# 2025
# Harris
# California
# Manufacturers Directory

Published January 2025 next update January 2026

**WARNING:** Purchasers and users of this directory may not use this directory to compile mailing lists, other marketing aids and other types of data, which are sold or otherwise provided to third parties. Such use is wrongful, illegal and a violation of the federal copyright laws.

**CAUTION:** Because of the many thousands of establishment listings contained in this directory and the possibilities of both human and mechanical error in processing this information, Mergent Inc. cannot assume liability for the correctness of the listings or information on which they are based. Hence, no information contained in this work should be relied upon in any instance where there is a possibility of any loss or damage as a consequence of any error or omission in this volume.

*Publisher*

Mergent Inc.
444 Madison Ave
New York, NY 10022

©Mergent Inc All Rights Reserved
2025 Mergent Business Press
ISSN 1080-2614
ISBN 978-1-63053-006-8

# TABLE OF CONTENTS

Summary of Contents & Explanatory Notes ................................................................................................ 4
User's Guide to Listings ................................................................................................................................ 6

**Products & Services**
**Standard Industrial Classification (SIC) Section**
SIC Numerical Index ..................................................................................................................................... 9
SIC Alphabetical Index ................................................................................................................................. 13
Firms Listed by SIC ....................................................................................................................................... 17

**Alphabetic Section**
Firms listed alphabetically by company name ............................................................................................ 945

**Geographic Section**
County/City Cross-Reference Index ............................................................................................................ 1285
Firms Listed by Location City ...................................................................................................................... 1289

# SUMMARY OF CONTENTS

Number of Companies ..................................................... 19,577
Number of Decision Makers ............................................. 35,164
Minimum Number of Employees ........................................... 15

# EXPLANATORY NOTES

### How to Cross-Reference in This Directory

This directory includes manufacturing establishments and corporate offices of manufacturing establishments. All of these firms are listed under Standard Industrial Classifications (SIC codes) 1011-1499 and 2011 through 3999. In addition, Prepackaged Software (SIC 7372), Tire Retreading & Repair Shops (SIC 7534), Welding Repair (SIC 7692), and Armature Rewinding Shops (SIC 7694) are also included in this directory because they frequently provide valueadded services that can be considered a manufacturing process.

### Source Suggestions Welcome

Although all known sources were used to compile this directory, it is possible that companies were inadvertently omitted. Your assistance in calling attention to such omissions would be greatly appreciated. A special form on the facing page will help you in the reporting process.

### Analysis

Every effort has been made to contact all firms to verify their information. The one exception to this rule is the annual sales figure, which is considered by many companies to be confidential information. Therefore, estimated sales have been calculated by multiplying the nationwide average sales per employee for the firm's major SIC code by the firm's number of employees. Nationwide averages for sales per employee by 4-digit SIC code are provided by the U.S. Department of Commerce and are updated annually. All sales—sales (est)—have been estimated by this method. The exceptions are parent companies (PA), division headquarters (DH) and headquarter locations (HQ) which may include an actual corporate sales figure—sales (corporate-wide) if available.

### Types of Companies

Descriptive and statistical data are included for companies in the entire state. These comprise manufacturers, machine shops, fabricators, assemblers and printers. Also identified are corporate offices in the state.

### Employment Data

This directory contains companies with 15 or more employees. The employment figure shown in the Products & Services Section includes male and female employees and embraces all levels of the company: administrative, clerical, sales and maintenance. This figure is for the facility listed and does not include other plants or offices. It should be recognized that these figures represent an approximate year-round average. These employment figures are broken into codes A through E and used in the Alphabetic and Geographic Sections to further help you in qualifying a company. Be sure to check the footnotes at the bottom of the page for the code breakdowns.

## Standard Industrial Classification (SIC)

The Standard Industrial Classification (SIC) system used in this directory was developed by the federal government for use in classifying establishments by the type of activity they are engaged in. The SIC classifications used in this directory are from the 1987 edition published by the U.S. Government's Office of Management and Budget. The SIC system separates all activities into broad industrial divisions (e.g., manufacturing, mining, retail trade). It further subdivides each division. The range of manufacturing industry classes extends from two-digit codes (major industry group) to four-digit codes (product).

For example:

| Industry Breakdown | Code | Industry, Product, etc. |
|---|---|---|
| *Major industry group | 20 | Food and kindred products |
| Industry group | 203 | Canned and frozen foods |
| *Industry | 2033 | Fruits and vegetables, etc. |

*Classifications used in this directory

Only two-digit and four-digit codes are used in this directory.

## Arrangement

1. The **Product & Services Section** contains complete in-depth corporate data. This section lists companies under their primary SIC. SIC codes are in numerical order with companies listed alphabetically under each code. A numerical and alphabetical index precedes this section.

> IMPORTANT NOTICE: It is a violation of both federal and state law to transmit an unsolicited advertisement to a facsimile machine. Any user of this product that violates such laws may be subject to civil and criminal penalties, which may exceed $500 for each transmission of an unsolicited facsimile. Mergent Inc. provides fax numbers for lawful purposes only and expressly forbids the use of these numbers in any unlawful manner.

2. The **Alphabetic Section** lists all companies with their full physical or mailing addresses and telephone number.

3. The **Geographic Section** is sorted by cities listed in alphabetic order and companies listed alphabetically within each city.

## Selectory®Online Business Database

Get unlimited online access to the most accurate, up-to-date company profiles for ALL companies in the U.S., Mexico and Canada, as well as 200 countries worldwide. Build targeted lists and find new opportunities for sales in minutes! Register for your free trial at **mergentprivateonline.com**.

# USER'S GUIDE TO LISTINGS

## PRODUCT & SERVICES SECTION

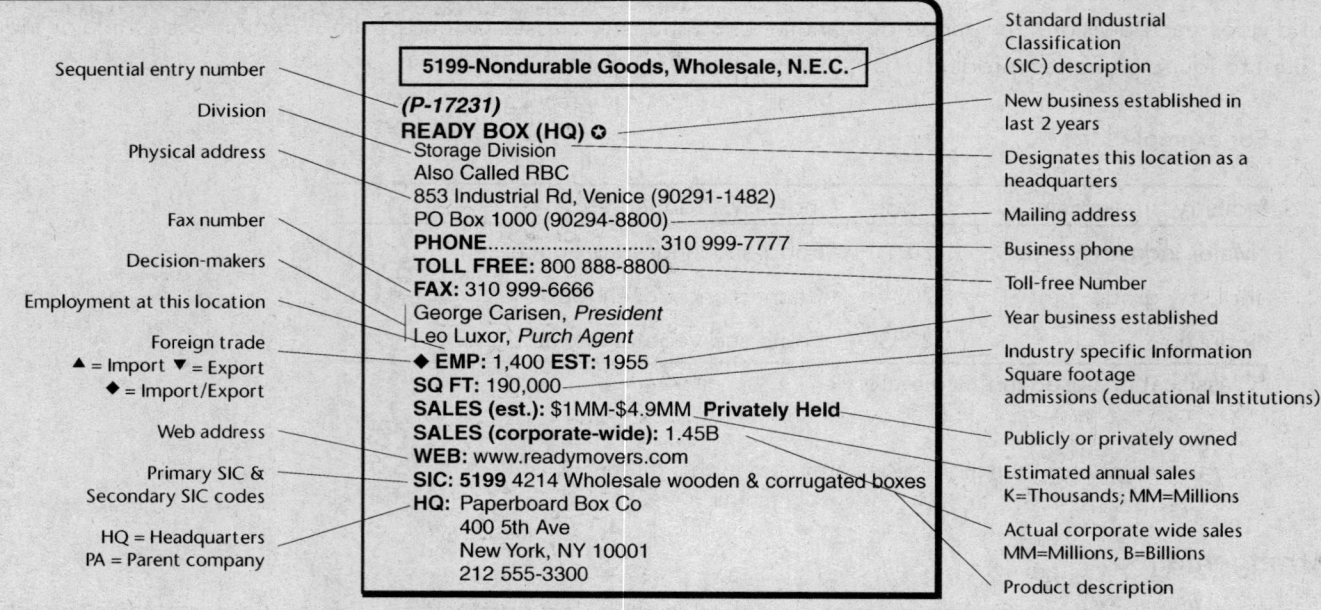

## ALPHABETIC SECTION

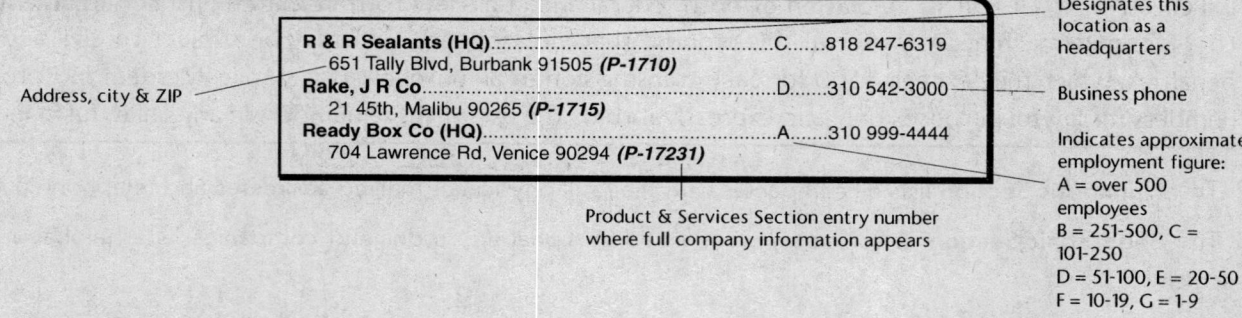

## GEOGRAPHIC SECTION

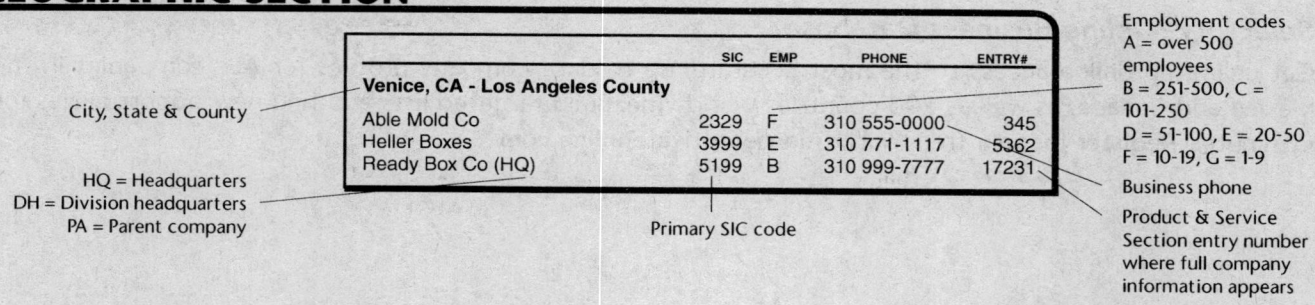

# NUMERICAL INDEX of SIC DESCRIPTIONS
# ALPHABETICAL INDEX of SIC DESCRIPTIONS

## PRODUCTS & SERVICES SECTION
Companies listed alphabetically under their primary SIC
In-depth company data listed

## ALPHABETIC SECTION
Company listings in alphabetical order

## GEOGRAPHIC INDEX
Companies sorted by city in alphabetical order

SIC INDEX

PRDTS & SVCS

ALPHABETIC

GEOGRAPHIC

# SIC INDEX

**Standard Industrial Classification Numerical Index**

| SIC NO | PRODUCT |

**01 agricultural production - crops**
0131 Cotton
0139 Field crops, except cash grain
0161 Vegetables and melons
0172 Grapes
0173 Tree nuts
0174 Citrus fruits
0175 Deciduous tree fruits
0179 Fruits and tree nuts, nec
0181 Ornamental nursery products
0182 Food crops grown under cover
0191 General farms, primarily crop

**02 agricultural production - livestock and animal specialties**
0241 Dairy farms
0252 Chicken eggs
0254 Poultry hatcheries
0279 Animal specialties, nec

**07 agricultural services**
0722 Crop harvesting
0723 Crop preparation services for market
0751 Livestock services, except veterinary
0762 Farm management services
0781 Landscape counseling and planning
0782 Lawn and garden services
0783 Ornamental shrub and tree services

**08 forestry**
0851 Forestry services

**10 metal mining**
1021 Copper ores
1041 Gold ores
1081 Metal mining services
1099 Metal ores, nec

**12 coal mining**
1221 Bituminous coal and lignite-surface mining
1231 Anthracite mining
1241 Coal mining services

**13 oil and gas extraction**
1311 Crude petroleum and natural gas
1321 Natural gas liquids
1381 Drilling oil and gas wells
1382 Oil and gas exploration services
1389 Oil and gas field services, nec

**14 mining and quarrying of nonmetallic minerals, except fuels**
1411 Dimension stone
1422 Crushed and broken limestone
1429 Crushed and broken stone, nec
1442 Construction sand and gravel
1446 Industrial sand
1455 Kaolin and ball clay
1474 Potash, soda, and borate minerals
1479 Chemical and fertilizer mining
1481 Nonmetallic mineral services
1499 Miscellaneous nonmetallic mining

**15 construction - general contractors & operative builders**
1521 Single-family housing construction
1531 Operative builders
1541 Industrial buildings and warehouses
1542 Nonresidential construction, nec

**16 heamy construction, except building construction, contractor**
1611 Highway and street construction
1622 Bridge, tunnel, and elevated highway
1623 Water, sewer, and utility lines

1629 Heavy construction, nec

**17 construction - special trade contractors**
1711 Plumbing, heating, air-conditioning
1721 Painting and paper hanging
1731 Electrical work
1742 Plastering, drywall, and insulation
1743 Terrazzo, tile, marble, mosaic work
1751 Carpentry work
1752 Floor laying and floor work, nec
1761 Roofing, siding, and sheetmetal work
1771 Concrete work
1781 Water well drilling
1791 Structural steel erection
1793 Glass and glazing work
1794 Excavation work
1796 Installing building equipment
1799 Special trade contractors, nec

**20 food and kindred products**
2011 Meat packing plants
2013 Sausages and other prepared meats
2015 Poultry slaughtering and processing
2021 Creamery butter
2022 Cheese; natural and processed
2023 Dry, condensed, evaporated products
2024 Ice cream and frozen deserts
2026 Fluid milk
2032 Canned specialties
2033 Canned fruits and specialties
2034 Dehydrated fruits, vegetables, soups
2035 Pickles, sauces, and salad dressings
2037 Frozen fruits and vegetables
2038 Frozen specialties, nec
2041 Flour and other grain mill products
2043 Cereal breakfast foods
2044 Rice milling
2045 Prepared flour mixes and doughs
2046 Wet corn milling
2047 Dog and cat food
2048 Prepared feeds, nec
2051 Bread, cake, and related products
2052 Cookies and crackers
2053 Frozen bakery products, except bread
2061 Raw cane sugar
2062 Cane sugar refining
2063 Beet sugar
2064 Candy and other confectionery products
2066 Chocolate and cocoa products
2068 Salted and roasted nuts and seeds
2076 Vegetable oil mills, nec
2077 Animal and marine fats and oils
2079 Edible fats and oils
2082 Malt beverages
2083 Malt
2084 Wines, brandy, and brandy spirits
2085 Distilled and blended liquors
2086 Bottled and canned soft drinks
2087 Flavoring extracts and syrups, nec
2091 Canned and cured fish and seafoods
2092 Fresh or frozen packaged fish
2095 Roasted coffee
2096 Potato chips and similar snacks
2097 Manufactured ice
2098 Macaroni and spaghetti
2099 Food preparations, nec

**21 tobacco products**
2111 Cigarettes
2131 Chewing and smoking tobacco

**22 textile mill products**
2211 Broadwoven fabric mills, cotton
2221 Broadwoven fabric mills, manmade
2231 Broadwoven fabric mills, wool

2241 Narrow fabric mills
2252 Hosiery, nec
2253 Knit outerwear mills
2257 Weft knit fabric mills
2259 Knitting mills, nec
2261 Finishing plants, cotton
2262 Finishing plants, manmade
2269 Finishing plants, nec
2273 Carpets and rugs
2281 Yarn spinning mills
2284 Thread mills
2295 Coated fabrics, not rubberized
2296 Tire cord and fabrics
2297 Nonwoven fabrics
2298 Cordage and twine
2299 Textile goods, nec

**23 apparel, finished products from fabrics & similar materials**
2311 Men's and boy's suits and coats
2321 Men's and boy's furnishings
2323 Men's and boy's neckwear
2325 Men's and boy's trousers and slacks
2326 Men's and boy's work clothing
2329 Men's and boy's clothing, nec
2331 Women's and misses' blouses and shirts
2335 Women's, junior's, and misses' dresses
2337 Women's and misses' suits and coats
2339 Women's and misses' outerwear, nec
2341 Women's and children's underwear
2342 Bras, girdles, and allied garments
2353 Hats, caps, and millinery
2361 Girl's and children's dresses, blouses
2369 Girl's and children's outerwear, nec
2371 Fur goods
2381 Fabric dress and work gloves
2384 Robes and dressing gowns
2386 Leather and sheep-lined clothing
2387 Apparel belts
2389 Apparel and accessories, nec
2391 Curtains and draperies
2392 Household furnishings, nec
2393 Textile bags
2394 Canvas and related products
2395 Pleating and stitching
2396 Automotive and apparel trimmings
2399 Fabricated textile products, nec

**24 lumber and wood products, except furniture**
2411 Logging
2421 Sawmills and planing mills, general
2426 Hardwood dimension and flooring mills
2429 Special product sawmills, nec
2431 Millwork
2434 Wood kitchen cabinets
2435 Hardwood veneer and plywood
2439 Structural wood members, nec
2441 Nailed wood boxes and shook
2448 Wood pallets and skids
2449 Wood containers, nec
2451 Mobile homes
2452 Prefabricated wood buildings
2491 Wood preserving
2493 Reconstituted wood products
2499 Wood products, nec

**25 furniture and fixtures**
2511 Wood household furniture
2512 Upholstered household furniture
2514 Metal household furniture
2515 Mattresses and bedsprings
2517 Wood television and radio cabinets
2519 Household furniture, nec
2521 Wood office furniture
2522 Office furniture, except wood

# SIC INDEX

2531 Public building and related furniture
2541 Wood partitions and fixtures
2542 Partitions and fixtures, except wood
2591 Drapery hardware and blinds and shades
2599 Furniture and fixtures, nec

### 26 paper and allied products

2611 Pulp mills
2621 Paper mills
2631 Paperboard mills
2652 Setup paperboard boxes
2653 Corrugated and solid fiber boxes
2655 Fiber cans, drums, and similar products
2656 Sanitary food containers
2657 Folding paperboard boxes
2671 Paper; coated and laminated packaging
2672 Paper; coated and laminated, nec
2673 Bags: plastic, laminated, and coated
2674 Bags: uncoated paper and multiwall
2675 Die-cut paper and board
2676 Sanitary paper products
2677 Envelopes
2678 Stationery products
2679 Converted paper products, nec

### 27 printing, publishing and allied industries

2711 Newspapers
2721 Periodicals
2731 Book publishing
2732 Book printing
2741 Miscellaneous publishing
2752 Commercial printing, lithographic
2754 Commercial printing, gravure
2759 Commercial printing, nec
2761 Manifold business forms
2771 Greeting cards
2782 Blankbooks and looseleaf binders
2789 Bookbinding and related work
2791 Typesetting
2796 Platemaking services

### 28 chemicals and allied products

2812 Alkalies and chlorine
2813 Industrial gases
2816 Inorganic pigments
2819 Industrial inorganic chemicals, nec
2821 Plastics materials and resins
2822 Synthetic rubber
2824 Organic fibers, noncellulosic
2833 Medicinals and botanicals
2834 Pharmaceutical preparations
2835 Diagnostic substances
2836 Biological products, except diagnostic
2841 Soap and other detergents
2842 Polishes and sanitation goods
2843 Surface active agents
2844 Toilet preparations
2851 Paints and allied products
2861 Gum and wood chemicals
2865 Cyclic crudes and intermediates
2869 Industrial organic chemicals, nec
2873 Nitrogenous fertilizers
2875 Fertilizers, mixing only
2879 Agricultural chemicals, nec
2891 Adhesives and sealants
2892 Explosives
2893 Printing ink
2895 Carbon black
2899 Chemical preparations, nec

### 29 petroleum refining and related industries

2911 Petroleum refining
2951 Asphalt paving mixtures and blocks
2952 Asphalt felts and coatings
2992 Lubricating oils and greases
2999 Petroleum and coal products, nec

### 30 rubber and miscellaneous plastic products

3011 Tires and inner tubes
3021 Rubber and plastics footwear
3052 Rubber and plastics hose and beltings
3053 Gaskets; packing and sealing devices
3061 Mechanical rubber goods
3069 Fabricated rubber products, nec
3081 Unsupported plastics film and sheet
3082 Unsupported plastics profile shapes
3083 Laminated plastics plate and sheet
3084 Plastics pipe
3085 Plastics bottles
3086 Plastics foam products
3087 Custom compound purchased resins
3088 Plastics plumbing fixtures
3089 Plastics products, nec

### 31 leather and leather products

3111 Leather tanning and finishing
3131 Footwear cut stock
3143 Men's footwear, except athletic
3144 Women's footwear, except athletic
3149 Footwear, except rubber, nec
3161 Luggage
3171 Women's handbags and purses
3172 Personal leather goods, nec
3199 Leather goods, nec

### 32 stone, clay, glass, and concrete products

3211 Flat glass
3221 Glass containers
3229 Pressed and blown glass, nec
3231 Products of purchased glass
3241 Cement, hydraulic
3251 Brick and structural clay tile
3253 Ceramic wall and floor tile
3259 Structural clay products, nec
3261 Vitreous plumbing fixtures
3262 Vitreous china table and kitchenware
3263 Semivitreous table and kitchenware
3264 Porcelain electrical supplies
3269 Pottery products, nec
3271 Concrete block and brick
3272 Concrete products, nec
3273 Ready-mixed concrete
3274 Lime
3275 Gypsum products
3281 Cut stone and stone products
3291 Abrasive products
3292 Asbestos products
3295 Minerals, ground or treated
3296 Mineral wool
3299 Nonmetallic mineral products,

### 33 primary metal industries

3312 Blast furnaces and steel mills
3313 Electrometallurgical products
3315 Steel wire and related products
3316 Cold finishing of steel shapes
3317 Steel pipe and tubes
3321 Gray and ductile iron foundries
3322 Malleable iron foundries
3324 Steel investment foundries
3325 Steel foundries, nec
3331 Primary copper
3334 Primary aluminum
3339 Primary nonferrous metals, nec
3341 Secondary nonferrous metals
3351 Copper rolling and drawing
3353 Aluminum sheet, plate, and foil
3354 Aluminum extruded products
3355 Aluminum rolling and drawing, nec
3356 Nonferrous rolling and drawing, nec
3357 Nonferrous wiredrawing and insulating
3363 Aluminum die-castings
3364 Nonferrous die-castings except aluminum
3365 Aluminum foundries
3366 Copper foundries
3369 Nonferrous foundries, nec
3398 Metal heat treating
3399 Primary metal products

### 34 fabricated metal products

3411 Metal cans
3412 Metal barrels, drums, and pails
3421 Cutlery
3423 Hand and edge tools, nec
3425 Saw blades and handsaws
3429 Hardware, nec
3431 Metal sanitary ware
3432 Plumbing fixture fittings and trim
3433 Heating equipment, except electric
3441 Fabricated structural metal
3442 Metal doors, sash, and trim
3443 Fabricated plate work (boiler shop)
3444 Sheet metalwork
3446 Architectural metalwork
3448 Prefabricated metal buildings
3449 Miscellaneous metalwork
3451 Screw machine products
3452 Bolts, nuts, rivets, and washers
3462 Iron and steel forgings
3463 Nonferrous forgings
3465 Automotive stampings
3466 Crowns and closures
3469 Metal stampings, nec
3471 Plating and polishing
3479 Metal coating and allied services
3483 Ammunition, except for small arms, nec
3484 Small arms
3489 Ordnance and accessories, nec
3491 Industrial valves
3492 Fluid power valves and hose fittings
3493 Steel springs, except wire
3494 Valves and pipe fittings, nec
3495 Wire springs
3496 Miscellaneous fabricated wire products
3498 Fabricated pipe and fittings
3499 Fabricated metal products, nec

### 35 industrial and commercial machinery and computer equipment

3511 Turbines and turbine generator sets
3519 Internal combustion engines, nec
3523 Farm machinery and equipment
3524 Lawn and garden equipment
3531 Construction machinery
3532 Mining machinery
3533 Oil and gas field machinery
3534 Elevators and moving stairways
3535 Conveyors and conveying equipment
3536 Hoists, cranes, and monorails
3537 Industrial trucks and tractors
3541 Machine tools, metal cutting type
3542 Machine tools, metal forming type
3544 Special dies, tools, jigs, and fixtures
3545 Machine tool accessories
3546 Power-driven handtools
3547 Rolling mill machinery
3548 Welding apparatus
3549 Metalworking machinery, nec
3552 Textile machinery
3553 Woodworking machinery
3554 Paper industries machinery
3555 Printing trades machinery
3556 Food products machinery
3559 Special industry machinery, nec
3561 Pumps and pumping equipment
3562 Ball and roller bearings
3563 Air and gas compressors
3564 Blowers and fans
3565 Packaging machinery
3566 Speed changers, drives, and gears
3567 Industrial furnaces and ovens
3568 Power transmission equipment, nec
3569 General industrial machinery,
3571 Electronic computers
3572 Computer storage devices
3575 Computer terminals
3577 Computer peripheral equipment, nec
3578 Calculating and accounting equipment
3579 Office machines, nec
3581 Automatic vending machines
3582 Commercial laundry equipment
3585 Refrigeration and heating equipment
3589 Service industry machinery, nec
3592 Carburetors, pistons, rings, valves
3593 Fluid power cylinders and actuators
3594 Fluid power pumps and motors

# SIC INDEX

3596 Scales and balances, except laboratory
3599 Industrial machinery, nec

### 36 electronic & other electrical equipment & components

3612 Transformers, except electric
3613 Switchgear and switchboard apparatus
3621 Motors and generators
3624 Carbon and graphite products
3625 Relays and industrial controls
3629 Electrical industrial apparatus
3631 Household cooking equipment
3632 Household refrigerators and freezers
3634 Electric housewares and fans
3635 Household vacuum cleaners
3639 Household appliances, nec
3641 Electric lamps
3643 Current-carrying wiring devices
3644 Noncurrent-carrying wiring devices
3645 Residential lighting fixtures
3646 Commercial lighting fixtures
3647 Vehicular lighting equipment
3648 Lighting equipment, nec
3651 Household audio and video equipment
3652 Prerecorded records and tapes
3661 Telephone and telegraph apparatus
3663 Radio and t.v. communications equipment
3669 Communications equipment, nec
3671 Electron tubes
3672 Printed circuit boards
3674 Semiconductors and related devices
3675 Electronic capacitors
3676 Electronic resistors
3677 Electronic coils and transformers
3678 Electronic connectors
3679 Electronic components, nec
3691 Storage batteries
3692 Primary batteries, dry and wet
3694 Engine electrical equipment
3695 Magnetic and optical recording media
3699 Electrical equipment and supplies, nec

### 37 transportation equipment

3711 Motor vehicles and car bodies
3713 Truck and bus bodies
3714 Motor vehicle parts and accessories
3715 Truck trailers
3716 Motor homes
3721 Aircraft
3724 Aircraft engines and engine parts
3728 Aircraft parts and equipment, nec
3731 Shipbuilding and repairing
3732 Boatbuilding and repairing
3743 Railroad equipment
3751 Motorcycles, bicycles, and parts
3761 Guided missiles and space vehicles
3764 Space propulsion units and parts
3769 Space vehicle equipment, nec
3792 Travel trailers and campers
3795 Tanks and tank components
3799 Transportation equipment, nec

### 38 measuring, photographic, medical, & optical goods, & clocks

3812 Search and navigation equipment
3821 Laboratory apparatus and furniture
3822 Environmental controls
3823 Process control instruments
3824 Fluid meters and counting devices
3825 Instruments to measure electricity
3826 Analytical instruments
3827 Optical instruments and lenses
3829 Measuring and controlling devices, nec
3841 Surgical and medical instruments
3842 Surgical appliances and supplies
3843 Dental equipment and supplies
3844 X-ray apparatus and tubes
3845 Electromedical equipment
3851 Ophthalmic goods
3861 Photographic equipment and supplies
3873 Watches, clocks, watchcases, and parts

### 39 miscellaneous manufacturing industries

3911 Jewelry, precious metal
3914 Silverware and plated ware
3915 Jewelers' materials and lapidary work
3931 Musical instruments
3942 Dolls and stuffed toys
3944 Games, toys, and children's vehicles
3949 Sporting and athletic goods, nec
3951 Pens and mechanical pencils
3952 Lead pencils and art goods
3953 Marking devices
3955 Carbon paper and inked ribbons
3961 Costume jewelry
3965 Fasteners, buttons, needles, and pins
3991 Brooms and brushes
3993 Signs and advertising specialties
3995 Burial caskets
3996 Hard surface floor coverings, nec
3999 Manufacturing industries, nec

### 41 local & suburban transit & interurban highway transportation

4111 Local and suburban transit
4119 Local passenger transportation, nec

### 42 motor freight transportation

4212 Local trucking, without storage
4215 Courier services, except by air
4221 Farm product warehousing and storage
4222 Refrigerated warehousing and storage
4225 General warehousing and storage
4226 Special warehousing and storage, nec

### 44 water transportation

4491 Marine cargo handling
4499 Water transportation services, nec

### 45 transportation by air

4581 Airports, flying fields, and services

### 47 transportation services

4724 Travel agencies
4725 Tour operators
4731 Freight transportation arrangement
4783 Packing and crating
4785 Inspection and fixed facilities

### 48 communications

4812 Radiotelephone communication
4813 Telephone communication, except radio
4832 Radio broadcasting stations
4833 Television broadcasting stations
4841 Cable and other pay television services
4899 Communication services, nec

### 49 electric, gas and sanitary services

4911 Electric services
4923 Gas transmission and distribution
4931 Electric and other services combined
4939 Combination utilities, nec
4941 Water supply
4952 Sewerage systems
4953 Refuse systems
4959 Sanitary services, nec
4971 Irrigation systems

### 50 wholesale trade - durable goods

5012 Automobiles and other motor vehicles
5013 Motor vehicle supplies and new parts
5014 Tires and tubes
5021 Furniture
5023 Homefurnishings
5031 Lumber, plywood, and millwork
5032 Brick, stone, and related material
5033 Roofing, siding, and insulation
5039 Construction materials, nec
5043 Photographic equipment and supplies
5044 Office equipment
5045 Computers, peripherals, and software
5046 Commercial equipment, nec
5047 Medical and hospital equipment
5048 Ophthalmic goods
5049 Professional equipment, nec
5051 Metals service centers and offices
5063 Electrical apparatus and equipment
5064 Electrical appliances, television and radio
5065 Electronic parts and equipment, nec
5072 Hardware
5074 Plumbing and hydronic heating supplies
5075 Warm air heating and air conditioning
5078 Refrigeration equipment and supplies
5082 Construction and mining machinery
5083 Farm and garden machinery
5084 Industrial machinery and equipment
5085 Industrial supplies
5087 Service establishment equipment
5088 Transportation equipment and supplies
5091 Sporting and recreation goods
5092 Toys and hobby goods and supplies
5093 Scrap and waste materials
5094 Jewelry and precious stones
5099 Durable goods, nec

### 51 wholesale trade - nondurable goods

5112 Stationery and office supplies
5113 Industrial and personal service paper
5122 Drugs, proprietaries, and sundries
5131 Piece goods and notions
5136 Men's and boy's clothing
5137 Women's and children's clothing
5139 Footwear
5141 Groceries, general line
5142 Packaged frozen goods
5143 Dairy products, except dried or canned
5144 Poultry and poultry products
5145 Confectionery
5146 Fish and seafoods
5147 Meats and meat products
5148 Fresh fruits and vegetables
5149 Groceries and related products, nec
5153 Grain and field beans
5159 Farm-product raw materials, nec
5162 Plastics materials and basic shapes
5169 Chemicals and allied products, nec
5172 Petroleum products, nec
5181 Beer and ale
5182 Wine and distilled beverages
5191 Farm supplies
5192 Books, periodicals, and newspapers
5193 Flowers and florists supplies
5198 Paints, varnishes, and supplies
5199 Nondurable goods, nec

### 52 building materials, hardware, garden supplies & mobile homes

5211 Lumber and other building materials
5231 Paint, glass, and wallpaper stores
5251 Hardware stores
5261 Retail nurseries and garden stores

### 53 general merchandise stores

5311 Department stores

### 54 food stores

5411 Grocery stores
5421 Meat and fish markets
5431 Fruit and vegetable markets
5441 Candy, nut, and confectionery stores
5461 Retail bakeries
5499 Miscellaneous food stores

### 55 automotive dealers and gasoline service stations

5511 New and used car dealers
5531 Auto and home supply stores
5541 Gasoline service stations
5551 Boat dealers
5571 Motorcycle dealers
5599 Automotive dealers, nec

### 56 apparel and accessory stores

5621 Women's clothing stores
5632 Women's accessory and specialty stores
5651 Family clothing stores
5661 Shoe stores
5699 Miscellaneous apparel and accessories

# SIC INDEX

### 57 home furniture, furnishings and equipment stores
5712 Furniture stores
5713 Floor covering stores
5714 Drapery and upholstery stores
5719 Miscellaneous homefurnishings
5722 Household appliance stores
5731 Radio, television, and electronic stores
5734 Computer and software stores
5736 Musical instrument stores

### 58 eating and drinking places
5812 Eating places
5813 Drinking places

### 59 miscellaneous retail
5921 Liquor stores
5932 Used merchandise stores
5941 Sporting goods and bicycle shops
5942 Book stores
5943 Stationery stores
5944 Jewelry stores
5945 Hobby, toy, and game shops
5946 Camera and photographic supply stores
5947 Gift, novelty, and souvenir shop
5949 Sewing, needlework, and piece goods
5961 Catalog and mail-order houses
5963 Direct selling establishments
5993 Tobacco stores and stands
5994 News dealers and newsstands
5995 Optical goods stores
5999 Miscellaneous retail stores, nec

### 61 nondepository credit institutions
6162 Mortgage bankers and correspondents
6163 Loan brokers

### 62 security & commodity brokers, dealers, exchanges & services
6211 Security brokers and dealers
6221 Commodity contracts brokers, dealers
6282 Investment advice

### 63 insurance carriers
6324 Hospital and medical service plans

### 64 insurance agents, brokers and service
6411 Insurance agents, brokers, and service

### 65 real estate
6512 Nonresidential building operators
6531 Real estate agents and managers

### 67 holding and other investment offices
6719 Holding companies, nec
6722 Management investment, open-ended
6726 Investment offices, nec
6794 Patent owners and lessors
6799 Investors, nec

### 70 hotels, rooming houses, camps, and other lodging places
7011 Hotels and motels
7033 Trailer parks and campsites

### 72 personal services
7212 Garment pressing and cleaners' agents
7213 Linen supply
7216 Drycleaning plants, except rugs
7218 Industrial launderers
7221 Photographic studios, portrait
7231 Beauty shops
7299 Miscellaneous personal services

### 73 business services
7311 Advertising agencies
7312 Outdoor advertising services
7313 Radio, television, publisher representatives
7319 Advertising, nec
7331 Direct mail advertising services
7334 Photocopying and duplicating services
7335 Commercial photography
7336 Commercial art and graphic design
7338 Secretarial and court reporting
7342 Disinfecting and pest control services
7349 Building maintenance services, nec
7353 Heavy construction equipment rental
7359 Equipment rental and leasing, nec
7363 Help supply services
7371 Custom computer programming services
7372 Prepackaged software
7373 Computer integrated systems design
7374 Data processing and preparation
7375 Information retrieval services
7378 Computer maintenance and repair
7379 Computer related services, nec
7381 Detective and armored car services
7382 Security systems services
7383 News syndicates
7389 Business services, nec

### 75 automotive repair, services and parking
7532 Top and body repair and paint shops
7534 Tire retreading and repair shops
7537 Automotive transmission repair shops
7538 General automotive repair shops
7539 Automotive repair shops, nec
7542 Carwashes
7549 Automotive services, nec

### 76 miscellaneous repair services
7622 Radio and television repair
7623 Refrigeration service and repair
7629 Electrical repair shops
7641 Reupholstery and furniture repair
7692 Welding repair
7694 Armature rewinding shops
7699 Repair services, nec

### 78 motion pictures
7812 Motion picture and video production
7819 Services allied to motion pictures

### 79 amusement and recreation services
7922 Theatrical producers and services
7929 Entertainers and entertainment groups
7948 Racing, including track operation
7992 Public golf courses
7993 Coin-operated amusement devices
7997 Membership sports and recreation clubs
7999 Amusement and recreation, nec

### 80 health services
8011 Offices and clinics of medical doctors
8042 Offices and clinics of optometrists
8062 General medical and surgical hospitals
8071 Medical laboratories
8072 Dental laboratories
8093 Specialty outpatient clinics, nec
8099 Health and allied services, nec

### 81 legal services
8111 Legal services

### 82 educational services
8211 Elementary and secondary schools
8231 Libraries
8243 Data processing schools
8249 Vocational schools, nec
8299 Schools and educational services

### 83 social services
8322 Individual and family services
8331 Job training and related services
8351 Child day care services
8361 Residential care

### 84 museums, art galleries and botanical and zoological gardens
8422 Botanical and zoological gardens

### 86 membership organizations
8661 Religious organizations
8699 Membership organizations, nec

### 87 engineering, accounting, research, and management services
8711 Engineering services
8712 Architectural services
8721 Accounting, auditing, and bookkeeping
8731 Commercial physical research
8732 Commercial nonphysical research
8733 Noncommercial research organizations
8734 Testing laboratories
8741 Management services
8742 Management consulting services
8743 Public relations services
8744 Facilities support services
8748 Business consulting, nec

### 89 services, not elsewhere classified
8999 Services, nec

### 91 executive, legislative & general government, except finance
9199 General government, nec

### 92 justice, public order and safety
9224 Fire protection

# SIC INDEX

**Standard Industrial Classification Alphabetical Index**

SIC NO    PRODUCT

## A

3291 Abrasive products
8721 Accounting, auditing, and bookkeeping
2891 Adhesives and sealants
7311 Advertising agencies
7319 Advertising, nec
2879 Agricultural chemicals, nec
3563 Air and gas compressors
3721 Aircraft
3724 Aircraft engines and engine parts
3728 Aircraft parts and equipment, nec
4581 Airports, flying fields, and services
2812 Alkalies and chlorine
3363 Aluminum die-castings
3354 Aluminum extruded products
3365 Aluminum foundries
3355 Aluminum rolling and drawing, nec
3353 Aluminum sheet, plate, and foil
3483 Ammunition, except for small arms, nec
7999 Amusement and recreation, nec
3826 Analytical instruments
2077 Animal and marine fats and oils
0279 Animal specialties, nec
1231 Anthracite mining
2389 Apparel and accessories, nec
2387 Apparel belts
3446 Architectural metalwork
8712 Architectural services
7694 Armature rewinding shops
3292 Asbestos products
2952 Asphalt felts and coatings
2951 Asphalt paving mixtures and blocks
5531 Auto and home supply stores
3581 Automatic vending machines
5012 Automobiles and other motor vehicles
2396 Automotive and apparel trimmings
5599 Automotive dealers, nec
7539 Automotive repair shops, nec
7549 Automotive services, nec
3465 Automotive stampings
7537 Automotive transmission repair shops

## B

2673 Bags: plastic, laminated, and coated
2674 Bags: uncoated paper and multiwall
3562 Ball and roller bearings
7231 Beauty shops
5181 Beer and ale
2063 Beet sugar
2836 Biological products, except diagnostic
1221 Bituminous coal and lignite-surface mining
2782 Blankbooks and looseleaf binders
3312 Blast furnaces and steel mills
3564 Blowers and fans
5551 Boat dealers
3732 Boatbuilding and repairing
3452 Bolts, nuts, rivets, and washers
2732 Book printing
2731 Book publishing
5942 Book stores
2789 Bookbinding and related work
5192 Books, periodicals, and newspapers
8422 Botanical and zoological gardens
2086 Bottled and canned soft drinks
2342 Bras, girdles, and allied garments
2051 Bread, cake, and related products
3251 Brick and structural clay tile
5032 Brick, stone, and related material
1622 Bridge, tunnel, and elevated highway
2211 Broadwoven fabric mills, cotton
2221 Broadwoven fabric mills, manmade
2231 Broadwoven fabric mills, wool
3991 Brooms and brushes
7349 Building maintenance services, nec
3995 Burial caskets
8748 Business consulting, nec

7389 Business services, nec

## C

4841 Cable and other pay television services
3578 Calculating and accounting equipment
5946 Camera and photographic supply stores
2064 Candy and other confectionery products
5441 Candy, nut, and confectionery stores
2062 Cane sugar refining
2091 Canned and cured fish and seafoods
2033 Canned fruits and specialties
2032 Canned specialties
2394 Canvas and related products
3624 Carbon and graphite products
2895 Carbon black
3955 Carbon paper and inked ribbons
3592 Carburetors; pistons, rings, valves
1751 Carpentry work
2273 Carpets and rugs
7542 Carwashes
5961 Catalog and mail-order houses
3241 Cement, hydraulic
3253 Ceramic wall and floor tile
2043 Cereal breakfast foods
2022 Cheese; natural and processed
1479 Chemical and fertilizer mining
2899 Chemical preparations, nec
5169 Chemicals and allied products, nec
2131 Chewing and smoking tobacco
0252 Chicken eggs
8351 Child day care services
2066 Chocolate and cocoa products
2111 Cigarettes
0174 Citrus fruits
1241 Coal mining services
2295 Coated fabrics, not rubberized
7993 Coin-operated amusement devices
3316 Cold finishing of steel shapes
4939 Combination utilities, nec
7336 Commercial art and graphic design
5046 Commercial equipment, nec
3582 Commercial laundry equipment
3646 Commercial lighting fixtures
8732 Commercial nonphysical research
7335 Commercial photography
8731 Commercial physical research
2754 Commercial printing, gravure
2752 Commercial printing, lithographic
2759 Commercial printing, nec
6221 Commodity contracts brokers, dealers
4899 Communication services, nec
3669 Communications equipment, nec
5734 Computer and software stores
7373 Computer integrated systems design
7378 Computer maintenance and repair
3577 Computer peripheral equipment, nec
7379 Computer related services, nec
3572 Computer storage devices
3575 Computer terminals
5045 Computers, peripherals, and software
3271 Concrete block and brick
3272 Concrete products, nec
1771 Concrete work
5145 Confectionery
5082 Construction and mining machinery
3531 Construction machinery
5039 Construction materials, nec
1442 Construction sand and gravel
2679 Converted paper products, nec
3535 Conveyors and conveying equipment
2052 Cookies and crackers
3366 Copper foundries
1021 Copper ores
3351 Copper rolling and drawing
2298 Cordage and twine
2653 Corrugated and solid fiber boxes

3961 Costume jewelry
0131 Cotton
4215 Courier services, except by air
2021 Creamery butter
0722 Crop harvesting
0723 Crop preparation services for market
3466 Crowns and closures
1311 Crude petroleum and natural gas
1422 Crushed and broken limestone
1429 Crushed and broken stone, nec
3643 Current-carrying wiring devices
2391 Curtains and draperies
3087 Custom compound purchased resins
7371 Custom computer programming services
3281 Cut stone and stone products
3421 Cutlery
2865 Cyclic crudes and intermediates

## D

0241 Dairy farms
5143 Dairy products, except dried or canned
7374 Data processing and preparation
8243 Data processing schools
0175 Deciduous tree fruits
2034 Dehydrated fruits, vegetables, soups
3843 Dental equipment and supplies
8072 Dental laboratories
5311 Department stores
7381 Detective and armored car services
2835 Diagnostic substances
2675 Die-cut paper and board
1411 Dimension stone
7331 Direct mail advertising services
5963 Direct selling establishments
7342 Disinfecting and pest control services
2085 Distilled and blended liquors
2047 Dog and cat food
3942 Dolls and stuffed toys
5714 Drapery and upholstery stores
2591 Drapery hardware and blinds and shades
1381 Drilling oil and gas wells
5813 Drinking places
5122 Drugs, proprietaries, and sundries
2023 Dry, condensed, evaporated products
7216 Drycleaning plants, except rugs
5099 Durable goods, nec

## E

5812 Eating places
2079 Edible fats and oils
4931 Electric and other services combined
3634 Electric housewares and fans
3641 Electric lamps
4911 Electric services
5063 Electrical apparatus and equipment
5064 Electrical appliances, television and radio
3699 Electrical equipment and supplies, nec
3629 Electrical industrial apparatus
7629 Electrical repair shops
1731 Electrical work
3845 Electromedical equipment
3313 Electrometallurgical products
3671 Electron tubes
3675 Electronic capacitors
3677 Electronic coils and transformers
3679 Electronic components, nec
3571 Electronic computers
3678 Electronic connectors
5065 Electronic parts and equipment, nec
3676 Electronic resistors
8211 Elementary and secondary schools
3534 Elevators and moving stairways
3694 Engine electrical equipment
8711 Engineering services
7929 Entertainers and entertainment groups
2677 Envelopes

# SIC INDEX

3822 Environmental controls
7359 Equipment rental and leasing, nec
1794 Excavation work
2892 Explosives

## F

2381 Fabric dress and work gloves
3499 Fabricated metal products, nec
3498 Fabricated pipe and fittings
3443 Fabricated plate work (boiler shop)
3069 Fabricated rubber products, nec
3441 Fabricated structural metal
2399 Fabricated textile products, nec
8744 Facilities support services
5651 Family clothing stores
5083 Farm and garden machinery
3523 Farm machinery and equipment
0762 Farm management services
4221 Farm product warehousing and storage
5191 Farm supplies
5159 Farm-product raw materials, nec
3965 Fasteners, buttons, needles, and pins
2875 Fertilizers, mixing only
2655 Fiber cans, drums, and similar products
0139 Field crops, except cash grain
2261 Finishing plants, cotton
2262 Finishing plants, manmade
2269 Finishing plants, nec
9224 Fire protection
5146 Fish and seafoods
3211 Flat glass
2087 Flavoring extracts and syrups, nec
5713 Floor covering stores
1752 Floor laying and floor work, nec
2041 Flour and other grain mill products
5193 Flowers and florists supplies
3824 Fluid meters and counting devices
2026 Fluid milk
3593 Fluid power cylinders and actuators
3594 Fluid power pumps and motors
3492 Fluid power valves and hose fittings
2657 Folding paperboard boxes
0182 Food crops grown under cover
2099 Food preparations, nec
3556 Food products machinery
5139 Footwear
3131 Footwear cut stock
3149 Footwear, except rubber, nec
0851 Forestry services
4731 Freight transportation arrangement
5148 Fresh fruits and vegetables
2092 Fresh or frozen packaged fish
2053 Frozen bakery products, except bread
2037 Frozen fruits and vegetables
2038 Frozen specialties, nec
5431 Fruit and vegetable markets
0179 Fruits and tree nuts, nec
2371 Fur goods
5021 Furniture
2599 Furniture and fixtures, nec
5712 Furniture stores

## G

3944 Games, toys, and children's vehicles
7212 Garment pressing and cleaners' agents
4923 Gas transmission and distribution
3053 Gaskets; packing and sealing devices
5541 Gasoline service stations
7538 General automotive repair shops
0191 General farms, primarily crop
9199 General government, nec
3569 General industrial machinery,
8062 General medical and surgical hospitals
4225 General warehousing and storage
5947 Gift, novelty, and souvenir shop
2361 Girl's and children's dresses, blouses
2369 Girl's and children's outerwear, nec
1793 Glass and glazing work
3221 Glass containers
1041 Gold ores
5153 Grain and field beans
0172 Grapes

3321 Gray and ductile iron foundries
2771 Greeting cards
5149 Groceries and related products, nec
5141 Groceries, general line
5411 Grocery stores
3761 Guided missiles and space vehicles
2861 Gum and wood chemicals
3275 Gypsum products

## H

3423 Hand and edge tools, nec
3996 Hard surface floor coverings, nec
5072 Hardware
5251 Hardware stores
3429 Hardware, nec
2426 Hardwood dimension and flooring mills
2435 Hardwood veneer and plywood
2353 Hats, caps, and millinery
8099 Health and allied services, nec
3433 Heating equipment, except electric
7353 Heavy construction equipment rental
1629 Heavy construction, nec
7363 Help supply services
1611 Highway and street construction
5945 Hobby, toy, and game shops
3536 Hoists, cranes, and monorails
6719 Holding companies, nec
5023 Homefurnishings
2252 Hosiery, nec
6324 Hospital and medical service plans
7011 Hotels and motels
5722 Household appliance stores
3639 Household appliances, nec
3651 Household audio and video equipment
3631 Household cooking equipment
2392 Household furnishings, nec
2519 Household furniture, nec
3632 Household refrigerators and freezers
3635 Household vacuum cleaners

## I

2024 Ice cream and frozen deserts
8322 Individual and family services
5113 Industrial and personal service paper
1541 Industrial buildings and warehouses
3567 Industrial furnaces and ovens
2813 Industrial gases
2819 Industrial inorganic chemicals, nec
7218 Industrial launderers
5084 Industrial machinery and equipment
3599 Industrial machinery, nec
2869 Industrial organic chemicals, nec
1446 Industrial sand
5085 Industrial supplies
3537 Industrial trucks and tractors
3491 Industrial valves
7375 Information retrieval services
2816 Inorganic pigments
4785 Inspection and fixed facilities
1796 Installing building equipment
3825 Instruments to measure electricity
6411 Insurance agents, brokers, and service
3519 Internal combustion engines, nec
6282 Investment advice
6726 Investment offices, nec
6799 Investors, nec
3462 Iron and steel forgings
4971 Irrigation systems

## J

3915 Jewelers' materials and lapidary work
5094 Jewelry and precious stones
5944 Jewelry stores
3911 Jewelry, precious metal
8331 Job training and related services

## K

1455 Kaolin and ball clay
2253 Knit outerwear mills
2259 Knitting mills, nec

## L

3821 Laboratory apparatus and furniture
3083 Laminated plastics plate and sheet
0781 Landscape counseling and planning
3524 Lawn and garden equipment
0782 Lawn and garden services
3952 Lead pencils and art goods
2386 Leather and sheep-lined clothing
3199 Leather goods, nec
3111 Leather tanning and finishing
8111 Legal services
8231 Libraries
3648 Lighting equipment, nec
3274 Lime
7213 Linen supply
5921 Liquor stores
0751 Livestock services, except veterinary
6163 Loan brokers
4111 Local and suburban transit
4119 Local passenger transportation, nec
4212 Local trucking, without storage
2411 Logging
2992 Lubricating oils and greases
3161 Luggage
5211 Lumber and other building materials
5031 Lumber, plywood, and millwork

## M

2098 Macaroni and spaghetti
3545 Machine tool accessories
3541 Machine tools, metal cutting type
3542 Machine tools, metal forming type
3695 Magnetic and optical recording media
3322 Malleable iron foundries
2083 Malt
2082 Malt beverages
8742 Management consulting services
6722 Management investment, open-ended
8741 Management services
2761 Manifold business forms
2097 Manufactured ice
3999 Manufacturing industries, nec
4491 Marine cargo handling
3953 Marking devices
2515 Mattresses and bedsprings
3829 Measuring and controlling devices, nec
5421 Meat and fish markets
2011 Meat packing plants
5147 Meats and meat products
3061 Mechanical rubber goods
5047 Medical and hospital equipment
8071 Medical laboratories
2833 Medicinals and botanicals
8699 Membership organizations, nec
7997 Membership sports and recreation clubs
5136 Men's and boy's clothing
2329 Men's and boy's clothing, nec
2321 Men's and boy's furnishings
2323 Men's and boy's neckwear
2311 Men's and boy's suits and coats
2325 Men's and boy's trousers and slacks
2326 Men's and boy's work clothing
3143 Men's footwear, except athletic
3412 Metal barrels, drums, and pails
3411 Metal cans
3479 Metal coating and allied services
3442 Metal doors, sash, and trim
3398 Metal heat treating
2514 Metal household furniture
1081 Metal mining services
1099 Metal ores, nec
3431 Metal sanitary ware
3469 Metal stampings, nec
5051 Metals service centers and offices
3549 Metalworking machinery, nec
2431 Millwork
3296 Mineral wool
3295 Minerals, ground or treated
3532 Mining machinery
5699 Miscellaneous apparel and accessories
3496 Miscellaneous fabricated wire products
5499 Miscellaneous food stores
5719 Miscellaneous homefurnishings

# SIC INDEX

3449 Miscellaneous metalwork
1499 Miscellaneous nonmetallic mining
7299 Miscellaneous personal services
2741 Miscellaneous publishing
5999 Miscellaneous retail stores, nec
2451 Mobile homes
6162 Mortgage bankers and correspondents
7812 Motion picture and video production
3716 Motor homes
3714 Motor vehicle parts and accessories
5013 Motor vehicle supplies and new parts
3711 Motor vehicles and car bodies
5571 Motorcycle dealers
3751 Motorcycles, bicycles, and parts
3621 Motors and generators
5736 Musical instrument stores
3931 Musical instruments

## N

2441 Nailed wood boxes and shook
2241 Narrow fabric mills
1321 Natural gas liquids
5511 New and used car dealers
5994 News dealers and newsstands
7383 News syndicates
2711 Newspapers
2873 Nitrogenous fertilizers
8733 Noncommercial research organizations
3644 Noncurrent-carrying wiring devices
5199 Nondurable goods, nec
3364 Nonferrous die-castings except aluminum
3463 Nonferrous forgings
3369 Nonferrous foundries, nec
3356 Nonferrous rolling and drawing, nec
3357 Nonferrous wiredrawing and insulating
3299 Nonmetallic mineral products,
1481 Nonmetallic mineral services
6512 Nonresidential building operators
1542 Nonresidential construction, nec
2297 Nonwoven fabrics

## O

5044 Office equipment
2522 Office furniture, except wood
3579 Office machines, nec
8011 Offices and clinics of medical doctors
8042 Offices and clinics of optometrists
1382 Oil and gas exploration services
3533 Oil and gas field machinery
1389 Oil and gas field services, nec
1531 Operative builders
3851 Ophthalmic goods
5048 Ophthalmic goods
5995 Optical goods stores
3827 Optical instruments and lenses
3489 Ordnance and accessories, nec
2824 Organic fibers, noncellulosic
0181 Ornamental nursery products
0783 Ornamental shrub and tree services
7312 Outdoor advertising services

## P

5142 Packaged frozen goods
3565 Packaging machinery
4783 Packing and crating
5231 Paint, glass, and wallpaper stores
1721 Painting and paper hanging
2851 Paints and allied products
5198 Paints, varnishes, and supplies
3554 Paper industries machinery
2621 Paper mills
2671 Paper; coated and laminated packaging
2672 Paper; coated and laminated, nec
2631 Paperboard mills
2542 Partitions and fixtures, except wood
6794 Patent owners and lessors
3951 Pens and mechanical pencils
2721 Periodicals
3172 Personal leather goods, nec
2999 Petroleum and coal products, nec
5172 Petroleum products, nec
2911 Petroleum refining

2834 Pharmaceutical preparations
7334 Photocopying and duplicating services
3861 Photographic equipment and supplies
5043 Photographic equipment and supplies
7221 Photographic studios, portrait
2035 Pickles, sauces, and salad dressings
5131 Piece goods and notions
1742 Plastering, drywall, and insulation
3085 Plastics bottles
3086 Plastics foam products
5162 Plastics materials and basic shapes
2821 Plastics materials and resins
3084 Plastics pipe
3088 Plastics plumbing fixtures
3089 Plastics products, nec
2796 Platemaking services
3471 Plating and polishing
2395 Pleating and stitching
5074 Plumbing and hydronic heating supplies
3432 Plumbing fixture fittings and trim
1711 Plumbing, heating, air-conditioning
2842 Polishes and sanitation goods
3264 Porcelain electrical supplies
1474 Potash, soda, and borate minerals
2096 Potato chips and similar snacks
3269 Pottery products, nec
5144 Poultry and poultry products
0254 Poultry hatcheries
2015 Poultry slaughtering and processing
3568 Power transmission equipment, nec
3546 Power-driven handtools
3448 Prefabricated metal buildings
2452 Prefabricated wood buildings
7372 Prepackaged software
2048 Prepared feeds, nec
2045 Prepared flour mixes and doughs
3652 Prerecorded records and tapes
3229 Pressed and blown glass, nec
3334 Primary aluminum
3692 Primary batteries, dry and wet
3331 Primary copper
3399 Primary metal products
3339 Primary nonferrous metals, nec
3672 Printed circuit boards
2893 Printing ink
3555 Printing trades machinery
3823 Process control instruments
3231 Products of purchased glass
5049 Professional equipment, nec
2531 Public building and related furniture
7992 Public golf courses
8743 Public relations services
2611 Pulp mills
3561 Pumps and pumping equipment

## R

7948 Racing, including track operation
3663 Radio and t.v. communications equipment
7622 Radio and television repair
4832 Radio broadcasting stations
5731 Radio, television, and electronic stores
7313 Radio, television, publisher representatives
4812 Radiotelephone communication
3743 Railroad equipment
2061 Raw cane sugar
3273 Ready-mixed concrete
6531 Real estate agents and managers
2493 Reconstituted wood products
4222 Refrigerated warehousing and storage
3585 Refrigeration and heating equipment
5078 Refrigeration equipment and supplies
7623 Refrigeration service and repair
4953 Refuse systems
3625 Relays and industrial controls
8661 Religious organizations
7699 Repair services, nec
8361 Residential care
3645 Residential lighting fixtures
5461 Retail bakeries
5261 Retail nurseries and garden stores
7641 Reupholstery and furniture repair
2044 Rice milling

2095 Roasted coffee
2384 Robes and dressing gowns
3547 Rolling mill machinery
5033 Roofing, siding, and insulation
1761 Roofing, siding, and sheetmetal work
3021 Rubber and plastics footwear
3052 Rubber and plastics hose and beltings

## S

2068 Salted and roasted nuts and seeds
2656 Sanitary food containers
2676 Sanitary paper products
4959 Sanitary services, nec
2013 Sausages and other prepared meats
3425 Saw blades and handsaws
2421 Sawmills and planing mills, general
3596 Scales and balances, except laboratory
8299 Schools and educational services
5093 Scrap and waste materials
3451 Screw machine products
3812 Search and navigation equipment
3341 Secondary nonferrous metals
7338 Secretarial and court reporting
6211 Security brokers and dealers
7382 Security systems services
3674 Semiconductors and related devices
3263 Semivitreous table and kitchenware
5087 Service establishment equipment
3589 Service industry machinery, nec
7819 Services allied to motion pictures
8999 Services, nec
2652 Setup paperboard boxes
4952 Sewerage systems
5949 Sewing, needlework, and piece goods
3444 Sheet metalwork
3731 Shipbuilding and repairing
5661 Shoe stores
3993 Signs and advertising specialties
3914 Silverware and plated ware
1521 Single-family housing construction
3484 Small arms
2841 Soap and other detergents
3764 Space propulsion units and parts
3769 Space vehicle equipment, nec
3544 Special dies, tools, jigs, and fixtures
3559 Special industry machinery, nec
2429 Special product sawmills
1799 Special trade contractors, nec
4226 Special warehousing and storage, nec
8093 Specialty outpatient clinics, nec
3566 Speed changers, drives, and gears
3949 Sporting and athletic goods, nec
5091 Sporting and recreation goods
5941 Sporting goods and bicycle shops
5112 Stationery and office supplies
2678 Stationery products
5943 Stationery stores
3325 Steel foundries, nec
3324 Steel investment foundries
3317 Steel pipe and tubes
3493 Steel springs, except wire
3315 Steel wire and related products
3691 Storage batteries
3259 Structural clay products, nec
1791 Structural steel erection
2439 Structural wood members, nec
2843 Surface active agents
3841 Surgical and medical instruments
3842 Surgical appliances and supplies
3613 Switchgear and switchboard apparatus
2822 Synthetic rubber

## T

3795 Tanks and tank components
3661 Telephone and telegraph apparatus
4813 Telephone communication, except radio
4833 Television broadcasting stations
1743 Terrazzo, tile, marble, mosaic work
8734 Testing laboratories
2393 Textile bags
2299 Textile goods, nec
3552 Textile machinery

# SIC INDEX
## Manufacturers Directory

7922 Theatrical producers and services
2284 Thread mills
2296 Tire cord and fabrics
7534 Tire retreading and repair shops
3011 Tires and inner tubes
5014 Tires and tubes
5993 Tobacco stores and stands
2844 Toilet preparations
7532 Top and body repair and paint shops
4725 Tour operators
5092 Toys and hobby goods and supplies
7033 Trailer parks and campsites
3612 Transformers, except electric
5088 Transportation equipment and supplies
3799 Transportation equipment, nec
4724 Travel agencies
3792 Travel trailers and campers
0173 Tree nuts
3713 Truck and bus bodies
3715 Truck trailers
3511 Turbines and turbine generator sets
2791 Typesetting

## U

3081 Unsupported plastics film and sheet
3082 Unsupported plastics profile shapes
2512 Upholstered household furniture
5932 Used merchandise stores

## V

3494 Valves and pipe fittings, nec
2076 Vegetable oil mills, nec
0161 Vegetables and melons
3647 Vehicular lighting equipment
3262 Vitreous china table and kitchenware
3261 Vitreous plumbing fixtures
8249 Vocational schools, nec

## W

5075 Warm air heating and air conditioning
3873 Watches, clocks, watchcases, and parts
4941 Water supply
4499 Water transportation services, nec
1781 Water well drilling
1623 Water, sewer, and utility lines
2257 Weft knit fabric mills
3548 Welding apparatus
7692 Welding repair
2046 Wet corn milling
5182 Wine and distilled beverages
2084 Wines, brandy, and brandy spirits
3495 Wire springs
5632 Women's accessory and specialty stores
5137 Women's and children's clothing
2341 Women's and children's underwear
2331 Women's and misses' blouses and shirts
2339 Women's and misses' outerwear, nec
2337 Women's and misses' suits and coats
5621 Women's clothing stores
3144 Women's footwear, except athletic
3171 Women's handbags and purses
2335 Women's, junior's, and misses' dresses
2449 Wood containers, nec
2511 Wood household furniture
2434 Wood kitchen cabinets
2521 Wood office furniture
2448 Wood pallets and skids
2541 Wood partitions and fixtures
2491 Wood preserving
2499 Wood products, nec
2517 Wood television and radio cabinets
3553 Woodworking machinery

## X

3844 X-ray apparatus and tubes

## Y

2281 Yarn spinning mills

# PRODUCTS & SERVICES SECTION

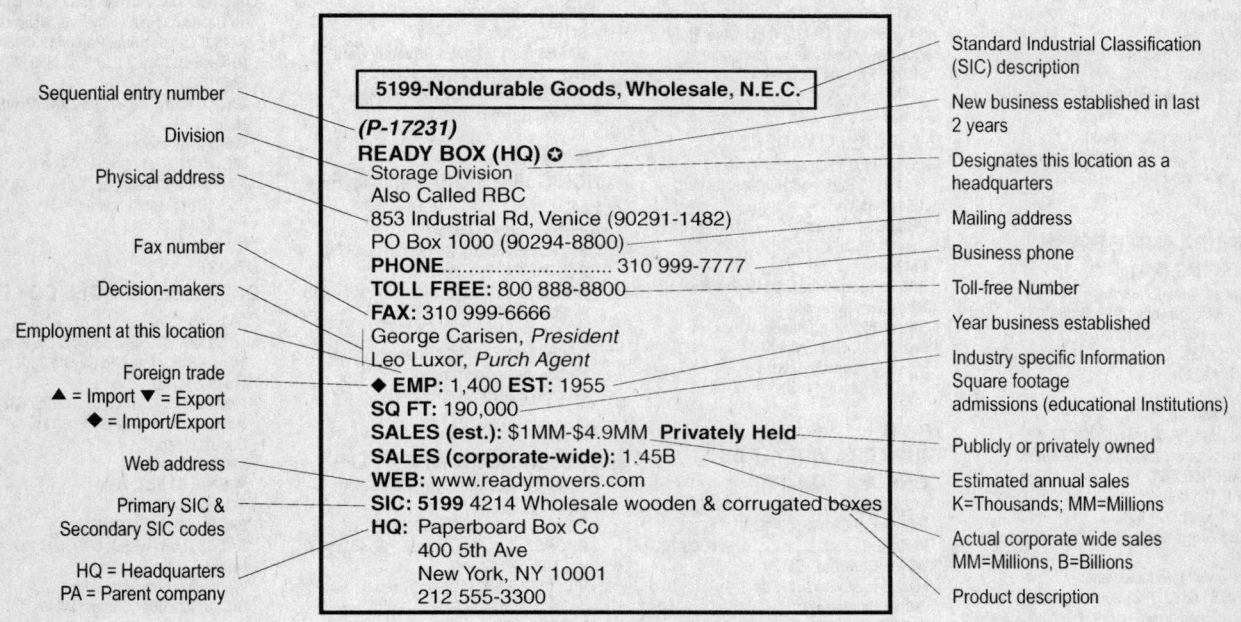

- Companies in this section are listed numerically under their primary SIC Companies are in alphabetical order under each code.
- A numerical and alphabetical index precedes this section.
- **Sequential Entry Numbers.** Each establishment in this section is numbered sequentially. The number assigned to each establishment's Entry Number. To make cross-referencing easier, each listing in the Product's & Services, Alphabetic and Geographical Section includes the establishment's entry number. To facilitate locating an entry in this section, the entry numbers for the first listing on the left page and the last listing on the right page are printed at the top of the page next to the Standard Industrial Classification (SIC) description.
- Further information can be found in the Explanatory Notes starting on page 5.
- See the footnotes for symbols and abbreviations.

**IMPORTANT NOTICE:** It is a violation of both federal and state law to transmit an unsolicited advertisement to a facsimile machine. Any user of this product that violates such laws may be subject to civil and criminal penalties which may exceed $500 for each transmission of an unsolicited facsimile. Harris InfoSource provides fax numbers for lawful purposes only and expressly forbids the use of these numbers in any unlawful manner.

---

### 0131 Cotton

**(P-1)**
**OLAM LLC**
Also Called: Olam Food Ingredients
205 E River Park Cir Ste 310, Fresno (93720-1572)
PHONE.....................559 446-6420
Sandip Sharma, *Pr*
**EMP:** 50 **EST:** 2007
**SALES (est)** 10.55MM **Privately Held**
Web: www.olamgroup.com
**SIC: 0131** 0722 0182 2281  Cotton; Peanuts, machine harvesting services; Tomatoes, grown under cover; Cotton yarn, spun

### 0139 Field Crops, Except Cash Grain

**(P-2)**
**GARLIC COMPANY (PA)**
18602 Zerker Rd, Shafter (93263-9101)
PHONE.............................661 393-4212
John Layous, *Mng Pt*
Joe Lane, *
◆ **EMP:** 80 **EST:** 1980
**SQ FT:** 150,000
**SALES (est):** 158.69MM
**SALES (corp-wide):** 158.69MM **Privately Held**
Web: www.thegarliccompany.com
**SIC: 0139** 2099 0191  Herb or spice farm; Food preparations, nec; General farms, primarily crop

**(P-3)**
**GRUPO FLOR CORPORATION**
514 Work St, Salinas (93901-4350)
PHONE..............................559 940-1070
Gavin Kogan, *Prin*
**EMP:** 86 **EST:** 2016
**SALES (est):** 3.9MM **Privately Held**
Web: www.grupoflor.com
**SIC: 0139** 3999 5159

**(P-4)**
**PAX LABS INC**
660 Alabama St Ste 2, San Francisco (94110-2190)
PHONE..............................415 829-2336
Michael Murphy, *Pr*
**EMP:** 175 **EST:** 2017
**SALES (est):** 9.49MM **Privately Held**
Web: www.paxvapor.com
**SIC: 0139** 3999

### 0161 Vegetables And Melons

**(P-5)**
**GENERIS HOLDINGS LP (PA)**
7200 E Brundage Ln, Bakersfield (93307-3016)
PHONE..............................661 366-7209
Jeffrey Dunn, *CEO*
**EMP:** 247 **EST:** 2019
**SALES (est):** 562.6MM
**SALES (corp-wide):** 562.6MM **Privately Held**
Web: www.bolthouse.com
**SIC: 0161** 2037 2033 2099  Carrot farm; Fruit juices; Vegetable juices: packaged in cans, jars, etc.; Sauce, gravy, dressing, and dip mixes

**(P-6)**
**MERRILL FARMS LLC (PA)**
18900 Portola Dr Ste 100, Salinas (93908-1268)

## 0161 - Vegetables And Melons (P-7)

P.O. Box 659 (93902-0659)
PHONE.............................831 424-7365
Lauren Merrill, *
Glen Dupree, *
**EMP:** 31 **EST:** 1933
**SALES (est):** 9.49MM
**SALES (corp-wide):** 9.49MM **Privately Held**
Web: www.merrillfarms.com
**SIC:** 0161 2097 Vegetables and melons; Manufactured ice

**(P-7)**
**TANIMURA ANTLE FRESH FOODS INC (PA)**
Also Called: Tanimura & Antle
1 Harris Rd, Salinas (93908-8608)
P.O. Box 4070 (93912-4070)
PHONE.............................831 455-2950
Rick Antle, *Pr*
Mike Antle, *
Robert Nielsen, *
Steve Bassi, *FARM PRODUCTION**
Carmen Ponce, *Land Vice President**
◆ **EMP:** 100 **EST:** 1982
**SQ FT:** 135,000
**SALES (est):** 321.47MM
**SALES (corp-wide):** 321.47MM **Privately Held**
Web: www.taproduce.com
**SIC:** 0161 0182 0723 2099 Lettuce farm; Food crops grown under cover; Vegetable packing services; Food preparations, nec

## 0172 Grapes

**(P-8)**
**BABCOCK ENTERPRISES INC**
Also Called: Babcock Vineyards
5175 E Highway 246, Lompoc (93436-9613)
P.O. Box 637 (93438-0637)
PHONE.............................805 736-1455
Bryan Babcock, *Pr*
Walter Babcock, *
Bryan Babcock, *VP*
Mona Babcock, *
**EMP:** 25 **EST:** 1979
**SALES (est):** 2.42MM **Privately Held**
Web: www.babcockwinery.com
**SIC:** 0172 2084 8734 Grapes; Wines; Food testing service

**(P-9)**
**CALIFORNIA WINE COMPANY**
Also Called: Stonegate Winery
2785 Napa Valley Corporate Dr, Napa (94558-6216)
PHONE.............................707 603-2203
Paul Croft, *Pr*
**EMP:** 24 **EST:** 1980
**SALES (est):** 178.16K **Privately Held**
**SIC:** 0172 2084 Grapes; Wines

**(P-10)**
**DAVE J MENDRIN INC**
4876 W Athens Ave, Fresno (93722-2119)
PHONE.............................559 352-1700
Jack Mendrin, *Pr*
**EMP:** 18 **EST:** 1991
**SALES (est):** 1.07MM **Privately Held**
**SIC:** 0172 2034 Grapes; Raisins

**(P-11)**
**DOMAINE CARNEROS LTD**
1240 Duhig Rd, Napa (94559-9713)
P.O. Box P O Box 5420 (94581-0420)
PHONE.............................707 257-0101
Eileen Crane, *

Robert Aldridge, *Prin*
◆ **EMP:** 80 **EST:** 1986
**SQ FT:** 50,000
**SALES (est):** 19.77MM **Privately Held**
Web: www.domainecarneros.com
**SIC:** 0172 2084 Grapes; Wines

**(P-12)**
**E & J GALLO WINERY**
Also Called: J Vineyards & Winery
11447 Old Redwood Hwy, Healdsburg (95448-9523)
PHONE.............................707 431-5400
Joseph Gallo, *CEO*
**EMP:** 15
**SALES (corp-wide):** 2.11B **Privately Held**
Web: www.jwine.com
**SIC:** 0172 2084 Grapes; Wines
**PA:** E. & J. Gallo Winery
600 Yosemite Blvd
209 341-3111

**(P-13)**
**GIUMARRA VINEYARDS CORPORATION (PA)**
11220 Edison Hwy, Edison (93220)
P.O. Box 1969 (93303-1969)
PHONE.............................661 395-7000
Wayne Childress, *CEO*
Mimi Corsaro-dorsey, *Sec*
Jeffrey Giumarra, *
◆ **EMP:** 500 **EST:** 1946
**SQ FT:** 10,000
**SALES (est):** 72.36MM
**SALES (corp-wide):** 72.36MM **Privately Held**
Web: www.giumarravineyards.com
**SIC:** 0172 2084 2086 Grapes; Wines; Fruit drinks (less than 100% juice): packaged in cans, etc.

**(P-14)**
**GOLDEN STATE VINTNERS**
Also Called: Golden State Winery
7409 W Central Ave, Fresno (93706-9449)
PHONE.............................559 266-6548
John Stout, *Brnch Mgr*
**EMP:** 38
**SALES (corp-wide):** 79.06K **Privately Held**
**SIC:** 0172 2084 Grapes; Wines
**PA:** Golden State Vintners
4596 S Tracy Blvd
707 254-4900

**(P-15)**
**GROTH VINEYARDS AND WINERY**
750 Oakville Cross Rd, Oakville (94562)
P.O. Box 390 (94562-0390)
PHONE.............................707 944-0290
Dennis Groth, *Managing Member*
Judith Groth, *
Christina Appleby, *
◆ **EMP:** 27 **EST:** 1982
**SQ FT:** 50,000
**SALES (est):** 4.76MM **Privately Held**
Web: www.grothwines.com
**SIC:** 0172 2084 Grapes; Wines

**(P-16)**
**GUGLIELMO EMILO WINERY INC**
Also Called: Emile's Table Wines
1480 E Main Ave, Morgan Hill (95037-3201)
PHONE.............................408 779-2145
George E Guglielmo, *Pr*
Madeline Guglielmo, *VP*
Eugene R Guglielmo, *Sec*

Gary J Guglielmo, *Treas*
Julie Bradford, *CFO*
**EMP:** 15 **EST:** 1925
**SQ FT:** 56,000
**SALES (est):** 2.44MM **Privately Held**
Web: www.guglielmowinery.com
**SIC:** 0172 2084 5921 7999 Grapes; Wines; Wine; Recreation center

**(P-17)**
**HONIG VINEYARD AND WINERY LLC**
Also Called: Honig Cellars
850 Rutherford Rd, Rutherford (94573)
P.O. Box 406 (94573-0406)
PHONE.............................707 963-5618
▲ **EMP:** 20 **EST:** 1982
**SQ FT:** 8,000
**SALES (est):** 7.43MM **Privately Held**
Web: www.honigwine.com
**SIC:** 0172 2084 Grapes; Wines

**(P-18)**
**J VINEYARDS & WINERY LP**
11447 Old Redwood Hwy, Healdsburg (95448)
P.O. Box 6009 (95448-6009)
PHONE.............................707 431-5400
▲ **EMP:** 52
**SIC:** 0172 2084 Grapes; Wines

**(P-19)**
**KLEIN FOODS INC**
Also Called: Rodney Strong Vineyards
11455 Old Redwood Hwy, Healdsburg (95448)
P.O. Box 6010 (95448)
PHONE.............................707 431-1533
Thomas B Klein, *Pr*
Tobin Ginter, *
◆ **EMP:** 100 **EST:** 1988
**SQ FT:** 20,000
**SALES (est):** 24.37MM **Privately Held**
Web: www.rodneystrong.com
**SIC:** 0172 2084 5182 Grapes; Wines; Wine and distilled beverages

**(P-20)**
**KVL HOLDINGS INC (PA)**
Also Called: Saint Nicolas Vineyard
37700 Foothill Rd, Soledad (93960-9620)
P.O. Box C (93960-0167)
PHONE.............................831 678-2132
Nicholaus Hahn, *CEO*
**EMP:** 50 **EST:** 1980
**SQ FT:** 30,000
**SALES (est):** 7.17MM
**SALES (corp-wide):** 7.17MM **Privately Held**
Web: www.hahnwines.com
**SIC:** 0172 2084 6719 Grapes; Wines; Investment holding companies, except banks

**(P-21)**
**MATCHBOOK WINE COMPANY**
12300 Co. Road 92b, Zamora (95698)
P.O. Box 493 (95698-0493)
PHONE.............................530 662-1032
Lane Giguiere, *Owner*
**EMP:** 32 **EST:** 2018
**SALES (est):** 2.35MM **Privately Held**
Web: www.matchbookwines.com
**SIC:** 0172 0762 2084 Grapes; Vineyard management and maintenance services; Wine cellars, bonded: engaged in blending wines

**(P-22)**
**ONEILL BEVERAGES CO LLC**
Also Called: O'Neill Vintners & Distillers
8418 S Lac Jac Ave, Parlier (93648-9708)
PHONE.............................559 638-3544
**EMP:** 200
**SALES (est):** 89.03MM **Privately Held**
Web: www.oneillwine.com
**SIC:** 0172 2084 Grapes; Wines
**PA:** O'neill Beverages Co. Llc
101 Lrkspur Lnding Cir St
559 638-3544

**(P-23)**
**ONEILL BEVERAGES CO LLC (PA)**
Also Called: O'Neill Vintners & Distillers
101 Larkspur Landing Cir Ste 350, Larkspur (94939-1749)
PHONE.............................559 638-3544
Jeffrey B O'Neill, *CEO*
Donald Heer, *
Matthew Towers, *
◆ **EMP:** 63 **EST:** 2004
**SQ FT:** 5,000
**SALES (est):** 89.03MM
**SALES (corp-wide):** 89.03MM **Privately Held**
Web: www.oneillwine.com
**SIC:** 0172 2084 Grapes; Wines

**(P-24)**
**R & G SCHATZ FARMS INC**
Also Called: Peltier Winery
22150 N Kennefick Rd, Acampo (95220-9242)
PHONE.............................209 367-4881
Rodney Schatz, *Pr*
Gayla Schatz, *CFO*
▲ **EMP:** 15 **EST:** 1986
**SQ FT:** 6,802
**SALES (est):** 1.77MM **Privately Held**
Web: www.peltierwinery.com
**SIC:** 0172 2084 Grapes; Wines

**(P-25)**
**RAYMOND VINEYARD & CELLAR INC (DH)**
Also Called: Healdsburg Wine Co.
849 Zinfandel Ln, Saint Helena (94574-1645)
PHONE.............................707 963-3141
Alain Leonnet, *CEO*
Jean C Boisset, *
Phil Marquand, *
▲ **EMP:** 26 **EST:** 1971
**SQ FT:** 70,000
**SALES (est):** 6.86MM **Privately Held**
Web: www.raymondvineyards.com
**SIC:** 0172 2084 Grapes; Wines
**HQ:** Jean-Claude Boisset Wines U.S.A., Inc.
849 Zinfandel Ln
Saint Helena CA 94574
707 963-6913

**(P-26)**
**RENZONI VINEYARDS INC**
Also Called: Robert Rnzoni Vineyards Winery
37350 De Portola Rd, Temecula (92592-9024)
PHONE.............................951 302-8466
Robert Renzoni, *Pr*
Fred Renzoni, *
▲ **EMP:** 37 **EST:** 2007
**SALES (est):** 2.03MM **Privately Held**
Web: www.robertrenzonivineyards.com
**SIC:** 0172 2084 Grapes; Wines

## PRODUCTS & SERVICES SECTION
### 0179 - Fruits And Tree Nuts, Nec (P-46)

**(P-27)**
**ROEDERER ESTATE INC**
Also Called: Roederer Estate Winery
4501 Highway 128, Philo (95466)
P.O. Box 67 (95466-0067)
PHONE.............................707 895-2288
Gregory Balogh, *CEO*
▲ **EMP:** 18 **EST:** 1982
**SALES (est):** 2.4MM **Privately Held**
Web: www.roedererestate.com
**SIC: 0172** 2084 Grapes; Wines
HQ: Mendocino Land Company, Inc.
383 4th St Ste 400
Oakland CA 94607
510 286-2000

**(P-28)**
**SAN BERNABE VINEYARDS**
53001 Oasis Rd, King City (93930-9667)
PHONE.............................831 385-4897
Claude Hoover, *Pr*
Dorothy Indelicato, *
Frank Indelicato, *
**EMP:** 24 **EST:** 1988
**SQ FT:** 15,000
**SALES (est):** 2.15MM
**SALES (corp-wide):** 498.29MM **Privately Held**
**SIC: 0172** 2084 Grapes; Wines, brandy, and brandy spirits
PA: Delicato Vineyards, Llc
12001 S Highway 99
209 824-3600

**(P-29)**
**SCHEID VINEYARDS INC (PA)**
Also Called: Scheid Family Wines
305 Hilltown Rd, Salinas (93908-8902)
PHONE.............................831 455-9990
Scott D Scheid, *Pr*
Alfred G Scheid, *
Heidi M Scheid, *
Kurt J Gollnick, *
Michael S Thomsen, *
**EMP:** 96 **EST:** 1997
**SQ FT:** 6,700
**SALES (est):** 54.23MM
**SALES (corp-wide):** 54.23MM **Publicly Held**
Web: www.scheidvineyards.com
**SIC: 0172** 2084 Grapes; Wines

**(P-30)**
**SCHRAMSBERG VINEYARDS COMPANY**
1400 Schramsberg Rd, Calistoga (94515-9624)
PHONE.............................707 942-4558
Hugh Davies, *Pr*
▲ **EMP:** 50 **EST:** 1965
**SQ FT:** 20,000
**SALES (est):** 10.14MM **Privately Held**
Web: www.schramsberg.com
**SIC: 0172** 2084 Grapes; Wines

**(P-31)**
**SONOMA-CUTRER VINEYARDS LLC (DH)**
4401 Slusser Rd, Windsor (95492-7601)
P.O. Box 9 (95439-0009)
PHONE.............................707 528-1181
Steve Dorfman, *Pr*
David Perata, *
◆ **EMP:** 50 **EST:** 1973
**SALES (est):** 22.65MM
**SALES (corp-wide):** 405.48MM **Publicly Held**
Web: www.sonomacutrer.com
**SIC: 0172** 2084 5921 Grapes; Wines; Liquor stores

HQ: The Duckhorn Portfolio Inc
1201 Dowdell Ln
Saint Helena CA 94574
707 302-2658

**(P-32)**
**TOPOLOS AT RSSIAN RIVER VINYRD**
Also Called: Russian River Vineyards
5700 Hwy 116, Forestville (95436-9393)
P.O. Box 920 (95436-0920)
PHONE.............................707 887-1575
Michael Topolos, *CEO*
Jerry Topolos, *Pt*
Christine Topolos, *Pt*
**EMP:** 25 **EST:** 1978
**SQ FT:** 2,000
**SALES (est):** 2.31MM **Privately Held**
Web: www.russianrivervineyards.com
**SIC: 0172** 2084 5813 5812 Grapes; Wines; Beer garden (drinking places); American restaurant

**(P-33)**
**TREASURY WINE ESTATES AMERICAS**
Also Called: Meridian Vineyards
7000 E Highway 46, Paso Robles (93446-7390)
P.O. Box 3289 (93447-3289)
PHONE.............................805 237-6000
Jim Schaefer, *Mgr*
**EMP:** 27
Web: www.treasurywineestates.com
**SIC: 0172** 2084 Grapes; Wines, brandy, and brandy spirits
HQ: Treasury Wine Estates Americas Company
555 Gateway Dr
Napa CA 94558
707 259-4500

**(P-34)**
**VIRGINIA SARABIAN**
Also Called: Sarabian Farms
2816 S Leonard Ave, Sanger (93657-9754)
PHONE.............................559 493-2900
Virginia Sarabian, *Owner*
Michael Sarabian, *
Sarkis Sarabian, *
**EMP:** 50 **EST:** 1956
**SQ FT:** 1,200
**SALES (est):** 4.85MM **Privately Held**
Web: www.sarabianfarms.com
**SIC: 0172** 4222 2033 0175 Grapes; Warehousing, cold storage or refrigerated; Fruits: packaged in cans, jars, etc.; Nectarine orchard

### 0173 Tree Nuts

**(P-35)**
**AGRESERVES INC**
Also Called: Deseret Farms of California
6100 Wilson Landing Rd, Chico (95973-8902)
PHONE.............................530 343-5365
Travis Reid, *Brnch Mgr*
**EMP:** 20
**SALES (corp-wide):** 4.54B **Privately Held**
Web: www.agreserves.com
**SIC: 0175** 0175 2096 Almond grove; Prune orchard; Cheese curls and puffs
HQ: Agreserves, Inc.
60 E South Temple # 1600
Salt Lake City UT 84111

**(P-36)**
**BATTH FARMS INC**
Also Called: Batth Farms
5434 W Kamm Ave, Caruthers (93609-9400)
PHONE.............................559 864-9421
Charanjit Singh Batth, *CEO*
**EMP:** 90 **EST:** 1969
**SQ FT:** 1,200
**SALES (est):** 9.76MM **Privately Held**
Web: www.batthfarms.com
**SIC: 0173** 0175 0172 2034 Almond grove; Prune orchard; Grapes; Raisins

**(P-37)**
**BAUGHER RANCH ORGANICS INC**
7030 County Road 25, Orland (95963-9719)
PHONE.............................530 865-4015
Nisha Carrow, *CEO*
Kelsey Hatcher, *COO*
Rania Heaney, *Dir Opers*
Ron Lautrup, *Business Relations*
Spencer Dykstra, *Opers Mgr*
▼ **EMP:** 40 **EST:** 1984
**SQ FT:** 45,000
**SALES (est):** 1.2MM **Privately Held**
Web: www.baugherranchorganics.com
**SIC: 0173** 2068 Almond grove; Nuts: dried, dehydrated, salted or roasted

**(P-38)**
**BENTON ENTERPRISES LLC**
Also Called: Elk Ridge Almonds
18252 Avenue 20, Madera (93637-9730)
P.O. Box 417 (93639-0417)
PHONE.............................559 664-0800
William B Pittmann, *Managing Member*
**EMP:** 30 **EST:** 2015
**SALES (est):** 2.24MM **Privately Held**
Web: www.elkridgealmonds.com
**SIC: 0173** 2068 5441 Tree nuts; Salted and roasted nuts and seeds; Nuts

**(P-39)**
**KEENAN FARMS INC**
31510 Plymouth Ave, Kettleman City (93239-9721)
P.O. Box 99 (93204-0099)
PHONE.............................559 945-1400
Robert M Keenan, *CEO*
Charles J Keenan Iii, *VP*
Mitchell Keenan, *
◆ **EMP:** 100 **EST:** 1972
**SALES (est):** 9.71MM **Privately Held**
Web: www.keenanfarms.com
**SIC: 0173** 2068 Pistachio grove; Nuts: dried, dehydrated, salted or roasted

**(P-40)**
**MONTE VISTA FARMING CO LLC**
5043 N Montpelier Rd, Denair (95316-9608)
P.O. Box 579 (95316-0579)
PHONE.............................209 874-1866
Jonathan Hoff, *CEO*
◆ **EMP:** 35 **EST:** 2014
**SALES (est):** 5.16MM **Privately Held**
Web: www.montevistafarming.com
**SIC: 0173** 0723 2034 Almond grove; Tree nut crops market preparation services; Dried and dehydrated fruits

**(P-41)**
**RIDDLE RANCHES INC**
Also Called: Waterford Almond Hller Sheller
12013 El Pomar Ave, Waterford (95386-9735)
PHONE.............................209 874-9784

Robert Riddle, *Pr*
Pamela Riddle Machado, *Sec*
Lane M Riddle, *VP*
**EMP:** 20 **EST:** 1967
**SALES (est):** 893.61K **Privately Held**
**SIC: 0173** 0175 2068 Almond grove; Peach orchard; Nuts: dried, dehydrated, salted or roasted

### 0174 Citrus Fruits

**(P-42)**
**WONDERFUL COMPANY LLC**
Also Called: Paramount Citrus
1901 S Lexington St, Delano (93215-9207)
PHONE.............................661 720-2400
Freddie Hernandez, *Mgr*
**EMP:** 273
**SALES (corp-wide):** 2.04B **Privately Held**
Web: www.wonderful.com
**SIC: 0174** 3911 Citrus fruits; Jewelry, precious metal
PA: The Wonderful Company Llc
11444 W Olympic Blvd Fl 1
310 966-5700

### 0175 Deciduous Tree Fruits

**(P-43)**
**MIKE JENSEN FARMS LLC**
13138 S Bethel Ave, Kingsburg (93631-9216)
PHONE.............................559 897-4192
**EMP:** 200 **EST:** 1984
**SQ FT:** 14,000
**SALES (est):** 3.04MM **Privately Held**
Web: www.hmcfarms.com
**SIC: 0175** 2033 2099 Apricot orchard; Fruits: packaged in cans, jars, etc.; Food preparations, nec

### 0179 Fruits And Tree Nuts, Nec

**(P-44)**
**DOLE FOOD COMPANY INC**
Also Called: Dole Food
639 Sanborn Pl, Salinas (93901-4517)
P.O. Box 1759 (93902-1759)
PHONE.............................831 422-8871
Lawrence Kern, *Prin*
**EMP:** 17
Web: www.dole.com
**SIC: 0179** 0174 0175 0161 Pineapple farm; Citrus fruits; Deciduous tree fruits; Lettuce farm
HQ: Dole Food Company, Inc.
200 S Tyron St Ste 600
Charlotte NC 28202
818 874-4000

**(P-45)**
**DOLE HOLDING COMPANY LLC**
1 Dole Dr, Westlake Village (91362-7300)
PHONE.............................818 879-6600
David H Murdock, *Ch Bd*
**EMP:** 74999 **EST:** 2004
**SALES (est):** 443.07K **Privately Held**
**SIC: 0179** 0174 0175 0161 Pineapple farm; Citrus fruits; Deciduous tree fruits; Lettuce farm
PA: Dhm Holding Company, Inc.
One Dole Drive

**(P-46)**
**MUNGER BROS LLC**
Also Called: Munger Farm

# 0181 - Ornamental Nursery Products (P-47)

786 Road 188, Delano (93215-9508)
PHONE..................................661 721-0390
Kewel K Munger, *
▲ EMP: 600 EST: 1998
SQ FT: 50,000
SALES (est): 5.61MM Privately Held
SIC: 0179 2033 Avocado orchard; Canned fruits and specialties

## 0181 Ornamental Nursery Products

**(P-47)**
**FLORAL GIFT HM DECOR INTL INC**
3200 Golf Course Dr Ste B, Ventura (93003-7615)
P.O. Box 2673 (93011-2673)
PHONE..................................818 849-8832
Dolly Ives, CEO
Edwin M Ives, *
▲ EMP: 25 EST: 1973
SALES (est): 762.4K Privately Held
SIC: 0181 3999 Florists' greens, cultivated: growing of; Foliage, artificial and preserved

**(P-48)**
**FRANTZ WHOLESALE NURSERY LLC**
12161 Delaware Rd, Hickman (95323-9602)
PHONE..................................209 874-1459
Mitzi Frantz, *
▲ EMP: 42 EST: 2001
SALES (est): 8.27MM Privately Held
Web: www.frantznursery.com
SIC: 0181 3999 Nursery stock, growing of; Plants, artificial and preserved

**(P-49)**
**HMCLAUSE INC (DH)**
260 Cousteau Pl Ste 210, Davis (95618-5490)
PHONE..................................800 320-4672
Remi Bastien, CEO
Matthew M Johnston, *
Andre Cariou, *
◆ EMP: 133 EST: 1856
SQ FT: 200,000
SALES (est): 69.01MM
SALES (corp-wide): 293.45MM Privately Held
Web: www.hmclause.com
SIC: 0181 3999 Seeds, vegetable: growing of; Seeds, coated or treated, from purchased seeds
HQ: Groupe Limagrain Holding
Biopole Clermont Limagne
Saint-Beauzire 63360
473634000

**(P-50)**
**PLANTEL NURSERIES INC (PA)**
Also Called: Plantel Tranplanting Services
2775 E Clark Ave, Santa Maria (93455-5813)
PHONE..................................805 349-8952
Scott Nicholson, Pr
Les Graulich, Sec
Craig Reade, VP
EMP: 20 EST: 1985
SQ FT: 1,300,000
SALES (est): 2.01MM
SALES (corp-wide): 2.01MM Privately Held
Web: www.plantelnurseries.com
SIC: 0181 5193 3523 Seeds, vegetable: growing of; Nursery stock; Transplanters

**(P-51)**
**TWIN OAKS GROWERS INTL INC**
Also Called: Twin Oaks Growers Intl
1969 Marilyn Ln, San Marcos (92069-9769)
PHONE..................................760 744-5581
Bas Denbraver, Pr
Mady Denbraver, VP
EMP: 20 EST: 1978
SQ FT: 120,000
SALES (est): 2.06MM Privately Held
Web: www.twinoaksgrowers.com
SIC: 0181 3999 Nursery stock, growing of; Plants, artificial and preserved

## 0182 Food Crops Grown Under Cover

**(P-52)**
**MONTEREY MUSHROOMS LLC**
Also Called: Monterey Mushrooms-Morgan Hill
642 Hale Ave, Morgan Hill (95037-9221)
P.O. Box 818 (95038-0818)
PHONE..................................408 779-4191
Clark Smith, Brnch Mgr
EMP: 34
SQ FT: 5,000
SALES (corp-wide): 304.31MM Privately Held
Web: www.montereymushrooms.com
SIC: 0182 2034 Mushrooms, grown under cover; Dried and dehydrated fruits, vegetables and soup mixes
PA: Monterey Mushrooms, Llc
260 Westgate Dr
831 763-5300

## 0191 General Farms, Primarily Crop

**(P-53)**
**BELLA VIVA ORCHARDS INC**
7030 Hughson Ave, Hughson (95326-8014)
P.O. Box 1014 (95326-1014)
PHONE..................................209 883-9015
Cristina Ribeiro, Mgr
EMP: 28
Web: www.bellaviva.com
SIC: 0191 2034 General farms, primarily crop; Dried and dehydrated fruits, vegetables and soup mixes
PA: Viva Bella Orchards Inc
3019 S Quincy Rd

**(P-54)**
**CENTRAL COAST AGRICULTURE INC (PA)**
8701 Santa Rosa Rd, Buellton (93427-8406)
PHONE..................................805 694-8594
Thomas Martin, CEO
EMP: 25 EST: 2015
SALES (est): 21.85MM Privately Held
Web: www.ccagriculture.com
SIC: 0191 2099 General farms, primarily crop; Food preparations, nec

**(P-55)**
**HARRIS FARMS INC (PA)**
Also Called: Harris Ranch Beef Co
29475 Fresno Coalinga Rd, Coalinga (93210-9699)
Rural Route 1 Box 400 (93210-9222)
PHONE..................................559 884-2435
EMP: 200 EST: 1938
SALES (est): 25.71MM
SALES (corp-wide): 25.71MM Privately Held
Web: www.harrisfarms.com
SIC: 0191 0211 2011 7011 General farms, primarily crop; Beef cattle feedlots; Meat packing plants; Hotels

**(P-56)**
**PLENTY UNLIMITED INC (PA)**
570 Eccles Ave, South San Francisco (94080-1905)
PHONE..................................650 735-3737
Matt Barnard, CEO
Nate Storey, CSO
Nick Kalajian, Sr VP
Mike Gupta, CFO
Kurt Kelty, COO
EMP: 74 EST: 2014
SQ FT: 200,000
SALES (est): 99.96MM
SALES (corp-wide): 99.96MM Privately Held
Web: www.plenty.ag
SIC: 0191 2099 General farms, primarily crop; Salads, fresh or refrigerated

**(P-57)**
**SILLS FARMS INC**
Also Called: Pleasant Grove Farms
5072 Pacific Ave, Pleasant Grove (95668-9719)
P.O. Box 636 (95668-0636)
PHONE..................................916 655-3391
Edward M Sills, Pr
Wynette Sills, Sec
Edward M Sills, VP
EMP: 20 EST: 1947
SQ FT: 4,000
SALES (est): 2.21MM Privately Held
Web: www.pleasantgrovefarms.com
SIC: 0191 3523 2099 5153 General farms, primarily crop; Farm machinery and equipment; Food preparations, nec; Grain and field beans

**(P-58)**
**THOMSON INTERNATIONAL INC**
11220 S Vineland Rd, Bakersfield (93307-9489)
PHONE..................................661 845-1111
Jack Thomson, Pr
EMP: 16
SALES (corp-wide): 2.54MM Privately Held
Web: www.thomsoninternational.net
SIC: 0191 2099 0723 0172 General farms, primarily crop; Food preparations, nec; Crop preparation services for market; Grapes
PA: Thomson International, Incorporated
9852 Buena Vista Blvd
661 845-1166

## 0241 Dairy Farms

**(P-59)**
**RAW FARM LLC**
7221 S Jameson Ave, Fresno (93706-9386)
PHONE..................................559 846-9732
Aaron Mcafee, Pr
Mark L Mcafee, Managing Member
EMP: 50 EST: 1998
SALES (est): 2.95MM Privately Held
Web: www.rawfarmusa.com
SIC: 0241 2021 2022 2026 Dairy farms; Creamery butter; Cheese; natural and processed; Milk processing (pasteurizing, homogenizing, bottling)

**(P-60)**
**VALLEY MILK LLC**
400 N Washington Rd, Turlock (95380-9550)
PHONE..................................209 410-6701
Donald A Machado, Managing Member
▼ EMP: 65 EST: 2016
SALES (est): 2.09MM Privately Held
Web: www.valleymilkca.com
SIC: 0241 2026 Milk production; Fluid milk

## 0252 Chicken Eggs

**(P-61)**
**FOSTER FARMS LLC**
Also Called: Foster Farms
770 N Plano Rd, Porterville (93257-6329)
PHONE..................................559 793-5501
Paul Bravinder, Mgr
EMP: 55
SQ FT: 81,000
SALES (corp-wide): 8.23B Privately Held
Web: www.fosterfarms.com
SIC: 0252 2015 Chicken eggs; Poultry slaughtering and processing
HQ: Foster Farms, Llc
1000 Davis St
Livingston CA 95334

**(P-62)**
**FOSTER FARMS LLC (HQ)**
1000 Davis St, Livingston (95334-1526)
P.O. Box 457 (95334-0457)
PHONE..................................209 394-7901
EMP: 90 EST: 2000
SALES (est): 488.82MM
SALES (corp-wide): 8.23B Privately Held
Web: www.fosterfarms.com
SIC: 0252 2015 Chicken eggs; Poultry slaughtering and processing
PA: Atlas Holdings, Llc
100 Northfield St
203 622-9138

**(P-63)**
**GEMPERLE ENTERPRISES**
Also Called: Gemperle Farms
10218 Lander Ave, Turlock (95380-9627)
PHONE..................................209 667-2651
Steve Gemperle, Managing Member
◆ EMP: 90 EST: 1952
SQ FT: 8,000
SALES (est): 8.8MM Privately Held
Web: www.gemperle.com
SIC: 0252 5144 2015 Chicken eggs; Eggs; Egg processing

**(P-64)**
**S K S ENTERPRISES INC (PA)**
11830 French Camp Rd, Manteca (95336-9732)
PHONE..................................209 599-4095
Wen Chang Su, Pr
EMP: 30 EST: 1980
SALES (est): 2.5MM
SALES (corp-wide): 2.5MM Privately Held
Web: www.sksenterprisesinc.com
SIC: 0252 2015 Chicken eggs; Poultry slaughtering and processing

**(P-65)**
**VALLEY FRESH FOODS INC**
Nest Best Egg Company
3600 E Linwood Ave, Turlock (95380-9109)
P.O. Box 370 (98579-0370)
PHONE..................................209 669-5600
Duane Olsen, Brnch Mgr
EMP: 46
SALES (corp-wide): 46.83MM Privately Held

# PRODUCTS & SERVICES SECTION

## 0723 - Crop Preparation Services For Market (P-84)

Web: www.valleyfreshfoods.com
SIC: 0252 2048 Chicken eggs; Prepared feeds, nec
PA: Valley Fresh Foods, Inc.
3600 E Linwood Ave
209 669-5600

### (P-66)
**VALLEY FRESH FOODS INC**
Also Called: Rainbow Farms
1220 Hall Rd, Denair (95316-9617)
P.O. Box 910 (95381-0910)
PHONE..................209 669-5510
Danny O'day, Mgr
EMP: 45
SQ FT: 1,216
SALES (corp-wide): 46.83MM Privately Held
Web: www.valleyfreshfoods.com
SIC: 0252 2015 Started pullet farm; Poultry slaughtering and processing
PA: Valley Fresh Foods, Inc.
3600 E Linwood Ave
209 669-5600

### (P-67)
**VALLEY FRESH FOODS INC (PA)**
Also Called: Skylane Farms
3600 E Linwood Ave, Turlock (95380-9109)
P.O. Box 910 (95381-0910)
PHONE..................209 669-5600
▲ EMP: 15 EST: 1969
SALES (est): 46.83MM
SALES (corp-wide): 46.83MM Privately Held
Web: www.valleyfreshfoods.com
SIC: 0252 2015 Chicken eggs; Egg processing

## 0254 Poultry Hatcheries

### (P-68)
**FOSTER POULTRY FARMS LLC**
834 Davis St, Livingston (95334)
P.O. Box 457 (95334-0457)
PHONE..................209 394-7901
Chris Carter, Brnch Mgr
EMP: 383
SALES (corp-wide): 1.25B Privately Held
Web: www.fosterfarms.com
SIC: 0254 2015 Poultry hatcheries; Poultry, processed, nsk
PA: Foster Poultry Farms, Llc
1000 Davis St
209 394-7901

## 0279 Animal Specialties, Nec

### (P-69)
**HONEY ISABELLS INC**
Also Called: Isabell's Honey Farm
539 N Glenoaks Blvd Ste 207b, Burbank (91502-3201)
PHONE..................800 708-8485
Oganes Kabakchuzyan, CEO
EMP: 46 EST: 2019
SALES (est): 2.16MM Privately Held
Web: www.isabellshoneyfarm.com
SIC: 0279 2099 Apiary (bee and honey farm); Honey, strained and bottled

### (P-70)
**OLIVAREZ HONEY BEES INC**
6398 County Road 20, Orland (95963-9475)
P.O. Box 847 (95963)
PHONE..................530 865-0298
Ray A Olivarez Junior, CEO

EMP: 97 EST: 2002
SALES (est): 5.02MM Privately Held
Web: www.ohbees.com
SIC: 0279 2099 Apiary (bee and honey farm); Almond pastes

## 0722 Crop Harvesting

### (P-71)
**ALPINE PACIFIC NUT CO INC**
Also Called: Alpine Pacific Nut Co.
6413 E Keyes Rd, Hughson (95326-9552)
P.O. Box 999 (95326-0999)
PHONE..................209 667-8688
John Mundt, CEO
Catherine Hendley-mundt, VP
◆ EMP: 40 EST: 2000
SQ FT: 90,000
SALES (est): 6.93MM Privately Held
Web: www.alpinepacificnut.com
SIC: 0722 2099 5411 Tree nuts, machine harvesting services; Food preparations, nec; Convenience stores, independent

### (P-72)
**CARNEROS VINTNERS INC**
4202 Stage Gulch Rd, Sonoma (95476-9739)
PHONE..................707 933-9349
Dennis Rippey, Pr
EMP: 17 EST: 2008
SALES (est): 1.2MM Privately Held
Web: www.carnerosvintners.com
SIC: 0722 2084 Grapes, machine harvesting services; Wines

## 0723 Crop Preparation Services For Market

### (P-73)
**APEEL TECHNOLOGY INC (PA)**
Also Called: Apeel Sciences
71 S Los Carneros Rd, Goleta (93117-5506)
PHONE..................805 203-0146
Luiz Beling, CEO
William Strong, *
EMP: 283 EST: 2012
SALES (est): 48.97MM
SALES (corp-wide): 48.97MM Privately Held
Web: www.apeel.com
SIC: 0723 2099 Crop preparation services for market; Almond pastes

### (P-74)
**BLUE DIAMOND GROWERS**
4800 Sisk Rd, Modesto (95356-8730)
PHONE..................209 545-6221
Bruce Mickelson, Mgr
EMP: 200
SALES (corp-wide): 661.89MM Privately Held
Web: www.bluediamondstore.com
SIC: 0723 2068 Almond hulling and shelling services; Nuts: dried, dehydrated, salted or roasted
PA: Diamond Blue Growers
1802 C St
800 987-2329

### (P-75)
**BOGHOSIAN RAISIN PKG CO INC**
726 S 8th St, Fowler (93625-2506)
P.O. Box 338 (93625-0338)
PHONE..................559 834-5348
Phillip Boghosian, Pr

Philip Boghosian, *
Cheryl Kennedy, *
Peter Boghosian, *
◆ EMP: 49 EST: 1972
SQ FT: 50,000
SALES (est): 12.2MM Privately Held
Web: www.boghosianraisin.com
SIC: 0723 2034 Fruit (farm-dried) packing services; Dried and dehydrated fruits, vegetables and soup mixes

### (P-76)
**CALIFORNIA ROYALE LLC**
Also Called: Monte Vista Farming Company
5043 N Montpelier Rd, Denair (95316-9608)
P.O. Box 579 (95316-0579)
PHONE..................209 874-1866
Jonathan Hoff, Managing Member
Elizabeth Nunez, Treas
▼ EMP: 22 EST: 2004
SQ FT: 60
SALES (est): 2.57MM Privately Held
Web: www.californiaroyale.com
SIC: 0723 2068 Tree nut crops market preparation services; Salted and roasted nuts and seeds

### (P-77)
**CENTRAL CAL ALMOND GRWERS ASSN (PA)**
8325 S Madera Ave, Kerman (93630-8953)
P.O. Box 338 (93630-0338)
PHONE..................559 846-5377
Michael Kelley, Pr
Geri Bartsch, *
Jim Sears, *
EMP: 36 EST: 1963
SQ FT: 22,000
SALES (est): 8.73MM
SALES (corp-wide): 8.73MM Privately Held
Web: www.ccaga.com
SIC: 0723 2068 Almond hulling and shelling services; Nuts: dried, dehydrated, salted or roasted

### (P-78)
**CENTRAL VALLEY AG GRINDING LLC (PA)**
Also Called: Cvag
5509 Langworth Rd, Oakdale (95361-7909)
PHONE..................209 869-1721
Paul Konzen, *
Todd Lush, *
EMP: 109 EST: 1998
SQ FT: 80,000
SALES (est): 85MM
SALES (corp-wide): 85MM Privately Held
Web: www.cv-ag.com
SIC: 0723 2041 2048 Grain milling; custom services; Flour and other grain mill products; Prepared feeds, nec

### (P-79)
**CHOOLJIAN & SONS INC (PA)**
Also Called: Del Rey Packing Co
5287 S Del Rey Ave, Del Rey (93616-9700)
P.O. Box 160 (93616-0160)
PHONE..................559 888-2031
Gerald Chooljian, CEO
Courtney Chooljian, *
▼ EMP: 50 EST: 1929
SQ FT: 14,400
SALES (est): 9.53MM
SALES (corp-wide): 9.53MM Privately Held
Web: www.delreypacking.com
SIC: 0723 2034 Fruit (farm-dried) packing services; Raisins

### (P-80)
**EARTHBOUND FARM LLC (PA)**
Also Called: Taylor Farms
1721 San Juan Hwy, San Juan Bautista (95045-9780)
PHONE..................831 623-7880
◆ EMP: 995 EST: 1988
SQ FT: 15,000
SALES (est): 52.46MM Privately Held
Web: www.earthboundfarm.com
SIC: 0723 2037 2099 Vegetable packing services; Frozen fruits and vegetables; Food preparations, nec

### (P-81)
**FARMERS RICE COOPERATIVE**
4937 Hwy 45, Colusa (95932-4008)
P.O. Box 265 (95970-0265)
PHONE..................530 439-2244
Joseph Alves, Mgr
EMP: 42
SQ FT: 1,378
SALES (corp-wide): 71.89MM Privately Held
Web: www.farmersrice.com
SIC: 0723 2044 Rice drying services; Rice milling
PA: Farmers' Rice Cooperative
2566 River Plaza Dr
916 923-5100

### (P-82)
**JUST TOMATOES INC**
Also Called: Tomato Press
2103 W Hamilton Rd, Westley (95387)
P.O. Box 807 (95387-0807)
PHONE..................209 894-5371
Bill Cox, Pr
Karen Cox, *
William Cox, *
EMP: 31 EST: 1985
SALES (est): 4.5MM Privately Held
Web: www.shopkarensnaturals.com
SIC: 0723 5961 2731 2771 Vegetable drying services; Fruit, mail order; Book publishing; Greeting cards

### (P-83)
**MARIANI PACKING CO INC (PA)**
500 Crocker Dr, Vacaville (95688-8706)
PHONE..................707 452-2800
Mark A Mariani, CEO
George Sousa Junior, Pr
Marian Ciabattari, *
George Sousa Senior, VP
Paul Mariani, *
◆ EMP: 275 EST: 1982
SALES (est): 114.7MM
SALES (corp-wide): 114.7MM Privately Held
Web: www.mariani.com
SIC: 0723 2034 5148 Fruit (farm-dried) packing services; Dried and dehydrated fruits; Fresh fruits and vegetables

### (P-84)
**MOONEY FARMS**
Also Called: Bella Sun Luci
1220 Fortress St, Chico (95973-9029)
PHONE..................530 899-2661
Mary Mooney, Pr
▲ EMP: 60 EST: 1987
SQ FT: 100,000
SALES (est): 10.88MM Privately Held
Web: www.bellasunluci.com
SIC: 0723 2034 2033 Fruit crops market preparation services; Dried and dehydrated fruits; Canned fruits and specialties

# 0723 - Crop Preparation Services For Market (P-85)

## (P-85)
**REYNOLDS PACKING CO (PA)**
Also Called: M & R Company
33 E Tokay St, Lodi (95240-4149)
PHONE..................209 369-2725
◆ **EMP:** 15 **EST:** 1955
**SALES (est):** 17.44MM
**SALES (corp-wide):** 17.44MM **Privately Held**
**Web:** www.mandrcherries.com
**SIC:** 0723 5148 2449 Fruit (fresh) packing services; Fruits, fresh; Fruit crates, wood: wirebound

## (P-86)
**SEED DYNAMICS INC**
1081b Harkins Rd, Salinas (93901-4406)
P.O. Box 6069 (93912-6069)
PHONE..................831 424-1177
David Holly, *CEO*
Curtis J Vaughan, *
Mel Bachman, *CRO*
**EMP:** 53 **EST:** 1985
**SQ FT:** 34,000
**SALES (est):** 4.18MM **Privately Held**
**Web:** www.seeddynamics.com
**SIC:** 0723 3999 Crop preparation services for market; Seeds, coated or treated, from purchased seeds

## (P-87)
**SUNKIST GROWERS INC**
531 W Poplar Ave, Tipton (93272-9646)
P.O. Box 3720 (91761-0993)
PHONE..................909 983-9811
Owen Belletto, *Brnch Mgr*
**EMP:** 23
**SALES (corp-wide):** 81.32MM **Privately Held**
**Web:** www.sunkist.com
**SIC:** 0723 5149 2099 Fruit crops market preparation services; Juices; Food preparations, nec
**PA:** Sunkist Growers, Inc.
27770 Entertainment Dr
661 290-8900

## (P-88)
**VALLEY FIG GROWERS**
2028 S 3rd St, Fresno (93702-4156)
PHONE..................559 349-1686
Gary Jue, *Pr*
Michael N Emigh, *
Linda Cain, *Marketing*
Paul Mesple, *
◆ **EMP:** 50 **EST:** 1959
**SQ FT:** 100,000
**SALES (est):** 13MM **Privately Held**
**Web:** www.valleyfig.com
**SIC:** 0723 2033 Fruit (fresh) packing services; Fruits and fruit products, in cans, jars, etc.

## (P-89)
**WILBUR PACKING COMPANY INC**
1500 Eager Rd, Live Oak (95953)
P.O. Box 3730 (95992-3730)
PHONE..................530 671-4911
Richard G Wilbur, *Pr*
Randy Baucom, *
Emily L Friend, *CAO*
Richard R Wilbur, *
◆ **EMP:** 100 **EST:** 1944
**SQ FT:** 60,650
**SALES (est):** 7.46MM **Privately Held**
**Web:** www.wilburpacking.com
**SIC:** 0723 2034 Crop preparation services for market; Dried and dehydrated fruits, vegetables and soup mixes

## (P-90)
**WONDERFUL CITRUS PACKING LLC (HQ)**
Also Called: Paramount Citrus Packing Co
1901 S Lexington St, Delano (93215-9207)
PHONE..................661 720-2400
Craig B Cooper, *Managing Member*
◆ **EMP:** 273 **EST:** 1950
**SQ FT:** 400,000
**SALES (est):** 280.36MM
**SALES (corp-wide):** 2.04B **Privately Held**
**Web:** www.wonderfulcitrus.com
**SIC:** 0723 0174 2033 Fruit (fresh) packing services; Orange grove; Fruit juices: fresh
**PA:** The Wonderful Company Llc
11444 W Olympic Blvd Fl 1
310 966-5700

## 0751 Livestock Services, Except Veterinary

## (P-91)
**AMERICAN BEEF PACKERS INC**
13677 Yorba Ave, Chino (91710-5059)
PHONE..................909 628-4888
Lawrence Miller, *Pr*
**EMP:** 250 **EST:** 2008
**SALES (est):** 20.7MM **Privately Held**
**SIC:** 0751 2011 5147 Slaughtering: custom livestock services; Beef products, from beef slaughtered on site; Meats and meat products

## 0762 Farm Management Services

## (P-92)
**ILLUME AGRICULTURE LLC**
9100 Ming Ave Ste 200, Bakersfield (93311-1329)
P.O. Box 22020 (93390-2020)
PHONE..................661 587-5198
Jeffrey Fabbri, *Managing Member*
**EMP:** 120 **EST:** 1939
**SALES (est):** 4.7MM **Privately Held**
**Web:** www.illumeag.com
**SIC:** 0762 5963 2099 Farm management services; Food services, direct sales; Box lunches, for sale off premises

## (P-93)
**KENZO ESTATE INC**
3200 Monticello Rd, Napa (94558-9655)
PHONE..................707 254-7572
Jude Radeski, *Pr*
Kenzo Tfujimoto, *
▲ **EMP:** 29 **EST:** 2000
**SQ FT:** 972
**SALES (est):** 4.49MM **Privately Held**
**Web:** www.kenzoestate.com
**SIC:** 0762 2084 Vineyard management and maintenance services; Wine cellars, bonded: engaged in blending wines

## (P-94)
**PINA VINEYARD MANAGEMENT LLC**
7960 Silverado Trl, Napa (94558-9433)
P.O. Box 373 (94562-0373)
PHONE..................707 944-2229
Davie Pina, *Managing Member*
**EMP:** 38 **EST:** 1960
**SQ FT:** 290
**SALES (est):** 2.8MM **Privately Held**
**Web:** www.pinavineyards.com
**SIC:** 0762 0723 2084 Vineyard management and maintenance services; Crop preparation services for market; Wines, brandy, and brandy spirits

## (P-95)
**VINO FARMS INC (PA)**
1377 E Lodi Ave, Lodi (95240-0840)
PHONE..................209 334-6975
James D Ledbetter, *Pr*
James D Ledbetter, *Pr*
Craig Ledbetter, *
Marissa Ledbetter, *
Kimberly Bronson, *
**EMP:** 50 **EST:** 1976
**SQ FT:** 6,000
**SALES (est):** 21.95MM
**SALES (corp-wide):** 21.95MM **Privately Held**
**Web:** www.vinofarms.com
**SIC:** 0762 8748 2084 Vineyard management and maintenance services; Agricultural consultant; Wines

## 0781 Landscape Counseling And Planning

## (P-96)
**GREENSCREEN**
Also Called: Atmospheric-Greenscreen
725 S Figueroa St Ste 1825, Los Angeles (90017-2827)
PHONE..................310 837-0526
Ruth Katzenstein, *Pr*
John Souza, *CEO*
**EMP:** 34 **EST:** 1995
**SQ FT:** 1,200
**SALES (est):** 784.07K **Privately Held**
**Web:** www.tournesol.com
**SIC:** 0781 7363 3446 Landscape planning services; Help supply services; Architectural metalwork

## (P-97)
**NN JAESCHKE INC**
9610 Waples St, San Diego (92121-2955)
PHONE..................858 550-7900
Ned Heiskell, *Pr*
Kelley Brewster, *Ex VP*
**EMP:** 48 **EST:** 2004
**SALES (est):** 4.16MM **Privately Held**
**Web:** www.nnj.com
**SIC:** 0781 7349 1389 Landscape services; Janitorial service, contract basis; Construction, repair, and dismantling services

## 0782 Lawn And Garden Services

## (P-98)
**H&GBYGISELLECO**
Also Called: Laborer
626 Mission Bay Blvd N Apt 114, San Francisco (94158-2496)
PHONE..................415 829-3867
Alston Sheppard Senior, *Owner*
**EMP:** 15 **EST:** 2019
**SALES (est):** 251.94K **Privately Held**
**SIC:** 0782 7359 0781 1629 Landscape contractors; Work zone traffic equipment (flags, cones, barrels, etc.); Landscape architects; Land clearing contractor

## 0783 Ornamental Shrub And Tree Services

## (P-99)
**OLD DURHAM WOOD INC**
1156 Oroville Chico Hwy, Durham (95938-9708)
PHONE..................530 342-7381
Michael Randall Mclaughlin, *CEO*
Sean Casey, *
**EMP:** 33 **EST:** 1981
**SQ FT:** 1,800
**SALES (est):** 2.75MM **Privately Held**
**SIC:** 0783 2611 5099 Ornamental shrub and tree services; Pulp manufactured from waste or recycled paper; Wood and wood by-products

## (P-100)
**TSU/TREE SERVICE UNLIMITED INC**
Also Called: Tree Service Unlimited
4080 Plaza Goldorado Cir, Cameron Park (95682-7455)
PHONE..................530 626-8733
Ashley Harpine, *CEO*
Tammie Van Bebber, *
Dale Van Bebber, *
**EMP:** 40 **EST:** 1979
**SQ FT:** 500
**SALES (est):** 2.25MM **Privately Held**
**Web:** www.tsutrees.com
**SIC:** 0783 2411 Planting, pruning, and trimming services; Timber, cut at logging camp

## 0851 Forestry Services

## (P-101)
**MARKIT FORESTRY MGT LLC**
14330 Musso Rd, Auburn (95603-9300)
PHONE..................279 444-0033
**EMP:** 16
**SALES (corp-wide):** 21.94MM **Privately Held**
**Web:** www.markitforestry.com
**SIC:** 0851 2411 4212 Forestry services; Timber, cut at logging camp; Timber trucking, local
**PA:** Markit Forestry Management Llc
2424 Grdn Of The Gods Rd
719 593-2365

## 1021 Copper Ores

## (P-102)
**LUSTROS INC**
9025 Carlton Hills Blvd Ste A, Santee (92071-7905)
PHONE..................619 449-4800
William Farley, *Ch Bd*
**EMP:** 44 **EST:** 2012
**SQ FT:** 1,530
**SALES (est):** 896.23K **Privately Held**
**Web:** www.perfectdomain.com
**SIC:** 1021 Copper ore mining and preparation

## 1041 Gold Ores

## (P-103)
**GOLDEN QUEEN MINING CO LLC**
2818 Silver Queen Rd, Mojave (93501-7021)
P.O. Box 1030 (93502-1030)

# PRODUCTS & SERVICES SECTION
## 1311 - Crude Petroleum And Natural Gas (P-122)

PHONE..............................661 824-4300
Thomas Clay, *Ch Bd*
Robert Walish, *
Andree St-germain, *CFO*
**EMP:** 180 **EST:** 2014
**SQ FT:** 2,500
**SALES (est):** 27.73MM
**SALES (corp-wide):** 57.04MM **Privately Held**
Web: www.goldenqueenllc.com
**SIC: 1041** Gold ores mining
**PA:** Golden Queen Mining Co. Ltd
   880-580 Hornby St
   604 417-7952

### (P-104)
### LOST DUTCHMANS MININGS ASSN (DH)
43445 Business Park Dr Ste 113, Temecula (92590-3671)
P.O. Box 891509 (92589-1509)
PHONE..............................951 699-4749
Perry Massie, *Pr*
Tom Massie, *
▲ **EMP:** 30 **EST:** 1995
**SQ FT:** 3,200
**SALES (est):** 2.78MM
**SALES (corp-wide):** 28.81MM **Privately Held**
Web: www.goldprospectors.org
**SIC: 1041** Gold ores
**HQ:** Outdoor Channel Holdings, Inc.
   1000 Chopper Cir
   Denver CO 80204

### (P-105)
### MERIDIAN GOLD INC
Also Called: Royal Mountain King
4461 Rock Creek Rd, Copperopolis (95228-7059)
PHONE..............................209 785-3222
Edgar Smith, *Brnch Mgr*
**EMP:** 474
**SALES (corp-wide):** 2.32B **Privately Held**
**SIC: 1041** Gold ores
**HQ:** Meridian Gold Inc.
   4635 Longley Ln Ste 110
   Reno NV 89502

### (P-106)
### STAVATTI INDUSTRIES LTD
3670 El Camino Dr, San Bernardino (92404-2025)
P.O. Box 211258 (55121-2658)
PHONE..............................651 238-5369
Christopher R Beskar, *Brnch Mgr*
**EMP:** 42
**SALES (corp-wide):** 887.61K **Privately Held**
Web: www.stavatti.com
**SIC: 1041** 1081 3511 3533  Gold ores mining; Metal mining exploration and development services; Turbines and turbine generator set units, complete; Oil and gas field machinery
**PA:** Stavatti Industries Ltd
   1061 Tiffany Dr
   651 238-5369

## 1081 Metal Mining Services

### (P-107)
### INYOAG LLC
13 Utah Dr, Darwin (93522)
P.O. Box 29 (93522-0029)
PHONE..............................775 427-8345
Jack Stone, *Pr*
Linda Stone, *CFO*
Nicholas Stone, *COO*
**EMP:** 20 **EST:** 2019

**SALES (est):** 788.13K **Privately Held**
**SIC: 1081** 2048  Metal mining services; Prepared feeds, nec

### (P-108)
### NATIONAL EWP INC
Also Called: National Explrtion Wells Pumps
5566 Arrow Hwy, Montclair (91763-1606)
PHONE..............................909 931-4014
Tom Moreland, *Brnch Mgr*
**EMP:** 17
**SALES (corp-wide):** 44.63MM **Privately Held**
Web: www.nationalewp.com
**SIC: 1081** Metal mining exploration and development services
**PA:** National Ewp, Inc.
   3707 Manzanita Ln
   775 753-7355

### (P-109)
### PERERA CNSTR & DESIGN INC
2890 Inland Empire Blvd Ste 102, Ontario (91764-4649)
PHONE..............................909 484-6350
Henry Perera Junior, *CEO*
Henry Perera, *CFO*
**EMP:** 35 **EST:** 1989
**SQ FT:** 20,000
**SALES (est):** 35.16MM **Privately Held**
Web: www.pererainc.com
**SIC: 1081** Metal mining exploration and development services

## 1099 Metal Ores, Nec

### (P-110)
### MP MATERIALS CORP
67750 Bailey Rd, Mountain Pass (92366)
PHONE..............................702 844-6111
**EMP:** 66
**SALES (corp-wide):** 253.44MM **Publicly Held**
Web: www.mpmaterials.com
**SIC: 1099** Rare-earth ores mining
**PA:** Mp Materials Corp.
   1700 S Pvlion Ctr Dr Ste
   702 844-6111

## 1221 Bituminous Coal And Lignite-surface Mining

### (P-111)
### CHEVRON MINING INC
Moly
67750 Bailey Rd, Mountain Pass (92366)
PHONE..............................760 856-7625
**EMP:** 245
**SALES (corp-wide):** 162.47B **Publicly Held**
**SIC: 1221** Surface mining, bituminous, nec
**HQ:** Chevron Mining Inc.
   116 Invrneco Dr E Ste 207
   Englewood CO 80112
   303 930-3600

### (P-112)
### CUSTOM CRUSHING INDUSTRIES INC
2409 E Oberlin Rd, Yreka (96097-9577)
P.O. Box 357 (96038-0357)
PHONE..............................530 842-5544
Clara Goodwin, *Sec*
Paul Goodwin, *Pr*
**EMP:** 24 **EST:** 2005
**SALES (est):** 2.48MM **Privately Held**

**SIC: 1221** 3295 3281 1499  Strip mining, bituminous; Minerals, ground or treated; Stone, quarrying and processing of own stone products; Peat mining and processing

## 1231 Anthracite Mining

### (P-113)
### GRUBB & NADLER INC
1719 Rainbow Valley Blvd, Fallbrook (92028-9774)
PHONE..............................760 728-0040
Thomas Emery, *Mgr*
**EMP:** 30
Web: www.floragrubb.com
**SIC: 1231** Preparation plants, anthracite
**PA:** Grubb & Nadler, Inc.
   1634 Jerrold Ave

### (P-114)
### GRUBB & NADLER INC (PA)
1634 Jerrold Ave, San Francisco (94124-2135)
PHONE..............................415 694-6441
Saul Nadler, *Pr*
**EMP:** 20 **EST:** 2003
**SALES (est):** 3.1MM **Privately Held**
Web: www.floragrubb.com
**SIC: 1231** Preparation plants, anthracite

### (P-115)
### MIDSTREAM ENERGY PARTNERS USA
9224 Tupman Rd, Tupman (93276)
PHONE..............................661 765-4087
**EMP:** 37 **EST:** 2012
**SALES (est):** 7.01MM **Privately Held**
Web: www.midstreamenergy.us
**SIC: 1231** 1382 1311 1321  Anthracite mining; Oil and gas exploration services; Crude petroleum and natural gas; Natural gas liquids

## 1241 Coal Mining Services

### (P-116)
### COLOMBIA ENERGY RESOURCES INC
Also Called: (An Exploration Stage Company)
1 Embarcadero Ctr Ste 500, San Francisco (94111-3610)
**EMP:** 133
**SIC: 1241** 1221 1222  Coal mining exploration and test boring; Bituminous coal and lignite-surface mining; Bituminous coal-underground mining

### (P-117)
### RIO TINTO MINERALS INC
Also Called: Reno Tenco
14486 Borax Rd, Boron (93516-2017)
PHONE..............................760 762-7121
Xiaoling Liu, *CEO*
Hugo Bague, *
Preston Chiaro, *
◆ **EMP:** 150 **EST:** 2006
**SALES (est):** 42.27MM
**SALES (corp-wide):** 54.04B **Privately Held**
Web: www.borax.com
**SIC: 1241** Coal mining services
**HQ:** U.S. Borax Inc.
   200 E Randolph St # 7100
   Chicago IL 60601
   773 270-6500

### (P-118)
### TAFT PRODUCTION COMPANY
950 Petroleum Club Rd, Taft (93268-9748)
P.O. Box 1277 (93268-1277)
PHONE..............................661 765-7194
Daniel S Jaffee, *Pr*
**EMP:** 95 **EST:** 2002
**SALES (est):** 16.23MM
**SALES (corp-wide):** 437.59MM **Publicly Held**
Web: www.oildri.com
**SIC: 1241** 1081  Coal mining services; Metal mining services
**PA:** Oil-Dri Corporation Of America
   410 N Mich Ave Ste 400
   312 321-1515

## 1311 Crude Petroleum And Natural Gas

### (P-119)
### AERA ENERGY LLC
10000 Ming Ave, Bakersfield (93389)
P.O. Box 11164 (93389)
PHONE..............................661 665-5000
Erik Bartsch, *Pr*
Ted Witt, *COO*
Sergio De Castro, *CFO*
Lynne Carrithers, *Legal*
Sara Oneill-bouton Senior, *External Affairs Vice President*
**EMP:** 918 **EST:** 1994
**SALES (est):** 4.51MM **Privately Held**
**SIC: 1311** Crude petroleum production

### (P-120)
### AERA ENERGY LLC
Also Called: Kernridge Division
19590 7th Standard Rd, Mc Kittrick (93251-9709)
PHONE..............................661 334-3100
Marie Crosby, *Prin*
**EMP:** 142
**SALES (corp-wide):** 316.62B **Privately Held**
Web: www.aeraenergy.com
**SIC: 1311** Natural gas production
**HQ:** Aera Energy Services Company
   10000 Ming Ave
   Bakersfield CA 93311
   661 665-5000

### (P-121)
### BERRY PETROLEUM COMPANY LLC
25121 Sierra Hwy, Newhall (91321-2007)
PHONE..............................661 255-6066
Eddie Azevedo, *Mgr*
**EMP:** 51
**SALES (corp-wide):** 903.46MM **Publicly Held**
Web: www.berrypetroleum.com
**SIC: 1311** Crude petroleum production
**HQ:** Berry Petroleum Company, Llc
   11117 River Run Blvd
   Bakersfield CA 93311
   661 616-3900

### (P-122)
### BERRY PETROLEUM COMPANY LLC
28700 Hovey Hills Rd, Taft (93268)
P.O. Box 925 (93268-0925)
PHONE..............................661 769-8820
Tom Cruise, *Mgr*
**EMP:** 51
**SALES (corp-wide):** 903.46MM **Publicly Held**

# 1311 - Crude Petroleum And Natural Gas (P-123)

**PRODUCTS & SERVICES SECTION**

Web: www.berrypetroleum.com
SIC: 1311 Crude petroleum production
HQ: Berry Petroleum Company, Llc
11117 River Run Blvd
Bakersfield CA 93311
661 616-3900

### (P-123)
**BERRY PETROLEUM COMPANY LLC (HQ)**
11117 River Run Blvd, Bakersfield (93311-8957)
PHONE.................................661 616-3900
Trem Smith, *Pr*
EMP: 24 EST: 1985
SALES (est): 130.26MM
SALES (corp-wide): 903.46MM **Publicly Held**
Web: www.berrypetroleum.com
SIC: 1311 Crude petroleum production
PA: Berry Corporation (Bry)
16000 Dallas Pkwy Ste 500
661 616-3900

### (P-124)
**BETA OPERATING COMPANY LLC**
Also Called: Beta Offshore
111 W Ocean Blvd, Long Beach (90802-4633)
PHONE.................................562 628-1526
EMP: 54
SALES (corp-wide): 307.6MM **Publicly Held**
Web: www.betaoffshore.com
SIC: 1311 Crude petroleum production
HQ: Beta Operating Company, Llc
500 Dallas St Ste 1600
Houston TX 77002

### (P-125)
**BEVERLY HILLCREST OIL CORP**
27241 Burbank, El Toro (92610-2500)
PHONE.................................949 598-7300
Morris Hodges, *Pr*
Katherine Hodges, *VP*
EMP: 15 EST: 1979
SALES (est): 1.21MM **Privately Held**
SIC: 1311 1321 Crude petroleum production; Natural gas liquids production

### (P-126)
**BREA CANON OIL CO INC**
18000 Studebaker Rd, Cerritos (90703-2679)
PHONE.................................310 326-4002
Andrew Barkler, *Pr*
Rod Benny, *Mgr*
Ray Javier, *VP*
Andrew Barkler, *Pr*
EMP: 17 EST: 2004
SALES (est): 2.98MM **Privately Held**
SIC: 1311 Crude petroleum production

### (P-127)
**BREITBURN ENERGY PARTNERS LP**
707 Wilshire Blvd Ste 4600, Los Angeles (90017-3501)
PHONE.................................213 225-5900
EMP: 671
SIC: 1311 Crude petroleum production

### (P-128)
**BREITBURN GP LLC**
707 Wilshire Blvd Ste 4600, Los Angeles (90017-3501)
PHONE.................................213 225-5900
Halbert S Washburn, *CEO*
EMP: 26 EST: 2006
SALES (est): 1.07MM **Privately Held**
SIC: 1311 Crude petroleum and natural gas

### (P-129)
**CALIFORNIA RESOURCES CORP (PA)**
1 World Trade Ctr Ste 1500, Long Beach (90831-1500)
PHONE.................................888 848-4754
Francisco J Leon, *Pr*
Tiffany Thom Cepak, *Ch Bd*
Manuela Molina, *Ex VP*
Michael L Preston, *Chief Strategy Officer*
Jay A Bys, *CCO*
EMP: 63 EST: 2014
SALES (est): 2.8B
SALES (corp-wide): 2.8B **Publicly Held**
Web: www.crc.com
SIC: 1311 Crude petroleum and natural gas

### (P-130)
**CALIFORNIA RESOURCES PROD CORP**
4900 W Lokern Rd, Mc Kittrick (93251-9764)
PHONE.................................661 869-8000
EMP: 25
SALES (corp-wide): 2.8B **Publicly Held**
Web: www.crc.com
SIC: 1311 1382 Crude petroleum production; Oil and gas exploration services
HQ: California Resources Production Corporation
27200 Tourney Rd Ste 200
Santa Clarita CA 91355

### (P-131)
**CALIFORNIA RESOURCES PROD CORP (HQ)**
Also Called: Vintage Production California
27200 Tourney Rd Ste 200, Santa Clarita (91355-4910)
PHONE.................................661 869-8000
EMP: 125 EST: 2005
SALES (est): 25.65MM
SALES (corp-wide): 2.8B **Publicly Held**
Web: www.crc.com
SIC: 1311 1382 Crude petroleum production; Oil and gas exploration services
PA: California Resources Corporation
1 World Trade Ctr Ste 150
888 848-4754

### (P-132)
**CALNRG OPERATING LLC (PA)**
1536 Eastman Ave, Ventura (93003-7773)
PHONE.................................805 477-9805
Clif Simonson, *COO*
EMP: 22 EST: 2010
SALES (est): 9.08MM
SALES (corp-wide): 9.08MM **Privately Held**
SIC: 1311 Natural gas production

### (P-133)
**CARBON CALIFORNIA COMPANY LLC**
270 Quail Ct Ste 201, Santa Paula (93060-9206)
PHONE.................................805 933-1901
Patrick R Mcdonald, *CEO*
Mark D Pierce, *Pr*
Kevin D Struzeski, *CFO*
EMP: 22 EST: 2016
SALES (est): 3.52MM
SALES (corp-wide): 116.63MM **Privately Held**
Web: www.carbonenergycorp.com
SIC: 1311 Crude petroleum and natural gas
PA: Carbon Energy Corporation
1700 Broadway Ste 1170
720 407-7043

### (P-134)
**HATHAWAY LLC**
4205 Atlas Ct, Bakersfield (93308-4510)
P.O. Box 81385 (93380-1385)
PHONE.................................661 393-2004
Charles Hathaway,
EMP: 38 EST: 2000
SQ FT: 4,500
SALES (est): 7.95MM **Privately Held**
Web: www.hathawayllc.com
SIC: 1311 Crude petroleum production

### (P-135)
**HELLMAN PROPERTIES LLC**
711 First St, Seal Beach (90740)
P.O. Box 2398 (90740-1398)
PHONE.................................562 431-6022
EMP: 15 EST: 1920
SQ FT: 200
SALES (est): 7.18MM **Privately Held**
SIC: 1311 Crude petroleum production

### (P-136)
**OCCIDENTAL PETROLEUM CORPORATION OF CALIFORNIA**
Also Called: OXY
10889 Wilshire Blvd, Los Angeles (90024-4213)
EMP: 3600
SIC: 1311 Crude petroleum production

### (P-137)
**PETROLEUM SALES INC**
2066 Redwood Hwy, Greenbrae (94904-2467)
PHONE.................................415 256-1600
Stephanie Shimk, *Brnch Mgr*
EMP: 16
SALES (corp-wide): 8.86MM **Privately Held**
Web: www.shineology.com
SIC: 1311 Crude petroleum and natural gas
PA: Petroleum Sales, Inc.
1475 2nd St
415 256-1600

### (P-138)
**SILURIA TECHNOLOGIES INC**
409 Illinois St, San Francisco (94158-2509)
PHONE.................................415 978-2170
Robert Trout, *CEO*
Karl Kurz, *Ch*
Alex Tkachenko, *Pr*
Erik Scher, *COO*
EMP: 30 EST: 2007
SALES (est): 10.38MM **Privately Held**
Web: www.siluria.com
SIC: 1311 Natural gas production

### (P-139)
**THE STRAND ENERGY COMPANY**
515 S Flower St Ste 4800, Los Angeles (90071-2241)
PHONE.................................213 225-5900
EMP: 380
SIC: 1311 Crude petroleum and natural gas production

### (P-140)
**THUMS LONG BEACH COMPANY**
111 W Ocean Blvd Ste 800, Long Beach (90802-7930)
PHONE.................................562 624-3400
EMP: 205
SIC: 1311 Crude petroleum production

### (P-141)
**TIDELANDS OIL PRODUCTION INC**
Also Called: Partnrship Prmnt Ptro Chnse En
301 E Ocean Blvd St 300, Long Beach (90802-4830)
PHONE.................................562 436-9918
EMP: 30
SIC: 1311 8748 4925 Crude petroleum production; Business consulting, nec; Gas production and/or distribution

### (P-142)
**TPG PARTNERS III LP (DH)**
Also Called: Tpg Growth
345 California St Ste 3300, San Francisco (94104-2640)
PHONE.................................415 743-1500
William E Mcglashan, *Mng Pt*
James G Coulter, *Pt*
William S Price, *Pt*
David Bonderman, *Pt*
EMP: 40 EST: 1999
SALES (est): 25.04MM
SALES (corp-wide): 3.2B **Publicly Held**
Web: www.tpg.com
SIC: 1311 1389 4922 5082 Crude petroleum production; Oil field services, nec; Natural gas transmission; Oil field equipment
HQ: Tpg Capital Management, L.P.
301 Commerce St Ste 3300
Fort Worth TX 76102

### (P-143)
**TRI-VALLEY CORPORATION**
4927 Calloway Dr Ste 101, Bakersfield (93312-9719)
PHONE.................................661 864-0500
EMP: 25
Web: www.tri-valleycorp.com
SIC: 1311 1382 1041 Crude petroleum and natural gas; Oil and gas exploration services ; Gold ores

### (P-144)
**UNIFIED FIELD SERVICES CORP**
6906 Downing Ave, Bakersfield (93308-5812)
PHONE.................................661 325-8962
Wesley R Furrh Junior, *Pr*
EMP: 39 EST: 2015
SALES (est): 7.57MM **Privately Held**
Web: www.unifiedfsc.com
SIC: 1311 Crude petroleum and natural gas

### (P-145)
**VAQUERO ENERGY INCORPORATED**
15545 Hermosa Rd, Bakersfield (93307-9477)
PHONE.................................661 363-7240
Ken Hunter, *Pr*
EMP: 50 EST: 2007
SALES (est): 9.9MM **Privately Held**
Web: www.vaqueroenergy.com
SIC: 1311 Crude petroleum production

### (P-146)
**WEST NEWPORT OIL COMPANY**
5800 W Coast Hwy, Newport Beach (92663-2002)
P.O. Box 1487 (92659-0487)
PHONE.................................949 631-1100
Robert A Armstrong, *Pr*
Jay Stair, *VP*
Margaret Armstrong, *Sec*

**PRODUCTS & SERVICES SECTION**

**1381 - Drilling Oil And Gas Wells (P-166)**

EMP: 24 EST: 1975
SALES (est): 4.91MM
SALES (corp-wide): 4.91MM **Privately Held**
SIC: **1311** Crude petroleum production
PA: Armstrong Petroleum Corporation
5800 W Coast Hwy
949 650-4000

**(P-147)**
**WORLD OIL CORP**
9302 Garfield Ave, South Gate (90280-3896)
P.O. Box 1 (90280-0001)
PHONE.................................562 928-0100
Robert S Roth, *CEO*
EMP: 147 EST: 1973
SALES (est): 31.37MM **Privately Held**
Web: www.worldoilcorp.com
SIC: **1311** Crude petroleum and natural gas

## 1321 Natural Gas Liquids

**(P-148)**
**BLYTHE ENERGY INC**
385 N Buck Blvd, Blythe (92225-3301)
P.O. Box 1210 (92226-1210)
PHONE.................................760 922-9950
David M Harris, *CEO*
Paul Thessen, *Pr*
Mark Brennan, *Treas*
Scott Carver, *Sec*
EMP: 15 EST: 1998
SALES (est): 7.45MM
SALES (corp-wide): 9.46B **Privately Held**
Web: www.altagas.ca
SIC: **1321 4939** Natural gas liquids production; Combination utilities, nec
HQ: Altagas Power Holdings (U.S.) Inc.
1411 3rd St Ste A
Port Huron MI 48060
810 887-4105

**(P-149)**
**HEXAGON AGILITY INC**
3335 Susan St Ste 100, Costa Mesa (92626-1647)
PHONE.................................949 236-5520
Hans Peter Havdal, *CEO*
Seung Baik, *Pr*
EMP: 46 EST: 2016
SALES (est): 20.16MM **Privately Held**
Web: www.hexagongroup.com
SIC: **1321** Natural gas liquids production
PA: Hexagon Composites Asa
Korsegata 4b

## 1381 Drilling Oil And Gas Wells

**(P-150)**
**AA PRODUCTION SERVICES INC**
8032 County Road 61, Princeton (95970-9501)
PHONE.................................530 982-0123
EMP: 31
SALES (corp-wide): 4.51MM **Privately Held**
SIC: **1381** Drilling oil and gas wells
PA: Aa Production Services, Inc.
433 2nd St Ste 103
530 668-7525

**(P-151)**
**AERA ENERGY SERVICES COMPANY (HQ)**
10000 Ming Ave, Bakersfield (93311-1301)
P.O. Box 11164 (93389-1164)
PHONE.................................661 665-5000
Erik Bartsch, *Pr*
EMP: 800 EST: 1994
SALES (est): 490.16MM
SALES (corp-wide): 316.62B **Privately Held**
Web: www.aeraenergy.com
SIC: **1381** Directional drilling oil and gas wells
PA: Shell Plc
Shell Centre
207 934-3363

**(P-152)**
**AERA ENERGY SERVICES COMPANY**
Also Called: Security Front Desk
59231 Main Camp Rd, Mc Kittrick (93251-9740)
PHONE.................................661 665-4400
Mike Brown, *Prin*
EMP: 126
SALES (corp-wide): 316.62B **Privately Held**
Web: www.aeraenergy.com
SIC: **1381** Directional drilling oil and gas wells
HQ: Aera Energy Services Company
10000 Ming Ave
Bakersfield CA 93311
661 665-5000

**(P-153)**
**AERA ENERGY SERVICES COMPANY**
Also Called: Aera Energy South Midway
29235 Highway 33, Maricopa (93252-9793)
PHONE.................................661 665-3200
Andy Anderson, *Mgr*
EMP: 77
SALES (corp-wide): 316.62B **Privately Held**
Web: www.aeraenergy.com
SIC: **1381** Directional drilling oil and gas wells
HQ: Aera Energy Services Company
10000 Ming Ave
Bakersfield CA 93311
661 665-5000

**(P-154)**
**ASTA CONSTRUCTION CO INC (PA)**
Also Called: Asta Construction
1090 Saint Francis Way, Rio Vista (94571-1200)
P.O. Box 758 (94571-0758)
PHONE.................................707 374-6472
Walt Koenig, *CEO*
Christien Koenig, *
Joan Brown, *
Schmitt V Scott, *
▲ EMP: 24 EST: 1943
SQ FT: 1,200
SALES (est): 5.67MM
SALES (corp-wide): 5.67MM **Privately Held**
Web: www.astaconstruction.com
SIC: **1381 1611 5032** Drilling oil and gas wells; General contractor, highway and street construction; Sand, construction

**(P-155)**
**DICK BROWNS TECHNICAL SERVICE**
Also Called: Aera Energy
553 Airport Rd Ste B, Rio Vista (94571-1293)
P.O. Box 1035 (94571-3035)
PHONE.................................707 374-2133
Richard Brown, *Pr*
EMP: 18 EST: 1984
SALES (est): 2.45MM **Privately Held**
SIC: **1381** Drilling oil and gas wells

**(P-156)**
**DICK HOWELLS HOLE DRLG SVC INC**
Also Called: Howell Drilling
2579 E 67th St, Long Beach (90805-1701)
PHONE.................................562 633-9898
Richard Howell Junior, *Pr*
Paul Howell, *VP*
Patty Howell, *Sec*
EMP: 18 EST: 1971
SALES (est): 773.47K **Privately Held**
Web: www.howelldrilling.com
SIC: **1381 1629 1741** Drilling oil and gas wells; Blasting contractor, except building demolition; Foundation building

**(P-157)**
**ELYSIUM JENNINGS LLC**
1600 Norris Rd, Bakersfield (93308-2234)
PHONE.................................661 679-1700
EMP: 125 EST: 2003
SALES (est): 6.21MM **Privately Held**
SIC: **1381** Drilling oil and gas wells
PA: E & B Natural Resources Management Corporation
1608 Norris Rd

**(P-158)**
**EXCALIBUR WELL SERVICES CORP**
22034 Rosedale Hwy, Bakersfield (93314-9704)
PHONE.................................661 589-5338
Stephen Layton, *Pr*
Stephen Layton, *CEO*
Frachsco Galesi, *
Gordon Isbel, *
EMP: 120 EST: 2006
SALES (est): 8.54MM **Privately Held**
Web: www.excaliburwellservices.com
SIC: **1381 1389** Drilling oil and gas wells; Fishing for tools, oil and gas field

**(P-159)**
**GEO GUIDANCE DRILLING SVCS INC (PA)**
200 Old Yard Dr, Bakersfield (93307-4268)
P.O. Box 42647 (93384-2647)
PHONE.................................661 833-9999
Joseph Williams, *CEO*
Matt Lemke, *
Charles B Peters, *
EMP: 25 EST: 2011
SQ FT: 3,000
SALES (est): 8.04MM **Privately Held**
Web: www.geoguidancedrilling.com
SIC: **1381** Drilling oil and gas wells

**(P-160)**
**GOLDEN STATE DRILLING INC**
3500 Fruitvale Ave, Bakersfield (93308-5106)
PHONE.................................661 589-0730
Philip F Phelps, *Pr*
Velma Phelps, *
James Phelps, *
EMP: 75 EST: 1977
SALES (est): 4.75MM **Privately Held**
Web: www.gsdrilling.com
SIC: **1381** Directional drilling oil and gas wells

**(P-161)**
**GUNNAR LLLP**
3600 Pegasus Dr, Bakersfield (93308-7088)
PHONE.................................281 690-0322
Clinton Moss, *Prin*
EMP: 16 EST: 2020
SALES (est): 1.35MM **Privately Held**
SIC: **1381** Directional drilling oil and gas wells

**(P-162)**
**LEGEND PUMP & WELL SERVICE INC**
1324 W Rialto Ave, San Bernardino (92410-1611)
PHONE.................................909 384-1000
Keith Collier, *Pr*
EMP: 20 EST: 2010
SALES (est): 4.87MM **Privately Held**
Web: www.legendpump.net
SIC: **1381 1781** Service well drilling; Servicing, water wells

**(P-163)**
**LEON KROUS DRILLING INC**
9300 Borden Ave, Sun Valley (91352-2006)
PHONE.................................818 833-4654
Leon Krus, *Pr*
EMP: 25 EST: 1981
SQ FT: 1,000
SALES (est): 11.47MM **Privately Held**
Web: leonkrousdrilling.thebluebook.com
SIC: **1381** Directional drilling oil and gas wells

**(P-164)**
**PAUL GRAHAM DRILLING & SVC CO**
Also Called: Paul Graham Drilling
2500 Airport Rd, Rio Vista (94571-1034)
P.O. Box 669 (94571-0669)
PHONE.................................707 374-5123
Kevin P Graham, *Pr*
Clarence Santos, *
Jill Graham, *
EMP: 170 EST: 1968
SQ FT: 30,000
SALES (est): 24.14MM **Privately Held**
Web: www.paulgrahamdrilling.com
SIC: **1381 7389 7359** Drilling oil and gas wells; Crane and aerial lift service; Industrial truck rental

**(P-165)**
**PETRO-LUD INC**
12625 Jomani Dr Ste 104, Bakersfield (93312-3454)
PHONE.................................661 747-4779
Clayton Ludington, *Prin*
EMP: 24 EST: 2012
SALES (est): 2.57MM **Privately Held**
Web: www.petro-lud.com
SIC: **1381** Drilling oil and gas wells

**(P-166)**
**SCIENTIFIC DRILLING INTL INC**
31101 Coberly Rd, Shafter (93263-9702)
PHONE.................................661 831-0636
Joe Williams, *Mgr*
EMP: 21
SALES (corp-wide): 400.64MM **Privately Held**
Web: www.scientificdrilling.com
SIC: **1381** Drilling oil and gas wells
PA: Scientific Drilling International, Inc.
1450 Lk Rbbins Dr Ste 200
281 443-3300

# 1381 - Drilling Oil And Gas Wells (P-167)

**(P-167)**
**WOODWARD DRILLING COMPANY INC**
550 River Rd, Rio Vista (94571-1216)
P.O. Box 336 (94571-0336)
PHONE.................................707 374-4300
Concing Woodward, *Pr*
Wayne G Woodward, *
**EMP:** 28 **EST:** 1990
**SQ FT:** 40,000
**SALES (est):** 4.16MM **Privately Held**
**Web:** www.woodwarddrilling.net
**SIC: 1381** 1781 Service well drilling; Water well drilling

## 1382 Oil And Gas Exploration Services

**(P-168)**
**ARGUELLO INC**
17100 Calle Mariposa Reina, Goleta (93117-9737)
PHONE.................................805 567-1632
James C Flores, *Pr*
John F Wombwell, *
Doss Dourgeois, *
Winston Taldert, *
**EMP:** 29 **EST:** 1999
**SALES (est):** 5.57MM
**SALES (corp-wide):** 22.86B **Publicly Held**
**SIC: 1382** Oil and gas exploration services
**HQ:** Freeport-Mcmoran Oil & Gas Llc
  21 Waterway Ave Ste 250
  Spring TX 77380
  713 579-6000

**(P-169)**
**BNK PETROLEUM (US) INC**
925 Broadbeck Dr Ste 220, Newbury Park (91320-1272)
PHONE.................................805 484-3613
Wolf E Regener, *Pr*
Gary W Johnson, *
Ray W Payne, *OF US Operations**
Steven M Warshauer, *Exploration Vice President**
**EMP:** 25 **EST:** 2006
**SALES (est):** 9.64MM **Privately Held**
**Web:** www.bnkpetroleum.com
**SIC: 1382** Oil and gas exploration services

**(P-170)**
**BOP RENEWABLES INC**
Also Called: Bird of Paradise Renewables
14111 La Gloria St, La Mirada (90638-3418)
PHONE.................................714 418-4420
David Yoo, *CEO*
Jaewon Jeong, *Sec*
**EMP:** 15 **EST:** 2013
**SALES (est):** 1.15MM **Privately Held**
**SIC: 1382** Oil and gas exploration services

**(P-171)**
**BREITBURN ENERGY HOLDINGS LLC**
707 Wilshire Blvd Ste 4600, Los Angeles (90017-3501)
PHONE.................................213 225-5900
**EMP:** 47 **EST:** 2009
**SALES (est):** 5.51MM **Privately Held**
**Web:** www.breitburn.com
**SIC: 1382** Oil and gas exploration services

**(P-172)**
**CALIFORNIA RESOURCES CORP**
5000 Stockdale Hwy, Bakersfield (93309-2650)
PHONE.................................661 395-8000
**EMP:** 98
**SALES (corp-wide):** 2.8B **Publicly Held**
**Web:** www.crc.com
**SIC: 1382** Oil and gas exploration services
**PA:** California Resources Corporation
  1 World Trade Ctr Ste 150
  888 848-4754

**(P-173)**
**CALIFRNIA RSRCES ELK HILLS LLC**
27200 Tourney Rd Ste 200, Santa Clarita (91355-4910)
PHONE.................................661 412-0000
Michael L Preston, *
Marshall D Smith, *
**EMP:** 400 **EST:** 1997
**SALES (est):** 22.28MM
**SALES (corp-wide):** 2.8B **Publicly Held**
**SIC: 1382** Oil and gas exploration services
**PA:** California Resources Corporation
  1 World Trade Ctr Ste 150
  888 848-4754

**(P-174)**
**CMBLU ENERGY INC**
621 2nd St Ste A, Petaluma (94952-5123)
PHONE.................................650 272-8804
Benjamin Kaun, *CEO*
**EMP:** 20 **EST:** 2022
**SALES (est):** 2.19MM **Privately Held**
**SIC: 1382** Oil and gas exploration services

**(P-175)**
**CRC SERVICES LLC**
27200 Tourney Rd Ste 200, Santa Clarita (91355-4910)
PHONE.................................888 848-4754
**EMP:** 18 **EST:** 2014
**SALES (est):** 9.89MM
**SALES (corp-wide):** 2.8B **Publicly Held**
**SIC: 1382** Oil and gas exploration services
**PA:** California Resources Corporation
  1 World Trade Ctr Ste 150
  888 848-4754

**(P-176)**
**DCOR LLC (PA)**
Also Called: Dcor
1000 Town Center Dr Fl 6, Oxnard (93036-1132)
P.O. Box 3401 (93006-3401)
PHONE.................................805 535-2000
Andrew Prestridge, *
Alan C Templeton, *
Jeff Warren, *
Bob Garcia, *
**EMP:** 100 **EST:** 2001
**SALES (est):** 44.53MM
**SALES (corp-wide):** 44.53MM **Privately Held**
**Web:** www.dcorllc.com
**SIC: 1382** Oil and gas exploration services

**(P-177)**
**DEMENNO KERDOON**
2000 N Alameda St, Compton (90222-2799)
PHONE.................................310 537-7100
Shane Bamelin, *Prin*
Jim Tice, *
Shane Bamelin, *Ch*
Jim Ennis, *
**EMP:** 16 **EST:** 2007
**SQ FT:** 11,614
**SALES (est):** 4.06MM **Privately Held**
**SIC: 1382** Oil and gas exploration services

**(P-178)**
**DRILLMEC INC**
8140 Rosecrans Ave, Paramount (90723-2754)
PHONE.................................281 885-0777
Paulo Brando Ballerini, *Pr*
Massimo Tartagni, *
♦ **EMP:** 74 **EST:** 1998
**SALES (est):** 5.14MM
**SALES (corp-wide):** 632.33MM **Privately Held**
**Web:** www.drillmecinc.com
**SIC: 1382** Oil and gas exploration services
**HQ:** Soilmec Spa
  Via Dismano 5819
  Cesena FC 47522
  054 731-9111

**(P-179)**
**E & B NTRAL RESOURCES MGT CORP**
1848 Perkins Rd, New Cuyama (93254)
P.O. Box 179 (93254-0179)
PHONE.................................661 766-2501
Edward Fetterman, *Brnch Mgr*
**EMP:** 39
**Web:** www.ebresources.com
**SIC: 1382** Oil and gas exploration services
**PA:** E & B Natural Resources Management Corporation
  1608 Norris Rd

**(P-180)**
**E & B NTRAL RESOURCES MGT CORP (PA)**
1608 Norris Rd, Bakersfield (93308-2234)
PHONE.................................661 387-8500
Steve Layton, *Pr*
Zac Hale, *
Hany Francis, *
**EMP:** 65 **EST:** 1972
**SALES (est):** 40.75MM **Privately Held**
**Web:** www.ebresources.com
**SIC: 1382** Oil and gas exploration services

**(P-181)**
**EAGLE DOMINION ENERGY CORP**
Also Called: Eagle Dominion Trust
3020 W Olive Ave, Burbank (91505-4537)
P.O. Box 7004 (93031-7004)
PHONE.................................270 366-4817
Roger H Shears, *Mgr*
Roger H Shears, *Pr*
Nancy Davis, *
Mary Pickford, *Prin*
**EMP:** 35 **EST:** 1997
**SQ FT:** 1,500
**SALES (est):** 474.13K **Privately Held**
**SIC: 1382** Oil and gas exploration services

**(P-182)**
**FREEPORT-MCMORAN OIL & GAS LLC**
760 W Hueneme Rd, Oxnard (93033-9013)
PHONE.................................805 567-1601
Eric Vang, *Brnch Mgr*
**EMP:** 29
**SALES (corp-wide):** 22.86B **Publicly Held**
**Web:** www.fcx.com
**SIC: 1382** Oil and gas exploration services
**HQ:** Freeport-Mcmoran Oil & Gas Llc
  21 Waterway Ave Ste 250
  Spring TX 77380
  713 579-6000

**(P-183)**
**FREEPORT-MCMORAN OIL & GAS LLC**
3252 W Crocker Springs Rd, Fellows (93224)
PHONE.................................661 768-4831
Tom Kaldenberg, *Brnch Mgr*
**EMP:** 21
**SALES (corp-wide):** 22.86B **Publicly Held**
**Web:** www.fcx.com
**SIC: 1382** Oil and gas exploration services
**HQ:** Freeport-Mcmoran Oil & Gas Llc
  21 Waterway Ave Ste 250
  Spring TX 77380
  713 579-6000

**(P-184)**
**FREEPORT-MCMORAN OIL & GAS LLC**
1200 Discovery Dr Ste 500, Bakersfield (93309-7038)
PHONE.................................661 322-7600
Kiran Leal, *Mgr*
**EMP:** 111
**SALES (corp-wide):** 22.86B **Publicly Held**
**Web:** www.fcx.com
**SIC: 1382** Oil and gas exploration services
**HQ:** Freeport-Mcmoran Oil & Gas Llc
  21 Waterway Ave Ste 250
  Spring TX 77380
  713 579-6000

**(P-185)**
**FREEPORT-MCMORAN OIL & GAS LLC**
Pxp Business Unit
17100 Calle Mariposa Reina, Goleta (93117-9737)
PHONE.................................805 567-1667
James C Flores, *Mgr*
**EMP:** 17
**SALES (corp-wide):** 22.86B **Publicly Held**
**Web:** www.fcx.com
**SIC: 1382** Oil and gas exploration services
**HQ:** Freeport-Mcmoran Oil & Gas Llc
  21 Waterway Ave Ste 250
  Spring TX 77380
  713 579-6000

**(P-186)**
**FREEPORT-MCMORAN OIL & GAS LLC**
5640 S Fairfax Ave, Los Angeles (90056-1266)
PHONE.................................323 298-2200
Charlotte Hargett, *Dir*
**EMP:** 103
**SALES (corp-wide):** 22.86B **Publicly Held**
**Web:** www.fcx.com
**SIC: 1382** Oil and gas exploration services
**HQ:** Freeport-Mcmoran Oil & Gas Llc
  21 Waterway Ave Ste 250
  Spring TX 77380
  713 579-6000

**(P-187)**
**GREKA INTEGRATED INC**
Also Called: Greka
1700 Sinton Rd, Santa Maria (93458-9708)
P.O. Box 5489 (93456-5489)
PHONE.................................805 347-8700
Randeep S Grewal, *CEO*
Susan Whalen, *
Ken Miller, *
▲ **EMP:** 145 **EST:** 2000
**SALES (est):** 23.58MM **Privately Held**
**Web:** www.greka.com
**SIC: 1382** Oil and gas exploration services

# PRODUCTS & SERVICES SECTION
## 1389 - Oil And Gas Field Services, Nec (P-210)

**(P-188)**
**LINN ENERGY LLC**
Also Called: Linn Western Operating
2000 Tonner Canyon Rd, Brea
(92821-2659)
PHONE.................714 257-1600
EMP: 20
SALES (corp-wide): 917.71MM **Privately Held**
SIC: 1382 Oil and gas exploration services
PA: Linn Energy, Inc.
   600 Travis St Ste 5100
   281 840-4000

**(P-189)**
**LINNCO LLC**
5201 Truxtun Ave, Bakersfield
(93309-0421)
PHONE.................661 616-3900
EMP: 888
SALES (corp-wide): 7.91MM **Privately Held**
SIC: 1382 Oil and gas exploration services
PA: Linnco, Llc
   600 Travis St Ste 5100
   281 840-4000

**(P-190)**
**MACPHERSON OIL COMPANY LLC**
24118 Round Mountain Rd, Bakersfield
(93308-9115)
P.O. Box 5368 (93388-5368)
PHONE.................661 556-6096
Wes Duncan, Mgr
EMP: 22
SALES (corp-wide): 903.46MM **Publicly Held**
Web: www.macphersonenergy.com
SIC: 1382 1311 Oil and gas exploration services; Crude petroleum and natural gas production
HQ: Macpherson Oil Company Llc
   11117 River Run Blvd
   Bakersfield CA 93311
   310 452-3880

**(P-191)**
**MAGNETRON POWER INVENTIONS INC**
2226 W 232nd St, Torrance (90501-5720)
PHONE.................310 462-6970
Ninan N Johnson, CEO
EMP: 22 EST: 1999
SQ FT: 2,500
SALES (est): 4.57MM **Privately Held**
Web: www.magnetronusa.com
SIC: 1382 Oil and gas exploration services

**(P-192)**
**NEWPORT ENERGY**
19200 Von Karman Ave Ste 400, Irvine
(92612-1541)
PHONE.................408 230-7545
Nyle Khan, CEO
Gordon Burk, COO
EMP: 25 EST: 1984
SQ FT: 5,000
SALES (est): 1.64MM **Privately Held**
SIC: 1382 Oil and gas exploration services

**(P-193)**
**OCCIDENTAL PETROLEUM INVESTMENT CO INC**
10889 Wilshire Blvd Fl 10, Los Angeles
(90024-4200)
PHONE.................310 208-8800
EMP: 4000
SIC: 1382 8744 Oil and gas exploration services; Facilities support services

**(P-194)**
**PHOENIX CPITL GROUP HLDNGS LLC**
18575 Jamboree Rd Ste 830, Irvine
(92612-2557)
PHONE.................303 749-0074
Dam Ferrari, CEO
Lindsey Wilson, COO
Curtis Allen, CFO
EMP: 50 EST: 2019
SALES (est): 9.33MM **Privately Held**
Web: www.phxcapitalgroup.com
SIC: 1382 Oil and gas exploration services

**(P-195)**
**QRE OPERATING LLC**
707 Wilshire Blvd Ste 4600, Los Angeles
(90017-3501)
PHONE.................213 225-5900
Alan L Smith, Managing Member
EMP: 81 EST: 2010
SALES (est): 931.85K **Privately Held**
SIC: 1382 Oil and gas exploration services
PA: Qr Energy, Lp
   707 Wlshire Blvd Ste 4600

**(P-196)**
**SAMEDAN OIL CORPORATION**
Also Called: Noble Energy
1360 Landing Ave, Seal Beach
(90740-6525)
PHONE.................661 319-5038
EMP: 449
SALES (corp-wide): 7.36MM **Privately Held**
Web: www.chevron.com
SIC: 1382 Oil and gas exploration services
PA: Samedan Oil Corporation
   1001 Noble Energy Way
   580 223-4110

**(P-197)**
**SANTA MARIA ENRGY HOLDINGS LLC**
2811 Airpark Dr, Santa Maria (93455-1417)
P.O. Box 7202 (93456-7202)
PHONE.................805 938-3320
EMP: 20 EST: 2008
SALES (est): 1.27MM **Privately Held**
Web: www.santamaria.com
SIC: 1382 Oil and gas exploration services

**(P-198)**
**SENTINEL PEAK RSOURCES CAL LLC**
1200 Discovery Dr Ste 100, Bakersfield
(93309-7033)
PHONE.................661 395-5214
EMP: 79
SALES (corp-wide): 83.66MM **Privately Held**
Web: www.sentinelpeakresources.com
SIC: 1382 Oil and gas exploration services
HQ: Sentinel Peak Resources California Llc
   6501 E Belleview Ave # 400
   Englewood CO 80111
   720 749-1105

**(P-199)**
**SENTINEL PEAK RSOURCES CAL LLC**
5640 S Fairfax Ave, Los Angeles
(90056-1266)
PHONE.................323 298-2200
EMP: 79
SALES (corp-wide): 83.66MM **Privately Held**
Web: www.sentinelpeakresources.com
SIC: 1382 Oil and gas exploration services
HQ: Sentinel Peak Resources California Llc
   6501 E Belleview Ave # 400
   Englewood CO 80111
   720 749-1105

**(P-200)**
**SIGNAL HILL PETROLEUM INC**
2633 Cherry Ave, Signal Hill (90755-2008)
PHONE.................562 595-6440
Jerrel Barto, Ch Bd
Craig C Barto, *
EMP: 49 EST: 1984
SALES (est): 27.28MM **Privately Held**
Web: www.shpi.net
SIC: 1382 Geological exploration, oil and gas field

**(P-201)**
**TERMO COMPANY**
3275 Cherry Ave, Long Beach
(90807-5213)
P.O. Box 2767 (90801-2767)
PHONE.................562 595-7401
David E Combs, Pr
Donna Sheaffer, Sec
Francis Roth, VP
Norbert Buss, VP
EMP: 21 EST: 1933
SQ FT: 18,034
SALES (est): 11.38MM **Privately Held**
Web: www.termoco.com
SIC: 1382 Oil and gas exploration services

**(P-202)**
**WARREN E&P INC**
Also Called: Warren E & P
400 Oceangate Ste 200, Long Beach
(90802-4306)
PHONE.................214 393-9688
James A Watt, CEO
Romy Massey, Contact Person*
EMP: 67 EST: 1973
SQ FT: 7,000
SALES (est): 22.04K **Privately Held**
Web: www.warrenresources.com
SIC: 1382 Oil and gas exploration services
PA: Warren Resources, Inc.
   14131 Midway Rd Ste 500

---
## 1389 Oil And Gas Field Services, Nec
---

**(P-203)**
**ALL RISK SHIELD INC**
1244 Pine St Ste 211, Paso Robles
(93446-7241)
P.O. Box 300 (93465-0300)
PHONE.................866 991-7190
Joe Torres, CEO
EMP: 20 EST: 2017
SALES (est): 2.78MM **Privately Held**
Web: www.allriskshield.com
SIC: 1389 7389 0851 Construction, repair, and dismantling services; Fire protection service other than forestry or public; Fire prevention services, forest

**(P-204)**
**ALLY ENTERPRISES**
5001 E Commercecenter Dr Ste 260, Bakersfield (93309-1659)
P.O. Box 20580 (93390-0580)
PHONE.................661 412-9933
Rick Noland, Pr
EMP: 20 EST: 2016
SALES (est): 6.26MM **Privately Held**
SIC: 1389 Oil field services, nec

**(P-205)**
**ANATESCO INC**
128 Bedford Way, Bakersfield (93308-1702)
P.O. Box 5694 (93388-5694)
PHONE.................661 399-6990
Douglas Paul Denesha, Pr
Jean Denesha, VP
EMP: 16 EST: 1978
SQ FT: 3,000
SALES (est): 2.24MM **Privately Held**
Web: www.anatesco.com
SIC: 1389 Oil field services, nec

**(P-206)**
**B & B PIPE AND TOOL CO (PA)**
3035 Walnut Ave, Long Beach
(90807-5221)
PHONE.................562 424-0704
Craig Braly, Pr
Stephanie Braly, *
▲ EMP: 23 EST: 1951
SQ FT: 2,000
SALES (est): 7.08MM
SALES (corp-wide): 7.08MM **Privately Held**
Web: www.bbpipe.com
SIC: 1389 Oil field services, nec

**(P-207)**
**BASIC ENERGY SERVICES INC**
6710 Stewart Way, Bakersfield (93308)
PHONE.................661 588-3800
EMP: 34
SALES (corp-wide): 411.38MM **Privately Held**
Web: www.basicenergyservices.com
SIC: 1389 Oil field services, nec
PA: Basic Energy Services, Inc.
   801 Cherry St Ste 2100
   817 334-4100

**(P-208)**
**BLACK GOLD PUMP & SUPPLY INC**
2459 Lewis Ave, Signal Hill (90755-3427)
PHONE.................323 298-0077
Michael L Bair, CEO
Michael L Bair, VP
Thomas E Casec, Sec
James L Hurd, Pr
▲ EMP: 17 EST: 1982
SALES (est): 11.84MM **Privately Held**
Web: www.blackgoldpump.com
SIC: 1389 Oil field services, nec

**(P-209)**
**C & H TESTING SERVICE INC (PA)**
6224 Price Way, Bakersfield (93308-5117)
P.O. Box 9907 (93389-1907)
PHONE.................661 589-4030
Donald T Hoover, Pr
Karen K Hoover, *
EMP: 20 EST: 1981
SQ FT: 1,500
SALES (est): 4.54MM
SALES (corp-wide): 4.54MM **Privately Held**
SIC: 1389 Oil field services, nec

**(P-210)**
**C&J WELL SERVICES LLC**
3752 Allen Rd, Bakersfield (93314-9242)
PHONE.................661 589-5220
Joana Lerma, Managing Member
Danielle Hunter, *
EMP: 900 EST: 2021

# 1389 - Oil And Gas Field Services, Nec (P-211)

SALES (est): 12.43MM **Privately Held**
Web: www.cjwellservices.com
**SIC: 1389** Servicing oil and gas wells

### (P-211)
### CAL-QUAKE CONSTRUCTION INC
636 N Formosa Ave, Los Angeles (90036-1943)
PHONE..................323 931-2969
Sheldon Perluss, *Pr*
Sheldon Perluss, *Pr*
John Taferner, *VP*
**EMP:** 28 **EST:** 2000
SALES (est): 2.12MM **Privately Held**
Web: www.cal-quake.com
**SIC: 1389** Construction, repair, and dismantling services

### (P-212)
### CAPSULE MANUFACTURING INC
Also Called: Capsule Mfg
1399 N Miller St, Anaheim (92806-1412)
PHONE..................949 245-4151
Chad Bowker, *Pr*
**EMP:** 68 **EST:** 2015
SALES (est): 1.33MM **Privately Held**
Web: www.capsulemfg.com
**SIC: 1389** Construction, repair, and dismantling services

### (P-213)
### CASING SPECIALTIES INC
12454 Snow Rd, Bakersfield (93314-8015)
PHONE..................661 399-5522
Russell C Davis, *Owner*
**EMP:** 25 **EST:** 2010
SALES (est): 4.98MM **Privately Held**
Web: www.casingspecialties.com
**SIC: 1389** Cementing oil and gas well casings

### (P-214)
### CASTRO CONSTRUCTION LLC
18375 Ventura Blvd, Tarzana (91356-4218)
PHONE..................689 220-9145
Ghil Castro, *Pr*
**EMP:** 25 **EST:** 2020
SALES (est): 1.43MM **Privately Held**
**SIC: 1389** Construction, repair, and dismantling services

### (P-215)
### CENTRAL CALIFORNIA CNSTR INC
7221 Downing Ave, Bakersfield (93308-5817)
PHONE..................661 978-8230
Dereke Gerecke, *Prin*
Tammie K Rankin-gerecke, *Prin*
**EMP:** 23 **EST:** 2005
SALES (est): 2.27MM **Privately Held**
**SIC: 1389** Construction, repair, and dismantling services

### (P-216)
### CHARGING TREE CORPORATION
35788 Highway 41, Coarsegold (93614-9786)
PHONE..................559 760-5473
**EMP:** 19
SALES (est): 983.01K **Privately Held**
Web: www.chargingtree.com
**SIC: 1389** Construction, repair, and dismantling services

### (P-217)
### CJ BERRY WELL SERVICES MGT LLC
3752 Allen Rd, Bakersfield (93314-9242)
PHONE..................661 589-5220
Joana Lerma, *Prin*
Danielle Hunter, *
Stacy Urbina, *
**EMP:** 900 **EST:** 2021
SALES (est): 7.6MM **Privately Held**
**SIC: 1389** Servicing oil and gas wells

### (P-218)
### CJD CONSTRUCTION SVCS INC
503 E Route 66, Glendora (91740-3506)
PHONE..................626 335-1116
Diego A Debenedetto, *Pr*
Diego Dibenedetto, *
**EMP:** 40 **EST:** 2004
SALES (est): 1.2MM **Privately Held**
Web: www.canyonair.com
**SIC: 1389** Construction, repair, and dismantling services

### (P-219)
### CL KNOX INC
Also Called: Advanced Industrial Services
34933 Imperial Ave, Bakersfield (93308-9579)
PHONE..................661 837-0477
Leslie Knox, *Pr*
Chris Knox, *
**EMP:** 80 **EST:** 1992
SALES (est): 10MM **Privately Held**
Web: www.clknoxinc.com
**SIC: 1389** 8742 Oil field services, nec; Industrial consultant

### (P-220)
### COMPOUND FOCUS INC
385 Oyster Point Blvd Ste 1, South San Francisco (94080-1970)
PHONE..................650 228-1400
**EMP:** 21 **EST:** 2006
SALES (est): 1.88MM
SALES (corp-wide): 849.39MM **Privately Held**
**SIC: 1389** Testing, measuring, surveying, and analysis services
PA: Evotec Se
Essener Bogen 7
40560810

### (P-221)
### CUMMINGS VACUUM SERVICE INC
Also Called: Cummings Transportation
112 El Paso Rd, Bakersfield (93314-3718)
PHONE..................661 746-1786
Pam Cummings, *Pr*
Ted Cummings, *
**EMP:** 60 **EST:** 1980
SALES (est): 8.4MM **Privately Held**
Web: www.cummings2.com
**SIC: 1389** Oil field services, nec

### (P-222)
### DE VRIES INTERNATIONAL INC (PA)
17671 Armstrong Ave, Irvine (92614-5727)
PHONE..................949 252-1212
Don Devries, *Pr*
◆ **EMP:** 27 **EST:** 1984
SALES (est): 9.93MM
SALES (corp-wide): 9.93MM **Privately Held**
Web: www.devriesintl.com
**SIC: 1389** Lease tanks, oil field: erecting, cleaning, and repairing

### (P-223)
### DRI CLEAN & RESTORATION
2918 N Blackstone Ave, Fresno (93703-1014)
PHONE..................559 292-1100
Lee Dannie, *Prin*
**EMP:** 25 **EST:** 2012
SALES (est): 3.85MM **Privately Held**
Web: www.drirestoration.com
**SIC: 1389** 1521 7699 Construction, repair, and dismantling services; Single-family housing construction; Cleaning services

### (P-224)
### DTE STOCKTON LLC
2526 W Washington St, Stockton (95203-2952)
PHONE..................209 467-3838
Nelson Nail, *Managing Member*
**EMP:** 34 **EST:** 2007
SALES (est): 11.74MM **Publicly Held**
**SIC: 1389** Construction, repair, and dismantling services
HQ: Dte Energy Services, Inc.
1 Energy Plz
Detroit MI 48226

### (P-225)
### DWAYNES ENGINEERING & CNSTR
3559 Addie Ave, Fellows (93224-9634)
PHONE..................661 762-7261
Dwayne Emfinger, *Pr*
**EMP:** 23 **EST:** 1979
SALES (est): 968.29K **Privately Held**
**SIC: 1389** Construction, repair, and dismantling services

### (P-226)
### ELI KISELMAN
Also Called: Dreamhome Remodeling and Bldrs
98 N 1st St Unit 725, San Jose (95113-1253)
PHONE..................832 886-3743
Eli Kiselman, *Owner*
**EMP:** 31 **EST:** 2021
SALES (est): 748.02K **Privately Held**
**SIC: 1389** Construction, repair, and dismantling services

### (P-227)
### ENGEL & GRAY INC
745 W Betteravia Rd Ste A, Santa Maria (93455-1298)
P.O. Box 5020 (93456-5020)
PHONE..................805 925-2771
Carl W Engel Junior, *Pr*
Robert Engel, *
**EMP:** 35 **EST:** 1946
**SQ FT:** 3,000
SALES (est): 4.9MM **Privately Held**
Web: www.engelandgray.com
**SIC: 1389** 1623 7389 2875 Construction, repair, and dismantling services; Pipeline construction, nsk; Crane and aerial lift service; Compost

### (P-228)
### ENGINEERED WELL SVC INTL INC
3120 Standard St, Bakersfield (93308-6241)
PHONE..................866 913-6283
Paul Sturgeon, *CEO*
John E Powell Junior, *Prin*
**EMP:** 19 **EST:** 2009
SALES (est): 1.64MM **Privately Held**

**SIC: 1389** Oil field services, nec

### (P-229)
### ETHOSENERGY FIELD SERVICES LLC (DH)
10455 Slusher Dr # 12, Santa Fe Springs (90670-3750)
PHONE..................310 639-3523
Mark Jones, *Pr*
Patricia Lelito, *CFO*
Mike Fieldhouse, *VP Opers*
**EMP:** 45 **EST:** 1970
SALES (est): 20.2MM
SALES (corp-wide): 5.9B **Privately Held**
Web: www.ethosenergyfs.com
**SIC: 1389** 8711 3462 Oil consultants; Industrial engineers; Pump, compressor, and turbine forgings
HQ: Ethosenergy Gts Holdings (Us), Llc
3100 S Sam Houston Pkwy E
Houston TX 77047

### (P-230)
### FIRST ENERGY SERVICES INC
1031 Carrier Parkway Ave, Bakersfield (93308-9670)
P.O. Box 80844 (93380-0844)
PHONE..................661 387-1972
Richard Chase, *Pr*
Jack Chase, *VP*
Charlotte Maddon, *Treas*
**EMP:** 20 **EST:** 1996
**SQ FT:** 7,000
SALES (est): 2.65MM **Privately Held**
**SIC: 1389** Oil field services, nec

### (P-231)
### GRAYSON SERVICE INC
1845 Greeley Rd, Bakersfield (93314-9547)
PHONE..................661 589-5444
Carol A Grayson, *Pr*
Cheryl Grayson, *
**EMP:** 18 **EST:** 1969
SALES (est): 1.02MM **Privately Held**
**SIC: 1389** Servicing oil and gas wells

### (P-232)
### GROUNDMETRICS INC
Also Called: GMI
7514 Girard Ave Ste 1306, La Jolla (92037-5149)
PHONE..................619 786-8023
George A Eiskamp, *CEO*
Jeffrey Symington, *CFO*
Carlos Heredia, *Corporate Secretary*
Svein Kjellesvik, *Dir*
John T Mcdougal, *Dir*
**EMP:** 15 **EST:** 2010
SALES (est): 2.34MM **Privately Held**
Web: www.groundmetrics.com
**SIC: 1389** 3829 Oil field services, nec; Surveying instruments and accessories

### (P-233)
### GROUP H ENGINEERING
2030 Vista Ave, Sierra Madre (91024-1554)
PHONE..................818 999-0999
Michael Karaiban, *Pt*
Anke Hamalian, *Pt*
**EMP:** 30 **EST:** 2001
SALES (est): 368.43K **Privately Held**
**SIC: 1389** Construction, repair, and dismantling services

### (P-234)
### HALLIBURTON COMPANY
34722 7th Standard Rd, Bakersfield (93314-9435)
PHONE..................661 393-8111
Dennis Lovett, *Brnch Mgr*

## PRODUCTS & SERVICES SECTION
## 1389 - Oil And Gas Field Services, Nec (P-257)

EMP: 52
Web: www.halliburton.com
SIC: 1389 Oil field services, nec
PA: Halliburton Company
3000 N Sam Houston Pkwy E

### (P-235)
### HALLIBURTON LEGAL
315 Bay St, San Francisco (94133-1993)
PHONE..................415 955-1155
EMP: 27 EST: 2019
SALES (est): 3.79MM Privately Held
Web: www.halliburtonlegal.com
SIC: 1389 Oil field services, nec

### (P-236)
### HAMO CONSTRUCTION
3650 Altura Ave, La Crescenta (91214-2463)
PHONE..................818 415-3334
Hamlet Karamyan, Owner
EMP: 47 EST: 2013
SALES (est): 525K Privately Held
SIC: 1389 Construction, repair, and dismantling services

### (P-237)
### HILLS WLDG & ENGRG CONTR INC
Also Called: Hwe Mechanical
22038 Stockdale Hwy, Bakersfield (93314-8889)
PHONE..................661 746-5400
Debora M Hill, VP
Robert Hill, Stockholder*
EMP: 92 EST: 1999
SALES (est): 9.58MM Privately Held
Web: www.hillswelding.com
SIC: 1389 Testing, measuring, surveying, and analysis services

### (P-238)
### HIRSH INC
Also Called: Better Mens Clothes
860 S Los Angeles St # 900, Los Angeles (90014-3311)
PHONE..................213 622-9441
EMP: 50
SALES (est): 1.09MM Privately Held
SIC: 1389 Lease tanks, oil field: erecting, cleaning, and repairing

### (P-239)
### HORIZON WELL LOGGING INC
711 Saint Andrews Way, Lompoc (93436-1326)
PHONE..................805 733-0972
Doug Milham, Pr
William Gilmore, Dir
James Eastes, Dir
▲ EMP: 22 EST: 1992
SALES (est): 6.6MM Privately Held
Web: www.horizon-well-logging.com
SIC: 1389 Oil field services, nec

### (P-240)
### INSTRUMENT CONTROL SERVICES
Also Called: I C S
6085 King Dr Unit 100, Ventura (93003-7178)
PHONE..................805 642-1999
Michael Leblanc, CEO
Joseph Edward Locklear, *
Michael Leblanc, VP
EMP: 45 EST: 1995
SQ FT: 6,100
SALES (est): 11.33MM Privately Held
Web: www.instrumentcontrol.com

SIC: 1389 7699 7373 7299 Construction, repair, and dismantling services; Industrial equipment services; Systems integration services; Banquet hall facilities

### (P-241)
### JAGUAR ENERGY LLC (PA)
2404 Colony Plz, Newport Beach (92660-6357)
PHONE..................949 706-7060
EMP: 27 EST: 2016
SALES (est): 925.83K
SALES (corp-wide): 925.83K Privately Held
SIC: 1389 Oil field services, nec

### (P-242)
### JERRY MELTON & SONS CNSTR INC
Also Called: Jerry Melton & Sons Cnstr
100 Jamison Ln, Taft (93268-4329)
PHONE..................661 765-5546
Jerry W Melton, Pr
Judy Melton, *
Steven Melton, *
Karen Melton, *
EMP: 85 EST: 1971
SALES (est): 4.08MM Privately Held
SIC: 1389 Oil and gas wells: building, repairing and dismantling

### (P-243)
### JOHN M PHILLIPS LLC
Also Called: John M Phillips Oil Field Eqp
2800 Gibson St, Bakersfield (93308-6106)
PHONE..................661 327-3118
Melody Shamaker, Off Mgr
EMP: 35
SALES (corp-wide): 4.47MM Privately Held
Web: www.johnmphillips.com
SIC: 1389 Oil field services, nec
PA: John M. Phillips, Llc
2755 Dawson Ave
562 595-7363

### (P-244)
### K C RESTORATION CO INC
1514 W 130th St, Gardena (90249-2104)
PHONE..................310 280-0597
Carolyn Lehne Macleod, Pr
Steve Lehne, *
Katherine Cecilia Lehne, *
EMP: 35 EST: 1991
SALES (est): 5.04MM Privately Held
Web: www.kcrestorationinc.com
SIC: 1389 2431 1752 1741 Construction, repair, and dismantling services; Windows and window parts and trim, wood; Wood floor installation and refinishing; Masonry and other stonework

### (P-245)
### KEY ENERGY SERVICES INC
62391 Sargents Rd, San Ardo (93450-8907)
PHONE..................831 627-2404
EMP: 46
SALES (corp-wide): 413.85MM Privately Held
Web: www.keyenergy.com
SIC: 1389 Servicing oil and gas wells
PA: Key Energy Services, Inc.
1500 Ctywest Blvd Ste 800
713 651-4300

### (P-246)
### KILGORE ENTERPRISES LLC
2005 San Jose Dr Unit 258, Antioch (94509-8607)

PHONE..................925 885-8999
EMP: 27 EST: 2015
SALES (est): 1.37MM Privately Held
Web: kilgore-enterprises-llc.business.site
SIC: 1389 Construction, repair, and dismantling services

### (P-247)
### KUSTER CO OIL WELL SERVICES
Also Called: Kuster Company
2900 E 29th St, Long Beach (90806-2315)
PHONE..................562 595-0661
John Davidson, CEO
▲ EMP: 23 EST: 1996
SALES (est): 1.58MM Privately Held
Web: www.probe1.com
SIC: 1389 Oil field services, nec
PA: Probe Holdings, Inc.
1132 Everman Pkwy Ste 100

### (P-248)
### LINDEN STEEL & CNSTR INC
17863 Ideal Pkwy, Manteca (95336-9477)
PHONE..................209 239-2160
Joe Orgon, Pr
EMP: 25 EST: 2004
SALES (est): 5.03MM Privately Held
SIC: 1389 Construction, repair, and dismantling services

### (P-249)
### M-I LLC
Also Called: M-I Swaco
4400 Fanucchi Way, Shafter (93263-9552)
PHONE..................661 321-5400
Forest Purpiance, Brnch Mgr
EMP: 31
Web: www.slb.com
SIC: 1389 Mud service, oil field drilling
HQ: M-I L.L.C.
5950 N Course Dr
Houston TX 77072
281 561-1300

### (P-250)
### MDM SOLUTIONS LLC
575 Anton Blvd Ste 300, Costa Mesa (92626-7161)
PHONE..................800 669-6361
Michael Flower, Managing Member
Michael Bryant, *
Cynthia Williams, *
Doug Sipe, *
EMP: 310 EST: 2015
SALES (est): 5.17MM Privately Held
Web: www.mdmcorp.com
SIC: 1389 Oil and gas wells: building, repairing and dismantling

### (P-251)
### MMI SERVICES INC
4042 Patton Way, Bakersfield (93308-5030)
PHONE..................661 589-9366
Steve Mcgowan, CEO
Steve Mcgowan, Pr
Mel Mcgowan, CEO
Eric Olson, *
EMP: 250 EST: 1985
SQ FT: 4,500
SALES (est): 24.14MM Privately Held
Web: www.mmi-services.com
SIC: 1389 Oil field services, nec

### (P-252)
### MTS STIMULATION SERVICES INC (PA)
Also Called: M T S

7131 Charity Ave, Bakersfield (93308-5870)
PHONE..................661 589-5804
Monda Dyrd, Pr
Craig Barto, Ch Bd
John Johnston, Sec
Polly Clark, Stockholder
Gary Starling, Stockholder
EMP: 15 EST: 1983
SQ FT: 1,400
SALES (est): 8MM
SALES (corp-wide): 8MM Privately Held
Web: www.mts-stim.com
SIC: 1389 Oil field services, nec

### (P-253)
### NABORS WELL SERVICES CO
2567 N Ventura Ave # C, Ventura (93001-1201)
PHONE..................805 648-2731
Paul Smith, Mgr
EMP: 75
Web: www.nabors.com
SIC: 1389 Oil field services, nec
HQ: Nabors Well Services Co.
515 W Greens Rd Ste 1000
Houston TX 77067
281 874-0035

### (P-254)
### NABORS WELL SERVICES CO
1025 Earthmover Ct, Bakersfield (93314-9529)
PHONE..................661 588-6140
Tom Jaquez, Mgr
EMP: 158
Web: www.nabors.com
SIC: 1389 Oil field services, nec
HQ: Nabors Well Services Co.
515 W Greens Rd Ste 1000
Houston TX 77067
281 874-0035

### (P-255)
### NABORS WELL SERVICES CO
19431 S Santa Fe Ave, Compton (90221-5912)
PHONE..................310 639-7074
EMP: 75
Web: www.nabors.com
SIC: 1389 Oil field services, nec
HQ: Nabors Well Services Co.
515 W Greens Rd Ste 1000
Houston TX 77067
281 874-0035

### (P-256)
### NABORS WELL SERVICES CO
1954 James Rd, Bakersfield (93308-9749)
PHONE..................661 392-7668
Dave Warner, Dist Mgr
EMP: 218
Web: www.nabors.com
SIC: 1389 Oil field services, nec
HQ: Nabors Well Services Co.
515 W Greens Rd Ste 1000
Houston TX 77067
281 874-0035

### (P-257)
### NABORS WELL SERVICES CO
7515 Rosedale Hwy, Bakersfield (93308-5727)
PHONE..................661 589-3970
Alan Pounds, Mgr
EMP: 211
Web: www.nabors.com
SIC: 1389 1382 Servicing oil and gas wells; Oil and gas exploration services
HQ: Nabors Well Services Co.
515 W Greens Rd Ste 1000

(PA)=Parent Co (HQ)=Headquarters
✪ = New Business established in last 2 years

## 1389 - Oil And Gas Field Services, Nec (P-258)

Houston TX 77067
281 874-0035

**(P-258)**
**OIL WELL SERVICE COMPANY**
10255 Enos Ln, Shafter (93263-9572)
PHONE..................661 746-4809
Rick Hobbs, *Off Mgr*
EMP: 60
SALES (corp-wide): 15.71MM **Privately Held**
Web: www.ows1.com
SIC: **1389** Swabbing wells
PA: Oil Well Service Company
  1241 E Burnett St
  562 612-0600

**(P-259)**
**OIL WELL SERVICE COMPANY (PA)**
1241 E Burnett St, Signal Hill (90755-3594)
PHONE..................562 612-0600
Jack Frost, *Pr*
Matt Hensley, *
Connie Laws, *
Richard Laws, *
EMP: 105 EST: 1940
SALES (est): 15.71MM
SALES (corp-wide): 15.71MM **Privately Held**
Web: www.ows1.com
SIC: **1389** Oil field services, nec

**(P-260)**
**OIL WELL SERVICE COMPANY**
Also Called: Oil Well Service
1015 Mission Rock Rd, Santa Paula (93060-9730)
PHONE..................805 525-2103
Harvey Himinell, *Mgr*
EMP: 60
SALES (corp-wide): 35.06MM **Privately Held**
Web: www.ows1.com
SIC: **1389** Oil field services, nec
PA: Oil Well Service Company
  1241 E Burnett St
  562 612-0600

**(P-261)**
**ONE STRUCTURAL INC**
19326 Ventura Blvd Ste 200, Tarzana (91356-3016)
PHONE..................626 252-0778
David Tashroudian, *Pr*
EMP: 35 EST: 2015
SALES (est): 2.68MM **Privately Held**
SIC: **1389** Construction, repair, and dismantling services

**(P-262)**
**OWEN OIL TOOLS LP**
5001 Standard St, Bakersfield (93308-4500)
PHONE..................661 637-1380
Frank Isbell, *Mgr*
EMP: 62
SALES (corp-wide): 509.79MM **Privately Held**
Web: www.ocsresponds.com
SIC: **1389** Oil field services, nec
HQ: Owen Oil Tools Lp
  12001 County Rd 1000
  Godley TX 76044
  817 551-0540

**(P-263)**
**PACIFIC PERFORATING INC**
25090 Highway 33, Fellows (93224-9777)
PHONE..................661 768-9224
Troy Ducharme, *Pr*
Perry Parker, *
▼ EMP: 25 EST: 1969
SQ FT: 4,000
SALES (est): 4.5MM **Privately Held**
Web: www.variperm.com
SIC: **1389** Oil field services, nec

**(P-264)**
**PACIFIC PETROLEUM CALIFORNIA INC**
Also Called: Oil Field Services
1615 E Betteravia Rd Ste A, Santa Maria (93454-9000)
P.O. Box 2646 (93457)
PHONE..................805 925-1947
EMP: 285 EST: 2005
SALES (est): 16.78MM **Privately Held**
Web: www.ppcinc.biz
SIC: **1389** 7353 Lease tanks, oil field: erecting, cleaning, and repairing; Oil field equipment, rental or leasing

**(P-265)**
**PACIFIC PROCESS SYSTEMS INC (PA)**
7401 Rosedale Hwy, Bakersfield (93308-5736)
PHONE..................661 321-9681
Jerry Wise, *CEO*
Alan George, *
Robert Peterson, *
▼ EMP: 90 EST: 1995
SQ FT: 7,000
SALES (est): 25.6MM **Privately Held**
Web: www.pps-equipment.com
SIC: **1389** 7353 5082 Testing, measuring, surveying, and analysis services; Oil field equipment, rental or leasing; Oil field equipment

**(P-266)**
**PALMER TANK & CONSTRUCTION INC**
2464 S Union Ave, Bakersfield (93307-5007)
PHONE..................661 834-1110
Jerry Palmer, *Pr*
EMP: 32 EST: 1971
SQ FT: 1,200
SALES (est): 4.58MM **Privately Held**
Web: www.palmertanks.com
SIC: **1389** 5731 Oil and gas wells: building, repairing and dismantling; Antennas

**(P-267)**
**PC MECHANICAL INC**
2803 Industrial Pkwy, Santa Maria (93455-1811)
PHONE..................805 925-2888
Lew Parker, *Pr*
Mitch Caron, *
Mary Parker, *
Brandon Burginger, *
EMP: 50 EST: 1991
SQ FT: 67,000
SALES (est): 10.07MM **Privately Held**
Web: www.pcmechanical.com
SIC: **1389** Oil field services, nec

**(P-268)**
**PENGO WIRELINE OF CALIFORNIA INC**
3529 Standard St, Bakersfield (93308-5224)
PHONE..................661 327-9900
EMP: 15 EST: 1981
SALES (est): 6.97MM **Privately Held**
Web: www.pengowireline.com
SIC: **1389** Oil field services, nec

**(P-269)**
**PRODUCTION DATA INC**
1210 33rd St, Bakersfield (93301-2124)
P.O. Box 3266 (93385-3266)
PHONE..................661 327-4776
Gerald Tonnelli, *Pr*
EMP: 35 EST: 1972
SQ FT: 1,800
SALES (est): 6.36MM **Privately Held**
Web: www.productiondatainc.com
SIC: **1389** Oil field services, nec

**(P-270)**
**PROS INCORPORATED**
3400 Patton Way, Bakersfield (93308-5722)
P.O. Box 20996 (93390-0996)
PHONE..................661 589-5400
Robert Lewis, *Pr*
EMP: 58 EST: 2007
SALES (est): 22.32MM **Privately Held**
Web: www.proswelltesting.com
SIC: **1389** Oil field services, nec

**(P-271)**
**PSC INDUSTRIAL OUTSOURCING LP**
Also Called: Hydrochempsc
200 Old Yard Dr, Bakersfield (93307-4268)
PHONE..................661 833-9991
Peter Burger, *Prin*
EMP: 72
SALES (corp-wide): 5.41B **Publicly Held**
Web: www.hpc-industrial.com
SIC: **1389** Oil field services, nec
HQ: Psc Industrial Outsourcing, Lp
  900 Georgia Ave
  Deer Park TX 77536
  713 393-5600

**(P-272)**
**REV VAC 7777 INC**
1907 Nute St, Bakersfield (93312-3512)
PHONE..................661 392-0355
Robin Brassfield-cooper, *Pr*
EMP: 20 EST: 2014
SALES (est): 2.3MM **Privately Held**
Web: www.revvac7777.com
SIC: **1389** Cleaning wells

**(P-273)**
**ROBERT HEELY CONSTRUCTION LP (PA)**
Also Called: Robert Heely Construction
5401 Woodmere Dr, Bakersfield (93313-2777)
PHONE..................661 617-1400
Robert Heely, *Ch*
Craig Bonna, *Pr*
EMP: 20 EST: 1974
SQ FT: 7,000
SALES (est): 23.04MM
SALES (corp-wide): 23.04MM **Privately Held**
Web: www.rhcteam.com
SIC: **1389** Oil field services, nec

**(P-274)**
**RPC INC**
1100 N Magnolia Ave Ste H, El Cajon (92020-1953)
PHONE..................619 334-6244
Roger Ramos, *Prin*
EMP: 29 EST: 2008
SALES (est): 5.18MM **Privately Held**
Web: www.usrpc.com
SIC: **1389** Oil field services, nec

**(P-275)**
**SCHLUMBERGER TECHNOLOGY CORP**
Also Called: Dowell Schlumberger
6120 Snow Rd, Bakersfield (93308-9531)
P.O. Box 81437 (93380-1437)
PHONE..................661 864-4721
Ron Melnyk, *Brnch Mgr*
EMP: 100
Web: www.slb.com
SIC: **1389** 1382 Oil field services, nec; Oil and gas exploration services
HQ: Schlumberger Technology Corp
  300 Schlumberger Dr
  Sugar Land TX 77478
  281 285-8500

**(P-276)**
**SOLI-BOND INC**
4230 Foster Ave, Bakersfield (93308-4559)
PHONE..................661 631-1633
Dwight Hartley, *Pr*
EMP: 15
Web: www.soli-bond.com
SIC: **1389** Oil field services, nec
PA: Soli-Bond, Inc.
  2377 2 Mile Rd

**(P-277)**
**STRATEGIC INDUSTRY INC**
1440 Draper St Ste C, Kingsburg (93631-1945)
P.O. Box 496 (93631-0496)
PHONE..................559 419-9481
Charles Miller, *Pr*
Jason Miller, *VP*
Rick Arteaga, *VP*
EMP: 20 EST: 2007
SALES (est): 4.94MM **Privately Held**
Web: www.strategicindustry.us
SIC: **1389** 1542 1541 Construction, repair, and dismantling services; Commercial and office building, new construction; Factory construction

**(P-278)**
**THETA OILFIELD SERVICES INC**
5201 California Ave Ste 370, Bakersfield (93309-1674)
PHONE..................661 633-2792
Dan A Newman, *Pr*
EMP: 44 EST: 2007
SALES (est): 2.92MM
SALES (corp-wide): 3.76B **Publicly Held**
Web: www.thetaportal.com
SIC: **1389** Oil field services, nec
PA: Championx Corporation
  2445 Tech Frest Blvd Bldg
  281 403-5772

**(P-279)**
**TIGER CASED HOLE SERVICES INC**
Also Called: Tiger Case Hole Services
2828 Junipero Ave, Signal Hill (90755-2112)
PHONE..................562 426-4044
Minnie P Baxter, *Sec*
Joseph S Baxter, *Treas*
▲ EMP: 43 EST: 1994
SQ FT: 6,000
SALES (est): 10.95MM
SALES (corp-wide): 4.15B **Publicly Held**
SIC: **1389** Oil field services, nec
HQ: Nextier Oilfield Solutions Llc
  3990 Rogerdale Rd
  Houston TX 77042
  713 325-6000

## PRODUCTS & SERVICES SECTION
### 1422 - Crushed And Broken Limestone (P-301)

**(P-280)**
**TITAN OILFIELD SERVICES INC**
Also Called: Titan Oilfield Services
21535 Kratzmeyer Rd, Bakersfield (93314-9482)
PHONE....................661 861-1630
Terry Hibbitts, CEO
Terry Hibbitts, Pr
Tim Barman, *
Tony Palacpac, *
**EMP:** 68 **EST:** 2011
**SALES (est):** 9.95MM **Privately Held**
Web: www.vinemarketing.com
**SIC: 1389** Oil field services, nec

**(P-281)**
**TOTAL-WESTERN INC**
3985 Teal Ct, Benicia (94510-1212)
PHONE....................707 747-5506
**EMP:** 40
**SALES (corp-wide):** 489.53MM **Privately Held**
Web: www.total-western.com
**SIC: 1389** Oil field services, nec
HQ: Total-Western, Inc.
8049 Somerset Blvd
Paramount CA 90723
562 220-1450

**(P-282)**
**TOTAL-WESTERN INC (HQ)**
Also Called: Roberts Engineers
8049 Somerset Blvd, Paramount (90723-4396)
PHONE....................562 220-1450
Paul F Conrad, CEO
Earl Grebing, *
Mary A Pool, *
Jerry Balos, *
Payman Farrokhyar, *
**EMP:** 49 **EST:** 1972
**SQ FT:** 13,000
**SALES (est):** 44.04MM
**SALES (corp-wide):** 489.53MM **Privately Held**
Web: www.total-western.com
**SIC: 1389** Oil field services, nec
PA: Bragg Investment Company, Inc.
6251 N Paramount Blvd
562 984-2400

**(P-283)**
**TRUITT OILFIELD MAINT CORP**
1051 James Rd, Bakersfield (93308-9753)
P.O. Box 5066 (93388-5066)
PHONE....................661 871-4099
Kimberly Sue New, Pr
Steve New, *
**EMP:** 300 **EST:** 1978
**SQ FT:** 3,000
**SALES (est):** 23.72MM **Privately Held**
Web: www.truittcorp.com
**SIC: 1389** Oil field services, nec

**(P-284)**
**TRYAD SERVICE CORPORATION**
5900 E Lerdo Hwy, Shafter (93263-4023)
PHONE....................661 391-1524
James Varner, Pr
Danny Seely, *
▲ **EMP:** 90 **EST:** 1933
**SALES (est):** 9.18MM **Privately Held**
Web: www.jdrush.com
**SIC: 1389** Oil and gas wells: building, repairing and dismantling

**(P-285)**
**TUBOSCOPE PIPELINE SVCS INC**
Also Called: Tuboscope
3003 Fairhaven Dr Ste B, Bakersfield (93308-6114)
PHONE....................661 328-5500
Scott Sprague, Mgr
**EMP:** 19
**SALES (corp-wide):** 8.58B **Publicly Held**
Web: www.nov.com
**SIC: 1389** Pipe testing, oil field service
HQ: Tuboscope Pipeline Services Inc.
2835 Holmes Rd
Houston TX 77051

**(P-286)**
**TUBOSCOPE PIPELINE SVCS INC**
Also Called: Tuboscope Nat Oilwell Varco
4621 Burr St, Bakersfield (93308-6143)
PHONE....................661 321-3400
Bill Grahm, Mgr
**EMP:** 16
**SALES (corp-wide):** 8.58B **Publicly Held**
Web: www.nov.com
**SIC: 1389** Oil field services, nec
HQ: Tuboscope Pipeline Services Inc.
2835 Holmes Rd
Houston TX 77051

**(P-287)**
**U S WEATHERFORD L P**
2815 Fruitvale Ave, Bakersfield (93308-5907)
PHONE....................661 589-9483
Rick Benton, Brnch Mgr
**EMP:** 231
Web: www.weatherford.com
**SIC: 1389** Oil field services, nec
HQ: U S Weatherford L P
1221 Evangeline Thruway
Broussard LA 70518
337 347-5300

**(P-288)**
**UPWING ENERGY INC**
16323 Shoemaker Ave, Cerritos (90703-2244)
PHONE....................562 293-1660
Herman Artinian, CEO
**EMP:** 15 **EST:** 2016
**SALES (est):** 9.99MM
**SALES (corp-wide):** 100.4MM **Privately Held**
Web: www.upwingenergy.com
**SIC: 1389** Oil field services, nec
HQ: Calnetix Technologies, Llc
16323 Shoemaker Ave
Cerritos CA 90703

**(P-289)**
**VANDERRA RESOURCES LLC**
1801 Century Park E Ste 2400, Los Angeles (90067-2326)
PHONE....................817 439-2220
**EMP:** 500
**SIC: 1389** Oil field services, nec

**(P-290)**
**VAQUERO ENERGY INC**
Also Called: Vaquero Hunter Inc.
4700 Stockdale Hwy Ste 120, Bakersfield (93309-2654)
P.O. Box 13550 (93389-3550)
PHONE....................661 616-0600
Kenneth H Hunter, CEO
Seth Hunter, VP
Cary Nikkel, Sec
**EMP:** 21 **EST:** 2000
**SALES (est):** 9.55MM **Privately Held**
Web: www.vaqueroenergy.com
**SIC: 1389** Testing, measuring, surveying, and analysis services

**(P-291)**
**WEATHERFORD INTERNATIONAL LLC**
201 Hallock Dr, Santa Paula (93060-9647)
P.O. Box 31 (93061-0031)
PHONE....................805 933-0242
Larry Brixey, Mgr
**EMP:** 18
Web: www.weatherford.com
**SIC: 1389** Oil field services, nec
HQ: Weatherford International, Llc
2000 St James Pl
Houston TX 77056
713 693-4000

**(P-292)**
**WELBILT INC**
3835 E Thousand Oaks Blvd Unit 315, Westlake Village (91362-3637)
PHONE....................310 339-1555
Ben Hunter, CEO
**EMP:** 25 **EST:** 2022
**SALES (est):** 1.64MM **Privately Held**
Web: www.welbiltsc.com
**SIC: 1389** Construction, repair, and dismantling services

### 1411 Dimension Stone

**(P-293)**
**BO DEAN CO INC (DH)**
Also Called: Bo Dean A Crh Company
1060 N Dutton Ave, Santa Rosa (95401-5011)
PHONE....................707 576-8205
Ricardo P Linares, CEO
**EMP:** 29 **EST:** 1988
**SQ FT:** 5,000
**SALES (est):** 19.44MM
**SALES (corp-wide):** 34.95B **Privately Held**
Web: www.bodeancompany.com
**SIC: 1411** 2951 Greenstone, dimension-quarrying; Concrete, asphaltic (not from refineries)
HQ: Crh Americas Materials, Inc.
900 Ashwood Pkwy Ste 600
Atlanta GA 30338

**(P-294)**
**CHANDLER AGGREGATES INC (PA)**
24867 Maitri Rd, Corona (92883-5136)
P.O. Box 78450 (92877-0148)
PHONE....................951 277-1341
Larry Werner, Pr
**EMP:** 20 **EST:** 1994
**SALES (est):** 4.38MM **Privately Held**
Web: www.wernercorp.net
**SIC: 1411** 1422 Dimension stone; Crushed and broken limestone

**(P-295)**
**TAKE IT FOR GRANITE INC**
Also Called: Tifg
345 Phelan Ave, San Jose (95112-4104)
PHONE....................408 790-2812
Jason Krulee, Pr
▲ **EMP:** 20 **EST:** 1997
**SQ FT:** 32,000
**SALES (est):** 3.33MM **Privately Held**
Web: www.tifgranite.com
**SIC: 1411** Dimension stone

### 1422 Crushed And Broken Limestone

**(P-296)**
**AZUSA ROCK LLC**
3605 Dehesa Rd, El Cajon (92019-2903)
PHONE....................619 440-2363
Tom Nelson, Mgr
**EMP:** 44
Web: www.azusaca.gov
**SIC: 1422** Crushed and broken limestone
HQ: Azusa Rock, Llc
3901 Fish Canyon Rd
Azusa CA 91702
858 530-9444

**(P-297)**
**AZUSA ROCK LLC**
Also Called: Los Banos Rock and Ready Mix
22101 W Sunset Ave, Los Banos (93635-9683)
P.O. Box 1111 (93635-1111)
PHONE....................209 826-5066
Wayne Stoughton, Mgr
**EMP:** 44
Web: www.azusaca.gov
**SIC: 1422** Crushed and broken limestone
HQ: Azusa Rock, Llc
3901 Fish Canyon Rd
Azusa CA 91702
858 530-9444

**(P-298)**
**CALMAT CO**
16101 Hwy 156, Maricopa (93252)
P.O. Box 22800 (93390-2800)
PHONE....................661 858-2673
Angela Bailey, Mgr
**EMP:** 360
Web: www.vulcanmaterials.com
**SIC: 1422** Crushed and broken limestone
HQ: Calmat Co.
1200 Urban Center Dr
Birmingham AL 35242
818 553-8821

**(P-299)**
**DUMBARTON QUARRY ASSOCIATES (PA)**
2000 Scott Creek Rd, Milpitas (95035)
PHONE....................510 793-8861
East E Co, Prin
**EMP:** 15 **EST:** 1968
**SQ FT:** 2,000
**SALES (est):** 6.43MM
**SALES (corp-wide):** 6.43MM **Privately Held**
**SIC: 1422** 3531 Cement rock, crushed and broken-quarrying; Asphalt plant, including gravel-mix type

**(P-300)**
**NORTHERN AGGREGATES INC**
500 Cropley Ln, Willits (95490-4140)
P.O. Box 1566 (95490-1566)
PHONE....................707 459-3929
Frank Dutra, Pr
Randy Lucchetti, *
**EMP:** 25 **EST:** 1990
**SQ FT:** 10,000
**SALES (est):** 6.25MM **Privately Held**
**SIC: 1422** Crushed and broken limestone

**(P-301)**
**PORTOLA MINERALS COMPANY**
Also Called: Blue Mountain Minerals
24599 Marble Quarry Rd, Columbia (95310-9772)

# 1422 - Crushed And Broken Limestone (P-302)

PHONE.................................209 533-0127
**EMP:** 52 **EST:** 1983
**SALES (est):** 21.63MM **Privately Held**
**Web:** www.bluemountainminerals.com
**SIC: 1422** Limestones, ground

## (P-302)
### SYAR INDUSTRIES INC
Also Called: SYAR INDUSTRIES, INC.
885 Lake Herman Rd, Vallejo (94591-8324)
P.O. Box 2540 (94558-0524)
PHONE.................................707 643-3261
Mike Burneson, *Mgr*
**EMP:** 21
**Web:** www.syarindustriesinc.com
**SIC: 1422** 5211 Crushed and broken limestone; Cement
**HQ:** Syar Industries, Llc
2301 Napa Vallejo Hwy
Napa CA 94558
707 252-8711

## 1429 Crushed And Broken Stone, Nec

### (P-303)
### OLIVER DE SILVA INC (PA)
Also Called: Gallagher & Burk
11555 Dublin Blvd, Dublin (94568-2854)
P.O. Box 2922 (94568-0922)
PHONE.................................925 829-9220
Edwin O De Silva, *Ch*
Richard B Gates, *Pr*
David De Silva, *Ex VP*
Ernest Lampkin, *VP*
J Scott Archibald, *VP*
**EMP:** 20 **EST:** 1931
**SQ FT:** 60,000
**SALES (est):** 9.39MM
**SALES (corp-wide):** 9.39MM **Privately Held**
**Web:** www.desilvagates.com
**SIC: 1429** Igneous rock, crushed and broken-quarrying

### (P-304)
### PAUL HUBBS CONSTRUCTION CO INC (PA)
542 W C St, Colton (92324-2140)
PHONE.................................951 360-3990
Jay P Hubbs, *Pr*
John L Hubbs, *
Lucile M Hubbs, *
Pat Hubbs, *
**EMP:** 18 **EST:** 1961
**SQ FT:** 4,000
**SALES (est):** 2.76MM
**SALES (corp-wide):** 2.76MM **Privately Held**
**SIC: 1429** Riprap quarrying

### (P-305)
### SAN RAFAEL ROCK QUARRY INC (HQ)
Also Called: Dutra Materials
2350 Kerner Blvd Ste 200, San Rafael (94901-5595)
PHONE.................................415 459-7740
Bill Toney Dutra, *CEO*
**EMP:** 70 **EST:** 1994
**SALES (est):** 17.72MM
**SALES (corp-wide):** 99.82MM **Privately Held**
**Web:** www.sanrafaelrockquarry.com
**SIC: 1429** 1629 Basalt, crushed and broken-quarrying; Marine construction
**PA:** The Dutra Group
2350 Kerner Blvd Ste 200
415 258-6876

### (P-306)
### TRIANGLE ROCK PRODUCTS LLC
500 N Brand Blvd Ste 500, Glendale (91203)
PHONE.................................818 553-8820
Stanley G Bass, *Pr*
**EMP:** 180 **EST:** 1978
**SQ FT:** 20,000
**SALES (est):** 804.46K **Publicly Held**
**SIC: 1429** 1442 2951 3273 Igneous rock, crushed and broken-quarrying; Construction sand and gravel; Asphalt paving mixtures and blocks; Ready-mixed concrete
**HQ:** Calmat Co.
1200 Urban Center Dr
Birmingham AL 35242
818 553-8821

## 1442 Construction Sand And Gravel

### (P-307)
### ALAMEDA CONSTRUCTION SVCS INC
2528 E 125th St, Compton (90222-1502)
PHONE.................................310 635-3277
Kevin Ramsey, *CEO*
Tracey Watson, *VP*
**EMP:** 20 **EST:** 1992
**SQ FT:** 8,000
**SALES (est):** 6.3MM **Privately Held**
**Web:** www.alamedaconstruction.com
**SIC: 1442** Construction sand and gravel

### (P-308)
### BALDWIN CONTRACTING CO INC
400 S Lincoln St, Stockton (95203-3312)
PHONE.................................209 460-3785
**EMP:** 16
**SALES (corp-wide):** 2.83B **Publicly Held**
**SIC: 1442** Construction sand and gravel
**HQ:** Baldwin Contracting Company, Inc.
1764 Skyway
Chico CA 95928
530 891-6555

### (P-309)
### BUTTE SAND AND GRAVEL
10373 S Butte Rd, Sutter (95982-9316)
P.O. Box 749 (95982-0749)
PHONE.................................530 755-0225
Darren Morehead, *Pr*
Joseph Morehead Ii, *VP*
Martin Morehead, *CFO*
**EMP:** 20 **EST:** 1963
**SQ FT:** 1,000
**SALES (est):** 9.3MM **Privately Held**
**Web:** www.buttesand.com
**SIC: 1442** 5211 Gravel mining; Sand and gravel

### (P-310)
### CANYON ROCK CO INC
Also Called: River Ready Mix
7525 Hwy 116, Forestville (95436-9227)
P.O. Box 639 (95436-0639)
PHONE.................................707 887-2207
Wendell Trappe, *Pr*
Gwen Trappe, *VP*
**EMP:** 20 **EST:** 1949
**SQ FT:** 3,000
**SALES (est):** 9.81MM **Privately Held**
**Web:** www.canyonrockinc.com
**SIC: 1442** 3273 Construction sand and gravel; Ready-mixed concrete

### (P-311)
### ENNISS INC
12535 Vigilante Rd, Lakeside (92040-1167)
P.O. Box 1769 (92040-0917)
PHONE.................................619 561-1101
David Von Bhren, *Pr*
D Lois Miller, *
**EMP:** 40 **EST:** 2002
**SQ FT:** 4,700
**SALES (est):** 9.43MM **Privately Held**
**Web:** www.ennissinc.com
**SIC: 1442** 4212 3271 4953 Sand mining; Local trucking, without storage; Architectural concrete: block, split, fluted, screen, etc.; Recycling, waste materials

### (P-312)
### GAIL MATERIALS INC
10060 Dawson Canyon Rd, Corona (92883-2112)
PHONE.................................951 667-6106
▲ **EMP:** 24 **EST:** 1987
**SQ FT:** 5,000
**SALES (est):** 3.74MM **Privately Held**
**Web:** www.gailmaterials.net
**SIC: 1442** Construction sand and gravel

### (P-313)
### GRANITE ROCK CO
Also Called: AR Wilson Quarry
Quarry Rd, Aromas (95004)
P.O. Box 699 (95004-0699)
PHONE.................................831 768-2300
Bruce Wollepert, *Pr*
**EMP:** 30
**SALES (corp-wide):** 501.14MM **Privately Held**
**Web:** www.graniterock.com
**SIC: 1442** 2951 Gravel mining; Asphalt paving mixtures and blocks
**PA:** Granite Rock Company
350 Technology Dr
831 768-2000

### (P-314)
### GRANITE ROCK COMPANY (PA)
350 Technology Dr, Watsonville (95076-2488)
P.O. Box 50001 (95077-5001)
PHONE.................................831 768-2000
Peter Lemon, *Pr*
Mary E Woolpert, *
Bruce G Woolpert, *Vice Chairman*
Rita Alves, *
**EMP:** 100 **EST:** 1900
**SQ FT:** 10,000
**SALES (est):** 501.14MM
**SALES (corp-wide):** 501.14MM **Privately Held**
**Web:** www.graniterock.com
**SIC: 1442** 3273 5032 2951 Gravel mining; Ready-mixed concrete; Sand, construction; Asphalt and asphaltic paving mixtures (not from refineries)

### (P-315)
### HANSEN BROS ENTERPRISES (PA)
Also Called: Hbe Rental
11727 La Barr Meadows Rd, Grass Valley (95949-7722)
P.O. Box 1599 (95945-1599)
PHONE.................................530 273-3100
Orson Hansen, *Pr*
Sue Peterson, *
Frank Bennallack, *
**EMP:** 70 **EST:** 1953
**SQ FT:** 20,000
**SALES (est):** 23.07MM
**SALES (corp-wide):** 23.07MM **Privately Held**
**Web:** www.gohbe.com
**SIC: 1442** 3273 1794 7359 Gravel mining; Ready-mixed concrete; Excavation work; Equipment rental and leasing, nec

### (P-316)
### KAUFMAN BUILDING & MGT INC
1834 Soscol Ave Ste C, Napa (94559-1352)
PHONE.................................707 732-3770
Jeff Kaufman, *CEO*
**EMP:** 16 **EST:** 2016
**SALES (est):** 947.88K **Privately Held**
**SIC: 1442** Construction sand and gravel

### (P-317)
### LHOIST NORTH AMERICA ARIZ INC
Also Called: Natividad Plant Us24
11771 Old Stage Road, Salinas (93908)
P.O. Box 1938 (93902-1938)
PHONE.................................831 449-9117
Chris Randall, *Manager*
**EMP:** 29
**SALES (corp-wide):** 127.31MM **Privately Held**
**SIC: 1442** Construction sand and gravel
**HQ:** Lhoist North America Of Arizona, Inc.
5600 Clearfork Main St # 300
Fort Worth TX 76101
817 732-8164

### (P-318)
### NORTH COUNTY SAND AND GRAV INC
26160 Jackson Ave, Murrieta (92563-9721)
PHONE.................................951 928-2881
M J La Paglia Iii, *Pr*
Michael J La Paglia Iii, *Pr*
Tracy Paglia, *CFO*
**EMP:** 18 **EST:** 1985
**SALES (est):** 4.43MM **Privately Held**
**Web:** www.northcountysandandgravel.com
**SIC: 1442** 5032 Construction sand and gravel; Sand, construction

### (P-319)
### PECK ROAD GRAVEL PIT
128 Live Oak Ave, Monrovia (91016-5050)
P.O. Box 1286 (91017-1286)
PHONE.................................626 574-7570
Steve Bubalo, *Pr*
Stephanie Bubalo Becerra, *
Louise Bubalo, *
**EMP:** 17 **EST:** 1995
**SALES (est):** 3.53MM **Privately Held**
**SIC: 1442** Construction sand and gravel

### (P-320)
### PTI SAND & GRAVEL INC
14925 River Rd, Eastvale (92880-8935)
P.O. Box 6019 (92860-8034)
PHONE.................................951 272-0140
Michael Ellena, *Pr*
Mark Horner, *
**EMP:** 28 **EST:** 1948
**SALES (est):** 4.15MM **Privately Held**
**Web:** www.ptisag.com
**SIC: 1442** Construction sand and gravel

### (P-321)
### TEICHERT INC
Also Called: Teichert Aggregates
13879 Butterfield Dr, Truckee (96161-3331)
P.O. Box 447 (96160-0447)
PHONE.................................530 587-3811
Ed Herrnberger, *Manager*
**EMP:** 113

## 1499 - Miscellaneous Nonmetallic Mining (P-339)

SALES (corp-wide): 827.08MM **Privately Held**
Web: www.teichert.com
SIC: **1442** Construction sand and gravel
HQ: A. Teichert & Son, Inc.
3500 American River Dr
Sacramento CA 95864

**(P-322)**
**TEICHERT INC**
Also Called: Teichert Aggregates
36314 S Bird Rd, Tracy (95304-8678)
PHONE.............................209 832-4150
Jerry Hansen, *Manager*
EMP: 81
SALES (corp-wide): 827.08MM **Privately Held**
Web: www.teichert.com
SIC: **1442** Construction sand and gravel
HQ: A. Teichert & Son, Inc.
3500 American River Dr
Sacramento CA 95864

**(P-323)**
**TEICHERT INC**
Also Called: Teichert Aggregates
27944 County Road 19a, Esparto (95627-2237)
PHONE.............................530 787-3468
Bill Cruickshank, *Manager*
EMP: 40
SALES (corp-wide): 827.08MM **Privately Held**
Web: www.teichert.com
SIC: **1442** Construction sand and gravel
HQ: A. Teichert & Son, Inc.
3500 American River Dr
Sacramento CA 95864

**(P-324)**
**TEICHERT INC**
Also Called: Teichert Aggregates
2601 State Highway 49, Cool (95614-9528)
P.O. Box 280 (95614-0280)
PHONE.............................530 885-4244
Ed Herrnberger, *Manager*
EMP: 115
SALES (corp-wide): 827.08MM **Privately Held**
Web: www.teichert.com
SIC: **1442** Construction sand and gravel
HQ: A. Teichert & Son, Inc.
3500 American River Dr
Sacramento CA 95864

**(P-325)**
**TEICHERT INC**
Also Called: Teichert Aggregates
3331 Walnut Ave, Marysville (95901-9421)
PHONE.............................530 749-1230
Brandon Stauffer, *Manager*
EMP: 87
SALES (corp-wide): 827.08MM **Privately Held**
Web: www.teichert.com
SIC: **1442** Construction sand and gravel
HQ: A. Teichert & Son, Inc.
3500 American River Dr
Sacramento CA 95864

**(P-326)**
**TEICHERT INC**
Also Called: Teichert Aggregates
4249 Hammonton Smartville Rd, Marysville (95901)
PHONE.............................530 743-6111
Brandon Stauffer, *Manager*
EMP: 109
SALES (corp-wide): 827.08MM **Privately Held**
Web: www.teichert.com
SIC: **1442** Construction sand and gravel
HQ: A. Teichert & Son, Inc.
3500 American River Dr
Sacramento CA 95864

**(P-327)**
**TEICHERT INC**
Also Called: Teichert Aggregates
3417 Grant Line Rd, Rancho Cordova (95742-7000)
P.O. Box 981 (95763-0981)
PHONE.............................916 351-0123
Mike Cunnigham, *Manager*
EMP: 116
SALES (corp-wide): 827.08MM **Privately Held**
Web: www.teichert.com
SIC: **1442** Construction sand and gravel
HQ: A. Teichert & Son, Inc.
3500 American River Dr
Sacramento CA 95864

**(P-328)**
**TEICHERT INC**
Also Called: Teichert Aggregates
8760 Kiefer Blvd, Sacramento (95826-3917)
P.O. Box 15002 (95851-0002)
PHONE.............................916 386-6900
Mike Cunnigham, *Manager*
EMP: 97
SALES (corp-wide): 827.08MM **Privately Held**
Web: www.teichert.com
SIC: **1442** Construction sand and gravel
HQ: A. Teichert & Son, Inc.
3500 American River Dr
Sacramento CA 95864

### 1446 Industrial Sand

**(P-329)**
**PIONEER SANDS LLC**
9952 Enos Lane, Bakersfield (93314)
PHONE.............................661 746-5789
Donna Bartlett, *Brnch Mgr*
EMP: 29
SALES (corp-wide): 344.58B **Publicly Held**
Web: www.pwgillibrand.com
SIC: **1446** Silica mining
HQ: Pioneer Sands Llc
777 Hidden Rdg
Irving TX 75038
972 444-9001

**(P-330)**
**PIONEER SANDS LLC**
31302 Ortega Hwy, San Juan Capistrano (92675)
PHONE.............................949 728-0171
Mike Miclette, *Brnch Mgr*
EMP: 32
SALES (corp-wide): 344.58B **Publicly Held**
SIC: **1446** Silica sand mining
HQ: Pioneer Sands Llc
777 Hidden Rdg
Irving TX 75038
972 444-9001

**(P-331)**
**PW GILLIBRAND CO INC (PA)**
4537 Ish Dr, Simi Valley (93063-7667)
P.O. Box 1019 (93062-1019)
PHONE.............................805 526-2195
Celine Gillibrand, *CEO*
Richard Valencia, *

Jim Costello, *
EMP: 48 EST: 1957
SQ FT: 11,000
SALES (est): 24.25MM
SALES (corp-wide): 24.25MM **Privately Held**
Web: www.pwgillibrand.com
SIC: **1446** Grinding sand mining

### 1455 Kaolin And Ball Clay

**(P-332)**
**CP KELCO US INC**
Also Called: CP Kelco
2025 Harbor Dr, San Diego (92113-2214)
PHONE.............................619 595-5000
Andrew Currie, *Brnch Mgr*
EMP: 20
SALES (corp-wide): 1.24B **Privately Held**
Web: www.cpkelco.com
SIC: **1455** Kaolin mining
HQ: Cp Kelco U.S., Inc.
3100 Cumberland Blvd Se # 600
Atlanta GA 30339
678 247-7300

### 1474 Potash, Soda, And Borate Minerals

**(P-333)**
**5E BORON AMERICAS LLC**
27555 Hector Rd, Newberry Springs (92365-8905)
PHONE.............................442 292-2120
Michael Schlumpberger, *CEO*
EMP: 38
Web: www.5eadvancedmaterials.com
SIC: **1474** Borate compounds (natural) mining
HQ: 5e Boron Americas, Llc
9329 Mariposa Rd Ste 210
Hesperia CA 92344
419 371-3331

### 1479 Chemical And Fertilizer Mining

**(P-334)**
**SEARLES VALLEY MINERALS INC**
80201 Trona Rd, Trona (93562)
PHONE.............................760 372-2259
Burnell Blanchard, *VP*
EMP: 122
Web: www.svminerals.com
SIC: **1479** Salt and sulfur mining
HQ: Searles Valley Minerals Inc.
9401 Indian Creek Pkwy
Overland Park KS 66210

**(P-335)**
**SEARLES VALLEY MINERALS INC**
13068 Main St, Trona (93562-1911)
PHONE.............................760 672-2053
EMP: 122
Web: www.svminerals.com
SIC: **1479** Salt and sulfur mining
HQ: Searles Valley Minerals Inc.
9401 Indian Creek Pkwy
Overland Park KS 66210

### 1481 Nonmetallic Mineral Services

**(P-336)**
**MP MINE OPERATIONS LLC**
67750 Bailey Rd, Mountain Pass (92366)
PHONE.............................702 277-0848
James H Litinsky, *CEO*
Michael Rosethal, *
EMP: 108 EST: 2017
SALES (est): 63.28MM
SALES (corp-wide): 253.44MM **Publicly Held**
SIC: **1481** 1099 Mine exploration, nonmetallic minerals; Rare-earth ores mining
PA: Mp Materials Corp.
1700 S Pvlion Ctr Dr Ste
702 844-6111

### 1499 Miscellaneous Nonmetallic Mining

**(P-337)**
**ATLAS LITHIUM CORPORATION**
433 N Camden Dr Ste 810, Beverly Hills (90210-4412)
PHONE.............................833 661-7900
Marc Fogassa, *Ch*
Tiago Moreira De Miranda, *Principal Accounting Officer*
Brian W Bernier, *Investor Relations Vice President*
Joel De Paiva Monteiro Esg, *Operations*
Areli Nogueira Da Silva Jr Geol, *MINERAL EXPLORATION*
EMP: 76 EST: 2012
SIC: **1499** Diamond mining, industrial

**(P-338)**
**DICAPERL CORPORATION (DH)**
Also Called: Grefco Dicaperl
23705 Crenshaw Blvd Ste 101, Torrance (90505)
PHONE.............................610 667-6640
Ray Perelman, *CEO*
Glenn Jones, *
Mike Cull, *
Barry Katz, *
▼ EMP: 90 EST: 1992
SQ FT: 5,000
SALES (est): 1.99MM **Privately Held**
Web: www.dicalite.com
SIC: **1499** 3677 Perlite mining; Filtration devices, electronic
HQ: Grefco Minerals Inc.
1 Bala Ave Ste 310
Bala Cynwyd PA 19004
610 660-8820

**(P-339)**
**FEATHEROCK INC (PA)**
20219 Bahama St, Chatsworth (91311-6204)
PHONE.............................818 882-3888
Eric Anderson, *Pr*
Bob Campagna, *Contrlr*
EMP: 15 EST: 1941
SQ FT: 20,000
SALES (est): 3.95MM
SALES (corp-wide): 3.95MM **Privately Held**
Web: www.featherock.com
SIC: **1499** Pumice mining

# 1499 - Miscellaneous Nonmetallic Mining (P-340)

## PRODUCTS & SERVICES SECTION

**(P-340)**
**H LIMA COMPANY INC**
704 E Yosemite Ave, Manteca (95336-5827)
PHONE.....................209 239-6787
Michael Lima, *Pr*
Henry Frank Lima Junior, *VP*
Mark Lima, *
Debbie Enos, *
Frank Lima, *
**EMP:** 26 **EST:** 1962
**SQ FT:** 1,300
**SALES (est):** 1.82MM **Privately Held**
**SIC: 1499** Gypsum mining

**(P-341)**
**IMERYS MINERALS CALIFORNIA INC (HQ)**
2500 San Miguelito Rd, Lompoc (93436-9743)
P.O. Box 519 (93438-0519)
PHONE.....................805 736-1221
Douglas A Smith, *Pr*
John Oskam, *
John Leichty, *
◆ **EMP:** 67 **EST:** 1991
**SQ FT:** 11,600
**SALES (est):** 88.71MM
**SALES (corp-wide):** 88.71MM **Privately Held**
**Web:** www.imerys.com
**SIC: 1499 3295** Diatomaceous earth mining; Minerals, ground or treated
**PA:** Imerys Filtration Minerals, Inc.
2500 San Miguelito Rd
805 736-1221

## 1521 Single-family Housing Construction

**(P-342)**
**1ST CENTURY BUILDERS INC**
5737 Kanan Rd, Agoura Hills (91301-1601)
PHONE.....................818 254-7183
Colin Pratt, *CEO*
**EMP:** 18 **EST:** 2017
**SALES (est):** 2.64MM **Privately Held**
**SIC: 1521 1389** New construction, single-family houses; Construction, repair, and dismantling services

**(P-343)**
**CALVILLO CONSTRUCTION CORP**
Also Called: Tiling and Stone Counter Tops
1133 Brooks St Ste C, Ontario (91762-3662)
PHONE.....................310 985-3911
Luciano Calvillo, *Owner*
Luciano Calvillo, *Pr*
**EMP:** 26 **EST:** 2011
**SALES (est):** 1.56MM **Privately Held**
**Web:** www.calvilloconstructioncorp.com
**SIC: 1521 1522 1411 1743** Single-family housing construction; Hotel/motel and multi-family home construction; Limestone and marble dimension stone; Tile installation, ceramic

**(P-344)**
**CHAMPION HOME BUILDERS INC**
299 N Smith Ave, Corona (92878-3241)
PHONE.....................951 256-4617
**EMP:** 105
**SALES (corp-wide):** 2.02B **Publicly Held**
**Web:** www.championhomes.com
**SIC: 1521 2451** New construction, single-family houses; Mobile homes, except recreational
**HQ:** Champion Home Builders, Inc.
755 W Big Beavr Rd # 1000
Troy MI 48084
248 614-8200

**(P-345)**
**NLMS ELITE CONSTRUCTION CO**
1254 S Waterman Ave, San Bernardino (92408-2855)
PHONE.....................626 205-8417
Nathan Murphy, *Owner*
**EMP:** 15 **EST:** 2008
**SALES (est):** 315.68K **Privately Held**
**SIC: 1521 1389 1542 1531** Single-family housing construction; Construction, repair, and dismantling services; Commercial and office building contractors; Speculative builder, multi-family dwellings

**(P-346)**
**PACIFIC CAST CNSTR WTRPROOFING**
390 Oak Ave Ste A, Carlsbad (92008-2966)
PHONE.....................760 298-3170
James Schilling, *Pr*
**EMP:** 23 **EST:** 2012
**SALES (est):** 2.53MM **Privately Held**
**Web:** www.pacificcoastcorporate.com
**SIC: 1521 1389** Single-family housing construction; Construction, repair, and dismantling services

**(P-347)**
**PGC CONSTRUCTION INC**
Also Called: Architectural Shtmtl Contr
41731 Corporate Center Ct, Murrieta (92562-7084)
PHONE.....................760 549-4121
Philip G Chapman, *CEO*
**EMP:** 20 **EST:** 2008
**SALES (est):** 4MM **Privately Held**
**SIC: 1521 3444 1761** Single-family housing construction; Skylights, sheet metal; Architectural sheet metal work

**(P-348)**
**PREFAB INNOVATIONS INC**
1801 Santa Clara St, Fresno (93721-2825)
PHONE.....................559 582-3871
David George Clevenger Junior, *CEO*
Melissa Westcoat, *Asstg*
**EMP:** 23 **EST:** 2021
**SALES (est):** 5MM **Privately Held**
**SIC: 1521 2452** Prefabricated single-family house erection; Prefabricated wood buildings

**(P-349)**
**STEVEN N LEDSON**
Also Called: Ledson Winery & Vineyards
7335 Sonoma Hwy, Santa Rosa (95409-6269)
P.O. Box 653 (95452-0653)
PHONE.....................707 537-3810
Steven N Ledson, *Owner*
**EMP:** 60 **EST:** 1976
**SALES (est):** 2.48MM **Privately Held**
**Web:** www.ledson.com
**SIC: 1521 2084** Single-family housing construction; Wines

## 1531 Operative Builders

**(P-350)**
**HOFMANN CONSTRUCTION CO (PA)**
Also Called: Hofmann Company
3000 Oak Rd Ste 300, Walnut Creek (94597-7775)
P.O. Box 907 (94522-0907)
PHONE.....................925 478-2000
Thomas Whalen, *CEO*
Albert Shaw, *
John Amaral, *
Patrick S Simons, *
**EMP:** 40 **EST:** 1959
**SQ FT:** 12,000
**SALES (est):** 10.56MM
**SALES (corp-wide):** 10.56MM **Privately Held**
**SIC: 1531 2439** Speculative builder, single-family houses; Structural wood members, nec

**(P-351)**
**JAIME ENTERPRISE GROUP**
Also Called: Shelter & Indus Svcs Mexico
3200 Paseo Village Way, San Diego (92130-3209)
PHONE.....................619 454-7681
Alfredo Jaime, *CEO*
**EMP:** 15 **EST:** 2012
**SALES (est):** 703.47K **Privately Held**
**SIC: 1531 3999 2452 7389** ; Manufacturing industries, nec; Modular homes, prefabricated, wood; Financial services

**(P-352)**
**MANDEVILLE MODULAR INC**
39510 Middleton St, Palmdale (93551-1046)
PHONE.....................888 662-8458
Heith Bibby, *Pr*
**EMP:** 15 **EST:** 2021
**SALES (est):** 2.6MM **Privately Held**
**SIC: 1531 8712 3448** ; Architectural engineering; Prefabricated metal buildings

**(P-353)**
**TRIAMID CNSTR CENTL CAL INC**
Also Called: Facility Maintenance & Cnstr
3130 Fite Cir Ste 1, Sacramento (95827-1817)
P.O. Box 1995 (95741)
PHONE.....................916 858-0397
Matt Defazio, *Pr*
Anthony Brizzi, *
Michael Blixt, *
**EMP:** 40 **EST:** 2011
**SQ FT:** 1,500
**SALES (est):** 5.16MM **Privately Held**
**Web:** www.triamid.com
**SIC: 1531 1542 1389 1731** ; Commercial and office building contractors; Construction, repair, and dismantling services; Electrical work

## 1541 Industrial Buildings And Warehouses

**(P-354)**
**BAKELL LLC**
Also Called: Jdi Distribution
824 Lytle St, Redlands (92374-6230)
PHONE.....................800 292-2137
Deborah Blevins, *Managing Member*
Justin Jordan, *
**EMP:** 65 **EST:** 2015
**SALES (est):** 4.58MM **Privately Held**
**Web:** www.bakell.com
**SIC: 1541 5149 2051 3299** Food products manufacturing or packing plant construction; Baking supplies; Bakery: wholesale or wholesale/retail combined; Mica products

**(P-355)**
**BIOTIX**
6995 Calle De Linea Ste 106, San Diego (92154-8015)
PHONE.....................858 875-5479
Mel Johnson, *Mgr*
**EMP:** 40
**Web:** www.biotix.com
**SIC: 1541 2869** Industrial buildings and warehouses; Laboratory chemicals, organic
**HQ:** Biotix
10636 Scripps Summit Ct # 130
San Diego CA 92131
858 875-7696

**(P-356)**
**CALIFORNIA CUSTOM PROC LLC**
3211 Aviation Dr, Madera (93637-8678)
PHONE.....................559 416-5122
Grant Willits, *Managing Member*
**EMP:** 24 **EST:** 2012
**SALES (est):** 15.07MM **Privately Held**
**Web:** www.californiacustomprocessing.com
**SIC: 1541 3556** Food products manufacturing or packing plant construction; Food products machinery

**(P-357)**
**CALIFORNIA SHTMTL WORKS INC**
Also Called: California Sheet Metal
1020 N Marshall Ave, El Cajon (92020-1829)
PHONE.....................619 562-7010
Robin Hoffos, *Pr*
Joe Isom, *
▲ **EMP:** 90 **EST:** 1913
**SQ FT:** 15,000
**SALES (est):** 41.52MM **Privately Held**
**Web:** www.califsheetmetal.com
**SIC: 1541 3444** Renovation, remodeling and repairs: industrial buildings; Sheet metalwork

**(P-358)**
**KUSTOM KANOPIES INC**
210 Senior Cir, Lompoc (93436-1491)
PHONE.....................801 399-3400
**TOLL FREE:** 800
Wesley R Robison, *Pr*
Ronald E Schwartz, *
Sharee Robison, *
**EMP:** 30 **EST:** 1987
**SQ FT:** 56,000
**SALES (est):** 541.36K **Privately Held**
**SIC: 1541 5999 3444** Industrial buildings and warehouses; Awnings; Sheet metalwork

**(P-359)**
**PROTECTIVE WTHER STRCTURES INC**
Also Called: P W S
5290 Orcutt Rd, San Luis Obispo (93401-8336)
PHONE.....................805 547-8797
Timothy Perozzi, *Pr*
John Hunter, *VP*
**EMP:** 16 **EST:** 1994
**SQ FT:** 4,000
**SALES (est):** 4.43MM **Privately Held**

▲ = Import ▼ = Export
◆ = Import/Export

## PRODUCTS & SERVICES SECTION
## 1611 - Highway And Street Construction (P-378)

Web: www.pwssteelbuildings.com
SIC: **1541** 3792 Steel building construction; Travel trailers and campers

### (P-360)
### PURE SIMPLE FOODS LLC
Also Called: Lark Ellen Farm
420 Bryant Cir Ste B, Ojai (93023-4209)
PHONE..................805 272-8448
Kelley D'angelo, *CEO*
**EMP:** 25 **EST:** 2021
**SALES (est):** 3.43MM **Privately Held**
**SIC: 1541** 5149 2068 Food products manufacturing or packing plant construction; Health foods; Nuts: dried, dehydrated, salted or roasted

### (P-361)
### SYNEAR FOODS USA LLC
Also Called: Synear Foods
9601 Canoga Ave, Chatsworth (91311-4115)
PHONE..................818 341-3588
**EMP:** 36 **EST:** 2015
**SALES (est):** 49.08MM **Privately Held**
Web: www.synearusa.com
**SIC: 1541** 2038 Food products manufacturing or packing plant construction; Breakfasts, frozen and packaged
**PA:** Zhengzhou Synear Food Co., Ltd. No. 13 Yingcai Street, Huiji District

### (P-362)
### VITA FORTE INC (PA)
19350 Cachagua Rd, Carmel Valley (93924-9376)
P.O. Box 1713 (93921-1713)
PHONE..................831 626-0555
Carlos Forte, *Pr*
▲ **EMP:** 18 **EST:** 2011
**SALES (est):** 11.84MM
**SALES (corp-wide):** 11.84MM **Privately Held**
Web: www.vitaforteinc.com
**SIC: 1541** 2034 3999 7389 Food products manufacturing or packing plant construction; Dried and dehydrated fruits, vegetables and soup mixes; Barber and beauty shop equipment; Business services, nec

---

## 1542 Nonresidential Construction, Nec

### (P-363)
### ANCHOR-41 CONSTRUCTION LLC
9301 W Airport Dr Ste A, Visalia (93277-9500)
PHONE..................559 740-7776
David Ruiz, *Managing Member*
**EMP:** 15 **EST:** 2017
**SALES (est):** 3.8MM **Privately Held**
Web: www.anchor41.com
**SIC: 1542** 1389 Commercial and office building contractors; Construction, repair, and dismantling services

### (P-364)
### CHINA PACIFIC INC
Also Called: China Pac Sheet Metal Mfg
1777 N Main St, Los Angeles (90031-2516)
PHONE..................323 222-9580
Kenneth Tsan, *Pr*
Frank Ho, *VP*
**EMP:** 15 **EST:** 1984
**SQ FT:** 10,000
**SALES (est):** 1.72MM **Privately Held**
Web: www.chinapacificcoinc.com

**SIC: 1542** 3444 3589 Restaurant construction; Restaurant sheet metalwork; Cooking equipment, commercial

### (P-365)
### CLAY CORONA COMPANY (PA)
22079 Knabe Rd, Corona (92883-7111)
PHONE..................951 277-2667
Gerald K Deleo, *Pr*
Craig Deleo, *
Joyce Deleo, *
**EMP:** 23 **EST:** 1947
**SALES (est):** 9.48MM
**SALES (corp-wide):** 9.48MM **Privately Held**
Web: www.coronaclayco.com
**SIC: 1542** 3295 8711 1794 Commercial and office building contractors; Minerals, ground or treated; Construction and civil engineering; Excavation work

### (P-366)
### CM CONSTRUCTION SERVICES INC (PA)
8300 W Doe Ave, Visalia (93291-9261)
P.O. Box 6237 (93290-6237)
PHONE..................559 735-9556
Monique Miron, *Pr*
**EMP:** 24 **EST:** 2002
**SALES (est):** 5.03MM
**SALES (corp-wide):** 5.03MM **Privately Held**
Web: www.cmconstructionservices.com
**SIC: 1542** 1522 3999 8741 Nonresidential construction, nec; Residential construction, nec; Carpet tackles; Construction management

### (P-367)
### DESIGNED MBL SYSTEMS INDS INC
800 S State Highway 33, Patterson (95363-9148)
P.O. Box 367 (95363-0367)
PHONE..................209 892-6298
David W Smith, *Pr*
Edward Smith, *
**EMP:** 16 **EST:** 1973
**SQ FT:** 100,000
**SALES (est):** 2.09MM **Privately Held**
Web: www.dmsi-inc.com
**SIC: 1542** 2451 3448 2452 Design and erection, combined: non-residential; Mobile classrooms; Prefabricated metal buildings and components; Prefabricated wood buildings

### (P-368)
### G HARTLEY INC
Also Called: SC Barns
3224 Dutton Ave, Santa Rosa (95407-7866)
PHONE..................707 523-3513
Gary E Hartley, *CEO*
**EMP:** 22 **EST:** 2019
**SALES (est):** 8.14MM **Privately Held**
Web: www.scbarns.com
**SIC: 1542** 3448 Nonresidential construction, nec; Prefabricated metal buildings

### (P-369)
### PENWAL INDUSTRIES INC
10611 Acacia St, Rancho Cucamonga (91730-5410)
PHONE..................909 466-1555
Chris A Pennington, *Prin*
▲ **EMP:** 100 **EST:** 1981
**SQ FT:** 65,000
**SALES (est):** 20.73MM **Privately Held**
Web: www.penwal.com

**SIC: 1542** 3999 8742 3993 Shopping center construction; Advertising display products; Management consulting services; Signs and advertising specialties

### (P-370)
### SILVER CREEK INDUSTRIES LLC
2830 Barrett Ave, Perris (92571-3258)
PHONE..................951 943-5393
Brett D Bashaw, *CEO*
Micheal Rhodes, *
**EMP:** 175 **EST:** 2005
**SQ FT:** 25,000
**SALES (est):** 91.07MM **Privately Held**
Web: www.silvercreekmodular.com
**SIC: 1542** 2452 Commercial and office building contractors; Prefabricated wood buildings

### (P-371)
### TRACY RENEWABLE ENERGY
4750 Holly Dr, Tracy (95304-1666)
P.O. Box 583 (95378-0583)
PHONE..................831 224-2513
Frank Schubert, *CEO*
Frank Schubert, *Pr*
**EMP:** 20 **EST:** 2017
**SALES (est):** 4.46MM **Privately Held**
Web: www.cstgreen.com
**SIC: 1542** 3589 Custom builders, non-residential; Water treatment equipment, industrial

### (P-372)
### WOODYS POULTRY SUPPLY
Also Called: Woody's
2900 E Monte Vista Ave, Denair (95316-8540)
P.O. Box 1628 (95381-1628)
PHONE..................209 634-2948
Richard Dias, *Pr*
Rita Dias, *Sec*
**EMP:** 15 **EST:** 1947
**SQ FT:** 25,000
**SALES (est):** 2.74MM **Privately Held**
Web: www.woodysgolfandindustrial.com
**SIC: 1542** 1541 3523 7699 Farm building construction; Steel building construction; Barn, silo, poultry, dairy, and livestock machinery; Recreational vehicle repair services

---

## 1611 Highway And Street Construction

### (P-373)
### BALDWIN CONTRACTING CO INC (DH)
Also Called: Knife River Construction
1764 Skyway, Chico (95928-8833)
PHONE..................530 891-6555
David C Barney, *CEO*
Steve Essoyan, *
Rene' J Vercruyssen, *
**EMP:** 28 **EST:** 1946
**SALES (est):** 40.89MM
**SALES (corp-wide):** 2.83B **Publicly Held**
**SIC: 1611** 2951 5032 1442 Highway and street construction; Concrete, asphaltic (not from refineries); Sand, construction; Construction sand and gravel
**HQ:** Krc Materials, Inc.
1150 W Century Ave
Bismarck ND 58506
701 530-1400

### (P-374)
### HARDY & HARPER INC
32 Rancho Cir, Lake Forest (92630-8325)
PHONE..................714 444-1851
Daniel Thomas Maas, *CEO*
Fred T Maas Senior, *Dir*
**EMP:** 200 **EST:** 1946
**SALES (est):** 24.53MM **Privately Held**
Web: www.hardyandharper.com
**SIC: 1611** 2951 Surfacing and paving; Asphalt paving mixtures and blocks

### (P-375)
### MATICH CORPORATION (PA)
1596 E Harry Shepard Blvd, San Bernardino (92408-0197)
P.O. Box 10 (92346-1010)
PHONE..................909 382-7400
Stephen A Matich, *CEO*
Martin A Matich, *
Randall Valadez, *
Robert M Matich, *
Patrick A Matich, *
**EMP:** 60 **EST:** 1918
**SQ FT:** 10,000
**SALES (est):** 48.1MM
**SALES (corp-wide):** 48.1MM **Privately Held**
Web: www.matichcorp.com
**SIC: 1611** 2951 General contractor, highway and street construction; Asphalt paving mixtures and blocks

### (P-376)
### MICHAEL TELFER (PA)
Also Called: Western Oil & Spreading
211 Foster St, Martinez (94553-1029)
P.O. Box 709 (94553-0151)
PHONE..................925 228-1515
Michael Telfer, *Owner*
**EMP:** 55 **EST:** 1992
**SQ FT:** 5,000
**SALES (est):** 6.95MM **Privately Held**
Web: www.telferpavements.com
**SIC: 1611** 2951 4213 4212 Highway and street paving contractor; Paving mixtures; Liquid petroleum transport, non-local; Local trucking, without storage

### (P-377)
### PAVER DECOR MASONRY INC
Also Called: Alpha & Omega Pavers
987 Calimesa Blvd, Calimesa (92320-1138)
P.O. Box 727 (92320-0727)
PHONE..................909 795-8474
Adam Cuevas, *Pr*
Mary Cuevas, *
**EMP:** 25 **EST:** 1995
**SQ FT:** 2,500
**SALES (est):** 10.17MM **Privately Held**
Web: www.paverdecor.com
**SIC: 1611** 3531 Highway and street paving contractor; Pavers

### (P-378)
### REED FAMILY COMPANIES (PA)
928 12th St Ste 700, Modesto (95354-2330)
P.O. Box 3191 (95353-3191)
PHONE..................209 521-9771
Jeffrey Reed, *CEO*
Margaret Reed, *
Casey Razma, *
▲ **EMP:** 50 **EST:** 1973
**SALES (est):** 163.99MM
**SALES (corp-wide):** 163.99MM **Privately Held**
Web: www.macropaver.com

---

(PA)=Parent Co (HQ)=Headquarters
✪ = New Business established in last 2 years

# 1611 - Highway And Street Construction (P-379)

SIC: **1611** 3273 2951 3532 Highway and street paving contractor; Ready-mixed concrete; Asphalt and asphaltic paving mixtures (not from refineries); Mining machinery

### (P-379)
### REED GROUP (HQ)
Also Called: Munn & Perkins
928 12th St Ste 700, Modesto (95354-2330)
PHONE..................209 521-7423
Wendell G Reed, *Pr*
John Shodun, *
**EMP:** 40 **EST:** 1944
**SQ FT:** 1,000
**SALES (est):** 23.04MM
**SALES (corp-wide):** 163.99MM **Privately Held**
Web: www.georgereed.com
SIC: **1611** 3273 2951 5032 Highway and street paving contractor; Ready-mixed concrete; Asphalt and asphaltic paving mixtures (not from refineries); Aggregate
PA: Reed Family Companies
928 12th St Ste 700
209 521-9771

### (P-380)
### S & S PAVING INC
23875 Ventura Blvd Ste 202, Calabasas (91302-1464)
PHONE..................818 591-0668
Jose Hurtado, *Pr*
Virginia Martinez, *
Jan Pick, *
**EMP:** 20 **EST:** 1971
**SQ FT:** 1,600
**SALES (est):** 1.89MM **Privately Held**
Web: www.sspavinginc.com
SIC: **1611** 2951 1629 Grading; Asphalt paving mixtures and blocks; Land leveling

### (P-381)
### SKANSKA USA CVIL W CAL DST INC (DH)
1995 Agua Mansa Rd, Riverside (92509-2405)
PHONE..................951 684-5360
Richard Cavallero, *CEO*
Michael Aparicio, *
Todd Sutton, *
Joseph Nogues, *
Michael Cobelli, *
**EMP:** 700 **EST:** 1919
**SQ FT:** 15,000
**SALES (est):** 139.9MM
**SALES (corp-wide):** 115.37MM **Privately Held**
Web: usa.skanska.com
SIC: **1611** 1622 1629 8711 General contractor, highway and street construction; Bridge construction; Dam construction; Engineering services
HQ: Skanska Usa Civil Inc.
7520 Astoria Blvd Ste 200
East Elmhurst NY 11370
718 340-0777

### (P-382)
### STEVENS CREEK QUARRY INC (PA)
Also Called: Scq Construction
21771 Stevens Creek Blvd Ste 100, Cupertino (95014-1164)
PHONE..................408 253-2512
Richard A Voss, *Pr*
Bob Romano, *
Richard Voss, *
Diana Voss, *
**EMP:** 60 **EST:** 1954
**SALES (est):** 20.92MM
**SALES (corp-wide):** 20.92MM **Privately Held**
Web: www.scqinc.com
SIC: **1611** 7353 1442 General contractor, highway and street construction; Heavy construction equipment rental; Construction sand mining

### (P-383)
### TALLEY OIL INC
12483 Road 29, Madera (93638-8401)
P.O. Box 568 (93639-0568)
PHONE..................559 673-9011
Kenneth William Talley, *CEO*
**EMP:** 32 **EST:** 2004
**SALES (est):** 14.25MM **Privately Held**
Web: www.talleyoil.com
SIC: **1611** 2951 Highway and street maintenance; Asphalt and asphaltic paving mixtures (not from refineries)

### (P-384)
### VSS INTERNATIONAL INC (HQ)
Also Called: V S S
3785 Channel Dr, West Sacramento (95691-3421)
P.O. Box 981330 (95798-1330)
PHONE..................916 373-1500
Jeffrey Reed, *Pr*
Alan Berger, *
Diane Minor, *Corporate Secretary**
John Shoden, *
Ron Bolles, *
▲ **EMP:** 62 **EST:** 1974
**SQ FT:** 5,000
**SALES (est):** 23.61MM
**SALES (corp-wide):** 163.99MM **Privately Held**
Web: www.slurry.com
SIC: **1611** 3531 2951 Highway and street paving contractor; Construction machinery; Asphalt paving mixtures and blocks
PA: Reed Family Companies
928 12th St Ste 700
209 521-9771

## 1622 Bridge, Tunnel, And Elevated Highway

### (P-385)
### GRANITE CONSTRUCTION INC (PA)
Also Called: GRANITE
585 W Beach St, Watsonville (95076-5123)
P.O. Box 50085 (95076)
PHONE..................831 724-1011
Kyle T Larkin, *Pr*
Michael F Mcnally, *Ch Bd*
James A Radich, *Ex VP*
Elizabeth L Curtis, *Ex VP*
Staci M Woolsey, *CAO*
**EMP:** 268 **EST:** 1922
**SALES (est):** 3.51B **Publicly Held**
Web: www.graniteconstruction.com
SIC: **1622** 1629 1442 1611 Bridge construction; Dam construction; Construction sand and gravel; General contractor, highway and street construction

## 1623 Water, Sewer, And Utility Lines

### (P-386)
### AIRX UTILITY SURVEYORS INC (PA)
785 E Mission Rd # 100, San Marcos (92069-1903)
PHONE..................760 480-2347
Gail Mcmorran, *Pr*
**EMP:** 55 **EST:** 1999
**SALES (est):** 9.17MM
**SALES (corp-wide):** 9.17MM **Privately Held**
Web: www.airxutility.com
SIC: **1623** 1389 3272 1611 Underground utilities contractor; Testing, measuring, surveying, and analysis services; Monuments, concrete; Highway and street construction

### (P-387)
### CONSTRUCTION SPECIALTY SVC INC
Also Called: C S S
4550 Buck Owens Blvd, Bakersfield (93308-4948)
P.O. Box 9429 (93389-9429)
PHONE..................661 864-7573
Daniel I George, *Pr*
Denise George, *
**EMP:** 53 **EST:** 2008
**SQ FT:** 1,000
**SALES (est):** 9.48MM **Privately Held**
Web: www.cssincorp.biz
SIC: **1623** 3271 Pipeline construction, nsk; Concrete block and brick

### (P-388)
### SCW CONTRACTING CORPORATION
2525 Old Highway 395, Fallbrook (92028-8794)
PHONE..................760 728-1308
Jeffrey Dean Scrape, *CEO*
Susanne Scrape, *
**EMP:** 70 **EST:** 1980
**SQ FT:** 3,000
**SALES (est):** 15.39MM **Privately Held**
Web: www.scwcompanies.com
SIC: **1623** 1791 3449 Underground utilities contractor; Structural steel erection; Miscellaneous metalwork

### (P-389)
### SOUTHWEST CONTRACTORS (PA)
Also Called: Bowman Pipeline Contractors
136 Allen Rd # 100, Bakersfield (93314-3710)
PHONE..................661 588-0484
Floyd E Bowman Junior, *CEO*
Kathy Bowman, *
**EMP:** 25 **EST:** 1981
**SALES (est):** 23.28MM
**SALES (corp-wide):** 23.28MM **Privately Held**
Web: www.southwestcontractors.net
SIC: **1623** 3443 Oil and gas pipeline construction; Industrial vessels, tanks, and containers

### (P-390)
### THERMAL ENERGY SOLUTIONS INC
100 Quantico Ave, Bakersfield (93307-2839)
PHONE..................661 489-4100
Nelson Ivan Ayala, *CEO*
Gabriela Lopez De Ayala, *
Nelson Ayala, *
**EMP:** 27 **EST:** 2008
**SALES (est):** 5.11MM **Privately Held**
Web: www.thermalenergyinc.com
SIC: **1623** 1711 3494 7699 Oil and gas line and compressor station construction; Process piping contractor; Line strainers, for use in piping systems; Tank and boiler cleaning service

### (P-391)
### TNH DEVELOPMENT LLC
1990 Olivera Rd Ste B, Concord (94520-5455)
PHONE..................847 525-3960
Heather Borst, *Managing Member*
Thomas Borst, *Managing Member*
**EMP:** 16 **EST:** 2014
**SALES (est):** 5.66MM **Privately Held**
Web: www.tnhdev.com
SIC: **1623** 1751 1541 3548 Transmitting tower (telecommunication) construction; Framing contractor; Steel building construction; Welding and cutting apparatus and accessories, nec

## 1629 Heavy Construction, Nec

### (P-392)
### ANAERGIA SERVICES LLC
705 Palomar Airport Rd Ste 200, Carlsbad (92011-1060)
PHONE..................760 436-8870
Andrew Benedek, *CEO*
Arun Sharma, *Pr*
Hani Kaissi, *CFO*
**EMP:** 22 **EST:** 2011
**SALES (est):** 24.83MM
**SALES (corp-wide):** 107.18MM **Privately Held**
Web: www.anaergia.com
SIC: **1629** 4911 7699 4953 Waste water and sewage treatment plant construction; Distribution, electric power; Waste cleaning services; Recycling, waste materials
PA: Anaergia Inc
4210 South Service Rd
905 766-3333

### (P-393)
### BELLINGHAM MARINE INDS INC
8810 Sparling Ln, Dixon (95620-9605)
PHONE..................707 678-2385
James R Puder, *Genl Mgr*
**EMP:** 45
**SALES (corp-wide):** 69.69MM **Privately Held**
Web: www.bellingham-marine.com
SIC: **1629** 3272 Marine construction; Concrete products, precast, nec
HQ: Bellingham Marine Industries, Inc.
144 River Rd
Lynden WA 98264
360 676-2800

### (P-394)
### CLARK BROS INC
745 Broadway St, Fresno (93721-2807)
PHONE..................209 392-6144
Lawrence A Clark, *CEO*
Sarah Woolf, *
Adrew Clark, *Stockholder**
Allan W Clark, *
**EMP:** 100 **EST:** 1949
**SQ FT:** 5,000
**SALES (est):** 55.94MM **Privately Held**
Web: www.clarkbrosinc.com
SIC: **1629** 3589 Trenching contractor; Water treatment equipment, industrial

### (P-395)
### DUTRA GROUP (PA)
Also Called: Dutra Group, The

# PRODUCTS & SERVICES SECTION
## 1711 - Plumbing, Heating, Air-conditioning (P-414)

2350 Kerner Blvd Ste 200, San Rafael (94901-5595)
PHONE..................415 258-6876
Harry K Stewart, *CEO*
Bill T Dutra, *
James Hagood, *
▲ EMP: 100 EST: 1973
SQ FT: 22,000
SALES (est): 99.82MM
SALES (corp-wide): 99.82MM Privately Held
Web: www.dutragroup.com
SIC: 1629 8711 1429 Marine construction; Civil engineering; Igneus rock, crushed and broken-quarrying

### (P-396)
### HAROLD SMITH & SON INC
800 Crane Ave, Saint Helena (94574)
PHONE..................707 963-7977
Pam Raybould, *Pr*
Irene Varozza, *
Tom Johnston, *
EMP: 25 EST: 1917
SQ FT: 800
SALES (est): 4.81MM Privately Held
Web: www.hsandson.com
SIC: 1629 3273 1611 4212 Earthmoving contractor; Ready-mixed concrete; Highway and street paving contractor; Dump truck haulage

### (P-397)
### HERON INNOVATORS INC
10624 Industrial Ave, Roseville (95678-5902)
PHONE..................916 408-6601
John Barsotti, *Pr*
EMP: 17 EST: 1998
SALES (est): 894.45K Privately Held
Web: www.heroninnovators.com
SIC: 1629 3589 Waste water and sewage treatment plant construction; Sewage treatment equipment

### (P-398)
### T T S CONSTRUCTION CORPORATION
1220 E Pine St, Lodi (95240-0812)
PHONE..................209 333-7788
Nathan Howard, *Pr*
Rudge Wynn, *
Reinie Naeb, *
EMP: 40 EST: 2004
SQ FT: 4,200
SALES (est): 6.06MM Privately Held
Web: www.ttsconstruction.com
SIC: 1629 3589 Power plant construction; Water treatment equipment, industrial

### (P-399)
### US JOINER LLC
Also Called: Marine Interiors
2800 Harbor Dr, San Diego (92113)
P.O. Box 13117 (92170-3117)
PHONE..................619 233-3993
Andy How, *Brnch Mgr*
EMP: 28
SALES (corp-wide): 449.31MM Privately Held
Web: www.tridentllc.com
SIC: 1629 5551 5091 3731 Marine construction; Boat dealers; Sporting and recreation goods; Shipbuilding and repairing
HQ: Us Joiner Llc
5690 Three Notch D Rd # 200
Crozet VA 22932
434 220-8500

### (P-400)
### VISTA STEEL CO INC
Also Called: VISTA STEEL CO INC
331 W Lewis St, Ventura (93001-1394)
PHONE..................805 653-1189
John Swaffar, *Brnch Mgr*
EMP: 24
SALES (corp-wide): 1.87MM Privately Held
Web: www.vistasteelco.com
SIC: 1629 3449 Dams, waterways, docks, and other marine construction; Miscellaneous metalwork
PA: Vista Steel Company
6100 Frncis Btllo Rd Ste
805 964-4732

### (P-401)
### WARREN COLLINS AND ASSOC INC (PA)
Also Called: Collins Company
300 E Eucalyptus Ave, Ontario (91762)
PHONE..................909 548-6708
Larry W Collins, *Pr*
Nancy Collins, *
▲ EMP: 23 EST: 1975
SQ FT: 8,000
SALES (est): 15.72MM
SALES (corp-wide): 15.72MM Privately Held
Web: www.collinscompany.com
SIC: 1629 3949 1799 3446 Athletic and recreation facilities construction; Sporting and athletic goods, nec; Scaffolding; Scaffolds, mobile or stationary: metal

## 1711 Plumbing, Heating, Air-conditioning

### (P-402)
### ACCO ENGINEERED SYSTEMS INC (PA)
Also Called: Acco
888 E Walnut St, Pasadena (91101-1895)
PHONE..................818 244-6571
EMP: 900 EST: 1934
SALES (est): 1.51B
SALES (corp-wide): 1.51B Privately Held
Web: www.accoes.com
SIC: 1711 7623 3448 Process piping contractor; Air conditioning repair; Buildings, portable: prefabricated metal

### (P-403)
### AIRE SHEET METAL INC
1973 E Bayshore Rd, Redwood City (94063-4149)
P.O. Box 5217 (94063-0217)
PHONE..................650 364-8081
Eugene Bramlett, *CEO*
Bobby E Bramlett, *
Marlo Bramlett, *
EMP: 40 EST: 1971
SALES (est): 8.8MM Privately Held
Web: www.airesm.com
SIC: 1711 3444 1761 Warm air heating and air conditioning contractor; Sheet metalwork; Sheet metal work, nec

### (P-404)
### ATLAS MECHANICAL INC (PA)
Also Called: Honeywell Authorized Dealer
8260 Camino Santa Fe Ste B, San Diego (92121-3255)
PHONE..................858 554-0700
EMP: 74 EST: 1991
SALES (est): 35.68MM Privately Held
Web: www.atlasmechanical.com

SIC: 1711 3531 Ventilation and duct work contractor; Construction machinery

### (P-405)
### BAYWA RE OPERATION SVCS LLC
Also Called: Baywa R.E.
18575 Jamboree Rd Ste 850, Irvine (92612-2558)
PHONE..................949 398-3915
Jam Attari, *CEO*
EMP: 21 EST: 2019
SALES (est): 3.95MM Privately Held
Web: us.baywa-re.com
SIC: 1711 8711 3621 Solar energy contractor; Energy conservation engineering; Windmills, electric generating

### (P-406)
### BENNETT & BENNETT INC
Also Called: Bennett Bnnett Irrgtion System
955 S Commerce Way, Lemoore (93245-9039)
P.O. Box 190 (93662-0150)
PHONE..................559 582-9336
EMP: 50
Web: www.garbennett.com
SIC: 1711 3272 Irrigation sprinkler system installation; Pipe, concrete or lined with concrete

### (P-407)
### BREEZE AIR CONDITIONING LLC
75145 Saint Charles Pl Ste A, Palm Desert (92211-9048)
PHONE..................760 346-0855
Joe Coker, *Managing Member*
EMP: 59 EST: 1980
SQ FT: 33,000
SALES (est): 4.48MM Privately Held
Web: www.breezeac.com
SIC: 1711 3444 5075 3433 Warm air heating and air conditioning contractor; Sheet metalwork; Warm air heating and air conditioning; Logs, gas fireplace

### (P-408)
### CASCADE COMFORT SERVICE INC
5203 Industrial Way, Anderson (96007-4954)
PHONE..................530 365-5350
Randy Downey, *Pr*
Andrew Dempsey, *VP*
Richard Boudro, *Sec*
EMP: 22 EST: 1984
SQ FT: 12,800
SALES (est): 3.44MM Privately Held
Web: www.cascadecomfort.com
SIC: 1711 3444 Warm air heating and air conditioning contractor; Sheet metalwork

### (P-409)
### CASCADE THERMAL SOLUTIONS LLC (PA)
1890 Cordell Ct Ste 102, El Cajon (92020-0913)
PHONE..................619 562-8852
Romulo Lambert Smith, *CEO*
Romulo Lambert Smith, *Pr*
Kay Smith, *
EMP: 49 EST: 1989
SQ FT: 55,000
SALES (est): 19.03MM Privately Held
Web: www.fullspectrumlabservices.com
SIC: 1711 3821 7699 Refrigeration contractor; Laboratory apparatus and furniture; Scientific equipment repair service

### (P-410)
### CENTRAL VALLEY CONCRETE INC
4200 Lester Rd, Denair (95316-9411)
PHONE..................209 667-0161
Don Klikna, *Mgr*
EMP: 34
SALES (corp-wide): 34.42MM Privately Held
Web: www.centralvalleyconcrete.com
SIC: 1711 3273 5032 7699 Septic system construction; Ready-mixed concrete; Brick, stone, and related material; Waste cleaning services
PA: Central Valley Concrete, Inc.
3823 N State Highway 59
209 723-8846

### (P-411)
### CHAMPION INDUSTRIAL CONTRS INC (PA)
1420 Coldwell Ave, Modesto (95350-5704)
P.O. Box 4399 (95352-4399)
PHONE..................209 524-6601
Darrell Frederick Champion, *CEO*
Darrell Frederick Champion, *Pr*
James C Champion, *
Charles M Vanwey, *
Eulala Jo Champion, *
EMP: 38 EST: 1933
SQ FT: 62,000
SALES (est): 33.09MM
SALES (corp-wide): 33.09MM Privately Held
Web: www.championindustrial.com
SIC: 1711 1761 3444 Mechanical contractor; Sheet metal work, nec; Sheet metalwork

### (P-412)
### CHAMPION INDUSTRIAL CONTRS INC
451 Tully Rd, Modesto (95350-5856)
PHONE..................209 579-5478
Charles Vanwey, *Mgr*
EMP: 42
SALES (corp-wide): 33.09MM Privately Held
Web: www.championindustrial.com
SIC: 1711 1761 3444 Mechanical contractor; Sheet metal work, nec; Sheet metalwork
PA: Champion Industrial Contractors, Inc.
1420 Coldwell Ave
209 524-6601

### (P-413)
### CONEJO VALLEY HEATING & AC INC
Also Called: Conejo Valley Air
2639 Lavery Ct Ste 7, Newbury Park (91320-2277)
PHONE..................833 538-9810
Branden Dickey, *CEO*
EMP: 18 EST: 2004
SALES (est): 4.3MM Privately Held
Web: www.conejoservices.com
SIC: 1711 3621 Plumbing, heating, air-conditioning; Electric motor and generator parts

### (P-414)
### CONTROL AIR CONDITIONING CORPORATION
Also Called: Honeywell Authorized Dealer
5200 E La Palma Ave, Anaheim (92807-2019)
PHONE..................714 777-8600
EMP: 360

# 1711 - Plumbing, Heating, Air-conditioning (P-415)

SIC: 1711 3444 Warm air heating and air conditioning contractor; Ducts, sheet metal

**(P-415)**
**DAC HEATING AND AC**
Also Called: Dac Heating and Air
190 Sierra Ct Ste B3, Palmdale (93550-7608)
PHONE..................661 441-2787
Alex Beltran, *CEO*
**EMP:** 18 **EST:** 2017
**SALES (est):** 2.02MM **Privately Held**
Web: www.dacheatingandair.com
SIC: 1711 8711 3634 3564 Plumbing, heating, air-conditioning; Heating and ventilation engineering; Heating units, electric (radiant heat): baseboard or wall; Filters, air: furnaces, air conditioning equipment, etc.

**(P-416)**
**ECB CORP (PA)**
Also Called: Omniduct
6400 Artesia Blvd, Buena Park (90620-1006)
PHONE..................714 385-8900
Robert Brumleu, *Pr*
▲ **EMP:** 100 **EST:** 1980
**SQ FT:** 56,000
**SALES (est):** 47.72MM
**SALES (corp-wide):** 47.72MM **Privately Held**
Web: www.omniduct.com
SIC: 1711 3444 Ventilation and duct work contractor; Ducts, sheet metal

**(P-417)**
**ENVIRNMNTAL SYSTEMS INC NTHRN (PA)**
Also Called: Honeywell Authorized Dealer
3353 De La Cruz Blvd, Santa Clara (95054-2636)
PHONE..................408 980-1711
V C Enfantino, *Pr*
Eugene L Enfantino, *
**EMP:** 83 **EST:** 1975
**SQ FT:** 13,800
**SALES (est):** 22.56MM
**SALES (corp-wide):** 22.56MM **Privately Held**
Web: www.esite.net
SIC: 1711 7623 3444 Mechanical contractor; Refrigeration service and repair; Sheet metalwork

**(P-418)**
**FRANK M BOOTH INC**
Also Called: Valley Sheet Metal
251 Michelle Ct, South San Francisco (94080-6202)
PHONE..................650 871-8292
F Martin Booth, *CEO*
**EMP:** 77
**SQ FT:** 70,000
**SALES (corp-wide):** 110MM **Privately Held**
Web: www.frankbooth.com
SIC: 1711 8712 3444 1761 Mechanical contractor; Architectural services; Sheet metalwork; Sheet metal work, nec
PA: Frank M. Booth, Inc.
222 3rd St
530 742-7134

**(P-419)**
**FRESCHI AIR SYSTEMS INC**
Also Called: Freschi Service Experts
715 Fulton Shipyard Rd, Antioch (94509-7557)
PHONE..................925 827-9361
TOLL FREE: 800
John R Freschi Junior, *Pr*
**EMP:** 55 **EST:** 1980
**SQ FT:** 5,000
**SALES (est):** 974.11K
**SALES (corp-wide):** 17.93B **Privately Held**
Web: www.freschiserviceexperts.com
SIC: 1711 3444 Warm air heating and air conditioning contractor; Sheet metalwork
HQ: Service Experts Llc
1840 N Grnvlle Ave Ste 12
Richardson TX 75081

**(P-420)**
**GAR BENNETT LLC**
955 S Commerce Way, Lemoore (93245-9001)
PHONE..................559 582-9336
Greg Musson, *Brnch Mgr*
**EMP:** 50
**SALES (corp-wide):** 27.6MM **Privately Held**
Web: www.garbennett.com
SIC: 1711 3272 Irrigation sprinkler system installation; Pipe, concrete or lined with concrete
PA: Gar Bennett, Llc
8246 S Crawford Ave
559 638-6311

**(P-421)**
**GEORGE M ROBINSON & CO (PA)**
1461 Atteberry Ln, San Jose (95131-1409)
PHONE..................510 632-7017
John P Joyce, *Pr*
Ned Raudsep, *
**EMP:** 26 **EST:** 1932
**SQ FT:** 20,000
**SALES (est):** 1.9MM
**SALES (corp-wide):** 1.9MM **Privately Held**
SIC: 1711 3498 Fire sprinkler system installation; Fabricated pipe and fittings

**(P-422)**
**GREINER HEATING AIR & ELC INC**
Also Called: Greiner Heating & AC
8235 Pedrick Rd, Dixon (95620)
PHONE..................707 678-1784
Patricia Greiner, *CEO*
David Krueger, *
**EMP:** 37 **EST:** 1991
**SQ FT:** 10,000
**SALES (est):** 6.2MM **Privately Held**
Web: www.ghac.com
SIC: 1711 3444 Warm air heating and air conditioning contractor; Ducts, sheet metal

**(P-423)**
**HEATHORN & ASSOC CONTRS INC**
Also Called: American Air Conditioning Co
500 Old Farm Rd, Danville (94526-4134)
PHONE..................510 351-7578
Norman T R Heathorn Junior, *Pr*
Mark Defranco, *VP*
Lisa Heathorn, *Sec*
**EMP:** 20 **EST:** 1992
**SALES (est):** 5.02MM **Privately Held**
Web: www.aacph.com
SIC: 1711 3444 Warm air heating and air conditioning contractor; Sheet metalwork

**(P-424)**
**LIVE ACTION GENERAL ENGRG INC**
2972 Larkin Ave, Clovis (93612-3986)
PHONE..................559 292-2900
Bobby Tracy, *Pr*
**EMP:** 130 **EST:** 2014
**SALES (est):** 60MM **Privately Held**
Web: www.eliteteamoffices.com
SIC: 1711 1771 1611 3531 Solar energy contractor; Concrete work; Surfacing and paving; Plows: construction, excavating, and grading

**(P-425)**
**MARELICH MECHANICAL CO INC (HQ)**
24041 Amador St, Hayward (94544-1201)
P.O. Box 1710 (94560)
PHONE..................510 785-5500
Keith R Atteberry, *Pr*
Terry J Kvochak, *
Andrew Ostrowski, *
John Powell, *
Chad Johnston, *
**EMP:** 65 **EST:** 1946
**SQ FT:** 40,000
**SALES (est):** 19.01MM
**SALES (corp-wide):** 12.58B **Publicly Held**
Web: www.marelich.com
SIC: 1711 1623 3822 Mechanical contractor; Pipeline construction, nsk; Environmental controls
PA: Emcor Group, Inc.
301 Merritt 7
203 849-7800

**(P-426)**
**MONTEREY MECHANICAL CO (PA)**
Also Called: Contra Costa Metal Fabricators
8275 San Leandro St, Oakland (94621-1972)
PHONE..................510 632-3173
Milton C Burleson, *CEO*
Jim Troup, *
Paul Moreira, *
▲ **EMP:** 50 **EST:** 1942
**SQ FT:** 40,000
**SALES (est):** 45.98MM
**SALES (corp-wide):** 45.98MM **Privately Held**
Web: www.montmech.com
SIC: 1711 1761 3444 3441 Mechanical contractor; Sheet metal work, nec; Sheet metalwork; Fabricated structural metal

**(P-427)**
**NICRO INC**
635 Delano Dr, Oakdale (95361-9756)
PHONE..................209 848-8826
**EMP:** 30 **EST:** 1989
**SALES (est):** 6.43MM **Privately Held**
Web: www.nicro.net
SIC: 1711 3441 Mechanical contractor; Fabricated structural metal

**(P-428)**
**O C MCDONALD CO INC**
1150 W San Carlos St, San Jose (95126-3440)
P.O. Box 26560 (95159-6560)
PHONE..................408 295-2182
James Mc Donald, *Pr*
**EMP:** 150 **EST:** 1906
**SQ FT:** 10,500
**SALES (est):** 22.37MM **Privately Held**
Web: www.ocmcdonald.com
SIC: 1711 3585 3541 3444 Mechanical contractor; Refrigeration and heating equipment; Machine tools, metal cutting type; Sheet metalwork

**(P-429)**
**OAKVILLE PUMP SERVICE INC**
2310 Laurel St Ste 1, Napa (94559-3155)
PHONE..................707 944-2471
Roger Lutz Junior, *Pr*
Marlys Lutz, *
▲ **EMP:** 17 **EST:** 1983
**SALES (est):** 2.31MM **Privately Held**
Web: www.oakvillepump.com
SIC: 1711 3594 5084 Plumbing contractors; Pumps, hydraulic power transfer; Pumps and pumping equipment, nec

**(P-430)**
**RAM MECHANICAL INC**
3506 Moore Rd, Ceres (95307-9402)
PHONE..................209 531-9155
Neil Hodgson, *Pr*
Neil Hodgson, *Prin*
James A Frias, *Prin*
**EMP:** 60 **EST:** 2004
**SQ FT:** 22,500
**SALES (est):** 25.17MM **Privately Held**
Web: www.ram-mechanical.com
SIC: 1711 8711 3599 3535 Mechanical contractor; Engineering services; Custom machinery; Conveyors and conveying equipment

**(P-431)**
**RANDO AAA HVAC INC**
Also Called: A A A Furnace Company
1712 Stone Ave Ste 1, San Jose (95125-1309)
PHONE..................408 293-4717
Jim Rando, *Pr*
**EMP:** 50 **EST:** 1951
**SQ FT:** 5,000
**SALES (est):** 6.19MM **Privately Held**
Web: www.aaa-furnace.com
SIC: 1711 3444 3433 Warm air heating and air conditioning contractor; Sheet metalwork; Heating equipment, except electric

**(P-432)**
**RIGHT ANGLE SOLUTIONS INC**
6315 Pedley Rd, Jurupa Valley (92509-6007)
P.O. Box 965 (91752-0965)
PHONE..................951 934-3081
Duane Eric Cook, *CEO*
**EMP:** 25 **EST:** 2009
**SALES (est):** 9.28MM **Privately Held**
Web: www.rightanglesolutionsinc.com
SIC: 1711 3569 4959 8744 Plumbing contractors; Filters and strainers, pipeline; Environmental cleanup services; Facilities support services

**(P-433)**
**RUSSELL MECHANICAL INC**
3251 Monier Cir Ste A, Rancho Cordova (95742-6812)
PHONE..................916 635-2522
Danny L Russell, *Pr*
Steve Russell, *
Karen Russell, *
**EMP:** 90 **EST:** 1982
**SQ FT:** 22,000
**SALES (est):** 4.98MM **Privately Held**
Web: www.russellmechanical.com
SIC: 1711 1799 7389 3441 Mechanical contractor; Welding on site; Design services; Fabricated structural metal

**(P-434)**
**SILEVO INC**
Also Called: Silevo
1055 Page Ave, Fremont (94538-7341)
PHONE..................510 771-1360

▲ EMP: 39
SIC: 1711 3674 Solar energy contractor; Solar cells

**(P-435)**
**SKI AIR CONDITIONING COMPANY**
5528 Merchant Cir, Placerville (95667-8625)
P.O. Box 1054 (95623-1054)
PHONE..................530 626-4010
Michael Lubinski, Pr
Nannette Lubinski, Sec
EMP: 20 EST: 1978
SQ FT: 6,000
SALES (est): 2.92MM Privately Held
Web: www.skiair.com
SIC: 1711 3444 Warm air heating and air conditioning contractor; Sheet metalwork

**(P-436)**
**STRATEGIC MECHANICAL INC**
4661 E Commerce Ave, Fresno (93725-2204)
PHONE..................559 291-1952
Lonnie F Petty, Pr
Donn Petty, *
Chad Petty, *
EMP: 120 EST: 2004
SQ FT: 60,000
SALES (est): 41MM Privately Held
Web: www.strategicmechanical.com
SIC: 1711 3444 3441 Mechanical contractor; Awnings and canopies; Fabricated structural metal

**(P-437)**
**SUNRUN INC (PA)**
Also Called: SUNRUN
600 California St Fl 18, San Francisco (94108-2711)
PHONE..................415 580-6900
Mary Powell, CEO
Lynn Jurich, C Executive
Edward Fenster, C Executive
Paul Dickson, Pr
Danny Abajian, CFO
EMP: 482 EST: 2007
SQ FT: 44,000
SALES (est): 2.26B Publicly Held
Web: www.sunrun.com
SIC: 1711 4911 5074 3433 Solar energy contractor; Heating equipment and panels, solar; Solar heaters and collectors

**(P-438)**
**TANCO INC**
Also Called: Tenney A Norquist
2310 N Walnut Rd, Turlock (95382-8910)
P.O. Box 4776 (95352-4776)
PHONE..................209 523-8365
Richard Norquist, Pr
Thomas Norquist, *
EMP: 26 EST: 1957
SQ FT: 10,000
SALES (est): 2.9MM Privately Held
Web: www.thornorinc.com
SIC: 1711 3444 Warm air heating and air conditioning contractor; Sheet metalwork

**(P-439)**
**TRENDSETTER SOLAR PRODUCTS INC**
818 Broadway, Eureka (95501-0122)
PHONE..................707 443-5652
TOLL FREE: 800
Dirk Atkinson, CEO
Brian Fretter, VP
Norman Ehrlich, VP
▲ EMP: 17 EST: 1980

SQ FT: 2,000
SALES (est): 903.95K Privately Held
Web: www.trendsetterindustries.com
SIC: 1711 3433 5074 Solar energy contractor; Solar heaters and collectors; Heating equipment and panels, solar

**(P-440)**
**WEEKS DRILLING AND PUMP CO (PA)**
6100 Sebastopol Ave, Sebastopol (95472-3821)
PHONE..................707 823-3184
Chris A Thompson, CEO
Charles Judson, *
EMP: 45 EST: 1906
SQ FT: 13,000
SALES (est): 9.18MM
SALES (corp-wide): 9.18MM Privately Held
Web: www.weeksdrilling.com
SIC: 1711 5251 5084 3589 Plumbing, heating, air-conditioning; Pumps and pumping equipment; Pumps and pumping equipment, nec; Water treatment equipment, industrial

**(P-441)**
**WEST-TECH MECHANICAL INC**
5589 Brooks St Ste A, Montclair (91763-4519)
PHONE..................909 635-1170
Gus Wahid, Pr
Samir Wahid, VP
EMP: 15 EST: 1989
SQ FT: 3,500
SALES (est): 5.29MM Privately Held
Web: www.westtechmechanical.com
SIC: 1711 3444 Mechanical contractor; Awnings and canopies

**(P-442)**
**WESTERN ALLIED CORPORATION**
Also Called: Honeywell Authorized Dealer
12046 Florence Ave, Santa Fe Springs (90670-4406)
P.O. Box 3628 (90670-1628)
PHONE..................562 944-6341
Howell L Poe, CEO
EMP: 45 EST: 1960
SQ FT: 15,000
SALES (est): 36.08MM Privately Held
Web: www.wasocal.com
SIC: 1711 3433 3432 Warm air heating and air conditioning contractor; Heating equipment, except electric; Plumbing fixture fittings and trim

## 1721 Painting And Paper Hanging

**(P-443)**
**CHAY & HARRIS PNTG CONTRS INC**
2520 Wyandotte St Ste E, Mountain View (94043-2381)
PHONE..................650 966-1472
Ron L Harris, Pr
Thomas E Chay, *
EMP: 30 EST: 1974
SQ FT: 5,000
SALES (est): 1.04MM Privately Held
Web: www.chayharris.com
SIC: 1721 3479 Commercial painting; Coating of metals and formed products

**(P-444)**
**DZ-FDT LLC**
Also Called: D. Zelinsky & Sons Inc
5301 Adeline St, Oakland (94608-3107)
PHONE..................510 215-5253
James G Mccloskey, Pr
Richard B Mccloskey, VP
Kathleen Mccloskey, Sec
EMP: 50 EST: 1884
SQ FT: 11,800
SALES (est): 4.39MM
SALES (corp-wide): 2.72B Privately Held
Web: www.dzelinskyandsons.com
SIC: 1721 1799 2391 Exterior commercial painting contractor; Window treatment installation; Draperies, plastic and textile: from purchased materials
HQ: F. D. Thomas, Inc.
217 Bateman Dr
Central Point OR 97502
541 664-3010

**(P-445)**
**EUROPEAN PAVING DESIGNS INC**
1474 Berger Dr, San Jose (95112-2701)
PHONE..................408 283-5230
Randy Hays, CEO
EMP: 55 EST: 1980
SQ FT: 3,000
SALES (est): 6.77MM Privately Held
Web: www.europeanpavingdesigns.com
SIC: 1721 2951 Pavement marking contractor; Asphalt and asphaltic paving mixtures (not from refineries)

**(P-446)**
**JEFFCO PAINTING & COATING INC**
1260 Railroad Ave, Vallejo (94592-1012)
P.O. Box 1888 (94590-0655)
PHONE..................707 562-1900
Steve Jeffress, Pr
Gene Glockner, *
EMP: 100 EST: 1978
SALES (est): 11.3MM Privately Held
Web: www.jeffcoptg.com
SIC: 1721 3471 Industrial painting; Sand blasting of metal parts

**(P-447)**
**LEADING EDGE AVIATION SVCS INC**
5251 California Ave Ste 170, Irvine (92617-3077)
PHONE..................714 556-0576
EMP: 800
SIC: 1721 4581 3721 Aircraft painting; Aircraft maintenance and repair services; Motorized aircraft

**(P-448)**
**R & M PAINTING INC**
Also Called: Gold Star Painting
2928 Yosemite Blvd, Modesto (95354-4138)
PHONE..................209 576-2576
Robert E Wright, Pr
EMP: 16 EST: 1977
SQ FT: 10,000
SALES (est): 1.63MM Privately Held
Web: www.goldstarmodesto.com
SIC: 1721 3479 Commercial painting; Painting, coating, and hot dipping

## 1731 Electrical Work

**(P-449)**
**ALBD ELECTRIC AND CABLE**
Also Called: A Lighting By Design
1031 S Leslie St, La Habra (90631-6843)
PHONE..................949 440-1216
Chad Lambert, CEO
James Black, *
EMP: 100 EST: 2002
SALES (est): 28.02MM Privately Held
Web: www.albdinc.com
SIC: 1731 3651 General electrical contractor; Household audio and video equipment

**(P-450)**
**ALLTECH INDUSTRIES INC**
301 E Pomona Blvd, Monterey Park (91755-7300)
PHONE..................323 450-2168
Hilda Perez, Pr
EMP: 30 EST: 2010
SQ FT: 2,000
SALES (est): 519.29K Privately Held
Web: alltechindustriesinc.wordpress.com
SIC: 1731 7381 3669 7382 Fire detection and burglar alarm systems specialization; Security guard service; Burglar alarm apparatus, electric; Fire alarm maintenance and monitoring

**(P-451)**
**BUILDING ELCTRONIC CONTRLS INC (PA)**
2246 Lindsay Way, Glendora (91740-5398)
PHONE..................909 305-1600
Richard Taylor, Pr
Shelley Taylor, *
EMP: 48 EST: 1996
SQ FT: 13,000
SALES (est): 18.43MM Privately Held
Web: www.becinc.net
SIC: 1731 3699 General electrical contractor; Security control equipment and systems

**(P-452)**
**C G SYSTEMS LLC**
Also Called: California Gate Entry Systems
1470 N Hundley St, Anaheim (92806-1322)
PHONE..................714 632-8882
Kevin Squire, CEO
EMP: 27 EST: 1982
SALES (est): 6.22MM Privately Held
Web: www.californiagate.com
SIC: 1731 3699 3315 5731 Fire detection and burglar alarm systems specialization; Security devices; Fence gates, posts, and fittings: steel; Video cameras, recorders, and accessories

**(P-453)**
**CLEANTEK ELECTRIC INC**
403 W 21st St, San Pedro (90731-5509)
PHONE..................424 400-3315
Carl Pancutt, CEO
Carl James Mark Pancutt, CEO
EMP: 20 EST: 2019
SALES (est): 4.38MM Privately Held
Web: www.cleantek.co
SIC: 1731 3621 3694 General electrical contractor; Generators for gas-electric or oil-electric vehicles; Battery charging generators, automobile and aircraft

**(P-454)**
**COSCO FIRE PROTECTION INC**
7455 Longard Rd, Livermore (94551-8238)
PHONE..................925 455-2751

# 1731 - Electrical Work (P-455)

Phil Raya, *Mgr*
**EMP**: 65
**Web**: www.coscofire.com
**SIC**: **1731** 3494 8711 7382  General electrical contractor; Sprinkler systems, field; Engineering services; Security systems services
**HQ**: Cosco Fire Protection, Inc.
29222 Rancho Viejo Rd # 205
San Juan Capistrano CA 92675

### (P-455)
### DONCO & SONS INC
Also Called: Donco Associates & Sons
2871 E Blue Star St, Anaheim (92806-2508)
**PHONE**..............................714 779-0099
Donavon W Fink, *Pr*
Mark Fink, *
Dave Fink, *
Diane Fink, *
**EMP**: 28 **EST**: 1980
**SALES (est)**: 5.45MM **Privately Held**
**Web**: www.donco.com
**SIC**: **1731** 3993  Electrical work; Electric signs

### (P-456)
### ELECTRIC INNOVATIONS INC
3711 Meadow View Dr Ste 100, Redding (96002-9795)
**PHONE**..............................530 222-3366
Theodore Paul Thompson, *CEO*
**EMP**: 51 **EST**: 2013
**SQ FT**: 2,000
**SALES (est)**: 13.23MM **Privately Held**
**Web**: www.electricinnovationsca.com
**SIC**: **1731** 3511  General electrical contractor; Steam turbine generator set units, complete

### (P-457)
### HIMCO NATIONAL INC
Also Called: Himco Security Products
120 E 33rd St, Los Angeles (90011-2313)
**PHONE**..............................323 231-9104
Markos Cerna, *Mgr*
**EMP**: 16
**SALES (corp-wide)**: 4.7MM **Privately Held**
**Web**: www.himcosecurity.com
**SIC**: **1731** 3496 3442  Electrical work; Miscellaneous fabricated wire products; Metal doors, sash, and trim
**PA**: Himco National, Inc.
3326 S Main St
323 232-2222

### (P-458)
### INDUSTRIAL ELCTRNIC SYSTEMS IN (PA)
3250 Monier Cir Ste F, Rancho Cordova (95742-6839)
**PHONE**..............................916 638-1000
Edward L Lane, *Pr*
Alan Steele, *
**EMP**: 35 **EST**: 1980
**SQ FT**: 3,000
**SALES (est)**: 9.25MM
**SALES (corp-wide)**: 9.25MM **Privately Held**
**Web**: www.iesi.net
**SIC**: **1731** 3699  Fire detection and burglar alarm systems specialization; Security control equipment and systems

### (P-459)
### KDC INC (HQ)
Also Called: Kdc Systems
4462 Corporate Center Dr, Los Alamitos (90720-2539)
**PHONE**..............................714 828-7000
Earnest Lee Brown, *Pr*
Ben Martin, *
Dusty Lord, *
**EMP**: 207 **EST**: 1976
**SQ FT**: 57,000
**SALES (est)**: 31.89MM
**SALES (corp-wide)**: 12.58B **Publicly Held**
**Web**: www.kdc-systems.com
**SIC**: **1731** 1611 3823  General electrical contractor; General contractor, highway and street construction; Process control instruments
**PA**: Emcor Group, Inc.
301 Merritt 7
203 849-7800

### (P-460)
### LA SIGNAL
155 N Eucla Ave, La Puente (91744)
P.O. Box 610 (91773-0610)
**PHONE**..............................909 599-2201
Ray Morales, *Prin*
**EMP**: 15 **EST**: 2011
**SALES (est)**: 1.34MM **Privately Held**
**Web**: www.lasignal.com
**SIC**: **1731** 3648 3669  Electrical work; Street lighting fixtures; Traffic signals, electric

### (P-461)
### LITTLEJOHN-REULAND CORPORATION
4575 Pacific Blvd, Vernon (90058-2207)
P.O. Box 58487 (90058-0487)
**PHONE**..............................323 587-5255
Richard Pena, *Pr*
Dolores Robinson, *
Barry Mileski, *
**EMP**: 45 **EST**: 1926
**SQ FT**: 50,000
**SALES (est)**: 10.03MM **Privately Held**
**Web**: www.littlejohn-reuland.com
**SIC**: **1731** 7694 5063 5511  General electrical contractor; Armature rewinding shops; Electrical supplies, nec; New and used car dealers

### (P-462)
### MODESTO INDUSTRIAL ELEC CO INC
Also Called: Industrial Electrical Co
2516 N Sunnyside Ave, Fresno (93727-1371)
**PHONE**..............................559 292-4714
Ron Forthun, *Mgr*
**EMP**: 91
**SALES (corp-wide)**: 51.76MM **Privately Held**
**Web**: www.industrialelectricalco.com
**SIC**: **1731** 5063 7694  General electrical contractor; Motors, electric; Electric motor repair
**PA**: Modesto Industrial Electrical Co., Inc.
1417 Coldwell Ave
209 527-2800

### (P-463)
### MODESTO INDUSTRIAL ELECTRICAL CO INC (PA)
Also Called: Industrial Electrical Company
1417 Coldwell Ave, Modesto (95350-5703)
**PHONE**..............................209 527-2800
**EMP**: 89 **EST**: 1935
**SALES (est)**: 51.76MM
**SALES (corp-wide)**: 51.76MM **Privately Held**
**Web**: www.industrialelectricalco.com
**SIC**: **1731** 5063 7694 7699  General electrical contractor; Motors, electric; Electric motor repair; Industrial machinery and equipment repair

### (P-464)
### NETRONIX INTEGRATION INC (HQ)
360 Turtle Creek Ct, San Jose (95125-1315)
**PHONE**..............................800 600-3939
Craig E Jarrett, *Pr*
Kimberly Jarrett, *
Kevin Thompson, *
**EMP**: 92 **EST**: 2007
**SALES (est)**: 41.9MM
**SALES (corp-wide)**: 686.58MM **Privately Held**
**Web**: www.netronixint.com
**SIC**: **1731** 3699  General electrical contractor; Security control equipment and systems
**PA**: Pavion Corp.
4151 Lfytte Ctr Dr Ste 70
703 631-3377

### (P-465)
### PACIFIC COAST CABLING INC (PA)
Also Called: PCC Network Solutions
20717 Prairie St, Chatsworth (91311-6011)
**PHONE**..............................818 407-1911
**EMP**: 50 **EST**: 1985
**SALES (est)**: 12.05MM
**SALES (corp-wide)**: 12.05MM **Privately Held**
**Web**: www.pccinc.com
**SIC**: **1731** 3613  Computer installation; Control panels, electric

### (P-466)
### PATRIC COMMUNICATIONS INC (PA)
Also Called: Advanced Electronic Solutions
15215 Alton Pkwy Ste 200, Irvine (92618-2613)
**PHONE**..............................619 579-2898
Sean P Mcdermott, *Pr*
Richard P Apgar, *
Kathy Alford, *
**EMP**: 70 **EST**: 1981
**SALES (est)**: 9.91MM **Privately Held**
**SIC**: **1731** 1751 3699  Fire detection and burglar alarm systems specialization; Carpentry work; Security devices

### (P-467)
### PRESIDIO SYSTEMS INC (PA)
159 Wright Brothers Ave, Livermore (94551-9466)
P.O. Box 886 (94551-0886)
**PHONE**..............................925 362-8400
Joe Schratz, *Pr*
Kris Schratz, *
**EMP**: 20 **EST**: 2002
**SALES (est)**: 3.91MM
**SALES (corp-wide)**: 3.91MM **Privately Held**
**Web**: www.presidiosystemsinc.com
**SIC**: **1731** 3589  Electrical work; Sewer cleaning equipment, power

### (P-468)
### QUALITY TECHNOLOGY SOLUTIONS
788 S Peach Ave, Reedley (93654-9348)
**PHONE**..............................559 804-4522
Quetzal Pena, *Pr*
**EMP**: 15 **EST**: 2016
**SALES (est)**: 1.21MM **Privately Held**
**Web**: www.qtspro.com
**SIC**: **1731** 3651 7819 5063  Electrical work; Video camera-audio recorders, household use; Cameraman, freelance; Fire alarm systems

### (P-469)
### SHADOW SECURITY APP INC
19709 Ventura Blvd Pmb 105-1017, Woodland Hills (91364-2623)
**PHONE**..............................310 388-9371
Daniel Krikorian, *CEO*
Keith Mcpherson, *Dir*
**EMP**: 15 **EST**: 2020
**SALES (est)**: 347.42K **Privately Held**
**SIC**: **1731** 7379 2761 7371  Safety and security specialization; Online services technology consultants; Computer forms, manifold or continuous; Custom computer programming services

### (P-470)
### TURNUPSEED ELECTRIC SERVICE
1580 S K St, Tulare (93274-6400)
P.O. Box 26 (93275-0026)
**PHONE**..............................559 686-1541
Wallace J Nelson, *Pr*
David Turnupseed, *
Terri Grant, *
**EMP**: 55 **EST**: 1949
**SQ FT**: 8,000
**SALES (est)**: 8.94MM **Privately Held**
**Web**: www.turnupseed.com
**SIC**: **1731** 7694 5063  General electrical contractor; Rewinding stators; Motors, electric

### (P-471)
### TWIN POWER USA LLC
Also Called: Twin Power Indus Solutions
40424 Jacob Way, Murrieta (92563-4916)
**PHONE**..............................714 609-6014
Michael Darwish, *CEO*
David Darwich, *Mgr*
David Darwish, *VP*
**EMP**: 20 **EST**: 2014
**SALES (est)**: 750.14K **Privately Held**
**Web**: www.twinpowerusa.com
**SIC**: **1731** 8748 8711 8742  General electrical contractor; Systems analysis and engineering consulting services; Consulting engineer; Management engineering

### (P-472)
### VALLEY COMMUNICATIONS INC (PA)
6921 Roseville Rd, Sacramento (95842-1660)
**PHONE**..............................916 349-7300
Ken Hurst, *Pr*
Kate Dewitt, *
Jeff Frydenlund, *
**EMP**: 60 **EST**: 1983
**SQ FT**: 12,000
**SALES (est)**: 22.67MM
**SALES (corp-wide)**: 22.67MM **Privately Held**
**Web**: www.valley-com.com
**SIC**: **1731** 3699  Voice, data, and video wiring contractor; Security control equipment and systems

### (P-473)
### VECTOR RESOURCES INC (PA)
Also Called: Vectorusa
20917 Higgins Ct, Torrance (90501-1723)
**PHONE**..............................310 436-1000
**TOLL FREE**: 800
David Zukerman, *Pr*
Robert Messinger, *
John Schuman, *Dist Vice President*
Jeffrey Zukerman, *
**EMP**: 167 **EST**: 1988
**SALES (est)**: 60.03MM
**SALES (corp-wide)**: 60.03MM **Privately Held**

Web: www.vectorusa.com
SIC: 1731 3651 7373 Communications specialization; Clock radio and telephone combinations; Systems engineering, computer related

**(P-474)**
**WORLD WIND ELECTRICAL SVCS INC**
Also Called: World Wind & Solar
228 W Tehachapi Blvd, Tehachapi (93561-1634)
PHONE..............................661 822-4877
Edward Cummings, *Pr*
EMP: 584 EST: 2009
SALES (est): 3.76MM
SALES (corp-wide): 503.06MM **Privately Held**
SIC: 1731 3621 8742 Electrical work; Windmills, electric generating; Maintenance management consultant
HQ: Pearce Services, Llc
1222 Vine St
Paso Robles CA 93446
805 467-2528

**(P-475)**
**WORLDWIND SERVICES LLC**
Also Called: World Wind & Solar
1222 Vine St Ste 301, Paso Robles (93446-2333)
PHONE..............................661 822-4877
Mark Mclanahan, *CEO*
Kristin Osborn, *
Matthew Gillette, *
EMP: 700 EST: 2007
SALES (est): 14.54MM
SALES (corp-wide): 503.06MM **Privately Held**
Web: www.worldwindsolar.com
SIC: 1731 1389 8742 Electrical work; Construction, repair, and dismantling services; Maintenance management consultant
HQ: Pearce Services, Llc
1222 Vine St
Paso Robles CA 93446
805 467-2528

## 1742 Plastering, Drywall, And Insulation

**(P-476)**
**LANCASTER BURNS CNSTR INC**
Also Called: L B Construction
8655 Washington Blvd, Roseville (95678-5945)
PHONE..............................916 624-8404
Jordan Edward Burns, *Pr*
Vance Lancaster, *
Christine Lancaster, *
EMP: 150 EST: 1992
SQ FT: 43,000
SALES (est): 27.57MM **Privately Held**
Web: www.lbconstructioninc.com
SIC: 1742 1751 1791 3449 Drywall; Framing contractor; Building front installation, metal; Bars, concrete reinforcing: fabricated steel

**(P-477)**
**MARTIN INTEGRATED SYSTEMS**
Also Called: Martin Integrated
1525 W Orange Grove Ave Ste D, Orange (92868-1109)
PHONE..............................714 998-9100
Cory Hovivian, *Pr*
Marshall Hovivian, *
Anne Reizer, *
EMP: 30 EST: 1989

SALES (est): 3.47MM **Privately Held**
Web: www.martinintegrated.com
SIC: 1742 3446 3296 Acoustical and ceiling work; Acoustical suspension systems, metal; Acoustical board and tile, mineral wool

**(P-478)**
**MGM DRYWALL INC**
1050 Commercial St Ste 102, San Jose (95112-1419)
PHONE..............................408 292-4085
Miguel Guillen, *Pr*
Martina Guillen, *
EMP: 100 EST: 2000
SALES (est): 9.32MM **Privately Held**
Web: www.mgmdrywall.com
SIC: 1742 1721 3446 Drywall; Residential painting; Acoustical suspension systems, metal

**(P-479)**
**ORANGE COUNTY THERMAL INDS INC (PA)**
1940 N Glassell St, Orange (92865-4314)
PHONE..............................714 279-9416
Eduardo Olivares, *Pr*
EMP: 51 EST: 2010
SQ FT: 10,000
SALES (est): 8.06MM
SALES (corp-wide): 8.06MM **Privately Held**
Web: www.teamocti.com
SIC: 1742 3296 Insulation, buildings; Acoustical board and tile, mineral wool

**(P-480)**
**PETROCHEM INSULATION INC**
Also Called: Petrochem
3117 E South St, Long Beach (90805-3742)
PHONE..............................310 638-6663
Erich Freudenthaler, *Mgr*
EMP: 111
SALES (corp-wide): 2.72B **Privately Held**
Web: www.petrocheminc.com
SIC: 1742 3531 Insulation, buildings; Construction machinery
HQ: Petrochem Insulation, Inc.
1501 W Ftnhead Pkwy # 550
Tempe AZ 85282
707 644-7455

**(P-481)**
**THERMO POWER INDUSTRIES**
Also Called: Thermo Power Industries
10570 Humbolt St, Los Alamitos (90720-2439)
PHONE..............................562 799-0087
Edward Lydic, *CEO*
John G Carroll, *
EMP: 50 EST: 1986
SQ FT: 5,500
SALES (est): 5.87MM **Privately Held**
Web: www.thermopowerindustries.com
SIC: 1742 1721 3479 Insulation, buildings; Commercial painting; Coating, rust preventive

## 1743 Terrazzo, Tile, Marble, Mosaic Work

**(P-482)**
**ALEXS TILE WORKS INC**
5920 Matthews St, Goleta (93117-3922)
P.O. Box 810 (93102-0810)
PHONE..............................805 967-5308
Vitali Drohomyrecky, *Pr*
Ruthe Drohomyrecky, *
Leonid Bondarenko, *
EMP: 25 EST: 1989

SALES (est): 2.48MM **Privately Held**
Web: www.alexstile.com
SIC: 1743 3272 Tile installation, ceramic; Floor slabs and tiles, precast concrete

**(P-483)**
**MANTELS & MORE CORP**
2909 Tanager Ave, Commerce (90040-2723)
PHONE..............................323 869-9764
Raffi Gourdikian, *CEO*
Tahlene Gourkikian, *
EMP: 43 EST: 1999
SQ FT: 25,000
SALES (est): 1.86MM **Privately Held**
SIC: 1743 3281 Terrazzo, tile, marble and mosaic work; Granite, cut and shaped

**(P-484)**
**PARAGON INDUSTRIES INC**
Also Called: Bedrosian's Tile
16450 Foothill Blvd Ste 100, Sylmar (91342-1087)
PHONE..............................818 833-0550
Josie Cox, *Brnch Mgr*
EMP: 31
SQ FT: 108,362
SALES (corp-wide): 251.57MM **Privately Held**
Web: www.bedrosians.com
SIC: 1743 3253 5032 5211 Tile installation, ceramic; Ceramic wall and floor tile; Ceramic wall and floor tile, nec; Tile, ceramic
PA: Paragon Industries, Inc.
4285 N Golden State Blvd
559 275-5000

**(P-485)**
**TILE & MARBLE DESIGN CO INC**
Also Called: Marbleworks
7421 Vincent Cir, Huntington Beach (92648-1246)
PHONE..............................714 847-6472
David Blataric, *CEO*
EMP: 32 EST: 2005
SALES (est): 3.2MM **Privately Held**
SIC: 1743 3281 Tile installation, ceramic; Marble, building: cut and shaped

## 1751 Carpentry Work

**(P-486)**
**ALEKSANDAR INC**
1542 W 130th St, Gardena (90249-2104)
PHONE..............................310 516-7700
Aleksandar Radovanovic, *CEO*
EMP: 15 EST: 1993
SALES (est): 2.76MM **Privately Held**
SIC: 1751 2431 1721 Cabinet and finish carpentry; Millwork; Wallcovering contractors

**(P-487)**
**ARCHITECTURAL WOODWORKING CO**
582 Monterey Pass Rd, Monterey Park (91754-2417)
PHONE..............................626 570-4125
John K Jack Heydorff, *Pr*
John F Heydorff, *Stockholder*
Richard A Schaub, *
Edward Illig, *
Thomas C Heydorff, *
EMP: 100 EST: 1963
SQ FT: 60,000
SALES (est): 4.69MM **Privately Held**
Web: www.awcla.com

SIC: 1751 2431 Carpentry work; Millwork

**(P-488)**
**CWP CABINETS INC**
15447 Anacapa Rd Ste 102, Victorville (92392-2481)
PHONE..............................760 246-4530
Michael Rodriguez, *CEO*
EMP: 115 EST: 2011
SALES (est): 1.34MM **Privately Held**
SIC: 1751 2434 2541 5712 Cabinet building and installation; Wood kitchen cabinets; Wood partitions and fixtures; Cabinet work, custom

**(P-489)**
**GARAGE CABINET WAREHOUSE INC (PA)**
Also Called: We're Organized Northern Cal
2700 Mercantile Dr Ste 800, Rancho Cordova (95742-7211)
P.O. Box 428 (95741-0428)
PHONE..............................916 638-0123
Joseph Rawlings, *Owner*
EMP: 22 EST: 1987
SQ FT: 10,000
SALES (est): 5.04MM
SALES (corp-wide): 5.04MM **Privately Held**
Web: www.wereorganized.com
SIC: 1751 2434 Cabinet building and installation; Wood kitchen cabinets

**(P-490)**
**GOLDFIRE CORPORATION**
Also Called: Metro Caseworks
4882 Davenport Pl, Fremont (94538-6304)
PHONE..............................510 354-3666
Arthur Howard Amon, *Pr*
EMP: 15 EST: 2008
SQ FT: 22,000
SALES (est): 4.12MM **Privately Held**
Web: www.metrocaseworks.com
SIC: 1751 2431 Cabinet building and installation; Millwork

**(P-491)**
**GRESEAN INDUSTRIES INC**
6320 Caballero Blvd, Buena Park (90620-1126)
P.O. Box 928 (92075-0928)
EMP: 25 EST: 1986
SALES (est): 2.73MM **Privately Held**
Web: www.cabinetsystems.com
SIC: 1751 2421 Cabinet and finish carpentry; Flooring (dressed lumber), softwood

**(P-492)**
**HAKES SASH & DOOR INC**
31945 Corydon St, Lake Elsinore (92530-8524)
PHONE..............................951 674-2414
Allen J Hakes, *Pr*
EMP: 190 EST: 2005
SQ FT: 2,000
SALES (est): 7.7MM **Privately Held**
Web: www.hakesdoor.net
SIC: 1751 3442 5211 Window and door installation and erection; Window and door frames; Sash, wood or metal

**(P-493)**
**HERITAGE INTERESTS LLC (PA)**
4300 Jetway Ct, North Highlands (95660-5702)
P.O. Box 214609 (95821-0609)
PHONE..............................916 481-5030
Edward Zuckerman, *Pr*
Charlie Gardemeyer, *
Dennis Gardemeyer, *

## 1751 - Carpentry Work

**(P-494)**
EMP: 90 EST: 2011
SQ FT: 80,000
SALES (est): 30.55MM
SALES (corp-wide): 30.55MM Privately Held
Web: www.heritageinterests.com
SIC: 1751 5031 2431 Cabinet and finish carpentry; Lumber, plywood, and millwork; Windows and window parts and trim, wood

**(P-494)**
**HOME ORGANIZERS INC**
Also Called: Closet World, The
3860 Capitol Ave, City Of Industry (90601-1733)
PHONE..................................562 699-9945
Frank Melkonian, Pr
EMP: 660 EST: 2001
SALES (est): 11.12MM Privately Held
Web: www.closetworld.com
SIC: 1751 2541 Cabinet building and installation; Cabinets, lockers, and shelving

**(P-495)**
**KEYSTONE DOOR & BLDG SUP INC**
Also Called: Keystone Door & Building Sup
1037 N Market Blvd Ste 9, Sacramento (95834-1917)
PHONE..................................916 623-8100
Dale Winchester, CEO
Dale Winchester, Ch
Thaddeus Carpenter, *
David Herron, *
EMP: 40 EST: 2013
SQ FT: 35,000
SALES (est): 2.03MM Privately Held
Web: www.keystonedoor.com
SIC: 1751 3429 Carpentry work; Furniture, builders' and other household hardware

**(P-496)**
**LOZANO CASEWORKS INC**
242 W Hanna St, Colton (92324-2772)
PHONE..................................909 783-7530
EMP: 70
SIC: 1751 2522 Cabinet building and installation; Cabinets, office: except wood

**(P-497)**
**MFI CONSTRUCTION INC**
417 E San Bernardino Rd, Covina (91723-1705)
PHONE..................................626 565-2015
Karmen Ochoa, CEO
Karmen Ochoa, Pr
EMP: 20 EST: 2004
SALES (est): 3.15MM Privately Held
Web: www.mficon.com
SIC: 1751 2431 Carpentry work; Millwork

**(P-498)**
**MISSION BELL MFG CO INC**
16100 Jacqueline Ct, Morgan Hill (95037-5526)
PHONE..................................408 778-2036
Bret Sisney, Pr
Nicolette Faultner, *
EMP: 280 EST: 2022
SALES (est): 7.04MM Privately Held
Web: www.missionbell.com
SIC: 1751 2421 2541 1799 Cabinet and finish carpentry; Building and structural materials, wood; Cabinets, lockers, and shelving; Building site preparation

**(P-499)**
**NORTHWEST EXTERIORS INC (PA)**
Also Called: Windows Hawaii
11200 Sun Center Dr, Rancho Cordova (95670-6145)
PHONE..................................916 851-1632
Thomas Orr, Pr
Thomas Marvin Orr, *
Todd Mckinstry, Ex VP
EMP: 45 EST: 1996
SQ FT: 5,000
SALES (est): 2.35MM Privately Held
Web: www.northwestexteriors.com
SIC: 1751 5074 1761 2434 Window and door (prefabricated) installation; Heating equipment and panels, solar; Roofing, siding, and sheetmetal work; Wood kitchen cabinets

**(P-500)**
**SEGALE BROS WOOD PRODUCTS INC**
1705 Sabre St, Hayward (94545-1015)
PHONE..................................510 300-1170
Donald A Segale, CEO
Christine Segale, *
EMP: 28 EST: 1976
SQ FT: 40,000
SALES (est): 6.41MM Privately Held
Web: www.segalebros.com
SIC: 1751 2434 Cabinet building and installation; Wood kitchen cabinets

**(P-501)**
**SIERRA TRIM INC**
Also Called: Construction
3137 Swetzer Rd Ste B, Loomis (95650-7611)
PHONE..................................916 259-2966
William D Snow, CEO
EMP: 25 EST: 2009
SALES (est): 4.75MM Privately Held
Web: www.sierratrim.com
SIC: 1751 2431 Finish and trim carpentry; Door frames, wood

**(P-502)**
**VORTEX INDUSTRIES LLC (PA)**
Also Called: Vortex Doors
20 Odyssey, Irvine (92618-3144)
PHONE..................................714 434-8000
Elizabeth Turner Everett, CEO
▲ EMP: 25 EST: 1937
SQ FT: 10,000
SALES (est): 144.97MM
SALES (corp-wide): 144.97MM Privately Held
Web: www.vortexdoors.com
SIC: 1751 3441 7699 Garage door, installation or erection; Fabricated structural metal; Door and window repair

**(P-503)**
**WIN-DOR INC (PA)**
450 Delta Ave, Brea (92821-2935)
PHONE..................................714 576-2030
TOLL FREE: 800
Gary Templin, CEO
Wolfgang Wirthgen, *
EMP: 170 EST: 1994
SQ FT: 73,000
SALES (est): 46.75MM Privately Held
Web: www.windorsystems.com
SIC: 1751 3446 Window and door (prefabricated) installation; Guards, made from pipe

## 1752 Floor Laying And Floor Work, Nec

**(P-504)**
**FLOOR SEAL TECHNOLOGY INC (PA)**
Also Called: Fst Design Build Concrete
1566 S 7th St, San Jose (95112-5929)
PHONE..................................408 436-8181
William Clyne, CEO
William Terry Ireland, *
Theresa Luu, *
EMP: 50 EST: 1980
SALES (est): 2.42MM
SALES (corp-wide): 2.42MM Privately Held
Web: www.floorseal.com
SIC: 1752 2891 3829 Wood floor installation and refinishing; Sealants; Measuring and controlling devices, nec

**(P-505)**
**PRO INSTALLATIONS INC (HQ)**
Also Called: Prospectra Contract Flooring
10948 Willow Ct Ste 100, San Diego (92127-2425)
▲ EMP: 20 EST: 1997
SALES (est): 4.86MM
SALES (corp-wide): 557.41MM Privately Held
SIC: 1752 2273 Carpet laying; Carpets and rugs
PA: Diverzify+ Llc
865 W Irving Park Rd
847 250-4600

**(P-506)**
**TERA-LITE INC**
Also Called: Revolan Systems
1631 S 10th St, San Jose (95112-2594)
PHONE..................................408 288-8655
David Palomino, Pr
EMP: 35 EST: 1964
SQ FT: 10,000
SALES (est): 5.93MM Privately Held
Web: www.tera-lite.com
SIC: 1752 5023 2851 Floor laying and floor work, nec; Floor coverings; Paints and allied products

**(P-507)**
**WEST COAST SURFACES INC**
27620 Commerce Center Dr Ste 107, Temecula (92590-2539)
PHONE..................................951 699-0600
Thomas Lahood, Pr
Kristi Lewis, Off Mgr
EMP: 20 EST: 2011
SQ FT: 2,400
SALES (est): 1.48MM Privately Held
SIC: 1752 1743 3281 3253 Ceramic floor tile installation; Terrazzo, tile, marble and mosaic work; Granite, cut and shaped; Ceramic wall and floor tile

## 1761 Roofing, Siding, And Sheetmetal Work

**(P-508)**
**A CLASS PRECISION INC**
13395 Estelle St, Corona (92879-1881)
PHONE..................................951 549-9706
Scott Broadbent, Managing Member
Kim Vasile, Managing Member
Rene Acero, Managing Member
EMP: 18 EST: 2006
SQ FT: 9,000
SALES (est): 2.4MM Privately Held
Web: www.classprecision.com
SIC: 1761 3599 Sheet metal work, nec; Machine and other job shop work

**(P-509)**
**A PLUS CUSTOM METAL SUPPLY INC**
Also Called: A Plus Custom Shtmtl & Sup
1891 1st St, Norco (92860-3139)
P.O. Box 178 (92860-0178)
PHONE..................................951 736-7900
TOLL FREE: 800
David Maizland, Owner
EMP: 16 EST: 1984
SQ FT: 6,700
SALES (est): 627.71K Privately Held
SIC: 1761 3444 5074 1799 Sheet metal work, nec; Metal roofing and roof drainage equipment; Fireplaces, prefabricated; Closet organizers, installation and design

**(P-510)**
**AEP SPAN INC**
2110 Enterprise Blvd, West Sacramento (95691-3428)
PHONE..................................916 372-0933
Al Price, Mgr
EMP: 29 EST: 2001
SQ FT: 16,000
SALES (est): 963.67K Privately Held
Web: www.ascprofiles.com
SIC: 1761 3448 3444 3443 Roofing contractor; Prefabricated metal buildings and components; Sheet metalwork; Fabricated plate work (boiler shop)
HQ: Asc Profiles Llc
2110 Enterprise Blvd
West Sacramento CA 95691
916 376-2800

**(P-511)**
**ALL FAB PRCSION SHEETMETAL INC**
1980 Senter Rd, San Jose (95112-2603)
PHONE..................................408 279-1099
Son P Ho, CEO
Kelly T Ho, *
▲ EMP: 100 EST: 2000
SALES (est): 26.98MM Privately Held
Web: www.allfabprecision.com
SIC: 1761 3444 Sheet metal work, nec; Sheet metalwork

**(P-512)**
**CROWN SHTMTL & SKYLIGHTS INC**
Also Called: Crown Sheet Metal & Skylights
855 Stanton Rd, Burlingame (94010-1403)
PHONE..................................415 467-5008
Beverly Dennehy, Pr
Donald Dennehy Senior, VP
Donald Dennehy Junior, Sec
EMP: 25 EST: 1971
SQ FT: 5,000
SALES (est): 1.03MM Privately Held
Web: www.crownsheetmetal.com
SIC: 1761 1796 3444 Skylight installation; Installing building equipment; Skylights, sheet metal

**(P-513)**
**EHMCKE SHEET METAL CORP**
840 W 19th St, National City (91950-5406)
P.O. Box 13010 (92170-3010)
PHONE..................................619 477-6484
John F Cornell, CEO
Dennis Isaacs, *
Dennis Stainbrook, *

Richard Parra, *
▲ **EMP:** 55 **EST:** 1927
**SQ FT:** 25,000
**SALES (est):** 9.66MM **Privately Held**
Web: www.ehmckesheetmetal.com
**SIC: 1761** 8712 3446 Sheet metal work, nec; Architectural services; Architectural metalwork

**(P-514)**
**FONCO INC**
Also Called: Broadway Sheet Metal & Mfg
133 Starlite St, South San Francisco (94080-6313)
**PHONE**.................................650 873-4585
John Fontaine, *Pr*
Steve Fontaine, *VP*
Mitch Fontaine, *Sec*
**EMP:** 18 **EST:** 1970
**SQ FT:** 14,000
**SALES (est):** 3.46MM **Privately Held**
Web: www.broadwaysheetmetal.com
**SIC: 1761** 3444 3441 Sheet metal work, nec; Sheet metalwork; Fabricated structural metal

**(P-515)**
**KAISER AIR CONDITIONING AND SHEET METAL INC**
Also Called: Kaiser Air Conditioning
600 Pacific Ave, Oxnard (93030-7318)
**PHONE**.................................805 988-1800
**EMP:** 25 **EST:** 1981
**SALES (est):** 7.97MM **Privately Held**
Web: www.kaiserac.com
**SIC: 1761** 1711 3444 Architectural sheet metal work; Warm air heating and air conditioning contractor; Sheet metalwork

**(P-516)**
**THORSENS-NORQUIST INC**
Also Called: Thorsens Plumbing & AC
2310 N Walnut Rd, Turlock (95382-8910)
**PHONE**.................................209 524-5296
Craig Vernon Pitau, *CEO*
Esther Thorsen, *Sec*
**EMP:** 55 **EST:** 1911
**SQ FT:** 19,500
**SALES (est):** 6.3MM **Privately Held**
Web: www.thornorinc.com
**SIC: 1761** 1711 5722 5075 Sheet metal work, nec; Plumbing contractors; Household appliance stores; Warm air heating equipment and supplies

**(P-517)**
**VAN-MULDER SHEET METAL INC**
2437 Radley Ct, Hayward (94545-1128)
**PHONE**.................................510 569-9123
**EMP:** 50 **EST:** 1972
**SALES (est):** 18MM **Privately Held**
Web: www.vanmulder.com
**SIC: 1761** 3444 Architectural sheet metal work; Sheet metalwork

**(P-518)**
**WEISS SHEET METAL COMPANY**
Also Called: Metcoe Skylight Specialties
1715 W 135th St, Gardena (90249-2507)
**PHONE**.................................310 354-2700
Andre Sarai, *Pr*
Steve Linder, *
Morris Saraie, *
▼ **EMP:** 45 **EST:** 1937
**SQ FT:** 33,000
**SALES (est):** 8.82MM **Privately Held**
Web: www.metcoe.com
**SIC: 1761** 3211 Skylight installation; Skylight glass

## 1771 Concrete Work

**(P-519)**
**BEACH PAVING INC**
749 N Poplar St, Orange (92868-1013)
P.O. Box 10442 (92627-0162)
**PHONE**.................................714 978-2414
Curtis Rummel, *Pr*
**EMP:** 17 **EST:** 1979
**SQ FT:** 1,000
**SALES (est):** 4.1MM **Privately Held**
Web: www.beachpavinginc.com
**SIC: 1771** 2951 Blacktop (asphalt) work; Asphalt paving mixtures and blocks

**(P-520)**
**CRAWFORD ASSOCIATES**
2635 E Chanslor Way, Blythe (92225-9805)
P.O. Box 807 (92226-0807)
**PHONE**.................................760 922-6804
Bill Crawford, *Pt*
Tommy Crawford, *Pt*
Cody Crawford, *Pt*
**EMP:** 27 **EST:** 1975
**SQ FT:** 1,500
**SALES (est):** 5.96MM **Privately Held**
Web: www.crawfordconcrete.com
**SIC: 1771** 3273 Concrete work; Ready-mixed concrete

**(P-521)**
**DE LA CRUZ LATH AND PLASTER CO**
3480 Carpenter Rd, Stockton (95215-8100)
**PHONE**.................................209 368-8658
Enrique De La Cruz S, *Pr*
**EMP:** 16 **EST:** 2011
**SALES (est):** 3.22MM **Privately Held**
**SIC: 1771** 3541 Exterior concrete stucco contractor; Lathes

**(P-522)**
**GEORGE REED INC (HQ)**
Also Called: Western Pavement Preservation
140 Empire Ave, Modesto (95354-3804)
P.O. Box 4760 (95352-4760)
**PHONE**.................................877 823-2305
Wendel Reed, *CEO*
Ed Berlier, *
C T Tutthill, *Mgr*
▲ **EMP:** 25 **EST:** 1962
**SQ FT:** 7,004
**SALES (est):** 33.34MM
**SALES (corp-wide):** 163.99MM **Privately Held**
Web: www.georgereed.com
**SIC: 1771** 3272 Concrete work; Concrete products, nec
**PA:** Reed Family Companies
928 12th St Ste 700
209 521-9771

**(P-523)**
**KP CONCRETE & STEEL INC**
3835 E 9th St, Pomona (91766-3916)
**PHONE**.................................909 461-4163
**EMP:** 15 **EST:** 2014
**SALES (est):** 2.41MM **Privately Held**
**SIC: 1771** 3312 Concrete work; Stainless steel

**(P-524)**
**PETERSON BROTHERS CNSTR INC**
Also Called: Pbc Companies
2929 E White Star Ave, Anaheim (92806-2628)
**PHONE**.................................714 278-0488
Elden Peterson, *CEO*
Robert K Peterson, *
Patrick Burns, *
Mike Hoefnagels, *
Jack Saldate, *
▲ **EMP:** 600 **EST:** 1983
**SALES (est):** 38.06MM **Privately Held**
Web: www.pbccompanies.com
**SIC: 1771** 3531 1741 Concrete work; Pavers; Concrete block masonry laying

**(P-525)**
**SOUTHLAND PAVING INC**
361 N Hale Ave, Escondido (92029-1716)
**PHONE**.................................760 747-6895
Richard Fleck, *CEO*
Daniel Devlin, *
Robert Kennedy, *
Anne Fleck, *
**EMP:** 75 **EST:** 1983
**SQ FT:** 35,000
**SALES (est):** 24.66MM **Privately Held**
Web: www.southlandpaving.com
**SIC: 1771** 2951 Blacktop (asphalt) work; Asphalt paving mixtures and blocks

## 1781 Water Well Drilling

**(P-526)**
**BRAX COMPANY INC**
Also Called: Frederick Pump Company
31248 Valley Center Rd, Valley Center (92082-6757)
**PHONE**.................................760 749-2209
Steven Tweed, *Pr*
**EMP:** 37 **EST:** 1985
**SQ FT:** 3,000
**SALES (est):** 1.69MM **Privately Held**
Web: www.braxcompany.com
**SIC: 1781** 5084 3563 Water well drilling; Water pumps (industrial); Air and gas compressors

## 1791 Structural Steel Erection

**(P-527)**
**ALLIED STEEL CO INC**
1027 Palmyrita Ave, Riverside (92507-1701)
**PHONE**.................................951 241-7000
Brian P Chapman, *Pr*
Perry K Chapman, *
Nicky Chapman, *
Jeanette Chapman, *
**EMP:** 60 **EST:** 1944
**SQ FT:** 48,000
**SALES (est):** 6.7MM **Privately Held**
Web: www.alliedsteelco.com
**SIC: 1791** 3441 Structural steel erection; Fabricated structural metal

**(P-528)**
**BAPKO METAL INC**
721 S Parker St Ste 300, Orange (92868-4732)
**PHONE**.................................714 639-9380
Fred Bagatourian, *Pr*
Heather Wiliams, *
Clint Rieber, *
**EMP:** 80 **EST:** 1978
**SALES (est):** 22.73MM **Privately Held**
Web: www.bapko.com
**SIC: 1791** 3441 Structural steel erection; Fabricated structural metal

**(P-529)**
**COAST IRON & STEEL CO**
12300 Lakeland Rd, Santa Fe Springs (90670-3869)
P.O. Box 2846 (90670-0846)
**PHONE**.................................562 946-4421
Greg White, *Pr*
Cyndi White Cramer, *Stockholder**
Carrie White, *Stockholder**
Jared White, *Stockholder**
Duane Westrup, *
▲ **EMP:** 50 **EST:** 1953
**SQ FT:** 360,000
**SALES (est):** 10.34MM **Privately Held**
Web: www.rsac.com
**SIC: 1791** 3441 Structural steel erection; Fabricated structural metal

**(P-530)**
**HEAVY METAL STEEL COMPANY INC**
Also Called: Heavy Metal Steel
12130 Lomica Dr, San Diego (92128-2716)
**PHONE**.................................858 433-4800
Linda Rosenberg, *Pr*
Linda D Rosenberg, *
Arnold Rosenberg, *
**EMP:** 25 **EST:** 2014
**SALES (est):** 2MM **Privately Held**
Web: www.heavymetalsteel.com
**SIC: 1791** 3449 Structural steel erection; Fabricated bar joists and concrete reinforcing bars

**(P-531)**
**KCB TOWERS INC**
27260 Meines St, Highland (92346-4223)
P.O. Box 100 (92346-0100)
**PHONE**.................................909 862-0322
S Lynn Bogh, *CEO*
Miles Bogh, *
Sharon Bogh, *
**EMP:** 100 **EST:** 1982
**SQ FT:** 12,000
**SALES (est):** 7.14MM **Privately Held**
Web: www.kcbtowers.com
**SIC: 1791** 3441 Concrete reinforcement, placing of; Fabricated structural metal

**(P-532)**
**LEGACY REINFORCING STEEL LLC**
1057 Tierra Del Rey Ste F, Chula Vista (91910-7882)
**PHONE**.................................619 646-0205
Brian Briggs, *Pr*
**EMP:** 75 **EST:** 2019
**SALES (est):** 2.65MM **Privately Held**
**SIC: 1791** 3449 Structural steel erection; Bars, concrete reinforcing: fabricated steel

**(P-533)**
**LHL CONSTRUCTION INC**
Also Called: Rankin and Rankin
1370 Furneaux Rd, Olivehurst (95961-7466)
**PHONE**.................................916 782-9001
Len Lewis Junior, *Pr*
Lenond B Lewis Junior, *Pr*
Lenond B Lewis Senior, *VP*
Chris Koski, *
**EMP:** 30 **EST:** 1984
**SALES (est):** 1.36MM **Privately Held**
Web: www.lhlconstruction.com
**SIC: 1791** 3448 2394 Structural steel erection; Prefabricated metal buildings and components; Canvas and related products

**(P-534)**
**SCHUFF STEEL COMPANY**
10100 Trinity Pkwy Ste 400, Stockton (95219-7240)
**PHONE**.................................209 938-0869
Chase Abbott, *Brnch Mgr*

# 1791 - Structural Steel Erection

**(P-535)**
EMP: 33
Web: www.schuff.com
SIC: 1791 3441  Structural steel erection; Fabricated structural metal
HQ: Schuff Steel Company
3003 N Centl Ave Ste 1500
Phoenix AZ 85012
602 252-7787

**(P-535)**
**SOS STEEL COMPANY INC**
Also Called: Somers Orear Stphan Stl Fbrcto
1160 Richard Ave, Santa Clara (95050-2873)
PHONE.................408 727-6363
EMP: 47 EST: 1946
SALES (est): 16.48MM  Privately Held
Web: www.sossteelco.com
SIC: 1791 3441  Structural steel erection; Fabricated structural metal

**(P-536)**
**STROCAL INC**
4651 Quail Lakes Dr, Stockton (95207-5258)
P.O. Box 77937 (95267-1237)
PHONE.................209 948-4646
▲ EMP: 336
Web: www.strocal.com
SIC: 1791 3441  Structural steel erection; Fabricated structural metal

**(P-537)**
**VALLEY IRON WORKS INC**
127 E Harney Ln, Lodi (95240-8836)
PHONE.................209 368-7037
Joseph M Coubal, Pr
Deborah Coubal, *
EMP: 30 EST: 1979
SQ FT: 20,000
SALES (est): 8.49MM  Privately Held
Web: www.valleyironworks.com
SIC: 1791 3449  Iron work, structural; Miscellaneous metalwork

**(P-538)**
**WHITES STEEL INC (PA)**
45524 Towne St, Indio (92201-4446)
P.O. Box 846 (92274-0846)
PHONE.................760 347-3401
Edwin Neumeyer, CEO
EMP: 17 EST: 1995
SALES (est): 10.92MM
SALES (corp-wide): 10.92MM  Privately Held
Web: www.whitessteel.com
SIC: 1791 3446 3599  Structural steel erection; Architectural metalwork; Machine shop, jobbing and repair

## 1793 Glass And Glazing Work

**(P-539)**
**BAGATELOS GLASS SYSTEMS INC (PA)**
Also Called: Bagatlos Archtctral GL Systems
2750 Redding Ave, Sacramento (95820-2156)
PHONE.................916 364-3600
Chris Bagatelos, CEO
▲ EMP: 38 EST: 1999
SQ FT: 50,000
SALES (est): 18.52MM
SALES (corp-wide): 18.52MM  Privately Held
Web: www.bagatelos.com
SIC: 1793 3229  Glass and glazing work; Glassware, industrial

**(P-540)**
**DELTA SPECIALTIES INC**
1374 E Turner Rd Ste A, Lodi (95240-0758)
PHONE.................209 937-9650
Tanya Watters, Pr
Robert Couillard, Sec
Gene Watters, VP
EMP: 15 EST: 2008
SALES (est): 2.18MM  Privately Held
Web: www.deltaspecialties.net
SIC: 1793 2452  Glass and glazing work; Prefabricated wood buildings

**(P-541)**
**NATIONAL GLASS SYSTEMS INC**
Also Called: Architctral Coml Glzing Alum P
258 Boulay Ct, Morgan Hill (95037-9348)
PHONE.................408 835-5124
Octavio Martinez, CEO
EMP: 23 EST: 2019
SALES (est): 1.88MM  Privately Held
SIC: 1793 1761 1799 3446  Glass and glazing work; Skylight installation; Glass tinting, architectural or automotive; Architectural metalwork

**(P-542)**
**SOUTH BAY SHOWERS INC**
Also Called: Shower Glass & Mirror Co
540 Martin Ave, Santa Clara (95050-2954)
PHONE.................408 988-3484
TOLL FREE: 800
Ron Ebel, Pr
Bob Sutton, *
Susan Ebel, *
Helen Sutton, *
▲ EMP: 25 EST: 1970
SQ FT: 15,800
SALES (est): 2.34MM  Privately Held
Web: www.southbayshowers.com
SIC: 1793 5039 5231 3231  Glass and glazing work; Glass construction materials; Glass; Products of purchased glass

## 1794 Excavation Work

**(P-543)**
**ARNETT CONSTRUCTION INC**
Also Called: A A Construction
626 W 1st St, Rialto (92376-5715)
P.O. Box 488 (92377-0488)
PHONE.................909 421-7960
Albert Arnett, Pr
Shirley Arnett, VP
Lea Ann Hibbetts, Sec
Wayne Arnett, Treas
EMP: 20 EST: 1983
SQ FT: 1,200
SALES (est): 2.55MM  Privately Held
SIC: 1794 1611 1542 3531  Excavation and grading, building construction; Concrete construction: roads, highways, sidewalks, etc.; Nonresidential construction, nec; Plows: construction, excavating, and grading

**(P-544)**
**GALLAGHER PROPERTIES INC (PA)**
344 High St, Oakland (94601-3902)
P.O. Box 779 (94549-0779)
PHONE.................510 261-0466
Allen Mckeen, VP
Denise Barger, *
EMP: 25 EST: 1946
SQ FT: 20,000
SALES (est): 6.24MM
SALES (corp-wide): 6.24MM  Privately Held
Web: www.gallagherburk.com
SIC: 1794 1611 2951 1771  Excavation and grading, building construction; Highway and street construction; Asphalt paving mixtures and blocks; Concrete work

**(P-545)**
**MACHADO BACKHOE INC**
22332 Third Ave, Stevinson (95374-9745)
PHONE.................209 634-4836
Daniel Machado, CEO
Daniel Machado, Pr
Corinne Machado, *
Natalie Pires, *
EMP: 25 EST: 1971
SQ FT: 1,100
SALES (est): 5.22MM  Privately Held
Web: www.machadobackhoe.com
SIC: 1794 3272  Excavation and grading, building construction; Solid containing units, concrete

**(P-546)**
**PACIFIC GOLD MARKETING INC**
Also Called: Mechanical Associates
745 Broadway St, Fresno (93721-2807)
PHONE.................559 272-8168
Sarah Woolf, CEO
Andrew Clark, *
Lawrence Clark, *
EMP: 35 EST: 1990
SQ FT: 9,400
SALES (est): 5.04MM  Privately Held
Web: www.pgmpower.com
SIC: 1794 1623 8711 3271  Excavation and grading, building construction; Water and sewer line construction; Civil engineering; Paving blocks, concrete

**(P-547)**
**PARMETER LOGGING AND EXCAV INC**
6040 Cazadero Hwy, Cazadero (95421-9513)
P.O. Box 128 (95421-0128)
PHONE.................707 632-5610
Steven Parmeter, Pr
Harriet Parmeter, Sec
Kenneth Parmeter, VP
Dana Radtkey, Treas
EMP: 18 EST: 1979
SQ FT: 5,400
SALES (est): 1.93MM  Privately Held
Web: www.parmeterlogging.com
SIC: 1794 2411  Excavation and grading, building construction; Logging

## 1796 Installing Building Equipment

**(P-548)**
**AMERICORE INC**
Also Called: Americore
19705 August Ave, Hilmar (95324-9302)
P.O. Box 1353 (95324-1353)
PHONE.................209 632-5679
Ryan Cunha, Pr
Ryan Marques Cunha, *
EMP: 60 EST: 2007
SALES (est): 5.92MM  Privately Held
Web: www.americoremechanical.com
SIC: 1796 3498 1711  Millwright; Fabricated pipe and fittings; Mechanical contractor

**(P-549)**
**CALIFORNIA AIR CONVEYING CORP**
16260 Minnesota Ave, Paramount (90723-4916)
PHONE.................562 531-4570
John De Long Junior, Pr
Leslie De Long, Sec
EMP: 15 EST: 1978
SQ FT: 5,000
SALES (est): 3.66MM  Privately Held
Web: www.calaircon.com
SIC: 1796 3444  Pollution control equipment installation; Machine guards, sheet metal

**(P-550)**
**MAINTECH RESOURCES INC**
5042 Northwestern Way, Westminster (92683-2729)
PHONE.................562 804-0664
John Ellen, Pr
EMP: 36 EST: 1984
SALES (est): 2.46MM  Privately Held
Web: www.maintech-hq.com
SIC: 1796 1731 8711 3498  Installing building equipment; General electrical contractor; Structural engineering; Coils, pipe: fabricated from purchased pipe

**(P-551)**
**WEST COAST IRON INC**
Also Called: Westcoast Iron
9302 Jamacha Rd, Spring Valley (91977-4203)
PHONE.................619 464-8456
EMP: 75 EST: 1988
SALES (est): 18.68MM  Privately Held
Web: www.westcoastiron.com
SIC: 1796 1541 3441  Installing building equipment; Steel building construction; Building components, structural steel

## 1799 Special Trade Contractors, Nec

**(P-552)**
**A-1 ENTERPRISES INC**
Also Called: A-1 Fence
2831 E La Cresta Ave, Anaheim (92806-1817)
PHONE.................714 630-3390
TOLL FREE: 800
Norman Shepherd, Pr
James Sypitkowski, *
EMP: 45 EST: 1953
SQ FT: 39,000
SALES (est): 9.56MM  Privately Held
Web: www.a1fence.com
SIC: 1799 3446  Fence construction; Acoustical suspension systems, metal

**(P-553)**
**AHLBORN FENCE & STEEL INC (PA)**
Also Called: Ahlborn Companies
1230 Century Ct, Santa Rosa (95403-1042)
PHONE.................707 573-0742
Thomas C Ahlborn, CEO
Cathy Ahlborn, Sec
EMP: 22 EST: 1991
SQ FT: 20,000
SALES (est): 6.4MM  Privately Held
Web: www.ahlbornfence.com
SIC: 1799 3449 3493  Fence construction; Miscellaneous metalwork; Steel springs, except wire

**(P-554)**
**B-F GLASS INC**
Also Called: Fresno Shower Door and Mirror
3603 W Gettysburg Ave, Fresno (93722-7817)
PHONE.................559 221-4100
EMP: 36

## PRODUCTS & SERVICES SECTION
### 1799 - Special Trade Contractors, Nec (P-575)

SIC: **1799** 3231 5231 Home/office interiors finishing, furnishing and remodeling; Doors, glass: made from purchased glass; Glass

**(P-555)**
### BIG BEAR BOWLING BARN INC
Also Called: Fun Flex
40625 Big Bear Blvd, Big Bear Lake (92315)
P.O. Box 1152 (92315)
PHONE..................................909 878-2695
William D Ross, *Pr*
William Douglas Ross, *Pr*
**EMP:** 20 **EST:** 2010
**SALES (est):** 908.88K **Privately Held**
Web: www.bowlingbarn.com
SIC: **1799** 3949 Bowling alley installation; Bowling alleys and accessories

**(P-556)**
### BRAVO SIGN & DESIGN INC
520 S Central Park Ave E, Anaheim (92802-1472)
PHONE..................................714 284-0500
Frank Fiore, *Pr*
**EMP:** 18 **EST:** 1990
**SQ FT:** 12,000
**SALES (est):** 2.59MM **Privately Held**
Web: www.bravosign.com
SIC: **1799** 3993 Sign installation and maintenance; Signs and advertising specialties

**(P-557)**
### CALIFORNIA COUNTERTOP INC (PA)
7811 Alvarado Rd, La Mesa (91942-0665)
PHONE..................................619 460-0205
Wayne J Krumenacker, *Pr*
**EMP:** 19 **EST:** 1984
**SQ FT:** 8,300
**SALES (est):** 5.39MM
**SALES (corp-wide):** 5.39MM **Privately Held**
Web: www.californiacountertop.com
SIC: **1799** 2541 5211 Counter top installation; Wood partitions and fixtures; Cabinets, kitchen

**(P-558)**
### CALIFRNIA CSTM SNROMS PTIO CVE
Also Called: California Sun Rooms
3160 Gold Valley Dr Ste 300, Rancho Cordova (95742-6577)
PHONE..................................800 834-3211
Abe Alvi, *Pr*
**EMP:** 19 **EST:** 1991
**SALES (est):** 4.66MM **Privately Held**
Web: www.californiasunrooms.com
SIC: **1799** 3448 Spa or hot tub installation or construction; Sunrooms, prefabricated metal

**(P-559)**
### CLEAR SIGN & DESIGN INC
170 Navajo St, San Marcos (92078-2506)
PHONE..................................760 736-8111
Steve Weddell, *Pr*
Gabe Griffin, *Genl Mgr*
**EMP:** 19 **EST:** 1981
**SQ FT:** 18,000
**SALES (est):** 6.61MM **Privately Held**
Web: www.clearsigns.com
SIC: **1799** 3993 Sign installation and maintenance; Signs and advertising specialties

**(P-560)**
### DAVIDSON ENTERPRISES INC
3223 Brittan St, Bakersfield (93308-4902)
PHONE..................................661 325-2145
Robert Davidson, *Ch Bd*
Philip R Davidson, *Pr*
Donna Davidson, *Sec*
Margaret Davidson, *Treas*
▲ **EMP:** 20 **EST:** 1959
**SALES (est):** 3.21MM **Privately Held**
Web: www.davidsontank.com
SIC: **1799** 3531 7699 Petroleum storage tanks, pumping and draining; Trucks, off-highway; Industrial equipment services

**(P-561)**
### DEMOR ENTERPRISES INC
Also Called: 911 Restoration of San Diego
4174 Sorrento Valley Blvd Ste H, San Diego (92121-1424)
PHONE..................................858 625-0003
Roni Dahar, *CEO*
**EMP:** 20 **EST:** 2009
**SALES (est):** 2.39MM **Privately Held**
Web: www.911restorationofsandiego.com
SIC: **1799** 1389 8322 1742 Fireproofing buildings; Construction, repair, and dismantling services; Disaster service; Insulation, buildings

**(P-562)**
### DEVELOPERS GENERAL CONTRACTING
10 Hughes, Irvine (92618-1911)
PHONE..................................949 351-7872
Abdul E Mohtasebzada, *CEO*
**EMP:** 18 **EST:** 2016
**SALES (est):** 846.26K **Privately Held**
SIC: **1799** 1389 1541 Special trade contractors, nec; Construction, repair, and dismantling services; General contractor, highway and street construction; Renovation, remodeling and repairs: industrial buildings

**(P-563)**
### HARTMARK CAB DESIGN & MFG INC
Also Called: Hartmark Cabinet Design
3575 Grapevine St, Jurupa Valley (91752-3505)
P.O. Box 54204 (92619-4204)
PHONE..................................909 591-9153
Gary Allen Hartmark, *Pr*
Gary Allen Hartmark, *Pr*
Marnell Hartmark, *
**EMP:** 45 **EST:** 1986
**SQ FT:** 44,000
**SALES (est):** 16.27MM **Privately Held**
Web: www.hartmark.com
SIC: **1799** 2434 1751 Kitchen cabinet installation; Wood kitchen cabinets; Cabinet and finish carpentry

**(P-564)**
### IN-LINE FENCE & RAILING CO INC
Also Called: In-Line Construction
1307 Walnut St, Ramona (92065-1840)
P.O. Box 2637 (92065-0945)
PHONE..................................760 789-0282
David Ortiz, *Pr*
**EMP:** 28 **EST:** 1998
**SALES (est):** 3.61MM **Privately Held**
Web: www.inlinerail.com

SIC: **1799** 1611 3441 1542 Fence construction; General contractor, highway and street construction; Building components, structural steel; Commercial and office building, new construction

**(P-565)**
### INSTALLTION DGTAL TRNSMSSONS I
Also Called: Idt Telecomm Data
517 Jacoby St Ste C, San Rafael (94901-5343)
PHONE..................................415 226-0020
Theresa Benecchi, *Pr*
James Mcgowan, *VP*
Frank Hernandez, *Prin*
**EMP:** 15 **EST:** 2008
**SALES (est):** 1.32MM **Privately Held**
SIC: **1799** 3612 Special trade contractors, nec; Line voltage regulators

**(P-566)**
### KITCHEN EXPO
7458 La Jolla Blvd, La Jolla (92037-5029)
**EMP:** 18 **EST:** 1984
**SALES (est):** 1.34MM **Privately Held**
Web: www.kitchenexpo.com
SIC: **1799** 5211 2434 1752 Kitchen and bathroom remodeling; Lumber and other building materials; Wood kitchen cabinets; Floor laying and floor work, nec

**(P-567)**
### MP AERO LLC
7701 Woodley Ave, Van Nuys (91406-1721)
PHONE..................................818 901-9828
**EMP:** 85 **EST:** 2013
**SQ FT:** 165,000
**SALES (est):** 10.62MM **Privately Held**
Web: www.mpaero.com
SIC: **1799** 3721 Renovation of aircraft interiors; Research and development on aircraft by the manufacturer

**(P-568)**
### NAVAL COATING INC
2080 Cambridge Ave, Cardiff By The Sea (92007-1708)
PHONE..................................619 234-8366
Alan Lerchbacker, *Pr*
**EMP:** 149 **EST:** 1969
**SALES (est):** 9.01MM **Privately Held**
Web: www.navalcoating.us
SIC: **1799** 1721 2851 Sandblasting of building exteriors; Industrial painting; Paints and allied products

**(P-569)**
### PROGRESSIVE DESIGN PLAYGROUNDS
Also Called: Pdplay
2235 Meyers Ave, Escondido (92029-1005)
PHONE..................................760 597-5990
John M Ogden, *CEO*
Margaret Ryan, *VP*
Tami Nelson, *Contrlr*
▲ **EMP:** 16 **EST:** 1989
**SQ FT:** 10,000
**SALES (est):** 2.29MM **Privately Held**
Web: www.pdplay.com
SIC: **1799** 5941 3949 Playground construction and equipment installation; Playground equipment; Ammunition belts, sporting type

**(P-570)**
### REPUBLIC FENCE CO INC (PA)
11309 Danube Ave, Granada Hills (91344-4323)
PHONE..................................818 341-5323
David Woolf, *Pr*
Bonnie Woolf, *
**EMP:** 26 **EST:** 1973
**SQ FT:** 11,000
**SALES (est):** 4.31MM
**SALES (corp-wide):** 4.31MM **Privately Held**
Web: www.republicfenceco.com
SIC: **1799** 3312 5085 Fence construction; Structural shapes and pilings, steel; Fasteners and fastening equipment

**(P-571)**
### ROWAR CORPORATION
Also Called: Arrow Fence Co
4025 Cincinnatti Ave, Sacramento (94203-0001)
PHONE..................................916 626-3030
Alan Harris, *Pr*
Kim Harris, *VP*
**EMP:** 17 **EST:** 1978
**SQ FT:** 2,200
**SALES (est):** 454.52K **Privately Held**
SIC: **1799** 3699 3446 Fence construction; Security devices; Architectural metalwork

**(P-572)**
### RT WESTERN INC
Also Called: Rt Western Construction Svcs
160 Mendell St, San Francisco (94124-1740)
PHONE..................................415 677-9202
Thomas P Pua, *CEO*
**EMP:** 40 **EST:** 2006
**SALES (est):** 8.05MM **Privately Held**
Web: www.rtwestern.com
SIC: **1799** 1751 2431 Cleaning new buildings after construction; Cabinet and finish carpentry; Doors and door parts and trim, wood

**(P-573)**
### SCENIC EXPRESS INC
9380 San Fernando Rd, Sun Valley (91352-1419)
PHONE..................................323 254-4351
Kevin Gadd, *Pr*
**EMP:** 20 **EST:** 1978
**SQ FT:** 25,000
**SALES (est):** 2.18MM **Privately Held**
Web: cmflores72.wixsite.com
SIC: **1799** 2541 Prop, set or scenery construction, theatrical; Wood partitions and fixtures

**(P-574)**
### SUPER WELDING SOUTHERN CAL INC
1668 Newton Ave, San Diego (92113-1013)
PHONE..................................619 239-8003
Roberto Victoria, *Pr*
Amelia Victoria, *VP*
Manuel Victoria, *Probation Officer*
**EMP:** 20 **EST:** 1987
**SALES (est):** 2.17MM **Privately Held**
Web: www.swsc-inc.com
SIC: **1799** 7692 Welding on site; Welding repair

**(P-575)**
### SUTTER BUTTES MFG LLC
Also Called: Sutter Buttes Mfg
1221 Independence Pl, Gridley (95948-9341)
PHONE..................................530 846-9960
Nevada Smith, *Mgr*
**EMP:** 16 **EST:** 2015
**SALES (est):** 4.75MM **Privately Held**
Web: www.tuffboyequip.com

# 1799 - Special Trade Contractors, Nec (P-576)

SIC: **1799** 3999 Athletic and recreation facilities construction; Atomizers, toiletry

### (P-576)
**TLS PRODUCTIONS INC**
6 Venture, Irvine (92618-3340)
PHONE..................................810 220-8577
William Ross, *Pr*
Brad Hayes, *
**EMP:** 24 **EST:** 1996
**SALES (est):** 3.81MM **Privately Held**
Web: www.tlsproductionsinc.com
SIC: **1799** 3648 7922 Rigging, theatrical; Stage lighting equipment; Lighting, theatrical

### (P-577)
**TORRES FENCE CO INC**
2357 S Orange Ave, Fresno (93725-1021)
P.O. Box 10137 (93745-0137)
PHONE..................................559 237-4141
Ralph Torres, *Pr*
Rene J Torres, *
Ralph Torres Junior, *VP*
Rebecca Torres, *
Mari Salas, *
▲ **EMP:** 50 **EST:** 1963
**SQ FT:** 6,000
**SALES (est):** 8.88MM **Privately Held**
Web: www.torresfence.com
SIC: **1799** 3315 3496 Fence construction; Chain link fencing; Barbed wire, made from purchased wire

### (P-578)
**TOURNESOL SITEWORKS LLC (PA)**
2930 Faber St, Union City (94587-1214)
PHONE..................................800 542-2282
Christopher J Lyon, *Managing Member*
▲ **EMP:** 55 **EST:** 2007
**SQ FT:** 10,000
**SALES (est):** 39.97MM
**SALES (corp-wide):** 39.97MM **Privately Held**
Web: www.tournesol.com
SIC: **1799** 5023 3444 1521 Fiberglass work; Home furnishings, wicker, rattan or reed; Metal roofing and roof drainage equipment; Patio and deck construction and repair

### (P-579)
**WASHINGTON ORNA IR WORKS INC (PA)**
Also Called: Washington Iron Works
17926 S Broadway, Gardena (90248-3540)
P.O. Box 460 (90247-0846)
PHONE..................................310 327-8660
Daniel Welsh, *CEO*
Tom Pederson, *
Luke Welsh, *
Chris Powell, *
**EMP:** 97 **EST:** 1966
**SQ FT:** 141,240
**SALES (est):** 25.46MM
**SALES (corp-wide):** 25.46MM **Privately Held**
SIC: **1799** 3446 Ornamental metal work; Architectural metalwork

### (P-580)
**WATER RESTORATION INC**
31855 Date Palm Dr Ste 3, Cathedral City (92234-3100)
PHONE..................................760 673-7374
Illes Borcsa, *Pr*
Illes Borcsa, *Prin*
**EMP:** 15 **EST:** 2012
**SALES (est):** 2.14MM **Privately Held**

SIC: **1799** 1389 Waterproofing; Construction, repair, and dismantling services

### (P-581)
**YYK ENTERPRISES OPERATIONS LLC (PA)**
3475 E St, San Diego (92102-3335)
PHONE..................................619 474-6229
Ted Kines, *CEO*
Steve Johnstone, *
**EMP:** 190 **EST:** 1981
**SQ FT:** 4,000
**SALES (est):** 9.58MM
**SALES (corp-wide):** 9.58MM **Privately Held**
Web: www.yykenterprises.com
SIC: **1799** 1721 3731 Sandblasting of building exteriors; Ship painting; Shipbuilding and repairing

---

## 2011 Meat Packing Plants

### (P-582)
**BEEF PACKERS INC**
Also Called: Fresno Meat Company
3115 S Fig Ave, Fresno (93706-5647)
PHONE..................................559 268-5586
**EMP:** 500
Web: www.beefpackers.com
SIC: **2011** Meat packing plants

### (P-583)
**BLOOMFIELD FOOD INC**
Also Called: Manufacturing
4740 E Hunter Ave, Anaheim (92807-1939)
PHONE..................................714 779-7273
Matthew Kang, *Pr*
**EMP:** 20 **EST:** 2011
**SALES (est):** 2.23MM **Privately Held**
Web: www.bloomfieldfood.com
SIC: **2011** Meat packing plants

### (P-584)
**BURNETT & SON MEAT CO INC**
Also Called: Burnett Fine Foods
1420 S Myrtle Ave, Monrovia (91016-4153)
PHONE..................................626 357-2165
Donald L Burnett, *Pr*
▲ **EMP:** 80 **EST:** 1978
**SQ FT:** 20,000
**SALES (est):** 23.89MM **Privately Held**
Web: www.burnettandson.com
SIC: **2011** Meat by-products, from meat slaughtered on site

### (P-585)
**CARGILL MEAT SOLUTIONS CORP**
13034 Excelsior Dr, Norwalk (90650-6687)
PHONE..................................562 345-5240
**EMP:** 39
**SALES (corp-wide):** 159.59B **Privately Held**
Web: distributors.cargill.com
SIC: **2011** Meat packing plants
HQ: Cargill Meat Solutions Corp
    825 E Douglas Ave
    Wichita KS 67202
    316 291-2500

### (P-586)
**CARGILL MEAT SOLUTIONS CORP**
2350 Academy Ave, Sanger (93657-9559)
PHONE..................................559 875-2232
Robert Case, *Brnch Mgr*
**EMP:** 51

**SALES (corp-wide):** 159.59B **Privately Held**
Web: www.cargill.com
SIC: **2011** Meat packing plants
HQ: Cargill Meat Solutions Corp
    825 E Douglas Ave
    Wichita KS 67202
    316 291-2500

### (P-587)
**CARGILL MEAT SOLUTIONS CORP**
3115 S Fig Ave, Fresno (93706-5647)
P.O. Box 12503 (93778-2503)
PHONE..................................559 268-5586
Tod Ventura, *Mgr*
**EMP:** 1338
**SALES (corp-wide):** 159.59B **Privately Held**
Web: www.cargillmeatsolutions.com
SIC: **2011** Beef products, from beef slaughtered on site
HQ: Cargill Meat Solutions Corp
    825 E Douglas Ave
    Wichita KS 67202
    316 291-2500

### (P-588)
**CARGILL MEAT SOLUTIONS CORP**
Cargill Food Distribution
10602 N Trademark Pkwy Ste 500, Rancho Cucamonga (91730-5937)
PHONE..................................909 476-3120
Guy Milam, *Genl Mgr*
**EMP:** 51
**SALES (corp-wide):** 159.59B **Privately Held**
Web: www.cargill.com
SIC: **2011** Meat by-products, from meat slaughtered on site
HQ: Cargill Meat Solutions Corp
    825 E Douglas Ave
    Wichita KS 67202
    316 291-2500

### (P-589)
**CENTRAL VALLEY MEAT CO INC (PA)**
10431 8 3/4 Ave, Hanford (93230-9248)
PHONE..................................559 583-9624
Brian Coelho, *CEO*
Lawrence Coelho, *
Steve Coelho, *
Clarence Gregory, *
Brain Cohen, *
▲ **EMP:** 200 **EST:** 1989
**SQ FT:** 30,000
**SALES (est):** 168.83MM **Privately Held**
Web: www.centralvalleymeat.com
SIC: **2011** Meat packing plants

### (P-590)
**CERTIFIED MEAT PRODUCTS INC**
Also Called: Commerce Ave Meat
4586 E Commerce Ave, Fresno (93725-2203)
P.O. Box 12502 (93778-2502)
PHONE..................................559 256-1433
Cassi Maxey, *CEO*
**EMP:** 75 **EST:** 2005
**SALES (est):** 11.66MM **Privately Held**
Web: www.certifiedmeatproducts.com
SIC: **2011** Meat packing plants

### (P-591)
**CLAUSEN MEAT COMPANY INC**
19455 W Clausen Rd, Turlock (95380)

P.O. Box 1826 (95381-1826)
PHONE..................................209 667-8690
Ping Lau, *CEO*
Ying Hung Vinh, *
▲ **EMP:** 40 **EST:** 1983
**SQ FT:** 15,000
**SALES (est):** 8.9MM **Privately Held**
Web: www.clausenmeat.com
SIC: **2011** Meat packing plants

### (P-592)
**CLOUGHERTY PACKING LLC (DH)**
Also Called: Smithfield Foods
3049 E Vernon Ave, Los Angeles (90058-1800)
P.O. Box 58870 (90058-0870)
PHONE..................................323 583-4621
Kenneth J Baptist, *Pr*
**EMP:** 300 **EST:** 1937
**SQ FT:** 1,000,000
**SALES (est):** 65.83MM **Privately Held**
Web: farmerjohn.sfdbrands.com
SIC: **2011** 2013 Meat packing plants; Sausages and other prepared meats
HQ: Smithfield Foods, Inc.
    200 Commerce St
    Smithfield VA 23430
    757 365-3000

### (P-593)
**COLUMBUS FOODS LLC**
30977 San Antonio St, Hayward (94544-7109)
PHONE..................................510 921-3400
Ralph Denisco, *CEO*
John Piccetti, *
Adam Ferrif, *
▲ **EMP:** 345 **EST:** 1917
**SALES (est):** 19.92MM **Privately Held**
SIC: **2011** 5143 5147 Luncheon meat, from meat slaughtered on site; Cheese; Meats and meat products

### (P-594)
**ELLENSBURG LAMB COMPANY INC**
Also Called: Superior Packing Co
7390 Rio Dixon Rd, Dixon (95620-9665)
P.O. Box 940 (95620-0940)
PHONE..................................707 678-3091
Martin Ducken, *Mgr*
**EMP:** 80
Web: www.superiorfarms.com
SIC: **2011** Meat packing plants
HQ: Ellensburg Lamb Company, Inc.
    2530 River Plaza Dr # 200
    Sacramento CA 95833

### (P-595)
**ELLENSBURG LAMB COMPANY INC (HQ)**
Also Called: Superior Farms
2530 River Plaza Dr Ste 200, Sacramento (95833-3675)
PHONE..................................530 758-3091
Les Oestereich, *Pr*
Jeff Evanson, *CFO*
Gary Pfeiffer, *Ex VP*
▼ **EMP:** 18 **EST:** 1996
**SQ FT:** 7,500
**SALES (est):** 23.6MM **Privately Held**
Web: www.superiorfarms.com
SIC: **2011** Lamb products, from lamb slaughtered on site
PA: Transhumance Holding Company, Inc.
    2530 River Plz Dr Ste 200

## PRODUCTS & SERVICES SECTION
## 2011 - Meat Packing Plants (P-618)

**(P-596)**
**FIRSTCLASS FOODS - TROJAN INC**
Also Called: First Class Foods
12500 Inglewood Ave, Hawthorne (90250-4217)
P.O. Box 2397 (90251-2397)
PHONE..................................310 676-2500
Salomon Benzimra, *Pr*
Felix Benzimra, *VP Sls*
Albert Benzimra, *Sec*
Lucy Benzimra, *CFO*
EMP: 135 EST: 1963
SQ FT: 45,000
SALES (est): 28.77MM **Publicly Held**
SIC: **2011** 5147 Meat packing plants; Meats and meat products
HQ: Us Foods, Inc.
    9399 W Higgins Rd Ste 500
    Rosemont IL 60018

**(P-597)**
**GAYLORDS HRI MEATS**
Also Called: Gaylord's Meat Co
1100 E Ash Ave Ste C, Fullerton (92831-5004)
PHONE..................................714 526-2278
Michael Smith, *Ch Bd*
Vance Dixon, *Pr*
EMP: 18 EST: 1975
SQ FT: 10,000
SALES (est): 1.93MM **Privately Held**
Web: www.gaylordsmeatcompany.com
SIC: **2011** 5147 5144 Meat packing plants; Meats and meat products; Poultry and poultry products

**(P-598)**
**GOLDEN VALLEY INDUSTRIES INC**
960 Lone Palm Ave, Modesto (95351-1533)
PHONE..................................209 939-3370
Mike Sullivan, *Pr*
EMP: 40 EST: 1997
SQ FT: 40,000
SALES (est): 1.73MM **Privately Held**
Web: www.goldenvalleyindustries.com
SIC: **2011** Meat packing plants

**(P-599)**
**GOLDEN WEST FOOD GROUP INC (PA)**
4401 S Downey Rd, Vernon (90058-2518)
PHONE..................................888 807-3663
Erik Litmanovich, *CEO*
EMP: 38 EST: 2011
SALES (est): 966.1MM
SALES (corp-wide): 966.1MM **Privately Held**
Web: www.gwfg.com
SIC: **2011** 2013 2015 Meat packing plants; Sausages and other prepared meats; Poultry, slaughtered and dressed

**(P-600)**
**HARRIS RANCH BEEF COMPANY**
16277 S Mccall Ave, Selma (93662-9458)
P.O. Box 220 (93662-0220)
PHONE..................................559 896-3081
John Harris, *Ch Bd*
▼ EMP: 700 EST: 2003
SALES (est): 85.93MM **Privately Held**
Web: www.harrisranchbeef.com
SIC: **2011** 2013 Meat packing plants; Sausages and other prepared meats
PA: Central Valley Meat Co., Inc.
    10431 8 3/4 Ave

**(P-601)**
**HEATHERFIELD FOODS INC**
Also Called: Villa Roma Sausage Co
1150 Brooks St, Ontario (91762-3606)
PHONE..................................877 460-3060
EMP: 25 EST: 1987
SALES (est): 9.9MM **Privately Held**
Web: www.villaromasausage.com
SIC: **2011** Sausages, from meat slaughtered on site

**(P-602)**
**HORMEL FOODS CORPORATION**
Also Called: Hormel
3656 Perlman Dr, Stockton (95206-4212)
PHONE..................................800 523-4635
Mike Devine, *Mgr*
EMP: 58
SQ FT: 130,000
SALES (corp-wide): 12.11B **Publicly Held**
Web: www.hormelfoods.com
SIC: **2011** Meat packing plants
PA: Hormel Foods Corporation
    1 Hormel Pl
    507 437-5611

**(P-603)**
**JOBBERS MEAT PACKING CO LLC**
Also Called: Wilmar
3336 Fruitland Ave, Vernon (90058-3714)
P.O. Box 58368 (90058)
PHONE..................................323 585-6328
Martin Evanson, *CEO*
EMP: 234 EST: 1978
SQ FT: 19,000
SALES (est): 25.04MM
SALES (corp-wide): 63.43MM **Privately Held**
SIC: **2011** Beef products, from beef slaughtered on site
PA: Hv Randall Foods Llc
    2900 Ayers
    323 261-6565

**(P-604)**
**LA PACHANGA FOODS INC**
708 L St, Modesto (95354-2240)
PHONE..................................209 522-2222
Gabriel Villa, *CEO*
EMP: 34 EST: 2013
SALES (est): 3.2MM **Privately Held**
SIC: **2011** Meat packing plants

**(P-605)**
**LOS BANOS ABATTOIR CO**
1312 W Pacheco Blvd, Los Banos (93635-7807)
P.O. Box 949 (93635-0949)
PHONE..................................209 826-2212
Steven La Salvia, *Pr*
Laura La Salvia, *
EMP: 35 EST: 1920
SQ FT: 7,500
SALES (est): 4.71MM **Privately Held**
Web: www.losbanosabattoir.com
SIC: **2011** 5147 Beef products, from beef slaughtered on site; Meats and meat products

**(P-606)**
**MARIN SUN FARMS INC (PA)**
Also Called: Mindful Meats
1522 Petaluma Blvd N, Petaluma (94952-1956)
P.O. Box 1136 (94956-1136)
PHONE..................................415 663-8997
David Evans, *CEO*
EMP: 21 EST: 2004
SQ FT: 1,500
SALES (est): 16.44MM **Privately Held**
Web: www.marinsunfarms.com
SIC: **2011** Meat packing plants

**(P-607)**
**MOHAWK LAND & CATTLE CO INC**
1660 Old Bayshore Hwy, San Jose (95112-4304)
P.O. Box 601 (95106-0601)
PHONE..................................408 436-1800
Steve Tognoli, *Pr*
▼ EMP: 64 EST: 1957
SQ FT: 50,000
SALES (est): 1.69MM **Privately Held**
SIC: **2011** Meat packing plants
HQ: Smithfield Packaged Meats Corp.
    805 E Kemper Rd
    Cincinnati OH 45246
    513 782-3800

**(P-608)**
**NAGLES VEAL INC**
1411 E Base Line St, San Bernardino (92410-4113)
PHONE..................................909 383-7075
Michael Lemler, *Pr*
▲ EMP: 50 EST: 1983
SQ FT: 12,500
SALES (est): 2.99MM **Privately Held**
Web: www.nagleveal.com
SIC: **2011** Veal, from meat slaughtered on site

**(P-609)**
**OLLI SALUMERIA AMERICANA LLC**
1301 Rocky Point Dr, Oceanside (92056)
▲ EMP: 65 EST: 2010
SALES (est): 25.13MM **Privately Held**
Web: www.olli.com
SIC: **2011** Meat packing plants

**(P-610)**
**OLSON MEAT COMPANY**
7301 Cutler Ave, Orland (95963-9601)
PHONE..................................530 865-8111
James Olson, *CEO*
Fred Olson, *
EMP: 35 EST: 1969
SALES (est): 7MM **Privately Held**
Web: olson-meat-company.business.site
SIC: **2011** Meat packing plants

**(P-611)**
**OWB PACKERS LLC**
57 Shank Rd, Brawley (92227-9616)
PHONE..................................760 351-2700
Eric W Brandt, *Managing Member*
EMP: 79 EST: 2016
SALES (est): 10.35MM **Privately Held**
Web: www.owbpackers.com
SIC: **2011** Meat packing plants

**(P-612)**
**PACIFIC PRIME MEATS LLC ✪**
3501 E Vernon Ave, Vernon (90058-1813)
PHONE..................................310 523-3664
Paul Guiliano, *CEO*
Dawn Allen, *
EMP: 100 EST: 2024
SALES (est): 7MM **Privately Held**
SIC: **2011** Meat packing plants

**(P-613)**
**R B R MEAT COMPANY INC**
Also Called: Rightway
5151 Alcoa Ave, Vernon (90058-3715)
P.O. Box 58225 (90058-0225)
PHONE..................................323 973-4868
Irwin Miller, *Pr*
Larry Vanden Bos, *
James Craig, *
EMP: 23 EST: 1951
SQ FT: 65,000
SALES (est): 10.43MM **Privately Held**
SIC: **2011** Meat packing plants

**(P-614)**
**RAMAR INTERNATIONAL CORP**
Also Called: Orientex
539 Garcia Ave Ste E, Pittsburg (94565-7403)
PHONE..................................925 432-4267
Tito Sanchez, *Mgr*
EMP: 24
SALES (corp-wide): 53.48MM **Privately Held**
Web: www.ramarfoods.com
SIC: **2011** Sausages, from meat slaughtered on site
PA: Ramar International Corp
    1101 Railroad Ave
    925 439-9009

**(P-615)**
**RICHWOOD MEAT COMPANY INC**
2751 N Santa Fe Ave, Merced (95348-4109)
P.O. Box 2599 (95344-0599)
PHONE..................................209 722-8171
Michael J Wood, *Pr*
Hellen Diane Inks-fragie, *CFO*
Carol J Wood, *Stockholder*
Steven J Wood, *
EMP: 100 EST: 1964
SQ FT: 43,000
SALES (est): 57.73MM **Privately Held**
Web: www.richwoodmeat.com
SIC: **2011** 5147 5421 Meat packing plants; Meats, fresh; Meat and fish markets

**(P-616)**
**SERV-RITE MEAT COMPANY INC**
Also Called: Packers Bar M
2515 N San Fernando Rd, Los Angeles (90065-1325)
P.O. Box 65026 (90065-0026)
PHONE..................................323 227-1911
Gary Marks, *CEO*
Norman Marks, *
Norma Marks, *
EMP: 55 EST: 1976
SQ FT: 55,000
SALES (est): 10.79MM **Privately Held**
Web: www.bar-m.com
SIC: **2011** Meat packing plants

**(P-617)**
**SSRE HOLDINGS LLC**
Also Called: Signature Fresh
18901 Railroad St, City Of Industry (91748)
PHONE..................................800 314-2098
Stanley J Wetch, *Managing Member*
Stanley Joseph Wetch, *Managing Member*
EMP: 100 EST: 2014
SALES (est): 3.01MM **Privately Held**
SIC: **2011** Meat by-products, from meat slaughtered on site

**(P-618)**
**TRANSHUMANCE HOLDING CO INC (PA)**
Also Called: Superior Farms
2530 River Plaza Dr Ste 200, Sacramento (95833-3675)
PHONE..................................530 758-3091
Rick Stott, *Pr*

## 2011 - Meat Packing Plants

**(P-619)** *(continued)*
Seth Robinson, *
◆ **EMP:** 50 **EST:** 1997
**SQ FT:** 16,000
**SALES (est):** 118.56MM **Privately Held**
**SIC: 2011** Meat packing plants

**(P-619)**
**TRANSHUMANCE HOLDING CO INC**
Also Called: Superior Farms
7390 Rio Dixon Rd, Dixon (95620-9665)
P.O. Box 940 (95620-0940)
**PHONE**.................................707 693-2303
Julie Angel, *Mgr*
**EMP:** 200
**SIC: 2011** Lamb products, from lamb slaughtered on site
**PA:** Transhumance Holding Company, Inc.
2530 River Plz Dr Ste 200

**(P-620)**
**TRANSHUMANCE INC**
Also Called: Superior Farms
2530 River Plaza Dr Ste 200, Sacramento (95833-3675)
**PHONE**.................................530 758-3091
◆ **EMP:** 430
**SIC: 2011** Meat packing plants

**(P-621)**
**VALLEY FRESH INC (HQ)**
1404 S Fresno Ave, Stockton (95206-1174)
**PHONE**.................................209 943-5411
Ronald W Fielding, *CEO*
Eugene Carney, *
**EMP:** 50 **EST:** 1956
**SQ FT:** 120,000
**SALES (est):** 4.16MM
**SALES (corp-wide):** 12.11B **Publicly Held**
**Web:** www.hormel.com
**SIC: 2011** Meat packing plants
**PA:** Hormel Foods Corporation
1 Hormel Pl
507 437-5611

**(P-622)**
**VEAL CONNECTION CORPORATION**
Also Called: Velsam
1987 Grosse Ave, Santa Rosa (95404)
P.O. Box 2247 (95405)
**PHONE**.................................707 992-0932
Simon Samson, *Pr*
Hanneke Samson, *Sec*
**EMP:** 22 **EST:** 1964
**SALES (est):** 2.34MM **Privately Held**
**SIC: 2011** Veal, from meat slaughtered on site

**(P-623)**
**VENUS FOODS INC**
770 S Stimson Ave, City Of Industry (91745-1638)
**PHONE**.................................626 369-5188
Gin Shen Wu, *Ch Bd*
Robert Y Tsai, *Pr*
T K Chow, *VP*
Shih-ai Meng, *Treas*
▲ **EMP:** 20 **EST:** 1980
**SQ FT:** 20,000
**SALES (est):** 5.66MM **Privately Held**
**Web:** www.venusfoods.com
**SIC: 2011 2099** Meat packing plants; Food preparations, nec

**(P-624)**
**VIZ CATTLE CORPORATION**
Also Called: Sukarne
17800 Castleton St Ste 435, City Of Industry (91748-5748)
**PHONE**.................................310 884-5260
Edwin Botero, *CEO*
Eddy Gutierrez, *
▲ **EMP:** 39 **EST:** 1992
**SALES (est):** 11.29MM **Privately Held**
**SIC: 2011** 5154 Meat packing plants; Cattle
**HQ:** Grupo Viz, S.A.P.I. De C.V.
Av. Diana Tang No. 59 - A
Culiacan SIN 80199

**(P-625)**
**WEST LAKE FOOD CORPORATION (PA)**
Also Called: Tay Ho
301 N Sullivan St, Santa Ana (92703-3417)
**PHONE**.................................714 973-2286
Jayce Yenson, *CEO*
Chieu Nguyen, *
Chuong Nguyen, *
Jayce Yenson, *Sec*
◆ **EMP:** 39 **EST:** 1986
**SALES (est):** 7.89MM
**SALES (corp-wide):** 7.89MM **Privately Held**
**SIC: 2011** Beef products, from beef slaughtered on site

**(P-626)**
**WESTERN MEAT PROCESSING INC**
725 Zeff Rd, Modesto (95351-3941)
**PHONE**.................................209 521-1843
Frank Lopes, *Prin*
Brad Nyman, *
R Malkassian, *
**EMP:** 41 **EST:** 2014
**SALES (est):** 1.98MM **Privately Held**
**SIC: 2011** Meat packing plants

**(P-627)**
**YOSEMITE VLY BEEF PKG CO INC**
970 E Sandy Mush Rd, Merced (95341-7903)
P.O. Box 1828 (91009-4828)
**PHONE**.................................626 435-0170
Michael Ban, *Pr*
E K Ban, *
**EMP:** 28 **EST:** 1965
**SQ FT:** 5,000
**SALES (est):** 5.43MM **Privately Held**
**Web:** www.yvbeef.com
**SIC: 2011** Meat packing plants

## 2013 Sausages And Other Prepared Meats

**(P-628)**
**AIDELLS SAUSAGE COMPANY INC**
Also Called: Aidells Sausage
2411 Baumann Ave, San Lorenzo (94580-1801)
**PHONE**.................................510 614-5450
**TOLL FREE:** 800
Ernie Gabiati, *Pr*
**EMP:** 900 **EST:** 2007
**SQ FT:** 15,000
**SALES (est):** 6.24MM
**SALES (corp-wide):** 53.31B **Publicly Held**
**Web:** www.aidells.com
**SIC: 2013** 5147 Sausages, from purchased meat; Meats and meat products
**HQ:** The Hillshire Brands Company
400 S Jefferson St Ste 1n
Chicago IL 60607
312 614-6000

**(P-629)**
**ALPINE MEATS INC**
9850 Lower Sacramento Rd, Stockton (95210-3915)
**PHONE**.................................209 477-2691
Rick Martin, *CEO*
**EMP:** 50 **EST:** 2009
**SALES (est):** 7.67MM **Privately Held**
**Web:** www.alpinemeats.com
**SIC: 2013** Smoked meats, from purchased meat

**(P-630)**
**AMERICAN CUSTOM MEATS LLC**
4276 N Tracy Blvd, Tracy (95304-1501)
**PHONE**.................................209 839-8800
Neil Kinney, *Pr*
**EMP:** 88 **EST:** 2011
**SQ FT:** 75,000
**SALES (est):** 32.04MM **Privately Held**
**Web:** www.acmeats.com
**SIC: 2013** 2015 2032 Prepared beef products, from purchased beef; Poultry slaughtering and processing; Puddings, except meat: packaged in cans, jars, etc.

**(P-631)**
**ARIES BEEF LLC**
17 W Magnolia Blvd, Burbank (91502-1781)
**PHONE**.................................818 526-4855
Steven Zoll, *Managing Member*
**EMP:** 36 **EST:** 2021
**SALES (est):** 17.3MM
**SALES (corp-wide):** 143.99MM **Privately Held**
**SIC: 2013** Sausages and other prepared meats
**PA:** United Deli Holdings Llc
1143 W Lake St

**(P-632)**
**BAR-S FOODS CO**
392 Railroad Ct, Milpitas (95035-4339)
**PHONE**.................................408 941-9958
Olga Vasquez, *Brnch Mgr*
**EMP:** 38
**Web:** www.bar-s.com
**SIC: 2013** Sausages and other prepared meats
**HQ:** Bar-S Foods Co.
18700 N Hayden Rd Ste 545
Scottsdale AZ 85255
602 264-7272

**(P-633)**
**BAR-S FOODS CO**
Also Called: Bar-S Foods Co. Los Angeles
4919 Alcoa Ave, Vernon (90058-3022)
**PHONE**.................................323 589-3600
**EMP:** 22
**Web:** www.bar-s.com
**SIC: 2013** Sausages and other prepared meats
**HQ:** Bar-S Foods Co.
18700 N Hayden Rd Ste 545
Scottsdale AZ 85255
602 264-7272

**(P-634)**
**BOYD SPECIALTIES LLC**
1016 E Cooley Dr Ste N, Colton (92324-3962)
**PHONE**.................................909 219-5120
Jae Boyd, *CEO*
▲ **EMP:** 64 **EST:** 2008
**SQ FT:** 10,000
**SALES (est):** 11.55MM **Privately Held**
**Web:** www.boydspecialtiesjerky.com
**SIC: 2013** Snack sticks, including jerky: from purchased meat

**(P-635)**
**CATTANEO BROS INC**
Also Called: Cattaneo Bros
769 Caudill St, San Luis Obispo (93401-5729)
**PHONE**.................................805 543-7188
Mike Kaney, *Pr*
Jayne Kaney, *Sec*
**EMP:** 20 **EST:** 1946
**SQ FT:** 5,500
**SALES (est):** 3.65MM **Privately Held**
**Web:** www.cattaneobros.com
**SIC: 2013** 5961 Beef, dried: from purchased meat; Food, mail order

**(P-636)**
**COLUMBUS MANUFACTURING INC (HQ)**
30977 San Antonio St, Hayward (94544-7109)
**PHONE**.................................510 921-3423
Joe Ennen, *CEO*
Randy Sieve, *
▼ **EMP:** 100 **EST:** 2006
**SQ FT:** 121,000
**SALES (est):** 21.73MM
**SALES (corp-wide):** 12.11B **Publicly Held**
**Web:** www.columbuscraftmeats.com
**SIC: 2013** Sausages and related products, from purchased meat
**PA:** Hormel Foods Corporation
1 Hormel Pl
507 437-5611

**(P-637)**
**COURAGE PRODUCTION LLC**
2475 Courage Dr, Fairfield (94533-6723)
**PHONE**.................................707 422-6300
Philip Gatto, *Managing Member*
**EMP:** 100 **EST:** 1962
**SALES (est):** 16.17MM **Privately Held**
**Web:** www.courageproduction.com
**SIC: 2013** Sausages, from purchased meat

**(P-638)**
**CTI FOODS AZUSA LLC**
Also Called: S & S Foods LLC
1120 W Foothill Blvd, Azusa (91702-2818)
**PHONE**.................................626 633-1609
Robert Horowitz, *CEO*
Horst Sieben, *CFO*
Pam Cardinale, *Dir Fin*
▲ **EMP:** 220 **EST:** 1998
**SQ FT:** 115,000
**SALES (est):** 24.29MM
**SALES (corp-wide):** 972MM **Privately Held**
**SIC: 2013** Cooked meats, from purchased meat
**HQ:** Cti Foods Holding Co., Llc
2106 E State Hwy 114 Ste
Southlake TX 76092

**(P-639)**
**DEREK AND CONSTANCE LEE CORP (PA)**
Also Called: Great River Food
19355 San Jose Ave, City Of Industry (91748-1420)
**PHONE**.................................909 595-8831
Derek E Lee, *Pr*
Eric Lee, *
▲ **EMP:** 95 **EST:** 1985
**SQ FT:** 50,000
**SALES (est):** 14.7MM
**SALES (corp-wide):** 14.7MM **Privately Held**

# PRODUCTS & SERVICES SECTION
## 2013 - Sausages And Other Prepared Meats (P-660)

Web: www.greatriverfood.com
SIC: 2013 1541 Sausages and other prepared meats; Food products manufacturing or packing plant construction

**(P-640)**
**FORMOSA MEAT COMPANY INC**
Also Called: Universal Meat Company
10646 Fulton Ct, Rancho Cucamonga (91730-4848)
PHONE..................909 987-0470
Cheng-ting Shih, VP
Hsiu-o Kan, Treas
▲ EMP: 40 EST: 1995
SQ FT: 23,000
SALES (est): 1.63MM Privately Held
Web: www.formosa.com
SIC: 2013 Snack sticks, including jerky: from purchased meat

**(P-641)**
**FRATELLI BERETTA USA INC**
Also Called: Busseto Foods
1090 W Church Ave, Fresno (93706-3917)
PHONE..................559 237-9591
G Grazier, Pr
EMP: 30
Web: www.busseto.com
SIC: 2013 Sausages, from purchased meat
HQ: Fratelli Beretta Usa, Inc.
750 Clark Dr
Budd Lake NJ 07828
201 438-0723

**(P-642)**
**FRATELLI BERETTA USA INC**
Also Called: Busseto Foods
1351 N Crystal Ave, Fresno (93728-1142)
P.O. Box 12403 (93777-2403)
PHONE..................201 438-0723
EMP: 30
Web: www.fratelliberetta.com
SIC: 2013 Cured meats, from purchased meat
HQ: Fratelli Beretta Usa, Inc.
750 Clark Dr
Budd Lake NJ 07828
201 438-0723

**(P-643)**
**FULLFILLMENT SYSTEMS INC**
Also Called: D'Ambrosio Bros
1228 Reamwood Ave, Sunnyvale (94089-2225)
PHONE..................408 745-7675
Pasquale Vitonti, Mgr
EMP: 36
SALES (corp-wide): 36.83MM Privately Held
Web: www.newyorkstylesausage.com
SIC: 2013 2011 Sausages, from purchased meat; Sausages, from meat slaughtered on site
PA: Fullfillment Systems, Inc.
1228 Reamwood Ave
408 745-7675

**(P-644)**
**FULLFILLMENT SYSTEMS INC (PA)**
Also Called: Giorgio's Pizza House
1228 Reamwood Ave, Sunnyvale (94089-2225)
PHONE..................408 745-7675
EMP: 90 EST: 1983
SALES (est): 36.83MM
SALES (corp-wide): 36.83MM Privately Held
Web: www.newyorkstylesausage.com

SIC: 2013 5812 Sausages and related products, from purchased meat; Eating places

**(P-645)**
**GAYTAN FOODS LLC**
15430 Proctor Ave, City Of Industry (91745-1024)
P.O. Box 3385 (91744-0385)
PHONE..................626 330-4553
EMP: 100
Web: www.benestarbrands.com
SIC: 2013 2099 2022 2011 Sausages and other prepared meats; Food preparations, nec; Cheese; natural and processed; Meat packing plants

**(P-646)**
**HAWA CORPORATION (PA)**
Also Called: Beef Jerky Factory
125 E Laurel St, Colton (92324-2462)
PHONE..................909 825-8882
Waleed Saab, VP
EMP: 18 EST: 2009
SQ FT: 34,500
SALES (est): 12.02MM
SALES (corp-wide): 12.02MM Privately Held
Web: www.enjoybeefjerky.com
SIC: 2013 Beef, dried: from purchased meat

**(P-647)**
**HORMEL FOODS CORP SVCS LLC**
Also Called: Hormel
2 Venture Ste 250, Irvine (92618-7408)
PHONE..................949 753-5350
Randy Kemmipz, Mgr
EMP: 20
SALES (corp-wide): 12.11B Publicly Held
Web: www.hormelfoods.com
SIC: 2013 Canned meats (except baby food), from purchased meat
HQ: Hormel Foods Corporate Services, Llc
1 Hormel Pl
Austin MN 55912

**(P-648)**
**KITCHEN CUTS LLC**
6045 District Blvd, Maywood (90270-3560)
PHONE..................323 560-7415
Raul Tapia Senior, CEO
EMP: 66 EST: 2011
SALES (est): 8.49MM
SALES (corp-wide): 87.04MM Privately Held
Web: www.kitchen-cuts.com
SIC: 2013 Beef stew, from purchased meat
PA: Tapia Enterprises, Inc.
6067 District Blvd
323 560-7415

**(P-649)**
**KMB FOODS INC (PA)**
1010 S Sierra Way, San Bernardino (92408-2124)
PHONE..................626 447-0545
Scott Biedermann, Pr
Sam Mangiaterra, COO
▲ EMP: 20 EST: 1998
SQ FT: 6,000
SALES (est): 12.78MM
SALES (corp-wide): 12.78MM Privately Held
Web: www.kmbfoods.com
SIC: 2013 2099 Prepared beef products, from purchased beef; Food preparations, nec

**(P-650)**
**KRAVE PURE FOODS INC**
Also Called: Krave Jerky
117 W Napa St Ste A, Sonoma (95476-6691)
PHONE..................707 939-9176
Jonathan A Sebastiani, CEO
EMP: 58 EST: 2009
SALES (est): 9.64MM Privately Held
Web: www.kravejerky.com
SIC: 2013 5147 Snack sticks, including jerky: from purchased meat; Meats and meat products

**(P-651)**
**KRUSE AND SON INC**
235 Kruse Ave, Monrovia (91016-4899)
P.O. Box 945 (91017-0945)
PHONE..................626 358-4536
David R Kruse, CEO
EMP: 25 EST: 1949
SQ FT: 20,000
SALES (est): 16.15MM Privately Held
Web: www.kruseandson.com
SIC: 2013 Ham, smoked: from purchased meat

**(P-652)**
**LA ESPANOLA MEATS INC**
25020 Doble Ave, Harbor City (90710-3155)
PHONE..................310 539-0455
Alex Motamedi, CEO
Juana Faraone, *
Frank Faraone, *
◆ EMP: 25 EST: 1975
SQ FT: 8,800
SALES (est): 6.9MM Privately Held
Web: www.laespanolameats.com
SIC: 2013 5421 Sausages and related products, from purchased meat; Meat markets, including freezer provisioners

**(P-653)**
**MILLER PACKING COMPANY**
Also Called: Miller Hot Dogs
1122 Industrial Way, Lodi (95240-3119)
PHONE..................209 339-2310
Michael A De Benedetti, Pr
Staige P Debenedetti, *
EMP: 50 EST: 1965
SQ FT: 40,000
SALES (est): 6.03MM Privately Held
Web: www.millerhotdogs.com
SIC: 2013 Sausages and other prepared meats

**(P-654)**
**MONDELEZ GLOBAL LLC**
Also Called: Kraft Foods
6201 Knott Ave, Buena Park (90620-1010)
PHONE..................714 690-7428
Jeferey Orchard, Brnch Mgr
EMP: 18
Web: www.mondelezinternational.com
SIC: 2013 Sausages and other prepared meats
HQ: Mondelez Global Llc
905 W Fulton Mkt Ste 200
Chicago IL 60607
847 943-4000

**(P-655)**
**OLD BBH INC**
280 10th Ave, San Diego (92101-7406)
P.O. Box 85362 (92186-5362)
PHONE..................858 715-4000
◆ EMP: 550
Web: www.bumblebee.com

SIC: 2013 2032 2033 Beef stew, from purchased meat; Chili, with or without meat: packaged in cans, jars, etc.; Vegetables and vegetable products, in cans, jars, etc.

**(P-656)**
**ONE WORLD MEAT COMPANY LLC**
6363 Knott Ave, Buena Park (90620-1021)
PHONE..................800 782-1670
Eric Brandt, CEO
EMP: 15 EST: 2019
SALES (est): 2.47MM Privately Held
Web: www.oneworldmeatco.com
SIC: 2013 Prepared beef products, from purchased beef

**(P-657)**
**PAMPANGA FOOD COMPANY INC**
1835 N Orangethorpe Park Ste A, Anaheim (92801-1143)
PHONE..................714 773-0537
Ray Reyes, Pr
Coni Reyes, VP
EMP: 30 EST: 1984
SQ FT: 11,000
SALES (est): 13.84MM Privately Held
Web: www.pampangafood.com
SIC: 2013 5812 8742 2011 Sausages and other prepared meats; Eating places; Food and beverage consultant; Sausages, from meat slaughtered on site

**(P-658)**
**PAPA CANTELLAS INCORPORATED**
Also Called: Papa Cantella's Sausage Plant
3341 E 50th St, Vernon (90058-3003)
PHONE..................323 584-7272
Thomas P Cantella, CEO
Chris Stafford, *
EMP: 60 EST: 1981
SQ FT: 13,000
SALES (est): 13.3MM Privately Held
Web: www.papacantella.com
SIC: 2013 Sausages, from purchased meat

**(P-659)**
**POCINO FOODS COMPANY**
14250 Lomitas Ave, City Of Industry (91746-3014)
P.O. Box 2219 (91746-0219)
PHONE..................626 968-8000
Naoki Higuchi, CEO
Luciana Obrien, *
▲ EMP: 100 EST: 1933
SQ FT: 70,000
SALES (est): 60.29MM Privately Held
Web: www.pocinofoods.com
SIC: 2013 Sausages, from purchased meat
PA: Zensho Holdings Co., Ltd.
2-18-1, Konan

**(P-660)**
**PROVENA FOODS INC (HQ)**
5010 Eucalyptus Ave, Chino (91710-9216)
PHONE..................909 627-1082
Theodore L Arena, Pr
Santo Zito, *
Ronald A Provera, *
Thomas J Mulroney, CAO*
▲ EMP: 60 EST: 1960
SALES (est): 24.3MM
SALES (corp-wide): 12.11B Publicly Held
SIC: 2013 2032 2098 Sausages and other prepared meats; Canned specialties; Macaroni and spaghetti
PA: Hormel Foods Corporation
1 Hormel Pl

## 2013 - Sausages And Other Prepared Meats (P-661)

**(P-661)**
**PROVENA FOODS INC**
Swiss-American Sausage
251 Darcy Pkwy, Lathrop (95330-8756)
**PHONE**..................................209 858-5555
Theodore Arena, *Brnch Mgr*
**EMP:** 188
**SQ FT:** 49,000
**SALES (corp-wide):** 12.11B **Publicly Held**
**SIC: 2013** Sausages and other prepared meats
**HQ:** Provena Foods Inc.
5010 Eucalyptus Ave
Chino CA 91710
909 627-1082

**(P-662)**
**RAEMICA INC**
Also Called: Far West Meats
7759 Victoria Ave, Highland (92346-5637)
P.O. Box 190 (92324-0190)
**PHONE**..................................909 864-1990
Thomas R Serrato, *CEO*
Wade Snyder, *
Michael Serrato, *
**EMP:** 41 **EST:** 1978
**SQ FT:** 35,000
**SALES (est):** 2.58MM **Privately Held**
**Web:** www.farwestmeat.com
**SIC: 2013** 5421 Cured meats, from purchased meat; Meat markets, including freezer provisioners

**(P-663)**
**RICE FIELD CORPORATION**
14500 Valley Blvd, City Of Industry (91746-2918)
**PHONE**..................................626 968-6917
Derek Lee, *Pr*
▲ **EMP:** 120 **EST:** 1997
**SQ FT:** 100,000
**SALES (est):** 9.28MM **Privately Held**
**Web:** www.ricefieldcorporation.com
**SIC: 2013** Sausages and other prepared meats

**(P-664)**
**SAAGS PRODUCTS LLC**
1799 Factor Ave, San Leandro (94577-5617)
P.O. Box 2078 (94577-0207)
**PHONE**..................................510 678-3412
Jim Mosle, *CEO*
Timothy Dam, *
▲ **EMP:** 22 **EST:** 2006
**SQ FT:** 40,000
**SALES (est):** 2.3MM
**SALES (corp-wide):** 12.11B **Publicly Held**
**SIC: 2013** Sausages, from purchased meat
**PA:** Hormel Foods Corporation
1 Hormel Pl
507 437-5611

**(P-665)**
**SAPAR USA INC (HQ)**
Also Called: Fabrique Delices
1610 Delta Ct Unit 1, Hayward (94544-7043)
**PHONE**..................................510 441-9500
Marc Poinsignon, *Pr*
Antonio Pinheiro, *
David Kemp, *
**EMP:** 25 **EST:** 1985
**SQ FT:** 20,000
**SALES (est):** 9.95MM
**SALES (corp-wide):** 61.56MM **Privately Held**
**Web:** www.fabriquedelices.com

**SIC: 2013** Spreads, sandwich: meat, from purchased meat
**PA:** Village Gourmet Holdco, Llc
32 W 39th St Ph 16
212 219-1230

**(P-666)**
**SETTLERS JERKY INC**
307 Paseo Sonrisa, Walnut (91789-2721)
**PHONE**..................................909 444-3999
Cherron L Hart, *CEO*
Aaron J Anderson, *
**EMP:** 27 **EST:** 2011
**SQ FT:** 20,000
**SALES (est):** 6.52MM **Privately Held**
**Web:** www.settlersjerky.com
**SIC: 2013** Snack sticks, including jerky: from purchased meat

**(P-667)**
**SILVA SAUSAGE CO**
5935 Rossi Ln, Gilroy (95020-7014)
**PHONE**..................................408 293-5437
**EMP:** 50 **EST:** 1968
**SALES (est):** 17.86MM **Privately Held**
**Web:** www.silvasausage.com
**SIC: 2013** Sausages and related products, from purchased meat

**(P-668)**
**SPAR SAUSAGE CO**
Also Called: Caspers
688 Williams St, San Leandro (94577-2624)
**PHONE**..................................510 614-8100
Jack Dorian, *Mgr*
**EMP:** 19
**SQ FT:** 9,750
**SALES (corp-wide):** 4.69MM **Privately Held**
**Web:** www.sparsausage.com
**SIC: 2013** Sausages, from purchased meat
**PA:** Spar Sausage Co.
3508 Mt Diablo Blvd Ste J
925 283-6877

**(P-669)**
**SQUARE H BRANDS INC (PA)**
Also Called: Hoffy
2731 S Soto St, Vernon (90058-8026)
**PHONE**..................................323 267-4600
Henry Haskell, *CEO*
William Hannigan, *CFO*
◆ **EMP:** 50 **EST:** 1995
**SQ FT:** 100,000
**SALES (est):** 25.94MM
**SALES (corp-wide):** 25.94MM **Privately Held**
**Web:** www.hoffybrand.com
**SIC: 2013** Sausages, from purchased meat

**(P-670)**
**STAR FOOD SNACKS INTL INC**
Also Called: Star Food Snacks
125 E Laurel St, Colton (92324-2462)
**PHONE**..................................909 825-8882
Aida Hawa, *CEO*
Waleed Saab, *
Asber Hawa, *
**EMP:** 80 **EST:** 2010
**SALES (est):** 3.28MM **Privately Held**
**Web:** www.enjoybeefjerky.com
**SIC: 2013** Beef, dried: from purchased meat

**(P-671)**
**SUNNYVALLEY SMOKED MEATS INC**
2475 W Yosemite Ave, Manteca (95337-9641)
P.O. Box 2158 (95336-1159)

**PHONE**..................................209 825-0288
William Andreetta, *Pr*
▲ **EMP:** 250 **EST:** 1990
**SQ FT:** 41,000
**SALES (est):** 147.88MM **Publicly Held**
**Web:** www.sunnyvalleysmokedmeats.com
**SIC: 2013** Bacon, side and sliced: from purchased meat
**HQ:** Plumrose Usa, Inc.
651 W Wash Blvd Ste 304
Chicago IL 60661

**(P-672)**
**SWIFT BEEF COMPANY**
Also Called: Jbs Case Ready
15555 Meridian Pkwy, Riverside (92518-3046)
**PHONE**..................................951 571-2237
Andre Nogueira, *CEO*
**EMP:** 200 **EST:** 2015
**SALES (est):** 49.99MM **Publicly Held**
**SIC: 2013** Beef, dried: from purchased meat
**HQ:** Jbs Usa Food Company
1770 Promontory Cir
Greeley CO 80634
970 506-8000

**(P-673)**
**T&J SAUSAGE KITCHEN INC**
Also Called: T & J Sausage Kitchen
2831 E Miraloma Ave, Anaheim (92806-1804)
**PHONE**..................................714 632-8350
Tom Drozdowski, *CEO*
David Armendariz, *
**EMP:** 45 **EST:** 1984
**SQ FT:** 20,000
**SALES (est):** 9.22MM **Privately Held**
**Web:** www.tandjsausage.com
**SIC: 2013** Sausages and other prepared meats

**(P-674)**
**TFI OF CALIFORNIA INC (DH)**
Also Called: Golden Island Jerky Co Inc
10646 Fulton Ct, Rancho Cucamonga (91730-4848)
**PHONE**..................................844 362-3222
Cheng Shih, *Pr*
▲ **EMP:** 20 **EST:** 2012
**SALES (est):** 5.04MM
**SALES (corp-wide):** 53.31B **Publicly Held**
**Web:** www.goldenislandjerky.com
**SIC: 2013** Snack sticks, including jerky: from purchased meat
**HQ:** The Hillshire Brands Company
400 S Jefferson St Ste 1n
Chicago IL 60607
312 614-6000

**(P-675)**
**VALLEY PROTEIN LLC**
1828 E Hedges Ave, Fresno (93703-3633)
**PHONE**..................................559 498-7115
Robert Coyle, *Managing Member*
**EMP:** 95 **EST:** 2010
**SALES (est):** 9.85MM **Privately Held**
**Web:** www.valleyproteinfresno.com
**SIC: 2013** Prepared beef products, from purchased beef

**(P-676)**
**WYCEN FOODS INC (PA)**
560 Estabrook St, San Leandro (94577-3512)
**PHONE**..................................510 351-1987
Arthur Leong, *Pr*
Nancy Leong, *Sec*
▲ **EMP:** 17 **EST:** 1981

**SQ FT:** 25,000
**SALES (est):** 5.67MM
**SALES (corp-wide):** 5.67MM **Privately Held**
**Web:** www.wycenfoods.com
**SIC: 2013** 2038 Sausages, from purchased meat; Ethnic foods, nec, frozen

**(P-677)**
**YONEKYU USA INC**
611 N 20th St, Montebello (90640-3135)
**PHONE**..................................323 581-4194
Osamu Saito, *Pr*
Kenji Ikeda, *
Don Ferris, *
▼ **EMP:** 52 **EST:** 1992
**SALES (est):** 2.27MM **Privately Held**
**Web:** www.yqusa.com
**SIC: 2013** Sausages, from purchased meat
**HQ:** Yonekyu Corp. Inc.
1259, Terabayashi, Okanomiya
Numazu SZO 410-0

## 2015 Poultry Slaughtering And Processing

**(P-678)**
**CENCAL FOODS LLC**
Also Called: Valley Protein
1828 E Hedges Ave, Fresno (93703-3633)
**PHONE**..................................559 341-5742
Robert Coyle, *Managing Member*
**EMP:** 17 **EST:** 2016
**SALES (est):** 11.65MM **Privately Held**
**SIC: 2015** Chicken slaughtering and processing

**(P-679)**
**COMMODITY SALES CO**
517 S Clarence St, Los Angeles (90033-4225)
**PHONE**..................................323 980-5463
William T Zant, *Pr*
**EMP:** 120 **EST:** 1967
**SQ FT:** 14,522
**SALES (est):** 2.48MM **Privately Held**
**SIC: 2015** 5144 5142 Poultry slaughtering and processing; Poultry and poultry products; Packaged frozen goods

**(P-680)**
**FOSTER FARMS LLC**
1900 Kern St, Kingsburg (93631-9687)
**PHONE**..................................559 897-1081
Donald Jones, *Brnch Mgr*
**EMP:** 30
**SALES (corp-wide):** 8.23B **Privately Held**
**Web:** www.fosterfarms.com
**SIC: 2015** Poultry slaughtering and processing
**HQ:** Foster Farms, Llc
1000 Davis St
Livingston CA 95334

**(P-681)**
**FOSTER FARMS LLC**
1111 Navy Dr, Stockton (95206-1125)
**PHONE**..................................209 948-0129
**EMP:** 20
**SALES (corp-wide):** 8.23B **Privately Held**
**Web:** www.fosterfarms.com
**SIC: 2015** Chicken slaughtering and processing
**HQ:** Foster Farms, Llc
1000 Davis St
Livingston CA 95334

# PRODUCTS & SERVICES SECTION
## 2015 - Poultry Slaughtering And Processing (P-703)

**(P-682)**
**FOSTER FARMS LLC**
2222 S East Ave, Fresno (93721-3405)
P.O. Box 12556 (93778-2556)
PHONE..................559 443-2750
EMP: 40
SALES (corp-wide): 8.23B Privately Held
Web: www.fosterfarms.com
SIC: 2015 Poultry, processed, nsk
HQ: Foster Farms, Llc
  1000 Davis St
  Livingston CA 95334

**(P-683)**
**FOSTER POULTRY FARMS**
Also Called: Foster Farms
1307 Ellenwood Rd, Waterford (95386-8702)
PHONE..................209 394-7901
Jay Husman, Mgr
EMP: 329
SQ FT: 68,316
SALES (corp-wide): 1.25B Privately Held
Web: www.fosterfarms.com
SIC: 2015 Poultry slaughtering and processing
PA: Foster Poultry Farms, Llc
  1000 Davis St
  209 394-7901

**(P-684)**
**FOSTER POULTRY FARMS**
Also Called: Foster Farms
1333 Swan St, Livingston (95334-1559)
P.O. Box 457 (95334-0457)
PHONE..................209 394-7901
Brent Allen, Brnch Mgr
EMP: 1844
SALES (corp-wide): 1.25B Privately Held
Web: www.fosterfarms.com
SIC: 2015 Poultry slaughtering and processing
PA: Foster Poultry Farms, Llc
  1000 Davis St
  209 394-7901

**(P-685)**
**FOSTER POULTRY FARMS**
Also Called: Foster Poultry Farms
843 Davis St Unit 1p, Livingston (95334-1525)
PHONE..................209 394-7901
EMP: 192
SALES (corp-wide): 1.25B Privately Held
Web: www.fosterfarms.com
SIC: 2015 Poultry slaughtering and processing
PA: Foster Poultry Farms, Llc
  1000 Davis St
  209 394-7901

**(P-686)**
**FOSTER POULTRY FARMS**
Also Called: Foster Turkey Live Haul
1033 S Center St, Turlock (95380-5568)
PHONE..................209 668-5922
Steve Page, Mgr
EMP: 100
SALES (corp-wide): 1.25B Privately Held
Web: www.fosterfarms.com
SIC: 2015 Poultry slaughtering and processing
PA: Foster Poultry Farms, Llc
  1000 Davis St
  209 394-7901

**(P-687)**
**FOSTER POULTRY FARMS**
Also Called: FOSTER POULTRY FARMS
1805 N Santa Fe Ave, Compton (90221-1009)
PHONE..................310 223-1499
Ronald Altman, Brnch Mgr
EMP: 470
SALES (corp-wide): 1.25B Privately Held
Web: www.fosterfarms.com
SIC: 2015 Poultry slaughtering and processing
PA: Foster Poultry Farms, Llc
  1000 Davis St
  209 394-7901

**(P-688)**
**FOSTER POULTRY FARMS**
Also Called: Foster Farms
2960 S Cherry Ave, Fresno (93706-5445)
PHONE..................559 442-3771
Bob Hansen, Mgr
EMP: 766
SALES (corp-wide): 1.25B Privately Held
Web: www.fosterfarms.com
SIC: 2015 Poultry slaughtering and processing
PA: Foster Poultry Farms, Llc
  1000 Davis St
  209 394-7901

**(P-689)**
**FOSTER POULTRY FARMS**
Also Called: FOSTER POULTRY FARMS
900 W Belgravia Ave, Fresno (93706-3909)
PHONE..................559 265-2000
Jessi Amezcua, Brnch Mgr
EMP: 470
SALES (corp-wide): 1.25B Privately Held
Web: www.fosterfarms.com
SIC: 2015 5812 0173 5191 Chicken slaughtering and processing; Chicken restaurant; Almond grove; Animal feeds
PA: Foster Poultry Farms, Llc
  1000 Davis St
  209 394-7901

**(P-690)**
**FOSTER POULTRY FARMS**
Also Called: FOSTER POULTRY FARMS
770 N Plano St, Porterville (93257-6329)
PHONE..................559 793-5501
Paul Bravinder, Mgr
EMP: 174
SALES (corp-wide): 1.25B Privately Held
Web: www.fosterfarms.com
SIC: 2015 5421 Chicken, processed: fresh; Meat and fish markets
PA: Foster Poultry Farms, Llc
  1000 Davis St
  209 394-7901

**(P-691)**
**FOSTER POULTRY FARMS LLC (PA)**
1000 Davis St, Livingston (95334-1526)
P.O. Box 457 (95334)
PHONE..................209 394-7901
Dan Huber, CEO
Ron M Foster, Pr
George Foster, Prin
Caryn Doyle, CFO
◆ EMP: 250 EST: 1939
SQ FT: 40,000
SALES (est): 1.25B
SALES (corp-wide): 1.25B Privately Held
Web: www.fosterfarms.com
SIC: 2015 Poultry slaughtering and processing

**(P-692)**
**GFI POULTRY LLC (PA)**
2495 W Shaw Ave Ste 102, Fresno (93711-3302)
EMP: 26 EST: 2006
SQ FT: 3,800
SALES (est): 14.24MM Privately Held
SIC: 2015 Poultry, processed: canned

**(P-693)**
**GLENOAKS FOOD INC**
11030 Randall St, Sun Valley (91352-2621)
PHONE..................818 768-9091
John J Fallon Iii, CEO
Marvin Caeser, Stockholder*
Katty Majailovic, Stockholder*
John J Fallon Iii, Pr
EMP: 40 EST: 1996
SQ FT: 30,000
SALES (est): 4.51MM Privately Held
Web: www.jcrivers.com
SIC: 2015 2013 3999 2091 Poultry slaughtering and processing; Beef, dried: from purchased meat; Pet supplies; Fish, dried

**(P-694)**
**GRIMAUD FARMS CALIFORNIA INC (DH)**
1320 S Aurora St Ste A, Stockton (95206-1616)
PHONE..................209 466-3200
Rheal Cayer, Pr
Fricrick Grimaud, Ch Bd
▲ EMP: 20 EST: 1985
SQ FT: 42,000
SALES (est): 12.14MM Privately Held
Web: www.grimaudfarms.com
SIC: 2015 Poultry slaughtering and processing
HQ: Groupe Grimaud La Corbiere
  Roussay
  Sevremoine PDL 49450
  241703690

**(P-695)**
**INGENUE INC**
Also Called: Qc Poultry
1111 W Olympic Blvd, Montebello (90640-5123)
P.O. Box 17238 (92817-7238)
PHONE..................323 726-8084
Nick Macis, Pr
Michelle Macis, Sec
EMP: 100 EST: 1998
SQ FT: 10,000
SALES (est): 17.13MM Privately Held
Web: www.qcpoultry.com
SIC: 2015 Poultry slaughtering and processing

**(P-696)**
**KIFUKI USA CO INC (HQ)**
15547 1st St, Irwindale (91706-6201)
PHONE..................626 334-8090
Kuniaki Ishikaiwa, Pr
▲ EMP: 90 EST: 1989
SQ FT: 52,000
SALES (est): 52.69MM Privately Held
Web: kifukiusa.openfos.com
SIC: 2015 2013 2035 Eggs, processed: dehydrated; Beef, dried: from purchased meat; Seasonings and sauces, except tomato and dry
PA: Kewpie Corporation
  1-4-13, Shibuya

**(P-697)**
**LOS ANGELES POULTRY CO INC**
4816 Long Beach Ave, Los Angeles (90058-1915)
P.O. Box 58328 (90058-0328)
PHONE..................323 232-1619
David Dahan, Pr
Dror Dahan, *
EMP: 88 EST: 1988
SQ FT: 32,000
SALES (est): 8.35MM Privately Held
Web: www.lapoultry.com
SIC: 2015 Poultry slaughtering and processing

**(P-698)**
**OLIVERA EGG RANCH LLC**
Also Called: Olivera Foods
3315 Sierra Rd, San Jose (95132-3099)
P.O. Box 32126 (95152-2126)
PHONE..................408 258-8074
▲ EMP: 60 EST: 1949
SQ FT: 35,000
SALES (est): 4.51MM Privately Held
SIC: 2015 5143 5142 5144 Egg processing; Cheese; Packaged frozen goods; Eggs

**(P-699)**
**PETALUMA ACQUISITIONS LLC**
2700 Lakeville Hwy, Petaluma (94954-5606)
PHONE..................707 763-1904
EMP: 59 EST: 2001
SALES (est): 2.42MM
SALES (corp-wide): 1.24B Privately Held
Web: www.cityofpetaluma.org
SIC: 2015 Chicken slaughtering and processing
PA: Perdue Farms Incorporated
  31149 Old Ocean City Rd
  800 473-7383

**(P-700)**
**PETALUMA ACQUISTION LLC**
Also Called: Petaluma Poultry Processors
1500 Cader Ln, Petaluma (94954-6953)
P.O. Box 7368 (94955-7368)
PHONE..................707 763-1904
EMP: 237
SIC: 2015 Chicken slaughtering and processing

**(P-701)**
**RICH CHICKS LLC**
13771 Gramercy Pl, Gardena (90249-2470)
PHONE..................209 879-4104
Charlie Brust, VP Opers
EMP: 20
Web: www.richchicks.com
SIC: 2015 Chicken, processed: frozen
PA: Rich Chicks, Llc
  4276 N Tracy Blvd

**(P-702)**
**WESTERN SUPREME INC**
Also Called: California Poultry
846 Produce Ct, Los Angeles (90021-1832)
P.O. Box 21441 (90021-0441)
PHONE..................213 627-3861
Frank Fogarty, Pr
Marlene Fogarty, *
EMP: 125 EST: 1991
SQ FT: 10,000
SALES (est): 9.81MM Privately Held
SIC: 2015 Chicken slaughtering and processing

**(P-703)**
**ZF IN LIQUIDATION LLC**
Also Called: Zacky Farms
2020 S East Ave, Fresno (93721-3328)
P.O. Box 12556 (93778-2556)
PHONE..................559 486-2310
▼ EMP: 700
SIC: 2015 Poultry slaughtering and processing

(PA)=Parent Co (HQ)=Headquarters
✪ = New Business established in last 2 years

## 2021 Creamery Butter

**(P-704)**
**CALIFORNIA DAIRIES INC**
Also Called: San Joaquin Valley Dairymen
475 S Tegner Rd, Turlock (95380-9406)
**PHONE**..................209 656-1942
Tamara Staggs, *Brnch Mgr*
**EMP:** 143
**SALES (corp-wide):** 3.32B **Privately Held**
**Web:** www.californiadairies.com
**SIC: 2021** 2023 2026 Creamery butter; Dry, condensed and evaporated dairy products; Fluid milk
**PA:** California Dairies, Inc.
2000 N Plz Dr
559 625-2200

**(P-705)**
**MIYOKOS KITCHEN**
Also Called: Miyoko's Creamery
1622 Corporate Cir, Petaluma (94954-6912)
**PHONE**..................415 521-5313
Stuart Kronauge, *CEO*
Shonn Tom, *
◆ **EMP:** 50 **EST:** 2013
**SALES (est):** 10.84MM **Privately Held**
**Web:** www.miyokoskitchen.com
**SIC: 2021** 2022 Creamery butter; Cheese; natural and processed

**(P-706)**
**STRAUS FAMILY CREAMERY INC (PA)**
1105 Industrial Ave Ste 200, Petaluma (94952-1141)
**PHONE**..................707 776-2887
Albert Straus, *CEO*
Deborah Parrish, *
**EMP:** 63 **EST:** 1994
**SQ FT:** 40,000
**SALES (est):** 24.17MM **Privately Held**
**Web:** www.strausfamilycreamery.com
**SIC: 2021** 2023 2026 Creamery butter; Ice cream mix, unfrozen: liquid or dry; Yogurt

**(P-707)**
**VENTURA FOODS LLC**
Also Called: Saffola Quality Foods
2900 Jurupa St, Ontario (91761-2915)
**PHONE**..................323 262-9157
Tom Bospic, *Mgr*
**EMP:** 42
**Web:** www.venturafoods.com
**SIC: 2021** 2035 5199 2079 Creamery butter; Dressings, salad: raw and cooked (except dry mixes); Oils, animal or vegetable; Edible fats and oils
**PA:** Ventura Foods, Llc
40 Pointe Dr

## 2022 Cheese; Natural And Processed

**(P-708)**
**ARIZA CHEESE CO INC**
7602 Jackson St, Paramount (90723-4912)
**PHONE**..................562 630-4144
Fatima Cristina Ariza, *CEO*
Ausencio Ariza, *
**EMP:** 40 **EST:** 1970
**SQ FT:** 8,000
**SALES (est):** 2.72MM **Privately Held**
**Web:** www.arizacheeseco.com
**SIC: 2022** Natural cheese

**(P-709)**
**ARIZA GLOBAL FOODS INC**
7602 Jackson St, Paramount (90723-4912)
**PHONE**..................562 630-4144
Pablo Gonzalez, *CEO*
**EMP:** 23 **EST:** 2015
**SALES (est):** 885.19K **Privately Held**
**SIC: 2022** Cheese; natural and processed

**(P-710)**
**CYPRESS GROVE CHEVRE INC**
1330 Q St, Arcata (95521-5740)
**PHONE**..................707 825-1100
Pamela Dressler, *Pr*
▲ **EMP:** 52 **EST:** 2000
**SQ FT:** 12,500
**SALES (est):** 8.9MM **Privately Held**
**Web:** www.cypressgrovecheese.com
**SIC: 2022** Natural cheese
**HQ:** Emmi Ag
Landenbergstrasse 1
Luzern LU 6005

**(P-711)**
**DAIRY FARMERS AMERICA INC**
600 Trade Way, Turlock (95380-9433)
**PHONE**..................209 667-9627
Thomas Baker, *Mgr*
**EMP:** 25
**SQ FT:** 63,976
**SALES (corp-wide):** 21.72B **Privately Held**
**Web:** www.dfamilk.com
**SIC: 2022** 2026 Natural cheese; Fluid milk
**PA:** Dairy Farmers Of America, Inc.
1405 N 98th St
816 801-6455

**(P-712)**
**EINSTEIN NOAH REST GROUP INC**
Also Called: Noah's New York Bagels
16304 Beach Blvd, Westminster (92683-7857)
**PHONE**..................714 847-4609
Fransico Valdez, *Mgr*
**EMP:** 197
**Web:** www.bagelbrands.com
**SIC: 2022** 5812 Spreads, cheese; Cafe
**PA:** Einstein Noah Restaurant Group, Inc.
555 Zang St Ste 300

**(P-713)**
**EINSTEIN NOAH REST GROUP INC**
Also Called: Noah's
15996 Los Gatos Blvd, Los Gatos (95032-3424)
**PHONE**..................408 358-5895
Susan Asef, *Mgr*
**EMP:** 181
**Web:** www.bagelbrands.com
**SIC: 2022** 5812 Spreads, cheese; Cafe
**PA:** Einstein Noah Restaurant Group, Inc.
555 Zang St Ste 300

**(P-714)**
**EXCELPRO INC (PA)**
1630 Amapola Ave, Torrance (90501-3101)
**PHONE**..................323 415-8544
Peter Ernster, *Pr*
Gregg Rowland, *CFO*
John H Ernster Junior, *Sec*
**EMP:** 19 **EST:** 1973
**SQ FT:** 36,000
**SALES (est):** 2.06MM
**SALES (corp-wide):** 2.06MM **Privately Held**
**SIC: 2022** 2023 Processed cheese; Dietary supplements, dairy and non-dairy based

**(P-715)**
**G&G SPECIALTY FOODS INC**
Also Called: G & G Foods
322 Bellevue Ave, Santa Rosa (95407-7711)
P.O. Box 282 (53076-0282)
**EMP:** 135
**SIC: 2022** Spreads, cheese

**(P-716)**
**GOLDEN VALLEY DAIRY PRODUCTS**
1025 E Bardsley Ave, Tulare (93274-5752)
**PHONE**..................559 687-1188
John Prince, *CEO*
**EMP:** 23 **EST:** 1996
**SALES (est):** 610.61K
**SALES (corp-wide):** 2.89B **Privately Held**
**SIC: 2022** Cheese; natural and processed
**PA:** Land O'lakes, Inc.
4001 Lexington Ave N
651 375-2222

**(P-717)**
**GREEN VALLEY FOODS PRODUCT**
25684 Community Blvd, Barstow (92311-9671)
**PHONE**..................760 964-1105
Hector Huerta, *Pr*
**EMP:** 15 **EST:** 1996
**SQ FT:** 10,000
**SALES (est):** 951.53K **Privately Held**
**SIC: 2022** Cheese; natural and processed

**(P-718)**
**HILMAR CHEESE COMPANY INC**
3600 W Canal Dr, Turlock (95380-8507)
P.O. Box 910 (95324-0910)
**PHONE**..................209 667-6076
David Ahlem, *CEO*
**EMP:** 324
**SALES (corp-wide):** 264.32MM **Privately Held**
**Web:** www.hilmar.com
**SIC: 2022** Natural cheese
**PA:** Hilmar Cheese Company, Inc.
8901 N Lander Ave
209 667-6076

**(P-719)**
**HILMAR CHEESE COMPANY INC (PA)**
8901 Lander Ave, Hilmar (95324-9327)
P.O. Box 910 (95324-0910)
**PHONE**..................209 667-6076
David Ahlem, *CEO*
Charles Ahlem, *
James Ahlem, *
Grant Ahlem, *
Vance Ahlem, *
◆ **EMP:** 323 **EST:** 1984
**SALES (est):** 264.32MM
**SALES (corp-wide):** 264.32MM **Privately Held**
**Web:** www.hilmar.com
**SIC: 2022** Natural cheese

**(P-720)**
**IDB HOLDINGS INC (DH)**
601 S Rockefeller Ave, Ontario (91761-7871)
**PHONE**..................909 390-5624
Jim Dekeyser, *CEO*
Peter Dolan, *Sec*
Daniel O'connell, *Sec*
◆ **EMP:** 15 **EST:** 1989
**SQ FT:** 4,000
**SALES (est):** 77.25MM
**SALES (corp-wide):** 2.77B **Privately Held**
**SIC: 2022** 5143 Processed cheese; Cheese
**HQ:** Ornua Foods Uk Limited
Sunnyhills Road
Leek STAFFS ST13
153 839-9111

**(P-721)**
**JOSEPH GALLO CHEESE COMPANY LP**
Also Called: Joseph Gallo Farms
10561 State Highway 140, Atwater (95301-9309)
P.O. Box 775 (95301-0775)
**PHONE**..................209 394-7984
Mike Gallo, *Pt*
**EMP:** 217 **EST:** 2022
**SALES (est):** 15.22MM **Privately Held**
**Web:** www.josephfarms.com
**SIC: 2022** Natural cheese

**(P-722)**
**KAROUN DAIRIES INC (PA)**
Also Called: Karoun Cheese
13023 Arroyo St, San Fernando (91340-1540)
**PHONE**..................818 767-7000
Anto Baghdassarian, *Pr*
Ohan Baghdassarian, *
Rostom Baghdassarian, *
Seta Baghdassarian, *
Tsolak Khatcherian, *
▲ **EMP:** 40 **EST:** 1991
**SQ FT:** 70,000
**SALES (est):** 43.03MM **Privately Held**
**Web:** www.karouncheese.com
**SIC: 2022** 5143 Natural cheese; Cheese

**(P-723)**
**LACTALIS HERITAGE DAIRY INC**
10800 Avenue 184, Tulare (93274-9514)
**PHONE**..................559 685-0790
Kristine Smith, *Asstg*
**EMP:** 199
**SALES (corp-wide):** 355.83K **Privately Held**
**Web:** www.lactalisheritagedairy.com
**SIC: 2022** Cheese; natural and processed
**HQ:** Lactalis Heritage Dairy, Inc.
540 W Madison St
Chicago IL 60661
312 934-2480

**(P-724)**
**LAND OLAKES INC**
Also Called: Land O'Lakes
400 S M St, Tulare (93274-5431)
**PHONE**..................559 687-8287
Jack Gherty, *Brnch Mgr*
**EMP:** 96
**SALES (corp-wide):** 2.89B **Privately Held**
**Web:** www.landolakes-ingredients.com
**SIC: 2022** Cheese; natural and processed
**PA:** Land O'lakes, Inc.
4001 Lexington Ave N
651 375-2222

**(P-725)**
**LAND OLAKES INC**
Also Called: Land O'Lakes
3601 County Road C, Orland (95963-9117)
**PHONE**..................530 865-7626
**EMP:** 29
**SALES (corp-wide):** 6.83B **Privately Held**
**SIC: 2022** Cheese; natural and processed
**PA:** Land O'lakes, Inc.
4001 Lexington Ave N

651 375-2222

**(P-726)**
**LEPRINO FOODS COMPANY**
2401 N Macarthur Dr, Tracy (95376-2095)
PHONE..................209 835-8340
Joel Crane, Genl Mgr
**EMP:** 404
**SALES (corp-wide):** 214.38MM **Privately Held**
Web: www.leprinofoods.com
**SIC: 2022** Natural cheese
**PA:** Leprino Foods Company
1830 W 38th Ave
303 480-2600

**(P-727)**
**LEPRINO FOODS COMPANY**
490 F St, Lemoore (93245-2661)
PHONE..................559 924-7722
Dave Direking, Brnch Mgr
**EMP:** 247
**SALES (corp-wide):** 214.38MM **Privately Held**
Web: www.leprinofoods.com
**SIC: 2022** Natural cheese
**PA:** Leprino Foods Company
1830 W 38th Ave
303 480-2600

**(P-728)**
**LEPRINO FOODS COMPANY**
351 Belle Haven Dr, Lemoore (93245-9247)
PHONE..................559 924-7939
James Leprino, Pr
**EMP:** 200
**SALES (corp-wide):** 214.38MM **Privately Held**
Web: www.leprinofoods.com
**SIC: 2022** Natural cheese
**PA:** Leprino Foods Company
1830 W 38th Ave
303 480-2600

**(P-729)**
**LIFE IS LIFE LLC**
Also Called: Parmela Creamery
2611 Cottonwood Ave, Moreno Valley (92553-8089)
PHONE..................310 584-7541
Ryan Hayes Salomone, Managing Member
**EMP:** 28 **EST:** 2012
**SALES (est):** 9.24MM **Privately Held**
**SIC: 2022** Imitation cheese

**(P-730)**
**RIZO-LOPEZ FOODS INC**
Also Called: Don Francisco Cheese
201 S Mcclure Rd, Modesto (95357-0519)
P.O. Box 1689 (95319-1689)
PHONE..................800 626-5587
Edwin Rizo, Pr
Ivan Rizo, *
▲ **EMP:** 313 **EST:** 1990
**SQ FT:** 3,800
**SALES (est):** 41.06MM **Privately Held**
Web: www.tiofranciscocheese.com
**SIC: 2022** 5143 2023 5141 Natural cheese; Dairy products, except dried or canned; Dry, condensed and evaporated dairy products; Groceries, general line

**(P-731)**
**ROMALV GROUP LLC**
Also Called: Peluso Cheese
429 H St, Los Banos (93635-4113)
PHONE..................213 272-1026
Joseph Reynoso, Prin
**EMP:** 25 **EST:** 2011
**SALES (est):** 3.83MM **Privately Held**
**SIC: 2022** Cheese; natural and processed

**(P-732)**
**RUMIANO CHEESE CO (PA)**
101 Harvest Dr, Willows (95988-3252)
P.O. Box 863 (95988-0863)
PHONE..................530 934-5438
Baird Rumiano, Pr
John F Rumiano, *
▲ **EMP:** 106 **EST:** 1921
**SQ FT:** 30,000
**SALES (est):** 53.02MM
**SALES (corp-wide):** 53.02MM **Privately Held**
Web: www.rumianocheese.com
**SIC: 2022** Natural cheese

**(P-733)**
**RUMIANO CHEESE CO**
511 9th St, Crescent City (95531-3408)
P.O. Box 305 (95531-0305)
PHONE..................707 465-1535
Baird Rumiano, Mgr
**EMP:** 44
**SALES (corp-wide):** 53.02MM **Privately Held**
Web: www.rumianocheese.com
**SIC: 2022** Natural cheese
**PA:** Rumiano Cheese Co.
101 Harvest Dr
530 934-5438

**(P-734)**
**SAPUTO CHEESE USA INC**
800 E Paige Ave, Tulare (93274-6863)
PHONE..................559 687-8411
**EMP:** 300
**SALES (corp-wide):** 3.79B **Privately Held**
Web: www.saputousafoodservice.com
**SIC: 2022** Cheese spreads, dips, pastes, and other cheese products
**HQ:** Saputo Cheese Usa Inc.
10700 W Res Dr Ste 400
Milwaukee WI 53226

**(P-735)**
**SAPUTO CHEESE USA INC**
691 Inyo Ave, Newman (95360-1403)
PHONE..................262 307-6738
Sikma Evan, Brnch Mgr
**EMP:** 100
**SALES (corp-wide):** 3.79B **Privately Held**
Web: www.saputo.com
**SIC: 2022** Natural cheese
**HQ:** Saputo Cheese Usa Inc.
10700 W Res Dr Ste 400
Milwaukee WI 53226

**(P-736)**
**SAPUTO CHEESE USA INC**
901 E Levin Ave, Tulare (93274-6525)
PHONE..................559 687-9999
Bob Timmons, Mgr
**EMP:** 476
**SALES (corp-wide):** 3.79B **Privately Held**
Web: www.stellacheese.com
**SIC: 2022** Natural cheese
**HQ:** Saputo Cheese Usa Inc.
10700 W Res Dr Ste 400
Milwaukee WI 53226

**(P-737)**
**SAPUTO CHEESE USA INC**
5611 Imperial Hwy, South Gate (90280-7419)
PHONE..................562 862-7686
Rick Mckenney, Brnch Mgr
**EMP:** 508
**SALES (corp-wide):** 3.79B **Privately Held**
Web: www.saputo.com
**SIC: 2022** 5143 Natural cheese; Cheese
**HQ:** Saputo Cheese Usa Inc.
10700 W Res Dr Ste 400
Milwaukee WI 53226

**(P-738)**
**SIERRA CHEESE MANUFACTURING COMPANY INC**
Also Called: Sierra
916 S Santa Fe Ave, Compton (90221-4333)
PHONE..................310 635-1216
**EMP:** 39 **EST:** 1959
**SALES (est):** 4.77MM **Privately Held**
Web: www.sierracheese.com
**SIC: 2022** Natural cheese

**(P-739)**
**SIERRA NEVADA CHEESE CO INC (PA)**
6505 County Road 39, Willows (95988-9709)
PHONE..................530 934-8660
Ben Gregersen, Pr
John Dundon, *
Racheloriana Schraeder, *
**EMP:** 58 **EST:** 1997
**SQ FT:** 27,000
**SALES (est):** 15.64MM
**SALES (corp-wide):** 15.64MM **Privately Held**
Web: www.sierranevadacheese.com
**SIC: 2022** Natural cheese

**(P-740)**
**STEPLADDER FARMSTEAD CRMRY LLC**
Also Called: Stepladder Creamery
4450 San Simeon Creek Rd, Cambria (93428-1836)
PHONE..................415 606-8559
**EMP:** 22 **EST:** 2015
**SALES (est):** 487.95K **Privately Held**
Web: www.stepladdercreamery.com
**SIC: 2022** Natural cheese

**(P-741)**
**TOP BRANDS DISTRIBUTION INC**
9675 Distribution Ave, San Diego (92121-2307)
PHONE..................858 578-0319
Steve Kwon, CEO
**EMP:** 15 **EST:** 2013
**SALES (est):** 2.96MM **Privately Held**
**SIC: 2022** Cheese spreads, dips, pastes, and other cheese products

## 2023 Dry, Condensed, Evaporated Products

**(P-742)**
**APHRO-D LLC**
548 Market St, San Francisco (94104-5401)
PHONE..................201 574-1875
Katrina Licudine, Managing Member
**EMP:** 30 **EST:** 2020
**SALES (est):** 2MM **Privately Held**
Web: www.aphro-d.com
**SIC: 2023** Dietary supplements, dairy and non-dairy based

**(P-743)**
**ARMOR DERMALOGICS LLC**
9151 Atlanta Ave Unit 5864, Huntington Beach (92615-2639)
PHONE..................714 202-6424
**EMP:** 50 **EST:** 2018
**SALES (est):** 306.03K **Privately Held**
**SIC: 2023** Dietary supplements, dairy and non-dairy based

**(P-744)**
**AUSSIE BUBS INC**
1390 Market St Ste 200, San Francisco (94102-5404)
PHONE..................888 685-1508
Kristy Carr, Pr
**EMP:** 50 **EST:** 2021
**SALES (est):** 1.65MM **Privately Held**
Web: www.aussiebubs.com
**SIC: 2023** Baby formulas

**(P-745)**
**BETTER BAR MANUFACTURING LLC**
6975 Arlington Ave, Riverside (92503-1537)
PHONE..................951 525-3111
**EMP:** 20 **EST:** 2018
**SALES (est):** 243.3K **Privately Held**
**SIC: 2023** Dietary supplements, dairy and non-dairy based

**(P-746)**
**BETTER NUTRITIONALS LLC (PA)**
3390 Horseless Carriage Dr, Norco (92860-3635)
PHONE..................310 356-9019
Sharon Hoffman, CEO
▼ **EMP:** 90 **EST:** 2015
**SQ FT:** 100,000
**SALES (est):** 34.31MM
**SALES (corp-wide):** 34.31MM **Privately Held**
**SIC: 2023** Dietary supplements, dairy and non-dairy based

**(P-747)**
**BETTER NUTRITIONALS LLC**
17120 S Figueroa St Ste B, Gardena (90248-3024)
PHONE..................310 356-9019
Sharon Hoffman, Brnch Mgr
**EMP:** 50
**SALES (corp-wide):** 34.31MM **Privately Held**
Web: www.betternutritionals.com
**SIC: 2023** Dietary supplements, dairy and non-dairy based
**PA:** Better Nutritionals, Llc
3390 Hrseless Carriage Dr
310 356-9019

**(P-748)**
**BETTER NUTRITIONALS LLC**
3380 Horseless Carriage Rd, Norco (92860-3635)
PHONE..................310 356-9019
Roger Tyre, Brnch Mgr
**EMP:** 100
**SALES (corp-wide):** 34.31MM **Privately Held**
**SIC: 2023** Dietary supplements, dairy and non-dairy based
**PA:** Better Nutritionals, Llc
3390 Hrseless Carriage Dr
310 356-9019

**(P-749)**
**BETTER NUTRITIONALS LLC**
3350 Horseless Carriage Rd, Norco (92860-3635)
PHONE..................310 356-9019

Roger Tyre, *Brnch Mgr*
**EMP:** 100
**SALES (corp-wide):** 34.31MM **Privately Held**
**SIC: 2023** Dietary supplements, dairy and non-dairy based
**PA:** Better Nutritionals, Llc
3390 Hrseless Carriage Dr
310 356-9019

### (P-750)
### BIO-NUTRITIONAL RES GROUP INC
Also Called: Power Crunch
6 Morgan Ste 100, Irvine (92618-1920)
P.O. Box 3669 (90510-3669)
**PHONE**.................................714 427-6990
Kevin Lawrence, *CEO*
Karen L Stensby, *Sec*
Curtis Steinhaus, *CFO*
**EMP:** 185 **EST:** 1991
**SQ FT:** 3,000
**SALES (est):** 49.64MM **Privately Held**
Web: www.powercrunch.com
**SIC: 2023** Dietary supplements, dairy and non-dairy based

### (P-751)
### BIORAY INC
10 Mason Ste 150, Irvine (92618-2705)
**PHONE**.................................949 305-7454
Stephanie Ray, *Pr*
Stephanie Ray, *VP*
Tim Ray, *Pr*
**EMP:** 15 **EST:** 1990
**SALES (est):** 2.63MM **Privately Held**
Web: www.bioray.com
**SIC: 2023** Dietary supplements, dairy and non-dairy based

### (P-752)
### CAMPER PACKAGING LLC
Also Called: Phoenix Custom Packaging
13208 Arctic Cir, Santa Fe Springs (90670-5510)
**PHONE**.................................562 239-6167
**EMP:** 19 **EST:** 2019
**SALES (est):** 943.96K **Privately Held**
**SIC: 2023** Dry, condensed and evaporated dairy products

### (P-753)
### CYTOSPORT INC
1340 Treat Blvd Ste 350, Walnut Creek (94597-2140)
**PHONE**.................................707 751-3942
Rahul Pinto, *CEO*
Cynthia Nastanski, *
Ada Cheng, *
▲ **EMP:** 190 **EST:** 1997
**SALES (est):** 90.43MM
**SALES (corp-wide):** 86.39B **Publicly Held**
Web: www.musclemilk.com
**SIC: 2023** 2086 Dry, condensed and evaporated dairy products; Soft drinks: packaged in cans, bottles, etc.
**PA:** Pepsico, Inc.
700 Anderson Hill Rd
914 253-2000

### (P-754)
### EL INDIO SHOPS INCORPORATED
Also Called: El Indio Mexican Restaurant
3695 India St, San Diego (92103-4799)
**PHONE**.................................619 299-0333
Ralph R Pesqueira Junior, *Pr*
Eva Sanchez, *
**EMP:** 55 **EST:** 1940
**SQ FT:** 10,000
**SALES (est):** 4.56MM **Privately Held**
Web: www.elindiosandiego.net
**SIC: 2023** 5812 Evaporated buttermilk; Mexican restaurant

### (P-755)
### ESPERER WEBSTORES LLC
Also Called: Diatomaceous Earth.com
3820 State St Ste B, Santa Barbara (93105-3182)
**PHONE**.................................805 880-1900
David Stephen Sorensen, *Managing Member*
**EMP:** 19 **EST:** 2016
**SALES (est):** 2.32MM **Privately Held**
**SIC: 2023** 5499 Dietary supplements, dairy and non-dairy based; Vitamin food stores

### (P-756)
### FEIHE INTERNATIONAL INC (PA)
2275 Huntington Dr Pmb 278, San Marino (91108-2640)
**PHONE**.................................626 757-8885
You-bin Leng, *Pr*
Hua Liu, *
**EMP:** 1932 **EST:** 1985
**SALES (est):** 362.97MM **Privately Held**
**SIC: 2023** Dry, condensed and evaporated dairy products

### (P-757)
### FENCHEM INC (HQ)
Also Called: Fenchem
15308 El Prado Rd Bldg 8, Chino (91710-7659)
**PHONE**.................................909 597-8880
Shufeng Fan, *CEO*
▲ **EMP:** 22 **EST:** 2007
**SALES (est):** 11.75MM **Privately Held**
Web: www.fenchem.com
**SIC: 2023** Dietary supplements, dairy and non-dairy based
**PA:** Fenchem Biotek Ltd.
Room 1917, No. 359, Hongwu Road, Qinhuai District

### (P-758)
### FOREVER RICH INTERNATIONAL LLC
14622 Ventura Blvd, Sherman Oaks (91403-3600)
**PHONE**.................................310 867-4723
Leon Katz, *Pr*
**EMP:** 25 **EST:** 2013
**SALES (est):** 262.87K **Privately Held**
**SIC: 2023** Dietary supplements, dairy and non-dairy based

### (P-759)
### FREAL FOODS LLC
Also Called: Freal
2100 Powell St Ste 700, Emeryville (94608-1873)
**PHONE**.................................800 483-3218
Dinsh Guzdar, *Pr*
◆ **EMP:** 100 **EST:** 1997
**SALES (est):** 25.1MM
**SALES (corp-wide):** 4.81B **Privately Held**
Web: www.freal.com
**SIC: 2023** Milkshake mix
**PA:** Rich Products Corporation
1 Robert Rich Way
716 878-8000

### (P-760)
### GSL TECH INC
172 W Pomona Ave, Monrovia (91016-4558)
**PHONE**.................................877 572-9617
Weihua Zhang, *Pr*
Shu Zhang, *VP*
▲ **EMP:** 16 **EST:** 1997
**SALES (est):** 283.25K **Privately Held**
Web: www.gslsupplements.com
**SIC: 2023** 5499 2834 Dietary supplements, dairy and non-dairy based; Vitamin food stores; Pharmaceutical preparations

### (P-761)
### HERITAGE DISTRIBUTING COMPANY
Also Called: Ninth Avenue Foods
425 S 9th Ave, City Of Industry (91746-3314)
**PHONE**.................................626 333-9526
Ted De Groot, *Brnch Mgr*
**EMP:** 22
**SIC: 2023** 2026 Dry, condensed and evaporated dairy products; Fluid milk
**PA:** Heritage Distributing Company
5743 Smithway St Ste 105

### (P-762)
### HILMAR WHEY PROTEIN INC (PA)
9001 Lander Ave, Hilmar (95324-8320)
P.O. Box 910 (95324-0910)
**PHONE**.................................209 667-6076
John J Jeter, *Pr*
**EMP:** 40 **EST:** 1991
**SALES (est):** 24.67MM
**SALES (corp-wide):** 24.67MM **Privately Held**
Web: www.hilmar.com
**SIC: 2023** Concentrated whey

### (P-763)
### HILMAR WHEY PROTEIN INC
Also Called: HILMAR WHEY PROTEIN INC
8901 Lander Ave, Hilmar (95324-8355)
P.O. Box 910 (95324-0910)
**PHONE**.................................209 667-6076
**EMP:** 360
**SALES (corp-wide):** 478.87K **Privately Held**
Web: www.hilmar.com
**SIC: 2023** Concentrated whey
**PA:** Hilmar Whey Protein, Inc.
9001 Lander Ave
209 667-6076

### (P-764)
### HUMBOLDT CREAMERY LLC
Also Called: Humboldt Creamery Association
572 Fernbridge Dr, Fortuna (95540-9711)
**PHONE**.................................209 576-3400
▼ **EMP:** 250
Web: www.humboldtcreamery.com
**SIC: 2023** 2024 2026 Powdered milk; Ice cream, packaged: molded, on sticks, etc.; Milk processing (pasteurizing, homogenizing, bottling)

### (P-765)
### KERRY INC
64405 Lincoln St, Mecca (92254-6501)
P.O. Box 398 (92254-0398)
**PHONE**.................................760 396-2116
Darren Worden, *Pr*
**EMP:** 63
Web: www.kerry.com
**SIC: 2023** Dry, condensed and evaporated dairy products
**HQ:** Kerry Inc.
3400 Millington Rd
Beloit WI 53511
608 363-1200

### (P-766)
### LIEF ORGANICS LLC (PA)
Also Called: Lief Labs
28903 Avenue Paine, Valencia (91355-4169)
**PHONE**.................................661 775-2500
Adel Villalobos, *CEO*
Adel Villalobos, *Pr*
Steve Chopp, *
Victor Leyson, *
Nathan Cox, *Development*
**EMP:** 25 **EST:** 2008
**SALES (est):** 43.84MM
**SALES (corp-wide):** 43.84MM **Privately Held**
Web: www.lieforganics.com
**SIC: 2023** Dietary supplements, dairy and non-dairy based

### (P-767)
### LONIX PHARMACEUTICAL INC
5001 Earle Ave, Rosemead (91770-1169)
**PHONE**.................................626 287-4700
Chak Yeung Chan, *Pr*
Chak Yeung Chan, *Pr*
Wendy Cheung, *Off Mgr*
**EMP:** 18 **EST:** 2013
**SQ FT:** 5,000
**SALES (est):** 615.33K **Privately Held**
**SIC: 2023** Dietary supplements, dairy and non-dairy based

### (P-768)
### MIRACLE GREENS INC
8477 Steller Dr, Culver City (90232-2424)
**PHONE**.................................800 521-5867
Michael G Dave, *Pr*
Jr Ortiz, *VP*
**EMP:** 15 **EST:** 2004
**SALES (est):** 506.86K **Privately Held**
**SIC: 2023** Dietary supplements, dairy and non-dairy based

### (P-769)
### MISSION AG RESOURCES LLC
Also Called: Sierra Feeds
6801 Avenue 430 Unit A, Reedley (93654-9002)
**PHONE**.................................559 591-3333
Al Cumin, *Managing Member*
Therald Benevedo, *Managing Member*
**EMP:** 20 **EST:** 2005
**SALES (est):** 2.42MM **Privately Held**
Web: www.techag.com
**SIC: 2023** Dietary supplements, dairy and non-dairy based

### (P-770)
### NATURAL ALTERNATIVES INTL INC
5928 Farnsworth Ct, Carlsbad (92008-7303)
**PHONE**.................................800 848-2646
Mark Ledoux, *CEO*
**EMP:** 16
**SALES (corp-wide):** 113.8MM **Publicly Held**
Web: www.nai-online.com
**SIC: 2023** Dietary supplements, dairy and non-dairy based
**PA:** Natural Alternatives International, Inc.
1535 Faraday Ave
760 736-7700

### (P-771)
### NATURALIFE ECO VITE LABS
Also Called: Paragon Laboratories
20433 Earl St, Torrance (90503-2414)
**PHONE**.................................310 370-1563
Jay Kaufman, *CEO*

## PRODUCTS & SERVICES SECTION
### 2024 - Ice Cream And Frozen Deserts (P-794)

Richard Kaufman, *
Claire Kaufman, *
Steven Billis, *
▲ EMP: 100 EST: 1971
SQ FT: 25,000
SALES (est): 25.51MM Privately Held
Web: www.paragonlabsusa.com
SIC: 2023 2844 2834 5122 Dietary supplements, dairy and non-dairy based; Toilet preparations; Suppositories; Vitamins and minerals

### (P-772)
### NESTLE USA INC
Also Called: Nestle Dsd
4065 E Therese Ave, Fresno (93725-8920)
PHONE.................................559 834-2554
Miguel Alvarez, Brnch Mgr
EMP: 79
Web: www.nestleusa.com
SIC: 2023 Evaporated milk
HQ: Nestle Usa, Inc.
1812 N Moore St
Arlington VA 22209
800 225-2270

### (P-773)
### NESTLE USA INC
3285 De Forest Cir, Jurupa Valley (91752-3239)
PHONE.................................877 463-7853
EMP: 76
Web: www.nestleusa.com
SIC: 2023 Evaporated milk
HQ: Nestle Usa, Inc.
1812 N Moore St
Arlington VA 22209
800 225-2270

### (P-774)
### NESTLE USA INC
7301 District Blvd, Bakersfield (93313-2042)
PHONE.................................661 398-3536
EMP: 145
Web: www.nestleusa.com
SIC: 2023 Evaporated milk
HQ: Nestle Usa, Inc.
1812 N Moore St
Arlington VA 22209
800 225-2270

### (P-775)
### NESTLE USA INC
800 N Brand Blvd, Glendale (91203-1245)
PHONE.................................818 549-6000
EMP: 145
Web: www.nestle.com
SIC: 2023 Evaporated milk
HQ: Nestle Usa, Inc.
1812 N Moore St
Arlington VA 22209
800 225-2270

### (P-776)
### NESTLE USA INC
Also Called: Nestle Confections Factory
736 Garner Rd, Modesto (95357-0515)
PHONE.................................209 574-2000
Stephanie Hart, Brnch Mgr
EMP: 448
Web: www.nestleusa.com
SIC: 2023 2033 2064 2099 Evaporated milk; Fruits: packaged in cans, jars, etc.; Candy and other confectionery products; Pasta, uncooked: packaged with other ingredients
HQ: Nestle Usa, Inc.
1812 N Moore St
Arlington VA 22209
800 225-2270

### (P-777)
### NOVOTECH NUTRACEUTICALS INC
Also Called: Manufacturer
2897 Palma Dr, Ventura (93003-7653)
PHONE.................................805 676-1098
Jennifer L Li, Pr
Jennifer Lihhwa Li, CEO
EMP: 42 EST: 2007
SALES (est): 5.94MM Privately Held
Web: www.novotechnutra.com
SIC: 2023 2833 2911 2048 Dietary supplements, dairy and non-dairy based; Vitamins, natural or synthetic: bulk, uncompounded; Mineral oils, natural; Mineral feed supplements

### (P-778)
### NUTRASUMMA INC
1315 John Reed Ct, City Of Industry (91745-2407)
PHONE.................................866 866-3993
Dongning Li, CEO
EMP: 20 EST: 2014
SALES (est): 485.85K Privately Held
Web: www.nutrasumma.com
SIC: 2023 Dietary supplements, dairy and non-dairy based

### (P-779)
### PHARMACHEM LABORATORIES LLC
Also Called: PHARMACHEM LABORATORIES, LLC
2929 E White Star Ave, Anaheim (92806-2628)
PHONE.................................714 630-6000
George Joseph, VP
EMP: 42
SALES (corp-wide): 2.19B Publicly Held
Web: www.ashland.com
SIC: 2023 Dietary supplements, dairy and non-dairy based
HQ: Pharmachem Laboratories Llc
265 Harrison Tpke
Kearny NJ 07032

### (P-780)
### PROLACTA BIOSCIENCE INC
1800 Highland Ave, Duarte (91010-2837)
PHONE.................................626 599-9260
Scott A Elster, CEO
EMP: 304
SALES (corp-wide): 91.91MM Privately Held
Web: www.prolacta.com
SIC: 2023 Dried and powdered milk and milk products
PA: Prolacta Bioscience, Inc.
757 Baldwin Pk Blvd
626 599-9260

### (P-781)
### SANTINI FOODS INC
Also Called: Santini Fine Wines
16505 Worthley Dr, San Lorenzo (94580-1811)
PHONE.................................510 317-8888
Bruce Liu, Pr
Anna M Liu, Prin
◆ EMP: 133 EST: 1987
SQ FT: 105,000
SALES (est): 54.3MM Privately Held
Web: www.santinifoods.com
SIC: 2023 2026 2032 2087 Condensed, concentrated, and evaporated milk products; Milk processing (pasteurizing, homogenizing, bottling); Ethnic foods, canned, jarred, etc.; Beverage bases, concentrates, syrups, powders and mixes

### (P-782)
### THORNE RESEARCH INC
533 Stone Rd, Benicia (94510-1057)
PHONE.................................707 297-3458
Liza Alma, Brnch Mgr
EMP: 15
Web: www.thorne.com
SIC: 2023 Dietary supplements, dairy and non-dairy based
HQ: Thorne Research, Inc.
620 Omni Industrial Blvd
Summerville SC 29486
208 263-1337

### (P-783)
### TRIPLE FIVE NUTRITION LLC ✪
17120 S Figueroa St Ste B, Gardena (90248-3016)
PHONE.................................310 502-2277
Sharon Hoffman, Owner
EMP: 20 EST: 2023
SALES (est): 368.11K Privately Held
SIC: 2023 Dietary supplements, dairy and non-dairy based

### (P-784)
### TROPICAL FUNCTIONAL LABS LLC
Also Called: Tahiti Trading Company
7111 Arlington Ave Ste F, Riverside (92503-1522)
PHONE.................................951 688-2619
▲ EMP: 22 EST: 1999
SALES (est): 969.28K Privately Held
SIC: 2023 Dietary supplements, dairy and non-dairy based

### (P-785)
### UQORA INC
4250 Executive Sq, La Jolla (92037-8404)
PHONE.................................888 313-1372
Vivian Rhoads, Pr
Jenna Ryan, *
Spencer Gordon, *
EMP: 43 EST: 2017
SALES (est): 23.57MM Privately Held
Web: www.uqora.com
SIC: 2023 Dietary supplements, dairy and non-dairy based
HQ: Pharmavite Llc
8531 Fallbrook Ave
West Hills CA 91304
818 221-6200

### (P-786)
### VITALBULK INC
440 Kings Village Rd, Scotts Valley (95066-4027)
PHONE.................................855 885-2855
EMP: 18
SQ FT: 1,800
SALES (est): 4MM Privately Held
SIC: 2023 Dietary supplements, dairy and non-dairy based

### (P-787)
### VITAWEST NUTRACEUTICALS INC
Also Called: Chocolates and Health
1502 Arrow Hwy, La Verne (91750-5318)
PHONE.................................888 557-8012
Iraiz Gomez, CEO
EMP: 25 EST: 2016
SALES (est): 2.13MM Privately Held
Web: www.vitawestnutra.com
SIC: 2023 Dietary supplements, dairy and non-dairy based

### (P-788)
### WAYNE
Also Called: Molaniki Distributor
640 W California Ave, Sunnyvale (94086-3624)
PHONE.................................669 206-2179
EMP: 30 EST: 2020
SALES (est): 331.46K Privately Held
SIC: 2023 Baby formulas

### (P-789)
### WELLINGTON FOODS INC (PA)
1930 California Ave, Corona (92881-6491)
PHONE.................................951 547-7000
Anthony E Harnack Senior, Ch
Tony Mauer, CFO
▲ EMP: 144 EST: 1974
SQ FT: 50,000
SALES (est): 21.82MM
SALES (corp-wide): 21.82MM Privately Held
Web: www.wellingtonfoods.com
SIC: 2023 Dietary supplements, dairy and non-dairy based

### (P-790)
### YBCC INC
17800 Castleton St Ste 386, City Of Industry (91748-1791)
PHONE.................................626 213-3945
Xiuhua Song, Pr
EMP: 38 EST: 1986
SALES (est): 352.06K Privately Held
SIC: 2023 Dietary supplements, dairy and non-dairy based

## 2024 Ice Cream And Frozen Deserts

### (P-791)
### AMPERSAND ICE CREAM LLC
3188 N Marks Ave Ste 110, Fresno (93722-4940)
PHONE.................................559 264-8000
EMP: 16 EST: 2015
SALES (est): 1.58MM Privately Held
Web: www.ampersandicecream.com
SIC: 2024 Ice cream and frozen deserts

### (P-792)
### ANITA GELATO CALIFORNIA INC
18700 Ventura Blvd, Tarzana (91356-6306)
PHONE.................................818 987-4055
Tomy Telio, Prin
EMP: 15 EST: 2021
SALES (est): 150K Privately Held
SIC: 2024 Ice cream and frozen deserts

### (P-793)
### BERENICE 2 AM CORP
Also Called: Bobboi Natural Gelato
8008 Girard Ave Ste 150, La Jolla (92037-4159)
PHONE.................................858 255-8693
Andrea Racca, CEO
Andrea Racca, Ofcr
EMP: 50 EST: 2014
SQ FT: 900
SALES (est): 1.83MM Privately Held
Web: www.bobboi.com
SIC: 2024 Ice cream and frozen deserts

### (P-794)
### BIG TRAIN INC
Also Called: Big T Industries
25392 Commercentre Dr, Lake Forest (92630-8823)
PHONE.................................949 340-8800

## 2024 - Ice Cream And Frozen Deserts (P-795)

◆ **EMP:** 150
**Web:** www.kerryfoodservice.com
**SIC: 2024** 2086 Ice cream and frozen deserts; Fruit drinks (less than 100% juice): packaged in cans, etc.

**(P-795)**
**BINDI NORTH AMERICA INC**
14502 Garfield Ave, Paramount (90723-3426)
**PHONE** .................................. 562 531-4301
Attilio Bindi, *Brnch Mgr*
**EMP:** 16
**SALES (corp-wide):** 244.57K **Privately Held**
**Web:** www.bindiusa.com
**SIC: 2024** Dairy based frozen desserts
**HQ:** Bindi North America, Inc.
   630 Belleville Tpke
   Kearny NJ 07032
   973 812-8118

**(P-796)**
**BROTHERS INTL DESSERTS (PA)**
Also Called: Brothers Desserts
3400 W Segerstrom Ave, Santa Ana (92704-6405)
**PHONE** .................................. 949 655-0080
Gary M Winkler, *CEO*
▲ **EMP:** 200 **EST:** 1974
**SALES (est):** 44.34MM
**SALES (corp-wide):** 44.34MM **Privately Held**
**Web:** www.brothersdesserts.com
**SIC: 2024** Ice cream, bulk

**(P-797)**
**DANONE US LLC**
3500 Barranca Pkwy Ste 240, Irvine (92606-8226)
**PHONE** .................................. 949 474-9670
John Mastrotaolo, *Dir*
**EMP:** 45
**SALES (corp-wide):** 967.79MM **Privately Held**
**Web:** www.dannon.com
**SIC: 2024** Ice cream and frozen deserts
**HQ:** Danone Us, Llc
   1 Maple Ave
   White Plains NY 10605
   914 872-8400

**(P-798)**
**DOLCE DOLCI LLC**
Also Called: Villa Dolce Gelato
16745 Saticoy St Ste 112, Van Nuys (91406-2710)
**PHONE** .................................. 818 343-8400
**EMP:** 19
**SALES (corp-wide):** 12.67MM **Privately Held**
**Web:** www.villadolcegelato.com
**SIC: 2024** Ice cream and ice milk
**PA:** Dolce Dolci, Llc
   23055 Sherman Way
   818 343-8400

**(P-799)**
**EDYS GRAND ICE CREAM**
Also Called: Windy City Express
5929 College Ave, Oakland (94618-1325)
**PHONE** .................................. 510 652-8187
▼ **EMP:** 3700
**SIC: 2024** 5143 Ice cream and ice milk; Ice cream and ices

**(P-800)**
**FARCHITECTURE BB LLC**
Also Called: Coolhaus
8588 Washington Blvd, Culver City (90232-7463)
**PHONE** .................................. 917 701-2777
Natasha Case, *Managing Member*
Daniel Fishman, *Pr*
**EMP:** 30 **EST:** 2009
**SALES (est):** 4.94MM **Privately Held**
**SIC: 2024** Ice cream, packaged: molded, on sticks, etc.

**(P-801)**
**FONO UNLIMITED (PA)**
Also Called: Bravo Fono
99 Stanford Shopping Ctr, Palo Alto (94304-1424)
**PHONE** .................................. 650 322-4664
Paulette Fono, *Pr*
Laslo Fono, *
**EMP:** 30 **EST:** 1972
**SALES (est):** 521.27K
**SALES (corp-wide):** 521.27K **Privately Held**
**SIC: 2024** 5812 5813 Ice cream, bulk; Italian restaurant; Drinking places

**(P-802)**
**GLASS JAR INC**
Also Called: Picnic Basket, The
125 Beach St, Santa Cruz (95060-5412)
**PHONE** .................................. 831 427-9946
Zachary Davis, *CEO*
**EMP:** 69
**SALES (corp-wide):** 5.02MM **Privately Held**
**Web:** www.thepicnicbasketsc.com
**SIC: 2024** Ice cream and frozen deserts
**PA:** The Glass Jar Inc
   913 Cedar St
   831 227-2247

**(P-803)**
**GLASS JAR INC (PA)**
Also Called: Penny Ice Creamery, The
913 Cedar St, Santa Cruz (95060-3801)
**PHONE** .................................. 831 227-2247
Zachary Davis, *CEO*
**EMP:** 31 **EST:** 2010
**SALES (est):** 5.02MM
**SALES (corp-wide):** 5.02MM **Privately Held**
**Web:** www.thepennyicecreamery.com
**SIC: 2024** 5812 Ice cream and frozen deserts; Ice cream stands or dairy bars

**(P-804)**
**HELADOS LA TAPATIA INC**
4495 W Shaw Ave, Fresno (93722-6206)
**PHONE** .................................. 559 441-1105
Emilio Sandoval, *Prin*
Emilio Sandoval, *Prin*
Sergio Sandoval, *
**EMP:** 40 **EST:** 1984
**SQ FT:** 8,800
**SALES (est):** 5.02MM **Privately Held**
**Web:** www.heladoslatapatia.com
**SIC: 2024** 5143 Ice cream and frozen deserts; Ice cream and ices

**(P-805)**
**HIGH ROAD CRAFT ICE CREAM INC (PA)**
12243 Branford St, Sun Valley (91352-1010)
**PHONE** .................................. 678 701-7623
Keith M Schroeder, *CEO*
Nicki Schroeder, *CMO**
Christian Rodrigue, *

Justine Zarch, *Chief Supply Chain Officer**
Danielle O'connor, *CFO*
**EMP:** 25 **EST:** 2010
**SALES (est):** 20.81MM **Privately Held**
**Web:** www.highroadcraft.com
**SIC: 2024** Ice cream and frozen deserts

**(P-806)**
**LOCO VENTURES INC**
Also Called: Loard's Ice Cream and Candies
2000 Wayne Ave, San Leandro (94577-3333)
**PHONE** .................................. 510 351-0405
Steven Cohen, *Pr*
Scott Cohen, *VP*
**EMP:** 20 **EST:** 1950
**SQ FT:** 16,000
**SALES (est):** 469.25K **Privately Held**
**Web:** www.loards.com
**SIC: 2024** 2064 5812 5441 Ice cream, bulk; Candy and other confectionery products; Ice cream stands or dairy bars; Candy

**(P-807)**
**LUTHMAN BACKLUND FOODS USA INC**
Also Called: N Ck's
214 Main St Pmb 300, El Segundo (90245-3803)
**PHONE** .................................. 310 994-9444
Tony Auger, *CEO*
Lars Johansson, *Sec*
**EMP:** 15 **EST:** 2018
**SALES (est):** 3.55MM **Privately Held**
**SIC: 2024** 5441 Ice cream, packaged: molded, on sticks, etc.; Candy

**(P-808)**
**MACKIE INTERNATIONAL INC (PA)**
Also Called: Sun Ice USA
4193 Flat Rock Dr Ste 200, Riverside (92505-7113)
**PHONE** .................................. 951 346-0530
Ernesto U Dacay Junior, *Pr*
◆ **EMP:** 40 **EST:** 1983
**SALES (est):** 4.8MM
**SALES (corp-wide):** 4.8MM **Privately Held**
**Web:** www.mackieinternational.net
**SIC: 2024** 2086 5199 Ices, flavored (frozen dessert); Fruit drinks (less than 100% juice): packaged in cans, etc.; Baskets

**(P-809)**
**MARIANNES ICE CREAM LLC (PA)**
1201 Fair Ave, Santa Cruz (95060)
**PHONE** .................................. 831 457-1447
Charles Wilcox, *Managing Member*
▲ **EMP:** 25 **EST:** 1993
**SALES (est):** 4.58MM **Privately Held**
**Web:** www.mariannesicecream.com
**SIC: 2024** 5812 Ice cream and frozen deserts; Ice cream stands or dairy bars

**(P-810)**
**MARIANNES ICE CREAM LLC**
218 State Park Dr, Aptos (95003-4324)
**PHONE** .................................. 831 713-4746
Charles Wilcox, *Managing Member*
**EMP:** 25
**Web:** www.mariannesicecream.com
**SIC: 2024** Custard, frozen
**PA:** Marianne's Ice Cream, Llc
   1201 Fair Ave

**(P-811)**
**MAVENS CREAMERY LLC**
1701 S 7th St Ste 7, San Jose (95112-6024)

**PHONE** .................................. 408 216-9270
Kim Lam, *Managing Member*
Tony Lam, *Managing Member*
**EMP:** 30 **EST:** 2015
**SQ FT:** 5,000
**SALES (est):** 3.66MM **Privately Held**
**Web:** www.mavenscreamery.com
**SIC: 2024** Ice cream and frozen deserts

**(P-812)**
**N7 CREAMERY INC**
35458 Byron Trl, Beaumont (92223-6218)
**PHONE** .................................. 909 922-8422
Brett Bingaman, *Pr*
Andrew Cox, *Sec*
**EMP:** 18 **EST:** 2012
**SALES (est):** 246.13K **Privately Held**
**Web:** www.n7creamery.com
**SIC: 2024** 2052 7389 Ice cream and frozen deserts; Bakery products, dry; Business services, nec

**(P-813)**
**NAIA INC**
Also Called: Gelateria Naia
736 Alfred Nobel Dr, Hercules (94547-1805)
**PHONE** .................................. 510 724-2479
Christopher Tan, *Pr*
Christopher C Tan, *Prin*
**EMP:** 21 **EST:** 2002
**SALES (est):** 6.17MM **Privately Held**
**Web:** www.gelaterianaia.com
**SIC: 2024** Ice cream, bulk

**(P-814)**
**RAMAR INTERNATIONAL CORP (PA)**
Also Called: Orientex Foods
1101 Railroad Ave, Pittsburg (94565-2641)
P.O. Box 111 (94565)
**PHONE** .................................. 925 439-9009
Susan Quesada, *CEO*
◆ **EMP:** 40 **EST:** 1968
**SALES (est):** 53.48MM
**SALES (corp-wide):** 53.48MM **Privately Held**
**Web:** www.ramarfoods.com
**SIC: 2024** 2013 5141 Ice cream and frozen deserts; Sausages and other prepared meats; Groceries, general line

**(P-815)**
**ROSA BROTHERS MILK CO INC (PA)**
10090 2nd Ave, Hanford (93230-9370)
**PHONE** .................................. 559 582-8825
Noel M Rosa, *Pr*
Rolland Rosa, *
**EMP:** 35 **EST:** 2011
**SALES (est):** 3.54MM
**SALES (corp-wide):** 3.54MM **Privately Held**
**Web:** www.rosabrothers.com
**SIC: 2024** 2026 Ice cream and frozen deserts; Half and half

**(P-816)**
**SUPER STORE INDUSTRIES**
Also Called: Mid Valley Dairy
2600 Spengler Way, Turlock (95380-8591)
**PHONE** .................................. 209 668-2100
Joe Mc Gill, *Mgr*
**EMP:** 100
**Web:** www.ssica.com
**SIC: 2024** 5143 Ice cream and frozen deserts; Ice cream and ices
**PA:** Super Store Industries
   16888 Mckinley Ave

▲ = Import ▼ = Export
◆ = Import/Export

PRODUCTS & SERVICES SECTION                                              2026 - Fluid Milk (P-839)

**(P-817)**
**TROPICALE FOODS LLC (PA)**
1237 W State St, Ontario (91762-4015)
P.O. Box 2224 (91708)
PHONE..................................909 635-1000
Steven C Schiller, *CEO*
▲ **EMP:** 46 **EST:** 1999
**SALES (est):** 181.55MM
**SALES (corp-wide):** 181.55MM **Privately Held**
Web: www.tropicalefoods.com
**SIC: 2024** Ice milk, packaged: molded, on sticks, etc.

**(P-818)**
**VON HOPPEN ICE CREAM**
Also Called: Frutstix Company
8221 Arjons Dr Ste A, San Diego (92126-6319)
PHONE..................................858 695-9111
Jim Elwel, *Mgr*
**EMP:** 15
**SALES (corp-wide):** 7.39MM **Privately Held**
**SIC: 2024** Ice cream, bulk
**HQ:** Von Hoppen Ice Cream
  1525 State St Ste 203
  Santa Barbara CA 93101
  805 965-2009

**(P-819)**
**WALLABY YOGURT COMPANY LLC**
Also Called: Wallaby Organic
110 Mezzetta Ct Ste B, American Canyon (94503-9691)
PHONE..................................855 925-4636
▲ **EMP:** 40 **EST:** 2016
**SALES (est):** 2.43MM **Privately Held**
Web: www.wallabyyogurt.com
**SIC: 2024** Dairy based frozen desserts

**(P-820)**
**WE THE PIE PEOPLE LLC**
Also Called: Jc's Pie Pops
9909 Topanga Canyon Blvd # 159, Chatsworth (91311-3602)
PHONE..................................818 349-1880
Jennifer Constantine, *Managing Member*
Thomas Spler, *
▲ **EMP:** 50 **EST:** 2012
**SALES (est):** 769.51K **Privately Held**
Web: www.piepops.com
**SIC: 2024** Nondairy based frozen desserts

**(P-821)**
**WONDER ICE CREAM INC (PA)**
Also Called: Circus Ice Cream
2338 Waish Ave, Santa Clara (95051-1301)
P.O. Box 304 (94560-0304)
PHONE..................................510 818-9102
▲ **EMP:** 40 **EST:** 1979
**SALES (est):** 35.99MM
**SALES (corp-wide):** 35.99MM **Privately Held**
Web: www.wonderic.com
**SIC: 2024** Ice cream, bulk

**(P-822)**
**ZIEGENFELDER COMPANY**
12290 Colony Ave, Chino (91710-2095)
PHONE..................................909 590-0493
Allan Hawthorne, *Brnch Mgr*
**EMP:** 65
Web: www.twinpops.com
**SIC: 2024** Ice cream, packaged: molded, on sticks, etc.
**HQ:** The Ziegenfelder Company
  87 18th St
  Wheeling WV 26003
  304 232-6360

**(P-823)**
**ZIEGENFELDER COMPANY**
12262 Colony Ave, Chino (91710-2095)
PHONE..................................909 509-0493
Donovan Arriaga, *Dir*
**EMP:** 65
Web: www.twinpops.com
**SIC: 2024** Fruit pops, frozen
**HQ:** The Ziegenfelder Company
  87 18th St
  Wheeling WV 26003
  304 232-6360

## 2026 Fluid Milk

**(P-824)**
**AFP ADVANCED FOOD PRODUCTS LLC**
900 N Plaza Dr, Visalia (93291-8826)
PHONE..................................559 651-1737
Corky Fortin, *Brnch Mgr*
**EMP:** 42
**SALES (corp-wide):** 355.83K **Privately Held**
Web: www.afpllc.com
**SIC: 2026** Fluid milk
**HQ:** Afp Advanced Food Products Llc
  402 S Custer Ave
  New Holland PA 17557
  717 355-8667

**(P-825)**
**AYO FOODS LLC**
Also Called: Ayo Food
927 Main St, Delano (93215-1729)
P.O. Box 1987 (93216-1987)
PHONE..................................661 345-5457
Matt Billings, *Managing Member*
**EMP:** 50 **EST:** 2018
**SALES (est):** 100K **Privately Held**
Web: www.ayoyogurt.com
**SIC: 2026** Yogurt

**(P-826)**
**BEBER INC**
Also Called: Beber Almond Milk
144 Meyers St Ste 140, Chico (95928-7153)
PHONE..................................530 487-8676
Arielle Danan, *CEO*
**EMP:** 45 **EST:** 2012
**SALES (est):** 4.44MM **Privately Held**
Web: www.freshalmondmilk.com
**SIC: 2026** Fluid milk

**(P-827)**
**BERKELEY FARMS LLC**
Also Called: Buds Ice Cream San Francisco
17637 E Valley Blvd, City Of Industry (91744-5731)
P.O. Box 4616 (94540-4616)
PHONE..................................510 265-8600
▲ **EMP:** 400
Web: www.berkeleyfarms.com
**SIC: 2026** 0241 5143 Fluid milk; Dairy farms; Butter

**(P-828)**
**CALIFORNIA DAIRIES INC (PA)**
2000 N Plaza Dr, Visalia (93291-9358)
PHONE..................................559 625-2200
Brad Anderson, *CEO*
Michael Burdeny, *
Phil Girard, *
Barb Rohrer, *Chief Counsel**
Dennis Bentoncourt Senior, *VP Mfg*
◆ **EMP:** 80 **EST:** 1938
**SQ FT:** 7,878,400
**SALES (est):** 3.32B
**SALES (corp-wide):** 3.32B **Privately Held**
Web: www.californiadairies.com
**SIC: 2026** 2021 2023 Fluid milk; Creamery butter; Dry, condensed and evaporated dairy products

**(P-829)**
**CALIFORNIA DAIRIES INC**
755 F St, Fresno (93706-3416)
P.O. Box 11865 (93775-1865)
PHONE..................................559 233-5154
Robert Ray, *Brnch Mgr*
**EMP:** 99
**SALES (corp-wide):** 3.32B **Privately Held**
Web: www.californiadairies.com
**SIC: 2026** 2021 2023 Fluid milk; Creamery butter; Dried milk
**PA:** California Dairies, Inc.
  2000 N Plz Dr
  559 625-2200

**(P-830)**
**CALIFORNIA DAIRIES INC**
11709 Artesia Blvd, Artesia (90701-3803)
PHONE..................................562 809-2595
Joe Heffington, *Brnch Mgr*
**EMP:** 65
**SALES (corp-wide):** 3.32B **Privately Held**
Web: www.californiadairies.com
**SIC: 2026** Milk processing (pasteurizing, homogenizing, bottling)
**PA:** California Dairies, Inc.
  2000 N Plz Dr
  559 625-2200

**(P-831)**
**CRYSTAL CREAM & BUTTER CO (HQ)**
8340 Belvedere Ave, Sacramento (95826-5902)
PHONE..................................916 444-7200
Donald K Hansen, *Ch*
Michael J Newell, *
Dan Kosewski, *
**EMP:** 100 **EST:** 1901
**SQ FT:** 100,000
**SALES (est):** 3.11MM
**SALES (corp-wide):** 2.21B **Privately Held**
Web: www.crystalcreamery.com
**SIC: 2026** 2021 2024 Milk processing (pasteurizing, homogenizing, bottling); Creamery butter; Ice cream and ice milk
**PA:** Hp Hood Llc
  6 Kimball Ln Ste 400
  617 887-3000

**(P-832)**
**DAIRY FARMERS AMERICA INC**
4375 N Ventura Ave, Ventura (93001-1124)
PHONE..................................805 653-0042
Kevin Clark, *Mgr*
**EMP:** 28
**SALES (corp-wide):** 21.72B **Privately Held**
Web: www.dfamilk.com
**SIC: 2026** 2022 2021 2023 Milk processing (pasteurizing, homogenizing, bottling); Natural cheese; Creamery butter; Condensed milk
**PA:** Dairy Farmers Of America, Inc.
  1405 N 98th St
  816 801-6455

**(P-833)**
**DEAN SOCAL LLC**
Also Called: Swiss Dairy
17637 E Valley Blvd, City Of Industry (91744-5731)
PHONE..................................951 734-3950
**EMP:** 140
**SIC: 2026** Fluid milk

**(P-834)**
**FARMDALE CREAMERY LLC**
Also Called: Farmdale
1049 W Base Line St, San Bernardino (92411)
PHONE..................................909 888-4938
Norman R Shotts Ii, *CEO*
Nicholas J Sibilio, *
Norman R Shotts Iii, *Genl Mgr*
Michael Shotts, *General Vice President**
Florence Shotts, *
▲ **EMP:** 100 **EST:** 1978
**SQ FT:** 110,000
**SALES (est):** 7.34MM **Privately Held**
Web: www.farmdale.net
**SIC: 2026** 2022 Buttermilk, cultured; Natural cheese

**(P-835)**
**GENERAL MILLS INC**
Also Called: General Mills
1055 Sandhill Ave, Carson (90746-1312)
P.O. Box 4589 (90749-4589)
PHONE..................................310 605-6108
Jeff Crandle, *Mgr*
**EMP:** 98
**SQ FT:** 62,497
**SALES (corp-wide):** 19.86B **Publicly Held**
Web: www.generalmills.com
**SIC: 2026** 2041 Yogurt; Flour mixes
**PA:** General Mills, Inc.
  1 General Mills Blvd
  763 764-7600

**(P-836)**
**GOLDEN STATE MIXING INC**
415 D St, Turlock (95380-5452)
P.O. Box 3046 (95381-3046)
PHONE..................................209 632-3656
Tim D Brewster, *Pr*
Brant Enoch, *
**EMP:** 30 **EST:** 2009
**SALES (est):** 7.96MM **Privately Held**
Web: www.goldenstatemixing.com
**SIC: 2026** Fluid milk

**(P-837)**
**GOOD CULTURE LLC**
22 Corporate Park, Irvine (92606-3117)
PHONE..................................949 545-9945
Jesse Merrill, *Managing Member*
Anders Eisner, *Managing Member**
**EMP:** 25 **EST:** 2014
**SALES (est):** 2MM **Privately Held**
Web: www.goodculture.com
**SIC: 2026** 2023 Fluid milk; Dry, condensed and evaporated dairy products

**(P-838)**
**HERITAGE DISTRIBUTING COMPANY (PA)**
Also Called: Rex Creamery
5743 Smithway St Ste 105, Commerce (90040)
P.O. Box 668 (90241)
PHONE..................................323 838-1225
Ted S Degroot, *Pr*
**EMP:** 24 **EST:** 1998
**SALES (est):** 68.56MM **Privately Held**
**SIC: 2026** Milk processing (pasteurizing, homogenizing, bottling)

**(P-839)**
**HP HOOD LLC**
8340 Belvedere Ave, Sacramento (95826-5902)
PHONE..................................916 379-9266
Gary Saavedra, *Brnch Mgr*
**EMP:** 296
**SALES (corp-wide):** 2.21B **Privately Held**

## 2026 - Fluid Milk (P-840)

**PRODUCTS & SERVICES SECTION**

Web: www.hood.com
SIC: **2026** Fluid milk
PA: Hp Hood Llc
6 Kimball Ln Ste 400
617 887-3000

### (P-840)
### JACKSON-MITCHELL INC (PA)
Also Called: Meyenburg Goat Milk Products
1240 South Ave, Turlock (95380-5113)
P.O. Box 934 (95381-0934)
PHONE..............................209 667-0786
Robert Jackson, *Ch Bd*
Jonathan Mitchell, *Sec*
Carol Jackson, *Treas*
Doug Buehrle, *CFO*
**EMP:** 22 **EST:** 1934
**SQ FT:** 11,200
**SALES (est):** 14.5MM
**SALES (corp-wide):** 14.5MM **Privately Held**
SIC: **2026** 2023 Milk, ultra-high temperature (longlife); Evaporated milk

### (P-841)
### PAC FILL INC
Also Called: Sun Dairy Co
5471 W San Fernando Rd, Los Angeles (90039-1014)
PHONE..............................818 409-0117
Vahik Sarkissian, *CEO*
Edward Sarkissian, *
Jerry Nicoghosian, *
**EMP:** 25 **EST:** 1977
**SQ FT:** 22,000
**SALES (est):** 9.23MM **Privately Held**
Web: www.sundairy.com
SIC: **2026** 2086 Yogurt; Carbonated soft drinks, bottled and canned

### (P-842)
### PARAMOUNT DAIRY INC
15255 Texaco Ave, Paramount (90723-3917)
PHONE..............................562 361-1800
Phillip C Chang, *Brnch Mgr*
**EMP:** 135
**SALES (corp-wide):** 3.07MM **Privately Held**
Web: www.paramount-dairy.com
SIC: **2026** Yogurt
PA: Paramount Dairy, Inc.
17801 Cartwright Rd
949 265-8077

### (P-843)
### REBBL INC
Also Called: Rebbl
5900 Hollis St Ste L, Emeryville (94608-2000)
PHONE..............................855 732-2500
Michele Kessler, *CEO*
**EMP:** 25 **EST:** 2011
**SALES (est):** 21.65MM
**SALES (corp-wide):** 35.69MM **Privately Held**
Web: www.rebbl.com
SIC: **2026** 2086 Milk drinks, flavored; Fruit drinks (less than 100% juice): packaged in cans, etc.
PA: Systm Brands Llc
3 Corporate Plaza Dr # 100

### (P-844)
### SAPUTO CHEESE USA INC
299 5th Ave, Gustine (95322-1202)
PHONE..............................209 854-6461
Richard Rosemire, *Brnch Mgr*
**EMP:** 175
**SQ FT:** 5,000

**SALES (corp-wide):** 3.79B **Privately Held**
Web: www.saputo.com
SIC: **2026** Milk processing (pasteurizing, homogenizing, bottling)
HQ: Saputo Cheese Usa Inc.
10700 W Res Dr Ste 400
Milwaukee WI 53226

### (P-845)
### STREMICKS HERITAGE FOODS LLC (HQ)
Also Called: Heritage Foods
4002 Westminster Ave, Santa Ana (92703-1310)
PHONE..............................714 775-5000
Louis J Stremick, *Managing Member*
Michael W Malone, *
Jack P Noenickx, *Managing Member**
▼ **EMP:** 300 **EST:** 1916
**SALES (est):** 574.58MM
**SALES (corp-wide):** 21.72B **Privately Held**
Web: www.heritage-foods.com
SIC: **2026** Cream, sour
PA: Dairy Farmers Of America, Inc.
1405 N 98th St
816 801-6455

### (P-846)
### WIN SOON INC
Also Called: Epoca Yocoool
4569 Firestone Blvd, South Gate (90280-3343)
PHONE..............................323 564-5070
Junsang Lee, *Pr*
Jun Sang Lee, *
▲ **EMP:** 52 **EST:** 1993
**SQ FT:** 7,000
**SALES (est):** 8.66MM **Privately Held**
Web: www.winsoonepoca.com
SIC: **2026** 5149 Yogurt; Soft drinks

---

## 2032 Canned Specialties

### (P-847)
### AFP ADVANCED FOOD PRODUCTS LLC
Also Called: Advanced Food Products
1211 E Noble Ave, Visalia (93292-3040)
PHONE..............................559 627-2070
Barry Ritchard, *Brnch Mgr*
**EMP:** 54
**SALES (corp-wide):** 355.83K **Privately Held**
Web: www.afpllc.com
SIC: **2032** 2022 2026 Puddings, except meat: packaged in cans, jars, etc.; Cheese spreads, dips, pastes, and other cheese products; Fluid milk
HQ: Afp Advanced Food Products Llc
402 S Custer Ave
New Holland PA 17557
717 355-8667

### (P-848)
### AMY LACEY PROJECT
Also Called: Cali'flour Foods
1057 Village Ln, Chico (95926-2812)
PHONE..............................866 422-3568
**EMP:** 22 **EST:** 2017
**SALES (est):** 2.54MM **Privately Held**
Web: www.soursopnutrition.com
SIC: **2032** Italian foods, nec: packaged in cans, jars, etc.

### (P-849)
### BELLISSIMO DISTRIBUTION LLC
Also Called: Greco and Sons
1389 Park Center Dr, Vista (92081-8338)

PHONE..............................760 292-9100
**EMP:** 49
**SALES (corp-wide):** 78.84B **Publicly Held**
Web: www.grecoandsons.com
SIC: **2032** Italian foods, nec: packaged in cans, jars, etc.
HQ: Bellissimo Distribution, Llc
1550 Hecht Dr
Bartlett IL 60103

### (P-850)
### BOBBY SLZARS MXCAN FD PDTS INC (PA)
Also Called: Bobby Salazar Corporate
2810 San Antonio Dr, Fowler (93625-9799)
PHONE..............................559 834-4787
Robert Salazar, *CEO*
Bobby Salazar, *
Charles Gamoian, *
**EMP:** 25 **EST:** 1996
**SQ FT:** 16,375
**SALES (est):** 9.66MM **Privately Held**
Web: www.bobbysalazar.com
SIC: **2032** 5812 Mexican foods, nec: packaged in cans, jars, etc.; Mexican restaurant

### (P-851)
### CAER INC
Also Called: Yumi
8070 Melrose Ave, Los Angeles (90046-7015)
PHONE..............................415 879-9864
Angela Sutherland, *CEO*
Evelyn Rusli, *
▲ **EMP:** 27 **EST:** 2015
**SALES (est):** 5.86MM **Privately Held**
Web: www.helloyumi.com
SIC: **2032** 7389 Baby foods, including meats: packaged in cans, jars, etc.; Business Activities at Non-Commercial Site

### (P-852)
### CG FINANCIAL LLC
Also Called: SD Fresh Products
7020 Alamitos Ave Ste B, San Diego (92154-4710)
P.O. Box 212996 (91921-2996)
PHONE..............................619 656-2919
Gustavo Gonzalez Junior, *Managing Member*
Catherine Gonzalez, *Pr*
**EMP:** 15 **EST:** 2011
**SALES (est):** 1.6MM **Privately Held**
SIC: **2032** Mexican foods, nec: packaged in cans, jars, etc.

### (P-853)
### CORN MAIDEN FOODS INC
24201 Frampton Ave, Harbor City (90710-2105)
PHONE..............................310 784-0400
Pascal Dropsy, *Pr*
**EMP:** 65 **EST:** 1995
**SQ FT:** 40,000
**SALES (est):** 3.49MM **Privately Held**
Web: www.cornmaidenfoods.com
SIC: **2032** Canned specialties

### (P-854)
### DOLORES CANNING CO INC
1020 N Eastern Ave, Los Angeles (90063-3214)
P.O. Box 63187 (90063-0187)
PHONE..............................323 263-9155
David Munoz, *Pr*
Steve A Munoz, *
Frank T Munoz, *
**EMP:** 25 **EST:** 1956
**SQ FT:** 5,000

**SALES (est):** 6.09MM **Privately Held**
Web: www.dolorescanning.com
SIC: **2032** 2011 Mexican foods, nec: packaged in cans, jars, etc.; Meat packing plants

### (P-855)
### EXPRO MANUFACTURING CORPORATION
2800 Ayers Ave, Vernon (90058-4302)
PHONE..............................323 415-8544
▲ **EMP:** 20
SIC: **2032** Canned specialties

### (P-856)
### FRESH PACKING CORPORATION
4333 S Maywood Ave, Vernon (90058-2521)
P.O. Box 3009 (91803-0009)
PHONE..............................213 612-0136
Monica Zambada Lopez, *CEO*
**EMP:** 20 **EST:** 2009
**SALES (est):** 6.11MM **Privately Held**
Web: www.freshpacking.net
SIC: **2032** Chili, with or without meat: packaged in cans, jars, etc.

### (P-857)
### GIORGIOS RESTAURANT ITALIANO
99 Rock Rd, Greenbrae (94904-2644)
PHONE..............................415 925-0808
George Dexter, *Owner*
**EMP:** 30 **EST:** 2002
**SALES (est):** 490.14K **Privately Held**
Web: www.giorgiosrestaurant.com
SIC: **2032** Italian foods, nec: packaged in cans, jars, etc.

### (P-858)
### IF COPACK LLC
Also Called: Initiative Foods
1912 Industrial Way, Sanger (93657-9508)
PHONE..............................559 875-3354
John Ypma, *Pr*
Jeff Jankovic, *
**EMP:** 42 **EST:** 2017
**SQ FT:** 51,348
**SALES (est):** 1.76MM **Privately Held**
Web: www.initiativefoods.com
SIC: **2032** Baby foods, including meats: packaged in cans, jars, etc.

### (P-859)
### INITIATIVE FOODS LLC
1912 Industrial Way, Sanger (93657-9508)
PHONE..............................559 875-3354
Richard Turner, *
**EMP:** 130 **EST:** 2007
**SALES (est):** 20.8MM
**SALES (corp-wide):** 20.8MM **Privately Held**
Web: www.initiativefoods.com
SIC: **2032** Baby foods, including meats: packaged in cans, jars, etc.
PA: If Holding, Inc.
1912 Industrial Way
559 875-3354

### (P-860)
### JIMENEZ MEXICAN FOODS INC
20343 Harvill Ave, Perris (92570-7237)
PHONE..............................951 351-0102
Veronica Jimenez, *Admn*
Roberto Jimenez, *CEO*
**EMP:** 20 **EST:** 2001
**SALES (est):** 4.9MM **Privately Held**
Web: www.jimenezfoods.com

# 2033 - Canned Fruits And Specialties (P-882)

SIC: 2032 Mexican foods, nec: packaged in cans, jars, etc.

### (P-861)
**JUANITAS FOODS**
Also Called: Pico Pica Foods
645 George De La Torre Jr Ave, Wilmington (90744-6055)
P.O. Box 847 (90748-0847)
PHONE..................................310 834-5339
Aaron De La Torre, CEO
Mark De La Torre, *
James Steveson, *
EMP: 125 EST: 1946
SQ FT: 85,000
SALES (est): 54.62MM Privately Held
Web: www.juanitas.com
SIC: 2032 Mexican foods, nec: packaged in cans, jars, etc.

### (P-862)
**KINGS ASIAN GOURMET INC**
683 Brannan St Unit 304, San Francisco (94107-1592)
PHONE..................................415 222-6100
Inja Wang, Pr
▲ EMP: 37 EST: 1963
SQ FT: 25,000
SALES (est): 2.31MM Privately Held
Web: www.kingsasian.com
SIC: 2032 Ethnic foods, canned, jarred, etc.

### (P-863)
**KRAFT HEINZ FOODS COMPANY**
Heinz
2450 White Rd, Irvine (92614-6250)
PHONE..................................949 250-4080
Dan Foss, Brnch Mgr
EMP: 26
SALES (corp-wide): 26.64B Publicly Held
Web: www.kraftheinzcompany.com
SIC: 2032 2035 Soups, except seafood: packaged in cans, jars, etc.; Seasonings and sauces, except tomato and dry
HQ: Kraft Heinz Foods Company
1 Ppg Pl Ste 3400
Pittsburgh PA 15222
412 456-5700

### (P-864)
**LA CASCADA INC**
1940 Union St Ste 10, Oakland (94607-2352)
PHONE..................................510 452-3663
Mohammad Bahrani, Pr
Asad Bahrani, Sec
Mohsen Bahrani, CFO
EMP: 19 EST: 2018
SQ FT: 2,500
SALES (est): 794.78K Privately Held
SIC: 2032 Mexican foods, nec: packaged in cans, jars, etc.

### (P-865)
**LA INDIANA TAMALES INC**
1142 S Indiana St, Los Angeles (90023-3215)
PHONE..................................323 262-4682
Raul Ramos, Pr
EMP: 15 EST: 1999
SQ FT: 8,000
SALES (est): 719.89K Privately Held
Web: www.laindianatamales.com
SIC: 2032 Tamales: packaged in cans, jars, etc.

### (P-866)
**MARIN FOOD SPECIALTIES INC**
14800 Byron Hwy, Byron (94514-0017)
P.O. Box 609 (94514-0609)
PHONE..................................925 634-6106
Ma De Lourdes Medina Ortega, CEO
Ana Ivette Garcia, *
Maria De Lourdes Campos, *
◆ EMP: 35 EST: 1974
SQ FT: 27,000
SALES (est): 4.84MM Privately Held
Web: www.marinfoods.com
SIC: 2032 Canned specialties

### (P-867)
**MASONGATE INC**
2800 Ayers Ave, Vernon (90058-4302)
PHONE..................................323 415-8544
EMP: 20
SIC: 2032 6552 Canned specialties; Subdividers and developers, nec

### (P-868)
**SALICO FARMS INC**
4231 Us Highway 86 Ste 4, Brawley (92227-9648)
P.O. Box 1531 (92227-0229)
PHONE..................................760 344-5375
Niaz Mohamed Junior, Pr
Sara Ann Mohamed, *
Martin Mohamed, *
EMP: 120 EST: 1981
SQ FT: 2,400
SALES (est): 472.61K Privately Held
SIC: 2032 Beans and bean sprouts, canned, jarred, etc.

### (P-869)
**SHINE FOOD INC (PA)**
19216 Normandie Ave, Torrance (90502-1011)
PHONE..................................310 329-3829
Stephen Y S Lee, CEO
Tracy Lee, *
▲ EMP: 50 EST: 1986
SQ FT: 30,000
SALES (est): 13.37MM
SALES (corp-wide): 13.37MM Privately Held
Web: www.shinefoods.com
SIC: 2032 Canned specialties

### (P-870)
**SUPERIOR QUALITY FOODS INC**
Also Called: Superior Touch
2355 E Francis St, Ontario (91761-7727)
P.O. Box 908 (30162-0908)
PHONE..................................909 923-4733
▲ EMP: 63
SIC: 2032 2034 Canned specialties; Dried and dehydrated soup mixes

### (P-871)
**T & T FOODS INC**
Also Called: Colonel Lee's Enterprises
3080 E 50th St, Vernon (90058-2918)
PHONE..................................323 588-2158
Michelle Ma, CEO
David Ma, VP
EMP: 50 EST: 1967
SQ FT: 19,000
SALES (est): 4.88MM Privately Held
Web: www.tandtfoods.net
SIC: 2032 2099 Ethnic foods, canned, jarred, etc.; Food preparations, nec

### (P-872)
**WEI LABORATORIES INC**
3002 Scott Blvd, Santa Clara (95054-3723)
PHONE..................................408 970-8700
Jeffery Wei, CEO
Jeffrey Horan, *
Sarah Li, VP
EMP: 25 EST: 2002
SALES (est): 3.28MM Privately Held
Web: www.weilab.com
SIC: 2032 Chinese foods, nec: packaged in cans, jars, etc.

### (P-873)
**WING HING FOODS LLC**
Also Called: Wing Hing
1659 E 23rd St, Los Angeles (90011-1803)
PHONE..................................323 232-8899
▲ EMP: 90
Web: www.winghing.com
SIC: 2032 Ethnic foods, canned, jarred, etc.

## 2033 Canned Fruits And Specialties

### (P-874)
**ABSINTHE GROUP INC**
2043 Airpark Ct Ste 30, Auburn (95602-9009)
PHONE..................................530 823-8527
Kim Sullivan, Dir
EMP: 47
SALES (corp-wide): 17.52MM Privately Held
Web: www.absinthe.com
SIC: 2033 2099 8742 2035 Barbecue sauce: packaged in cans, jars, etc.; Food preparations, nec; Food and beverage consultant; Pickles, sauces, and salad dressings
PA: The Absinthe Group Inc
368 Hayes St
415 864-2693

### (P-875)
**AMAZON PRSRVATION PARTNERS INC**
Also Called: Zola Acai
1550 Leigh Ave, San Jose (95125-5301)
PHONE..................................415 775-6355
Chris Cuvelier, CEO
▲ EMP: 24 EST: 2002
SALES (est): 2.1MM Privately Held
Web: www.livezola.com
SIC: 2033 Fruit juices: fresh

### (P-876)
**ASEPTIC TECHNOLOGY LLC**
Also Called: Aseptic Technology
24855 Corbit Pl, Yorba Linda (92887-5543)
PHONE..................................714 694-0168
Julie Hodson, *
Noel Calma, *
Clay White, *
Lan Pham, *
EMP: 117 EST: 2013
SQ FT: 59,300
SALES (est): 6.53MM Privately Held
Web: www.asepticllc.com
SIC: 2033 Canned fruits and specialties

### (P-877)
**BEAUMONT JUICE LLC**
Also Called: Perricone Juices
550 B St, Beaumont (92223)
PHONE..................................951 769-7171
Robert Paul Rovzar, CEO
Thomas M Carmody, *
Joe Perricone, *
Paul Golub, *
▲ EMP: 98 EST: 1994
SQ FT: 30,000
SALES (est): 37.91MM
SALES (corp-wide): 37.91MM Privately Held
Web: www.perriconefarms.com

SIC: 2033 Fruit juices: fresh
PA: G B & P Citrus Co Inc
1601 E Olympic Blvd Ste 1
213 312-1380

### (P-878)
**BELL-CARTER FOODS INC**
Also Called: BELL-CARTER FOODS, INC.
20497 Avenue 184, Strathmore (93267-9585)
PHONE..................................559 568-1650
EMP: 158
SALES (corp-wide): 114.98MM Privately Held
Web: www.bellcarter.com
SIC: 2033 Olives: packaged in cans, jars, etc.
PA: Bell-Carter Olive Packing Company, Inc.
590 Ygncio Vly Rd Ste 300
209 549-5939

### (P-879)
**BELL-CARTER FOODS INC**
Also Called: Bell-Carter Packaging
4207 Finch Rd, Modesto (95357-4101)
PHONE..................................209 549-5939
Bill Floyd, Mgr
EMP: 20
SALES (corp-wide): 98.01MM Privately Held
Web: www.bellcarter.com
SIC: 2033 Olives: packaged in cans, jars, etc.
PA: Bell-Carter Olive Packing Company, Inc.
590 Ygncio Vly Rd Ste 300
209 549-5939

### (P-880)
**BELL-CARTER OLIVE PACKING CO (PA)**
Also Called: Bell-Carter Olive Company
590 Ygnacio Valley Rd Ste 300, Walnut Creek (94596-3807)
PHONE..................................209 549-5939
Francisco J Escalente, CEO
Paul Adcock, *
Paul Mcginty, VP
Marie Flanigan, *
◆ EMP: 105 EST: 1912
SQ FT: 9,000
SALES (est): 114.98MM
SALES (corp-wide): 114.98MM Privately Held
Web: www.bellcarter.com
SIC: 2033 Olives: packaged in cans, jars, etc.

### (P-881)
**COBBLESTONE FRUIT**
730 N Oliver Ave, Sanger (93657-8918)
P.O. Box 275 (93657-0275)
PHONE..................................559 524-1005
Robert Hives, CEO
EMP: 150 EST: 2022
SALES (est): 9.35MM Privately Held
SIC: 2033 7389 Fruits and fruit products, in cans, jars, etc.; Business services, nec

### (P-882)
**DEL MAR FOOD PRODUCTS CORP**
1720 Beach Rd, Watsonville (95076-9536)
P.O. Box 891 (95077-0891)
PHONE..................................831 722-3516
Paul Joseph Mecozzi, CEO
Paul Wendt, *
Carolyn Mecozzi, *
Robert D Hayes, *
◆ EMP: 100 EST: 1955
SQ FT: 53,408
SALES (est): 23.06MM Privately Held

## 2033 - Canned Fruits And Specialties (P-883)

Web: www.delmarfoods.com
SIC: **2033** 2099 Canned fruits and specialties; Food preparations, nec

**(P-883)**
**DEL MONTE FOODS INC**
Also Called: Del Monte Foods
10652 Jackson Ave, Hanford (93230-9552)
PHONE......................559 639-6160
Ted Leaman, *Mgr*
**EMP:** 64
Web: www.delmontefoods.com
SIC: **2033** 2035 Tomato paste: packaged in cans, jars, etc.; Pickles, sauces, and salad dressings
HQ: Del Monte Foods, Inc.
205 N Wiget Ln
Walnut Creek CA 94598
925 949-2772

**(P-884)**
**DEL MONTE FOODS INC**
Also Called: Del Monte Foods
4000 Yosemite Blvd, Modesto (95357-1580)
P.O. Box 576008 (95357-6008)
PHONE......................209 548-5509
Jim Fullmer, *Mgr*
**EMP:** 62
**SQ FT:** 5,000
Web: www.delmontefoods.com
SIC: **2033** Tomato purees: packaged in cans, jars, etc.
HQ: Del Monte Foods, Inc.
205 N Wiget Ln
Walnut Creek CA 94598
925 949-2772

**(P-885)**
**DEL MONTE FOODS INC**
Also Called: Del Monte Foods
1509 Draper St Ste A, Kingsburg (93631-1950)
P.O. Box 7 (93631-0007)
PHONE......................559 419-9214
Brian Okland, *Mgr*
**EMP:** 18
**SQ FT:** 111,920
Web: www.delmontefoods.com
SIC: **2033** Fruits: packaged in cans, jars, etc.
HQ: Del Monte Foods, Inc.
205 N Wiget Ln
Walnut Creek CA 94598
925 949-2772

**(P-886)**
**DIANA FRUIT CO INC**
651 Mathew St, Santa Clara (95050-2928)
P.O. Box 268 (95052-0268)
PHONE......................408 727-9631
◆ **EMP:** 100
Web: www.dianafruit.com
SIC: **2033** 2099 Fruits and fruit products, in cans, jars, etc.; Food preparations, nec

**(P-887)**
**ESCALON PREMIER BRANDS INC**
1905 Mchenry Ave, Escalon (95320-9361)
PHONE......................209 838-7341
▼ **EMP:** 75
Web: www.kraftheinzcompany.ccm
SIC: **2033** Tomato sauce: packaged in cans, jars, etc.

**(P-888)**
**FRESHSOURCE NORTH INC**
16478 Beach Blvd # 391, Westminster (92683-7860)
PHONE......................805 878-6567
Robert F Thompson, *CEO*
Shawn Dagen, *Pr*
Leith Anderson, *VP*
**EMP:** 18 **EST:** 2012
**SALES (est):** 123.67K **Privately Held**
Web: www.freshsource.info
SIC: **2033** Vegetables and vegetable products, in cans, jars, etc.

**(P-889)**
**G L MEZZETTA INC**
2200 Larkspur Landing Cir, Larkspur (94939-1821)
PHONE......................707 648-1050
Jeffery Mezzetta, *CEO*
**EMP:** 80
**SALES (corp-wide):** 137.64MM **Privately Held**
Web: www.mezzetta.com
SIC: **2033** Pizza sauce: packaged in cans, jars, etc.
PA: G. L. Mezzetta, Inc.
105 Mezzetta Ct
707 648-1050

**(P-890)**
**G L MEZZETTA INC (PA)**
Also Called: Mezzetta
105 Mezzetta Ct, American Canyon (94503-9604)
PHONE......................707 648-1050
Jeffery Mezzetta, *CEO*
Ronald J Mezzetta, *
◆ **EMP:** 114 **EST:** 1957
**SALES (est):** 137.64MM
**SALES (corp-wide):** 137.64MM **Privately Held**
Web: www.mezzetta.com
SIC: **2033** Pizza sauce: packaged in cans, jars, etc.

**(P-891)**
**GEORGE DELALLO COMPANY INC**
Also Called: Delallo Italian Foods
1800 Idora St, Oroville (95966-6767)
PHONE......................530 533-3303
George Hoag, *Mgr*
**EMP:** 15
**SQ FT:** 48,750
**SALES (corp-wide):** 102.3MM **Privately Held**
Web: www.delallo.com
SIC: **2033** Canned fruits and specialties
PA: George Delallo Company, Inc.
1 Delallo Way
877 335-2556

**(P-892)**
**HK CANNING INC (PA)**
130 N Garden St, Ventura (93001-2529)
PHONE......................805 652-1392
Henry Knaust, *Pr*
Carol Knaust, *VP*
**EMP:** 39 **EST:** 1996
**SQ FT:** 91,552
**SALES (est):** 3.35MM **Privately Held**
SIC: **2033** Vegetables: packaged in cans, jars, etc.

**(P-893)**
**HUY FONG FOODS INC**
4800 Azusa Canyon Rd, Irwindale (91706-1938)
PHONE......................626 286-8328
David Tran, *Pr*
Ada Tran, *VP*
Donna Lam, *Sec*
◆ **EMP:** 20 **EST:** 1980
**SQ FT:** 68,000
**SALES (est):** 5.75MM **Privately Held**
Web: www.huyfong.com
SIC: **2033** Chili sauce, tomato: packaged in cans, jars, etc.

**(P-894)**
**INGOMAR PACKING COMPANY LLC (PA)**
9950 S Ingomar Grade, Los Banos (93635)
P.O. Box 1448 (93635-1448)
PHONE......................209 826-9494
Gregory Pruett, *CEO*
John F Bennett, *
William B Cahill Junior, *VP*
◆ **EMP:** 100 **EST:** 1982
**SQ FT:** 10,000
**SALES (est):** 93.45MM
**SALES (corp-wide):** 93.45MM **Privately Held**
Web: www.ingomarpacking.com
SIC: **2033** Tomato paste: packaged in cans, jars, etc.

**(P-895)**
**J M SMUCKER COMPANY**
800 Commercial Ave, Oxnard (93030-7234)
P.O. Box 5161 (93031-5161)
PHONE......................805 487-5483
Al Yamamoto, *Mgr*
**EMP:** 47
**SQ FT:** 20,000
**SALES (corp-wide):** 8.18B **Publicly Held**
Web: www.smuckers.com
SIC: **2033** Canned fruits and specialties
PA: The J M Smucker Company
1 Strawberry Ln
330 682-3000

**(P-896)**
**JACKSON MANUFACTURING LLC**
Also Called: Bear State Kitchen
3515 W Washington Blvd, Los Angeles (90018-1122)
PHONE......................213 399-9300
**EMP:** 18 **EST:** 2020
**SALES (est):** 1.17MM **Privately Held**
SIC: **2033** Canned fruits and specialties

**(P-897)**
**KAGOME INC (HQ)**
333 Johnson Rd, Los Banos (93635-9768)
PHONE......................209 826-8850
Luis De Oliviera, *Pr*
Ann Hall, *
◆ **EMP:** 22 **EST:** 1998
**SQ FT:** 175,000
**SALES (est):** 120.34MM **Privately Held**
Web: www.kagomeusa.com
SIC: **2033** Tomato products, packaged in cans, jars, etc.
PA: Kagome Co., Ltd.
3-21-1, Nihombashihamacho

**(P-898)**
**KRAFT HEINZ FOODS COMPANY**
Also Called: Kraft Foods
1500 E Walnut Ave, Fullerton (92831-4731)
PHONE......................714 870-8235
Robert Pech, *Brnch Mgr*
**EMP:** 65
**SQ FT:** 2,878
**SALES (corp-wide):** 26.64B **Publicly Held**
Web: www.kraftheinzcompany.com
SIC: **2033** Canned fruits and specialties
HQ: Kraft Heinz Foods Company
1 Ppg Pl Ste 3400
Pittsburgh PA 15222
412 456-5700

**(P-899)**
**KRAFT HEINZ FOODS COMPANY**
Also Called: Kraft Foods
2494 S Orange Ave, Fresno (93725-1328)
PHONE......................559 441-8515
Mark Librizzi, *Brnch Mgr*
**EMP:** 32
**SQ FT:** 167,590
**SALES (corp-wide):** 26.64B **Publicly Held**
Web: www.kraftheinzcompany.com
SIC: **2033** Fruit juices: packaged in cans, jars, etc.
HQ: Kraft Heinz Foods Company
1 Ppg Pl Ste 3400
Pittsburgh PA 15222
412 456-5700

**(P-900)**
**LLC LYONS MAGNUS (PA)**
3158 E Hamilton Ave, Fresno (93702)
PHONE......................559 268-5966
Ed Carolan, *CEO*
◆ **EMP:** 285 **EST:** 1967
**SQ FT:** 63,000
**SALES (est):** 927.25MM
**SALES (corp-wide):** 927.25MM **Privately Held**
Web: www.lyonsmagnus.com
SIC: **2033** 2026 2087 Jams, including imitation: packaged in cans, jars, etc.; Yogurt; Syrups, flavoring (except drink)

**(P-901)**
**LLC LYONS MAGNUS**
1636 S 2nd St, Fresno (93702-4143)
PHONE......................559 268-5966
Robert E Smittcamp, *Brnch Mgr*
**EMP:** 174
**SALES (corp-wide):** 927.25MM **Privately Held**
Web: www.lyonsmagnus.com
SIC: **2033** 2026 2087 Jams, including imitation: packaged in cans, jars, etc.; Yogurt; Syrups, flavoring (except drink)
PA: Lyons Magnus, Llc
3158 E Hamilton Ave
559 268-5966

**(P-902)**
**LOS GATOS TOMATO PRODUCTS LLC (PA)**
7041 N Van Ness Blvd, Fresno (93711-7169)
P.O. Box 429 (93234-0429)
PHONE......................559 945-2700
Reuben Peterson, *Managing Member*
◆ **EMP:** 19 **EST:** 1990
**SQ FT:** 35,000
**SALES (est):** 12.58MM **Privately Held**
Web: www.losgatostomato.com
SIC: **2033** Tomato paste: packaged in cans, jars, etc.

**(P-903)**
**LUDFORDS INC**
3038 Pleasant St, Riverside (92507-5554)
PHONE......................909 948-0797
**EMP:** 40 **EST:** 1926
**SALES (est):** 35.84MM **Privately Held**
Web: www.ludfordsinc.com
SIC: **2033** Fruit juices: packaged in cans, jars, etc.

**(P-904)**
**MANZANA PRODUCTS CO INC**
9141 Green Valley Rd, Sebastopol (95472-2245)
P.O. Box 209 (95473-0209)
PHONE......................707 823-5313
Jean-jacques Ducom, *CEO*

Suzanne C Kaido, *
Ralph E Sandborn, *
Edith Norton, *
Richard H Norton, *
◆ **EMP:** 40 **EST:** 1920
**SQ FT:** 91,000
**SALES (est):** 12.72MM **Privately Held**
Web: www.manzanaproductsco.com
**SIC: 2033** 2099 Apple sauce: packaged in cans, jars, etc.; Vinegar

### (P-905)
### MORNING STAR PACKING CO LP
12045 Ingomar Grade, Los Banos (93635-9796)
**PHONE**...............................209 826-8000
**EMP:** 45
Web: www.morningstarco.com
**SIC: 2033** Tomato paste: packaged in cans, jars, etc.
**PA:** The Morning Star Packing Company LP
   13448 Volta Rd

### (P-906)
### MORNING STAR PACKING CO LP
Also Called: Morning Star Packing
2211 Old Highway 99w, Williams (95987-5146)
**PHONE**...............................530 473-3600
Rich Rostomily, *Brnch Mgr*
**EMP:** 30
Web: www.morningstarco.com
**SIC: 2033** Tomato paste: packaged in cans, jars, etc.
**PA:** The Morning Star Packing Company LP
   13448 Volta Rd

### (P-907)
### NASCO GOURMET FOODS INC
Also Called: Platinum Distribution
22720 Savi Ranch Pkwy, Yorba Linda (92887-4608)
**PHONE**...............................714 279-2100
Burhan Nasser, *Pr*
Jerry Pascoe, *
Mary Beth Nasser, *
**EMP:** 90 **EST:** 1990
**SQ FT:** 42,000
**SALES (est):** 3.67MM
**SALES (corp-wide):** 44.16MM **Privately Held**
Web: www.nasserco.com
**SIC: 2033** Seasonings, tomato: packaged in cans, jars, etc.
**PA:** Nasser Company, Inc.
   22720 Savi Ranch Pkwy
   714 279-2100

### (P-908)
### NEIL JONES FOOD COMPANY
San Benito Foods
711 Sally St, Hollister (95023-3934)
P.O. Box 100 (95024-0100)
**PHONE**...............................831 637-0573
Steven Arnoldy, *Mgr*
**EMP:** 42
**SALES (corp-wide):** 133.7MM **Privately Held**
Web: www.neiljonesfoodcompany.com
**SIC: 2033** Canned fruits and specialties
**PA:** The Neil Jones Food Company
   1701 W 16th St
   360 696-4356

### (P-909)
### NEIL JONES FOOD COMPANY
Also Called: Toma Tek
2502 N St, Firebaugh (93622-2456)
P.O. Box 8 (93622-0008)
**PHONE**...............................559 659-5100
Steve Arnoldy, *VP*
**EMP:** 25
**SALES (corp-wide):** 133.7MM **Privately Held**
Web: www.neiljonesfoodcompany.com
**SIC: 2033** Tomato products, packaged in cans, jars, etc.
**PA:** The Neil Jones Food Company
   1701 W 16th St
   360 696-4356

### (P-910)
### OH JUICE INC
5631 Palmer Way Ste A, Carlsbad (92010-7243)
**PHONE**...............................619 318-0207
Hanna Gregor, *CEO*
Michael Mendoza, *Stockholder*
**EMP:** 15 **EST:** 2013
**SALES (est):** 348.56K **Privately Held**
Web: www.ohjuicecleanse.com
**SIC: 2033** Fruit juices: packaged in cans, jars, etc.

### (P-911)
### OLAM TOMATO PROCESSORS INC
1175 S 19th Ave, Lemoore (93245-9747)
**PHONE**...............................559 447-1390
**EMP:** 428
**SALES (corp-wide):** 174.1MM **Privately Held**
Web: www.olamnet.com
**SIC: 2033** Tomato sauce: packaged in cans, jars, etc.
**HQ:** Olam Tomato Processors, Inc.
   205 E River Park Cir # 310
   Fresno CA 93720

### (P-912)
### OLAM TOMATO PROCESSORS INC (DH)
205 E River Park Cir Ste 310, Fresno (93720-1571)
P.O. Box 160 (93245-0160)
**PHONE**...............................559 447-1390
Sunny Verghese, *CEO*
John Gibbons, *
Greg Estep, *
◆ **EMP:** 25 **EST:** 2009
**SALES (est):** 4.25MM
**SALES (corp-wide):** 174.1MM **Privately Held**
Web: www.olamus.com
**SIC: 2033** 0723 Tomato sauce: packaged in cans, jars, etc.; Crop preparation services for market
**HQ:** Olam Americas, Llc
   205 E River Pk Pl Ste 310
   Fresno CA 93720
   559 447-1390

### (P-913)
### OLAM WEST COAST INC
Also Called: Olam Spices and Vegetables
1400 Churchill Downs Ave, Woodland (95776-6146)
**PHONE**...............................530 473-4290
Rich Freidas, *Brnch Mgr*
**EMP:** 109
**SALES (corp-wide):** 174.1MM **Privately Held**
Web: www.olamgroup.com
**SIC: 2033** Tomato products, packaged in cans, jars, etc.
**HQ:** Olam West Coast, Inc.
   205 E Rver Pk Cir Ste 310
   Fresno CA 93720
   559 256-6224

### (P-914)
### OLIVE MUSCO PRODUCTS INC (PA)
Also Called: Musco Family Olive Co
17950 Via Nicolo, Tracy (95377-9767)
**PHONE**...............................866 965-4837
Nicholas Musco, *CEO*
Felix Musco, *
Scott Hamilton, *
▲ **EMP:** 180 **EST:** 1943
**SQ FT:** 350,000
**SALES (est):** 78.47MM
**SALES (corp-wide):** 78.47MM **Privately Held**
Web: www.olives.com
**SIC: 2033** 2035 Canned fruits and specialties; Olives, brined: bulk

### (P-915)
### OM MUSHROOM SUPERFOOD ✪
5931 Priestly Dr Ste 101, Carlsbad (92008-8810)
**PHONE**...............................858 779-1275
**EMP:** 50 **EST:** 2023
**SALES (est):** 397.88K **Privately Held**
Web: www.ommushrooms.com
**SIC: 2033** Mushrooms: packaged in cans, jars, etc.

### (P-916)
### PACIFIC COAST PRODUCERS
Also Called: Contadina Foods
1376 Lemen Ave, Woodland (95776-3369)
**PHONE**...............................530 662-8661
Craig Powell, *Brnch Mgr*
**EMP:** 108
**SALES (corp-wide):** 1.06B **Privately Held**
Web: www.pacificcoastproducers.com
**SIC: 2033** Canned fruits and specialties
**PA:** Pacific Coast Producers
   631 N Cluff Ave
   209 367-8800

### (P-917)
### PACIFIC COAST PRODUCERS (PA)
631 N Cluff Ave, Lodi (95240)
P.O. Box 1600 (95241)
**PHONE**...............................209 367-8800
Matt Strong, *CEO*
Neil Dougherty, *Vice Chairman*
Mona Shulman, *
Aaron Smith, *VP*
Andy Russick, *VP*
◆ **EMP:** 300 **EST:** 1971
**SQ FT:** 20,000
**SALES (est):** 1.06B
**SALES (corp-wide):** 1.06B **Privately Held**
Web: www.pacificcoastproducers.com
**SIC: 2033** Fruits: packaged in cans, jars, etc.

### (P-918)
### PACIFIC COAST PRODUCERS
1601 Mitchell Ave, Oroville (95965-5863)
P.O. Box 311 (95965-0311)
**PHONE**...............................530 533-4311
Niraj Raj, *Prin*
**EMP:** 156
**SQ FT:** 60,000
**SALES (corp-wide):** 1.06B **Privately Held**
Web: www.pacificcoastproducers.com
**SIC: 2033** Fruits: packaged in cans, jars, etc.
**PA:** Pacific Coast Producers
   631 N Cluff Ave
   209 367-8800

### (P-919)
### PACIFIC COAST PRODUCERS
741 S Stockton St, Lodi (95240-4809)
P.O. Box 880 (95241-0880)
**PHONE**...............................209 334-3352
Mike Van Gundy, *Brnch Mgr*
**EMP:** 137
**SALES (corp-wide):** 1.06B **Privately Held**
Web: www.pacificcoastproducers.com
**SIC: 2033** Vegetables: packaged in cans, jars, etc.
**PA:** Pacific Coast Producers
   631 N Cluff Ave
   209 367-8800

### (P-920)
### PURVEYORS KITCHEN
2043 Airpark Ct Ste 30, Auburn (95602-9009)
**PHONE**...............................530 823-8527
Karen Foley, *CEO*
John Foley, *Prin*
**EMP:** 20 **EST:** 2012
**SALES (est):** 4.86MM
**SALES (corp-wide):** 17.52MM **Privately Held**
Web: www.madwills.com
**SIC: 2033** 2099 8742 2035 Barbecue sauce: packaged in cans, jars, etc.; Food preparations, nec; Food and beverage consultant; Pickles, sauces, and salad dressings
**PA:** The Absinthe Group Inc
   368 Hayes St
   415 864-2693

### (P-921)
### REFRESCO BEVERAGES US INC
Also Called: Crosby Fruit Products
11751 Pacific Ave, Fontana (92337-6961)
**PHONE**...............................951 685-0481
Kirk Karassa, *Brnch Mgr*
**EMP:** 150
**SQ FT:** 99,500
Web: www.refresco-na.com
**SIC: 2033** Fruit juices: packaged in cans, jars, etc.
**HQ:** Refresco Beverages Us Inc.
   8112 Woodland Center Blvd
   Tampa FL 33614

### (P-922)
### RIO PLUMA COMPANY LLC (HQ)
1900 State Highway 99, Gridley (95948-9401)
P.O. Box 948 (95948-0948)
**PHONE**...............................530 846-5200
Brad Stapleton, *Pr*
Eric Heitman, *
Gavin Heitman, *
◆ **EMP:** 21 **EST:** 1978
**SQ FT:** 100,000
**SALES (est):** 4.68MM
**SALES (corp-wide):** 18.06MM **Privately Held**
Web: www.stapleton-spence.com
**SIC: 2033** 2034 2068 0723 Fruits and fruit products, in cans, jars, etc.; Dried and dehydrated fruits; Nuts: dried, dehydrated, salted or roasted; Fruit crops market preparation services
**PA:** Stapleton - Spence Packing Co.
   1900 Highway 99
   408 297-8815

### (P-923)
### S MARTINELLI & COMPANY
257 Kearney Ext, Watsonville (95076-4223)
**PHONE**...............................831 768-3958
Emma Kitchen, *Brnch Mgr*
**EMP:** 33
**SALES (corp-wide):** 77.16MM **Privately Held**
Web: www.martinellis.com

# 2033 - Canned Fruits And Specialties (P-924)

SIC: **2033** Canned fruits and specialties
PA: S. Martinelli & Company
735 W Beach St
831 724-1126

### (P-924)
**S MARTINELLI & COMPANY**
1260 W Beach St, Watsonville (95076-5124)
PHONE..............................831 768-3958
Emma Kitchen, *Brnch Mgr*
**EMP:** 33
**SALES (corp-wide):** 77.16MM **Privately Held**
Web: www.martinellis.com
SIC: **2033** Canned fruits and specialties
PA: S. Martinelli & Company
735 W Beach St
831 724-1126

### (P-925)
**SATICOY FOODS CORPORATION**
554 Todd Rd, Santa Paula (93060-9725)
P.O. Box 4547 (93007-0547)
PHONE..............................805 647-5266
**EMP:** 40 **EST:** 1967
**SALES (est):** 12.19MM
**SALES (corp-wide):** 63.59MM **Privately Held**
SIC: **2033** Vegetables: packaged in cans, jars, etc.
PA: Moody Dunbar, Inc.
2000 Waters Edge Dr # 21
423 952-0100

### (P-926)
**SK FOODS LP**
1175 19th Ave, Lemoore (93245-9747)
P.O. Box 160 (93245-0160)
PHONE..............................559 924-6500
◆ **EMP:** 165
SIC: **2033** Tomato products, packaged in cans, jars, etc.

### (P-927)
**STANISLAUS FOOD PRODUCTS CO (PA)**
1202 D St, Modesto (95354-2407)
P.O. Box 3951 (95352-3951)
PHONE..............................209 548-3537
Thomas A Cortopassi, *CEO*
William D Butler, *
Rick Serpa, *
Dino Cortopassi, *Stockholder*
▲ **EMP:** 100 **EST:** 1942
**SQ FT:** 50,000
**SALES (est):** 148.53MM
**SALES (corp-wide):** 148.53MM **Privately Held**
Web: www.stanislaus.com
SIC: **2033** Tomato paste: packaged in cans, jars, etc.

### (P-928)
**STAPLETON - SPENCE PACKING CO (PA)**
Also Called: Stapleton
1900 State Highway 99, Gridley (95948-9401)
PHONE..............................408 297-8815
Martin Bradley Stapleton, *Pr*
Gavin Heitman, *
◆ **EMP:** 79 **EST:** 1951
**SQ FT:** 105,000
**SALES (est):** 18.06MM
**SALES (corp-wide):** 18.06MM **Privately Held**
Web: www.stapleton-spence.com

SIC: **2033** 5085 Fruits and fruit products, in cans, jars, etc.; Cans for fruits and vegetables

### (P-929)
**SUNDOWN FOODS USA INC**
Also Called: Sundown Foods
10891 Business Dr, Fontana (92337-8235)
PHONE..............................909 606-6797
Jeff Wartell, *Pr*
▲ **EMP:** 30 **EST:** 1998
**SALES (est):** 4.14MM **Privately Held**
Web: www.sundownfoods.com
SIC: **2033** Vegetables and vegetable products, in cans, jars, etc.

### (P-930)
**SUNNYGEM LLC (PA)**
Also Called: Sunnygem
500 N F St, Wasco (93280-1435)
PHONE..............................661 758-0491
John Vidovich, *Managing Member*
Ajit Sidhu, *
◆ **EMP:** 116 **EST:** 2005
**SQ FT:** 270,000
**SALES (est):** 41.45MM **Privately Held**
Web: www.sunnygem.com
SIC: **2033** 3556 Fruit juices: fresh; Juice extractors, fruit and vegetable: commercial type

### (P-931)
**TAPATIO FOODS LLC**
Also Called: Tapatio Hot Sauce
4685 District Blvd, Vernon (90058-2731)
PHONE..............................323 587-8933
Jose Luis Saavedra, *Managing Member*
**EMP:** 16 **EST:** 1971
**SQ FT:** 30,000
**SALES (est):** 5.37MM **Privately Held**
Web: www.tapatiohotsauce.com
SIC: **2033** Canned fruits and specialties

### (P-932)
**THE MORNING STAR PACKING COMPANY L P (PA)**
Also Called: Morning Star
13448 Volta Rd, Los Banos (93635-9785)
PHONE..............................209 826-8000
◆ **EMP:** 35 **EST:** 1970
**SALES (est):** 78.13MM **Privately Held**
Web: www.morningstarco.com
SIC: **2033** Tomato paste: packaged in cans, jars, etc.

### (P-933)
**TROPICAL PRESERVING CO INC**
5 Lewiston Ct, Ladera Ranch (92694-0532)
PHONE..............................213 748-5108
Ronald Randall, *Pr*
**EMP:** 23 **EST:** 1928
**SALES (est):** 2.67MM **Privately Held**
Web: www.tropicalpreserving.com
SIC: **2033** Jams, jellies, and preserves, packaged in cans, jars, etc.

### (P-934)
**TROPICANA PRODUCTS INC**
Also Called: Tropicana
240 N Orange Ave, City Of Industry (91744-3433)
PHONE..............................626 968-1299
Kevin Frebert, *Manager*
**EMP:** 21
**SQ FT:** 1,512
**SALES (corp-wide):** 1.11B **Privately Held**
Web: www.tropicana.com
SIC: **2033** Fruit juices: fresh
PA: Tropicana Products, Inc.
433 W Van Buren St Ste 3n

941 747-4461

### (P-935)
**VALLEY VIEW FOODS INC**
7547 Sawtelle Ave, Yuba City (95991-9514)
PHONE..............................530 673-7356
Jaswant Bains, *Pr*
Satwant Bains, *Sec*
**EMP:** 70 **EST:** 2016
**SQ FT:** 80,000
**SALES (est):** 2.47MM **Privately Held**
Web: www.valleyviewfoods.com
SIC: **2033** Fruit juices: fresh

### (P-936)
**VIE-DEL COMPANY (PA)**
11903 S Chestnut Ave, Fresno (93725-9618)
P.O. Box 2908 (93745-2908)
PHONE..............................559 834-2525
Dianne S Nury, *Pr*
Massud S Nury, *
Richard D Watson, *
▲ **EMP:** 75 **EST:** 1946
**SQ FT:** 500,000
**SALES (est):** 28.37MM
**SALES (corp-wide):** 28.37MM **Privately Held**
Web: www.vie-delequipmentsales.com
SIC: **2033** 2084 Fruit juices: concentrated, hot pack; Brandy

### (P-937)
**VITA JUICE CORPORATION**
10725 Sutter Ave, Pacoima (91331-2553)
PHONE..............................818 899-1195
**EMP:** 100
SIC: **2033** Fruit juices: concentrated, hot pack

### (P-938)
**VITA-PAKT CITRUS PRODUCTS CO (PA)**
10000 Stockdale Hwy Ste 390, Bakersfield (93311-3601)
P.O. Box 309 (91723-0309)
PHONE..............................626 332-1101
James R Boyles, *CEO*
Lloyd Shimizu, *
◆ **EMP:** 50 **EST:** 1957
**SALES (est):** 47.18MM
**SALES (corp-wide):** 47.18MM **Privately Held**
Web: www.vita-pakt.com
SIC: **2033** 2037 Apple sauce: packaged in cans, jars, etc.; Fruit juices, frozen

### (P-939)
**VIVE ORGANIC INC**
2554 Lincoln Blvd Ste 772, Venice (90291-5043)
PHONE..............................877 774-9291
Wyatt Taubman, *CEO*
**EMP:** 35 **EST:** 2015
**SALES (est):** 5.27MM
**SALES (corp-wide):** 59.64MM **Privately Held**
Web: www.viveorganic.com
SIC: **2033** Fruit juices: packaged in cans, jars, etc.
PA: Suja Life, Llc
3841 Ocean Ranch Blvd
855 879-7852

### (P-940)
**WALKER FOODS INC**
Also Called: La Flora Del Sur
237 N Mission Rd, Los Angeles (90033-2103)
PHONE..............................323 268-5191

Robert L Walker Junior, *Pr*
Denise Walker, *
**EMP:** 65 **EST:** 1914
**SQ FT:** 150,000
**SALES (est):** 15.06MM **Privately Held**
Web: www.walkerfoods.net
SIC: **2033** 2032 2099 Canned fruits and specialties; Canned specialties; Ready-to-eat meals, salads, and sandwiches

### (P-941)
**WILDBRINE LLC (PA)**
Also Called: Wildbrine
322 Bellevue Ave, Santa Rosa (95407-7711)
PHONE..............................707 657-7607
Chris Glab, *Managing Member*
Richard Goldberg, *
**EMP:** 24 **EST:** 2012
**SQ FT:** 9,000
**SALES (est):** 5.33MM
**SALES (corp-wide):** 5.33MM **Privately Held**
Web: www.wildbrine.com
SIC: **2033** 5149 Sauerkraut: packaged in cans, jars, etc.; Beverages, except coffee and tea

### (P-942)
**WONDERFUL CITRUS PACKING LLC**
1701 S Lexington St, Delano (93215-9200)
PHONE..............................661 720-2400
**EMP:** 17
**SALES (corp-wide):** 2.04B **Privately Held**
Web: www.wonderfulcitrus.com
SIC: **2033** Fruit juices: fresh
HQ: Wonderful Citrus Packing Llc
1901 S Lexington St
Delano CA 93215

---

## 2034 Dehydrated Fruits, Vegetables, Soups

### (P-943)
**AMERICAN FOOD INGREDIENTS INC**
4021 Avenida De La Plata Ste 501, Oceanside (92056-5849)
PHONE..............................760 967-6287
Karen Koppenhaver, *CEO*
▲ **EMP:** 30 **EST:** 1993
**SQ FT:** 2,000
**SALES (est):** 7.73MM **Privately Held**
Web: www.americanfoodingredients.com
SIC: **2034** Dried and dehydrated vegetables

### (P-944)
**B & R FARMS LLC**
5280 Fairview Rd, Hollister (95023-9009)
PHONE..............................831 637-9168
Jim Rossey, *Prin*
Mari Rossi, *Prin*
▲ **EMP:** 34 **EST:** 1979
**SALES (est):** 3.31MM **Privately Held**
Web: www.brfarms.com
SIC: **2034** 0191 Dried and dehydrated fruits; General farms, primarily crop

### (P-945)
**BASIC AMERICAN INC (PA)**
Also Called: Basic American Foods
1676 N California Blvd Ste 525, Walnut Creek (94596-5170)
PHONE..............................800 227-4050
Bryan Reese, *Pr*
James Collins, *
Amanda Neel, *

# PRODUCTS & SERVICES SECTION

## 2034 - Dehydrated Fruits, Vegetables, Soups (P-967)

John Barnecut, *
▼ EMP: 60 EST: 1986
SALES (est): 354.03MM
SALES (corp-wide): 354.03MM Privately Held
Web: www.baf.com
SIC: 2034 2099 Potato products, dried and dehydrated; Potatoes, peeled for the trade

### (P-946) CAL RANCH INC (PA)
Also Called: Cal Ranch Wines
4070 Nelson Ave Ste D, Concord (94520-1231)
P.O. Box 608 (94517)
PHONE.....................925 429-2900
Juliana Colline, Pr
Charles Deng, *
◆ EMP: 36 EST: 1998
SALES (est): 8.27MM
SALES (corp-wide): 8.27MM Privately Held
Web: www.calranchfood.com
SIC: 2034 2084 5146 Dried and dehydrated fruits; Wine cellars, bonded: engaged in blending wines; Seafoods

### (P-947) CARO NUT COMPANY
2904 S Angus Ave Ste 106, Fresno (93725-1939)
PHONE.....................559 475-5471
EMP: 176
SALES (corp-wide): 99.6MM Privately Held
Web: www.caro-nut.com
SIC: 2034 Dried and dehydrated fruits
HQ: Caro Nut Company
2885 S Cherry Ave
Fresno CA 93706
559 475-5400

### (P-948) CARUTHERS RAISIN PKG CO INC (PA)
12797 S Elm Ave, Caruthers (93609-9711)
PHONE.....................559 864-9448
Donald Kizirian, Pr
Don Kizirian, *
Dennis Housepian, *
Gina Elsea, *
◆ EMP: 68 EST: 1985
SQ FT: 4,000
SALES (est): 10.19MM
SALES (corp-wide): 10.19MM Privately Held
Web: www.caruthersraisinpacking.com
SIC: 2034 5084 4513 Dried and dehydrated fruits, vegetables and soup mixes; Processing and packaging equipment; Air courier services

### (P-949) CLARA FOODS CO
1 Tower Pl Fl 8, South San Francisco (94080-1828)
PHONE.....................650 733-4015
Arturo Elizondo, CEO
EMP: 18 EST: 2015
SALES (est): 5.2MM Privately Held
Web: www.clarafoods.com
SIC: 2034 Dried and dehydrated fruits, vegetables and soup mixes

### (P-950) CULINARY FARMS INC
1244 E Beamer St, Woodland (95776-6002)
PHONE.....................916 375-3000
Kirk Bewley, Pr

▲ EMP: 50 EST: 1994
SALES (est): 9.15MM Privately Held
Web: www.culinaryfarms.com
SIC: 2034 Dried and dehydrated vegetables

### (P-951) INLAND EMPIRE FOODS INC (PA)
5425 Wilson St, Riverside (92509-2434)
PHONE.....................951 682-8222
Mark H Sterner, Pr
Paul Stiritz, *
▼ EMP: 35 EST: 1985
SQ FT: 85,000
SALES (est): 10.57MM
SALES (corp-wide): 10.57MM Privately Held
Web: www.inlandempirefoods.com
SIC: 2034 Vegetables, dried or dehydrated (except freeze-dried)

### (P-952) JAIN FARM FRESH FOODS INC (DH)
Also Called: White Oak Frozen Foods
2525 Cooper Ave, Merced (95348-4313)
PHONE.....................541 481-2522
Jack Sollazzo, Pr
Frank Wells Stkldr, Prin
Mike Kilfoy Stkldr, Prin
Narinder Gupta, *
Suvan Sharma, *
◆ EMP: 22 EST: 1993
SQ FT: 75,000
SALES (est): 24.98MM Privately Held
Web: www.jainfarmfresh.us
SIC: 2034 Dried and dehydrated vegetables
HQ: Jain America Foods, Inc.
1819 Walcutt Rd Ste 1
Columbus OH 43228

### (P-953) KERN DELTA CO LLC
2513 W Shaw Ave Ste 101, Fresno (93711-3322)
PHONE.....................559 276-2855
Dwight J Wiegand, Managing Member
Walter R Fisher Junior, Managing Member
Leslie Sagouspe, Prin
EMP: 28 EST: 2014
SALES (est): 6.34MM Privately Held
Web: www.mesaverdetrading.com
SIC: 2034 Dried and dehydrated fruits, vegetables and soup mixes

### (P-954) LAUMIERE GOURMET FRUITS CO LLC
3331 Pegasus Dr Ste 101, Bakersfield (93308-6870)
PHONE.....................661 218-9768
EMP: 18 EST: 2019
SALES (est): 2.16MM Privately Held
Web: www.laumieregourmet.com
SIC: 2034 Dried and dehydrated fruits, vegetables and soup mixes

### (P-955) LION RAISINS INC (PA)
Also Called: Lion Packing Co
9500 S De Wolf Ave, Selma (93662-9534)
P.O. Box 1350 (93662-1350)
PHONE.....................559 834-6677
Alfred Lion Junior, Pr
Bruce Lion, *
Isabel Lion, *
Larry Lion, *
◆ EMP: 220 EST: 1903
SQ FT: 130,000

SALES (est): 48.01MM
SALES (corp-wide): 48.01MM Privately Held
Web: www.lionraisins.com
SIC: 2034 Raisins

### (P-956) MARIANI PACKING CO INC
Also Called: Mariani Bros
9281 State Highway 70, Marysville (95901-3064)
PHONE.....................530 749-6565
Mark Kettmann, Mgr
EMP: 237
SALES (corp-wide): 114.7MM Privately Held
Web: www.mariani.com
SIC: 2034 Prunes, dried
PA: Mariani Packing Co., Inc.
500 Crocker Dr
707 452-2800

### (P-957) MELKONIAN ENTERPRISES INC
Also Called: California Fruit Basket
2730 S De Wolf Ave, Sanger (93657-9770)
PHONE.....................559 217-0749
Mark Melkonian, CEO
Douglas Melkonian, VP
Dennis Melkonian, VP
EMP: 20 EST: 1951
SQ FT: 160,000
SALES (est): 4.11MM Privately Held
SIC: 2034 0172 5431 Raisins; Grapes; Fruit stands or markets

### (P-958) MERCER FOODS LLC (PA)
Also Called: Mercer Foods
1836 Lapham Dr, Modesto (95354-3900)
PHONE.....................877 743-5373
Hendrik Jacobs, CEO
▲ EMP: 254 EST: 1988
SQ FT: 160,000
SALES (est): 52.41MM
SALES (corp-wide): 52.41MM Privately Held
Web: www.thrivefoods.com
SIC: 2034 Dried and dehydrated fruits, vegetables and soup mixes

### (P-959) NAMAR FOODS
Also Called: Namar Company
6830 Walthall Way, Paramount (90723-2028)
PHONE.....................562 531-2744
EMP: 38 EST: 1962
SALES (est): 5.11MM Privately Held
Web: www.namar.com
SIC: 2034 Dried and dehydrated fruits, vegetables and soup mixes

### (P-960) RAY MOLES FARMS INC (PA)
9503 S Hughes Ave, Fresno (93706-9731)
PHONE.....................559 444-0324
Ray Moles, Pr
EMP: 29 EST: 1975
SALES (est): 8.53MM
SALES (corp-wide): 8.53MM Privately Held
SIC: 2034 Raisins

### (P-961) RIVER RANCH RAISINS INC
4087 N Howard Ave, Kerman (93630-9674)
P.O. Box 27 (93606-0027)
PHONE.....................559 843-2294
Troy Gillespie, Pr

Troy Gillespie, CEO
Barbara Gillespie, *
Linda Kay Abdulian, *
EMP: 46 EST: 2015
SALES (est): 5.91MM Privately Held
Web: www.rrraisins.com
SIC: 2034 Raisins

### (P-962) SACRAMENTO PACKING INC
833 Tudor Rd, Yuba City (95991-9532)
P.O. Box 3540 (95992-3540)
PHONE.....................530 671-4488
Jaswant S Bains, Pr
◆ EMP: 300 EST: 1991
SQ FT: 80,000
SALES (est): 23.78MM Privately Held
Web: www.sacramentopacking.com
SIC: 2034 Dried and dehydrated fruits, vegetables and soup mixes

### (P-963) SAN JOAQUIN FIGS INC
Also Called: Nutra-Figs
3564 N Hazel Ave, Fresno (93722-4912)
P.O. Box 9547 (93793-9547)
PHONE.....................559 224-4492
Keith Jura, Pr
Mary Jura, *
◆ EMP: 50 EST: 1989
SQ FT: 18,000
SALES (est): 10.57MM Privately Held
Web: www.nutrafig.com
SIC: 2034 2099 Dried and dehydrated fruits, vegetables and soup mixes; Food preparations, nec

### (P-964) SENSIENT DEHYDRATED FLAVORS COMPANY
151 S Walnut Rd, Turlock (95380-5127)
P.O. Box 1524 (95381-1524)
PHONE.....................209 667-2777
◆ EMP: 550
SIC: 2034 Dried and dehydrated fruits, vegetables and soup mixes

### (P-965) SUN VLLEY RSINS INC A CAL CORP
9595 S Hughes Ave, Fresno (93706-9731)
PHONE.....................559 233-8070
Ermel Ray Moles, Pr
Debra Moles, VP
▼ EMP: 15 EST: 2007
SQ FT: 18,000
SALES (est): 5.61MM Privately Held
Web: www.sunvalleyraisins.com
SIC: 2034 Dried and dehydrated fruits

### (P-966) SUNRISE FRESH LLC
Also Called: Sunrise Fresh Fruit and Nut Co
237 N Golden Gate Ave, Stockton (95205-4768)
P.O. Box 128 (95236-0128)
PHONE.....................209 932-0192
James Samuel, *
EMP: 70 EST: 2003
SQ FT: 42,000
SALES (est): 5.11MM Privately Held
Web: www.sunrisefresh.com
SIC: 2034 Dried and dehydrated fruits, vegetables and soup mixes

### (P-967) SUNSWEET DRYERS
23760 Loleta Ave, Corning (96021-9699)
P.O. Box 201 (96021-0201)

## 2034 - Dehydrated Fruits, Vegetables, Soups (P-968)

PHONE.................................530 824-5854
Dan Lima, *Mgr*
**EMP:** 238
**SALES (corp-wide):** 244.87MM **Privately Held**
Web: www.sunsweet.com
**SIC: 2034** Prunes, dried
HQ: Sunsweet Dryers
901 N Walton Ave
Yuba City CA 95993
530 846-5578

**(P-968)**
**SUNSWEET DRYERS**
26 E Evans Reimer Rd, Gridley (95948-9544)
PHONE.................................530 846-5578
Jeff Wilson, *Mgr*
**EMP:** 238
**SALES (corp-wide):** 244.87MM **Privately Held**
Web: www.sunsweet.com
**SIC: 2034** Prunes, dried
HQ: Sunsweet Dryers
901 N Walton Ave
Yuba City CA 95993
530 846-5578

**(P-969)**
**SUNSWEET GROWERS INC**
23760 Loleta Ave, Corning (96021-9699)
P.O. Box 201 (96021-0201)
PHONE.................................530 824-5376
Robert Safford, *Mgr*
**EMP:** 60
**SALES (corp-wide):** 244.87MM **Privately Held**
Web: www.sunsweet.com
**SIC: 2034** Dried and dehydrated fruits, vegetables and soup mixes
PA: Sunsweet Growers Inc.
901 N Walton Ave
800 417-2253

**(P-970)**
**SUNSWEET GROWERS INC (PA)**
901 N Walton Ave, Yuba City (95993-9370)
PHONE.................................800 417-2253
Brad Schuler, *CEO*
Brendon S Flynn, *
Ana Klein, *
Matt Kelly, *
Melvin Ward, *
◆ **EMP:** 600 **EST:** 1917
**SQ FT:** 1,200,000
**SALES (est):** 244.87MM
**SALES (corp-wide):** 244.87MM **Privately Held**
Web: www.sunsweet.com
**SIC: 2034** 2037 2086 Dried and dehydrated fruits; Fruit juices; Fruit drinks (less than 100% juice); packaged in cans, etc.

**(P-971)**
**TRUE LEAF FARMS LLC (PA)**
1275 San Justo Rd, San Juan Bautista (95045-9733)
P.O. Box 509 (93902-0509)
PHONE.................................831 623-4667
Rio Farms, *Managing Member*
**EMP:** 102 **EST:** 2002
**SALES (est):** 88.83MM
**SALES (corp-wide):** 88.83MM **Privately Held**
Web: www.trueleaffarms.com
**SIC: 2034** Vegetables, dried or dehydrated (except freeze-dried)

**(P-972)**
**VACAVILLE FRUIT CO INC (PA)**
2055 Cessna Dr Ste 200, Vacaville (95688-8838)
P.O. Box 1537 (95696-1537)
PHONE.................................707 448-5292
Nicole Ciarabellini, *Prin*
◆ **EMP:** 40 **EST:** 1960
**SQ FT:** 15,000
**SALES (est):** 10.67MM
**SALES (corp-wide):** 10.67MM **Privately Held**
Web: www.vacavillefruit.com
**SIC: 2034** Prunes, dried

**(P-973)**
**VICTOR PACKING INC**
11687 Rd 27 1/2, Madera (93637-9440)
PHONE.................................559 673-5908
Victor Sahatdjian, *Pr*
Margaret Sahatdjian, *
◆ **EMP:** 50 **EST:** 1963
**SQ FT:** 150,000
**SALES (est):** 1.66MM **Privately Held**
Web: www.victorpacking.com
**SIC: 2034** Raisins

**(P-974)**
**ZORIA FARMS INC (PA)**
3487 Mckee Rd Ste 54, San Jose (95127-2269)
PHONE.................................559 673-6368
FAX: 408 673-7508
◆ **EMP:** 450 **EST:** 1921
**SALES (est):** 35.51MM
**SALES (corp-wide):** 35.51MM **Privately Held**
Web: www.zoria.com
**SIC: 2034** Fruits, dried or dehydrated, except freeze-dried

## 2035 Pickles, Sauces, And Salad Dressings

**(P-975)**
**BELL-CARTER FOODS LLC**
1012 2nd St, Corning (96021-3248)
PHONE.................................530 528-4820
Steve Henderson, *Brnch Mgr*
**EMP:** 300
Web: www.bellcarter.com
**SIC: 2035** 2033 Olives, brined: bulk; Canned fruits and specialties
HQ: Bell-Carter Foods, Llc
590 Yngcio Vly Rd Ste 220
Walnut Creek CA 94596
530 528-4883

**(P-976)**
**CALCHEF FOODS LLC (HQ)**
Also Called: Kevin's Natural Foods
4221 E Mariposa Rd Ste B, Stockton (95215-8139)
PHONE.................................888 638-7083
Kevin Mccray, *Pr*
Valerie Ellis, *CFO*
**EMP:** 20 **EST:** 2012
**SALES (est):** 80.78MM
**SALES (corp-wide):** 42.84B **Privately Held**
Web: www.kevinsnaturalfoods.com
**SIC: 2035** 2032 5142 Pickles, sauces, and salad dressings; Ethnic foods, canned, jarred, etc.; Dinners, frozen
PA: Mars, Incorporated
6885 Elm St
703 821-4900

**(P-977)**
**EAT JUST INC (PA)**
Also Called: Just Egg
1145 Atlantic Ave, Alameda (94501)
PHONE.................................844 423-6637
Joshua Tetrick, *CEO*
**EMP:** 55 **EST:** 2011
**SALES (est):** 100.92MM
**SALES (corp-wide):** 100.92MM **Privately Held**
Web: www.ju.st
**SIC: 2035** 2052 5147 Mayonnaise; Cookies; Meats and meat products

**(P-978)**
**GEDNEY FOODS COMPANY**
12243 Branford St, Sun Valley (91352-1010)
P.O. Box 8 (55318-0008)
PHONE.................................952 448-2612
Charles Weil, *CEO*
Barry Stecter, *
Carl Tuttle, *
James R Cook, *Technology Vice President*
▲ **EMP:** 125 **EST:** 1881
**SALES (est):** 2.32MM **Privately Held**
Web: www.gedneyfoods.com
**SIC: 2035** Pickles, vinegar

**(P-979)**
**GFF INC**
Also Called: Girard Food Service
145 Willow Ave, City Of Industry (91746-2047)
PHONE.................................323 232-6255
Emanuel Marti, *CEO*
Bill Perry, *Pr*
William Perry, *Pr*
▲ **EMP:** 89 **EST:** 1981
**SQ FT:** 92,000
**SALES (est):** 24.54MM **Privately Held**
Web: www.girardsdressings.com
**SIC: 2035** Pickles, sauces, and salad dressings
PA: Haco Holding Ag
Worbstrasse 262

**(P-980)**
**KIKKOMAN FOODS INC**
1000 Glenn Dr, Folsom (95630-3164)
PHONE.................................916 355-8078
Masashi Kasuga, *Pr*
**EMP:** 15
Web: www.kikkoman.com
**SIC: 2035** Pickles, sauces, and salad dressings
HQ: Kikkoman Foods, Inc.
N1365 Six Corners Rd
Walworth WI 53184
262 275-6181

**(P-981)**
**KRUGER FOODS INC**
18362 E Highway 4, Stockton (95215-9433)
P.O. Box 220 (95230-0220)
PHONE.................................209 941-8518
Kara Kruger, *CEO*
Leslie Kruger, *
Eric Kruger, *
▼ **EMP:** 155 **EST:** 1930
**SQ FT:** 80,000
**SALES (est):** 38.57MM **Privately Held**
Web: www.krugerfoods.com
**SIC: 2035** Pickles, vinegar

**(P-982)**
**LEE BROTHERS INC**
Also Called: Four In One Company
1011 Timothy Dr, San Jose (95133-1043)
PHONE.................................650 964-9650
Gene Lee, *CEO*
Gene Lee, *Pr*
Jim Lee, *
Jay Lee, *
**EMP:** 30 **EST:** 1974
**SQ FT:** 46,000
**SALES (est):** 1.79MM **Privately Held**
Web: www.fourinone.com
**SIC: 2035** Dressings, salad: raw and cooked (except dry mixes)

**(P-983)**
**LEE KUM KEE (USA) FOODS INC (PA)**
14455 Don Julian Rd, City Of Industry (91746-3102)
PHONE.................................626 709-1888
Simon Wu, *Pr*
Dickson Chan, *
**EMP:** 99 **EST:** 1996
**SQ FT:** 54,000
**SALES (est):** 17.13MM
**SALES (corp-wide):** 17.13MM **Privately Held**
Web: corporate.lkk.com
**SIC: 2035** Seasonings and sauces, except tomato and dry

**(P-984)**
**MAJESTIC GARLIC INC**
2222 Foothill Blvd Ste E, La Canada (91011-1485)
PHONE.................................951 677-0555
Lucie Sabounjian, *Owner*
**EMP:** 15 **EST:** 2006
**SALES (est):** 990.88K **Privately Held**
Web: www.majesticgarlic.com
**SIC: 2035** Spreads, garlic

**(P-985)**
**MOREHOUSE FOODS INC**
760 Epperson Dr, City Of Industry (91748-1336)
PHONE.................................626 854-1655
David L Latter Senior, *Ch*
David L Latter Junior, *Pr*
◆ **EMP:** 50 **EST:** 1898
**SQ FT:** 65,000
**SALES (est):** 9.72MM **Privately Held**
Web: www.morehousefoods.com
**SIC: 2035** 5149 Mustard, prepared (wet); Seasonings, sauces, and extracts

**(P-986)**
**OCINET INC**
8718 Cleta St, Downey (90241-5203)
PHONE.................................213 280-0989
Jennifer Oh, *CEO*
Aesook Oh, *Prin*
Nathaniel Law, *Ofcr*
**EMP:** 15 **EST:** 2001
**SALES (est):** 1.52MM **Privately Held**
**SIC: 2035** 2099 Pickles, sauces, and salad dressings; Food preparations, nec

**(P-987)**
**OLIVE MUSCO PRODUCTS INC**
Swift & 5th St, Orland (95963)
P.O. Box 368 (95963-0368)
PHONE.................................530 865-4111
Dennis Burreson, *Manager*
**EMP:** 40
**SALES (corp-wide):** 78.47MM **Privately Held**
Web: www.olives.com
**SIC: 2035** 2033 Pickles, sauces, and salad dressings; Olives: packaged in cans, jars, etc.
PA: Olive Musco Products Inc
17950 Via Nicolo

▲ = Import ▼ = Export
◆ = Import/Export

## PRODUCTS & SERVICES SECTION
## 2037 - Frozen Fruits And Vegetables (P-1007)

866 965-4837

**(P-988)**
**PACIFIC CHOICE BRANDS INC (PA)**
4652 E Date Ave, Fresno (93725-2123)
PHONE..................559 892-5365
Allan R Andrews, *CEO*
◆ **EMP:** 200 **EST:** 1930
**SQ FT:** 225,000
**SALES (est):** 44.04MM
**SALES (corp-wide):** 44.04MM **Privately Held**
**Web:** www.pcbrands.com
**SIC: 2035** Pickled fruits and vegetables

**(P-989)**
**PACIFICA FOODS LLC**
Also Called: Stir Foods
1581 N Main St, Orange (92867)
PHONE..................951 371-3123
Ming Milton Liu, *
**EMP:** 140 **EST:** 2000
**SALES (est):** 60MM
**SALES (corp-wide):** 249.44MM **Privately Held**
**Web:** www.stirfoods.com
**SIC: 2035** 5149 2033 Seasonings and sauces, except tomato and dry; Sauces; Tomato products, packaged in cans, jars, etc.
**PA:** Corona-Orange Foods Intermediate Holdings Llc
1581 N Main St
714 637-6050

**(P-990)**
**Q & B FOODS INC (DH)**
15547 1st St, Irwindale (91706-6201)
PHONE..................626 334-8090
Kuniaki Ishikaiwa, *Pr*
Jerry Shepherd, *Ex VP*
Akio Okumura, *CEO*
◆ **EMP:** 69 **EST:** 1982
**SQ FT:** 52,000
**SALES (est):** 41.31MM **Privately Held**
**Web:** www.qbfoods.com
**SIC: 2035** Dressings, salad: raw and cooked (except dry mixes)
**HQ:** Kifuki U.S.A. Co., Inc.
15547 1st St
Irwindale CA 91706

**(P-991)**
**S M S BRINERS INC**
17750 E Highway 4, Stockton (95215-9721)
PHONE..................209 941-8515
Kara Kruger, *CEO*
Frances Sousa, *Pr*
Arnold Sousa, *VP*
Laurie Flatter, *Sec*
**EMP:** 45 **EST:** 1966
**SQ FT:** 5,000
**SALES (est):** 2.19MM **Privately Held**
**Web:** s-m-s-briners-inc.hub.biz
**SIC: 2035** Vegetables, brined

**(P-992)**
**SONOMA GOURMET INC**
Also Called: Pometta's
21684 8th St E Ste 100, Sonoma (95476-2816)
PHONE..................707 939-3700
William K Weber, *Pr*
Rodger C Declercq, *VP*
**EMP:** 26 **EST:** 1990
**SQ FT:** 50,000
**SALES (est):** 3.22MM **Privately Held**
**Web:** www.sonomagourmet.com
**SIC: 2035** Pickles, sauces, and salad dressings

**(P-993)**
**SOY SAUCE PRODUCTIONS LLC** ✪
30700 Russell Ranch Rd Ste 250, Westlake Village (91362-9507)
PHONE..................818 213-1092
Derek Johnson, *CEO*
**EMP:** 17 **EST:** 2023
**SALES (est):** 1.05MM **Privately Held**
**SIC: 2035** Soy sauce

**(P-994)**
**SUNOPTA GLOBL ORGNIC INGRDNTS (HQ)**
Also Called: Sunopta Food Solutions
100 Enterprise Way Ste B101, Scotts Valley (95066-3248)
PHONE..................831 685-6506
Joseph Stern, *Pr*
Loren Morr, *VP*
◆ **EMP:** 20 **EST:** 1996
**SQ FT:** 2,800
**SALES (est):** 6.77MM
**SALES (corp-wide):** 630.3MM **Publicly Held**
**Web:** www.sunopta.com
**SIC: 2035** 2033 Relishes, vinegar; Fruit nectars: packaged in cans, jars, etc.
**PA:** Sunopta Inc.
7078 Shady Oak Rd
952 820-2518

**(P-995)**
**U S ENTERPRISE CORPORATION**
Also Called: Wing Nien Company
30560 San Antonio St, Hayward (94544-7102)
PHONE..................510 487-8877
David H Hall, *Pr*
Ken Jue Md, *VP*
Gregory Hall, *Sec*
▲ **EMP:** 19 **EST:** 1942
**SQ FT:** 40,000
**SALES (est):** 3.54MM **Privately Held**
**Web:** www.wnfoods.com
**SIC: 2035** 5141 Seasonings and sauces, except tomato and dry; Groceries, general line

**(P-996)**
**VALLEY GARLIC LLC**
500 Enterprise Pkwy, Coalinga (93210-9513)
PHONE..................559 934-1763
Chris Kiser, *CEO*
**EMP:** 20 **EST:** 2002
**SALES (est):** 3.95MM **Privately Held**
**SIC: 2035** Spreads, garlic

**(P-997)**
**VANLAW FOOD PRODUCTS INC (HQ)**
Also Called: Coron-Rnge Fods Intrmdate Hldn
2325 Moore Ave, Fullerton (92833-2510)
P.O. Box 2388 (92837-0388)
PHONE..................714 870-9091
**EMP:** 72 **EST:** 1945
**SALES (est):** 49.69MM
**SALES (corp-wide):** 249.44MM **Privately Held**
**Web:** www.stirfoods.com
**SIC: 2035** 2087 Pickles, sauces, and salad dressings; Syrups, drink
**PA:** Corona-Orange Foods Intermediate Holdings.Llc
1581 N Main St
714 637-6050

## 2037 Frozen Fruits And Vegetables

**(P-998)**
**CALIFORNIA CONCENTRATE COMPANY**
Also Called: Kimberley Wine Vinegars
18678 N Highway 99, Acampo (95220-9557)
PHONE..................209 334-9112
Thomas Alexander, *Pr*
Dennis Alexander, *
Andy Alexander, *
Thomas P Alexander, *
◆ **EMP:** 24 **EST:** 1969
**SQ FT:** 17,000
**SALES (est):** 20.64MM **Privately Held**
**Web:** www.californiaconcentrate.com
**SIC: 2037** 2082 Fruit juice concentrates, frozen; Extract, malt

**(P-999)**
**CALIFRNIA CITRUS PRODUCERS INC**
525 E Lindmore St, Lindsay (93247-2559)
P.O. Box 6940 (93290-6940)
PHONE..................559 562-5169
Frank T Elliott Iv, *Pr*
**EMP:** 93 **EST:** 1983
**SQ FT:** 40,000
**SALES (est):** 773.75K
**SALES (corp-wide):** 90.25MM **Privately Held**
**SIC: 2037** Fruit juice concentrates, frozen
**PA:** Wileman Bros. & Elliott, Inc.
40232 Road 128
559 651-8378

**(P-1000)**
**CANADAS FINEST FOODS INC**
Also Called: Reliant Foodservice
26290 Ynez Rd, Temecula (92591-6000)
PHONE..................951 296-1040
David Canada, *Pr*
▲ **EMP:** 70 **EST:** 1996
**SQ FT:** 102,000
**SALES (est):** 2.06MM **Privately Held**
**Web:** 051ef4c.netsolhost.com
**SIC: 2037** 2024 Fruit juices; Dairy based frozen desserts

**(P-1001)**
**CLEUGHS FROZEN FOODS INC**
6571 Altura Blvd Ste 200, Buena Park (90620-1020)
**EMP:** 20 **EST:** 1933
**SALES (est):** 916.4K
**SALES (corp-wide):** 630.3MM **Publicly Held**
**SIC: 2037** Frozen fruits and vegetables
**PA:** Sunopta Inc.
7078 Shady Oak Rd
952 820-2518

**(P-1002)**
**CROWN CITRUS COMPANY INC**
407 S Industrial Ave, Calipatria (92233)
PHONE..................760 348-9755
Mark Mcbroom, *Pr*
**EMP:** 17 **EST:** 2007
**SALES (est):** 826.5K **Privately Held**
**Web:** www.fivecrowns.com
**SIC: 2037** Citrus pulp, dried

**(P-1003)**
**DOLE PACKAGED FOODS LLC (HQ)**
Also Called: Glacier Foods Division
1 Baxter Way, Westlake Village (91362)
P.O. Box 5700 (91359)
PHONE..................800 232-8888
David A Delorenzo, *Managing Member*
Gregory Costley, *Managing Member**
Ann Wiese, *
Jim Johnston, *
Tim Nelson, *
◆ **EMP:** 550 **EST:** 1967
**SQ FT:** 81,000
**SALES (est):** 256.93MM **Privately Held**
**Web:** www.dolesunshine.com
**SIC: 2037** Fruits, quick frozen and cold pack (frozen)
**PA:** Itochu Corporation
2-5-1, Kitaaoyama

**(P-1004)**
**DOLE PACKAGED FOODS LLC**
Also Called: Glacier Foods Division
1117 K St, Sanger (93657-3200)
PHONE..................559 875-3354
Alvin Mc Avoy, *Mgr*
**EMP:** 170
**Web:** www.dolesunshine.com
**SIC: 2037** 2033 2095 2032 Fruits, quick frozen and cold pack (frozen); Canned fruits and specialties; Roasted coffee; Canned specialties
**HQ:** Dole Packaged Foods, Llc
1 Baxter Way
Westlake Village CA 91362
800 232-8888

**(P-1005)**
**ECKERT COLD STORAGE COMPANY (PA)**
905 Clough Rd, Escalon (95320-8647)
PHONE..................209 838-4040
**EMP:** 400 **EST:** 1936
**SALES (est):** 141.5MM
**SALES (corp-wide):** 141.5MM **Privately Held**
**Web:** www.eckertcs.com
**SIC: 2037** Frozen fruits and vegetables

**(P-1006)**
**FORAGER PROJECT LLC (PA)**
Also Called: Forager Project
235 Montgomery St Ste 420, San Francisco (94104-2921)
PHONE..................855 729-5253
Stephen Williamson, *Managing Member*
John Charles Hanley, *
Alexis Hager, *
**EMP:** 73 **EST:** 2014
**SALES (est):** 35MM
**SALES (corp-wide):** 35MM **Privately Held**
**Web:** www.foragerproject.com
**SIC: 2037** Fruit juices

**(P-1007)**
**IMPERIAL VALLEY FOODS INC**
1961 Buchanan Ave, Calexico (92231-4306)
P.O. Box 233 Paulin Ave (92231)
PHONE..................760 203-1896
Gustavo Cabellero, *CEO*
Gustavo Cabellero Junior, *Pr*
Fernando Cabellero, *
Edna Cabellero, *
▲ **EMP:** 300 **EST:** 2006
**SALES (est):** 21.48MM **Privately Held**

(PA)=Parent Co (HQ)=Headquarters
✪ = New Business established in last 2 years

## 2037 - Frozen Fruits And Vegetables (P-1008)

**(P-1008)**
**J HELLMAN FROZEN FOODS INC (PA)**
1601 E Olympic Blvd Ste 200, Los Angeles (90021-1941)
P.O. Box 86267 (90086-0267)
PHONE..................213 243-9105
Tracy Hellman, *CEO*
Bryce Hellman, *
EMP: 50 EST: 1990
SQ FT: 21,000
SALES (est): 4.92MM
SALES (corp-wide): 4.92MM **Privately Held**
Web: www.jhellmanfrozenfoods.com
SIC: 2037 Frozen fruits and vegetables

**(P-1009)**
**JR SIMPLOT COMPANY**
4863 Carpenter Rd, Stockton (95215-8106)
P.O. Box 31870 (95213-1870)
PHONE..................209 941-4456
EMP: 46
SALES (corp-wide): 4.42B **Privately Held**
SIC: 2037 Frozen fruits and vegetables
PA: J.R. Simplot Company
  1099 W Front St
  208 336-2110

**(P-1010)**
**LA ALOE LLC**
2301 E 7th St Ste A152, Los Angeles (90023-1044)
PHONE..................888 968-2563
▲ EMP: 21 EST: 2011
SQ FT: 47,000
SALES (est): 1.99MM **Privately Held**
Web: www.lalibations.com
SIC: 2037 Fruit juices

**(P-1011)**
**LANGER JUICE COMPANY INC**
16185 Stephens St, City Of Industry (91744)
PHONE..................626 336-3100
EMP: 300 EST: 2016
SALES (est): 2.88MM **Privately Held**
Web: www.langers.com
SIC: 2037 Fruit juices

**(P-1012)**
**LIVE FRESH CORPORATION**
1055 E Cooley Ave, San Bernardino (92408-2819)
PHONE..................909 478-0895
▲ EMP: 180 EST: 1993
SALES (est): 8.89MM **Privately Held**
SIC: 2037 Fruit juices

**(P-1013)**
**NATURE QULTY A CAL LTD PARTNR**
9351 Fairview Rd, Hollister (95023-9426)
P.O. Box 1230 (95046-1230)
EMP: 18 EST: 1984
SQ FT: 30,000
SALES (est): 3.01MM **Privately Held**
SIC: 2037 Frozen fruits and vegetables

**(P-1014)**
**OXNARD LEMON COMPANY**
2001 Sunkist Cir, Oxnard (93033-3902)
P.O. Box 2240 (93034-2240)
PHONE..................805 483-1173
Sam Mayhew, *Genl Mgr*
Nancy Low, *Off Mgr*
Tom Mayhew, *Superintnt*
EMP: 17 EST: 1996
SALES (est): 2.95MM **Privately Held**
Web: www.oxnardlemon.com
SIC: 2037 0723 5148 Frozen fruits and vegetables; Crop preparation services for market; Fresh fruits and vegetables

**(P-1015)**
**PERFECT PUREE OF NAPA VLY LLC**
2700 Napa Valley Corporate Dr, Napa (94558-7557)
PHONE..................707 261-5100
Kevin Zeigler, *Pr*
▲ EMP: 19 EST: 2006
SALES (est): 1.24MM **Privately Held**
Web: www.perfectpuree.com
SIC: 2037 Frozen fruits and vegetables

**(P-1016)**
**RAW JUICERY INC**
915 Mateo St Ste 207, Los Angeles (90021-1786)
PHONE..................213 221-6081
Ryan Davidson, *CEO*
EMP: 15 EST: 2017
SALES (est): 884.31K **Privately Held**
Web: www.rawjuicery.com
SIC: 2037 Fruit juices

**(P-1017)**
**SUN TROPICS INC**
4000 Executive Pkwy Ste 190, San Ramon (94583-4316)
P.O. Box 407 (94583-0407)
PHONE..................925 202-2221
Sharon Sy, *VP*
◆ EMP: 16 EST: 2002
SALES (est): 4.6MM **Privately Held**
Web: www.suntropics.com
SIC: 2037 Fruit juices

**(P-1018)**
**SUNSATION INC**
100 S Cambridge Ave, Claremont (91711-4842)
PHONE..................909 542-0280
Perry Eichor, *CEO*
Perry Eichor, *Pr*
David Bryant, *
Saul Kusnier, *Prin*
EMP: 48 EST: 2003
SQ FT: 30,000
SALES (est): 6.08MM **Privately Held**
SIC: 2037 Fruit juices

**(P-1019)**
**VENTURA COASTAL LLC (PA)**
2325 Vista Del Mar Dr, Ventura (93001-3700)
P.O. Box 69 (93002-0069)
PHONE..................805 653-7000
Donald Dames, *
Bill Borgers, *Managing Member**
Rolph Scherer, *
Don Uhlrich, *
◆ EMP: 50 EST: 1951
SQ FT: 25,000
SALES (est): 31.97K
SALES (corp-wide): 31.97K **Privately Held**
Web: www.venturacoastal.com
SIC: 2037 Fruit juice concentrates, frozen

**(P-1020)**
**WM BOLTHOUSE FARMS INC (HQ)**
Also Called: Bolthouse Farms
7200 E Brundage Ln, Bakersfield (93307-3099)
PHONE..................800 467-4683
Jeffrey Dunn, *CEO*
Mike Rosenthal, *
Matthew Ayres, *
◆ EMP: 1000 EST: 1970
SQ FT: 700,000
SALES (est): 562.6MM
SALES (corp-wide): 562.6MM **Privately Held**
Web: www.bolthouse.com
SIC: 2037 0161 2033 2099 Fruit juices; Carrot farm; Vegetable juices: packaged in cans, jars, etc.; Sauce, gravy, dressing, and dip mixes
PA: Generis Holdings, Lp
  7200 E Brundage Ln
  661 366-7209

## 2038 Frozen Specialties, Nec

**(P-1021)**
**AJINOMOTO FOODS NORTH AMER INC**
Also Called: Windsor Foods
2395 American Ave, Hayward (94545-1807)
PHONE..................510 293-1838
Venita Darien, *Brnch Mgr*
EMP: 375
Web: www.ajinomotofoods.com
SIC: 2038 2037 Frozen specialties, nec; Frozen fruits and vegetables
HQ: Ajinomoto Foods North America, Inc.
  4200 E Concours Ste 100
  Ontario CA 91764

**(P-1022)**
**AJINOMOTO FOODS NORTH AMER INC**
Also Called: Windsor Foods
4200 Concours Ste 100, Ontario (91764-4982)
PHONE..................909 477-4700
Steve Charles, *Mgr*
EMP: 244
Web: www.ajinomotofoods.com
SIC: 2038 5142 Frozen specialties, nec; Packaged frozen goods
HQ: Ajinomoto Foods North America, Inc.
  4200 E Concours Ste 100
  Ontario CA 91764

**(P-1023)**
**AJINOMOTO FOODS NORTH AMER INC (DH)**
4200 Concours Ste 100, Ontario (91764-4982)
PHONE..................909 477-4700
Sumio Maeda, *Pr*
Taro Komura, *
James Caltabiano, *
Daniel O'brien, *CIO*
Brett Buatti Csco, *Prin*
▲ EMP: 100 EST: 2015
SQ FT: 56,000
SALES (est): 844.87MM **Privately Held**
Web: www.ajinomotofoods.com
SIC: 2038 2037 Frozen specialties, nec; Frozen fruits and vegetables
HQ: Ajinomoto North America Holdings, Inc.
  7124 N Marine Dr
  Portland OR 97203
  503 505-5783

**(P-1024)**
**AMYS KITCHEN INC (PA)**
109 Kentucky St, Petaluma (94952-2303)
P.O. Box P.O. Box 4759 (94955)
PHONE..................707 578-7188
Andrew R Berliner, *CEO*
Peter Wong, *
Michael L Resch, *
Amy Michele Berliner-ricafrente, *Dir*
Goretti Hamlin, *
◆ EMP: 800 EST: 1988
SALES (est): 466.41MM
SALES (corp-wide): 466.41MM **Privately Held**
Web: www.amys.com
SIC: 2038 2053 Dinners, frozen and packaged; Frozen bakery products, except bread

**(P-1025)**
**ARMANINO FOODS DISTINCTION INC**
5976 W Las Positas Blvd Ste 200, Pleasanton (94588-8511)
PHONE..................510 441-9300
Tim Anderson, *CEO*
Edgar Estonina, *
Reba Gong Ctrl, *Prin*
▼ EMP: 34 EST: 1986
SQ FT: 31,783
SALES (est): 60MM **Privately Held**
Web: www.armaninofoods.com
SIC: 2038 2099 Frozen specialties, nec; Sauce, gravy, dressing, and dip mixes

**(P-1026)**
**ASTROCHEF LLC**
Also Called: Pegasus Foods
1111 Mateo St, Los Angeles (90021-1717)
P.O. Box 86404 (90086-0404)
PHONE..................213 627-9860
Jim Zaferis, *CEO*
Evangelos Ambatielos, *
Steve Koufoudakis, *
EMP: 55 EST: 1998
SQ FT: 60,000
SALES (est): 9.81MM **Privately Held**
Web: www.pegasusfoodsinc.com
SIC: 2038 Frozen specialties, nec

**(P-1027)**
**BABA SMALL BATCH LLC**
103 Santa Felicia Dr, Goleta (93117-2804)
P.O. Box 8125 (93118-8125)
PHONE..................805 439-2250
Cecilia Voettcher, *Genl Mgr*
EMP: 16 EST: 2009
SQ FT: 4,000
SALES (est): 1.53MM **Privately Held**
Web: www.babasmallbatch.com
SIC: 2038 Ethnic foods, nec, frozen

**(P-1028)**
**BEYOND MEAT INC (PA)**
Also Called: BEYOND MEAT
888 N Douglas St Ste 100, El Segundo (90245-2569)
PHONE..................866 756-4112
Ethan Brown, *Pr*
Seth Goldman, *Ch Bd*
Lubi Kutua, *CFO*
Jonathan Nelson, *COO*
Dariush Ajami, *CIO*
▲ EMP: 20 EST: 2009
SQ FT: 282,000
SALES (est): 343.38MM
SALES (corp-wide): 343.38MM **Publicly Held**
Web: www.beyondmeat.com
SIC: 2038 2013 Frozen specialties, nec; Frozen meats, from purchased meat

**(P-1029)**
**CARDENAS MARKETS LLC**
1621 E Francis St, Ontario (91761-8324)

# PRODUCTS & SERVICES SECTION
## 2038 - Frozen Specialties, Nec (P-1050)

PHONE..................909 923-7426
Javier Ramirez, COO
**EMP:** 200
**SALES (corp-wide):** 142.12MM **Privately Held**
Web: www.cardenasmarkets.com
**SIC: 2038** 5411 Frozen specialties, nec; Grocery stores
**HQ:** Cardenas Markets Llc
2501 E Guasti Rd
Ontario CA 91761
909 923-7426

### (P-1030)
### CRAVE FOODS INC
Also Called: Crave Foods
2043 Imperial St, Los Angeles (90021-3203)
PHONE..................562 900-7272
Shaheda Sayed, Pr
Riaz A Surti, *
▲ **EMP:** 40 **EST:** 1992
**SQ FT:** 20,000
**SALES (est):** 3.54MM **Privately Held**
Web: www.cravefoods.com
**SIC: 2038** Frozen specialties, nec

### (P-1031)
### CULINARY BRANDS INC (PA)
3280 E 44th St, Vernon (90058-2426)
PHONE..................626 289-3000
Frank Calma, Pr
Mohsen Ganeian, Prin
**EMP:** 41 **EST:** 2011
**SQ FT:** 2,000
**SALES (est):** 8.29MM
**SALES (corp-wide):** 8.29MM **Privately Held**
Web: www.culinaryinternational.com
**SIC: 2038** Frozen specialties, nec

### (P-1032)
### DEL REAL LLC (PA)
Also Called: Del Real Foods
11041 Inland Ave, Jurupa Valley (91752-1155)
PHONE..................951 681-0395
Michael Axelrod, CEO
Jesus Cardenas, Pr
Jose Cardenas, VP
Viviano Del Villar Junior, COO
Manuel Martinez, CFO
**EMP:** 72 **EST:** 2003
**SQ FT:** 175,000
**SALES (est):** 104.79MM
**SALES (corp-wide):** 104.79MM **Privately Held**
Web: www.delrealfoods.com
**SIC: 2038** Ethnic foods, nec, frozen

### (P-1033)
### DON MIGUEL MEXICAN FOODS INC (HQ)
Also Called: Don Miguel Foods
333 S Anita Dr Ste 1000, Orange (92868-3318)
PHONE..................714 385-4500
Jeff Frank, CEO
Saralyn Brown, *
Mike Elliott, *
Terry Girch, *
Michael Chaignot, *
▲ **EMP:** 45 **EST:** 1908
**SQ FT:** 80,000
**SALES (est):** 114.82MM **Privately Held**
Web: www.donmiguel.com
**SIC: 2038** Frozen specialties, nec
**PA:** Megamex Foods, Llc
333 S Anita Dr Ste 1000

### (P-1034)
### EXCELLINE FOOD PRODUCTS LLC
833 N Hollywood Way, Burbank (91505-2814)
PHONE..................818 701-7710
**EMP:** 29 **EST:** 1979
**SQ FT:** 23,000
**SALES (est):** 2.56MM **Privately Held**
Web: www.excellinefoods.com
**SIC: 2038** Ethnic foods, nec, frozen

### (P-1035)
### GOLDEN STATE FOODS CORP
640 S 6th Ave, City Of Industry (91746-3086)
PHONE..................626 465-7500
Chad Buechel, Brnch Mgr
**EMP:** 350
**SALES (corp-wide):** 1.5MM **Privately Held**
Web: www.goldenstatefoods.com
**SIC: 2038** 2087 2026 2051 Frozen specialties, nec; Flavoring extracts and syrups, nec; Fluid milk; Bread, cake, and related products
**PA:** Golden State Foods Corp.
18301 Von Krman Ave Ste 1
949 247-8000

### (P-1036)
### HARVEST FARMS INC
45000 Yucca Ave, Lancaster (93534-2526)
PHONE..................661 945-3636
Craig Shugert, CEO
Eric Shiring, *
▲ **EMP:** 100 **EST:** 1947
**SQ FT:** 18,000
**SALES (est):** 19.81MM
**SALES (corp-wide):** 519.54MM **Privately Held**
Web: www.harvestfarms.com
**SIC: 2038** 5144 Lunches, frozen and packaged; Poultry and poultry products
**HQ:** Good Source Solutions, Inc.
3115 Melrose Dr Ste 160
Carlsbad CA 92010
858 455-4800

### (P-1037)
### LA MEXICANA LLC
6535 Caballero Blvd Unit A, Buena Park (90620-8106)
PHONE..................323 277-3660
Angelo Fraggos, CEO
**EMP:** 40 **EST:** 2006
**SALES (est):** 1MM
**SALES (corp-wide):** 471.74MM **Privately Held**
**SIC: 2038** Ethnic foods, nec, frozen
**PA:** Blue Point Capital Partners Llc
127 Public Sq Ste 5100
216 535-4700

### (P-1038)
### LA MOUSSE DESSERTS INC
Also Called: La Mousse
18211 S Broadway, Gardena (90248-3535)
PHONE..................310 478-6051
Leah Noble, Pr
**EMP:** 29 **EST:** 2017
**SQ FT:** 11,000
**SALES (est):** 5.91MM **Privately Held**
Web: www.lamoussedesserts.com
**SIC: 2038** Frozen specialties, nec

### (P-1039)
### LANGLOIS FANCY FROZEN FOODS INC
2975 Laguna Canyon Rd, Laguna Beach (92651-1148)
PHONE..................949 497-1741
**EMP:** 49 **EST:** 1951
**SALES (est):** 4.49MM **Privately Held**
Web: www.langloisfoods.com
**SIC: 2038** Dinners, frozen and packaged

### (P-1040)
### NATES FINE FOODS LLC
8880 Industrial Ave Ste 100, Roseville (95678-6237)
PHONE..................310 897-2690
Nathan Barker, CEO
**EMP:** 28 **EST:** 2012
**SQ FT:** 50,000
**SALES (est):** 5.2MM **Privately Held**
Web: www.natesfinefood.com
**SIC: 2038** Ethnic foods, nec, frozen

### (P-1041)
### NESTLE USA INC
Also Called: Nestle Dist Ctr & Logistics
3450 Dulles Dr, Jurupa Valley (91752-3242)
PHONE..................951 360-7200
Dean Ingram, Brnch Mgr
**EMP:** 345
Web: www.nestleusa.com
**SIC: 2038** Frozen specialties, nec
**HQ:** Nestle Usa, Inc.
1812 N Moore St
Arlington VA 22209
800 225-2270

### (P-1042)
### NIPPON INDUSTRIES INC
2430 S Watney Way, Fairfield (94533-6730)
PHONE..................707 427-3127
Eric D Wong, Pr
◆ **EMP:** 31 **EST:** 1999
**SQ FT:** 30,000
**SALES (est):** 7.46MM **Privately Held**
Web: www.nipponindustries.com
**SIC: 2038** Dinners, frozen and packaged

### (P-1043)
### PICTSWEET COMPANY
732 Hanson Way, Santa Maria (93458-9710)
P.O. Box 5878 (93456-5878)
PHONE..................805 928-4414
Thomas Kerulas, Brnch Mgr
**EMP:** 300
**SALES (corp-wide):** 403.32MM **Privately Held**
Web: www.pictsweetfarms.com
**SIC: 2038** 2099 Frozen specialties, nec; Food preparations, nec
**PA:** The Pictsweet Company
10 Pictsweet Dr
731 663-7600

### (P-1044)
### REAL VISION FOODS LLC
Also Called: Real Vision Foods
72 Knollglen, Irvine (92614-7485)
PHONE..................253 228-5050
Joseph H Ertman, Pr
Joseph Ertman, *
**EMP:** 50 **EST:** 2019
**SALES (est):** 1.05MM **Privately Held**
Web: www.realvisionfoods.com
**SIC: 2038** Snacks, incl. onion rings, cheese sticks, etc.

### (P-1045)
### SAN FRANCISCO FOODS INC
14054 Catalina St, San Leandro (94577-5508)
PHONE..................510 357-7343
Hamad M Malak, CEO
Robert F Steel, *
Bernard K Ludwig, *
▲ **EMP:** 55 **EST:** 1998
**SQ FT:** 12,000
**SALES (est):** 10MM **Privately Held**
Web: www.sanfranciscofoods.com
**SIC: 2038** Pizza, frozen

### (P-1046)
### SHINE FOOD INC
Jesse Lord
21100 S Western Ave, Torrance (90501-1700)
PHONE..................310 533-6010
John Freschi, Mgr
**EMP:** 90
**SALES (corp-wide):** 13.37MM **Privately Held**
Web: www.shinefoods.com
**SIC: 2038** 2053 2052 2051 Frozen specialties, nec; Frozen bakery products, except bread; Cookies and crackers; Bread, cake, and related products
**PA:** Shine Food, Inc.
19216 Normandie Ave
310 329-3829

### (P-1047)
### SPECIALTY BRANDS INCORPORATED
4200 Concours Ste 100, Ontario (91764-4982)
P.O. Box 51467 (91761-1057)
PHONE..................909 477-4851
**EMP:** 1900
**SIC: 2038** 5142 Frozen specialties, nec; Packaged frozen goods

### (P-1048)
### STIR FOODS LLC
1851 N Delilah St, Corona (92879-1800)
PHONE..................714 871-9231
Phil Decarion, CEO
**EMP:** 27
**SALES (corp-wide):** 249.44MM **Privately Held**
Web: www.stirfoods.com
**SIC: 2038** 2099 Frozen specialties, nec; Food preparations, nec
**HQ:** Stir Foods, Llc
1581 N Main St
Orange CA 92867

### (P-1049)
### TAWA SUPERMARKET INC (PA)
Also Called: 99 Ranch Market
6281 Regio Ave, Buena Park (90620)
PHONE..................714 521-8899
Chang Hua K Chen, CEO
▲ **EMP:** 102 **EST:** 1985
**SQ FT:** 117,000
**SALES (est):** 490.41MM
**SALES (corp-wide):** 490.41MM **Privately Held**
Web: www.99ranch.com
**SIC: 2038** 5411 Breakfasts, frozen and packaged; Supermarkets, chain

### (P-1050)
### WESTECH INV ADVISORS LLC (HQ)
104 La Mesa Dr Ste 102, Portola Valley (94028-7510)
PHONE..................650 234-4300
Jay Cohan, Managing Member
Ronald W Swenson, *
**EMP:** 28 **EST:** 1980
**SQ FT:** 1,500
**SALES (est):** 4.97MM
**SALES (corp-wide):** 241.73MM **Publicly Held**

# 2038 - Frozen Specialties, Nec (P-1051)

**SIC: 2038** 7359 6141  Frozen specialties, nec
; Equipment rental and leasing, nec;
Personal credit institutions
**PA:** P10, Inc.
4514 Cole Ave Ste 1600
214 865-7998

### (P-1051)
### WINDSOR QUALITY FOOD COMPANY LTD
Also Called: Windsor Foods
4200 Concours Ste 100, Ontario (91764-4982)
**PHONE**..................713 843-5200
**EMP:** 3300
**Web:** www.ajinomotofoods.com
**SIC: 2038** Frozen specialties, nec

## 2041 Flour And Other Grain Mill Products

### (P-1052)
### ANDREW LLC
Also Called: Sanluisina
17058 Lagos Dr, Chino Hills  (91709-3998)
**PHONE**..................909 270-9356
Miriam Navarro, *Managing Member*
**EMP:** 18 **EST:** 2012
**SALES (est):** 581.29K **Privately Held**
**SIC: 2041**  Corn meal

### (P-1053)
### ARCHER-DANIELS-MIDLAND COMPANY
Also Called: ADM
350 N Guild Ave, Lodi  (95240-0803)
P.O. Box 2675 (95241-2675)
**PHONE**..................209 339-1252
**EMP:** 15
**SALES (corp-wide):** 93.94B **Publicly Held**
**Web:** www.adm.com
**SIC: 2041**  Flour and other grain mill products
**PA:** Archer-Daniels-Midland Company
77 W Wacker Dr Ste 4600
312 634-8100

### (P-1054)
### ARDENT MILLS  LLC
2020 E Steel Rd, Colton  (92324-4008)
**PHONE**..................951 201-1170
Brad Beckwith, *Brnch Mgr*
**EMP:** 22
**SALES (corp-wide):** 571.31MM **Privately Held**
**Web:** www.ardentmills.com
**SIC: 2041**  Flour and other grain mill products
**PA:** Ardent Mills, Llc
1875 Lawrence St Ste 1200
866 477-3544

### (P-1055)
### ARDENT MILLS  LLC
Also Called: Cargill Flour Milling Division
19684 Cajon Blvd, San Bernardino (92407-1813)
**PHONE**..................909 887-3407
Nelson Selmer, *Brnch Mgr*
**EMP:** 21
**SQ FT:** 26,180
**SALES (corp-wide):** 571.31MM **Privately Held**
**Web:** www.ardentmills.com
**SIC: 2041**  Flour mills, cereal (except rice)
**PA:** Ardent Mills, Llc
1875 Lawrence St Ste 1200
866 477-3544

### (P-1056)
### ARDENT MILLS LLC
Also Called: Ardent Mills
3939 Producers Dr, Stockton  (95206-4204)
**PHONE**..................209 983-6551
**EMP:** 15
**SALES (corp-wide):** 571.31MM **Privately Held**
**Web:** www.ardentmills.com
**SIC: 2041**  Flour and other grain mill products
**PA:** Ardent Mills, Llc
1875 Lawrence St Ste 1200
866 477-3544

### (P-1057)
### BAY STATE MILLING COMPANY
360 Hanson Way, Woodland  (95776-6212)
**PHONE**..................530 666-6565
Vanderliet Joseph, *Owner*
**EMP:** 39
**SALES (corp-wide):** 131.82MM **Privately Held**
**Web:** www.baystatemilling.com
**SIC: 2041**  Flour
**PA:** Bay State Milling Company
100 Congress St
617 328-4400

### (P-1058)
### GENERAL MILLS  INC
Also Called: General Mills
4309 Fruitland Ave, Vernon  (90058-3176)
**PHONE**..................323 584-3433
Jeff Shapiro, *Brnch Mgr*
**EMP:** 26
**SQ FT:** 81,186
**SALES (corp-wide):** 19.86B **Publicly Held**
**Web:** www.generalmills.com
**SIC: 2041**  Flour mills, cereal (except rice)
**PA:** General Mills, Inc.
1 General Mills Blvd
763 764-7600

### (P-1059)
### GIUSTOS SPECIALTY FOODS LLC (PA)
344 Littlefield Ave, South San Francisco (94080-6103)
**PHONE**..................650 873-6566
Craig A Moore, *Managing Member*
Jarjeet Bahia, *COO*
Ann Moore, *CFO*
▲ **EMP:** 43 **EST:** 1940
**SQ FT:** 5,000
**SALES (est):** 10.89MM
**SALES (corp-wide):** 10.89MM **Privately Held**
**Web:** www.giustos.com
**SIC: 2041**  Flour mills, cereal (except rice)

### (P-1060)
### GK FOODS  INC
Also Called: San Marcos Trading Company
133 Mata Way Ste 101, San Marcos (92069-2946)
**PHONE**..................760 752-5230
Laurence Hickerson, *CEO*
Laurence James Hickerson, *CEO*
John Bartelt, *Sec*
**EMP:** 20 **EST:** 2002
**SQ FT:** 15,000
**SALES (est):** 4.81MM **Privately Held**
**Web:** www.globalkaizen.com
**SIC: 2041** 7389 5149  Flour and other grain mill products; Packaging and labeling services; Organic and diet food

### (P-1061)
### LT FOODS AMERICAS  INC (HQ)
11130 Warland Dr, Cypress  (90630-5032)
**PHONE**..................562 340-4040
Abhinav Arora, *CEO*
Mukesh Agrawal, *
◆ **EMP:** 17 **EST:** 1992
**SQ FT:** 30,000
**SALES (est):** 26.46MM **Privately Held**
**Web:** www.ltfoodsglobal.com
**SIC: 2041** 5149  Flour and other grain mill products; Pasta and rice
**PA:** Lt Foods Limited
4th Floor, Mvl-I Park, Sector 15

### (P-1062)
### PILLSBURY COMPANY  LLC
Also Called: Pillsbury
220 S Kenwood St Ste 202, Glendale (91205-1671)
**PHONE**..................818 522-3952
Linda Goodman, *Brnch Mgr*
**EMP:** 32
**SALES (corp-wide):** 19.86B **Publicly Held**
**Web:** www.lgpillsbury.com
**SIC: 2041**  Doughs and batters
**HQ:** The Pillsbury Company Llc
1 General Mills Blvd
Minneapolis MN 55426

### (P-1063)
### SING KUNG CORP
12061 Clark St, Arcadia  (91006-5829)
**PHONE**..................626 358-5838
Louis Choy, *Pr*
◆ **EMP:** 25 **EST:** 1997
**SQ FT:** 7,000
**SALES (est):** 2.1MM **Privately Held**
**Web:** www.singkung.com
**SIC: 2041**  Flour and other grain mill products

### (P-1064)
### SUNOPTA GRAINS AND FOODS INC
12128 Center St, South Gate  (90280-8046)
**PHONE**..................323 774-6000
**EMP:** 62
**SALES (corp-wide):** 630.3MM **Publicly Held**
**Web:** www.sunopta.com
**SIC: 2041** 5153  Flour and other grain mill products; Grains
**HQ:** Sunopta Grains And Foods Inc.
7078 Shady Oak Rd
Eden Prairie MN 55344

### (P-1065)
### THE SWEET LIFE ENTERPRISES INC
Also Called: Aryzta Sweet Life
2350 Pullman St, Santa Ana  (92705-5507)
**PHONE**..................949 261-7400
**EMP:** 115
**Web:** www.sweetlifeinc.com
**SIC: 2041** 5149  Doughs and batters; Crackers, cookies, and bakery products

### (P-1066)
### VALLEY FINE FOODS COMPANY  LLC (PA)
Also Called: Pasta Prima
3909 Park Rd Ste H, Benicia  (94510-1167)
**PHONE**..................707 746-6888
Todd Nettleton, *Managing Member*
Ryan Tu, *
Wayne Tu, *
Brian Cullen, *
▲ **EMP:** 100 **EST:** 1992
**SQ FT:** 83,598
**SALES (est):** 92.98MM **Privately Held**
**Web:** www.pastaprima.com
**SIC: 2041** 2038  Doughs, frozen or refrigerated; Frozen specialties, nec

### (P-1067)
### VICOLO WHOLESALE LLC (PA)
Also Called: Vicolo Pizza
31112 San Clemente St, Hayward (94544-7802)
**PHONE**..................510 475-6019
Eric Mount, *Pt*
Richard Sander, *Pt*
**EMP:** 49 **EST:** 1998
**SQ FT:** 1,400
**SALES (est):** 5.28MM
**SALES (corp-wide):** 5.28MM **Privately Held**
**Web:** www.vicolopizza.com
**SIC: 2041**  Flour and other grain mill products

### (P-1068)
### WESTERN FOODS  LLC
440 N Pioneer Ave Ste 200, Woodland (95776-6138)
**PHONE**..................530 601-5991
Miguel Reyna, *Managing Member*
**EMP:** 106
**SALES (corp-wide):** 311.5MM **Privately Held**
**Web:** www.westernfoodsco.com
**SIC: 2041**  Flour
**HQ:** Western Foods, Llc
420 N Pioneer Ave
Woodland CA 95776
530 601-5991

## 2043 Cereal Breakfast Foods

### (P-1069)
### CALIFRNIA NUTRITIONAL PDTS INC
64405 Lincoln St, Mecca  (92254-6501)
**PHONE**..................760 625-3884
Minh Tuan Nguyen, *CEO*
Roy Nguyen, *
Douglas Scott Scharinger, *
**EMP:** 65 **EST:** 2022
**SALES (est):** 5.5MM **Privately Held**
**SIC: 2043**  Cereal breakfast foods

### (P-1070)
### EAST WEST TEA COMPANY  LLC
Also Called: Golden Temple
1616 Preuss Rd, Los Angeles (90035-4212)
**PHONE**..................310 275-9891
Gurudhan S Khalsa, *Mgr*
**EMP:** 226
**SALES (corp-wide):** 63.9MM **Privately Held**
**Web:** www.yogiproducts.com
**SIC: 2043** 2099 2064 8721  Cereal breakfast foods; Tea blending; Candy and other confectionery products; Billing and bookkeeping service
**PA:** East West Tea Company, Llc
1325 Westec Dr
800 964-4832

### (P-1071)
### INTELLIGENT BLENDS LLC
5330 Eastgate Mall, San Diego (92121-2804)
**PHONE**..................858 888-7937
Michael Ishayik, *Pr*
▲ **EMP:** 38 **EST:** 2013
**SALES (est):** 15.05MM **Privately Held**
**Web:** www.intelligentblends.com

PRODUCTS & SERVICES SECTION  2047 - Dog And Cat Food (P-1092)

SIC: 2043  Cereal breakfast foods

## 2044 Rice Milling

**(P-1072)**
**CALIFORNIA FAMILY FOODS LLC**
6550 Struckmeyer Rd, Arbuckle (95912)
PHONE.....................530 476-3326
David Myers, *Pr*
Bruce Meyers, *Managing Member*
Tom Charter, *Managing Member*
Perry Charter, *
▼ EMP: 75 EST: 1995
SQ FT: 75,000
SALES (est): 20.07MM Privately Held
Web: www.californiafamilyfoods.com
SIC: 2044 0723  Rice milling; Rice drying services

**(P-1073)**
**CALIFORNIA HERITAGE MILLS INC**
15 Comet Ln, Maxwell (95955-8062)
P.O. Box 152 (95955-0152)
PHONE.....................530 438-2100
Paul Richter, *Pr*
Steven Sutter, *
◆ EMP: 30 EST: 2011
SALES (est): 7.36MM Privately Held
Web: www.chmrice.com
SIC: 2044  Rice milling

**(P-1074)**
**FAR WEST RICE INC**
3455 Nelson Rd, Nelson (95958)
P.O. Box 370 (95938-0370)
PHONE.....................530 891-1339
C W Johnson, *CEO*
Gregory Johnson, *
Charles Schwab, *
◆ EMP: 35 EST: 1985
SQ FT: 3,000
SALES (est): 4.96MM Privately Held
Web: www.farwestrice.com
SIC: 2044 5141 2099  Rice milling; Groceries, general line; Food preparations, nec

**(P-1075)**
**FARMERS RICE COOPERATIVE (PA)**
Also Called: Frc
2566 River Plaza Dr, Sacramento (95833-3673)
P.O. Box 15223 (95851-0223)
PHONE.....................916 923-5100
Frank Bragg, *CEO*
H Kirk Messick, *
Keith Hargrove, *
Rob Paschoal, *
Bill Tanimoto, *
◆ EMP: 35 EST: 1944
SQ FT: 12,000
SALES (est): 71.89MM
SALES (corp-wide): 71.89MM Privately Held
Web: www.farmersrice.com
SIC: 2044  Rice milling

**(P-1076)**
**FARMERS RICE COOPERATIVE**
845 Kentucky Ave, Woodland (95695-2744)
PHONE.....................530 666-1691
EMP: 62
SALES (corp-wide): 71.89MM Privately Held
Web: www.farmersrice.com

PA: Farmers' Rice Cooperative
2566 River Plaza Dr
916 923-5100

**(P-1077)**
**FARMERS RICE COOPERATIVE**
2224 Industrial Blvd, West Sacramento (95691-3429)
P.O. Box 15223 (95851-0223)
PHONE.....................916 373-5500
Keith Hargrove, *Mgr*
EMP: 63
SALES (corp-wide): 71.89MM Privately Held
Web: www.farmersrice.com
SIC: 2044  Rice milling
PA: Farmers' Rice Cooperative
2566 River Plaza Dr
916 923-5100

**(P-1078)**
**FARMERS RICE COOPERATIVE**
Also Called: Pacific Intl Rice Mills
845 Kentucky Ave, Woodland (95695-2744)
P.O. Box 652 (95776-0652)
PHONE.....................530 666-1691
Melveryn Anderson, *Pr*
EMP: 58
SALES (corp-wide): 71.89MM Privately Held
Web: www.pirmirice.com
SIC: 2044  Rice milling
PA: Farmers' Rice Cooperative
2566 River Plaza Dr
916 923-5100

**(P-1079)**
**GOLD RIVER MILLS LLC (PA)**
1620 E Kentucky Ave, Woodland (95776-6110)
P.O. Box 8729 (95776-8729)
PHONE.....................530 661-1923
◆ EMP: 29 EST: 2001
SALES (est): 1.21MM
SALES (corp-wide): 1.21MM Privately Held
Web: www.hinoderice.com
SIC: 2044  Rice milling

**(P-1080)**
**KODA FARMS INC**
22540 Russell Ave, South Dos Palos (93665)
P.O. Box 10 (93665-0010)
PHONE.....................209 392-2191
Edward K Koda, *Pr*
Tama T Koda, *
Robin Koda, *
Laura Koda, *
Ross Koda, *
▲ EMP: 24 EST: 1946
SQ FT: 20,000
SALES (est): 4.32MM Privately Held
Web: www.kodafarms.com
SIC: 2044 0112  Rice milling; Rice

**(P-1081)**
**RICE CORPORATION (PA)**
Also Called: Krohn Division
11140 Fair Oaks Blvd Ste 101, Fair Oaks (95628-5126)
PHONE.....................916 784-7745
Jay Kapila, *Pr*
Praveen K Kaps, *VP*
Xavier Verspieren, *CFO*
◆ EMP: 20 EST: 1991
SQ FT: 7,000
SALES (est): 7.79MM Privately Held
Web: www.therice.ca
SIC: 2044  Rice milling

**(P-1082)**
**SUN VALLEY RICE COMPANY LLC**
Also Called: Sun Valley Rice
7050 Eddy Rd, Arbuckle (95912-9789)
P.O. Box 8 (95937-0008)
PHONE.....................530 476-3000
Kenneth M Lagrande, *Managing Member*
Michael La Grande, *
Kart Thomas, *
◆ EMP: 98 EST: 1999
SQ FT: 20,000
SALES (est): 23.66MM Privately Held
Web: www.sunvalleyrice.com
SIC: 2044  Rice milling

**(P-1083)**
**SUNWEST MILLING INC**
507 Bannock St, Biggs (95917)
P.O. Box 70 (95917-0070)
PHONE.....................530 868-5421
James R Errecarte, *Pr*
EMP: 70 EST: 1991
SALES (est): 530.94K Privately Held
SIC: 2044  Rice milling

**(P-1084)**
**TAMAKI RICE CORPORATION**
1701 Abel Rd, Williams (95987-5156)
PHONE.....................530 473-2862
Masami Kitagawa, *Pr*
◆ EMP: 20 EST: 1988
SQ FT: 14,000
SALES (est): 2.28MM Privately Held
Web: www.tamakimai.com
SIC: 2044  Rice milling

**(P-1085)**
**WEHAH FARM INC**
Also Called: Lundberg Family Farms
5311 Midway, Richvale (95974)
P.O. Box 369 (95974-0369)
PHONE.....................530 538-3500
Grant Lundberg, *CEO*
EMP: 255 EST: 1974
SALES (est): 38.86MM Privately Held
Web: www.lundberg.com
SIC: 2044  Rice milling

**(P-1086)**
**WEHAH-LUNDBERG INC**
Also Called: Lundberg Family Farms
5311 Midway, Richvale (95974)
P.O. Box 369 (95974-0369)
PHONE.....................530 882-4551
▼ EMP: 220
SIC: 2044 0723 4221  Rice milling; Rice drying services; Farm product warehousing and storage

## 2045 Prepared Flour Mixes And Doughs

**(P-1087)**
**LANGLOIS COMPANY**
Also Called: Langlois Flour Company
10810 San Sevaine Way, Jurupa Valley (91752-1116)
PHONE.....................951 360-3900
Richard W Langlois, *Pr*
Sally Langlois, *
Lynn Langlois Nye, *
▼ EMP: 50 EST: 1950
SQ FT: 48,000
SALES (est): 7.88MM Privately Held
Web: www.langloiscompany.com

SIC: 2045 2035 2079 2099  Blended flour: from purchased flour; Mayonnaise; Vegetable refined oils (except corn oil); Gelatin dessert preparations

**(P-1088)**
**POPLA INTERNATIONAL INC**
1740 S Sacramento Ave, Ontario (91761-7744)
PHONE.....................909 923-6899
Mike Shinozaki, *Pr*
Ashley Shinozaki, *
◆ EMP: 41 EST: 1986
SQ FT: 8,000
SALES (est): 4.17MM Privately Held
Web: www.popla.com
SIC: 2045  Prepared flour mixes and doughs

## 2046 Wet Corn Milling

**(P-1089)**
**CORN PRODUCTS DEVELOPMENT INC (HQ)**
1021 Industrial Dr, Stockton (95206-3928)
P.O. Box 6129 (95206-0129)
PHONE.....................209 982-1920
Samuel Scott, *Prin*
EMP: 27 EST: 2011
SALES (est): 686.1K
SALES (corp-wide): 8.16B Publicly Held
SIC: 2046  Wet corn milling
PA: Ingredion Incorporated
5 Westbrook Corporate Ctr
708 551-2600

**(P-1090)**
**INGREDION INCORPORATED**
Also Called: Corn Products-Stockton Plant
1021 Industrial Dr, Stockton (95206-3928)
P.O. Box 6129 (95206-0129)
PHONE.....................209 982-1920
Mark Madsen, *Mgr*
EMP: 85
SALES (corp-wide): 8.16B Publicly Held
Web: www.ingredion.com
SIC: 2046  Corn sugars and syrups
PA: Ingredion Incorporated
5 Westbrook Corporate Ctr
708 551-2600

## 2047 Dog And Cat Food

**(P-1091)**
**ARCHEYY & FRIENDS LLC**
3630 Andrews Dr Apt 114, Pleasanton (94588-3015)
PHONE.....................703 579-7649
EMP: 20 EST: 2017
SALES (est): 848.74K Privately Held
SIC: 2047 0752  Dog food; Animal boarding services

**(P-1092)**
**ARIES PREPARED BEEF COMPANY**
11850 Sheldon St, Sun Valley (91352-1507)
PHONE.....................818 771-0181
EMP: 18
SALES (corp-wide): 10.06MM Privately Held
Web: www.registrar-transfers.com
SIC: 2047  Dog food
PA: Aries Prepared Beef Company
17 W Magnolia Blvd
818 526-4855

## 2047 - Dog And Cat Food (P-1093)

### (P-1093)
**ARTHUR DOGSWELL LLC (PA)**
Also Called: Dogswell
11301 W Olympic Blvd Ste 520, Los Angeles (90064-1603)
PHONE................................888 559-8833
Brad Casper, *Managing Member*
Gianmarco Giannini, *Managing Member**
Berenice Officer, *
▲ **EMP:** 33 **EST:** 2003
**SQ FT:** 2,000
**SALES (est):** 21.2MM
**SALES (corp-wide):** 21.2MM **Privately Held**
Web: www.dogswell.com
**SIC: 2047** 5149  Dog food; Pet foods

### (P-1094)
**BIG HEART PET BRANDS INC (HQ)**
1 Maritime Plz Fl 2, San Francisco (94111-3407)
P.O. Box 193575 (94119-3575)
PHONE................................415 247-3000
Tucker Marshall, *CEO*
Robert Ferguson, *
◆ **EMP:** 300 **EST:** 2002
**SALES (est):** 426.39MM
**SALES (corp-wide):** 8.18B **Publicly Held**
**SIC: 2047**  Dog food
PA: The J M Smucker Company
 1 Strawberry Ln
 330 682-3000

### (P-1095)
**CANINE CAVIAR PET FOODS DE INC**
4131 Tigris Way, Riverside (92503-4844)
PHONE................................714 223-1800
Jeff A Baker, *Prin*
**EMP:** 18 **EST:** 2019
**SALES (est):** 609.65K **Privately Held**
Web: www.caninecaviar.com
**SIC: 2047**  Dog and cat food

### (P-1096)
**GARMON CORPORATION**
Also Called: Naturvet
43350 Business Park Dr Unit 2, Temecula (92590-3665)
PHONE................................951 296-6308
**EMP:** 15
**SALES (corp-wide):** 24.1MM **Privately Held**
Web: www.naturvet.com
**SIC: 2047**  Dog and cat food
PA: The Garmon Corporation
 27461 Via Industria
 888 628-8783

### (P-1097)
**GARMON CORPORATION**
Also Called: Naturvet
27497 Via Industria, Temecula (92590-3752)
PHONE................................951 296-6308
**EMP:** 15
**SALES (corp-wide):** 24.1MM **Privately Held**
Web: www.naturvet.com
**SIC: 2047**  Dog and cat food
PA: The Garmon Corporation
 27461 Via Industria
 888 628-8783

### (P-1098)
**GARMON CORPORATION**
Also Called: Naturvet
27503 Via Industria Unit Q2, Temecula (92590-3753)
PHONE................................951 296-6308
**EMP:** 15
**SALES (corp-wide):** 24.1MM **Privately Held**
Web: www.naturvet.com
**SIC: 2047**  Dog and cat food
PA: The Garmon Corporation
 27461 Via Industria
 888 628-8783

### (P-1099)
**GARMON CORPORATION**
Also Called: Naturvet
41995 Remington Ave, Temecula (92590-2543)
PHONE................................951 296-6308
**EMP:** 15
**SALES (corp-wide):** 24.1MM **Privately Held**
Web: www.naturvet.com
**SIC: 2047**  Dog and cat food
PA: The Garmon Corporation
 27461 Via Industria
 888 628-8783

### (P-1100)
**HILLSIDE FARMS CORPORATION**
16330 Bake Pkwy, Irvine (92618)
PHONE................................888 846-9653
Victor Wu, *CEO*
**EMP:** 15 **EST:** 2020
**SALES (est):** 31.21MM
**SALES (corp-wide):** 32.87MM **Privately Held**
Web: www.hillside-farms.com
**SIC: 2047**  Dog food
PA: Globalinx Corporation
 16330 Bake Pkwy
 714 531-9812

### (P-1101)
**HONEST KITCHEN INC**
1785 Hancock St Ste 100, San Diego (92110)
PHONE................................619 544-0018
Michael Greenwell, *CEO*
Jacob Fuller, *CFO*
Nathan Kredich, *COO*
Mike Steck, *Mktg Dir*
Kirk Jensen, *COO*
**EMP:** 73 **EST:** 2002
**SALES (est):** 20.68MM **Privately Held**
Web: www.thehonestkitchen.com
**SIC: 2047**  Dog and cat food

### (P-1102)
**INABA FOODS (USA) INC**
19191 S Vermont Ave Ste 1050, Torrance (90502-1054)
PHONE................................310 818-2270
Tomohide Inagaki, *CEO*
▲ **EMP:** 15 **EST:** 2015
**SALES (est):** 9.99MM **Privately Held**
Web: www.inabafoods.com
**SIC: 2047**  Dog and cat food

### (P-1103)
**J&R TAYLOR BROTHERS ASSOC INC**
Also Called: Premium Pet Foods
16321 Arrow Hwy, Irwindale (91706-2018)
PHONE................................626 334-9301
Rick Taylor, *Pr*
◆ **EMP:** 58 **EST:** 1967
**SALES (est):** 1.38MM
**SALES (corp-wide):** 3.31B **Publicly Held**
**SIC: 2047** 2048  Dog food; Prepared feeds, nec
PA: Central Garden & Pet Company
 1340 Treat Blvd Ste 600
 925 948-4000

### (P-1104)
**JE RICH COMPANY**
Also Called: Sittin Pretty Natural Dog Bky
7225 Edison Ave, Ontario (91762-7507)
PHONE................................909 464-1872
**EMP:** 21
**SALES (corp-wide):** 273.93K **Privately Held**
Web: www.adlvet.com
**SIC: 2047**  Dog and cat food
PA: J.E. Rich Company
 7225 Edison Ave
 714 368-1895

### (P-1105)
**JUSTFOODFORDOGS LLC (PA)**
1787 Flight Way, Tustin (92782-1838)
PHONE................................949 722-3647
Richard Shawn Buckley, *Managing Member*
**EMP:** 15 **EST:** 2006
**SALES (est):** 30.8MM
**SALES (corp-wide):** 30.8MM **Privately Held**
Web: www.justfoodfordogs.com
**SIC: 2047** 5149  Dog food; Dog food

### (P-1106)
**KRUSE PET HOLDINGS LLC (HQ)**
Also Called: Perfection Pet Foods, LLC
1111 N Miller Park Ct, Visalia (93291-9454)
PHONE................................559 302-4880
Kevin Kruse, *CEO*
Jeremy Wilhelm, *Pr*
Mike Gagene, *VP*
Brian Ubegin, *CFO*
**EMP:** 20 **EST:** 2011
**SALES (est):** 76.3MM **Publicly Held**
Web: www.perfectionpetfoods.com
**SIC: 2047**  Dog food
PA: Post Holdings, Inc.
 2503 S Hanley Rd

### (P-1107)
**MARS PETCARE US INC**
13243 Nutro Way, Victorville (92395-7789)
PHONE................................760 261-7900
**EMP:** 61
**SALES (corp-wide):** 42.84B **Privately Held**
Web: www.marspetcare.com
**SIC: 2047**  Cat food
HQ: Mars Petcare Us, Inc.
 2013 Ovation Pkwy
 Franklin TN 37067
 615 807-4626

### (P-1108)
**MARS PETCARE US INC**
2765 Lexington Way, San Bernardino (92407-1842)
PHONE................................909 887-8131
Ed Skokan, *Mgr*
**EMP:** 50
**SQ FT:** 76,000
**SALES (corp-wide):** 42.84B **Privately Held**
Web: www.marspetcare.com
**SIC: 2047** 2048  Dog food; Prepared feeds, nec
HQ: Mars Petcare Us, Inc.
 2013 Ovation Pkwy
 Franklin TN 37067
 615 807-4626

### (P-1109)
**NESTLE PURINA PETCARE COMPANY**
Also Called: Nestle Purina Factory
1710 Golden Cat Rd, Maricopa (93252)
PHONE................................661 769-8261
Mike Ashmore, *Mgr*
**EMP:** 103
Web: www.purina.com
**SIC: 2047**  Dog and cat food
HQ: Nestle Purina Petcare Company
 800 Chouteau Ave
 Saint Louis MO 63102
 314 982-1000

### (P-1110)
**NESTLE PURINA PETCARE COMPANY**
800 N Brand Blvd Fl 5, Glendale (91203-4281)
PHONE................................314 982-1000
**EMP:** 46
Web: www.purina.com
**SIC: 2047**  Dog and cat food
HQ: Nestle Purina Petcare Company
 800 Chouteau Ave
 Saint Louis MO 63102
 314 982-1000

### (P-1111)
**NOMNOMNOW INC**
371 3rd St, Oakland (94607-4103)
PHONE................................415 991-0669
Nathan Phillips, *Brnch Mgr*
**EMP:** 88
**SALES (corp-wide):** 42.84B **Privately Held**
Web: www.nomnomnow.com
**SIC: 2047**  Dog and cat food
HQ: Nomnomnow Inc.
 1605 County Hospital Rd
 Nashville TN 37218
 415 991-0669

### (P-1112)
**PRIMAL PET FOODS**
5100 Fulton Dr, Fairfield (94534-1639)
PHONE................................415 642-7400
Tim Simonds, *CEO*
**EMP:** 25
**SALES (est):** 767.47K **Privately Held**
**SIC: 2047**  Dog and cat food

### (P-1113)
**PRIMAL PET FOODS INC**
801 Chadbourne Rd Ste 103, Fairfield (94534-4189)
PHONE................................415 642-7400
**EMP:** 50
**SALES (corp-wide):** 33.39MM **Privately Held**
Web: www.primalpetfoods.com
**SIC: 2047** 4225  Dog and cat food; General warehousing and storage
PA: Primal Pet Foods, Inc.
 535 Watt Dr Ste B
 415 642-7400

### (P-1114)
**PRIMAL PET FOODS INC (PA)**
535 Watt Dr Ste B, Fairfield (94534-1790)
PHONE................................415 642-7400
Matthew Koss, *CEO*
▲ **EMP:** 97 **EST:** 2001
**SQ FT:** 5,000
**SALES (est):** 33.39MM
**SALES (corp-wide):** 33.39MM **Privately Held**
Web: www.primalpetfoods.com
**SIC: 2047**  Dog food

### (P-1115)
**SCHELL & KAMPETER INC**
250 Roth Rd, Lathrop (95330-9724)
PHONE................................209 983-4900

# PRODUCTS & SERVICES SECTION

## 2048 - Prepared Feeds, Nec (P-1136)

Gary Schell, *Brnch Mgr*
**EMP:** 61
**SALES (corp-wide):** 113.89MM Privately Held
**Web:** www.diamondpet.com
**SIC:** 2047 Dog food
**PA:** Schell & Kampeter, Inc.
103 N Olive St
573 229-4203

### (P-1116)
**WILD EARTH INC**
2865 7th St, Berkeley (94710-2704)
**PHONE**..................................510 206-6559
**EMP:** 24 **EST:** 2018
**SALES (est):** 6MM Privately Held
**Web:** www.wildearth.com
**SIC:** 2047 Dog food

## 2048 Prepared Feeds, Nec

### (P-1117)
**A SHOC BEVERAGE LLC**
844 Production Pl, Newport Beach (92663-2810)
**PHONE**..................................949 490-1612
Lance Collins, *Managing Member*
Kyle Ostrowsky, *
**EMP:** 50 **EST:** 2018
**SALES (est):** 11.06MM Privately Held
**Web:** www.drinkaccelerator.com
**SIC:** 2048 Mineral feed supplements

### (P-1118)
**ASSOCIATED FEED & SUPPLY CO (PA)**
Also Called: Farwest Trading
5213 W Main St, Turlock (95381)
P.O. Box 2367 (95381)
**PHONE**..................................209 667-2708
Matt Swanson, *Pr*
Jim Hyer, *Ex VP*
Kurt Hertlein, *VP*
▲ **EMP:** 16 **EST:** 1971
**SQ FT:** 1,800
**SALES (est):** 73.55MM
**SALES (corp-wide):** 73.55MM Privately Held
**Web:** www.associatedfeed.com
**SIC:** 2048 Prepared feeds, nec

### (P-1119)
**ASSOCIATED FEED & SUPPLY CO**
4107 Avenue 360, Traver (93673)
P.O. Box 2367 (95381)
**PHONE**..................................209 664-3323
Lastiri Anastacio, *Mgr*
**EMP:** 250
**SALES (corp-wide):** 73.55MM Privately Held
**SIC:** 2048 Prepared feeds, nec
**PA:** Associated Feed & Supply Co.
5213 W Main St
209 667-2708

### (P-1120)
**BAR ALE INC (PA)**
1011 5th St, Williams (95987-8003)
P.O. Box 699 (95987-0699)
**PHONE**..................................530 473-3333
▲ **EMP:** 25 **EST:** 1946
**SALES (est):** 9.77MM
**SALES (corp-wide):** 9.77MM Privately Held
**Web:** www.baraleinc.com
**SIC:** 2048 Poultry feeds

### (P-1121)
**CALVA PRODUCTS LLC (PA)**
4351 E Winery Rd, Acampo (95220-9506)
**PHONE**..................................800 328-9680
Beth Ford, *CEO*
**EMP:** 25 **EST:** 2016
**SALES (est):** 4.67MM
**SALES (corp-wide):** 4.67MM Privately Held
**Web:** www.calvaproducts.com
**SIC:** 2048 Prepared feeds, nec

### (P-1122)
**CALVA PRODUCTS CO INC**
4351 E Winery Rd, Acampo (95220-9506)
P.O. Box 126 (95220-0126)
**PHONE**..................................209 339-1516
Jim Cook Senior, *CEO*
Bill Cook, *VP*
◆ **EMP:** 39 **EST:** 1975
**SQ FT:** 62,000
**SALES (est):** 12.68MM
**SALES (corp-wide):** 2.89B Privately Held
**Web:** www.calvaproducts.com
**SIC:** 2048 Prepared feeds, nec
**HQ:** Purina Animal Nutrition Llc
100 Danforth Dr
Gray Summit MO 63039

### (P-1123)
**CANINE CAVIAR PET FOODS INC**
Also Called: Canine Caviar
4131 Tigris Way, Riverside (92503-4844)
P.O. Box 5872 (92860-8029)
**PHONE**..................................714 223-1800
Jeff Baker, *Pr*
Gary Ward, *
◆ **EMP:** 30 **EST:** 1996
**SQ FT:** 6,000
**SALES (est):** 5.56MM Privately Held
**Web:** www.caninecaviar.com
**SIC:** 2048 Canned pet food (except dog and cat)

### (P-1124)
**DEXT COMPANY OF MARYLAND (DH)**
Also Called: Reconserve of Maryland
2811 Wilshire Blvd Ste 410, Santa Monica (90403-4803)
P.O. Box 2211 (90407-2211)
**PHONE**..................................310 458-1574
Meyer Luskin, *Ch Bd*
Robert Mcmullen, *Pr*
Rida Hamed, *VP Fin*
Gerald Truelove, *General Vice President*
**EMP:** 20 **EST:** 1985
**SQ FT:** 4,000
**SALES (est):** 3.69MM
**SALES (corp-wide):** 203.79MM Privately Held
**Web:** www.reconserve.com
**SIC:** 2048 Prepared feeds, nec
**HQ:** Reconserve, Inc.
2811 Wlshire Blvd Ste 410
Santa Monica CA 90403
310 458-1574

### (P-1125)
**ELK GROVE MILLING INC**
8320 Eschinger Rd, Elk Grove (95757-9739)
**PHONE**..................................916 684-2056
Robert Lent, *Pr*
▲ **EMP:** 25 **EST:** 1985
**SQ FT:** 400,000
**SALES (est):** 7.66MM Privately Held
**Web:** www.elkgrovemilling.com

**SIC:** 2048 3541 5191 Livestock feeds; Machine tools, metal cutting type; Animal feeds

### (P-1126)
**FOSTER POULTRY FARMS**
Also Called: FOSTER POULTRY FARMS
221 Stefani Ave, Livingston (95334-1543)
**PHONE**..................................209 394-7950
Jeremiah Nord, *Mgr*
**EMP:** 244
**SALES (corp-wide):** 1.25B Privately Held
**Web:** www.fosterfarms.com
**SIC:** 2048 Poultry feeds
**PA:** Foster Poultry Farms, Llc
1000 Davis St
209 394-7901

### (P-1127)
**GARMON CORPORATION (PA)**
Also Called: Naturvet
27461 Via Industria, Temecula (92590-3752)
**PHONE**..................................888 628-8783
Scott Garmon, *CEO*
Debra O'brien, *CFO*
Jodi Hoefler, *Sec*
▲ **EMP:** 60 **EST:** 1979
**SQ FT:** 18,500
**SALES (est):** 24.1MM
**SALES (corp-wide):** 24.1MM Privately Held
**Web:** www.naturvet.com
**SIC:** 2048 Feed supplements

### (P-1128)
**GEORGE VERHOEVEN GRAIN INC (PA)**
301 E 6th St, Hanford (93230-4651)
**PHONE**..................................909 605-1531
Randall Verhoeven, *Pr*
Robert Verhoeven, *VP*
**EMP:** 15 **EST:** 1988
**SALES (est):** 2.68MM Privately Held
**Web:** www.verhoevengraininc.com
**SIC:** 2048 5153 Livestock feeds; Grain elevators

### (P-1129)
**HARBOR GREEN GRAIN LP**
13181 Crossroads Pkwy N Ste 200, City Of Industry (91746-3451)
**PHONE**..................................310 991-8089
Shing Lo, *Pr*
Zach Xu, *CEO*
Kevin Yoon, *COO*
◆ **EMP:** 45 **EST:** 2014
**SALES (est):** 4.96MM Privately Held
**SIC:** 2048 Alfalfa, cubed

### (P-1130)
**HRK PET FOOD PRODUCTS INC**
12924 Pierce St, Pacoima (91331-2526)
**PHONE**..................................818 897-2521
Joey Herrick, *Pr*
Lynnda Herrick, *VP*
▲ **EMP:** 19 **EST:** 1999
**SQ FT:** 30,000
**SALES (est):** 628.71K Privately Held
**SIC:** 2048 Canned pet food (except dog and cat)

### (P-1131)
**INTEGRATED GRAIN & MILLING INC**
Also Called: I G M
7910 N Ingram Ave Ste 101, Fresno (93711-5828)
P.O. Box 27200 (93729-7200)

**PHONE**..................................559 443-6500
**EMP:** 42
**SIC:** 2048 5153 Cereal-, grain-, and seed-based feeds; Grains

### (P-1132)
**INTERNATIONAL PROCESSING CORP (DH)**
233 Wilshire Blvd Ste 310, Santa Monica (90401-1206)
P.O. Box 2211 (90407-2211)
**PHONE**..................................310 458-1574
Bob Mcmullen, *Pr*
**EMP:** 25 **EST:** 1953
**SALES (est):** 3.02MM
**SALES (corp-wide):** 203.79MM Privately Held
**SIC:** 2048 Prepared feeds, nec
**HQ:** Reconserve, Inc.
2811 Wlshire Blvd Ste 410
Santa Monica CA 90403
310 458-1574

### (P-1133)
**LAWLEYS INC**
Also Called: Lawley's Trucking
4554 Qantas Ln, Stockton (95206-5002)
P.O. Box 31447 (95213-1447)
**PHONE**..................................209 337-1170
Casey Lawley, *CEO*
Ron Lawley, *Bd of Dir*
Desirea Hernandez, *CFO*
**EMP:** 37 **EST:** 1984
**SQ FT:** 40,000
**SALES (est):** 9.45MM Privately Held
**Web:** www.lawleys.com
**SIC:** 2048 Feed premixes

### (P-1134)
**LAYNE LABORATORIES INC**
Also Called: Patina Products
4303 Huasna Rd, Arroyo Grande (93420-6175)
P.O. Box 1259 (93421-1259)
**PHONE**..................................805 242-7918
John Waterman, *CEO*
Patricia Moffitt, *
◆ **EMP:** 18 **EST:** 1990
**SQ FT:** 40,000
**SALES (est):** 1.73MM Privately Held
**Web:** www.laynelabs.com
**SIC:** 2048 Frozen pet food (except dog and cat)

### (P-1135)
**LEGACY EPOCH LLC**
21011 Warner Center Ln Ste A, Woodland Hills (91367-6509)
**PHONE**..................................844 673-7305
Shawn Lipman, *CEO*
Gary Puterman, *
Robert Roizen, *
Brian Roizen, *Chief Architect**
Igor Roizen, *Chief Scientist**
**EMP:** 83 **EST:** 2015
**SALES (est):** 11.31MM
**SALES (corp-wide):** 309.39MM Publicly Held
**Web:** www.feedonomics.com
**SIC:** 2048 Chicken feeds, prepared
**PA:** Bigcommerce Holdings, Inc.
11305 Four Pnts Dr Bldg I
512 865-4500

### (P-1136)
**LIND MARINE INCORPORATED (PA)**
1175 Nimitz Ave Ste 120, Vallejo (94592-1003)
**PHONE**..................................707 762-7251

## 2048 - Prepared Feeds, Nec (P-1137)

Mike Lind, *Pr*
Christian Lind, *VP*
**EMP:** 22 **EST:** 1920
**SQ FT:** 18,500
**SALES (est):** 14.01MM
**SALES (corp-wide):** 14.01MM **Privately Held**
**Web:** www.lindmarine.com
**SIC: 2048** 1629 Oyster shells, ground: prepared as animal feed; Dredging contractor

**(P-1137)**
**MODESTO MILLING INC**
Also Called: Empire Milling
142 Linley Ave, Empire (95319)
P.O. Box A (95319-0015)
**PHONE**.....................209 523-9167
**EMP:** 20 **EST:** 1974
**SALES (est):** 5.35MM **Privately Held**
**Web:** www.modestomilling.com
**SIC: 2048** Livestock feeds

**(P-1138)**
**NATURAL BALANCE PET FOODS LLC**
1224 Montague Unit 1, Pacoima (91331)
**PHONE**.....................800 829-4493
**EMP:** 68
**Web:** www.naturalbalanceinc.com
**SIC: 2048** Prepared feeds, nec
**PA:** Natural Balance Pet Foods, Llc
  19425 Soledad Cyn Rd #302

**(P-1139)**
**NATURAL BALANCE PET FOODS LLC (PA)**
19425 Soledad Canyon Rd # 302, Canyon Country (91351-2632)
P.O. Box 397 (91785-0397)
**PHONE**.....................800 829-4493
Brian Connolly, *CEO*
▲ **EMP:** 65 **EST:** 1989
**SQ FT:** 55,000
**SALES (est):** 26.42MM **Privately Held**
**Web:** www.naturalbalanceinc.com
**SIC: 2048** 5199 Prepared feeds, nec; Pet supplies

**(P-1140)**
**NUTRA-BLEND LLC**
Also Called: Thomas Products
2140 W Industrial Ave, Madera (93637-5210)
**PHONE**.....................559 661-6161
Mike Osborne, *Brnch Mgr*
**EMP:** 420
**SALES (corp-wide):** 2.89B **Privately Held**
**Web:** www.nutrablend.com
**SIC: 2048** 5191 Pulverized oats, prepared as animal feed; Animal feeds
**HQ:** Nutra-Blend, L.L.C.
  3200 E 2nd St
  Neosho MO 64850
  800 657-5657

**(P-1141)**
**NUTRIUS LLC (PA)**
Also Called: Nutrius
39494 Clarkson Dr, Kingsburg (93631-9100)
**PHONE**.....................559 897-5862
▲ **EMP:** 27 **EST:** 2005
**SALES (est):** 9.86MM **Privately Held**
**Web:** www.nutrius.com
**SIC: 2048** Prepared feeds, nec

**(P-1142)**
**NUWEST MILLING LLC**
4636 Geer Rd, Hughson (95326-9403)
P.O. Box 1031 (95326-1031)
**PHONE**.....................209 883-1163
Gary West, *Managing Member*
◆ **EMP:** 16 **EST:** 1998
**SQ FT:** 1,250
**SALES (est):** 7.15MM **Privately Held**
**Web:** www.nuwestmilling.com
**SIC: 2048** Prepared feeds, nec

**(P-1143)**
**PACIFIC CATCH INC**
Also Called: Pacific Catch
770 Tamalpais Dr Ste 210, Corte Madera (94925-1736)
**PHONE**.....................415 504-6905
Keith M Cox, *Pr*
**EMP:** 23 **EST:** 2011
**SALES (est):** 9.24MM **Privately Held**
**Web:** www.pacificcatch.com
**SIC: 2048** Prepared feeds, nec

**(P-1144)**
**PITMAN FARMS**
Pitman Farms
10365 Iona Ave, Hanford (93230-9553)
**PHONE**.....................559 585-3330
Al Ward, *Manager*
**EMP:** 55
**SALES (corp-wide):** 100.1MM **Privately Held**
**Web:** www.pitmanfarms.com
**SIC: 2048** Livestock feeds
**PA:** Pitman Family Farms
  1075 N Ave
  559 875-9300

**(P-1145)**
**RECONSERVE INC (HQ)**
Also Called: Dext Company
2811 Wilshire Blvd Ste 410, Santa Monica (90403-4805)
P.O. Box 2211 (90407-2211)
**PHONE**.....................310 458-1574
Meyer Luskin, *CEO*
David Luskin, *
**EMP:** 25 **EST:** 1966
**SQ FT:** 5,000
**SALES (est):** 99.3MM
**SALES (corp-wide):** 203.79MM **Privately Held**
**Web:** www.reconserve.com
**SIC: 2048** Livestock feeds
**PA:** Scope Industries
  2811 Wilshire Blvd # 410
  310 458-1574

**(P-1146)**
**REED MARICULTURE INC**
Also Called: Instant Algae
900 E Hamilton Ave Ste 100, Campbell (95008-0613)
P.O. Box 1049 (95019-1049)
**PHONE**.....................408 377-1065
Timothy Allen Reed, *CEO*
Shawn Neverve, *VP*
Lyn Reed, *COO*
Edwin Reed, *Sec*
◆ **EMP:** 18 **EST:** 1995
**SQ FT:** 217,800
**SALES (est):** 4.88MM **Privately Held**
**Web:** www.reedmariculture.com
**SIC: 2048** Fish food

**(P-1147)**
**ROBINSON FARMS FEED COMPANY**
7000 S Inland Dr, Stockton (95206-9688)

**PHONE**.....................209 466-7915
**TOLL FREE:** 800
Michael S Robinson, *Pr*
Jerry N Robinson, *VP*
Dale L Drury, *Sec*
**EMP:** 60 **EST:** 1943
**SQ FT:** 10,000
**SALES (est):** 3.83MM **Privately Held**
**Web:** www.robinsonfarmsfeedco.com
**SIC: 2048** 0139 0119 0115 Feed premixes; Alfalfa farm; Safflower farm; Corn

**(P-1148)**
**S & M PROFESSIONALS INC (PA)**
Also Called: Sales & Mktg Professionals
710 Graves Ave, Oxnard (93030-8049)
**PHONE**.....................805 988-7677
Stephen M Prange, *CEO*
▲ **EMP:** 20 **EST:** 1999
**SALES (est):** 7.62MM **Privately Held**
**Web:** www.savoryprimepet.com
**SIC: 2048** Prepared feeds, nec

**(P-1149)**
**SAN FRANCISCO BAY BRAND INC (PA)**
8239 Enterprise Dr, Newark (94560-3305)
**PHONE**.....................510 792-7200
Andreas Schmidt, *Pr*
Anthony Schmidt, *
◆ **EMP:** 35 **EST:** 1969
**SQ FT:** 30,000
**SALES (est):** 6.61MM
**SALES (corp-wide):** 6.61MM **Privately Held**
**Web:** www.sfbb.com
**SIC: 2048** Fish food

**(P-1150)**
**SEED FACTORY NORTHWEST INC (PA)**
4319 Jessup Rd, Ceres (95307-9604)
P.O. Box 245 (95307-0245)
**PHONE**.....................209 634-8522
Randall Steele, *Pr*
Lynda Blakemore, *Sec*
▲ **EMP:** 20 **EST:** 2000
**SQ FT:** 30,000
**SALES (est):** 4.64MM
**SALES (corp-wide):** 4.64MM **Privately Held**
**Web:** www.volkmanpet.com
**SIC: 2048** Bird food, prepared

**(P-1151)**
**STAR MILLING CO**
23901 Water St, Perris (92570-9094)
P.O. Box 1987 (92572-1987)
**PHONE**.....................951 657-3143
William R Cramer Junior, *Pr*
Paul R Cramer, *
Greg W Carls, *
◆ **EMP:** 99 **EST:** 1952
**SALES (est):** 26.43MM **Privately Held**
**Web:** www.starmilling.com
**SIC: 2048** Poultry feeds

**(P-1152)**
**SUN-GRO COMMODITIES INC (PA)**
34575 Famoso Rd, Bakersfield (93308-9769)
**PHONE**.....................661 393-2612
Donald G Smith, *CEO*
Scott Smith, *
Lori Melendez, *
Wendy Smith, *
**EMP:** 25 **EST:** 1974

**SQ FT:** 1,400
**SALES (est):** 7.25MM
**SALES (corp-wide):** 7.25MM **Privately Held**
**Web:** www.sun-gro.com
**SIC: 2048** 4212 Livestock feeds; Local trucking, without storage

**(P-1153)**
**THOMAS PRODUCTS LLC**
Also Called: Tpi
2140 W Industrial Ave, Madera (93637-5210)
P.O. Box 64101 (55164-0101)
**PHONE**.....................559 661-6161
▲ **EMP:** 55
**SIC: 2048** Feed supplements

**(P-1154)**
**VIVOTEIN LLC**
231 S Pleasant Ave, Ontario (91761-1730)
**PHONE**.....................918 344-8742
Harout Ajaryan, *Managing Member*
**EMP:** 16 **EST:** 2016
**SALES (est):** 2.59MM **Privately Held**
**Web:** www.vivotein.com
**SIC: 2048** Prepared feeds, nec

## 2051 Bread, Cake, And Related Products

**(P-1155)**
**ALEXANDER INTERNATIONAL INC** ✪
150 S Rodeo Dr Ste 290, Beverly Hills (90212-2409)
**PHONE**.....................424 285-8080
Anna Menedjian, *Pr*
Susanna Sisakyan, *CFO*
Polina Levant, *CMO*
**EMP:** 20 **EST:** 2024
**SALES (est):** 1.13MM **Privately Held**
**SIC: 2051** Bakery: wholesale or wholesale/retail combined

**(P-1156)**
**ANDRE-BOUDIN BAKERIES INC**
67 Broadway Ln, Walnut Creek (94596-5104)
**PHONE**.....................925 935-4375
Andrew Friedman, *Mgr*
**EMP:** 27
**Web:** www.boudinbakery.com
**SIC: 2051** 5812 Bread, cake, and related products; Cafe
**HQ:** Andre-Boudin Bakeries, Inc.
  50 Francisco St Ste 200
  San Francisco CA 94133
  415 882-1849

**(P-1157)**
**ANDRE-BOUDIN BAKERIES INC (HQ)**
Also Called: Boudin Sourdough Bakery & Cafe
50 Francisco St Ste 200, San Francisco (94133-2132)
**PHONE**.....................415 882-1849
**EMP:** 25 **EST:** 1849
**SALES (est):** 151.13MM **Privately Held**
**Web:** www.boudinbakery.com
**SIC: 2051** 5812 5961 5461 Breads, rolls, and buns; Cafe; Food, mail order; Bread
**PA:** Boudin Holdings, Inc.
  221 Main St Ste 1230

## PRODUCTS & SERVICES SECTION
## 2051 - Bread, Cake, And Related Products (P-1180)

**(P-1158)**
**ASPIRE BAKERIES LLC**
Also Called: Fresh Start Bakeries
920 Shaw Rd, Stockton (95215-4014)
PHONE.................................209 469-4920
Dan Bailey, Brnch Mgr
**EMP:** 234
**SALES (corp-wide):** 1.78B Privately Held
Web: www.aspirebakeries.com
**SIC:** 2051 Bakery: wholesale or wholesale/retail combined
HQ: Aspire Bakeries Llc
6701 Center Dr W Ste 850
Los Angeles CA 90045
844 992-7747

**(P-1159)**
**ATHENS BAKING COMPANY INC**
1847 International Blvd, Oakland (94606-4804)
PHONE.................................510 533-5705
Dave Smart, Mgr
**EMP:** 15
**SALES (corp-wide):** 3.17MM Privately Held
Web: www.athensbaking.com
**SIC:** 2051 Bread, cake, and related products
PA: Athens Baking Company, Inc.
7080 N Whitney Ave # 103
559 324-8535

**(P-1160)**
**ATHENS BAKING COMPANY INC (PA)**
Also Called: Shannon's Imperial Brand
7080 N Whitney Ave Ste 103, Fresno (93720-0155)
PHONE.................................559 324-8535
**EMP:** 25 **EST:** 1910
**SALES (est):** 3.17MM
**SALES (corp-wide):** 3.17MM Privately Held
Web: www.athensbaking.com
**SIC:** 2051 5461 5142 Bakery: wholesale or wholesale/retail combined; Retail bakeries; Bakery products, frozen

**(P-1161)**
**ATORIAS BAKING COMPANY**
Also Called: Atoria's Family Bakery
101 Leavesley Rd, Gilroy (95020)
PHONE.................................408 846-0876
Rene Eshco, CEO
Lilea Eshoo, Prin
**EMP:** 20 **EST:** 2015
**SALES (est):** 1.33MM Privately Held
Web: www.atoriasfamilybakery.com
**SIC:** 2051 Bread, cake, and related products

**(P-1162)**
**BAGELRY INC (PA)**
320 Cedar St Ste A, Santa Cruz (95060-4362)
PHONE.................................831 429-8049
John Hamstra, Pr
Laurie Rivin, *
**EMP:** 35 **EST:** 1977
**SQ FT:** 3,000
**SALES (est):** 1.79MM
**SALES (corp-wide):** 1.79MM Privately Held
Web: www.bagelrysantacruz.com
**SIC:** 2051 5812 2052 Bakery: wholesale or wholesale/retail combined; Eating places; Cookies and crackers

**(P-1163)**
**BAKE R US INC**
Also Called: Dave's Baking Goods
2632 Wilshire Blvd Ste 463, Santa Monica (90403-4623)

PHONE.................................310 630-5873
**EMP:** 15
**SALES (corp-wide):** 3.37MM Privately Held
Web: www.davesbaking.com
**SIC:** 2051 Doughnuts, except frozen
PA: Bake R Us, Inc.
13400 S Western Ave
310 630-5873

**(P-1164)**
**BAKE USA INC**
Also Called: Retail
10250 Santa Monica Blvd, Los Angeles (90067-6404)
PHONE.................................415 629-8274
Jun Kawachi, CEO
**EMP:** 20 **EST:** 2017
**SALES (est):** 1MM Privately Held
Web: us.cheesetart.com
**SIC:** 2051 5461 Cakes, pies, and pastries; Pastries

**(P-1165)**
**BAKED IN THE SUN**
Also Called: S & S Bakery
2560 Progress St, Vista (92081-8465)
PHONE.................................760 591-9045
**EMP:** 250
Web: www.bakedinthesun.com
**SIC:** 2051 Bagels, fresh or frozen

**(P-1166)**
**BAKERS KNEADED LLC**
148 W 132nd St Ste D, Los Angeles (90061-1649)
PHONE.................................310 819-8700
Carlos Enriquez, CEO
Carlos Enriquez, Managing Member
Paul Cox, *
**EMP:** 28 **EST:** 2017
**SALES (est):** 2.45MM Privately Held
**SIC:** 2051 Bread, all types (white, wheat, rye, etc); fresh or frozen

**(P-1167)**
**BAKERY DEPOT INC**
4489 Bandini Blvd, Vernon (90058-4309)
PHONE.................................323 261-8388
Wilton Thinh Thai, CEO
◆ **EMP:** 15 **EST:** 2005
**SALES (est):** 10.04MM Privately Held
Web: www.bakerydepotinc.com
**SIC:** 2051 Bakery: wholesale or wholesale/retail combined

**(P-1168)**
**BECKMANNS OLD WORLD BAKERY LTD**
Also Called: Beckmann's Bakery
1053 17th Ave, Santa Cruz (95062-3053)
PHONE.................................831 423-9242
Beth Holland, CEO
Peter Beckmann, *
Sharon May, *
▲ **EMP:** 100 **EST:** 1985
**SQ FT:** 17,000
**SALES (est):** 9.04MM Privately Held
Web: www.beckmannsbakery.com
**SIC:** 2051 5461 Bakery: wholesale or wholesale/retail combined; Retail bakeries

**(P-1169)**
**BEST EXPRESS FOODS INC**
2651 S Airport Way, Stockton (95206-3522)
PHONE.................................209 465-5540
**EMP:** 260
Web: www.bestxfoods.com

**SIC:** 2051 Bread, cake, and related products
PA: Best Express Foods, Inc.
1718 Boeing Way Ste 100

**(P-1170)**
**BESTWAY SANDWICHES INC (PA)**
Also Called: Bestway Foods
28209 Avenue Stanford, Valencia (91355-3984)
PHONE.................................818 361-1800
Khachatur Budagyan, CEO
**EMP:** 46 **EST:** 2008
**SALES (est):** 12.2MM Privately Held
**SIC:** 2051 Bread, all types (white, wheat, rye, etc); fresh or frozen

**(P-1171)**
**BIMBO BAKERIES USA INC**
Also Called: Bimbo Bakeries USA, Inc
2007 N Main St, Manteca (95336-9629)
PHONE.................................209 825-8647
Jesus Mendoza, Brnch Mgr
**EMP:** 16
Web: www.arnoldbread.com
**SIC:** 2051 Bread, cake, and related products
HQ: Bimbo Bakeries Usa, Inc.
355 Business Center Drive
Horsham PA 19044
215 347-5500

**(P-1172)**
**BIMBO BAKERIES USA INC**
Also Called: Bimbo Bakeries USA, Inc
480 S Vail Ave, Montebello (90640-4947)
PHONE.................................323 720-6099
Edgar Jaramillo, Brnch Mgr
**EMP:** 18
Web: www.arnoldbread.com
**SIC:** 2051 Bakery: wholesale or wholesale/retail combined
HQ: Bimbo Bakeries Usa, Inc.
355 Business Center Drive
Horsham PA 19044
215 347-5500

**(P-1173)**
**BREAD SRSLY LLC**
3310 Peralta St, Oakland (94608-4132)
PHONE.................................646 244-9553
Sadie Scheffer, CEO
Sadie Sosha Scheffer, CEO
**EMP:** 17 **EST:** 2014
**SALES (est):** 1.09MM Privately Held
Web: www.breadsrsly.com
**SIC:** 2051 Bakery: wholesale or wholesale/retail combined

**(P-1174)**
**BUBBLES BAKING COMPANY**
15215 Keswick St, Van Nuys (91405-1014)
P.O. Box 2a (93287-0002)
PHONE.................................818 786-1700
FAX: 818 786-3617
**EMP:** 50
**SQ FT:** 23,000
**SALES (est):** 13.38MM Privately Held
**SIC:** 2051 Cakes, bakery: except frozen

**(P-1175)**
**CALIFORNIA CHURROS CORPORATION**
751 Via Lata, Colton (92324-3930)
PHONE.................................909 370-4777
Jorge D Martinez, CEO
Jorge D Martinez Senior, Pr
Eva A Martinez, *
Frank Ruvalcaba, *
**EMP:** 264 **EST:** 1980

**SQ FT:** 54,800
**SALES (est):** 8.34MM
**SALES (corp-wide):** 1.56B Publicly Held
Web: www.churros.com
**SIC:** 2051 Pastries, e.g. danish: except frozen
HQ: J & J Snack Foods Corp. Of California
5353 Downey Rd
Los Angeles CA 90058
323 581-0171

**(P-1176)**
**CENTRAL CALIFORNIA BAKING CO**
701 Industrial Dr Ca, Exeter (93221-2102)
PHONE.................................559 592-2270
Ken Hall, Admn
Diana Philips, Acctg Mgr
**EMP:** 178 **EST:** 2019
**SALES (est):** 171K
**SALES (corp-wide):** 497.81MM Privately Held
**SIC:** 2051 Bakery: wholesale or wholesale/retail combined
PA: United States Bakery
315 Ne 10th Ave
503 232-2191

**(P-1177)**
**CITY BAKING COMPANY**
1373 Lowrie Ave, South San Francisco (94080-6403)
PHONE.................................650 332-8730
Alex Bulazo, Pr
**EMP:** 55 **EST:** 1991
**SALES (est):** 5.56MM Privately Held
Web: www.citybaking.com
**SIC:** 2051 Bread, cake, and related products

**(P-1178)**
**COTTAGE BAKERY INC**
Also Called: Frozen Bakery
1831 S Stockton St, Lodi (95240-6302)
P.O. Box 1720 (95241-1720)
PHONE.................................209 334-3616
◆ **EMP:** 400 **EST:** 1972
**SALES (est):** 185.49MM
**SALES (corp-wide):** 3.43B Publicly Held
**SIC:** 2051 2053 5149 Bread, cake, and related products; Frozen bakery products, except bread; Bakery products
PA: Treehouse Foods, Inc.
2021 Spring Rd Ste 600
708 483-1300

**(P-1179)**
**DANISH BAKING CO INC**
Also Called: Bubbles Baking Company
15215 Keswick St, Van Nuys (91405-1014)
PHONE.................................818 786-1700
**EMP:** 70
**SIC:** 2051 Bread, cake, and related products

**(P-1180)**
**DAWN FOOD PRODUCTS INC**
Also Called: Dawn Bakery Service Center
2845 Faber St, Union City (94587-1203)
PHONE.................................510 487-9007
Paul Lawrence, Brnch Mgr
**EMP:** 29
**SALES (corp-wide):** 1.73B Privately Held
Web: www.dawnfoods.com
**SIC:** 2051 2045 5046 Bread, cake, and related products; Prepared flour mixes and doughs; Bakery equipment and supplies
HQ: Dawn Food Products, Inc.
3333 Sargent Rd
Jackson MI 49201

## 2051 - Bread, Cake, And Related Products (P-1181)

**(P-1181)**
**DAWN FOOD PRODUCTS INC**
15601 Mosher Ave Ste 230, Tustin (92780-6426)
PHONE..................714 258-1223
Joe Barsoppi, Genl Mgr
**EMP:** 150
**SALES (corp-wide):** 1.73B **Privately Held**
**Web:** www.dawnfoods.com
**SIC:** 2051 Pastries, e.g. danish: except frozen
**HQ:** Dawn Food Products, Inc.
  3333 Sargent Rd
  Jackson MI 49201

**(P-1182)**
**DESSERTS ON US INC**
57 Belle Falor Ct, Arcata (95521-9234)
PHONE..................707 822-0160
Emran Essa, CEO
Emran Essa, Pr
Kathleen Essa, Sec
▲ **EMP:** 15 **EST:** 1990
**SQ FT:** 20,000
**SALES (est):** 5.69MM **Privately Held**
**Web:** www.dessertsonus.com
**SIC:** 2051 2099 2052 Pastries, e.g. danish: except frozen; Dessert mixes and fillings; Cookies

**(P-1183)**
**DISTINCT INDULGENCE INC**
Also Called: Mrs Appletree's Bakery
5018 Lante St, Baldwin Park (91706-1839)
PHONE..................818 546-1700
Robert W Gray, Pr
Suzanne Gray, *
▲ **EMP:** 38 **EST:** 1985
**SQ FT:** 10,000
**SALES (est):** 8.28MM **Privately Held**
**Web:** www.mrsappletree.com
**SIC:** 2051 5499 Bakery: wholesale or wholesale/retail combined; Health and dietetic food stores

**(P-1184)**
**DOBAKE BAKERIES INC**
Also Called: Happy Doughnuts
810 81st Ave, Oakland (94621-2569)
P.O. Box 1447 (95476-1447)
PHONE..................510 834-3134
**EMP:** 100 **EST:** 1990
**SALES (est):** 2.04MM **Privately Held**
**Web:** www.dobake.com
**SIC:** 2051 Cakes, bakery: except frozen
**PA:** Gold Coast Baking Company, Llc
  21250 Califa St Ste 104

**(P-1185)**
**DONSUEMOR INC**
2080 N Loop Rd, Alameda (94502-8012)
PHONE..................888 420-4441
**EMP:** 100 **EST:** 1976
**SALES (est):** 13.85MM **Privately Held**
**Web:** www.donsuemor.com
**SIC:** 2051 Bakery: wholesale or wholesale/retail combined

**(P-1186)**
**DOUCE DE FRANCE**
686 Brdwy St, Redwood City (94063)
PHONE..................650 369-9644
Mauro Ferreira, Mgr
**EMP:** 15
**SALES (corp-wide):** 394.84K **Privately Held**
**Web:** www.cafedoucefrance.com
**SIC:** 2051 Bread, cake, and related products
**PA:** Douce De France
  104 Town And Country Vlg
  650 322-3601

**(P-1187)**
**DOUGHTRONICS INC (PA)**
Also Called: Acme Bread Company
1601 San Pablo Ave, Berkeley (94702-1317)
PHONE..................510 524-1327
Steven Sullivan, Pr
Susan Sullivan, *
Doug Volkmer, *
**EMP:** 30 **EST:** 1983
**SALES (est):** 15.74MM
**SALES (corp-wide):** 15.74MM **Privately Held**
**Web:** www.acmebread.com
**SIC:** 2051 5461 Bakery: wholesale or wholesale/retail combined; Bread

**(P-1188)**
**DOUGHTRONICS INC**
Also Called: Acme Bread Co Div II
2730 9th St, Berkeley (94710-2633)
PHONE..................510 843-2978
Rick Kirkby, Mgr
**EMP:** 40
**SQ FT:** 4,372
**SALES (corp-wide):** 15.74MM **Privately Held**
**Web:** www.acmebread.com
**SIC:** 2051 Bakery: wholesale or wholesale/retail combined
**PA:** Doughtronics, Inc.
  1601 San Pablo Ave
  510 524-1327

**(P-1189)**
**EDNER CORPORATION**
Also Called: Wayfarers
528 Oakshire Pl, Alamo (94507-2325)
PHONE..................925 831-1248
**EMP:** 15 **EST:** 1977
**SQ FT:** 21,408
**SALES (est):** 938.63K **Privately Held**
**SIC:** 2051 5149 Bread, cake, and related products; Groceries and related products, nec

**(P-1190)**
**EL METATE INC**
Also Called: El Metate Market
817 W 19th St, Costa Mesa (92627-3518)
PHONE..................949 646-9362
Brian Murrieta, Brnch Mgr
**EMP:** 190
**SALES (corp-wide):** 3.68MM **Privately Held**
**Web:** www.elmetate.com
**SIC:** 2051 2052 2099 5812 Breads, rolls, and buns; Cookies; Tortillas, fresh or refrigerated; Mexican restaurant
**PA:** El Metate, Inc.
  838 E 1st St
  714 542-3913

**(P-1191)**
**EL SEGUNDO BREAD BAR LLC**
Also Called: Bread Bar
701 E El Segundo Blvd, El Segundo (90245-4108)
PHONE..................310 615-9898
Myrna Al-midani, Managing Member
▲ **EMP:** 32 **EST:** 2004
**SQ FT:** 8,000
**SALES (est):** 2.28MM **Privately Held**
**Web:** www.breadbar.la
**SIC:** 2051 5149 Bread, all types (white, wheat, rye, etc); fresh or frozen; Bakery products

**(P-1192)**
**FEEMSTER CO INC**
Also Called: Some Crust Bakery
119 Yale Ave, Claremont (91711-4723)
PHONE..................909 621-9772
Larry Feemster, Pr
Sandra Feemster, *
**EMP:** 26 **EST:** 1997
**SQ FT:** 3,000
**SALES (est):** 894.14K **Privately Held**
**Web:** www.somecrust.com
**SIC:** 2051 5461 Bread, cake, and related products; Retail bakeries

**(P-1193)**
**FIESTA MEXICAN FOODS INC**
979 G St, Brawley (92227-2615)
PHONE..................760 344-3580
Raymond Armenta, Pr
**EMP:** 30 **EST:** 1956
**SQ FT:** 4,000
**SALES (est):** 2.5MM **Privately Held**
**SIC:** 2051 2099 Pastries, e.g. danish: except frozen; Tortillas, fresh or refrigerated

**(P-1194)**
**FIREBRAND PBC**
707 W Tower Ave, Alameda (94501-5073)
PHONE..................510 594-9213
Matt Kreutz, CEO
**EMP:** 63 **EST:** 2007
**SALES (est):** 8.79MM **Privately Held**
**Web:** www.firebrandbread.com
**SIC:** 2051 Bakery: wholesale or wholesale/retail combined

**(P-1195)**
**FLOWERS BAKERIES SLS SOCAL LLC** ◆
10625 Poplar Ave, Fontana (92337-7335)
PHONE..................702 281-4797
Mallyn Kong, Admn
**EMP:** 34 **EST:** 2024
**SALES (est):** 2.46MM **Privately Held**
**SIC:** 2051 Bread, all types (white, wheat, rye, etc); fresh or frozen

**(P-1196)**
**FLOWERS BAKING CO MODESTO LLC**
906 N Carpenter Rd, Modesto (95351-1195)
PHONE..................209 526-5512
Mallyn Kong, Mgr
**EMP:** 16
**SALES (corp-wide):** 5.09B **Publicly Held**
**Web:** www.flowersfoods.com
**SIC:** 2051 Breads, rolls, and buns
**HQ:** Flowers Baking Co. Of Modesto, Llc
  736 Mariposa Rd
  Modesto CA 95354
  209 857-4600

**(P-1197)**
**FLOWERS BAKING CO MODESTO LLC (HQ)**
736 Mariposa Rd, Modesto (95354-4115)
PHONE..................209 857-4600
**EMP:** 62 **EST:** 2013
**SQ FT:** 250,000
**SALES (est):** 21.5MM
**SALES (corp-wide):** 5.09B **Publicly Held**
**Web:** www.flowersfoods.com
**SIC:** 2051 Breads, rolls, and buns
**PA:** Flowers Foods, Inc.
  1919 Flowers Cir
  229 226-9110

**(P-1198)**
**FLOWERS BKG CO HENDERSON LLC**
21540 Blythe St, Canoga Park (91304-4910)
PHONE..................818 884-8970
**EMP:** 67
**SALES (corp-wide):** 5.09B **Publicly Held**
**Web:** www.flowersfoods.com
**SIC:** 2051 Breads, rolls, and buns
**HQ:** Flowers Baking Co. Of Henderson, Llc
  501 Conestoga Way
  Henderson NV 89002
  702 567-6401

**(P-1199)**
**FLOWERS BKG CO HENDERSON LLC**
3800 W Century Blvd, Inglewood (90303-1011)
PHONE..................310 695-9846
**EMP:** 67
**SALES (corp-wide):** 5.09B **Publicly Held**
**Web:** www.flowersfoods.com
**SIC:** 2051 Breads, rolls, and buns
**HQ:** Flowers Baking Co. Of Henderson, Llc
  501 Conestoga Way
  Henderson NV 89002
  702 567-6401

**(P-1200)**
**FLOWERS BKG CO HENDERSON LLC**
7311 Doig Dr, Garden Grove (92841-1806)
PHONE..................702 281-4797
**EMP:** 67
**SALES (corp-wide):** 5.09B **Publicly Held**
**Web:** www.flowersfoods.com
**SIC:** 2051 Breads, rolls, and buns
**HQ:** Flowers Baking Co. Of Henderson, Llc
  501 Conestoga Way
  Henderson NV 89002
  702 567-6401

**(P-1201)**
**FOOD FOR LIFE BAKING CO INC (PA)**
Also Called: Natural Food Mill
2991 Doherty St, Corona (92879-5811)
P.O. Box 1434 (92878-1434)
PHONE..................951 279-5090
R James Torres, Pr
Charles Torres, *
▲ **EMP:** 100 **EST:** 1970
**SQ FT:** 170,000
**SALES (est):** 36.34MM
**SALES (corp-wide):** 36.34MM **Privately Held**
**Web:** www.foodforlife.com
**SIC:** 2051 Bakery: wholesale or wholesale/retail combined

**(P-1202)**
**FREEPORT BAKERY INC**
2966 Freeport Blvd, Sacramento (95818-3855)
PHONE..................916 442-4256
Marlene Goetzeler, Pr
Walter Goetzeler, *
**EMP:** 38 **EST:** 1982
**SALES (est):** 2.57MM **Privately Held**
**Web:** www.freeportbakery.com
**SIC:** 2051 5461 5812 Bread, cake, and related products; Retail bakeries; Eating places

## PRODUCTS & SERVICES SECTION
## 2051 - Bread, Cake, And Related Products (P-1224)

**(P-1203)**
**FRESH START BAKERIES INC**
Also Called: Fresh Start Bakeries N Amer
145 S State College Blvd Ste 200, Brea (92821-5806)
PHONE.................................714 256-8900
▲ EMP: 600
SIC: 2051 Bread, cake, and related products

**(P-1204)**
**FRESNO FRENCH BREAD BAKERY INC**
Also Called: Basque French Bakery
2625 Inyo St, Fresno (93721-2732)
PHONE.................................559 268-7088
Al Lewis, Pr
Rita Ingmire, *
EMP: 34 EST: 1963
SQ FT: 32,000
SALES (est): 4.53MM Privately Held
Web: www.fresnobread.com
SIC: 2051 Bakery: wholesale or wholesale/retail combined

**(P-1205)**
**FRISCO BAKING COMPANY INC**
Also Called: Frisco Baking Company
621 W Avenue 26, Los Angeles (90065-1095)
PHONE.................................323 225-6111
Aldo Pricco Junior, CEO
James Pricco, *
Ronald Perata, *
John Pricco, *
Mary Anne Fetter, *
EMP: 115 EST: 1938
SQ FT: 18,000
SALES (est): 5.8MM Privately Held
Web: www.friscobakingcompany.com
SIC: 2051 Bread, all types (white, wheat, rye, etc); fresh or frozen

**(P-1206)**
**FULLBLOOM BAKING COMPANY INC**
6500 Overlake Pl, Newark (94560-1083)
PHONE.................................510 456-3638
Karen Trilevsky, CEO
▲ EMP: 68 EST: 1989
SQ FT: 95,000
SALES (est): 4.75MM
SALES (corp-wide): 1.78B Privately Held
Web: www.fullbloom.com
SIC: 2051 Bread, cake, and related products
HQ: Aspire Bakeries Llc
6701 Center Dr W Ste 850
Los Angeles CA 90045
844 992-7747

**(P-1207)**
**FUSION FOOD FACTORY**
Also Called: La Jolla Baking Co
8980 Crestmar Pt, San Diego (92121-3222)
PHONE.................................858 578-8001
Steve Kwon, Pr
EMP: 20 EST: 1998
SALES (est): 4.1MM Privately Held
Web: www.lajollabaking.com
SIC: 2051 Bread, cake, and related products

**(P-1208)**
**GALASSOS BAKERY (PA)**
10820 San Sevaine Way, Mira Loma (91752-1116)
PHONE.................................951 360-1211
Jeannette Galasso, CEO
Jeannette Galasso, Pr
Mark Bailey, *
Pearl Denault, *
Rick Vargas, Operations*
EMP: 180 EST: 1968
SQ FT: 110,000
SALES (est): 33.21MM
SALES (corp-wide): 33.21MM Privately Held
Web: www.galassos.com
SIC: 2051 Bread, cake, and related products

**(P-1209)**
**GALAXY DESSERTS**
1100 Marina Way S Ste D, Richmond (94804-3727)
PHONE.................................510 439-3160
Paul Levitan, CEO
Jean-yves Charon, VP
▲ EMP: 160 EST: 1991
SQ FT: 56,000
SALES (est): 26.41MM
SALES (corp-wide): 6.34MM Privately Held
Web: www.galaxydesserts.com
SIC: 2051 Bread, cake, and related products
HQ: Brioche Pasquier Cerqueux
Route D'yzernay
Les Cerqueux PDL 49360
241637500

**(P-1210)**
**GIULIANO-PAGANO CORPORATION**
Also Called: Giuliano's Bakery
1264 E Walnut St, Carson (90746-1319)
PHONE.................................310 537-7700
Nancy Ritmire Giuliano, Ch Bd
Gregory Ritmire, *
EMP: 100 EST: 1952
SQ FT: 40,000
SALES (est): 1.69MM Privately Held
Web: www.giulianos.com
SIC: 2051 Bakery: wholesale or wholesale/retail combined

**(P-1211)**
**GLOBAL IMPACT INV PARTNERS LLC**
1410 Westwood Blvd Apt 260, Los Angeles (90024-4974)
PHONE.................................310 592-2000
EMP: 25 EST: 2014
SQ FT: 16,400
SALES (est): 283.46K Privately Held
SIC: 2051 Cakes, bakery: except frozen

**(P-1212)**
**GOLD COAST BAKING COMPANY LLC**
1590 E Saint Gertrude Pl, Santa Ana (92705-5310)
PHONE.................................714 545-2253
Eli Cooperstein, Mgr
EMP: 26
Web: www.goldcoastbakery.com
SIC: 2051 Bread, cake, and related products
PA: Gold Coast Baking Company, Llc
21250 Califa St Ste 104

**(P-1213)**
**GOLD COAST BAKING COMPANY LLC**
21160 Califa St, Woodland Hills (91367-5002)
PHONE.................................818 575-7280
Carla Costa, Mgr
EMP: 16
Web: www.goldcoastbakery.com
SIC: 2051 Bakery: wholesale or wholesale/retail combined
PA: Gold Coast Baking Company, Llc
21250 Califa St Ste 104

**(P-1214)**
**GOLD COAST BAKING COMPANY LLC (PA)**
Also Called: Kanan Baking Company
21250 Califa St Ste 104, Woodland Hills (91367-5040)
PHONE.................................818 575-7280
Edward H Rogers Iii, CEO
EMP: 57 EST: 2003
SQ FT: 60,000
SALES (est): 104.72MM Privately Held
Web: www.goldcoastbakery.com
SIC: 2051 Bakery: wholesale or wholesale/retail combined

**(P-1215)**
**GOLDILOCKS CORPORATION CALIF (PA)**
Also Called: Goldilocks Bakeshop and Rest
30865 San Clemente St, Hayward (94544-7136)
PHONE.................................510 476-0700
Mendrei Leelin, Pr
Menard Leelin, Pr
Mendrei Leelin, VP
Cecilia Leelin, Treas
EMP: 50 EST: 2000
SQ FT: 12,000
SALES (est): 4.51MM
SALES (corp-wide): 4.51MM Privately Held
Web: www.goldilocks-usa.com
SIC: 2051 Bread, cake, and related products

**(P-1216)**
**HANNAHMAX BAKING INC**
14601 S Main St, Gardena (90248)
PHONE.................................310 380-6778
Joanne Adirim, CEO
Stuart Scwartz, *
EMP: 145 EST: 1993
SQ FT: 15,000
SALES (est): 10.18MM Privately Held
Web: www.hannahmax.com
SIC: 2051 Bakery: wholesale or wholesale/retail combined

**(P-1217)**
**HOUSE OF BAGELS INC (PA)**
1007 Washington St, San Carlos (94070-5318)
PHONE.................................650 595-4700
Larry Chassy, Pr
EMP: 15 EST: 1962
SALES (est): 5.52MM
SALES (corp-wide): 5.52MM Privately Held
Web: www.houseofbagels.co
SIC: 2051 5461 Bread, cake, and related products; Retail bakeries

**(P-1218)**
**JEANNINES BKG CO SANTA BARBARA (PA)**
Also Called: Jeannine's Bakery
3607 State St, Santa Barbara (93105-2521)
P.O. Box 8929 (93118-8929)
PHONE.................................805 687-8701
Gordon Hardey, CEO
Gordon W Hardey, CEO
Eleanor Hardey, Pr
EMP: 19 EST: 1991
SQ FT: 1,800
SALES (est): 4.52MM Privately Held
Web: www.jeannines.com
SIC: 2051 5812 Bread, cake, and related products; American restaurant

**(P-1219)**
**JULIANS FOODS LLC**
3021 Industry St, Oceanside (92054-4834)
PHONE.................................760 583-9358
Mauricio Gomory, Admn
Sergio Rosado, Managing Member
EMP: 20 EST: 2022
SALES (est): 1.13MM Privately Held
Web: www.julianbakery.com
SIC: 2051 1541 Bakery: wholesale or wholesale/retail combined; Food products manufacturing or packing plant construction

**(P-1220)**
**LA BREA BAKERY CAFE INC**
14490 Catalina St, San Leandro (94577-5516)
PHONE.................................818 742-4242
◆ EMP: 1200
SIC: 2051 2052 2053 Bread, cake, and related products; Cookies and crackers; Frozen bakery products, except bread

**(P-1221)**
**LAURAS ORGNAL BSTON BRWNIES IN**
Also Called: Bhu Food
2735 Cactus Rd Ste 101, San Diego (92154-8024)
PHONE.................................619 855-3258
Laura Katleman, CEO
EMP: 18 EST: 2013
SQ FT: 4,000
SALES (est): 6.11MM Privately Held
Web: www.bhufoods.com
SIC: 2051 2052 Bread, cake, and related products; Cookies and crackers

**(P-1222)**
**LAVASH CORPORATION OF AMERICA**
Also Called: Tonenel Lavash
2835 Newell St, Los Angeles (90039-3817)
PHONE.................................323 663-5249
Edmond Hartounin, Pr
EMP: 25 EST: 1980
SQ FT: 10,000
SALES (est): 2.44MM Privately Held
Web: www.organicflatbread.net
SIC: 2051 Bakery: wholesale or wholesale/retail combined

**(P-1223)**
**LITTLE BROTHERS BAKERY LLC**
Also Called: Little Brothers Bakery
320 W Alondra Blvd, Gardena (90248-2423)
PHONE.................................310 225-3790
Paul C Giuliano, Managing Member
Anthony S Giuliano, *
Joann Giuliano, *
▲ EMP: 65 EST: 1999
SQ FT: 15,000
SALES (est): 10.19MM Privately Held
Web: www.littlebrothersbakery.com
SIC: 2051 5149 Bakery: wholesale or wholesale/retail combined; Bakery products

**(P-1224)**
**LUPITAS BAKERY INC (PA)**
1848 W Florence Ave, Los Angeles (90047-2123)
PHONE.................................323 752-2391
Able Diaz, Pr
Martha Diaz, Sec
EMP: 18 EST: 1985
SQ FT: 8,000
SALES (est): 1.78MM
SALES (corp-wide): 1.78MM Privately Held

## 2051 - Bread, Cake, And Related Products (P-1225)

**(P-1225)**
**LY BROTHERS CORPORATION (PA)**
Also Called: Sugar Bowl Bakery
1963 Sabre St, Hayward (94545-1021)
PHONE..................510 782-2118
Joel Feldman, *
Andrew A Ly, *
Joel Feldman, *
Sam Ly, *
Binh Ly, *
◆ EMP: 99 EST: 1954
SQ FT: 100,000
SALES (est): 97.67MM
SALES (corp-wide): 97.67MM Privately Held
Web: www.sugarbowlbakery.com
SIC: 2051 Bakery: wholesale or wholesale/retail combined

**(P-1226)**
**LY BROTHERS CORPORATION**
Also Called: Sugar Bowl Bakery
20389 Corsair Blvd, Hayward (94545-1026)
PHONE..................510 782-2118
Andrew A Ly, Pr
EMP: 76
SALES (corp-wide): 97.67MM Privately Held
Web: www.sugarbowlbakery.com
SIC: 2051 Bakery: wholesale or wholesale/retail combined
PA: Ly Brothers Corporation
1963 Sabre St
510 782-2118

**(P-1227)**
**MARY ANNS BAKING CO INC**
Also Called: Mary Ann's
8371 Carbide Ct, Sacramento (95828-5636)
PHONE..................916 681-7444
George A Demas, Pr
John Demas, *
John Schell, *
EMP: 200 EST: 1961
SQ FT: 75,000
SALES (est): 33.48MM Privately Held
Web: www.maryannsbaking.com
SIC: 2051 Doughnuts, except frozen

**(P-1228)**
**MOCHI ICE CREAM COMPANY LLC (PA)**
Also Called: Mikawaya
5563 Alcoa Ave, Vernon (90058-3730)
PHONE..................323 587-5504
Jerry Bucan, CEO
Joel Friedman, Ofcr
◆ EMP: 30 EST: 1910
SQ FT: 10,000
SALES (est): 19.62MM
SALES (corp-wide): 19.62MM Privately Held
Web: www.mymochi.com
SIC: 2051 2024 5451 Cakes, pies, and pastries; Ice cream and frozen deserts; Ice cream (packaged)

**(P-1229)**
**MRP INC**
150 S La Cadena Dr, Colton (92324-3416)
P.O. Box 555 (92324-0555)
PHONE..................909 825-4800
Nick Telliard, Pr
Tom P Telliard, Pr
Nick Telliard, VP
EMP: 20 EST: 1956
SQ FT: 76,030
SALES (est): 6.46MM Privately Held
SIC: 2051 Cakes, bakery: except frozen

**(P-1230)**
**NOUSHIG INC**
Also Called: Amoretti
451 Lombard St, Oxnard (93030)
PHONE..................805 983-2903
Jack Barsoumian, CEO
Hayop L Barsoumian, *
Maral Barsoumian, *
◆ EMP: 50 EST: 1998
SQ FT: 10,000
SALES (est): 10.86MM Privately Held
Web: www.amoretti.com
SIC: 2051 5149 Bread, cake, and related products; Soft drinks

**(P-1231)**
**OLD NEW YORK BAGEL DELI CO INC (PA)**
Also Called: Old New York Deli & Bagel Co
4972 Verdugo Way, Camarillo (93012-8632)
P.O. Box 1288 (93066-1288)
PHONE..................805 484-3354
Michael J Raimondo, Pr
Julie Raimondo, VP
EMP: 15 EST: 1994
SQ FT: 2,400
SALES (est): 4.28MM Privately Held
Web: www.oldnewyork.com
SIC: 2051 5812 6794 Bakery: wholesale or wholesale/retail combined; Coffee shop; Franchises, selling or licensing

**(P-1232)**
**ORANGE BAKERY INC (HQ)**
17751 Cowan, Irvine (92614-6064)
PHONE..................949 863-1377
Yukinobu Saito, CEO
Yokinobu Saito, *
Mikio Kobayashi, *
Yoshiaki Okazaki, *
Kota Ueki, *
▲ EMP: 19 EST: 1978
SQ FT: 45,000
SALES (est): 49.04MM Privately Held
Web: www.orangebakery.com
SIC: 2051 Bread, cake, and related products
PA: Rheon Automatic Machinery Co.,Ltd.
2-3, Nozawamachi

**(P-1233)**
**OVEN FRESH BAKERY INCORPORATED**
23188 Foley St, Hayward (94545-1602)
PHONE..................650 366-9201
Juanita Casillas, Pr
Jorge A Alfonso, Treas
EMP: 15 EST: 1951
SQ FT: 18,000
SALES (est): 1.91MM Privately Held
Web: www.ovenfresh-bakery.com
SIC: 2051 2053 Bakery: wholesale or wholesale/retail combined; Frozen bakery products, except bread

**(P-1234)**
**PAMELAS PRODUCTS INCORPORATED**
Also Called: Pamela's Products
1 Carousel Ln Ste D, Ukiah (95482-9509)
PHONE..................707 462-6605
EMP: 85
Web: www.pamelasproducts.com

**(P-1235)**
**PAN-O-RAMA BAKING INC**
500 Florida St, San Francisco (94110-1415)
PHONE..................415 522-5500
Bill Upson, Pr
EMP: 16 EST: 1993
SALES (est): 2.14MM Privately Held
Web: www.panoramabaking.com
SIC: 2051 Bakery: wholesale or wholesale/retail combined

**(P-1236)**
**PASCAL PATISSERIE**
21040 Victory Blvd, Woodland Hills (91367-2601)
PHONE..................818 712-9375
Bruno Marcy, Pr
EMP: 18 EST: 2015
SALES (est): 1.08MM Privately Held
SIC: 2051 Bakery: wholesale or wholesale/retail combined

**(P-1237)**
**PETITS PAINS & CO LP**
1730 Gilbreth Rd, Burlingame (94010-1305)
PHONE..................650 692-6000
Alain Bourgade, Prin
EMP: 26 EST: 2013
SALES (est): 6.12MM Privately Held
Web: www.petitspains.com
SIC: 2051 Bakery: wholesale or wholesale/retail combined

**(P-1238)**
**PIN HSIAO & ASSOCIATES LLC**
Also Called: Antonina's Bakery
1316 Dupont Ct, Manteca (95336-6004)
P.O. Box 40177 (98015-4177)
PHONE..................209 665-4176
Todd Wetherell, Manager
EMP: 52
Web: www.antoninasglutenfreebakery.com
SIC: 2051 Bakery: wholesale or wholesale/retail combined
PA: Pin Hsiao & Associates L.L.C.
5501 W Vly Hwy E Ste A101

**(P-1239)**
**QUINOA CORPORATION**
Also Called: Ancient Harvest
1 Carousel Ln Ste D, Ukiah (95482-9509)
PHONE..................707 462-6605
Dave Schnorr, Brnch Mgr
EMP: 44
SALES (corp-wide): 24.46MM Privately Held
Web: www.ancientharvest.com
SIC: 2051 2052 Bakery products, partially cooked (except frozen); Cookies and crackers
HQ: Quinoa Corporation
4653 Tbl Muntian Dr Ste A
Golden CO 80403
310 217-8125

**(P-1240)**
**RISE BAKING COMPANY LLC**
2111 W Valley Blvd, Colton (92324-1814)
PHONE..................909 825-7343
Bret Weaver, Brnch Mgr
EMP: 72
Web: www.risebakingcompany.com
SIC: 2051 2053 Bread, cake, and related products; Pies, bakery; frozen
HQ: Rise Baking Company, Llc
3001 Brdway St Ne Ste 400
Minneapolis MN 55413
612 455-7500

**(P-1241)**
**ROSSMOOR PASTRIES MGT INC**
2325 Redondo Ave, Signal Hill (90755-4019)
PHONE..................562 498-2253
Charles Feder, CEO
Janice Ahlgren, *
EMP: 80 EST: 2000
SALES (est): 3.95MM Privately Held
Web: www.rossmoorpastries.com
SIC: 2051 Bread, cake, and related products

**(P-1242)**
**SGB BETTER BAKING CO LLC**
14528 Blythe St, Van Nuys (91402-6006)
PHONE..................818 787-9992
Chris Botticella, CEO
Ash Aghasi, *
EMP: 57 EST: 2019
SALES (est): 1.54MM
SALES (corp-wide): 22.41MM Privately Held
SIC: 2051 5149 Bakery: wholesale or wholesale/retail combined; Bakery products
PA: Surge Global Bakeries Holdings Llc
13336 Paxton St
818 896-0525

**(P-1243)**
**SGB BUBBLES BAKING CO LLC**
15215 Keswick St, Van Nuys (91405-1014)
PHONE..................818 786-1700
Lewis Sharp, *
EMP: 100 EST: 2019
SQ FT: 50,000
SALES (est): 1.26MM Privately Held
SIC: 2051 5461 Bread, cake, and related products; Retail bakeries

**(P-1244)**
**SUGAR FOODS LLC**
6190 E Slauson Ave, Commerce (90040-3010)
PHONE..................323 727-8290
Harland Gray, Mgr
EMP: 100
SALES (corp-wide): 677.96MM Privately Held
Web: www.sugarfoods.com
SIC: 2051 2052 2099 Bread, cake, and related products; Cookies and crackers; Food preparations, nec
HQ: Sugar Foods Llc
3059 Townsgate Rd Ste 101
Westlake Village CA 91361
805 396-5000

**(P-1245)**
**SWEETIE PIES LLC**
520 Main St, Napa (94559-3353)
PHONE..................707 257-7280
EMP: 19 EST: 1994
SQ FT: 600
SALES (est): 3.18MM Privately Held
Web: www.sweetiepies.com
SIC: 2051 5812 Bakery: wholesale or wholesale/retail combined; Eating places

**(P-1246)**
**TALLGRASS PICTURES LLC**
Also Called: Izola
710 13th St Ste 300, San Diego (92101-7351)
PHONE..................619 227-2701
Jeffrey Lamont Brown, Managing Member
EMP: 29 EST: 2004
SALES (est): 2.5MM Privately Held

# PRODUCTS & SERVICES SECTION
## 2052 - Cookies And Crackers (P-1267)

Web: www.izolabakery.com
SIC: 2051 Bakery: wholesale or wholesale/retail combined

**(P-1247)**
**TARTINE LP**
Also Called: Tartine Bakery & Cafe
600 Guerrero St, San Francisco (94110-1528)
PHONE.................................415 487-2600
Frederic Soulies, CEO
Chad Robertson, *
Elisabeth Prueitt, *
EMP: 45 EST: 2002
SALES (est): 9.27MM Privately Held
Web: www.tartinebakery.com
SIC: 2051 5812 5921 Breads, rolls, and buns; Cafe; Wine and beer

**(P-1248)**
**THIRD CULTURE FOOD GROUP INC**
2701 8th St, Berkeley (94710-2675)
PHONE.................................650 479-4585
Raymundus Butarbutar, CEO
EMP: 26 EST: 2017
SALES (est): 2.34MM Privately Held
Web: www.thirdculturebakery.com
SIC: 2051 Bakery: wholesale or wholesale/retail combined

**(P-1249)**
**UNITED STATES BAKERY**
Also Called: Franz Family Bakeries
457 E Martin Luther King Jr Blvd, Los Angeles (90011-5650)
PHONE.................................323 232-6124
EMP: 26
SALES (corp-wide): 497.81MM Privately Held
Web: www.franzbakery.com
SIC: 2051 Bread, cake, and related products
PA: United States Bakery
315 Ne 10th Ave
503 232-2191

**(P-1250)**
**VALLEY LAHVOSH BAKING CO INC**
502 M St, Fresno (93721-3013)
PHONE.................................559 485-2700
Janet F Saghatelian, Pr
Agnes Wilson, *
▲ EMP: 30 EST: 1922
SQ FT: 27,000
SALES (est): 5.44MM Privately Held
Web: www.valleylahvosh.com
SIC: 2051 5461 Bread, all types (white, wheat, rye, etc); fresh or frozen; Bread

**(P-1251)**
**VBC HOLDINGS INC**
134 Main St, El Segundo (90245-3801)
PHONE.................................310 322-7357
James N Desisto, CEO
Larry De Sisto, *
EMP: 40 EST: 1959
SQ FT: 35,000
SALES (est): 1.07MM Privately Held
Web: www.venicebakery.com
SIC: 2051 5149 Bread, all types (white, wheat, rye, etc); fresh or frozen; Baking supplies

**(P-1252)**
**VURGER CO (USA) CORP**
1800 Century Park E Ste 600, Los Angeles (90067-1501)
PHONE.................................929 318-9546

Rachel Hugh, CEO
EMP: 50 EST: 2022
SALES (est): 803.26K Privately Held
SIC: 2051 Bakery: wholesale or wholesale/retail combined

**(P-1253)**
**WESTERN BAGEL BAKING CORP (PA)**
7814 Sepulveda Blvd, Van Nuys (91405-1020)
PHONE.................................818 786-5847
Steven Ustin, Pr
▼ EMP: 225 EST: 1946
SQ FT: 23,500
SALES (est): 44.04MM
SALES (corp-wide): 44.04MM Privately Held
Web: www.westernbagel.com
SIC: 2051 5461 Bagels, fresh or frozen; Bagels

**(P-1254)**
**WESTERN BAGEL BAKING CORP**
21749 Ventura Blvd, Woodland Hills (91364-1835)
PHONE.................................818 887-5451
Tim Brennen, Prin
EMP: 24
SALES (corp-wide): 44.04MM Privately Held
Web: www.westernbagel.com
SIC: 2051 5461 Bagels, fresh or frozen; Bagels
PA: Western Bagel Baking Corp
7814 Sepulveda Blvd
818 786-5847

**(P-1255)**
**WINDMILL CORPORATION**
Also Called: Wedemeyer Bakery
314 Harbor Way, South San Francisco (94080-6900)
PHONE.................................650 873-1000
Larry Strain, Pr
EMP: 17 EST: 2004
SALES (est): 2.71MM Privately Held
Web: www.wedemeyerbakery.com
SIC: 2051 5461 5149 Bread, all types (white, wheat, rye, etc); fresh or frozen; Retail bakeries; Groceries and related products, nec

**(P-1256)**
**YAMAZAKI BAKING CO LTD**
335 E 2nd St Ste 223, Los Angeles (90012-4220)
PHONE.................................323 581-5218
Yoshinaga Nagano, Admn
EMP: 33
Web: www.yamazakipan.co.jp
SIC: 2051 Bakery: wholesale or wholesale/retail combined
PA: Yamazaki Baking Co., Ltd.
3-10-1, Iwamotocho

## 2052 Cookies And Crackers

**(P-1257)**
**ADRIENNES GOURMET FOODS**
849 Ward Dr, Santa Barbara (93111-2920)
PHONE.................................805 964-6848
▲ EMP: 60
SIC: 2052 2099 2098 Cookies and crackers; Food preparations, nec; Macaroni and spaghetti

**(P-1258)**
**AMAYS BAKERY & NOODLE CO INC (PA)**
837 E Commercial St, Los Angeles (90012-3413)
PHONE.................................213 626-2713
Kee Hom, CEO
▲ EMP: 63 EST: 1968
SQ FT: 20,000
SALES (est): 9.6MM
SALES (corp-wide): 9.6MM Privately Held
Web: www.amaysbakery.com
SIC: 2052 2098 Cookies; Noodles (e.g. egg, plain, and water), dry

**(P-1259)**
**ASPIRE BAKERIES HOLDCO LLC (HQ)**
6701 Center Dr W Ste 850, Los Angeles (90045-1695)
PHONE.................................844 992-7747
Tyson Yu, Pr
Didier Vinamont, *
Chris Woo, *
EMP: 135 EST: 2021
SALES (est): 1.62B
SALES (corp-wide): 1.78B Privately Held
SIC: 2052 2053 2051 Cookies; Frozen bakery products, except bread; Cakes, pies, and pastries
PA: Goldberg Lindsay & Co. Llc
630 Fifth Ave 30th Fl
212 651-1100

**(P-1260)**
**ASPIRE BAKERIES LLC (DH)**
6701 Center Dr W Ste 850, Los Angeles (90045)
PHONE.................................844 992-7747
Tyson Yu, CEO
◆ EMP: 235 EST: 1977
SQ FT: 90,000
SALES (est): 1.6B
SALES (corp-wide): 1.78B Privately Held
Web: www.aspirebakeries.com
SIC: 2052 2053 2051 Cookies; Frozen bakery products, except bread; Cakes, pies, and pastries
HQ: Aspire Bakeries Holdings Llc
6701 Center Dr W Ste 850
Los Angeles CA 90045
844 992-7747

**(P-1261)**
**ASPIRE BAKERIES LLC**
15963 Strathern St, Van Nuys (91406-1313)
PHONE.................................818 904-8230
Marcus Garcia, Brnch Mgr
EMP: 390
SALES (corp-wide): 1.78B Privately Held
Web: www.aspirebakeries.com
SIC: 2052 Cookies
HQ: Aspire Bakeries Llc
6701 Center Dr W Ste 850
Los Angeles CA 90045
844 992-7747

**(P-1262)**
**ASPIRE BAKERIES LLC**
357 W Santa Ana Ave, Bloomington (92316-2901)
PHONE.................................714 478-4656
Armando Villalpando, Mgr
EMP: 121
SALES (corp-wide): 1.78B Privately Held
Web: www.aspirebakeries.com
SIC: 2052 Cookies
HQ: Aspire Bakeries Llc
6701 Center Dr W Ste 850
Los Angeles CA 90045
844 992-7747

**(P-1263)**
**ASPIRE BAKERIES MIDCO LLC (DH)**
6701 Center Dr W Ste 850, Los Angeles (90045-1695)
PHONE.................................844 992-7747
Tyson Yu, Pr
Didier Vinamont, *
Chris Woo, *
EMP: 17 EST: 2021
SALES (est): 1.62B
SALES (corp-wide): 1.78B Privately Held
Web: www.aspirebakeries.com
SIC: 2052 2053 2051 Cookies; Frozen bakery products, except bread; Cakes, pies, and pastries
HQ: Aspire Bakeries Holdco Llc
6701 Center Dr W Ste 850
Los Angeles CA 90045
844 992-7747

**(P-1264)**
**BETTER BAKERY LLC**
Also Called: Better Bakery Co
444 E Santa Clara St, Ventura (93001-2749)
PHONE.................................661 294-9882
EMP: 212
Web: www.betterbakery.com
SIC: 2052 Bakery products, dry

**(P-1265)**
**BISCOMERICA CORP**
565 West Slover Ave, Rialto (92377)
P.O. Box 1070 (92376)
PHONE.................................909 877-5997
Nadi Soltan, Ch Bd
Ayad Fargo, *
◆ EMP: 252 EST: 1979
SQ FT: 250,000
SALES (est): 55.15MM Privately Held
Web: www.biscomericacorp.com
SIC: 2052 2064 Cookies; Candy and other confectionery products

**(P-1266)**
**BLOOMFIELD BAKERS**
Also Called: Bloomfield Bakers
10711 Bloomfield St, Los Alamitos (90720-2503)
PHONE.................................626 610-2253
William R Ross, Genl Pt
Gary Marx, Brnch Mgr
▼ EMP: 600 EST: 1992
SQ FT: 75,000
SALES (est): 104.92MM
SALES (corp-wide): 3.43B Publicly Held
Web: www.bloomfieldbakers.com
SIC: 2052 2064 Cookies; Candy and other confectionery products
HQ: Treehouse Private Brands, Inc.
2021 Spring Rd Ste 600
Oak Brook IL 60523

**(P-1267)**
**BROWNIE BAKER INC**
4870 W Jacquelyn Ave, Fresno (93722-5027)
PHONE.................................559 277-7070
Dennis Perkins, CEO
▲ EMP: 70 EST: 1979
SQ FT: 30,000
SALES (est): 1.77MM Privately Held
Web: www.browniebaker.com
SIC: 2052 2051 Cookies; Bread, cake, and related products

# 2052 - Cookies And Crackers (P-1268)

## (P-1268)
**CHARLIES SPECIALTIES INC**
501 Airpark Dr, Fullerton (92833-2501)
PHONE........................724 346-2350
Jay Thier, Pr
Edward G Byrnes Junior, Ch
Thomas C Byrnes, *
**EMP:** 93 **EST:** 1967
**SALES (est):** 1.31MM
**SALES (corp-wide):** 38.32MM **Privately Held**
**Web:** www.bkcompany.com
**SIC:** 2052 5149 5142 2045 Cookies; Groceries and related products, nec; Packaged frozen goods; Prepared flour mixes and doughs
**PA:** Byrnes And Kiefer Company
  131 Kline Ave
  724 538-5200

## (P-1269)
**CRUMBL COOKIES**
23702 El Toro Rd Ste B, Lake Forest (92630-8905)
PHONE........................949 519-0791
Spencer Hanks, Owner
**EMP:** 70 **EST:** 2021
**SALES (est):** 1.7MM **Privately Held**
**Web:** www.crumblcookies.com
**SIC:** 2052 Cookies

## (P-1270)
**D F STAUFFER BISCUIT CO INC**
Laguna Cookie Company
4041 W Garry Ave, Santa Ana (92704-6315)
PHONE........................714 546-6855
Albert Ovalle, Mgr
**EMP:** 50
**Web:** www.meijiamerica.com
**SIC:** 2052 Cookies
**HQ:** D F Stauffer Biscuit Co Inc
  360 S Belmont St
  York PA 17403
  717 815-4600

## (P-1271)
**DAWN FOOD PRODUCTS INC**
2455 Tenaya Dr, Modesto (95354-3918)
PHONE........................517 789-4400
Ty Hackman, Mgr
**EMP:** 26
**SALES (corp-wide):** 1.73B **Privately Held**
**Web:** www.dawnfoods.com
**SIC:** 2052 Bakery products, dry
**HQ:** Dawn Food Products, Inc.
  3333 Sargent Rd
  Jackson MI 49201

## (P-1272)
**DIBELLA BAKING COMPANY INC**
Also Called: Dibella
3524 Seagate Way Ste 110, Oceanside (92056-2673)
PHONE........................951 797-4144
**EMP:** 65
**Web:** www.dibellafamiglia.com
**SIC:** 2052 Cookies

## (P-1273)
**ELEMENTS FOOD GROUP INC**
5560 Brooks St, Montclair (91763-4522)
P.O. Box 4020 (92661-4020)
PHONE........................909 983-2011
Wayne Sorensen, Pr
**EMP:** 60 **EST:** 2004
**SQ FT:** 23,000
**SALES (est):** 506.35K **Privately Held**
**Web:** www.elementsfoods.com
**SIC:** 2052 2038 Bakery products, dry; Breakfasts, frozen and packaged

## (P-1274)
**FANTASY COOKIE CORPORATION (PA)**
Also Called: Fantasy Cookie Company
12322 Gladstone Ave, Sylmar (91342-5318)
PHONE........................818 361-6901
▲ **EMP:** 34 **EST:** 1979
**SALES (est):** 11.57MM
**SALES (corp-wide):** 11.57MM **Privately Held**
**Web:** www.fantasycookie.com
**SIC:** 2052 Cookies and crackers

## (P-1275)
**FREDS FOODS, INC**
2300 S Watney Way Ste J, Fairfield (94533-6737)
P.O. Box 21302 (94521-0302)
PHONE........................707 639-9438
Fred Vuylsteke, CEO
Fred Vuylstele, Pr
**EMP:** 15 **EST:** 2020
**SALES (est):** 1.27MM **Privately Held**
**Web:** www.fredsfoods.com
**SIC:** 2052 Cookies

## (P-1276)
**GRANDVILLE LLC**
Also Called: Jihwaja Rice Bakery
1670 Cordova St, Los Angeles (90007-1112)
PHONE........................213 382-3878
**EMP:** 17
**SALES (corp-wide):** 373.44K **Privately Held**
**Web:** www.jihwajaricebakery.com
**SIC:** 2052 Rice cakes
**PA:** Grandville, Llc.
  1001 S Vermont Ave # 110
  213 382-3878

## (P-1277)
**INTERNTNAL DESSERTS DELICACIES (PA)**
Also Called: Cookie Lovers
4700 District Blvd, Vernon (90058-2714)
PHONE........................818 549-0056
Robbie Jacobs, Pr
Bonnie Jacobs, VP
Jeffrey Jacobs, Sec
**EMP:** 18 **EST:** 1983
**SQ FT:** 4,000
**SALES (est):** 2.85MM
**SALES (corp-wide):** 2.85MM **Privately Held**
**Web:** www.uncleeddiesvegancookies.com
**SIC:** 2052 Cookies

## (P-1278)
**J & J SNACK FOODS CORP CAL (HQ)**
5353 S Downey Rd, Los Angeles (90058-3725)
PHONE........................323 581-0171
Dan Fachner, Ch Bd
Ken Plunk, *
Lynwood Mallard, CMO*
Michael Pollner, *
Steve Every, *
▲ **EMP:** 96 **EST:** 1978
**SQ FT:** 132,000
**SALES (est):** 103.41MM
**SALES (corp-wide):** 1.56B **Publicly Held**
**Web:** www.jjsnack.com
**SIC:** 2052 5149 Pretzels; Cookies
**PA:** J&J Snack Foods Corp.
  350 Fellowship Rd
  856 665-9533

## (P-1279)
**KEEBLER COMPANY**
Also Called: Keebler
1550 N Chrisman Rd, Tracy (95304-9396)
PHONE........................209 836-0302
**EMP:** 101
**SALES (corp-wide):** 15.31B **Publicly Held**
**Web:** www.keebler.com
**SIC:** 2052 Cookies
**HQ:** Keebler Company
  1 Kellogg Sq
  Battle Creek MI 49017
  269 961-2000

## (P-1280)
**LAGUNA COOKIE COMPANY INC**
4041 W Garry Ave, Santa Ana (92704-6315)
PHONE........................714 546-6855
Takeshi Izumi, CEO
**EMP:** 100 **EST:** 1981
**SQ FT:** 55,000
**SALES (est):** 11.13MM **Privately Held**
**SIC:** 2052 Cookies
**HQ:** D F Stauffer Biscuit Co Inc
  360 S Belmont St
  York PA 17403
  717 815-4600

## (P-1281)
**PAK GROUP LLC**
Also Called: Dellarise
236 N Chester Ave Ste 200, Pasadena (91106-5166)
PHONE........................626 316-6555
Walter Postelwait, Managing Member
▲ **EMP:** 24 **EST:** 2012
**SQ FT:** 6,200
**SALES (est):** 1.2MM
**SALES (corp-wide):** 2.5MM **Privately Held**
**Web:** www.bellarise.com
**SIC:** 2052 2099 5149 Bakery products, dry; Food preparations, nec; Yeast
**PA:** Tech Us Corp
  236 N Chester Ave Ste 200
  626 316-6555

## (P-1282)
**PHENIX GOURMET LLC**
Also Called: Monaco Baking Company
4225 N Palm St, Fullerton (92835-1045)
PHONE........................562 404-5028
▲ **EMP:** 135
**SIC:** 2052 Cookies

## (P-1283)
**SOOJIANS INC**
Also Called: AK Mak Bakeries Division
89 Academy Ave, Sanger (93657-2104)
PHONE........................559 875-5511
Manoog Soojian, Pr
Hagop Soojian, VP
**EMP:** 21 **EST:** 1936
**SQ FT:** 8,000
**SALES (est):** 3.53MM **Privately Held**
**Web:** www.akmakbakeries.com
**SIC:** 2052 5046 Crackers, dry, nec; Bakery equipment and supplies

## (P-1284)
**SOUTH COAST BAKING LLC (PA)**
Also Called: South Coast Baking Co.
1711 Kettering, Irvine (92614-5615)
PHONE........................949 851-9654
Kent Hayden, CEO
Rick Ptak, *
◆ **EMP:** 55 **EST:** 2011
**SALES (est):** 88.26MM **Privately Held**
**SIC:** 2052 5149 Cookies; Cookies

---

## 2053 Frozen Bakery Products, Except Bread

## (P-1285)
**BENNETTS BAKING COMPANY**
Also Called: Bennett's Bakery
2530 Tesla Way, Sacramento (95825-1912)
PHONE........................916 481-3349
Michael Bennett, Pr
**EMP:** 15 **EST:** 1993
**SQ FT:** 3,000
**SALES (est):** 788.74K **Privately Held**
**Web:** www.bennettsbakery.com
**SIC:** 2053 Frozen bakery products, except bread

## (P-1286)
**BONERTS INCORPORATED**
Also Called: Bonert's Slice of Pie
3144 W Adams St, Santa Ana (92704-5808)
PHONE........................714 540-3535
Tim Rooney, Mgr
**EMP:** 50
**Web:** www.bonertspies.com
**SIC:** 2053 2051 Frozen bakery products, except bread; Bread, cake, and related products
**PA:** Bonert's Incorporated
  273 S Canon Dr

## (P-1287)
**HORIZON SNACK FOODS INC**
Also Called: Cutie Pie Snack Pies
197 Darcy Pkwy, Lathrop (95330-9222)
PHONE........................925 373-7700
William D Reynolds, Pr
Lee Rucker, *
Andrew Kunkler, *
Betty Blakely, *
**EMP:** 62 **EST:** 1957
**SQ FT:** 9,000
**SALES (est):** 9.14MM **Privately Held**
**Web:** www.getcutiepie.com
**SIC:** 2053 Pies, bakery; frozen
**PA:** Horizon Holdings, Llc
  1 Bush St

## (P-1288)
**MARYS COUNTRY KITCHEN**
Also Called: Malibu Kitchen
3900 Cross Creek Rd Ste 3, Malibu (90265-4962)
P.O. Box 153 (90265-0153)
PHONE........................310 456-7845
William Miller, Owner
**EMP:** 15 **EST:** 2000
**SALES (est):** 423.35K **Privately Held**
**Web:** www.malibucountrymart.com
**SIC:** 2053 Pies, bakery; frozen

## (P-1289)
**NATURAL DECADENCE LLC**
5720 West End Rd Ste 2, Arcata (95521-9395)
P.O. Box 644 (95524-0644)
PHONE........................707 444-2629
**EMP:** 17 **EST:** 2012
**SALES (est):** 2.4MM **Privately Held**
**Web:** www.raisedglutenfree.com
**SIC:** 2053 2052 Pies, bakery; frozen; Cookies

## PRODUCTS & SERVICES SECTION
## 2064 - Candy And Other Confectionery Products (P-1309)

**(P-1290)**
**NEMOS BAKERY INC (HQ)**
Also Called: Ne-Mo's
416 N Hale Ave, Escondido (92029-1496)
PHONE.................................760 741-5725
Phillip S Estes, *CEO*
Bob Yurick, *VP*
Sam Delucca Junior, *Sr VP*
James M Shorin, *Sec*
Michael J Chaignot, *CFO*
▲ **EMP:** 70 **EST:** 1975
**SALES (est):** 24.63MM **Privately Held**
Web: www.nemosbakery.com
**SIC: 2053** Cakes, bakery: frozen
**PA:** Horizon Holdings, Llc
    1 Bush St

**(P-1291)**
**OPERA PATISSERIE**
Also Called: Opera Patisserie
8480 Redwood Creek Ln, San Diego (92126-1067)
PHONE.................................858 536-5800
Diane Anderson, *Prin*
Vincent Garcia, *
**EMP:** 61 **EST:** 2002
**SQ FT:** 9,000
**SALES (est):** 5.19MM **Privately Held**
Web: www.operapatisserie.com
**SIC: 2053** 5812 Pastries, e.g. danish: frozen; Cafe

**(P-1292)**
**RICH PRODUCTS CORPORATION**
3401 W Segerstrom Ave, Santa Ana (92704-6404)
PHONE.................................714 338-1145
**EMP:** 28
**SALES (corp-wide):** 4.81B **Privately Held**
Web: www.richs.com
**SIC: 2053** Frozen bakery products, except bread
**PA:** Rich Products Corporation
    1 Robert Rich Way
    716 878-8000

## 2061 Raw Cane Sugar

**(P-1293)**
**AZUMEX CORP**
2320 Paseo De Las Americas, San Diego (92154-7276)
PHONE.................................619 710-8855
Fabian Gomez-ibarra, *CEO*
**EMP:** 28 **EST:** 2011
**SALES (est):** 4.28MM **Privately Held**
Web: www.azumexsugar.com
**SIC: 2061** Granulated cane sugar

## 2062 Cane Sugar Refining

**(P-1294)**
**CALIFORNIA SUGARS LLC**
1465 Tanforan Ave, Woodland (95776-6108)
P.O. Box 64799 (46401-0799)
PHONE.................................800 333-9666
John B Yonover, *Pr*
Matthew Yonover, *Mgr*
**EMP:** 28 **EST:** 2022
**SALES (est):** 1.86MM **Privately Held**
Web: www.sugars.com
**SIC: 2062** Cane sugar refining

## 2063 Beet Sugar

**(P-1295)**
**C&H SUGAR COMPANY INC**
Also Called: C&H Sugar
830 Loring Ave, Crockett (94525-1104)
PHONE.................................510 787-2121
Antonio L Contreras, *CEO*
Gabriel Buenaventura, *
Armando A Tabernilla, *
▲ **EMP:** 550 **EST:** 1998
**SQ FT:** 385,000
**SALES (est):** 100.42MM **Privately Held**
**SALES (corp-wide):** 2.16B **Privately Held**
Web: www.asr-group.com
**SIC: 2063** Beet sugar
**HQ:** American Sugar Refining, Inc.
    1 N Clematis St Ste 200
    West Palm Beach FL 33401
    561 366-5100

**(P-1296)**
**SPRECKELS SUGAR COMPANY INC**
395 W Keystone Rd, Brawley (92227-9759)
P.O. Box 581 (92227-0581)
PHONE.................................760 344-3110
John Richmond, *Pr*
John Richmond, *CEO*
Neil Rudeen, *
Jeff Plathe, *
▲ **EMP:** 260 **EST:** 1905
**SALES (est):** 25.24MM
**SALES (corp-wide):** 112.01MM **Privately Held**
Web: www.spreckelssugar.com
**SIC: 2063** Beet sugar, from beet sugar refinery
**PA:** Southern Minnesota Beet Sugar Cooperative
    83550 County Rd 21
    320 329-8305

## 2064 Candy And Other Confectionery Products

**(P-1297)**
**180 SNACKS INC**
Also Called: Mareblu Naturals
1173 N Armando St, Anaheim (92806-2609)
PHONE.................................714 238-1192
Michael Kim, *Pr*
Katherine Kim, *
▲ **EMP:** 47 **EST:** 2004
**SALES (est):** 9.16MM **Privately Held**
Web: www.180snacks.com
**SIC: 2064** 2034 2068 Granola and muesli, bars and clusters; Dried and dehydrated fruits; Salted and roasted nuts and seeds

**(P-1298)**
**ADAMS AND BROOKS INC**
4345 Hallmark Pkwy, San Bernardino (92407-1829)
P.O. Box 9940 (92427-0940)
PHONE.................................909 880-2305
▲ **EMP:** 160 **EST:** 1932
**SALES (est):** 23MM **Privately Held**
Web: www.adams-brooks.com
**SIC: 2064** Nuts, candy covered

**(P-1299)**
**AMERICAN LICORICE COMPANY**
2477 Liston Way, Union City (94587-1979)
P.O. Box 826 (94587-0826)
PHONE.................................510 487-5500
John Sullivan, *Prin*
**EMP:** 350
**SALES (corp-wide):** 96.11MM **Privately Held**
Web: www.americanlicorice.com
**SIC: 2064** Licorice candy
**PA:** American Licorice Company
    1914 Happiness Way
    219 324-1400

**(P-1300)**
**ANETTES CHOCOLATE FACTORY INC**
1321 1st St, Napa (94559-2958)
PHONE.................................707 252-4228
Anette M Madsen, *Pr*
Brent Madsen, *VP*
**EMP:** 15 **EST:** 1991
**SQ FT:** 4,500
**SALES (est):** 1.05MM **Privately Held**
Web: www.anettes.com
**SIC: 2064** 2024 5441 5812 Candy and other confectionery products; Ice cream, bulk; Confectionery; Ice cream stands or dairy bars

**(P-1301)**
**CALIFORNIA SNACK FOODS INC**
Also Called: California Candy
2131 Tyler Ave, South El Monte (91733-2754)
PHONE.................................626 444-4508
Murl W Nelson, *CEO*
Steve Nelson, *
Paul Mullen, *
Mary Nelson, *
**EMP:** 45 **EST:** 1961
**SQ FT:** 30,000
**SALES (est):** 6.91MM **Privately Held**
Web: www.californiasnackfoods.com
**SIC: 2064** 2024 2099 2051 Fruits candied, crystallized, or glazed; Juice pops, frozen; Popcorn, packaged: except already popped ; Cakes, pies, and pastries

**(P-1302)**
**CHOCOLATES A LA CARTE INC**
24836 Avenue Rockefeller, Valencia (91355-3467)
PHONE.................................661 257-3700
▲ **EMP:** 165
Web: www.candymaker.com
**SIC: 2064** 2066 Chocolate candy, except solid chocolate; Chocolate and cocoa products

**(P-1303)**
**CLIF BAR & COMPANY LLC (HQ)**
1451 66th St, Emeryville (94608)
PHONE.................................510 596-6300
Sally Grimes, *CEO*
Hari Avula, *
Kevin Cleary, *
▲ **EMP:** 213 **EST:** 1986
**SQ FT:** 120,000
**SALES (est):** 445.93MM **Publicly Held**
Web: www.clifbar.com
**SIC: 2064** 5149 Candy bars, including chocolate covered bars; Specialty food items
**PA:** Mondelez International, Inc.
    905 W Fulton Mkt Ste 200

**(P-1304)**
**ED & DONS OF HAWAII INC**
Also Called: Ed & Don's Candies
1555 Bayshore Hwy, Burlingame (94010-1661)
PHONE.................................808 423-8200
Vladimir Grave, *Pr*
Tony Nakashima, *
▲ **EMP:** 75 **EST:** 1956
**SALES (est):** 2.82MM
**SALES (corp-wide):** 8.37MM **Privately Held**
Web: www.edanddons.com
**SIC: 2064** 5441 Candy and other confectionery products; Candy
**PA:** Oritz Corporation
    1555 Old Byshore Hwy Ste
    650 692-8000

**(P-1305)**
**EL SUPER LEON PNCHIN SNCKS INC**
2545 Britannia Blvd Ste A, San Diego (92154-7427)
PHONE.................................619 426-2968
Alfonso Guerrero, *Pr*
**EMP:** 21
Web: www.elsuperleoninc.com
**SIC: 2064** Candy and other confectionery products
**PA:** El Super Leon Ponchin Snacks, Inc.
    2545 Britannia Blvd

**(P-1306)**
**EZAKI GLICO USA CORPORATION**
Also Called: Ezaki Glico
18022 Cowan Ste 110, Irvine (92614-6805)
PHONE.................................949 251-0144
Akitoshi Oku, *Pr*
▲ **EMP:** 19 **EST:** 1996
**SALES (est):** 9.93MM **Privately Held**
Web: www.glicousa.com
**SIC: 2064** 8111 Candy and other confectionery products; General practice attorney, lawyer
**PA:** Ezaki Glico Co.,Ltd.
    4-6-5, Utajima, Nishiyodogawa-Ku

**(P-1307)**
**FOOD TECHNOLOGY AND DESIGN LLC (PA)**
Also Called: Food Pharma
10012 Painter Ave, Santa Fe Springs (90670-3016)
PHONE.................................562 944-7821
Glen Marinelli, *Managing Member*
Remmell Gopez, *Managing Member*
**EMP:** 27 **EST:** 2001
**SQ FT:** 20,000
**SALES (est):** 16.28MM
**SALES (corp-wide):** 16.28MM **Privately Held**
Web: www.foodpharma.com
**SIC: 2064** Candy and other confectionery products

**(P-1308)**
**GENESIS FOODS CORPORATION**
Also Called: Garvey Nut & Candy
8825 Mercury Ln, Pico Rivera (90660-6707)
PHONE.................................323 890-5890
**TOLL FREE:** 800
▲ **EMP:** 60
Web: www.garveycandy.com
**SIC: 2064** 5149 Candy and other confectionery products; Cookies

**(P-1309)**
**HGC HOLDINGS INC**
3303 Martin Luther King Jr Blvd, Lynwood (90262-1905)
PHONE.................................323 567-2226
Robert I Hadgraft, *CEO*
David Worth, *

## 2064 - Candy And Other Confectionery Products (P-1310)

Robert Worth, *
▲ **EMP:** 21 **EST:** 1944
**SQ FT:** 90,000
**SALES (est):** 1.13MM **Privately Held**
**SIC: 2064** 5441 Chocolate candy, except solid chocolate; Candy

**(P-1310)**
**HIRA PARIS INC**
Also Called: Andy Anand Chocolates
3811 Schaefer Ave Ste B, Chino (91710-5400)
**PHONE**.....................909 634-3900
Thaminder Singh Anand, *Pr*
Sing Datu, *VP*
**EMP:** 200 **EST:** 2020
**SALES (est):** 2.19MM **Privately Held**
Web: www.andyanand.com
**SIC: 2064** 5149 Candy bars, including chocolate covered bars; Chocolate

**(P-1311)**
**HOTLIX (PA)**
Also Called: Hotlix Candy
966 Griffin St, Grover Beach (93433-3019)
P.O. Box 447 (93483-0447)
**PHONE**.....................805 473-0596
Larry Peterman, *Pr*
▼ **EMP:** 25 **EST:** 1983
**SQ FT:** 1,500
**SALES (est):** 5.8MM
**SALES (corp-wide):** 5.8MM **Privately Held**
Web: www.hotlix.com
**SIC: 2064** Lollipops and other hard candy

**(P-1312)**
**INTERNATIONAL GLACE INC (PA)**
4067 W Shaw Ave, Fresno (93722-6214)
**PHONE**.....................559 385-7675
Allen Sipole, *Pr*
**EMP:** 24 **EST:** 2017
**SALES (est):** 6.9MM
**SALES (corp-wide):** 6.9MM **Privately Held**
Web: www.internationalglace.com
**SIC: 2064** Nuts, glace

**(P-1313)**
**INW LIVING ECOLOGY OPCO LLC (DH)**
Also Called: Interntnal Ntrtn Wllness Hldng
240 Crouse Dr, Corona (92879-8093)
**PHONE**.....................951 371-4982
Aman Chogle, *Managing Member*
**EMP:** 28 **EST:** 2020
**SALES (est):** 1.81MM
**SALES (corp-wide):** 358.89MM **Privately Held**
Web: www.inwmfg.com
**SIC: 2064** 2023 Granola and muesli, bars and clusters; Dietary supplements, dairy and non-dairy based
HQ: International Nutrition & Wellness Holdings, Llc
1270 Champion Cir
Carrollton TX 75006
972 490-3300

**(P-1314)**
**ISLAND SNACKS INC**
Also Called: Island Products
7650 Stage Rd, Buena Park (90621-1226)
**PHONE**.....................714 994-1228
Alin Barak, *Pr*
◆ **EMP:** 20 **EST:** 1980
**SQ FT:** 6,600
**SALES (est):** 6.26MM **Privately Held**
Web: www.islandsnacksinc.com
**SIC: 2064** Candy and other confectionery products

**(P-1315)**
**JNR CONFECTION SPECIALTY CORP**
Also Called: Funway Snack Foods
2399 Walnut Ave, Signal Hill (90755-6400)
**EMP:** 15 **EST:** 1958
**SALES (est):** 486.65K **Privately Held**
**SIC: 2064** 5441 2096 2066 Candy and other confectionery products; Candy, nut, and confectionery stores; Potato chips and similar snacks; Chocolate and cocoa products

**(P-1316)**
**LB BEADELS LLC**
70 Atlantic Ave, Long Beach (90802-5202)
**PHONE**.....................562 726-1700
Joshua Beadel, *Prin*
**EMP:** 32 **EST:** 2013
**SALES (est):** 4.93MM **Privately Held**
Web: www.the-breakfast-bar.com
**SIC: 2064** Breakfast bars

**(P-1317)**
**LE BELGE CHOCOLATIER INC**
761 Skyway Ct, Napa (94558-7510)
**PHONE**.....................707 258-9200
David Grunhut, *CEO*
Debby Kelly, *
◆ **EMP:** 25 **EST:** 1984
**SQ FT:** 15,000
**SALES (est):** 9.89MM
**SALES (corp-wide):** 82.16MM **Privately Held**
Web: www.lebelgechocolatier.com
**SIC: 2064** 2066 Chocolate candy, except solid chocolate; Chocolate candy, solid
PA: Astor Chocolate Corp.
651 New Hampshire Ave
732 901-1000

**(P-1318)**
**MANHATTAN CONFECTIONERS INC**
Also Called: Jo's Candies
2530 W 237th St, Torrance (90505-5217)
**PHONE**.....................310 257-0260
Thomas King, *Pr*
▲ **EMP:** 16 **EST:** 1946
**SQ FT:** 20,000
**SALES (est):** 1.33MM **Privately Held**
**SIC: 2064** 5145 Candy and other confectionery products; Candy

**(P-1319)**
**MARICH CONFECTIONERY CO INC**
2101 Bert Dr, Hollister (95023-2562)
**PHONE**.....................831 634-4700
Bradley M Van Dam, *Pr*
Ronald B Packard, *
Von Packard, *Stockholder**
▲ **EMP:** 150 **EST:** 1983
**SQ FT:** 60,000
**SALES (est):** 21.54MM **Privately Held**
Web: www.marich.com
**SIC: 2064** 2099 2068 Candy and other confectionery products; Food preparations, nec; Salted and roasted nuts and seeds

**(P-1320)**
**MAVE ENTERPRISES INC**
Also Called: It's Delish
11555 Cantara St Ste B-E, North Hollywood (91605-1652)
P.O. Box 480620 (90048-1620)
**PHONE**.....................818 767-4533
Amy Grawitzky, *CEO*
Moshe Grawitzky, *

Rochell Legarreta, *
▲ **EMP:** 35 **EST:** 1992
**SQ FT:** 35,000
**SALES (est):** 8.08MM **Privately Held**
Web: www.itsdelish.com
**SIC: 2064** 2099 2033 2068 Candy and other confectionery products; Seasonings and spices; Canned fruits and specialties; Salted and roasted nuts and seeds

**(P-1321)**
**MCKEEVER DANLEE CONFECTIONARY**
760 N Mckeever Ave, Azusa (91702-2349)
**PHONE**.....................626 334-8964
Gerald Morris, *Pr*
Brian Halpert, *
David A Pistole, *
**EMP:** 103 **EST:** 1994
**SQ FT:** 10,000
**SALES (est):** 963.87K
**SALES (corp-wide):** 179.18MM **Privately Held**
**SIC: 2064** Candy and other confectionery products
HQ: Morris National, Inc.
760 N Mckeever Ave
Azusa CA 91702
626 385-2000

**(P-1322)**
**NO NUTS LLC**
Also Called: No Nuts
750 Calle Plano, Camarillo (93012-8555)
**PHONE**.....................805 309-2420
Spencer Thompson, *Managing Member*
**EMP:** 15 **EST:** 2020
**SALES (est):** 1.34MM **Privately Held**
Web: www.gononuts.com
**SIC: 2064** Granola and muesli, bars and clusters

**(P-1323)**
**ROBERTS FERRY NUT COMPANY INC**
20493 Yosemite Blvd, Waterford (95386-9506)
**PHONE**.....................209 874-3247
Nic West, *Pr*
Brad Humble, *VP*
Stacey Humble, *Sec*
Kim West, *Treas*
**EMP:** 20 **EST:** 1981
**SQ FT:** 10,000
**SALES (est):** 5.89MM **Privately Held**
Web: www.robertsferrygourmet.com
**SIC: 2064** 5145 Nuts, candy covered; Nuts, salted or roasted

**(P-1324)**
**SAIYR SWEETS LLC**
10292 Marlaw Way, Elk Grove (95757-1653)
**PHONE**.....................916 667-1407
**EMP:** 15
**SALES (est):** 356.02K **Privately Held**
**SIC: 2064** Fruit, chocolate covered (except dates)

**(P-1325)**
**SANDERS CANDY FACTORY INC**
Also Called: Zander
5051 Calmview Ave, Baldwin Park (91706-1802)
**PHONE**.....................626 814-2038
Timothy Sanders, *CEO*
Mark Sanders, *VP*
Steven L Peralez, *Sec*
**EMP:** 20 **EST:** 1989
**SQ FT:** 40,000

**SALES (est):** 9.5MM **Privately Held**
Web: www.zanderfinechocolates.com
**SIC: 2064** Candy and other confectionery products

**(P-1326)**
**SCONZA CANDY COMPANY**
1 Sconza Candy Ln, Oakdale (95361-7899)
**PHONE**.....................209 845-3700
James R Sconza, *Pr*
Ronald J Sconza, *
▲ **EMP:** 100 **EST:** 1939
**SQ FT:** 40,000
**SALES (est):** 28.26MM **Privately Held**
Web: www.sconza.com
**SIC: 2064** Lollipops and other hard candy

**(P-1327)**
**SEES CANDIES INC (DH)**
Also Called: See's Candies
210 El Camino Real S, San Francisco (94132)
**PHONE**.....................800 347-7337
Patrick Egan, *CEO*
Ken Scott, *Treas*
▲ **EMP:** 500 **EST:** 1935
**SQ FT:** 250,000
**SALES (est):** 337.6MM
**SALES (corp-wide):** 364.48B **Publicly Held**
Web: www.sees.com
**SIC: 2064** 5441 Candy and other confectionery products; Candy
HQ: See's Candy Shops, Incorporated
210 El Camino Real
South San Francisco CA 94080
650 761-2490

**(P-1328)**
**SEES CANDY SHOPS INCORPORATED (HQ)**
Also Called: See's Candies
210 El Camino Real S, South San Francisco (94080-5968)
**PHONE**.....................650 761-2490
▲ **EMP:** 40 **EST:** 1921
**SQ FT:** 250,000
**SALES (est):** 584.96MM
**SALES (corp-wide):** 364.48B **Publicly Held**
Web: chocolateshops.sees.com
**SIC: 2064** 5441 Candy and other confectionery products; Candy
PA: Berkshire Hathaway Inc.
3555 Farnam St Ste 1440
402 346-1400

**(P-1329)**
**SENCHA NATURALS INC**
1101 Monterey Pass Rd Ste A, Monterey Park (91754-3629)
**PHONE**.....................213 353-9908
David Kerdoon, *Pr*
▲ **EMP:** 15 **EST:** 2008
**SALES (est):** 7.26MM **Privately Held**
Web: www.senchanaturals.com
**SIC: 2064** Candy and other confectionery products

**(P-1330)**
**SUGARFINA INC**
377 Santana Row, San Jose (95128-2053)
**PHONE**.....................855 784-2734
**EMP:** 22
**SALES (corp-wide):** 8.2MM **Privately Held**
Web: www.sugarfina.com
**SIC: 2064** Candy and other confectionery products
PA: Sugarfina, Inc.
5275 W Diablo Dr 1

## PRODUCTS & SERVICES SECTION
### 2068 - Salted And Roasted Nuts And Seeds (P-1352)

424 256-9489

**(P-1331)**
**SUGARFINA INC**
840 S Pacific Coast Hwy, El Segundo (90245-4834)
PHONE...............................424 290-0777
**EMP:** 22
**SALES (corp-wide):** 8.2MM **Privately Held**
Web: www.sugarfina.com
**SIC: 2064** Candy and other confectionery products
**PA:** Sugarfina, Inc.
5275 W Diablo Dr 1
424 256-9489

**(P-1332)**
**SUGARFINA INC**
20 Hugus Aly, Pasadena (91103-3644)
PHONE...............................424 284-8518
**EMP:** 22
**SALES (corp-wide):** 8.2MM **Privately Held**
Web: www.sugarfina.com
**SIC: 2064** Candy and other confectionery products
**PA:** Sugarfina, Inc.
5275 W Diablo Dr 1
424 256-9489

**(P-1333)**
**SUGARFINA INC**
9495 Santa Monica Blvd, Beverly Hills (90210-4620)
PHONE...............................855 784-2734
Josh Resnick, *Brnch Mgr*
**EMP:** 22
**SALES (corp-wide):** 8.2MM **Privately Held**
Web: www.sugarfina.com
**SIC: 2064** 5441 Candy and other confectionery products; Candy
**PA:** Sugarfina, Inc.
5275 W Diablo Dr 1
424 256-9489

**(P-1334)**
**SUGARFINA INC**
4353 La Jolla Village Dr, San Diego (92122-1242)
PHONE...............................949 301-9482
**EMP:** 22
**SALES (corp-wide):** 8.2MM **Privately Held**
Web: www.sugarfina.com
**SIC: 2064** Candy and other confectionery products
**PA:** Sugarfina, Inc.
5275 W Diablo Dr 1
424 256-9489

**(P-1335)**
**SUGARFINA INC**
779 Americana Way, Glendale (91210-1507)
PHONE...............................818 302-0765
**EMP:** 22
**SALES (corp-wide):** 10.38MM **Privately Held**
Web: www.sugarfina.com
**SIC: 2064** Candy and other confectionery products
**PA:** Sugarfina, Inc.
5275 W Diablo Dr 1
424 256-9489

**(P-1336)**
**TORN RANCH INC (PA)**
2198 S Mcdowell Boulevard Ext, Petaluma (94954-6902)
PHONE...............................415 506-3000
Su Morrow, *CEO*
Dean Morrow, *Pr*

◆ **EMP:** 77 **EST:** 1991
**SALES (est):** 12.97MM
**SALES (corp-wide):** 12.97MM **Privately Held**
Web: www.tornranch.com
**SIC: 2064** Candy and other confectionery products

### 2066 Chocolate And Cocoa Products

**(P-1337)**
**BARRY CALLEBAUT USA LLC**
1175 Commerce Blvd Ste D, American Canyon (94503-9626)
PHONE...............................707 642-8200
**EMP:** 108
Web: www.barry-callebaut.com
**SIC: 2066** Chocolate
**HQ:** Barry Callebaut U.S.A. Llc
600 W Chicago Ave Ste 860
Chicago IL 60654

**(P-1338)**
**BLOMMER CHOCOLATE COMPANY CAL**
1515 Pacific St, Union City (94587-2041)
PHONE...............................510 471-4300
Henry J Blommer Junior, *CEO*
Joseph W Blommer, *
Martin Krueger, *
Peter W Blommer, *
Jack S Larsen, *
◆ **EMP:** 200 **EST:** 1902
**SQ FT:** 142,000
**SALES (est):** 22.84MM **Privately Held**
Web: www.blommer.com
**SIC: 2066** Chocolate coatings and syrup
**HQ:** The Blommer Chocolate Company
222 Merchandise Mart Plz
Chicago IL 60654
800 825-8181

**(P-1339)**
**G DEBBAS CHOCOLATIER INC**
5877 E Brown Ave, Fresno (93727-1364)
PHONE...............................559 294-2071
▲ **EMP:** 37
Web: www.madeinnature.com
**SIC: 2066** Chocolate

**(P-1340)**
**GUITTARD CHOCOLATE HOLDINGS CO**
10 Guittard Rd, Burlingame (94010-2203)
P.O. Box 4308 (94011-4308)
PHONE...............................650 697-4427
**TOLL FREE:** 800
Gary W Guittard, *Pr*
◆ **EMP:** 240 **EST:** 1868
**SALES (est):** 39.81MM **Privately Held**
Web: www.guittard.com
**SIC: 2066** 2064 Chocolate; Candy and other confectionery products

**(P-1341)**
**IRCA GROUP USA LLC**
33063 Western Ave, Union City (94587-2156)
PHONE...............................678 679-3292
Serhat Unsal, *Brnch Mgr*
**EMP:** 100
**SALES (corp-wide):** 113.11MM **Privately Held**
Web: www.kerry.com
**SIC: 2066** Cocoa and cocoa products
**PA:** Irca Group Usa Llc
1775 Brcknrdge Pkwy Ste 6

678 679-3292

**(P-1342)**
**KIVA BRANDS INC**
2300 N Loop Rd, Alameda (94502-8009)
PHONE...............................510 592-8711
Scott Palmer, *CEO*
**EMP:** 17 **EST:** 2014
**SALES (est):** 5.85MM **Privately Held**
Web: www.kivaconfections.com
**SIC: 2066** Chocolate and cocoa products

**(P-1343)**
**POCO DOLCE CHOCOLATES**
Also Called: Poco Dolce
2419 3rd St, San Francisco (94107-3110)
PHONE...............................415 255-1443
Kathy Wiley, *Pr*
**EMP:** 15 **EST:** 2007
**SALES (est):** 265.99K **Privately Held**
Web: www.pocodolce.com
**SIC: 2066** Chocolate and cocoa products

**(P-1344)**
**SHELTON INC**
Also Called: Judy's Candy Company
1225 8th St, Berkeley (94710-1413)
**EMP:** 25 **EST:** 1972
**SQ FT:** 7,400
**SALES (est):** 645.7K **Privately Held**
Web: www.judyscandy.com
**SIC: 2066** 2064 Chocolate candy, solid; Candy and other confectionery products

**(P-1345)**
**SSI G DEBBAS CHOCOLATIER LLC**
2794 N Larkin Ave, Fresno (93727-1315)
PHONE...............................559 294-2071
**EMP:** 37 **EST:** 2015
**SALES (est):** 1.4MM **Privately Held**
Web: www.madeinnature.com
**SIC: 2066** Chocolate and cocoa products

**(P-1346)**
**TCHO VENTURES INC**
Also Called: Tcho
1900 Powell St Ste 600, Emeryville (94608-1885)
PHONE...............................415 981-0189
Marcel Bens, *CEO*
**EMP:** 31
Web: www.tcho.com
**SIC: 2066** Chocolate
**HQ:** Tcho Ventures, Inc.
3100 San Pablo Ave
Berkeley CA 94702

**(P-1347)**
**VERY SPECIAL CHOCOLATS INC**
760 N Mckeever Ave, Azusa (91702-2349)
PHONE...............................626 334-7838
Gerry Morris Zubatoff, *CEO*
Gerald Morris, *
Bram Morris, *
David Pistole, *
▲ **EMP:** 171 **EST:** 1986
**SQ FT:** 40,000
**SALES (est):** 3.6MM
**SALES (corp-wide):** 179.18MM **Privately Held**
**SIC: 2066** Chocolate and cocoa products
**HQ:** Morris National, Inc.
760 N Mckeever Ave
Azusa CA 91702
626 385-2000

### 2068 Salted And Roasted Nuts And Seeds

**(P-1348)**
**CAL TREEHOUSE ALMONDS LLC (PA)**
6914 Road 160, Earlimart (93219-9627)
P.O. Box 12150 (93219-2150)
PHONE...............................559 757-5020
Mauro Trevisani, *CEO*
Jonathan Meyer, *
Carl Tristao, *
Keith B Gardiner, *
◆ **EMP:** 26 **EST:** 2002
**SALES (est):** 24.96MM
**SALES (corp-wide):** 24.96MM **Privately Held**
Web: www.treehousealmonds.com
**SIC: 2068** 2041 0173 Nuts: dried, dehydrated, salted or roasted; Flour; Almond grove

**(P-1349)**
**CARO NUT COMPANY (HQ)**
Also Called: Caro Nut
2885 S Cherry Ave, Fresno (93706-5406)
PHONE...............................559 475-5400
Munish Minocha, *CEO*
▲ **EMP:** 24 **EST:** 2008
**SALES (est):** 80.23MM
**SALES (corp-wide):** 99.6MM **Privately Held**
Web: www.caro-nut.com
**SIC: 2068** Salted and roasted nuts and seeds
**PA:** Candor-Ags, Inc.
2885 S Cherry Ave
559 439-2365

**(P-1350)**
**CUSTOM ALMONDS**
Also Called: Sequoia Nut Company
7014 Road 160, Earlimart (93219-9689)
PHONE...............................559 346-8212
Bikram Hundal, *Owner*
▼ **EMP:** 24 **EST:** 2009
**SALES (est):** 670.94K **Privately Held**
Web: www.customalmonds.com
**SIC: 2068** Nuts: dried, dehydrated, salted or roasted

**(P-1351)**
**DIAMOND FOODS LLC (PA)**
Also Called: Diamond of California*
1050 Diamond St, Stockton (95205-7020)
P.O. Box 1727 (95201)
PHONE...............................209 467-6000
Gary Ford, *CEO*
Ray Silcock, *V PES**
David Colo, *
Lloyd J Johnson, *
Linda Segre, *Executive Strategy Vice President**
◆ **EMP:** 575 **EST:** 2005
**SALES (est):** 725.47MM
**SALES (corp-wide):** 725.47MM **Privately Held**
Web: www.diamondnuts.com
**SIC: 2068** 2096 Salted and roasted nuts and seeds; Potato chips and similar snacks

**(P-1352)**
**HORMEL FOODS CORPORATION**
Also Called: Hormel
4343 E Florence Ave, Fresno (93725-1151)
PHONE...............................559 237-9206
F Chavez, *Brnch Mgr*
**EMP:** 29
**SQ FT:** 55,200
**SALES (corp-wide):** 12.11B **Publicly Held**

## 2068 - Salted And Roasted Nuts And Seeds (P-1353)

Web: www.hormelfoods.com
SIC: 2068 2096 Nuts: dried, dehydrated, salted or roasted; Potato chips and similar snacks
PA: Hormel Foods Corporation
1 Hormel Pl
507 437-5611

**(P-1353)**
**HUGHSON NUT INC (DH)**
1825 Verduga Rd, Hughson (95326-9675)
P.O. Box 1150 (95326-1150)
PHONE..................209 883-0403
Martin Pohl, Pr
◆ EMP: 64 EST: 1985
SQ FT: 40,000
SALES (est): 24.25MM
SALES (corp-wide): 174.1MM Privately Held
SIC: 2068 Salted and roasted nuts and seeds
HQ: Olam International Limited
7 Straits View
Singapore 01893

**(P-1354)**
**JOHN B SANFILIPPO & SON INC**
29241 Cottonwood Rd, Gustine (95322-9574)
PHONE..................209 854-2455
Isidro Cortez, Mgr
EMP: 257
SQ FT: 1,286
SALES (corp-wide): 1.07B Publicly Held
Web: www.jbssinc.com
SIC: 2068 Nuts: dried, dehydrated, salted or roasted
PA: John B. Sanfilippo & Son, Inc.
1703 N Randall Rd
847 289-1800

**(P-1355)**
**KENNFOODS USA LLC**
Also Called: Latitude 1
861 Performance Dr, Stockton (95206-4974)
PHONE..................209 932-8132
▲ EMP: 30
SIC: 2068 Nuts: dried, dehydrated, salted or roasted

**(P-1356)**
**KLEIN BROS HOLDINGS LTD**
Also Called: Klein Bros Snacks
3101 W March Ln Ste B, Stockton (95219-2385)
PHONE..................209 465-5033
EMP: 39 EST: 1977
SALES (est): 1.41MM Privately Held
Web: www.kleinbroswhse.com
SIC: 2068 4783 5141 Seeds: dried, dehydrated, salted or roasted; Packing and crating; Groceries, general line

**(P-1357)**
**MELLACE FAMILY BRANDS CAL INC**
6195 El Camino Real, Carlsbad (92009-1602)
P.O. Box 22831 (92192-2831)
PHONE..................760 448-1940
V Pulla, Pr
J Pulla, *
Vincent Cosentino, *
EMP: 50 EST: 2011
SQ FT: 50,000
SALES (est): 922.07K
SALES (corp-wide): 394.19MM Privately Held
SIC: 2068 Salted and roasted nuts and seeds
PA: Johnvince Foods
555 Steeprock Dr

416 663-6146

**(P-1358)**
**MERIDIAN GROWERS PROC INC**
13559 Firebaugh Blvd, Madera (93637)
PHONE..................559 458-7272
Jim Zion, Pr
EMP: 16 EST: 2020
SALES (est): 3.02MM Privately Held
Web: www.meridiangrowers.com
SIC: 2068 Nuts: dried, dehydrated, salted or roasted

**(P-1359)**
**MFB LIQUIDATION INC**
Also Called: Mama Mellaces Old World Treats
6195 El Camino Real, Carlsbad (92009-1602)
PHONE..................760 448-1940
▲ EMP: 50 EST: 1962
SALES (est): 1.16MM Privately Held
SIC: 2068 Salted and roasted nuts and seeds

**(P-1360)**
**MIXED NUTS INC**
7909 Crossway Dr, Pico Rivera (90660)
PHONE..................323 587-6887
Vanik Hartounian, Pr
◆ EMP: 25 EST: 1986
SALES (est): 6.96MM Privately Held
Web: www.mixednutsinc.com
SIC: 2068 5145 Nuts: dried, dehydrated, salted or roasted; Nuts, salted or roasted

**(P-1361)**
**NEW CENTURY SNACKS LLC**
5560 E Slauson Ave, Commerce (90040-2921)
PHONE..................323 278-9578
▲ EMP: 25
SIC: 2068 2099 Salted and roasted nuts and seeds; Food preparations, nec

**(P-1362)**
**NICHOLS PISTACHIO**
Also Called: Nichols Farms
13762 1st Ave, Hanford (93230-9316)
PHONE..................559 584-6811
Chuck Nichols, CEO
Chuck Nichols, Prin
Susan Nichols, *
◆ EMP: 200 EST: 1990
SQ FT: 110,000
SALES (est): 43.99MM Privately Held
Web: www.nicholsfarms.com
SIC: 2068 Salted and roasted nuts and seeds

**(P-1363)**
**PREMIER ORGANICS**
Also Called: Artisana
810 81st Ave Ste B, Oakland (94621-2571)
P.O. Box 6057 (94603-0057)
PHONE..................866 237-8688
▲ EMP: 35 EST: 2002
SALES (est): 5.08MM Privately Held
Web: www.artisanafoods.com
SIC: 2068 Nuts: dried, dehydrated, salted or roasted

**(P-1364)**
**PRIMEX FARMS LLC (PA)**
16070 Wildwood Rd, Wasco (93280-9210)
PHONE..................661 758-7790
Ali Amin, CEO
Ignasius Handoko, *
EMP: 30 EST: 2002
SQ FT: 136,837
SALES (est): 264.21MM
SALES (corp-wide): 264.21MM Privately Held

Web: www.primex.us
SIC: 2068 Nuts: dried, dehydrated, salted or roasted

**(P-1365)**
**SELECT HARVEST USA LLC**
7418 County Road 24, Orland (95963-9796)
PHONE..................530 865-7286
Paula Jones, Sls Mgr
EMP: 65
SALES (corp-wide): 47.55MM Privately Held
Web: www.selectharvestusa.com
SIC: 2068 Nuts: dried, dehydrated, salted or roasted
PA: Select Harvest Usa, Llc
14827 W Harding Rd
209 668-2471

**(P-1366)**
**SNAK CLUB LLC**
Also Called: New Century Snacks
5560 E Slauson Ave, Commerce (90040-2921)
PHONE..................323 278-9578
Farhad Morshed, Pr
EMP: 117
SALES (corp-wide): 118.93MM Privately Held
Web: www.snakclub.com
SIC: 2068 2099 Salted and roasted nuts and seeds; Food preparations, nec
HQ: Snak Club, Llc
607 N Nash St
El Segundo CA 90245
310 322-4400

**(P-1367)**
**STEWART & JASPER MARKETING INC (PA)**
Also Called: Stewart & Jasper Orchards
3500 Shiells Rd, Newman (95360-9798)
PHONE..................209 862-9600
Jim Jasper, Pr
Susan Dompe, *
Jason Jasper, *
◆ EMP: 175 EST: 1993
SQ FT: 225,000
SALES (est): 49.66MM
SALES (corp-wide): 49.66MM Privately Held
Web: www.stewartandjasper.com
SIC: 2068 0723 0173 5148 Nuts: dried, dehydrated, salted or roasted; Crop preparation services for market; Tree nuts; Fresh fruits and vegetables

**(P-1368)**
**TEAAROMA INC**
Also Called: Beyond Nature Company
841 E Artesia Blvd, Carson (90746-1203)
PHONE..................310 525-3400
Young Kim, Ch Bd
Young Kim, CEO
Simon Kim, Dir
Jay Kim, Dir
Logan Moon, Prin
◆ EMP: 15 EST: 2003
SQ FT: 23,000
SALES (est): 23.65MM Privately Held
Web: www.teaaroma.com
SIC: 2068 5141 5149 Nuts: dried, dehydrated, salted or roasted; Food brokers; Coffee and tea

**(P-1369)**
**TORN & GLASSER INC**
1845 W Mt Vernon Ave, Pomona (91768-3348)

PHONE..................909 706-4100
Greg Glasser, Pr
EMP: 25
SALES (corp-wide): 129.37MM Privately Held
Web: www.tornandglasser.com
SIC: 2068 Salted and roasted nuts and seeds
PA: Torn & Glasser, Inc.
1622 E Olympic Blvd
213 593-1332

**(P-1370)**
**WONDERFUL PSTCHIOS ALMONDS LLC (HQ)**
Also Called: Paramount Farms
11444 W Olympic Blvd Fl 10, Los Angeles (90064-1557)
P.O. Box 200937 (75320)
PHONE..................310 966-5700
Stewart Resnick, Pr
Michael Hohmann, *
Craig B Cooper, Senior Vice President Managing*
Bill Phillimore, *
◆ EMP: 25 EST: 1989
SQ FT: 15,000
SALES (est): 915.31MM
SALES (corp-wide): 2.04B Privately Held
Web: www.wonderful.com
SIC: 2068 Salted and roasted nuts and seeds
PA: The Wonderful Company Llc
11444 W Olympic Blvd Fl 1
310 966-5700

## 2076 Vegetable Oil Mills, Nec

**(P-1371)**
**GLOBAL AGRI-TRADE (PA)**
Also Called: Gatc Ghq
15500 S Avalon Blvd, Rancho Dominguez (90220-3205)
PHONE..................562 320-8550
Haresh Kumar Bhatt, CEO
Jignesh Bhatt, VP
Lynn Willis, Contrlr
▲ EMP: 21 EST: 2006
SQ FT: 2,500
SALES (est): 1.79MM
SALES (corp-wide): 1.79MM Privately Held
Web: www.globalagritrade.com
SIC: 2076 5199 Palm kernel oil; Oils, animal or vegetable

**(P-1372)**
**PEARL CROP INC**
Also Called: Turkhan Nuts
17641 French Camp Rd, Ripon (95366-9799)
PHONE..................209 982-9933
EMP: 23
SALES (corp-wide): 90MM Privately Held
Web: www.pearlcrop.com
SIC: 2076 Walnut oil
PA: Pearl Crop, Inc.
1550 Industrial Dr
209 808-7575

**(P-1373)**
**SMART FOODS LLC**
3398 Leonis Blvd, Vernon (90058-3014)
PHONE..................800 284-2250
◆ EMP: 25 EST: 2015
SALES (est): 3.11MM Privately Held
Web: www.avocadooilusa.com
SIC: 2076 2046 Vegetable oil mills, nec; Corn oil, refined

## 2079 - Edible Fats And Oils (P-1395)

**(P-1374)**
**TERVIVA INC**
980 Atlantic Ave Ste 105, Alameda (94501-1098)
PHONE..........................510 501-3707
Naveen Sikka, *CEO*
▲ **EMP:** 65 **EST:** 2010
**SALES (est):** 10.06MM **Privately Held**
Web: www.terviva.com
**SIC: 2076** Vegetable oil mills, nec

**(P-1375)**
**WILMAR OILS FATS STOCKTON LLC**
2008 Port Road B, Stockton (95203-2923)
PHONE..........................925 627-1600
Thomas Lim, *Managing Member*
Mike Fargas, *
▲ **EMP:** 25 **EST:** 2013
**SALES (est):** 6.66MM **Privately Held**
**SIC: 2076** Palm kernel oil

## 2077 Animal And Marine Fats And Oils

**(P-1376)**
**BAKER COMMODITIES INC**
3001 Sierra Pine Ave, Vernon (90058-4120)
PHONE..........................323 318-8260
**EMP:** 27
**SALES (corp-wide):** 153.63MM **Privately Held**
Web: www.bakercommodities.com
**SIC: 2077** Animal and marine fats and oils
PA: Baker Commodities, Inc.
    4020 Bandini Blvd
    323 268-2801

**(P-1377)**
**BAKER COMMODITIES INC (PA)**
Also Called: Corenco
4020 Bandini Blvd, Vernon (90058-4274)
PHONE..........................323 268-2801
TOLL FREE: 800
James M Andreoli, *Pr*
Mitchell Ebright, *
Denis Luckey, *
◆ **EMP:** 150 **EST:** 1948
**SQ FT:** 12,000
**SALES (est):** 153.63MM
**SALES (corp-wide):** 153.63MM **Privately Held**
Web: www.bakercommodities.com
**SIC: 2077** 2048 Tallow rendering, inedible; Poultry feeds

**(P-1378)**
**BAKER COMMODITIES INC**
16801 W Jensen Ave, Kerman (93630-9194)
P.O. Box 416 (93630-0416)
PHONE..........................559 237-4320
Manuel Ponte, *Dir*
**EMP:** 37
**SQ FT:** 28,690
**SALES (corp-wide):** 153.63MM **Privately Held**
Web: www.bakercommodities.com
**SIC: 2077** Tallow rendering, inedible
PA: Baker Commodities, Inc.
    4020 Bandini Blvd
    323 268-2801

**(P-1379)**
**BAKER COMMODITIES INC**
7480 Hanford Armona Rd, Hanford (93230-9343)
P.O. Box 1286 (93232-1286)
PHONE..........................559 686-4797
Doug Fletcher, *Mgr*
**EMP:** 29
**SALES (corp-wide):** 153.63MM **Privately Held**
Web: www.bakercommodities.com
**SIC: 2077** 2048 Tallow rendering, inedible; Prepared feeds, nec
PA: Baker Commodities, Inc.
    4020 Bandini Blvd
    323 268-2801

**(P-1380)**
**D & D SERVICES INC**
Also Called: D & D Cremations Service
4105 Bandini Blvd, Vernon (90058-4208)
P.O. Box 55338 (91385-0338)
PHONE..........................323 261-4176
William M Gorman, *Pr*
Vincent Gorman, *
Roseanne Gorman, *
**EMP:** 41 **EST:** 1967
**SQ FT:** 100,000
**SALES (est):** 4.67MM **Privately Held**
**SIC: 2077** Animal and marine fats and oils

**(P-1381)**
**DARLING INGREDIENTS INC**
795 W Belgravia Ave, Fresno (93706)
P.O. Box 11445 (93773-1445)
PHONE..........................559 268-5325
Edward H Jenkins, *Mgr*
**EMP:** 25
**SQ FT:** 10,500
**SALES (corp-wide):** 6.79B **Publicly Held**
Web: www.darlingii.com
**SIC: 2077** 2048 Animal and marine fats and oils; Prepared feeds, nec
PA: Darling Ingredients Inc.
    5601 N Macarthur Blvd
    972 717-0300

**(P-1382)**
**DARLING INGREDIENTS INC**
2626 E 25th St, Los Angeles (90058-1212)
P.O. Box 58725 (90058-0725)
PHONE..........................323 583-6311
Thomas Nunley, *Genl Mgr*
**EMP:** 44
**SALES (corp-wide):** 6.79B **Publicly Held**
Web: www.darlingii.com
**SIC: 2077** 2048 Animal and marine fats and oils; Prepared feeds, nec
PA: Darling Ingredients Inc.
    5601 N Macarthur Blvd
    972 717-0300

**(P-1383)**
**DARLING INGREDIENTS INC**
429 Amador St Pier 92, San Francisco (94124-1232)
P.O. Box 880006 (94188-0006)
PHONE..........................415 647-4890
Gene Hanson, *Genl Mgr*
**EMP:** 47
**SALES (corp-wide):** 6.79B **Publicly Held**
Web: www.darlingii.com
**SIC: 2077** 2048 5172 Grease rendering, inedible; Prepared feeds, nec; Lubricating oils and greases
PA: Darling Ingredients Inc.
    5601 N Macarthur Blvd
    972 717-0300

**(P-1384)**
**DARLING INGREDIENTS INC**
Also Called: Turlock Rendering
11946 Carpenter Rd, Crows Landing (95313-9749)
P.O. Box 1608 (95381-1608)
PHONE..........................209 667-9153
Dick Labuga, *Genl Mgr*
**EMP:** 27
**SQ FT:** 43,498
**SALES (corp-wide):** 6.79B **Publicly Held**
Web: www.darlingii.com
**SIC: 2077** 2048 Grease rendering, inedible; Prepared feeds, nec
PA: Darling Ingredients Inc.
    5601 N Macarthur Blvd
    972 717-0300

**(P-1385)**
**JR GREASE SERVICES INC**
5900 S Eastern Ave Ste 150, Commerce (90040-4018)
P.O. Box 226894 (90022-0594)
PHONE..........................323 318-2096
**EMP:** 20 **EST:** 2011
**SALES (est):** 961.98K **Privately Held**
Web: www.greaseservices.com
**SIC: 2077** Grease rendering, inedible

**(P-1386)**
**NORDIC NATURALS INC**
Also Called: Westport Scandinavia
111 Jennings Way, Watsonville (95076)
PHONE..........................800 662-2544
John Stockman, *CEO*
Michele Opheim, *
▲ **EMP:** 150 **EST:** 2002
**SALES (est):** 58.14MM **Privately Held**
Web: www.nordic.com
**SIC: 2077** Fish oil

**(P-1387)**
**NORTH STATE RENEWABLES LLC**
15 Shippee Rd, Oroville (95965-9297)
P.O. Box 239 (95938-0239)
PHONE..........................530 343-6076
Chris Ottone, *Pr*
Patrick Ottone, *
William Ottone, *
**EMP:** 23 **EST:** 1969
**SQ FT:** 15,000
**SALES (est):** 2.21MM **Privately Held**
Web: www.rendering.com
**SIC: 2077** Tallow rendering, inedible

**(P-1388)**
**PARK WEST ENTERPRISES INC**
Also Called: Co-West Commodities
2586 Shenandoah Way, San Bernardino (92407-1845)
PHONE..........................909 383-8341
Sergio Perez, *CEO*
Freddie Peterson, *
**EMP:** 18 **EST:** 1996
**SALES (est):** 1.02MM **Privately Held**
Web: www.co-west.com
**SIC: 2077** Animal and marine fats and oils

**(P-1389)**
**SACRAMENTO RENDERING CO**
11350 Kiefer Blvd, Sacramento (95830-9498)
P.O. Box 276424 (95827-6424)
PHONE..........................916 363-4821
TOLL FREE: 800
Michael P Koewler, *CEO*
**EMP:** 52 **EST:** 1913
**SALES (est):** 200.8K **Privately Held**
Web: www.srccompanies.com
**SIC: 2077** Animal and marine fats and oils

**(P-1390)**
**SRC MILLING CO LLC**
Also Called: Sacramento Rendering Co
11350 Kiefer Blvd, Sacramento (95830-9405)
PHONE..........................916 363-4821
Jim Walsh, *Managing Member*
Dennis J Breen, *Managing Member*
▲ **EMP:** 20 **EST:** 1996
**SALES (est):** 4.57MM **Privately Held**
Web: www.srccompanies.com
**SIC: 2077** Rendering

## 2079 Edible Fats And Oils

**(P-1391)**
**AAK USA RICHMOND CORP (DH)**
Also Called: California Oils
1145 Harbour Way S, Richmond (94804-3618)
PHONE..........................510 233-7660
◆ **EMP:** 60 **EST:** 1982
**SALES (est):** 19.87MM
**SALES (corp-wide):** 39.28MM **Privately Held**
Web: www.betterwithaak.com
**SIC: 2079** Edible fats and oils
HQ: Aak Denmark Holding A/S
    Slipvej 4
    Aarhus C
    87306000

**(P-1392)**
**BOUNDARY BEND INC**
Also Called: Boundary Bend Olives
455 Harter Ave, Woodland (95776-6105)
PHONE..........................844 626-2726
Adam Englehardt, *CEO*
▲ **EMP:** 20 **EST:** 2014
**SALES (est):** 14.82MM **Privately Held**
Web: www.cobramestate.com
**SIC: 2079** Olive oil
PA: Cobram Estate Olives Limited
    151 Broderick Rd

**(P-1393)**
**BUNGE OILS INC**
Also Called: Bunge North America
436 S Mcclure Rd, Modesto (95357-0519)
PHONE..........................209 574-9981
Dale Casky, *Mgr*
**EMP:** 119
**SQ FT:** 76,824
Web: www.bunge.com
**SIC: 2079** Cooking oils, except corn: vegetable refined
HQ: Bunge Oils, Inc.
    1391 Tmbarlake Manor Pkwy
    Chesterfield MO 63017
    314 292-2000

**(P-1394)**
**CALIFORNIA OLIVE AND VINE LLC**
Also Called: Sutter Buttes Olive Oil
1670 Poole Blvd, Yuba City (95993-2610)
PHONE..........................530 763-7921
Alka Kumar, *Pr*
**EMP:** 15 **EST:** 2011
**SQ FT:** 10,000
**SALES (est):** 4.85MM **Privately Held**
Web: www.sutterbuttesoliveoil.com
**SIC: 2079** 5921 Olive oil; Liquor stores

**(P-1395)**
**CALIFORNIA OLIVE RANCH INC (PA)**
265 Airpark Blvd Ste 200, Chico (95973-9518)

## 2079 - Edible Fats And Oils (P-1396)

PHONE..................................530 846-8000
Gregory B Kelly, *CEO*
Pedro Olabrria, *
Guillermo Romero, *Vice Chairman*
Antonio Valla, *VP*
Mike Forbes, *VP*
◆ **EMP:** 53 **EST:** 1998
**SALES (est):** 36.71MM **Privately Held**
Web: www.californiaoliveranch.com
**SIC: 2079** Olive oil

### (P-1396)
### COAST PACKING COMPANY
3275 E Vernon Ave, Vernon  (90058-1820)
P.O. Box 58918  (90058-0918)
PHONE..................................323 277-7700
**EMP:** 60 **EST:** 1922
**SALES (est):** 22.23MM **Privately Held**
Web: www.coastpacking.com
**SIC: 2079** Edible fats and oils

### (P-1397)
### ELDORADO USA  LLC
1405 Stonewood Pl, Concord  (94520-2821)
PHONE..................................925 285-4572
**EMP:** 15 **EST:** 2014
**SALES (est):** 217.83K **Privately Held**
**SIC: 2079** Olive oil

### (P-1398)
### GEMSA ENTERPRISES  LLC
Also Called: Gemsa Oils
14370 Gannet St, La Mirada  (90638-5221)
P.O. Box 1447  (90637-1447)
PHONE..................................714 521-1736
▲ **EMP:** 20 **EST:** 1996
**SQ FT:** 60,000
**SALES (est):** 13.05MM **Privately Held**
Web: www.gemsaoils.com
**SIC: 2079** Olive oil

### (P-1399)
### LIBERTY VEGETABLE OIL COMPANY
15760 Ventura Blvd, Encino  (91436-3000)
P.O. Box 4207  (90703-4207)
PHONE..................................562 921-3567
Irwin Field, *Pr*
Ronald Field, *
◆ **EMP:** 40 **EST:** 1948
**SQ FT:** 30,000
**SALES (est):** 5.36MM **Privately Held**
Web: www.libertyvegetableoil.com
**SIC: 2079** Olive oil

### (P-1400)
### MCEVOY OF MARIN  LLC
1600 Barlow Ln, Sebastopol  (95472-2511)
PHONE..................................707 467-1999
Dan Mosley, *Mgr*
**EMP:** 27
Web: www.mcevoyranch.com
**SIC: 2079** Olive oil
PA: Mcevoy Of Marin, Llc
   5935 Red Hill Rd

### (P-1401)
### MCEVOY OF MARIN LLC (PA)
Also Called: McEvoy Ranch
5935 Red Hill Rd, Petaluma  (94952-9437)
P.O. Box 341  (94953-0341)
PHONE..................................707 778-2307
Dan Mosley, *Mgr*
◆ **EMP:** 46 **EST:** 1998
**SALES (est):** 13.44MM **Privately Held**
Web: www.mcevoyranch.com
**SIC: 2079** Olive oil

### (P-1402)
### NICK SCIABICA & SONS A CORP
Also Called: Sciabica's
2150 Yosemite Blvd, Modesto  (95354-3931)
PHONE..................................209 577-5067
Gemma Sciabica, *CEO*
Joseph N Sciabica, *Pr*
Daniel R Sciabica, *Sec*
▲ **EMP:** 20 **EST:** 1925
**SQ FT:** 68,728
**SALES (est):** 5.23MM **Privately Held**
Web: www.sunshineinabottle.com
**SIC: 2079** 5149  Olive oil; Cooking oils

### (P-1403)
### OLIVE CORTO L P
10201 Live Oak Rd, Stockton  (95212-9319)
P.O. Box 1706  (95241-1706)
PHONE..................................888 832-0051
Brady Whitlow, *Pr*
▲ **EMP:** 15 **EST:** 2006
**SALES (est):** 4.72MM **Privately Held**
Web: www.corto-olive.com
**SIC: 2079** Olive oil

### (P-1404)
### OLIVE OIL FACTORY  LLC (PA)
770 Chadbourne Rd, Fairfield  (94534-9643)
PHONE..................................707 426-3400
Francine Brossier, *Managing Member*
▲ **EMP:** 21 **EST:** 2004
**SALES (est):** 14MM **Privately Held**
Web: www.critelli.com
**SIC: 2079** Olive oil

### (P-1405)
### SOGNO TOSCANO TUSCAN DREAM
820 Aladdin Ave, San Leandro  (94577)
PHONE..................................718 581-9494
**EMP:** 5000
**SALES (est):** 474.13K
**SALES (corp-wide):** 18.83MM **Privately Held**
**SIC: 2079** Olive oil
PA: Sogno Toscano Tuscan Dream, Inc.
   1445 W 12th Pl Ste 101
   480 281-1818

### (P-1406)
### SPECTRUM ORGANIC PRODUCTS  LLC
Also Called: Spectrum Naturals
2201 S Mcdowell Boulevard Ext, Petaluma  (94954-7624)
PHONE..................................888 343-6637
Neil G Blomquist, *Pr*
Jethren P Phillips, *
Nils Michael Langenborg, *
Randall H Sias, *
◆ **EMP:** 21 **EST:** 1980
**SQ FT:** 18,600
**SALES (est):** 2.01MM **Publicly Held**
Web: www.spectrumorganics.com
**SIC: 2079** 2035 2099 2834  Edible fats and oils; Dressings, salad: raw and cooked (except dry mixes); Vinegar; Vitamin, nutrient, and hematinic preparations for human use
PA: The Hain Celestial Group Inc
   221 River St Ste 12

### (P-1407)
### STRATAS FOODS LLC
3390 S Chestnut Ave, Fresno  (93725-2609)
PHONE..................................559 495-4506
**EMP:** 99
Web: www.stratasfoods.com
**SIC: 2079** Edible fats and oils
PA: Stratas Foods Llc
   7000 Gdlett Frms Pkwy Ste

### (P-1408)
### VENTURA FOODS  LLC
2900 Jurupa St, Ontario  (91761-2915)
PHONE..................................714 257-3700
Wayne Kess, *Mgr*
**EMP:** 68
Web: www.venturafoods.com
**SIC: 2079** 2035  Vegetable shortenings (except corn oil); Pickles, sauces, and salad dressings
PA: Ventura Foods, Llc
   40 Pointe Dr

### (P-1409)
### VENTURA FOODS  LLC (PA)
Also Called: Lou Ana Foods
40 Pointe Dr, Brea  (92821-3652)
PHONE..................................714 257-3700
Christopher Furman, *Pr*
Rebecca J Walsh, *
Andy Euser, *CAO*
Erika Noonburg-morgan, *Ex VP*
Luis Andrade, *Executive Commercial Vice President*
◆ **EMP:** 200 **EST:** 1996
**SALES (est):** 2.05B **Privately Held**
Web: www.venturafoods.com
**SIC: 2079** 2035  Vegetable shortenings (except corn oil); Pickles, sauces, and salad dressings

### (P-1410)
### VERONICA FOODS COMPANY
Also Called: Veronica Foods
1991 Dennison St, Oakland  (94606-5225)
P.O. Box P.O. Box 2225  (94621-0125)
PHONE..................................510 535-6833
Michael Bradley, *CEO*
Veronica Bradley, *
◆ **EMP:** 50 **EST:** 1940
**SALES (est):** 8.23MM **Privately Held**
Web: www.evoliveoil.com
**SIC: 2079** 5149  Cooking oils, except corn: vegetable refined; Cooking oils and shortenings

### (P-1411)
### WILSEY FOODS  INC
40 Pointe Dr, Brea  (92821-3652)
PHONE..................................714 257-3700
Takashi Fukunaga, *CEO*
Steve Takagi, *
Hiro Matsumura, *
◆ **EMP:** 1000 **EST:** 1919
**SQ FT:** 103,378
**SALES (est):** 4.08MM **Privately Held**
Web: www.venturafoods.com
**SIC: 2079** 5149  Cooking oils, except corn: vegetable refined; Shortening, vegetable
HQ: Mbk Usa Holdings, Inc.
   200 Park Ave Fl 36
   New York NY 10166
   212 878-6773

## 2082 Malt Beverages

### (P-1412)
### ANDERSON VALLEY BREWING INC
Also Called: ANDERSON VALLEY BREWING COMPAN
17700 Hwy 253, Boonville  (95415)
P.O. Box 505  (95415-0505)
PHONE..................................707 895-2337
Kenneth D Allen, *Pr*
◆ **EMP:** 45 **EST:** 1987
**SQ FT:** 5,000
**SALES (est):** 6.58MM **Privately Held**
Web: www.avbc.com
**SIC: 2082** 5812  Ale (alcoholic beverage); Cafe

### (P-1413)
### ANHEUSER-BUSCH  LLC
Also Called: Anheuser-Busch
12065 Pike St, Santa Fe Springs  (90670-2964)
P.O. Box 3988  (90670-1988)
PHONE..................................562 699-3424
**EMP:** 32
**SALES (corp-wide):** 1.7B **Privately Held**
Web: www.anheuser-busch.com
**SIC: 2082** 5181  Malt beverage products; Beer and ale
HQ: Anheuser-Busch, Llc
   1 Busch Pl
   Saint Louis MO 63118
   800 342-5283

### (P-1414)
### ANHEUSER-BUSCH  LLC
Also Called: Anheuser-Busch
5959 Santa Fe St, San Diego  (92109-1623)
P.O. Box 80758  (92138-0758)
PHONE..................................858 581-7000
Denise Cooper, *Genl Mgr*
**EMP:** 54
**SALES (corp-wide):** 1.7B **Privately Held**
Web: www.budweisertours.com
**SIC: 2082**  Beer (alcoholic beverage)
HQ: Anheuser-Busch, Llc
   1 Busch Pl
   Saint Louis MO 63118
   800 342-5283

### (P-1415)
### ANHEUSER-BUSCH  LLC
Also Called: Anheuser-Busch
3101 Busch Dr, Fairfield  (94534-9726)
PHONE..................................707 429-7595
Kevin Finger, *Mgr*
**EMP:** 450
**SALES (corp-wide):** 1.7B **Privately Held**
Web: www.budweisertours.com
**SIC: 2082**  Beer (alcoholic beverage)
HQ: Anheuser-Busch, Llc
   1 Busch Pl
   Saint Louis MO 63118
   800 342-5283

### (P-1416)
### ANHEUSER-BUSCH  LLC
Also Called: Anheuser-Busch
2800 S Reservoir St, Pomona  (91766-6525)
PHONE..................................951 782-3935
**TOLL FREE:** 800
Yo Sanchez, *Mgr*
**EMP:** 115
**SALES (corp-wide):** 1.7B **Privately Held**
Web: www.budweisertours.com
**SIC: 2082**  Beer (alcoholic beverage)
HQ: Anheuser-Busch, Llc
   1 Busch Pl
   Saint Louis MO 63118
   800 342-5283

### (P-1417)
### ANHEUSER-BUSCH  LLC
Also Called: Anheuser-Busch
20499 S Reeves Ave, Carson  (90810-1011)
PHONE..................................310 761-4600
Damian Bonnenfant, *Mgr*
**EMP:** 48
**SALES (corp-wide):** 1.7B **Privately Held**

## PRODUCTS & SERVICES SECTION
### 2082 - Malt Beverages (P-1439)

Web: www.budweisertours.com
SIC: 2082 Beer (alcoholic beverage)
HQ: Anheuser-Busch, Llc
   1 Busch Pl
   Saint Louis MO 63118
   800 342-5283

**(P-1418)**
**ARTISAN BREWERS LLC**
Also Called: Drake's Brewing Company
1933 Davis St Ste 177, San Leandro (94577-1256)
PHONE...............510 567-4926
◆ EMP: 44 EST: 2008
SALES (est): 12.21MM Privately Held
SIC: 2082 Beer (alcoholic beverage)

**(P-1419)**
**ASSOCIATED MICROBREWERIES INC**
9675 Scranton Rd, San Diego (92121-1761)
PHONE...............858 587-2739
Bryan King, Brnch Mgr
EMP: 89
SALES (corp-wide): 22.36MM Privately Held
Web: www.karlstrauss.com
SIC: 2082 Beer (alcoholic beverage)
PA: Associated Microbreweries, Inc.
   5985 Santa Fe St
   858 273-2739

**(P-1420)**
**ASSOCIATED MICROBREWERIES INC**
901 S Coast Dr Ste A, Costa Mesa (92626-7790)
PHONE...............714 546-2739
David Sadeler, Mgr
EMP: 86
SALES (corp-wide): 22.36MM Privately Held
Web: www.karlstrauss.com
SIC: 2082 Beer (alcoholic beverage)
PA: Associated Microbreweries, Inc.
   5985 Santa Fe St
   858 273-2739

**(P-1421)**
**ASSOCIATED MICROBREWERIES INC (PA)**
Also Called: Karl Strauss Brewery Garden
5985 Santa Fe St, San Diego (92109-1623)
PHONE...............858 273-2739
Christopher W Cramer, Pr
Matthew H Rattner, *
EMP: 50 EST: 1988
SQ FT: 2,000
SALES: 22.36MM
SALES (corp-wide): 22.36MM Privately Held
Web: www.karlstrauss.com
SIC: 2082 5812 Beer (alcoholic beverage); Eating places

**(P-1422)**
**ASSOCIATED MICROBREWERIES INC**
Also Called: Karl Strauss Brewery & Rest
1157 Columbia St, San Diego (92101-3511)
PHONE...............619 234-2739
Shawn Phaby, Mgr
EMP: 90
SALES (corp-wide): 22.36MM Privately Held
Web: www.karlstrauss.com
SIC: 2082 5812 Beer (alcoholic beverage); Eating places

PA: Associated Microbreweries, Inc.
   5985 Santa Fe St
   858 273-2739

**(P-1423)**
**ASSOCTED MCRBRWRIES LTD A CAL**
Also Called: Karl Strauss Brewing Company
5985 Santa Fe St, San Diego (92109-1623)
PHONE...............858 273-2739
Christopher W Cramer, Prin
EMP: 27 EST: 1988
SALES (est): 1.51MM Privately Held
Web: www.karlstrauss.com
SIC: 2082 Beer (alcoholic beverage)

**(P-1424)**
**BAREBOTTLE BREWING COMPANY INC**
1525 Cortland Ave, San Francisco (94110-5714)
PHONE...............415 926-8617
Michael Seitz, CEO
Lester Koga, *
Ben Sterling, *
EMP: 60 EST: 2011
SQ FT: 17,000
SALES (est): 8.51MM Privately Held
Web: www.barebottle.com
SIC: 2082 Ale (alcoholic beverage)

**(P-1425)**
**BU LLC**
9073 Pulsar Ct Ste A, Corona (92883-7357)
PHONE...............951 277-7470
Ryan Mason, Managing Member
EMP: 15 EST: 2018
SALES (est): 934.5K Privately Held
SIC: 2082 Malt beverages

**(P-1426)**
**CHAPMAN CBC LLC**
123 N Cypress St, Orange (92866-1309)
PHONE...............844 855-2337
Wil Dee, CEO
Randy Nelson, CFO
EMP: 20 EST: 2013
SALES (est): 5.69MM Privately Held
Web: www.chapmancrafted.beer
SIC: 2082 Beer (alcoholic beverage)

**(P-1427)**
**DUDES BREWING COMPANY**
1840 W 208th St, Somis (93066)
P.O. Box 276 (93066-0276)
PHONE...............424 271-2915
Toby Humes, Owner
EMP: 20 EST: 2013
SALES (est): 1.17MM Privately Held
Web: www.thedudesbrew.com
SIC: 2082 5921 Beer (alcoholic beverage); Beer (packaged)

**(P-1428)**
**FIRESTONE WALKER INC**
1332 Vendels Cir, Paso Robles (93446-3802)
PHONE...............805 226-8514
Adam Firestone, Brnch Mgr
EMP: 86
SALES (corp-wide): 97.18MM Privately Held
Web: www.firestonewalker.com
SIC: 2082 Beer (alcoholic beverage)
PA: Firestone Walker, Inc.
   1400 Ramada Dr
   805 225-5911

**(P-1429)**
**FIRESTONE WALKER INC**
Also Called: Firestone Walker Brewing Co
620 Mc Murray Rd, Buellton (93427-2511)
PHONE...............805 254-4205
Patrick Mcalary, Genl Mgr
EMP: 86
SALES (corp-wide): 97.18MM Privately Held
Web: www.firestonewalker.com
SIC: 2082 Beer (alcoholic beverage)
PA: Firestone Walker, Inc.
   1400 Ramada Dr
   805 225-5911

**(P-1430)**
**FIRESTONE WALKER INC (PA)**
Also Called: Firestone Walker Brewing Co
1400 Ramada Dr, Paso Robles (93446-3993)
PHONE...............805 225-5911
David Walker, CEO
Adam Firestone, *
◆ EMP: 156 EST: 1997
SALES (est): 97.18MM
SALES (corp-wide): 97.18MM Privately Held
Web: www.firestonewalker.com
SIC: 2082 Beer (alcoholic beverage)

**(P-1431)**
**FIRESTONE WALKER LLC**
Also Called: Firestone Walker Brewing Co
10130 Commercial Ave, Penn Valley (95946-9466)
PHONE...............805 225-5911
David Walker, CEO
EMP: 86
SALES (corp-wide): 97.18MM Privately Held
Web: www.firestonewalker.com
SIC: 2082 Beer (alcoholic beverage)
PA: Firestone Walker, Inc.
   1400 Ramada Dr
   805 225-5911

**(P-1432)**
**FULL CIRCLE BREWING CO LTD LLC**
Also Called: Los Californias Winery
620 F St, Fresno (93704)
PHONE...............559 264-6323
Jeff Haak, Managing Member
EMP: 18 EST: 1998
SALES (est): 4.6MM Privately Held
Web: www.fullcirclebrewing.com
SIC: 2082 Beer (alcoholic beverage)

**(P-1433)**
**GORDON BIERSCH BREWING COMPANY (PA)**
Also Called: Gordon Biersch Brewing Company
357 E Taylor St, San Jose (95112-3148)
PHONE...............408 278-1008
Daniel Gordon, CEO
William Bullard, CFO
Paul Michels, CFO
Lorenzon Fertitta, Dir
Frank Fertitta Iii, Dir
▲ EMP: 15 EST: 1987
SQ FT: 1,500
SALES (est): 15.19MM
SALES (corp-wide): 15.19MM Privately Held
Web: www.gordonbirschbrewing.com
SIC: 2082 Malt beverages

**(P-1434)**
**HOME BREW MART INC**
9045 Carroll Way, San Diego (92121-2405)
PHONE...............858 790-6900
Jim Buechler, CEO
Jack White, *
Yuseff Cherney, *
Rick Morgan, *
Julie Buechler, *
▲ EMP: 425 EST: 1992
SQ FT: 107,000
SALES (est): 6.98MM
SALES (corp-wide): 9.96B Publicly Held
Web: www.ballastpoint.com
SIC: 2082 5999 Ale (alcoholic beverage); Alcoholic beverage making equipment and supplies
PA: Constellation Brands, Inc.
   50 E Broad St
   585 678-7100

**(P-1435)**
**INNOVATION BREWWORKS**
3650 W Temple Ave Ste 100, Pomona (91768-2583)
PHONE...............909 979-6197
EMP: 18 EST: 2014
SALES (est): 131.89K Privately Held
Web: www.ibrewworks.com
SIC: 2082 Malt beverages

**(P-1436)**
**J&L EPPIG BREWING LLC**
Also Called: Eppig Brewing
1347 Keystone Way Ste C, Vista (92081-8311)
PHONE...............760 295-2009
Todd Warshaw, Mgr
Clayton Leblanc, Mgr
Stephanie Eppig, Mgr
EMP: 18 EST: 2015
SALES (est): 989.73K Privately Held
Web: www.eppigbrewing.com
SIC: 2082 Beer (alcoholic beverage)

**(P-1437)**
**JDZ INC**
Also Called: Alesmith Brewing Company
9990 Alesmith Ct, San Diego (92126-4200)
P.O. Box 993 (92038-0993)
PHONE...............858 549-9888
Peter Zien, CEO
EMP: 54 EST: 2014
SALES (est): 4.79MM Privately Held
SIC: 2082 Beer (alcoholic beverage)

**(P-1438)**
**K A MCNAIR BREWING CO LLC**
Also Called: North Park Beer Co.
3038 University Ave, San Diego (92104-3002)
PHONE...............858 254-3238
EMP: 20 EST: 2013
SALES (est): 3.72MM Privately Held
Web: www.northparkbeerco.com
SIC: 2082 Malt beverages

**(P-1439)**
**KARL STRAUSS BREWING COMPANY**
600 Wilshire Blvd Ste 100, Los Angeles (90017-3214)
PHONE...............213 228-2739
EMP: 15
Web: www.karlstrauss.com
SIC: 2082 Beer (alcoholic beverage)
PA: Karl Strauss Brewing Company
   5985 Santa Fe St

## 2082 - Malt Beverages (P-1440)

**(P-1440)**
**KARL STRAUSS BREWING COMPANY (PA)**
5985 Santa Fe St, San Diego (92109-1623)
P.O. Box 5965 (92109)
PHONE..................................858 273-2739
Chris Cramer, *CEO*
Matt Rattner, *Prin*
**EMP:** 50 **EST:** 1989
**SALES (est):** 15.92MM **Privately Held**
**Web:** www.karlstrauss.com
**SIC: 2082** Beer (alcoholic beverage)

**(P-1441)**
**KINGS & CONVICTS BP LLC (HQ)**
Also Called: Ballast Point Brewing Company
9045 Carroll Way, San Diego (92121-2405)
PHONE..................................858 790-6900
Braden Watters, *CEO*
Chris Bradley, *COO*
**EMP:** 22 **EST:** 2019
**SALES (est):** 116.07MM
**SALES (corp-wide):** 116.07MM **Privately Held**
**Web:** www.ballastpoint.com
**SIC: 2082** Beer (alcoholic beverage)
**PA:** Hopmaniacs Llc
523 Bank Ln
224 707-0117

**(P-1442)**
**KINGS & CONVICTS BP LLC**
2215 India St, San Diego (92101-1725)
PHONE..................................619 255-7213
**EMP:** 193
**SALES (corp-wide):** 116.07MM **Privately Held**
**Web:** www.ballastpoint.com
**SIC: 2082** Malt beverages
**HQ:** Kings & Convicts Bp, Llc
9045 Carroll Way
San Diego CA 92121
858 790-6900

**(P-1443)**
**KINGS & CONVICTS BP LLC**
5401 Linda Vista Rd Ste 406, San Diego (92110-2402)
PHONE..................................619 295-2337
Jim Johnson, *Brnch Mgr*
**EMP:** 91
**SALES (corp-wide):** 116.07MM **Privately Held**
**Web:** www.ballastpoint.com
**SIC: 2082** Malt beverages
**HQ:** Kings & Convicts Bp, Llc
9045 Carroll Way
San Diego CA 92121
858 790-6900

**(P-1444)**
**LA QUINTA BREWING COMPANY LLC**
74714 Technology Dr, Palm Desert (92211-5803)
PHONE..................................760 200-2597
Scott Stokes, *Managing Member*
Scott Stoaks, *
**EMP:** 55 **EST:** 2013
**SALES (est):** 6.23MM **Privately Held**
**Web:** www.laquintabrewing.com
**SIC: 2082** 5813 Beer (alcoholic beverage); Beer garden (drinking places)

**(P-1445)**
**LEFT COAST BREWING COMPANY**
Also Called: Left Coast Brewing Company
1245 Puerta Del Sol, San Clemente (92673-6310)
PHONE..................................949 218-3961
George Hadjis, *Pr*
Dora Hadjis, *CFO*
**EMP:** 15 **EST:** 2004
**SQ FT:** 7,500
**SALES (est):** 3.93MM **Privately Held**
**Web:** www.leftcoastbrewing.com
**SIC: 2082** Beer (alcoholic beverage)

**(P-1446)**
**LIQUID GOLD**
1040 Hyde St, San Francisco (94109-4917)
PHONE..................................415 660-5142
**EMP:** 22 **EST:** 2014
**SALES (est):** 306.83K **Privately Held**
**Web:** www.liquidgoldsf.com
**SIC: 2082** Beer (alcoholic beverage)

**(P-1447)**
**MENDOCINO BREWING COMPANY INC (HQ)**
1601 Airport Rd, Ukiah (95482-6456)
PHONE..................................707 744-1015
Yashpal Singh, *Pr*
Vijay Mallya, *
Mahadevan Narayanan, *
▲ **EMP:** 19 **EST:** 1983
**SALES (est):** 7.91MM **Privately Held**
**Web:** www.mendobrew.com
**SIC: 2082** Beer (alcoholic beverage)
**PA:** United Breweries (Holdings) Limited
Level 12-16, Ub Tower, Ub City 24

**(P-1448)**
**MILLER BREWING CO**
15801 1st St, Irwindale (91706-2069)
PHONE..................................626 353-1604
**EMP:** 19 **EST:** 2016
**SALES (est):** 2.37MM **Privately Held**
**Web:** www.molsoncoors.com
**SIC: 2082** Beer (alcoholic beverage)

**(P-1449)**
**MOREFLAVOR INC (PA)**
Also Called: Beer Beer & More Beer
701 Willow Pass Rd Unit 1, Pittsburg (94565-1803)
PHONE..................................800 600-0033
Olin Schultz, *CEO*
Dan Lipscomb, *CFO*
◆ **EMP:** 21 **EST:** 1995
**SQ FT:** 10,000
**SALES (est):** 10.04MM **Privately Held**
**Web:** www.moreflavor.com
**SIC: 2082** 2084 2095 Beer (alcoholic beverage); Wine coolers (beverages); Roasted coffee

**(P-1450)**
**NORTH COAST BREWING CO INC (PA)**
Also Called: Brew Building
455 N Main St, Fort Bragg (95437-3215)
PHONE..................................707 964-2739
Jennifer Owen, *CEO*
Mark E Ruedrich, *
Tom Allen, *
Sheila Martins, *
▲ **EMP:** 50 **EST:** 1988
**SQ FT:** 3,000
**SALES (est):** 14.69MM
**SALES (corp-wide):** 14.69MM **Privately Held**
**Web:** www.northcoastbrewing.com
**SIC: 2082** 5812 5813 Beer (alcoholic beverage); Eating places; Bars and lounges

**(P-1451)**
**NORTH COAST BREWING CO INC**
444 N Main St, Fort Bragg (95437-3216)
PHONE..................................707 964-3400
**EMP:** 25
**SALES (corp-wide):** 14.69MM **Privately Held**
**Web:** www.northcoastbrewing.com
**SIC: 2082** Beer (alcoholic beverage)
**PA:** North Coast Brewing Co., Inc.
455 N Main St
707 964-2739

**(P-1452)**
**OTAY LAKES BREWERY LLC**
Also Called: Novo Brasil Brewing Co.
901 Lane Ave Ste 100, Chula Vista (91914-3536)
PHONE..................................619 768-0172
**EMP:** 38 **EST:** 2014
**SALES (est):** 6.49MM **Privately Held**
**Web:** www.novobrew.com
**SIC: 2082** Ale (alcoholic beverage)

**(P-1453)**
**OUTLAW BEVERAGE INC**
3945 Freedom Cir Ste 560, Santa Clara (95054-1269)
PHONE..................................310 424-5077
Douglas Weekes, *CEO*
**EMP:** 18 **EST:** 2015
**SALES (est):** 401.13K **Privately Held**
**SIC: 2082** Malt beverages

**(P-1454)**
**POWER BRANDS CONSULTING LLC**
Also Called: Bevpack
5805 Sepulveda Blvd Ste 501, Van Nuys (91411-2551)
PHONE..................................818 989-9646
**EMP:** 40 **EST:** 2006
**SQ FT:** 5,000
**SALES (est):** 8.53MM **Privately Held**
**Web:** www.powerbrands.us
**SIC: 2082** 8742 Malt beverage products; Food and beverage consultant

**(P-1455)**
**PROST LLC**
Also Called: Bolt Brewery
8179 Center St, La Mesa (91942-2907)
PHONE..................................619 954-4189
**EMP:** 25 **EST:** 2013
**SALES (est):** 931.3K **Privately Held**
**SIC: 2082** Malt beverages

**(P-1456)**
**PURE PROJECT LLC**
1305 Hot Springs Way, Vista (92081-7876)
PHONE..................................760 552-7873
Mat Robar, *Managing Member*
**EMP:** 67 **EST:** 2015
**SALES (est):** 6MM **Privately Held**
**Web:** www.purebrewing.org
**SIC: 2082** Beer (alcoholic beverage)

**(P-1457)**
**RARE BARREL LLC**
Also Called: Rare Barrel, The
216 Amherst Ave, San Mateo (94402-2202)
PHONE..................................510 984-6585
Brad Goodwin, *Managing Member*
▲ **EMP:** 23 **EST:** 2012
**SALES (est):** 2.3MM **Privately Held**
**Web:** www.therarebarrel.com
**SIC: 2082** Beer (alcoholic beverage)

**(P-1458)**
**SIERRA NEVADA BREWING CO (PA)**
1075 E 20th St, Chico (95928-6722)
PHONE..................................530 893-3520
Ken Grossman, *Interim Chief Executive Officer*
Kenneth Grossman, *
Paul Janicki, *
◆ **EMP:** 475 **EST:** 1979
**SALES (est):** 300MM
**SALES (corp-wide):** 300MM **Privately Held**
**Web:** www.sierranevada.com
**SIC: 2082** 5812 Beer (alcoholic beverage); Eating places

**(P-1459)**
**SPEAKEASY ALES & LAGERS INC**
1195 Evans Ave, San Francisco (94124-1704)
P.O. Box 882724 (94188-2724)
PHONE..................................415 642-3371
▲ **EMP:** 33
**Web:** www.goodbeer.com
**SIC: 2082** Beer (alcoholic beverage)

**(P-1460)**
**STEINBECK BREWING COMPANY**
Also Called: Buffalo Bills Brewery
1082 B St, Hayward (94541-4108)
P.O. Box 150 (94543-0150)
PHONE..................................510 886-9823
Geoffrey A Harries, *Pr*
**EMP:** 84 **EST:** 1994
**SQ FT:** 4,000
**SALES (est):** 8.44MM **Privately Held**
**SIC: 2082** 5812 Beer (alcoholic beverage); Eating places

**(P-1461)**
**STONE BREWING CO LLC**
2816 Historic Decatur Rd Ste 116, San Diego (92106-6164)
PHONE..................................619 269-2100
**EMP:** 219
**Web:** www.stonebrewing.com
**SIC: 2082** Malt beverages
**HQ:** Stone Brewing Co., Llc
1999 Citracado Pkwy
Escondido CA 92029

**(P-1462)**
**STONE BREWING CO LLC**
1977 Citracado Pkwy, Escondido (92029-4158)
PHONE..................................760 294-7899
**EMP:** 219
**Web:** www.stonebrewing.com
**SIC: 2082** Malt beverages
**HQ:** Stone Brewing Co., Llc
1999 Citracado Pkwy
Escondido CA 92029

**(P-1463)**
**TABLE BLUFF BREWING INC (PA)**
Also Called: Lost Coast Brewery & Cafe
617 4th St, Eureka (95501-1013)
PHONE..................................707 445-4480
Barbara Groom, *CEO*
Wendy Pound, *
Kurt Kovacs, *
◆ **EMP:** 30 **EST:** 1989
**SALES (est):** 13.77MM **Privately Held**
**Web:** www.lostcoast.com

# PRODUCTS & SERVICES SECTION

## 2084 - Wines, Brandy, And Brandy Spirits (P-1488)

SIC: 2082 5812 5813 Beer (alcoholic beverage); Eating places; Bar (drinking places)

### (P-1464)
**TAPROOM BEER CO**
2000 El Cajon Blvd, San Diego (92104-1007)
PHONE..................619 539-7738
Kevin Conover, Pt
EMP: 30 EST: 2020
SALES (est): 585.28K Privately Held
Web: www.taproombeerco.com
SIC: 2082 Beer (alcoholic beverage)

### (P-1465)
**TEMBLOR BREWING LLC**
3200 Buck Owens Blvd, Bakersfield (93308-6318)
PHONE..................661 489-4855
Donald Bynum, CEO
EMP: 49 EST: 2014
SQ FT: 19,000
SALES (est): 4.15MM Privately Held
Web: www.temblorbrewing.com
SIC: 2082 5813 Ale (alcoholic beverage); Bars and lounges

### (P-1466)
**W CELLARS INC**
333 S Grand Ave Ste 3400, Los Angeles (90071-1538)
PHONE..................714 655-2025
Maria Thomas, Prin
EMP: 15 EST: 2018
SALES (est): 784.7K Privately Held
SIC: 2082 Beer (alcoholic beverage)

### (P-1467)
**W G BARR BEVERAGE COMPANY LP**
Also Called: Two Pitchers Brewing Company
2344 Webster St, Oakland (94612-3116)
PHONE..................510 999-4939
Wilson Barr, Mgr
Wilson G Barr, CEO
EMP: 25 EST: 2011
SALES (est): 1.87MM Privately Held
Web: www.twopitchers.com
SIC: 2082 5181 5921 Beer (alcoholic beverage); Beer and ale; Beer (packaged)

## 2083 Malt

### (P-1468)
**GREAT WESTERN MALTING CO**
995 Joshua Way Ste B, Vista (92081-7856)
PHONE..................360 991-0888
Mike O'toole, Pr
EMP: 99
Web: www.greatwesternmalting.com
SIC: 2083 Malt
HQ: Great Western Malting Co.
1705 Nw Harborside Dr
Vancouver WA 98660
360 693-3661

## 2084 Wines, Brandy, And Brandy Spirits

### (P-1469)
**3 BADGE BEVERAGE CORPORATION**
Also Called: 3 Badge Enology
32 Patten St, Sonoma (95476-6727)
PHONE..................707 343-1167
Richard Zeller, CEO
Keith Casale, COO
August David Sebastiani, CEO
EMP: 15 EST: 2009
SALES (est): 5.2MM Privately Held
Web: www.3badge.com
SIC: 2084 5182 Wine cellars, bonded: engaged in blending wines; Bottling wines and liquors

### (P-1470)
**ADAMS WINERY LLC**
9711 W Dry Creek Rd, Healdsburg (95448-8113)
PHONE..................707 395-6126
Scott Adams, *
Lynn Adams, *
EMP: 50 EST: 1999
SALES (est): 1.77MM Privately Held
SIC: 2084 Wines

### (P-1471)
**ADOBE ROAD WINERY**
6 Petaluma Blvd N Ste A1, Petaluma (94952-3051)
PHONE..................707 939-9099
EMP: 19 EST: 2018
SALES (est): 256.31K Privately Held
Web: www.adoberoadwines.com
SIC: 2084 Wines

### (P-1472)
**AGNES COVE LLC (PA)**
Also Called: Agnes Cove
50 Technology Ct, Napa (94558)
P.O. Box 10724 (94581)
PHONE..................707 266-6899
EMP: 40
SALES (est): 321.56K
SALES (corp-wide): 321.56K Privately Held
SIC: 2084 Wines

### (P-1473)
**AGUA DULCE VINEYARDS LLC**
9640 Sierra Hwy, Agua Dulce (91390-4622)
PHONE..................661 268-7402
EMP: 20 EST: 2001
SALES (est): 1.79MM Privately Held
Web: www.aguadulcewinery.com
SIC: 2084 5921 Wines; Wine

### (P-1474)
**AKASH WINERY & VINEYARDS LLC**
39730 Calle Contento, Temecula (92591-4014)
PHONE..................714 306-9966
EMP: 18 EST: 2017
SALES (est): 1.08MM Privately Held
Web: www.akashwinery.com
SIC: 2084 Wines

### (P-1475)
**ALMA ROSA WINERY VINEYARDS LLC**
1607 Mission Dr Ste 300, Solvang (93463-3640)
PHONE..................805 688-9090
J Richard Sanford, Managing Member
EMP: 26 EST: 2006
SALES (est): 1.18MM Privately Held
Web: www.almarosawinery.com
SIC: 2084 Wines

### (P-1476)
**ANTINORI CALIFORNIA**
Also Called: Antica NAPA Valley
3149 Soda Canyon Rd, Napa (94558-9448)
PHONE..................707 265-8866
Marchase P Antinori, Pr
▲ EMP: 22 EST: 1993
SALES (est): 2.5MM Privately Held
Web: www.antinorinapavalley.com
SIC: 2084 5921 Wines; Wine

### (P-1477)
**ARC VINEYARDS LLC**
5391 Presquile Dr, Santa Maria (93455-5811)
PHONE..................805 937-3901
EMP: 30
SALES (corp-wide): 950.07K Privately Held
Web: www.presquilewine.com
SIC: 2084 Wines
PA: Arc Vineyards, Llc
2529b Professional Pkwy
805 310-9322

### (P-1478)
**ARCHERY SUMMIT WINERY**
5901 Silverado Trl, Napa (94558-9417)
PHONE..................707 252-9777
EMP: 15
Web: www.archerysummit.com
SIC: 2084 Wines
PA: Archery Summit Winery
18599 Ne Archery Smmit Rd

### (P-1479)
**ARTISTE MANAGEMENT COMPANY LLC**
Also Called: Artiste Management Company
2948 Grand Ave, Los Olivos (93441-4403)
P.O. Box 1796 (93460-1796)
PHONE..................805 686-2626
EMP: 16 EST: 2020
SALES (est): 946.61K Privately Held
Web: www.artisteart.com
SIC: 2084 Wines

### (P-1480)
**ASV WINES INC (PA)**
Also Called: Asv Wines
1998 Road 152, Delano (93215-9437)
PHONE..................661 792-3159
Marko B Zaninovich, Pr
Kent Stephens, *
◆ EMP: 15 EST: 1981
SQ FT: 4,000
SALES (est): 9.81MM
SALES (corp-wide): 9.81MM Privately Held
Web: www.asvwines.com
SIC: 2084 Wines

### (P-1481)
**AVV WINERY CO LLC**
Also Called: Alexander Valley Vineyards
8644 Highway 128, Healdsburg (95448-9021)
P.O. Box 175 (95448-0175)
PHONE..................707 433-7209
Harry H Wetzel Iii, Managing Member
Linda Wetzel, *
John Wetzel, *
▲ EMP: 25 EST: 1975
SQ FT: 32,000
SALES (est): 5.11MM Privately Held
Web: www.avvwine.com
SIC: 2084 Wines

### (P-1482)
**BARREL TEN QARTER CIR LAND INC**
33 Harlow Ct, Napa (94558-7520)
P.O. Box 789 (95307-0789)
PHONE..................209 538-3131
Fred T Franzia, Prin
EMP: 23
SALES (corp-wide): 69.71MM Privately Held
SIC: 2084 Wines
HQ: Barrel Ten Quarter Circle Land Company, Inc.
6342 Bystrum Rd
Ceres CA 95307
707 258-0550

### (P-1483)
**BAYWOOD CELLARS INC**
Also Called: Hook or Crook Cellars
5573 W Woodbridge Rd, Lodi (95242-9497)
PHONE..................415 606-4640
William Stokes, CEO
Allen Lambardi, *
John Healy, *
EMP: 30 EST: 2012
SALES (est): 4.51MM Privately Held
Web: www.baywood-cellars.com
SIC: 2084 Wines

### (P-1484)
**BERNARDO WINERY INC (PA)**
13330 Paseo Del Verano Norte, San Diego (92128-1899)
PHONE..................858 487-1866
Ross Rizzo, Pr
EMP: 16 EST: 1932
SALES (est): 3MM
SALES (corp-wide): 3MM Privately Held
Web: www.bernardowinery.com
SIC: 2084 5921 7941 Wines; Wine; Sports field or stadium operator, promoting sports events

### (P-1485)
**BFW ASSOCIATES LLC (HQ)**
Also Called: Benziger Family Winery
1883 London Ranch Rd, Glen Ellen (95442-9728)
PHONE..................707 935-3000
▲ EMP: 30 EST: 1980
SQ FT: 6,000
SALES (est): 9.35MM Privately Held
Web: www.benziger.com
SIC: 2084 5921 Wines; Wine
PA: The Wine Group Llc
17000 E State Highway 120

### (P-1486)
**BOEGER WINERY INC**
Also Called: Boeger
1709 Carson Rd, Placerville (95667-4906)
PHONE..................530 622-8094
Greg Boeger, Pr
Susan Boeger, *
EMP: 50 EST: 1972
SQ FT: 8,000
SALES (est): 4.6MM Privately Held
Web: www.boegerwinery.com
SIC: 2084 0172 Wines; Grapes

### (P-1487)
**BONNY DOON WINERY INC**
328 Ingalls St, Santa Cruz (95060-5882)
PHONE..................831 425-3625
Randall Grahm, Pr
Lisa Kohrs, *
◆ EMP: 15 EST: 1983
SQ FT: 20,000
SALES (est): 2.59MM Privately Held
Web: www.bonnydoonvineyard.com
SIC: 2084 Wines

### (P-1488)
**BOTTAIA WINES LP**
35601 Rancho California Rd, Temecula (92591-4024)

## 2084 - Wines, Brandy, And Brandy Spirits (P-1489)

PHONE..............................951 252-1799
**EMP:** 40 **EST:** 2016
**SALES (est):** 5.09MM **Privately Held**
**Web:** www.bottaiawinery.com
**SIC: 2084** Wines

**(P-1489)**
**BOUCHAINE VINEYARDS INC**
Also Called: Bouchaine Winery
1075 Buchli Station Rd, Napa (94559-9716)
PHONE..............................707 252-9065
Tatiana Copeland, *Pr*
Gerret Copeland, *Ch*
**EMP:** 18 **EST:** 1980
**SQ FT:** 35,000
**SALES (est):** 4.06MM **Privately Held**
**Web:** www.bouchaine.com
**SIC: 2084** 5812 Wines; Eating places

**(P-1490)**
**BURGESS CELLARS INC**
1108 Deer Park Rd, Saint Helena (94574-9728)
P.O. Box 282 (94574-0282)
PHONE..............................707 963-4766
Thomas E Burgess, *Pr*
**EMP:** 23 **EST:** 1972
**SQ FT:** 20,000
**SALES (est):** 1.97MM **Privately Held**
**Web:** www.burgesscellars.com
**SIC: 2084** 0172 Wines; Grapes

**(P-1491)**
**BWSC LLC**
1 Winemaster Way Ste D, Lodi (95240-0860)
PHONE..............................424 353-1767
**EMP:** 48
**SALES (corp-wide):** 72.07MM **Privately Held**
**SIC: 2084** Wines, brandy, and brandy spirits
**HQ:** Bwsc, Llc
    1751 Berkeley St Ste 3
    Santa Monica CA 90404

**(P-1492)**
**C MONDAVI & FAMILY (PA)**
Also Called: Charles Krug Winery
2800 Main St, Saint Helena (94574-2600)
P.O. Box 191 (94574-0191)
PHONE..............................707 967-2200
John Lennon, *Pr*
Mark Mondavi, *
Peter Mondavi Junior, *Treas*
Mike Spiegel, *
▲ **EMP:** 85 **EST:** 1866
**SQ FT:** 175,000
**SALES (est):** 23.64MM
**SALES (corp-wide):** 23.64MM **Privately Held**
**Web:** www.charleskrug.com
**SIC: 2084** 0172 Wine cellars, bonded: engaged in blending wines; Grapes

**(P-1493)**
**CAKEBREAD CELLARS**
Also Called: Cakebread Cellar Vineyards
8300 Saint Helena Hwy, Rutherford (94573)
P.O. Box 216 (94573-0216)
PHONE..............................707 963-5221
Jack E Cakebread, *CEO*
Bruce Cakebread, *
Dennis Cakebread, *
Dolores Cakebread, *
Michael W Thomas, *
▲ **EMP:** 60 **EST:** 1973
**SQ FT:** 100,000
**SALES (est):** 21.64MM **Privately Held**
**Web:** www.cakebread.com
**SIC: 2084** Wines

**(P-1494)**
**CALCAREOUS VINEYARD LLC**
3430 Peachy Canyon Rd, Paso Robles (93446-7685)
PHONE..............................805 239-0289
▲ **EMP:** 15 **EST:** 2000
**SALES (est):** 2.28MM **Privately Held**
**Web:** www.calcareous.com
**SIC: 2084** Wines

**(P-1495)**
**CALDWELL VINEYARD LLC**
Also Called: Caldwell Winery
169 Kreuzer Ln, Napa (94559-3604)
PHONE..............................707 255-1294
John Caldwell, *Owner*
▲ **EMP:** 15 **EST:** 1988
**SALES (est):** 2.71MM **Privately Held**
**Web:** www.caldwellvineyard.com
**SIC: 2084** Wines

**(P-1496)**
**CALLAWAY VINEYARD & WINERY**
32720 Rancho California Rd, Temecula (92591-4925)
P.O. Box 9014 (92589-9014)
PHONE..............................951 676-4001
Mike Jellison, *Pr*
▲ **EMP:** 70 **EST:** 1969
**SALES (est):** 5.13MM **Privately Held**
**Web:** www.callawaywinery.com
**SIC: 2084** Wine cellars, bonded: engaged in blending wines

**(P-1497)**
**CAMPOS VINEYARDS LLC**
Also Called: Campos Family Vineyards
3501 Byer Rd, Byron (94514-1506)
PHONE..............................925 308-7963
**EMP:** 24 **EST:** 2017
**SALES (est):** 705.46K **Privately Held**
**Web:** www.camposfamilyvineyards.com
**SIC: 2084** Wines

**(P-1498)**
**CAYMUS VINEYARDS**
Also Called: Wagner Wine Company
8700 Conn Creek Rd, Rutherford (94573)
P.O. Box 268 (94573)
PHONE..............................707 963-4204
◆ **EMP:** 45 **EST:** 1943
**SALES (est):** 11.21MM **Privately Held**
**Web:** www.caymus.com
**SIC: 2084** Wines

**(P-1499)**
**CEDAR KNOLL VINEYARDS INC**
Also Called: Palmaz Vineyards
4029 Hagen Rd, Napa (94558-3818)
PHONE..............................707 226-5587
Amalia Palmaze, *Pr*
▲ **EMP:** 30 **EST:** 1998
**SALES (est):** 4.28MM **Privately Held**
**Web:** www.palmazvineyards.com
**SIC: 2084** Wines

**(P-1500)**
**CENTRAL COAST WINE WAREHOUSE (PA)**
Also Called: Central Coast Wine Services
2717 Aviation Way Ste 101, Santa Maria (93455-1506)
PHONE..............................805 928-9210
Jim Lunt, *Ltd Pt*
Jeff Maiken, *Ltd Pt*
▲ **EMP:** 17 **EST:** 1988
**SQ FT:** 35,000
**SALES (est):** 4.81MM **Privately Held**
**SIC: 2084** 5182 7389 Wines; Bottling wines and liquors; Field warehousing

**(P-1501)**
**CHAMISAL VINEYARDS LLC**
Also Called: Burtech Family Wines
7525 Orcutt Rd, San Luis Obispo (93401-8341)
PHONE..............................866 808-9463
Andrea De Palo, *Prin*
Norman L Goss, *Prin*
▲ **EMP:** 15 **EST:** 1972
**SALES (est):** 2.34MM
**SALES (corp-wide):** 72.4MM **Publicly Held**
**Web:** www.chamisalvineyards.com
**SIC: 2084** 0172 Wines; Grapes
**PA:** Crimson Wine Group, Ltd.
    5901 Silverado Trl
    800 486-0503

**(P-1502)**
**CHAPPELLET VINEYARD**
1581 Sage Canyon Rd, Saint Helena (94574-9628)
PHONE..............................707 286-4219
**EMP:** 53 **EST:** 2009
**SALES (est):** 3.11MM **Privately Held**
**Web:** www.chappellet.com
**SIC: 2084** Wines

**(P-1503)**
**CHAPPELLET WINERY INC (PA)**
1581 Sage Canyon Rd, Saint Helena (94574-9628)
PHONE..............................707 286-4219
Cyril Donn Chappellet, *CEO*
Mary Alice Chappellet, *
David Francke, *
▲ **EMP:** 34 **EST:** 1967
**SQ FT:** 22,472
**SALES (est):** 5.13MM
**SALES (corp-wide):** 5.13MM **Privately Held**
**Web:** www.chappellet.com
**SIC: 2084** Wines

**(P-1504)**
**CHATEAU DIANA LLC (PA)**
Also Called: US Megano Wine
6195 Dry Creek Rd, Healdsburg (95448)
P.O. Box 1013 (95448)
PHONE..............................707 433-6992
Corey Manning, *Managing Member*
Dawn Manning, *Managing Member*
▲ **EMP:** 15 **EST:** 1978
**SQ FT:** 8,000
**SALES (est):** 6.24MM
**SALES (corp-wide):** 6.24MM **Privately Held**
**Web:** www.chateaud.com
**SIC: 2084** Wines

**(P-1505)**
**CHATEAU MASSON LLC**
Also Called: Mountain Winery
14831 Pierce Rd, Saratoga (95070-9724)
PHONE..............................408 741-7002
**EMP:** 25 **EST:** 1999
**SQ FT:** 1,500
**SALES (est):** 4.33MM **Privately Held**
**Web:** www.mountainwinery.com
**SIC: 2084** Wines

**(P-1506)**
**CHATEAU MONTELENA LLC**
Also Called: Chateau Montelena Winery
1429 Tubbs Ln, Calistoga (94515-9726)
PHONE..............................707 942-5105
Bo Barrett, *Managing Member*
▲ **EMP:** 30 **EST:** 2015
**SQ FT:** 22,000
**SALES (est):** 6.55MM **Privately Held**
**Web:** www.montelena.com
**SIC: 2084** 0172 Wines; Grapes

**(P-1507)**
**CLINE CELLARS INC (PA)**
Also Called: Cline Cellars Winery
24737 Arnold Dr, Sonoma (95476-9216)
PHONE..............................707 940-4000
◆ **EMP:** 30 **EST:** 1982
**SALES (est):** 6.22MM
**SALES (corp-wide):** 6.22MM **Privately Held**
**Web:** www.clinecellars.com
**SIC: 2084** Wines

**(P-1508)**
**CLOS DE LA TECH LLC**
1000 Fern Hollow Rd, La Honda (94020)
PHONE..............................650 722-3038
Thurman J Rodgers, *Managing Member*
Valeta Massey, *Managing Member*
**EMP:** 20 **EST:** 2001
**SALES (est):** 3.69MM **Privately Held**
**Web:** www.closdelatech.com
**SIC: 2084** Wines

**(P-1509)**
**CLOS DU BOIS WINES INC**
Also Called: Constlltion Brnds US Oprations
19410 Geyserville Ave, Geyserville (95441-9603)
PHONE..............................707 857-1651
Jon Moramarco, *Pr*
Mike Jellison, *
Tom Hobart, *
▲ **EMP:** 18 **EST:** 1982
**SALES (est):** 8.44MM **Privately Held**
**Web:** www.closdubois.com
**SIC: 2084** Wines
**HQ:** Suntory Global Spirits
    11 Madison Ave 12th Fl
    New York NY 10010
    312 964-6999

**(P-1510)**
**CLOS DU VAL WINE COMPANY LTD**
Also Called: Golet Wine Estates
5330 Silverado Trl, Napa (94558)
PHONE..............................707 259-2200
Bernard Portet, *Ch*
Adam Torpy, *
Jon-mark Chappellet, *Pr*
◆ **EMP:** 50 **EST:** 1972
**SQ FT:** 32,000
**SALES (est):** 9.95MM **Privately Held**
**Web:** www.closduval.com
**SIC: 2084** Wines

**(P-1511)**
**CLOS LA CHANCE WINES INC**
1 Hummingbird Ln, San Martin (95046-9473)
PHONE..............................408 686-1050
Bill Murphy, *CEO*
Brenda Murphy, *
Bob Dunnett, *
▲ **EMP:** 45 **EST:** 1992
**SQ FT:** 25,000
**SALES (est):** 7.26MM **Privately Held**
**Web:** www.clos.com
**SIC: 2084** Wines

**(P-1512)**
**CLOS LACHANCE WINES LLC**
Also Called: Hayes Valley Wine
1 Hummingbird Ln, San Martin (95046-9473)

## PRODUCTS & SERVICES SECTION
### 2084 - Wines, Brandy, And Brandy Spirits (P-1535)

PHONE..................408 686-1050
Brenda Murphy, *Prin*
EMP: 19
SALES (est): 1.32MM **Privately Held**
SIC: 2084 Wines

**(P-1513)**
### COASTAL VINEYARD SERVICES LLC
120 Callie Ct, Arroyo Grande (93420-2939)
PHONE..................805 441-4465
Kevin Wilkinson, *Prin*
EMP: 22 EST: 2013
SALES (est): 236.11K **Privately Held**
Web: www.coastalvineyardservices.com
SIC: 2084 Wines

**(P-1514)**
### CODORNIU NAPA INC
Also Called: Artesa
1345 Henry Rd, Napa (94559-9705)
PHONE..................707 254-2148
Sergio Fuster, *CEO*
Xavier Pages, *
Arthur O'connor, *Pr*
Michael Kenton, *
David Gilbreath, *
▲ EMP: 47 EST: 1988
SQ FT: 120,000
SALES (est): 8.35MM
SALES (corp-wide): 872.89K **Privately Held**
Web: www.artesawinery.com
SIC: 2084 Wines
HQ: Codorniu Sa
    Avenida Jaume De Codorniu, S/N
    Sant Sadurni D'anoia B 08770

**(P-1515)**
### CONETECH CUSTOM SERVICES LLC
Also Called: Martini Prati Winery
2191 Laguna Rd, Santa Rosa (95401-3705)
PHONE..................707 823-2404
Wayne Salk, *Prin*
EMP: 40 EST: 2000
SQ FT: 1,280
SALES (est): 193.94K **Privately Held**
Web: www.martinraywinery.com
SIC: 2084 Wines

**(P-1516)**
### CONSTLLTION BRNDS US OPRTONS I
Also Called: Dunnewood Vineyards
2399 N State St, Ukiah (95482)
P.O. Box 698 (95448)
PHONE..................707 467-4840
George Phelan, *Mgr*
EMP: 42
SALES (corp-wide): 9.96B **Publicly Held**
Web: www.cbrands.com
SIC: 2084 Wines
HQ: Constellation Brands U.S. Operations, Inc.
    235 N Bloomfield Rd
    Canandaigua NY 14424
    585 396-7600

**(P-1517)**
### CONSTLLTION BRNDS US OPRTONS I
Also Called: Beam Wine Estates
349 Healdsburg Ave, Healdsburg (95448-4137)
PHONE..................707 433-8268
EMP: 33
SALES (corp-wide): 9.96B **Publicly Held**
Web: www.cbrands.com
SIC: 2084 0172 Wines; Grapes
HQ: Constellation Brands U.S. Operations, Inc.
    235 N Bloomfield Rd
    Canandaigua NY 14424
    585 396-7600

**(P-1518)**
### CORBETT VINEYARDS LLC
Also Called: Kitchen and Rail
2195 Corbett Canyon Rd, Arroyo Grande (93420-4974)
PHONE..................805 782-9463
William Swanson, *Managing Member*
Bill Swanson, *
Rob Rossi, *
▲ EMP: 25 EST: 2008
SALES (est): 1.83MM **Privately Held**
Web: www.coewine.com
SIC: 2084 Wines

**(P-1519)**
### COSENTINO SIGNATURE WINERIES
Also Called: Cosentino Winery
7415 St Helena Hwy, Yountville (94599)
P.O. Box 2818 (94599-2818)
PHONE..................707 921-2809
Mitch Cosentino, *Pr*
Larry J Soldinger, *
▲ EMP: 25 EST: 1981
SQ FT: 7,000
SALES (est): 738.1K **Privately Held**
SIC: 2084 Wines

**(P-1520)**
### COURTSIDE CELLARS LLC (PA)
Also Called: Tolosa Winery
4910 Edna Rd, San Luis Obispo (93401-7938)
PHONE..................805 782-0500
James Efird, *
Robin Baggett, *
▲ EMP: 30 EST: 1998
SQ FT: 70,000
SALES (est): 10.2MM
SALES (corp-wide): 10.2MM **Privately Held**
Web: www.tolosawinery.com
SIC: 2084 Wines

**(P-1521)**
### COURTSIDE CELLARS LLC
2425 Mission St, San Miguel (93451-9556)
PHONE..................805 467-2882
David Mchenry, *Genl Mgr*
EMP: 17
SALES (corp-wide): 10.2MM **Privately Held**
Web: www.tolosawinery.com
SIC: 2084 Wine cellars, bonded: engaged in blending wines
PA: Courtside Cellars, Llc
    4910 Edna Rd
    805 782-0500

**(P-1522)**
### CRIMSON WINE GROUP LTD (PA)
Also Called: CRIMSON
5901 Silverado Trl, Napa (94558-9417)
PHONE..................800 486-0503
Jennifer L Locke, *CEO*
John D Cumming, *Ch Bd*
Nicolas M E Quille, *WINEMAKING*
Adam D Howell, *CFO*
▲ EMP: 110 EST: 1991
SALES (est): 72.4MM
SALES (corp-wide): 72.4MM **Publicly Held**
Web: www.cbrands.com
SIC: 2084 5182 Wines, brandy, and brandy spirits; Wine and distilled beverages

**(P-1523)**
### CYDEA INC
Also Called: Beveragefactory.com
8510 Miralani Dr, San Diego (92126-4351)
PHONE..................800 710-9939
Craig Costanzo, *CEO*
Michael Costanzo, *
Barbara Costanzo, *
◆ EMP: 49 EST: 1997
SQ FT: 12,000
SALES (est): 10.41MM **Privately Held**
Web: www.beveragefactory.com
SIC: 2084 2082 5046 5078 Wines, brandy, and brandy spirits; Beer (alcoholic beverage); Coffee brewing equipment and supplies; Refrigeration equipment and supplies

**(P-1524)**
### DANA ESTATES INC (PA)
1500 Whitehall Ln, Saint Helena (94574-9685)
P.O. Box 153 (94573-0153)
PHONE..................707 963-4365
Hi Sang Lee, *Pr*
▲ EMP: 24 EST: 2005
SALES (est): 4.77MM **Privately Held**
Web: www.danaestates.com
SIC: 2084 Wines

**(P-1525)**
### DANZA DEL SOL WINERY INC
39050 De Portola Rd, Temecula (92592-8833)
P.O. Box 892889 (92589-2889)
PHONE..................951 302-6363
Robert Olson, *Pr*
EMP: 27 EST: 2015
SALES (est): 3.11MM **Privately Held**
Web: www.danzadelsolwinery.com
SIC: 2084 Wines

**(P-1526)**
### DAOU VINEYARDS LLC
Also Called: Daou Vineyards
2740 Hidden Mountain Rd, Paso Robles (93446-8712)
PHONE..................805 226-5460
Ben Dollard, *Brnch Mgr*
EMP: 29
Web: www.daouvineyards.com
SIC: 2084 Wines
PA: Daou Vineyards, Llc
    2777 Hidden Mountain Rd

**(P-1527)**
### DARCIE KENT VINEYARDS LLC
4590 Tesla Rd, Livermore (94550-9002)
PHONE..................925 243-9040
Darcie Kent, *Prin*
▲ EMP: 28 EST: 2011
SALES (est): 3.82MM **Privately Held**
Web: www.darciekentvineyards.com
SIC: 2084 Wines

**(P-1528)**
### DARIOUSH KHALEDI WINERY LLC
4240 Silverado Trl, Napa (94558-1117)
PHONE..................707 257-2345
Darioush Khaledi, *Managing Member*
Hahpar Khaledi, *Managing Member*
▲ EMP: 21 EST: 1998
SALES (est): 5.23MM **Privately Held**
Web: www.darioush.com
SIC: 2084 Wines

**(P-1529)**
### DAVERO FARMS & WINERY LLC
766 Westside Rd, Healdsburg (95448-9334)
PHONE..................707 431-8000
Ridgely Evers, *Mgr*
EMP: 16 EST: 2010
SALES (est): 200.89K **Privately Held**
Web: www.davero.com
SIC: 2084 Wines

**(P-1530)**
### DAVID BRUCE WINERY INC
21439 Bear Creek Rd, Los Gatos (95033-9429)
PHONE..................408 354-4214
TOLL FREE: 800
David Bruce, *Ch Bd*
EMP: 15 EST: 1963
SQ FT: 12,000
SALES (est): 2.36MM **Privately Held**
Web: www.davidbrucewinery.com
SIC: 2084 0172 Wines; Grapes

**(P-1531)**
### DAVID JAMES LLC
21660 8th St E Ste A, Sonoma (95476-2828)
PHONE..................925 817-9215
David Sinegal, *Mgr*
EMP: 28
SALES (corp-wide): 4.05MM **Privately Held**
Web: www.sinegalestate.com
SIC: 2084 Wines
PA: David James, Llc
    2125 Inglewood Ave
    925 817-9215

**(P-1532)**
### DEL DOTTO VINEYARDS
1445 Saint Helena Hwy S, Saint Helena (94574-9775)
PHONE..................707 603-1084
EMP: 29
Web: www.deldottovineyards.com
SIC: 2084 Wines
PA: Del Dotto Vineyards
    1291 Zinfandel Ln

**(P-1533)**
### DEL DOTTO VINEYARDS
1055 Atlas Peak Rd, Napa (94558-1501)
PHONE..................707 963-2134
EMP: 29
Web: www.deldottovineyards.com
SIC: 2084 Wines
PA: Del Dotto Vineyards
    1291 Zinfandel Ln

**(P-1534)**
### DEL DOTTO VINEYARDS
Also Called: Del Dotto
540 Technology Way, Napa (94558-7513)
PHONE..................707 963-2134
Desiree Del Dotto, *Managing Member*
Dave Del Dotto, *
▲ EMP: 100 EST: 2000
SALES (est): 10.43MM **Privately Held**
Web: www.deldottovineyards.com
SIC: 2084 Wines

**(P-1535)**
### DELICATO VINEYARDS LLC (PA)
Also Called: Costal Brands
12001 S Highway 99, Manteca (95336-8499)
PHONE..................209 824-3600
Christopher Indelicato, *Managing Member*

## 2084 - Wines, Brandy, And Brandy Spirits (P-1536)

Frank Indelicato, *Managing Member**
Juan Valdes, *Managing Member**
◆ **EMP:** 120 **EST:** 1924
**SQ FT:** 12,000
**SALES (est):** 498.29MM
**SALES (corp-wide):** 498.29MM **Privately Held**
**Web:** www.delicato.com
**SIC: 2084** Wines

**(P-1536)**
### DELICATO VINEYARDS LLC
Also Called: Dfv Wines
455 Devlin Rd Ste 201, Napa (94558-6274)
**PHONE**....................707 265-1700
Chris Indelicato, *Mgr*
**EMP:** 42
**SALES (corp-wide):** 498.29MM **Privately Held**
**Web:** www.delicato.com
**SIC: 2084** Wines
**PA:** Delicato Vineyards, Llc
  12001 S Highway 99
  209 824-3600

**(P-1537)**
### DEMEINE ESTATES LLC
1380 Main St Ste 200, Saint Helena (94574-1905)
**PHONE**....................707 531-7838
**EMP:** 38 **EST:** 2019
**SALES (est):** 4.43MM **Privately Held**
**Web:** www.demeineestates.com
**SIC: 2084** Wine cellars, bonded: engaged in blending wines

**(P-1538)**
### DIAGEO NORTH AMERICA INC
Also Called: United Distlrs Vintners N Amer
1160 Battery St Ste 30, San Francisco (94111-1215)
**PHONE**....................415 835-7300
Karen Cass, *Brnch Mgr*
**EMP:** 85
**SALES (corp-wide):** 20.27B **Privately Held**
**SIC: 2084** 2082 Wines, brandy, and brandy spirits; Malt beverages
**HQ:** Diageo North America, Inc.
  175 Grnwich St Fl 41-42 3
  New York NY 10007
  212 202-1800

**(P-1539)**
### DIAMOND CREEK VINEYARD
1500 Diamond Mountain Rd, Calistoga (94515-9669)
**PHONE**....................707 942-6926
Adelle Brounstein, *Owner*
▲ **EMP:** 17 **EST:** 1968
**SQ FT:** 1,799
**SALES (est):** 3.29MM **Privately Held**
**Web:** www.diamondcreekvineyards.com
**SIC: 2084** 0172 Wines; Grapes

**(P-1540)**
### DOMAINE CHANDON INC (DH)
1 California Dr, Yountville (94599-1426)
**PHONE**....................707 944-8844
Matthew Wood, *CEO*
◆ **EMP:** 100 **EST:** 1973
**SQ FT:** 240,000
**SALES (est):** 63.36MM
**SALES (corp-wide):** 667.51MM **Privately Held**
**Web:** www.chandon.com
**SIC: 2084** 5812 0762 5813 Wines; Eating places; Vineyard management and maintenance services; Drinking places
**HQ:** Moet Hennessy Usa, Inc.
  7 World Trade Ctr Fl 250
  New York NY 10007
  212 251-8200

**(P-1541)**
### DOMINUS ESTATE CORPORATION
2570 Napa Nook Rd, Yountville (94599-1455)
**PHONE**....................707 944-8954
Christian Moueix, *Pr*
▲ **EMP:** 18 **EST:** 1982
**SQ FT:** 4,000
**SALES (est):** 2.72MM **Privately Held**
**Web:** www.dominusestate.com
**SIC: 2084** Wines

**(P-1542)**
### DON SBSTANI SONS INTL WINE NGC
520 Airpark Rd, Napa (94558-7535)
**PHONE**....................707 337-1961
John Nicolette, *Brnch Mgr*
**EMP:** 40
**SALES (corp-wide):** 19.85MM **Privately Held**
**Web:** www.donsebastianandsons.com
**SIC: 2084** Wines
**PA:** Don Sebastiani & Sons International Wine Negociants
  19150 Sonoma Hwy 12
  707 224-0410

**(P-1543)**
### DRY CREEK VINEYARD INC
Also Called: Dry Creek Vineyard
3770 Lambert Bridge Rd, Healdsburg (95448-9713)
P.O. Box T (95448-0107)
**PHONE**....................707 433-1000
Kim Wallace, *
Debbie Detrick, *
▲ **EMP:** 35 **EST:** 1972
**SQ FT:** 11,000
**SALES (est):** 7.92MM **Privately Held**
**Web:** www.drycreekvineyard.com
**SIC: 2084** 0172 Wines; Grapes

**(P-1544)**
### DRY FARM WINES LLC (PA)
2114 W Park Ave, Napa (94558-4655)
P.O. Box 3566 (94599-3566)
**PHONE**....................707 944-1500
Todd White, *CEO*
David Allred, *CEO*
Mark Moschel, *Pr*
**EMP:** 25 **EST:** 2015
**SALES (est):** 4.27MM
**SALES (corp-wide):** 4.27MM **Privately Held**
**Web:** www.dryfarmwines.com
**SIC: 2084** Wines

**(P-1545)**
### DUCKHORN WINE COMPANY (DH)
Also Called: Goldeneye
1000 Lodi Ln, Saint Helena (94574-9410)
**PHONE**....................707 963-7108
Zach Rasmuson, *COO*
Lori Beaudoin, *CFO*
◆ **EMP:** 40 **EST:** 1976
**SALES (est):** 45.77MM
**SALES (corp-wide):** 405.48MM **Publicly Held**
**Web:** www.duckhorn.com
**SIC: 2084** 0172 Wines; Grapes
**HQ:** The Duckhorn Portfolio Inc
  1201 Dowdell Ln
  Saint Helena CA 94574
  707 302-2658

**(P-1546)**
### E & J GALLO WINERY (PA)
Also Called: New Amsterdam Spirits
600 Yosemite Blvd, Modesto (95354-2760)
P.O. Box 1130 (95353-1130)
**PHONE**....................209 341-3111
Joseph E Gallo, *CEO*
◆ **EMP:** 2500 **EST:** 1942
**SALES (est):** 2.11B
**SALES (corp-wide):** 2.11B **Privately Held**
**Web:** www.gallo.com
**SIC: 2084** 0172 Wines; Grapes

**(P-1547)**
### E & J GALLO WINERY
5610 E Olive Ave, Fresno (93727-2707)
P.O. Box 1081 (93714-1081)
**PHONE**....................559 458-0807
Joe Rossi, *Brnch Mgr*
**EMP:** 123
**SALES (corp-wide):** 2.11B **Privately Held**
**Web:** www.gallo.com
**SIC: 2084** 0172 Wines; Grapes
**PA:** E. & J. Gallo Winery
  600 Yosemite Blvd
  209 341-3111

**(P-1548)**
### E & J GALLO WINERY
Also Called: Gallo Os Sonoma
3387 Dry Creek Rd, Healdsburg (95448-9740)
**PHONE**....................707 431-1946
Wayne Van Wagner, *Dir*
**EMP:** 39
**SQ FT:** 2,700
**SALES (corp-wide):** 2.11B **Privately Held**
**Web:** www.gallo.com
**SIC: 2084** 0172 Wines; Grapes
**PA:** E. & J. Gallo Winery
  600 Yosemite Blvd
  209 341-3111

**(P-1549)**
### E & J GALLO WINERY
2101 Yosemite Blvd, Modesto (95354-3024)
**PHONE**....................209 341-3111
Joseph E Gallo, *CEO*
**EMP:** 41
**SALES (corp-wide):** 2.11B **Privately Held**
**Web:** www.gallo.com
**SIC: 2084** Wines
**PA:** E. & J. Gallo Winery
  600 Yosemite Blvd
  209 341-3111

**(P-1550)**
### E & J GALLO WINERY
Also Called: Lerexa Winery
18000 River Rd, Livingston (95334-9514)
**PHONE**....................209 394-6200
Kent Mann, *Mgr*
**EMP:** 94
**SALES (corp-wide):** 2.11B **Privately Held**
**Web:** www.gallo.com
**SIC: 2084** 0172 Wines; Grapes
**PA:** E. & J. Gallo Winery
  600 Yosemite Blvd
  209 341-3111

**(P-1551)**
### EDMEADES LLC
Also Called: Edmeades Estate Winery
18700 Geyserville Ave, Geyserville (95441-9526)
**PHONE**....................707 895-3232
▲ **EMP:** 20 **EST:** 2001
**SQ FT:** 3,736
**SALES (est):** 1.99MM **Privately Held**
**Web:** www.edmeades.com
**SIC: 2084** Wines

**(P-1552)**
### EGO ONE LLC
Also Called: Ru Vango Winery
1285 Dealy Ln, Napa (94559-9706)
**PHONE**....................707 253-1615
**EMP:** 18 **EST:** 2021
**SALES (est):** 1.59MM **Privately Held**
**SIC: 2084** Wines, brandy, and brandy spirits

**(P-1553)**
### ELLISTON VINEYARDS INC
463 Kilkare Rd, Sunol (94586-9415)
**PHONE**....................925 862-2377
Donna Flavetta, *Pr*
**EMP:** 55 **EST:** 1983
**SQ FT:** 1,000
**SALES (est):** 1.66MM **Privately Held**
**Web:** www.ellistonvineyards.com
**SIC: 2084** Wines

**(P-1554)**
### EMILIO GUGLIELMO WINERY INC
1480 E Main Ave, Morgan Hill (95037-3201)
**PHONE**....................408 779-2145
**EMP:** 15 **EST:** 1973
**SALES (est):** 3.41MM **Privately Held**
**Web:** www.guglielmowinery.com
**SIC: 2084** Wines

**(P-1555)**
### ENTERPRISE VINEYARDS INC
16600 Norrbom Rd, Sonoma (95476-4780)
P.O. Box 233 (95487-0233)
**PHONE**....................707 996-6513
Philip Coturri, *Pr*
Arden Kremer, *VP*
**EMP:** 21 **EST:** 1979
**SALES (est):** 1.18MM **Privately Held**
**Web:** www.enterprisevineyards.com
**SIC: 2084** Wines

**(P-1556)**
### EOS ESTATE WINERY
Also Called: Eos
2300 Airport Rd, Paso Robles (93446-8549)
P.O. Box 1287 (93447-1287)
**PHONE**....................805 239-2562
**TOLL FREE:** 800
Frank Arciero, *Pt*
Phil Arciero, *Pt*
Fern Underwood, *Pt*
▲ **EMP:** 47 **EST:** 1986
**SALES (est):** 2.58MM **Privately Held**
**Web:** www.eosvintage.com
**SIC: 2084** 0172 3172 Wines; Grapes; Personal leather goods, nec

**(P-1557)**
### EUROBIZUSA INC
Also Called: Terravino
572 E Green St Ste 301, Pasadena (91101-2080)
**PHONE**....................626 793-0032
Valerio Chiarotti, *CEO*
**EMP:** 18 **EST:** 2006
**SALES (est):** 813K **Privately Held**
**SIC: 2084** Wines, brandy, and brandy spirits

**(P-1558)**
### EUROPA VILLAGE LLC
Also Called: Europa Village
33475 La Serena Way, Temecula (92591-5104)

## PRODUCTS & SERVICES SECTION
## 2084 - Wines, Brandy, And Brandy Spirits (P-1579)

PHONE..................951 506-1818
John Goldsmith, *General*
▲ **EMP:** 140
**SALES (corp-wide):** 1.6MM **Privately Held**
Web: www.europavillage.com
**SIC: 2084** Wines
**PA:** Europa Village Llc
41150 Vua Europa
951 506-1818

### (P-1559)
### F KORBEL & BROS (PA)
Also Called: Korbel Champagne Cellers
13250 River Rd, Guerneville (95446-9593)
PHONE..................707 824-7000
Gary B Heck, *Pr*
Danny Baker, *Ex VP*
Matthew Healey, *VP Fin*
Harold Duncan, *VP Opers*
David Faris, *Treas*
◆ **EMP:** 200 **EST:** 1882
**SQ FT:** 66,000
**SALES (est):** 42.09MM
**SALES (corp-wide):** 42.09MM **Privately Held**
Web: www.korbel.com
**SIC: 2084** 0172 Wines; Grapes

### (P-1560)
### FAIRWINDS ESTATE WINERY LLC
4550 Silverado Trl, Calistoga (94515-9647)
PHONE..................707 341-5300
Brandon Chaney, *CEO*
**EMP:** 16 **EST:** 2015
**SALES (est):** 2.38MM **Privately Held**
Web: www.fewinery.com
**SIC: 2084** Wines

### (P-1561)
### FALKNER WINERY INC
40620 Calle Contento, Temecula (92591-5041)
PHONE..................951 676-6741
Ray Falkner, *CEO*
Loretta Falkner, *
**EMP:** 65 **EST:** 1993
**SALES (est):** 5.05MM **Privately Held**
Web: www.falknerwinery.com
**SIC: 2084** 7299 Wines; Banquet hall facilities

### (P-1562)
### FAR NIENTE WINERY INC
Also Called: Far Niente Wine Estates
1350 Acacia Dr, Oakville (94562)
P.O. Box 327 (94562-0327)
PHONE..................707 944-2861
Larry Maguire, *CEO*
Laura Harwood, *CFO*
▲ **EMP:** 100 **EST:** 1979
**SQ FT:** 30,000
**SALES (est):** 12.07MM **Privately Held**
Web: www.farniente.com
**SIC: 2084** Wines

### (P-1563)
### FAZELI VINEYARDS LLC
37320 De Portola Rd, Temecula (92592-9024)
PHONE..................951 303-3366
Bizhan Fazeli, *Owner*
**EMP:** 15 **EST:** 2015
**SALES (est):** 1.44MM **Privately Held**
Web: www.fazelicellars.com
**SIC: 2084** Wines

### (P-1564)
### FERRAR-CRANO VNYRDS WINERY LLC (PA)
Also Called: Ferrari-Carano Winery
8761 Dry Creek Rd, Healdsburg (95448-9133)
P.O. Box 1549 (95448-1549)
PHONE..................707 433-6700
Rhonda Carano, *CEO*
▲ **EMP:** 99 **EST:** 1981
**SQ FT:** 46,000
**SALES (est):** 9.34MM
**SALES (corp-wide):** 9.34MM **Privately Held**
Web: www.ferrari-carano.com
**SIC: 2084** 0172 Wines; Grapes

### (P-1565)
### FETZER VINEYARDS (HQ)
Also Called: Vina Concha Y Tora USA
12901 Old River Rd, Hopland (95449)
P.O. Box 611 (95449)
PHONE..................707 744-1250
Eduardo Guilisasti Gana, *CEO*
Dennis Martin, *
Sid Goldstein, *
◆ **EMP:** 242 **EST:** 1960
**SALES (est):** 48.95MM **Privately Held**
Web: www.fetzer.com
**SIC: 2084** Wines
**PA:** Vina Concha Y Toro S.A.
Av. Nueva Tajamar 481, Piso 15

### (P-1566)
### FIOR DI SOLE LLC (PA)
2511 Napa Valley Corporate Dr, Napa (94558-7574)
P.O. Box 6829 (94581)
PHONE..................707 259-1477
Stefano Migotto, *
◆ **EMP:** 43 **EST:** 2012
**SQ FT:** 52,118
**SALES (est):** 117.81MM
**SALES (corp-wide):** 117.81MM **Privately Held**
Web: www.fiordisole.com
**SIC: 2084** Wines

### (P-1567)
### FIOR DI SOLE LLC
Also Called: Fior Di Sole 504 Devlin
504 Devlin Rd, Napa (94558-7591)
PHONE..................707 492-3506
**EMP:** 26
**SALES (corp-wide):** 117.81MM **Privately Held**
Web: www.fiordisole.com
**SIC: 2084** Wines
**PA:** Fior Di Sole, Llc
2511 Napa Valley Corp Dr
707 259-1477

### (P-1568)
### FIOR DI SOLE LLC
2515 Napa Valley Corporate Dr, Napa (94558-7541)
PHONE..................707 204-8268
Amanda Gonsalves, *Mgr*
**EMP:** 26
**SALES (corp-wide):** 117.81MM **Privately Held**
Web: www.fiordisole.com
**SIC: 2084** Wines
**PA:** Fior Di Sole, Llc
2511 Napa Valley Corp Dr
707 259-1477

### (P-1569)
### FIRESTONE VINEYARD LP
Also Called: Curtis Winery
5000 Zaca Station Rd, Los Olivos (93441)
P.O. Box 244 (93441)
PHONE..................805 688-3940
Michael L Gravelle, *Pt*
Adam Firestone, *Pt*
▲ **EMP:** 85 **EST:** 1976
**SQ FT:** 45,000
**SALES (est):** 2.76MM
**SALES (corp-wide):** 69.09MM **Privately Held**
Web: www.firestonewine.com
**SIC: 2084** 0172 Wines; Grapes
**HQ:** Foley Family Wines, Inc.
200 Concourse Blvd
Santa Rosa CA 95403

### (P-1570)
### FLOOD RANCH COMPANY
Also Called: Rancho Sisquoc Winery
6600 Foxen Canyon Rd, Santa Maria (93454-9656)
PHONE..................805 937-3616
Ed A Holt, *Mgr*
**EMP:** 33
**SALES (corp-wide):** 4.59MM **Privately Held**
Web: www.ranchosisquoc.com
**SIC: 2084** Wines
**PA:** Flood Ranch Company
870 Market St Ste 1100
415 982-5645

### (P-1571)
### FLORA SPRINGS WINE COMPANY
677 Saint Helena Hwy S, Saint Helena (94574-2209)
PHONE..................707 963-5711
John Komes, *Pr*
Patrick Garvey, *VP*
Martha Komes, *Treas*
Julie Garvey, *Sec*
▲ **EMP:** 19 **EST:** 1978
**SALES (est):** 3.21MM **Privately Held**
Web: www.florasprings.com
**SIC: 2084** Wines

### (P-1572)
### FN CELLARS LLC
1350 Acacia Dr, Oakville (94562)
P.O. Box 327 (94562-0327)
PHONE..................707 944-2861
Larry Maguire, *CEO*
**EMP:** 16
**SALES (corp-wide):** 20.89MM **Privately Held**
Web: www.farniente.com
**SIC: 2084** Wines
**PA:** Fn Cellars, Llc
27000 Ramal Rd
707 944-2412

### (P-1573)
### FN CELLARS LLC
Also Called: Bella Union Winery
1695 Saint Helena Hwy S, Saint Helena (94574-9777)
PHONE..................707 967-9600
**EMP:** 16
**SALES (corp-wide):** 20.89MM **Privately Held**
**SIC: 2084** Wines
**PA:** Fn Cellars, Llc
27000 Ramal Rd
707 944-2412

### (P-1574)
### FOLEY FMLY WINES HOLDINGS INC
90 Easy St, Buellton (93427-9566)
PHONE..................805 450-7225
**EMP:** 93
**SALES (corp-wide):** 69.09MM **Privately Held**
Web: www.foleyfoodandwinesociety.com
**SIC: 2084** Wines
**PA:** Foley Family Wines Holdings, Inc.
200 Concourse Blvd
707 708-7600

### (P-1575)
### FOX BARREL CIDER COMPANY INC
1213 S Auburn St Ste A, Colfax (95713-9773)
P.O. Box 753 (95713-0753)
PHONE..................530 346-9699
Bruce Nissen, *Pr*
Sean Deorsey, *
**EMP:** 50 **EST:** 2004
**SALES (est):** 667.03K
**SALES (corp-wide):** 11.7B **Publicly Held**
Web: www.crispincider.com
**SIC: 2084** Wines
**HQ:** Crispin Cider Company
3939 W Highland Blvd
Milwaukee WI 53208
530 346-9699

### (P-1576)
### FOXEN VINEYARD INC
Also Called: Foxen Canyon Winery & Vineyard
7600 Foxen Canyon Rd, Santa Maria (93454-9170)
PHONE..................805 937-4251
Richard Dore, *Pr*
William Wathen, *
**EMP:** 35 **EST:** 1987
**SQ FT:** 4,000
**SALES (est):** 4.98MM **Privately Held**
Web: www.foxenvineyard.com
**SIC: 2084** Wines

### (P-1577)
### FRANCIS COPPOLA WINERY LLC
Also Called: Countess Walewska, The
300 Via Archimedes, Geyserville (95441-9325)
P.O. Box 208 (94573-0208)
PHONE..................707 857-1400
Francis Coppola, *Managing Member*
▲ **EMP:** 35 **EST:** 2006
**SALES (est):** 9.39MM **Privately Held**
Web: www.francisfordcoppolawinery.com
**SIC: 2084** Wines

### (P-1578)
### FRANCIS FORD CPPOLA PRSNTS LLC
Also Called: Francis Ford Coppola Winery
300 Via Archimedes, Geyserville (95441-9325)
P.O. Box 208 (94573-0208)
PHONE..................707 251-3200
Francis Coppola, *Managing Member*
◆ **EMP:** 20 **EST:** 2006
**SALES (est):** 8.1MM **Privately Held**
Web: www.francisfordcoppolawinery.com
**SIC: 2084** Wines

### (P-1579)
### FREIXENET SONOMA CAVES INC
Also Called: Gloria Ferrer Winery
23555 Arnold Dr, Sonoma (95476-9285)
P.O. Box 1427 (95476-1427)
PHONE..................707 996-4981

## 2084 - Wines, Brandy, And Brandy Spirits (P-1580)

### PRODUCTS & SERVICES SECTION

Jose M Ferrer, *CEO*
Diego Jimenez, *
▲ EMP: 40 EST: 1982
SQ FT: 4,000
SALES (est): 17.05MM **Privately Held**
Web: www.gloriaferrer.com
SIC: **2084** 5812 Wines; Eating places
PA: Freixenet Sa
  Plaza Joan Sala 2

**(P-1580)**
### FROGS LEAP WINERY
8815 Conn Creek Rd, Rutherford (94573)
P.O. Box 189 (94573-0189)
PHONE.................................707 963-4704
John T Williams, *Pr*
◆ EMP: 36 EST: 1981
SQ FT: 8,000
SALES (est): 6.11MM **Privately Held**
Web: www.frogsleap.com
SIC: **2084** Wines

**(P-1581)**
### GAINEY VINEYARD
3950 E Highway 246, Santa Ynez (93460)
P.O. Box 910 (93460-0910)
PHONE.................................805 688-0558
Daniel H Gainey, *Pr*
▲ EMP: 22 EST: 1983
SQ FT: 20,000
SALES (est): 4.31MM **Privately Held**
Web: www.gaineyvineyard.com
SIC: **2084** Wines

**(P-1582)**
### GALLO SALES COMPANY INC (DH)
30825 Wiegman Rd, Hayward (94544-7893)
PHONE.................................510 476-5000
Joseph E Gallo, *Pr*
▲ EMP: 225 EST: 1952
SQ FT: 59,000
SALES (est): 21.72MM
SALES (corp-wide): 2.11B **Privately Held**
Web: www.gallocareers.com
SIC: **2084** Wines
HQ: Gallo Glass Company
  605 S Santa Cruz Ave
  Modesto CA 95354
  209 341-3710

**(P-1583)**
### GALLO VINEYARDS INC
5595 Creston Rd, Paso Robles (93446-9480)
PHONE.................................209 394-6281
Allan Reynolds, *Dir*
Javier Pulido, *Mgr*
EMP: 143 EST: 2000
SQ FT: 2,624
SALES (est): 4.66MM **Privately Held**
Web: www.gallo.com
SIC: **2084** Wines

**(P-1584)**
### GARRE VINEYARD AND WINERY INC
7986 Tesla Rd, Livermore (94550-9353)
P.O. Box 1048 (94566-1048)
PHONE.................................925 371-8200
Gina Molinaro-cardera, *Prin*
EMP: 26 EST: 2008
SALES (est): 2.36MM **Privately Held**
Web: www.garrewinery.com
SIC: **2084** Wines

**(P-1585)**
### GEKKEIKAN SAKE (USA) INC
1136 Sibley St, Folsom (95630-3223)
PHONE.................................916 985-3111
Kengo Matsumura, *Pr*
Masahiro Namise, *
Yu Hyodo, *
◆ EMP: 25 EST: 1989
SQ FT: 390,000
SALES (est): 9.95MM **Privately Held**
Web: www.gekkeikan.com
SIC: **2084** Wines
PA: Gekkeikan Sake Company, Ltd.
  247, Minamimihamacho, Fushimi-Ku

**(P-1586)**
### GEYSER PEAK WINERY
Also Called: Canyon Road Winery
1300 1st St Ste 368, Napa (94559-2956)
PHONE.................................707 857-9463
TOLL FREE: 800
Stephen Brower, *Pr*
Tim Matz, *
▲ EMP: 21 EST: 1989
SALES (est): 1.22MM **Privately Held**
Web: www.geyserpeakwinery.com
SIC: **2084** Wines

**(P-1587)**
### GIBSON WINE COMPANY
Also Called: Jfc International Vineyards
1720 Academy Ave, Sanger (93657-3704)
PHONE.................................559 875-2505
Keith D Nilmeier, *CEO*
Duane Metzger, *
James D Karle, *
Henry Mayeda, *
EMP: 39 EST: 1939
SQ FT: 2,000
SALES (est): 9.2MM **Privately Held**
Web: www.gibsonwinecompany.com
SIC: **2084** Wines

**(P-1588)**
### GIUMARRA VINEYARDS CORPORATION
11220 Edison Hwy, Bakersfield (93307-8431)
P.O. Box 1968 (93303-1968)
PHONE.................................661 395-7000
EMP: 117
SALES (corp-wide): 72.36MM **Privately Held**
Web: www.giumarravineyards.com
SIC: **2084** Wines, brandy, and brandy spirits
PA: Giumarra Vineyards Corporation
  11220 Edison Hwy
  661 395-7000

**(P-1589)**
### GLOBAL WINE GROUP
Also Called: Triad Global Group
3750 E Woodbridge Rd, Acampo (95220-8700)
P.O. Box 576097 (95357-6097)
PHONE.................................209 340-8500
Jeffery Hansen, *Pr*
Rod Moniz, *VP*
James R Grant Iii, *CFO*
▼ EMP: 22 EST: 2000
SQ FT: 50,000
SALES (est): 611.41K **Privately Held**
SIC: **2084** Wine cellars, bonded: engaged in blending wines

**(P-1590)**
### GMIC VINEYARDS LLC
Also Called: Hanzell Vineyards
18596 Lomita Ave, Sonoma (95476-4619)
PHONE.................................707 996-3860

Jean L Arnold, *Pr*
Alexander De Brye, *Treas*
EMP: 20 EST: 1958
SALES (est): 2.17MM **Privately Held**
Web: www.hanzell.com
SIC: **2084** Wines

**(P-1591)**
### GOLDEN STATE VINTNERS (PA)
4596 S Tracy Blvd, Tracy (95377-8106)
PHONE.................................707 254-4900
Brian Jay Vos, *CEO*
John Oliver Sutton, *Sec*
▼ EMP: 15 EST: 1995
SQ FT: 8,000
SALES (est): 79.06K
SALES (corp-wide): 79.06K **Privately Held**
SIC: **2084** Wines

**(P-1592)**
### GOLDEN STATE VINTNERS
1777 Metz Rd, Soledad (93960-2805)
PHONE.................................831 678-3991
Jay Clark, *Mgr*
EMP: 38
SALES (corp-wide): 79.06K **Privately Held**
SIC: **2084** 0172 Wines; Grapes
PA: Golden State Vintners
  4596 S Tracy Blvd
  707 254-4900

**(P-1593)**
### GOLDEN STATE VINTNERS
1175 Commerce Blvd, Vallejo (94503-9626)
PHONE.................................707 553-6480
Jeff Neil, *Brnch Mgr*
EMP: 23
SALES (corp-wide): 79.06K **Privately Held**
SIC: **2084** Wines
PA: Golden State Vintners
  4596 S Tracy Blvd
  707 254-4900

**(P-1594)**
### GOLDEN STATE VINTNERS
1075 Golden Gate Dr, Napa (94558-6187)
PHONE.................................707 254-1985
EMP: 23
SALES (corp-wide): 79.06K **Privately Held**
SIC: **2084** Wine cellars, bonded: engaged in blending wines
PA: Golden State Vintners
  4596 S Tracy Blvd
  707 254-4900

**(P-1595)**
### GOLDEN VLY GRAPE JICE WINE LLC (PA)
11770 Road 27 1/2, Madera (93637-9108)
PHONE.................................559 661-4657
Gerard Pantaleo, *Managing Member*
Frank Pantaleo, *
Nicholas Pantaleo, *
Jerry Pantaleo, *
▲ EMP: 20 EST: 1997
SALES (est): 12.51MM
SALES (corp-wide): 12.51MM **Privately Held**
Web: www.goldenvalleywine.com
SIC: **2084** Wines

**(P-1596)**
### GOLDEN VLY GRAPE JICE WINE LLC
11770 Road 27 And Half, Madera (93637)
PHONE.................................559 661-4657
Gerald D Homolka, *Genl Mgr*
EMP: 20
SALES (corp-wide): 12.51MM **Privately Held**

Web: www.goldenvalleywine.com
SIC: **2084** 2033 Wines; Fruit juices: fresh
PA: Golden Valley Grape Juice And Wine, Llc
  11770 Road 27 1/2
  559 661-4657

**(P-1597)**
### GOLDLINE BRANDS INC
7449 Fairplay Rd, Somerset (95684-9539)
PHONE.................................818 319-7038
EMP: 24 EST: 2019
SALES (est): 229.79K **Privately Held**
Web: www.goldlinebrands.com
SIC: **2084** Wines

**(P-1598)**
### GOLDRIDGEPINOTCOM LLC
Also Called: Emeritus Vineyards
2500 Gravenstein Hwy N, Sebastopol (95472-6470)
P.O. Box 749 (95473-0749)
PHONE.................................707 823-4464
▲ EMP: 57 EST: 1999
SALES (est): 3.66MM **Privately Held**
Web: www.emeritusvineyards.com
SIC: **2084** Wines

**(P-1599)**
### GOLDSTONE LAND COMPANY LLC
Also Called: Bear Creek Winery
11900 Furry Rd, Lodi (95240-7201)
PHONE.................................209 368-3113
Joan M Kautz, *Managing Member*
Stephen J Kautz, *Managing Member*
◆ EMP: 30 EST: 1995
SALES (est): 6.05MM **Privately Held**
Web: www.bearcreekwinery.net
SIC: **2084** Wines

**(P-1600)**
### GRAPE LINKS INC
Also Called: Barefoot Cellars
420 Aviation Blvd Ste 106, Santa Rosa (95403-1039)
P.O. Box 1130 (95353-1130)
PHONE.................................707 524-8000
Michael C Houlihan, *Pr*
Michael C Houlihan, *Pr*
Bonnie Harvey, *
Jennifer Wall, *
Martin A Jones, *
EMP: 35 EST: 1986
SQ FT: 4,200
SALES (est): 585.46K
SALES (corp-wide): 2.11B **Privately Held**
Web: www.barefootwine.com
SIC: **2084** Wines
PA: E. & J. Gallo Winery
  600 Yosemite Blvd
  209 341-3111

**(P-1601)**
### GREAT AMERICAN WINERIES INC
2511 Garden Rd Ste B100, Monterey (93940-5344)
P.O. Box 444 (10272-0444)
PHONE.................................831 920-4736
Robert S Brower Senior, *Pr*
Robert S Brower, *Pr*
Patricia Brower, *VP*
Robert Brower Junior, *Prin*
Michael Brennan, *Prin*
EMP: 20 EST: 1982
SQ FT: 14,000
SALES (est): 1.52MM **Privately Held**
SIC: **2084** 5182 Wines; Wine

## PRODUCTS & SERVICES SECTION
## 2084 - Wines, Brandy, And Brandy Spirits (P-1625)

**(P-1602)**
**GRGICH HILLS CELLAR**
Also Called: G and H Vineyards
1829 St Helena Hwy, Rutherford (94573)
P.O. Box 450 (94573-0450)
PHONE..................707 963-2784
Miljenko Mike Grgich, *Pr*
Austin E Hills, *
Violet Grgich, *
Ivo Jeramaz, *
▲ **EMP:** 35 **EST:** 1977
**SQ FT:** 43,000
**SALES (est):** 8.97MM **Privately Held**
Web: www.grgich.com
**SIC: 2084** 5812 0172 Wines; Eating places; Grapes

**(P-1603)**
**GRINDSTONE WINES LLC**
130 Cortina School Rd, Arbuckle (95912)
PHONE..................530 393-2162
Michael Doherty, *Pt*
**EMP:** 20 **EST:** 2019
**SALES (est):** 676.22K **Privately Held**
Web: www.grindstonewines.com
**SIC: 2084** Wines

**(P-1604)**
**GROSKOPF WAREHOUSE & LOGISTICS**
20580 8th St E, Sonoma (95476-9590)
P.O. Box 128 (95487-0128)
PHONE..................707 939-3100
Alec Merriam, *Owner*
▲ **EMP:** 41 **EST:** 2001
**SALES (est):** 4.87MM **Privately Held**
Web: www.groskopf.com
**SIC: 2084** Wines

**(P-1605)**
**GROWEST INC (PA)**
Also Called: Growest Development
1660 Chicago Ave Ste M11, Riverside (92507-2033)
PHONE..................951 638-1000
John Bremer, *Pr*
**EMP:** 15 **EST:** 1998
**SALES (est):** 7.46MM
**SALES (corp-wide):** 7.46MM **Privately Held**
Web: www.growest.com
**SIC: 2084** 5193 Wines; Nursery stock

**(P-1606)**
**H DE V LLC**
588 Trancas St, Napa (94558-3143)
PHONE..................541 386-9119
Rick Hyde, *Brnch Mgr*
**EMP:** 35
**SALES (corp-wide):** 515.04K **Privately Held**
Web: www.hdvwines.com
**SIC: 2084** Wines
PA: H De V, Llc
1101 Sherman Ave
541 386-9119

**(P-1607)**
**HAGAFEN CELLARS INC**
4160 Silverado Trl, Napa (94558-1118)
PHONE..................707 252-0781
Ernie Weir, *Pr*
Irit Weir, *VP*
▲ **EMP:** 17 **EST:** 1979
**SQ FT:** 6,000
**SALES (est):** 3.26MM **Privately Held**
Web: www.hagafen.com
**SIC: 2084** Wines

**(P-1608)**
**HALL WINES LLC**
Also Called: Walt
401 Saint Helena Hwy S, Saint Helena (94574-2200)
P.O. Box 25 (94573-0025)
PHONE..................707 967-2626
Kathryn Hall, *
Craig Hall, *
Donald L Braun, *
Larry E Levey, *
▲ **EMP:** 50 **EST:** 2003
**SQ FT:** 20,000
**SALES (est):** 18.27MM **Privately Held**
Web: www.hallwines.com
**SIC: 2084** Wines

**(P-1609)**
**HALTER PROPERTIES LLC**
Also Called: Halter Ranch Vineyard
8910 Adelaida Rd, Paso Robles (93446-8798)
PHONE..................805 226-9455
Hanjorg Wyss, *Prin*
▲ **EMP:** 17 **EST:** 2000
**SALES (est):** 871.78K **Privately Held**
Web: www.halterranch.com
**SIC: 2084** Wines

**(P-1610)**
**HALTER WINERY LLC (PA)**
Also Called: Chaparral Blend
8910 Adelaida Rd, Paso Robles (93446-8798)
PHONE..................805 226-9455
**EMP:** 22 **EST:** 2002
**SALES (est):** 8.5MM **Privately Held**
Web: www.halterranch.com
**SIC: 2084** Wines

**(P-1611)**
**HAUS BEVERAGE INC**
1377 Grove St Ste D, Healdsburg (95448-4774)
PHONE..................503 939-5298
**EMP:** 30 **EST:** 2019
**SALES (est):** 2.02MM **Privately Held**
**SIC: 2084** Wines

**(P-1612)**
**HESS COLLECTION WINERY**
1166 Commerce Blvd, American Canyon (94503-9621)
PHONE..................707 255-1144
John Bulleri, *Mgr*
**EMP:** 95
Web: www.hesspersonestates.com
**SIC: 2084** Wines
HQ: The Hess Collection Winery
4411 Redwood Rd
Napa CA 94558
707 255-1144

**(P-1613)**
**HESS COLLECTION WINERY (DH)**
Also Called: Hess Collection Import Co
4411 Redwood Rd, Napa (94558-9708)
P.O. Box 4140 (94558-0565)
PHONE..................707 255-1144
Timothy Persson, *CEO*
Tom Selfridge, *
Clement J Firko, *
Brian Dunn, *
John Grant, *
◆ **EMP:** 25 **EST:** 1978
**SQ FT:** 100,000
**SALES (est):** 54.18MM **Privately Held**
Web: www.hesspersonestates.com
**SIC: 2084** Wines

HQ: Colome Holding Ag
Hohle Gasse 4
Liebefeld BE 3097

**(P-1614)**
**HILLIARD BRUCE VINEYARDS LLC (PA)**
2097 Vineyard View Ln, Lompoc (93436-2628)
PHONE..................805 736-5366
John C Hilliard, *Managing Member*
**EMP:** 19 **EST:** 2006
**SALES (est):** 585.3K **Privately Held**
Web: www.hellinthearmory.com
**SIC: 2084** Wines

**(P-1615)**
**HIRSCH WINERY LLC**
57 Front St, Healdsburg (95448-4437)
PHONE..................707 847-3001
David Hirsch, *Managing Member*
**EMP:** 15 **EST:** 2001
**SALES (est):** 471.42K **Privately Held**
Web: www.hirschvineyards.com
**SIC: 2084** Wine cellars, bonded: engaged in blending wines

**(P-1616)**
**HUDSON WINES LLC**
5398 Sonoma Hwy, Napa (94559-9710)
PHONE..................707 255-1345
**EMP:** 18 **EST:** 2004
**SALES (est):** 514K **Privately Held**
Web: www.hudsonranch.com
**SIC: 2084** Wines

**(P-1617)**
**HUNEEUS VINTNERS LLC (PA)**
Also Called: Quintessa Vinyards
1224 Adams St Ste B, Saint Helena (94574-1950)
P.O. Box 505 (94573-0505)
PHONE..................707 286-2724
Agustin Huneeus, *Managing Member*
Valeria Huneeus, *
▲ **EMP:** 19 **EST:** 1999
**SALES (est):** 9.85MM
**SALES (corp-wide):** 9.85MM **Privately Held**
Web: www.quintessa.com
**SIC: 2084** Wines

**(P-1618)**
**HUSCH VINEYARDS INC (PA)**
4400 Highway 128, Philo (95466-9476)
P.O. Box 189 (95481-0189)
PHONE..................707 895-3216
Zac Robinson, *Pr*
Richard Robinson, *
**EMP:** 30 **EST:** 1979
**SALES (est):** 4.9MM
**SALES (corp-wide):** 4.9MM **Privately Held**
Web: www.huschvineyards.com
**SIC: 2084** 0172 Wines; Grapes

**(P-1619)**
**INGLENOOK**
1991 St Helena Hwy, Rutherford (94573)
PHONE..................707 968-1100
Francis Ford Coppola, *Prin*
▲ **EMP:** 53 **EST:** 2011
**SALES (est):** 4.61MM **Privately Held**
Web: www.inglenook.com
**SIC: 2084** Wines

**(P-1620)**
**IRON HORSE VINEYARDS**
Also Called: Vineyards and Winery
9786 Ross Station Rd, Sebastopol (95472-2179)

PHONE..................707 887-1909
Joy Sterling, *Pt*
Barry H Sterling, *
Laurence Sterling, *
▲ **EMP:** 35 **EST:** 1979
**SQ FT:** 19,000
**SALES (est):** 4.72MM **Privately Held**
Web: www.ironhorsevineyards.com
**SIC: 2084** Wines

**(P-1621)**
**IVES BAY LLC (PA)**
Also Called: Ives Bay
50 Technology Ct, Napa (94558)
P.O. Box 10724 (94581)
PHONE..................707 266-6899
Philip James, *CEO*
**EMP:** 37
**SALES (est):** 1.05MM
**SALES (corp-wide):** 1.05MM **Privately Held**
**SIC: 2084** Wines

**(P-1622)**
**J LOHR WINERY CORPORATION**
6169 Airport Rd, Paso Robles (93446-9547)
PHONE..................805 239-8900
J Lohr, *Owner*
**EMP:** 31
**SALES (corp-wide):** 49.49MM **Privately Held**
Web: www.jlohr.com
**SIC: 2084** Wines
PA: J. Lohr Winery Corporation
1000 Lenzen Ave
408 288-5057

**(P-1623)**
**J LOHR WINERY CORPORATION (PA)**
Also Called: J Lohr Viney
1000 Lenzen Ave, San Jose (95126-2739)
PHONE..................408 288-5057
Steven W Lohr, *CEO*
Jerome J Lohr, *
Bruce Arkley, *
James Schuett, *
◆ **EMP:** 50 **EST:** 1974
**SQ FT:** 47,000
**SALES (est):** 49.49MM
**SALES (corp-wide):** 49.49MM **Privately Held**
Web: www.jlohr.com
**SIC: 2084** Wines

**(P-1624)**
**J LOHR WINERY CORPORATION**
Also Called: J Lohr Warehouse
1935 S 10th St, San Jose (95112-4111)
PHONE..................408 293-1345
Albert Perez, *Brnch Mgr*
**EMP:** 31
**SALES (corp-wide):** 24.9MM **Privately Held**
Web: www.jlohr.com
**SIC: 2084** Wines
PA: J. Lohr Winery Corporation
1000 Lenzen Ave
408 288-5057

**(P-1625)**
**J PEDRONCELLI WINERY INC**
Also Called: Grapeseed Wines
1220 Canyon Rd, Geyserville (95441-9639)
PHONE..................707 857-3531
John A Pedroncelli, *Pr*
James A Pedroncelli, *VP*
**EMP:** 22 **EST:** 1927
**SQ FT:** 25,000

## 2084 - Wines, Brandy, And Brandy Spirits (P-1626)

SALES (est): 4.38MM **Privately Held**
Web: www.pedroncelli.com
SIC: **2084** 0172 Wine cellars, bonded: engaged in blending wines; Grapes

### (P-1626)
### JACKSON FAMILY FARMS LLC
5660 Skylane Blvd, Santa Rosa (95403-1086)
PHONE.................................707 836-2047
Jeff Jackson, *Mgr*
EMP: 17
SALES (corp-wide): 9.96MM **Privately Held**
Web: www.jacksonfamilywines.com
SIC: **2084** Wines
PA: Jackson Family Farms Llc
425 Aviation Blvd
707 837-1000

### (P-1627)
### JACKSON FAMILY WINES INC
1190 Kittyhawk Blvd, Santa Rosa (95403-1013)
PHONE.................................707 836-2035
Barbara Banke, *Pr*
EMP: 21
Web: www.kj.com
SIC: **2084** Wines
PA: Jackson Family Wines, Inc.
425 Aviation Blvd

### (P-1628)
### JACKSON FAMILY WINES INC (PA)
Also Called: Vineyards of Monterey
425 Aviation Blvd, Santa Rosa (95403-1069)
PHONE.................................707 544-4000
Barbara Banke, *Dir*
Charles Shea, *Product Vice President**
Viviann Stapp, **
▲ EMP: 100 EST: 1987
SQ FT: 25,000
SALES (est): 280.96MM **Privately Held**
Web: www.jacksonfamilywines.com
SIC: **2084** 0172 5813 Wines; Grapes; Wine bar

### (P-1629)
### JACUZZI FAMILY VINEYARDS LLC
Also Called: Jacuzzi Family Winery
24724 Arnold Dr, Sonoma (95476-2814)
PHONE.................................707 931-7500
▲ EMP: 16 EST: 2008
SALES (est): 3.75MM **Privately Held**
Web: www.jacuzziwines.com
SIC: **2084** Wines

### (P-1630)
### JADA VINEYARDS & WINERY
5520 Vineyard Dr, Paso Robles (93446-9685)
PHONE.................................805 226-4200
Jada Vineyard, *Owner*
▲ EMP: 16 EST: 2007
SALES (est): 270.36K **Privately Held**
Web: www.jadavineyard.com
SIC: **2084** Wines

### (P-1631)
### JAMES TOBIN CELLARS INC
8950 Union Rd, Paso Robles (93446-9356)
PHONE.................................805 239-2204
Tcbin J Shumrick, *Pr*
Claire Silver, *Stockholder**
EMP: 23 EST: 1987
SQ FT: 10,000

SALES (est): 4.59MM **Privately Held**
Web: www.tobinjames.com
SIC: **2084** Wines

### (P-1632)
### JARVIS
Also Called: Jarvis Winery
2970 Monticello Rd, Napa (94558-9615)
PHONE.................................707 255-5280
William R Jarvis, *Pr*
Leticia Jarvis, **
Deanna Martinez, **
William E Jarvis, **
EMP: 30 EST: 1991
SQ FT: 45,000
SALES (est): 5.79MM **Privately Held**
Web: www.jarviswines.com
SIC: **2084** Wines

### (P-1633)
### JEAN-CLUDE BSSET WINES USA INC
124 Matheson St, Healdsburg (95448-4118)
PHONE.................................707 963-6903
EMP: 16
Web: www.boissetcollection.com
SIC: **2084** Wines
HQ: Jean-Claude Boisset Wines U.S.A., Inc.
849 Zinfandel Ln
Saint Helena CA 94574
707 963-6913

### (P-1634)
### JEAN-CLUDE BSSET WINES USA INC
Buena Vista Carneros Winery
18000 Old Winery Rd, Sonoma (95476-4840)
PHONE.................................800 926-1266
Harry Parsley, *Mgr*
EMP: 22
Web: www.buenavistawinery.com
SIC: **2084** Wine cellars, bonded: engaged in blending wines
HQ: Jean-Claude Boisset Wines U.S.A., Inc.
849 Zinfandel Ln
Saint Helena CA 94574
707 963-6913

### (P-1635)
### JEPSON VINEYARD LTD
Also Called: Jepson Vnyrds-Wnery-Distillery
10400 S Highway 101, Ukiah (95482)
PHONE.................................707 468-8936
Robert S Jepson Junior, *Ch Bd*
EMP: 15 EST: 1985
SQ FT: 13,000
SALES (est): 628.13K **Privately Held**
Web: www.jepsonwine.com
SIC: **2084** 0172 Wines; Grapes

### (P-1636)
### JESSUP CELLARS INC
6740 Washington St, Yountville (94599-1304)
PHONE.................................707 944-8523
Dan Blue, *Managing Member*
EMP: 19 EST: 2000
SALES (est): 442.43K **Privately Held**
Web: www.jessupcellars.com
SIC: **2084** Wines

### (P-1637)
### JORDAN VINEYARD & WINERY LP
1474 Alexander Valley Rd, Healdsburg (95448-9003)

PHONE.................................707 431-5250
Jordan John, *Pr*
▲ EMP: 81 EST: 2011
SALES (est): 5.19MM **Privately Held**
Web: www.jordanwinery.com
SIC: **2084** Wines

### (P-1638)
### JOSEPH PHELPS VINEYARDS LLC
1625 Freestone Flat Rd, Sebastopol (95472-9521)
PHONE.................................707 967-3717
EMP: 39
SALES (corp-wide): 667.51MM **Privately Held**
Web: www.josephphelps.com
SIC: **2084** Wines
HQ: Joseph Phelps Vineyards Llc
200 Taplin Rd
Saint Helena CA 94574
707 963-2745

### (P-1639)
### JOSEPH PHELPS VINEYARDS LLC (DH)
200 Taplin Rd, Saint Helena (94574)
PHONE.................................707 963-2745
David Pearson, *CEO*
EMP: 31 EST: 1983
SQ FT: 50,000
SALES (est): 2.58MM
SALES (corp-wide): 667.51MM **Privately Held**
Web: www.josephphelps.com
SIC: **2084** Wines
HQ: Moet Hennessy
24 A 32
Paris Cedex 08 75382
144132222

### (P-1640)
### JOULLIAN VINEYARDS LTD
2 Village Dr Ste A, Carmel Valley (93924-9766)
PHONE.................................831 659-8100
Debra Monnastes, *Mgr*
EMP: 42
SALES (corp-wide): 4.86MM **Privately Held**
Web: www.joullian.com
SIC: **2084** Wines
PA: Joullian Vineyards Ltd.
5653 N Pennsylvania Ave
405 848-4585

### (P-1641)
### JUSTIN VINEYARDS & WINERY LLC
2265 Wisteria Ln, Paso Robles (93446-9820)
PHONE.................................805 238-6932
EMP: 17
SALES (corp-wide): 2.04B **Privately Held**
Web: www.justinwine.com
SIC: **2084** Wines
HQ: Justin Vineyards & Winery Llc
11680 Chimney Rock Rd
Paso Robles CA 93446

### (P-1642)
### JUSTIN VINEYARDS & WINERY LLC
6050 Westside Rd, Healdsburg (95448-8318)
PHONE.................................805 591-3260
EMP: 17
SALES (corp-wide): 2.04B **Privately Held**
Web: www.landmarkwine.com

SIC: **2084** Wines
HQ: Justin Vineyards & Winery Llc
11680 Chimney Rock Rd
Paso Robles CA 93446

### (P-1643)
### JVW CORPORATION
Also Called: Jordan Vineyard & Winery
1474 Alexander Valley Rd, Healdsburg (95448-9003)
P.O. Box 878 (95448-0878)
PHONE.................................707 431-5250
John Jordan, *CEO*
Thomas N Jordan Junior, *Pr*
◆ EMP: 75 EST: 1972
SQ FT: 50,000
SALES (est): 10.02MM **Privately Held**
Web: www.jordanwinery.com
SIC: **2084** 0172 Wines; Grapes

### (P-1644)
### KAUTZ VINEYARDS INC
6111 E Armstrong Rd, Lodi (95240-7224)
PHONE.................................209 369-1911
John Kautz, *Owner*
EMP: 20
SQ FT: 2,062
Web: www.ironstonevineyards.com
SIC: **2084** Wines
PA: Kautz Vineyards, Inc.
1894 6 Mile Rd

### (P-1645)
### KB WINES LLC
Also Called: Kosta Browne
220 Morris St, Sebastopol (95472-3801)
P.O. Box 1959 (95473-1959)
PHONE.................................707 823-7430
Wine Co, *Managing Member*
▼ EMP: 15 EST: 2003
SALES (est): 3.24MM **Privately Held**
Web: www.kostabrowne.com
SIC: **2084** Wines

### (P-1646)
### KENDALL-JACKSON WINE ESTATES (HQ)
425 Aviation Blvd, Santa Rosa (95403-1069)
PHONE.................................707 544-4000
Edward Pitlik, *CEO*
Jess Jackson, *Pr*
Tyler Comstock, *Treas*
EMP: 275 EST: 1995
SQ FT: 10,000
SALES (est): 91.83MM **Privately Held**
Web: www.jacksonfamilywines.com
SIC: **2084** Wines
PA: Jackson Family Wines, Inc.
425 Aviation Blvd

### (P-1647)
### KENEFICK RANCHES LLC
2200 Pickett Rd, Calistoga (94515-1805)
PHONE.................................707 942-6175
Thomas Kenefick, *Managing Member*
Chris Kenefick, **
Caitlin Kenefick Innes, *Prin*
EMP: 25 EST: 1981
SALES (est): 1.76MM **Privately Held**
Web: www.kenefickranch.com
SIC: **2084** 7389 Wines; Business services, nec

### (P-1648)
### KIEU HOANG WINERY LLC
1285 Dealy Ln, Napa (94559-9706)
PHONE.................................707 253-1615
EMP: 20 EST: 2014
SALES (est): 993.81K **Privately Held**

# PRODUCTS & SERVICES SECTION
## 2084 - Wines, Brandy, And Brandy Spirits (P-1673)

Web: www.kieuhoangwinery.com
SIC: 2084 Wines

**(P-1649)**
**KOSTA BROWNE WINES LLC**
Also Called: Kosta Browne Winery
220 Morris St, Sebastopol (95472-3801)
P.O. Box 1959 (95473-1959)
PHONE.....................707 823-7430
▲ EMP: 29 EST: 2001
SALES (est): 1.96MM Privately Held
Web: www.kostabrowne.com
SIC: 2084 Wines

**(P-1650)**
**KRUPP BROTHERS LLC (PA)**
1345 Hestia Way, Napa (94558-2105)
PHONE.....................707 226-2215
EMP: 17 EST: 1999
SALES (est): 1.13MM
SALES (corp-wide): 1.13MM Privately Held
Web: www.premierenapavalley.com
SIC: 2084 Wines

**(P-1651)**
**KSSM LLC**
Also Called: Michel-Schlumberger
4155 Wine Creek Rd, Healdsburg (95448-9112)
PHONE.....................707 433-7427
Jacques Schlumberger, Pt
EMP: 15 EST: 2013
SALES (est): 2.16MM Privately Held
Web: www.michelschlumberger.com
SIC: 2084 Wines

**(P-1652)**
**KUGLER WINES LLC**
300 N 12th St Ste 4b, Lompoc (93436-9444)
PHONE.....................630 306-4634
EMP: 20
SALES (corp-wide): 332.05K Privately Held
SIC: 2084 Wines
PA: Kugler Wines Llc
    3506 Newridge Dr
    310 345-2934

**(P-1653)**
**KUNDE ENTERPRISES INC**
Also Called: Kunde Estate Winery
9825 Sonoma Hwy, Kenwood (95452)
P.O. Box 639 (95452-0639)
PHONE.....................707 833-5501
Don Chase, Pr
▲ EMP: 60 EST: 1989
SQ FT: 15,000
SALES (est): 9.88MM Privately Held
Web: www.kunde.com
SIC: 2084 Wines

**(P-1654)**
**L FOPPIANO WINE CO**
Also Called: Foppiano Vineyards
12707 Old Redwood Hwy, Healdsburg (95448-9241)
P.O. Box 606 (95448-0606)
PHONE.....................707 433-2736
Louis J Foppiano, Pr
▲ EMP: 31 EST: 1896
SQ FT: 140,000
SALES (est): 4.16MM Privately Held
Web: www.foppiano.com
SIC: 2084 Wines

**(P-1655)**
**LADERA VINEYARDS LLC**
150 White Cottage Rd S, Angwin (94508-9615)
P.O. Box 313 (94574-0313)
PHONE.....................707 965-2445
▲ EMP: 18 EST: 1998
SALES (est): 842.89K Privately Held
Web: www.laderavineyards.com
SIC: 2084 Wines

**(P-1656)**
**LADERA WINERY LLC**
Also Called: Chateau Woltner
150 White Cottage Rd S, Angwin (94508-9615)
P.O. Box 313 (94574-0313)
PHONE.....................707 965-2445
Patrick L Stotesbery, Managing Member
Christopher Rye, *
▲ EMP: 30 EST: 1998
SALES (est): 1.93MM Privately Held
Web: www.laderavineyards.com
SIC: 2084 Wines

**(P-1657)**
**LADY FAMILY WINES**
Also Called: Fel Wines
1473 Yountville Cross Rd, Yountville (94599-9471)
PHONE.....................707 944-8642
Remi Cohen, VP
EMP: 16 EST: 2019
SALES (est): 491.58K Privately Held
Web: www.cliffledevineyards.com
SIC: 2084 Wines

**(P-1658)**
**LAETITIA VINEYARD & WINERY INC**
Also Called: Laetitia Winery
453 Laetitia Vineyard Dr, Arroyo Grande (93420-9701)
PHONE.....................805 481-1772
Selim K Zilkha, Pr
▲ EMP: 65 EST: 1994
SALES (est): 4.04MM Privately Held
Web: www.laetitiawine.com
SIC: 2084 Wines

**(P-1659)**
**LAGUNA OAKS VNYARDS WINERY INC**
Also Called: Balletto Vineyards
5700 Occidental Rd, Santa Rosa (95401-5533)
P.O. Box 2579 (95473-2579)
PHONE.....................707 568-2455
John G Balleto, Pr
Teresa M Balleto, VP
▲ EMP: 26 EST: 1999
SQ FT: 9,600
SALES (est): 2.99MM Privately Held
Web: www.ballettovineyards.com
SIC: 2084 Wines

**(P-1660)**
**LAIRD FAMILY ESTATE LLC (PA)**
5055 Solano Ave, Napa (94558-1326)
PHONE.....................707 257-0360
Rebecca A Laird, Managing Member
Ken Laird, Managing Member*
Gail Laird, *
▲ EMP: 19 EST: 1998
SQ FT: 64,000
SALES (est): 14.15MM
SALES (corp-wide): 14.15MM Privately Held
Web: www.lairdfamilyestate.com

SIC: 2084 Wines

**(P-1661)**
**LANGETWINS INC**
1298 E Jahant Rd, Acampo (95220)
PHONE.....................209 339-4055
Randy Lange, Pr
Charlene Lange, *
Brad Lange, *
Susan Lange, *
EMP: 40 EST: 1970
SALES (est): 7.3MM Privately Held
Web: www.langetwins.com
SIC: 2084 Wines

**(P-1662)**
**LANGETWINS WINE COMPANY INC**
Also Called: Langetwins Winery & Vineyards
1525 E Jahant Rd, Acampo (95220-9187)
PHONE.....................209 334-9780
Marissa Lange, Pr
Aaron Lange, CFO
Kendra Altnow, VP
Philip Lange, Sec
Joseph Lange, Sec
EMP: 22 EST: 2005
SALES (est): 7.33MM Privately Held
Web: www.langetwins.com
SIC: 2084 Wines

**(P-1663)**
**LANGTRY FARMS LLC**
21000 Butts Canyon Rd, Middletown (95461-9606)
PHONE.....................707 987-2772
Eason Manson, Managing Member
EMP: 15 EST: 2007
SALES (est): 2.46MM Privately Held
Web: www.langtryfarms.com
SIC: 2084 Wines, brandy, and brandy spirits

**(P-1664)**
**LAVA SPRINGS INC**
Also Called: Lava Cap Winery
2221 Fruitridge Rd, Placerville (95667-3700)
PHONE.....................530 621-0175
Thomas D Jones, Pr
Jeanne H Jones, *
▲ EMP: 30 EST: 1981
SQ FT: 18,000
SALES (est): 4.48MM Privately Held
Web: www.lavacap.com
SIC: 2084 Wines

**(P-1665)**
**LAVENDER RIDGE VINEYARD INC**
Also Called: Tasting Room
425a Main St, Murphys (95247-9628)
PHONE.....................209 728-2441
Richard Gilpin, Pr
EMP: 20 EST: 2004
SALES (est): 766.47K Privately Held
Web: www.lavenderridgevineyard.com
SIC: 2084 Wines

**(P-1666)**
**LCF WINE COMPANY LLC**
1525 E Jahant Rd, Acampo (95220-9187)
PHONE.....................209 334-9782
Ficeli J David, Mgr
▲ EMP: 17 EST: 2014
SALES (est): 3.79MM Privately Held
Web: www.langetwins.com
SIC: 2084 Wines

**(P-1667)**
**LEONESSE CELLARS LLC**
38311 De Portola Rd, Temecula (92592-8923)
P.O. Box 1371 (92593-1371)
PHONE.....................951 302-7601
Gary Winder, Managing Member
Michael Rennie, *
▲ EMP: 25 EST: 2003
SQ FT: 6,000
SALES (est): 5MM Privately Held
Web: www.leonesscellars.com
SIC: 2084 Wines

**(P-1668)**
**LEVECKE LLC**
Also Called: Chaco Flaco Drinks
10810 Inland Ave, Jurupa Valley (91752-3235)
PHONE.....................951 681-8600
Tim Levecke, Managing Member
Reed Levecke, Managing Member*
Neil Levecke, Managing Member*
▲ EMP: 23 EST: 1949
SQ FT: 150,000
SALES (est): 971.07K Privately Held
Web: www.levecke.com
SIC: 2084 Wines, brandy, and brandy spirits

**(P-1669)**
**LOUIDAR LLC**
Also Called: Mount Palomar Winery
33820 Rancho California Rd, Temecula (92591-4930)
P.O. Box 891510 (92589-1510)
PHONE.....................951 676-5047
Peter Poole, Prin
Louis Darwish, Managing Member
EMP: 30 EST: 1997
SQ FT: 4,000
SALES (est): 4.33MM Privately Held
Web: www.mountpalomarwinery.com
SIC: 2084 Wines

**(P-1670)**
**LUNA VINEYARDS INC**
2921 Silverado Trl, Napa (94558-2016)
PHONE.....................707 255-2474
Andre Crisp, Pr
Mary Ann Tsai, Pr
Janel Sizelove, Sec
▲ EMP: 20 EST: 1995
SALES (est): 1.72MM Privately Held
Web: www.lunavineyards.com
SIC: 2084 5182 5921 Wines; Wine; Wine

**(P-1671)**
**MACCHIA INC**
7099 E Peltier Rd, Acampo (95220-9605)
PHONE.....................209 333-2600
Tim Holdener, Pr
EMP: 15 EST: 2007
SALES (est): 1.69MM Privately Held
Web: www.macchiawines.com
SIC: 2084 Wines

**(P-1672)**
**MADRIGAL FAMILY WINERY LLC**
3718 Saint Helena Hwy, Calistoga (94515-9651)
PHONE.....................415 887-9539
EMP: 15 EST: 2012
SALES (est): 942.5K Privately Held
Web: www.madrigalfamilywinery.com
SIC: 2084 Wines

**(P-1673)**
**MARIETTA CELLARS INCORPORATED**

## 2084 - Wines, Brandy, And Brandy Spirits (P-1674)

### PRODUCTS & SERVICES SECTION

Also Called: Marietta Marketing
22295 Chianti Rd, Geyserville
(95441-9702)
P.O. Box 800 (95441-0800)
PHONE..................707 433-2747
Chris Bilbro, Pr
▲ **EMP:** 15 **EST:** 1980
**SALES (est):** 2.24MM **Privately Held**
Web: www.mariettacellars.com
**SIC: 2084** Wines

### (P-1674)
### MATHY WINERY LLC
Also Called: Small City Cider Co.
8533 Dry Creek Rd, Geyserville
(95441-9480)
PHONE..................707 431-2700
**EMP:** 22 **EST:** 2007
**SALES (est):** 2.3MM **Privately Held**
Web: www.dutchercrossingwinery.com
**SIC: 2084** Wines

### (P-1675)
### MCBRIDE SISTERS COLLECTIONS
Also Called: McBride Sisters Collection
6114 La Salle Ave Pmb 280, Oakland
(94611)
PHONE..................510 671-0739
Andrea Mcbride, CEO
Robin Mcbride, CFO
**EMP:** 47 **EST:** 2017
**SALES (est):** 9.33MM **Privately Held**
Web: www.mcbridesisters.com
**SIC: 2084** Wines

### (P-1676)
### MCMANIS FAMILY VINEYARDS INC
Also Called: Dearly Beloved Wines
18700 E River Rd, Ripon (95366-9711)
PHONE..................209 599-1186
Ronald W Mcmanis, Admn
▲ **EMP:** 26 **EST:** 2014
**SALES (est):** 5.51MM **Privately Held**
Web: www.mcmanisfamilyvineyards.com
**SIC: 2084** Wines

### (P-1677)
### MCNAB RIDGE WINERY LLC
Also Called: McNab Ridge
2350 Mcnab Ranch Rd, Ukiah
(95482-9350)
PHONE..................707 462-2423
John A Parducci, Managing Member
**EMP:** 15 **EST:** 1999
**SALES (est):** 500.78K **Privately Held**
Web: www.mcnabridge.com
**SIC: 2084** Wines

### (P-1678)
### MEREDITH VINEYARD ESTATE INC
Also Called: Merry Edwards Wines
636 Gold Ridge Rd, Sebastopol
(95472-3932)
PHONE..................707 823-7466
Merideth Edwards, CEO
Richard Privet, Ch Bd
Einer Sunde, Treas
**EMP:** 15 **EST:** 1997
**SALES (est):** 2.97MM **Privately Held**
Web: www.merryedwards.com
**SIC: 2084** Wines

### (P-1679)
### MERRYVALE VINEYARDS LLC
Also Called: Starmont Winery
1000 Main St, Saint Helena (94574-2011)
PHONE..................707 963-2225
Glenn Ochsner, *
Mark Evans, *
◆ **EMP:** 40 **EST:** 1983
**SQ FT:** 30,850
**SALES (est):** 9.35MM **Privately Held**
Web: www.merryvale.com
**SIC: 2084** 0172 Wines; Grapes

### (P-1680)
### MONTEREY WINE COMPANY LLC
1010 Industrial Way, King City
(93930-2506)
PHONE..................831 386-1100
**EMP:** 19 **EST:** 2002
**SALES (est):** 5.81MM **Privately Held**
Web: www.montereywinecompany.com
**SIC: 2084** Wines

### (P-1681)
### MONTICELLO CELLARS INC
4242 Big Ranch Rd, Napa (94558-1396)
P.O. Box 2486 (94558-0248)
PHONE..................707 253-2802
John Kevin Corley, Pr
**EMP:** 20 **EST:** 1980
**SQ FT:** 25,000
**SALES (est):** 1.06MM
**SALES (corp-wide):** 4.12MM **Privately Held**
Web: www.monticellonapa.com
**SIC: 2084** Wines
PA: Monticello Vineyards
4242 Big Ranch Rd
707 253-2802

### (P-1682)
### MPL BRANDS INC (PA)
71 Liberty Ship Way, Sausalito
(94965-1731)
PHONE..................888 513-3022
Michael Patane, CEO
**EMP:** 40 **EST:** 2016
**SQ FT:** 5,000
**SALES (est):** 17.32MM
**SALES (corp-wide):** 17.32MM **Privately Held**
Web: www.patcobrands.com
**SIC: 2084** Wines, brandy, and brandy spirits

### (P-1683)
### MUNSELLE VINEYARDS LLC
2859 Dry Creek Rd, Healdsburg
(95448-8230)
P.O. Box 617 (95441-0617)
PHONE..................707 857-9988
Reta Munselle, Managing Member
**EMP:** 15 **EST:** 2011
**SALES (est):** 1MM **Privately Held**
Web: www.munsellevineyards.com
**SIC: 2084** Wines

### (P-1684)
### NAPA SELECT VINEYARD SVCS INC
5 Financial Plz Ste 200, Napa
(94558-6419)
PHONE..................707 294-2637
Jason Ray, Pr
**EMP:** 18 **EST:** 2017
**SALES (est):** 1.65MM **Privately Held**
Web: www.sterlingvineyards.com
**SIC: 2084** Wines

### (P-1685)
### NAPA WINE COMPANY LLC
7830 St Helena Hwy # 40, Oakville
(94562-9200)
P.O. Box 434 (94562-0434)
PHONE..................707 944-8669
▲ **EMP:** 35 **EST:** 1993
**SQ FT:** 100,000
**SALES (est):** 5.73MM **Privately Held**
Web: www.napawineco.com
**SIC: 2084** Wines

### (P-1686)
### NAVARRO VINEYARDS LLC
Also Called: Navarro Vineyard
5601 Highway 128, Philo (95466-9513)
P.O. Box 47 (95466-0047)
PHONE..................707 895-3686
Sarah Cahn Bennett, *
▲ **EMP:** 32 **EST:** 1974
**SQ FT:** 10,000
**SALES (est):** 4.08MM **Privately Held**
Web: www.navarrowine.com
**SIC: 2084** 0172 5921 Wine cellars, bonded: engaged in blending wines; Grapes; Wine

### (P-1687)
### NELSON & SONS INC
Also Called: Nelson Family Vineyard
550 Nelson Ranch Rd, Ukiah (95482-9316)
PHONE..................707 462-3755
Gregory Nelson, Pr
Christopher Nelson, VP
Tyler Nelson, VP
**EMP:** 19 **EST:** 1932
**SALES (est):** 2.11MM **Privately Held**
Web: www.nelsonfamilyvineyards.com
**SIC: 2084** 0172 Wines; Grapes

### (P-1688)
### NEW VAVIN INC
Also Called: Ehlers Estate
3222 Ehlers Ln, Saint Helena (94574-9657)
PHONE..................707 963-5972
Steven Folb, Genl Mgr
▲ **EMP:** 20 **EST:** 1996
**SALES (est):** 3.25MM **Privately Held**
Web: www.ehlersestate.com
**SIC: 2084** Wines

### (P-1689)
### NEWTON VINEYARD LLC (DH)
Also Called: Newton Vineyard
1040 Main St Ste 204, Napa (94559-2605)
P.O. Box 540 (94574-5040)
PHONE..................707 204-7423
▲ **EMP:** 40 **EST:** 1979
**SALES (est):** 11.54MM
**SALES (corp-wide):** 667.51MM **Privately Held**
Web: www.newtonvineyard.com
**SIC: 2084** 0172 Wines; Grapes
HQ: Moet Hennessy
24 A 32
Paris Cedex 08 IDF 75382
144132222

### (P-1690)
### NEWTON VINEYARD LLC
1 California Dr, Yountville (94599-1426)
PHONE..................707 204-7410
**EMP:** 159
**SALES (corp-wide):** 667.51MM **Privately Held**
Web: www.newtonvineyard.com
**SIC: 2084** 0172 Wines; Grapes
HQ: Newton Vineyard Llc
1040 Main St Ste 204
Napa CA 94559
707 204-7423

### (P-1691)
### NIEBAM-CPPOLA ESTATE WINERY LP
Also Called: Cafe Niebaum Coppola
916 Kearny St, San Francisco
(94133-5107)
PHONE..................415 291-1700
Krista Voisin, Mgr
**EMP:** 50
Web: www.cafezoetrope.com
**SIC: 2084** Wines
PA: Niebaum-Coppola Estate Winery, L.P.
1991 St Helena Hwy

### (P-1692)
### NIEBAM-CPPOLA ESTATE WINERY LP (PA)
1991 St Helena Hwy, Rutherford (94573)
P.O. Box 208 (94573-0208)
PHONE..................707 968-1100
Gordon Wang, CFO
American Zoetrope, *
Earl Martin, *
◆ **EMP:** 150 **EST:** 1992
**SALES (est):** 23.39MM **Privately Held**
Web: www.inglenook.com
**SIC: 2084** Wines

### (P-1693)
### NINER WINE ESTATES LLC
2400 W Highway 46, Paso Robles
(93446-8602)
PHONE..................805 239-2233
▲ **EMP:** 22 **EST:** 2004
**SALES (est):** 4.53MM **Privately Held**
Web: www.ninerwine.com
**SIC: 2084** Wines

### (P-1694)
### OAK RIDGE WINERY LLC
Also Called: Maggio Estates
6100 E. Hwy 12 Victor Rd, Lodi (95240)
PHONE..................209 369-4768
Jason Dodge, Genl Mgr
◆ **EMP:** 50 **EST:** 2002
**SALES (est):** 10.93MM **Privately Held**
Web: www.oakridgewinery.com
**SIC: 2084** Wines

### (P-1695)
### OBSIDIAN RIDGE WINE COMPANY
21684 8th St E, Sonoma (95476-2815)
PHONE..................707 939-7625
Arpad Molnar, Mng Pt
**EMP:** 24 **EST:** 2011
**SALES (est):** 953.37K **Privately Held**
Web: www.obsidianwineco.com
**SIC: 2084** Wines

### (P-1696)
### ONEILL BEVERAGES CO LLC
2975 Mitchell Ranch Way, Paso Robles
(93446)
PHONE..................805 239-1616
Jeffrey O'neill, Pr
**EMP:** 22
**SALES (corp-wide):** 89.03MM **Privately Held**
Web: www.oneillwine.com
**SIC: 2084** Wines
PA: O'Neill Beverages Co. Llc
101 Lrkspur Lnding Cir St
559 638-3544

### (P-1697)
### OPAL MOON WINERY LLC
Also Called: Artisans & Vines
21660 8th St E Ste A, Sonoma (95476)
PHONE..................707 996-0420
**EMP:** 15 **EST:** 2011
**SQ FT:** 30,000

▲ = Import ▼ = Export
◆ = Import/Export

## PRODUCTS & SERVICES SECTION
## 2084 - Wines, Brandy, And Brandy Spirits (P-1720)

SALES (est): 1.26MM **Privately Held**
Web: www.opalmooncrush.com
SIC: **2084** Wines

**(P-1698)**
**OPOLO VINEYARDS INC**
2801 Townsgate Rd Ste 123, Westlake Village (91361-3033)
P.O. Box 277 (93447-0277)
PHONE..................805 238-9593
EMP: 19
SALES (corp-wide): 3.37MM **Privately Held**
Web: www.opolo.com
SIC: **2084** Wines
PA: Opolo Vineyards, Inc.
  7110 Vineyard Dr
  805 238-9593

**(P-1699)**
**OPUS ONE WINERY LLC (PA)**
Also Called: Opus One
7900 St Helena Hwy, Oakville (94562)
P.O. Box 6 (94562-0006)
PHONE..................707 944-9442
Christopher Lynch, CEO
Robert Fowles, *
Roger Asleson, *
Robert Ruex, *
Larunt Telassus, *
◆ EMP: 75 EST: 1979
SQ FT: 85,000
SALES (est): 19.74MM **Privately Held**
Web: www.opusonewinery.com
SIC: **2084** Wines

**(P-1700)**
**ORFILA VINEYARDS INC (PA)**
Also Called: Orfila Vineyards & Winery
13455 San Pasqual Rd, Escondido (92025-7833)
PHONE..................760 738-6500
Alejandro Orfila, Pr
Helga Orfila, *
Justin Mund, *
Danica Gvozden, *
▲ EMP: 19 EST: 1989
SQ FT: 12,000
SALES (est): 6.47MM **Privately Held**
Web: www.orfila.com
SIC: **2084** 0172 7299 Wines; Grapes; Wedding chapel, privately operated

**(P-1701)**
**OTSUKA AMERICA INC**
80 Railroad Ave, Milpitas (95035-4333)
PHONE..................408 867-3233
EMP: 40
Web: www.otsuka-america.com
SIC: **2084** Wines
HQ: Otsuka America, Inc.
  1 Embrcadero Ctr Ste 2020
  San Francisco CA 94111

**(P-1702)**
**OZEKI SAKE (USA) INC (HQ)**
Also Called: Jfcmirin Inc
249 Hillcrest Rd, Hollister (95023-4921)
PHONE..................831 637-9217
Bunjiro Osabe, Ch Bd
Masaru Ogihara, *
Norio Sumomogi, *
▲ EMP: 25 EST: 1979
SQ FT: 22,000
SALES (est): 4.66MM **Privately Held**
Web: www.ozekisake.com
SIC: **2084** Wines
PA: Ozeki Co., Ltd.
  1-14-1, Shintomi

**(P-1703)**
**PARDUCCI WINE ESTATES LLC**
Also Called: Mendicino Wine Company
501 Parducci Rd, Ukiah (95482-3015)
PHONE..................707 463-5350
▲ EMP: 35 EST: 1986
SALES (est): 2.44MM **Privately Held**
Web: www.mendocinowineco.com
SIC: **2084** Wines

**(P-1704)**
**PERNOD RICARD USA LLC**
Also Called: Kenwood Vineyards
9592 Sonoma Hwy, Kenwood (95452-8028)
P.O. Box 669 (95452-0669)
PHONE..................707 833-5891
EMP: 75
SQ FT: 1,414
SALES (corp-wide): 452.86MM **Privately Held**
Web: www.pernod-ricard-usa.com
SIC: **2084** 0172 Wines; Grapes
HQ: Pernod Ricard Usa, Llc
  250 Park Ave 17th Fl
  New York NY 10177
  212 372-5400

**(P-1705)**
**PERNOD RICARD USA LLC**
Also Called: Mumm NAPA Valley
8445 Silverado Trl, Rutherford (94573)
PHONE..................707 967-7770
Samuel Bronfman Ii, Brnch Mgr
EMP: 65
SALES (corp-wide): 452.86MM **Privately Held**
Web: www.pernod-ricard-usa.com
SIC: **2084** Wines
HQ: Pernod Ricard Usa, Llc
  250 Park Ave 17th Fl
  New York NY 10177
  212 372-5400

**(P-1706)**
**PETALUMAIDENCE OPCO LLC**
Also Called: Vineyard Post Acute
101 Monroe St, Petaluma (94954-2328)
PHONE..................707 763-4109
Jason Murray, Prin
Mark Hancock, *
EMP: 124 EST: 2016
SALES (est): 12.32MM
SALES (corp-wide): 2.56B **Publicly Held**
Web: www.vineyardpostacute.com
SIC: **2084** 8051 Wines; Skilled nursing care facilities
HQ: Providence Group Wine Country, Llc
  262 N University Ave
  Farmington UT
  801 447-9829

**(P-1707)**
**PHASE 2 CELLARS LLC**
Also Called: Bezel
4910 Edna Rd, San Luis Obispo (93401-7938)
PHONE..................805 782-0300
Kenneth Robin Baggett, Managing Member
EMP: 18 EST: 2015
SALES (est): 3.2MM **Privately Held**
Web: www.phase2cellars.com
SIC: **2084** Wines

**(P-1708)**
**PINE RIDGE WINERY LLC (HQ)**
Also Called: Pine Ridge Vineyards
5901 Silverado Trl, Napa (94558-9417)
P.O. Box 2508 (94599-2508)
PHONE..................707 253-7500
◆ EMP: 20 EST: 1978
SQ FT: 17,000
SALES (est): 10.8MM
SALES (corp-wide): 72.4MM **Publicly Held**
Web: www.pineridgevineyards.com
SIC: **2084** 5812 0172 Wines; Eating places; Grapes
PA: Crimson Wine Group, Ltd.
  5901 Silverado Trl
  800 486-0503

**(P-1709)**
**PINE RIDGE WINERY LLC**
Also Called: Seghesio Family Vineyards
700 Grove St, Healdsburg (95448-4753)
PHONE..................707 260-0330
EMP: 80
SALES (corp-wide): 72.4MM **Publicly Held**
Web: www.seghesio.com
SIC: **2084** Wines
HQ: Pine Ridge Winery, Llc
  5901 Silverado Trl
  Napa CA 94558
  707 253-7500

**(P-1710)**
**PJK WINERY LLC**
Also Called: Quivira Vineyards
4900 W Dry Creek Rd, Healdsburg (95448-9721)
PHONE..................707 431-8333
Pete Kight, Managing Member
EMP: 25 EST: 1981
SQ FT: 5,400
SALES (est): 2.8MM **Privately Held**
Web: www.quivirawine.com
SIC: **2084** Wines

**(P-1711)**
**PORTHOS VENTURES INC**
33 Filbert Ave, Sausalito (94965-1878)
PHONE..................415 339-2790
Emmett H Oates, Pr
EMP: 17
SALES (corp-wide): 3.11MM **Privately Held**
Web: www.porthos.com
SIC: **2084** Wine cellars, bonded: engaged in blending wines
PA: Porthos Ventures, Inc.
  4326 Redwood Hwy Ste 300
  415 454-2115

**(P-1712)**
**PRESTON VINEYARDS INC**
Also Called: Preston Vineyards & Winery
9282 W Dry Creek Rd, Healdsburg (95448-9134)
PHONE..................707 433-3372
Louis Preston, Pr
Susan Preston, VP
EMP: 15 EST: 1973
SALES (est): 3.24MM **Privately Held**
Web: www.prestonfarmandwinery.com
SIC: **2084** 5812 5182 Wines; Eating places; Wine

**(P-1713)**
**PROMONTORY LLC**
1601 Oakville Grade Rd, Oakville (94562)
PHONE..................707 944-1441
EMP: 16 EST: 2017
SALES (est): 1.62MM **Privately Held**
Web: www.promontory.wine
SIC: **2084** Wines

**(P-1714)**
**PURPLE WINE PRODUCTION COMPANY**
Also Called: Sonomay Wine
9119 Graton Rd, Graton (95444-9373)
Rural Route 9119 Gratn (95444)
PHONE..................707 829-6100
EMP: 160
SIC: **2084** Wine cellars, bonded: engaged in blending wines

**(P-1715)**
**QUADY WINERY INC**
13181 Road 24, Madera (93637-9087)
P.O. Box 728 (93639-0728)
PHONE..................559 673-8068
Andrew K Quady, Pr
Laurel Quady, VP
EMP: 16 EST: 1979
SQ FT: 16,000
SALES (est): 3.3MM **Privately Held**
Web: www.quadywinery.com
SIC: **2084** Wines

**(P-1716)**
**RAMADOR INC**
Also Called: Renwood Winery
12225 Steiner Rd, Plymouth (95669-9502)
P.O. Box 399 (95669-0399)
PHONE..................209 245-6979
▲ EMP: 90
SIC: **2084** Wines

**(P-1717)**
**RAMS GATE WINERY LLC**
28700 Arnold Dr, Sonoma (95476-9700)
PHONE..................707 721-8700
Jeffrey O'neill, Managing Member
Peter Mullin, *
Paul Violich, *
Michael J John, *
▲ EMP: 38 EST: 2006
SALES (est): 4.42MM **Privately Held**
Web: www.ramsgatewinery.com
SIC: **2084** Wines

**(P-1718)**
**RB WINE ASSOCIATES LLC**
1 Winemaster Way Ste D, Lodi (95240-0860)
PHONE..................209 365-9463
EMP: 35
Web: www.rackandriddle.com
SIC: **2084** Wines
PA: Rb Wine Associates, Llc
  499 Moore Ln

**(P-1719)**
**RB WINE ASSOCIATES LLC (PA)**
Also Called: Rack & Riddle
499 Moore Ln, Healdsburg (95448-4825)
P.O. Box 2400 (95448)
PHONE..................707 433-8400
EMP: 80 EST: 2007
SQ FT: 100,000
SALES (est): 11MM **Privately Held**
Web: www.rackandriddle.com
SIC: **2084** Wines

**(P-1720)**
**RBZ VINEYARDS LLC**
Also Called: Sextant Wines
2324 W Highway 46, Paso Robles (93446-8602)
P.O. Box 391 (93447-0391)
PHONE..................805 542-0133
Craig Stoller, Prin
EMP: 30 EST: 2006
SALES (est): 4.36MM **Privately Held**
Web: www.sextantwines.com
SIC: **2084** Wines

## 2084 - Wines, Brandy, And Brandy Spirits (P-1721)

### (P-1721)
**REGUSCI VINEYARD MGT INC**
Also Called: Regusci Winery
5584 Silverado Trl, Napa (94558-9411)
PHONE..............................707 254-0403
James Regusci, *Pr*
Diana Regusci, *
**EMP:** 30 **EST:** 1995
**SALES (est):** 5.11MM **Privately Held**
Web: www.regusciwinery.com
**SIC: 2084** 0762 Wines; Vineyard management and maintenance services

### (P-1722)
**RHYS VINEYARDS LLC**
11715 Skyline Blvd, Los Gatos (95033-9588)
PHONE..............................650 419-2050
▲ **EMP:** 24 **EST:** 2004
**SALES (est):** 4.64MM **Privately Held**
Web: www.rhysvineyards.com
**SIC: 2084** Wines

### (P-1723)
**RIOS-LOVELL ESTATE WINERY**
Also Called: Rios-Lovell Winery
6500 Tesla Rd, Livermore (94550-9123)
PHONE..............................925 443-0434
Max Rios, *Pt*
Katie Lovell, *Pt*
**EMP:** 20 **EST:** 1994
**SALES (est):** 2.25MM **Privately Held**
Web: www.rioslovellwinery.com
**SIC: 2084** Wines

### (P-1724)
**RIVERBENCH LLC**
137 Anacapa St, Santa Barbara (93101-1848)
PHONE..............................805 324-4100
Laura Booras, *Brnch Mgr*
**EMP:** 44
Web: www.riverbench.com
**SIC: 2084** 0172 Wines; Grapes
**PA:** Riverbench Llc
6020 Foxen Canyon Rd

### (P-1725)
**ROBERT MONDAVI CORPORATION (HQ)**
166 Gateway Rd E, Napa (94558-7576)
P.O. Box 407 (94573-0407)
PHONE..............................707 967-2100
Gregory Evans, *Pr*
Gregory M Evans, *
Timothy J Mondavi, *
Henry J Salvo Junior, *CFO*
▲ **EMP:** 75 **EST:** 1966
**SQ FT:** 5,000
**SALES (est):** 6.41MM
**SALES (corp-wide):** 9.96B **Publicly Held**
Web: www.robertmondaviwinery.com
**SIC: 2084** Wines
**PA:** Constellation Brands, Inc.
50 E Broad St
585 678-7100

### (P-1726)
**ROBERT MONDAVI CORPORATION**
770 N Guild Ave, Lodi (95240-0861)
PHONE..............................209 365-2995
Rick Anderson, *Mgr*
**EMP:** 844
**SALES (corp-wide):** 9.96B **Publicly Held**
Web: www.robertmondaviwinery.com
**SIC: 2084** Wines
**HQ:** The Robert Mondavi Corporation
166 Gateway Rd E
Napa CA 94558
707 967-2100

### (P-1727)
**ROBERT MONDAVI WINERY**
7801 St. Helena Hwy, Oakville (94562)
PHONE..............................707 738-5727
**EMP:** 97 **EST:** 2017
**SALES (est):** 4.63MM **Privately Held**
Web: www.robertmondaviwinery.com
**SIC: 2084** Wines

### (P-1728)
**ROBERT TAYLOR**
Also Called: Retzlaff Vineyards
1356 S Livermore Ave, Livermore (94550-9505)
PHONE..............................925 447-8941
Robert Taylor, *Owner*
**EMP:** 16 **EST:** 1976
**SQ FT:** 2,000
**SALES (est):** 975.57K **Privately Held**
Web: www.retzlaffvineyards.com
**SIC: 2084** Wines

### (P-1729)
**ROCK WALL WINE COMPANY INC**
2301 Monarch St, Alameda (94501-7582)
PHONE..............................510 522-5700
Shauna Michelle Rosenblum, *CEO*
**EMP:** 20 **EST:** 2008
**SQ FT:** 200
**SALES (est):** 2.42MM **Privately Held**
Web: www.rockwallwines.com
**SIC: 2084** Wines

### (P-1730)
**ROLLING HILLS VINEYARD INC**
4213 Pascal Pl, Pls Vrds Pnsl (90274-3943)
PHONE..............................310 541-5098
**EMP:** 23
**SALES (corp-wide):** 211.41K **Privately Held**
**SIC: 2084** Wines, brandy, and brandy spirits
**PA:** Rolling Hills Vineyard, Inc.
6200 E Canyon Rim Rd # 201

### (P-1731)
**ROMBAUER VINEYARDS LLC (HQ)**
3522 Silverado Trl N, Saint Helena (94574-9663)
PHONE..............................707 963-5170
Koerner Rombauer, *Pr*
Matthew Owings, *
◆ **EMP:** 52 **EST:** 1980
**SQ FT:** 25,000
**SALES (est):** 24.21MM
**SALES (corp-wide):** 2.11B **Privately Held**
Web: www.rombauer.com
**SIC: 2084** Wines
**PA:** E. & J. Gallo Winery
600 Yosemite Blvd
209 341-3111

### (P-1732)
**ROUND HILL CELLARS**
Also Called: Rutherford Wine Company
1680 Silverado Trl S, Saint Helena (94574-9542)
P.O. Box 387 (94573-0387)
PHONE..............................707 968-3200
Marko B Zaninovich, *Pr*
Theo Zaninovich, *
▼ **EMP:** 55 **EST:** 1978
**SQ FT:** 31,000
**SALES (est):** 7.12MM **Privately Held**
Web: www.rutherfordranch.com
**SIC: 2084** Wines

### (P-1733)
**ROYAL WINE CORPORATION**
Also Called: Herzog Wine Cellars
3201 Camino Del Sol, Oxnard (93030-8915)
PHONE..............................805 983-1560
Joseph Herzog, *Brnch Mgr*
**EMP:** 20
**SALES (corp-wide):** 44.27MM **Privately Held**
Web: www.herzogwine.com
**SIC: 2084** 5182 Wines; Wine
**PA:** Royal Wine Corporation
63 Lefante Dr
718 384-2400

### (P-1734)
**RUDD WINES INC (PA)**
Also Called: Rudd Winery
500 Oakville Crossroad, Oakville (94562)
P.O. Box 105 (94562-0105)
PHONE..............................707 944-8577
Leslei Rudd, *Pr*
▲ **EMP:** 20 **EST:** 1996
**SALES (est):** 5.36MM
**SALES (corp-wide):** 5.36MM **Privately Held**
Web: www.ruddwines.com
**SIC: 2084** Wines

### (P-1735)
**RUSSIAN RIVER WINERY INC**
2191 Laguna Rd, Santa Rosa (95401-3705)
PHONE..............................707 824-2005
Courtney M Benham, *CEO*
**EMP:** 16 **EST:** 2003
**SQ FT:** 76,000
**SALES (est):** 1.28MM **Privately Held**
Web: www.martinraywinery.com
**SIC: 2084** Wines

### (P-1736)
**RUTHERFORD HILL WINERY**
200 Rutherford Hill Rd, Rutherford (94573)
P.O. Box 427 (94573-0427)
PHONE..............................707 963-1871
**EMP:** 350 **EST:** 1976
**SALES (est):** 8.82MM
**SALES (corp-wide):** 54.49MM **Privately Held**
Web: www.rutherfordhill.com
**SIC: 2084** Wines
**PA:** Terlato Wine Group, Ltd.
900 Armour Dr
847 604-8900

### (P-1737)
**SAINTSBURY LLC**
1500 Los Carneros Ave, Napa (94559-9742)
PHONE..............................707 252-0592
Richard Ward, *Genl Mgr*
**EMP:** 18 **EST:** 1981
**SQ FT:** 32,500
**SALES (est):** 2.63MM **Privately Held**
Web: www.saintsbury.com
**SIC: 2084** Wines

### (P-1738)
**SAMSARA WINERY AND TASTING RM**
6485 Calle Real Ste E, Goleta (93117-1539)
PHONE..............................805 845-8001
**EMP:** 22 **EST:** 2019
**SALES (est):** 490.38K **Privately Held**
Web: www.samsarawine.com
**SIC: 2084** Wines

### (P-1739)
**SAN ANTONIO WINERY INC (PA)**
Also Called: San Antonio Gift Shop
737 Lamar St, Los Angeles (90031-2591)
PHONE..............................323 223-1401
Santo Riboli, *CEO*
Maddelena Riboli, *
Cathey Riboli, *
◆ **EMP:** 101 **EST:** 1917
**SQ FT:** 310,000
**SALES (est):** 27.28MM
**SALES (corp-wide):** 27.28MM **Privately Held**
Web: www.sanantoniowinery.com
**SIC: 2084** 5182 5812 Wines; Wine; Eating places

### (P-1740)
**SAN BERNABE VINEYARDS LLC**
12001 S Highway 99, Manteca (95336-8499)
PHONE..............................209 824-3501
Delicato Vineyards, *Prin*
▼ **EMP:** 22 **EST:** 2001
**SALES (est):** 1.12MM **Privately Held**
Web: www.delicatowineshop.com
**SIC: 2084** Wines

### (P-1741)
**SAVANNAH CHANELLE VINEYARDS**
Also Called: Mariani Winery
23600 Big Basin Way, Saratoga (95070-9755)
PHONE..............................301 758-2338
Michael Ballard, *Pr*
Kellie Ballard, *CFO*
**EMP:** 17 **EST:** 1992
**SALES (est):** 744.09K **Privately Held**
Web: www.savannahchanelle.com
**SIC: 2084** 5812 0172 Wines; Eating places; Grapes

### (P-1742)
**SBRAGIA FAMILY VINEYARDS LLC**
Also Called: West Grant Vineyards
9990 Dry Creek Rd, Geyserville (95441-9686)
PHONE..............................707 473-2992
Edward Sbargia, *Managing Member*
**EMP:** 18 **EST:** 2006
**SALES (est):** 5.08MM **Privately Held**
Web: www.sbragia.com
**SIC: 2084** Wines

### (P-1743)
**SEBASTIANI VINEYARDS INC**
Also Called: Sebastiani Vineyards & Winery
389 4th St E, Sonoma (95476)
PHONE..............................707 933-3200
Mary Ann Sebastiani Cuneo, *CEO*
Richard Cuneo, *
Paul Bergena, *
Emma Swain, *
Omar Percich, *
◆ **EMP:** 100 **EST:** 1972
**SQ FT:** 2,000
**SALES (est):** 7.07MM
**SALES (corp-wide):** 69.09MM **Privately Held**
Web: www.sebastiani.com
**SIC: 2084** Wines
**HQ:** Foley Family Wines, Inc.
200 Concourse Blvd
Santa Rosa CA 95403

## PRODUCTS & SERVICES SECTION
## 2084 - Wines, Brandy, And Brandy Spirits (P-1766)

**(P-1744)**
**SEGHESIO WINERIES INC**
Also Called: Family Vineyards
700 Grove St, Healdsburg (95448-4753)
PHONE.................707 433-3579
Eugene Peter Seghesio, CEO
Raymond Seghesio, VP
Amy Seghesio, Treas
Edward H Seghesio Junior, Sec
▼ **EMP:** 20 **EST:** 1942
**SQ FT:** 6,000
**SALES (est):** 2.2MM Privately Held
Web: www.seghesio.com
**SIC: 2084** 0172 Wines; Grapes

**(P-1745)**
**SHAFER VINEYARDS**
6154 Silverado Trl, Napa (94558-9748)
PHONE.................707 944-2877
John Shafer, Ch
Douglas S Shafer, Pr
Bradford J Shafer, Stockholder
Elizabeth S Cafaro, Stockholder
◆ **EMP:** 17 **EST:** 1979
**SQ FT:** 2,000
**SALES (est):** 5.98MM Privately Held
Web: www.shafervineyards.com
**SIC: 2084** Wines
PA: Shinsegae Inc.
  63 Sogong-Ro, Jung-Gu

**(P-1746)**
**SHANNON RIDGE INC (PA)**
2150 Argonaut Rd, Lakeport (95453-9368)
P.O. Box 279 (95451-0279)
PHONE.................707 281-6780
Clay Shannon, Pr
Mark Altrecht, *
**EMP:** 40 **EST:** 2003
**SALES (est):** 12.9MM
**SALES (corp-wide):** 12.9MM Privately Held
Web: www.shannonfamilyofwines.com
**SIC: 2084** 5921 Wines; Wine

**(P-1747)**
**SHANNON RIDGE INC**
4350 Thomas Dr, Lakeport (95453-8777)
PHONE.................707 281-6780
Clay Shannon, Pr
**EMP:** 30
**SALES (corp-wide):** 12.9MM Privately Held
Web: www.shannonfamilyofwines.com
**SIC: 2084** Wines
PA: Shannon Ridge, Inc.
  2150 Argonaut Rd
  707 281-6780

**(P-1748)**
**SILVER OAK WINE CELLARS LLC**
Also Called: Alexander Valley Winery
7300 Highway 128, Healdsburg (95448-8018)
PHONE.................707 942-7082
Timothy E Duncan, Prin
**EMP:** 19 **EST:** 2019
**SALES (est):** 1.33MM Privately Held
Web: www.silveroak.com
**SIC: 2084** Wines

**(P-1749)**
**SILVER OAK WINE CELLARS LLC (PA)**
Also Called: Silver Oak
915 Oakville Cross Rd, Oakville (94562)
P.O. Box 414 (94562-0414)
PHONE.................707 942-7022

David R Duncan, Pt
Raymond Duncan, Pr
**EMP:** 15 **EST:** 1972
**SALES (est):** 24.74MM
**SALES (corp-wide):** 24.74MM Privately Held
Web: www.silveroak.com
**SIC: 2084** Wines

**(P-1750)**
**SILVERADO VINEYARDS**
6121 Silverado Trl, Napa (94558-9415)
PHONE.................707 257-1770
Ronald W Miller, CEO
Walter Miller, VP
Robert Wilson, Treas
Ron Miller, Prin
▲ **EMP:** 23 **EST:** 1980
**SALES (est):** 4.9MM
**SALES (corp-wide):** 14.15MM Privately Held
Web: www.silveradovineyards.com
**SIC: 2084** Wines
PA: Laird Family Estate Llc
  5055 Solano Ave
  707 257-0360

**(P-1751)**
**SLO CIDER LLC**
3419 Roberto Ct, San Luis Obispo (93401-7289)
PHONE.................805 439-0865
**EMP:** 16 **EST:** 2019
**SALES (est):** 245.3K Privately Held
Web: www.slociderco.com
**SIC: 2084** Wines

**(P-1752)**
**SMALL VINES VITICULTURE INC**
2160 Green Hill Rd, Sebastopol (95472-9306)
PHONE.................707 823-0886
Paul Sloan, Pr
Catherine Sloan, Sec
Cathryn Sloan, Prin
**EMP:** 18 **EST:** 1998
**SALES (est):** 2.49MM Privately Held
Web: www.smallvines.com
**SIC: 2084** Wines

**(P-1753)**
**SOBON WINE COMPANY LLC**
12300 Steiner Rd, Plymouth (95669-9503)
PHONE.................209 245-4457
Robert F Sobon, Prin
**EMP:** 16 **EST:** 2016
**SALES (est):** 881.55K Privately Held
Web: www.sobonwine.com
**SIC: 2084** Wines

**(P-1754)**
**SONOMA COUNTY WINEGROWERS**
3245 Guerneville Rd, Santa Rosa (95401-4030)
PHONE.................707 522-5860
**EMP:** 28
**SALES (est):** 233.16K Privately Held
Web: www.sonomawinegrape.org
**SIC: 2084** Wines

**(P-1755)**
**SONOMA WINE HARDWARE INC**
360 Swift Ave Ste 34, South San Francisco (94080-6220)
PHONE.................650 866-3020
James Mackey, Pr
**EMP:** 20 **EST:** 2005
**SALES (est):** 324.74K Privately Held

**SIC: 2084** Wines, brandy, and brandy spirits

**(P-1756)**
**SOUTH COAST WINERY INC**
Also Called: South Coast Winery Resort Spa
34843 Rancho California Rd, Temecula (92591-4006)
PHONE.................951 587-9463
James A Carter, Pr
▲ **EMP:** 32 **EST:** 2001
**SALES (est):** 11.2MM
**SALES (corp-wide):** 24.46MM Privately Held
Web: www.southcoastwinery.com
**SIC: 2084** 7011 7991 Wines; Resort hotel; Spas
PA: Spruce Grove, Inc.
  3719 S Plaza Dr
  714 546-4255

**(P-1757)**
**SPRING MOUNTAIN VINEYARDS INC**
2805 Spring Mountain Rd, Saint Helena (94574-1798)
P.O. Box 991 (94574)
PHONE.................707 967-4188
Don Yannias, Pr
Jean-pierre Boustany, VP
**EMP:** 42 **EST:** 1992
**SQ FT:** 16,000
**SALES (est):** 3.65MM Privately Held
Web: www.springmountainvineyard.com
**SIC: 2084** 0762 Wines; Vineyard management and maintenance services

**(P-1758)**
**ST GEORGE SPIRITS INC (PA)**
2601 Monarch St, Alameda (94501-7541)
PHONE.................510 769-1601
Lance Winters, Pr
Jorg Rupf, Prin
▲ **EMP:** 18 **EST:** 1982
**SQ FT:** 65,000
**SALES (est):** 4.67MM
**SALES (corp-wide):** 4.67MM Privately Held
Web: www.stgeorgespirits.com
**SIC: 2084** 2085 Brandy spirits; Distilled and blended liquors

**(P-1759)**
**ST SUPERY INC (DH)**
Also Called: Skalli Vineyards
8440 St Helena Hwy, Rutherford (94573)
P.O. Box 38 (94573-0038)
PHONE.................707 963-4507
Emma Swain, CEO
◆ **EMP:** 50 **EST:** 1982
**SQ FT:** 20,000
**SALES (est):** 14.37MM Privately Held
Web: www.stsupery.com
**SIC: 2084** Wines
HQ: Chanel, Inc.
  9 W 57th St Bsmt 2b
  New York NY 10019
  212 303-5978

**(P-1760)**
**STAGS LEAP WINE CELLARS LLC (PA)**
Also Called: Hawk Crest
5766 Silverado Trl, Napa (94558-9413)
PHONE.................707 944-2020
Warren Winiarski, Prin
▲ **EMP:** 110 **EST:** 1970
**SQ FT:** 40,000
**SALES (est):** 14.12MM
**SALES (corp-wide):** 14.12MM Privately Held

Web: www.stagsleapwinecellars.com
**SIC: 2084** Wines

**(P-1761)**
**STEELE WINES INC**
Also Called: Steele Wines
4350 Thomas Dr, Kelseyville (95451)
P.O. Box 190 (95451-0190)
PHONE.................707 279-9475
Jedediah T Steele, Pr
Naomi Key, *
**EMP:** 25 **EST:** 1989
**SALES (est):** 2.77MM Privately Held
Web: www.shannonfamilyofwines.com
**SIC: 2084** Wines

**(P-1762)**
**STEVEN KENT LLC**
Also Called: La- Rochelle
2245 S Vasco Rd, Livermore (94550-8314)
PHONE.................925 243-6442
Steven Mirassou, Managing Member
▲ **EMP:** 16 **EST:** 2001
**SALES (est):** 4.36MM Privately Held
Web: www.stevenkent.com
**SIC: 2084** Wines

**(P-1763)**
**STEVENOT WINERY & IMPORTS INC (PA)**
2690 San Domingo Rd, Murphys (95247-9646)
PHONE.................209 728-0638
Barden Stevenot, Pr
▲ **EMP:** 20 **EST:** 2000
**SALES (est):** 672.73K
**SALES (corp-wide):** 672.73K Privately Held
Web: www.stevenotwinery.com
**SIC: 2084** Wines

**(P-1764)**
**STONE BRIDGE CELLARS INC (PA)**
Also Called: Joseph Phelps Vineyards
200 Taplin Rd, Saint Helena (94574-9544)
P.O. Box 1031 (94574-0531)
PHONE.................707 963-2745
Joseph Phelps, Ch Bd
William H Phelps, *
Craig Williams, *
Robert Boyd, *
Clarice Turner, *
▲ **EMP:** 50 **EST:** 1984
**SQ FT:** 50,000
**SALES (est):** 17.48MM
**SALES (corp-wide):** 17.48MM Privately Held
Web: www.josephphelps.com
**SIC: 2084** Wines

**(P-1765)**
**STONECUSHION INC (PA)**
Also Called: Wilson Artisan Wineries
1400 Lytton Springs Rd, Healdsburg (95448-9695)
P.O. Box 487 (95441-0487)
PHONE.................707 433-1911
Kenneth C Wilson, Pr
**EMP:** 23 **EST:** 2005
**SALES (est):** 6.98MM Privately Held
Web: www.mazzocco.com
**SIC: 2084** Wines

**(P-1766)**
**SUGARLOAF FARMING CORPORATION**
Also Called: Peter Michael Winery
12400 Ida Clayton Rd, Calistoga (94515-9507)

## 2084 - Wines, Brandy, And Brandy Spirits (P-1767)

**PRODUCTS & SERVICES SECTION**

PHONE....................707 942-4459
Scott Rodde, CEO
Scott Rodde, Pr
Bill Vyenielo, General Vice President*
Stuart Bockman, *
◆ **EMP:** 25 **EST:** 1982
**SQ FT:** 1,000
**SALES (est):** 6.84MM
**SALES (corp-wide):** 53.35MM **Privately Held**
**Web:** www.petermichaelwinery.com
**SIC:** 2084 Wines
**PA:** Stockford Limited
Sheet Street

### (P-1767)
### SUTTER HOME WINERY INC (PA)
Also Called: Trinchero Family Estates
100 St Helena Hwy (Hwy. 29) S, Saint Helena (94574)
P.O. Box 248 (94574)
PHONE....................707 963-3104
Bob Torkelson, Pr
◆ **EMP:** 200 **EST:** 1946
**SQ FT:** 17,000
**SALES (est):** 188.11MM
**SALES (corp-wide):** 188.11MM **Privately Held**
**Web:** www.tfewines.com
**SIC:** 2084 0172 Wines; Grapes

### (P-1768)
### SUTTER HOME WINERY INC
Also Called: Trinchero Family Estates
18655 Jacob Brack Rd, Lodi (95242-9185)
PHONE....................707 963-5928
**EMP:** 19
**SALES (corp-wide):** 188.11MM **Privately Held**
**Web:** www.tfewines.com
**SIC:** 2084 Wines
**PA:** Sutter Home Winery, Inc.
100 St Hlena Hwy S
707 963-3104

### (P-1769)
### SUTTER HOME WINERY INC
560 Gateway Dr, Napa (94558-7517)
PHONE....................707 963-3104
**EMP:** 31
**SALES (corp-wide):** 188.11MM **Privately Held**
**Web:** www.tfewines.com
**SIC:** 2084 Wines
**PA:** Sutter Home Winery, Inc.
100 St Hlena Hwy S
707 963-3104

### (P-1770)
### SUTTER HOME WINERY INC
Also Called: NAPA Cellars
7481 St Helena Hwy S, Oakville (94562)
PHONE....................707 944-2565
Erin Redding, Prin
**EMP:** 28
**SALES (corp-wide):** 188.11MM **Privately Held**
**Web:** www.onestopwineshop.com
**SIC:** 2084 Wines
**PA:** Sutter Home Winery, Inc.
100 St Hlena Hwy S
707 963-3104

### (P-1771)
### SUTTER HOME WINERY INC
277 Saint Helena Hwy S Hwy29, Saint Helena (94574-2202)
PHONE....................800 967-4663
Barry Wiss, Mgr

**EMP:** 20
**SALES (corp-wide):** 188.11MM **Privately Held**
**Web:** www.tfewines.com
**SIC:** 2084 Wines
**PA:** Sutter Home Winery, Inc.
100 St Hlena Hwy S
707 963-3104

### (P-1772)
### SWANSON FAMILY ESTATE (DH)
1271 Manley Ln, Rutherford (94573)
P.O. Box 148 (94562-0148)
PHONE....................707 754-4018
Clarke Swanson Junior, CEO
Michael Jellison, Pr
Bill Cole, CFO
▲ **EMP:** 28 **EST:** 1987
**SQ FT:** 3,500
**SALES (est):** 16.95K
**SALES (corp-wide):** 283.23MM **Privately Held**
**SIC:** 2084 Wines
**HQ:** Vintage Wine Estates, Inc. (Ca)
205 Concourse Blvd
Santa Rosa CA 95403

### (P-1773)
### TABLAS CREEK VNYRD A CAL LTD P
9339 Adelaida Rd, Paso Robles (93446-9785)
PHONE....................805 237-1231
Bob Haas, Mng Pt
▲ **EMP:** 18 **EST:** 1990
**SQ FT:** 40,000
**SALES (est):** 3.67MM **Privately Held**
**Web:** www.tablascreek.com
**SIC:** 2084 Wines

### (P-1774)
### TAFT STREET INC
Also Called: Taft Street Winery
2030 Barlow Ln, Sebastopol (95472)
PHONE....................707 823-2049
Michael Tierney, Pr
Mike Martini, CFO
Martin Tierney Junior, VP
**EMP:** 20 **EST:** 1982
**SQ FT:** 30,000
**SALES (est):** 2.28MM **Privately Held**
**Web:** www.taftstreetwinery.com
**SIC:** 2084 Wines

### (P-1775)
### TALLEY VINEYARDS
3031 Lopez Dr, Arroyo Grande (93420-4999)
P.O. Box 360 (93421-0360)
PHONE....................805 489-0446
Brian Talley, Pr
▲ **EMP:** 15 **EST:** 1989
**SQ FT:** 2,000
**SALES (est):** 2.05MM **Privately Held**
**Web:** www.talleyvineyards.com
**SIC:** 2084 Wines

### (P-1776)
### TEMECULA VALLEY WINERY MGT LLC
Also Called: Leonesse Cellars
27495 Diaz Rd, Temecula (92590-3414)
PHONE....................951 699-8896
**EMP:** 56 **EST:** 2008
**SQ FT:** 40,000
**SALES (est):** 11.86MM **Privately Held**
**Web:** www.tvwinerymanagement.com
**SIC:** 2084 Wines

### (P-1777)
### TERRAVANT WINE COMPANY LLC
Also Called: Terravant Wine
35 Industrial Way, Buellton (93427-9565)
PHONE....................805 688-4245
Lew Eisaguirre, Pr
Diane Turner, *
Fred Kayne, Managing Member*
Eric J Guerra, *
▲ **EMP:** 110 **EST:** 2006
**SQ FT:** 25,000
**SALES (est):** 23.54MM **Privately Held**
**Web:** www.summerlandwinebrands.com
**SIC:** 2084 Wines

### (P-1778)
### TESLA VINEYARDS LP
Also Called: Concannon Vineyard
4590 Tesla Rd, Livermore (94550-9002)
PHONE....................925 456-2500
TOLL FREE: 800
Eric Wente, Pt
Henry Wilder, Pt
Michael Wood, Pt
Timothy Wood, Pt
Dennis Wood, Pt
▲ **EMP:** 20 **EST:** 1883
**SALES (est):** 1.85MM **Privately Held**
**Web:** www.concannonvineyard.com
**SIC:** 2084 0721 Wines; Vines, cultivation of

### (P-1779)
### TESTAROSSA VINEYARDS LLC
Also Called: Testarossa Winery
300 College Ave Ste A, Los Gatos (95030-7066)
P.O. Box 969 (95031-0969)
PHONE....................408 354-6150
Robert Jensen, *
▲ **EMP:** 25 **EST:** 1994
**SQ FT:** 10,000
**SALES (est):** 6.61MM **Privately Held**
**Web:** www.testarossa.com
**SIC:** 2084 Wines

### (P-1780)
### THE WONDERFUL COMPANY LLC (PA)
Also Called: Teleflora
11444 W Olympic Blvd Fl 10, Los Angeles (90064-1557)
P.O. Box 30119 (90030-0119)
PHONE....................310 966-5700
◆ **EMP:** 250 **EST:** 2010
**SALES (est):** 2.04B
**SALES (corp-wide):** 2.04B **Privately Held**
**Web:** www.wonderful.com
**SIC:** 2084 0723 Wines; Fruit crops market preparation services

### (P-1781)
### THOMAS ALLEN VNYRDS WINERY LLC
Also Called: Ray Road Vineyards
5573 W Woodbridge Rd, Lodi (95242-9497)
PHONE....................209 288-7880
Allen Lombardi, Mgr
**EMP:** 31 **EST:** 2015
**SALES (est):** 7.15MM **Privately Held**
**Web:** www.thomasallenwine.com
**SIC:** 2084 Wines

### (P-1782)
### THOMAS FOGARTY WINERY LLC
19501 Skyline Blvd, Woodside (94062)
PHONE....................650 851-6777
▲ **EMP:** 25 **EST:** 1979

**SQ FT:** 4,000
**SALES (est):** 4.69MM **Privately Held**
**Web:** www.fogartywinery.com
**SIC:** 2084 0172 7299 Wines; Grapes; Facility rental and party planning services

### (P-1783)
### THOMAS LEONARDINI
Also Called: Whitehall Lane Winery
1563 Saint Helena Hwy S, Saint Helena (94574-9775)
PHONE....................707 963-9454
Thomas Leonardini, Owner
▲ **EMP:** 15 **EST:** 1988
**SQ FT:** 24,000
**SALES (est):** 3.74MM **Privately Held**
**Web:** www.whitehalllane.com
**SIC:** 2084 0172 Wines; Grapes

### (P-1784)
### THORNTON WINERY
Also Called: Cafe Champagne
32575 Rancho California Rd, Temecula (92591-4935)
P.O. Box 9008 (92589-9008)
PHONE....................951 699-0099
John M Thornton, Ch Bd
Steve Thornton, *
**EMP:** 98 **EST:** 1975
**SQ FT:** 41,000
**SALES (est):** 4.89MM **Privately Held**
**Web:** www.thorntonwine.com
**SIC:** 2084 5812 5947 Wine cellars, bonded: engaged in blending wines; Eating places; Gift shop

### (P-1785)
### THREE STICKS WINES LLC
143 W Spain St, Sonoma (95476-5638)
P.O. Box 1869 (95476-1869)
PHONE....................707 996-3328
Bill Price, Owner
**EMP:** 21 **EST:** 2006
**SALES (est):** 2.24MM **Privately Held**
**Web:** www.threestickswines.com
**SIC:** 2084 Wines

### (P-1786)
### TOOTH AND NAIL WINERY
3090 Anderson Rd, Paso Robles (93446-9616)
PHONE....................805 369-6100
Kim Walker, Pr
**EMP:** 38 **EST:** 2014
**SALES (est):** 523.14K **Privately Held**
**Web:** www.toothandnailwine.com
**SIC:** 2084 Wines

### (P-1787)
### TPWC INC (HQ)
Also Called: Franciscan Vineyards Inc.
1178 Galleron Rd, Saint Helena (94574-9790)
PHONE....................877 283-5934
Agustin Francisco Huneeus, Pr
Bill Skowronski, *
▲ **EMP:** 75 **EST:** 1971
**SQ FT:** 110,000
**SALES (est):** 22.92MM
**SALES (corp-wide):** 9.96B **Publicly Held**
**Web:** www.franciscan.com
**SIC:** 2084 Wines
**PA:** Constellation Brands, Inc.
50 E Broad St
585 678-7100

### (P-1788)
### TPWC INC
Also Called: Mount Veeder Winery
1999 Mount Veeder Rd, Napa (94558-9773)

## PRODUCTS & SERVICES SECTION
## 2084 - Wines, Brandy, And Brandy Spirits (P-1808)

P.O. Box 407  (94573-0407)
PHONE.................................707 224-4039
Chris Fehrnstrom, *Prin*
**EMP:** 94
**SQ FT:** 1,728
**SALES (corp-wide):** 9.96B **Publicly Held**
Web: www.franciscan.com
**SIC:** 2084  Wines
HQ: Tpwc, Inc.
1178 Galleron Rd
Saint Helena CA 94574
877 283-5934

### (P-1789)
### TREANA WINERY LLC
Also Called: Liberty School
4280 Second Wind Way, Paso Robles (93447)
P.O. Box 3260  (93447-3260)
PHONE.................................805 237-2932
Charles Wagner, *
▲ **EMP:** 30 **EST:** 1996
**SALES (est):** 6.85MM **Privately Held**
Web: www.hopefamilywines.com
**SIC:** 2084  Wines

### (P-1790)
### TREASURY CHATEAU & ESTATES
Also Called: Chalone Vineyard
10300 Chalk Hill Rd, Healdsburg (95448-9558)
P.O. Box 518  (93960-0518)
PHONE.................................707 299-2600
▲ **EMP:** 170
Web: www.chalonevineyard.com
**SIC:** 2084  5182  Wines; Wine

### (P-1791)
### TREASURY WINE ESTATES AMERICAS
630 Airpark Rd, Napa  (94558-7527)
P.O. Box 3382  (94558-0338)
PHONE.................................707 880-9967
**EMP:** 51
Web: www.treasurywineestates.com
**SIC:** 2084  Wines
HQ: Treasury Wine Estates Americas Company
555 Gateway Dr
Napa CA 94558
707 259-4500

### (P-1792)
### TREASURY WINE ESTATES AMERICAS
6480 Finnell Rd, Yountville  (94599-9409)
PHONE.................................707 312-0081
**EMP:** 15
Web: www.tweglobal.com
**SIC:** 2084  Wines
HQ: Treasury Wine Estates Americas Company
555 Gateway Dr
Napa CA 94558
707 259-4500

### (P-1793)
### TREASURY WINE ESTATES AMERICAS (HQ)
Also Called: Beringer
555 Gateway Dr, Napa  (94558)
PHONE.................................707 259-4500
Michael Clarke, *CEO*
Robert Foye, *
Walter Klenz, *
Martin Foster, *
Doug Roberts, *
◆ **EMP:** 400 **EST:** 1973

**SQ FT:** 26,000
**SALES (est):** 498.43MM **Privately Held**
Web: www.treasurywineestates.com
**SIC:** 2084  Wines
PA: Treasury Wine Estates Limited
L 8 161 Collins St

### (P-1794)
### TREASURY WINE ESTATES AMERICAS
Also Called: Cellar 360
21468 8th St E Ste A, Sonoma (95476-9767)
PHONE.................................707 935-1357
**EMP:** 26
Web: www.treasurywineestates.com
**SIC:** 2084  Wines
HQ: Treasury Wine Estates Americas Company
555 Gateway Dr
Napa CA 94558
707 259-4500

### (P-1795)
### TREASURY WINE ESTATES AMERICAS
2010 Diamond Mountain Rd, Calistoga (94515-9638)
PHONE.................................707 942-4945
**EMP:** 16
Web: www.tweglobal.com
**SIC:** 2084  Wines
HQ: Treasury Wine Estates Americas Company
555 Gateway Dr
Napa CA 94558
707 259-4500

### (P-1796)
### TREASURY WINE ESTATES AMERICAS
Also Called: Sterling Vineyards
1111 Dunaweal Ln, Calistoga  (94515)
PHONE.................................707 564-8477
Ben Dollard, *Brnch Mgr*
**EMP:** 16
Web: www.tweglobal.com
**SIC:** 2084  Wines
HQ: Treasury Wine Estates Americas Company
555 Gateway Dr
Napa CA 94558
707 259-4500

### (P-1797)
### TREASURY WINE ESTATES AMERICAS
300 Lakeside Dr 25th Fl, Oakland (94612-3534)
PHONE.................................707 299-3112
**EMP:** 17
Web: www.treasurywineestates.com
**SIC:** 2084  Wines
HQ: Treasury Wine Estates Americas Company
555 Gateway Dr
Napa CA 94558
707 259-4500

### (P-1798)
### TREASURY WINE ESTATES AMERICAS
Also Called: Etude Wines
1250 Cuttings Wharf Rd, Napa (94559-9738)
PHONE.................................707 257-5300
Ben Dollard, *Brnch Mgr*
**EMP:** 35
Web: www.winebusiness.com

**SIC:** 2084  Wines
HQ: Treasury Wine Estates Americas Company
555 Gateway Dr
Napa CA 94558
707 259-4500

### (P-1799)
### TREASURY WINE ESTATES AMERICAS
Also Called: Beringer Vineyards
1000 Pratt Ave, Saint Helena  (94574-1020)
P.O. Box 111  (94574-0111)
PHONE.................................707 963-4812
Ben Dollard, *Brnch Mgr*
**EMP:** 41
Web: www.tweglobal.com
**SIC:** 2084  5182  5921  Wines; Wine; Liquor stores
HQ: Treasury Wine Estates Americas Company
555 Gateway Dr
Napa CA 94558
707 259-4500

### (P-1800)
### TREASURY WINE ESTATES AMERICAS
Also Called: St Clement Vineyards
2867 Saint Helena Hwy N, Saint Helena (94574-9655)
PHONE.................................707 963-7221
FAX: 707 963-1412
**EMP:** 25
**SALES (corp-wide):** 1.72B **Privately Held**
**SIC:** 2084  0172  Wines; Grapes
HQ: Treasury Wine Estates Americas Company
555 Gateway Dr
Napa CA 94558
707 259-4500

### (P-1801)
### TREASURY WINE ESTATES AMERICAS
2000 Saint Helena Hwy N, Saint Helena (94574)
PHONE.................................707 963-7115
TOLL FREE: 800
**EMP:** 81
**SIC:** 2084  Wines
HQ: Treasury Wine Estates Americas Company
555 Gateway Dr
Napa CA 94558
707 259-4500

### (P-1802)
### TREFETHEN VINEYARDS WINERY INC
Also Called: Trefethen Family Vineyards
1160 Oak Knoll Ave, Napa  (94558-1398)
P.O. Box 2460  (94558-0291)
PHONE.................................707 255-7700
Jon Ruel, *Pr*
Janet Trefethen, *
David Whitehouse, *
Carla Trefethen, *Stockholder*
Robert Helmer, *
▲ **EMP:** 50 **EST:** 1973
**SQ FT:** 4,000
**SALES (est):** 12.46MM **Privately Held**
Web: www.trefethen.com
**SIC:** 2084  5921  Wines; Wine

### (P-1803)
### TURLEY WINE CELLARS
11076 Bell Rd, Plymouth  (95669-9516)
P.O. Box 189  (95669-0189)

PHONE.................................209 245-3938
Lawrence Cobb, *Owner*
**EMP:** 34
**SALES (corp-wide):** 2.08MM **Privately Held**
Web: www.turleywinecellars.com
**SIC:** 2084  Wines
PA: Turley Wine Cellars
2900 Vineyard Dr
805 434-1030

### (P-1804)
### TURLEY WINE CELLARS INC
Also Called: Pesenti Winery
3358 Saint Helena Hwy N, Saint Helena (94574-9660)
PHONE.................................707 968-2700
Larry Turley, *Pr*
**EMP:** 50 **EST:** 1994
**SALES (est):** 8.96MM **Privately Held**
Web: www.turleywinecellars.com
**SIC:** 2084  Wines

### (P-1805)
### TURNBULL WINE CELLARS
8210 St Helena Hwy, Oakville  (94562)
P.O. Box 29  (94562-0029)
PHONE.................................707 963-5839
Patrick O'dell, *Pr*
▲ **EMP:** 35 **EST:** 1977
**SQ FT:** 1,600
**SALES (est):** 5.65MM
**SALES (corp-wide):** 11.04MM **Privately Held**
Web: www.turnbullwines.com
**SIC:** 2084  Wines
PA: Humboldt Group
180 S Fortuna Blvd
707 725-6661

### (P-1806)
### TWIN PEAKS WINERY INC
Also Called: Cliff Lede Vineyards
1473 Yountville Cross Rd, Yountville (94599-9471)
PHONE.................................707 944-8642
Cliff Lede, *Pr*
▲ **EMP:** 54 **EST:** 1971
**SALES (est):** 9.26MM **Privately Held**
Web: www.cliffledevineyards.com
**SIC:** 2084  Wines

### (P-1807)
### TWISTED OAK WINERY LLC (PA)
4280 Red Hill Rd, Vallecito  (95251)
P.O. Box 2385  (95247-2385)
PHONE.................................209 728-3000
**EMP:** 15 **EST:** 2001
**SQ FT:** 1,000
**SALES (est):** 2.05MM
**SALES (corp-wide):** 2.05MM **Privately Held**
Web: www.twistedoak.com
**SIC:** 2084  Wine cellars, bonded: engaged in blending wines

### (P-1808)
### VALLEY OF MOON WINERY
134 Church St, Sonoma  (95476-6612)
P.O. Box 1951  (95442-1951)
PHONE.................................707 939-4500
Gary Heck, *Pr*
◆ **EMP:** 23 **EST:** 1945
**SALES (est):** 477.69K
**SALES (corp-wide):** 42.09MM **Privately Held**
Web: www.valleyofthemoonwinery.com
**SIC:** 2084  0172  Wines; Grapes
PA: F. Korbel & Bros.
13250 River Rd

## 2084 - Wines, Brandy, And Brandy Spirits (P-1809)

### PRODUCTS & SERVICES SECTION

707 824-7000

**(P-1809)**
**VIE-DEL COMPANY**
13363 S Indianola Ave, Kingsburg (93631-9268)
PHONE..................559 896-3065
Richard Watson, *Prin*
**EMP:** 24
**SALES (corp-wide):** 28.37MM **Privately Held**
Web: www.vie-del.com
**SIC: 2084** 2037 Brandy; Frozen fruits and vegetables
PA: Vie-Del Company
   11903 S Chestnut Ave
   559 834-2525

**(P-1810)**
**VILLA AMOROSA**
Also Called: Castello Diamorosa
4045 Saint Helena Hwy, Calistoga (94515-9609)
PHONE..................707 967-6272
Georg Falzner, *Pr*
▲ **EMP:** 100 **EST:** 1994
**SALES (est):** 8.09MM **Privately Held**
Web: www.castellodiamorosa.com
**SIC: 2084** Wines

**(P-1811)**
**VILLA DEL LAGO LLC (PA)**
540 Technology Way, Napa (94558-7513)
PHONE..................707 963-2134
David Del Dotto, *Managing Member*
**EMP:** 22 **EST:** 2007
**SALES (est):** 628.29K
**SALES (corp-wide):** 628.29K **Privately Held**
Web: www.deldottovineyards.com
**SIC: 2084** Wines

**(P-1812)**
**VILLA TOSCANO WINERY**
10600 Shenandoah Rd, Plymouth (95669-9513)
P.O. Box 1029 (95669-1029)
PHONE..................209 245-3800
Jerry Wright, *Owner*
▲ **EMP:** 17 **EST:** 1996
**SQ FT:** 18,000
**SALES (est):** 2.87MM **Privately Held**
Web: www.villatoscano.com
**SIC: 2084** Wines

**(P-1813)**
**VINEBURG WINE COMPANY INC (PA)**
Also Called: Bartholomew Park Winery
2000 Denmark St, Sonoma (95476-9615)
P.O. Box 1 (95487-0001)
PHONE..................707 938-5277
Jim Bundschu, *CEO*
Nancy Bundschu, *
▲ **EMP:** 25 **EST:** 1858
**SQ FT:** 4,000
**SALES (est):** 8.89MM
**SALES (corp-wide):** 8.89MM **Privately Held**
Web: www.gunbun.com
**SIC: 2084** 0172 Wines; Grapes

**(P-1814)**
**VINO VAULT INC (PA)**
5800 W 3rd St, Los Angeles (90036-2830)
PHONE..................323 937-9463
Jeffrey Anthony, *CEO*
Jim Ancavo, *COO*
**EMP:** 15 **EST:** 2019
**SALES (est):** 55.2MM

**SALES (corp-wide):** 55.2MM **Privately Held**
Web: www.vinovaultwine.com
**SIC: 2084** Wine coolers (beverages)

**(P-1815)**
**VINTAGE WINE ESTATES INC CA**
Also Called: B.R. Cohn Winery
15000 Hwy 12, Glen Ellen (95442-9454)
PHONE..................800 330-4064
**EMP:** 80
**SALES (corp-wide):** 283.23MM **Privately Held**
Web: www.brcohn.com
**SIC: 2084** 0172 5921 Wines; Grapes; Wine
HQ: Vintage Wine Estates, Inc. (Ca)
   205 Concourse Blvd
   Santa Rosa CA 95403

**(P-1816)**
**VINTAGE WINE ESTATES INC CA**
Also Called: Delectus Winery
1091 Saint Helena Hwy S, Saint Helena (94574-2268)
PHONE..................707 921-2600
**EMP:** 55
**SALES (corp-wide):** 283.23MM **Privately Held**
Web: www.vintagewineestates.com
**SIC: 2084** Wines
HQ: Vintage Wine Estates, Inc. (Ca)
   205 Concourse Blvd
   Santa Rosa CA 95403

**(P-1817)**
**VINTAGE WINE ESTATES INC CA**
251 Rhode Island St Ste 203, San Francisco (94103-5168)
PHONE..................415 495-1350
**EMP:** 30
**SALES (corp-wide):** 283.23MM **Privately Held**
Web: www.vintagewineestates.com
**SIC: 2084** Wines
HQ: Vintage Wine Estates, Inc. (Ca)
   205 Concourse Blvd
   Santa Rosa CA 95403

**(P-1818)**
**VINTAGE WINE ESTATES INC CA**
3070 Limestone Way Unit C, Paso Robles (93446-5988)
PHONE..................805 503-9660
**EMP:** 22
**SALES (corp-wide):** 283.23MM **Privately Held**
Web: www.vintagewineestates.com
**SIC: 2084** Wines
HQ: Vintage Wine Estates, Inc. (Ca)
   205 Concourse Blvd
   Santa Rosa CA 95403

**(P-1819)**
**VINTAGE WINE ESTATES INC CA (HQ)**
Also Called: Vintage Wine Estates
205 Concourse Blvd, Santa Rosa (95403-8258)
PHONE..................877 289-9463
Kristina Johnston, *Dir*
Terry Wheatley, *Pr*
Kathy Devillers, *CFO*
Jeff Nicholson, *COO*
Ejnar Knudsen, *Dir*
▲ **EMP:** 42 **EST:** 2000
**SALES (est):** 189.92MM
**SALES (corp-wide):** 283.23MM **Privately Held**
Web: www.vintagewineestates.com
**SIC: 2084** Wines

PA: Vintage Wine Estates, Inc. (Nv)
   937 Tahoe Blvd Ste 210
   707 346-3640

**(P-1820)**
**VINTNERS DISTRIBUTORS INC**
Also Called: Oakdale Shell
1728 Oakdale Rd, Modesto (95355-3010)
PHONE..................209 551-6422
**EMP:** 62
**SALES (corp-wide):** 15.85MM **Privately Held**
Web: www.vintnersdistributors.net
**SIC: 2084** Wines, brandy, and brandy spirits
PA: Vintners Distributors, Inc.
   41805 Albrae St Ste 2
   510 657-9150

**(P-1821)**
**WALT PINOT NOIR**
380 1st St W, Sonoma (95476-5631)
PHONE..................707 933-4440
**EMP:** 16 **EST:** 2019
**SALES (est):** 196.26K **Privately Held**
Web: www.waltwines.com
**SIC: 2084** Wines

**(P-1822)**
**WATERS EDGE WINERIES INC**
Also Called: Waters Edge Winery
8560 Vineyard Ave Ste 408, Rancho Cucamonga (91730-4351)
PHONE..................909 468-9463
Ken Lineberger, *Prin*
**EMP:** 20 **EST:** 2012
**SALES (est):** 1.58MM **Privately Held**
Web: www.watersedgewineries.com
**SIC: 2084** 6794 Wines; Franchises, selling or licensing

**(P-1823)**
**WENTE BROS**
Also Called: Wente Family Estates
7701 Las Positas Rd, Livermore (94551-8205)
PHONE..................925 456-2286
**EMP:** 21
**SALES (corp-wide):** 47.28MM **Privately Held**
Web: www.wentevineyards.com
**SIC: 2084** Wines
PA: Wente Bros.
   5050 Arroyo Rd
   925 456-2300

**(P-1824)**
**WENTE BROS**
Also Called: Wente Brothers Winery
37995 Elm Ave, Greenfield (93927-9794)
PHONE..................831 674-5642
Keith Roberts, *Mgr*
**EMP:** 20
**SALES (corp-wide):** 47.28MM **Privately Held**
Web: www.wentevineyards.com
**SIC: 2084** Wines
PA: Wente Bros.
   5050 Arroyo Rd
   925 456-2300

**(P-1825)**
**WG BEST WEINKELLEREI INC**
Also Called: Montesquieu Winery
888 W E St, San Diego (92101-5915)
PHONE..................858 627-1747
Fonda Hopkins, *CEO*
Fonda Hopkins, *Pr*
Frank Kryger, *Sec*
▲ **EMP:** 18 **EST:** 1985
**SALES (est):** 2.25MM **Privately Held**

**SIC: 2084** 5182 5921 Wine cellars, bonded: engaged in blending wines; Wine; Wine

**(P-1826)**
**WIENS CELLARS LLC**
35055 Via Del Ponte, Temecula (92592-8022)
PHONE..................951 694-9892
**EMP:** 45 **EST:** 2001
**SALES (est):** 9.52MM **Privately Held**
Web: www.wienscellars.com
**SIC: 2084** Wines

**(P-1827)**
**WILLIAMS & SELYEM LLC**
981 Airway Ct Ste E-F, Santa Rosa (95403-1983)
PHONE..................707 536-9685
**EMP:** 19
**SALES (corp-wide):** 9.9MM **Privately Held**
Web: www.williamselyem.com
**SIC: 2084** Wines
PA: Williams & Selyem, Llc
   7227 Westside Rd
   707 433-6425

**(P-1828)**
**WILSON CREEK WNERY VNYARDS INC**
Also Called: Wilson Creek Winery
35960 Rancho California Rd, Temecula (92591-5088)
PHONE..................951 699-9463
William J Wilson, *CEO*
Michael Wilson, *
Craig Johns, *
**EMP:** 110 **EST:** 2000
**SQ FT:** 6,000
**SALES (est):** 24.19MM **Privately Held**
Web: www.wilsoncreekwinery.com
**SIC: 2084** 8999 Wines; Personal services

**(P-1829)**
**WINC INC**
927 S Santa Fe Ave, Los Angeles (90021-1726)
PHONE..................855 282-5829
Alexander Oxman, *CEO*
**EMP:** 146 **EST:** 2007
**SALES (est):** 2.47MM **Privately Held**
Web: www.winc.com
**SIC: 2084** Wines

**(P-1830)**
**WINDSOR OAKS VINEYARDS LLP**
Also Called: Windsor Oaks Vineyards
10810 Hillview Rd, Windsor (95492-7519)
P.O. Box 883 (95492-0883)
PHONE..................707 433-4050
Windsor Oaks, *Pt*
◆ **EMP:** 25 **EST:** 1992
**SALES (est):** 1.13MM **Privately Held**
Web: www.windsoroaks.com
**SIC: 2084** Wines

**(P-1831)**
**WINE GROUP INC (HQ)**
Also Called: Mogan David Wine
17000 E State Highway 120, Ripon (95366-9412)
PHONE..................209 599-4111
Brian Jay Vos, *CEO*
Arthur Ciocca, *
Stephen Hughes, *
Louis Quaccia, *
Morris Ball, *Field Operations Vice President*
◆ **EMP:** 200 **EST:** 1933

# PRODUCTS & SERVICES SECTION
## 2086 - Bottled And Canned Soft Drinks (P-1852)

SQ FT: 3,000
SALES (est): 114.75MM **Privately Held**
Web: www.thewinegroup.com
SIC: 2084 Wines
PA: The Wine Group Llc
 17000 E State Highway 120

### (P-1832)
### WOODBRIDGE WINERY
5950 E Woodbridge Rd, Acampo (95220-9429)
PHONE..................................209 369-5861
EMP: 17 EST: 2010
SALES (est): 3.96MM **Privately Held**
SIC: 2084 Wines, brandy, and brandy spirits

## 2085 Distilled And Blended Liquors

### (P-1833)
### BAR NONE INC
1302 Santa Fe Dr, Tustin (92780-6434)
PHONE..................................714 259-8450
John Underwood, Pr
Elizabeth Underwood, Sec
EMP: 18 EST: 1963
SQ FT: 20,000
SALES (est): 4.8MM
SALES (corp-wide): 763.76MM **Publicly Held**
Web: www.barnoneinc.com
SIC: 2085 2087 3565 Cocktails, alcoholic; Beverage bases, concentrates, syrups, powders and mixes; Bottling machinery: filling, capping, labeling
PA: First Advantage Corporation
 1 Concrse Pkwy Ne Ste 200
 888 314-9761

### (P-1834)
### BOOCHERY INC
Also Called: Boochcraft
684 Anita St Ste F, Chula Vista (91911-7170)
PHONE..................................619 207-0530
Michael Kent, CEO
Adam Hiner, *
Andrew Clark, *
Michael Kent, Sec
EMP: 65 EST: 2015
SQ FT: 5,000
SALES (est): 10.81MM **Privately Held**
Web: www.boochcraft.com
SIC: 2085 Distilled and blended liquors

### (P-1835)
### DENNY BAR COMPANY LLC
511 Main St, Etna (96027-8014)
PHONE..................................530 467-5115
EMP: 22 EST: 2016
SALES (est): 405.79K **Privately Held**
Web: www.dennybarcompany.com
SIC: 2085 Distilled and blended liquors

### (P-1836)
### DIAGEO NORTH AMERICA INC
Also Called: DIAGEO NORTH AMERICA INC.
6130 Stoneridge Mall Rd Ste 250, Pleasanton (94588-3279)
PHONE..................................925 520-3116
Lisa Buell, Mgr
EMP: 20
SALES (corp-wide): 20.27B **Privately Held**
SIC: 2085 Distilled and blended liquors
HQ: Diageo North America, Inc.
 175 Grnwich St Fl 41-42 3
 New York NY 10007
 212 202-1800

### (P-1837)
### DIAGEO NORTH AMERICA INC
Also Called: DIAGEO NORTH AMERICA INC.
151 Commonwealth Dr, Menlo Park (94025-1105)
PHONE..................................650 329-3220
Del Kruse, Brnch Mgr
EMP: 42
SALES (corp-wide): 20.27B **Privately Held**
SIC: 2085 2084 Distilled and blended liquors; Wines, brandy, and brandy spirits
HQ: Diageo North America, Inc.
 175 Grnwich St Fl 41-42 3
 New York NY 10007
 212 202-1800

### (P-1838)
### HAMMOND INC WHICH WILL DO BUS
404 S Coast Hwy, Oceanside (92054-4007)
PHONE..................................925 381-5392
Nicholas Hammond, Pr
EMP: 25 EST: 2018
SALES (est): 2.35MM **Privately Held**
Web: www.paccoastspirits.com
SIC: 2085 Ethyl alcohol for beverage purposes

### (P-1839)
### HEMILANE INC
Also Called: Cerk Beverage
909 E El Segundo Blvd, El Segundo (90245)
PHONE..................................424 277-1134
Robert Rubens, CFO
EMP: 15 EST: 2015
SALES (est): 1.18MM **Privately Held**
SIC: 2085 Distilled and blended liquors

### (P-1840)
### LIN FRANK DISTILLERS
2455 Huntington Dr, Fairfield (94533-9734)
PHONE..................................707 437-1092
Frank Lin, Prin
EMP: 30 EST: 2010
SALES (est): 5.29MM **Privately Held**
SIC: 2085 Distilled and blended liquors

### (P-1841)
### RARE BREED DISTILLING LLC (HQ)
Also Called: Wild Turkey Distillery
55 Francisco St Ste 100, San Francisco (94133-2136)
PHONE..................................415 315-8060
Francesca Mazzoleni, Prin
▼ EMP: 21 EST: 2009
SALES (est): 24.69MM
SALES (corp-wide): 1.02B **Privately Held**
SIC: 2085 Distilled and blended liquors
PA: Davide Campari Milano N.V.
 Via Franco Sacchetti 20
 0262251

### (P-1842)
### SANTA CROCE LLC
Also Called: Savage & Cooke
1097 Nimitz Ave, Vallejo (94592-1025)
P.O. Box 2020 (94574-2018)
PHONE..................................707 227-7834
EMP: 15
SALES (corp-wide): 2.61MM **Privately Held**
Web: www.savageandcooke.com
SIC: 2085 Distilled and blended liquors
PA: Santa Croce Llc
 1352 Main St
 707 967-9179

### (P-1843)
### SAZERAC COMPANY INC
Barton Brands of California
2202 E Del Amo Blvd, Carson (90749)
P.O. Box 6263 (90749-6263)
PHONE..................................310 604-8717
Michael Dominick, Mgr
EMP: 55
SALES (corp-wide): 1.28B **Privately Held**
Web: www.sazerac.com
SIC: 2085 Distilled and blended liquors
PA: Sazerac Company, Inc.
 101 Magazine St Fl 5
 866 729-3722

### (P-1844)
### SELTZER REVOLUTIONS INC
Also Called: Mexi
2911 Branciforte Dr, Santa Cruz (95065-9774)
PHONE..................................604 765-9966
Alice Chen, CEO
Kevin Finkas, COO
EMP: 15 EST: 2020
SALES (est): 402.23K **Privately Held**
SIC: 2085 7389 Distilled and blended liquors; Business services, nec

### (P-1845)
### STILLHOUSE LLC
8201 Beverly Blvd Ste 300, Los Angeles (90048-4542)
PHONE..................................323 498-1111
Brad Beckerman, CEO
Paul Sheppard, COO
EMP: 32 EST: 2009
SALES (est): 1.51MM **Privately Held**
Web: www.stillhouse.com
SIC: 2085 Corn whiskey
PA: Bacardi Limited
 C/O Conyers Corporate Services
 (Bermuda) Limited

### (P-1846)
### TAKARA SAKE USA INC (DH)
Also Called: Numano Sake Company
708 Addison St, Berkeley (94710-1925)
PHONE..................................510 540-8250
Yoshihiro Naka, CEO
Yoichiro Miyakuni, *
◆ EMP: 16 EST: 1977
SQ FT: 15,000
SALES (est): 13.19MM **Privately Held**
Web: www.takarasake.com
SIC: 2085 5182 Grain alcohol for beverage purposes; Wine
HQ: Usa Takara Holding Company
 708 Addison St
 Berkeley CA 94710

### (P-1847)
### TEQUILAS PREMIUM INC
Also Called: Tequila Clase Azul
470 Columbus Ave Ste 210, San Francisco (94133-3930)
PHONE..................................415 399-0496
Sergio Arturo Lomeli, CEO
Patrick Carney, CFO
Juan J Sanchez, Pr
Patrick T Carney, CFO
▲ EMP: 17 EST: 2004
SALES (est): 4.89MM **Privately Held**
SIC: 2085 Distilled and blended liquors
PA: Casa Tradicion, S.A. De C.V.
 Av. Prolongacion Lopez Mateos Sur
 No. 7201 Nave 2

### (P-1848)
### TREASURY WINE ESTATES AMERICAS
Also Called: Beaulieu Vineyard
1960 Saint Helena Hwy, Rutherford (94573)
P.O. Box 219 (94573)
PHONE..................................707 967-5200
Armond Rist, Dir
EMP: 30
Web: www.bvwines.com
SIC: 2085 2084 0172 Distilled and blended liquors; Wines, brandy, and brandy spirits; Grapes
HQ: Treasury Wine Estates Americas Company
 555 Gateway Dr
 Napa CA 94558
 707 259-4500

## 2086 Bottled And Canned Soft Drinks

### (P-1849)
### AMCAN BEVERAGES INC
Also Called: Pokka Beverages
1201 Commerce Blvd, American Canyon (94503-9611)
PHONE..................................707 557-0500
Don Soetaert, Pr
EMP: 58 EST: 1976
SQ FT: 250,000
SALES (est): 5.33MM
SALES (corp-wide): 45.75B **Publicly Held**
SIC: 2086 Iced tea and fruit drinks, bottled and canned
PA: The Coca-Cola Company
 1 Coca Cola Plz
 404 676-2121

### (P-1850)
### AMERICAN BOTTLING COMPANY
Also Called: Dr Pepper Snapple Group
1188 Mt Vernon Ave, Riverside (92507-1829)
PHONE..................................951 341-7500
Vince Spurgeon, Mgr
EMP: 79
Web: www.keurigdrpepper.com
SIC: 2086 5149 Soft drinks: packaged in cans, bottles, etc.; Soft drinks
HQ: The American Bottling Company
 6425 Hall Of Fame Ln
 Frisco TX 75034

### (P-1851)
### AMERICAN BOTTLING COMPANY
Also Called: Seven-Up Bottling
2210 S Mcdowell Boulevard Ext, Petaluma (94954-5659)
PHONE..................................707 766-9750
Ray Gutendorf, Mgr
EMP: 75
SQ FT: 1,600
Web: www.keurigdrpepper.com
SIC: 2086 Soft drinks: packaged in cans, bottles, etc.
HQ: The American Bottling Company
 6425 Hall Of Fame Ln
 Frisco TX 75034

### (P-1852)
### AMERICAN BOTTLING COMPANY
Also Called: Seven-Up Bottling
100 Wabash Ave, Ukiah (95482-6313)
PHONE..................................707 462-8871
Allen Brown, Mgr
EMP: 83
Web: www.keurigdrpepper.com

## 2086 - Bottled And Canned Soft Drinks (P-1853)

SIC: **2086** Soft drinks: packaged in cans, bottles, etc.
HQ: The American Bottling Company
6425 Hall Of Fame Ln
Frisco TX 75034

### (P-1853)
### AMERICAN BOTTLING COMPANY
230 E 18th St, Bakersfield (93305-5609)
PHONE..................................661 323-7921
Brian Sutton, *Mgr*
**EMP:** 79
Web: www.keurigdrpepper.com
SIC: **2086** 5149 Soft drinks: packaged in cans, bottles, etc.; Soft drinks
HQ: The American Bottling Company
6425 Hall Of Fame Ln
Frisco TX 75034

### (P-1854)
### AMERICAN BOTTLING COMPANY
2012 S Pearl St, Fresno (93721-3312)
PHONE..................................559 442-1553
Mariel Guardado, *Mgr*
**EMP:** 56
**SQ FT:** 25,000
Web: www.keurigdrpepper.com
SIC: **2086** Soft drinks: packaged in cans, bottles, etc.
HQ: The American Bottling Company
6425 Hall Of Fame Ln
Frisco TX 75034

### (P-1855)
### AMERICAN BOTTLING COMPANY
1555 Heartwood Dr, Mckinleyville (95519-3989)
PHONE..................................707 840-9727
Ron Ellis, *Genl Mgr*
**EMP:** 52
Web: www.keurigdrpepper.com
SIC: **2086** Soft drinks: packaged in cans, bottles, etc.
HQ: The American Bottling Company
6425 Hall Of Fame Ln
Frisco TX 75034

### (P-1856)
### AMERICAN BOTTLING COMPANY
1166 Arroyo St, San Fernando (91340-1824)
PHONE..................................818 898-1471
Ed Nemecek, *Brnch Mgr*
**EMP:** 79
Web: www.keurigdrpepper.com
SIC: **2086** 5149 Soft drinks: packaged in cans, bottles, etc.; Soft drinks
HQ: The American Bottling Company
6425 Hall Of Fame Ln
Frisco TX 75034

### (P-1857)
### AMERICAN BOTTLING COMPANY
1166 Arroyo St, Orange (92865)
PHONE..................................714 974-8560
Mark Jones, *Mgr*
**EMP:** 185
Web: www.keurigdrpepper.com
SIC: **2086** 5149 Soft drinks: packaged in cans, bottles, etc.; Soft drinks
HQ: The American Bottling Company
6425 Hall Of Fame Ln
Frisco TX 75034

### (P-1858)
### AMERICAN BOTTLING COMPANY
618 Hanson Way, Santa Maria (93458-9734)
PHONE..................................805 928-1001
Richard Roese, *Brnch Mgr*
**EMP:** 52
Web: www.keurigdrpepper.com
SIC: **2086** Soft drinks: packaged in cans, bottles, etc.
HQ: The American Bottling Company
6425 Hall Of Fame Ln
Frisco TX 75034

### (P-1859)
### AMERICAN BOTTLING COMPANY
Also Called: 7 Up / R C Bottling Co
3220 E 26th St, Vernon (90058-8008)
PHONE..................................323 268-7779
Russ Wolfe, *Cntrlr*
**EMP:** 115
Web: www.keurigdrpepper.com
SIC: **2086** 5149 Soft drinks: packaged in cans, bottles, etc.; Groceries and related products, nec
HQ: The American Bottling Company
6425 Hall Of Fame Ln
Frisco TX 75034

### (P-1860)
### AMERICAN BOTTLING COMPANY
Also Called: Seven-Up Btlg Co Marysville
2720 Land Ave, Sacramento (95815-1834)
PHONE..................................916 929-3575
Jim Hough, *Mgr*
**EMP:** 52
Web: www.americanbottle.com
SIC: **2086** Soft drinks: packaged in cans, bottles, etc.
HQ: The American Bottling Company
6425 Hall Of Fame Ln
Frisco TX 75034

### (P-1861)
### AMERICAN BOTTLING COMPANY
2670 Land Ave, Sacramento (95815-2380)
PHONE..................................916 929-7777
**EMP:** 75
Web: www.keurigdrpepper.com
SIC: **2086** Soft drinks: packaged in cans, bottles, etc.
HQ: The American Bottling Company
6425 Hall Of Fame Ln
Frisco TX 75034

### (P-1862)
### AMERICAN BOTTLING COMPANY
11205 Commercial Pkwy, Castroville (95012-3205)
PHONE..................................831 632-0777
**EMP:** 40
Web: www.keurigdrpepper.com
SIC: **2086** Soft drinks: packaged in cans, bottles, etc.
HQ: The American Bottling Company
6425 Hall Of Fame Ln
Frisco TX 75034

### (P-1863)
### AMERICAN BOTTLING COMPANY
6160 Stoneridge Mall Rd Ste 280, Pleasanton (94588-3285)
PHONE..................................925 251-3001
**EMP:** 40
Web: www.keurigdrpepper.com
SIC: **2086** Soft drinks: packaged in cans, bottles, etc.
HQ: The American Bottling Company
6425 Hall Of Fame Ln
Frisco TX 75034

### (P-1864)
### AMERIPEC INC
6965 Aragon Cir, Buena Park (90620-1118)
PHONE..................................714 690-9191
Ping C Wu, *CEO*
Ed Muratori, *
**EMP:** 150 **EST:** 1988
**SQ FT:** 215,000
**SALES (est):** 2.56MM **Privately Held**
Web: www.ameripec.com
SIC: **2086** Carbonated soft drinks, bottled and canned
HQ: President Global Corporation
6965 Aragon Cir
Buena Park CA 90620

### (P-1865)
### ANOMALIES INTERNATIONAL INC
Also Called: Partyaid
2833 Mission St, Santa Cruz (95060-5755)
P.O. Box 761 (95061-0761)
PHONE..................................800 855-1113
Orion Melehan, *CEO*
Aaron Hinde, *COO*
▲ **EMP:** 55 **EST:** 2011
**SQ FT:** 9,105
**SALES (est):** 4.43MM **Privately Held**
Web: www.lifeaidbevco.com
SIC: **2086** Bottled and canned soft drinks

### (P-1866)
### AQUAHYDRATE INC
5870 W Jefferson Blvd Ste D, Los Angeles (90016-3159)
P.O. Box 69798 (90069-0798)
PHONE..................................310 559-5058
John Cochran, *CEO*
David Loewen, *
Mark Loeffler, *
Mark Wahlberg, *
Matthew Howison, *
◆ **EMP:** 38 **EST:** 2003
**SALES (est):** 3.04MM **Privately Held**
Web: www.aquahydrate.com
SIC: **2086** Mineral water, carbonated: packaged in cans, bottles, etc.

### (P-1867)
### BEVERAGES & MORE INC
Also Called: Bevmo
28011 Greenfield Dr, Laguna Niguel (92677-4428)
PHONE..................................949 643-3020
Christoph Killin, *Brnch Mgr*
**EMP:** 135
**SALES (corp-wide):** 1.61B **Privately Held**
Web: www.bevmo.com
SIC: **2086** 5149 5921 Bottled and canned soft drinks; Beverages, except coffee and tea; Beer (packaged)
HQ: Beverages & More, Inc.
1401 Wllow Pass Rd Ste 90
Concord CA 94520

### (P-1868)
### BLK INTERNATIONAL LLC
12410 Clark St, Santa Fe Springs (90670-3916)
PHONE..................................424 282-3443
Sara Bergstein, *CEO*
Jacqueline Wilkie, *
Louise Wilkie, *
John Kim, *
**EMP:** 27 **EST:** 2016
**SQ FT:** 5,500
**SALES (est):** 1.44MM **Privately Held**
Web: www.getblk.com
SIC: **2086** Water, natural: packaged in cans, bottles, etc.

### (P-1869)
### BOTTLING GROUP LLC
Also Called: Pepsi Beverages
3440 S East Ave, Fresno (93725-9481)
PHONE..................................914 767-6000
**EMP:** 1462
**SALES (corp-wide):** 86.39B **Publicly Held**
Web: www.pepsico.com
SIC: **2086** Bottled and canned soft drinks
HQ: Bottling Group, Llc
1111 Westchester Ave
White Plains NY 10604
914 253-2000

### (P-1870)
### BOTTLING GROUP LLC
29000 Hesperian Blvd, Hayward (94545-5014)
PHONE..................................510 781-3723
**EMP:** 1219
**SALES (corp-wide):** 86.39B **Publicly Held**
Web: www.pepsico.com
SIC: **2086** Carbonated soft drinks, bottled and canned
HQ: Bottling Group, Llc
1111 Westchester Ave
White Plains NY 10604
914 253-2000

### (P-1871)
### BOTTLING GROUP LLC
Also Called: Pepsi Beverages
1150 E North Ave, Fresno (93725-1929)
PHONE..................................559 485-5050
**EMP:** 1706
**SALES (corp-wide):** 86.39B **Publicly Held**
Web: www.pepsico.com
SIC: **2086** Carbonated soft drinks, bottled and canned
HQ: Bottling Group, Llc
1111 Westchester Ave
White Plains NY 10604
914 253-2000

### (P-1872)
### BOTTLING GROUP LLC
Also Called: Pepsico
6659 Sycamore Canyon Blvd, Riverside (92507-0733)
PHONE..................................951 697-3200
Jon Hess, *Prin*
**EMP:** 55 **EST:** 2011
**SALES (est):** 19.61MM **Privately Held**
Web: www.pepsico.com
SIC: **2086** Carbonated soft drinks, bottled and canned

### (P-1873)
### CALIFORNIA BOTTLING COMPANY
Also Called: High Country Water
8250 Industrial Ave, Roseville (95678-5900)
PHONE..................................916 772-1000
Robert Wikse, *Pr*
Christopher Crain, *
L Douglas Mckenzie, *VP*
**EMP:** 50 **EST:** 1992
**SQ FT:** 50,000
**SALES (est):** 3.42MM **Privately Held**

## PRODUCTS & SERVICES SECTION
### 2086 - Bottled And Canned Soft Drinks (P-1896)

Web: www.cbcwater.com
SIC: 2086 Water, natural: packaged in cans, bottles, etc.

**(P-1874)**
**CALIFORNIA SPIRITS COMPANY LLC**
2946 Norman Strasse Rd, San Marcos (92069-5933)
PHONE..................................619 677-7066
Sam Alexander, *Managing Member*
Kyle Clarke, *Managing Member*✪
Casey Miles, *Managing Member*✪
Justin Wilkinson, *Managing Member*✪
**EMP:** 30 **EST:** 2016
**SALES (est):** 5.7MM **Privately Held**
Web: www.calspirits.com
SIC: 2086 Carbonated soft drinks, bottled and canned

**(P-1875)**
**CASTLE ROCK SPRING WATER CO**
4121 Dunsmuir Ave, Dunsmuir (96025-1704)
PHONE..................................530 678-4444
Ed Lauth, *Pr*
Clark Wright, *VP*
Scott Lidster, *VP*
**EMP:** 23 **EST:** 1990
**SQ FT:** 42,000
**SALES (est):** 262.41K **Privately Held**
Web: www.castlerockwatercompany.com
SIC: 2086 Water, natural: packaged in cans, bottles, etc.

**(P-1876)**
**CCE**
1334 S Central Ave, Los Angeles (90021-2210)
PHONE..................................213 744-8909
**EMP:** 31 **EST:** 2011
**SALES (est):** 158.19K **Privately Held**
SIC: 2086 Bottled and canned soft drinks

**(P-1877)**
**CG ROXANE LLC**
Also Called: Cg Roxane Shasta
1400 Marys Dr, Weed (96094-9643)
P.O. Box 560 (96094-0560)
PHONE..................................530 225-1260
Rick Moore, *Mgr*
**EMP:** 18
Web: www.crystalgeyserplease.com
SIC: 2086 Bottled and canned soft drinks
PA: Cg Roxane Llc
1210 South Hwy 395

**(P-1878)**
**CHAMELEON BEVERAGE COMPANY INC (PA)**
6444 E 26th St, Commerce (90040-3214)
PHONE..................................323 724-8223
Derek Reineman, *CEO*
Walter Corrigan, *
◆ **EMP:** 68 **EST:** 1995
**SQ FT:** 100,000
**SALES (est):** 12.42MM **Privately Held**
Web: www.chameleonbeverage.com
SIC: 2086 5149 Water, natural: packaged in cans, bottles, etc.; Soft drinks

**(P-1879)**
**CLEAN WATER STORES INC**
2806 Soquel Ave Ste A, Santa Cruz (95062-1435)
PHONE..................................888 600-5426
Peter Bulfin, *CEO*
Peter G Bulfin, *Pr*
▲ **EMP:** 18 **EST:** 2001
**SALES (est):** 493.9K **Privately Held**
Web: www.cleanwaterstore.com
SIC: 2086 Water, natural: packaged in cans, bottles, etc.

**(P-1880)**
**COCA-COLA COMPANY**
Also Called: Coca-Cola
1650 S Vintage Ave, Ontario (91761-3656)
PHONE..................................909 975-5200
Melvin Robinson, *Mgr*
**EMP:** 63
**SALES (corp-wide):** 45.75B **Publicly Held**
Web: www.coca-colacompany.com
SIC: 2086 Bottled and canned soft drinks
PA: The Coca-Cola Company
1 Coca Cola Plz
404 676-2121

**(P-1881)**
**COCA-COLA COMPANY AMERICAN CYN**
Also Called: Coca-Cola
1201 Commerce Blvd, American Canyon (94503-9611)
PHONE..................................707 556-1220
**EMP:** 28 **EST:** 2014
**SALES (est):** 8.93MM **Privately Held**
Web: careers.coca-colacompany.com
SIC: 2086 Bottled and canned soft drinks

**(P-1882)**
**CRYSTAL GEYSER WATER COMPANY (DH)**
501 Washington St, Calistoga (94515-1425)
P.O. Box 304 (94515-0304)
PHONE..................................888 424-1977
◆ **EMP:** 50 **EST:** 1977
**SALES (est):** 45.03MM **Privately Held**
Web: www.crystalgeyserwatercompany.com
SIC: 2086 Mineral water, carbonated: packaged in cans, bottles, etc.
HQ: Otsuka Pharmaceutical Co., Ltd.
2-16-4, Konan
Minato-Ku TKY 108-0

**(P-1883)**
**CRYSTAL GEYSER WATER COMPANY**
1233 E California Ave, Bakersfield (93307-1205)
PHONE..................................661 323-6296
Gerhard Gaugel, *Brnch Mgr*
**EMP:** 46
Web: www.crystalgeyser.com
SIC: 2086 5141 2099 2033 Mineral water, carbonated: packaged in cans, bottles, etc.; Groceries, general line; Food preparations, nec; Canned fruits and specialties
HQ: Crystal Geyser Water Company
501 Washington St
Calistoga CA 94515
888 424-1977

**(P-1884)**
**CRYSTAL GEYSER WATER COMPANY**
2351 E Brundage Ln Ste A, Bakersfield (93307-3063)
PHONE..................................661 321-0896
Robert Hofferd, *Mgr*
**EMP:** 46
Web: www.crystalgeyserwatercompany.com
SIC: 2086 Mineral water, carbonated: packaged in cans, bottles, etc.
HQ: Crystal Geyser Water Company
501 Washington St
Calistoga CA 94515
888 424-1977

**(P-1885)**
**DR PEPPER/SEVEN UP INC**
1901 Russell Ave, Santa Rosa (95403-2646)
PHONE..................................707 545-7797
Ray Gutendorf, *Prin*
**EMP:** 16
Web: www.drpepper.com
SIC: 2086 Soft drinks: packaged in cans, bottles, etc.
HQ: Dr Pepper/Seven Up, Inc.
6425 Hall Of Fame Ln
Frisco TX 75034
800 527-7096

**(P-1886)**
**DRINKPAK LLC**
21375 Needham Ranch Pkwy, Santa Clarita (91321-5528)
PHONE..................................833 376-5725
Nathaniel Patena, *Managing Member*
Jon Ballas, *
Ben Rush, *
**EMP:** 600 **EST:** 2020
**SALES (est):** 74MM **Privately Held**
Web: www.drinkpak.com
SIC: 2086 Carbonated beverages, nonalcoholic: pkged. in cans, bottles

**(P-1887)**
**DS SERVICES OF AMERICA INC**
Also Called: Sparkletts Water
1449 N Avenue 46, Los Angeles (90041-3410)
PHONE..................................323 551-5724
Reggie Doster, *Mgr*
**EMP:** 15
**SALES (corp-wide):** 1.77B **Privately Held**
Web: www.water.com
SIC: 2086 5499 Bottled and canned soft drinks; Beverage stores
HQ: Ds Services Of America, Inc.
1150 Assembly Dr Ste 800
Tampa FL 33607
770 933-1400

**(P-1888)**
**FAST TRACK ENERGY DRINK LLC**
8447 Wilshire Blvd Ste 401, Beverly Hills (90211-3209)
PHONE..................................310 281-2045
Brian Slover Senior, *Pr*
**EMP:** 25 **EST:** 2010
**SALES (est):** 366.71K **Privately Held**
SIC: 2086 Carbonated beverages, nonalcoholic: pkged. in cans, bottles

**(P-1889)**
**GENIUS PRODUCTS NT INC**
556 N Diamond Bar Blvd Ste 101, Diamond Bar (91765-1000)
PHONE..................................510 671-0219
Chris Clifford, *CEO*
**EMP:** 110 **EST:** 2019
**SALES (est):** 1.23MM **Privately Held**
SIC: 2086 Carbonated beverages, nonalcoholic: pkged. in cans, bottles

**(P-1890)**
**GREEN SPOT PACKAGING INC**
Also Called: Green Spot USA
100 S Cambridge Ave, Claremont (91711-4842)
PHONE..................................909 625-8771
Greg Saust, *CEO*
**EMP:** 20 **EST:** 1934
**SQ FT:** 100,000
**SALES (est):** 8.44MM **Privately Held**
Web: www.greenspotusa.com
SIC: 2086 Fruit drinks (less than 100% juice): packaged in cans, etc.
PA: Green Spot International
C/O Grand Pavilion Main Entrance

**(P-1891)**
**GTS LIVING FOODS LLC**
4646 Hampton St, Vernon (90058-2116)
PHONE..................................323 581-7787
Gt Dave, *Mgr*
**EMP:** 20
Web: www.gtslivingfoods.com
SIC: 2086 Bottled and canned soft drinks
PA: Gt's Living Foods, Llc
4415 Bandini Blvd

**(P-1892)**
**GTS LIVING FOODS LLC (PA)**
Also Called: Synergy Beverages
4415 Bandini Blvd, Vernon (90058-4309)
P.O. Box 2352 (90213-2352)
PHONE..................................323 581-7787
Kim Bates, *CMO*
**EMP:** 700 **EST:** 1994
**SALES (est):** 172.15MM **Privately Held**
Web: www.gtslivingfoods.com
SIC: 2086 Bottled and canned soft drinks

**(P-1893)**
**HA RIDER & SONS INC**
2482 Freedom Blvd, Watsonville (95076-1025)
PHONE..................................831 722-3882
George C Rider, *Pt*
Thomas Rider, *
▲ **EMP:** 45 **EST:** 1940
**SQ FT:** 168,000
**SALES (est):** 4.52MM **Privately Held**
Web: www.hariderandsons.com
SIC: 2086 Soft drinks: packaged in cans, bottles, etc.

**(P-1894)**
**HINT INC**
625 Market St Ste 1000, San Francisco (94105-3312)
P.O. Box 29078 (94129-0078)
PHONE..................................415 513-4051
Kara Goldin, *CEO*
Theodore Goldin, *
**EMP:** 250 **EST:** 2005
**SALES (est):** 45.41MM **Privately Held**
Web: www.drinkhint.com
SIC: 2086 Mineral water, carbonated: packaged in cans, bottles, etc.

**(P-1895)**
**J & R BOTTLING AND DISTRIBUTING INC**
1130 S Vail Ave, Montebello (90640-6021)
PHONE..................................323 724-4076
**EMP:** 20
SIC: 2086 Soft drinks: packaged in cans, bottles, etc.

**(P-1896)**
**JOHN FITZPATRICK & SONS**
Also Called: Pepsico
1480 Beltline Rd, Redding (96003-1410)
PHONE..................................530 241-3216
John Fitzpatrick Junior, *CEO*
Jerome Fitzpatrick, *VP*
**EMP:** 22 **EST:** 1958
**SQ FT:** 2,000
**SALES (est):** 958.42K **Privately Held**
Web: www.pepsico.com

## 2086 - Bottled And Canned Soft Drinks (P-1897)

**PRODUCTS & SERVICES SECTION**

SIC: 2086 Carbonated soft drinks, bottled and canned

### (P-1897)
**KEURIG GREEN MOUNTAIN INC**
26875 Pioneer Ave, Redlands (92374-2026)
PHONE..................909 557-6513
Jeffery Jenkins, *Brnch Mgr*
EMP: 20
Web: www.keurigdrpepper.com
SIC: 2086 Soft drinks: packaged in cans, bottles, etc.
HQ: Keurig Green Mountain, Inc.
1 Rotarian Pl
Waterbury VT 05676
877 879-2326

### (P-1898)
**KEVITA INC (HQ)**
Also Called: Kevita
2220 Celsius Ave Ste A, Oxnard (93030-5181)
PHONE..................805 200-2250
Chakra Earthsong, *CEO*
Cynthia Nastanski, *
Ada Cheng, *
EMP: 58 EST: 2009
SQ FT: 17,000
SALES (est): 21.55MM
SALES (corp-wide): 86.39B **Publicly Held**
Web: www.kevita.com
SIC: 2086 Bottled and canned soft drinks
PA: Pepsico, Inc.
700 Anderson Hill Rd
914 253-2000

### (P-1899)
**LA BOTTLEWORKS INC**
1605 Beach St, Montebello (90640-5432)
PHONE..................323 724-4076
Ryan Marsh, *CEO*
Matthew Marsh, *VP*
EMP: 20 EST: 2013
SALES (est): 1.73MM
SALES (corp-wide): 15.47MM **Privately Held**
Web: www.labottleworks.com
SIC: 2086 Bottled and canned soft drinks
PA: Entertainment Arts Research, Inc.
19109 W Ctwba Ave Ste 200
980 999-0270

### (P-1900)
**LIFEAID BEVERAGE COMPANY LLC (PA)**
2833 Mission St, Santa Cruz (95060-5755)
PHONE..................888 558-1113
Orion Melehan, *CFO*
EMP: 41 EST: 2015
SALES (est): 11.61MM
SALES (corp-wide): 11.61MM **Privately Held**
Web: www.lifeaidbevco.com
SIC: 2086 Bottled and canned soft drinks

### (P-1901)
**LIQUID DEATH MOUNTAIN WATER**
1447 2nd St Ste 200, Santa Monica (90401-3404)
PHONE..................818 521-5500
EMP: 35 EST: 2022
SALES (est): 10.62MM **Privately Held**
Web: www.liquiddeath.com
SIC: 2086 Water, natural: packaged in cans, bottles, etc.

### (P-1902)
**MANANALU INC**
8605 Santa Monica Blvd Pmb 82374, West Hollywood (90069-4109)
PHONE..................805 222-0046
David Cuthburt, *CEO*
Ilyse Kaplan, *CFO*
EMP: 21 EST: 2019
SALES (est): 8.42MM **Privately Held**
Web: www.mananalu.com
SIC: 2086 Water, natural: packaged in cans, bottles, etc.

### (P-1903)
**MONSTER BEVERAGE 1990 CORPORATION**
1 Monster Way, Corona (92879-7101)
PHONE..................951 739-6200
◆ EMP: 2001
SIC: 2086 Soft drinks: packaged in cans, bottles, etc.

### (P-1904)
**MONSTER BEVERAGE COMPANY**
1990 Pomona Rd, Corona (92878-4355)
PHONE..................866 322-4466
Mark Hall, *Prin*
EMP: 25 EST: 2010
SALES (est): 3.24MM
SALES (corp-wide): 7.14B **Publicly Held**
Web: www.monsterbevcorp.com
SIC: 2086 Soft drinks: packaged in cans, bottles, etc.
PA: Monster Beverage Corporation
1 Monster Way
951 739-6200

### (P-1905)
**MONSTER BEVERAGE CORPORATION (PA)**
Also Called: MONSTER
1 Monster Way, Corona (92879-7101)
PHONE..................951 739-6200
Rodney C Sacks, *Ch Bd*
Hilton H Schlosberg, *
Thomas J Kelly, *CFO*
EMP: 2367 EST: 1985
SALES (est): 7.14B
SALES (corp-wide): 7.14B **Publicly Held**
Web: www.monsterbevcorp.com
SIC: 2086 Carbonated beverages, nonalcoholic: pkgd. in cans, bottles

### (P-1906)
**NOR-CAL BEVERAGE CO INC**
1375 Terminal St, West Sacramento (95691-3514)
PHONE..................916 372-1700
Larry Buban, *Mgr*
EMP: 21
SALES (corp-wide): 53.99MM **Privately Held**
Web: www.mannabev.com
SIC: 2086 5181 Carbonated beverages, nonalcoholic: pkgd. in cans, bottles; Beer and ale
PA: Nor-Cal Beverage Co., Inc.
2150 Stone Blvd
916 372-0600

### (P-1907)
**OLIPOP INC**
360 Grand Ave # 259, Oakland (94610-4840)
PHONE..................510 560-5709
David Matthew Lester, *CEO*
EMP: 52 EST: 2018
SALES (est): 53.97MM **Privately Held**
Web: www.drinkolipop.com
SIC: 2086 Carbonated beverages, nonalcoholic: pkged. in cans, bottles

### (P-1908)
**ORANGE BANG INC**
13115 Telfair Ave, Sylmar (91342-3574)
PHONE..................818 833-1000
David Fox, *Pr*
EMP: 40 EST: 1971
SQ FT: 33,000
SALES (est): 2.3MM **Privately Held**
Web: www.orangebang.com
SIC: 2086 Soft drinks: packaged in cans, bottles, etc.

### (P-1909)
**PATHWATER INC**
Also Called: Pathwater
44137 Fremont Blvd, Fremont (94538)
PHONE..................510 518-0014
Shadi Bakour, *CEO*
Amer Orabi, *
EMP: 40 EST: 2020
SALES (est): 2.94MM **Privately Held**
Web: www.drinkpathwater.com
SIC: 2086 Pasteurized and mineral waters, bottled and canned

### (P-1910)
**PEPSI-COLA BOTTLING GROUP**
Also Called: Pepsico
215 E 21st St, Bakersfield (93305-5186)
PHONE..................661 635-1100
Steve Longfield, *Brnch Mgr*
EMP: 62
SALES (corp-wide): 86.39B **Publicly Held**
Web: www.pepsi-ny.com
SIC: 2086 Carbonated soft drinks, bottled and canned
HQ: Pepsi-Cola Bottling Group
700 Anderson Hill Rd
Purchase NY 10577

### (P-1911)
**PEPSI-COLA METRO BTLG CO INC**
Also Called: Pepsi-Cola
2471 Nadeau St, Mojave (93501-1507)
PHONE..................661 824-2051
Blaine Sherritt, *Mgr*
EMP: 33
SALES (corp-wide): 86.39B **Publicly Held**
Web: www.pepsico.com
SIC: 2086 5149 Bottled and canned soft drinks; Soft drinks
HQ: Pepsi-Cola Metropolitan Bottling Company, Inc.
700 Anderson Hill Rd
Purchase NY 10577
914 767-6000

### (P-1912)
**PEPSI-COLA METRO BTLG CO INC**
Also Called: Pepsico
2345 Thompson Way, Santa Maria (93455-1050)
PHONE..................805 739-2160
Joe Pearson, *Brnch Mgr*
EMP: 50
SALES (corp-wide): 86.39B **Publicly Held**
Web: www.pepsico.com
SIC: 2086 Carbonated soft drinks, bottled and canned
HQ: Pepsi-Cola Metropolitan Bottling Company, Inc.
700 Anderson Hill Rd
Purchase NY 10577
914 767-6000

### (P-1913)
**PEPSI-COLA METRO BTLG CO INC**
Also Called: Pepsi-Cola
6261 Caballero Blvd, Buena Park (90620-1191)
PHONE..................714 522-9635
Margaret Gramann, *Mgr*
EMP: 123
SALES (corp-wide): 86.39B **Publicly Held**
Web: www.pepsico.com
SIC: 2086 5149 Carbonated soft drinks, bottled and canned; Soft drinks
HQ: Pepsi-Cola Metropolitan Bottling Company, Inc.
700 Anderson Hill Rd
Purchase NY 10577
914 767-6000

### (P-1914)
**PEPSI-COLA METRO BTLG CO INC**
Also Called: Pepsi-Cola
4699 Old Ironsides Dr Ste 150, Santa Clara (95054-1824)
PHONE..................408 617-2200
Jerry Titwell, *Brnch Mgr*
EMP: 47
SALES (corp-wide): 86.39B **Publicly Held**
Web: www.pepsico.com
SIC: 2086 Carbonated soft drinks, bottled and canned
HQ: Pepsi-Cola Metropolitan Bottling Company, Inc.
700 Anderson Hill Rd
Purchase NY 10577
914 767-6000

### (P-1915)
**PEPSI-COLA METRO BTLG CO INC**
Also Called: Pepsi-Cola
19700 Figueroa St, Carson (90745-1098)
PHONE..................310 327-4222
Stefan Freeman, *Mgr*
EMP: 228
SALES (corp-wide): 86.39B **Publicly Held**
Web: www.pepsico.com
SIC: 2086 5149 Carbonated soft drinks, bottled and canned; Soft drinks
HQ: Pepsi-Cola Metropolitan Bottling Company, Inc.
700 Anderson Hill Rd
Purchase NY 10577
914 767-6000

### (P-1916)
**PEPSI-COLA METRO BTLG CO INC**
Also Called: Pepsico
4225 Pepsi Pl, Stockton (95215-2316)
PHONE..................209 367-7140
Sydney Van Vusan, *Prin*
EMP: 57
SALES (corp-wide): 86.39B **Publicly Held**
Web: www.pepsico.com
SIC: 2086 Carbonated soft drinks, bottled and canned
HQ: Pepsi-Cola Metropolitan Bottling Company, Inc.
700 Anderson Hill Rd
Purchase NY 10577
914 767-6000

### (P-1917)
**PEPSI-COLA METRO BTLG CO INC**
Also Called: Pepsi-Cola
4701 Park Rd, Benicia (94510-1125)

## 2086 - Bottled And Canned Soft Drinks (P-1936)

PHONE.....................707 746-5404
Neal Sturrock, *Owner*
**EMP:** 58
**SQ FT:** 5,000
**SALES (corp-wide):** 86.39B **Publicly Held**
Web: www.pepsico.com
**SIC: 2086** 5149 Carbonated soft drinks, bottled and canned; Groceries and related products, nec
**HQ:** Pepsi-Cola Metropolitan Bottling Company, Inc.
700 Anderson Hill Rd
Purchase NY 10577
914 767-6000

### (P-1918)
### PEPSI-COLA METRO BTLG CO INC
Also Called: Pepsico
10057 Marathon Pkwy, Lakeside (92040-2771)
PHONE.....................858 560-6735
Art Brennan, *Brnch Mgr*
**EMP:** 103
**SALES (corp-wide):** 86.39B **Publicly Held**
Web: www.pepsico.com
**SIC: 2086** Carbonated soft drinks, bottled and canned
**HQ:** Pepsi-Cola Metropolitan Bottling Company, Inc.
700 Anderson Hill Rd
Purchase NY 10577
914 767-6000

### (P-1919)
### PEPSI-COLA METRO BTLG CO INC
Also Called: Pepsi-Cola
1200 Arroyo St, San Fernando (91340-1545)
PHONE.....................818 898-3829
Bob Simpson, *Brnch Mgr*
**EMP:** 59
**SALES (corp-wide):** 86.39B **Publicly Held**
Web: www.pepsico.com
**SIC: 2086** Carbonated soft drinks, bottled and canned
**HQ:** Pepsi-Cola Metropolitan Bottling Company, Inc.
700 Anderson Hill Rd
Purchase NY 10577
914 767-6000

### (P-1920)
### PEPSI-COLA METRO BTLG CO INC
Also Called: Pepsi-Cola
29000 Hesperian Blvd, Hayward (94545-5014)
PHONE.....................510 781-3600
**TOLL FREE:** 877
Greg Knabe, *Mgr*
**EMP:** 246
**SALES (corp-wide):** 86.39B **Publicly Held**
Web: www.pepsico.com
**SIC: 2086** Carbonated soft drinks, bottled and canned
**HQ:** Pepsi-Cola Metropolitan Bottling Company, Inc.
700 Anderson Hill Rd
Purchase NY 10577
914 767-6000

### (P-1921)
### PEPSI-COLA METRO BTLG CO INC
Also Called: Pepsico
27717 Aliso Creek Rd, Aliso Viejo (92656-3804)
PHONE.....................949 643-5700
Natolie Daniel, *Mgr*
**EMP:** 92
**SALES (corp-wide):** 86.39B **Publicly Held**
Web: www.pepsico.com
**SIC: 2086** Carbonated soft drinks, bottled and canned
**HQ:** Pepsi-Cola Metropolitan Bottling Company, Inc.
700 Anderson Hill Rd
Purchase NY 10577
914 767-6000

### (P-1922)
### PEPSI-COLA METRO BTLG CO INC
Also Called: Pepsi-Cola
7550 Reese Rd, Sacramento (95828-3707)
PHONE.....................916 423-1000
Randy Kieser, *Mgr*
**EMP:** 130
**SALES (corp-wide):** 86.39B **Publicly Held**
Web: www.pepsico.com
**SIC: 2086** 5962 Soft drinks: packaged in cans, bottles, etc.; Merchandising machine operators
**HQ:** Pepsi-Cola Metropolitan Bottling Company, Inc.
700 Anderson Hill Rd
Purchase NY 10577
914 767-6000

### (P-1923)
### PEPSICO
1650 E Central Ave, San Bernardino (92408-2611)
PHONE.....................562 818-9429
**EMP:** 28 **EST:** 2015
**SALES (est):** 1.08MM **Privately Held**
Web: www.pepsico.com
**SIC: 2086** Carbonated soft drinks, bottled and canned

### (P-1924)
### PEPSICO INC
Also Called: Pepsico
8530 Wilshire Blvd Ste 300, Beverly Hills (90211-3122)
PHONE.....................323 785-2820
Taylor Liptak, *Mktg Mgr*
**EMP:** 18
**SALES (corp-wide):** 86.39B **Publicly Held**
Web: www.pepsico.com
**SIC: 2086** Carbonated soft drinks, bottled and canned
**PA:** Pepsico, Inc.
700 Anderson Hill Rd
914 253-2000

### (P-1925)
### PEPSICO INC
Also Called: Pepsico
4416 Azusa Canyon Rd, Baldwin Park (91706-2740)
PHONE.....................626 338-5531
Kip Zaughan, *Mgr*
**EMP:** 23
**SALES (corp-wide):** 86.39B **Publicly Held**
Web: www.pepsico.com
**SIC: 2086** Carbonated soft drinks, bottled and canned
**PA:** Pepsico, Inc.
700 Anderson Hill Rd
914 253-2000

### (P-1926)
### PEPSICO INC
Also Called: Pepsico
20445 Business Pkwy, Walnut (91789-2939)
PHONE.....................909 718-8229
**EMP:** 21 **EST:** 2015
**SALES (est):** 227.48K **Privately Held**
Web: www.pepsico.com
**SIC: 2086** Carbonated soft drinks, bottled and canned

### (P-1927)
### PURE-FLO WATER CO (PA)
Also Called: Pure Flo Water
2169 Orange Ave, Escondido (92029-4302)
P.O. Box 660579 (75266-0579)
PHONE.....................619 596-4130
Braian Grant, *CEO*
Marian Grant, *
**EMP:** 75 **EST:** 1969
**SALES (est):** 5.47MM
**SALES (corp-wide):** 5.47MM **Privately Held**
Web: www.water.com
**SIC: 2086** Water, natural: packaged in cans, bottles, etc.

### (P-1928)
### RED BULL MEDIA HSE N AMER INC
1630 Stewart St Ste A, Santa Monica (90404-4020)
PHONE.....................310 393-4647
Jennifer Barney, *Brnch Mgr*
**EMP:** 54
**SALES (corp-wide):** 11.47B **Privately Held**
**SIC: 2086** Carbonated beverages, nonalcoholic: pkged. in cans, bottles
**HQ:** Red Bull Media House North America, Inc.
1740 Stewart St
Santa Monica CA 90404
310 393-4647

### (P-1929)
### REFRESCO BEVERAGES US INC
631 S Waterman Ave, San Bernardino (92408-2329)
PHONE.....................909 915-1400
Armando Martinez, *Brnch Mgr*
**EMP:** 26
Web: www.refresco-na.com
**SIC: 2086** Carbonated beverages, nonalcoholic: pkged. in cans, bottles
**HQ:** Refresco Beverages Us Inc.
8112 Woodland Ctr Blvd
Tampa FL 33614

### (P-1930)
### REFRESCO BEVERAGES US INC
Also Called: San Bernardino Canning Co.
499 E Mill St, San Bernardino (92408-1523)
PHONE.....................909 915-1430
Ed Williams, *Mgr*
**EMP:** 35
**SQ FT:** 76,180
Web: www.refresco-na.com
**SIC: 2086** 5149 Carbonated beverages, nonalcoholic: pkged. in cans, bottles; Soft drinks
**HQ:** Refresco Beverages Us Inc.
8112 Woodland Ctr Blvd
Tampa FL 33614

### (P-1931)
### REFRESCO BEVERAGES US INC
1455 Research Dr Unit A, Redlands (92374-4584)
PHONE.....................909 915-1432
**EMP:** 17
Web: www.refresco-na.com
**SIC: 2086** Bottled and canned soft drinks
**HQ:** Refresco Beverages Us Inc.
8112 Woodland Ctr Blvd
Tampa FL 33614

### (P-1932)
### REYES COCA-COLA BOTTLING LLC (PA)
Also Called: Coca-Cola
3 Park Plz Ste 600, Irvine (92614-2575)
PHONE.....................213 744-8616
James Quincy, *CEO*
Nehal Desai, *
◆ **EMP:** 300 **EST:** 1902
**SQ FT:** 80,000
**SALES (est):** 850.14MM
**SALES (corp-wide):** 850.14MM **Privately Held**
Web: www.reyescocacola.com
**SIC: 2086** Bottled and canned soft drinks

### (P-1933)
### REYES COCA-COLA BOTTLING LLC
4320 Ride St, Bakersfield (93313-4831)
PHONE.....................661 324-6531
Ed Shell, *Mgr*
**EMP:** 75
**SALES (corp-wide):** 850.14MM **Privately Held**
Web: www.reyescocacola.com
**SIC: 2086** Bottled and canned soft drinks
**PA:** Reyes Coca-Cola Bottling, L.L.C.
3 Park Plz Ste 600
213 744-8616

### (P-1934)
### REYES COCA-COLA BOTTLING LLC
Also Called: Coca-Cola
1555 Old Bayshore Hwy, San Jose (95112-4303)
PHONE.....................408 436-3700
Larry Loeffer, *Mgr*
**EMP:** 102
**SALES (corp-wide):** 850.14MM **Privately Held**
Web: www.reyescocacola.com
**SIC: 2086** Bottled and canned soft drinks
**PA:** Reyes Coca-Cola Bottling, L.L.C.
3 Park Plz Ste 600
213 744-8616

### (P-1935)
### REYES COCA-COLA BOTTLING LLC
Also Called: Coca-Cola
8729 Cleta St, Downey (90241-5202)
PHONE.....................562 803-8100
Kim Curtis, *Mgr*
**EMP:** 90
**SQ FT:** 76,395
**SALES (corp-wide):** 850.14MM **Privately Held**
Web: www.coca-cola.com
**SIC: 2086** 5149 Bottled and canned soft drinks; Groceries and related products, nec
**PA:** Reyes Coca-Cola Bottling, L.L.C.
3 Park Plz Ste 600
213 744-8616

### (P-1936)
### REYES COCA-COLA BOTTLING LLC
Also Called: Coca-Cola
14655 Wicks Blvd, San Leandro (94577-6715)
PHONE.....................510 667-6300
Ron King, *Brnch Mgr*
**EMP:** 110
**SALES (corp-wide):** 850.14MM **Privately Held**
Web: www.reyescocacola.com

## 2086 - Bottled And Canned Soft Drinks (P-1937)

SIC: 2086 2087 2037 2095 Bottled and canned soft drinks; Syrups, drink; Fruit juice concentrates, frozen; Roasted coffee
PA: Reyes Coca-Cola Bottling, L.L.C.
3 Park Plz Ste 600
213 744-8616

**(P-1937)**
**REYES COCA-COLA BOTTLING LLC**
Also Called: Coca-Cola
3220 E Malaga Ave, Fresno (93725-9353)
PHONE..................559 264-4631
Mike Lozier, Brnch Mgr
EMP: 76
SQ FT: 62,365
SALES (corp-wide): 850.14MM **Privately Held**
Web: www.reyescocacola.com
SIC: 2086 Bottled and canned soft drinks
PA: Reyes Coca-Cola Bottling, L.L.C.
3 Park Plz Ste 600
213 744-8616

**(P-1938)**
**REYES COCA-COLA BOTTLING LLC**
Also Called: Coca-Cola
5335 Walker St, Ventura (93003-7406)
PHONE..................805 644-2211
Jim Donelson, Mgr
EMP: 34
SALES (corp-wide): 850.14MM **Privately Held**
Web: www.reyescocacola.com
SIC: 2086 5149 Bottled and canned soft drinks; Groceries and related products, nec
PA: Reyes Coca-Cola Bottling, L.L.C.
3 Park Plz Ste 600
213 744-8616

**(P-1939)**
**REYES COCA-COLA BOTTLING LLC**
Also Called: Coca-Cola
4101 Gateway Park Blvd, Sacramento (95834-1951)
PHONE..................209 466-9501
Clay Frenzel, Mgr
EMP: 69
SALES (corp-wide): 850.14MM **Privately Held**
Web: www.reyescocacola.com
SIC: 2086 Bottled and canned soft drinks
PA: Reyes Coca-Cola Bottling, L.L.C.
3 Park Plz Ste 600
213 744-8616

**(P-1940)**
**REYES COCA-COLA BOTTLING LLC**
Also Called: Coca-Cola
86375 Industrial Way, Coachella (92236-2729)
PHONE..................760 396-4500
Andrell Gritley, Genl Mgr
EMP: 69
SALES (corp-wide): 850.14MM **Privately Held**
Web: www.reyescocacola.com
SIC: 2086 Bottled and canned soft drinks
PA: Reyes Coca-Cola Bottling, L.L.C.
3 Park Plz Ste 600
213 744-8616

**(P-1941)**
**REYES COCA-COLA BOTTLING LLC**
Also Called: Coca-Cola
120 E Jones St, Santa Maria (93454-5101)
PHONE..................805 925-2629
Dan Suchecki, Mgr
EMP: 21
SQ FT: 50
SALES (corp-wide): 850.14MM **Privately Held**
Web: www.reyescocacola.com
SIC: 2086 Bottled and canned soft drinks
PA: Reyes Coca-Cola Bottling, L.L.C.
3 Park Plz Ste 600
213 744-8616

**(P-1942)**
**REYES COCA-COLA BOTTLING LLC**
Also Called: Coca-Cola
715 Vandenberg St, Salinas (93905-3355)
P.O. Box 3978 (93912-3978)
PHONE..................831 755-8300
Bill Neighbors, Brnch Mgr
EMP: 76
SALES (corp-wide): 850.14MM **Privately Held**
Web: www.reyescocacola.com
SIC: 2086 Bottled and canned soft drinks
PA: Reyes Coca-Cola Bottling, L.L.C.
3 Park Plz Ste 600
213 744-8616

**(P-1943)**
**REYES COCA-COLA BOTTLING LLC**
Also Called: Coca-Cola
11900 Cabernet Dr, Fontana (92337-7707)
PHONE..................909 980-3121
Sid Campa, Mgr
EMP: 179
SALES (corp-wide): 850.14MM **Privately Held**
Web: www.reyescocacola.com
SIC: 2086 5149 Bottled and canned soft drinks; Groceries and related products, nec
PA: Reyes Coca-Cola Bottling, L.L.C.
3 Park Plz Ste 600
213 744-8616

**(P-1944)**
**REYES COCA-COLA BOTTLING LLC**
Also Called: Coca-Cola
1000 Fairway Dr, Santa Maria (93455-1512)
PHONE..................805 614-3702
Dan Suchecki, Mgr
EMP: 28
SALES (corp-wide): 850.14MM **Privately Held**
Web: www.reyescocacola.com
SIC: 2086 Bottled and canned soft drinks
PA: Reyes Coca-Cola Bottling, L.L.C.
3 Park Plz Ste 600
213 744-8616

**(P-1945)**
**REYES COCA-COLA BOTTLING LLC**
Also Called: Coca-Cola
971 E North Ave, Fresno (93725-1931)
PHONE..................559 264-4631
EMP: 28
SALES (corp-wide): 850.14MM **Privately Held**
Web: www.reyescocacola.com
SIC: 2086 Bottled and canned soft drinks
PA: Reyes Coca-Cola Bottling, L.L.C.
3 Park Plz Ste 600
213 744-8616

**(P-1946)**
**REYES COCA-COLA BOTTLING LLC**
Also Called: Coca-Cola
1580 Beltline Rd, Redding (96003-1408)
PHONE..................530 241-4315
David Hallagan, Mgr
EMP: 62
SQ FT: 75,000
SALES (corp-wide): 850.14MM **Privately Held**
Web: www.reyescocacola.com
SIC: 2086 Bottled and canned soft drinks
PA: Reyes Coca-Cola Bottling, L.L.C.
3 Park Plz Ste 600
213 744-8616

**(P-1947)**
**REYES COCA-COLA BOTTLING LLC**
Also Called: Coca-Cola
5255 Federal Blvd, San Diego (92105-5710)
PHONE..................619 266-6300
Randy Cleveland, Mgr
EMP: 372
SALES (corp-wide): 850.14MM **Privately Held**
Web: www.reyescocacola.com
SIC: 2086 5149 Bottled and canned soft drinks; Groceries and related products, nec
PA: Reyes Coca-Cola Bottling, L.L.C.
3 Park Plz Ste 600
213 744-8616

**(P-1948)**
**REYES COCA-COLA BOTTLING LLC**
Also Called: Coca-Cola
666 Union St, Montebello (90640-6624)
PHONE..................323 278-2600
Gary Drees, Mgr
EMP: 221
SQ FT: 127,556
SALES (corp-wide): 850.14MM **Privately Held**
Web: www.reyescocacola.com
SIC: 2086 Bottled and canned soft drinks
PA: Reyes Coca-Cola Bottling, L.L.C.
3 Park Plz Ste 600
213 744-8616

**(P-1949)**
**REYES COCA-COLA BOTTLING LLC**
Also Called: Coca-Cola
1430 Melody Rd, Marysville (95901)
PHONE..................530 743-6533
Tom Quilty, Mgr
EMP: 34
SALES (corp-wide): 850.14MM **Privately Held**
Web: www.reyescocacola.com
SIC: 2086 Bottled and canned soft drinks
PA: Reyes Coca-Cola Bottling, L.L.C.
3 Park Plz Ste 600
213 744-8616

**(P-1950)**
**REYES COCA-COLA BOTTLING LLC**
Also Called: Coca-Cola
700 W Grove Ave, Orange (92865-3214)
PHONE..................714 974-1901
Thomas Murphy, Brnch Mgr
EMP: 69
SQ FT: 7,043
SALES (corp-wide): 850.14MM **Privately Held**
Web: www.reyescocacola.com
SIC: 2086 Bottled and canned soft drinks
PA: Reyes Coca-Cola Bottling, L.L.C.
3 Park Plz Ste 600
213 744-8616

**(P-1951)**
**REYES COCA-COLA BOTTLING LLC**
Also Called: Coca-Cola
530 Getty Ct, Benicia (94510-1139)
PHONE..................707 747-2000
TOLL FREE: 800
Gerold Henderickson, Mgr
EMP: 34
SALES (corp-wide): 850.14MM **Privately Held**
Web: www.reyescocacola.com
SIC: 2086 Bottled and canned soft drinks
PA: Reyes Coca-Cola Bottling, L.L.C.
3 Park Plz Ste 600
213 744-8616

**(P-1952)**
**REYES COCA-COLA BOTTLING LLC**
Also Called: Coca-Cola
1338 E 14th St, Los Angeles (90021-2344)
PHONE..................213 744-8659
Perry Fitch, Genl Mgr
EMP: 28
SALES (corp-wide): 850.14MM **Privately Held**
Web: www.reyescocacola.com
SIC: 2086 Bottled and canned soft drinks
PA: Reyes Coca-Cola Bottling, L.L.C.
3 Park Plz Ste 600
213 744-8616

**(P-1953)**
**REYES COCA-COLA BOTTLING LLC**
Also Called: Coca-Cola
2633 Camino Ramon Ste 300, San Ramon (94583-2570)
PHONE..................925 830-6500
Jim Hegenbart, Mgr
EMP: 110
SALES (corp-wide): 850.14MM **Privately Held**
Web: www.reyescocacola.com
SIC: 2086 Bottled and canned soft drinks
PA: Reyes Coca-Cola Bottling, L.L.C.
3 Park Plz Ste 600
213 744-8616

**(P-1954)**
**REYES COCA-COLA BOTTLING LLC**
Also Called: Coca-Cola
17220 Nutro Way, Victorville (92395-7714)
PHONE..................760 241-2653
Rose Wols, Mgr
EMP: 28
SALES (corp-wide): 850.14MM **Privately Held**
Web: www.reyescocacola.com
SIC: 2086 Bottled and canned soft drinks
PA: Reyes Coca-Cola Bottling, L.L.C.
3 Park Plz Ste 600
213 744-8616

**(P-1955)**
**REYES COCA-COLA BOTTLING LLC**
Also Called: Coca-Cola
126 S 3rd St, El Centro (92243-2542)
PHONE..................760 352-1561
Jose Chaira, Mgr
EMP: 21
SALES (corp-wide): 850.14MM **Privately Held**

## PRODUCTS & SERVICES SECTION — 2086 - Bottled And Canned Soft Drinks (P-1975)

Web: www.reyescocacola.com
SIC: **2086** Bottled and canned soft drinks
PA: Reyes Coca-Cola Bottling, L.L.C.
3 Park Plz Ste 600
213 744-8616

**(P-1956)**
**ROGER ENRICO**
Also Called: Pepsi-Cola
1150 E North Ave, Fresno  (93725-1929)
PHONE...............................559 485-5050
Eric Foss, *CEO*
Robert King, *Pr*
Craig Weatherup, *Ch Bd*
**EMP:** 39 **EST:** 1900
**SQ FT:** 250,000
**SALES (est):** 6.02MM **Privately Held**
Web: www.pepsico.com
SIC: **2086** Soft drinks: packaged in cans, bottles, etc.

**(P-1957)**
**SACRAMENTO COCA-COLA BTLG INC (HQ)**
Also Called: Coca-Cola
4101 Gateway Park Blvd, Sacramento  (95834-1951)
PHONE...............................916 928-2300
Steven A Cahillane, *CEO*
David Etheridge, *
**EMP:** 365 **EST:** 1927
**SQ FT:** 260,000
**SALES (est):** 17.33MM
**SALES (corp-wide):** 850.14MM **Privately Held**
Web: previewsaccoke.weebly.com
SIC: **2086** Bottled and canned soft drinks
PA: Reyes Coca-Cola Bottling, L.L.C.
3 Park Plz Ste 600
213 744-8616

**(P-1958)**
**SACRAMENTO COCA-COLA BTLG INC**
Also Called: Coca-Cola
1733 Morgan Rd Ste 200, Modesto  (95358-5841)
PHONE...............................209 541-3200
Rex Mcgowen, *Prin*
**EMP:** 78
**SALES (corp-wide):** 850.14MM **Privately Held**
Web: previewsaccoke.weebly.com
SIC: **2086** Bottled and canned soft drinks
HQ: Sacramento Coca-Cola Bottling Co., Inc.
4101 Gateway Park Blvd
Sacramento CA 95834
916 928-2300

**(P-1959)**
**SBM DAIRIES INC**
Also Called: Heartland Farms
17851 Railroad St, City Of Industry  (91748-1118)
PHONE...............................626 923-3000
▼ **EMP:** 300
Web: www.gcd.com
SIC: **2086** 2026 2033 Fruit drinks (less than 100% juice): packaged in cans, etc.; Fluid milk; Canned fruits and specialties

**(P-1960)**
**SEVEN UP BTLG CO SAN FRANCISCO (HQ)**
Also Called: Seven-Up Bottling
2875 Prune Ave, Fremont  (94539-6731)
PHONE...............................925 938-8777
Roger Easley, *Ch Bd*

Linda Orsi, *
**EMP:** 175 **EST:** 1935
**SALES (est):** 16.47MM **Publicly Held**
Web: www.7up.com
SIC: **2086** 5149 4225 Soft drinks: packaged in cans, bottles, etc.; Groceries and related products, nec; General warehousing and storage
PA: Keurig Dr Pepper Inc.
53 South Ave

**(P-1961)**
**SEVEN UP BTLG CO SAN FRANCISCO**
Also Called: Seven-Up Bottling
11205 Commercial Pkwy, Castroville  (95012-3205)
PHONE...............................831 632-0777
Frank Reyes, *Genl Mgr*
**EMP:** 145
Web: www.7up.com
SIC: **2086** Soft drinks: packaged in cans, bottles, etc.
HQ: Seven Up Bottling Company Of San Francisco
2875 Prune Ave
Fremont CA 94539
925 938-8777

**(P-1962)**
**SEVEN UP BTLG CO SAN FRANCISCO**
Also Called: Seven-Up Bottling
2670 Land Ave, Sacramento  (95815-2380)
P.O. Box 15820  (95852-0820)
PHONE...............................916 929-7777
Tom Tontes, *Mgr*
**EMP:** 199
Web: www.drpepper.com
SIC: **2086** 5078 Soft drinks: packaged in cans, bottles, etc.; Refrigerated beverage dispensers
HQ: Seven Up Bottling Company Of San Francisco
2875 Prune Ave
Fremont CA 94539
925 938-8777

**(P-1963)**
**SHASTA BEVERAGES  INC (DH)**
Also Called: National Bevpak
26901 Indl Blvd, Hayward  (94545)
PHONE...............................954 581-0922
Joseph G Caporella, *CEO*
Nick Caporella, *
John Minton, *
Dean Mccoy, *VP*
◆ **EMP:** 80 **EST:** 1889
**SQ FT:** 156,000
**SALES (est):** 92.86MM
**SALES (corp-wide):** 1.19B **Publicly Held**
Web: www.shastapop.com
SIC: **2086** Soft drinks: packaged in cans, bottles, etc.
HQ: Newbevco, Inc.
8100 Sw 10th St
Plantation FL 33324

**(P-1964)**
**SHASTA BEVERAGES  INC**
14405 Artesia Blvd, La Mirada  (90638-5886)
PHONE...............................714 523-2280
Bruce Mcdowell, *Mgr*
**EMP:** 66
**SALES (corp-wide):** 1.19B **Publicly Held**
Web: www.shastapop.com
SIC: **2086** 5149 Soft drinks: packaged in cans, bottles, etc.; Soft drinks
HQ: Shasta Beverages, Inc.
26901 Indl Blvd

Hayward CA 94545
954 581-0922

**(P-1965)**
**SMUCKER NATURAL FOODS INC (HQ)**
37 Speedway Ave, Chico  (95928-9554)
PHONE...............................530 899-5000
Richard K Smucker, *CEO*
Julia Sabin, *
Timothy P Smucker, *
Steven Oakland, *Prin*
◆ **EMP:** 130 **EST:** 1971
**SQ FT:** 85,000
**SALES (est):** 300.07MM
**SALES (corp-wide):** 8.18B **Publicly Held**
SIC: **2086** 2033 2087 Iced tea and fruit drinks, bottled and canned; Canned fruits and specialties; Syrups, drink
PA: The J M Smucker Company
1 Strawberry Ln
330 682-3000

**(P-1966)**
**STRATUS GROUP DUO LLC**
4401 S Downey Rd, Vernon  (90058-2518)
PHONE...............................323 581-3663
Dara Killilea, *Managing Member*
**EMP:** 30 **EST:** 2018
**SALES (est):** 833.97K **Privately Held**
SIC: **2086** Bottled and canned soft drinks

**(P-1967)**
**SVC MFG INC A CORP**
Also Called: Pepsi Co
5625 International Blvd, Oakland  (94621-4403)
PHONE...............................510 261-5800
David Chu, *Prin*
▲ **EMP:** 23 **EST:** 2005
**SALES (est):** 4.16MM **Privately Held**
Web: www.pepsico.com
SIC: **2086** Carbonated soft drinks, bottled and canned

**(P-1968)**
**TOGNAZZINI BEVERAGE SERVICE**
Also Called: Coca-Cola
241 Roemer Way, Santa Maria  (93454-1129)
PHONE...............................805 928-1144
**TOLL FREE:** 800
Jim Tognazzini, *Owner*
**EMP:** 16 **EST:** 1965
**SQ FT:** 18,000
**SALES (est):** 5.09MM **Privately Held**
Web: www.togbev.com
SIC: **2086** 7699 Bottled and canned soft drinks; Fountain repair

**(P-1969)**
**TRACTOR BEVERAGE CO**
512 Briarwood Ter, Ventura  (93001-2438)
PHONE...............................909 855-4106
Kristin Carlisle, *Prin*
**EMP:** 20 **EST:** 2019
**SALES (est):** 168.9K **Privately Held**
Web: www.drinktractor.com
SIC: **2086** Iced tea and fruit drinks, bottled and canned

**(P-1970)**
**UNIX PACKAGING  LLC (PA)**
Also Called: Mammoth Water
9 Minson Way, Montebello  (90640)
PHONE...............................213 627-5050
Bobby Melamed, *CEO*
Shawn Arianpour, *

Kourosh Melamed, *
▲ **EMP:** 75 **EST:** 2010
**SQ FT:** 125,000
**SALES (est):** 90.43MM
**SALES (corp-wide):** 90.43MM **Privately Held**
Web: www.unixpackaging.com
SIC: **2086** Pasteurized and mineral waters, bottled and canned

**(P-1971)**
**VARNI BROTHERS CORPORATION**
Also Called: 7 Up
1109 W Anderson St, Stockton  (95206-1158)
PHONE...............................209 464-7778
Larry Varni, *Mgr*
**EMP:** 85
Web: www.7up.com
SIC: **2086** Bottled and canned soft drinks
HQ: Varni Brothers Corporation
400 Hosmer Ave
Modesto CA 95351
209 521-1777

**(P-1972)**
**WATERCO OF CENTRAL STATES INC**
Also Called: Brookcrest By Culligan
1908 D St, Sacramento  (95811)
PHONE...............................916 290-4591
**EMP:** 20
**SALES (corp-wide):** 2.51MM **Privately Held**
SIC: **2086** Water, natural: packaged in cans, bottles, etc.
PA: Waterco Of The Central States, Inc.
1200 Arden Way
408 988-8661

**(P-1973)**
**WISER FOODS INC**
5405 E Village Rd Unit 8219, Long Beach  (90808-7030)
P.O. Box 8219  (90808-0219)
PHONE...............................310 895-0888
Jeri Powers, *CEO*
Jeri Diane Powers, *
**EMP:** 100 **EST:** 2017
**SALES (est):** 890.62K **Privately Held**
Web: www.wiserfoods.global
SIC: **2086** 5169 1541 8742 Bottled and canned soft drinks; Alcohols; Food products manufacturing or packing plant construction; Administrative services consultant

**(P-1974)**
**WIT GROUP**
1822 Buenaventura Blvd Ste 101, Redding  (96001-6313)
PHONE...............................530 243-4447
Paul A Kassis, *Pr*
James Akers, *
▼ **EMP:** 35 **EST:** 2001
**SQ FT:** 1,100
**SALES (est):** 2.88MM **Privately Held**
SIC: **2086** Water, natural: packaged in cans, bottles, etc.

**(P-1975)**
**ZEVIA LLC**
15821 Ventura Blvd Ste 145, Encino  (91436)
PHONE...............................310 202-7000
Padraic Spence, *Managing Member*
**EMP:** 75 **EST:** 2007
**SALES (est):** 110.03MM
**SALES (corp-wide):** 166.42MM **Publicly Held**

# 2086 - Bottled And Canned Soft Drinks (P-1976)

Web: www.zevia.com
SIC: **2086** Bottled and canned soft drinks
PA: Zevia Pbc
  15821 Vntura Blvd Ste 135
  424 343-2654

**(P-1976)**
**ZEVIA PBC (PA)**
Also Called: Zevia
15821 Ventura Blvd Ste 135, Encino (91436-4787)
PHONE.................................424 343-2654
Amy Taylor, *Pr*
Padraic L Spence, *Non-Executive Chairman of the Board*
Girish Satya, *CAO*
Alfred A Guarino, *CCO*
Lorna R Simms, *Corporate Secretary*
**EMP:** 40 **EST:** 2007
**SQ FT:** 20,185
**SALES (est):** 166.42MM
**SALES (corp-wide):** 166.42MM **Publicly Held**
Web: www.zevia.com
SIC: **2086** Bottled and canned soft drinks

**(P-1977)**
**ZICO BEVERAGES LLC (HQ)**
Also Called: Zico
2101 E El Segundo Blvd Ste 403, El Segundo (90245-4518)
P.O. Box 1734 (30301-1734)
PHONE.................................866 729-9426
Ronald J Lewis, *Managing Member*
Marie D Quintero-johnson, *Managing Member*
▲ **EMP:** 20 **EST:** 2009
**SQ FT:** 10,000
**SALES (est):** 3.38MM
**SALES (corp-wide):** 45.75B **Publicly Held**
Web: www.zico.com
SIC: **2086** Bottled and canned soft drinks
PA: The Coca-Cola Company
  1 Coca Cola Plz
  404 676-2121

# 2087 Flavoring Extracts And Syrups, Nec

**(P-1978)**
**AMERICAN FRUITS & FLAVORS LLC (HQ)**
Also Called: Juice Division
10725 Sutter Ave, Pacoima (91331-2553)
P.O. Box 331060 (91333-1060)
PHONE.................................818 899-9574
Jack Haddad, *
◆ **EMP:** 125 **EST:** 1975
**SQ FT:** 10,000
**SALES (est):** 40.37MM
**SALES (corp-wide):** 7.14B **Publicly Held**
Web: www.americanfruits-flavors.com
SIC: **2087** Concentrates, drink
PA: Monster Beverage Corporation
  1 Monster Way
  951 739-6200

**(P-1979)**
**AMERICAN FRUITS & FLAVORS LLC**
1527 Knowles Ave, Los Angeles (90063-1606)
PHONE.................................818 899-9574
Daron Canales, *Mgr*
**EMP:** 25
**SALES (corp-wide):** 7.14B **Publicly Held**
Web: www.americanfruits-flavors.com
SIC: **2087** Concentrates, drink
HQ: American Fruits And Flavors, Llc
  10725 Sutter Ave
  Pacoima CA 91331
  818 899-9574

**(P-1980)**
**AMERICAN FRUITS & FLAVORS LLC**
1565 Knowles Ave, Los Angeles (90063-1606)
PHONE.................................818 899-9574
Daron Canales, *Mgr*
**EMP:** 25
**SALES (corp-wide):** 7.14B **Publicly Held**
Web: www.americanfruits-flavors.com
SIC: **2087** Concentrates, drink
HQ: American Fruits And Flavors, Llc
  10725 Sutter Ave
  Pacoima CA 91331
  818 899-9574

**(P-1981)**
**AMERICAN FRUITS & FLAVORS LLC**
400 S Central Ave, Los Angeles (90013-1712)
PHONE.................................213 624-1831
Terry Miller, *Mgr*
**EMP:** 64
**SALES (corp-wide):** 7.14B **Publicly Held**
Web: www.americanfruits-flavors.com
SIC: **2087** Concentrates, drink
HQ: American Fruits And Flavors, Llc
  10725 Sutter Ave
  Pacoima CA 91331
  818 899-9574

**(P-1982)**
**AMERICAN FRUITS & FLAVORS LLC**
Also Called: Ability
22560 Lucerne St, Carson (90745-4303)
PHONE.................................310 522-1844
Ricardo Velasquez, *Mgr*
**EMP:** 55
**SALES (corp-wide):** 7.14B **Publicly Held**
Web: www.americanfruits-flavors.com
SIC: **2087** Concentrates, drink
HQ: American Fruits And Flavors, Llc
  10725 Sutter Ave
  Pacoima CA 91331
  818 899-9574

**(P-1983)**
**AMERICAN FRUITS & FLAVORS LLC**
Also Called: Lineage
3001 Sierra Pine Ave, Vernon (90058-4120)
PHONE.................................323 881-8321
Julio Tovar, *Mgr*
**EMP:** 47
**SALES (corp-wide):** 7.14B **Publicly Held**
Web: www.americanfruits-flavors.com
SIC: **2087** Concentrates, drink
HQ: American Fruits And Flavors, Llc
  10725 Sutter Ave
  Pacoima CA 91331
  818 899-9574

**(P-1984)**
**AMERICAN FRUITS & FLAVORS LLC**
Also Called: Weber
9345 Santa Anita Ave, Rancho Cucamonga (91730-6126)
PHONE.................................909 291-2620
Brian Martin, *Mgr*
**EMP:** 48
**SALES (corp-wide):** 7.14B **Publicly Held**
Web: www.americanfruits-flavors.com
SIC: **2087** Concentrates, drink
HQ: American Fruits And Flavors, Llc
  10725 Sutter Ave
  Pacoima CA 91331
  818 899-9574

**(P-1985)**
**AMERICAN FRUITS & FLAVORS LLC**
13530 Rosecrans Ave, Santa Fe Springs (90670-5023)
PHONE.................................562 320-2802
Michael Mallette, *Mgr*
**EMP:** 34
**SALES (corp-wide):** 7.14B **Publicly Held**
Web: www.americanfruits-flavors.com
SIC: **2087** Concentrates, drink
HQ: American Fruits And Flavors, Llc
  10725 Sutter Ave
  Pacoima CA 91331
  818 899-9574

**(P-1986)**
**BERRI PRO INC**
840 Apollo St Ste 100, El Segundo (90245-4641)
PHONE.................................781 929-8288
Jerome Joseph Tse, *CEO*
**EMP:** 19 **EST:** 2015
**SALES (est):** 2.25MM **Privately Held**
Web: www.berriorganics.com
SIC: **2087** Concentrates, drink

**(P-1987)**
**BETTER BEVERAGES INC (PA)**
Also Called: Chem-Mark of Orange County
10624 Midway Ave, Cerritos (90703-1581)
P.O. Box 1399 (90707-1399)
PHONE.................................562 924-8321
H Ronald Harris, *CEO*
Tricia Harris, *
William Kendig, *General Vice President**
Patrick Dickson, *
▲ **EMP:** 40 **EST:** 1946
**SQ FT:** 15,000
**SALES (est):** 8.26MM
**SALES (corp-wide):** 8.26MM **Privately Held**
Web: www.betbev.com
SIC: **2087** 7359 5169 Beverage bases; Equipment rental and leasing, nec; Industrial gases

**(P-1988)**
**BI NUTRACEUTICALS INC**
2384 E Pacifica Pl, Rancho Dominguez (90220-6214)
PHONE.................................310 669-2100
◆ **EMP:** 120
Web: www.botanicals.com
SIC: **2087** 2833 5122 5149 Flavoring extracts and syrups, nec; Medicinals and botanicals; Vitamins and minerals; Seasonings, sauces, and extracts

**(P-1989)**
**BLOSSOM VALLEY FOODS INC**
Also Called: Pepper Plant, The
20 Casey Ln, Gilroy (95020-4539)
PHONE.................................408 848-5520
Robert M Wagner, *Pr*
**EMP:** 25 **EST:** 1933
**SQ FT:** 27,000
**SALES (est):** 3.98MM **Privately Held**
Web: www.blossomvalleyfoods.com
SIC: **2087** 2099 Cocktail mixes, nonalcoholic ; Food preparations, nec

**(P-1990)**
**BLUE PACIFIC FLAVORS INC**
1354 Marion Ct, City Of Industry (91745-2418)
PHONE.................................626 934-0099
Donald F Wilkes, *Pr*
▲ **EMP:** 35 **EST:** 1993
**SQ FT:** 40,000
**SALES (est):** 9.05MM **Privately Held**
Web: www.bluepacificflavors.com
SIC: **2087** 2869 Extracts, flavoring; Perfumes, flavorings, and food additives

**(P-1991)**
**BYRNES & KIEFER CO**
501 Airpark Dr, Fullerton (92833-2501)
PHONE.................................714 554-4000
**EMP:** 55 **EST:** 2012
**SALES (est):** 2.47MM **Privately Held**
Web: www.bkcompany.com
SIC: **2087** Colorings, confectioners'

**(P-1992)**
**CALIFRNIA CSTM FRITS FLVORS LL (PA)**
Also Called: California Cstm Frt & Flavors
15800 Tapia St, Irwindale (91706-2178)
PHONE.................................626 736-4130
Mike Mulhausen, *Pr*
◆ **EMP:** 35 **EST:** 1984
**SALES (est):** 27.98MM
**SALES (corp-wide):** 27.98MM **Privately Held**
Web: www.ccff.com
SIC: **2087** 2033 2099 5083 Extracts, flavoring ; Fruits: packaged in cans, jars, etc.; Food preparations, nec; Dairy machinery and equipment

**(P-1993)**
**CARMI FLVR & FRAGRANCE CO INC (PA)**
Also Called: Carmi Flavors
6030 Scott Way, Commerce (90040-3516)
PHONE.................................323 888-9240
Eliot Carmi, *Pr*
▲ **EMP:** 40 **EST:** 1980
**SQ FT:** 35,000
**SALES (est):** 19.68MM
**SALES (corp-wide):** 19.68MM **Privately Held**
Web: www.carmiflavors.com
SIC: **2087** 2844 Extracts, flavoring; Perfumes, cosmetics and other toilet preparations

**(P-1994)**
**COMMON COLLABS LLC (PA)**
Also Called: Hangar 1
1820 E Walnut Ave, Fullerton (92831-4844)
PHONE.................................714 519-3245
Freddy Lopez, *Managing Member*
**EMP:** 17 **EST:** 2019
**SALES (est):** 2.12MM
**SALES (corp-wide):** 2.12MM **Privately Held**
Web: www.commoncollabs.com
SIC: **2087** Beverage bases

**(P-1995)**
**CUSTOM INGREDIENTS INC (PA)**
Also Called: Custom Flavors
160 Calle Iglesia Ste 102, San Clemente (92672-7551)
PHONE.................................949 276-7995
Michael L Wendling, *CEO*
Steven Bishop, *CFO*
Alexander Wendling, *Pr*
**EMP:** 24 **EST:** 2000

## 2087 - Flavoring Extracts And Syrups, Nec (P-2016)

SALES (est): 21.22MM **Privately Held**
**Web:** www.customflavors.com
**SIC: 2087** Beverage bases, concentrates, syrups, powders and mixes

**(P-1996)**
**DE LA CALLE CO (PA)**
5701 W Adams Blvd, Los Angeles (90016-2401)
**PHONE**.................650 465-0093
Alex Matthews, *CEO*
Erin Kelley, *VP*
**EMP:** 16 **EST:** 2019
**SALES (est):** 2.13MM
**SALES (corp-wide):** 2.13MM **Privately Held**
**Web:** www.delacalle.mx
**SIC: 2087** Beverage bases

**(P-1997)**
**DELANO GROWERS GRAPE PRODUCTS**
32351 Bassett Ave, Delano (93215-9699)
**PHONE**.................661 725-3255
Jim Cesare, *Pr*
▲ **EMP:** 55 **EST:** 1940
**SQ FT:** 40,000
**SALES (est):** 8.82MM **Privately Held**
**Web:** www.delanogrowersgrapeproducts.com
**SIC: 2087** Concentrates, drink

**(P-1998)**
**DISTRIBUTORS PROCESSING INC**
Also Called: D P I
17656 Avenue 168, Porterville (93257-9263)
**PHONE**.................559 781-0297
Randy Walker, *Pr*
Gary Jacinto, *Ch Bd*
William Blatnick, *Sec*
▼ **EMP:** 17 **EST:** 1965
**SQ FT:** 23,050
**SALES (est):** 3.96MM **Privately Held**
**Web:** www.impactmb-compost.com
**SIC: 2087** Extracts, flavoring

**(P-1999)**
**DR SMOOTHIE BRANDS LLC**
Also Called: Sunny Sky Products
1730 Raymer Ave, Fullerton (92833-2530)
**PHONE**.................714 449-9787
Sam Lteif, *CEO*
▼ **EMP:** 25 **EST:** 2006
**SQ FT:** 30,000
**SALES (est):** 2.53MM
**SALES (corp-wide):** 42.45MM **Privately Held**
**Web:** www.drsmoothie.com
**SIC: 2087** Beverage bases, concentrates, syrups, powders and mixes
**PA:** Juice Tyme, Inc.
4401 S Oakley Ave
773 579-1291

**(P-2000)**
**DR SMOOTHIE ENTERPRISES LLC**
Also Called: Sunny Sky Products
1730 Raymer Ave, Fullerton (92833-2530)
**PHONE**.................714 449-9787
Bill Haugh, *Pr*
William P Haugh, *Prin*
▼ **EMP:** 21 **EST:** 1998
**SQ FT:** 30,000
**SALES (est):** 168K
**SALES (corp-wide):** 168.71MM **Privately Held**
**Web:** www.drsmoothie.com

**SIC: 2087** Beverage bases, concentrates, syrups, powders and mixes
**HQ:** Lx/Jt Intermediate Holdings, Inc.
4401 S Oakley Ave
Chicago IL 60609
773 579-1291

**(P-2001)**
**DRYWATER INC**
3901 Westerly Pl Ste 111, Newport Beach (92660-2306)
**PHONE**.................844 434-0829
Bryan Appio, *CEO*
**EMP:** 25 **EST:** 2021
**SALES (est):** 2.49MM **Privately Held**
**Web:** www.drywater.com
**SIC: 2087** Beverage bases

**(P-2002)**
**FELBRO FOOD PRODUCTS INC**
Also Called: Felbro
5700 W Adams Blvd, Los Angeles (90016-2402)
**PHONE**.................323 936-5266
**TOLL FREE:** 800
Michael Feldman, *CEO*
Barton J Feldman, *
Barton Feldman, *
**EMP:** 49 **EST:** 1946
**SQ FT:** 35,000
**SALES (est):** 10.89MM **Privately Held**
**Web:** www.felbro.com
**SIC: 2087** Syrups, drink

**(P-2003)**
**FLAVOR FACTORY INC**
2058 2nd St, Norco (92860-2804)
**PHONE**.................951 273-9877
Daniel S Wixted, *Pr*
Mary J Wixted, *Sec*
**EMP:** 15 **EST:** 2005
**SQ FT:** 13,750
**SALES (est):** 2.49MM **Privately Held**
**Web:** www.flavorfactory.net
**SIC: 2087** Concentrates, flavoring (except drink)

**(P-2004)**
**FLAVOR HOUSE INC**
16378 Koala Rd, Adelanto (92301-3916)
**PHONE**.................760 246-9131
Richard Staley, *Owner*
Richard Staley, *Pr*
▲ **EMP:** 45 **EST:** 1977
**SQ FT:** 23,600
**SALES (est):** 7.35MM **Privately Held**
**Web:** www.flavorhouseinc.com
**SIC: 2087** Flavoring extracts and syrups, nec

**(P-2005)**
**FLAVOR INFUSION LLC**
Also Called: Fisa
332 Forest Ave Ste 19, Laguna Beach (92651-2100)
**PHONE**.................949 715-4369
◆ **EMP:** 40
**SIC: 2087** Syrups, drink

**(P-2006)**
**FLAVOR PRODUCERS LLC (PA)**
Also Called: Flavor Producers
8521 Fallbrook Ave Ste 380, West Hills (91304-3239)
**PHONE**.................661 257-3400
**EMP:** 47 **EST:** 1981
**SALES (est):** 57.58MM
**SALES (corp-wide):** 57.58MM **Privately Held**
**Web:** www.flavorproducers.com

**SIC: 2087** Concentrates, flavoring (except drink)

**(P-2007)**
**FROZEN BEAN INC**
9238 Bally Ct, Rancho Cucamonga (91730-5313)
**PHONE**.................855 837-6936
John Bae, *CEO*
▼ **EMP:** 30 **EST:** 2011
**SALES (est):** 5.39MM **Privately Held**
**Web:** www.thefrozenbean.com
**SIC: 2087** Beverage bases, concentrates, syrups, powders and mixes

**(P-2008)**
**GOLDEN STATE FOODS CORP (PA)**
Also Called: Golden State Foods
18301 Von Karman Ave Ste 1100, Irvine (92612-0133)
**PHONE**.................949 247-8000
Brian Dick, *Pr*
Mark Wetterau, *Ch Bd*
John E Page, *
Ed Rodriguez, *Chief Human Resources Officer*
William Sanderson, *
◆ **EMP:** 35 **EST:** 1969
**SALES (est):** 1.5MM
**SALES (corp-wide):** 1.5MM **Privately Held**
**Web:** www.goldenstatefoods.com
**SIC: 2087** 5142 5148 5149 Syrups, drink; Packaged frozen goods; Vegetables; Condiments

**(P-2009)**
**HERBALIFE MANUFACTURING LLC (DH)**
800 W Olympic Blvd Ste 406, Los Angeles (90015)
**PHONE**.................866 866-4744
Richard Caloca, *
◆ **EMP:** 36 **EST:** 2008
**SQ FT:** 145,000
**SALES (est):** 49.5MM **Privately Held**
**Web:** www.herbalife.com
**SIC: 2087** 2023 Beverage bases, concentrates, syrups, powders and mixes; Dietary supplements, dairy and non-dairy based
**HQ:** Herbalife International, Inc.
800 W Olympic Blvd Ste 40
Los Angeles CA 90015
310 410-9600

**(P-2010)**
**J & J PROCESSING INC**
Also Called: Custom Foods
14715 Anson Ave, Santa Fe Springs (90670-5305)
**PHONE**.................562 926-2333
James B Nelson, *CEO*
Paul Nelson, *
▲ **EMP:** 50 **EST:** 1972
**SQ FT:** 44,000
**SALES (est):** 8.65MM **Privately Held**
**Web:** www.custom-foods.com
**SIC: 2087** 2041 2099 Beverage bases; Flour and other grain mill products; Seasonings: dry mixes

**(P-2011)**
**JAVO BEVERAGE COMPANY INC**
1311 Specialty Dr, Vista (92081)
**PHONE**.................760 560-5286
Dennis Riley, *Pr*
Dennis Riley, *Pr*

Gerry Anderson, *CFO*
Chris Johnson, *Ex VP*
▲ **EMP:** 100 **EST:** 2002
**SQ FT:** 39,000
**SALES (est):** 39.27MM
**SALES (corp-wide):** 33.16MM **Privately Held**
**Web:** www.javobeverage.com
**SIC: 2087** Extracts, flavoring
**HQ:** Florida Food Products, Llc
1025 Grnwood Blvd Ste 500
Lake Mary FL 32746
855 337-1633

**(P-2012)**
**KEY ESSENTIALS INC**
Also Called: Agilex Flavors & Fragrances
1916 S Tubeway Ave, Commerce (90040-1612)
▲ **EMP:** 60
**SIC: 2087** Flavoring extracts and syrups, nec

**(P-2013)**
**LA PAZ PRODUCTS INC**
345 Oak Pl, Brea (92821-4122)
P.O. Box 459 (92822-0459)
**PHONE**.................714 990-0982
Suanne Casey, *CEO*
▼ **EMP:** 18 **EST:** 1968
**SQ FT:** 18,000
**SALES (est):** 3.4MM **Privately Held**
**Web:** www.lapazproducts.com
**SIC: 2087** Cocktail mixes, nonalcoholic

**(P-2014)**
**MARTIN BAUER INC**
Also Called: Martin Bauer Inc.
20710 S Alameda St, Long Beach (90810-1107)
**PHONE**.................310 669-2100
Peter Hafermann, *Mgr*
**EMP:** 15
**SALES (corp-wide):** 768.56MM **Privately Held**
**Web:** www.botanicals.com
**SIC: 2087** 2099 Flavoring extracts and syrups, nec; Spices, including grinding
**HQ:** Martin Bauer, Inc.
400 Plaza Dr Ste 303
Secaucus NJ 07094
201 659-3100

**(P-2015)**
**METAROM USA INC**
1725 Gillespie Way Ste 101, El Cajon (92020-1044)
**PHONE**.................619 449-0299
Christophe Dugas, *Pr*
Brandon Brown, *
**EMP:** 46 **EST:** 2016
**SALES (est):** 1.48MM **Privately Held**
**SIC: 2087** Extracts, flavoring

**(P-2016)**
**MISSION FLAVORS FRAGRANCES INC**
25882 Wright, El Toro (92610-3503)
**PHONE**.................949 461-3344
Patrick S Imburgia, *CEO*
**EMP:** 15 **EST:** 1987
**SALES (est):** 4.69MM **Privately Held**
**Web:** www.missionflavors.com
**SIC: 2087** Extracts, flavoring
**HQ:** T. Hasegawa U.S.A. Inc.
14017 E 183rd St
Cerritos CA 90703
714 522-1900

## 2087 - Flavoring Extracts And Syrups, Nec (P-2017)

**(P-2017)**
**NEWPORT FLAVORS & FRAGRANCES**
Also Called: Nature's Flavors
833 N Elm St, Orange (92867-7909)
PHONE..........................714 771-2200
William R Sabo, *CEO*
Jeanne A Rossman, *
▲ **EMP:** 30 **EST:** 1984
**SALES (est):** 3.32MM **Privately Held**
Web: www.newportflavours.com
**SIC: 2087** Extracts, flavoring

**(P-2018)**
**PACIFIC COAST INGREDIENTS (PA)**
Also Called: Perfumer's Apprentice
170 Technology Cir, Scotts Valley (95066-3520)
PHONE..........................831 316-7137
Linda Andrews, *CEO*
**EMP:** 15 **EST:** 2004
**SQ FT:** 50,000
**SALES (est):** 12.74MM
**SALES (corp-wide):** 12.74MM **Privately Held**
Web: shop.perfumersapprentice.com
**SIC: 2087** 5141 8741 Extracts, flavoring; Food brokers; Administrative management

**(P-2019)**
**PACIFIC COAST INGREDIENTS**
Also Called: Perfumer's Apprentice
200 Technology Cir, Scotts Valley (95066-3500)
PHONE..........................831 316-7137
David Hertzberg, *Prod Manager*
**EMP:** 32
**SQ FT:** 26,000
**SALES (corp-wide):** 12.74MM **Privately Held**
Web: shop.perfumersapprentice.com
**SIC: 2087** 2844 Extracts, flavoring; Concentrates, perfume
**PA:** Pacific Coast Ingredients
170 Technology Cir
831 316-7137

**(P-2020)**
**PRINCE KONA FOOD LLC**
2284 Britton Ct, Valley Springs (95252-8597)
PHONE..........................209 430-7814
Joseph T Collette, *Managing Member*
**EMP:** 100 **EST:** 2020
**SALES (est):** 588.4K **Privately Held**
**SIC: 2087** 2035 Flavoring extracts and syrups, nec; Pickles, sauces, and salad dressings

**(P-2021)**
**QUAKER OATS COMPANY**
Also Called: Quaker Oats
5625 International Blvd, Oakland (94621-4403)
PHONE..........................510 261-5800
Joan Parrott Sheffer, *Brnch Mgr*
**EMP:** 214
**SALES (corp-wide):** 86.39B **Publicly Held**
**SIC: 2087** 2086 Beverage bases, concentrates, syrups, powders and mixes; Bottled and canned soft drinks
**HQ:** The Quaker Oats Company
433 W Van Buren St Ste 3n
Chicago IL 60607
312 821-1000

**(P-2022)**
**R TORRE & COMPANY INC (PA)**
Also Called: Torani Syrups & Flavors
2000 Marina Blvd, San Leandro (94577-3208)
PHONE..........................800 775-1925
**TOLL FREE:** 800
Melanie Dulbecco, *CEO*
Lisa Lucheta,
Paul Lucheta, *
◆ **EMP:** 100 **EST:** 1979
**SQ FT:** 110,000
**SALES (est):** 101.91MM
**SALES (corp-wide):** 101.91MM **Privately Held**
Web: www.torani.com
**SIC: 2087** Syrups, drink

**(P-2023)**
**R TORRE & COMPANY INC**
1952 Williams St, San Leandro (94577-2304)
PHONE..........................800 775-1925
Hamid Farzi Qa, *Mgr*
**EMP:** 30
**SALES (corp-wide):** 101.91MM **Privately Held**
Web: www.torani.com
**SIC: 2087** Syrups, drink
**PA:** R. Torre & Company, Inc.
2000 Marina Blvd
800 775-1925

**(P-2024)**
**SCISOREK & SON FLAVORS INC**
Also Called: S&S Flavours
2951 Enterprise St, Brea (92821-6212)
PHONE..........................714 524-0550
Mark Tuerffs, *Pr*
Dan Hart, *
**EMP:** 50 **EST:** 1928
**SQ FT:** 33,000
**SALES (est):** 6.23MM **Privately Held**
Web: www.ssflavors.com
**SIC: 2087** Extracts, flavoring

**(P-2025)**
**SPORTS STREET MARKETING A CALIFORNIA LIMITED PARTNERSHIP**
Also Called: Gu Pure Performing Energy
1609 4th St, Berkeley (94710-1708)
PHONE..........................510 527-4664
**EMP:** 30 **EST:** 1994
**SALES (est):** 5.79MM **Privately Held**
Web: www.guenergy.com
**SIC: 2087** 5149 Powders, drink; Diet foods

**(P-2026)**
**STILL ROOM LLC**
Also Called: Small Hand Foods
2624 Barrington Ct, Hayward (94545-1100)
PHONE..........................510 847-1930
**EMP:** 33 **EST:** 2018
**SALES (est):** 1.84MM **Privately Held**
**SIC: 2087** Beverage bases, concentrates, syrups, powders and mixes

**(P-2027)**
**SUNOPTA FRUIT GROUP INC**
12128 Center St, South Gate (90280-8046)
P.O. Box 2218 (90280-9218)
PHONE..........................323 774-6000
◆ **EMP:** 62
**SIC: 2087** Flavoring extracts and syrups, nec

**(P-2028)**
**T HASEGAWA USA INC**
25882 Wright, Foothill Ranch (92610-3503)
PHONE..........................949 461-3344
**EMP:** 20
**SIC: 2087** Flavoring extracts and syrups, nec
**HQ:** T. Hasegawa U.S.A. Inc.
14017 E 183rd St
Cerritos CA 90703
714 522-1900

**(P-2029)**
**T HASEGAWA USA INC**
8720 Rochester Ave, Rancho Cucamonga (91730-4907)
PHONE..........................714 522-1900
Tom Damiano, *Prin*
**EMP:** 20
Web: www.thasegawa.com
**SIC: 2087** Flavoring extracts and syrups, nec
**HQ:** T. Hasegawa U.S.A. Inc.
14017 E 183rd St
Cerritos CA 90703
714 522-1900

**(P-2030)**
**T HASEGAWA USA INC (HQ)**
14017 183rd St, Cerritos (90703-7000)
PHONE..........................714 522-1900
Tom Damiano, *CEO*
Tokujiro Hasegawa, *
▲ **EMP:** 50 **EST:** 1978
**SQ FT:** 56,000
**SALES (est):** 68.18MM **Privately Held**
Web: www.thasegawa.com
**SIC: 2087** Extracts, flavoring
**PA:** T.Hasegawa Co., Ltd.
4-4-14, Nihombashihoncho

**(P-2031)**
**UNITED BRANDS COMPANY INC**
5930 Cornerstone Ct W Ste 170, San Diego (92121-3772)
PHONE..........................619 461-5220
Michael Michail, *Pr*
Philip W Oneil, *CRO*
**EMP:** 43 **EST:** 2001
**SQ FT:** 1,800
**SALES (est):** 2.18MM **Privately Held**
Web: www.unitedbrandsco.com
**SIC: 2087** 2082 Beverage bases; Ale (alcoholic beverage)

**(P-2032)**
**WEIDER HEALTH AND FITNESS**
21100 Erwin St, Woodland Hills (91367-3772)
PHONE..........................818 884-6800
Eric Weider, *Pr*
George Lengvari, *
Bernard J Cartoon, *
Lian Katz, *
Tonja Fuller, *
**EMP:** 466 **EST:** 1940
**SQ FT:** 6,000
**SALES (est):** 5.22MM **Privately Held**
**SIC: 2087** 7991 7999 Beverage bases, concentrates, syrups, powders and mixes; Physical fitness facilities; Physical fitness instruction

**(P-2033)**
**WEST COAST NATURALS LLC**
4585 Firestone Blvd, South Gate (90280-3343)
PHONE..........................310 467-3007
**EMP:** 20 **EST:** 2017
**SALES (est):** 2.18MM **Privately Held**
Web: www.wcnfoods.com
**SIC: 2087** Bitters (flavoring concentrates)

## 2091 Canned And Cured Fish And Seafoods

**(P-2034)**
**AQUAMAR INC**
10888 7th St, Rancho Cucamonga (91730)
PHONE..........................909 481-4700
Hugo Yamakawa, *Pr*
Taka Iwasaki, *
◆ **EMP:** 150 **EST:** 1987
**SQ FT:** 42,000
**SALES (est):** 24.99MM **Privately Held**
Web: www.aquamarseafood.com
**SIC: 2091** 2092 Shellfish, canned and cured; Fresh or frozen packaged fish
**PA:** Lm Foods, Llc
100 Raskulinecz Rd

**(P-2035)**
**BUMBLE BEE FOODS LLC**
13100 Arctic Cir, Santa Fe Springs (90670-5508)
PHONE..........................562 483-7474
Jan Tharp, *Brnch Mgr*
**EMP:** 41
Web: www.thebumblebeecompany.com
**SIC: 2091** Canned and cured fish and seafoods
**HQ:** Bumble Bee Foods, Llc
280 10th Ave
San Diego CA 92101
800 800-8572

**(P-2036)**
**BUMBLE BEE FOODS LLC (HQ)**
280 10th Ave, San Diego (92101-7406)
PHONE..........................800 800-8572
Andrew Choe, *CEO*
**EMP:** 17 **EST:** 2019
**SALES (est):** 366.7MM **Privately Held**
Web: www.thebumblebeecompany.com
**SIC: 2091** Tuna fish: packaged in cans, jars, etc.
**PA:** Fcf Co., Ltd.
28f, No. 8, Minquan 2nd Rd.

**(P-2037)**
**BUMBLE BEE SEAFOODS LP**
280 10th Ave, San Diego (92101-7406)
P.O. Box 85362 (92186-5362)
PHONE..........................858 715-4000
Christopher Lischewsky, *Pt*
◆ **EMP:** 150 **EST:** 1997
**SALES (est):** 18.34MM **Privately Held**
Web: www.bumblebee.com
**SIC: 2091** 2047 Tuna fish: packaged in cans, jars, etc.; Dog and cat food

**(P-2038)**
**CANNERY SEAFOOD OF PACIFIC LLC**
3010 Lafayette Rd, Newport Beach (92663-3808)
PHONE..........................949 566-0060
Creed Salisbury, *Managing Member*
**EMP:** 18 **EST:** 2000
**SALES (est):** 426.8K **Privately Held**
Web: www.cannerynewport.com
**SIC: 2091** Seafood products: packaged in cans, jars, etc.

**(P-2039)**
**COAST SEAFOODS COMPANY**
25 Waterfront Dr, Eureka (95501-0370)
PHONE..........................707 442-2947
Greg Dale, *Mgr*
**EMP:** 62
**SALES (corp-wide):** 22.05MM **Privately Held**

PRODUCTS & SERVICES SECTION  2092 - Fresh Or Frozen Packaged Fish (P-2059)

SIC: **2091** 0913 2092 Oysters: packaged in cans, jars, etc.; Oyster beds; Fresh or frozen packaged fish
HQ: Coast Seafoods Company
1200 Robert Bush Drive
Bellevue WA 98007

### (P-2040)
### OCEAN FRESH LLC (PA)
Also Called: Ocean Fresh Seafood Products
344 N Franklin St, Fort Bragg (95437-3402)
PHONE....................707 964-1389
Robert S Juntz, *Managing Member*
▲ **EMP**: 23 **EST**: 1981
**SALES (est)**: 2.35MM
**SALES (corp-wide)**: 2.35MM **Privately Held**
Web: of.mcn.org
SIC: **2091** Fish, canned and cured

### (P-2041)
### PACIFIC AMERICAN FISH CO INC (PA)
Also Called: Pafco
5525 S Santa Fe Ave, Vernon (90058-3523)
PHONE....................323 319-1551
Peter Huh, *CEO*
Paul Huh, *
◆ **EMP**: 150 **EST**: 1977
**SQ FT**: 100,000
**SALES (est)**: 54.66MM
**SALES (corp-wide)**: 54.66MM **Privately Held**
Web: www.pafco.net
SIC: **2091** 5146 Fish, filleted (boneless); Fish, fresh

### (P-2042)
### PACIFIC PLAZA IMPORTS INC (PA)
Also Called: Plaze De Caviar
3018 Willow Pass Rd Ste 102, Concord (94519)
PHONE....................925 349-4000
Mark Bolourchi, *Pr*
Sharon Bolourchi, *VP*
Ali Bolourchi, *VP*
◆ **EMP**: 17 **EST**: 1985
**SQ FT**: 24,000
**SALES (est)**: 9.49MM
**SALES (corp-wide)**: 9.49MM **Privately Held**
Web: www.plazadecaviar.com
SIC: **2091** Caviar: packaged in cans, jars, etc.

### (P-2043)
### SOUTHWIND FOODS LLC (PA)
Also Called: Great Amercn Seafood Import Co
20644 S Fordyce Ave, Carson (90810-1018)
P.O. Box 86021 (90086)
PHONE....................323 262-8222
Sebastiano Buddy Galletti, *CEO*
Jim Lee, *
Paul Galletti, *
Sam Galletti, *
Salvatori Perri, *
▲ **EMP**: 125 **EST**: 1999
**SQ FT**: 80,000
**SALES (est)**: 136.02MM
**SALES (corp-wide)**: 136.02MM **Privately Held**
Web: www.southwindfoods.com
SIC: **2091** Seafood products: packaged in cans, jars, etc.

### (P-2044)
### THAI UNION NORTH AMERICA INC (HQ)
2150 E Grand Ave, El Segundo (90245-5024)
PHONE....................424 397-8556
Bryan Rosenberg, *Pr*
◆ **EMP**: 16 **EST**: 1996
**SALES (est)**: 154.18MM **Privately Held**
Web: www.thaiunion.com
SIC: **2091** Tuna fish: packaged in cans, jars, etc.
PA: Thai Union Group Public Company Limited
72/1 Moo 7, Sethakit 1 Road

### (P-2045)
### YAMASA ENTERPRISES
Also Called: Yamasa Fish Cake
515 Stanford Ave, Los Angeles (90013-2189)
PHONE....................213 626-2211
Frank Kawana, *CEO*
Yuji Kawana, *
Sachie Kawana, *
▲ **EMP**: 27 **EST**: 1939
**SQ FT**: 20,000
**SALES (est)**: 4.77MM **Privately Held**
Web: www.yamasafishcake.com
SIC: **2091** Fish and seafood cakes: packaged in cans, jars, etc.

## 2092 Fresh Or Frozen Packaged Fish

### (P-2046)
### ADVANCED FRESH CNCPTS FRNCHISE
Also Called: Afcfc
19700 Mariner Ave, Torrance (90503-1648)
PHONE....................310 604-3200
Jeffery Seiler, *CEO*
▲ **EMP**: 60 **EST**: 2002
**SALES (est)**: 10.19MM
**SALES (corp-wide)**: 48.2MM **Privately Held**
Web: www.advancedfreshconcepts.com
SIC: **2092** 6794 Fresh or frozen packaged fish; Franchises, selling or licensing
PA: Advanced Fresh Concepts Corp.
19205 S Laurel Park Rd
310 604-3630

### (P-2047)
### ATLANTIS SEAFOOD LLC
Also Called: Seacatch Seafoods
10501 Valley Blvd Ste 1820, El Monte (91731-3623)
PHONE....................626 626-4900
**EMP**: 85
SIC: **2092** Seafoods, frozen: prepared

### (P-2048)
### AZUMA FOODS INTL INC USA (HQ)
Also Called: Azuma Foods Internatl
20201 Mack St, Hayward (94545-1224)
PHONE....................510 782-1112
Takahiro Tamura, *CEO*
Toshinobu Azuma, *
Takahiro Tamura, *Pr*
Toshie Azuma, *
◆ **EMP**: 72 **EST**: 1990
**SQ FT**: 70,000
**SALES (est)**: 21.27MM **Privately Held**
Web: www.azumafoods.com
SIC: **2092** 5146 Fresh or frozen packaged fish; Seafoods

PA: Azuma Foods Co., Ltd.
3095-45, Nagai, Komonocho

### (P-2049)
### BLUE NALU INC
Also Called: Bluenalu
6060 Nancy Ridge Dr Ste 100, San Diego (92121-3218)
PHONE....................858 703-8703
Henry Louis Cooperhouse, *CEO*
Chris Somogyi, *
Deja Westerson, *
**EMP**: 42 **EST**: 2017
**SALES (est)**: 11.85MM **Privately Held**
Web: www.bluenalu.com
SIC: **2092** Fresh or frozen packaged fish

### (P-2050)
### CFWF INC
842 Flint Ave, Wilmington (90744-3739)
PHONE....................310 221-6280
▲ **EMP**: 102
SIC: **2092** 5146 Fresh or frozen packaged fish; Fish and seafoods

### (P-2051)
### ETHOS SEAFOOD GROUP LLC
18531 S Broadwick St, Rancho Dominguez (90220-6440)
PHONE....................312 858-3474
**EMP**: 54 **EST**: 2012
**SALES (est)**: 1.79MM
**SALES (corp-wide)**: 142.04MM **Privately Held**
Web: www.smseafoodcr.com
SIC: **2092** 5146 Fresh or frozen packaged fish; Fish and seafoods
PA: Santa Monica Seafood Company
18531 S Broadwick St
310 886-7900

### (P-2052)
### FISH HOUSE FOODS INC
1263 Linda Vista Dr, San Marcos (92078-3827)
PHONE....................760 597-1270
Ron Butler, *Pr*
Ronald J Butler, *
Rex Butler, *
Karen Butler, *
**EMP**: 240 **EST**: 1985
**SQ FT**: 52,000
**SALES (est)**: 1.15MM
**SALES (corp-wide)**: 2.24MM **Privately Held**
Web: www.fishhousefoods.com
SIC: **2092** 5149 Seafoods, fresh: prepared; Groceries and related products, nec
PA: The Fish House Vera Cruz Inc
3585 Main St Ste 212
760 744-8000

### (P-2053)
### FISHERMANS PRIDE PRCESSORS INC
Also Called: Neptune Foods
4510 S Alameda St, Vernon (90058-2011)
PHONE....................323 232-1980
Howard Choi, *CEO*
Hector Poon, *
◆ **EMP**: 300 **EST**: 1954
**SQ FT**: 125,000
**SALES (est)**: 25.9MM **Privately Held**
SIC: **2092** Fresh or frozen packaged fish

### (P-2054)
### INLAND COLD STORAGE
2356 Fleetwood Dr, Riverside (92509-2409)
PHONE....................951 369-0230
**EMP**: 38 **EST**: 2013

**SALES (est)**: 259.82K **Privately Held**
Web: www.inlandcold.com
SIC: **2092** Fresh or frozen packaged fish

### (P-2055)
### J DELUCA FISH COMPANY INC
Also Called: Nautilus Seafood
505 E Harry Bridges Blvd, Wilmington (90744-6607)
PHONE....................310 221-6500
Wayne Berman, *Brnch Mgr*
**EMP**: 38
**SALES (corp-wide)**: 23.11MM **Privately Held**
Web: www.jdelucafishco.com
SIC: **2092** Fresh or frozen packaged fish
PA: J Deluca Fish Company, Inc.
2194 Signal Pl
310 684-5180

### (P-2056)
### MONTEREY FISH COMPANY INC (PA)
960 S Sanborn Rd, Salinas (93901-4530)
PHONE....................831 775-0522
◆ **EMP**: 30 **EST**: 1938
**SALES (est)**: 12.26MM
**SALES (corp-wide)**: 12.26MM **Privately Held**
Web: www.montereyfishcompany.com
SIC: **2092** 2091 Fish, fresh: prepared; Fish: packaged in cans, jars, etc.

### (P-2057)
### MS INTERTRADE INC (PA)
Also Called: Sonoma Foods
2221 Bluebell Dr Ste A, Santa Rosa (95403-2545)
P.O. Box 6083 (95406-0083)
PHONE....................707 837-8057
Matthew J Mariani, *CEO*
Scott A Gray, *
Charles Hansen, *
**EMP**: 44 **EST**: 1993
**SQ FT**: 8,000
**SALES (est)**: 666.45K **Privately Held**
Web: www.sonomaseafoods.com
SIC: **2092** Fresh or frozen fish or seafood chowders, soups, and stews

### (P-2058)
### NIKKO ENTERPRISE CORPORATION
Also Called: Hanna Fuji Sushi
13168 Sandoval St, Santa Fe Springs (90670-6600)
PHONE....................562 941-6080
Tlang T Mawii, *CEO*
Robby Sharma, *
Sein Myint, *Stockholder**
**EMP**: 23 **EST**: 1995
**SQ FT**: 5,000
**SALES (est)**: 1.14MM **Privately Held**
Web: www.necsushi.com
SIC: **2092** Fresh or frozen fish or seafood chowders, soups, and stews

### (P-2059)
### OCEAN DIRECT LLC (HQ)
Also Called: Boardwalk Solutions
13771 Gramercy Pl, Gardena (90249-2470)
PHONE....................424 266-9300
▼ **EMP**: 184 **EST**: 2003
**SQ FT**: 20,000
**SALES (est)**: 52.1MM
**SALES (corp-wide)**: 113.36MM **Privately Held**
Web: www.oceandirect.com

## 2092 - Fresh Or Frozen Packaged Fish (P-2060)

**SIC: 2092** 2022 2037 2033  Fresh or frozen fish or seafood chowders, soups, and stews ; Natural cheese; Frozen fruits and vegetables; Vegetables and vegetable products, in cans, jars, etc.
- **PA:** Richmond Wholesale Meat, Llc
  2920 Regatta Blvd
  510 233-5111

### (P-2060)
### RICH PRODUCTS CORPORATION
320 O St, Fresno  (93721-3024)
P.O. Box 631  (93709-0631)
**PHONE**..................................559 486-7380
Gary Rogers, *Brnch Mgr*
**EMP:** 45
**SQ FT:** 64,413
**SALES (corp-wide):** 4.81B **Privately Held**
**Web:** www.richs.com
**SIC: 2092** 2045 2038  Fresh or frozen packaged fish; Prepared flour mixes and doughs; Frozen specialties, nec
- **PA:** Rich Products Corporation
  1 Robert Rich Way
  716 878-8000

### (P-2061)
### SANTA MONICA SEAFOOD COMPANY (PA)
Also Called: Santa Monica Seafood
18531 S Broadwick St, Rancho Dominguez  (90220-6440)
**PHONE**..................................310 886-7900
**TOLL FREE:** 888
Roger O'brien, *CEO*
Michael Cigliano Ii, *VP*
▲ **EMP:** 100 **EST:** 1939
**SQ FT:** 65,000
**SALES (est):** 142.04MM
**SALES (corp-wide):** 142.04MM **Privately Held**
**Web:** www.santamonicaseafood.com
**SIC: 2092** 5146  Seafoods, frozen: prepared; Seafoods

### (P-2062)
### SCOTTS SEAFOOD ROUNDHOUSE
824 Sutter St, Folsom  (95630-2440)
P.O. Box 1042  (95763-1042)
**PHONE**..................................916 989-6711
**EMP:** 82 **EST:** 2018
**SALES (est):** 1.67MM **Privately Held**
**Web:** www.scottsseafoodroundhouse.com
**SIC: 2092**  Fresh or frozen packaged fish

### (P-2063)
### SIMPLY FRESH  LLC
Also Called: Rojo's
11215 Knott Ave Ste A, Cypress  (90630-5495)
**PHONE**..................................714 562-5000
Dale Jabour, *CEO*
▼ **EMP:** 160 **EST:** 1987
**SQ FT:** 20,000
**SALES (est):** 44.28MM
**SALES (corp-wide):** 113.55MM **Privately Held**
**Web:** www.simplyff.com
**SIC: 2092**  Fresh or frozen packaged fish
- **PA:** Lakeview Farms, Llc
  1600 Gressel Dr
  419 695-9225

### (P-2064)
### STATE FISH CO INC
624 W 9th St Ste 100, San Pedro  (90731-7288)
**PHONE**..................................310 547-9530
◆ **EMP:** 230
**Web:** www.statefish.com
**SIC: 2092** 5146  Fresh or frozen packaged fish; Fish, frozen, unpackaged

### (P-2065)
### TARDIO ENTERPRISES  INC
Also Called: Newport Fish
457 S Canal St, South San Francisco  (94080-4607)
**PHONE**..................................650 877-7200
Andrew Tardio, *Pr*
**EMP:** 25 **EST:** 1985
**SALES (est):** 4.81MM **Privately Held**
**SIC: 2092** 5421  Fresh or frozen packaged fish; Fish and seafood markets

## 2095 Roasted Coffee

### (P-2066)
### AMERICAS BEST BEVERAGE INC
600 50th Ave, Oakland  (94601-5004)
**PHONE**..................................800 723-8808
Hovik Azadkhanian, *CEO*
**EMP:** 25 **EST:** 2018
**SALES (est):** 7.92MM **Privately Held**
**Web:** www.americasbestbeverage.com
**SIC: 2095** 2086  Roasted coffee; Tea, iced: packaged in cans, bottles, etc.

### (P-2067)
### APFFELS COFFEE  INC
Also Called: Apffels Coffee
12115 Pacific St, Santa Fe Springs  (90670-2989)
P.O. Box 2506  (90670-0506)
**PHONE**..................................562 309-0400
Darryl Blunk, *CEO*
Alvin Apffel, *
Edward Apffel, *
Mike Rogers, *
◆ **EMP:** 37 **EST:** 1914
**SQ FT:** 100,000
**SALES (est):** 4.03MM **Privately Held**
**Web:** www.apffels.com
**SIC: 2095** 5149  Coffee roasting (except by wholesale grocers); Coffee, green or roasted

### (P-2068)
### CAFFE DAMORE INC
1916 S Tubeway Ave, Commerce  (90040-1612)
▲ **EMP:** 105
**Web:** www.kerryfoodservice.com
**SIC: 2095** 5046  Instant coffee; Coffee brewing equipment and supplies

### (P-2069)
### EBERINE ENTERPRISES INC
Also Called: Euro Coffee
3360 Fruitland Ave, Los Angeles  (90058-3714)
**PHONE**..................................323 587-1111
▲ **EMP:** 29 **EST:** 1983
**SALES (est):** 3.08MM **Privately Held**
**Web:** www.eurocoffee.com
**SIC: 2095**  Roasted coffee

### (P-2070)
### EQUAL EXCHANGE  INC
2920 Norman Strasse Rd, San Marcos  (92069-5935)
**PHONE**..................................619 335-6259
Nanelle Newbom, *Mgr*
**EMP:** 79
**SALES (corp-wide):** 1.57MM **Privately Held**
**Web:** shop.equalexchange.coop
**SIC: 2095**  Coffee roasting (except by wholesale grocers)
- **PA:** Equal Exchange, Inc.
  3401 Se 17th Ave
  503 847-2000

### (P-2071)
### F GAVINA & SONS INC
Also Called: Gavia
2700 Fruitland Ave, Vernon  (90058-2893)
**PHONE**..................................323 582-0671
Pedro Gavina, *Pr*
Francisco M Gavina, *
Leonora Gavina, *
Jose Gavina, *
▲ **EMP:** 295 **EST:** 1870
**SQ FT:** 239,000
**SALES (est):** 32.94MM **Privately Held**
**Web:** www.gavina.com
**SIC: 2095**  Coffee roasting (except by wholesale grocers)

### (P-2072)
### GOURMET COFFEE WAREHOUSE  INC (PA)
Also Called: Groundwork Coffee Company
920 N Formosa Ave, Los Angeles  (90046-6702)
**PHONE**..................................323 871-8930
Richard Karno, *Pr*
**EMP:** 20 **EST:** 1991
**SQ FT:** 10,000
**SALES (est):** 2.81MM **Privately Held**
**Web:** www.groundworkcoffee.com
**SIC: 2095** 5149 5499  Coffee roasting (except by wholesale grocers); Coffee and tea; Coffee

### (P-2073)
### GROUNDWORK COFFEE ROASTERS LLC
Also Called: Groundwork Coffee
5457 Cleon Ave, North Hollywood  (91601-2834)
**PHONE**..................................818 506-6020
**EMP:** 160 **EST:** 2011
**SQ FT:** 4,650
**SALES (est):** 16.69MM **Privately Held**
**Web:** www.groundworkcoffee.com
**SIC: 2095** 5812 5149  Roasted coffee; Contract food services; Coffee, green or roasted

### (P-2074)
### JEREMIAHS PICK COFFEE COMPANY
1495 Evans Ave, San Francisco  (94124-1706)
**PHONE**..................................415 206-9900
Jeremiah Pick, *Pr*
Mike Ahmadi, *Stockholder*
▲ **EMP:** 19 **EST:** 1993
**SQ FT:** 11,000
**SALES (est):** 2.2MM **Privately Held**
**Web:** www.jeremiahspick.com
**SIC: 2095** 5149  Coffee roasting (except by wholesale grocers); Coffee, green or roasted

### (P-2075)
### NOBLE BREWER BEER COMPANY
Also Called: Office Libations
562 Whitney St, San Leandro  (94577-1114)
**PHONE**..................................510 766-2337
Claude Burns, *CEO*
**EMP:** 40 **EST:** 2014
**SALES (est):** 9.29MM **Privately Held**
**Web:** www.noblebrewer.com
**SIC: 2095** 5149 5963 5812  Coffee roasting (except by wholesale grocers); Coffee and tea; Direct selling establishments; Contract food services

### (P-2076)
### PEERLESS COFFEE COMPANY INC
Also Called: Peerles Coffee and Tea
260 Oak St, Oakland  (94607-4512)
**PHONE**..................................510 763-1763
**TOLL FREE:** 800
George J Vukasin Junior, *CEO*
Kristina V Brouhard, *
John Ziglar, *
**EMP:** 85 **EST:** 1924
**SQ FT:** 65,000
**SALES (est):** 22.58MM **Privately Held**
**Web:** www.peerlesscoffee.com
**SIC: 2095** 5149  Coffee roasting (except by wholesale grocers); Tea

### (P-2077)
### PEETS COFFEE & TEA  LLC (DH)
1400 Park Ave, Emeryville  (94608-3520)
**PHONE**..................................510 594-2100
David Burwick, *CEO*
Shawn Conway, *
▲ **EMP:** 29 **EST:** 1971
**SQ FT:** 60,000
**SALES (est):** 1.53B
**SALES (corp-wide):** 2.67MM **Privately Held**
**Web:** www.peets.com
**SIC: 2095** 5149  Roasted coffee; Coffee, green or roasted
- **HQ:** Jab Holding Company S.A.R.L.
  Rue Jean Monnet 4
  Luxembourg 2180

### (P-2078)
### PEETS COFFEE & TEA  LLC
1875 S Bascom Ave, Campbell  (95008-2310)
**PHONE**..................................408 558-9535
**EMP:** 30
**SALES (corp-wide):** 2.67MM **Privately Held**
**Web:** www.peets.com
**SIC: 2095** 5499  Roasted coffee; Beverage stores
- **HQ:** Peet's Coffee & Tea, Llc
  1400 Park Ave
  Emeryville CA 94608
  510 594-2100

### (P-2079)
### RED BAY COFFEE COMPANY INC
3098 E 10th St, Oakland  (94601-2960)
**PHONE**..................................510 409-1076
**EMP:** 50 **EST:** 2020
**SALES (est):** 5.06MM **Privately Held**
**Web:** www.redbaycoffee.com
**SIC: 2095**  Coffee roasting (except by wholesale grocers)

### (P-2080)
### SON OF A BARISTA USA  LLC
5125 Wheeler Ridge Rd, Arvin  (93203-9629)
**PHONE**..................................323 788-8718
**EMP:** 37
**SALES (corp-wide):** 962.14K **Privately Held**
**SIC: 2095**  Roasted coffee
- **PA:** Son Of A Barista Usa, Llc
  5401 S Soto St
  323 780-8250

**PRODUCTS & SERVICES SECTION**  2096 - Potato Chips And Similar Snacks (P-2102)

**(P-2081)**
**STOBLE LLC**
418 Broadway St, Chico (95928-5323)
PHONE....................................530 990-3607
EMP: 20 EST: 2018
SALES (est): 269.33K Privately Held
Web: www.stoblecoffee.com
SIC: 2095 Roasted coffee

**(P-2082)**
**TAYLOR MAID FARMS LLC**
6790 Mckinley Ave, Sebastopol (95472-3496)
PHONE....................................707 824-9110
EMP: 30 EST: 2000
SALES (est): 945.33K Privately Held
Web: www.stoblecoffee.com
SIC: 2095 Roasted coffee

## 2096 Potato Chips And Similar Snacks

**(P-2083)**
**4505 MEATS INC**
548 Market St, San Francisco (94104-5401)
PHONE....................................415 255-3094
Ryan Farr, CEO
EMP: 20 EST: 2017
SALES (est): 2.46MM Privately Held
Web: www.4505meats.com
SIC: 2096 Pork rinds

**(P-2084)**
**ANITAS MEXICAN FOODS CORP (PA)**
3454 N Mike Daley Dr, San Bernardino (92407-1890)
PHONE....................................909 884-8706
Ricardo Alvarez, Pr
Ricardo Robles, *
Rene Robles, *
Jacqueline Robles, *
▲ EMP: 57 EST: 1936
SQ FT: 330,000
SALES (est): 65.3MM
SALES (corp-wide): 65.3MM Privately Held
Web: www.anitasmfc.com
SIC: 2096 Potato chips and similar snacks

**(P-2085)**
**ANITAS MEXICAN FOODS CORP**
3392 N Mike Daley Dr, San Bernardino (92407-1892)
PHONE....................................909 884-8706
EMP: 32
SALES (corp-wide): 65.3MM Privately Held
Web: www.anitasmfc.com
SIC: 2096 Potato chips and similar snacks
PA: Anita's Mexican Foods Corp.
    3454 N Mike Daley Dr
    909 884-8706

**(P-2086)**
**CA CREAMERY HOLDINGS LLC**
21750 8th St E, Sonoma (95476-9803)
PHONE....................................270 861-5956
Aaron Greenwald, Managing Member
EMP: 38
SALES (est): 1.34MM Privately Held
SIC: 2096 Potato chips and other potato-based snacks

**(P-2087)**
**CALBEE AMERICA INCORPORATED**
17577 Road 24, Madera (93638-9646)
PHONE....................................559 661-4845
Kevin Davar, Mgr
EMP: 83
Web: www.calbeeamerica.com
SIC: 2096 Tortilla chips
HQ: Calbee America Incorporated
    2600 Maxwell Way
    Fairfield CA 94534
    707 427-2500

**(P-2088)**
**CALIFORNIA NUGGETS INC**
23073 S Frederick Rd, Ripon (95366-9616)
PHONE....................................209 599-7131
Steve Gikas, CEO
Barbara Bain, *
Lori Gikas, *
Richard Piercefield, *
◆ EMP: 40 EST: 1998
SQ FT: 50,000
SALES (est): 4.44MM Privately Held
Web: www.californianuggets.com
SIC: 2096 2068 Potato chips and similar snacks; Nuts: dried, dehydrated, salted or roasted

**(P-2089)**
**DON VITO OZUNA FOOD CORP**
180 Cochrane Cir, Morgan Hill (95037-2807)
PHONE....................................408 465-2010
Severo Ozuna, Pr
Cevero Ozuna, Pr
EMP: 22 EST: 2006
SQ FT: 12,000
SALES (est): 6.62MM Privately Held
Web: www.ozunatortillafactory.com
SIC: 2096 2099 Tortilla chips; Tortillas, fresh or refrigerated

**(P-2090)**
**FANTE INC (PA)**
Also Called: Casa Sanchez Foods
2898 W Winton Ave, Hayward (94545-1122)
P.O. Box 12582 (94112-0582)
PHONE....................................650 697-7525
Robert C Sanchez, Pr
Robert Sanchez, *
▲ EMP: 30 EST: 1972
SALES (est): 16MM
SALES (corp-wide): 16MM Privately Held
Web: www.casassanchezfoods.com
SIC: 2096 2099 Tortilla chips; Dips, except cheese and sour cream based

**(P-2091)**
**FRITO-LAY NORTH AMERICA INC**
Also Called: Frito-Lay
1190 Spreckels Rd, Manteca (95336-8962)
PHONE....................................209 824-3700
Keith Prather, Mgr
EMP: 17
SALES (corp-wide): 86.39B Publicly Held
Web: www.fritolay.com
SIC: 2096 5145 Potato chips and similar snacks; Confectionery
HQ: Frito-Lay North America, Inc.
    7701 Legacy Dr
    Plano TX 75024

**(P-2092)**
**FRITO-LAY NORTH AMERICA INC**
Also Called: Frito-Lay
635 W Valley Blvd, Bloomington (92316-2200)
PHONE....................................909 877-0902
Fred Schmidt, Brnch Mgr
EMP: 17
SQ FT: 18,220
SALES (corp-wide): 86.39B Publicly Held
Web: www.fritolay.com
SIC: 2096 5145 5149 4226 Potato chips and similar snacks; Confectionery; Groceries and related products, nec; Special warehousing and storage, nec
HQ: Frito-Lay North America, Inc.
    7701 Legacy Dr
    Plano TX 75024

**(P-2093)**
**FRITO-LAY NORTH AMERICA INC**
Also Called: Frito-Lay
600 Garner Rd, Modesto (95357-0514)
PHONE....................................209 544-5400
Bob Schreck, Mgr
EMP: 450
SALES (corp-wide): 86.39B Publicly Held
Web: www.fritolay.com
SIC: 2096 2099 Potato chips and similar snacks; Food preparations, nec
HQ: Frito-Lay North America, Inc.
    7701 Legacy Dr
    Plano TX 75024

**(P-2094)**
**GRUMA CORPORATION**
Also Called: Mission Foods
5505 E Olympic Blvd, Commerce (90022-5129)
PHONE....................................323 803-1400
Bob Solano, Brnch Mgr
EMP: 500
Web: www.missionfoods.com
SIC: 2096 Tortilla chips
HQ: Gruma Corporation
    5601 Executive Dr Ste 800
    Irving TX 75038
    972 232-5000

**(P-2095)**
**GRUMA CORPORATION**
Also Called: Mission Foods
11559 Jersey Blvd Ste A, Rancho Cucamonga (91730-4924)
PHONE....................................909 980-3566
Victor Cervantes, Manager
EMP: 85
Web: www.missionfoods.com
SIC: 2096 Tortilla chips
HQ: Gruma Corporation
    5601 Executive Dr Ste 800
    Irving TX 75038
    972 232-5000

**(P-2096)**
**KING HENRYS INC**
Also Called: Manufacturing
29124 Hancock Pkwy 1, Valencia (91355-1066)
PHONE....................................818 536-3692
Trina Davidian, CEO
◆ EMP: 45 EST: 1989
SQ FT: 44,000
SALES (est): 11.67MM Privately Held
Web: www.kinghenrys.com
SIC: 2096 2064 Cheese curls and puffs; Breakfast bars

**(P-2097)**
**MARQUEZ MARQUEZ INC**
Also Called: Marquez & Marquez Food PR
11821 Industrial Ave, South Gate (90280-7914)
PHONE....................................562 408-0960
Elias Marquez, Pr
EMP: 29 EST: 1993
SALES (est): 2.33MM Privately Held
Web: www.marquezmarquez.com
SIC: 2096 2041 Corn chips and other corn-based snacks; Flour

**(P-2098)**
**NEW FRONTIER FOODS INC**
Also Called: Ocean's Halo
1424 Chapin Ave, Burlingame (94010-4003)
PHONE....................................713 501-0292
Robert Mock, CEO
Shin Rhee, Pr
Grace Mok, CFO
▲ EMP: 17 EST: 2011
SQ FT: 5,000
SALES (est): 6.25MM Privately Held
Web: www.oceanshalo.com
SIC: 2096 2032 Potato chips and similar snacks; Broth, except seafood: packaged in cans, jars, etc.

**(P-2099)**
**POPSALOT LLC**
Also Called: Popsalot Gourmet Popcorn
7723 Somerset Blvd, Paramount (90723-4104)
P.O. Box 7040 (90212-7040)
PHONE....................................213 761-0156
Victoria Ho, Prin
▼ EMP: 20 EST: 2005
SQ FT: 8,400
SALES (est): 3.22MM Privately Held
Web: www.popsalot.com
SIC: 2096 Popcorn, already popped (except candy covered)

**(P-2100)**
**PURE NATURE FOODS LLC**
700 Santa Anita Dr Ste A, Woodland (95776-6102)
P.O. Box 2387 (95776)
PHONE....................................530 723-5269
Miguel Reyna, Pr
Shan Staka, *
Dan Miller, *
EMP: 30 EST: 2016
SQ FT: 60,000
SALES (est): 4.89MM Privately Held
Web: www.purenaturefoodsco.com
SIC: 2096 Rice chips

**(P-2101)**
**RAISON DETRE BAKERY LLC**
Also Called: Joyfull Cheese Co.
179 Starlite St, South San Francisco (94080-6313)
PHONE....................................650 952-8889
David Borgan, CEO
Mark Borden, CFO
EMP: 58 EST: 2020
SALES (est): 6.04MM Privately Held
Web: www.raisondetrebakery.com
SIC: 2096 Potato chips and similar snacks

**(P-2102)**
**SNACK IT FORWARD LLC**
Also Called: World Peas Brand
6080 Center Dr Ste 600, Los Angeles (90045-1574)
PHONE....................................310 242-5517
Nick Desai, CEO
Bryan Cameron, COO
EMP: 23 EST: 2011
SQ FT: 500
SALES (est): 6.79MM Privately Held
Web: www.snackitforward.com
SIC: 2096 Cheese curls and puffs

# 2096 - Potato Chips And Similar Snacks (P-2103)

**(P-2103)**
**SNAK-KING LLC (PA)**
16150 Stephens St, City Of Industry (91745-1718)
PHONE..................626 336-7711
◆ **EMP:** 500 **EST:** 1978
**SALES (est):** 174.35MM
**SALES (corp-wide):** 174.35MM **Privately Held**
Web: www.snakking.com
SIC: 2096 Potato chips and similar snacks

**(P-2104)**
**TACO WORKS INC**
3424 Sacramento Dr, San Luis Obispo (93401-7128)
PHONE..................805 541-1556
Roy D Bayly, *Pr*
Theresa Bayly, *Sec*
**EMP:** 20 **EST:** 1976
**SQ FT:** 9,900
**SALES (est):** 3.32MM **Privately Held**
Web: www.tacoworks.net
SIC: 2096 5145 Tortilla chips; Snack foods

**(P-2105)**
**TACUPETO CHIPS & SALSA INC**
1330 Distribution Way Ste A, Vista (92081-8837)
PHONE..................760 597-9400
Gilberto Pablo Fajardo, *Pr*
Gilberto Ramon Fajardo, *VP*
**EMP:** 18 **EST:** 2009
**SALES (est):** 1.65MM **Privately Held**
Web: www.tacupetochipsandsalsa.com
SIC: 2096 Corn chips and other corn-based snacks

## 2097 Manufactured Ice

**(P-2106)**
**ARCTIC GLACIER USA INC**
17011 Central Ave, Carson (90746-1303)
PHONE..................310 638-0321
Sharon Cooper, *Mgr*
**EMP:** 200
**SALES (corp-wide):** 253.92MM **Privately Held**
Web: www.arcticglacier.com
SIC: 2097 Manufactured ice
HQ: Arctic Glacier U.S.A., Inc.
    307 23rd Street Ext
    Pittsburgh PA 15251
    800 562-1990

**(P-2107)**
**ARCTIC GLACIER USA INC**
8710 Park St, Bellflower (90706-5527)
PHONE..................800 562-1990
**EMP:** 20
**SALES (corp-wide):** 253.92MM **Privately Held**
Web: www.arcticglacier.com
SIC: 2097 Manufactured ice
HQ: Arctic Glacier U.S.A., Inc.
    307 23rd Street Ext
    Pittsburgh PA 15251
    800 562-1990

**(P-2108)**
**GLACIER VALLEY ICE COMPANY LP (PA)**
Also Called: Glacier Ice Company
8580 Laguna Station Rd, Elk Grove (95758-9550)
PHONE..................916 394-2939
Sarah Demartini, *Prin*
**EMP:** 40 **EST:** 1972
**SQ FT:** 72,000
**SALES (est):** 3.99MM **Privately Held**
SIC: 2097 5199 Manufactured ice; Ice, manufactured or natural

**(P-2109)**
**GROWERS ICE CO**
1124 Abbott St, Salinas (93901-4502)
P.O. Box 298 (93902-0298)
PHONE..................831 424-5781
Susan Merrill, *Ch Bd*
**EMP:** 36 **EST:** 1935
**SQ FT:** 200,000
**SALES (est):** 8.82MM **Privately Held**
Web: www.postharvesttechnologies.com
SIC: 2097 4222 7623 6512 Manufactured ice ; Warehousing, cold storage or refrigerated; Ice making machinery repair service; Commercial and industrial building operation

**(P-2110)**
**KAR ICE SERVICE INC (PA)**
2521 Solar Way, Barstow (92311-3616)
P.O. Box 1197 (92312-1197)
PHONE..................760 256-2648
Tom Lewis, *Pr*
Carol Lewis, *Sec*
Micheal Lewis, *CFO*
**EMP:** 18 **EST:** 1980
**SQ FT:** 14,400
**SALES (est):** 1.2MM
**SALES (corp-wide):** 1.2MM **Privately Held**
Web: www.arcticglacier.com
SIC: 2097 Ice cubes

**(P-2111)**
**MOUNTAIN WATER ICE COMPANY INC (PA)**
17011 Central Ave, Carson (90746-1303)
PHONE..................310 638-0321
**EMP:** 54 **EST:** 1925
**SALES (est):** 4.83MM
**SALES (corp-wide):** 4.83MM **Privately Held**
SIC: 2097 Manufactured ice

**(P-2112)**
**PELTON-SHEPHERD INDUSTRIES INC (PA)**
812 W Luce St Ste B, Stockton (95203-4937)
P.O. Box 30218 (95213-0218)
PHONE..................209 460-0893
Alicia M Shepherd, *Pr*
▲ **EMP:** 35 **EST:** 1950
**SQ FT:** 30,000
**SALES (est):** 16.5MM
**SALES (corp-wide):** 16.5MM **Privately Held**
Web: www.peltonshepherd.com
SIC: 2097 Manufactured ice

## 2098 Macaroni And Spaghetti

**(P-2113)**
**FUNGS VILLAGE INC**
5339 E Washington Blvd, Commerce (90040-2111)
PHONE..................323 881-1600
Albert Lee, *Pr*
▲ **EMP:** 20 **EST:** 1984
**SQ FT:** 18,000
**SALES (est):** 2.15MM **Privately Held**
Web: www.fungsvillage.com
SIC: 2098 Noodles (e.g. egg, plain, and water), dry

**(P-2114)**
**GOODER FOODS INC**
Also Called: Goodles
415 River St Ste A, Santa Cruz (95060-2724)
PHONE..................773 541-4108
Jennifer Zeszut, *CEO*
Paul Earle, *Board Director*
Greg Peterson, *COO*
Deb Luster, *IMPACT*
Gal Gadot, *Founding Partner*
**EMP:** 27 **EST:** 2020
**SALES (est):** 8.29MM **Privately Held**
SIC: 2098 Noodles (e.g. egg, plain, and water), dry

**(P-2115)**
**MARUCHAN INC**
1902 Deere Ave, Irvine (92606-4819)
PHONE..................949 789-2300
Shino Saki, *Mgr*
**EMP:** 220
Web: www.maruchan.com
SIC: 2098 5146 Noodles (e.g. egg, plain, and water), dry; Fish, cured
HQ: Maruchan, Inc.
    15800 Laguna Canyon Rd
    Irvine CA 92618
    949 789-2300

**(P-2116)**
**MYOJO USA INC**
6220 Prescott Ct, Chino (91710-7111)
PHONE..................909 464-1411
Yoshie Nakamura, *Pr*
Takuro Okada, *CFO*
▲ **EMP:** 16 **EST:** 1991
**SQ FT:** 20,759
**SALES (est):** 9.46MM **Privately Held**
Web: www.myojousa.com
SIC: 2098 Noodles (e.g. egg, plain, and water), dry
PA: Nissin Foods Holdings Co., Ltd.
    6-28-1, Shinjuku

**(P-2117)**
**NISSIN FOODS USA COMPANY INC (DH)**
2001 W Rosecrans Ave, Gardena (90249-2931)
PHONE..................310 327-8478
Brian Huff, *Pr*
Takahiro Enomoto, *
◆ **EMP:** 200 **EST:** 1970
**SQ FT:** 200,000
**SALES (est):** 123.55MM **Privately Held**
Web: www.nissinfoods.com
SIC: 2098 2038 Noodles (e.g. egg, plain, and water), dry; Ethnic foods, nec, frozen
HQ: Nissin Food Products Co., Ltd.
    6-28-1, Shinjuku
    Shinjuku-Ku TKY 160-0

**(P-2118)**
**PEKING NOODLE CO INC**
1514 N San Fernando Rd, Los Angeles (90065-1282)
PHONE..................323 223-0897
Frank Tong, *Pr*
Stephen Tong, *
Donna Tong, *
▲ **EMP:** 40 **EST:** 1928
**SQ FT:** 40,000
**SALES (est):** 5.94MM **Privately Held**
Web: www.pekingnoodle.com
SIC: 2098 2052 Noodles (e.g. egg, plain, and water), dry; Cookies and crackers

**(P-2119)**
**SANYO FOODS CORP AMERICA (DH)**
Also Called: Yorba Linda Country Club
11955 Monarch St, Garden Grove (92841-2194)
PHONE..................714 891-3671
Yuko Takahashi, *CEO*
Yumei Mugita, *
◆ **EMP:** 30 **EST:** 1978
**SQ FT:** 130,000
**SALES (est):** 13.18MM **Privately Held**
Web: www.sanyofoodsamerica.com
SIC: 2098 7997 Noodles (e.g. egg, plain, and water), dry; Golf club, membership
HQ: Sanyo Foods Co., Ltd.
    1-1-1, Higashihama
    Ichikawa CHI 272-0

## 2099 Food Preparations, Nec

**(P-2120)**
**AGUSA**
1055 S 19th Ave, Lemoore (93245-9747)
PHONE..................559 924-4785
Joel Delira, *CEO*
Javier Souchard, *
Inigo Martinez, *
◆ **EMP:** 36 **EST:** 2000
**SQ FT:** 28,000
**SALES (est):** 8.2MM **Privately Held**
Web: www.agusa.biz
SIC: 2099 Food preparations, nec

**(P-2121)**
**AIR PROTEIN INC**
2020 Williams St Ste B1, San Leandro (94577-2335)
PHONE..................510 285-9097
Lisa Dyson, *CEO*
**EMP:** 44 **EST:** 2020
**SALES (est):** 13.38MM **Privately Held**
Web: www.airprotein.com
SIC: 2099 Food preparations, nec

**(P-2122)**
**ALBANY FARMS INC**
625 Fair Oaks Ave Ste 125, South Pasadena (91030-2688)
PHONE..................213 330-6573
William Saller, *CEO*
**EMP:** 39
**SALES (corp-wide):** 1.5MM **Privately Held**
Web: www.albanyfarms.com
SIC: 2099 Food preparations, nec
PA: Albany Farms Inc.
    10680 W Pico Blvd Ste 230
    877 832-8269

**(P-2123)**
**ALBANY FARMS INC (PA)**
10680 W Pico Blvd Ste 230, Los Angeles (90064-7203)
PHONE..................877 832-8269
William Saller, *CEO*
**EMP:** 22 **EST:** 2014
**SQ FT:** 50,000
**SALES (est):** 1.5MM
**SALES (corp-wide):** 1.5MM **Privately Held**
Web: www.albanyfarms.com
SIC: 2099 Noodles, uncooked: packaged with other ingredients

**(P-2124)**
**ALEXANDER VALLEY GOURMET LLC**
256 Sutton Pl, Santa Rosa (95407-8163)
PHONE..................707 473-0116

## 2099 - Food Preparations, Nec (P-2146)

EMP: 20 EST: 2013
SALES (est): 3.4MM Privately Held
SIC: 2099 Food preparations, nec

**(P-2125)**
**ALFRED LOUIE INCORPORATED**
4501 Shepard St, Bakersfield (93313-2310)
PHONE..............................661 831-2520
Victor Louie, Pr
Gordon Louie, Sec
Samuel Louie, Stockholder
Maryann Louie, Stockholder
EMP: 26 EST: 1979
SQ FT: 28,000
SALES (est): 2.97MM Privately Held
SIC: 2099 0182 Noodles, fried (Chinese); Bean sprouts, grown under cover

**(P-2126)**
**AMERICAN YEAST CORPORATION**
5455 District Blvd, Bakersfield (93313-2123)
PHONE..............................661 834-1050
Lloyd Fry, Mgr
EMP: 28
SALES (corp-wide): 300K Privately Held
SIC: 2099 Food preparations, nec
HQ: American Yeast Corporation
8215 Beachwood Rd
Baltimore MD 21222
410 477-3700

**(P-2127)**
**ANNIES INC (HQ)**
Also Called: Homegrown Naturals
1610 5th St, Berkeley (94710-1715)
PHONE..............................510 558-7500
John Foraker, CEO
Kelly J Kennedy, CFO
Mark Mortimer, Executive Sales & Marketing Vice President
Amanda K Martinez, Ofcr
Molly F Ashby, Ch Bd
EMP: 67 EST: 2004
SQ FT: 33,500
SALES (est): 21.12MM
SALES (corp-wide): 19.86B Publicly Held
Web: www.annies.com
SIC: 2099 Food preparations, nec
PA: General Mills, Inc.
1 General Mills Blvd
763 764-7600

**(P-2128)**
**ARANDAS TORTILLA COMPANY INC**
1450 E Scotts Ave, Stockton (95205-6250)
PHONE..............................209 464-8675
EMP: 19
Web: www.arandastortillacompany.com
SIC: 2099 Tortillas, fresh or refrigerated
PA: Aranda's Tortilla Company, Incorporated
1318 E Scotts Ave

**(P-2129)**
**ARANDAS TORTILLA COMPANY INC (PA)**
1318 E Scotts Ave, Stockton (95205-6152)
PHONE..............................209 464-8675
Victor Aranda, CEO
Vicent Aranda, VP
Javier Aranda, Treas
EMP: 29 EST: 1982
SQ FT: 20,000
SALES (est): 9.09MM Privately Held
Web: www.arandastortillacompany.com
SIC: 2099 Tortillas, fresh or refrigerated

**(P-2130)**
**AREVALO TORTILLERIA INC (PA)**
1537 W Mines Ave, Montebello (90640-5414)
P.O. Box 788 (90640-0788)
PHONE..............................323 888-1711
Jose Luis Arevalo, CEO
Emilia Arevalo, *
▲ EMP: 82 EST: 1985
SQ FT: 20,000
SALES (est): 18.86MM
SALES (corp-wide): 18.86MM Privately Held
Web: www.arevalos.com
SIC: 2099 Food preparations, nec

**(P-2131)**
**AREVALO TORTILLERIA INC**
3033 Supply Ave, Commerce (90040-2709)
P.O. Box 788 (90078-0788)
PHONE..............................323 888-1711
Edward Arello, Mgr
EMP: 30
SALES (corp-wide): 18.86MM Privately Held
Web: www.arevalos.com
SIC: 2099 Tortillas, fresh or refrigerated
PA: Arevalo Tortilleria, Inc.
1537 W Mines Ave
323 888-1711

**(P-2132)**
**ASIANA CUISINE ENTERPRISES INC**
Also Called: Ace Sushi
22771 S Western Ave Ste 100, Torrance (90501-5196)
PHONE..............................310 327-2223
Harlan Chin, Pr
Gary Chin, *
▲ EMP: 560 EST: 1990
SQ FT: 6,000
SALES (est): 23.02MM Privately Held
Web: www.acesushi.com
SIC: 2099 5812 8741 Ready-to-eat meals, salads, and sandwiches; Fast food restaurants and stands; Management services

**(P-2133)**
**BAKEMARK USA LLC**
32621 Central Ave, Union City (94587-2008)
PHONE..............................510 487-8188
Dean Chavez, Mgr
EMP: 23
SALES (corp-wide): 563.73MM Privately Held
Web: www.yourbakemark.com
SIC: 2099 Food preparations, nec
PA: Bakemark Usa Llc
7351 Crider Ave
562 949-1054

**(P-2134)**
**BARNEY & CO CALIFORNIA LLC**
2925 S Elm Ave Ste 101, Fresno (93706-5411)
PHONE..............................559 442-1752
EMP: 18 EST: 2006
SQ FT: 37,000
SALES (est): 6.34MM Privately Held
Web: www.barneybutter.com
SIC: 2099 Almond pastes

**(P-2135)**
**BCD FOOD INC**
320 W Carob St, Compton (90220)
PHONE..............................310 323-1200
Tae Ro Lee, Pr
▲ EMP: 40 EST: 2006
SALES (est): 2.21MM Privately Held
SIC: 2099 Box lunches, for sale off premises

**(P-2136)**
**BENEVOLENCE FOOD PRODUCTS LLC**
Also Called: Bfp
2761 Saturn St Ste D, Brea (92821-6707)
PHONE..............................888 832-3738
EMP: 24 EST: 2010
SALES (est): 343.91K Privately Held
SIC: 2099 Food preparations, nec

**(P-2137)**
**BERBER FOOD MANUFACTURING LLC**
Also Called: Ml Rancho Tortilla Factory
10115 Iron Rock Way Ste 1, Elk Grove (95624)
PHONE..............................510 553-0444
Manuel Berber, Pr
Robert Berber Junior, Sec
▼ EMP: 150 EST: 1994
SALES (est): 34.07MM Privately Held
Web: www.mirancho.com
SIC: 2099 Tortillas, fresh or refrigerated

**(P-2138)**
**BEST FORMULATIONS LLC**
938 Radecki Ct, City Of Industry (91748-1132)
PHONE..............................626 912-9998
EMP: 111
Web: www.bestformulations.com
SIC: 2099 8748 5149 2834 Food preparations, nec; Business consulting, nec; Health foods; Pharmaceutical preparations
HQ: Best Formulations Llc
17758 Rowland St
City Of Industry CA 91748
626 912-9998

**(P-2139)**
**BEST FORMULATIONS LLC (HQ)**
Also Called: Best Formulations
17758 Rowland St, City Of Industry (91748-1148)
PHONE..............................626 912-9998
Jeffrey Goh, CEO
Eugene Ung, Executive Manager*
Kelly Ung, *
◆ EMP: 39 EST: 1984
SQ FT: 50,000
SALES (est): 106.95MM Privately Held
Web: www.bestformulations.com
SIC: 2099 8748 5149 2834 Food preparations, nec; Business consulting, nec; Health foods; Pharmaceutical preparations
PA: Sirio Pharma Co., Ltd.
No.83, Taishan Rd.

**(P-2140)**
**BETTER MEAT CO**
2939 Promenade St Ste 100, West Sacramento (95691-6403)
PHONE..............................916 893-8777
Paul Shapiro, CEO
Joanna Bromley, COO
EMP: 18 EST: 2018
SALES (est): 6.19MM Privately Held
Web: www.bettermeat.co
SIC: 2099 Food preparations, nec

**(P-2141)**
**BITCHIN INC (PA)**
Also Called: Bitchin Sauce
6211 Yarrow Dr Ste C, Carlsbad (92011-1538)
PHONE..............................760 224-7447
Starr Edwards, CEO
Harrison Edwards, CMO
EMP: 30 EST: 2012
SALES (est): 10.16MM
SALES (corp-wide): 10.16MM Privately Held
Web: www.bitchinsauce.com
SIC: 2099 Sauce, gravy, dressing, and dip mixes

**(P-2142)**
**BITCHIN SAUCE LLC**
Also Called: Bitchin' Sauce
4509 Adams St, Carlsbad (92008-4208)
P.O. Box 130610 (92013-0610)
PHONE..............................737 248-2446
Starr Edwards, CEO
Starr Edwards, Ch Bd
EMP: 75 EST: 2020
SALES (est): 1.33MM
SALES (corp-wide): 10.16MM Privately Held
Web: www.bitchinsauce.com
SIC: 2099 Sauce, gravy, dressing, and dip mixes
PA: Bitchin' Inc.
6211 Yarrow Dr Ste C
760 224-7447

**(P-2143)**
**BLUE DIAMOND GROWERS**
1701 C St, Sacramento (95811-1029)
PHONE..............................916 446-8464
EMP: 149
SALES (corp-wide): 661.89MM Privately Held
Web: www.bluediamondstore.com
SIC: 2099 Food preparations, nec
PA: Diamond Blue Growers
1802 C St
800 987-2329

**(P-2144)**
**BLUE DIAMOND GROWERS**
Also Called: Blue Diamond
1300 N Washington Rd, Turlock (95380-9506)
PHONE..............................209 604-1501
EMP: 114
SALES (corp-wide): 319.04MM Privately Held
Web: www.bdingredients.com
SIC: 2099 Food preparations, nec
PA: Diamond Blue Growers
1802 C St
800 987-2329

**(P-2145)**
**BOTANAS MEXICO INC**
11122 Rush St, South El Monte (91733-3549)
PHONE..............................626 279-1512
Carlos Aleman, Pr
Miriam Aleman, VP
◆ EMP: 16 EST: 2008
SALES (est): 2.34MM Privately Held
SIC: 2099 5499 Seasonings and spices; Spices and herbs

**(P-2146)**
**BRAGA FRESH FOODS LLC (PA)**
121 Spreckels Blvd Bldg 10, Salinas (93962-2405)
PHONE..............................831 756-7614

## 2099 - Food Preparations, Nec (P-2147)

### PRODUCTS & SERVICES SECTION

Kolby Pereira, *Managing Member*
▲ **EMP:** 48 **EST:** 2016
**SALES (est):** 28.26MM
**SALES (corp-wide):** 28.26MM **Privately Held**
**Web:** www.bragafresh.com
**SIC:** 2099 Food preparations, nec

**(P-2147)**
### BRAGA FRESH FOODS LLC
Also Called: Braga Fresh Foods Gonzales
180 Katherine St, Gonzales (93926)
**PHONE**.................................831 751-5573
**EMP:** 685
**SALES (corp-wide):** 28.26MM **Privately Held**
**Web:** www.bragafresh.com
**SIC:** 2099 Food preparations, nec
**PA:** Braga Fresh Foods, Llc
  121 Spreckels Blvd # 10
  831 756-7614

**(P-2148)**
### BRIGHT PEOPLE FOODS INC (PA)
Also Called: Dr McDougall's Right Foods
1640 Tide Ct, Woodland (95776-6210)
P.O. Box 2205 (95776-2205)
**PHONE**.................................530 669-6870
Michael L Vinnicombe, *Pr*
Carolyn Vinnicombe, *
▼ **EMP:** 24 **EST:** 1953
**SQ FT:** 30,000
**SALES (est):** 15.1MM
**SALES (corp-wide):** 15.1MM **Privately Held**
**Web:** www.rightfoods.com
**SIC:** 2099 Spices, including grinding

**(P-2149)**
### BRISTOL FARMS (HQ)
915 E 230th St, Carson (90745-5005)
**PHONE**.................................310 233-4700
Adam Caldecott, *CEO*
**EMP:** 100 **EST:** 1982
**SQ FT:** 73,667
**SALES (est):** 94.53MM **Privately Held**
**Web:** www.bristolfarms.com
**SIC:** 2099 5411 Ready-to-eat meals, salads, and sandwiches; Grocery stores, chain
**PA:** The Endeavour Capital Fund Limited Partnership
  920 Sw 6th Ave Ste 1400

**(P-2150)**
### C & F FOODS INC
12400 Wilshire Blvd Ste 1180, Los Angeles (90025-1058)
**PHONE**.................................626 723-1000
◆ **EMP:** 400
**Web:** www.cnf-foods.com
**SIC:** 2099 Food preparations, nec

**(P-2151)**
### CACHE CREEK FOODS LLC
411 N Pioneer Ave, Woodland (95776-6122)
P.O. Box 180 (95776-0180)
**PHONE**.................................530 662-1764
Matthew Morehart, *CEO*
Connie Stephens, *
▲ **EMP:** 60 **EST:** 1993
**SQ FT:** 40,000
**SALES (est):** 9.94MM **Privately Held**
**Web:** www.cachecreekfoods.com
**SIC:** 2099 2064 Almond pastes; Nuts, glace

**(P-2152)**
### CADENCE GOURMET LLC (PA)
Also Called: Cadence Gourmet Involve Foods
155 Klug Cir, Corona (92878-5424)
**PHONE**.................................951 444-9269
Brian J Wynn, *CEO*
David Wells, *
▲ **EMP:** 18 **EST:** 2004
**SQ FT:** 12,000
**SALES (est):** 7.98MM
**SALES (corp-wide):** 7.98MM **Privately Held**
**Web:** www.cadencekitchen.com
**SIC:** 2099 Food preparations, nec

**(P-2153)**
### CALAVO GROWERS INC (PA)
Also Called: Calavo
1141 Cummings Rd Ste A, Santa Paula (93060-9118)
**PHONE**.................................805 525-1245
Lecil Cole, *Pr*
Steven Hollister, *
Danny Dumas, *Sr VP*
Shawn Munsell, *CFO*
**EMP:** 91 **EST:** 1924
**SALES (est):** 971.95MM
**SALES (corp-wide):** 971.95MM **Publicly Held**
**Web:** www.calavo.com
**SIC:** 2099 5148 Salads, fresh or refrigerated; Fruits

**(P-2154)**
### CALIFORNIA NATURAL PRODUCTS
Also Called: Power Automation Systems
1250 Lathrop Rd, Lathrop (95330-9709)
P.O. Box 1219 (95330-1219)
**PHONE**.................................209 858-2525
Craig Lemieux, *CEO*
Timothy Preuninger, *
David Stott, *
◆ **EMP:** 375 **EST:** 1976
**SQ FT:** 220,000
**SALES (est):** 88.5MM
**SALES (corp-wide):** 176.71MM **Privately Held**
**Web:** www.gehlfoodandbeverage.com
**SIC:** 2099 7389 Food preparations, nec; Packaging and labeling services
**PA:** Gehl Foods, Llc
  N116 W15970 Main St
  262 251-8570

**(P-2155)**
### CALIFORNIA NEW FOODS LLC
1101 Roosevelt St, Monterey (93940-2146)
**PHONE**.................................831 444-1872
**EMP:** 25 **EST:** 2018
**SALES (est):** 1.57MM **Privately Held**
**SIC:** 2099 Food preparations, nec

**(P-2156)**
### CAMINO REAL FOODS INC (PA)
Also Called: Camino Real Kitchens
2638 E Vernon Ave, Los Angeles (90058-1825)
P.O. Box 30729 (90030-0729)
**PHONE**.................................323 585-6599
Rob Cross, *Pr*
Richard Lunsford, *
**EMP:** 150 **EST:** 1980
**SALES (est):** 55.44MM
**SALES (corp-wide):** 55.44MM **Privately Held**
**Web:** www.caminorealkitchens.com
**SIC:** 2099 Food preparations, nec

**(P-2157)**
### CANTARE FOODS INC
900 Glenneyre St, Laguna Beach (92651-2707)
▲ **EMP:** 42 **EST:** 1992
**SALES (est):** 1.86MM **Privately Held**
**Web:** www.cantarefoods.com
**SIC:** 2099 2022 Food preparations, nec; Cheese; natural and processed

**(P-2158)**
### CARGILL MEAT SOLUTIONS CORP
3501 E Vernon Ave, Vernon (90058-1813)
**PHONE**.................................515 735-9800
Hans Kabat, *Pr*
**EMP:** 219
**SALES (corp-wide):** 159.59B **Privately Held**
**Web:** www.cargill.com
**SIC:** 2099 Food preparations, nec
**HQ:** Cargill Meat Solutions Corp
  825 E Douglas Ave
  Wichita KS 67202
  316 291-2500

**(P-2159)**
### CARMEL FOOD GROUP INC
31128 San Clemente St, Hayward (94544-7802)
**PHONE**.................................510 471-4889
▲ **EMP:** 31
**SIC:** 2099 Pasta, uncooked: packaged with other ingredients

**(P-2160)**
### CEDARLANE NATURAL FOODS INC (PA)
Also Called: Cedarlane Foods
717 E Artesia Blvd Ste A, Carson (90746-1228)
**PHONE**.................................310 886-7720
Robert Atallah, *CEO*
Neil Holmes, *
▲ **EMP:** 100 **EST:** 1981
**SALES (est):** 81.29MM
**SALES (corp-wide):** 81.29MM **Privately Held**
**Web:** www.cedarlanefoods.com
**SIC:** 2099 Food preparations, nec

**(P-2161)**
### CFARMS INC
1244 E Beamer St, Woodland (95776-6002)
**PHONE**.................................916 375-3000
Baljit Pattar, *Brnch Mgr*
**EMP:** 28
**SALES (corp-wide):** 4.63MM **Privately Held**
**Web:** www.culinaryfarms.com
**SIC:** 2099 5149 Food preparations, nec; Flavorings and fragrances
**PA:** Cfarms, Inc.
  1330 N Dutton Ave Ste 100
  916 375-3000

**(P-2162)**
### CFARMS INC (PA)
Also Called: Culinary Farms
1330 N Dutton Ave Ste 100, Santa Rosa (95401-4646)
**PHONE**.................................916 375-3000
Christopher Adam Lee, *CEO*
Petra Iris Horlbeck, *CFO*
**EMP:** 28 **EST:** 2017
**SALES (est):** 4.63MM
**SALES (corp-wide):** 4.63MM **Privately Held**
**SIC:** 2099 5149 Food preparations, nec; Flavorings and fragrances

**(P-2163)**
### CHEF MERITO INC
Also Called: Chef Merito, Inc.
15355 Raymer St, Van Nuys (91406-2033)
**PHONE**.................................818 781-0470
**EMP:** 15
**SALES (corp-wide):** 26.51MM **Privately Held**
**Web:** www.chefmerito.com
**SIC:** 2099 Food preparations, nec
**PA:** Chef Merito, Llc
  7915 Sepulveda Blvd
  818 787-0100

**(P-2164)**
### CHEF MERITO LLC (PA)
Also Called: Merito.com
7915 Sepulveda Blvd, Van Nuys (91405-1032)
**PHONE**.................................818 787-0100
Margaret Crow, *CEO*
Jose J Corugedo, *
Natt Hasson, *
▲ **EMP:** 43 **EST:** 1985
**SQ FT:** 30,000
**SALES (est):** 26.51MM
**SALES (corp-wide):** 26.51MM **Privately Held**
**Web:** www.chefmerito.com
**SIC:** 2099 2033 2032 2044 Spices, including grinding; Jellies, edible, including imitation: in cans, jars, etc.; Soups, except seafood: packaged in cans, jars, etc.; Enriched rice (vitamin and mineral fortified)

**(P-2165)**
### CHEFMASTER
501 Airpark Dr, Fullerton (92833-2501)
**PHONE**.................................714 554-4000
Aaron G Byrnes, *Pr*
▲ **EMP:** 35 **EST:** 1939
**SALES (est):** 6.66MM **Privately Held**
**Web:** www.chefmaster.com
**SIC:** 2099 Sugar powdered, from purchased ingredients

**(P-2166)**
### CHEFSATTRACTION LLC
3400 Cottage Way, Sacramento (95825-1474)
**PHONE**.................................310 800-3778
Dustin Taylor, *Pr*
**EMP:** 40 **EST:** 2021
**SALES (est):** 269.74K **Privately Held**
**SIC:** 2099 Ready-to-eat meals, salads, and sandwiches

**(P-2167)**
### CJ FOODS INC (HQ)
Also Called: CJ America
4 Centerpointe Dr Ste 100, La Palma (90623-1074)
**PHONE**.................................714 367-7200
Pious Jung, *CEO*
**EMP:** 78 **EST:** 1995
**SALES (est):** 48.39MM **Privately Held**
**Web:** www.cjfoods.com
**SIC:** 2099 Food preparations, nec
**PA:** Cj Cheiljedang Corporation
  330 Dongho-Ro, Jung-Gu

**(P-2168)**
### CLARMIL MANUFACTURING CORP (PA)
Also Called: Goldilocks
30865 San Clemente St, Hayward (94544-7136)

## PRODUCTS & SERVICES SECTION
## 2099 - Food Preparations, Nec (P-2190)

PHONE..............................510 476-0700
Mary-ann Yee Ortiz-luis, *Pr*
Mary Ann Yee Ortiz Luis, *
Freddie L Go Junior, *COO*
Mannette Roxas, *
Cherrimel Yuzon, *
▲ **EMP:** 39 **EST:** 1991
**SQ FT:** 57,000
**SALES (est):** 8.88MM **Privately Held**
**Web:** www.goldilocks-usa.com
**SIC: 2099** 5149 2051  Food preparations, nec ; Bakery products; Bread, cake, and related products

### (P-2169)
### CLASSIC SALADS LLC
525 Old Natividad Rd, Salinas (93908-9540)
P.O. Box 3800  (93912-3800)
PHONE..............................831 763-4520
Lance Batistich, *Managing Member*
Christina Batistich, *
▲ **EMP:** 44 **EST:** 2000
**SALES (est):** 7.66MM **Privately Held**
**Web:** www.classicsalads.com
**SIC: 2099**  Salads, fresh or refrigerated

### (P-2170)
### CLW FOODS LLC
3425 E Vernon Ave, Vernon  (90058-1811)
PHONE..............................323 432-4600
**EMP:** 17
**SALES (corp-wide):** 1.28MM **Privately Held**
**Web:** www.clwfoods.com
**SIC: 2099**  Dessert mixes and fillings
**PA:**  Clw Foods, Llc
   8765 3rd St
   559 639-6661

### (P-2171)
### CNC NOODLE CORPORATION
1787 Sabre St, Hayward  (94545-1015)
PHONE..............................510 732-1318
Betty Lim, *Pr*
▲ **EMP:** 19 **EST:** 1984
**SQ FT:** 12,000
**SALES (est):** 2.34MM **Privately Held**
**SIC: 2099**  Noodles, fried (Chinese)

### (P-2172)
### CORBION BIOTECH INC (HQ)
1 Tower Pl Ste 600, South San Francisco (94080-1832)
PHONE..............................650 780-4777
Tjerk De Ruiter, *CEO*
**EMP:** 30 **EST:** 2017
**SALES (est):** 13.41MM
**SALES (corp-wide):** 1.57B **Privately Held**
**Web:** www.corbion.com
**SIC: 2099**  Emulsifiers, food
**PA:**  Corbion N.V.
   Piet Heinkade 127
   205906911

### (P-2173)
### COSMOS FOOD CO INC
17501 Mondino Dr, Rowland Heights (91748-4160)
PHONE..............................323 221-9142
David Kim, *Pr*
**EMP:** 45 **EST:** 1971
**SALES (est):** 5.97MM **Privately Held**
**Web:** www.cosmosfood.com
**SIC: 2099** 5149  Tortillas, fresh or refrigerated ; Groceries and related products, nec

### (P-2174)
### COUNTERTOP
230 W Avenue 26 Unit 256, Los Angeles (90031-1812)
PHONE..............................323 788-3591
**EMP:** 22 **EST:** 2017
**SALES (est):** 148.15K **Privately Held**
**Web:** www.kitchenambition.com
**SIC: 2099**  Food preparations, nec

### (P-2175)
### CREATIVE FOODS LLC
12622 Poway Rd # A, Poway  (92064-4451)
PHONE..............................858 748-0070
Frank Interlandi, *Managing Member*
**EMP:** 25 **EST:** 2007
**SALES (est):** 471.29K **Privately Held**
**SIC: 2099** 5812  Food preparations, nec; Eating places

### (P-2176)
### CULINARY INTERNATIONAL LLC (PA)
3280 E 44th St, Vernon  (90058)
PHONE..............................626 289-3000
**EMP:** 249 **EST:** 2017
**SALES (est):** 23.83MM
**SALES (corp-wide):** 23.83MM **Privately Held**
**Web:** www.culinaryinternational.com
**SIC: 2099** 2038 5149  Food preparations, nec ; Ethnic foods, nec, frozen; Natural and organic foods

### (P-2177)
### CULINARY SPECIALTIES INC
Also Called: Culinary Specialties
1231 Linda Vista Dr, San Marcos (92078-3809)
PHONE..............................760 744-8220
Chris Schragner, *Pr*
Patrick O Farrell, *
**EMP:** 53 **EST:** 1997
**SQ FT:** 6,400
**SALES (est):** 7.94MM **Privately Held**
**Web:** www.culinaryspecialties.net
**SIC: 2099** 2038  Emulsifiers, food; Frozen specialties, nec

### (P-2178)
### CURATION FOODS INC (HQ)
2811 Airpark Dr, Santa Maria  (93455-1417)
P.O. Box 727  (93434)
PHONE..............................800 454-1355
◆ **EMP:** 80 **EST:** 1979
**SQ FT:** 200,000
**SALES (est):** 67.97MM
**SALES (corp-wide):** 128.26MM **Publicly Held**
**Web:** www.apioinc.com
**SIC: 2099** 0723  Food preparations, nec; Vegetable packing services
**PA:**  Lifecore Biomedical, Inc.
   3515 Lyman Blvd
   952 368-4300

### (P-2179)
### DAD INVESTMENTS
2929 Halladay St, Santa Ana  (92705-5622)
PHONE..............................714 751-8500
**EMP:** 22
**SALES (est):** 959.12K **Privately Held**
**SIC: 2099** 5812  Food preparations, nec; Caterers

### (P-2180)
### DEAN DISTRIBUTORS INC
5015 Hallmark Pkwy, San Bernardino (92407-1871)
PHONE..............................323 587-8147
John D Garinger, *Brnch Mgr*
**EMP:** 21
**SALES (corp-wide):** 4.55MM **Privately Held**
**Web:** www.deandistributors.com
**SIC: 2099** 2087 2834  Sauces: dry mixes; Syrups, flavoring (except drink); Pharmaceutical preparations
**PA:**  Dean Distributors, Inc.
   899 Northgate Dr Ste 405
   800 792-0816

### (P-2181)
### DEL CASTILLO FOODS INC
Also Called: Lili Panaderia
2346 Maggio Cir, Lodi  (95240-8812)
PHONE..............................209 369-2877
Marciano Del Castillo, *Pr*
Rosario Del Castillo, *
Bertha Del Castillo, *
**EMP:** 40 **EST:** 1981
**SQ FT:** 16,200
**SALES (est):** 2.99MM **Privately Held**
**SIC: 2099** 5461 5411 2096  Tortillas, fresh or refrigerated; Retail bakeries; Grocery stores ; Potato chips and similar snacks

### (P-2182)
### DELORI-NUTIFOOD PRODUCTS INC
Also Called: Delori Foods
17043 Green Dr, City Of Industry (91745-1812)
P.O. Box 92668  (91715-2668)
PHONE..............................626 965-3006
Jaime Brown, *CEO*
Blanca Brown, *
▲ **EMP:** 32 **EST:** 1991
**SALES (est):** 5.42MM **Privately Held**
**Web:** www.deloriproducts.com
**SIC: 2099**  Jelly, corncob (gelatin)

### (P-2183)
### DIAMOND BLUE GROWERS (PA)
Also Called: California Almond Growers Exch
1802 C St, Sacramento  (95811-1099)
P.O. Box 1768  (95812-1768)
PHONE..............................800 987-2329
◆ **EMP:** 650 **EST:** 1910
**SALES (est):** 661.89MM
**SALES (corp-wide):** 661.89MM **Privately Held**
**Web:** www.bdingredients.com
**SIC: 2099**  Food preparations, nec

### (P-2184)
### DIAMOND CRYSTAL BRANDS INC
Also Called: Diamond Crystal Brands-Hormel
8700 W Doe Ave, Visalia  (93291-8900)
PHONE..............................559 651-7782
Robert Elderdice, *Brnch Mgr*
**EMP:** 40
**SALES (corp-wide):** 155.99MM **Privately Held**
**Web:** www.dymabrands.com
**SIC: 2099**  Food preparations, nec
**PA:**  Diamond Crystal Brands, Inc
   2000 Rvredge Pkwy Ste 950
   800 654-5115

### (P-2185)
### DIANAS MEXICAN FOOD PDTS INC (PA)
Also Called: La Bonita
16330 Pioneer Blvd, Norwalk  (90650-7042)
P.O. Box 369  (90651-0369)
PHONE..............................562 926-5802
Samuel Magana, *CEO*
Hortensia Magana, *
**EMP:** 50 **EST:** 1975
**SQ FT:** 4,068
**SALES (est):** 23.78MM
**SALES (corp-wide):** 23.78MM **Privately Held**
**Web:** www.dianas.net
**SIC: 2099** 5812  Tortillas, fresh or refrigerated ; Ethnic food restaurants

### (P-2186)
### DIANAS MEXICAN FOOD PDTS INC
2905 Durfee Ave, El Monte  (91732-3517)
PHONE..............................626 444-0555
Samuel Magana, *Owner*
**EMP:** 59
**SQ FT:** 13,530
**SALES (corp-wide):** 25.69MM **Privately Held**
**Web:** www.dianas.net
**SIC: 2099** 5812  Tortillas, fresh or refrigerated ; Mexican restaurant
**PA:**  Diana's Mexican Food Products, Inc.
   16330 Pioneer Blvd
   562 926-5802

### (P-2187)
### DIVINE PASTA COMPANY
140 W Providencia Ave, Burbank (91502-2121)
P.O. Box 15425  (90209-1425)
PHONE..............................818 559-7440
**EMP:** 42
**SIC: 2099**  Pasta, rice, and potato, packaged combination products

### (P-2188)
### DOLE FRESH VEGETABLES INC (HQ)
Also Called: Dole
2959 Salinas Hwy, Monterey  (93940-6400)
P.O. Box 2018  (93942-2018)
PHONE..............................831 422-8871
Howard Roeder, *CEO*
Timothy Escamilla, *
Ray Riggi, *
David H Murdock, *
Roger Billingsly, *
◆ **EMP:** 150 **EST:** 1983
**SQ FT:** 15,000
**SALES (est):** 131.69MM
**SALES (corp-wide):** 3.83B **Privately Held**
**Web:** www.dole.com
**SIC: 2099** 0723  Food preparations, nec; Fruit (fresh) packing services
**PA:**  Chiquita Holdings Limited
   3rd Floor, 25 Park Lane

### (P-2189)
### EARTH ISLAND LLC (HQ)
Also Called: Follow Your Heart
9201 Owensmouth Ave, Chatsworth (91311-5854)
P.O. Box 9400  (91309)
PHONE..............................818 725-2820
▲ **EMP:** 35 **EST:** 1988
**SALES (est):** 11.79MM
**SALES (corp-wide):** 967.79MM **Privately Held**
**Web:** www.followyourheart.com
**SIC: 2099**  Food preparations, nec
**PA:**  Danone
   17 Boulevard Haussmann
   149485000

### (P-2190)
### EARTHRISE NUTRITIONALS LLC
113 E Hoober Rd, Calipatria  (92233-9703)
P.O. Box 270  (92233-0270)
PHONE..............................760 348-5027
Jose Perez, *Mgr*
**EMP:** 29
**Web:** www.earthrise.com

## 2099 - Food Preparations, Nec (P-2191)

**SIC: 2099** Chicory root, dried
**HQ:** Earthrise Nutritionals Llc
3333 Michelson Dr Ste 300
Irvine CA 92612
949 623-0980

### (P-2191)
### EL GALLITO MARKET INC
12242 Valley Blvd, El Monte (91732-3108)
**PHONE**.................................626 442-1190
Sandra Veisaga, *Pr*
Mario Rodriguez, *
**EMP:** 35 **EST:** 1974
**SQ FT:** 1,200
**SALES (est):** 2.36MM **Privately Held**
**Web:** www.elgallitomkt.com
**SIC: 2099** 5421 5411 Tortillas, fresh or refrigerated; Meat and fish markets; Grocery stores

### (P-2192)
### ESPERANZAS TORTILLERIA
750 Rock Springs Rd, Escondido (92025-1625)
**PHONE**.................................760 743-5908
Victor Martinez, *Pr*
Teresa Martinez, *
Hugo Martinez, *
Leonor Batista, *
**EMP:** 46 **EST:** 1980
**SALES (est):** 1.77MM **Privately Held**
**Web:** www.esperanzastortilleria.com
**SIC: 2099** Tortillas, fresh or refrigerated

### (P-2193)
### EVERSON SPICE COMPANY INC
2667 Gundry Ave, Long Beach (90755-1808)
**PHONE**.................................562 595-4785
Kim Everson, *CEO*
Ken Hopkins, *
Thomas L Everson, *Prin*
▲ **EMP:** 35 **EST:** 1987
**SQ FT:** 35,000
**SALES (est):** 5.6MM **Privately Held**
**Web:** www.eversonspice.com
**SIC: 2099** Spices, including grinding

### (P-2194)
### EVERYTABLE PBC
Also Called: Everytable
3650 W Martin Luther King Jr Blvd, Los Angeles (90008-1700)
**PHONE**.................................323 296-0311
**EMP:** 38
**SALES (corp-wide):** 70.66MM **Privately Held**
**Web:** www.everytable.com
**SIC: 2099** Box lunches, for sale off premises
**PA:** Everytable, Pbc
18901 Railroad St
917 319-6156

### (P-2195)
### F I O IMPORTS INC
Also Called: Contessa Premium Foods
5980 Alcoa Ave, Vernon (90058-3925)
**PHONE**.................................323 263-5100
Dirk Leuenberger, *Pr*
Bob Nielsen, *CFO*
**EMP:** 180 **EST:** 2002
**SALES (est):** 24.31MM **Privately Held**
**SIC: 2099** Food preparations, nec
**HQ:** Aqua Star (Usa), Corp.
2025 1st Ave Ste 200
Seattle WA 98121
800 232-6280

### (P-2196)
### FALCON TRADING COMPANY (PA)
Also Called: Sunridge Farms
423 Salinas Rd, Royal Oaks (95076-5232)
**PHONE**.................................831 786-7000
Morton Cohen, *CEO*
Rebecca Cohen, *
Ronald Giannini, *
◆ **EMP:** 150 **EST:** 1977
**SQ FT:** 24,500
**SALES (est):** 45.97MM
**SALES (corp-wide):** 45.97MM **Privately Held**
**Web:** www.shopsunridgefarms.com
**SIC: 2099** 5149 Food preparations, nec; Natural and organic foods

### (P-2197)
### FAMILY LOOMPYA CORPORATION
2626 Southport Way Ste F, National City (91950-8753)
**PHONE**.................................619 477-2125
Alen Enriquez, *Pr*
▲ **EMP:** 25 **EST:** 1973
**SQ FT:** 10,000
**SALES (est):** 3.94MM **Privately Held**
**Web:** www.familyloompya.com
**SIC: 2099** 5149 Food preparations, nec; Specialty food items

### (P-2198)
### FINE MEXICAN FOOD PRODUCTS INC
7025 Old 215 Frontage Rd, Moreno Valley (92553-7901)
P.O. Box 8019 (92552-8019)
**PHONE**.................................714 476-7104
Marcos Doddoli, *CEO*
Marcos Guido Doddoli, *CEO*
▲ **EMP:** 15 **EST:** 2002
**SALES (est):** 15.13MM **Privately Held**
**Web:** www.finemexicanproducts.com
**SIC: 2099** Food preparations, nec

### (P-2199)
### FIORE DI PASTA INC
Also Called: Primavera Foods USA
4776 E Jensen Ave, Fresno (93725-1704)
**PHONE**.................................559 457-0431
Bernadetta Primavera, *Pr*
Anthony Primavera, *
▲ **EMP:** 67 **EST:** 1994
**SQ FT:** 59,000
**SALES (est):** 9.7MM **Privately Held**
**Web:** www.fioredipasta.com
**SIC: 2099** Pasta, uncooked: packaged with other ingredients

### (P-2200)
### FIVE STAR GOURMET FOODS INC (PA)
3880 Ebony St, Ontario (91761-1500)
**PHONE**.................................909 390-0032
Tal Shoshan, *CEO*
Michelle Eoff, *Ex VP*
Masha Simonian, *CFO*
Michael Solomon, *Pr*
**EMP:** 199 **EST:** 1999
**SQ FT:** 130,000
**SALES (est):** 52.52MM
**SALES (corp-wide):** 52.52MM **Privately Held**
**Web:** www.fivestargourmetfoods.com
**SIC: 2099** Ready-to-eat meals, salads, and sandwiches

### (P-2201)
### FLEISCHMANNS VINEGAR COMPANY INC (DH)
12604 Hiddencreek Way Ste A, Cerritos (90703-2137)
**PHONE**.................................562 483-4619
**EMP:** 20 **EST:** 1920
**SALES (est):** 46.81MM **Privately Held**
**Web:** www.fleischmannsvinegar.com
**SIC: 2099** 2087 Vinegar; Flavoring extracts and syrups, nec
**HQ:** Kerry Inc.
3400 Millington Rd
Beloit WI 53511
608 363-1200

### (P-2202)
### FOODOLOGY LLC
Also Called: Sproutime
8920 Norris Ave, Sun Valley (91352-2740)
**PHONE**.................................818 252-1888
**EMP:** 75 **EST:** 1980
**SQ FT:** 20,000
**SALES (est):** 1.48MM **Privately Held**
**SIC: 2099** Ready-to-eat meals, salads, and sandwiches

### (P-2203)
### FOODS ON FLY LLC
7004 Carroll Rd, San Diego (92121-2213)
**PHONE**.................................858 404-0642
Peter Didomizio, *Managing Member*
Budy Kubursi, *
**EMP:** 38 **EST:** 2019
**SALES (est):** 2.41MM **Privately Held**
**SIC: 2099** Sandwiches, assembled and packaged: for wholesale market

### (P-2204)
### FOUR SEASONS HUMMUS INC
11030 Randall St, Sun Valley (91352-2621)
**PHONE**.................................305 409-0449
Claudia Mejia, *Pr*
Francisco Mejia, *Dir*
**EMP:** 17 **EST:** 2019
**SALES (est):** 354.69K **Privately Held**
**SIC: 2099** 1541 Sauce, gravy, dressing, and dip mixes; Food products manufacturing or packing plant construction

### (P-2205)
### FRESH & READY FOODS LLC (PA)
1145 Arroyo St Ste B, San Fernando (91340-1842)
**PHONE**.................................818 837-7600
Art Sezgin, *Pr*
John Saladino, *
**EMP:** 99 **EST:** 2015
**SALES (est):** 23.22MM
**SALES (corp-wide):** 23.22MM **Privately Held**
**Web:** www.freshandreadyfoods.com
**SIC: 2099** Salads, fresh or refrigerated

### (P-2206)
### FRESH EXPRESS INC
Also Called: Fresh Express
900 E Blanco Rd, Salinas (93901-4419)
**PHONE**.................................831 770-7600
**EMP:** 52 **EST:** 1989
**SALES (est):** 16.58MM **Privately Held**
**Web:** www.freshexpress.com
**SIC: 2099** Food preparations, nec

### (P-2207)
### FRESHREALM INC (PA)
1330 Calle Avanzado, San Clemente (92673-6351)
P.O. Box 5317 (92674-5317)
**PHONE**.................................800 264-1297
Michael R Lippold, *CEO*
Salomi Varma, *
**EMP:** 125 **EST:** 2013
**SQ FT:** 5,000
**SALES (est):** 212.4MM
**SALES (corp-wide):** 212.4MM **Privately Held**
**Web:** www.freshrealm.com
**SIC: 2099** Food preparations, nec

### (P-2208)
### FRESHREALM INC
3151 Regatta Ave Pmb B60, Richmond (94804-6411)
**PHONE**.................................888 278-4349
**EMP:** 450
**SALES (corp-wide):** 212.4MM **Privately Held**
**Web:** www.freshrealm.com
**SIC: 2099** Food preparations, nec
**PA:** Freshrealm, Inc.
1330 Calle Avanzado
800 264-1297

### (P-2209)
### FRESHREALM INC
2900 N Macarthur Dr Unit 300, Tracy (95376-2068)
**PHONE**.................................800 264-1297
**EMP:** 455
**SALES (corp-wide):** 212.4MM **Privately Held**
**Web:** www.freshrealm.com
**SIC: 2099** Food preparations, nec
**PA:** Freshrealm, Inc.
1330 Calle Avanzado
800 264-1297

### (P-2210)
### FUJI FOOD PRODUCTS INC (PA)
14420 Bloomfield Ave, Santa Fe Springs (90670-5410)
**PHONE**.................................562 404-2590
Farrell Hirsch, *CEO*
Javier Aceves, *
▲ **EMP:** 100 **EST:** 2010
**SQ FT:** 90,000
**SALES (est):** 46.24MM
**SALES (corp-wide):** 46.24MM **Privately Held**
**Web:** www.fujisansushi.com
**SIC: 2099** Food preparations, nec

### (P-2211)
### FUJI FOOD PRODUCTS INC
8660 Miramar Rd Ste N, San Diego (92126-4362)
**PHONE**.................................619 268-3118
Kenny Sung, *Brnch Mgr*
**EMP:** 152
**SALES (corp-wide):** 46.24MM **Privately Held**
**Web:** www.fujisansushi.com
**SIC: 2099** Food preparations, nec
**PA:** Fuji Food Products, Inc.
14420 Bloomfield Ave
562 404-2590

### (P-2212)
### FUJI NATURAL FOODS INC (HQ)
13500 S Hamner Ave, Ontario (91761-2605)
P.O. Box 3728 (91761-0973)
**PHONE**.................................909 947-1008
Katsushiro Nakagawa, *CEO*
Ikuzo Sugiyama, *
◆ **EMP:** 72 **EST:** 1979
**SQ FT:** 65,000

# PRODUCTS & SERVICES SECTION
## 2099 - Food Preparations, Nec (P-2234)

SALES (est): 9.09MM Privately Held
Web: www.fujinf.com
SIC: 2099 Food preparations, nec
PA: Taiyo Foodstuffs Industry Co., Ltd.
2618-6, Naegicho

### (P-2213)
### GH FOODS CA LLC (DH)
8425 Carbide Ct, Sacramento (95828-5609)
PHONE.................................916 844-1140
EMP: 330 EST: 2007
SQ FT: 60,000
SALES (est): 46.95MM
SALES (corp-wide): 971.95MM Publicly Held
SIC: 2099 Salads, fresh or refrigerated
HQ: Renaissance Food Group, Llc
500 W Elmer Rd
Vineland NJ 08360
916 638-8825

### (P-2214)
### GHIRINGHLLI SPCIALTY FOODS INC
101 Benicia Rd, Vallejo (94590-7003)
PHONE.................................707 561-7670
Mike Ghiringhelli, Pr
Ed Ferrero, *
EMP: 145 EST: 1984
SQ FT: 55,000
SALES (est): 23.81MM Privately Held
Web: www.gfoods.net
SIC: 2099 Ready-to-eat meals, salads, and sandwiches

### (P-2215)
### GLUTEN FREE FOODS MFG LLC (PA)
5010 Eucalyptus Ave, Chino (91710-9216)
PHONE.................................909 823-8230
Luis Faura, Managing Member
EMP: 16 EST: 2015
SALES (est): 6.13MM
SALES (corp-wide): 6.13MM Privately Held
Web: www.glutenfreefoodsmfg.com
SIC: 2099 Pasta, uncooked: packaged with other ingredients

### (P-2216)
### GOBBLE INC
Also Called: Gobble
18675 Madrone Pkwy, Morgan Hill (95037)
PHONE.................................650 847-1258
Ooshma Garg, CEO
EMP: 170 EST: 2010
SALES (est): 20.92MM Privately Held
Web: www.gobble.com
SIC: 2099 Food preparations, nec

### (P-2217)
### GOLD COAST INGREDIENTS INC
2429 Yates Ave, Commerce (90040-1917)
PHONE.................................323 724-8935
Clarence H Brasher, CEO
James A Sgro, *
Laurie Goddard, *
◆ EMP: 53 EST: 1985
SQ FT: 50,000
SALES (est): 20.06MM Privately Held
Web: www.goldcoastinc.com
SIC: 2099 Almond pastes

### (P-2218)
### GOLD STAR FOODS INC
Also Called: Gold Star Foods
1000 Vaughn Rd, Dixon (95620-4553)
PHONE.................................909 843-9600

EMP: 32
SALES (corp-wide): 519.54MM Privately Held
Web: www.goldstarfoods.com
SIC: 2099 Ready-to-eat meals, salads, and sandwiches
HQ: Gold Star Foods, Inc.
3781 E Airport Dr
Ontario CA 91761
909 843-9600

### (P-2219)
### GOLD STAR FOODS INC (HQ)
3781 E Airport Dr, Ontario (91761-1558)
P.O. Box 4328 (91761-8828)
PHONE.................................909 843-9600
Sean Leer, Pr
C Scott Salmon, Strategy Vice President*
Joe Villarreal, *
Greg Johnson, *
Les Wong, *
▲ EMP: 64 EST: 2007
SQ FT: 38,000
SALES (est): 329.25MM
SALES (corp-wide): 519.54MM Privately Held
Web: www.goldstarfoods.com
SIC: 2099 Ready-to-eat meals, salads, and sandwiches
PA: Highview Capital, Llc
11755 Wlshire Blvd Ste 14
310 806-9780

### (P-2220)
### GOLDEN SPECIALTY FOODS LLC
14605 Best Ave, Norwalk (90650-5258)
PHONE.................................562 802-2537
Philip Pisciotta, CEO
Philip Pisciotta, Managing Member
Jeff Chan, *
Deryk Howard, *
◆ EMP: 25 EST: 1979
SQ FT: 31,000
SALES (est): 5.06MM Privately Held
Web: www.goldenspecialtyfoods.com
SIC: 2099 2032 Food preparations, nec; Canned specialties

### (P-2221)
### GOOD VIEW FUTURE GROUP INC
277 S B St, San Mateo (94401-4017)
PHONE.................................408 834-5698
William Jiang, CEO
EMP: 18 EST: 2019
SALES (est): 413.65K Privately Held
SIC: 2099 Desserts, ready-to-mix

### (P-2222)
### GOODMAN FOOD PRODUCTS INC (PA)
Also Called: Don Lee Farms
200 E Beach Ave Fl 1, Inglewood (90302-3404)
PHONE.................................310 674-3180
Donald Goodman, CEO
▲ EMP: 250 EST: 1982
SQ FT: 55,000
SALES (est): 49.19MM
SALES (corp-wide): 49.19MM Privately Held
Web: www.donleefarms.com
SIC: 2099 Food preparations, nec

### (P-2223)
### GPDE SLVA SPCES INCRPORATION (PA)
Also Called: Peterson's Spices

8531 Loch Lomond Dr, Pico Rivera (90660-2509)
PHONE.................................562 407-2643
Ravi De Silva, Pr
Rupa De Silva, *
Binuka De Silva, *
Nalin Kulasooriya, *
◆ EMP: 80 EST: 2008
SQ FT: 60,000
SALES (est): 19.85MM Privately Held
Web: www.cinnamononline.com
SIC: 2099 5149 Chili pepper or powder; Spices and seasonings

### (P-2224)
### GRUMA CORPORATION
Also Called: Mission Foods
2849 E Edgar Ave, Fresno (93706-5454)
PHONE.................................559 498-7820
Kathy Trout, Manager
EMP: 68
Web: www.missionfoods.com
SIC: 2099 Food preparations, nec
HQ: Gruma Corporation
5601 Executive Dr Ste 800
Irving TX 75038
972 232-5000

### (P-2225)
### HAIGS DELICACIES LLC
25673 Nickel Pl, Hayward (94545-3221)
PHONE.................................510 782-6285
Rita Takvorian, Managing Member
EMP: 20 EST: 1958
SQ FT: 1,200
SALES (est): 4.55MM Privately Held
Web: www.haigs.com
SIC: 2099 Dips, except cheese and sour cream based

### (P-2226)
### HALIBURTON INTERNATIONAL FOODS INC
3855 Jurupa St, Ontario (91761-1404)
PHONE.................................909 428-8520
▲ EMP: 278 EST: 1992
SALES (est): 49.38MM Privately Held
Web: www.haliburton.net
SIC: 2099 Food preparations, nec

### (P-2227)
### HANA GROUP OPS LLC
5919 3rd St, San Francisco (94124-3103)
PHONE.................................628 280-9401
EMP: 20
SALES (est): 835.08K Privately Held
SIC: 2099 Food preparations, nec

### (P-2228)
### HARMLESS HARVEST INC
Also Called: Harmless Harvest
1814 Franklin St Ste 1000, Oakland (94612-3461)
PHONE.................................347 688-6286
Ben Mand, CEO
Giannella Alvarez, *
Justin Guilbert, *
Brad Paris, *
▲ EMP: 45 EST: 2010
SALES (est): 15.92MM
SALES (corp-wide): 967.79MM Privately Held
Web: www.harmlessharvest.com
SIC: 2099 Coconut, desiccated and shredded
PA: Danone
17 Boulevard Haussmann
149485000

### (P-2229)
### HEALTHY TIMES INC
Also Called: Healthy Tmes Ntral Pdts For Ch
225 Broadway Ste 450, San Diego (92101-5027)
PHONE.................................858 513-1550
Rondi Prescott, CEO
Richard Prescott, Pr
EMP: 15 EST: 1994
SQ FT: 2,800
SALES (est): 919.77K Privately Held
SIC: 2099 2844 Food preparations, nec; Cosmetic preparations

### (P-2230)
### HEARTLAND HARVEST
1174 Pierre Way, El Cajon (92021-4606)
PHONE.................................619 729-1604
Pamela Leathers, Pr
EMP: 19 EST: 2005
SALES (est): 205.88K Privately Held
Web: www.heartlandharvestinc.com
SIC: 2099 Food preparations, nec

### (P-2231)
### HESPERIA UNIFIED SCHOOL DST
Also Called: Hesperia Usd Food Service
11176 G Ave, Hesperia (92345-8315)
PHONE.................................760 948-1051
Janet Clesceri, Brnch Mgr
EMP: 63
SALES (corp-wide): 450.24MM Privately Held
Web: www.cottonwoodelementary.org
SIC: 2099 8322 8299 Box lunches, for sale off premises; Geriatric social service; Arts and crafts schools
PA: Hesperia Unified School District
15576 Main St
760 244-4411

### (P-2232)
### HONEY BENNETTS FARM
3176 Honey Ln, Fillmore (93015-2026)
PHONE.................................805 521-1375
Gilebert Vannoy, Pr
Ann Lindsay Bennett, *
EMP: 25 EST: 1978
SQ FT: 20,000
SALES (est): 2.66MM Privately Held
Web: www.bennethoney.com
SIC: 2099 5191 0279 Honey, strained and bottled; Farm supplies; Apiary (bee and honey farm)

### (P-2233)
### HOUSE FOODS AMERICA CORP (HQ)
Also Called: Hinoichi Tofu
7351 Orangewood Ave, Garden Grove (92841-1411)
PHONE.................................714 901-4350
Atsushi Tomohara, Pr
Masakazu Nishida, *
▲ EMP: 41 EST: 1947
SQ FT: 30,000
SALES (est): 74.4MM Privately Held
Web: www.house-foods.com
SIC: 2099 Food preparations, nec
PA: House Foods Group Inc.
1-5-7, Mikuriyasakaemachi

### (P-2234)
### HUGHSON NUT INC
11173 Mercedes Ave, Livingston (95334-9707)
PHONE.................................209 394-6005
Luis Ma, Prin

## 2099 - Food Preparations, Nec (P-2235)

**EMP:** 156
**SALES (corp-wide):** 174.1MM **Privately Held**
**SIC: 2099** Food preparations, nec
**HQ:** Hughson Nut, Inc.
  1825 Verduga Rd
  Hughson CA 95326
  209 883-0403

### (P-2235)
### HUSKS UNLIMITED (PA)
9925 Airway Rd # C, San Diego (92154-7932)
**PHONE** .................................. 619 476-8301
Luis Duenas, *CEO*
Eric Brenk, *Pr*
**EMP:** 30 **EST:** 2012
**SALES (est):** 7.1MM
**SALES (corp-wide):** 7.1MM **Privately Held**
**Web:** www.husksunlimitedinc.com
**SIC: 2099** 0723 5159 2013 Food preparations, nec; Corn drying services; Corn husks; Cooked meats, from purchased meat

### (P-2236)
### IF HOLDING INC (PA)
Also Called: Initiative Food Company
1912 Industrial Way, Sanger (93657-9508)
**PHONE** .................................. 559 875-3354
John Ypma, *Pr*
John P Mulvaney, *
David F Markle, *
**EMP:** 52 **EST:** 2002
**SQ FT:** 200,094
**SALES (est):** 20.8MM
**SALES (corp-wide):** 20.8MM **Privately Held**
**Web:** www.initiativefoods.com
**SIC: 2099** Food preparations, nec

### (P-2237)
### IMPERFECT FOODS INC (HQ)
Also Called: Imperfect Produce
351 Cheryl Ln, Walnut (91789)
**PHONE** .................................. 510 595-6683
Abhi Ramesh, *CEO*
**EMP:** 75 **EST:** 2017
**SALES (est):** 24.28MM
**SALES (corp-wide):** 25MM **Privately Held**
**Web:** www.imperfectfoods.com
**SIC: 2099** Vegetables, peeled for the trade
**PA:** Misfits Market, Inc.
  7481 Coca Cola Dr
  678 559-7970

### (P-2238)
### IMPOSSIBLE FOODS INC (PA)
400 Saginaw Dr, Redwood City (94063-4749)
**PHONE** .................................. 650 461-4385
Peter Mcguinness, *CEO*
David J Lipman, *CSO*
Dana Wagner, *CLO*
Dennis Woodside, *Pr*
▲ **EMP:** 210 **EST:** 2011
**SALES (est):** 173.73MM **Privately Held**
**Web:** www.impossiblefoods.com
**SIC: 2099** Food preparations, nec

### (P-2239)
### INGREDIENTS BY NATURE LLC
5555 Brooks St, Montclair (91763-4547)
**PHONE** .................................. 909 230-6200
Matt Outz, *Pr*
**EMP:** 19 **EST:** 2010
**SALES (est):** 3.42MM **Privately Held**
**Web:** www.ingredientsbynature.com
**SIC: 2099** Molasses, mixed or blended: from purchased ingredients

### (P-2240)
### INTERNTIONAL TEA IMPORTERS INC (PA)
Also Called: India Tea Importers
2140 Davie Ave, Commerce (90040-1706)
**PHONE** .................................. 562 801-9600
Brendan Shah, *CEO*
Bianca Shah, *
Reena Shah, *
◆ **EMP:** 32 **EST:** 1992
**SQ FT:** 21,500
**SALES (est):** 9.68MM **Privately Held**
**Web:** www.teavendor.com
**SIC: 2099** 5149 Tea blending; Coffee and tea

### (P-2241)
### J W FLOOR COVERING INC
3401 Enterprise Ave, Hayward (94545-3201)
**PHONE** .................................. 858 444-1214
Decklan Donohue, *Mgr*
**EMP:** 134
**SALES (corp-wide):** 48.9MM **Privately Held**
**Web:** www.jwfloors.com
**SIC: 2099** Food preparations, nec
**PA:** J. W. Floor Covering, Inc.
  9881 Carroll Centre Rd
  858 536-8565

### (P-2242)
### JAYONE FOODS INC
7212 Alondra Blvd, Paramount (90723-3902)
**PHONE** .................................. 562 633-7400
Seung Hoon Lee, *Pr*
Chil Park, *
◆ **EMP:** 50 **EST:** 1999
**SQ FT:** 28,000
**SALES (est):** 8.94MM **Privately Held**
**Web:** www.jayonefoods.com
**SIC: 2099** Food preparations, nec

### (P-2243)
### JBR INC (PA)
Also Called: San Francisco Bay Coffee Co
1731 Aviation Blvd, Lincoln (95648-9317)
**PHONE** .................................. 916 258-8000
Peter Rogers, *CEO*
Barbara Rogers, *VP*
Albert Troutman, *CFO*
◆ **EMP:** 124 **EST:** 1979
**SQ FT:** 400,000
**SALES (est):** 44.2MM
**SALES (corp-wide):** 44.2MM **Privately Held**
**Web:** www.sfbaycoffee.com
**SIC: 2099** 2095 Tea blending; Coffee roasting (except by wholesale grocers)

### (P-2244)
### JIMENES FOOD INC
7046 Jackson St, Paramount (90723-4835)
**PHONE** .................................. 562 602-2505
Reyna Jimenez, *Pr*
Juan Jimenez, *
**EMP:** 30 **EST:** 1998
**SQ FT:** 11,000
**SALES (est):** 11.35MM **Privately Held**
**Web:** www.juanjs.com
**SIC: 2099** Tortillas, fresh or refrigerated

### (P-2245)
### JSL FOODS INC (PA)
3550 Pasadena Ave, Los Angeles (90031-1946)
**PHONE** .................................. 323 223-2484
Teiji Kawana, *Pr*
Koji Kawana, *
◆ **EMP:** 71 **EST:** 1990
**SALES (est):** 59.68MM **Privately Held**
**Web:** www.jslfoods.com
**SIC: 2099** 5142 2052 Pasta, uncooked: packaged with other ingredients; Packaged frozen goods; Cookies

### (P-2246)
### KATE FARMS INC
101 Innovation Pl, Santa Barbara (93108-2268)
P.O. Box 50840 (93150-0840)
**PHONE** .................................. 805 845-2446
Richard Laver, *Pr*
Richard Laver, *Prin*
Michelle Laver, *
Tom Beecher, *Executive Corporate Development Vice President*
**EMP:** 123 **EST:** 2015
**SALES (est):** 40.72MM **Privately Held**
**Web:** www.katefarms.com
**SIC: 2099** Ready-to-eat meals, salads, and sandwiches

### (P-2247)
### KTS KITCHENS INC
1065 E Walnut St Ste C, Carson (90746-1384)
**PHONE** .................................. 310 764-0850
Kathleen D Taggares, *CEO*
Joan Paris, *
**EMP:** 250 **EST:** 1987
**SALES (est):** 20.32MM **Privately Held**
**Web:** www.ktskitchens.com
**SIC: 2099** 2035 Pizza, refrigerated: except frozen; Dressings, salad: raw and cooked (except dry mixes)

### (P-2248)
### LA BARCA TORTILLERIA INC
3047 Whittier Blvd, Los Angeles (90023-1651)
P.O. Box 23548 (90023-0548)
**PHONE** .................................. 323 268-1744
Jose Luis Arevalo, *CEO*
Antonio Arevalo, *
Alexander Arevalo, *
**EMP:** 50 **EST:** 1988
**SQ FT:** 6,000
**SALES (est):** 4.6MM **Privately Held**
**SIC: 2099** Tortillas, fresh or refrigerated

### (P-2249)
### LA CHAPALITA INC (PA)
1724 Chico Ave, El Monte (91733-2942)
**PHONE** .................................. 626 443-8556
Luis E Moya Senior, *Pr*
Luis E Moya Junior, *Genl Mgr*
**EMP:** 20 **EST:** 1981
**SQ FT:** 15,000
**SALES (est):** 4.28MM
**SALES (corp-wide):** 4.28MM **Privately Held**
**Web:** www.lachapalita.com
**SIC: 2099** Tortillas, fresh or refrigerated

### (P-2250)
### LA COLONIAL TORTILLA PDTS INC
Also Called: La Colonial Mexican Foods
543 Monterey Pass Rd, Monterey Park (91754-2416)
**PHONE** .................................. 626 289-3647
Daniel Robles, *Pr*
**EMP:** 185 **EST:** 1950
**SQ FT:** 27,000
**SALES (est):** 7.95MM **Privately Held**
**Web:** www.lacolonial-la.com
**SIC: 2099** Tortillas, fresh or refrigerated

### (P-2251)
### LA COPA DE ORO
Also Called: Productos Oropeza
3321 W 1st St, Santa Ana (92703-3423)
**PHONE** .................................. 714 554-9925
Jose Oropeza, *Owner*
**EMP:** 20 **EST:** 1975
**SQ FT:** 2,400
**SALES (est):** 850.37K **Privately Held**
**SIC: 2099** Tortillas, fresh or refrigerated

### (P-2252)
### LA FE TORTILLERIA INC (PA)
Also Called: La Fe Tortilleria Factory
1512 Linda Vista Dr, San Marcos (92078)
P.O. Box 787 (92079)
**PHONE** .................................. 760 752-8350
Jesus Martinez, *Pr*
Isabel Delgado, *
Hoxsie Smith, *
Andrea Smith, *
**EMP:** 30 **EST:** 2005
**SQ FT:** 4,000
**SALES (est):** 2.76MM
**SALES (corp-wide):** 2.76MM **Privately Held**
**Web:** www.lafetortilleria.com
**SIC: 2099** 5812 5046 5461 Tortillas, fresh or refrigerated; Mexican restaurant; Bakery equipment and supplies; Retail bakeries

### (P-2253)
### LA FORTALEZA INC
525 N Ford Blvd, Los Angeles (90022-1104)
**PHONE** .................................. 323 261-1211
Hermila Josefina Ortiz, *CEO*
David Ortiz, *
Ramiro Ortiz Junior, *VP*
**EMP:** 98 **EST:** 1990
**SQ FT:** 40,000
**SALES (est):** 10.08MM **Privately Held**
**Web:** www.lafortalezaproducts.net
**SIC: 2099** 2096 Tortillas, fresh or refrigerated; Potato chips and similar snacks

### (P-2254)
### LA GLORIA FOODS CORP (PA)
Also Called: La Gloria Tortilleria
3455 E 1st St, Los Angeles (90063-2945)
**PHONE** .................................. 323 262-0410
Maria De La Luz Vera, *CEO*
▼ **EMP:** 80 **EST:** 1954
**SQ FT:** 8,000
**SALES (est):** 4.45MM
**SALES (corp-wide):** 4.45MM **Privately Held**
**Web:** www.lagloriafoods.com
**SIC: 2099** 5461 5812 Tortillas, fresh or refrigerated; Bread; Mexican restaurant

### (P-2255)
### LA GLORIA FOODS CORP
Also Called: La Gloria Flour Tortillas
3285 E Cesar E Chavez Ave, Los Angeles (90063-2853)
**PHONE** .................................. 323 263-6755
Daniel Torrez, *Mgr*
**EMP:** 20
**SALES (corp-wide):** 4.45MM **Privately Held**
**Web:** www.lagloriafoods.com
**SIC: 2099** 5461 Tortillas, fresh or refrigerated; Retail bakeries
**PA:** La Gloria Foods Corp.
  3455 E 1st St
  323 262-0410

## PRODUCTS & SERVICES SECTION
## 2099 - Food Preparations, Nec (P-2277)

**(P-2256)**
**LA MEJOR INC**
Also Called: La Mejor Restaurant
684 S Farmersville Blvd, Farmersville
(93223-2042)
P.O. Box 657 (93223-0657)
PHONE..................................559 747-0739
Rafael Vasquez, *Admn*
Rafael Vasquez, *Owner*
Octaviana Vasquez, *
**EMP:** 35 **EST:** 1970
**SALES (est):** 2.75MM **Privately Held**
**Web:** www.lamejorfarmersville.com
**SIC:** 2099 5411 Tortillas, fresh or refrigerated
; Grocery stores, independent

**(P-2257)**
**LA PRINCESITA TORTILLERIA INC (PA)**
Also Called: Abalquiga
3432 E Cesar E Chavez Ave, Los Angeles
(90063-4146)
PHONE..................................323 267-0673
Francisco Ramirez, *Pr*
**EMP:** 19 **EST:** 1974
**SQ FT:** 2,195
**SALES (est):** 2.46MM
**SALES (corp-wide):** 2.46MM **Privately Held**
**Web:** www.la-princesita.com
**SIC:** 2099 Tortillas, fresh or refrigerated

**(P-2258)**
**LA ROSA TORTILLA FACTORY INC**
26 Menker St, Watsonville (95076-4915)
PHONE..................................831 728-5332
Alfonso Solorio, *Owner*
**EMP:** 118
**Web:** www.larosatortillafactory.com
**SIC:** 2099 Tortillas, fresh or refrigerated
**PA:** La Rosa Tortilla Factory, Inc.
142 2nd St

**(P-2259)**
**LA TAPATIA TORTILLERIA INC**
Also Called: Sol De Oro
104 E Belmont Ave, Fresno (93701-1403)
PHONE..................................559 441-1030
Helen Chavez-hansen, *Prin*
John Hansen, *
Dan Soleno, *Prin*
**EMP:** 170 **EST:** 1944
**SQ FT:** 40,000
**SALES (est):** 24.89MM **Privately Held**
**Web:** www.tortillas4u.com
**SIC:** 2099 Tortillas, fresh or refrigerated

**(P-2260)**
**LABRUCHERIE PRODUCE LLC**
1407 S La Brucherie Rd, El Centro
(92243-9677)
PHONE..................................760 352-2170
Jean Labrucherie, *Managing Member*
Tim Labrucherie, *Prin*
**EMP:** 42 **EST:** 2011
**SALES (est):** 11.3MM
**SALES (corp-wide):** 11.3MM **Privately Held**
**Web:** www.lbproduce.com
**SIC:** 2099 0191 Vegetables, peeled for the trade; General farms, primarily crop
**PA:** Tjl Capital, Inc.
1407 S La Brucherie Rd
760 352-2170

**(P-2261)**
**LASELVA BEACH SPICE CO INC**
453 Mcquaide Dr, Watsonville
(95076-1908)
PHONE..................................831 724-4500
Floyd W Brady, *CEO*
**EMP:** 18 **EST:** 2018
**SALES (est):** 2.25MM **Privately Held**
**Web:** www.laselvabeachspice.com
**SIC:** 2099 Seasonings and spices

**(P-2262)**
**LASSONDE PAPPAS AND CO INC**
1755 E Acacia St, Ontario (91761-7702)
PHONE..................................909 923-4041
Rick Jochums, *Mgr*
**EMP:** 30
**SALES (corp-wide):** 402.06MM **Privately Held**
**Web:** www.lassondepappas.com
**SIC:** 2099 Food preparations, nec
**HQ:** Lassonde Pappas And Company, Inc.
3 Executive Campus
Cherry Hill NJ 08002
856 455-1000

**(P-2263)**
**LEHMAN FOODS INC**
Also Called: Fresh & Ready
1145 Arroyo St Ste B, San Fernando
(91340-1842)
PHONE..................................818 837-7600
Charles Lehman, *CEO*
Art Sezgin, *
Harry Iknadosian, *
Lisa Lehman, *
Cameron Childs, *
**EMP:** 25 **EST:** 1990
**SQ FT:** 15,000
**SALES (est):** 6.29MM **Privately Held**
**SIC:** 2099 Salads, fresh or refrigerated

**(P-2264)**
**LETS DO LUNCH**
Also Called: Integrated Food Service
310 W Alondra Blvd, Gardena
(90248-2423)
PHONE..................................310 523-3664
Paul G Giuliano, *CEO*
Paul G Giuliano, *Pr*
Jon Sugimoto, *
David Watzke, *
▲ **EMP:** 300 **EST:** 1991
**SQ FT:** 57,000
**SALES (est):** 26.22MM **Privately Held**
**Web:** www.integratedfoodservice.com
**SIC:** 2099 Sandwiches, assembled and packaged: for wholesale market

**(P-2265)**
**LEY GRAND FOODS CORPORATION**
287 S 6th Ave, La Puente (91746-2916)
PHONE..................................626 336-2244
Frank Chen, *Pr*
J J Chen, *Sec*
Chien Chen, *VP*
▲ **EMP:** 23 **EST:** 1989
**SQ FT:** 4,000
**SALES (est):** 2.01MM **Privately Held**
**Web:** www.leygrandfoods.com
**SIC:** 2099 Food preparations, nec

**(P-2266)**
**LIDESTRI FOODS INC**
Also Called: International Co-Packing Co
568 S Temperance Ave, Fresno
(93727-6601)
PHONE..................................559 251-1000
Willie Bynum, *Brnch Mgr*
**EMP:** 347
**SALES (corp-wide):** 474.82MM **Privately Held**
**Web:** www.lidestrifoodanddrink.com
**SIC:** 2099 Food preparations, nec
**PA:** Lidestri Foods, Inc.
815 W Whitney Rd
585 377-7700

**(P-2267)**
**LIVING WELLNESS PARTNERS LLC**
Also Called: Buddha Teas
3305 Tyler St, Carlsbad (92008-3056)
PHONE..................................800 642-3754
John Boyd, *CEO*
Nicholas Narier, *
**EMP:** 30 **EST:** 2013
**SQ FT:** 10,000
**SALES (est):** 4.53MM **Privately Held**
**Web:** www.buddhateas.com
**SIC:** 2099 Tea blending

**(P-2268)**
**LOS PERICOS FOOD PRODUCTS LLC**
2301 Valley Blvd, Pomona (91768-1105)
PHONE..................................909 623-5625
Marcelino Ortega, *Pt*
Luis Ortega, *Pt*
Guadalupe Ortega, *Pt*
**EMP:** 46 **EST:** 1962
**SQ FT:** 20,000
**SALES (est):** 2.51MM **Privately Held**
**Web:** www.lospericosfood.com
**SIC:** 2099 Tortillas, fresh or refrigerated

**(P-2269)**
**LUCERNE FOODS INC**
5918 Stoneridge Mall Rd, Pleasanton
(94588-3229)
PHONE..................................925 951-4724
Kenneth Gott, *Pr*
Peggy Han, *
▼ **EMP:** 3001 **EST:** 1979
**SALES (est):** 1.95MM
**SALES (corp-wide):** 79.24B **Publicly Held**
**Web:** www.lucernefoods.com
**SIC:** 2099 Food preparations, nec
**HQ:** Safeway Inc.
5918 Stoneridge Mall Rd
Pleasanton CA 94588
925 226-5000

**(P-2270)**
**LYRICAL FOODS INC**
Also Called: Kite Hill
3180 Corporate Pl, Hayward (94545-3916)
PHONE..................................510 784-0955
John Haugen, *CEO*
Jean Prebot, *
Kristin Hites, *
▲ **EMP:** 108 **EST:** 2012
**SQ FT:** 20,000
**SALES (est):** 24.64MM **Privately Held**
**Web:** www.kite-hill.com
**SIC:** 2099 Food preparations, nec

**(P-2271)**
**MARS FOOD US LLC (HQ)**
Also Called: Mars Food North America
2001 E Cashdan St Ste 201, Rancho Dominguez (90220-6438)
PHONE..................................310 933-0670
Vincent Howell, *Managing Member*
◆ **EMP:** 500 **EST:** 1936
**SALES (est):** 221.15MM
**SALES (corp-wide):** 42.84B **Privately Held**
**SIC:** 2099 Food preparations, nec
**PA:** Mars, Incorporated
6885 Elm St
703 821-4900

**(P-2272)**
**MARUCHAN INC (HQ)**
15800 Laguna Canyon Rd, Irvine (92618)
PHONE..................................949 789-2300
Noritaka Sumimoto, *CEO*
Mutsuhiko Oda, *
◆ **EMP:** 450 **EST:** 1972
**SQ FT:** 300,000
**SALES (est):** 243.06MM **Privately Held**
**Web:** www.maruchan.com
**SIC:** 2099 Food preparations, nec
**PA:** Toyo Suisan Kaisha, Ltd.
2-13-40, Konan

**(P-2273)**
**MARUKAN VINEGAR U S A INC (HQ)**
Also Called: Marukan Vinegar
16203 Vermont Ave, Paramount
(90723-5042)
PHONE..................................562 630-6060
Yasuo Sasada, *Ch Bd*
Denzaemon Sasada, *
Toshio Takeuchi, *
Shugi Yamada, *General Vice President**
Junichi Oyama, *
◆ **EMP:** 20 **EST:** 1649
**SQ FT:** 20,000
**SALES (est):** 41.64MM **Privately Held**
**Web:** www.marukan-usa.com
**SIC:** 2099 Vinegar
**PA:** Marukan Vinegar Co.,Ltd.
5-6, Koyochonishi, Higashinada-Ku

**(P-2274)**
**MARUKAN VINEGAR U S A INC**
7755 Monroe St, Paramount (90723-5020)
PHONE..................................562 630-6060
Yasuo Sasada, *Ch Bd*
**EMP:** 42
**Web:** www.marukan-usa.com
**SIC:** 2099 Vinegar
**HQ:** Marukan Vinegar (U. S. A.) Inc.
16203 Vermont Ave
Paramount CA 90723
562 630-6060

**(P-2275)**
**MARUKOME USA INC (HQ)**
17132 Pullman St, Irvine (92614-5524)
PHONE..................................949 863-0110
Takeshi Azuma, *CEO*
Toshio Abe, *Sec*
Kazuhiko Fushimi, *S&M/Dir*
Shigeru Kiuchi, *Ofcr*
▲ **EMP:** 17 **EST:** 2004
**SQ FT:** 134,172
**SALES (est):** 7.58MM **Privately Held**
**Web:** www.marukomeusa.com
**SIC:** 2099 Seasonings and spices
**PA:** Marukome Co.,Ltd.
883, Amori

**(P-2276)**
**MCCORMICK & CO**
340 El Camino Real S, Salinas
(93901-4553)
PHONE..................................831 775-3485
**EMP:** 55 **EST:** 1996
**SALES (est):** 1.79MM **Privately Held**
**SIC:** 2099 Seasonings and spices

**(P-2277)**
**MCCORMICK & COMPANY INC**
340 El Camino Real S Ste 20, Salinas
(93901-4556)
PHONE..................................831 775-3350
David Sasaki, *Brnch Mgr*
**EMP:** 16
**SALES (corp-wide):** 6.66B **Publicly Held**

(PA)=Parent Co (HQ)=Headquarters
✪ = New Business established in last 2 years

## 2099 - Food Preparations, Nec (P-2278)

Web: www.mccormickcorporation.com
SIC: 2099 Spices, including grinding
PA: Mccormick & Company Incorporated
24 Schilling Rd Ste 1
410 771-7301

### (P-2278)
### MCI FOODS INC
Also Called: Los Cabos Mexican Foods
13013 Molette St, Santa Fe Springs (90670-5521)
PHONE.................................562 977-4000
Daniel Southard, Pr
Alberta Southard, *
John M Southard, *
EMP: 140 EST: 1970
SQ FT: 15,000
SALES (est): 22.81MM Privately Held
Web: www.loscabosmexicanfoods.com
SIC: 2099 Food preparations, nec

### (P-2279)
### MCK ENTERPRISES INC
Also Called: Valley Spuds
910 Commercial Ave, Oxnard (93030-7232)
PHONE.................................805 483-5292
Evelyn Gardiner, Pr
Al Melino, *
Travis Dergan, *
Evelyn Gardner, *
EMP: 87 EST: 2004
SQ FT: 60,000
SALES (est): 2MM Privately Held
Web: www.valleyspuds.com
SIC: 2099 Food preparations, nec

### (P-2280)
### MINSLEY INC
989 S Monterey Ave, Ontario (91761-3463)
PHONE.................................909 458-1100
Song Tae Jin, CEO
▲ EMP: 40 EST: 2002
SQ FT: 42,000
SALES (est): 5.21MM Privately Held
Web: www.minsley.com
SIC: 2099 Pasta, rice, and potato, packaged combination products

### (P-2281)
### MIZKAN AMERICA INC
46 Walker St, Watsonville (95076-4925)
PHONE.................................831 728-2061
David Shields, Mgr
EMP: 69
Web: www.mizkan.com
SIC: 2099 Vinegar
HQ: Mizkan America, Inc.
1661 Fhanville Dr Ste 200
Mount Prospect IL 60056
847 590-0059

### (P-2282)
### MIZKAN AMERICA INC
Also Called: Indian Summer
10037 8th St, Rancho Cucamonga (91750-5210)
PHONE.................................909 484-8743
Pete Marsing, Brnch Mgr
EMP: 101
SQ FT: 58,500
Web: www.mizkan.com
SIC: 2099 Vinegar
HQ: Mizkan America, Inc.
1661 Fhanville Dr Ste 200
Mount Prospect IL 60056
847 590-0059

### (P-2283)
### MOJAVE FOODS CORPORATION (HQ)
6200 E Slauson Ave, Los Angeles (90040)
PHONE.................................323 890-8900
Richard D Lipka, CEO
Craig M Berger, *
◆ EMP: 96 EST: 1953
SQ FT: 110,000
SALES (est): 32.29MM
SALES (corp-wide): 6.66B Publicly Held
SIC: 2099 Butter, renovated and processed
PA: Mccormick & Company Incorporated
24 Schilling Rd Ste 1
410 771-7301

### (P-2284)
### MOJAVE FOODS CORPORATION
6000 E Slauson Ave, Commerce (90040-3008)
PHONE.................................323 890-8900
EMP: 104
SALES (corp-wide): 6.66B Publicly Held
SIC: 2099 Butter, renovated and processed
HQ: Mojave Foods Corporation
6200 E Slauson Ave
Los Angeles CA 90040
323 890-8900

### (P-2285)
### MOORE FARMS INC
916 S Derby St, Arvin (93203-2312)
P.O. Box 698 (93203-0698)
PHONE.................................661 854-5588
John Moore, Pr
EMP: 15 EST: 1955
SQ FT: 2,000
SALES (est): 840.14K Privately Held
Web: www.moorefarmsca.com
SIC: 2099 0134 Potatoes, peeled for the trade; Irish potatoes

### (P-2286)
### MORINAGA NUTRITIONAL FOODS INC (HQ)
3838 Del Amo Blvd Ste 201, Torrance (90503)
P.O. Box 7969 (90504)
PHONE.................................310 787-0200
Hiroyuki Imanishi, Pr
Tetsuhisa Tato, VP
▼ EMP: 19 EST: 1985
SQ FT: 2,782
SALES (est): 48.29MM Privately Held
Web: www.morinaga-usa.com
SIC: 2099 Food preparations, nec
PA: Morinaga Milk Industry Co.,Ltd.
1-5-2, Higashishimbashi

### (P-2287)
### MR TORTILLA INC
1112 Arroyo St, San Fernando (91340-1850)
PHONE.................................818 233-8932
Anthony Alcazar, CEO
Ronald Alcazar, *
EMP: 50 EST: 2012
SALES (est): 1.7MM Privately Held
Web: www.mrtortilla.com
SIC: 2099 Tortillas, fresh or refrigerated

### (P-2288)
### MRS FOODS INCORPORATED (PA)
Also Called: La Rancherita Tortilleria Deli
4406 W 5th St, Santa Ana (92703-3224)
PHONE.................................714 554-2791
Laura Perez, Pr
Shirley Serna, *
Roxana Perez, *
▲ EMP: 40 EST: 1981
SQ FT: 4,000
SALES (est): 1.78MM
SALES (corp-wide): 1.78MM Privately Held
SIC: 2099 5812 Tortillas, fresh or refrigerated ; Fast-food restaurant, independent

### (P-2289)
### NANCYS SPECIALTY FOODS
2400 Olympic Blvd Ste 8, Lafayette (94595-1500)
PHONE.................................510 494-1100
Adam Ferrif, COO
David M Joiner, VP
R Larry Booth, VP Sls
EMP: 375 EST: 1977
SQ FT: 86,000
SALES (est): 2.09MM
SALES (corp-wide): 26.64B Publicly Held
Web: www.kraftheinzcompany.com
SIC: 2099 Food preparations, nec
HQ: Kraft Heinz Foods Company
1 Ppg Pl Ste 3400
Pittsburgh PA 15222
412 456-5700

### (P-2290)
### NATREN INC
3105 Willow Ln, Thousand Oaks (91361-4919)
PHONE.................................805 371-4737
Yordan Trenev, CEO
Natasha Trenev, *
Odessa Braza, *
EMP: 60 EST: 1983
SQ FT: 22,000
SALES (est): 8.31MM Privately Held
Web: www.natren.com
SIC: 2099 8011 Food preparations, nec; Offices and clinics of medical doctors

### (P-2291)
### NATURES FLAVORS
833 N Elm St, Orange (92867-7909)
PHONE.................................714 744-3700
Bill Sabo, Prin
▲ EMP: 44 EST: 1998
SALES (est): 4.89MM Privately Held
Web: www.naturesflavors.com
SIC: 2099 Food preparations, nec

### (P-2292)
### NECTAVE INC
3309 E Miraloma Ave Ste 105, Anaheim (92806-1942)
PHONE.................................714 736-9811
Robert Chavez, CEO
Richard Ellinghausen, Pr
EMP: 15 EST: 2011
SQ FT: 30,000
SALES (est): 990.31K Privately Held
Web: www.nectave.com
SIC: 2099 Sorghum syrups, for sweetening

### (P-2293)
### NELLSON NUTRACEUTICAL LLC
1000 Etiwanda Ave, Ontario (91761-8612)
PHONE.................................626 812-6522
EMP: 18
Web: www.nellsonllc.com
SIC: 2099 Food preparations, nec
PA: Nellson Nutraceutical, Llc
5115 E La Palma Ave

### (P-2294)
### NEW HONG KONG NOODLE CO INC
360 Swift Ave Ste 22, South San Francisco (94080-6220)
PHONE.................................650 588-6425
Steven Lum, Pr
Richard Lum, *
Lam Wai Lum, *
Wai-kui England Lum, Treas
◆ EMP: 40 EST: 1971
SQ FT: 26,000
SALES (est): 4.67MM Privately Held
Web: www.nhknoodle.com
SIC: 2099 Food preparations, nec

### (P-2295)
### NEW HORIZON FOODS INC
Also Called: New Horizon Foods
33440 Western Ave, Union City (94587-3202)
PHONE.................................510 489-8600
Kenneth Crawford, Pr
EMP: 25 EST: 1998
SQ FT: 20,000
SALES (est): 5.12MM Privately Held
Web: www.newhorizonfoodsinc.com
SIC: 2099 Food preparations, nec

### (P-2296)
### NEWLY WEDS FOODS INC
Also Called: Heller Seasoning
437 S Mcclure Rd, Modesto (95357-0519)
PHONE.................................209 491-7777
Allen Holzmen, Mgr
EMP: 65
SALES (corp-wide): 2.07B Privately Held
Web: www.newlywedsfoods.com
SIC: 2099 Spices, including grinding
HQ: Newly Weds Foods, Llc
4140 W Fullerton Ave
Chicago IL 60639
800 621-7521

### (P-2297)
### NINA MIA INC
Also Called: Pasta Mia
826 Enterprise Way, Fullerton (92831-5015)
PHONE.................................714 773-5588
Diego Mazza, Pr
▲ EMP: 80 EST: 1984
SQ FT: 32,000
SALES (est): 14.99MM Privately Held
Web: www.pastamia.com
SIC: 2099 Pasta, uncooked: packaged with other ingredients

### (P-2298)
### NINAS MEXICAN FOODS INC
20631 Valley Blvd Ste A, Walnut (91789-2751)
PHONE.................................909 468-5888
Ruben Vasquez, Pr
▲ EMP: 40 EST: 1989
SQ FT: 14,000
SALES (est): 2.09MM Privately Held
SIC: 2099 Tortillas, fresh or refrigerated

### (P-2299)
### NIPPON TRENDS FOOD SERVICE INC (PA)
631 Giguere Ct Ste A1, San Jose (95133-1745)
PHONE.................................408 479-0558
Hideyuki Yamashita, Pr
Tomoko Yamashita, *
▲ EMP: 59 EST: 2000
SQ FT: 5,000
SALES (est): 7.72MM Privately Held
Web: www.yamachanramen.com
SIC: 2099 Noodles, uncooked: packaged with other ingredients

## 2099 - Food Preparations, Nec (P-2324)

**(P-2300)**
**NUTIVA**
213 W Cutting Blvd, Richmond (94804-2015)
P.O. Box 2717 (94531)
PHONE....................510 255-2700
John Roulac, *Ch Bd*
Steven Naccarato, *
◆ **EMP:** 115 **EST:** 1999
**SQ FT:** 1,300
**SALES (est):** 43.19MM **Privately Held**
Web: www.nutiva.com
**SIC: 2099** Vegetables, peeled for the trade

**(P-2301)**
**ORGANIC MILLING INC (PA)**
505 W Allen Ave, San Dimas (91773-1487)
PHONE....................800 638-8686
Wolfgang Buehler, *CEO*
Lupe Martinez, *
**EMP:** 89 **EST:** 2009
**SALES (est):** 10.66MM **Privately Held**
Web: www.organicmilling.com
**SIC: 2099** Food preparations, nec

**(P-2302)**
**ORGANIC MILLING CORPORATION**
505 W Allen Ave, San Dimas (91773-1487)
PHONE....................909 599-0961
◆ **EMP:** 33
Web: www.organicmilling.com
**SIC: 2099** Food preparations, nec

**(P-2303)**
**ORGANIC SPICES (PA)**
4180 Business Center Dr, Fremont (94538-6354)
PHONE....................510 440-1044
Bijan Chansari, *CEO*
Clara Bonner, *
Bijan Chansari, *CFO*
Chris Cole, *
◆ **EMP:** 20 **EST:** 2002
**SQ FT:** 27,000
**SALES (est):** 9.08MM
**SALES (corp-wide):** 9.08MM **Privately Held**
Web: www.organicspices.com
**SIC: 2099** Seasonings and spices

**(P-2304)**
**ORGANICGIRL LLC**
900 Work St, Salinas (93901-4386)
P.O. Box 5999 (93901)
PHONE....................831 758-7800
Mark Drever, *CEO*
**EMP:** 650 **EST:** 2007
**SQ FT:** 125,000
**SALES (est):** 43.98MM **Privately Held**
Web: www.iloveorganicgirl.com
**SIC: 2099** 5148 Ready-to-eat meals, salads, and sandwiches; Fresh fruits and vegetables

**(P-2305)**
**OSI INDUSTRIES LLC**
1155 Mt Vernon Ave, Riverside (92507-1830)
PHONE....................951 684-4500
Sheldon Lavin, *CEO*
▲ **EMP:** 414
Web: www.osigroup.com
**SIC: 2099** Ready-to-eat meals, salads, and sandwiches
HQ: Osi Industries, Llc
  1225 Corp Blvd Ste 105
  Aurora IL 60505
  630 851-6600

**(P-2306)**
**OTAFUKU FOODS INC**
13117 Molette St, Santa Fe Springs (90670-5523)
PHONE....................562 404-4700
Naoyoshi Saki, *Ch*
Takamitsu Ozawa, *Pr*
▲ **EMP:** 22 **EST:** 1998
**SQ FT:** 2,000
**SALES (est):** 5MM **Privately Held**
Web: www.otafukufoods.com
**SIC: 2099** Food preparations, nec
PA: Otafuku Holdings Co., Ltd.
  7-4-27, Shoko Center, Nishi-Ku

**(P-2307)**
**OUT OF SHELL LLC**
Also Called: Ling's
9658 Remer St, South El Monte (91733-3033)
PHONE....................626 401-1923
Bing Yang, *
**EMP:** 200 **EST:** 1999
**SALES (est):** 14.12MM **Privately Held**
Web: www.outoftheshell.com
**SIC: 2099** Food preparations, nec

**(P-2308)**
**OVERHILL FARMS INC (DH)**
Also Called: Chicago Brothers
2727 E Vernon Ave, Vernon (90058-1822)
P.O. Box 58806 (90058-0806)
PHONE....................323 582-9977
James Rudis, *Pr*
Robert C Bruning, *
Robert A Olivarez, *
Rick Alvarez, *
**EMP:** 113 **EST:** 1995
**SQ FT:** 170,000
**SALES (est):** 104.91MM **Privately Held**
Web: www.overhillfarms.com
**SIC: 2099** Food preparations, nec
HQ: Bellisio Foods, Inc
  701 N Wash St Ste 400
  Minneapolis MN 55401

**(P-2309)**
**PACIFIC CULINARY GROUP INC**
566 Monterey Pass Rd, Monterey Park (91754-2417)
PHONE....................626 284-1328
Bingham Lee, *CEO*
Lin Ma, *Pr*
**EMP:** 20 **EST:** 2013
**SALES (est):** 1.06MM **Privately Held**
**SIC: 2099** Food preparations, nec

**(P-2310)**
**PACIFIC HOLDINGS 137 COMPANY**
Also Called: Fisher Nut Company
137 N Hart Rd, Modesto (95358)
PHONE....................209 527-0108
Ronald Fisher, *Pr*
◆ **EMP:** 15 **EST:** 1980
**SALES (est):** 6.23MM **Privately Held**
Web: www.fishernut.com
**SIC: 2099** Food preparations, nec

**(P-2311)**
**PACIFIC SPICE COMPANY INC**
Also Called: Pacific Natural Spices
6430 E Slauson Ave, Commerce (90040-3108)
PHONE....................323 726-9190
Gershon Schlussel, *CEO*
Gershon D Schlussel, *
Akiba E Schlussel, *
Sharon Schlussel, *
◆ **EMP:** 130 **EST:** 1966
**SQ FT:** 150,000
**SALES (est):** 23.1MM **Privately Held**
Web: www.pacificspice.com
**SIC: 2099** 5149 Spices, including grinding; Spices and seasonings

**(P-2312)**
**PALERMO FAMILY LP (PA)**
Also Called: Divine Pasta Company
140 W Providencia Ave, Burbank (91502-2121)
PHONE....................213 542-3300
Alexander Palermo, *Prin*
**EMP:** 27 **EST:** 1991
**SQ FT:** 30,000
**SALES (est):** 4.36MM **Privately Held**
Web: www.divinepasta.com
**SIC: 2099** Pasta, rice, and potato, packaged combination products

**(P-2313)**
**PAPPYS MEAT COMPANY INC**
Also Called: Pappy's Fine Foods
5663 E Fountain Way, Fresno (93727-7813)
P.O. Box 5257 (93755-5257)
PHONE....................559 291-0218
Marie Papulias, *Pr*
Edward Papulias, *
Patricia Papulias, *
**EMP:** 23 **EST:** 1964
**SQ FT:** 10,000
**SALES (est):** 2.86MM **Privately Held**
Web: www.pappysfinefoods.com
**SIC: 2099** Seasonings and spices

**(P-2314)**
**PASSPORT FOOD GROUP LLC**
Also Called: Wing Hing Noodle Company
2539 E Philadelphia St, Ontario (91761-7774)
PHONE....................909 627-7312
▲ **EMP:** 150
**SIC: 2099** Pasta, rice, and potato, packaged combination products

**(P-2315)**
**PASSPORT FOODS (SVC) LLC**
2539 E Philadelphia St, Ontario (91761-7774)
PHONE....................909 627-7312
Mark Thomson, *CEO*
**EMP:** 150 **EST:** 2019
**SALES (est):** 5.43MM **Privately Held**
**SIC: 2099** Pasta, rice, and potato, packaged combination products

**(P-2316)**
**PEARL CROP INC**
Also Called: Linden Nut
8452 Demartini Ln, Linden (95236-9446)
PHONE....................209 887-3731
Halil Ulas Turkhan, *Pr*
**EMP:** 22
**SALES (corp-wide):** 90MM **Privately Held**
Web: www.pearlcrop.com
**SIC: 2099** 2068 Food preparations, nec; Salted and roasted nuts and seeds
PA: Pearl Crop, Inc.
  1550 Industrial Dr
  209 808-7575

**(P-2317)**
**PENGUIN NATURAL FOODS INC**
5659 Mansfield Way, Bell (90201-6300)
PHONE....................323 488-6000
**EMP:** 28
Web: www.penguinfoods.com
**SIC: 2099** Food preparations, nec
PA: Penguin Natural Foods, Inc.
  4400 Alcoa Ave

**(P-2318)**
**PENGUIN NATURAL FOODS INC (PA)**
4400 Alcoa Ave, Vernon (90058-2412)
PHONE....................323 727-7980
▲ **EMP:** 45 **EST:** 1993
**SALES (est):** 13.73MM **Privately Held**
Web: www.penguinfoods.com
**SIC: 2099** Pasta, rice, and potato, packaged combination products

**(P-2319)**
**PENSIEVE FOODS**
Also Called: Eatgud
1782 Industrial Way, Los Angeles (90023-4319)
P.O. Box 995 (91711-0995)
PHONE....................323 938-8666
David Alan Medak, *Managing Member*
**EMP:** 45 **EST:** 2015
**SALES (est):** 4.04MM **Privately Held**
**SIC: 2099** 2037 Food preparations, nec; Frozen fruits and vegetables

**(P-2320)**
**PETIT POT LLC**
4221 Horton St, Emeryville (94608-3533)
PHONE....................650 488-7432
Maxime Pouvreau, *CEO*
**EMP:** 20 **EST:** 2015
**SQ FT:** 20,000
**SALES (est):** 6.08MM **Privately Held**
Web: www.petitpot.com
**SIC: 2099** Dessert mixes and fillings

**(P-2321)**
**PGP INTERNATIONAL INC (DH)**
351 Hanson Way, Woodland (95776-6224)
P.O. Box 2060 (95776-2060)
PHONE....................530 662-5056
Angelica Horst, *CEO*
Carmen Sciackitano, *Sec*
◆ **EMP:** 180 **EST:** 1998
**SALES (est):** 49.29MM
**SALES (corp-wide):** 25.28B **Privately Held**
Web: www.pgpint.com
**SIC: 2099** Almond pastes
HQ: Abf Ingredients Limited
  British Sugar Building
  Peterborough CAMBS PE7 8

**(P-2322)**
**PLANT RANCH LLC**
242 N Avenue 25 Ste 114, Los Angeles (90031-1881)
PHONE....................818 384-9727
Gary Robert Huerta, *Managing Member*
**EMP:** 17 **EST:** 2016
**SALES (est):** 413.93K **Privately Held**
Web: www.plantranchfoods.com
**SIC: 2099** Food preparations, nec

**(P-2323)**
**PLENTY UNLIMITED INC**
126 E Oris St, Compton (90222-2714)
PHONE....................415 735-3737
**EMP:** 16
**SALES (corp-wide):** 99.96MM **Privately Held**
Web: www.plenty.ag
**SIC: 2099** Ready-to-eat meals, salads, and sandwiches
PA: Plenty Unlimited Inc.
  570 Eccles Ave
  650 735-3737

**(P-2324)**
**PRODUCE WORLD INC**
37293 3rd St, Fremont (94536-2841)

## 2099 - Food Preparations, Nec (P-2325)

**PHONE**..................510 441-1449
Joseph Fereira, *Pr*
Dennis Dahlin, *
**EMP:** 75 **EST:** 1979
**SALES (est):** 4.8MM **Privately Held**
**SIC: 2099** Vegetables, peeled for the trade

### (P-2325)
### PSW INC
Also Called: Taste Nirvana International
281 Corporate Terrace St, Corona (92879-6000)
**PHONE**..................951 371-7100
Jack Wattanaporn, *Pr*
▲ **EMP:** 15 **EST:** 1989
**SALES (est):** 2.34MM **Privately Held**
**Web:** www.tastenirvana.com
**SIC: 2099** 2095 5141 Tea blending; Roasted coffee; Groceries, general line

### (P-2326)
### PULMUONE FOODS USA INC
Also Called: Monterey Pasta Company
340 El Camino Real S Ste 35, Salinas (93901-4553)
**PHONE**..................831 753-6262
▲ **EMP:** 340
**Web:** www.montereygourmetfoods.com
**SIC: 2099** 2098 2035 Pasta, rice, and potato, packaged combination products; Macaroni and spaghetti; Pickles, sauces, and salad dressings

### (P-2327)
### QST INGREDIENTS AND PACKG INC
9734 6th St, Rancho Cucamonga (91730-5713)
**PHONE**..................909 989-4343
Marc J Rinehart Senior, *CEO*
▲ **EMP:** 15 **EST:** 2005
**SALES (est):** 4.73MM **Privately Held**
**Web:** www.qsting.com
**SIC: 2099** 5046 Seasonings and spices; Commercial cooking and food service equipment

### (P-2328)
### QUOC VIET FOODS
830 Williamson Ave, Fullerton (92832-2134)
**PHONE**..................714 519-3199
Tuan Nguyen, *Brnch Mgr*
**EMP:** 16
**SALES (corp-wide):** 18.03MM **Privately Held**
**Web:** www.quocviet.com
**SIC: 2099** 2095 2034 5149 Seasonings and spices; Coffee, ground: mixed with grain or chicory; Soup mixes; Coffee and tea
**PA:** Quoc Viet Foods
  12221 Monarch St
  714 283-3663

### (P-2329)
### QUOC VIET FOODS
1967 N Glassell St, Orange (92865-4320)
**PHONE**..................714 283-3663
Tuan V Nguyen, *Brnch Mgr*
**EMP:** 16
**SALES (corp-wide):** 18.03MM **Privately Held**
**Web:** www.quocviet.com
**SIC: 2099** 2095 2034 5149 Seasonings and spices; Coffee, ground: mixed with grain or chicory; Soup mixes; Coffee and tea
**PA:** Quoc Viet Foods
  12221 Monarch St
  714 283-3663

### (P-2330)
### QUOC VIET FOODS (PA)
Also Called: Cafvina Coffee & Tea
12221 Monarch St, Garden Grove (92841-2906)
**PHONE**..................714 283-3663
Tuan Nguyen, *CEO*
Tuan Nguyen, *Pr*
Theresa Nguyen, *Ex VP*
Kim Vu, *Stockholder*
Khanh Nguyen, *Stockholder*
▲ **EMP:** 32 **EST:** 2002
**SQ FT:** 2,000
**SALES (est):** 18.03MM
**SALES (corp-wide):** 18.03MM **Privately Held**
**Web:** www.quocviet.com
**SIC: 2099** 2095 5149 2034 Seasonings and spices; Coffee roasting (except by wholesale grocers); Coffee and tea; Soup mixes

### (P-2331)
### RAMA FOOD MANUFACTURE CORP (PA)
1486 E Cedar St, Ontario (91761-8300)
P.O. Box 4045 (91761-1002)
**PHONE**..................909 923-5305
Karen Trang Ving, *CEO*
▲ **EMP:** 18 **EST:** 1984
**SQ FT:** 25,000
**SALES (est):** 6.57MM
**SALES (corp-wide):** 6.57MM **Privately Held**
**Web:** www.ramafood.com
**SIC: 2099** Noodles, fried (Chinese)

### (P-2332)
### READY PAC FOODS INC (HQ)
4401 Foxdale St, Irwindale (91706-2161)
**PHONE**..................626 856-8686
Mary Thompson, *CEO*
Tim Clark, *Chief*
Jay Ellis, *SO*
Dan Redfern, *CFO*
Scott Mcguire, *SCO*
◆ **EMP:** 2000 **EST:** 2000
**SQ FT:** 135,000
**SALES (est):** 973.11MM
**SALES (corp-wide):** 2.67MM **Privately Held**
**Web:** www.readypac.com
**SIC: 2099** 5148 Salads, fresh or refrigerated; Vegetables, fresh
**PA:** Bonduelle
  La Woestyne
  328426060

### (P-2333)
### READY PAC PRODUCE INC (DH)
Also Called: Ready Pac Foods
4401 Foxdale St, Irwindale (91706-2161)
**PHONE**..................800 800-4088
Tony Sarsam, *CEO*
Jay Ellis, *Sls Mgr*
Bob Estes, *CIO*
Dan Redfern, *CFO*
Tristan Simpson, *CMO*
▲ **EMP:** 32 **EST:** 1969
**SQ FT:** 480,000
**SALES (est):** 78.85MM
**SALES (corp-wide):** 2.67MM **Privately Held**
**Web:** www.readypac.com
**SIC: 2099** 5148 Salads, fresh or refrigerated; Fresh fruits and vegetables
**HQ:** Ready Pac Foods, Inc.
  4401 Foxdale St
  Irwindale CA 91706
  626 856-8686

### (P-2334)
### RESERS FINE FOODS INC
15100 Jack Tone Rd, Manteca (95336-9729)
**PHONE**..................503 643-6431
Mark Reser, *CEO*
**EMP:** 21
**SALES (corp-wide):** 347.92MM **Privately Held**
**Web:** www.resers.com
**SIC: 2099** Salads, fresh or refrigerated
**PA:** Reser's Fine Foods, Inc.
  15570 Sw Jenkins Rd
  503 643-6431

### (P-2335)
### REYNALDOS MEXICAN FOOD CO LLC (PA)
3301 E Vernon Ave, Vernon (90058-1809)
**PHONE**..................562 803-3188
Douglas Reed, *CFO*
Marisol Scrugham, *
Al Soto, *Managing Member*
**EMP:** 160 **EST:** 2006
**SALES (est):** 31.26MM **Privately Held**
**Web:** www.sabrosurafoods.com
**SIC: 2099** Food preparations, nec

### (P-2336)
### RICH PRODUCTS CORPORATION
12805 Busch Pl, Santa Fe Springs (90670-3023)
**PHONE**..................562 946-6396
Mike Ball, *Mgr*
**EMP:** 106
**SALES (corp-wide):** 4.81B **Privately Held**
**Web:** www.richs.com
**SIC: 2099** 2051 Desserts, ready-to-mix; Bread, cake, and related products
**PA:** Rich Products Corporation
  1 Robert Rich Way
  716 878-8000

### (P-2337)
### RISING TIDE BOTTLEWORKS LLC
Also Called: Bivouac Ciderworks
3986 30th St, San Diego (92104-3005)
**PHONE**..................619 725-0844
Lara Worm, *CEO*
**EMP:** 18 **EST:** 2016
**SALES (est):** 253.81K **Privately Held**
**SIC: 2099** Cider, nonalcoholic

### (P-2338)
### RISVOLDS INC
1234 W El Segundo Blvd, Gardena (90247-1522)
**PHONE**..................323 770-2674
Tim Brandon, *CEO*
Ed Scoullar, *
**EMP:** 65 **EST:** 1937
**SQ FT:** 30,000
**SALES (est):** 9.1MM **Privately Held**
**Web:** www.risvolds.com
**SIC: 2099** Salads, fresh or refrigerated

### (P-2339)
### ROBLES BROS INC (PA)
Also Called: La Colonial
1700 Rogers Ave, San Jose (95112-1107)
**PHONE**..................408 436-5551
George Robles, *Pr*
Hector Robles, *
Claudia Robles, *
**EMP:** 34 **EST:** 1976
**SQ FT:** 7,000
**SALES (est):** 5.92MM
**SALES (corp-wide):** 5.92MM **Privately Held**
**Web:** www.roblesbros.com
**SIC: 2099** Tortillas, fresh or refrigerated

### (P-2340)
### ROMEROS FOOD PRODUCTS INC (PA)
15155 Valley View Ave, Santa Fe Springs (90670-5323)
**PHONE**..................562 802-1858
Richard Scandalito, *CEO*
Leon Romero Senior, *Pr*
Raul Romero Senior, *VP*
Leon S Romero, *
**EMP:** 100 **EST:** 1971
**SQ FT:** 20,000
**SALES (est):** 21.87MM
**SALES (corp-wide):** 21.87MM **Privately Held**
**Web:** www.romerosfood.com
**SIC: 2099** 2096 5461 Tortillas, fresh or refrigerated; Tortilla chips; Retail bakeries

### (P-2341)
### ROSKAM BAKING COMPANY LLC
505 W Allen Ave, San Dimas (91773-1445)
**PHONE**..................909 599-0961
Robert Roskam, *Pr*
**EMP:** 140
**SALES (corp-wide):** 280.97MM **Privately Held**
**Web:** www.roskamfoods.com
**SIC: 2099** Food preparations, nec
**PA:** Roskam Baking Company, Llc
  4880 Corp Exch Blvd Se
  616 574-5757

### (P-2342)
### ROSKAM BAKING COMPANY LLC
305 S Acacia St Ste A, San Dimas (91773-2928)
**PHONE**..................909 305-0185
Lupe Martinez, *Brnch Mgr*
**EMP:** 409
**SALES (corp-wide):** 280.97MM **Privately Held**
**Web:** www.organicmilling.com
**SIC: 2099** Food preparations, nec
**PA:** Roskam Baking Company, Llc
  4880 Corp Exch Blvd Se
  616 574-5757

### (P-2343)
### RUIZ MEXICAN FOODS INC (PA)
Also Called: Ruiz Flour Tortillas
1200 Marlborough Ave Ste A, Riverside (92507-2158)
**PHONE**..................909 947-7811
Dolores C Ruiz, *CEO*
▼ **EMP:** 120 **EST:** 1976
**SQ FT:** 38,000
**SALES (est):** 5.26MM
**SALES (corp-wide):** 5.26MM **Privately Held**
**Web:** www.ruizflourtortillas.com
**SIC: 2099** 3556 Tortillas, fresh or refrigerated ; Food products machinery

### (P-2344)
### S MARTINELLI & COMPANY (PA)
735 W Beach St, Watsonville (95076-5141)
P.O. Box 1868 (95077-1868)
**PHONE**..................831 724-1126
Stephen C Martinelli, *Ch*
Stephen John Martinelli, *
Doris M Brown, *

▲ = Import ▼ = Export ◆ = Import/Export

Gun Ruder, *
Alice M Kett, *
▲ **EMP:** 96 **EST:** 1868
**SALES (est):** 77.16MM
**SALES (corp-wide):** 77.16MM **Privately Held**
**Web:** www.martinellis.com
**SIC: 2099** Food preparations, nec

### (P-2345)
### S MARTINELLI & COMPANY
345 Harvest Dr, Watsonville (95076-5102)
**PHONE**..................................831 724-1126
**EMP:** 33
**SALES (corp-wide):** 77.16MM **Privately Held**
**Web:** www.martinellis.com
**SIC: 2099** Food preparations, nec
**PA:** S. Martinelli & Company
 735 W Beach St
 831 724-1126

### (P-2346)
### SABATER USA INC (PA)
Also Called: Npms Natural Products Mil Svcs
14824 S Main St, Gardena (90248-1919)
**PHONE**..................................310 518-2227
Jose Sabater Sanchez, *CEO*
David Solomon, *Prin*
▲ **EMP:** 33 **EST:** 1999
**SQ FT:** 80,000
**SALES (est):** 8.6MM
**SALES (corp-wide):** 8.6MM **Privately Held**
**Web:** www.bdsnatural.com
**SIC: 2099** 5149 Seasonings and spices; Natural and organic foods

### (P-2347)
### SALAD COSMO USA CORPORATION
Also Called: Salad Cosmo
5944 Dixon Ave W, Dixon (95620-9730)
**PHONE**..................................707 678-6633
Masahiro Nakada, *Pr*
Isaura Nakada, *Sec*
▲ **EMP:** 20 **EST:** 1995
**SQ FT:** 50,000
**SALES (est):** 3.65MM **Privately Held**
**Web:** www.saladcosmo.com
**SIC: 2099** Food preparations, nec

### (P-2348)
### SAUER BRANDS INC
184 Suburban Rd, San Luis Obispo (93401-7502)
**PHONE**..................................805 597-8900
William W Lovette, *CEO*
**EMP:** 65
**SALES (corp-wide):** 700.62MM **Privately Held**
**Web:** www.sauerbrandsinc.com
**SIC: 2099** Seasonings and spices
**PA:** Sauer Brands, Inc.
 2000 W Broad St
 804 359-5786

### (P-2349)
### SENECA
2801 Finch Rd, Modesto (95354-4120)
**PHONE**..................................209 815-3023
**EMP:** 28 **EST:** 2019
**SALES (est):** 997.09K **Privately Held**
**Web:** www.senecafoods.com
**SIC: 2099** Food preparations, nec

### (P-2350)
### SENSIENT NTRAL INGREDIENTS LLC (HQ)
Also Called: Sensient Dehydrated Flavors
151 S Walnut Rd, Turlock (95380-5127)
P.O. Box 1524 (95381-1524)
**PHONE**..................................209 667-2777
Craig Mitchel, *Pr*
**EMP:** 46 **EST:** 2007
**SALES (est):** 59.29MM
**SALES (corp-wide):** 1.46B **Publicly Held**
**Web:** www.sensientnaturalingredients.com
**SIC: 2099** Food preparations, nec
**PA:** Sensient Technologies Corporation
 777 E Wisconsin Ave
 414 271-6755

### (P-2351)
### SENSIENT NTRAL INGREDIENTS LLC
1700 Kibby Rd, Merced (95341-9301)
**PHONE**..................................209 667-2777
Mauricio Lupi, *Mgr*
**EMP:** 20
**SALES (corp-wide):** 1.46B **Publicly Held**
**Web:** www.sensientnaturalingredients.com
**SIC: 2099** Food preparations, nec
**HQ:** Sensient Natural Ingredients Llc
 151 S Walnut Rd
 Turlock CA 95380
 209 667-2777

### (P-2352)
### SHORE FRONT LLC
3973 Trolley Ct, Brea (92823-1054)
**PHONE**..................................714 612-3751
Anil Kumar, *
Ajay Maini, *CEO*
**EMP:** 40 **EST:** 2009
**SALES (est):** 4.29MM **Privately Held**
**Web:** www.subway.com
**SIC: 2099** 5812 Ready-to-eat meals, salads, and sandwiches; Eating places

### (P-2353)
### SILAO TORTILLERIA INC
Also Called: Silao Tortilleria
18316 Senteno St, Rowland Heights (91748-4433)
**PHONE**..................................626 961-0761
Leandro Espinosa Senior, *Pr*
Leandro Espinosa Junior, *VP*
**EMP:** 44 **EST:** 1955
**SALES (est):** 4.21MM **Privately Held**
**SIC: 2099** Tortillas, fresh or refrigerated

### (P-2354)
### SINCERE ORIENT COMMERCIAL CORP
Also Called: Sincere Orient Food Company
15222 Valley Blvd, City Of Industry (91746-3323)
**PHONE**..................................626 333-8882
Andy Khun, *Pr*
▲ **EMP:** 70 **EST:** 1984
**SQ FT:** 12,000
**SALES (est):** 5.61MM **Privately Held**
**Web:** www.sincereorient.com
**SIC: 2099** Pasta, rice, and potato, packaged combination products

### (P-2355)
### SIP & SONDER LLC
108 S Market St, Inglewood (90301-1712)
**PHONE**..................................908 309-3739
**EMP:** 16 **EST:** 2017
**SALES (est):** 210.54K **Privately Held**
**Web:** www.sipandsonder.com
**SIC: 2099** Food preparations, nec

### (P-2356)
### SONORA MILLS FOODS INC (PA)
Also Called: Pop Chips
3064 E Maria St, E Rncho Dmngz (90221-5804)
**PHONE**..................................310 639-5333
Patrick Turpin, *CEO*
Martin Basch, *
▲ **EMP:** 191 **EST:** 1991
**SQ FT:** 80,000
**SALES (est):** 22.58MM
**SALES (corp-wide):** 22.58MM **Privately Held**
**SIC: 2099** Food preparations, nec

### (P-2357)
### SOUP BASES LOADED INC
2355 E Francis St, Ontario (91761-7727)
**PHONE**..................................909 230-6890
Alan Portney, *Pr*
**EMP:** 45 **EST:** 1997
**SQ FT:** 27,000
**SALES (est):** 10.28MM **Privately Held**
**Web:** www.soupbasesloaded.com
**SIC: 2099** 2034 Seasonings: dry mixes; Dried and dehydrated soup mixes

### (P-2358)
### SOUTHWEST PRODUCTS LLC
8411 Siempre Viva Rd, San Diego (92154-6299)
**PHONE**..................................619 263-8000
▲ **EMP:** 250
**Web:** www.assemblysystems.com
**SIC: 2099** Tortillas, fresh or refrigerated

### (P-2359)
### SOYFOODS OF AMERICA
1091 Hamilton Rd, Duarte (91010-2743)
**PHONE**..................................626 358-3836
Ka Nin Lee, *Pr*
**EMP:** 27 **EST:** 1981
**SQ FT:** 15,000
**SALES (est):** 3.1MM **Privately Held**
**Web:** www.soyfoods-usa.com
**SIC: 2099** Food preparations, nec

### (P-2360)
### STANESS JONEKOS ENTPS INC
Also Called: Eat Like A Woman
4000 W Magnolia Blvd Ste D, Burbank (91505-2827)
**PHONE**..................................818 606-2710
Staness Jonekos, *Owner*
**EMP:** 27 **EST:** 1988
**SALES (est):** 239.42K **Privately Held**
**Web:** www.eatlikeawoman.com
**SIC: 2099** Food preparations, nec

### (P-2361)
### SUN BASKET INC (PA)
501 Folsom St Fl 3, San Francisco (94105-3175)
**PHONE**..................................866 786-2758
Adam Zbar, *CEO*
Don Barnett, *
Isobel Jones, *
Jessica Jensen, *CMO**
Marc Friend, *
**EMP:** 200 **EST:** 2012
**SALES (est):** 106.83MM
**SALES (corp-wide):** 106.83MM **Privately Held**
**Web:** www.sunbasket.com
**SIC: 2099** Food preparations, nec

### (P-2362)
### SUN BASKET INC
1 Clarence Pl Unit 14, San Francisco (94107-2577)
**PHONE**..................................408 669-4418
Todd Smith, *Corporate Controller*
**EMP:** 78
**SALES (corp-wide):** 106.83MM **Privately Held**
**Web:** www.sunbasket.com
**SIC: 2099** Almond pastes
**PA:** Sun Basket, Inc.
 501 Folsom St
 866 786-2758

### (P-2363)
### SUN BASKET INC
18675 Madrone Pkwy, Morgan Hill (95037-2868)
**PHONE**..................................925 240-1512
**EMP:** 78
**SALES (corp-wide):** 106.83MM **Privately Held**
**Web:** www.sunbasket.com
**SIC: 2099** Almond pastes
**PA:** Sun Basket, Inc.
 501 Folsom St
 866 786-2758

### (P-2364)
### SUN RICH FOODS INTL CORP
1240 N Barsten Way, Anaheim (92806-1822)
**PHONE**..................................714 632-7577
Walid A Barakat, *
Shirley Barakat, *CFO*
Alex Barakat, *VP*
**EMP:** 19 **EST:** 1981
**SQ FT:** 6,500
**SALES (est):** 861.42K **Privately Held**
**Web:** www.sunrichfoods.com
**SIC: 2099** Food preparations, nec

### (P-2365)
### SUNRISE GROWERS INC
Also Called: Oxnard 2 Warehouse
2640 Sturgis Rd, Oxnard (93030-7931)
**PHONE**..................................612 619-9545
Jill Barnett, *Pr*
**EMP:** 1129 **EST:** 2011
**SALES (est):** 2.41MM
**SALES (corp-wide):** 630.3MM **Publicly Held**
**SIC: 2099** Food preparations, nec
**HQ:** Sunopta Foods Inc.
 7078 Shady Oak Rd
 Eden Prairie MN 55344

### (P-2366)
### SUPHERB FARMS
Also Called: Supherb Farms
300 Dianne Dr, Turlock (95380)
P.O. Box 610 (95381)
**PHONE**..................................209 633-3600
Frederic Jaubert, *Mgr*
Michael Finete, *
Sally Smedal, *
Don Douglas, *
Maurice Barrera, *
◆ **EMP:** 220 **EST:** 1992
**SQ FT:** 65,190
**SALES (est):** 47.83MM **Privately Held**
**Web:** www.supherbfarms.com
**SIC: 2099** 5149 2037 2034 Seasonings and spices; Sauces; Vegetables, quick frozen & cold pack, excl. potato products; Vegetables, freeze-dried

## 2099 - Food Preparations, Nec (P-2367)

**(P-2367)**
**T HASEGAWA USA INC**
2026 Cecilia Cir, Corona (92881-3389)
PHONE...................................951 264-1121
**EMP:** 20
**Web:** www.thasegawa.com
**SIC:** 2099 Food preparations, nec
**HQ:** T. Hasegawa U.S.A. Inc.
14017 E 183rd St
Cerritos CA 90703
714 522-1900

**(P-2368)**
**TAMPICO SPICE CO INCORPORATED**
Also Called: Tampico Spice Company
5901 S Central Ave # 5941, Los Angeles (90001-1128)
P.O. Box 1229 (90001-0229)
PHONE...................................323 235-3154
George Martinez, *CEO*
Delia Navarro, *Sec*
▲ **EMP:** 40 **EST:** 1946
**SQ FT:** 150,000
**SALES (est):** 8.37MM **Privately Held**
**Web:** www.tampicospice.com
**SIC:** 2099 Spices, including grinding

**(P-2369)**
**TATTOOED CHEF INC (PA)**
6305 Alondra Blvd, Paramount (90723-3750)
PHONE...................................562 602-0822
Salvatore Galletti, *CEO*
Salvatore Galletti, *Ch Bd*
Gaspare Guarrasi, *COO*
Stephanie Dieckmann, *CFO*
Matthew Williams, *CGO*
**EMP:** 30 **EST:** 2018
**SALES (est):** 230.93MM
**SALES (corp-wide):** 230.93MM **Publicly Held**
**Web:** www.tattooedchef.com
**SIC:** 2099 Food preparations, nec

**(P-2370)**
**TEASDALE FOODS INC**
Also Called: Teasdale Foods
901 Packers St, Atwater (95301-4614)
PHONE...................................209 358-5616
**EMP:** 79 **EST:** 2011
**SALES (est):** 7.95MM **Privately Held**
**SIC:** 2099 Food preparations, nec

**(P-2371)**
**TERRAVIA HOLDINGS INC**
1 Tower Pl Ste 600, South San Francisco (94080-1828)
**EMP:** 50
**Web:** www.corbion.com
**SIC:** 2099 Emulsifiers, food

**(P-2372)**
**THE HUNTER SPICE INC**
184 Suburban Rd, San Luis Obispo (93401-7502)
P.O. Box 8110 (93403-8110)
PHONE...................................805 597-8900
▲ **EMP:** 65
**Web:** www.sauers.com
**SIC:** 2099 Seasonings and spices

**(P-2373)**
**THG BRANDS INC**
Also Called: Hummus Guy, The
1810 Abalone Ave, Torrance (90501-3703)
P.O. Box 1039 (90278-0039)
PHONE...................................844 694-8327
Noel D Bonn, *CEO*

John Molino, *CFO*
Mohamed Cherif, *COO*
**EMP:** 20 **EST:** 2014
**SQ FT:** 4,000
**SALES (est):** 2.49MM **Privately Held**
**SIC:** 2099 Food preparations, nec

**(P-2374)**
**THISTLE HEALTH INC**
1000 Van Ness Ave Ste 10004, San Francisco (94109-6971)
PHONE...................................917 587-2341
Ashwin Ninan Cheriyan, *CEO*
**EMP:** 400 **EST:** 2013
**SALES (est):** 14.83MM **Privately Held**
**Web:** www.thistle.co
**SIC:** 2099 Food preparations, nec

**(P-2375)**
**THREE STONE HEARTH LLC**
Also Called: Three Stone Hearth
1581 University Ave, Berkeley (94703-1422)
PHONE...................................510 981-1334
Larry Wisch, *Prin*
**EMP:** 34 **EST:** 2006
**SALES (est):** 1.03MM **Privately Held**
**Web:** www.threestonehearth.com
**SIC:** 2099 Ready-to-eat meals, salads, and sandwiches

**(P-2376)**
**TRADIN ORGANICS USA LLC**
Also Called: Big Basin Foods
15 Parade St Ste A, Aptos (95003)
PHONE...................................831 685-6565
Gerard Versteegh, *CEO*
◆ **EMP:** 30 **EST:** 2000
**SALES (est):** 3.7MM
**SALES (corp-wide):** 274.72MM **Privately Held**
**Web:** www.tradinorganic.com
**SIC:** 2099 Food preparations, nec
**PA:** Acomo N.V.
Beursplein 37 21e Etage
104051195

**(P-2377)**
**TRADITIONAL MEDICINALS INC (PA)**
4515 Ross Rd, Sebastopol (95472-2250)
P.O. Box 239 (94931-0239)
PHONE...................................707 823-8911
Joe Stanziano, *CEO*
Drake Sadler, *
Jane C Howard, *
Teal Tasso, *
◆ **EMP:** 148 **EST:** 1979
**SQ FT:** 20,000
**SALES (est):** 1.18MM
**SALES (corp-wide):** 1.18MM **Privately Held**
**Web:** www.traditionalmedicinals.com
**SIC:** 2099 Tea blending

**(P-2378)**
**TRADITIONS PREPARED MEALS LLC**
849 F St, West Sacramento (95605-2313)
PHONE...................................916 534-4937
Alan Farrar, *Brnch Mgr*
**EMP:** 25
**SIC:** 2099 Food preparations, nec
**HQ:** Traditions Prepared Meals, Llc
300 S Tryon St Ste 400
Charlotte NC 28202
704 424-1071

**(P-2379)**
**TRIPLE H FOOD PROCESSORS LLC**
5821 Wilderness Ave, Riverside (92504-1004)
PHONE...................................951 352-5700
Richard J Harris, *
▲ **EMP:** 60 **EST:** 1976
**SQ FT:** 120,000
**SALES (est):** 17.18MM **Privately Held**
**Web:** www.triplehfoods.com
**SIC:** 2099 2035 2033 Food preparations, nec ; Pickles, sauces, and salad dressings; Jams, jellies, and preserves, packaged in cans, jars, etc.

**(P-2380)**
**TRUROOTS LLC**
Also Called: Chico Site
37 Speedway Ave, Chico (95928-9554)
PHONE...................................530 899-5000
**EMP:** 43
**SALES (corp-wide):** 93.57MM **Privately Held**
**Web:** www.truroots.com
**SIC:** 2099 2032 Rice, uncooked: packaged with other ingredients; Ethnic foods, canned, jarred, etc.
**PA:** Truroots, Llc
770 Legacy Pl
800 288-3637

**(P-2381)**
**TU MADRE ROMANA INC**
13633 S Western Ave, Gardena (90249-2503)
P.O. Box 1275 (90249-0275)
PHONE...................................323 321-6041
**EMP:** 215
**Web:** www.ramonas.com
**SIC:** 2099 5812 Tortillas, fresh or refrigerated ; Delicatessen (eating places)

**(P-2382)**
**UCE HOLDINGS INC**
411 Center St, Los Angeles (90012-3435)
PHONE...................................213 217-4235
Gary Kawaguchi, *CEO*
Edward Shelley, *
◆ **EMP:** 87 **EST:** 2006
**SQ FT:** 45,000
**SALES (est):** 164.91K **Privately Held**
**Web:** www.uppercrustent.com
**SIC:** 2099 Bread crumbs, except made in bakeries

**(P-2383)**
**UNITED FOODS INTL USA INC (DH)**
Also Called: Senba USA
23447 Cabot Blvd, Hayward (94545-1665)
PHONE...................................510 264-5850
Takeo Shimura, *Pr*
◆ **EMP:** 24 **EST:** 1988
**SQ FT:** 24,000
**SALES (est):** 30.96MM **Privately Held**
**Web:** www.ufiusa.com
**SIC:** 2099 Seasonings: dry mixes
**HQ:** United Foods International Co., Ltd.
1-5-18, Kandasarugakucho
Chiyoda-Ku TKY 101-0

**(P-2384)**
**UPSIDE FOODS INC**
Also Called: Upside Fods Engrg Prod Innvtio
6001 Shellmound St Ste 115 # 125, Emeryville (94608-1968)
PHONE...................................510 588-1224
**EMP:** 52

**SALES (corp-wide):** 47.8MM **Privately Held**
**Web:** www.upsidefoods.com
**SIC:** 2099 Food preparations, nec
**PA:** Upside Foods, Inc.
804 Heinz Ave # 200

**(P-2385)**
**VALLEY FINE FOODS COMPANY INC**
Also Called: VALLEY FINE FOODS COMPANY, INC.
300 Epley Dr, Yuba City (95991-7221)
PHONE...................................530 671-7200
**EMP:** 138
**Web:** www.valleyfine.com
**SIC:** 2099 Food preparations, nec
**PA:** Valley Fine Foods Company, Llc
3909 Park Rd Ste H

**(P-2386)**
**VALLEY SUN PRODUCTS INC**
3324 Orestimba Rd, Newman (95360-9628)
PHONE...................................209 862-1200
Chris J Rufer, *Pr*
Robert Benech, *
Chris J Rufer, *CEO*
▲ **EMP:** 53 **EST:** 2007
**SQ FT:** 27,000
**SALES (est):** 7.86MM
**SALES (corp-wide):** 79.78MM **Privately Held**
**Web:** www.valleysun.com
**SIC:** 2099 Food preparations, nec
**PA:** The Morning Star Company
724 Main St
530 666-6600

**(P-2387)**
**VILLAGE GREEN FOODS INC**
1732 Kaiser Ave, Irvine (92614-5706)
PHONE...................................949 261-0111
**EMP:** 25 **EST:** 1970
**SALES (est):** 3.19MM **Privately Held**
**Web:** www.villagegreenfoods.com
**SIC:** 2099 Food preparations, nec

**(P-2388)**
**VIRGINIA PARK LLC**
Also Called: Virginia Park Foods
2225 Via Cerro Ste A, Riverside (92509-2440)
P.O. Box 1567 (10159-1567)
PHONE...................................816 592-0776
Manoj Venugopal, *Managing Member*
**EMP:** 15 **EST:** 2015
**SQ FT:** 35,000
**SALES (est):** 2.92MM
**SALES (corp-wide):** 24.3MM **Privately Held**
**Web:** www.virginiaparkfoods.com
**SIC:** 2099 Pasta, uncooked: packaged with other ingredients
**PA:** Banza Llc
760 Virginia Park St
914 338-8009

**(P-2389)**
**WAWONA FROZEN FOODS (PA)**
100 W Alluvial Ave, Clovis (93611-9176)
PHONE...................................559 299-2901
William Smittcamp, *Pr*
Earl Smittcamp, *
Muriel Smittcamp, *
▲ **EMP:** 123 **EST:** 1953
**SQ FT:** 125,000
**SALES (est):** 419.54MM
**SALES (corp-wide):** 419.54MM **Privately Held**

**PRODUCTS & SERVICES SECTION**  
**2211 - Broadwoven Fabric Mills, Cotton (P-2412)**

Web: www.wawona.com
SIC: 2099  Food preparations, nec

**(P-2390)**
**WIN FOODS CORPORATION**
Also Called: Wing Nien Foods
30560 San Antonio St, Hayward (94544-7102)
PHONE..................510 487-8877
Gregory D Hall, Pr
▲ EMP: 87 EST: 2001
SALES (est): 7.88MM Privately Held
Web: wingnien.wordpress.com
SIC: 2099  Food preparations, nec

**(P-2391)**
**WOOLERY ENTERPRISES INC**
Also Called: Will's Fresh Foods
1991 Republic Ave, San Leandro (94577-4220)
PHONE..................510 357-5700
Daniel C Woolery, CEO
Susan Woolery, *
EMP: 43 EST: 1949
SQ FT: 23,000
SALES (est): 1.36MM Privately Held
Web: www.willsfreshfoods.com
SIC: 2099  Salads, fresh or refrigerated

**(P-2392)**
**WORLDWIDE SPECIALTIES INC**
Also Called: California Specialty Farms
2420 Modoc St, Los Angeles (90021-2916)
PHONE..................323 587-2200
Mady Joes, Mgr
EMP: 120
Web: www.newcsf.com
SIC: 2099  Almond pastes
PA: Worldwide Specialties, Inc.
 2421 E 16th St 1

**(P-2393)**
**YBP HOLDINGS LLC**
Also Called: Yagi Brothers Produce LLC
5614 Lincoln Blvd, Livingston (95334-9642)
PHONE..................209 394-7311
EMP: 45 EST: 2019
SALES (est): 3.28MM Privately Held
Web: www.yagibros.com
SIC: 2099  Potatoes, dried: packaged with other ingredients

## 2111 Cigarettes

**(P-2394)**
**HEMPACCO CO INC (HQ)**
9925 Airway Rd, San Diego (92154-7932)
PHONE..................619 779-0715
Sandro Piancone, Pr
Sandro Piancone, Pr
Stuart Titus, *
Neville Pearson, CFO
Jorge Olson, CMO*
EMP: 15 EST: 2019
SALES (est): 4.05MM
SALES (corp-wide): 5.1MM Publicly Held
Web: www.hempacco.com
SIC: 2111  Cigarettes
PA: Green Globe International, Inc.
 12009 Sterns Ave
 619 202-7456

**(P-2395)**
**HOOK IT UP**
1513 S Grand Ave, Santa Ana (92705-4410)
PHONE..................714 600-0100
Zack Zakari, CEO
EMP: 23 EST: 2014
SQ FT: 5,000
SALES (est): 461.15K Privately Held
SIC: 2111  Cigarettes

**(P-2396)**
**R J REYNOLDS TOBACCO COMPANY**
8380 Miramar Mall Ste 117, San Diego (92121-2548)
PHONE..................858 625-8453
Ken Stevens, Prin
EMP: 92
Web: www.rjrt.com
SIC: 2111  Cigarettes
HQ: R. J. Reynolds Tobacco Company
 401 N Main St
 Winston Salem NC 27101
 336 741-5000

**(P-2397)**
**USA SALES INC**
Also Called: Statewide Distributors
1560 S Archibald Ave, Ontario (91761-7629)
PHONE..................909 390-9606
Kabiruddin Ali, CEO
EMP: 20 EST: 2005
SALES (est): 4.41MM Privately Held
Web: www.mystatewide.com
SIC: 2111 2121  Cigarettes; Cigars

## 2131 Chewing And Smoking Tobacco

**(P-2398)**
**FANTASIA DISTRIBUTION INC**
Also Called: Fantasia Hookah Tobacco
2400 E Katella Ave Ste 800, Anaheim (92806-5945)
PHONE..................714 817-8300
Randy Jacob Bahbah, CEO
Issa Bahbah, CFO
◆ EMP: 17 EST: 2007
SALES (est): 2.48MM Privately Held
Web: www.fantasiadistribution.com
SIC: 2131  Smoking tobacco

## 2211 Broadwoven Fabric Mills, Cotton

**(P-2399)**
**ALLBIRDS INC (PA)**
Also Called: ALLBIRDS
730 Montgomery St, San Francisco (94111-2104)
PHONE..................628 225-4848
Joe Vernachio, Pr
Timothy Brown, CIO*
Annie Mitchell, CFO
EMP: 200 EST: 2015
SQ FT: 39,000
SALES (est): 254.06MM
SALES (corp-wide): 254.06MM Publicly Held
Web: www.allbirds.com
SIC: 2211 3143 3144  Apparel and outerwear fabrics, cotton; Men's footwear, except athletic; Women's footwear, except athletic

**(P-2400)**
**ALSTYLE APPAREL LLC**
1501 E Cerritos Ave, Anaheim (92805-6400)
PHONE..................714 765-0400
EMP: 1163 EST: 2014
SALES (est): 1.06MM
SALES (corp-wide): 3.2B Privately Held
SIC: 2211  Apparel and outerwear fabrics, cotton
HQ: Alstyle Apparel & Activewear Management Co.
 1501 E Cerritos Ave
 Anaheim CA 92805
 714 765-0400

**(P-2401)**
**AVITEX INC (PA)**
Also Called: Veratex
20362 Plummer St, Chatsworth (91311-5371)
PHONE..................818 994-6487
Avi Cohen, CEO
▲ EMP: 250 EST: 1992
SQ FT: 15,000
SALES (est): 2.53MM Privately Held
Web: www.veratex.com
SIC: 2211 5131  Sheets, bedding and table cloths: cotton; Linen piece goods, woven

**(P-2402)**
**BABYLON INTERNATIONAL LLC**
16520 Bake Pkwy Ste 230, Irvine (92618-4689)
PHONE..................323 433-4104
Ayse G Erkovan, Opers Mgr
EMP: 50 EST: 2005
SALES (est): 1.61MM Privately Held
SIC: 2211  Twills, drills, denims and other ribbed fabrics: cotton

**(P-2403)**
**BELAGIO ENTERPRISES INC**
3737 Ross St, Vernon (90058-1635)
PHONE..................323 731-6934
Ruben Melamed, CEO
▲ EMP: 20 EST: 2002
SALES (est): 1.74MM Privately Held
Web: www.belagioenterprises.com
SIC: 2211 2269  Decorative trim and specialty fabrics, including twist weave; Decorative finishing of narrow fabrics

**(P-2404)**
**BONDED FIBERLOFT INC**
2748 Tanager Ave, Commerce (90040-2721)
PHONE..................323 726-7820
Mark Bidner, CEO
Mike Wood, CFO
EMP: 299 EST: 1998
SQ FT: 96,000
SALES (est): 806.93K Privately Held
SIC: 2211 2823 2299  Broadwoven fabric mills, cotton; Cellulosic manmade fibers; Batts and batting: cotton mill waste and related material
PA: Western Synthetic Fiber Inc
 2 Atlantic Ave Fl 4

**(P-2405)**
**BTS TRADING INC**
Also Called: Manufacture
2052 E Vernon Ave, Vernon (90058-1613)
PHONE..................213 800-6755
Euisoo Kim, Pr
EMP: 35 EST: 2020
SALES (est): 553.95K Privately Held
SIC: 2211  Apparel and outerwear fabrics, cotton

**(P-2406)**
**CALA ACTION INC**
2440 Troy Ave, South El Monte (91733-1432)
PHONE..................213 272-9759
Hongfang Li, CEO
EMP: 20 EST: 2017
SALES (est): 322.1K Privately Held
SIC: 2211  Apparel and outerwear fabrics, cotton

**(P-2407)**
**CENTRIC BRANDS INC**
Also Called: Joe's Dsert Hlls Prmium Otlets
48650 Seminole Dr Ste 170, Cabazon (92230-2118)
PHONE..................951 797-5077
EMP: 40
Web: www.centricbrands.com
SIC: 2211  Denims
PA: Centric Brands Llc
 350 5th Ave Fl 6

**(P-2408)**
**CENTRIC BRANDS INC**
Also Called: CENTRIC BRANDS INC.
5630 Paseo Del Norte Ste 144, Carlsbad (92008-4470)
PHONE..................760 603-8520
EMP: 39
Web: www.joesjeans.com
SIC: 2211  Denims
PA: Centric Brands Llc
 350 5th Ave Fl 6

**(P-2409)**
**CENTRIC BRANDS INC**
Also Called: Joe's Jeans
1500 N El Centro Ave Ste 150, Los Angeles (90025-3303)
PHONE..................323 837-3700
EMP: 17
Web: www.centricbrands.com
SIC: 2211  Denims
PA: Centric Brands Llc
 350 5th Ave Fl 6

**(P-2410)**
**COLORMAX INDUSTRIES INC (PA)**
1627 Paloma St, Los Angeles (90021)
PHONE..................213 748-6600
Gholamreza Amighi, Pr
Goodarz Haydarzadeh, *
EMP: 25 EST: 1988
SQ FT: 64,000
SALES (est): 1.25MM
SALES (corp-wide): 1.25MM Privately Held
SIC: 2211 2269 2261 2254  Broadwoven fabric mills, cotton; Finishing plants, nec; Finishing plants, cotton; Dyeing and finishing knit underwear

**(P-2411)**
**CREATIVE COSTUMING DESIGNS INC**
Also Called: Creative Costuming & Designs
15402 Electronic Ln, Huntington Beach (92649-1334)
PHONE..................714 895-0982
Noreen Roberts, Pr
Noreen Roberts, CEO
Kevin Roberts, *
EMP: 35 EST: 2009
SQ FT: 5,300
SALES (est): 2.49MM Privately Held
Web: www.creative-costuming.com
SIC: 2211  Apparel and outerwear fabrics, cotton

**(P-2412)**
**EAST SHORE GARMENT COMPANY LLC**
3250 E Olympic Blvd, Los Angeles (90023-3709)

## 2211 - Broadwoven Fabric Mills, Cotton (P-2413)

PHONE...............................323 923-4454
EMP: 20 EST: 2017
SALES (est): 2.28MM
SALES (corp-wide): 40.59MM Privately Held
Web: www.eastshoregarment.com
SIC: 2211 Broadwoven fabric mills, cotton
PA: Lakeshirts Llc
    750 Randolph Rd
    800 627-2780

### (P-2413)
### EVERYBODY WORLD LLC
Also Called: Everybody.world
5718 S Santa Fe Ave, Vernon (90058-3528)
PHONE...............................213 305-9450
EMP: 15 EST: 2016
SALES (est): 1.81MM Privately Held
Web: www.everybody.world
SIC: 2211 Shirting fabrics, cotton

### (P-2414)
### FACTORY ONE STUDIO INC
6700 Avalon Blvd Ste 101, Los Angeles (90003-1920)
PHONE...............................323 752-1670
Steve C Rhee, CEO
EMP: 52 EST: 2017
SALES (est): 1.8MM Privately Held
Web: www.factoryonestudio.com
SIC: 2211 Denims

### (P-2415)
### FIRST FINISH INC
11126 Wright Rd, Lynwood (90262-3122)
PHONE...............................310 631-6717
Keyomars Fard, Pr
▲ EMP: 25 EST: 2003
SQ FT: 10,000
SALES (est): 1.09MM Privately Held
SIC: 2211 Jean fabrics

### (P-2416)
### G KAGAN AND SONS INC (PA)
Also Called: Kagan Trim Center
3957 S Hill St, Los Angeles (90037-1313)
PHONE...............................323 583-1400
Jed Kagan, Pr
Rod Kagan, *
◆ EMP: 25 EST: 1946
SQ FT: 50,000
SALES (est): 2.76MM
SALES (corp-wide): 2.76MM Privately Held
Web: www.kagantrim.com
SIC: 2211 Apparel and outerwear fabrics, cotton

### (P-2417)
### GREY STUDIO INC
Also Called: Grey Studio
629 S Clarence St, Los Angeles (90023-1107)
PHONE...............................323 780-8111
Kendrick D Kim, Pr
EMP: 15 EST: 2005
SALES (est): 361.28K Privately Held
SIC: 2211 Denims

### (P-2418)
### HIDDEN JEANS INC
Also Called: Cello Jeans
7210 Dominion Cir, Commerce (90040-3647)
PHONE...............................213 746-4223
Kenny Park, CEO
Adam Lee, *
◆ EMP: 30 EST: 2007
SQ FT: 4,000
SALES (est): 4.92MM Privately Held
Web: www.hiddenjeans.com
SIC: 2211 2339 Denims; Jeans: women's, misses', and juniors'

### (P-2419)
### INTERNATIONAL TEX GROUP INC
Also Called: B Green
3097 E Ana St, East Rancho Domingue (90221)
PHONE...............................310 667-9030
Mike Ferid, Owner
EMP: 16 EST: 2008
SALES (est): 1.72MM Privately Held
Web: www.natureusa.net
SIC: 2211 Apparel and outerwear fabrics, cotton

### (P-2420)
### KNIT GENERATION GROUP INC
3818 S Broadway, Los Angeles (90037-1412)
PHONE...............................213 221-5081
Joseph Dania, CEO
EMP: 25 EST: 2013
SALES (est): 2.38MM Privately Held
Web: www.knitgeneration.net
SIC: 2211 Broadwoven fabric mills, cotton

### (P-2421)
### LINKSOUL LLC
530 S Coast Hwy, Oceanside (92054-4009)
PHONE...............................760 231-7069
Dave Seymour Cfo, COO
EMP: 29 EST: 2013
SALES (est): 2.52MM Privately Held
Web: www.linksoul.com
SIC: 2211 Apparel and outerwear fabrics, cotton

### (P-2422)
### MASTERPIECE ARTIST CANVAS LLC
Also Called: Canvas Concepts
1401 Air Wing Rd, San Diego (92154-7705)
PHONE...............................619 710-2500
John M Sooklaris, Pr
◆ EMP: 50 EST: 1965
SQ FT: 1,000
SALES (est): 2.44MM Privately Held
Web: www.masterpiecearts.com
SIC: 2211 Canvas

### (P-2423)
### NUX GROUP INC
5164 Alcoa Ave, Vernon (90058-3716)
P.O. Box 58102 (90058)
PHONE...............................323 780-4700
Malek S Neman, Pr
EMP: 20 EST: 2010
SALES (est): 3.7MM Privately Held
Web: www.nuxactive.com
SIC: 2211 Apparel and outerwear fabrics, cotton

### (P-2424)
### PJY LLC
Also Called: Intimo Industry
3251 Leonis Blvd, Vernon (90058-3018)
PHONE...............................323 583-7737
Ryan Fisher, CEO
▲ EMP: 40 EST: 2001
SALES (est): 5.69MM Privately Held
Web: www.intimoindustry.com
SIC: 2211 Long cloth, cotton

### (P-2425)
### SAITEX (USA) LLC
6074 Malburg Way, Vernon (90058-3946)
PHONE...............................323 391-6116
Sanjeev Bahl, CEO
EMP: 18 EST: 2019
SALES (est): 6.58MM Privately Held
Web: www.sai-tex.com
SIC: 2211 Denims

### (P-2426)
### SOCAL GARMENT WORKS LLC
4700 S Boyle Ave Ste C, Vernon (90058-3032)
PHONE...............................323 300-5717
Michael Burns, Managing Member
Joseph Burns, Managing Member
Sho Kato, Managing Member
EMP: 43 EST: 2020
SALES (est): 1.1MM Privately Held
SIC: 2211 2221 Apparel and outerwear fabrics, cotton; Apparel and outerwear fabric, manmade fiber or silk

### (P-2427)
### STANDARD FIBER LLC
919 E Hillsdale Blvd Ste 100, Foster City (94404-2112)
PHONE...............................650 872-6528
Chad Altbaier, Mgr
EMP: 27
SALES (corp-wide): 26.26MM Privately Held
Web: www.standardfiber.com
SIC: 2211 Sheets, bedding and table cloths: cotton
PA: Standard Fiber, Llc
    12010 Bermuda Rd
    702 761-2600

### (P-2428)
### STANZINO INC
17937 Santa Rita St, Encino (91316-3602)
PHONE...............................818 602-5171
David Ghods, Brnch Mgr
EMP: 120
SALES (corp-wide): 3.85MM Privately Held
SIC: 2211 Apparel and outerwear fabrics, cotton
PA: Stanzino, Inc.
    16325 S Avalon Blvd
    213 746-8822

### (P-2429)
### STANZINO INC (PA)
Also Called: Apparel House USA
16325 S Avalon Blvd, Gardena (90248-2909)
PHONE...............................213 746-8822
David Ghods, CEO
EMP: 25 EST: 2011
SALES (est): 3.85MM
SALES (corp-wide): 3.85MM Privately Held
SIC: 2211 Apparel and outerwear fabrics, cotton

### (P-2430)
### TRITEX TRADING INC
7171 Warner Ave Ste B348, Huntington Beach (92647-5478)
PHONE...............................949 413-8454
Joe Alame, CEO
▲ EMP: 15 EST: 2011
SQ FT: 1,800
SALES (est): 453.79K Privately Held
Web: www.tritextrading.com
SIC: 2211 Denims

### (P-2431)
### TWIN DRAGON MARKETING INC (PA)
Also Called: Tdmi
14600 S Broadway, Gardena (90248-1812)
PHONE...............................310 715-7070
Dominic Poon, CEO
Joseph Tse, Treas
◆ EMP: 49 EST: 1980
SQ FT: 39,000
SALES (est): 21.88MM
SALES (corp-wide): 21.88MM Privately Held
Web: www.tdmi-us.com
SIC: 2211 Denims

### (P-2432)
### XCVI LLC (PA)
15236 Burbank Blvd, Sherman Oaks (91411-3504)
PHONE...............................213 749-2661
Alon Zeltzer, CEO
Mordechia Zelter, *
Gita Zeltzer, *
▲ EMP: 60 EST: 1996
SALES (est): 9.68MM
SALES (corp-wide): 9.68MM Privately Held
Web: www.xcvi.com
SIC: 2211 Apparel and outerwear fabrics, cotton

## 2221 Broadwoven Fabric Mills, Manmade

### (P-2433)
### AGRICULTURE BAG MFG USA INC (PA)
Also Called: Agriculture Bag Manufacturing,
960 98th Ave, Oakland (94603-2347)
PHONE...............................510 632-5637
Jeff C Kuo, CEO
▲ EMP: 44 EST: 1984
SALES (est): 1.56MM
SALES (corp-wide): 1.56MM Privately Held
SIC: 2221 2673 2393 Polypropylene broadwoven fabrics; Plastic and pliofilm bags; Textile bags

### (P-2434)
### DAE SHIN USA INC
610 N Gilbert St, Fullerton (92833-2555)
PHONE...............................714 578-8900
Jae Weon Lee, CEO
▲ EMP: 100 EST: 1999
SQ FT: 10,000
SALES (est): 5.93MM Privately Held
SIC: 2221 Textile mills, broadwoven: silk and manmade, also glass
PA: Daeshin Textile Co., Ltd.
    16 Haean-Ro 397beon-Gil, Danwon-Gu

### (P-2435)
### DOOL FNA INC
Also Called: Grand Textile
16624 Edwards Rd, Cerritos (90703-2438)
PHONE...............................562 483-4100
Jae Weon Lee, CEO
▲ EMP: 120 EST: 1999
SALES (est): 3.11MM Privately Held
SIC: 2221 Textile mills, broadwoven: silk and manmade, also glass

### (P-2436)
### FABRICMATE SYSTEMS INC
Also Called: Fabricmate
2781 Golf Course Dr Unit A, Ventura (93003-7939)

# PRODUCTS & SERVICES SECTION

## 2252 - Hosiery, Nec (P-2458)

PHONE..................805 642-7470
Craig Lanuza, Pr
Manoj Pradhan, *
▲ EMP: 30 EST: 1995
SQ FT: 16,116
SALES (est): 4.92MM **Privately Held**
Web: www.fabricmate.com
SIC: 2221  Upholstery, tapestry, and wall covering fabrics

### (P-2437)
### FABTEX INC
Also Called: Ft Textiles
615 S State College Blvd, Fullerton (92831-5115)
PHONE..................714 538-0877
William P Friese, Brnch Mgr
EMP: 105
SALES (corp-wide): 49.37MM **Privately Held**
Web: www.fabtex.com
SIC: 2221 2515 2392 2391  Draperies and drapery fabrics, manmade fiber and silk; Mattresses and bedsprings; Household furnishings, nec; Curtains and draperies
PA: Fabtex, Inc.
    111 Woodbine Ln
    800 778-2791

### (P-2438)
### GROUND CONTROL BUSINESS MGT (DH)
Also Called: Savitsky Stin Bcon Bcci A Cal
2049 Century Park E Ste 1400, Los Angeles (90067-3116)
PHONE..................310 315-6200
Chris Bucci, CEO
EMP: 25 EST: 1997
SALES (est): 20.94MM **Privately Held**
Web: www.gcbm.com
SIC: 2221  Satins
HQ: Nfp Corp.
    200 Park Ave Fl 32
    New York NY 10166
    212 301-4001

### (P-2439)
### JUICY COUTURE INC
1580 Jesse St, Los Angeles (90021-1317)
PHONE..................888 824-8826
Pamela Levy, CEO
Edgar O Huber, Pr
Lisa Rodericks, *
Ellen Rodriguez, *
▲ EMP: 160 EST: 1990
SALES (est): 48.81K **Publicly Held**
Web: www.juicycouture.com
SIC: 2221  Broadwoven fabric mills, manmade
HQ: Kate Spade Holdings Llc
    5822 Haverford Ave Ste 2
    Philadelphia PA 19131
    212 354-4900

### (P-2440)
### POP 82 INC
Also Called: Pop 82
8211 Orangethorpe Ave, Buena Park (90621-3811)
PHONE..................714 523-8500
Steven North, CEO
Bill Blandin, VP
Marisela Ramos, Sec
EMP: 15 EST: 2013
SQ FT: 15,000
SALES (est): 1.61MM **Privately Held**
Web: www.pop82.com
SIC: 2221 7389  Acrylic broadwoven fabrics; Printing broker

### (P-2441)
### S&B DEVELOPMENT GROUP LLC
1901 Avenue Of The Stars 235, Los Angeles (90067-6064)
PHONE..................213 446-2818
Nathalio Ortez, CEO
EMP: 48 EST: 2008
SQ FT: 50,000
SALES (est): 703.71K **Privately Held**
SIC: 2221 5023  Broadwoven fabric mills, manmade; Sheets, textile

### (P-2442)
### SPD MANUFACTURING INC
1101 E Truslow Ave, Fullerton (92831-4625)
PHONE..................985 302-1902
Debra Macaluso, CEO
EMP: 19 EST: 2018
SALES (est): 1.24MM **Privately Held**
SIC: 2221  Apparel and outerwear fabric, manmade fiber or silk

## 2231 Broadwoven Fabric Mills, Wool

### (P-2443)
### CALIFORNIA INDUSTRIAL FABRICS
2325 Marconi Ct, San Diego (92154-7241)
PHONE..................619 661-7166
TOLL FREE: 800
Michael Kent Lindsey, Pr
Patrick Dickey, *
Erin Mcnamara, CFO
◆ EMP: 30 EST: 1978
SQ FT: 24,000
SALES (est): 5.66MM **Privately Held**
Web: www.cifabrics.com
SIC: 2231  Broadwoven fabric mills, wool

### (P-2444)
### CMK MANUFACTURING LLC
Also Called: Green Dragon
10375 Wilshire Blvd Apt 2h, Los Angeles (90024-4728)
▲ EMP: 31 EST: 2003
SALES (est): 2.49MM **Privately Held**
Web: www.freesocietyclothing.com
SIC: 2231 5632  Cloth, wool: mending; Apparel accessories

### (P-2445)
### COMFORT INDUSTRIES INC
301 W Las Tunas Dr, San Gabriel (91776-1201)
PHONE..................562 692-8288
Kevin D.o.s., CEO
Ken Quach, *
Mike D.o.s., Treas
Kevin Deal, *
◆ EMP: 35 EST: 1998
SALES (est): 821.69K **Privately Held**
SIC: 2231  Upholstery fabrics, wool

### (P-2446)
### FAM LLC (PA)
Also Called: Fam Brands
5553 Bandini Blvd B, Bell (90201-6421)
PHONE..................323 888-7755
Frank Zarabi, Pr
Rich Campanelli, *
Rich Lyons, *
Nazy Salamat, *
Carrie Henley, *
▲ EMP: 64 EST: 1985
SQ FT: 75,000
SALES (est): 77.14MM **Privately Held**
Web: www.fambrands.com
SIC: 2231 2221  Apparel and outerwear broadwoven fabrics; Apparel and outerwear fabric, manmade fiber or silk

### (P-2447)
### ICON APPAREL GROUP LLC
2989 Promenade St Ste 100, West Sacramento (95691-6419)
PHONE..................916 372-4266
Juan Carlos Ceja, CEO
Juan Carlos Ceja, Managing Member
Ronnie Leavitt, *
Jerrad Fiore, *
EMP: 45 EST: 2002
SQ FT: 10,000
SALES (est): 2.25MM **Privately Held**
Web: www.iconapparel.com
SIC: 2231 7389 2759  Apparel and outerwear broadwoven fabrics; Apparel designers, commercial; Screen printing

### (P-2448)
### LEKOS DYE & FINISHING INC (PA)
3131 E Harcourt St, Compton (90221-5505)
P.O. Box 2245 (90621)
PHONE..................310 763-0900
Ilgun Lee, Pr
▲ EMP: 65 EST: 2003
SQ FT: 72,000
SALES (est): 6.57MM
SALES (corp-wide): 6.57MM **Privately Held**
SIC: 2231  Dyeing and finishing: wool or similar fibers

### (P-2449)
### ROSHAN TRADING INC
Also Called: Envirofabrics
3631 Union Pacific Ave, Los Angeles (90023-3255)
PHONE..................213 622-9904
David Roshan, CEO
◆ EMP: 40 EST: 1986
SALES (est): 5.08MM **Privately Held**
Web: www.lagunafabrics.com
SIC: 2231 5131  Broadwoven fabric mills, wool; Textiles, woven, nec

### (P-2450)
### TRI-STAR DYEING & FINSHG INC
15125 Marquardt Ave, Santa Fe Springs (90670-5705)
PHONE..................562 483-0123
Jang You, Prin
▲ EMP: 63 EST: 2006
SQ FT: 60,000
SALES (est): 2.81MM **Privately Held**
Web: www.tristar-df.com
SIC: 2231  Dyeing and finishing: wool or similar fibers

## 2241 Narrow Fabric Mills

### (P-2451)
### CHUA & SONS CO INC
Also Called: Reliable Tape Products
3300 E 50th St, Vernon (90058-3004)
P.O. Box 58261 (90058-0261)
PHONE..................323 588-8044
Shirley Chua, Pr
▲ EMP: 23 EST: 1984
SQ FT: 67,000
SALES (est): 778.13K **Privately Held**
SIC: 2241  Fabric tapes

### (P-2452)
### HOLLYWOOD RIBBON INDUSTRIES INC
9000 Rochester Ave, Rancho Cucamonga (91730-5522)
P.O. Box 428 (18063-0428)
PHONE..................323 266-0670
◆ EMP: 400
Web: www.hollywoodribbon.com
SIC: 2241  Ribbons, nec

### (P-2453)
### HORVATH HOLDINGS INC
Also Called: Clayborn Lab
12755 Rainbow Dr, Truckee (96161-2645)
PHONE..................530 587-4700
Justin Horvath, Pr
Amy Horvath, Corporate Secretary
EMP: 15 EST: 2019
SALES (est): 462.3K **Privately Held**
Web: www.claybornlab.com
SIC: 2241  Electric insulating tapes and braids, except plastic

### (P-2454)
### KEYSTONE TEXTILE INC
1201 Mateo St, Los Angeles (90021-1737)
PHONE..................213 622-7755
▲ EMP: 15
Web: www.keystonetextile.com
SIC: 2241  Manmade fiber narrow woven fabrics

### (P-2455)
### UNIVERSAL ELASTIC & GARMENT SUPPLY INC
2200 S Alameda St, Vernon (90058-1308)
PHONE..................213 748-2995
▲ EMP: 23 EST: 1991
SALES (est): 3.91MM **Privately Held**
Web: www.universalelastic.com
SIC: 2241 5131  Narrow fabric mills; Piece goods and notions

### (P-2456)
### WEST COAST TRIMMING CORP
7100 Wilson Ave, Los Angeles (90001-2249)
PHONE..................323 587-0701
Arnold F Pretz Junior, Pr
James R Mcbride, VP
Robert D Clarke, Sec
▲ EMP: 21 EST: 1922
SQ FT: 12,000
SALES (est): 1.3MM **Privately Held**
Web: www.westcoasttrimming.com
SIC: 2241 5131  Trimmings, textile; Drapery material, woven

## 2252 Hosiery, Nec

### (P-2457)
### GILDAN USA INC
Also Called: GILDAN USA INC.
28200 Highway 189, Lake Arrowhead (92352-9700)
PHONE..................909 485-1475
EMP: 46
SALES (corp-wide): 3.2B **Privately Held**
Web: www.gildancorp.com
SIC: 2252  Hosiery, nec
HQ: Gildan Usa Llc
    1980 Clements Ferry Rd
    Charleston SC 29492

### (P-2458)
### K B SOCKS INC (DH)
Also Called: K Bell

## 2252 - Hosiery, Nec (P-2459)

550 N Oak St, Inglewood  (90302-2942)
PHONE..............................310 670-3235
▲ EMP: 51  EST: 1985
SALES (est): 2.89MM
SALES (corp-wide): 3.26B  Privately Held
Web: www.kbellsocks.com
SIC: 2252  Socks
HQ: Renfro Llc
661 Linville Rd
Mount Airy NC 27030
336 719-8000

**(P-2459)**
**SOCKSMITH DESIGN  INC (PA)**
1515 Pacific Ave, Santa Cruz  (95060-3911)
PHONE..............................831 426-6416
Eric Gil, *Pr*
Ellen Gil, *
Cassandra Aaron, *
▲ EMP: 24  EST: 2009
SQ FT: 10,000
SALES (est): 2.45MM  Privately Held
Web: www.socksmith.com
SIC: 2252  Socks

**(P-2460)**
**SOXNET  INC**
235 S 6th Ave, La Puente  (91746-2916)
PHONE..............................626 934-9400
Miri Ryu, *CEO*
▲ EMP: 17  EST: 2002
SQ FT: 30,434
SALES (est): 1.57MM  Privately Held
Web: www.soxnetinc.com
SIC: 2252  Men's, boys', and girls' hosiery

**(P-2461)**
**UNIVERSAL HOSIERY  INC**
28337 Constellation Rd, Valencia  (91355-5048)
PHONE..............................661 702-8444
Johnathan Ekizian, *Pr*
▲ EMP: 75  EST: 1994
SQ FT: 44,000
SALES (est): 3.2MM  Privately Held
Web: www.universalhosiery.com
SIC: 2252  Socks

## 2253 Knit Outerwear Mills

**(P-2462)**
**BALBOA MANUFACTURING CO  LLC (PA)**
Also Called: Bobster Eyewear
4909 Murphy Canyon Rd Ste 310, San Diego  (92123-4301)
PHONE..............................858 715-0060
John Smaller, *Managing Member*
Jennifer Struebing, *
▲ EMP: 26  EST: 1996
SQ FT: 40,000
SALES (est): 4.8MM  Privately Held
Web: www.bobster.com
SIC: 2253  2211  Hats and headwear, knit; Apparel and outerwear fabrics, cotton

**(P-2463)**
**BYER CALIFORNIA**
Alfred Paquette Division
1201 Rio Vista Ave, Los Angeles  (90023-2609)
PHONE..............................323 780-7615
Jan Shostak, *Mgr*
EMP: 114
SQ FT: 10,000
SALES (corp-wide): 124.12MM  Privately Held
Web: www.byerca.com
SIC: 2253  2339  2335  Dresses, knit; Women's and misses' outerwear, nec; Women's, junior's, and misses' dresses
PA: Byer California
66 Potrero Ave
415 626-7844

**(P-2464)**
**CREW KNITWEAR  LLC**
2155 E 7th St Ste 125, Los Angeles  (90023-1031)
PHONE..............................323 526-3888
Fredrick Ken, *Mgr*
EMP: 66
Web: www.crewknitwear.com
SIC: 2253  Dresses, knit
PA: Crew Knitwear, Llc
660 S Myers St

**(P-2465)**
**CUT AND SEW CO  INC**
1939 S Susan St, Santa Ana  (92704-3901)
PHONE..............................714 981-7244
Arturo Martinez, *CEO*
EMP: 107  EST: 2020
SALES (est): 3.35MM  Privately Held
SIC: 2253  T-shirts and tops, knit

**(P-2466)**
**DELTA PACIFIC ACTIVEWEAR  INC**
331 S Hale Ave, Fullerton  (92831-4805)
PHONE..............................714 871-9281
Imran Parekh, *Pr*
▲ EMP: 80  EST: 1998
SALES (est): 1.25MM  Privately Held
Web: www.delpacific.com
SIC: 2253  2331  2321  T-shirts and tops, knit; Women's and misses' blouses and shirts; Men's and boy's furnishings

**(P-2467)**
**DESIGN KNIT INC**
Also Called: DK
1636 Staunton Ave, Los Angeles  (90021-3132)
PHONE..............................213 742-1234
▲ EMP: 21  EST: 1985
SALES (est): 2.74MM  Privately Held
Web: www.designknit.com
SIC: 2253  Knit outerwear mills

**(P-2468)**
**FANTASY ACTIVEWEAR  INC (PA)**
Also Called: Fantasy Manufacturing
5383 Alcoa Ave, Vernon  (90058-3734)
PHONE..............................213 705-4111
Anwar Gajiani, *CEO*
Yassmin Gajiani, *
▲ EMP: 38  EST: 1991
SQ FT: 20,000
SALES (est): 10.99MM  Privately Held
SIC: 2253  2331  2321  T-shirts and tops, knit; Women's and misses' blouses and shirts; Men's and boy's furnishings

**(P-2469)**
**FANTASY DYEING & FINISHING  INC**
5383 Alcoa Ave, Vernon  (90058)
PHONE..............................323 983-9988
Anwar M Gajiani, *CEO*
EMP: 36  EST: 2003
SALES (est): 1.56MM  Privately Held
SIC: 2253  Dyeing and finishing knit outerwear, excl. hosiery and glove

**(P-2470)**
**FORTUNE SWIMWEAR  LLC (HQ)**
Also Called: Palisades Beach Club
2340 E Olympic Blvd Ste A, Los Angeles  (90021-2544)
PHONE..............................310 733-2130
Stephen Soller, *Managing Member*
Craig Soller, *
Gary Bub, *
Ann Kennedy, *
◆ EMP: 30  EST: 2002
SQ FT: 10,000
SALES (est): 34.7MM  Privately Held
Web: www.fortuneswimwear.com
SIC: 2253  2335  Bathing suits and swimwear, knit; Women's, junior's, and misses' dresses
PA: Coast Style Group, Llc
860 S Los Angeles St # 540

**(P-2471)**
**FUTURESTITCH INC**
144 Avenida Serra, San Clemente  (92672-4759)
PHONE..............................760 707-2003
Taylor Shupe, *CEO*
EMP: 15  EST: 2018
SALES (est): 23.5MM  Privately Held
Web: www.futurestitch.com
SIC: 2253  Knit outerwear mills

**(P-2472)**
**GRAND WEST  INC (PA)**
Also Called: Crown Fashion
1441 E Adams Blvd, Los Angeles  (90011-1819)
PHONE..............................323 235-2700
Dae Hyun Kim, *Pr*
EMP: 22  EST: 1985
SQ FT: 52,000
SALES (est): 299.98K
SALES (corp-wide): 299.98K  Privately Held
SIC: 2253  Jerseys, knit

**(P-2473)**
**INSTA-LETTERING MACHINE CO  (PA)**
Also Called: Insta Graphic Systems
13925 166th St, Cerritos  (90703-2431)
P.O. Box 7900  (90702-7900)
PHONE..............................562 404-3000
◆ EMP: 90  EST: 1959
SALES (est): 8.72MM
SALES (corp-wide): 8.72MM  Privately Held
Web: www.instagraph.com
SIC: 2253  2752  2396  T-shirts and tops, knit; Transfers, decalcomania or dry: lithographed; Screen printing on fabric articles

**(P-2474)**
**ISIQALO LLC**
Also Called: Spectra USA
5610 Daniels St, Chino  (91710-9024)
PHONE..............................714 683-2820
Nick Agakanian, *
▼ EMP: 350  EST: 2012
SALES (est): 8.81MM  Privately Held
Web: www.spectrausa.net
SIC: 2253  5136  5137  2321  T-shirts and tops, knit; Men's and boy's clothing; Women's and children's clothing; Sport shirts, men's and boys': from purchased materials

**(P-2475)**
**LATIGO INC**
4371 E 49th St, Vernon  (90058-3122)
PHONE..............................323 583-8000
Mandana Vasseghi, *CEO*
Nazanine Farshidan, *
EMP: 30  EST: 2011
SQ FT: 18,000
SALES (est): 2.66MM  Privately Held
Web: www.latigousa.com
SIC: 2253  Knit outerwear mills

**(P-2476)**
**LSPACE AMERICA  LLC**
Also Called: L Space
14420 Myford Rd, Irvine  (92606-1017)
PHONE..............................949 750-2292
Lauren Kula, *
◆ EMP: 62  EST: 2008
SALES (est): 5.9MM  Privately Held
Web: www.lspace.com
SIC: 2253  2331  Bathing suits and swimwear, knit; Women's and misses' blouses and shirts

**(P-2477)**
**MAD ENGINE GLOBAL  LLC (HQ)**
Also Called: Mad Engine
7 Studebaker, Irvine  (92618-2013)
PHONE..............................858 558-5270
Danish Gajiani, *CEO*
Faizan Bakali, *
Erik Johnson, *
◆ EMP: 54  EST: 1987
SALES (est): 638.25MM
SALES (corp-wide): 638.25MM  Privately Held
Web: www.madengine.com
SIC: 2253  2261  T-shirts and tops, knit; Screen printing of cotton broadwoven fabrics
PA: Mad Acquisition Corporation
360 N Crescent Dr
858 558-5270

**(P-2478)**
**MJCK CORPORATION**
Also Called: Xzavier
3222 E Washington Blvd, Vernon  (90058-8022)
PHONE..............................888 992-8437
Tae Y Choi, *Pr*
EMP: 16  EST: 2010
SALES (est): 726.75K  Privately Held
SIC: 2253  2361  T-shirts and tops, knit; T-shirts and tops: girls', children's, and infants'

**(P-2479)**
**SNOWFLAKE DESIGNS  CORPORATION**
2893 Larkin Ave, Clovis  (93612-3908)
PHONE..............................559 291-6234
EMP: 22  EST: 1995
SQ FT: 7,100
SALES (est): 2.45MM  Privately Held
Web: www.snowflakedesigns.com
SIC: 2253  5632  Leotards, knit; Dancewear

**(P-2480)**
**STUDIO9D8  INC**
9743 Alesia St, South El Monte  (91733-3008)
PHONE..............................626 350-0832
Ann Lem, *CEO*
EMP: 30  EST: 2011
SALES (est): 2.52MM  Privately Held
Web: www.studio9d8.com
SIC: 2253  2515  T-shirts and tops, knit; Studio couches

**(P-2481)**
**SUNSETS INC**
Also Called: Sunsets Separates
24511 Frampton Ave, Harbor City  (90710-2108)

## PRODUCTS & SERVICES SECTION

### 2269 - Finishing Plants, Nec (P-2502)

PHONE...............................310 784-3600
▲ EMP: 35 EST: 1984
SALES (est): 5.39MM Privately Held
Web: www.sunsetsinc.com
SIC: 2253 Bathing suits and swimwear, knit

### 2257 Weft Knit Fabric Mills

**(P-2482)**
**SHARA-TEX INC**
3338 E Slauson Ave, Vernon (90058-3915)
PHONE...............................323 587-7200
Shahram Fahimian, *Ch Bd*
S Tony Souferian, *
▲ EMP: 45 EST: 1989
SQ FT: 55,000
SALES (est): 2.8MM Privately Held
Web: www.shara-tex.com
SIC: 2257 Weft knit fabric mills

**(P-2483)**
**TENENBLATT CORPORATION**
Also Called: Antex Knitting Mills
3750 Broadway Pl, Los Angeles (90007-4400)
PHONE...............................323 232-2061
William Tenenblatt, *Pr*
Anna Tenenblatt, *
✦ EMP: 104 EST: 1973
SQ FT: 60,000
SALES (est): 1.41MM
SALES (corp-wide): 66.31MM Privately Held
SIC: 2257 Dyeing and finishing circular knit fabrics
PA: Matchmaster Dyeing & Finishing, Inc.
3750 S Broadway
323 232-2061

### 2259 Knitting Mills, Nec

**(P-2484)**
**AZITEX TRADING CORP**
Also Called: Azitex Knitting Mills
1850 E 15th St, Los Angeles (90021-2820)
PHONE...............................213 745-7072
Michael Azizi, *Pr*
Mozie Azizi, *
Andrew Azizi, *
▲ EMP: 60 EST: 1986
SQ FT: 50,000
SALES (est): 3.3MM Privately Held
Web: azitex-trading-co-knitting-mills.business.site
SIC: 2259 2253 Convertors, knit goods; Knit outerwear mills

**(P-2485)**
**MIDTHRUST IMPORTS INC**
Also Called: Midthrust
830 E 14th Pl, Los Angeles (90021-2120)
PHONE...............................213 749-6651
Kamran Noman, *CEO*
▲ EMP: 20 EST: 1983
SALES (est): 2.8MM Privately Held
Web: kiosk.midthrust.com
SIC: 2259 Convertors, knit goods

**(P-2486)**
**PIERCAN USA INC**
160 Bosstick Blvd, San Marcos (92069-5930)
PHONE...............................760 599-4543
Vincent Lucas, *CEO*
Vincent Lucas, *Pr*
Gean-christopher Lucas, *Treas*
Antoine Dobrowolski, *
▲ EMP: 62 EST: 1995
SALES (est): 10.05MM Privately Held
Web: www.piercanusa.com
SIC: 2259 3842 3089 2673 Work gloves, knit; Gloves, safety; Gloves or mittens, plastics; Plastic and pliofilm bags

**(P-2487)**
**SAS TEXTILES INC**
3100 E 44th St, Vernon (90058-2406)
PHONE...............................323 277-5555
Sohrab Sassounian, *Pr*
Soheil Sassounian, *
Albert Sassounian, *
▲ EMP: 70 EST: 1991
SQ FT: 40,000
SALES (est): 9.5MM Privately Held
Web: www.sastextile.com
SIC: 2259 2257 7389 Convertors, knit goods; Weft knit fabric mills; Textile and apparel services

**(P-2488)**
**SW SUSTAINABILITY SOLUTIONS INC**
33278 Central Ave Ste 102, Union City (94587-2016)
PHONE...............................510 429-8692
Belle Chou, *Pr*
▼ EMP: 26 EST: 2010
SALES (est): 4.78MM Privately Held
Web: www.swssglobal.com
SIC: 2259 Gloves and mittens, knit

### 2261 Finishing Plants, Cotton

**(P-2489)**
**CAITAC GARMENT PROCESSING INC**
14725 S Broadway, Gardena (90248-1813)
PHONE...............................310 217-9888
Muneyuki Ishii, *CEO*
Azusa Sahara, *
▲ EMP: 270 EST: 1991
SQ FT: 200,000
SALES (est): 23.61MM Privately Held
Web: www.caitacgarment.com
SIC: 2261 2339 2325 5651 Screen printing of cotton broadwoven fabrics; Women's and misses' outerwear, nec; Men's and boy's trousers and slacks; Jeans stores
PA: Caitac Holdings Corp.
3-12, Showacho, Kita-Ku

**(P-2490)**
**CINDER BLOCK LLC**
2220 W Winton Ave, Hayward (94545-1212)
PHONE...............................510 957-1333
▲ EMP: 17 EST: 1989
SALES (est): 380.41K Privately Held
SIC: 2261 5699 Screen printing of cotton broadwoven fabrics; T-shirts, custom printed

**(P-2491)**
**CUSTOM LOGOS INC**
7889 Clairemont Mesa Blvd, San Diego (92111-1618)
PHONE...............................858 277-1886
▲ EMP: 44 EST: 1982
SALES (est): 13.86MM Privately Held
Web: www.customlogos.com
SIC: 2261 Screen printing of cotton broadwoven fabrics

**(P-2492)**
**HARRYS DYE AND WASH INC**
Also Called: Harry's Dye & Wash
1015 E Orangethorpe Ave, Anaheim (92801-1135)
PHONE...............................714 446-0300
Harry Choung, *Pr*
Kang Ho Lee, *
▲ EMP: 30 EST: 1994
SQ FT: 20,000
SALES (est): 2.02MM Privately Held
SIC: 2261 2269 Finishing plants, cotton; Finishing plants, nec

**(P-2493)**
**INDUSTRY THREADWORKS**
8902 Activity Rd Ste C, San Diego (92126-4471)
PHONE...............................858 265-6177
Ryan Williams, *Prin*
▲ EMP: 20 EST: 2015
SALES (est): 1.48MM Privately Held
Web: www.industrythreadworks.com
SIC: 2261 Printing of cotton broadwoven fabrics

**(P-2494)**
**SILK SCREEN SHIRTS INC**
Also Called: SSS
6185 El Camino Real, Carlsbad (92009-1602)
PHONE...............................760 233-3900
Stephen H Taylor, *Pr*
Laura D Wile, *
William Regan, *
▲ EMP: 30 EST: 1969
SQ FT: 20,000
SALES (est): 4.42MM Privately Held
Web: www.silkscreenshirtsinc.com
SIC: 2261 2396 Screen printing of cotton broadwoven fabrics; Automotive and apparel trimmings

**(P-2495)**
**SRL APPAREL INC**
Also Called: Printed Image, The
2209 Park Ave, Chico (95928-6704)
PHONE...............................530 898-9525
Scott Laursen, *Pr*
Marie Halvorsen, *Stockholder*
▲ EMP: 26 EST: 1980
SQ FT: 14,130
SALES (est): 2.57MM Privately Held
Web: www.printedimagechico.com
SIC: 2261 5137 5136 2396 Screen printing of cotton broadwoven fabrics; Women's and children's sportswear and swimsuits; Men's and boys' sportswear and work clothing; Automotive and apparel trimmings

**(P-2496)**
**SUPER DYEING LLC**
Also Called: Super Dyeing and Finishing
8825 Millergrove Dr, Santa Fe Springs (90670-2003)
PHONE...............................562 692-9500
▲ EMP: 75 EST: 1995
SALES (est): 1.91MM Privately Held
Web: www.superdyeing.com
SIC: 2261 Dyeing cotton broadwoven fabrics

**(P-2497)**
**TOMORROWS LOOK INC**
Also Called: Dimensions In Screen Printing
17462 Von Karman Ave, Irvine (92614-6206)
PHONE...............................949 596-8400
Steven E Mellgren, *CEO*
Torrey Mellgren, *
EMP: 70 EST: 1986
SQ FT: 36,000
SALES (est): 7.39MM Privately Held
SIC: 2261 Screen printing of cotton broadwoven fabrics

**(P-2498)**
**WASHINGTON GRMENT DYG FNSHG IN**
1332 E 18th St, Los Angeles (90021-3027)
PHONE...............................213 747-1111
Pradip Shah, *Mgr*
EMP: 35
SALES (corp-wide): 1.34MM Privately Held
Web: www.washingtongarment.com
SIC: 2261 2262 Finishing plants, cotton; Finishing plants, manmade
PA: Washington Garment Dyeing & Finishing, Inc.
1341 E Washington Blvd
213 747-1111

### 2262 Finishing Plants, Manmade

**(P-2499)**
**INX PRINTS INC**
1802 Kettering, Irvine (92614-5618)
PHONE...............................949 660-9190
Harold A Haase Junior, *CEO*
David Van Steenhuyse, *
▼ EMP: 100 EST: 2004
SQ FT: 26,000
SALES (est): 15.72MM Privately Held
Web: inx-prints-inc.hub.biz
SIC: 2262 Screen printing: manmade fiber and silk broadwoven fabrics

**(P-2500)**
**SPREADCO INC**
803 Us Highway 78, Brawley (92227-9514)
P.O. Box 1400 (92227-1320)
PHONE...............................760 351-0747
Mario Valenzuela, *Pr*
Roque Valenzuela, *Sec*
EMP: 20 EST: 2005
SALES (est): 1.92MM Privately Held
Web: www.spreadco.net
SIC: 2262 Chemical coating or treating of manmade broadwoven fabrics

**(P-2501)**
**WASHINGTON GARMENT DYEING (PA)**
1341 E Washington Blvd, Los Angeles (90021-3037)
PHONE...............................213 747-1111
Vijay Shah, *Pr*
Pradip Shah, *
EMP: 25 EST: 1988
SQ FT: 20,000
SALES (est): 1.34MM
SALES (corp-wide): 1.34MM Privately Held
Web: www.washingtongarment.com
SIC: 2262 2261 2269 Dyeing: manmade fiber and silk broadwoven fabrics; Dyeing cotton broadwoven fabrics; Finishing plants, nec

### 2269 Finishing Plants, Nec

**(P-2502)**
**EXPO DYEING & FINISHING INC**
8898 Los Coyotes Ct Unit 320, Buena Park (90621-3875)
PHONE...............................714 220-9583
Eduardo J Kim, *Pr*
▲ EMP: 170 EST: 1987
SALES (est): 8.06MM Privately Held
Web: www.expodye.com

## 2269 - Finishing Plants, Nec (P-2503)

SIC: 2269 Dyeing: raw stock, yarn, and narrow fabrics

**(P-2503)**
**GEARMENT INC (PA)**
Also Called: Gearment
14801 Able Ln Ste 102, Huntington Beach (92647-2059)
PHONE.....................866 236-5476
Ton Le, *Pr*
Tom Le, *Pr*
Sang D.o.s., *CMO*
EMP: 195 EST: 2016
SALES (est): 33.6MM
SALES (corp-wide): 33.6MM **Privately Held**
Web: www.gearment.com
SIC: 2269 Printing of narrow fabrics

**(P-2504)**
**MATCHMASTER DYG & FINSHG INC (PA)**
Also Called: Antex Knitting Mills
3750 S Broadway, Los Angeles (90007-4436)
PHONE.....................323 232-2061
William Tenenblatt, *Pr*
◆ EMP: 250 EST: 1977
SQ FT: 66,000
SALES (est): 66.31MM
SALES (corp-wide): 66.31MM **Privately Held**
Web: www.antex.com
SIC: 2269 Dyeing: raw stock, yarn, and narrow fabrics

**(P-2505)**
**PACIFIC COAST BACH LABEL INC**
3015 S Grand Ave, Los Angeles (90007-3814)
PHONE.....................213 612-0314
Dan Finnegan, *Pr*
▲ EMP: 23 EST: 1989
SALES (est): 2.12MM **Privately Held**
Web: www.pcblabel.com
SIC: 2269 2679 Labels, cotton: printed; Labels, paper: made from purchased material

**(P-2506)**
**PACIFIC CONTNTL TEXTILES INC**
Also Called: Pct
2880 E Ana St, Compton (90221-5602)
P.O. Box 1330 (90801)
PHONE.....................310 639-1500
Edmund Kim, *CEO*
◆ EMP: 98 EST: 1983
SALES (est): 5.98MM
SALES (corp-wide): 23.03MM **Privately Held**
SIC: 2269 2329 Finishing plants, nec; Men's and boys' sportswear and athletic clothing
PA: Edmund Kim International, Inc.
2880 E Ana St
310 604-1100

**(P-2507)**
**REZEX CORPORATION**
Also Called: Geltman Industries
1930 E 51st St, Vernon (90058-2804)
PHONE.....................213 622-2015
EMP: 25 EST: 1981
SALES (est): 2.49MM **Privately Held**
Web: www.geltman.com
SIC: 2269 Finishing plants, nec

## 2273 Carpets And Rugs

**(P-2508)**
**AMERICAN COVER DESIGN 26 INC**
2131 E 52nd St, Vernon (90058-3498)
PHONE.....................323 582-8666
Daniel Mahgerefteh, *CEO*
Elyas Myers, *
EMP: 25 EST: 2001
SALES (est): 6.76MM **Privately Held**
Web: www.americancoverdesign.com
SIC: 2273 5023 Rugs, machine woven; Rugs

**(P-2509)**
**ATLAS CARPET MILLS INC**
3201 S Susan St, Santa Ana (92704-6838)
P.O. Box 11467 (36671-0467)
PHONE.....................323 724-7930
James Horwich, *Pr*
Ada Horwich, *
Stan Dunford, *
Mark Hesther, *
Markos Varpas, *
▲ EMP: 229 EST: 1969
SALES (est): 3.72MM
SALES (corp-wide): 276.34MM **Publicly Held**
Web: www.atlascarpetmills.com
SIC: 2273 Rugs, tufted
HQ: Tdg Operations, Llc
716 Bill Myles Dr
Saraland AL 36571
251 679-3512

**(P-2510)**
**BENTLEY MILLS INC (PA)**
Also Called: Bentley Mills
14641 Don Julian Rd, City Of Industry (91746-3106)
PHONE.....................626 333-4585
Jay Brown, *Pr*
Nancy Agger-nielsen, *CFO*
◆ EMP: 250 EST: 1980
SQ FT: 390,000
SALES (est): 99.82MM
SALES (corp-wide): 99.82MM **Privately Held**
Web: www.bentleymills.com
SIC: 2273 2299 Carpets, textile fiber; Batting, wadding, padding and fillings

**(P-2511)**
**CATALINA CARPET MILLS INC (PA)**
Also Called: Catalina Home
14418 Best Ave, Santa Fe Springs (90670-5133)
PHONE.....................562 926-5811
Duane Jensen, *Pr*
Jack Heinrich, *
▲ EMP: 38 EST: 1975
SQ FT: 60,000
SALES (est): 9.4MM
SALES (corp-wide): 9.4MM **Privately Held**
Web: www.catalinahome.com
SIC: 2273 5023 Finishers of tufted carpets and rugs; Floor coverings

**(P-2512)**
**CREATIVE ACCENTS**
6294 Curtis Pl, California City (93505-6006)
P.O. Box 2510 (93581-2510)
PHONE.....................760 373-1222
Mike Hensler, *Pr*
▲ EMP: 20 EST: 1967
SQ FT: 22,000
SALES (est): 1.95MM **Privately Held**
Web: www.creativeaccents.com
SIC: 2273 Carpets and rugs

**(P-2513)**
**DURKAN PATTERNED CARPETS INC**
3633 Lenawee Ave # 120, Los Angeles (90016-4319)
PHONE.....................310 838-2898
Kathy Stein, *Mgr*
EMP: 248
SIC: 2273 Carpets, hand and machine made
HQ: Durkan Patterned Carpets, Inc.
121 Goodwill Dr
Dalton GA 30721
706 278-7037

**(P-2514)**
**FABRICA INTERNATIONAL INC**
Also Called: Fabrica Fine Carpet
3201 S Susan St, Santa Ana (92704-6838)
P.O. Box 2007 (30722-2007)
PHONE.....................949 261-7181
Greg Uttecht, *Pr*
Jon A Faulkner, *
▲ EMP: 167 EST: 1974
SQ FT: 107,000
SALES (est): 7.21MM
SALES (corp-wide): 276.34MM **Publicly Held**
SIC: 2273 Carpets, hand and machine made
PA: The Dixie Group Inc
475 Reed Rd
706 876-5800

**(P-2515)**
**INTERFACEFLOR LLC**
1111 S Grand Ave Ste 103, Los Angeles (90015-2164)
PHONE.....................213 741-2139
EMP: 81
SALES (corp-wide): 1.26B **Publicly Held**
Web: www.interface.com
SIC: 2273 Finishers of tufted carpets and rugs
HQ: Interfaceflor, Llc
1503 Orchard Hill Rd
Lagrange GA 30240

**(P-2516)**
**MARSPRING CORPORATION (PA)**
Also Called: Marflex
4920 S Boyle Ave, Vernon (90058-3017)
P.O. Box 58643 (90058-0643)
PHONE.....................323 589-5637
Ronald J Greitzer, *Pr*
Stan Greitzer, *
▲ EMP: 34 EST: 1950
SQ FT: 54,008
SALES (est): 6.62MM
SALES (corp-wide): 6.62MM **Privately Held**
Web: www.reliancecarpetcushion.com
SIC: 2273 Carpets, textile fiber

**(P-2517)**
**MAT CACTUS MFG CO**
930 W 10th St, Azusa (91702-1936)
PHONE.....................626 969-0444
Debra Hartranft-dering, *Pr*
Cailey Dering, *Treas*
▲ EMP: 20 EST: 1934
SQ FT: 35,000
SALES (est): 2.59MM **Privately Held**
Web: www.cactusmat.com
SIC: 2273 5023 3069 Carpets and rugs; Floor coverings; Mats or matting, rubber, nec

**(P-2518)**
**MOHAWK INDUSTRIES INC**
9687 Transportation Way, Fontana (92335-2604)
PHONE.....................909 357-1064
Lisa Gomez, *Brnch Mgr*
EMP: 26
SIC: 2273 3253 Finishers of tufted carpets and rugs; Ceramic wall and floor tile
PA: Mohawk Industries, Inc.
160 S Industrial Blvd

**(P-2519)**
**ROYALTY CARPET MILLS INC**
Also Called: Royalty
17111 Red Hill Ave, Irvine (92614-5607)
PHONE.....................949 474-4000
▲ EMP: 800
SIC: 2273 Carpets, hand and machine made

**(P-2520)**
**SHAW INDUSTRIES GROUP INC**
Also Called: Carriage Carpet Mills
11411 Valley View St, Cypress (90630-5368)
PHONE.....................562 430-4445
Stan Diehl, *Mgr*
EMP: 30
SALES (corp-wide): 364.48B **Publicly Held**
Web: www.shawinc.com
SIC: 2273 5713 5023 Finishers of tufted carpets and rugs; Floor covering stores; Homefurnishings
HQ: Shaw Industries Group, Inc.
616 E Walnut Ave
Dalton GA 30722
706 278-3812

**(P-2521)**
**STANTON CARPET CORP**
Also Called: Hibernia Woolen Mills
2209 Pine Ave, Manhattan Beach (90266-2832)
PHONE.....................562 945-8711
Debbie Dearo, *Mgr*
EMP: 50
SALES (corp-wide): 49.28MM **Privately Held**
Web: www.stantoncarpet.com
SIC: 2273 Carpets and rugs
PA: Stanton Carpet Corp.
100 Snnyside Blvd Ste 100
516 822-5878

**(P-2522)**
**STUDENT SPORTS LLC**
23954 Madison St, Torrance (90505-6011)
PHONE.....................310 791-1142
Andy Bark, *Prin*
EMP: 15 EST: 2008
SALES (est): 1.82MM **Privately Held**
Web: www.areacodebaseball.com
SIC: 2273 Carpets and rugs

## 2281 Yarn Spinning Mills

**(P-2523)**
**TDG OPERATIONS LLC**
Also Called: Candlewick-Porterville
600 Se St, Porterville (93257-5318)
PHONE.....................559 781-4116
Dennis Johnson, *Brnch Mgr*
EMP: 60
SQ FT: 144,964
SALES (corp-wide): 276.34MM **Publicly Held**

# PRODUCTS & SERVICES SECTION
## 2299 - Textile Goods, Nec (P-2543)

SIC: 2281 2221 Yarn spinning mills; Broadwoven fabric mills, manmade
HQ: Tdg Operations, Llc
475 Reed Rd
Dalton GA 30720
706 876-5851

### 2284 Thread Mills

**(P-2524)**
**AMERICAN & EFIRD LLC**
6098 Rickenbacker Rd, Commerce (90040-3030)
PHONE..................323 724-6884
Juan Anbric, Mgr
EMP: 18
SALES (corp-wide): 1.98B Privately Held
Web: www.amefird.com
SIC: 2284 Thread mills
HQ: American & Efird Llc
24 American St
Mount Holly NC 28120
704 827-4311

### 2295 Coated Fabrics, Not Rubberized

**(P-2525)**
**AOC LLC**
Also Called: AOC California Plant
19991 Seaton Ave, Perris (92570-8724)
PHONE..................951 657-5161
John Mulrine, Mgr
EMP: 100
Web: www.aocresins.com
SIC: 2295 2821 5169 Resin or plastic coated fabrics; Plastics materials and resins; Synthetic resins, rubber, and plastic materials
PA: Aoc, Llc
955 Hwy 57

**(P-2526)**
**CALIFORNIA COMBINING CORP**
5607 S Santa Fe Ave, Vernon (90058-3525)
P.O. Box 509 (90280-0509)
PHONE..................323 589-5727
Charlette Heller, CEO
Vincent Rosato, *
Kathy Diaz, *
▲ EMP: 37 EST: 1947
SQ FT: 68,000
SALES (est): 2.53MM Privately Held
Web: www.flamelaminatingcorp.com
SIC: 2295 Coated fabrics, not rubberized

**(P-2527)**
**FLEXFIRM HOLDINGS LLC**
2300 Chico Ave, El Monte (91733-1611)
PHONE..................323 283-1173
Barry Eichorn, Pr
EMP: 15 EST: 1968
SQ FT: 10,000
SALES (est): 1MM Privately Held
Web: www.flexfirmproducts.com
SIC: 2295 Resin or plastic coated fabrics

**(P-2528)**
**J MILLER CANVAS LLC**
2429 S Birch St, Santa Ana (92707-3406)
PHONE..................714 641-0052
EMP: 26 EST: 2018
SALES (est): 2.35MM Privately Held
Web: www.jmillercanvas.com
SIC: 2295 Waterproofing fabrics, except rubberizing

**(P-2529)**
**KASLEN TEXTILES LLC**
Also Called: Kaslen Textiles
2140 E 51st St, Vernon (90058-2817)
PHONE..................323 588-7700
David Raminfard, CEO
Jennifer Raminfard Net, Mktg Dir
▲ EMP: 16 EST: 2010
SQ FT: 36,000
SALES (est): 5.44MM Privately Held
Web: www.kaslentextiles.com
SIC: 2295 Coated fabrics, not rubberized

**(P-2530)**
**SOLECTA INC (PA)**
4113 Avenida De La Plata, Oceanside (92056)
PHONE..................760 630-9643
Jim Ford, CEO
Michael Ahearn, *
▲ EMP: 24 EST: 2014
SALES (est): 11.03MM
SALES (corp-wide): 11.03MM Privately Held
Web: www.solecta.com
SIC: 2295 Chemically coated and treated fabrics

**(P-2531)**
**SPECILTY MTALS FABRICATION INC**
11222 Woodside Ave N, Santee (92071-4716)
PHONE..................619 937-6100
Richard Buxton, Pr
Tom Buxton, CFO
Larry Hendry, Sec
Sandy Fousek, Off Mgr
EMP: 16 EST: 2004
SALES (est): 2.2MM Privately Held
Web: www.specialtymetalsfab.com
SIC: 2295 Metallizing of fabrics

### 2296 Tire Cord And Fabrics

**(P-2532)**
**BEBOP SENSORS INC**
970 Miller Ave, Berkeley (94708-1406)
P.O. Box 408 (97034-0408)
PHONE..................503 875-4990
Keith A Mcmillen, CEO
Michelle Cook, *
EMP: 24 EST: 2014
SALES (est): 2.41MM Privately Held
Web: www.bebopsensors.com
SIC: 2296 Tire cord and fabrics

### 2297 Nonwoven Fabrics

**(P-2533)**
**TEXOLLINI INC**
2575 E El Presidio St, Long Beach (90810-1114)
PHONE..................310 537-3400
Daniel Kadisha, Pr
◆ EMP: 250 EST: 1989
SQ FT: 200,000
SALES (est): 22.96MM Privately Held
Web: www.texollini.com
SIC: 2297 2262 2269 2221 Nonwoven fabrics; Dyeing: manmade fiber and silk broadwoven fabrics; Finishing plants, nec; Broadwoven fabric mills, manmade

### 2298 Cordage And Twine

**(P-2534)**
**BAY ASSOCIATES WIRE TECH CORP (DH)**
46840 Lakeview Blvd, Fremont (94538-6543)
PHONE..................510 988-3800
Harry Avonti, CEO
Mark Rotner, *
Jack Sanford, *
◆ EMP: 31 EST: 2008
SQ FT: 45,000
SALES (est): 42.08MM
SALES (corp-wide): 99.1MM Privately Held
Web: www.baycable.com
SIC: 2298 3351 3357 Cable, fiber; Copper rolling and drawing; Nonferrous wiredrawing and insulating
HQ: New England Wire Technologies Corporation
130 N Main St
Lisbon NH 03585
603 838-6624

**(P-2535)**
**DYNAMEX CORPORATION**
155 E Albertoni St, Carson (90746-1405)
PHONE..................310 329-0399
Ben Bravin, Pr
◆ EMP: 20 EST: 1975
SALES (est): 3.27MM Privately Held
SIC: 2298 Cable, fiber

**(P-2536)**
**LIFT-IT MANUFACTURING CO INC**
Also Called: Lift It
1603 W 2nd St, Pomona (91766-1252)
PHONE..................909 469-2251
▲ EMP: 46 EST: 1979
SALES (est): 6.47MM Privately Held
Web: www.lift-it.com
SIC: 2298 Slings, rope

**(P-2537)**
**PACIFIC FIBRE & ROPE CO INC**
2700 Rose Ave Ste R, Signal Hill (90755-1931)
P.O. Box 187 (90748-0187)
PHONE..................310 834-4567
Mark Goldman, Pr
Allen Goldman, Pr
Ronald Goldman, VP
Michael Goldman, Sec
▲ EMP: 15 EST: 1930
SQ FT: 45,000
SALES (est): 890.61K Privately Held
Web: www.pacificfibre.com
SIC: 2298 5085 Cordage: abaca, sisal, henequen, hemp, jute, or other fiber; Rope, except wire rope

**(P-2538)**
**PELICAN ROPE WORKS**
1600 E Mcfadden Ave, Santa Ana (92705-4310)
PHONE..................714 545-0116
Gaylord C Whipple, Pr
Jacob Williams, Ex VP
◆ EMP: 15 EST: 1981
SQ FT: 20,000
SALES (est): 2.84MM Privately Held
Web: www.pelicanrope.com
SIC: 2298 Ropes and fiber cables

**(P-2539)**
**RIP-TIE INC**
883 San Leandro Blvd, San Leandro (94577-1530)
P.O. Box 549 (94577-0549)
PHONE..................510 577-0200
Michael Paul Fennell, Pr
▲ EMP: 18 EST: 1985
SQ FT: 45,000
SALES (est): 2.43MM Privately Held
Web: www.riptie.com
SIC: 2298 Cordage and twine

### 2299 Textile Goods, Nec

**(P-2540)**
**ALANIC INTERNATIONAL CORP**
Also Called: Dioz Group, The
8730 Wilshire Blvd Ph, Beverly Hills (90211-2709)
PHONE..................855 525-2642
Farhan Beig, Pr
Johnny Beig, CEO
Tony Beig, Sr VP
▲ EMP: 38 EST: 2013
SALES (est): 7.55MM Privately Held
Web: www.alanic.com
SIC: 2299 2329 2339 Broadwoven fabrics: linen, jute, hemp, and ramie; Athletic clothing, except uniforms: men's, youths' and boys'; Athletic clothing: women's, misses', and juniors'

**(P-2541)**
**AMERICAN DAWN INC (PA)**
Also Called: ADI
401 W Artesia Blvd, Compton (90220)
PHONE..................800 821-2221
Adnan Rawjee, Pr
Mahmud G Rawjee, *
◆ EMP: 60 EST: 1980
SQ FT: 212,000
SALES (est): 25.02MM
SALES (corp-wide): 25.02MM Privately Held
Web: www.americandawn.com
SIC: 2299 5023 5131 2393 Linen fabrics; Linens and towels; Textiles, woven, nec; Cushions, except spring and carpet: purchased materials

**(P-2542)**
**AMERICAN FOAM FIBER & SUPS INC (PA)**
Also Called: Foam Depot
255 S 7th Ave Ste A, City Of Industry (91746-3256)
PHONE..................626 969-7268
Jack Hung, Pr
Irene Hung, VP
▲ EMP: 26 EST: 2006
SALES (est): 3.82MM Privately Held
Web: www.affsinc.com
SIC: 2299 Hair, curled: for upholstery, pillow, and quilt filling

**(P-2543)**
**AMPM MAINTENANCE CORPORATION**
1010 E 14th St, Los Angeles (90021-2212)
PHONE..................424 230-1300
Mohammad Saderi, Pr
EMP: 48 EST: 2020
SALES (est): 165.06K Privately Held
Web: www.ampmmaintenance.com
SIC: 2299 Textile goods, nec

## 2299 - Textile Goods, Nec (P-2544)

**(P-2544)**
**AMRAPUR OVERSEAS INCORPORATED (PA)**
Also Called: Colonial Home Textiles
1560 E 6th St Ste 101, Corona (92879-1712)
PHONE..................714 893-8808
Chandru H Wadhwani, CEO
Laxmi Wadhwani, *
◆ EMP: 25 EST: 1983
SQ FT: 130,000
SALES (est): 9.2MM
SALES (corp-wide): 9.2M Privately Held
Web: www.amrapur.com
SIC: 2299 2269 5023 Linen fabrics; Linen fabrics: dyeing, finishing, and printing; Linens and towels

**(P-2545)**
**DECCOFELT CORPORATION**
555 S Vermont Ave, Glendora (91741-6206)
P.O. Box 156 (91740-0156)
PHONE..................626 963-8511
Gerald L Heinrich, CEO
▲ EMP: 24 EST: 1951
SQ FT: 33,000
SALES (est): 4.69MM Privately Held
Web: www.deccofelt.com
SIC: 2299 Felts and felt products

**(P-2546)**
**ETRADE 24 INC**
16600 Calneva Dr, Encino (91436-3140)
PHONE..................818 712-0574
EMP: 25 EST: 2018
SALES (est): 2.06MM Privately Held
Web: us.etrade.com
SIC: 2299 2326 7389 Batting, wadding, padding and fillings; Medical and hospital uniforms, men's; Brokers' services

**(P-2547)**
**J H TEXTILES INC**
2301 E 55th St, Vernon (90058-3435)
PHONE..................323 585-4124
Jong Soon Hur, CEO
▲ EMP: 25 EST: 2003
SQ FT: 80,000
SALES (est): 1MM Privately Held
Web: www.jhtextilesinc.com
SIC: 2299 Textile mill waste and remnant processing

**(P-2548)**
**LF VISUALS INC**
Also Called: Little Folk Visuals
39620 Entrepreneur Ln, Palm Desert (92211-0400)
P.O. Box 14243 (92255-4243)
PHONE..................760 345-5571
Michael Firman, CEO
▲ EMP: 15 EST: 1982
SQ FT: 7,300
SALES (est): 1.73MM Privately Held
Web: www.littlefolkvisuals.com
SIC: 2299 Felts and felt products

**(P-2549)**
**MFB WORLDWIDE INC (PA)**
4901 Patata St Ste 201-204, Cudahy (90201-5942)
PHONE..................323 562-2339
Daniel Holmes, CEO
Pedro Garcia, COO
Robert Harrison, CMO
EMP: 15 EST: 2013
SQ FT: 20,000
SALES (est): 653.18K
SALES (corp-wide): 653.18K Privately Held
SIC: 2299 Fabrics: linen, jute, hemp, ramie

**(P-2550)**
**MISTO LINO**
3585 Mt Diablo Blvd, Lafayette (94549)
PHONE..................925 284-6565
EMP: 15 EST: 2020
SALES (est): 46.58K Privately Held
Web: www.mistolino.com
SIC: 2299 Textile goods, nec

**(P-2551)**
**NEW HAVEN COMPANIES INC**
13571 Vaughn St Unit E, San Fernando (91340-3006)
PHONE..................818 686-7020
Alex Franco, Mgr
EMP: 55
Web: www.newhaven-usa.com
SIC: 2299 3537 2298 2273 Batting, wadding, padding and fillings; Industrial trucks and tractors; Cordage and twine; Carpets and rugs
PA: The New Haven Companies Inc
3951 Sw 30th Ave

**(P-2552)**
**NEXTRADE INC (PA)**
Also Called: Nextex International
12411 Industrial Ave, South Gate (90280-8221)
PHONE..................562 944-9950
Jang R Cho, CEO
◆ EMP: 20 EST: 1998
SQ FT: 40,000
SALES (est): 1.9MM
SALES (corp-wide): 1.9MM Privately Held
SIC: 2299 Batting, wadding, padding and fillings

**(P-2553)**
**PACESETTER FABRICS LLC (HQ)**
11450 Sheldon St, Sun Valley (91352-1121)
PHONE..................213 741-9999
◆ EMP: 17 EST: 1997
SQ FT: 36,000
SALES (est): 4.66MM Privately Held
SIC: 2299 Tops and top processing, manmade or other fiber
PA: Unitex Industries, Inc.
1401 Griffith Ave

**(P-2554)**
**REDWOOD WELLNESS LLC**
1950 W Corporate Way, Anaheim (92801-5373)
PHONE..................323 843-2676
Robert Rosenheck, CEO
EMP: 38 EST: 2017
SALES (est): 3.41MM Privately Held
SIC: 2299 Hemp yarn, thread, roving, and textiles

**(P-2555)**
**STONE HARBOR INC**
5015 District Blvd, Vernon (90058-2719)
PHONE..................323 277-2777
▲ EMP: 18 EST: 2003
SALES (est): 1.98MM Privately Held
SIC: 2299 Textile mill waste and remnant processing

## 2311 Men's And Boy's Suits And Coats

**(P-2556)**
**AMWEAR USA INC**
Also Called: Tactsquad
250 Benjamin Dr, Corona (92879-6508)
PHONE..................800 858-6755
Hong Li Hawkins, CEO
Hang Guo, Prin
EMP: 29 EST: 2017
SALES (est): 1.6MM Privately Held
Web: www.tactsquad.com
SIC: 2311 5699 Men's and boys' uniforms; Uniforms

**(P-2557)**
**BARCO UNIFORMS INC**
350 W Rosecrans Ave, Gardena (90248-1728)
PHONE..................310 323-7315
Ron Wagensiel, CEO
Danny Robertson, *
David Ayers, *
Kathy Peterson, *
David Aquino, *
◆ EMP: 372 EST: 1929
SQ FT: 74,000
SALES (est): 32.56MM Privately Held
Web: www.barcomade.com
SIC: 2311 2326 2337 Men's and boys' uniforms; Men's and boy's work clothing; Uniforms, except athletic: women's, misses', and juniors'

**(P-2558)**
**BLUE SPHERE INC**
Also Called: Lucky-13 Apparel
10869 Portal Dr, Los Alamitos (90720-2508)
PHONE..................714 953-7555
Robert Kloetzly, Pr
▲ EMP: 33 EST: 1989
SALES (est): 748.18K Privately Held
Web: www.bluespheremfg.com
SIC: 2311 2331 2369 Men's and boy's suits and coats; Women's and misses' blouses and shirts; Girl's and children's outerwear, nec

**(P-2559)**
**CROSSPORT MOCEAN**
Also Called: Mocean
1611 Babcock St, Newport Beach (92663-2805)
PHONE..................949 646-1701
Bill Levitt, Pr
Tim Hindman, Sec
Pamela Green, Treas
▲ EMP: 18 EST: 1991
SQ FT: 3,000
SALES (est): 543.81K Privately Held
Web: www.mocean.net
SIC: 2311 Policemen's uniforms: made from purchased materials

**(P-2560)**
**FIRST TACTICAL LLC**
Also Called: First Tactical
496 E Whitmore Ave Bldg 4, Modesto (95358)
PHONE..................209 482-7255
Dan J Costa, *
Denise L Costa, *
EMP: 901 EST: 2015
SALES (est): 15.15MM Privately Held
Web: www.firsttactical.com
SIC: 2311 Military uniforms, men's and youths': purchased materials

**(P-2561)**
**MILITARY ADVANTAGE INC**
Also Called: Beale Afb
17600 25th St Bldg 2434, Beale Afb (95903)
PHONE..................530 788-0221
Gail Lecour, Genl Mgr
EMP: 20
SALES (corp-wide): 27.64B Privately Held
Web: www.military.com
SIC: 2311 Military uniforms, men's and youths': purchased materials
HQ: Military Advantage, Inc.
799 Market St Fl 7
San Francisco CA 94103
415 820-3434

**(P-2562)**
**NEW CHEF FASHION INC**
3223 E 46th St, Los Angeles (90058-2407)
PHONE..................323 581-0300
Chantal Salama, CEO
Guy Lucien Salama, *
▲ EMP: 70 EST: 1989
SALES (est): 8.66MM Privately Held
Web: www.newchef.com
SIC: 2311 2339 2326 5137 Men's and boys' uniforms; Women's and misses' outerwear, nec; Men's and boy's work clothing; Uniforms, women's and children's

**(P-2563)**
**NO SECOND THOUGHTS INC**
Also Called: Nst
1333 30th St Ste D, San Diego (92154-3487)
PHONE..................619 428-5992
Audrey Swirsky, Pr
Onnie Ramos, *
EMP: 52 EST: 1999
SALES (est): 2.2MM Privately Held
Web: www.nst2.com
SIC: 2311 2329 2326 Men's and boys' uniforms; Men's and boys' sportswear and athletic clothing; Medical and hospital uniforms, men's

**(P-2564)**
**RDD ENTERPRISES INC**
Also Called: Americawear
4638 E Washington Blvd, Commerce (90040-1026)
PHONE..................213 746-0020
Tony Lomeli, Brnch Mgr
EMP: 16
SALES (corp-wide): 3.12MM Privately Held
Web: www.rddusa.com
SIC: 2311 Military uniforms, men's and youths': purchased materials
PA: R.D.D. Enterprises, Inc.
4638 E Washington Blvd
213 742-0666

**(P-2565)**
**ROBERT TALBOTT INC (PA)**
Also Called: Talbott Ties
24560 Silver Cloud Ct Ste 201, Monterey (93940-6560)
PHONE..................831 649-6000
Robert J Corliss, CEO
Robert Corliss Ii, Pr
▲ EMP: 28 EST: 1950
SQ FT: 77,000
SALES (est): 9.5MM
SALES (corp-wide): 9.5MM Privately Held
Web: www.roberttalbottofficial.com
SIC: 2311 2321 2322 2323 Men's and boy's suits and coats; Men's and boy's furnishings; Men's and boy's underwear and nightwear; Men's and boy's neckwear

**(P-2566)**
**SANTANA FORMAL ACCESSORIES INC**
707 Arroyo St Ste B, San Fernando (91340-1855)

# PRODUCTS & SERVICES SECTION

## 2325 - Men's And Boy's Trousers And Slacks (P-2588)

P.O. Box 2248 (91376-2248)
PHONE..................818 898-3677
Delores Tennant, Pr
Doug Freed, *
EMP: 15 EST: 1970
SQ FT: 18,000
SALES (est): 439.97K **Privately Held**
Web: www.santanaapparel.com
SIC: 2311 2339 2323 2389 Vests: made from purchased materials; Women's and misses' outerwear, nec; Bow ties, men's and boys': made from purchased materials; Cummerbunds

### (P-2567)
### STRINGKING INC (PA)
19100 S Vermont Ave, Gardena (90248-4413)
PHONE..................310 503-8901
Jake Mccampbell, CEO
EMP: 23 EST: 2020
SALES (est): 50MM
SALES (corp-wide): 50MM **Privately Held**
Web: www.stringking.com
SIC: 2311 Men's and boys' uniforms

### (P-2568)
### TRUMAKER INC
Also Called: Trumaker & Co.
228 Grant Ave Fl 2, San Francisco (94108-4647)
PHONE..................415 662-3836
Mark Lovas, CEO
Michael Zhang, *
▲ EMP: 50 EST: 2011
SALES (est): 1.55MM **Privately Held**
Web: www.trumaker.com
SIC: 2311 2321 2325 Men's and boy's suits and coats; Men's and boy's furnishings; Men's and boy's trousers and slacks

### (P-2569)
### TYLER TRAFFICANTE INC (PA)
Also Called: Richard Tyler
700 S Palm Ave, Alhambra (91803-1528)
PHONE..................323 869-9299
Lisa Trafficante, Pr
Richard Tyler, *
EMP: 23 EST: 1986
SQ FT: 30,000
SALES (est): 3.83MM
SALES (corp-wide): 3.83MM **Privately Held**
Web: www.hbpta.org
SIC: 2311 2335 5611 5621 Tailored suits and formal jackets; Gowns, formal; Suits, men's; Dress shops

## 2321 Men's And Boy's Furnishings

### (P-2570)
### COTTON LINKS LLC
2990 Grace Ln, Costa Mesa (92626-4120)
PHONE..................714 444-4700
Robby Khalek, Managing Member
EMP: 25 EST: 2011
SALES (est): 1.64MM **Privately Held**
Web: www.clca.us
SIC: 2321 Men's and boy's furnishings

### (P-2571)
### CREATIVE DESIGN INDUSTRIES
2587 Otay Center Dr, San Diego (92154-7612)
PHONE..................619 710-2525
Sylvia Habchi, Pt
Elie Habchi, *
▲ EMP: 125 EST: 1982

SQ FT: 15,000
SALES (est): 1.76MM **Privately Held**
SIC: 2321 5137 Men's and boy's furnishings; Sportswear, women's and children's

### (P-2572)
### DISTRO WORLDWIDE LLC
Also Called: Get Primped
3400 S Main St, Los Angeles (90007-4412)
PHONE..................818 849-0953
Jessica Raben, Managing Member
EMP: 25 EST: 2020
SALES (est): 466.96K **Privately Held**
SIC: 2321 Men's and boys' dress shirts

### (P-2573)
### GINO CORPORATION
Also Called: Shaka Wear
555 E Jefferson Blvd, Los Angeles (90011-2430)
PHONE..................323 234-7979
Sung Uk Park, CEO
Eugene Park, Ex VP
◆ EMP: 28 EST: 2004
SALES (est): 6.73MM **Privately Held**
Web: www.shakawear.com
SIC: 2321 5136 Men's and boys' dress shirts; Shirts, men's and boys'

### (P-2574)
### JL DESIGN ENTERPRISES INC
Also Called: Jl Racing.com
37407 Industry Way, Murrieta (92563-3103)
PHONE..................714 479-0240
Jolene Sparza, Pr
Kenneth Mills, *
▲ EMP: 63 EST: 1983
SALES (est): 3.91MM **Privately Held**
Web: www.jlrowing.com
SIC: 2321 Sport shirts, men's and boys': from purchased materials

### (P-2575)
### JUST FOR FUN INC
Also Called: Jff Uniforms
557 Van Ness Ave, Torrance (90501-1424)
P.O. Box 9012 (90508-9012)
PHONE..................310 320-1327
Corinne Stolz, Pr
Gary Stolz, *
▲ EMP: 24 EST: 1975
SQ FT: 11,000
SALES (est): 877.79K **Privately Held**
Web: www.jffuniforms.com
SIC: 2321 2337 2339 2326 Uniform shirts: made from purchased materials; Uniforms, except athletic: women's, misses', and juniors'; Women's and misses' outerwear, nec; Men's and boy's work clothing

### (P-2576)
### LISA FACTORY INC
144 N Swall Dr, Beverly Hills (90211-1943)
PHONE..................213 536-5326
Abrar Ahmed, CEO
EMP: 52 EST: 2020
SALES (est): 48.66MM **Privately Held**
SIC: 2321 5199 Men's and boys' dress shirts; General merchandise, non-durable

### (P-2577)
### SIMO HOLDINGS INC
611 Gateway Blvd Ste 120, South San Francisco (94080-7066)
PHONE..................760 931-9550
George Blanco, CRO
Brian Simo, VP
▲ EMP: 300 EST: 1990
SALES (est): 2.85MM **Privately Held**
Web: www.simo.co

SIC: 2321 Men's and boy's furnishings

### (P-2578)
### TEXTILE UNLIMITED CORPORATION (PA)
20917 Higgins Ct, Torrance (90501-1723)
PHONE..................310 263-7400
James Y Kim, CEO
Sam Lee, Pr
Stanley Kim, Pr
Yumi Park, Sec
◆ EMP: 61 EST: 1994
SALES (est): 1.84MM **Privately Held**
Web: www.tuc.net
SIC: 2321 2339 2329 2331 Men's and boy's furnishings; Women's and misses' athletic clothing and sportswear; Men's and boys' athletic uniforms; Women's and misses' blouses and shirts

### (P-2579)
### TOP HEAVY CLOTHING COMPANY INC (PA)
28381 Vincent Moraga Dr, Temecula (92590-3653)
PHONE..................951 442-8839
Tadd D Chilcott, Pr
Douglas Lo, *
▲ EMP: 65 EST: 1995
SQ FT: 40,000
SALES (est): 9.9MM **Privately Held**
Web: www.topheavyclothing.com
SIC: 2321 Men's and boys' dress shirts

### (P-2580)
### TRUE CLASSIC TEES LLC
26635 Agoura Rd Ste 105, Calabasas (91302-3807)
PHONE..................323 419-1092
Ryan Bartlett, Managing Member
EMP: 22 EST: 2018
SALES (est): 1.2MM **Privately Held**
Web: www.trueclassictees.com
SIC: 2321 Men's and boys' dress shirts

## 2323 Men's And Boy's Neckwear

### (P-2581)
### ADAPTIVE INSIGHTS LLC
14 W Central Ave, Los Gatos (95030-7121)
PHONE..................408 656-4229
EMP: 46
Web: www.workday.com
SIC: 2323 Men's and boy's neckwear
HQ: Adaptive Insights Llc
2300 Geng Rd Ste 100
Palo Alto CA 94303
650 528-7500

### (P-2582)
### ARMY OF HAPPY LLC
4580 Euclid Ave, San Diego (92115-3223)
PHONE..................704 517-9890
Sean Brunle, Prin
EMP: 46 EST: 2013
SALES (est): 287.49K **Privately Held**
SIC: 2323 Men's and boy's neckwear

### (P-2583)
### FASHIONGO
2250 Maple Ave, Los Angeles (90011-1190)
PHONE..................213 745-2667
EMP: 38
SALES (est): 1.06MM **Privately Held**
Web: www.fashiongo.net
SIC: 2323 Men's and boy's neckwear

### (P-2584)
### SOPHIE BUHAI LLC
2658 Griffith Park Blvd # 417, Los Angeles (90039-2520)
PHONE..................949 302-8762
Sophie Buhai, Prin
EMP: 16 EST: 2015
SALES (est): 418.61K **Privately Held**
Web: www.sophiebuhai.com
SIC: 2323 Men's and boy's neckwear

## 2325 Men's And Boy's Trousers And Slacks

### (P-2585)
### AG ADRIANO GOLDSCHMIED INC (PA)
Also Called: AG Jeans
2741 Seminole Ave Ste A, South Gate (90280-5550)
PHONE..................323 357-1111
U Yul Ku, CEO
Adriano Suarez, *
▲ EMP: 44 EST: 2000
SQ FT: 150,000
SALES (est): 22.87MM
SALES (corp-wide): 22.87MM **Privately Held**
Web: www.agjeans.com
SIC: 2325 2339 5136 5137 Men's and boy's trousers and slacks; Women's and misses' outerwear, nec; Men's and boy's clothing; Women's and children's clothing

### (P-2586)
### LEVI STRAUSS & CO (PA)
Also Called: Levi Strauss
1155 Battery St, San Francisco (94111-1264)
PHONE..................415 501-6000
Michelle Gass, Pr
Robert A Eckert, Ex VP
Elizabeth O'neill, *
Harmit Singh, Chief Financial GROWTH
Tracy Layney, Chief Human Resource Officer
◆ EMP: 1100 EST: 1853
SALES (est): 6.18B
SALES (corp-wide): 6.18B **Publicly Held**
Web: www.levistrauss.com
SIC: 2325 2339 2321 2331 Jeans: men's, youths', and boys'; Jeans: women's, misses', and juniors'; Men's and boy's furnishings; Shirts, women's and juniors': made from purchased materials

### (P-2587)
### RCRV INC (PA)
Also Called: Rock Revival
4715 S Alameda St, Vernon (90058-2014)
PHONE..................323 235-8070
Eric S Choi, Pr
Young S Cho, *
Kheim Nguyen, Design Vice President*
◆ EMP: 23 EST: 2008
SQ FT: 70,000
SALES (est): 1.56MM
SALES (corp-wide): 1.56MM **Privately Held**
Web: www.rockrevival.com
SIC: 2325 5699 Men's and boys' jeans and dungarees; Customized clothing and apparel

### (P-2588)
### ROB INC
Also Called: Robin's Jeans
6760 Foster Bridge Blvd, Bell Gardens (90201-2030)

## 2325 - Men's And Boy's Trousers And Slacks (P-2589)

PHONE.....................562 806-5589
Robert Chretien, *CEO*
Gilberto Jimenez, *
◆ **EMP:** 90 **EST:** 2005
**SQ FT:** 26,000
**SALES (est):** 9.62MM **Privately Held**
**Web:** www.robinsjean.com
**SIC: 2325** 2339 2369  Jeans: men's, youths', and boys'; Women's and misses' culottes, knickers and shorts; Shorts (outerwear): girls' and children's

**(P-2589)**
**TRUE RELIGION APPAREL INC (HQ)**
Also Called: True Religion Brand Jeans
500 W 190th St Ste 300, Gardena (90248-4269)
PHONE.....................323 266-3072
Michael Buckley, *CEO*
Lynne Koplin, *Pr*
Peter F Collins, *CFO*
Kelly Gvildys, *VP Opers*
David Chiovetti, *Sr VP*
▲ **EMP:** 300 **EST:** 2005
**SALES (est):** 270.02MM
**SALES (corp-wide):** 350MM **Privately Held**
**Web:** www.truereligion.com
**SIC: 2325** 2339 2369  Men's and boy's trousers and slacks; Women's and misses' outerwear, nec; Jeans: girls', children's, and infants'
**PA:** Trlg Corporate Holdings, Llc
1888 Rosecrans Ave
323 266-3072

**(P-2590)**
**UNSPUN INC**
6655 Hollis St, Emeryville (94608-1031)
PHONE.....................207 577-8745
Elizabeth Faith Esponnette, *CEO*
**EMP:** 34 **EST:** 2018
**SALES (est):** 11.64MM **Privately Held**
**Web:** www.unspun.io
**SIC: 2325**  Jeans: men's, youths', and boys'

## 2326 Men's And Boy's Work Clothing

**(P-2591)**
**BRING ROKK LLC**
Also Called: Rock World Merchandise
1275 N Manassero St, Anaheim (92807-1933)
PHONE.....................714 904-2243
Joseph David Jacobs, *CEO*
Joseph David Jacobs, *Managing Member*
**EMP:** 15 **EST:** 2007
**SALES (est):** 2.5MM **Privately Held**
**Web:** www.rockworldmerch.com
**SIC: 2326** 2335  Men's and boy's work clothing; Women's, junior's, and misses' dresses

**(P-2592)**
**FANTASY ACTIVEWEAR INC**
3420 W Maywood Ave, Santa Ana (92704-4423)
PHONE.....................714 751-0137
**EMP:** 19 **EST:** 2020
**SALES (est):** 67.05K **Privately Held**
**SIC: 2326**  Men's and boy's work clothing

**(P-2593)**
**FIGS INC**
Also Called: Figs
2834 Colorado Ave Ste 100, Santa Monica (90404-3644)
PHONE.....................424 300-8330
Catherine Spear, *CEO*
Heather Hasson, *
Sarah Oughtred, *CFO*
▲ **EMP:** 354 **EST:** 2013
**SALES (est):** 545.65MM **Privately Held**
**Web:** www.wearfigs.com
**SIC: 2326** 5699  Work apparel, except uniforms; Work clothing

**(P-2594)**
**IMAGE APPAREL FOR BUSINESS INC**
1618 E Edinger Ave, Santa Ana (92705-5019)
PHONE.....................714 541-5247
Keith Knerr, *CEO*
Robert Duffield, *
**EMP:** 25 **EST:** 2009
**SALES (est):** 2.87MM **Privately Held**
**Web:** www.ia4biz.com
**SIC: 2326** 2339 2353 7213  Men's and boy's work clothing; Uniforms, athletic: women's, misses', and juniors'; Uniform hats and caps ; Linen supply

**(P-2595)**
**IMAGE SOLUTIONS APPAREL INC**
Also Called: Image Solutions
19571 Magellan Dr, Torrance (90502-1136)
PHONE.....................310 464-8991
Christopher Kelley, *Pr*
Paula Fox, *
▲ **EMP:** 111 **EST:** 1997
**SQ FT:** 4,500
**SALES (est):** 24.41MM **Privately Held**
**Web:** www.eimagesolutions.com
**SIC: 2326** 2337  Work uniforms; Uniforms, except athletic: women's, misses', and juniors'

**(P-2596)**
**INDIE SOURCE**
940 Venice Blvd, Venice (90291-4979)
PHONE.....................424 200-2027
Jesse Dombrowiak, *Pr*
**EMP:** 20 **EST:** 2014
**SALES (est):** 2.24MM **Privately Held**
**Web:** www.indiesource.com
**SIC: 2326** 7336  Men's and boy's work clothing; Graphic arts and related design

**(P-2597)**
**LA TRIUMPH INC**
Also Called: Medgear
13336 Alondra Blvd, Cerritos (90703-2205)
PHONE.....................562 404-7657
Hasina Lakhani, *CEO*
Amin Lakhani, *
▲ **EMP:** 24 **EST:** 2003
**SQ FT:** 40,000
**SALES (est):** 2.39MM **Privately Held**
**Web:** www.pacuniforms.com
**SIC: 2326**  Medical and hospital uniforms, men's

**(P-2598)**
**MED COUTURE INC**
Also Called: Peaches
15301 Ventura Blvd, Sherman Oaks (91403-3102)
PHONE.....................214 231-2500
Barry Rothschild, *Pr*
Mark Wilcoxson, *
▲ **EMP:** 87 **EST:** 1987
**SALES (est):** 22.53MM **Privately Held**
**Web:** www.medcouture.com
**SIC: 2326**  Work uniforms

**(P-2599)**
**MEXAPPAREL INC (PA)**
2344 E 38th St, Vernon (90058-1627)
PHONE.....................323 364-8600
Maria Maniatis, *Pr*
Hubert Guez, *
Fred Kalmar, *
Nomaan Yousef, *
**EMP:** 21 **EST:** 1991
**SQ FT:** 277,000
**SALES (est):** 4.37MM **Privately Held**
**SIC: 2326**  Service apparel (baker, barber, lab, etc.), washable: men's

**(P-2600)**
**OFFLINE INC (PA)**
Also Called: Inspira
2931 S Alameda St, Vernon (90058-1326)
PHONE.....................213 742-9001
Charles Park, *Pr*
Karen Park, *CFO*
▲ **EMP:** 45 **EST:** 2002
**SALES (est):** 10.14MM
**SALES (corp-wide):** 10.14MM **Privately Held**
**Web:** www.offlineinc.com
**SIC: 2326** 2342  Industrial garments, men's and boys'; Foundation garments, women's

**(P-2601)**
**PPD HOLDING LLC (PA)**
10119 Jefferson Blvd, Culver City (90232-3519)
PHONE.....................310 733-2100
Paige Adams-geller, *Chief Design Officer*
**EMP:** 63 **EST:** 2012
**SALES (est):** 49.17MM
**SALES (corp-wide):** 49.17MM **Privately Held**
**SIC: 2326** 2331 6719  Men's and boy's work clothing; Women's and misses' blouses and shirts; Investment holding companies, except banks

**(P-2602)**
**ROF LLC**
Also Called: Ring of Fire
7800 Airport Business Pkwy, Van Nuys (91406-1731)
PHONE.....................818 933-4000
Eran Bitton, *
▲ **EMP:** 45 **EST:** 2007
**SQ FT:** 60,000
**SALES (est):** 4.97MM **Privately Held**
**Web:** www.ringoffireclothing.com
**SIC: 2326** 5651 5136  Men's and boy's work clothing; Jeans stores; Men's and boys' outerwear

**(P-2603)**
**STRATEGIC DISTRIBUTION L P**
Also Called: Cherokee Uniforms
15301 Ventura Blvd, Sherman Oaks (91403-3102)
▲ **EMP:** 240 **EST:** 2003
**SALES (est):** 36.27MM
**SALES (corp-wide):** 609.92MM **Privately Held**
**Web:** www.strategicpartners.net
**SIC: 2326** 2337 3143 3144  Work uniforms; Uniforms, except athletic: women's, misses', and juniors'; Men's footwear, except athletic; Women's footwear, except athletic
**HQ:** Careismatic Brands, Llc
15301 Ventura Blvd
Sherman Oaks CA 91403

**(P-2604)**
**WAY OUT WEST INC**
1440 W 135th St, Gardena (90249-2218)
PHONE.....................310 769-6937
Michael C Goldberg, *Pr*
Mark J Goldberg, *
Michael Goldberg, *
▲ **EMP:** 18 **EST:** 1979
**SALES (est):** 5.1MM **Privately Held**
**Web:** www.wayoutwestinc.com
**SIC: 2326** 2385  Industrial garments, men's and boys'; Waterproof outerwear

## 2329 Men's And Boy's Clothing, Nec

**(P-2605)**
**4 WHAT ITS WORTH INC (PA)**
Also Called: Tyte Jeans
5815 Smithway St, Commerce (90040-1605)
PHONE.....................323 728-4503
Alden J Halpern, *Dir*
Kyle Soladay, *CFO*
◆ **EMP:** 50 **EST:** 1993
**SQ FT:** 38,000
**SALES (est):** 15.35MM **Privately Held**
**Web:** www.rewash.com
**SIC: 2329** 5961 5651 5699  Knickers, dress (separate): men's and boys'; Electronic shopping; Jeans stores; Designers, apparel

**(P-2606)**
**A AND G INC (HQ)**
Also Called: Alstyle Apparel
11296 Harrel St, Jurupa Valley (91752-3715)
PHONE.....................714 765-0400
Keith S Walters, *Pr*
Keith S Walters, *Prin*
Michael D Magill Same, *Sec*
◆ **EMP:** 627 **EST:** 1978
**SALES (est):** 17.04MM
**SALES (corp-wide):** 3.2B **Privately Held**
**Web:** www.americanapparel.com
**SIC: 2329** 2253  Athletic clothing, except uniforms: men's, youths' and boys'; T-shirts and tops, knit
**PA:** Les Vetements De Sport Gildan Inc
600 Boul De Maisonneuve O 33eme Etage
514 735-2023

**(P-2607)**
**ACTIVEAPPAREL INC (PA)**
11076 Venture Dr, Jurupa Valley (91752-3234)
PHONE.....................951 361-0060
Wasif M Siddique, *Pr*
Khan Baloch, *Sec*
▲ **EMP:** 19 **EST:** 1993
**SQ FT:** 30,000
**SALES (est):** 9.7MM **Privately Held**
**Web:** www.activeapparel.net
**SIC: 2329** 2339 7389  Men's and boys' sportswear and athletic clothing; Women's and misses' athletic clothing and sportswear ; Sewing contractor

**(P-2608)**
**ADIDAS NORTH AMERICA INC**
Also Called: Adidas Outlet Store Camarillo
950 Camarillo Center Dr Ste 956, Camarillo (93010-7747)
PHONE.....................805 482-3475
Joshua Bowler, *Mgr*
**EMP:** 16
**SALES (corp-wide):** 23.29B **Privately Held**

## 2329 - Men's And Boy's Clothing, Nec (P-2629)

SIC: 2329 Athletic clothing, except uniforms: men's, youths' and boys'
HQ: Adidas North America, Inc.
3449 N Anchor St Ste 500
Portland OR 97217
971 234-2300

### (P-2609)
### ANDARI FASHION INC
Also Called: Andari
9626 Telstar Ave, El Monte (91731-3004)
PHONE..................................626 575-2759
Wei Chen Wang, *Pr*
Lillian Wang, *
Charles Chang, *
◆ EMP: 120 EST: 1991
SQ FT: 50,000
SALES (est): 9.37MM Privately Held
Web: www.andari.com
SIC: 2329 2339 2253 5199 Sweaters and sweater jackets, men's and boys'; Women's and misses' accessories; Sweaters and sweater coats, knit; Art goods and supplies

### (P-2610)
### ANTAEUS FASHIONS GROUP INC
740 S 5th Ave, City Of Industry (91746-3012)
PHONE..................................626 452-0797
Yungchieh Lin, *CEO*
Shangwen Lin, *
Peter Lin, *
▲ EMP: 19 EST: 1991
SALES (est): 518.97K Privately Held
Web: www.atfusa.com
SIC: 2329 2339 Men's and boys' sportswear and athletic clothing; Women's and misses' athletic clothing and sportswear

### (P-2611)
### ARIES 33 LLC
3400 S Main St, Los Angeles (90007-4412)
PHONE..................................310 355-8330
Daniel Guez, *CEO*
Robin Saeks, *CFO*
EMP: 20 EST: 2017
SQ FT: 28,000
SALES (est): 2.46MM Privately Held
SIC: 2329 7389 2339 Men's and boys' sportswear and athletic clothing; Apparel designers, commercial; Women's and misses' outerwear, nec

### (P-2612)
### ASHWORTH INC
Also Called: Ashworth Studio
2765 Loker Ave W, Carlsbad (92010-6601)
PHONE..................................760 438-6610
◆ EMP: 598
Web: www.ashworth-golf.com
SIC: 2329 2339 2353 Men's and boys' sportswear and athletic clothing; Athletic clothing: women's, misses', and juniors'; Hats, caps, and millinery

### (P-2613)
### BIRDWELL ENTERPRISES INC
Also Called: Birdwell Beach Britches
8801 Research Dr, Irvine (92618-4236)
PHONE..................................714 557-7040
Vivian Richardson, *Pr*
William Robert Mann, *
EMP: 25 EST: 1962
SALES (est): 2.39MM Privately Held
Web: www.birdwellbeachbritches.com
SIC: 2329 2339 2326 Bathing suits and swimwear: men's and boys'; Women's and misses' outerwear, nec; Men's and boy's work clothing

### (P-2614)
### BOA INC
580 W Lambert Rd Ste L, Brea (92821-3913)
PHONE..................................714 256-8960
David Fleming, *Pr*
Pamela Fleming, *
▲ EMP: 34 EST: 1992
SQ FT: 6,000
SALES (est): 3.18MM Privately Held
Web: www.boausa.com
SIC: 2329 2337 2339 Men's and boys' sportswear and athletic clothing; Women's and misses' suits and coats; Women's and misses' outerwear, nec

### (P-2615)
### BODY GLOVE INTERNATIONAL LLC
Also Called: Body Glove
6255 W Sunset Blvd Ste 650, Hollywood (90028-7403)
PHONE..................................310 374-3441
Cory M Baker, *COO*
Warren Clamen, *CFO*
◆ EMP: 44 EST: 1997
SALES (est): 1.56MM Privately Held
Web: www.bodyglove.com
SIC: 2329 2339 2369 3069 Bathing suits and swimwear: men's and boys'; Bathing suits: women's, misses', and juniors'; Bathing suits and swimwear: girls', children's, and infants'; Wet suits, rubber

### (P-2616)
### DC SHOES LLC (PA)
Also Called: DC
5600 Argosy Ave Ste 100, Huntington Beach (92649-1063)
PHONE..................................714 889-4206
Arne Arens, *CEO*
Francis Roy, *CFO*
Maryn Miller, *Sec*
◆ EMP: 87 EST: 1993
SQ FT: 100,000
SALES (est): 9.63MM Privately Held
Web: www.dcshoes.com
SIC: 2329 5136 5137 5139 Men's and boys' sportswear and athletic clothing; Men's and boy's clothing; Women's and children's clothing; Footwear

### (P-2617)
### DOH QUEST LLC
8939 S Sepulveda Blvd Ste 102, Los Angeles (90045-3631)
PHONE..................................213 651-3441
EMP: 20
SALES (est): 681.28K Privately Held
SIC: 2329 Riding clothes: men's, youths', and boys'

### (P-2618)
### EDMUND KIM INTERNATIONAL INC (PA)
2880 E Ana St, Compton (90221-5602)
P.O. Box 1330 (90801-1330)
PHONE..................................310 604-1100
Edmund K Kim, *Pr*
Reza Farmehr, *Sec*
◆ EMP: 20 EST: 1997
SALES (est): 23.03MM
SALES (corp-wide): 23.03MM Privately Held
Web: www.ekii.com
SIC: 2329 2261 7218 2253 Athletic clothing, except uniforms: men's, youths' and boys'; Dyeing cotton broadwoven fabrics; Industrial launderers; Dresses and skirts

### (P-2619)
### FEAR OF GOD LLC
558 S Alameda St, Los Angeles (90013-1726)
PHONE..................................213 235-7985
Bastien Daguzan, *CEO*
Jerry Manuel, *Managing Member*
EMP: 99 EST: 2011
SALES (est): 5.56MM Privately Held
Web: www.fearofgod.com
SIC: 2329 Sweaters and sweater jackets, men's and boys'

### (P-2620)
### FETISH GROUP INC (PA)
Also Called: Tag Rag
1013 S Los Angeles St Ste 700, Los Angeles (90015-1782)
PHONE..................................323 587-7873
Raphael Sabbah, *CEO*
Orly Dahan, *
▲ EMP: 39 EST: 1986
SQ FT: 28,000
SALES (est): 2.3MM
SALES (corp-wide): 2.3MM Privately Held
Web: www.goldhawkclothing.com
SIC: 2329 2339 2369 Men's and boys' sportswear and athletic clothing; Women's and misses' athletic clothing and sportswear; Girl's and children's outerwear, nec

### (P-2621)
### GLOBAL CASUALS INC
18505 S Broadway, Gardena (90248-4632)
PHONE..................................310 817-2828
Jack Tsao, *Genl Mgr*
▲ EMP: 47 EST: 1995
SQ FT: 2,000
SALES (est): 423.63K
SALES (corp-wide): 49.41MM Privately Held
SIC: 2329 Men's and boys' sportswear and athletic clothing
PA: Seattle Pacific Industries, Inc.
1633 Wstlake Ave N Ste 30
253 872-8822

### (P-2622)
### HOT SHOPPE DESIGNS INC
Also Called: Hot Shoppe Design
1323 Calle Avanzado, San Clemente (92673-6351)
PHONE..................................949 487-2828
David Marietti, *CEO*
▲ EMP: 15 EST: 1982
SQ FT: 6,500
SALES (est): 788.01K Privately Held
Web: www.hotshoppedesigns.com
SIC: 2329 5136 7336 7389 Riding clothes: men's, youths', and boys'; Shirts, men's and boys'; Package design; Lettering and sign painting services

### (P-2623)
### HURLEY INTERNATIONAL LLC (PA)
Also Called: Hurley
3080 Bristol St, Costa Mesa (92626-3093)
PHONE..................................855 655-2515
Adrian L Bell, *
Ann M Miller, *
◆ EMP: 200 EST: 2001
SALES (est): 47.52MM
SALES (corp-wide): 47.52MM Privately Held
Web: www.hurley.com
SIC: 2329 5137 Knickers, dress (separate): men's and boys'; Women's and children's clothing

### (P-2624)
### J2 LLC
Also Called: Mx No Fear
2251 Faraday Ave Ste A, Carlsbad (92008-7209)
P.O. Box 130040 (92013-0040)
PHONE..................................760 930-1738
Jeff Surwall, *Pr*
▲ EMP: 16 EST: 1999
SQ FT: 30,000
SALES (est): 7MM Privately Held
Web: www.nofear.com
SIC: 2329 Riding clothes: men's, youths', and boys'

### (P-2625)
### JH DESIGN GROUP
940 W Washington Blvd, Los Angeles (90015-3312)
PHONE..................................213 747-5700
▲ EMP: 60 EST: 1987
SALES (est): 9.91MM Privately Held
Web: www.shopjhdesign.com
SIC: 2329 2337 Jackets (suede, leatherette, etc.), sport: men's and boys'; Women's and misses' capes and jackets

### (P-2626)
### JOE WELLS ENTERPRISES INC
Also Called: Max Muscle
1500 S Sunkist St Ste D, Anaheim (92806-5815)
P.O. Box 825 (92781-0825)
◆ EMP: 26
Web: www.maxmuscle.com
SIC: 2329 2023 2339 6794 Men's and boys' sportswear and athletic clothing; Dietary supplements, dairy and non-dairy based; Sportswear, women's; Franchises, selling or licensing

### (P-2627)
### JS APPAREL INC
1751 E Del Amo Blvd, Carson (90746-2938)
PHONE..................................310 631-6333
Ki S Kim, *Pr*
▲ EMP: 99 EST: 2004
SALES (est): 1.4MM Privately Held
Web: www.jsapparel.net
SIC: 2329 2339 Men's and boys' sportswear and athletic clothing; Women's and misses' outerwear, nec

### (P-2628)
### KORAL LLC
Also Called: Koral Activewear
1334 3rd Street Promenade Ste 200, Santa Monica (90401-1313)
PHONE..................................323 391-1060
Marcelo Kugel, *Managing Member*
Peter Koral, *
Liz Hampshire, *
Ilana Kugel, *
EMP: 36 EST: 2002
SALES (est): 2.2MM Privately Held
Web: www.koral.com
SIC: 2329 2339 Men's and boys' sportswear and athletic clothing; Women's and misses' athletic clothing and sportswear

### (P-2629)
### L A CSTM AP & PROMOTIONS INC (PA)
2680 Temple Ave, Long Beach (90806-2209)
PHONE..................................562 595-1770
Chris Roybal, *Pr*
EMP: 33 EST: 1984
SQ FT: 10,000

## 2329 - Men's And Boy's Clothing, Nec (P-2630)

SALES (est): 5.26MM **Privately Held**
**Web:** www.lacustomapparel.com
**SIC: 2329** 5136 Athletic clothing, except uniforms: men's, youths' and boys'; Men's and boy's clothing

### (P-2630)
### LEEMARC INDUSTRIES LLC
Also Called: Canari
340 Rancheros Dr Ste 172, San Marcos (92069-2980)
**PHONE**..................760 598-0505
Christopher Robinson, *Managing Member*
▲ **EMP:** 55 **EST:** 2000
**SALES (est):** 5.32MM **Privately Held**
**Web:** www.canari.com
**SIC: 2329** 2339 Athletic clothing, except uniforms: men's, youths' and boys'; Women's and misses' outerwear, nec

### (P-2631)
### LEVI STRAUSS INTERNATIONAL (HQ)
1155 Battery St, San Francisco (94111-1203)
**PHONE**..................415 501-6000
Michael Howard, *Pr*
Michael Howard, *OF EUROPE DIVISION*
S Lindsay Webbe, *OF ASIA PACIFIC DIVISION*
John Anderson, *Pr*
▲ **EMP:** 51 **EST:** 1965
**SQ FT:** 25,000
**SALES (est):** 2.06MM
**SALES (corp-wide):** 6.18B **Publicly Held**
**Web:** www.levistrauss.com
**SIC: 2329** 2339 Men's and boys' sportswear and athletic clothing; Women's and misses' outerwear, nec
**PA:** Levi Strauss & Co.
1155 Battery St
415 501-6000

### (P-2632)
### LIQUID GRAPHICS INC
2701 S Harbor Blvd Unit A, Santa Ana (92704-5803)
**PHONE**..................949 486-3588
Josh Merrell, *Pr*
Mark Hyman, *
◆ **EMP:** 130 **EST:** 1997
**SQ FT:** 100,000
**SALES (est):** 29.19MM **Privately Held**
**Web:** www.liquidgraphicsmfg.com
**SIC: 2329** Men's and boys' sportswear and athletic clothing

### (P-2633)
### MARMOT MOUNTAIN LLC (HQ)
Also Called: Marmot Mountain
5789 State Farm Dr Ste 100, Rohnert Park (94928-6308)
**PHONE**..................888 357-3262
▲ **EMP:** 120 **EST:** 2004
**SALES (est):** 66.12MM
**SALES (corp-wide):** 8.13B **Publicly Held**
**Web:** www.marmot.com
**SIC: 2329** Men's and boys' sportswear and athletic clothing
**PA:** Newell Brands Inc.
6655 Pachtree Dunwoody Rd
770 418-7000

### (P-2634)
### MORTEX CORPORATION
Also Called: Mortex Apparel
40 E Verdugo Ave, Burbank (91502-1931)
P.O. Box 127 (27591-0127)
**EMP:** 225

**SIC: 2329** 2339 5699 Men's and boys' sportswear and athletic clothing; Sportswear, women's; Sports apparel

### (P-2635)
### NAUTICA OPCO LLC
950 Barrington Ave, Ontario (91764-5111)
**PHONE**..................909 297-7243
**EMP:** 371
**SALES (corp-wide):** 3.08B **Privately Held**
**SIC: 2329** 2834 5136 5137 Men's and boys' sportswear and athletic clothing; Pharmaceutical preparations; Men's and boys' sportswear and work clothing; Women's and children's lingerie and undergarments
**HQ:** Nautica Opco Llc
125 Chubb Ave Fl 5
Lyndhurst NJ 07071
866 376-4184

### (P-2636)
### PATAGONIA INC (HQ)
Also Called: Great Pacific Patagonia
259 W Santa Clara St, Ventura (93001-2545)
P.O. Box 150 (93002-0150)
**PHONE**..................805 643-8616
◆ **EMP:** 500 **EST:** 1979
**SALES (est):** 342.14MM
**SALES (corp-wide):** 415.44MM **Privately Held**
**Web:** www.patagoniaprovisions.com
**SIC: 2329** 2339 Athletic clothing, except uniforms: men's, youths' and boys'; Athletic clothing: women's, misses', and juniors'
**PA:** Patagonia Works
259 W Santa Clara St
805 643-8616

### (P-2637)
### RYTE VENTURES LLC (PA)
Also Called: Ryte Sport
15471 Red Hill Ave, Tustin (92780-7315)
**PHONE**..................925 323-7195
Alex Young, *Managing Member*
**EMP:** 16 **EST:** 2018
**SALES (est):** 2.01MM
**SALES (corp-wide):** 2.01MM **Privately Held**
**Web:** www.rytesport.com
**SIC: 2329** 2339 2369 Men's and boys' sportswear and athletic clothing; Women's and misses' athletic clothing and sportswear; Bathing suits and swimwear: girls', children's, and infants'

### (P-2638)
### SAUVAGE INC (PA)
7717 Formula Pl, San Diego (92121-2419)
**PHONE**..................858 408-0100
Elizabeth Southwood, *Pr*
Simon Southwood, *Sec*
**EMP:** 17 **EST:** 1981
**SQ FT:** 10,000
**SALES (est):** 2.41MM
**SALES (corp-wide):** 2.41MM **Privately Held**
**Web:** www.sauvagewear.com
**SIC: 2329** 2339 Men's and boys' sportswear and athletic clothing; Bathing suits: women's, misses', and juniors'

### (P-2639)
### SPEEDO USA INC
Also Called: Speedo USA
6251 Katella Ave, Cypress (90630-5234)
**PHONE**..................657 465-3800
Jim Gerson, *Pr*
◆ **EMP:** 400 **EST:** 1990

**SQ FT:** 10,000
**SALES (est):** 17.93MM **Privately Held**
**Web:** us.speedo.com
**SIC: 2329** 2339 2321 3949 Athletic clothing, except uniforms: men's, youths' and boys'; Bathing suits: women's, misses', and juniors'; Men's and boys sports and polo shirts; Water sports equipment
**HQ:** Pentland Capital Limited
8 Manchester Square
London W1U 3
207 535-3820

### (P-2640)
### SPIRIT CLOTHING COMPANY
2137 E 37th St, Vernon (90058-1416)
**PHONE**..................213 784-5372
**EMP:** 70
**SALES (corp-wide):** 9.71MM **Privately Held**
**Web:** www.spiritjersey.com
**SIC: 2329** 5651 Men's and boys' sportswear and athletic clothing; Unisex clothing stores
**PA:** Spirit Clothing Company
2211 E 37th St
213 784-0251

### (P-2641)
### SPIRIT CLOTHING COMPANY (PA)
Also Called: Spirit Active Wear
2211 E 37th St, Los Angeles (90058-1427)
**PHONE**..................213 784-0251
**TOLL FREE:** 800
Jake Ptasznik, *CEO*
▼ **EMP:** 102 **EST:** 1983
**SQ FT:** 19,000
**SALES (est):** 9.71MM
**SALES (corp-wide):** 9.71MM **Privately Held**
**Web:** www.spiritjersey.com
**SIC: 2329** 5651 5621 Men's and boys' sportswear and athletic clothing; Unisex clothing stores; Ready-to-wear apparel, women's

### (P-2642)
### SPORTSROBE INC
8654 Hayden Pl, Culver City (90232-2902)
**PHONE**..................310 559-3999
Allen Ruegsegger, *Pr*
Mary Ann Ruegsegger, *
**EMP:** 49 **EST:** 1979
**SQ FT:** 14,000
**SALES (est):** 535.57K **Privately Held**
**SIC: 2329** Baseball uniforms: men's, youths', and boys'

### (P-2643)
### STEADY CLOTHING INC
2851 E White Star Ave Ste A, Anaheim (92806-2550)
**PHONE**..................714 444-2058
Eric Anthony, *Pr*
Joshua Brownfield, *VP*
▲ **EMP:** 17 **EST:** 1994
**SALES (est):** 2.45MM **Privately Held**
**Web:** www.steadyclothing.com
**SIC: 2329** 2339 Men's and boys' sportswear and athletic clothing; Sportswear, women's

### (P-2644)
### STRAIGHT DOWN ENTERPRISES (PA)
Also Called: Straight Down Clothing Company
625 Clarion Ct, San Luis Obispo (93401-8177)
**PHONE**..................805 543-3086
Michael Rowley, *CEO*
▲ **EMP:** 20 **EST:** 1989

**SQ FT:** 21,000
**SALES (est):** 7.73MM
**SALES (corp-wide):** 7.73MM **Privately Held**
**Web:** www.straightdown.com
**SIC: 2329** 2339 Men's and boys' sportswear and athletic clothing; Women's and misses' outerwear, nec

### (P-2645)
### STREAMLINE DSIGN SLKSCREEN INC (PA)
Also Called: Old Guys Rule
1299 S Wells Rd, Ventura (93004-1901)
**PHONE**..................805 884-1025
Thom Hill, *CEO*
▲ **EMP:** 60 **EST:** 1995
**SQ FT:** 33,000
**SALES (est):** 1.41MM **Privately Held**
**Web:** www.oldguysrule.com
**SIC: 2329** 5136 5611 Men's and boys' sportswear and athletic clothing; Men's and boy's clothing; Men's and boys' clothing stores

### (P-2646)
### SURF RIDE
1909 S Coast Hwy, Oceanside (92054-6432)
**PHONE**..................760 433-4020
**EMP:** 15
**SALES (est):** 4.98MM **Privately Held**
**Web:** www.surfride.com
**SIC: 2329** 5941 Men's and boys' sportswear and athletic clothing; Skateboarding equipment

### (P-2647)
### TARTAN FASHION INC
4357 Rowland Ave, El Monte (91731-1119)
**PHONE**..................626 575-2828
Joann Sun, *Pr*
◆ **EMP:** 20 **EST:** 2002
**SQ FT:** 20,363
**SALES (est):** 641.62K **Privately Held**
**SIC: 2329** Men's and boys' sportswear and athletic clothing

### (P-2648)
### THIRTY THREE THREADS INC (PA)
Also Called: Toesox
1330 Park Center Dr, Vista (92081-8300)
**PHONE**..................877 486-3769
Barry Buchholtz, *CEO*
Joseph Patterson, *Dir*
Deedee Wilson, *Dir*
▲ **EMP:** 34 **EST:** 2004
**SALES (est):** 10.8MM
**SALES (corp-wide):** 10.8MM **Privately Held**
**Web:** www.thirtythreethreads.com
**SIC: 2329** 2252 Athletic clothing, except uniforms: men's, youths' and boys'; Socks

### (P-2649)
### TRAVISMATHEW LLC (HQ)
15202 Graham St, Huntington Beach (92649-1109)
**PHONE**..................562 799-6900
Ryan Ellis, *CEO*
▲ **EMP:** 38 **EST:** 2007
**SALES (est):** 37.91MM
**SALES (corp-wide):** 4.28B **Publicly Held**
**Web:** www.travismathew.com
**SIC: 2329** 5699 5651 5661 Athletic clothing, except uniforms: men's, youths' and boys'; Sports apparel; Unisex clothing stores; Men's shoes
**PA:** Topgolf Callaway Brands Corp.
2180 Rutherford Rd

## PRODUCTS & SERVICES SECTION
### 2331 - Women's And Misses' Blouses And Shirts (P-2671)

760 931-1771

**(P-2650)**
**WATERFRONT DESIGN GROUP LLC**
122 E Washington Blvd, Los Angeles (90015-3601)
PHONE..................213 746-5800
**EMP:** 23 **EST:** 2001
**SALES (est):** 275.57K **Privately Held**
**SIC: 2329** Men's and boys' sportswear and athletic clothing

**(P-2651)**
**ZK ENTERPRISES INC**
Also Called: Unique Sales
4368 District Blvd, Vernon (90058-3124)
PHONE..................213 622-7012
Ron Kelfer, *Pr*
Kathy Kelfer, *
**EMP:** 40 **EST:** 1985
**SQ FT:** 13,000
**SALES (est):** 1.59MM **Privately Held**
Web: www.uniquesalesco.com
**SIC: 2329** 2339 Athletic clothing, except uniforms: men's, youths' and boys'; Jogging and warmup suits: women's, misses', and juniors'

### 2331 Women's And Misses' Blouses And Shirts

**(P-2652)**
**ABGB DESIGNS INC**
Also Called: Storm Tee's
6351 Regent St Ste 226, Huntington Park (90255-3823)
**EMP:** 16 **EST:** 1990
**SALES (est):** 274.09K **Privately Held**
**SIC: 2331** Women's and misses' blouses and shirts

**(P-2653)**
**ALLIANCE APPAREL INC**
Also Called: Blu Heaven
3422 Garfield Ave, Commerce (90040-3104)
PHONE..................323 888-8900
Tae Hoo Shin, *Pr*
Michael Park, *
▲ **EMP:** 40 **EST:** 1999
**SQ FT:** 17,500
**SALES (est):** 1.09MM **Privately Held**
Web: www.imagenationapparel.com
**SIC: 2331** Blouses, women's and juniors': made from purchased material

**(P-2654)**
**ALPINESTARS USA**
Also Called: Alpinestars USA
2780 W 237th St, Torrance (90505-5270)
PHONE..................310 891-0222
Giovanni Mazzarolo, *CEO*
▲ **EMP:** 82 **EST:** 1986
**SQ FT:** 28,380
**SALES (est):** 9.27MM
**SALES (corp-wide):** 333.6MM **Privately Held**
Web: www.asbydf.com
**SIC: 2331** 2326 3751 5571 Women's and misses' blouses and shirts; Men's and boy's work clothing; Motorcycle accessories; Motorcycle parts and accessories
**HQ:** Alpinestars Spa
Viale Enrico Fermi 5
Asolo TV 31011
042 352-9571

**(P-2655)**
**AU MERROW CORPORATION**
Also Called: Daniel Rainn
7210 Dominion Cir, Commerce (90040-3647)
**EMP:** 16
Web: www.danielrainn.com
**SIC: 2331** Women's and misses' blouses and shirts

**(P-2656)**
**BLTEE LLC**
7101 Telegraph Rd, Montebello (90640-6511)
P.O. Box 2762 (90670-0762)
PHONE..................213 802-1736
Elano Miguel Elias, *Managing Member*
**EMP:** 45 **EST:** 2013
**SQ FT:** 4,900
**SALES (est):** 812.84K **Privately Held**
**SIC: 2331** 5136 Women's and misses' blouses and shirts; Shirts, men's and boys'

**(P-2657)**
**BLUPRINT CLOTHING CORP**
4851 S Santa Fe Ave, Vernon (90058-2103)
PHONE..................323 780-4347
Ju Hyun Kim, *CEO*
Liz Lee, *
▲ **EMP:** 75 **EST:** 2005
**SALES (est):** 30MM **Privately Held**
Web: www.bluprintcorp.com
**SIC: 2331** Women's and misses' blouses and shirts

**(P-2658)**
**BYER CALIFORNIA (PA)**
66 Potrero Ave, San Francisco (94103-4800)
PHONE..................415 626-7844
Philip Byer, *CEO*
Ed Manburg, *
Marian Byer, *
Max Curry, *
Barbara Berling, *
▲ **EMP:** 575 **EST:** 1964
**SQ FT:** 230,000
**SALES (est):** 124.12MM
**SALES (corp-wide):** 124.12MM **Privately Held**
Web: www.byerca.com
**SIC: 2331** Women's and misses' blouses and shirts

**(P-2659)**
**C-QUEST INC**
Also Called: Ava James
1439 S Herbert Ave, Los Angeles (90023-4047)
PHONE..................323 980-1400
Nam H Paik, *CEO*
◆ **EMP:** 22 **EST:** 2003
**SQ FT:** 100,000
**SALES (est):** 4.68MM **Privately Held**
**SIC: 2331** Women's and misses' blouses and shirts

**(P-2660)**
**COLON MANUFACTURING INC (PA)**
Also Called: Coc Inc
1100 S San Pedro St Ste 0-08, Los Angeles (90015-2328)
PHONE..................213 749-6149
Thomas T Byun, *Pr*
Julia Anna Byun, *Sec*
**EMP:** 19 **EST:** 1991
**SALES (est):** 943.11K **Privately Held**
**SIC: 2331** 2335 2337 Women's and misses' blouses and shirts; Women's, junior's, and misses' dresses; Women's and misses' suits and coats

**(P-2661)**
**CRESTONE LLC**
Also Called: Hazel Clothes
2511 S Alameda St, Vernon (90058-1309)
PHONE..................323 588-8857
Robert A Cho, *CEO*
▲ **EMP:** 20 **EST:** 2005
**SQ FT:** 10,000
**SALES (est):** 2.41MM **Privately Held**
**SIC: 2331** 2361 Women's and misses' blouses and shirts; Girl's and children's dresses, blouses

**(P-2662)**
**CURE APPAREL LLC**
Also Called: Liberty Love
3338 S Malt Ave, Commerce (90040-3126)
PHONE..................562 927-7460
Amir Seilabi, *Managing Member*
▲ **EMP:** 15 **EST:** 2008
**SQ FT:** 5,000
**SALES (est):** 1.98MM **Privately Held**
**SIC: 2331** Blouses, women's and juniors': made from purchased material

**(P-2663)**
**EASTWEST CLOTHING INC (PA)**
Also Called: Language Los Angeles
40 E Verdugo Ave, Burbank (91502-1931)
PHONE..................323 980-1177
Michael Schreier, *CEO*
Arvril Ozen, *COO*
▲ **EMP:** 19 **EST:** 1995
**SQ FT:** 10,000
**SALES (est):** 3.68MM **Privately Held**
Web: www.languagelosangeles.com
**SIC: 2331** Women's and misses' blouses and shirts

**(P-2664)**
**ETRO USA INCORPORATED**
9501 Wilshire Blvd, Beverly Hills (90212-2404)
PHONE..................310 248-2855
Janine Masaki, *Mgr*
▲ **EMP:** 21 **EST:** 2007
**SALES (est):** 490.95K **Privately Held**
Web: www.etro.com
**SIC: 2331** 2339 2341 5137 Women's and misses' blouses and shirts; Women's and misses' outerwear, nec; Women's and children's underwear; Women's and children's clothing

**(P-2665)**
**FORTUNE CASUALS LLC (PA)**
Also Called: Judy Ann
10119 Jefferson Blvd, Culver City (90232-3519)
PHONE..................310 733-2100
Fred Kayne, *Managing Member*
◆ **EMP:** 100 **EST:** 1999
**SQ FT:** 40,000
**SALES (est):** 9.52MM
**SALES (corp-wide):** 9.52MM **Privately Held**
**SIC: 2331** 2339 2321 T-shirts and tops, women's: made from purchased materials; Slacks: women's, misses', and juniors'; Men's and boy's furnishings

**(P-2666)**
**GLORIA LANCE INC (PA)**
Also Called: Electric Designs
15616 S Broadway, Gardena (90248-2211)
P.O. Box 3941 (90247-7519)
PHONE..................310 767-4400
Robert Hempling, *Pr*
Zvia Hempling, *
Miguel Lopez, *
Gloria Lopez, *
◆ **EMP:** 90 **EST:** 1983
**SQ FT:** 25,000
**SALES (est):** 4.49MM
**SALES (corp-wide):** 4.49MM **Privately Held**
**SIC: 2331** 2339 2335 Blouses, women's and juniors': made from purchased material; Sportswear, women's; Bridal and formal gowns

**(P-2667)**
**GURU KNITS INC**
Also Called: Antex Knitting Mills
225 W 38th St, Los Angeles (90037-1405)
PHONE..................323 235-9424
Kevin Port, *CEO*
William Tenenblatt, *
◆ **EMP:** 60 **EST:** 2007
**SALES (est):** 4.08MM **Privately Held**
Web: www.aceross.com
**SIC: 2331** 2361 Women's and misses' blouses and shirts; Blouses: girls', children's, and infants'

**(P-2668)**
**GUSB INC**
219 E 32nd St, Los Angeles (90011-1917)
PHONE..................323 233-0044
Scott Changsup Lee, *CEO*
▲ **EMP:** 15 **EST:** 2006
**SQ FT:** 10,000
**SALES (est):** 565.57K **Privately Held**
**SIC: 2331** 2335 2337 2339 Women's and misses' blouses and shirts; Women's, junior's, and misses' dresses; Women's and misses' suits and coats; Women's and misses' outerwear, nec

**(P-2669)**
**HARARI INC (PA)**
9646 Brighton Way, Los Angeles (90016)
PHONE..................323 734-5302
**EMP:** 45 **EST:** 1979
**SALES (est):** 1.29MM
**SALES (corp-wide):** 1.29MM **Privately Held**
Web: www.harariinc.com
**SIC: 2331** 5621 Women's and misses' blouses and shirts; Women's clothing stores

**(P-2670)**
**HARKHAM INDUSTRIES INC (PA)**
Also Called: Jonathan Martin
857 S San Pedro St Ste 300, Los Angeles (90014-2432)
PHONE..................323 586-4600
Uri Harkham, *Pr*
◆ **EMP:** 50 **EST:** 1974
**SQ FT:** 140,000
**SALES (est):** 6MM
**SALES (corp-wide):** 6MM **Privately Held**
Web: www.jonathanmartin.com
**SIC: 2331** 2335 2337 2339 Blouses, women's and juniors': made from purchased material; Women's, junior's, and misses' dresses; Skirts, separate: women's, misses, and juniors'; Women's and misses' outerwear, nec

**(P-2671)**
**J HEYRI INC**
Also Called: Everleigh
219 E 32nd St, Los Angeles (90011-1917)

## 2331 - Women's And Misses' Blouses And Shirts (P-2672)

**PHONE**.....................323 588-1234
Tiffany Lin, *Pr*
Sunny Choi, *VP*
Alexis Kwak, *VP*
◆ **EMP:** 20 **EST:** 2010
**SALES (est):** 2.41MM **Privately Held**
**SIC: 2331** Women's and misses' blouses and shirts

### (P-2672)
### JUDY ANN OF CALIFORNIA INC
Also Called: Landing Gear
1936 Mateo St, Los Angeles (90021-2833)
**PHONE**.....................213 623-9233
Michael Geller, *Pr*
**EMP:** 150 **EST:** 1985
**SALES (est):** 2.31MM **Privately Held**
**SIC: 2331** 2339 T-shirts and tops, women's: made from purchased materials; Slacks: women's, misses', and juniors'

### (P-2673)
### K TOO
Also Called: K-Too
800 E 12th St Ste 117, Los Angeles (90021)
**PHONE**.....................213 747-7766
Jae Hee Kim, *CEO*
Kelley Kim, *
◆ **EMP:** 41 **EST:** 2007
**SALES (est):** 2.68MM **Privately Held**
**Web:** www.ktoousa.com
**SIC: 2331** Women's and misses' blouses and shirts

### (P-2674)
### KANDY KISS OF CALIFORNIA INC
14761 Califa St, Van Nuys (91411-3107)
▲ **EMP:** 60
**Web:** www.perfectdomain.com
**SIC: 2331** 2335 2361 Women's and misses' blouses and shirts; Women's, junior's, and misses' dresses; Shirts: girls', children's, and infants'

### (P-2675)
### KOMEX INTERNATIONAL INC
Also Called: Bubblegum USA
736 E 29th St, Los Angeles (90011-2014)
**PHONE**.....................323 233-9005
John J Inn, *Pr*
Paul Sanghyon Inn, *VP*
Laura Hong, *VP*
◆ **EMP:** 16 **EST:** 1994
**SQ FT:** 60,000
**SALES (est):** 2.51MM **Privately Held**
**SIC: 2331** 2329 2339 2325 Women's and misses' blouses and shirts; Men's and boy's sportswear and athletic clothing; Women's and misses' outerwear, nec; Men's and boy's trousers and slacks

### (P-2676)
### KSM GARMENT INC
Also Called: Alex and Jane
5613 Maywood Ave, Maywood (90270-2503)
**PHONE**.....................323 585-8811
**EMP:** 42
**SIC: 2331** Women's and misses' blouses and shirts

### (P-2677)
### LA MAMBA LLC
150 N Myers St, Los Angeles (90033-2109)
**PHONE**.....................323 526-3526
Fabian Oberfeld, *Managing Member*
Denni Kopelan, *
Stephen Brown, *

▲ **EMP:** 31 **EST:** 2008
**SALES (est):** 3.36MM **Privately Held**
**SIC: 2331** Blouses, women's and juniors': made from purchased material

### (P-2678)
### LEEBE APPAREL INC
Also Called: Leebe
3499 S Main St, Los Angeles (90007-4413)
**PHONE**.....................323 897-5585
Won Joo Lee, *Pr*
▲ **EMP:** 25 **EST:** 2007
**SQ FT:** 8,000
**SALES (est):** 895.68K **Privately Held**
**Web:** www.leebeapparel.com
**SIC: 2331** Women's and misses' blouses and shirts

### (P-2679)
### LF SPORTSWEAR INC (PA)
Also Called: Furst
13336 Beach Ave, Marina Del Rey (90292-5622)
**PHONE**.....................310 437-4100
Phillip L Furst, *CEO*
Marsha Furst, *
Steve Katz, *
◆ **EMP:** 30 **EST:** 1980
**SALES (est):** 9.4MM
**SALES (corp-wide):** 9.4MM **Privately Held**
**Web:** www.lfstores.com
**SIC: 2331** 5137 2211 Women's and misses' blouses and shirts; Women's and children's dresses, suits, skirts, and blouses; Denims

### (P-2680)
### MF INC
Also Called: Welovefine
2010 E 15th St, Los Angeles (90021-2823)
**PHONE**.....................213 627-2498
Danish Gajiani, *CEO*
Faizan Bakali, *Pr*
Bill Bussiere, *CFO*
Dean Allen, *CMO*
◆ **EMP:** 120 **EST:** 1999
**SQ FT:** 700,000
**SALES (est):** 3.55MM
**SALES (corp-wide):** 638.25MM **Privately Held**
**SIC: 2331** 2253 T-shirts and tops, women's: made from purchased materials; T-shirts and tops, knit
**HQ:** Mad Engine Global, Llc
7 Studebaker
Irvine CA 92618
858 558-5270

### (P-2681)
### MONROW LLC
Also Called: Monrow
1404 S Main St Ste C, Los Angeles (90015-2566)
**PHONE**.....................213 741-6007
Megan George, *Pr*
**EMP:** 29 **EST:** 2007
**SALES (est):** 4.19MM **Privately Held**
**Web:** www.monrow.com
**SIC: 2331** T-shirts and tops, women's: made from purchased materials

### (P-2682)
### MXF DESIGNS INC
Also Called: Nally & Millie
5327 Valley Blvd, Los Angeles (90032-3930)
**PHONE**.....................323 266-1451
James Park, *Pr*
Nally Park, *Stockholder*
▼ **EMP:** 95 **EST:** 1994
**SALES (est):** 2.21MM **Privately Held**

**Web:** www.nallyandmillie.com
**SIC: 2331** Blouses, women's and juniors': made from purchased material

### (P-2683)
### MYMICHELLE COMPANY LLC (HQ)
Also Called: My Michelle
13077 Temple Ave, La Puente (91746-1418)
**PHONE**.....................626 934-4166
Arthur Gordon, *Pr*
Arthur Gordon, *Pr*
Roger D Joseph, *
◆ **EMP:** 300 **EST:** 1948
**SQ FT:** 600,000
**SALES (est):** 2.44MM
**SALES (corp-wide):** 373.66MM **Privately Held**
**SIC: 2331** 2337 2335 2361 Blouses, women's and juniors': made from purchased material; Skirts, separate: women's, misses', and juniors'; Dresses,paper, cut and sewn; Blouses: girls', children's, and infants'
**PA:** Kellwood Company, Llc
13071 Temple Ave
626 934-4122

### (P-2684)
### NOTHING TO WEAR INC
Also Called: Subtle Luxury
630 Maple Ave, Torrance (90503-5001)
**PHONE**.....................310 328-0408
**EMP:** 19
**Web:** www.shopsubtleluxury.com
**SIC: 2331** Women's and misses' blouses and shirts
**PA:** Nothing To Wear, Inc.
630 Maple Ave

### (P-2685)
### NOTHING TO WEAR INC (PA)
Also Called: Figure 8
630 Maple Ave, Torrance (90503-5001)
**PHONE**.....................310 328-0408
Cindy Nunes Freeman, *Pr*
Darrin Freeman, *
◆ **EMP:** 35 **EST:** 1991
**SQ FT:** 18,000
**SALES (est):** 2.19MM **Privately Held**
**Web:** www.goldensunbrand.com
**SIC: 2331** 2335 2339 Women's and misses' blouses and shirts; Women's, junior's, and misses' dresses; Women's and misses' accessories

### (P-2686)
### PAIGE LLC (HQ)
Also Called: Paige Premium Denim
10119 Jefferson Blvd, Culver City (90232-3519)
**PHONE**.....................310 733-2100
Paige Adams-geller, *Chief Design Officer*
Walter Lacher, *
Michael Henschel, *
Caroline Blanchard, *
◆ **EMP:** 150 **EST:** 2004
**SQ FT:** 40,000
**SALES (est):** 49.17MM
**SALES (corp-wide):** 49.17MM **Privately Held**
**Web:** www.paige.com
**SIC: 2331** 2326 Women's and misses' blouses and shirts; Men's and boy's work clothing
**PA:** Ppd Holding, Llc
10119 Jefferson Blvd
310 733-2100

### (P-2687)
### PROJECT SOCIAL T LLC
615 S Clarence St, Los Angeles (90023-1107)
**PHONE**.....................323 266-4500
Mike Chodler, *Managing Member*
**EMP:** 30 **EST:** 2011
**SALES (est):** 2.96MM **Privately Held**
**Web:** www.projectsocialt.com
**SIC: 2331** 5137 5621 Women's and misses' blouses and shirts; Women's and children's clothing; Women's clothing stores

### (P-2688)
### RIKI FASHION INC
Also Called: Riki
815 Sweetbriar Rd, Davis (95616-3729)
**PHONE**.....................530 756-8048
Ursula Labermeier, *Pr*
Peter Labermeier, *Sec*
**EMP:** 17 **EST:** 1985
**SQ FT:** 1,300
**SALES (est):** 339.89K **Privately Held**
**SIC: 2331** 5621 5137 Women's and misses' blouses and shirts; Women's clothing stores; Women's and children's clothing

### (P-2689)
### STONY APPAREL CORP (PA)
Also Called: Eyeshadow
1201 S Grand Ave, Los Angeles (90015-2105)
**PHONE**.....................323 981-9080
Lu Kong, *CEO*
Anthony Millar, *CFO*
Sarah Van Zee, *Sec*
▲ **EMP:** 175 **EST:** 1996
**SALES (est):** 32.12MM **Privately Held**
**Web:** www.stonyapparel.com
**SIC: 2331** 2335 7389 Women's and misses' blouses and shirts; Women's, junior's, and misses' dresses; Apparel designers, commercial

### (P-2690)
### T2C INC
1348 S Flower St, Los Angeles (90015-2908)
**PHONE**.....................213 741-5232
Shawn Janet, *Pr*
**EMP:** 18 **EST:** 2002
**SQ FT:** 3,500
**SALES (est):** 298.66K **Privately Held**
**SIC: 2331** Women's and misses' blouses and shirts

### (P-2691)
### TIANELLO INC
Also Called: Tianello By Steve Barraza
138 W 38th St, Los Angeles (90037-1404)
**PHONE**.....................323 231-0599
Steven Barraza, *Pr*
▲ **EMP:** 185 **EST:** 1992
**SQ FT:** 25,000
**SALES (est):** 1.55MM **Privately Held**
**Web:** www.tianello.com
**SIC: 2331** 5621 2339 Women's and misses' blouses and shirts; Women's clothing stores; Women's and misses' outerwear, nec

### (P-2692)
### UMGEE USA INC
Also Called: Umgee
1565 E 23rd St, Los Angeles (90011-1801)
**PHONE**.....................323 526-9138
Boyng Ki Gi, *Pr*
◆ **EMP:** 18 **EST:** 2001
**SALES (est):** 865.07K **Privately Held**
**Web:** www.umgeeusa.com

# PRODUCTS & SERVICES SECTION
## 2335 - Women's, Junior's, And Misses' Dresses (P-2714)

SIC: 2331 2335 Women's and misses' blouses and shirts; Women's, junior's, and misses' dresses

### (P-2693)
### UNGER FABRIK LLC (PA)
18525 Railroad St, City Of Industry (91748-1316)
PHONE.................................626 469-8080
Yongbin Luo, CEO
◆ EMP: 110 EST: 1998
SQ FT: 300,000
SALES (est): 5.56MM
SALES (corp-wide): 5.56MM Privately Held
Web: www.oneworldapparel.com
SIC: 2331 Women's and misses' blouses and shirts

### (P-2694)
### VEEZEE INC
Also Called: Honulua Surf Co
121 Waterworks Way, Irvine (92618-7719)
PHONE.................................949 265-0800
Paul Naude, Pr
▲ EMP: 20 EST: 2001
SALES (est): 9.2MM Privately Held
SIC: 2331 5099 Women's and misses' blouses and shirts; Sunglasses
HQ: Billabong International Pty Ltd
    5 Billabong Place
    Burleigh Waters QLD 4220

### (P-2695)
### W5 CONCEPTS INC
2049 E 38th St, Vernon (90058-1614)
PHONE.................................323 231-2415
Kyung Eun Kim, CEO
EMP: 20 EST: 2014
SQ FT: 3,800
SALES (est): 2.43MM Privately Held
Web: www.w5concepts.com
SIC: 2331 Women's and misses' blouses and shirts

### (P-2696)
### YS GARMENTS LLC (HQ)
Also Called: Next Level Apparel
588 Crenshaw Blvd, Torrance (90503-1705)
PHONE.................................310 631-4955
▲ EMP: 18 EST: 2003
SALES (est): 49.47MM
SALES (corp-wide): 49.47MM Privately Held
Web: www.nextlevelapparel.com
SIC: 2331 2326 5136 5137 Women's and misses' blouses and shirts; Men's and boy's work clothing; Men's and boy's clothing; Blouses
PA: Next Level Holdings Company Llc
    588 Crenshaw Blvd
    310 631-4955

## 2335 Women's, Junior's, And Misses' Dresses

### (P-2697)
### AGS USA LLC
Also Called: American Garment Sewing
1210 Rexford Ave, Pasadena (91107-1713)
PHONE.................................323 588-2200
▲ EMP: 150
Web: www.agsusallc.com
SIC: 2335 2326 2331 2339 Women's, junior's, and misses' dresses; Men's and boy's work clothing; Women's and misses' blouses and shirts; Jeans: women's, misses', and juniors'

### (P-2698)
### AQUARIUS RAGS LLC (PA)
Also Called: ABS By Allen Schwartz
15821 Ventura Blvd Ste 270, Encino (91436-4775)
PHONE.................................213 895-4400
Allen Schwartz, Managing Member
▲ EMP: 75 EST: 2003
SALES (est): 5.35MM
SALES (corp-wide): 5.35MM Privately Held
SIC: 2335 Women's, junior's, and misses' dresses

### (P-2699)
### AVALON APPAREL LLC
1901 W Center St, Colton (92324-6509)
PHONE.................................323 440-4344
EMP: 93
Web: www.avalonapparel.com
SIC: 2335 Ensemble dresses: women's, misses', and juniors'
PA: Avalon Apparel, Llc
    2520 W 6th St

### (P-2700)
### AVALON APPAREL LLC (PA)
Also Called: Disorderly Kids
2520 W 6th St, Los Angeles (90057-3174)
PHONE.................................323 581-3511
Elliot Schutzer, Managing Member
Jason Schutzer, *
Jill Grossman, *
Terri Cohen, *
EMP: 165 EST: 2004
SQ FT: 5,000
SALES (est): 24.58MM Privately Held
Web: www.avalonapparel.com
SIC: 2335 Ensemble dresses: women's, misses', and juniors'

### (P-2701)
### CALIFORNIA BLUE APPAREL INC
Also Called: Ever Blue
245 W 28th St, Los Angeles (90007-3312)
PHONE.................................213 745-5400
▲ EMP: 30
Web: www.californiablue.com
SIC: 2335 2339 2331 Women's, junior's, and misses' dresses; Women's and misses' outerwear, nec; Women's and misses' blouses and shirts

### (P-2702)
### CAROL ANDERSON INC (PA)
Also Called: Carol Anderson By Invitation
18700 S Laurel Park Rd, Rancho Dominguez (90220-6003)
PHONE.................................310 638-3333
Jan Janura, Pr
Carol M Anderson, *
Jan A Janura, *
◆ EMP: 25 EST: 1977
SQ FT: 50,000
SALES (est): 4.69MM
SALES (corp-wide): 4.69MM Privately Held
Web: www.cabionline.com
SIC: 2335 2339 Women's, junior's, and misses' dresses; Shorts (outerwear): women's, misses', and juniors'

### (P-2703)
### CHOON INC (PA)
Also Called: Pezeme
1443 E 4th St, Los Angeles (90033-4214)
PHONE.................................213 225-2500
Choon S Nakamura, Pr
Daniel Nakamura, *
◆ EMP: 31 EST: 1972
SALES (est): 2.32MM
SALES (corp-wide): 2.32MM Privately Held
Web: www.choon.com
SIC: 2335 Women's, junior's, and misses' dresses

### (P-2704)
### COMPLETE CLOTHING COMPANY (PA)
Also Called: Willow
4950 E 49th St, Vernon (90058-2736)
PHONE.................................213 892-1188
Eleanor M Sanchez, CEO
▲ EMP: 43 EST: 1995
SQ FT: 30,000
SALES (est): 10.67MM Privately Held
Web: www.shopwillow.com
SIC: 2335 2339 2337 2331 Women's, junior's, and misses' dresses; Sportswear, women's; Women's and misses' suits and coats; Women's and misses' blouses and shirts

### (P-2705)
### J C TRIMMING COMPANY INC
Also Called: JC Industries
3800 S Hill St, Los Angeles (90037-1416)
PHONE.................................323 235-4458
Eric Shin, CEO
◆ EMP: 65 EST: 1993
SALES (est): 7.54MM Privately Held
SIC: 2335 2326 Women's, junior's, and misses' dresses; Men's and boy's work clothing

### (P-2706)
### JODI KRISTOPHER LLC (PA)
Also Called: City Triangles
1950 Naomi Ave, Los Angeles (90011-1342)
PHONE.................................323 890-8000
Adir Haroni, CEO
Juduth Naka, *
▲ EMP: 83 EST: 1990
SQ FT: 100,000
SALES (est): 25.48MM Privately Held
Web: www.davidkristopher.com
SIC: 2335 Women's, junior's, and misses' dresses

### (P-2707)
### JWC STUDIO INC (PA)
Also Called: Johnny Was Showroom
2423 E 23rd St, Los Angeles (90058-1201)
PHONE.................................323 231-8222
Eli Levite, Pr
▼ EMP: 26 EST: 1994
SQ FT: 30,000
SALES (est): 2.3MM
SALES (corp-wide): 2.3MM Privately Held
Web: www.johnnywas.com
SIC: 2335 Women's, junior's, and misses' dresses

### (P-2708)
### L A GLO INC
Also Called: Roberta
1451 Hi Point St, Los Angeles (90035-4100)
PHONE.................................323 932-0091
Elaine Johnson, Pr
Alan Johnson, *
▲ EMP: 50 EST: 1979
SQ FT: 25,000
SALES (est): 1.35MM Privately Held
SIC: 2335 Women's, junior's, and misses' dresses

### (P-2709)
### L Y Z LTD (PA)
Also Called: Lily Samii Collection
210 Post St, San Francisco (94108-5102)
PHONE.................................415 445-9505
Lily Samii, Pr
Laleh Eskandari, Sec
▲ EMP: 17 EST: 1969
SQ FT: 7,200
SALES (est): 913.06K
SALES (corp-wide): 913.06K Privately Held
Web: www.lilysamii.com
SIC: 2335 5621 Women's, junior's, and misses' dresses; Dress shops

### (P-2710)
### LOTUS ORIENT CORP (PA)
Also Called: Venus Bridal Gowns
411 S California St, San Gabriel (91776-2527)
P.O. Box 280 (91778-0280)
PHONE.................................626 285-5796
Eugene Wu, Pr
▲ EMP: 18 EST: 1985
SQ FT: 6,400
SALES (est): 534.12K
SALES (corp-wide): 534.12K Privately Held
Web: www.lotusorient.com
SIC: 2335 5621 Wedding gowns and dresses; Bridal shops

### (P-2711)
### MISS KIM INC
Also Called: Miss Cristina
363 Patton St Apt 3, Los Angeles (90026-6606)
PHONE.................................213 741-0888
Leticia Alvarez, CEO
Sung H Kim, CFO
EMP: 16 EST: 2012
SALES (est): 377.9K Privately Held
SIC: 2335 5137 Ensemble dresses: women's, misses', and juniors'; Dresses

### (P-2712)
### OLA NATION LLC
Also Called: Go Sales.us
915 W Barbara Ave, West Covina (91790-4135)
PHONE.................................310 256-0638
Oscar Linares, Pr
EMP: 20 EST: 2007
SALES (est): 1.05MM Privately Held
SIC: 2335 Bridal and formal gowns

### (P-2713)
### PRIVATE BRAND MDSG CORP
Also Called: Jody of California
214 W Olympic Blvd, Los Angeles (90015-1605)
P.O. Box 260923 (91426-0923)
PHONE.................................213 749-0191
William Berman, Pr
Rochelle Berman, *
John Berman, *
EMP: 23 EST: 1954
SQ FT: 6,000
SALES (est): 1.33MM Privately Held
Web: privatebm.openfos.com
SIC: 2335 2339 Women's, junior's, and misses' dresses; Sportswear, women's

### (P-2714)
### PROMISES PROMISES INC
3121 S Grand Ave, Los Angeles (90007-3816)
PHONE.................................213 749-7725
Eugene M Hardy, CEO

# 2335 - Women's, Junior's, And Misses' Dresses (P-2715)

Sean Hardy, *
▲ **EMP:** 29 **EST:** 1978
**SALES (est):** 3.58MM **Privately Held**
**SIC: 2335** Women's, junior's, and misses' dresses

### (P-2715)
### SEWBY LLC
5066 W Jefferson Blvd, Los Angeles (90016-3925)
**PHONE**..................310 494-7705
Jaleh Factor, *Pr*
**EMP:** 20 **EST:** 2019
**SALES (est):** 1.52MM **Privately Held**
**Web:** www.sewby.com
**SIC: 2335** 2389 2211 2221 Dresses,paper, cut and sewn; Men's miscellaneous accessories; Apparel and outerwear fabrics, cotton; Apparel and outerwear fabric, manmade fiber or silk

### (P-2716)
### SUBLITEX INC
Also Called: Sublitex Sublimation Tech
1515 E 15th St, Los Angeles (90021-2711)
**PHONE**..................323 582-9596
**EMP:** 35 **EST:** 2008
**SALES (est):** 3.4MM **Privately Held**
**SIC: 2335** 7389 Women's, junior's, and misses' dresses; Printing broker

### (P-2717)
### TLMF INC
Also Called: Big Strike
1515 E 15th St, Los Angeles (90021-2711)
**PHONE**..................212 764-2334
▲ **EMP:** 100
**Web:** www.heartsoul.org
**SIC: 2335** 2337 Women's, junior's, and misses' dresses; Women's and misses' suits and coats

### (P-2718)
### TONY MARTERIE & ASSOCIATES INC
Also Called: North Coast Industries
28 Liberty Ship Way Fl 2, Sausalito (94965-3320)
P.O. Box 2018 (94966-2018)
**PHONE**..................415 331-7150
Tony Marterie, *Pr*
Roxanne Marterie, *
▲ **EMP:** 25 **EST:** 1965
**SQ FT:** 27,000
**SALES (est):** 2.26MM **Privately Held**
**Web:** www.blast-usa.com
**SIC: 2335** 2339 Women's, junior's, and misses' dresses; Women's and misses' outerwear, nec

### (P-2719)
### TRINITY SPORTS INC
2067 E 55th St, Vernon (90058-3441)
**PHONE**..................323 277-9288
▲ **EMP:** 300
**Web:** www.trinitysportsinc.com
**SIC: 2335** 2339 2325 Women's, junior's, and misses' dresses; Women's and misses' outerwear, nec; Men's and boy's trousers and slacks

### (P-2720)
### TRIXXI CLOTHING COMPANY INC (PA)
Also Called: Ash & Violet
6817 E Acco St, Commerce (90040-1901)
**PHONE**..................323 585-4200
Annette Soufrine, *CEO*
Leslie Flores, *Pr*

▲ **EMP:** 49 **EST:** 2001
**SQ FT:** 35,000
**SALES (est):** 10.09MM
**SALES (corp-wide):** 10.09MM **Privately Held**
**Web:** www.trixxi.com
**SIC: 2335** 2331 Women's, junior's, and misses' dresses; Blouses, women's and juniors': made from purchased material

## 2337 Women's And Misses' Suits And Coats

### (P-2721)
### ANN LILLI CORP (PA)
1010 B St Ste 333, San Rafael (94901-2920)
**PHONE**..................415 482-9444
Don Kamler, *Prin*
Jo Schuman, *
**EMP:** 63 **EST:** 1969
**SALES (est):** 10.35MM
**SALES (corp-wide):** 10.35MM **Privately Held**
**SIC: 2337** Women's and misses' suits and coats

### (P-2722)
### DANOC MANUFACTURING CORP
Also Called: Danoc Embroidery
6015 Power Inn Rd Ste A, Sacramento (95824-2336)
**PHONE**..................916 455-2876
Tom Land, *Pr*
**EMP:** 16 **EST:** 1910
**SQ FT:** 1,500
**SALES (est):** 1.5MM **Privately Held**
**Web:** www.motowear.com
**SIC: 2337** 2326 Uniforms, except athletic: women's, misses', and juniors'; Industrial garments, men's and boys'

### (P-2723)
### EVA FRANCO INC
1509 Mission St, South Pasadena (91030-3215)
**PHONE**..................213 746-4776
Eva Franco, *CEO*
Robert Arbogast, *CFO*
▲ **EMP:** 15 **EST:** 2004
**SALES (est):** 3.31MM **Privately Held**
**Web:** www.evafranco.com
**SIC: 2337** 2331 2335 Skirts, separate: women's, misses', and juniors'; Women's and misses' blouses and shirts; Women's, junior's, and misses' dresses

### (P-2724)
### KOMAROV ENTERPRISES INC
Also Called: Kisca
10939 Venice Blvd, Los Angeles (90034-7015)
**PHONE**..................213 244-7000
Dimitri Komarov, *Pr*
Dimitri Leiberman, *
Shelley Komvarov, *
▲ **EMP:** 75 **EST:** 1997
**SALES (est):** 9.52MM **Privately Held**
**Web:** www.komarov.com
**SIC: 2337** 2331 Women's and misses' suits and coats; Women's and misses' blouses and shirts

### (P-2725)
### R B III ASSOCIATES INC
Also Called: Teamwork Athletic Apparel
2386 Faraday Ave Ste 125, Carlsbad (92008-7263)
**PHONE**..................760 471-5370

Matthew Lehrer, *CEO*
Dave Caserta, *
Andy Lehrer, *
▲ **EMP:** 150 **EST:** 1976
**SALES (est):** 24.58MM **Privately Held**
**SIC: 2337** 2329 Uniforms, except athletic: women's, misses', and juniors'; Men's and boys' athletic uniforms

### (P-2726)
### S STUDIO INC
Also Called: Sue Wong
3030 W 6th St, Los Angeles (90020-1506)
**PHONE**..................213 388-7400
Dieter Raabe, *Pr*
Dieter Raabe, *Pr*
Sue Wong, *Ch Bd*
▲ **EMP:** 15 **EST:** 1995
**SQ FT:** 28,000
**SALES (est):** 2.57MM **Privately Held**
**Web:** www.ncastudio.com
**SIC: 2337** Women's and misses' suits and skirts

### (P-2727)
### SCHOOL APPAREL INC (PA)
Also Called: A School Apparel
838 Mitten Rd, Burlingame (94010-1304)
**PHONE**..................650 777-4500
Ryan K Knoss, *CEO*
Kenneth Knoss, *
Bernice B Knoss, *
Dave Weil, *
Vince Knoss, *
◆ **EMP:** 54 **EST:** 1976
**SALES (est):** 25.09MM
**SALES (corp-wide):** 25.09MM **Privately Held**
**Web:** www.schoolapparel.com
**SIC: 2337** 2311 2326 Uniforms, except athletic: women's, misses', and juniors'; Men's and boys' uniforms; Work uniforms

### (P-2728)
### THEORY LLC
412 Jackson St, San Francisco (94111-1602)
**PHONE**..................415 376-9065
**EMP:** 18
**Web:** www.theory.com
**SIC: 2337** Women's and misses' suits and coats
HQ: Theory Llc
   38 Gansevoort St
   New York NY 10014

### (P-2729)
### TOPSON DOWNS CALIFORNIA INC
Also Called: TOPSON DOWNS OF CALIFORNIA, INC.
3545 Motor Ave, Los Angeles (90034-4806)
**PHONE**..................310 558-0300
Kris Scott, *Brnch Mgr*
**EMP:** 131
**SALES (corp-wide):** 45.02MM **Privately Held**
**Web:** www.topsondowns.com
**SIC: 2337** 5621 Women's and misses' suits and coats; Ready-to-wear apparel, women's
PA: Topson Downs Of California, Llc
   3840 Watseka Ave
   310 558-0300

## 2339 Women's And Misses' Outerwear, Nec

### (P-2730)
### AARON CORPORATION
Also Called: J P Sportswear
2645 Industry Way, Lynwood (90262-4007)
**PHONE**..................323 235-5959
Paul Shechet, *Pr*
Francisco Balleste, *
▲ **EMP:** 170 **EST:** 1955
**SALES (est):** 3.38MM **Privately Held**
**Web:** www.jpsportswear.us
**SIC: 2339** Women's and misses' athletic clothing and sportswear

### (P-2731)
### ABS BY ALLEN SCHWARTZ LLC (HQ)
15821 Ventura Blvd Ste 270, Encino (91436-4775)
**PHONE**..................213 895-4400
Allen Schwartz, *Managing Member*
Kirk Foster, *
▲ **EMP:** 22 **EST:** 2004
**SALES (est):** 5.35MM
**SALES (corp-wide):** 5.35MM **Privately Held**
**Web:** www.absstyle.com
**SIC: 2339** 5621 Women's and misses' outerwear, nec; Women's clothing stores
PA: Aquarius Rags, Llc
   15821 Ventura Blvd # 270
   213 895-4400

### (P-2732)
### AMBIANCE USA INC
2465 E 23rd St, Los Angeles (90058-1201)
**PHONE**..................323 587-0007
**EMP:** 16
**SALES (corp-wide):** 11.13MM **Privately Held**
**Web:** www.waxjean.com
**SIC: 2339** Women's and misses' outerwear, nec
PA: Ambiance U.S.A., Inc.
   2415 E 15th St
   323 587-0007

### (P-2733)
### AMBIANCE USA INC (PA)
Also Called: Ambiance Apparel
2415 E 15th St, Los Angeles (90021-2936)
**PHONE**..................323 587-0007
Sang Noh, *CEO*
◆ **EMP:** 22 **EST:** 1999
**SALES (est):** 11.13MM
**SALES (corp-wide):** 11.13MM **Privately Held**
**Web:** www.ambianceapparel.com
**SIC: 2339** 5137 Women's and misses' outerwear, nec; Women's and children's clothing

### (P-2734)
### AMBIANCE USA INC
Also Called: Wax Jean By Ambiance
930 Towne Ave, Los Angeles (90021-2022)
**PHONE**..................213 765-9600
**EMP:** 16
**SALES (corp-wide):** 11.13MM **Privately Held**
**Web:** www.waxjean.com
**SIC: 2339** Jeans: women's, misses', and juniors'
PA: Ambiance U.S.A., Inc.
   2415 E 15th St
   323 587-0007

# PRODUCTS & SERVICES SECTION
## 2339 - Women's And Misses' Outerwear, Nec (P-2755)

**(P-2735)**
**APPAREL PROD SVCS GLOBL LLC**
Also Called: APS Global
8954 Lurline Ave, Chatsworth (91311-6103)
P.O. Box 5011 (91365-5011)
PHONE.................................818 700-3700
◆ EMP: 42 EST: 2013
SQ FT: 15,000
SALES (est): 5.56MM Privately Held
SIC: 2339 2329 Women's and misses' athletic clothing and sportswear; Men's and boys' sportswear and athletic clothing

**(P-2736)**
**BARE NOTHINGS INC (PA)**
17705 Sampson Ln, Huntington Beach (92647-6790)
PHONE.................................714 848-8532
Ann Mase, Pr
Ronald Mase, VP
EMP: 22 EST: 1977
SALES (est): 546.8K
SALES (corp-wide): 546.8K Privately Held
Web: www.barenothings.com
SIC: 2339 Bathing suits: women's, misses', and juniors'

**(P-2737)**
**BB CO INC**
Also Called: Wild Lizard
1753 E 21st St, Los Angeles (90058-1006)
PHONE.................................213 550-1158
Kyoung K Frazier, Pr
Kyoung K Frazier, Pr
Cecy Mendoza, *
▲ EMP: 30 EST: 1998
SQ FT: 22,000
SALES (est): 7.5MM Privately Held
SIC: 2339 Women's and misses' athletic clothing and sportswear

**(P-2738)**
**BE BOP CLOTHING**
Also Called: Rebel Jeans
5833 Avalon Blvd, Los Angeles (90003-1307)
PHONE.................................323 846-0121
Guillermo Granados, Pr
Marcus Sphatt, *
Michael Harb, *
EMP: 350 EST: 1987
SQ FT: 100,000
SALES (est): 19.8MM Privately Held
SIC: 2339 Sportswear, women's

**(P-2739)**
**BOARDRIDERS WHOLESALE LLC**
Dakine
6201 Oak Cyn Ste 100, Irvine (92618-5232)
PHONE.................................949 916-3060
EMP: 45
SALES (corp-wide): 106.29MM Privately Held
Web: www.quiksilver.com
SIC: 2339 2331 Women's and misses' outerwear, nec; Women's and misses' blouses and shirts
PA: Boardriders Wholesale, Llc
5600 Argosy Ave Ste 100

**(P-2740)**
**BURNING TORCH INC**
1738 Cordova St, Los Angeles (90007-1129)
PHONE.................................323 733-7700
Karyn Craven, Pr
▲ EMP: 20 EST: 1999
SQ FT: 5,000
SALES (est): 2.12MM Privately Held
Web: www.burningtorchinc.com
SIC: 2339 Sportswear, women's

**(P-2741)**
**C P SHADES INC (PA)**
Also Called: C P Shades
403 Coloma St, Sausalito (94965-2827)
PHONE.................................415 331-4581
David Weinstein, Pr
Alison Pownall, VP
Denise Weinstein, Treas
▲ EMP: 17 EST: 1973
SQ FT: 40,405
SALES (est): 21.66MM
SALES (corp-wide): 21.66MM Privately Held
Web: www.cpshades.com
SIC: 2339 5621 Women's and misses' athletic clothing and sportswear; Women's sportswear

**(P-2742)**
**CAMP SMIDGEMORE INC (DH)**
Also Called: Renee Claire Inc
3641 10th Ave, Los Angeles (90018-4114)
PHONE.................................323 634-0333
Wendy Luttrel, CEO
Renee Bertrand, Pr
▲ EMP: 22 EST: 2001
SQ FT: 13,000
SALES (est): 1.75MM
SALES (corp-wide): 359.75MM Privately Held
Web: www.bedheadpjs.com
SIC: 2339 2341 Women's and misses' outerwear, nec; Pajamas and bedjackets: women's and children's
HQ: Komar Intimates, Llc
90 Hudson St
Jersey City NJ 07302
212 725-1500

**(P-2743)**
**CARBON 38 INC**
2866 Westbrook Ave, Los Angeles (90046-1249)
PHONE.................................888 723-5838
Katherine Johnson, CEO
EMP: 90 EST: 2012
SALES (est): 11.76MM
SALES (corp-wide): 25.07MM Privately Held
Web: www.carbon38.com
SIC: 2339 Sportswear, women's
PA: Bc Brands, Llc
38 E 29th St

**(P-2744)**
**CAROL WIOR INC**
Also Called: Slimsuit
7533 Garfield Ave, Bell (90201-4817)
PHONE.................................562 927-0052
Carol Wior, Pr
Niki Wior, *
Lucy Weddell, *
Troy Berg, *
Julie Wilson, *
▲ EMP: 30 EST: 1991
SQ FT: 77,000
SALES (est): 1.1MM Privately Held
Web: www.carolwiorinc.com
SIC: 2339 5699 Bathing suits: women's, misses', and juniors'; Bathing suits

**(P-2745)**
**CITIZENS OF HUMANITY LLC (PA)**
Also Called: Goldsign
5715 Bickett St, Huntington Park (90255-2624)
PHONE.................................323 923-1240
Jerome Dahan, CEO
Amy Williams, Pr
◆ EMP: 158 EST: 2005
SQ FT: 70,000
SALES (est): 47.21MM
SALES (corp-wide): 47.21MM Privately Held
Web: www.citizensofhumanity.com
SIC: 2339 Jeans: women's, misses', and juniors'

**(P-2746)**
**CLOTHING ILLUSTRATED INC (PA)**
Also Called: Love Stitch
836 Traction Ave, Los Angeles (90013-1816)
PHONE.................................213 403-9950
Danny Hanasab Foruzesh, CEO
▲ EMP: 35 EST: 2002
SALES (est): 9.58MM Privately Held
Web: www.shoplovestitch.com
SIC: 2339 Women's and misses' accessories

**(P-2747)**
**CLUE CLOTHING CORP**
Also Called: Testament Apparel
2325 E 55th St, Vernon (90058-3435)
PHONE.................................323 277-4500
EMP: 16 EST: 1995
SALES (est): 1.9MM Privately Held
SIC: 2339 Women's and misses' athletic clothing and sportswear

**(P-2748)**
**CREW KNITWEAR LLC (PA)**
Also Called: Hiatus
660 S Myers St, Los Angeles (90023-1015)
PHONE.................................323 526-3888
Tricia Franklin, CEO
Chris Y Jung, Pr
Peter Jung, CFO
▲ EMP: 58 EST: 2001
SQ FT: 39,000
SALES (est): 13.6MM Privately Held
Web: www.crewknitwear.com
SIC: 2339 Women's and misses' outerwear, nec

**(P-2749)**
**CUT LOOSE (PA)**
101 Williams Ave, San Francisco (94124-2619)
PHONE.................................415 822-2031
Will Wenham, Pr
Rosemarie Ovian, *
◆ EMP: 55 EST: 1984
SQ FT: 17,000
SALES (est): 9.66MM
SALES (corp-wide): 9.66MM Privately Held
Web: www.cutloose.com
SIC: 2339 5621 2331 Sportswear, women's; Women's clothing stores; Women's and misses' blouses and shirts

**(P-2750)**
**DAKINE EQUIPMENT LLC**
19400 Harborgate Way, Torrance (90501-1354)
PHONE.................................424 276-3618
Shane Wallace, *
EMP: 25 EST: 2018
SALES (est): 4.19MM
SALES (corp-wide): 4.91MM Privately Held
SIC: 2339 2329 Snow suits: women's, misses', and juniors'; Ski and snow clothing: men's and boys'
PA: Jr286, Inc.
20100 S Vermont Ave
877 464-5301

**(P-2751)**
**DAVID GRMENT CTNG FSING SVC IN**
Also Called: Clothng/Pparel/Uniform/ppe Mfg
5008 S Boyle Ave, Vernon (90058-3904)
PHONE.................................323 216-1574
Mario Alvarado, CEO
David Alvarado, *
Mario Alvarado, VP
▲ EMP: 45 EST: 1987
SQ FT: 15,000
SALES (est): 4.97MM Privately Held
SIC: 2339 2326 2329 Women's and misses' athletic clothing and sportswear; Men's and boy's work clothing; Men's and boys' sportswear and athletic clothing

**(P-2752)**
**DDA HOLDINGS INC**
Also Called: A Commom Thread
834 S Broadway Ste 600, Los Angeles (90014-3217)
PHONE.................................213 624-5200
Anthony Graham, CEO
Sandra Balestier, *
▲ EMP: 25 EST: 2007
SQ FT: 15,000
SALES (est): 8.47MM Privately Held
Web: www.ddaholdings.com
SIC: 2339 Women's and misses' athletic clothing and sportswear

**(P-2753)**
**DE SOTO CLOTHING INC**
Also Called: De Soto Sport
7584 Trade St, San Diego (92121-2412)
PHONE.................................858 578-6672
Emilio De Soto Ii, Pr
Dan Neyenhuis, Stockholder
Marta Lundgren, Sec
▲ EMP: 15 EST: 1990
SQ FT: 5,600
SALES (est): 1.42MM Privately Held
Web: www.desotosport.com
SIC: 2339 2329 Women's and misses' athletic clothing and sportswear; Men's and boys' sportswear and athletic clothing

**(P-2754)**
**DESIGN TODAYS INC (PA)**
11707 Cetona Way, Porter Ranch (91326-4604)
PHONE.................................213 745-3091
Sung Ok Hong, Pr
EMP: 26 EST: 1987
SALES (est): 980.05K Privately Held
SIC: 2339 Women's and misses' outerwear, nec

**(P-2755)**
**DMBM LLC**
2445 E 12th St Ste C, Los Angeles (90021-2954)
PHONE.................................714 321-6032
David Chong, Owner
EMP: 23
SIC: 2339 2369 Women's and misses' outerwear, nec; Girl's and children's outerwear, nec
PA: Dmbm, Llc
2701 S Santa Fe Ave

## 2339 - Women's And Misses' Outerwear, Nec (P-2756)

**(P-2756)**
**DNAM APPAREL INDUSTRIES LLC**
Also Called: Ed Hardy
4938 Triggs St, Commerce (90022-4832)
PHONE..............................323 859-0114
Henri Levy, *Managing Member*
Michael Cohen, *
▲ **EMP:** 32 **EST:** 2004
**SALES (est):** 1.22MM **Privately Held**
**SIC: 2339** 5137 Service apparel, washable: women's; Women's and children's clothing

**(P-2757)**
**ESKA INC**
1370 Mirasol St, Los Angeles (90023-3109)
PHONE..............................323 846-3700
Suk Cho, *Pr*
**EMP:** 25 **EST:** 2014
**SALES (est):** 983.78K **Privately Held**
**SIC: 2339** Athletic clothing: women's, misses', and juniors'

**(P-2758)**
**EV R INC**
Also Called: Skinny Minnie
3400 Slauson Ave, Maywood (90270-2525)
PHONE..............................323 312-5400
▲ **EMP:** 50
**SIC: 2339** Athletic clothing: women's, misses', and juniors'

**(P-2759)**
**FINESSE APPAREL INC**
Also Called: Finesse
815 Fairview Ave Unit 101, South Pasadena (91030-2490)
PHONE..............................213 747-7077
▲ **EMP:** 45
Web: www.finesseusa.com
**SIC: 2339** Women's and misses' athletic clothing and sportswear

**(P-2760)**
**GAZE USA INC**
2011 E 25th St, Vernon (90058-1127)
PHONE..............................213 622-0022
Ji S Hong, *CEO*
Stephen S Whang, *
**EMP:** 25 **EST:** 2010
**SALES (est):** 816.98K **Privately Held**
**SIC: 2339** 5651 3999 Women's and misses' athletic clothing and sportswear; Unisex clothing stores; Bristles, dressing of

**(P-2761)**
**GOOD AMERICAN LLC (PA)**
1601 Vine St, Los Angeles (90028-8806)
P.O. Box 888 (90232-0888)
PHONE..............................213 357-5100
Emma Grede, *CEO*
Khloe Kardashian, *
**EMP:** 42 **EST:** 2016
**SALES (est):** 19.95MM
**SALES (corp-wide):** 19.95MM **Privately Held**
Web: www.goodamerican.com
**SIC: 2339** 5137 5621 Jeans: women's, misses', and juniors'; Women's and children's clothing; Women's clothing stores

**(P-2762)**
**GYPSY 05 INC**
3200 Union Pacific Ave, Los Angeles (90023-4203)
PHONE..............................323 265-2700
Dotan Shoham, *Pr*
▲ **EMP:** 44 **EST:** 2005
**SALES (est):** 426.57K **Privately Held**

Web: www.gypsy05.com
**SIC: 2339** Women's and misses' athletic clothing and sportswear

**(P-2763)**
**HEARTS DELIGHT**
4035 N Ventura Ave, Ventura (93001-1163)
PHONE..............................805 648-7123
Deborah Mesker, *Owner*
**EMP:** 27 **EST:** 1986
**SQ FT:** 2,000
**SALES (est):** 765.29K **Privately Held**
Web: shop.heartsdelightclothiers.com
**SIC: 2339** 5621 Women's and misses' outerwear, nec; Boutiques

**(P-2764)**
**HEATHER BY BORDEAUX INC**
Also Called: Bordeaux
5983 Malburg Way, Vernon (90058-3945)
PHONE..............................213 622-0555
Afshin Raminfar, *CEO*
▲ **EMP:** 39 **EST:** 2003
**SALES (est):** 1.69MM **Privately Held**
Web: www.heatherfashion.com
**SIC: 2339** Service apparel, washable: women's

**(P-2765)**
**HYLETE INC**
Also Called: Hylete
11622 El Camino Real Ste 100, San Diego (92130-2051)
PHONE..............................858 225-8998
Adam Colton, *CEO*
Ron L Wilson Ii, *Interim Chief Financial Officer*
Matthew Paulson, *VP*
**EMP:** 20 **EST:** 2012
**SQ FT:** 4,300
**SALES (est):** 5.54MM **Privately Held**
Web: www.hylete.com
**SIC: 2339** 5091 2329 Women's and misses' athletic clothing and sportswear; Athletic goods; Athletic clothing, except uniforms: men's, youths' and boys'

**(P-2766)**
**IT JEANS INC**
Also Called: It Campus
2425 E 38th St, Vernon (90058-1708)
PHONE..............................323 588-2156
▲ **EMP:** 23
Web: www.itjeans.com
**SIC: 2339** 2369 Jeans: women's, misses', and juniors'; Girl's and children's outerwear, nec

**(P-2767)**
**J & F DESIGN INC**
Also Called: Next Generation
2042 Garfield Ave, Commerce (90040-1804)
PHONE..............................323 526-4444
Jack Farshi, *Pr*
◆ **EMP:** 75 **EST:** 1991
**SQ FT:** 100,000
**SALES (est):** 18MM **Privately Held**
Web: www.bobbyjackbrand.com
**SIC: 2339** Sportswear, women's

**(P-2768)**
**JANIN**
10031 Hunt Ave, South Gate (90280-6310)
PHONE..............................323 564-0995
Jose Estevez, *Owner*
**EMP:** 210 **EST:** 1987
**SQ FT:** 10,000
**SALES (est):** 821.28K **Privately Held**

**SIC: 2339** Neckwear and ties: women's, misses', and juniors'

**(P-2769)**
**JAPANESE WEEKEND INC (PA)**
496 S Airport Blvd, South San Francisco (94080-6911)
PHONE..............................415 621-0555
Barbara White, *Pr*
▲ **EMP:** 25 **EST:** 1979
**SQ FT:** 6,000
**SALES (est):** 4.99MM
**SALES (corp-wide):** 4.99MM **Privately Held**
**SIC: 2339** 5621 Maternity clothing; Maternity wear

**(P-2770)**
**JAYA APPAREL GROUP LLC**
Likely
2761 Fruitland Ave, Vernon (90058-3607)
PHONE..............................323 584-3500
**EMP:** 18
**SALES (corp-wide):** 24.28MM **Privately Held**
Web: www.jayaapparelgroup.com
**SIC: 2339** Women's and misses' jackets and coats, except sportswear
**PA:** Jaya Apparel Group Llc
2761 Frtland Ave Fl 2 Ste
323 584-3500

**(P-2771)**
**JAYA APPAREL GROUP LLC (PA)**
2761 Fruitland Ave Fl 2, Los Angeles (90058-3607)
PHONE..............................323 584-3500
Jane Siskin, *Managing Member*
Don Lewis, *
Jalal Elbasri, *
◆ **EMP:** 67 **EST:** 2005
**SALES (est):** 24.28MM
**SALES (corp-wide):** 24.28MM **Privately Held**
Web: www.jayaapparelgroup.com
**SIC: 2339** 2337 Women's and misses' jackets and coats, except sportswear; Women's and misses' suits and skirts

**(P-2772)**
**JD/CMC INC**
Also Called: Color ME Cotton
2834 E 11th St, Los Angeles (90023-3406)
PHONE..............................818 767-2260
Mari Tatevosian, *Pr*
Anait Grigorian, *
◆ **EMP:** 35 **EST:** 1991
**SQ FT:** 12,000
**SALES (est):** 2.15MM **Privately Held**
Web: www.cmcclick.com
**SIC: 2339** Women's and misses' outerwear, nec

**(P-2773)**
**JJS MAE INC (PA)**
Also Called: Rainbeau
1812 Harrison St, San Francisco (94103-4228)
PHONE..............................415 255-7047
▲ **EMP:** 76 **EST:** 1980
**SALES (est):** 6.51MM
**SALES (corp-wide):** 6.51MM **Privately Held**
Web: www.rainbeau.com
**SIC: 2339** Women's and misses' athletic clothing and sportswear

**(P-2774)**
**JNJ APPAREL INC**
18788 Fairfield Rd, Porter Ranch (91326-3922)

PHONE..............................323 584-9700
Chan Hyoung Park, *Pr*
▲ **EMP:** 30 **EST:** 2001
**SALES (est):** 604.29K **Privately Held**
**SIC: 2339** Women's and misses' athletic clothing and sportswear

**(P-2775)**
**JOLYN CLOTHING COMPANY LLC**
16390 Pacific Coast Hwy Ste 201, Huntington Beach (92649-1851)
PHONE..............................714 794-2149
Warren Lief Pedersen, *Pr*
Ann Dawson, *
Brandon Molina, *
**EMP:** 30 **EST:** 2007
**SALES (est):** 3.03MM **Privately Held**
Web: www.jolyn.com
**SIC: 2339** 5621 Women's and misses' athletic clothing and sportswear; Women's sportswear

**(P-2776)**
**JOWETT GARMENTS FACTORY INC**
Also Called: Jowett Group
10359 Rush St, South El Monte (91733-3341)
PHONE..............................626 350-0515
◆ **EMP:** 40
Web: www.jowett.com
**SIC: 2339** Athletic clothing: women's, misses', and juniors'

**(P-2777)**
**JT DESIGN STUDIO INC (PA)**
Also Called: 860, Shameless, Hot Wire
860 S Los Angeles St Ste 912, Los Angeles (90014-3319)
PHONE..............................213 891-1500
Ted Cooper, *Pr*
Robert Grossman, *
▲ **EMP:** 24 **EST:** 1998
**SALES (est):** 2.97MM
**SALES (corp-wide):** 2.97MM **Privately Held**
Web: www.jtdesignstudio.com
**SIC: 2339** Women's and misses' athletic clothing and sportswear

**(P-2778)**
**JUST FOR WRAPS INC (PA)**
Also Called: A-List
4871 S Santa Fe Ave, Vernon (90058-2103)
PHONE..............................213 239-0503
Vrajesh Lal, *CEO*
Rakesh Lal, *
▲ **EMP:** 130 **EST:** 1980
**SALES (est):** 9.93MM
**SALES (corp-wide):** 9.93MM **Privately Held**
Web: muralsjustforkids.weebly.com
**SIC: 2339** 2335 2337 Sportswear, women's; Women's, junior's, and misses' dresses; Women's and misses' suits and coats

**(P-2779)**
**KAYO OF CALIFORNIA (PA)**
Also Called: Kayo Clothing Company
11854 Alameda St, Lynwood (90262-4019)
PHONE..............................323 233-6107
Jack Ostrovsky, *Ch Bd*
Jeffrey Michaels, *
Jonathan Kaye, *
Annabelle Wall, *
▲ **EMP:** 45 **EST:** 1968
**SALES (est):** 7.93MM
**SALES (corp-wide):** 7.93MM **Privately Held**

## 2339 - Women's And Misses' Outerwear, Nec (P-2802)

Web: www.kayo.com
SIC: **2339** 2337 Sportswear, women's; Skirts, separate: women's, misses', and juniors'

**(P-2780)**
### KIM & CAMI PRODUCTIONS INC
2950 Leonis Blvd, Vernon (90058-2916)
PHONE..................323 584-1300
Kimberly A Hiatt, *Pr*
Cami Gasmer, *
▲ **EMP:** 40 **EST:** 1999
**SQ FT:** 1,000
**SALES (est):** 2.41MM **Privately Held**
**SIC: 2339** Sportswear, women's

**(P-2781)**
### KLK FORTE INDUSTRY INC (PA)
Also Called: Honey Punch
1535 Rio Vista Ave, Los Angeles (90023-2619)
PHONE..................323 415-9181
Katherine Kim, *CEO*
◆ **EMP:** 45 **EST:** 2012
**SQ FT:** 30,000
**SALES (est):** 1.79MM
**SALES (corp-wide):** 1.79MM **Privately Held**
**SIC: 2339** Women's and misses' outerwear, nec

**(P-2782)**
### KOKATAT INC
5350 Ericson Way, Arcata (95521-9277)
PHONE..................707 822-7621
Mark Loughmiller, *CEO*
Stephen O Meara, *
Kit Mann, *
▲ **EMP:** 150 **EST:** 1982
**SQ FT:** 30,000
**SALES (est):** 7.37MM **Privately Held**
Web: www.kokatat.com
**SIC: 2339** 2329 3842 Women's and misses' athletic clothing and sportswear; Men's and boys' sportswear and athletic clothing; Clothing, fire resistant and protective

**(P-2783)**
### KORAL INDUSTRIES LLC (PA)
Also Called: Koral Los Angeles
1334 3rd Street Promenade Ste 200, Santa Monica (90401-1310)
PHONE..................323 585-5343
Peter Koral, *
▲ **EMP:** 31 **EST:** 2012
**SALES (est):** 8.71MM
**SALES (corp-wide):** 8.71MM **Privately Held**
Web: www.koral.com
**SIC: 2339** Service apparel, washable: women's

**(P-2784)**
### L&L MANUFACTURING CO INC
Also Called: L & L Distributors
12400 Wilshire Blvd Ste 360, Los Angeles (90025-1059)
**EMP:** 270
**SIC: 2339** 2329 2369 8741 Sportswear, women's; Men's and boys' sportswear and athletic clothing; Girl's and children's outerwear, nec; Management services

**(P-2785)**
### LAT LLC
Also Called: G Girl Clothing
2618 Fruitland Ave, Vernon (90058-2220)
PHONE..................323 233-3017
Simon Cho, *Managing Member*
Sung H Cho, *
▲ **EMP:** 40 **EST:** 1999
**SALES (est):** 3.04MM **Privately Held**
Web: www.latapparel.com
**SIC: 2339** Women's and misses' outerwear, nec

**(P-2786)**
### LEE THOMAS INC (PA)
13800 S Figueroa St, Los Angeles (90061-1026)
PHONE..................310 532-7560
Lee Opolinsky, *Pr*
Thomas Mahoney, *
**EMP:** 30 **EST:** 1981
**SQ FT:** 45,000
**SALES (est):** 2.27MM
**SALES (corp-wide):** 2.27MM **Privately Held**
**SIC: 2339** Women's and misses' athletic clothing and sportswear

**(P-2787)**
### LEFTY PRODUCTION CO LLC
318 W 9th St Ste 1010, Los Angeles (90015-1546)
PHONE..................323 515-9266
Marta Abrams, *Managing Member*
**EMP:** 36 **EST:** 2012
**SALES (est):** 561.67K **Privately Held**
Web: www.leftyproductionco.com
**SIC: 2339** Athletic clothing: women's, misses', and juniors'

**(P-2788)**
### MARGARET OLEARY INC (PA)
Also Called: Margaret O'Leary
50 Dorman Ave, San Francisco (94124-1807)
PHONE..................415 354-6663
Margaret O'leary, *CEO*
▲ **EMP:** 70 **EST:** 1991
**SQ FT:** 16,000
**SALES (est):** 17.62MM **Privately Held**
Web: www.margaretoleary.com
**SIC: 2339** 2253 Sportswear, women's; Knit outerwear mills

**(P-2789)**
### MARIKA LLC
5553 Bandini Blvd B, Bell (90201-6421)
PHONE..................323 888-7755
▲ **EMP:** 100 **EST:** 1982
**SQ FT:** 160,000
**SALES (est):** 3.83MM **Privately Held**
Web: www.marika.com
**SIC: 2339** 5137 Athletic clothing: women's, misses', and juniors'; Women's and children's outerwear

**(P-2790)**
### MAX LEON INC (PA)
Also Called: Max Studio.com
3100 New York Dr Ste 100, Pasadena (91107-1554)
P.O. Box 70879 (91117-7879)
PHONE..................626 797-6886
Leon Max, *CEO*
Ernest E Hoffer, *
Kerri Specker, *
▲ **EMP:** 100 **EST:** 1979
**SQ FT:** 65,000
**SALES (est):** 37.65MM
**SALES (corp-wide):** 37.65MM **Privately Held**
Web: www.maxstudio.com
**SIC: 2339** 5632 Sportswear, women's; Apparel accessories

**(P-2791)**
### MGT INDUSTRIES INC (PA)
Also Called: California Dynasty
13889 S Figueroa St, Los Angeles (90061-1025)
PHONE..................310 516-5900
Jeffrey P Mirvis, *CEO*
Alessandra Strahl, *
Mike Brooks, *
Phil Nathanson, *
▲ **EMP:** 68 **EST:** 1983
**SQ FT:** 82,000
**SALES (est):** 4.18K
**SALES (corp-wide):** 4.18K **Privately Held**
Web: www.mgtind.com
**SIC: 2339** Women's and misses' outerwear, nec

**(P-2792)**
### MONTEREY CANYON LLC (PA)
1515 E 15th St, Los Angeles (90021-2711)
PHONE..................213 741-0209
Richard Sneider, *
▲ **EMP:** 70 **EST:** 1977
**SALES (est):** 5.41MM
**SALES (corp-wide):** 5.41MM **Privately Held**
**SIC: 2339** Sportswear, women's

**(P-2793)**
### NEW FASHION PRODUCTS INC
3600 E Olympic Blvd, Los Angeles (90023-3121)
PHONE..................310 354-0090
▲ **EMP:** 170 **EST:** 1975
**SALES (est):** 3.59MM **Privately Held**
**SIC: 2339** 2325 Slacks: women's, misses', and juniors'; Men's and boy's trousers and slacks

**(P-2794)**
### NEW GENERATION ATHLETE LLC ✪
680 Lighthouse Ave Unit 51688, Pacific Grove (93950-8099)
PHONE..................661 316-2209
Desmond Early, *Managing Member*
**EMP:** 15 **EST:** 2023
**SALES (est):** 213.85K **Privately Held**
**SIC: 2339** Athletic clothing: women's, misses', and juniors'

**(P-2795)**
### NEXXEN APPAREL INC (PA)
Also Called: Check It Out
1555 Los Palos St, Los Angeles (90023-3218)
PHONE..................323 267-9900
Jai Sim, *Pr*
Carol Chang, *VP*
Billy Sim, *VP*
**EMP:** 18 **EST:** 1998
**SQ FT:** 10,000
**SALES (est):** 2.38MM
**SALES (corp-wide):** 2.38MM **Privately Held**
**SIC: 2339** Women's and misses' outerwear, nec

**(P-2796)**
### NILS INC (PA)
Also Called: Nils Skiwear
12572 Western Ave, Garden Grove (92841-4013)
PHONE..................714 755-1600
Nils Andersson, *CEO*
Richard Leffler, *Pr*
▲ **EMP:** 15 **EST:** 1953
**SALES (est):** 2.59MM
**SALES (corp-wide):** 2.59MM **Privately Held**
Web: www.nils.us
**SIC: 2339** Women's and misses' athletic clothing and sportswear

**(P-2797)**
### PACIFIC ATHLETIC WEAR INC
7340 Lampson Ave, Garden Grove (92841-2902)
PHONE..................714 751-8006
John Hillenbrand, *Pr*
Gabriela Hillenbrand, *
▲ **EMP:** 70 **EST:** 1994
**SALES (est):** 6.47MM **Privately Held**
Web: www.pacificathleticwear.com
**SIC: 2339** Uniforms, athletic: women's, misses', and juniors'

**(P-2798)**
### PATTERSON KINCAID LLC
5175 S Soto St, Vernon (90058-3620)
PHONE..................323 584-3559
Jane Siskin, *Managing Member*
Jilali Elbasri, *
◆ **EMP:** 42 **EST:** 2010
**SQ FT:** 35,000
**SALES (est):** 994.83K
**SALES (corp-wide):** 24.28MM **Privately Held**
**SIC: 2339** Women's and misses' outerwear, nec
**PA:** Jaya Apparel Group Llc
2761 Frtland Ave Fl 2 Ste
323 584-3500

**(P-2799)**
### PIERRE MITRI (PA)
Also Called: Watch L.A.
1138 Wall St, Los Angeles (90015-2320)
P.O. Box 2100 (90632-2100)
PHONE..................213 747-1838
Pierre D Mitri, *Owner*
▲ **EMP:** 17 **EST:** 1989
**SQ FT:** 6,000
**SALES (est):** 1.91MM **Privately Held**
Web: www.lashowroom.com
**SIC: 2339** Jeans: women's, misses', and juniors'

**(P-2800)**
### PIET RETIEF INC
Also Called: Peter Cohen Companies
1914 6th Ave, Los Angeles (90018-1124)
PHONE..................323 732-8312
Peter Cohen, *Pr*
Lee Stuart Cox, *
Anna Cohen, *
**EMP:** 34 **EST:** 1983
**SQ FT:** 4,800
**SALES (est):** 894.56K **Privately Held**
**SIC: 2339** Sportswear, women's

**(P-2801)**
### POINT CONCEPTION INC
Also Called: Kechika
23121 Arroyo Vis Ste A, Rcho Sta Marg (92688-2633)
PHONE..................949 589-6890
Jeff Jung, *CEO*
Jamie Jung, *
Victoria Jung, *
◆ **EMP:** 35 **EST:** 1979
**SQ FT:** 20,000
**SALES (est):** 974.67K **Privately Held**
Web: www.kechika.com
**SIC: 2339** Bathing suits: women's, misses', and juniors'

**(P-2802)**
### RAJ MANUFACTURING LLC
Also Called: Rajswim

## 2339 - Women's And Misses' Outerwear, Nec (P-2803)

2712 Dow Ave, Tustin (92780-7210)
PHONE.....................714 838-3110
Barinder Bhathal, Pr
Jennifer Renish, Contrlr
**EMP:** 25 **EST:** 2006
**SALES (est):** 2.14MM Privately Held
Web: www.rajswim.com
**SIC: 2339** Bathing suits: women's, misses', and juniors'

### (P-2803)
### RAJ MANUFACTURING INC (PA)
Also Called: Athena Pick Your Fit
2712 Dow Ave, Tustin (92780-7210)
PHONE.....................714 838-3110
Raghbir S Bhathal, CEO
◆ **EMP:** 17 **EST:** 1963
**SALES (est):** 4.91MM
**SALES (corp-wide):** 4.91MM Privately Held
Web: www.rajswim.com
**SIC: 2339** Athletic clothing: women's, misses', and juniors'

### (P-2804)
### RHAPSODY CLOTHING INC
Also Called: Epilogue and Arrested
810 E Pico Blvd Ste 24, Los Angeles (90021-2375)
PHONE.....................213 614-8887
Bryan Kang, CEO
Yoon Mi Kang, VP
▲ **EMP:** 65 **EST:** 1994
**SALES (est):** 5.28MM Privately Held
Web: www.rhapsodyclothing.com
**SIC: 2339** Shorts (outerwear): women's, misses', and juniors'

### (P-2805)
### ROTAX INCORPORATED
Also Called: Gamma
2940 Leonis Blvd, Vernon (90058-2916)
P.O. Box 58071 (90058-0071)
PHONE.....................323 589-5999
Arthur Torssien, Pr
Ripsick Kepenekian, *
▲ **EMP:** 40 **EST:** 1993
**SALES (est):** 1.93MM Privately Held
Web: www.rotax1.com
**SIC: 2339** 2329 Women's and misses' outerwear, nec; Men's and boys' sportswear and athletic clothing

### (P-2806)
### SECOND GENERATION INC
Also Called: Fish Bowl
21650 Oxnard St Ste 500, Woodland Hills (91367-4911)
▲ **EMP:** 68 **EST:** 1996
**SQ FT:** 11,000
**SALES (est):** 9.88MM Privately Held
Web: www.bebopjeans.com
**SIC: 2339** 5621 Women's and misses' athletic clothing and sportswear; Women's clothing stores

### (P-2807)
### SFO APPAREL
41 Park Pl # 43, Brisbane (94005-1306)
PHONE.....................415 468-8816
Peter Mou, Pr
▲ **EMP:** 140 **EST:** 1994
**SQ FT:** 20,000
**SALES (est):** 4.55MM Privately Held
**SIC: 2339** Women's and misses' athletic clothing and sportswear

### (P-2808)
### SOLOW
2907 Glenview Ave, Los Angeles (90039-2823)
PHONE.....................323 664-7772
▲ **EMP:** 30 **EST:** 1999
**SQ FT:** 20,000
**SALES (est):** 662.01K Privately Held
**SIC: 2339** Sportswear, women's

### (P-2809)
### SPLITS 59 LLC
527 Colyton St, Los Angeles (90013-2212)
PHONE.....................310 827-5200
**EMP:** 15 **EST:** 2006
**SALES (est):** 1.04MM Privately Held
**SIC: 2339** Women's and misses' athletic clothing and sportswear

### (P-2810)
### ST JOHN KNITS INC (DH)
Also Called: St John Knits
5515 E La Palma Ave Ste 100, Anaheim (92807)
PHONE.....................877 750-1171
Andy Lew, CEO
Andrew Wong, *
Christina Zabat-fran, Sec
**EMP:** 262 **EST:** 1962
**SALES (est):** 34.22MM
**SALES (corp-wide):** 239.44MM Privately Held
Web: www.stjohncafe.com
**SIC: 2339** 2253 2389 Women's and misses' accessories; Knit outerwear mills; Men's miscellaneous accessories
HQ: St. John Knits International, Incorporated
17522 Armstrong Ave
Irvine CA 92614
949 863-1171

### (P-2811)
### ST JOHN KNITS INTL INC (HQ)
Also Called: St John Knits
17522 Armstrong Ave, Irvine (92614)
PHONE.....................949 863-1171
Geoffroy Van Raemdonck, CEO
Glenn Mcmahon, CEO
Bernd Beetz, *
Tammy Storino, *
Bruce Fetter, *
◆ **EMP:** 150 **EST:** 1962
**SQ FT:** 71,100
**SALES (est):** 239.44MM
**SALES (corp-wide):** 239.44MM Privately Held
Web: www.stjohnknits.com
**SIC: 2339** Sportswear, women's
PA: Gray Vestar Investors Llc
17622 Armstrong Ave
949 863-1171

### (P-2812)
### TCJ MANUFACTURING LLC
Also Called: Velvet Heart
2744 E 11th St, Los Angeles (90023)
PHONE.....................213 488-8400
▲ **EMP:** 43 **EST:** 2008
**SALES (est):** 2.84MM Privately Held
Web: www.velvetheart.com
**SIC: 2339** Athletic clothing: women's, misses', and juniors'

### (P-2813)
### TCW TRENDS INC
2886 Columbia St, Torrance (90503-3808)
PHONE.....................310 533-5177
Charanjit Mansingh, CEO
▲ **EMP:** 28 **EST:** 2001
**SQ FT:** 10,000
**SALES (est):** 4.95MM Privately Held
Web: www.tcwusa.com

**SIC: 2339** 2326 5137 Aprons, except rubber or plastic: women's, misses', juniors'; Men's and boy's work clothing; Coordinate sets: women's, children's, and infants'

### (P-2814)
### TEMPTED APPAREL CORP
4516 Loma Vista Ave, Vernon (90058-2602)
PHONE.....................323 859-2480
Don X Ho, CEO
Tsun Kit Luk, *
▲ **EMP:** 58 **EST:** 1996
**SALES (est):** 4.4MM Privately Held
Web: www.temptedapparel.com
**SIC: 2339** Women's and misses' outerwear, nec

### (P-2815)
### THE ORIGINAL CULT INC
Also Called: Lip Service
40 E Verdugo Ave, Burbank (91502-1931)
PHONE.....................323 260-7308
▲ **EMP:** 71
**SIC: 2339** 2311 2399 Women's and misses' outerwear, nec; Men's and boy's suits and coats; Emblems, badges, and insignia

### (P-2816)
### TOAD & CO INTERNATIONAL INC (PA)
Also Called: Toad & Co
2020 Alameda Padre Serra Ste 125, Santa Barbara (93103-1756)
P.O. Box 21508 (93121-1508)
PHONE.....................800 865-8623
Gordon Seabury, Pr
▲ **EMP:** 35 **EST:** 1991
**SQ FT:** 7,000
**SALES (est):** 17.72MM Privately Held
Web: www.toadandco.com
**SIC: 2339** 2329 Women's and misses' athletic clothing and sportswear; Men's and boys' sportswear and athletic clothing

### (P-2817)
### TOSKA INC
Also Called: Tz
1100 S San Pedro St Ste I6, Los Angeles (90015-2387)
PHONE.....................213 746-0088
Nancy Choi, Pr
▲ **EMP:** 15 **EST:** 1998
**SALES (est):** 362.1K Privately Held
Web: www.toska4u.com
**SIC: 2339** 5137 Women's and misses' outerwear, nec; Women's and children's clothing

### (P-2818)
### TREIVUSH INDUSTRIES INC
Also Called: B B Blu
940 W Washington Blvd, Los Angeles (90015-3312)
PHONE.....................213 745-7774
Menachem Treivush, Pr
**EMP:** 100 **EST:** 1983
**SQ FT:** 125,000
**SALES (est):** 2.18MM Privately Held
Web: www.treivush.com
**SIC: 2339** 5137 Sportswear, women's; Sportswear, women's and children's

### (P-2819)
### VICTORY CUSTOM ATHLETICS
2001 Anchor Ct Ste A, Newbury Park (91320-1615)
PHONE.....................818 349-8476
Mike Le Cocq, Pt
Carlos Yniguez, *

**EMP:** 24 **EST:** 1985
**SQ FT:** 5,500
**SALES (est):** 366.54K Privately Held
Web: www.victoryathletics.com
**SIC: 2339** 2329 Athletic clothing: women's, misses', and juniors'; Athletic clothing, except uniforms: men's, youths' and boys'

### (P-2820)
### VICTORY PROFESSIONAL PDTS INC
Also Called: Victory Koredrry
5601 Engineer Dr, Huntington Beach (92649-1123)
PHONE.....................714 887-0621
Marc V Spitaleri, CEO
Marc Spitaleri, *
▲ **EMP:** 28 **EST:** 1979
**SQ FT:** 8,500
**SALES (est):** 3MM Privately Held
Web: www.victorybuiltusa.com
**SIC: 2339** 2329 2393 Women's and misses' athletic clothing and sportswear; Men's and boys' sportswear and athletic clothing; Textile bags

### (P-2821)
### VXB & ORFWID INC
Also Called: Lost & Wander
5041 S Santa Fe Ave Unit B, Vernon (90058-2123)
PHONE.....................213 222-0030
Jillian J Yoo, CEO
**EMP:** 20 **EST:** 2014
**SALES (est):** 2.43MM Privately Held
Web: www.lostandwander.com
**SIC: 2339** Sportswear, women's

### (P-2822)
### W & W CONCEPT INC
Also Called: Perseption
4890 S Alameda St, Vernon (90058-2806)
PHONE.....................323 803-3090
Wonsook Chong, Pr
Jay Joo, *
▲ **EMP:** 55 **EST:** 1996
**SQ FT:** 45,000
**SALES (est):** 8.3MM Privately Held
Web: www.perseption.com
**SIC: 2339** 5137 Sportswear, women's; Women's and children's outerwear

### (P-2823)
### YMI JEANSWEAR INC
1015 Wall St Ste 115, Los Angeles (90015-2392)
PHONE.....................213 746-6681
Ronan Vered, Brnch Mgr
**EMP:** 54
**SALES (corp-wide):** 7.52MM Privately Held
Web: www.ymijeans.com
**SIC: 2339** 2325 Jeans: women's, misses', and juniors'; Men's and boys' jeans and dungarees
PA: Y.M.I Jeanswear, Inc.
1155 S Boyle Ave
323 581-7700

### (P-2824)
### ZOOEY APPAREL INC
1526 Cloverfield Blvd Ste C, Santa Monica (90404-3772)
PHONE.....................310 315-2880
Alice Heller, *
Viet D.o.s., COO
**EMP:** 24 **EST:** 2003
**SQ FT:** 5,000
**SALES (est):** 285.74K Privately Held

SIC: 2339 Women's and misses' outerwear, nec

**(P-2825)**
**ZOOT SPORTS INC**
2719 Loker Ave W Ste B, Carlsbad (92010-6679)
PHONE.................................760 681-3587
Erik Vervloet, Pr
EMP: 22 EST: 2000
SALES (est): 753.52K
SALES (corp-wide): 116.17MM Privately Held
Web: www.zootsports.com
SIC: 2339 2329 Athletic clothing: women's, misses', and juniors'; Men's and boys' sportswear and athletic clothing
PA: Manifattura Valcismon Spa
Via Guglielmo Marconi 81/83
04395711

## 2341 Women's And Children's Underwear

**(P-2826)**
**402 SHOES INC**
Also Called: Trashy Lingerie
402 N La Cienega Blvd, West Hollywood (90048-1907)
PHONE.................................323 655-5437
Mitchell Shrier, Pr
Tracy Shrier, Sec
EMP: 23 EST: 1974
SQ FT: 6,000
SALES (est): 832.64K Privately Held
Web: www.trashy.com
SIC: 2341 5632 2322 Women's and children's nightwear; Lingerie and corsets (underwear); Men's and boy's underwear and nightwear

**(P-2827)**
**AFR APPAREL INTERNATIONAL INC**
Also Called: Parisa Lingerie & Swim Wear
25365 Prado De La Felicidad, Calabasas (91302-3652)
PHONE.................................818 773-5000
Amir Moghadam, Pr
Brenda J Moghadam, *
▲ EMP: 60 EST: 1992
SALES (est): 25MM Privately Held
Web: www.parisausa.com
SIC: 2341 2342 2369 5137 Women's and children's nightwear; Bras, girdles, and allied garments; Bathing suits and swimwear: girls', children's, and infants'; Lingerie

**(P-2828)**
**CHARLES KOMAR & SONS INC**
Also Called: Komar Distribution Services
11850 Riverside Dr, Jurupa Valley (91752-1001)
PHONE.................................951 934-1377
Lisa Casillas, Brnch Mgr
EMP: 307
SALES (corp-wide): 359.75MM Privately Held
Web: www.komarbrands.com
SIC: 2341 Women's and children's underwear
PA: Charles Komar & Sons, Inc.
90 Hudson St Fl 9
212 725-1500

**(P-2829)**
**DELTA GALIL USA INC**
777 S Alameda St Fl 3, Los Angeles (90021-1657)
PHONE.................................213 488-4859
EMP: 305
Web: www.deltagalil.com
SIC: 2341 Women's and children's undergarments
HQ: Delta Galil Usa Inc.
1 Harmon Plz Fl 5
Secaucus NJ 07094
201 902-0055

**(P-2830)**
**GUESS INC (PA)**
Also Called: Guess
1444 S Alameda St, Los Angeles (90021-2433)
PHONE.................................213 765-3100
Carlos Alberini, CEO
Alex Yemenidjian, Non-Executive Chairman of the Board*
Paul Marciano, CCO*
Dennis Secor, Interim Chief Financial Officer
Fabrice Benarouche, CAO
◆ EMP: 700 EST: 1981
SQ FT: 341,700
SALES (est): 2.78B
SALES (corp-wide): 2.78B Publicly Held
Web: www.guess.com
SIC: 2341 2325 2369 6794 Women's and children's underwear; Men's and boy's trousers and slacks; Girl's and children's outerwear, nec; Copyright buying and licensing

**(P-2831)**
**HONEST COMPANY INC (PA)**
Also Called: HONEST
12130 Millennium Ste 500, Los Angeles (90094-2946)
PHONE.................................310 917-9199
Nikolaos Vlahos, CEO
Carla Vernon, CEO
James D White, Ch Bd
Rick Rexing, CRO
▲ EMP: 156 EST: 2011
SQ FT: 46,518
SALES (est): 344.37MM Publicly Held
Web: www.honest.com
SIC: 2341 2833 5961 Panties: women's, misses, children's, and infants'; Vitamins, natural or synthetic: bulk, uncompounded; Catalog and mail-order houses

**(P-2832)**
**HONEYDEW APPAREL GROUP INC**
20830 Dearborn St, Chatsworth (91311-5915)
PHONE.................................818 717-9717
Benny Zafrani, CEO
Jim Zafrani, Sec
Liron Zafrani, Dir
▲ EMP: 15 EST: 2011
SALES (est): 1.73MM Privately Held
Web: www.honeydewintimates.com
SIC: 2341 Women's and children's undergarments

**(P-2833)**
**NATIONAL CORSET SUPPLY HOUSE (PA)**
Also Called: Louden Madelon
3240 E 26th St, Vernon (90058-8008)
PHONE.................................323 261-0265
Roy Schlobohm, CEO
◆ EMP: 65 EST: 1948
SQ FT: 25,000
SALES (est): 6.24MM
SALES (corp-wide): 6.24MM Privately Held
Web: www.shirleyofhollywood.com
SIC: 2341 5137 Women's and children's undergarments; Corsets

**(P-2834)**
**SELECTRA INDUSTRIES CORP**
5166 Alcoa Ave, Vernon (90058-3716)
PHONE.................................323 581-8500
John Neman, Pr
Mark Neman, *
Malek Neman, *
▲ EMP: 85 EST: 2000
SQ FT: 30,000
SALES (est): 4.77MM Privately Held
Web: www.selectraindustries.com
SIC: 2341 2339 Women's and children's underwear; Sportswear, women's

**(P-2835)**
**SPICY CHIX INC**
1753 E 21st St, Los Angeles (90058-1006)
PHONE.................................562 293-7690
Kyoung Frazire, Pr
Cecy Mendoza, Contrlr
EMP: 15 EST: 2021
SALES (est): 1.28MM Privately Held
SIC: 2341 Women's and children's undergarments

## 2342 Bras, Girdles, And Allied Garments

**(P-2836)**
**BRAGEL INTERNATIONAL INC**
Also Called: Brava
3383 Pomona Blvd, Pomona (91768-3297)
PHONE.................................909 598-8808
Clotilde Chen, CEO
Alice Chen, *
Kenny Chen, Stockholder*
▲ EMP: 45 EST: 1989
SQ FT: 30,000
SALES (est): 5.03MM Privately Held
Web: www.bragel.com
SIC: 2342 Brassieres

**(P-2837)**
**FOH GROUP INC (PA)**
Also Called: Fredericks.com
6255 W Sunset Blvd Ste 2212, Los Angeles (90028-7403)
PHONE.................................310 815-9000
◆ EMP: 38 EST: 1935
SQ FT: 23,000
SALES (est): 24.88MM
SALES (corp-wide): 24.88MM Privately Held
SIC: 2342 2339 5621 5632 Bras, girdles, and allied garments; Women's and misses' outerwear, nec; Women's clothing stores; Women's accessory and specialty stores

**(P-2838)**
**METRIC PRODUCTS INC (PA)**
4630 Leahy St, Culver City (90232-3515)
PHONE.................................310 815-9000
Shirley Magidson, Pr
Debra Magidson, Sec
Rita Haft, VP
▲ EMP: 20 EST: 1948
SQ FT: 25,000
SALES (est): 7.94MM
SALES (corp-wide): 7.94MM Privately Held
Web: www.metric-products.com
SIC: 2342 3496 Brassieres; Fabrics, woven wire

**(P-2839)**
**NOBBE ORTHOPEDICS INC**
3010 State St, Santa Barbara (93105-3304)
PHONE.................................805 687-7508
Ralph W Nobbe, Pr
Rolf Schiefel, *
Erwin Nobbe, *
◆ EMP: 37 EST: 1964
SQ FT: 2,850
SALES (est): 2.49MM
SALES (corp-wide): 1.12B Privately Held
Web: www.nobbeorthopedics.com
SIC: 2342 5999 Corsets and allied garments; Orthopedic and prosthesis applications
PA: Hanger, Inc.
10910 Domain Dr Ste 300
512 777-3800

## 2353 Hats, Caps, And Millinery

**(P-2840)**
**AGRON INC (PA)**
2440 S Sepulveda Blvd Ste 201, Los Angeles (90064-1748)
PHONE.................................310 473-7223
Wade Siegel, Pr
Anton Schiff, *
◆ EMP: 57 EST: 1989
SQ FT: 10,000
SALES (est): 9.84MM Privately Held
Web: sales.agron.com
SIC: 2353 2393 3949 3171 Hats, caps, and millinery; Canvas bags; Sporting and athletic goods, nec; Women's handbags and purses

**(P-2841)**
**AUGUST HAT COMPANY INC (PA)**
Also Called: August Accessories
2021 Calle Yucca, Thousand Oaks (91360-2257)
PHONE.................................805 983-4651
Roque Valladares, Pr
Ann Valladares, Sec
▲ EMP: 23 EST: 1990
SALES (est): 1.66MM Privately Held
SIC: 2353 2381 2339 Hats, caps, and millinery; Fabric dress and work gloves; Scarves, hoods, headbands, etc.: women's

**(P-2842)**
**CALI-FAME LOS ANGELES INC**
Also Called: Kennedy Athletics
20934 S Santa Fe Ave, Carson (90810-1131)
PHONE.................................310 747-5263
Michael G Kennedy, CEO
Brian Kennedy, *
Timothy Kennedy, *
Linelle Kennedy, *
▲ EMP: 92 EST: 1925
SQ FT: 30,000
SALES (est): 9.11MM Privately Held
Web: www.caliheadwear.com
SIC: 2353 Uniform hats and caps

**(P-2843)**
**HEADMASTER INC (PA)**
3000 S Croddy Way, Santa Ana (92704-6305)
PHONE.................................714 556-5244
Dong J Park, Pr
Jimmy J Park, VP
◆ EMP: 16 EST: 1985
SQ FT: 35,000
SALES (est): 580.13K
SALES (corp-wide): 580.13K Privately Held

# 2353 - Hats, Caps, And Millinery (P-2844)

Web: www.headmaster.com
SIC: 2353 Hats: cloth, straw, and felt

**(P-2844)**
**HEMLOCK HAT COMPANY**
2793 Loker Ave W, Carlsbad (92010-6601)
PHONE.................................888 490-6440
Anthony Lora, Pr
EMP: 22 EST: 2017
SALES (est): 1.36MM **Privately Held**
Web: www.hemlockhatco.com
SIC: 2353 Hats: cloth, straw, and felt

**(P-2845)**
**LEGENDARY HOLDINGS INC**
Also Called: Legendary Headwear
2295 Paseo De Las Americas Ste 19, San Diego (92154-7909)
PHONE.................................619 872-6100
◆ EMP: 38
Web: www.legendaryholdings.com
SIC: 2353 Hats, caps, and millinery

**(P-2846)**
**MAGIC APPAREL GROUP INC**
Also Called: Magic Apparel & Magic Headwear
1100 W Walnut St, Compton (90220-5114)
P.O. Box 2308 (90274-8308)
PHONE.................................310 223-4000
◆ EMP: 30
SIC: 2353 Baseball caps

**(P-2847)**
**NIKE INC**
Nike
20001 Ellipse, Foothill Ranch (92610-3001)
PHONE.................................949 616-4042
Matt Ross, Mgr
EMP: 17
SALES (corp-wide): 51.36B **Publicly Held**
Web: www.nike.com
SIC: 2353 5137 5136 Baseball caps; Women's and children's clothing; Men's and boy's clothing
PA: Nike, Inc.
   1 Sw Bowerman Dr
   503 671-6453

**(P-2848)**
**ONE HAT ONE HAND LLC**
1335 Yosemite Ave, San Francisco (94124-3319)
PHONE.................................415 822-2020
Marcus Guillard, *
EMP: 42 EST: 2008
SQ FT: 19,000
SALES (est): 5.59MM **Privately Held**
Web: www.onehatonehand.com
SIC: 2353 Hats, caps, and millinery

**(P-2849)**
**PETER GRIMM LTD**
Also Called: Gold Coast Sunwear
550 Rancheros Dr, San Marcos (92069-2911)
PHONE.................................800 664-4287
Peter Niedermeyer, Pr
Glen Walker, VP
Peter Grimm, Prin
◆ EMP: 20 EST: 1989
SQ FT: 6,000
SALES (est): 4.35MM **Privately Held**
Web: www.petergrimm.com
SIC: 2353 5136 Hats, caps, and millinery; Hats, men's and boys'

## 2361 Girl's And Children's Dresses, Blouses

**(P-2850)**
**A THANKS MILLION INC**
8195 Mercury Ct Ste 140, San Diego (92111-1231)
PHONE.................................858 432-7744
Lowell J Cohen, CEO
Peter Mouostaos, Pr
Ian Barrow, CFO
◆ EMP: 19 EST: 2003
SALES (est): 1.68MM **Privately Held**
Web: www.justaddakid.com
SIC: 2361 2329 T-shirts and tops: girls', children's, and infants'; Shirt and slack suits: men's, youths', and boys'

**(P-2851)**
**ALL ACCESS APPAREL INC (PA)**
Also Called: Self Esteem
1515 Gage Rd, Montebello (90640-6613)
PHONE.................................323 889-4300
Richard Claremen, CEO
Andrea Rankin, *
Michael Conway, *
◆ EMP: 130 EST: 1997
SQ FT: 122,000
SALES (est): 17.6MM **Privately Held**
Web: www.selfesteemclothing.com
SIC: 2361 2335 2331 Girl's and children's dresses, blouses; Women's, junior's, and misses' dresses; Women's and misses' blouses and shirts

**(P-2852)**
**AST SPORTSWEAR INC (PA)**
2701 E Imperial Hwy, Brea (92821-6713)
P.O. Box 17219 (92817-7219)
PHONE.................................714 223-2030
Shoaib Dadabhoy, CEO
Taher Dadabhoy, Sec
Abdul Rashid, COO
▲ EMP: 85 EST: 1995
SQ FT: 42,000
SALES (est): 18.52MM **Privately Held**
Web: www.astsportswear.com
SIC: 2361 2331 5699 T-shirts and tops: girls', children's, and infants'; T-shirts and tops, women's: made from purchased materials; Sports apparel

**(P-2853)**
**EVY OF CALIFORNIA INC**
2042 Garfield Ave, Commerce (90040-1804)
P.O. Box 812030 (90081-0018)
PHONE.................................213 746-4647
▲ EMP: 140
Web: www.evy.com
SIC: 2361 2369 Dresses: girls', children's, and infants'; Warm-up, jogging, and sweat suits: girls' and children's

**(P-2854)**
**JESSICA MCCLINTOCK INC (PA)**
2307 Bdwy St, San Francisco (94115-1291)
PHONE.................................415 553-8200
Jessica Mc Clintock, Pr
▲ EMP: 150 EST: 1970
SQ FT: 120,000
SALES (est): 24.61MM
SALES (corp-wide): 24.61MM **Privately Held**
Web: www.jessicamcclintock.com
SIC: 2361 2335 2844 Dresses: girls', children's, and infants'; Women's, junior's, and misses' dresses; Perfumes, natural or synthetic

**(P-2855)**
**KWDZ MANUFACTURING LLC (PA)**
337 S Anderson St, Los Angeles (90033-3742)
PHONE.................................323 526-3526
Gene Bonilla, *
◆ EMP: 75 EST: 1999
SQ FT: 45,000
SALES (est): 1.7MM
SALES (corp-wide): 1.7MM **Privately Held**
Web: www.calfashion.org
SIC: 2361 T-shirts and tops: girls', children's, and infants'

**(P-2856)**
**LEIGH JERRY CALIFORNIA INC (PA)**
Also Called: Jerry Leigh Entertainment AP
7860 Nelson Rd, Van Nuys (91402-6044)
PHONE.................................818 909-6200
Andrew Leigh, CEO
Barbara Leigh, *
◆ EMP: 245 EST: 1962
SQ FT: 40,000
SALES (est): 95.93MM
SALES (corp-wide): 95.93MM **Privately Held**
Web: www.jerryleigh.com
SIC: 2361 5137 Girl's and children's dresses, blouses; Sportswear, women's and children's

**(P-2857)**
**MISYD CORP (PA)**
Also Called: Ruby Rox
30 Fremont Pl, Los Angeles (90005-3858)
PHONE.................................213 742-1800
Robert Borman, Pr
Joseph Hanasab, *
▲ EMP: 79 EST: 1993
SQ FT: 35,000
SALES (est): 3.02MM **Privately Held**
Web: www.misyd.com
SIC: 2361 Shirts: girls', children's, and infants'

## 2369 Girl's And Children's Outerwear, Nec

**(P-2858)**
**BABY GUESS INC**
Also Called: Guess
1444 S Alameda St, Los Angeles (90021-2433)
PHONE.................................213 765-3100
Maurice Marciano, Ch Bd
EMP: 22 EST: 1999
SALES (est): 1.33MM
SALES (corp-wide): 2.78B **Publicly Held**
Web: www.guess.com
SIC: 2369 Jackets: girls', children's, and infants'
PA: Guess , Inc.
   1444 S Alameda St
   213 765-3100

**(P-2859)**
**BODYWAVES INC (PA)**
Also Called: Aks, Amy K Su
12362 Knott St, Garden Grove (92841-2802)
PHONE.................................714 898-9900
EMP: 47 EST: 1986
SALES (est): 3.16MM
SALES (corp-wide): 3.16MM **Privately Held**
Web: www.elleven.com

SIC: 2369 2335 2331 2325 Girl's and children's outerwear, nec; Dresses,paper, cut and sewn; Women's and misses' blouses and shirts; Men's and boy's trousers and slacks

**(P-2860)**
**FRANKIES BIKINIS LLC**
Also Called: Frankies Bikinis
4030 Del Rey Ave, Venice (90292-5602)
PHONE.................................323 354-4133
Francheska Aiello, CEO
Miriam Aiello, *
Frank Messmann, *
EMP: 36 EST: 2013
SALES (est): 5.68MM **Privately Held**
Web: www.frankiesbikinis.com
SIC: 2369 Bathing suits and swimwear: girls', children's, and infants'

**(P-2861)**
**GRACING BRAND MANAGEMENT INC**
Also Called: Gbm
1108 W Valley Blvd Ste 660, Alhambra (91803)
PHONE.................................626 297-2472
Sabrina Yam, CEO
Vico Yam, *
EMP: 492 EST: 2017
SALES (est): 1.34MM **Privately Held**
SIC: 2369 5137 5131 2211 Bathing suits and swimwear: girls', children's, and infants'; Swimsuits: women's, children's, and infants' ; Trimmings, apparel; Apparel and outerwear fabrics, cotton

**(P-2862)**
**IMPERIAL GARMENT INDS INC**
Also Called: United Garment
831 International Blvd, Oakland (94606-3628)
PHONE.................................510 834-7771
Sin Man Tang, Pr
Irene Cheung, VP
Pui Ying S Tang, Sec
Patrick Cheung, Treas
EMP: 15 EST: 1985
SQ FT: 10,000
SALES (est): 190.5K **Privately Held**
SIC: 2369 2339 Girl's and children's outerwear, nec; Women's and misses' outerwear, nec

**(P-2863)**
**KHARMA CLOTHING LLC**
Also Called: Lezat
5066 W Jefferson Blvd, Los Angeles (90016-3925)
PHONE.................................323 494-7705
Jaleh Factor, Pr
EMP: 15 EST: 2020
SALES (est): 105.58K **Privately Held**
SIC: 2369 5621 2389 5137 Girl's and children's outerwear, nec; Ready-to-wear apparel, women's; Apparel and accessories, nec; Apparel belts, women's and children's

**(P-2864)**
**MACK & REISS INC**
Also Called: Biscotti and Kate Mack
5601 San Leandro St Ste 3, Oakland (94621-4433)
PHONE.................................510 434-9122
Bernadette Reiss, Pr
Robert Mack, *
▲ EMP: 85 EST: 1986
SQ FT: 75,000
SALES (est): 2.31MM **Privately Held**

## PRODUCTS & SERVICES SECTION
### 2387 - Apparel Belts (P-2885)

Web: www.biscottiinc.com
SIC: 2369 Girl's and children's outerwear, nec

**(P-2865)**
**MANHATTAN BEACHWEAR LLC (PA)**
10855 Business Center Dr Ste C, Cypress (90630-5252)
PHONE..............................657 384-2110
EMP: 65 EST: 2020
SALES (est): 24.1MM
SALES (corp-wide): 24.1MM Privately Held
Web: www.mbwswim.com
SIC: 2369 2329 Bathing suits and swimwear: girls', children's, and infants'; Bathing suits and swimwear: men's and boys'

**(P-2866)**
**THE LUNADA BAY CORPORATION (PA)**
Also Called: Becca
2000 E Winston Rd, Anaheim (92806-5546)
PHONE..............................714 490-1313
▲ EMP: 49 EST: 1980
SALES (est): 12.73MM
SALES (corp-wide): 12.73MM Privately Held
Web: www.lunadabayswim.com
SIC: 2369 Bathing suits and swimwear: girls', children's, and infants'

**(P-2867)**
**TRLG CORPORATE HOLDINGS LLC (PA)**
1888 Rosecrans Ave, Manhattan Beach (90266-3712)
PHONE..............................323 266-3072
Dalli Snyder, CFO
Alan Weiss, VP
Eugene Davis, Dir
Steve Perrella, Dir
◆ EMP: 101 EST: 2017
SQ FT: 119,000
SALES (est): 350MM
SALES (corp-wide): 350MM Privately Held
Web: deluxeductcleaners.yolasite.com
SIC: 2369 2325 2339 Girl's and children's outerwear, nec; Men's and boy's trousers and slacks; Women's and misses' outerwear, nec

**(P-2868)**
**UN DEUX TROIS INC (PA)**
2301 E 7th St, Los Angeles (90023-1043)
PHONE..............................323 588-1067
Colin Shorkend, Pr
Cydney Shorkend, *
Beverly Shorkend, *
Erin Shorkend, *
▲ EMP: 24 EST: 1988
SALES (est): 4.97MM Privately Held
Web: www.udtfashion.com
SIC: 2369 5137 Girl's and children's outerwear, nec; Fur clothing, women's and children's

**(P-2869)**
**VESTURE GROUP INCORPORATED**
Also Called: Pinky Los Angeles
3405 W Pacific Ave, Burbank (91505-1555)
PHONE..............................818 842-0200
Robert Galishoff, CEO
Gayle Lupacchini, *
▲ EMP: 72 EST: 2007
SQ FT: 3,500
SALES (est): 9.41MM Privately Held
Web: www.vesturegroupinc.com
SIC: 2369 2335 Skirts: girls', children's, and infants'; Women's, junior's, and misses' dresses

### 2371 Fur Goods

**(P-2870)**
**FUR ACCENTS LLC**
349 W Grove Ave, Orange (92865-3205)
PHONE..............................714 403-5286
Steven Goodyear, Managing Member
EMP: 15 EST: 2016
SALES (est): 300.84K Privately Held
Web: www.furaccents.com
SIC: 2371 5632 Fur goods; Fur apparel

### 2381 Fabric Dress And Work Gloves

**(P-2871)**
**ORBITA CORP (PA)**
Also Called: Estam
1136 Crocker St, Los Angeles (90021-2014)
PHONE..............................213 746-4783
Dae Seung Park, Pr
▲ EMP: 15 EST: 1997
SALES (est): 1.31MM Privately Held
SIC: 2381 Fabric dress and work gloves

**(P-2872)**
**SVO ENTERPRISE LLC**
9854 Baldwin Pl, El Monte (91731-2202)
PHONE..............................626 406-4770
Scott Streitfld C.p.a., Admn
EMP: 25 EST: 2013
SALES (est): 498.37K Privately Held
Web: www.svoenterprises.com
SIC: 2381 Fabric dress and work gloves

### 2384 Robes And Dressing Gowns

**(P-2873)**
**TERRY TOWN CORPORATION**
8851 Kerns St Ste 100, San Diego (92154-6298)
PHONE..............................619 421-5354
Saip Ereren, CEO
◆ EMP: 100 EST: 1988
SALES (est): 33.19MM Privately Held
Web: www.terrytown.com
SIC: 2384 5023 5719 Bathrobes, men's and women's: made from purchased materials; Linens and towels; Bedding (sheets, blankets, spreads, and pillows)

### 2386 Leather And Sheep-lined Clothing

**(P-2874)**
**AJG INC**
Also Called: Astrologie California
7220 E Slauson Ave, Commerce (90040-3625)
PHONE..............................323 346-0171
Angelo Ghailian, CEO
▲ EMP: 20 EST: 2003
SALES (est): 2.1MM Privately Held
Web: www.ajg.com
SIC: 2386 5131 5199 Leather and sheep-lined clothing; Knit fabrics; Fabrics, yarns, and knit goods

**(P-2875)**
**CHROME HEARTS LLC (PA)**
Also Called: Chrome Hearts
915 N Mansfield Ave, Los Angeles (90038-2311)
PHONE..............................323 957-7544
Richard Stark, Managing Member
Robert Bowman, *
Mario D Lejtman, *
▲ EMP: 50 EST: 2005
SQ FT: 50,000
SALES (est): 21.87MM
SALES (corp-wide): 21.87MM Privately Held
Web: www.chromehearts.com
SIC: 2386 3911 2511 2371 Leather and sheep-lined clothing; Jewelry, precious metal; Wood household furniture; Fur goods

**(P-2876)**
**CORONADO LEATHER CO INC**
1961 Main St, San Diego (92113-2129)
PHONE..............................619 238-0265
Brent Laulom, Pr
EMP: 15 EST: 1981
SQ FT: 2,100
SALES (est): 907.84K Privately Held
Web: www.coronadoleather.com
SIC: 2386 3111 Garments, leather; Handbag leather

**(P-2877)**
**DISTINCTIVE INDS TEXAS INC**
Also Called: Roadwire Distinctive Inds
10618 Shoemaker Ave, Santa Fe Springs (90670-4038)
PHONE..............................512 491-3500
Dwight Forrester, Prin
EMP: 22
Web: www.distinctiveindustries.com
SIC: 2386 Leather and sheep-lined clothing
PA: Distinctive Industries Of Texas, Inc. 4516 Seton Center Pkwy # 13

**(P-2878)**
**DISTINCTIVE INDS TEXAS INC**
9419 Ann St, Santa Fe Springs (90670-2613)
PHONE..............................323 889-5766
Dwight Forrester, Brnch Mgr
EMP: 30
Web: www.distinctiveindustries.com
SIC: 2386 Coats and jackets, leather and sheep-lined
PA: Distinctive Industries Of Texas, Inc. 4516 Seton Center Pkwy # 13

**(P-2879)**
**FLIGHT SUITS**
Also Called: Gibson & Barnes
1900 Weld Blvd Ste 140, El Cajon (92020-0503)
PHONE..............................619 440-2700
▲ EMP: 100 EST: 1977
SALES (est): 15.33MM Privately Held
Web: www.gibson-barnes.com
SIC: 2386 Coats and jackets, leather and sheep-lined

**(P-2880)**
**GB SPORT SF LLC**
Also Called: Golden Bear Sportswear
200 Potrero Ave, San Francisco (94103-4815)
PHONE..............................415 863-6171
Ronald Gilmere, Managing Member
EMP: 20 EST: 2018
SALES (est): 718.49K Privately Held
Web: www.goldenbearsportswear.com

SIC: 2386 Leather and sheep-lined clothing

**(P-2881)**
**KRASNES INC**
Also Called: Cop Shopper
2222 Commercial St, San Diego (92113-1111)
PHONE..............................619 232-2066
Jerry Krasne, Pr
Gail Wilson, *
Kurt Krasne, *
▲ EMP: 90 EST: 1947
SQ FT: 28,000
SALES (est): 1.51MM Privately Held
Web: www.triplek.com
SIC: 2386 3484 Leather and sheep-lined clothing; Small arms

**(P-2882)**
**MR S LEATHER**
Also Called: Fetters U.S.A.
385 8th St, San Francisco (94103-4423)
PHONE..............................415 863-7764
Richard Hunter, Pr
Tchukon Hunter, *
▲ EMP: 45 EST: 1979
SQ FT: 15,000
SALES (est): 4.98MM Privately Held
Web: www.mr-s-leather.com
SIC: 2386 5699 5136 Garments, leather; Leather garments; Men's and boy's clothing

**(P-2883)**
**SCULLY SPORTSWEAR INC (PA)**
Also Called: Scully Leather Wear
1701 Pacific Ave, Oxnard (93033-1879)
PHONE..............................805 483-6339
Daniel Scully Iii, CEO
Robert Swink, *
▲ EMP: 50 EST: 1906
SQ FT: 80,000
SALES (est): 10.39MM
SALES (corp-wide): 10.39MM Privately Held
Web: www.scullyleather.com
SIC: 2386 5099 Coats and jackets, leather and sheep-lined; Luggage

### 2387 Apparel Belts

**(P-2884)**
**SHIRINIAN-SHAW INC**
Also Called: Lejon Tulliani
1229 Railroad St, Corona (92882-1838)
PHONE..............................951 736-1229
John W Shirinian, Pr
Jack Shirinian, *
▲ EMP: 40 EST: 1968
SQ FT: 33,000
SALES (est): 10.68MM Privately Held
Web: www.lejon.com
SIC: 2387 3172 Apparel belts; Personal leather goods, nec

**(P-2885)**
**STREETS AHEAD INC**
Also Called: Hyde
5510 S Soto St Unit B, Vernon (90058-3623)
PHONE..............................323 277-0860
David Sack, CEO
Michael Fructuoso, Contrlr
▲ EMP: 20 EST: 1982
SQ FT: 28,000
SALES (est): 1.17MM Privately Held
Web: www.streetsaheadinc.com
SIC: 2387 Apparel belts

# 2387 - Apparel Belts (P-2886)

## PRODUCTS & SERVICES SECTION

**(P-2886)**
**WESTSIDE ACCESSORIES INC (PA)**
8920 Vernon Ave Ste 128, Montclair (91763-1663)
PHONE..................626 858-5452
Carol Cantagallo, Pr
▲ EMP: 17 EST: 1991
SALES (est): 1.16MM Privately Held
Web: www.belts-etc.com
SIC: 2387 Apparel belts

## 2389 Apparel And Accessories, Nec

**(P-2887)**
**ACADEMIC CH CHOIR GWNS MFG INC**
Also Called: Academic Cap & Gown
8944 Mason Ave, Chatsworth (91311-6107)
PHONE..................818 886-8697
TOLL FREE: 800
Michael Cronan, Pr
Mike Cronan, *
Evelyn Cronan, *
Mark Cronan, *
◆ EMP: 30 EST: 1947
SQ FT: 13,000
SALES (est): 1.34MM Privately Held
Web: www.academicapparel.com
SIC: 2389 2353 Clergymen's vestments; Hats, caps, and millinery

**(P-2888)**
**AHS TRINITY GROUP INC (PA)**
11041 Vanowen St, North Hollywood (91605-6314)
PHONE..................818 508-2105
Eddie Marks, Pr
Bill Haber, CFO
EMP: 25 EST: 1989
SALES (est): 8.87MM Privately Held
Web: www.westerncostume.com
SIC: 2389 7299 6512 Costumes; Costume rental; Commercial and industrial building operation

**(P-2889)**
**ANAYA BROTHERS CUTTING LLC**
3130 Leonis Blvd, Vernon (90058-3012)
PHONE..................323 582-5758
Martin Anaya Junior, Owner
EMP: 90
SALES (est): 4.82MM Privately Held
SIC: 2389 Apparel and accessories, nec

**(P-2890)**
**APP WINDDOWN LLC (HQ)**
Also Called: American Apparel
747 Warehouse St, Los Angeles (90021-1106)
P.O. Box 5129 (39047-5129)
◆ EMP: 141 EST: 2005
SALES (est): 45.89MM
SALES (corp-wide): 3.2B Privately Held
Web: www.greenmanairductcleaning.com
SIC: 2389 2311 2331 Men's miscellaneous accessories; Men's and boy's suits and coats; Women's and misses' blouses and shirts
PA: Les Vetements De Sport Gildan Inc
600 Boul De Maisonneuve O 33eme Etage
514 735-2023

**(P-2891)**
**B2 APPAREL INC**
Also Called: Bb Apparel
219 E 32nd St, Los Angeles (90011-1917)
PHONE..................323 233-0044
Scott Lee, Pr
EMP: 15 EST: 2000
SQ FT: 20,000
SALES (est): 1.53MM Privately Held
Web: www.gusbinc.com
SIC: 2389 Footlets

**(P-2892)**
**CALIFRNIA CSTUME CLLCTIONS INC (PA)**
Also Called: California Costume Int'l
210 S Anderson St, Los Angeles (90033-3205)
PHONE..................323 262-8383
Tak Kwan Woo, CEO
Peter Woo, Pr
Charles C K Woo, Sec
◆ EMP: 280 EST: 1992
SQ FT: 300,000
SALES (est): 24.56MM Privately Held
Web: www.californiacostumes.com
SIC: 2389 5699 Costumes; Costumes, masquerade or theatrical

**(P-2893)**
**CHARADES LLC**
20579 Valley Blvd, Walnut (91789-2730)
PHONE..................626 435-0077
▲ EMP: 240 EST: 2000
SALES (est): 2MM Privately Held
Web: www.rubies.com
SIC: 2389 Costumes

**(P-2894)**
**CONQUER NATION INC**
Also Called: Conquer Nation Staffing
2651 E 12th St, Los Angeles (90023-2618)
PHONE..................310 651-5555
Jerry Saeedian, CEO
EMP: 142 EST: 2022
SALES (est): 1.99MM Privately Held
Web: www.conquernation.com
SIC: 2389 Hospital gowns

**(P-2895)**
**CUSTOM CHARACTERS INC**
621 Thompson Ave, Glendale (91201-2032)
PHONE..................818 507-5940
Ryan Lin Rhodes, Pr
Drew Jonathan Herron, CFO
EMP: 18 EST: 1985
SQ FT: 5,200
SALES (est): 1.88MM Privately Held
Web: www.customcharacters.com
SIC: 2389 3999 Costumes; Stage hardware and equipment, except lighting

**(P-2896)**
**DECKERS OUTDOOR CORPORATION (PA)**
Also Called: DECKERS
250 Coromar Dr, Goleta (93117-3697)
PHONE..................805 967-7611
Stefano Caroti, Pr
Michael F Devine Iii, Ch Bd
Steven J Fasching, CFO
Angela Ogbechie, Chief Supply Chain Officer
Thomas Garcia, Chief
▲ EMP: 2758 EST: 1975
SALES (est): 4.29B
SALES (corp-wide): 4.29B Publicly Held
Web: www.deckers.com

SIC: 2389 2339 3021 Men's miscellaneous accessories; Women's and misses' accessories; Sandals, rubber

**(P-2897)**
**DIAMOND COLLECTION LLC**
Also Called: Charades
20579 Valley Blvd, Walnut (91789)
PHONE..................626 435-0077
EMP: 30 EST: 2016
SALES (est): 400.89K Privately Held
SIC: 2389 5137 Costumes; Dresses

**(P-2898)**
**DIANA DID-IT DESIGNS INC**
Also Called: Princess Paradise
20579 Valley Blvd, Walnut (91789-2730)
PHONE..................970 226-5062
Diana Clements, Pr
Brad Clements, *
◆ EMP: 26 EST: 1980
SALES (est): 351.16K Privately Held
Web: www.rubies.com
SIC: 2389 7299 Costumes; Costume rental

**(P-2899)**
**DISGUISE INC (HQ)**
12120 Kear Pl, Poway (92064-7132)
PHONE..................858 391-3600
Stephen Berman, CEO
Benoit Pousset, Pr
◆ EMP: 69 EST: 1987
SQ FT: 206,000
SALES (est): 27.92MM Publicly Held
Web: www.disguise.com
SIC: 2389 7299 Costumes; Costume rental
PA: Jakks Pacific, Inc.
2951 28th St

**(P-2900)**
**GILLI INC**
1100 S San Pedro St Ste C07, Los Angeles (90015-2385)
PHONE..................213 744-9808
Hae Yun Suh, Brnch Mgr
EMP: 18
SALES (corp-wide): 13.44MM Privately Held
Web: www.gilliclothing.com
SIC: 2389 5137 Uniforms and vestments; Women's and children's clothing
PA: Gilli, Inc.
2939 Bandini Blvd
323 235-3722

**(P-2901)**
**HAVUNI LLC ✪**
2701 S Harcourt Ave, Los Angeles (90016)
PHONE..................917 428-1183
EMP: 22 EST: 2023
SALES (est): 379.45K Privately Held
SIC: 2389 Apparel and accessories, nec

**(P-2902)**
**IMMORTAL MASKS INC**
261 W Allen Ave, San Dimas (91773-1439)
PHONE..................909 599-5391
EMP: 20 EST: 2014
SALES (est): 672.47K Privately Held
Web: www.immortalmasks.com
SIC: 2389 Masquerade costumes

**(P-2903)**
**LAVA ATHLETICA INC**
Also Called: Wholesale and Retail
9661 Garvey Ave Ste 112-528, South El Monte (91733-4634)
PHONE..................909 859-1287
Jian Cai, CEO

EMP: 16 EST: 2019
SALES (est): 508.35K Privately Held
SIC: 2389 Apparel and accessories, nec

**(P-2904)**
**LOS ANGELES APPAREL INC (PA)**
Also Called: La Apparel
1020 E 59th St, Los Angeles (90001-1010)
PHONE..................213 275-3120
Dov Charney, CEO
Morris Charney, Dir
David Nisenbaum, Dir
EMP: 70 EST: 2016
SALES (est): 33.41MM
SALES (corp-wide): 33.41MM Privately Held
Web: www.losangelesapparel.net
SIC: 2389 Uniforms and vestments

**(P-2905)**
**MDC INTERIOR SOLUTIONS LLC**
Also Called: Komar Apparel Supply
6900 E Washington Blvd, Los Angeles (90040-1908)
PHONE..................800 621-4006
Gary Rothschild, Mgr
EMP: 23
SALES (corp-wide): 26.25MM Privately Held
Web: www.mdcwall.com
SIC: 2389 Men's miscellaneous accessories
PA: Mdc Interior Solutions, Llc
400 High Grove Blvd
847 437-4000

**(P-2906)**
**ML KISHIGO MFG CO LLC**
11250 Slater Ave, Fountain Valley (92708-5421)
PHONE..................949 852-1963
Loren H Wall, CEO
Karen Wall, *
▲ EMP: 86 EST: 1971
SALES (est): 14.09MM
SALES (corp-wide): 14.7B Privately Held
Web: www.catricking.com
SIC: 2389 5099 Men's miscellaneous accessories; Safety equipment and supplies
PA: Bunzl Public Limited Company
York House
208 560-1244

**(P-2907)**
**OUTER REBEL INC**
Also Called: Green Room Oc
3211 W Macarthur Blvd, Santa Ana (92704-6801)
PHONE..................949 246-2421
Michael A Carlson, CEO
EMP: 18 EST: 2008
SALES (est): 2.97MM Privately Held
SIC: 2389 5651 Apparel for handicapped; Unisex clothing stores

**(P-2908)**
**R & R INDUSTRIES INC**
204 Avenida Fabricante, San Clemente (92672-7538)
PHONE..................800 234-5611
Robert Pare, Pr
Roger Poulin, *
▲ EMP: 30 EST: 1978
SQ FT: 8,150
SALES (est): 3.61MM Privately Held
Web: www.rrind.com
SIC: 2389 2759 Uniforms and vestments; Promotional printing

## PRODUCTS & SERVICES SECTION
### 2392 - Household Furnishings, Nec (P-2931)

**(P-2909)**
**RG COSTUMES & ACCESSORIES INC**
726 Arrow Grand Cir, Covina (91722-2147)
PHONE...............626 858-9559
Roger Lee, *Pr*
Michael Lee, *
◆ EMP: 30 EST: 1982
SQ FT: 21,000
SALES (est): 747.44K **Privately Held**
Web: www.rgcostume.com
SIC: 2389 7299 Costumes; Costume rental

**(P-2910)**
**SUSPENDER FACTORY INC**
Also Called: Suspender Factory of S F
1425 63rd St, Emeryville (94608-2188)
PHONE...............510 547-5400
John Nemec, *Pr*
▲ EMP: 35 EST: 1976
SQ FT: 6,000
SALES (est): 2.04MM **Privately Held**
Web: www.suspenderfactory.com
SIC: 2389 2387 Suspenders; Apparel belts

**(P-2911)**
**TRUE WARRIOR LLC**
21226 Lone Star Way, Santa Clarita (91390-4226)
PHONE...............661 237-6588
EMP: 20 EST: 2017
SALES (est): 508.62K **Privately Held**
SIC: 2389 3069 Apparel and accessories, nec; Boot or shoe products, rubber

**(P-2912)**
**UNDERWRAPS COSTUME CORPORATION**
Also Called: Underwraps Costumes
9600 Irondale Ave, Chatsworth (91311-5008)
P.O. Box 9603 (91309-0603)
PHONE...............818 349-5300
Payman Shaffa, *CEO*
Irene Shaffa, *VP*
▲ EMP: 16 EST: 2004
SQ FT: 45,000
SALES (est): 2.44MM **Privately Held**
Web: www.underwraps.net
SIC: 2389 Costumes

**(P-2913)**
**WALT DSNEY IMGNRING RES DEV IN**
Also Called: Disney
1200 N Miller St Unit D, Anaheim (92806-1954)
PHONE...............714 781-3152
Mark Hollingworth, *Brnch Mgr*
EMP: 41
SALES (corp-wide): 88.9B **Publicly Held**
Web: www.disneyimaginations.com
SIC: 2389 Masquerade costumes
HQ: Walt Disney Imagineering Research & Development, Inc.
1401 Flower St
Glendale CA 91201
818 544-6500

### 2391 Curtains And Draperies

**(P-2914)**
**AMTEX CALIFORNIA INC**
Also Called: Ameritex International
113 S Utah St, Los Angeles (90033-3213)
PHONE...............323 859-2200
Saq Hafeez, *Pr*
Alia Hafeez, *

◆ EMP: 45 EST: 1991
SQ FT: 40,000
SALES (est): 1.85MM **Privately Held**
Web: ameritexinternational.americommerce.com
SIC: 2391 2392 5023 Draperies, plastic and textile: from purchased materials; Bedspreads and bed sets: made from purchased materials; Curtains

**(P-2915)**
**MBF INTERIORS INC**
Also Called: Modern Blind Factory
7831 Ostrow St, San Diego (92111-3602)
PHONE...............858 565-2944
Behrooz Barry Farhood, *Pr*
EMP: 16 EST: 1973
SQ FT: 24,000
SALES (est): 411.09K **Privately Held**
SIC: 2391 2591 5714 5719 Draperies, plastic and textile: from purchased materials; Blinds vertical; Draperies; Vertical blinds

**(P-2916)**
**RYAN MC TEER**
Also Called: Sierra Finish Carpentry
5920 E Shields Ave Ste 103, Fresno (93727-8065)
PHONE...............559 217-1450
Ryan Mc Teer, *Pr*
Ryan Mc Teer, *Managing Member*
EMP: 16 EST: 2008
SALES (est): 1.19MM **Privately Held**
Web: www.sierrafinishcarpentry.com
SIC: 2391 2431 5031 5719 Curtains, window: made from purchased materials; Doors and door parts and trim, wood; Doors and windows; Venetian blinds

**(P-2917)**
**S & K THEATRICAL DRAP INC**
Also Called: Sk Drapes
7313 Varna Ave, North Hollywood (91605-4009)
PHONE...............818 503-0596
Carmela Skogman, *Pr*
EMP: 16 EST: 1965
SALES (est): 2.26MM **Privately Held**
Web: www.skdrapes.com
SIC: 2391 Draperies, plastic and textile: from purchased materials

**(P-2918)**
**SANDYS DRAPERY INC (PA)**
48374 Milmont Dr Bldg A, Fremont (94538-7324)
PHONE...............510 445-0112
Donald L Yauger, *Pr*
Harry Yauger, *VP*
Cindy Yauger, *Sec*
EMP: 25 EST: 1955
SQ FT: 27,500
SALES (est): 2.23MM
SALES (corp-wide): 2.23MM **Privately Held**
Web: www.sandysdrapery.net
SIC: 2391 2591 2211 Draperies, plastic and textile: from purchased materials; Drapery hardware and window blinds and shades; Draperies and drapery fabrics, cotton

**(P-2919)**
**SEW WHAT INC**
Also Called: Rent What
1978 E Gladwick St, Compton (90220-6201)
PHONE...............310 639-6000
Megan Duckett, *Pr*
Adam Duckett, *
◆ EMP: 35 EST: 1997

SQ FT: 15,000
SALES (est): 4.85MM **Privately Held**
Web: www.sewwhatinc.com
SIC: 2391 5049 Curtains and draperies; Theatrical equipment and supplies

**(P-2920)**
**SUPERIOR WINDOW COVERINGS INC**
7683 N San Fernando Rd, Burbank (91505-1073)
PHONE...............818 762-6685
Marco Bonilla, *Pr*
▲ EMP: 35 EST: 1979
SQ FT: 4,000
SALES (est): 2.4MM **Privately Held**
Web: www.superiorshades.com
SIC: 2391 2591 Draperies, plastic and textile: from purchased materials; Blinds vertical

### 2392 Household Furnishings, Nec

**(P-2921)**
**ANATOMIC GLOBAL INC**
1241 Old Temescal Rd Ste 103, Corona (92881-7266)
PHONE...............800 874-7237
▲ EMP: 115 EST: 1991
SALES (est): 1.54MM **Privately Held**
SIC: 2392 Bedspreads and bed sets: made from purchased materials

**(P-2922)**
**BEME INTERNATIONAL LLC**
7333 Ronson Rd, San Diego (92111-1404)
PHONE...............858 751-0580
▲ EMP: 15 EST: 1998
SALES (est): 2.23MM **Privately Held**
Web: www.beme.net
SIC: 2392 Household furnishings, nec

**(P-2923)**
**BOJER INC**
177 S Peckham Rd, Azusa (91702-3237)
PHONE...............626 334-1711
Doris Gabai, *Pr*
Joey Gabai, *VP*
EMP: 20 EST: 1991
SQ FT: 12,974
SALES (est): 2.35MM **Privately Held**
Web: www.bojeroutdoor.com
SIC: 2392 Cushions and pillows

**(P-2924)**
**BRENTWOOD ORIGINALS INC (PA)**
Also Called: Brentwood Originals
3780 Kilroy Airport Way Ste 540, Long Beach (90806)
PHONE...............310 637-6804
Joy Stewart, *CEO*
Loren Sweet, *
Bill Bronstein, *
Craig Torrey, *
Tom Rose, *
◆ EMP: 35 EST: 1958
SALES (est): 96.27MM
SALES (corp-wide): 96.27MM **Privately Held**
Web: www.brentwoodoriginals.com
SIC: 2392 Cushions and pillows

**(P-2925)**
**CJ PRODUCTS INC**
Also Called: Pillow Pets
310 Via Vera Cruz Ste 211, San Marcos (92078-2632)

PHONE...............760 444-4217
Clint Telfer, *Pr*
◆ EMP: 15 EST: 2008
SALES (est): 2.98MM **Privately Held**
Web: www.pillowpets.com
SIC: 2392 Cushions and pillows

**(P-2926)**
**COOP HOME GOODS LLC**
Also Called: Coop
9 Executive Cir, Irvine (92614-6734)
PHONE...............888 316-1886
Zachary Kramer, *Managing Member*
EMP: 50 EST: 2021
SALES (est): 7.06MM **Privately Held**
Web: www.coopsleepgoods.com
SIC: 2392 Pillows, bed: made from purchased materials

**(P-2927)**
**CUSTOM QUILTING INC**
2832 Walnut Ave Ste D, Tustin (92780-7002)
PHONE...............714 731-7271
Alfredo Zermeno, *Owner*
Elda Zermeno, *
EMP: 28 EST: 1983
SALES (est): 689.37K **Privately Held**
Web: www.customquiltinginc.com
SIC: 2392 5719 Bedspreads and bed sets: made from purchased materials; Bedding (sheets, blankets, spreads, and pillows)

**(P-2928)**
**DV KAP INC**
Also Called: Canaan Company
426 W Bedford Ave, Fresno (93711-6858)
PHONE...............559 435-5575
Dan Sivas, *CEO*
◆ EMP: 50 EST: 2002
SQ FT: 25,000
SALES (est): 9.86MM **Privately Held**
Web: www.dvkap.com
SIC: 2392 Cushions and pillows

**(P-2929)**
**INSTANT TUCK INC**
9663 Santa Monica Blvd, Beverly Hills (90210-4303)
PHONE...............310 955-8824
Adrian Gluck, *CEO*
EMP: 30 EST: 2019
SALES (est): 472.88K **Privately Held**
SIC: 2392 Mattress pads

**(P-2930)**
**JLA HOME INC**
Also Called: Jla Home
45875 Northport Loop E, Fremont (94538-6414)
PHONE...............510 490-9788
EMP: 42
SIC: 2392 5021 5023 Household furnishings, nec; Household furniture; Sheets, textile

**(P-2931)**
**JOMAR TABLE LINENS INC**
Also Called: Linen Lovers
4000 E Airport Dr Ste A, Ontario (91761-1566)
PHONE...............909 390-1444
EMP: 80 EST: 1982
SALES (est): 4.14MM **Privately Held**
Web: www.jomaronline.com
SIC: 2392 7336 Tablecloths: made from purchased materials; Silk screen design

# 2392 - Household Furnishings, Nec (P-2932)

**(P-2932)**
**KIDS LINE LLC**
10541 Humbolt St, Los Alamitos (90720-5401)
P.O. Box 16712 (92623-6712)
PHONE.................310 660-0110
◆ **EMP:** 140
**SIC: 2392** Blankets, comforters and beddings

**(P-2933)**
**KLEEN MAID INC**
11450 Sheldon St, Sun Valley (91352-1121)
PHONE.................323 581-3000
Sean Solouki, *CEO*
Kamyar Solouki, *
Hamid Moghaven, *
◆ **EMP:** 15 **EST:** 2000
**SALES (est):** 471.76K **Privately Held**
**SIC: 2392** 3991 Mops, floor and dust; Brushes, household or industrial

**(P-2934)**
**LA PILLOW & FIBER INC**
7633 Bequette Ave, Pico Rivera (90660-4501)
PHONE.................323 724-7969
**EMP:** 57
**SALES (corp-wide):** 10.53MM **Privately Held**
**SIC: 2392** Cushions and pillows
**PA:** L.A. Pillow & Fiber, Inc.
2331 S Tubeway Ave
323 724-7969

**(P-2935)**
**LAMBS & IVY INC**
Also Called: Bed Time Originals
2042 E Maple Ave, El Segundo (90245-5008)
PHONE.................310 322-3800
Barbara Laiken, *Pr*
Cathy Ravdin, *
◆ **EMP:** 39 **EST:** 1979
**SQ FT:** 30,000
**SALES (est):** 5.57MM **Privately Held**
Web: www.lambsivy.com
**SIC: 2392** Blankets, comforters and beddings

**(P-2936)**
**LOFTA**
9225 Brown Deer Rd, San Diego (92121-2268)
PHONE.................858 299-8000
Jay B Levitt, *CEO*
**EMP:** 35 **EST:** 2016
**SALES (est):** 11.09MM **Publicly Held**
Web: www.lofta.com
**SIC: 2392** Mattress pads
**HQ:** Apria, Inc.
7353 Company Dr
Indianapolis IN 46237
800 990-9799

**(P-2937)**
**MATTEO LLC**
1000 E Cesar E Chavez Ave, Los Angeles (90033-1204)
PHONE.................213 617-2813
Matthew Lenoci, *Managing Member*
▲ **EMP:** 50 **EST:** 1996
**SQ FT:** 25,000
**SALES (est):** 2.76MM **Privately Held**
Web: www.matteola.com
**SIC: 2392** Blankets, comforters and beddings

**(P-2938)**
**MEADOW DECOR INC**
1477 E Cedar St Ste F, Ontario (91761-8330)
PHONE.................909 923-2558
Jun Chen, *CEO*
David Mok, *Ch Bd*
John Chen, *Pr*
Jiali Zhang, *Prin*
▲ **EMP:** 15 **EST:** 2000
**SALES (est):** 992.19K **Privately Held**
Web: www.legacycustomcushions.com
**SIC: 2392** 2519 Cushions and pillows; Lawn and garden furniture, except wood and metal

**(P-2939)**
**MICRONOVA MANUFACTURING INC**
3431 Lomita Blvd, Torrance (90505-5010)
PHONE.................310 784-6990
Audrey J Reynolds Lowman, *CEO*
▲ **EMP:** 30 **EST:** 1984
**SQ FT:** 28,310
**SALES (est):** 7.37MM **Privately Held**
Web: www.micronova-mfg.com
**SIC: 2392** Mops, floor and dust

**(P-2940)**
**NORTHWESTERN CONVERTING CO**
Also Called: Premier Mop & Broom
2395 Railroad St, Corona (92878-5411)
P.O. Box 78328 (92877-0144)
PHONE.................800 959-3402
Tom Buckles, *Pr*
Thomas M Buckles, *
▲ **EMP:** 100 **EST:** 1935
**SALES (est):** 10.27MM **Privately Held**
Web: northwesternc.openfos.com
**SIC: 2392** Household furnishings, nec

**(P-2941)**
**OMNIA LEATHER MOTION INC**
Also Called: Cathy Ireland Home
4950 Edison Ave, Chino (91710-5713)
PHONE.................909 393-4400
Peter Zolferino, *Pr*
Luie Nastri, *
▲ **EMP:** 200 **EST:** 1989
**SALES (est):** 9.21MM **Privately Held**
Web: www.omnialeather.com
**SIC: 2392** Household furnishings, nec

**(P-2942)**
**ONE BELLA CASA INC**
Also Called: Artehouse
101 Lucas Valley Rd Ste 130, San Rafael (94903-1791)
PHONE.................707 746-8300
Gary Sattin, *CEO*
▲ **EMP:** 24 **EST:** 2013
**SQ FT:** 10,000
**SALES (est):** 444.21K **Privately Held**
Web: www.onebellacasa.com
**SIC: 2392** 3952 Pillows, bed: made from purchased materials; Canvas, prepared on frames: artists'

**(P-2943)**
**PACIFIC CAST FTHER CUSHION LLC (HQ)**
Also Called: Pacific Coast Feather Cushion
7600 Industry Ave, Pico Rivera (90660-4302)
PHONE.................562 801-9995
Neil Puro, *Managing Member*
◆ **EMP:** 110 **EST:** 1986
**SALES (est):** 12.84MM
**SALES (corp-wide):** 60.19MM **Privately Held**
Web: www.pcfcushion.com

**SIC: 2392** Cushions and pillows
**PA:** Pacific Coast Feather, Llc
901 W Yamato Rd Ste 250
206 624-1057

**(P-2944)**
**PACIFIC COAST HOME FURN INC (PA)**
Also Called: Sherry Kline
2424 Saybrook Ave, Commerce (90040-2510)
PHONE.................323 838-7808
Parviz Banafshe, *Pr*
Shahrokh Samani, *VP*
▲ **EMP:** 19 **EST:** 1988
**SQ FT:** 35,000
**SALES (est):** 3.75MM
**SALES (corp-wide):** 3.75MM **Privately Held**
Web: www.pacificcoasthomefurnishings.com
**SIC: 2392** 3261 Cushions and pillows; Bathroom accessories/fittings, vitreous china or earthenware

**(P-2945)**
**PACIFIC URETHANES LLC**
Also Called: Pacific Urethanes
1671 Champagne Ave Ste A, Ontario (91761-3660)
PHONE.................909 390-8400
Darrell Nance, *Managing Member*
Neil Silverman, *
▲ **EMP:** 200 **EST:** 2010
**SQ FT:** 250,000
**SALES (est):** 23.84MM
**SALES (corp-wide):** 5.15B **Publicly Held**
Web: www.pacificurethanes.com
**SIC: 2392** 5021 Blankets, comforters and beddings; Beds and bedding
**PA:** Leggett & Platt, Incorporated
1 Leggett Rd
417 358-8131

**(P-2946)**
**PARACHUTE HOME INC**
3525 Eastham Dr, Culver City (90232-2440)
PHONE.................310 903-0353
Ariel Kaye, *CEO*
Jeff Barker, *
**EMP:** 250 **EST:** 2013
**SQ FT:** 13,000
**SALES (est):** 57.14MM **Privately Held**
Web: www.parachutehome.com
**SIC: 2392** 5719 Sheets, fabric: made from purchased materials; Bedding (sheets, blankets, spreads, and pillows)

**(P-2947)**
**PRO-MART INDUSTRIES INC**
Also Called: Promart Dazz
17421 Von Karman Ave, Irvine (92614-6205)
PHONE.................949 428-7700
Azad Sabounjian, *CEO*
▲ **EMP:** 40 **EST:** 1970
**SQ FT:** 120,000
**SALES (est):** 8.94MM **Privately Held**
Web: www.shopsmartdesign.com
**SIC: 2392** 1799 5085 Bags, laundry: made from purchased materials; Closet organizers, installation and design; Bins and containers, storage

**(P-2948)**
**RELIANCE UPHOLSTERY SUP CO INC**
Also Called: Reliance Carpet Cushion
4920 S Boyle Ave, Huntington Park (90255)

P.O. Box 58584 (90058-0584)
PHONE.................323 321-2300
Ronald J Greitzer, *CEO*
Stanley Grietzer, *
Sheldon P Wallach, *
▲ **EMP:** 95 **EST:** 1931
**SQ FT:** 360,000
**SALES (est):** 3.44MM **Privately Held**
Web: www.reliancecarpetcushion.com
**SIC: 2392** Linings, carpet: textile, except felt

**(P-2949)**
**ROYAL BLUE INC**
9025 Wilshire Blvd Ste 301, Beverly Hills (90211-1831)
PHONE.................310 888-0156
Diana Moinian, *Pr*
▲ **EMP:** 21 **EST:** 2005
**SALES (est):** 1.76MM **Privately Held**
Web: www.royalblueintl.com
**SIC: 2392** 2299 Household furnishings, nec; Towels and towelings, linen and linen-and-cotton mixtures

**(P-2950)**
**THOMAS WEST INC (PA)**
Also Called: T W I
470 Mercury Dr, Sunnyvale (94085-4706)
PHONE.................408 481-3850
Tom West, *CEO*
Doctor Steve Kirtley, *COO*
▲ **EMP:** 23 **EST:** 1981
**SQ FT:** 43,000
**SALES (est):** 6.29MM
**SALES (corp-wide):** 6.29MM **Privately Held**
Web: www.perfectdomain.com
**SIC: 2392** Towels, dishcloths and dust cloths

**(P-2951)**
**UNIVERSAL CUSHION COMPANY INC (PA)**
Also Called: Cloud Nine Comforts
1610 Mandeville Canyon Rd, Los Angeles (90049-2524)
PHONE.................323 887-8000
Sharyl G Bloom, *Pr*
Sharyl Bloom, *
▲ **EMP:** 34 **EST:** 1989
**SALES (est):** 1.27MM **Privately Held**
Web: www.cloudninecomforts.com
**SIC: 2392** 2221 2211 Cushions and pillows; Comforters and quilts, manmade fiber and silk; Sheets and sheetings, cotton

**(P-2952)**
**VFT INC**
Also Called: Vertical Fiber Technologies
1040 S Vail Ave, Montebello (90640-6020)
PHONE.................323 728-2280
John Chang, *Pr*
▲ **EMP:** 40 **EST:** 1998
**SQ FT:** 70,000
**SALES (est):** 5.77MM **Privately Held**
**SIC: 2392** Household furnishings, nec

## 2393 Textile Bags

**(P-2953)**
**ACTION BAG & COVER INC**
18401 Mount Langley St, Fountain Valley (92708-6904)
PHONE.................714 965-7777
Byung Ki Lee, *Pr*
▲ **EMP:** 80 **EST:** 1978
**SQ FT:** 15,000
**SALES (est):** 2.22MM **Privately Held**
Web: www.actionbaginc.com
**SIC: 2393** Canvas bags

## PRODUCTS & SERVICES SECTION
## 2394 - Canvas And Related Products (P-2976)

**(P-2954)**
**CHICOECO INC**
Also Called: Chicobag
747 Fortress St, Chico (95973-9012)
PHONE..................530 342-4426
Andrew Keller, *Pr*
▲ **EMP:** 30 **EST:** 2005
**SALES (est):** 4.67MM **Privately Held**
**Web:** www.chicobag.com
**SIC: 2393** Textile bags

**(P-2955)**
**CONTINENTAL MARKETING SVC INC**
Also Called: Continental Marketing
15381 Proctor Ave, City Of Industry (91745-1022)
PHONE..................626 626-8888
Dawn Du, *Pr*
**EMP:** 17 **EST:** 1986
**SALES (est):** 2.48MM **Privately Held**
**SIC: 2393** Bags and containers, except sleeping bags: textile

**(P-2956)**
**CTA MANUFACTURING INC**
Also Called: Bagmasters
1160 California Ave, Corona (92881-3324)
PHONE..................951 280-2400
Richard Whittier, *Pr*
Gayne Whittier, *
▲ **EMP:** 40 **EST:** 1922
**SQ FT:** 23,000
**SALES (est):** 5.1MM **Privately Held**
**Web:** www.bagmasters.com
**SIC: 2393** Textile bags

**(P-2957)**
**GMI INC**
Also Called: GARY MANUFACTURING
2626 Southport Way Ste E, National City (91950-8754)
PHONE..................619 429-4479
Kathryn Smith, *CEO*
Andrea Beagle, *
**EMP:** 26 **EST:** 2022
**SALES (est):** 272.42K **Privately Held**
**SIC: 2393** 2392 2394 2385 Textile bags; Tablecloths: made from purchased materials; Liners and covers, fabric: made from purchased materials; Diaper covers, waterproof: made from purchased materials

**(P-2958)**
**GOLD CREST INDUSTRIES INC**
1018 E Acacia St, Ontario (91761-4553)
P.O. Box 939 (91769-0939)
PHONE..................909 930-9069
Jose Garcia, *Pr*
**EMP:** 40 **EST:** 1963
**SQ FT:** 14,000
**SALES (est):** 2.47MM **Privately Held**
**Web:** www.goldcrestind.com
**SIC: 2393** 3999 2392 Cushions, except spring and carpet: purchased materials; Umbrellas, garden or wagon; Household furnishings, nec

**(P-2959)**
**KEEPCOOL USA LLC (PA)**
25 Orinda Way Ste 210, Orinda (94563-4403)
PHONE..................925 962-1832
▲ **EMP:** 18 **EST:** 2001
**SQ FT:** 2,000
**SALES (est):** 51MM
**SALES (corp-wide):** 51MM **Privately Held**
**Web:** www.keepcoolbags.com
**SIC: 2393** Canvas bags

**(P-2960)**
**OUTDOOR RCRTION GROUP HLDNGS L (PA)**
Also Called: Outdoor Products
3450 Mount Vernon Dr, Los Angeles (90008-4936)
PHONE..................323 226-0830
Andrew Altshule, *CEO*
Joel Altshule, *
George Aba, *
◆ **EMP:** 37 **EST:** 1946
**SQ FT:** 90,000
**SALES (est):** 14MM
**SALES (corp-wide):** 14MM **Privately Held**
**Web:** www.outdoorproducts.com
**SIC: 2393** 3949 Textile bags; Camping equipment and supplies

**(P-2961)**
**RICKSHAW BAGWORKS INC**
904 22nd St, San Francisco (94107-3427)
PHONE..................415 904-8368
Mark Dwight, *CEO*
▲ **EMP:** 26 **EST:** 2007
**SALES (est):** 2.34MM **Privately Held**
**Web:** www.rickshawbags.com
**SIC: 2393** Textile bags

**(P-2962)**
**TIMBUK2 DESIGNS INC (HQ)**
Also Called: Timbuk2
400 Alabama St Ste 201, San Francisco (94110-1315)
PHONE..................415 252-4300
Paul Devries, *CEO*
◆ **EMP:** 15 **EST:** 1997
**SALES (est):** 4MM **Privately Held**
**Web:** www.timbuk2.com
**SIC: 2393** 5632 5948 Textile bags; Handbags; Leather goods, except luggage and shoes
**PA:** Exemplis Llc
6415 Katella Ave

**(P-2963)**
**TIMBUK2 DESIGNS INC**
2031 Cessna Dr, Vacaville (95688-8903)
PHONE..................800 865-2513
Chris Garcia, *Mgr*
**EMP:** 25
**Web:** www.timbuk2.com
**SIC: 2393** Canvas bags
**HQ:** Timbuk2 Designs, Inc.
400 Alabama St Ste 201
San Francisco CA 94110

## 2394 Canvas And Related Products

**(P-2964)**
**A&R TARPAULINS INC**
Also Called: AR Tech Aerospace
16246 Valley Blvd, Fontana (92335-7831)
P.O. Box 1400 (92334-1400)
PHONE..................909 829-4444
Carmen Weisbart, *Pr*
Bud Weisbart, *
Charles Rosselet, *
**EMP:** 34 **EST:** 1977
**SQ FT:** 15,000
**SALES (est):** 7.53MM **Privately Held**
**Web:** www.artarpaulins.com
**SIC: 2394** Awnings, fabric: made from purchased materials

**(P-2965)**
**A-AZTEC RENTS & SELLS INC (PA)**
Also Called: Aztec Tents
2665 Columbia St, Torrance (90503-3801)
PHONE..................310 347-3010
**TOLL FREE:** 800
Chuck Miller, *CEO*
Alex Kouzmanoff, *
◆ **EMP:** 125 **EST:** 1967
**SQ FT:** 70,000
**SALES (est):** 18.63MM
**SALES (corp-wide):** 18.63MM **Privately Held**
**Web:** www.aztectent.com
**SIC: 2394** Canvas and related products

**(P-2966)**
**ABC SUN CONTROL LLC**
7241 Ethel Ave, North Hollywood (91605-4215)
PHONE..................818 982-6989
▲ **EMP:** 16 **EST:** 1979
**SQ FT:** 30,000
**SALES (est):** 775.95K **Privately Held**
**Web:** www.abcsuncontrolsystems.com
**SIC: 2394** Awnings, fabric: made from purchased materials

**(P-2967)**
**AIRCRAFT COVERS INC**
Also Called: Bruce's Custom Covers
18850 Adams Ct, Morgan Hill (95037-2816)
PHONE..................408 738-3959
Bruce Perlitch, *Pr*
**EMP:** 31
**SQ FT:** 21,909
**SALES (corp-wide):** 10.38MM **Privately Held**
**Web:** www.aircraftcovers.com
**SIC: 2394** Canvas and related products
**PA:** Aircraft Covers, Inc.
18850 Adams Ct
408 738-3959

**(P-2968)**
**AIRCRAFT COVERS INC (PA)**
Also Called: Bruce's Custom Covers
18850 Adams Ct, Morgan Hill (95037-2816)
PHONE..................408 738-3959
**EMP:** 34 **EST:** 1979
**SALES (est):** 10.38MM
**SALES (corp-wide):** 10.38MM **Privately Held**
**Web:** www.aircraftcovers.com
**SIC: 2394** Canvas and related products

**(P-2969)**
**CANVAS CONCEPTS INC**
649 Anita St Ste A2, Chula Vista (91911-4658)
PHONE..................619 424-3428
Robert A Mackenzie, *Pr*
Anton Silvernagel, *
Olivia Appel, *
**EMP:** 34 **EST:** 2000
**SQ FT:** 9,600
**SALES (est):** 901.24K **Privately Held**
**Web:** www.canvasstore.com
**SIC: 2394** Awnings, fabric: made from purchased materials

**(P-2970)**
**CANVAS SPECIALTY INC**
1309 S Eastern Ave, Commerce (90040-5610)
▲ **EMP:** 25 **EST:** 1942
**SQ FT:** 84,000
**SALES (est):** 829.03K **Privately Held**
**Web:** www.can-spec.com
**SIC: 2394** 5199 Tarpaulins, fabric: made from purchased materials; Canvas products

**(P-2971)**
**CARAVAN CANOPY INTL INC**
Also Called: Caravan Canopy
17510-17512 Studebaker Rd, Cerritos (90703)
PHONE..................714 367-3000
Lindy Jung Park, *CEO*
David Hudrlik, *
◆ **EMP:** 70 **EST:** 1999
**SQ FT:** 50,000
**SALES (est):** 9.76MM **Privately Held**
**Web:** www.caravancanopy.com
**SIC: 2394** 3444 2392 Canvas and related products; Awnings and canopies; Chair covers and pads: made from purchased materials

**(P-2972)**
**CASTILLO MARITESS**
Also Called: American Supply
1490 S Vineyard Ave Ste G, Ontario (91761-8043)
P.O. Box 2322 (91708-2322)
PHONE..................949 216-0468
Maritess Castillo, *Owner*
**EMP:** 16 **EST:** 2013
**SQ FT:** 1,600
**SALES (est):** 362.95K **Privately Held**
**SIC: 2394** Liners and covers, fabric: made from purchased materials

**(P-2973)**
**EIDE INDUSTRIES INC**
Also Called: Awnings.com
16215 Piuma Ave, Cerritos (90703-1528)
PHONE..................562 402-8335
Don Araiza, *Pr*
Jesus Borrego, *
Dan Neill, *
Joe Belli, *
◆ **EMP:** 80 **EST:** 1938
**SQ FT:** 41,000
**SALES (est):** 8.97MM **Privately Held**
**Web:** www.eideindustries.com
**SIC: 2394** Tents: made from purchased materials

**(P-2974)**
**FRAMETENT INC**
Also Called: Central Tent
26480 Summit Cir, Santa Clarita (91350-2991)
PHONE..................661 290-3375
Nattha Chunapongse, *Pr*
◆ **EMP:** 30 **EST:** 1994
**SALES (est):** 1.94MM **Privately Held**
**SIC: 2394** 5999 Tents: made from purchased materials; Tents

**(P-2975)**
**GMA COVER CORP**
1170 Somera Rd, Los Angeles (90077-2628)
▲ **EMP:** 179
**SIC: 2394** 3812 Canvas and related products; Defense systems and equipment

**(P-2976)**
**INTERNATIONAL E-Z UP INC (PA)**
1900 2nd St, Norco (92860-2803)
PHONE..................800 742-3363
Leonardo Pais, *CEO*
Katie Melzer, *
◆ **EMP:** 89 **EST:** 1983
**SQ FT:** 115,000
**SALES (est):** 24.62MM
**SALES (corp-wide):** 24.62MM **Privately Held**
**Web:** www.ezup.com

## 2394 - Canvas And Related Products (P-2977)

SIC: **2394** 5999 Shades, canvas: made from purchased materials; Tents

**(P-2977)**
**LARSENS INC**
1041 17th Ave Ste A, Santa Cruz (95062-3070)
PHONE..................831 476-3009
Kurt W Larsen, *Pr*
Susan Larsen, *VP*
EMP: 15 EST: 1972
SQ FT: 6,000
SALES (est): 2.45MM **Privately Held**
Web: www.larsensinc.com
SIC: **2394** Sails: made from purchased materials

**(P-2978)**
**MOUNTAIN HARDWEAR INC**
Also Called: Montrail
1414 Harbour Way S Ste 1005, Richmond (94804-3632)
PHONE..................510 558-3000
▲ EMP: 1500 EST: 1993
SALES (est): 19.87MM
SALES (corp-wide): 3.49B **Publicly Held**
Web: www.mountainhardwear.com
SIC: **2394** 2399 5651 Canvas and related products; Sleeping bags; Unisex clothing stores
HQ: Columbia Brands Usa, Llc
    14375 Nw Science Park Dr
    Portland OR 97229
    503 985-4000

**(P-2979)**
**OVERLAND VEHICLE SYSTEMS LLC**
9830 Norwalk Blvd Ste 130, Santa Fe Springs (90670)
PHONE..................833 226-4863
Sean Angues, *Managing Member*
EMP: 20 EST: 2022
SALES (est): 5.31MM **Privately Held**
Web: www.overlandvehiclesystems.com
SIC: **2394** 5999 Awnings, fabric: made from purchased materials; Tents

**(P-2980)**
**PACIFIC PLAY TENTS INC**
2801 E 12th St, Los Angeles (90023-3621)
PHONE..................323 269-0431
Victor Preisler, *CEO*
Brian Jablan, *VP*
◆ EMP: 15 EST: 1993
SQ FT: 75,000
SALES (est): 484.77K **Privately Held**
Web: www.pacificplaytents.com
SIC: **2394** 5941 5092 3944 Tents: made from purchased materials; Sporting goods and bicycle shops; Toys, nec; Games, toys, and children's vehicles

**(P-2981)**
**ROLL-RITE LLC**
Also Called: Pulltarps Manufacturing
1404 N Marshall Ave, El Cajon (92020-1521)
PHONE..................619 449-8860
EMP: 48
Web: www.rollrite.com
SIC: **2394** 3479 Tarpaulins, fabric: made from purchased materials; Bonderizing of metal or metal products
HQ: Roll-Rite Llc
    650 Industrial Dr
    Gladwin MI 48624

**(P-2982)**
**SAN JOSE AWNING COMPANY INC**
Also Called: San Jose Awning
755 Chestnut St Ste E, San Jose (95110-1832)
PHONE..................408 350-7000
Michael Yaholkovsky, *Pr*
EMP: 22 EST: 1983
SQ FT: 8,800
SALES (est): 2.54MM **Privately Held**
Web: www.sanjoseawning.com
SIC: **2394** Awnings, fabric: made from purchased materials

**(P-2983)**
**STARK MFG CO**
Also Called: Stark Awning & Canvas
76 Broadway, Chula Vista (91910-1422)
PHONE..................619 425-5880
Turner Stark, *Ch*
EMP: 29 EST: 1953
SQ FT: 3,500
SALES (est): 2.62MM **Privately Held**
Web: www.starkmfgco.com
SIC: **2394** 3444 Awnings, fabric: made from purchased materials; Sheet metalwork

**(P-2984)**
**SUPERIOR AWNING INC**
14555 Titus St, Panorama City (91402-4920)
PHONE..................818 780-7200
Brian Hotchkiss, *Pr*
Julie Hotchkiss, *
EMP: 40 EST: 1984
SQ FT: 11,776
SALES (est): 8.38MM **Privately Held**
Web: www.superiorawning.com
SIC: **2394** 5999 3444 Awnings, fabric: made from purchased materials; Awnings; Sheet metalwork

**(P-2985)**
**TRANSPORTATION EQUIPMENT INC**
Also Called: Pulltarps Manufacturing
1404 N Marshall Ave, El Cajon (92020-1521)
PHONE..................619 449-8860
TOLL FREE: 800
▲ EMP: 48
Web: www.pulltarps.com
SIC: **2394** 3479 Tarpaulins, fabric: made from purchased materials; Bonderizing of metal or metal products

**(P-2986)**
**ULLMAN SAILS INC (PA)**
2710 S Croddy Way, Santa Ana (92704-5206)
PHONE..................714 432-1860
Bruce Cooper, *Owner*
Bruce Cooper, *Pr*
EMP: 15 EST: 1967
SQ FT: 10,900
SALES (est): 2.17MM
SALES (corp-wide): 2.17MM **Privately Held**
Web: newportbeach.ullmansails.com
SIC: **2394** Sails: made from purchased materials

**(P-2987)**
**VAE INDUSTRIES CORPORATION**
Also Called: Vitabri Canopies
5402 Research Dr, Huntington Beach (92649-1542)
PHONE..................714 842-7500
Damien Vieille, *CEO*
Mathieu Hayaud, *VP*
◆ EMP: 22 EST: 2010
SQ FT: 7,500
SALES (est): 2.13MM **Privately Held**
Web: www.instent.com
SIC: **2394** 5999 Canopies, fabric: made from purchased materials; Banners

## 2395 Pleating And Stitching

**(P-2988)**
**AMERICAN QUILTING COMPANY INC**
Also Called: Antaky Quilting Company
1540 Calzona St, Los Angeles (90023-3254)
PHONE..................323 233-2500
Derek Antaky, *CEO*
Elias Antaky Junior, *VP*
▲ EMP: 30 EST: 1917
SALES (est): 2.06MM **Privately Held**
Web: www.antakyquilting.com
SIC: **2395** Quilting: for the trade

**(P-2989)**
**BEST- IN- WEST**
Also Called: Best-In-West Emblem Co
2279 Eagle Glen Pkwy Ste 112, Corona (92883-0785)
PHONE..................909 947-6507
Eric Roberts, *Pr*
Heriberto Perez, *
Beatriz Roberts, *
EMP: 23 EST: 1980
SQ FT: 15,000
SALES (est): 530.35K **Privately Held**
SIC: **2395** 2759 Embroidery products, except Schiffli machine; Commercial printing, nec

**(P-2990)**
**ENRICH ENTERPRISES INC** ✪
Also Called: National Emblem
3925 E Vernon St, Long Beach (90815-1727)
PHONE..................310 515-5055
Rich Rozycki, *CEO*
EMP: 25 EST: 2024
SALES (est): 4.67MM **Privately Held**
SIC: **2395** Embroidery and art needlework

**(P-2991)**
**J & M RICHMAN CORPORATION**
1501 Beach St, Montebello (90640-5431)
PHONE..................800 422-9646
James D Richman, *Pr*
Tom Shapiro, *
Maury Rice, *
EMP: 25 EST: 1992
SALES (est): 3.92MM **Privately Held**
Web: www.academydesign.co
SIC: **2395** 5999 3448 Quilted fabrics or cloth ; Awnings; Buildings, portable: prefabricated metal

**(P-2992)**
**LA PALM FURNITURES & ACC INC (PA)**
Also Called: Royal Plasticware
1650 W Artesia Blvd, Gardena (90248-3217)
PHONE..................310 217-2700
Dorra Ngan, *CEO*
Donna Sada, *VP*
Gino Lam, *Dir*
John Lee, *Dir*
Shawn Morse, *Sls Dir*
▲ EMP: 27 EST: 1996
SQ FT: 30,000
SALES (est): 5.9MM
SALES (corp-wide): 5.9MM **Privately Held**
SIC: **2395** Embroidery products, except Schiffli machine

**(P-2993)**
**LAKESHIRTS LLC**
Also Called: Yesterdays Sportswear
1400 Railroad St Ste 104, Paso Robles (93446-1771)
PHONE..................805 239-1290
Mark Fritz, *Brnch Mgr*
EMP: 45
SALES (corp-wide): 33.08MM **Privately Held**
Web: www.yessport.com
SIC: **2395** Embroidery and art needlework
PA: Lakeshirts Llc
    750 Randolph Rd
    800 627-2780

**(P-2994)**
**MANHATTAN STITCHING CO INC**
Also Called: Manhattan Stitching Co
8362 Artesia Blvd Ste E, Buena Park (90621-4179)
PHONE..................714 521-9479
Maxine Jossel, *Pr*
Lynne Miller, *
Cory Miller, *
EMP: 37 EST: 2005
SQ FT: 750
SALES (est): 1.85MM **Privately Held**
Web: www.manhattanstitching.com
SIC: **2395** 2759 7389 Embroidery products, except Schiffli machine; Promotional printing ; Advertising, promotional, and trade show services

**(P-2995)**
**MELMARC PRODUCTS INC**
752 S Campus Ave, Ontario (91761-1728)
PHONE..................714 549-2170
Brian Hirth, *Pr*
Leila Drager, *
Harish Naran, *
▲ EMP: 160 EST: 1987
SQ FT: 85,000
SALES (est): 24.5MM **Privately Held**
Web: www.melmarc.com
SIC: **2395** 2396 Pleating and stitching; Screen printing on fabric articles

**(P-2996)**
**MODERN EMBROIDERY INC**
3701 W Moore Ave, Santa Ana (92704-6836)
PHONE..................714 436-9960
Gene Lee, *Pr*
EMP: 42 EST: 1996
SALES (est): 3.59MM **Privately Held**
Web: www.modernembroidery.com
SIC: **2395** Embroidery and art needlework

**(P-2997)**
**NATIONAL EMBLEM INC (PA)**
3925 E Vernon St, Long Beach (90815)
P.O. Box 15680 (90815)
PHONE..................310 515-5055
TOLL FREE: 800
Milton H Lubin Senior, *Pr*
Milton H Lubin Junior, *VP*
▲ EMP: 250 EST: 1972
SQ FT: 60,000
SALES (est): 4.09MM
SALES (corp-wide): 4.09MM **Privately Held**
Web: www.nationalemblem.com

# PRODUCTS & SERVICES SECTION
## 2396 - Automotive And Apparel Trimmings (P-3019)

SIC: **2395** 2396 Emblems, embroidered; Automotive and apparel trimmings

**(P-2998)**
### OUTLOOK RESOURCES INC
Also Called: Leftbank Art
14930 Alondra Blvd, La Mirada (90638-5752)
PHONE..................................562 623-9328
Chris Hyun, *Pr*
◆ **EMP:** 100 **EST:** 2008
**SALES (est):** 9.48MM **Privately Held**
Web: www.leftbankart.com
SIC: **2395** 5999 Pleating and stitching; Art dealers

**(P-2999)**
### REBECCA INTERNATIONAL INC
4587 E 48th St, Vernon (90058-3201)
PHONE..................................323 973-2602
Eli Kahen, *Owner*
**EMP:** 25 **EST:** 2015
**SQ FT:** 1,500
**SALES (est):** 801.72K **Privately Held**
Web: www.rebeccainternational.com
SIC: **2395** 2759 7299 Embroidery products, except Schiffli machine; Screen printing; Stitching services

---

## 2396 Automotive And Apparel Trimmings

**(P-3000)**
### ABSOLUTE SCREENPRINT INC
333 Cliffwood Park St, Brea (92821-4104)
P.O. Box 9069 (92822-9069)
PHONE..................................714 529-2120
Steven Restivo, *CEO*
Andrea Restivo, *
▲ **EMP:** 250 **EST:** 1991
**SQ FT:** 65,000
**SALES (est):** 24.87MM **Privately Held**
Web: www.absolutescreenprint.com
SIC: **2396** 3993 2759 Screen printing on fabric articles; Signs and advertising specialties; Screen printing

**(P-3001)**
### ATELIER LUXURY GROUP LLC
Also Called: Amiri
1330 Channing St, Los Angeles (90021-2411)
PHONE..................................310 751-2444
Michael Amiri, *Managing Member*
**EMP:** 45 **EST:** 2019
**SQ FT:** 30,000
**SALES (est):** 13.58MM **Privately Held**
SIC: **2396** 2311 2321 2331 Apparel and other linings, except millinery; Men's and boy's suits and coats; Men's and boy's furnishings; Women's and misses' blouses and shirts

**(P-3002)**
### BANDMERCH LLC
3945 Freedom Cir Ste 560, Santa Clara (95054-1269)
PHONE..................................818 736-4800
Joseph Bongiovi, *Pr*
▲ **EMP:** 33 **EST:** 2003
**SALES (est):** 3.27MM **Privately Held**
Web: www.bandmerch.com
SIC: **2396** Fabric printing and stamping
HQ: Aeg Presents Llc
425 W 11th St
Los Angeles CA 90015
323 930-5700

**(P-3003)**
### C S DASH COVER INC
14020 Paramount Blvd, Paramount (90723-2606)
PHONE..................................562 790-8300
Cameron Zada, *Pr*
▲ **EMP:** 16 **EST:** 1992
**SQ FT:** 3,200
**SALES (est):** 964.55K **Privately Held**
Web: www.csdashcovers.com
SIC: **2396** 5521 Automotive trimmings, fabric; Used car dealers

**(P-3004)**
### D AND J MARKETING INC
Also Called: DJM Suspension
580 W 184th St, Gardena (90248-4202)
PHONE..................................310 538-1583
Jeffery J Ullmann, *Pr*
Mark Dunham, *
▲ **EMP:** 32 **EST:** 1985
**SQ FT:** 18,000
**SALES (est):** 2.07MM **Privately Held**
Web: www.djmsuspension.com
SIC: **2396** 2531 3714 Automotive trimmings, fabric; Public building and related furniture; Motor vehicle parts and accessories

**(P-3005)**
### DISTINCTIVE INDUSTRIES
Also Called: Specialty Division
10618 Shoemaker Ave, Santa Fe Springs (90670-4038)
PHONE..................................800 421-9777
Dwight Forrister, *CEO*
Aaron Forrister, *
▲ **EMP:** 410 **EST:** 1969
**SQ FT:** 110,000
**SALES (est):** 3.72MM **Privately Held**
Web: www.distinctiveindustries.com
SIC: **2396** 3086 Automotive trimmings, fabric; Plastics foam products
PA: Distinctive Industries Of Texas, Inc.
4516 Seton Center Pkwy # 13

**(P-3006)**
### DUDS BY DUDES LLC
Also Called: Duds By Dudes
7855 Ostrow St Ste A, San Diego (92111-3634)
PHONE..................................858 442-5613
Brian Geffen, *Managing Member*
**EMP:** 15 **EST:** 2007
**SALES (est):** 1.34MM **Privately Held**
Web: www.dudsbydudes.com
SIC: **2396** Screen printing on fabric articles

**(P-3007)**
### FOUR SEASONS DESIGN INC (PA)
2451 Britannia Blvd, San Diego (92154-7405)
PHONE..................................619 761-5151
John Borsini, *Pr*
▲ **EMP:** 25 **EST:** 2000
**SALES (est):** 20.15MM
**SALES (corp-wide):** 20.15MM **Privately Held**
Web: www.fourseasonsdesign.com
SIC: **2396** Screen printing on fabric articles

**(P-3008)**
### GRAPHIC PRINTS INC
Also Called: Pipeline
904 Silver Spur Rd Ste 415, Rolling Hills Estate (90274-3800)
P.O. Box 459 (90248)
PHONE..................................310 870-1239
Alan Greenberg, *CEO*
Tamotsu Inouye, *
Richard Greenberg, *
▲ **EMP:** 45 **EST:** 1971
**SQ FT:** 22,000
**SALES (est):** 3.18MM **Privately Held**
Web: www.pipelinegear.com
SIC: **2396** 2339 2329 Screen printing on fabric articles; Women's and misses' athletic clothing and sportswear; Men's and boys' sportswear and athletic clothing

**(P-3009)**
### I D BRAND LLC
3185 Airway Ave Ste A, Costa Mesa (92626-4601)
PHONE..................................949 422-7057
▲ **EMP:** 44 **EST:** 1995
**SQ FT:** 6,400
**SALES (est):** 2.81MM **Privately Held**
Web: www.brandid.com
SIC: **2396** Apparel findings and trimmings

**(P-3010)**
### J & H PRODUCTION
4481 S Santa Fe Ave, Vernon (90058-2101)
PHONE..................................323 261-6600
Joseph Hendifar, *Pt*
Sassan Kohan, *Pt*
**EMP:** 20 **EST:** 1988
**SQ FT:** 8,000
**SALES (est):** 220.79K **Privately Held**
SIC: **2396** Pads, shoulder: for coats, suits, etc.

**(P-3011)**
### KAMM INDUSTRIES INC
Also Called: Prp Seats
43352 Business Park Dr, Temecula (92590-3665)
PHONE..................................800 317-6253
Aaron Wedeking, *CEO*
Mike Doherty, *
▲ **EMP:** 43 **EST:** 2009
**SALES (est):** 5.38MM **Privately Held**
Web: www.prpseats.com
SIC: **2396** Automotive trimmings, fabric

**(P-3012)**
### KAPAN - KENT COMPANY INC
3540 Seagate Way Ste 100, Oceanside (92056-2672)
PHONE..................................760 631-1716
Arnold Kapen Senior, *Pr*
▲ **EMP:** 35 **EST:** 1958
**SALES (est):** 4.02MM **Privately Held**
Web: www.kapankent.com
SIC: **2396** 3231 Screen printing on fabric articles; Decorated glassware: chipped, engraved, etched, etc.

**(P-3013)**
### NEXT DAY PRINTED TEES
Also Called: Swim Cap Company, The
3523 Main St Ste 601, Chula Vista (91911-0803)
PHONE..................................619 420-8618
Timothy B Lewis, *Pr*
Mary Jane Lewis, *Sr VP*
Carmen Nichols, *VP*
Jane Lewis, *VP*
Christopher Lewis, *VP*
**EMP:** 16 **EST:** 1991
**SQ FT:** 9,000
**SALES (est):** 2.23MM **Privately Held**
Web: www.nextdayprintedtees.com
SIC: **2396** 5699 Screen printing on fabric articles; Customized clothing and apparel

**(P-3014)**
### ORBO MANUFACTURING INC
1000 S Euclid St, La Habra (90631-6806)
PHONE..................................562 222-4535
Roberto Galvez, *CEO*
**EMP:** 25 **EST:** 2021
**SALES (est):** 1.42MM **Privately Held**
SIC: **2396** Furniture trimmings, fabric

**(P-3015)**
### PARTSFLEX INC
1775 Park St Ste 77, Selma (93662-3659)
PHONE..................................408 677-7121
Max Alsedda, *Pr*
**EMP:** 25 **EST:** 2017
**SALES (est):** 413.75K **Privately Held**
SIC: **2396** 5013 Automotive and apparel trimmings; Automotive supplies and parts

**(P-3016)**
### SECURITY TEXTILE CORPORATION
1457 E Washington Blvd, Los Angeles (90021-3039)
PHONE..................................213 747-2673
Doug Weitman, *CEO*
Brian Weitman, *
▲ **EMP:** 20 **EST:** 1972
**SQ FT:** 85,000
**SALES (est):** 638.81K **Privately Held**
Web: www.stc-qst.com
SIC: **2396** 5131 Automotive and apparel trimmings; Sewing supplies and notions

**(P-3017)**
### SIMSO TEX SUBLIMATION (PA)
Also Called: Simso Tex
3028 E Las Hermanas St, Compton (90221-5511)
PHONE..................................310 885-9717
Joe Simsoly, *CEO*
Eli Simsollo, *
Kaden Simsollo, *
▲ **EMP:** 36 **EST:** 2001
**SQ FT:** 38,000
**SALES (est):** 3.18MM
**SALES (corp-wide):** 3.18MM **Privately Held**
SIC: **2396** Fabric printing and stamping

**(P-3018)**
### SMOOTHREADS INC
Also Called: 2.95 Guys
13750 Stowe Dr Ste A, Poway (92064-8828)
PHONE..................................800 536-5959
Lance Beesley, *Pr*
▲ **EMP:** 28 **EST:** 1987
**SQ FT:** 12,000
**SALES (est):** 2.3MM **Privately Held**
Web: www.295guys.com
SIC: **2396** 2395 Screen printing on fabric articles; Embroidery products, except Schiffli machine

**(P-3019)**
### TESCA USA INC
Also Called: Tesca
333 S Grand Ave Ste 4100, Los Angeles (90071-1571)
PHONE..................................586 991-0744
Christopher Glinka, *Genl Mgr*
**EMP:** 43 **EST:** 2004
**SALES (est):** 8.03MM **Privately Held**
Web: www.tescagroup.com
SIC: **2396** 3089 3465 3714 Automotive trimmings, fabric; Injection molding of plastics; Automotive stampings; Automotive wiring harness sets

---

(PA)=Parent Co (HQ)=Headquarters
✪ = New Business established in last 2 years

## 2396 - Automotive And Apparel Trimmings (P-3020)

**(P-3020)**
**WESTIN AUTOMOTIVE PRODUCTS INC (PA)**
Also Called: Westin
320 W Covina Blvd, San Dimas (91773-2907)
PHONE.................626 960-6762
Robert West, *CEO*
▲ **EMP:** 35 **EST:** 1994
**SQ FT:** 10,000
**SALES (est):** 15.59MM **Privately Held**
Web: www.westinautomotive.com
**SIC: 2396** Automotive and apparel trimmings

---

### 2399 Fabricated Textile Products, Nec

**(P-3021)**
**A LOT TO SAY INC**
1541 S Vineyard Ave, Ontario (91761-7717)
PHONE.................877 366-8448
Jennifer Spannich Danmiller, *CEO*
Alisson Spannich Powers, *COO*
**EMP:** 20 **EST:** 2008
**SALES (est):** 1.23MM **Privately Held**
**SIC: 2399** Banners, made from fabric

**(P-3022)**
**ACTION EMBROIDERY CORP (PA)**
Also Called: Action
1315 Brooks St, Ontario (91762-3612)
PHONE.................909 983-1359
Ira Newman, *Pr*
Steven Mendelow, *
Ozzie Silna Stkhlr, *Prin*
▲ **EMP:** 120 **EST:** 1986
**SQ FT:** 12,000
**SALES (est):** 9.24MM
**SALES (corp-wide):** 9.24MM **Privately Held**
Web: www.actionembroiderycorp.com
**SIC: 2399** 2395 Emblems, badges, and insignia: from purchased materials; Pleating and stitching

**(P-3023)**
**AIRBORNE SYSTEMS N AMER CA INC**
3100 W Segerstrom Ave, Santa Ana (92704-5812)
PHONE.................714 662-1400
Bryce Wiedeman, *Pr*
Sean P Maroney, *
Halle F Terrion, *
Terrance M Paradie, *
▼ **EMP:** 200 **EST:** 1919
**SQ FT:** 160,000
**SALES (est):** 48.12MM
**SALES (corp-wide):** 7.94B **Publicly Held**
Web: www.airborne-sys.com
**SIC: 2399** Parachutes
HQ: Airborne Systems North America Inc.
5800 Magnolia Ave
Pennsauken NJ 08109
856 663-1275

**(P-3024)**
**AUTOLIV ASP INC**
Also Called: Autoliv Akr Fcilty -Casa Whse
9355 Airway Rd, San Diego (92154-7931)
PHONE.................619 662-8018
Alberto Garcia, *Brnch Mgr*
**EMP:** 41
**SALES (corp-wide):** 10.47B **Publicly Held**
**SIC: 2399** Seat belts, automobile and aircraft
HQ: Autoliv Asp, Inc.
1320 Pacific Dr
Auburn Hills MI 48326

**(P-3025)**
**AUTOLIV SAFETY TECHNOLOGY INC**
2475 Paseo De Las Americas Ste A, San Diego (92154-7255)
PHONE.................619 662-8000
Bradley J Murray, *Pr*
Anthony J Nellis, *
Raymond B Pekar, *
**EMP:** 1003 **EST:** 1989
**SALES (est):** 3.14MM
**SALES (corp-wide):** 10.47B **Publicly Held**
Web: www.autoliv.com
**SIC: 2399** Seat belts, automobile and aircraft
PA: Autoliv, Inc.
3350 Airport Rd
801 629-9800

**(P-3026)**
**DISPLAY FABRICATION GROUP INC**
1231 N Miller St Ste 100, Anaheim (92806-1950)
PHONE.................714 373-2100
Luis Ocampo, *Pr*
Luis Ocampo, *Pr*
◆ **EMP:** 50 **EST:** 2002
**SQ FT:** 100,000
**SALES (est):** 5.08MM **Privately Held**
Web: www.displayfg.com
**SIC: 2399** Belting, fabric: made from purchased materials

**(P-3027)**
**EEVELLE LLC**
5928 Balfour Ct, Carlsbad (92008-7304)
PHONE.................760 434-2231
Charles Mckee, *Managing Member*
▲ **EMP:** 24 **EST:** 1994
**SALES (est):** 4.28MM **Privately Held**
Web: www.eevelle.com
**SIC: 2399** Automotive covers, except seat and tire covers

**(P-3028)**
**EXXEL OUTDOORS INC**
343 Baldwin Park Blvd, City Of Industry (91746-1406)
PHONE.................626 369-7278
**EMP:** 158
**SALES (corp-wide):** 122.95MM **Privately Held**
Web: www.exxel.com
**SIC: 2399** Sleeping bags
PA: Exxel Outdoors, Inc.
300 American Blvd
205 486-5258

**(P-3029)**
**FXC CORPORATION**
Guardian Parachute Division
3050 Red Hill Ave, Costa Mesa (92626-4524)
PHONE.................714 557-8032
Frank X Chevrier, *Mgr*
**EMP:** 64
**SALES (corp-wide):** 11.45MM **Privately Held**
Web: www.fxcguardian.com
**SIC: 2399** 3429 Parachutes; Parachute hardware
PA: Fxc Corporation
3050 Red Hill Ave
714 556-7400

**(P-3030)**
**HITEX DYEING & FINISHING INC**
355 Vineland Ave, City Of Industry (91746-2321)
PHONE.................626 363-0160
Young C Kim, *Pr*
▲ **EMP:** 25 **EST:** 2010
**SALES (est):** 466.71K **Privately Held**
Web: www.hitexdye.com
**SIC: 2399** 2257 Nets, launderers and dyers; Dyeing and finishing circular knit fabrics

**(P-3031)**
**JUANITA F WADE**
Also Called: Seaborn Canvas
435 N Harbor Blvd Ste B1, San Pedro (90731-2271)
PHONE.................310 519-1208
Juanita F Wade, *Owner*
Juanita Wade, *Owner*
▼ **EMP:** 25 **EST:** 1987
**SQ FT:** 5,000
**SALES (est):** 463.33K **Privately Held**
**SIC: 2399** 2394 Banners, pennants, and flags; Canvas and related products

**(P-3032)**
**NORTH BAY RHBLITATION SVCS INC (PA)**
Also Called: NORTH BAY INDUSTRIES
649 Martin Ave, Rohnert Park (94928-2050)
PHONE.................707 585-1991
Robert Hutt, *CEO*
William Stewart, *
▲ **EMP:** 229 **EST:** 1968
**SQ FT:** 18,000
**SALES (est):** 14.66MM
**SALES (corp-wide):** 14.66MM **Privately Held**
Web: www.nbrs.org
**SIC: 2399** 0782 8331 Banners, pennants, and flags; Lawn services; Community service employment training program

**(P-3033)**
**PRESTIGE FLAG & BANNER CO INC**
Also Called: Prestige Flag
591 Camino De La Reina Ste 917, San Diego (92108-3146)
PHONE.................619 497-2220
▼ **EMP:** 100 **EST:** 1991
**SALES (est):** 7.19MM **Privately Held**
Web: www.prestigeflag.com
**SIC: 2399** Flags, fabric

**(P-3034)**
**REFLEX CORPORATION**
2401 Mountain View Dr, Carlsbad (92008-2221)
PHONE.................760 931-9009
John C Levy Junior, *Pr*
▲ **EMP:** 20 **EST:** 1976
**SALES (est):** 1.07MM **Privately Held**
Web: www.premiumtufflock.com
**SIC: 2399** Horse and pet accessories, textile

**(P-3035)**
**SCOTTEX INC**
12828 S Broadway, Los Angeles (90061-1116)
PHONE.................310 516-1411
Stanley Jung, *Pr*
▲ **EMP:** 25 **EST:** 1995
**SQ FT:** 19,000
**SALES (est):** 503.72K **Privately Held**
Web: www.scottex.es
**SIC: 2399** Hand woven and crocheted products

**(P-3036)**
**SEVENTH HEAVEN INC**
Also Called: Western Mountaineering
1025 S 5th St, San Jose (95112-3927)
PHONE.................408 287-8945
Gary Schaezlein, *Mktg Dir*
▲ **EMP:** 30 **EST:** 1970
**SQ FT:** 12,000
**SALES (est):** 5.61MM **Privately Held**
Web: www.westernmountaineering.com
**SIC: 2399** 2392 2329 Sleeping bags; Comforters and quilts: made from purchased materials; Down-filled clothing: men's and boys'

**(P-3037)**
**VANGUARD INDUSTRIES EAST INC**
2440 Impala Dr, Carlsbad (92010-7226)
PHONE.................800 433-1334
William M Gershen, *Brnch Mgr*
**EMP:** 30
**SALES (corp-wide):** 12.95MM **Privately Held**
Web: www.vanguardmil.com
**SIC: 2399** Military insignia, textile
PA: Vanguard Industries East, Inc.
1172 Azalea Garden Rd
757 665-8405

**(P-3038)**
**VANGUARD INDUSTRIES WEST INC (PA)**
2440 Impala Dr, Carlsbad (92010-7226)
PHONE.................760 438-4437
William M Gershen, *Pr*
Michael Harrison, *
Bill Gershen, *
▲ **EMP:** 107 **EST:** 1980
**SQ FT:** 36,000
**SALES (est):** 8.92MM
**SALES (corp-wide):** 8.92MM **Privately Held**
Web: www.vanguardmil.com
**SIC: 2399** 2395 Military insignia, textile; Pleating and stitching

**(P-3039)**
**WESSCO INTL LTD A CAL LTD PRTN (PA)**
Also Called: Wessco International
11400 W Olympic Blvd Ste 450, Los Angeles (90064-1550)
PHONE.................310 477-4272
Robert Bregman, *Pr*
Tyler Shepodd, *CFO*
Nick Bregman, *COO*
◆ **EMP:** 54 **EST:** 1979
**SQ FT:** 7,000
**SALES (est):** 60MM
**SALES (corp-wide):** 60MM **Privately Held**
Web: www.wessco.net
**SIC: 2399** 2393 3161 2273 Sleeping bags; Textile bags; Traveling bags; Bathmats and sets, textile

**(P-3040)**
**YOUNG SUNG (USA) INC**
1122 S Alvarado St, Los Angeles (90006-4110)
PHONE.................213 427-2580
Pyung Kwon, *Pr*
▲ **EMP:** 15 **EST:** 1985
**SQ FT:** 15,600
**SALES (est):** 892.74K **Privately Held**
Web: www.youngsungusa.com

# PRODUCTS & SERVICES SECTION

## 2411 - Logging (P-3062)

SIC: 2399 Seat covers, automobile

## 2411 Logging

**(P-3041)**
**ANDERSON LOGGING INC**
1296 N Main St, Fort Bragg (95437-8407)
P.O. Box 1266 (95437-1266)
PHONE ................. 707 964-2770
Michael Anderson, *Pr*
Joseph Anderson, *
Maribelle Anderson, *
**EMP:** 100 **EST:** 1977
**SQ FT:** 3,000
**SALES (est):** 5.15MM **Privately Held**
**Web:** www.andersonlogging.com
**SIC:** 2411 4212 Logging camps and contractors; Lumber (log) trucking, local

**(P-3042)**
**APEX ENTERPRISES INC**
461 Ophir Rd, Oroville (95966-9596)
PHONE ................. 530 871-0723
Kristin Rabe, *Admn*
Debbie Mccann, *Off Mgr*
Logan Bamford, *
**EMP:** 25 **EST:** 2017
**SALES (est):** 6.27MM **Privately Held**
**Web:** www.apexenterprisesinc.com
**SIC:** 2411 Logging

**(P-3043)**
**BIG HILL LOG & RD BLDG CO INC (PA)**
680 Sutter St, Yuba City (95991-4218)
PHONE ................. 530 673-4155
Macarthur Siller, *Pr*
Janet Siller, *
Dane Siller, *
Mcarthur Siller, *Pr*
**EMP:** 25 **EST:** 1986
**SQ FT:** 1,726
**SALES (est):** 775.51K **Privately Held**
**SIC:** 2411 1611 Logging camps and contractors; Highway and street construction

**(P-3044)**
**ELIZABETH HEADRICK**
Also Called: Headrick Logging
7194 Bridge St, Anderson (96007-9496)
PHONE ................. 530 247-8000
Elizabeth Headrick, *Owner*
**EMP:** 19 **EST:** 1986
**SQ FT:** 4,500
**SALES (est):** 2.17MM **Privately Held**
**SIC:** 2411 Logging camps and contractors

**(P-3045)**
**FORD LOGGING INC**
Also Called: Pacific Earthscape
1225 Central Ave Ste 11, Mckinleyville (95519-5301)
PHONE ................. 707 840-9442
Delman Ford, *Pr*
Glenn Ford, *VP*
Derek Ford, *Sec*
Heath Ford, *Treas*
**EMP:** 18 **EST:** 1995
**SALES (est):** 1.58MM **Privately Held**
**Web:** www.pacificearthscape.com
**SIC:** 2411 1611 Logging camps and contractors; Gravel or dirt road construction

**(P-3046)**
**HOOPA FOREST INDUSTRIES**
778 Marshall Ln, Hoopa (95546-9762)
P.O. Box 759 (95546-0759)
PHONE ................. 530 625-4281
Merwin Clark, *CEO*
Wendell White Woodboss, *Prin*
**EMP:** 29 **EST:** 2014
**SALES (est):** 916.04K **Privately Held**
**Web:** www.hoopaforestry.com
**SIC:** 2411 Logging
**PA:** The Hoopa Valley Tribe
11860 State Highway 96
530 625-4211

**(P-3047)**
**J W BAMFORD INC**
Also Called: Bamford Equipment
4288 State Highway 70, Oroville (95965-8340)
PHONE ................. 530 533-0732
Joel Bamford, *Pr*
James Bamford, *VP*
Nathan Bamford, *Sec*
**EMP:** 16 **EST:** 1980
**SQ FT:** 8,000
**SALES (est):** 4.81MM **Privately Held**
**Web:** www.bamfordinc.net
**SIC:** 2411 Logging

**(P-3048)**
**JOHN WHEELER LOGGING INC**
13570 State Highway 36 E, Red Bluff (96080-8878)
P.O. Box 339 (96080-0339)
PHONE ................. 530 527-2993
Dave Holder, *Pr*
Vern Mc Coshum, *
**EMP:** 105 **EST:** 1966
**SQ FT:** 3,500
**SALES (est):** 9.09MM **Privately Held**
**SIC:** 2411 4212 Logging camps and contractors; Local trucking, without storage

**(P-3049)**
**LEONARDO LOGGING AND CNSTR INC**
Also Called: Anthony Leonardo Logging
604 L St, Fortuna (95540-1900)
P.O. Box 875 (95540-0875)
PHONE ................. 707 725-1809
Anthony Leonardo, *CEO*
Janice Leonardo, *
Shannon Leonardo, *
**EMP:** 40 **EST:** 1993
**SALES (est):** 4.95MM **Privately Held**
**SIC:** 2411 4212 Logging camps and contractors; Lumber and timber trucking

**(P-3050)**
**LITE ON LAND INC**
35846 Powerhouse Rd, Auberry (93602)
P.O. Box 936 (93602)
PHONE ................. 559 203-2322
Ryan Day, *CEO*
**EMP:** 23 **EST:** 2006
**SALES (est):** 4.5MM **Privately Held**
**Web:** www.liteontheland.com
**SIC:** 2411 Wooden logs

**(P-3051)**
**MOUNTAIN F ENTERPRISES INC**
Also Called: Tree Service
950 Iron Point Rd Ste 210, Folsom (95630-8338)
P.O. Box 1040 (95651)
PHONE ................. 530 626-4127
Raul Gomez, *Pr*
Marcos A Gomez, *
Raul Gomez, *COO*
**EMP:** 40 **EST:** 1989
**SQ FT:** 4,000
**SALES (est):** 22.18MM **Privately Held**
**Web:** www.mtfent.com

**SIC:** 2411 0851 0783 5099 Logging; Forestry services; Tree trimming services for public utility lines; Firewood

**(P-3052)**
**ROACH BROS INC**
23550 Shady Ln, Fort Bragg (95437-8421)
PHONE ................. 707 964-9240
Leroy Roach, *Pr*
Gary Roach, *
Sybil Roach, *
Sally Roach, *
**EMP:** 70 **EST:** 1968
**SALES (est):** 494.24K **Privately Held**
**SIC:** 2411 Logging camps and contractors

**(P-3053)**
**ROBINSON ENTERPRISES INVESTMENT CO INC**
Also Called: Robinson Timber
293 Lower Grass Valley Rd Ste 201, Nevada City (95959-3120)
PHONE ................. 530 265-5844
**EMP:** 75 **EST:** 1971
**SALES (est):** 4.86MM **Privately Held**
**Web:** www.robinsonenterprises.com
**SIC:** 2411 5171 7353 Logging camps and contractors; Petroleum bulk stations; Heavy construction equipment rental

**(P-3054)**
**SANDERS PRCSION TMBER FLLING I (PA)**
9509 N Old Stage Rd, Weed (96094-9516)
PHONE ................. 530 938-4120
Ross Sanders, *Owner*
Forest Sanders, *VP*
Tom Midget, *Sec*
Bernard Cilione, *Treas*
**EMP:** 20 **EST:** 1981
**SALES (est):** 416.94K **Privately Held**
**SIC:** 2411 Timber, cut at logging camp

**(P-3055)**
**SHASTA GREEN INC**
Also Called: Franklin Logging
35856a State Highway 299 E, Burney (96013-4048)
PHONE ................. 530 335-4924
Diane Franklin, *Pr*
Keith Tiner, *
**EMP:** 50 **EST:** 2002
**SQ FT:** 1,500
**SALES (est):** 9.92MM **Privately Held**
**SIC:** 2411 Logging camps and contractors

**(P-3056)**
**SIERRA RESOURCE MANAGEMENT INC**
Also Called: Sierra Resource Management
12015 La Grange Rd, Jamestown (95327-9724)
PHONE ................. 209 984-1146
Mike Albrecht, *Pr*
Stacy Dodge, *
**EMP:** 18 **EST:** 1993
**SQ FT:** 4,500
**SALES (est):** 973.3K **Privately Held**
**Web:** www.sierraresource.org
**SIC:** 2411 Logging camps and contractors

**(P-3057)**
**SILLER BROTHERS INC (PA)**
Also Called: Siller Aviation
1250 Smith Rd, Yuba City (95991-6948)
P.O. Box 1585 (95992-1585)
PHONE ................. 530 673-0734
Tom Siller, *Pr*
Andrew Jansen, *

Hunt Norris, *
Jack Parnell, *
**EMP:** 50 **EST:** 1943
**SALES (est):** 5.92MM
**SALES (corp-wide):** 5.92MM **Privately Held**
**Web:** www.sillerhelicopters.com
**SIC:** 2411 2421 Logging camps and contractors; Sawmills and planing mills, general

**(P-3058)**
**SKYLINE ALTERATIONS INC (PA)**
5626 Riverland Dr, Anderson (96007-8378)
PHONE ................. 530 549-4010
Dawn Sherman, *Pr*
Jody Sherman, *VP*
Brian Parnell, *Sec*
**EMP:** 24 **EST:** 2003
**SALES (est):** 2.25MM
**SALES (corp-wide):** 2.25MM **Privately Held**
**SIC:** 2411 Logging

**(P-3059)**
**TUBIT ENTERPRISES INC**
21640 S Vallejo St, Burney (96013-9778)
P.O. Box 1019 (96013-1019)
PHONE ................. 530 335-5085
Douglas Lindgren, *CEO*
Richard Lindgren, *
**EMP:** 40 **EST:** 1995
**SQ FT:** 3,000
**SALES (est):** 5.46MM **Privately Held**
**Web:** tubit-enterprises-inc.business.site
**SIC:** 2411 Logging camps and contractors

**(P-3060)**
**WARNER ENTERPRISES INC**
1577 Beltline Rd, Redding (96003-1407)
PHONE ................. 530 241-4000
Paul Warner, *Pr*
Gary Warner, *
**EMP:** 30 **EST:** 1978
**SQ FT:** 9,000
**SALES (est):** 4.64MM **Privately Held**
**SIC:** 2411 Wood chips, produced in the field

**(P-3061)**
**WELL ANALYSIS CORPORATION INC (PA)**
Also Called: Welaco
5500 Woodmere Dr, Bakersfield (93313-2776)
P.O. Box 20008 (93390-0008)
PHONE ................. 661 283-9510
Judy L Bebout, *CEO*
Brenda Muniozguren, *
Robert Muniozguren, *
Dan Bebout, *
▲ **EMP:** 26 **EST:** 1989
**SQ FT:** 1,400
**SALES (est):** 5.02MM **Privately Held**
**Web:** www.welacogroup.com
**SIC:** 2411 1389 Logging; Oil field services, nec

**(P-3062)**
**WILLIAM R SCHMITT**
Also Called: Schmitt Superior Classics
18135 Clear Creek Rd, Redding (96001-5233)
PHONE ................. 530 243-3069
William R Schmitt, *Owner*
**EMP:** 20 **EST:** 1950
**SALES (est):** 353.97K **Privately Held**
**Web:** www.superiorclassics.com

## 2411 - Logging (P-3063)

### PRODUCTS & SERVICES SECTION

SIC: **2411** 4212 5521 Logging; Lumber (log) trucking, local; Automobiles, used cars only

**(P-3063)**
**WYLATTI RESOURCE MGT INC**
23601 Cemetery Ln, Covelo (95428-9773)
P.O. Box 575 (95428-0575)
PHONE.................707 983-8135
Brian K Hurt, *Pr*
EMP: 20 EST: 1999
SALES (est): 1.29MM Privately Held
SIC: **2411** 1611 1622 1442 Logging; General contractor, highway and street construction; Bridge construction; Construction sand and gravel

---

### 2421 Sawmills And Planing Mills, General

**(P-3064)**
**ARTESIA SAWDUST PRODUCTS INC**
13434 S Ontario Ave, Ontario (91761-7956)
PHONE.................909 947-5983
TOLL FREE: 800
Brigitte De Laura-espinoza, *Pr*
Anthony Espinoza, *
EMP: 35 EST: 1960
SQ FT: 2,700
SALES (est): 4.4MM Privately Held
Web: www.artesiasawdust.com
SIC: **2421** Sawdust and shavings

**(P-3065)**
**BURGESS LUMBER**
8800 West Rd, Redwood Valley (95470-6199)
PHONE.................707 485-8072
Bobby Puga, *Mgr*
EMP: 26
SALES (corp-wide): 4.51MM Privately Held
Web: www.goldenstatelumber.com
SIC: **2421** Resawing lumber into smaller dimensions
PA: Burgess Lumber
3610 Copperhill Ln
707 542-5091

**(P-3066)**
**CABINETS GLORE ORANGE CNTY INC**
Also Called: Cabinets Galore Oc
9279 Cabot Dr Ste D, San Diego (92126-4364)
PHONE.................858 586-0555
Barry Jacobs, *Pr*
Adi Jacobs, *VP*
Luke Breandt, *Prin*
EMP: 20 EST: 1986
SQ FT: 10,000
SALES (est): 1.77MM Privately Held
Web: www.cabinetsgalore.net
SIC: **2421** 1751 Furniture dimension stock, softwood; Cabinet and finish carpentry

**(P-3067)**
**COLLINS PINE COMPANY**
500 Main St, Chester (96020)
P.O. Box 796 (96020-0796)
PHONE.................530 258-2111
Chris Verderber, *Brnch Mgr*
EMP: 37
SALES (corp-wide): 47.32MM Privately Held
Web: www.collinsco.com
SIC: **2421** Sawmills and planing mills, general
PA: Collins Pine Company
29100 Sw Town Ctr Loop W
503 227-1219

**(P-3068)**
**COLLINS PINE COMPANY**
Builders Sup Div Collinspine
540 Main St, Chester (96020)
P.O. Box 990 (96020-0990)
PHONE.................530 258-2131
Mike Stelzriede, *Mgr*
EMP: 83
SALES (corp-wide): 47.32MM Privately Held
Web: www.collinsco.com
SIC: **2421** Sawmills and planing mills, general
PA: Collins Pine Company
29100 Sw Town Ctr Loop W
503 227-1219

**(P-3069)**
**FULGHUM FIBRES INC (HQ)**
Also Called: Fulghum Fibres
333 S Grand Ave Ste 4100, Los Angeles (90071-1571)
PHONE.................706 651-1000
O T Fulghum Junior, *Pr*
H Heyward Wells, *Junior President*
Jeff B Boatright, *VP*
Heyward T H T Fulghum, *VP*
Anthony M Hauff, *CFO*
EMP: 16 EST: 1956
SALES (est): 25.11MM
SALES (corp-wide): 133.06MM Privately Held
Web: www.thepricecompanies.com
SIC: **2421** Chipper mill
PA: Rentech, Inc.
10880 Wlshire Blvd Ste 11
310 571-9800

**(P-3070)**
**HMR BUILDING SYSTEMS LLC**
620 Newport Center Dr Fl 12, Newport Beach (92660-6420)
PHONE.................951 749-4700
▲ EMP: 67 EST: 2008
SQ FT: 90,000
SALES (est): 688.35K Privately Held
SIC: **2421** Building and structural materials, wood
PA: Rsi Holding Llc
620 Nwport Ctr Dr 12th Fl

**(P-3071)**
**INTERNATIONAL WOOD INDUSTRIES INC**
Also Called: International Wood Industries
250 D St, Turlock (95380-5431)
P.O. Box 398 (95686-0398)
PHONE.................209 632-3300
▼ EMP: 29
Web: www.iwiproducts.com
SIC: **2421** 5031 Sawmills and planing mills, general; Plywood

**(P-3072)**
**LAUSMANN LUMBER & MOULDING CO**
3370 Rippey Rd, Loomis (95650-7655)
P.O. Box 65 (95650-0065)
PHONE.................916 652-9201
EMP: 20
Web: www.lausmannlumber.com
SIC: **2421** 5031 Sawmills and planing mills, general; Lumber, plywood, and millwork

**(P-3073)**
**MALLARD CREEK INC**
4095 Duluth Ave, Rocklin (95765-1401)
PHONE.................916 645-1681
EMP: 15 EST: 1982
SALES (est): 5.74MM Privately Held
Web: www.mallardcreekinc.com
SIC: **2421** 3271 3532 Sawdust, shavings, and wood chips; Blocks, concrete: landscape or retaining wall; Pellet mills (mining machinery)

**(P-3074)**
**NORTH CAL WOOD PRODUCTS INC**
700 Kunzler Ranch Rd, Ukiah (95482-3264)
P.O. Box 1534 (95482-1534)
PHONE.................707 462-0686
Frank Van Vranken, *Pr*
Charles Currey, *
Tony Fernandez, *Operations**
EMP: 50 EST: 1984
SQ FT: 8,000
SALES (est): 5.03MM Privately Held
Web: www.northcal.com
SIC: **2421** 2431 2435 Lumber: rough, sawed, or planed; Panel work, wood; Hardwood veneer and plywood

**(P-3075)**
**PLUM VALLEY INC**
Also Called: Pacwood
3308 Cyclone Ct, Cottonwood (96022-8077)
P.O. Box 1485 (96022-1485)
PHONE.................530 262-6262
Clinton Heiss, *CEO*
Donald E Frank, *CEO*
EMP: 20 EST: 2003
SQ FT: 5,000
SALES (est): 2.53MM Privately Held
SIC: **2421** Lumber: rough, sawed, or planed

**(P-3076)**
**RAFAEL SANDOVAL**
Also Called: Lathrop Woodworks
16175 Mckinley Ave, Lathrop (95330-9703)
PHONE.................209 858-4173
Rafael Sandoval, *Owner*
▲ EMP: 45 EST: 1984
SQ FT: 1,000
SALES (est): 5.01MM Privately Held
SIC: **2421** Outdoor wood structural products

**(P-3077)**
**REUSER INC**
370 Santana Dr, Cloverdale (95425-4224)
PHONE.................707 894-4224
Bruce Reuser, *Pr*
John Reuser, *VP*
EMP: 15 EST: 1978
SQ FT: 5,000
SALES (est): 2.68MM Privately Held
Web: www.reuserinc.com
SIC: **2421** 2875 Sawdust and shavings; Fertilizers, mixing only

**(P-3078)**
**SCHMIDBAUER LUMBER INC (PA)**
Also Called: Pacific Clears
1099 W Waterfront Dr, Eureka (95501)
P.O. Box 152 (95502-0152)
PHONE.................707 443-7024
Frank Schmidbauer, *Prin*
Frank Schmidbauer, *VP*
Mary Schmidbauer, *
Duane Martin, *

▲ EMP: 110 EST: 1972
SQ FT: 200,000
SALES (est): 21.43MM
SALES (corp-wide): 21.43MM Privately Held
Web: www.schmidbauerlumber.com
SIC: **2421** 5211 Sawmills and planing mills, general; Lumber and other building materials

**(P-3079)**
**SCHMIDBAUER LUMBER INC**
Pacific Clears
1017 Samoa Blvd, Arcata (95521-6605)
P.O. Box 1141 (95518-1141)
PHONE.................707 822-7607
Lee Iorg, *Mgr*
EMP: 100
SQ FT: 3,000
SALES (corp-wide): 21.43MM Privately Held
Web: www.schmidbauerlumber.com
SIC: **2421** 5211 Resawing lumber into smaller dimensions; Planing mill products and lumber
PA: Schmidbauer Lumber, Inc.
1099 W Waterfront Dr
707 443-7024

**(P-3080)**
**SETZER FOREST PRODUCTS INC**
Also Called: Millwork Div
1980 Kusel Rd, Oroville (95966-9528)
PHONE.................530 534-8100
Terry Dunn, *Mgr*
EMP: 118
SALES (corp-wide): 49.51MM Privately Held
Web: www.setzerforest.com
SIC: **2421** 2431 Cut stock, softwood; Millwork
PA: Setzer Forest Products, Inc.
2555 3rd St Ste 200
916 442-2555

**(P-3081)**
**SIERRA PACIFIC INDUSTRIES**
Also Called: SIERRA PACIFIC INDUSTRIES
1538 Lee Rd, Quincy (95971-9687)
PHONE.................530 283-2820
Randy Lilburn, *Brnch Mgr*
EMP: 225
SQ FT: 216
SALES (corp-wide): 542.23MM Privately Held
Web: www.spi-ind.com
SIC: **2421** 4939 Sawmills and planing mills, general; Combination utilities, nec
PA: Sierra Pacific Industries Inc.
19794 Riverside Ave
530 378-8000

**(P-3082)**
**SIERRA PACIFIC INDUSTRIES**
Also Called: SIERRA PACIFIC INDUSTRIES
14980 Camage Ave, Sonora (95370-9287)
P.O. Box 247 (95373-0247)
PHONE.................530 378-8301
Rod Johnson, *Mgr*
EMP: 119
SALES (corp-wide): 542.23MM Privately Held
Web: www.spi-ind.com
SIC: **2421** Lumber: rough, sawed, or planed
PA: Sierra Pacific Industries Inc.
19794 Riverside Ave
530 378-8000

## PRODUCTS & SERVICES SECTION
## 2426 - Hardwood Dimension And Flooring Mills (P-3103)

**(P-3083)**
**SIERRA PACIFIC INDUSTRIES**
Also Called: SIERRA PACIFIC INDUSTRIES
Hwy 299 E, Burney (96013)
P.O. Box 2677 (96013-2677)
PHONE..............................530 335-3681
Ed Fisher, Brnch Mgr
**EMP:** 42
**SQ FT:** 1,000
**SALES (corp-wide):** 542.23MM **Privately Held**
Web: www.spi-ind.com
**SIC: 2421** Lumber: rough, sawed, or planed
**PA:** Sierra Pacific Industries Inc.
19794 Riverside Ave
530 378-8000

**(P-3084)**
**SIERRA PACIFIC INDUSTRIES**
Also Called: SIERRA PACIFIC INDUSTRIES
19758 Riverside Ave, Anderson (96007-4908)
P.O. Box 10939 (96007-1939)
PHONE..............................530 365-3721
Shane Young, Mgr
**EMP:** 110
**SALES (corp-wide):** 542.23MM **Privately Held**
Web: www.spi-ind.com
**SIC: 2421** Lumber: rough, sawed, or planed
**PA:** Sierra Pacific Industries Inc.
19794 Riverside Ave
530 378-8000

**(P-3085)**
**SIERRA PACIFIC INDUSTRIES**
Also Called: SIERRA PACIFIC INDUSTRIES
3950 Carson Rd, Camino (95709-9347)
P.O. Box 680 (95709-0680)
PHONE..............................530 644-2311
Brian Coyle, Brnch Mgr
**EMP:** 29
**SALES (corp-wide):** 542.23MM **Privately Held**
Web: www.spi-ind.com
**SIC: 2421** Lumber: rough, sawed, or planed
**PA:** Sierra Pacific Industries Inc.
19794 Riverside Ave
530 378-8000

**(P-3086)**
**SIERRA PACIFIC INDUSTRIES**
Also Called: SIERRA PACIFIC INDUSTRIES
1440 Lincoln Blvd, Lincoln (95648-9105)
P.O. Box 670 (95648-0670)
PHONE..............................916 645-1631
Dan Quarton, Brnch Mgr
**EMP:** 53
**SALES (corp-wide):** 542.23MM **Privately Held**
Web: www.spi-ind.com
**SIC: 2421** Lumber: rough, sawed, or planed
**PA:** Sierra Pacific Industries Inc.
19794 Riverside Ave
530 378-8000

**(P-3087)**
**SIERRA PACIFIC INDUSTRIES INC**
Sierra Pacific Windows
11605 Reading Rd, Red Bluff (96080-6702)
P.O. Box 8489 (96080-8489)
PHONE..............................530 527-9620
Bob Taylor, Brnch Mgr
**EMP:** 500
**SALES (corp-wide):** 542.23MM **Privately Held**
Web: www.sierrapacificwindows.com
**SIC: 2421** Sawmills and planing mills, general
**PA:** Sierra Pacific Industries Inc.
19794 Riverside Ave
530 378-8000

**(P-3088)**
**SIERRA PACIFIC INDUSTRIES INC (PA)**
19794 Riverside Ave, Anderson (96007-4908)
P.O. Box 496028 (96049)
PHONE..............................530 378-8000
Mark Emmerson, CEO
George Emmerson, *
Todd Payne, *
◆ **EMP:** 100 **EST:** 1949
**SQ FT:** 37,000
**SALES (est):** 542.23MM
**SALES (corp-wide):** 542.23MM **Privately Held**
Web: www.spi-ind.com
**SIC: 2421** 2431 Lumber: rough, sawed, or planed; Millwork

**(P-3089)**
**STRATA FOREST PRODUCTS INC (PA)**
Also Called: Profile Planing Mill
2600 S Susan St, Santa Ana (92704-5816)
PHONE..............................714 751-0800
TOLL FREE: 800
Richard W Hormuth, Pr
John Hormuth, *
▲ **EMP:** 50 **EST:** 1991
**SQ FT:** 38,000
**SALES (est):** 8.61MM
**SALES (corp-wide):** 8.61MM **Privately Held**
Web: www.strataforest.com
**SIC: 2421** Planing mills, nec

**(P-3090)**
**SUNSET MOULDING CO (PA)**
2231 Paseo Rd, Live Oak (95953-9721)
P.O. Box 326 (95992-0326)
PHONE..............................530 790-2700
John A Morrison, CEO
Wendy Forren, CFO
Michel Morrison, VP
Mark Westlake, VP
▲ **EMP:** 50 **EST:** 1946
**SALES (est):** 10.11MM
**SALES (corp-wide):** 10.11MM **Privately Held**
Web: www.sunsetmoulding.com
**SIC: 2421** 2431 Cut stock, softwood; Moldings, wood: unfinished and prefinished

**(P-3091)**
**WILLITS REDWOOD COMPANY INC**
220 Franklin Ave, Willits (95490-4132)
PHONE..............................707 459-4549
Bruce Burton, Pr
Chris Baldo, VP
**EMP:** 38 **EST:** 1975
**SQ FT:** 500
**SALES (est):** 2.17MM **Privately Held**
Web: www.willitsredwood.com
**SIC: 2421** Sawmills and planing mills, general

## 2426 Hardwood Dimension And Flooring Mills

**(P-3092)**
**FURNITURE TECHNOLOGIES INC**
17227 Columbus St, Adelanto (92301)
P.O. Box 1076 (92301-1076)
PHONE..............................760 246-9180
Kenneth Drum, CEO
**EMP:** 24 **EST:** 1998
**SQ FT:** 31,000
**SALES (est):** 2.88MM **Privately Held**
Web: www.ftical.com
**SIC: 2426** Furniture stock and parts, hardwood

**(P-3093)**
**HALLMARK HOME INTERIORS INC (PA)**
Also Called: Hallmark Floors
2360 S Archibald Ave, Ontario (91761-8520)
PHONE..............................909 947-7736
Zheng Qing Pan, Pr
**EMP:** 17 **EST:** 2020
**SALES (est):** 1.74MM
**SALES (corp-wide):** 1.74MM **Privately Held**
**SIC: 2426** Flooring, hardwood

**(P-3094)**
**HARDWOOD FLRG LIQUIDATORS INC (PA)**
Also Called: Republic Flooring
7227 Telegraph Rd, Montebello (90640-6512)
PHONE..............................323 201-4200
Eliyahu Shuat, CEO
▲ **EMP:** 100 **EST:** 2008
**SALES (est):** 76.09MM
**SALES (corp-wide):** 76.09MM **Privately Held**
Web: www.republicfloor.com
**SIC: 2426** Flooring, hardwood

**(P-3095)**
**HOGUE BROS INC**
Also Called: Hogue Grips
550 Linne Rd, Paso Robles (93446-8454)
P.O. Box 1138 (93447-1138)
PHONE..............................805 239-1440
▲ **EMP:** 36
Web: www.hogueinc.com
**SIC: 2426** 3489 Hardwood dimension and flooring mills; Guns, howitzers, mortars, and related equipment

**(P-3096)**
**LA HARDWOOD FLOORING INC (PA)**
Also Called: Eternity Floors
9880 San Fernando Rd, Pacoima (91331-2603)
PHONE..............................818 361-0099
Doron Gal, CEO
Eliyahu Shuat, Prin
▲ **EMP:** 17 **EST:** 2005
**SQ FT:** 12,000
**SALES (est):** 9.37MM
**SALES (corp-wide):** 9.37MM **Privately Held**
Web: www.eternityflooring.com
**SIC: 2426** 5211 Flooring, hardwood; Flooring, wood

**(P-3097)**
**MONIKER GENERAL LLC**
Also Called: Moniker General
2860 Sims Rd, San Diego (92106-6170)
PHONE..............................619 255-8772
Ryan Sisson, CEO
**EMP:** 15 **EST:** 2015
**SALES (est):** 595.98K **Privately Held**
Web: www.monikergeneral.com

**SIC: 2426** 5099 5499 Carvings, furniture: wood; Brass goods; Coffee

**(P-3098)**
**MOTOMOTION USA CORPORATION**
Also Called: Blue Berry Health Care
1008 S Baldwin Ave Ste G, Arcadia (91007-7203)
PHONE..............................626 538-4866
Xiaoqin Li, CEO
Jack Copley, Pr
**EMP:** 16 **EST:** 2011
**SALES (est):** 6.19MM **Privately Held**
**SIC: 2426** Furniture stock and parts, hardwood

**(P-3099)**
**N M FLOOR COVERINGS INC**
Also Called: Pacific Coast Coml Interiors
5651 Palmer Way Ste D, Carlsbad (92010-7244)
PHONE..............................760 931-8274
**EMP:** 15 **EST:** 2007
**SALES (est):** 820.74K **Privately Held**
**SIC: 2426** 2599 Hardwood dimension and flooring mills; Factory furniture and fixtures

**(P-3100)**
**O INDUSTRIES CORPORATION**
1930 W 139th St, Gardena (90249-2490)
P.O. Box 779 (92629-0779)
PHONE..............................310 719-2289
Rhonda Oerding, CEO
William Oerding, COO
▼ **EMP:** 15 **EST:** 2010
**SQ FT:** 40,000
**SALES (est):** 3MM **Privately Held**
Web: www.oindcorp.com
**SIC: 2426** Flooring, hardwood

**(P-3101)**
**PARQUET BY DIAN**
16601 S Main St, Gardena (90248-2722)
PHONE..............................310 527-3779
Anatoli Efros, CEO
Dima Efros, Pr
**EMP:** 92 **EST:** 1993
**SALES (est):** 5.19MM **Privately Held**
Web: www.parquet.com
**SIC: 2426** Parquet flooring, hardwood

**(P-3102)**
**RTMEX INC**
Also Called: Best Redwood
1202 Piper Ranch Rd, San Diego (92154-7714)
P.O. Box 8662 (91912-8662)
PHONE..............................619 391-9913
Jorje Sampietro, Pr
**EMP:** 108 **EST:** 2010
**SQ FT:** 15,000
**SALES (est):** 1.88MM **Privately Held**
Web: www.best-redwood.com
**SIC: 2426** Carvings, furniture: wood

**(P-3103)**
**WEST COAST FURN FRAMERS INC**
24006 Tahquitz Rd, Apple Valley (92307-2236)
PHONE..............................760 669-5275
Katelynn Galiana-baca, Pr
Katelynn Baca, *
Javier Galiana, *
**EMP:** 27 **EST:** 2017
**SALES (est):** 2.52MM **Privately Held**
**SIC: 2426** Frames for upholstered furniture, wood

(PA)=Parent Co (HQ)=Headquarters
✪ = New Business established in last 2 years

## 2429 Special Product Sawmills, Nec

**(P-3104)**
**CEDAR VALLEY MANUFACTURING INC**
943 San Felipe Rd, Hollister (95023-2807)
PHONE...............................831 636-8110
EMP: 130 EST: 1997
SALES (est): 5.31MM Privately Held
Web: cedarvalleyshisyslpc.openfos.com
SIC: 2429 Shingles, wood: sawed or hand split

## 2431 Millwork

**(P-3105)**
**ABC CUSTOM WOOD SHUTTERS INC**
Also Called: Golden West Shutters
20561 Pascal Way, Lake Forest (92630-8119)
PHONE...............................949 595-0300
David Harris, VP
John Stahman, *
EMP: 35 EST: 1991
SALES (est): 874.78K Privately Held
Web: www.gwshutters.com
SIC: 2431 Door shutters, wood

**(P-3106)**
**ALL-WEATHER ARCHITECTURAL ALUMINUM INC**
777 Aldridge Rd, Vacaville (95688-9282)
PHONE...............................707 452-1600
▲ EMP: 56 EST: 1969
SALES (est): 10.03MM Privately Held
Web: www.allweatheraa.com
SIC: 2431 Windows and window parts and trim, wood

**(P-3107)**
**AMERICAN CABINET WORKS INC**
13518 S Normandie Ave, Gardena (90249-2606)
PHONE...............................310 715-6815
Alex Medrano, Owner
EMP: 22 EST: 1999
SQ FT: 5,000
SALES (est): 2.48MM Privately Held
Web: www.americancabinetworks.com
SIC: 2431 Millwork

**(P-3108)**
**ANDERCO INC**
540 Airpark Dr, Fullerton (92833-2503)
PHONE...............................714 446-9508
Peter Johnson, Pr
Ralph Johnson, *
▲ EMP: 50 EST: 1983
SQ FT: 70,000
SALES (est): 7.03MM
SALES (corp-wide): 183.49MM Privately Held
SIC: 2431 5031 Door frames, wood; Doors and windows
HQ: Metrie Inc.
2200 140th Ave E Ste 600
Sumner WA 98390
253 470-5050

**(P-3109)**
**ARCHITCTRAL MLLWK SLUTIONS INC**
2565 Progress St, Vista (92081-8423)
PHONE...............................760 510-6440
Ricardo Alcantara, Pr
Ricardo E Alcantara, Pr
Terry Alcantara, CFO
EMP: 15 EST: 2004
SQ FT: 8,850
SALES (est): 1.58MM Privately Held
Web: www.archmilsol.com
SIC: 2431 Millwork

**(P-3110)**
**ARCHITCTRAL MLLWK SNTA BARBARA**
Also Called: Manufacturers of Wood Products
8 N Nopal St, Santa Barbara (93103-3317)
P.O. Box 4699 (93140-4699)
PHONE...............................805 965-7011
Thomas G Mathews, Pr
Glenice Mathews, *
Joseph J Mathews, *
Ronald Mathews, Stockholder*
EMP: 40 EST: 1968
SQ FT: 10,000
SALES (est): 4.87MM Privately Held
Web: www.archmill.com
SIC: 2431 Millwork

**(P-3111)**
**ART GLASS ETC INC**
Also Called: AG Millworks
3111 Golf Course Dr, Ventura (93003-7604)
PHONE...............................805 644-4494
Rachid El Etel, Pr
Aida El Etel, *
▲ EMP: 50 EST: 1986
SALES (est): 4.55MM Privately Held
Web: www.agmillworks.com
SIC: 2431 Doors and door parts and trim, wood

**(P-3112)**
**AVALON SHUTTERS INC**
3407 N Perris Blvd, Perris (92571-3100)
PHONE...............................909 937-4900
Douglas Noel Serbin, Pr
Douglas Noel Serbin, CEO
▲ EMP: 90 EST: 1986
SQ FT: 85,000
SALES (est): 14.73MM Privately Held
Web: www.avalonshutters.com
SIC: 2431 Window shutters, wood

**(P-3113)**
**CALIFORNIA CAB & STORE FIX**
8472 Carbide Ct, Sacramento (95828-5609)
PHONE...............................916 386-1340
Bruce D Nicolson, Pr
EMP: 30 EST: 1989
SQ FT: 20,640
SALES (est): 590.87K Privately Held
SIC: 2431 2541 Millwork; Table or counter tops, plastic laminated

**(P-3114)**
**CALIFORNIA MILLWORKS CORP**
Also Called: California Classics
27772 Avenue Scott, Santa Clarita (91355-3417)
PHONE...............................661 294-2345
Steven Gadol, Pr
Lay Cho, Pr
Edmond Cho, VP
Steven Godol, Pr
EMP: 22 EST: 1981
SQ FT: 149,000
SALES (est): 1.09MM
SALES (corp-wide): 1.09MM Privately Held
Web: www.california-classics.com
SIC: 2431 Doors, wood
PA: Old English Milling & Woodworks, Inc.
27772 Avenue Scott
661 294-9171

**(P-3115)**
**CALIFORNIA WOOD CSTM SOLUTIONS (PA)**
4857 Schaefer Ave, Chino (91710-5546)
PHONE...............................909 364-2440
Cindy Huong Giang Dang, CEO
Gustavo Ureta, CFO
▲ EMP: 16 EST: 2012
SALES (est): 3MM
SALES (corp-wide): 3MM Privately Held
SIC: 2431 Millwork

**(P-3116)**
**CALIFRNIA DLUXE WNDOWS INDS IN (PA)**
20735 Superior St, Chatsworth (91311-4416)
PHONE...............................818 349-5566
Aaron Adirim, Pr
EMP: 46 EST: 1999
SQ FT: 60,000
SALES (est): 12.36MM
SALES (corp-wide): 12.36MM Privately Held
Web: www.cdwindows.com
SIC: 2431 2824 Windows and window parts and trim, wood; Vinyl fibers

**(P-3117)**
**CALIFRNIA MANTEL FIREPLACE INC (PA)**
4141 N Freeway Blvd, Sacramento (95834-1209)
P.O. Box 340037 (95834-0037)
PHONE...............................916 925-5775
Stephen Casey, Pr
EMP: 37 EST: 1988
SQ FT: 7,000
SALES (est): 10.83MM Privately Held
Web: www.calmantel.com
SIC: 2431 3272 Mantels, wood; Mantels, concrete

**(P-3118)**
**CANYON GRAPHICS INC**
3738 Ruffin Rd, San Diego (92123)
PHONE...............................858 646-0444
Scott Moncrieff, CEO
EMP: 60 EST: 1981
SALES (est): 9.26MM Privately Held
Web: www.canyongraphics.com
SIC: 2431 2754 Moldings and baseboards, ornamental and trim; Labels: gravure printing

**(P-3119)**
**CHARLES GEMEINER CABINETS**
3225 Exposition Pl, Los Angeles (90018-4032)
PHONE...............................323 299-8696
Charles Gemeiner, Owner
EMP: 16 EST: 1984
SQ FT: 20,000
SALES (est): 748.65K Privately Held
SIC: 2431 1751 Millwork; Cabinet building and installation

**(P-3120)**
**COMMERCIAL CASEWORK INC (PA)**
Also Called: Madera Fina
41780 Christy St, Fremont (94538-5106)
PHONE...............................510 657-7933
William M Palmer, CEO
EMP: 73 EST: 1976
SQ FT: 35,000
SALES (est): 11.59MM
SALES (corp-wide): 11.59MM Privately Held
Web: www.commercialcasework.com
SIC: 2431 2541 Millwork; Office fixtures, wood

**(P-3121)**
**COMPOSITE TECHNOLOGY INTL INC**
Also Called: Composite Technology Intl
622 20th St, Sacramento (95811-2107)
PHONE...............................916 551-1850
Griff Reid, CEO
Griffin Reid V, US Operations President
Joseph Falmer, *
Cynthia Reid, *
Todd Stemler, *
▲ EMP: 55 EST: 2004
SALES (est): 11.33MM Privately Held
Web: www.cti-web.com
SIC: 2431 5023 8711 3999 Moldings, wood: unfinished and prefinished; Frames and framing, picture and mirror; Sanitary engineers; Barber and beauty shop equipment

**(P-3122)**
**CONTRACTORS WARDROBE INC (PA)**
Also Called: Contractors Wardrobe
26121 Avenue Hall, Valencia (91355-3490)
P.O. Box 800790 (91380)
PHONE...............................661 257-1177
▲ EMP: 200 EST: 1972
SALES (est): 110.99MM
SALES (corp-wide): 110.99MM Privately Held
Web: www.cwdoors.com
SIC: 2431 3088 Doors, wood; Shower stalls, fiberglass and plastics

**(P-3123)**
**CRESTMARK MILLWORK INC**
5640 West End Rd, Arcata (95521-9202)
PHONE...............................707 822-4034
Scott David Olsen, CEO
EMP: 35 EST: 1997
SALES (est): 3.68MM Privately Held
Web: www.crestmarkmillwork.com
SIC: 2431 Millwork

**(P-3124)**
**DANMER INC**
Also Called: Danmer Custom Shutters
8000 Woodley Ave, Van Nuys (91406-1226)
PHONE...............................516 670-5125
▲ EMP: 250
Web: www.danmer.com
SIC: 2431 5023 Window shutters, wood; Window covering parts and accessories

**(P-3125)**
**DAY STAR INDUSTRIES**
13727 Excelsior Dr, Santa Fe Springs (90670-5104)
PHONE...............................562 926-8800
Dan R Prigmore, Pr
Anne Prigmore, Treas
EMP: 19 EST: 1985
SALES (est): 2.54MM Privately Held
Web: www.daystarindustries.com
SIC: 2431 Millwork

## PRODUCTS & SERVICES SECTION
## 2431 - Millwork (P-3148)

**(P-3126)**
**DECORE-ATIVE SPC NC LLC (PA)**
2772 Peck Rd, Monrovia (91016-5005)
PHONE..................626 254-9191
Jack Lansford Senior, *CEO*
Jack Lansford Junior, *Pr*
Eric Lansford, *
Billie Lansford, *
▲ EMP: 650 EST: 1969
SALES (est): 106.28MM
SALES (corp-wide): 106.28MM **Privately Held**
Web: www.decore.com
SIC: 2431 Millwork

**(P-3127)**
**DECORE-ATIVE SPC NC LLC**
4414 Azusa Canyon Rd, Irwindale (91706-2740)
PHONE..................626 960-7731
David Thompson, *Brnch Mgr*
EMP: 111
SALES (corp-wide): 106.28MM **Privately Held**
Web: www.decore.com
SIC: 2431 Millwork
PA: Decore-Ative Specialties Nc Llc
2772 Peck Rd
626 254-9191

**(P-3128)**
**DECORE-ATIVE SPC NC LLC**
104 Gate Eats Stock Blvd, Elk Grove (95624)
PHONE..................916 686-4700
Jack Albright, *Mgr*
EMP: 111
SALES (corp-wide): 106.28MM **Privately Held**
Web: www.decore.com
SIC: 2431 Doors, wood
PA: Decore-Ative Specialties Nc Llc
2772 Peck Rd
626 254-9191

**(P-3129)**
**DESIGN SYNTHESIS INC**
9855 Black Mountain Rd, San Diego (92126-4512)
PHONE..................858 271-8480
EMP: 20 EST: 1976
SALES (est): 5.36MM **Privately Held**
Web: www.designsynthesis.net
SIC: 2431 2434 Doors, wood; Wood kitchen cabinets

**(P-3130)**
**DESIGN WOODWORKING INC (PA)**
709 N Sacramento St, Lodi (95240-1255)
PHONE..................209 334-6674
David Worfolk, *Pr*
Stefan I Sekula, *Sec*
EMP: 20 EST: 1976
SQ FT: 22,000
SALES (est): 1.62MM
SALES (corp-wide): 1.62MM **Privately Held**
Web: www.deswood.com
SIC: 2431 Millwork

**(P-3131)**
**DORRIS LUMBER AND MOULDING CO (PA)**
3453 Ramona Ave Ste 5, Sacramento (95826-3828)
PHONE..................916 452-7531
Joshua Tyler, *Pr*
E Chase Israelson, *
Nels Israelson, *Stockholder**
Dennis Murcko, *
▲ EMP: 75 EST: 1924
SALES (est): 10.5MM
SALES (corp-wide): 10.5MM **Privately Held**
Web: www.dorrismoulding.com
SIC: 2431 Moldings, wood: unfinished and prefinished

**(P-3132)**
**DYNAMIC WOODWORKS INC**
Also Called: K & D Contracting
3509 Crooked Creek Dr, Diamond Bar (91765-3722)
PHONE..................562 483-8400
Gloria C Vigil, *Pr*
EMP: 15 EST: 2007
SALES (est): 1.79MM **Privately Held**
Web: www.dynamicwoodworks.com
SIC: 2431 Millwork

**(P-3133)**
**ECMD INC**
4722 Skyway Dr, Marysville (95901)
PHONE..................530 741-0769
Don Mays, *Mgr*
EMP: 145
SQ FT: 85,960
SALES (corp-wide): 186.49MM **Privately Held**
Web: www.ecmd.com
SIC: 2431 Millwork
PA: Ecmd, Inc.
2 Grandview St
336 667-5976

**(P-3134)**
**ECMD INC**
10863 Jersey Blvd 100, Rancho Cucamonga (91730-5151)
PHONE..................909 980-1775
EMP: 47
SALES (corp-wide): 186.49MM **Privately Held**
Web: www.ecmd.com
SIC: 2431 Moldings, wood: unfinished and prefinished
PA: Ecmd, Inc.
2 Grandview St
336 667-5976

**(P-3135)**
**EEW HOLDINGS INC**
10149 Iron Rock Way, Elk Grove (95624-2700)
PHONE..................916 685-1855
Cathy Vidas, *Pr*
EMP: 47
SQ FT: 100,000
SALES (corp-wide): 23.61MM **Privately Held**
Web: www.elandelwoodproducts.com
SIC: 2431 Millwork
PA: Eew Holdings, Inc.
6011 Schaffer Ave
916 685-1855

**(P-3136)**
**EQUINOX MILLWORKS INC**
Also Called: Equinox Construction
1440 Whipple Rd, Union City (94587-2045)
PHONE..................510 946-9729
Oscar Sillas, *CEO*
EMP: 35 EST: 2022
SALES (est): 1.68MM **Privately Held**
Web: www.equinoxmillworks.com
SIC: 2431 Millwork

**(P-3137)**
**FINELINE WOODWORKING INC**
Also Called: Fineline Architectural Mllwk
1139 Baker St, Costa Mesa (92626-4114)
PHONE..................714 540-5468
Marc Butman, *CEO*
Jon Muller, *
Tom Crone, *
Julie Butman, *OF EVENTS & SOCIAL MEDIA**
EMP: 60 EST: 2006
SQ FT: 20,000
SALES (est): 6.44MM **Privately Held**
Web: www.finelinewood.com
SIC: 2431 Millwork

**(P-3138)**
**GARAGE DOORS INCORPORATED**
147 Martha St, San Jose (95112-5814)
PHONE..................408 293-7443
Scott Jensen, *Pr*
Nancy Jensen, *
EMP: 15 EST: 1987
SQ FT: 45,000
SALES (est): 4.64MM **Privately Held**
Web: www.garagedoorsinc.com
SIC: 2431 5031 Garage doors, overhead, wood; Doors, garage

**(P-3139)**
**GL WOODWORKING INC**
Also Called: Millers Woodworking
14341 Franklin Ave, Tustin (92780-7010)
PHONE..................949 515-2192
Grant Miller, *Owner*
EMP: 63 EST: 2004
SALES (est): 7.02MM **Privately Held**
SIC: 2431 Millwork

**(P-3140)**
**GONZALEZ FELICIANO**
Also Called: Paradise Kitchen Doors
1583 E Grand Ave, Pomona (91766-3808)
PHONE..................909 236-1372
Feliciano Gonzalez, *Owner*
EMP: 15 EST: 2015
SALES (est): 165.69K **Privately Held**
SIC: 2431 Doors, wood

**(P-3141)**
**HALEY BROS INC**
1575 Riverview Dr, San Bernardino (92408-2922)
PHONE..................800 854-5951
EMP: 110
SALES (corp-wide): 103.49MM **Privately Held**
Web: www.haleybros.com
SIC: 2431 Doors, wood
HQ: Haley Bros., Inc.
6291 Orangethorpe Ave
Buena Park CA 90620

**(P-3142)**
**HALEY BROS INC (HQ)**
6291 Orangethorpe Ave, Buena Park (90620-1339)
PHONE..................714 670-2112
Thomas J Cobb, *CEO*
Thomas Cobb, *Sec*
▲ EMP: 90 EST: 1987
SQ FT: 24,000
SALES (est): 18.16MM
SALES (corp-wide): 103.49MM **Privately Held**
Web: www.haleybros.com
SIC: 2431 Doors, wood
PA: T. M. Cobb Company
500 Palmyrita Ave
951 248-2400

**(P-3143)**
**HAND CRFTED DUTCHMAN DOORS INC**
Also Called: Dutchman Doors
770 Stonebridge Dr, Tracy (95376-2812)
PHONE..................209 833-7378
Larry B Vis, *Pr*
Donna Vis, *
EMP: 40 EST: 1982
SQ FT: 16,000
SALES (est): 5.62MM **Privately Held**
Web: www.dutchmandoors.com
SIC: 2431 2434 Doors, wood; Wood kitchen cabinets

**(P-3144)**
**HARWOOD PRODUCTS**
Branscomb Rd, Branscomb (95417)
P.O. Box 224 (95417-0224)
PHONE..................707 984-1601
Art Harwood, *CEO*
EMP: 230 EST: 2000
SALES (est): 1.59MM **Privately Held**
Web: www.rootsofmotivepower.com
SIC: 2431 Millwork

**(P-3145)**
**HIGHLAND LUMBER SALES INC**
300 E Santa Ana St, Anaheim (92805-3953)
PHONE..................714 778-2293
Richard Phillips, *Pr*
Daniel Lobue, *
▲ EMP: 31 EST: 1991
SQ FT: 2,000
SALES (est): 8.52MM **Privately Held**
Web: www.highlandlumber.com
SIC: 2431 5031 2493 5211 Millwork; Lumber: rough, dressed, and finished; Reconstituted wood products; Lumber products

**(P-3146)**
**HOSPITALITY WOOD PRODUCTS INC**
7206 E Gage Ave, Commerce (90040-3813)
PHONE..................562 806-5564
Michael Romero, *Pr*
Victor Garcia, *VP*
Carlos Escalante, *Treas*
EMP: 17 EST: 2001
SALES (est): 2.46MM **Privately Held**
SIC: 2431 Interior and ornamental woodwork and trim

**(P-3147)**
**ICI ARCHITECTURAL MILLWORK INC**
14059 Garfield Ave, Paramount (90723-2143)
PHONE..................323 759-4993
Izhak Korin, *CEO*
Robert A Babayan, *Pr*
EMP: 15 EST: 2007
SALES (est): 877.85K **Privately Held**
Web: www.icimillwork.com
SIC: 2431 Millwork

**(P-3148)**
**J & J QUALITY DOOR INC**
Also Called: Quality Door & Trim
1233 E Ronald St, Stockton (95205-3331)
PHONE..................209 948-5013
Jeffery Dean Cannon, *CEO*
Steve Cantrell, *
Debbie Sue Cantrell, *

## 2431 - Millwork (P-3149)

**EMP:** 35 **EST:** 1964
**SALES (est):** 6.12MM **Privately Held**
**Web:** www.jandjqualitydoor.com
**SIC:** 2431  Doors, wood

### (P-3149)
### J SUMMITT INC
Also Called: Summit Forest Products
13834 Bettencourt St, Cerritos
(90703-1010)
**PHONE**.................................562 236-5744
Jim Summit, *Brnch Mgr*
**EMP:** 19
**Web:** www.summittforestproducts.com
**SIC:** 2431  Millwork
**PA:** J. Summitt, Inc.
   12200 Los Nietos Rd

### (P-3150)
### JELD-WEN INC
Also Called: International Wood Products
3760 Convoy St Ste 111, San Diego
(92111-3743)
**PHONE**.................................800 468-3667
Hugo Hernadez, *Off Mgr*
**EMP:** 140
**Web:** www.jeld-wen.ca
**SIC:** 2431  Doors, wood
**HQ:** Jeld-Wen, Inc.
   2645 Silver Crescent Dr
   Charlotte NC 28273
   800 535-3936

### (P-3151)
### JELD-WEN INC
Jeld-Wen Doors
3901 Cincinnati Ave, Rocklin  (95765-1303)
**PHONE**.................................916 782-4900
Roald Pederson, *Mgr*
**EMP:** 211
**Web:** www.jeld-wen.com
**SIC:** 2431 5211  Doors, wood; Door and window products
**HQ:** Jeld-Wen, Inc.
   2645 Silver Crescent Dr
   Charlotte NC 28273
   800 535-3936

### (P-3152)
### KL DECORATOR SALES
Also Called: K & L Shutters
10120 Artesia Pl, Bellflower  (90706-6729)
**PHONE**.................................562 920-0268
**FAX:** 562 920-3865
**EMP:** 20
**SIC:** 2431  Window shutters, wood
**PA:** Kl Decorator Sales
   3848 N Mckinley St 11o

### (P-3153)
### LEEPERS WOOD TURNING CO INC (PA)
Also Called: Leeper's Stair Products
341 Bonnie Cir Ste 104, Corona
(92878-5195)
P.O. Box 17098  (90807-7098)
**PHONE**.................................562 422-6525
Michael Skinner, *Pr*
Barbara Skinner, *
Molly Rubio, *
◆ **EMP:** 38 **EST:** 1946
**SQ FT:** 29,000
**SALES (est):** 1.82MM
**SALES (corp-wide):** 1.82MM **Privately Held**
**Web:** www.ljsmith.com
**SIC:** 2431  Staircases and stairs, wood

### (P-3154)
### LOWPENSKY MOULDING
Also Called: Maple Clamp
900 Palou Ave, San Francisco
(94124-3429)
**PHONE**.................................415 822-7422
Theodore M Lowpensky, *Owner*
**EMP:** 15 **EST:** 1949
**SQ FT:** 13,000
**SALES (est):** 2.61MM **Privately Held**
**Web:** www.lowpenskymoulding.com
**SIC:** 2431  Moldings, wood: unfinished and prefinished

### (P-3155)
### MASONITE INTERNATIONAL CORP
3632 Petersen Rd, Stockton  (95215-7966)
**PHONE**.................................209 463-3503
**EMP:** 25
**Web:** www.masonite.com
**SIC:** 2431 3442  Doors, wood; Metal doors
**HQ:** Masonite International Corporation
   1242 E 5th Ave
   Tampa FL 33605
   813 877-2726

### (P-3156)
### METRIE EL & EL LLC (DH)
9129 Remington Ave, Chino  (91710-9350)
**PHONE**.................................909 591-0339
**EMP:** 17 **EST:** 2022
**SALES (est):** 2.94MM
**SALES (corp-wide):** 183.49MM **Privately Held**
**Web:** www.elandelwoodproducts.com
**SIC:** 2431  Millwork
**HQ:** Metrie Inc.
   2200 140th Ave E Ste 600
   Sumner WA 98390
   253 470-5050

### (P-3157)
### MILLCRAFT INC
2850 E White Star Ave, Anaheim
(92806-2517)
**PHONE**.................................714 632-9621
Lars Eppick, *Pr*
Ray Pfeifer, *
Philip De Marco, *
Reginald Skipcott, *
**EMP:** 70 **EST:** 1983
**SQ FT:** 34,000
**SALES (est):** 1.28MM **Privately Held**
**Web:** www.millcraft.com
**SIC:** 2431 2434  Doors, wood; Wood kitchen cabinets

### (P-3158)
### MILLER WOODWORKING INC
1429 259th St, Harbor City  (90710-3326)
**PHONE**.................................310 257-6806
Steve Miller, *Pr*
**EMP:** 20 **EST:** 1986
**SQ FT:** 17,000
**SALES (est):** 4.73MM **Privately Held**
**Web:** www.millerwoodworking.com
**SIC:** 2431  Millwork

### (P-3159)
### MILLWORK COMPANY INC
Also Called: Cabinet Manufacturing
607 Brazos St Ste C, Ramona
(92065-1884)
**PHONE**.................................760 788-1533
Gregory Lucas, *Pr*
Gregory J Lucas, *CEO*
**EMP:** 16 **EST:** 2002
**SALES (est):** 2.23MM **Privately Held**
**Web:** www.themillworkcompany.com

**SIC:** 2431  Millwork

### (P-3160)
### MILLWORKS BY DESIGN INC
4525 Runway St, Simi Valley  (93063-3479)
**PHONE**.................................818 597-1326
Daniel S Parish, *CEO*
Zachary D Eglit, *Pr*
▲ **EMP:** 66 **EST:** 2007
**SALES (est):** 2.46MM **Privately Held**
**Web:** www.millworksbydesign.com
**SIC:** 2431  Millwork

### (P-3161)
### MOLDINGS PLUS INC
1856 S Grove Ave, Ontario  (91761-5613)
**PHONE**.................................909 947-3310
Robert Bryant, *Pr*
Steve Totri, *VP*
▲ **EMP:** 20 **EST:** 1972
**SQ FT:** 13,500
**SALES (est):** 2.43MM **Privately Held**
**Web:** www.moldingsplus.com
**SIC:** 2431  Moldings, wood: unfinished and prefinished

### (P-3162)
### MOULDING COMPANY
5117 Commercial Cir, Concord
(94520-8523)
**PHONE**.................................925 798-7525
Sara Randle, *Prin*
▲ **EMP:** 51 **EST:** 2003
**SALES (est):** 4.03MM **Privately Held**
**Web:** www.themouldingcompany.com
**SIC:** 2431  Millwork

### (P-3163)
### MTD KITCHEN INC
13213 Sherman Way, North Hollywood
(91605-4649)
**PHONE**.................................818 764-2254
Gil Alkoby, *CEO*
**EMP:** 85 **EST:** 2012
**SALES (est):** 10.54MM **Privately Held**
**Web:** www.mtdkitchen.com
**SIC:** 2431 2441 1799 2434  Millwork; Cases, wood; Kitchen cabinet installation; Vanities, bathroom: wood

### (P-3164)
### NEWMAN BROS CALIFORNIA INC (PA)
Also Called: A-1 Grit Co
1901 Massachusetts Ave, Riverside
(92507-2618)
P.O. Box 5675  (92517-5675)
**PHONE**.................................951 782-0102
Harold Newman, *CEO*
**EMP:** 19 **EST:** 1973
**SALES (est):** 5.01MM **Privately Held**
**Web:** www.a1grit.com
**SIC:** 2431 3291 5199 8711  Millwork; Grit, steel; Architects' supplies (non-durable); Consulting engineer

### (P-3165)
### NICKS DOOR CORPORATION
Also Called: Nick's Cabinet Doors
1052 W Kirkwall Rd, Azusa  (91702-5126)
**PHONE**.................................626 812-6491
Nicolas Huizar, *Pr*
Sal Huizar, *VP*
Socorro Huizar, *Sec*
Anna Huizar, *Treas*
**EMP:** 15 **EST:** 1984
**SQ FT:** 32,000
**SALES (est):** 3.71MM **Privately Held**

**SIC:** 2431 5211  Doors, wood; Door and window products

### (P-3166)
### NORTH BAY PLYWOOD INC
510 Northbay Dr, Napa  (94559-1426)
P.O. Box 2338  (94558-0518)
**PHONE**.................................707 224-7849
Thomas H Lowenstein, *Pr*
Janice Leann Lowenstein, *
**EMP:** 20 **EST:** 1958
**SQ FT:** 24,000
**SALES (est):** 8.62MM **Privately Held**
**Web:** www.northbayplywood.com
**SIC:** 2431 2599 5211 2434  Doors, wood; Cabinets, factory; Cabinets, kitchen; Wood kitchen cabinets

### (P-3167)
### NORTHWESTERN INC
10153-1/2 Riverside Dr #250, Toluca Lake
(91602-2561)
**PHONE**.................................818 786-1581
▲ **EMP:** 40
**SIC:** 2431  Woodwork, interior and ornamental, nec

### (P-3168)
### NOVO MANUFACTURING LLC
Also Called: Lj Smith Stair Systems
341 Bonnie Cir Ste 104, Corona
(92878-5195)
**PHONE**.................................951 479-4620
Rob Brown, *CEO*
**EMP:** 59
**SALES (corp-wide):** 2.58B **Privately Held**
**Web:** www.ljsmith.com
**SIC:** 2431  Millwork
**HQ:** Novo Manufacturing, Llc
   35280 Scio-Bowerston Rd
   Bowerston OH 44695
   740 269-2221

### (P-3169)
### NOVO MANUFACTURING LLC
25956 Commercentre Dr, Lake Forest
(92630-8815)
**PHONE**.................................949 609-0544
Danny Umemoto, *Mgr*
**EMP:** 47
**SALES (corp-wide):** 2.58B **Privately Held**
**Web:** www.ljsmith.com
**SIC:** 2431  Millwork
**HQ:** Novo Manufacturing, Llc
   35280 Scio-Bowerston Rd
   Bowerston OH 44695
   740 269-2221

### (P-3170)
### OHLINE CORPORATION
1930 W 139th St, Gardena  (90249-2408)
**PHONE**.................................310 327-4630
**EMP:** 33
**SIC:** 2431  Door shutters, wood

### (P-3171)
### OLD ENGLISH MIL WOODWORKS INC (PA)
Also Called: Old English Mil & Woodworks
27772 Avenue Scott, Santa Clarita
(91355-3417)
**PHONE**.................................661 294-9171
Lay Cho, *Pr*
Edmond Cho, *
**EMP:** 30 **EST:** 1977
**SQ FT:** 30,000
**SALES (est):** 1.09MM
**SALES (corp-wide):** 1.09MM **Privately Held**
**Web:** www.oldenglishmilling.com

PRODUCTS & SERVICES SECTION
2431 - Millwork (P-3194)

SIC: 2431 2439 1751 Staircases and stairs, wood; Structural wood members, nec; Carpentry work

**(P-3172)**
**ORANGE WOODWORKS INC**
1215 N Parker St, Orange (92867-4613)
PHONE..................714 997-2600
Jeff Mcmillian, Pr
EMP: 45 EST: 1984
SQ FT: 120,000
SALES (est): 4.68MM Privately Held
Web: www.orangewoodworks.com
SIC: 2431 Millwork

**(P-3173)**
**PACIFIC ARCHTECTURAL MLLWK INC**
1435 Pioneer St, Brea (92821-3721)
PHONE..................562 905-9282
EMP: 43
SALES (est): 1.4MM Privately Held
Web: www.pacmillwork.com
SIC: 2431 Millwork

**(P-3174)**
**PACIFIC ARCHTECTURAL MLLWK INC**
101 E Commwl Ave Ste A, Fullerton (92832)
PHONE..................714 525-2059
EMP: 62
Web: www.pacmillwork.com
SIC: 2431 Window shutters, wood
PA: Pacific Architectural Millwork, Inc.
  101 E Commwl Ave Ste A

**(P-3175)**
**PACIFIC ARCHTECTURAL MLLWK INC**
Also Called: Reveal Windows & Doors
1031 S Leslie St, La Habra (90631-6843)
PHONE..................562 905-3200
John Higman, CEO
Roy Gustin, *
Alice Vanberpool, *
◆ EMP: 100 EST: 2007
SALES (est): 9.04MM Privately Held
Web: www.pacmillwork.com
SIC: 2431 Planing mill, millwork

**(P-3176)**
**PACIFIC DOOR & CABINET COMPANY**
7050 N Harrison Ave, Pinedale (93650-1008)
PHONE..................559 439-3822
Duane Failla, Pr
EMP: 30 EST: 1968
SQ FT: 16,000
SALES (est): 3.9MM Privately Held
Web: www.pacificdoorinc.com
SIC: 2431 3442 Doors, wood; Metal doors, sash, and trim

**(P-3177)**
**PARAMOUNT WINDOWS & DOORS**
Also Called: Paramount Window & Doors
723 W Mill St, San Bernardino (92410-3347)
PHONE..................909 888-4688
Don Mc Farland, CEO
EMP: 17 EST: 1999
SQ FT: 10,000
SALES (est): 1.79MM Privately Held
Web: www.paramountwindowsanddoors.com

SIC: 2431 5211 Windows and window parts and trim, wood; Door and window products

**(P-3178)**
**PINNACLE STAIR GROUP INC**
1875 N Macarthur Dr, Tracy (95376-2820)
PHONE..................209 832-3200
Brian D Wagner, CEO
Eric Yocius, *
Janet Wagner, *
Alan Bentley, *
EMP: 35 EST: 1997
SQ FT: 14,500
SALES (est): 2.59MM Privately Held
SIC: 2431 Staircases, stairs and railings

**(P-3179)**
**PLANT/ALLISON CORPORATION**
Also Called: Plant
300 Newhall St, San Francisco (94124-1498)
PHONE..................415 285-0500
EMP: 28 EST: 2016
SALES (est): 2.53MM Privately Held
Web: www.plantconstruction.com
SIC: 2431 Millwork

**(P-3180)**
**PRECISION COMPANIES INC**
Also Called: Precision Doors & Millwork Co
15088 La Palma Dr, Chino (91710-9669)
PHONE..................909 548-2700
Joseph J Felix, Pr
Marcia Felix, Sec
EMP: 15 EST: 1994
SQ FT: 5,000
SALES (est): 2.25MM Privately Held
SIC: 2431 3441 3442 Millwork; Fabricated structural metal; Metal doors, sash, and trim

**(P-3181)**
**PRECISION MILLWORK LLC**
14300 Davenport Rd Ste 4a, Agua Dulce (91390-5000)
PHONE..................661 402-5021
Ardith Swanger, Managing Member
EMP: 15 EST: 2012
SQ FT: 5,000
SALES (est): 6.77MM Privately Held
Web: www.precisionmillworkllc.com
SIC: 2431 Millwork

**(P-3182)**
**PREMIER WOODWORKING LLC**
5800 Alder Ave, Sacramento (95828-1108)
PHONE..................916 999-0050
Satpal Singh Brar, Managing Member
EMP: 41 EST: 2018
SALES (est): 2.92MM Privately Held
SIC: 2431 Millwork

**(P-3183)**
**QUALITY SHUTTERS INC**
3359 Chicago Ave Ste A, Riverside (92507-6820)
PHONE..................951 683-4939
Agustin Flores, Owner
EMP: 49 EST: 2002
SALES (est): 1.81MM Privately Held
SIC: 2431 Window frames, wood

**(P-3184)**
**RENAISSNCE FRNCH DORS SASH INC (PA)**
Also Called: Renaissance Doors & Windows
38 Segada, Rcho Sta Marg (92688-2744)
PHONE..................714 578-0090
Michael Jenkins, Pr
Thomas Jenkins, *

James Jenkins, *
EMP: 129 EST: 1982
SQ FT: 75,000
SALES (est): 2.84MM
SALES (corp-wide): 2.84MM Privately Held
Web: www.renaissancewindowsanddoors.com
SIC: 2431 Doors, wood

**(P-3185)**
**RIVER CITY MILLWORK INC**
3045 Fite Cir, Sacramento (95827-1814)
PHONE..................916 364-8981
Paul Parks, Pr
Valerie Parks, *
EMP: 33 EST: 1984
SQ FT: 24,000
SALES (est): 6.04MM Privately Held
Web: www.rcmill.com
SIC: 2431 2434 Moldings, wood: unfinished and prefinished; Wood kitchen cabinets

**(P-3186)**
**RJP FRAMING HOLDING CO**
1139 Sibley St Ste 100, Folsom (95630-3572)
PHONE..................916 817-1427
EMP: 18 EST: 2017
SALES (est): 1.72MM Privately Held
Web: www.rjpframing.com
SIC: 2431 Millwork

**(P-3187)**
**SETZER FOREST PRODUCTS INC (PA)**
2555 3rd St Ste 200, Sacramento (95818-1196)
PHONE..................916 442-2555
D Mark Kable, CEO
Garner Setzer, *
Hardie Setzer, Stockholder*
Jeff Setzer, *
▲ EMP: 160 EST: 1927
SALES (est): 20.85MM
SALES (corp-wide): 20.85MM Privately Held
Web: www.setzerforest.com
SIC: 2431 2441 Moldings, wood: unfinished and prefinished; Box shook, wood

**(P-3188)**
**SIERRA PACIFIC INDUSTRIES**
Also Called: SIERRA PACIFIC INDUSTRIES
Alameda Rd, Corning (96021)
PHONE..................530 824-2474
Kendall Pierson, VP
EMP: 45
SALES (corp-wide): 542.23MM Privately Held
Web: www.spi-ind.com
SIC: 2431 2426 2421 Millwork; Hardwood dimension and flooring mills; Sawmills and planing mills, general
PA: Sierra Pacific Industries Inc.
  19794 Riverside Ave
  530 378-8000

**(P-3189)**
**SIERRA PACIFIC INDUSTRIES INC**
11400 Reading Rd, Red Bluff (96080-6705)
P.O. Box 8460 (96080-8460)
PHONE..................530 529-5108
Greg Thom, Brnch Mgr
EMP: 51
SALES (corp-wide): 542.23MM Privately Held
Web: www.spi-ind.com

SIC: 2431 2421 Millwork; Sawmills and planing mills, general
PA: Sierra Pacific Industries Inc.
  19794 Riverside Ave
  530 378-8000

**(P-3190)**
**SIERRAPINE A CALIFORNIA LIMITED PARTNERSHIP**
1050 Melody Ln Ste 160, Roseville (95678-5196)
PHONE..................800 676-3339
▼ EMP: 447
Web: www.timberproducts.com
SIC: 2431 Panel work, wood

**(P-3191)**
**SIMMONS STAIRWAYS INC**
Also Called: Stair Service
255 Apollo Way # B, Hollister (95023-2522)
PHONE..................408 920-0105
Howard Simmons, CEO
Charles Simmons, VP
EMP: 20 EST: 1995
SQ FT: 15,000
SALES (est): 2.47MM Privately Held
Web: www.simmonsstairways.com
SIC: 2431 Millwork

**(P-3192)**
**SISKIYOU FOREST PRODUCTS (PA)**
6275 State Highway 273, Anderson (96007-9418)
PHONE..................530 378-6980
Fred Duchi, Pr
Bill Duchi, *
▲ EMP: 47 EST: 1974
SQ FT: 2,280
SALES (est): 8.49MM
SALES (corp-wide): 8.49MM Privately Held
Web: www.siskiyouforestproducts.com
SIC: 2431 5031 Millwork; Lumber, plywood, and millwork

**(P-3193)**
**SOUTH COAST STAIRS INC**
30251 Tomas, Rcho Sta Marg (92688-2123)
PHONE..................949 858-1685
Chris Galloway, Pr
Mary Galloway, *
Tamera Selchau, *
EMP: 40 EST: 1980
SQ FT: 2,000
SALES (est): 2.78MM Privately Held
Web: www.scstairs.com
SIC: 2431 2439 5211 Staircases and stairs, wood; Structural wood members, nec; Millwork and lumber

**(P-3194)**
**T M COBB COMPANY (PA)**
Also Called: Haley Bros
500 Palmyrita Ave, Riverside (92507-1801)
PHONE..................951 248-2400
Jeffrey Cobb, Pr
Thomas J Cobb, *
▲ EMP: 23 EST: 1947
SALES (est): 103.49MM
SALES (corp-wide): 103.49MM Privately Held
Web: www.tmcobb.com
SIC: 2431 3442 Door frames, wood; Window and door frames

## 2431 - Millwork (P-3195)

**(P-3195)**
**T M COBB COMPANY**
Also Called: Haley Brothers
2651 E Roosevelt St, Stockton
(95205-3825)
PHONE.................209 948-5358
John Jenkins, Brnch Mgr
EMP: 55
SQ FT: 1,200
SALES (corp-wide): 103.49MM Privately Held
Web: www.tmcobb.com
SIC: 2431 Doors, wood
PA: T. M. Cobb Company
500 Palmyrita Ave
951 248-2400

**(P-3196)**
**TABER COMPANY INC**
121 Waterworks Way Ste 100, Irvine
(92618-7719)
PHONE.................714 543-7100
Brian Taber, Pr
EMP: 65 EST: 2002
SALES (est): 22.63MM Privately Held
Web: www.taberco.net
SIC: 2431 Millwork

**(P-3197)**
**TALBERT ARCHTCTRAL PANL DOOR I**
711 S Stimson Ave, City Of Industry
(91745-1627)
PHONE.................714 671-9700
Jeff Tustin, Pr
Nick Parrino, *
Angie Talbert, Corporate Secretary*
Heidi Gordon Ctrl, Prin
EMP: 65 EST: 2005
SALES (est): 18MM Privately Held
Web: www.talbertusa.com
SIC: 2431 Millwork

**(P-3198)**
**THE ENKEBOLL CO**
Also Called: Enkeboll Design
16506 Avalon Blvd, Carson (90746-1007)
PHONE.................310 532-1400
EMP: 27 EST: 1955
SALES (est): 2.44MM Privately Held
Web: www.enkebolldesigns.com
SIC: 2431 Ornamental woodwork: cornices, mantels, etc.

**(P-3199)**
**TOLLHOUSE WINDOW COMPANY**
Also Called: Anlin Window Systems
1665 Tollhouse Rd, Clovis (93611-0523)
PHONE.................800 287-7996
Thomas Anton Vidmar, Prin
Stan Fikes, *
Greg Vidmar, *
Harry Parisi, *
Eric Vidmar, *
EMP: 250 EST: 1990
SQ FT: 188,000
SALES (est): 24.55MM Privately Held
Web: www.anlin.com
SIC: 2431 Windows and window parts and trim, wood

**(P-3200)**
**TRINITY WOODWORKS INC**
2620 Temple Heights Dr, Oceanside
(92056-3152)
PHONE.................760 639-5351
Jeffrey D Hollenbeck, CEO
EMP: 23 EST: 2011
SALES (est): 4.21MM Privately Held
Web: www.trinitywoodworksinc.com
SIC: 2431 Millwork

**(P-3201)**
**UNITY FOREST PRODUCTS INC**
1162 Putman Ave, Yuba City (95991-7216)
P.O. Box 1849 (95992-1849)
PHONE.................530 671-7152
Enita Elphick, Pr
Michael Smith, *
Shawn Nelson, *
Ryan Smith, *
EMP: 48 EST: 1988
SQ FT: 4,200
SALES (est): 11MM Privately Held
Web: www.unityforest.com
SIC: 2431 Millwork

**(P-3202)**
**W B POWELL INC**
630 Parkridge Ave, Norco (92860-3124)
PHONE.................951 270-0095
Charles G Mayhew, CEO
Chuck Mayhew, *
Doug Westra, *
EMP: 57 EST: 1993
SALES (est): 12.79MM
SALES (corp-wide): 44.51MM Privately Held
Web: www.wbpowell.com
SIC: 2431 2439 Millwork; Structural wood members, nec
PA: Plymold, Inc.
615 Centennial Dr
507 789-5111

**(P-3203)**
**WESTERN INTEGRATED MTLS INC (PA)**
3310 E 59th St, Long Beach (90805-4504)
PHONE.................562 634-2823
Larry Farrah, Pr
Edward G Farrah, *
Jim Halbrook, *
Alex Rojas, *
Debra Price, *
▲ EMP: 30 EST: 1975
SQ FT: 20,000
SALES (est): 5.36MM
SALES (corp-wide): 5.36MM Privately Held
Web: www.aluminumdoorframes.com
SIC: 2431 3442 Millwork; Window and door frames

**(P-3204)**
**WESTGATE HARDWOODS INC (PA)**
9296 Midway, Durham (95938-9779)
PHONE.................530 892-0300
Ivan Hoath, Pr
Becky Hoath, Sec
Ivan Hoath Iii, VP
EMP: 22 EST: 1986
SQ FT: 10,000
SALES (est): 6.63MM Privately Held
Web: www.westgatehardwoods.com
SIC: 2431 5031 Millwork; Lumber: rough, dressed, and finished

**(P-3205)**
**WINDSOR WILLITS COMPANY (PA)**
Also Called: Windsor One
737 Southpoint Blvd Ste H, Petaluma
(94954-1495)
PHONE.................707 665-9663
Craig Flynn, Pr
Alrene Flynn, *
Douglas Sherer, *
◆ EMP: 29 EST: 1976
SQ FT: 50,000
SALES (est): 32.49MM
SALES (corp-wide): 32.49MM Privately Held
Web: www.windsorone.com
SIC: 2431 Moldings, wood: unfinished and prefinished

**(P-3206)**
**WINDSOR WILLITS COMPANY**
Also Called: Windsor Mill
661 Railroad Ave, Willits (95490-3942)
PHONE.................707 459-8568
John Hankins, Mgr
EMP: 59
SALES (corp-wide): 32.49MM Privately Held
Web: www.windsorone.com
SIC: 2431 2439 Moldings, wood: unfinished and prefinished; Structural wood members, nec
PA: Windsor Willits Company
737 Southpoint Blvd Ste H
707 665-9663

**(P-3207)**
**WOOD CONNECTION INC**
4701 N Star Way, Modesto (95356-9567)
PHONE.................209 577-1044
William W Fenstermacher, Pr
Judy L Fenstermacher, Sec
EMP: 21 EST: 1982
SQ FT: 11,400
SALES (est): 5.36MM Privately Held
Web: www.woodcon.com
SIC: 2431 2434 Millwork; Wood kitchen cabinets

**(P-3208)**
**WOODEN WINDOW INC**
849 29th St, Oakland (94608-4507)
PHONE.................510 893-1157
William P Essert, Pr
Priscilla Call Essert, *
Robert D Essert, *
Mark Christiansen, Co-Principal*
EMP: 30 EST: 1980
SALES (est): 941.51K Privately Held
Web: www.kinneywoodworks.com
SIC: 2431 Millwork

**(P-3209)**
**WOODWORK PIONEERS CORP**
1757 S Claudina Way, Anaheim
(92805-6544)
PHONE.................714 991-1017
Karina Avalos, Pr
EMP: 50 EST: 2016
SALES (est): 749.13K Privately Held
Web: www.woodworkpioneers.com
SIC: 2431 Millwork

**(P-3210)**
**YOUNG & FAMILY INC**
Also Called: Quality Doors & Trim
64 Soda Bay Rd, Lakeport (95453-5609)
P.O. Box 897 (95453-0897)
PHONE.................707 263-8877
Hilary Young, Pr
Andrew Young, *
EMP: 25 EST: 1988
SQ FT: 11,400
SALES (est): 2.39MM Privately Held
SIC: 2431 2434 Doors, wood; Wood kitchen cabinets

**(P-3211)**
**YUBA RVER MLDING MILL WORK INC (PA)**
Also Called: Cal Yuba Investments
3757 Feather River Blvd, Olivehurst
(95961-9615)
P.O. Box 1078 (95992-1078)
PHONE.................530 742-2168
Thomas C Williams Senior, Ch Bd
Thomas C Williams Junior, Pr
Jolyne Williams, Sec
▲ EMP: 33 EST: 1977
SQ FT: 200,000
SALES (est): 8.35MM
SALES (corp-wide): 8.35MM Privately Held
Web: www.yubarivermoulding.com
SIC: 2431 6512 Moldings, wood: unfinished and prefinished; Commercial and industrial building operation

## 2434 Wood Kitchen Cabinets

**(P-3212)**
**ACCURATE LAMINATED PDTS INC**
1826 Dawns Way, Fullerton (92831-5323)
PHONE.................714 632-2773
Daniel Dunn, Pr
Patricia Dunn, *
EMP: 30 EST: 1989
SQ FT: 5,000
SALES (est): 4.99MM Privately Held
Web: www.accuratelaminated.com
SIC: 2434 Wood kitchen cabinets

**(P-3213)**
**AMBERWOOD PRODUCTS INC**
Also Called: Amberwood Installation
1555 S 7th St Bldg 7, San Jose
(95112-5926)
PHONE.................408 938-1600
EMP: 150
SIC: 2434 Vanities, bathroom: wood

**(P-3214)**
**AMERICAN WOODMARK CORPORATION**
Also Called: Timberlake Cabinet
3146 Gold Camp Dr, Rancho Cordova
(95670-6035)
PHONE.................916 851-7400
John Eldredge, Mgr
EMP: 205
SALES (corp-wide): 1.85B Publicly Held
Web: www.americanwoodmark.com
SIC: 2434 Wood kitchen cabinets
PA: American Woodmark Corporation
561 Shady Elm Rd
540 665-9100

**(P-3215)**
**AMERICAN WOODMARK CORPORATION**
Also Called: RSI Home Products
400 E Orangethorpe Ave, Anaheim
(92801-1046)
PHONE.................714 449-2200
EMP: 280
SALES (corp-wide): 1.85B Publicly Held
Web: www.americanwoodmark.com
SIC: 2434 Vanities, bathroom: wood
PA: American Woodmark Corporation
561 Shady Elm Rd
540 665-9100

# PRODUCTS & SERVICES SECTION

## 2434 - Wood Kitchen Cabinets (P-3240)

**(P-3216)**
**ARCHITECTURAL WOOD DESIGN INC**
Also Called: Carpentry Millwork
5672 E Dayton Ave, Fresno (93727-7801)
PHONE..................559 292-9104
Phillip D Farnsworth, *Pr*
Corey Farnsworth, *
**EMP:** 40 **EST:** 1984
**SQ FT:** 16,000
**SALES (est):** 6.57MM **Privately Held**
Web: www.awdfresno.com
**SIC: 2434** Wood kitchen cabinets

**(P-3217)**
**ARTCRAFTERS CABINETS**
5446 Cleon Ave, North Hollywood (91601-2897)
PHONE..................818 752-8960
Jack R Walter, *Pr*
Sharon E Walter, *
**EMP:** 50 **EST:** 1949
**SQ FT:** 20,000
**SALES (est):** 2.34MM **Privately Held**
Web: www.artcrafter.com
**SIC: 2434** 2521 2431 Wood kitchen cabinets; Wood office furniture; Millwork

**(P-3218)**
**B YOUNG ENTERPRISES INC**
Also Called: Mission Vly Cab / Counter Tech
12254 Iavelli Way, Poway (92064-6818)
PHONE..................858 748-0935
**EMP:** 75
**SIC: 2434** 2521 5031 5211 Wood kitchen cabinets; Cabinets, office: wood; Kitchen cabinets; Cabinets, kitchen

**(P-3219)**
**B-K MILL AND FIXTURES INC**
37523 Sycamore St, Newark (94560-3944)
PHONE..................510 713-8657
Sandra Barclay, *CEO*
Sandra Marie Barclay, *CEO*
Jim Korhummel, *Pr*
Tom Korhummel, *VP*
Sussy Korhummel, *Stockholder*
**EMP:** 15 **EST:** 1976
**SQ FT:** 23,000
**SALES (est):** 4.12MM **Privately Held**
**SIC: 2434** 2431 Wood kitchen cabinets; Millwork

**(P-3220)**
**BARBOSA CABINETS INC**
2020 E Grant Line Rd, Tracy (95304-8525)
PHONE..................209 836-2501
Edward Barbosa, *Pr*
Ron Barbosa, *
▲ **EMP:** 346 **EST:** 1978
**SQ FT:** 300,000
**SALES (est):** 39.56MM **Privately Held**
Web: www.barcab.com
**SIC: 2434** Wood kitchen cabinets

**(P-3221)**
**BRASSINGTON CASEWORKS**
1035 Pioneer Way Ste 150, El Cajon (92020-1965)
PHONE..................619 442-7277
Mike Brassington, *Pr*
**EMP:** 15 **EST:** 2003
**SALES (est):** 3.13MM **Privately Held**
Web: www.brassingtoncaseworks.com
**SIC: 2434** Wood kitchen cabinets

**(P-3222)**
**BROMACK COMPANY**
3005 Humboldt St, Los Angeles (90031-1830)
PHONE..................323 227-5000
Kurt Webster, *Managing Member*
Kurt Webster, *Prin*
Brown Mcpherson Iii, *Prin*
**EMP:** 24 **EST:** 2010
**SALES (est):** 1.02MM **Privately Held**
Web: www.bromack.com
**SIC: 2434** Wood kitchen cabinets

**(P-3223)**
**CABINETS 2000 LLC**
11100 Firestone Blvd, Norwalk (90650-2269)
PHONE..................562 868-0909
Afshin Abdollahi, *CEO*
Nematollah Abdollahi, *
Sherwood Prusso, *
Sue Abdollahi, *
Frank Hamadani, *
**EMP:** 180 **EST:** 1988
**SQ FT:** 103,000
**SALES (est):** 27.21MM
**SALES (corp-wide):** 2.54B **Privately Held**
Web: www.cabinets2000.com
**SIC: 2434** 1751 Wood kitchen cabinets; Cabinet and finish carpentry
**PA:** Cabinetworks Group, Inc.
20000 Victor Pkwy
734 205-4600

**(P-3224)**
**CABINETS BY PRCISION WORKS INC**
Also Called: Precision Works
81101 Indio Blvd Ste D22, Indio (92201-1922)
PHONE..................760 342-1133
Pierre Letellier, *Pr*
Katherine Letellier, *
**EMP:** 50 **EST:** 1993
**SQ FT:** 16,000
**SALES (est):** 4.8MM **Privately Held**
Web: www.cabinetsbyprecision.com
**SIC: 2434** 2431 Wood kitchen cabinets; Millwork

**(P-3225)**
**CABINETS R US**
1240 N Fee Ana St, Anaheim (92807-1817)
PHONE..................562 483-6886
Stephanie Chang, *Admn*
◆ **EMP:** 20 **EST:** 2013
**SALES (est):** 1.56MM **Privately Held**
Web: www.cabinetsrus.us
**SIC: 2434** Wood kitchen cabinets

**(P-3226)**
**CALIFORNIA CABINET & STR FIXS**
Also Called: California Cabinet & Storage
8472 Carbide Ct, Sacramento (95828-5609)
PHONE..................916 681-0901
Bruce Nichols, *Pr*
**EMP:** 20 **EST:** 1985
**SALES (est):** 2.32MM **Privately Held**
Web: www.californiacabinets.net
**SIC: 2434** Wood kitchen cabinets

**(P-3227)**
**CALIFORNIA KIT CAB DOOR CORP (PA)**
Also Called: California Door
610 Jarvis Dr, Morgan Hill (95037-2889)
PHONE..................408 782-5700
Edward Joseph Rossi, *Prin*
◆ **EMP:** 94 **EST:** 1988
**SALES (est):** 44.1MM
**SALES (corp-wide):** 44.1MM **Privately Held**
Web: www.caldoor.com
**SIC: 2434** 2431 Wood kitchen cabinets; Millwork

**(P-3228)**
**CALIFORNIA WOODWORKING INC**
1726 Ives Ave, Oxnard (93033-4072)
PHONE..................805 982-9090
Edward Vickery, *Pr*
Lucas Vickery, *
Susan Vickery, *
**EMP:** 30 **EST:** 1990
**SQ FT:** 8,000
**SALES (est):** 2.31MM **Privately Held**
Web: www.calwoodinc.com
**SIC: 2434** Wood kitchen cabinets

**(P-3229)**
**CALIFRNIA DSGNERS CHICE CSTM C**
547 Constitution Ave Ste F, Camarillo (93012-8572)
PHONE..................805 987-5820
Mark Mulchay, *Pr*
Russell Leavitt, *
**EMP:** 38 **EST:** 1989
**SALES (est):** 4.37MM **Privately Held**
Web: www.cdcc-inc.com
**SIC: 2434** Wood kitchen cabinets

**(P-3230)**
**CARPET WAGON-GLENDALE INC (PA)**
Also Called: Payless Kitchen Cabinets
3614 San Fernando Rd, Glendale (91204-2944)
PHONE..................818 937-9545
Avedis Barsoumian, *Pr*
**EMP:** 15 **EST:** 2004
**SALES (est):** 6.23MM
**SALES (corp-wide):** 6.23MM **Privately Held**
Web: www.paylesskitchencabinets.com
**SIC: 2434** Wood kitchen cabinets

**(P-3231)**
**CHAMPION INSTALLS INC**
11075 Jeff Brian Ln, Wilton (95693-9514)
PHONE..................916 627-0929
Brock Rhodes, *Prin*
**EMP:** 16 **EST:** 2014
**SALES (est):** 4.84MM **Privately Held**
Web: www.championinstalls.com
**SIC: 2434** Wood kitchen cabinets

**(P-3232)**
**CLASSIC MILL & CABINET LLC**
Also Called: Classic Innovations
590 Santana Dr, Cloverdale (95425-4296)
PHONE..................707 894-9800
Tony Mertes, *Pr*
Ms. Billie Siemsen, *Mgr*
▲ **EMP:** 37 **EST:** 1967
**SQ FT:** 35,000
**SALES (est):** 2.15MM **Privately Held**
Web: www.classicmill.com
**SIC: 2434** Wood kitchen cabinets

**(P-3233)**
**CORONA MILLWORKS COMPANY (PA)**
5572 Edison Ave, Chino (91710-6936)
PHONE..................909 606-3288
Jose Corona, *CEO*
▲ **EMP:** 63 **EST:** 1995
**SQ FT:** 8,700
**SALES (est):** 26MM
**SALES (corp-wide):** 26MM **Privately Held**
Web: www.coronamillworks.com
**SIC: 2434** Wood kitchen cabinets

**(P-3234)**
**D & D CBNETS - SVAGE DSGNS INC**
1478 Sky Harbor Dr, Olivehurst (95961-7418)
PHONE..................530 634-9713
Peter D Giordano, *Pr*
**EMP:** 32 **EST:** 2006
**SALES (est):** 3.02MM **Privately Held**
Web: www.savagecabinets.com
**SIC: 2434** Wood kitchen cabinets

**(P-3235)**
**DREES WOOD PRODUCTS INC**
14020 Orange Ave, Paramount (90723-2018)
PHONE..................562 633-7337
Ed Drees, *Pr*
**EMP:** 100 **EST:** 1982
**SALES (est):** 6.09MM **Privately Held**
Web: www.dreeswoodproducts.com
**SIC: 2434** Wood kitchen cabinets

**(P-3236)**
**ELEMENTS MANUFACTURING INC**
115 Harvey West Blvd Ste C, Santa Cruz (95060-2168)
PHONE..................831 421-9440
Ken Ketch, *Pr*
Alan Stormes, *Sec*
**EMP:** 20 **EST:** 1995
**SQ FT:** 15,000
**SALES (est):** 2.52MM **Privately Held**
Web: www.elementsmfg.com
**SIC: 2434** Wood kitchen cabinets

**(P-3237)**
**ELITE STONE GROUP INC**
1205 S Dupont Ave, Ontario (91761-1536)
PHONE..................909 629-6988
Yiyong Huang, *CEO*
**EMP:** 30 **EST:** 2015
**SALES (est):** 2.56MM **Privately Held**
Web: www.elitestonegroup.com
**SIC: 2434** 5032 1741 Wood kitchen cabinets; Building stone; Stone masonry

**(P-3238)**
**EMERZIAN WOODWORKING INC**
2555 N Argyle Ave, Fresno (93727-1378)
PHONE..................559 292-2448
Tom Emerzian, *Owner*
**EMP:** 40 **EST:** 1984
**SQ FT:** 46,000
**SALES (est):** 5.29MM **Privately Held**
Web: www.emerzianwoodworking.com
**SIC: 2434** 2431 Wood kitchen cabinets; Millwork

**(P-3239)**
**EXCEL CABINETS INC**
225 Jason Ct, Corona (92879-6199)
PHONE..................951 279-4545
Charles W Ketzel, *CEO*
Kevin Ketzel, *
Sandra Ketzel, *
▲ **EMP:** 35 **EST:** 1990
**SALES (est):** 7.45MM **Privately Held**
Web: www.excelcabinetsinc.com
**SIC: 2434** Wood kitchen cabinets

**(P-3240)**
**FINELINE CARPENTRY INC**
1297 Old County Rd, Belmont (94002-3920)

---

(PA)=Parent Co (HQ)=Headquarters
✪ = New Business established in last 2 years

## 2434 - Wood Kitchen Cabinets (P-3241)

PHONE..................650 592-2442
Mac Bean, Pr
Cheryl Bean, *
EMP: 25 EST: 1982
SQ FT: 15,000
SALES (est): 2.14MM **Privately Held**
Web: www.finelinecarpentry.com
SIC: 2434 Wood kitchen cabinets

### (P-3241)
### FINISHING TOUCH MOULDING INC
Also Called: Finishing Touch Millwork
6190 Corte Del Cedro, Carlsbad (92011-1515)
PHONE..................760 444-1019
Roland Chaney, Pr
EMP: 55 EST: 2013
SALES (est): 4.82MM **Privately Held**
Web: www.ftmillwork.com
SIC: 2434 1751 Wood kitchen cabinets; Carpentry work

### (P-3242)
### HOME PLUS GROUP INC
Also Called: 405 Cabinets & Stone
18315 Mount Baldy Cir, Fountain Valley (92708-6115)
PHONE..................714 500-3855
Tin Phan, CEO
Jenny Phan, CFO
▲ EMP: 17 EST: 2006
SQ FT: 4,000
SALES (est): 4.86MM **Privately Held**
Web: www.405cs.com
SIC: 2434 Wood kitchen cabinets

### (P-3243)
### I AND E CABINETS INC
14660 Raymer St, Van Nuys (91405-1217)
PHONE..................818 933-6480
Israel Chlomovitz, CEO
Ettie Chlomovitz, *
EMP: 34 EST: 1981
SQ FT: 9,000
SALES (est): 2.4MM **Privately Held**
Web: www.iecabinets.com
SIC: 2434 Wood kitchen cabinets

### (P-3244)
### JOHN C DESTEFANO
Also Called: Destefano Design Group
7325 Reese Rd, Sacramento (95828-3704)
PHONE..................916 276-4056
John Destefano, Owner
EMP: 30 EST: 1982
SQ FT: 1,500
SALES (est): 400K **Privately Held**
SIC: 2434 Wood kitchen cabinets

### (P-3245)
### JR STEPHENS COMPANY
5208 Boyd Rd, Arcata (95521-4410)
PHONE..................707 825-0100
Jim Stephens, Pr
Rosalie Stephens, *
Bryan Stephens, *
Josh Stephens, *
EMP: 23 EST: 1978
SALES (est): 788.71K **Privately Held**
SIC: 2434 Wood kitchen cabinets

### (P-3246)
### K & Z CABINET CO INC
1450 S Grove Ave, Ontario (91761-4523)
PHONE..................909 947-3567
Dennis Chan, Pr
EMP: 60 EST: 1975
SQ FT: 59,000
SALES (est): 4.85MM **Privately Held**

Web: www.kzcabt.com
SIC: 2434 2431 Wood kitchen cabinets; Millwork

### (P-3247)
### KENEY MANUFACTURING CO (PA)
Also Called: Keney's Cabinets
586 Broadway Ave, Atwater (95301-4408)
P.O. Box 518 (95301-0518)
PHONE..................209 358-6474
Robert Hernandez, Pt
Rodney Haygood, Pt
EMP: 16 EST: 1952
SALES (est): 603.77K
SALES (corp-wide): 603.77K **Privately Held**
SIC: 2434 Wood kitchen cabinets

### (P-3248)
### KITCHEN PRO CABINETRY INC
11347 Vanowen St, North Hollywood (91605-6321)
PHONE..................877 210-6361
Yaron Goren, Pr
Ben Guttman, VP
▼ EMP: 20 EST: 2006
SALES (est): 1.8MM **Privately Held**
Web: www.kpmoderncabinetry.com
SIC: 2434 Wood kitchen cabinets

### (P-3249)
### KITCHENS NOW INC
6047 Power Inn Rd, Sacramento (95824-2320)
PHONE..................916 229-8224
Douglas Carl Schubert, CEO
Kevin Sexton, COO
EMP: 25 EST: 2007
SALES (est): 5.79MM **Privately Held**
Web: www.kitchensnow.com
SIC: 2434 Wood kitchen cabinets

### (P-3250)
### KOBIS WINDOWS & DOORS MFG INC
7326 Laurel Canyon Blvd, North Hollywood (91605-3710)
PHONE..................818 764-6400
Kobi Louria, CEO
▲ EMP: 25 EST: 1999
SALES (est): 2.62MM **Privately Held**
Web: www.kobiwindows.net
SIC: 2434 2431 1522 Vanities, bathroom: wood; Millwork; Residential construction, nec

### (P-3251)
### LA BATH VANITY INC (PA)
1071 W 9th St, Upland (91786-5702)
PHONE..................909 303-3323
Lingcong Luo, CEO
EMP: 18 EST: 2018
SALES (est): 928.79K **Privately Held**
SIC: 2434 Vanities, bathroom: wood

### (P-3252)
### MASTERBRAND CABINETS LLC
3700 S Riverside Ave, Colton (92324-3329)
PHONE..................951 682-1535
Michael Mejia, Mgr
EMP: 46
SALES (corp-wide): 2.73B **Publicly Held**
Web: www.masterbrand.com
SIC: 2434 Wood kitchen cabinets
HQ: Masterbrand Cabinets Llc
3300 Entp Pkwy Ste 300
Beachwood OH 44122
812 482-2527

### (P-3253)
### MASTERBRAND CABINETS LLC
Also Called: Aristikraft
5576 Inland Empire Blvd, Ontario (91764)
PHONE..................909 989-2992
Jim Krogman, Brnch Mgr
EMP: 20
SALES (corp-wide): 2.73B **Publicly Held**
Web: www.masterbrand.com
SIC: 2434 Wood kitchen cabinets
HQ: Masterbrand Cabinets Llc
3300 Entp Pkwy Ste 300
Beachwood OH 44122
812 482-2527

### (P-3254)
### MCCONNELL CABINETS INC
Also Called: Coastal Wood Products
13110 Louden Ln, City Of Industry (91746-1507)
PHONE..................626 937-2200
▲ EMP: 740
Web: www.mcconnellinc.com
SIC: 2434 Wood kitchen cabinets

### (P-3255)
### MEYER & REEDER INC
2800 S Main St Ste I, Santa Ana (92707-3443)
PHONE..................714 388-0146
Jeff Oskins, Pr
EMP: 17 EST: 2007
SALES (est): 2.2MM **Privately Held**
Web: www.meyerandreederinc.com
SIC: 2434 Wood kitchen cabinets

### (P-3256)
### MIKADA CABINETS LLC
Also Called: Mikada Cabinets
11777 San Vicente Blvd, Los Angeles (90049-5067)
PHONE..................713 681-6116
Tom Moodie, CEO
Kevin Horton, *
Monette Stephens, *
Debbie Thompson, *
EMP: 60 EST: 1965
SALES (est): 3.92MM **Privately Held**
Web: www.mikadacabinets.com
SIC: 2434 Wood kitchen cabinets

### (P-3257)
### MILLWOOD CABINET CO INC
2321 Virginia Ave, Bakersfield (93307-2545)
PHONE..................661 327-0371
David T Millwood Junior, Pr
Sandra Millwood, Treas
Diana Shackelford, Sec
EMP: 16 EST: 1973
SQ FT: 18,000
SALES (est): 439.02K **Privately Held**
Web: www.millwoodcabinet.com
SIC: 2434 2541 Wood kitchen cabinets; Wood partitions and fixtures

### (P-3258)
### MULTITASKR
2576 Catamaran Way, Chula Vista (91914-4533)
PHONE..................619 391-3371
EMP: 19 EST: 2020
SALES (est): 2.84MM **Privately Held**
Web: www.gomultitaskr.com
SIC: 2434 1799 1522 1521 Wood kitchen cabinets; Special trade contractors, nec; Residential construction, nec; Single-family housing construction

### (P-3259)
### N K CABINETS INC
Also Called: Universal Custom Cabinets
13290 Paxton St, Pacoima (91331)
PHONE..................818 897-7909
Arno Yesayan, CEO
Norik Kayramanyon, *
EMP: 34 EST: 1995
SALES (est): 2.18MM **Privately Held**
Web: www.nkcabinets.com
SIC: 2434 2521 3843 2599 Wood kitchen cabinets; Cabinets, office: wood; Cabinets, dental; Cabinets, factory

### (P-3260)
### PROFESSIONAL CABINET SOLUTIONS
2111 Eastridge Ave, Riverside (92507-0778)
PHONE..................909 614-2900
M Scott Culbreth, CEO
Paul Joachimczyk, CFO
EMP: 250 EST: 1996
SALES (est): 9.28MM
SALES (corp-wide): 1.85B **Publicly Held**
Web: www.pcscabinetry.com
SIC: 2434 Wood kitchen cabinets
HQ: Rsi Home Products Llc
400 E Orangethorpe Ave
Anaheim CA 92801
714 449-2200

### (P-3261)
### QUALITY CABINET AND FIXTURE CO (HQ)
7955 Saint Andrews Ave, San Diego (92154-8224)
PHONE..................619 266-1011
Donald Paradise, Ch Bd
Tim Paradise, *
Andrew Meek, *
Nicholas P Willems, *
Mike Bonde, *
▲ EMP: 23 EST: 1966
SQ FT: 55,000
SALES (est): 2.08MM
SALES (corp-wide): 20.34MM **Privately Held**
Web: www.glennrieder.com
SIC: 2434 Wood kitchen cabinets
PA: Glenn Rieder, Llc
6520 W Becher Pl
414 449-2888

### (P-3262)
### QUALITY CABINET SHOP INC
3256 Tomahawk Dr, Stockton (95205-2436)
PHONE..................209 948-0431
John Droge, Pr
Steve Andersen, VP
EMP: 20 EST: 1977
SQ FT: 16,000
SALES (est): 337.23K **Privately Held**
Web: s483664495.initial-website.com
SIC: 2434 Wood kitchen cabinets

### (P-3263)
### RAWSON CUSTOM CABINETS INC
1115 Holly Oak Cir, San Jose (95120)
PHONE..................408 779-9838
Dennis Rawson, Pr
Patricia Rawson, *
EMP: 24 EST: 1975
SALES (est): 654.34K **Privately Held**
Web: www.rawson-cabinets.com
SIC: 2434 Wood kitchen cabinets

**PRODUCTS & SERVICES SECTION**

**2435 - Hardwood Veneer And Plywood (P-3288)**

**(P-3264)**
**REBORN CABINETS LLC (PA)**
Also Called: Reborn Bath Solutions
5515 E La Palma Ave Ste 250, Anaheim (92807-2131)
PHONE.................714 630-2220
TOLL FREE: 800
Vincent Nardolillo, *Managing Member*
Anthony Nardolillo, *
EMP: 484 EST: 1983
SALES (est): 114.99MM
SALES (corp-wide): 114.99MM **Privately Held**
Web: www.reborncabinets.com
SIC: 2434 2431 Wood kitchen cabinets; Millwork

**(P-3265)**
**ROBERT C WORTH INC**
15846 Liggett St, North Hills (91343-3142)
PHONE.................661 942-6601
Robert C Worth, *Prin*
EMP: 60 EST: 2011
SALES (est): 1.77MM **Privately Held**
Web: www.worthcabinets.com
SIC: 2434 Wood kitchen cabinets

**(P-3266)**
**ROYAL CABINETS INC**
Also Called: Royal Cabinets
1299 E Phillips Blvd, Pomona (91766-5429)
PHONE.................909 629-8565
Clay Smith, *Pr*
Bill Roan, *
▲ EMP: 600 EST: 1984
SQ FT: 70,000
SALES (est): 19.15MM **Privately Held**
Web: www.royalcabinets.com
SIC: 2434 2511 Wood kitchen cabinets; Wood household furniture

**(P-3267)**
**ROYAL INDUSTRIES INC**
Also Called: Royal Cabinets
1299 E Phillips Blvd, Pomona (91766-5429)
PHONE.................909 629-8565
Clay R Smith, *Ch Bd*
Eric Vanderheyden, *
Gary Silverman, *
William Roan, *
Gustavo Danjoi, *
EMP: 130 EST: 1985
SALES (est): 11.23MM **Privately Held**
Web: www.royalcabinets.com
SIC: 2434 Vanities, bathroom: wood

**(P-3268)**
**SAN DIEGO CUSTOM CABINETS**
683 Vernon Way, El Cajon (92020)
PHONE.................858 256-0933
Nicanor Gonzales Iii, *Pr*
EMP: 21 EST: 2007
SALES (est): 582.62K **Privately Held**
Web: www.sdcustomcabinets.com
SIC: 2434 Wood kitchen cabinets

**(P-3269)**
**SANTA MONICA MILLWORKS**
2568 Channel Dr, Ventura (93003-4548)
PHONE.................805 643-0010
William Lunche, *Pr*
EMP: 20 EST: 1996
SALES (est): 304.59K **Privately Held**
SIC: 2434 Wood kitchen cabinets

**(P-3270)**
**SOUTHCOAST CABINET INC (PA)**
755 Pinefalls Ave, Walnut (91789-3027)
PHONE.................909 594-3089
Dante M Senese, *CEO*
John Lopez, *
EMP: 42 EST: 1983
SQ FT: 108,000
SALES (est): 10.57MM
SALES (corp-wide): 10.57MM **Privately Held**
Web: www.southcoastcabinet.com
SIC: 2434 Wood kitchen cabinets

**(P-3271)**
**SUPERIOR KITCHEN CABINETS INC**
1703 Voumard Ranch Dr, Turlock (95382-7426)
PHONE.................209 247-0097
Noah Ramirez, *Pr*
EMP: 22 EST: 2011
SALES (est): 1.33MM **Privately Held**
SIC: 2434 Wood kitchen cabinets

**(P-3272)**
**TAMALPAIS COML CABINETRY INC**
200 9th St, Richmond (94801-3146)
P.O. Box 2169 (94802-1169)
PHONE.................510 231-6800
John Kenner, *Pr*
EMP: 30 EST: 1985
SQ FT: 23,000
SALES (est): 3.02MM **Privately Held**
Web: www.tamcab.com
SIC: 2434 Wood kitchen cabinets

**(P-3273)**
**TESSA MIA CORP**
9565 Vassar Ave, Chatsworth (91311-4141)
PHONE.................877 740-5757
Zack Karni, *CEO*
Yom Tov Yohanan, *
EMP: 27 EST: 2019
SALES (est): 5.5MM **Privately Held**
SIC: 2434 Wood kitchen cabinets

**(P-3274)**
**TONUSA LLC**
Also Called: Contemporary Bath.com
16770 E Johnson Dr, City Of Industry (91745-2414)
PHONE.................626 961-8700
◆ EMP: 15 EST: 2006
SQ FT: 4,000
SALES (est): 537.39K **Privately Held**
Web: www.tonusa.com
SIC: 2434 Vanities, bathroom: wood

**(P-3275)**
**TRUE DESIGN INC**
9427 Norwalk Blvd, Santa Fe Springs (90670-2943)
PHONE.................562 699-2001
Hani Abi Naked, *CEO*
Thomas Cavelti, *CFO*
EMP: 15 EST: 2014
SQ FT: 17,000
SALES (est): 1.75MM **Privately Held**
SIC: 2434 Wood kitchen cabinets

**(P-3276)**
**ULTRA BUILT KITCHENS INC**
1814 E 43rd St, Los Angeles (90058-1517)
PHONE.................323 232-3762
Iris Yanes, *Pr*
Eduardo Yanes, *
Daisy Blanco, *
EMP: 28 EST: 1993
SQ FT: 18,000
SALES (est): 2.35MM **Privately Held**
Web: www.ultrabuiltkitchens.net
SIC: 2434 Vanities, bathroom: wood

**(P-3277)**
**UNITED CABINET COMPANY INC**
1510 S Mountain View Ave, San Bernardino (92408-3134)
PHONE.................909 796-3015
Dennis Rice, *Pr*
Jeffery Westrom, *VP*
Doris Rice, *Sec*
Gayle L Rice, *Stockholder*
EMP: 20 EST: 1963
SQ FT: 10,000
SALES (est): 2.36MM **Privately Held**
SIC: 2434 Wood kitchen cabinets

**(P-3278)**
**VALET ORGANIZERS INC**
Also Called: Valet Cstm Cabiners & Closets
1190 Dell Ave Ste J, Campbell (95008-6614)
PHONE.................408 370-1041
TOLL FREE: 800
Scott Heeb, *Pr*
EMP: 31 EST: 1987
SQ FT: 15,000
SALES (est): 3.75MM **Privately Held**
Web: www.valetcustom.com
SIC: 2434 Wood kitchen cabinets

**(P-3279)**
**VCSD INC**
Also Called: Valley Cabinet
585 Vernon Way, El Cajon (92020-1934)
PHONE.................619 579-6886
Larry Doyle, *Pr*
Susan Raymond, *
EMP: 49 EST: 2011
SALES (est): 5.08MM **Privately Held**
Web: www.vcsdinc.com
SIC: 2434 Wood kitchen cabinets

**(P-3280)**
**W L RUBOTTOM CO**
320 W Lewis St, Ventura (93001-1335)
PHONE.................805 648-6943
Gary Mccoy, *Pr*
Lawrence Rubottom, *
EMP: 55 EST: 1946
SQ FT: 40,000
SALES (est): 5.01MM **Privately Held**
Web: www.wlrubottom.com
SIC: 2434 Wood kitchen cabinets

**(P-3281)**
**WOODLINE PARTNERS INC**
Also Called: Woodline Cabinets
5165 Fulton Dr, Fairfield (94534-1638)
PHONE.................707 864-5445
Grant Paxton, *Pr*
Paul Mckay, *CFO*
EMP: 49 EST: 1982
SQ FT: 37,500
SALES (est): 5.47MM **Privately Held**
SIC: 2434 Wood kitchen cabinets

**(P-3282)**
**WOODPECKER CABINETS INC**
21512 Nordhoff St, Chatsworth (91311-5822)
PHONE.................310 404-4805
Izaac Sananes, *CEO*
River Cook, *Mgr*
EMP: 20 EST: 2005
SALES (est): 1.76MM **Privately Held**
SIC: 2434 1799 Wood kitchen cabinets; Kitchen cabinet installation

**(P-3283)**
**WYNDHAM COLLECTION LLC**
1175 Aviation Pl, San Fernando (91340-1460)
PHONE.................888 522-8476
Martin Symes, *Managing Member*
EMP: 26 EST: 2011
SQ FT: 100,000
SALES (est): 5.92MM **Privately Held**
Web: www.wyndhamcollection.com
SIC: 2434 Vanities, bathroom: wood

## 2435 Hardwood Veneer And Plywood

**(P-3284)**
**G - L VENEER CO INC (PA)**
2224 E Slauson Ave, Huntington Park (90255-2793)
PHONE.................323 582-5203
▲ EMP: 96 EST: 1977
SALES (est): 21.28MM
SALES (corp-wide): 21.28MM **Privately Held**
Web: www.glveneer.com
SIC: 2435 Hardwood veneer and plywood

**(P-3285)**
**GENERAL VENEER MFG CO**
8652 Otis St, South Gate (90280-3220)
P.O. Box 1607 (90280-1607)
PHONE.................323 564-2661
William Dewitt, *Pr*
Ed Bewitt, *
Douglas Bradley, *
EMP: 50 EST: 1942
SQ FT: 200,000
SALES (est): 8.74MM **Privately Held**
Web: www.generalveneer.com
SIC: 2435 3365 Hardwood veneer and plywood; Aerospace castings, aluminum

**(P-3286)**
**MALAKAN INC (PA)**
11035 Sherman Way, Sun Valley (91352-4928)
PHONE.................310 910-9270
Radik Khachatryan, *Pr*
▲ EMP: 16 EST: 2014
SQ FT: 8,000
SALES (est): 2.83MM
SALES (corp-wide): 2.83MM **Privately Held**
SIC: 2435 7389 Hardwood veneer and plywood; Business services, nec

**(P-3287)**
**PLYCRAFT INDUSTRIES INC**
Also Called: Concepts & Wood
2100 E Slauson Ave, Huntington Park (90255-2727)
PHONE.................323 587-8101
Ashley Joffe, *Pr*
Nathan Joffe, *
Donald R Greenberg, *
▲ EMP: 180 EST: 1979
SQ FT: 71,187
SALES (est): 4.55MM **Privately Held**
Web: www.plycraft.com
SIC: 2435 Plywood, hardwood or hardwood faced

**(P-3288)**
**SWANER HARDWOOD CO INC (PA)**
5 W Magnolia Blvd, Burbank (91502-1719)
PHONE.................818 953-5350
Gary Swaner, *Pr*

## 2435 - Hardwood Veneer And Plywood (P-3289)

Keith M Swaner, *
Beverly Swaner, *
Stephen Haag, *
▲ EMP: 70 EST: 1967
SQ FT: 4,500
SALES (est): 21.83MM
SALES (corp-wide): 21.83MM Privately Held
Web: www.swanerhardwood.com
SIC: 2435 5031 Hardwood veneer and plywood; Lumber: rough, dressed, and finished

**(P-3289)**
**TIMBER PRODUCTS CO LTD PARTNR**
Also Called: Yreka Division
130 N Phillipe Ln, Yreka (96097-9014)
P.O. Box 766 (96097-0766)
PHONE..............................530 842-2310
Pete Himmel, Brnch Mgr
EMP: 51
SALES (corp-wide): 376.24MM Privately Held
Web: www.timberproducts.com
SIC: 2435 2436 Veneer stock, hardwood; Softwood veneer and plywood
PA: Timber Products Co. Limited Partnership
305 S 4th St
541 747-4577

---

## 2439 Structural Wood Members, Nec

**(P-3290)**
**ADVANTAGE TRUSS COMPANY LLC**
Also Called: Manufacturer
2025 San Juan Rd, Hollister (95023-9601)
PHONE..............................831 635-0377
Jennifer Pfeiffer, Pr
Jennifer Pfeiffer, CEO
EMP: 35 EST: 2000
SALES (est): 3.74MM Privately Held
Web: www.advantagetruss.com
SIC: 2439 1522 Trusses, wooden roof; Residential construction, nec

**(P-3291)**
**ALL-TRUSS INC**
22700 Bdwy, Sonoma (95476-8233)
PHONE..............................707 938-5595
Robert L Biggs, Pr
EMP: 20 EST: 1992
SALES (est): 2.56MM Privately Held
Web: www.alltrussinc.com
SIC: 2439 Trusses, wooden roof

**(P-3292)**
**ALPINE TRUSS LLC** ◆
800 S State Highway 33, Patterson (95363-9148)
PHONE..............................209 345-0831
EMP: 20 EST: 2024
SALES (est): 1.25MM Privately Held
SIC: 2439 Trusses, wooden roof

**(P-3293)**
**AUTOMATED BLDG COMPONENTS INC**
4949 W Spruce Ave, Fresno (93722-3443)
PHONE..............................559 485-8232
David Cervantes, Pr
Gabriel Cervantes, VP
Violet Cervantes, Treas
EMP: 15 EST: 1991
SALES (est): 816.97K Privately Held
SIC: 2439 Trusses, wooden roof

**(P-3294)**
**BETTER BUILT TRUSS INC**
251 E 4th St, Ripon (95366-2774)
P.O. Box 1319 (95366-1319)
PHONE..............................209 869-4545
Jeff Qualle, CEO
David Sanders, *
EMP: 50 EST: 2010
SALES (est): 5.23MM
SALES (corp-wide): 141.88MM Privately Held
Web: www.betterbuilttruss.com
SIC: 2439 Trusses, wooden roof
HQ: Us Lbm Holdings, Inc.
2150 E Lk Cook Rd Ste 101
Buffalo Grove IL 60089
847 353-7800

**(P-3295)**
**BROWN HNYCUTT TRUSS SYSTEMS IN**
16775 Smoke Tree St, Hesperia (92345-6165)
P.O. Box 401804 (92340-1804)
PHONE..............................760 244-8887
Michael Hough, Pr
Pedro Sanchez, Stockholder*
EMP: 18 EST: 1968
SQ FT: 1,800
SALES (est): 939.29K Privately Held
SIC: 2439 Trusses, wooden roof

**(P-3296)**
**CAL-ASIA TRUSS INC**
10547 E Stockton Blvd, Elk Grove (95624-9743)
PHONE..............................916 685-5648
Richard Avery, Mgr
EMP: 47
SIC: 2439 Trusses, wooden roof
PA: Cal-Asia Truss, Inc.
2300 Clayton Rd Ste 1400

**(P-3297)**
**CALIFORNIA TRUSFRAME LLC**
1144 Commerce Way, Sanger (93657-8726)
PHONE..............................559 876-3630
EMP: 206
SALES (corp-wide): 17.1B Publicly Held
Web: www.bldr.com
SIC: 2439 Trusses, wooden roof
HQ: California Trusframe, Llc
23665 Cajalco Rd
Perris CA 92570

**(P-3298)**
**CALIFORNIA TRUSFRAME LLC**
23447 Cajalco Rd, Perris (92570-8435)
PHONE..............................951 657-7491
EMP: 206
SALES (corp-wide): 17.1B Publicly Held
Web: www.bldr.com
SIC: 2439 Trusses, wooden roof
HQ: California Trusframe, Llc
23665 Cajalco Rd
Perris CA 92570

**(P-3299)**
**CALIFORNIA TRUSFRAME LLC**
2800 Tully Rd, Hughson (95326-9640)
PHONE..............................209 883-8000
EMP: 206
SALES (corp-wide): 17.1B Publicly Held
Web: www.bldr.com
SIC: 2439 Trusses, wooden roof
HQ: California Trusframe, Llc
23665 Cajalco Rd
Perris CA 92570

**(P-3300)**
**CALIFORNIA TRUSFRAME LLC (HQ)**
Also Called: Ctf
23665 Cajalco Rd, Perris (92570-8181)
PHONE..............................951 350-4880
Shawn Overholtzer, Pr
Steve Stroder, *
Mark Rome, *
EMP: 90 EST: 2011
SALES (est): 52.82MM
SALES (corp-wide): 17.1B Publicly Held
Web: www.bldr.com
SIC: 2439 Trusses, wooden roof
PA: Builders Firstsource, Inc.
6031 Cnnection Dr Ste 400
214 880-3500

**(P-3301)**
**CALIFORNIA TRUSS COMPANY (PA)**
23665 Cajalco Rd, Perris (92570-8181)
PHONE..............................951 657-7491
Kenneth M Cloyd, Pr
Mike Ruede, VP
Jim Butler, CFO
EMP: 87 EST: 1970
SQ FT: 5,000
SALES (est): 4.86MM
SALES (corp-wide): 4.86MM Privately Held
Web: www.caltruss.com
SIC: 2439 Trusses, wooden roof

**(P-3302)**
**CALIFORNIA TRUSS COMPANY**
2800 Tully Rd, Hughson (95326-9640)
PHONE..............................209 883-8000
Kenneth Cloyd, Pr
EMP: 163
SALES (corp-wide): 4.86MM Privately Held
Web: www.caltruss.com
SIC: 2439 Trusses, wooden roof
PA: California Truss Company
23665 Cajalco Rd
951 657-7491

**(P-3303)**
**CENTRAL VALLEY TRUSS**
1804 Soscol Ave Ste 205, Napa (94559-1300)
PHONE..............................707 963-3622
EMP: 19 EST: 2010
SALES (est): 875.86K Privately Held
Web: www.central-valley.com
SIC: 2439 Structural wood members, nec

**(P-3304)**
**COMPU-TECH LUMBER PRODUCTS INC**
1980 Huntington Ct, Fairfield (94533-9753)
PHONE..............................707 437-6683
Walter L Young, Pr
Greg Young, VP
Michael Blazer, CFO
EMP: 34 EST: 1995
SQ FT: 94,657
SALES (est): 2.28MM Privately Held
SIC: 2439 2431 1742 Trusses, wooden roof; Doors and door parts and trim, wood; Plastering, plain or ornamental

**(P-3305)**
**CY TRUSS**
10715 E American Ave, Del Rey (93616-9703)
P.O. Box 188 (93616-0188)
PHONE..............................559 888-2160
Dave Campos, Owner
EMP: 30 EST: 2012
SALES (est): 2.44MM Privately Held
Web: www.centralvalleytruss.com
SIC: 2439 Trusses, wooden roof

**(P-3306)**
**EL DORADO TRUSS CO INC**
300 Industrial Dr, Placerville (95667-6828)
PHONE..............................530 622-1264
TOLL FREE: 800
Steve Stewart, Pr
Edith Stewart, *
EMP: 45 EST: 1978
SQ FT: 15,000
SALES (est): 4.02MM Privately Held
Web: www.eldoradotruss.com
SIC: 2439 Trusses, wooden roof

**(P-3307)**
**GENERAL TRUSS COMPANY INC**
6947 Power Inn Rd, Sacramento (95828-2402)
PHONE..............................916 388-9300
EMP: 18 EST: 1999
SALES (est): 2.36MM Privately Held
Web: www.thetrussco.com
SIC: 2439 Trusses, wooden roof

**(P-3308)**
**GOLDENWOOD TRUSS CORPORATION**
11032 Nardo St, Ventura (93004-3210)
PHONE..............................805 659-2520
Kevin Tollefson, Pr
Darin Ranson, *
Myron Hodgson, *
EMP: 80 EST: 1998
SALES (est): 9.74MM Privately Held
Web: www.goldenwoodtruss.com
SIC: 2439 Trusses, wooden roof

**(P-3309)**
**HAISCH CONSTRUCTION CO INC**
Also Called: Systems Plus Lumber
1800 S Barney Rd, Anderson (96007-9703)
PHONE..............................530 378-6800
Matthew C Haisch, CEO
Bill Ivey, Sec
Douglas C Haisch, Prin
EMP: 18 EST: 1968
SQ FT: 10,000
SALES (est): 2.44MM Privately Held
Web: www.systplus.com
SIC: 2439 3441 Trusses, wooden roof; Fabricated structural metal

**(P-3310)**
**HANSON TRUSS INC**
13950 Yorba Ave, Chino (91710-5520)
PHONE..............................909 591-9256
Donald R Hanson, Pr
Tom Hanson, *
EMP: 300 EST: 1985
SQ FT: 4,000
SALES (est): 10.44MM Privately Held
Web: www.hansontruss.com
SIC: 2439 Trusses, wooden roof

**(P-3311)**
**HESPERIA HOLDING INC**
9780 E Ave, Hesperia (92345-6174)
PHONE..............................760 244-8787
William Nalls, Pr
Mark Presgraves, *
Don Shimp, *
EMP: 74 EST: 2000
SALES (est): 1.73MM Privately Held

## PRODUCTS & SERVICES SECTION
## 2448 - Wood Pallets And Skids (P-3332)

Web: www.capitalholdingsinc.com
SIC: 2439 Structural wood members, nec

### (P-3312)
### INLAND TRUSS INC (PA)
275 W Rider St, Perris (92571-3225)
PHONE.................................951 300-1758
Dan Irwin, Pr
Ernie Castro, *
EMP: 66 EST: 1991
SQ FT: 1,200
SALES (est): 7MM Privately Held
Web: www.inlandempiretruss.com
SIC: 2439 Trusses, wooden roof

### (P-3313)
### LASSEN FOREST PRODUCTS INC
22829 Casale Rd, Red Bluff (96080)
P.O. Box 8520 (96080-8520)
PHONE.................................530 527-7677
Peter Brunello Junior, Pr
EMP: 42 EST: 1960
SQ FT: 30,000
SALES (est): 5.95MM Privately Held
Web: www.lassenforestproducts.com
SIC: 2439 5031 Structural wood members, nec; Lumber, plywood, and millwork

### (P-3314)
### MC TRUSS INC
1144 Academy Ave, Sanger (93657-3113)
PHONE.................................559 876-3630
EMP: 80
SQ FT: 480
SALES (est): 6.87MM Privately Held
SIC: 2439 Trusses, wooden roof

### (P-3315)
### NORCAL TRIANGLES INC
4476 Skyway Dr, Olivehurst (95961)
P.O. Box 31 (95901)
PHONE.................................530 740-7750
Steven L Hanson, Pr
EMP: 60 EST: 2012
SALES (est): 5.78MM Privately Held
Web: www.hansontruss.com
SIC: 2439 Trusses, wooden roof

### (P-3316)
### PACIFIC COAST SUPPLY LLC
Also Called: Pacific Supply
5550 Roseville Rd, North Highlands (95660-5038)
PHONE.................................916 339-8100
Alo Taueleele, Brnch Mgr
EMP: 15
SALES (corp-wide): 1.21B Privately Held
Web: www.paccoastsupply.com
SIC: 2439 Trusses, wooden roof
HQ: Pacific Coast Supply, Llc
4290 Roseville Rd
North Highlands CA 95660
916 971-2301

### (P-3317)
### SIMPSON STRONG-TIE COMPANY INC
12246 Holly St, Riverside (92509-2314)
PHONE.................................714 871-8373
Dave Bastian, Brnch Mgr
EMP: 250
SQ FT: 40,845
SALES (corp-wide): 2.21B Publicly Held
Web: www.strongtie.com
SIC: 2439 3429 Structural wood members, nec; Hardware, nec
HQ: Simpson Strong-Tie Company Inc.
5956 W Las Positos Blvd

Pleasanton CA 94588
925 560-9000

### (P-3318)
### SPATES FABRICATORS INC
Also Called: Spates Fabricators
85435 Middleton St, Thermal (92274-9619)
PHONE.................................760 397-4122
Tom Spates, Pr
David Spates, *
Frankie Spates, *
EMP: 51 EST: 1976
SQ FT: 40,000
SALES (est): 9.52MM Privately Held
Web: www.spates.com
SIC: 2439 Trusses, except roof: laminated lumber

### (P-3319)
### T L TIMMERMAN CNSTR INC
Also Called: Timco
9845 Santa Fe Ave E, Hesperia (92345-6216)
P.O. Box 402563 (92340-2563)
PHONE.................................760 244-2532
Timothy L Timmerman, Pr
Anita Timmerman, *
EMP: 30 EST: 1976
SQ FT: 7,700
SALES (est): 2.15MM Privately Held
SIC: 2439 Trusses, wooden roof

### (P-3320)
### TRUSS ENGINEERING INC
477 Zeff Rd, Modesto (95351-3943)
P.O. Box 580210 (95358-0005)
PHONE.................................209 527-6387
Lawrence O Brien, Pr
EMP: 20 EST: 1978
SQ FT: 14,000
SALES (est): 2.3MM Privately Held
SIC: 2439 Trusses, wooden roof

### (P-3321)
### VOLUMETRIC BLDG COMPANIES LLC
2302 Paradise Rd, Tracy (95304-8530)
PHONE.................................623 236-5322
Matt Ryan, Brnch Mgr
EMP: 24
SALES (corp-wide): 33.83MM Privately Held
Web: www.vbc.co
SIC: 2439 2421 2434 Trusses, wooden roof; Lumber: rough, sawed, or planed; Wood kitchen cabinets
PA: Volumetric Building Companies Llc
6128 Ridge Ave
800 674-9340

## 2441 Nailed Wood Boxes And Shook

### (P-3322)
### A & J INDUSTRIES INC
Also Called: A & J Manufacturing
1430 240th St, Harbor City (90710-1307)
P.O. Box 90596 (90009-0596)
PHONE.................................310 216-2170
TOLL FREE: 800
Patrick Doucette, CEO
Keith Bell, Sec
◆ EMP: 18 EST: 1945
SQ FT: 40,000
SALES (est): 2.47MM Privately Held
Web: www.ajcases.com
SIC: 2441 Chests and trunks, wood

### (P-3323)
### BASAW MANUFACTURING INC (PA)
Also Called: Basaw Manufacturing
11323 Hartland St, North Hollywood (91605-6310)
PHONE.................................818 765-6650
Robert Allen, Pr
Hugh Mullen, *
Eleazar Padilla, *
Jorge Cea, *
Martha Rivera, *
▲ EMP: 32 EST: 1990
SALES (est): 9.51MM
SALES (corp-wide): 9.51MM Privately Held
Web: www.basaw.com
SIC: 2441 7389 Shipping cases, wood: nailed or lock corner; Packaging and labeling services

### (P-3324)
### BASAW MANUFACTURING INC
Also Called: Basaw
13340 Raymer, North Hollywood (91605-4101)
PHONE.................................818 765-6650
Robert Allen, Mgr
EMP: 22
SALES (corp-wide): 9.51MM Privately Held
Web: www.basaw.com
SIC: 2441 Shipping cases, wood: nailed or lock corner
PA: Basaw Manufacturing, Inc.
11323 Hartland St
818 765-6650

### (P-3325)
### CAL-COAST PKG & CRATING INC
2040 E 220th St, Carson (90810-1603)
PHONE.................................310 518-7215
Dale Loughry, Pr
▲ EMP: 35 EST: 1957
SQ FT: 58,000
SALES (est): 2.55MM Privately Held
Web: www.calcoastpacking.com
SIC: 2441 2449 Shipping cases, wood: nailed or lock corner; Wood containers, nec

### (P-3326)
### LARSON PACKAGING COMPANY LLC
1000 Yosemite Dr, Milpitas (95035-5410)
PHONE.................................408 946-4971
TOLL FREE: 800
Mark A Hoffman, Managing Member
Arnold Hoffman, *
Gold Hoffman, *
Greg Wayman, *
Anna Trujillo, *
EMP: 48 EST: 1967
SQ FT: 30,000
SALES (est): 4.27MM Privately Held
Web: www.larsonpkg.com
SIC: 2441 2448 5199 Nailed wood boxes and shook; Pallets, wood; Packaging materials

### (P-3327)
### NEFAB PACKAGING INC
8477 Central Ave, Newark (94560-3431)
PHONE.................................408 678-2500
Ana Gonzales, Brnch Mgr
EMP: 98
SALES (corp-wide): 977.18MM Privately Held
Web: www.nefab.com

SIC: 2441 5113 5199 Shipping cases, wood: nailed or lock corner; Cardboard and products; Packaging materials
HQ: Nefab Packaging, Inc.
204 Airline Dr Ste 100
Coppell TX 75019
469 444-5268

### (P-3328)
### NELSON CASE CORPORATION
Also Called: Nelson Case
650 S Jefferson St Ste A, Placentia (92870-6640)
PHONE.................................714 528-2215
Edward Bobadilla, CEO
John Bovadilla Junior, CEO
Virginia Sandburg, CFO
EMP: 20 EST: 1995
SALES (est): 2.8MM Privately Held
Web: www.nelsoncasecorp.com
SIC: 2441 5199 5099 2449 Packing cases, wood: nailed or lock corner; Bags, baskets, and cases; Carrying cases; Shipping cases, wood: wirebound

## 2448 Wood Pallets And Skids

### (P-3329)
### AAA PALLET RECYCLING & MFG INC
Also Called: AAA Pallet
1346 Stirrup Way, Norco (92860-3864)
PHONE.................................951 681-7748
Tyson Paulis, CEO
EMP: 22 EST: 1994
SQ FT: 152,460
SALES (est): 1.74MM Privately Held
SIC: 2448 Pallets, wood

### (P-3330)
### ALL BAY PALLET COMPANY INC (PA)
24993 Tarman Ave, Hayward (94544-2119)
PHONE.................................510 636-4131
Eladio Garcia Padilla, Pr
EMP: 36 EST: 1991
SQ FT: 50,000
SALES (est): 2.55MM Privately Held
Web: www.allbaymovers.com
SIC: 2448 2449 Pallets, wood; Wood containers, nec

### (P-3331)
### ALL GOOD PALLETS INC
1055 Diamond St, Stockton (95205-7020)
PHONE.................................209 467-7000
Jasbir Nagra, Pr
Jack Singh Nagra, *
Jagdev Singh, *
EMP: 40 EST: 1995
SALES (est): 6.93MM Privately Held
Web: www.allgoodpallets.com
SIC: 2448 7699 Pallets, wood and metal combination; Pallet repair

### (P-3332)
### AMERICAN PALLET & LUMBER INC
1001 Knox Rd, Oakdale (95361-9463)
P.O. Box 1413 (95361-1413)
PHONE.................................209 847-6122
EMP: 40 EST: 1975
SALES (est): 8.76MM Privately Held
Web: www.americanpallet.com
SIC: 2448 2441 Pallets, wood; Nailed wood boxes and shook

## 2448 - Wood Pallets And Skids (P-3333)

**(P-3333)**
**ARNIES SUPPLY SERVICE LTD (PA)**
1541 N Ditman Ave, Los Angeles (90063-2501)
P.O. Box 26 (91754-0026)
PHONE.................................323 263-1696
Arnold Espino, *Pr*
Madeline Espino, *
Maria Espino, *
EMP: 25 EST: 1975
SALES (est): 4.4MM
SALES (corp-wide): 4.4MM **Privately Held**
Web: www.arniessupply.com
SIC: 2448 Pallets, wood

**(P-3334)**
**CHEP (USA) INC**
Also Called: Bay Area Palette Company
2276 Wilbur Ln, Antioch (94509-8510)
PHONE.................................925 234-4970
Vince Sheldon, *Mgr*
EMP: 18
Web: www.chep.com
SIC: 2448 5085 Pallets, wood; Industrial supplies
HQ: Chep (U.S.A.) Inc.
5897 Windward Pkwy
Alpharetta GA 30005
770 668-8100

**(P-3335)**
**COMMERCIAL LBR & PALLET CO INC (PA)**
135 Long Ln, City Of Industry (91746-2633)
PHONE.................................626 968-0631
Raymond Gutierrez, *Pr*
EMP: 150 EST: 1941
SQ FT: 10,000
SALES (est): 25.14MM
SALES (corp-wide): 25.14MM **Privately Held**
Web: www.clcpallets.com
SIC: 2448 5031 Pallets, wood; Lumber: rough, dressed, and finished

**(P-3336)**
**CORREA PALLET INC (PA)**
Also Called: National Wholesale Lumber
13036 Avenue 76, Pixley (93256-9458)
PHONE.................................559 757-1790
Martin Correa, *Pr*
EMP: 23 EST: 2002
SALES (est): 10.69MM **Privately Held**
Web: www.correapallets.com
SIC: 2448 Pallets, wood

**(P-3337)**
**CORTEZ PALLETS SERVICE INC (PA)**
14739 Proctor Ave, La Puente (91746-3203)
P.O. Box 2552 (91746-0552)
PHONE.................................626 961-8891
Salvadore Cortez, *Pr*
Julia Cortez, *VP*
Salvadore Cortez Junior, *Sec*
EMP: 18 EST: 1976
SQ FT: 2,000
SALES (est): 2.16MM
SALES (corp-wide): 2.16MM **Privately Held**
Web: www.industrypallets.com
SIC: 2448 Pallets, wood

**(P-3338)**
**CUTTER LUMBER PRODUCTS**
4004 S El Dorado St, Stockton (95206-3759)
PHONE.................................209 982-4477
Tony Palma, *Mgr*
EMP: 38
SALES (corp-wide): 9.78MM **Privately Held**
Web: www.cutterlumber.com
SIC: 2448 Pallets, wood
PA: Cutter Lumber Products
10 Rickenbacker Cir
925 443-5959

**(P-3339)**
**D L B PALLETS (PA)**
4510 Rutile St, Riverside (92509-2649)
P.O. Box 10513 (92423-0513)
PHONE.................................951 360-9896
Daniel Bodbyl, *Pr*
Anna Bodbyl, *Treas*
EMP: 15 EST: 1986
SALES (est): 1.86MM **Privately Held**
SIC: 2448 5031 Pallets, wood; Pallets, wood

**(P-3340)**
**E VASQUEZ DISTRIBUTORS INC**
Also Called: Oxnard Pallet Company
4524 E Pleasant Valley Rd, Oxnard (93033-2309)
P.O. Box 1748 (93032-1748)
PHONE.................................805 487-8458
Elias Vasquez Junior, *Pr*
Beatrice Vasquez, *
EMP: 30 EST: 1989
SQ FT: 480
SALES (est): 5.26MM **Privately Held**
Web: www.oxnardpalletco.com
SIC: 2448 4214 Pallets, wood; Local trucking with storage

**(P-3341)**
**FIVE STAR LUMBER COMPANY LLC (PA)**
Also Called: Five Star Pallet Co
6899 Smith Ave, Newark (94560-4223)
PHONE.................................510 795-7204
Marco Beretta, *Managing Member*
David Beretta, *
Bruce Beretta, *
Sandra Beretta, *
▲ EMP: 25 EST: 1981
SQ FT: 20,000
SALES (est): 4.21MM
SALES (corp-wide): 4.21MM **Privately Held**
Web: www.fivestarpallet.com
SIC: 2448 5031 Pallets, wood; Lumber: rough, dressed, and finished

**(P-3342)**
**G C PALLETS INC**
5490 26th St, Riverside (92509-2212)
PHONE.................................909 357-8515
Mayra Gaona, *CEO*
Sebastian Gaona, *
EMP: 30 EST: 2001
SALES (est): 2.45MM **Privately Held**
Web: www.gcpalletsusa.com
SIC: 2448 Pallets, wood

**(P-3343)**
**GARCIAS PALLETS INC**
Also Called: Garcia Pallet
4125 S Golden State Blvd, Fresno (93725-9356)
PHONE.................................559 485-8182
Guadalupe Garcia, *CEO*
EMP: 31 EST: 1997
SQ FT: 19,600
SALES (est): 5.94MM **Privately Held**
SIC: 2448 Pallets, wood

**(P-3344)**
**GO PALLETS INC**
15642 Slover Ave, Fontana (92337-7362)
PHONE.................................909 823-4663
Guatalupe Ojeda, *Pr*
EMP: 15 EST: 1983
SALES (est): 460.9K **Privately Held**
SIC: 2448 Pallets, wood

**(P-3345)**
**GONZALEZ PALLETS INC (PA)**
1261 Yard Ct, San Jose (95133-1048)
PHONE.................................408 999-0280
Rafael Gomez, *CEO*
Jaime Silva, *
Rafael Gomez Junior, *Sec*
EMP: 35 EST: 1994
SQ FT: 85,000
SALES (est): 8.84MM **Privately Held**
Web: www.gonzalezpallets.com
SIC: 2448 Pallets, wood

**(P-3346)**
**HARDING CONTAINERS INTL INC**
4000 Santa Fe Ave, Long Beach (90810-1832)
PHONE.................................310 549-7272
Victor Hsing, *Pr*
Keith R Mayer, *VP*
▲ EMP: 16 EST: 1992
SQ FT: 1,000
SALES (est): 2.37MM **Privately Held**
SIC: 2448 Cargo containers, wood and wood with metal

**(P-3347)**
**IFCO SYSTEMS US LLC**
8950 Rochester Ave Ste 150, Rancho Cucamonga (91730-5541)
PHONE.................................909 484-4332
Mike Ellis, *Prin*
EMP: 56
Web: www.ifco.com
SIC: 2448 Pallets, wood
PA: Ifco Systems Us, Llc
3030 N Rcky Pt Dr Ste 300

**(P-3348)**
**JOSE GARCIA ASTORGA**
26820 Hansen Rd, Tracy (95377-8846)
PHONE.................................559 500-9338
Jose Garcia Astorga, *Owner*
EMP: 34 EST: 2022
SALES (est): 688.85K **Privately Held**
SIC: 2448 Pallets, wood

**(P-3349)**
**LOPEZ PALLET INC**
11080 Redwood Ave, Fontana (92337-7130)
P.O. Box 847 (91729-0847)
PHONE.................................909 823-0865
Jesus M Lopez, *Pr*
EMP: 16 EST: 1995
SQ FT: 700
SALES (est): 875.55K **Privately Held**
Web: www.lopezpallets.com
SIC: 2448 7699 Pallets, wood; Pallet repair

**(P-3350)**
**MEZA PALLETS INC**
14619 Merrill Ave, Fontana (92335-4219)
PHONE.................................909 829-0223
Leodegario G Meza, *Pr*
Michael Meza, *Pr*
EMP: 15 EST: 1988
SALES (est): 769.28K **Privately Held**
Web: www.mezapalletsinc.com
SIC: 2448 Pallets, wood

**(P-3351)**
**PACIFIC PALLET EXCHANGE INC**
3350 51st Ave, Sacramento (95823-1014)
PHONE.................................916 448-5589
Ricardo Zepeda, *Pr*
Douglas Schnabel, *
Glenna Schnabel, *
EMP: 30 EST: 1989
SQ FT: 77,537
SALES (est): 3.61MM **Privately Held**
Web: www.pacificpalletexchange.com
SIC: 2448 Pallets, wood

**(P-3352)**
**PALLET DEPOT INC**
19049 Avenue 242, Lindsay (93247-9698)
PHONE.................................916 645-0490
Jamie Anderson, *Pr*
Mike Anderson, *
Sharon Anderson, *
EMP: 70 EST: 1994
SALES (est): 745.31K **Privately Held**
SIC: 2448 Pallets, wood and wood with metal

**(P-3353)**
**PALLET MASTERS INC**
655 E Florence Ave, Los Angeles (90001-2319)
PHONE.................................323 758-1713
Stephen H Anderson, *Pr*
EMP: 55 EST: 1991
SQ FT: 105,000
SALES (est): 1.69MM **Privately Held**
Web: www.palletmasters.com
SIC: 2448 2441 2439 Pallets, wood; Boxes, wood; Structural wood members, nec

**(P-3354)**
**PALLETMASTERS LLC**
Also Called: Palletmasters
104 Matmor Rd, Woodland (95776-6006)
PHONE.................................510 715-1242
Austin Golden, *Prin*
EMP: 18 EST: 2021
SALES (est): 1.13MM **Privately Held**
SIC: 2448 Wood pallets and skids

**(P-3355)**
**PALLETS UNLIMITED INC**
2390 Athens Ave, Lincoln (95648-9508)
P.O. Box 1656 (95648-1443)
PHONE.................................916 408-1914
Nick Mehalakis, *Pr*
EMP: 18 EST: 2010
SALES (est): 2.08MM **Privately Held**
SIC: 2448 Pallets, wood

**(P-3356)**
**RAMIREZ PALLETS INC**
8431 Sultana Ave, Fontana (92335-3298)
PHONE.................................909 822-2066
Cresencio Ramirez, *Pr*
EMP: 35 EST: 1977
SALES (est): 2.65MM **Privately Held**
Web: www.ramirezpallets.com
SIC: 2448 Pallets, wood

**(P-3357)**
**RM PALLETS INC**
Also Called: Rm Pallets
2512 Paulson Rd, Turlock (95380-9757)
PHONE.................................209 632-9887
Georgina Ceja, *CEO*
EMP: 15 EST: 2015
SALES (est): 936.73K **Privately Held**
SIC: 2448 Pallets, wood

## 2449 - Wood Containers, Nec

**(P-3358)**
**ROGER R CARUSO ENTERPRISES INC**
Also Called: Century Pallets
2911 Norton Ave, Lynwood (90262-1810)
PHONE..................714 778-6006
Roger R Caruso, *Pr*
Rose Caruso, *Sec*
▲ EMP: 20 EST: 1973
SQ FT: 92,000
SALES (est): 1.99MM **Privately Held**
Web: www.centurypallets.com
SIC: 2448  Pallets, wood

**(P-3359)**
**SATCO INC (PA)**
Also Called: Satco
1601 E El Segundo Blvd, El Segundo (90245-4334)
PHONE..................310 322-4719
Glenn M Proctor, *CEO*
Vincent Voong, *
Richard Weis, *
▲ EMP: 125 EST: 1968
SQ FT: 27,000
SALES (est): 56.12MM
SALES (corp-wide): 56.12MM **Privately Held**
Web: www.satco-inc.com
SIC: 2448 3537  Pallets, wood and metal combination; Containers (metal), air cargo

**(P-3360)**
**SELMA PALLET INC**
1651 Pacific St, Selma (93662-9336)
P.O. Box 615 (93662-0615)
PHONE..................559 896-7171
Lupe Romero, *Pr*
Vera Romero, *
Lynette Romero Wilson, *
EMP: 90 EST: 1980
SQ FT: 1,000
SALES (est): 9.7MM **Privately Held**
Web: www.selmapallet.com
SIC: 2448  Pallets, wood

**(P-3361)**
**SUN PAC STORAGE CONTAINERS INC**
23222 Olive Ave Ste A, Lake Forest (92630-5301)
P.O. Box 339 (92609-0339)
PHONE..................949 458-2347
Tom Harris, *Prin*
EMP: 15 EST: 2004
SALES (est): 3.7MM **Privately Held**
Web: www.sunpaccontainers.com
SIC: 2448 4225  Cargo containers, wood and wood with metal; Warehousing, self storage

**(P-3362)**
**TRANPAK INC**
1209 Victory Ln, Madera (93637)
PHONE..................800 827-2474
Martin Ueland, *Pr*
Donna Ueland, *Treas*
Christian Ueland, *Sec*
◆ EMP: 21 EST: 1994
SQ FT: 80,000
SALES (est): 6.69MM **Privately Held**
Web: www.tranpak.com
SIC: 2448  Pallets, wood

**(P-3363)**
**UNITED PALLET SERVICES INC**
4043 Crows Landing Rd, Modesto (95358-9404)
PHONE..................209 538-5844
Wayne Randall, *Pr*

Darrel Roberson, *
Amber Mcmahon, *Sec*
EMP: 150 EST: 1976
SQ FT: 46,884
SALES (est): 8.71MM **Privately Held**
Web: www.unitedpalletservices.com
SIC: 2448 7699  Pallets, wood; Pallet repair

**(P-3364)**
**VALLEY PALLET INC**
6060 Midway St, Sacramento (95828-0924)
PHONE..................916 381-7954
Jose Barajas, *Brnch Mgr*
EMP: 17
Web: www.plasolutions.com
SIC: 2448  Pallets, wood
PA: Valley Pallet, Inc.
    522 El Camino Real S

**(P-3365)**
**VOTAW WOOD PRODUCTS INC**
Also Called: Pomona Box Co
301 W Imperial Hwy, La Habra (90631-7263)
P.O. Box 536 (90633-0536)
PHONE..................714 871-0932
EMP: 30 EST: 1929
SALES (est): 2.23MM **Privately Held**
Web: www.pomonabox.com
SIC: 2448 2441 5085  Pallets, wood; Boxes, wood; Boxes, crates, etc., other than paper

**(P-3366)**
**WESTSIDE PALLET INC**
2138 L St, Newman (95360-9765)
P.O. Box 786 (95360-0786)
PHONE..................209 862-3941
Bernadine Rocha, *Pr*
Carolyn Beach, *
EMP: 28 EST: 1994
SQ FT: 10,000
SALES (est): 2.7MM **Privately Held**
Web: www.westsidepallet.net
SIC: 2448  Pallets, wood

---

### 2449 Wood Containers, Nec

**(P-3367)**
**A & S CASE COMPANY INC**
5260 Vineland Ave, North Hollywood (91601-3221)
PHONE..................800 394-6181
TOLL FREE: 800
FAX: 818 509-1397
EMP: 22
SQ FT: 21,000
SALES (est): 1.5MM **Privately Held**
Web: www.ascase.com
SIC: 2449 3089  Shipping cases and drums, wood: wirebound and plywood; Cases, plastics

**(P-3368)**
**APEX DRUM COMPANY INC**
Also Called: Apex Container Services
6226 Ferguson Dr, Commerce (90022-5399)
PHONE..................323 721-8994
Abe Michlin, *CEO*
Sybil Flom, *Sec*
EMP: 19 EST: 1946
SQ FT: 40,000
SALES (est): 4.07MM **Privately Held**
Web: www.apexdrum.com
SIC: 2449 5085  Containers, plywood and veneer wood; Cooperage stock

**(P-3369)**
**CORRWOOD CONTAINERS**
7182 Rasmussen Ave, Visalia (93291-9405)
P.O. Box 670 (93227-0670)
PHONE..................559 651-0335
▲ EMP: 31
Web: www.corrwoodcontainers.com
SIC: 2449  Shipping cases, wood: wirebound

**(P-3370)**
**FIRST CLASS PACKAGING INC**
280 Cypress Ln Ste D, El Cajon (92020-1662)
PHONE..................619 579-7166
Sandra L Brock, *Pr*
EMP: 22 EST: 1987
SQ FT: 18,500
SALES (est): 982.11K
SALES (corp-wide): 12MM **Privately Held**
Web: www.larsonpkg.com
SIC: 2449 3086 5085 2653  Rectangular boxes and crates, wood; Plastics foam products; Bins and containers, storage; Corrugated and solid fiber boxes
PA: Larson Packaging Holdings, Inc.
    280 Cypress Ln
    408 946-4971

**(P-3371)**
**GREIF INC**
6001 S Eastern Ave, Commerce (90040-3413)
PHONE..................323 724-7500
EMP: 26
SALES (corp-wide): 5.22B **Publicly Held**
Web: www.greif.com
SIC: 2449 2655  Shipping cases and drums, wood: wirebound and plywood; Fiber cans, drums, and similar products
PA: Greif, Inc.
    425 Winter Rd
    740 549-6000

**(P-3372)**
**JOHN DANIEL GONZALEZ**
Also Called: Custom Wood Products
13458 E Industrial Dr, Parlier (93648-9678)
P.O. Box 783 (93648-0783)
PHONE..................559 646-6621
John Daniel Gonzalez, *Owner*
EMP: 43 EST: 2005
SQ FT: 14,000
SALES (est): 2.59MM **Privately Held**
Web: www.customwoodproductsinc.com
SIC: 2449  Wood containers, nec

**(P-3373)**
**JOHNSTONS TRADING POST INC**
11 N Pioneer Ave, Woodland (95776-5907)
PHONE..................530 661-6152
James B Johnston, *CEO*
Cary Johnston, *
Gloria Johnston, *
EMP: 50 EST: 1980
SQ FT: 112,000
SALES (est): 4.75MM **Privately Held**
Web: www.johnstontrading.com
SIC: 2449 4225  Wood containers, nec; General warehousing and storage

**(P-3374)**
**PICNIC AT ASCOT INC**
3237 W 131st St, Hawthorne (90250-5514)
PHONE..................310 674-3098
Paul Whitlock, *Pr*
Jill Brown, *
◆ EMP: 30 EST: 1992
SQ FT: 20,000

SALES (est): 2.25MM **Privately Held**
Web: www.picnicatascot.com
SIC: 2449 5947  Baskets: fruit and vegetable, round stave, till, etc.; Gift, novelty, and souvenir shop

**(P-3375)**
**SPECILIZED PACKG SOLUTIONS INC (PA)**
Also Called: Specilized Packg Solutions-Wood
38505 Cherry St Ste H, Newark (94560-4700)
P.O. Box P.O. Box 3042 (94539-0304)
PHONE..................510 494-5670
Karen Besso, *CEO*
Terrence Besso, *VP*
▲ EMP: 61 EST: 1994
SQ FT: 63,000
SALES (est): 19.17MM **Privately Held**
Web: www.specializedpackagingsolutions.com
SIC: 2449 2653 5113 3086  Rectangular boxes and crates, wood; Sheets, corrugated: made from purchased materials; Corrugated and solid fiber boxes; Plastics foam products

**(P-3376)**
**TONNELLERIE FRANCAISE FRENCH C**
Also Called: Nadalie USA
1401 Tubbs Ln, Calistoga (94515-9726)
P.O. Box 798 (94515-0798)
PHONE..................707 942-9301
Jean Jacques Nadalie, *CEO*
Alain Poisson, *General Vice President*
▲ EMP: 18 EST: 1980
SQ FT: 12,000
SALES (est): 9.58MM
SALES (corp-wide): 32.46MM **Privately Held**
Web: www.nadalie.com
SIC: 2449  Barrels: wood, coopered
PA: Tonnelerie Nadalie
    99 Rue Lafont
    557100202

**(P-3377)**
**TONNELLERIE RADOUX USA INC**
480 Aviation Blvd, Santa Rosa (95403-1069)
PHONE..................707 284-2888
Christen Liarg, *Pr*
Phillip Doray, *Sec*
▲ EMP: 17 EST: 1994
SQ FT: 25,000
SALES (est): 2.48MM
SALES (corp-wide): 43.11MM **Privately Held**
Web: www.tonnellerieradoux.com
SIC: 2449  Vats, wood: coopered
HQ: Tonnelerie Radoux
    Avenue Faidherbe
    Jonzac 17500
    546480065

**(P-3378)**
**WINE COUNTRY CASES INC**
621 Airpark Rd, Napa (94558)
P.O. Box 26 (94573)
PHONE..................707 967-4805
Dan C Pina, *Pr*
EMP: 87 EST: 1988
SQ FT: 5,500
SALES (est): 3.51MM **Privately Held**
Web: www.winecountrycases.com
SIC: 2449 2657  Butter crates, wood: wirebound; Folding paperboard boxes

# 2449 - Wood Containers, Nec

**(P-3379)**
**WOOD-N-WOOD PRODUCTS CAL INC (PA)**
2247 W Birch Ave, Fresno (93711-0442)
PHONE..................559 896-3636
Rodney Allen Scary, *CEO*
Susan Scarry, *Treas*
**EMP:** 20 **EST:** 1982
**SQ FT:** 15,000
**SALES (est):** 2.26MM
**SALES (corp-wide):** 2.26MM **Privately Held**
**SIC: 2449** Wood containers, nec

**(P-3380)**
**WOOD-N-WOOD PRODUCTS CAL INC**
13598 S Golden State Blvd, Selma (93662)
PHONE..................559 896-3636
Rick Murillo, *Mgr*
**EMP:** 15
**SALES (corp-wide):** 2.26MM **Privately Held**
**SIC: 2449** Containers, plywood and veneer wood
**PA:** Wood-N-Wood Products Of California, Inc.
2247 W Birch Ave
559 896-3636

## 2451 Mobile Homes

**(P-3381)**
**CALIFORNIA TINY HOUSE INC**
Also Called: California Tiny House
3337 W Sussex Way, Fresno (93722-4993)
PHONE..................559 316-4500
Nicholas A Mosley, *Owner*
Bell Lisa Sales, *Prin*
**EMP:** 15 **EST:** 2017
**SALES (est):** 1.01MM **Privately Held**
Web: www.californiatinyhouse.com
**SIC: 2451** 2452 Mobile buildings: for commercial use; Prefabricated wood buildings

**(P-3382)**
**CAVCO INDUSTRIES INC**
Also Called: Fleetwood Homes
7007 Jurupa Ave, Riverside (92504-1015)
P.O. Box 49991 (92514-1991)
PHONE..................951 688-5353
Mike Hayes, *Brnch Mgr*
**EMP:** 46
**SALES (corp-wide):** 1.79B **Publicly Held**
Web: www.cavco.com
**SIC: 2451** 2452 Mobile homes; Prefabricated buildings, wood
**PA:** Cavco Industries, Inc.
3636 N Centl Ave Ste 1200
602 256-6263

**(P-3383)**
**D-MAC INC**
1105 E Discovery Ln, Anaheim (92801-1121)
PHONE..................714 808-3918
David A Wade, *Prin*
**EMP:** 26 **EST:** 1998
**SALES (est):** 1.77MM **Privately Held**
Web: www.d-macinc.com
**SIC: 2451** 5039 5032 Mobile home frames; Structural assemblies, prefabricated: non-wood; Paving materials

**(P-3384)**
**DVELE INC**
25525 Redlands Blvd, Loma Linda (92354-2009)
P.O. Box 1710 (92354-0150)
PHONE..................909 796-2561
**EMP:** 45
**SALES (corp-wide):** 8.07MM **Privately Held**
Web: www.dvele.com
**SIC: 2451** 2452 Mobile homes, except recreational; Prefabricated buildings, wood
**PA:** Dvele, Inc.
5521 La Jolla Blvd
805 323-3711

**(P-3385)**
**DVELE OMEGA CORPORATION**
Also Called: Hallmark Southwest
25525 Redlands Blvd, Loma Linda (92354-2009)
P.O. Box 1710 (92354-0150)
PHONE..................909 796-2561
Luca Brammer, *Pr*
**EMP:** 100 **EST:** 2018
**SQ FT:** 5,000
**SALES (est):** 12.27MM **Privately Held**
Web: www.dvele.com
**SIC: 2451** 2452 Mobile homes, personal or private use; Prefabricated wood buildings

**(P-3386)**
**FLEETWOOD HOMES CALIFORNIA INC (DH)**
Also Called: Fleetwood Homes
7007 Jurupa Ave, Riverside (92504-1015)
P.O. Box 7638 (92513-7638)
PHONE..................951 351-2494
Elvin Smith, *Pr*
Boyd R Plowman, *
Forrest D Theobald, *
Lyle N Larkin, *
Roger L Howsmon, *
▲ **EMP:** 176 **EST:** 1963
**SQ FT:** 262,900
**SALES (est):** 10.39MM **Privately Held**
**SIC: 2451** Mobile homes
**HQ:** Fleetwood Enterprises, Inc.
1351 Pomona Rd Ste 230
Corona CA 92882
951 354-3000

**(P-3387)**
**NEXTMOD INC**
6361 Box Springs Blvd, Riverside (92507-0716)
P.O. Box 2008 (91709-0067)
PHONE..................909 740-3120
Melina Corona, *CEO*
Sean Khan, *
Elvia Chavez, *
**EMP:** 45 **EST:** 2012
**SALES (est):** 8.71MM **Privately Held**
Web: www.nextmodinc.com
**SIC: 2451** 7519 Mobile buildings: for commercial use; Mobile offices and commercial units, rental

**(P-3388)**
**SKYLINE HOMES INC**
499 W Esplanade Ave, San Jacinto (92583-5001)
P.O. Box 670 (92581-0670)
PHONE..................951 654-9321
Jim Claverie, *Genl Mgr*
**EMP:** 115
**SALES (corp-wide):** 2.02B **Publicly Held**
Web: www.skylinehomes.com
**SIC: 2451** Mobile homes
**HQ:** Skyline Homes, Inc.
2520 Bypass Rd
Elkhart IN 46514
574 294-6521

**(P-3389)**
**SKYLINE HOMES INC**
Also Called: Buddy Homes 355
1720 E Beamer St, Woodland (95776-6218)
P.O. Box 1870 (95776-1870)
PHONE..................530 666-0974
Tim Howard, *Prin*
**EMP:** 191
**SALES (corp-wide):** 2.02B **Publicly Held**
Web: www.skylinehomes.com
**SIC: 2451** Mobile homes
**HQ:** Skyline Homes, Inc.
2520 Bypass Rd
Elkhart IN 46514
574 294-6521

## 2452 Prefabricated Wood Buildings

**(P-3390)**
**ALAN PRE-FAB BUILDING CORP**
Also Called: Alan Portable Buildings
17817 Evelyn Ave, Gardena (90248-3735)
PHONE..................310 538-0333
**TOLL FREE:** 888
John W Andrus, *Pr*
Bill Andrus, *VP*
Bret Andrus, *VP*
Ann Andrus, *Sec*
**EMP:** 16 **EST:** 1971
**SQ FT:** 49,000
**SALES (est):** 915.98K **Privately Held**
Web: www.alanprefab.com
**SIC: 2452** 7359 Prefabricated wood buildings; Equipment rental and leasing, nec

**(P-3391)**
**AMERICAN MODULAR SYSTEMS INC**
Also Called: AMS
787 Spreckels Ave, Manteca (95336-6002)
PHONE..................209 825-1921
Daniel Sarich, *Pr*
Tony Sarich, *
**EMP:** 100 **EST:** 1982
**SQ FT:** 85,000
**SALES (est):** 36.42MM **Privately Held**
Web: www.americanmodular.com
**SIC: 2452** 1542 Modular homes, prefabricated, wood; Nonresidential construction, nec

**(P-3392)**
**APPLIED POLYTECH SYSTEMS INC**
Also Called: A P S
26000 Springbrook Ave Ste 102, Santa Clarita (91350-2590)
PHONE..................818 504-9261
Christine Wagner, *Pr*
**EMP:** 30 **EST:** 1988
**SQ FT:** 6,000
**SALES (est):** 772.85K **Privately Held**
Web: www.apsincprecast.com
**SIC: 2452** Prefabricated wood buildings

**(P-3393)**
**DVELE INC (PA)**
5521 La Jolla Blvd, La Jolla (92037-7612)
PHONE..................805 323-3711
Kurt Goodjohn, *CEO*
Luca Bramme, *COO*
**EMP:** 17 **EST:** 2016
**SALES (est):** 8.07MM
**SALES (corp-wide):** 8.07MM **Privately Held**
Web: www.dvele.com
**SIC: 2452** 2451 Prefabricated buildings, wood; Mobile homes, except recreational

**(P-3394)**
**ENTEKRA LLC**
945 E Whitmore Ave, Modesto (95358-9408)
PHONE..................209 624-1630
**EMP:** 78 **EST:** 2018
**SQ FT:** 200,000
**SALES (est):** 6.44MM **Privately Held**
Web: www.entekra.com
**SIC: 2452** Prefabricated wood buildings

**(P-3395)**
**GARY DOUPNIK MANUFACTURING INC**
3237 Rippey Rd, Loomis (95650-7654)
P.O. Box 527 (95650-0527)
PHONE..................916 652-9291
Sherie Edgar, *Pr*
Gary Doupnik Junior, *VP*
Kirtus Doupnik, *
Jt Doupnik, *
Gary Doupnik Senior, *Treas*
**EMP:** 23 **EST:** 1976
**SQ FT:** 4,000
**SALES (est):** 322.51K **Privately Held**
**SIC: 2452** 3448 Prefabricated buildings, wood; Prefabricated metal buildings and components

**(P-3396)**
**GLOBAL DIVERSIFIED INDS INC (PA)**
450 Commerce Ave, Atwater (95301-9412)
P.O. Box 32 (95301-0032)
PHONE..................559 665-5800
Phillip Hamilton, *Pr*
Adam N Debard, *Sec*
**EMP:** 15 **EST:** 1990
**SQ FT:** 100,000
**SALES (est):** 16.97MM
**SALES (corp-wide):** 16.97MM **Privately Held**
Web: www.gdvi.net
**SIC: 2452** Modular homes, prefabricated, wood

**(P-3397)**
**HOME FACTORIES INC (HQ)**
225 Elm Ave, Galt (95632-1558)
PHONE..................209 745-3001
Jeffrey Gore, *CEO*
**EMP:** 16 **EST:** 2000
**SALES (est):** 9.91MM
**SALES (corp-wide):** 145.11MM **Privately Held**
Web: www.bmdusa.com
**SIC: 2452** Prefabricated wood buildings
**PA:** Building Material Distributors, Inc.
225 Elm Ave
800 356-3001

**(P-3398)**
**PLH PRODUCTS INC**
10541 Calle Lee Ste 119, Los Alamitos (90720-6782)
PHONE..................714 739-6622
Seung Woo Lee, *Ch Bd*
Kyung Min Park, *
Won Yong Lee, *
◆ **EMP:** 405 **EST:** 1992
**SALES (est):** 24.43MM **Privately Held**
Web: www.plhproducts.com
**SIC: 2452** 2449 5999 Sauna rooms, prefabricated, wood; Hot tubs, wood; Sauna equipment and supplies

## PRODUCTS & SERVICES SECTION
## 2499 - Wood Products, Nec (P-3419)

**(P-3399)**
**VBC TRACY LLC (PA)**
2302 Paradise Rd, Tracy (95304-8530)
PHONE.....................215 259-7509
Vaughan Buckley, *CEO*
EMP: 25 EST: 2021
SALES (est): 7.65MM
SALES (corp-wide): 7.65MM **Privately Held**
Web: www.vbc.co
SIC: 2452 Prefabricated wood buildings

**(P-3400)**
**WALDEN STRUCTURES INC**
1000 Bristol St N # 126, Newport Beach (92660-8916)
PHONE.....................909 389-9100
Charlie Walden, *Owner*
Michael J Dominici, *
Curtis H Claire, *
EMP: 400 EST: 1996
SQ FT: 150,000
SALES (est): 48.47MM **Privately Held**
Web: www.silvercreekmodular.com
SIC: 2452 Modular homes, prefabricated, wood

### 2491 Wood Preserving

**(P-3401)**
**CALIFORNIA CASCADE INDUSTRIES**
7512 14th Ave, Sacramento (95820-3539)
P.O. Box 130026 (95853-0026)
PHONE.....................916 736-3353
Stuart D Heath, *Pr*
Stu Heath, *
Kyle Keaton, *
Richard Rose, *
EMP: 200 EST: 1975
SQ FT: 6,500
SALES (est): 45.08MM
SALES (corp-wide): 1.81B **Privately Held**
Web: www.californiacascade.com
SIC: 2491 2421 Wood preserving; Sawmills and planing mills, general
PA: Doman Building Materials Group Ltd
1600-1100 Melville St
604 432-1400

**(P-3402)**
**EAST BAY FIXTURE COMPANY**
941 Aileen St, Oakland (94608-2805)
PHONE.....................510 652-4421
Richard Laible, *Pr*
Frances Laible, *
EMP: 50 EST: 1923
SQ FT: 32,000
SALES (est): 4.4MM **Privately Held**
Web: www.eastbayfixture.com
SIC: 2491 2541 Millwork, treated wood; Office fixtures, wood

**(P-3403)**
**HOOVER TREATED WOOD PDTS INC**
Also Called: Hoover Treated Wood Pdts Plant
5601 District Blvd, Bakersfield (93313-2129)
PHONE.....................661 833-0429
EMP: 23
SALES (corp-wide): 4.41B **Publicly Held**
Web: www.frtw.com
SIC: 2491 Structural lumber and timber, treated wood
HQ: Hoover Treated Wood Products, Inc.
154 Wire Rd
Thomson GA 30824
706 595-5058

**(P-3404)**
**THUNDERBOLT SALES INC**
3400 Patterson Rd, Riverbank (95367-2998)
P.O. Box 890 (95367-0890)
PHONE.....................209 869-4561
T W Ted Seybold, *Pr*
Don De Vries, *VP*
Leonard Lovalvo, *VP*
EMP: 17 EST: 1982
SALES (est): 589.01K
SALES (corp-wide): 6.85MM **Privately Held**
Web: www.thunderboltwoodtreating.com
SIC: 2491 Wood preserving
PA: Thunderbolt Wood Treating Co., Inc.
3400 Patterson Rd
209 869-4561

**(P-3405)**
**WEST COAST WOOD PRESERVING LLC**
5601 District Blvd, Bakersfield (93313-2129)
PHONE.....................661 833-0429
▲ EMP: 125
SIC: 2491 Preserving (creosoting) of wood

### 2493 Reconstituted Wood Products

**(P-3406)**
**CALPLANT I LLC**
Also Called: Eureka
6101 State Hwy 162, Willows (95988)
P.O. Box 1338 (95988)
PHONE.....................530 361-0003
Jeffrey N Wagner, *Managing Member*
EMP: 23 EST: 2008
SALES (est): 10.72MM
SALES (corp-wide): 10.72MM **Privately Held**
Web: www.calplant1.com
SIC: 2493 Reconstituted wood products
PA: Calplant I Holdco, Llc
6101 State Hwy 162
530 570-0542

**(P-3407)**
**CALPLANT I HOLDCO LLC (PA)**
6101 State Hwy 162, Willows (95988)
P.O. Box 1338 (95988)
PHONE.....................530 570-0542
Gerald Uhland, *CEO*
Chris Motley, *CFO*
EMP: 23 EST: 2017
SALES (est): 10.72MM
SALES (corp-wide): 10.72MM **Privately Held**
Web: www.calplant1.com
SIC: 2493 Reconstituted wood products

**(P-3408)**
**REGARDS ENTERPRISES INC**
Also Called: Quality Marble & Granite
731 S Taylor Ave, Ontario (91761-1847)
PHONE.....................909 983-0655
Evan Cohen, *CEO*
▲ EMP: 19 EST: 2013
SQ FT: 95,000
SALES (est): 2.58MM **Privately Held**
SIC: 2493 3281 Marbleboard (stone face hard board); Granite, cut and shaped

### 2499 Wood Products, Nec

**(P-3409)**
**ALACO LADDER COMPANY**
5167 G St, Chino (91710-5143)
PHONE.....................909 591-7561
Gil Jacobs, *Pr*
Mario Garcia, *
▼ EMP: 25 EST: 1946
SQ FT: 26,000
SALES (est): 669.22K
SALES (corp-wide): 6.72MM **Privately Held**
Web: www.alacoladder.com
SIC: 2499 3354 3499 Ladders, wood; Aluminum extruded products; Metal ladders
PA: B, E & P Enterprises, Llc
5167 G St
909 591-7561

**(P-3410)**
**APPLIED SILVER INC**
26254 Eden Landing Rd, Hayward (94545-3717)
PHONE.....................888 939-4747
Sean Morham, *CEO*
Elizabeth Hutt Pollard, *Ch Bd*
EMP: 28 EST: 2011
SALES (est): 2.88MM **Privately Held**
Web: www.appliedsilver.com
SIC: 2499 5719 Laundry products, wood; Linens

**(P-3411)**
**B E & P ENTERPRISES LLC (PA)**
Also Called: Alaco Ladder Company
5167 G St, Chino (91710-5143)
PHONE.....................909 591-7561
Fred Evans, *
Gil Jacobs, *
Stephen Bernstein, *
EMP: 24 EST: 1946
SALES (est): 4.72MM
SALES (corp-wide): 4.72MM **Privately Held**
Web: www.alacoladder.com
SIC: 2499 3499 3354 Ladders, wood; Ladders, portable: metal; Aluminum extruded products

**(P-3412)**
**BRENT-WOOD PRODUCTS INC**
17071 Hercules St, Hesperia (92345-7621)
P.O. Box 17037 (90807-7037)
PHONE.....................800 400-7335
Lawrence D Hobbs, *CEO*
Birgitta Olin, *
Anna Pinili, *
▼ EMP: 30 EST: 1963
SQ FT: 26,000
SALES (est): 1.34MM **Privately Held**
Web: www.brent-wood.com
SIC: 2499 Reels, plywood

**(P-3413)**
**CALIFORNIA CEDAR PRODUCTS CO (PA)**
Also Called: Blackwing
2385 Arch Airport Rd Ste 500, Stockton (95206-4403)
PHONE.....................209 932-5002
Charles Berolzheimer, *Pr*
Susan Macintyre, *CFO*
◆ EMP: 50 EST: 1920
SQ FT: 10,000
SALES (est): 39.61K
SALES (corp-wide): 39.61K **Privately Held**
Web: www.calcedar.com

SIC: 2499 Pencil slats, wood

**(P-3414)**
**CARRIS REELS CALIFORNIA INC (HQ)**
2100 W Almond Ave, Madera (93637-5203)
P.O. Box 88 (93639-0088)
PHONE.....................802 733-9111
William Carris, *Ch Bd*
Dave Ferraro, *Pr*
David Fitzgerald, *
Linda Gallipo, *Sec*
David Ferraro, *
▲ EMP: 30 EST: 1966
SALES (est): 12.38MM **Privately Held**
Web: www.carris.com
SIC: 2499 2448 Spools, reels, and pulleys: wood; Pallets, wood
PA: Carris Financial Corp.
49 Main St

**(P-3415)**
**CORK SUPPLY USA INC**
531 Stone Rd, Benicia (94510-1113)
PHONE.....................707 746-0353
EMP: 60
SALES (est): 7.01MM **Privately Held**
SIC: 2499 Cork and cork products

**(P-3416)**
**CRI 2000 LP (PA)**
Also Called: Lso
2245 San Diego Ave Ste 125, San Diego (92110-2942)
PHONE.....................619 542-1975
Mitchell G Lynn, *Pt*
◆ EMP: 50 EST: 2002
SQ FT: 10,000
SALES (est): 10.42MM **Privately Held**
Web: www.cri2000.com
SIC: 2499 5112 5049 5092 Picture frame molding, finished; Office supplies, nec; School supplies; Arts and crafts equipment and supplies

**(P-3417)**
**GARRETT MOULDING COMPANY INC**
200 Coral St, Santa Cruz (95060-2105)
PHONE.....................831 426-2020
◆ EMP: 20
SIC: 2499 Picture frame molding, finished

**(P-3418)**
**HANDLE INC**
580 Howard St Unit 404, San Francisco (94105-3025)
PHONE.....................650 863-6113
Yvette Ma, *Prin*
EMP: 44 EST: 2018
SALES (est): 6.29MM **Privately Held**
Web: www.handle.today
SIC: 2499 Handles, wood

**(P-3419)**
**LARSON-JUHL US LLC**
Also Called: Larson Picture Frames
12206 Bell Ranch Dr, Santa Fe Springs (90670-3361)
PHONE.....................562 946-6873
Anthony Eikenberry, *Mgr*
EMP: 31
SALES (corp-wide): 364.48B **Publicly Held**
Web: www.artmaterialsservice.com
SIC: 2499 Picture frame molding, finished
HQ: Larson-Juhl Us L L C
990 Pchtree Indus Blvd Un
Suwanee GA 30024
770 279-5200

## 2499 - Wood Products, Nec (P-3420)

**(P-3420)**
**MARTIN GROUP INC (PA)**
Also Called: C T R
1470 Grove St, Healdsburg (95448-4700)
P.O. Box P.O. Box 159 (95448)
PHONE.................................707 433-3900
Gordon Martin, *CEO*
Terri Martin, *Sec*
▲ **EMP:** 20 **EST:** 1997
**SQ FT:** 1,200
**SALES (est):** 8.93MM
**SALES (corp-wide):** 8.93MM Privately Held
Web: www.themartingroup.com
**SIC:** 2499 Cooling towers, wood or wood and sheet metal combination

**(P-3421)**
**OUTDOOR DIMENSIONS LLC**
5325 E Hunter Ave, Anaheim (92807)
PHONE.................................714 578-9555
Brian Pickler, *Managing Member*
Donald Pickler, *
Brian Pickler, *VP*
**EMP:** 160 **EST:** 1974
**SQ FT:** 80,000
**SALES (est):** 39.28MM Privately Held
Web: www.outdoordimensions.com
**SIC:** 2499 3993 3281 Signboards, wood; Signs and advertising specialties; Cut stone and stone products

**(P-3422)**
**PACIFIC PANEL PRODUCTS CORP**
Also Called: Pacific Panel Products
15601 Arrow Hwy, Irwindale (91706-2004)
P.O. Box 2204 (91706-1126)
PHONE.................................626 851-0444
Jon R Dickey, *CEO*
▲ **EMP:** 39 **EST:** 1994
**SQ FT:** 79,800
**SALES (est):** 4.76MM Privately Held
Web: www.pacificpanel.com
**SIC:** 2499 Decorative wood and woodwork

**(P-3423)**
**PRO TOUR MEMORABILIA LLC**
Also Called: Ptm Images
700 N San Vicente Blvd Ste G696, West Hollywood (90069-5073)
P.O. Box 15084 (90209-1084)
PHONE.................................424 303-7200
◆ **EMP:** 25 **EST:** 1995
**SQ FT:** 8,000
**SALES (est):** 2.48MM Privately Held
Web: pro-tour-memorabilia-llc.hub.biz
**SIC:** 2499 Picture and mirror frames, wood

**(P-3424)**
**QUALITY FIRST WOODWORKS INC**
1264 N Lakeview Ave, Anaheim (92807-1831)
PHONE.................................714 632-0480
Mark Nappy, *Pr*
Chad Nappy, *
**EMP:** 115 **EST:** 1989
**SQ FT:** 30,000
**SALES (est):** 10.53MM Privately Held
Web: www.qfwinc.com
**SIC:** 2499 1751 Decorative wood and woodwork; Cabinet building and installation

**(P-3425)**
**RAPHAELS INC**
4460 Braeburn Rd, San Diego (92116-2126)
▲ **EMP:** 17 **EST:** 1976
**SALES (est):** 487.8K Privately Held
Web: www.raphaelsap.com
**SIC:** 2499 Picture and mirror frames, wood

**(P-3426)**
**ROMA MOULDING INC**
6230 N Irwindale Ave, Irwindale (91702-3208)
PHONE.................................626 334-2539
Jon Mathews, *Opers Mgr*
**EMP:** 44
**SALES (corp-wide):** 28.86MM Privately Held
Web: www.romamoulding.com
**SIC:** 2499 5023 Picture frame molding, finished; Frames and framing, picture and mirror
**PA:** Roma Moulding Inc
360 Hanlan Rd
905 850-1500

**(P-3427)**
**SHASTA FOREST PRODUCTS INC**
1423 Montague Rd, Yreka (96097-9659)
P.O. Box 777 (96097-0777)
PHONE.................................530 842-2787
Bill Hall, *Mgr*
**EMP:** 38
**SALES (corp-wide):** 10.7MM Privately Held
Web: www.shastabark.com
**SIC:** 2499 2421 Mulch, wood and bark; Sawmills and planing mills, general
**PA:** Shasta Forest Products, Inc.
1412 Montague Rd
530 842-0527

**(P-3428)**
**SHASTA WOOD PRODUCTS INC**
19751 Hirsch Ct, Anderson (96007-4945)
P.O. Box 1101 (96022-1101)
PHONE.................................530 378-6880
Jeff Aboud, *Pr*
Thomas Aboud, *
Tamara Aboud, *
Cheryl Aboud, *
**EMP:** 35 **EST:** 1986
**SQ FT:** 12,000
**SALES (est):** 6.36MM Privately Held
Web: www.shastawoodproducts.com
**SIC:** 2499 2434 2541 1751 Kitchen, bathroom, and household ware: wood; Wood kitchen cabinets; Cabinets, lockers, and shelving; Cabinet building and installation

**(P-3429)**
**UNIVERSITY FRAMES INC**
Also Called: Campus Images
3060 E Miraloma Ave, Anaheim (92806-1810)
PHONE.................................714 575-5100
John G Winn, *CEO*
Diane Winn, *
▲ **EMP:** 50 **EST:** 1996
**SQ FT:** 20,000
**SALES (est):** 4.92MM Privately Held
Web: www.universityframes.com
**SIC:** 2499 5999 Picture frame molding, finished; Picture frames, ready made

**(P-3430)**
**WALTON COMPANY INC**
17900 Sampson Ln, Huntington Beach (92647-7149)
PHONE.................................714 847-8800
Don Walton, *CEO*
◆ **EMP:** 20 **EST:** 1960
**SQ FT:** 12,000
**SALES (est):** 955.25K Privately Held
Web: www.thewaltoncompany.com
**SIC:** 2499 Cork and cork products

**(P-3431)**
**WHOLESALE ART AND FRAMING INC**
3068 Sunrise Blvd Ste E, Rancho Cordova (95742-6525)
PHONE.................................916 851-0770
Ranell Carpenter, *Brnch Mgr*
**EMP:** 17
Web: www.wholesaleartandframing.com
**SIC:** 2499 Picture frame molding, finished
**PA:** Wholesale Art And Framing Inc
1774 Broadway

**(P-3432)**
**YTI ENTERPRISES INC**
Also Called: Laminating Technologies
1260 S State College Pkwy, Anaheim (92806-5240)
PHONE.................................714 632-8696
Judith Rochverger, *Pr*
Jair N Rochverger, *CFO*
**EMP:** 15 **EST:** 1996
**SQ FT:** 16,500
**SALES (est):** 7.8MM Privately Held
**SIC:** 2499 Seats, toilet

---

## 2511 Wood Household Furniture

**(P-3433)**
**BAU FURNITURE MFG INC**
21 Kelly Ln, Ladera Ranch (92694-1463)
PHONE.................................949 643-2729
Thomas Bau, *Pr*
Linda Bau, *
**EMP:** 52 **EST:** 1978
**SALES (est):** 589.1K Privately Held
**SIC:** 2511 2512 2521 Tables, household: wood; Upholstered household furniture; Tables, office: wood

**(P-3434)**
**BEAUTY CRAFT FURNITURE CORP**
Also Called: California House
3316 51st Ave, Sacramento (95823-1089)
PHONE.................................916 428-2238
Steven Start, *Pr*
Dee Start, *
▲ **EMP:** 44 **EST:** 1953
**SQ FT:** 65,000
**SALES (est):** 4.56MM Privately Held
Web: www.californiahouse.com
**SIC:** 2511 Wood game room furniture

**(P-3435)**
**BERKELEY MLLWK & FURN CO INC**
Also Called: Berkeley Mills
2830 7th St, Berkeley (94710-2703)
PHONE.................................510 549-2854
Eugene Agress, *Pr*
Scott Pew, *
Luong Lee Dinh, *
**EMP:** 43 **EST:** 1989
**SQ FT:** 18,000
**SALES (est):** 3.36MM Privately Held
Web: www.berkeleymills.com
**SIC:** 2511 2541 2434 Wood household furniture; Wood partitions and fixtures; Wood kitchen cabinets

**(P-3436)**
**BIG TREE FURNITURE & INDS INC (PA)**
760 S Vail Ave, Montebello (90640-4954)
PHONE.................................310 894-7500
Joe Ho, *CEO*
◆ **EMP:** 47 **EST:** 1985
**SALES (est):** 8.58MM Privately Held
**SIC:** 2511 Wood household furniture

**(P-3437)**
**BROWNWOOD FURNITURE INC**
9805 6th St Ste 104, Rancho Cucamonga (91730-5751)
PHONE.................................909 945-5613
Rick Vartanian, *Pr*
Pat Eberly, *
Jose Navarro, *
◆ **EMP:** 150 **EST:** 1979
**SQ FT:** 107,000
**SALES (est):** 5.36MM Privately Held
Web: www.brownwoodfurniture.com
**SIC:** 2511 Wood bedroom furniture

**(P-3438)**
**DEDON INC**
8687 Melrose Ave Ste B188, West Hollywood (90069-5708)
PHONE.................................310 388-4721
**EMP:** 16
**SALES (corp-wide):** 355.83K Privately Held
Web: www.dedon.de
**SIC:** 2511 Lawn furniture: wood
**HQ:** Dedon, Inc.
657 Brigham Rd Ste C
Greensboro NC 27409

**(P-3439)**
**DOREL HOME FURNISHINGS INC**
5400 Shea Center Dr, Ontario (91761-7892)
PHONE.................................909 390-5705
**EMP:** 67
**SALES (corp-wide):** 1.39B Privately Held
Web: www.ameriwoodhome.com
**SIC:** 2511 Console tables: wood
**HQ:** Dorel Home Furnishings, Inc.
410 E 1st St S
Wright City MO 63390
636 745-3351

**(P-3440)**
**DOUG MOCKETT & COMPANY INC**
1915 Abalone Ave, Torrance (90501-3706)
P.O. Box 3333 (90266-1333)
PHONE.................................310 318-2491
Tyra Cunningham, *Pr*
Susan Darby Gordon, *
Sonia Marie H Mockett, *
◆ **EMP:** 65 **EST:** 1984
**SALES (est):** 9.82MM Privately Held
Web: www.mockett.com
**SIC:** 2511 5072 Unassembled or unfinished furniture, household: wood; Furniture hardware, nec

**(P-3441)**
**FREMARC INDUSTRIES INC (PA)**
Also Called: Fremarc Designs
18810 San Jose Ave, City Of Industry (91748-1325)
P.O. Box 1086 (91788-1086)
PHONE.................................626 965-0802
Maurice M Donenfeld, *Pr*
Harriette Donenfeld, *
▲ **EMP:** 78 **EST:** 1971

# PRODUCTS & SERVICES SECTION
## 2512 - Upholstered Household Furniture (P-3464)

SQ FT: 45,000
SALES (est): 4.12MM
SALES (corp-wide): 4.12MM Privately Held
Web: www.fremarc.com
SIC: 2511 Wood household furniture

### (P-3442)
### FRENCH TRADITION INC (PA)
2413 Moreton St, Torrance (90505-5310)
PHONE..................................310 719-9977
Franck Valles, Pr
EMP: 15 EST: 1984
SALES (est): 2MM Privately Held
Web: www.thefrenchtradition.com
SIC: 2511 Wood household furniture

### (P-3443)
### FURNITURE TECHNICS INC
Also Called: Furniture Techniques
2900 Supply Ave, Commerce (90040-2708)
PHONE..................................562 802-0261
Cesar Rousseau, Pr
Ricardo Flores, *
EMP: 25 EST: 1988
SALES (est): 823.21K Privately Held
SIC: 2511 2426 Wood household furniture; Furniture stock and parts, hardwood

### (P-3444)
### HOLLYWOOD CHAIRS (PA)
Also Called: Totally Bamboo
120 W Grand Ave Ste 102, Escondido (92025-2642)
PHONE..................................760 471-6600
Joanne Sullivan, CEO
Thomas Sullivan, Sec
◆ EMP: 24 EST: 1999
SQ FT: 10,000
SALES (est): 6.86MM Privately Held
Web: www.totallybamboo.com
SIC: 2511 Wood household furniture

### (P-3445)
### JP PRODUCTS LLC
2054 Davie Ave, Commerce (90040-1705)
PHONE..................................310 237-6237
Patrick Mooney, Managing Member
Jacqueline Mooney, Managing Member*
EMP: 46 EST: 2010
SQ FT: 35,000
SALES (est): 1.11MM Privately Held
SIC: 2511 Wood household furniture

### (P-3446)
### LAUREN ANTHONY & CO INC
11425 Woodside Ave Ste B, Santee (92071-4726)
PHONE..................................619 590-1141
Randy T Passanisi, Pr
EMP: 23 EST: 2004
SALES (est): 233.05K Privately Held
Web: www.anthonylauren.com
SIC: 2511 Wood household furniture

### (P-3447)
### LEGACY COMMERCIAL HOLDINGS INC
Also Called: Armen Living
28939 Avenue Williams, Valencia (91355-4183)
PHONE..................................818 767-6626
Kevin Kevonian, Pr
Kevon Kevonian, Pr
Honigsfeld Lee, VP
▲ EMP: 35 EST: 2007
SALES (est): 1.1MM Privately Held
Web: www.armenliving.com

SIC: 2511 2514 2531 2521 Kitchen and dining room furniture; Metal lawn and garden furniture; Public building and related furniture; Wood office furniture

### (P-3448)
### LOTUS BED SOLUTIONS LLC
4600 Greenholme Dr Apt 3, Sacramento (95842-3473)
PHONE..................................415 756-5099
Katrina Smith, Prin
EMP: 19 EST: 2021
SALES (est): 354.02K Privately Held
SIC: 2511 Wood household furniture

### (P-3449)
### MIKHAIL DARAFEEV INC (PA)
5075 Edison Ave, Chino (91710-5716)
PHONE..................................909 613-1818
Antonina Darafeev, Pr
Paul Darafeev, *
George Darafeev, *
▲ EMP: 50 EST: 1957
SALES (est): 9.95MM
SALES (corp-wide): 9.95MM Privately Held
Web: www.darafeev.com
SIC: 2511 Stools, household: wood

### (P-3450)
### MORETTIS DESIGN COLLECTION INC
16926 Keegan Ave Ste C, Carson (90746-1322)
PHONE..................................310 638-5555
Mori Afshar, Pr
▲ EMP: 30 EST: 1992
SALES (est): 691.66K Privately Held
Web: www.morettisdesign.com
SIC: 2511 Wood household furniture

### (P-3451)
### NELSON ADAMS NACO CORPORATION
420 S E St, San Bernardino (92401-2013)
PHONE..................................909 256-8938
Rafael Rangel, Pr
EMP: 20 EST: 2008
SALES (est): 3.94MM Privately Held
Web: www.nelsonadamsnaco.com
SIC: 2511 Coffee tables: wood

### (P-3452)
### NOVA LIFESTYLE INC (PA)
6565 E Washington Blvd, Commerce (90040-1821)
PHONE..................................323 888-9999
Thanh H Lam, Ch Bd
Min Su, Corporate Secretary*
Jeffery Chuang, CFO
Mark Chapman, VP Mktg
Steven Qiang Liu, VP
EMP: 24 EST: 2011
SALES (est): 11.09MM
SALES (corp-wide): 11.09MM Publicly Held
Web: www.novalifestyle.com
SIC: 2511 2512 Wood household furniture; Upholstered household furniture

### (P-3453)
### RADFORD CABINETS INC
216 E Avenue K8, Lancaster (93535-4527)
PHONE..................................661 729-8931
Steven Radford, Pr
Robert Mendoza, *
Sharon Radford, *
EMP: 70 EST: 1992
SQ FT: 20,000

SALES (est): 4.12MM Privately Held
Web: www.radfordcabinetsinc.com
SIC: 2511 2434 2521 Kitchen and dining room furniture; Wood kitchen cabinets; Cabinets, bffice: wood

### (P-3454)
### RUSS BASSETT CORP
Also Called: Group Five
8189 Byron Rd, Whittier (90606-2615)
PHONE..................................562 945-2445
Mike Dressendorfer, CEO
Peter Fink, *
▲ EMP: 115 EST: 1959
SQ FT: 112,000
SALES (est): 21.9MM Privately Held
Web: www.russbassett.com
SIC: 2511 Wood household furniture

### (P-3455)
### SAN DIEGO ARCFT INTERIORS INC
2381 Boswell Rd, Chula Vista (91914-3509)
PHONE..................................619 474-1997
Juan Carlos Vasquez, Pr
▲ EMP: 23 EST: 2009
SALES (est): 2.38MM Privately Held
Web: www.sdaircraftinteriors.com
SIC: 2511 Chairs, household, except upholstered: wood

### (P-3456)
### SANDBERG FURNITURE MFG CO INC (PA)
Also Called: Sandberg Furniture
5705 Alcoa Ave, Vernon (90058-3794)
P.O. Box 58291 (90058-0291)
PHONE..................................323 582-0711
John Sandberg, CEO
Mark Nixon, Sr VP
▲ EMP: 225 EST: 1918
SALES (est): 24.72MM
SALES (corp-wide): 24.72MM Privately Held
Web: www.sandbergfurniture.com
SIC: 2511 Wood bedroom furniture

### (P-3457)
### STUART DAVID INC (PA)
Also Called: Stuart's Fine Furniture
3419 Railroad Ave, Ceres (95307-3623)
P.O. Box 1009 (95307-1009)
PHONE..................................209 537-7449
David Neilson, Pr
EMP: 26 EST: 1962
SQ FT: 79,000
SALES (est): 5.66MM
SALES (corp-wide): 5.66MM Privately Held
Web: www.stuartdavid.com
SIC: 2511 Wood household furniture

### (P-3458)
### TREND MANOR FURN MFG CO INC
17047 Gale Ave, City Of Industry (91745-1808)
PHONE..................................626 964-6493
Theodore Vecchione, Pr
▲ EMP: 42 EST: 1946
SQ FT: 63,000
SALES (est): 2.83MM Privately Held
Web: www.trendmanor.com
SIC: 2511 Wood household furniture

### (P-3459)
### WEST COAST CATRG TRCKS MFG INC
1217 Goodrich Blvd, Commerce (90022-5124)
PHONE..................................323 278-1279
Juan Gomez, Pr
Jesus Gomez, Dir
EMP: 15 EST: 2004
SQ FT: 18,000
SALES (est): 492.04K Privately Held
Web: www.westcoastcateringtrucks.com
SIC: 2511 Stands, household, nec: wood

### (P-3460)
### WESTCOTT DESIGNS INC
4455 Park Rd, Benicia (94510-1124)
PHONE..................................510 367-7229
Michael Westcott Isheim, CEO
Sheryl Isheim, VP
▲ EMP: 20 EST: 1990
SQ FT: 40,000
SALES (est): 2.42MM Privately Held
Web: www.westcottdesigns.net
SIC: 2511 Wood household furniture

### (P-3461)
### WESTERN DOVETAIL INCORPORATED
Also Called: Manufacturing
1101 Nimitz Ave Ste 209, Vallejo (94592-1034)
P.O. Box 1592 (94590-0159)
PHONE..................................707 556-3683
Maxfield Hunter, CEO
Maxfield Hunter, Prin
Joshua Hunter, Dir
EMP: 22 EST: 1993
SQ FT: 1,000
SALES (est): 4.09MM Privately Held
Web: www.drawer.com
SIC: 2511 Wood household furniture

### (P-3462)
### WHALEN LLC (DH)
Also Called: Whalen Furniture Manufacturing
1578 Air Wing Rd, San Diego (92154-7706)
PHONE..................................619 423-9948
Jose Luis Laparte, Pr
David Levinson, *
◆ EMP: 26 EST: 1991
SQ FT: 100,000
SALES (est): 24.78MM Privately Held
Web: www.whalenfurniture.com
SIC: 2511 Wood household furniture
HQ: Li & Fung Development (China) Limited
10/F Lifung Twr
Cheung Sha Wan KLN

### (P-3463)
### WOOD TECH INC
4611 Malat St, Oakland (94601-4903)
PHONE..................................510 534-4930
Juan D Figueroa, CEO
EMP: 70 EST: 1993
SQ FT: 92,000
SALES (est): 9.43MM Privately Held
Web: www.woodtechonline.com
SIC: 2511 2521 Wood household furniture; Wood office furniture

## 2512 Upholstered Household Furniture

### (P-3464)
### A RUDIN INC (PA)
Also Called: A Rudin Designs
6062 Alcoa Ave, Vernon (90058-3902)
PHONE..................................323 589-5547
Arnold Rudin, Pr
Ralph Rudin, *
◆ EMP: 92 EST: 1918

## 2512 - Upholstered Household Furniture (P-3465)

SQ FT: 117,000
SALES (est): 8.06MM
SALES (corp-wide): 8.06MM **Privately Held**
Web: www.arudin.com
SIC: **2512** 5021  Upholstered household furniture; Household furniture

### (P-3465)
### ARDMORE HOME DESIGN INC (PA)
Also Called: Pigeon and Poodle
918 S Stimson Ave, City Of Industry (91745-1640)
PHONE......................626 803-7769
Chris Dewitt, *CEO*
Oscar Yague, *
◆ EMP: 49 EST: 2012
SALES (est): 22.93MM
SALES (corp-wide): 22.93MM **Privately Held**
Web: www.madegoods.com
SIC: **2512**  Upholstered household furniture

### (P-3466)
### BJ LIQUIDATION INC
Also Called: Burton James
428 Turnbull Canyon Rd, City Of Industry (91745-1011)
PHONE......................626 961-7221
Harold Zoref, *CEO*
Norman Zoref, *
EMP: 80 EST: 1983
SQ FT: 28,000
SALES (est): 4.24MM **Privately Held**
Web: www.burtonjames.com
SIC: **2512**  Upholstered household furniture

### (P-3467)
### CHROMCRAFT RVNGTON DOUGLAS IND (PA)
Also Called: Douglas Casual Living
1011 S Grove Ave, Ontario (91761-3437)
PHONE......................909 930-9891
Willa Li, *CEO*
▲ EMP: 16 EST: 2008
SQ FT: 45,000
SALES (est): 7.5MM
SALES (corp-wide): 7.5MM **Privately Held**
Web: www.chromcrafthome.com
SIC: **2512** 5021  Upholstered household furniture; Household furniture

### (P-3468)
### CISCO BROS CORP (PA)
Also Called: Cisco & Brothers Designs
474 S Arroyo Pkwy, Pasadena (91105-2530)
PHONE......................323 778-8612
Francisco Pinedo, *CEO*
Alba E Pinedo, *
◆ EMP: 145 EST: 1993
SALES (est): 22.04MM **Privately Held**
Web: www.ciscohome.net
SIC: **2512**  Upholstered household furniture

### (P-3469)
### COMMERCIAL INTR RESOURCES INC
Also Called: Contract Resources
6077 Rickenbacker Rd, Commerce (90040-3031)
PHONE......................562 926-5885
Roberta Tuchman, *CEO*
Stanley Rice, *
Barbara Rice, *
Stephanie Lesko, *
EMP: 65 EST: 1982
SQ FT: 28,000

SALES (est): 1.42MM **Privately Held**
Web: www.villahallmark.com
SIC: **2512**  Upholstered household furniture

### (P-3470)
### DELLAROBBIA INC (PA)
119 Waterworks Way, Irvine (92618-3110)
PHONE......................949 251-9532
David Soonlan, *Pr*
Sunee Soonlan, *
▲ EMP: 48 EST: 1979
SQ FT: 27,000
SALES (est): 673K
SALES (corp-wide): 673K **Privately Held**
Web: www.dellarobbia.com
SIC: **2512**  Upholstered household furniture

### (P-3471)
### E J LAUREN LLC
Also Called: Ejl
2690 Pellissier Pl, City Of Industry (90601-1507)
PHONE......................562 803-1113
Antonio Ocampo, *Managing Member*
◆ EMP: 50 EST: 2009
SALES (est): 3.94MM **Privately Held**
Web: www.ejlauren.com
SIC: **2512**  Upholstered household furniture

### (P-3472)
### ELITE LEATHER LLC
1620 5th Ave Ste 400, San Diego (92101-2738)
PHONE......................909 548-8600
▲ EMP: 100
Web: www.oneforvictory.com
SIC: **2512**  Living room furniture: upholstered on wood frames

### (P-3473)
### GENESIS TC INC
Also Called: Genesis 2000
524 Hofgaarden St, La Puente (91744-5529)
PHONE......................626 968-4455
Anthony Moreno, *Pr*
EMP: 22 EST: 2003
SALES (est): 509.67K **Privately Held**
SIC: **2512**  Wood upholstered chairs and couches

### (P-3474)
### GOMEN FURNITURE MFG INC
11612 Wright Rd, Lynwood (90262-3945)
PHONE......................310 635-4894
Leonardo Gonzalez, *Pr*
▲ EMP: 30 EST: 1990
SALES (est): 928.02K **Privately Held**
Web: www.gomenfurnmfg.com
SIC: **2512** 7641  Upholstered household furniture; Upholstery work

### (P-3475)
### HARBOR FURNITURE MFG INC (PA)
Also Called: Harbor House
15817 Whitepost Ln, La Mirada (90638-3126)
PHONE......................323 636-1201
Malcolm Tuttleton Junior, *Pr*
Brent Tuttleton, *
▲ EMP: 25 EST: 1929
SALES (est): 1.9MM
SALES (corp-wide): 1.9MM **Privately Held**
SIC: **2512** 2511 6514 2521  Upholstered household furniture; Wood household furniture; Dwelling operators, except apartments; Wood office furniture

### (P-3476)
### HUNTINGTON INDUSTRIES INC
12520 Chadron Ave, Hawthorne (90250-4808)
PHONE......................323 772-5575
▲ EMP: 150
SIC: **2512**  Upholstered household furniture

### (P-3477)
### KAY CHESTERFIELD INC
3109 Adeline St, Emeryville (94608-4411)
PHONE......................510 533-5565
Kriss Kokoefer, *Pr*
EMP: 15 EST: 1921
SALES (est): 861.16K **Privately Held**
Web: www.kaychesterfield.com
SIC: **2512** 7641  Upholstered household furniture; Upholstery work

### (P-3478)
### LITTLE CASTLE FURNITURE CO INC
301 Todd Ct, Oxnard (93030-5192)
P.O. Box 4254 (91359-1254)
PHONE......................805 278-4646
Kayvan Torabian, *Pr*
▲ EMP: 35 EST: 1998
SQ FT: 9,000
SALES (est): 7.64MM **Privately Held**
Web: www.littlecastleinc.com
SIC: **2512**  Upholstered household furniture

### (P-3479)
### M&J DESIGN INC
Also Called: M&J Design Furniture
1303 S Claudina St, Anaheim (92805-6235)
PHONE......................714 687-9918
Jorge Mojica, *CEO*
EMP: 23 EST: 2018
SALES (est): 2.71MM **Privately Held**
Web: www.mjdesignus.com
SIC: **2512** 2541 5712  Upholstered household furniture; Wood partitions and fixtures; Custom made furniture, except cabinets

### (P-3480)
### MARGE CARSON INC (PA)
555 W 5th St, Los Angeles (90013-2670)
P.O. Box 1283 (91769-1283)
PHONE......................626 571-1111
James Labarge, *CEO*
Dominic Ching, *
▲ EMP: 82 EST: 1951
SALES (est): 9.82MM
SALES (corp-wide): 9.82MM **Privately Held**
Web: www.margecarson.com
SIC: **2512** 2511  Living room furniture: upholstered on wood frames; Wood household furniture

### (P-3481)
### MARLIN DESIGNS LLC
13845 Alton Pkwy Ste C, Irvine (92618-1643)
PHONE......................949 637-7257
Ronald Whitlock, *Managing Member*
EMP: 150 EST: 1995
SALES (est): 2.03MM **Privately Held**
Web: www.marlin-designs.com
SIC: **2512**  Upholstered household furniture

### (P-3482)
### MARTIN/BRATTRUD INC
1231 W 134th St, Gardena (90247-1902)
PHONE......................323 770-4171
Allan G Stratford, *Pr*
Patrick Baxter, *

EMP: 95 EST: 1946
SQ FT: 38,000
SALES (est): 9.12MM **Privately Held**
Web: www.martinbrattrud.com
SIC: **2512** 2511  Upholstered household furniture; Tables, household: wood

### (P-3483)
### MINSON CORPORATION
Also Called: Mallin Casual Furniture
11701 Wilshire Blvd Ste 15a, Los Angeles (90025-1599)
PHONE......................323 513-1041
▲ EMP: 300
Web: www.minson.com
SIC: **2512** 2514  Wood upholstered chairs and couches; Lawn furniture: metal

### (P-3484)
### MULHOLLAND BROTHERS (PA)
1710 4th St, Berkeley (94710-1711)
PHONE......................415 824-5995
Jay Holland, *Pr*
Guy Holland, *
▲ EMP: 49 EST: 1996
SALES (est): 3.7MM
SALES (corp-wide): 3.7MM **Privately Held**
Web: www.shopmulholland.com
SIC: **2512** 5199 3161  Upholstered household furniture; Leather, leather goods, and furs; Cases, carrying, nec

### (P-3485)
### NEW CLASSIC HM FURNISHING INC (PA)
Also Called: New Classic Furniture
7351 Mcguire Ave, Fontana (92336-1668)
PHONE......................909 484-7676
Jean Tong, *CEO*
◆ EMP: 44 EST: 2001
SALES (est): 104.06MM
SALES (corp-wide): 104.06MM **Privately Held**
Web: www.newclassicfurniture.com
SIC: **2512** 5023  Living room furniture: upholstered on wood frames; Decorative home furnishings and supplies

### (P-3486)
### R C FURNITURE INC
1111 Jellick Ave, City Of Industry (91748-1212)
PHONE......................626 964-4100
Rene Cazares, *Pr*
▲ EMP: 81 EST: 1986
SQ FT: 25,000
SALES (est): 1.67MM **Privately Held**
Web: www.renecazares.com
SIC: **2512** 5021  Upholstered household furniture; Furniture

### (P-3487)
### ROBERT MICHAEL LTD
10035 Geary Ave, Santa Fe Springs (90670-3237)
P.O. Box 2397 (90670-0397)
PHONE......................562 758-6789
◆ EMP: 263
Web: www.robertmichaellimited.com
SIC: **2512**  Upholstered household furniture

### (P-3488)
### ROYAL CUSTOM DESIGNS LLC
Also Called: Custom Furniture Designs, LLC
13951 Monte Vista Ave, Chino (91710-5536)
PHONE......................909 591-8990
Jeff Sladick, *Pr*
▲ EMP: 133 EST: 1970
SQ FT: 35,000

**PRODUCTS & SERVICES SECTION**  **2514 - Metal Household Furniture (P-3509)**

SALES (est): 17.44MM
SALES (corp-wide): 17.44MM **Privately Held**
Web: www.royalcustomdesigns.com
SIC: **2512** Upholstered household furniture
PA: Makers & Craftsmen Llc
 396 E Jefferson Ave
 909 525-5181

*(P-3489)*
**RTMH INC (PA)**
Also Called: Rose Tarlow-Melrose House
425 N Robertson Blvd, West Hollywood (90048-1735)
PHONE.....................323 651-2202
Rose Tarlow, *CEO*
▲ EMP: 17 EST: 1981
SALES (est): 2.81MM
SALES (corp-wide): 2.81MM **Privately Held**
Web: www.rosetarlow.com
SIC: **2512** 2511 Upholstered household furniture; Wood household furniture

*(P-3490)*
**SOFA U LOVE LLC (PA)**
Also Called: Factory Showroom Exchange
1207 N Western Ave, Los Angeles (90029-1018)
PHONE.....................323 464-3397
Varougan Karapetian, *Pr*
EMP: 22 EST: 1976
SQ FT: 22,000
SALES (est): 3.22MM
SALES (corp-wide): 3.22MM **Privately Held**
Web: www.sofaulove.com
SIC: **2512** 5712 Upholstered household furniture; Furniture stores

*(P-3491)*
**SOLE DESIGNS INC**
11685 Mcbean Dr, El Monte (91732-1104)
PHONE.....................626 452-8642
Linda Le, *CEO*
Lam Tran, *Pr*
▲ EMP: 17 EST: 1996
SQ FT: 8,000
SALES (est): 926.73K **Privately Held**
Web: www.soledesigns.com
SIC: **2512** Upholstered household furniture

*(P-3492)*
**STITCH INDUSTRIES INC**
Also Called: Joybird
767 S Alameda St Ste 360, Los Angeles (90021-1633)
PHONE.....................888 282-0842
Kurt L Darrow, *CEO*
EMP: 50 EST: 2013
SALES (est): 27.55MM
SALES (corp-wide): 2.05B **Publicly Held**
Web: www.joybird.com
SIC: **2512** 5961 5712 Upholstered household furniture; Catalog and mail-order houses; Furniture stores
PA: La-Z-Boy Incorporated
 1 Lazboy Dr
 734 242-1444

*(P-3493)*
**TERRA FURNITURE INC**
549 E Edna Pl, Hacienda Heights (91745-4209)
▲ EMP: 41 EST: 1964
SALES (est): 2.46MM **Privately Held**
Web: www.terrafurniture.com

SIC: **2512** 2514 2522 2511 Upholstered household furniture; Metal household furniture; Office furniture, except wood; Wood lawn and garden furniture

*(P-3494)*
**VAN SARK INC (PA)**
Also Called: Dependable Furniture Mfg Co
410 Harriet St, San Francisco (94103-4915)
PHONE.....................510 635-1111
Kevin Sarkisian, *Pr*
Eniko Sarkisian, *Prin*
▲ EMP: 87 EST: 1991
SQ FT: 75,000
SALES (est): 9.03MM **Privately Held**
Web: www.dependablefm.com
SIC: **2512** Wood upholstered chairs and couches

*(P-3495)*
**YEN-NHAI INC**
Also Called: Nathan Anthony Furniture
4940 District Blvd, Vernon (90058-2718)
PHONE.....................323 584-1315
Khai Mai, *Pr*
EMP: 40 EST: 1995
SALES (est): 3.65MM **Privately Held**
Web: www.nafurniture.com
SIC: **2512** Upholstered household furniture

---

## 2514 Metal Household Furniture

*(P-3496)*
**A A CATER TRUCK MFG CO INC**
Also Called: Hizco Truck Body
750 E Slauson Ave, Los Angeles (90011-5236)
PHONE.....................323 233-2343
Vahe Karapetian, *Pr*
EMP: 24 EST: 1971
SQ FT: 60,000
SALES (est): 768.54K **Privately Held**
Web: www.aacatertruck.com
SIC: **2514** 7538 Metal household furniture; General truck repair

*(P-3497)*
**ATLANTIC REPRESENTATIONS INC (PA)**
Also Called: Snowsound USA
10018 Santa Fe Springs Rd, Santa Fe Springs (90670-2922)
P.O. Box 2399 (90670-0399)
PHONE.....................562 903-9550
Shahriar Dardashti, *Pr*
Farnaz Dardashti, *
Leo Dardashti, *
▲ EMP: 30 EST: 1984
SQ FT: 150,000
SALES (est): 8.62MM **Privately Held**
Web: www.snowsoundusa.com
SIC: **2514** 2511 Metal household furniture; Wood household furniture

*(P-3498)*
**ATLAS SURVIVAL SHELTERS LLC**
7407 Telegraph Rd, Montebello (90640-6515)
PHONE.....................323 727-7084
Ronal D Hubbard, *Managing Member*
EMP: 25 EST: 2011
SQ FT: 30,000
SALES (est): 2.34MM **Privately Held**
Web: www.atlassurvivalshelters.com
SIC: **2514** Beds, including folding and cabinet, household: metal

*(P-3499)*
**CASUALWAY USA LLC**
Also Called: Casualway Home & Garden
1623 Lola Way, Oxnard (93030-5080)
PHONE.....................805 660-7408
Guoxiang Wu, *Pr*
Ralph Ybarra, *VP*
EMP: 99
SALES (est): 492.58K **Privately Held**
SIC: **2514** Garden furniture, metal

*(P-3500)*
**COSMO IMPORT & EXPORT LLC**
3771 Channel Dr, West Sacramento (95691-3421)
PHONE.....................916 209-5500
Jennifer Hayes, *CEO*
EMP: 20 EST: 2013
SQ FT: 100,000
SALES (est): 227.62K **Privately Held**
SIC: **2514** Garden furniture, metal

*(P-3501)*
**DOUGLAS FURNITURE OF CALIFORNIA LLC**
809 Tyburn Rd, Palos Verdes Estates (90274-2843)
PHONE.....................310 749-0003
▲ EMP: 2400
SIC: **2514** 2512 Dinette sets: metal; Recliners: upholstered on wood frames

*(P-3502)*
**EARTHLITE LLC (DH)**
Also Called: Earthlite
990 Joshua Way, Vista (92081-7855)
P.O. Box 51245 (90051-5545)
PHONE.....................760 599-1112
James Chenevey, *CEO*
Philippe Barret, *
Tara Grodjesk, *WELLNESS**
◆ EMP: 86 EST: 1987
SQ FT: 68,000
SALES (est): 42.65MM
SALES (corp-wide): 47.43MM **Privately Held**
Web: www.earthlite.com
SIC: **2514** 5091 2531 Tables, household: metal; Spa equipment and supplies; Chairs, portable folding
HQ: Earthlite Holdings, Llc
 150 E 58th St Fl 37
 New York NY 10155
 212 317-2004

*(P-3503)*
**ELLIOTTS DESIGNS INC**
2473 E Rancho Del Amo Pl, Compton (90220-6311)
PHONE.....................310 631-4931
Elliott Jones, *Pr*
Julie Jones, *
EMP: 30 EST: 1974
SQ FT: 127,000
SALES (est): 399.15K **Privately Held**
SIC: **2514** 5021 Beds, including folding and cabinet, household: metal; Furniture

*(P-3504)*
**GRACO CHILDRENS PRODUCTS INC**
17182 Nevada St, Victorville (92394-7806)
PHONE.....................770 418-7200
EMP: 293
SALES (corp-wide): 8.13B **Publicly Held**
SIC: **2514** Juvenile furniture, household: metal
HQ: Graco Children's Products Inc.
 6655 Pachtree Dunwoody Rd
 Atlanta GA 30328
 770 418-7200

*(P-3505)*
**JBI LLC**
Also Called: Buchbinder, Jay Industries
18521 S Santa Fe Ave, Compton (90221-5624)
PHONE.....................310 537-2910
Claudio Luna, *Mgr*
EMP: 48
SALES (corp-wide): 54.78MM **Privately Held**
Web: www.jbi-interiors.com
SIC: **2514** 2221 2511 Tables, household: metal; Fiberglass fabrics; Wood household furniture
PA: Jbi, Llc
 2650 E El Presidio St
 310 886-8034

*(P-3506)*
**M724 INC**
949 N Cataract Ave Ste E, San Dimas (91773-1464)
PHONE.....................951 314-1333
EMP: 17
SALES (est): 1.05MM **Privately Held**
SIC: **2514** Metal household furniture

*(P-3507)*
**MURRAYS IRON WORKS INC (PA)**
7355 E Slauson Ave, Commerce (90040-3626)
PHONE.....................323 521-1100
▲ EMP: 165 EST: 1966
SALES (est): 2.54MM
SALES (corp-wide): 2.54MM **Privately Held**
Web: www.murraysiw.com
SIC: **2514** 3446 5021 5961 Metal household furniture; Fences or posts, ornamental iron or steel; Furniture; Furniture and furnishings, mail order

*(P-3508)*
**PACIFIC CASUAL LLC**
1060 Avenida Acaso, Camarillo (93012-8712)
PHONE.....................805 445-8310
Dale Boles, *CEO*
Jay Weber, *Pr*
▲ EMP: 16 EST: 2002
SQ FT: 29,000
SALES (est): 2.58MM **Privately Held**
Web: www.pacificcasual.com
SIC: **2514** Metal lawn and garden furniture

*(P-3509)*
**RSI HOME PRODUCTS INC**
RSI HOME PRODUCTS, INC.
620 Newport Center Dr Ste 1030, Newport Beach (92660-8048)
PHONE.....................949 720-1116
Terri Stevens, *Brnch Mgr*
EMP: 184
SALES (corp-wide): 1.85B **Publicly Held**
Web: www.americanwoodmark.com
SIC: **2514** 2541 1751 Metal household furniture; Wood partitions and fixtures; Cabinet and finish carpentry
HQ: Rsi Home Products Llc
 400 E Orangethorpe Ave
 Anaheim CA 92801
 714 449-2200

# 2514 - Metal Household Furniture (P-3510)

## (P-3510)
### RSI HOME PRODUCTS LLC (HQ)
Also Called: RSI
400 E Orangethorpe Ave, Anaheim (92801-1046)
PHONE...............................714 449-2200
Alex Calabrese, *CEO*
Jeff Hoeft, *
David Lowrie, *
▲ **EMP:** 700 **EST:** 1994
**SQ FT:** 675,000
**SALES (est):** 559.01MM
**SALES (corp-wide):** 1.85B **Publicly Held**
**Web:** www.americanwoodmark.com
**SIC: 2514** 2541 3281 2434 Kitchen cabinets: metal; Counter and sink tops; Cut stone and stone products; Wood kitchen cabinets
**PA:** American Woodmark Corporation
561 Shady Elm Rd
540 665-9100

## (P-3511)
### SANDUSKY LEE LLC
16125 Widmere Rd, Arvin (93203-9307)
P.O. Box 517 (93203-0517)
PHONE...............................661 854-5551
Jim Coontz, *Brnch Mgr*
**EMP:** 26
**SALES (corp-wide):** 279.66MM **Privately Held**
**Web:** www.sanduskycabinets.com
**SIC: 2514** 2522 Metal household furniture; Office furniture, except wood
**HQ:** Sandusky Lee Llc
80 Keystone St
Littlestown PA 17340
717 359-4111

## (P-3512)
### SURROUNDING ELEMENTS LLC
33051 Calle Aviador Ste A, San Juan Capistrano (92675-4780)
PHONE...............................949 582-9000
Moss Shacter, *Managing Member*
**EMP:** 20 **EST:** 2001
**SQ FT:** 15,000
**SALES (est):** 2.48MM **Privately Held**
**Web:** www.surroundingelements.com
**SIC: 2514** Lawn furniture: metal

## (P-3513)
### THOMAS LUNDBERG
Also Called: Lundberg Designs
2620 3rd St, San Francisco (94107-3115)
PHONE...............................415 695-0110
Thomas Lundberg, *Owner*
**EMP:** 34 **EST:** 1987
**SQ FT:** 5,000
**SALES (est):** 1.99MM **Privately Held**
**Web:** www.lundbergdesign.com
**SIC: 2514** Metal household furniture

## (P-3514)
### TK CLASSICS LLC
3771 Channel Dr Ste 100, West Sacramento (95691-3421)
PHONE...............................916 209-5500
Jennifer Hayes, *Managing Member*
**EMP:** 20 **EST:** 2017
**SQ FT:** 100,000
**SALES (est):** 4.68MM
**SALES (corp-wide):** 33.02MM **Privately Held**
**SIC: 2514** 5712 Garden furniture, metal; Outdoor and garden furniture
**PA:** Twin-Star International, Inc.
750 Park Of Commerce Blvd # 400
866 661-1218

## (P-3515)
### TROPITONE FURNITURE CO INC (DH)
5 Marconi, Irvine (92618-2594)
PHONE...............................949 595-2010
Randy Danielson, *Ex VP*
◆ **EMP:** 300 **EST:** 1954
**SQ FT:** 100,000
**SALES (est):** 100MM
**SALES (corp-wide):** 133.42MM **Privately Held**
**Web:** www.tropitone.com
**SIC: 2514** 2522 Garden furniture, metal; Office furniture, except wood
**HQ:** Jordan Brown Inc
475 W Town Pl Ste 200
Saint Augustine FL 32092

## (P-3516)
### WESLEY ALLEN INC
Also Called: Iron Beds of America
1001 E 60th St, Los Angeles (90001-1018)
PHONE...............................323 231-4275
Victor Sawan, *CEO*
▲ **EMP:** 150 **EST:** 1976
**SQ FT:** 100,000
**SALES (est):** 19.05MM **Privately Held**
**Web:** www.wesleyallen.com
**SIC: 2514** Metal household furniture

---

## 2515 Mattresses And Bedsprings

## (P-3517)
### ADVANCED INNVTIVE RCVERY TECH (PA)
Also Called: Smart Foam Pads
23615 El Toro Rd, Lake Forest (92630-4707)
PHONE...............................949 273-8100
Robert Doherty, *CEO*
Michael Seffer, *CFO*
Timothy G Woodward, *COO*
**EMP:** 15 **EST:** 2011
**SQ FT:** 4,000
**SALES (est):** 14.06MM
**SALES (corp-wide):** 14.06MM **Privately Held**
**Web:** www.bebetterfoam.com
**SIC: 2515** Mattresses, containing felt, foam rubber, urethane, etc.

## (P-3518)
### ADVANCED INNVTIVE RCVERY TECH
3401 Space Center Ct Ste 811b, Jurupa Valley (91752-1128)
PHONE...............................949 273-8100
Brad Bannister, *Mgr*
**EMP:** 30
**SALES (corp-wide):** 14.06MM **Privately Held**
**Web:** www.airtechfoam.com
**SIC: 2515** Mattresses, containing felt, foam rubber, urethane, etc.
**PA:** Advanced Innovative Recovery Technologies, Inc.
23615 El Toro Rd
949 273-8100

## (P-3519)
### AMERICAN NATIONAL MFG INC
252 Mariah Cir, Corona (92879-1751)
PHONE...............................951 273-7888
Eve Miller, *Pr*
Craig Miller, *VP*
◆ **EMP:** 65 **EST:** 1993
**SQ FT:** 75,000
**SALES (est):** 8.59MM **Privately Held**
**Web:** www.americannationalmfg.com
**SIC: 2515** 5712 Mattresses and bedsprings; Furniture stores

## (P-3520)
### AMF SUPPORT SURFACES INC (DH)
1691 N Delilah St, Corona (92879-1885)
PHONE...............................951 549-6800
Fredrick Kohnke, *CEO*
Curt Wyatt, *
Charles C Wyatt, *
Carole A Wyatt, *
▲ **EMP:** 162 **EST:** 1932
**SQ FT:** 40,000
**SALES (est):** 9.42MM
**SALES (corp-wide):** 14.81B **Publicly Held**
**SIC: 2515** Mattresses, containing felt, foam rubber, urethane, etc.
**HQ:** Anodyne Medical Device, Inc.
1069 State Road 46 E
Batesville IN 47006

## (P-3521)
### BANNER MATTRESS INC
1501 E Cooley Dr Ste B, Colton (92324-3991)
PHONE...............................909 835-4200
▲ **EMP:** 57
**Web:** www.bannermattressonline.com
**SIC: 2515** 5021 Bedsprings, assembled; Mattresses

## (P-3522)
### BRENTWOOD HOME LLC (PA)
Also Called: Silverrest
621 Burning Tree Rd, Fullerton (92833-1448)
PHONE...............................562 949-3759
Vy Nguyen, *CEO*
**EMP:** 128 **EST:** 2015
**SQ FT:** 80,000
**SALES (est):** 26.71MM
**SALES (corp-wide):** 26.71MM **Privately Held**
**Web:** www.brentwoodhome.com
**SIC: 2515** 5021 5712 Mattresses, containing felt, foam rubber, urethane, etc.; Mattresses; Mattresses

## (P-3523)
### CRISTAL MATERIALS INC
6825 Mckinley Ave, Los Angeles (90001-1525)
PHONE...............................323 855-1688
Luis Ponce, *CEO*
**EMP:** 15 **EST:** 2013
**SALES (est):** 3.29MM **Privately Held**
**SIC: 2515** 5999 3086 Mattresses, containing felt, foam rubber, urethane, etc.; Foam and foam products; Plastics foam products

## (P-3524)
### DELLA ROBBIA INC
Also Called: Focus One Home
796 E Harrison St, Corona (92879-1348)
PHONE...............................951 372-9199
David Soonlan, *Pr*
▲ **EMP:** 20 **EST:** 1980
**SQ FT:** 72,000
**SALES (est):** 2.38MM **Privately Held**
**Web:** www.dellarobbia.com
**SIC: 2515** Sofa beds (convertible sofas)

## (P-3525)
### ES KLUFT & COMPANY INC (DH)
Also Called: Aireloom
11096 Jersey Blvd Ste 101, Rancho Cucamonga (91730-5158)
PHONE...............................909 373-4211
Jon Stowe, *CEO*
Brad Goodshaw, *CFO*
◆ **EMP:** 174 **EST:** 2004
**SALES (est):** 110.87MM **Privately Held**
**Web:** www.aireloom.com
**SIC: 2515** Mattresses, innerspring or box spring
**HQ:** Vi - Spring Limited
Ernesettle Lane
Plymouth PL5 2
175 236-6311

## (P-3526)
### G & M MATTRESS AND FOAM CORPORATION
Also Called: Fun Furnishings
1943 N White Ave, La Verne (91750-5663)
P.O. Box 7220 (91750-7220)
PHONE...............................909 593-1000
**EMP:** 80 **EST:** 1987
**SALES (est):** 13MM **Privately Held**
**SIC: 2515** Mattresses, containing felt, foam rubber, urethane, etc.

## (P-3527)
### GATEWAY MATTRESS CO INC
624 S Vail Ave, Montebello (90640-4952)
PHONE...............................323 725-1923
**EMP:** 65 **EST:** 1961
**SALES (est):** 6.41MM **Privately Held**
**Web:** www.gatewaymattress.com
**SIC: 2515** Mattresses, innerspring or box spring

## (P-3528)
### GOLDEN MATTRESS CO INC
11680 Wright Rd, Lynwood (90262-3945)
PHONE...............................323 887-1888
San Dang, *CEO*
Phuc Nguyen, *
◆ **EMP:** 52 **EST:** 1980
**SALES (est):** 772.76K **Privately Held**
**Web:** www.goldenmattressus.com
**SIC: 2515** 5021 Mattresses and foundations; Mattresses

## (P-3529)
### IDEAL MATTRESS COMPANY INC
1901 Main St, San Diego (92113-2129)
PHONE...............................619 595-0003
Jesse Hernandez, *Pr*
John Hernandez, *
Patrick Goularte, *
Estella Goularte, *
**EMP:** 25 **EST:** 1929
**SQ FT:** 10,000
**SALES (est):** 388.95K **Privately Held**
**SIC: 2515** Mattresses, containing felt, foam rubber, urethane, etc.

## (P-3530)
### KINGDOM MATTRESS CO INC
Also Called: Kingdom Matress Company
2425 S Malt Ave, Commerce (90040-3201)
PHONE...............................562 630-5531
Jose Flores, *Pr*
**EMP:** 17 **EST:** 1999
**SALES (est):** 3.07MM **Privately Held**
**Web:** www.kingdommattress.com
**SIC: 2515** Mattresses and bedsprings

## (P-3531)
### LEGGETT & PLATT INCORPORATED
2015 N Macarthur Dr, Tracy (95376-2850)
PHONE...............................209 839-8230
**EMP:** 17
**SALES (corp-wide):** 5.15B **Publicly Held**

# PRODUCTS & SERVICES SECTION

## 2519 - Household Furniture, Nec (P-3553)

Web: www.leggett.com
SIC: 2515 Mattresses and bedsprings
PA: Leggett & Platt, Incorporated
1 Leggett Rd
417 358-8131

**(P-3532)**
**LEGGETT & PLATT INCORPORATED**
Also Called: Lpcc 6008
1050 S Dupont Ave, Ontario (91761-1578)
PHONE.................909 937-1010
Barry Kubasak, *Mgr*
EMP: 96
SALES (corp-wide): 5.15B **Publicly Held**
Web: www.leggett.com
SIC: 2515 Mattresses, innerspring or box spring
PA: Leggett & Platt, Incorporated
1 Leggett Rd
417 358-8131

**(P-3533)**
**MARSPRING CORPORATION**
Also Called: Los Angeles Fiber Co
5190 S Santa Fe Ave, Vernon (90058-3532)
P.O. Box 58643 (90058-0643)
PHONE.................310 484-6849
Ronald Greitzer, *Pr*
EMP: 56
SALES (corp-wide): 6.62MM **Privately Held**
Web: www.reliancecarpetcushion.com
SIC: 2515 Spring cushions
PA: Marspring Corporation
4920 S Boyle Ave
323 589-5637

**(P-3534)**
**MCROSKEY MATTRESS COMPANY**
1400 Minnesota St, San Francisco (94107-3520)
PHONE.................415 861-4532
▲ EMP: 39
Web: www.mcroskey.com
SIC: 2515 Mattresses and foundations

**(P-3535)**
**PURA NATURALS INC**
3401 Space Center Ct Ste 811a, Jurupa Valley (91752-1128)
PHONE.................949 273-8100
Brad Bannister, *Mgr*
EMP: 30
SALES (corp-wide): 14.06MM **Privately Held**
Web: www.puranaturalsproducts.com
SIC: 2515 Mattresses, containing felt, foam rubber, urethane, etc.
HQ: Pura Naturals, Inc.
23615 El Toro Rd Ste X300
Lake Forest CA 92630
949 273-8100

**(P-3536)**
**SEALY MATTRESS MFG CO LLC**
Also Called: Sealy Mattress
1130 7th St, Richmond (94801-2103)
PHONE.................510 235-7171
Curt Maszun, *Brnch Mgr*
EMP: 56
SQ FT: 238,000
SALES (corp-wide): 4.93B **Publicly Held**
Web: www.tempursealy.com
SIC: 2515 Mattresses and bedsprings
HQ: Sealy Mattress Manufacturing Company, Llc
1000 Tempur Way
Lexington KY 40511
859 455-1000

**(P-3537)**
**SERTA SIMMONS BEDDING LLC**
23700 Cactus Ave, Moreno Valley (92553-8900)
PHONE.................951 807-8467
Stephanie Mckibbon, *Brnch Mgr*
EMP: 50
SALES (corp-wide): 4.59B **Privately Held**
Web: www.sertasimmons.com
SIC: 2515 Mattresses and bedsprings
HQ: Serta Simmons Bedding, Llc
2451 Industry Ave
Doraville GA 30360

**(P-3538)**
**SKY RIDER EQUIPMENT CO INC**
1180 N Blue Gum St, Anaheim (92806-2409)
PHONE.................714 632-6890
Martin Villegas, *CEO*
Carl Gray, *
Dev Donnelley, *
Karl Keranen, *
▲ EMP: 30 EST: 1984
SQ FT: 12,000
SALES (est): 5.37MM **Privately Held**
Web: www.sky-rider.com
SIC: 2515 7349 5719 Foundations and platforms; Window cleaning; Window shades, nec

**(P-3539)**
**SLEEP TECHNOLOGIES INC**
Also Called: Natural Latex Company, The
3233 Mission Oaks Blvd Ste C, Camarillo (93012-5138)
PHONE.................866 931-1964
Michael Hughes, *Pr*
Carmelita Hughes, *Dir*
EMP: 15 EST: 2012
SQ FT: 40,000
SALES (est): 5.88MM **Privately Held**
SIC: 2515 Mattresses, containing felt, foam rubber, urethane, etc.

**(P-3540)**
**SOUTH BAY INTERNATIONAL INC**
Also Called: Cariloha
8570 Hickory Ave, Rancho Cucamonga (91739)
PHONE.................909 718-5000
Guohai Tang, *Pr*
Daniella Serven, *
Weijun She, *
Wendiao Hou, *
▲ EMP: 25 EST: 1993
SALES (est): 50.07MM **Privately Held**
Web: www.southbayinternational.com
SIC: 2515 Mattresses and bedsprings

**(P-3541)**
**SQUARE DEAL MATTRESS FACTORY**
Also Called: Square Deal Mat Fctry & Uphl
1354 Humboldt Ave, Chico (95928-5952)
PHONE.................530 342-2510
Lois Lash, *Pr*
Richard Lash, *
Lois Lash, *Treas*
EMP: 24 EST: 1920
SQ FT: 6,000
SALES (est): 2.35MM **Privately Held**
Web: www.squaredealmattress.com
SIC: 2515 5712 Mattresses and bedsprings; Furniture stores

**(P-3542)**
**STRESS-O-PEDIC MATTRESS CO INC**
Also Called: Stress-O-Pedic
2060 S Wineville Ave Ste A, Ontario (91761-3633)
PHONE.................909 605-2010
▲ EMP: 58
Web: www.stressopedic.com
SIC: 2515 Mattresses, innerspring or box spring

**(P-3543)**
**SUPRACOR INC**
2050 Corporate Ct, San Jose (95131-1753)
PHONE.................408 432-1616
▼ EMP: 48 EST: 1982
SALES (est): 9.14MM **Privately Held**
Web: www.supracor.com
SIC: 2515 Mattresses, containing felt, foam rubber, urethane, etc.

**(P-3544)**
**TEMPO INDUSTRIES INC**
2137 E 55th St, Vernon (90058-3439)
P.O. Box 1822 (91353-1822)
PHONE.................415 552-8074
▲ EMP: 134
Web: www.tempofurniture.com
SIC: 2515 Sleep furniture

**(P-3545)**
**VISIONARY SLEEP LLC**
2060 S Wineville Ave Ste A, Ontario (91761-3633)
PHONE.................909 605-2010
Carter Gronbach, *Mgr*
EMP: 58
SALES (corp-wide): 7.4MM **Privately Held**
SIC: 2515 Mattresses, innerspring or box spring
PA: Visionary Sleep, Llc
1721 Moon Lake Blvd # 205
812 945-4155

**(P-3546)**
**WIDLY INC**
Also Called: American Furniture Alliance
785 E Harrison St Ste 100, Corona (92879-1350)
PHONE.................951 279-0900
▲ EMP: 130
SIC: 2515 5021 Mattresses and bedsprings; Furniture

**(P-3547)**
**XTRACTION INC**
3688 E Central Ave Ste 103, Fresno (93725-9339)
PHONE.................800 273-4137
Robert Michael Gurnee, *CEO*
Frank Sentous, *COO*
EMP: 19 EST: 2018
SALES (est): 3.05MM **Privately Held**
SIC: 2515 Mattresses and bedsprings

**(P-3548)**
**ZINUS INC (HQ)**
5731 Promontory Pkwy, Tracy (95377-9200)
PHONE.................925 417-2100
Youn Jae Lee, *Pr*
◆ EMP: 36 EST: 1987
SQ FT: 155,000
SALES (est): 20.15MM **Privately Held**
Web: www.zinus.com
SIC: 2515 Chair and couch springs, assembled
PA: Zinus Inc.
10 Yatap-Ro 81beon-Gil, Bundang-Gu

## 2517 Wood Television And Radio Cabinets

**(P-3549)**
**ANA GLOBAL LLC (PA)**
2360 Marconi Ct, San Diego (92154-7241)
PHONE.................619 482-9990
▲ EMP: 90 EST: 1953
SALES (est): 9.69MM
SALES (corp-wide): 9.69MM **Privately Held**
Web: www.anaglb.com
SIC: 2517 5999 Television cabinets, wood; Medical apparatus and supplies

**(P-3550)**
**GILBERT MARTIN WDWKG CO INC (PA)**
Also Called: Martin Furniture
2345 Britannia Blvd, San Diego (92154-8313)
PHONE.................800 268-5669
Gilbert Martin, *CEO*
Mark Mitchell, *CFO*
◆ EMP: 30 EST: 1980
SQ FT: 210,000
SALES (est): 10.01MM
SALES (corp-wide): 10.01MM **Privately Held**
Web: www.martinfurniture.com
SIC: 2517 2511 2521 5021 Home entertainment unit cabinets, wood; Wood household furniture; Wood office furniture; Furniture

## 2519 Household Furniture, Nec

**(P-3551)**
**ACRYLIC DISTRIBUTION CORP**
Also Called: Acrylic Distribution
8421 Lankershim Blvd, Sun Valley (91352-3125)
PHONE.................818 767-8448
Shlomi Haziza, *Prin*
Soli Amor, *
Nick Enriques, *
▲ EMP: 20 EST: 1992
SALES (est): 1.61MM **Privately Held**
SIC: 2519 Furniture, household: glass, fiberglass, and plastic

**(P-3552)**
**ARKTURA LLC (HQ)**
966 Sandhill Ave, Carson (90746-1217)
PHONE.................310 532-1050
Chris Kabatsi, *Managing Member*
▲ EMP: 30 EST: 2008
SALES (est): 10.35MM
SALES (corp-wide): 1.3B **Publicly Held**
Web: www.arktura.com
SIC: 2519 Furniture, household: glass, fiberglass, and plastic
PA: Armstrong World Industries, Inc.
2500 Columbia Ave
717 397-0611

**(P-3553)**
**CALIFRNIA FURN COLLECTIONS INC**
Also Called: Artifacts International
150 Reed Ct Ste A, Chula Vista (91911-5890)
PHONE.................619 621-2455
Eric Vogt, *Pr*
EMP: 114 EST: 1986
SQ FT: 40,000

## 2519 - Household Furniture, Nec (P-3554)

SALES (est): 1.5MM **Privately Held**
Web: www.artifactsinternational.com
SIC: **2519** 2514 2511 2512  Household furniture, except wood or metal: upholstered; Metal household furniture; Wood household furniture; Upholstered household furniture

### (P-3554)
### DON ALDERSON ASSOCIATES INC
3327 La Cienega Pl, Los Angeles (90016-3116)
PHONE....................310 837-5141
Juan Guardado, *Prin*
EMP: 40 EST: 1979
SALES (est): 580.16K **Privately Held**
SIC: **2519**  Household furniture, except wood or metal: upholstered

### (P-3555)
### NEXT DAY FRAME INC
11560 Wright Rd, Lynwood (90262-3944)
PHONE....................310 886-0851
Nancy Abelar, *CEO*
EMP: 65 EST: 2012
SALES (est): 2.17MM **Privately Held**
SIC: **2519**  Household furniture, except wood or metal: upholstered

### (P-3556)
### NICHOLAS MICHAEL DESIGNS LLC
2330 Raymer Ave, Fullerton (92833-2515)
PHONE....................714 562-8101
Michael A Cimarusti Senior, *CEO*
Michael J Cimarusti I, *
▲ EMP: 120 EST: 2003
SALES (est): 21.79MM **Privately Held**
Web: www.mndca.com
SIC: **2519**  Household furniture, except wood or metal: upholstered

### (P-3557)
### RECYCLED SPACES INC
Also Called: High Camp Home
10157 Donner Pass Rd, Truckee (96161-0495)
P.O. Box 10358 (96162-0358)
PHONE....................530 587-3394
Diana Vincent, *CEO*
Teresa Mersky, *Pr*
▲ EMP: 15 EST: 1997
SALES (est): 3.95MM **Privately Held**
Web: www.highcamphome.com
SIC: **2519** 5712  Lawn and garden furniture, except wood and metal; Furniture stores

### (P-3558)
### STANDDESK INC
5042 Wilshire Blvd # 44689, Los Angeles (90036-4305)
PHONE....................213 634-0665
Steven Yu, *Pr*
▲ EMP: 20 EST: 2013
SQ FT: 1,300
SALES (est): 600.33K **Privately Held**
Web: www.standdesk.com
SIC: **2519** 2522  Household furniture, except wood or metal: upholstered; Benches, office: except wood

## 2521 Wood Office Furniture

### (P-3559)
### A M CABINETS  INC (PA)
239 E Gardena Blvd, Gardena (90248-2813)
PHONE....................310 532-1919
Alex H Mc Kay Junior, *CEO*
Alex H Mc Kay Junior, *Pr*
Nancy Wolfinger, *
EMP: 88 EST: 1975
SQ FT: 35,000
SALES (est): 14.89MM
SALES (corp-wide): 14.89MM **Privately Held**
Web: www.amcabinets.com
SIC: **2521** 2434 2541  Wood office furniture; Wood kitchen cabinets; Counters or counter display cases, wood

### (P-3560)
### AMERICON
1690 Larkfield Ave, Westlake Village (91362-4281)
PHONE....................805 987-0412
Bill Farrah, *Pr*
EMP: 17 EST: 1982
SALES (est): 2.69MM **Privately Held**
Web: www.americon-usa.com
SIC: **2521** 3663  Wood office furniture; Radio and t.v. communications equipment

### (P-3561)
### BLEAU CONSULTING  INC (PA)
555 Raven St, San Diego (92102)
PHONE....................619 263-5550
Ron P Montbleau, *Pr*
Marti Montbleau, *
David Zammit, *
Barton Ward, *
EMP: 57 EST: 1980
SQ FT: 32,000
SALES (est): 25.72MM
SALES (corp-wide): 25.72MM **Privately Held**
Web: www.montbleau.com
SIC: **2521** 1751 2434  Wood office furniture; Cabinet building and installation; Wood kitchen cabinets

### (P-3562)
### CAPITOL STORE FIXTURES
Also Called: Capitol Components
4220 Pell Dr Ste C, Sacramento (95838-2575)
PHONE....................916 646-9096
TOLL FREE: 888
Jim Pelc, *Pr*
Vicki Pelc, *
EMP: 25 EST: 1985
SQ FT: 24,000
SALES (est): 878.22K **Privately Held**
Web: www.csfixtures.com
SIC: **2521** 5046  Cabinets, office: wood; Shelving, commercial and industrial

### (P-3563)
### CASEWORX  INC (PA)
Also Called: Caseworx
1130 Research Dr, Redlands (92374-4562)
PHONE....................909 799-8550
Bruce Humphrey, *Pr*
Gregg Schneider, *Sec*
▲ EMP: 25 EST: 1992
SQ FT: 28,000
SALES (est): 5.45MM **Privately Held**
Web: www.caseworx.com
SIC: **2521**  Cabinets, office: wood

### (P-3564)
### CREATIVE WOOD PRODUCTS INC
900 77th Ave, Oakland (94621-2526)
PHONE....................510 635-5399
Jose Mendes, *Pr*
Polly Peggs Mendes, *
▲ EMP: 120 EST: 1964
SQ FT: 85,000
SALES (est): 19.88MM **Privately Held**
Web: www.creativewood.net
SIC: **2521**  Desks, office: wood

### (P-3565)
### CRI SUB 1 (DH)
Also Called: E O C
1715 S Anderson Ave, Compton (90220-5005)
PHONE....................310 537-1657
Ken Bodger, *CEO*
Richard L Sinclair Junior, *Pr*
Charles Hess, *VP*
▲ EMP: 27 EST: 1969
SQ FT: 120,000
SALES (est): 1.79MM
SALES (corp-wide): 11.48MM **Privately Held**
SIC: **2521**  Cabinets, office: wood
HQ: Chromcraft Revington, Inc.
140 Bradford Dr Ste A
West Berlin NJ 08091

### (P-3566)
### DESKMAKERS  INC
6525 Flotilla St, Commerce (90040-1713)
PHONE....................323 264-2260
Philip Polishook, *CEO*
John Bornstein, *
◆ EMP: 50 EST: 1982
SQ FT: 105,000
SALES (est): 12.55MM **Privately Held**
Web: www.deskmakers.com
SIC: **2521**  Desks, office: wood

### (P-3567)
### FORTRESS  INC
Also Called: Off Broadway
1721 Wright Ave, La Verne (91750-5841)
PHONE....................909 593-8600
Donald I Wolper, *Pr*
▲ EMP: 35 EST: 1959
SQ FT: 100
SALES (est): 6.66MM **Privately Held**
Web: www.fortresseating.com
SIC: **2521** 2522  Chairs, office: padded, upholstered, or plain: wood; Chairs, office: padded or plain: except wood

### (P-3568)
### FURNITURE SOLUTIONS INC
1347 N Blue Gum St, Anaheim (92806-1750)
P.O. Box 3578 (92834-3578)
PHONE....................714 666-0424
Karen Valverde, *Ex VP*
Karen Valverde, *VP*
Daniel Nolazco, *Pr*
EMP: 24 EST: 1993
SQ FT: 25,000
SALES (est): 470.84K **Privately Held**
Web: www.furnituresolutions.us
SIC: **2521** 2511  Wood office furniture; Wood household furniture

### (P-3569)
### GALTECH COMPUTER CORPORATION
Also Called: Galtech International
501 Flynn Rd, Camarillo (93012-8756)
P.O. Box 305 (91319-0305)
PHONE....................805 376-1060
Fei Lin Ko, *CEO*
Robert Ko, *Pr*
Jim Lai, *Stockholder*
▲ EMP: 20 EST: 1991
SQ FT: 32,000
SALES (est): 2.2MM **Privately Held**
Web: www.galtechcorp.com
SIC: **2521**  Benches, office: wood

### (P-3570)
### HPL CONTRACT  INC
525 Baldwin Rd, Patterson (95363-8859)
PHONE....................209 892-1717
Frank Stratiotis, *Pr*
Jim Robertson, *VP*
EMP: 17 EST: 1997
SQ FT: 7,200
SALES (est): 4.72MM **Privately Held**
Web: www.hplcontract.com
SIC: **2521**  Wood office furniture

### (P-3571)
### IRONIES
2200 Central St Ste D, Richmond (94801-1213)
PHONE....................510 644-2100
Kathleen Mcintyre, *Pr*
EMP: 35 EST: 1989
SALES (est): 4.28MM **Privately Held**
Web: www.ironies.com
SIC: **2521**  Wood office furniture

### (P-3572)
### J & C CUSTOM CABINETS  INC
11451 Elks Cir, Rancho Cordova (95742-7355)
PHONE....................916 638-3400
Chris Christie, *Ch Bd*
James E Farrell, *Pr*
EMP: 18 EST: 2011
SQ FT: 20,000
SALES (est): 1.18MM **Privately Held**
Web: www.jandccustomcabinets.com
SIC: **2521** 2434  Cabinets, office: wood; Wood kitchen cabinets

### (P-3573)
### LUXER CORPORATION
Also Called: Luxer One
5040 Dudley Blvd, Mcclellan (95652-1029)
PHONE....................415 390-0123
Arik Levy, *CEO*
EMP: 130 EST: 2014
SALES (est): 50.5MM **Privately Held**
Web: www.luxerone.com
SIC: **2521** 5712  Wood office furniture; Furniture stores
PA: Assa Abloy Ab
Klarabergsviadukten 90
850648500

### (P-3574)
### NAKAMURA-BEEMAN INC
8520 Wellsford Pl, Santa Fe Springs (90670-2226)
PHONE....................562 696-1400
Mike Beeman, *Pr*
EMP: 40 EST: 1978
SQ FT: 20,000
SALES (est): 4.91MM **Privately Held**
Web: www.nbifixtures.com
SIC: **2521** 3429 2541  Wood office furniture; Cabinet hardware; Display fixtures, wood

### (P-3575)
### NEW MAVERICK DESK  INC
Also Called: Maverick Desk
15100 S Figueroa St, Gardena (90248-1724)
PHONE....................310 217-1554
John Long, *CEO*
Ted Jaroszewicz, *
Rich Mealey, *
▲ EMP: 150 EST: 1997
SQ FT: 1,000
SALES (est): 20.65MM **Privately Held**

▲ = Import  ▼ = Export
◆ = Import/Export

## 2522 - Office Furniture, Except Wood (P-3598)

Web: www.maverickdesk.com
SIC: 2521 Wood office furniture
HQ: Workstream Inc.
3158 Production Dr
Fairfield OH 45014

**(P-3576)**
**NORSTAR OFFICE PRODUCTS INC (PA)**
Also Called: Boss
5353 Jillson St, Commerce (90040-2115)
PHONE.................................323 262-1919
William W Huang, *Pr*
◆ EMP: 40 EST: 1991
SQ FT: 150,000
SALES (est): 97.07MM **Privately Held**
Web: www.boss-chair.com
SIC: 2521 2522 Chairs, office: padded, upholstered, or plain: wood; Chairs, office: padded or plain: except wood

**(P-3577)**
**NORTHWOOD DESIGN PARTNERS INC**
1550 Atlantic St, Union City (94587-2006)
PHONE.................................510 731-6505
Michael Hayes, *CEO*
Josh Michael Hayes, *
EMP: 38 EST: 2010
SQ FT: 2,000
SALES (est): 8.91MM **Privately Held**
Web: www.northwooddp.com
SIC: 2521 2431 Wood office furniture; Millwork

**(P-3578)**
**OFFICE CHAIRS INC**
Also Called: Oci
14815 Radburn Ave, Santa Fe Springs (90670-5319)
PHONE.................................562 802-0464
Sharon Klapper, *Pr*
Donald J Simek, *
Joseph J Klapper Junior, *Sec*
▲ EMP: 60 EST: 1974
SQ FT: 60,000
SALES (est): 2.92MM **Privately Held**
Web: www.ocicontract.com
SIC: 2521 2512 Wood office furniture; Chairs: upholstered on wood frames

**(P-3579)**
**OFS BRANDS HOLDINGS INC**
5559 Mcfadden Ave, Huntington Beach (92649-1317)
P.O. Box 100 (47542-0100)
PHONE.................................714 903-2257
Craig Baker, *Pr*
EMP: 628 EST: 2018
SALES (est): 2.5MM
SALES (corp-wide): 228.87MM **Privately Held**
SIC: 2521 Wood office furniture
PA: Ofs Brands Holdings Inc.
1204 E 6th St
800 521-5381

**(P-3580)**
**OHIO INC**
Also Called: Ohio
630 Treat Ave, San Francisco (94110-2016)
PHONE.................................415 647-6446
David Pierce, *Pr*
EMP: 17 EST: 1996
SQ FT: 7,000
SALES (est): 7.82MM **Privately Held**
Web: www.ohiodesign.com
SIC: 2521 Wood office furniture

**(P-3581)**
**PARKINSON ENTERPRISES INC**
Also Called: Salman
135 S State College Blvd Ste 625, Brea (92821-5811)
PHONE.................................714 626-0275
Michael Parkinson, *CEO*
Carolyn Parkinson, *
EMP: 70 EST: 1993
SQ FT: 75,000
SALES (est): 2.69MM **Privately Held**
SIC: 2521 Wood office furniture

**(P-3582)**
**PCT ENTERPRISES INC**
Also Called: Precision Design Source
4255 Hopyard Rd, Pleasanton (94588-2770)
PHONE.................................925 412-3341
EMP: 192
Web: www.precisioncabinets.com
SIC: 2521 Cabinets, office: wood
PA: Pct Enterprises, Inc.
145 Middlefield Ct

**(P-3583)**
**PCT ENTERPRISES INC (PA)**
Also Called: Precision Cabinets
145 Middlefield Ct, Brentwood (94513-4023)
PHONE.................................925 634-5552
EMP: 58 EST: 1996
SALES (est): 21.97MM **Privately Held**
Web: www.precisioncabinets.com
SIC: 2521 Cabinets, office: wood

**(P-3584)**
**RBF GROUP INTERNATIONAL**
Also Called: Rbf Lifestyle Holdings
1441 W 2nd St, Pomona (91766-1202)
PHONE.................................626 333-5700
Robert Brown, *CEO*
▲ EMP: 18 EST: 2007
SALES (est): 1.11MM **Privately Held**
SIC: 2521 Chairs, office: padded, upholstered, or plain: wood

**(P-3585)**
**RBF LIFESTYLE HOLDINGS LLC**
Also Called: Beverly Furniture
1441 W 2nd St, Pomona (91766-1202)
PHONE.................................626 333-5700
▲ EMP: 45
SIC: 2521 2511 Chairs, office: padded, upholstered, or plain: wood; Dining room furniture: wood

**(P-3586)**
**S & H CABINETS AND MFG INC**
10860 Mulberry Ave, Fontana (92337-7027)
PHONE.................................909 357-0551
Michael Hansen, *CEO*
EMP: 40 EST: 1954
SQ FT: 22,000
SALES (est): 4.87MM **Privately Held**
Web: www.shcabinets.com
SIC: 2521 2541 2431 Cabinets, office: wood; Table or counter tops, plastic laminated; Millwork

**(P-3587)**
**SPACESTOR INC**
16411 Carmenita Rd, Cerritos (90703-2216)
PHONE.................................310 410-0220
Charles Hubert Kingston, *CEO*
▲ EMP: 23 EST: 2013
SALES (est): 24.74MM **Privately Held**
Web: www.spacestor.com
SIC: 2521 2522 5712 Wood office furniture; Office furniture, except wood; Office furniture

**(P-3588)**
**STOLO CABINETS INC (PA)**
Also Called: Stolo Custom Cabinets
860 Challenger St, Brea (92821-2946)
PHONE.................................714 529-7303
Gary Stolo, *VP*
Justin Stolo, *
Robert F Stolo, *
EMP: 45 EST: 1953
SQ FT: 15,000
SALES (est): 9.55MM
SALES (corp-wide): 9.55MM **Privately Held**
Web: www.stolocabinets.com
SIC: 2521 Cabinets, office: wood

**(P-3589)**
**VALLEY OAKS INDUSTRIES**
Also Called: Valley Oak Cabinets
3550 E Highway 246 Ste Ae, Santa Ynez (93460-9480)
P.O. Box 1097 (93460-1097)
PHONE.................................805 688-2754
Tom Carlson, *Pr*
Kim Carlson, *VP*
EMP: 17 EST: 1982
SALES (est): 4.14MM **Privately Held**
Web: www.valleyoakindustries.com
SIC: 2521 2511 Wood office furniture; Wood household furniture

**(P-3590)**
**WORKRITE ERGONOMICS LLC**
Also Called: Workrite Ergonomics
2277 Pine View Way Ste 100, Petaluma (94954-5827)
PHONE.................................707 780-6400
▲ EMP: 153 EST: 1998
SALES (est): 22.16MM
SALES (corp-wide): 3.63B **Privately Held**
Web: www.workriteergo.com
SIC: 2521 3577 Wood office furniture; Computer peripheral equipment, nec
HQ: Knape & Vogt Manufacturing Company
2700 Oak Industrial Dr Ne
Grand Rapids MI 49505
616 459-3311

**(P-3591)**
**ZENBOOTH INC**
650 University Ave Unit 10, Berkeley (94710-1947)
PHONE.................................510 646-8368
Sam Johnson, *CEO*
EMP: 21 EST: 2016
SALES (est): 1.74MM **Privately Held**
Web: www.zenbooth.net
SIC: 2521 Wood office furniture

## 2522 Office Furniture, Except Wood

**(P-3592)**
**ANGELL & GIROUX INC**
2727 Alcazar St, Los Angeles (90033-1196)
P.O. Box 33156 (90033)
PHONE.................................323 269-8596
Richard M Hart, *CEO*
Carol A Hart, *
Kenneth Hart, *
EMP: 52 EST: 1956
SQ FT: 13,000
SALES (est): 5.41MM **Privately Held**
Web: www.angellandgiroux.com

SIC: 2522 3479 Cabinets, office: except wood; Painting, coating, and hot dipping

**(P-3593)**
**ARTE DE MEXICO INC (PA)**
1000 Chestnut St, Burbank (91506-1623)
PHONE.................................818 753-4559
Gerald J Stoffers, *CEO*
▲ EMP: 90 EST: 1982
SQ FT: 103,000
SALES (est): 8.01MM
SALES (corp-wide): 8.01MM **Privately Held**
Web: www.artedemexico.com
SIC: 2522 3645 Office furniture, except wood; Residential lighting fixtures

**(P-3594)**
**AUTONOMOUS INC**
21800 Opportunity Way, Riverside (92518-3100)
PHONE.................................844 949-3879
Geoffrey Handley, *Pr*
EMP: 28 EST: 2021
SALES (est): 8.61MM **Privately Held**
Web: www.autonomous.ai
SIC: 2522 Office furniture, except wood

**(P-3595)**
**CARTERS METAL FABRICATORS INC**
935 W 5th St, Azusa (91702-3311)
PHONE.................................626 815-4225
EMP: 30
Web: www.cartersmetal.com
SIC: 2522 Office furniture, except wood

**(P-3596)**
**CRAFTWOOD INDUSTRIES INC**
222 Shelbourne, Irvine (92620-2176)
P.O. Box 2068 (49422-2068)
PHONE.................................616 796-1209
Terry W Beckering, *Pr*
Roger Steensma, *
Kathy Prominski, *Corporate Secretary*
EMP: 35 EST: 1995
SALES (est): 1.45MM **Privately Held**
Web: www.craftwoodindustries.com
SIC: 2522 2531 2426 2511 Office furniture, except wood; Public building and related furniture; Hardwood dimension and flooring mills; Wood household furniture

**(P-3597)**
**ELITE MFG CORP**
Also Called: Elite Modern
12143 Altamar Pl, Santa Fe Springs (90670-2501)
PHONE.................................888 354-8356
Peter Luong, *CEO*
Robinson Ho, *
▲ EMP: 102 EST: 1988
SQ FT: 62,000
SALES (est): 16.12MM **Privately Held**
Web: www.elitemodern.com
SIC: 2522 2514 Office furniture, except wood; Metal household furniture

**(P-3598)**
**ERGOCRAFT CONTRACT SOLUTIONS**
Also Called: Ergocraft Office Furniture
6055 E Washington Blvd Ste 500, Commerce (90040-2426)
▲ EMP: 25 EST: 2001
SALES (est): 1.37MM **Privately Held**
Web: www.ecs-designs.com
SIC: 2522 Office furniture, except wood

## 2522 - Office Furniture, Except Wood (P-3599)

**(P-3599)**
**ERGONONMIC COMFORT DESIGN INC**
9140 Stellar Ct Ste B, Corona (92883-4902)
P.O. Box 79018 (92877-0167)
PHONE..................................951 277-1558
Aldolfo Agramonte, *Pr*
Patricia Agramonte, *VP*
▲ **EMP:** 18 **EST:** 1994
**SQ FT:** 22,000
**SALES (est):** 2.24MM **Privately Held**
Web: www.ecdergo.com
**SIC: 2522** Office chairs, benches, and stools, except wood

**(P-3600)**
**EXEMPLIS LLC**
Also Called: Sit On It
6280 Artesia Blvd, Buena Park (90620-1004)
PHONE..................................714 995-4800
Paul Devries, *Mgr*
**EMP:** 147
Web: www.exemplis.com
**SIC: 2522** 2521 2512 Chairs, office: padded or plain: except wood; Wood office furniture; Upholstered household furniture
PA: Exemplis Llc
6415 Katella Ave

**(P-3601)**
**EXEMPLIS LLC**
Also Called: Ideon
6280 Artesia Blvd, Buena Park (90620-1004)
PHONE..................................714 898-5500
Craig Dumity, *Dir*
**EMP:** 43
Web: www.exemplis.com
**SIC: 2522** 5021 Chairs, office: padded or plain: except wood; Furniture
PA: Exemplis Llc
6415 Katella Ave

**(P-3602)**
**EXEMPLIS LLC (PA)**
Also Called: Sitonit
6415 Katella Ave, Cypress (90630-5245)
PHONE..................................714 995-4800
Paul Devries, *CEO*
Mike Mekjian, *
Patrick Sommerfield, *
◆ **EMP:** 40 **EST:** 1996
**SQ FT:** 20,000
**SALES (est):** 157.5MM **Privately Held**
Web: www.exemplis.com
**SIC: 2522** Chairs, office: padded or plain: except wood

**(P-3603)**
**HIGHMARK SMART RELIABLE SEATING INC**
Also Called: Highmark
5559 Mcfadden Ave, Huntington Beach (92649-1317)
PHONE..................................714 903-2257
◆ **EMP:** 200
**SIC: 2522** Chairs, office: padded or plain: except wood

**(P-3604)**
**KORDEN INC**
601 S Milliken Ave Ste H, Ontario (91761-8103)
PHONE..................................909 988-8979
Barjona S Meek, *Prin*
Thomas Mc Cormick, *Pr*
Jim Ethridge, *Ex VP*
**EMP:** 25 **EST:** 1949
**SALES (est):** 7.79MM **Privately Held**
Web: www.modernspace.com
**SIC: 2522** Stools, office: except wood

**(P-3605)**
**MCDOWELL CRAIG OFF SYSTEMS INC**
Also Called: McDowell-Craig Office Furn
13146 Firestone Blvd, Norwalk (90650)
P.O. Box 349 (90651-0349)
PHONE..................................562 921-4441
Brent G Mcdowell, *Pr*
Jeffrey C Mcdowell, *Sec*
**EMP:** 70 **EST:** 1995
**SQ FT:** 117,000
**SALES (est):** 2.52MM **Privately Held**
Web: www.mcdowellcraig.com
**SIC: 2522** Office furniture, except wood

**(P-3606)**
**MODULAR OFFICE SOLUTIONS INC**
11701 6th St, Rancho Cucamonga (91730-6030)
PHONE..................................909 476-4200
Daniel G Coelho, *CEO*
Jorge E Robles, *
▲ **EMP:** 40 **EST:** 1999
**SQ FT:** 173,000
**SALES (est):** 899.26K **Privately Held**
Web: www.chicagoofficefurniture.com
**SIC: 2522** 2521 Office furniture, except wood; Wood office furniture

**(P-3607)**
**SISNEROS INC**
Also Called: Sisneros Office Furntiure
12717 Los Nietos Rd, Santa Fe Springs (90670-3007)
PHONE..................................562 777-9797
Luis Sisneros, *Pr*
Margarita Sisneros, *VP*
**EMP:** 16 **EST:** 1994
**SQ FT:** 20,000
**SALES (est):** 874K **Privately Held**
**SIC: 2522** Office furniture, except wood

**(P-3608)**
**SUPER STRUCT BLDG SYSTEMS INC**
1251 Montalvo Way Ste F, Palm Springs (92263)
P.O. Box 1014 (92247-1014)
PHONE..................................760 322-2522
John G Kalogeris, *Pr*
Chris Kalogeris, *
**EMP:** 40 **EST:** 1960
**SQ FT:** 10,000
**SALES (est):** 598.29K **Privately Held**
**SIC: 2522** 2439 Panel systems and partitions, office: except wood; Trusses, wooden roof

**(P-3609)**
**VERSA PRODUCTS (PA)**
Also Called: Versatables.com
14105 Avalon Blvd, Los Angeles (90061-2637)
PHONE..................................310 353-7100
Christopher Laudadio, *CEO*
▲ **EMP:** 108 **EST:** 2000
**SQ FT:** 35,000
**SALES (est):** 21.68MM
**SALES (corp-wide):** 21.68MM **Privately Held**
Web: www.versatables.com
**SIC: 2522** Office desks and tables, except wood

**(P-3610)**
**X-CHAIR LLC**
6415 Katella Ave Ste 200, Cypress (90630-5245)
PHONE..................................844 492-4247
Anthony Mazlish, *Managing Member*
**EMP:** 39 **EST:** 2015
**SALES (est):** 2.56MM **Privately Held**
Web: www.xchair.com
**SIC: 2522** Office furniture, except wood
PA: Exemplis Llc
6415 Katella Ave

**(P-3611)**
**Z-LINE DESIGNS INC**
181 Pullman St, Livermore (94551-5128)
PHONE..................................925 743-4000
◆ **EMP:** 100
Web: www.z-linedesigns.com
**SIC: 2522** Office furniture, except wood

## 2531 Public Building And Related Furniture

**(P-3612)**
**AEROFOAM INDUSTRIES INC**
Also Called: Quality Foam Packaging
31855 Corydon St, Lake Elsinore (92530-8501)
PHONE..................................951 245-4429
Noel Castellon, *Pr*
Noel Castellon Junior, *VP*
Jim Barrett, *
Ruth Castellon, *
Darlene Garay, *
▲ **EMP:** 80 **EST:** 2010
**SQ FT:** 150,000
**SALES (est):** 9.82MM **Privately Held**
Web: www.aerofoams.com
**SIC: 2531** Seats, aircraft

**(P-3613)**
**AIRO INDUSTRIES COMPANY**
429 Jessie St, San Fernando (91340-2541)
PHONE..................................818 838-1008
Bahram Salem, *Pr*
Mike Salem, *
▲ **EMP:** 25 **EST:** 1989
**SQ FT:** 20,000
**SALES (est):** 2.45MM **Privately Held**
Web: www.airoindustries.com
**SIC: 2531** 4581 Seats, aircraft; Aircraft upholstery repair

**(P-3614)**
**CITY OF STOCKTON**
Also Called: Public Works
22 E Weber Ave Ste 301, Stockton (95202-2326)
PHONE..................................209 937-8339
Jim Giotonini, *Brnch Mgr*
**EMP:** 113
**SALES (corp-wide):** 484.6MM **Privately Held**
Web: www.stocktonlive.com
**SIC: 2531** Public building and related furniture
PA: City Of Stockton
425 N El Dorado St
209 937-8212

**(P-3615)**
**CLARIOS LLC**
Also Called: Johnson Controls
2100 Chicago Ave, Riverside (92507-2202)
PHONE..................................951 222-0284
**EMP:** 23
**SALES (corp-wide):** 69.83B **Privately Held**
Web: www.clarios.com
**SIC: 2531** Public building and related furniture
HQ: Clarios, Llc
5757 N Green Bay Ave Flor
Glendale WI 53209

**(P-3616)**
**CLARIOS LLC**
Also Called: Johnson Controls
3526 Breakwater Ct Bldg E, Hayward (94545-3611)
PHONE..................................510 783-4000
**EMP:** 32
**SALES (corp-wide):** 69.83B **Privately Held**
Web: www.clarios.com
**SIC: 2531** Seats, automobile
HQ: Clarios, Llc
5757 N Green Bay Ave Flor
Glendale WI 53209

**(P-3617)**
**CLARIOS LLC**
Also Called: Johnson Controls
4100 Guardian St, Simi Valley (93063-6717)
PHONE..................................805 522-5555
Dimitri Dorfan, *Mgr*
**EMP:** 36
**SALES (corp-wide):** 69.83B **Privately Held**
Web: www.clarios.com
**SIC: 2531** Seats, automobile
HQ: Clarios, Llc
5757 N Green Bay Ave Flor
Glendale WI 53209

**(P-3618)**
**CLARIOS LLC**
Also Called: Johnson Controls
39312 Leopard St Ste A, Palm Desert (92211-1129)
PHONE..................................760 200-5225
**EMP:** 38
**SALES (corp-wide):** 69.83B **Privately Held**
Web: www.clarios.com
**SIC: 2531** Seats, automobile
HQ: Clarios, Llc
5757 N Green Bay Ave Flor
Glendale WI 53209

**(P-3619)**
**CLARIOS LLC**
Also Called: Johnson Controls
103 Woodmere Rd Ste 110, Folsom (95630-4731)
PHONE..................................916 294-8866
Allon Corron, *Brnch Mgr*
**EMP:** 85
**SALES (corp-wide):** 69.83B **Privately Held**
Web: www.clarios.com
**SIC: 2531** Seats, automobile
HQ: Clarios, Llc
5757 N Green Bay Ave Flor
Glendale WI 53209

**(P-3620)**
**CLERPREM USA CORP**
1330 Del Paso Rd Ste 300, Sacramento (95834-7771)
PHONE..................................415 856-9001
Gian Roberto Marchesi, *CEO*
Davide Baratti, *CFO*
Antonio Valla, *Sec*
**EMP:** 21 **EST:** 2018
**SALES (est):** 3.98MM
**SALES (corp-wide):** 146.72MM **Privately Held**
Web: www.clerprem.com
**SIC: 2531** Seats, automobile
HQ: Clerprem Spa
Via Bianche 10

Carre' VI 36010
044 586-9700

### (P-3621)
### COD USA INC
Also Called: Creative Outdoor Distrs USA
25954 Commercentre Dr, Lake Forest (92630-8815)
PHONE..................................949 381-7367
Heather Smulson, *Pr*
Brian Horowitz, *CEO*
Barbara Tolbert, *COO*
◆ **EMP:** 23 **EST:** 2016
**SQ FT:** 34,000
**SALES (est):** 1.15MM **Privately Held**
**SIC: 2531** Chairs, portable folding

### (P-3622)
### DEFOE FURNITURE FOR KIDS INC
Also Called: Defoe Furniture
723 W Mill St, San Bernardino (92410-3347)
PHONE..................................909 947-4459
John G Defoe, *Pr*
Narcisa Defoe, *Sec*
**EMP:** 16 **EST:** 1980
**SALES (est):** 796.99K **Privately Held**
**Web:** www.defoefurniture4kids.com
**SIC: 2531** School furniture

### (P-3623)
### ECR4KIDS LP
Also Called: Early Childhood Resources
5630 Kearny Mesa Rd Ste B, San Diego (92111-1323)
PHONE..................................619 323-2005
Lee Siegel, *Pt*
◆ **EMP:** 25 **EST:** 2003
**SALES (est):** 5.26MM **Privately Held**
**Web:** www.ecr4kids.com
**SIC: 2531** 3944 2511 5021 Chairs, table and arm; Craft and hobby kits and sets; Children's wood furniture; Chairs
**PA:** Cri 2000, L.P.
2245 San Diego Ave # 125

### (P-3624)
### ERA PRODUCTS INC
1130 Benedict Canyon Dr, Beverly Hills (90210-2726)
PHONE..................................310 324-4908
Marlene Alter, *Pr*
Roy H Alter, *VP*
**EMP:** 16 **EST:** 1972
**SQ FT:** 56,792
**SALES (est):** 554K **Privately Held**
**Web:** www.eraproducts.com
**SIC: 2531** Vehicle furniture

### (P-3625)
### EUROTEC SEATING INCORPORATED
1000 S Euclid St, La Habra (90631-6806)
PHONE..................................562 806-6171
◆ **EMP:** 50
**SIC: 2531** Seats, automobile

### (P-3626)
### HOLGUIN & HOLGUIN INC
Also Called: Seating Resource
968 W Foothill Blvd, Azusa (91702-2842)
PHONE..................................626 815-0168
Gilda Vega, *Pr*
John H Holguin, *
**EMP:** 45 **EST:** 1994
**SQ FT:** 25,000
**SALES (est):** 1.57MM **Privately Held**
**Web:** www.seatingresource.com

**SIC: 2531** Public building and related furniture

### (P-3627)
### J L FURNISHINGS LLC
Also Called: J L F/Lone Meadow
1620 5th Ave Ste 400, San Diego (92101-2738)
PHONE..................................310 605-6600
◆ **EMP:** 300
**Web:** www.thestandardbyrcd.com
**SIC: 2531** 2521 Chairs, table and arm; Wood office chairs, benches and stools

### (P-3628)
### JOHNSON CONTROLS INC
Also Called: Johnson Controls
5770 Warland Dr Ste A, Cypress (90630-5047)
PHONE..................................562 594-3200
Dough Beebe, *Mgr*
**EMP:** 150
**Web:** www.johnsoncontrols.com
**SIC: 2531** 1711 5075 5065 Seats, automobile ; Heating systems repair and maintenance; Warm air heating and air conditioning; Electronic parts and equipment, nec
**HQ:** Johnson Controls, Inc.
5757 N Green Bay Ave
Milwaukee WI 53209
866 496-1999

### (P-3629)
### JOHNSON CONTROLS INC
Also Called: Johnson Controls
12393 Slauson Ave, Whittier (90606-2824)
PHONE..................................562 698-8301
Stephen Roell, *Brnch Mgr*
**EMP:** 27
**Web:** www.johnsoncontrols.com
**SIC: 2531** 1711 Seats, automobile; Warm air heating and air conditioning contractor
**HQ:** Johnson Controls, Inc.
5757 N Green Bay Ave
Milwaukee WI 53209
866 496-1999

### (P-3630)
### JOHNSON CONTROLS INC
Also Called: Johnson Controls
2226 Northpoint Pkwy, Santa Rosa (95407-7398)
PHONE..................................707 546-3042
Glen Nold, *Brnch Mgr*
**EMP:** 21
**Web:** www.johnsoncontrols.com
**SIC: 2531** 7623 Seats, automobile; Air conditioning repair
**HQ:** Johnson Controls, Inc.
5757 N Green Bay Ave
Milwaukee WI 53209
866 496-1999

### (P-3631)
### JOHNSON CONTROLS INC
Also Called: Johnson Controls
1828 34th St #c, Bakersfield (93301)
PHONE..................................661 862-5706
**EMP:** 15
**Web:** www.johnsoncontrols.com
**SIC: 2531** Seats, automobile
**HQ:** Johnson Controls, Inc.
5757 N Green Bay Ave
Milwaukee WI 53209
866 496-1999

### (P-3632)
### JOSEPH MANUFACTURING CO INC
Also Called: Mortech Manufacturing

411 N Aerojet Dr, Azusa (91702)
PHONE..................................626 334-1471
Gino Joseph, *Pr*
Gino Joseph, *CEO*
Paul Joseph, *
Christy Haines, *
◆ **EMP:** 82 **EST:** 1986
**SQ FT:** 43,000
**SALES (est):** 11.64MM **Privately Held**
**Web:** www.mortechmfg.com
**SIC: 2531** 5087 Altars and pulpits; Funeral director's equipment and supplies

### (P-3633)
### KINGS RIVER CASTING INC
1350 North Ave, Sanger (93657-3742)
PHONE..................................559 875-8250
Patrick Henry, *Pr*
Merry Henry, *Sec*
▼ **EMP:** 18 **EST:** 1978
**SQ FT:** 30,000
**SALES (est):** 3.66MM **Privately Held**
**Web:** www.kingsrivercasting.com
**SIC: 2531** 3648 2599 Benches for public buildings; Street lighting fixtures; Bar furniture

### (P-3634)
### KRUEGER INTERNATIONAL INC
16510 Bake Pkwy Ste 100, Irvine (92618-4663)
PHONE..................................949 748-7000
**EMP:** 42
**SALES (corp-wide):** 484.48MM **Privately Held**
**Web:** www.ki.com
**SIC: 2531** School furniture
**PA:** Krueger International, Inc.
1330 Bellevue St
920 468-8100

### (P-3635)
### LOUIS SARDO UPHOLSTERY INC (PA)
Also Called: Sardo Bus & Coach Upholstery
512 W Rosecrans Ave, Gardena (90248-1515)
PHONE..................................310 327-0532
Louis Sardo, *Pr*
Jeanie Sardo, *
**EMP:** 55 **EST:** 1916
**SQ FT:** 10,000
**SALES (est):** 5MM
**SALES (corp-wide):** 5MM **Privately Held**
**Web:** www.sardobus.com
**SIC: 2531** 3713 7641 Seats, automobile; Truck and bus bodies; Reupholstery and furniture repair

### (P-3636)
### ORBO CORPORATION (PA)
Also Called: Eurotec Seating
1000 S Euclid St, La Habra (90631-6806)
PHONE..................................562 806-6171
Oscar Galvez, *Pr*
**EMP:** 37 **EST:** 2001
**SALES (est):** 1.86MM
**SALES (corp-wide):** 1.86MM **Privately Held**
**Web:** www.4seating.com
**SIC: 2531** Seats, automobile

### (P-3637)
### PACIFIC HOSPITALITY DESIGN INC
Also Called: PH Design
2620 S Malt Ave, Commerce (90040-3206)
PHONE..................................323 278-7998
Gilberto Martinez, *CEO*
Ana Martinez, *

**EMP:** 25 **EST:** 1979
**SQ FT:** 14,000
**SALES (est):** 2.31MM **Privately Held**
**Web:** www.phdesign.com
**SIC: 2531** Public building and related furniture

### (P-3638)
### SEATING CONCEPTS LLC
4229 Ponderosa Ave Ste B, San Diego (92123-1519)
PHONE..................................619 491-3159
Juan Carlos Letayf, *Managing Member*
Bill Overton, *
Jose Letayf, *
◆ **EMP:** 30 **EST:** 1982
**SALES (est):** 3.57MM **Privately Held**
**Web:** www.scicustom.com
**SIC: 2531** 5021 Theater furniture; Chairs

### (P-3639)
### SERIOUS ENERGY INC
Also Called: Serious Windows
1250 Elko Dr, Sunnyvale (94089-2213)
PHONE..................................408 541-8000
▲ **EMP:** 100
**Web:** www.seriousenergy.com
**SIC: 2531** Public building and related furniture

### (P-3640)
### TALIMAR SYSTEMS INC
3105 W Alpine St, Santa Ana (92704-6911)
PHONE..................................714 557-4884
David G Wesdell, *Pr*
▲ **EMP:** 37 **EST:** 1988
**SQ FT:** 11,000
**SALES (est):** 4.11MM **Privately Held**
**Web:** www.talimarsystems.com
**SIC: 2531** 5712 7389 5932 Public building and related furniture; Furniture stores; Merchandise liquidators; Office furniture, secondhand

### (P-3641)
### VILLA FURNITURE MFG CO
Also Called: Villa International
16440 Manning Way, Cerritos (90703-2225)
PHONE..................................714 535-7272
Andrew M Greenthal, *Pr*
▲ **EMP:** 125 **EST:** 1949
**SALES (est):** 9.91MM **Privately Held**
**Web:** www.villainternational.com
**SIC: 2531** 2522 Vehicle furniture; Office furniture, except wood

### (P-3642)
### VIRCO MFG CORPORATION (PA)
2027 Harpers Way, Torrance (90501-1524)
PHONE..................................310 533-0474
Robert A Virtue, *Ch Bd*
Douglas A Virtue, *
J Scott Bell, *Sr VP*
Robert E Dose, *Sr VP*
Patricia Quinones, *Sr VP*
◆ **EMP:** 88 **EST:** 1950
**SQ FT:** 560,000
**SALES (est):** 269.12MM
**SALES (corp-wide):** 269.12MM **Publicly Held**
**Web:** www.virco.com
**SIC: 2531** 2522 2511 School furniture; Office furniture, except wood; Wood household furniture

## 2541 Wood Partitions And Fixtures

**(P-3643)**
**ALCO DESIGNS**
15117 S Broadway, Gardena (90248-1821)
PHONE................................310 353-2300
Dick Warden, *National Accounts Manager*
**EMP:** 15 **EST:** 1988
**SALES (est):** 295.58K **Privately Held**
Web: www.alcodesigns.com
**SIC: 2541** Wood partitions and fixtures

**(P-3644)**
**AMTREND CORPORATION**
1458 Manhattan Ave, Fullerton (92831-5222)
PHONE................................714 630-2070
Hamid A Malik, *Pr*
Javeeda Malik, *
**EMP:** 85 **EST:** 1980
**SQ FT:** 45,000
**SALES (est):** 16.52MM **Privately Held**
Web: www.amtrend.com
**SIC: 2541** 2521 7641 2512 Wood partitions and fixtures; Wood office furniture; Upholstery work; Upholstered household furniture

**(P-3645)**
**ARNOLD AND EGAN MFG CO**
1515 Griffith St, San Francisco (94124-3412)
PHONE................................415 822-2700
Kenneth Egan, *CEO*
Rose Egan, *CFO*
Donna Egan, *Sec*
**EMP:** 20 **EST:** 1977
**SQ FT:** 10,000
**SALES (est):** 2.81MM **Privately Held**
Web: www.arnoldandegan.com
**SIC: 2541** 2521 2434 2431 Wood partitions and fixtures; Wood office furniture; Wood kitchen cabinets; Millwork

**(P-3646)**
**BLOCK TOPS INC (PA)**
Also Called: Top Source, The
1321 S Sunkist St, Anaheim (92806-5614)
PHONE................................714 978-5080
Vanessa Bates, *CEO*
Nate Kolenski, *
▲ **EMP:** 34 **EST:** 1977
**SQ FT:** 10,000
**SALES (est):** 7.19MM
**SALES (corp-wide):** 7.19MM **Privately Held**
Web: www.blocktops.com
**SIC: 2541** 2519 3281 2821 Table or counter tops, plastic laminated; Furniture, household: glass, fiberglass, and plastic; Cut stone and stone products; Plastics materials and resins

**(P-3647)**
**BORODIAN INC (PA)**
Also Called: J P B Jewelry Box Co
2428 Dallas St, Los Angeles (90031-1013)
PHONE................................323 225-0360
Jerry Borodian, *Pt*
Josephine Borodian, *Pt*
▲ **EMP:** 15 **EST:** 1978
**SQ FT:** 14,000
**SALES (est):** 1.67MM
**SALES (corp-wide):** 1.67MM **Privately Held**
Web: www.jpbbox.com
**SIC: 2541** 2441 3172 Wood partitions and fixtures; Nailed wood boxes and shook; Cases, jewelry

**(P-3648)**
**BRISTOL OMEGA INC**
9441 Opal Ave Ste 2, Mentone (92359-9900)
PHONE................................909 794-6862
Ralf G Zacky, *CEO*
**EMP:** 27 **EST:** 1993
**SALES (est):** 2.03MM **Privately Held**
Web: www.bristolomega.com
**SIC: 2541** 1611 Wood partitions and fixtures; General contractor, highway and street construction

**(P-3649)**
**CALIFORNIA MFG CABINETRY INC**
Also Called: C M C
1474 E Francis St, Ontario (91761-5791)
PHONE................................909 930-3632
Miguel Jimenez, *Pr*
Mike Jimmez, *VP*
**EMP:** 15 **EST:** 1988
**SALES (est):** 2.03MM **Privately Held**
**SIC: 2541** 2434 2431 Cabinets, except refrigerated: show, display, etc.: wood; Wood kitchen cabinets; Millwork

**(P-3650)**
**CCM ENTERPRISES (PA)**
10848 Wheatlands Ave, Santee (92071-2855)
PHONE................................619 562-2605
Cody L Nosko, *CEO*
Duane Nosco, *
Virginia Jaggi, *
**EMP:** 60 **EST:** 1995
**SQ FT:** 67,543
**SALES (est):** 5MM **Privately Held**
Web: www.ccmmfg.com
**SIC: 2541** 1799 Counter and sink tops; Kitchen and bathroom remodeling

**(P-3651)**
**CK MANUFACTURING & TRADING INC**
Also Called: Kosakura Associates
3 Holland, Irvine (92618-2506)
P.O. Box 1190 (75483-1190)
PHONE................................949 529-3400
▲ **EMP:** 35
**SIC: 2541** Display fixtures, wood

**(P-3652)**
**COLUMBIA SHOWCASE & CAB CO INC**
11034 Sherman Way Ste A, Sun Valley (91352-4927)
PHONE................................818 765-9710
Samuel M Patterson Junior, *CEO*
▲ **EMP:** 125 **EST:** 1950
**SQ FT:** 170,000
**SALES (est):** 8.6MM **Privately Held**
**SIC: 2541** 1542 Cabinets, except refrigerated: show, display, etc.: wood; Commercial and office building contractors

**(P-3653)**
**COMPATICO INC**
1901 S Archibald Ave, Ontario (91761-8548)
PHONE................................616 940-1772
John Rea, *Pr*
Richard Posthumus, *
William Boer, *
Cheryl Daniels, *
Carrie Boer, *
◆ **EMP:** 45 **EST:** 1989
**SALES (est):** 4.55MM **Privately Held**
Web: www.compatico.com
**SIC: 2541** Wood partitions and fixtures

**(P-3654)**
**DISPLAY SUPPLY CHAIN CONS LLC**
1237 Muirlands Vista Way, La Jolla (92037-6212)
PHONE................................512 577-3672
Ross Young, *CEO*
Robert J Obrien, *CFO*
**EMP:** 16 **EST:** 2016
**SALES (est):** 2.09MM **Privately Held**
Web: www.displaysupplychain.com
**SIC: 2541** Store and office display cases and fixtures
HQ: Counterpoint Research Hk Limited 26/F Prosperity Twr Central District HK

**(P-3655)**
**EUROPEAN WHOLESALE COUNTER**
10051 Prospect Ave, Santee (92071-4321)
PHONE................................619 562-0565
Pete Sciarrino, *CEO*
**EMP:** 150 **EST:** 2008
**SQ FT:** 40,000
**SALES (est):** 3.59MM **Privately Held**
Web: www.europeancompany.com
**SIC: 2541** 1799 Counter and sink tops; Counter top installation

**(P-3656)**
**F-J-E INC**
Also Called: Jf Fixtures & Design
546 W Esther St, Long Beach (90813-1529)
PHONE................................562 437-7466
Frank Ernandes, *Pr*
Barbara Ernandes, *
**EMP:** 25 **EST:** 1983
**SQ FT:** 26,000
**SALES (est):** 1.99MM **Privately Held**
Web: www.jffixtures.com
**SIC: 2541** 2542 Store fixtures, wood; Fixtures, store: except wood

**(P-3657)**
**IDEAL PRODUCTS INC**
4025 Garner Rd, Riverside (92501-1043)
P.O. Box 4090 (91761-1006)
PHONE................................951 727-8600
Robert L Martin Junior, *CEO*
Virginia Martin, *
**EMP:** 35 **EST:** 1976
**SALES (est):** 5.6MM **Privately Held**
Web: www.ideallockers.com
**SIC: 2541** Lockers, except refrigerated: wood

**(P-3658)**
**IVARS DISPLAY (PA)**
Also Called: Ivar's Displays
2314 E Locust Ct, Ontario (91761-7613)
PHONE................................909 923-2761
Ivan Gundersen, *CFO*
Karl Gundersen, *
Linda Pulice, *
Jason Gundersen, *
▲ **EMP:** 87 **EST:** 1966
**SQ FT:** 95,000
**SALES (est):** 18.21MM
**SALES (corp-wide):** 18.21MM **Privately Held**
Web: www.ivarsdisplay.com
**SIC: 2541** 2542 Store fixtures, wood; Shelving, office and store, except wood

**(P-3659)**
**JBE INC**
Also Called: Dimensions Unlimited
1080 Nimitz Ave Ste 400, Vallejo (94592-1009)
PHONE................................707 552-6800
John Ewer, *Pr*
Jane Ewer, *Sec*
**EMP:** 15 **EST:** 1971
**SQ FT:** 9,300
**SALES (est):** 662.25K **Privately Held**
Web: www.ducabinetry.com
**SIC: 2541** 1751 5712 Cabinets, except refrigerated: show, display, etc.: wood; Cabinet and finish carpentry; Customized furniture and cabinets

**(P-3660)**
**JUDITH VON HOPF INC**
1525 W 13th St Ste H, Upland (91786-7528)
PHONE................................909 481-1884
Judith P Hopf, *CEO*
▲ **EMP:** 25 **EST:** 1976
**SALES (est):** 4.06MM **Privately Held**
Web: www.judithvonhopf.com
**SIC: 2541** Display fixtures, wood

**(P-3661)**
**KILLION INDUSTRIES INC (PA)**
1380 Poinsettia Ave, Vista (92081-8504)
PHONE................................760 727-5102
Richard W Killion, *Pr*
Larry Edward, *
◆ **EMP:** 80 **EST:** 1981
**SQ FT:** 185,000
**SALES (est):** 23.59MM
**SALES (corp-wide):** 23.59MM **Privately Held**
Web: www.killionindustries.com
**SIC: 2541** Store and office display cases and fixtures

**(P-3662)**
**L & N FIXTURES INC**
2214 Tyler Ave, El Monte (91733-2710)
PHONE................................626 442-4778
Louis Pierotti, *Pr*
**EMP:** 16 **EST:** 1970
**SQ FT:** 16,000
**SALES (est):** 1.3MM **Privately Held**
**SIC: 2541** 1799 2521 2434 Store fixtures, wood; Office furniture installation; Wood office furniture; Wood kitchen cabinets

**(P-3663)**
**LA CABINET & MILLWORK INC**
Also Called: Bromack
3005 Humboldt St, Los Angeles (90031-1830)
PHONE................................323 227-5000
**EMP:** 25 **EST:** 2005
**SQ FT:** 17,000
**SALES (est):** 3.71MM **Privately Held**
**SIC: 2541** 1799 2434 1751 Counters or counter display cases, wood; Counter top installation; Wood kitchen cabinets; Carpentry work

**(P-3664)**
**LEONARDS CARPET SERVICE INC (PA)**
Also Called: Xgrass Turf Direct
1121 N Red Gum St, Anaheim (92806-2582)
PHONE................................714 630-1930
Leonard Nagel, *Pr*
Joel Nagel, *
▲ **EMP:** 75 **EST:** 1970
**SQ FT:** 52,000

## PRODUCTS & SERVICES SECTION
## 2542 - Partitions And Fixtures, Except Wood (P-3686)

SALES (est): 23.06MM
SALES (corp-wide): 23.06MM **Privately Held**
Web: www.leonardscarpetservice.com
SIC: **2541** 1771 1799 Table or counter tops, plastic laminated; Flooring contractor; Artificial turf installation

**(P-3665)**
**NICO NAT MFG CORP**
Also Called: Niconat Manufacturing
2624 Yates Ave, Commerce (90040-2622)
PHONE..................323 721-1900
Jose Valdez, *CEO*
Francisco Valdez, *Stockholder**
EMP: 45 EST: 2008
SALES (est): 9.42MM **Privately Held**
Web: www.niconatmfg.com
SIC: **2541** Store and office display cases and fixtures

**(P-3666)**
**OLDE WORLD CORPORATION**
Also Called: Great Spaces USA
360 Grogan Ave, Merced (95341-6446)
PHONE..................209 384-1337
Richard T Conas, *Pr*
Jan Conas, *VP*
EMP: 20 EST: 1979
SQ FT: 35,000
SALES (est): 3.32MM **Privately Held**
Web: www.oldeworldcorp.com
SIC: **2541** Store and office display cases and fixtures

**(P-3667)**
**OMNI ENCLOSURES INC**
Also Called: Omni Pacific
505 Raleigh Ave, El Cajon (92020-3139)
PHONE..................619 579-6664
Thomas P Burke, *Pr*
▲ EMP: 27 EST: 1981
SQ FT: 20,000
SALES (est): 8.75MM **Privately Held**
Web: www.omnilabsolutions.com
SIC: **2541** Office fixtures, wood

**(P-3668)**
**PG EMMINGER INC**
4036 Pacheco Blvd # A, Martinez (94553-2224)
PHONE..................925 313-5830
Philip G Emminger, *Pr*
EMP: 22 EST: 1971
SQ FT: 10,000
SALES (est): 2.5MM **Privately Held**
Web: www.emminger.com
SIC: **2541** Wood partitions and fixtures

**(P-3669)**
**PLANET ONE PRODUCTS INC (PA)**
Also Called: Cellarpro Cooling Systems
1445 N Mcdowell Blvd, Petaluma (94954-6516)
PHONE..................707 794-8000
Ben Z Argov, *Pr*
Keith Sedwick, *
Bruce Kirsten, *
▲ EMP: 19 EST: 2004
SQ FT: 18,000
SALES (est): 9.53MM
SALES (corp-wide): 9.53MM **Privately Held**
Web: www.lecachewinecabinets.com
SIC: **2541** Cabinets, except refrigerated: show, display, etc.: wood

**(P-3670)**
**SCIENTIFIC SURFACE INDS INC**
Also Called: Ssi Surfaces
855 Rancho Conejo Blvd, Newbury Park (91320-1714)
PHONE..................805 499-5100
David Marquez, *VP*
EMP: 16 EST: 2009
SQ FT: 10,000
SALES (est): 1.11MM **Privately Held**
Web: www.ssisurfaces.com
SIC: **2541** Counter and sink tops

**(P-3671)**
**SPOONERS WOODWORKS INC**
Also Called: Spooners Woodworks
12460 Kirkham Ct, Poway (92064-6819)
PHONE..................858 679-9086
Tom Spooner, *Admn*
Thomas Spooner, *
Stephen Spooner, *
Valerie Spooner, *
Rosemary Spooner, *
EMP: 120 EST: 1979
SQ FT: 22,000
SALES (est): 23.76MM **Privately Held**
Web: www.spoonerwoodworks.com
SIC: **2541** Store fixtures, wood

**(P-3672)**
**SURFACE TECHNIQUES CORPORATION (PA)**
Also Called: Surface Technology
25673 Nickel Pl, Hayward (94545-3221)
PHONE..................510 887-6000
Howard Berger, *Pr*
EMP: 30 EST: 1986
SQ FT: 13,000
SALES (est): 1.73MM
SALES (corp-wide): 1.73MM **Privately Held**
SIC: **2541** Counters or counter display cases, wood

**(P-3673)**
**SW FIXTURES INC**
3940 Valley Blvd Ste C, Walnut (91789-1541)
PHONE..................909 595-2506
Daniel Zachary, *Pr*
EMP: 18 EST: 1985
SQ FT: 22,500
SALES (est): 2.48MM **Privately Held**
Web: www.swfixtures.com
SIC: **2541** 2431 Display fixtures, wood; Planing mill, millwork

**(P-3674)**
**TEMEKA ADVERTISING INC**
Also Called: Temeka Group
9073 Pulsar Ct, Corona (92883)
PHONE..................951 277-2525
Michael D Wilson, *CEO*
Paul Mieboer, *Stockholder**
Marlene Kelly, *
▲ EMP: 55 EST: 1991
SQ FT: 24,000
SALES (est): 10.27MM **Privately Held**
Web: www.temekagroup.com
SIC: **2541** Store and office display cases and fixtures

**(P-3675)**
**V TWEST INC**
16222 Phoebe Ave, La Mirada (90638-5610)
PHONE..................714 521-2167
Douglas Edward Clausen, *Brnch Mgr*
EMP: 17
SALES (corp-wide): 434.93MM **Privately Held**
Web: www.vtindustries.com
SIC: **2541** Counter and sink tops
HQ: V T.West Inc.
1000 Industrial Park
Holstein IA 51025

**(P-3676)**
**VIEW RITE MANUFACTURING**
455 Allan St, Daly City (94014-1627)
PHONE..................415 468-3856
Brad Somberg, *Pr*
Nha Nguyen, *
EMP: 40 EST: 1969
SQ FT: 78,000
SALES (est): 1.15MM **Privately Held**
SIC: **2541** 2542 Store fixtures, wood; Fixtures, store: except wood

**(P-3677)**
**WALLACE WOOD PRODUCTS**
Also Called: Corte Custom Case
1247 S Buena Vista St Ste C, San Jacinto (92583-4664)
PHONE..................951 654-9311
Roy Wallace, *Owner*
EMP: 16
Web: www.spinolution.com
SIC: **2541** Wood partitions and fixtures
PA: Wallace Wood Products
1247 S Buena Vista St C

**(P-3678)**
**YOSHIMASA DISPLAY CASE INC**
Also Called: Yoshimasa
10808 Weaver Ave, South El Monte (91733-2751)
PHONE..................213 637-9999
Toro Hayashi, *Pr*
Michael Y Yoo, *
Alma Kim Oprtn, *Mgr*
▲ EMP: 35 EST: 2011
SALES (est): 1.56MM **Privately Held**
Web: www.yoshimasausa.com
SIC: **2541** 3564 Store and office display cases and fixtures; Aircurtains (blower)

## 2542 Partitions And Fixtures, Except Wood

**(P-3679)**
**ADVANCED EQUIPMENT CORPORATION (PA)**
2401 W Commonwealth Ave, Fullerton (92833-2999)
PHONE..................714 635-5350
Wesley B Dickson, *Ch*
W Scott Dickson, *Senior President**
W Dickson, *
Bryan Dickson, *
Frank Manning, *
◆ EMP: 50 EST: 1957
SQ FT: 51,000
SALES (est): 15.89MM
SALES (corp-wide): 15.89MM **Privately Held**
Web: www.advancedequipment.com
SIC: **2542** 2541 Partitions for floor attachment, prefabricated: except wood; Wood partitions and fixtures

**(P-3680)**
**BOBRICK WASHROOM EQUIPMENT INC (HQ)**
Also Called: Gamco
6901 Tujunga Ave, North Hollywood (91605-5882)
PHONE..................818 764-1000
◆ EMP: 100 EST: 1906
SALES (est): 129.48MM
SALES (corp-wide): 132.97MM **Privately Held**
Web: www.bobrick.com
SIC: **2542** Partitions for floor attachment, prefabricated: except wood
PA: The Bobrick Corporation
6901 Tujunga Ave
818 764-1000

**(P-3681)**
**BRITCAN INC**
Also Called: Rich Limited
3809 Ocean Ranch Blvd Ste 110, Oceanside (92056-8606)
PHONE..................760 722-2300
James B Hollen, *CEO*
◆ EMP: 20 EST: 1992
SQ FT: 23,000
SALES (est): 8.25MM **Privately Held**
Web: www.richltd.com
SIC: **2542** 3089 Racks, merchandise display or storage: except wood; Air mattresses, plastics

**(P-3682)**
**CTA FIXTURES INC**
5721 Santa Ana St Ste B, Ontario (91761-8617)
PHONE..................909 390-6744
Carlos Gutierrez, *CEO*
▲ EMP: 62 EST: 1994
SQ FT: 90,000
SALES (est): 1.5MM **Privately Held**
Web: www.ctafixtures.com
SIC: **2542** Partitions and fixtures, except wood

**(P-3683)**
**CUTTING EDGE CREATIVE LLC**
9944 Flower St, Bellflower (90706-5411)
PHONE..................562 907-7007
Jennifer Franklin, *Managing Member*
Ward Lookabaugh, *
▲ EMP: 75 EST: 1996
SALES (est): 1.8MM **Privately Held**
SIC: **2542** 3496 7319 Racks, merchandise display or storage: except wood; Miscellaneous fabricated wire products; Display advertising service

**(P-3684)**
**DC LOCKER INC**
160 Commerce Way, Walnut (91789-2714)
PHONE..................909 480-0066
Yang Zhao, *CEO*
EMP: 16 EST: 2018
SALES (est): 673.33K **Privately Held**
Web: www.dclocker.com
SIC: **2542** Partitions and fixtures, except wood

**(P-3685)**
**EVOLV SURFACES INC**
Also Called: Fox Marble & Granite
825 Potter St, Berkeley (94710-2745)
PHONE..................415 767-4600
Charles Mclaughlin, *Pr*
▲ EMP: 122 EST: 1986
SALES (est): 19.65MM **Privately Held**
Web: www.evolvsurfaces.com
SIC: **2542** 5032 Counters or counter display cases, except wood; Marble building stone

**(P-3686)**
**FELBRO INC**
3666 E Olympic Blvd, Los Angeles (90023-3147)
PHONE..................323 263-8686
Howard Feldner, *Ch Bd*

## 2542 - Partitions And Fixtures, Except Wood (P-3687)

Norman Feldner, *
Jeffrey Feldner, *
▲ **EMP:** 180 **EST:** 1945
**SQ FT:** 75,000
**SALES (est):** 8.59MM **Privately Held**
**Web:** www.felbrodisplays.com
**SIC: 2542** Racks, merchandise display or storage: except wood

### (P-3687)
### FIELD MANUFACTURING CORP (PA)
1751 Torrance Blvd Ste N, Torrance (90501-1726)
**PHONE**.................................310 781-9292
Patrick Field, Pr
▲ **EMP:** 36 **EST:** 1955
**SQ FT:** 20,000
**SALES (est):** 8.23MM
**SALES (corp-wide):** 8.23MM **Privately Held**
**Web:** www.field-manufacturing.com
**SIC: 2542** 3089 Partitions and fixtures, except wood; Injection molding of plastics

### (P-3688)
### FRESNO RACK & SHELVING INC
Also Called: Rack Shelves
711 N Armstrong Ave Ste 107, Fresno (93727-2938)
**PHONE**.................................559 275-7225
**EMP:** 25 **EST:** 1989
**SALES (est):** 6.39MM **Privately Held**
**Web:** www.fresnorack.com
**SIC: 2542** Racks, merchandise display or storage: except wood

### (P-3689)
### GALINDO INSTLLTION MVG SVCS IN
Also Called: G.I.M.S.
2901 Mariposa St Ste 3, San Francisco (94110-1339)
**PHONE**.................................415 861-4230
Wilfredo Galindo, Owner
Marjorie Lovell, CEO
**EMP:** 19 **EST:** 1995
**SQ FT:** 3,000
**SALES (est):** 5.09MM **Privately Held**
**Web:** www.gims-sf.com
**SIC: 2542** 1799 7641 7389 Partitions for floor attachment, prefabricated: except wood; Office furniture installation; Office furniture repair and maintenance; Relocation service

### (P-3690)
### GLOBAL STEEL PRODUCTS CORP
Also Called: Global Specialties Direct
1030 Riverside Pkwy, West Sacramento (95605-1523)
**PHONE**.................................510 652-2060
Steve Allen, Mgr
**EMP:** 37
**SALES (corp-wide):** 105.52MM **Privately Held**
**Web:** www.specialtiesdirect.com
**SIC: 2542** 5023 5021 5046 Partitions for floor attachment, prefabricated: except wood; Homefurnishings; Furniture; Partitions
**HQ:** Global Steel Products Corp
95 Marcus Blvd
Deer Park NY 11729
631 586-3455

### (P-3691)
### IDX LOS ANGELES LLC
Also Called: West Coast Mfg & Whsng
5005 E Philadelphia St, Ontario (91761-2816)
**PHONE**.................................909 212-8333
Graham Fownes, Genl Mgr
◆ **EMP:** 109 **EST:** 2012
**SALES (est):** 24.8MM
**SALES (corp-wide):** 7.22B **Publicly Held**
**Web:** www.idxcorporation.com
**SIC: 2542** Partitions and fixtures, except wood
**PA:** Ufp Industries, Inc.
2801 E Beltline Ave Ne
616 364-6161

### (P-3692)
### JCM INDUSTRIES INC (PA)
Also Called: Advance Storage Products
15302 Pipeline Ln, Huntington Beach (92649-1138)
**PHONE**.................................714 902-9000
John Vr Krummell, Pr
Ken Blankenhorn, Pr
John Warren, CFO
▼ **EMP:** 21 **EST:** 1970
**SQ FT:** 10,000
**SALES (est):** 44.06MM
**SALES (corp-wide):** 44.06MM **Privately Held**
**Web:** www.advancestorageproducts.com
**SIC: 2542** Racks, merchandise display or storage: except wood

### (P-3693)
### JOHNS FORMICA INC
Also Called: John's Formica Shop
2439 Piner Rd, Santa Rosa (95403-2356)
**PHONE**.................................707 544-8585
John Deas, Pr
Ellen Deas, VP
**EMP:** 24 **EST:** 1966
**SQ FT:** 4,500
**SALES (est):** 5.65MM **Privately Held**
**Web:** www.johnsformicashop.com
**SIC: 2542** 2434 Counters or counter display cases, except wood; Wood kitchen cabinets

### (P-3694)
### K-JACK ENGINEERING CO INC
5672 Buckingham Dr, Huntington Beach (92649-1160)
P.O. Box 2320 (90249)
**PHONE**.................................310 327-8389
▲ **EMP:** 60 **EST:** 1963
**SALES (est):** 1.85MM **Privately Held**
**Web:** www.kjack.com
**SIC: 2542** Racks, merchandise display or storage: except wood

### (P-3695)
### LIBERTY DIVERSIFIED INTL INC
Also Called: Liberty Packaging
13100 Danielson St, Poway (92064-6840)
**PHONE**.................................858 391-7302
**EMP:** 245
**SALES (corp-wide):** 1.02B **Privately Held**
**Web:** www.libertydiversified.com
**SIC: 2542** 5112 3089 2952 Fixtures, office: except wood; Stationery and office supplies ; Plastics containers, except foam; Roofing materials
**PA:** Liberty Diversified International, Inc.
5600 Highway 169 N
763 536-6600

### (P-3696)
### LLC WALKER WEST
Also Called: Impac International
5500 Jurupa St, Ontario (91761-3668)
**PHONE**.................................800 767-9378
Kory Levoy, Brnch Mgr
**EMP:** 53
**Web:** www.premierenclosuresystems.com
**SIC: 2542** 3444 Cabinets: show, display, or storage: except wood; Sheet metalwork
**PA:** Walker West, Llc
1555 S Vintage Ave

### (P-3697)
### M3 PRODUCTS INC
Also Called: J Roberts Design
15134 Matisse Cir, La Mirada (90638-4738)
**PHONE**.................................626 371-1900
Heejung Yu, Pr
**EMP:** 20 **EST:** 1997
**SALES (est):** 229.7K **Privately Held**
**Web:** www.jrobertscorp.com
**SIC: 2542** Fixtures, store: except wood

### (P-3698)
### MSF INC
5763 Drakes Dr, Discovery Bay (94505-9381)
**PHONE**.................................650 592-0239
Sabino F Madariaga, Pr
Brian Madariaga, VP
Mike Jaca, VP
**EMP:** 16 **EST:** 1986
**SALES (est):** 426.12K **Privately Held**
**Web:** www.slaymakerchiropractic.com
**SIC: 2542** Partitions and fixtures, except wood

### (P-3699)
### ONQ SOLUTIONS INC (PA)
25821 Industrial Blvd, Hayward (94545-2996)
**PHONE**.................................650 351-4245
Paul Chapuis, CEO
Paul Chapuis, Pr
Jack Lester, *
**EMP:** 45 **EST:** 2007
**SALES (est):** 24.74MM **Privately Held**
**Web:** www.onqsolutions.com
**SIC: 2542** Stands, merchandise display: except wood

### (P-3700)
### PACIFIC MANUFACTURING MGT INC
Also Called: Greneker Solutions
3110 E 12th St, Los Angeles (90023-3616)
**PHONE**.................................323 263-9000
Erik Johnson, Pr
Steven Beckman, *
▲ **EMP:** 60 **EST:** 2003
**SQ FT:** 60,000
**SALES (est):** 4.63MM **Privately Held**
**Web:** www.greneker.com
**SIC: 2542** 2541 Fixtures: display, office, or store: except wood; Display fixtures, wood

### (P-3701)
### RACK INSTALLATION SERVICES INC
1256 Brooks St Ste E, Ontario (91762-3663)
**PHONE**.................................909 261-2243
Gabriel Caliana, CEO
**EMP:** 20 **EST:** 2018
**SALES (est):** 931.54K **Privately Held**
**SIC: 2542** 1796 Partitions and fixtures, except wood; Installing building equipment

### (P-3702)
### RAP SECURITY INC
4630 Cecilia St, Cudahy (90201-5814)
**PHONE**.................................323 560-3493
Angelo Palmer, Pr
Bob Palmer, *
◆ **EMP:** 55 **EST:** 1984
**SQ FT:** 40,000
**SALES (est):** 2.02MM **Privately Held**
**SIC: 2542** Fixtures, store: except wood

### (P-3703)
### RAPID RACK HOLDINGS INC
1370 Valley Vista Dr Ste 100, Diamond Bar (91765-3950)
**EMP:** 618
**Web:** www.rapidrack.com
**SIC: 2542** Postal lock boxes, mail racks, and related products

### (P-3704)
### RAPID RACK INDUSTRIES INC
1370 Valley Vista Dr Ste 100, Diamond Bar (91765-3911)
▲ **EMP:** 75
**SIC: 2542** Partitions and fixtures, except wood

### (P-3705)
### REEVE STORE EQUIPMENT COMPANY (PA)
9131 Bermudez St, Pico Rivera (90660-4507)
**PHONE**.................................562 949-2535
**TOLL FREE:** 800
John Frackelton, Pr
Robert Frackelton, *
Mary Ann Crysler, *
▲ **EMP:** 100 **EST:** 1932
**SQ FT:** 170,000
**SALES (est):** 16.22MM
**SALES (corp-wide):** 16.22MM **Privately Held**
**Web:** www.reeveco.com
**SIC: 2542** 3471 Counters or counter display cases, except wood; Electroplating of metals or formed products

### (P-3706)
### SALSBURY INDUSTRIES INC
1010 E 62nd St, Los Angeles (90001-1510)
**PHONE**.................................323 846-6700
**EMP:** 95
**Web:** www.salsburyindustries.com
**SIC: 2542** Locker boxes, postal service: except wood
**PA:** Salsbury Industries, Inc.
18300 Central Ave

### (P-3707)
### SALSBURY INDUSTRIES INC (PA)
Also Called: Salsbury Industries
18300 Central Ave, Carson (90746-4008)
**PHONE**.................................800 624-5269
**TOLL FREE:** 800
Dennis Fraher, Pr
Brian Fraher, VP
John Fraher, Ch
Michael N Lobasso, CFO
◆ **EMP:** 250 **EST:** 1936
**SQ FT:** 600,000
**SALES (est):** 94.73MM **Privately Held**
**Web:** www.mailboxes.com
**SIC: 2542** Locker boxes, postal service: except wood

### (P-3708)
### SPECTRUM INTL HOLDINGS
14421 Bonelli St, City Of Industry (91746-3021)
**PHONE**.................................626 333-7225

## PRODUCTS & SERVICES SECTION
### 2591 - Drapery Hardware And Blinds And Shades (P-3728)

Matthew Harrison, *Ch Bd*
Robert A Davies, *
**EMP:** 620 **EST:** 1997
**SALES (est):** 2.74MM **Privately Held**
**SIC:** 2542 Postal lock boxes, mail racks, and related products

**(P-3709)**
### STEVES PLATING CORPORATION
3111 N San Fernando Blvd, Burbank (91504-2527)
**PHONE**..................................818 842-2184
Terry Knezevich, *CEO*
Roger C Knezevich, *
**EMP:** 140 **EST:** 1956
**SQ FT:** 80,000
**SALES (est):** 2.21MM **Privately Held**
Web: www.stevesplating.com
**SIC:** 2542 3446 3471 7692 Fixtures, store: except wood; Ladders, for permanent installation: metal; Plating of metals or formed products; Welding repair

**(P-3710)**
### TEICHMAN ENTERPRISES INC
Also Called: T & H Store Fixtures
6100 Bandini Blvd, Commerce (90040-3112)
**PHONE**..................................323 278-9000
Ruth Teichman, *Pr*
Steve Teichman, *
Bernard Teichman, *
Sidney Teichman, *
Alan Teichman, *
▲ **EMP:** 50 **EST:** 1956
**SALES (est):** 5.16MM **Privately Held**
Web: www.teichman.net
**SIC:** 2542 Fixtures: display, office, or store: except wood

**(P-3711)**
### THE BOBRICK CORPORATION (PA)
6901 Tujunga Ave, North Hollywood (91605-6213)
**PHONE**..................................818 764-1000
◆ **EMP:** 100 **EST:** 1906
**SALES (est):** 132.97MM
**SALES (corp-wide):** 132.97MM **Privately Held**
Web: www.bobrick.com
**SIC:** 2542 Partitions for floor attachment, prefabricated: except wood

**(P-3712)**
### TURTLE STORAGE LTD
Also Called: American Bicycle Security Co
401 S Beckwith Rd, Santa Paula (93060-3047)
P.O. Box 7359 (93006-7359)
**PHONE**..................................805 933-3688
Thomas Volk, *CEO*
Thomas M Volk, *CEO*
Thomas Volk, *Pr*
**EMP:** 20 **EST:** 1986
**SQ FT:** 16,000
**SALES (est):** 4.97MM **Privately Held**
Web: www.ameribike.com
**SIC:** 2542 1799 Lockers (not refrigerated): except wood; Fiberglass work

**(P-3713)**
### UNIWEB INC (PA)
Also Called: Uniweb
222 S Promenade Ave, Corona (92879-1743)
**PHONE**..................................951 279-7999
Karl F Weber, *CEO*
▲ **EMP:** 90 **EST:** 1979

**SQ FT:** 170,000
**SALES (est):** 14.27MM
**SALES (corp-wide):** 14.27MM **Privately Held**
Web: www.uniwebinc.com
**SIC:** 2542 Fixtures: display, office, or store: except wood

**(P-3714)**
### WESTERN PCF STOR SOLUTIONS INC (PA)
300 E Arrow Hwy, San Dimas (91773-3339)
**PHONE**..................................909 451-0303
Tom Rogers, *Pr*
Peter G Dunn, *
Angie Bosley, *
Soheir Hakim, *
Paul Bautista, *
**EMP:** 100 **EST:** 1985
**SQ FT:** 165,000
**SALES (est):** 24.79MM
**SALES (corp-wide):** 24.79MM **Privately Held**
Web: www.wpss.com
**SIC:** 2542 Shelving, office and store, except wood

---

## 2591 Drapery Hardware And Blinds And Shades

**(P-3715)**
### ALL STRONG INDUSTRY (USA) INC (PA)
326 Paseo Tesoro, Walnut (91789-2725)
**PHONE**..................................909 598-6494
Pei-hsiang Hsu, *Ch Bd*
Frank Hsu, *
◆ **EMP:** 30 **EST:** 1992
**SQ FT:** 52,000
**SALES (est):** 7.29MM **Privately Held**
**SIC:** 2591 Mini blinds

**(P-3716)**
### BONDED WINDOW COVERINGS INC
7831 Ostrow St, San Diego (92111-3602)
P.O. Box 710130 (92171-0130)
**PHONE**..................................858 576-8400
Lee Howard Tandet, *Pr*
**EMP:** 21 **EST:** 1976
**SALES (est):** 459.64K **Privately Held**
Web: www.bondedwindowcoverings.com
**SIC:** 2591 Drapery hardware and window blinds and shades

**(P-3717)**
### CENTURY BLINDS INC
300 S Promenade Ave, Corona (92879-1754)
P.O. Box 77940 (92877-0131)
**PHONE**..................................951 734-3762
Mitch Shapiro, *CEO*
▲ **EMP:** 100 **EST:** 1992
**SALES (est):** 21.47MM **Privately Held**
Web: www.altawindowfashions.com
**SIC:** 2591 3429 5719 5023 Blinds vertical; Hardware, nec; Vertical blinds; Vertical blinds
HQ: Hunter Douglas Scandinavia Ab
Kristineholmsvagen 14a
AlingsAs 441 3
32277500

**(P-3718)**
### DIAMANTE WORLDWIDE INC
387 Magnolia Ave Ste 103, Corona (92879)
**PHONE**..................................714 822-7458
Adam Jurlin, *CEO*

Christina Olson, *Sec*
**EMP:** 17 **EST:** 2021
**SALES (est):** 2.72MM **Privately Held**
**SIC:** 2591 Drapery hardware and window blinds and shades

**(P-3719)**
### ELWIN INC
6910 8th St, Buena Park (90620-1036)
**PHONE**..................................714 752-6962
Josh W Kim, *CEO*
**EMP:** 20 **EST:** 2015
**SALES (est):** 1.75MM **Privately Held**
**SIC:** 2591 5719 Window blinds; Window shades, nec

**(P-3720)**
### HD WINDOW FASHIONS INC (DH)
Also Called: M & B Window Fashions
1818 Oak St, Los Angeles (90015-3302)
**PHONE**..................................213 749-6333
Wayne Gourlay, *Pr*
Dominique Au Yeung, *
▲ **EMP:** 500 **EST:** 1975
**SQ FT:** 200,000
**SALES (est):** 2.54MM **Privately Held**
**SIC:** 2591 Mini blinds
HQ: Hunter Douglas Inc.
1 Blue Hill Plz
Pearl River NY 10965
845 664-7000

**(P-3721)**
### HUNTER DOUGLAS INC
Hunter Douglas Contract
9900 Gidley St, El Monte (91731-1112)
**PHONE**..................................858 679-7500
Rich Ries, *Brnch Mgr*
**EMP:** 438
Web: www.hunterdouglasarchitectural.com
**SIC:** 2591 3446 Drapery hardware and window blinds and shades; Architectural metalwork
HQ: Hunter Douglas Inc.
1 Blue Hill Plz
Pearl River NY 10965
845 664-7000

**(P-3722)**
### JC WINDOW FASHIONS INC
Also Called: JC Window Fashions
2438 Peck Rd, Whittier (90601-1604)
**PHONE**..................................909 364-8888
Jennifer Chiao, *CEO*
▲ **EMP:** 28 **EST:** 2011
**SALES (est):** 4.79MM **Privately Held**
Web: www.jcwindowfashions.com
**SIC:** 2591 Drapery hardware and window blinds and shades

**(P-3723)**
### KITTRICH CORPORATION (PA)
1585 W Mission Blvd, Pomona (91766-1233)
**PHONE**..................................714 736-1000
Robert Friedland, *CEO*
◆ **EMP:** 130 **EST:** 1978
**SQ FT:** 237,000
**SALES (est):** 125.59MM
**SALES (corp-wide):** 125.59MM **Privately Held**
Web: www.kittrich.com
**SIC:** 2591 2392 2381 Blinds vertical; Household furnishings, nec; Fabric dress and work gloves

**(P-3724)**
### L C PRINGLE SALES INC (PA)
Also Called: Pringle's Draperies
12020 Western Ave, Garden Grove (92841-2913)
**PHONE**..................................714 892-1524
Larry C Pringle, *Pr*
Carolyn Pringle, *
Curtis L Pringle, *
Susan Pringle Kusinsky, *
Pamela Pringle Skinner, *
**EMP:** 30 **EST:** 1968
**SQ FT:** 11,000
**SALES (est):** 2.57MM
**SALES (corp-wide):** 2.57MM **Privately Held**
Web: www.pringlesdraperies.com
**SIC:** 2591 7216 2391 7211 Blinds vertical; Drapery, curtain drycleaning; Draperies, plastic and textile; from purchased materials; Power laundries, family and commercial

**(P-3725)**
### PHASE II PRODUCTS INC (PA)
Also Called: Phase II
16875 W Bernardo Dr, San Diego (92127-1675)
**PHONE**..................................619 236-9699
Charles Hunt, *CEO*
Gordon Peiper, *
John Bowie, *
▲ **EMP:** 18 **EST:** 1999
**SALES (est):** 7.23MM
**SALES (corp-wide):** 7.23MM **Privately Held**
Web: www.phaseii.com
**SIC:** 2591 Drapery hardware and window blinds and shades

**(P-3726)**
### ROBERSON CONSTRUCTION
Also Called: Architectural Window Shades
22 Central Ct, Pasadena (91105-2060)
P.O. Box 3286 (91731)
**PHONE**..................................626 578-1936
▲ **EMP:** 35
Web: www.openinfo.com
**SIC:** 2591 Window shades

**(P-3727)**
### ROLL-A-SHADE LLC (PA)
12101 Madera Way, Riverside (92503-4849)
**PHONE**..................................951 245-5077
Tyrone Pereira, *Pr*
Ric Berg, *VP*
◆ **EMP:** 22 **EST:** 1996
**SQ FT:** 10,000
**SALES (est):** 12.17MM **Privately Held**
Web: www.rollashade.com
**SIC:** 2591 1799 Window shades; Window treatment installation

**(P-3728)**
### SHEWARD & SON & SONS (PA)
Also Called: Solar Shading Systems
14352 Chambers Rd, Tustin (92780-6912)
**PHONE**..................................714 556-6055
▲ **EMP:** 25 **EST:** 1986
**SALES (est):** 5.21MM
**SALES (corp-wide):** 5.21MM **Privately Held**
Web: www.shewards.com
**SIC:** 2591 1799 2221 1752 Curtain and drapery rods, poles, and fixtures; Window treatment installation; Draperies and drapery fabrics, manmade fiber and silk; Carpet laying

## 2591 - Drapery Hardware And Blinds And Shades (P-3729)

**(P-3729)**
**SHOWDOGS INC**
Also Called: Wholesale Shade
168 S Pacific St, San Marcos (92078-2527)
PHONE................................760 603-3269
Patrick Howe, Pr
EMP: 30 EST: 2013
SQ FT: 10,000
SALES (est): 2.32MM **Privately Held**
Web: www.wholesaleshade.com
SIC: 2591 Blinds vertical

**(P-3730)**
**SOLEFFECT**
10125 Freeman Ave, Santa Fe Springs (90670-3407)
PHONE................................323 275-9945
EMP: 15 EST: 2019
SALES (est): 1.91MM **Privately Held**
Web: www.soleffectshades.com
SIC: 2591 Drapery hardware and window blinds and shades

---

## 2599 Furniture And Fixtures, Nec

**(P-3731)**
**1PERFECTCHOICE**
21908 Valley Blvd, Walnut (91789-0938)
PHONE................................909 594-8855
Chi Ching Lin, CEO
Brian Lin, CFO
EMP: 18 EST: 2014
SQ FT: 5,000
SALES (est): 862.96K **Privately Held**
Web: www.1perfectchoice.com
SIC: 2599 5021 5712 Hospital furniture, except beds; Furniture; Furniture stores

**(P-3732)**
**6TH STREET PARTNERS LLC**
3950 W 6th St 201, Los Angeles (90020-4251)
PHONE................................213 377-5277
EMP: 17 EST: 2015
SALES (est): 550.75K **Privately Held**
SIC: 2599 Bar, restaurant and cafeteria furniture

**(P-3733)**
**ALEGACY FDSRVICE PDTS GROUP IN**
Also Called: Alegacy
12683 Corral Pl, Santa Fe Springs (90670-4748)
PHONE................................562 320-3100
Jesse Gross, Prin
Brett Gross, *
Eric Gross, *
◆ EMP: 60 EST: 2000
SQ FT: 130,000
SALES (est): 9.66MM **Privately Held**
Web: www.alegacy.com
SIC: 2599 3263 Carts, restaurant equipment; Cookware, fine earthenware

**(P-3734)**
**ARTISTRY IN WOOD**
24350 Road 19, Chowchilla (93610-9577)
PHONE................................559 665-7171
Primitivo Nuno, Prin
EMP: 18 EST: 2010
SALES (est): 164.42K **Privately Held**
SIC: 2599 Furniture and fixtures, nec

**(P-3735)**
**COMMERCIAL CSTM STING UPHL INC**
12601 Western Ave, Garden Grove (92841-4014)
PHONE................................714 850-0520
Robert Francis, CEO
Lynn D.o.s., Sec
▲ EMP: 90 EST: 1988
SQ FT: 50,000
SALES (est): 21.05MM **Privately Held**
Web: www.ccs-ind.com
SIC: 2599 Restaurant furniture, wood or metal

**(P-3736)**
**DAVID HAID**
8619 Crocker St, Los Angeles (90003-3516)
PHONE................................323 752-8096
EMP: 20
Web: www.oasisimports.com
SIC: 2599 5199 Factory furniture and fixtures; Advertising specialties
PA: David Haid
3931 Topanga Canyon Blvd

**(P-3737)**
**EARLY MORNING INC**
2180 Golden Centre Ln Ste 100, Gold River (95670-4479)
PHONE................................916 871-9005
Louis Dedier, CEO
EMP: 35 EST: 2014
SALES (est): 306.55K **Privately Held**
SIC: 2599 Bar, restaurant and cafeteria furniture

**(P-3738)**
**ELEGANCE UPHOLSTERY INC**
11803 Slauson Ave Unit A, Ontario (91762)
PHONE................................562 698-2584
Ricardo Vargas, CEO
EMP: 16 EST: 2010
SALES (est): 2.03MM **Privately Held**
Web: www.eleganceupholsteryinc.com
SIC: 2599 7641 Bar, restaurant and cafeteria furniture; Reupholstery and furniture repair

**(P-3739)**
**ERGONOM CORPORATION (PA)**
Also Called: E R G International
361 Bernoulli Cir, Oxnard (93030-5164)
PHONE................................805 981-9978
George Zaki, CEO
Roy Zaki, *
▲ EMP: 90 EST: 1981
SALES (est): 24.86MM
SALES (corp-wide): 24.86MM **Privately Held**
Web: www.erginternational.com
SIC: 2599 2531 Hospital furniture, except beds; School furniture

**(P-3740)**
**ERGONOM CORPORATION**
Also Called: Erg International
390 Lombard St, Oxnard (93030-7209)
PHONE................................805 981-9978
Roy Zaki, Pr
EMP: 70
SALES (corp-wide): 24.86MM **Privately Held**
Web: www.erginternational.com
SIC: 2599 2531 Hospital furniture, except beds; School furniture
PA: Ergonom Corporation
361 Bernoulli Cir
805 981-9978

**(P-3741)**
**FORBES INDUSTRIES DIV**
1933 E Locust St, Ontario (91761-7608)
PHONE................................909 923-4559
Tim Sweetland, Pr
Peter Sweetland, *
▼ EMP: 210 EST: 1919
SQ FT: 110,000
SALES (est): 3.96MM
SALES (corp-wide): 48.01MM **Privately Held**
Web: www.forbesindustries.com
SIC: 2599 Carts, restaurant equipment
PA: The Winsford Corporation
1933 E Locust St
909 923-4559

**(P-3742)**
**FURY HOT CHICKEN LLC**
Also Called: Food and Beverage
3035 E Malaga Ave, Fresno (93725-9212)
PHONE................................559 944-8061
Marcel Mcalister, CEO
Marcel Mcalister, Managing Member
EMP: 15 EST: 2021
SALES (est): 1.02MM **Privately Held**
Web: www.furyhotchicken.com
SIC: 2599 7389 Food wagons, restaurant; Business services, nec

**(P-3743)**
**HARMONY INFINITE INC**
Also Called: Best Slip Cover Company
12918 Bloomfield St, Studio City (91604-1401)
EMP: 16 EST: 1986
SALES (est): 1.86MM **Privately Held**
SIC: 2599 Factory furniture and fixtures

**(P-3744)**
**HIRE ELEGANCE**
8333 Arjons Dr Ste E, San Diego (92126-6320)
PHONE................................858 740-7862
Stuart Simble, Prin
EMP: 17 EST: 2010
SALES (est): 4.69MM **Privately Held**
Web: www.hire-elegance.com
SIC: 2599 Furniture and fixtures, nec

**(P-3745)**
**I2K LLC**
Also Called: I2k Defense
748 N Mckeever Ave, Azusa (91702-2349)
PHONE................................626 788-0247
Stephen Gray, Managing Member
EMP: 20 EST: 2015
SALES (est): 347.39K **Privately Held**
Web: www.i2kairpad.com
SIC: 2599 Inflatable beds

**(P-3746)**
**JBI LLC (PA)**
Also Called: Jbi Interiors
2650 E El Presidio St, Long Beach (90810-1115)
PHONE................................310 886-8034
Pete Jensen, Music Manager
Bonnie Holt, *
Michael Buchbinder, *
Gregg Buchbinder, *
◆ EMP: 200 EST: 1968
SQ FT: 270,000
SALES (est): 54.78MM
SALES (corp-wide): 54.78MM **Privately Held**
Web: www.jbi-interiors.com
SIC: 2599 5046 Restaurant furniture, wood or metal; Restaurant equipment and supplies, nec

**(P-3747)**
**PTM IMAGES LLC**
555 W 5th St, Los Angeles (90013-2670)
PHONE................................310 881-8053
Jonathan Bass, Mgr
EMP: 15 EST: 1995
SALES (est): 908.11K **Privately Held**
Web: www.ptmmovers.com
SIC: 2599 Factory furniture and fixtures

**(P-3748)**
**R & J FABRICATORS INC**
1121 Railroad St Ste 102, Corona (92882-8219)
PHONE................................951 817-0300
James Ciarletta, CEO
Jay Warren Ciarletta, VP
EMP: 20 EST: 1982
SQ FT: 20,000
SALES (est): 2.52MM **Privately Held**
SIC: 2599 Restaurant furniture, wood or metal

**(P-3749)**
**ROTH WOOD PRODUCTS LTD**
2260 Canoas Garden Ave, San Jose (95125-2007)
PHONE................................408 723-8888
Robert E Roth, CEO
Marilyn Roth, *
EMP: 22 EST: 1974
SQ FT: 12,800
SALES (est): 4.59MM **Privately Held**
Web: www.rothwoodproducts.com
SIC: 2599 2434 Cabinets, factory; Wood kitchen cabinets

**(P-3750)**
**STAINLESS FIXTURES INC**
1250 E Franklin Ave, Pomona (91766-5449)
PHONE................................909 622-1615
Randy Rodriguez, Pr
EMP: 35 EST: 1989
SQ FT: 36,000
SALES (est): 1.63MM **Privately Held**
SIC: 2599 Restaurant furniture, wood or metal

**(P-3751)**
**TAHITI CABINETS INC**
5419 E La Palma Ave, Anaheim (92807-2022)
PHONE................................714 693-0618
Mark Ramsey, Pr
Doreen Ramsey, *
EMP: 58 EST: 1975
SQ FT: 32,000
SALES (est): 3.12MM **Privately Held**
Web: www.tahiticabinets.com
SIC: 2599 2431 2434 Cabinets, factory; Millwork; Wood kitchen cabinets

**(P-3752)**
**TRESTON IAC LLC**
8175 E Brookdale Ln, Anaheim (92807-2526)
PHONE................................714 990-8997
EMP: 28
Web: www.iacindustries.com
SIC: 2599 Bar furniture
HQ: Treston Iac Llc
3831 S Bullard Ave
Goodyear AZ 85338
714 989-5363

**(P-3753)**
**WESTERN MILL FABRICATORS INC**

670 S Jefferson St Ste B, Placentia (92870-6638)
PHONE..................714 993-3667
Kimball Boyack, *CEO*
**EMP:** 30 **EST:** 1987
**SALES (est):** 506.44K **Privately Held**
**Web:** www.wmfinc.com
**SIC: 2599** Bar, restaurant and cafeteria furniture

## 2611 Pulp Mills

### (P-3754)
### ARNA TRADING INC (PA)
Also Called: Simba Recycling
2892 S Santa Fe Ave Ste 109, San Marcos (92069-6022)
PHONE..................760 940-2775
Ash Shah, *Pr*
◆ **EMP:** 15 **EST:** 1992
**SQ FT:** 20,000
**SALES (est):** 2.48MM **Privately Held**
**SIC: 2611** Pulp mills, mechanical and recycling processing

### (P-3755)
### CENCAL RECYCLING LLC
501 Port Road 22, Stockton (95203-2909)
PHONE..................209 546-8000
Steve Sutta, *Managing Member*
**EMP:** 16 **EST:** 2004
**SQ FT:** 104,400
**SALES (est):** 2.23MM **Privately Held**
**Web:** www.cencalrecycling.com
**SIC: 2611** Pulp mills, mechanical and recycling processing

### (P-3756)
### EVERGREEN PAPER AND ENERGY LLC (PA)
Also Called: Evergreen-Energy
353 Rio Del Oro Ln, Sacramento (95825-6311)
PHONE..................802 357-1003
**EMP:** 64 **EST:** 1993
**SALES (est):** 1.78MM **Privately Held**
**SIC: 2611 2621** Pulp mills; Paper mills

### (P-3757)
### GO2ZERO STRATEGIES LLC
6625 N Calle Eva Miranda Ste A, Irwindale (91702-2870)
PHONE..................626 840-1850
Judi Gregory, *Brnch Mgr*
**EMP:** 15
**SALES (corp-wide):** 3.42MM **Privately Held**
**Web:** www.go2zero.net
**SIC: 2611** Pulp mills, mechanical and recycling processing
**PA:** Go2zero Strategies, Llc
   6625 N Calle Eva Miranda
   877 462-9376

### (P-3758)
### NEW GREEN DAY LLC
1710 E 111th St, Los Angeles (90059-1910)
P.O. Box 72147 (90002-0147)
PHONE..................323 566-7603
Brian Kelly, *CEO*
David Holt, *
Kirk Sanford, *Managing Member**
Daniel Montoya, *
Randi Yamamoto, *
**EMP:** 25 **EST:** 2004
**SQ FT:** 25,000
**SALES (est):** 5.06MM **Privately Held**
**Web:** www.ngdla.com

**SIC: 2611** Pulp manufactured from waste or recycled paper

## 2621 Paper Mills

### (P-3759)
### ACME UNITED CORPORATION
630 Young St, Santa Ana (92705-5633)
PHONE..................714 557-2001
**EMP:** 22
**SALES (corp-wide):** 191.5MM **Publicly Held**
**Web:** www.acmeunited.com
**SIC: 2621** Absorbent paper
**PA:** Acme United Corporation
   1 Waterview Dr Ste 200
   203 254-6060

### (P-3760)
### ALLIED WEST PAPER CORP
11101 Etiwanda Ave Unit 100, Fontana (92337-6986)
PHONE..................909 349-0710
Ray Ovanessian, *CEO*
Mike Ovanessian, *
Eric Ovanessian, *
◆ **EMP:** 95 **EST:** 1989
**SQ FT:** 300,000
**SALES (est):** 40.47MM **Privately Held**
**Web:** www.alliedwestpaper.com
**SIC: 2621** Paper mills

### (P-3761)
### BOISE CASCADE COMPANY
3221 Hutchison Ave, Los Angeles (90034-3246)
PHONE..................310 815-2200
Paul Hurty, *Brnch Mgr*
**EMP:** 19
**SALES (corp-wide):** 8.39B **Publicly Held**
**Web:** www.bc.com
**SIC: 2621** Paper mills
**PA:** Boise Cascade Company
   1111 W Jffrson St Ste 300
   208 384-6161

### (P-3762)
### BOISE CASCADE COMPANY
Also Called: Boise Cascade
12030 S Harlan Rd, Lathrop (95330-8768)
PHONE..................209 983-4114
Brad Terrell, *Brnch Mgr*
**EMP:** 192
**SALES (corp-wide):** 8.39B **Publicly Held**
**Web:** www.bc.com
**SIC: 2621 2679** Paper mills; Building paper, laminated: made from purchased material
**PA:** Boise Cascade Company
   1111 W Jffrson St Ste 300
   208 384-6161

### (P-3763)
### BRISTOL MANAGEMENT SVCS INC
4621 Teller Ave Ste 130, Newport Beach (92660-2165)
PHONE..................714 267-7346
Kurt Caillier, *CEO*
**EMP:** 17 **EST:** 2022
**SALES (est):** 6.06MM **Privately Held**
**Web:** www.bristolmsi.com
**SIC: 2621** Bristols

### (P-3764)
### CROWN PAPER CONVERTING INC
Also Called: Crown Paper Converting
1380 S Bon View Ave, Ontario (91761-4403)

P.O. Box 3277 (91761-0928)
PHONE..................909 923-5226
Bruce Hale, *Prin*
Lisa Hale, *
**EMP:** 40 **EST:** 1983
**SQ FT:** 34,000
**SALES (est):** 1.8MM **Privately Held**
**Web:** www.crownpaperconverting.com
**SIC: 2621** Paper mills

### (P-3765)
### D D OFFICE PRODUCTS INC
Also Called: Liberty Paper
5025 Hampton St, Los Angeles (90058-2133)
P.O. Box 58026 (90058-0026)
PHONE..................323 582-3400
Alex Ismail, *CEO*
Anwar Lalani, *Pr*
Benazir Ismael, *CFO*
▲ **EMP:** 15 **EST:** 1986
**SQ FT:** 22,000
**SALES (est):** 11.14MM **Privately Held**
**Web:** www.libertypp.com
**SIC: 2621 5112 5044 5045** Printing paper; Stationery and office supplies; Office equipment; Computers and accessories, personal and home entertainment

### (P-3766)
### DOCUMENT PROC SOLUTIONS INC
535 Main St Ste 317, Martinez (94553-1102)
PHONE..................925 839-1182
**EMP:** 35
**SALES (corp-wide):** 4.87MM **Privately Held**
**Web:** www.perfectdomain.com
**SIC: 2621** Paper mills
**PA:** Document Processing Solutions, Inc.
   590 W Lambert Rd
   714 482-2060

### (P-3767)
### DYNAMIC RESOURCES INC
7894 Dagget St Ste 202e, San Diego (92111-2323)
PHONE..................619 268-3070
Kwang Kim, *CFO*
Cheong Won Bae, *CEO*
**EMP:** 60 **EST:** 2010
**SQ FT:** 9,000
**SALES (est):** 769.86K **Privately Held**
**Web:** www.dynamicresources.biz
**SIC: 2621 2672** Lithograph paper; Adhesive papers, labels, or tapes: from purchased material

### (P-3768)
### ENVELOPMENTS INC
13091 Sandhurst Pl, Santa Ana (92705-2135)
PHONE..................714 569-3300
Mark A Smith, *CEO*
Holly Jakobs, *
Deborah Hefter, *
▲ **EMP:** 39 **EST:** 1993
**SALES (est):** 3.56MM **Privately Held**
**Web:** www.envelopments.com
**SIC: 2621 5112** Stationary, envelope and tablet papers; Stationery

### (P-3769)
### FRINGE STUDIO LLC
6029 W Slauson Ave, Culver City (90230-6507)
P.O. Box 3663 (90230)
PHONE..................310 390-9900
Scott Kingsland, *Managing Member*

▲ **EMP:** 30 **EST:** 2004
**SALES (est):** 4.94MM **Privately Held**
**Web:** www.fringestudio.com
**SIC: 2621 3999** Stationary, envelope and tablet papers; Pet supplies
**PA:** Punch Studio, Llc
   6025 W Slauson Ave

### (P-3770)
### GEORGIA-PACIFIC LLC
Also Called: Georgia-Pacific
1988 Marina Blvd, San Leandro (94577-3207)
PHONE..................510 483-7580
Fred Curcio, *Brnch Mgr*
**EMP:** 50
**SALES (corp-wide):** 64.37B **Privately Held**
**Web:** www.gp.com
**SIC: 2621 3275** Paper mills; Gypsum products
**HQ:** Georgia-Pacific Llc
   133 Peachtree St Nw
   Atlanta GA 30303
   404 652-4000

### (P-3771)
### HARVARD LABEL LLC
Also Called: Harvard Card Systems
111 Baldwin Park Blvd, City Of Industry (91746-1402)
PHONE..................626 333-8881
Michael Tang, *CEO*
David Banducci, *
▲ **EMP:** 115 **EST:** 1996
**SQ FT:** 125,000
**SALES (est):** 24.81MM **Privately Held**
**SIC: 2621 2675 2752** Greeting card paper; Stencil cards, die-cut: made from purchased materials; Cards, lithographed
**PA:** Plasticard - Locktech International, Llc
   1220 Trade Dr

### (P-3772)
### INTERNATIONAL PAPER COMPANY
Also Called: International Paper
42305 Albrae St, Fremont (94538-3392)
PHONE..................510 490-5887
Jay Casos, *Mgr*
**EMP:** 53
**SQ FT:** 60,805
**SALES (corp-wide):** 18.92B **Publicly Held**
**Web:** www.internationalpaper.com
**SIC: 2621** Paper mills
**PA:** International Paper Company
   6400 Poplar Ave
   901 419-7000

### (P-3773)
### INTERNATIONAL PAPER COMPANY
International Paper
601 E Ball Rd, Anaheim (92805-5910)
PHONE..................714 776-6060
Terry Tockey, *Brnch Mgr*
**EMP:** 117
**SALES (corp-wide):** 18.92B **Publicly Held**
**Web:** www.internationalpaper.com
**SIC: 2621** Paper mills
**PA:** International Paper Company
   6400 Poplar Ave
   901 419-7000

### (P-3774)
### INTERNATIONAL PAPER COMPANY
Also Called: International Paper
1111 N Anderson Rd, Exeter (93221-9370)
PHONE..................559 592-7279

## 2621 - Paper Mills (P-3775)

Rick Goddard, *Genl Mgr*
**EMP:** 60
**SALES (corp-wide):** 18.92B **Publicly Held**
**Web:** www.internationalpaper.com
**SIC:** 2621 Paper mills
**PA:** International Paper Company
6400 Poplar Ave
901 419-7000

### (P-3775)
### INTERNATIONAL PAPER COMPANY
Also Called: International Paper
10268 Waterman Rd, Elk Grove (95624-9403)
**PHONE**.................916 685-9000
Dave Carpenter, *Brnch Mgr*
**EMP:** 52
**SALES (corp-wide):** 18.92B **Publicly Held**
**Web:** www.internationalpaper.com
**SIC:** 2621 Paper mills
**PA:** International Paper Company
6400 Poplar Ave
901 419-7000

### (P-3776)
### INTERNATIONAL PAPER COMPANY
Also Called: International Paper
2000 Pleasant Valley Rd, Camarillo (93010-8543)
**PHONE**.................805 933-4347
**EMP:** 22
**SALES (corp-wide):** 18.92B **Publicly Held**
**Web:** www.internationalpaper.com
**SIC:** 2621 Paper mills
**PA:** International Paper Company
6400 Poplar Ave
901 419-7000

### (P-3777)
### INTERNATIONAL PAPER COMPANY
Also Called: International Paper
19615 S Susana Rd, Compton (90221-5717)
**PHONE**.................310 639-2310
Joseph Winters, *Genl Mgr*
**EMP:** 38
**SALES (corp-wide):** 18.92B **Publicly Held**
**Web:** www.internationalpaper.com
**SIC:** 2621 Paper mills
**PA:** International Paper Company
6400 Poplar Ave
901 419-7000

### (P-3778)
### INTERNATIONAL PAPER COMPANY
Also Called: International Paper
1000 Muscat Ave, Sanger (93657-4001)
**PHONE**.................559 875-3311
**EMP:** 64
**SALES (corp-wide):** 18.92B **Publicly Held**
**Web:** www.internationalpaper.com
**SIC:** 2621 Paper mills
**PA:** International Paper Company
6400 Poplar Ave
901 419-7000

### (P-3779)
### INTERNATIONAL PAPER COMPANY
Also Called: International Paper
1345 Harkins Rd, Salinas (93901-4408)
**PHONE**.................831 755-2100
**EMP:** 45
**SALES (corp-wide):** 18.92B **Publicly Held**
**Web:** www.internationalpaper.com
**SIC:** 2621 Paper mills
**PA:** International Paper Company
6400 Poplar Ave
901 419-7000

### (P-3780)
### INTERNATIONAL PAPER COMPANY
Also Called: International Paper
6400 Jamieson Way, Gilroy (95020-6620)
**PHONE**.................408 847-6400
Michael Hayford, *Brnch Mgr*
**EMP:** 104
**SALES (corp-wide):** 18.92B **Publicly Held**
**Web:** www.internationalpaper.com
**SIC:** 2621 Paper mills
**PA:** International Paper Company
6400 Poplar Ave
901 419-7000

### (P-3781)
### INTERNATIONAL PAPER COMPANY
International Paper
1714 Cebrian St, West Sacramento (95691-3819)
**PHONE**.................916 371-4634
Clark Weiss, *Opers Mgr*
**EMP:** 62
**SALES (corp-wide):** 18.92B **Publicly Held**
**Web:** www.internationalpaper.com
**SIC:** 2621 Paper mills
**PA:** International Paper Company
6400 Poplar Ave
901 419-7000

### (P-3782)
### INTERNATIONAL PAPER COMPANY
Also Called: International Paper
9211 Norwalk Blvd, Santa Fe Springs (90670-2923)
**PHONE**.................562 692-9465
Lee Bekiarian, *Brnch Mgr*
**EMP:** 64
**SALES (corp-wide):** 18.92B **Publicly Held**
**Web:** www.internationalpaper.com
**SIC:** 2621 Paper mills
**PA:** International Paper Company
6400 Poplar Ave
901 419-7000

### (P-3783)
### INTERNATIONAL PAPER COMPANY
Also Called: International Paper
1350 E 223rd St, Carson (90745-4381)
**PHONE**.................310 549-5525
Melanie Kastner, *Brnch Mgr*
**EMP:** 66
**SALES (corp-wide):** 18.92B **Publicly Held**
**Web:** www.internationalpaper.com
**SIC:** 2621 Paper mills
**PA:** International Paper Company
6400 Poplar Ave
901 419-7000

### (P-3784)
### INTERNATIONAL PAPER COMPANY
Also Called: International Paper
6791 Alexander St, Gilroy (95020-6679)
**PHONE**.................408 846-2060
David Washer, *Genl Mgr*
**EMP:** 26
**SALES (corp-wide):** 18.92B **Publicly Held**
**Web:** www.internationalpaper.com
**SIC:** 2621 Printing paper
**PA:** International Paper Company
6400 Poplar Ave
901 419-7000

### (P-3785)
### LD PRODUCTS INC
Also Called: 4inkjets
2501 E 28th St, Signal Hill (90755-2138)
**PHONE**.................888 321-2552
Aaron Leon, *CEO*
Patrick Devane, *
◆ **EMP:** 193 **EST:** 1999
**SALES (est):** 36.58MM **Privately Held**
**Web:** www.ldproducts.com
**SIC:** 2621 5045 Stationary, envelope and tablet papers; Printers, computer

### (P-3786)
### NAKAGAWA MANUFACTURING USA INC
1709 Junction Ct, San Jose (95112-1044)
**PHONE**.................510 782-0197
Yuzuru Isshiki, *CEO*
Tetsuya Isshiki, *
Shinji Aoki, *
◆ **EMP:** 40 **EST:** 1987
**SALES (est):** 9.17MM **Privately Held**
**Web:** www.nakagawa-usa.com
**SIC:** 2621 Specialty papers
**HQ:** Nakagawa Mfg.Co., Ltd.
2-5-21, Nishikicho
Warabi STM 335-0

### (P-3787)
### NEW-INDY CONTAINERBOARD LLC (DH)
Also Called: International Paper
3500 Porsche Way Ste 150, Ontario (91764-4969)
P.O. Box 519 (93044-0519)
**PHONE**.................909 296-3400
Richard Hartman, *CEO*
Mike Conkey, *
▲ **EMP:** 95 **EST:** 2012
**SALES (est):** 319.18MM
**SALES (corp-wide):** 586.01MM **Privately Held**
**Web:** www.newindycontainerboard.com
**SIC:** 2621 Paper mills
**HQ:** New-Indy Containerboard Hold Co Llc
1 Patriot Pl
Foxborough MA 02035

### (P-3788)
### NEW-INDY ONTARIO LLC
Also Called: New-Indy Containerboard
5100 Jurupa St, Ontario (91761-3618)
**PHONE**.................909 390-1055
Richard Hartman, *CEO*
Mike Conkey, *
**EMP:** 110 **EST:** 2012
**SALES (est):** 56.01MM
**SALES (corp-wide):** 586.01MM **Privately Held**
**Web:** www.newindycontainerboard.com
**SIC:** 2621 Paper mills
**HQ:** New-Indy Containerboard Llc
3500 Porsche Wy Ste 150
Ontario CA 91764
909 296-3400

### (P-3789)
### NEW-INDY OXNARD LLC
Also Called: New-Indy Containerboard
5936 Perkins Rd, Oxnard (93033-9044)
P.O. Box 519 (93044-0519)
**PHONE**.................805 986-3881
Richard Hartman, *CEO*
Mike Conkey, *
▲ **EMP:** 224 **EST:** 2012
**SALES (est):** 18.14MM
**SALES (corp-wide):** 586.01MM **Privately Held**
**Web:** www.newindycontainerboard.com
**SIC:** 2621 Paper mills
**HQ:** New-Indy Containerboard Llc
3500 Porsche Wy Ste 150
Ontario CA 91764
909 296-3400

### (P-3790)
### OEM MATERIALS & SUPPLIES INC
Also Called: OEM Materials
1500 Ritchey St, Santa Ana (92705-4731)
**PHONE**.................714 564-9600
Wendy King, *CEO*
Randall K Johnson, *Pr*
Michael Cavazos, *Acctg Mgr*
Gloria Montoya, *Acctnt*
**EMP:** 20 **EST:** 2008
**SALES (est):** 9.6MM **Privately Held**
**Web:** www.oemmaterials.com
**SIC:** 2621 2631 5084 2671 Wrapping and packaging papers; Container, packaging, and boxboard; Processing and packaging equipment; Paper; coated and laminated packaging

### (P-3791)
### PACON INC
4249 Puente Ave, Baldwin Park (91706-3420)
**PHONE**.................626 814-4654
Robert M Austin, *CEO*
Michael Austin, *
◆ **EMP:** 103 **EST:** 1977
**SQ FT:** 44,000
**SALES (est):** 20.6MM **Privately Held**
**Web:** www.paconinc.com
**SIC:** 2621 Paper mills

### (P-3792)
### PAPER PROCESSORS INC
Also Called: P P I
2583 Mercantile Dr, Rancho Cordova (95742-6217)
P.O. Box 1893 (95741-1893)
**EMP:** 35 **EST:** 1984
**SQ FT:** 94,600
**SALES (est):** 1.4MM **Privately Held**
**Web:** www.paperprocessorsinc.com
**SIC:** 2621 Paper mills

### (P-3793)
### PAPER SURCE CONVERTING MFG INC
Also Called: Soft-Touch Tissue
4800 S Santa Fe Ave, Vernon (90058-2104)
**PHONE**.................323 583-3800
Jacob Khobian, *CEO*
Jonathan Khodabakhsh, *
Fery Khodabakhsh, *
▲ **EMP:** 50 **EST:** 1996
**SQ FT:** 55,000
**SALES (est):** 24.53MM **Privately Held**
**Web:** www.papersourcemfg.com
**SIC:** 2621 Tissue paper

### (P-3794)
### PRATT INDUSTRIES INC
2131 E Louise Ave, Lathrop (95330-9607)
**PHONE**.................770 922-0117
Ron Mccomas, *Genl Mgr*
**EMP:** 110
**Web:** www.prattindustries.com
**SIC:** 2621 Packaging paper
**PA:** Pratt Industries, Inc.
4004 Smmit Blvd Ne Ste 10

**(P-3795)**
**SAN DIEGO DAILY TRANSCRIPT**
Also Called: Daily Transcript
34 Emerald Gln, Laguna Niguel
(92677-9379)
P.O. Box 85469 (92186-5469)
PHONE...................................619 232-4381
Ed Frederickson, Pr
EMP: 63 EST: 1886
SQ FT: 30,000
SALES (est): 2.88MM
SALES (corp-wide): 3.92MM Privately Held
SIC: 2621 4813 Printing paper; Online service providers
PA: Calcomco, Inc.
5544 S Red Pine Cir
313 885-9228

**(P-3796)**
**SAPPI NORTH AMERICA INC**
21700 Copley Dr Ste 165, Diamond Bar (91765-4434)
PHONE...................................714 456-0600
Brent Demichael, Brnch Mgr
EMP: 44
Web: www.sappi.com
SIC: 2621 Paper mills
HQ: Sappi North America, Inc.
255 State St Ste 4
Boston MA 02109
617 423-7300

**(P-3797)**
**SOLUT INC**
4645 North Ave Ste 102, Oceanside (92056-3593)
PHONE...................................760 758-7240
EMP: 43
Web: www.gosolut.com
SIC: 2621 2656 Packaging paper; Sanitary food containers
PA: Solut , Inc.
7787 Graphics Way

**(P-3798)**
**SPECIALTY PAPER MILLS INC**
8844 Millergrove Dr, Santa Fe Springs (90670-2004)
P.O. Box 3188 (90670-0188)
PHONE...................................562 692-8737
Ronald Gabriel, Pr
Aldo De Soto, *
Agnes Gabriel, *
EMP: 200 EST: 1959
SQ FT: 45,000
SALES (est): 2.42MM
SALES (corp-wide): 15.93MM Privately Held
Web: www.gabrielcontainer.com
SIC: 2621 2631 Paper mills; Paperboard mills
PA: Gabriel Container
8844 Millergrove Dr
562 699-1051

**(P-3799)**
**SPILL MAGIC INC**
630 Young St, Santa Ana (92705-5633)
PHONE...................................714 557-2001
Susan Wampler, Pr
David Wampler, VP
▲ EMP: 22 EST: 1995
SQ FT: 30,000
SALES (est): 5.42MM
SALES (corp-wide): 191.5MM Publicly Held
Web: www.firstaidonly.com
SIC: 2621 Absorbent paper
PA: Acme United Corporation
1 Waterview Dr Ste 200

203 254-6060

## 2631 Paperboard Mills

**(P-3800)**
**CALIFRNIA TRADE CONVERTERS INC**
9816 Variel Ave, Chatsworth (91311-4316)
PHONE...................................818 899-1455
Carlos Martinez, Pr
EMP: 25 EST: 1997
SALES (est): 2.02MM Privately Held
SIC: 2631 2675 Paperboard mills; Paper die-cutting

**(P-3801)**
**CARAUSTAR INDUSTRIES INC**
4502 E Airport Dr, Ontario (91761-7820)
PHONE...................................951 685-5544
D Wever Paul Potter, Mgr
EMP: 21
SALES (corp-wide): 5.22B Publicly Held
Web: www.greif.com
SIC: 2631 Paperboard mills
HQ: Caraustar Industries, Inc.
5000 Astell Pwdr Sprng Rd
Austell GA 30106
770 948-3101

**(P-3802)**
**EASTWEST CONTAINER GROUP INC**
5521 Schaefer Ave, Chino (91710-9070)
PHONE...................................626 523-1523
Nongwang Lai, CEO
Jialin Wu, CFO
EMP: 20 EST: 2019
SALES (est): 2.01MM Privately Held
Web: www.2eastwest.com
SIC: 2631 Container, packaging, and boxboard

**(P-3803)**
**INTERNATIONAL PAPER COMPANY**
Also Called: International Paper
660 Mariposa Rd, Modesto (95354-4130)
P.O. Box 3171 (95353-3171)
PHONE...................................209 526-4700
Rick Fritz, Brnch Mgr
EMP: 165
SQ FT: 165,196
SALES (corp-wide): 18.92B Publicly Held
Web: www.internationalpaper.com
SIC: 2631 2653 Corrugating medium; Corrugated and solid fiber boxes
PA: International Paper Company
6400 Poplar Ave
901 419-7000

**(P-3804)**
**MAXCO SUPPLY INC**
2059 E Olsen Ave, Reedley (93654)
P.O. Box 814 (93648-0814)
PHONE...................................559 638-8449
Roy Ortega, Mgr
EMP: 101
SQ FT: 50,550
SALES (corp-wide): 103.6MM Privately Held
Web: www.maxcopackaging.com
SIC: 2631 Cardboard
PA: Maxco Supply, Inc.
605 S Zediker
559 646-8449

**(P-3805)**
**ONE UP MANUFACTURING LLC**
550 E Airline Way, Gardena (90248-2502)
PHONE...................................310 749-8347
Nielson Ballon, Managing Member
Kavish Mehta, *
Nathan Miller, *
EMP: 25 EST: 2017
SALES (est): 3.46MM Privately Held
SIC: 2631 Container, packaging, and boxboard

**(P-3806)**
**PREFERRED PRINTING & PACKAGING INC**
1493 E Philadelphia St, Ontario (91761-5729)
PHONE...................................909 923-2053
EMP: 30 EST: 1991
SALES (est): 4.99MM Privately Held
Web: www.preferredpnp.com
SIC: 2631 Folding boxboard

**(P-3807)**
**SONOCO PRODUCTS COMPANY**
Also Called: Sonoco Industrial Products Div
166 Baldwin Park Blvd, City Of Industry (91746-1498)
PHONE...................................626 369-6611
Dhamo Srinivasan, Mgr
EMP: 93
SALES (corp-wide): 6.78B Publicly Held
Web: www.sonoco.com
SIC: 2631 2611 Paperboard mills; Pulp mills
PA: Sonoco Products Company
1 N 2nd St
843 383-7000

**(P-3808)**
**SONOCO PRODUCTS COMPANY**
12851 Leyva St, Norwalk (90650-6853)
PHONE...................................562 921-0881
Jeff Blaine, Mgr
EMP: 63
SQ FT: 164,934
SALES (corp-wide): 6.78B Publicly Held
Web: www.sonoco.com
SIC: 2631 2655 Paperboard mills; Fiber cans, drums, and similar products
PA: Sonoco Products Company
1 N 2nd St
843 383-7000

**(P-3809)**
**TAYLORD PRODUCTS INTL INC (PA)**
4505 Lister St, San Diego (92110-3333)
PHONE...................................619 247-6544
Adela S Taylor, CEO
Thomas N Taylor, Pr
EMP: 155 EST: 1990
SALES (est): 4.19MM
SALES (corp-wide): 4.19MM Privately Held
SIC: 2631 Container, packaging, and boxboard

**(P-3810)**
**UNION CARBIDE CORPORATION**
19206 Hawthorne Blvd, Torrance (90503-1590)
PHONE...................................310 214-5300
Patrick E Gottschalk, Prin
EMP: 34
SQ FT: 15,269
SALES (corp-wide): 44.62B Publicly Held
Web: www.unioncarbide.com
SIC: 2631 Latex board
HQ: Union Carbide Corporation
7501 State Hwy 185 N
Seadrift TX 77983
361 553-2997

**(P-3811)**
**WRKCO INC**
1025 W 190th St Ste 450, Gardena (90248-4339)
PHONE...................................310 532-8988
EMP: 32
SIC: 2631 Paperboard mills
HQ: Wrkco Inc.
1000 Abrnthy Rd Ne Ste 12
Atlanta GA 30328
770 448-2193

**(P-3812)**
**WRKCO INC**
14103 Borate St, Santa Fe Springs (90670-5342)
PHONE...................................770 448-2193
EMP: 27
SIC: 2631 Paperboard mills
HQ: Wrkco Inc.
1000 Abrnthy Rd Ne Ste 12
Atlanta GA 30328
770 448-2193

**(P-3813)**
**ZAPP PACKAGING INC**
1921 S Business Pkwy, Ontario (91761-8539)
PHONE...................................909 930-1500
Vincent Randazzo, CEO
William L Finn, *
Bruce Altshuler, *
▲ EMP: 60 EST: 1931
SQ FT: 80,000
SALES (est): 9.15MM Privately Held
Web: www.autajon.com
SIC: 2631 Folding boxboard

## 2652 Setup Paperboard Boxes

**(P-3814)**
**CUSTOM PAPER PRODUCTS LP**
2360 Teagarden St, San Leandro (94577-4341)
PHONE...................................510 352-6880
Robert W Field Junior, Pr
Peggy Field, Stockholder*
R E Birtel, Stockholder*
Kendall Field, Stockholder*
EMP: 70 EST: 1950
SQ FT: 100,000
SALES (est): 9.46MM Privately Held
Web: www.custompaperproducts.com
SIC: 2652 3089 Filing boxes, paperboard: made from purchased materials; Boxes, plastics

**(P-3815)**
**MOZAIK LLC**
245 W Carl Karcher Way, Anaheim (92801-2499)
PHONE...................................562 207-1900
Sharon Carton Ctrl, Prin
▲ EMP: 24 EST: 2006
SQ FT: 27,000
SALES (est): 8.12MM Privately Held
Web: www.mozaik.net
SIC: 2652 Filing boxes, paperboard: made from purchased materials

**(P-3816)**
**WESTROCK RKT LLC**
1854 E Home Ave, Fresno (93703-3636)
PHONE...................................559 441-1181

# 2653 - Corrugated And Solid Fiber Boxes (P-3817)

Wes Gentles, *Genl Mgr*
**EMP:** 151
**SQ FT:** 50,000
**Web:** www.westrock.com
**SIC: 2652** 2631 Setup paperboard boxes; Paperboard mills
**HQ:** Westrock Rkt, Llc
  1000 Abernathy Rd Ste 125
  Atlanta GA 30328
  770 448-2193

## 2653 Corrugated And Solid Fiber Boxes

### (P-3817)
### ABEX DISPLAY SYSTEMS INC (PA)
Also Called: Abex Exhibit Systems
355 Parkside Dr, San Fernando (91340-3036)
**PHONE**.................................800 537-0231
Robbie Blumenfeld, *Pr*
Max Candiotty, *
◆ **EMP:** 105 **EST:** 1982
**SQ FT:** 85,000
**SALES (est):** 2.78MM
**SALES (corp-wide):** 2.78MM **Privately Held**
**Web:** www.abex.com
**SIC: 2653** 2541 Display items, solid fiber: made from purchased materials; Store and office display cases and fixtures

### (P-3818)
### ADVANCE PAPER BOX COMPANY
Also Called: Packaging Spectrum
6100 S Gramercy Pl, Los Angeles (90047-1397)
**PHONE**.................................323 750-2550
Martin Gardner, *CEO*
Martin Gardner, *Pr*
Nick Silk, *
Carlo Mendoza, *
Devan Gardner, *
▲ **EMP:** 250 **EST:** 1924
**SQ FT:** 500,000
**SALES (est):** 23.18MM **Privately Held**
**Web:** www.advancepaperbox.com
**SIC: 2653** 3082 2657 Boxes, corrugated: made from purchased materials; Unsupported plastics profile shapes; Folding paperboard boxes

### (P-3819)
### ANDROP PACKAGING INC
Also Called: Ontario Foam Products
4400 E Francis St, Ontario (91761-2327)
**PHONE**.................................909 605-8842
Cesar Flores, *Pr*
▲ **EMP:** 23 **EST:** 1974
**SQ FT:** 52,000
**SALES (est):** 8.63MM **Privately Held**
**Web:** www.androppkg.com
**SIC: 2653** 3086 Boxes, corrugated: made from purchased materials; Plastics foam products

### (P-3820)
### BAY CITIES CONTAINER CORP (PA)
Also Called: Bay Cities Packaging & Design
5138 Industry Ave, Pico Rivera (90660-2550)
**PHONE**.................................562 948-3751
Greg A Tucker, *CEO*
Patrick Donohoe, *
Michael Musgrave, *
▲ **EMP:** 96 **EST:** 1956

**SALES (est):** 150.82MM
**SALES (corp-wide):** 150.82MM **Privately Held**
**Web:** www.bay-cities.com
**SIC: 2653** 3993 5113 Boxes, corrugated: made from purchased materials; Signs and advertising specialties; Corrugated and solid fiber boxes

### (P-3821)
### BAY CITIES CONTAINER CORP
9206 Santa Fe Springs Rd, Santa Fe Springs (90670-2618)
**PHONE**.................................562 302-2552
**EMP:** 18
**SALES (corp-wide):** 150.82MM **Privately Held**
**Web:** www.bay-cities.com
**SIC: 2653** Boxes, corrugated: made from purchased materials
**PA:** Bay Cities Container Corp
  5138 Industry Ave Frnt
  562 948-3751

### (P-3822)
### BLOWER-DEMPSAY CORPORATION (PA)
Also Called: Pak West Paper & Packaging
4042 W Garry Ave, Santa Ana (92704-6300)
**PHONE**.................................714 481-3800
James Blower, *Pr*
Linda Dempsay, *
Serge Poirier, *
▲ **EMP:** 217 **EST:** 1973
**SQ FT:** 190,000
**SALES (est):** 107.24MM
**SALES (corp-wide):** 107.24MM **Privately Held**
**Web:** pakwest.blowerdempsay.com
**SIC: 2653** Boxes, corrugated: made from purchased materials

### (P-3823)
### BLUE RIBBON CONT & DISPLAY INC
5450 Dobbs Ave, Buena Park (90621)
**PHONE**.................................562 944-1217
Kenneth G Overfield, *Pr*
**EMP:** 22 **EST:** 1991
**SQ FT:** 32,000
**SALES (est):** 2.8MM **Privately Held**
**Web:** www.brcbox.com
**SIC: 2653** 5199 5113 2621 Boxes, corrugated: made from purchased materials; Packaging materials; Boxes and containers; Paper mills

### (P-3824)
### BOXES R US INC
Also Called: Ultimate Paper Box Company
15051 Don Julian Rd, City Of Industry (91746-3302)
**PHONE**.................................626 820-5410
Janak P Patel, *Pr*
Dipak Patel, *
▲ **EMP:** 70 **EST:** 1996
**SQ FT:** 38,000
**SALES (est):** 9.64MM **Privately Held**
**SIC: 2653** Boxes, corrugated: made from purchased materials

### (P-3825)
### C B SHEETS INC
13901 Carmenita Rd, Santa Fe Springs (90670-4916)
**PHONE**.................................562 921-1223
John Widera, *CEO*
Mackey Davis, *Pr*
**EMP:** 21 **EST:** 2001

**SALES (est):** 15.19MM
**SALES (corp-wide):** 78.02MM **Privately Held**
**Web:** www.calbox.com
**SIC: 2653** Boxes, corrugated: made from purchased materials
**PA:** California Box Company
  13901 Carmenita Rd
  562 921-1223

### (P-3826)
### CAL SHEETS LLC
1212 Performance Dr, Stockton (95206-4925)
P.O. Box 30370 (95213-0370)
**PHONE**.................................209 234-3300
Rick Goddard, *CEO*
Scott Sherman, *
Joe Escobar, *Managing Member*
Pete Brodie, *
◆ **EMP:** 68 **EST:** 1998
**SQ FT:** 203,000
**SALES (est):** 28.36MM
**SALES (corp-wide):** 792.6MM **Privately Held**
**Web:** www.goldenwestpackaging.com
**SIC: 2653** Boxes, corrugated: made from purchased materials
**PA:** Golden West Packaging Group Llc
  15250 Don Julian Rd
  888 501-5893

### (P-3827)
### CALIFORNIA BOX COMPANY (PA)
13901 Carmenita Rd, Santa Fe Springs (90670-4916)
**PHONE**.................................562 921-1223
▲ **EMP:** 67 **EST:** 1990
**SALES (est):** 78.02MM
**SALES (corp-wide):** 78.02MM **Privately Held**
**Web:** www.calbox.com
**SIC: 2653** Corrugated and solid fiber boxes

### (P-3828)
### CAPITAL CORRUGATED LLC
Also Called: Capital Corrugated and Carton
8333 24th Ave, Sacramento (95826-4809)
P.O. Box P.O. Box 278060 (95827-8060)
**PHONE**.................................916 388-7848
Dennis D Watson, *Pr*
▲ **EMP:** 80 **EST:** 1995
**SQ FT:** 124,000
**SALES (est):** 20.12MM
**SALES (corp-wide):** 792.6MM **Privately Held**
**Web:** www.goldenwestpackaging.com
**SIC: 2653** Boxes, corrugated: made from purchased materials
**PA:** Golden West Packaging Group Llc
  15250 Don Julian Rd
  888 501-5893

### (P-3829)
### CD CONTAINER INC
Also Called: Carton Design
7343 Paramount Blvd, Pico Rivera (90660-3713)
**PHONE**.................................562 948-1910
Juan De La Cruz, *Pr*
Juan De La Cruz, *Pr*
Jose De La Cruz, *
▲ **EMP:** 70 **EST:** 1987
**SQ FT:** 46,000
**SALES (est):** 9.46MM **Privately Held**
**Web:** www.cdcontainerinc.com
**SIC: 2653** Boxes, corrugated: made from purchased materials

### (P-3830)
### CFLUTE CORP
Also Called: Montebello Container
13220 Molette St, Santa Fe Springs (90670-5526)
P.O. Box 788 (90637-0788)
**PHONE**.................................562 404-6221
▲ **EMP:** 170
**Web:** www.montcc.com
**SIC: 2653** Boxes, corrugated: made from purchased materials

### (P-3831)
### CITY PAPER BOX CO
652 E 61st St, Los Angeles (90001-1021)
**PHONE**.................................323 231-5990
Stanley Goodrich, *Pr*
Frieda Goodrich, *VP*
Abe Friedman, *Ex VP*
Maurey Friedman, *VP Sls*
Michael Goodrich, *VP Opers*
**EMP:** 16 **EST:** 1962
**SQ FT:** 9,000
**SALES (est):** 936.89K **Privately Held**
**Web:** www.citypaperbox.com
**SIC: 2653** Boxes, corrugated: made from purchased materials

### (P-3832)
### COMMANDER PACKAGING WEST INC
602 S Rockefeller Ave Ste D, Ontario (91761-8191)
**PHONE**.................................714 921-9350
Joseph F Kindlon, *Ch Bd*
Brian R Webber, *
**EMP:** 37 **EST:** 1987
**SQ FT:** 48,000
**SALES (est):** 866.79K **Privately Held**
**SIC: 2653** 7389 5113 Boxes, corrugated: made from purchased materials; Packaging and labeling services; Corrugated and solid fiber boxes
**PA:** Cano Container Corporation
  3920 Enterprise Ct Ste A

### (P-3833)
### CORRU-KRAFT IV
1911 E Rosslynn Ave, Fullerton (92831-5141)
**PHONE**.................................714 773-0124
Bob Dunford, *Prin*
**EMP:** 17 **EST:** 2008
**SALES (est):** 10.93MM **Privately Held**
**Web:** www.ororacorrugated.com
**SIC: 2653** Boxes, corrugated: made from purchased materials

### (P-3834)
### CORRUGADOS DE BAJA CALIFORNIA
2475 Paseo De Las A, San Diego (92154)
**PHONE**.................................619 662-8672
Smurfit Kappa, *Owner*
**EMP:** 900 **EST:** 2008
**SALES (est):** 39.19MM **Privately Held**
**SIC: 2653** Corrugated and solid fiber boxes

### (P-3835)
### CORRUGATED PACKAGING PDTS INC
21615 Hesperian Blvd Ste B, Hayward (94541-7026)
**PHONE**.................................650 615-9180
Christopher Grandov, *Pr*
Linda Grandov, *Sec*
**EMP:** 16 **EST:** 1960
**SALES (est):** 5.67MM **Privately Held**

# PRODUCTS & SERVICES SECTION
## 2653 - Corrugated And Solid Fiber Boxes (P-3854)

SIC: 2653 2631 Corrugated and solid fiber boxes; Paperboard mills

### (P-3836)
### CROCKETT GRAPHICS INC (PA)
Also Called: Folding Cartons
980 Avenida Acaso, Camarillo (93012-8759)
PHONE..................................805 987-8577
Edward Randall Crockett, *Pr*
Edward Randall Crockett, *Pr*
Rod K Rieth, *
▲ **EMP:** 60 **EST:** 1994
**SALES (est):** 17.11MM
**SALES (corp-wide):** 17.11MM **Privately Held**
Web: www.garedgraphics.com
SIC: 2653 Corrugated boxes, partitions, display items, sheets, and pad

### (P-3837)
### CROWN CARTON COMPANY INC
1820 E 48th Pl, Vernon (90058-1946)
PHONE..................................323 582-3053
Jeffrey P Marks, *Pr*
**EMP:** 20 **EST:** 1953
**SQ FT:** 28,000
**SALES (est):** 2.41MM **Privately Held**
Web: www.crowncarton.com
SIC: 2653 Boxes, corrugated: made from purchased materials

### (P-3838)
### CUSTOM PAD AND PARTITION INC
1100 Richard Ave, Santa Clara (95050-2800)
PHONE..................................408 970-9711
James L Jones, *CEO*
Janice Jones, *
**EMP:** 65 **EST:** 1976
**SQ FT:** 60,000
**SALES (est):** 9.78MM **Privately Held**
Web: www.custompad.com
SIC: 2653 Boxes, corrugated: made from purchased materials

### (P-3839)
### ECKO PRODUCTS GROUP LLC
Also Called: Ecko Print & Packaging
740 S Milliken Ave Ste C, Ontario (91761-7829)
P.O. Box 4117 (91761-1007)
PHONE..................................909 628-5678
Eric Rogers, *CFO*
Christopher Hively, *Pr*
◆ **EMP:** 23 **EST:** 2002
**SQ FT:** 17,000
**SALES (est):** 5.41MM **Privately Held**
Web: www.eckopg.com
SIC: 2653 5085 2759 Boxes, corrugated: made from purchased materials; Abrasives and adhesives; Commercial printing, nec

### (P-3840)
### EMPIRE CONTAINER CORPORATION
1161 E Walnut St, Carson (90746-1382)
PHONE..................................310 537-8190
Donald Simmons, *Pr*
Gregory V Hall, *
Patrick Fox, *Stockholder*
▲ **EMP:** 66 **EST:** 1970
**SQ FT:** 61,000
**SALES (est):** 2.49MM **Privately Held**
Web: www.empirecfs.com

SIC: 2653 3578 Boxes, corrugated: made from purchased materials; Point-of-sale devices

### (P-3841)
### EXPRESS CONTAINER INC
5450 Dodds Ave, Buena Park (90621-1209)
P.O. Box 230 (92373-0064)
PHONE..................................909 798-3857
Gilles Roy, *Pr*
**EMP:** 22 **EST:** 1984
**SALES (est):** 2.42MM **Privately Held**
Web: www.expresscontainerline.com
SIC: 2653 Boxes, corrugated: made from purchased materials

### (P-3842)
### FLEETWOOD FIBRE LLC
Also Called: Fleetwood Fibre Pkg & Graphics
15250 Don Julian Rd, City Of Industry (91745-1001)
PHONE..................................626 968-8503
**EMP:** 225 **EST:** 1952
**SALES (est):** 24.05MM
**SALES (corp-wide):** 792.6MM **Privately Held**
Web: www.goldenwestpackaging.com
SIC: 2653 Boxes, corrugated: made from purchased materials
PA: Golden West Packaging Group Llc
15250 Don Julian Rd
888 501-5893

### (P-3843)
### FRUIT GROWERS SUPPLY COMPANY (PA)
Also Called: Fgs Packing Services
27770 Entertainment Dr Ste 120, Valencia (91355-1093)
PHONE..................................888 997-4855
Jim Phillips, *CEO*
Charles Boyce, *
William O Knox, *
◆ **EMP:** 50 **EST:** 1907
**SQ FT:** 10,000
**SALES (est):** 122.9MM
**SALES (corp-wide):** 122.9MM **Privately Held**
Web: www.fruitgrowerssupply.com
SIC: 2653 0811 5191 2448 Boxes, corrugated: made from purchased materials; Timber tracts; Farm supplies; Pallets, wood

### (P-3844)
### FRUIT GROWERS SUPPLY COMPANY
Also Called: F G S Packing Services
674 E Myer Ave, Exeter (93221-9644)
PHONE..................................559 592-6550
Bruce Adams, *Mgr*
**EMP:** 15
**SQ FT:** 5,240
**SALES (corp-wide):** 122.9MM **Privately Held**
Web: www.fruitgrowers.com
SIC: 2653 Boxes, corrugated: made from purchased materials
PA: Fruit Growers Supply Company Inc
27770 N Entrmt Dr Fl 3 Flr 3
888 997-4855

### (P-3845)
### GABRIEL CONTAINER (PA)
Also Called: Recycled Paper Products
8844 Millergrove Dr, Santa Fe Springs (90670-2004)
P.O. Box 3188 (90670-0188)
PHONE..................................562 699-1051

Ronald H Gabriel, *Pr*
Agnes Gabriel, *
▲ **EMP:** 199 **EST:** 1935
**SQ FT:** 72,000
**SALES (est):** 15.93MM
**SALES (corp-wide):** 15.93MM **Privately Held**
Web: www.gabrielcontainer.com
SIC: 2653 2621 Boxes, corrugated: made from purchased materials; Paper mills

### (P-3846)
### GENERAL CONTAINER
235 Radio Rd, Corona (92879-1725)
PHONE..................................714 562-8700
Tim G Black, *CEO*
Scott Black, *
**EMP:** 72 **EST:** 1976
**SALES (est):** 19.64MM
**SALES (corp-wide):** 50.43MM **Privately Held**
Web: www.gcbox.com
SIC: 2653 Boxes, corrugated: made from purchased materials
PA: U.S. Display Group, Inc.
810 S Washington St
931 455-9585

### (P-3847)
### GEORGIA-PACIFIC LLC
Georgia-Pacific
2400 Lapham Dr, Modesto (95354-4003)
PHONE..................................209 522-5201
David Rieser, *Genl Mgr*
**EMP:** 88
**SALES (corp-wide):** 64.37B **Privately Held**
Web: www.gp.com
SIC: 2653 Boxes, corrugated: made from purchased materials
HQ: Georgia-Pacific Llc
133 Peachtree St Nw
Atlanta GA 30303
404 652-4000

### (P-3848)
### GEORGIA-PACIFIC LLC
Georgia-Pacific
24600 Avenue 13, Madera (93637-9019)
P.O. Box 1327 (93639-1327)
PHONE..................................559 674-4685
Steve Mindt, *Genl Mgr*
**EMP:** 93
**SALES (corp-wide):** 64.37B **Privately Held**
Web: www.gp.com
SIC: 2653 5113 Boxes, corrugated: made from purchased materials; Corrugated and solid fiber boxes
HQ: Georgia-Pacific Llc
133 Peachtree St Nw
Atlanta GA 30303
404 652-4000

### (P-3849)
### GLOBAL PACKAGING SOLUTIONS INC
6259 Progressive Dr Ste 200, San Diego (92154-6644)
PHONE..................................619 710-2661
Jawed Ghias, *CEO*
Anila Parikh, *
Rajnikanth Parikh, *
Tariq Butt, *
Henry Romo, *Stockholder*
▲ **EMP:** 280 **EST:** 2006
**SALES (est):** 8.19MM **Privately Held**
Web: www.globsoln.com
SIC: 2653 3089 Corrugated and solid fiber boxes; Injection molding of plastics

PA: Global Packaging Solutions, S.A. De C.V.
Calle 7 Norte No.108

### (P-3850)
### GOLDEN BEAR PACKAGING INC
6645 Las Positas Rd, Livermore (94551-5107)
P.O. Box 6940 (93290-6940)
PHONE..................................925 455-4283
**EMP:** 26 **EST:** 2011
**SALES (est):** 2.45MM
**SALES (corp-wide):** 90.25MM **Privately Held**
SIC: 2653 3086 3993 Boxes, corrugated: made from purchased materials; Packaging and shipping materials, foamed plastics; Signs and advertising specialties
HQ: Kaweah Container, Inc.
7101 Ave 304
Visalia CA 93291

### (P-3851)
### GOLDEN WEST PACKG GROUP LLC (PA)
15250 Don Julian Rd, City Of Industry (91745-1001)
PHONE..................................888 501-5893
Mark J Favre, *CEO*
Brad Jordan, *
Brian Mcdonnell, *CFO*
**EMP:** 381 **EST:** 2017
**SALES (est):** 792.6MM
**SALES (corp-wide):** 792.6MM **Privately Held**
Web: www.goldenwestpackaging.com
SIC: 2653 Boxes, corrugated: made from purchased materials

### (P-3852)
### GOLDENCORR SHEETS LLC
13890 Nelson Ave, City Of Industry (91746-2050)
P.O. Box 90968 (91715-0968)
PHONE..................................626 369-6446
Tom Anderson, *Managing Member*
John Webb, *Managing Member*
Glen Tucker, *Managing Member*
Jeffrey Erseluis, *Managing Member*
John Perullo, *
▲ **EMP:** 150 **EST:** 1999
**SALES (est):** 26.57MM **Privately Held**
Web: www.goldencorr.net
SIC: 2653 Corrugated boxes, partitions, display items, sheets, and pad

### (P-3853)
### HARVEST CONTAINER COMPANY
24476 Road 216, Lindsay (93247-8222)
P.O. Box 697 (93247-0697)
PHONE..................................559 562-1394
Dennis A Del Rio, *Prin*
Fred Lo Bue, *
Dennis A Del Rio, *Ex VP*
Robert Reniers, *
▲ **EMP:** 45 **EST:** 1983
**SQ FT:** 104,000
**SALES (est):** 10.01MM **Privately Held**
Web: www.harvestcontainer.com
SIC: 2653 Boxes, corrugated: made from purchased materials

### (P-3854)
### HERITAGE CONTAINER INC
4777 Felspar St, Riverside (92509-3040)
P.O. Box 605 (91752-0605)
PHONE..................................951 360-1900
Richard Gabriel, *CEO*
Thomas Gabriel, *

## 2653 - Corrugated And Solid Fiber Boxes (P-3855)

Nancy Zuniga, *
**EMP:** 100 **EST:** 1988
**SQ FT:** 95,000
**SALES (est):** 16.5MM Privately Held
**Web:** www.heritagecontainer.com
**SIC: 2653** 5199 Boxes, corrugated: made from purchased materials; Packaging materials

### (P-3855)
### HERITAGE PAPER CO (HQ)
2400 S Grand Ave, Santa Ana (92705-5211)
**PHONE**..................714 540-9737
Ron Scagliotti, *CEO*
Lenet Derksen, *
▲ **EMP:** 75 **EST:** 1976
**SQ FT:** 150,000
**SALES (est):** 24.68MM
**SALES (corp-wide):** 44.54MM Privately Held
**Web:** www.heritagepaper.net
**SIC: 2653** 5199 Boxes, corrugated: made from purchased materials; Packaging materials
**PA:** Pioneer Packing, Inc.
2430 S Grand Ave
714 540-9751

### (P-3856)
### HERITAGE PAPER LLC (PA)
Also Called: Heritage Paper Co
6850 Brisa St, Livermore (94550-2566)
P.O. Box 44441 (94144-0001)
**PHONE**..................925 449-1148
John Tatum, *CEO*
Richard Heinz, *
▲ **EMP:** 130 **EST:** 1986
**SQ FT:** 129,000
**SALES (est):** 22.83MM
**SALES (corp-wide):** 22.83MM Privately Held
**Web:** www.goldenwestpackaging.com
**SIC: 2653** 5113 Boxes, corrugated: made from purchased materials; Corrugated and solid fiber boxes

### (P-3857)
### HOOD CONTAINER CORPORATION
Hood Container
25014 Avenue Kearny, Santa Clarita (91355-1253)
**PHONE**..................818 848-1648
Craig Lutes, *Genl Mgr*
**EMP:** 15
**Web:** www.hoodcontainer.com
**SIC: 2653** Boxes, corrugated: made from purchased materials
**HQ:** Hood Container Corporation
2100 Rvredge Pkwy Ste 650
Atlanta GA 30328
855 605-6317

### (P-3858)
### HOOVER CONTAINERS INC
19570 San Jose Ave, City Of Industry (91748-1404)
P.O. Box 10366 (92838-6366)
**PHONE**..................909 444-9454
▲ **EMP:** 60
**SIC: 2653** 5113 Boxes, corrugated: made from purchased materials; Corrugated and solid fiber boxes

### (P-3859)
### HPI LIQUIDATIONS INC
13100 Danielson St, Poway (92064-6840)
**PHONE**..................858 391-7302
**EMP:** 245

**SIC: 2653** 5199 Boxes, corrugated: made from purchased materials; Packaging materials

### (P-3860)
### INTERNATIONAL PAPER COMPANY
Also Called: International Paper
11211 Greenstone Ave, Santa Fe Springs (90670-4616)
**PHONE**..................323 946-6100
Marc Bailey, *Genl Mgr*
**EMP:** 24
**SALES (corp-wide):** 18.92B Publicly Held
**Web:** www.internationalpaper.com
**SIC: 2653** Boxes, corrugated: made from purchased materials
**PA:** International Paper Company
6400 Poplar Ave
901 419-7000

### (P-3861)
### JELLCO CONTAINER INC
1151 N Tustin Ave, Anaheim (92807-1736)
**PHONE**..................714 666-2728
Jeff Erseluis, *Pr*
Rick Leininger, *
**EMP:** 72 **EST:** 1977
**SQ FT:** 42,000
**SALES (est):** 10.44MM Privately Held
**Web:** www.jellco.com
**SIC: 2653** Boxes, corrugated: made from purchased materials

### (P-3862)
### JKV INC
Also Called: Atlantic Box & Carton Company
8343 Loch Lomond Dr, Pico Rivera (90660-2507)
**PHONE**..................562 948-3000
Michael Valov, *Pr*
Jack Valov, *
Elena Valov, *
**EMP:** 40 **EST:** 1971
**SQ FT:** 30,000
**SALES (est):** 4.72MM Privately Held
**Web:** www.atlanticboxncarton.com
**SIC: 2653** Boxes, corrugated: made from purchased materials

### (P-3863)
### KAWEAH CONTAINER INC (HQ)
7101 Avenue 304, Visalia (93291-9479)
P.O. Box 6940 (93290-6940)
**PHONE**..................559 651-7846
Frank T Elliott Iv, *CEO*
▲ **EMP:** 35 **EST:** 1988
**SQ FT:** 30,000
**SALES (est):** 56.9MM
**SALES (corp-wide):** 90.25MM Privately Held
**Web:** www.kcboxes.com
**SIC: 2653** Boxes, corrugated: made from purchased materials
**PA:** Wileman Bros. & Elliott, Inc.
40232 Road 128
559 651-8378

### (P-3864)
### LIBERTY CONTAINER COMPANY
Also Called: Key Container
4224 Santa Ana St, South Gate (90280-2557)
**PHONE**..................323 564-4211
Robert J Watts, *Pr*
William J Watts, *
▲ **EMP:** 110 **EST:** 1956
**SQ FT:** 300,000
**SALES (est):** 20.42MM Privately Held
**Web:** www.keycontainer.com

**SIC: 2653** Boxes, corrugated: made from purchased materials

### (P-3865)
### LIFOAM INDUSTRIES LLC
15671 Industry Ln, Huntington Beach (92649-1536)
**PHONE**..................714 891-5035
**EMP:** 48
**SALES (corp-wide):** 1.86B Privately Held
**Web:** www.lifoam.com
**SIC: 2653** Corrugated and solid fiber boxes
**HQ:** Lifoam Industries, Llc
1303 S Batesville Rd
Greer SC 29650
410 889-1023

### (P-3866)
### MARFRED INDUSTRIES
Also Called: Amatix
12708 Branford St, Sun Valley (91353)
▲ **EMP:** 300
**SIC: 2653** 5113 Boxes, solid fiber: made from purchased materials; Shipping supplies

### (P-3867)
### MENASHA PACKAGING COMPANY LLC
Also Called: Menasha
1550 N Chrisman Rd, Tracy (95304-9396)
**PHONE**..................951 660-5361
Esther Martinez, *Brnch Mgr*
**EMP:** 20
**SALES (corp-wide):** 1.94B Privately Held
**Web:** www.menasha.com
**SIC: 2653** Boxes, corrugated: made from purchased materials
**HQ:** Menasha Packaging Company, Llc
1645 Bergstrom Rd
Neenah WI 54956
920 751-1000

### (P-3868)
### NEXGEN CONTAINER LLC
7182 Rasmussen Ave, Visalia (93291-9405)
**PHONE**..................559 553-7500
Bobby Marina, *CEO*
Christie Marina, *
**EMP:** 55 **EST:** 2019
**SALES (est):** 13.5MM Privately Held
**Web:** www.ngcontainer.com
**SIC: 2653** 4225 Corrugated and solid fiber boxes; General warehousing and storage

### (P-3869)
### NORTHWEST PALLETS LLC
Also Called: Northwest Pallets
3264 Ramona Ave, Sacramento (95826-3815)
**PHONE**..................916 736-2787
Ricardo Ochoa, *Managing Member*
**EMP:** 25 **EST:** 2002
**SQ FT:** 17,500
**SALES (est):** 3.75MM Privately Held
**SIC: 2653** 2448 Pallets, corrugated: made from purchased materials; Wood pallets and skids

### (P-3870)
### NUMATECH WEST (KMP) LLC
Also Called: Kmp Numatech Pacific
1201 E Lexington Ave, Pomona (91766-5520)
P.O. Box 357 (92871-0357)
**PHONE**..................909 706-3627
John Neate, *Managing Member*
▲ **EMP:** 100 **EST:** 1986
**SQ FT:** 65,000
**SALES (est):** 2.36MM

**SALES (corp-wide):** 2.36MM Privately Held
**SIC: 2653** Boxes, corrugated: made from purchased materials
**PA:** Nw Packaging Llc
1201 E Lexington Ave
909 706-3627

### (P-3871)
### PACIFIC QUALITY PACKAGING CORP
660 Neptune Ave, Brea (92821-2909)
**PHONE**..................714 257-1234
Frederick H Chau, *Pr*
▲ **EMP:** 65 **EST:** 1984
**SQ FT:** 44,000
**SALES (est):** 8.04MM Privately Held
**SIC: 2653** 3993 Boxes, corrugated: made from purchased materials; Signs and advertising specialties

### (P-3872)
### PACIFIC SOUTHWEST CONT LLC
Also Called: PSC
9525 W Nicholas Ct, Visalia (93291-9468)
**PHONE**..................559 651-5500
**EMP:** 45
**SALES (corp-wide):** 123.49MM Privately Held
**Web:** www.teampsc.com
**SIC: 2653** Boxes, corrugated: made from purchased materials
**PA:** Pacific Southwest Container, Llc
4530 Leckron Rd
209 526-0444

### (P-3873)
### PACKAGING CORPORATION AMERICA
Also Called: PCA/Los Angeles 349
4240 Bandini Blvd, Vernon (90058-4207)
**PHONE**..................323 263-7581
Mark Beyma, *Brnch Mgr*
**EMP:** 91
**SALES (corp-wide):** 8.48B Publicly Held
**Web:** www.packagingcorp.com
**SIC: 2653** Boxes, corrugated: made from purchased materials
**PA:** Packaging Corporation Of America
1 N Field Ct
847 482-3000

### (P-3874)
### PACKAGING CORPORATION AMERICA
Also Called: San Bernardino Sheet Plant
879 E Rialto Ave, San Bernardino (92408-1202)
**PHONE**..................909 888-7008
**EMP:** 24
**SALES (corp-wide):** 8.48B Publicly Held
**Web:** www.packagingcorp.com
**SIC: 2653** Boxes, corrugated: made from purchased materials
**PA:** Packaging Corporation Of America
1 N Field Ct
847 482-3000

### (P-3875)
### PACKAGING CORPORATION AMERICA
Also Called: PCA/South Gate 378
9700 E Frontage Rd Ste 20, South Gate (90280-5421)
**PHONE**..................562 927-7741
Eric Thorntoon, *Brnch Mgr*
**EMP:** 114
**SALES (corp-wide):** 8.48B Publicly Held
**Web:** www.packagingcorp.com

# PRODUCTS & SERVICES SECTION
## 2653 - Corrugated And Solid Fiber Boxes (P-3898)

**SIC: 2653** Boxes, corrugated: made from purchased materials
**PA:** Packaging Corporation Of America
1 N Field Ct
847 482-3000

### (P-3876)
### PACTIV LLC
4545 Qantas Ln, Stockton (95206-3982)
**PHONE**..................209 983-1930
**EMP:** 99
**Web:** www.pactivevergreen.com
**SIC: 2653** 2656 2652 Boxes, corrugated: made from purchased materials; Sanitary food containers; Setup paperboard boxes
**HQ:** Pactiv Llc
1900 W Field Ct
Lake Forest IL 60045
847 482-2000

### (P-3877)
### PCA CENTRAL CAL CORRUGATED LLC
Also Called: Packaging America - Sacramento
4841 Urbani Ave, Mcclellan (95652-2025)
**PHONE**..................916 614-0580
Bob Bruna, *Genl Mgr*
**EMP:** 52
**SALES (corp-wide):** 8.48B **Publicly Held**
**Web:** www.packagingcorp.com
**SIC: 2653** Boxes, corrugated: made from purchased materials
**HQ:** Pca Central California Corrugated, Llc
1955 W Field Ct
Lake Forest IL 60045
847 482-3000

### (P-3878)
### PK1 INC (HQ)
Also Called: American River Packaging
401 S Granada Dr, Madera (93637-5054)
**PHONE**..................559 662-1910
Thomas Kandris, *CEO*
Ronald Frederick, *
▲ **EMP:** 100 **EST:** 1980
**SQ FT:** 240,000
**SALES (est):** 32.21MM
**SALES (corp-wide):** 792.6MM **Privately Held**
**Web:** www.goldenwestpackaging.com
**SIC: 2653** 5113 4783 Boxes, corrugated: made from purchased materials; Industrial and personal service paper; Packing goods for shipping
**PA:** Golden West Packaging Group Llc
15250 Don Julian Rd
888 501-5893

### (P-3879)
### PNC PROACTIVE NTHRN CONT LLC
Also Called: Proactive Northern Container
602 S Rockefeller Ave Ste A, Ontario (91761-8190)
**PHONE**..................909 390-5624
Gary Hartog, *Managing Member*
▲ **EMP:** 44 **EST:** 2005
**SQ FT:** 362,000
**SALES (est):** 1.92MM **Privately Held**
**SIC: 2653** Boxes, corrugated: made from purchased materials
**PA:** Fourth Third Llc
375 Park Ave Ste 3304

### (P-3880)
### PRATT LATHROP CORRUGATING LLC
2131 E Louise Ave, Lathrop (95330-9607)
**PHONE**..................209 670-0900
Brian Mcpheely, *CEO*
**EMP:** 18 **EST:** 2017
**SALES (est):** 4.51MM **Privately Held**
**Web:** www.prattindustries.com
**SIC: 2653** Boxes, corrugated: made from purchased materials

### (P-3881)
### PRATT ROBERT MANN PACKG LLC
340 El Camino Real S Ste 36, Salinas (93901-4553)
**PHONE**..................831 789-8300
Brian Mcpheely, *CEO*
**EMP:** 25 **EST:** 2015
**SALES (est):** 33.92MM **Privately Held**
**SIC: 2653** Boxes, corrugated: made from purchased materials
**PA:** Pratt Industries, Inc.
4004 Smmit Blvd Ne Ste 10

### (P-3882)
### RELIABLE CONTAINER CORPORATION
9206 Santa Fe Springs Rd, Santa Fe Springs (90670-2618)
**PHONE**..................562 861-6226
**EMP:** 275
**SIC: 2653** 5113 Boxes, corrugated: made from purchased materials; Corrugated and solid fiber boxes

### (P-3883)
### RM ESOP INC
340 El Camino Real S Ste 36, Salinas (93901-4554)
**PHONE**..................831 789-8300
◆ **EMP:** 175
**SIC: 2653** 5113 Boxes, solid fiber: made from purchased materials; Corrugated and solid fiber boxes

### (P-3884)
### SACRAMENTO CONTAINER CORP
4841 Urbani Ave, Mcclellan (95652-2025)
**PHONE**..................916 614-0580
▲ **EMP:** 180
**SIC: 2653** Corrugated and solid fiber boxes

### (P-3885)
### SAN DIEGO CRATING & PKG INC
12678 Brookprinter Pl, Poway (92064-6809)
**PHONE**..................858 748-0100
Jacqueline H Peterson, *Prin*
Jacqueline H Peterson, *CEO*
Lee Peterson, *Pr*
**EMP:** 17 **EST:** 1975
**SQ FT:** 12,000
**SALES (est):** 5.65MM **Privately Held**
**Web:** www.sdcrate.com
**SIC: 2653** 4783 Boxes, corrugated: made from purchased materials; Crating goods for shipping

### (P-3886)
### SCOPE PACKAGING INC
Also Called: Sp
13400 Nelson Ave, City Of Industry (91746-2331)
**PHONE**..................714 998-4411
**TOLL FREE:** 800
Mike E Flinn, *CEO*
Cindy Baker, *
▲ **EMP:** 47 **EST:** 1966
**SQ FT:** 70,000
**SALES (est):** 2.79MM **Privately Held**
**SIC: 2653** 7389 Boxes, corrugated: made from purchased materials; Packaging and labeling services

### (P-3887)
### SONOCO PRTECTIVE SOLUTIONS INC
3466 Enterprise Ave, Hayward (94545-3219)
**PHONE**..................510 785-0220
Rob Hazelton, *Mgr*
**EMP:** 60
**SQ FT:** 125,975
**SALES (corp-wide):** 6.78B **Publicly Held**
**Web:** www.sonoco.com
**SIC: 2653** 3086 Boxes, corrugated: made from purchased materials; Plastics foam products
**HQ:** Sonoco Protective Solutions, Inc.
3930 N Ventura Dr
Arlington Heights IL 60004
847 398-0110

### (P-3888)
### SOUTHLAND BOX COMPANY
4201 Fruitland Ave, Vernon (90058-3118)
P.O. Box 512214 (90051-0214)
**PHONE**..................323 583-2231
▲ **EMP:** 170 **EST:** 1945
**SALES (est):** 69.74MM **Privately Held**
**Web:** www.southlandbox.com
**SIC: 2653** 5113 Corrugated boxes, partitions, display items, sheets, and pad; Corrugated and solid fiber boxes
**PA:** Tomoku Co., Ltd.
2-2-2, Marunouchi

### (P-3889)
### SOUTHLAND CONTAINER CORP
Also Called: Concept Packaging Group
1600 Champagne Ave, Ontario (91761-3612)
**PHONE**..................909 937-9781
Tom Heinz, *Brnch Mgr*
**EMP:** 239
**SALES (corp-wide):** 93.13MM **Privately Held**
**Web:** www.southlandcontainer.com
**SIC: 2653** Boxes, corrugated: made from purchased materials
**PA:** Southland Container Corporation
60 Fairview Church Rd
864 578-0085

### (P-3890)
### ST WORTH CONTAINER LLC
727 S Wanamaker Ave, Ontario (91761-8116)
**PHONE**..................909 390-4550
**EMP:** 82 **EST:** 1994
**SALES (est):** 14.75MM **Privately Held**
**Web:** www.goldenwestpackaging.com
**SIC: 2653** Corrugated boxes, partitions, display items, sheets, and pad

### (P-3891)
### THARCO CONTAINER INC
2222 Grant Ave, San Lorenzo (94580-1804)
**PHONE**..................510 276-8600
▲ **EMP:** 1000
**SIC: 2653** Corrugated and solid fiber boxes

### (P-3892)
### THARCO HOLDINGS INC
Also Called: Tharco
2222 Grant Ave, San Lorenzo (94580-1804)
P.O. Box 990050 (83799-0050)
**PHONE**..................303 373-1860
▲ **EMP:** 1001
**SIC: 2653** 3086 2675 Corrugated and solid fiber boxes; Plastics foam products; Die-cut paper and board

### (P-3893)
### TRIPLE A CONTAINERS INC
16069 Shoemaker Ave, Cerritos (90703-2234)
P.O. Box 6111 (90702-6111)
**PHONE**..................562 404-7433
**EMP:** 88 **EST:** 1957
**SALES (est):** 3.18MM **Privately Held**
**Web:** www.newindypackaging.com
**SIC: 2653** 3993 Corrugated boxes, partitions, display items, sheets, and pad; Signs and advertising specialties

### (P-3894)
### WESTERN CORRUGATED DESIGN INC
8741 Pioneer Blvd, Santa Fe Springs (90670-2021)
**PHONE**..................562 695-9295
John Brendlinger, *CEO*
▲ **EMP:** 50 **EST:** 2004
**SALES (est):** 10.93MM **Privately Held**
**Web:** www.wcd1.com
**SIC: 2653** Boxes, corrugated: made from purchased materials

### (P-3895)
### WESTROCK RKT LLC
749 N Poplar St, Orange (92868-1013)
**PHONE**..................714 978-2895
Bob Appoloney, *Brnch Mgr*
**EMP:** 29
**Web:** www.westrock.com
**SIC: 2653** Boxes, corrugated: made from purchased materials
**HQ:** Westrock Rkt, Llc
1000 Abernathy Rd Ste 125
Atlanta GA 30328
770 448-2193

### (P-3896)
### WESTROCK RKT LLC
3366 E Muscat Ave, Fresno (93725-2624)
**PHONE**..................559 497-1662
Thomas Bernardo, *Brnch Mgr*
**EMP:** 31
**Web:** www.westrock.com
**SIC: 2653** Boxes, corrugated: made from purchased materials
**HQ:** Westrock Rkt, Llc
1000 Abernathy Rd Ste 125
Atlanta GA 30328
770 448-2193

### (P-3897)
### WESTROCK RKT LLC
Also Called: Alliance Display & Packaging
100 E Tujunga Ave Ste 102, Burbank (91502-1963)
**PHONE**..................818 729-0610
Allen Kinder, *Brnch Mgr*
**EMP:** 51
**Web:** www.westrock.com
**SIC: 2653** Boxes, corrugated: made from purchased materials
**HQ:** Westrock Rkt, Llc
1000 Abernathy Rd Ste 125
Atlanta GA 30328
770 448-2193

### (P-3898)
### WESTROCK RKT LLC
1401 S Madera Ave, Kerman (93630-9139)
**PHONE**..................559 567-3501
**EMP:** 59

## 2655 Fiber Cans, Drums, And Similar Products

Web: www.westrock.com
SIC: 2653 Boxes, corrugated: made from purchased materials
HQ: Westrock Rkt, Llc
1000 Abernathy Rd Ste 125
Atlanta GA 30328
770 448-2193

### (P-3899)
**ADMAIL WEST INC**
800 N 10th St Ste F, Sacramento (95811-0342)
PHONE.................916 554-5755
Mike Mc Bride, *Mgr*
EMP: 95
SALES (corp-wide): 14.17MM **Privately Held**
Web: www.admailwest.com
SIC: 2655 Fiber shipping and mailing containers
PA: Admail West, Inc.
4130 S Market Ct
916 442-3613

### (P-3900)
**CARAUSTAR INDUSTRIES INC**
Newark Recovery & Recycling
800b W Church St, Stockton (95203-3206)
P.O. Box 58044 (95052-8044)
PHONE.................209 464-6590
Mark Vincent, *Mgr*
EMP: 25
SQ FT: 480,000
SALES (corp-wide): 5.22B **Publicly Held**
Web: www.caraustar.com
SIC: 2655 Fiber cans, drums, and similar products
HQ: Caraustar Industries, Inc.
5000 Astell Pwdr Sprng Rd
Austell GA 30106
770 948-3101

### (P-3901)
**CARAUSTAR INDUSTRIES INC**
Also Called: California Paperboard
525 Mathew St, Santa Clara (95050-3001)
P.O. Box 58044 (95052-8044)
PHONE.................408 845-7600
Stephen G Blankenship, *Mgr*
EMP: 81
SQ FT: 61,005
SALES (corp-wide): 5.22B **Publicly Held**
Web: www.greif.com
SIC: 2655 Fiber cans, drums, and similar products
HQ: Caraustar Industries, Inc.
5000 Astell Pwdr Sprng Rd
Austell GA 30106
770 948-3101

### (P-3902)
**COMPOSITE SUPPORT AND SLTNS IN**
767 W Channel St, San Pedro (90731-1411)
PHONE.................310 514-3162
Clem Hill, *Pr*
Hilde Hiel, *Sec*
EMP: 16 EST: 2003
SALES (est): 261.39K **Privately Held**
SIC: 2655 Cans, composite: foil-fiber and other: from purchased fiber

### (P-3903)
**DORCO ELECTRONICS INC**
Also Called: Dorco Fiberglass Products
13540 Larwin Cir, Santa Fe Springs (90670-5031)
PHONE.................562 623-1133
Ted Casmer, *Pr*
Gary Dexter, *VP*
EMP: 16 EST: 1958
SQ FT: 7,000
SALES (est): 2.46MM **Privately Held**
Web: www.dorco.com
SIC: 2655 Bobbins, fiber: made from purchased material

### (P-3904)
**GREIF INC**
2400 Cooper Ave, Merced (95348-4310)
P.O. Box 2146 (95344-0146)
PHONE.................209 383-4396
Farrell Smith, *Mgr*
EMP: 94
SALES (corp-wide): 5.22B **Publicly Held**
Web: www.greif.com
SIC: 2655 Fiber cans, drums, and similar products
PA: Greif, Inc.
425 Winter Rd
740 549-6000

### (P-3905)
**GREIF INC**
Western Division
235 San Pedro Ave, Morgan Hill (95037-5236)
PHONE.................408 779-2161
John Saldate, *Mgr*
EMP: 86
SQ FT: 105,731
SALES (corp-wide): 5.22B **Publicly Held**
Web: www.greif.com
SIC: 2655 Drums, fiber: made from purchased material
PA: Greif, Inc.
425 Winter Rd
740 549-6000

### (P-3906)
**MAUSER USA LLC**
Also Called: California Fiber Drum Co
2777 N State Highway 59 Bldg C, Merced (95348-4346)
PHONE.................209 205-1135
EMP: 33
SALES (corp-wide): 3.82B **Privately Held**
Web: www.mauserpackaging.com
SIC: 2655 Fiber cans, drums, and containers
HQ: Mauser Usa, Llc
1515 W 22nd St Ste 1100
Oak Brook IL 60523

### (P-3907)
**PACIFIC PAPER TUBE LLC (PA)**
4343 E Fremont St, Stockton (95215-4032)
PHONE.................510 562-8823
TOLL FREE: 888
Patrick Wallace, *Pr*
Colleen Wallace, *
Nancy Wallace, *
▲ EMP: 50 EST: 1989
SQ FT: 85,000
SALES (est): 25.5MM **Privately Held**
Web: www.pacificpapertube.com
SIC: 2655 Tubes, fiber or paper: made from purchased material

### (P-3908)
**PLASTOPAN INDUSTRIES INC (PA)**
Also Called: Plastopan
812 E 59th St, Los Angeles (90001-1006)
PHONE.................323 231-2225
Ronald D Miller, *Pr*
Catherine M Bump, *
Sofia G Miller, *
Martin L Miller, *
EMP: 30 EST: 1992
SQ FT: 48,000
SALES (est): 5.55MM **Privately Held**
SIC: 2655 Fiber cans, drums, and similar products

### (P-3909)
**SGL COMPOSITES INC (DH)**
1551 W 139th St, Gardena (90249-2603)
PHONE.................424 329-5250
David Otterson, *CEO*
Jeff Schade, *
▼ EMP: 90 EST: 1995
SALES (est): 49.48MM
SALES (corp-wide): 1.18B **Privately Held**
Web: www.sglcarbon.com
SIC: 2655 Fiber cans, drums, and similar products
HQ: Sgl Carbon, Llc
10715 Dvid Taylor Dr Ste 4
Charlotte NC 28262
704 593-5100

### (P-3910)
**SPIRAL PPR TUBE & CORE CO INC**
5200 Industry Ave, Pico Rivera (90660-2506)
PHONE.................562 801-9705
George Hibard, *CEO*
Summer Hibard, *
▲ EMP: 45 EST: 1949
SQ FT: 40,000
SALES (est): 1.41MM **Privately Held**
Web: www.spiralpaper.com
SIC: 2655 Fiber cans, drums, and similar products

### (P-3911)
**TUBE-TAINER INC**
8174 Byron Rd, Whittier (90606-2616)
PHONE.................562 945-3711
Mike Mundia, *Pr*
▲ EMP: 45 EST: 1967
SQ FT: 44,000
SALES (est): 10.5MM **Privately Held**
Web: www.tubetainer.com
SIC: 2655 Tubes, fiber or paper: made from purchased material

## 2656 Sanitary Food Containers

### (P-3912)
**AMSCAN INC**
Ampro
804 W Town & Country Rd, Orange (92868-4712)
PHONE.................714 972-2626
James Bell, *Brnch Mgr*
EMP: 62
SALES (corp-wide): 2.17B **Privately Held**
Web: www.amscan.com
SIC: 2656 Cups, paper: made from purchased material
HQ: Amscan Inc.
1 Celebration Sq
Woodcliff Lake NJ 07677
800 444-8887

### (P-3913)
**CJ UNITED FOOD CORPORATION (PA)**
Also Called: C & J Food
155 98th Ave, Oakland (94603-1003)
PHONE.................510 895-6868
John J Huang, *Pr*
▲ EMP: 19 EST: 2001
SALES (est): 8.53MM
SALES (corp-wide): 8.53MM **Privately Held**
Web: www.cj78.com
SIC: 2656 5046 Sanitary food containers; Restaurant equipment and supplies, nec

### (P-3914)
**FINELINE SETTINGS LLC**
2041 S Turner Ave Unit 30, Ontario (91761-8510)
PHONE.................845 369-6100
Abraham Feig, *Brnch Mgr*
▲ EMP: 27
SALES (corp-wide): 384.87MM **Privately Held**
Web: www.finelinesettings.com
SIC: 2656 Sanitary food containers
HQ: Fineline Settings, Llc
135 Crotty Rd Ste 1
Middletown NY 10941
845 369-6100

### (P-3915)
**HARVEST PACK INC**
12336 Lower Azusa Rd, Arcadia (91006-5872)
PHONE.................888 727-7225
Christina Pou, *CEO*
EMP: 17 EST: 2013
SALES (est): 2.6MM **Privately Held**
Web: www.harvest-pack.com
SIC: 2656 Plates, paper: made from purchased material

## 2657 Folding Paperboard Boxes

### (P-3916)
**ABSOLUTE PACKAGING INC**
1201 N Miller St, Anaheim (92806-1933)
PHONE.................714 630-3020
Ramin Kohan, *Pr*
EMP: 35 EST: 2020
SALES (est): 2.64MM **Privately Held**
Web: www.absolutepackaginginc.com
SIC: 2657 5199 Folding paperboard boxes; Packaging materials

### (P-3917)
**EVERETT GRAPHICS INC**
7300 Edgewater Dr, Oakland (94621-3006)
PHONE.................510 577-6777
Munson Wittman Everett, *Pr*
Munson Wittman Everett, *Pr*
John F Everett, *
Mark Carlson, *
▲ EMP: 75 EST: 1980
SQ FT: 100,000
SALES (est): 24.38MM **Privately Held**
Web: www.everettgraphics.com
SIC: 2657 Folding paperboard boxes

### (P-3918)
**GOLDEN W PPR CONVERTING CORP**
2480 Grant Ave, San Lorenzo (94580-1808)
PHONE.................510 317-0646
Shirley Hooi, *Pr*

# PRODUCTS & SERVICES SECTION

## 2671 - Paper; Coated And Laminated Packaging (P-3938)

Henry Hooi, *
David Hooi, *
Michelle Walker, *
▼ EMP: 26 EST: 1984
SQ FT: 42,000
SALES (est): 9.58MM Privately Held
SIC: 2657 3565 Folding paperboard boxes; Carton packing machines

**(P-3919)**
**T & T BOX COMPANY INC**
Also Called: Thomas Container & Packaging
602 N Cypress St, Orange (92867-6604)
PHONE.....................909 465-0848
Thomas Murphy, CEO
Andy Murphy, VP
EMP: 22 EST: 1972
SALES (est): 2.02MM Privately Held
Web: www.thomascontainer.com
SIC: 2657 2653 Folding paperboard boxes; Corrugated and solid fiber boxes

**(P-3920)**
**YAVAR MANUFACTURING CO INC**
Also Called: National Packaging Products
1900 S Tubeway Ave, Commerce (90040-1612)
PHONE.....................323 722-2040
Massoud Afari, CEO
Ben Afari, *
▲ EMP: 48 EST: 1998
SQ FT: 50,000
SALES (est): 14.43MM Privately Held
Web: www.nationalpkg.com
SIC: 2657 2631 Folding paperboard boxes; Folding boxboard

## 2671 Paper; Coated And Laminated Packaging

**(P-3921)**
**AMCOR FLEXIBLES LLC**
Also Called: Amcor Flexibles Healthcare
5425 Broadway St, American Canyon (94503-9678)
PHONE.....................707 257-6481
Richard Evans, Brnch Mgr
EMP: 135
SALES (corp-wide): 14.69B Privately Held
SIC: 2671 2621 2821 3081 Plastic film, coated or laminated for packaging; Packaging paper; Plastics materials and resins; Packing materials, plastics sheet
HQ: Amcor Flexibles Llc
3 Parkway North Blvd # 300
Deerfield IL 60015
224 313-7000

**(P-3922)**
**AMCOR FLEXIBLES LLC**
Also Called: Amcor Flexibles Healthcare
5416 Union Pacific Ave, Commerce (90022-5117)
PHONE.....................323 721-6777
Graeme Liebelt, Brnch Mgr
EMP: 1118
SALES (corp-wide): 14.69B Privately Held
SIC: 2671 2621 2821 3081 Plastic film, coated or laminated for packaging; Packaging paper; Plastics materials and resins; Packing materials, plastics sheet
HQ: Amcor Flexibles Llc
3 Parkway North Blvd # 300
Deerfield IL 60015
224 313-7000

**(P-3923)**
**AUDIO VIDEO COLOR CORPORATION (PA)**
17707 S Santa Fe Ave, E Rncho Dmngz (90221-5419)
PHONE.....................424 213-7500
Kali J Limath, CEO
Guy Marrom, *
Michael Baker, Prin
▲ EMP: 145 EST: 1990
SQ FT: 78,000
SALES (est): 15.02MM Privately Held
Web: www.avccorp.com
SIC: 2671 Paper; coated and laminated packaging

**(P-3924)**
**BADGER PAPERBOARD CAL LLC**
14657 Industry Cir, La Mirada (90638-5816)
PHONE.....................657 529-0456
▲ EMP: 18 EST: 2014
SQ FT: 47,000
SALES (est): 2.43MM Privately Held
Web: www.badgerpaperboard.com
SIC: 2671 Paper; coated and laminated packaging

**(P-3925)**
**BAY CITIES CONTAINER CORP**
9206 Santa Fe Springs Rd, Santa Fe Springs (90670-2618)
PHONE.....................562 551-2946
Greg Tucker, CEO
EMP: 32
SALES (corp-wide): 150.82MM Privately Held
Web: www.bay-cities.com
SIC: 2671 Paper; coated and laminated packaging
PA: Bay Cities Container Corp
5138 Industry Ave
562 948-3751

**(P-3926)**
**DREAMFIELDS CALIFORNIA LLC**
65000 Two Bunch Palms Trl, Desert Hot Springs (92240-5429)
PHONE.....................310 691-9739
Scot Garrambone, CFO
Sebastian Solano, Managing Member*
Lukasz Tracz, Managing Member*
EMP: 300 EST: 2022
SALES (est): 3.35MM Privately Held
SIC: 2671 Paper; coated and laminated packaging

**(P-3927)**
**FEDERATED DIVERSIFIED SLS INC**
Also Called: FDS Manufacturing Company Svcs
2200 S Reservoir St, Pomona (91766-6408)
P.O. Box 45 (91769-0045)
PHONE.....................909 591-1733
Robert B Stevenson, CEO
EMP: 89 EST: 1957
SALES (est): 3.89MM Privately Held
SIC: 2671 2631 2653 3086 Paper; coated and laminated packaging; Container, packaging, and boxboard; Corrugated and solid fiber boxes; Cups and plates, foamed plastics

**(P-3928)**
**GLOBAL LINK SOURCING INC**
41690 Corporate Center Ct, Murrieta (92562-7084)
PHONE.....................951 698-1977
Jullie Annet, Pr
▲ EMP: 70 EST: 2006
SQ FT: 80,000
SALES (est): 4.77MM Privately Held
Web: www.globallinksourcing.com
SIC: 2671 Paper; coated and laminated packaging

**(P-3929)**
**IRONWOOD PACKAGING LLC**
8975 Cottage Ave, Rancho Cucamonga (91730-5235)
PHONE.....................909 581-0077
Bill O'melveny, CEO
William O'melveny, Managing Member
▲ EMP: 21 EST: 1998
SQ FT: 35,000
SALES (est): 5.14MM Privately Held
Web: www.ironwoodpackaging.com
SIC: 2671 Plastic film, coated or laminated for packaging

**(P-3930)**
**MICHELSEN PACKAGING CO CAL**
Also Called: Michelsen Packaging California
4165 S Cherry Ave, Fresno (93706-5709)
P.O. Box 10109 (93745-0109)
PHONE.....................559 237-3819
Dan Keck, Pr
EMP: 36
SALES (corp-wide): 39.61MM Privately Held
Web: www.michelsenpackaging.com
SIC: 2671 2674 Paper; coated and laminated packaging; Paper bags: made from purchased materials
PA: Michelsen Packaging Company Of California
202 N 2nd Ave
509 248-6270

**(P-3931)**
**PACIFIC SOUTHWEST CONT LLC (PA)**
4530 Leckron Rd, Modesto (95357-0517)
PHONE.....................209 526-0444
TOLL FREE: 800
John W Mayol, Managing Member
James D Mayol, Managing Member*
Lester H Mangold, *
Bryan Smith, *
▲ EMP: 347 EST: 1973
SQ FT: 129,600
SALES (est): 123.49MM
SALES (corp-wide): 123.49MM Privately Held
Web: www.teampsc.com
SIC: 2671 2657 3086 2653 Paper; coated and laminated packaging; Folding paperboard boxes; Packaging and shipping materials, foamed plastics; Boxes, corrugated: made from purchased materials

**(P-3932)**
**PACIFIC SOUTHWEST CONT LLC**
671 Mariposa Rd, Modesto (95354-4145)
PHONE.....................209 526-0444
EMP: 39
SALES (corp-wide): 123.49MM Privately Held
Web: www.teampsc.com
SIC: 2671 2657 3086 2653 Paper; coated and laminated packaging; Folding paperboard boxes; Packaging and shipping materials, foamed plastics; Boxes, corrugated: made from purchased materials
PA: Pacific Southwest Container, Llc
4530 Leckron Rd

209 526-0444

**(P-3933)**
**PAPERBOARD PACKAGING CORP**
Also Called: Deluxe Pckges An Amcor Flexble
800 N Walton Ave, Yuba City (95993-9352)
P.O. Box 3057 (95992-3057)
PHONE.....................530 671-9000
▲ EMP: 92
SIC: 2671 2759 Paper; coated and laminated packaging; Flexographic printing

**(P-3934)**
**PAPERCUTTERS INC**
6900 Washington Blvd, Montebello (90640-5424)
PHONE.....................323 888-1330
Susan Feinstein, Pr
Beth Feinstein, VP
Joyce Feinstein, Sec
▲ EMP: 21 EST: 1983
SALES (est): 7.89MM Privately Held
Web: www.papercutters.net
SIC: 2671 5113 Paper; coated and laminated packaging; Paper, wrapping or coarse, and products

**(P-3935)**
**PGAC CORP (PA)**
Also Called: Pgi
9630 Ridgehaven Ct Ste B, San Diego (92123-5605)
PHONE.....................858 560-8213
Mark Grantham, Pr
Florentina Shields, *
EMP: 75 EST: 1975
SALES (est): 19.79MM Privately Held
Web: www.pgisd.com
SIC: 2671 Paper, coated or laminated for packaging

**(P-3936)**
**PRECISION LABEL LLC**
659 Benet Rd, Oceanside (92058-1208)
P.O. Box 766 (92075-0766)
PHONE.....................760 757-7533
Robert A Wilcox, Pr
EMP: 30 EST: 1991
SQ FT: 7,000
SALES (est): 10.88MM
SALES (corp-wide): 4.71B Privately Held
Web: www.p-label.com
SIC: 2671 2759 Paper; coated and laminated packaging; Labels and seals: printing, nsk
HQ: Inovar Packaging Group, Llc
9001 Sterling St
Irving TX 75063

**(P-3937)**
**SHERPA CLINICAL PACKAGING LLC**
6920 Carroll Rd, San Diego (92121-2211)
PHONE.....................858 282-0928
Derek Truninger, Prin
EMP: 20 EST: 2010
SALES (est): 561.99K Privately Held
SIC: 2671 Plastic film, coated or laminated for packaging

**(P-3938)**
**SHIP SMART INC**
783 Rio Del Mar Blvd Ste 9, Aptos (95003-4702)
PHONE.....................831 661-4841
John Kessler, Pr
Carole-anne Kessler, Treas
EMP: 25 EST: 1999

## 2671 - Paper; Coated And Laminated Packaging (P-3939)

SQ FT: 1,200
SALES (est): 18.14MM **Privately Held**
Web: www.shipsmart.com
SIC: 2671 4783 Paper; coated and laminated packaging; Packing goods for shipping

### (P-3939)
### THERMECH CORPORATION
Also Called: Thermech Engineering
1773 W Lincoln Ave Ste I, Anaheim (92801-6713)
PHONE..................................714 533-3183
Jim Shah, *CEO*
Richard Gorman, *
**EMP:** 23 **EST:** 1949
**SQ FT:** 24,000
**SALES (est):** 5.1MM **Privately Held**
Web: www.thermech.com
SIC: 2671 3083 Paper; coated and laminated packaging; Plastics finished products, laminated

### (P-3940)
### TRIUNE ENTERPRISES INC
Also Called: Triune Enterprises Mfg
13711 S Normandie Ave, Gardena (90249-2609)
PHONE..................................310 719-1600
John Christman, *CEO*
Sidney Arouh, *VP*
Donald Alhanati, *Sec*
◆ **EMP:** 23 **EST:** 1996
**SQ FT:** 29,000
**SALES (est):** 1.65MM **Privately Held**
Web: www.triuneent.com
SIC: 2671 5162 Plastic film, coated or laminated for packaging; Plastics materials and basic shapes

### (P-3941)
### VINYL TECHNOLOGY LLC (PA)
200 Railroad Ave, Monrovia (91016-4643)
PHONE..................................626 443-5257
Carlos A Mollura, *Ch Bd*
Daniel Mullora, *
Carlos Mollura Junior, *VP*
Rodney Mollura, *
Haydee Mollura, *
◆ **EMP:** 199 **EST:** 1981
**SQ FT:** 68,000
**SALES (est):** 46.38MM
**SALES (corp-wide):** 46.38MM **Privately Held**
Web: www.vinyltechnology.com
SIC: 2671 7389 Plastic film, coated or laminated for packaging; Sewing contractor

## 2672 Paper; Coated And Laminated, Nec

### (P-3942)
### AVERY DENNISON CORPORATION
50 Pointe Dr, Brea (92821-3648)
PHONE..................................714 674-8500
Rick Alonzo, *Mgr*
**EMP:** 400
**SALES (corp-wide):** 8.36B **Publicly Held**
Web: www.averydennison.com
SIC: 2672 3081 3497 2678 Adhesive papers, labels, or tapes: from purchased material; Unsupported plastics film and sheet; Metal foil and leaf; Stationery products
PA: Avery Dennison Corporation
8080 Norton Pkwy
440 534-6000

### (P-3943)
### AVERY DENNISON CORPORATION
2900 Bradley St, Pasadena (91107-1560)
PHONE..................................626 304-2000
Dave Edwards, *VP*
**EMP:** 120
**SQ FT:** 67,580
**SALES (corp-wide):** 8.36B **Publicly Held**
Web: www.averydennison.com
SIC: 2672 2679 Adhesive papers, labels, or tapes: from purchased material; Labels, paper: made from purchased material
PA: Avery Dennison Corporation
8080 Norton Pkwy
440 534-6000

### (P-3944)
### AVERY DENNISON CORPORATION
11195 Eucalyptus St, Rancho Cucamonga (91730-3836)
PHONE..................................909 987-4631
Marta E Corfaelb, *Mgr*
**EMP:** 62
**SALES (corp-wide):** 8.36B **Publicly Held**
Web: www.averydennison.com
SIC: 2672 Tape, pressure sensitive: made from purchased materials
PA: Avery Dennison Corporation
8080 Norton Pkwy
440 534-6000

### (P-3945)
### AVERY DENNISON FOUNDATION
207 N Goode Ave Ste 500, Glendale (91203-1301)
PHONE..................................626 304-2000
Alicia Maddox, *Pr*
**EMP:** 26 **EST:** 1978
**SALES (est):** 1.24MM **Privately Held**
SIC: 2672 Paper; coated and laminated, nec

### (P-3946)
### BECKERS FABRICATION INC
Also Called: B F I Labels
22465 La Palma Ave, Yorba Linda (92887-3803)
PHONE..................................714 692-1600
Mark Becker, *CEO*
Dan Becker, *
**EMP:** 24 **EST:** 1981
**SQ FT:** 6,500
**SALES (est):** 5.71MM **Privately Held**
Web: www.beckersfab.com
SIC: 2672 2759 Paper; coated and laminated, nec; Screen printing

### (P-3947)
### CINTON LLC
Also Called: West Coast Labels
620 Richfield Rd, Placentia (92870-6727)
PHONE..................................714 961-8808
Salvatore Scaffide, *Pr*
Romona Scaffide, *
Cindi Montgomery, *
**EMP:** 46 **EST:** 1972
**SQ FT:** 23,000
**SALES (est):** 9.63MM **Privately Held**
Web: www.fortissolutionsgroup.com
SIC: 2672 2679 Paper; coated and laminated, nec; Labels, paper: made from purchased material
PA: Fortis Solutions Group, Llc
2505 Hawkeye Ct

### (P-3948)
### CLARIANT CORPORATION
926 S 8th St, Colton (92324-3500)
P.O. Box 610 (92324-0610)
PHONE..................................909 825-1793
Kenneth Golder, *Pr*
**EMP:** 32
Web: www.clariant.com
SIC: 2672 7389 5199 Paper; coated and laminated, nec; Packaging and labeling services; Packaging materials
HQ: Clariant Corporation
500 E Morehead St Ste 400
Charlotte NC 28202
704 331-7000

### (P-3949)
### EDWARDS ASSOC CMMNICATIONS INC (PA)
Also Called: Edwards Label
2277 Knoll Dr Ste A, Ventura (93003-5878)
PHONE..................................805 658-2626
Joel Horacio Gomez-avila, *Pr*
John Edwards, *
**EMP:** 150 **EST:** 1984
**SQ FT:** 44,000
**SALES (est):** 17.08MM
**SALES (corp-wide):** 17.08MM **Privately Held**
Web: www.edwardslabel.com
SIC: 2672 Labels (unprinted), gummed: made from purchased materials

### (P-3950)
### FELIX SCHOELLER NORTH AMER INC
1260 N Lakeview Ave, Anaheim (92807-1831)
PHONE..................................315 298-8425
**EMP:** 25
**SALES (corp-wide):** 29.22MM **Privately Held**
Web: www.felix-schoeller.com
SIC: 2672 Paper; coated and laminated, nec
HQ: Felix Schoeller North America Inc.
179 County Route 2a
Pulaski NY 13142
315 298-8425

### (P-3951)
### HARRIS INDUSTRIES INC (PA)
5181 Argosy Ave, Huntington Beach (92649-1058)
P.O. Box 3269 (92605-3269)
PHONE..................................714 898-8048
William Helzer, *Pr*
Gail Helzer, *
◆ **EMP:** 50 **EST:** 1987
**SQ FT:** 25,000
**SALES (est):** 9.97MM
**SALES (corp-wide):** 9.97MM **Privately Held**
Web: www.harrisind.com
SIC: 2672 Tape, pressure sensitive: made from purchased materials

### (P-3952)
### MILLER PRODUCTS INC
Also Called: Mpi Label Systems
2315 Station Dr, Stockton (95215-7928)
P.O. Box 5543 (95205-0543)
PHONE..................................209 467-2470
**TOLL FREE:** 800
Spencer Cser, *Prin*
**EMP:** 67
**SALES (corp-wide):** 70.41MM **Privately Held**
Web: www.mpilabels.com
SIC: 2672 2679 2759 Adhesive papers, labels, or tapes: from purchased material; Labels, paper: made from purchased material; Commercial printing, nec
PA: Miller Products, Inc.
450 Courtney Rd

330 938-2134

### (P-3953)
### PRECISION DYNAMICS CORPORATION (HQ)
Also Called: Pdc-Identicard
25124 Springfield Ct Ste 200, Valencia (91355-1087)
PHONE..................................818 897-1111
J Michael Nauman, *CEO*
Robin Barber, *
Robert Case, *
John Park, *
◆ **EMP:** 161 **EST:** 1956
**SQ FT:** 75,000
**SALES (est):** 34.6MM
**SALES (corp-wide):** 1.34B **Publicly Held**
Web: www.pdcorp.com
SIC: 2672 2754 5047 3069 Adhesive papers, labels, or tapes: from purchased material; Labels: gravure printing; Instruments, surgical and medical; Tape, pressure sensitive: rubber
PA: Brady Corporation
6555 W Good Hope Rd
414 358-6600

### (P-3954)
### SC LIQUIDATION COMPANY LLC
566 Vanguard Way, Brea (92821-3928)
PHONE..................................714 482-1006
**EMP:** 103
Web: www.spinps.com
SIC: 2672 Labels (unprinted), gummed: made from purchased materials
HQ: Sc Liquidation Company, Llc
550 Summit Ave
Troy OH 45373
937 332-6500

### (P-3955)
### SEAL METHODS INC (PA)
11915 Shoemaker Ave, Santa Fe Springs (90670)
P.O. Box 2604 (90670)
PHONE..................................562 944-0291
Darin Welter, *CEO*
Geraldine Welter, *
Douglas Kraus, *
◆ **EMP:** 90 **EST:** 1974
**SQ FT:** 75,000
**SALES (est):** 35.55MM
**SALES (corp-wide):** 35.55MM **Privately Held**
Web: www.sealmethodsinc.com
SIC: 2672 3053 5085 Masking tape: made from purchased materials; Gaskets, all materials; Gaskets

### (P-3956)
### TAPE AND LABEL CONVERTERS INC
8231 Allport Ave, Santa Fe Springs (90670-2105)
P.O. Box 398 (90660-0398)
PHONE..................................562 945-3486
**TOLL FREE:** 888
Robert Varela Senior, *Pr*
Jeanette Verela, *Sec*
**EMP:** 20 **EST:** 1996
**SQ FT:** 3,625
**SALES (est):** 2.32MM **Privately Held**
Web: www.stickybiz.com
SIC: 2672 2782 2752 2671 Labels (unprinted), gummed: made from purchased materials; Blankbooks and looseleaf binders; Commercial printing, lithographic; Paper; coated and laminated packaging

# PRODUCTS & SERVICES SECTION
## 2673 - Bags: Plastic, Laminated, And Coated (P-3976)

### (P-3957) UPM RAFLATAC INC
1105 Auto Center Dr, Ontario (91761-2213)
PHONE..................................909 390-4657
Alan Punch, Mgr
EMP: 19
Web: www.upmraflatac.com
SIC: 2672 2679 Paper; coated and laminated, nec; Labels, paper: made from purchased material
HQ: Upm Raflatac, Inc.
  400 Broadpointe Dr
  Mills River NC 28759
  828 651-4800

### (P-3958) VALMARK INDUSTRIES INC
Also Called: Valmark Interface Solutions
7900 National Dr, Livermore (94550-8811)
PHONE..................................925 960-9900
▲ EMP: 190 EST: 1993
SALES (est): 19.66MM Privately Held
Web: www.valmarkfg.com
SIC: 2672 2759 Paper; coated and laminated, nec; Commercial printing, nec
PA: Nidec Corporation
  338, Kuzetonoshirocho, Minami-Ku

### (P-3959) VINTAGE 99 LABEL MFG INC (PA)
Also Called: Label Innovators
611 Enterprise Ct, Livermore (94550-5200)
PHONE..................................925 294-5270
Mark Gonzales, CEO
Kathy Gonzales, Pr
EMP: 20 EST: 1998
SALES (est): 6.44MM
SALES (corp-wide): 6.44MM Privately Held
Web: www.vintage99.com
SIC: 2672 2752 Labels (unprinted), gummed: made from purchased materials; Commercial printing, lithographic

---

## 2673 Bags: Plastic, Laminated, And Coated

### (P-3960) AGRIBAG INC
3925 Alameda Ave, Oakland (94601-3931)
PHONE..................................510 533-2388
Hsieh Liang, Pr
Wen-ping Liang, VP
▲ EMP: 25 EST: 1987
SQ FT: 20,000
SALES (est): 1.87MM Privately Held
Web: www.agribag.com
SIC: 2673 5199 Bags: plastic, laminated, and coated; Packaging materials

### (P-3961) ASIA PLASTICS INC
9347 Rush St, South El Monte (91733-2544)
PHONE..................................626 448-8100
Kent Ung, CEO
Hung Tran, CFO
Tracy Ung, Sec
▲ EMP: 20 EST: 1982
SQ FT: 11,000
SALES (est): 2.94MM Privately Held
SIC: 2673 Plastic bags: made from purchased materials

### (P-3962) BAGCRAFTPAPERCON III LLC
515 Turnbull Canyon Rd, City Of Industry (91745-1118)
PHONE..................................626 961-6766
EMP: 122
SALES (corp-wide): 32.64B Publicly Held
Web: www.novolex.com
SIC: 2673 Plastic bags: made from purchased materials
HQ: Bagcraftpapercon Iii, Llc
  3436 Trıngdon Way Ste 100
  Charlotte NC 28277
  800 845-6051

### (P-3963) CALIFORNIA PLASTIX INC
1319 E 3rd St, Pomona (91766-2212)
PHONE..................................909 629-8288
Danny Farshadfar, Pr
Touraj Tour, *
▼ EMP: 25 EST: 1994
SQ FT: 44,000
SALES (est): 4MM Privately Held
Web: www.californiaplastix.com
SIC: 2673 3089 Garment and wardrobe bags, (plastic film); Extruded finished plastics products, nec

### (P-3964) CF&B MANUFACTURING INC
Also Called: Cleanroom Film & Bags
1700 Barcelona Cir, Placentia (92870-6630)
P.O. Box 807 (92811-0807)
PHONE..................................714 744-8361
Michael Hoffman, CEO
Kyle Purcell, CFO
EMP: 20 EST: 2004
SQ FT: 10,000
SALES (est): 8.65MM Privately Held
Web: www.cleanroomfilm.com
SIC: 2673 Plastic bags: made from purchased materials
HQ: C. P. Converters, Inc.
  15 Grumbacher Rd
  York PA 17406
  717 764-1193

### (P-3965) CROWN POLY INC
Also Called: Pull-N-Pac
5700 Bickett St, Huntington Park (90255)
PHONE..................................323 585-5522
Ebrahim Simhaee, CEO
◆ EMP: 150 EST: 1991
SQ FT: 40,000
SALES (est): 25.6MM Privately Held
Web: www.crownpoly.com
SIC: 2673 Plastic bags: made from purchased materials

### (P-3966) DURABAG COMPANY INC
Also Called: Superpak
1432 Santa Fe Dr, Tustin (92780-6417)
PHONE..................................714 259-8811
Frank C S Huang, VP
Daniel Huang, *
Feng Jung Huang, *
▲ EMP: 70 EST: 1985
SQ FT: 150,000
SALES (est): 10.17MM Privately Held
Web: www.durabag.net
SIC: 2673 Food storage and frozen food bags, plastic

### (P-3967) EARTHWISE BAG COMPANY INC
207 N Goode Ave Ste 340, Glendale (91203-1364)
PHONE..................................818 396-5025
Stanley Ekstrom, Pr

James Anthony Mccool, CEO
Daniel J Let, Sec
Anh Phuong Katy Vu, CFO
EMP: 16 EST: 2006
SALES (est): 8.19MM Privately Held
Web: www.earthwisebags.com
SIC: 2673 Food storage and trash bags (plastic)

### (P-3968) GREAT AMERICAN PACKAGING
4361 S Soto St, Vernon (90058-2311)
PHONE..................................323 582-2247
Greg Gurewitz, Pr
Marlene Gurewitz, *
Bruce Carter, *
Bob Clarke, *
Fito Perez Outside Sales, Prin
EMP: 50 EST: 1966
SQ FT: 40,000
SALES (est): 8.97MM Privately Held
Web: www.greatampack.com
SIC: 2673 3081 3082 Plastic bags: made from purchased materials; Plastics film and sheet; Unsupported plastics profile shapes

### (P-3969) HIGH TEK USA INC
12420 Gold Flake Ct, Rancho Cordova (95742-6900)
PHONE..................................800 504-7120
Jason Sigman, Pr
EMP: 16 EST: 2004
SALES (est): 10.16MM Privately Held
Web: www.hightekusa.com
SIC: 2673 Food storage and frozen food bags, plastic

### (P-3970) LIBERTY PACKG & EXTRUDING INC
Also Called: Liberty Film
3015 Supply Ave, Commerce (90040-2709)
PHONE..................................323 722-5124
Derek De Heras, CEO
Derek De Heras, Pr
Bonnie Hudson, *
Mary Hudson, *
Mary Anne Bove, *
EMP: 40 EST: 1986
SQ FT: 25,000
SALES (est): 5.11MM Privately Held
Web: www.libertypkg.com
SIC: 2673 7389 Plastic and pliofilm bags; Packaging and labeling services

### (P-3971) MERCURY PLASTICS INC (HQ)
14825 Salt Lake Ave, City Of Industry (91746-3131)
PHONE..................................626 961-0165
Benjamin Deutsch, CEO
Stanley Tzenkov, *
Kamyar Mirdamadi, *
Yathira Munoz, *
▲ EMP: 415 EST: 1987
SQ FT: 140,000
SALES (est): 92.41MM Privately Held
Web: www.mercplastics.com
SIC: 2673 2759 3089 Plastic bags: made from purchased materials; Bags, plastic: printing, nsk; Plastics containers, except foam
PA: Alpha Industries Management, Inc.
  2919 Center Port Cir

### (P-3972) METRO POLY CORPORATION
1651 Aurora Dr, San Leandro (94577-3101)
PHONE..................................510 357-9898

Peter Kung, Prin
▲ EMP: 48 EST: 1990
SQ FT: 40,000
SALES (est): 7.99MM Privately Held
Web: www.metropolybag.com
SIC: 2673 Plastic bags: made from purchased materials

### (P-3973) MOHAWK WESTERN PLASTICS INC
1496 Arrow Hwy, La Verne (91750-5297)
P.O. Box 463 (91750-0463)
PHONE..................................909 593-7547
John R Mordoff, CEO
J Christopher Mordoff, *
EMP: 40 EST: 1965
SQ FT: 28,000
SALES (est): 10.66MM Privately Held
Web: www.mohawkwestern.com
SIC: 2673 3081 Plastic bags: made from purchased materials; Unsupported plastics film and sheet

### (P-3974) NORMAN PAPER AND FOAM CO INC
Also Called: Norman International
4501 S Santa Fe Ave, Vernon (90058-2129)
PHONE..................................323 582-7132
Norman Levine, Pr
Dawnn Winter, *
Christopher Werner, *
Ellen Levine, *
▲ EMP: 23 EST: 1980
SQ FT: 40,000
SALES (est): 6.76MM Privately Held
Web: www.normaninternational.com
SIC: 2673 2671 3086 Bags: plastic, laminated, and coated; Paper; coated and laminated packaging; Packaging and shipping materials, foamed plastics

### (P-3975) NOVOLEX BAGCRAFT INC
Also Called: Zenith Specialty Bag
17625 Railroad St, Rowland Heights (91748-1110)
PHONE..................................626 912-2481
Stanley Bikulege, Mgr
EMP: 88
SALES (corp-wide): 32.64B Publicly Held
Web: www.novolex.com
SIC: 2673 2674 Bags: plastic, laminated, and coated; Bags: uncoated paper and multiwall
HQ: Novolex Bagcraft, Inc.
  3436 Trıngdon Way Ste 100
  Charlotte NC 28277
  800 845-6051

### (P-3976) PRINTPACK INC
5870 Stoneridge Mall Rd Ste 200, Pleasanton (94588-3704)
PHONE..................................925 469-0601
Doug Brow, Mgr
EMP: 73
SALES (corp-wide): 684.49MM Privately Held
Web: www.printpack.com
SIC: 2673 3081 Bags: plastic, laminated, and coated; Plastics film and sheet
HQ: Printpack, Inc.
  2800 Overlook Pkwy Ne
  Atlanta GA 30339
  404 460-7000

## 2673 - Bags: Plastic, Laminated, And Coated (P-3977)

**(P-3977)**
**REPUBLIC BAG INC (PA)**
580 E Harrison St, Corona (92879)
PHONE.....................951 734-9740
Richard Schroeder, *CEO*
Steven Fritz, *
Mark Teo, *
▲ EMP: 80 EST: 1976
SQ FT: 59,000
SALES (est): 18.95MM
SALES (corp-wide): 18.95MM **Privately Held**
Web: www.republicbag.com
SIC: 2673  Plastic bags: made from purchased materials

**(P-3978)**
**ROPLAST INDUSTRIES INC**
3155 S 5th Ave, Oroville (95965-5858)
PHONE.....................530 532-9500
Robert Berman, *Ch*
Robert Bateman, *
◆ EMP: 164 EST: 1989
SQ FT: 160,000
SALES (est): 12.1MM
SALES (corp-wide): 3.49B **Privately Held**
Web: www.roplast.com
SIC: 2673 5199  Plastic bags: made from purchased materials; Packaging materials
HQ: Prezero Us, Inc.
   4388 Serrano Dr
   Jurupa Valley CA 91752
   858 677-0884

**(P-3979)**
**SIUS PRODUCTS AND DISTR INC (PA)**
1065 46th Ave, Oakland (94601)
PHONE.....................510 382-1700
Kuai Cheong Siu, *CEO*
Peter Siu, *VP*
▲ EMP: 15 EST: 1980
SALES (est): 2.29MM
SALES (corp-wide): 2.29MM **Privately Held**
SIC: 2673  Plastic bags: made from purchased materials

**(P-3980)**
**SORMA USA LLC**
231 S Kelsey St, Visalia (93291-7973)
PHONE.....................559 651-1269
Tracy Hart, *CEO*
Rick Goddard, *
▲ EMP: 350 EST: 1993
SALES (est): 19.79MM **Privately Held**
Web: www.sormausa.com
SIC: 2673 3565  Bags: plastic, laminated, and coated; Packaging machinery
HQ: Sorma Spa
   Via Delle Mele 65
   Cesena FC 47522
   054 741-8613

**(P-3981)**
**SUN PLASTICS INC**
7140 E Slauson Ave, Commerce (90040-3663)
PHONE.....................323 888-6999
Vahan Bagamian, *Pr*
Movses Shirikian, *
EMP: 50 EST: 1979
SQ FT: 60,000
SALES (est): 8.75MM **Privately Held**
Web: www.sunplastics.com
SIC: 2673  Plastic bags: made from purchased materials

**(P-3982)**
**SUNSHINE FPC INC**
Also Called: Sunshine
1600 Gage Rd, Montebello (90640)
PHONE.....................323 721-8168
▲ EMP: 65 EST: 1981
SALES (est): 8.99MM **Privately Held**
Web: www.sunshinefpc.com
SIC: 2673  Plastic bags: made from purchased materials

**(P-3983)**
**TDI2 CUSTOM PACKAGING INC**
17391 Mount Cliffwood Cir, Fountain Valley (92708-4102)
PHONE.....................714 751-6782
Stephen Deniger, *CEO*
Catharina Deniger, *Sec*
EMP: 17 EST: 1975
SQ FT: 19,000
SALES (est): 2.53MM **Privately Held**
Web: www.tdicustompackaging.com
SIC: 2673  Plastic bags: made from purchased materials

**(P-3984)**
**THE HEAT FACTORY INC**
2793 Loker Ave W, Carlsbad (92010-6601)
PHONE.....................760 893-8300
Chris Treptow, *CEO*
▲ EMP: 35 EST: 1980
SALES (est): 2.1MM **Privately Held**
Web: shop.heatfactory.com
SIC: 2673 2381  Bags: plastic, laminated, and coated; Fabric dress and work gloves

**(P-3985)**
**TRANS WESTERN POLYMERS INC**
7539 Las Positas Rd, Livermore (94551-8202)
P.O. Box 2399 (54912-2399)
PHONE.....................925 449-7800
◆ EMP: 400
Web: www.twpoly.com
SIC: 2673 5023 3089  Plastic bags: made from purchased materials; Kitchen tools and utensils, nec; Tableware, plastics

**(P-3986)**
**TRANSCONTINENTAL US LLC**
Also Called: Coveris
5601 Santa Ana St, Ontario (91761-8622)
PHONE.....................909 390-8866
EMP: 20
SALES (corp-wide): 2.18B **Privately Held**
SIC: 2673  Bags: plastic, laminated, and coated
HQ: Transcontinental Us Llc
   8700 W Bryn Mawr Ave
   Chicago IL 60631
   773 877-3300

**(P-3987)**
**UNI POLY INC**
2040 Williams, San Leandro (94577-2306)
PHONE.....................510 357-9898
Alex Eduardo, *Mgr*
EMP: 18
SALES (corp-wide): 733.1K **Privately Held**
Web: www.metropolybag.com
SIC: 2673  Plastic and pliofilm bags
PA: Uni Poly, Inc.
   1651 Aurora Dr
   510 357-9898

**(P-3988)**
**WESTERN STATES PACKAGING INC**
13276 Paxton St, Pacoima (91331-2356)
PHONE.....................818 686-6045
Richard Joyce, *Pr*
Mark Pickrell, *
▲ EMP: 50 EST: 1995
SQ FT: 35,000
SALES (est): 8.18MM **Privately Held**
Web: www.wspusa.com
SIC: 2673 5113 5162  Plastic bags: made from purchased materials; Bags, paper and disposable plastic; Plastics materials, nec

## 2674 Bags: Uncoated Paper And Multiwall

**(P-3989)**
**ACME BAG CO INC (PA)**
Also Called: California Bag
440 N Pioneer Ave Ste 300, Woodland (95776-6139)
PHONE.....................530 662-6130
TOLL FREE: 800
David Rosenberg, *CEO*
◆ EMP: 15 EST: 1923
SQ FT: 40,000
SALES (est): 1.63MM
SALES (corp-wide): 1.63MM **Privately Held**
Web: www.cherokeemfg.com
SIC: 2674 5199 5191 2673  Bags: uncoated paper and multiwall; Bags, textile; Greenhouse equipment and supplies; Bags: plastic, laminated, and coated

**(P-3990)**
**ENDPAK PACKAGING INC**
9101 Perkins St, Pico Rivera (90660-4512)
PHONE.....................562 801-0281
Edgar A Garcia, *CEO*
Carlos Garcia, *
EMP: 90 EST: 1992
SQ FT: 45,600
SALES (est): 17.91MM **Privately Held**
Web: www.endpak.com
SIC: 2674 5199  Paper bags: made from purchased materials; Packaging materials

**(P-3991)**
**LANGSTON COMPANIES INC**
2500 S K St, Tulare (93274-6874)
PHONE.....................559 688-3839
Joe Hart, *Brnch Mgr*
EMP: 172
SQ FT: 26,000
SALES (corp-wide): 101.56MM **Privately Held**
Web: www.langstonbag.com
SIC: 2674  Bags: uncoated paper and multiwall
PA: Langston Companies, Inc.
   1760 S 3rd St
   901 774-4440

**(P-3992)**
**PACOBOND INC**
9344 Glenoaks Blvd, Sun Valley (91352-1533)
PHONE.....................818 768-5002
Arsine Seraydarian, *CEO*
Gerard Seradarian, *
▲ EMP: 50 EST: 1985
SALES (est): 2.17MM **Privately Held**
Web: www.pacobond.com
SIC: 2674 5162  Shopping bags: made from purchased materials; Plastics materials, nec

**(P-3993)**
**PETER**
Also Called: Shlbao Distributors
2850 Gateway Oaks Dr, Sacramento (95833-4347)
PHONE.....................916 588-9954
EMP: 30 EST: 2020
SALES (est): 909.6K **Privately Held**
SIC: 2674  Shipping and shopping bags or sacks

**(P-3994)**
**ROMEO PACKING COMPANY**
106 Princeton Ave, Half Moon Bay (94019-4035)
PHONE.....................650 728-3393
Charles Romeo, *Pr*
Joey Romeo, *VP*
Constance Romeo, *Sec*
Frank Romeo, *Treas*
EMP: 22 EST: 1947
SQ FT: 40,000
SALES (est): 8.88MM **Privately Held**
Web: www.romeopacking.com
SIC: 2674 2873  Paper bags: made from purchased materials; Fertilizers: natural (organic), except compost

## 2675 Die-cut Paper And Board

**(P-3995)**
**APEX DIE CORPORATION**
840 Cherry Ln, San Carlos (94070-3307)
PHONE.....................650 592-6350
Thomas J Cullen, *Ch*
Kevin Cullen, *
Chris J Cullen, *
Eva Cummings, *
Judy Grilli, *
EMP: 55 EST: 1956
SQ FT: 33,800
SALES (est): 6.87MM **Privately Held**
Web: www.apexdie.com
SIC: 2675 2759 2672  Die-cut paper and board; Embossing on paper; Paper; coated and laminated, nec

**(P-3996)**
**IMPERIAL TRADE BINDERY INC**
300 N 12th St, Sacramento (95811-0510)
PHONE.....................916 443-6142
Brent Rabe, *Pr*
Jennifer Rabe, *
EMP: 35 EST: 1991
SALES (est): 1.87MM **Privately Held**
Web: www.imperialtradebindery.com
SIC: 2675 3469 2759  Die-cut paper and board; Metal stampings, nec; Commercial printing, nec

**(P-3997)**
**J J FOIL COMPANY INC**
1734 W Sequoia Ave, Orange (92868-1016)
PHONE.....................714 998-9920
Tiffany Dang, *Pr*
EMP: 24 EST: 1991
SALES (est): 971K **Privately Held**
Web: www.jjfoil.com
SIC: 2675 2759  Paper die-cutting; Embossing on paper

**(P-3998)**
**K & D GRAPHICS**
Also Called: K & D Graphics Prtg & Packg
1432 N Main St Ste C, Orange (92867-3450)
PHONE.....................714 639-8900
Don Chew, *CEO*
Kim Chew, *
Montri Chew, *
Bebe Chew, *

Gus Chew, *
▲ EMP: 48 EST: 1981
SQ FT: 75,500
SALES (est): 9.07MM Privately Held
Web: www.kdgpp.com
SIC: 2675 2752 Die-cut paper and board; Offset printing

### (P-3999)
### OUTFORM GROUP INC
Also Called: Rapid Displays
30526 San Antonio St, Hayward (94544-7102)
PHONE.................................510 431-5872
EMP: 33
SALES (corp-wide): 77.61MM Privately Held
Web: www.cadaco.com
SIC: 2675 Die-cut paper and board
PA: Outform Group, Inc.
   4300 W 47th St
   773 927-5000

### (P-4000)
### OUTFORM GROUP INC
Also Called: Rapid Displays
33195 Lewis St, Union City (94587-2201)
PHONE.................................510 433-1586
EMP: 49
SALES (corp-wide): 77.61MM Privately Held
Web: www.cadaco.com
SIC: 2675 3944 Die-cut paper and board; Board games, children's and adults'
PA: Outform Group, Inc.
   4300 W 47th St
   773 927-5000

### (P-4001)
### PRESENTATION FOLDER INC
1130 N Main St, Orange (92867-3421)
PHONE.................................714 289-7000
Joseph Tardie Junior, Pr
Joseph Tardie Senior, VP
◆ EMP: 45 EST: 1988
SQ FT: 70,000
SALES (est): 8.56MM Privately Held
Web: www.presentationfolder.com
SIC: 2675 2759 2672 Folders, filing, die-cut: made from purchased materials; Embossing on paper; Paper; coated and laminated, nec

## 2676 Sanitary Paper Products

### (P-4002)
### JOHNSON & JOHNSON
3509 Langdon Cmn, Fremont (94538-5403)
PHONE.................................650 237-4878
Phil Palin, Prin
EMP: 80
SALES (corp-wide): 85.16B Publicly Held
Web: www.jnj.com
SIC: 2676 Feminine hygiene paper products
PA: Johnson & Johnson
   1 Johnson & Johnson Plz
   732 524-0400

### (P-4003)
### PRINCESS PAPER INC
4455 Fruitland Ave, Vernon (90058-3222)
PHONE.................................323 588-4777
Abraham Hakimi, Pr
▲ EMP: 45 EST: 1989
SQ FT: 150,000
SALES (est): 4.69MM Privately Held
Web: www.princesspaper.com
SIC: 2676 Towels, napkins, and tissue paper products

### (P-4004)
### PROCTER & GAMBLE PAPER PDTS CO
Also Called: Procter & Gamble
800 N Rice Ave, Oxnard (93030-8910)
PHONE.................................805 485-8871
Shirley Boone, Mgr
EMP: 2498
SALES (corp-wide): 84.04B Publicly Held
Web: us.pg.com
SIC: 2676 Towels, paper: made from purchased paper
HQ: The Procter & Gamble Paper Products Company
   1 Procter And Gamble Plz
   Cincinnati OH 45202
   513 983-1100

### (P-4005)
### RAEL INC
6940 Beach Blvd Unit D301, Buena Park (90621-6827)
PHONE.................................800 573-1516
Aness Han, CEO
Yanghee Park, Pr
EMP: 20 EST: 2017
SALES (est): 15.19MM Privately Held
Web: www.getrael.com
SIC: 2676 Feminine hygiene paper products

### (P-4006)
### UI MEDICAL LLC
1670 W Park Ave, Redlands (92373-8048)
PHONE.................................562 453-1515
Joseph Baum Harris, Ex Dir
Wade Johnson, *
Nicolas Soichet, *
Christian Bluhm, *
Aaron Johnson, *
EMP: 25 EST: 2016
SALES (est): 1.59MM Privately Held
Web: www.quickchange.com
SIC: 2676 Diapers, paper (disposable): made from purchased paper

## 2677 Envelopes

### (P-4007)
### ASTRO CONVERTERS INC (PA)
Also Called: Astro Paper & Envelopes
2370 Oak Ridge Way Ste B, Vista (92081-8345)
PHONE.................................800 752-5003
EMP: 22 EST: 1970
SALES (est): 4.7MM
SALES (corp-wide): 4.7MM Privately Held
Web: www.astropaper.com
SIC: 2677 2621 2678 Envelopes; Paper mills ; Stationery products

### (P-4008)
### GOLDEN WEST ENVELOPE CORP
1009 Morton St, Alameda (94501-3904)
PHONE.................................510 452-5419
Raymond Mazur, Pr
Gert Mazur, *
EMP: 25 EST: 1970
SQ FT: 17,000
SALES (est): 2.4MM Privately Held
Web: www.goldenwestenvelope.com
SIC: 2677 2752 Envelopes; Offset printing

### (P-4009)
### INLAND ENVELOPE COMPANY
Also Called: Alna Envelope Company
150 N Park Ave, Pomona (91768-3835)
PHONE.................................909 622-2016
Bernard Kloenne, CEO
Otilia Kloenne, Corporate Secretary*
EMP: 55 EST: 1966
SQ FT: 45,000
SALES (est): 16.61MM Privately Held
Web: www.inlandenvelope.com
SIC: 2677 Envelopes

### (P-4010)
### LA ENVELOPE INCORPORATED
1053 S Vail Ave, Montebello (90640-6019)
PHONE.................................323 838-9300
Gary T Earls, Pr
Louise Earls, *
EMP: 35 EST: 1986
SQ FT: 25,000
SALES (est): 6.46MM Privately Held
Web: www.laenvelope.com
SIC: 2677 2752 Envelopes; Offset printing

### (P-4011)
### SEABOARD ENVELOPE CO INC
15601 Cypress Ave, Irwindale (91706-2120)
P.O. Box 721 (92625-0721)
PHONE.................................626 960-4559
Ronald Neidringhaus, Pr
Richard Riggle, *
Valerie Niedringhaus, Prin
EMP: 25 EST: 1939
SQ FT: 72,000
SALES (est): 872.08K Privately Held
Web: www.seaboardenvelope.com
SIC: 2677 Envelopes

### (P-4012)
### SOUTHLAND ENVELOPE LLC
8830 Siempre Viva Rd, San Diego (92154-6278)
P.O. Box 1570 (92040-0913)
PHONE.................................619 449-3553
David Gonzalez, CEO
Frank Soloman Junior, Pr
Rita Soloman, *
EMP: 115 EST: 1970
SQ FT: 80,000
SALES (est): 19.55MM Privately Held
Web: www.marketing.com
SIC: 2677 Envelopes

### (P-4013)
### VISION ENVELOPE & PRTG CO INC (PA)
13707 S Figueroa St, Los Angeles (90061-1045)
PHONE.................................310 324-7062
Mark Fisher, Prin
Michael J Leeny, *
Ericka Fisher, Prin
Joe Barretto, Prin
Kraig Herrera, Prin
EMP: 50 EST: 1993
SQ FT: 45,000
SALES (est): 8.37MM Privately Held
Web: www.vision-envelope.com
SIC: 2677 2752 Envelopes; Offset printing

## 2678 Stationery Products

### (P-4014)
### AVERY DENNISON OFFICE PRODUCTS CO INC
Also Called: Dennison Division
50 Pointe Dr, Brea (92821-3652)
▼ EMP: 2410
SIC: 2678 3951 2672 2891 Notebooks: made from purchased paper; Markers, soft tip (felt, fabric, plastic, etc.); Labels (unprinted), gummed: made from purchased materials; Adhesives

### (P-4015)
### AVERY DNNSON RET INFO SVCS LLC (HQ)
207 N Goode Ave Fl 6, Glendale (91203-1364)
PHONE.................................626 304-2000
EMP: 51 EST: 2008
SALES (est): 23.41MM
SALES (corp-wide): 8.36B Publicly Held
SIC: 2678 3497 Notebooks: made from purchased paper; Metal foil and leaf
PA: Avery Dennison Corporation
   8080 Norton Pkwy
   440 534-6000

### (P-4016)
### AVERY PRODUCTS CORPORATION
6987 Calle De Linea Ste 101, San Diego (92154-8016)
PHONE.................................619 671-1022
Geoff Martin, Pr
EMP: 133
SALES (corp-wide): 4.84B Privately Held
Web: www.avery.com
SIC: 2678 Stationery products
HQ: Avery Products Corporation
   50 Pointe Dr
   Brea CA 92821
   714 674-8500

### (P-4017)
### AVERY PRODUCTS CORPORATION (DH)
Also Called: ID&c
50 Pointe Dr, Brea (92821-3648)
PHONE.................................714 674-8500
Mark Cooper, CEO
Jeff Lattanzio, *
Bohdan Sirota, *
◆ EMP: 101 EST: 2012
SALES (est): 325.82MM
SALES (corp-wide): 4.84B Privately Held
Web: www.avery.com
SIC: 2678 3951 2672 2891 Notebooks: made from purchased paper; Markers, soft tip (felt, fabric, plastic, etc.); Labels (unprinted), gummed: made from purchased materials; Adhesives
HQ: Ccl Industries Corporation
   161 Worcester Rd Ste 403
   Framingham MA 01701

### (P-4018)
### BAVARIAN NORDIC INC
6275 Nancy Ridge Dr Ste 110, San Diego (92121-2245)
PHONE.................................919 600-1260
EMP: 25 EST: 2005
SALES (est): 5.23MM Privately Held
SIC: 2678 Stationery products

### (P-4019)
### COAST INDEX CO INC
Also Called: Coast Index 965
850 Lawrence Dr, Newbury Park (91320-1508)
PHONE.................................805 499-6844
EMP: 75 EST: 1982
SALES (est): 1.96MM Privately Held
Web: www.coastindex.com

# 2678 - Stationery Products (P-4020)

SIC: 2678 2782 Stationery: made from purchased materials; Library binders, looseleaf

**(P-4020)**
**CONTIXO INC**
13947 Central Ave, Chino (91710-5556)
PHONE................................909 465-5668
Tao Zhang, *CEO*
EMP: 20 EST: 2013
SALES (est): 1.36MM **Privately Held**
Web: www.contixo.com
SIC: 2678 5092 Tablets and pads, book and writing: from purchased materials; Educational toys

**(P-4021)**
**PENCIL GRIP INC (PA)**
21200 Superior St Ste A, Chatsworth (91311-4324)
P.O. Box 3787 (91313-3787)
PHONE................................310 315-3545
Alexander Provda, *CEO*
Alexander Provda, *Pr*
Asher Provda, *CEO*
Steve George, *Dir*
Julia Boyle, *VP*
◆ EMP: 17 EST: 1991
SQ FT: 12,000
SALES (est): 11.85MM **Privately Held**
Web: www.tpgcreations.com
SIC: 2678 Stationery products

**(P-4022)**
**PIPSTICKS INC**
Also Called: Pipsticks
872 Higuera St, San Luis Obispo (93401-3610)
P.O. Box 13260 (93406-3260)
PHONE................................805 439-1692
Nathan Vazquez, *CEO*
Maureen D Vazquez, *Prin*
EMP: 22 EST: 2016
SALES (est): 7.97MM **Privately Held**
Web: www.pipsticks.com
SIC: 2678 Stationery products

**(P-4023)**
**TREE HOUSE PAD & PAPER INC**
2341 Pomona Rd Ste 108, Corona (92878-4330)
PHONE................................800 213-4184
David Moncrief, *Pr*
Darrin Monroe, *
EMP: 55 EST: 1998
SQ FT: 50,000
SALES (est): 8.84MM **Privately Held**
Web: www.treehousepaper.com
SIC: 2678 Stationery products

**(P-4024)**
**VIVA HOLDINGS LLC (PA)**
Also Called: Viva Concepts
4210 Charter St, Vernon (90058-2520)
PHONE................................818 243-1363
EMP: 18 EST: 2011
SALES (est): 14.77MM
SALES (corp-wide): 14.77MM **Privately Held**
Web: www.vivaconcepts.com
SIC: 2678 Memorandum books, except printed: purchased materials

**(P-4025)**
**VIVA PRINT LLC (HQ)**
1025 N Brand Blvd Ste 300, Glendale (91202-3633)
PHONE................................818 243-1363
EMP: 17 EST: 2013
SQ FT: 28,000
SALES (est): 4.77MM
SALES (corp-wide): 14.77MM **Privately Held**
SIC: 2678 Memorandum books, except printed: purchased materials
PA: Viva Holdings, Llc
4210 Charter St
818 243-1363

---

## 2679 Converted Paper Products, Nec

**(P-4026)**
**88 SPECIAL SWEET INC**
10488 Hickson St, El Monte (91731-4900)
PHONE................................909 525-7055
Stella Sotoodeh, *CEO*
EMP: 78 EST: 2005
SALES (est): 2.56MM **Privately Held**
Web: www.stellateaproducts.com
SIC: 2679 Cups, pressed and molded pulp: made from purchased material

**(P-4027)**
**A A LABEL INC (PA)**
Also Called: All American Label
6958 Sierra Ct, Dublin (94568-2641)
PHONE................................925 803-5709
Bradley Brown, *CEO*
Cynthia Brown, *
▲ EMP: 22 EST: 1995
SQ FT: 25,000
SALES (est): 16.52MM **Privately Held**
Web: www.imprimus.com
SIC: 2679 Labels, paper: made from purchased material

**(P-4028)**
**A PLUS LABEL INC**
3215 W Warner Ave, Santa Ana (92704-5314)
PHONE................................714 229-9811
Nick Phan, *Pr*
EMP: 50 EST: 1995
SQ FT: 6,400
SALES (est): 5.72MM **Privately Held**
Web: apluslabel.wpcomstaging.com
SIC: 2679 Tags and labels, paper

**(P-4029)**
**APPLE PAPER CONVERTING INC**
3800 E Miraloma Ave, Anaheim (92806-2108)
P.O. Box 768 (92811-0768)
PHONE................................714 632-3195
Jorge Daniel Podboj, *Pr*
Louis Salavar, *Pr*
George Podboj, *VP*
EMP: 20 EST: 2001
SALES (est): 2.1MM **Privately Held**
Web: www.applepaperconverting.com
SIC: 2679 Paper products, converted, nec

**(P-4030)**
**ARTISSIMO DESIGNS LLC (HQ)**
2100 E Grand Ave Ste 400, El Segundo (90245-5169)
PHONE................................310 906-3700
Ravi Bhagavatula, *Managing Member*
▲ EMP: 50 EST: 2015
SQ FT: 13,000
SALES (est): 41.71MM
SALES (corp-wide): 42.13MM **Privately Held**
SIC: 2679 Wallboard, decorated: made from purchased material
PA: Excelsior Capital Partners, Llc
4695 Mcarthur Crt Ste 370
949 566-8110

**(P-4031)**
**ARTISTRY IN MOTION INC**
19411 Londelius St, Northridge (91324-3512)
PHONE................................818 994-7388
Roger Wachtell, *CEO*
Richard Graves, *Pr*
▼ EMP: 22 EST: 1995
SALES (est): 3.5MM **Privately Held**
Web: www.artistryinmotion.com
SIC: 2679 5947 Confetti: made from purchased material; Gifts and novelties

**(P-4032)**
**BOYD GMN INC**
2095 Otoole Ave, San Jose (95131-1303)
PHONE................................408 435-1666
Bruce Cleckley, *Mgr*
EMP: 208
SQ FT: 24,600
Web: www.boydcorp.com
SIC: 2679 3479 3993 2752 Labels, paper: made from purchased material; Name plates: engraved, etched, etc.; Signs and advertising specialties; Commercial printing, lithographic
HQ: Boyd Gmn, Inc.
2040 15th Ave W
Seattle WA 98119
206 284-2200

**(P-4033)**
**CALPACO PAPERS INC (PA)**
3155 Universe Dr, Jurupa Valley (91752-3252)
PHONE................................323 767-2800
Paul Maier, *Pr*
Francis A Maier, *
▲ EMP: 136 EST: 1968
SQ FT: 606,000
SALES (est): 1.83MM
SALES (corp-wide): 1.83MM **Privately Held**
Web: www.actfulfillment.com
SIC: 2679 5111 Paper products, converted, nec; Printing and writing paper

**(P-4034)**
**CAMEO SONOMA LIMITED**
Also Called: Cameo Crafts
21684 8th St E Ste 700, Sonoma (95476-2818)
PHONE................................707 935-0202
▲ EMP: 75
SIC: 2679 Tags and labels, paper

**(P-4035)**
**CONTINENTAL DATALABEL INC**
Also Called: American Single Sheets
211 Business Center Ct, Redlands (92373-4404)
PHONE................................909 307-3600
Patrick Flynn, *Brnch Mgr*
EMP: 16
SALES (corp-wide): 24.95MM **Privately Held**
Web: www.datalabel.com
SIC: 2679 2672 Labels, paper: made from purchased material; Paper; coated and laminated, nec
PA: Continental Datalabel, Inc.
1855 Fox Ln
847 742-1600

**(P-4036)**
**DIGITAL LABEL SOLUTIONS LLC**
1177 N Grove St, Anaheim (92806-2110)
PHONE................................714 982-5000
Joel H Mark, *CEO*
Sandy Petersen, *
Suzie Dobyns, *
EMP: 29 EST: 2006
SALES (est): 1.71MM **Privately Held**
Web: www.digitallabelsolutions.com
SIC: 2679 Tags and labels, paper
PA: Brook & Whittle Limited
20 Carter Dr

**(P-4037)**
**ENCORR SHEETS LLC**
5171 E Francis St, Ontario (91761-3661)
PHONE................................626 523-4661
EMP: 44 EST: 2016
SALES (est): 2.41MM **Privately Held**
Web: www.encorrsheetsllc.com
SIC: 2679 Corrugated paper: made from purchased material

**(P-4038)**
**FDS MANUFACTURING COMPANY (PA)**
2200 S Reservoir St, Pomona (91766-6408)
P.O. Box 3120 (91769-3120)
PHONE................................909 591-1733
Robert B Stevenson, *CEO*
Samuel B Stevenson, *
Chuck O'connor, *VP*
Kevin Stevenson, *
▲ EMP: 100 EST: 1950
SQ FT: 240,000
SALES (est): 21.08MM
SALES (corp-wide): 21.08MM **Privately Held**
Web: www.fdsmfg.com
SIC: 2679 3089 Corrugated paper: made from purchased material; Plastics containers, except foam

**(P-4039)**
**FLEENOR COMPANY INC (PA)**
Also Called: Fleenor Paper Company
2225 Harbor Bay Pkwy, Alameda (94502-3026)
P.O. Box 14438 (94614-2438)
PHONE................................800 433-2531
Rebecca Fleenor, *Pr*
Janine Rochex, *
John Rochex, *Marketing*
◆ EMP: 40 EST: 1962
SALES (est): 42.34MM
SALES (corp-wide): 42.34MM **Privately Held**
Web: www.fleenorpaper.com
SIC: 2679 Paper products, converted, nec

**(P-4040)**
**GLEASON INDUSTRIES**
1277 Santa Anita Ct, Woodland (95776-6100)
PHONE................................800 488-3471
▲ EMP: 70
SIC: 2679 Paperboard products, converted, nec

**(P-4041)**
**GOLDEN KRAFT INC**
15500 Valley View Ave, La Mirada (90638-5230)
PHONE................................562 926-8888
Dan August, *Genl Mgr*
▲ EMP: 254 EST: 1982
SQ FT: 63,200
SALES (est): 4.25MM
SALES (corp-wide): 64.37B **Privately Held**
SIC: 2679 2631 Corrugated paper: made from purchased material; Paperboard mills
HQ: Georgia-Pacific Corrugated Iii Llc
5645 W 82nd St

## PRODUCTS & SERVICES SECTION

## 2711 - Newspapers (P-4062)

Indianapolis IN 46278

**(P-4042)**
**NCLA INC**
1388 W Foothill Blvd, Azusa (91702-2846)
**PHONE**..................................562 926-6252
John Mcgee, *Pr*
**EMP:** 16 **EST:** 1997
**SALES (est):** 406.53K **Privately Held**
**Web:** www.nclainc.com
**SIC: 2679** 3083 Paper products, converted, nec; Plastics finished products, laminated

**(P-4043)**
**P & R PAPER SUPPLY CO INC**
1350 Piper Ranch Rd, San Diego (92154-7708)
**PHONE**..................................619 671-2400
Bruce Overmeyer, *Mgr*
**EMP:** 180
**SALES (corp-wide):** 1.65B **Privately Held**
**Web:** www.prpaper.com
**SIC: 2679** 2621 Paper products, converted, nec; Paper mills
**HQ:** P. & R. Paper Supply Company, Inc.
1898 E Colton Ave
Redlands CA 92374
909 389-1807

**(P-4044)**
**PACIFIC PPRBD CONVERTING LLC (PA)**
Also Called: Pacific Paper
8865 Utica Ave Ste A, Rancho Cucamonga (91730-5144)
**PHONE**..................................909 476-6466
William F Donahue, *Managing Member*
**EMP:** 24 **EST:** 2016
**SALES (est):** 14.94MM
**SALES (corp-wide):** 14.94MM **Privately Held**
**Web:** www.pacificpaper.com
**SIC: 2679** Paperboard products, converted, nec

**(P-4045)**
**PAPER PULP & FILM**
Also Called: Fresno Paper Express
2822 S Maple Ave, Fresno (93725-2207)
**PHONE**..................................559 233-1151
G Carol Jones, *CEO*
Tal Cloud, *
Meredith Orman, *
▲ **EMP:** 40 **EST:** 1986
**SQ FT:** 120,000
**SALES (est):** 10K **Privately Held**
**Web:** www.paperconverter.com
**SIC: 2679** 4213 Wrappers, paper (unprinted): made from purchased material; Heavy hauling, nec

**(P-4046)**
**POSITIVE CONCEPTS INC (PA)**
Also Called: Ameri-Fax
2021 N Glassell St, Orange (92865-3305)
**PHONE**..................................714 685-5800
Lambert C Thom, *CEO*
▼ **EMP:** 22 **EST:** 1989
**SQ FT:** 20,000
**SALES (est):** 7.95MM
**SALES (corp-wide):** 7.95MM **Privately Held**
**Web:** www.posconcepts.com
**SIC: 2679** 5084 Paper products, converted, nec; Machine tools and accessories

**(P-4047)**
**PRIME CONVERTING CORPORATION**
9121 Pittsburgh Ave Ste 100, Rancho Cucamonga (91730-5550)
P.O. Box 3207 (91729)
**PHONE**..................................909 476-9500
Robert J Nielsen, *Pr*
▲ **EMP:** 24 **EST:** 2003
**SALES (est):** 2.02MM **Privately Held**
**Web:** www.primecc.com
**SIC: 2679** Paper products, converted, nec

**(P-4048)**
**PROGRESSIVE LABEL INC**
2545 Yates Ave, Commerce (90040-2619)
P.O. Box 911430 (90091-1238)
**PHONE**..................................323 415-9770
Gus Garcia, *Pr*
Adam Flores, *
Julie Lawrence, *
David Lawrence, *Stockholder*
▲ **EMP:** 39 **EST:** 1988
**SQ FT:** 18,000
**SALES (est):** 4.48MM **Privately Held**
**Web:** www.progressivelabel.com
**SIC: 2679** 2672 2671 2241 Tags and labels, paper; Paper; coated and laminated, nec; Paper; coated and laminated packaging; Narrow fabric mills

**(P-4049)**
**SALINAS VALLEY WAX PAPER CO**
Also Called: Salinas Valley Wax Paper
1111 Abbott St, Salinas (93901-4501)
P.O. Box Po Box 68 (93902-0068)
**PHONE**..................................831 424-2747
Charles Nelson, *CEO*
Bill Zimmerman, *VP*
Chris Zimmerman, *Sec*
▲ **EMP:** 49 **EST:** 1928
**SQ FT:** 50,000
**SALES (est):** 1.67MM **Privately Held**
**Web:** www.svwpco.com
**SIC: 2679** 2672 Paper products, converted, nec; Paper; coated and laminated, nec

**(P-4050)**
**SIGNODE INDUSTRIAL GROUP LLC**
Also Called: Down River
3901 Navone Rd, Stockton (95215-9311)
**PHONE**..................................209 931-0917
Humberto Laguna, *Brnch Mgr*
**EMP:** 44
**SALES (corp-wide):** 12.01B **Publicly Held**
**Web:** www.signode.com
**SIC: 2679** 2655 Paper products, converted, nec; Ammunition cans or tubes, board laminated with metal foil
**HQ:** Signode Industrial Group Llc
14025 Rveredge Dr Ste 500
Tampa FL 33637
800 323-2464

**(P-4051)**
**SUMMIT ENTERPRISES INC**
Also Called: Summit Erosion Control
2471 Montecito Rd Ste A, Ramona (92065-1641)
P.O. Box 880335 (92168-0335)
**PHONE**..................................858 679-2100
Larry Holley, *CEO*
Timothy R Binder, *
**EMP:** 50 **EST:** 2005
**SALES (est):** 9.14MM **Privately Held**
**Web:** www.summiterosion.com
**SIC: 2679** Book covers, paper

**(P-4052)**
**SUNRISE MFG INC (PA)**
2665 Mercantile Dr, Rancho Cordova (95742)
**PHONE**..................................916 635-6262
James Sewell, *CEO*
◆ **EMP:** 25 **EST:** 1981
**SQ FT:** 72,000
**SALES (est):** 15.14MM
**SALES (corp-wide):** 15.14MM **Privately Held**
**Web:** www.sunrisemfg.com
**SIC: 2679** Building, insulating, and packaging paper

**(P-4053)**
**TAGTIME USA INC**
4601 District Blvd, Vernon (90058-2731)
**PHONE**..................................323 587-1555
Cort Johnson, *Pr*
Darryl Rudnick, *
Mindy Knox, *
David Scott, *
▲ **EMP:** 480 **EST:** 2001
**SQ FT:** 23,000
**SALES (est):** 16.66MM **Privately Held**
**Web:** www.tagtimeusa.com
**SIC: 2679** Labels, paper: made from purchased material

**(P-4054)**
**TEKNI-PLEX INC**
Also Called: Natvar
19555 Arenth Ave, City Of Industry (91748-1403)
**PHONE**..................................909 589-4366
Joleen Kennelley, *Brnch Mgr*
**EMP:** 97
**SALES (corp-wide):** 996.3MM **Privately Held**
**Web:** www.tekni-plex.com
**SIC: 2679** 3061 Egg cartons, molded pulp: made from purchased material; Medical and surgical rubber tubing (extruded and lathe-cut)
**PA:** Tekni-Plex, Inc.
460 E Swedesford Rd # 300
484 690-1520

**(P-4055)**
**THOMPSON PIPE GROUP INC (PA)**
3011 N Laurel Ave, Rialto (92377-3725)
**PHONE**..................................909 822-0200
Kenneth D Thompson, *CEO*
**EMP:** 26 **EST:** 2018
**SALES (est):** 30.07MM
**SALES (corp-wide):** 30.07MM **Privately Held**
**Web:** www.thompsonpipegroup.com
**SIC: 2679** Pipes and fittings, fiber: made from purchased material

**(P-4056)**
**TRIPLE D AND DS**
Also Called: Baron Paper Company
4040 Calle Platino Ste 105, Oceanside (92056-5833)
**EMP:** 23 **EST:** 2002
**SALES (est):** 854.87K **Privately Held**
**SIC: 2679** Paper products, converted, nec

**(P-4057)**
**W/S PACKAGING GROUP INC**
W/S Packaging Fullerton
531 Airpark Dr, Fullerton (92833-2501)
**PHONE**..................................714 992-2574
Mathew Edwards, *Genl Mgr*
**EMP:** 28
**SALES (corp-wide):** 14.54B **Privately Held**
**SIC: 2679** 2671 2759 Labels, paper: made from purchased material; Paper; coated and laminated packaging; Labels and seals: printing, nsk
**HQ:** W/S Packaging Group, Inc.
2571 S Hemlock Rd
Green Bay WI 54229
800 818-5481

**(P-4058)**
**WORLD CENTRIC**
Also Called: World Centric
1500 Valley House Dr Ste 210, Rohnert Park (94928-4938)
**PHONE**..................................707 241-9190
Aseem Das, *CEO*
Eugene Cordero, *
Paul Schmitt, *
◆ **EMP:** 65 **EST:** 2005
**SALES (est):** 18.92MM **Privately Held**
**Web:** www.worldcentric.com
**SIC: 2679** 2675 5113 Plates, pressed and molded pulp: from purchased material; Die-cut paper and board; Industrial and personal service paper

## 2711 Newspapers

**(P-4059)**
**13 STARS**
5860 El Camino Real Ste G, Atascadero (93422-3303)
P.O. Box 6068 (93422)
**PHONE**..................................805 466-4086
Nicholas Mattson, *CEO*
Hayley Elizabeth Mattson, *Ch Bd*
**EMP:** 19 **EST:** 2018
**SALES (est):** 1.2MM **Privately Held**
**Web:** www.pasoroblespress.com
**SIC: 2711** Newspapers, publishing and printing

**(P-4060)**
**2100 FREEDOM INC (HQ)**
625 N Grand Ave, Santa Ana (92701-4347)
**PHONE**..................................714 796-7000
Richard E Mirman, *CEO*
Aaron Kushner, *CEO*
**EMP:** 100 **EST:** 2012
**SALES (est):** 3.4MM
**SALES (corp-wide):** 9.3MM **Privately Held**
**SIC: 2711** 2721 7313 2741 Newspapers, publishing and printing; Periodicals; Newspaper advertising representative; Miscellaneous publishing
**PA:** 2100 Trust, Llc
625 N Grand Ave
877 469-7344

**(P-4061)**
**ACORN NEWSPAPER INC**
29800 Agoura Rd, Agoura Hills (91301-2576)
**PHONE**..................................818 706-0266
Jim Rule, *Pr*
**EMP:** 16 **EST:** 1974
**SALES (est):** 336.72K **Privately Held**
**Web:** www.theacorn.com
**SIC: 2711** Newspapers: publishing only, not printed on site

**(P-4062)**
**ALAMEDA NEWSPAPERS INC (DH)**
Also Called: Times Herald
22533 Foothill Blvd, Hayward (94541-4109)
**PHONE**..................................510 783-6111
Joh Schueler, *Pr*
P Scott Mckibben, *Pr*

## 2711 - Newspapers (P-4063)

EMP: 250 EST: 1985
SQ FT: 50,000
SALES (est): 2.77MM
SALES (corp-wide): 499.57MM **Privately Held**
SIC: 2711 Newspapers, publishing and printing
HQ: Medianews Group, Inc.
5990 Washington St
Denver CO 80216

### (P-4063)
### ALAMEDA NEWSPAPERS INC
Also Called: San Mateo Times
1080 S Amphlett Blvd, San Mateo (94402-1802)
PHONE...............................650 348-4321
Dan Cruey, *Mgr*
EMP: 214
SALES (corp-wide): 499.57MM **Privately Held**
SIC: 2711 Newspapers: publishing only, not printed on site
HQ: Alameda Newspapers, Inc
22533 Foothill Blvd
Hayward CA 94541
510 783-6111

### (P-4064)
### AMERICAN CITY BUS JOURNALS INC
Also Called: Sacramento Business Journal
555 Capitol Mall Ste 200, Sacramento (95814-4557)
P.O. Box 189249 (95818-9249)
PHONE...............................916 447-7661
Mike Trainor, *Genl Mgr*
EMP: 106
SALES (corp-wide): 2.88B **Privately Held**
Web: www.acbj.com
SIC: 2711 Newspapers: publishing only, not printed on site
HQ: American City Business Journals, Inc.
120 W Morehead St Ste 400
Charlotte NC 28202
704 973-1000

### (P-4065)
### ANTELOPE VALLEY NEWSPAPERS INC
Also Called: Antelope Valley Press
44939 10th St W, Lancaster (93534-2313)
PHONE...............................661 940-1000
Tammy Valdes, *Mgr*
EMP: 29
SALES (corp-wide): 9.82MM **Privately Held**
Web: www.avpress.com
SIC: 2711 7313 2741 Newspapers: publishing only, not printed on site; Newspaper advertising representative; Miscellaneous publishing
PA: Antelope Valley Newspapers Inc.
37404 Sierra Hwy
661 273-2700

### (P-4066)
### ARGONAUT
5355 Mcconnell Ave, Los Angeles (90066-7025)
PHONE...............................310 822-1629
David Asper Johnson, *Pr*
George Drury Smith, *
EMP: 37 EST: 1971
SQ FT: 10,000
SALES (est): 494.68K **Privately Held**
Web: www.argonautnews.com
SIC: 2711 Newspapers: publishing only, not printed on site

### (P-4067)
### ASIA-PACIFIC CALIFORNIA INC (PA)
Also Called: China Press, The
2121 W Mission Rd Ste 207, Alhambra (91803-1431)
PHONE...............................323 318-2254
Yining Xie, *Pr*
▲ EMP: 17 EST: 1991
SQ FT: 13,000
SALES (est): 2.5MM **Privately Held**
SIC: 2711 Newspapers, publishing and printing

### (P-4068)
### ASIA-PACIFIC CALIFORNIA INC
Also Called: The China Press
1710 S Del Mar Ave, San Gabriel (91776)
PHONE...............................626 281-8500
Non Hiand, *Genl Mgr*
EMP: 35
SIC: 2711 Newspapers, publishing and printing
PA: Asia-Pacific California, Inc.
2121 W Mission Rd Ste 207

### (P-4069)
### ASSOCIATED DESERT NEWSPAPER (DH)
Also Called: Imperial Valley Press
205 N 8th St, El Centro (92243-2301)
P.O. Box 2641 (92244-2641)
PHONE...............................760 337-3400
Mayer Malone, *Pr*
David Leone, *
Teresa Zimmer, *
Clifford James, *
John Yanni, *
EMP: 40 EST: 1950
SQ FT: 30,000
SALES (est): 9.91MM
SALES (corp-wide): 3.28B **Publicly Held**
Web: www.ivpressonline.com
SIC: 2711 Newspapers, publishing and printing
HQ: Schurz Communications, Inc.
1301 E Douglas Rd Ste 200
Mishawaka IN 46545
574 247-7237

### (P-4070)
### ASSOCIATED STUDENTS UCLA
Also Called: Asucla Publications
308 Westwood Plz Ste 118, Los Angeles (90095-8355)
PHONE...............................310 825-2787
Arvli Ward, *Mgr*
EMP: 153
SALES (corp-wide): 55.96MM **Privately Held**
Web: asucla.ucla.edu
SIC: 2711 2741 2721 Newspapers: publishing only, not printed on site; Miscellaneous publishing; Periodicals
PA: Associated Students U.C.L.A.
308 Westwood Plz
310 794-8836

### (P-4071)
### AUBURN TRADER INC (DH)
1115 Grass Valley Hwy, Auburn (95603-3439)
P.O. Box 5910 (95604-5910)
PHONE...............................530 888-7653
Bill Brehm, *Pr*
Kim Christen, *Mgr*
EMP: 20 EST: 1981
SALES (est): 46.15MM
SALES (corp-wide): 106.45MM **Privately Held**
Web: www.goldcountrymedia.com
SIC: 2711 Newspapers, publishing and printing
HQ: Auburn Journal Inc
1030 High St
Auburn CA 95603
530 885-5656

### (P-4072)
### BALITA MEDIA INC
Also Called: Weekend Balita
2629 Foothill Blvd, La Crescenta (91214-3511)
PHONE...............................818 552-4503
Luchie Allen, *CEO*
Ramonsito Mendoza, *Sec*
Ruby Allen, *Prin*
EMP: 18 EST: 1993
SALES (est): 887.29K **Privately Held**
Web: www.balita.com
SIC: 2711 Newspapers, publishing and printing

### (P-4073)
### BAR MEDIA INC
Also Called: Bay Area Reporter
44 Gough St Ste 302, San Francisco (94103-5423)
PHONE...............................415 861-5019
Michael Yamashita, *Pr*
Thomas E Horn, *Ch Bd*
Todd Vogt, *Sec*
Patrick Brown, *Chief Financial*
EMP: 15 EST: 2013
SALES (est): 1.12MM **Privately Held**
Web: www.ebar.com
SIC: 2711 Newspapers, publishing and printing

### (P-4074)
### BAY GUARDIAN COMPANY
Also Called: San Francisco Bay Guardian
135 Micaicaippi St, San Francisco (94107)
PHONE...............................415 255-3100
Bruce Brugman, *Pr*
Jean Brugman, *
EMP: 42 EST: 1966
SQ FT: 28,000
SALES (est): 214.57K **Privately Held**
Web: www.sfbg.com
SIC: 2711 Newspapers, publishing and printing

### (P-4075)
### BERKELEYSIDE LLC
2120 University Ave, Berkeley (94704-1026)
PHONE...............................510 671-0380
EMP: 22 EST: 2012
SALES (est): 432.56K **Privately Held**
Web: www.berkeleyside.org
SIC: 2711 Newspapers, publishing and printing

### (P-4076)
### BIOCENTURY INC (PA)
1235 Radio Rd Ste 100, Redwood City (94065-1315)
P.O. Box 1246 (94070-1246)
PHONE...............................650 595-5333
David Flores, *Pr*
EMP: 17 EST: 1992
SALES (est): 8.88MM **Privately Held**
Web: www.biocentury.com
SIC: 2711 2721 Newspapers; Periodicals

### (P-4077)
### BRENTWOOD PRESS & PUBG CO LLC
Also Called: Brentwood Yellow Pages
248 Oak St, Brentwood (94513-1337)
PHONE...............................925 516-4757
Jimmy Chamores, *Managing Member*
EMP: 45 EST: 1997
SQ FT: 3,500
SALES (est): 917.24K **Privately Held**
Web: www.thepress.net
SIC: 2711 Newspapers, publishing and printing

### (P-4078)
### BUSINESS JRNL PUBLICATIONS INC
125 S Market St Ste 1100 # 11, San Jose (95113-2292)
PHONE...............................408 295-3800
Italo Jimenez, *Mgr*
EMP: 507
SALES (corp-wide): 2.88B **Privately Held**
SIC: 2711 Newspapers: publishing only, not printed on site
HQ: Business Journal Publications, Inc.
4350 W Cypress St Ste 800
Tampa FL 33607

### (P-4079)
### BUSINESS JRNL PUBLICATIONS INC
Also Called: San Francisco Business Times
275 Battery St Ste 250, San Francisco (94111-3318)
PHONE...............................415 989-2522
Mary Huss, *Prin*
EMP: 45
SALES (corp-wide): 2.88B **Privately Held**
Web: www.databirdjournal.com
SIC: 2711 Newspapers: publishing only, not printed on site
HQ: Business Journal Publications, Inc.
4350 W Cypress St Ste 800
Tampa FL 33607

### (P-4080)
### CALIFORNIA COMMUNITY NEWS LLC (DH)
2000 E 8th St, Los Angeles (90021-2474)
PHONE...............................626 388-1017
Eddy Hartenstein, *Pr*
Judy Kendall, *
Julie Xanders, *
EMP: 349 EST: 1993
SALES (est): 5.27MM **Privately Held**
SIC: 2711 Newspapers, publishing and printing
HQ: Tribune Publishing Company
1000 Albion Ave
Schaumburg IL 60193
312 222-9100

### (P-4081)
### CALIFORNIA COMMUNITY NEWS LLC
Also Called: Burbank Leader
221 N Brand Blvd Fl 2, Glendale (91203-2609)
PHONE...............................818 843-8700
Danette Goulet, *Mgr*
EMP: 56
SIC: 2711 Newspapers: publishing only, not printed on site
HQ: California Community News, Llc
2000 E 8th St
Los Angeles CA 90021

### (P-4082)
### CALIFORNIA NEWSPAPERS INC
Also Called: Marin Independent Journal
150 Alameda Del Prado, Novato (94949-6665)

## PRODUCTS & SERVICES SECTION
## 2711 - Newspapers (P-4100)

PHONE..............................415 883-8600
Roger Grossman, *Pr*
Mario Bendingan, *
**EMP:** 1584 **EST:** 1861
**SQ FT:** 60,000
**SALES (est):** 1.1MM
**SALES (corp-wide):** 499.57MM **Privately Held**
**SIC: 2711** Commercial printing and newspaper publishing combined
**HQ:** California Newspapers Limited Partnership
605 E Huntington Dr # 100
Monrovia CA 91016
626 962-8811

### (P-4083)
### CALIFORNIA NEWSPAPERS PARTNR (PA)
Also Called: Mng Newspapers
4 N 2nd St Ste 700, San Jose (95113-1308)
PHONE..............................408 920-5333
Steven B Rossi, *Pr*
**EMP:** 50 **EST:** 2004
**SALES (est):** 23.25MM
**SALES (corp-wide):** 23.25MM **Privately Held**
Web: www.mercurynews.com
**SIC: 2711** Newspapers, publishing and printing

### (P-4084)
### CALIFORNIA NEWSPPR SVC BUR INC
Also Called: California Newspaper Service
915 E 1st St, Los Angeles (90012-4050)
P.O. Box 60460 (90060-0460)
PHONE..............................213 229-5500
**EMP:** 17 **EST:** 1990
**SALES (est):** 2.26MM
**SALES (corp-wide):** 67.71MM **Publicly Held**
Web: www.journaltech.com
**SIC: 2711** Newspapers, publishing and printing
**PA:** Daily Journal Corporation
915 E 1st St
213 229-5300

### (P-4085)
### CALIFRNIA NWSPAPERS LTD PARTNR (DH)
Also Called: Inland Valley Daily Bulletin
605 E Huntington Dr Ste 100, Monrovia (91016-3636)
P.O. Box 1259 (91722-0259)
PHONE..............................626 962-8811
Ron Hasse, *Pr*
Mark Welches, *VP*
**EMP:** 450 **EST:** 1997
**SALES (est):** 15.7MM
**SALES (corp-wide):** 499.57MM **Privately Held**
Web: www.sgvtribune.com
**SIC: 2711** Newspapers, publishing and printing
**HQ:** Medianews Group, Inc.
5990 Washington St
Denver CO 80216

### (P-4086)
### CALIFRNIA NWSPAPERS LTD PARTNR
Also Called: Inland Valley Daily Bulletin
3200 E Guasti Rd Ste 100, Ontario (91761-8661)
PHONE..............................909 987-6397
Bob Balzer, *Mgr*
**EMP:** 288
**SALES (corp-wide):** 499.57MM **Privately Held**

Web: www.sgvtribune.com
**SIC: 2711** Newspapers, publishing and printing
**HQ:** California Newspapers Limited Partnership
605 E Huntington Dr # 100
Monrovia CA 91016
626 962-8811

### (P-4087)
### CALIFRNIA NWSPAPERS LTD PARTNR
Also Called: Redlands Daily Facts
19 E Citrus Ave Ste 102, Redlands (92373-4763)
PHONE..............................909 793-3221
Peggy Del Torro, *Mgr*
**EMP:** 288
**SQ FT:** 8,301
**SALES (corp-wide):** 499.57MM **Privately Held**
Web: www.sgvtribune.com
**SIC: 2711** 7313 Newspapers, publishing and printing; Newspaper advertising representative
**HQ:** California Newspapers Limited Partnership
605 E Huntington Dr # 100
Monrovia CA 91016
626 962-8811

### (P-4088)
### CALIFRNIA NWSPAPERS LTD PARTNR
Also Called: Media News
5399 Clark Rd, Paradise (95969-6325)
P.O. Box 70 (95967-0070)
PHONE..............................530 877-4413
Steve Mccormick, *Contrlr*
**EMP:** 288
**SALES (corp-wide):** 499.57MM **Privately Held**
Web: www.paradisepost.com
**SIC: 2711** 2796 2791 2789 Newspapers: publishing only, not printed on site; Platemaking services; Typesetting; Bookbinding and related work
**HQ:** California Newspapers Limited Partnership
605 E Huntington Dr # 100
Monrovia CA 91016
626 962-8811

### (P-4089)
### CHICKEN RNCH ECONOMIC DEV CORP
Also Called: Cred-Corp
16929 Chicken Ranch Rd, Jamestown (95327-9779)
PHONE..............................209 984-9066
**EMP:** 25 **EST:** 2021
**SALES (est):** 471.65K **Privately Held**
**SIC: 2711** Newspapers

### (P-4090)
### CHICO COMMUNITY PUBLISHING (PA)
Also Called: Reno News & Review
603 Orange St, Chico (95928-5020)
P.O. Box 13370 (95813-3370)
PHONE..............................530 894-2300
Deborah Redmond, *CEO*
Jeff Vonkaenel, *
Valentina Flynn, *
Charles Marcks, *
Deborah Redmond, *Sec*
**EMP:** 40 **EST:** 1977
**SQ FT:** 7,200
**SALES (est):** 3.6MM
**SALES (corp-wide):** 3.6MM **Privately Held**

Web: sacramento.newsreview.com
**SIC: 2711** Newspapers, publishing and printing

### (P-4091)
### CHICO COMMUNITY PUBLISHING
Also Called: Sacramento News & Review
3925 Power Inn Rd, Sacramento (95826-4334)
P.O. Box 13370 (95813-3370)
PHONE..............................916 498-1234
Deborah Redmond, *Prin*
**EMP:** 101
**SALES (corp-wide):** 7.81MM **Privately Held**
Web: www.newsreview.com
**SIC: 2711** Newspapers, publishing and printing
**PA:** Chico Community Publishing Inc
603 Orange St
530 894-2300

### (P-4092)
### CHURM PUBLISHING INC (PA)
Also Called: O.C. Metro Magazine
1451 Quail St Ste 201, Newport Beach (92660-2741)
PHONE..............................714 796-7000
Steve Churm, *Pr*
Peter Churm, *
Brian O'neill, *CFO*
**EMP:** 47 **EST:** 1982
**SQ FT:** 7,000
**SALES (est):** 457.3K
**SALES (corp-wide):** 457.3K **Privately Held**
Web: www.ocmetro.com
**SIC: 2711** Newspapers, publishing and printing

### (P-4093)
### CITY NEWS GROUP INC
22797 Barton Rd, Grand Terrace (92313-5207)
PHONE..............................909 370-1200
Margie Miller, *CEO*
**EMP:** 20 **EST:** 2006
**SALES (est):** 221.51K **Privately Held**
Web: www.citynewsgroup.com
**SIC: 2711** 2621 7311 Newspapers: publishing only, not printed on site; Catalog, magazine, and newsprint papers; Advertising agencies

### (P-4094)
### CLAREMONT COURIER INC
114 Olive St, Claremont (91711-4924)
P.O. Box 878 (91711)
PHONE..............................909 621-4761
Peter Weinberger, *Pr*
**EMP:** 18 **EST:** 1955
**SQ FT:** 4,000
**SALES (est):** 474.92K **Privately Held**
Web: www.claremont-courier.com
**SIC: 2711** Newspapers, publishing and printing

### (P-4095)
### COAST NEWS INC
Also Called: Beach News
531 Encinitas Blvd Ste 204, Encinitas (92024-3773)
P.O. Box 232550 (92023-2550)
PHONE..............................760 436-9737
James Kydd, *CEO*
**EMP:** 70 **EST:** 1987
**SALES (est):** 4MM **Privately Held**
Web: www.thecoastnews.com

**SIC: 2711** 2741 Newspapers, publishing and printing; Miscellaneous publishing

### (P-4096)
### COMMUNITY MEDIA CORPORATION
19100 Crest Ave Apt 26, Castro Valley (94546-2864)
PHONE..............................657 337-0200
Alene Renne Whiten, *Brnch Mgr*
**EMP:** 43
Web: www.communitymediaus.com
**SIC: 2711** Newspapers, publishing and printing
**PA:** Community Media Corporation
15005 S Vermont Ave

### (P-4097)
### COMMUNITY MEDIA CORPORATION (PA)
Also Called: San Dego Nghborhood Newspapers
15005 S Vermont Ave, Gardena (90247-3004)
PHONE..............................714 220-0292
Kathy Verdugo, *Pr*
**EMP:** 37 **EST:** 1993
**SALES (est):** 4.65MM **Privately Held**
Web: www.communitymediaus.com
**SIC: 2711** Newspapers, publishing and printing

### (P-4098)
### CONTRA COSTA NEWSPAPERS INC (DH)
Also Called: Contra Costa Times
175 Lennon Ln Ste 100, Walnut Creek (94598-2466)
PHONE..............................925 935-2525
George Riggs, *CEO*
John Armstrong, *
**EMP:** 1000 **EST:** 1947
**SQ FT:** 180,000
**SALES (est):** 9.93MM
**SALES (corp-wide):** 499.57MM **Privately Held**
**SIC: 2711** Newspapers, publishing and printing
**HQ:** Medianews Group, Inc.
5990 Washington St
Denver CO 80216

### (P-4099)
### CONTRA COSTA NEWSPAPERS INC
4301 Lakeside Dr, San Pablo (94806-5281)
PHONE..............................510 758-8400
Kathy Edwards, *Prin*
**EMP:** 100
**SQ FT:** 8,000
**SALES (corp-wide):** 499.57MM **Privately Held**
**SIC: 2711** Newspapers, publishing and printing
**HQ:** Contra Costa Newspapers, Inc.
175 Lennon Ln Ste 100
Walnut Creek CA 94598
925 935-2525

### (P-4100)
### CYCLE NEWS INC (PA)
Also Called: CN Publishing Group
17771 Mitchell N, Irvine (92614-6028)
PHONE..............................949 863-7082
Sharon Clayton, *Pr*
**EMP:** 32 **EST:** 1965
**SQ FT:** 10,000
**SALES (est):** 4.75MM
**SALES (corp-wide):** 4.75MM **Privately Held**

Web: www.cyclenews.com
SIC: 2711  Newspapers, publishing and printing

**(P-4101)**
**DAILY JOURNAL CORPORATION (PA)**
915 E 1st St, Los Angeles  (90012-4042)
PHONE..............................213 229-5300
Steven Myhill-jones, *Interim Chief Executive Officer*
Tu To, *CFO*
EMP: 69 EST: 1888
SQ FT: 34,000
SALES (est): 67.71MM
SALES (corp-wide): 67.71MM **Publicly Held**
Web: www.dailyjournal.com
SIC: 2711 2721 7313 7372  Newspapers, publishing and printing; Magazines: publishing and printing; Newspaper advertising representative; Prepackaged software

**(P-4102)**
**DAILYMEDIA  INC (PA)**
8 E Figueroa St Ste 220, Santa Barbara  (93101-2716)
PHONE..............................541 821-5207
Scott Blum, *Pr*
EMP: 19 EST: 2005
SQ FT: 5,000
SALES (est): 264.21K **Privately Held**
SIC: 2711  Newspapers, publishing and printing

**(P-4103)**
**DESERT SUN PUBLISHING CO (DH)**
Also Called: Desert Sun The
750 N Gene Autry Trl, Palm Springs  (92262-5463)
P.O. Box 2734 (92263-2734)
PHONE..............................760 322-8889
EMP: 200 EST: 1974
SQ FT: 30,621
SALES (est): 2.23MM
SALES (corp-wide): 2.66B **Publicly Held**
Web: www.desertsun.com
SIC: 2711  Newspapers, publishing and printing
HQ: Gannett Media Corp.
     7950 Jones Branch Dr
     Mclean VA 22102
     703 854-6000

**(P-4104)**
**DOW JONES & COMPANY  INC**
Also Called: Dow Jones
201 California St Ste 1350, San Francisco  (94111-5022)
PHONE..............................415 765-6131
Steve Yoder, *Chief*
EMP: 22
SALES (corp-wide): 10.09B **Publicly Held**
Web: www.dowjones.com
SIC: 2711  Newspapers, publishing and printing
HQ: Dow Jones & Company, Inc.
     1211 Ave Of The Americas
     New York NY 10036
     800 369-5663

**(P-4105)**
**DOW JONES LMG STOCKTON INC**
Also Called: Record The
530 E Market St, Stockton  (95202-3009)
P.O. Box 900  (95201-0900)
PHONE..............................209 943-6397
Deitra Kenoly, *Pr*
Roger Coover, *
EMP: 223 EST: 2003
SALES (est): 1.85MM
SALES (corp-wide): 2.66B **Publicly Held**
Web: www.recordnet.com
SIC: 2711  Newspapers, publishing and printing
HQ: Local Media Group, Inc.
     90 Crystal Run Rd Ste 310
     Middletown NY 10941
     845 341-1100

**(P-4106)**
**E Z BUY & E Z SELL RECYCL CORP (DH)**
Also Called: Recycler Classified
4954 Van Nuys Blvd Ste 201, Sherman Oaks  (91403-1719)
PHONE..............................310 886-7808
Niki Ruokosuo, *Pr*
Jim Fullmer, *
EMP: 200 EST: 1973
SQ FT: 13,000
SALES (est): 48.09MM
SALES (corp-wide): 4.93B **Publicly Held**
Web: recyclerclassifieds.blogspot.com
SIC: 2711 2741  Newspapers: publishing only, not printed on site; Miscellaneous publishing
HQ: Tribune Media Company
     515 N State St Ste 2400
     Chicago IL 60654
     312 222-3394

**(P-4107)**
**EAST BAY PUBLISHING LLC**
Also Called: East Bay Express
318 Harrison St Ste 302, Oakland  (94607-4134)
PHONE..............................510 879-3708
EMP: 15
SALES (est): 225.68K **Privately Held**
Web: www.eastbayexpress.com
SIC: 2711  Newspapers, publishing and printing

**(P-4108)**
**EL CLASIFICADO (PA)**
11205 Imperial Hwy, Norwalk  (90650-2229)
PHONE..............................323 837-4095
Martha C Dela Torre, *Pr*
Gil Garcia, *
Joseph Badame, *
EMP: 42 EST: 1988
SALES (est): 24.96MM **Privately Held**
Web: www.elclasificado.com
SIC: 2711  Newspapers, publishing and printing

**(P-4109)**
**EL DORADO NEWSPAPERS (DH)**
Also Called: Clovis Independent
2100 Q St, Sacramento  (95816-6816)
P.O. Box 15779 (95852-0779)
PHONE..............................916 321-1826
Karole Morgan-prager, *Sec*
EMP: 200 EST: 1979
SALES (est): 44.71MM
SALES (corp-wide): 709.52MM **Privately Held**
Web: www.mcclatchy.com
SIC: 2711  Commercial printing and newspaper publishing combined
HQ: Mcclatchy Newspapers, Inc.
     1601 Alhambra Blvd # 100
     Sacramento CA 95816
     916 321-1855

**(P-4110)**
**EMBARCADERO MEDIA**
Also Called: Country Almanac
3525 Alameda De Las Pulgas, Menlo Park  (94025-6544)
PHONE..............................650 854-2626
Tom Gibboney, *Publisher*
EMP: 25
SALES (corp-wide): 6.89MM **Privately Held**
Web: www.embarcaderomediagroup.com
SIC: 2711  Newspapers, publishing and printing
PA: Embarcadero Media
     450 Cambridge Ave
     650 964-6300

**(P-4111)**
**EMBARCADERO MEDIA (PA)**
Also Called: Country Almanac
450 Cambridge Ave, Palo Alto  (94306-1507)
P.O. Box 1610  (94302-1610)
PHONE..............................650 964-6300
William Johnson, *Pr*
EMP: 100 EST: 1979
SQ FT: 4,500
SALES (est): 6.89MM
SALES (corp-wide): 6.89MM **Privately Held**
Web: www.embarcaderomediagroup.com
SIC: 2711  Commercial printing and newspaper publishing combined

**(P-4112)**
**EPOCH TIMES LOS ANGELES**
9550 Flair Dr, El Monte  (91731-2900)
PHONE..............................626 401-1828
Joseph Cheng, *Prin*
EMP: 17 EST: 2010
SALES (est): 9.52MM **Privately Held**
Web: www.epochtimes.com
SIC: 2711  Newspapers, publishing and printing

**(P-4113)**
**FEATHER PUBLISHING COMPANY INC (PA)**
Also Called: Feather River Bulletin
287 Lawrence St, Quincy  (95971-9477)
P.O. Box B  (95971-3586)
PHONE..............................530 283-0800
Michael C Taborski, *Pr*
Keri B Taborski, *
EMP: 30 EST: 1866
SALES (est): 3.47MM
SALES (corp-wide): 3.47MM **Privately Held**
Web: www.plumasnews.com
SIC: 2711 2752  Newspapers, publishing and printing; Lithographing on metal

**(P-4114)**
**FOOTHILLS SUN-GAZETTE**
Also Called: Foothills Advertiser
120 Ne St, Exeter  (93221-1729)
P.O. Box 7  (93221-0007)
PHONE..............................559 592-3171
Katie Byrne, *Pr*
Reggie Ellis, *VP*
Wsley Byrne, *Treas*
William Brown, *Prin*
EMP: 20 EST: 1984
SQ FT: 5,000
SALES (est): 837.51K **Privately Held**
Web: www.thesungazette.com
SIC: 2711  Newspapers, publishing and printing

**(P-4115)**
**FREEDOM COMMUNICATIONS INC**
Also Called: Freedom Newspapers
625 N Grand Ave, Santa Ana  (92701-4347)
P.O. Box 11450  (92711-1450)
PHONE..............................714 796-7000
▲ EMP: 7542
SIC: 2711 2721 7313 2741  Newspapers, publishing and printing; Periodicals; Newspaper advertising representative; Miscellaneous publishing

**(P-4116)**
**GANNETT STLLITE INFO NTWRK LLC**
6060 Center Dr, Los Angeles  (90045-1587)
PHONE..............................310 846-5870
EMP: 18
SALES (corp-wide): 2.66B **Publicly Held**
Web: www.usatoday.com
SIC: 2711  Newspapers, publishing and printing
HQ: Gannett Satellite Information Network, Llc
     1675 Broadway Fl 23
     New York NY 10019
     703 854-6000

**(P-4117)**
**GARDENA VALLEY NEWS  INC**
Also Called: Valley News Gardens
15005 S Vermont Ave, Gardena  (90247-3004)
P.O. Box 219  (90248-0219)
PHONE..............................310 329-6351
George D Algie, *Pr*
Ruriko Yatabe, *
EMP: 40 EST: 1904
SQ FT: 8,200
SALES (est): 695.81K **Privately Held**
Web: www.gardenavalleynews.org
SIC: 2711  Commercial printing and newspaper publishing combined

**(P-4118)**
**GATEHOUSE MEDIA  LLC**
Also Called: Fort Bragg Advocate-News
617 S State St, Ukiah  (95482-4912)
P.O. Box 1188  (95437-1188)
PHONE..............................707 964-5642
Stan Andreson, *Mgr*
EMP: 35
SALES (corp-wide): 2.66B **Publicly Held**
Web: www.mendocinobeacon.com
SIC: 2711  Newspapers, publishing and printing
HQ: Gatehouse Media, Llc
     175 Sllys Trl Fl 3 Corp C
     Pittsford NY 14534
     585 598-0030

**(P-4119)**
**GATEHOUSE MEDIA  LLC**
Also Called: Siskiyou Daily News
309 S Broadway St, Yreka  (96097-2905)
P.O. Box 127  (96067-0127)
PHONE..............................530 842-5777
Rod Ows, *Brnch Mgr*
EMP: 35
SALES (corp-wide): 2.66B **Publicly Held**
Web: www.gannett.com
SIC: 2711  Newspapers, publishing and printing
HQ: Gatehouse Media, Llc
     175 Sllys Trl Fl 3 Corp C
     Pittsford NY 14534
     585 598-0030

## PRODUCTS & SERVICES SECTION
### 2711 - Newspapers (P-4138)

**(P-4120)**
**GATEHOUSE MEDIA LLC**
Also Called: Chico Enterprise Record
400 E Park Ave, Chico (95928-7127)
P.O. Box 9 (95927-0009)
PHONE...................530 891-1234
Wolf Rosenberg, *Brnch Mgr*
**EMP:** 123
**SALES (corp-wide):** 2.66B **Publicly Held**
Web: www.gannett.com
**SIC:** 2711 Newspapers, publishing and printing
**HQ:** Gatehouse Media, Llc
 175 Sllys Trl Fl 3 Corp C
 Pittsford NY 14534
 585 598-0030

**(P-4121)**
**GATEHOUSE MEDIA LLC**
Also Called: Victorville Daily Press
13891 Park Ave, Victorville (92392-2435)
PHONE...................760 241-7744
**EMP:** 26
**SALES (corp-wide):** 2.66B **Publicly Held**
Web: www.vvdailypress.com
**SIC:** 2711 Commercial printing and newspaper publishing combined
**HQ:** Gatehouse Media, Llc
 175 Sllys Trl Fl 3 Corp C
 Pittsford NY 14534
 585 598-0030

**(P-4122)**
**GIBSON PRINTING & PUBG INC**
Also Called: Benicia Herald
820 1st St, Benicia (94510-3216)
P.O. Box 65 (94510-0065)
PHONE...................707 745-0733
Pam Poppee, *Mgr*
**EMP:** 25
**SALES (corp-wide):** 774.83K **Privately Held**
Web: www.gibsondunn.com
**SIC:** 2711 7313 Newspapers: publishing only, not printed on site; Newspaper advertising representative
**PA:** Gibson Printing & Publishing, Inc.
 544 Curtola Pkwy

**(P-4123)**
**GRACE COMMUNICATIONS INC (PA)**
Also Called: Metropolitan News Company
210 S Spring St, Los Angeles (90012-3710)
P.O. Box 86308 (90086-0308)
PHONE...................213 628-4384
Joann W Grace, *Pr*
Roger M Grace, *
**EMP:** 43 **EST:** 1901
**SQ FT:** 21,000
**SALES (est):** 8.87MM
**SALES (corp-wide):** 8.87MM **Privately Held**
Web: www.mnc.net
**SIC:** 2711 Newspapers, publishing and printing

**(P-4124)**
**GUM SUN TIMES INC (PA)**
Also Called: Chinese Times
625 Kearny St, San Francisco (94108-1849)
PHONE...................415 379-6788
Michael Lamm, *Pr*
See B Stanley Hom, *Pr*
Harrison Lim, *Pr*
**EMP:** 17 **EST:** 1920
**SQ FT:** 9,000
**SALES (est):** 397.61K
**SALES (corp-wide):** 397.61K **Privately Held**
Web: www.bestofsfchinatown.com
**SIC:** 2711 Newspapers: publishing only, not printed on site

**(P-4125)**
**HANFORD SENTINEL INC**
Also Called: Pulitzer Community Newspapers
300 W 6th St, Hanford (93230-4518)
P.O. Box 9 (93232-0009)
PHONE...................559 582-0471
Randy Rickman, *Pr*
Mark Daniel, *
**EMP:** 304 **EST:** 1900
**SQ FT:** 16,000
**SALES (est):** 861.03K
**SALES (corp-wide):** 691.14MM **Publicly Held**
Web: www.hanfordsentinel.com
**SIC:** 2711 Commercial printing and newspaper publishing combined
**HQ:** Pulitzer Inc
 900 N Tucker Blvd
 Saint Louis MO 63101
 314 340-8000

**(P-4126)**
**HARRELL HOLDINGS (PA)**
1707 Eye St Ste 102, Bakersfield (93301-5208)
P.O. Box 440 (93302-0440)
PHONE...................661 322-5627
Richard Beene, *Pr*
Virginia Fritts Moorhouse, *
Gizel Bermudez, *
Michelle Hirst, *
Logan Molen, *
**EMP:** 188 **EST:** 1897
**SALES (est):** 13.61MM
**SALES (corp-wide):** 13.61MM **Privately Held**
Web: www.bakersfield.com
**SIC:** 2711 Commercial printing and newspaper publishing combined

**(P-4127)**
**HEARST COMMUNICATIONS INC**
Chronicle Books
680 2nd St, San Francisco (94107-2015)
PHONE...................415 537-4200
Nion Mcevoy, *Mgr*
**EMP:** 23
**SALES (corp-wide):** 4.29B **Privately Held**
Web: www.hearst.com
**SIC:** 2711 Newspapers, publishing and printing
**HQ:** Hearst Communications, Inc.
 300 W 57th St
 New York NY 10019
 212 649-2000

**(P-4128)**
**HERBURGER PUBLICATIONS INC (PA)**
Also Called: Galt Herald
604 N Lincoln Way, Galt (95632-8601)
P.O. Box 307 (95632-0307)
PHONE...................916 685-5533
Roy Herburger, *Pr*
David Herburger, *General Vice President*
**EMP:** 60 **EST:** 1903
**SQ FT:** 10,000
**SALES (est):** 2.57MM
**SALES (corp-wide):** 2.57MM **Privately Held**
Web: www.herburger.net
**SIC:** 2711 Commercial printing and newspaper publishing combined

**(P-4129)**
**HI-DESERT PUBLISHING COMPANY**
Also Called: Yucaipa & Calimesa News Mirror
35154 Yucaipa Blvd, Yucaipa (92399-4339)
P.O. Box 760 (92399-0760)
PHONE...................909 795-8145
Jerry Bean, *Mgr*
**EMP:** 27
**SALES (corp-wide):** 21.91MM **Privately Held**
Web: www.newsmirror.net
**SIC:** 2711 Newspapers, publishing and printing
**HQ:** Hi-Desert Publishing Company
 56445 29 Palms Hwy
 Yucca Valley CA 92284

**(P-4130)**
**HI-DESERT PUBLISHING COMPANY (HQ)**
56445 29 Palms Hwy, Yucca Valley (92284-2861)
PHONE...................760 365-3315
Cindy Melland, *Publisher*
Stacy Moore, *
**EMP:** 70 **EST:** 1990
**SALES (est):** 10.35MM
**SALES (corp-wide):** 106.45MM **Privately Held**
Web: www.hidesertstar.com
**SIC:** 2711 Newspapers, publishing and printing
**PA:** Brehm Communications, Inc.
 16644 W Bernardo Dr # 300
 858 451-6200

**(P-4131)**
**HI-DESERT PUBLISHING COMPANY**
Also Called: Mountain News & Shopper
28200 Highway 189 Bldg O-1, Lake Arrowhead (92352-9700)
P.O. Box 2410 (92352-2410)
PHONE...................909 336-3555
Harry Bradley, *Mgr*
**EMP:** 41
**SALES (corp-wide):** 21.91MM **Privately Held**
Web: www.hidesertstar.com
**SIC:** 2711 Commercial printing and newspaper publishing combined
**HQ:** Hi-Desert Publishing Company
 56445 29 Palms Hwy
 Yucca Valley CA 92284

**(P-4132)**
**HOMES & LAND OF VENTURA**
Also Called: Publishers Distribution Svcs
2193 Portola Rd, Ventura (93003-7723)
PHONE...................805 644-9816
Donald J Wilkinson, *Owner*
**EMP:** 20 **EST:** 1987
**SALES (est):** 271.71K **Privately Held**
**SIC:** 2711 8742 Newspapers; Marketing consulting services

**(P-4133)**
**INDEPNDENT BRKLEY STDNT PUBG I**
Also Called: DAILY CALIFORNIAN
2483 Hearst Ave, Berkeley (94709-1320)
P.O. Box 1949 (94701-1949)
PHONE...................510 548-8300
Karim Doumar, *Pr*
**EMP:** 42 **EST:** 1871
**SQ FT:** 4,100
**SALES (est):** 237.64K **Privately Held**
Web: www.dailycal.org

**(P-4134)**
**INDIA-WEST PUBLICATIONS INC (PA)**
933 Macarthur Blvd, San Leandro (94577-3062)
PHONE...................510 383-1140
Ramesh Murarka, *Pr*
Bina Murarka, *Sec*
**EMP:** 21 **EST:** 1975
**SQ FT:** 7,000
**SALES (est):** 869.05K
**SALES (corp-wide):** 869.05K **Privately Held**
Web: www.indiawest.com
**SIC:** 2711 Newspapers, publishing and printing

**(P-4135)**
**INTERNATIONAL DAILY NEWS INC (PA)**
870 Monterey Pass Rd, Monterey Park (91754-3688)
PHONE...................323 265-1317
Jessica G Elnitiarta, *Pr*
▲ **EMP:** 20 **EST:** 1981
**SQ FT:** 10,000
**SALES (est):** 3.33MM
**SALES (corp-wide):** 3.33MM **Privately Held**
Web: www.chinesetoday.com
**SIC:** 2711 Newspapers, publishing and printing

**(P-4136)**
**INVESTORS BUSINESS DAILY INC (HQ)**
5900 Wilshire Blvd Ste 2950, Los Angeles (90036-5013)
PHONE...................800 831-2525
William O'neil, *Pr*
Kathy Sherman, *
Edward Skolarus, *CDO*
▲ **EMP:** 200 **EST:** 1984
**SQ FT:** 180,000
**SALES (est):** 11.48MM
**SALES (corp-wide):** 335.64MM **Privately Held**
Web: www.investors.com
**SIC:** 2711 Newspapers, publishing and printing
**PA:** Data Analysis Inc.
 12655 Beatrice St
 310 448-6800

**(P-4137)**
**JCK LEGACY COMPANY (HQ)**
1601 Alhambra Blvd Ste 100, Sacramento (95816-7165)
P.O. Box 15779 (95852)
PHONE...................916 321-1844
Tony Hunter, *CEO*
**EMP:** 97 **EST:** 1857
**SALES (est):** 709.52MM
**SALES (corp-wide):** 709.52MM **Privately Held**
Web: www.mcclatchy.com
**SIC:** 2711 Newspapers, publishing and printing
**PA:** Sij Holdings, Llc
 1601 Alhmbra Blvd Ste 100

**(P-4138)**
**JOONG-ANG DAILY NEWS CAL INC**
Also Called: JOONG-ANG DAILY NEWS CALIFORNIA, INC.

## 2711 - Newspapers (P-4139)

7750 Dagget St Ste 208, San Diego (92111-2236)
**PHONE**.................................858 573-1111
Kwong Luk Chang, *Brnch Mgr*
▲ **EMP:** 56
**Web:** www.koreadaily.com
**SIC: 2711** Newspapers, publishing and printing
**HQ:** Joongangilbo Usa, Inc.
690 Wilshire Pl
Los Angeles CA 90005
213 368-2512

### (P-4139)
### JOONG-ANG DAILY NEWS CAL INC
Also Called: JOONG-ANG DAILY NEWS CALIFORNIA, INC.
23575 Cabot Blvd Ste 201, Hayward (94545-1657)
**PHONE**.................................510 487-3333
Joung Sihn, *Brnch Mgr*
**EMP:** 56
**Web:** www.koreadaily.com
**SIC: 2711** Commercial printing and newspaper publishing combined
**HQ:** Joongangilbo Usa, Inc.
690 Wilshire Pl
Los Angeles CA 90005
213 368-2512

### (P-4140)
### JOONGANGILBO USA INC (DH)
Also Called: Joong-Ang Daily News Cal Inc
690 Wilshire Pl, Los Angeles (90005-3930)
**PHONE**.................................213 368-2512
Kae Hong Ko, *CEO*
In Taek Park, *
◆ **EMP:** 200 **EST:** 1974
**SQ FT:** 70,000
**SALES (est):** 20.81MM **Privately Held**
**Web:** www.koreadaily.com
**SIC: 2711** Commercial printing and newspaper publishing combined
**HQ:** Joongang Ilbo Co.,Ltd.
48-6 Sangamsan-Ro, Mapo-Gu
Seoul 03909

### (P-4141)
### KAAR DRECT MAIL FLFILLMENT LLC
1225 Exposition Way Ste 160, San Diego (92154-6667)
**PHONE**.................................619 382-3670
**EMP:** 25 **EST:** 2013
**SALES (est):** 5.1MM **Privately Held**
**Web:** www.kaardm.com
**SIC: 2711** 5963 2752 8742 Commercial printing and newspaper publishing combined; Direct sales, telemarketing; Publication printing, lithographic; Marketing consulting services

### (P-4142)
### KEVIN WHITE
Also Called: Habit Homes
9918 Ramona St Apt 1, Bellflower (90706-6947)
**PHONE**.................................562 231-6642
Kevin White, *Prin*
**EMP:** 15 **EST:** 2017
**SALES (est):** 161.04K **Privately Held**
**SIC: 2711** Newspapers, publishing and printing

### (P-4143)
### LA OPINION LP (HQ)
Also Called: Lozano Enterprises
915 Wilshire Blvd Ste 915, Los Angeles (90017-3474)

P.O. Box 71847 (90071-0847)
**PHONE**.................................213 891-9191
Monica C Lozano, *CEO*
**EMP:** 54 **EST:** 1926
**SALES (est):** 3.9MM
**SALES (corp-wide):** 28.44MM **Privately Held**
**Web:** www.laopinion.com
**SIC: 2711** Newspapers, publishing and printing
**PA:** Impremedia, Llc
41 Flatbush Ave Ste 1
212 807-4600

### (P-4144)
### LA OPINION LP
210 E Washington Blvd, Los Angeles (90015-3603)
**PHONE**.................................213 896-2222
Carlos Marina, *Mgr*
**EMP:** 359
**SALES (corp-wide):** 28.44MM **Privately Held**
**Web:** www.laopinion.com
**SIC: 2711** Newspapers, publishing and printing
**HQ:** La Opinion, L.P.
915 Wilshire Blvd Ste 915 # 915
Los Angeles CA 90017
213 891-9191

### (P-4145)
### LA TIMES
202 W 1st St Ste 500, Los Angeles (90012-4401)
**PHONE**.................................213 237-2279
Raymond Jansen, *CEO*
**EMP:** 51 **EST:** 2008
**SALES (est):** 2.5MM **Privately Held**
**Web:** www.onnitimessquare.com
**SIC: 2711** Newspapers, publishing and printing

### (P-4146)
### LAKE COUNTY PUBLISHING CO INC
Also Called: Lake County Record-Bee
415 Talmage Rd Ste A, Ukiah (95482-7486)
P.O. Box 849 (95453-0849)
**PHONE**.................................707 263-5636
Edward Mead, *Pr*
**EMP:** 75 **EST:** 1981
**SALES (est):** 760.12K
**SALES (corp-wide):** 499.57MM **Privately Held**
**Web:** www.record-bee.com
**SIC: 2711** Newspapers, publishing and printing
**HQ:** Medianews Group, Inc.
5990 Washington St
Denver CO 80216

### (P-4147)
### LATINA & ASSOCIATES INC (PA)
Also Called: El Latino Newspaper
1031 Bay Blvd, Chula Vista (91911-1625)
P.O. Box 120550 (92112-0550)
**PHONE**.................................619 426-1491
Fanny Miller, *CEO*
**EMP:** 25 **EST:** 1985
**SALES (est):** 831.55K
**SALES (corp-wide):** 831.55K **Privately Held**
**Web:** www.ellatinoonline.com
**SIC: 2711** Newspapers: publishing only, not printed on site

### (P-4148)
### LEE PUBLISHING COMPANY
Also Called: Sacramento Observer, The

1825 Del Paso Blvd Ste 2, Sacramento (95815-3018)
P.O. Box 209 (95812-0209)
**PHONE**.................................916 284-0022
Lawrence Lee, *CEO*
William Lee, *Pr*
**EMP:** 16 **EST:** 1962
**SALES (est):** 2.38MM **Privately Held**
**Web:** www.sacobserver.com
**SIC: 2711** Newspapers: publishing only, not printed on site

### (P-4149)
### LIVE JOURNAL INC
6363 Skyline Blvd, Oakland (94611-1042)
**PHONE**.................................415 230-3600
Andrew Paulson, *Pr*
Steffanie Gravelle, *CFO*
**EMP:** 33 **EST:** 1999
**SALES (est):** 669.28K **Privately Held**
**Web:** www.livejournal.com
**SIC: 2711** Newspapers, publishing and printing

### (P-4150)
### LOS ANGELES SENTINEL INC
Also Called: La Sentinel Newspaper
3800 Crenshaw Blvd, Los Angeles (90008-1813)
**PHONE**.................................323 299-3800
Jennifer Thomas, *Pr*
Brik Booker, *
**EMP:** 51 **EST:** 1933
**SALES (est):** 1.11MM **Privately Held**
**Web:** www.lasentinel.net
**SIC: 2711** Newspapers, publishing and printing

### (P-4151)
### LOS ANGLES TMES CMMNCTIONS LLC (PA)
Also Called: Los Angeles Times
2300 E Imperial Hwy, El Segundo (90245-2813)
**PHONE**.................................213 237-5000
Ross Levinsohn, *CEO*
Scott Mckibben, *Pr*
Don Reis S, *VP*
▲ **EMP:** 3955 **EST:** 1884
**SQ FT:** 162,000
**SALES (est):** 216MM
**SALES (corp-wide):** 216MM **Privately Held**
**Web:** www.latimes.com
**SIC: 2711** Newspapers, publishing and printing

### (P-4152)
### MAINSTREET MEDIA GROUP LLC
6400 Monterey Rd, Gilroy (95020-6663)
P.O. Box 516 (95021-0516)
**PHONE**.................................408 842-6400
**EMP:** 180
**Web:** www.mainstreetmg.com
**SIC: 2711** Newspapers, publishing and printing

### (P-4153)
### MAMMOTH MEDIA INC
1447 2nd St, Santa Monica (90401-3404)
**PHONE**.................................832 315-0833
Benoit Vatere, *CEO*
Mike Jones, *
**EMP:** 64 **EST:** 2016
**SALES (est):** 2.18MM **Privately Held**
**Web:** www.mammoth.la
**SIC: 2711** Newspapers

### (P-4154)
### MCCLATCHY NEWSPAPERS INC (DH)
Also Called: Sacramento Bee
1601 Alhambra Blvd Ste 100, Sacramento (95816-7164)
P.O. Box 15779 (95852-0779)
**PHONE**.................................916 321-1855
Tony W Hunter, *CEO*
Jeffrey Dorsey, *
◆ **EMP:** 2500 **EST:** 1857
**SALES (est):** 424.7MM
**SALES (corp-wide):** 709.52MM **Privately Held**
**Web:** www.mcclatchy.com
**SIC: 2711** 2759 7375 Newspapers, publishing and printing; Commercial printing, nec; On-line data base information retrieval
**HQ:** Jck Legacy Company
1601 Alhmbra Blvd Ste 100
Sacramento CA 95816
916 321-1844

### (P-4155)
### MCNAUGHTON NEWSPAPERS
Also Called: D Davis Enterprise
325 G St, Davis (95616-4119)
P.O. Box 1470 (95617-1470)
**PHONE**.................................530 756-0800
Foy Mcnaughton, *Owner*
Richard B Mc Naughton, *
**EMP:** 36 **EST:** 1966
**SALES (est):** 447.69K **Privately Held**
**Web:** www.davisenterprise.com
**SIC: 2711** Commercial printing and newspaper publishing combined

### (P-4156)
### MCNAUGHTON NEWSPAPERS INC (PA)
Also Called: Daily Republic
1250 Texas St, Fairfield (94533-5748)
P.O. Box 47 (94533-0747)
**PHONE**.................................707 425-4646
Foy Mc Naughton, *Pr*
R Burt Mc Naughton, *
▲ **EMP:** 99 **EST:** 1855
**SQ FT:** 35,000
**SALES (est):** 4.01MM
**SALES (corp-wide):** 4.01MM **Privately Held**
**Web:** www.mcnaughton.media
**SIC: 2711** Commercial printing and newspaper publishing combined

### (P-4157)
### MEDIANEWS GROUP INC
Also Called: Convertly
4 N 2nd St Ste 800, San Jose (95113-1317)
**PHONE**.................................408 920-5713
Michael Koren, *CFO*
**EMP:** 500
**SALES (corp-wide):** 499.57MM **Privately Held**
**Web:** www.medianewsgroup.com
**SIC: 2711** Newspapers, publishing and printing
**HQ:** Medianews Group, Inc.
5990 Washington St
Denver CO 80216

### (P-4158)
### METRO PUBLISHING INC
Also Called: Metrosa
445 Center St, Healdsburg (95448-3807)
**PHONE**.................................707 527-1200
Rosemary Olson, *Mgr*
**EMP:** 32
**SALES (corp-wide):** 4.41MM **Privately Held**

## PRODUCTS & SERVICES SECTION

### 2711 - Newspapers (P-4177)

Web: www.metronews.com
SIC: 2711 8611 Newspapers, publishing and printing; Business associations
PA: Metro Publishing, Inc.
380 S 1st St
408 298-8000

**(P-4159)**
**METROPOLITAN NEWS COMPANY**
Also Called: Riverside Blltin Jrupa This We
3540 12th St, Riverside (92501-3802)
P.O. Box 60859 (90060-0859)
PHONE.................................951 369-5890
Roger Gray, Pr
EMP: 29 EST: 1998
SALES (est): 167.25K Privately Held
Web: www.mnc.net
SIC: 2711 Newspapers, publishing and printing

**(P-4160)**
**MONTEREY COUNTY HERALD COMPANY (DH)**
Also Called: Monterey Herald
2200 Garden Rd # 101, Monterey (93940-5329)
PHONE.................................831 372-3311
Gary Omerick, Pr
EMP: 30 EST: 1922
SALES (est): 1.56MM
SALES (corp-wide): 499.57MM Privately Held
Web: www.montereyherald.com
SIC: 2711 Commercial printing and newspaper publishing combined
HQ: Medianews Group, Inc.
5990 Washington St
Denver CO 80216

**(P-4161)**
**MORRIS MULTIMEDIA INC**
Also Called: Signal Newspaper, The
26330 Diamond Pl Ste 100, Santa Clarita (91350-5819)
PHONE.................................661 259-1234
Jay Harn, Brnch Mgr
EMP: 20
SALES (corp-wide): 44.73MM Privately Held
Web: www.morrismultimedia.com
SIC: 2711 Newspapers: publishing only, not printed on site
PA: Morris Multimedia, Inc.
27 Abercorn St
912 233-1281

**(P-4162)**
**MORRIS NEWSPAPER CORP CAL (HQ)**
Also Called: Manteca Bulletin
531 E Yosemite Ave, Manteca (95336-5806)
P.O. Box 1958 (95336-1156)
PHONE.................................209 249-3500
Jennifer Merrick, Dir
Dennis Wyatt, *
EMP: 65 EST: 1972
SQ FT: 8,000
SALES (est): 2.78MM
SALES (corp-wide): 44.73MM Privately Held
Web: www.mantecabulletin.com
SIC: 2711 6531 Newspapers, publishing and printing; Real estate agents and managers
PA: Morris Multimedia, Inc.
27 Abercorn St
912 233-1281

**(P-4163)**
**MORRIS PUBLICATIONS (PA)**
Also Called: Advertiser, The
122 S 3rd Ave, Oakdale (95361-3935)
P.O. Box 278 (95361-0278)
PHONE.................................209 847-3021
Drew Savage, Genl Mgr
EMP: 40 EST: 1888
SQ FT: 5,000
SALES (est): 812.18K
SALES (corp-wide): 812.18K Privately Held
Web: www.theriverbanknews.com
SIC: 2711 2752 8999 Commercial printing and newspaper publishing combined; Photo-offset printing; Newspaper column writing

**(P-4164)**
**MOTHER LODE PRTG & PUBG CO INC**
Also Called: Mountain Democrat
2889 Ray Lawyer Dr, Placerville (95667-3914)
P.O. Box 1088 (95667-1088)
PHONE.................................530 344-5030
James Webb, Publisher
EMP: 35 EST: 1851
SQ FT: 19,400
SALES (est): 936.79K Privately Held
Web: www.mtdemocrat.com
SIC: 2711 Commercial printing and newspaper publishing combined

**(P-4165)**
**NAPA VALLEY PUBLISHING CO**
Also Called: NAPA Register
1615 Soscol Ave, Napa (94559)
PHONE.................................707 226-3711
E W Scripps, Ch Bd
Betty Knight Scripps, Vice Chairman*
Jay Scott, *
EMP: 100 EST: 1958
SALES (est): 891.23K Privately Held
Web: www.napavalleyregister.com
SIC: 2711 Newspapers: publishing only, not printed on site

**(P-4166)**
**NATIONAL MEDIA INC**
Also Called: Beach Reporter, The
2615 Pacific Coast Hwy Ste 329, Hermosa Beach (90254-2229)
PHONE.................................310 372-0388
Richard Frank, Publisher
EMP: 16
SALES (corp-wide): 499.57MM Privately Held
Web: www.dailybreeze.com
SIC: 2711 Newspapers, publishing and printing
HQ: National Media, Inc.
609 Deep Valley Dr # 200
Rlng Hls Est CA 90274
310 377-6877

**(P-4167)**
**NATIONAL MEDIA INC (HQ)**
Also Called: Beach Reporter
609 Deep Valley Dr Ste 200, Rlng Hls Est (90274-3629)
P.O. Box 2609 (90274-8609)
PHONE.................................310 377-6877
Stephen C Laxineta, Pr
Simon M Tam, *
William Dean Singleton, *
EMP: 30 EST: 1983
SQ FT: 12,000
SALES (est): 4.27MM
SALES (corp-wide): 499.57MM Privately Held

Web: www.dailybreeze.com
SIC: 2711 Newspapers: publishing only, not printed on site
PA: Digital First Media, Llc
101 W Colfax Ave Fl 11
303 954-6360

**(P-4168)**
**NEWLON ROUGE LLC**
Also Called: Santa Monica Daily Press
1640 5th St Ste 218, Santa Monica (90401-3325)
P.O. Box 1380 (90406-1380)
PHONE.................................310 458-7737
Ross Furukawa, Pr
EMP: 20 EST: 2001
SALES (est): 846.97K Privately Held
Web: www.smdp.com
SIC: 2711 Commercial printing and newspaper publishing combined

**(P-4169)**
**NGUOI VIET VTNAMESE PEOPLE INC (PA)**
Also Called: Nguoi Viet Newspaper
14771 Moran St, Westminster (92683-5553)
PHONE.................................714 892-9414
Dat Pham, Ch
Hoang Tong, *
Dieu Le, *
▲ EMP: 30 EST: 1978
SQ FT: 10,000
SALES (est): 4.83MM
SALES (corp-wide): 4.83MM Privately Held
Web: www.nguoi-viet.com
SIC: 2711 5994 2741 Newspapers: publishing only, not printed on site; News dealers and newsstands; Miscellaneous publishing

**(P-4170)**
**NOOZHAWK**
1327a State St, Santa Barbara (93101-2609)
PHONE.................................805 456-7267
EMP: 19 EST: 2017
SALES (est): 223.56K Privately Held
Web: www.noozhawk.com
SIC: 2711 Newspapers, publishing and printing

**(P-4171)**
**NORTH AREA NEWS (PA)**
2612 El Camino Ave, Sacramento (95821-5937)
P.O. Box 214245 (95821-0245)
PHONE.................................916 486-1248
Tom Hoey, Pr
John Hoey, VP
Joanne Hoey, Sec
EMP: 24 EST: 1961
SQ FT: 2,400
SALES (est): 1.89MM
SALES (corp-wide): 1.89MM Privately Held
Web: north-area-news.hub.biz
SIC: 2711 Newspapers, publishing and printing

**(P-4172)**
**NORTH COUNTY TIMES (DH)**
Also Called: Californian, The
350 Camino De La Reina, San Diego (92108-3007)
PHONE.................................800 533-8830
▲ EMP: 250 EST: 1962
SQ FT: 45,000
SALES (est): 1.17MM

SALES (corp-wide): 691.14MM Publicly Held
Web: www.caseybrownco.com
SIC: 2711 Newspapers, publishing and printing
HQ: Lee Publications, Inc.
4600 E 53rd St
Davenport IA 52807
563 383-2100

**(P-4173)**
**NORTH COUNTY TIMES**
28441 Rancho California Rd Ste 103, Temecula (92590-3618)
PHONE.................................951 676-4315
Claude Reinke, Mgr
EMP: 45
SALES (corp-wide): 691.14MM Publicly Held
Web: www.caseybrownco.com
SIC: 2711 Newspapers, publishing and printing
HQ: North County Times
350 Camino De La Reina
San Diego CA 92108
800 533-8830

**(P-4174)**
**NORTHEAST NEWSPAPERS INC**
621 W Beverly Blvd, Montebello (90640-3623)
PHONE.................................213 727-1117
Art Aguilar, Pr
Tom Morrison, *
EMP: 32 EST: 1905
SALES (est): 2.58MM Privately Held
SIC: 2711 Newspapers, publishing and printing

**(P-4175)**
**NOTICIERO SEMANAL ADVERTISING**
Also Called: Porterville Recorder
115 E Oak Ave, Porterville (93257-3807)
P.O. Box 151 (93258-0151)
PHONE.................................559 784-5000
Paul Mauney, Prin
EMP: 18 EST: 2005
SALES (est): 487.72K Privately Held
Web: www.recorderonline.com
SIC: 2711 7313 Newspapers, publishing and printing; Newspaper advertising representative

**(P-4176)**
**OLYMPIC CASCADE PUBLISHING (DH)**
Also Called: Puyallup Herald
2100 Q St, Sacramento (95816-6816)
P.O. Box 15779 (95852-0779)
PHONE.................................916 321-1000
R Elaine Lintecum, VP
Marion Dodd, *
EMP: 22 EST: 1965
SQ FT: 5,100
SALES (est): 1.23MM
SALES (corp-wide): 709.52MM Privately Held
Web: www.thenewstribune.com
SIC: 2711 Commercial printing and newspaper publishing combined
HQ: Mcclatchy Newspapers, Inc.
1601 Alhambra Blvd # 100
Sacramento CA 95816
916 321-1855

**(P-4177)**
**PACIFIC NORTHWEST PUBG CO INC**

## 2711 - Newspapers (P-4178)

2100 Q St, Sacramento (95816-6816)
**PHONE**..................................916 321-1828
R Elaine Lintecum, *VP*
Patrick Talmantes, *
**EMP:** 311 **EST:** 1905
**SQ FT:** 100,000
**SALES (est):** 871.16K
**SALES (corp-wide):** 2.66B **Publicly Held**
**SIC:** 2711 Newspapers, publishing and printing
**HQ:** Gannett River States Publishing Corporation
7950 Jones Branch Dr
Mc Lean VA 22102
703 284-6000

### (P-4178)
### PARADISE POST INC
5399 Clark Rd, Paradise (95969-6325)
P.O. Box 70 (95967-0070)
**PHONE**..................................530 872-5581
**FAX:** 530 877-5213
**EMP:** 250
**SQ FT:** 64,823
**SALES (est):** 21.45MM **Privately Held**
**Web:** www.paradisepost.com
**SIC:** 2711 2796 2791 2789 Newspapers; Platemaking services; Typesetting; Bookbinding and related work

### (P-4179)
### PASADENA NEWSPAPERS INC
Also Called: Daily News, The
6737 Bright Ave Ste 109, Whittier (90601-4313)
**PHONE**..................................562 698-0955
Bill Dell, *Mgr*
**EMP:** 15
**Web:** www.pasadenastarnews.com
**SIC:** 2711 7313 Newspapers; Newspaper advertising representative
**PA:** Pasadena Newspapers Inc
605 E Huntington Dr # 100

### (P-4180)
### PASADENA NEWSPAPERS INC (PA)
Also Called: Pasadena Star-News
605 E Huntington Dr Ste 100, Monrovia (91016-6352)
**PHONE**..................................626 578-6300
Dean Singleton, *Pr*
▲ **EMP:** 190 **EST:** 1884
**SALES (est):** 827.87K **Privately Held**
**Web:** www.pasadenastarnews.com
**SIC:** 2711 7313 Commercial printing and newspaper publishing combined; Newspaper advertising representative

### (P-4181)
### PASADENA NEWSPAPERS INC
Also Called: Eureka Times-Standard
930 6th St, Eureka (95501-1112)
P.O. Box 3580 (95502-3580)
**PHONE**..................................707 442-1711
Gerry Adolph, *Mgr*
**EMP:** 160
**SQ FT:** 49,872
**Web:** www.pasadenastarnews.com
**SIC:** 2711 2752 Newspapers: publishing only, not printed on site; Commercial printing, lithographic
**PA:** Pasadena Newspapers Inc
605 E Huntington Dr # 100

### (P-4182)
### PRESS-ENTERPRISE COMPANY (PA)
3450 14th St, Riverside (92501-3862)
P.O. Box 792 (92502-0792)
**PHONE**..................................951 684-1200
Ronald Redfern, *Pr*
Kathy Weiermiller, *VP*
Sue Barry, *VP*
Ed Lasak, *CFO*
▲ **EMP:** 700 **EST:** 2011
**SQ FT:** 190,000
**SALES (est):** 18.62MM
**SALES (corp-wide):** 18.62MM **Privately Held**
**Web:** www.pressenterprise.com
**SIC:** 2711 Commercial printing and newspaper publishing combined

### (P-4183)
### RECORDER
1035 Market St, San Francisco (94103-1600)
**PHONE**..................................877 256-2472
**EMP:** 21 **EST:** 2018
**SALES (est):** 143.23K **Privately Held**
**Web:** www.law.com
**SIC:** 2711 Newspapers: publishing only, not printed on site

### (P-4184)
### REPORTER
Also Called: Media News Groups
916 Cotting Ln, Vacaville (95688-9338)
**PHONE**..................................707 448-6401
Jody Lodevick, *Pr*
**EMP:** 15 **EST:** 1883
**SQ FT:** 40,000
**SALES (est):** 352.59K **Privately Held**
**Web:** www.thereporter.com
**SIC:** 2711 Commercial printing and newspaper publishing combined

### (P-4185)
### RUNWAY BEAUTY INC
Also Called: Runway
6075 Rodgerton Dr, Los Angeles (90068-1961)
**PHONE**..................................844 240-2250
Vincent Mazzotta, *CEO*
**EMP:** 18 **EST:** 2022
**SALES (est):** 619.14K **Privately Held**
**Web:** www.runway.net
**SIC:** 2711 Newspapers, publishing and printing

### (P-4186)
### SAN DIEGO UNION-TRIBUNE LLC
San Diego Union Tribune
1920 Main St, Irvine (92614-7223)
P.O. Box 120191 (92112-0191)
**PHONE**..................................619 299-3131
Roy E Gene Bell, *CEO*
**EMP:** 39
**Web:** www.sandiegouniontribune.com
**SIC:** 2711 7313 Newspapers: publishing only, not printed on site; Newspaper advertising representative
**PA:** The San Diego Union-Tribune Llc
600 B St Ste 1201

### (P-4187)
### SAN DIEGO UNION-TRIBUNE LLC (PA)
Also Called: San Diego Union Tribune, The
600 B St Ste 1201, San Diego (92101-4505)
P.O. Box 120191 (92112-0191)
**PHONE**..................................619 299-3131
Jeff Light, *Pr*
**EMP:** 600 **EST:** 2009
**SALES (est):** 11.96MM **Privately Held**
**Web:** www.sandiegouniontribune.com
**SIC:** 2711 7313 7383 Newspapers: publishing only, not printed on site; Newspaper advertising representative; News reporting services for newspapers and periodicals

### (P-4188)
### SAN JOSE BUSINESS JOURNAL
125 S Market St Fl 11, San Jose (95113-2292)
**PHONE**..................................408 295-3800
Dick Kruez, *Publisher*
Italo Jimenez, *
**EMP:** 124 **EST:** 1980
**SALES (est):** 548.43K
**SALES (corp-wide):** 2.88B **Privately Held**
**Web:** www.sjbjudo.org
**SIC:** 2711 2741 Newspapers, publishing and printing; Miscellaneous publishing
**HQ:** American City Business Journals, Inc.
120 W Morehead St Ste 400
Charlotte NC 28202
704 973-1000

### (P-4189)
### SAN JOSE MERCURY-NEWS LLC (DH)
Also Called: DIGITAL FIRST MEDIA
4 N 2nd St Fl 8, San Jose (95113-1308)
P.O. Box 65190 (80962-5190)
**PHONE**..................................408 920-5000
Joseph T Natoli, *
Michael Tully, *
Mindy Kiernan, *
David Yarnold, *
**EMP:** 1000 **EST:** 2006
**SQ FT:** 400,000
**SALES (est):** 683.47K
**SALES (corp-wide):** 499.57MM **Privately Held**
**Web:** www.mercurynews.com
**SIC:** 2711 Commercial printing and newspaper publishing combined
**HQ:** Medianews Group, Inc.
5990 Washington St
Denver CO 80216

### (P-4190)
### SAN LUIS OBSPO COCMMNTY CLGDST
2800 Buena Vista Dr, Paso Robles (93446-8556)
**PHONE**..................................805 591-6200
**EMP:** 17 **EST:** 2015
**SALES (est):** 99.54K **Privately Held**
**Web:** www.cuesta.edu
**SIC:** 2711 Newspapers, publishing and printing

### (P-4191)
### SANTA BARBARA INDEPENDENT INC
Also Called: Independent
1715 State St, Santa Barbara (93101-2521)
**PHONE**..................................805 965-5205
M Partridge Poette, *Pr*
Marianne Partridge Poette, *
Brandi Rivera, *
**EMP:** 40 **EST:** 1984
**SALES (est):** 2.19MM **Privately Held**
**Web:** www.independent.com
**SIC:** 2711 Newspapers, publishing and printing

### (P-4192)
### SANTA ROSA PRESS DEMOCRAT INC (HQ)
Also Called: Press Democrat, The
427 Mendocino Ave, Santa Rosa (95401-5391)
P.O. Box 569 (95402-0569)
**PHONE**..................................707 546-2020
Michael J Parman, *Pr*
**EMP:** 270 **EST:** 1998
**SALES (est):** 6.86MM
**SALES (corp-wide):** 13.51MM **Privately Held**
**Web:** www.pressdemocrat.com
**SIC:** 2711 Newspapers, publishing and printing
**PA:** Sonoma Media Investments, Llc
416 B St Ste C
707 526-8563

### (P-4193)
### SCALABLE PRESS
41454 Christy St, Fremont (94538-5105)
**PHONE**..................................877 752-9060
**EMP:** 16 **EST:** 2015
**SALES (est):** 3.11MM **Privately Held**
**Web:** www.scalablepress.com
**SIC:** 2711 Newspapers

### (P-4194)
### SIGNAL
Also Called: Newhall Signal
26330 Diamond Pl Ste 100, Santa Clarita (91350-5819)
P.O. Box 801870 (91380-1870)
**PHONE**..................................661 259-1234
Charles Morris, *Pr*
**EMP:** 29 **EST:** 1919
**SQ FT:** 32,000
**SALES (est):** 2.02MM
**SALES (corp-wide):** 44.73MM **Privately Held**
**Web:** www.signalscv.com
**SIC:** 2711 Newspapers, publishing and printing
**PA:** Morris Multimedia, Inc.
27 Abercom St
912 233-1281

### (P-4195)
### SING TAO NEWSPAPERS (DH)
Also Called: Sing Tao Daily
1818 Gilbreth Rd Ste 108, Burlingame (94010-1217)
**PHONE**..................................650 808-8800
Robin Mui, *CEO*
Charles Fu, *
▲ **EMP:** 75 **EST:** 1977
**SQ FT:** 22,000
**SALES (est):** 4.88MM
**SALES (corp-wide):** 779.52K **Privately Held**
**Web:** www.singtaousa.com
**SIC:** 2711 Commercial printing and newspaper publishing combined
**HQ:** Sing Tao Newspapers New York Ltd.
188 Lafayette St
New York NY 10013

### (P-4196)
### SING TAO NEWSPAPERS LTD
Also Called: Sing Tao Nwspapers Los Angeles
17059 Green Dr, City Of Industry (91745-1812)
**PHONE**..................................626 956-8200
Sau K Cheung, *Mgr*
**EMP:** 52
**Web:** std.stheadline.com
**SIC:** 2711 Newspapers, publishing and printing
**HQ:** Sing Tao Limited
8/F Sing Tao News Corporation Bldg
Tseung Kwan O NT

▲ = Import ▼ = Export
◆ = Import/Export

## PRODUCTS & SERVICES SECTION
## 2711 - Newspapers (P-4218)

**(P-4197)**
**SLO NEW TIMES INC**
Also Called: New Times Media Group
1010 Marsh St, San Luis Obispo
(93401-3630)
PHONE..................805 546-8208
Bob Rucker, *CEO*
**EMP:** 20 **EST:** 1987
**SALES (est):** 788.07K **Privately Held**
Web: www.newtimesslo.com
**SIC: 2711** Newspapers, publishing and printing

**(P-4198)**
**SONOMA MEDIA INVESTMENTS LLC (PA)**
Also Called: Sonoma Magazine
416 B St Ste C, Santa Rosa (95401-8540)
PHONE..................707 526-8563
Steven B Falk, *Mgr*
Steven B Falk, *Managing Member*
Stephen Daniels, *CFO*
**EMP:** 79 **EST:** 2012
**SALES (est):** 13.51MM
**SALES (corp-wide):** 13.51MM **Privately Held**
Web: www.sonomamediainvestments.com
**SIC: 2711** Newspapers

**(P-4199)**
**SOUTHWEST JOURNAL INC**
Also Called: Minnesota Premier Publications
3727 Burnside Rd, Sebastopol (95472-9459)
PHONE..................612 825-9205
Janis Hall, *Pr*
Terry Gahan, *VP*
**EMP:** 15 **EST:** 1990
**SALES (est):** 360.48K **Privately Held**
Web: www.mnpubs.com
**SIC: 2711** Newspapers, publishing and printing

**(P-4200)**
**ST LOUIS POST-DISPATCH LLC**
Also Called: Novato Advance Newspaper
1068 Machin Ave, Novato (94945-2458)
P.O. Box 8 (94948-0008)
PHONE..................415 892-1516
William C Haigwood, *Mgr*
**EMP:** 121
**SALES (corp-wide):** 691.14MM **Publicly Held**
Web: www.stltoday.com
**SIC: 2711** Newspapers, publishing and printing
**HQ:** St. Louis Post-Dispatch Llc
901 N 10th St
Saint Louis MO 63101
314 340-8000

**(P-4201)**
**ST LOUIS POST-DISPATCH LLC**
Also Called: Argus Courier
830 Petaluma Blvd N, Petaluma (94952-2109)
P.O. Box 1091 (94953-1091)
PHONE..................707 762-4541
John Burnes, *Brnch Mgr*
**EMP:** 97
**SQ FT:** 10,000
**SALES (corp-wide):** 691.14MM **Publicly Held**
Web: www.stltoday.com
**SIC: 2711** Newspapers, publishing and printing
**HQ:** St. Louis Post-Dispatch Llc
901 N 10th St
Saint Louis MO 63101
314 340-8000

**(P-4202)**
**STANFORD DAILY PUBLISHING CORP**
Also Called: Stanford Daily, The
456 Panama Mall, Stanford (94305-5294)
PHONE..................650 723-2555
Alice Brown, *Pr*
Wes Radez, *
**EMP:** 40 **EST:** 1973
**SQ FT:** 2,300
**SALES (est):** 3.88MM **Privately Held**
Web: www.stanforddaily.com
**SIC: 2711** Newspapers: publishing only, not printed on site

**(P-4203)**
**SUN CMPANY OF SAN BRNRDINO CAL (HQ)**
Also Called: San Bernardino County Sun, The
4030 Georgia Blvd, San Bernardino (92407-1847)
PHONE..................909 889-9666
Bob Balzer, *Pr*
Douglass H Mccorkindale, *Prin*
**EMP:** 400 **EST:** 1964
**SQ FT:** 110,000
**SALES (est):** 140.1MM
**SALES (corp-wide):** 2.66B **Publicly Held**
Web: www.sbsun.com
**SIC: 2711** Newspapers, publishing and printing
**PA:** Gannett Co., Inc.
1675 Broadway Fl 23
703 854-6000

**(P-4204)**
**TAKE A BREAK PAPER**
1048 W Gardena Blvd, Gardena (90247-4956)
PHONE..................323 333-7773
Albert Moran, *Pt*
**EMP:** 30 **EST:** 2013
**SALES (est):** 198.49K **Privately Held**
Web: www.takeabreakpaper.com
**SIC: 2711** Newspapers, publishing and printing

**(P-4205)**
**TAKUYO CORPORATION**
Also Called: Light House
970 W 190th St Ste 620, Torrance (90502-1070)
PHONE..................310 782-6927
Yoichi Komiyama, *Pr*
Yuzo Komiyama, *VP*
**EMP:** 15 **EST:** 1989
**SALES (est):** 2.43MM **Privately Held**
Web: www.us-utopia.com
**SIC: 2711** Newspapers, publishing and printing

**(P-4206)**
**TAMARACK SPRNG MUTL WTR CO INC (PA)**
125 N Church St, Lodi (95240-2102)
P.O. Box 1360 (95241-1360)
PHONE..................209 369-2761
Melissa Harris, *Mgr*
**EMP:** 38 **EST:** 1967
**SALES (est):** 469.04K **Privately Held**
Web: www.tamaracksprings.org
**SIC: 2711** Newspapers, publishing and printing

**(P-4207)**
**TEHACHAPI NEWS INC (PA)**
Also Called: Southeast Kern Weekender
411 N Mill St, Tehachapi (93561-1351)
P.O. Box 1840 (93581-1840)
PHONE..................661 822-6828
Al Criseli, *Pr*
William J Mead, *Pr*
Elizabeth S Mead, *Sec*
**EMP:** 15 **EST:** 1943
**SQ FT:** 2,400
**SALES (est):** 1.15MM
**SALES (corp-wide):** 1.15MM **Privately Held**
Web: www.tehachapinews.com
**SIC: 2711** Newspapers, publishing and printing

**(P-4208)**
**THE KOREA TIMES LOS ANGELES INC (PA)**
Also Called: Korea Times
3731 Wilshire Blvd Ste 1000, Los Angeles (90010-2819)
PHONE..................323 692-2000
▲ **EMP:** 200 **EST:** 1969
**SALES (est):** 23.89MM
**SALES (corp-wide):** 23.89MM **Privately Held**
Web: www.koreatimes.com
**SIC: 2711** Newspapers, publishing and printing

**(P-4209)**
**THE SUN**
852 Hollister St Unit B, San Diego (92154-1334)
PHONE..................619 405-7702
Lindsey Bosch, *Prin*
**EMP:** 15 **EST:** 2010
**SALES (est):** 70.13K **Privately Held**
Web: www.the-sun.com
**SIC: 2711** Newspapers, publishing and printing

**(P-4210)**
**THEWRAP**
2260 S Centinela Ave Ste 150, Los Angeles (90064-1007)
PHONE..................424 273-4787
**EMP:** 41 **EST:** 2016
**SALES (est):** 1.17MM **Privately Held**
Web: www.thewrap.com
**SIC: 2711** Newspapers

**(P-4211)**
**TIDINGS**
Also Called: VIDA NUEVA
3424 Wilshire Blvd, Los Angeles (90010-2263)
PHONE..................213 637-7360
Roger Mahoney, *Pr*
**EMP:** 23 **EST:** 1895
**SALES (est):** 2.09MM **Privately Held**
Web: www.angelusnews.com
**SIC: 2711** Newspapers: publishing only, not printed on site

**(P-4212)**
**TIMES MEDIA INCORPORATED**
Also Called: Bellou Publishing
1900 Camden Ave, San Jose (95124-2942)
PHONE..................408 494-7000
William D Bellou, *CEO*
**EMP:** 48 **EST:** 1982
**SALES (est):** 406.2K **Privately Held**
Web: www.timesmediainc.com
**SIC: 2711** Newspapers, publishing and printing

**(P-4213)**
**TRACY PRESS INC**
145 W 10th St, Tracy (95376-3952)
P.O. Box 419 (95378-0419)
PHONE..................209 835-3030

Robert S Matthews, *Pr*
Tom Matthews, *
**EMP:** 29 **EST:** 1896
**SQ FT:** 20,000
**SALES (est):** 3.02MM **Privately Held**
Web: www.ttownmedia.com
**SIC: 2711** Commercial printing and newspaper publishing combined

**(P-4214)**
**TRIBE MDIA CORP A CAL NNPRFIT**
Also Called: Jewish Journal, The
3250 Wilshire Blvd, Los Angeles (90010-1577)
PHONE..................213 368-1661
Rob Eshman, *Publisher*
**EMP:** 27 **EST:** 1985
**SQ FT:** 4,500
**SALES (est):** 773.01K **Privately Held**
Web: www.jewishjournal.com
**SIC: 2711** Newspapers, publishing and printing

**(P-4215)**
**TURLOCK JOURNAL**
121 S Center St # 2, Turlock (95380-4507)
P.O. Box 800 (95381-0800)
PHONE..................209 634-9141
Olaf Frandsen, *Prin*
**EMP:** 15 **EST:** 2013
**SALES (est):** 225.77K **Privately Held**
Web: www.turlockjournal.com
**SIC: 2711** Commercial printing and newspaper publishing combined

**(P-4216)**
**TXD INTERNATIONAL USA INC**
2336 S Vineyard Ave # A, Ontario (91761-7767)
PHONE..................909 947-6568
Rodolfo J Galvez Cordova, *CEO*
Francisco Galvez Vernis, *VP*
Armando Herrera, *Sec*
▲ **EMP:** 15 **EST:** 2003
**SQ FT:** 8,500
**SALES (est):** 729.72K **Privately Held**
Web: www.txdinternational.com
**SIC: 2711** 2752 2211 2262 Commercial printing and newspaper publishing combined; Promotional printing, lithographic; Print cloths, cotton; Printing, manmade fiber and silk broadwoven fabrics

**(P-4217)**
**VILLAGE NEWS INC**
Also Called: Fallbrook Bonsall Village News
41740 Enterprise Cir S, Temecula (92590-4881)
PHONE..................760 451-3488
Julie Reeder, *Pr*
Michelle Howard, *Advt Dir*
**EMP:** 26 **EST:** 1997
**SQ FT:** 1,500
**SALES (est):** 2.35MM **Privately Held**
Web: www.villagenews.com
**SIC: 2711** Newspapers, publishing and printing

**(P-4218)**
**VOICE OF SAN DIEGO**
110 W A St Ste 650, San Diego (92101-3708)
PHONE..................619 325-0525
Scott Lewis, *CEO*
Julianne Markow, *COO*
**EMP:** 53 **EST:** 2004
**SALES (est):** 2.34MM **Privately Held**
Web: www.voiceofsandiego.org

## 2711 - Newspapers (P-4219)

SIC: 2711 Newspapers: publishing only, not printed on site

### (P-4219)
**WAVE COMMUNITY NEWSPAPERS INC (PA)**
Also Called: The Wave
1007 N Sepulveda Blvd, Manhattan Beach (90266-5964)
PHONE..................323 290-3000
Pluria Marshall, *Pr*
Andy Wiedlin, *Chief Business Officer*
▲ EMP: 30 EST: 1970
SALES (est): 4.92MM
SALES (corp-wide): 4.92MM **Privately Held**
SIC: 2711 Commercial printing and newspaper publishing combined

### (P-4220)
**WESTERN OUTDOORS PUBLICATIONS (PA)**
Also Called: Western Outdoor News
901 Calle Amanecer Ste 115, San Clemente (92673-4216)
P.O. Box 73370 (92673-0113)
PHONE..................949 366-0030
Robert Twilegar, *Pr*
Lori Twilegar, *
EMP: 28 EST: 1953
SALES (est): 2.38MM
SALES (corp-wide): 2.38MM **Privately Held**
Web: www.wonews.com
SIC: 2711 2721 Newspapers: publishing only, not printed on site; Periodicals

### (P-4221)
**WICK COMMUNICATIONS CO**
Also Called: Kern Valley Sun
6404 Lake Isabella Blvd, Lake Isabella (93240-9475)
P.O. Box 3074 (93240-3074)
PHONE..................760 379-3667
Cliff Urfeth, *Mgr*
EMP: 27
SALES (corp-wide): 37.72MM **Privately Held**
Web: www.wickcommunications.com
SIC: 2711 Newspapers, publishing and printing
HQ: Wick Communications Co.
333 W Wilcox Dr Ste 302
Sierra Vista AZ 85635
520 458-0200

### (P-4222)
**WICK COMMUNICATIONS CO**
Also Called: Half Moon Bay Review
714 Kelly St, Half Moon Bay (94019-1919)
P.O. Box 68 (94019-0068)
PHONE..................650 726-4424
Debra Godshall, *Prin*
EMP: 23
SALES (corp-wide): 37.72MM **Privately Held**
Web: www.wickcommunications.com
SIC: 2711 6531 Newspapers, publishing and printing; Real estate agents and managers
HQ: Wick Communications Co.
333 W Wilcox Dr Ste 302
Sierra Vista AZ 85635
520 458-0200

### (P-4223)
**WORLD JOURNAL INC (PA)**
1633 Bayshore Hwy Ste 231, Burlingame (94010-1533)
PHONE..................650 692-9936
Pi Ly Wang, *Pr*
Shiun Yi Hsia, *
▲ EMP: 98 EST: 1975
SALES (est): 995.19K
SALES (corp-wide): 995.19K **Privately Held**
SIC: 2711 Newspapers, publishing and printing

### (P-4224)
**WORLD JOURNAL LA LLC (HQ)**
1588 Corporate Center Dr, Monterey Park (91754-7624)
PHONE..................323 268-4982
James Guon, *CEO*
▲ EMP: 170 EST: 1981
SQ FT: 45,000
SALES (est): 6.03MM **Privately Held**
SIC: 2711 Newspapers, publishing and printing
PA: United Daily News Co., Ltd.
No. 369, Datong Rd., Sec. 1

## 2721 Periodicals

### (P-4225)
**ADAMS TRADE PRESS LP (PA)**
Also Called: Adams Business Media
420 S Palm Canyon Dr, Palm Springs (92262-7304)
PHONE..................760 318-7000
Mark Adams, *Pt*
EMP: 30 EST: 1994
SQ FT: 2,000
SALES (est): 1.01MM **Privately Held**
SIC: 2721 Magazines: publishing only, not printed on site

### (P-4226)
**ADVANSTAR COMMUNICATIONS INC**
6200 Canoga Ave Fl 3, Woodland Hills (91367-2450)
PHONE..................818 593-5000
Nora Ellingwood, *Brnch Mgr*
EMP: 17
SALES (corp-wide): 3.98B **Privately Held**
Web: epay.advanstar.com
SIC: 2721 Magazines: publishing only, not printed on site
HQ: Advanstar Communications Inc.
2501 Colorado Ave Ste 280
Santa Monica CA 90404
310 857-7500

### (P-4227)
**ADVANSTAR COMMUNICATIONS INC**
2525 Main St Ste 300, Irvine (92614-6680)
PHONE..................714 513-8400
FAX: 714 513-8403
EMP: 80
SALES (corp-wide): 1.06B **Privately Held**
SIC: 2721 7389 Magazines: publishing only, not printed on site; Trade show arrangement
HQ: Advanstar Communications Inc.
2501 Colorado Ave Ste 280
Santa Monica CA 90404
310 857-7500

### (P-4228)
**AEROTECH NEWS AND REVIEW INC (PA)**
Also Called: Astro News
220 E Avenue K4 Ste 4, Lancaster (93535-4687)
P.O. Box 1332 (93584-1332)
PHONE..................661 945-5634
Paul Kinison, *Pr*
EMP: 42 EST: 1986
SALES (est): 911.65K
SALES (corp-wide): 911.65K **Privately Held**
Web: www.aerotechnews.com
SIC: 2721 2741 2752 Trade journals: publishing only, not printed on site; Miscellaneous publishing; Commercial printing, lithographic

### (P-4229)
**AFFLUENT TARGET MARKETING INC**
Also Called: Affluent Living Publication
3855 E La Palma Ave Ste 250, Anaheim (92807-1765)
P.O. Box 18507 (92817-8507)
PHONE..................714 446-6280
Wally Hicks, *Pr*
EMP: 20 EST: 1980
SQ FT: 3,500
SALES (est): 238.07K **Privately Held**
Web: www.affluenttargetmarketing.com
SIC: 2721 Magazines: publishing only, not printed on site

### (P-4230)
**ARSENIC INC**
530 S Hewitt St Unit 119, Los Angeles (90013-2290)
PHONE..................310 701-7559
Amanda Micallef, *Pr*
EMP: 17 EST: 2015
SALES (est): 237.63K **Privately Held**
Web: www.arsenic.tv
SIC: 2721 Magazines: publishing only, not printed on site

### (P-4231)
**BBM FAIRWAY INC (PA)**
3520 Challenger St, Torrance (90503-1640)
P.O. Box 2703 (90509-2703)
EMP: 120 EST: 1961
SALES (est): 7.75MM
SALES (corp-wide): 7.75MM **Privately Held**
Web: www.bobit.com
SIC: 2721 7319 8742 Magazines: publishing only, not printed on site; Media buying service; Marketing consulting services

### (P-4232)
**BOBIT BUSINESS MEDIA INC**
21250 Hawthorne Blvd Ste 360, Torrance (90503-5540)
PHONE..................310 533-2400
Richard Rivera, *CEO*
EMP: 245 EST: 2018
SALES (est): 2.79MM
SALES (corp-wide): 957.36MM **Privately Held**
Web: www.bobit.com
SIC: 2721 Magazines: publishing only, not printed on site
PA: Gemspring Capital, Llc
54 Wilton Rd
203 842-8886

### (P-4233)
**BUSINESS EXTENSION BUREAU LTD**
Also Called: Western Real Estate News
500 S Airport Blvd, South San Francisco (94080-6912)
PHONE..................650 737-5700
Gil Chin, *Pr*
EMP: 18 EST: 1927
SQ FT: 7,000
SALES (est): 957.42K **Privately Held**
SIC: 2721 7331 2752 Trade journals: publishing and printing; Direct mail advertising services; Commercial printing, lithographic

### (P-4234)
**BUSINESS JOURNAL**
Also Called: Fresno Business Journal
1315 Van Ness Ave Ste 200, Fresno (93721-1729)
P.O. Box 126 (93707-0126)
PHONE..................559 490-3400
Gordon M Webster Junior, *Pr*
EMP: 24 EST: 1886
SALES (est): 838.07K **Privately Held**
Web: www.thebusinessjournal.com
SIC: 2721 2711 Trade journals: publishing only, not printed on site; Newspapers

### (P-4235)
**CAVIAR AFFAIR LLC**
637 Homer Ave, Palo Alto (94301-2828)
PHONE..................415 235-4169
Polina Steier, *Managing Member*
EMP: 21 EST: 2004
SQ FT: 2,000
SALES (est): 183.21K **Privately Held**
Web: www.caviaraffair.com
SIC: 2721 Periodicals

### (P-4236)
**CBJ LP**
Also Called: Los Angeles Business Journal
11150 Santa Monica Blvd, Los Angeles (90025-3314)
PHONE..................323 549-5225
Matt Toledo, *Brnch Mgr*
EMP: 40
SALES (corp-wide): 23.64MM **Privately Held**
Web: www.labusinessjournal.com
SIC: 2721 2711 8742 Periodicals, publishing only; Newspapers; General management consultant
PA: Cbj, L.P.
7101 College Blvd # 1100
913 451-9000

### (P-4237)
**CBJ LP**
Also Called: San Fernando Valley Bus Jurnl
11150 Santa Monica Blvd Ste 350, Los Angeles (90025-3314)
PHONE..................818 676-1750
Pegi Matsuda, *Mgr*
EMP: 76
SALES (corp-wide): 23.64MM **Privately Held**
Web: www.sfvbj.com
SIC: 2721 Magazines: publishing only, not printed on site
PA: Cbj, L.P.
7101 College Blvd # 1100
913 451-9000

### (P-4238)
**CBJ LP**
Also Called: Orange County Business Journal
18500 Von Karman Ave Ste 150, Irvine (92612-0504)
PHONE..................949 833-8373
Janet Cox, *Mgr*
EMP: 40
SALES (corp-wide): 23.64MM **Privately Held**
Web: www.ocbj.com
SIC: 2721 2711 7313 Trade journals: publishing only, not printed on site; Newspapers; Newspaper advertising representative

## PRODUCTS & SERVICES SECTION — 2721 - Periodicals (P-4259)

PA: Cbj, L.P.
7101 College Blvd # 1100
913 451-9000

**(P-4239)**
**CBJ LP**
Also Called: San Diego Business Journal
4909 Murphy Canyon Rd Ste 200, San Diego (92123-4349)
PHONE..................858 277-6359
Armon Mills, *Prin*
EMP: 25
SQ FT: 10,000
SALES (corp-wide): 23.64MM **Privately Held**
Web: www.sdbj.com
SIC: **2721** 2741 2711 Trade journals: publishing and printing; Miscellaneous publishing; Newspapers
PA: Cbj, L.P.
7101 College Blvd # 1100
913 451-9000

**(P-4240)**
**CLIQUE BRANDS INC**
Also Called: Who What Wear
750 N San Vicente Blvd Ste 800, West Hollywood (90069-5788)
PHONE..................310 623-6916
Katherine Power, *CEO*
Hilary Kerr, *Pr*
Mika Onishi, *COO*
David Thomas, *Dir*
EMP: 32 EST: 2007
SQ FT: 2,200
SALES (est): 4.89MM **Privately Held**
SIC: **2721** 5621 Magazines: publishing only, not printed on site; Women's specialty clothing stores

**(P-4241)**
**COMSTOCK PUBLISHING INC**
Also Called: Comstock's Magazine
2335 American River Dr Ste 301, Sacramento (95825-7088)
PHONE..................916 364-1000
Winnie Comstockcarlson, *Ex VP*
EMP: 15 EST: 1989
SQ FT: 1,600
SALES (est): 2.43MM **Privately Held**
Web: www.comstocksmag.com
SIC: **2721** Magazines: publishing only, not printed on site

**(P-4242)**
**CREATIVE AGE PUBLICATIONS INC**
Also Called: Nailpro
15975 High Knoll Rd, Encino (91436-3426)
PHONE..................818 782-7328
Deborah Carver, *Pr*
Mindy Rosiejka, *
EMP: 50 EST: 1972
SALES (est): 4.13MM **Privately Held**
Web: www.creativeage.com
SIC: **2721** 2731 Magazines: publishing only, not printed on site; Book publishing

**(P-4243)**
**CURTCO MEDIA GROUP**
29160 Heathercliff Rd Fl 1, Malibu (90265-6310)
P.O. Box 6934 (90264-6934)
PHONE..................310 589-7700
Samantha Brooks, *Prin*
EMP: 18 EST: 2010
SALES (est): 3.07MM **Privately Held**
Web: www.curtco.com
SIC: **2721** Magazines: publishing and printing

**(P-4244)**
**CURTCO ROBB MEDIA LLC (PA)**
29160 Heathercliff Rd Ste 200, Malibu (90265-6310)
PHONE..................310 589-7700
Stephen Colvin, *CEO*
William J Curtis, *
Christopher Fabian, *
David Arnold, *
EMP: 30 EST: 2001
SALES (est): 5.1MM
SALES (corp-wide): 5.1MM **Privately Held**
Web: www.curtco.com
SIC: **2721** Magazines: publishing and printing

**(P-4245)**
**CYPRESS MAGAZINES INC**
Also Called: National Jurist
5715 Kearny Villa Rd Ste 107, San Diego (92123-1133)
P.O. Box 939039 (92193-9039)
PHONE..................858 503-7572
Jack Crittenden, *Pr*
EMP: 16 EST: 1991
SALES (est): 351.59K **Privately Held**
Web: www.crittendenresearch.com
SIC: **2721** Magazines: publishing and printing

**(P-4246)**
**DESERT PUBLICATIONS INC (PA)**
Also Called: Desert Grafics
303 N Indian Canyon Dr, Palm Springs (92262-6015)
P.O. Box 2724 (92263-2724)
PHONE..................760 325-2333
Franklin Jones, *VP*
EMP: 47 EST: 1965
SQ FT: 25,000
SALES (est): 4.19MM
SALES (corp-wide): 4.19MM **Privately Held**
Web: www.palmspringslife.com
SIC: **2721** 7311 Magazines: publishing only, not printed on site; Advertising agencies

**(P-4247)**
**DIABLO COUNTRY MAGAZINE INC**
Also Called: Diablo Custom Publishing
2520 Camino Diablo, Walnut Creek (94597-3939)
PHONE..................925 943-1111
Steven J Rivera, *Pr*
▲ EMP: 40 EST: 1979
SQ FT: 7,640
SALES (est): 5.18MM **Privately Held**
Web: www.dcpubs.com
SIC: **2721** 2741 Magazines: publishing only, not printed on site; Miscellaneous publishing

**(P-4248)**
**DISNEY PUBLISHING WORLDWIDE (DH)**
Also Called: Disney Editions
500 S Buena Vista St, Burbank (91521-0001)
PHONE..................212 633-4400
R Russell Hampton Junior, *Ch*
▲ EMP: 100 EST: 1992
SALES (est): 52.93MM
SALES (corp-wide): 88.9B **Publicly Held**
Web: jobs.disneycareers.com
SIC: **2721** Magazines: publishing only, not printed on site
HQ: Disney Enterprises, Inc.
500 S Buena Vista St
Burbank CA 91521
818 560-1000

**(P-4249)**
**DUNCAN MCINTOSH COMPANY INC (PA)**
Also Called: Sea Magazine
18475 Bandilier Cir, Fountain Valley (92708-7012)
P.O. Box 1337 (92659-0337)
PHONE..................949 660-6150
Duncan R Mcintosh, *CEO*
Teresa Mcintosh, *Sec*
EMP: 35 EST: 1967
SQ FT: 15,728
SALES (est): 5.36MM
SALES (corp-wide): 5.36MM **Privately Held**
Web: www.duncanmcintoshco.com
SIC: **2721** 7389 Magazines: publishing and printing; Trade show arrangement

**(P-4250)**
**DWELL LIFE INC (PA)**
Also Called: Dwell
595 Pacific Ave Fl 4, San Francisco (94133-4685)
P.O. Box 40608 (94140-0608)
PHONE..................415 373-5100
Michela Abrams, *Managing Member*
Lara H Deam, *
David Morin, *
▲ EMP: 40 EST: 2002
SALES (est): 3.44MM
SALES (corp-wide): 3.44MM **Privately Held**
Web: www.dwell.com
SIC: **2721** 7389 Magazines: publishing and printing; Advertising, promotional, and trade show services

**(P-4251)**
**ELISID MAGAZINE**
1485 Spruce St, Riverside (92507-2445)
PHONE..................619 990-9999
Anthony R Vasquez, *Pt*
EMP: 20 EST: 2010
SALES (est): 1.16MM **Privately Held**
SIC: **2721** Periodicals

**(P-4252)**
**EMERALD X LLC**
Also Called: Vnu Business
31910 Del Obispo St Ste 200, San Juan Capistrano (92675-3182)
PHONE..................949 226-5754
Denise Bashem, *Brnch Mgr*
EMP: 30
SALES (corp-wide): 385.6MM **Publicly Held**
Web: www.emeraldx.com
SIC: **2721** 7389 Trade journals: publishing only, not printed on site; Promoters of shows and exhibitions
HQ: Emerald X, Llc
31910 Del Obspo St Ste 20
San Juan Capistrano CA 92675

**(P-4253)**
**ENTREPRENEUR MEDIA LLC (PA)** ✪
Also Called: Entrepeneur Magazine
1651 E 4th St Ste 125, Santa Ana (92701-5141)
P.O. Box 19787 (92623-9787)
PHONE..................949 261-2325
Ryan Shea, *CEO*
Bill Shaw, *
Chris Damore, *
Michael Le Du, *
▲ EMP: 80 EST: 2023
SQ FT: 30,000
SALES (est): 18.87MM **Privately Held**
Web: www.entrepreneur.com
SIC: **2721** Magazines: publishing only, not printed on site

**(P-4254)**
**EXCELLENCE MAGAZINE INC**
Also Called: Ross Periodicals
42 Digital Dr Ste 5, Novato (94949-5762)
PHONE..................415 382-0582
Tom Toldrian, *Pr*
Tom Toldrian, *Pt*
EMP: 16 EST: 1986
SQ FT: 2,850
SALES (est): 241.69K **Privately Held**
Web: www.excellence-mag.com
SIC: **2721** Magazines: publishing only, not printed on site

**(P-4255)**
**FINE MAGAZINE**
905 1/2 Crest Rd, Del Mar (92014-2617)
PHONE..................858 261-0963
John Winfield, *Prin*
EMP: 17 EST: 2019
SALES (est): 73.79K **Privately Held**
Web: www.finehomesandliving.com
SIC: **2721** Magazines: publishing only, not printed on site

**(P-4256)**
**FLAUNT MAGAZINE**
1418 N Highland Ave, Los Angeles (90028-7611)
PHONE..................323 836-1044
Luis A Barajas Junior, *Pr*
▲ EMP: 18 EST: 1998
SALES (est): 2.47MM **Privately Held**
Web: www.flaunt.com
SIC: **2721** Magazines: publishing only, not printed on site

**(P-4257)**
**FOUNDATION FOR NAT PROGRESS**
Also Called: Mother Jones
222 Sutter St Ste 600, San Francisco (94108-4457)
PHONE..................415 321-1700
Monika Bauerlein, *CEO*
Madeleine Buckingham, *CFO*
Sara Frankel, *Sec*
EMP: 39 EST: 1975
SQ FT: 13,500
SALES (est): 16.53MM **Privately Held**
Web: www.motherjones.com
SIC: **2721** Magazines: publishing and printing

**(P-4258)**
**FRANCHISE UPDATE INC**
Also Called: Franchise Update Media Group
6489 Camden Ave Ste 204, San Jose (95120-2851)
P.O. Box 20547 (95160-0547)
PHONE..................408 402-5681
Therese Thilgen, *CEO*
EMP: 15 EST: 1988
SALES (est): 2.27MM **Privately Held**
Web: www.franchising.com
SIC: **2721** Magazines: publishing only, not printed on site

**(P-4259)**
**FREEDOM OF PRESS FOUNDATION**
601 Van Ness Ave Ste E731, San Francisco (94102-3242)
PHONE..................510 995-0780
Trevor Timm, *Ex Dir*
EMP: 16 EST: 2012

## 2721 - Periodicals (P-4260)

**SALES (est):** 393.23K **Privately Held**
**Web:** www.freedom.press
**SIC:** 2721 Periodicals

**(P-4260)**
**GOLD PROSPECTORS ASSN AMER LLC**
Also Called: Gold Prospectors Assn Amer
25819 Jefferson Ave Ste 110, Murrieta (92562-6964)
P.O. Box 891509 (92589-1509)
**PHONE**..................951 699-4749
Thomas Massie, *Managing Member*
Richard Dixon, *Managing Member*
**EMP:** 60 **EST:** 1966
**SALES (est):** 2.39MM **Privately Held**
**Web:** www.goldprospectors.org
**SIC:** 2721 4833 Magazines: publishing only, not printed on site; Television broadcasting stations

**(P-4261)**
**GRAPHIC FILM GROUP LLC (PA)**
1901 Avenue Of The Stars, Los Angeles (90067-6001)
**PHONE**..................310 887-6330
Randy Mendhlsohn, *Prin*
**EMP:** 15 **EST:** 2016
**SALES (est):** 377.69K
**SALES (corp-wide):** 377.69K **Privately Held**
**Web:** www.graphicfilmgroup.com
**SIC:** 2721 7812 Television schedules: publishing and printing; Video production

**(P-4262)**
**HARTLE MEDIA VENTURES LLC**
Also Called: 7x7
680 2nd St, San Francisco (94107-2015)
**PHONE**..................415 362-7797
**EMP:** 18 **EST:** 2000
**SQ FT:** 2,000
**SALES (est):** 328.79K **Privately Held**
**Web:** www.7x7.com
**SIC:** 2721 Magazines: publishing only, not printed on site

**(P-4263)**
**HAYMARKET WORLDWIDE INC**
17030 Red Hill Ave, Irvine (92614-5626)
**PHONE**..................949 417-6700
Peter Foubister, *CEO*
▲ **EMP:** 31 **EST:** 1992
**SQ FT:** 4,000
**SALES (est):** 2.08MM
**SALES (corp-wide):** 226.37MM **Privately Held**
**SIC:** 2721 Magazines: publishing only, not printed on site
**HQ:** Haymarket Media, Inc.
275 7th Ave Fl 10
New York NY 10001
646 638-6000

**(P-4264)**
**HIC CORPORATION (PA)**
Also Called: Heavy Duty Trucking
38 Executive Park Ste 300, Irvine (92614-6755)
**PHONE**..................949 261-1636
Doug Condra, *Pr*
**EMP:** 15 **EST:** 1947
**SALES (est):** 563.44K
**SALES (corp-wide):** 563.44K **Privately Held**
**Web:** www.newportcommunicationsgroup.com
**SIC:** 2721 Magazines: publishing only, not printed on site

**(P-4265)**
**ID MATTERS LLC**
7060 Hollywood Blvd 8th Fl, Los Angeles (90028-6021)
**PHONE**..................323 822-4800
Kelly Novak, *Managing Member*
**EMP:** 36 **EST:** 2012
**SALES (est):** 1.11MM **Privately Held**
**SIC:** 2721 Magazines: publishing and printing

**(P-4266)**
**IDG CONSUMER & SMB INC (DH)**
Also Called: PC World Magazine
501 2nd St, San Francisco (94107-1469)
**PHONE**..................415 243-0500
Colin Crawford, *Pr*
Miriam Karlin, *
Michael Kisseberth, *
Edward B Bloom, *
Kevin C Krull, *
**EMP:** 116 **EST:** 1982
**SQ FT:** 21,000
**SALES (est):** 7.32MM
**SALES (corp-wide):** 8.02B **Publicly Held**
**Web:** www.idg.com
**SIC:** 2721 Magazines: publishing only, not printed on site
**HQ:** Idg Communications, Inc.
140 Kendrick St Ste A110
Needham MA 02494
508 872-8200

**(P-4267)**
**INFOWORLD MEDIA GROUP INC (DH)**
Also Called: Infoworld
501 2nd St Ste 500, San Francisco (94107-4133)
**PHONE**..................415 243-4344
Robert Ostrow, *CEO*
Patrick J Mc Govern, *
William P Murphy, *
Derek Butcher, *
Miles Dennison, *Associate Publisher*
▲ **EMP:** 75 **EST:** 1979
**SQ FT:** 50,000
**SALES (est):** 5.56MM
**SALES (corp-wide):** 8.02B **Publicly Held**
**Web:** www.infoworld.com
**SIC:** 2721 2741 7389 Magazines: publishing only, not printed on site; Newsletter publishing; Trade show arrangement
**HQ:** Idg Communications, Inc.
140 Kendrick St Ste A110
Needham MA 02494
508 872-8200

**(P-4268)**
**INLAND EMPIRE MEDIA GROUP INC**
Also Called: Inland Empire Magazine
36095 Monte De Oro Rd, Temecula (92592-8123)
**PHONE**..................951 682-3026
Don Lorenzi, *Pr*
Don Lorenzi, *Pr*
Richard Lorenzi, *Sec*
**EMP:** 49 **EST:** 1972
**SALES (est):** 1.64MM **Privately Held**
**Web:** www.inlandempiremagazine.com
**SIC:** 2721 Magazines: publishing and printing

**(P-4269)**
**KELLEY BLUE BOOK CO INC (DH)**
195 Technology Dr, Irvine (92618-2402)
P.O. Box 19691 (92623)
**PHONE**..................949 770-7704
Jared Rowe, *CEO*
John Morrison, *
**EMP:** 92 **EST:** 1926
**SALES (est):** 25.19MM
**SALES (corp-wide):** 16.61B **Privately Held**
**Web:** www.kbb.com
**SIC:** 2721 Trade journals: publishing only, not printed on site
**HQ:** Autotrader.Com, Inc.
6205 Pachtree Dunwoody Rd
Atlanta GA 30328
404 568-8000

**(P-4270)**
**L F P INC (PA)**
Also Called: Flynt, Larry Publishing
8484 Wilshire Blvd Ste 900, Beverly Hills (90211-3211)
**PHONE**..................323 651-3525
Larry Flynt, *Ch Bd*
Michael H Klein, *
▲ **EMP:** 100 **EST:** 1976
**SQ FT:** 10,000
**SALES (est):** 33.18MM
**SALES (corp-wide):** 33.18MM **Privately Held**
**Web:** www.hustlermagazine.com
**SIC:** 2721 Magazines: publishing only, not printed on site

**(P-4271)**
**LA PARENT MAGAZINE (PA)**
5855 Topanga Canyon Blvd Ste 150, Woodland Hills (91367-4671)
P.O. Box 8275 (91372-8275)
**PHONE**..................818 264-2222
Madelyn Calabrese, *Mgr*
**EMP:** 15 **EST:** 1978
**SQ FT:** 2,500
**SALES (est):** 378.97K
**SALES (corp-wide):** 378.97K **Privately Held**
**Web:** www.laparent.com
**SIC:** 2721 Magazines: publishing only, not printed on site

**(P-4272)**
**LANDSCAPE COMMUNICATIONS INC**
Also Called: Landscape Contract National
14771 Plaza Dr Ste A, Tustin (92780-2779)
P.O. Box 1126 (92781-1126)
**PHONE**..................714 979-5276
George Schmok, *Pr*
**EMP:** 25 **EST:** 1991
**SQ FT:** 1,618
**SALES (est):** 3.11MM **Privately Held**
**Web:** www.landscapearchitect.com
**SIC:** 2721 Trade journals: publishing only, not printed on site

**(P-4273)**
**LOS ANGELES BUS JURNL ASSOC**
11150 Santa Monica Blvd Ste 350, Los Angeles (90025-3314)
**PHONE**..................323 549-5225
Matt Toledo, *Pr*
**EMP:** 15 **EST:** 1975
**SALES (est):** 903.64K **Privately Held**
**Web:** www.labusinessjournal.com
**SIC:** 2721 Magazines: publishing only, not printed on site

**(P-4274)**
**LUNDBERG SURVEY INCORPORATED**
911 Via Alondra, Camarillo (93012-8048)
**PHONE**..................805 383-2400
Trilby Lundberg, *Pr*
**EMP:** 34 **EST:** 1949
**SALES (est):** 755.94K **Privately Held**
**Web:** www.lundbergsurvey.com
**SIC:** 2721 8748 2741 Statistical reports (periodicals): publishing only; Business consulting, nec; Miscellaneous publishing

**(P-4275)**
**MAC PUBLISHING LLC (DH)**
Also Called: Macworld Magazine
501 2nd St Ste 600, San Francisco (94107-4133)
**PHONE**..................415 243-0505
Colin Crawford, *Pr*
**EMP:** 20 **EST:** 1997
**SALES (est):** 896.72K
**SALES (corp-wide):** 8.02B **Publicly Held**
**SIC:** 2721 Magazines: publishing only, not printed on site
**HQ:** International Data Group, Inc.
140 Kendrick St Bldg B
Needham MA 02494
508 875-5000

**(P-4276)**
**MAKE COMMUNITY LLC**
150 Todd Rd Ste 100, Santa Rosa (95407-8412)
P.O. Box 239 (95473-0239)
**PHONE**..................707 200-3714
**EMP:** 20 **EST:** 2019
**SALES (est):** 2.76MM **Privately Held**
**Web:** www.make.co
**SIC:** 2721 Magazines: publishing only, not printed on site

**(P-4277)**
**MAXWELL PETERSEN ASSOCIATES**
Also Called: Dynamic Chiropractic
412 Olive Ave Ste 208, Huntington Beach (92648-5142)
**PHONE**..................714 230-3150
Donald M Petersen, *Pr*
**EMP:** 19 **EST:** 1977
**SQ FT:** 2,000
**SALES (est):** 2.63MM **Privately Held**
**Web:** www.mpamedia.com
**SIC:** 2721 Magazines: publishing only, not printed on site

**(P-4278)**
**MINORITY SUCCESS PUBG GROUP**
Also Called: Minorities & Success
23505 Crenshaw Blvd, Torrance (90505-5223)
**PHONE**..................310 736-2462
Farimah Farahpour, *Pr*
Ali F Chegini, *VP*
**EMP:** 20 **EST:** 1990
**SALES (est):** 668.3K **Privately Held**
**Web:** www.minoritysuccess.us
**SIC:** 2721 Magazines: publishing only, not printed on site

**(P-4279)**
**MNM CORPORATION (PA)**
Also Called: Apparel Newsgroup, The
110 E 9th St Ste A777, Los Angeles (90079-1777)
**PHONE**..................213 627-3737
Martin Wernicke, *CEO*
▲ **EMP:** 25 **EST:** 1985
**SQ FT:** 11,000
**SALES (est):** 963.99K
**SALES (corp-wide):** 963.99K **Privately Held**
**Web:** www.apparelnews.net

# PRODUCTS & SERVICES SECTION

## 2721 - Periodicals (P-4299)

SIC: 2721 8721 Magazines: publishing only, not printed on site; Accounting, auditing, and bookkeeping

### (P-4280)
**MODEL LYFE**
Also Called: Model Lyfe Magazine
5405 Wilshire Blvd, Los Angeles (90036-4203)
PHONE.................................224 325-5933
EMP: 15
SALES (est): 950K Privately Held
SIC: 2721 Periodicals

### (P-4281)
**MODERN LUXURY MEDIA LLC (HQ)**
Also Called: Angeleno Magazine
243 Vallejo St, San Francisco (94111-1511)
PHONE.................................404 443-0004
Michael B Kong, Managing Member
▲ EMP: 40 EST: 1993
SALES (est): 2.44MM
SALES (corp-wide): 6.38MM Privately Held
Web: www.lamodernmedia.com
SIC: 2721 Magazines: publishing only, not printed on site
PA: Dickey Publishing, Inc.
3280 Peachtree Rd Ne # 23
404 949-0700

### (P-4282)
**OMICS GROUP INC**
5716 Corsa Ave Ste 110, Westlake Village (91362-7354)
PHONE.................................650 268-9744
Srinu B Gedela, Brnch Mgr
EMP: 460
SALES (corp-wide): 791.73K Privately Held
Web: www.omicsonline.org
SIC: 2721 Trade journals: publishing and printing
PA: Omics Group Inc
2360 Corp Cir Ste 400
888 843-8169

### (P-4283)
**OMICS GROUP INC**
731 Gull Ave, Foster City (94404-1329)
PHONE.................................650 268-9744
Srinu B Gedela, Brnch Mgr
EMP: 460
SALES (corp-wide): 791.73K Privately Held
Web: www.omicsonline.org
SIC: 2721 Trade journals: publishing and printing
PA: Omics Group Inc
2360 Corp Cir Ste 400
888 843-8169

### (P-4284)
**ORANGE COAST MAGAZINE LLC**
Also Called: Orange Coast Magazine
5900 Wilshire Blvd # 10, Los Angeles (90036-5013)
PHONE.................................949 862-1133
Gary Thoe, Pr
EMP: 61 EST: 1975
SALES (est): 998.78K
SALES (corp-wide): 39.71MM Privately Held
Web: www.orangecoast.com
SIC: 2721 5812 Magazines: publishing only, not printed on site; Eating places
HQ: Emmis Publishing, L.P.
40 Monument Cir Ste 100
Indianapolis IN 46204

### (P-4285)
**PAISANO PUBLICATIONS LLC (PA)**
Also Called: V Twin Magazine
28210 Dorothy Dr, Agoura Hills (91301-2693)
PHONE.................................818 889-8740
John Lagana, CEO
John Lagana, Publisher
Joseph Teresi, *
Robert Davis, *
EMP: 60 EST: 1971
SQ FT: 40,000
SALES (est): 1.24MM
SALES (corp-wide): 1.24MM Privately Held
Web: www.v-twin.com
SIC: 2721 Magazines: publishing only, not printed on site

### (P-4286)
**PAISANO PUBLICATIONS INC**
Also Called: V/ Twins
28210 Dorothy Dr, Agoura Hills (91301-2693)
P.O. Box 3000 (91376-3000)
PHONE.................................818 889-8740
Bill Prather, Pr
Allen Ribakoff, *
Joseph Teresi, *
Robert Davis, *
EMP: 52 EST: 1993
SALES (est): 941.32K
SALES (corp-wide): 1.24MM Privately Held
SIC: 2721 7812 Magazines: publishing and printing; Commercials, television: tape or film
PA: Paisano Publications, Llc
28210 Dorothy Dr
818 889-8740

### (P-4287)
**PARTNER CONCEPTS INC**
811 Camino Viejo, Santa Barbara (93108-2313)
PHONE.................................805 745-7199
William J Kasch, Pr
William L Coulson, *
EMP: 75 EST: 1983
SALES (est): 18.57MM Privately Held
SIC: 2721 Magazines: publishing only, not printed on site

### (P-4288)
**PLAYBOY ENTERPRISES INC**
10960 Wilshire Blvd Fl 22, Los Angeles (90024-3808)
PHONE.................................310 424-1800
John Luther, Mgr
EMP: 79
SALES (corp-wide): 142.95MM Publicly Held
Web: www.powersergefitness.com
SIC: 2721 Magazines: publishing and printing
HQ: Playboy Enterprises, Inc.
10960 Wlshire Blvd Ste 22
Los Angeles CA 90024
310 424-1800

### (P-4289)
**PLAYBOY JAPAN INC**
9346 Civic Center Dr # 200, Beverly Hills (90210-3604)
PHONE.................................310 424-1800
EMP: 16 EST: 2010
SALES (est): 299.9K
SALES (corp-wide): 142.95MM Publicly Held
SIC: 2721 Magazines: publishing and printing
HQ: Playboy Enterprises, Inc.
10960 Wlshire Blvd Ste 22
Los Angeles CA 90024
310 424-1800

### (P-4290)
**PUBLISHERS DEVELOPMENT CORP**
Also Called: American Handgunner and Guns
225 W Valley Pkwy Ste 100, Escondido (92025-2613)
PHONE.................................858 605-0200
Thomas Von Rosen, CEO
Thomas M Hollander, *
EMP: 40 EST: 1941
SALES (est): 1.39MM Privately Held
Web: www.americanhandgunner.com
SIC: 2721 Magazines: publishing only, not printed on site

### (P-4291)
**QG PRINTING CORP**
6688 Box Springs Blvd, Riverside (92507-0726)
PHONE.................................951 571-2500
Ken Eazell, Mgr
EMP: 50
SALES (corp-wide): 2.96B Publicly Held
SIC: 2721 2752 Periodicals; Commercial printing, lithographic
HQ: Qg Printing Corp.
N61w23044 Harrys Way
Sussex WI 53089

### (P-4292)
**R T C GROUP**
Also Called: Cots Journal Magazine
905 Calle Amanecer Ste 250, San Clemente (92673-6226)
PHONE.................................949 226-2000
John Reardon, Owner
EMP: 22 EST: 1985
SALES (est): 744.79K Privately Held
Web: www.rtcgroup.com
SIC: 2721 Magazines: publishing only, not printed on site

### (P-4293)
**RECRUITMENT SERVICES INC**
Also Called: Working Nurse
3600 Wilshire Blvd Ste 1526, Los Angeles (90010-2603)
PHONE.................................213 364-1960
Randy Goldring, Pr
EMP: 33 EST: 2008
SALES (est): 194.64K Privately Held
Web: www.workingnurse.com
SIC: 2721 Periodicals

### (P-4294)
**REFINITIV US LLC**
Also Called: Refinitiv
50 California St, San Francisco (94111-4624)
PHONE.................................415 344-6000
Andrea Lavoie, Prin
EMP: 168
SALES (corp-wide): 3.04B Privately Held
Web: www.lseg.com
SIC: 2721 Periodicals
HQ: Refinitiv Us Llc
28 Liberty St Fl 58
New York NY 10005
212 314-1100

### (P-4295)
**ROBB CURTCO MEDIA LLC**
22741 Pacific Coast Hwy Ste 401, Malibu (90265-5876)
PHONE.................................310 589-7700
EMP: 33
SALES (corp-wide): 5.1MM Privately Held
Web: www.curtco.com
SIC: 2721 Magazines: publishing and printing
PA: Curtco Robb Media Llc
29160 Heathercliff Rd # 1
310 589-7700

### (P-4296)
**SABOT PUBLISHING INC (PA)**
Also Called: A Media
300 Continental Blvd Ste 650, El Segundo (90245-5042)
PHONE.................................310 356-4100
Gibb Zimbalist, Pr
William Berry, CFO
EMP: 20 EST: 1999
SQ FT: 4,400
SALES (est): 1.95MM
SALES (corp-wide): 1.95MM Privately Held
SIC: 2721 2731 Magazines: publishing and printing; Book publishing

### (P-4297)
**SAN DIEGO MAGAZINE PUBG CO**
Also Called: San Diego Magazine
1230 Columbia St Ste 800, San Diego (92101-3571)
PHONE.................................619 230-9292
James Fitzpatrick, CEO
Claire Johnson, *
EMP: 30 EST: 1948
SALES (est): 2.49MM
SALES (corp-wide): 11.2MM Privately Held
Web: www.sandiegomagazine.com
SIC: 2721 Magazines: publishing only, not printed on site
PA: Curtco, Publishing
29160 Heathercliff Rd # 1
310 589-7700

### (P-4298)
**STYLE MEDIA GROUP INC**
909 Mormon St, Folsom (95630-2412)
P.O. Box 925 (95763-0925)
PHONE.................................916 988-9888
Terence Carroll, CEO
Wendy Sipple, COO
EMP: 24 EST: 2003
SALES (est): 762.09K Privately Held
Web: www.stylemg.com
SIC: 2721 Magazines: publishing only, not printed on site

### (P-4299)
**SUNSET PUBLISHING CORPORATION (HQ)**
Also Called: Sunset Magazine
55 Harrison St Ste 200, Oakland (94607-3772)
PHONE.................................800 777-0117
Kevin Lynch, VP
Lorinda Reichert, VP
Katie Tamony, VP
Mark Okean, VP
Christopher Kevorkian, VP
EMP: 150 EST: 1928
SQ FT: 56,000
SALES (est): 3.82MM
SALES (corp-wide): 921.67MM Privately Held
Web: www.sunset.com
SIC: 2721 2731 Magazines: publishing only, not printed on site; Books, publishing only
PA: Regent, Lp
9720 Wilshire Blvd Fl 6

## 2721 - Periodicals (P-4300)

310 299-4100

**(P-4300)**
**TEN PUBLISHING MEDIA LLC**
Transworld Snowboarding
2052 Corte Del Nogal Ste 100, Carlsbad (92011-1427)
PHONE..................760 722-7777
Scott Dickey, CEO
EMP: 17
SIC: 2721 Magazines: publishing only, not printed on site
PA: Ten Publishing Media, Llc
831 S Douglas St Ste 100

**(P-4301)**
**TL ENTERPRISES LLC**
Also Called: Highways Magazine
2750 Park View Ct Ste 240, Oxnard (93036-5458)
PHONE..................805 981-8393
EMP: 200
Web: rv.campingworld.com
SIC: 2721 Magazines: publishing only, not printed on site

**(P-4302)**
**TOTAL BEAUTY MEDIA INC**
1158 26th St Ste 535, Santa Monica (90403-4621)
PHONE..................310 295-9593
Emrah Kovacoglu, CEO
Beth Mayall, VP
Ivan Ivankovich, CFO
Ann Marie Macdougall, VP
EMP: 15 EST: 2007
SALES (est): 36.59K
SALES (corp-wide): 18.63MM Privately Held
SIC: 2721 7231 Magazines: publishing and printing; Beauty shops
PA: Evolve Media, Llc
5140 Goldleaf Cir 3rd Fl
310 449-1890

**(P-4303)**
**UBM CANON LLC (DH)**
2901 28th St Ste 100, Santa Monica (90405-2975)
PHONE..................310 445-4200
Sally Shankland, CEO
Scott Schulman, *
Sally Shankland, Pr
Stephen Corrick, *
Fred Gysi, *
EMP: 31 EST: 1996
SQ FT: 50,000
SALES (est): 5.88MM
SALES (corp-wide): 3.98B Privately Held
Web: www.informamarkets.com
SIC: 2721 7389 Magazines: publishing only, not printed on site; Trade show arrangement
HQ: Informa Tech Holdings Llc
1983 Marcus Ave Ste 250
New Hyde Park NY 11042
516 562-7800

**(P-4304)**
**VIDEOMAKER INC**
Also Called: Smart TV & Sound
645 Mangrove Ave, Chico (95926-3946)
P.O. Box 4591 (95927-4591)
PHONE..................530 891-8410
Matthew York, Pr
Patrice York, *
EMP: 36 EST: 1985
SQ FT: 8,000
SALES (est): 1.89MM Privately Held
Web: www.videomaker.com

SIC: 2721 7812 Magazines: publishing only, not printed on site; Motion picture and video production

**(P-4305)**
**VIZ MEDIA LLC**
Also Called: Viz Media Music
1355 Market St Ste 200, San Francisco (94103-1460)
P.O. Box 77010 (94107-0010)
PHONE..................415 546-7073
Brad Woods, *
▲ EMP: 200 EST: 1986
SALES (est): 32.24MM Privately Held
Web: www.viz.com
SIC: 2721 2731 7819 6794 Comic books: publishing only, not printed on site; Books, publishing only; Video tape or disk reproduction; Copyright buying and licensing
PA: Shogakukan Inc.
2-3-1, Hitotsubashi

**(P-4306)**
**WIRED VENTURES INC**
Also Called: Wired
520 3rd St Ste 305, San Francisco (94107-6805)
PHONE..................415 276-8400
Louis Rossetto, Ch Bd
Jane Metcalfe, Prin
EMP: 175 EST: 1992
SALES (est): 1.57MM Privately Held
Web: www.wired.com
SIC: 2721 6719 Magazines: publishing only, not printed on site; Investment holding companies, except banks

**(P-4307)**
**WORLD HISTORY GROUP LLC**
Also Called: Historynet
9720 Wilshire Blvd, Beverly Hills (90212-2021)
PHONE..................703 779-8322
EMP: 27 EST: 2015
SALES (est): 198.99K Privately Held
Web: www.historynet.com
SIC: 2721 7389 Magazines: publishing only, not printed on site; Business services, nec

## 2731 Book Publishing

**(P-4308)**
**80LV LLC**
15260 Ventura Blvd Ste 2230, Sherman Oaks (91403-5307)
PHONE..................818 435-6613
EMP: 38 EST: 2015
SALES (est): 247.44K Privately Held
Web: www.80.lv
SIC: 2731 Book publishing

**(P-4309)**
**ABC - CLIO INC (HQ)**
Also Called: ABC-Clio
75 Aero Camino, Goleta (93117-3134)
P.O. Box 1911 (93116-1911)
PHONE..................805 968-1911
Ronald Boehm, CEO
EMP: 115 EST: 1955
SALES (est): 21.96MM
SALES (corp-wide): 434.48MM Privately Held
Web: www.abc-clio.com
SIC: 2731 Books, publishing only
PA: Bloomsbury Publishing Plc
50 Bedford Square
207 631-5600

**(P-4310)**
**ACCESS BOOKS**
1800 Century Park E Ste 600, Los Angeles (90067-1501)
PHONE..................310 920-1694
Mark Constantino, Pr
Mark Constantino, Pr
EMP: 148 EST: 1999
SQ FT: 36,000
SALES (est): 697.48K Privately Held
Web: www.accessbooks.net
SIC: 2731 Book publishing

**(P-4311)**
**AMAZING FACTS INC**
Also Called: Amazing Facts Ministries
1203 W Sunset Blvd, Rocklin (95765-1305)
P.O. Box 1058 (95678-8058)
PHONE..................916 434-3880
Doug Batchelor, Pr
Steve Keiser, *
Allen Hrenyk, *
EMP: 70 EST: 1966
SQ FT: 28,000
SALES (est): 4.32MM Privately Held
Web: www.afcoe.org
SIC: 2731 4832 4833 Pamphlets: publishing and printing; Religious; Television broadcasting stations

**(P-4312)**
**AVN MEDIA NETWORK INC**
Also Called: Adult Video News
9400 Penfield Ave, Chatsworth (91311-6549)
PHONE..................818 718-5788
Tony Rios, CEO
EMP: 30 EST: 1982
SQ FT: 15,000
SALES (est): 2.42MM Privately Held
Web: www.avn.com
SIC: 2731 2721 Book publishing; Periodicals

**(P-4313)**
**BERRETT-KOEHLER PUBLISHERS INC (PA)**
1333 Broadway Ste 1000, Oakland (94612-1926)
PHONE..................510 817-2277
Steven Piersanti, Pr
▲ EMP: 16 EST: 1991
SALES (est): 2.5MM Privately Held
Web: www.bkconnection.com
SIC: 2731 Books, publishing only

**(P-4314)**
**BERTELSMANN INC**
Also Called: Arvato Services
29011 Commerce Center Dr, Valencia (91355-4195)
PHONE..................661 702-2700
Janet Adams, Mgr
EMP: 9820
SALES (corp-wide): 147.78MM Privately Held
Web: www.arvato.com
SIC: 2731 Books, publishing only
HQ: Bertelsmann, Inc.
1745 Broadway
New York NY 10019
212 782-1000

**(P-4315)**
**BLURB INC**
580 California St Fl 3, San Francisco (94104-1024)
PHONE..................415 364-6300
Eileen Gittins, CEO
Elizabeth Allen, CMO
Kelly Leach, Co-Vice President

EMP: 28 EST: 2004
SALES (est): 3.47MM Privately Held
Web: www.blurb.com
SIC: 2731 Books, publishing only

**(P-4316)**
**BOOK BUDDY DIGITAL MEDIA INC**
42982 Osgood Rd, Fremont (94539-5627)
PHONE..................510 226-9074
Alex Woo, CEO
EMP: 46 EST: 2011
SALES (est): 99.82K Privately Held
Web: www.bookbuddymedia.com
SIC: 2731 Book publishing

**(P-4317)**
**BRIDGE PUBLICATIONS INC (PA)**
Also Called: Bpi Records
5600 E Olympic Blvd, Commerce (90022-5128)
PHONE..................323 888-6200
Blake Silber, CEO
Lis Astrupgaard, *
Marilyn Pisani, *
Suzanne Riley, *
▲ EMP: 40 EST: 1981
SQ FT: 15,000
SALES (est): 20.95MM
SALES (corp-wide): 20.95MM Privately Held
Web: www.bridgepub.com
SIC: 2731 3652 Books, publishing only; Prerecorded records and tapes

**(P-4318)**
**CALLISTO MEDIA INC**
Also Called: Rockridge Press
1955 Broadway # 400, Oakland (94612-2205)
PHONE..................510 253-0500
Benjamin Wayne, CEO
Mary Amicucci, *
Timothy Musgrove, *
Brian Cooper, *
EMP: 162 EST: 2011
SALES (est): 9.1MM Privately Held
Web: www.callistopublishing.com
SIC: 2731 Books, publishing only

**(P-4319)**
**CENTER FOR CLLBRTIVE CLASSROOM**
1001 Marina Village Pkwy Ste 110, Alameda (94501-1091)
PHONE..................510 533-0213
Roger King, CEO
Victor Young, *
Peter Brunn, *
Barbra Radcliffe, *
Brent Welling, *
▲ EMP: 99 EST: 1975
SQ FT: 15,000
SALES (est): 17.69MM Privately Held
Web: www.collaborativeclassroom.org
SIC: 2731 8299 Book publishing; Personal development school

**(P-4320)**
**CHICK PUBLICATIONS INC**
8780 Archibald Ave, Rancho Cucamonga (91730-4697)
P.O. Box 3500 (91761-1019)
PHONE..................909 987-0771
Jack T Chick, Pr
George A Collins, *
Ronald Rockney, *
◆ EMP: 21 EST: 1961
SQ FT: 10,000
SALES (est): 839.21K Privately Held

# PRODUCTS & SERVICES SECTION

## 2731 - Book Publishing (P-4341)

Web: www.chick.com
SIC: 2731 5961 Books, publishing only; Mail order house, nec

**(P-4321)**
**CHRONICLE BOOKS LLC (HQ)**
680 2nd St, San Francisco (94107-2015)
PHONE....................................415 537-4200
Jack Jensen, *
◆ EMP: 62 EST: 1999
SALES (est): 9.81MM
SALES (corp-wide): 12.64MM **Privately Held**
Web: www.chroniclebooks.com
SIC: 2731 Books, publishing only
PA: The Mcevoy Group Llc
    680 2nd St
    415 537-4200

**(P-4322)**
**CPP INC**
185 N Wolfe Rd, Sunnyvale (94086-5212)
PHONE....................................650 969-8901
EMP: 18 EST: 2020
SALES (est): 1.19MM **Privately Held**
Web: www.themyersbriggs.com
SIC: 2731 Book publishing

**(P-4323)**
**CPP/BELWIN INC**
16320 Roscoe Blvd Ste 100, Van Nuys (91406-1216)
P.O. Box 10003 (91410-0003)
PHONE....................................818 891-5999
Steven Manus, Pr
▲ EMP: 57 EST: 1988
SQ FT: 142,000
SALES (est): 481.55K **Privately Held**
SIC: 2731 Book music: publishing only, not printed on site
PA: Alfred Music Group Inc.
    16320 Roscoe Blvd Ste 100

**(P-4324)**
**CREATIVE TEACHING PRESS INC (PA)**
11145 Knott Ave, Cypress (90630-5140)
PHONE....................................714 799-2100
James M Connelly, CEO
Luella Connelly, *
Susan Connelly, *
Patrick Connelly, *
◆ EMP: 95 EST: 1965
SALES (est): 5.46MM
SALES (corp-wide): 5.46MM **Privately Held**
Web: www.creativeteaching.com
SIC: 2731 Books, publishing only

**(P-4325)**
**DAWN SIGN PRESS INC**
6130 Nancy Ridge Dr, San Diego (92121-3223)
PHONE....................................858 625-0600
Joe Dannis, CEO
Thomas Schlegel, *
Tina Jo Breindel, *
◆ EMP: 28 EST: 1977
SQ FT: 16,500
SALES (est): 2.46MM **Privately Held**
Web: www.dawnsign.com
SIC: 2731 Books, publishing only

**(P-4326)**
**DHARMA MUDRANALAYA (PA)**
Also Called: Dharma Publishing
35788 Hauser Bridge Rd, Cazadero (95421-9611)
PHONE....................................707 847-3380
Arnaud Maitland, CEO
Tarthang Tulku, Pr
Debbie Black, VP
▲ EMP: 21 EST: 1971
SQ FT: 16,000
SALES (est): 111.38K
SALES (corp-wide): 111.38K **Privately Held**
Web: www.dharmapublishing.com
SIC: 2731 7336 Books, publishing and printing; Commercial art and graphic design

**(P-4327)**
**DISNEY BOOK GROUP LLC (DH)**
Also Called: Hyperion Books For Children
500 S Buena Vista St, Burbank (91521-0001)
PHONE....................................818 560-1000
Russell R Hampton Junior, Pr
Marsha L Reed, Sec
EMP: 28 EST: 1999
SALES (est): 2.94MM
SALES (corp-wide): 88.9B **Publicly Held**
Web: www.thewaltdisneycompany.com
SIC: 2731 Book publishing
HQ: Twdc Enterprises 18 Corp.
    500 S Buena Vista St
    Burbank CA 91521

**(P-4328)**
**EDUCATIONAL IDEAS INCORPORATED**
Also Called: Ballard & Tighe Publishers
950 W Central Ave, Brea (92821-2261)
P.O. Box 219 (92822-0219)
PHONE....................................714 990-4332
Dorothy Roberts, Ch Bd
Mark Espinola, CEO
Kent Roberts, Sec
◆ EMP: 48 EST: 1976
SALES (est): 2.77MM **Privately Held**
Web: www.ballard-tighe.com
SIC: 2731 Books, publishing only

**(P-4329)**
**EVAN-MOOR CORPORATION (HQ)**
Also Called: Evan-Moor Educational Publr
18 Lower Ragsdale Dr, Monterey (93940-5746)
PHONE....................................831 649-5901
William E Evans, Pr
▲ EMP: 30 EST: 1979
SQ FT: 20,000
SALES (est): 8.04MM **Privately Held**
Web: www.evan-moor.com
SIC: 2731 Books, publishing and printing
PA: Lincoln Learning Solutions, Inc.
    2139 Brodhead Rd

**(P-4330)**
**HAWKEYE ACQUISITION INC**
Also Called: Meredith Publishing
201 Mission St Fl 12, San Francisco (94105-1888)
PHONE....................................415 249-2362
Tamara Marcsisak, Mgr
EMP: 80
SALES (corp-wide): 3.28B **Publicly Held**
Web: www.dotdashmeredith.com
SIC: 2731 2721 Book publishing; Periodicals
HQ: Hawkeye Acquisition, Inc.
    1716 Locust St
    Des Moines IA 50309
    515 284-3000

**(P-4331)**
**HESPERIAN HEALTH GUIDES (PA)**
2860 Telegraph Ave, Oakland (94609-3607)
PHONE....................................510 845-1447
Sarah Shannon, Dir
EMP: 20 EST: 1962
SQ FT: 1,600
SALES (est): 1.91MM
SALES (corp-wide): 1.91MM **Privately Held**
Web: www.hesperian.org
SIC: 2731 2741 8399 8641 Books, publishing only; Miscellaneous publishing; Community development groups; Civic and social associations

**(P-4332)**
**HOUGHTON MIFFLIN HARCOURT PUBG**
Also Called: Harcourt Trade Publishers
525 B St Ste 1900, San Diego (92101-4495)
PHONE....................................617 351-5000
Barbara Fisch, Brnch Mgr
EMP: 26
SALES (corp-wide): 1.97B **Privately Held**
Web: www.hmhco.com
SIC: 2731 Textbooks: publishing only, not printed on site
HQ: Houghton Mifflin Harcourt Publishing Company
    125 High St Ste 900
    Boston MA 02110
    617 351-5000

**(P-4333)**
**INSIGHT EDITIONS LP**
Also Called: Insight Editions
800 A St, San Rafael (94901-3011)
P.O. Box 3088 (94912-3088)
PHONE....................................415 526-1370
Raoul Goff, Pt
Michael Madden, Pt
▲ EMP: 89 EST: 2005
SALES (est): 14.57MM **Privately Held**
Web: www.insighteditions.com
SIC: 2731 2721 Books, publishing only; Comic books: publishing only, not printed on site

**(P-4334)**
**JUDY O PRODUCTIONS INC**
4858 W Pico Blvd Ste 331, Los Angeles (90019-4225)
PHONE....................................323 938-8513
Judy Ostarch, Pr
▲ EMP: 28 EST: 1999
SALES (est): 503.12K **Privately Held**
SIC: 2731 Book publishing

**(P-4335)**
**MANSON WESTERN LLC**
Also Called: Western Psychological Services
625 Alaska Ave, Torrance (90503-5124)
PHONE....................................424 201-8800
EMP: 117 EST: 1996
SALES (est): 32.55MM **Privately Held**
Web: www.wpspublish.com
SIC: 2731 Book publishing

**(P-4336)**
**MIKE MURACH & ASSOCIATES INC**
3730 W Swift Ave, Fresno (93722-6350)
PHONE....................................559 440-9071
Michael Murach, Pr
EMP: 22 EST: 1972
SALES (est): 776.98K **Privately Held**
Web: www.murach.com
SIC: 2731 Textbooks: publishing only, not printed on site

**(P-4337)**
**NARCOTICS ANYMOUS WRLD SVCS I (PA)**
Also Called: WORLD SERVICE OFFICE
19737 Nordhoff Pl, Chatsworth (91311-6606)
P.O. Box 9999 (91409-9099)
PHONE....................................818 773-9999
Anthony Edmondson, CEO
▲ EMP: 44 EST: 1953
SQ FT: 35,000
SALES (est): 9.92MM
SALES (corp-wide): 9.92MM **Privately Held**
Web: www.naws.org
SIC: 2731 Books, publishing only

**(P-4338)**
**NEW HARBINGER PUBLICATIONS INC (PA)**
5674 Shattuck Ave, Oakland (94609-1662)
PHONE....................................510 652-0215
Matt Mckay, Pr
▲ EMP: 33 EST: 1975
SQ FT: 6,500
SALES (est): 4.94MM
SALES (corp-wide): 4.94MM **Privately Held**
Web: www.newharbinger.com
SIC: 2731 3652 Books, publishing only; Master records or tapes, preparation of

**(P-4339)**
**NOLO**
6801 Koll Center Pkwy Ste 300, Pleasanton (94566-7047)
PHONE....................................510 549-1976
Bob Dubow, CEO
Annika Rogers, *
Jackie Thompson, Bridge Division Vice President*
John Plessas, Lawyer*
Laurence Nathanson, Business Division Vice President*
EMP: 120 EST: 1981
SALES (est): 6.15MM
SALES (corp-wide): 111.07MM **Privately Held**
Web: www.nolo.com
SIC: 2731 8111 8742 Books, publishing only; Legal services; Marketing consulting services
PA: Autodata Solutions Group, Llc
    909 N Pacific Coast Hwy # 11
    310 280-4000

**(P-4340)**
**PLURAL PUBLISHING INC**
9177 Aero Dr, San Diego (92123-2400)
PHONE....................................858 492-1555
Sadanand Singh, Pr
▲ EMP: 44 EST: 2004
SALES (est): 3.46MM **Privately Held**
Web: www.pluralpublishing.com
SIC: 2731 Textbooks: publishing only, not printed on site

**(P-4341)**
**PRACTICE MANAGEMENT INFO CORP (PA)**
Also Called: Pmic
4727 Wilshire Blvd Ste 302, Los Angeles (90010-3933)
PHONE....................................323 954-0224
James B Davis, Pr
◆ EMP: 15 EST: 1988
SQ FT: 6,000
SALES (est): 4.32MM
SALES (corp-wide): 4.32MM **Privately Held**

## 2731 - Book Publishing (P-4342)

**Web:** www.pmionline.com
**SIC:** 2731 7372 Book publishing; Business oriented computer software

**(P-4342)**
**QUITE POWERFUL ENTERPRISES LLC** ○
626 Wilshire Blvd Ste 410, Los Angeles (90017-2915)
**PHONE**.................................800 782-0915
Quan Lawson Paxton, *CEO*
**EMP:** 15 **EST:** 2024
**SALES (est):** 592.99K **Privately Held**
**SIC:** 2731 Books, publishing only

**(P-4343)**
**ROBERT W CAMERON & CO INC**
Also Called: Cameroncompany
149 Kentucky St Ste 7, Petaluma (94952-2940)
**PHONE**.................................707 769-1617
Robert Cameron, *Ch Bd*
Christopher Roger Gruener, *CEO*
Linda Henry, *Sec*
Tracy Davis, *Treas*
▲ **EMP:** 20 **EST:** 1965
**SQ FT:** 8,000
**SALES (est):** 552.15K **Privately Held**
**Web:** www.abramsbooks.com
**SIC:** 2731 Books, publishing only

**(P-4344)**
**SADDLEBACK EDUCATIONAL INC**
Also Called: Saddleback Educational Pubg
3130 Clay St, Newport Beach (92663-4112)
P.O. Box 6533 (91109-6501)
**PHONE**.................................714 640-5200
Arianne M Mchugh, *Pr*
Arianne M Mchugh, *Pr*
Tim Mchugh, *VP Sls*
▲ **EMP:** 19 **EST:** 1982
**SQ FT:** 5,000
**SALES (est):** 4.83MM **Privately Held**
**Web:** www.sdlback.com
**SIC:** 2731 5192 Books, publishing only; Books

**(P-4345)**
**SAGE PUBLICATIONS INC (PA)**
Also Called: Cq Press Fairfax Co
2455 Teller Rd, Thousand Oaks (91320-2234)
**PHONE**.................................805 499-0721
▲ **EMP:** 104 **EST:** 1965
**SALES (est):** 89.37MM
**SALES (corp-wide):** 89.37MM **Privately Held**
**Web:** us.sagepub.com
**SIC:** 2731 Book publishing

**(P-4346)**
**SOCIETY FOR THE STUDY NTIV ART**
Also Called: NORTH ATLANTIC BOOKS
2526 Martin Luther King Jr Way, Berkeley (94704-2607)
**PHONE**.................................510 549-4270
Douglas Reil, *CEO*
Richard Grossinger, *
Lindy Hough, *
Alla Spector, *
▲ **EMP:** 25 **EST:** 1964
**SQ FT:** 6,000
**SALES (est):** 5.62MM **Privately Held**
**Web:** www.northatlanticbooks.com
**SIC:** 2731 Books, publishing only

**(P-4347)**
**TEACHER CREATED RESOURCES INC**
Also Called: Blue Star Education
12621 Western Ave, Garden Grove (92841-4014)
**PHONE**.................................714 230-7060
Darin Smith, *Pr*
Sarah Fournier, *
◆ **EMP:** 103 **EST:** 2004
**SALES (est):** 24.2MM **Privately Held**
**Web:** www.teachercreated.com
**SIC:** 2731 Books, publishing and printing

**(P-4348)**
**TEACHERS CURRICULUM INST LLC (PA)**
2440 W El Camino Real Ste 400, Mountain View (94040-1498)
P.O. Box 1327 (95741-1327)
**PHONE**.................................800 497-6138
Bert Bower, *Managing Member*
**EMP:** 24 **EST:** 1989
**SQ FT:** 7,994
**SALES (est):** 4.69MM **Privately Held**
**Web:** www.teachtci.com
**SIC:** 2731 8748 Books, publishing only; Educational consultant

**(P-4349)**
**THE FULL VOID 2 INC**
Also Called: Alfred Music Publishing
16320 Roscoe Blvd Ste 100, Van Nuys (91406-1216)
P.O. Box 10003 (91410-0003)
**PHONE**.................................818 891-5999
◆ **EMP:** 275
**SIC:** 2731 Book publishing

**(P-4350)**
**THE WINE APPRECIATION GUILD LTD**
Also Called: Vintage Image
360 Swift Ave Unit 3040, South San Francisco (94080-6228)
**PHONE**.................................650 866-3020
**TOLL FREE:** 800
▲ **EMP:** 18
**Web:** www.wineappreciation.com
**SIC:** 2731 2542 5149 Books, publishing only; Racks, merchandise display or storage: except wood; Wine makers' equipment and supplies

**(P-4351)**
**TOKYOPOP INC (PA)**
4136 Del Rey Ave, Marina Del Rey (90292-5604)
**PHONE**.................................323 920-5967
Stuart J Levy, *Pr*
John Parker, *
Victor Chin, *
◆ **EMP:** 66 **EST:** 1997
**SALES (est):** 5.28MM
**SALES (corp-wide):** 5.28MM **Privately Held**
**Web:** www.tokyopop.com
**SIC:** 2731 3652 7812 7371 Books, publishing only; Compact laser discs, prerecorded; Video tape production; Custom computer programming services

**(P-4352)**
**UNIVERSITY CAL PRESS FUNDATION (PA)**
155 Grand Ave Ste 400, Oakland (94612-3764)
**PHONE**.................................510 642-4247
Lynne Withey, *Pr*
Richard C Atkinson, *
Tim Sullivan, *
Steven Jenkins, *
▲ **EMP:** 100 **EST:** 1893
**SALES (est):** 1.16MM
**SALES (corp-wide):** 1.16MM **Privately Held**
**Web:** www.ucpress.edu
**SIC:** 2731 Books, publishing only

**(P-4353)**
**WALTER FOSTER PUBLISHING INC**
6 Orchard Ste 100, Lake Forest (92630-8351)
**PHONE**.................................949 380-7510
▲ **EMP:** 26
**Web:** www.walterfoster.com
**SIC:** 2731 Books, publishing only

**(P-4354)**
**WEST PUBLISHING CORPORATION**
Also Called: The Rutter Group
5161 Lankershim Blvd, North Hollywood (91601-4962)
**PHONE**.................................800 747-3161
William Rutter, *Brnch Mgr*
**EMP:** 1767
**SALES (corp-wide):** 10.66B **Publicly Held**
**Web:** home.westacademic.com
**SIC:** 2731 8111 Book publishing; General practice attorney, lawyer
**HQ:** West Publishing Corporation
2900 Ames Crssing Rd Ste
Eagan MN 55121
651 687-7000

**(P-4355)**
**WIXEN MUSIC PUBLISHING INC**
27200 Agoura Rd Ste 201, Agoura Hills (91301-5138)
**PHONE**.................................818 591-7355
Randall Wixen, *Pr*
**EMP:** 15 **EST:** 1978
**SALES (est):** 2.11MM **Privately Held**
**Web:** www.wixenmusic.com
**SIC:** 2731 8111 Book music: publishing and printing; Legal services

## 2732 Book Printing

**(P-4356)**
**CONSOLIDATED PRINTERS INC**
2459 Radley Ct, Hayward (94545-1128)
**PHONE**.................................510 843-8524
Lawrence A Hawkins, *CEO*
**EMP:** 50 **EST:** 1952
**SALES (est):** 8.6MM **Privately Held**
**Web:** www.consoprinters.com
**SIC:** 2732 2752 Books, printing and binding; Commercial printing, lithographic

## 2741 Miscellaneous Publishing

**(P-4357)**
**418 MEDIA LLC**
Also Called: 418 Media
1875 Century Park E Ste 370, Los Angeles (90067-2253)
**PHONE**.................................614 350-3960
**EMP:** 20 **EST:** 2010
**SALES (est):** 633.67K **Privately Held**
**Web:** www.lewishowes.com
**SIC:** 2741 Internet publishing and broadcasting

**(P-4358)**
**ACCEPTEDCOM LLC**
2229 S Canfield Ave, Los Angeles (90034-1114)
**PHONE**.................................310 815-9553
Linda Abraham, *Pr*
**EMP:** 22 **EST:** 2002
**SALES (est):** 918.89K **Privately Held**
**Web:** www.accepted.com
**SIC:** 2741 Miscellaneous publishing

**(P-4359)**
**ACORN PUBLISHING LLC**
115 Quiet Pl, Irvine (92602-1809)
**PHONE**.................................714 471-6973
Jessica Therrien, *Prin*
**EMP:** 15 **EST:** 2019
**SALES (est):** 142.36K **Privately Held**
**Web:** www.acornpublishingllc.com
**SIC:** 2741 Miscellaneous publishing

**(P-4360)**
**ADVANCED PUBLISHING TECH INC**
1105 N Hollywood Way, Burbank (91505-2528)
**PHONE**.................................818 557-3035
D Kraai, *Owner*
**EMP:** 18
**Web:** www.advpubtech.com
**SIC:** 2741 Miscellaneous publishing
**PA:** Advanced Publishing Technology, Inc.
140 S Buena Vista St M

**(P-4361)**
**AIO ACQUISITION INC (HQ)**
Also Called: Personnel Concepts
3200 E Guasti Rd Ste 300, Ontario (91761-8661)
P.O. Box 5750 (60197)
**PHONE**.................................800 333-3795
▲ **EMP:** 92 **EST:** 1989
**SALES (est):** 20.83MM
**SALES (corp-wide):** 1.34B **Publicly Held**
**Web:** www.personnelconcepts.com
**SIC:** 2741 7319 Posters: publishing and printing; Circular and handbill distribution
**PA:** Brady Corporation
6555 W Good Hope Rd
414 358-6600

**(P-4362)**
**ALG INC**
120 Broadway Ste 200, Santa Monica (90401-2385)
P.O. Box 61207 (93160-1207)
**PHONE**.................................424 258-8026
James Nguyen, *Pr*
Michael Guthrie, *
Jeff Swart, *
Scott Watkinson, *
Bernard Brenner, *
**EMP:** 97 **EST:** 1972
**SALES (est):** 2.31MM **Publicly Held**
**Web:** www.automotiveleaseguide.com
**SIC:** 2741 Guides: publishing only, not printed on site
**PA:** Truecar, Inc.
225 Snta Mnica Blvd Fl 12

**(P-4363)**
**ALMADEN PRESS AND PUBG LLC (PA)**
Also Called: Almaden
2549 Scott Blvd, Santa Clara (95050-2508)
**PHONE**.................................408 450-7910
Eric T Stern, *Pr*
Chris Siebert, *
**EMP:** 110 **EST:** 1998

SQ FT: 100,000
SALES (est): 20.12MM **Privately Held**
Web: www.almadenpress.com
SIC: **2741** Miscellaneous publishing

**(P-4364)**
**AMERICAN SOC CMPSERS ATHORS PB**
Also Called: Ascap
7920 W Sunset Blvd Ste 300, Los Angeles (90046-3300)
PHONE.....................323 883-1000
Daniel Gonzales, *Genl Mgr*
EMP: 123
SALES (corp-wide): 49.06MM **Privately Held**
Web: www.ascap.com
SIC: **2741** Miscellaneous publishing
PA: American Society Of Composers, Authors And Publishers
250 W 57th St Ste 1300
212 621-6000

**(P-4365)**
**ART BRAND STUDIOS LLC (PA)**
Also Called: Art of Entertainment
381 Cannery Row, Monterey (93940)
PHONE.....................408 201-5000
Mark Mickelson, *
EMP: 50 EST: 2014
SALES (est): 13.95MM
SALES (corp-wide): 13.95MM **Privately Held**
Web: www.artbrand.com
SIC: **2741** 6794 Art copy and poster publishing; Copyright buying and licensing

**(P-4366)**
**ART19 LLC (DH)**
1999 Harrison St Ste 2675, Oakland (94612-4722)
PHONE.....................866 882-7819
Sean Carr, *CEO*
EMP: 21 EST: 2011
SALES (est): 1.59MM **Publicly Held**
SIC: **2741** Internet publishing and broadcasting
HQ: Amazon Technologies, Inc.
410 Terry Ave N
Seattle WA 98109
206 266-4064

**(P-4367)**
**ASSOCIATED DESERT SHOPPERS INC (DH)**
Also Called: The White Sheet
73400 Highway 111, Palm Desert (92260-3908)
PHONE.....................760 346-1729
Harold Paradis, *Pr*
Esperanza Barrett, *
Rey Verdugo Senior, *Dir Opers*
EMP: 75 EST: 1987
SQ FT: 4,000
SALES (est): 9.72MM
SALES (corp-wide): 3.28B **Publicly Held**
Web: www.greenandwhitesheet.com
SIC: **2741** 7313 Shopping news: publishing and printing; Newspaper advertising representative
HQ: Schurz Communications, Inc.
1301 E Douglas Rd Ste 200
Mishawaka IN 46545
574 247-7237

**(P-4368)**
**ASSOCTED STDNTS OF THE UNIV CA**
Also Called: Bsr
112 Hearst Gym Rm 4520, Berkeley (94720-3611)
P.O. Box 40140 (94704-4140)
PHONE.....................510 590-7874
Asako Miyakawa, *Project Head*
EMP: 100
SALES (corp-wide): 804.77K **Privately Held**
Web: www.asuc.org
SIC: **2741** 8299 Miscellaneous publishing; Educational services
PA: Associated Students Of The University Of California
Bancroft Way 400 Eshlman St Bancroft W
510 642-5420

**(P-4369)**
**AUTHORS PRESS**
1321 Buchanan Rd, Pittsburg (94565-6406)
PHONE.....................925 698-2619
Maribelle Birao, *Pr*
EMP: 16 EST: 2019
SALES (est): 188.19K **Privately Held**
Web: www.authorspress.com
SIC: **2741** Miscellaneous publishing

**(P-4370)**
**BINGO PUBLISHERS INCORPORATED**
24881 Alicia Pkwy Ste E, Laguna Hills (92653-4617)
PHONE.....................949 581-5410
Charles Sloan, *Pr*
EMP: 22 EST: 1990
SQ FT: 3,000
SALES (est): 499.64K **Privately Held**
Web: www.localbingohalls.com
SIC: **2741** Miscellaneous publishing

**(P-4371)**
**BIRDEYE INC (PA)**
2479 E Bayshore Rd Ste 188, Palo Alto (94303-3245)
PHONE.....................800 561-3357
Navee Gupta, *CEO*
Dave Lehman, *
Jeff Foster, *
Chris Aker, *CRO*
EMP: 50 EST: 2012
SALES (est): 21.91MM
SALES (corp-wide): 21.91MM **Privately Held**
Web: www.birdeye.com
SIC: **2741** Internet publishing and broadcasting

**(P-4372)**
**BROWNTROUT PUBLISHERS INC (PA)**
Also Called: Browntrout
201 Continental Blvd Ste 200, El Segundo (90245-4514)
PHONE.....................424 290-6122
William Michael Brown, *CEO*
Gray Peterson, *
▲ EMP: 40 EST: 1993
SQ FT: 11,000
SALES (est): 13.98MM **Privately Held**
Web: www.browntrout.com
SIC: **2741** Miscellaneous publishing

**(P-4373)**
**BRUD INC**
837 N Spring St Ste 101, Los Angeles (90012-2594)
PHONE.....................310 806-2283
Trevor Mcfedries, *Pr*
EMP: 17 EST: 2017
SALES (est): 1.15MM **Privately Held**
Web: www.dapperlabs.com
SIC: **2741** Internet publishing and broadcasting

**(P-4374)**
**C PUBLISHING LLC**
Also Called: C Magazine
1543 7th St Ste 202, Santa Monica (90401-2645)
PHONE.....................310 393-3800
Jennifer Smith Hale, *Managing Member*
Jennifer Smith Hale, *Mgr*
Jenny Murray, *IN*
Lesley Canpoy, *Publisher*
EMP: 25 EST: 2005
SALES (est): 1.2MM **Privately Held**
Web: www.magazinec.com
SIC: **2741** Miscellaneous publishing

**(P-4375)**
**C&T PUBLISHING INC**
1651 Challenge Dr, Concord (94520-5206)
PHONE.....................925 677-0377
J Todd Hensley, *CEO*
Tony Hensley, *
▲ EMP: 33 EST: 1983
SQ FT: 12,250
SALES (est): 3.91MM **Privately Held**
Web: www.ctpub.com
SIC: **2741** Miscellaneous publishing

**(P-4376)**
**CENTER OF MEDIA JUSTICE**
1300 Clay St Ste 600, Oakland (94612-1427)
PHONE.....................510 698-3800
Steven Renderos, *Ex Dir*
EMP: 25 EST: 2009
SALES (est): 262.84K **Privately Held**
SIC: **2741** Miscellaneous publishing

**(P-4377)**
**CHINESE OVERSEAS MKTG SVC CORP**
33420 Alvarado Niles Rd, Union City (94587-3110)
PHONE.....................510 476-0880
Alan Kao, *Pr*
EMP: 20
SALES (corp-wide): 4.76MM **Privately Held**
Web: www.ccyp.com
SIC: **2741** 7389 Directories, telephone: publishing only, not printed on site; Trade show arrangement
PA: Chinese Overseas Marketing Service Corporation
3940 Rosemead Blvd
626 280-8588

**(P-4378)**
**CHINESE OVERSEAS MKTG SVC CORP**
Also Called: Chinese Consumer Yellow Pages
46292 Warm Springs Blvd Unit 614, Fremont (94539-7997)
PHONE.....................626 280-8588
Gorden Kao, *Brnch Mgr*
EMP: 20
SALES (corp-wide): 4.76MM **Privately Held**
Web: www.ccyp.com
SIC: **2741** 7389 8742 Directories, telephone: publishing only, not printed on site; Trade show arrangement; Marketing consulting services
PA: Chinese Overseas Marketing Service Corporation
3940 Rosemead Blvd
626 280-8588

**(P-4379)**
**CHINESE OVERSEAS MKTG SVC CORP (PA)**
Also Called: Chinese Consumer Yellow Pages
3940 Rosemead Blvd, Rosemead (91770-1952)
PHONE.....................626 280-8588
Alan Kao, *Pr*
Gorden Kao, *Dir*
▲ EMP: 60 EST: 1982
SQ FT: 9,298
SALES (est): 4.76MM
SALES (corp-wide): 4.76MM **Privately Held**
Web: www.ccyp.com
SIC: **2741** 7389 8742 Directories, telephone: publishing only, not printed on site; Trade show arrangement; Marketing consulting services

**(P-4380)**
**COGNELLA INC**
Also Called: University Readers
320 S Cedros Ave Ste 400, Solana Beach (92075-1996)
PHONE.....................858 552-1120
Bassin Hamadeh, *CEO*
EMP: 65 EST: 1997
SQ FT: 8,000
SALES (est): 8.06MM **Privately Held**
Web: www.cognella.com
SIC: **2741** Miscellaneous publishing

**(P-4381)**
**COLBI TECHNOLOGIES INC**
13891 Newport Ave Ste 150, Tustin (92780-7897)
PHONE.....................714 505-9544
Charles Olsen, *Prin*
Larry Goshorn, *
Francisco Javier Oseguera, *
Jamin Boggs, *
Lettie Cowie, *
EMP: 43 EST: 2008
SALES (est): 1.35MM **Privately Held**
Web: www.colbitech.com
SIC: **2741** Miscellaneous publishing

**(P-4382)**
**COMPARENETWORKS INC (PA)**
Also Called: Biocompare
164 Townsend St Unit 2, San Francisco (94107-1990)
PHONE.....................518 238-6617
Paul Gatti, *CEO*
Andy Miller, *COO*
Kelly Valmore, *CFO*
Joan Boyce, *VP*
Mike Okimoto, *CCO*
EMP: 58 EST: 2000
SQ FT: 16,152
SALES (est): 13.24MM
SALES (corp-wide): 13.24MM **Privately Held**
Web: www.comparenetworks.com
SIC: **2741** Internet publishing and broadcasting

**(P-4383)**
**CORWIN PRESS INC**
2455 Teller Rd, Newbury Park (91320-2218)
PHONE.....................805 499-9734
Douglas Rife, *Pr*
Leigh Peake, *
Johnnie A James, *
EMP: 52 EST: 1990
SALES (est): 3.75MM
SALES (corp-wide): 89.37MM **Privately Held**

## 2741 - Miscellaneous Publishing (P-4384)

Web: us.corwin.com
SIC: 2741 Miscellaneous publishing
PA: Sage Publications, Inc.
2455 Teller Rd
805 499-0721

**(P-4384)**
**CRAZY MAPLE STUDIO INC (PA)**
1277 Borregas Ave Ste C, Sunnyvale (94089-1311)
PHONE...................972 757-1283
Yi Jia, *CEO*
Ruizhi Yang, *Dir*
Zhilei Tong, *Dir*
EMP: 24 EST: 2016
SALES (est): 1.04MM
SALES (corp-wide): 1.04MM **Privately Held**
Web: www.crazymaplestudios.com
SIC: 2741 Internet publishing and broadcasting

**(P-4385)**
**CYP ONLINE INC**
4500 Great America Pkwy Ste 93, Santa Clara (95054-1283)
PHONE...................510 516-6589
Taiyi Li, *Admn*
Taiyi Li, *Dir*
EMP: 15 EST: 2021
SALES (est): 288.92K **Privately Held**
Web: www.chineseyellowpages.net
SIC: 2741 7311 7379 Directories, nec: publishing only, not printed on site; Advertising consultant; Online services technology consultants

**(P-4386)**
**DAISY PUBLISHING COMPANY INC**
Also Called: Hi-Torque Publications
25233 Anza Dr, Santa Clarita (91355-1289)
P.O. Box 957 (91380-9057)
PHONE...................661 295-1910
Roland Hinz, *Pr*
Lila Hinz, *
EMP: 55 EST: 1969
SQ FT: 16,000
SALES (est): 4.12MM **Privately Held**
Web: www.hi-torque.com
SIC: 2741 Miscellaneous publishing

**(P-4387)**
**DANIELS INC (PA)**
Also Called: Big Nickel
74745 Leslie Ave, Palm Desert (92260-2030)
PHONE...................801 621-3355
Daniel Murphy, *Pr*
Dennis Porter, *
EMP: 23 EST: 1968
SQ FT: 10,000
SALES (est): 2.1MM
SALES (corp-wide): 2.1MM **Privately Held**
Web: www.danielsdki.com
SIC: 2741 Shopping news: publishing and printing

**(P-4388)**
**DIVERSIFIED PRINTERS INC**
12834 Maxwell Dr, Tustin (92782-0914)
PHONE...................714 994-3400
Kenneth Bittner, *Pr*
Jerry Tominaga, *
Paul R Nassar, *
EMP: 51 EST: 1986
SQ FT: 105,000
SALES (est): 891.92K **Privately Held**
SIC: 2741 2759 2789 Directories, nec: publishing and printing; Commercial printing, nec; Bookbinding and related work

**(P-4389)**
**DOLEX DOLLAR EXPRESS INC**
12727 Sherman Way, North Hollywood (91605-5032)
PHONE...................818 982-2852
Gira Chang, *Prin*
EMP: 16
SALES (corp-wide): 436MM **Privately Held**
Web: www.dolex.com
SIC: 2741 Miscellaneous publishing
PA: Dolex Dollar Express, Inc.
10777 Wsthmer Rd Ste 1040
888 246-2527

**(P-4390)**
**DWELL LIFE INC**
Also Called: Dwell Store The
548 Market St, San Francisco (94104-5401)
P.O. Box 160171 (11216-0171)
PHONE...................212 382-2010
Regina Flynn, *Off Mgr*
EMP: 17
SALES (corp-wide): 3.44MM **Privately Held**
Web: www.dwell.com
SIC: 2741 Miscellaneous publishing
PA: Dwell Life, Inc.
595 Pacific Ave Fl 4
415 373-5100

**(P-4391)**
**ECONODAY INC**
3730 Mt Diablo Blvd Ste 340, Lafayette (94549-3641)
P.O. Box 954 (94549-0954)
PHONE...................925 299-5350
Cynthia Parker, *Pr*
June Moberg, *Sec*
EMP: 17 EST: 1990
SQ FT: 1,200
SALES (est): 1.7MM **Privately Held**
Web: www.econoday.com
SIC: 2741 Miscellaneous publishing

**(P-4392)**
**ECT NEWS NETWORK INC**
16133 Ventura Blvd Ste 700, Encino (91436-2403)
P.O. Box 18500 (91416-8500)
PHONE...................818 461-9700
Richard Kern, *Prin*
EMP: 16 EST: 2004
SALES (est): 410.67K **Privately Held**
Web: www.ectnews.com
SIC: 2741 Internet publishing and broadcasting

**(P-4393)**
**ELECTRIC SOLIDUS LLC**
26565 Agoura Rd Ste 200, Calabasas (91302-1990)
PHONE...................917 692-7764
EMP: 25 EST: 2019
SALES (est): 1.09MM **Privately Held**
SIC: 2741 Internet publishing and broadcasting

**(P-4394)**
**ELSEVIER INC**
Also Called: Elsevier Academic Press
525 B St, San Diego (92101-4420)
PHONE...................619 231-6616
EMP: 30
SALES (corp-wide): 11.42B **Privately Held**

Web: www.elsevier.com
SIC: 2741 Technical manuals: publishing only, not printed on site
HQ: Elsevier Inc.
230 Park Ave Fl 7
New York NY 10169
212 309-8100

**(P-4395)**
**ELSEVIER INC**
Also Called: Elsevier
10620 Treena St, San Diego (92131-1140)
PHONE...................619 231-6616
Kristen Chrisman, *Brnch Mgr*
EMP: 67
SALES (corp-wide): 11.42B **Privately Held**
Web: www.elsevier.com
SIC: 2741 Miscellaneous publishing
HQ: Elsevier Inc.
230 Park Ave Fl 7
New York NY 10169
212 309-8100

**(P-4396)**
**EXPRESS PRESS**
12021 Jefferson Blvd, Culver City (90230-6219)
PHONE...................424 228-2261
EMP: 20 EST: 2017
SALES (est): 1.12MM **Privately Held**
SIC: 2741 Miscellaneous publishing

**(P-4397)**
**EXTREME REACH INC**
Also Called: Extreme Reach
1048 N Lake St, Burbank (91502-1624)
PHONE...................818 588-3635
Kris Estrella, *Brnch Mgr*
EMP: 21
Web: www.xr.global
SIC: 2741 Miscellaneous publishing
PA: Extreme Reach, Inc.
3 Allied Dr Ste 130

**(P-4398)**
**FEDERATED MEDIA PUBLISHING LLC**
350 Sansome St Ste 925, San Francisco (94104-1314)
PHONE...................415 332-6955
▲ EMP: 249
Web: www.nexstardigital.com
SIC: 2741 Miscellaneous publishing

**(P-4399)**
**FOODBEAST INC**
220 E 4th St Ste 202, Santa Ana (92701-4652)
PHONE...................949 344-2634
Geoff Kutnick, *CEO*
Elie Ayrouth, *Pr*
Patrick Fraioli, *Chief Counsel*
EMP: 16 EST: 2014
SALES (est): 552.7K **Privately Held**
Web: www.foodbeast.com
SIC: 2741 Internet publishing and broadcasting

**(P-4400)**
**FUNDX INVESTMENT GROUP LLC**
Also Called: Fundex Investment Group
101 Montgomery St 2400, San Francisco (94104-4151)
PHONE...................415 986-7979
Janet Brown, *Pr*
Jeffrey Smith, *Prin*
EMP: 18 EST: 1969
SQ FT: 2,000

SALES (est): 1.92MM **Privately Held**
Web: www.fundx.com
SIC: 2741 6282 Newsletter publishing; Investment advisory service

**(P-4401)**
**G R LEONARD & CO INC**
Also Called: Leonard's Guide
181 N Vermont Ave, Glendora (91741-3321)
PHONE...................847 797-8101
David Ercolani, *CEO*
Ahmed Hawari, *
Elizabeth Stern, *
▲ EMP: 26 EST: 1912
SALES (est): 2.19MM **Privately Held**
Web: www.leonardsguide.com
SIC: 2741 Directories, nec: publishing only, not printed on site

**(P-4402)**
**GAME INSIGHT PUBLISHING**
211 Gough St Ste 116, San Francisco (94102-6802)
PHONE...................415 412-5064
Leonid Sirotin, *Prin*
EMP: 21 EST: 2012
SALES (est): 180.86K **Privately Held**
SIC: 2741 Miscellaneous publishing

**(P-4403)**
**GLOBAL COMPLIANCE INC**
Also Called: Compliance Poster
438 W Chestnut Ave Ste A, Monrovia (91016-1129)
P.O. Box 607 (91017-0607)
PHONE...................626 303-6855
Patricia A Blum, *Pr*
EMP: 25 EST: 1990
SALES (est): 4.39MM **Privately Held**
Web: www.accupostdocs.com
SIC: 2741 Posters: publishing and printing

**(P-4404)**
**GLOBAL PUBLISHING INC**
4415 Technology Dr, Fremont (94538-6343)
EMP: 50 EST: 2005
SALES (est): 868.78K **Publicly Held**
Web: www.globalpublishinginc.net
SIC: 2741 Miscellaneous publishing
PA: Anything Technologies Media Inc.
4710 Oak Hill Rd

**(P-4405)**
**GLS US FREIGHT INC**
3561 Philadelphia St, Chino (91710-2089)
PHONE...................909 627-2538
Erin Craig, *Mgr*
EMP: 21
SALES (corp-wide): 117.33MM **Privately Held**
Web: freight.gls-us.com
SIC: 2741 Miscellaneous publishing
PA: Gls Us Freight, Inc.
6750 S Longe St Ste 100
209 823-2168

**(P-4406)**
**GOFF INVESTMENT GROUP LLC**
Also Called: Global Printing Sourcing & Dev
135 3rd St Ste 150, San Rafael (94901-3531)
PHONE...................415 456-2934
▲ EMP: 24 EST: 2004
SQ FT: 3,000
SALES (est): 494.14K **Privately Held**
Web: www.touchstoneeditions.com
SIC: 2741 Miscellaneous publishing

## 2741 - Miscellaneous Publishing (P-4430)

**(P-4407)**
**GOOD WORLDWIDE LLC**
6380 Wilshire Blvd # 15, Los Angeles (90048-5003)
PHONE..................323 206-6495
Michelle Medlock, *Mgr*
**EMP:** 44 **EST:** 2010
**SALES (est):** 1.3MM **Privately Held**
Web: www.good.is
**SIC:** 2741 Miscellaneous publishing

**(P-4408)**
**GRAPHIQ LLC**
101a Innovation Pl, Santa Barbara (93108-2268)
P.O. Box 1259 (93067-1259)
PHONE..................805 335-2433
Kevin Oconnor, *Pr*
Scott Leonard, *
**EMP:** 120 **EST:** 2009
**SALES (est):** 9.26MM **Publicly Held**
Web: www.graphiq.com
**SIC:** 2741 4813 Internet publishing and broadcasting; Web search portals
**PA:** Amazon.Com, Inc.
   410 Terry Ave N

**(P-4409)**
**GREAT EASTERN ENTERTAINMENT CO**
610 W Carob St, Compton (90220-5210)
PHONE..................310 638-5058
Kent Hsu, *Pr*
▲ **EMP:** 24 **EST:** 1995
**SQ FT:** 6,000
**SALES (est):** 2.28MM **Privately Held**
Web: www.geanimation.com
**SIC:** 2741 Posters: publishing and printing

**(P-4410)**
**GUADALUPE ASSOCIATES INC (PA)**
Also Called: Ignatius Press
1348 10th Ave, San Francisco (94122-2304)
PHONE..................415 387-2324
Mark Brumley, *CEO*
◆ **EMP:** 15 **EST:** 1976
**SQ FT:** 1,500
**SALES (est):** 2.52MM
**SALES (corp-wide):** 2.52MM **Privately Held**
Web: www.ignatius.com
**SIC:** 2741 2731 Miscellaneous publishing; Books, publishing only

**(P-4411)**
**HAGADONE DIRECTORIES INC**
555 H St Ste E, Eureka (95501-1045)
PHONE..................707 444-0255
Jim Hail, *Pr*
**EMP:** 129
**SALES (corp-wide):** 290.98MM **Privately Held**
Web: www.blackphonebook.com
**SIC:** 2741 Directories, nec: publishing and printing
**HQ:** Hagadone Directories Inc
   201 N 2nd St
   Coeur D Alene ID 83814
   208 667-8744

**(P-4412)**
**HANLEY WOOD MEDIA INC (HQ)**
Also Called: Zonda Media
4000 Macarthur Blvd Ste 400, Newport Beach (92660-2543)
PHONE..................202 736-3300
Jeffrey Meyers, *CEO*
**EMP:** 26 **EST:** 2013
**SALES (est):** 39.77MM
**SALES (corp-wide):** 179.03MM **Privately Held**
Web: www.jlconline.com
**SIC:** 2741 Business service newsletters: publishing and printing
**PA:** Hw Holdco, Llc
   1 Thomas Cir Nw # 600
   202 452-0800

**(P-4413)**
**HEAT PRESS NATION**
2300 E Walnut Ave, Fullerton (92831-4937)
PHONE..................800 215-0894
**EMP:** 34 **EST:** 2018
**SALES (est):** 309.11K **Privately Held**
Web: www.heatpressnation.com
**SIC:** 2741 Miscellaneous publishing

**(P-4414)**
**HOPSCOTCH PRESS INC**
21 Orinda Way Ste C428, Orinda (94563-2530)
PHONE..................510 548-0400
Meredith Monday Schwartz, *CEO*
**EMP:** 32 **EST:** 2017
**SALES (est):** 965.76K **Privately Held**
Web: www.herecomestheguide.com
**SIC:** 2741 Miscellaneous publishing

**(P-4415)**
**INFORMA BUSINESS MEDIA INC**
Sourceesb
16815 Von Karman Ave # 150, Irvine (92606-2406)
PHONE..................949 252-1146
**EMP:** 30
**SALES (corp-wide):** 3.12B **Privately Held**
**SIC:** 2741 Directories, nec: publishing only, not printed on site
**HQ:** Informa Business Media, Inc.
   605 3rd Ave
   New York NY 10158
   212 204-4200

**(P-4416)**
**INKITT INC**
50 Francisco St Ste 100, San Francisco (94133-2108)
PHONE..................978 844-1074
**EMP:** 21 **EST:** 2017
**SALES (est):** 1.23MM **Privately Held**
Web: www.inkitt.com
**SIC:** 2741 Miscellaneous publishing

**(P-4417)**
**INSIDE EAST SACRAMENTO**
625 33rd St, Sacramento (95816-3815)
PHONE..................916 443-5087
**EMP:** 15 **EST:** 2010
**SALES (est):** 248.36K **Privately Held**
Web: www.insidesacramento.com
**SIC:** 2741 Miscellaneous publishing

**(P-4418)**
**INSTITUTIONAL REAL ESTATE INC (PA)**
1475 N Broadway Ste 300, Walnut Creek (94596-4643)
PHONE..................925 933-4040
Geoffrey Dohrmann, *CEO*
Nyia Dohrmann, *Pr*
Erika Cohen, *COO*
**EMP:** 20 **EST:** 1986
**SQ FT:** 3,000
**SALES (est):** 3.52MM **Privately Held**
Web: www.irei.com
**SIC:** 2741 8742 8748 2721 Newsletter publishing; Real estate consultant; Business consulting, nec; Periodicals

**(P-4419)**
**ISSUU INC (PA)**
131 Lytton Ave, Palo Alto (94301-1045)
PHONE..................844 477-8800
Joseph Hyrkin, *CEO*
**EMP:** 20 **EST:** 2007
**SALES (est):** 8.23MM
**SALES (corp-wide):** 8.23MM **Privately Held**
Web: www.issuu.com
**SIC:** 2741 Miscellaneous publishing

**(P-4420)**
**JIGSAW DATA CORPORATION**
900 Concar Dr, San Mateo (94402-2600)
PHONE..................650 235-8400
James Fowler, *Pr*
Garth Moulton, *VP*
Steven Klei, *CFO*
**EMP:** 29 **EST:** 2004
**SALES (est):** 1.66MM
**SALES (corp-wide):** 34.86B **Publicly Held**
**SIC:** 2741 Telephone and other directory publishing
**PA:** Salesforce, Inc.
   415 Mission St Fl 3
   415 901-7000

**(P-4421)**
**JOURNEYWORKS PUBLISHING**
763 Chestnut St, Santa Cruz (95060-3751)
P.O. Box 8466 (95061-8466)
PHONE..................831 423-1400
Steven Bignell, *Pr*
Judith Carey, *VP*
Mary Bignell, *Sec*
**EMP:** 16 **EST:** 1995
**SQ FT:** 5,200
**SALES (est):** 2.49MM **Privately Held**
Web: www.journeyworks.com
**SIC:** 2741 Miscellaneous publishing

**(P-4422)**
**JUMPER MEDIA LLC**
Also Called: Jumper Media
1719 Alta La Jolla Dr, La Jolla (92037-7103)
PHONE..................831 333-6202
Colton Bollinger, *CEO*
**EMP:** 99 **EST:** 2016
**SALES (est):** 5.53MM **Privately Held**
Web: www.jumpermedia.co
**SIC:** 2741 Internet publishing and broadcasting

**(P-4423)**
**JUNGOTV LLC**
1800 Vine St, Los Angeles (90028-5250)
PHONE..................650 207-6227
George Chung, *CEO*
**EMP:** 60 **EST:** 2015
**SALES (est):** 945.26K **Privately Held**
Web: www.jungotv.com
**SIC:** 2741 Internet publishing and broadcasting

**(P-4424)**
**KUDOS&CO INC**
470 Ramona St, Palo Alto (94301-1707)
PHONE..................650 799-9104
Ole Vidar Hestaas, *CEO*
**EMP:** 15 **EST:** 2018
**SALES (est):** 9MM **Privately Held**
Web: www.kudos.com
**SIC:** 2741 Internet publishing and broadcasting

**(P-4425)**
**LA XPRESS AIR & HEATING SVCS**
6400 E Washington Blvd Ste 121, Commerce (90040-1820)
PHONE..................310 856-9678
Jesus A Chavez, *CEO*
**EMP:** 67 **EST:** 2013
**SALES (est):** 1.08MM **Privately Held**
Web: www.laxpressairheating.com
**SIC:** 2741 Miscellaneous publishing

**(P-4426)**
**LELAND STANFORD JUNIOR UNIV**
Also Called: Stanford University Libraries
557 Escondido Mall, Stanford (94305-6001)
PHONE..................650 723-5553
Robert Phillips, *Brnch Mgr*
**EMP:** 44
**SQ FT:** 10,000
**SALES (corp-wide):** 15.13B **Privately Held**
Web: www.stanford.edu
**SIC:** 2741 8221 Miscellaneous publishing; University
**PA:** Leland Stanford Junior University
   450 Jane Stanford Way
   650 723-2300

**(P-4427)**
**LINQUIP CORPORATION**
440 N Wolfe Rd, Sunnyvale (94085-3869)
PHONE..................925 998-2480
Syd Hashemi, *Prin*
**EMP:** 15 **EST:** 2022
**SALES (est):** 483.6K **Privately Held**
Web: www.linquip.com
**SIC:** 2741 Internet publishing and broadcasting

**(P-4428)**
**LOG(N) LLC**
Also Called: Mismo
5651 Dreyer Pl, Oakland (94619-3109)
PHONE..................323 839-4538
Jinal Jhaveri, *Managing Member*
Forum Desai, *COO*
**EMP:** 40 **EST:** 2010
**SALES (est):** 1.06MM **Privately Held**
Web: www.mismo.team
**SIC:** 2741 7379 Internet publishing and broadcasting; Computer related consulting services

**(P-4429)**
**LONELY PLANET PUBLICATIONS INC**
124 Linden St, Oakland (94607-2538)
PHONE..................510 250-6400
◆ **EMP:** 70 **EST:** 1984
**SALES (est):** 5.77MM
**SALES (corp-wide):** 6.84B **Privately Held**
Web: www.lonelyplanet.com
**SIC:** 2741 Guides: publishing only, not printed on site
**HQ:** Bbc Studios Distribution Limited
   1 Television Centre
   London W12 7
   370 010-0222

**(P-4430)**
**M G A INVESTMENT CO INC**
Also Called: Easy Ad Magazine
3211 Broad St Ste 201, San Luis Obispo (93401-6770)
PHONE..................805 543-9050
Jackie Koda, *Admn*
**EMP:** 15 **EST:** 1975
**SQ FT:** 2,000

## 2741 - Miscellaneous Publishing (P-4431)

SALES (est): 140.53K **Privately Held**
SIC: 2741 2721 Shopping news: publishing only, not printed on site; Magazines: publishing only, not printed on site

**(P-4431)**
**MARCOA MEDIA LLC (PA)**
9955 Black Mountain Rd, San Diego (92126-4514)
P.O. Box 509100 (92150-9100)
PHONE..................................858 635-9627
Michael Martella, *Managing Member*
Matt Benedict, *
EMP: 40 EST: 1967
SQ FT: 40,000
SALES (est): 5.7MM
SALES (corp-wide): 5.7MM **Privately Held**
Web: www.mybaseguide.com
SIC: 2741 Atlas, map, and guide publishing

**(P-4432)**
**MITCHELL REPAIR INFO CO LLC (HQ)**
Also Called: Mitchell1
16067 Babcock St, San Diego (92127-3690)
PHONE..................................858 391-5000
EMP: 20 EST: 1996
SALES (est): 87.41MM
SALES (corp-wide): 4.73B **Publicly Held**
Web: www.mitchell1.com
SIC: 2741 2731 5251 Technical manuals: publishing only, not printed on site; Book publishing; Hardware stores
PA: Snap-On Incorporated
2801 80th St
262 656-5200

**(P-4433)**
**MOTHERLY INC**
1725 Oakdell Dr, Menlo Park (94025-5735)
PHONE..................................917 860-9926
Jill Kozio, *CEO*
Christina Cubeta, *
EMP: 24 EST: 2018
SALES (est): 856.34K **Privately Held**
Web: www.mother.ly
SIC: 2741 Internet publishing and broadcasting

**(P-4434)**
**MYANIMELIST LLC**
Also Called: Mal
8445 Camino Santa Fe Ste 210, San Diego (92121-2650)
PHONE..................................714 423-8289
Kyohei Tomida, *Managing Member*
EMP: 15 EST: 2010
SALES (est): 463.71K **Privately Held**
Web: www.myanimelist.net
SIC: 2741 Internet publishing and broadcasting
PA: Media Do Co., Ltd.
1-1-1, Hitotsubashi

**(P-4435)**
**NATIONAL APPRAISAL GUIDES INC**
Also Called: Nada Appraisal Guide
3186 Airway Ave Ste K, Costa Mesa (92626-4650)
PHONE..................................714 556-8511
Donald D Christy Junior, *Pr*
Jody Christy, *
Robin Lewis, *
EMP: 33 EST: 1968
SQ FT: 20,000
SALES (est): 4.41MM **Privately Held**
Web: www.jdpower.com

SIC: 2741 Guides: publishing and printing

**(P-4436)**
**NEIL A KJOS MUSIC COMPANY (PA)**
Also Called: Kjos Music
4382 Jutland Dr, San Diego (92117-3642)
P.O. Box 178270 (92177-8270)
PHONE..................................858 270-9800
Neil A Kjos Junior, *Ch Bd*
Ryan Nowlin, *
Barbara G Kjos, *
▲ EMP: 40 EST: 1985
SQ FT: 72,000
SALES (est): 4.21MM
SALES (corp-wide): 4.21MM **Privately Held**
Web: www.kjos.com
SIC: 2741 Music, book: publishing and printing

**(P-4437)**
**NETMARBLE US INC**
600 Wilshire Blvd Ste 1100, Los Angeles (90005-3983)
PHONE..................................213 222-7712
Chul Min Sim, *CEO*
EMP: 66 EST: 2012
SQ FT: 2,500
SALES (est): 2.36MM **Privately Held**
SIC: 2741 5734 Miscellaneous publishing; Software, computer games
PA: Netmarble Corporation
G-Tower

**(P-4438)**
**NETWORK TELEVISION TIME INC**
3929 Clearford Ct, Westlake Village (91361-4106)
PHONE..................................877 468-8899
Bruce Arditte, *Pr*
EMP: 26 EST: 1999
SQ FT: 200
SALES (est): 384.33K **Privately Held**
SIC: 2741 7374 7371 Internet publishing and broadcasting; Data processing and preparation; Custom computer programming services

**(P-4439)**
**NEXTCLIENTCOM INC**
25000 Avenue Stanford, Valencia (91355-4553)
PHONE..................................661 222-7755
EMP: 30 EST: 2000
SALES (est): 2.07MM **Privately Held**
Web: www.nextclient.com
SIC: 2741 8742 7336 Newsletter publishing; Marketing consulting services; Commercial art and graphic design

**(P-4440)**
**NO STARCH PRESS INC**
329 Primrose Rd, Burlingame (94010-4093)
PHONE..................................415 863-9900
William Pollock, *Pr*
▲ EMP: 18 EST: 1994
SALES (est): 202.41K **Privately Held**
Web: www.nostarch.com
SIC: 2741 Miscellaneous publishing

**(P-4441)**
**OREILLY MEDIA INC (PA)**
1005 Gravenstein Hwy N, Sebastopol (95472-2811)
PHONE..................................707 827-7000
Timothy O'reilly, *Pr*
Maria Manrique, *

▲ EMP: 150 EST: 1983
SQ FT: 90,000
SALES (est): 38.46MM
SALES (corp-wide): 38.46MM **Privately Held**
Web: www.oreilly.com
SIC: 2741 2731 8231 Internet publishing and broadcasting; Books, publishing only; Libraries

**(P-4442)**
**OWSLA TOURING LLC**
16000 Ventura Blvd Ste 600, Encino (91436-2744)
PHONE..................................818 385-1933
Tim Smith, *Prin*
EMP: 29 EST: 2013
SALES (est): 882.91K **Privately Held**
SIC: 2741 Miscellaneous publishing

**(P-4443)**
**PACIFIC BELL DIRECTORY**
Also Called: SBC
101 Spear St Fl 5, San Francisco (94105-1554)
PHONE..................................800 303-3000
▲ EMP: 2400
SIC: 2741 Directories, nec: publishing only, not printed on site

**(P-4444)**
**PARROT COMMUNICATIONS INTL INC**
Also Called: Parrot Media Network
25461 Rye Canyon Rd, Valencia (91355-1206)
PHONE..................................818 567-4700
Robert W Mertz, *CEO*
▲ EMP: 50 EST: 1989
SALES (est): 4.1MM **Privately Held**
Web: www.parrotmedia.com
SIC: 2741 7331 4822 7375 Directories, nec: publishing only, not printed on site; Direct mail advertising services; Facsimile transmission services; Information retrieval services

**(P-4445)**
**PENINSULA PUBLISHING INC**
1602 Monrovia Ave, Newport Beach (92663-2808)
PHONE..................................949 631-1307
Nick Slevin, *Pr*
EMP: 22 EST: 1998
SALES (est): 727.62K **Privately Held**
Web: www.builder.media
SIC: 2741 Miscellaneous publishing

**(P-4446)**
**PENNYSAVER USA PUBLISHING LLC**
Also Called: Original Pennysaver, The
2830 Orbiter St, Brea (92821-6224)
P.O. Box 8900 (92822-8900)
PHONE..................................866 640-3900
EMP: 1000
Web: www.pennysaverusa.com
SIC: 2741 Shopping news: publishing only, not printed on site

**(P-4447)**
**PENROSE STUDIOS INC**
223 Mississippi St Ste 3, San Francisco (94107-2501)
P.O. Box 2507 (34786-2507)
PHONE..................................703 354-1801
Eugene Chung, *CEO*
EMP: 15 EST: 2015
SALES (est): 277.91K **Privately Held**

Web: www.penrosestudios.com
SIC: 2741 Internet publishing and broadcasting

**(P-4448)**
**PEOPLEFINDERS NGT POR PRIOF**
1915 21st St, Sacramento (95811-6813)
PHONE..................................916 341-0227
Rob Miller, *Prin*
EMP: 23 EST: 2014
SALES (est): 1.24MM **Privately Held**
Web: www.peoplefinders.com
SIC: 2741 Miscellaneous publishing

**(P-4449)**
**PLANETIZEN INC**
Also Called: Planetizen
3530 Wilshire Blvd Ste 1285, Los Angeles (90010-2328)
PHONE..................................877 260-7526
Chris Steins, *Pr*
EMP: 32 EST: 2011
SALES (est): 283.75K **Privately Held**
Web: www.planetizen.com
SIC: 2741 Internet publishing and broadcasting

**(P-4450)**
**PLAYBOY ENTERPRISES INTL INC**
Also Called: Peei
10960 Wilshire Blvd Ste 2200, Los Angeles (90024-3702)
PHONE..................................310 424-1800
Christopher Pachler, *Ex VP*
Christopher Pachler, *CAO*
Hugh Heffner, *Chief Creative Officer* *
EMP: 100 EST: 1964
SALES (est): 12.01MM
SALES (corp-wide): 142.95MM **Publicly Held**
Web: www.playboy.com
SIC: 2741 Miscellaneous publishing
HQ: Playboy Enterprises, Inc.
10960 Wlshire Blvd Ste 22
Los Angeles CA 90024
310 424-1800

**(P-4451)**
**POLLSTAR LLC**
Also Called: Pollstar.com
1100 Glendon Ave Ste 2100, Los Angeles (90024-3592)
PHONE..................................559 271-7900
Gary Bongiovanni, *Pr*
Gary Smith, *
EMP: 58 EST: 1981
SALES (est): 3.25MM **Privately Held**
Web: store.pollstar.com
SIC: 2741 Miscellaneous publishing

**(P-4452)**
**PRIORITY POSTING AND PUBG INC**
17501 Irvine Blvd Ste 1, Tustin (92780-3103)
PHONE..................................714 338-2568
Thomas Haacker, *Pr*
Maureen Haacker, *VP*
EMP: 17 EST: 1993
SQ FT: 3,000
SALES (est): 1.31MM **Privately Held**
Web: www.priorityposting.com
SIC: 2741 Miscellaneous publishing

**(P-4453)**
**PROTOTYPE INDUSTRIES INC (PA)**

## PRODUCTS & SERVICES SECTION
## 2741 - Miscellaneous Publishing (P-4476)

26035 Acero Ste 100, Mission Viejo (92691-7951)
PHONE...........................949 680-4890
Irene Grigoriadis, CEO
EMP: 15 EST: 1991
SQ FT: 4,000
SALES (est): 491.51K Privately Held
Web: www.prototypeindustries.com
SIC: 2741 2752 Miscellaneous publishing; Offset printing

### (P-4454)
### PROVIDENCE PUBLICATIONS LLC
1620 Santa Clara Dr Ste 115, Roseville (95661-3559)
P.O. Box 2610 (95746-2610)
PHONE...........................916 774-4000
EMP: 30 EST: 1998
SQ FT: 7,904
SALES (est): 563.74K Privately Held
Web: www.cal-osha.com
SIC: 2741 Miscellaneous publishing

### (P-4455)
### PUBLISH BRAND INC
15731 Graham St, Huntington Beach (92649-1612)
PHONE...........................714 890-1908
Chuong Huynh, Prin
EMP: 16 EST: 2013
SALES (est): 764.97K Privately Held
Web: www.publishbrand.com
SIC: 2741 Miscellaneous publishing

### (P-4456)
### QUADRIGA AMERICAS LLC
17800 S Main St Ste 113, Gardena (90248-3511)
PHONE...........................424 634-4900
EMP: 21
SALES (corp-wide): 1.66MM Privately Held
SIC: 2741 Internet publishing and broadcasting
PA: Quadriga Americas, Llc
 480 Olde Worthington Rd
 614 890-6090

### (P-4457)
### QWILT INC
275 Shoreline Dr Ste 510, Redwood City (94065-1413)
PHONE...........................650 249-6521
Alon Maor, CEO
Yoni Mizrahi, CFO
Jesper Knutsson, CCO
Jonathan Candee, CCO
EMP: 20 EST: 2010
SALES (est): 5.81MM Privately Held
SIC: 2741 Internet publishing and broadcasting

### (P-4458)
### RANGEME USA LLC
821 Folsom St, San Francisco (94107-1190)
PHONE...........................510 688-0995
Nicky Jackson, CEO
EMP: 21 EST: 2016
SALES (est): 233.43K Privately Held
Web: www.rangeme.com
SIC: 2741 Miscellaneous publishing

### (P-4459)
### RASPADOXPRESS
8610 Van Nuys Blvd, Panorama City (91402-7205)
PHONE...........................818 892-6969
Oscar Limon, Brnch Mgr

EMP: 77
SALES (corp-wide): 1.42MM Privately Held
Web: www.raspadxpress.com
SIC: 2741 Miscellaneous publishing
PA: Raspadoxpress
 9765 Laurel Canyon Blvd
 818 890-4111

### (P-4460)
### REAL MARKETING
8470 Redwood Creek Ln Ste 200, San Diego (92126-1000)
PHONE...........................858 847-0335
David Collins, Pr
▼ EMP: 28 EST: 2007
SALES (est): 3.93MM Privately Held
Web: www.realmarketing4you.com
SIC: 2741 2759 2721 Newsletter publishing; Promotional printing; Magazines: publishing and printing

### (P-4461)
### RETAIL CONTENT SERVICE INC
440 N Wolfe Rd, Sunnyvale (94085-3869)
PHONE...........................415 890-2097
Zakhar Dikhtyar, CEO
EMP: 45 EST: 2017
SALES (est): 173.52K Privately Held
SIC: 2741 Internet publishing and broadcasting

### (P-4462)
### RIYE GROUP LLC
2110 W 103rd St, Los Angeles (90047-4113)
PHONE...........................820 203-9215
Lanon Johnson, Pr
EMP: 49 EST: 2021
SALES (est): 150.2K Privately Held
SIC: 2741 8742 8741 7514 Internet publishing and broadcasting; Marketing consulting services; Administrative management; Passenger car rental

### (P-4463)
### SELLER BEST PUBLISHING
253 N San Gabriel Blvd, Pasadena (91107-3429)
PHONE...........................626 765-9750
EMP: 34 EST: 2014
SALES (est): 444.29K Privately Held
Web: www.bestsellerpublishing.org
SIC: 2741 Miscellaneous publishing

### (P-4464)
### SERVICE EXPRESS INC
Also Called: Logistics
3619 S Fowler Ave, Fresno (93725-9327)
P.O. Box 565 (93625-0565)
PHONE...........................559 495-4790
Harninder Gill, Prin
Harninder S Gill, Pr
EMP: 20 EST: 1996
SALES (est): 1.5MM Privately Held
Web: www.serviceexpress.com
SIC: 2741 Miscellaneous publishing

### (P-4465)
### SIEMENS ENERGY INC
6 Journey Ste 200, Aliso Viejo (92656-5321)
PHONE...........................949 448-0600
Ralph Sonnseld, Brnch Mgr
EMP: 21
SALES (corp-wide): 33.81B Privately Held
Web: www.siemens.com
SIC: 2741 Miscellaneous publishing
HQ: Siemens Energy, Inc.
 4400 N Alafaya Trl

Orlando FL 32826
407 736-2000

### (P-4466)
### SONGS MUSIC PUBLISHING LLC
7656 W Sunset Blvd, Los Angeles (90046-2724)
PHONE...........................323 939-3511
Carianne Marshall, Brnch Mgr
EMP: 15
Web: www.songspub.com
SIC: 2741 Miscellaneous publishing
PA: Songs Music Publishing, Llc
 307 7th Ave Rm 904

### (P-4467)
### SPARKCENTRAL INC (HQ)
535 Mission St Fl 14, San Francisco (94105-2903)
PHONE...........................866 559-6229
Tom Keiser, CEO
EMP: 53 EST: 2012
SQ FT: 1,400
SALES (est): 2.48MM
SALES (corp-wide): 207.89MM Privately Held
Web: www.hootsuite.com
SIC: 2741 4899 Miscellaneous publishing; Data communication services
PA: Hootsuite Inc
 111 5 Ave E
 604 681-4668

### (P-4468)
### SPEED SOCIETY LLC
4122 Sorrento Valley Blvd Ste 104, San Diego (92121-1431)
PHONE...........................760 402-6838
EMP: 16 EST: 2015
SALES (est): 1.13MM Privately Held
Web: www.speedsociety.com
SIC: 2741 Internet publishing and broadcasting

### (P-4469)
### SPIDELL PUBLISHING INC
1134 N Gilbert St, Anaheim (92801-1401)
P.O. Box 61044 (92803-6144)
PHONE...........................714 776-7850
Lynn Freer, Pr
EMP: 30 EST: 1975
SQ FT: 2,500
SALES (est): 1.96MM
SALES (corp-wide): 13.95MM Privately Held
Web: www.caltax.com
SIC: 2741 Guides: publishing only, not printed on site
PA: Cerifi, Llc
 3625 Brookside Pkwy # 450
 877 850-9291

### (P-4470)
### STAFFING INDUSTRY ANALYSTS INC
Also Called: Staffing Industry Report
1975 W El Camino Real Ste 304, Mountain View (94040-2218)
PHONE...........................650 390-6200
Ron Mester, CEO
Barry Asin, *
EMP: 28 EST: 1990
SQ FT: 4,307
SALES (est): 1.67MM
SALES (corp-wide): 249.16MM Privately Held
Web: www.staffingindustry.com
SIC: 2741 Newsletter publishing
PA: Crain Communications, Inc.
 1155 Gratiot Ave

313 446-6000

### (P-4471)
### STORIES INTERNATIONAL INC
400 Corporate Pointe, Culver City (90230-7615)
PHONE...........................310 242-8409
Tomoya Suzuki, CEO
EMP: 20 EST: 2013
SALES (est): 384.24K Privately Held
Web: www.stories-llc.com
SIC: 2741 Miscellaneous publishing

### (P-4472)
### STUDIO SYSTEMS INC (PA)
5700 Wilshire Blvd Ste 600, Los Angeles (90036-3659)
PHONE...........................323 634-3400
Gary Hiller, Pr
EMP: 20 EST: 1999
SQ FT: 13,000
SALES (est): 1.28MM
SALES (corp-wide): 1.28MM Privately Held
Web: www.studiosystem.com
SIC: 2741 Miscellaneous publishing

### (P-4473)
### SUPERBAM INC
214 Main St, El Segundo (90245-3803)
PHONE...........................310 845-5784
Rian Bosak, CEO
EMP: 27 EST: 2018
SALES (est): 783.65K Privately Held
Web: www.superbam.com
SIC: 2741 Internet publishing and broadcasting

### (P-4474)
### SUPERMEDIA LLC
Also Called: Verizon
3131 Katella Ave, Los Alamitos (90720-2335)
P.O. Box 3770 (90720-0377)
PHONE...........................562 594-5101
Del Humenik, Mgr
EMP: 50
SQ FT: 150,078
SALES (corp-wide): 916,96MM Publicly Held
SIC: 2741 7372 2791 Directories, telephone: publishing only, not printed on site; Prepackaged software; Typesetting
HQ: Supermedia Llc
 2200 W Airfield Dr
 Dfw Airport TX 75261
 972 453-7000

### (P-4475)
### TABOR COMMUNICATIONS INC
Also Called: Hpcwire
8445 Camino Santa Fe Ste 101, San Diego (92121-2649)
PHONE...........................858 625-0070
Debra Goldfarb, Pr
Thomas Taber, Ch Bd
Lara Kisielewska, CMO
EMP: 37 EST: 2002
SQ FT: 15,000
SALES (est): 4.19MM Privately Held
Web: www.hpcwire.com
SIC: 2741 Miscellaneous publishing

### (P-4476)
### TEACHER CREATED MATERIALS INC
5301 Oceanus Dr, Huntington Beach (92649-1030)
P.O. Box 1040 (92647-1040)
PHONE...........................714 891-2273

## 2741 - Miscellaneous Publishing (P-4477)

Rachelle Cracchiolo, *CEO*
Corinne Burton, *
Deanne Mendoza, *
Rich Levitt, *
◆ **EMP:** 110 **EST:** 1979
**SQ FT:** 10,000
**SALES (est):** 24.31MM **Privately Held**
**Web:** www.teachercreatedmaterials.com
**SIC: 2741** Miscellaneous publishing

### (P-4477)
### TECHTURE INC
Also Called: Estech Digital
1010 Wilshire Blvd Apt 1206, Los Angeles (90017-5662)
**PHONE**.................................323 347-6209
Muhammad Zubair Khan, *Pr*
Chris M Joseph, *
**EMP:** 35 **EST:** 2021
**SALES (est):** 379.2K **Privately Held**
**Web:** www.techture.co
**SIC: 2741** Internet publishing and broadcasting

### (P-4478)
### TELLME NETWORKS INC
1065 La Avenida St, Mountain View (94043-1421)
**PHONE**.................................650 693-1009
John Lamacchia, *Ch*
Robert Komin, *
▲ **EMP:** 330 **EST:** 1999
**SALES (est):** 3.68MM
**SALES (corp-wide):** 245.12B **Publicly Held**
**Web:** www.247.ai
**SIC: 2741** 4812 Telephone and other directory publishing; Radiotelephone communication
**PA:** Microsoft Corporation
1 Microsoft Way
425 882-8080

### (P-4479)
### THINK SOCIAL PUBLISHING INC
Also Called: Social Thinking
404 Saratoga Ave Ste 200, Santa Clara (95050-7000)
**PHONE**.................................408 557-8595
Michelle Winner, *CEO*
▲ **EMP:** 20 **EST:** 2006
**SALES (est):** 2.43MM **Privately Held**
**Web:** www.socialthinking.com
**SIC: 2741** Miscellaneous publishing

### (P-4480)
### THOMSON REUTERS CORPORATION
3280 Motor Ave Ste 200, Los Angeles (90034-3700)
**PHONE**.................................310 287-2360
Ayanna Chambliss, *Brnch Mgr*
**EMP:** 29
**SQ FT:** 900
**SALES (corp-wide):** 10.66B **Publicly Held**
**Web:** www.thomsonreuters.com
**SIC: 2741** Miscellaneous publishing
**HQ:** Thomson Reuters Corporation
333 Bay St
Toronto ON M5H 2
416 687-7500

### (P-4481)
### THOMSON REUTERS CORPORATION
163 Albert Pl, Costa Mesa (92627-1744)
**PHONE**.................................949 400-7782
**EMP:** 26
**SALES (corp-wide):** 10.66B **Publicly Held**
**Web:** www.thomsonreuters.com

**SIC: 2741** Miscellaneous publishing
**HQ:** Thomson Reuters Corporation
333 Bay St
Toronto ON M5H 2
416 687-7500

### (P-4482)
### TRANSWESTERN PUBLISHING COMPANY LLC
Also Called: Transwestern Publishing
8344 Clairemont Mesa Blvd, San Diego (92111-1307)
**PHONE**.................................858 467-2800
**EMP:** 1869
**SIC: 2741** Directories, telephone: publishing and printing

### (P-4483)
### TURBO DEBT RELIEF
23181 Verdugo Dr Ste 100a, Laguna Hills (92653-1313)
**PHONE**.................................949 244-1907
Roozbeh Vishkaei, *Pr*
**EMP:** 17 **EST:** 2019
**SALES (est):** 111.3K **Privately Held**
**Web:** www.turbodebt.com
**SIC: 2741** Internet publishing and broadcasting

### (P-4484)
### TWITCH INTERACTIVE INC
350 Bush St Fl 2, San Francisco (94104-2879)
**PHONE**.................................
**EMP:** 1146 **EST:** 2006
**SALES (est):** 65.02MM **Publicly Held**
**Web:** www.twitch.tv
**SIC: 2741** Internet publishing and broadcasting
**PA:** Amazon.Com, Inc.
410 Terry Ave N

### (P-4485)
### UCC GUIDE INC
Also Called: Ernst Publishing Co
225 Cabrillo Hwy S Ste 200c, Half Moon Bay (94019-7200)
**PHONE**.................................800 345-3822
Gregory E Teal, *Brnch Mgr*
**EMP:** 15
**SALES (corp-wide):** 7.99B **Publicly Held**
**Web:** www.gamenguide.com
**SIC: 2741** Miscellaneous publishing
**HQ:** The Ucc Guide Inc
99 Washngton Ave Ste 309
Albany NY 12210

### (P-4486)
### UNIVERSAL MUS GROUP DIST CORP (DH)
Also Called: Umgd
2220 Colorado Ave, Santa Monica (90404-3506)
**PHONE**.................................310 235-4700
Jim Urie, *Pr*
Kevin Lipson, *
**EMP:** 76 **EST:** 1989
**SALES (est):** 14.91MM **Privately Held**
**Web:** www.universalmusic.com
**SIC: 2741** Miscellaneous publishing
**HQ:** Vivendi Holding I Llc
1755 Broadway Fl 2
New York NY 10019
212 445-3800

### (P-4487)
### UNIVERSAL MUSIC PUBLISHING INC
Also Called: Universal Christian Music Pubg
1601 Cloverfield Blvd, Santa Monica (90404-4082)

**PHONE**.................................310 235-4700
Jody Gerson, *CEO*
**EMP:** 92 **EST:** 1999
**SALES (est):** 3.71MM **Privately Held**
**Web:** www.spandauballetstore.com
**SIC: 2741** Miscellaneous publishing
**HQ:** Universal Music Group, Inc.
2220 Colorado Ave
Santa Monica CA 90404
310 865-0770

### (P-4488)
### UPPER DECK COMPANY (PA)
5830 El Camino Real, Carlsbad (92008-8816)
**PHONE**.................................800 873-7332
Jason Masherah, *Pr*
Don Utic, *Treas*
**EMP:** 30 **EST:** 2003
**SQ FT:** 33,424
**SALES (est):** 25.3MM **Privately Held**
**Web:** www.upperdeckstore.com
**SIC: 2741** Music, book: publishing and printing

### (P-4489)
### VISION COLLECTIVE INC
Also Called: Vision Design Studio
109 Wappo Ave, Calistoga (94515-1136)
**PHONE**.................................562 597-4000
Carl Patrick Dene, *Pr*
**EMP:** 28 **EST:** 2000
**SALES (est):** 1.55MM **Privately Held**
**Web:** www.vdsla.com
**SIC: 2741** 7311 Miscellaneous publishing; Advertising agencies

### (P-4490)
### WARNER CHAPPELL MUSIC INC (DH)
Also Called: Warner Geometric Music
777 S Santa Fe Ave, Los Angeles (90021-1750)
**PHONE**.................................310 441-8600
Cameron Strang, *CEO*
Ira Pianko, *
Jay Morgenstern, *
Brian Roberts, *
Scott Francis, *
**EMP:** 110 **EST:** 1984
**SALES (est):** 14.57MM **Publicly Held**
**Web:** www.warnerrecords.com
**SIC: 2741** Music book and sheet music publishing
**HQ:** Warner Music Inc.
1633 Broadway
New York NY 10019

### (P-4491)
### WB MUSIC CORP (DH)
Also Called: Wc Music Corp.
10585 Santa Monica Blvd Ste 200, Los Angeles (90025-4950)
**PHONE**.................................310 441-8600
Leslie Bider, *CEO*
**EMP:** 125 **EST:** 1994
**SALES (est):** 1.86MM **Publicly Held**
**SIC: 2741** Music, sheet: publishing only, not printed on site
**HQ:** Warner Music Inc.
1633 Broadway
New York NY 10019

### (P-4492)
### WEBTOON ENTERTAINMENT INC (PA)
5700 Wilshire Blvd Ste 220, Los Angeles (90036-7205)
**PHONE**.................................323 297-3410
Junkoo Kim, *Ch Bd*

David J Lee, *
Yongsoo Kim, *CSO*
Chankyu Park, *
Hyeeun Son, *CDO*
**EMP:** 739 **EST:** 2016
**SQ FT:** 22,296
**SALES (est):** 14.01MM
**SALES (corp-wide):** 14.01MM **Publicly Held**
**Web:** apply.workable.com
**SIC: 2741** Miscellaneous publishing

### (P-4493)
### WEST PUBLISHING CORPORATION
2801 Camino Del Rio S, San Diego (92108-3800)
**PHONE**.................................619 296-7862
Wes Askins, *Brnch Mgr*
**EMP:** 505
**SALES (corp-wide):** 10.66B **Publicly Held**
**Web:** store.legal.thomsonreuters.com
**SIC: 2741** Miscellaneous publishing
**HQ:** West Publishing Corporation
2900 Ames Crssing Rd Ste
Eagan MN 55121
651 687-7000

### (P-4494)
### WHATEVER PUBLISHING INC
Also Called: New World Library
14 Pamaron Way Ste 1, Novato (94949-6215)
**PHONE**.................................415 884-2100
Marc Allen, *Pr*
Victoria Clarke, *CEO*
▲ **EMP:** 18 **EST:** 1977
**SQ FT:** 6,000
**SALES (est):** 2.1MM **Privately Held**
**Web:** www.newworldlibrary.com
**SIC: 2741** Miscellaneous publishing

### (P-4495)
### WORKBOOK INC
110 N Doheny Dr, Beverly Hills (90211-1811)
**PHONE**.................................323 856-0008
Alexis Scott, *Prin*
◆ **EMP:** 28 **EST:** 2008
**SALES (est):** 6.82MM **Privately Held**
**Web:** www.workbook.com
**SIC: 2741** Miscellaneous publishing

### (P-4496)
### YAMAGATA AMERICA INC
3760 Convoy St Ste 219, San Diego (92111-3744)
**PHONE**.................................858 751-1010
Yasuhide Fujimoto, *Pr*
**EMP:** 101 **EST:** 2009
**SQ FT:** 4,630
**SALES (est):** 804.67K **Privately Held**
**Web:** www.yamagatadsa.com
**SIC: 2741** Technical manuals: publishing and printing
**HQ:** Yamagata Holdings America, Inc.
3760 Convoy St Ste 219
San Diego CA 92111

### (P-4497)
### YB MEDIA LLC
1534 Plaza Ln # 146, Burlingame (94010-3204)
**PHONE**.................................310 467-5804
Benjamin Maggin, *CEO*
**EMP:** 20 **EST:** 2017
**SALES (est):** 610.17K **Privately Held**
**Web:** www.yardbarker.com
**SIC: 2741** Internet publishing and broadcasting

# PRODUCTS & SERVICES SECTION
## 2752 - Commercial Printing, Lithographic (P-4521)

## 2752 Commercial Printing, Lithographic

**(P-4498)**
**365 PRINTING INC**
8475 Artesia Blvd, Buena Park (90621-8423)
PHONE..................714 752-6990
Chang Lee, *Pr*
**EMP:** 15 **EST:** 2014
**SALES (est):** 617.8K **Privately Held**
**Web:** www.365inlove.com
**SIC:** 2752 Commercial printing, lithographic

**(P-4499)**
**ABC PRINTING INC**
Also Called: ABC Printing
1090 S Milpitas Blvd, Milpitas (95035-6307)
PHONE..................408 263-1118
Danny Luong, *Pr*
Diana Wong, *Treas*
**EMP:** 15 **EST:** 1986
**SQ FT:** 8,000
**SALES (est):** 2.24MM **Privately Held**
**Web:** www.goabcprint.com
**SIC:** 2752 7389 Offset printing; Mailbox rental and related service

**(P-4500)**
**ACE COMMERCIAL INC**
Also Called: Press Colorcom
10310 Pioneer Blvd Ste 1, Santa Fe Springs (90670-3737)
PHONE..................562 946-6664
Andrew H Choi, *CEO*
**EMP:** 40 **EST:** 1988
**SQ FT:** 22,000
**SALES (est):** 5.72MM **Privately Held**
**Web:** www.acecommercial.com
**SIC:** 2752 7331 2791 2789 Offset printing; Direct mail advertising services; Typesetting; Bookbinding and related work

**(P-4501)**
**ACME PRESS INC**
Also Called: California Lithographers
2312 Stanwell Dr, Concord (94520-4809)
P.O. Box 5698 (94524-0698)
PHONE..................925 682-1111
Mardjan Taheripour, *CEO*
Bahman Taheripour, *
**EMP:** 87 **EST:** 1976
**SQ FT:** 36,000
**SALES (est):** 20.04MM **Privately Held**
**Web:** www.calitho.com
**SIC:** 2752 Offset printing

**(P-4502)**
**ACP VENTURES**
Also Called: Allegro Copy & Print
3340 Mt Diablo Blvd Ste B, Lafayette (94549-4076)
PHONE..................925 297-0100
Peter Smyth, *Pr*
Karen Smyth, *VP*
**EMP:** 19 **EST:** 1987
**SQ FT:** 6,300
**SALES (est):** 2.16MM **Privately Held**
**Web:** www.allegrocp.com
**SIC:** 2752 2791 2789 7331 Offset printing; Typesetting; Bookbinding and related work; Mailing service

**(P-4503)**
**ADMAIL-EXPRESS INC**
31640 Hayman St, Hayward (94544-7122)
PHONE..................510 471-6200
Brian M Schott, *CEO*
**EMP:** 45 **EST:** 1973
**SQ FT:** 55,000
**SALES (est):** 8.74MM **Privately Held**
**Web:** www.admail.com
**SIC:** 2752 Offset printing

**(P-4504)**
**ADVANCED COLOR GRAPHICS**
Also Called: Acg Ecopack
1921 S Business Pkwy, Ontario (91761-8539)
PHONE..................909 930-1500
Steve Thompson, *Pr*
Mike Mullens, *
**EMP:** 60 **EST:** 1992
**SQ FT:** 70,000
**SALES (est):** 1.39MM **Privately Held**
**SIC:** 2752 Offset printing

**(P-4505)**
**ADVANCED VSUAL IMAGE DSIGN LLC**
Also Called: Avid Ink
229 N Sherman Ave, Irvine (92614)
PHONE..................951 279-2138
Jennie Enholm, *
▲ **EMP:** 26 **EST:** 1997
**SQ FT:** 20,000
**SALES (est):** 2.12MM **Privately Held**
**SIC:** 2752 Offset printing

**(P-4506)**
**AKIDO PRINTING INC**
Also Called: Promotion Xpress Prtg Graphics
2096 Merced St, San Leandro (94577-3230)
PHONE..................510 357-0238
Thanh D.o.s., *Pr*
Stella Phan, *CFO*
**EMP:** 18 **EST:** 1992
**SQ FT:** 12,000
**SALES (est):** 523.37K **Privately Held**
**SIC:** 2752 Offset printing

**(P-4507)**
**ALLIANCE PRINTING ASSOC I**
11807 Slauson Ave, Santa Fe Springs (90670-2219)
PHONE..................562 594-7975
**EMP:** 18 **EST:** 2020
**SALES (est):** 991.65K **Privately Held**
**Web:** www.apabrandu.com
**SIC:** 2752 Offset printing

**(P-4508)**
**ALPHA PRINTING & GRAPHICS INC**
12758 Schabarum Ave, Irwindale (91706-6801)
PHONE..................626 851-9800
Stacey Chen, *Pr*
Kelly Ngo, *CEO*
▲ **EMP:** 20 **EST:** 1990
**SQ FT:** 5,000
**SALES (est):** 2.39MM **Privately Held**
**Web:** www.alphaprinting.com
**SIC:** 2752 Offset printing

**(P-4509)**
**AMERICAN LITHOGRAPHERS INC**
Also Called: Pacific Standard Print
1281 National Dr, Sacramento (95834-1902)
PHONE..................916 441-5392
**EMP:** 70 **EST:** 2001
**SALES (est):** 15.18MM
**SALES (corp-wide):** 15B **Privately Held**
**Web:** www.printpsp.com
**SIC:** 2752 2759 Offset printing; Commercial printing, nec
**HQ:** R. R. Donnelley & Sons Company
35 W Wacker Dr
Chicago IL 60601
312 326-8000

**(P-4510)**
**AMERICAN PCF PRTRS COLLEGE INC**
Also Called: Kenny The Printer
675 N Main St, Orange (92868-1103)
PHONE..................949 250-3212
**TOLL FREE:** 800
David Smith, *CEO*
Cal Laird, *
**EMP:** 36 **EST:** 1981
**SALES (est):** 3.99MM **Privately Held**
**Web:** www.westprint.com
**SIC:** 2752 Offset printing

**(P-4511)**
**AMERICHIP INC (PA)**
Also Called: Americhip
19032 S Vermont Ave, Gardena (90248-4412)
PHONE..................310 323-3697
Timothy Clegg, *CEO*
Kevin Clegg, *Pr*
John Clegg, *VP*
Primoz Samardzija, *Ex VP*
Francis Logan, *Corporate Counsel*
▲ **EMP:** 45 **EST:** 1995
**SQ FT:** 30,000
**SALES (est):** 4.35MM
**SALES (corp-wide):** 4.35MM **Privately Held**
**Web:** www.americhip.com
**SIC:** 2752 Promotional printing, lithographic

**(P-4512)**
**AMP PRINTING INC**
Also Called: Gold Medal Press
6955 Sierra Ct, Dublin (94568-2641)
PHONE..................925 556-9000
**EMP:** 80 **EST:** 1979
**SALES (est):** 7.89MM **Privately Held**
**Web:** www.ampprinting.com
**SIC:** 2752 Offset printing

**(P-4513)**
**ANCHORED PRINTS**
1199 N Grove St, Anaheim (92806-2110)
PHONE..................714 929-9317
Samuel I Schinhofen, *CEO*
Samuel Schinhofen, *CEO*
**EMP:** 23 **EST:** 2018
**SALES (est):** 2.5MM **Privately Held**
**Web:** home.anchoredprints.com
**SIC:** 2752 Commercial printing, lithographic

**(P-4514)**
**ANDERSON LA INC**
Also Called: Anderson Printing
3550 Tyburn St, Los Angeles (90065-1427)
PHONE..................323 460-4115
▲ **EMP:** 95
**SIC:** 2752 2759 Commercial printing, lithographic; Letterpress printing

**(P-4515)**
**API MARKETING**
Also Called: Auburn Printers and Mfg
13020 Earhart Ave, Auburn (95602-9536)
PHONE..................916 632-1946
Merrill Kagan-weston, *Pr*
Brad Weston, *VP*
Kelley Buxton, *Opers Mgr*
**EMP:** 17 **EST:** 1946
**SQ FT:** 10,000
**SALES (est):** 916.04K **Privately Held**
**Web:** www.api-marketing.com
**SIC:** 2752 Offset printing

**(P-4516)**
**APPLE GRAPHICS INC**
3550 Tyburn St, Los Angeles (90065-1427)
PHONE..................626 301-4287
**EMP:** 50
**SIC:** 2752 2791 2789 Lithographing on metal; Typesetting; Bookbinding and related work

**(P-4517)**
**ASIA AMERICA ENTERPRISE INC**
Also Called: America Printing
1321 N Carolan Ave, Burlingame (94010-2401)
PHONE..................650 348-2333
Macy Mak, *CEO*
Ryan Mak, *Sec*
**EMP:** 20 **EST:** 1980
**SQ FT:** 27,000
**SALES (est):** 2.07MM **Privately Held**
**Web:** www.maxwellmortgage.com
**SIC:** 2752 Offset printing

**(P-4518)**
**ASL PRINT FX LTD**
Also Called: Asl Print Fx
871 Latour Ct, Napa (94558-6258)
PHONE..................707 927-3096
Chavis Pollard, *Brnch Mgr*
**EMP:** 15
**SALES (corp-wide):** 28.01MM **Privately Held**
**Web:** www.aslprintfx.com
**SIC:** 2752 Commercial printing, lithographic
**HQ:** Asl Print Fx Ltd
A-1 Royal Gate Blvd
Woodbridge ON L4L 8
416 798-7310

**(P-4519)**
**AUTUMN PRESS INC**
Also Called: Autumn Press
945 Camelia St, Berkeley (94710-1437)
PHONE..................510 654-4545
Miguel Alson, *Pr*
Theresa Thornton, *
**EMP:** 27 **EST:** 1978
**SQ FT:** 15,000
**SALES (est):** 6.8MM **Privately Held**
**Web:** www.autumnpress.com
**SIC:** 2752 Offset printing

**(P-4520)**
**AVION GRAPHICS INC**
27192 Burbank, Foothill Ranch (92610-2503)
PHONE..................949 472-0438
Craig Greiner, *Pr*
Michele Morris, *
Mary Kay Swanson, *Stockholder*
**EMP:** 33 **EST:** 1984
**SQ FT:** 6,800
**SALES (est):** 6.12MM **Privately Held**
**Web:** www.aviongraphics.com
**SIC:** 2752 7336 3993 5999 Decals, lithographed; Commercial art and graphic design; Signs and advertising specialties; Decals

**(P-4521)**
**AXIOMPRINT INC**
Also Called: Axiom Designs & Printing
4544 San Fernando Rd Ste 210, Glendale (91204-5014)
PHONE..................747 888-7777
Garnik Bayatyan, *CEO*
▼ **EMP:** 17 **EST:** 2009

---

(PA)=Parent Co (HQ)=Headquarters
✪ = New Business established in last 2 years

## 2752 - Commercial Printing, Lithographic (P-4522)

SALES (est): 6.52MM **Privately Held**
**Web**: www.axiomprint.com
**SIC**: **2752** 5999 2741 7312  Offset printing; Banners, flags, decals, and posters; Posters: publishing and printing; Poster advertising, outdoor

**(P-4522)**
**AZALEA SYSTEMS CORP INC**
Also Called: Handbill Printers
820 E Parkridge Ave, Corona  (92879-6611)
**PHONE**......................951 547-5910
Ralph Azar, *Pr*
**EMP**: 26 **EST**: 2018
**SALES (est)**: 5.28MM **Privately Held**
**SIC**: **2752**  Offset printing

**(P-4523)**
**B AND Z PRINTING  INC**
1300 E Wakeham Ave # B, Santa Ana  (92705-4145)
**PHONE**......................714 892-2000
Frank Buono, *Pr*
James Zimmer, *
**EMP**: 45 **EST**: 1984
**SQ FT**: 40,000
**SALES (est)**: 947.08K **Privately Held**
**Web**: www.bandzprinting.com
**SIC**: **2752** 2789  Offset printing; Bookbinding and related work

**(P-4524)**
**B R PRINTERS  INC (PA)**
Also Called: B R
665 Lenfest Rd, San Jose  (95133-1615)
**PHONE**......................408 278-7711
Jorge Velasco, *Pr*
Cristy Abella, *
**EMP**: 65 **EST**: 1992
**SQ FT**: 90,000
**SALES (est)**: 161.36MM **Privately Held**
**Web**: www.brprinters.com
**SIC**: **2752**  Commercial printing, lithographic

**(P-4525)**
**BABYLON PRINTING INC**
Also Called: Medius
15850 Concord Cir Ste B, Morgan Hill  (95037-7143)
**PHONE**......................408 519-5000
Daisy Zaia, *CEO*
George Zaia, *
◆ **EMP**: 43 **EST**: 1982
**SALES (est)**: 8.44MM **Privately Held**
**Web**: www.mediuscorp.com
**SIC**: **2752**  Offset printing

**(P-4526)**
**BACCHUS PRESS  INC (PA)**
1287 66th St, Emeryville  (94608-1198)
**PHONE**......................510 420-5800
Monsoor Assadi, *Pr*
**EMP**: 20 **EST**: 1975
**SQ FT**: 10,000
**SALES (est)**: 1.94MM
**SALES (corp-wide)**: 1.94MM **Privately Held**
**Web**: www.bacchuspress.com
**SIC**: **2752**  Offset printing

**(P-4527)**
**BARLOW AND SONS PRINTING INC**
Also Called: Barlow Printing
481 Aaron St, Cotati  (94931-3081)
**PHONE**......................707 664-9773
Patrick Barlow, *Pr*
Ken Reed, *VP*
**EMP**: 15 **EST**: 1961
**SQ FT**: 20,000
**SALES (est)**: 2.06MM **Privately Held**
**Web**: www.barlowprinting.com
**SIC**: **2752**  Letters, circular or form: lithographed

**(P-4528)**
**BARRYS PRINTING  INC**
Also Called: All About Printing
9005 Eton Ave Ste D, Canoga Park  (91304-1617)
**PHONE**......................818 998-8600
Barry Shapiro, *CEO*
**EMP**: 30 **EST**: 1996
**SALES (est)**: 1.01MM **Privately Held**
**Web**: barrysprinting.mfgpages.com
**SIC**: **2752** 7334  Offset printing; Photocopying and duplicating services

**(P-4529)**
**BEN FRANKLIN PRESS & LABEL CO**
Also Called: Ben Franklin Press
480 Technology Way, Napa  (94558-7564)
**PHONE**......................707 253-8250
**EMP**: 35
**SIC**: **2752**  Offset printing

**(P-4530)**
**BERGIN SCREEN PRTG & ETCHING**
451 Technology Way, Napa  (94558-7571)
**PHONE**......................707 224-0111
**EMP**: 28 **EST**: 2018
**SALES (est)**: 413.94K **Privately Held**
**Web**: www.berginglass.com
**SIC**: **2752**  Commercial printing, lithographic

**(P-4531)**
**BERT-CO INDUSTRIES INC**
Also Called: Bert-Co
2150 S Parco Ave, Ontario  (91761-5768)
P.O. Box 4150  (91761-1068)
**PHONE**......................323 669-5700
▲ **EMP**: 154
**SIC**: **2752**  Commercial printing, lithographic

**(P-4532)**
**BIG HORN WEALTH MANAGEMENT INC**
2577 Research Dr, Corona  (92882-7607)
**PHONE**......................951 273-7900
▲ **EMP**: 64
**SIC**: **2752**  Offset printing

**(P-4533)**
**BOONE PRINTING & GRAPHICS INC**
70 S Kellogg Ave Ste 8, Goleta  (93117-6408)
**PHONE**......................805 683-2349
Andrew Ochsner, *Pr*
Dave Tanner, *
Jim Petrini Acctn, *Mgr*
**EMP**: 52 **EST**: 1988
**SQ FT**: 15,000
**SALES (est)**: 10.92MM **Privately Held**
**Web**: www.boonegraphics.net
**SIC**: **2752**  Offset printing

**(P-4534)**
**BOSS LITHO  INC**
1544 Hauser Blvd, Los Angeles  (90019)
**PHONE**......................626 912-7088
Jean Paul Nataf, *Pr*
**EMP**: 48 **EST**: 2010
**SALES (est)**: 4.16MM **Privately Held**
**Web**: www.bosslitho.com
**SIC**: **2752**  Offset printing

**(P-4535)**
**BOX CO INC**
7575 Britannia Park Pl, San Diego  (92154-7418)
**PHONE**......................619 661-8090
Richard Barragan, *Pr*
Maggie Barragan, *Sec*
◆ **EMP**: 16 **EST**: 1984
**SQ FT**: 16,000
**SALES (est)**: 2.43MM **Privately Held**
**Web**: www.theboxpkg.com
**SIC**: **2752** 2657  Commercial printing, lithographic; Folding paperboard boxes

**(P-4536)**
**BREAKAWAY PRESS INC**
9620 Topanga Canyon Pl Ste A, Chatsworth  (91311-0868)
**PHONE**......................818 727-7388
Cynthia Friedman, *Pr*
Marc Friedman, *VP*
**EMP**: 20 **EST**: 1993
**SQ FT**: 3,000
**SALES (est)**: 971.17K **Privately Held**
**Web**: www.breakawaypress.com
**SIC**: **2752**  Offset printing

**(P-4537)**
**BREHM COMMUNICATIONS  INC (PA)**
Also Called: B C I
16644 W Bernardo Dr Ste 300, San Diego  (92127-1901)
P.O. Box 28429  (92198-0429)
**PHONE**......................858 451-6200
Bill Brehm Junior, *Pr*
Tom Taylor, *
Mona Brehm, *
W J Brehm, *
**EMP**: 29 **EST**: 1919
**SQ FT**: 6,000
**SALES (est)**: 21.91MM
**SALES (corp-wide)**: 21.91MM **Privately Held**
**Web**: www.brehmcommunications.com
**SIC**: **2752** 2711  Offset printing; Commercial printing and newspaper publishing combined

**(P-4538)**
**BUSINESS CARDS TOMORROW**
Also Called: B C T
546 S Pacific St Ste 104, San Marcos  (92078-4070)
**PHONE**......................760 471-2012
Creston Cain, *Pr*
Barbara Cain, *Sec*
**EMP**: 19 **EST**: 1986
**SQ FT**: 3,800
**SALES (est)**: 390.71K **Privately Held**
**Web**: www.evoprint.com
**SIC**: **2752** 6221  Visiting cards, lithographed; Commodity contracts brokers, dealers

**(P-4539)**
**C & L GRAPHICS  INC**
16461 Sherman Way, Van Nuys  (91406-3842)
**PHONE**......................818 785-8310
Charles Ball, *Pr*
Laurie Ball, *Sec*
**EMP**: 18 **EST**: 1985
**SALES (est)**: 2.54MM **Privately Held**
**Web**: www.clgraphicsinc.com
**SIC**: **2752**  Offset printing

**(P-4540)**
**C4 LITHO  LLC**
27020 Daisy Cir, Yorba Linda  (92887-4233)
**PHONE**......................714 259-1073
Su T Dang, *Managing Member*
**EMP**: 24 **EST**: 2006
**SALES (est)**: 965.57K **Privately Held**
**Web**: www.c4usa.com
**SIC**: **2752**  Offset printing

**(P-4541)**
**CAL SOUTHERN GRAPHICS CORP (HQ)**
Also Called: California Graphics
9655 De Soto Ave, Chatsworth  (91311-5013)
**PHONE**......................310 559-3600
Timothy Toomey, *CEO*
▲ **EMP**: 91 **EST**: 1959
**SALES (est)**: 20.03MM
**SALES (corp-wide)**: 25.12MM **Privately Held**
**Web**: www.socalgraph.com
**SIC**: **2752** 2759 2754  Lithographing on metal ; Commercial printing, nec; Commercial printing, gravure
**PA**: Gpa Printing Ca Llc
9655 De Soto Ave
818 237-9771

**(P-4542)**
**CALIFORNIA OFFSET PRINTERS INC (PA)**
Also Called: Cop Communications
5075 Brooks St, Montclair  (91763-4804)
**PHONE**......................818 291-1100
**TOLL FREE**: 800
John Hedlund, *Ch Bd*
William R Rittwage, *Pr*
**EMP**: 68 **EST**: 1962
**SQ FT**: 55,000
**SALES (est)**: 11.72MM
**SALES (corp-wide)**: 11.72MM **Privately Held**
**Web**: www.copprints.com
**SIC**: **2752** 2741 2721  Offset printing; Miscellaneous publishing; Periodicals

**(P-4543)**
**CASEY PRINTING  INC**
398 E San Antonio Dr, King City  (93930-2509)
P.O. Box 913  (93930-0913)
**PHONE**......................831 385-3221
Richard Casey, *Pr*
Bill Casey, *
Sharon Casey, *
**EMP**: 48 **EST**: 1901
**SQ FT**: 31,000
**SALES (est)**: 4.66MM **Privately Held**
**Web**: www.caseyprinting.com
**SIC**: **2752**  Offset printing

**(P-4544)**
**CDR GRAPHICS  INC (PA)**
1207 E Washington Blvd, Los Angeles  (90021-3035)
P.O. Box 15311  (90015-0311)
**PHONE**......................310 474-7600
Homan Hadawi, *Pr*
**EMP**: 23 **EST**: 2010
**SALES (est)**: 2.33MM
**SALES (corp-wide)**: 2.33MM **Privately Held**
**Web**: www.cdrgraphics.com
**SIC**: **2752**  Offset printing

**(P-4545)**
**CELEBRATION WEST INC**
2505 N Shirk Rd, Visalia  (93291-8605)
**EMP**: 124
**SIC**: **2752**  Commercial printing, lithographic

## PRODUCTS & SERVICES SECTION
## 2752 - Commercial Printing, Lithographic (P-4569)

**(P-4546)**
**CENTRAL BUSINESS FORMS INC**
Also Called: Central Printing Group
289 Foster City Blvd Ste B, Foster City (94404-1100)
PHONE.................................650 548-0918
Jeanine M Morgan, *Pr*
Michelle L Cabral, *Sec*
EMP: 21 EST: 1982
SQ FT: 22,800
SALES (est): 430.68K **Privately Held**
Web: www.bannerprinting.com
SIC: **2752** Offset printing

**(P-4547)**
**CERTIFIED AD SERVICES**
909 W Nielsen Ave, Fresno (93706-1308)
P.O. Box 12025 (93776-2025)
PHONE.................................559 233-1891
▲ EMP: 185
SIC: **2752** Circulars, lithographed

**(P-4548)**
**CHECCHI ENTERPRISES INC**
Also Called: Harvest Printing Company
19849 Riverside Ave, Anderson (96007-4909)
PHONE.................................530 378-1207
Tom Watega, *Pr*
EMP: 15 EST: 1976
SQ FT: 10,200
SALES (est): 1.89MM **Privately Held**
Web: www.harvestprinting.com
SIC: **2752** Offset printing

**(P-4549)**
**CHROMATIC INC LITHOGRAPHERS**
127 Concord St, Glendale (91203-2456)
PHONE.................................818 242-5785
Keith Sevigny, *Pr*
Michael Sevigny, *
Mary Gene Sevigny, *
Marlene Lunn, *
▲ EMP: 32 EST: 1969
SALES (est): 4.97MM **Privately Held**
Web: www.chromaticinc.com
SIC: **2752** Offset printing

**(P-4550)**
**CHUP CORPORATION**
Also Called: Color Digit
2990 Airway Ave Ste A, Costa Mesa (92626-6037)
PHONE.................................949 455-0676
Mohsen Kaeni, *Pr*
Hadi Kaeni, *VP*
Hamid Kaeni, *Sec*
EMP: 15 EST: 1990
SQ FT: 11,000
SALES (est): 6.46MM **Privately Held**
SIC: **2752** 2796 Offset printing; Color separations, for printing

**(P-4551)**
**CITATION PRESS**
2050 Junction Ave, San Jose (95131-2104)
PHONE.................................408 957-9900
EMP: 52
SQ FT: 25,500
SALES (est): 5.05MM **Privately Held**
Web: www.citationpress.com
SIC: **2752** Offset printing

**(P-4552)**
**CLASSIC LITHO & DESIGN INC**
340 Maple Ave, Torrance (90503-2600)
PHONE.................................310 224-5200
Masoud Nikravan, *CEO*
Firouzeh Nikravan, *
EMP: 30 EST: 1976
SQ FT: 12,500
SALES (est): 5.21MM **Privately Held**
Web: www.classiclitho.com
SIC: **2752** Offset printing

**(P-4553)**
**CLEAR IMAGE PRINTING INC**
12744 San Fernando Rd, Sylmar (91342-3853)
PHONE.................................818 547-4684
Anthony Toven, *Pr*
EMP: 28 EST: 2007
SQ FT: 18,000
SALES (est): 5.04MM **Privately Held**
Web: www.clearimageprinting.com
SIC: **2752** Offset printing

**(P-4554)**
**CLIC LLC**
Also Called: Andresen
855 Stanton Rd Ste 300, Burlingame (94010-1403)
PHONE.................................415 421-2900
Michael Hicks, *Managing Member*
EMP: 24 EST: 2004
SALES (est): 4.71MM **Privately Held**
Web: www.clic.es
SIC: **2752** 7374 Commercial printing, lithographic; Computer graphics service

**(P-4555)**
**CMY IMAGE CORPORATION**
Also Called: Compandsave
33268 Central Ave, Union City (94587-2010)
PHONE.................................510 516-6668
Andrew Yeung, *CEO*
EMP: 15 EST: 2013
SALES (est): 262.22K **Privately Held**
Web: www.compandsave.com
SIC: **2752** Photo-offset printing

**(P-4556)**
**COAST SPECIALTY PRINTING CO**
Also Called: Coast Specialty
403 S Gertruda Ave, Redondo Beach (90277-3809)
PHONE.................................626 359-2451
Richard Petrosino, *Pr*
Joe Juliano, *Sec*
EMP: 22 EST: 1978
SQ FT: 2,000
SALES (est): 271.43K **Privately Held**
SIC: **2752** 2761 Commercial printing, lithographic; Manifold business forms

**(P-4557)**
**COLOR INC**
1600 Flower St, Glendale (91201-2319)
PHONE.................................818 240-1350
Barry D Hamm, *Pr*
James E Hamm, *
EMP: 35 EST: 1968
SQ FT: 16,000
SALES (est): 2.54MM **Privately Held**
Web: www.colorincorporated.com
SIC: **2752** 2796 Color lithography; Platemaking services

**(P-4558)**
**COLOR FX INC**
8000 Haskell Ave, Van Nuys (91406-1321)
PHONE.................................877 763-7671
EMP: 34 EST: 1995
SALES (est): 194.43K **Privately Held**
Web: www.colorfxweb.com
SIC: **2752** Offset printing

**(P-4559)**
**COLOR WEST INC**
Also Called: Color West Printing & Packg
2228 N Hollywood Way, Burbank (91505-1112)
P.O. Box 10879 (91510-0879)
PHONE.................................818 840-8881
EMP: 170
Web: www.colorwestprinting.com
SIC: **2752** Commercial printing, lithographic

**(P-4560)**
**COLORCOM INC**
2437 S Eastern Ave, Commerce (90040-1414)
PHONE.................................323 246-4640
John Youn, *Pr*
Young Kim, *Stockholder*
EMP: 18 EST: 1992
SALES (est): 3.12MM **Privately Held**
Web: www.colorcom.net
SIC: **2752** Offset printing

**(P-4561)**
**COLORFX INC**
11050 Randall St, Sun Valley (91352-2621)
P.O. Box 12357 (91224-5357)
PHONE.................................818 767-7671
Razmik Avedissian, *CEO*
Arby Avedissan, *
Yolanda Avedissan, *
EMP: 50 EST: 1996
SQ FT: 28,000
SALES (est): 1.26MM **Privately Held**
Web: www.colorfxweb.com
SIC: **2752** Offset printing

**(P-4562)**
**COLOUR CONCEPTS INC**
Also Called: Partner Printing
1225 Los Angeles St, Glendale (91204-2403)
EMP: 150 EST: 1989
SQ FT: 36,000
SALES (est): 2.44MM **Privately Held**
Web: www.partnerprinting.com
SIC: **2752** 7371 Offset printing; Computer software development

**(P-4563)**
**COMMERCE PRINTING SERVICES**
322 N 12th St, Sacramento (95811-0528)
PHONE.................................916 442-8100
EMP: 58 EST: 1988
SALES (est): 2MM **Privately Held**
Web: www.commerceprinting.com
SIC: **2752** Offset printing

**(P-4564)**
**COMMUNICATION SERVICES CTR INC**
Also Called: Direct Mail Center
1099 Mariposa St, San Francisco (94107-2519)
PHONE.................................415 252-1600
Mely Leung, *Pr*
Wendy Chien, *
Pierre Smit, *
EMP: 25 EST: 1984
SALES (est): 3.76MM **Privately Held**
Web: www.directmailctr.com
SIC: **2752** Offset printing

**(P-4565)**
**COMMUNITY PRINTERS INC**
1827 Soquel Ave, Santa Cruz (95062-1385)
PHONE.................................831 426-4682
Joe Chavez, *Pr*
Ross Newport, *Prin*
Shelly D'amour, *Treas*
Mischa Kandinksy, *
EMP: 32 EST: 1977
SQ FT: 10,000
SALES (est): 63.95K
SALES (corp-wide): 119.91K **Privately Held**
Web: www.comprinters.com
SIC: **2752** Offset printing
PA: Eschaton Foundation
612 Ocean St
831 423-1626

**(P-4566)**
**CONNECTED TRNSP PRTNERS STHERN**
1035 22nd Ave Unit 19, Oakland (94606-5271)
PHONE.................................510 542-5446
Marvin Wilcher, *CEO*
EMP: 36 EST: 2021
SALES (est): 351.04K **Privately Held**
SIC: **2752** Schedules, transportation: lithographed

**(P-4567)**
**CONTINENTAL GRAPHICS CORP**
Also Called: Continental Engineering Svcs
6910 Carroll Rd, San Diego (92121-2211)
PHONE.................................858 552-6520
Manuel Defaria, *Brnch Mgr*
EMP: 53
SALES (corp-wide): 77.79B **Publicly Held**
Web: services.boeing.com
SIC: **2752** 7336 Promotional printing, lithographic; Graphic arts and related design
HQ: Continental Graphics Corporation
4060 N Lkwood Blvd Bldg 8
Long Beach CA 90808
714 503-4200

**(P-4568)**
**CONTINENTAL GRAPHICS CORP**
Also Called: Continental Data Graphics
4060 N Lakewood Blvd Bldg 801, Long Beach (90808-1700)
PHONE.................................714 827-1752
Warren Smith, *Mgr*
EMP: 53
SALES (corp-wide): 77.79B **Publicly Held**
Web: www.cdgnow.com
SIC: **2752** 7336 Promotional printing, lithographic; Graphic arts and related design
HQ: Continental Graphics Corporation
4060 N Lkwood Blvd Bldg 8
Long Beach CA 90808
714 503-4200

**(P-4569)**
**CONTINENTAL GRAPHICS CORP**
Also Called: Continental Data Graphics
9302 Pittsburgh Ave Ste 100, Rancho Cucamonga (91730-5564)
PHONE.................................909 758-9800
Steve Meade, *Brnch Mgr*
EMP: 53
SALES (corp-wide): 77.79B **Publicly Held**
Web: services.boeing.com
SIC: **2752** 7336 Promotional printing, lithographic; Graphic arts and related design
HQ: Continental Graphics Corporation
4060 N Lkwood Blvd Bldg 8
Long Beach CA 90808
714 503-4200

## 2752 - Commercial Printing, Lithographic (P-4570)

**(P-4570)**
**CONTINENTAL GRAPHICS CORP**
Also Called: Continental Data Graphics
4000 N Lakewood Blvd, Long Beach (90808-1700)
PHONE.................................714 503-4200
Steve Meade, Mgr
**EMP:** 53
**SALES (corp-wide):** 77.79B **Publicly Held**
Web: www.cdgnow.com
**SIC: 2752** Promotional printing, lithographic
HQ: Continental Graphics Corporation
   4060 N Lkwood Blvd Bldg 8
   Long Beach CA 90808
   714 503-4200

**(P-4571)**
**CONTINENTAL GRAPHICS CORP**
Also Called: Continental Data Graphics
222 N Pacific Coast Hwy Ste 300, El Segundo (90245-5648)
PHONE.................................310 662-2307
Mike Parvin, Mgr
**EMP:** 53
**SALES (corp-wide):** 77.79B **Publicly Held**
Web: www.cdgnow.com
**SIC: 2752** 7336 Promotional printing, lithographic; Graphic arts and related design
HQ: Continental Graphics Corporation
   4060 N Lkwood Blvd Bldg 8
   Long Beach CA 90808
   714 503-4200

**(P-4572)**
**COPY SOLUTIONS INC**
919 S Fremont Ave Ste 398, Alhambra (91803-4701)
PHONE.................................323 307-0900
Roger Zhao, Pr
**EMP:** 20 **EST:** 1995
**SQ FT:** 5,000
**SALES (est):** 3.42MM **Privately Held**
Web: www.copysolution.com
**SIC: 2752** Offset printing

**(P-4573)**
**CORPORATE GRAPHICS & PRINTING**
335 Science Dr, Moorpark (93021-2092)
PHONE.................................805 529-5333
Harry A Stidham, Pr
Harry Stidham, Pr
**EMP:** 17 **EST:** 2002
**SQ FT:** 20,000
**SALES (est):** 2.37MM **Privately Held**
Web: www.corgfx.com
**SIC: 2752** Offset printing

**(P-4574)**
**CORPORATE GRAPHICS INTL INC**
Also Called: Corporate Graphics West
4909 Alcoa Ave, Vernon (90058-3022)
PHONE.................................323 826-3440
Robert Gonynor, Genl Mgr
**EMP:** 65
**SALES (corp-wide):** 3.81B **Privately Held**
Web: www.taylor.com
**SIC: 2752** 2759 Offset printing; Embossing on paper
HQ: Corporate Graphics International, Inc.
   1750 Tower Blvd
   North Mankato MN 56003

**(P-4575)**
**COYLE REPRODUCTIONS INC (PA)**
2850 Orbiter St, Brea (92821-6224)
PHONE.................................866 269-5373
Frank T Cutrone Junior, CEO
Frank T Cutrone, Ch Bd
**EMP:** 112 **EST:** 1963
**SQ FT:** 85,000
**SALES (est):** 11.25MM
**SALES (corp-wide):** 11.25MM **Privately Held**
Web: www.coylerepro.com
**SIC: 2752** 2759 Offset printing; Screen printing

**(P-4576)**
**CREATIVE PRESS LLC**
1600 E Ball Rd, Anaheim (92805-5990)
PHONE.................................714 774-5060
**EMP:** 36
Web: www.creativepressinc.net
**SIC: 2752** 2791 2789 Offset printing; Typesetting; Bookbinding and related work
PA: Creative Press, L.L.C.
   1350 S Caldwell Cir

**(P-4577)**
**CREATIVE PRESS LLC (PA)**
Also Called: Creative Press
1350 S Caldwell Cir, Anaheim (92805-6408)
PHONE.................................714 774-5060
**EMP:** 29 **EST:** 2007
**SQ FT:** 31,000
**SALES (est):** 9.23MM **Privately Held**
Web: www.creativepressinc.net
**SIC: 2752** 2791 2789 Offset printing; Typesetting; Bookbinding and related work

**(P-4578)**
**CRESCENT INC**
Also Called: Print Printing
670 S Jefferson St, Placentia (92870-6638)
PHONE.................................714 992-6030
Reza Mohkami, Pr
Ira Heshmati, *
Tahereh Mohkami, *
**EMP:** 25 **EST:** 1980
**SALES (est):** 2.04MM **Privately Held**
Web: www.printprinting.com
**SIC: 2752** 7549 Offset printing; Do-it-yourself garages

**(P-4579)**
**CRESTEC USA INC**
Also Called: Crestec Los Angeles
2410 Mira Mar Ave, Long Beach (90815-1756)
PHONE.................................310 327-9000
Takeomi Kurisawa, CEO
Mike Burk, *
▲ **EMP:** 50 **EST:** 1967
**SALES (est):** 8.74MM **Privately Held**
Web: www.crestecusa.com
**SIC: 2752** Offset printing
PA: Crestec Inc.
   69, Higashimikatacho, Chuo-Ku

**(P-4580)**
**CYU LITHOGRAPHICS INC**
Also Called: Choice Lithographics
6951 Oran Cir, Buena Park (90621-3305)
PHONE.................................888 878-9898
Michael Wang, Pr
▲ **EMP:** 25 **EST:** 1983
**SQ FT:** 13,000
**SALES (est):** 2.41MM **Privately Held**
**SIC: 2752** 2721 Color lithography; Magazines: publishing only, not printed on site

**(P-4581)**
**D & J PRINTING INC**
Also Called: Bang Printing
600 W Technology Dr, Palmdale (93551-3748)
PHONE.................................661 265-1995
**EMP:** 69
**SALES (corp-wide):** 611.15MM **Privately Held**
Web: www.sheridan.com
**SIC: 2752** Offset printing
HQ: D. & J. Printing, Inc.
   3323 Oak St
   Brainerd MN 56401
   218 829-2877

**(P-4582)**
**D & R SCREEN PRINTING INC**
7314 Pierce Ave, Whittier (90602-1111)
PHONE.................................562 458-6443
Jose D Rios, Pr
**EMP:** 31 **EST:** 2008
**SALES (est):** 781.65K **Privately Held**
**SIC: 2752** Commercial printing, lithographic

**(P-4583)**
**DAKOTA PRESS INC**
14400 Doolittle Dr, San Leandro (94577-5546)
PHONE.................................510 895-1300
Mary Reid, CEO
Mary Reid, Pr
Gary Reid, VP
**EMP:** 15 **EST:** 2010
**SALES (est):** 2.94MM **Privately Held**
Web: www.dakotapress.com
**SIC: 2752** Offset printing

**(P-4584)**
**DAVID B ANDERSON**
Also Called: Central Coast Printing
174 Suburban Rd Ste 100, San Luis Obispo (93401-7522)
PHONE.................................805 489-0661
David B Anderson, Owner
**EMP:** 26 **EST:** 1978
**SALES (est):** 2MM **Privately Held**
Web: www.boonegraphics.net
**SIC: 2752** Offset printing

**(P-4585)**
**DELTA PRINT GROUP LLC**
4251 Gateway Park Blvd, Sacramento (95834-1975)
PHONE.................................916 928-0801
**EMP:** 30 **EST:** 2019
**SALES (est):** 3.47MM **Privately Held**
Web: www.deltaprintgroup.com
**SIC: 2752** Offset printing

**(P-4586)**
**DELTA PRINTING SOLUTIONS INC**
28210 Avenue Stanford, Valencia (91355-3983)
PHONE.................................661 257-0584
Tony Richardson, Pr
**EMP:** 130 **EST:** 2003
**SQ FT:** 100,000
**SALES (est):** 2.03MM **Privately Held**
Web: www.deltaprintingsolutions.com
**SIC: 2752** Offset printing

**(P-4587)**
**DENNIS BOLTON ENTERPRISES INC**
7285 Coldwater Canyon Ave, North Hollywood (91605-4204)
PHONE.................................818 982-1800
Dennis Bolton, Pr
Max Guerrero, VP
Carlo Bernal, Sec
Osvaldo Acosta, Treas
**EMP:** 17 **EST:** 1971
**SQ FT:** 14,780
**SALES (est):** 655.33K **Privately Held**
Web: www.printingbydbe.com
**SIC: 2752** 7334 7311 Offset printing; Photocopying and duplicating services; Advertising consultant

**(P-4588)**
**DIEGO & SON PRINTING INC**
2277 National Ave, San Diego (92113-3614)
P.O. Box 13100 (92170)
PHONE.................................619 233-5373
Nicholas Aguilera, Pr
Rebecca Aguilera, VP
Isabelle Aguilera, Sec
**EMP:** 22 **EST:** 1972
**SALES (est):** 1.88MM **Privately Held**
Web: www.diegoandson.com
**SIC: 2752** 2759 Offset printing; Commercial printing, nec

**(P-4589)**
**DIGITAL MANIA INC**
Also Called: Copymat
455 Market St Ste 180, San Francisco (94105-2476)
PHONE.................................415 896-0500
Darius Meykadah, Pr
**EMP:** 20 **EST:** 1994
**SALES (est):** 2.61MM **Privately Held**
Web: www.copymat1.com
**SIC: 2752** Offset printing

**(P-4590)**
**DIGITAL PRINTING SYSTEMS INC (PA)**
2350 Panorama Ter, Los Angeles (90039-2536)
PHONE.................................626 815-1888
Donald J Nores, Ch
Donald J Nores, Ch Bd
Peter Young, *
Jim Nores, *
Joyce Nores, *
◆ **EMP:** 68 **EST:** 1971
**SALES (est):** 2.13MM
**SALES (corp-wide):** 2.13MM **Privately Held**
Web: www.southlandprinting.com
**SIC: 2752** Offset printing

**(P-4591)**
**DIGITAL SUPERCOLOR INC**
Also Called: Supercolor
PHONE.................................949 622-0010
▲ **EMP:** 55
Web: www.supercolor.com
**SIC: 2752** 7336 2759 Commercial printing, lithographic; Commercial art and graphic design; Commercial printing, nec

**(P-4592)**
**DIGITALPRO INC**
Also Called: Dpi Direct
13257 Kirkham Way, Poway (92064-7116)
PHONE.................................858 874-7750
Sam Mousavi, Pr
Mohammed Khaki, VP Opers
Paul Moebius, Development*
**EMP:** 65 **EST:** 2001
**SQ FT:** 38,000
**SALES (est):** 3.27MM **Privately Held**
Web: www.dpidirect.com
**SIC: 2752** Offset printing

## PRODUCTS & SERVICES SECTION — 2752 - Commercial Printing, Lithographic (P-4614)

**(P-4593)**
**DOCUMOTION RESEARCH INC**
Also Called: Stickypos
2020 S Eastwood Ave, Santa Ana (92705-5208)
PHONE.................714 662-3800
Joel Van Boom, Pr
EMP: 17 EST: 2010
SQ FT: 10,000
SALES (est): 4.93MM Privately Held
Web: www.documotion.com
SIC: 2752 Commercial printing, lithographic

**(P-4594)**
**DOME PRINTING & PACKAGING LLC (HQ)**
Also Called: PM Packaging
2031 Dome Ln, Mcclellan (95652-2033)
PHONE.................800 343-3139
EMP: 23 EST: 2022
SALES (est): 3.35MM
SALES (corp-wide): 150.21MM Privately Held
Web: www.pmpackaging.com
SIC: 2752 Offset printing
PA: Pm Corporate Group Inc.
2285 Mchael Frday Dr Ste
800 343-3139

**(P-4595)**
**DOT CORP**
1801 S Standard Ave, Santa Ana (92707-2465)
PHONE.................714 708-5960
EMP: 17
SALES (corp-wide): 4.43MM Privately Held
Web: www.thedotcorp.com
SIC: 2752 Offset printing
PA: The Dot Corp
2525 Pullman St
714 708-5800

**(P-4596)**
**DOT PRINTER INC (PA)**
2424 Mcgaw Ave, Irvine (92614-5834)
PHONE.................949 474-1100
Bruce M Carson, Pr
Jim Voss, *
Stan Lowe, *
▲ EMP: 95 EST: 1980
SQ FT: 40,000
SALES (est): 29.08MM
SALES (corp-wide): 29.08MM Privately Held
Web: www.thedotcorp.com
SIC: 2752 2732 3555 Offset printing; Book printing; Printing trades machinery

**(P-4597)**
**DUMONT PRINTING INC**
Also Called: Dumont Printing & Mailing
1333 G St, Fresno (93706-1634)
P.O. Box 12726 (93779-2726)
PHONE.................559 485-6311
Susan Denise Moore, CEO
Susan Moore, *
▼ EMP: 42 EST: 1950
SQ FT: 21,000
SALES (est): 6.46MM Privately Held
Web: www.dumontprinting.com
SIC: 2752 2759 7331 7334 Offset printing; Commercial printing, nec; Direct mail advertising services; Photocopying and duplicating services

**(P-4598)**
**EAGLE GRAPHICS INC (PA)**
Also Called: Eagle Print Dynamics
1430 W Katella Ave, Orange (92867-3409)
PHONE.................714 978-2200
Tim Smith, Pr
Jeff Carte, VP
Kevin Welch, VP
EMP: 15 EST: 1971
SALES (est): 4.64MM
SALES (corp-wide): 4.64MM Privately Held
Web: www.eagle411.com
SIC: 2752 Commercial printing, lithographic

**(P-4599)**
**EARTH PRINT INC**
Also Called: Cr Print
31115 Via Colinas Ste 301, Westlake Village (91362-4507)
PHONE.................818 879-6050
Jim Friedl, Pr
Edward Corridori, Sec
EMP: 19 EST: 1994
SQ FT: 7,500
SALES (est): 2.42MM Privately Held
Web: www.crprint.com
SIC: 2752 7334 Offset printing; Photocopying and duplicating services

**(P-4600)**
**ECLIPSE PRTG & GRAPHICS LLC**
Also Called: James Litho
9145 Milliken Ave, Rancho Cucamonga (91730-5509)
PHONE.................909 390-2452
Jeffrey James, Managing Member
Sue James, *
EMP: 23 EST: 1999
SALES (est): 4.47MM Privately Held
Web: www.jameslitho.com
SIC: 2752 Offset printing

**(P-4601)**
**ECON-O-PLATE INC**
Also Called: Pacific Rim Printers & Mailers
5731 W Slauson Ave Ste 175, Culver City (90230-6509)
PHONE.................310 342-5900
Robert Brothers, Pr
Brad Carl, Treas
EMP: 15 EST: 1969
SALES (est): 2.51MM Privately Held
Web: www.pacificrimprinters.com
SIC: 2752 7331 Offset printing; Mailing service

**(P-4602)**
**EDELSTEIN PRINTING CO**
Also Called: Service Printing Co
2725 Miller St, San Leandro (94577-5619)
PHONE.................510 352-7890
Jerome Edelstein, Ch Bd
James Edelstein, *
EMP: 35 EST: 1925
SQ FT: 24,000
SALES (est): 661.63K Privately Held
SIC: 2752 Lithographing on metal

**(P-4603)**
**ELITE 4 PRINT INC**
851 E Walnut St, Carson (90746-1214)
PHONE.................310 366-1344
Keith Kyong, Prin
▲ EMP: 20 EST: 2008
SALES (est): 2.25MM Privately Held
Web: www.elite4print.com
SIC: 2752 Offset printing

**(P-4604)**
**ELUM DESIGNS INC**
Also Called: Elum
8969 Kenamar Dr Ste 113, San Diego (92121-2441)
PHONE.................858 650-3586
Bradley Foster, CEO
Melissa Foster, *
Craig Ross, *
▲ EMP: 27 EST: 2002
SALES (est): 2.27MM Privately Held
Web: www.elumdesigns.com
SIC: 2752 Offset printing

**(P-4605)**
**EPAC LOS ANGELES LLC**
Also Called: Epac Flexible Packaging
5475 Daniels St, Chino (91710-9009)
PHONE.................844 623-8603
EMP: 15 EST: 2018
SALES (est): 2.54MM Privately Held
SIC: 2752 Wrapper and seal printing, lithographic

**(P-4606)**
**EPAC TECHNOLOGIES INC (PA)**
2561 Grant Ave, San Leandro (94579-2501)
PHONE.................510 317-7979
Sasha Dobrovolsky, CEO
James Gentilcore, *
▲ EMP: 124 EST: 1998
SALES (est): 40.04MM
SALES (corp-wide): 40.04MM Privately Held
Web: www.epac.com
SIC: 2752 Commercial printing, lithographic

**(P-4607)**
**ESSENCE PRINTING INC (PA)**
270 Oyster Point Blvd, South San Francisco (94080-1911)
PHONE.................650 952-5072
Sue Wei, Pr
Herbert Wei, VP
Edwin Wei Junior, VP
EMP: 48 EST: 1988
SQ FT: 40,000
SALES (est): 6.25MM
SALES (corp-wide): 6.25MM Privately Held
Web: www.essenceprinting.com
SIC: 2752 Offset printing

**(P-4608)**
**FGS-WI LLC**
5401 Jurupa St, Ontario (91761-3621)
PHONE.................909 467-8300
Ron Roger, Mgr
EMP: 21
SALES (corp-wide): 143.76MM Privately Held
Web: www.fgs.com
SIC: 2752 Offset printing
HQ: Fgs-Wi, Llc
1101 S Janesville St
Milton WI 53563
608 373-6500

**(P-4609)**
**FIREBRAND MEDIA LLC**
Also Called: Laguna Beach Magazine
900 Glenneyre St, Laguna Beach (92651-2707)
PHONE.................949 715-4100
Vincent Zepezauer, Managing Member
Steve Zepezauer, CEO
Carrie Robles, Dir
Cindy Mendaros, Off Mgr
EMP: 36 EST: 2015
SALES (est): 1.71MM Privately Held
Web: www.firebrandmediainc.com
SIC: 2752 Commercial printing, lithographic

**(P-4610)**
**FIRST IMPRESSIONS PRINTING INC**
25030 Viking St, Hayward (94545-2704)
PHONE.................510 784-0811
Gary E Stang, Pr
Nancy Stang, Treas
Jennifer Stang, Sec
EMP: 21 EST: 1988
SQ FT: 10,000
SALES (est): 892.13K Privately Held
Web: www.firstimpressionsprinting.com
SIC: 2752 Offset printing

**(P-4611)**
**FISHER PRINTING INC (PA)**
2257 N Pacific St, Orange (92865-2615)
PHONE.................714 998-9200
Thomas Fischer, Ch
Will Fischer, *
Tom Scarpati, *
EMP: 150 EST: 1933
SQ FT: 60,000
SALES (est): 47.46K
SALES (corp-wide): 47.46K Privately Held
Web: www.gofisher.net
SIC: 2752 Offset printing

**(P-4612)**
**FONG BROTHERS PRINTING INC (PA)**
320 Valley Dr, Brisbane (94005-1208)
PHONE.................415 467-1050
Tony D Fong, Pr
Paul Fong, *
Eugene Fong, *
Peter Fong, *
Nancy Wong, *
▲ EMP: 150 EST: 1971
SQ FT: 105,000
SALES (est): 23.49MM
SALES (corp-wide): 23.49MM Privately Held
Web: www.fbp.com
SIC: 2752 Offset printing

**(P-4613)**
**FONG FONG PRTRS LTHGRPHERS INC**
3009 65th St, Sacramento (95820-2021)
PHONE.................916 739-1313
TOLL FREE: 800
Karen Cotton, CEO
May L Fong, *
Marsha Fong, *
EMP: 43 EST: 1958
SQ FT: 50,000
SALES (est): 2.27MM Privately Held
Web: www.fongprinters.com
SIC: 2752 Offset printing

**(P-4614)**
**FOREST INVESTMENT GROUP INC**
Also Called: Unicorn Group
83 Hamilton Dr Ste 100, Novato (94949-5674)
PHONE.................415 459-2330
David A Brooks, CEO
Mark Schmidt, VP
EMP: 15 EST: 2003
SQ FT: 8,000
SALES (est): 2.32MM Privately Held
Web: www.unicornprintmail.com
SIC: 2752 2791 2789 7334 Offset printing; Typesetting; Bookbinding and related work; Photocopying and duplicating services

## 2752 - Commercial Printing, Lithographic (P-4615)

**(P-4615)**
**FOSTER PRINTING COMPANY INC**
700 E Alton Ave, Santa Ana (92705-5610)
**PHONE**..................................714 731-2000
Dennis M Blackburn, *CEO*
**EMP:** 18 **EST:** 1988
**SQ FT:** 35,000
**SALES (est):** 2.99MM **Privately Held**
**Web:** www.fosterprint.com
**SIC:** 2752 Offset printing

**(P-4616)**
**FRANCHISE SERVICES INC (PA)**
26722 Plaza, Mission Viejo (92691-8051)
**PHONE**..................................949 348-5400
Don F Lowe, *Ch Bd*
Daniel J Conger, *CFO*
**EMP:** 20 **EST:** 1968
**SQ FT:** 44,000
**SALES (est):** 19.99MM
**SALES (corp-wide):** 19.99MM **Privately Held**
**Web:** www.franserv.com
**SIC:** 2752 6159 Commercial printing, lithographic; Machinery and equipment finance leasing

**(P-4617)**
**FRICKE-PARKS PRESS INC**
Also Called: F-P Press
33250 Transit Ave, Union City (94587-2035)
P.O. Box 59390 (95159)
**PHONE**..................................510 489-6543
Robert C Parks, *Ch Bd*
David Brown, *
**EMP:** 22 **EST:** 1972
**SQ FT:** 50,000
**SALES (est):** 2.9MM **Privately Held**
**Web:** www.fricke-parks.com
**SIC:** 2752 Offset printing

**(P-4618)**
**FRUITRIDGE PRTG LITHOGRAPH INC (PA)**
3258 Stockton Blvd, Sacramento (95820-1418)
**PHONE**..................................916 452-9213
**TOLL FREE:** 800
Susan Hausmann, *Pr*
Karen Young, *
**EMP:** 39 **EST:** 1965
**SQ FT:** 28,500
**SALES (est):** 4.04MM
**SALES (corp-wide):** 4.04MM **Privately Held**
**Web:** www.deltaprintgroup.com
**SIC:** 2752 2796 Color lithography; Platemaking services

**(P-4619)**
**GORMAN CATALOG PRINTING INC**
492 Koller St, San Francisco (94110)
**EMP:** 25
**SIC:** 2752 Catalogs, lithographed

**(P-4620)**
**GORMAN MANUFACTURING COMPANY INC (PA)**
492 Koller St, San Francisco (94110)
**PHONE**..................................650 555-0000
**FAX:** 000 000-0000
**EMP:** 120 **EST:** 1985
**SALES (est):** 50.23MM **Privately Held**
**SIC:** 2752 Commercial printing, lithographic

**(P-4621)**
**GPA PRINTING CA LLC (PA)**
9655 De Soto Ave, Chatsworth (91311-5013)
**PHONE**..................................818 237-9771
Tom Wang, *Pr*
**EMP:** 15 **EST:** 2019
**SALES (est):** 25.12MM
**SALES (corp-wide):** 25.12MM **Privately Held**
**Web:** www.gpaglobal.net
**SIC:** 2752 Commercial printing, lithographic

**(P-4622)**
**GRAPHIC COLOR SYSTEMS INC**
Also Called: Continental Colorcraft
1166 W Garvey Ave, Monterey Park (91754-2511)
**PHONE**..................................323 283-3000
Andy Scheidegger, *Pr*
Linda Clarke, *
Maria Donhauser, *
**EMP:** 52 **EST:** 1968
**SQ FT:** 28,000
**SALES (est):** 4.97MM **Privately Held**
**Web:** www.continentalcolorcraft.com
**SIC:** 2752 2796 2791 2759 Offset printing; Color separations, for printing; Typesetting; Commercial printing, nec

**(P-4623)**
**GRAPHIC ENTERPRISES INC**
Also Called: Chromagraphics
440 Tesconi Cir, Santa Rosa (95401-4620)
**PHONE**..................................707 528-2644
**EMP:** 38 **EST:** 1981
**SALES (est):** 6.93MM **Privately Held**
**Web:** www.chromaprints.com
**SIC:** 2752 Offset printing

**(P-4624)**
**GRAPHIC VISIONS INC**
7119 Fair Ave, North Hollywood (91605-6304)
**PHONE**..................................818 845-8393
Randall Avazian, *CEO*
Kenneth Langer, *
▲ **EMP:** 23 **EST:** 1940
**SALES (est):** 4.36MM **Privately Held**
**Web:** www.graphicvisionsla.com
**SIC:** 2752 Offset printing

**(P-4625)**
**GSG PRINTING INC (PA)**
Also Called: Golden State Graphics
2304 Faraday Ave, Carlsbad (92008-7216)
**PHONE**..................................760 752-9500
David Hyman, *
▲ **EMP:** 20 **EST:** 2000
**SALES (est):** 2.28MM
**SALES (corp-wide):** 2.28MM **Privately Held**
**Web:** www.goldenstategraphics.com
**SIC:** 2752 Offset printing

**(P-4626)**
**GSL FINE LITHOGRAPHERS**
Also Called: Gsl
1281 National Dr, Sacramento (95834-1902)
**PHONE**..................................916 231-1410
Joe R Davis, *Ch Bd*
Chanel Decker, *
Darian Koberl, *
**EMP:** 38 **EST:** 1985
**SALES (est):** 1.63MM
**SALES (corp-wide):** 15B **Privately Held**
**Web:** www.gslitho.com
**SIC:** 2752 Offset printing
**HQ:** Consolidated Graphics, Inc. 5858 Westheimer Rd # 200 Houston TX 77057

**(P-4627)**
**GW REED PRINTING INC**
4071 Greystone Dr, Ontario (91761-3100)
**PHONE**..................................909 947-0599
**EMP:** 40
**SIC:** 2752 7336 Offset printing; Commercial art and graphic design

**(P-4628)**
**HANDBILL PRINTERS LP**
Also Called: Handbill Printers
820 E Parkridge Ave, Corona (92879-6611)
**PHONE**..................................951 547-5910
Don J Messick, *Pr*
Kenneth Messick, *Pt*
Michael Messick, *Pt*
Mark Messick, *Pt*
Dane Messick, *Pt*
**EMP:** 45 **EST:** 1984
**SQ FT:** 62,500
**SALES (est):** 5.59MM **Privately Held**
**Web:** www.handbillprinters.com
**SIC:** 2752 7336 Offset printing; Graphic arts and related design

**(P-4629)**
**HARMAN PRESS INC**
Also Called: Harman Envelopes
6840 Vineland Ave, North Hollywood (91605-6409)
**PHONE**..................................818 432-0570
Jay Goldner, *Pr*
Phillip Goldner, *
Deborah Goldner-watson, *Sec*
**EMP:** 38 **EST:** 1963
**SQ FT:** 10,000
**SALES (est):** 4.36MM **Privately Held**
**Web:** www.harmanpress.com
**SIC:** 2752 Offset printing

**(P-4630)**
**HERALD PRINTING LTD**
3536 Aliso Canyon Rd, Santa Paula (93060-9702)
**PHONE**..................................805 647-1870
Eric Linquist, *Pr*
Cathy Linquist, *Sec*
**EMP:** 15 **EST:** 1962
**SALES (est):** 2.46MM **Privately Held**
**Web:** www.precisiongraphicsolutions.com
**SIC:** 2752 Offset printing

**(P-4631)**
**HERDELL PRTG & LITHOGRAPHY INC**
340 Mccormick St, Saint Helena (94574-1419)
P.O. Box 72 (94574-0072)
**PHONE**..................................707 963-3634
Michael Herdell, *Pr*
Michael Herdell, *Pr*
Patricia A Herdell, *
**EMP:** 15 **EST:** 1951
**SQ FT:** 22,200
**SALES (est):** 1.27MM **Privately Held**
**Web:** www.herdellprinting.com
**SIC:** 2752 Offset printing

**(P-4632)**
**HJS GRAPHICS**
Also Called: Printing Connection , The
3533 Old Conejo Rd Ste 104, Newbury Park (91320-2156)
**PHONE**..................................818 782-5490
Henry Steenackers, *Pr*
**EMP:** 15 **EST:** 1983
**SALES (est):** 907.48K **Privately Held**
**SIC:** 2752 Offset printing

**(P-4633)**
**HNC PRINTING SERVICES LLC**
Also Called: Business Point Impressions
2490 Arnold Industrial Way Ste B, Concord (94520-5371)
**PHONE**..................................925 771-2080
**EMP:** 17 **EST:** 2006
**SALES (est):** 1.72MM **Privately Held**
**Web:** www.bpiprinting.com
**SIC:** 2752 Offset printing

**(P-4634)**
**HOUSE OF PRINTING INC**
3336 E Colorado Blvd, Pasadena (91107-3885)
**PHONE**..................................626 793-7034
Eugene F Pittroff Senior, *Pr*
Walter E Pittroff, *VP*
Edna Pittroff, *Sec*
Marguerite Pittroff, *Treas*
**EMP:** 22 **EST:** 1942
**SQ FT:** 6,500
**SALES (est):** 3.04MM **Privately Held**
**Web:** www.thehouseofprinting.com
**SIC:** 2752 2791 2789 Offset printing; Typesetting; Bookbinding and related work

**(P-4635)**
**IDEAL PRINTING COMPANY**
17855 Maclaren St, City Of Industry (91744-5799)
**PHONE**..................................626 964-2019
Richard Mancino, *Pr*
Yolanda Mancino, *VP*
**EMP:** 20 **EST:** 1961
**SQ FT:** 30,000
**SALES (est):** 947.54K **Privately Held**
**Web:** www.idealprintingcompany.com
**SIC:** 2752 Offset printing

**(P-4636)**
**IKONICK LLC**
705 W 9th St Apt 1404, Los Angeles (90015-1696)
**PHONE**..................................516 680-7765
Mark Mastrandrea, *Pr*
**EMP:** 35 **EST:** 2017
**SALES (est):** 675.54K **Privately Held**
**Web:** www.ikonick.com
**SIC:** 2752 7336 Commercial printing, lithographic; Commercial art and graphic design

**(P-4637)**
**IMAGEMOVER INC**
13031 Bradley Ave, Sylmar (91342-3832)
**PHONE**..................................818 485-8840
Ben Taylor, *Pr*
**EMP:** 17 **EST:** 2009
**SALES (est):** 3.49MM **Privately Held**
**Web:** www.imagemoverinc.com
**SIC:** 2752 Commercial printing, lithographic

**(P-4638)**
**IMAGEX INC**
5990 Stoneridge Dr Ste 112, Pleasanton (94588-4517)
**PHONE**..................................925 474-8100
Stan Poitras, *Pr*
**EMP:** 17 **EST:** 1986
**SALES (est):** 982.92K **Privately Held**
**Web:** www.thesourcinggroup.com
**SIC:** 2752 Offset printing

**(P-4639)**
**IMAGIC**
2810 N Lima St, Burbank (91504-2510)

## PRODUCTS & SERVICES SECTION
### 2752 - Commercial Printing, Lithographic (P-4663)

PHONE.................818 333-1670
**EMP:** 59
**SIC:** 2752 Commercial printing, lithographic

**(P-4640)**
**IMPACT CREATIVE LLC**
155 Dubois St Ste G, Santa Cruz (95060-2108)
PHONE.................831 824-9660
**EMP:** 15 **EST:** 2020
**SALES (est):** 83.91K **Privately Held**
**Web:** www.impactcreative.com
**SIC:** 2752 Offset printing

**(P-4641)**
**IMPACT PRINTING & GRAPHICS**
15150 Sierra Bonita Ln, Chino (91710-8903)
PHONE.................909 614-1678
Bill Mcginley, *Pr*
**EMP:** 25 **EST:** 1995
**SQ FT:** 14,000
**SALES (est):** 3.79MM **Privately Held**
**Web:** www.impactpkgco.com
**SIC:** 2752 Offset printing

**(P-4642)**
**IMPERIAL PRINTERS (PA)**
Also Called: Imperial Printers Rocket Copy
430 W Main St, El Centro (92243-3019)
PHONE.................760 352-4374
Rudy Rodgruegos, *Pr*
Marvin Wieben Junior, *VP*
Rodolfo Rodriguez, *VP*
**EMP:** 18 **EST:** 1977
**SQ FT:** 8,725
**SALES (est):** 2.37MM
**SALES (corp-wide):** 2.37MM **Privately Held**
**Web:** www.imperialprinters.com
**SIC:** 2752 2796 Offset printing; Letterpress plates, preparation of

**(P-4643)**
**IMPRESS COMMUNICATIONS LLC**
9320 Lurline Ave, Chatsworth (91311)
PHONE.................818 701-8800
Paul Marino, *CEO*
▲ **EMP:** 92 **EST:** 1974
**SQ FT:** 50,000
**SALES (est):** 10.5MM **Privately Held**
**Web:** www.impress1.com
**SIC:** 2752 7336 7319 Offset printing; Commercial art and graphic design; Display advertising service

**(P-4644)**
**INK & COLOR INC**
Also Called: Acuprint
5920 Bowcroft St, Los Angeles (90016-4302)
PHONE.................310 280-6060
Saman Sowlaty, *CEO*
Mojgan Sowalty, *
▲ **EMP:** 30 **EST:** 1985
**SQ FT:** 17,000
**SALES (est):** 5.19MM **Privately Held**
**Web:** www.acuprint.net
**SIC:** 2752 Offset printing

**(P-4645)**
**INK SPOT INC**
9737 Bell Ranch Dr, Santa Fe Springs (90670-2951)
PHONE.................626 338-4500
Somsak Reuanglith, *CEO*
**EMP:** 26 **EST:** 2004
**SALES (est):** 4.66MM **Privately Held**
**Web:** www.inkspotinc.com

**SIC:** 2752 Offset printing

**(P-4646)**
**INKOVATION INC**
Also Called: Signsusa.com
13659 Excelsior Dr, Santa Fe Springs (90670-5103)
PHONE.................800 465-4174
Janak Savaliya, *Pr*
**EMP:** 16 **EST:** 2010
**SALES (est):** 859.12K **Privately Held**
**Web:** www.inkovation.net
**SIC:** 2752 Offset printing

**(P-4647)**
**INKWRIGHT LLC**
5822 Research Dr, Huntington Beach (92649-1348)
PHONE.................714 892-3300
**EMP:** 30 **EST:** 2010
**SALES (est):** 4.17MM **Privately Held**
**Web:** www.inkwright.com
**SIC:** 2752 Offset and photolithographic printing

**(P-4648)**
**INLAND LITHO LLC**
Also Called: Inland Group
4305 E La Palma Ave, Anaheim (92807-1843)
PHONE.................714 993-6000
**EMP:** 60 **EST:** 1984
**SQ FT:** 40,000
**SALES (est):** 9.15MM **Privately Held**
**Web:** www.inlandgroupllc.com
**SIC:** 2752 Offset printing

**(P-4649)**
**INSTANT WEB LLC**
Also Called: Iwco Direct - Downey
7300 Flores St, Downey (90242-4010)
PHONE.................562 658-2020
Jake Hertel, *Brnch Mgr*
**EMP:** 130
**SALES (corp-wide):** 6.55B **Privately Held**
**Web:** www.iwco.com
**SIC:** 2752 Commercial printing, lithographic
**HQ:** Instant Web, Llc
7951 Powers Blvd
Chanhassen MN 55317
952 474-0961

**(P-4650)**
**INSUA GRAPHICS INCORPORATED**
9121 Glenoaks Blvd, Sun Valley (91352-2612)
PHONE.................818 767-7007
Jose Miguel Insua, *CEO*
Eric Insua, *
Albert Insua, *
◆ **EMP:** 35 **EST:** 1996
**SQ FT:** 28,000
**SALES (est):** 6.22MM **Privately Held**
**Web:** www.insua.com
**SIC:** 2752 Offset printing

**(P-4651)**
**INTEGRATED COMMUNICATIONS INC**
208 N Broadway, Santa Ana (92701-4863)
PHONE.................310 851-8066
Peter Levshin, *CEO*
David Humphrey, *
▲ **EMP:** 24 **EST:** 1986
**SALES (est):** 2.34MM **Privately Held**
**Web:** www.icla.com
**SIC:** 2752 Commercial printing, lithographic

**(P-4652)**
**INTEGRATED DIGITAL MEDIA**
Also Called: AlphaGraphics
14 Avila St, San Francisco (94123-2008)
PHONE.................415 627-8310
Manuel Torres, *Brnch Mgr*
**EMP:** 16
**Web:** www.alphagraphics.com
**SIC:** 2752 Commercial printing, lithographic
**HQ:** Integrated Digital Media
530 Howard St Ste 100
San Francisco CA 94105
415 986-4091

**(P-4653)**
**INTER-CITY PRINTING CO INC**
Also Called: Madison Street Press
614 Madison St, Oakland (94607-4726)
PHONE.................510 451-4775
Paul Murai, *Pr*
Miok Murai, *Sec*
**EMP:** 17 **EST:** 1909
**SQ FT:** 6,500
**SALES (est):** 3.76MM **Privately Held**
**Web:** www.madisonstreetpress.com
**SIC:** 2752 Offset printing

**(P-4654)**
**INTERLINK INC**
Also Called: Precision Plastics Packaging
3845 E Coronado St, Anaheim (92807-1606)
PHONE.................714 905-7700
Bob Bhagat, *Pr*
Hathin Bhagat, *
▲ **EMP:** 85 **EST:** 1963
**SQ FT:** 50,000
**SALES (est):** 11.23MM **Privately Held**
**Web:** www.pppc.com
**SIC:** 2752 Commercial printing, lithographic

**(P-4655)**
**J P GRAPHICS INC**
Also Called: JP
3310 Woodward Ave, Santa Clara (95054-2627)
PHONE.................408 235-8821
Joan Escover, *CEO*
▲ **EMP:** 40 **EST:** 1998
**SQ FT:** 14,000
**SALES (est):** 5.23MM **Privately Held**
**Web:** www.jp-graphics.com
**SIC:** 2752 Offset printing

**(P-4656)**
**JAMES ALLYN INC**
6575 Trinity Ct Ste B, Dublin (94568-2643)
**EMP:** 16 **EST:** 2001
**SALES (est):** 2.6MM **Privately Held**
**Web:** www.jamesallyn.com
**SIC:** 2752 Offset printing

**(P-4657)**
**JEB-PHI INC**
Also Called: PIP Printing
10417 Lakewood Blvd, Downey (90241-2744)
PHONE.................562 861-0863
Bruce Pansky, *Pr*
Phillip Pansky, *VP*
Belinda Pansky, *Sec*
**EMP:** 16 **EST:** 1970
**SQ FT:** 2,900
**SALES (est):** 1.97MM **Privately Held**
**Web:** www.pip.com
**SIC:** 2752 Offset printing

**(P-4658)**
**K-1 PACKAGING GROUP**
Also Called: K-1 Packaging Group
2001 W Mission Blvd, Pomona (91766-1020)
PHONE.................626 964-9384
**EMP:** 134
**Web:** www.k1packaging.com
**SIC:** 2752 Offset and photolithographic printing
**PA:** K-1 Packaging Group Llc
17989 Arenth Ave

**(P-4659)**
**K-1 PACKAGING GROUP LLC (PA)**
17989 Arenth Ave, City Of Industry (91748-1126)
PHONE.................626 964-9384
Mike Tsai, *Pr*
◆ **EMP:** 77 **EST:** 1992
**SALES (est):** 23.05MM **Privately Held**
**Web:** www.k1packaging.com
**SIC:** 2752 Offset and photolithographic printing

**(P-4660)**
**KELMSCOTT COMMUNICATIONS LLC**
Also Called: Orange County Printing
2485 Da Vinci, Irvine (92614-5844)
PHONE.................949 475-1900
Paz Calaci, *Brnch Mgr*
**EMP:** 320
**SALES (corp-wide):** 15B **Privately Held**
**Web:** www.rrd.com
**SIC:** 2752 Offset printing
**HQ:** Kelmscott Communications Llc
5858 Westheimer Rd # 410
Houston TX 77057
713 787-0977

**(P-4661)**
**KINDRED LITHO INCORPORATED**
10833 Bell Ct, Rancho Cucamonga (91730-4835)
PHONE.................909 944-4015
Kurt Kindred, *Pr*
Cherie Kindred, *Sec*
**EMP:** 36 **EST:** 1971
**SQ FT:** 8,000
**SALES (est):** 1.18MM **Privately Held**
**Web:** www.kindredcorp.com
**SIC:** 2752 Offset printing

**(P-4662)**
**KM PRINTING PRODUCTION INC**
218 Longden Ave, Irwindale (91706-1328)
PHONE.................626 821-0008
Chim Moon Ming, *Pr*
Kerwin Ngo, *VP*
Wendy Lui, *Acctg Mgr*
**EMP:** 18 **EST:** 1994
**SQ FT:** 600
**SALES (est):** 909.03K **Privately Held**
**Web:** www.kmppi.com
**SIC:** 2752 Offset printing

**(P-4663)**
**KOVIN CORPORATION INC**
Also Called: Neb Cal Printing
9240 Mira Este Ct, San Diego (92126-6336)
PHONE.................858 558-0100
Mervin Kodesh, *Pr*
Sandra Kodesh, *
Debbie Dykstra, *
**EMP:** 30 **EST:** 1984

## 2752 - Commercial Printing, Lithographic (P-4664)

SQ FT: 10,000
SALES (est): 2.08MM **Privately Held**
SIC: **2752** 2789  Offset printing; Bookbinding and related work

**(P-4664)**
**KP LLC (PA)**
13951 Washington Ave, San Leandro (94578)
PHONE..................510 346-0729
Brett Olszewski, *CEO*
▲ EMP: 80 EST: 1929
SQ FT: 12,000
SALES (est): 100.08MM
SALES (corp-wide): 100.08MM **Privately Held**
Web: www.kpcorp.com
SIC: **2752** 7334 7331 7374  Offset printing; Photocopying and duplicating services; Direct mail advertising services; Computer graphics service

**(P-4665)**
**KP LLC**
K/P Graphics-Salem Division
13951 Washington Ave, San Leandro (94578-3220)
PHONE..................510 346-0729
TOLL FREE: 800
Keith Whittier, *Mgr*
EMP: 22
SALES (corp-wide): 100.08MM **Privately Held**
Web: www.kpcorporation.com
SIC: **2752** 8742 7331 2796  Offset printing; Management consulting services; Direct mail advertising services; Platemaking services
PA: Kp Llc
  13951 Washington Ave
  510 346-0729

**(P-4666)**
**KP LLC**
Also Called: K P Graphics
1134 Enterprise St, Stockton (95204-2316)
P.O. Box 8900 (95208-0900)
PHONE..................209 466-6761
Roberta Morris, *Mgr*
EMP: 25
SQ FT: 10,000
SALES (corp-wide): 100.08MM **Privately Held**
Web: www.kpcorporation.com
SIC: **2752**  Offset printing
PA: Kp Llc
  13951 Washington Ave
  510 346-0729

**(P-4667)**
**L & L PRINTERS CARLSBAD LLC**
Also Called: Specialist Media Group
6200 Yarrow Dr, Carlsbad (92011-1537)
PHONE..................760 477-0321
William Anderson, *Pr*
EMP: 50 EST: 2006
SALES (est): 5.02MM **Privately Held**
Web: www.llprinters.com
SIC: **2752**  Offset printing

**(P-4668)**
**L T LITHO & PRINTING CO**
16811 Noyes Ave, Irvine (92606-5122)
PHONE..................949 466-8584
Craig Thomas, *Pr*
Mark Thomas, *
EMP: 22 EST: 1970
SQ FT: 16,000
SALES (est): 598.7K **Privately Held**

Web: www.ltlitho.net
SIC: **2752** 2759  Offset printing; Commercial printing, nec

**(P-4669)**
**LA PRINTING & GRAPHICS  INC**
Also Called: L A Press
13951 S Main St, Los Angeles (90061-2140)
PHONE..................310 527-4526
Kevin Sheu Chhim Kaing, *CEO*
Sheu C Kevin Kaing, *
Lor Yik, *Corporate Secretary*
EMP: 26 EST: 1989
SQ FT: 32,000
SALES (est): 2.22MM **Privately Held**
SIC: **2752**  Offset printing

**(P-4670)**
**LABOR LAW CENTER INC**
Also Called: Laborlawcenter.com
3501 W Garry Ave, Santa Ana (92704-6422)
PHONE..................800 745-9970
Duyen La, *Pr*
EMP: 25 EST: 2004
SALES (est): 5.71MM **Privately Held**
Web: www.laborlawcenter.com
SIC: **2752**  Commercial printing, lithographic

**(P-4671)**
**LAHLOUH  INC (PA)**
Also Called: Lahlouh
1649 Adrian Rd, Burlingame (94010-2103)
P.O. Box 4345 (94011-4345)
PHONE..................650 692-6600
John Lahlouh, *Pr*
Fadi Lahlouh, *
Michael Lahlouh, *
▲ EMP: 176 EST: 1981
SALES (est): 48.85MM
SALES (corp-wide): 48.85MM **Privately Held**
Web: www.lahlouh.com
SIC: **2752**  Offset printing

**(P-4672)**
**LAYTON PRINTING & MAILING**
Also Called: Layton Printing
1538 Arrow Hwy, La Verne (91750-5318)
PHONE..................909 592-4419
Michael Layton, *Pr*
Mary Ellen Layton, *Sec*
EMP: 18 EST: 1996
SQ FT: 20,000
SALES (est): 970.71K **Privately Held**
Web: www.laytonprinting.com
SIC: **2752**  Offset printing

**(P-4673)**
**LEEWOOD PRESS  INC**
398 Beach Rd, Burlingame (94010-2004)
PHONE..................415 896-0513
Tom W Lee, *Pr*
EMP: 20 EST: 1992
SALES (est): 768.6K **Privately Held**
Web: www.leewoodpress.com
SIC: **2752**  Offset printing

**(P-4674)**
**LEGAL VISION GROUP  LLC**
2030 Paddock Ln, Norco (92860-2663)
PHONE..................310 945-5550
EMP: 30 EST: 2018
SALES (est): 521.33K **Privately Held**
Web: www.legalvisiongroup.com
SIC: **2752** 7389 7374 7335  Commercial printing, lithographic; Mailing and messenger services; Data processing and preparation; Commercial photography

**(P-4675)**
**LEO LAM  INC**
Also Called: A & M Printing
1348 Terminal St, West Sacramento (95691-3515)
PHONE..................925 484-3690
Leo Lam, *Pr*
Amy Chan, *
EMP: 30 EST: 1983
SALES (est): 2.51MM **Privately Held**
Web: www.lppprints.com
SIC: **2752** 7331 2789  Offset printing; Direct mail advertising services; Bookbinding and related work

**(P-4676)**
**LESTER LITHOGRAPH  INC**
1128 N Gilbert St, Anaheim (92801-1401)
PHONE..................714 491-3981
Robert Miller, *CEO*
Georgiana Lester, *
Larry Lester, *
Larita Miller, *
James Jim Witt, *VP*
EMP: 50 EST: 1980
SQ FT: 25,000
SALES (est): 4.31MM **Privately Held**
Web: www.lesterlitho.com
SIC: **2752**  Offset printing

**(P-4677)**
**LETTERHEAD FACTORY  INC**
1007 E Dominguez St Ste H, Carson (90746-7252)
PHONE..................310 538-3321
Richard W Rice, *CEO*
EMP: 15 EST: 1986
SQ FT: 5,000
SALES (est): 797.81K **Privately Held**
Web: www.letterheadfactory.com
SIC: **2752**  Offset printing

**(P-4678)**
**LICHER DIRECT MAIL  INC**
980 Seco St, Pasadena (91103-2816)
PHONE..................626 795-3333
Wayne Licher Senior, *Pr*
Wayne Licher Junior, *VP*
Besse Licher, *Sec*
EMP: 35 EST: 1946
SQ FT: 17,000
SALES (est): 5.35MM **Privately Held**
Web: www.licherdm.com
SIC: **2752** 7331  Offset printing; Direct mail advertising services

**(P-4679)**
**LITHOGRAPHIX  INC (PA)**
12250 Crenshaw Blvd, Hawthorne (90250-3332)
PHONE..................323 770-1000
Herbert Zebrack, *Pr*
Jeffrey Zebrack, *
Victor Wolfe, *
▲ EMP: 305 EST: 1949
SQ FT: 250,000
SALES (est): 45.78MM
SALES (corp-wide): 45.78MM **Privately Held**
Web: lithographix.com.lithographix.com
SIC: **2752** 2759  Offset printing; Commercial printing, nec

**(P-4680)**
**LITHOTYPE COMPANY  INC (PA)**
333 Point San Bruno Blvd, South San Francisco (94080-4917)
PHONE..................650 871-1750
Aphos Ikonomou, *Pr*
Penelope Rich, *

Robert Shoreen, *
Carl Haynes, *Parts Vice President*
Greg Edwall, *
▲ EMP: 65 EST: 1940
SQ FT: 41,000
SALES (est): 5.46MM
SALES (corp-wide): 5.46MM **Privately Held**
Web: www.lithotype.com
SIC: **2752**  Wrappers, lithographed

**(P-4681)**
**LIVING WAY INDUSTRIES  INC**
Also Called: Creative Graphic Services
20734 Centre Pointe Pkwy, Santa Clarita (91350-2966)
PHONE..................661 298-3200
Ronald Niner, *Pr*
Charlene E Niner, *Sec*
EMP: 18 EST: 1970
SQ FT: 22,500
SALES (est): 3.16MM **Privately Held**
Web: www.creativegraphicservices.com
SIC: **2752**  Commercial printing, lithographic

**(P-4682)**
**LOBCOM  INC**
Also Called: Lob.com
2261 Market St Pmb 5668, San Francisco (94114-1612)
PHONE..................415 894-9979
Leore Avidar, *CEO*
Ryan Ferrier, *
Madhu Jagannathan, *
EMP: 141 EST: 2013
SALES (est): 39.06MM **Privately Held**
Web: www.lob.com
SIC: **2752**  Offset and photolithographic printing

**(P-4683)**
**LOMBARD ENTERPRISES  INC**
Also Called: Lombard Graphics
3619 San Gabriel River Pkwy, Pico Rivera (90660-1403)
PHONE..................562 692-7070
Stephen R Lombard, *Pr*
Ross Lombard, *VP*
EMP: 20 EST: 1993
SQ FT: 10,000
SALES (est): 2.46MM **Privately Held**
Web: www.lombardgraphics.com
SIC: **2752**  Offset printing

**(P-4684)**
**LUMAPRINTS**
955 E Ball Rd, Anaheim (92805-5916)
PHONE..................800 380-6038
EMP: 18 EST: 2017
SALES (est): 3.14MM **Privately Held**
Web: www.lumaprints.com
SIC: **2752**  Commercial printing, lithographic

**(P-4685)**
**MADISN/GRHAM CLOR GRAPHICS INC**
Also Called: Colorgraphics
150 N Myers St, Los Angeles (90033-2109)
PHONE..................323 261-7171
Cappy Childs, *CEO*
Arthur Bell, *
Chris Madison, *
Terry Bell, *
▲ EMP: 380 EST: 1953
SQ FT: 96,000
SALES (est): 4.63MM **Privately Held**
Web: www.advantageinc.com
SIC: **2752** 7336 2796  Offset printing; Graphic arts and related design; Platemaking services

## PRODUCTS & SERVICES SECTION
## 2752 - Commercial Printing, Lithographic (P-4709)

**(P-4686)**
**MAIL HANDLING GROUP INC**
Also Called: Mail Handling Services
2840 Madonna Dr, Fullerton (92835-1830)
PHONE..................................952 975-5000
Brian Ostenso, President COOC
Michael Murphy, *
EMP: 120 EST: 1977
SALES (est): 1.87MM Privately Held
SIC: 2752 7331 7374 Offset printing; Mailing service; Data processing service

**(P-4687)**
**MAJESTIC PRINT INC**
Also Called: Majestic Printing Systems
4017 Trail Creek Rd, Riverside (92505-5863)
P.O. Box 7912 (92375-1112)
PHONE..................................951 509-2539
Isaiah Rudy, Pr
EMP: 15 EST: 1981
SQ FT: 6,500
SALES (est): 2.14MM Privately Held
Web: www.majesticprintinc.com
SIC: 2752 2759 Offset printing; Commercial printing, nec

**(P-4688)**
**MAN-GROVE INDUSTRIES INC**
Also Called: Lithocraft Co
1201 N Miller St, Anaheim (92806-1933)
PHONE..................................714 630-3020
EMP: 64
Web: www.lithocraft-files.com
SIC: 2752 Offset printing

**(P-4689)**
**MARINA GRAPHIC CENTER INC**
Also Called: Brotherwise Games
12901 Cerise Ave, Hawthorne (90250-5520)
PHONE..................................310 970-1777
EMP: 115 EST: 1964
SALES (est): 8.13MM Privately Held
Web: www.marinagraphics.com
SIC: 2752 Offset printing

**(P-4690)**
**MARRS PRINTING INC**
Also Called: Mars Printing and Packaging
860 Tucker Ln, City Of Industry (91789-2914)
PHONE..................................909 594-9459
Walter H Marrs, CEO
Scott Marrs, *
Teresa Grisby, *
Jackie Marrs, *
EMP: 82 EST: 1971
SQ FT: 27,000
SALES (est): 9.96MM Privately Held
Web: www.marrs.com
SIC: 2752 Offset printing

**(P-4691)**
**MATSUDA HOUSE PRINTING INC**
Also Called: B & G House of Printing
1825 W 169th St Ste A, Gardena (90247-5270)
PHONE..................................310 532-1533
Benjamin Matsuda, CEO
Darren Matsuda, *
Patsy Matsuda, *
▲ EMP: 31 EST: 1975
SALES (est): 2.35MM Privately Held
Web: www.bgprinting.com
SIC: 2752 Lithographing on metal

**(P-4692)**
**MEKONG PRINTING INC**
Also Called: Mk Printing
2421 W 1st St, Santa Ana (92703-3509)
PHONE..................................714 558-9595
Hoan Truong, CEO
Hoan Truong, Pr
Nancy Luu, VP
EMP: 22 EST: 1986
SQ FT: 20,000
SALES (est): 2.16MM Privately Held
SIC: 2752 Offset printing

**(P-4693)**
**MERIDIAN GRAPHICS INC**
2652 Dow Ave, Tustin (92780-7208)
PHONE..................................949 833-3500
David R Melin, Pr
Paul Valencia, Pr
David Melin, *
Craig Miller, *
▲ EMP: 65 EST: 2000
SQ FT: 40,000
SALES (est): 3.84MM Privately Held
Web: www.mglitho.com
SIC: 2752 2759 Offset printing; Letterpress printing

**(P-4694)**
**MIDNIGHT OIL AGENCY LLC**
Also Called: Midnight Oil Agency, Inc.
3800 W Vanowen St Ste 101, Burbank (91505-1173)
PHONE..................................818 295-6100
EMP: 285 EST: 1989
SALES (est): 17.06MM
SALES (corp-wide): 430.34MM Privately Held
Web: www.moagency.com
SIC: 2752 8742 Commercial printing, lithographic; Marketing consulting services
PA: The Imagine Group Llc
1000 Valley Park Dr
800 942-7088

**(P-4695)**
**MINALOAS INC**
Also Called: Lava Products
2358 E Walnut Ave, Fullerton (92831-4937)
PHONE..................................949 951-7191
Michael Freitas, CEO
▲ EMP: 22 EST: 1997
SALES (est): 4.73MM Privately Held
Web: www.lavapartners.com
SIC: 2752 Offset printing

**(P-4696)**
**MITTERA GROUP INC**
Also Called: Mittera-CA
3791 Catalina St, Los Alamitos (90720-2402)
PHONE..................................562 598-2446
EMP: 26 EST: 2020
SALES (est): 2.6MM Privately Held
Web: www.mittera.com
SIC: 2752 Offset printing

**(P-4697)**
**MODERN PRINTING & MAILING INC**
3535 Enterprise St, San Diego (92110-3211)
PHONE..................................619 222-0535
Steve Hire, Pr
Alice Hire, *
EMP: 28 EST: 1962
SQ FT: 12,000
SALES (est): 663.34K Privately Held
Web: modern-printing-and-mailing-in-san-diego-ca.cityfos.com
SIC: 2752 7331 2759 Offset printing; Mailing service; Commercial printing, nec

**(P-4698)**
**MODY ENTREPRENEURS INC**
Also Called: Copy 2 Copy
8975 Complex Dr, San Diego (92123-1405)
PHONE..................................858 292-8100
Nimish Mody, Pr
EMP: 15 EST: 2000
SQ FT: 4,300
SALES (est): 2.67MM Privately Held
Web: www.copy2copy.com
SIC: 2752 Offset printing

**(P-4699)**
**MOLINO COMPANY**
Also Called: Melcast
13712 Alondra Blvd, Cerritos (90703-2316)
PHONE..................................323 726-1000
Melchor Castano, Pr
EMP: 85 EST: 1976
SQ FT: 200,000
SALES (est): 6.22MM Privately Held
SIC: 2752 Offset printing

**(P-4700)**
**MONARCH LITHO INC (PA)**
1501 Date St, Montebello (90640-6324)
PHONE..................................323 727-0300
Robert Lopez, CEO
George Lopez, VP
Victor Neri, Sec
EMP: 50 EST: 1974
SQ FT: 153,000
SALES (est): 18.21MM
SALES (corp-wide): 18.21MM Privately Held
Web: www.monarchlitho.com
SIC: 2752 Offset printing

**(P-4701)**
**MOQUIN PRESS INC**
555 Harbor Blvd, Belmont (94002-4020)
PHONE..................................650 592-0575
EMP: 60 EST: 1985
SQ FT: 22,000
SALES (est): 8.39MM Privately Held
Web: www.moquinpress.com
SIC: 2752 Offset printing

**(P-4702)**
**NANOGRAFIX CORPORATION**
3820 Valley Centre Dr Ste 705, San Diego (92130-2331)
PHONE..................................858 524-3295
Dan Lieberman, CEO
EMP: 18 EST: 2015
SALES (est): 205.75K Privately Held
Web: www.nanografix.com
SIC: 2752 Commercial printing, lithographic

**(P-4703)**
**NATIONAL GRAPHICS LLC**
Also Called: Jano Graphics
200 N Elevar St, Oxnard (93030-7969)
PHONE..................................805 644-9212
Mike Scher, Pr
EMP: 40 EST: 1960
SALES (est): 12.42MM Privately Held
Web: www.janoprint.com
SIC: 2752 Offset printing

**(P-4704)**
**NATIONAL PRINT + PROMO**
2321 Circadian Way, Santa Rosa (95407-5416)
P.O. Box 3109 (94927-3109)
PHONE..................................707 576-6375
EMP: 40 EST: 2018
SALES (est): 527.22K Privately Held
Web: www.nationalprintpromo.net
SIC: 2752 Offset printing

**(P-4705)**
**NEYENESCH PRINTERS INC**
2750 Kettner Blvd, San Diego (92101-1295)
P.O. Box 81184 (92138-1184)
PHONE..................................619 297-2281
Carl A Bentley, CEO
Clifford Neyenesch, *
Dave Pauley, *
Kandy Neyenesch, *
EMP: 70 EST: 1899
SQ FT: 30,000
SALES (est): 18.65MM Privately Held
Web: www.neyenesch.com
SIC: 2752 Offset printing

**(P-4706)**
**NIKNEJAD INC**
Also Called: Colornet Press
6855 Hayvenhurst Ave, Van Nuys (91406-4718)
PHONE..................................310 477-0407
Kamran Niknejad, Pr
Rashid Yassamy, *
Sima Fouladi, *
EMP: 40 EST: 1981
SQ FT: 5,000
SALES (est): 3.31MM Privately Held
Web: www.colornetpress.com
SIC: 2752 7336 2791 Offset printing; Graphic arts and related design; Typesetting

**(P-4707)**
**NO BOUNDARIES INC**
Also Called: Greenbox Art and Culture
789 Gateway Center Way, San Diego (92102-4539)
PHONE..................................619 266-2349
Thomas Capp, CEO
Karen Capp, *
▲ EMP: 50 EST: 2002
SQ FT: 3,500
SALES (est): 1.81MM Privately Held
Web: www.shopgreenboxart.com
SIC: 2752 Offset printing

**(P-4708)**
**NSS ENTERPRISES**
Also Called: Cyber Press
3380 Viso Ct, Santa Clara (95054-2625)
PHONE..................................408 970-9200
Chuck Nijmeh, Pr
Adam Zeno, VP
EMP: 22 EST: 1996
SALES (est): 6.37MM Privately Held
Web: www.cyberpress.net
SIC: 2752 Offset printing

**(P-4709)**
**OAKMEAD PRTG REPRODUCTION INC**
Also Called: Oakmead Printing
233 E Weddell Dr Ste G, Sunnyvale (94089-1659)
PHONE..................................408 734-5505
TOLL FREE: 888
Tony Ngo, Pr
EMP: 50 EST: 1978
SQ FT: 2,000
SALES (est): 2.12MM Privately Held
Web: www.oakmead.com
SIC: 2752 2791 Offset printing; Typesetting, computer controlled

## 2752 - Commercial Printing, Lithographic (P-4710)

**(P-4710)**
**OCPC INC**
Also Called: The Orange County Printing Co
2485 Da Vinci, Irvine (92614-5844)
PHONE.................................949 475-1900
Miguel Jacobowitz, Prin
**EMP:** 60 **EST:** 1986
**SQ FT:** 18,000
**SALES (est):** 4.91MM **Privately Held**
Web: www.rrd.com
**SIC: 2752** Offset printing

**(P-4711)**
**ODCOMBE PRESS (NASHVILLE)**
Also Called: Haynes Publications
2801 Townsgate Rd, Westlake Village (91361-3010)
PHONE.................................615 793-5414
John H Haynes, Ch Bd
▲ **EMP:** 26 **EST:** 1993
**SALES (est):** 2.07MM **Privately Held**
Web: www.haynes.com
**SIC: 2752** Offset printing
HQ: Haynes Group Limited
Sparkford
Yeovil BA22
196 344-0635

**(P-4712)**
**ONEIL DIGITAL SOLUTIONS LLC**
12655 Beatrice St, Los Angeles (90066-7300)
PHONE.................................310 448-6407
David Woodley, Contrlr
**EMP:** 201
**SALES (corp-wide):** 335.64MM **Privately Held**
Web: www.oneildigitalsolutions.com
**SIC: 2752** 5045 7379 Commercial printing, lithographic; Computer software; Computer related consulting services
HQ: O'neil Digital Solutions, Llc
3100 E Plano Pkwy
Plano TX 75074
972 881-1282

**(P-4713)**
**ORANGE COAST REPROGRAPHICS INC**
Also Called: Mouse Graphics
659 W 19th St, Costa Mesa (92627-2715)
PHONE.................................949 548-5571
Constance Mary Lane, CEO
**EMP:** 22 **EST:** 1947
**SQ FT:** 9,000
**SALES (est):** 3.22MM **Privately Held**
Web: www.sendmouse.com
**SIC: 2752** 7336 2789 2759 Commercial printing, lithographic; Commercial art and graphic design; Bookbinding and related work; Commercial printing, nec

**(P-4714)**
**PACER PRINT**
4101 Guardian St, Simi Valley (93063-3382)
PHONE.................................888 305-3144
Peter Varady, CEO
Naomi Gonzalez, *
**EMP:** 35 **EST:** 2016
**SALES (est):** 7.27MM **Privately Held**
Web: www.pacerprint.com
**SIC: 2752** Offset printing

**(P-4715)**
**PACIFIC WEST LITHO INC**
Also Called: Pacific West
3291 E Miraloma Ave, Anaheim (92806-1910)
PHONE.................................714 579-0868
Chang Che Chou, CEO
**EMP:** 70 **EST:** 1984
**SQ FT:** 24,000
**SALES (est):** 6.39MM **Privately Held**
Web: www.pacificwestlitho.com
**SIC: 2752** Lithographing on metal

**(P-4716)**
**PACKAGING MANUFACTURING INC**
2285 Michael Faraday Dr Ste 12, San Diego (92154-7926)
PHONE.................................619 498-9199
Salvatore Anza, CEO
Jim Belcher, *
Gayle Cronin, *
**EMP:** 240 **EST:** 2009
**SALES (est):** 30MM **Privately Held**
Web: www.pmpackaging.com
**SIC: 2752** Commercial printing, lithographic

**(P-4717)**
**PAN PACIFIC PRINTING PRESS INC**
Also Called: Pacific Printing
1899 N Helm Ave, Fresno (93727-1612)
PHONE.................................559 252-1624
**EMP:** 35
Web: www.pacificprinting.net
**SIC: 2752** Commercial printing, lithographic

**(P-4718)**
**PARKS GROUP EY**
1515 10th St, Modesto (95354-0726)
PHONE.................................209 576-2568
**EMP:** 25 **EST:** 2018
**SALES (est):** 1.08MM **Privately Held**
Web: www.theparksgroup.com
**SIC: 2752** Offset printing

**(P-4719)**
**PATSONS PRESS**
Also Called: Patsons Media Group
3000 Scott Blvd Ste 101, Santa Clara (95054-3321)
PHONE.................................408 567-0911
Patricia Dellamano, Pr
Mark Dellamano, *
Joseph Dellamano, *
**EMP:** 50 **EST:** 1968
**SALES (est):** 1.19MM **Privately Held**
Web: www.advantageinc.com
**SIC: 2752** Offset printing

**(P-4720)**
**PAUL BAKER PRINTING INC**
4251 Gateway Park Blvd, Sacramento (95834-1975)
PHONE.................................916 969-8317
Kasey Cotulla, Pr
James Davis, *
**EMP:** 32 **EST:** 1990
**SALES (est):** 2.44MM **Privately Held**
Web: www.deltaprintgroup.com
**SIC: 2752** Offset printing

**(P-4721)**
**PDF PRINT COMMUNICATIONS INC (PA)**
2630 E 28th St, Long Beach (90755-2202)
PHONE.................................562 426-6978
Robert Albert Mullaney, CEO
Kevin J Mullaney, *
Shirley Mullaney, *
**EMP:** 52 **EST:** 1973
**SQ FT:** 23,000
**SALES (est):** 16.91MM
**SALES (corp-wide):** 16.91MM **Privately Held**
Web: www.pdfpc.com
**SIC: 2752** 2761 Offset printing; Manifold business forms

**(P-4722)**
**PEGASUS INTERPRINT INC**
7111 Hayvenhurst Ave, Van Nuys (91406-3807)
PHONE.................................800 926-9873
▲ **EMP:** 24
**SIC: 2752** Offset printing

**(P-4723)**
**PGI PACIFIC GRAPHICS INTL**
Also Called: Pgi
14938 Nelson Ave, City Of Industry (91744-4330)
PHONE.................................626 336-7707
Yvonne Castillo Wasson, CEO
Ricardo Wasson, *
**EMP:** 25 **EST:** 1989
**SQ FT:** 17,000
**SALES (est):** 4.6MM **Privately Held**
Web: www.pacgraphics.com
**SIC: 2752** 2759 8742 7331 Offset printing; Commercial printing, nec; Marketing consulting services; Mailing service

**(P-4724)**
**PHOENIX MARKETING SERVICES INC**
651 Wharton Dr, Claremont (91711-4819)
PHONE.................................909 399-4000
▲ **EMP:** 95
Web: www.phoenixmarketing.net
**SIC: 2752** 5199 Offset printing; Advertising specialties

**(P-4725)**
**PINNACLE DIVERSIFIED INC**
Also Called: Pinnacle Press
1248 San Luis Obispo St, Hayward (94544-7916)
PHONE.................................510 400-7929
Jason Kim, Pr
Rui Wang, VP
**EMP:** 17 **EST:** 1994
**SQ FT:** 13,000
**SALES (est):** 1.3MM **Privately Held**
**SIC: 2752** Offset printing

**(P-4726)**
**PJ PRINTERS INC**
1530 Lakeview Loop, Anaheim (92807-1819)
PHONE.................................714 779-8484
**EMP:** 45 **EST:** 1983
**SALES (est):** 7.02MM **Privately Held**
Web: www.pjprinters.com
**SIC: 2752** Commercial printing, lithographic

**(P-4727)**
**PM CORPORATE GROUP INC (PA)**
Also Called: PM Packaging
2285 Michael Faraday Dr Ste 12, San Diego (92154-7926)
PHONE.................................800 343-3139
Salvatore Anza, CEO
Jim Belcher, Pr
Gayle Cronin, COO
**EMP:** 56 **EST:** 2007
**SALES (est):** 150.21MM
**SALES (corp-wide):** 150.21MM **Privately Held**
Web: www.pmpackaging.com
**SIC: 2752** Offset printing

**(P-4728)**
**POSTAL INSTANT PRESS INC (HQ)**
Also Called: PIP Printing
26722 Plaza, Mission Viejo (92691-8051)
P.O. Box 9077 (92690-9077)
PHONE.................................949 348-5000
Don F Lowe, CEO
Dan F Lowe, *
Richard Low, *
Thomas Muller, *
Dan Conger, *
**EMP:** 40 **EST:** 1996
**SQ FT:** 25,000
**SALES (est):** 2.61MM
**SALES (corp-wide):** 19.99MM **Privately Held**
Web: www.pip.com
**SIC: 2752** 6159 Offset printing; Machinery and equipment finance leasing
PA: Franchise Services, Inc.
26722 Plaza
949 348-5400

**(P-4729)**
**PRECISION LITHO INC**
Also Called: Rrd Pckaging Solutions - Vista
1185 Joshua Way, Vista (92081-7840)
PHONE.................................760 727-9400
Daniel Knotts, Pr
Elif Sagsen-ercel, Ex VP
**EMP:** 35 **EST:** 1981
**SQ FT:** 40,000
**SALES (est):** 6.97MM
**SALES (corp-wide):** 15B **Privately Held**
Web: www.plitho.com
**SIC: 2752** Offset printing
HQ: Consolidated Graphics, Inc.
5858 Westheimer Rd # 200
Houston TX 77057

**(P-4730)**
**PRECISION OFFSET INC**
Also Called: Precision Services Group
15201 Woodlawn Ave, Tustin (92780-6418)
PHONE.................................949 752-1714
Lawrence Smith, CEO
**EMP:** 75 **EST:** 1979
**SQ FT:** 15,000
**SALES (est):** 9.24MM **Privately Held**
Web: www.precisionservicesgroup.com
**SIC: 2752** Offset printing

**(P-4731)**
**PRIMARY COLOR SYSTEMS CORP**
3500 W Burbank Blvd, Burbank (91505-2268)
PHONE.................................818 643-5944
**EMP:** 53
**SALES (corp-wide):** 47.93MM **Privately Held**
Web: www.pchagencyla.com
**SIC: 2752** Offset printing
PA: Primary Color Systems Corporation
11130 Holder St Ste 210
949 660-7080

**(P-4732)**
**PRINTERY INC**
1762 Kaiser Ave, Irvine (92614-5706)
PHONE.................................949 757-1930
Massis Chahbazian, CEO
▲ **EMP:** 15 **EST:** 1989
**SQ FT:** 10,000
**SALES (est):** 2.19MM **Privately Held**
Web: www.theprintery.com
**SIC: 2752** Offset printing

## PRODUCTS & SERVICES SECTION
### 2752 - Commercial Printing, Lithographic (P-4755)

**(P-4733)**
**PRINTING MANAGEMENT ASSOCIATES**
17128 Edwards Rd, Cerritos (90703-2424)
P.O. Box 5037 (90703-5037)
PHONE.................................562 407-9977
Jeffrey Brady, *CEO*
Michael Lane, *Pr*
Rich Russell, *VP*
Clif Mcdougall, *Ex VP*
▲ **EMP:** 19 **EST:** 1991
**SQ FT:** 12,600
**SALES (est):** 4.4MM **Privately Held**
**Web:** www.printmgt.com
**SIC: 2752** 5111 Offset printing; Printing paper

**(P-4734)**
**PRINTING PALACE INC (PA)**
2300 Lincoln Blvd, Santa Monica (90405-2530)
PHONE.................................310 451-5151
Eli Albek, *Pr*
**EMP:** 19 **EST:** 1982
**SQ FT:** 8,000
**SALES (est):** 2.35MM
**SALES (corp-wide):** 2.35MM **Privately Held**
**Web:** www.printingpalace.com
**SIC: 2752** Offset printing

**(P-4735)**
**PRINTIVITY LLC**
Also Called: Printivity
8840 Kenamar Dr Ste 405, San Diego (92121-2450)
PHONE.................................877 649-5463
Lawrence Chou, *CEO*
**EMP:** 30 **EST:** 2010
**SALES (est):** 7.13MM **Privately Held**
**Web:** www.printivity.com
**SIC: 2752** 2711 2721 Offset printing; Commercial printing and newspaper publishing combined; Magazines: publishing and printing

**(P-4736)**
**PRINTOGRAPH INC**
Also Called: Gotprint.com
7625 N San Fernando Rd, Burbank (91505-1073)
PHONE.................................818 252-3000
Kristina Keshishyan, *Prin*
**EMP:** 21 **EST:** 2014
**SALES (est):** 2.97MM **Privately Held**
**Web:** www.gotprint.com
**SIC: 2752** Offset printing

**(P-4737)**
**PRINTRUNNER LLC**
Also Called: U-Nited Printing and Copy Ctr
8000 Haskell Ave, Van Nuys (91406-1321)
PHONE.................................888 296-5760
Dean Rabbani, *Managing Member*
Mike Zaya, *
Adam Berger, *
Kamie Davison, *
**EMP:** 35 **EST:** 1999
**SQ FT:** 50,000
**SALES (est):** 1.23MM **Privately Held**
**Web:** www.printrunner.com
**SIC: 2752** Offset printing

**(P-4738)**
**PRINTS 4 LIFE**
43145 Business Ctr Pkwy, Lancaster (93535-4564)
PHONE.................................661 942-2233
**EMP:** 27
**Web:** www.learn4life.org
**SIC: 2752** Commercial printing, lithographic

**(P-4739)**
**PRO DOCUMENT SOLUTIONS INC (PA)**
Also Called: Pro Vote Solutions
1760 Commerce Way, Paso Robles (93446-3620)
PHONE.................................805 238-6680
George Phillips, *CEO*
Brad Stier, *
Noal Phillips, *
Molly Comin, *
Diana Phillips, *
▲ **EMP:** 43 **EST:** 1979
**SQ FT:** 35,000
**SALES (est):** 10.09MM
**SALES (corp-wide):** 10.09MM **Privately Held**
**Web:** www.prodocumentsolutions.com
**SIC: 2752** Forms, business: lithographed

**(P-4740)**
**PROFESSIONAL PRINT & MAIL INC**
Also Called: Professional Print & Mail
2818 E Hamilton Ave, Fresno (93721-3209)
PHONE.................................559 237-7468
Doug Carlile, *Pr*
Roberta L Carlile, *
**EMP:** 30 **EST:** 1985
**SQ FT:** 20,000
**SALES (est):** 4.86MM **Privately Held**
**Web:** www.printfresno.com
**SIC: 2752** 7331 5999 Offset printing; Mailing service; Banners, flags, decals, and posters

**(P-4741)**
**PROGRAPHICS INC**
9200 Lower Azusa Rd, Rosemead (91770-1593)
PHONE.................................626 287-0417
Christina Stevens, *CEO*
Timothy Stevens, *
Jaime Colacio, *
**EMP:** 28 **EST:** 1967
**SQ FT:** 23,000
**SALES (est):** 2.45MM **Privately Held**
**Web:** www.prographicsllc.com
**SIC: 2752** Offset printing

**(P-4742)**
**PRPCO**
Also Called: Poor Richard's Press
2226 Beebee St, San Luis Obispo (93401-5505)
PHONE.................................805 543-6844
Todd P Ventura, *Pr*
Richard C Blake, *
Mary Monroe, *
**EMP:** 35 **EST:** 2000
**SALES (est):** 4.08MM **Privately Held**
**Web:** www.prpco.com
**SIC: 2752** Offset printing

**(P-4743)**
**PYRAMID GRAPHICS**
Also Called: Pyramid Printing and Graphics
325 Harbor Way, South San Francisco (94080-6919)
PHONE.................................650 871-0290
Kingman Leung, *Pr*
Nancy Tam, *Treas*
**EMP:** 16 **EST:** 1988
**SQ FT:** 4,000
**SALES (est):** 2.03MM **Privately Held**
**Web:** www.pyramidgraphics.net
**SIC: 2752** 7374 7336 Offset printing; Data processing and preparation; Commercial art and graphic design

**(P-4744)**
**Q TEAM**
Also Called: Ryan Press
6400 Dale St, Buena Park (90621-3115)
PHONE.................................714 228-4465
Mike Quibodeaux, *CEO*
Donna Quibodeaux, *
Mike Quibodeaux, *VP*
James Quibodeaux, *
**EMP:** 45 **EST:** 1980
**SQ FT:** 13,000
**SALES (est):** 4.84MM **Privately Held**
**Web:** www.ryanpress.com
**SIC: 2752** Offset printing

**(P-4745)**
**QG LLC**
Worldcolor Merced
2201 Cooper Ave, Merced (95348-4307)
PHONE.................................209 384-0444
**EMP:** 585
**SALES (corp-wide):** 2.96B **Publicly Held**
**Web:** www.theqg.com
**SIC: 2752** Offset printing
**HQ:** Qg, Llc
N61 W23044 Harry's Way
Sussex WI 53089

**(P-4746)**
**QG PRINTING IL LLC**
Also Called: Quad Graphics
6688 Box Springs Blvd, Riverside (92507-0726)
PHONE.................................951 571-2500
Georg Decker, *Brnch Mgr*
**EMP:** 123
**SALES (corp-wide):** 2.96B **Publicly Held**
**SIC: 2752** Offset printing
**HQ:** Qg Printing Ii Llc
N61w23044 Harrys Way
Sussex WI 53089

**(P-4747)**
**QUAD/GRAPHICS INC**
Also Called: QUAD/GRAPHICS INC.
6688 Box Springs Blvd, Riverside (92507-0726)
PHONE.................................951 689-1122
Uli Oels, *Genl Mgr*
**EMP:** 62
**SALES (corp-wide):** 2.96B **Publicly Held**
**Web:** www.quad.com
**SIC: 2752** 7336 Offset printing; Commercial art and graphic design
**PA:** Quad/Graphics, Inc.
N61 W23044 Harry's Way
414 566-6000

**(P-4748)**
**QUEEN BEACH PRINTERS INC**
937 Pine Ave, Long Beach (90813-4375)
P.O. Box 540 (90801-0540)
PHONE.................................562 436-8201
Nicholas W Edwards, *CEO*
William L Edwards Senior, *Pr*
William L Edwards Junior, *VP*
Virginia Noyes, *
**EMP:** 30 **EST:** 1944
**SQ FT:** 25,000
**SALES (est):** 3.52MM **Privately Held**
**Web:** www.qbprinters.com
**SIC: 2752** 7336 Offset printing; Commercial art and graphic design

**(P-4749)**
**RAYMONDS LITTLE PRINT SHOP INC**
Also Called: Jim Little Raymonds Print Shop
41454 Christy St, Fremont (94538-5105)
PHONE.................................510 353-3608
Raymond Lei, *Pr*
**EMP:** 450 **EST:** 2012
**SQ FT:** 100,000
**SALES (est):** 2.38MM
**SALES (corp-wide):** 24.03MM **Privately Held**
**SIC: 2752** Commercial printing, lithographic
**PA:** Ooshirts Inc.
39899 Blentine Dr Ste 220
866 660-8667

**(P-4750)**
**READY INDUSTRIES INC**
Also Called: Ready Reproductions
1520 E 15th St, Los Angeles (90021-2712)
P.O. Box 39576 (90039)
PHONE.................................213 749-2041
E H Reitz, *CEO*
Chuck Nix, *Ex VP*
**EMP:** 16 **EST:** 1968
**SQ FT:** 15,000
**SALES (est):** 671.99K **Privately Held**
**Web:** www.readyrepro.com
**SIC: 2752** Offset printing

**(P-4751)**
**RED BRICK CORPORATION**
Also Called: Design Printing
5364 Venice Blvd, Los Angeles (90019-5240)
PHONE.................................323 549-9444
Parviz Bina, *CEO*
Bijan Bina, *VP*
**EMP:** 18 **EST:** 1984
**SQ FT:** 8,000
**SALES (est):** 2.56MM **Privately Held**
**Web:** www.dprintla.com
**SIC: 2752** Offset printing

**(P-4752)**
**REDDING PRINTING CO INC (PA)**
1130 Continental St, Redding (96001-0799)
PHONE.................................530 243-0525
Ken Peterson, *Pr*
Richard Peterson, *
**EMP:** 30 **EST:** 1937
**SQ FT:** 14,000
**SALES (est):** 5.15MM
**SALES (corp-wide):** 5.15MM **Privately Held**
**Web:** www.reddingprinting.com
**SIC: 2752** Offset printing

**(P-4753)**
**REDSTONE PRINT & MAIL INC**
910 Riverside Pkwy Ste 40, West Sacramento (95605-1510)
PHONE.................................925 335-9090
Andy Cody, *CEO*
**EMP:** 108 **EST:** 2015
**SALES (est):** 2.04MM **Privately Held**
**SIC: 2752** Commercial printing, lithographic

**(P-4754)**
**RIVER CITY PRINTERS LLC**
4251 Gateway Park Blvd, Sacramento (95834-1975)
PHONE.................................916 638-8400
Kasey Cotulla, *Managing Member*
Eric Fields, *VP*
**EMP:** 35 **EST:** 2011
**SALES (est):** 4.95MM **Privately Held**
**Web:** www.deltaprintgroup.com
**SIC: 2752** Offset printing

**(P-4755)**
**RNJ PRINTING CORPORATION**
116 23rd Pl, Manhattan Beach (90266-4301)
PHONE.................................310 638-7768

## 2752 - Commercial Printing, Lithographic (P-4756)

John Samuel Osten, *Pr*
Rose Cecola Osten, *CFO*
**EMP:** 16 **EST:** 1977
**SALES (est):** 742.26K **Privately Held**
**Web:** www.rnjprinting.com
**SIC: 2752** 2796 Offset printing; Letterpress plates, preparation of

**(P-4756)**
**ROBO 3D INC**
Also Called: Robo 3d Printer
5070 Santa Fe St Ste C, San Diego (92109-1610)
**PHONE**......................844 476-2233
Braydon Moreno, *CEO*
Randall Waynick, *
▲ **EMP:** 25 **EST:** 2013
**SALES (est):** 3.76MM **Privately Held**
**Web:** www.robo3d.com
**SIC: 2752** Commercial printing, lithographic

**(P-4757)**
**RUSH PRESS INC**
Also Called: Arts & Crafts Press
955 Gateway Center Way, San Diego (92102-4542)
**PHONE**......................619 296-7874
**EMP:** 48
**Web:** www.rushpress.com
**SIC: 2752** Offset printing

**(P-4758)**
**SAN DIEGUITO PUBLISHERS INC**
Also Called: San Dieguito Printers
1880 Diamond St, San Marcos (92078-5100)
P.O. Box 885 (92075-0885)
**PHONE**......................760 593-5139
▲ **EMP:** 59 **EST:** 1964
**SALES (est):** 1.64MM **Privately Held**
**Web:** www.sd-print.com
**SIC: 2752** Offset printing

**(P-4759)**
**SCHOLASTIC SPORTS INC**
4878 Ronson Ct Ste Kl, San Diego (92111-1806)
**PHONE**......................858 496-9221
**EMP:** 90
**SQ FT:** 5,500
**SALES (est):** 867.63K **Privately Held**
**SIC: 2752** Commercial printing, lithographic

**(P-4760)**
**SEDAS PRINTING INC**
5335 Santa Monica Blvd, Los Angeles (90029-1105)
**PHONE**......................323 469-1034
John Rashidi, *Pr*
Seda Rashidi, *VP*
**EMP:** 15 **EST:** 1984
**SQ FT:** 8,000
**SALES (est):** 2.27MM **Privately Held**
**Web:** www.sedasprinting.com
**SIC: 2752** Offset printing

**(P-4761)**
**SELECT IMAGING LLC**
6398 Dougherty Rd Ste 27, Dublin (94568-2645)
**PHONE**......................925 803-1210
**EMP:** 16 **EST:** 2020
**SALES (est):** 531.19K **Privately Held**
**Web:** www.selectimaging.com
**SIC: 2752** Offset printing

**(P-4762)**
**SHIFT CALENDARS INC**
Also Called: Graphics United
809 N Glendora Ave, Covina (91724-2529)
**PHONE**......................626 967-5862
Robert Breaux Junior, *Pr*
**EMP:** 15 **EST:** 1975
**SQ FT:** 6,500
**SALES (est):** 2.29MM **Privately Held**
**SIC: 2752** Offset printing

**(P-4763)**
**SIERRA OFFICE SYSTEMS PDTS INC (PA)**
Also Called: Sierra Office Supply & Prtg
9950 Horn Rd Ste 5, Sacramento (95827-1905)
**PHONE**......................916 369-0491
Michael Kipp, *CEO*
Mary Theis, *
**EMP:** 100 **EST:** 1981
**SQ FT:** 28,000
**SALES (est):** 32.5MM
**SALES (corp-wide):** 32.5MM **Privately Held**
**Web:** www.sierrabg.com
**SIC: 2752** 5712 5943 Offset printing; Office furniture; Office forms and supplies

**(P-4764)**
**SIR SPEEDY INC (HQ)**
Also Called: Sir Speedy
26722 Plaza, Mission Viejo (92691-6390)
P.O. Box 9077 (92690-9077)
**PHONE**......................949 348-5000
Don Lowe, *CEO*
Richard Lowe, *
Dan Conger, *
**EMP:** 43 **EST:** 1968
**SQ FT:** 44,000
**SALES (est):** 7.99MM
**SALES (corp-wide):** 19.99MM **Privately Held**
**Web:** www.sirspeedy.com
**SIC: 2752** Commercial printing, lithographic
**PA:** Franchise Services, Inc.
   26722 Plaza
   949 348-5400

**(P-4765)**
**SOCIAL PRINT STUDIO**
548 Market St # 16617, San Francisco (94104-5401)
**PHONE**......................805 551-5328
Tawny Holguin, *Owner*
**EMP:** 15 **EST:** 2010
**SALES (est):** 227.02K **Privately Held**
**Web:** www.socialprintstudio.com
**SIC: 2752** Commercial printing, lithographic

**(P-4766)**
**SOUTHWEST OFFSET PRTG CO INC (PA)**
13650 Gramercy Pl, Gardena (90249-2453)
**PHONE**......................310 965-9154
Greg Mcdonald, *CEO*
Jennifer Mcdonald, *VP*
Art Spear, *
▲ **EMP:** 275 **EST:** 1986
**SQ FT:** 45,000
**SALES (est):** 42.54MM
**SALES (corp-wide):** 42.54MM **Privately Held**
**Web:** www.southwestoffset.com
**SIC: 2752** Offset printing

**(P-4767)**
**SPECTRUM LITHOGRAPH INC**
4300 Business Center Dr, Fremont (94538-6358)
**PHONE**......................510 438-9192
Fernandino Pereira, *Pr*
Fernanda Pereira, *
**EMP:** 27 **EST:** 2006
**SQ FT:** 46,000
**SALES (est):** 7.94MM **Privately Held**
**Web:** www.spectrumlithograph.com
**SIC: 2752** Offset printing

**(P-4768)**
**SPORT CARD CO LLC**
5830 El Camino Real, Carlsbad (92008-8816)
**PHONE**......................800 873-7332
Richard Mc William, *CEO*
Jason Masherah, *
Roz Nowicki, *
◆ **EMP:** 400 **EST:** 1988
**SQ FT:** 247,000
**SALES (est):** 19MM **Privately Held**
**Web:** www.upperdeck.com
**SIC: 2752** 5947 Souvenir cards, lithographed ; Gift, novelty, and souvenir shop

**(P-4769)**
**SPYDER3D LLC**
620 Lunar Ave, Brea (92821-3131)
**PHONE**......................714 256-1122
**EMP:** 16 **EST:** 2014
**SALES (est):** 642.97K **Privately Held**
**Web:** www.spyder3d.com
**SIC: 2752** Commercial printing, lithographic

**(P-4770)**
**SS WHITTIER LLC**
Also Called: Sir Speedy
7240 Greenleaf Ave, Whittier (90602)
**PHONE**......................562 698-7513
George Coriaty, *Owner*
**EMP:** 32 **EST:** 1979
**SQ FT:** 12,000
**SALES (est):** 5.26MM **Privately Held**
**Web:** www.sswhittier.com
**SIC: 2752** 7334 Commercial printing, lithographic; Photocopying and duplicating services

**(P-4771)**
**STANFORD BUSINESS MAGAZINE** ✪
655 Knight Way, Stanford (94305-7216)
**PHONE**......................650 723-2146
**EMP:** 22 **EST:** 2023
**SALES (est):** 396.2K **Privately Held**
**SIC: 2752** Commercial printing, lithographic

**(P-4772)**
**STOUGHTON PRINTING CO**
130 N Sunset Ave, City Of Industry (91744-3595)
**PHONE**......................626 961-3678
Jack Stoughton Junior, *Pr*
Clay Stoughton, *
**EMP:** 18 **EST:** 1952
**SQ FT:** 21,000
**SALES (est):** 3.83MM **Privately Held**
**Web:** www.stoughtonprinting.com
**SIC: 2752** Offset printing

**(P-4773)**
**STREETER PRINTING INC**
9880 Via Pasar Ste C, San Diego (92126-4575)
**PHONE**......................858 566-0866
Adrienne Streeter, *Pr*
Jack Streeter, *VP*
**EMP:** 16 **EST:** 1980
**SQ FT:** 11,000
**SALES (est):** 2.02MM **Privately Held**
**Web:** www.streeterprinting.com
**SIC: 2752** Offset printing

**(P-4774)**
**SUPERIOR LITHOGRAPHICS INC**
3055 Bandini Blvd, Vernon (90058-4109)
**PHONE**......................323 263-8400
Douglas Rawson, *CEO*
Carol Rawson, *
▲ **EMP:** 90 **EST:** 1982
**SQ FT:** 60,000
**SALES (est):** 19.68MM **Privately Held**
**Web:** www.superiorlithographics.com
**SIC: 2752** Offset printing

**(P-4775)**
**SUPERPRINT LITHOGRAPHICS INC**
Also Called: Superprint Lithographics
8332 Secura Way, Santa Fe Springs (90670-2204)
**PHONE**......................562 698-8001
Chao-tung Chen, *CEO*
Roy Chen, *Pr*
Erika Delun, *Acctnt*
**EMP:** 15 **EST:** 1978
**SQ FT:** 30,000
**SALES (est):** 2.06MM **Privately Held**
**Web:** www.superprintla.com
**SIC: 2752** Offset printing

**(P-4776)**
**SUPREME GRAPHICS INC**
1201 N Miller St, Anaheim (92806-1933)
**PHONE**......................310 531-8300
Ramin Kohanteb, *Pr*
**EMP:** 18 **EST:** 2005
**SALES (est):** 3.03MM **Privately Held**
**Web:** www.supremegraphicsinc.com
**SIC: 2752** Offset printing

**(P-4777)**
**SYRIANI BROTHERS CORP**
Also Called: O'Dell Printing Company
237 Picnic Ave Apt 24, San Rafael (94901-5083)
**PHONE**......................707 585-2718
**EMP:** 48
**Web:** www.almadenglobal.com
**SIC: 2752** Offset printing

**(P-4778)**
**TACKETT VOLUME PRESS INC**
Also Called: Volume Press
1348 Terminal St, West Sacramento (95691-3515)
**PHONE**......................916 374-8991
Pinder Basi, *Pr*
Ron Tackett, *
**EMP:** 50 **EST:** 1998
**SQ FT:** 45,000
**SALES (est):** 1.63MM **Privately Held**
**Web:** www.lppprints.com
**SIC: 2752** Offset printing

**(P-4779)**
**TAILGATE PRINTING INC**
Also Called: Hip Hop Royalty
2930 S Fairview St, Santa Ana (92704-6503)
**PHONE**......................714 966-3035
Maria C Vega, *CEO*
**EMP:** 90 **EST:** 2008
**SQ FT:** 80,000
**SALES (est):** 7.76MM **Privately Held**
**Web:** www.tailgatela.com
**SIC: 2752** Offset printing

**(P-4780)**
**TAJEN GRAPHICS INC**
Also Called: Apollo Printing & Graphics

# PRODUCTS & SERVICES SECTION
## 2752 - Commercial Printing, Lithographic (P-4802)

2100 W Lincoln Ave Ste B, Anaheim (92801-5642)
PHONE..............................714 527-3122
Dhansukhlal Ratanjee, *Pr*
Ken Ratanjee, *
**EMP:** 30 **EST:** 1977
**SQ FT:** 1,800
**SALES (est):** 3.22MM **Privately Held**
**Web:** www.apganaheim.com
**SIC:** 2752 2791 Offset printing; Typesetting, computer controlled

### (P-4781)
### TAM PRINTING INC
2961 E White Star Ave, Anaheim (92806-2630)
PHONE..............................714 224-4488
Tam Bui, *Pr*
**EMP:** 19 **EST:** 1986
**SQ FT:** 10,000
**SALES (est):** 2.41MM **Privately Held**
**Web:** www.tamprinting.com
**SIC:** 2752 Offset printing

### (P-4782)
### TECHNOLOGY TRAINING CORP
Also Called: Avalon Communications
3238 W 131st St, Hawthorne (90250-5517)
PHONE..............................310 644-7777
Richard D Lytle, *Pr*
**EMP:** 54
**SALES (corp-wide):** 4.84MM **Privately Held**
**Web:** www.ttcus.com
**SIC:** 2752 7331 3577 Offset printing; Direct mail advertising services; Computer peripheral equipment, nec
**PA:** Technology Training Corp
369 Van Ness Way Ste 735
310 320-8110

### (P-4783)
### TERRY GRIMES GRAPHIC CENTER OF SACRAMENTO INC
Also Called: Graphic Center
3925 Power Inn Rd, Sacramento (95826-4334)
P.O. Box 15050 (95851-0050)
PHONE..............................916 453-1332
▲ **EMP:** 21 **EST:** 1972
**SALES (est):** 450.61K **Privately Held**
**Web:** www.graphiccenter.net
**SIC:** 2752 7334 3993 Commercial printing, lithographic; Photocopying and duplicating services; Signs and advertising specialties

### (P-4784)
### THE LIGATURE INC (HQ)
Also Called: Echelon Fine Printing
4909 Alcoa Ave, Vernon (90058-3022)
PHONE..............................323 585-6000
Linda H Pennell, *
Denyse Owens, *
Dave Meyer, *
Tom Clifford, *
**EMP:** 50 **EST:** 1920
**SQ FT:** 47,415
**SALES (est):** 6.93MM
**SALES (corp-wide):** 3.81B **Privately Held**
**Web:** www.echelonprint.com
**SIC:** 2752 2759 Offset printing; Invitation and stationery printing and engraving
**PA:** Taylor Corporation
1725 Roe Crest Dr
507 625-2828

### (P-4785)
### THERMCRAFT INC
3762 Bradview Dr, Sacramento (95827-9702)
PHONE..............................916 363-9411
Ray Summers, *Pr*
Maurine Summers, *VP*
**EMP:** 16 **EST:** 1988
**SQ FT:** 4,600
**SALES (est):** 776.44K **Privately Held**
**Web:** www.thermcraft.com
**SIC:** 2752 Offset printing

### (P-4786)
### THOMAS BURT
Also Called: Ink Spots
5095 Brooks St, Montclair (91763-4804)
P.O. Box 2086 (91077-2086)
PHONE..............................626 301-9065
Thomas Burt, *Owner*
**EMP:** 15 **EST:** 1987
**SQ FT:** 15,000
**SALES (est):** 368.63K **Privately Held**
**SIC:** 2752 Offset printing

### (P-4787)
### TOUCH LITHO COMPANY
7215 E Gage Ave, Commerce (90040-3812)
PHONE..............................562 927-8899
Michael Wu, *Pr*
▲ **EMP:** 15 **EST:** 1999
**SQ FT:** 6,000
**SALES (est):** 2.44MM **Privately Held**
**Web:** www.touchlitho.com
**SIC:** 2752 Offset printing

### (P-4788)
### TRADE LITHO INC
Also Called: Trade Lithography
110 L St Ste 1, Antioch (94509-1168)
PHONE..............................510 965-6501
John Lompa, *CEO*
**EMP:** 15 **EST:** 1998
**SALES (est):** 4.2MM **Privately Held**
**Web:** www.tradelitho.us
**SIC:** 2752 Offset printing

### (P-4789)
### TREND OFFSET PRINTING SERVICES INC (HQ)
Also Called: Trend Offset Printing
3701 Catalina St, Los Alamitos (90720-2402)
P.O. Box 3008 (90720-1308)
PHONE..............................562 598-2446
◆ **EMP:** 41 **EST:** 1986
**SALES (est):** 85.58MM
**SALES (corp-wide):** 487.58MM **Privately Held**
**Web:** www.mittera.com
**SIC:** 2752 Offset printing
**PA:** Mittera Group, Inc.
5085 Ne 17th St
515 343-5359

### (P-4790)
### TREND OFFSET PRINTING SVCS INC
Also Called: TREND OFFSET PRINTING SERVICES INCORPORATED
3791 Catalina St, Los Alamitos (90720-2402)
PHONE..............................562 598-2446
Paul Rhilindger, *Mgr*
**EMP:** 425
**SALES (corp-wide):** 487.58MM **Privately Held**
**Web:** www.mittera.com
**SIC:** 2752 2732 Offset printing; Books, printing and binding
**HQ:** Trend Offset Printing Services, Inc.
3701 Catalina St
Los Alamitos CA 90720
562 598-2446

### (P-4791)
### TSCG VENTURES INC
Also Called: JP Graphics
550 Santa Rosa Dr, Los Gatos (95032)
PHONE..............................408 409-3274
Adam Demaestri, *CEO*
Scott Detrick, *
**EMP:** 40 **EST:** 2020
**SALES (est):** 4.14MM **Privately Held**
**SIC:** 2752 Commercial printing, lithographic

### (P-4792)
### TULIP PUBG & GRAPHICS INC
Also Called: Greener Printer
1003 Canal Blvd, Richmond (94804-3549)
PHONE..............................510 898-0000
Mario Assadi, *Prin*
**EMP:** 28 **EST:** 1986
**SQ FT:** 40,000
**SALES (est):** 1.6MM **Privately Held**
**Web:** www.greenerprinter.com
**SIC:** 2752 Offset printing

### (P-4793)
### TULLY-WIHR COMPANY
148 Whitcomb Ave, Colfax (95713-9036)
PHONE..............................530 346-2649
**EMP:** 119
**Web:** www.tullywihr.com
**SIC:** 2752 8742 7371 Forms, business: lithographed; Management consulting services; Custom computer programming services

### (P-4794)
### TYPECRAFT INC
Also Called: Typecraft Wood & Jones
2040 E Walnut St, Pasadena (91107-5804)
PHONE..............................626 795-8093
D Harry Montgomery, *Pr*
Jeffrey J Gish, *
**EMP:** 38 **EST:** 1947
**SQ FT:** 19,000
**SALES (est):** 4.23MM **Privately Held**
**Web:** www.typecraft.com
**SIC:** 2752 Offset printing

### (P-4795)
### TYT LLC (HQ)
Also Called: PS Print, LLC
2861 Mandela Pkwy, Oakland (94608-4011)
PHONE..............................510 444-3933
Andy Comly, *Managing Member*
Frank Young, *Managing Member*
▼ **EMP:** 110 **EST:** 2003
**SQ FT:** 55,000
**SALES (est):** 3.21MM
**SALES (corp-wide):** 2.19B **Publicly Held**
**Web:** www.psprint.com
**SIC:** 2752 Offset printing
**PA:** Deluxe Corporation
801 Marquette Ave
651 483-7111

### (P-4796)
### ULTIMATE PRINT SOURCE INC
Also Called: Printing 4him
2070 S Hellman Ave, Ontario (91761-8018)
PHONE..............................909 947-5292
Jeffrey J Ferrazzano, *CEO*
Desiree Ferrazzano, *
Edith Le Leux, *
Jon Le Leux, *
**EMP:** 30 **EST:** 1987
**SQ FT:** 20,000
**SALES (est):** 4.74MM **Privately Held**
**Web:** www.ultimateprintsource.com
**SIC:** 2752 Offset printing

### (P-4797)
### UNI-SPORT INC
16933 Gramercy Pl, Gardena (90247-5207)
PHONE..............................310 217-4587
Thomas Hebert, *Pr*
◆ **EMP:** 25 **EST:** 2006
**SQ FT:** 10,000
**SALES (est):** 2.25MM **Privately Held**
**Web:** www.uni-sport.com
**SIC:** 2752 Commercial printing, lithographic

### (P-4798)
### UNIVERSAL PRINTING SVCS INC
Also Called: Color Tech Commercial Printing
26012 Atlantic Ocean Dr, Lake Forest (92630-8843)
PHONE..............................951 788-1500
Gregg Baxter, *Pr*
Sharon Baxter, *VP*
**EMP:** 16 **EST:** 1985
**SQ FT:** 2,800
**SALES (est):** 919.94K **Privately Held**
**SIC:** 2752 Offset printing

### (P-4799)
### UTAP PRINTING CO INC
1423 San Mateo Ave, South San Francisco (94080-6504)
PHONE..............................650 588-2818
Patrick Y Chin, *Pr*
**EMP:** 18 **EST:** 1986
**SQ FT:** 5,200
**SALES (est):** 1.78MM **Privately Held**
**Web:** www.utap.com
**SIC:** 2752 Offset printing

### (P-4800)
### V3 PRINTING CORPORATION
Also Called: V 3
200 N Elevar St, Oxnard (93030-7969)
PHONE..............................805 981-2600
David Wilson, *Pr*
Michael Szanger, *
**EMP:** 80 **EST:** 1959
**SQ FT:** 4,000
**SALES (est):** 9MM **Privately Held**
**Web:** www.printv3.com
**SIC:** 2752 Lithographing on metal

### (P-4801)
### VALLEY BUSINESS PRINTERS INC
Also Called: Valley Printers
6355 Topanga Canyon Blvd Ste 225, Woodland Hills (91367-2118)
PHONE..............................818 362-7771
Michael Flannery, *CEO*
Bruce Bolkin, *
Karen S Flannery, *
▲ **EMP:** 92 **EST:** 1965
**SALES (est):** 1.28MM **Privately Held**
**Web:** www.valleyprinters.net
**SIC:** 2752 2759 Offset printing; Commercial printing, nec

### (P-4802)
### VDP DIRECT LLC (PA)
5520 Ruffin Rd Ste 111, San Diego (92123-1320)
P.O. Box 910027 (92191-0027)
PHONE..............................858 300-4510
**EMP:** 24 **EST:** 2004
**SQ FT:** 12,500
**SALES (est):** 1.03MM
**SALES (corp-wide):** 1.03MM **Privately Held**
**Web:** www.vdpdirect.com
**SIC:** 2752 Offset printing

## 2752 - Commercial Printing, Lithographic (P-4803)

**(P-4803)**
**VENTURA PRINTING INC (PA)**
Also Called: V3
200 N Elevar St, Oxnard (93030-7969)
PHONE..................805 981-2600
David Wilson, Pr
▲ EMP: 99 EST: 1946
SALES (est): 4.26MM
SALES (corp-wide): 4.26MM **Privately Held**
Web: www.nationalgraphics.com
SIC: 2752 Offset printing

**(P-4804)**
**VILLAGE INSTANT PRINTING INC**
Also Called: Park's Prtg & Lithographical Co
1515 10th St, Modesto (95354-0726)
PHONE..................209 576-2568
Austin E Parks, Pr
Frank Parks, *
Michelle Neilsen, *
Patricia Parks Minnix, *
EMP: 40 EST: 1974
SQ FT: 10,000
SALES (est): 4.41MM **Privately Held**
SIC: 2752 Offset printing

**(P-4805)**
**VISTA WAY CORPORATION**
472 Vista Way, Milpitas (95035-5406)
PHONE..................408 586-8107
Jim Dibona, Pr
David Hinds, VP
Maryann Dibona, Sec
EMP: 25 EST: 2003
SALES (est): 4.98MM **Privately Held**
Web: www.resourcelabel.com
SIC: 2752 Commercial printing, lithographic

**(P-4806)**
**VOMELA SPECIALTY COMPANY**
Also Called: Vomela
9810 Bell Ranch Dr, Santa Fe Springs (90670-2952)
PHONE..................562 944-3853
Loren Maxwell, Brnch Mgr
EMP: 163
SALES (corp-wide): 258.06MM **Privately Held**
Web: www.vomela.com
SIC: 2752 7336 Poster and decal printing, lithographic; Commercial art and graphic design
PA: Vomela Specialty Company
845 Minnehaha Ave E
651 228-2200

**(P-4807)**
**WE DO GRAPHICS INC**
1150 N Main St, Orange (92867-3421)
PHONE..................714 997-7390
Douglas K Le Mieux, Pr
Steven I Lehrer, *
Heidi G Le Mieux, *
▲ EMP: 22 EST: 1980
SQ FT: 23,000
SALES (est): 2.79MM **Privately Held**
Web: www.wedographics.com
SIC: 2752 Offset printing

**(P-4808)**
**WEBER PRINTING COMPANY INC**
1124 E Del Amo Blvd, Long Beach (90807-1010)
PHONE..................310 639-5064
Richard M Weber, Pr
Steven Weber, *
Lynda Slack, *
EMP: 35 EST: 1946
SQ FT: 30,000
SALES (est): 2.84MM **Privately Held**
Web: www.weberprint.com
SIC: 2752 Offset printing

**(P-4809)**
**WESTERN WEB INC**
Also Called: Western Web
1900 Bendixsen St Ste 2, Samoa (95564-9525)
P.O. Box 278 (95564-0278)
PHONE..................707 444-6236
Stephen Jackson, Pr
Michael Morris, VP
EMP: 21 EST: 2010
SQ FT: 25,400
SALES (est): 2.46MM **Privately Held**
Web: www.western-web.net
SIC: 2752 Offset printing

**(P-4810)**
**WESTLABEL LLC (PA)**
Also Called: Western Printing and Label
675 N Main St, Orange (92868-1103)
PHONE..................714 532-3946
EMP: 22 EST: 1946
SALES (est): 2.47MM
SALES (corp-wide): 2.47MM **Privately Held**
Web: www.westprint.com
SIC: 2752 2791 2759 2741 Offset printing; Typesetting; Commercial printing, nec; Miscellaneous publishing

**(P-4811)**
**WESTROCK CP LLC**
MPS Corona
2577 Research Dr, Corona (92882-7607)
PHONE..................951 273-7900
EMP: 64
Web: www.westrock.com
SIC: 2752 Offset printing
HQ: Westrock Cp, Llc
1000 Abernathy Rd Ste 125
Atlanta GA 30328

**(P-4812)**
**WILLEY PRINTING COMPANY (PA)**
1405 10th St, Modesto (95354-0724)
P.O. Box 886 (95353-0886)
PHONE..................209 524-4811
Jerry Sauls, Pr
Mary Alice Willey, *
EMP: 20 EST: 1946
SQ FT: 20,000
SALES (est): 2.46MM
SALES (corp-wide): 2.46MM **Privately Held**
Web: www.willeyprinting.com
SIC: 2752 Offset printing

**(P-4813)**
**WIRZ & CO**
444 Colton Ave, Colton (92324-3019)
PHONE..................909 825-6970
Charles Fred Wirz, Owner
EMP: 18 EST: 1985
SQ FT: 8,000
SALES (est): 911.54K **Privately Held**
Web: www.wirzco.com
SIC: 2752 Offset printing

**(P-4814)**
**WOODRIDGE PRESS INC**
2485 Da Vinci, Irvine (92614-5844)
PHONE..................949 475-1900
EMP: 50
Web: www.woodridgepress.com
SIC: 2752 2796 Offset printing; Platemaking services

**(P-4815)**
**WS PACKAGING-BLAKE PRINTERY**
Also Called: Poor Richards Press
2224 Beebee St, San Luis Obispo (93401-5505)
PHONE..................805 543-6844
Bruce Dickinson, Brnch Mgr
EMP: 34
SQ FT: 3,500
SALES (corp-wide): 14.54B **Privately Held**
SIC: 2752 2621 2791 Offset printing; Wrapping paper; Typesetting, computer controlled
HQ: Ws Packaging-Blake Printery
2222 Beebee St
San Luis Obispo CA 93401
805 543-6843

**(P-4816)**
**WTPC INC**
Also Called: World Trade Printing Company
12082 Western Ave, Garden Grove (92841-2913)
PHONE..................714 903-2500
Joe Ratanjee, CEO
▲ EMP: 30 EST: 1991
SQ FT: 25,000
SALES (est): 14.46MM **Privately Held**
Web: www.wtpcenter.com
SIC: 2752 Offset printing

**(P-4817)**
**X-IGENT PRINTING INC**
1001 Goodrich Blvd, Commerce (90022-5102)
PHONE..................323 837-9779
Omar Rodriguez, Pr
Hugo Cervantes, Sec
EMP: 15 EST: 2001
SQ FT: 6,000
SALES (est): 2.23MM **Privately Held**
Web: www.xigentprints.com
SIC: 2752 Offset printing

**(P-4818)**
**ZAITUN PRINTING & GRAPHICS INC**
16260 Church St Ste 100, Morgan Hill (95037-7134)
PHONE..................402 305-0109
Sumana Murshed, CEO
EMP: 15 EST: 2020
SALES (est): 2.2MM **Privately Held**
Web: www.chasevp.com
SIC: 2752 Offset printing

**(P-4819)**
**ZOO PRINTING INC (PA)**
Also Called: Zoo Printing Trade Printer
1225 Los Angeles St, Glendale (91204-2403)
PHONE..................310 253-7751
Dan Doron, Pr
Maria Camins, *
▲ EMP: 43 EST: 2001
SALES (est): 9.87MM
SALES (corp-wide): 9.87MM **Privately Held**
Web: www.zooprinting.com
SIC: 2752 Offset printing

**(P-4820)**
**ZUZA LLC**
2304 Faraday Ave, Carlsbad (92008-7216)
PHONE..................760 494-9000
Philip M Lurie, CEO
Philip M Lurie, Pr
Martin Solarish, *
EMP: 72 EST: 1992
SQ FT: 23,000
SALES (est): 15.49MM **Privately Held**
Web: www.zuzaprint.com
SIC: 2752 Offset printing

## 2754 Commercial Printing, Gravure

**(P-4821)**
**EUROSTAMPA CALIFORNIA LLC**
1315 Airport Blvd Ste A, Napa (94558-6313)
PHONE..................707 927-4848
Gianmario Cillario, CEO
EMP: 43 EST: 2014
SALES (est): 17.42MM **Privately Held**
Web: www.eurostampa.com
SIC: 2754 Commercial printing, gravure
HQ: Industria Grafica Eurostampa Spa
Viale Rimembranza 20
Bene Vagienna CN 12041
017 265-1811

**(P-4822)**
**FERNQVIST RETAIL SYSTEMS INC (DH)**
Also Called: Fernqvist Labeling Solutions
2544 Leghorn St, Mountain View (94043-1614)
PHONE..................650 428-0330
EMP: 16 EST: 1989
SQ FT: 6,100
Web: www.fernqvist.com
SIC: 2754 5734 Labels: gravure printing; Printers and plotters: computers
HQ: Epic Labeling Solutions, Inc.
665 Lenfest Rd
San Jose CA 95133
650 428-0330

**(P-4823)**
**KMR LABEL LLC**
Also Called: Axiom Label Group
1360 W Walnut Pkwy, Compton (90220-5029)
PHONE..................310 603-8910
EMP: 50
Web: www.resourcelabel.com
SIC: 2754 2752 Labels: gravure printing; Commercial printing, lithographic

**(P-4824)**
**MC ALLISTER INDUSTRIES INC (PA)**
731 S Highway 101 Ste 2, Solana Beach (92075-2629)
PHONE..................858 755-0683
Robert Mc Allister, Pr
▲ EMP: 20 EST: 1998
SQ FT: 2,500
SALES (est): 417.6K **Privately Held**
Web: www.mcallisterindustries.com
SIC: 2754 Cards, except greeting: gravure printing

**(P-4825)**
**ONEIL CAPITAL MANAGEMENT INC**
12655 Beatrice St, Los Angeles (90066-7003)
PHONE..................310 448-6400
William O Neil, CEO
▲ EMP: 152 EST: 1973

## 2759 - Commercial Printing, Nec (P-4848)

SQ FT: 70,000
SALES (est): 25.29MM
SALES (corp-wide): 335.64MM **Privately Held**
Web: www.oneildigitalsolutions.com
SIC: 2754 2732 2741 2711 Catalogs: gravure printing, not published on site; Book printing; Miscellaneous publishing; Newspapers
PA: Data Analysis Inc.
 12655 Beatrice St
 310 448-6800

**(P-4826)**
**QPE INC**
Also Called: Quality Packaging and Engrg
1372 Mcgaw Ave, Irvine (92614-5539)
PHONE..................949 263-0381
Kirk Wei, *Pr*
Joseph S Chiang, *Sec*
▲ **EMP:** 18 **EST:** 1986
SQ FT: 10,000
SALES (est): 2.22MM **Privately Held**
Web: www.qpe-inc.com
SIC: 2754 7389 Labels: gravure printing; Packaging and labeling services

**(P-4827)**
**RESOURCE LABEL GROUP LLC**
Also Called: Axiom Label & Packaging
1360 W Walnut Pkwy, Compton (90220-5029)
PHONE..................310 603-8910
Kieron Delahunt, *Brnch Mgr*
EMP: 50
Web: www.resourcelabel.com
SIC: 2754 2752 Labels: gravure printing; Commercial printing, lithographic
PA: Resource Label Group, Llc
 2550 Mridian Blvd Ste 370

**(P-4828)**
**STUART F COOPER CO**
1565 E 23rd St, Los Angeles (90011-1801)
P.O. Box 11306 (90011-0306)
PHONE..................213 747-7141
EMP: 150
SIC: 2754 Announcements: gravure printing

**(P-4829)**
**WESTERN SHELD ACQUISITIONS LLC (PA)**
Also Called: Imprimus Labels and Packaging
3760 Kilroy Airport Way Ste 500, Long Beach (90806-2443)
PHONE..................310 527-6212
Nizar Elias, *CEO*
Frank Connelly, *VP*
Thomas Moyer, *Pr*
EMP: 15 EST: 1970
SALES (est): 33.67MM
SALES (corp-wide): 33.67MM **Privately Held**
Web: www.imprimus.com
SIC: 2754 3172 2752 Labels: gravure printing; Tobacco pouches; Coupons, lithographed

---

### 2759 Commercial Printing, Nec

**(P-4830)**
**4 OVER LLC (HQ)**
Also Called: 4 Over
1225 Los Angeles St, Glendale (91204-2403)
PHONE..................818 246-1170
Zarik Megerdichian, *CEO*
Tina Hartounian, *
▲ **EMP:** 50 **EST:** 2000

SQ FT: 172.36MM
SALES (est): 172.36MM
SALES (corp-wide): 172.36MM **Privately Held**
Web: www.4over.com
SIC: 2759 7336 Commercial printing, nec; Commercial art and graphic design
PA: Four Cents Holdings, Llc
 1225 Los Angeles St

**(P-4831)**
**A F E INDUSTRIES INC (PA)**
13233 Barton Cir, Whittier (90605-3255)
P.O. Box 3303 (90670-1303)
PHONE..................562 944-6889
Fred Elhami, *Pr*
Ruth Elhami, *Sec*
EMP: 15 EST: 1981
SQ FT: 27,000
SALES (est): 14.94MM **Privately Held**
Web: www.afeindustries.com
SIC: 2759 Screen printing

**(P-4832)**
**ABC IMAGING OF WASHINGTON**
17240 Red Hill Ave, Irvine (92614-5628)
PHONE..................949 419-3728
EMP: 23
SALES (corp-wide): 129.31MM **Privately Held**
Web: www.abcimaging.com
SIC: 2759 Commercial printing, nec
PA: Abc Imaging Of Washington, Inc
 5290 Shawnee Rd Ste 300
 202 429-8870

**(P-4833)**
**ABC IMAGING OF WASHINGTON**
2327 Union St, Oakland (94607-2320)
PHONE..................202 429-8870
EMP: 20
SALES (corp-wide): 129.31MM **Privately Held**
Web: www.abcimaging.com
SIC: 2759 Commercial printing, nec
PA: Abc Imaging Of Washington, Inc
 5290 Shawnee Rd Ste 300
 202 429-8870

**(P-4834)**
**ABC IMAGING OF WASHINGTON**
832 Folsom St, San Francisco (94107-4502)
PHONE..................415 525-3874
EMP: 20
SALES (corp-wide): 129.31MM **Privately Held**
Web: www.abcimaging.com
SIC: 2759 Advertising literature: printing, nsk
PA: Abc Imaging Of Washington, Inc
 5290 Shawnee Rd Ste 300
 202 429-8870

**(P-4835)**
**ABC IMAGING OF WASHINGTON**
Also Called: ABC Imaging
13573 Larwin Cir, Santa Fe Springs (90670-5032)
PHONE..................562 375-7280
EMP: 20
SALES (corp-wide): 129.31MM **Privately Held**
Web: www.abcimaging.com
SIC: 2759 Advertising literature: printing, nsk
PA: Abc Imaging Of Washington, Inc
 5290 Shawnee Rd Ste 300
 202 429-8870

**(P-4836)**
**ADCRAFT PRODUCTS CO INC**
Also Called: Adcraft Labels

1230 S Sherman St, Anaheim (92805-6455)
PHONE..................714 776-1230
Randy C Mottram, *Pr*
Keith A Mottram, *
EMP: 27 EST: 1977
SALES (est): 7.87MM **Privately Held**
Web: www.adcraftlabels.com
SIC: 2759 Labels and seals: printing, nsk

**(P-4837)**
**ADVANCED WEB OFFSET INC**
Also Called: Awo
2260 Oak Ridge Way, Vista (92081-8341)
PHONE..................760 727-1700
Stephen F Shoemaker, *Pr*
David Altomare, *
EMP: 75 EST: 1989
SQ FT: 65,000
SALES (est): 11.96MM **Privately Held**
Web: www.awoink.com
SIC: 2759 2752 Newspapers: printing, nsk; Offset and photolithographic printing

**(P-4838)**
**ALL OUT INC**
2121 S El Camino Real Ste B100, San Mateo (94403-1861)
EMP: 23
SIC: 2759 2754 Commercial printing, nec; Commercial printing, gravure

**(P-4839)**
**AMCOR FLEXIBLES LLC**
Also Called: Amcor Flexibles Healthcare
800 N Walton Ave, Yuba City (95993-9352)
P.O. Box 3057 (95992-3057)
PHONE..................530 671-9000
EMP: 85
SALES (corp-wide): 14.69B **Privately Held**
SIC: 2759 3497 2823 2752 Flexographic printing; Metal foil and leaf; Cellulosic manmade fibers; Commercial printing, lithographic
HQ: Amcor Flexibles Llc
 3 Parkway North Blvd # 300
 Deerfield IL 60015
 224 313-7000

**(P-4840)**
**AMERICAN FOOTHILL PUBG CO INC**
10009 Commerce Ave, Tujunga (91042-2303)
PHONE..................818 352-7878
Doris Horwith, *Pr*
Douglas Horwith, *
EMP: 40 EST: 1920
SQ FT: 13,000
SALES (est): 2.32MM **Privately Held**
Web: www.americanfoothillpublishing.com
SIC: 2759 Newspapers: printing, nsk

**(P-4841)**
**AMERICAN ZABIN INTL INC**
3933 S Hill St, Los Angeles (90037-1313)
PHONE..................213 746-3770
Alan Faiola, *CEO*
Alan Faiola, *CFO*
Steven Garfinkle, *
Eric Sedso, *Marketing*
◆ **EMP:** 32 **EST:** 1993
SQ FT: 18,000
SALES (est): 2.89MM **Privately Held**
Web: www.zabin.com
SIC: 2759 Tags: printing, nsk

**(P-4842)**
**ARACA MERCHANDISE LP**
Araca Ink
459 Park Ave, San Fernando (91340-2525)
PHONE..................818 743-5400
Judy Courney, *Mgr*
EMP: 97
Web: www.araca.com
SIC: 2759 Screen printing
HQ: Araca Merchandise L.P.
 545 W 45th St Fl 10
 New York NY 10036

**(P-4843)**
**ARTISAN NAMEPLATE AWARDS CORP**
Also Called: Weber Precision Graphics
2730 S Shannon St, Santa Ana (92704-5232)
PHONE..................714 556-6222
Henry G Weber, *Pr*
Margaret Weber, *
EMP: 33 EST: 1972
SQ FT: 12,160
SALES (est): 4.65MM **Privately Held**
Web: www.weberpg.com
SIC: 2759 3479 Labels and seals: printing, nsk; Coating of metals with plastic or resins

**(P-4844)**
**ARTISAN SCREEN PRINTING INC**
1055 W 5th St, Azusa (91702-3313)
PHONE..................626 815-2700
Vasant N Doabria, *Pr*
Praful Bajaria, *
C P Kheni, *
▲ **EMP:** 120 **EST:** 2004
SQ FT: 90,000
SALES (est): 3.52MM **Privately Held**
Web: www.artisanscreen.com
SIC: 2759 Screen printing

**(P-4845)**
**ASPE INC**
41658 Ivy St Ste 118, Murrieta (92562-9427)
PHONE..................951 296-2595
Alexander Szyszko, *CEO*
▲ **EMP:** 15 **EST:** 2011
SALES (est): 950.66K **Privately Held**
Web: www.aspesite.com
SIC: 2759 Screen printing

**(P-4846)**
**B A L**
Also Called: Bay Area Labels
1980 Lundy Ave, San Jose (95131-1831)
PHONE..................408 432-1980
▲ **EMP:** 85
Web: www.bal.com
SIC: 2759 Labels and seals: printing, nsk

**(P-4847)**
**BEL AIRE DISPLAYS**
506 W Ohio Ave, Richmond (94804-2040)
PHONE..................510 232-5100
▲ **EMP:** 60
Web: www.belairedisplays.com
SIC: 2759 3993 Screen printing; Signs and advertising specialties

**(P-4848)**
**BEYONDGREEN BIOTECH INC**
Also Called: Beyondgreen
1202 E Wakeham Ave, Santa Ana (92705-4145)
PHONE..................800 983-7221
Veejay Patell, *CEO*

## 2759 - Commercial Printing, Nec (P-4849)

### PRODUCTS & SERVICES SECTION

EMP: 15 EST: 2018
SQ FT: 8,500
SALES (est): 4.49MM
SALES (corp-wide): 5.31MM **Privately Held**
Web: www.byndgrn.com
SIC: **2759** 2875 3089 2656 Bags, plastic: printing, nsk; Compost; Injection molded finished plastics products, nec; Straws, drinking: made from purchased material
PA: Prosourcing, Inc.
 12 Santa Catrina
 949 246-6868

### (P-4849)
### BLACKBURN ALTON INVSTMENTS LLC
Also Called: Foster Print
700 E Alton Ave, Santa Ana (92705-5610)
PHONE.....................714 731-2000
EMP: 34 EST: 2011
SALES (est): 1.64MM **Privately Held**
SIC: **2759** Commercial printing, nec

### (P-4850)
### BLC WC INC (PA)
Also Called: Imperial Marking Systems
13260 Moore St, Cerritos (90703-2228)
PHONE.....................562 926-1452
TOLL FREE: 800
Ernest Wong, Pr
Donald Ingle, *
Timothy Koontz, *
EMP: 120 EST: 1989
SQ FT: 60,000
SALES (est): 11.19MM
SALES (corp-wide): 11.19MM **Privately Held**
Web: www.resourcelabel.com
SIC: **2759** Labels and seals: printing, nsk

### (P-4851)
### BLUE TEES ENTERPRISES LLC
1990 N California Blvd Ste 20 Pmb 1111, Walnut Creek (94596-3791)
PHONE.....................949 702-0564
Christopher Markham, Managing Member
EMP: 25 EST: 2019
SALES (est): 21MM **Privately Held**
Web: www.blueteesgolf.com
SIC: **2759** Screen printing

### (P-4852)
### BRAND MARINADE HOLDINGS LLC
Also Called: Brand Marinade
717 Whitney St, San Leandro (94577-1117)
PHONE.....................510 435-2002
Jeremy Castro, Prin
EMP: 16 EST: 2009
SALES (est): 2.04MM **Privately Held**
Web: www.brandmarinade.com
SIC: **2759** Letterpress and screen printing

### (P-4853)
### BRETKERI CORPORATION
Also Called: So Cal Graphics
8316 Clairemont Mesa Blvd Ste 105, San Diego (92111-1316)
P.O. Box 720386 (92172-0386)
PHONE.....................858 292-4919
Bret Catcott, Pr
Keri Catcott, Sec
EMP: 26 EST: 1982
SQ FT: 4,500
SALES (est): 2.93MM **Privately Held**
Web: www.socalgraphics.com
SIC: **2759** 7336 Commercial printing, nec; Graphic arts and related design

### (P-4854)
### BRIXEN & SONS INC
2100 S Fairview St, Santa Ana (92704-4516)
PHONE.....................714 566-1444
Martin Corey Brixen, Pr
Son Nguyen, *
▲ EMP: 27 EST: 1992
SQ FT: 32,000
SALES (est): 4.71MM **Privately Held**
Web: www.brixen.com
SIC: **2759** 3993 Screen printing; Signs and advertising specialties

### (P-4855)
### BROOK & WHITTLE LIMITED
Also Called: Label Impressions
1177 N Grove St, Anaheim (92806-2110)
PHONE.....................714 634-3466
Remy Zada, Brnch Mgr
EMP: 42
Web: www.brookandwhittle.com
SIC: **2759** Labels and seals: printing, nsk
PA: Brook & Whittle Limited
 20 Carter Dr

### (P-4856)
### BY QUEST LLC
Also Called: Quest Inds - Stockton Plant
2518 Boeing Way, Stockton (95206-3937)
PHONE.....................209 234-0202
Ryan Reid, Brnch Mgr
EMP: 18
SALES (corp-wide): 30.08MM **Privately Held**
Web: www.byquest.com
SIC: **2759** Labels and seals: printing, nsk
PA: By Quest, Llc
 15 Bleeker St Ste 202
 908 851-9070

### (P-4857)
### C T L PRINTING INDS INC
Also Called: Cal Tape & Label
1741 W Lincoln Ave Ste A, Anaheim (92801-6716)
PHONE.....................714 635-2980
James Edward Hudson, CEO
J J Hudson, *
Dave Adams, *
EMP: 25 EST: 1960
SQ FT: 8,950
SALES (est): 1.73MM **Privately Held**
Web: ctlprintingindustries.openfos.com
SIC: **2759** Labels and seals: printing, nsk

### (P-4858)
### CCL LABEL INC
Pharmaceutical Label Systems
576 College Commerce Way, Upland (91786-4377)
PHONE.....................909 608-2655
Kieron Delahunt, Brnch Mgr
EMP: 75
SQ FT: 43,000
SALES (corp-wide): 4.84B **Privately Held**
Web: www.cclind.com
SIC: **2759** Labels and seals: printing, nsk
HQ: Ccl Label, Inc.
 161 Worcester Rd Ste 403
 Framingham MA 01701
 508 872-4511

### (P-4859)
### CCL LABEL (DELAWARE) INC
576 College Commerce Way, Upland (91786-4377)
PHONE.....................909 608-2260
Kieron Delahunt, Mgr
EMP: 253

SALES (corp-wide): 4.84B **Privately Held**
SIC: **2759** Labels and seals: printing, nsk
HQ: Ccl Label (Delaware), Inc.
 15 Controls Dr
 Shelton CT 06484
 203 926-1253

### (P-4860)
### CNM MARKETING INC
Also Called: Blankstylcom Vision Sport Mtrs
2392 Morse Ave Unit 120, Irvine (92614-5232)
PHONE.....................866 792-5265
Mark Azzarito, Pr
EMP: 15 EST: 2008
SALES (est): 2.23MM **Privately Held**
Web: www.blankstyle.com
SIC: **2759** Screen printing

### (P-4861)
### COASTAL TAG & LABEL INC
13233 Barton Cir, Whittier (90605-3255)
P.O. Box 3303 (90670-1303)
PHONE.....................562 946-4318
Fred Elhami, Pr
Ruth Elhami, *
EMP: 94 EST: 1982
SALES (est): 10.04MM **Privately Held**
SIC: **2759** 2672 2671 Labels and seals: printing, nsk; Paper; coated and laminated, nec; Paper; coated and laminated packaging
PA: A F E Industries, Inc.
 13233 Barton Cir

### (P-4862)
### COLLOTYPE LABELS USA INC (DH)
Also Called: Multi-Color Napa/Sonama
21 Executive Way, Napa (94558-6271)
PHONE.....................707 603-2500
Nigel Vinecombe, CEO
David Buse, *
Mike Huntsinger, *
▲ EMP: 103 EST: 1997
SQ FT: 14,500
SALES (est): 29.41MM
SALES (corp-wide): 14.54B **Privately Held**
SIC: **2759** Labels and seals: printing, nsk
HQ: Multi-Color Corporation
 4053 Clough Woods Dr
 Batavia OH 45103
 513 381-1480

### (P-4863)
### COLMOL INC
Also Called: King Graphics
8517 Production Ave, San Diego (92121-2204)
PHONE.....................858 693-7575
Sean P Mundy, CEO
▲ EMP: 45 EST: 1991
SQ FT: 14,000
SALES (est): 4.77MM **Privately Held**
Web: www.kinggraph.com
SIC: **2759** Screen printing

### (P-4864)
### CONSOLIDATED EAGLE PRESS INC
Also Called: Eagle Press
2629 5th St, Sacramento (95818-2802)
PHONE.....................916 383-7850
EMP: 31
SIC: **2759** Commercial printing, nec

### (P-4865)
### CONSOLIDATED GRAPHICS INC
Anderson La

3550 Tyburn St, Los Angeles (90065-1427)
PHONE.....................323 460-4115
Luke Westlake, Grp VP
EMP: 110
SALES (corp-wide): 15B **Privately Held**
Web: www.rrd.com
SIC: **2759** 2752 Commercial printing, nec; Offset printing
HQ: Consolidated Graphics, Inc.
 5858 Westheimer Rd # 200
 Houston TX 77057

### (P-4866)
### CORPORATE IMPRESSIONS LA INC
Also Called: Dorado Pkg
10742 Burbank Blvd, North Hollywood (91601-2516)
PHONE.....................818 761-9295
Jennifer L Freund, Pr
EMP: 27 EST: 1982
SQ FT: 10,000
SALES (est): 2.39MM **Privately Held**
Web: www.impressionsla.com
SIC: **2759** 7389 Screen printing; Packaging and labeling services

### (P-4867)
### COSMO FIBER CORPORATION (PA)
1802 Santo Domingo Ave, Duarte (91010-2933)
PHONE.....................626 256-6098
Sidney Ru, Pr
Sissy Ru, Sec
◆ EMP: 26 EST: 1990
SQ FT: 4,000
SALES (est): 4.55MM **Privately Held**
Web: www.cosmopromos.com
SIC: **2759** 7389 Promotional printing; Advertising, promotional, and trade show services

### (P-4868)
### CR & A CUSTOM APPAREL INC
Also Called: Cr & A Custom
312 W Pico Blvd, Los Angeles (90015-2437)
PHONE.....................213 749-4440
Masoud Rad, COO
Carmen Rad, Pr
Dino Maquiddang, *
◆ EMP: 30 EST: 1993
SQ FT: 26,500
SALES (est): 5.87MM **Privately Held**
Web: www.cracustom.com
SIC: **2759** Posters, including billboards: printing, nsk

### (P-4869)
### CUPIX AMERICA INC
3003 N 1st St, San Jose (95134-2004)
PHONE.....................650 785-2122
Yeong Kim, Pr
EMP: 68 EST: 2017
SALES (est): 2.53MM **Privately Held**
Web: www.cupix.com
SIC: **2759** Commercial printing, nec

### (P-4870)
### CUSTOM LABEL & DECAL LLC
Also Called: Custom Label
3392 Investment Blvd, Hayward (94545-3809)
PHONE.....................510 876-0000
Colin Ho-tseung Junior, Managing Member
EMP: 20 EST: 1976
SQ FT: 25,000
SALES (est): 4.38MM **Privately Held**
Web: www.customlabel.com

▲ = Import ▼ = Export
◆ = Import/Export

# PRODUCTS & SERVICES SECTION  2759 - Commercial Printing, Nec (P-4894)

SIC: 2759 2752 2672 Labels and seals: printing, nsk; Commercial printing, lithographic; Paper; coated and laminated, nec

### (P-4871)
### DEAN HESKETH COMPANY INC
Also Called: Mpressions
2551 W La Palma Ave, Anaheim (92801-2622)
PHONE.................................714 236-2138
Matthew Hesketh, *Pr*
▲ EMP: 35 EST: 1956
SQ FT: 6,000
SALES (est): 1.67MM **Privately Held**
Web: www.mpressions.graphics
SIC: 2759 Commercial printing, nec

### (P-4872)
### DELTA WEB PRINTING INC
Also Called: Delta Web Printing & Bindery
4251 Gateway Park Blvd, Sacramento (95834-1975)
PHONE.................................916 375-0044
James Davis, *Pr*
Kasey Cotulla, *VP*
EMP: 22 EST: 1992
SALES (est): 2.31MM **Privately Held**
Web: www.deltaprintgroup.com
SIC: 2759 2789 Screen printing; Binding and repair of books, magazines, and pamphlets

### (P-4873)
### DIGITAL ROOM HOLDINGS INC (HQ)
Also Called: New Printing
8000 Haskell Ave, Van Nuys (91406-1321)
PHONE.................................310 575-4440
Michael Turner, *CEO*
Brett Zane, *
▲ EMP: 63 EST: 2016
SALES (est): 84.81MM **Publicly Held**
Web: www.digitalroominc.com
SIC: 2759 7336 Commercial printing, nec; Graphic arts and related design
PA: Sycamore Partners Management, L.P.
9 W 57th St Ste 3100

### (P-4874)
### DM LUXURY LLC
875 Prospect St Ste 300, La Jolla (92037-4264)
PHONE.................................858 366-9721
EMP: 107
SALES (corp-wide): 46.69MM **Privately Held**
Web: www.modernluxurymedia.com
SIC: 2759 Advertising literature: printing, nsk
PA: Dm Luxury, Llc
3414 Peachtree Rd Ne # 48
404 443-1780

### (P-4875)
### EAST PRIVATE HOLDINGS II LLC (PA)
6750 Dumbarton Cir, Fremont (94555-3616)
PHONE.................................650 357-3500
EMP: 44 EST: 2019
SALES (est): 1.1B
SALES (corp-wide): 1.1B **Privately Held**
SIC: 2759 Commercial printing, nec

### (P-4876)
### ECLECTIC PRINTING & DESIGN LLC
1030 Ortega Way Ste A, Placentia (92870-7161)
P.O. Box 6667 (92834-6667)
PHONE.................................714 528-8040
Jeffrey Abraham, *Pr*
Jeff Abraham, *Owner*
EMP: 18 EST: 2007
SALES (est): 823.2K **Privately Held**
Web: www.eclecticprinting.com
SIC: 2759 Screen printing

### (P-4877)
### ELECTRONIC PRTG SOLUTIONS LLC
4879 Ronson Ct Ste C, San Diego (92111-1811)
PHONE.................................858 576-3000
Grant Freeman, *Managing Member*
EMP: 20 EST: 1997
SQ FT: 7,600
SALES (est): 2.11MM **Privately Held**
Web: www.epsolution.com
SIC: 2759 2732 Magazines: printing, nsk; Book printing

### (P-4878)
### EXPRESS BUSINESS SYSTEMS INC
Also Called: Express
9155 Trade Pl, San Diego (92126-4377)
P.O. Box 537 (92038-0537)
PHONE.................................858 549-9828
Briggs Keiffer, *Pr*
Maureen O'malley, *Sec*
EMP: 37 EST: 1987
SQ FT: 7,000
SALES (est): 6.37MM **Privately Held**
Web: www.expresscorp.com
SIC: 2759 3993 2672 2671 Labels and seals: printing, nsk; Signs and advertising specialties; Paper; coated and laminated, nec; Paper; coated and laminated packaging

### (P-4879)
### FABFAD LLC
1901 E 7th Pl, Los Angeles (90021-1601)
PHONE.................................213 488-0456
Lolita Mejia, *VP Opers*
EMP: 19 EST: 2017
SALES (est): 991.51K **Privately Held**
Web: www.fabfad.com
SIC: 2759 Screen printing

### (P-4880)
### FORTIS SOLUTIONS GROUP LLC
1870 Wardrobe Ave, Merced (95341-6407)
PHONE.................................800 388-1990
EMP: 58
Web: www.fortissolutionsgroup.com
SIC: 2759 Labels and seals: printing, nsk
PA: Fortis Solutions Group, Llc
2505 Hawkeye Ct

### (P-4881)
### G-2 GRAPHIC SERVICE INC
5510 Cleon Ave, North Hollywood (91601-2835)
PHONE.................................818 623-3100
John C Beard, *CEO*
Joe Cotrupe, *
Pamela Beard-cotrupe, *VP*
Scott Dewinkeleer, *
◆ EMP: 52 EST: 1969
SQ FT: 35,000
SALES (est): 9.55MM **Privately Held**
Web: www.g2online.com
SIC: 2759 7331 Commercial printing, nec; Direct mail advertising services

### (P-4882)
### GOLDEN APPLEXX CO INC
19805 Harrison Ave, Walnut (91789-2849)
PHONE.................................909 594-9788
Peter Lee, *Pr*
Shio-ru Lee, *VP*
◆ EMP: 15 EST: 1986
SALES (est): 1.28MM **Privately Held**
Web: www.goldenapplexx.com
SIC: 2759 2396 Promotional printing; Automotive and apparel trimmings

### (P-4883)
### GOLDEN GROVE TRADING INC
Also Called: Crystal Castle
468 S Humane Way, Pomona (91766-1035)
PHONE.................................909 718-8000
Werner Schulz, *Pr*
Yung Schulz, *VP*
▲ EMP: 15 EST: 1983
SQ FT: 20,000
SALES (est): 3.09MM **Privately Held**
Web: www.ggtrading.com
SIC: 2759 2395 5699 Letterpress and screen printing; Embroidery and art needlework; Customized clothing and apparel

### (P-4884)
### GRAPHIC LAB INC
1263 Pioneer Way, El Cajon (92020-1623)
PHONE.................................858 437-9100
Rob Acosta, *CEO*
EMP: 20 EST: 2014
SALES (est): 419.86K **Privately Held**
Web: www.graphiclabpromotionalproducts.com
SIC: 2759 Screen printing

### (P-4885)
### GRAPHIC PACKAGING INTL LLC
Also Called: Sierra Pacific Packaging
525 Airport Pkwy, Oroville (95965-9248)
PHONE.................................530 533-1058
Allen Ennis, *Brnch Mgr*
EMP: 160
Web: www.graphicpkg.com
SIC: 2759 2752 2671 2631 Commercial printing, nec; Commercial printing, lithographic; Paper; coated and laminated packaging; Paperboard mills
HQ: Graphic Packaging International, Llc
1500 Rvredge Pkwy Ste 100
Atlanta GA 30328

### (P-4886)
### GRAPHIC SPORTSWEAR LLC
173 Utah Ave, South San Francisco (94080-6712)
P.O. Box 77193 (94107-0193)
PHONE.................................415 206-7200
Mike Smith, *
EMP: 52 EST: 1976
SQ FT: 20,000
SALES (est): 1.81MM **Privately Held**
Web: www.graphicsportswear.com
SIC: 2759 Screen printing

### (P-4887)
### GRAPHIC TRENDS INCORPORATED
7301 Adams St, Paramount (90723-4007)
PHONE.................................562 531-2339
Kieu V Tran, *Prin*
EMP: 40 EST: 1983
SQ FT: 20,984
SALES (est): 4.85MM **Privately Held**
Web: www.graphictrends.net
SIC: 2759 7336 Screen printing; Graphic arts and related design

### (P-4888)
### GRAPHICS 2000 LLC
1600 E Valencia Dr, Fullerton (92831-4735)
PHONE.................................714 879-1188
EMP: 54
SIC: 2759 2396 Letterpress and screen printing; Automotive and apparel trimmings

### (P-4889)
### GREAT WESTERN PACKAGING LLC
8230 Haskell Ave 8240, Van Nuys (91406-1322)
PHONE.................................818 464-3800
Michael C Warner, *Managing Member*
Victoria Warner Kaplan, *
EMP: 68 EST: 1970
SALES (est): 2.37MM **Privately Held**
Web: www.greatwesternpackaging.com
SIC: 2759 Commercial printing, nec

### (P-4890)
### HB PRODUCTS LLC
Also Called: Lean Merch
5671 Engineer Dr, Huntington Beach (92649-1123)
PHONE.................................714 799-6967
EMP: 20 EST: 2000
SALES (est): 2.13MM **Privately Held**
Web: www.hbapparel.com
SIC: 2759 Screen printing

### (P-4891)
### HEARTLAND LABEL PRINTERS LLC
9817 7th St Ste 703, Rancho Cucamonga (91730-7802)
PHONE.................................909 243-7151
John Wojcik, *Prin*
EMP: 575
Web: www.hrtlp.com
SIC: 2759 Labels and seals: printing, nsk
HQ: Heartland Label Printers, Llc
1700 Stephen St
Little Chute WI 54140
920 687-4145

### (P-4892)
### HIRONAKA PROMOTIONS LLC
Also Called: Garage Champs
2608 R St, Sacramento (95816-6915)
PHONE.................................916 631-8470
EMP: 20 EST: 2018
SALES (est): 1.34MM **Privately Held**
Web: www.garagechamps.com
SIC: 2759 Screen printing

### (P-4893)
### HUDSON PRINTING INC
Also Called: Hudson Printing
2780 Loker Ave W, Carlsbad (92010-6611)
PHONE.................................760 602-1260
James Fairweather, *Pr*
Tom Fairweather, *VP*
Anne Fairweather, *Treas*
EMP: 23 EST: 2004
SQ FT: 6,000
SALES (est): 5.41MM **Privately Held**
Web: www.hudsonsd.com
SIC: 2759 2752 Screen printing; Offset printing

### (P-4894)
### IC INK IMAGE CO INC
Also Called: Legends Apparel & I C Ink
4627 E Fremont St, Stockton (95215-4010)
P.O. Box 4487 (95204-0487)
PHONE.................................209 931-3040
Tom Sousa, *Pr*

## 2759 - Commercial Printing, Nec (P-4895)

EMP: 20 EST: 1991
SQ FT: 25,000
SALES (est): 1.84MM Privately Held
Web: www.icink.com
SIC: 2759 2396 2395 Screen printing; Automotive and apparel trimmings; Pleating and stitching

### (P-4895)
### ID SUPPLY
3183 Red Hill Ave, Costa Mesa (92626-3401)
PHONE.................................949 287-9200
Brandon Ruddach, CEO
Brandon Ruddach, *
EMP: 49 EST: 2017
SALES (est): 5.2MM Privately Held
Web: www.idsupplyco.com
SIC: 2759 Screen printing

### (P-4896)
### IGRAPHICS (PA)
Also Called: Precision Printers
165 Spring Hill Dr, Grass Valley (95945-5936)
PHONE.................................530 273-2200
James G Clay, Owner
James G Clay, Managing Member
David Clay, Managing Member
EMP: 24 EST: 1981
SQ FT: 15,000
SALES (est): 2.37MM
SALES (corp-wide): 2.37MM Privately Held
Web: www.igraphicspp.com
SIC: 2759 7389 3993 2671 Screen printing; Printing broker; Signs and advertising specialties; Paper; coated and laminated packaging

### (P-4897)
### INFOIMAGE OF CALIFORNIA INC (PA)
Also Called: Infoimage
175 S Hill Dr, Brisbane (94005-1343)
PHONE.................................650 473-6388
Howard Lee, Pr
Rose Lee, *
Calvin Fong, *
Eddie Yuen, *
Lilly Fong, *
EMP: 74 EST: 1984
SALES (est): 23.48MM
SALES (corp-wide): 23.48MM Privately Held
Web: www.infoimageinc.com
SIC: 2759 7331 7374 Laser printing; Mailing service; Data processing service

### (P-4898)
### INK FX CORPORATION
513 S La Serena Dr, Covina (91723)
PHONE.................................909 673-1950
Joe Metz, Pr
Mike Machrone, *
EMP: 25 EST: 1993
SALES (est): 2.35MM Privately Held
Web: www.inkfx.com
SIC: 2759 Screen printing

### (P-4899)
### INTERNTIONAL COLOR POSTERS INC
Also Called: ICP West
8081 Orangethorpe Ave, Buena Park (90621-3801)
PHONE.................................949 768-1005
Eric Guerineau, Pr
▲ EMP: 33 EST: 1985
SQ FT: 26,000
SALES (est): 1.81MM Privately Held
SIC: 2759 Screen printing

### (P-4900)
### INVESTMENT ENTERPRISES INC (PA)
Also Called: A2z Color Graphics
8230 Haskell Ave Ste 8240, Van Nuys (91406-1322)
PHONE.................................818 464-3800
Michael Warner, Pr
Denise Scanlon, *
Jack Wickson, *
EMP: 43 EST: 1970
SALES (est): 2.29MM
SALES (corp-wide): 2.29MM Privately Held
SIC: 2759 Magazines: printing, nsk

### (P-4901)
### IRIS GROUP INC
Also Called: Modern Postcard
1675 Faraday Ave, Carlsbad (92008-7314)
PHONE.................................760 431-1103
Steve Hoffman, CEO
EMP: 250 EST: 1977
SQ FT: 75,000
SALES (est): 17.97MM Privately Held
Web: www.modernpostcard.com
SIC: 2759 5961 Commercial printing, nec; Mail order house, nec

### (P-4902)
### ISLAND VIEW PRINT WORKS INC
Also Called: Island View Outfitters
6565 Trigo Rd Ste A, Goleta (93117-5036)
PHONE.................................805 845-1333
EMP: 20 EST: 2017
SALES (est): 305.99K Privately Held
Web: www.islandviewoutfitters.com
SIC: 2759 Screen printing

### (P-4903)
### J&D 2050 WARDROBE INC A CALIFORNIA CORPORATION
2050 Wardrobe Ave, Merced (95341-6409)
PHONE.................................209 384-1000
TOLL FREE: 800
▲ EMP: 105
SIC: 2759 Labels and seals: printing, nsk

### (P-4904)
### KIERAN LABEL CORP
2321 Siempre Viva Ct Ste 101, San Diego (92154-6301)
PHONE.................................619 449-4457
Denis Vanier, CEO
William Walker, *
Bill Walker, *
▲ EMP: 44 EST: 1979
SALES (est): 1.46MM Privately Held
Web: www.kieranlabel.com
SIC: 2759 Commercial printing, nec
PA: I.D. Images Llc
    1120 W 130th St

### (P-4905)
### L A SUPPLY CO
Also Called: Label House
4241 E Brickell St, Ontario (91761-1512)
PHONE.................................949 470-9900
Randolph William Austin, CEO
▲ EMP: 31 EST: 1947
SALES (est): 773.81K Privately Held

SIC: 2759 2752 2672 2396 Labels and seals: printing, nsk; Commercial printing, lithographic; Paper; coated and laminated, nec; Automotive and apparel trimmings

### (P-4906)
### LABEL ART - HM ES-E STIK LBELS
Also Called: Label Art of California
290 27th St, Oakland (94612-3821)
PHONE.................................510 465-1125
TOLL FREE: 800
David S Masri, Pr
Daniel Masri, General Vice President*
Elizabeth Masri, *
EMP: 25 EST: 1964
SALES (est): 3.02MM Privately Held
Web: label-art-home-of-ease-stik-labels-inc-in-oakland-ca.cityfos.com
SIC: 2759 Labels and seals: printing, nsk
PA: A A Label, Inc.
    6958 Sierra Ct

### (P-4907)
### LABEL ID TECHNOLOGIES INC
2275 Michael Faraday Dr Ste 4, San Diego (92154-7927)
PHONE.................................619 661-5566
Ricardo Tamborrell, Pr
Alex Nieves, CFO
▲ EMP: 15 EST: 2005
SQ FT: 12,000
SALES (est): 2MM Privately Held
Web: www.labelidtech.com
SIC: 2759 Labels and seals: printing, nsk

### (P-4908)
### LABEL IMPRESSIONS INC
1831 W Sequoia Ave, Orange (92868-1017)
PHONE.................................714 634-3466
EMP: 42
SIC: 2759 Labels and seals: printing, nsk

### (P-4909)
### LABEL SPECIALTIES INC
704 Dunn Way, Placentia (92870-6805)
PHONE.................................714 961-8074
Michael A Gyure, Pr
Tom Wetterhus, VP
EMP: 19 EST: 1981
SQ FT: 11,000
SALES (est): 4.86MM Privately Held
Web: www.labelspec.com
SIC: 2759 Labels and seals: printing, nsk

### (P-4910)
### LABELING HURST SYSTEMS LLC
Also Called: Hurst International
20747 Dearborn St, Chatsworth (91311-5914)
P.O. Box 5169 (91313-5169)
PHONE.................................818 701-0710
Aron Lichtenberg, Pr
▲ EMP: 18 EST: 1995
SQ FT: 12,875
SALES (est): 2.61MM Privately Held
Web: www.hurst-international.com
SIC: 2759 Labels and seals: printing, nsk

### (P-4911)
### LABELTRONIX LLC (HQ)
Also Called: Rethink Label Systems
2419 E Winston Rd, Anaheim (92806-5544)
PHONE.................................800 429-4321
▲ EMP: 73 EST: 1993
SQ FT: 48,000
SALES (est): 15.75MM
SALES (corp-wide): 28.01MM Privately Held
Web: www.awtlabelpack.com
SIC: 2759 Labels and seals: printing, nsk
PA: Advanced Web Technologies, Inc.
    600 Hoover St Ne Ste 500
    612 706-3700

### (P-4912)
### LCA PROMOTIONS INC
3073 Cicero Ct, Simi Valley (93063-1606)
PHONE.................................818 773-9170
Terrence R Aleck, Pr
EMP: 20 EST: 1992
SALES (est): 2.03MM Privately Held
Web: www.lcapromotions.com
SIC: 2759 Screen printing

### (P-4913)
### LEFT COAST T-SHIRT COMPANY
755 Fiero Ln Ste A, San Luis Obispo (93401-7902)
P.O. Box 728 (93406-0728)
PHONE.................................805 547-1622
Alexander Friend, Pr
EMP: 20 EST: 2017
SALES (est): 239.47K Privately Held
Web: www.leftcoast.com
SIC: 2759 Screen printing

### (P-4914)
### LEGION CREATIVE GROUP
500 N Brand Blvd Ste 1800, Glendale (91203-3305)
PHONE.................................323 498-1100
Kathleen Fliller, Owner
EMP: 25 EST: 2015
SALES (est): 6.7MM Privately Held
Web: www.legioncreative.us
SIC: 2759 Advertising literature: printing, nsk

### (P-4915)
### LOCAL SAVERS LLC
10535 Estckton Blvd Ste F, Elk Grove (95624)
PHONE.................................916 672-1006
EMP: 15 EST: 2012
SALES (est): 900K Privately Held
SIC: 2759 Coupons: printing, nsk

### (P-4916)
### LPS AGENCY SALES & POSTING INC
3210 El Camino Real Ste 200, Irvine (92602-1368)
PHONE.................................714 247-7500
Richard Teal, Brnch Mgr
EMP: 16
SALES (corp-wide): 658.5K Privately Held
SIC: 2759 Publication printing
PA: Lps Agency Sales And Posting, Inc.
    3210 El Cmino Real Ste 20
    714 247-7503

### (P-4917)
### LUSTRE-CAL LLC
715 S Guild Ave, Lodi (95240-3153)
PHONE.................................206 370-1600
Heather Chartrand, Prin
Chris Colbert, Prin
Avinash Pathak, Prin
Maxvell Smith, Prin
EMP: 65 EST: 2020
SALES (est): 4.89MM Privately Held
Web: www.lustrecal.com
SIC: 2759 Commercial printing, nec

## PRODUCTS & SERVICES SECTION
### 2759 - Commercial Printing, Nec (P-4942)

**(P-4918)**
**LUSTRE-CAL NAMEPLATE CORP**
Also Called: Lustre-Cal
715 S Guild Ave, Lodi (95240-3153)
P.O. Box 439 (95241-0439)
PHONE..................................209 370-1600
Clydene Hohenrieder, CEO
Joseph Hohenrieder, *
Heather Chartrand, *
▲ EMP: 65 EST: 1964
SQ FT: 50,000
SALES (est): 9.83MM Privately Held
Web: www.lustrecal.com
SIC: 2759 Labels and seals: printing, nsk

**(P-4919)**
**MARCO FINE ARTS GALLERIES INC**
4860 W 147th St, Hawthorne (90250-6706)
PHONE..................................310 615-1818
Al Marco, Pr
Kristoff Honeymany, *
▲ EMP: 22 EST: 1986
SQ FT: 10,000
SALES (est): 2.51MM Privately Held
Web: www.marcofinearts.com
SIC: 2759 5199 5023 Commercial printing, nec; Art goods; Frames and framing, picture and mirror

**(P-4920)**
**MARTIN E-Z STICK LABELS**
12921 Sunnyside Pl, Santa Fe Springs (90670-4645)
PHONE..................................562 906-1577
Francisco Martinez, Pr
Moncia Martinez, Sec
Sylvia Martinez, Treas
EMP: 18 EST: 1979
SQ FT: 14,800
SALES (est): 2.44MM Privately Held
Web: www.martinezsticklabels.com
SIC: 2759 Labels and seals: printing, nsk

**(P-4921)**
**MATRIX DOCUMENT IMAGING INC**
527 E Rowland St Ste 214, Covina (91723-3267)
PHONE..................................626 966-9959
Thomas Smith, Pr
Mercedes Uribe, *
EMP: 16 EST: 2006
SALES (est): 874.02K Privately Held
Web: www.legal-records.us
SIC: 2759 8111 Laser printing; Legal services

**(P-4922)**
**MEPCO LABEL SYSTEMS**
1313 S Stockton St, Lodi (95240-5942)
PHONE..................................209 946-0201
Jennifer Tracy, CEO
Alfred M Gassner, *
Carol Gassner, *
Tom Gassner, *
EMP: 96 EST: 1912
SQ FT: 83,000
SALES (est): 17.62MM Privately Held
Web: www.mepcolabel.com
SIC: 2759 Labels and seals: printing, nsk

**(P-4923)**
**MILLION CORPORATION**
Also Called: Able Card Corporation
1300 W Optical Dr Ste 600, Irwindale (91702-3285)
PHONE..................................626 969-1888
Herman Ho, CEO
Hector Dominguez, *
Donny Yu, *
EMP: 70 EST: 1989
SQ FT: 45,000
SALES (est): 7.93MM Privately Held
Web: www.ablecard.com
SIC: 2759 Commercial printing, nec
PA: First Nations Capital Partners, Llc
7676 Hazard Center Dr # 5

**(P-4924)**
**MORELAND MANUFACTURING INC**
Also Called: Coast Label Company
17406 Mount Cliffwood Cir, Fountain Valley (92708)
PHONE..................................714 426-1411
EMP: 20 EST: 1991
SALES (est): 4.7MM Privately Held
Web: www.coastlabel.com
SIC: 2759 Labels and seals: printing, nsk
PA: Resource Label Group, Llc
2550 Mridian Blvd Ste 370

**(P-4925)**
**MS CARITA INC**
2159 Research Dr, Livermore (94550-3805)
PHONE..................................925 243-1720
▲ EMP: 31 EST: 1975
SALES (est): 3.88MM Privately Held
Web: www.mscarita.com
SIC: 2759 Labels and seals: printing, nsk

**(P-4926)**
**MULTI-COLOR CORPORATION**
21 Executive Way, Napa (94558-6271)
PHONE..................................707 931-7400
EMP: 89
SALES (corp-wide): 14.54B Privately Held
Web: www.mcclabel.com
SIC: 2759 Labels and seals: printing, nsk
HQ: Multi-Color Corporation
4053 Clough Woods Dr
Batavia OH 45103
513 381-1480

**(P-4927)**
**NEFT VODKA USA INC**
144 Penn St, El Segundo (90245-3907)
PHONE..................................415 846-0359
Christopher Holtzer, Prin
EMP: 18 EST: 2017
SALES (est): 3.06MM Privately Held
Web: www.neftvodka.com
SIC: 2759 Screen printing

**(P-4928)**
**NO FRILL FRANCHISING INC**
7310 Miramar Rd, San Diego (92126-4225)
PHONE..................................858 642-4848
Ralph Askar, Pr
EMP: 19 EST: 2011
SALES (est): 481.89K Privately Held
Web: www.instantimprints.com
SIC: 2759 Imprinting

**(P-4929)**
**NOWDOCS INTERNATIONAL INC**
Also Called: Nowdocs
3230 E Imperial Hwy Ste 302, Brea (92821-6721)
PHONE..................................714 986-1559
EMP: 24
SIC: 2759 Commercial printing, nec

**(P-4930)**
**ONE STOP LABEL CORPORATION**
1641 S Baker Ave, Ontario (91761-8025)
PHONE..................................909 230-9380
Maria Navarro, Pr
Jorge Navarro, VP
EMP: 16 EST: 1996
SQ FT: 12,000
SALES (est): 1.27MM Privately Held
Web: www.onestoplabel.com
SIC: 2759 Labels and seals: printing, nsk

**(P-4931)**
**OOSHIRTS INC (PA)**
Also Called: Scalable
39899 Balentine Dr Ste 220, Newark (94560-5358)
P.O. Box 26099 (46226)
PHONE..................................866 660-8667
Raymond Lei, Pr
◆ EMP: 55 EST: 2011
SALES (est): 24.03MM
SALES (corp-wide): 24.03MM Privately Held
Web: www.ooshirts.com
SIC: 2759 Screen printing

**(P-4932)**
**OPTEC LASER SYSTEMS LLC**
11622 El Camino Real Ste 100, San Diego (92130-2049)
PHONE..................................858 220-1070
EMP: 25 EST: 2017
SALES (est): 900.51K Privately Held
Web: www.optec-laser-systems.com
SIC: 2759 Laser printing

**(P-4933)**
**ORANGE CIRCLE STUDIO CORP (PA)**
Also Called: Studio OH
2 Technology Dr, Irvine (92618-5317)
PHONE..................................949 727-0800
Kelly Carioti, CEO
Daniel H Whang, Sec
Scott Whang, Ch
◆ EMP: 77 EST: 2009
SALES (est): 38.5MM
SALES (corp-wide): 38.5MM Privately Held
Web: www.studiooh.com
SIC: 2759 5112 5199 2086 Calendars: printing, nsk; Social stationery and greeting cards; Candles; Bottled and canned soft drinks

**(P-4934)**
**ORBITEL INTERNATIONAL LLC**
Also Called: Weddingolala
15304 Valley Blvd, City Of Industry (91746-3324)
PHONE..................................626 369-7050
▲ EMP: 25 EST: 2008
SALES (est): 243.22K Privately Held
SIC: 2759 5199 Invitations: printing, nsk; Party favors, balloons, hats, etc.

**(P-4935)**
**ORORA VISUAL LLC**
1600 E Valencia Dr, Fullerton (92831-4735)
PHONE..................................714 879-2400
James R Hamel, Pr
▲ EMP: 100 EST: 1987
SALES (est): 10.03MM Privately Held
Web: www.ororagroup.com
SIC: 2759 Screen printing

**(P-4936)**
**PARADIGM LABEL INC**
1177 N Grove St, Anaheim (92806-2110)
PHONE..................................951 372-9212
Curtis Harton, CEO
EMP: 15 EST: 2006
SALES (est): 2.29MM Privately Held

Web: www.aguirresfightingsystem.com
SIC: 2759 Labels and seals: printing, nsk

**(P-4937)**
**PAW PRINTS INC**
3166 Bay Rd, Redwood City (94063-3907)
PHONE..................................650 365-4077
John Garibaldi, Pr
Antionette Garibaldi, VP
EMP: 16 EST: 1969
SALES (est): 415.51K Privately Held
Web: pawprints.espwebsite.com
SIC: 2759 5199 3993 Screen printing; Advertising specialties; Signs and advertising specialties

**(P-4938)**
**PAX TAG & LABEL INC**
9528 Rush St Ste C, El Monte (91733-1551)
PHONE..................................626 579-2000
Michael Brown, Pr
EMP: 20 EST: 1994
SQ FT: 10,000
SALES (est): 611.66K Privately Held
Web: www.paxtag.com
SIC: 2759 2679 Tags: printing, nsk; Tags, paper (unprinted): made from purchased paper

**(P-4939)**
**POLYCRAFT INC**
42075 Avenida Alvarado, Temecula (92590-3486)
PHONE..................................951 296-0860
William D Verstegen, Pr
Patricia Verstegen, Prin
Bryan Nealy, Prin
EMP: 20 EST: 1974
SQ FT: 21,000
SALES (est): 2.32MM Privately Held
Web: www.polycraftinc.com
SIC: 2759 2671 Screen printing; Paper; coated and laminated packaging

**(P-4940)**
**PRESIDENT ENTERPRISE LLC**
Also Called: Lotus Labels
655 Tamarack Ave, Brea (92821-3213)
PHONE..................................714 671-9577
George Wu, Pr
Shu-feng T Wu, VP
▲ EMP: 20 EST: 1992
SALES (est): 2.53MM Privately Held
Web: www.lotuslabels.net
SIC: 2759 Labels and seals: printing, nsk

**(P-4941)**
**PRIMARY COLOR SYSTEMS CORP (PA)**
11130 Holder St Ste 210, Cypress (90630-5162)
PHONE..................................949 660-7080
Daniel Hirt, CEO
Michael Hirt, *
▲ EMP: 305 EST: 1984
SQ FT: 40,000
SALES (est): 47.93MM
SALES (corp-wide): 47.93MM Privately Held
Web: www.primarycolor.com
SIC: 2759 2752 Commercial printing, nec; Offset printing

**(P-4942)**
**PRIMARY COLOR SYSTEMS CORP**
401 Coral Cir, El Segundo (90245-4622)
PHONE..................................310 841-0250

## 2759 - Commercial Printing, Nec (P-4943)

Ed Philipps, *Brnch Mgr*
**EMP:** 53
**SALES (corp-wide):** 47.93MM **Privately Held**
**Web:** www.primarycolor.com
**SIC: 2759** 2752 Commercial printing, nec; Commercial printing, lithographic
**PA:** Primary Color Systems Corporation
11130 Holder St Ste 210
949 660-7080

**(P-4943)**
**PRINT INK LLC**
Also Called: Build Your Own Garment
6918 Sierra Ct, Dublin (94568)
**PHONE**............................925 829-3950
Cathileen Marchese, *Pr*
**EMP:** 17 **EST:** 1993
**SALES (est):** 2.26MM **Privately Held**
**Web:** www.printinkinc.com
**SIC: 2759** Screen printing

**(P-4944)**
**PROGRAPHICS SCREENPRINTING INC**
1975 Diamond St, San Marcos (92078-5122)
**PHONE**............................760 744-4555
Bruce Heid, *Pr*
Barbara Heid, *
**EMP:** 41 **EST:** 1989
**SQ FT:** 18,000
**SALES (est):** 2.68MM **Privately Held**
**Web:** www.prografx.com
**SIC: 2759** 3993 2396 5112 Screen printing; Signs and advertising specialties; Automotive and apparel trimmings; Pens and/or pencils

**(P-4945)**
**PROGROUP**
Also Called: Pro Group
17622 Armstrong Ave, Irvine (92614)
**PHONE**............................949 748-5400
Cindy Kennedy, *Pr*
Thomas Brian Kennedy, *
**EMP:** 25 **EST:** 2008
**SALES (est):** 10.34MM **Privately Held**
**Web:** professionalreprographic.mfgpages.com
**SIC: 2759** Commercial printing, nec

**(P-4946)**
**PROGRSSIVE INTGRATED SOLUTIONS**
Also Called: Progressive Manufacturing
3291 E Miraloma Ave, Anaheim (92806-1910)
**PHONE**............................714 237-0980
Rodney Dean Boehme, *Pr*
**EMP:** 76 **EST:** 1988
**SALES (est):** 4.18MM **Privately Held**
**Web:** www.progressiveusa.com
**SIC: 2759** 2752 Envelopes: printing, nsk; Offset printing

**(P-4947)**
**R R DONNELLEY & SONS COMPANY**
Also Called: R R Donnelley
955 Gateway Center Way, San Diego (92102-4542)
**PHONE**............................619 527-4600
Boyd Richardson, *Brnch Mgr*
**EMP:** 39
**SALES (corp-wide):** 15B **Privately Held**
**Web:** www.rrd.com
**SIC: 2759** Commercial printing, nec
**HQ:** R. R. Donnelley & Sons Company
35 W Wacker Dr
Chicago IL 60601
312 326-8000

**(P-4948)**
**R R DONNELLEY & SONS COMPANY**
Los Angeles Manufacturing Div
19681 Pacific Gateway Dr, Torrance (90502-1116)
**PHONE**............................310 516-3100
Barbara Dowell, *Dir*
**EMP:** 70
**SQ FT:** 80,000
**SALES (corp-wide):** 15B **Privately Held**
**Web:** www.rrd.com
**SIC: 2759** 2752 Publication printing; Commercial printing, lithographic
**HQ:** R. R. Donnelley & Sons Company
35 W Wacker Dr
Chicago IL 60601
312 326-8000

**(P-4949)**
**RESOURCE LABEL GROUP LLC**
1511 E Edinger Ave, Santa Ana (92705-4907)
**PHONE**............................714 619-7100
Robert Simko, *Mgr*
**EMP:** 80
**Web:** www.resourcelabel.com
**SIC: 2759** 2752 Commercial printing, nec; Commercial printing, lithographic
**PA:** Resource Label Group, Llc
2550 Mridian Blvd Ste 370

**(P-4950)**
**RESOURCE LABEL GROUP LLC**
Also Called: Paragon Label
3810 Cypress Dr, Petaluma (94954-5613)
**PHONE**............................707 773-4363
**EMP:** 27
**Web:** www.resourcelabel.com
**SIC: 2759** Labels and seals: printing, nsk
**PA:** Resource Label Group, Llc
2550 Mridian Blvd Ste 370

**(P-4951)**
**RESOURCE LABEL GROUP LLC**
Also Called: Spectrum Label
39611 Eureka Dr, Newark (94560-4806)
**PHONE**............................510 477-0707
**EMP:** 49
**Web:** www.resourcelabel.com
**SIC: 2759** Labels and seals: printing, nsk
**PA:** Resource Label Group, Llc
2550 Mridian Blvd Ste 370

**(P-4952)**
**RESPONSE ENVELOPE INC (PA)**
1340 S Baker Ave, Ontario (91761-7742)
**PHONE**............................909 923-5855
Jonas Ulrich, *CEO*
Philip Ulrich, *
▲ **EMP:** 104 **EST:** 1986
**SQ FT:** 85,000
**SALES (est):** 11.55MM
**SALES (corp-wide):** 11.55MM **Privately Held**
**Web:** www.marketing.com
**SIC: 2759** 2677 Envelopes: printing, nsk; Envelopes

**(P-4953)**
**RETAIL PRINT MEDIA INC**
Also Called: RPM Media
2355 Crenshaw Blvd Ste 135, Torrance (90501-3329)
**PHONE**............................424 488-6950
Raymond Young, *CEO*
Karli Sikich, *

**EMP:** 35 **EST:** 2015
**SALES (est):** 3.01MM **Privately Held**
**Web:** www.retailprintmedia.com
**SIC: 2759** 7371 Advertising literature: printing, nsk; Computer software writing services

**(P-4954)**
**RJ ACQUISITION CORP (PA)**
Also Called: Ad Art Company
3260 E 26th St, Los Angeles (90058-8008)
**PHONE**............................323 318-1107
Joe M Demarco, *Pr*
Roger Keech, *
Eddie Leon, *Prin*
Jose Puentes Plant, *Prin*
▲ **EMP:** 215 **EST:** 1944
**SQ FT:** 200,000
**SALES (est):** 28.7MM
**SALES (corp-wide):** 28.7MM **Privately Held**
**Web:** www.adartco.com
**SIC: 2759** Screen printing

**(P-4955)**
**ROBERT R WIX INC (PA)**
Also Called: Valley Printing
2140 Pine St, Ceres (95307-3638)
P.O. Box 2671 (95307-7871)
**PHONE**............................209 537-4561
Robert R Wix, *Pr*
Tom Mink, *
Linny Goodrich, *
**EMP:** 32 **EST:** 1959
**SQ FT:** 31,000
**SALES (est):** 777.88K
**SALES (corp-wide):** 777.88K **Privately Held**
**SIC: 2759** 2752 2672 2671 Letterpress printing; Offset printing; Paper; coated and laminated, nec; Paper; coated and laminated packaging

**(P-4956)**
**ROBINSON PRINTING INC**
Also Called: Robinson Printing
42685 Rio Nedo, Temecula (92590-3711)
**PHONE**............................951 296-0300
David Robinson, *CEO*
Mike Robinson, *
▲ **EMP:** 38 **EST:** 1981
**SQ FT:** 24,000
**SALES (est):** 2.78MM **Privately Held**
**Web:** www.robinsonprinting.com
**SIC: 2759** 2621 Screen printing; Packaging paper

**(P-4957)**
**SAFE PUBLISHING COMPANY**
400 Del Norte Blvd, Oxnard (93030-7997)
**PHONE**............................805 973-1300
John Gooden, *Pr*
**EMP:** 70 **EST:** 1976
**SQ FT:** 96,000
**SALES (est):** 1.39MM **Privately Held**
**SIC: 2759** 8748 8742 8741 Promotional printing; Business consulting, nec; Management consulting services; Management services

**(P-4958)**
**SAN BRNRDINO CMNTY COLLEGE DST**
Also Called: Print Shop
701 S Mount Vernon Ave, San Bernardino (92410-2705)
**PHONE**............................909 888-6511
Louie Chavira, *Supervisor*
**EMP:** 85
**SALES (corp-wide):** 46.53MM **Privately Held**

**Web:** www.sbccd.edu
**SIC: 2759** Commercial printing, nec
**PA:** San Bernardino Community College District
550 E Hospitality Ln # 200
909 382-4000

**(P-4959)**
**SCREEN PRINTERS RESOURCE INC**
3164 E La Palma Ave, Anaheim (92806-2811)
**PHONE**............................714 441-1155
Frank Sator, *Pr*
◆ **EMP:** 16 **EST:** 2000
**SALES (est):** 5.22MM **Privately Held**
**Web:** www.silkscreen-supplies.com
**SIC: 2759** Screen printing

**(P-4960)**
**SHORETT PRINTING INC (PA)**
Also Called: Crown Printers
250 W Rialto Ave, San Bernardino (92408-1017)
**PHONE**............................714 545-4689
Charles D Shorett Junior, *CEO*
John Shorett, *
**EMP:** 30 **EST:** 1970
**SALES (est):** 6.4MM
**SALES (corp-wide):** 6.4MM **Privately Held**
**Web:** www.crownconnect.com
**SIC: 2759** 2752 Commercial printing, nec; Offset printing

**(P-4961)**
**SIRENA INCORPORATED**
Also Called: Los Angeles Wraps
22717 S Western Ave, Torrance (90501-4952)
**PHONE**............................866 548-5353
Brandon Park, *CEO*
**EMP:** 16 **EST:** 2010
**SQ FT:** 10,000
**SALES (est):** 1.16MM **Privately Held**
**Web:** www.lawraps.com
**SIC: 2759** Commercial printing, nec

**(P-4962)**
**SPECTRUM LABEL CORPORATION**
30803 San Clemente St, Hayward (94544-7136)
**PHONE**............................510 477-9374
▲ **EMP:** 49
**SIC: 2759** Flexographic printing

**(P-4963)**
**SUNSPORTS INC**
Also Called: Sun Sports Apparels
7 Holland, Irvine (92618-2506)
▲ **EMP:** 16 **EST:** 2005
**SALES (est):** 606.12K **Privately Held**
**SIC: 2759** Screen printing

**(P-4964)**
**SUPACOLOR USA INC**
Also Called: Supacolor
12705 Daphne Ave, Hawthorne (90250-3311)
**PHONE**............................844 973-2862
Ramneek Walia, *CEO*
**EMP:** 91 **EST:** 2019
**SALES (est):** 9.9MM **Privately Held**
**Web:** www.supacolor.com
**SIC: 2759** Letterpress and screen printing

**(P-4965)**
**SUPER COLOR DIGITAL LLC (PA)**

▲ = Import ▼ = Export
◆ = Import/Export

## PRODUCTS & SERVICES SECTION
### 2761 - Manifold Business Forms (P-4987)

Also Called: Super Color Digital
16761 Hale Ave, Irvine (92606-5006)
PHONE.................................949 622-0010
Peyman Rashtchi, *Managing Member*
▲ EMP: 25 EST: 2006
SQ FT: 48,043
SALES (est): 43.33MM **Privately Held**
Web: www.supercolor.com
SIC: 2759 Commercial printing, nec

**(P-4966)**
**SUPERIOR PRINTING INC**
Also Called: Superior Press
9440 Norwalk Blvd, Santa Fe Springs (90670-2928)
PHONE.................................888 590-7998
Robert Traut, *Pr*
Kevin Traut, *
Jason Traut, *
EMP: 95 EST: 1953
SQ FT: 32,000
SALES (est): 20.15MM **Privately Held**
Web: www.superiorpress.com
SIC: 2759 5112 Commercial printing, nec; Business forms

**(P-4967)**
**TARGET MDIA PRTNERS INTRCTIVE (HQ)**
Also Called: Target Mdia Prtners Intractive
5200 Lankershim Blvd Ste 350, North Hollywood (91601-3109)
PHONE.................................323 930-3123
Dave Duckwitz, *CEO*
EMP: 35 EST: 1998
SALES (est): 15.06MM
SALES (corp-wide): 25.03MM **Privately Held**
Web: www.targetmediapartners.com
SIC: 2759 7331 Commercial printing, nec; Direct mail advertising services
PA: Responselogix, Inc.
6900 E Camelback Rd
888 713-8958

**(P-4968)**
**TAYLOR DIGITAL**
101 W Avenida Vista Hermosa Ste 122, San Clemente (92672-7707)
PHONE.................................949 391-3333
EMP: 24 EST: 2019
SALES (est): 1.21MM **Privately Held**
SIC: 2759 Commercial printing, nec

**(P-4969)**
**TAYLOR GRAPHICS INC**
1582 Browning, Irvine (92606-4807)
PHONE.................................949 752-5200
Dean S Taylor, *CEO*
Carla Spicer, *
EMP: 23 EST: 1950
SQ FT: 7,500
SALES (est): 2.86MM **Privately Held**
SIC: 2759 Screen printing

**(P-4970)**
**TEC COLOR CRAFT (PA)**
Also Called: TEC Color Craft Products
1860 Wright Ave, La Verne (91750-5824)
PHONE.................................909 392-9000
Edgar A Frenkiel, *CEO*
▲ EMP: 40 EST: 1960
SQ FT: 8,000
SALES (est): 5.39MM
SALES (corp-wide): 5.39MM **Privately Held**
Web: www.teccolorcraft.com
SIC: 2759 Screen printing

**(P-4971)**
**TEE STYLED INC**
4640 E La Palma Ave, Anaheim (92807-1910)
PHONE.................................323 983-9988
Anwar Gajiani, *Pr*
EMP: 41 EST: 2019
SALES (est): 1.05MM **Privately Held**
Web: www.teestyled.com
SIC: 2759 Screen printing
PA: Fantasy Activewear, Inc.
5383 Alcoa Ave

**(P-4972)**
**TEMECULA T-SHIRT PRINTERS INC**
41607 Enterprise Cir N Ste A, Temecula (92590-5684)
PHONE.................................951 296-0184
Kenneth Dawkins, *Pr*
EMP: 15 EST: 2015
SALES (est): 728.37K **Privately Held**
Web: www.temeculatshirtprinters.com
SIC: 2759 Screen printing

**(P-4973)**
**THE/STUDIO**
360 E 2nd St Ste 800, Los Angeles (90012-4607)
PHONE.................................213 233-1633
EMP: 25 EST: 2018
SALES (est): 1.63MM **Privately Held**
Web: www.thestudio.com
SIC: 2759 Screen printing

**(P-4974)**
**THERAPEUTIC RES FACULTY LLC**
3120 W March Ln, Stockton (95219-2368)
PHONE.................................209 472-2240
Wes Crews, *CEO*
EMP: 200 EST: 2013
SALES (est): 503.32K **Privately Held**
SIC: 2759 Publication printing

**(P-4975)**
**THREE MAN CORPORATION**
Also Called: San Diego Printers
10025 Huennekens St, San Diego (92121-2967)
PHONE.................................858 684-5200
John Barros, *Pr*
Wayne Ihms, *VP*
EMP: 20 EST: 1999
SQ FT: 14,000
SALES (est): 6.5MM **Privately Held**
Web: www.sdprinters.com
SIC: 2759 2752 Commercial printing, nec; Commercial printing, lithographic

**(P-4976)**
**TRANSCONTINENTAL NRTHERN CA 20**
47540 Kato Rd, Fremont (94538-7303)
PHONE.................................510 580-7700
Brian Reid, *CEO*
Francois Olivier, *
Vivian Marzin Mckay, *Dir Fin*
▲ EMP: 200 EST: 2006
SALES (est): 5.45MM
SALES (corp-wide): 2.18B **Privately Held**
SIC: 2759 Magazines: printing, nsk
PA: Transcontinental Inc
1 Place Ville-Marie Bureau 3240
514 954-0500

**(P-4977)**
**TSHIRTGUYSCOM (PA)**
11264 Chula Vista Ave, San Jose (95127-1316)
PHONE.................................619 500-5271
Maria Rodriguez, *CEO*
EMP: 15 EST: 2000
SALES (est): 578.8K
SALES (corp-wide): 578.8K **Privately Held**
Web: www.tshirtguys.com
SIC: 2759 7389 Screen printing; Business services, nec

**(P-4978)**
**VALLEY IMAGES LLC**
Also Called: Valley Images
1925 Kyle Park Ct, San Jose (95125-1029)
PHONE.................................408 279-6777
Carlo Strangis, *Pt*
Robert Malik, *Pt*
EMP: 17 EST: 1990
SQ FT: 10,201
SALES (est): 2.4MM **Privately Held**
Web: www.valleyimages.com
SIC: 2759 Screen printing

**(P-4979)**
**VITACHROME GRAPHICS GROUP INC**
Also Called: Vitachrome Graphics
3710 Park Pl, Montrose (91020-1623)
P.O. Box 2924 (90670-0924)
PHONE.................................818 957-0900
Gary Durbin, *Pr*
Tony Won, *
EMP: 45 EST: 1971
SQ FT: 43,000
SALES (est): 4.82MM **Privately Held**
Web: www.adahotelsigns.com
SIC: 2759 Decals: printing, nsk

**(P-4980)**
**VOMAR PRODUCTS INC**
Also Called: Vomar
7800 Deering Ave, Canoga Park (91304-5005)
PHONE.................................818 610-5115
Paul Van Ostrand, *CEO*
Herbert Paul Van Ostrand, *
Jason Van Ostrand, *
EMP: 38 EST: 1961
SQ FT: 29,000
SALES (est): 6MM **Privately Held**
Web: www.vomarproducts.com
SIC: 2759 3993 Commercial printing, nec; Name plates: except engraved, etched, etc.: metal

**(P-4981)**
**WES GO INC**
Also Called: GP Color Imaging Group
8211 Lankershim Blvd, North Hollywood (91605-1614)
PHONE.................................818 504-1200
Wesley Adams, *CEO*
Thomas Wilhelm, *
▲ EMP: 24 EST: 2001
SALES (est): 4.45MM **Privately Held**
Web: www.gpcolor.com
SIC: 2759 Posters, including billboards: printing, nsk

**(P-4982)**
**WESTERN CONVERTING SPC INC**
Also Called: Consolidated Design West
15601 Cypress Ave, Baldwin Park (91706-2120)
PHONE.................................909 392-4578
Chad Junkin, *Pr*
EMP: 20 EST: 1980
SALES (est): 1.96MM **Privately Held**
Web: www.westernconverting.com
SIC: 2759 Commercial printing, nec

**(P-4983)**
**WESTERN ROTO ENGRAVERS INC**
Also Called: W R E Colortech
1225 6th St, Berkeley (94710-1401)
PHONE.................................510 525-2950
Bill Mackay, *Mgr*
EMP: 25
SALES (corp-wide): 12.93MM **Privately Held**
Web: www.wrecolor.com
SIC: 2759 2796 Engraving, nec; Plates and cylinders for rotogravure printing
PA: Western Roto Engravers, Incorporated
533 Banner Ave
336 275-9821

**(P-4984)**
**WESTERN STATES ENVELOPE CORP**
2301 Raymer Ave, Fullerton (92833-2514)
P.O. Box 2607 (92837)
PHONE.................................714 449-0909
Lisa Hoehle, *Pr*
EMP: 60 EST: 1968
SQ FT: 24,000
SALES (est): 1.09MM **Privately Held**
Web: www.wseca.com
SIC: 2759 Commercial printing, nec

**(P-4985)**
**WILSONS ART STUDIO INC**
Also Called: Solutions Unlimited
501 S Acacia Ave, Fullerton (92831-5101)
PHONE.................................714 870-7030
William L Goetsch, *Pr*
N Jim Goetsch, *
Roberta C Goetsch, *
EMP: 63 EST: 1958
SQ FT: 50,000
SALES (est): 4.49MM **Privately Held**
Web: www.solutions-unlimited.net
SIC: 2759 2396 Screen printing; Automotive and apparel trimmings

**(P-4986)**
**WIZARD GRAPHICS INC**
411 Otterson Dr Ste 20, Chico (95973)
P.O. Box 7650 (95927-7650)
PHONE.................................530 893-3636
Merlin Newkirk, *Pr*
EMP: 15 EST: 2003
SQ FT: 10,000
SALES (est): 279.56K **Privately Held**
Web: www.wgiprint.com
SIC: 2759 Commercial printing, nec

### 2761 Manifold Business Forms

**(P-4987)**
**APPERSON INC (PA)**
17315 Studebaker Rd Ste 211, Cerritos (90703-2563)
P.O. Box 480309 (28269-5338)
PHONE.................................562 356-3333
Kelly Doherty, *CEO*
Brian Apperson, *
William Apperson, *
▲ EMP: 70 EST: 1955
SQ FT: 80,080
SALES (est): 9.86MM

## 2761 - Manifold Business Forms (P-4988)

**SALES (corp-wide):** 9.86MM **Privately Held**
Web: www.apperson.com
SIC: 2761 Continuous forms, office and business

### (P-4988) BESTFORMS INC
1135 Avenida Acaso, Camarillo (93012-8740)
PHONE..........................805 388-0503
Joe Valdez, *Pr*
Patrick Valdez, *
**EMP:** 48 **EST:** 1985
**SQ FT:** 31,000
**SALES (est):** 8.36MM **Privately Held**
Web: www.bestforms.com
SIC: 2761 Manifold business forms

### (P-4989) COMPLYRIGHT DIST SVCS INC
3451 Jupiter Ct, Oxnard (93030-8957)
PHONE..........................805 981-0992
Richard Roddis, *CEO*
**EMP:** 44 **EST:** 2006
**SALES (est):** 10.92MM
**SALES (corp-wide):** 3.81B **Privately Held**
Web: www.complyrightdealer.com
SIC: 2761 Manifold business forms
PA: Taylor Corporation
1725 Roe Crest Dr
507 625-2828

### (P-4990) NBS SYSTEMS INC (PA)
2477 E Orangethorpe Ave, Fullerton (92831-5303)
PHONE..........................217 999-3472
Bill Gascon, *Pr*
**EMP:** 35 **EST:** 1963
**SALES (est):** 2.1MM
**SALES (corp-wide):** 2.1MM **Privately Held**
Web: www.nbschecks.com
SIC: 2761 2759 Continuous forms, office and business; Commercial printing, nec

### (P-4991) PRINTEGRA CORP
23281 La Palma Ave, Yorba Linda (92887-4768)
PHONE..........................714 692-2221
Terri Reynolds, *Mgr*
**EMP:** 65
**SQ FT:** 38,000
**SALES (corp-wide):** 420.11MM **Publicly Held**
Web: www.printegra.com
SIC: 2761 2782 Continuous forms, office and business; Blankbooks and looseleaf binders
HQ: Printegra Corp
1560 Westfork Dr
Lithia Springs GA 30122
770 319-9500

### (P-4992) TAYLOR COMMUNICATIONS INC
3885 Seaport Blvd Ste 40, West Sacramento (95691-3527)
PHONE..........................916 340-0200
John Joyce, *Brnch Mgr*
**EMP:** 20
**SALES (corp-wide):** 3.81B **Privately Held**
Web: www.taylor.com
SIC: 2761 Manifold business forms
HQ: Taylor Communications, Inc.
1725 Roe Crest Dr
North Mankato MN 56003
866 541-0937

### (P-4993) TST/IMPRESO INC
10589 Business Dr, Fontana (92337-8223)
PHONE..........................909 357-7190
▲ **EMP:** 42
**SALES (corp-wide):** 72.86MM **Privately Held**
Web: www.tstimpreso.com
SIC: 2761 Manifold business forms
HQ: Tst/Impreso, Inc.
652 Southwestern Blvd
Coppell TX 75019
972 462-0100

### (P-4994) WRIGHT BUSINESS GRAPHICS LLC
Also Called: Wright Business Graphics Calif
13602 12th St Ste A, Chino (91710-5200)
P.O. Box 20489 (97294-0489)
PHONE..........................909 614-6700
Gene Snitker, *Prin*
**EMP:** 28
**SALES (corp-wide):** 420.11MM **Publicly Held**
Web: www.wrightbg.com
SIC: 2761 Manifold business forms
HQ: Wright Business Graphics Llc
18440 Ne San Rafael St
Portland OR 97230
800 547-8397

## 2771 Greeting Cards

### (P-4995) FOUND IMAGE PRESS INC
5151 Santa Fe St, San Diego (92109-1618)
P.O. Box 16116 (92176-6116)
PHONE..........................619 282-3452
**EMP:** 16 **EST:** 1996
**SALES (est):** 695.29K **Privately Held**
Web: www.foundimage.com
SIC: 2771 5199 Greeting cards; Calendars

### (P-4996) PUNKPOST LLC
Also Called: Punkpost
41 Federal St Unit 4, San Francisco (94107)
PHONE..........................415 818-7677
Alexis Monson, *CEO*
Santiago Prieto, *Pr*
**EMP:** 28 **EST:** 2016
**SALES (est):** 240.39K **Privately Held**
Web: www.punkpost.co
SIC: 2771 7389 Greeting cards; Business Activities at Non-Commercial Site

### (P-4997) SCHURMAN FINE PAPERS
Also Called: Papyrus
36 Petaluma Blvd N, Petaluma (94952-3002)
PHONE..........................707 765-2514
FAX: 707 765-2970
**EMP:** 158
**SALES (corp-wide):** 1.3B **Privately Held**
SIC: 2771 Greeting cards
PA: Schurman Fine Papers
500 Chadbourne Rd
707 425-8006

## 2782 Blankbooks And Looseleaf Binders

### (P-4998) CHAMELEON LIKE INC
Also Called: Chameleon Books & Journals
345 Kishimura Dr, Gilroy (95020-3653)
PHONE..........................408 847-3661
Pierre Martichoux, *Pr*
Bradley Boggs, *
▲ **EMP:** 80 **EST:** 1998
**SQ FT:** 12,000
**SALES (est):** 10MM **Privately Held**
Web: www.chameleonlike.com
SIC: 2782 Blankbooks and looseleaf binders

### (P-4999) CHECKWORKS INC
315 Cloverleaf Dr Ste J, Baldwin Park (91706-6510)
P.O. Box 60065 (91716-0065)
PHONE..........................626 333-1444
Aloysious J Uniack, *Pr*
Aloysius J Uniack, *
Christen Mc Kiernan, *
**EMP:** 55 **EST:** 1995
**SQ FT:** 15,000
**SALES (est):** 4.52MM **Privately Held**
Web: www.checkworks.com
SIC: 2782 Checkbooks

### (P-5000) CONTINENTAL BDR SPECIALTY CORP (PA)
407 W Compton Blvd, Gardena (90248-1703)
PHONE..........................310 324-8227
Andrew Lisardi, *CEO*
Jack Gray, *
▼ **EMP:** 120 **EST:** 1978
**SQ FT:** 31,000
**SALES (est):** 6.14MM
**SALES (corp-wide):** 6.14MM **Privately Held**
Web: www.continentalbinder.com
SIC: 2782 2759 2675 2396 Looseleaf binders and devices; Commercial printing, nec; Die-cut paper and board; Automotive and apparel trimmings

### (P-5001) DOCUPAK INC
1702 Edinger Ave, Tustin (92780-6511)
PHONE..........................714 670-7944
William Lyons, *Pr*
Pat Lyons, *VP*
John Flores, *CFO*
**EMP:** 17 **EST:** 1993
**SALES (est):** 939.9K **Privately Held**
Web: www.docupakinc.com
SIC: 2782 Looseleaf binders and devices

### (P-5002) HANOVER ACCESSORIES CORP
6049 E Slauson Ave, Commerce (90040-3007)
▲ **EMP:** 120
SIC: 2782 Library binders, looseleaf

### (P-5003) PIONEER PHOTO ALBUMS INC (PA)
9801 Deering Ave, Chatsworth (91311-4398)
P.O. Box 2497 (91313-2497)
PHONE..........................818 882-2161
Shell Plutsky, *CEO*
Jason Reubens, *
Rick Collies, *
♦ **EMP:** 150 **EST:** 1972
**SQ FT:** 100,000
**SALES (est):** 16.64MM
**SALES (corp-wide):** 16.64MM **Privately Held**
Web: www.pioneerphotoalbums.com

SIC: 2782 Albums

### (P-5004) SHARON HAVRILUK
Also Called: American Mailing & Prtg Svc
1164 N Kraemer Pl, Anaheim (92806-1922)
PHONE..........................714 630-1313
Sharon Havriluk, *Owner*
**EMP:** 20 **EST:** 1966
**SQ FT:** 10,000
**SALES (est):** 948.57K **Privately Held**
Web: www.ampls.com
SIC: 2782 7331 Account books; Mailing list compilers

### (P-5005) TOTAL ACCNTNG BKKPING SLTIONS
6345 Balboa Blvd Ste 160, Encino (91316-1519)
PHONE..........................818 981-0600
**EMP:** 18 **EST:** 2019
**SALES (est):** 227.18K **Privately Held**
Web: www.taabs.la
SIC: 2782 Account books

### (P-5006) ULTRA PRO ACQUISITION LLC
6049 E Slauson Ave, Commerce (90040-3007)
PHONE..........................323 725-1975
▲ **EMP:** 21 **EST:** 2007
**SALES (est):** 2.04MM **Privately Held**
SIC: 2782 Library binders, looseleaf
PA: Marlin Equity Partners, Llc
1301 Manhattan Ave

### (P-5007) VAPOR DELUX INC
2148 Glendale Galleria, Glendale (91210-2101)
PHONE..........................818 370-8308
**EMP:** 20
**SALES (corp-wide):** 404.48K **Privately Held**
Web: www.vapordelux.com
SIC: 2782 Checkbooks
PA: Vapor Delux Inc
11152 Fleetwood St Ste 1
818 856-3750

### (P-5008) WE OWN EVERYTHING RECORDS LLC
620 W Huntington Dr Unit 103, Arcadia (91007-3437)
PHONE..........................323 208-9454
**EMP:** 15 **EST:** 2022
**SALES (est):** 193.64K **Privately Held**
SIC: 2782 Record albums

## 2789 Bookbinding And Related Work

### (P-5009) B J BINDERY INC
833 S Grand Ave, Santa Ana (92705-4117)
PHONE..........................714 835-7342
Naresh Arya, *CEO*
Renu Arya, *
▲ **EMP:** 80 **EST:** 1970
**SQ FT:** 29,000
**SALES (est):** 4.34MM **Privately Held**
Web: www.bjbindery.com
SIC: 2789 Binding only: books, pamphlets, magazines, etc.

▲ = Import ▼ = Export
♦ = Import/Export

# PRODUCTS & SERVICES SECTION
## 2812 - Alkalies And Chlorine (P-5031)

**(P-5010)**
**GENERAL REWINDING INC**
Also Called: General Newsprint
888 W Crowther Ave, Placentia (92870-6348)
PHONE.....................714 776-5561
▲ **EMP:** 20 **EST:** 1980
**SALES (est):** 774.72K **Privately Held**
**SIC: 2789** Paper cutting

**(P-5011)**
**GOLDEN RULE BINDERY INC**
Also Called: Golden Rule Packaging
221 Townsite Dr, Vista (92084-4331)
PHONE.....................760 471-2013
Jerry Kiley, *Pr*
Fred Antor, *Treas*
**EMP:** 22 **EST:** 1957
**SALES (est):** 1.41MM **Privately Held**
Web: www.goldenrulebindery.com
**SIC: 2789** Bookbinding and related work

**(P-5012)**
**KATER-CRAFTS INCORPORATED**
Also Called: Book Binders
3205 Weldon Ave, Los Angeles (90065-2312)
PHONE.....................562 692-0665
Bruce Kavin, *Pr*
Richard Kavin, *
**EMP:** 40 **EST:** 1948
**SALES (est):** 1.32MM **Privately Held**
Web: www.katercrafts.com
**SIC: 2789** Binding only: books, pamphlets, magazines, etc.

**(P-5013)**
**PEL MANUFACTURING AND LSG CORP**
Also Called: Pel Mfg & Leasing
3200 Kashiwa St, Torrance (90505-4021)
PHONE.....................310 530-7145
Phillis Pelezzare, *Pr*
Joseph A Pelezzare, *Pr*
**EMP:** 16 **EST:** 1981
**SQ FT:** 9,000
**SALES (est):** 1.87MM **Privately Held**
Web: www.pelspiral.com
**SIC: 2789** Bookbinding and related work

**(P-5014)**
**ROSS BINDERY INC**
15310 Spring Ave, Santa Fe Springs (90670-5644)
PHONE.....................562 623-4565
George Jackson, *CEO*
▲ **EMP:** 120 **EST:** 1969
**SQ FT:** 65,000
**SALES (est):** 7.97MM **Privately Held**
Web: www.rossbindery.com
**SIC: 2789** Pamphlets, binding

**(P-5015)**
**S & S BINDERY INC**
2366 1st St, La Verne (91750-5545)
PHONE.....................909 596-2213
Steve Thompson, *Pr*
Scott Fehrensen, *VP*
▼ **EMP:** 20 **EST:** 1998
**SQ FT:** 13,750
**SALES (est):** 668.4K **Privately Held**
**SIC: 2789** Binding only: books, pamphlets, magazines, etc.

## 2791 Typesetting

**(P-5016)**
**BARKERBLUE INC**
363 N Amphlett Blvd, San Mateo (94401-1806)
PHONE.....................650 696-2100
Eugene A Klein, *CEO*
Michael Callaghan, *
Konstantin Koshelev, *
**EMP:** 35 **EST:** 1961
**SALES (est):** 5.49MM **Privately Held**
Web: www.barkerblue.com
**SIC: 2791 7334** Typesetting; Blueprinting service

**(P-5017)**
**CASTLE PRESS**
1128 N Gilbert St, Anaheim (92801-1401)
PHONE.....................800 794-0858
Jay Bautista, *Mgr*
**EMP:** 48 **EST:** 2016
**SALES (est):** 1.27MM **Privately Held**
Web: www.castlepress.com
**SIC: 2791** Typesetting

**(P-5018)**
**DT123 (PA)**
13035 Hartsook St, Sherman Oaks (91423)
PHONE.....................213 488-1230
David Richard Tobman, *CEO*
Ann Tobman, *
**EMP:** 37 **EST:** 1949
**SALES (est):** 4.88MM
**SALES (corp-wide):** 4.88MM **Privately Held**
Web: www.automation-123.com
**SIC: 2791 2796 2759 2732** Typesetting; Platemaking services; Commercial printing, nec; Book printing

**(P-5019)**
**FOLGERGRAPHICS INC**
21093 Forbes Ave, Hayward (94545-1115)
PHONE.....................510 293-2294
Richard L Folger, *CEO*
Patricia A Folger, *
**EMP:** 40 **EST:** 1958
**SQ FT:** 16,000
**SALES (est):** 9.64MM **Privately Held**
Web: www.folgergraphics.com
**SIC: 2791 2752** Typesetting; Offset printing

**(P-5020)**
**GOLDING PUBLICATIONS**
Also Called: Friday Flier
31558 Railroad Canyon Rd, Canyon Lake (92587-9427)
PHONE.....................951 244-1966
Charles G Golding, *Owner*
**EMP:** 16 **EST:** 1990
**SALES (est):** 350.42K **Privately Held**
Web: www.goldingpublications.com
**SIC: 2791** Typesetting

**(P-5021)**
**NORCO PRINTING INC**
4588 Grenadier Pl, Castro Valley (94546-1275)
PHONE.....................510 569-2200
Ricky C Damiani, *Pr*
Rick C Damiani, *Pr*
Rose Damiani, *VP*
**EMP:** 15 **EST:** 1973
**SALES (est):** 1.05MM **Privately Held**
Web: www.norcoprint.com
**SIC: 2791 2759 2752 2789** Typesetting; Letterpress and screen printing; Offset printing; Bookbinding and related work

**(P-5022)**
**RAPID TYPOGRAPHERS COMPANY (PA)**
Also Called: Rapid Lasergraphics
836 Harrison St, San Francisco (94107-1125)
PHONE.....................415 957-5840
Bent Kjolby, *Pr*
John Perkins, *VP*
**EMP:** 15 **EST:** 1964
**SQ FT:** 12,000
**SALES (est):** 2.13MM
**SALES (corp-wide):** 2.13MM **Privately Held**
Web: www.rapidgraphics.com
**SIC: 2791 2752 7336 2759** Typesetting; Color lithography; Graphic arts and related design; Commercial printing, nec

## 2796 Platemaking Services

**(P-5023)**
**COAST ENGRAVING COMPANIES INC**
Also Called: Coast Creative Nameplates
18220 Bancroft Ave, Monte Sereno (95030-4106)
PHONE.....................408 297-2555
Ida Wool, *Pr*
Fred A Wool Junior, *CFO*
**EMP:** 40 **EST:** 1970
**SALES (est):** 1.75MM **Privately Held**
Web: www.coaste.com
**SIC: 2796 2752 2759** Engraving on copper, steel, wood, or rubber: printing plates; Commercial printing, lithographic; Commercial printing, nec

**(P-5024)**
**FLEXLINE INCORPORATED**
3727 S Meyler St, San Pedro (90731-6431)
PHONE.....................562 921-4141
John Bateman, *Pr*
William Hall, *
**EMP:** 28 **EST:** 1991
**SALES (est):** 654.1K **Privately Held**
**SIC: 2796 2759 3555** Platemaking services; Commercial printing, nec; Printing plates

**(P-5025)**
**GEMINI GEL LLC**
8365 Melrose Ave, Los Angeles (90069-5419)
PHONE.....................323 651-0513
Sidney B Felsen, *Pr*
Stanley Grinstein, *VP*
**EMP:** 32 **EST:** 1966
**SQ FT:** 6,000
**SALES (est):** 900.62K **Privately Held**
Web: www.geminigel.com
**SIC: 2796 2752** Etching on copper, steel, wood, or rubber: printing plates; Commercial printing, lithographic

**(P-5026)**
**GRAFICO INC**
15326 Cornet St, Santa Fe Springs (90670-5532)
PHONE.....................562 832-7601
Dan Koon, *CEO*
Daniel Koon, *Pr*
▲ **EMP:** 15 **EST:** 1967
**SQ FT:** 23,500
**SALES (est):** 2.31MM **Privately Held**
Web: www.grafico.com
**SIC: 2796 7336 2791** Color separations, for printing; Commercial art and graphic design; Typesetting

**(P-5027)**
**MASTER ARTS INC**
Also Called: Master Arts Engraving
3737 E Miraloma Ave, Anaheim (92806-2100)
PHONE.....................714 240-4550
Elgin Chalayan, *Pr*
**EMP:** 15 **EST:** 1962
**SQ FT:** 10,000
**SALES (est):** 2.32MM **Privately Held**
Web: www.masterartsgraphicsinc.com
**SIC: 2796 3555** Platemaking services; Printing plates

**(P-5028)**
**SGK LLC**
Also Called: Schawk
650 Townsend St Ste 160, San Francisco (94103-6258)
PHONE.....................415 438-6700
Leslie Ungar, *Mgr*
**EMP:** 38
**SALES (corp-wide):** 1.88B **Publicly Held**
Web: www.sgkinc.com
**SIC: 2796 7374** Color separations, for printing; Computer graphics service
**HQ:** Sgk, Llc
2 North Shore Center
Pittsburgh PA 15212
847 827-9494

## 2812 Alkalies And Chlorine

**(P-5029)**
**ARKEMA INC**
Also Called: Arkema Coating Resins
19206 Hawthorne Blvd, Torrance (90503-1505)
PHONE.....................310 214-5327
**EMP:** 43
**SALES (corp-wide):** 125.67MM **Privately Held**
Web: www.arkema.com
**SIC: 2812 2819 2869 2899** Chlorine, compressed or liquefied; Industrial inorganic chemicals, nec; Industrial organic chemicals, nec; Metal treating compounds
**HQ:** Arkema Inc.
900 1st Ave
King Of Prussia PA 19406
610 205-7000

**(P-5030)**
**CHURCH & DWIGHT CO INC**
31266 Avenue 12, Madera (93638-8328)
PHONE.....................559 661-2790
David Johnston, *Mgr*
**EMP:** 25
**SALES (corp-wide):** 5.87B **Publicly Held**
Web: www.churchdwight.com
**SIC: 2812** Sodium bicarbonate
**PA:** Church & Dwight Co., Inc.
500 Charles Ewing Blvd
609 806-1200

**(P-5031)**
**HASA INC (PA)**
23119 Drayton St, Saugus (91350-2599)
P.O. Box 761 (90213)
PHONE.....................661 259-5848
**EMP:** 95 **EST:** 1964
**SALES (est):** 149.04MM
**SALES (corp-wide):** 149.04MM **Privately Held**
Web: www.hasa.com
**SIC: 2812** Chlorine, compressed or liquefied

## 2812 - Alkalies And Chlorine (P-5032)

**(P-5032)**
**HILL BROTHERS CHEMICAL COMPANY**
Also Called: Desert Brand
15017 Clark Ave, City Of Industry (91745-1409)
PHONE.................................626 333-2251
TOLL FREE: 800
Ron Hill, Pr
EMP: 18
SQ FT: 17,203
SALES (corp-wide): 80.33MM Privately Held
Web: www.hillbrothers.com
SIC: 2812 2851 2819 Chlorine, compressed or liquefied; Paints and allied products; Industrial inorganic chemicals, nec
PA: Hill Brothers Chemical Company
3000 E Birch St Ste 108
714 998-8800

**(P-5033)**
**JCI JONES CHEMICALS INC**
Also Called: Jones Chemicals
1401 Del Amo Blvd, Torrance (90501-1630)
PHONE.................................310 523-1629
Mike Reddinton, Mgr
EMP: 21
SALES (corp-wide): 113.83MM Privately Held
Web: www.jcichem.com
SIC: 2812 2899 Alkalies; Chemical preparations, nec
PA: Jci Jones Chemicals, Inc.
1765 Ringling Blvd
941 330-1537

**(P-5034)**
**OLIN CHLOR ALKALI LOGISTICS**
Also Called: Chlor Alkali Products & Vinyls
11600 Pike St, Santa Fe Springs (90670-2938)
PHONE.................................562 692-0510
John Bilac, Brnch Mgr
EMP: 115
SALES (corp-wide): 6.83B Publicly Held
Web: www.olinchloralkali.com
SIC: 2812 Alkalies and chlorine
HQ: Olin Chlor Alkali Logistics Inc
490 Stuart Rd Ne
Cleveland TN 37312
423 336-4850

**(P-5035)**
**OLIN CHLOR ALKALI LOGISTICS**
Also Called: Chlor Alkali Products & Vinyls
26700 S Banta Rd, Tracy (95304-8157)
PHONE.................................209 835-5424
George Karscig, Mgr
EMP: 113
SALES (corp-wide): 6.83B Publicly Held
Web: www.olinchloralkali.com
SIC: 2812 Alkalies and chlorine
HQ: Olin Chlor Alkali Logistics Inc
490 Stuart Rd Ne
Cleveland TN 37312
423 336-4850

## 2813 Industrial Gases

**(P-5036)**
**AIR LIQUID HEALTHCARE**
12460 Arrow Rte, Rancho Cucamonga (91739-9682)
PHONE.................................909 899-4633
Gerald Berger, Prin
EMP: 28 EST: 2004
SALES (est): 2.61MM Privately Held
SIC: 2813 8099 Oxygen, compressed or liquefied; Health and allied services, nec

**(P-5037)**
**AIR LIQUIDE ELECTRONICS US LP**
1502 W Anaheim St, Wilmington (90744-2303)
PHONE.................................310 549-7079
EMP: 3930
SALES (corp-wide): 114.13MM Privately Held
Web: www.airliquide.com
SIC: 2813 3564 8631 2819 Industrial gases; Blowers and fans; Labor organizations; Industrial inorganic chemicals, nec
HQ: Air Liquide Electronics U.S. Lp
9101 Lyndon B Jhnson Fwy
Dallas TX 75243
972 301-5200

**(P-5038)**
**AIR LIQUIDE ELECTRONICS US LP**
11754 Rd 120, Pixley (93256-9727)
PHONE.................................559 685-2402
EMP: 3930
SALES (corp-wide): 114.13MM Privately Held
Web: www.airliquide.com
SIC: 2813 Industrial gases
HQ: Air Liquide Electronics U.S. Lp
9101 Lyndon B Jhnson Fwy
Dallas TX 75243
972 301-5200

**(P-5039)**
**AIR PRODUCTS AND CHEMICALS INC**
Air Products
1969 Palomar Oaks Way, Carlsbad (92011-1307)
PHONE.................................760 931-9555
EMP: 85
SALES (corp-wide): 12.6B Publicly Held
Web: www.airproducts.com
SIC: 2813 3625 2899 2865 Industrial gases; Relays and industrial controls; Chemical preparations, nec; Cyclic crudes and intermediates
PA: Air Products And Chemicals, Inc.
1940 Air Products Blvd
610 481-4911

**(P-5040)**
**AIRGAS INC**
Also Called: Airgas
3737 Worsham Ave, Long Beach (90808-1774)
P.O. Box 93500 (90809-3500)
PHONE.................................510 429-4216
EMP: 51
SALES (corp-wide): 114.13MM Privately Held
Web: www.airgas.com
SIC: 2813 Industrial gases
HQ: Airgas, Inc.
259 N Rdnor Chster Rd Ste
Radnor PA 19087
610 687-5253

**(P-5041)**
**AIRGAS USA LLC**
8832 Dice Rd, Santa Fe Springs (90670-2516)
PHONE.................................562 945-1383
Rafael Motta, Brnch Mgr
EMP: 45
SQ FT: 29,887
SALES (corp-wide): 114.13MM Privately Held
Web: www.airgas.com
SIC: 2813 5084 Industrial gases; Industrial machinery and equipment
HQ: Airgas Usa, Llc
259 N Radnor Chester Rd
Radnor PA 19087
216 642-6600

**(P-5042)**
**AIRGAS USA LLC**
9756 Santa Fe Springs Rd, Santa Fe Springs (90670-2920)
PHONE.................................562 906-8700
Cynthia Aragundi, Mgr
EMP: 23
SALES (corp-wide): 114.13MM Privately Held
Web: www.airgas.com
SIC: 2813 5169 Industrial gases; Oxygen
HQ: Airgas Usa, Llc
259 N Rdnor Chster Rd Ste
Radnor PA 19087
216 642-6600

**(P-5043)**
**AMERICAN AIR LIQUIDE INC (DH)**
46409 Landing Pkwy, Fremont (94538-6496)
PHONE.................................510 624-4000
Benoit Potier, Ch
Gregory Alexander, *
Pierre Dufour, *
Jean-pierre Duprieu, Ex VP
Scott Krapf, *
◆ EMP: 90 EST: 1940
SQ FT: 40,000
SALES (est): 11.17MM
SALES (corp-wide): 114.13MM Privately Held
SIC: 2813 5084 3533 4931 Industrial gases; Welding machinery and equipment; Oil and gas drilling rigs and equipment; Electric and other services combined
HQ: Air Liquide International
75 Quai D Orsay
Paris 7 IDF 75007
140625555

**(P-5044)**
**H2U TECHNOLOGIES INC**
20360 Plummer St, Chatsworth (91311-5371)
PHONE.................................626 344-0505
Mark Mcgough, Pr
EMP: 26 EST: 2021
SALES (est): 7.76MM Privately Held
Web: www.h2utechnologies.com
SIC: 2813 Hydrogen

**(P-5045)**
**LINDE GAS & EQUIPMENT INC**
Also Called: Praxair
2771 S Maple Ave, Fresno (93725-2117)
PHONE.................................559 237-5521
Keith Martinez, Brnch Mgr
EMP: 77
SQ FT: 11,800
Web: www.lindeus.com
SIC: 2813 Industrial gases
HQ: Linde Gas & Equipment Inc.
10 Riverview Dr
Danbury CT 06810
844 445-4633

**(P-5046)**
**LINDE GAS & EQUIPMENT INC**
Also Called: Praxair
203 Golden State Blvd, Turlock (95380-4956)
PHONE.................................800 225-8247
EMP: 23
Web: www.lindeus.com
SIC: 2813 Industrial gases
HQ: Linde Gas & Equipment Inc.
10 Riverview Dr
Danbury CT 06810
844 445-4633

**(P-5047)**
**LINDE INC**
Also Called: Praxair
2995 Atlas Rd, San Pablo (94806-1167)
PHONE.................................510 223-9593
Bill Holland, Brnch Mgr
EMP: 20
Web: www.lindeus.com
SIC: 2813 Industrial gases
HQ: Linde Inc.
10 Riverview Dr
Danbury CT 06810
203 837-2000

**(P-5048)**
**LINDE INC**
Praxair
5705 E Airport Dr, Ontario (91761-8611)
PHONE.................................909 390-0283
M M Stenberg, Brnch Mgr
EMP: 33
Web: www.lindeus.com
SIC: 2813 Industrial gases
HQ: Linde Inc.
10 Riverview Dr
Danbury CT 06810
203 837-2000

**(P-5049)**
**LINDE INC**
Also Called: Praxair
901 Embarcadero, Oakland (94606-5120)
PHONE.................................510 451-4100
Mike Tyler, Prin
EMP: 150
Web: www.lindeus.com
SIC: 2813 Carbon dioxide
HQ: Linde Inc.
10 Riverview Dr
Danbury CT 06810
203 837-2000

**(P-5050)**
**MATHESON TRI-GAS INC**
16125 Ornelas St, Irwindale (91706-2037)
PHONE.................................626 334-2905
Fermin Reyes, Mgr
EMP: 22
SQ FT: 19,472
Web: www.mathesongas.com
SIC: 2813 5169 Industrial gases; Industrial gases
HQ: Matheson Tri-Gas, Inc.
3 Mountainview Rd Ste 3 # 3
Warren NJ 07059
908 991-9200

**(P-5051)**
**MATHESON TRI-GAS INC**
6775 Central Ave, Newark (94560-3936)
PHONE.................................510 793-2559
Rob Peetz, Brnch Mgr
EMP: 43
SQ FT: 19,281
Web: www.mathesongas.com
SIC: 2813 5084 3494 Industrial gases; Welding machinery and equipment; Valves and pipe fittings, nec
HQ: Matheson Tri-Gas, Inc.
3 Mountainview Rd Ste 3 # 3

Warren NJ 07059
908 991-9200

**(P-5052)**
**MESSER LLC**
2535 Del Amo Blvd, Torrance (90503-1706)
**PHONE**................................310 533-8394
Jason Lacasella, *Brnch Mgr*
**EMP:** 95
**SALES (corp-wide):** 2.29B **Privately Held**
**Web:** www.messeramericas.com
**SIC: 2813** Carbon dioxide
**HQ:** Messer Llc
200 Smrst Corp Blvd # 7000
Bridgewater NJ 08807
800 755-9277

**(P-5053)**
**MESSER LLC**
5858 88th St, Sacramento (95828-1104)
**PHONE**................................916 381-1606
Steve Morgan, *Brnch Mgr*
**EMP:** 62
**SALES (corp-wide):** 1.63B **Privately Held**
**Web:** www.messeramericas.com
**SIC: 2813** Nitrogen
**HQ:** Messer Llc
200 Smrst Corp Blvd # 7000
Bridgewater NJ 08807
800 755-9277

**(P-5054)**
**MESSER LLC**
Also Called: Cryostar USA
13117 Meyer Rd, Whittier (90605-3555)
**PHONE**................................562 903-1290
Mark Sutton, *Brnch Mgr*
**EMP:** 43
**SALES (corp-wide):** 2.29B **Privately Held**
**Web:** www.messeramericas.com
**SIC: 2813** 3561 Oxygen, compressed or liquefied; Pumps and pumping equipment
**HQ:** Messer Llc
200 Smrst Corp Blvd # 7000
Bridgewater NJ 08807
800 755-9277

**(P-5055)**
**NEL HYDROGEN INC**
2389 Verna Ct, San Leandro (94577-4205)
**PHONE**................................650 543-3180
**EMP:** 27 **EST:** 2017
**SALES (est):** 12.7MM **Privately Held**
**Web:** www.nelhydrogen.com
**SIC: 2813** Hydrogen

**(P-5056)**
**NEON ROSE INC**
Also Called: Neon Rose
5158 Bristol Rd, San Diego (92116-2130)
**PHONE**................................619 218-6103
Erin Cutler, *Prin*
**EMP:** 26 **EST:** 2018
**SALES (est):** 286.52K **Privately Held**
**Web:** www.neonroseagency.com
**SIC: 2813** Neon

**(P-5057)**
**OHMIUM INTERNATIONAL INC (PA)**
39672 Eureka Dr, Newark (94560-4805)
**PHONE**................................775 237-2077
Arne Ballantine, *CEO*
**EMP:** 17 **EST:** 2019
**SALES (est):** 10.47MM
**SALES (corp-wide):** 10.47MM **Privately Held**
**Web:** www.ohmium.com
**SIC: 2813** Hydrogen

**(P-5058)**
**PLZ CORP**
840 Tourmaline Dr, Newbury Park (91320-1205)
**PHONE**................................805 498-4531
James Seastrom, *Brnch Mgr*
**EMP:** 43
**SALES (corp-wide):** 766.3MM **Privately Held**
**Web:** www.plzcorp.com
**SIC: 2813** Aerosols
**PA:** Plz Corp.
2651 Wrrnville Rd Ste 300
630 628-3000

**(P-5059)**
**PRAXAIR DISTRIBUTION INC**
Also Called: Praxair
1555 E Edinger Ave, Santa Ana (92705-4907)
**PHONE**................................714 564-7311
Vince Biagiotti, *Pr*
**EMP:** 19 **EST:** 1997
**SALES (est):** 229.77K **Privately Held**
**SIC: 2813** Oxygen, compressed or liquefied

**(P-5060)**
**VERDAGY INC**
11500 Dolan Rd Bldg 17, Moss Landing (95039-9715)
**PHONE**................................831 800-0250
Marty Neese, *CEO*
**EMP:** 15 **EST:** 2021
**SALES (est):** 1.67MM **Privately Held**
**Web:** www.verdagy.com
**SIC: 2813** Hydrogen

## 2816 Inorganic Pigments

**(P-5061)**
**DAY-GLO COLOR CORP**
Also Called: Day-Glo
4615 Ardine St, Cudahy (90201-5801)
**PHONE**................................323 560-2000
Joe Cummings, *Mgr*
**EMP:** 15
**SQ FT:** 100,000
**SALES (corp-wide):** 7.34B **Publicly Held**
**Web:** www.dayglo.com
**SIC: 2816** 5169 2865 2851 Inorganic pigments; Synthetic resins, rubber, and plastic materials; Color pigments, organic; Paints and allied products
**HQ:** Day-Glo Color Corp.
4515 St Clair Ave
Cleveland OH 44103
216 391-7070

**(P-5062)**
**OXERRA AMERICAS LLC**
Davis Colors
3700 E Olympic Blvd, Los Angeles (90023-3123)
P.O. Box 23100 (90023-0100)
**PHONE**................................323 269-7311
Nick Paris, *VP*
**EMP:** 70
**SQ FT:** 540,000
**Web:** americas.oxerra.com
**SIC: 2816** 2865 Inorganic pigments; Cyclic crudes and intermediates
**HQ:** Oxerra Americas, Llc
10001 Wdloch Frest Dr Ste
The Woodlands TX 77380
281 465-6700

**(P-5063)**
**RYVEC INC**
251 E Palais Rd, Anaheim (92805-6239)
**PHONE**................................714 520-5592
Michael Ryan, *CEO*
Aristeo Figueroa, *CFO*
◆ **EMP:** 23 **EST:** 1982
**SQ FT:** 43,000
**SALES (est):** 1.56MM **Privately Held**
**Web:** www.ryvec.com
**SIC: 2816** 2865 2821 Color pigments; Dyes and pigments; Polyurethane resins

**(P-5064)**
**SOLOMON COLORS INC**
1371 Laurel Ave, Rialto (92376-3011)
**PHONE**................................909 873-9444
Jeff Bowers, *Brnch Mgr*
**EMP:** 31
**SQ FT:** 80,000
**SALES (corp-wide):** 120MM **Privately Held**
**Web:** www.solomoncolors.com
**SIC: 2816** Inorganic pigments
**PA:** Solomon Colors, Inc.
4050 Color Plant Rd
217 522-3112

**(P-5065)**
**SPECTRA COLOR INC**
9116 Stellar Ct, Corona (92883-4923)
P.O. Box 79527 (92877-0184)
**PHONE**................................951 277-0200
Robert Shedd, *Pr*
John Shedd, *
▲ **EMP:** 42 **EST:** 1976
**SQ FT:** 40,000
**SALES (est):** 8.91MM **Privately Held**
**Web:** www.spectracolor.com
**SIC: 2816** 3089 2821 Color pigments; Coloring and finishing of plastics products; Plastics materials and resins

## 2819 Industrial Inorganic Chemicals, Nec

**(P-5066)**
**ADVANCED CHEMICAL TECHNOLOGY**
Also Called: Advanced Chemical Technology
3540 E 26th St, Vernon (90058-4103)
**PHONE**................................800 527-9607
Daniel Anthony Earley, *CEO*
**EMP:** 40 **EST:** 1996
**SALES (est):** 9.97MM **Privately Held**
**Web:** www.actglobal.net
**SIC: 2819** 2899 5169 Industrial inorganic chemicals, nec; Antiscaling compounds, boiler; Anti-corrosion products

**(P-5067)**
**AIR LIQUIDE ELECTRONICS US LP**
Also Called: Aloha
46401 Landing Pkwy, Fremont (94538-6496)
**PHONE**................................510 624-4338
Don Swetnam, *Brnch Mgr*
**EMP:** 3930
**SALES (corp-wide):** 114.13MM **Privately Held**
**Web:** www.airliquide.com
**SIC: 2819** Industrial inorganic chemicals, nec
**HQ:** Air Liquide Electronics U.S. Lp
9101 Lyndon B Jhnson Fwy
Dallas TX 75243
972 301-5200

**(P-5068)**
**AMBER CHEMICAL INC**
5201 Boylan St, Bakersfield (93308-4567)
**PHONE**................................661 325-2072
▲ **EMP:** 24 **EST:** 1983
**SALES (est):** 8.27MM **Privately Held**
**Web:** www.amberchem.com
**SIC: 2819** 5169 Industrial inorganic chemicals, nec; Industrial chemicals

**(P-5069)**
**AMCOR MANUFACTURING INC**
500 Winmoore Way, Modesto (95358-5750)
**PHONE**................................209 581-9687
Michael Harvey, *Pr*
Michael Archibald, *VP*
**EMP:** 16 **EST:** 1996
**SQ FT:** 36,000
**SALES (est):** 941.64K **Privately Held**
**SIC: 2819** Industrial inorganic chemicals, nec

**(P-5070)**
**AMERICAN LITHIUM ENERGY CORP**
2261 Rutherford Rd, Carlsbad (92008-8815)
**PHONE**................................760 599-7388
Jiang Fan, *Pr*
Danny Y Joe, *CFO*
▲ **EMP:** 15 **EST:** 2008
**SALES (est):** 2.59MM **Privately Held**
**Web:** www.americanlithiumenergy.com
**SIC: 2819** 3692 5063 Lithium compounds, inorganic; Dry cell batteries, single or multiple cell; Storage batteries, industrial

**(P-5071)**
**AMPAC FINE CHEMICALS LLC (DH)**
Highway 50 And Hazel Ave, Rancho Cordova (95670)
P.O. Box 1718 (95741-1718)
**PHONE**................................916 357-6880
Aslam Malik, *CEO*
Jeff Butler, *
Joe Warchol, *
▲ **EMP:** 54 **EST:** 2005
**SQ FT:** 235,000
**SALES (est):** 167.96MM **Privately Held**
**Web:** www.ampacfinechemicals.com
**SIC: 2819** Industrial inorganic chemicals, nec
**HQ:** Sk Pharmteco Inc.
12460 Akron St Ste 100
Rancho Cordova CA 95742
888 330-2232

**(P-5072)**
**AMPAC FINE CHEMICALS LLC**
12295 Hartford St, Rancho Cordova (95742-6444)
**PHONE**................................916 357-6221
Jary Xiong Traffic, *Contrlr*
**EMP:** 255
**Web:** www.ampacfinechemicals.com
**SIC: 2819** Industrial inorganic chemicals, nec
**HQ:** Ampac Fine Chemicals Llc
Highway 50 And Hazel Ave
Rancho Cordova CA 95670
916 357-6880

**(P-5073)**
**BASF CATALYSTS LLC**
Also Called: BASF Catalysts
46820 Fremont Blvd, Fremont (94538-6571)
**PHONE**................................510 490-2150
Teresa Concreras, *Admn*
**EMP:** 740
**SALES (corp-wide):** 74.89B **Privately Held**
**Web:** catalysts.basf.com
**SIC: 2819** Industrial inorganic chemicals, nec
**HQ:** Basf Catalysts Llc
33 Wood Ave

## 2819 - Industrial Inorganic Chemicals, Nec (P-5074)

Iselin NJ 08830
732 205-5000

**(P-5074)**
**CAL-PAC CHEMICAL CO INC**
6231 Maywood Ave, Huntington Park (90255-4530)
PHONE.................................323 585-2178
Charles F Duane, *Pr*
**EMP:** 17 **EST:** 1955
**SQ FT:** 37,000
**SALES (est):** 2.67MM **Privately Held**
Web: www.calpacchem.com
**SIC: 2819** Industrial inorganic chemicals, nec

**(P-5075)**
**CALIFORNIA SILICA PRODUCTS LLC**
12808 Rancho Rd, Adelanto (92301-2719)
PHONE.................................909 947-0028
Randall Humphreys, *Brnch Mgr*
**EMP:** 84
**SALES (corp-wide):** 813.38K **Privately Held**
Web: www.calsilica.net
**SIC: 2819** Silica compounds
**PA:** California Silica Products, Llc
1420 S Bon View Ave
760 885-5358

**(P-5076)**
**CALIFORNIA SULPHUR COMPANY**
2250 E Pacific Coast Hwy, Wilmington (90744-2917)
P.O. Box 176 (90748-0176)
PHONE.................................562 437-0768
John Babbitt, *Prin*
▼ **EMP:** 28 **EST:** 1958
**SQ FT:** 900
**SALES (est):** 6.8MM **Privately Held**
Web: www.california-sulphur-company.com
**SIC: 2819** Industrial inorganic chemicals, nec

**(P-5077)**
**CAR SOUND EXHAUST SYSTEM INC**
Environmental Catalyst Tech
1901 Corporate Centre Dr, Oceanside (92056-5831)
PHONE.................................949 888-1625
**EMP:** 145
**SALES (corp-wide):** 89.19MM **Privately Held**
Web: www.magnaflow.com
**SIC: 2819** Catalysts, chemical
**PA:** Car Sound Exhaust System, Inc.
1901 Corporate Centre
949 858-5900

**(P-5078)**
**CARBOMER INC**
6324 Ferris Sq Ste B, San Diego (92121-3238)
P.O. Box 261026 (92196-1026)
PHONE.................................858 552-0992
Manssur Yalpani, *Pr*
**EMP:** 85 **EST:** 1995
**SALES (est):** 5.55MM **Privately Held**
Web: www.carbomer.com
**SIC: 2819** Industrial inorganic chemicals, nec

**(P-5079)**
**CARBON ACTIVATED CORPORATION (PA)**
2250 S Central Ave, Compton (90220)
PHONE.................................310 885-4555
◆ **EMP:** 50 **EST:** 1993
**SALES (est):** 28.54MM **Privately Held**
Web: www.activatedcarbon.com
**SIC: 2819** 5074 Charcoal (carbon), activated ; Water purification equipment

**(P-5080)**
**CDTI ADVANCED MATERIALS INC (PA)**
Also Called: Cdti
1641 Fiske Pl, Oxnard (93033-1862)
PHONE.................................805 639-9458
Matthew Beale, *Pr*
Lon E Bell, *
Peter J Chase, *
Tracy A Kern, *Corporate Secretary**
Stephen J Golden, *
**EMP:** 47 **EST:** 1994
**SALES (est):** 22.85MM **Privately Held**
Web: www.cdti.com
**SIC: 2819** 3823 Catalysts, chemical; Process control instruments

**(P-5081)**
**CELITE CORPORATION**
2500 San Miguelito Rd, Lompoc (93436-9743)
PHONE.................................805 736-1221
**EMP:** 17 **EST:** 2015
**SALES (est):** 2.19MM **Privately Held**
Web: www.imerys.com
**SIC: 2819** Industrial inorganic chemicals, nec

**(P-5082)**
**CHAMPIONX LLC**
Also Called: Nalco Champion
6321 District Blvd, Bakersfield (93313-2143)
PHONE.................................661 834-0454
Tom Pappas, *Mgr*
**EMP:** 30
**SQ FT:** 5,000
**SALES (corp-wide):** 3.76B **Publicly Held**
Web: www.championx.com
**SIC: 2819** 7349 Industrial inorganic chemicals, nec; Chemical cleaning services
**HQ:** Championx Llc
2445 Tech Frest Blvd Bldg
The Woodlands TX 77381
281 632-6500

**(P-5083)**
**CHEMTRADE CHEMICALS US LLC**
525 Castro St, Richmond (94801-2104)
PHONE.................................510 232-7193
Thomas Brafford, *Mgr*
**EMP:** 77
**SALES (corp-wide):** 1.34B **Privately Held**
**SIC: 2819** Sulfuric acid, oleum
**HQ:** Chemtrade Chemicals Us Llc
90 E Halsey Rd
Parsippany NJ 07054

**(P-5084)**
**CODEXIS INC (PA)**
Also Called: Codexis
200 Penobscot Dr, Redwood City (94063-4718)
PHONE.................................650 421-8100
Stephen Dilly, *Pr*
Byron L Dorgan, *Ch Bd*
Kevin Norrett, *COO*
Georgia Erbez, *CFO*
Margaret Nell Fitzgerald, *CLO CCO*
**EMP:** 109 **EST:** 2002
**SQ FT:** 77,300
**SALES (est):** 70.14MM
**SALES (corp-wide):** 70.14MM **Publicly Held**
Web: www.codexis.com

**SIC: 2819** 2869 8731 Catalysts, chemical; Industrial organic chemicals, nec; Commercial research laboratory

**(P-5085)**
**CYTEC SOLVAY GROUP**
1440 N Kraemer Blvd, Anaheim (92806-1404)
PHONE.................................714 630-9400
**EMP:** 17 **EST:** 2020
**SALES (est):** 1.3MM **Privately Held**
Web: www.solvay.com
**SIC: 2819** Industrial inorganic chemicals, nec

**(P-5086)**
**DUPONT DE NEMOURS INC**
Also Called: Dupont Slcon Vly Innvation Ctr
965 W Maude Ave, Sunnyvale (94085-2802)
PHONE.................................408 419-4491
**EMP:** 36
**SALES (corp-wide):** 2.93B **Publicly Held**
Web: www.dupont.com
**SIC: 2819** Industrial inorganic chemicals, nec
**PA:** Dupont De Nemours, Inc.
974 Centre Rd Bldg 730
302 295-5783

**(P-5087)**
**ECO SERVICES OPERATIONS CORP**
100 Mococo Rd, Martinez (94553-1314)
PHONE.................................925 313-8224
Darrel Hodge, *Brnch Mgr*
**EMP:** 42
**SALES (corp-wide):** 691.12MM **Publicly Held**
Web: www.pqcorp.com
**SIC: 2819** Sulfuric acid, oleum
**HQ:** Eco Services Operations Corp.
300 Lindenwood Dr
Malvern PA 19355
610 251-9118

**(P-5088)**
**ECO SERVICES OPERATIONS CORP**
20720 S Wilmington Ave, Long Beach (90810-1034)
PHONE.................................310 885-6719
Stephen Caro, *Brnch Mgr*
**EMP:** 51
**SALES (corp-wide):** 691.12MM **Publicly Held**
Web: www.pqcorp.com
**SIC: 2819** Sulfuric acid, oleum
**HQ:** Eco Services Operations Corp.
300 Lindenwood Dr
Malvern PA 19355
610 251-9118

**(P-5089)**
**EKC TECHNOLOGY INC (HQ)**
Also Called: E K C Technology/Burmar Chem
2520 Barrington Ct, Hayward (94545-1163)
PHONE.................................510 784-9105
Young Bae, *CEO*
John Odom, *
Seng Wui Lim, *
David G Bills, *
Thomas M Connelly Junior, *Ex VP*
◆ **EMP:** 115 **EST:** 1963
**SQ FT:** 65,000
**SALES (est):** 39.13MM
**SALES (corp-wide):** 2.93B **Publicly Held**
Web: www.dupont.com
**SIC: 2819** Industrial inorganic chemicals, nec
**PA:** Dupont De Nemours, Inc.
974 Centre Rd Bldg 730
302 295-5783

**(P-5090)**
**ELEMENT SIX TECH US CORP**
3901 Burton Dr, Santa Clara (95054-1583)
PHONE.................................408 986-8184
Adrian Wilson, *Pr*
**EMP:** 17 **EST:** 2011
**SALES (est):** 8.71MM **Privately Held**
Web: www.e6cvd.com
**SIC: 2819** Industrial inorganic chemicals, nec

**(P-5091)**
**ELEMENTIS SPECIALTIES INC**
31763 Mountain View Rd, Newberry Springs (92365-9763)
PHONE.................................760 257-9112
Mike Mcgath, *Mgr*
**EMP:** 80
**SALES (corp-wide):** 713.4MM **Privately Held**
Web: www.elementis.com
**SIC: 2819** Industrial inorganic chemicals, nec
**HQ:** Elementis Specialties, Inc.
469 Old Trenton Rd
East Windsor NJ 08512

**(P-5092)**
**ENERGY SOLUTIONS (US) LLC**
Also Called: Marchem Solvay Group
20851 S Santa Fe Ave, Long Beach (90810-1130)
PHONE.................................310 669-5300
Maria Johnson, *Mgr*
**EMP:** 328
**SALES (corp-wide):** 8.01MM **Privately Held**
Web: www.solvay.com
**SIC: 2819** Industrial inorganic chemicals, nec
**HQ:** Solvay Usa Llc
504 Carnegie Ctr
Princeton NJ 08540
609 860-4000

**(P-5093)**
**ENVIRNMENTAL CATALYST TECH LLC**
3937 Ocean Ranch Blvd, Oceanside (92056-2670)
PHONE.................................949 459-3870
Gennaro Paolone, *Pr*
▲ **EMP:** 20 **EST:** 2000
**SALES (est):** 943.93K
**SALES (corp-wide):** 89.19MM **Privately Held**
Web: www.ect-catalyst.com
**SIC: 2819** Catalysts, chemical
**PA:** Car Sound Exhaust System, Inc.
1901 Corporate Centre
949 858-5900

**(P-5094)**
**GE-HITACHI NUCLEAR ENERGY**
Also Called: GE Vallecitos Nuclear Center
6705 Vallecitos Rd, Sunol (94586-9524)
PHONE.................................925 862-4382
David Turner, *Mgr*
**EMP:** 72
**SALES (corp-wide):** 4.68B **Publicly Held**
Web: nuclear.gepower.com
**SIC: 2819** Nuclear fuel and cores, inorganic
**HQ:** Ge-Hitachi Nuclear Energy Americas Llc
3901 Castle Hayne Rd
Castle Hayne NC 28429

**(P-5095)**
**HONEYWELL INTERNATIONAL INC**
Also Called: Honeywell
3500 Garrett Dr, Santa Clara (95054-2827)

# PRODUCTS & SERVICES SECTION
## 2819 - Industrial Inorganic Chemicals, Nec (P-5116)

PHONE.....................408 962-2000
Paul Raymond, *VP*
**EMP:** 89
**SALES (corp-wide):** 36.66B **Publicly Held**
Web: www.honeywell.com
**SIC: 2819** 3674 Chemicals, reagent grade: refined from technical grade; Semiconductors and related devices
**PA:** Honeywell International Inc.
855 S Mint St
704 627-6200

### (P-5096)
### JM HUBER CORPORATION
700 Kiernan Ave Ste D, Modesto (95356-9329)
PHONE.....................209 549-9771
Aaron Bolinger, *Mgr*
**EMP:** 87
**SALES (corp-wide):** 1.24B **Privately Held**
Web: www.huber.com
**SIC: 2819** Industrial inorganic chemicals, nec
**PA:** J.M. Huber Corporation
3100 Cmbrland Blvd Se Ste
678 247-7300

### (P-5097)
### JM HUBER MICROPOWDERS INC
Also Called: Nutri Granulations
16024 Phoebe Ave, La Mirada (90638-5606)
PHONE.....................714 994-7855
Mike Marberry, *Pr*
**EMP:** 35
**SQ FT:** 45,000
**SALES (corp-wide):** 1.24B **Privately Held**
Web: www.nutrigranulations.com
**SIC: 2819** Industrial inorganic chemicals, nec
**HQ:** J.M. Huber Micropowders Inc.
3100 Cumberland Blvd Se # 600
Atlanta GA 30339
732 549-8600

### (P-5098)
### KEMIRA WATER SOLUTIONS INC
14000 San Bernardino Ave, Fontana (92335-5258)
PHONE.....................909 350-5678
Keith Heasley, *Mgr*
**EMP:** 29
**SALES (corp-wide):** 3.68B **Privately Held**
Web: www.californiasteel.com
**SIC: 2819** Industrial inorganic chemicals, nec
**HQ:** Kemira Water Solutions, Inc.
200 Gllria Pkwy Se Ste 15
Atlanta GA 30339

### (P-5099)
### LICAP TECHNOLOGIES INC
9795 Business Park Dr Ste A, Sacramento (95827-1708)
PHONE.....................916 329-8099
Linda Zhong, *CEO*
Martin M Zea, *
**EMP:** 67 **EST:** 2016
**SALES (est):** 7.22MM **Privately Held**
Web: www.licaptech.com
**SIC: 2819** Elements

### (P-5100)
### MARCHEM TECHNOLOGIES LLC
20851 S Santa Fe Ave, Carson (90810-1130)
PHONE.....................310 638-9352
◆ **EMP:** 30
Web: www.marchemtechnologies.com

**SIC: 2819** 2899 Industrial inorganic chemicals, nec; Chemical preparations, nec

### (P-5101)
### MERELEX CORPORATION
Also Called: American Elements
10884 Weyburn Ave, Los Angeles (90024-2917)
PHONE.....................310 208-0551
Michael Silver, *Pr*
▲ **EMP:** 22 **EST:** 1996
**SALES (est):** 7.26MM **Privately Held**
Web: www.americanbiochemistry.com
**SIC: 2819** Chemicals, high purity: refined from technical grade

### (P-5102)
### MISSION PARK HOTEL LP
Also Called: Element Santa Clara
1950 Wyatt Dr, Santa Clara (95054-1544)
PHONE.....................408 809-3838
Mona Rigdon, *Prin*
Brent Lower, *
**EMP:** 38 **EST:** 2019
**SALES (est):** 2.62MM **Privately Held**
Web: www.elementsantaclara.com
**SIC: 2819** Elements

### (P-5103)
### MONOLITH MATERIALS INC
662 Laurel St, San Carlos (94070-3112)
PHONE.....................650 933-4957
Rob Hanson, *CEO*
Bill Brady, *
Roscoe Taylor, *
**EMP:** 26 **EST:** 2012
**SALES (est):** 4.59MM **Privately Held**
Web: www.monolithmaterials.com
**SIC: 2819** Chemicals, high purity: refined from technical grade

### (P-5104)
### MORAVEK BIOCHEMICALS INC (PA)
Also Called: Moravek
577 Mercury Ln, Brea (92821-4831)
P.O. Box 1716 (92822-1716)
PHONE.....................714 990-2018
Paul Moravek, *Pr*
Joseph Moravek, *
Helen Moravek, *
▲ **EMP:** 25 **EST:** 1976
**SQ FT:** 6,000
**SALES (est):** 8.57MM
**SALES (corp-wide):** 8.57MM **Privately Held**
Web: www.moravek.com
**SIC: 2819** Industrial inorganic chemicals, nec

### (P-5105)
### MORGAN ADVANCED CERAMICS INC
13079 Earhart Ave, Auburn (95602-9536)
PHONE.....................530 823-3401
John Stang, *CEO*
James A West, *
Chester Chiu, *
▲ **EMP:** 26 **EST:** 1986
**SQ FT:** 80,000
**SALES (est):** 22.87MM
**SALES (corp-wide):** 1.39B **Privately Held**
Web: www.morgantechnicalceramics.com
**SIC: 2819** 3356 3264 Aluminum oxide; Zirconium and zirconium alloy bars, sheets, strip, etc.; Porcelain electrical supplies
**HQ:** Morganite Industries Inc.
4000 Wstchase Blvd Ste 17
Raleigh NC 27607
919 821-1253

### (P-5106)
### OMYA CALIFORNIA INC
Also Called: O M Y A
7299 Crystal Creek Rd, Lucerne Valley (92356-8646)
PHONE.....................760 248-7306
▲ **EMP:** 100
**SIC: 2819** 8741 3281 Calcium compounds and salts, inorganic, nec; Management services; Cut stone and stone products

### (P-5107)
### OMYA INC
7299 Crystal Creek Rd, Lucerne Valley (92356-8646)
PHONE.....................760 248-5200
Rainer Seidler, *CEO*
**EMP:** 100
Web: www.omya.com
**SIC: 2819** 8741 3281 Calcium compounds and salts, inorganic, nec; Management services; Cut stone and stone products
**HQ:** Omya Inc.
9987 Carver Rd Ste 300
Cincinnati OH 45242
513 387-4600

### (P-5108)
### PCT-GW CARBIDE TOOLS USA INC
13701 Excelsior Dr, Santa Fe Springs (90670-5104)
PHONE.....................562 921-7898
Shamir Seth, *Pr*
▲ **EMP:** 17 **EST:** 2005
**SALES (est):** 598.06K **Privately Held**
**SIC: 2819** Carbides

### (P-5109)
### PERIMETER SOLUTIONS LP
Wildfire Control Division
10667 Jersey Blvd, Rancho Cucamonga (91730-5110)
PHONE.....................909 983-0772
Vinayak Sharma, *Mgr*
**EMP:** 20
Web: www.perimeter-solutions.com
**SIC: 2819** Industrial inorganic chemicals, nec
**HQ:** Perimeter Solutions Lp
8000 Maryland Ave Ste 350
Saint Louis MO 63105
314 983-7500

### (P-5110)
### PHIBRO-TECH INC
8851 Dice Rd, Santa Fe Springs (90670-2515)
PHONE.....................562 698-8036
Mark Alling, *Mgr*
**EMP:** 50
**SALES (corp-wide):** 1.02B **Publicly Held**
Web: www.pahc.com
**SIC: 2819** 2899 Inorganic metal compounds or salts, nec; Chemical preparations, nec
**HQ:** Phibro-Tech, Inc.
300 Frank W Burr Blvd
Teaneck NJ 07666

### (P-5111)
### PICKERING LABORATORIES INC
1280 Space Park Way, Mountain View (94043-1434)
PHONE.....................650 694-6700
Michael Pickering, *Pr*
Jim Murphy, *VP Opers*
Robert Borawski, *Sec*
David Mazawa, *Prin*
Mike Gottschalk, *Prin*

**EMP:** 22 **EST:** 1979
**SQ FT:** 17,000
**SALES (est):** 5.7MM **Privately Held**
Web: www.pickeringlabs.com
**SIC: 2819** 3826 2899 Chemicals, reagent grade: refined from technical grade; Liquid chromatographic instruments; Chemical preparations, nec

### (P-5112)
### PQ LLC
8401 Quartz Ave, South Gate (90280-2536)
PHONE.....................323 326-1100
Jim Olivier, *Mgr*
**EMP:** 107
**SALES (corp-wide):** 461.02MM **Privately Held**
Web: www.pqcorp.com
**SIC: 2819** Industrial inorganic chemicals, nec
**PA:** Pq Llc
300 Lindenwood Dr
610 651-4200

### (P-5113)
### REAGENT CHEMICAL & RES INC
Also Called: White Fire Tagets
1454 S Sunnyside Ave, San Bernardino (92408-2810)
PHONE.....................909 796-4059
Dan Sumnter, *Brnch Mgr*
**EMP:** 24
**SQ FT:** 99,400
**SALES (corp-wide):** 384.87MM **Privately Held**
Web: www.reagentchemical.com
**SIC: 2819** 3949 Sulfur, recovered or refined, incl. from sour natural gas; Targets, archery and rifle shooting
**HQ:** Reagent Chemical & Research, Llc
115 Us Hwy 202
Ringoes NJ 08551
908 284-2800

### (P-5114)
### SHELL CATALYSTS & TECH LP
10 Mococo Rd, Martinez (94553-1340)
PHONE.....................925 370-9675
▲ **EMP:** 71
**SALES (corp-wide):** 316.62B **Privately Held**
**SIC: 2819** Industrial inorganic chemicals, nec
**HQ:** Shell Catalysts & Technologies Lp
910 Louisiana St Fl 29
Houston TX 77002
888 737-2377

### (P-5115)
### SHELL CATALYSTS & TECH LP
2840 Willow Pass Rd, Pittsburg (94565)
P.O. Box 5159 (94565)
PHONE.....................925 458-9045
William Howell, *Mgr*
**EMP:** 90
**SALES (corp-wide):** 316.62B **Privately Held**
**SIC: 2819** Catalysts, chemical
**HQ:** Shell Catalysts & Technologies Lp
910 Louisiana St Fl 29
Houston TX 77002
888 737-2377

### (P-5116)
### SHELL CHEMICAL LP
10 Mococo Rd, Martinez (94553-1340)
PHONE.....................925 313-8601
Marj Leeds, *Mgr*
**EMP:** 21
**SALES (corp-wide):** 316.62B **Privately Held**
Web: www.shell.us

## 2819 - Industrial Inorganic Chemicals, Nec (P-5117)

SIC: 2819 Catalysts, chemical
HQ: Shell Chemical Lp
910 Louisiana St
Houston TX 77002
855 697-4355

**(P-5117)**
**SINGOD INVESTORS VI LLC**
Also Called: Element Anheim Rsort Cnvntion
1600 S Clementine St, Anaheim (92802-2901)
PHONE..................714 326-7800
Padmesh Patel, *Prin*
EMP: 55 EST: 2016
SALES (est): 6.9MM **Privately Held**
Web: www.marriott.com
SIC: 2819 Elements

**(P-5118)**
**SOLVAY AMERICA INC**
Also Called: SOLVAY AMERICA, INC.
1440 N Kraemer Blvd, Anaheim (92806-1404)
PHONE..................714 688-4403
Michele Jenkins, *Brnch Mgr*
EMP: 116
SALES (corp-wide): 120.79MM **Privately Held**
Web: www.solvay.com
SIC: 2819 Industrial inorganic chemicals, nec
HQ: Solvay America Llc
3737 Buffalo Spdwy Ste 80
Houston TX 77098
713 525-4000

**(P-5119)**
**SOLVAY AMERICA INC**
Also Called: SOLVAY AMERICA, INC.
645 N Cypress St, Orange (92867-6603)
PHONE..................225 361-3376
EMP: 52
SALES (corp-wide): 120.79MM **Privately Held**
Web: www.solvay.com
SIC: 2819 Industrial inorganic chemicals, nec
HQ: Solvay America Llc
3737 Buffalo Spdwy Ste 80
Houston TX 77098
713 525-4000

**(P-5120)**
**SOLVAY AMERICA INC**
Also Called: SOLVAY AMERICA, INC.
12801 Ann St, Santa Fe Springs (90670-3025)
PHONE..................562 906-3300
EMP: 90
SALES (corp-wide): 120.79MM **Privately Held**
Web: www.solvay.com
SIC: 2819 Industrial inorganic chemicals, nec
HQ: Solvay America Llc
3737 Buffalo Spdwy Ste 80
Houston TX 77098
713 525-4000

**(P-5121)**
**SOLVAY AMERICA LLC**
1191 N Hawk Cir, Anaheim (92807-1723)
PHONE..................713 525-4000
EMP: 82
SALES (corp-wide): 120.79MM **Privately Held**
Web: www.solvay.com
SIC: 2819 Industrial inorganic chemicals, nec
HQ: Solvay America Llc
3737 Buffalo Spdwy Ste 80
Houston TX 77098
713 525-4000

**(P-5122)**
**SOLVAY CHEMICALS INC**
645 N Cypress St, Orange (92867-6603)
PHONE..................714 744-5610
EMP: 27
SALES (corp-wide): 120.79MM **Privately Held**
Web: www.solvay.com
SIC: 2819 Industrial inorganic chemicals, nec
HQ: Solvay Chemicals, Inc.
1201 Fannin St Ste 262
Houston TX 77002
713 525-6500

**(P-5123)**
**SPECIALTY MINERALS INC**
Minerals Technology
6565 Meridian Rd, Lucerne Valley (92356-8602)
P.O. Box 558 (92356-0558)
PHONE..................760 248-5300
Doug Mayger, *Brnch Mgr*
EMP: 150
Web: www.mineralstech.com
SIC: 2819 Industrial inorganic chemicals, nec
HQ: Specialty Minerals Inc.
622 Third Ave 38th Fl
New York NY 10017

**(P-5124)**
**TESSENDERLO KERLEY INC**
5247 E Central Ave, Fresno (93725-9336)
PHONE..................559 485-0114
Vince Roggentine, *Genl Mgr*
EMP: 23
SALES (corp-wide): 250.72K **Privately Held**
Web: www.tkinet.com
SIC: 2819 Industrial inorganic chemicals, nec
HQ: Tessenderlo Kerley, Inc.
2910 N 44th St Ste 100
Phoenix AZ 85018
602 889-8300

**(P-5125)**
**TOKYO OHKA KOGYO AMERICA INC**
Also Called: Tok America
190 Topaz St, Milpitas (95035-5429)
PHONE..................408 956-9901
Yoshi Arai, *Mgr*
EMP: 42
SQ FT: 12,560
Web: www.tokamerica.com
SIC: 2819 3674 Industrial inorganic chemicals, nec; Semiconductors and related devices
HQ: Tokyo Ohka Kogyo America, Inc.
4600 Ne Brookwood Pkwy
Hillsboro OR 97124

**(P-5126)**
**TONBO BIOTECHNOLOGIES CORP**
Also Called: Tonbo Biosciences
10840 Thornmint Rd, San Diego (92127-2404)
PHONE..................858 888-7300
Todd Robert Nelson, *CEO*
Chrisopher Coarke, *CIO*
EMP: 20 EST: 2011
SALES (est): 4.47MM **Privately Held**
Web: www.cytekbio.com
SIC: 2819 Inorganic metal compounds or salts, nec

**(P-5127)**
**US BORAX INC**
14486 Borax Rd, Boron (93516-2017)
PHONE..................760 762-7000
Joe A Carrabba, *Brnch Mgr*
EMP: 900
SALES (corp-wide): 54.04B **Privately Held**
Web: www.borax.com
SIC: 2819 Industrial inorganic chemicals, nec
HQ: U.S. Borax Inc.
200 E Randolph St # 7100
Chicago IL 60601
773 270-6500

**(P-5128)**
**VACUUM ENGRG & MTLS CO INC**
390 Reed St, Santa Clara (95050-3108)
PHONE..................408 871-9900
John S Kavanaugh Junior, *Ch Bd*
Robert T Kavanaugh, *
Stephanie Mcconnell, *CFO*
EMP: 50 EST: 1986
SQ FT: 16,500
SALES (est): 23.09MM **Privately Held**
Web: www.vem-co.com
SIC: 2819 3399 3499 Chemicals, high purity: refined from technical grade; Powder, metal ; Friction material, made from powdered metal

**(P-5129)**
**VENUS LABORATORIES INC**
Earth Friendly Products
11150 Hope St, Cypress (90630-5236)
PHONE..................714 891-3100
Firas Jamal, *Mgr*
EMP: 70
SALES (corp-wide): 76.72MM **Privately Held**
Web: www.ecos.com
SIC: 2819 2844 2842 2841 Industrial inorganic chemicals, nec; Perfumes, cosmetics and other toilet preparations; Polishes and sanitation goods; Soap and other detergents
PA: Venus Laboratories, Inc.
111 S Rohlwing Rd
630 595-1900

**(P-5130)**
**W R GRACE & CO**
Also Called: W R Grace Construction Pdts
7237 E Gage Ave, Commerce (90040-3812)
PHONE..................562 927-8513
Suzanne Parsons, *Mgr*
EMP: 19
SQ FT: 18,595
SALES (corp-wide): 6.35B **Privately Held**
Web: www.grace.com
SIC: 2819 Industrial inorganic chemicals, nec
HQ: W. R. Grace & Co.
7500 Grace Dr
Columbia MD 21044
410 531-4000

## 2821 Plastics Materials And Resins

**(P-5131)**
**ACP NOXTAT INC**
1112 E Washington Ave, Santa Ana (92701-4221)
PHONE..................714 547-5477
Anthony Floyd Richard, *Pr*
EMP: 16 EST: 2004
SALES (est): 3.85MM **Privately Held**
Web: www.noxtat.com
SIC: 2821 Plastics materials and resins

**(P-5132)**
**ACUANTIA INC**
Also Called: Rotoplas
2651 Cooper Ave, Merced (95348-4315)
PHONE..................209 723-5000
Juan Negrete, *Brnch Mgr*
EMP: 15
Web: www.plastic-mart.com
SIC: 2821 Molding compounds, plastics
HQ: Acuantia Inc
1121 Riverside Dr
Fort Worth TX 76111

**(P-5133)**
**ALPHA CORPORATION OF TENNESSEE**
Also Called: Alpha-Owens Corning
19991 Seaton Ave, Perris (92570-8724)
PHONE..................951 657-5161
John Mulrine, *Mgr*
EMP: 136
SALES (corp-wide): 1.78B **Privately Held**
Web: www.aocresins.com
SIC: 2821 Polyethylene resins
HQ: The Alpha Corporation Of Tennessee
955 Highway 57
Piperton TN 38017
901 854-2800

**(P-5134)**
**AMERICAN LIQUID PACKAGING SYSTEMS INC (PA)**
Also Called: Chemtex International
440 N Wolfe Rd, Sunnyvale (94085-3869)
PHONE..................408 524-7474
◆ EMP: 60 EST: 1977
SALES (est): 10.35MM
SALES (corp-wide): 10.35MM **Privately Held**
Web: www.chemtexglobal.com
SIC: 2821 Plastics materials and resins

**(P-5135)**
**AMERICAN PACIFIC PLASTIC FABRICATORS INC**
Also Called: Sterling Sleep Systems
7130 Fenwick Ln, Westminster (92683-5248)
PHONE..................714 891-3191
▲ EMP: 15 EST: 1987
SALES (est): 13.81MM **Privately Held**
Web: www.appf.com
SIC: 2821 3089 5021 2515 Polyvinyl chloride resins, PVC; Air mattresses, plastics; Mattresses; Mattresses and bedsprings

**(P-5136)**
**AMERICAS STYRENICS LLC**
305 Crenshaw Blvd, Torrance (90503-1701)
PHONE..................424 488-3757
Brad Crocker, *Brnch Mgr*
EMP: 83
SALES (corp-wide): 7.42B **Privately Held**
Web: www.amsty.com
SIC: 2821 Plastics materials and resins
HQ: Americas Styrenics Llc
24 Waterway Ave Ste 1200
The Woodlands TX 77380

**(P-5137)**
**APTCO LLC (PA)**
31381 Pond Rd Bldg 2, Mc Farland (93250-9795)
PHONE..................661 792-2107
Jim Banuelos, *Managing Member*
◆ EMP: 99 EST: 1996
SALES (est): 16.07MM **Privately Held**
Web: www.aptcollc.com

# 2821 - Plastics Materials And Resins (P-5159)

SIC: 2821 Thermoplastic materials

**(P-5138)**
**AVIENT CORPORATION**
2104 E 223rd St, Carson (90810-1611)
P.O. Box 9077 (90810-0077)
PHONE...................310 513-7100
Rod Myers, Brnch Mgr
EMP: 19
Web: www.avient.com
SIC: 2821 Polyvinyl chloride resins, PVC
PA: Avient Corporation
  33587 Walker Rd

**(P-5139)**
**B & B PLASTICS INC**
1892 W Casmalia St, Rialto (92377-4112)
PHONE...................909 829-3606
Baltazar Mejia, CEO
EMP: 30 EST: 2014
SALES (est): 2.01MM Privately Held
Web: www.bbplasticsinc.com
SIC: 2821 Thermoplastic materials

**(P-5140)**
**BAYER CORPORATION**
800 Dwight Way, Berkeley (94710-2456)
PHONE...................412 777-2000
EMP: 43
SALES (corp-wide): 51.78B Privately Held
Web: cropscience.bayer.com
SIC: 2821 3841 Polypropylene resins; Surgical and medical instruments
HQ: Bayer Corporation
  100 Bayer Blvd
  Whippany NJ 07981
  412 777-2000

**(P-5141)**
**BDC EPOXY SYSTEMS INC**
12903 Sunshine Ave, Santa Fe Springs (90670-4732)
P.O. Box 2445 (90670-0445)
PHONE...................562 944-6177
Fred Benson, CEO
Matt Benson, *
Laura Benson, *
▲ EMP: 27 EST: 1976
SQ FT: 15,000
SALES (est): 5.28MM Privately Held
Web: www.bdcepoxysystems.com
SIC: 2821 Epoxy resins

**(P-5142)**
**BJB ENTERPRISES INC**
14791 Franklin Ave, Tustin (92780-7215)
PHONE...................714 734-8450
Brian Stransky, Pr
EMP: 27 EST: 1970
SQ FT: 38,000
SALES (est): 7.16MM Privately Held
Web: www.bjbenterprises.com
SIC: 2821 3087 5162 Polyurethane resins; Custom compound purchased resins; Plastics materials and basic shapes

**(P-5143)**
**CGPC AMERICA CORPORATION**
Also Called: Enduratex
4 Latitude Way Unit 108, Corona (92881-4918)
PHONE...................951 332-4100
Quentin Wu, Ch Bd
Doctor Dean Lee, VP
Amy Pan, CFO
▲ EMP: 22 EST: 1985
SALES (est): 13.68MM Privately Held
Web: www.enduratex.com
SIC: 2821 Plastics materials and resins
PA: China General Plastics Corporation
  12th Floor , No.37 , Ji-Hu Rd.

**(P-5144)**
**CHEVRON ORONITE COMPANY LLC**
100 Chevron Way, Richmond (94801-2016)
PHONE...................925 842-1000
EMP: 390
SALES (corp-wide): 200.95B Publicly Held
Web: www.oronite.com
SIC: 2821 Plastics materials and resins
HQ: Chevron Oronite Company Llc
  5001 Executive Pkwy
  San Ramon CA 94583

**(P-5145)**
**CHEVRON PHILLIPS CHEM CO LP**
Also Called: Performance Pipe Div
5001 Executive Pkwy, San Ramon (94583-5006)
PHONE...................909 420-5500
Phil Foley, Brnch Mgr
EMP: 29
SALES (corp-wide): 7.42B Privately Held
Web: www.cpchem.com
SIC: 2821 Plastics materials and resins
HQ: Chevron Phillips Chemical Company Lp
  10001 Six Pines Dr
  The Woodlands TX 77380
  832 813-4100

**(P-5146)**
**COASTAL ENTERPRISES**
Also Called: Coastal Enterprises Company
1925 W Collins Ave, Orange (92867-5426)
P.O. Box 4875 (92863-4875)
PHONE...................714 771-4969
Chuck Miller, Owner
▲ EMP: 20 EST: 1970
SQ FT: 25,000
SALES (est): 2.44MM Privately Held
Web: www.precisionboard.com
SIC: 2821 Plastics materials and resins

**(P-5147)**
**COMPOSITES HORIZONS LLC (DH)**
1629 W Industrial Park St, Covina (91722-3418)
PHONE...................626 331-0861
Renee Fahmy, *
▲ EMP: 140 EST: 1974
SQ FT: 25,000
SALES (est): 33.9MM
SALES (corp-wide): 364.48B Publicly Held
Web: www.pccstructurals.com
SIC: 2821 3844 3728 Plastics materials and resins; X-ray apparatus and tubes; Aircraft parts and equipment, nec
HQ: Precision Castparts Corp.
  5885 Meadows Rd Ste 620
  Lake Oswego OR 97035
  503 946-4800

**(P-5148)**
**COSMIC PLASTICS INC (PA)**
28410 Industry Dr, Valencia (91355-4108)
PHONE...................661 257-3274
George Luh, CEO
Edwin Luh, *
◆ EMP: 18 EST: 1960
SQ FT: 846,000
SALES (est): 6.08MM
SALES (corp-wide): 6.08MM Privately Held
Web: www.cosmicplastics.com

SIC: 2821 Thermosetting materials

**(P-5149)**
**CROSSFIELD PRODUCTS CORP (PA)**
Also Called: Dex-O-Tex Division
3000 E Harcourt St, Compton (90221-5589)
PHONE...................310 886-9100
Richard Watt, Ch Bd
W Brad Watt, *
Ronald Borum, *
◆ EMP: 47 EST: 1938
SQ FT: 23,000
SALES (est): 23.79MM
SALES (corp-wide): 23.79MM Privately Held
Web: www.crossfieldproducts.com
SIC: 2821 Plastics materials and resins

**(P-5150)**
**CYTEC ENGINEERED MATERIALS INC**
Also Called: Cytec
1191 N Hawk Cir, Anaheim (92807-1723)
PHONE...................714 632-8444
George Slayton, Brnch Mgr
EMP: 20
SALES (corp-wide): 8.01MM Privately Held
Web: www.syensqo.com
SIC: 2821 2822 Plastics materials and resins; Synthetic rubber
HQ: Cytec Engineered Materials Inc.
  2085 E Tech Cir Ste 102
  Tempe AZ 85284

**(P-5151)**
**DOW CHEMICAL COMPANY**
25500 Whitesell St, Hayward (94545-3615)
PHONE...................510 786-0100
◆ EMP: 69
SALES (corp-wide): 44.62B Publicly Held
Web: corporate.dow.com
SIC: 2821 Thermoplastic materials
HQ: The Dow Chemical Company
  2211 H H Dow Way
  Midland MI 48674
  989 636-1000

**(P-5152)**
**DOW COMPANY FOUNDATION**
Dow Chemical
11266 Jersey Blvd, Rancho Cucamonga (91730-5114)
P.O. Box 748 (91729-0748)
PHONE...................909 476-4127
Steve Rynders, Prin
EMP: 159
SALES (corp-wide): 44.62B Publicly Held
Web: corporate.dow.com
SIC: 2821 Thermoplastic materials
HQ: Dow Company Foundation
  2030 Dow Ctr
  Midland MI 48674
  989 636-1000

**(P-5153)**
**ECOWISE INC**
13538 Excelsior Dr Unit B, Santa Fe Springs (90670-5616)
PHONE...................626 759-3997
Sheng Xu, Pr
EMP: 30 EST: 2019
SALES (est): 5.93MM Privately Held
Web: www.ecowisepcr.com
SIC: 2821 Polyethylene resins

**(P-5154)**
**EEZER PRODUCTS INC**
4734 E Home Ave, Fresno (93703-4509)
PHONE...................559 255-4140
Leighton Sjostrand, Pr
◆ EMP: 21 EST: 1964
SQ FT: 20,000
SALES (est): 3.69MM Privately Held
Web: www.eezer.com
SIC: 2821 Plastics materials and resins

**(P-5155)**
**ELASCO INC**
Also Called: E Sales
11377 Markon Dr, Garden Grove (92841-1402)
PHONE...................714 373-4767
Henry Larrucea, Pr
Janet Lurrucea, *
Gary Stull, *
David Schindler, *
▲ EMP: 100 EST: 1979
SQ FT: 28,000
SALES (est): 4.68MM Privately Held
Web: www.elascourethane.com
SIC: 2821 2891 2822 Polyurethane resins; Adhesives and sealants; Synthetic rubber

**(P-5156)**
**ELASCO URETHANE INC**
11377 Markon Dr, Garden Grove (92841-1402)
PHONE...................714 895-7031
John Frasco, CEO
EMP: 34 EST: 2014
SALES (est): 3.84MM Privately Held
Web: www.elascourethane.com
SIC: 2821 2891 2822 Polyurethane resins; Adhesives and sealants; Synthetic rubber

**(P-5157)**
**FERCO COLOR INC (PA)**
Also Called: Ferco Plastic Products
5498 Vine St, Chino (91710-5247)
PHONE...................909 930-0773
Jennifer Thaw, Pr
EMP: 48 EST: 1989
SQ FT: 20,000
SALES (est): 1.2MM Privately Held
Web: www.fercocolor.com
SIC: 2821 2865 Polyethylene resins; Color pigments, organic

**(P-5158)**
**HOFFMAN PLASTIC COMPOUNDS INC**
16616 Garfield Ave, Paramount (90723-5305)
PHONE...................323 636-3346
Ronald P Hoffman, Pr
Susan Hoffman, *
▲ EMP: 66 EST: 1976
SQ FT: 46,000
SALES (est): 8.92MM Privately Held
Web: www.hoffmanplastic.com
SIC: 2821 3087 Polyvinyl chloride resins, PVC; Custom compound purchased resins

**(P-5159)**
**HOLCIM SOLUTIONS & PDTS US LLC**
Pacific Polymers
12271 Monarch St, Garden Grove (92841-2906)
PHONE...................714 898-0025
Robert Seiple, Brnch Mgr
EMP: 27
Web: www.holcimacs.com

## 2821 - Plastics Materials And Resins (P-5160)

SIC: **2821** 2822 2851 2891 Plastics materials and resins; Synthetic rubber; Paints and allied products; Adhesives and sealants
HQ: Holcim Solutions And Products Us, Llc
26 Century Blvd Ste 205
Nashville TN 37214

### (P-5160)
### HUNTSMAN ADVANCED MATERIALS AM
Also Called: Huntsman
5121 W San Fernando Rd, Los Angeles (90039-1011)
PHONE.................................818 265-7221
Glenn Bauernschmidt, *Mgr*
**EMP:** 120
**SALES (corp-wide):** 6.11B **Publicly Held**
Web: www.huntsman.com
SIC: **2821** Plastics materials and resins
HQ: Huntsman Advanced Materials Americas Llc
10003 Woodloch Forest Dr
The Woodlands TX 77380
281 719-6000

### (P-5161)
### HUNTSMAN ADVNCED MTLS AMRCAS L
4541 Electronics Pl, Los Angeles (90039-1007)
PHONE.................................818 265-7302
**EMP:** 20
**SALES (corp-wide):** 6.11B **Publicly Held**
Web: www.huntsman.com
SIC: **2821** Plastics materials and resins
HQ: Huntsman Advanced Materials Americas Llc
10003 Woodloch Forest Dr
The Woodlands TX 77380
281 719-6000

### (P-5162)
### INDORAMA VNTRES SSTNBLE SLTION
11591 Etiwanda Ave, Fontana (92337-6927)
PHONE.................................951 727-8318
John Wang, *CEO*
**EMP:** 39 **EST:** 2018
**SALES (est):** 25.55MM **Privately Held**
Web: www.indoramaventures.com
SIC: **2821** Plastics materials and resins
HQ: Indorama Ventures Public Company Limited
75/102 Soi Sukhumvit 19 (Vadhana), Asok Road
Vadhana 10110

### (P-5163)
### INDUSPAC CALIFORNIA INC
Also Called: Pacific Foam
1550 Champagne Ave, Ontario (91761-3600)
PHONE.................................909 390-4422
Keith Tatum, *Genl Mgr*
**EMP:** 30
Web: induspac.squarespace.com
SIC: **2821** Polyethylene resins
HQ: Induspac California, Inc.
38505 Cherry St Ste H
Newark CA 94560

### (P-5164)
### INDUSPAC CALIFORNIA INC (HQ)
Also Called: Western Foam
38505 Cherry St, Newark (94560-4700)
PHONE.................................510 324-3626
John Mcauslan, *CEO*
**EMP:** 16 **EST:** 1999
**SALES (est):** 4MM **Privately Held**
Web: www.induspacwest.com
SIC: **2821** Polyethylene resins
PA: Induspac Tijuana, S. De R.L. De C.V.
Av. De Los Cabos No. 8650

### (P-5165)
### INEOS COMPOSITES US LLC
6608 E 26th St, Los Angeles (90040-3216)
P.O. Box 22118 (90022-0118)
PHONE.................................323 767-1300
Reid Mork, *Brnch Mgr*
**EMP:** 60
**SQ FT:** 45,845
**SALES (corp-wide):** 950.17K **Privately Held**
Web: www.ineos.com
SIC: **2821** Plastics materials and resins
HQ: Ineos Composites Us, Llc
955 Yard St # 400
Columbus OH 43212
614 790-9299

### (P-5166)
### INEOS POLYPROPYLENE LLC
Also Called: Ineos
2384 E 223rd St, Carson (90810-1615)
PHONE.................................310 847-8523
Jim Ratcliffe, *Ch*
▲ **EMP:** 148 **EST:** 1998
**SALES (est):** 24.42MM
**SALES (corp-wide):** 950.17K **Privately Held**
Web: www.ineos.com
SIC: **2821** Plastics materials and resins
HQ: Ineos Usa Llc
2600 S Shore Blvd Ste 500
League City TX 77573

### (P-5167)
### IP CORPORATION
Also Called: Silmar Division
12335 S Van Ness Ave, Hawthorne (90250-3320)
PHONE.................................323 757-1801
Doug Johnson, *Brnch Mgr*
**EMP:** 29
**SQ FT:** 56,425
**SALES (corp-wide):** 608.16MM **Privately Held**
Web: www.interplastic.com
SIC: **2821** 5169 Plastics materials and resins; Synthetic resins, rubber, and plastic materials
PA: Ip Corporation
1225 Willow Lake Blvd
651 481-6860

### (P-5168)
### J-M MANUFACTURING COMPANY INC
7501 W Goshen Ave, Visalia (93291-7955)
PHONE.................................559 651-2100
Dave Christian, *Mgr*
**EMP:** 35
**SALES (corp-wide):** 304.63MM **Privately Held**
Web: www.jmeagle.com
SIC: **2821** Plastics materials and resins
PA: J-M Manufacturing Company, Inc.
5200 W Century Blvd
310 693-8200

### (P-5169)
### J-M MANUFACTURING COMPANY INC
Also Called: JM Eagle
23711 Rider St, Perris (92570-7114)
PHONE.................................951 657-7400
Robert Johnson, *Mgr*
**EMP:** 33
**SALES (corp-wide):** 304.63MM **Privately Held**
Web: www.jmeagle.com
SIC: **2821** Polyvinyl chloride resins, PVC
PA: J-M Manufacturing Company, Inc.
5200 W Century Blvd
310 693-8200

### (P-5170)
### J-M MANUFACTURING COMPANY INC
10990 Hemlock Ave, Fontana (92337-7250)
PHONE.................................909 822-3009
Stephen Yang, *Mgr*
**EMP:** 96
**SQ FT:** 72,000
**SALES (corp-wide):** 304.63MM **Privately Held**
Web: www.jmeagle.com
SIC: **2821** 3084 5051 3085 Polyvinyl chloride resins, PVC; Plastics pipe; Pipe and tubing, steel; Plastics bottles
PA: J-M Manufacturing Company, Inc.
5200 W Century Blvd
310 693-8200

### (P-5171)
### J-M MANUFACTURING COMPANY INC
1051 Sperry Rd, Stockton (95206-3931)
PHONE.................................209 982-1500
David Chen, *Mgr*
**EMP:** 74
**SALES (corp-wide):** 304.63MM **Privately Held**
Web: www.jmeagle.com
SIC: **2821** 3084 Polyvinyl chloride resins, PVC; Plastics pipe
PA: J-M Manufacturing Company, Inc.
5200 W Century Blvd
310 693-8200

### (P-5172)
### JOES PLASTICS INC
Also Called: Joes Plastics
5725 District Blvd, Vernon (90058-5590)
PHONE.................................323 771-8433
Joe La Fountain Junior, *CEO*
▼ **EMP:** 40 **EST:** 1974
**SQ FT:** 130,000
**SALES (est):** 4.27MM **Privately Held**
SIC: **2821** Plastics materials and resins

### (P-5173)
### LAMKIN CORPORATION (PA)
6530 Gateway Park Dr, San Diego (92154-7599)
PHONE.................................619 661-7090
▲ **EMP:** 17 **EST:** 1925
**SALES (est):** 4.91MM
**SALES (corp-wide):** 4.91MM **Privately Held**
Web: www.lamkingrips.com
SIC: **2821** 3069 Thermoplastic materials; Grips or handles, rubber

### (P-5174)
### LINCOLN COMPOSITE MTLS INC
5451 Commercial Dr, Huntington Beach (92649-1231)
PHONE.................................714 898-8350
Scott Lincoln, *Pr*
**EMP:** 19 **EST:** 2013
**SALES (est):** 3.75MM **Privately Held**
Web: www.lcmaterials.com

### (P-5175)
### MANGO MATERIALS INC
800 Buchanan St, Berkeley (94710-1105)
P.O. Box 11 (94302-0011)
PHONE.................................650 440-0430
Molly Morse, *CEO*
**EMP:** 19 **EST:** 2010
**SALES (est):** 2.64MM **Privately Held**
Web: www.mangomaterials.com
SIC: **2821** Plastics materials and resins

### (P-5176)
### MAPEI CORPORATION
5415 Industrial Pkwy, San Bernardino (92407-1803)
PHONE.................................909 475-4100
Jose Granillo, *Mgr*
**EMP:** 62
**SALES (corp-wide):** 4.55B **Privately Held**
Web: www.mapei.com
SIC: **2821** Acrylic resins
HQ: Mapei Corporation
1144 E Newport Ctr Dr
Deerfield Beach FL 33442
954 246-8888

### (P-5177)
### MER-KOTE PRODUCTS INC
4125 E La Palma Ave Ste 250, Anaheim (92807-1860)
P.O. Box 17866 (92817-7866)
PHONE.................................714 778-2266
**EMP:** 30
SIC: **2821** Thermoplastic materials

### (P-5178)
### MITSUBSHI CHEM ADVNCED MTLS IN
3837 Imperial Way, Stockton (95215-9691)
PHONE.................................209 464-2701
**EMP:** 22
Web: www.mcam.com
SIC: **2821** Plastics materials and resins
HQ: Mitsubishi Chemical Advanced Materials Inc.
2120 Fairmont Ave
Reading PA 19612
610 320-6600

### (P-5179)
### MULTI-PLASTICS INC
Also Called: Multi Plastics
11625 Los Nietos Rd, Santa Fe Springs (90670-2009)
PHONE.................................562 692-1202
Rafael Enriquez, *Brnch Mgr*
**EMP:** 24
**SALES (corp-wide):** 107.83MM **Privately Held**
Web: www.multi-plastics.com
SIC: **2821** Plastics materials and resins
PA: Multi-Plastics, Inc.
7770 N Central Dr
740 548-4894

### (P-5180)
### MUM INDUSTRIES INC
2320 Meyers Ave, Escondido (92029-1006)
PHONE.................................800 729-1314
**EMP:** 61
**SALES (corp-wide):** 40.62MM **Privately Held**
Web: www.mumindustries.com
SIC: **2821** Plasticizer/additive based plastic materials
PA: Mum Industries Inc.
8989 Tyler Blvd
440 269-4966

▲ = Import ▼ = Export
◆ = Import/Export

# 2821 - Plastics Materials And Resins (P-5202)

**(P-5181)**
**NATURAL ENVMTL PROTECTION CO**
Also Called: Nepco
750 S Reservoir St, Pomona (91766-3815)
**PHONE**..................909 620-8028
Young Su Shin, *Pr*
▲ **EMP:** 31 **EST:** 2006
**SQ FT:** 3,600
**SALES (est):** 9.42MM **Privately Held**
**SIC: 2821** Polystyrene resins
**PA:** Kumsung Industrial Co.Ltd
 57-6 Gubong-Gil, Donghwa-Myeon

**(P-5182)**
**NEW TECHNOLOGY PLASTICS INC**
7110 Fenwick Ln, Westminster (92683-5248)
**PHONE**..................562 941-6034
Gregory A Nelson, *CEO*
**EMP:** 35 **EST:** 1996
**SALES (est):** 5.12MM **Privately Held**
**Web:** www.newtechnologyplastics.com
**SIC: 2821** 5162 Molding compounds, plastics ; Plastics materials and basic shapes

**(P-5183)**
**NORTH AMRCN SPECIALTY PDTS LLC**
300 S Beckman Rd, Lodi (95240-3103)
**PHONE**..................209 365-7500
**EMP:** 17
**Web:** www.westlake.com
**SIC: 2821** Plastics materials and resins
**HQ:** North American Specialty Products Llc
 993 Old Eagle School Rd
 Wayne PA 19087
 484 253-4545

**(P-5184)**
**ORION PLASTICS CORPORATION**
700 W Carob St, Compton (90220-5225)
**PHONE**..................310 223-0370
Patricia Conkling, *Prin*
▲ **EMP:** 75 **EST:** 2000
**SQ FT:** 60,000
**SALES (est):** 18.4MM **Privately Held**
**Web:** www.orionplastics.net
**SIC: 2821** Plastics materials and resins

**(P-5185)**
**PERFORMANCE MATERIALS CORP (HQ)**
Also Called: Tencate Performance Composite
1150 Calle Suerte, Camarillo (93012-8051)
**PHONE**..................805 482-1722
Thomas W Smith, *Pr*
◆ **EMP:** 100 **EST:** 1986
**SQ FT:** 50,000
**SALES (est):** 23.82MM **Privately Held**
**Web:** www.toraytac.com
**SIC: 2821** Plastics materials and resins
**PA:** Toray Industries, Inc.
 2-1-1, Nihonbashimuromachi

**(P-5186)**
**PEXCO AEROSPACE INC**
5451 Argosy Ave, Huntington Beach (92649-1038)
**PHONE**..................714 894-9922
Julio Cuevas, *Manager*
**EMP:** 40
**SALES (corp-wide):** 7.94B **Publicly Held**
**Web:** www.pexcoaerospace.com
**SIC: 2821** Plastics materials and resins
**HQ:** Pexco Aerospace, Inc.
 2405 S 3rd Ave
 Union Gap WA 98903

**(P-5187)**
**PLASKOLITE WEST LLC**
Also Called: Continental Acrylics
2225 E Del Amo Blvd, Compton (90220-6303)
**PHONE**..................310 637-2103
Rick Larkin, *CFO*
▲ **EMP:** 30 **EST:** 2000
**SALES (est):** 9.44MM
**SALES (corp-wide):** 443.48MM **Privately Held**
**SIC: 2821** Acrylic resins
**PA:** Plaskolite, Llc
 400 W Ntnwide Blvd Ste 40
 614 294-3281

**(P-5188)**
**PLASTICS FAMILY HOLDINGS INC**
Also Called: Port Plastics
15317 Don Julian Rd, City Of Industry (91745-1034)
**PHONE**..................626 333-7678
Dustin Roberts, *Brnch Mgr*
**EMP:** 17
**Web:** www.portplastics.com
**SIC: 2821** Plastics materials and resins
**HQ:** Plastics Family Holdings, Inc.
 5800 Cmpus Cir Dr E Ste 1
 Irving TX 75063
 469 299-7000

**(P-5189)**
**POLY PROCESSING COMPANY LLC**
8055 Ash St, French Camp (95231-9667)
P.O. Box 80 (95231-0080)
**PHONE**..................209 982-4904
**EMP:** 34 **EST:** 1995
**SQ FT:** 75,000
**SALES (est):** 5.03MM
**SALES (corp-wide):** 49.05MM **Privately Held**
**Web:** www.polyprocessing.com
**SIC: 2821** 3443 Molding compounds, plastics ; Fabricated plate work (boiler shop)
**PA:** Abell Corporation
 2500 Sterlington Rd
 318 343-7565

**(P-5190)**
**POLYMER CONCEPTS TECH PBY INC**
13522 Manhasset Rd, Apple Valley (92308-5790)
P.O. Box 2738 (92307-0052)
**PHONE**..................760 240-4999
Rob Girman, *Pr*
Dean Anderson, *CFO*
**EMP:** 15 **EST:** 1995
**SQ FT:** 3,000
**SALES (est):** 1.9MM **Privately Held**
**Web:** www.polymerconcepts.com
**SIC: 2821** Plastics materials and resins

**(P-5191)**
**PROFESSIONAL PLASTICS INC (PA)**
1810 E Valencia Dr, Fullerton (92831-4847)
**PHONE**..................714 446-6500
**TOLL FREE:** 800
**EMP:** 50 **EST:** 1984
**SALES (est):** 110.43MM
**SALES (corp-wide):** 110.43MM **Privately Held**
**Web:** www.professionalplastics.com
**SIC: 2821** 5162 3083 3081 Plastics materials and resins; Plastics materials and basic shapes; Laminated plastics plate and sheet; Plastics film and sheet

**(P-5192)**
**QYCELL CORPORATION**
600 Etiwanda Ave, Ontario (91761-8635)
**PHONE**..................909 390-6644
Grant Kesler, *CEO*
▲ **EMP:** 25 **EST:** 1990
**SQ FT:** 45,000
**SALES (est):** 8.09MM **Privately Held**
**Web:** www.qycellfoam.com
**SIC: 2821** Plastics materials and resins

**(P-5193)**
**R K FABRICATION INC**
1283 N Grove St, Anaheim (92806-2114)
**PHONE**..................714 630-9654
Roger King, *CEO*
Sarah King, *Treas*
**EMP:** 18 **EST:** 1989
**SQ FT:** 10,000
**SALES (est):** 10.04MM **Privately Held**
**Web:** www.rkfabrication.com
**SIC: 2821** 3714 1799 Plastics materials and resins; Exhaust systems and parts, motor vehicle; Fiberglass work

**(P-5194)**
**RESINATE MATERIALS GROUP INC**
6451 El Camino Real Ste C, Carlsbad (92009-2800)
**PHONE**..................800 891-2955
Brian D Phillips, *CEO*
Brian J Chermside, *COO*
Rick Tabor, *Ex VP*
**EMP:** 16 **EST:** 2007
**SALES (est):** 396.43K **Privately Held**
**SIC: 2821** Plastics materials and resins

**(P-5195)**
**ROCK SPRINGS INDUSTRIES INC**
Also Called: Eti
300 S Bay Depot Rd, Fields Landing (95537)
P.O. Box 365 (95537-0365)
**PHONE**..................707 443-9323
David C Fonsen, *Pr*
◆ **EMP:** 25 **EST:** 1969
**SQ FT:** 3,000
**SALES (est):** 4.37MM
**SALES (corp-wide):** 55.55MM **Privately Held**
**Web:** www.eti-usa.com
**SIC: 2821** Thermoplastic materials
**PA:** Polytek Development Corp.
 55 Hilton St
 610 559-8620

**(P-5196)**
**ROCK WEST COMPOSITES INC (PA)**
Also Called: Performance Plastics
7625 Panasonic Way, San Diego (92154-8204)
**PHONE**..................858 537-6260
James P Gormican, *CEO*
**EMP:** 51 **EST:** 2006
**SALES (est):** 51.31MM **Privately Held**
**Web:** www.rockwestcomposites.com
**SIC: 2821** Plastics materials and resins

**(P-5197)**
**SABIC INNOVATIVE PLAS US LLC**
Also Called: Sabic Polymershapes
3311 E Central Ave, Fresno (93725-2539)
**PHONE**..................559 264-4100
**TOLL FREE:** 800
Laurie Couto, *Mgr*
**EMP:** 24
**Web:** www.polymershapes.com
**SIC: 2821** Plastics materials and resins
**HQ:** Sabic Innovative Plastics Us Llc
 2500 Ctyweb Blvd Ste 100
 Houston TX 77042

**(P-5198)**
**SAINT-GOBAIN PRFMCE PLAS CORP**
7301 Orangewood Ave, Garden Grove (92841-1411)
**PHONE**..................714 893-0470
Greg Maki, *Brnch Mgr*
**EMP:** 190
**SALES (corp-wide):** 402.18MM **Privately Held**
**Web:** plastics.saint-gobain.com
**SIC: 2821** Plastics materials and resins
**HQ:** Saint-Gobain Performance Plastics Corporation
 20 Moores Rd
 Malvern PA 19355
 440 836-6900

**(P-5199)**
**SAINT-GOBAIN PRFMCE PLAS CORP**
Also Called: High Performance Seals
7301 Orangewood Ave, Garden Grove (92841-1411)
**PHONE**..................714 630-5818
Thomas Kinisky, *CEO*
**EMP:** 91
**SALES (corp-wide):** 402.18MM **Privately Held**
**Web:** plastics.saint-gobain.com
**SIC: 2821** Plastics materials and resins
**HQ:** Saint-Gobain Performance Plastics Corporation
 20 Moores Rd
 Malvern PA 19355
 440 836-6900

**(P-5200)**
**SANDERS INDS HOLDINGS INC (PA)**
Also Called: Integrated Polymer Solutions
3701 E Conant St, Long Beach (90808-1783)
**PHONE**..................562 354-2920
Richard Mcmanus, *CEO*
Jean Marc Pesson, *CFO*
▲ **EMP:** 15 **EST:** 1985
**SQ FT:** 55,000
**SALES (est):** 150.17MM
**SALES (corp-wide):** 150.17MM **Privately Held**
**Web:** www.integratedpolymersolutions.com
**SIC: 2821** Plastics materials and resins

**(P-5201)**
**SK CHEMICALS AMERICA INC**
3 Park Plz Ste 430, Irvine (92614-2579)
**PHONE**..................949 336-8088
Michael Tae, *Pr*
▲ **EMP:** 15 **EST:** 2002
**SALES (est):** 1.97MM **Privately Held**
**SIC: 2821** Plastics materials and resins

**(P-5202)**
**SOUTHLAND POLYMERS INC**
14030 Gannet St, Santa Fe Springs (90670-5314)

## 2821 - Plastics Materials And Resins (P-5203)

PHONE.....................562 921-0444
Henry Hsi, *Pr*
◆ **EMP:** 22 **EST:** 1979
**SQ FT:** 64,000
**SALES (est):** 9.65MM **Privately Held**
Web: www.southlandpolymers.com
**SIC: 2821** 5162  Plastics materials and resins; Plastics resins

**(P-5203)**
**SPHERE ALLIANCE INC**
Also Called: Advanced Aircraft Seal
3087 12th St, Riverside  (92507-4904)
PHONE.....................951 352-2400
Daryl Silva, *CEO*
**EMP:** 37 **EST:** 2011
**SALES (est):** 3.85MM **Privately Held**
**SIC: 2821**  Plastics materials and resins

**(P-5204)**
**ST CLAIR PLASTICS INC**
10031 Freeman Ave, Santa Fe Springs (90670-3405)
PHONE.....................562 946-3115
**EMP:** 20 **EST:** 1988
**SALES (est):** 2.1MM **Privately Held**
**SIC: 2821**  Plastics materials and resins

**(P-5205)**
**STEPAN COMPANY**
Also Called: Anaheim Plant
1208 N Patt St, Anaheim  (92801-2549)
PHONE.....................714 776-9870
Tom Szczeblowski, *Mgr*
**EMP:** 247
**SQ FT:** 10,412
**SALES (corp-wide):** 2.33B **Publicly Held**
Web: www.stepan.com
**SIC: 2821** 2843  Plastics materials and resins; Surface active agents
**PA:** Stepan Company
    1101 Skokie Blvd Ste 500
    847 446-7500

**(P-5206)**
**STOROPACK  INC**
Strap-Lok
12007 Woodruff Ave, Downey (90241-5643)
P.O. Box 7007  (90242-8007)
PHONE.....................562 803-5582
Randy Nicholson, *VP*
**EMP:** 15
**SALES (corp-wide):** 635.28MM **Privately Held**
Web: www.storopack.us
**SIC: 2821** 5113 3086 2671  Plastics materials and resins; Industrial and personal service paper; Plastics foam products; Paper; coated and laminated packaging
**HQ:** Storopack, Inc.
    4758 Devitt Dr
    Cincinnati OH 45246
    513 874-0314

**(P-5207)**
**TA AEROSPACE CO**
Also Called: Ta Division
28065 Franklin Pkwy, Valencia (91355-4117)
PHONE.....................661 702-0448
Jim Sweeney, *Pr*
**EMP:** 180
**SQ FT:** 78,124
**SALES (corp-wide):** 7.94B **Publicly Held**
Web: www.transdigm.com
**SIC: 2821** 3429  Elastomers, nonvulcanizable (plastics); Clamps, metal
**HQ:** Ta Aerospace Co.
    28065 Franklin Pkwy

Valencia CA 91355
661 775-1100

**(P-5208)**
**TAMMY TAYLOR NAILS  INC**
2001 E Deere Ave, Santa Ana (92705-5724)
PHONE.....................949 250-9287
Tammy Taylor, *Pr*
▼ **EMP:** 45 **EST:** 1982
**SQ FT:** 11,500
**SALES (est):** 5.5MM **Privately Held**
Web: www.tammytaylornails.com
**SIC: 2821** 7231 5087  Acrylic resins; Beauty shops; Beauty parlor equipment and supplies

**(P-5209)**
**TAP PLASTICS INC A CAL CORP (PA)**
Also Called: Tap
3011 Alvarado St Ste A, San Leandro (94577-5707)
PHONE.....................510 357-3755
David Freeberg, *Pr*
Robert J Wilson, *VP*
Carole L Bremer, *CFO*
**EMP:** 15 **EST:** 1952
**SQ FT:** 4,000
**SALES (est):** 18.08MM
**SALES (corp-wide):** 18.08MM **Privately Held**
Web: www.tapplastics.com
**SIC: 2821** 5162  Acrylic resins; Resins, synthetic

**(P-5210)**
**TECHMER PM  INC**
18420 S Laurel Park Rd, Compton (90220-6015)
PHONE.....................310 632-9211
John R Manuck, *Pr*
◆ **EMP:** 500 **EST:** 1982
**SQ FT:** 40,000
**SALES (est):** 14.27MM **Privately Held**
Web: www.techmerpm.com
**SIC: 2821**  Plastics materials and resins

**(P-5211)**
**TEKNOR APEX COMPANY**
Maclin Company
420 S 6th Ave, City Of Industry (91746-3128)
P.O. Box 2307  (91746-0307)
PHONE.....................626 968-4656
Tony Patrizio, *Mgr*
**EMP:** 104
**SALES (corp-wide):** 731.88MM **Privately Held**
Web: www.teknorapex.com
**SIC: 2821** 3081 3089  Vinyl resins, nec; Unsupported plastics film and sheet; Plastics processing
**PA:** Teknor Apex Company
    505 Central Ave
    401 725-8000

**(P-5212)**
**TEKNOR COLOR COMPANY**
Also Called: Teknor Apex
420 S 6th Ave, City Of Industry (91746-3128)
P.O. Box 2307  (91746-0307)
PHONE.....................626 336-7709
Tony Patrizio, *Genl Mgr*
**EMP:** 29
**SALES (corp-wide):** 731.88MM **Privately Held**
Web: www.teknorapex.com

**SIC: 2821** 3089  Plastics materials and resins; Plastics processing
**HQ:** Teknor Color Company Llc
    505 Central Ave
    Pawtucket RI 02861

**(P-5213)**
**TORAY ADVANCED COMPOSITES USA INC (DH)**
18255 Sutter Blvd, Morgan Hill (95037-2820)
PHONE.....................408 465-8500
▲ **EMP:** 160 **EST:** 1990
**SALES (est):** 215.43MM
**SALES (corp-wide):** 600K **Privately Held**
Web: www.toraytac.com
**SIC: 2821**  Thermosetting materials
**HQ:** Toray Tcac Holding Usa Inc.
    365 S Holland Dr
    Pendergrass GA 30567
    706 693-2226

**(P-5214)**
**TORAY ADVNCED CMPSITES ADS LLC**
2450 Cordelia Rd, Fairfield  (94534-1651)
PHONE.....................707 359-3400
Terry Boboige, *Managing Member*
**EMP:** 53 **EST:** 2019
**SALES (est):** 22MM **Privately Held**
Web: www.toraytac.com
**SIC: 2821** 2891  Thermoplastic materials; Adhesives and sealants
**PA:** Toray Industries, Inc.
    2-1-1, Nihombashimuromachi

**(P-5215)**
**TUFF STUFF PRODUCTS**
Also Called: Tuff Stuff Products
9600 Road 256, Terra Bella  (93270-9732)
PHONE.....................559 535-5778
Maximilian B Lee, *Pr*
▲ **EMP:** 500 **EST:** 1999
**SALES (est):** 10.9MM **Privately Held**
Web: www.tufftubs.com
**SIC: 2821**  Plastics materials and resins

**(P-5216)**
**UREMET CORPORATION**
7012 Belgrave Ave, Garden Grove (92841-2808)
PHONE.....................657 257-4027
Steve Zamollo, *CEO*
Mark Moore, *
John Cockriel, *
▲ **EMP:** 26 **EST:** 1989
**SQ FT:** 9,500
**SALES (est):** 13.28MM **Privately Held**
Web: www.uremet.com
**SIC: 2821**  Polyurethane resins

**(P-5217)**
**US BLANKS  LLC (PA)**
14700 S San Pedro St, Gardena (90248-2001)
P.O. Box 486  (90248-0486)
PHONE.....................310 225-6774
Kimberly Thress, *
▲ **EMP:** 48 **EST:** 2006
**SALES (est):** 15.52MM
**SALES (corp-wide):** 15.52MM **Privately Held**
Web: www.usblanks.com
**SIC: 2821**  Plastics materials and resins

**(P-5218)**
**XERXES CORPORATION**
1210 N Tustin Ave, Anaheim  (92807-1617)
PHONE.....................714 630-0012

Rudy Tapia, *Mgr*
**EMP:** 119
**SALES (corp-wide):** 673.6MM **Privately Held**
Web: www.xerxes.com
**SIC: 2821** 5999 3444  Polystyrene resins; Fiberglass materials, except insulation; Sheet metalwork
**HQ:** Xerxes Corporation
    7901 Xerxes Ave S
    Minneapolis MN 55431
    952 887-1890

## 2822 Synthetic Rubber

**(P-5219)**
**ARNCO**
5141 Firestone Pl, South Gate (90280-3535)
PHONE.....................323 249-7500
◆ **EMP:** 50 **EST:** 1971
**SALES (est):** 5.76MM **Privately Held**
**SIC: 2822** 2821 3089  Synthetic rubber; Plastics materials and resins; Casting of plastics; Paint spray equipment, industrial

**(P-5220)**
**CRITICALPOINT CAPITAL  LLC**
Arlon Materials For Elec Div
9433 Hyssop Dr, Rancho Cucamonga (91730-6107)
PHONE.....................909 987-9533
Roy Baulmer, *Brnch Mgr*
**EMP:** 100
**SALES (corp-wide):** 19.26MM **Privately Held**
Web: www.criticalpointpartners.com
**SIC: 2822** 3672 2821  Silicone rubbers; Printed circuit boards; Plastics materials and resins
**PA:** Criticalpoint Capital, Llc
    2101 Rosecrans Ave
    310 321-4400

**(P-5221)**
**LTI HOLDINGS  INC (PA)**
Also Called: Boyd
5960 Inglewood Dr Ste 115, Pleasanton (94588-8611)
PHONE.....................925 271-8041
Doug Britt, *CEO*
▲ **EMP:** 15 **EST:** 2006
**SALES (est):** 661.75MM **Privately Held**
**SIC: 2822** 3069  Synthetic rubber; Hard rubber and molded rubber products

## 2824 Organic Fibers, Noncellulosic

**(P-5222)**
**MATCHES  INC**
1700 E Araby St Ste 64, Palm Springs (92264)
PHONE.....................760 899-1919
Jinle Chen, *Ch Bd*
Zhimeng Zhao, *CAO*
Xiqing Zhang, *COO*
**EMP:** 359 **EST:** 2009
**SALES (est):** 1.04MM **Privately Held**
**SIC: 2824**  Polyester fibers

**(P-5223)**
**ST PAUL BRANDS  INC**
11842 Monarch St, Garden Grove (92841-2113)
PHONE.....................714 903-1000
Jimmy Ngo, *Pr*
Henry Smith, *

Fred Evans, *
▲ **EMP:** 25 **EST:** 2004
**SALES (est):** 2.35MM **Privately Held**
**Web:** probactive.en.ec21.com
**SIC:** 2824 Protein fibers

**(P-5224)**
**TURNER FIBERFILL INC**
1600 Date St, Montebello (90640-6371)
P.O. Box 460 (90640-0460)
**PHONE**..................323 724-7957
Paul Turner, *Pr*
▲ **EMP:** 35 **EST:** 2003
**SALES (est):** 2.42MM **Privately Held**
**SIC:** 2824 Polyester fibers

**(P-5225)**
**UNITED FIBER INC**
1680 W Winton Ave Ste 7, Hayward (94545-1333)
**PHONE**..................510 783-6904
Pirut Saelao, *Pr*
Paul Sealao, *
Fah Saelao, *
Pirut Paul Saelao, *Pr*
**EMP:** 32 **EST:** 1988
**SALES (est):** 541.3K **Privately Held**
**SIC:** 2824 2395 2396 Polyester fibers; Quilting: for the trade; Automotive and apparel trimmings

**(P-5226)**
**VYBION INC**
584 Oak St, Monterey (93940-1321)
**PHONE**..................607 227-2502
Lee A Henderson, *Ch Bd*
**EMP:** 16 **EST:** 1993
**SQ FT:** 2,500
**SALES (est):** 641.99K **Privately Held**
**SIC:** 2824 Protein fibers

## 2833 Medicinals And Botanicals

**(P-5227)**
**ACE CREATIONS LLC**
2190 Grove St Apt 1, San Francisco (94117-1024)
**PHONE**..................248 762-9679
Ardalan Sedghi, *Managing Member*
**EMP:** 18 **EST:** 2017
**SALES (est):** 550.97K **Privately Held**
**Web:** www.elementalwellnesscenter.com
**SIC:** 2833 Medicinals and botanicals

**(P-5228)**
**AKESO HEALTH SCIENCES LLC**
822 Hampshire Rd Ste E, Westlake Village (91361-2847)
**PHONE**..................818 865-1046
Jenny Bolger, *Admn*
Jenny Bolger, *Dir Opers*
**EMP:** 15 **EST:** 2004
**SALES (est):** 593.18K **Privately Held**
**Web:** www.migrelief.com
**SIC:** 2833 Medicinals and botanicals

**(P-5229)**
**ALLERMED LABORATORIES INC**
7203 Convoy Ct, San Diego (92111-1020)
**PHONE**..................858 292-1060
H S Nielsen, *Pr*
**EMP:** 30 **EST:** 1972
**SQ FT:** 20,000
**SALES (est):** 4.5MM **Privately Held**
**Web:** www.stallergenesgreer.com
**SIC:** 2833 2836 Medicinals and botanicals; Biological products, except diagnostic

**(P-5230)**
**AMASS BRANDS INC**
860 E Stowell Rd, Santa Maria (93454-7006)
**PHONE**..................619 204-2560
Mark Thomas Lynn, *CEO*
**EMP:** 68 **EST:** 2019
**SALES (est):** 8.56MM **Privately Held**
**Web:** www.amass.com
**SIC:** 2833 Alkaloids and other botanical based products

**(P-5231)**
**B & C NUTRITIONAL PRODUCTS INC**
Also Called: Merical
2995 E Miraloma Ave, Anaheim (92806-1805)
**PHONE**..................714 238-7225
**EMP:** 77
**SIC:** 2833 2048 2834 Medicinals and botanicals; Prepared feeds, nec; Vitamin preparations

**(P-5232)**
**BEACON MANUFACTURING INC**
Also Called: North West Pharmanaturals
1000 Beacon St, Brea (92821-2938)
**PHONE**..................714 529-0980
Jack L Brown, *CEO*
Patrick D K Brown, *CFO*
**EMP:** 20 **EST:** 2015
**SQ FT:** 25,000
**SALES (est):** 3.19MM **Privately Held**
**Web:** www.northwestpn.com
**SIC:** 2833 Vitamins, natural or synthetic: bulk, uncompounded

**(P-5233)**
**BEIGENE USA INC**
1900 Powell St Ste 500, Emeryville (94608-1812)
**PHONE**..................619 733-1842
**EMP:** 362
**Web:** www.beigene.com
**SIC:** 2833 Medicinals and botanicals
**HQ:** Beigene Usa, Inc.
  55 Cambrdge Pkwy Ste 700w
  Cambridge MA 02142
  781 801-1800

**(P-5234)**
**BIO-RAD LABORATORIES INC**
Bio-RAD E C S
9500 Jeronimo Rd, Irvine (92618-2017)
**PHONE**..................949 598-1200
Kelly Knapps, *Brnch Mgr*
**EMP:** 187
**SALES (corp-wide):** 2.8B **Publicly Held**
**Web:** www.bio-rad.com
**SIC:** 2833 2835 Medicinals and botanicals; Diagnostic substances
**PA:** Bio-Rad Laboratories, Inc.
  1000 Alfred Nobel Dr
  510 724-7000

**(P-5235)**
**CARGILL INCORPORATED**
Also Called: Cargill
600 N Gilbert St, Fullerton (92833-2555)
**PHONE**..................714 449-6708
Steve Hoemoller, *Mgr*
**EMP:** 48
**SALES (corp-wide):** 159.59B **Privately Held**
**Web:** www.cargill.com
**SIC:** 2833 2079 5199 Vegetable oils, medicinal grade: refined or concentrated; Edible fats and oils; Oils, animal or vegetable
**PA:** Cargill, Incorporated
  15407 Mcginty Rd W
  800 227-4455

**(P-5236)**
**CHROMADEX CORPORATION (PA)**
Also Called: Chromadex
10900 Wilshire Blvd Ste 600, Los Angeles (90024-6534)
**PHONE**..................310 388-6706
Robert Fried, *CEO*
Frank L Jaksch Junior, *Ex Ch Bd*
James Lee, *Interim CAO*
Carlos Lopez, *Sr VP*
Ozan Pamir, *CFO*
**EMP:** 31 **EST:** 2000
**SQ FT:** 10,000
**SALES (est):** 83.57MM
**SALES (corp-wide):** 83.57MM **Publicly Held**
**Web:** www.chromadex.com
**SIC:** 2833 Medicinals and botanicals

**(P-5237)**
**ERBAVIVA INC**
Also Called: Erba Organics
19831 Nordhoff Pl Ste 116, Chatsworth (91311-6608)
**PHONE**..................818 998-7112
Robin Brown, *CEO*
Robin Brown, *Prin*
Anna C Brown, *VP*
▲ **EMP:** 20 **EST:** 2010
**SQ FT:** 10,000
**SALES (est):** 6.63MM **Privately Held**
**Web:** www.erbaviva.com
**SIC:** 2833 Organic medicinal chemicals: bulk, uncompounded

**(P-5238)**
**ESMOND NATURAL INC**
Also Called: Hopkins Labratory Co
5316 Irwindale Ave, Irwindale (91706-2034)
**PHONE**..................626 337-1588
Paul C Wei, *CEO*
Lindey Tseng, *
Midori H Wei, *Sec*
▲ **EMP:** 25 **EST:** 1994
**SALES (est):** 5.23MM **Privately Held**
**Web:** www.esmondnatural.com
**SIC:** 2833 Vitamins, natural or synthetic: bulk, uncompounded

**(P-5239)**
**EVERGREEN LICENSING LLC**
Also Called: Evergreen Licensing
5737 Kanan Rd, Agoura Hills (91301-1601)
**PHONE**..................844 270-2700
Bruce Friedman, *Managing Member*
**EMP:** 15 **EST:** 2014
**SALES (est):** 10MM **Privately Held**
**Web:** www.evergreen-licensing.com
**SIC:** 2833 8742 Vitamins, natural or synthetic: bulk, uncompounded; Business management consultant

**(P-5240)**
**EVOLIFE SCIENTIFIC LLC**
3150 Long Beach Blvd, Long Beach (90807-5061)
**PHONE**..................888 750-0310
**EMP:** 23 **EST:** 2019
**SALES (est):** 1.42MM **Privately Held**
**Web:** www.evolifescientific.com
**SIC:** 2833 Medicinals and botanicals

**(P-5241)**
**EXCELSIOR NUTRITION INC**
Also Called: 4excelsior
1206 N Miller St Unit D, Anaheim (92806-1960)
**PHONE**..................657 999-5188
Lin Yisheng, *Pr*
Jian Wu, *
**EMP:** 61 **EST:** 2014
**SQ FT:** 78,000
**SALES (est):** 10.36MM **Privately Held**
**Web:** www.4excelsior.com
**SIC:** 2833 Medicinals and botanicals

**(P-5242)**
**GLOBALRIDGE LLC**
Also Called: Nutribiotic
865 Parallel Dr, Lakeport (95453-5707)
**PHONE**..................800 225-4345
Kenneth Ridgeway, *CEO*
**EMP:** 19 **EST:** 2019
**SALES (est):** 2.77MM **Privately Held**
**Web:** www.nutribiotic.com
**SIC:** 2833 Medicinals and botanicals

**(P-5243)**
**GREEN DRAGON CAREGIVERS INC**
7236 Varna Ave, North Hollywood (91605-4102)
**PHONE**..................818 997-1368
Manuel Semerjian, *Prin*
**EMP:** 18 **EST:** 2007
**SALES (est):** 411.88K **Privately Held**
**Web:** www.greendragoncoop.com
**SIC:** 2833 Drugs and herbs: grading, grinding, and milling

**(P-5244)**
**GREEN STAR LABS INC**
Also Called: Covalent Cbd
4075 Ruffin Rd, San Diego (92123-1817)
**PHONE**..................619 489-9020
Sandro Piancone, *CEO*
Brooke Dang, *
**EMP:** 50 **EST:** 2022
**SALES (est):** 5MM
**SALES (corp-wide):** 5.1MM **Publicly Held**
**Web:** www.greenstarlabs.net
**SIC:** 2833 Medicinals and botanicals
**HQ:** The Hempacco Co Inc
  9925 Airway Rd
  San Diego CA 92154
  619 779-0715

**(P-5245)**
**HENLIUS USA INC**
430 N Mccarthy Blvd, Milpitas (95035-5112)
**PHONE**..................510 445-0305
Scott Liu, *CEO*
**EMP:** 104 **EST:** 2018
**SALES (est):** 6.29MM **Privately Held**
**Web:** www.hengenix.com
**SIC:** 2833 Medicinal chemicals

**(P-5246)**
**J & D LABORATORIES INC**
2710 Progress St, Vista (92081-8449)
**PHONE**..................760 734-6800
David Wood, *CEO*
Fon Wong, *CFO*
▲ **EMP:** 300 **EST:** 1988
**SQ FT:** 32,000
**SALES (est):** 10.33MM
**SALES (corp-wide):** 203.23MM **Privately Held**
**Web:** www.capteksoftgel.com

## 2833 - Medicinals And Botanicals (P-5247)

SIC: 2833 2834 Vitamins, natural or synthetic: bulk, uncompounded; Pharmaceutical preparations
HQ: Captek Softgel International, Inc.
16218 Arthur St
Cerritos CA 90703

**(P-5247)**
**MERCI LIFE LLC**
321 N Pass Ave Ste 144, Burbank (91505-3859)
PHONE.....................317 341-4109
Samantha Ford, *Mgr*
**EMP:** 15 **EST:** 2020
**SALES (est):** 239.13K **Privately Held**
Web: www.mercilifeco.com
SIC: 2833  Medicinals and botanicals

**(P-5248)**
**MIDNIGHT MANUFACTURING LLC**
Also Called: Loud Mfg
2535 Conejo Spectrum St Bldg 4, Thousand Oaks (91320-1453)
PHONE.....................714 833-6130
Kevin A Shaw, *Pr*
**EMP:** 25 **EST:** 2019
**SALES (est):** 5.59MM **Privately Held**
Web: www.midnightmanufacturing.com
SIC: 2833  Medicinals and botanicals

**(P-5249)**
**MRO MARYRUTH LLC**
1171 S Robertson Blvd Ste 148, Los Angeles (90035-1403)
PHONE.....................424 343-6650
Colleen Boehmer, *Managing Member*
Mary Boehmer, *
Dave Hsu, *
**EMP:** 195 **EST:** 2021
**SALES (est):** 2.93MM **Privately Held**
SIC: 2833  Medicinals and botanicals

**(P-5250)**
**MULTIVITAMIN DIRECT INC**
2178 Paragon Dr, San Jose (95131-1305)
PHONE.....................408 573-7292
Paul Huang, *CEO*
▲ **EMP:** 27 **EST:** 2010
**SQ FT:** 5,000
**SALES (est):** 1.1MM **Privately Held**
SIC: 2833  Vitamins, natural or synthetic: bulk, uncompounded

**(P-5251)**
**MYCELIUM ENTERPRISES LLC** ✪
10632 Trask Ave, Garden Grove (92843-2496)
PHONE.....................657 251-0016
Andrew Boyd Jones, *Managing Member*
Matthew Rhoden, *Managing Member**
Heather Norris, *
**EMP:** 25 **EST:** 2023
**SALES (est):** 1.04MM **Privately Held**
SIC: 2833  Medicinals and botanicals

**(P-5252)**
**NATURAL ALTERNATIVES INTL INC (PA)**
Also Called: NAI
1535 Faraday Ave, Carlsbad (92008-7319)
PHONE.....................760 736-7700
Mark A Ledoux, *Ch Bd*
Kenneth E Wolf, *Pr*
Michael E Fortin, *CFO*
▲ **EMP:** 178 **EST:** 1980
**SQ FT:** 20,981
**SALES (est):** 113.8MM
**SALES (corp-wide):** 113.8MM **Publicly Held**
Web: www.nai-online.com
SIC: 2833 2834  Medicinals and botanicals; Pharmaceutical preparations

**(P-5253)**
**NOAH PHARMACEUTICALS INC**
1380 San Andreas Rd, Watsonville (95076-9636)
PHONE.....................707 631-0921
Joshua Atiba, *CEO*
**EMP:** 20 **EST:** 2018
**SALES (est):** 276.15K **Privately Held**
SIC: 2833  Drugs and herbs: grading, grinding, and milling

**(P-5254)**
**NORDIC NATURALS MFG INC**
Also Called: Select Supplements
111 Jennings Way, Watsonville (95076-2054)
PHONE.....................800 662-2544
Joar A Opheim, *CEO*
Hector Gudino, *
Susan Valli, *
▲ **EMP:** 32 **EST:** 2007
**SALES (est):** 6.86MM **Privately Held**
Web: www.selectsupplements.com
SIC: 2833  Medicinals and botanicals

**(P-5255)**
**NORTH WEST PHARMANATURALS INC**
Also Called: Vitamins Unlimited
1000 Beacon St, Brea (92821-2938)
PHONE.....................714 529-0980
▲ **EMP:** 20
SIC: 2833  Vitamins, natural or synthetic: bulk, uncompounded

**(P-5256)**
**NORWAY TOPCO LP (PA)**
1950 University Ave, Palo Alto (94303-2250)
PHONE.....................435 655-6000
Monty Sharma, *CEO*
Ankit Dhawan, *CFO*
**EMP:** 15 **EST:** 2017
**SALES (est):** 319.31MM
**SALES (corp-wide):** 319.31MM **Privately Held**
SIC: 2833  Medicinals and botanicals

**(P-5257)**
**NU-HEALTH PRODUCTS CO**
Also Called: Nu Health Products
20875 Currier Rd, Walnut (91789-3081)
PHONE.....................909 869-0666
Lynn Leung, *Pr*
▲ **EMP:** 25 **EST:** 1991
**SQ FT:** 12,000
**SALES (est):** 2.59MM **Privately Held**
Web: www.nu-health.com
SIC: 2833 2048 5149  Vitamins, natural or synthetic: bulk, uncompounded; Prepared feeds, nec; Organic and diet food

**(P-5258)**
**ORGAIN LLC**
16631 Millikan Ave, Irvine (92606-5028)
P.O. Box 4918 (92616-4918)
PHONE.....................888 881-4246
Andrew Abraham, *CEO*
**EMP:** 47 **EST:** 2019
**SALES (est):** 36.76MM **Privately Held**
Web: www.orgain.com
SIC: 2833 5499  Medicinals and botanicals; Health and dietetic food stores
PA: Nestle S.A.
Avenue Nestle 55

**(P-5259)**
**ORGANIC BY NATURE INC (PA)**
Also Called: Organic
2610 Homestead Pl, Rancho Dominguez (90220-5610)
PHONE.....................562 901-0177
Amy L Venner Hamdi, *CEO*
David Sandoval, *
▲ **EMP:** 35 **EST:** 1993
**SQ FT:** 30,000
**SALES (est):** 10.32MM **Privately Held**
Web: www.organicbynatureinc.com
SIC: 2833  Adrenal derivatives

**(P-5260)**
**PALETTE LIFE SCIENCES INC (PA)**
27 E Cota St Ste 402, Santa Barbara (93101-7603)
PHONE.....................805 869-7020
Per Lango, *CEO*
Hank Courson, *
**EMP:** 71 **EST:** 2018
**SALES (est):** 5.44MM
**SALES (corp-wide):** 5.44MM **Privately Held**
Web: www.palettelifesciences.com
SIC: 2833  Medicinal chemicals

**(P-5261)**
**PHARMAVITE LLC (DH)**
8531 Fallbrook Ave, West Hills (91304-3232)
PHONE.....................818 221-6200
Jeff Boutelle, *CEO*
Tobe Cohen, *SPECIALTY BRANDS**
Christine Burdick-bell J.d., *Ex VP*
Rhonda Hoffman, *CGO**
Jerome Metivier, *
▲ **EMP:** 300 **EST:** 1971
**SQ FT:** 45,000
**SALES (est):** 519.52MM **Privately Held**
Web: www.pharmavite.com
SIC: 2833 2834  Vitamins, natural or synthetic: bulk, uncompounded; Pharmaceutical preparations
HQ: Otsuka America, Inc.
1 Embrcadero Ctr Ste 2020
San Francisco CA 94111

**(P-5262)**
**PHARMAVITE LLC**
1150 Aviation Pl, San Fernando (91340-1460)
PHONE.....................818 221-6200
Jim Jordan, *Ex VP*
**EMP:** 19
Web: www.pharmavite.com
SIC: 2833  Vitamins, natural or synthetic: bulk, uncompounded
HQ: Pharmavite Llc
8531 Fallbrook Ave
West Hills CA 91304
818 221-6200

**(P-5263)**
**PHILIP B INC**
Also Called: Philip B
9053 Nemo St, West Hollywood (90069-5511)
PHONE.....................888 376-8236
Philip Bloom, *CEO*
**EMP:** 20 **EST:** 2005
**SALES (est):** 2.45MM **Privately Held**
Web: www.philipb.com
SIC: 2833  Medicinals and botanicals

**(P-5264)**
**PROMEGA BIOSCIENCES LLC**
277 Granada Dr, San Luis Obispo (93401-7396)
PHONE.....................805 544-8524
**EMP:** 55 **EST:** 1999
**SQ FT:** 40,000
**SALES (est):** 21.39MM
**SALES (corp-wide):** 743.96MM **Privately Held**
Web: www.promega.com
SIC: 2833 2835  Medicinal chemicals; Diagnostic substances
PA: Promega Corporation
2800 Woods Hollow Rd
608 274-4330

**(P-5265)**
**PROTHENA CORP PUB LTD CO**
331 Oyster Point Blvd, South San Francisco (94080-1913)
PHONE.....................650 837-8550
**EMP:** 15 **EST:** 2021
**SALES (est):** 990.32K **Privately Held**
Web: www.prothena.com
SIC: 2833  Medicinals and botanicals

**(P-5266)**
**RAINBOW LIGHT**
125 Mcpherson St, Santa Cruz (95060-5883)
PHONE.....................831 429-9089
Linda Kahler, *Mgr*
**EMP:** 45
**SALES (corp-wide):** 7.09B **Publicly Held**
Web: www.betteryourhealth.com
SIC: 2833 2834  Vitamins, natural or synthetic: bulk, uncompounded; Pharmaceutical preparations
HQ: Rainbow Light Nutritional Systems, Inc.
1301 Sawgrass Corp Pkwy
Sunrise FL 33323
954 233-3300

**(P-5267)**
**RON TEEGUARDEN ENTERPRISES INC (PA)**
Also Called: Dragon Herbs
10940 Wilshire Blvd, Los Angeles (90024-3915)
PHONE.....................323 556-8188
Ron Teagarden, *Pr*
Yanlin Teeguarden, *
◆ **EMP:** 23 **EST:** 1994
**SALES (est):** 4.8MM
**SALES (corp-wide):** 4.8MM **Privately Held**
Web: www.dragonherbs.com
SIC: 2833 5122  Drugs and herbs: grading, grinding, and milling; Medicinals and botanicals

**(P-5268)**
**S&B PHARMA INC**
Also Called: Norac Pharma
405 S Motor Ave, Azusa (91702-3232)
PHONE.....................626 334-2908
Doctor Daniel Levin, *Pr*
▲ **EMP:** 66 **EST:** 2012
**SALES (est):** 10.36MM **Privately Held**
Web: www.noracpharma.com
SIC: 2833 8731 2834  Medicinals and botanicals; Commercial physical research; Pharmaceutical preparations
PA: Alkem Laboratories Limited
Devashish Building, Alkem House,

**(P-5269)**
**SABRE SCIENCES INC**
2233 Faraday Ave Ste K, Carlsbad (92008-7214)

PHONE.................760 448-2750
Victor Salerno, Pr
Anna Salerno, Treas
Michael Borkin, Prin
**EMP:** 18 **EST:** 1999
**SQ FT:** 8,000
**SALES (est):** 4.05MM **Privately Held**
Web: www.sabresciences.com
**SIC: 2833** 8731 Hormones or derivatives; Commercial physical research

### (P-5270)
### SAPPHIRE ENERGY INC
10996 Torreyana Rd Ste 280, San Diego (92121-1159)
PHONE.................858 768-4700
James Levine, CEO
Thomas Willardson, CFO
**EMP:** 55 **EST:** 2007
**SALES (est):** 10.46MM **Privately Held**
Web: www.sapphireenergy.com
**SIC: 2833** Medicinals and botanicals

### (P-5271)
### STAUBER CALIFORNIA INC
Also Called: Stauber USA
4120 N Palm St, Fullerton (92835-1026)
PHONE.................714 441-3900
▲ **EMP:** 95
**SIC: 2833** Medicinals and botanicals

### (P-5272)
### STAUBER PRFMCE INGREDIENTS INC (HQ)
Also Called: Stauber
4120 N Palm St, Fullerton (92835-1026)
PHONE.................714 441-3900
Patrick Hawkins, CEO
Dan Stauber, Chief Brand Officer
**EMP:** 66 **EST:** 1969
**SALES (est):** 34.06MM
**SALES (corp-wide):** 919.16MM **Publicly Held**
Web: www.stauberusa.com
**SIC: 2833** Medicinals and botanicals
**PA:** Hawkins, Inc.
2381 Rosegate
612 331-6910

### (P-5273)
### THRESHOLD ENTERPRISES LTD
165 Technology Dr, Watsonville (95076-2448)
PHONE.................831 425-3955
**EMP:** 30
**SALES (corp-wide):** 97.32MM **Privately Held**
Web: www.thresholdenterprises.com
**SIC: 2833** 2099 Vitamins, natural or synthetic: bulk, uncompounded; Food preparations, nec
**PA:** Threshold Enterprises Ltd.
23 Janis Way
831 438-6851

### (P-5274)
### THRESHOLD ENTERPRISES LTD (PA)
Also Called: Vanguard Marketing
23 Janis Way, Scotts Valley (95066-3546)
PHONE.................831 438-6851
Ira L Goldberg, CEO
Tom Grillea, *
◆ **EMP:** 231 **EST:** 1978
**SQ FT:** 100,000
**SALES (est):** 97.32MM
**SALES (corp-wide):** 97.32MM **Privately Held**
Web: www.thresholdenterprises.com

**SIC: 2833** 5499 Vitamins, natural or synthetic: bulk, uncompounded; Health and dietetic food stores

### (P-5275)
### THRESHOLD ENTERPRISES LTD
11 Janis Way, Scotts Valley (95066-3537)
PHONE.................831 461-6413
Scott Laforce, Contrlr
**EMP:** 30
**SALES (corp-wide):** 97.32MM **Privately Held**
Web: www.thresholdenterprises.com
**SIC: 2833** 5122 Vitamins, natural or synthetic: bulk, uncompounded; Vitamins and minerals
**PA:** Threshold Enterprises Ltd.
23 Janis Way
831 438-6851

### (P-5276)
### THRESHOLD ENTERPRISES LTD
19 Janis Way, Scotts Valley (95066-3506)
PHONE.................831 461-6343
**EMP:** 30
**SALES (corp-wide):** 97.32MM **Privately Held**
Web: www.thresholdenterprises.com
**SIC: 2833** Vitamins, natural or synthetic: bulk, uncompounded
**PA:** Threshold Enterprises Ltd.
23 Janis Way
831 438-6851

### (P-5277)
### THRESHOLD ENTERPRISES LTD
2280 Delaware Ave, Santa Cruz (95060-5707)
PHONE.................831 466-4014
Ryan Garcia, Mgr
**EMP:** 30
**SALES (corp-wide):** 97.32MM **Privately Held**
Web: www.thresholdenterprises.com
**SIC: 2833** Vitamins, natural or synthetic: bulk, uncompounded
**PA:** Threshold Enterprises Ltd.
23 Janis Way
831 438-6851

### (P-5278)
### TIKUN OLAM ADELANTO LLC
541 S Spring St Unit 213, Los Angeles (90013-1657)
PHONE.................833 468-4586
David Librush, Brnch Mgr
**EMP:** 32
**SALES (corp-wide):** 871.48K **Privately Held**
Web: www.tikuncannabis.com
**SIC: 2833** Medicinals and botanicals
**PA:** Tikun Olam Adelanto Llc
16605 Koala Rd
833 468-4586

### (P-5279)
### UNI-CAPS LLC
540 Lambert Rd, Brea (92821)
PHONE.................714 529-8400
Sang H Kim, Managing Member
▲ **EMP:** 22 **EST:** 2006
**SALES (est):** 9.31MM **Privately Held**
Web: www.unicapsllc.com
**SIC: 2833** Vitamins, natural or synthetic: bulk, uncompounded

### (P-5280)
### VERTOSA INC
1630 N Main St Ste 363, Walnut Creek (94596-4609)

PHONE.................510 550-5850
Harold Han, Pr
Benjamin Larson, CFO
**EMP:** 35 **EST:** 2018
**SALES (est):** 7.55MM **Privately Held**
Web: www.vertosa.com
**SIC: 2833** Medicinals and botanicals

### (P-5281)
### VITAJOY USA INC
14165 Ramona Ave, Chino (91710-5753)
PHONE.................626 965-8830
Dan Gu, CEO
Charles Kuo, CFO
▲ **EMP:** 22 **EST:** 2012
**SALES (est):** 8.78MM **Privately Held**
Web: www.vitajoyusa.com
**SIC: 2833** Vitamins, natural or synthetic: bulk, uncompounded

### (P-5282)
### VYTALOGY WELLNESS LLC
15233 Ventura Blvd, Sherman Oaks (91403-2201)
PHONE.................818 867-4440
Nina Barton, Managing Member
**EMP:** 130 **EST:** 2021
**SALES (est):** 14.75MM **Privately Held**
Web: www.natrol.com
**SIC: 2833** Vitamins, natural or synthetic: bulk, uncompounded

### (P-5283)
### WESTAR NUTRITION CORP (PA)
350 Paularino Ave, Costa Mesa (92626-4616)
PHONE.................949 645-6100
David Fan, Pr
Lucy Fan, VP
▼ **EMP:** 20 **EST:** 1973
**SQ FT:** 55,000
**SALES (est):** 8.44MM
**SALES (corp-wide):** 8.44MM **Privately Held**
Web: www.westarnutrition.com
**SIC: 2833** 2834 2844 7389 Vitamins, natural or synthetic: bulk, uncompounded; Pharmaceutical preparations; Cosmetic preparations; Packaging and labeling services

## 2834 Pharmaceutical Preparations

### (P-5284)
### 89BIO INC
Also Called: 89bio
655 Montgomery St Ste 1500, San Francisco (94111)
PHONE.................415 432-9270
Rohan Palekar, CEO
Steven M Altschuler, *
Ryan Martins, CFO
Hank Mansbach, CMO
Quoc Le-nguyen, Chief Technician
**EMP:** 70 **EST:** 2018
**SQ FT:** 21,216
Web: www.89bio.com
**SIC: 2834** Pharmaceutical preparations

### (P-5285)
### A Q PHARMACEUTICALS INC
11555 Monarch St Ste C, Garden Grove (92841-1814)
PHONE.................714 903-1000
Tracy Nguyen, Pr
Henry Smith, *
▲ **EMP:** 30 **EST:** 2001
**SQ FT:** 3,000

**SALES (est):** 3.97MM **Privately Held**
Web: www.aqpharmaceuticals.com
**SIC: 2834** Pharmaceutical preparations

### (P-5286)
### AADI BIOSCIENCE INC (PA)
Also Called: AADI
17383 W Sunset Blvd Ste A250, Pacific Palisades (90272-4181)
PHONE.................424 744-8055
David Lennon, Pr
Caley Castelein, Ch Bd
Scott Giacobello, CFO
**EMP:** 40 **EST:** 2007
**SQ FT:** 2,760
**SALES (est):** 24.35MM
**SALES (corp-wide):** 24.35MM **Publicly Held**
Web: www.aadibio.com
**SIC: 2834** Pharmaceutical preparations

### (P-5287)
### ABBOTT DIABETES CARE SLS CORP
Also Called: Abbott Diabetes Care
1360 S Loop Rd, Alameda (94502-7000)
PHONE.................510 749-5400
Robert Ford, CEO
**EMP:** 82 **EST:** 2006
**SALES (est):** 8.73MM
**SALES (corp-wide):** 40.11B **Publicly Held**
Web: www.diabetescare.abbott
**SIC: 2834** Pharmaceutical preparations
**PA:** Abbott Laboratories
100 Abbott Park Rd
224 667-6100

### (P-5288)
### ABBOTT LABORATORIES
15900 Valley View Ct, Sylmar (91342-3577)
PHONE.................818 493-2388
Dee Vetter, Prin
**EMP:** 22
**SALES (corp-wide):** 40.11B **Publicly Held**
Web: www.abbott.com
**SIC: 2834** Pharmaceutical preparations
**PA:** Abbott Laboratories
100 Abbott Park Rd
224 667-6100

### (P-5289)
### ABBOTT NUTRITION
2302 Courage Dr, Fairfield (94533-6713)
PHONE.................707 399-1100
**EMP:** 77 **EST:** 2014
**SALES (est):** 7.01MM **Privately Held**
Web: www.abbott.com
**SIC: 2834** Pharmaceutical preparations

### (P-5290)
### ABBOTT NUTRITION MFG INC (HQ)
2351 N Watney Way Ste C, Fairfield (94533-6726)
PHONE.................707 399-1100
Mark Shaffar, VP
Mel Williamson, *
▼ **EMP:** 183 **EST:** 2004
**SALES (est):** 64.12MM
**SALES (corp-wide):** 40.11B **Publicly Held**
Web: www.abbottstore.com
**SIC: 2834** Vitamin, nutrient, and hematinic preparations for human use
**PA:** Abbott Laboratories
100 Abbott Park Rd
224 667-6100

# 2834 - Pharmaceutical Preparations (P-5291)

**PRODUCTS & SERVICES SECTION**

**(P-5291)**
**ABBOTT VASCULAR INC**
26531 Ynez Rd, Temecula  (92591-4630)
**PHONE**...............................951 941-2400
Ronald Dollens, *Brnch Mgr*
**EMP:** 500
**SALES (corp-wide):** 40.11B **Publicly Held**
**Web:** www.cardiovascular.abbott
**SIC:** 2834  Pharmaceutical preparations
**HQ:** Abbott Vascular Inc.
   3200 Lakeside Dr
   Santa Clara CA 95054
   408 845-3000

**(P-5292)**
**ABCO LABORATORIES  INC (PA)**
Also Called: Baron Brand Spices
2450 S Watney Way, Fairfield  (94533-6730)
P.O. Box 2519  (94533)
**PHONE**...............................707 432-2200
Allen Baron, *Pr*
▲ **EMP:** 97 **EST:** 1963
**SQ FT:** 29,000
**SALES (est):** 24.75MM
**SALES (corp-wide):** 24.75MM **Privately Held**
**Web:** www.abcolabs.com
**SIC:** 2834  2099  Vitamin preparations; Spices, including grinding

**(P-5293)**
**ABRAXIS BIOSCIENCE  LLC (DH)**
11755 Wilshire Blvd Fl 20, Los Angeles  (90025-1543)
**PHONE**...............................800 564-0216
**EMP:** 232 **EST:** 2007
**SALES (est):** 16.97MM
**SALES (corp-wide):** 45.01B **Publicly Held**
**Web:** www.celgene.com
**SIC:** 2834  Pharmaceutical preparations
**HQ:** Abraxis Bioscience, Inc.
   86 Morris Ave
   Summit NJ 07901

**(P-5294)**
**ACADIA PHARMACEUTICALS INC (PA)**
Also Called: ACADIA
12830 El Camino Real Ste 400, San Diego  (92130-2976)
**PHONE**...............................858 558-2871
Catherine Owen Adams, *CEO*
Stephen R Biggar, *
Mark C Schneyer, *Ex VP*
Brendan P Teehan, *Ex VP*
Austin D Kim, *Ex VP*
▲ **EMP:** 563 **EST:** 1993
**SQ FT:** 98,000
**SALES (est):** 726.44MM **Publicly Held**
**Web:** www.acadia.com
**SIC:** 2834  Pharmaceutical preparations

**(P-5295)**
**ACCOLADE PHARMA USA**
13260 Temple Ave, City Of Industry  (91746-1511)
**PHONE**...............................626 279-9699
Spencer Liu, *CEO*
**EMP:** 20 **EST:** 2018
**SALES (est):** 4.11MM **Privately Held**
**Web:** www.accoladepharma.us
**SIC:** 2834  Pharmaceutical preparations

**(P-5296)**
**ACTAVIS LLC**
311 Bonnie Cir, Corona  (92878-5182)
P.O. Box 1149  (92878-1149)
**PHONE**...............................909 270-1400
Allen Chao, *Brnch Mgr*
**EMP:** 79

**Web:** www.actavis.com
**SIC:** 2834  Pharmaceutical preparations
**HQ:** Actavis Llc
   1150 S Northpoint Blvd
   Waukegan IL 60085
   862 261-7000

**(P-5297)**
**ACTELION US HOLDING COMPANY (HQ)**
5000 Shoreline Ct Ste 200, South San Francisco  (94080-1956)
**PHONE**...............................650 624-6900
Tina Kitt, *Pr*
Marian Borovsky, *VP*
Joerg Felix, *VP*
Andrew Oakley, *Treas*
**EMP:** 39 **EST:** 2006
**SALES (est):** 6.79MM
**SALES (corp-wide):** 85.16B **Publicly Held**
**SIC:** 2834  Pharmaceutical preparations
**PA:** Johnson & Johnson
   1 Johnson & Johnson Plz
   732 524-0400

**(P-5298)**
**ADAM NUTRITION INC**
11010 Hopkins St Ste B, Jurupa Valley  (91752-3279)
**PHONE**...............................951 361-1120
◆ **EMP:** 130
**Web:** www.adamnutrition.com
**SIC:** 2834  Vitamin, nutrient, and hematinic preparations for human use

**(P-5299)**
**ADIANA INC**
1240 Elko Dr, Sunnyvale  (94089-2212)
**PHONE**...............................650 421-2900
Paul Goeld, *CEO*
**EMP:** 307 **EST:** 1997
**SQ FT:** 12,000
**SALES (est):** 729.21K
**SALES (corp-wide):** 4.03B **Publicly Held**
**SIC:** 2834  8731  Pharmaceutical preparations ; Commercial physical research
**HQ:** Cytyc Corporation
   250 Campus Dr
   Marlborough MA 01752

**(P-5300)**
**ADURO GVAX INC**
740 Heinz Ave, Berkeley  (94710-2748)
**PHONE**...............................510 848-4400
Jennifer Lew, *CFO*
**EMP:** 23 **EST:** 2018
**SALES (est):** 3.5MM **Privately Held**
**Web:** www.adurolife.com
**SIC:** 2834  Pharmaceutical preparations
**HQ:** Chinook Therapeutics, Inc.
   1 Health Plz
   East Hanover NJ 07936

**(P-5301)**
**AEGIS LIFE INC**
Also Called: Aegis Biodefense
3033 Science Park Rd Ste 270, San Diego  (92121-1167)
**PHONE**...............................650 666-5287
Hong Jiang, *COO*
John Lewis, *CEO*
**EMP:** 30 **EST:** 2020
**SALES (est):** 885.44K **Privately Held**
**Web:** www.aegis.life
**SIC:** 2834  Pharmaceutical preparations

**(P-5302)**
**AGOURON PHARMACEUTICALS  INC (HQ)**
10777 Science Center Dr, San Diego  (92121-1111)
**PHONE**...............................858 622-3000
Catherine Mackey Ph.d., *Sr VP*
**EMP:** 50 **EST:** 1984
**SALES (est):** 10.11MM
**SALES (corp-wide):** 58.5B **Publicly Held**
**Web:** www.agi.org
**SIC:** 2834  5122  8731  Pharmaceutical preparations; Pharmaceuticals; Commercial physical research
**PA:** Pfizer Inc.
   66 Hudson Blvd E
   212 733-2323

**(P-5303)**
**AKCEA THERAPEUTICS  INC (HQ)**
Also Called: Akcea Therapeutics
2850 Gazelle Ct, Carlsbad  (92010)
**PHONE**...............................617 207-0202
Brett Monia, *Pr*
Elizabeth Hougen, *Treas*
Melissa Yoon, *Sec*
Michael Pollock, *Chief Commercial Officer*
Tracy Berns, *Chief Compliance Officer*
**EMP:** 73 **EST:** 2017
**SALES (est):** 488.54MM
**SALES (corp-wide):** 787.65MM **Publicly Held**
**Web:** www.ionispharma.com
**SIC:** 2834  8731  Pharmaceutical preparations ; Biological research
**PA:** Ionis Pharmaceuticals, Inc.
   2855 Gazelle Ct
   760 931-9200

**(P-5304)**
**ALECTOR LLC**
521 Cottonwood Dr Ste 112, Milpitas  (95035-7467)
**PHONE**...............................415 231-5660
**EMP:** 47
**SALES (corp-wide):** 97.06MM **Publicly Held**
**Web:** www.alector.com
**SIC:** 2834  Pharmaceutical preparations
**HQ:** Alector Llc
   131 Oyster Pt Blvd Ste 60
   South San Francisco CA 94080
   415 231-5660

**(P-5305)**
**ALEXZA PHARMACEUTICALS INC (HQ)**
6550 Dumbarton Cir Ste A, Fremont  (94555-3605)
**PHONE**...............................650 944-7000
Stacy Palermini, *Sr VP*
David Hasegawa, *
Wolfgang Schmidt, *
Daniel Myers, *
Matthew Pepe, *
**EMP:** 25 **EST:** 2000
**SQ FT:** 65,604
**SALES (est):** 45.21MM **Privately Held**
**Web:** www.alexza.com
**SIC:** 2834  Pharmaceutical preparations
**PA:** Grupo Ferrer Internacional Sa
   Avenida Diagonal, 549 - 5  Planta

**(P-5306)**
**ALLAKOS INC**
Also Called: ALLAKOS
825 Industrial Rd Ste 500, San Carlos  (94070-3323)
**PHONE**...............................650 597-5002
Robert Alexander, *Pr*
Daniel Janney, *
Adam Tomasi, *Pr*

Baird Radford, *CFO*
Chin Lee, *CMO*
**EMP:** 131 **EST:** 2012
**SQ FT:** 96,000
**SALES (est):** 28.67MM **Privately Held**
**Web:** www.allakos.com
**SIC:** 2834  Pharmaceutical preparations

**(P-5307)**
**ALLERGAN SALES LLC (DH)**
2525 Dupont Dr, Irvine  (92612-1599)
P.O. Box 19534  (92623-9534)
**PHONE**...............................862 261-7000
Brenton L Saunders, *Ch*
William Meury, *CCO*
Matthew M Walsh, *
A Robert D Bailey, *CLO*
Karen L Ling, *Chief Human Resource Officer*
▲ **EMP:** 600 **EST:** 1986
**SQ FT:** 10,000
**SALES (est):** 372.19MM
**SALES (corp-wide):** 54.32B **Publicly Held**
**Web:** www.abbvie.com
**SIC:** 2834  Pharmaceutical preparations
**HQ:** Allergan, Inc.
   1 N Waukegan Rd
   North Chicago IL 60064
   862 261-7000

**(P-5308)**
**ALLERGAN SPCLTY THRPEUTICS INC**
Also Called: Allergan
2525 Dupont Dr, Irvine  (92612-1599)
**PHONE**...............................714 246-4500
David Pyott, *Pr*
**EMP:** 1500 **EST:** 1997
**SALES (est):** 481.05MM
**SALES (corp-wide):** 54.32B **Publicly Held**
**Web:** www.allergandatalabs.com
**SIC:** 2834  Pharmaceutical preparations
**HQ:** Allergan, Inc.
   1 N Waukegan Rd
   North Chicago IL 60064
   862 261-7000

**(P-5309)**
**ALLERGAN USA  INC (DH)**
Also Called: Pacific Communications
18581 Teller Ave, Irvine  (92612-1627)
P.O. Box 19534  (92623-9534)
**PHONE**...............................714 427-1900
David E l Pyott, *CEO*
Craig Sullivan, *Pr*
Jeffrey L Edwards, *VP*
Douglas S Ingram, *Sec*
James M Hindman, *Treas*
**EMP:** 67 **EST:** 2007
**SALES (est):** 471.46MM
**SALES (corp-wide):** 54.32B **Publicly Held**
**Web:** www.pacificcommunications.com
**SIC:** 2834  Druggists' preparations (pharmaceuticals)
**HQ:** Allergan, Inc.
   1 N Waukegan Rd
   North Chicago IL 60064
   862 261-7000

**(P-5310)**
**ALX ONCOLOGY HOLDINGS INC (PA)**
Also Called: Alx Oncology
323 Allerton Ave, South San Francisco  (94080-4816)
**PHONE**...............................650 466-7125
Jason Lettmann, *CEO*
Jaume Pons, *CSO*
Corey Goodman, *Ex Ch Bd*
Peter Garcia, *CFO*

▲ = Import  ▼ = Export
◆ = Import/Export

## PRODUCTS & SERVICES SECTION
## 2834 - Pharmaceutical Preparations (P-5332)

Sophia Randolph, *CMO*
**EMP:** 54 **EST:** 2015
**SQ FT:** 10,000
**Web:** www.alxoncology.com
**SIC:** 2834 Pharmaceutical preparations

**(P-5311)**
### ALZA CORPORATION (HQ)
Also Called: Alza Pharmaceuticals
700 Eubanks Dr, Vacaville (95688-9470)
**PHONE**.............................707 453-6400
Katie Fitz Chaddock, *Pr*
▲ **EMP:** 800 **EST:** 1987
**SQ FT:** 74,500
**SALES (est):** 36.91MM
**SALES (corp-wide):** 85.16B **Publicly Held**
**Web:** www.alza.com
**SIC:** 2834 Pharmaceutical preparations
**PA:** Johnson & Johnson
   1 Johnson & Johnson Plz
   732 524-0400

**(P-5312)**
### AMARE GLOBAL LP
17872 Gillette Ave Ste 100, Irvine (92614-6573)
**PHONE**.............................888 898-8551
Jared Turner, *CEO*
Hiep Tran, *Ch*
Gabriel Sanchez, *OF SALES*
**EMP:** 27 **EST:** 2017
**SALES (est):** 2.71MM **Privately Held**
**SIC:** 2834 Vitamin preparations

**(P-5313)**
### AMBIT BIOSCIENCES CORPORATION
10201 Wateridge Cir Ste 200, San Diego (92121-5806)
**PHONE**.............................858 334-2100
Michael A Martino, *Pr*
Faheem Hasnain, *Ch Bd*
Alan Fuhrman, *CFO*
Annette North, *Sr VP*
Mario Orlando, *Sr VP*
**EMP:** 53 **EST:** 2000
**SQ FT:** 20,000
**SALES (est):** 6.5MM **Privately Held**
**Web:** www.ambitbio.com
**SIC:** 2834 Pharmaceutical preparations
**PA:** Daiichi Sankyo Company, Limited
   3-5-1, Nihombashihoncho

**(P-5314)**
### AMBRX INC (PA)
10975 N Torrey Pines Rd Ste 100, La Jolla (92037-1051)
**PHONE**.............................858 875-2400
Tiecheng Qiao, *CEO*
John D Diekman, *
John W Wallen Iii, *VP*
Ho Cho, *
Simon Allen, *Chief Business Officer*
**EMP:** 56 **EST:** 2003
**SALES (est):** 25MM
**SALES (corp-wide):** 25MM **Privately Held**
**Web:** www.ambrx.com
**SIC:** 2834 Druggists' preparations (pharmaceuticals)

**(P-5315)**
### AMERIPHARMA SPECIALTY PHRM DIV
132 S Anita Dr, Orange (92868-3317)
**PHONE**.............................877 778-3773
**EMP:** 21 **EST:** 2017
**SALES (est):** 345.97K **Privately Held**
**Web:** www.ameripharma.com
**SIC:** 2834 Pharmaceutical preparations

**(P-5316)**
### AMF PHARMA LLC
1909 S Campus Ave, Ontario (91761-5410)
**PHONE**.............................909 930-9599
**EMP:** 30 **EST:** 2012
**SALES (est):** 1.65MM **Privately Held**
**Web:** www.amfpharma.com
**SIC:** 2834 Pharmaceutical preparations

**(P-5317)**
### AMGEN INC
1840 De Havilland Dr, Newbury Park (91320-1789)
**PHONE**.............................805 447-1000
Gordon M Binder, *Mgr*
**EMP:** 169
**SALES (corp-wide):** 28.19B **Publicly Held**
**Web:** www.amgen.com
**SIC:** 2834 Pharmaceutical preparations
**PA:** Amgen Inc.
   1 Amgen Center Dr
   805 447-1000

**(P-5318)**
### AMGEN USA INC (HQ)
1 Amgen Center Dr, Thousand Oaks (91320-1799)
**PHONE**.............................805 447-1000
Kevin W Sharer, *CEO*
**EMP:** 96 **EST:** 2010
**SALES (est):** 27.37MM
**SALES (corp-wide):** 28.19B **Publicly Held**
**Web:** www.amgen.com
**SIC:** 2834 Pharmaceutical preparations
**PA:** Amgen Inc.
   1 Amgen Center Dr
   805 447-1000

**(P-5319)**
### AMPAC FINE CHEMICALS LLC
Also Called: Ampac Analytical
1100 Windfield Way, El Dorado Hills (95762-9622)
**PHONE**.............................916 245-6500
Renato Murrer, *Brnch Mgr*
**EMP:** 255
**Web:** www.ampacanalytical.com
**SIC:** 2834 Digitalis pharmaceutical preparations
**HQ:** Ampac Fine Chemicals Llc
   Highway 50 And Hazel Ave
   Rancho Cordova CA 95670
   916 357-6880

**(P-5320)**
### AMPHASTAR PHARMACEUTICALS INC (PA)
Also Called: AMPHASTAR
11570 6th St, Rancho Cucamonga (91730-6025)
**PHONE**.............................909 980-9484
Jack Yongfeng Zhang, *CSO*
Jack Yongfeng Zhang, *CSO*
Mary Ziping Luo, *Chief Scientist*
William J Peters, *
▲ **EMP:** 102 **EST:** 1996
**SQ FT:** 267,674
**SALES (est):** 644.39MM
**SALES (corp-wide):** 644.39MM **Publicly Held**
**Web:** www.amphastar.com
**SIC:** 2834 Pharmaceutical preparations

**(P-5321)**
### AMYLIN OHIO LLC
9360 Towne Centre Dr, San Diego (92121-3057)
**PHONE**.............................858 552-2200
**EMP:** 1300
**SIC:** 2834 Pharmaceutical preparations

**(P-5322)**
### ANACOR PHARMACEUTICALS INC
1060 E Meadow Cir, Palo Alto (94303-4230)
**PHONE**.............................650 543-7500
James Marconi, *Brnch Mgr*
**EMP:** 40
**SALES (corp-wide):** 58.5B **Publicly Held**
**Web:** www.pfizer.com
**SIC:** 2834 Pharmaceutical preparations
**HQ:** Anacor Pharmaceuticals, Inc.
   66 Hudson Blvd E
   New York NY 10001
   212 733-2323

**(P-5323)**
### ANAPTYSBIO INC (PA)
Also Called: ANAPTYSBIO
10770 Wateridge Cir Ste 210, San Diego (92121-5801)
**PHONE**.............................858 362-6295
John Orwin, *Ch Bd*
Hamza Suria, *Pr*
Eric Loumeau, *COO*
Dennis Mulroy, *CFO*
Paul F Lizzul, *CMO*
**EMP:** 116 **EST:** 2005
**SQ FT:** 45,000
**SALES (est):** 17.16MM **Publicly Held**
**Web:** www.anaptysbio.com
**SIC:** 2834 Pharmaceutical preparations

**(P-5324)**
### ANCHEN PHARMACEUTICALS INC
5 Goodyear, Irvine (92618-2000)
**PHONE**.............................949 639-8100
Phillip Brancazio, *Brnch Mgr*
**EMP:** 236
**Web:** www.parpharm.com
**SIC:** 2834 Druggists' preparations (pharmaceuticals)
**HQ:** Anchen Pharmaceuticals, Inc.
   300 Tice Blvd Ste 230
   Woodcliff Lake NJ 07677
   949 639-8100

**(P-5325)**
### ANNEXON INC (PA)
Also Called: Annexon
1400 Sierra Point Pkwy Ste 200, Brisbane (94005-1808)
**PHONE**.............................650 822-5500
Douglas E Love, *Pr*
Thomas G Wiggans, *Non-Executive Chairman of the Board*
Jennifer Lew, *Ex VP*
Rick Artis, *CSO*
Ted Yednock, *CIO*
**EMP:** 70 **EST:** 2011
**SQ FT:** 65,818
**Web:** www.annexonbio.com
**SIC:** 2834 8731 Pharmaceutical preparations ; Biotechnical research, commercial

**(P-5326)**
### ANTRIABIO DELAWARE INC
570 El Camino Real, Redwood City (94063-1200)
**PHONE**.............................303 222-2128
**EMP:** 30 **EST:** 2019
**SALES (est):** 253.9K **Publicly Held**
**SIC:** 2834 Pharmaceutical preparations
**PA:** Rezolute, Inc.
   275 Shoreline Dr Ste 500
   650 206-4507

**(P-5327)**
### AOE INTERNATIONAL INC
20611 Belshaw Ave, Carson (90746-3507)
▲ **EMP:** 35 **EST:** 1998
**SQ FT:** 12,500
**SALES (est):** 839.73K **Privately Held**
**SIC:** 2834 Vitamin, nutrient, and hematinic preparations for human use

**(P-5328)**
### APPLIED MLECULAR EVOLUTION INC (HQ)
10300 Campus Point Dr Ste 200, San Diego (92121-1504)
**PHONE**.............................858 597-4990
Thomas Bumol, *Pr*
**EMP:** 50 **EST:** 1990
**SQ FT:** 43,000
**SALES (est):** 3.03MM
**SALES (corp-wide):** 34.12B **Publicly Held**
**SIC:** 2834 Pharmaceutical preparations
**PA:** Eli Lilly And Company
   1 Lilly Corporate Ctr
   317 276-2000

**(P-5329)**
### APPLIED MOLECULAR TRNSPT INC
325 Sharon Park Dr # 1001, Menlo Park (94025-6805)
**PHONE**.............................650 392-0420
Scott Fine, *CEO*
**EMP:** 80 **EST:** 2010
**SQ FT:** 18,748
**SALES (corp-wide):** 1.08MM **Publicly Held**
**Web:** www.appliedmt.com
**SIC:** 2834 Pharmaceutical preparations
**PA:** Cyclo Therapeutics, Inc.
   6714 Nw 16th St Ste B
   386 418-8060

**(P-5330)**
### ARADIGM CORPORATION
Also Called: Aradigm
1613 Lyon St, San Francisco (94115-2414)
**PHONE**.............................510 265-9000
**EMP:** 23 **EST:** 1991
**SALES (est):** 4.14MM **Privately Held**
**Web:** www.aradigm.com
**SIC:** 2834 Drugs acting on the respiratory system

**(P-5331)**
### ARCTURUS THRPTICS HOLDINGS INC (PA)
Also Called: ARCTURUS
10628 Science Center Dr Ste 250, San Diego (92121-1132)
**PHONE**.............................858 900-2660
Joseph E Payne, *Pr*
Peter Farrell, *Ch Bd*
Andy Sassine, *CFO*
Padmanabh Chivukula, *CSO*
Lance Kurata, *CLO*
**EMP:** 26 **EST:** 2013
**SQ FT:** 24,700
**SALES (est):** 166.8MM
**SALES (corp-wide):** 166.8MM **Publicly Held**
**Web:** www.arcturusrx.com
**SIC:** 2834 Pharmaceutical preparations

**(P-5332)**
### ARDEA BIOSCIENCES INC
9390 Towne Centre Dr Ste 100, San Diego (92121-3026)
**PHONE**.............................858 625-0787
**EMP:** 25 **EST:** 2019

## 2834 - Pharmaceutical Preparations (P-5333)

SALES (est): 2.94MM **Privately Held**
SIC: 2834  Pharmaceutical preparations

**(P-5333)**
**ARIA PHARMACEUTICALS INC**
265 Cambridge Ave Unit 60099, Palo Alto (94306-5701)
PHONE..................................650 382-2605
Andrew A Radin, *CEO*
EMP: 19 EST: 2015
SALES (est): 2.46MM **Privately Held**
Web: www.ariapharmaceuticals.com
SIC: 2834  Pharmaceutical preparations

**(P-5334)**
**ARIDIS PHARMACEUTICALS INC (PA)**
983 University Ave Bldg B, Los Gatos (95032-7637)
PHONE..................................408 385-1742
Vu Truong, *CSO*
Eric Patzer, *Ex Ch Bd*
Michael A Nazak, *CFO*
Hasan Jafri, *CMO*
EMP: 21 EST: 2003
SQ FT: 15,129
SALES (est): 1.53MM
SALES (corp-wide): 1.53MM **Publicly Held**
Web: www.aridispharma.com
SIC: 2834  Pharmaceutical preparations

**(P-5335)**
**ARMO BIOSCIENCES INC**
Also Called: Armo
575 Chesapeake Dr, Redwood City (94063-4724)
PHONE..................................650 779-5075
Peter Van Vlasselaer, *Pr*
Herb Cross, *CFO*
Joseph Leveque, *CMO*
EMP: 21 EST: 2010
SQ FT: 11,388
SALES (est): 5.16MM
SALES (corp-wide): 34.12B **Publicly Held**
SIC: 2834  Pharmaceutical preparations
PA: Eli Lilly And Company
1 Lilly Corporate Ctr
317 276-2000

**(P-5336)**
**ARROWHEAD PHARMACEUTICALS INC**
10102 Hoyt Park Dr, San Diego (92131-3000)
PHONE..................................626 304-3400
EMP: 52
Web: www.arrowheadpharma.com
SIC: 2834  Pharmaceutical preparations
PA: Arrowhead Pharmaceuticals, Inc.
177 E Colo Blvd Ste 700

**(P-5337)**
**ARROWHEAD PHARMACEUTICALS INC (PA)**
Also Called: ARROWHEAD
177 E Colorado Blvd Ste 700, Pasadena (91105-1976)
PHONE..................................626 304-3400
Christopher Anzalone, *Pr*
Douglass Given, *
Kenneth A Myszkowski, *CFO*
Patrick O'brien, *COO*
Javier San Martin, *CMO*
EMP: 137 EST: 1989
SQ FT: 49,000
SALES (est): 240.74MM **Publicly Held**
Web: www.arrowheadpharma.com

SIC: 2834  8731  Pharmaceutical preparations; Biological research

**(P-5338)**
**ARS PHARMACEUTICALS INC (PA)**
11682 El Camino Real Ste 120, San Diego (92130-2092)
PHONE..................................858 771-9307
Richard Lowenthal, *Pr*
Pratik Shah, *Ch Bd*
Kathleen Scott, *CFO*
Sarina Tanimoto, *CMO*
Eric Karas, *CCO*
EMP: 21 EST: 2016
SALES (est): 30K
SALES (corp-wide): 30K **Publicly Held**
Web: www.ars-pharma.com
SIC: 2834  Pharmaceutical preparations

**(P-5339)**
**ASSEMBLY BIOSCIENCES INC**
Also Called: ASSEMBLY
2 Tower Pl Ste 700 # 2, South San Francisco (94080-1848)
PHONE..................................833 509-4583
Jason A Okazaki, *Pr*
William R Ringo Junior, *Non-Executive Chairman of the Board*
William E Delaney Iv, *CSO*
Jeanette M Bjorkquist, *CAO*
Anuj Gaggar, *CMO*
EMP: 65 EST: 2005
SALES (est): 7.16MM **Privately Held**
Web: www.assemblybio.com
SIC: 2834  Pharmaceutical preparations

**(P-5340)**
**ASTEX PHARMACEUTICALS INC (DH)**
4420 Rosewood Dr Ste 200, Pleasanton (94588-3008)
PHONE..................................925 560-0100
James Manuso, *Ch*
Harren Jhoti, *Pr*
Mohammad Azab, *CMO*
Michael Molkentin, *CFO*
Martin Buckland, *Chief Business Officer*
EMP: 118 EST: 2011
SQ FT: 37,000
SALES (est): 24.36MM **Privately Held**
Web: www.astx.com
SIC: 2834  Pharmaceutical preparations
HQ: Otsuka America, Inc.
1 Embrcadero Ctr Ste 2020
San Francisco CA 94111

**(P-5341)**
**ASTRAZENECA LP**
121 Oyster Point Blvd, South San Francisco (94080-1910)
PHONE..................................650 634-0103
EMP: 44 EST: 1998
SALES (est): 3.01MM **Privately Held**
SIC: 2834  Pharmaceutical preparations

**(P-5342)**
**ASTRAZENECA PHARMACEUTICALS LP**
200 Cardinal Way, Redwood City (94063-4702)
PHONE..................................650 305-2600
Ed Louie, *Brnch Mgr*
EMP: 26
SALES (corp-wide): 45.81B **Privately Held**
Web: www.astrazeneca.com
SIC: 2834  Druggists' preparations (pharmaceuticals)
HQ: Astrazeneca Pharmaceuticals Lp
1800 Concord Pike
Wilmington DE 19850

**(P-5343)**
**ATP CLINICAL RESEARCH INC**
3151 Airway Ave Ste T3, Costa Mesa (92626-4627)
PHONE..................................714 393-0787
EMP: 16 EST: 2005
SALES (est): 497.25K **Privately Held**
Web: www.atpcr.com
SIC: 2834  Pharmaceutical preparations

**(P-5344)**
**ATTRALUS INC**
337 Beach Rd Ste C, Burlingame (94010-2076)
PHONE..................................415 410-3268
Mark Timney, *CEO*
EMP: 32 EST: 2019
SALES (est): 5.16MM **Privately Held**
Web: www.attralus.com
SIC: 2834  Pharmaceutical preparations

**(P-5345)**
**ATXCO INC**
3030 Bunker Hill St Ste 325, San Diego (92109-5754)
PHONE..................................650 334-2079
Robert Williamson, *CEO*
EMP: 21 EST: 2019
SALES (est): 272.23K **Privately Held**
SIC: 2834  Pharmaceutical preparations

**(P-5346)**
**AUSPEX PHARMACEUTICALS INC**
3333 N Torrey Pines Ct Ste 400, La Jolla (92037-1022)
P.O. Box 49272  (90049-0272)
PHONE..................................858 558-2400
Larry Downey, *Pr*
Deborah A Griffin, *
Austin D Kim, *
EMP: 30 EST: 2001
SALES (est): 2.38MM **Privately Held**
Web: www.tevapharm.com
SIC: 2834  Pharmaceutical preparations
PA: Teva Pharmaceutical Industries Limited
124 Dvora Hanevia

**(P-5347)**
**AVANIR PHARMACEUTICALS INC (DH)**
30 Enterprise Ste 200, Aliso Viejo (92656-7112)
PHONE..................................949 389-6700
Rohan Palekar, *Pr*
Gregory J Flesher, *Sr VP*
Joao Siffert, *Sr VP*
Christine G Ocampo, *VP*
EMP: 67 EST: 1988
SALES (est): 64.98MM **Privately Held**
Web: www.otsuka-us.com
SIC: 2834  Pharmaceutical preparations
HQ: Otsuka Pharmaceutical Co., Ltd.
2-16-4, Konan
Minato-Ku TKY 108-0

**(P-5348)**
**AVID BIOSERVICES INC**
14272 Franklin Ave Ste 115, Tustin (92780-7064)
PHONE..................................714 508-6000
Steven W King, *Pr*
EMP: 97
SALES (corp-wide): 139.91MM **Publicly Held**
Web: www.avidbio.com

SIC: 2834  Pharmaceutical preparations
PA: Avid Bioservices, Inc.
14191 Myford Rd
714 508-6100

**(P-5349)**
**AVID BIOSERVICES INC**
14282 Franklin Ave, Tustin (92780-7009)
PHONE..................................714 508-6166
EMP: 48
SALES (corp-wide): 139.91MM **Publicly Held**
Web: www.avidbio.com
SIC: 2834  Pharmaceutical preparations
PA: Avid Bioservices, Inc.
14191 Myford Rd
714 508-6100

**(P-5350)**
**AVID BIOSERVICES INC (PA)**
Also Called: AVID BIOSERVICES
14191 Myford Rd, Tustin (92780-7020)
PHONE..................................714 508-6100
Nicholas S Green, *Pr*
Joseph Carleone, *Non-Executive Chairman of the Board*
Daniel R Hart, *CFO*
Matthew Kwietniak, *CCO*
Mark R Ziebell, *Corporate Secretary*
EMP: 120 EST: 1981
SALES (est): 139.91MM
SALES (corp-wide): 139.91MM **Publicly Held**
Web: www.avidbio.com
SIC: 2834  Pharmaceutical preparations

**(P-5351)**
**AVIDITY BIOSCIENCES INC (PA)**
Also Called: AVIDITY BIOSCIENCES
10578 Science Center Dr Ste 125, San Diego (92121-1145)
PHONE..................................858 401-7900
Sarah Boyce, *Pr*
Troy Wilson, *
Joseph Baroldi, *COO*
Michael F Maclean, *CFO*
Arthur A Levin, *CSO*
EMP: 23 EST: 2012
SQ FT: 8,561
SALES (est): 9.56MM
SALES (corp-wide): 9.56MM **Publicly Held**
Web: www.aviditybiosciences.com
SIC: 2834  Pharmaceutical preparations

**(P-5352)**
**BACHEM AMERICAS INC**
3131 Fujita St, Torrance (90505-4006)
PHONE..................................424 347-5600
EMP: 45
Web: www.bachem.com
SIC: 2834  Pharmaceutical preparations
HQ: Bachem Americas, Inc.
3132 Kashiwa St
Torrance CA 90505
310 784-4440

**(P-5353)**
**BACHEM AMERICAS INC**
Also Called: Bachem Vista BSD
1271 Avenida Chelsea, Vista  (92081-8315)
PHONE..................................888 422-2436
Brian Gregg, *Pr*
EMP: 45
Web: www.bachem.com
SIC: 2834  Pharmaceutical preparations
HQ: Bachem Americas, Inc.
3132 Kashiwa St
Torrance CA 90505
310 784-4440

## PRODUCTS & SERVICES SECTION
## 2834 - Pharmaceutical Preparations (P-5375)

**(P-5354)**
**BAUSCH HEALTH AMERICAS INC**
1330 Redwood Way Ste C, Petaluma (94954-7122)
PHONE.................707 793-2600
EMP: 140
SALES (corp-wide): 8.76B **Privately Held**
Web: www.valeant.com
SIC: **2834** Pharmaceutical preparations
HQ: Bausch Health Americas, Inc.
    400 Somerset Corp Blvd
    Bridgewater NJ 08807
    908 927-1400

**(P-5355)**
**BAXALTA US INC**
4501 Colorado Blvd, Los Angeles (90039-1103)
PHONE.................818 240-5600
Raul Navarro, *Brnch Mgr*
EMP: 644
SIC: **2834** Pharmaceutical preparations
HQ: Baxalta Us Inc.
    1200 Lakeside Dr
    Bannockburn IL

**(P-5356)**
**BAXCO PHARMACEUTICAL INC (PA)**
2393 Bateman Ave, Irwindale (91010-3313)
PHONE.................626 610-7088
Dennis Wong, *Pr*
Joseph Meuse, *COO*
Koki Luu, *CFO*
Rose Ibarra, *Genl Mgr*
▲ EMP: 17 EST: 2000
SALES (est): 6.21MM
SALES (corp-wide): 6.21MM **Privately Held**
Web: www.baxcoinc.com
SIC: **2834** Pharmaceutical preparations

**(P-5357)**
**BAYER CORPORATION**
7025 Angelo Ln, Gilroy (95020-9546)
PHONE.................408 406-8491
Patrick Mcbride, *Brnch Mgr*
EMP: 26
SALES (corp-wide): 51.78B **Privately Held**
Web: cropscience.bayer.com
SIC: **2834** Pharmaceutical preparations
HQ: Bayer Corporation
    100 Bayer Blvd
    Whippany NJ 07981
    412 777-2000

**(P-5358)**
**BAYER HEALTHCARE LLC**
5885 Hollis St, Emeryville (94608-2404)
PHONE.................510 597-6150
Anita Bawa, *Brnch Mgr*
EMP: 104
SALES (corp-wide): 51.78B **Privately Held**
Web: www.bayercare.com
SIC: **2834** Pharmaceutical preparations
HQ: Bayer Healthcare Llc
    100 Bayer Blvd
    Whippany NJ 07981
    862 404-3000

**(P-5359)**
**BAYER HEALTHCARE LLC**
800 Dwight Way, Berkeley (94710-2456)
PHONE.................510 705-7545
Paul Heiden, *Brnch Mgr*
EMP: 134
SALES (corp-wide): 51.78B **Privately Held**
Web: www.bayercare.com

SIC: **2834** Pharmaceutical preparations
HQ: Bayer Healthcare Llc
    100 Bayer Blvd
    Whippany NJ 07981
    862 404-3000

**(P-5360)**
**BAYER HEALTHCARE LLC**
747 Grayson St, Berkeley (94710-2678)
P.O. Box 6314 (26003-0734)
PHONE.................510 705-4421
EMP: 67
SQ FT: 1,964
SALES (corp-wide): 51.78B **Privately Held**
Web: www.bayercare.com
SIC: **2834** Pharmaceutical preparations
HQ: Bayer Healthcare Llc
    100 Bayer Blvd
    Whippany NJ 07981
    862 404-3000

**(P-5361)**
**BAYER HEALTHCARE LLC**
Also Called: Bayer Diabetes Care
510 Oakmead Pkwy, Sunnyvale (94085-4022)
PHONE.................408 499-0606
Joseph Ruggiero, *Brnch Mgr*
EMP: 30
SALES (corp-wide): 51.78B **Privately Held**
Web: www.bayercare.com
SIC: **2834** Pharmaceutical preparations
HQ: Bayer Healthcare Llc
    100 Bayer Blvd
    Whippany NJ 07981
    862 404-3000

**(P-5362)**
**BEAUTY & HEALTH INTERNATIONAL**
7541 Anthony Ave, Garden Grove (92841-4005)
P.O. Box 890 (92684-0890)
PHONE.................714 903-9730
Charles G Myung, *Pr*
▲ EMP: 50 EST: 1993
SQ FT: 12,000
SALES (est): 2.31MM **Privately Held**
SIC: **2834** 2844 5122 5149 Vitamin preparations; Cosmetic preparations; Vitamins and minerals; Health foods

**(P-5363)**
**BEIGENE USA INC**
1840 Gateway Dr Fl 3, San Mateo (94404-4027)
PHONE.................877 828-5568
EMP: 362
Web: www.beigene.com
SIC: **2834** 5122 8731 Pharmaceutical preparations; Pharmaceuticals; Commercial research laboratory
HQ: Beigene Usa, Inc.
    55 Cambrdge Pkwy Ste 700w
    Cambridge MA 02142
    781 801-1800

**(P-5364)**
**BEST FORMULATIONS LLC**
17775 Rowland St, City Of Industry (91748-1138)
PHONE.................626 912-9998
EMP: 111
Web: www.bestformulations.com
SIC: **2834** Pharmaceutical preparations
HQ: Best Formulations Llc
    17758 Rowland St
    City Of Industry CA 91748
    626 912-9998

**(P-5365)**
**BETTER THERAPEUTICS INC (PA)**
548 Market St # 49404, San Francisco (94104-5401)
PHONE.................415 887-2311
Kevin Appelbaum, *CEO*
David Perry, *Ex Ch Bd*
Mark Berman, *CMO*
Kristin Wynholds, *CPO*
Justin Zamirowski, *CCO*
EMP: 19 EST: 2020
Web: www.mcacquisition.com
SIC: **2834** Pharmaceutical preparations

**(P-5366)**
**BETTER THERAPEUTICS OPCO INC**
548 Market St # 49404, San Francisco (94104-5401)
PHONE.................415 887-2311
Kevin Appelbaum, *CEO*
EMP: 17 EST: 2020
SALES (est): 4.35MM **Publicly Held**
Web: www.bettertx.com
SIC: **2834** Pharmaceutical preparations
PA: Better Therapeutics, Inc.
    548 Market St # 49404
    415 887-2311

**(P-5367)**
**BF SUMA PHARMACEUTICALS INC**
5001 Earle Ave, Rosemead (91770-1169)
PHONE.................626 285-8366
Chak Yeung Chan, *Pr*
Annie Cheng, *Contrlr*
▲ EMP: 52 EST: 2006
SQ FT: 10,000
SALES (est): 6.63MM **Privately Held**
SIC: **2834** Pharmaceutical preparations

**(P-5368)**
**BIMEDA INC**
5539 Ayon Ave, Irwindale (91706-2057)
PHONE.................626 815-1680
Tim Tynan, *Brnch Mgr*
EMP: 187
SALES (corp-wide): 3.51B **Privately Held**
Web: www.bimedaus.com
SIC: **2834** 3841 Veterinary pharmaceutical preparations; Surgical and medical instruments
HQ: Bimeda Inc.
    475 N Martingale Rd # 120
    Schaumburg IL 60173
    630 928-0361

**(P-5369)**
**BIO-NUTRACEUTICALS INC (PA)**
Also Called: Bni
21820 Marilla St, Chatsworth (91311-4127)
PHONE.................818 727-0246
EMP: 17 EST: 2004
SALES (est): 8.61MM
SALES (corp-wide): 8.61MM **Privately Held**
Web: www.bnipure.com
SIC: **2834** Tablets, pharmaceutical

**(P-5370)**
**BIOAGE LABS INC**
Also Called: BIOAGE
1445 S 50th St Ste A, Richmond (94804-4605)
PHONE.................510 806-1445
Kristen Fortney, *Pr*
Jean-pierre Garnier, *Ch Bd*
Eric Morgen, *

Dov Goldstein, *CFO*
Paul Rubin, *CMO*
EMP: 60 EST: 2015
Web: www.bioagelabs.com
SIC: **2834** 8731 Pharmaceutical preparations; Biotechnical research, commercial

**(P-5371)**
**BIOMARIN PHARMACEUTICAL INC (PA)**
Also Called: BIOMARIN
770 Lindaro St, San Rafael (94901-3991)
PHONE.................415 506-6700
Jean-jacques Bienaime, *CEO*
Alexander Hardy, *
Richard A Meier, *
Brian R Mueller, *Ex VP*
C Greg Guyer, *Ex VP*
EMP: 255 EST: 1996
SQ FT: 407,300
SALES (est): 2.42B
SALES (corp-wide): 2.42B **Publicly Held**
Web: www.biomarin.com
SIC: **2834** Pharmaceutical preparations

**(P-5372)**
**BIOMEA FUSION INC (PA)**
Also Called: Biomea Fusion
900 Middlefield Rd Ste 4, Redwood City (94063-1681)
PHONE.................650 980-9099
Thomas Butler, *Ch Bd*
Rainer Erdtmann, *Pr*
Franco Valle, *CFO*
Juan Pablo Frias, *CMO*
EMP: 37 EST: 2017
SQ FT: 2,938
Web: www.biomeafusion.com
SIC: **2834** 8731 Pharmaceutical preparations; Biotechnical research, commercial

**(P-5373)**
**BIOMED CALIFORNIA INC**
Also Called: Soleo Health
721 S Glasgow Ave Ste C, Inglewood (90301-3016)
PHONE.................310 665-1121
John Ginzler, *CFO*
Drew Walk, *CEO*
EMP: 47 EST: 2007
SALES (est): 2.43MM **Privately Held**
SIC: **2834** 5912 Druggists' preparations (pharmaceuticals); Drug stores and proprietary stores
HQ: Biomed Healthcare, Inc.
    950 Calcon Hook Rd Ste 19
    Sharon Hill PA 19079
    888 244-2340

**(P-5374)**
**BIOMED INDUSTRIES INC (PA)**
2570 N 1st St Fl 2, San Jose (95131-1035)
PHONE.................800 824-5135
Lloyd Tran, *CEO*
EMP: 16 EST: 2020
SALES (est): 1.82MM
SALES (corp-wide): 1.82MM **Privately Held**
Web: www.biomedind.com
SIC: **2834** Pharmaceutical preparations

**(P-5375)**
**BIOPHARMACEUTICAL RES CO LLC**
11045 Commercial Pkwy, Castroville (95012-3209)
PHONE.................704 905-8703
George Hodgin, *CEO*
EMP: 50 EST: 2017
SQ FT: 8,400

## 2834 - Pharmaceutical Preparations (P-5376)

### PRODUCTS & SERVICES SECTION

SALES (est): 5.11MM **Privately Held**
Web: www.biopharmaresearchco.com
SIC: **2834** Pharmaceutical preparations

### (P-5376)
### BIOQ PHARMA INCORPORATED (PA)
1325 Howard St, San Francisco (94103-2612)
PHONE.................415 336-6496
Josh Kriesel, *CEO*
Serena Joshi, *VP*
Ronald Pauli, *CFO*
Walter Clerymans, *COO*
**EMP: 17 EST:** 2003
SALES (est): 4.46MM **Privately Held**
Web: www.bioqpharma.com
SIC: **2834** Pharmaceutical preparations

### (P-5377)
### BIORX PHARMACEUTICALS INC
Also Called: Biorx Laboratories
6320 Chalet Dr, Commerce (90040-3706)
PHONE.................323 725-3100
Amin Jack, *Pr*
**EMP: 32 EST:** 2010
SALES (est): 2.4MM **Privately Held**
Web: www.biorxlabs.com
SIC: **2834** 2844 Pharmaceutical preparations ; Perfumes, cosmetics and other toilet preparations

### (P-5378)
### BIOVAIL TECHNOLOGIES LTD
1 Enterprise, Aliso Viejo (92656-2606)
PHONE.................703 995-2400
David Tierney, *Pr*
**EMP: 61 EST:** 1988
**SQ FT:** 55,000
SALES (est): 5.42MM
SALES (corp-wide): 8.05B **Privately Held**
SIC: **2834** 8731 3841 2087 Pharmaceutical preparations; Commercial physical research ; Surgical and medical instruments; Flavoring extracts and syrups, nec
PA: Bausch Health Companies Inc
2150 Boul Saint-Elzear O
514 744-6792

### (P-5379)
### BLACKTHORN THERAPEUTICS INC
780 Brannan St, San Francisco (94103-4919)
PHONE.................510 828-4062
Paul Berns, *Ch*
**EMP: 35 EST:** 2013
SALES (est): 4.59MM **Publicly Held**
Web: www.blackthornrx.com
SIC: **2834** Pharmaceutical preparations
PA: Neumora Therapeutics, Inc.
490 Arsenal Way Ste 200
857 760-0900

### (P-5380)
### BLADE THERAPEUTICS INC
181 28th Ave, San Francisco (94121-1052)
PHONE.................650 334-2079
Wendye Robbins, *CEO*
Jean-frdric Viret, *CFO*
**EMP: 21 EST:** 2015
SALES (est): 3.76MM **Privately Held**
Web: www.blademed.com
SIC: **2834** Pharmaceutical preparations

### (P-5381)
### BOEHRNGER INGLHEIM FREMONT INC (DH)
6397 Kaiser Dr, Fremont (94555-3602)
PHONE.................510 608-6500
Lars Dreesmann, *CEO*
Christian Orth, *CFO*
Sheila Denton, *Sec*
**EMP: 158 EST:** 2011
SALES (est): 52.68MM
SALES (corp-wide): 23.34B **Privately Held**
SIC: **2834** Pharmaceutical preparations
HQ: Boehringer Ingelheim Corporation
900 Ridgebury Rd
Ridgefield CT 06877
203 798-9988

### (P-5382)
### BOLT BIOTHERAPEUTICS INC
Also Called: BOLT BIOTHERAPEUTICS
900 Chesapeake Dr, Redwood City (94063-4727)
PHONE.................650 665-9295
Willie Quinn, *CEO*
William P Quinn, *CEO*
David Dornan, *CSO*
Edith A Perez, *CMO*
Grant Yonehiro, *COO*
**EMP: 100 EST:** 2015
**SQ FT:** 80,500
SALES (est): 7.88MM **Privately Held**
Web: www.boltbio.com
SIC: **2834** Pharmaceutical preparations

### (P-5383)
### BRIDGEBIO PHARMA INC (PA)
Also Called: BRIDGEBIO
3160 Porter Dr Ste 250, Palo Alto (94304-1222)
PHONE.................650 391-9740
Neil Kumar, *Pr*
Brian C Stephenson, *CFO*
Thomas Trimarchi, *Pr*
**EMP: 248 EST:** 2015
**SQ FT:** 9,789
SALES (est): 9.3MM
SALES (corp-wide): 9.3MM **Publicly Held**
Web: www.bridgebio.com
SIC: **2834** 8731 Pharmaceutical preparations ; Biotechnical research, commercial

### (P-5384)
### BRIDGENE BIOSCIENCES INC
75 Nicholson Ln, San Jose (95134-1366)
PHONE.................626 632-3188
Ping Cao, *CEO*
Irene Yuan, *Ex VP*
Hang Chen, *VP*
**EMP: 33 EST:** 2021
SALES (est): 8.38MM **Privately Held**
Web: www.bridgenebio.com
SIC: **2834** Pharmaceutical preparations

### (P-5385)
### BRISTOL-MYERS SQUIBB COMPANY
Also Called: Bristol-Myers Squibb
700 Bay Rd, Redwood City (94063-2477)
PHONE.................800 332-2056
**EMP:** 61
SALES (corp-wide): 45.01B **Publicly Held**
Web: www.bms.com
SIC: **2834** Pharmaceutical preparations
PA: Bristol-Myers Squibb Company
Route 206/Prvince Line Rd
609 252-4621

### (P-5386)
### CAPNIA INC
1101 Chess Dr, Foster City (94404-1102)
PHONE.................650 213-8444
Anish Bhatnagar Md, *CEO*
David D O'toole, *CFO*
Kristen Yen, *VP*
Otho Boone, *Genl Mgr*
Anthony Wondka, *VP*
**EMP: 28 EST:** 2006
SALES (est): 6.24MM **Privately Held**
Web: www.capnia.com
SIC: **2834** Pharmaceutical preparations

### (P-5387)
### CAPRICOR
8700 Beverly Blvd, West Hollywood (90048-1804)
PHONE.................310 423-2104
**EMP: 38 EST:** 2018
SALES (est): 5.93MM **Privately Held**
Web: www.capricor.com
SIC: **2834** Pharmaceutical preparations

### (P-5388)
### CAPRICOR THERAPEUTICS INC (PA)
Also Called: Capricor
10865 Road To The Cure Ste 150, San Diego (92121-1156)
PHONE.................858 727-1755
Linda Marban, *Pr*
Frank Litvack, *Ex Ch Bd*
Anthony Bergmann, *CFO*
Karen G Krasney, *Ex VP*
**EMP: 19 EST:** 1996
SALES (est): 25.18MM
SALES (corp-wide): 25.18MM **Publicly Held**
Web: www.capricor.com
SIC: **2834** Pharmaceutical preparations

### (P-5389)
### CAPTEK MIDCO INC
2710 Progress St, Vista (92081-8449)
PHONE.................760 734-6800
**EMP:** 66
SALES (corp-wide): 203.23MM **Privately Held**
Web: www.capteksoftgel.com
SIC: **2834** Pharmaceutical preparations
HQ: Captek Midco, Inc.
16218 Arthur St
Cerritos CA 90703
562 921-9511

### (P-5390)
### CAPTEK SOFTGEL INTL INC (DH)
16218 Arthur St, Cerritos (90703)
PHONE.................562 921-9511
Carl Randall Bridges, *CEO*
Danielle Conner, *
Jan Fuh Miller, *
▲ **EMP: 300 EST:** 1995
**SQ FT:** 90,000
SALES (est): 203.23MM
SALES (corp-wide): 203.23MM **Privately Held**
Web: www.capteksoftgel.com
SIC: **2834** Vitamin, nutrient, and hematinic preparations for human use
HQ: Captek Midco, Inc.
16218 Arthur St
Cerritos CA 90703
562 921-9511

### (P-5391)
### CAPTEK SOFTGEL INTL INC
Also Called: Captek Pharma
14535 Industry Cir, La Mirada (90638-5814)
PHONE.................657 325-0412
Paul Hwang, *Genl Mgr*
**EMP:** 50
SALES (corp-wide): 203.23MM **Privately Held**
Web: www.capteksoftgel.com
SIC: **2834** Pharmaceutical preparations
HQ: Captek Softgel International, Inc.
16218 Arthur St
Cerritos CA 90703

### (P-5392)
### CARDIFF ONCOLOGY INC
Also Called: CARDIFF ONCOLOGY
11055 Flintkote Ave, San Diego (92121-1220)
PHONE.................858 952-7570
Mark Erlander, *CEO*
Rodney S Markin, *
James Levine, *CFO*
Tod Smeal, *CSO*
**EMP: 32 EST:** 2002
SALES (est): 488K **Privately Held**
Web: www.cardiffoncology.com
SIC: **2834** 2836 Pharmaceutical preparations ; Biological products, except diagnostic

### (P-5393)
### CARDINAL HEALTH 414 LLC
640 S Jefferson St, Placentia (92870-6600)
PHONE.................714 572-9900
Shanam Biglari, *Mgr*
**EMP:** 20
SALES (corp-wide): 226.83B **Publicly Held**
SIC: **2834** 5912 Pharmaceutical preparations ; Drug stores and proprietary stores
HQ: Cardinal Health 414, Llc
7000 Cardinal Pl
Dublin OH 43017
614 757-5000

### (P-5394)
### CARLSBAD TECHNOLOGY INC (DH)
Also Called: Carlsbad Tech
5922 Farnsworth Ct Ste 101, Carlsbad (92008)
PHONE.................760 431-8284
Robert Wan, *CEO*
Andy Cheng, *
▲ **EMP: 30 EST:** 1990
**SQ FT:** 27,000
SALES (est): 23.67MM **Privately Held**
Web: www.carlsbadtech.com
SIC: **2834** Druggists' preparations (pharmaceuticals)
HQ: Yung Shin Pharm. Ind. Co., Ltd.
No. 1191, Zhongshan Rd., Sec. 1,
Taichung City 43700

### (P-5395)
### CARLSBAD TECHNOLOGY INC
Also Called: Carlsbad Tech
5923 Balfour Ct, Carlsbad (92008-7304)
PHONE.................760 431-8284
Robert Wan, *CEO*
**EMP:** 70
Web: www.carlsbadtech.com
SIC: **2834** Druggists' preparations (pharmaceuticals)
HQ: Carlsbad Technology Inc.
5922 Frnsworth Ct Ste 101
Carlsbad CA 92008

### (P-5396)
### CARMOT THERAPEUTICS INC
740 Heinz Ave, Berkeley (94710-2748)
PHONE.................888 402-4674
Heather Turner, *CEO*
Michael Gray, *CFO*
**EMP: 15 EST:** 2008
SALES (est): 11.04MM **Privately Held**
Web: www.carmot.us
SIC: **2834** Pharmaceutical preparations
HQ: F. Hoffmann-La Roche Ag
Grenzacherstrasse 124

Basel BS 4058

**(P-5397)**
**CATALENT PHARMA SOLUTIONS INC**
Also Called: Pharmatek
7330 Carroll Rd Ste 200, San Diego (92121-2364)
PHONE..................................858 805-6383
EMP: 200
Web: www.catalent.com
SIC: 2834 Pharmaceutical preparations
HQ: Catalent Pharma Solutions, Inc.
14 Schoolhouse Rd
Somerset NJ 08873

**(P-5398)**
**CATALENT PHARMA SOLUTIONS INC**
8926 Ware Ct, San Diego (92121-2222)
PHONE..................................877 587-1835
EMP: 51
Web: www.catalent.com
SIC: 2834 Pharmaceutical preparations
HQ: Catalent Pharma Solutions, Inc.
14 Schoolhouse Rd
Somerset NJ 08873

**(P-5399)**
**CELGENE CORPORATION**
Also Called: Celgene Signal Research
10300 Campus Point Dr Ste 100, San Diego (92121-1504)
PHONE..................................858 795-4961
Alan Lewis, Brnch Mgr
EMP: 32
SALES (corp-wide): 45.01B Publicly Held
Web: www.bms.com
SIC: 2834 Pharmaceutical preparations
HQ: Celgene Corporation
86 Morris Ave
Summit NJ 07901
908 673-9000

**(P-5400)**
**CELL DESIGN LABS INC**
5858 Horton St Ste 240, Emeryville (94608-2018)
PHONE..................................510 398-0501
Brian Atwood, CEO
Peter Emtage, *
Roger Sidhu, Chief Medical Officer*
EMP: 50 EST: 2015
SQ FT: 19,000
SALES (est): 4.86MM
SALES (corp-wide): 27.12B Publicly Held
SIC: 2834 Pharmaceutical preparations
PA: Gilead Sciences, Inc.
333 Lakeside Dr
650 574-3000

**(P-5401)**
**CELLTHEON CORPORATION**
Also Called: Celltheon
32980 Alvarado Niles Rd Ste 826, Union City (94587-8104)
PHONE..................................650 743-3672
Amita S Goel, CEO
Anura Goel, CFO
EMP: 17 EST: 2012
SQ FT: 4,000
SALES (est): 3.03MM Privately Held
Web: www.celltheon.com
SIC: 2834 Pharmaceutical preparations

**(P-5402)**
**CEREXA**
2100 Franklin St Ste 900, Oakland (94612-3147)

PHONE..................................510 285-9200
EMP: 16 EST: 2019
SALES (est): 624.03K Privately Held
Web: www.abbvie.com
SIC: 2834 Pharmaceutical preparations

**(P-5403)**
**CH LABORATORIES INC (PA)**
1243 W 130th St, Gardena (90247-1501)
PHONE..................................310 516-8273
Brid Nolan, Pr
EMP: 24 EST: 2001
SQ FT: 30,000
SALES (est): 2.46MM
SALES (corp-wide): 2.46MM Privately Held
Web: www.chlabs.com
SIC: 2834 Vitamin preparations

**(P-5404)**
**CHEMOCENTRYX INC (HQ)**
750 Gateway Blvd, South San Francisco (94080-7020)
PHONE..................................650 210-2900
Thomas J Schall, Ch Bd
Tausif Butt, Ex VP
Susan M Kanaya, Chief Financial*
Jan L Hillson, Senior Vice President Drug Development
Rajinder Singh, Senior Vice President Research
EMP: 50 EST: 1997
SALES (est): 32.22MM
SALES (corp-wide): 28.19B Publicly Held
Web: www.chemocentryx.com
SIC: 2834 Drugs affecting parasitic and infective diseases
PA: Amgen Inc.
1 Amgen Center Dr
805 447-1000

**(P-5405)**
**CHEMPARTNER INC**
280 Utah Ave Ste 100, South San Francisco (94080-6883)
PHONE..................................215 720-6650
Michael Hui, CEO
EMP: 20 EST: 2014
SALES (est): 4.03MM Privately Held
Web: www.chempartner.com
SIC: 2834 Pharmaceutical preparations

**(P-5406)**
**CONCENTRIC ANALGESICS INC**
1824 Jackson St Apt A, San Francisco (94109-2871)
PHONE..................................415 771-5129
John F Donovan, Owner
Mike A Royal, Chief Medical Officer
EMP: 28 EST: 2015
SALES (est): 5.73MM Privately Held
Web: www.concentricanalgesics.com
SIC: 2834 Analgesics

**(P-5407)**
**CONFLUENT MEDICAL TECH INC**
47533 Westinghouse Dr, Fremont (94539-7463)
PHONE..................................510 683-2000
EMP: 24
Web: www.confluentmedical.com
SIC: 2834 Pharmaceutical preparations
PA: Confluent Medical Technologies, Inc.
6263 N Scttsdale Rd Ste 2

**(P-5408)**
**CONTINENTAL VITAMIN CO INC**
Also Called: Cvc Specialties
4510 S Boyle Ave, Vernon (90058-2418)
PHONE..................................323 581-0176

Ron Beckenfeld, Pr
Lillian Beckenfeld, *
EMP: 60 EST: 1969
SQ FT: 80,000
SALES (est): 9.54MM Privately Held
Web: www.cvc4health.com
SIC: 2834 5122 Vitamin preparations; Vitamins and minerals

**(P-5409)**
**COR THERAPEUTICS INC**
256 E Grand Ave, South San Francisco (94080-4811)
PHONE..................................650 244-6800
Vaughn M Kailian, Pr
Charles J Homcy, Executive Research & Development Vice President*
Patrick A Broderick, Corporate Secretary
Lee M Rauch, Senior Vice President Corporate Development
Peter S Roddy, VP Fin
EMP: 320 EST: 1988
SQ FT: 100,000
SALES (est): 1.28MM Privately Held
Web: www.integrilin.com
SIC: 2834 Drugs acting on the cardiovascular system, except diagnostic

**(P-5410)**
**CORCEPT THERAPEUTICS INC (PA)**
Also Called: CORCEPT
101 Redwood Shores Pkwy, Redwood City (94065-1176)
PHONE..................................650 327-3270
Joseph K Belanoff, Pr
James N Wilson, Ch Bd
G Charles Robb, Chief Business Officer
Robert S Fishman, CMO
Sean Maduck, Senior Vice President Commercial
EMP: 228 EST: 1998
SALES (est): 482.38MM
SALES (corp-wide): 482.38MM Publicly Held
Web: www.corcept.com
SIC: 2834 Pharmaceutical preparations

**(P-5411)**
**CORVUS PHARMACEUTICALS INC**
Also Called: CORVUS PHARMACEUTICALS
863 Mitten Rd Ste 102, Burlingame (94010-1311)
PHONE..................................650 900-4520
Richard A Miller, Ch Bd
Leiv Lea, CFO
Jeffrey Arcara, Chief Business Officer
William B Jones, Sr VP
EMP: 28 EST: 2014
SQ FT: 27,280
Web: www.corvuspharma.com
SIC: 2834 Pharmaceutical preparations

**(P-5412)**
**COSMEDX SCIENCE INC**
3550 Vine St Ste 210, Riverside (92507-4175)
P.O. Box 1925 (92878-1925)
PHONE..................................951 371-0509
▲ EMP: 50
Web: www.cosmedxscience.com
SIC: 2834 Dermatologicals

**(P-5413)**
**COTHERA BIOPHARMA INC**
1960 Noel Dr, Los Altos (94024-7060)
PHONE..................................510 364-1930
Yue Alexander Wu, CEO
EMP: 30 EST: 2018

SALES (est): 100K Privately Held
SIC: 2834 7389 Pharmaceutical preparations ; Business services, nec

**(P-5414)**
**COUGAR BIOTECHNOLOGY INC**
10990 Wilshire Blvd Ste 1200, Los Angeles (90024-3919)
PHONE..................................310 943-8040
Alan H Auerbach, Pr
Charles Eyler, VP Fin
Gloria Lee Md, Clinical Vice President
Arie S Belldegrun Md, Ch Bd
EMP: 58 EST: 2003
SQ FT: 7,300
SALES (est): 2.38MM
SALES (corp-wide): 85.16B Publicly Held
Web: www.pumabiotechnology.com
SIC: 2834 Drugs affecting neoplasms and endocrine systems
PA: Johnson & Johnson
1 Johnson & Johnson Plz
732 524-0400

**(P-5415)**
**CRINETICS PHARMACEUTICALS INC (PA)**
Also Called: CRINETICS
6055 Lusk Blvd, San Diego (92121-2700)
PHONE..................................858 450-6464
R Scott Struthers, Pr
Wendell Wierenga, Ch Bd
Jeff Knight, COO
Marc Wilson, CFO
Alan Krasner, CMO
EMP: 60 EST: 2008
SALES (est): 4.01MM Publicly Held
Web: www.crinetics.com
SIC: 2834 Pharmaceutical preparations

**(P-5416)**
**CURAE PHARMA360 INC**
49 Stevenson St Ste 1100, San Francisco (94105-2958)
PHONE..................................415 951-8700
Autumn Ehnow, CEO
EMP: 40 EST: 2017
SALES (est): 1.23MM Privately Held
Web: www.curaepharma.com
SIC: 2834 Pharmaceutical preparations

**(P-5417)**
**CV SCIENCES INC (PA)**
9530 Padgett St Ste 107, San Diego (92126-4449)
PHONE..................................866 290-2157
Joseph Dowling, CEO
Michael Mona Iii, Pr
Joerg Grasser, CFO
EMP: 38 EST: 2013
SALES (est): 16MM
SALES (corp-wide): 16MM Privately Held
Web: www.cvsciences.com
SIC: 2834 Pharmaceutical preparations

**(P-5418)**
**CYMABAY THERAPEUTICS INC (PA)**
333 Lakeside Dr, Foster City (94404)
PHONE..................................650 574-3000
Sujal Shah, Pr
Robert J Wills, Ch Bd
Charles Mcwherter, CSO
Klara Chief Regulatory Dickinson, Quality Assurance
Paul Quinlan, CCO
EMP: 83 EST: 1988
SALES (est): 31.07MM Privately Held
Web: www.cymabay.com

## 2834 - Pharmaceutical Preparations (P-5419)

SIC: 2834  Druggists' preparations (pharmaceuticals)

**(P-5419)**
**CYMBIOTIKA LLC (PA)**
5825 Oberlin Dr Ste 5, San Diego (92121-3777)
PHONE..........................770 910-4945
Shahab Elmi, *CEO*
EMP: 32  EST: 2018
SALES (est): 3.39MM
SALES (corp-wide): 3.39MM **Privately Held**
Web: www.cymbiotika.com
SIC: 2834  Pharmaceutical preparations

**(P-5420)**
**CYMBIOTIKA LLC**
8885 Rehco Rd, San Diego (92121-3261)
PHONE..........................949 652-8177
Anya Bytnar, *Mgr*
EMP: 58
SALES (corp-wide): 3.39MM **Privately Held**
Web: www.cymbiotika.com
SIC: 2834  Pharmaceutical preparations
PA: Cymbiotika Llc
5825 Oberlin Dr Ste 5
770 910-4945

**(P-5421)**
**CYTOKINETICS INCORPORATED (PA)**
Also Called: CYTOKINETICS
350 Oyster Point Blvd, South San Francisco (94080-1912)
PHONE..........................650 624-3000
Robert I Blum, *Pr*
John T Henderson, *
Andrew M Callos, *CCO*
Fady I Malik, *Ex VP*
Sung Lee, *Ex VP*
EMP: 415  EST: 1997
SQ FT: 234,892
SALES (est): 7.53MM
SALES (corp-wide): 7.53MM **Publicly Held**
Web: www.cytokinetics.com
SIC: 2834 8731  Pharmaceutical preparations; Biotechnical research, commercial

**(P-5422)**
**CYTOMX THERAPEUTICS INC**
Also Called: CYTOMX THERAPEUTICS
151 Oyster Point Blvd Ste 400, South San Francisco (94080-1841)
PHONE..........................650 515-3185
Sean A Mccarthy, *Ch Bd*
Marcia P Belvin, *CSO*
Jeff Landau, *Chief Business Officer*
Chris Ogden, *CAO*
EMP: 122  EST: 2008
SQ FT: 76,000
SALES (est): 101.21MM **Privately Held**
Web: www.cytomx.com
SIC: 2834  Pharmaceutical preparations

**(P-5423)**
**DANIEL LORIA NOVARTIS**
4560 Horton St, Emeryville (94608-2916)
PHONE..........................510 655-8729
Daniel Loria Novartis, *Prin*
EMP: 35  EST: 2010
SALES (est): 3.22MM **Privately Held**
Web: www.novartis.com
SIC: 2834  Pharmaceutical preparations

**(P-5424)**
**DENDREON PHARMACEUTICALS LLC (HQ)**
1700 Saturn Way, Seal Beach (90740)
PHONE..........................562 252-7500
Jason Oneill, *CEO*
Matthew Kemp, *CCO*
Christina Yi, *
Chris Carr, *
EMP: 50  EST: 2015
SALES (est): 115.38MM **Privately Held**
Web: www.dendreon.com
SIC: 2834  Pharmaceutical preparations
PA: Nanjing Xinjiekou Department Store Co., Ltd.
No.1, Zhongshan South Road, Qinhuai District

**(P-5425)**
**DERMIRA INC**
275 Middlefield Rd Ste 150, Menlo Park (94025-4008)
PHONE..........................650 421-7200
Heather Wasserman, *Pr*
Philip L Johnson, *
Katie Lodato, *
Bronwen Mantlo, *
EMP: 333  EST: 2010
SALES (est): 25.17MM
SALES (corp-wide): 34.12B **Publicly Held**
Web: www.dermira.com
SIC: 2834  Pharmaceutical preparations
PA: Eli Lilly And Company
1 Lilly Corporate Ctr
317 276-2000

**(P-5426)**
**DESIGN THERAPEUTICS INC**
Also Called: DESIGN THERAPEUTICS
6005 Hidden Valley Rd Ste 110, Carlsbad (92011-4223)
PHONE..........................858 293-4900
Pratik Shah, *Ch Bd*
Sean Jeffries, *COO*
Jae B Kim, *CMO*
EMP: 124  EST: 2017
Web: www.designtx.com
SIC: 2834  Pharmaceutical preparations

**(P-5427)**
**DIABLO CLINICAL RESEARCH INC**
2255 Ygnacio Valley Rd Ste M, Walnut Creek (94598-3347)
PHONE..........................925 930-7267
Richard Weinstein, *Pr*
EMP: 22  EST: 1995
SQ FT: 2,200
SALES (est): 3.93MM **Privately Held**
Web: www.diabloclinical.com
SIC: 2834 8011  Pharmaceutical preparations; Offices and clinics of medical doctors

**(P-5428)**
**DNIB UNWIND INC**
333 S Grand Ave Ste 4070, Los Angeles (90071-1544)
PHONE..........................213 617-2717
EMP: 114
SIC: 2834  Pharmaceutical preparations

**(P-5429)**
**EARTHRISE NUTRITIONALS LLC (HQ)**
3333 Michelson Dr Ste 300, Irvine (92612-1683)
PHONE..........................949 623-0980
Ichi Kato, *
▲ EMP: 25  EST: 1987
SALES (est): 21.94MM **Privately Held**
Web: www.earthrise.com
SIC: 2834 2023  Tablets, pharmaceutical; Dietary supplements, dairy and non-dairy based
PA: Dic Corporation
3-7-20, Nihombashi

**(P-5430)**
**EDWARDS LIFESCIENCES LLC (HQ)**
1 Edwards Way, Irvine (92614-5688)
PHONE..........................949 250-2500
Michael A Mussallem, *CEO*
John H Kehl Junior, *VP*
▲ EMP: 1700  EST: 1958
SALES (est): 488.01MM
SALES (corp-wide): 6B **Publicly Held**
Web: www.edwards.com
SIC: 2834  Pharmaceutical preparations
PA: Edwards Lifesciences Corp
1 Edwards Way
949 250-2500

**(P-5431)**
**ELITRA PHARMACEUTICALS**
3510 Dunhill St Ste A, San Diego (92121-1201)
PHONE..........................858 410-3030
Paul R Hamelin, *CEO*
Harry Hixson Junior, *Ch Bd*
J Gordon Foulkes, *Senior Vice President Research & Development*
EMP: 65  EST: 1997
SQ FT: 35,735
SALES (est): 4.81MM **Privately Held**
Web: www.elitra.net
SIC: 2834 8731  Pharmaceutical preparations; Commercial physical research

**(P-5432)**
**ENTOS PHARMACEUTICALS INC**
3040 Science Park Rd, San Diego (92121-1102)
PHONE..........................800 727-0884
John D Lewis, *CEO*
Jason Ding, *Chief Business Officer*
EMP: 18  EST: 2021
SALES (est): 6.31MM **Privately Held**
Web: www.entospharma.com
SIC: 2834  Pharmaceutical preparations

**(P-5433)**
**ENVIRONMENTAL SCIENCE US LLC**
Also Called: Envu
890 Embarcadero Dr, West Sacramento (95605-1503)
PHONE..........................800 331-2867
EMP: 232
SALES (corp-wide): 344.15MM **Privately Held**
Web: us.envu.com
SIC: 2834  Pharmaceutical preparations
HQ: Environmental Science U.S. Llc
5000 Cntre Green Way Ste
Cary NC 27513

**(P-5434)**
**EQRX INC (HQ)**
Also Called: Eqrx
700 Saginaw Dr, Redwood City (94063-4752)
PHONE..........................617 315-2255
Melanie Nallicheri, *Pr*
Alexis Borisy, *Ex Ch Bd*
Jami Rubin, *CFO*
EMP: 77  EST: 2019
SALES (corp-wide): 11.58MM **Publicly Held**
Web: www.eqrx.com
SIC: 2834  Pharmaceutical preparations
PA: Revolution Medicines, Inc.
700 Saginaw Dr
650 481-6801

**(P-5435)**
**EQUILLIUM INC (PA)**
2223 Avenida De La Playa Ste 105, La Jolla (92037-3217)
PHONE..........................858 412-5302
Bruce D Steel, *Pr*
Daniel M Bradbury, *Ex Ch Bd*
Stephen Connelly, *CSO*
Christine Zedelmayer, *Sr VP*
Penny Tom, *CAO*
EMP: 31  EST: 2017
SQ FT: 1,750
SALES (est): 36.08MM
SALES (corp-wide): 36.08MM **Publicly Held**
Web: www.equilliumbio.com
SIC: 2834 2836  Pharmaceutical preparations; Biological products, except diagnostic

**(P-5436)**
**ERASCA INC**
10835 Road To The Cure Ste 140, San Diego (92121-1130)
PHONE..........................858 465-6511
Jonathan E Lim, *Ch Bd*
David M Chacko, *Chief Business Officer*
Nik Chetwyn, *COO*
Ebun S Garner, *Corporate Secretary*
Shannon R Morris, *Chief Medical Officer*
EMP: 126  EST: 2018
SQ FT: 16,153
Web: www.erasca.com
SIC: 2834  Pharmaceutical preparations

**(P-5437)**
**ESSENTIAL PHARMACEUTICAL CORP**
1906 W Holt Ave, Pomona (91768-3351)
PHONE..........................909 623-4565
Bruce Lin, *CEO*
Po Chia Lin, *Sec*
▲ EMP: 20  EST: 1986
SQ FT: 7,642
SALES (est): 4.89MM **Privately Held**
Web: www.essentialpharmaceutical.com
SIC: 2834  Vitamin preparations

**(P-5438)**
**EVOLUS INC (PA)**
Also Called: EVOLUS
520 Newport Center Dr Ste 1200, Newport Beach (92660-7022)
PHONE..........................949 284-4555
David Moatazedi, *Pr*
Vikram Malik, *Ch Bd*
Sandra Beaver, *CFO*
Rui Avelar, *CMO*
EMP: 193  EST: 2012
SQ FT: 17,758
SALES (est): 202.09MM **Publicly Held**
Web: www.evolus.com
SIC: 2834  Pharmaceutical preparations

**(P-5439)**
**FIBROGEN INC (PA)**
Also Called: FIBROGEN
350 Bay St Ste 100, San Francisco (94133-1998)
P.O. Box 6009  (94133)
PHONE..........................415 978-1200
Thane Wettig, *CEO*
James A Schoeneck, *Ch Bd*

## PRODUCTS & SERVICES SECTION
### 2834 - Pharmaceutical Preparations (P-5460)

Juan Graham, *CFO*
Deyaa Adib, *CMO*
**EMP:** 204 **EST:** 1993
**SQ FT:** 234,000
**SALES (est):** 147.75MM **Publicly Held**
**Web:** www.fibrogen.com
**SIC: 2834** Pharmaceutical preparations

### (P-5440)
### FINE CHEMICALS HOLDINGS CORP
Hazel Ave Hwy 50 Bldg 05019, Rancho Cordova (95741)
P.O. Box 1718 (95741)
**PHONE**..................................916 357-6880
Fraser Preston, *Pr*
Michael Gallagher, *
John Sobchak, *
**EMP:** 584 **EST:** 2014
**SALES (est):** 1.28MM **Privately Held**
**Web:** www.ampacfinechemicals.com
**SIC: 2834** Pharmaceutical preparations

### (P-5441)
### FIRST PERSON INC
Also Called: First Person Group
611 N Brand Blvd Ste 1300, Glendale (91203-3213)
**PHONE**..................................609 760-0040
Cory Rosenberg, *CEO*
Chris Claussen, *CIO*
Darcy Campbell, *CFO*
**EMP:** 15 **EST:** 2021
**SALES (est):** 8MM
**SALES (corp-wide):** 423.55K **Privately Held**
**SIC: 2834** Vitamin, nutrient, and hematinic preparations for human use
**PA:** First Person Ltd
444 5 Ave Sw Suite 1840
587 577-9261

### (P-5442)
### FIVE PRIME THERAPEUTICS INC
Also Called: Five Prime
750 Gateway Blvd, South San Francisco (94080-7020)
**PHONE**..................................415 365-5600
Thomas Civik, *Pr*
William Ringo, *Interim Chief Executive Officer**
David V Smith, *CAO**
Francis W Sarena, *CSO**
Helen Collins, *CMO**
**EMP:** 87 **EST:** 2001
**SALES (est):** 13.18MM
**SALES (corp-wide):** 28.19B **Publicly Held**
**Web:** www.amgen.com
**SIC: 2834** 8733 Pharmaceutical preparations ; Biotechnical research, noncommercial
**PA:** Amgen Inc.
1 Amgen Center Dr
805 447-1000

### (P-5443)
### FORMEX LLC
9601 Jeronimo Rd, Irvine (92618-2025)
**PHONE**..................................858 529-6600
Cyrus K Mirsaidi, *Pr*
Ian Wisenberg, *
J Blair West, *CSO**
**EMP:** 32 **EST:** 2013
**SALES (est):** 4.49MM **Privately Held**
**Web:** www.formexllc.com
**SIC: 2834** 8731 8071 Tablets, pharmaceutical; Biological research; Testing laboratories
**PA:** Bioduro Llc
11011 Torreyana Rd

### (P-5444)
### FORMULATION TECHNOLOGY INC
571 Armstrong Way, Oakdale (95361-9367)
P.O. Box 1895 (95361-1895)
**PHONE**..................................209 847-0331
Keith W Hensley, *Pr*
Keith W Hensley, *Pr*
Jed Meese, *
Celia Meese, *
April Houck, *Stockholder**
▲ **EMP:** 49 **EST:** 1981
**SQ FT:** 15,000
**SALES (est):** 9.36MM **Privately Held**
**Web:** www.formulationtech.com
**SIC: 2834** Vitamin preparations

### (P-5445)
### FORTY SEVEN INC (HQ)
Also Called: Forty Seven
333 Lakeside Dr, Foster City (94404-1147)
**PHONE**..................................650 352-4150
Mark A Mccamish, *CEO*
Andrew D Dickinson, *Pr*
Ann D Rhoads, *CFO*
Chris H Takimoto, *CMO*
Craig S Gibbs, *Chief Business Officer*
**EMP:** 23 **EST:** 2014
**SALES (est):** 15.68MM
**SALES (corp-wide):** 27.12B **Publicly Held**
**Web:** www.gilead.com
**SIC: 2834** 8731 Pharmaceutical preparations ; Biotechnical research, commercial
**PA:** Gilead Sciences, Inc.
333 Lakeside Dr
650 574-3000

### (P-5446)
### FORTY SEVEN INC
1661 Page Mill Rd Ste C, Palo Alto (94304-1209)
**PHONE**..................................650 352-4150
**EMP:** 45
**SALES (corp-wide):** 27.12B **Publicly Held**
**Web:** www.gilead.com
**SIC: 2834** Pharmaceutical preparations
**HQ:** Forty Seven, Inc.
333 Lakeside Dr
Foster City CA 94404
650 352-4150

### (P-5447)
### FRONTAGE LABORATORIES INC
3825 Bay Center Pl, Hayward (94545-3619)
**PHONE**..................................510 626-9993
**EMP:** 16
**Web:** www.frontagelab.com
**SIC: 2834** 8731 Pharmaceutical preparations ; Biological research
**HQ:** Frontage Laboratories, Inc.
700 Pennsylvania Dr
Exton PA 19341
610 232-0100

### (P-5448)
### FRONTIER MEDICINES CORPORATION (PA)
151 Oyster Point Blvd Fl 2, South San Francisco (94080-1840)
**PHONE**..................................650 457-1005
Chris Varma, *CEO*
Gerardo Ubaghs, *CFO*
**EMP:** 22 **EST:** 2018
**SALES (est):** 19.79MM
**SALES (corp-wide):** 19.79MM **Privately Held**
**Web:** www.frontiermeds.com

SIC: 2834 Medicines, capsuled or ampuled

### (P-5449)
### GENENTECH INC
501 Dna Way, South San Francisco (94080-4943)
**PHONE**..................................650 467-0810
**EMP:** 3941
**Web:** www.gene.com
**SIC: 2834** Pharmaceutical preparations
**HQ:** Genentech, Inc.
1 Dna Way Stop 258a
South San Francisco CA 94080
650 225-1000

### (P-5450)
### GENENTECH INC
1 Antibody Way, Oceanside (92056-5701)
**PHONE**..................................760 231-2440
Amr Elkhayat, *Dir*
**EMP:** 5024
**Web:** www.gene.com
**SIC: 2834** Pharmaceutical preparations
**HQ:** Genentech, Inc.
1 Dna Way Stop 258a
South San Francisco CA 94080
650 225-1000

### (P-5451)
### GENENTECH INC
Also Called: Genentech
640 Forbes Blvd # B9, South San Francisco (94080-2020)
**PHONE**..................................650 225-1000
**EMP:** 690
**Web:** www.gene.com
**SIC: 2834** Pharmaceutical preparations
**HQ:** Genentech, Inc.
1 Dna Way Stop 258a
South San Francisco CA 94080
650 225-1000

### (P-5452)
### GENENTECH INC
1000 New Horizons Way, Vacaville (95688-9431)
**PHONE**..................................707 454-1000
Frank Jackson, *Brnch Mgr*
**EMP:** 25
**Web:** www.gene.com
**SIC: 2834** Pharmaceutical preparations
**HQ:** Genentech, Inc.
1 Dna Way Stop 258a
South San Francisco CA 94080
650 225-1000

### (P-5453)
### GENENTECH INC
340 Point San Bruno Blvd, South San Francisco (94080-4916)
P.O. Box 5712 (94705-0712)
**PHONE**..................................650 438-2626
**EMP:** 887
**Web:** www.gene.com
**SIC: 2834** Pharmaceutical preparations
**HQ:** Genentech, Inc.
1 Dna Way Stop 258a
South San Francisco CA 94080
650 225-1000

### (P-5454)
### GENENTECH USA INC
1 Dna Way, South San Francisco (94080-4990)
**PHONE**..................................650 225-1000
Ian T Clark, *Pr*
▲ **EMP:** 5169 **EST:** 2007
**SALES (est):** 24.47MM **Privately Held**
**Web:** www.gene.com

**SIC: 2834** Hormone preparations
**HQ:** Genentech, Inc.
1 Dna Way Stop 258a
South San Francisco CA 94080
650 225-1000

### (P-5455)
### GENETRONICS INC
10480 Wateridge Cir, San Diego (92121-5773)
**PHONE**..................................858 410-3112
**EMP:** 23 **EST:** 2019
**SALES (est):** 59.43K **Publicly Held**
**SIC: 2834** Pharmaceutical preparations
**PA:** Inovio Pharmaceuticals, Inc.
660 W Grmntown Pike Ste 1

### (P-5456)
### GENOMICS INST OF NVRTIS RES FN
10675 John J Hopkins Dr, San Diego (92121-1127)
**PHONE**..................................858 812-1805
Genevieve Welch, *Prin*
**EMP:** 64 **EST:** 2013
**SALES (est):** 3.51MM **Privately Held**
**Web:** www.novartis.com
**SIC: 2834** Pharmaceutical preparations

### (P-5457)
### GENVIVO INC
1981 E Locust St, Ontario (91761-7608)
**PHONE**..................................626 441-6695
Chris Bergman, *Brnch Mgr*
**EMP:** 38
**SALES (corp-wide):** 6.66MM **Privately Held**
**Web:** www.genvivoinc.com
**SIC: 2834** Pharmaceutical preparations
**PA:** Genvivo, Inc.
475 Huntington Dr
626 441-6695

### (P-5458)
### GENZYME CORPORATION
Also Called: Genzyme Genetics
655 E Huntington Dr, Monrovia (91016-3636)
**PHONE**..................................626 471-9922
Jane Willis, *Brnch Mgr*
**EMP:** 77
**Web:** www.genzyme.com
**SIC: 2834** Pharmaceutical preparations
**HQ:** Genzyme Corporation
450 Water St
Cambridge MA 02141
617 252-7500

### (P-5459)
### GERON CORPORATION (PA)
Also Called: GERON
919 E Hillsdale Blvd Ste 250, Foster City (94404-3296)
**PHONE**..................................650 473-7700
John A Scarlett, *Ch Bd*
Michelle Robertson, *Ex VP*
Faye Feller, *CMO*
Andrew Grethlein, *Interim Vice President*
Scott A Samuels, *CLO*
**EMP:** 125 **EST:** 1990
**SALES (est):** 237K **Publicly Held**
**Web:** www.geron.com
**SIC: 2834** Pharmaceutical preparations

### (P-5460)
### GILEAD PALO ALTO INC
4049 Avenida De La Plata, Oceanside (92056-5802)
**PHONE**..................................760 945-7701
**EMP:** 125

## 2834 - Pharmaceutical Preparations (P-5461)

SALES (corp-wide): 27.12B **Publicly Held**
Web: www.gilead.com
SIC: 2834 Pharmaceutical preparations
HQ: Alto Gilead Palo Inc
333 Lakeside Dr
Foster City CA 94404

**(P-5461)**
**GILEAD PALO ALTO INC**
Also Called: Gilead Scientist
550 Cliffside Dr, San Dimas (91773-2978)
PHONE.............................909 394-4000
Chris Beley, *CEO*
**EMP:** 125
**SALES (corp-wide):** 27.12B **Publicly Held**
Web: www.gilead.com
SIC: 2834 Pharmaceutical preparations
HQ: Alto Gilead Palo Inc
333 Lakeside Dr
Foster City CA 94404

**(P-5462)**
**GILEAD SCIENCES INC**
1800 Wheeler St, La Verne (91750-5801)
PHONE.............................650 522-2771
Michael Lee, *Prin*
**EMP:** 99 **EST:** 1987
**SALES (est):** 26.89MM **Privately Held**
Web: www.gilead.com
SIC: 2834 Pharmaceutical preparations

**(P-5463)**
**GILEAD SCIENCES INC (PA)**
Also Called: AMBISOME
333 Lakeside Dr, Foster City (94404-1394)
PHONE.............................650 574-3000
Daniel P O'day, *Ch Bd*
Andrew D Dickinson, *CFO*
Johanna Mercier, *CCO*
Merdad V Parsey, *CMO*
Deborah H Telman, *Ex VP*
▲ **EMP:** 289 **EST:** 1987
**SALES (est):** 27.12B
**SALES (corp-wide):** 27.12B **Publicly Held**
Web: www.gilead.com
SIC: 2834 2836 Pharmaceutical preparations
; Biological products, except diagnostic

**(P-5464)**
**GILEAD SCIENCES INC**
Also Called: Nexstar Pharmaceutical
650 Cliffside Dr, San Dimas (91773-2957)
PHONE.............................909 394-4000
Christin Eley, *Prin*
**EMP:** 19
**SALES (corp-wide):** 27.12B **Publicly Held**
Web: www.gilead.com
SIC: 2834 Pharmaceutical preparations
PA: Gilead Sciences, Inc.
333 Lakeside Dr
650 574-3000

**(P-5465)**
**GLOBAL BLOOD THERAPEUTICS INC (HQ)**
Also Called: Gbt
181 Oyster Point Blvd, South San Francisco (94080)
PHONE.............................650 741-7700
Ted W Love, *Pr*
Jeffrey Farrow, *CFO*
Eric Fink, *Chief Human Resources Officer*
David L Johnson, *CCO*
**EMP:** 275 **EST:** 2012
**SQ FT:** 164,150
**SALES (est):** 194.75MM
**SALES (corp-wide):** 58.5B **Publicly Held**
Web: www.globalbloodtx.com
SIC: 2834 8731 Pharmaceutical preparations
; Biological research

PA: Pfizer Inc.
66 Hudson Blvd E
212 733-2323

**(P-5466)**
**GMP LABORATORIES AMERICA INC (PA)**
Also Called: Gmp Laboratories of America
2931 E La Jolla St, Anaheim (92806-1306)
PHONE.............................714 630-2467
Mohammad Ishaq, *CEO*
Suhail Ishaq, *
▲ **EMP:** 92 **EST:** 1994
**SQ FT:** 90,000
**SALES (est):** 23MM **Privately Held**
Web: www.gmplabs.com
SIC: 2834 Pharmaceutical preparations

**(P-5467)**
**GOSSAMER BIO INC (PA)**
3013 Science Park Rd Ste 200, San Diego (92121-1101)
PHONE.............................858 684-1300
Faheem Hasnain, *Ch Bd*
Bryan Giraudo, *CFO*
Richard Aranda, *CMO*
Bob Smith, *CCO*
Christian Waage, *Ex VP*
**EMP:** 116 **EST:** 2015
**SQ FT:** 63,667
Web: www.gossamerbio.com
SIC: 2834 Pharmaceutical preparations

**(P-5468)**
**GRAIL INC (PA)**
1525a Obrien Dr, Menlo Park (94025-1463)
PHONE.............................833 694-2553
Robert Ragusa, *CEO*
Charles Dadswell, *
Josh Ofman, *Pr*
Aaron Freidin, *CFO*
**EMP:** 189 **EST:** 2015
**SQ FT:** 74,300
**SALES (est):** 93.11MM
**SALES (corp-wide):** 93.11MM **Publicly Held**
Web: www.grail.com
SIC: 2834 8731 Pharmaceutical preparations
; Biotechnical research, commercial

**(P-5469)**
**GREENWICH BIOSCIENCES LLC (DH)**
Also Called: Greenwich Biosciences, Inc.
5750 Fleet St Ste 200, Carlsbad (92008-4700)
PHONE.............................760 795-2200
Julian Gangolli, *Pr*
Justin Gover, *
Scott Giacobello, *
**EMP:** 23 **EST:** 2013
**SQ FT:** 4,911
**SALES (est):** 19.51MM **Privately Held**
Web: www.jazzpharma.com
SIC: 2834 Pharmaceutical preparations
HQ: Gw Pharmaceuticals Limited
Sovereign House
Cambridge CAMBS
122 326-6800

**(P-5470)**
**GSMS INC (PA)**
5187 Camino Ruiz, Camarillo (93012-8601)
PHONE.............................805 477-9866
Michael Bornitz, *Pr*
**EMP:** 22 **EST:** 2012
**SALES (est):** 47.53MM
**SALES (corp-wide):** 47.53MM **Privately Held**
Web: www.gsms.us

SIC: 2834 Pharmaceutical preparations

**(P-5471)**
**GU**
1204 10th St, Berkeley (94710-1509)
PHONE.............................510 527-4664
Bill Vaughn, *Owner*
**EMP:** 21 **EST:** 1994
**SALES (est):** 2.63MM **Privately Held**
Web: www.guenergy.com
SIC: 2834 Vitamin, nutrient, and hematinic preparations for human use

**(P-5472)**
**GUCKENHEIMER ENTERPRISES INC**
4010 Ocean Ranch Blvd, Oceanside (92056-5700)
PHONE.............................760 414-3659
**EMP:** 74
**SALES (corp-wide):** 44.25MM **Privately Held**
Web: www.gilead.com
SIC: 2834 Pharmaceutical preparations
PA: Guckenheimer Enterprises, Inc.
1850 Gateway Dr Ste 500
650 592-3800

**(P-5473)**
**GYRE THERAPEUTICS INC (PA)**
12730 High Bluff Dr Ste 250, San Diego (92130-3023)
PHONE.............................650 266-8674
Charles Wu, *CEO*
Ying Luo, *Ch Bd*
Songjiang Ma, *Pr*
Ruoyu Chen, *Interim Chief Financial Officer*
Weiguo Ye, *COO*
**EMP:** 450 **EST:** 2002
**SALES (est):** 113.45MM **Publicly Held**
Web: www.catalystbiosciences.com
SIC: 2834 Pharmaceutical preparations

**(P-5474)**
**H J HARKINS COMPANY INC**
Also Called: Pharma Pac
1400 W Grand Ave Ste F, Grover Beach (93433-4221)
PHONE.............................805 929-1333
Norma Jean Erenius, *CEO*
Charles Smith, *
**EMP:** 50 **EST:** 1984
**SQ FT:** 10,000
**SALES (est):** 2.24MM **Privately Held**
Web: www.pharmapac.com
SIC: 2834 Pharmaceutical preparations

**(P-5475)**
**HALEON US LP**
2020 E Vine Ave, Fresno (93706-5458)
PHONE.............................559 650-1550
Mark Bullard, *Brnch Mgr*
**EMP:** 91
**SALES (corp-wide):** 14.09B **Privately Held**
SIC: 2834 Pharmaceutical preparations
HQ: Haleon Us Lp
184 Liberty Corner Rd
Warren NJ 07059

**(P-5476)**
**HARMONY FOODS LLC (PA)**
Also Called: Scn Bestco
2200 Delaware Ave, Santa Cruz (95060-5707)
PHONE.............................831 457-3200
Carlyn Solomon, *Managing Member*
Michael Westhusing, *
▲ **EMP:** 270 **EST:** 2002
**SQ FT:** 200,000
**SALES (est):** 125.49MM

**SALES (corp-wide):** 125.49MM **Privately Held**
Web: www.scnbestco.com
SIC: 2834 2064 Vitamin, nutrient, and hematinic preparations for human use; Candy and other confectionery products

**(P-5477)**
**HARPERS PHARMACY INC**
Also Called: Ameripharma
132 S Anita Dr Ste 210, Orange (92868-3317)
PHONE.............................877 778-3773
Andrew A Harper, *CEO*
Gor Mnatsakanyan, *
**EMP:** 187 **EST:** 2016
**SALES (est):** 14.07MM **Privately Held**
Web: www.ameripharma.com
SIC: 2834 Pharmaceutical preparations

**(P-5478)**
**HEALTH ONE PHARMACEUTICAL INC**
Also Called: Escort Health
13260 Temple Ave, City Of Industry (91746-1511)
P.O. Box 5276 (91745-0276)
PHONE.............................626 279-9699
▲ **EMP:** 15
Web: www.healthonepharm.com
SIC: 2834 Pharmaceutical preparations

**(P-5479)**
**HERON THERAPEUTICS INC (PA)**
Also Called: HERON THERAPEUTICS
4242 Campus Point Ct Ste 200, San Diego (92121-1513)
PHONE.............................858 251-4400
Craig Collard, *CEO*
Adam Morgan, *
Ira Duarte, *Ex VP*
William Forbes, *CDO*
Brett Fleshman, *Chief Business Officer*
**EMP:** 122 **EST:** 1983
**SQ FT:** 52,148
**SALES (est):** 127.04MM
**SALES (corp-wide):** 127.04MM **Publicly Held**
Web: www.herontx.com
SIC: 2834 Pharmaceutical preparations

**(P-5480)**
**HIKMA PHARMACEUTICALS USA INC**
2325 Camino Vida Roble Ste B, Carlsbad (92011-1567)
PHONE.............................760 683-0901
Sigurdur Olafsson, *Brnch Mgr*
**EMP:** 45
**SALES (corp-wide):** 2.88B **Privately Held**
Web: www.hikma.com
SIC: 2834 Pharmaceutical preparations
HQ: Hikma Pharmaceuticals Usa Inc.
200 Connell Dr Ste 4000
Berkeley Heights NJ 07922
908 673-1030

**(P-5481)**
**HIMS & HERS HEALTH INC (PA)**
2269 Chestnut St # 523, San Francisco (94123-2600)
PHONE.............................415 851-0195
Andrew Dudum, *Ch Bd*
Melissa Baird, *COO*
Yemi Okupe, *CFO*
Soleil Boughton, *CLO*
Mike Chi, *CCO*
**EMP:** 24 **EST:** 2013

SALES (est): 872MM
SALES (corp-wide): 872MM **Publicly Held**
Web: www.hims.com
SIC: **2834** 5912 5122 8742  Pharmaceutical preparations; Proprietary (non-prescription medicine) stores; Cosmetics, perfumes, and hair products; Hospital and health services consultant

**(P-5482)**
## HYLANDS CONSUMER HEALTH INC (PA)
Also Called: Hyland's Homeopathic
13301 S Main St, Los Angeles (90061-1611)
P.O. Box 61067  (90061-0067)
PHONE.............................310 768-0700
Daniel Krombach, *Pr*
Daniel M Krombach, *
Will Righeimer, *
Dan Krombach, *
Stephen Schnack, *
▲ **EMP:** 300 **EST:** 1903
**SQ FT:** 150
**SALES (est):** 96.52MM
**SALES (corp-wide):** 96.52MM **Privately Held**
Web: www.hylands.com
SIC: **2834** 5912  Pharmaceutical preparations; Drug stores

**(P-5483)**
## IDEAYA BIOSCIENCES INC (PA)
Also Called: IDEAYA BIOSCIENCES
7000 Shoreline Ct Ste 350, South San Francisco  (94080-7604)
PHONE.............................650 443-6209
Yujiro Hata, *Pr*
John Diekman, *Ch Bd*
Jeffrey Hager, *Sr VP*
Julie Hambleton, *CMO*
Jason Throne, *VP*
**EMP:** 54 **EST:** 2015
**SALES (est):** 23.39MM
**SALES (corp-wide):** 23.39MM **Publicly Held**
Web: www.ideayabio.com
SIC: **2834**  Pharmaceutical preparations

**(P-5484)**
## IDEAYA BIOSCIENCES INC
5000 Shoreline Ct Ste 300, South San Francisco  (94080-1956)
PHONE.............................650 534-3568
**EMP:** 70
**SALES (corp-wide):** 23.39MM **Publicly Held**
Web: www.ideayabio.com
SIC: **2834**  Pharmaceutical preparations
PA: Ideaya Biosciences, Inc.
7000 Shoreline Ct Ste 350
650 443-6209

**(P-5485)**
## IGENCIA BIOTHERAPEUTICS INC
863 Mitten Rd Ste 102, Burlingame  (94010-1311)
PHONE.............................650 231-4320
**EMP:** 40
SIC: **2834**  Druggists' preparations (pharmaceuticals)

**(P-5486)**
## IGNYTA INC (DH)
Also Called: Ignyta
1 Dna Way, South San Francisco  (94080-4918)
PHONE.............................858 255-5959
Jonathan E Lim, *Ch Bd*
Zachary Hornby, *COO*

Jacob Chacko, *CFO*
William Mccarthy, *Chief Business Officer*
Pratik Multani, *CMO*
**EMP:** 96 **EST:** 2011
**SALES (est):** 8.33MM **Privately Held**
SIC: **2834**  Pharmaceutical preparations
HQ: Roche Holding Ag
Grenzacherstrasse 124
Basel BS 4058

**(P-5487)**
## IMIDOMICS INC
1000 4th St Ste 500, San Rafael  (94901-3134)
PHONE.............................415 652-4963
Juan Harrison, *CEO*
Manuel Lopez-figueroa, *COO*
Susan Vuong, *CFO*
**EMP:** 18 **EST:** 2021
**SALES (est):** 1.66MM **Privately Held**
Web: www.imidomics.com
SIC: **2834**  Proprietary drug products

**(P-5488)**
## IMPAX LABORATORIES LLC
Impax Generics
30831 Huntwood Ave, Hayward  (94544-7003)
PHONE.............................510 240-6000
**EMP:** 43
**SALES (corp-wide):** 2.39B **Publicly Held**
Web: www.impaxlabs.com
SIC: **2834**  Pharmaceutical preparations
HQ: Impax Laboratories, Llc
30831 Huntwood Ave
Hayward CA 94544

**(P-5489)**
## IMPAX LABORATORIES LLC (DH)
30831 Huntwood Ave, Hayward  (94544-7003)
▲ **EMP:** 600 **EST:** 1995
**SQ FT:** 45,000
**SALES (est):** 38.33MM
**SALES (corp-wide):** 2.39B **Publicly Held**
Web: www.impaxlabs.com
SIC: **2834**  Pharmaceutical preparations
HQ: Amneal Pharmaceuticals Llc
400 Crossing Blvd 3rd Fl
Bridgewater NJ 08807

**(P-5490)**
## IMPAX LABORATORIES LLC
31047 Genstar Rd, Hayward  (94544-7831)
PHONE.............................510 240-6000
Larry Hsu, *CEO*
**EMP:** 69
**SALES (corp-wide):** 2.39B **Publicly Held**
Web: www.impaxlabs.com
SIC: **2834**  Pharmaceutical preparations
HQ: Impax Laboratories, Llc
30831 Huntwood Ave
Hayward CA 94544

**(P-5491)**
## IMPAX LABORATORIES USA LLC
30831 Huntwood Ave, Hayward  (94544-7003)
PHONE.............................510 240-6000
Larry Hsu Ph.d., *CEO*
**EMP:** 27 **EST:** 2013
**SALES (est):** 1.86MM
**SALES (corp-wide):** 2.39B **Publicly Held**
SIC: **2834**  Pharmaceutical preparations
HQ: Impax Laboratories, Llc
30831 Huntwood Ave
Hayward CA 94544

**(P-5492)**
## IMPRIMISRX LLC
Also Called: Imprimisrx
1000 Aviara Dr Ste 220, Carlsbad  (92011-4218)
PHONE.............................844 446-6979
**EMP:** 86 **EST:** 2019
**SALES (est):** 17.1MM **Publicly Held**
Web: www.imprimisrx.com
SIC: **2834**  Pharmaceutical preparations
PA: Harrow, Inc.
102 Woodmont Blvd Ste 610

**(P-5493)**
## INCARDA THERAPEUTICS INC
Also Called: Incarda Therapeutics
39899 Balentine Dr Ste 185, Newark  (94560-5361)
PHONE.............................510 422-5522
Grace Colon, *Pr*
Luiz Belardinelli, *CMO*
Carlos Schuler, *COO*
Samantha Miller Senior Corporate, *Development*
Robert L Roden, *VP*
**EMP:** 20 **EST:** 2009
**SALES (est):** 2.51MM **Privately Held**
Web: www.incardatherapeutics.com
SIC: **2834**  Pharmaceutical preparations

**(P-5494)**
## INNOCOLL BIOTHERAPEUTICS NA
5163 Lakeview Canyon Rd, Westlake Village  (91362-5212)
PHONE.............................484 406-5200
Louis Pascarella, *CEO*
**EMP:** 100 **EST:** 2015
**SALES (est):** 2.42MM **Privately Held**
Web: www.innocoll.com
SIC: **2834**  Pharmaceutical preparations

**(P-5495)**
## INNOVIVA INC (PA)
Also Called: INNOVIVA
1350 Bayshore Hwy Ste 400, Burlingame  (94010-1813)
PHONE.............................650 238-9600
Pavel Raifeld, *CEO*
Stephen Basso, *CFO*
Marianne Zhen, *CAO*
**EMP:** 17 **EST:** 1997
**SQ FT:** 2,111
**SALES (est):** 310.46MM
**SALES (corp-wide):** 310.46MM **Publicly Held**
Web: www.inva.com
SIC: **2834**  Drugs acting on the respiratory system

**(P-5496)**
## INOVA DIAGNOSTICS INC
9889 Willow Creek Rd, San Diego  (92131-1119)
PHONE.............................858 586-9900
**EMP:** 143
Web: www.werfen.com
SIC: **2834**  Pharmaceutical preparations
HQ: Inova Diagnostics, Inc.
9900 Old Grove Rd
San Diego CA 92131
858 586-9900

**(P-5497)**
## INSTACURE HEALING PRODUCTS
235 N Moorpark Rd Unit 2022, Thousand Oaks  (91360-4311)
PHONE.............................818 222-9600

David Traub, *Owner*
**EMP:** 33 **EST:** 2015
**SQ FT:** 6,000
**SALES (est):** 476.4K **Privately Held**
Web: www.instacure.net
SIC: **2834**  Lip balms

**(P-5498)**
## INTERMUNE INC (DH)
1 Dna Way, South San Francisco  (94080-4918)
PHONE.............................415 466-4383
Daniel G Welch, *Pr*
John C Hodgman, *
Jonathan A Leff, *Executive Research & Development Vice President*
Sean P Nolan, *Chief Business Officer*
Andrew Powell, *CORP SE*
**EMP:** 215 **EST:** 1998
**SQ FT:** 56,000
**SALES (est):** 13.47MM **Privately Held**
Web: www.gene.com
SIC: **2834** 8731  Pharmaceutical preparations; Medical research, commercial
HQ: Roche Holdings, Inc.
1 Dna Way
South San Francisco CA 94080
650 225-1000

**(P-5499)**
## INTERNATIONAL VITAMIN CORP
Also Called: Adam Nutrition
1 Park Plz Ste 800, Irvine  (92614-5998)
PHONE.............................949 664-5500
Iliu Elisara, *Brnch Mgr*
**EMP:** 125
Web: www.ivcinc.com
SIC: **2834**  Vitamin, nutrient, and hematinic preparations for human use
PA: International Vitamin Corporation
4695 Mcarthur Ct Ste 1400

**(P-5500)**
## INTERNATIONAL VITAMIN CORPORAT (PA)
Also Called: I V C
4695 Macarthur Ct Ste 1400, Newport Beach  (92660-8896)
PHONE.............................949 664-5500
John Torphy, *CEO*
Bing Ma, *CFO*
Bence Rabo, *
▲ **EMP:** 72 **EST:** 2009
**SQ FT:** 166,000
**SALES (est):** 619.44MM **Privately Held**
Web: www.ivcinc.com
SIC: **2834** 5149 8099  Vitamin preparations; Organic and diet food; Nutrition services

**(P-5501)**
## INTERNTNAL MDCTION SYSTEMS LTD
Also Called: IMS
1886 Santa Anita Ave, South El Monte  (91733-3414)
PHONE.............................626 442-6757
Jack Zhang, *CEO*
William Peters, *
Mary Luo Zhang, *
▲ **EMP:** 720 **EST:** 1963
**SALES (est):** 28.78MM
**SALES (corp-wide):** 644.39MM **Publicly Held**
Web: www.amphastar.com
SIC: **2834** 2833 3841  Drugs acting on the central nervous system & sense organs; Anesthetics, in bulk form; Surgical and medical instruments
PA: Amphastar Pharmaceuticals Inc
11570 6th St

# 2834 - Pharmaceutical Preparations (P-5502)

**PRODUCTS & SERVICES SECTION**

909 980-9484

**(P-5502)**
**IONIS PHARMACEUTICALS INC**
1896 Rutherford Rd, Carlsbad
(92008-7326)
PHONE..............................760 931-9200
Alfred Chappell, *Brnch Mgr*
**EMP:** 100
**SALES (corp-wide):** 787.65MM **Publicly Held**
Web: www.ionispharma.com
**SIC: 2834** Pharmaceutical preparations
**PA:** Ionis Pharmaceuticals, Inc.
2855 Gazelle Ct
760 931-9200

**(P-5503)**
**IONIS PHARMACEUTICALS INC (PA)**
Also Called: IONIS
2855 Gazelle Ct, Carlsbad (92010-6670)
PHONE..............................760 931-9200
Brett P Monia, *CEO*
Joseph Loscalzo, *Non-Executive Chairman of the Board\**
Elizabeth L Hougen, *Ex VP*
Joseph T Baroldi, *Chief Business Officer*
C Frank Bennett, *CSO*
▲ **EMP:** 559 **EST:** 1989
**SALES (est):** 787.65MM
**SALES (corp-wide):** 787.65MM **Publicly Held**
Web: www.ionispharma.com
**SIC: 2834** 8731 3845 Pharmaceutical preparations; Medical research, commercial; Electromedical equipment

**(P-5504)**
**IONIS PHARMACEUTICALS INC**
2282 Faraday Ave, Carlsbad (92008-7208)
PHONE..............................760 603-3567
Stanley Crooke, *Brnch Mgr*
**EMP:** 103
**SALES (corp-wide):** 787.65MM **Publicly Held**
Web: www.ionispharma.com
**SIC: 2834** Pharmaceutical preparations
**PA:** Ionis Pharmaceuticals, Inc.
2855 Gazelle Ct
760 931-9200

**(P-5505)**
**IONIS PHARMACEUTICALS INC**
1767 Avenida Segovia, Oceanside (92056-6230)
PHONE..............................760 603-2631
Gregory Hardee, *Brnch Mgr*
**EMP:** 16
**SALES (corp-wide):** 787.65MM **Publicly Held**
Web: www.ionispharma.com
**SIC: 2834** Pharmaceutical preparations
**PA:** Ionis Pharmaceuticals, Inc.
2855 Gazelle Ct
760 931-9200

**(P-5506)**
**IOVANCE BIOTHERAPEUTICS INC (PA)**
825 Industrial Rd Fl 4, San Carlos (94070-3312)
PHONE..............................650 260-7120
Frederick G Vogt, *Pr*
Frederick G Vogt, *Pr*
Iain Dukes, *Ch Bd*
Igor Bilinsky, *COO*
Jean-marc Bellemin, *CFO*
**EMP:** 461 **EST:** 2011
**SQ FT:** 49,918

**SALES (est):** 1.19MM **Publicly Held**
Web: www.iovance.com
**SIC: 2834** Pharmaceutical preparations

**(P-5507)**
**ISTA PHARMACEUTICALS INC**
50 Technology Dr, Irvine (92618-2301)
P.O. Box 25169 (18002-5169)
PHONE..............................949 788-6000
**EMP:** 330
**SIC: 2834** Pharmaceutical preparations

**(P-5508)**
**IVC INC**
4695 Macarthur Ct Ste 1400, Newport Beach (92660-8896)
PHONE..............................215 671-1400
Brian I Rekos, *Pr*
**EMP:** 19 **EST:** 1995
**SALES (est):** 4.9MM **Privately Held**
Web: www.ivcinc.com
**SIC: 2834** Pharmaceutical preparations

**(P-5509)**
**JAGUAR HEALTH INC (PA)**
Also Called: JAGUAR ANIMAL HEALTH
200 Pine St Fl 4, San Francisco (94104-2710)
PHONE..............................415 371-8300
Lisa A Conte, *Pr*
James J Bochnowski, *Ch Bd*
Carol R Lizak, *CFO*
Steven R King, *SUSTAINBLE SUPP ETHNOBOTANICAL RES & INTEL*
Jonathan S Wolin, *Chief of Staff*
**EMP:** 43 **EST:** 2013
**SQ FT:** 10,526
**SALES (est):** 9.76MM
**SALES (corp-wide):** 9.76MM **Publicly Held**
Web: www.jaguar.health
**SIC: 2834** 0752 Pharmaceutical preparations; Animal specialty services

**(P-5510)**
**JANSSEN BIOPHARMA INC**
1600 Sierra Point Pkwy, Brisbane (94005-1809)
PHONE..............................650 452-0210
**EMP:** 26 **EST:** 2006
**SALES (est):** 4.07MM **Privately Held**
**SIC: 2834** Pharmaceutical preparations

**(P-5511)**
**JANSSEN BIOPHARMA INC**
260 E Grand Ave, South San Francisco (94080-4811)
PHONE..............................650 635-5500
Lawrence Blatt Md, *Pr*
Leonid Beigelman Md, *CSO*
John Donovan Md, *Chief Business Officer*
**EMP:** 26 **EST:** 2006
**SALES (est):** 8.4MM
**SALES (corp-wide):** 85.16B **Publicly Held**
**SIC: 2834** Pharmaceutical preparations
**PA:** Johnson & Johnson
1 Johnson & Johnson Plz
732 524-0400

**(P-5512)**
**JANSSEN RESEARCH & DEV LLC**
3210 Merryfield Row, San Diego (92121-1126)
PHONE..............................858 450-2000
Steve Schuetzle, *Mgr*
**EMP:** 228
**SALES (corp-wide):** 85.16B **Publicly Held**
Web: www.janssen.com

**SIC: 2834** Pharmaceutical preparations
**HQ:** Janssen Research & Development, Llc
920 Us Highway 202
Raritan NJ 08869
908 704-4000

**(P-5513)**
**JANUX THERAPEUTICS INC**
Also Called: JANUX
10955 Vista Sorrento Pkwy Ste 200, San Diego (92130-8699)
PHONE..............................858 751-4493
David Campbell, *Pr*
Ron Barrett, *Ch Bd*
Tommy Diraimondo, *CSO*
**EMP:** 69 **EST:** 2017
**SALES (est):** 8.08MM **Privately Held**
Web: www.januxrx.com
**SIC: 2834** Pharmaceutical preparations

**(P-5514)**
**JARROW INDUSTRIES LLC (PA)**
12246 Hawkins St, Santa Fe Springs (90670-3365)
PHONE..............................562 906-1919
Jarrow Rogovin, *Ch Bd*
Mohammed Khalid, *\**
Ben Khowong, *\**
David Chen, *\**
▲ **EMP:** 74 **EST:** 2000
**SQ FT:** 125,000
**SALES (est):** 46.12MM
**SALES (corp-wide):** 46.12MM **Privately Held**
Web: www.jarrowindustries.com
**SIC: 2834** Vitamin preparations

**(P-5515)**
**JARROW INDUSTRIES LLC**
12342 Hawkins St, Santa Fe Springs (90670-3367)
PHONE..............................562 631-9330
Jackie Kelley, *Mgr*
**EMP:** 22
**SALES (corp-wide):** 24.41MM **Privately Held**
Web: www.jarrowindustries.com
**SIC: 2834** Vitamin preparations
**PA:** Jarrow Industries, L.L.C.
12246 Hawkins St
562 906-1919

**(P-5516)**
**JARROW INDUSTRIES LLC**
10226 Palm Dr, Santa Fe Springs (90670-3368)
PHONE..............................562 631-9330
Jackie Kelley, *Mgr*
**EMP:** 22
**SALES (corp-wide):** 24.41MM **Privately Held**
Web: www.jarrowindustries.com
**SIC: 2834** Vitamin preparations
**PA:** Jarrow Industries, L.L.C.
12246 Hawkins St
562 906-1919

**(P-5517)**
**JARROW INDUSTRIES LLC**
12328 Hawkins St, Santa Fe Springs (90670-3367)
PHONE..............................562 631-9330
Jackie Kelley, *Mgr*
**EMP:** 22
**SALES (corp-wide):** 24.41MM **Privately Held**
Web: www.jarrowindustries.com
**SIC: 2834** Vitamin preparations
**PA:** Jarrow Industries, L.L.C.
12246 Hawkins St

562 906-1919

**(P-5518)**
**JAZZ PHARMACEUTICALS INC**
3180 Porter Dr, Palo Alto (94304-1288)
PHONE..............................650 496-3777
**EMP:** 122
Web: www.jazzpharma.com
**SIC: 2834** Pharmaceutical preparations
**HQ:** Jazz Pharmaceuticals, Inc.
3170 Porter Dr
Palo Alto CA 94304
650 496-3777

**(P-5519)**
**JAZZ PHARMACEUTICALS INC (HQ)**
3170 Porter Dr, Palo Alto (94304-1212)
PHONE..............................650 496-3777
Bruce C Cozadd, *Ch Bd*
Kathryn E Falberg, *\**
Russell J Cox, *\**
Neena Patil, *\**
▲ **EMP:** 17 **EST:** 2003
**SALES (est):** 269.17MM **Privately Held**
Web: www.jazzpharma.com
**SIC: 2834** Drugs acting on the central nervous system & sense organs
**PA:** Jazz Pharmaceuticals Public Limited Company
Waterloo Exchange

**(P-5520)**
**K-MAX HEALTH PRODUCTS CORP**
1468 E Mission Blvd, Pomona (91766-2229)
PHONE..............................909 455-0158
Lei Ye, *CEO*
**EMP:** 17 **EST:** 1999
**SALES (est):** 659.41K **Privately Held**
**SIC: 2834** Vitamin, nutrient, and hematinic preparations for human use

**(P-5521)**
**KAI PHARMACEUTICALS INC**
1120 Veterans Blvd, South San Francisco (94080-1985)
PHONE..............................650 328-9164
Paul Aeurbach, *Pr*
Kristine Ball, *CFO*
Gregory Bell, *CMO*
Stephen Harrison, *Research Vice President*
Dirk B Mendel, *VP*
**EMP:** 23 **EST:** 2003
**SALES (est):** 2.18MM
**SALES (corp-wide):** 28.19B **Publicly Held**
**SIC: 2834** Pharmaceutical preparations
**PA:** Amgen Inc.
1 Amgen Center Dr
805 447-1000

**(P-5522)**
**KARTOS THERAPEUTICS INC**
275 Shoreline Dr Ste 100, Redwood City (94065-1412)
PHONE..............................650 542-0130
Jesse Mcgreivy, *CEO*
Srdan Verstovsek, *Chief Medical Officer\**
**EMP:** 93 **EST:** 2017
**SALES (est):** 4.55MM **Privately Held**
Web: www.kartosthera.com
**SIC: 2834** Pharmaceutical preparations

**(P-5523)**
**KATE SOMERVILLE SKINCARE LLC (HQ)**
Also Called: Kate Smrvlle Skin Hlth Experts
2121 Park Pl Ste 100, El Segundo (90245-4180)

PHONE.................323 655-7546
Stuart Hill, CEO
Ambrus Seres, *
Lina Goodnight Ctrl, Prin
Kate Somerville, *
Michelle Taylor, *
▲ EMP: 51 EST: 2005
SALES (est): 24.1MM
SALES (corp-wide): 64.79B **Privately Held**
Web: www.katesomerville.com
SIC: **2834** 5122  Pharmaceutical preparations
; Toiletries
PA: Unilever Plc
Unilever House
207 572-1202

**(P-5524)**
**KC PHARMACEUTICALS INC (PA)**
3420 Pomona Blvd, Pomona  (91768-3236)
PHONE.................909 598-9499
Lieutenant Khouw, Ch Bd
Doctor Pramuditya Oen, CEO
Joseph Sutedjo, *
▲ EMP: 62 EST: 1987
SQ FT: 20,000
SALES (est): 44.57MM
SALES (corp-wide): 44.57MM **Privately Held**
Web: www.kc-ph.com
SIC: **2834**  Solutions, pharmaceutical

**(P-5525)**
**KEZAR LIFE SCIENCES INC (PA)**
Also Called: Kezar Life Sciences
4000 Shoreline Ct Ste 300, South San Francisco  (94080-2005)
PHONE.................650 822-5600
Christopher Kirk, CEO
Graham Cooper, Ch Bd
Marc L Belsky, CFO
Mark Schiller, CLO
EMP: 49 EST: 2015
SQ FT: 24,357
SALES (est): 7MM
SALES (corp-wide): 7MM **Publicly Held**
Web: www.kezarlifesciences.com
SIC: **2834** 8731  Pharmaceutical preparations
; Biotechnical research, commercial

**(P-5526)**
**KINDEVA DRUG DELIVERY LP**
Also Called: 3m/Pharmaceuticals
19901 Nordhoff St, Northridge  (91324)
P.O. Box 1001 (91328)
PHONE.................818 341-1300
Carol Beesley, Brnch Mgr
EMP: 400
Web: www.kindevadd.com
SIC: **2834**  Pharmaceutical preparations
PA: Kindeva Drug Delivery L.P.
42 Water St W Bldg 75

**(P-5527)**
**KINDREDBIO EQUINE INC**
1555 Bayshore Hwy Ste 200, Burlingame  (94010-1617)
PHONE.................888 608-2542
EMP: 29 EST: 2019
SALES (est): 3.26MM
SALES (corp-wide): 4.42B **Publicly Held**
SIC: **2834**  Pharmaceutical preparations
HQ: Kindred Biosciences, Inc.
2500 Innovation Way N
Greenfield IN 46140
650 701-7901

**(P-5528)**
**KODIAK SCIENCES INC (PA)**
Also Called: KODIAK
1200 Page Mill Rd, Palo Alto  (94304-1122)
PHONE.................650 281-0850
Victor Perlroth, Ch Bd
John A Borgeson, Ex VP
Pablo Velazquez-martin, CMO
Tracy Chien, Corporate Controller
Gorton Chiu, VP Fin
EMP: 87 EST: 2009
SQ FT: 155,000
Web: www.kodiak.com
SIC: **2834** 2836 8731  Pharmaceutical preparations; Biological products, except diagnostic; Biotechnical research, commercial

**(P-5529)**
**KOSHLAND PHARMACY INC**
Also Called: Koshland Pharm Cstm Cmpnding P
301 Folsom St Ste B, San Francisco  (94105-2309)
PHONE.................415 344-0600
Peter Koshland, Pr
Krista Koshland, Sec
EMP: 18 EST: 2009
SQ FT: 3,000
SALES (est): 2.68MM **Privately Held**
Web: www.koshlandpharm.com
SIC: **2834**  Druggists' preparations (pharmaceuticals)

**(P-5530)**
**KRONOS BIO INC (PA)**
Also Called: KRONOS BIO
1300 S El Camino Real Ste 400, San Mateo  (94402-2970)
PHONE.................650 781-5200
Norbert Bischofberger, Pr
Arie S Belldegrun, Ch Bd
Sandra A Gardiner, Interim Chief Financial Officer
Deborah Knobelman, COO
EMP: 23 EST: 2017
SQ FT: 17,340
SALES (est): 6.29MM
SALES (corp-wide): 6.29MM **Publicly Held**
Web: www.kronosbio.com
SIC: **2834**  Pharmaceutical preparations

**(P-5531)**
**KURA ONCOLOGY INC (PA)**
12730 High Bluff Dr Ste 400, San Diego  (92130-2079)
PHONE.................858 500-8800
Troy E Wilson, Ch Bd
Kathleen Ford, COO
Teresa Bair, CLO
Stephen Dale, CMO
EMP: 36 EST: 2007
SQ FT: 13,420
Web: www.kuraoncology.com
SIC: **2834**  Pharmaceutical preparations

**(P-5532)**
**KYOWA KIRIN INC**
9420 Athena Cir, La Jolla  (92037-1387)
PHONE.................858 952-7000
Steve Schaefer, Brnch Mgr
EMP: 50
Web: kkna.kyowakirin.com
SIC: **2834**  Pharmaceutical preparations
HQ: Kyowa Kirin, Inc.
510 Carnegie Ctr Ste 600
Princeton NJ 08540
609 919-1100

**(P-5533)**
**KYTHERA BIOPHARMACEUTICALS INC**
30930 Russell Ranch Rd Fl 3, Westlake Village  (91362-7378)
PHONE.................818 587-4500
A Robert D Bailey, Pr
John W Smither, CFO
Elisabeth A Sandoval, CCO
Frederick Beddingfield Iii, CMO
EMP: 106 EST: 2005
SQ FT: 33,198
SALES (est): 25.08MM
SALES (corp-wide): 54.32B **Publicly Held**
Web: www.mykybella.com
SIC: **2834**  Dermatologicals
HQ: Allergan Unlimited Company
Clonshaugh Business & Technology Park
Coolock D17 E

**(P-5534)**
**LEINER HEALTH PRODUCTS INC (DH)**
Also Called: Leiner Health Products
901 E 233rd St, Carson  (90745-6204)
PHONE.................631 200-2000
Jeffrey A Nagel, CEO
Michael Collins, *
Harvey Kamil, *
◆ EMP: 200 EST: 1952
SQ FT: 488,000
SALES (est): 22.13MM **Privately Held**
Web: www.leiner.com
SIC: **2834** 5122  Vitamin, nutrient, and hematinic preparations for human use; Vitamins and minerals
HQ: Nhs U.S., Llc
1041 Us-202
Bridgewater NJ 08807
800 422-2752

**(P-5535)**
**LEINER HEALTH PRODUCTS INC**
Also Called: Leiner Health Products
7366 Orangewood Ave, Garden Grove  (92841-1412)
PHONE.................714 898-9936
James Smith, Mgr
EMP: 46
Web: www.leiner.com
SIC: **2834** 2844 2833 5122  Vitamin, nutrient, and hematinic preparations for human use; Perfumes, cosmetics and other toilet preparations; Medicinals and botanicals; Vitamins and minerals
HQ: Leiner Health Products, Inc.
901 E 233rd St
Carson CA 90745
631 200-2000

**(P-5536)**
**LEVENA BIOPHARMA US INC**
11760 Sorrento Valley Rd Ste N, San Diego  (92121-1018)
PHONE.................858 720-1439
Hui Li, Pr
EMP: 33 EST: 2016
SALES (est): 286.31K
SALES (corp-wide): 62.84MM **Publicly Held**
Web: www.levenabiopharma.com
SIC: **2834**  Pharmaceutical preparations
PA: Sorrento Therapeutics, Inc.
4955 Directors Pl
858 203-4100

**(P-5537)**
**LONGBOARD PHARMACEUTICALS INC**
Also Called: LONGBOARD
4275 Executive Sq Ste 950, La Jolla  (92037-9208)
PHONE.................858 789-9283
Kevin R Lind, Pr
Paul J Sekhri, *
Brandi L Roberts, Ex VP
Randall E Kaye, Chief Medical Officer
EMP: 50 EST: 2020
SQ FT: 9,289
SALES (est): 1.24MM **Privately Held**
Web: www.longboardpharma.com
SIC: **2834**  Pharmaceutical preparations

**(P-5538)**
**LONZA BIOLOGICS INC**
21075 Alexander Ct, Hayward  (94545-1214)
PHONE.................510 265-3095
EMP: 17 EST: 2019
SALES (est): 635.31K **Privately Held**
Web: www.lonza.com
SIC: **2834**  Pharmaceutical preparations

**(P-5539)**
**M & L PHARMACEUTICAL INC**
629 S Allen St, San Bernardino  (92408-2250)
PHONE.................909 890-0078
Jorge Molina, Pr
Guadalupe Molina, Sec
Jorge Molina Junior, VP
EMP: 15 EST: 1991
SQ FT: 6,000
SALES (est): 1.02MM **Privately Held**
Web: www.mlpharmaceutical.com
SIC: **2834**  Vitamin preparations

**(P-5540)**
**MANNA HEALTH LLC**
Also Called: Manna
216 Nautilus St, La Jolla  (92037-5918)
PHONE.................877 576-2662
EMP: 20 EST: 2020
SALES (est): 3.02MM **Privately Held**
SIC: **2834**  Vitamin preparations

**(P-5541)**
**MANNKIND CORPORATION**
30930 Russell Ranch Rd Ste 300, Westlake Village  (91362-7378)
PHONE.................818 661-5000
EMP: 303
SALES (corp-wide): 198.96MM **Publicly Held**
Web: www.mannkindcorp.com
SIC: **2834**  Pharmaceutical preparations
PA: Mannkind Corporation
1 Casper St Ste 330
818 661-5000

**(P-5542)**
**MAP PHARMACEUTICALS INC**
Also Called: (A Development Stage Enterprise)
2400 Bayshore Pkwy Ste 200, Mountain View  (94043-1150)
P.O. Box 19534 (92623-9534)
PHONE.................650 625-8790
◆ EMP: 116
Web: agn.client.shareholder.com
SIC: **2834**  Pharmaceutical preparations

**(P-5543)**
**MAPLIGHT THERAPEUTICS INC**
800 Chesapeake Dr, Redwood City  (94063-4748)
PHONE.................207 653-8478
Jonathan Gills, Prin
EMP: 43 EST: 2019
SALES (est): 1.84MM **Privately Held**
Web: www.maplightrx.com

# 2834 - Pharmaceutical Preparations (P-5544)

SIC: 2834 Pharmaceutical preparations

**(P-5544)**
**MARAVAI LFSCENCES HOLDINGS INC (PA)**
Also Called: MARAVAI LIFESCIENCES
10770 Wateridge Cir Ste 200, San Diego (92121-5801)
PHONE..................858 546-0004
William Martin Iii, *CEO*
Eric Tardif, *Pr*
Kevin Herde, *CFO*
Brian Neel Coo Nucleic Acid Production, *Prin*
Christine Dolan Coo Biologics Safety Testing, *Prin*
**EMP:** 27 **EST:** 2014
**SQ FT:** 119,000
**SALES (est):** 288.94MM
**SALES (corp-wide):** 288.94MM **Publicly Held**
Web: www.maravai.com
SIC: 2834 Pharmaceutical preparations

**(P-5545)**
**MAVERICK THERAPEUTICS INC**
3260 Bayshore Blvd, Brisbane (94005-1021)
PHONE..................650 684-7140
James S Scibetta, *CEO*
Robert Dubridge, *Research*
**EMP:** 29 **EST:** 2017
**SALES (est):** 8.84MM **Privately Held**
SIC: 2834 Pharmaceutical preparations

**(P-5546)**
**MCGUFF OTSURCING SOLUTIONS INC**
2921 W Macarthur Blvd Ste 142, Santa Ana (92704-6909)
PHONE..................800 603-4795
Ron Mcguff, *CEO*
**EMP:** 20 **EST:** 2022
**SALES (est):** 320.59K **Privately Held**
SIC: 2834 Pharmaceutical preparations

**(P-5547)**
**MCKENNA LABS INC (PA)**
1601 E Orangethorpe Ave, Fullerton (92831-5230)
PHONE..................714 687-6888
Dennis Alexander Owen, *Pr*
◆ **EMP:** 38 **EST:** 1998
**SQ FT:** 62,000
**SALES (est):** 42.48MM
**SALES (corp-wide):** 42.48MM **Privately Held**
Web: www.mckennalabs.com
SIC: 2834 2844 Pharmaceutical preparations; Perfumes, cosmetics and other toilet preparations

**(P-5548)**
**MED-PHARMEX INC**
2727 Thompson Creek Rd, Pomona (91767-1861)
PHONE..................909 593-7875
Paul Hays, *CEO*
▲ **EMP:** 117 **EST:** 1982
**SQ FT:** 18,000
**SALES (est):** 17.68MM
**SALES (corp-wide):** 355.83K **Privately Held**
Web: www.medpharmex.com
SIC: 2834 Pharmaceutical preparations
HQ: Dechra Pharmaceuticals Limited
24 Cheshire Business Park
Northwich CW9 7

**(P-5549)**
**MEDIATECH INC**
Also Called: J R Scientific
1242 Commerce Ave, Woodland (95776-5916)
PHONE..................530 666-9868
Tomothy Kubit, *CEO*
Deanna Lynn Kubit, *
**EMP:** 30 **EST:** 2013
**SALES (est):** 2.6MM
**SALES (corp-wide):** 12.59B **Publicly Held**
SIC: 2834 Water, sterile: for injections
HQ: Mediatech, Inc.
9345 Discovery Blvd
Manassas VA 20109
978 221-7701

**(P-5550)**
**MEDIVATION INC**
499 Illinois St, San Francisco (94158-2518)
PHONE..................415 812-6345
**EMP:** 191
**SALES (corp-wide):** 58.5B **Publicly Held**
Web: www.pfizer.com
SIC: 2834 Pharmaceutical preparations
HQ: Medivation, Inc.
525 Market St Fl 36
San Francisco CA 94105
415 543-3470

**(P-5551)**
**MEDIVATION INC (HQ)**
Also Called: Xtandi
525 Market St Ste 2800, San Francisco (94105-2736)
PHONE..................415 543-3470
David T Hung, *Pr*
Jennifer Jarrett, *CFO*
Marion Mccourt, *COO*
Mohammad Hirmand, *Interim CMO*
Andrew Powell, *Corporate Secretary*
**EMP:** 54 **EST:** 1995
**SQ FT:** 143,000
**SALES (est):** 19.98MM
**SALES (corp-wide):** 58.5B **Publicly Held**
Web: www.pfizer.com
SIC: 2834 Pharmaceutical preparations
PA: Pfizer Inc.
66 Hudson Blvd E
212 733-2323

**(P-5552)**
**MEI PHARMA INC**
Also Called: MEI PHARMA
11455 El Camino Real Ste 250, San Diego (92130-2088)
PHONE..................858 369-7100
Frederick W Driscoll, *Ch Bd*
**EMP:** 46 **EST:** 2002
**SQ FT:** 45,100
**SALES (est):** 65.3MM **Privately Held**
Web: www.meipharma.com
SIC: 2834 Pharmaceutical preparations

**(P-5553)**
**MEREO BIOPHARMA 5 INC**
800 W El Camino Real Ste 180, Mountain View (94040-2586)
PHONE..................650 995-8200
Denise Scots-knight, *CEO*
**EMP:** 56 **EST:** 2004
**SALES (est):** 21.78MM
**SALES (corp-wide):** 9.86MM **Privately Held**
Web: www.mereobiopharma.com
SIC: 2834 Pharmaceutical preparations
HQ: Mereo Us Holdings Inc.
800 Chesapeake Dr
Redwood City CA 94063
650 995-8200

**(P-5554)**
**METACRINE INC**
Also Called: Metacrine
3985 Sorrento Valley Blvd Ste C, San Diego (92121-1497)
PHONE..................858 369-7800
Preston Klassen, *Pr*
Richard Heyman, *
Patricia Millican, *CFO*
Hubert Chen, *CMO*
**EMP:** 32 **EST:** 2014
**SQ FT:** 20,475
Web: www.metacrine.com
SIC: 2834 Pharmaceutical preparations

**(P-5555)**
**MILK SPECIALTIES COMPANY**
Also Called: Actus Nutrition
715 N Divisadero St, Visalia (93291-4607)
PHONE..................559 732-1220
▼ **EMP:** 39
**SALES (corp-wide):** 326.93MM **Privately Held**
Web: www.milkspecialties.com
SIC: 2834 2026 5149 Vitamin, nutrient, and hematinic preparations for human use; Fermented and cultured milk products; Health foods
PA: Milk Specialties Company
7500 Flying Cloud Dr Ste
952 942-7310

**(P-5556)**
**MIRUM PHARMACEUTICALS INC (PA)**
Also Called: MIRUM
989 E Hillsdale Blvd Ste 300, Foster City (94404-4260)
PHONE..................650 667-4085
Christopher Peetz, *CEO*
Michael Grey, *Ch Bd*
Peter Radovich, *Pr*
Eric Bjerkholt, *CFO*
Lara Longpre, *CDO*
**EMP:** 147 **EST:** 2018
**SQ FT:** 11,200
**SALES (est):** 186.37MM
**SALES (corp-wide):** 186.37MM **Publicly Held**
Web: www.mirumpharma.com
SIC: 2834 Pharmaceutical preparations

**(P-5557)**
**MOM ENTERPRISES LLC**
1001 Canal Blvd Unit C-1, Richmond (94804-3524)
P.O. Box 6524 (94903-0524)
PHONE..................415 694-3799
Yasmin Kaderali, *CEO*
Roshan Kaderali, *
Shiraz Kaderali, *
**EMP:** 45 **EST:** 1999
**SQ FT:** 3,000
**SALES (est):** 8.37MM **Privately Held**
Web: www.mommysbliss.com
SIC: 2834 Antacids

**(P-5558)**
**MURAD LLC (HQ)**
2121 Park Pl Fl 1, El Segundo (90245-4843)
PHONE..................310 726-0600
Elizabeth Ashmun, *
▲ **EMP:** 160 **EST:** 1990
**SQ FT:** 8,000
**SALES (est):** 52.4MM
**SALES (corp-wide):** 64.79B **Privately Held**
Web: www.murad.com
SIC: 2834 5122 Vitamin, nutrient, and hematinic preparations for human use; Pharmaceuticals
PA: Unilever Plc
Unilever House
207 572-1202

**(P-5559)**
**MURAD LLC**
Also Called: Murad
8207 W 3rd St, Los Angeles (90048-4302)
PHONE..................310 906-3100
**EMP:** 97
**SALES (corp-wide):** 64.79B **Privately Held**
Web: www.murad.com
SIC: 2834 Pharmaceutical preparations
HQ: Murad, Llc
2121 Park Pl Ste 1
El Segundo CA 90245

**(P-5560)**
**MYOKARDIA INC (HQ)**
1000 Sierra Point Pkwy, Brisbane (94005-1804)
PHONE..................650 741-0900
Tassos Gianakakos, *Pr*
Taylor C Harris, *CFO*
Robert S Mcdowell, *CSO*
Jake Bauer, *Chief Business Officer*
William Fairey, *CCO*
**EMP:** 64 **EST:** 2012
**SQ FT:** 34,400
**SALES (corp-wide):** 45.01B **Publicly Held**
Web: www.bms.com
SIC: 2834 Pharmaceutical preparations
PA: Bristol-Myers Squibb Company
Route 206/Prvince Line Rd
609 252-4621

**(P-5561)**
**NATALS INC**
Also Called: Ritual
1370 N St Andrews Pl, Los Angeles (90028-8529)
PHONE..................323 475-6033
Katerina Schneider, *CEO*
Elizabeth Reifsnyder, *
**EMP:** 110 **EST:** 2015
**SALES (est):** 9.94MM **Privately Held**
Web: www.ritual.com
SIC: 2834 Vitamin preparations

**(P-5562)**
**NATIONAL RESILIENCE INC (PA)**
Also Called: Resilience
3115 Merryfield Row Ste 200, San Diego (92121-1174)
PHONE..................888 737-2460
Rahul Singhvi, *CEO*
Sandy Mahatme, *Pr*
Elliot Menschik, *Chief Digital Officer*
Georgeta Puscalau, *Chief Quality Officer*
**EMP:** 23 **EST:** 2020
**SALES (est):** 535.8MM
**SALES (corp-wide):** 535.8MM **Privately Held**
Web: www.resilience.com
SIC: 2834 Pharmaceutical preparations

**(P-5563)**
**NATROL INC**
21411 Prairie St, Chatsworth (91311-5829)
PHONE..................818 739-6000
◆ **EMP:** 230
SIC: 2834 2833 Vitamin, nutrient, and hematinic preparations for human use; Medicinals and botanicals

## 2834 - Pharmaceutical Preparations (P-5584)

**(P-5564)**
**NATROL LLC (PA)**
15233 Ventura Blvd Fl 900, Sherman Oaks (91403)
PHONE..................800 262-8765
Nina Barton, CEO
◆ EMP: 130 EST: 2014
SALES (est): 85.54MM
SALES (corp-wide): 85.54MM **Privately Held**
Web: www.natrol.com
SIC: 2834 Pharmaceutical preparations

**(P-5565)**
**NBTY MANUFACTURING LLC**
Also Called: Omni-Pak Industries
5115 E La Palma Ave, Anaheim (92807-2018)
PHONE..................714 765-8323
Steve Cahillane, CEO
Harvey Kamil, *Managing Member**
Scott Rudolph, *
Hans Lindgren, *
▼ EMP: 224 EST: 1978
SALES (est): 9.73MM **Privately Held**
SIC: 2834 Vitamin preparations
HQ: Nhs U.S., Llc
1041 Us-202
Bridgewater NJ 08807
800 422-2752

**(P-5566)**
**NEILMED PHARMACEUTICALS INC (PA)**
498 Aviation Blvd, Santa Rosa (95403-1069)
PHONE..................707 525-3784
Kaetan Mehta Md, CEO
Nina Mehta, *
▲ EMP: 300 EST: 2001
SALES (est): 80.8MM **Privately Held**
Web: www.neilmed.com
SIC: 2834 Pharmaceutical preparations

**(P-5567)**
**NEKTAR THERAPEUTICS (PA)**
Also Called: NEKTAR
455 Mission Bay Blvd S, San Francisco (94158-2158)
PHONE..................415 482-5300
Howard W Robin, Pr
Robert B Chess, *
Mark A Wilson J.d., CLO
Sandra Gardiner, *Interim Chief Financial Officer*
Jonathan Zalevsky, *Research & Development*
EMP: 94 EST: 1990
SQ FT: 155,215
SALES (est): 90.12MM **Publicly Held**
Web: www.nektar.com
SIC: 2834 Pharmaceutical preparations

**(P-5568)**
**NEKTAR THERAPEUTICS**
150 Industrial Rd, San Carlos (94070-6256)
PHONE..................650 622-1790
EMP: 52
Web: www.nektar.com
SIC: 2834 Pharmaceutical preparations
PA: Nektar Therapeutics
455 Mission Bay Blvd S

**(P-5569)**
**NEURELIS INC (PA)**
3430 Carmel Mountain Rd Ste 300, San Diego (92121-1071)
PHONE..................858 251-2111
Craig Chambliss, CEO
George Stuart, CFO
Charles Dewildt, *Chief Commercial Officer*
Brittany Bradrick, CFO
Adrian L Rabinowicz, CMO
EMP: 30 EST: 2008
SQ FT: 100
SALES (est): 12.17MM
SALES (corp-wide): 12.17MM **Privately Held**
Web: www.neurelis.com
SIC: 2834 Druggists' preparations (pharmaceuticals)

**(P-5570)**
**NEUROGESX INC**
999 Baker Way Ste 200, San Mateo (94404-5047)
PHONE..................650 358-3300
EMP: 35
Web: www.neurogesx.com
SIC: 2834 Pharmaceutical preparations

**(P-5571)**
**NEW GENERATION WELLNESS INC (PA)**
Also Called: Nexgen Pharma
46 Corporate Park Ste 200, Irvine (92606-3120)
P.O. Box 19516 (92623-9516)
PHONE..................949 863-0340
Kyle Brown, Pr
Mark Nishi, *
Chris Limer, *OF DIETARY SUPPLEMENT**
EMP: 190 EST: 1935
SQ FT: 50,000
SALES (est): 52.38MM
SALES (corp-wide): 52.38MM **Privately Held**
Web: www.newgenerationwellness.com
SIC: 2834 Pharmaceutical preparations

**(P-5572)**
**NGM BIOPHARMACEUTICALS INC (PA)**
Also Called: Ngmbio
333 Oyster Point Blvd, South San Francisco (94080-1978)
PHONE..................650 243-5555
David J Woodhouse, CEO
William J Rieflin, *Non-Executive Chairman of the Board*
Jean-frederic Viret, CFO
Hsiao D Lieu, CMO
Valerie Pierce, CCO
EMP: 137 EST: 2008
SQ FT: 122,000
SALES (est): 4.42MM **Privately Held**
Web: www.ngmbio.com
SIC: 2834 Pharmaceutical preparations

**(P-5573)**
**NHK LABORATORIES INC (PA)**
12230 Florence Ave, Santa Fe Springs (90670-3806)
PHONE..................562 903-5835
Karim Amirul, CEO
Nasima A Karim, *
Mohammad H Haque, *
Shafiel Ahmed, *
▲ EMP: 35 EST: 1987
SQ FT: 90,000
SALES (est): 21.21MM **Privately Held**
Web: www.nhklabs.com
SIC: 2834 5122 Vitamin preparations; Vitamins and minerals

**(P-5574)**
**NHK LABORATORIES INC**
10603 Norwalk Blvd, Santa Fe Springs (90670-3821)
PHONE..................562 204-5002
Shafiel Ahmed, CEO
EMP: 55
Web: www.nhklabs.com
SIC: 2834 5122 Vitamin preparations; Vitamins and minerals
PA: Nhk Laboratories, Inc.
12230 Florence Ave

**(P-5575)**
**NITTO AVECIA PHARMA SVCS INC (DH)**
10 Vanderbilt, Irvine (92618-2010)
PHONE..................949 951-4425
Raymond Kaczmarek, Pr
EMP: 18 EST: 2016
SQ FT: 62,000
SALES (est): 25.49MM **Privately Held**
Web: www.aveciapharma.com
SIC: 2834 Pharmaceutical preparations
HQ: Nitto Denko Avecia Inc.
125 Fortune Blvd
Milford MA 01757

**(P-5576)**
**NIVAGEN PHARMACEUTICALS INC (PA)**
3050 Fite Cir Ste 100, Sacramento (95827-1818)
PHONE..................916 364-1662
Jwalant S Shukla, CEO
Ray Walker, Ex VP
Anand Shukla, *Research Vice President*
Tom Henry, VP Sls
Robert Miller, CFO
EMP: 64 EST: 2009
SALES (est): 9.84MM
SALES (corp-wide): 9.84MM **Privately Held**
Web: www.nivagen.com
SIC: 2834 7389 Pharmaceutical preparations ; Business Activities at Non-Commercial Site

**(P-5577)**
**NKARTA INC**
Also Called: NKARTA
1150 Veterans Blvd, South San Francisco (94080-1985)
PHONE..................925 407-1049
Paul Hastings, CEO
Ali Behbahani, *
Nadir Mahmood, Pr
Alyssa Levin, *Chief Business Officer*
EMP: 150 EST: 2015
SQ FT: 88,000
Web: www.nkartatx.com
SIC: 2834 Pharmaceutical preparations

**(P-5578)**
**NOVARTIS INSTTTES FOR BMDCAL R**
5959 Horton St, Emeryville (94608-2120)
PHONE..................510 923-4248
EMP: 236
Web: www.novartis.com
SIC: 2834 Pharmaceutical preparations
HQ: Novartis Institutes For Biomedical Research, Inc.
700 Main St
Cambridge MA 02139
617 777-8276

**(P-5579)**
**NOVARTIS PHARMACEUTICALS CORP**
1121 L St Ste 211, Sacramento (95814-3970)
PHONE..................862 778-8300
EMP: 163
Web: www.novartis.com
SIC: 2834 Pharmaceutical preparations
HQ: Novartis Pharmaceuticals Corporation
1 Health Plz
East Hanover NJ 07936
862 778-8300

**(P-5580)**
**NOVO NORDISK INC**
6300 Dumbarton Cir, Fremont (94555-3644)
PHONE..................510 299-9508
EMP: 597
SALES (corp-wide): 39.23B **Privately Held**
Web: www.novonordisk-us.com
SIC: 2834 Pharmaceutical preparations
HQ: Novo Nordisk Inc.
800 Scudders Mill Rd
Plainsboro NJ 08536
609 987-5800

**(P-5581)**
**NURA USA LLC**
Also Called: Nura
2652 White Rd, Irvine (92614-6248)
PHONE..................949 946-5700
Lily Ruan, Pr
EMP: 30 EST: 2018
SALES (est): 8.14MM **Privately Held**
Web: www.nurausa.com
SIC: 2834 Vitamin preparations

**(P-5582)**
**NUTRAWISE HEALTH & BEAUTY LLC**
Also Called: Nutrawise
9600 Toledo Way, Irvine (92618-1808)
PHONE..................888 271-8976
Darren Rude, CEO
Patty Terzo-rude, Pr
EMP: 95 EST: 2010
SQ FT: 130,000
SALES (est): 37.44MM
SALES (corp-wide): 492.26MM **Privately Held**
Web: www.youtheory.com
SIC: 2834 Vitamin, nutrient, and hematinic preparations for human use
PA: Jamieson Wellness Inc
1 Adelaide St E Suite 2200
416 960-0052

**(P-5583)**
**OCULEVE INC**
4410 Rosewood Dr, Pleasanton (94588-3050)
PHONE..................415 745-3784
Michael D Ackermann, Pr
EMP: 15 EST: 2011
SALES (est): 1.53MM
SALES (corp-wide): 54.32B **Publicly Held**
Web: www.abbvie.com
SIC: 2834 Pharmaceutical preparations
HQ: Allergan Unlimited Company
Clonshaugh Business & Technology Park
Coolock D17 E

**(P-5584)**
**OLEMA PHARMACEUTICALS INC (PA)**
Also Called: OLEMA ONCOLOGY
780 Brannan St, San Francisco (94103-4919)
PHONE..................415 651-3316
Sean Bohen, Pr
Ian Clark, *
Shane Kovacs, COO
Naseem Zojwalla, CMO
David C Myles, CDO CSCDO

## 2834 - Pharmaceutical Preparations (P-5585)

EMP: 88 EST: 2006
SQ FT: 20,500
SALES (est): 34.97MM
SALES (corp-wide): 34.97MM **Publicly Held**
Web: www.olema.com
SIC: 2834 Pharmaceutical preparations

**(P-5585)**
**ONYX PHARMACEUTICALS INC**
1 Amgen Center Dr, Newbury Park (91320-1730)
PHONE..................650 266-0000
Pablo Cagnoni, *Pr*
Bob Goeltz, *Ex Dir*
Matthew K Fust, *Ex VP*
Suzanne M Shema, *Ex VP*
Helen Torley, *Ex VP*
EMP: 741 EST: 2013
SQ FT: 297,111
SALES (est): 26.92MM
SALES (corp-wide): 28.19B **Publicly Held**
SIC: 2834 8049 Drugs affecting parasitic and infective diseases; Occupational therapist
PA: Amgen Inc.
  1 Amgen Center Dr
  805 447-1000

**(P-5586)**
**OREXIGEN THERAPEUTICS INC**
Also Called: Orexigen
3344 N Torrey Pines Ct Ste 200, La Jolla (92037-1024)
PHONE..................858 875-8600
Thomas P Lynch, *Pr*
Thomas P Lynch, *Pr*
Lota S Zoth, *
EMP: 100 EST: 2003
SQ FT: 29,935
SALES (est): 5.9MM
SALES (corp-wide): 50.13MM **Privately Held**
Web: www.curraxpharma.com
SIC: 2834 Pharmaceutical preparations
HQ: Nalpropion Pharmaceuticals, Llc
  155 Franklin Rd Ste 450
  Brentwood TN 37027
  800 793-2145

**(P-5587)**
**ORIC PHARMACEUTICALS INC**
240 E Grand Ave Fl 2, South San Francisco (94080-4811)
PHONE..................650 388-5600
Jacob M Chacko, *Pr*
Richard Heyman, *
Dominic Piscitelli, *CFO*
Pratik Multani, *CMO*
EMP: 100 EST: 2014
SQ FT: 33,663
Web: www.oricpharma.com
SIC: 2834 Pharmaceutical preparations

**(P-5588)**
**ORPHAN MEDICAL INC**
3180 Porter Dr, Palo Alto (94304-1287)
PHONE..................650 496-3777
Matthew Fust, *CFO*
EMP: 80 EST: 1994
SQ FT: 15,000
SALES (est): 891.09K **Privately Held**
Web: www.jazzpharma.com
SIC: 2834 8731 Pharmaceutical preparations ; Commercial physical research
HQ: Jazz Pharmaceuticals, Inc.
  3170 Porter Dr
  Palo Alto CA 94304
  650 496-3777

**(P-5589)**
**OTONOMY INC**
Also Called: Otonomy
4796 Executive Dr, San Diego (92121-3090)
PHONE..................619 323-2200
David A Weber, *Pr*
Jay Lichter, *
Paul E Cayer, *Chief Business Officer*
EMP: 56 EST: 2008
SQ FT: 62,000
SALES (est): 125K **Privately Held**
Web: www.otonomy.com
SIC: 2834 Pharmaceutical preparations

**(P-5590)**
**P & L DEVELOPMENT LLC**
Also Called: Pl Development
11865 Alameda St, Lynwood (90262-4022)
PHONE..................323 567-2482
Jim Smith, *Genl Mgr*
EMP: 123
Web: www.pldevelopments.com
SIC: 2834 2841 2844 Pharmaceutical preparations; Soap and other detergents; Perfumes, cosmetics and other toilet preparations
PA: P & L Development, Llc
  200 Hicks St

**(P-5591)**
**PACIFIC PHARMA INC**
18600 Von Karman Ave, Irvine (92612-1513)
PHONE..................714 246-4600
Roger Maffia, *Dir*
EMP: 2000 EST: 1997
SALES (est): 1.52MM
SALES (corp-wide): 54.32B **Publicly Held**
SIC: 2834 Pharmaceutical preparations
HQ: Allergan, Inc.
  1 N Waukegan Rd
  North Chicago IL 60064
  862 261-7000

**(P-5592)**
**PACIFIC SHORE HOLDINGS INC**
Also Called: Nature-Cide
8236 Remmet Ave, Canoga Park (91304-4156)
PHONE..................818 998-0996
Matthew Mills, *Pr*
Jennifer Mills, *
Ronald J Tchorzewski, *
David E Toomey, *
▲ EMP: 24 EST: 1981
SQ FT: 13,000
SALES (est): 5.25MM
SALES (corp-wide): 5.25MM **Privately Held**
Web: www.pac-sh.com
SIC: 2834 2879 Pharmaceutical preparations ; Pesticides, agricultural or household
PA: X Med Inc
  8236 Remmet Ave
  818 349-2870

**(P-5593)**
**PACIRA PHARMACEUTICALS INC**
10578 Science Center Dr, San Diego (92121-1149)
PHONE..................858 625-2424
Chuck Laranjeira, *Pr*
EMP: 73 EST: 2022
SALES (est): 7.63MM **Publicly Held**
Web: www.pacira.com
SIC: 2834 Pharmaceutical preparations
PA: Pacira Biosciences, Inc.
  5401 W Knnedy Blvd Lncoln

**(P-5594)**
**PARVUS THERAPEUTICS US INC**
750 Gateway Blvd, South San Francisco (94080-7020)
PHONE..................415 805-8251
Peter Strumph, *CFO*
EMP: 19 EST: 2018
SALES (est): 5.03MM **Privately Held**
Web: www.parvustx.com
SIC: 2834 Pharmaceutical preparations

**(P-5595)**
**PEARL THERAPEUTICS INC**
200 Cardinal Way, Redwood City (94063-4703)
PHONE..................650 305-2600
EMP: 51
SIC: 2834 Druggists' preparations (pharmaceuticals)

**(P-5596)**
**PEREZ DISTRIBUTING FRESNO INC (PA)**
103 S Academy Ave, Sanger (93657-2428)
P.O. Box 579 (93657-0579)
PHONE..................800 638-3512
Emeterio P Perez, *Pr*
Alma Perez, *VP*
▲ EMP: 16 EST: 2002
SQ FT: 16,000
SALES (est): 4.76MM **Privately Held**
Web: www.perezdistfresno.com
SIC: 2834 Druggists' preparations (pharmaceuticals)

**(P-5597)**
**PFENEX INC**
Also Called: Pfenex
10790 Roselle St, San Diego (92121-1508)
PHONE..................858 352-4400
Evert B Schimmelpennink, *
Evert B Schimmelpennink, *
Jason Grenfell-gardner, *Ch Bd*
Shawn A Scranton, *Sr VP*
Patrick K Lucy, *Chief Business Officer*
EMP: 81 EST: 2009
SQ FT: 46,959
SALES (est): 9.84MM
SALES (corp-wide): 131.31MM **Publicly Held**
Web: www.pelicanexpression.com
SIC: 2834 Pharmaceutical preparations
PA: Ligand Pharmaceuticals Incorporated
  555 Heritage Dr Ste 200
  858 550-7500

**(P-5598)**
**PFIZER INC**
Also Called: Pfizer
10777 Science Center Dr, San Diego (92121-1111)
PHONE..................858 622-3000
Karen Katen, *Brnch Mgr*
EMP: 92
SALES (corp-wide): 58.5B **Publicly Held**
Web: www.pfizer.com
SIC: 2834 Pharmaceutical preparations
PA: Pfizer Inc.
  66 Hudson Blvd E
  212 733-2323

**(P-5599)**
**PFIZER INC**
Also Called: Pfizer
10646 Science Center Dr, San Diego (92121-1150)
PHONE..................858 622-3001
Mary Mateja, *Mgr*

EMP: 57
SALES (corp-wide): 58.5B **Publicly Held**
Web: www.pfizer.com
SIC: 2834 Pharmaceutical preparations
PA: Pfizer Inc.
  66 Hudson Blvd E
  212 733-2323

**(P-5600)**
**PHARMACEUTIC LITHO LABEL INC**
3990 Royal Ave, Simi Valley (93063)
PHONE..................805 285-5162
Timothy Laurence, *Pr*
Tom Moore, *Pr*
Rick Machale, *VP*
▲ EMP: 85 EST: 1964
SQ FT: 32,000
SALES (est): 21.15MM **Privately Held**
Web: www.resourcelabel.com
SIC: 2834 Pharmaceutical preparations
PA: Resource Label Group, Llc
  2550 Mridian Blvd Ste 370

**(P-5601)**
**PHARMACYCLICS INC**
995 E Arques Ave, Sunnyvale (94085-4521)
PHONE..................408 774-0330
EMP: 607
SIC: 2834 Pharmaceutical preparations

**(P-5602)**
**PHARMACYCLICS LLC (HQ)**
1000 Gateway Blvd, South San Francisco (94080-7028)
PHONE..................408 215-3000
EMP: 57 EST: 2015
SALES (est): 301.88MM
SALES (corp-wide): 54.32B **Publicly Held**
Web: www.pharmacyclics.com
SIC: 2834 Pharmaceutical preparations
PA: Abbvie Inc.
  1 N Waukegan Rd
  847 932-7900

**(P-5603)**
**PHARMION CORPORATION**
12481 High Bluff Dr Ste 200, San Diego (92130-3585)
PHONE..................858 335-5744
Jeffry Howbert, *Brnch Mgr*
EMP: 48
SALES (corp-wide): 45.01B **Publicly Held**
Web: www.bms.com
SIC: 2834 Pharmaceutical preparations
HQ: Pharmion Corporation
  86 Morris Ave
  Summit NJ 07901
  908 673-9000

**(P-5604)**
**PHOENIX PHARMACEUTICALS INC**
330 Beach Rd, Burlingame (94010-2004)
PHONE..................650 558-8898
Jaw-kang Chang, *Pr*
Eng Tau, *Dir*
EMP: 20 EST: 1994
SQ FT: 5,000
SALES (est): 5.05MM **Privately Held**
Web: www.phoenixpeptide.com
SIC: 2834 8731 Pharmaceutical preparations ; Commercial physical research

**(P-5605)**
**PIONYR IMMUNOTHERAPEUTICS INC**
2 Tower Pl # 8, South San Francisco (94080-1826)

# PRODUCTS & SERVICES SECTION
## 2834 - Pharmaceutical Preparations (P-5625)

PHONE.............................415 226-7503
EMP: 49 EST: 2017
SALES (est): 9.43MM **Privately Held**
Web: www.pionyrtx.com
SIC: **2834** Pharmaceutical preparations

**(P-5606)**
**POLARIS PHARMACEUTICALS INC (PA)**
9990 Mesa Rim Rd, San Diego (92121-3932)
PHONE.............................858 452-6688
Bor Wen Wu, *CEO*
John Bomalaski, *VP*
Robert E Hoffman, *Mgr*
EMP: 15 EST: 2006
SALES (est): 6.06MM
SALES (corp-wide): 6.06MM **Privately Held**
Web: www.polarispharma.com
SIC: **2834** Pharmaceutical preparations

**(P-5607)**
**POLYPEPTIDE LABS SAN DIEGO LLC**
9395 Cabot Dr, San Diego (92126-4310)
PHONE.............................858 408-0808
EMP: 72 EST: 1986
SQ FT: 43,000
SALES (est): 9.12MM **Privately Held**
Web: www.polypeptide.com
SIC: **2834** 2833 8731 Pharmaceutical preparations; Medicinals and botanicals; Biotechnical research, commercial
HQ: Polypeptide Laboratories Inc.
365 Maple Ave
Torrance CA 90503

**(P-5608)**
**PRESCIENT HOLDINGS GROUP LLC**
10181 Scripps Gateway Ct, San Diego (92131-5152)
PHONE.............................858 790-7004
Christine Nguyen, *Pr*
Debra Minich, *Dir*
Ethan Dargie, *VP*
Mike Schneider, *VP*
Vasu Bobba, *VP*
EMP: 39 EST: 2021
SALES (est): 986.07K **Privately Held**
Web: www.prescientholdingsgroup.com
SIC: **2834** Pharmaceutical preparations

**(P-5609)**
**PRIMAPHARMA INC**
3443 Tripp Ct, San Diego (92121)
PHONE.............................858 259-0969
Mark Livingston, *Pr*
Tony Dziabo, *
Larry Braga, *
Nayaz Ahmed, *
Arshad Chaudry, *
EMP: 35 EST: 2015
SQ FT: 24,000
SALES (est): 5.2MM **Privately Held**
Web: www.primapharma.net
SIC: **2834** Pharmaceutical preparations

**(P-5610)**
**PROMETHEUS BIOSCIENCES INC**
3050 Science Park Rd, San Diego (92121-1102)
PHONE.............................858 422-4300
Mark C Mckenna, *Ch Bd*
Keith W Marshall, *CFO*
Mark Stenhouse, *COO*
EMP: 72 EST: 2016

SALES (est): 6.81MM
SALES (corp-wide): 60.12B **Publicly Held**
Web: www.prometheuslabs.com
SIC: **2834** Pharmaceutical preparations
PA: Merck & Co., Inc.
126 E Lincoln Ave
908 740-4000

**(P-5611)**
**PROMETHEUS LABORATORIES INC**
9410 Carroll Park Dr, San Diego (92121-5201)
PHONE.............................858 824-0895
Warren Cresswell, *CEO*
Peter Westlake, *
Robert Carlson, *
Bruce M Wagman, *
Larry Mimms Ph.d., *VP*
EMP: 405 EST: 1996
SQ FT: 99,000
SALES (est): 33.67MM **Privately Held**
Web: www.prometheuslabs.com
SIC: **2834** 8011 Pharmaceutical preparations; Offices and clinics of medical doctors

**(P-5612)**
**PROTAB LABORATORIES**
30321 Esperanza, Rcho Sta Marg (92688-2119)
PHONE.............................949 713-1301
Son Dao, *Brnch Mgr*
EMP: 85
Web: www.protablabs.com
SIC: **2834** Pharmaceutical preparations
PA: Protab Laboratories
25892 Towne Centre Dr

**(P-5613)**
**PROTAB LABORATORIES (PA)**
25892 Towne Centre Dr, Foothill Ranch (92610-3409)
PHONE.............................949 635-1930
Min W Chen, *CEO*
Randy L Pollan, *VP*
Shafiqul Islam, *VP*
Joanne Hsu, *Dir Opers*
▲ EMP: 65 EST: 2004
SALES (est): 31.26MM **Privately Held**
Web: www.protablabs.com
SIC: **2834** 2023 Vitamin preparations; Dietary supplements, dairy and non-dairy based

**(P-5614)**
**PROTAGONIST THERAPEUTICS INC (PA)**
Also Called: PROTAGONIST THERAPEUTICS
7707 Gateway Blvd Ste 140, Newark (94560-1160)
PHONE.............................510 474-0170
Dinesh V Patel, *Pr*
Harold E Selick, *Ch Bd*
Asif Ali, *Ex VP*
Suneel Gupta, *CDO*
Arturo Molina, *CMO*
EMP: 62 EST: 2006
SQ FT: 57,900
SALES (est): 60MM **Publicly Held**
Web: www.protagonist-inc.com
SIC: **2834** 8731 Pharmaceutical preparations; Commercial physical research

**(P-5615)**
**PROVISION HEALTH CORP**
Also Called: PH Labs
9760 Via De La Amistad, San Diego (92154-7210)
PHONE.............................619 240-3263

EMP: 16 EST: 2014
SALES (est): 2.52MM **Privately Held**
Web: www.phlabsca.com
SIC: **2834** Druggists' preparations (pharmaceuticals)

**(P-5616)**
**PSI PHARMA SUPPORT AMERICA INC**
401 California Dr, Burlingame (94010-4008)
PHONE.............................267 464-2500
EMP: 41
SIC: **2834** Pharmaceutical preparations
HQ: Psi Pharma Support America, Inc.
875 1st Ave
King Of Prussia PA 19406
267 464-2500

**(P-5617)**
**PUMA BIOTECHNOLOGY INC (PA)**
Also Called: PUMA BIOTECHNOLOGY
10880 Wilshire Blvd Ste 2150, Los Angeles (90024-4106)
P.O. Box 64945 (55164-0945)
PHONE.............................424 248-6500
Alan H Auerbach, *Ch Bd*
Maximo F Nougues, *CFO*
Alvin Wong, *CSO*
Jeff Ludwig, *CCO*
Douglas Hunt, *Regional AFF MED AFF PHARMA*
EMP: 185 EST: 2007
SQ FT: 65,656
SALES (est): 235.64MM
SALES (corp-wide): 235.64MM **Publicly Held**
Web: www.pumabiotechnology.com
SIC: **2834** Pharmaceutical preparations

**(P-5618)**
**PURETEK CORPORATION**
7900 Nelson Rd Unit A, Panorama City (91402-6828)
PHONE.............................818 361-3949
Jeff Pressman, *Brnch Mgr*
EMP: 130
Web: www.puretekcorp.com
SIC: **2834** 2844 Pharmaceutical preparations; Cosmetic preparations
PA: Puretek Corporation
1145 Arroyo Ave Unit D

**(P-5619)**
**PURETEK CORPORATION (PA)**
1145 Arroyo St Ste D, San Fernando (91340)
PHONE.............................818 361-3316
Barry Pressman, *CEO*
◆ EMP: 50 EST: 1991
SQ FT: 114,000
SALES (est): 55.92MM **Privately Held**
Web: www.puretekcorp.com
SIC: **2834** Pharmaceutical preparations

**(P-5620)**
**QUANTICEL PHARMACUETICALS INC**
9393 Towne Centre Dr Ste 110, San Diego (92121-3070)
PHONE.............................858 956-3747
Steve Kaldor, *Brnch Mgr*
EMP: 20
SIC: **2834** Pharmaceutical preparations
PA: Quanticel Pharmaceuticals, Inc.
1500 Owens St Ste 500

**(P-5621)**
**QUARK PHARMACEUTICALS INC (DH)**
495 N Whisman Rd Ste 100, Mountain View (94043-5725)
PHONE.............................510 402-4020
EMP: 25 EST: 1991
SALES (est): 10.26MM **Privately Held**
Web: www.quarkpharma.com
SIC: **2834** Pharmaceutical preparations
HQ: Sbi Biotech Co., Ltd.
1-6-1, Roppongi
Minato-Ku TKY 106-0

**(P-5622)**
**QUOREX PHARM INC (PA)**
2232 Rutherford Rd, Carlsbad (92008-8814)
PHONE.............................760 602-1910
Robert Robb, *Pr*
Robert Robb, *Pr*
Jeffrey Stein, *Chief Scientist*
Krzysztof Appelt, *Technology*
Gary J G Atkinson, *CFO*
EMP: 42 EST: 1999
SQ FT: 23,500
SALES (est): 1.99MM
SALES (corp-wide): 1.99MM **Privately Held**
SIC: **2834** Pharmaceutical preparations

**(P-5623)**
**RAIN ONCOLOGY INC (PA)**
Also Called: Rain Therapeutics
8000 Jarvis Ave Ste 204, Newark (94560-1154)
PHONE.............................510 953-5559
Avanish Vellanki, *Ch Bd*
Robert Doebele, *CSO*
Richard Bryce, *CMO*
Nelson Cabatuan, *VP Fin*
EMP: 63 EST: 2017
SQ FT: 3,900
Web: www.rainoncology.com
SIC: **2834** Pharmaceutical preparations

**(P-5624)**
**RANDAL OPTIMAL NUTRIENTS LLC**
Also Called: Vimco
1595 Hampton Way, Santa Rosa (95407-6844)
P.O. Box 7328 (95407-0328)
PHONE.............................707 528-1800
William A Robotham, *Pr*
Lynn J Brinker, *
Donna Coats, *
EMP: 32 EST: 1947
SQ FT: 22,500
SALES (est): 6.13MM **Privately Held**
Web: www.randaloptimal.com
SIC: **2834** 5122 Vitamin preparations; Drugs, proprietaries, and sundries

**(P-5625)**
**RANI THERAPEUTICS LLC**
2051 Ringwood Ave, San Jose (95131-1703)
PHONE.............................408 457-3700
Talat Imran, *CEO*
Svai Sanford, *CFO*
EMP: 71 EST: 2012
SQ FT: 22,000
SALES (est): 462K **Publicly Held**
Web: www.ranitherapeutics.com
SIC: **2834** Pharmaceutical preparations
PA: Rani Therapeutics Holdings, Inc.
2051 Ringwood Ave
408 457-3700

(PA)=Parent Co (HQ)=Headquarters
✪ = New Business established in last 2 years

## 2834 - Pharmaceutical Preparations (P-5626)

**(P-5626)**
**RANI THERAPEUTICS HOLDINGS INC (PA)**
Also Called: Rani Therapeutics
2051 Ringwood Ave, San Jose (95131-1703)
PHONE..................408 457-3700
Talat Imran, *CEO*
Mir Imran, *Ex Ch Bd*
Svai Sanford, *CFO*
Mir Hashim, *CSO*
Kate Mckinley, *Chief Business Officer*
EMP: 67 EST: 2012
SQ FT: 22,000
Web: www.ranitherapeutics.com
SIC: 2834 Pharmaceutical preparations

**(P-5627)**
**RANIR LLC**
Also Called: Dr. Fresh
6 Centerpointe Dr Ste 640, La Palma (90623-2587)
PHONE..................866 373-7374
Kevin Parekh, *Brnch Mgr*
EMP: 34
Web: www.perrigo.com
SIC: 2834 Pharmaceutical preparations
HQ: Ranir, Llc
  4701 E Paris Ave Se
  Grand Rapids MI 49512
  616 698-8880

**(P-5628)**
**RAPT THERAPEUTICS INC**
Also Called: RAPT THERAPEUTICS
561 Eccles Ave, South San Francisco (94080-1906)
PHONE..................650 489-9000
Brian Wong, *Pr*
William Rieflin, *
Rodney Young, *CFO*
Dirk Brockstedt, *CSO*
William Ho, *CMO*
EMP: 75 EST: 2015
SQ FT: 36,754
Web: www.rapt.com
SIC: 2834 8731 Pharmaceutical preparations; Biotechnical research, commercial

**(P-5629)**
**RASCAL THERAPEUTICS INC**
3000 El Camino Real Bldg 4, Palo Alto (94306-2100)
PHONE..................650 770-0192
Michael Mann, *CEO*
EMP: 20 EST: 2011
SALES (est): 539.27K Privately Held
SIC: 2834 Drugs affecting neoplasms and endocrine systems

**(P-5630)**
**RAY THERAPEUTICS INC**
1 Sansome St, San Francisco (94104-4448)
PHONE..................858 617-8610
EMP: 32 EST: 2021
SALES (est): 6.65MM Privately Held
Web: www.raytherapeutics.com
SIC: 2834 Pharmaceutical preparations

**(P-5631)**
**RAYZEBIO INC (HQ)**
5505 Morehouse Dr Ste 300, San Diego (92121-1720)
PHONE..................619 937-2754
Benjamin Hickey, *Pr*
Sandra Ramos-alves, *VP*
EMP: 18 EST: 2020
SQ FT: 28,000
SALES (corp-wide): 45.01B Publicly Held
Web: www.rayzebio.com
SIC: 2834 8731 Pharmaceutical preparations; Medical research, commercial
PA: Bristol-Myers Squibb Company
  Route 206/Prvince Line Rd
  609 252-4621

**(P-5632)**
**RECEPTOS INC**
3033 Science Park Rd Ste 300, San Diego (92121-1168)
PHONE..................858 652-5700
Faheem Hasnain, *Pr*
Marcus F Boehm, *
Graham Cooper, *
Shiela Gujrathi, *CMO**
Robert J Peach, *CSO**
EMP: 32 EST: 2009
SALES (est): 7.27MM
SALES (corp-wide): 45.01B Publicly Held
Web: www.celgene.com
SIC: 2834 Pharmaceutical preparations
HQ: Celgene Corporation
  86 Morris Ave
  Summit NJ 07901
  908 673-9000

**(P-5633)**
**REDWOOD SCIENTIFIC TECH INC**
245 E Main St Ste 115, Alhambra (91801-7507)
PHONE..................310 693-5401
Jason E Cardiff, *Pr*
Eunjung Cardiff, *
Jacques Poujade, *
Rhonda Pearlman, *
M Salah Zaki, *CMO**
EMP: 24 EST: 2014
SALES (est): 933.91K Privately Held
SIC: 2834 Druggists' preparations (pharmaceuticals)

**(P-5634)**
**REMPEX PHARMACEUTICALS INC**
3013 Science Park Rd 1st Fl, San Diego (92121-1101)
PHONE..................858 875-2840
Stuart Kingsley, *Pr*
William Oconner, *
EMP: 40 EST: 2013
SQ FT: 60
SALES (est): 3.13MM Privately Held
SIC: 2834 Pharmaceutical preparations
HQ: The Medicines Company
  8 Sylvan Way
  Parsippany NJ 07054
  973 290-6000

**(P-5635)**
**RENOVARO INC (PA)**
Also Called: Renovaro
2080 Century Park E Ste 906, Los Angeles (90067-2011)
PHONE..................305 918-1980
Mark Dybul, *Vice Chairman*
Rene Sindlev, *Ch Bd*
Francois Binette, *Ex VP*
Luisa Puche, *CFO*
EMP: 21 EST: 2011
SQ FT: 3,554
Web: www.renovarobio.com
SIC: 2834 8731 Pharmaceutical preparations; Biotechnical research, commercial

**(P-5636)**
**RESILIENCE US INC (HQ)**
3115 Merryfield Row Ste 200, San Diego (92121-1174)
PHONE..................984 202-0854
Rahul Singhvi, *CEO*
Sandy Mahatme, *Pr*
EMP: 23 EST: 2020
SALES (est): 98.63MM
SALES (corp-wide): 535.8MM Privately Held
SIC: 2834 3559 Pharmaceutical preparations; Pharmaceutical machinery
PA: National Resilience, Inc.
  3115 Mrryfeld Row Ste 200
  888 737-2460

**(P-5637)**
**REVIR THERAPEUTICS INC**
150 N Hill Dr Ste 19, Brisbane (94005-1018)
PHONE..................415 794-7166
EMP: 16 EST: 2020
SALES (est): 4.32MM Privately Held
SIC: 2834 Pharmaceutical preparations

**(P-5638)**
**REZO THERAPEUTICS INC**
455 Mission Bay Blvd S Ste 525, San Francisco (94158-2158)
PHONE..................650 704-5577
EMP: 23
SALES (est): 5.69MM Privately Held
Web: www.rezotx.com
SIC: 2834 Pharmaceutical preparations

**(P-5639)**
**REZOLUTE INC (PA)**
275 Shoreline Dr Ste 500, Redwood City (94065-1413)
PHONE..................650 206-4507
Nevan Charles Elam, *Ch Bd*
Nevan Charles Elam, *Ch Bd*
Brian Roberts, *CMO*
Daron Evans, *CFO*
EMP: 27 EST: 2010
SQ FT: 9,300
Web: www.rezolutebio.com
SIC: 2834 Pharmaceutical preparations

**(P-5640)**
**RIGEL PHARMACEUTICALS INC (PA)**
611 Gateway Blvd Ste 900, South San Francisco (94080-7029)
PHONE..................650 624-1100
Raul R Rodriguez, *Pr*
Gregg A Lapointe, *
Dean L Schorno, *Ex VP*
David A Santos, *CCO*
Raymond J Furey, *Corporate Secretary*
EMP: 151 EST: 1996
SQ FT: 13,670
SALES (est): 116.88MM Publicly Held
Web: www.rigel.com
SIC: 2834 8733 Pharmaceutical preparations; Medical research

**(P-5641)**
**ROBINSON PHARMA INC**
3701 W Warner Ave, Santa Ana (92704-5218)
PHONE..................714 241-0235
Tam H Nguyen, *CEO*
EMP: 121
Web: www.robinsonpharma.com
SIC: 2834 7389 Pharmaceutical preparations; Packaging and labeling services
PA: Robinson Pharma, Inc.
  3330 S Harbor Blvd

**(P-5642)**
**ROBINSON PHARMA INC**
3300 W Segerstrom Ave, Santa Ana (92704-6403)
PHONE..................714 241-0235
Gulfam Sheikh, *Mgr*
EMP: 120
Web: www.robinsonpharma.com
SIC: 2834 Medicines, capsuled or ampuled
PA: Robinson Pharma, Inc.
  3330 S Harbor Blvd

**(P-5643)**
**ROBINSON PHARMA INC (PA)**
3330 S Harbor Blvd, Santa Ana (92704-6831)
PHONE..................714 241-0235
Tuong Nguyen, *CEO*
Tam Nguyen, *
Elaine Phan, *
◆ EMP: 310 EST: 1989
SQ FT: 124,000
SALES (est): 91.87MM Privately Held
Web: www.robinsonpharma.com
SIC: 2834 Medicines, capsuled or ampuled

**(P-5644)**
**ROCHE DIAGNOSTICS CORPORATION**
1 Dna Way, South San Francisco (94080-4918)
PHONE..................650 491-7251
EMP: 204
Web: www.roche.com
SIC: 2834 Pharmaceutical preparations
HQ: Roche Diagnostics Corporation
  9115 Hague Rd
  Indianapolis IN 46256
  800 428-5076

**(P-5645)**
**ROCHE MOLECULAR SYSTEMS INC**
1 Dna Way, South San Francisco (94080-4918)
P.O. Box 45090 (94145-0090)
PHONE..................650 225-1000
EMP: 25
Web: www.gene.com
SIC: 2834 Pharmaceutical preparations
HQ: Roche Molecular Systems, Inc.
  4300 Hacienda Dr
  Pleasanton CA 94588

**(P-5646)**
**ROCHE SEQUENCING SOLUTIONS INC**
5945 Optical Ct, San Jose (95138-1400)
PHONE..................408 386-5414
Theodore Siquijor, *Mgr*
EMP: 15
Web: www.roche.com
SIC: 2834 Pharmaceutical preparations
HQ: Roche Sequencing Solutions, Inc.
  4300 Hacienda Dr
  Pleasanton CA 94588
  925 854-6246

**(P-5647)**
**S K LABORATORIES INC**
Also Called: S K Labs
5420 E La Palma Ave, Anaheim (92807-2023)
PHONE..................714 695-9800
Bansi Patel, *Pr*
Ramila B Patel, *
▲ EMP: 100 EST: 1992
SQ FT: 60,000
SALES (est): 25MM Privately Held

## 2834 - Pharmaceutical Preparations (P-5669)

**Web:** www.sklabs.com
**SIC: 2834** Pharmaceutical preparations

### (P-5648)
### SAMSON PHARMACEUTICALS INC
5635 Smithway St, Commerce (90040-1545)
**PHONE**.................323 722-3066
Jay Kassir, *Pr*
▲ **EMP:** 40 **EST:** 2001
**SALES (est):** 6.16MM **Privately Held**
**Web:** www.samsonpharmaceutical.com
**SIC: 2834** Pharmaceutical preparations

### (P-5649)
### SAMSUNG BIOLOGICS AMERICA INC
600 Gateway Blvd, South San Francisco (94080-7014)
**PHONE**.................650 898-9717
Yong Park, *CEO*
Do Young Heo, *CFO*
**EMP:** 17 **EST:** 2020
**SALES (est):** 7.16MM **Privately Held**
**Web:** www.samsungbiologics.com
**SIC: 2834** Pharmaceutical preparations

### (P-5650)
### SANTARUS INC
3611 Valley Centre Dr Ste 400, San Diego (92130-3331)
**PHONE**.................858 314-5700
Blake Boland, *Prin*
**EMP:** 15 **EST:** 2014
**SALES (est):** 2.53MM **Privately Held**
**SIC: 2834** 5122 Pharmaceutical preparations ; Pharmaceuticals

### (P-5651)
### SAPU BIOSCIENCE LLC
10840 Thornmint Rd Ste 118, San Diego (92127-2404)
**PHONE**.................650 635-7018
Vuong Trieu, *Managing Member*
Chao Hsiao, *
**EMP:** 25 **EST:** 2022
**SALES (est):** 5.49MM **Privately Held**
**SIC: 2834** Pharmaceutical preparations

### (P-5652)
### SCILEX PHARMACEUTICALS INC
960 San Antonio Rd, Palo Alto (94303-4922)
**PHONE**.................650 430-3238
Dmitri Lissin, *VP*
**EMP:** 30
**SALES (corp-wide):** 62.84MM **Publicly Held**
**Web:** www.scilexholding.com
**SIC: 2834** Pharmaceutical preparations
**HQ:** Scilex Pharmaceuticals Inc.
4955 Directors Pl
San Diego CA 92121
949 441-2270

### (P-5653)
### SENTYNL THERAPEUTICS INC
420 Stevens Ave Ste 200, Solana Beach (92075-2078)
**PHONE**.................888 227-8725
Matt Heck, *CEO*
Daniel Stokely, *
Michael Hercz, *General**
Darren Pincus, *
Shawn Scranton, *
**EMP:** 30 **EST:** 2011
**SALES (est):** 6.4MM **Privately Held**
**Web:** www.sentynl.com
**SIC: 2834** Pharmaceutical preparations
**HQ:** Zydus Lifesciences Limited
Zydus Corporate Park Scheme No. 63, Survey No. 536,
Ahmedabad GJ 38248

### (P-5654)
### SFJ PHARMACEUTICALS INC
5000 Hopyard Rd Ste 330, Pleasanton (94588-3349)
**PHONE**.................925 223-6233
Robert Debenedetto, *CEO*
**EMP:** 22 **EST:** 2009
**SALES (est):** 2.6MM **Privately Held**
**Web:** www.sfj-pharma.com
**SIC: 2834** Pharmaceutical preparations

### (P-5655)
### SHIRE
1445 Lawrence Dr, Newbury Park (91320-1311)
**PHONE**.................805 372-3000
John Sandstrom, *Prin*
**EMP:** 43 **EST:** 2018
**SALES (est):** 1.07MM **Privately Held**
**Web:** www.takeda.com
**SIC: 2834** Pharmaceutical preparations

### (P-5656)
### SHIRE RGENERATIVE MEDICINE INC
Also Called: Advanced Biohealing.com
11095 Torreyana Rd, San Diego (92121-1104)
**PHONE**.................858 754-5396
**EMP:** 50
**SIC: 2834** Pharmaceutical preparations
**HQ:** Shire Regenerative Medicine, Inc.
36 Church Ln
Westport CT 06880
877 422-4463

### (P-5657)
### SICOR INC (HQ)
19 Hughes, Irvine (92618-1902)
**PHONE**.................949 455-4700
Carlo Salvi, *Vice Chairman*
▲ **EMP:** 800 **EST:** 1986
**SQ FT:** 170,000
**SALES (est):** 17.49MM **Privately Held**
**Web:** www.tevausa.com
**SIC: 2834** 8731 Drugs acting on the cardiovascular system, except diagnostic; Medical research, commercial
**PA:** Teva Pharmaceutical Industries Limited
124 Dvora Hanevia

### (P-5658)
### SIERRA ONCOLOGY INC (HQ)
Also Called: Sierra Oncology
1820 Gateway Dr Ste 110, San Mateo (94404-4059)
**PHONE**.................650 376-8679
Stephen G Dilly, *Pr*
Robert Pelzer, *Ch Bd*
Sukhi Jagpal, *CFO*
Barbara Klencke, *CDO*
Mark Kowalski, *CMO*
**EMP:** 52 **EST:** 2003
**SQ FT:** 3,800
**SALES (est):** 300K
**SALES (corp-wide):** 37.8B **Privately Held**
**SIC: 2834** Pharmaceutical preparations
**PA:** Gsk Plc
980 Great West Road
208 047-5000

### (P-5659)
### SIGNAL PHARMACEUTICALS LLC
10300 Campus Point Dr Ste 100, San Diego (92121-1504)
**PHONE**.................858 795-4700
Alan J Lewis Ph.d., *Pr*
Shripad Bhagwat, *Drug Discovery Vice President**
David R Webb, *Research Vice President**
**EMP:** 134 **EST:** 1992
**SQ FT:** 78,202
**SALES (est):** 40.2MM
**SALES (corp-wide):** 45.01B **Publicly Held**
**SIC: 2834** Pharmaceutical preparations
**HQ:** Celgene Corporation
86 Morris Ave
Summit NJ 07901
908 673-9000

### (P-5660)
### SIMPSON INDUSTRIES INC
Also Called: Simpsonsimpson Industries
20611 Belshaw Ave, Carson (90746-3507)
**PHONE**.................310 605-1224
Rick Simpson, *CEO*
Robert Simpson, *
**EMP:** 35 **EST:** 2011
**SALES (est):** 4.07MM **Privately Held**
**Web:** www.simpsonindustries.com
**SIC: 2834** Proprietary drug products

### (P-5661)
### SIRNA THERAPEUTICS INC
1700 Owens St, San Francisco (94158-0004)
**PHONE**.................415 512-7200
**EMP:** 50 **EST:** 1992
**SALES (est):** 6.24MM
**SALES (corp-wide):** 844.29MM **Publicly Held**
**SIC: 2834** Pharmaceutical preparations
**PA:** Alnylam Pharmaceuticals, Inc.
675 W Kendall St
617 551-8200

### (P-5662)
### SK PHARMTECO INC (HQ)
12460 Akron St Ste 100, Rancho Cordova (95742-6447)
**PHONE**.................888 330-2232
Joerg Ahlgrimm, *CEO*
**EMP:** 25 **EST:** 2018
**SALES (est):** 527.24MM **Privately Held**
**Web:** www.skpharmteco.com
**SIC: 2834** Pharmaceutical preparations
**PA:** Sk Inc.
26 Jong-Ro, Jongno-Gu

### (P-5663)
### SKINMEDICA INC
18655 Teller Ave, Irvine (92612-1610)
P.O. Box 19534 (92623-9534)
**PHONE**.................760 929-2600
▲ **EMP:** 275
**Web:** www.skinmedica.com
**SIC: 2834** 2844 Dermatologicals; Perfumes, cosmetics and other toilet preparations

### (P-5664)
### SOCIETAL CDMO SAN DIEGO LLC
6828 Nancy Ridge Dr Ste 100, San Diego (92121-2224)
**PHONE**.................858 623-1520
J David Enloe Junior, *Pr*
Ryan Lake, *
Scott Rizzo, *
**EMP:** 55 **EST:** 2015
**SQ FT:** 24,100
**SALES (est):** 10.92MM **Privately Held**
**SIC: 2834** Druggists' preparations (pharmaceuticals)
**HQ:** Societal Cdmo, Inc.
490 Lapp Rd
Malvern PA 19355

### (P-5665)
### SOFIE CO
Also Called: Sofie
5900b Obata Way, Gilroy (95020-7065)
**PHONE**.................408 842-0520
Homan Jarrar, *Brnch Mgr*
**EMP:** 22
**Web:** www.sofie.com
**SIC: 2834** Pharmaceutical preparations
**HQ:** Sofie Co.
21000 Atl Blvd Ste 730
Dulles VA 20166

### (P-5666)
### SOFT GEL TECHNOLOGIES INC (HQ)
6982 Bandini Blvd, Los Angeles (90040)
**PHONE**.................323 726-0700
Ken Tsuchibe, *CEO*
Hiroshi Kishimoto, *CFO*
▲ **EMP:** 21 **EST:** 1994
**SQ FT:** 21,000
**SALES (est):** 27.28MM **Privately Held**
**Web:** www.soft-gel.com
**SIC: 2834** Medicines, capsuled or ampuled
**PA:** Kenko Corporation
3-1-2, Iwamotocho

### (P-5667)
### SOLENO THERAPEUTICS INC (PA)
100 Marine Pkwy Ste 400, Redwood City (94065-5204)
**PHONE**.................650 213-8444
Anish Bhatnagar, *Pr*
Ernest Mario, *Ch Bd*
Patricia Hirano, *Senior Vice President Regulatory Affairs*
Kristen Yen Senior, *Clinical Vice President*
James Mackaness, *CFO*
**EMP:** 17 **EST:** 1999
**SQ FT:** 10,509
**SALES (est):** 10.58MM
**SALES (corp-wide):** 10.58MM **Publicly Held**
**Web:** www.soleno.life
**SIC: 2834** Pharmaceutical preparations

### (P-5668)
### SOLEO HEALTH INC
1324 W Winton Ave, Hayward (94545-1408)
**PHONE**.................844 362-7360
John Ginzler, *CFO*
**EMP:** 19
**Web:** www.soleohealth.com
**SIC: 2834** 5912 Druggists' preparations (pharmaceuticals); Drug stores and proprietary stores
**HQ:** Soleo Health Inc.
950 Calcon Hook Rd Ste 19
Sharon Hill PA 19079
888 244-2340

### (P-5669)
### SPRING DISCOVERY INC
1121 Industrial Rd # 500, San Carlos (94070-4106)
**PHONE**.................917 572-1552
**EMP:** 21
**SALES (est):** 2.94MM **Privately Held**

## 2834 - Pharmaceutical Preparations (P-5670)

**SIC: 2834** Pharmaceutical preparations

**(P-5670)**
**SPRUCE BIOSCIENCES INC**
Also Called: SPRUCE
611 Gateway Blvd Ste 740, South San Francisco (94080-7029)
PHONE.................................415 655-4168
Javier Szwarcberg, CEO
Michael Grey, *
Samir Gharib, Pr
Ralph William Charlton Iii, Chief Medical Officer
**EMP:** 29 **EST:** 2014
**SQ FT:** 6,500
**SALES (est):** 10.09MM **Privately Held**
Web: www.sprucebio.com
**SIC: 2834** Pharmaceutical preparations

**(P-5671)**
**SPYGLASS PHARMA INC**
27061 Aliso Creek Rd Ste 100, Aliso Viejo (92656-5326)
PHONE.................................949 284-6904
Patrick Mooney, CEO
Margot Goodkin, CMO
James Dennewill, CFO
**EMP:** 23 **EST:** 2019
**SALES (est):** 3.56MM **Privately Held**
Web: www.spyglasspharma.com
**SIC: 2834** Pharmaceutical preparations

**(P-5672)**
**ST JUDE MEDICAL LLC**
Also Called: Sjm Facility
2375 Morse Ave, Irvine (92614-6233)
PHONE.................................949 769-5000
**EMP:** 24
**SALES (corp-wide):** 40.11B **Publicly Held**
Web: www.cardiovascular.abbott
**SIC: 2834** Pharmaceutical preparations
HQ: St. Jude Medical, Llc
   1 Saint Jude Medical Dr
   Saint Paul MN 55117
   651 756-2000

**(P-5673)**
**STA PHARMACEUTICAL US LLC**
6114 Nancy Ridge Dr, San Diego (92121-3223)
PHONE.................................609 606-6499
Chen Hui, CFO
**EMP:** 40 **EST:** 2016
**SALES (est):** 5.48MM **Privately Held**
Web: www.stapharma.com
**SIC: 2834** Pharmaceutical preparations

**(P-5674)**
**STAIDSON BIOPHARMA INC**
2600 Hilltop Dr Bldg A, San Pablo (94806-1971)
PHONE.................................800 345-1899
Zhiwen Zhou, Pr
Zhiwen Zhou, Prin
**EMP:** 18 **EST:** 2014
**SALES (est):** 4.99MM **Privately Held**
Web: www.staidsonbio.com
**SIC: 2834** Pharmaceutical preparations
PA: Staidson (Beijing) Biopharmaceuticals Co.,Ltd.
   No.36, Jinghai 2nd Road, Beijing Economic Technology Development

**(P-5675)**
**STASON PHARMACEUTICALS INC (PA)**
Also Called: IMT-Stason Laboratories
11 Morgan, Irvine (92618-2005)
PHONE.................................949 380-0752
Harry Fan, CEO
▲ **EMP:** 15 **EST:** 1994
**SQ FT:** 37,149
**SALES (est):** 11.92MM **Privately Held**
Web: www.stasonpharma.com
**SIC: 2834** Pharmaceutical preparations

**(P-5676)**
**STEADYMED THERAPEUTICS INC**
2603 Camino Ramon Ste 350, San Ramon (94583-9127)
P.O. Box 2147 (94583-7147)
PHONE.................................925 361-7111
Jonathan Rigby, Pr
Peter Noymer, Executive Research & Development Vice President
**EMP:** 23 **EST:** 2012
**SALES (est):** 3.64MM **Publicly Held**
**SIC: 2834** Tranquilizers or mental drug preparations
PA: United Therapeutics Corporation
   1000 Spring St

**(P-5677)**
**STERISYN INC**
Also Called: Sterisyn Scientific
11969 Challenger Ct, Moorpark (93021-7119)
PHONE.................................805 991-9694
Julie Anne, Admn
Timothy Henry, CEO
**EMP:** 30 **EST:** 2015
**SALES (est):** 789.15K **Privately Held**
Web: www.sterisyn.com
**SIC: 2834** Pharmaceutical preparations

**(P-5678)**
**STRUCTURE THERAPEUTICS INC**
611 Gateway Blvd Ste 223, South San Francisco (94080-7017)
PHONE.................................628 229-9277
Raymond Stevens, CEO
Daniel G Welch, *
Jun Yoon, CFO
Xichen Lin, CSO
Mark Bach, CMO
**EMP:** 68 **EST:** 2016
**SQ FT:** 200
Web: www.structuretx.com
**SIC: 2834** Pharmaceutical preparations

**(P-5679)**
**SUMITOMO PHARMA AMERICA INC**
2000 Sierra Point Pkwy, Brisbane (94005-1845)
PHONE.................................650 392-0222
Myrtle Potter, CEO
**EMP:** 132
Web: us.sumitomo-pharma.com
**SIC: 2834** Pharmaceutical preparations
HQ: Sumitomo Pharma America, Inc.
   84 Waterford Dr
   Marlborough MA 01752
   508 481-6700

**(P-5680)**
**SUMMIT THERAPEUTICS SUB INC**
2882 Sand Hill Rd Ste 106, Menlo Park (94025-7057)
PHONE.................................617 225-4455
Robert Duggan, CEO
Erik Ostrowski, *
David Roblin, CMO*
Mahkam Zanganeh, *
**EMP:** 113 **EST:** 2014
**SALES (est):** 7.68MM **Privately Held**
Web: www.smmtx.com
**SIC: 2834** Pharmaceutical preparations

**(P-5681)**
**SUN TEN LABORATORIES INC**
9250 Jeronimo Rd, Irvine (92618-1905)
PHONE.................................949 587-1238
Hong-yen Hsu, Prin
**EMP:** 30 **EST:** 2016
**SALES (est):** 1.08MM **Privately Held**
Web: www.sunten.com
**SIC: 2834** Medicines, capsuled or ampuled

**(P-5682)**
**SURROZEN OPERATING INC (HQ)**
171 Oyster Point Blvd, South San Francisco (94080-1936)
PHONE.................................650 918-8818
Craig Parker, CEO
Tim Kutzkey, *
Charles Williams, *
**EMP:** 46 **EST:** 2015
**SALES (est):** 8.77MM **Publicly Held**
Web: www.surrozen.com
**SIC: 2834** Adrenal pharmaceutical preparations
PA: Surrozen, Inc.
   171 Oyster Pt Blvd Ste 30
   650 489-9000

**(P-5683)**
**SYNTHORX INC**
Also Called: Synthorx
11099 N Torrey Pines Rd Ste 190, La Jolla (92037-1029)
PHONE.................................858 352-5100
John Reed, Pr
Marie Debans, *
**EMP:** 38 **EST:** 2014
**SQ FT:** 8,636
**SALES (est):** 7.66MM **Publicly Held**
Web: www.synthorx.com
**SIC: 2834** 8731 Pharmaceutical preparations ; Biotechnical research, commercial
HQ: Aventis Inc.
   55 Corporate Dr
   Bridgewater NJ 08807

**(P-5684)**
**TALPHERA INC**
Also Called: Talphera
1850 Gateway Dr Ste 175, San Mateo (94404-4084)
PHONE.................................650 216-3500
Vincent J Angotti, CEO
Adrian Adams, Ch Bd
Raffi Asadorian, CFO
Shakil Aslam, CDO CMO
Badri Dasu, Chief Engineering Officer
**EMP:** 15 **EST:** 2005
**SQ FT:** 4,012
**SALES (est):** 651K **Privately Held**
Web: www.talphera.com
**SIC: 2834** Pharmaceutical preparations

**(P-5685)**
**TEIKOKU PHARMA USA INC (HQ)**
Also Called: Teikoku Pharma USA
1718 Ringwood Ave, San Jose (95131-1711)
PHONE.................................408 501-1800
Masahisa Kitagawa, Pr
Atsumu Matsushita, *
Ichiro Mori, *
Larry Caldwell, *
Tetsuto Nagata, *
▲ **EMP:** 51 **EST:** 1997
**SALES (est):** 16.21MM **Privately Held**
Web: www.teikokuusa.com
**SIC: 2834** Pharmaceutical preparations
PA: Teikoku Seiyaku Co.,Ltd.
   567, Sambommatsu

**(P-5686)**
**TEON THERAPEUTICS INC**
555 Twin Dolphin Dr Ste 120, Redwood City (94065-2129)
PHONE.................................650 832-1421
**EMP:** 16 **EST:** 2018
**SALES (est):** 1.39MM **Privately Held**
Web: www.teontherapeutics.com
**SIC: 2834** Pharmaceutical preparations

**(P-5687)**
**TERNS PHARMACEUTICALS INC (PA)**
1065 E Hillsdale Blvd Ste 100, Foster City (94404-1688)
PHONE.................................650 525-5535
Amy Burroughs, CEO
David Fellows, Ch Bd
Erin Quirk, Head OF Research & Development
Mark Vignola, CFO
Elona Kogan, CLO
**EMP:** 24 **EST:** 2016
**SQ FT:** 9,750
**SALES (est):** 8.69MM
**SALES (corp-wide):** 8.69MM **Publicly Held**
Web: www.ternspharma.com
**SIC: 2834** Pharmaceutical preparations

**(P-5688)**
**TEVA PARENTERAL MEDICINES INC**
19 Hughes, Irvine (92618-1902)
P.O. Box 57049 (92618)
PHONE.................................949 455-4700
Phillip Frost, Ch Bd
Amir Elstein, *
Karin Shanahan, *
Nir Baron, *
Iris Beck-codner, VP
▲ **EMP:** 830 **EST:** 1990
**SQ FT:** 148,000
**SALES (est):** 30.16MM **Privately Held**
**SIC: 2834** Pills, pharmaceutical
HQ: Teva Pharmaceuticals Usa, Inc.
   400 Interpace Pkwy Bldg A
   Parsippany NJ 07054
   215 591-3000

**(P-5689)**
**THERAVANCE BIOPHARMA US INC**
901 Gateway Blvd, South San Francisco (94080-7024)
PHONE.................................650 808-6000
Rick Winningham, CEO
**EMP:** 244 **EST:** 2013
**SALES (est):** 76.14MM **Privately Held**
Web: www.theravance.com
**SIC: 2834** Pharmaceutical preparations
PA: Theravance Biopharma Inc
   C/O Maples Corporate Services Ltd

**(P-5690)**
**TIANCHENG INTL INC USA**
2851 E Philadelphia St, Ontario (91761-8553)
PHONE.................................909 947-5577
Lizhe Zhang, CEO
Zhang Guoji, Ch Bd
▲ **EMP:** 15 **EST:** 2000
**SQ FT:** 25,000
**SALES (est):** 1.76MM **Privately Held**

# PRODUCTS & SERVICES SECTION
## 2834 - Pharmaceutical Preparations (P-5710)

Web: tianchengusa.lookchem.com
SIC: 2834 Pharmaceutical preparations
PA: Tianjin Tiancheng Pharmaceutical Co.,Ltd.
No.9 Liuming Road, Yangliuqing Town, Xiqing District

### (P-5691)
### TITAN MEDICAL ENTERPRISES INC
Also Called: US Apothecary Crown Labs
11100 Greenstone Ave, Santa Fe Springs (90670-4640)
PHONE..................................562 903-7236
James L Mcdaniel, Pr
James Mcdaniel, Pr
EMP: 15 EST: 1990
SQ FT: 12,000
SALES (est): 406.13K Privately Held
SIC: 2834 Vitamin preparations

### (P-5692)
### TOTUS MEDICINES INC
1480 64th St, Emeryville (94608-1183)
PHONE..................................510 501-4832
Nassim Usman, CEO
EMP: 33 EST: 2019
SALES (est): 8.82MM Privately Held
Web: www.totusmedicines.com
SIC: 2834 Pharmaceutical preparations

### (P-5693)
### TRAVERE THERAPEUTICS INC (PA)
Also Called: TRAVERE
3611 Valley Centre Dr Ste 300, San Diego (92130-3331)
PHONE..................................888 969-7879
Eric Dube, Pr
Gary Lyons, Ch Bd
Christopher Cline, CFO
Peter Heerma, CCO
Elizabeth E Reed, Corporate Secretary
EMP: 331 EST: 2008
SQ FT: 149,123
SALES (est): 145.24MM Publicly Held
Web: www.travere.com
SIC: 2834 8731 Pharmaceutical preparations ; Biotechnical research, commercial

### (P-5694)
### TRIUS THERAPEUTICS LLC
4747 Executive Dr Ste 1100, San Diego (92121-3114)
PHONE..................................858 452-0370
Jeffrey Stein, Pr
John P Schmid, *
Michael Morneau, CAO*
Kenneth Bartizal, Chief Development Officer*
John Finn, *
EMP: 152 EST: 2007
SQ FT: 39,000
SALES (est): 4.15MM
SALES (corp-wide): 60.12B Publicly Held
Web: www.triusrx.com
SIC: 2834 Antibiotics, packaged
HQ: Cubist Pharmaceuticals Llc
2000 Galloping Hill Road
Kenilworth NJ 07033

### (P-5695)
### TRUEPILL INC (PA)
3121 Diablo Ave, Hayward (94545-2701)
PHONE..................................855 910-8606
Paul Greenall, CEO
Lorraine Guzman, Contrlr
EMP: 19 EST: 2019
SALES (est): 22.18MM
SALES (corp-wide): 22.18MM Privately Held
Web: www.truepill.com
SIC: 2834 Pharmaceutical preparations

### (P-5696)
### TYRA BIOSCIENCES INC
Also Called: TYRA
2656 State St, Carlsbad (92008-1626)
PHONE..................................619 728-4760
Todd Harris, Pr
Robert More, *
Daniel Bensen, COO
Alan Fuhrman, CFO
Hiroomi Tada, CMO
EMP: 49 EST: 2018
SQ FT: 4,734
Web: www.tyra.bio
SIC: 2834 Pharmaceutical preparations

### (P-5697)
### ULTRAGENYX PHARMACEUTICAL INC (PA)
Also Called: ULTRAGENYX
60 Leveroni Ct, Novato (94949-5746)
PHONE..................................415 483-8800
Emil D Kakkis, Pr
Daniel G Welch, *
Mardi C Dier, Ex VP
Dennis Huang, Chief Technician
Karah Parschauer, CLO
EMP: 1045 EST: 2010
SALES (est): 434.25MM Publicly Held
Web: www.ultragenyx.com
SIC: 2834 Pharmaceutical preparations

### (P-5698)
### UNITED PHARMA LLC
2317 Moore Ave, Fullerton (92833-2510)
PHONE..................................714 738-8999
Bill Wang, Pr
▲ EMP: 130 EST: 2006
SQ FT: 53,000
SALES (est): 25.22MM Privately Held
Web: www.unitedpharmallc.com
SIC: 2834 Pharmaceutical preparations

### (P-5699)
### UNIVERSAL PRTEIN SPPLMNTS CORP
3441 Gato Ct, Riverside (92507-6800)
PHONE..................................732 545-3130
Michael Rockoff, Pr
EMP: 18
SALES (corp-wide): 41.1MM Privately Held
Web: www.universalusa.com
SIC: 2834 2032 Vitamin, nutrient, and hematinic preparations for human use; Canned specialties
PA: Universal Protein Supplements Corporation
3 Terminal Rd
732 545-3130

### (P-5700)
### VALITOR INC
2956 San Pablo Ave, Berkeley (94702-2471)
PHONE..................................510 813-8611
Wesley Jackson, Pr
EMP: 15 EST: 2010
SALES (est): 4.31MM Privately Held
Web: www.valitorbio.com
SIC: 2834 Pharmaceutical preparations

### (P-5701)
### VALOR COMPOUNDING PHARMACY INC
Also Called: Valor Compounding Pharmacy
2461 Shattuck Ave, Berkeley (94704)
PHONE..................................855 554-2889
Rick Niemi, CEO
EMP: 55 EST: 2016
SALES (est): 10.7MM Privately Held
Web: www.valorcompounding.com
SIC: 2834 Druggists' preparations (pharmaceuticals)

### (P-5702)
### VAXART INC (PA)
Also Called: VAXART
170 Harbor Way Ste 300, South San Francisco (94080-6102)
PHONE..................................650 550-3500
Steven Lo, Pr
Michael J Finney, Ch Bd
Phillip E Lee, CAO
James Cummings, CMO
Sean N Tucker, CSO
EMP: 31 EST: 1969
SALES (est): 7.38MM
SALES (corp-wide): 7.38MM Publicly Held
Web: www.vaxart.com
SIC: 2834 2836 Pharmaceutical preparations ; Vaccines and other immunizing products

### (P-5703)
### VERA THERAPEUTICS INC (PA)
8000 Marina Blvd Ste 120, Brisbane (94005-1881)
PHONE..................................650 770-0077
Marshall Fordyce, Pr
Michael M Morrissey, Ch Bd
David Johnson, COO
Sean Grant, CFO
Robert Brenner, CMO
EMP: 49 EST: 2016
SQ FT: 24,606
Web: www.veratx.com
SIC: 2834 8731 Pharmaceutical preparations ; Biological research

### (P-5704)
### VERSEON CORPORATION (PA)
47000 Warm Springs Blvd Ste 3, Fremont (94539-7467)
PHONE..................................510 225-9000
Adityo Prakash, Pr
Eniko Fodor, COO
David Kita, VP
Kevin Short, Dir
David Williams, Dir
EMP: 27 EST: 2002
SALES (est): 5.86MM Privately Held
Web: www.verseon.com
SIC: 2834 Druggists' preparations (pharmaceuticals)

### (P-5705)
### VERSEON INTERNATIONAL CORP (PA)
47000 Warm Springs Blvd Ste 3, Fremont (94539-7467)
PHONE..................................510 225-9000
Adityo Prakash, CEO
Eniko Fodor, COO
EMP: 20 EST: 2020
SALES (est): 1.56MM
SALES (corp-wide): 1.56MM Privately Held
SIC: 2834 Pharmaceutical preparations

### (P-5706)
### VERTEX PHRMCTCALS SAN DEGO LLC (HQ)
3215 Merryfield Row, San Diego (92121-1126)
PHONE..................................858 404-6600
Joshua S Boger, Managing Member
Ian F Smith, *
▲ EMP: 235 EST: 2001
SQ FT: 81,000
SALES (est): 32.85MM Publicly Held
Web: www.vrtx.com
SIC: 2834 Pharmaceutical preparations
PA: Vertex Pharmaceuticals Incorporated
50 Northern Ave

### (P-5707)
### VIKING THERAPEUTICS INC (PA)
9920 Pacific Heights Blvd Ste 350, San Diego (92121-4306)
PHONE..................................858 704-4660
Brian Lian, Pr
Lawson Macartney, Ch Bd
Marianne Mancini, COO
Greg Zante, CFO
EMP: 26 EST: 2012
SQ FT: 7,940
Web: www.vikingtherapeutics.com
SIC: 2834 Pharmaceutical preparations

### (P-5708)
### VINCERX PHARMA INC (PA)
260 Sheridan Ave Ste 400, Palo Alto (94306-2011)
PHONE..................................650 800-6676
Ahmed M Hamdy, Ch Bd
Raquel E Izumi, Pr
Alexander A Seelenberger, CFO
Tom C Thomas, CLO
EMP: 17 EST: 2020
SALES (est): 9.53MM
SALES (corp-wide): 9.53MM Publicly Held
Web: www.vincerx.com
SIC: 2834 Pharmaceutical preparations

### (P-5709)
### VIRACTA THERAPEUTICS INC (PA)
Also Called: VIRACTA
2533 S Coast Highway 101 Ste 210, Cardiff (92007-2133)
PHONE..................................858 400-8470
Mark Rothera, Pr
Roger Pomerantz, Ch Bd
Melody Burcar, VP Fin
Michael Faerm, CFO
Darrel Cohen, Chief Medical Officer
EMP: 35 EST: 1998
SQ FT: 5,337
SALES (est): 4.09MM
SALES (corp-wide): 4.09MM Publicly Held
Web: www.sunesis.com
SIC: 2834 Pharmaceutical preparations

### (P-5710)
### VISTAGEN THERAPEUTICS INC (PA)
Also Called: VISTAGEN
343 Allerton Ave, South San Francisco (94080-4816)
PHONE..................................650 577-3600
Shawn K Singh, CEO
Jon S Saxe, Ch Bd
H Ralph Snodgrass, CSO
Mark A Smith, CMO
Jerrold D Dotson, Corporate Secretary
EMP: 30 EST: 1998
SQ FT: 10,900
SALES (est): 1.06MM Publicly Held
Web: www.vistagen.com
SIC: 2834 8731 Pharmaceutical preparations ; Biological research

(PA)=Parent Co (HQ)=Headquarters
✿ = New Business established in last 2 years

# 2834 - Pharmaceutical Preparations (P-5711)

**(P-5711)**
**VITABEST NUTRITION INC (HQ)**
Also Called: Vit Best
2802 Dow Ave, Tustin (92780)
PHONE..................................714 832-9700
Gale Bensussen, *Pr*
Toni Clubb, *CFO*
Bing Jiang, *Sec*
**EMP:** 16 **EST:** 2015
**SQ FT:** 200,000
**SALES (est):** 46.16MM **Privately Held**
**Web:** www.vit-best.com
**SIC: 2834** Vitamin preparations
**PA:** Xiamen Kingdomway Group Company
Xinyang Industrial Zone, Haicang

**(P-5712)**
**VITATECH NUTRITIONAL SCIENCES INC**
2802 Dow Ave, Tustin (92780-7212)
PHONE..................................714 832-9700
▲ **EMP:** 285
**SIC: 2834** Vitamin preparations

**(P-5713)**
**VIVUS LLC (PA)**
Also Called: Vivus
900 E Hamilton Ave Ste 550, Campbell (95008-0643)
PHONE..................................650 934-5200
John P Amos, *CEO*
David Y Norton, *
Mark K Oki, *CAO*
Santosh T Varghese, *CMO*
John L Slebir, *
**EMP:** 49 **EST:** 1991
**SQ FT:** 13,981
**SALES (est):** 69.76MM **Privately Held**
**Web:** www.vivus.com
**SIC: 2834** Druggists' preparations (pharmaceuticals)

**(P-5714)**
**WACKER BIOTECH US INC**
10390 Pacific Center Ct, San Diego (92121-4340)
PHONE..................................858 875-4700
Doctor Philippe Cronet, *CEO*
Keith Hall, *
**EMP:** 24 **EST:** 2018
**SQ FT:** 68,400
**SALES (est):** 9.07MM
**SALES (corp-wide):** 6.96B **Privately Held**
**Web:** www.wacker.com
**SIC: 2834** Pharmaceutical preparations
**HQ:** Wacker Chemical Corporation
3301 Sutton Rd
Adrian MI 49221
517 264-8500

**(P-5715)**
**WAKUNAGA OF AMERICA CO LTD (HQ)**
Also Called: Kyolic
23501 Madero, Mission Viejo (92691-2744)
PHONE..................................949 855-2776
Kazuhiko Nomura, *Pr*
Hiyoshi Sakai, *
◆ **EMP:** 64 **EST:** 1972
**SQ FT:** 36,000
**SALES (est):** 31.86MM **Privately Held**
**Web:** www.kyolic.com
**SIC: 2834** Pharmaceutical preparations
**PA:** Wakunaga Pharmaceutical Co., Ltd.
13-4, Arakicho

**(P-5716)**
**WEDGEWOOD CONNECT**
Also Called: Leiter's Compounding
17 Great Oaks Blvd, San Jose (95119-1359)
PHONE..................................855 321-3477
Paul Yamamoto, *Managing Member*
Paul Yamamoto, *VP*
Jim Cunniff, *
Charles Leiter, *
**EMP:** 50 **EST:** 2020
**SALES (est):** 9.33MM **Privately Held**
**Web:** www.wedgewood.com
**SIC: 2834** Druggists' preparations (pharmaceuticals)

**(P-5717)**
**WEST COAST LABORATORIES INC**
156 E 162nd St, Gardena (90248-2802)
PHONE..................................310 527-6163
Maurice Ovadia, *Mgr*
**EMP:** 35
**SQ FT:** 4,000
**SALES (corp-wide):** 10.66MM **Privately Held**
**Web:** www.westcoastlabsinc.com
**SIC: 2834** Vitamin preparations
**PA:** West Coast Laboratories, Inc.
116 E Alondra Blvd
323 321-4774

**(P-5718)**
**WEST COAST LABORATORIES INC (PA)**
116 E Alondra Blvd, Gardena (90248-2806)
PHONE..................................323 321-4774
Maurice Ovadia, *Pr*
Naim Abdullah, *VP*
Jamil Shad, *Treas*
Anwar Abdullah, *Sec*
**EMP:** 15 **EST:** 1967
**SQ FT:** 4,000
**SALES (est):** 10.66MM
**SALES (corp-wide):** 10.66MM **Privately Held**
**Web:** www.westcoastlabsinc.com
**SIC: 2834** Vitamin preparations

**(P-5719)**
**WRIGHT PHARMA INC**
700 Kiernan Ave Ste A, Modesto (95356-9329)
PHONE..................................209 549-9771
Eric Fogleman, *Brnch Mgr*
**EMP:** 20
**SALES (corp-wide):** 6.74MM **Privately Held**
**Web:** www.thewrightgroup.net
**SIC: 2834** 2023 Pharmaceutical preparations; Dietary supplements, dairy and non-dairy based
**PA:** Wright Pharma, Inc.
201 Energy Pkwy Ste 400
337 783-3096

**(P-5720)**
**XENCOR INC**
Also Called: Xencor
465 N Halstead St Ste 200, Pasadena (91107-3291)
PHONE..................................626 305-5900
Bassil I Dahiyat, *Pr*
John R Desjarlais, *CSO*
Nancy K Valente, *CDO*
Bart Jan Cornelissen, *Sr VP*
Celia E Eckert, *Corporate Secretary*
**EMP:** 256 **EST:** 1997
**SQ FT:** 83,083
**SALES (est):** 168.34MM **Privately Held**
**Web:** www.xencor.com
**SIC: 2834** Pharmaceutical preparations

**(P-5721)**
**YOUCARE PHARMA (USA) INC**
132 Business Center Dr, Corona (92878-3224)
P.O. Box 668 (92878-0668)
PHONE..................................951 258-3114
Weishi Yu, *CEO*
**EMP:** 60 **EST:** 2015
**SQ FT:** 160,000
**SALES (est):** 2.43MM **Privately Held**
**SIC: 2834** Pharmaceutical preparations
**PA:** Youcare Pharmaceutical Group Co., Ltd
No. 6, Hongda Middle Road, Economic And Technological Area

**(P-5722)**
**ZOETIS INC**
30411 Whipple Rd, Union City (94587-1531)
PHONE..................................510 474-9259
**EMP:** 152
**SALES (corp-wide):** 8.54B **Publicly Held**
**Web:** www.zoetis.com
**SIC: 2834** Pharmaceutical preparations
**PA:** Zoetis Inc.
10 Sylvan Way
973 822-7000

**(P-5723)**
**ZOGENIX INC (HQ)**
Also Called: Zogenix
5959 Horton St Ste 500, Emeryville (94608-2120)
PHONE..................................510 550-8300
Stephen J Farr, *Pr*
Cam L Garner, *Ch Bd*
Michael P Smith, *Ex VP*
Bradley S Galer, *CMO*
Gail M Farfel, *CDO*
**EMP:** 23 **EST:** 2006
**SQ FT:** 37,307
**SALES (est):** 42.88MM
**SALES (corp-wide):** 1.04B **Privately Held**
**Web:** www.ucb-usa.com
**SIC: 2834** Pharmaceutical preparations
**PA:** U C B
Allee De La Recherche 60
25599999

**(P-5724)**
**ZOSANO PHARMA CORPORATION (PA)**
Also Called: Zosano Pharma
34790 Ardentech Ct, Fremont (94555-3657)
PHONE..................................510 745-1200
Steven Lo, *Pr*
John P Walker, *
Christine Matthews, *CFO*
Hayley Lewis, *VP Opers*
Donald Kellerman, *Vice-President Clinical Development*
**EMP:** 36 **EST:** 2012
**SALES (est):** 785K
**SALES (corp-wide):** 785K **Privately Held**
**Web:** www.zosanopharma.com
**SIC: 2834** Pharmaceutical preparations

**(P-5725)**
**ZP OPCO INC**
Also Called: Zosano
34790 Ardentech Ct, Los Angeles (90071-3152)
PHONE..................................510 745-1200
Konstantinos Alataris, *CEO*
Konstantinos Alataris, *Pr*
Winnie W Tso, *CFO*
**EMP:** 32 **EST:** 2006
**SALES (est):** 448.57K
**SALES (corp-wide):** 785K **Privately Held**
**SIC: 2834** Pharmaceutical preparations
**PA:** Zosano Pharma Corporation
34790 Ardentech Ct
510 745-1200

**(P-5726)**
**ZS PHARMA INC**
1100 Park Pl Fl 3, San Mateo (94403-1599)
PHONE..................................650 753-1823
**EMP:** 43 **EST:** 2017
**SALES (est):** 3.41MM
**SALES (corp-wide):** 45.81B **Privately Held**
**Web:** www.zspharma.com
**SIC: 2834** Pharmaceutical preparations
**PA:** Astrazeneca Plc
1 Francis Crick Avenue
203 749-5000

## 2835 Diagnostic Substances

**(P-5727)**
**ABBOTT DIABETES CARE INC (HQ)**
Also Called: Medisense
1360 S Loop Rd, Alameda (94502-7000)
PHONE..................................855 632-8658
Jared Watkin, *CEO*
Tara Kaesebier, *
Robert Funck, *
▲ **EMP:** 250 **EST:** 1995
**SQ FT:** 54,500
**SALES (est):** 131.84MM
**SALES (corp-wide):** 40.11B **Publicly Held**
**Web:** www.abbott.com
**SIC: 2835** 3845 3823 In vitro diagnostics; Electromedical equipment; Process control instruments
**PA:** Abbott Laboratories
100 Abbott Park Rd
224 667-6100

**(P-5728)**
**ACON LABORATORIES INC (PA)**
9440 Carroll Park Dr, San Diego (92121-5201)
PHONE..................................858 875-8000
Jinn-nan Lin, *Pr*
▲ **EMP:** 46 **EST:** 1999
**SQ FT:** 36,000
**SALES (est):** 19.24MM **Privately Held**
**Web:** www.aconlabs.com
**SIC: 2835** Diagnostic substances

**(P-5729)**
**ACROMETRIX CORPORATION**
46500 Kato Rd, Fremont (94538-7310)
PHONE..................................707 746-8888
**EMP:** 45
**Web:** www.acrometrix.com
**SIC: 2835** Diagnostic substances

**(P-5730)**
**ADEZA BIOMEDICAL CORPORATION**
1240 Elko Dr, Sunnyvale (94089-2212)
PHONE..................................408 745-6491
Emory V Anderson, *Pr*
Andrew E Senyei, *Ch Bd*
Mark D Fischer Colbrie, *VP Fin*
Marian E Sacco, *Marketing*
**EMP:** 613 **EST:** 1985
**SQ FT:** 22,600
**SALES (est):** 1.42MM
**SALES (corp-wide):** 4.03B **Publicly Held**
**Web:** www.healthdxs.com
**SIC: 2835** Pregnancy test kits
**HQ:** Cytyc Corporation
250 Campus Dr

## PRODUCTS & SERVICES SECTION
## 2835 - Diagnostic Substances (P-5752)

Marlborough MA 01752

**(P-5731)**
**ALERE INC**
9975 Summers Ridge Rd, San Diego (92121-2997)
PHONE..............................858 805-2000
Sabina Roaldset, *Brnch Mgr*
EMP: 54
SALES (corp-wide): 40.11B **Publicly Held**
Web: www.globalpointofcare.abbott
SIC: **2835** Diagnostic substances
HQ: Alere Inc.
51 Sawyer Rd Ste 200
Waltham MA 02453
781 647-3900

**(P-5732)**
**ALERE INC**
Also Called: Alere of San Diego
5995 Pacific Center Blvd Ste 108, San Diego (92121-6309)
PHONE..............................858 805-3810
EMP: 17
SALES (corp-wide): 40.11B **Publicly Held**
Web: www.globalpointofcare.abbott
SIC: **2835** Diagnostic substances
HQ: Alere Inc.
51 Sawyer Rd Ste 200
Waltham MA 02453
781 647-3900

**(P-5733)**
**ALERE SAN DIEGO INC**
Also Called: Immunalysis
829 Towne Center Dr, Pomona (91767-5901)
PHONE..............................909 482-0840
Bob Funck, *Brnch Mgr*
EMP: 453
SALES (corp-wide): 40.11B **Publicly Held**
Web: www.globalpointofcare.abbott
SIC: **2835** 3841 Diagnostic substances; Diagnostic apparatus, medical
HQ: Alere San Diego, Inc.
9942 Mesa Rim Rd
San Diego CA 92121
858 805-2000

**(P-5734)**
**ALERE SAN DIEGO INC (DH)**
9942 Mesa Rim Rd, San Diego (92121-2910)
PHONE..............................858 805-2000
Christopher Scoggins, *CEO*
Karen Peterson, *
▲ EMP: 97 EST: 1988
SQ FT: 350,000
SALES (est): 92.79MM
SALES (corp-wide): 40.11B **Publicly Held**
Web: www.globalpointofcare.abbott
SIC: **2835** Diagnostic substances
HQ: Alere Inc.
51 Sawyer Rd Ste 200
Waltham MA 02453
781 647-3900

**(P-5735)**
**ALERE SAN DIEGO INC**
828 Towne Center Dr, Pomona (91767-5900)
PHONE..............................858 805-2000
EMP: 453
SALES (corp-wide): 40.11B **Publicly Held**
Web: www.globalpointofcare.abbott
SIC: **2835** In vitro diagnostics
HQ: Alere San Diego, Inc.
9942 Mesa Rim Rd
San Diego CA 92121
858 805-2000

**(P-5736)**
**ALFA SCIENTIFIC DESIGNS INC**
13200 Gregg St, Poway (92064-7121)
PHONE..............................858 513-3888
Chai Bunyagidj, *CEO*
Chai Bunyagidj, *Pr*
Naishu Wang, *
Angela Shen, *
Claudia Shen, *
▲ EMP: 94 EST: 1996
SQ FT: 39,000
SALES (est): 18.89MM **Privately Held**
Web: www.alfascientific.com
SIC: **2835** Diagnostic substances

**(P-5737)**
**ANAEROBE SYSTEMS**
15906 Concord Cir, Morgan Hill (95037-5451)
PHONE..............................408 782-7557
EMP: 20 EST: 1978
SALES (est): 4.64MM **Privately Held**
Web: www.anaerobesystems.com
SIC: **2835** Microbiology and virology diagnostic products

**(P-5738)**
**ANTIBODIES INCORPORATED**
25242 County Road 95, Davis (95616-9405)
P.O. Box 1560 (95617-1560)
PHONE..............................800 824-8540
Richard Krogsrud, *Pr*
EMP: 18 EST: 1962
SQ FT: 23,000
SALES (est): 4.49MM **Privately Held**
Web: www.antibodiesinc.com
SIC: **2835** 2836 Diagnostic substances; Serums

**(P-5739)**
**BIOCARE MEDICAL LLC (PA)**
60 Berry Dr, Pacheco (94553-5601)
PHONE..............................925 603-8000
Luis De Luzuriaga, *CEO*
Jamie Conroy, *
▼ EMP: 130 EST: 1997
SQ FT: 51,000
SALES (est): 49.89MM **Privately Held**
Web: www.biocare.net
SIC: **2835** 3841 5047 Diagnostic substances; Diagnostic apparatus, medical; Diagnostic equipment, medical

**(P-5740)**
**BIOCELL LABORATORIES INC**
2001 E University Dr, Rancho Dominguez (90220-6411)
PHONE..............................310 537-3300
▲ EMP: 35 EST: 1972
SALES (est): 2.53MM **Privately Held**
Web: www.biocell.com
SIC: **2835** 2836 Diagnostic substances; Biological products, except diagnostic

**(P-5741)**
**BIOMERICA INC (PA)**
Also Called: BIOMERICA
17571 Von Karman Ave, Irvine (92614-6207)
PHONE..............................949 645-2111
Zackary Irani, *CEO*
Allen Barbieri, *Executive Vice Chairman of the Board*
Gary Lu, *CAO*
Jack Kenny, *Ch Bd*
▲ EMP: 16 EST: 1971
SQ FT: 22,000
SALES (est): 5.42MM
SALES (corp-wide): 5.42MM **Publicly Held**
Web: www.biomerica.com
SIC: **2835** Diagnostic substances

**(P-5742)**
**BIOSERV CORPORATION**
Also Called: Bioserve
9380 Judicial Dr, San Diego (92121)
PHONE..............................917 817-1326
Henry Ji Ph.d., *Pr*
Kevin Herde, *
EMP: 27 EST: 2016
SALES (est): 5MM
SALES (corp-wide): 62.84MM **Publicly Held**
Web: www.bioservamerica.com
SIC: **2835** 2834 Diagnostic substances; Pharmaceutical preparations
PA: Sorrento Therapeutics, Inc.
4955 Directors Pl
858 203-4100

**(P-5743)**
**BIOSOURCE INTERNATIONAL INC**
5791 Van Allen Way, Carlsbad (92008-7321)
PHONE..............................805 659-5759
Terrance J Bieker, *Pr*
Alan Edrick, *Ex VP*
Kevin J Reagan Ph.d., *Executive Technical Vice President*
Jean-pierre L Conte, *Ch Bd*
Jozef Vangenechten, *Executive Commercial Vice President*
EMP: 30 EST: 1989
SQ FT: 51,821
SALES (est): 1.39MM **Privately Held**
SIC: **2835** Diagnostic substances

**(P-5744)**
**C S BIO CO**
20 Kelly Ct Ste 127, Menlo Park (94025-1418)
PHONE..............................650 322-1111
Jason Chang, *Pr*
EMP: 75
Web: www.csbio.com
SIC: **2835** Diagnostic substances
PA: C S Bio Co.
20 Kelly Ct

**(P-5745)**
**CELL MARQUE CORPORATION**
6600 Sierra College Blvd, Rocklin (95677-4306)
PHONE..............................916 746-8900
Nora Lacey, *Pr*
Paul Ardi, *
David Zembo, *
EMP: 42 EST: 1994
SALES (est): 12.81MM
SALES (corp-wide): 22.82B **Privately Held**
Web: www.cellmarque.com
SIC: **2835** Diagnostic substances
HQ: Sigma-Aldrich Corporation
3050 Spruce St
Saint Louis MO 63103
314 771-5765

**(P-5746)**
**DANISCO US INC (HQ)**
Also Called: Genencor International
925 Page Mill Rd, Palo Alto (94304-1013)
PHONE..............................650 846-7500
James C Collins, *CEO*
Mark A Goldsmith, *
◆ EMP: 200 EST: 1989
SQ FT: 128,000
SALES (est): 532.49MM
SALES (corp-wide): 11.48B **Publicly Held**

SIC: **2835** 8731 2899 2869 Diagnostic substances; Commercial physical research; Chemical preparations, nec; Industrial organic chemicals, nec
PA: International Flavors & Fragrances Inc.
521 W 57th St
212 765-5500

**(P-5747)**
**DERMTECH INC (PA)**
12340 El Camino Real, San Diego (92130-3078)
PHONE..............................866 450-4223
Bret Christensen, *Pr*
Matthew Posard, *Non-Executive Chairman of the Board*
Kevin Sun, *CFO*
Claudia Ibarra, *COO*
Todd Wood, *Chief Commercial Officer*
EMP: 207 EST: 1995
SQ FT: 28,655
SALES (est): 15.3MM
SALES (corp-wide): 15.3MM **Publicly Held**
Web: www.dermtechstratum.com
SIC: **2835** 8071 Diagnostic substances; Testing laboratories

**(P-5748)**
**DIADEXUS INC**
349 Oyster Point Blvd, South San Francisco (94080-1947)
PHONE..............................650 246-6400
EMP: 38
Web: www.diazyme.com
SIC: **2835** In vitro diagnostics

**(P-5749)**
**DIASORIN MOLECULAR LLC**
11331 Valley View St, Cypress (90630-5300)
PHONE..............................562 240-6500
Carlo Rosa, *CEO*
EMP: 200 EST: 2016
SALES (est): 34.34MM **Privately Held**
Web: int.diasorin.com
SIC: **2835** 5047 In vitro diagnostics; Diagnostic equipment, medical
HQ: Diasorin Inc.
1951 Northwestern Ave
Stillwater MN 55082
651 439-9710

**(P-5750)**
**EPICUREN DISCOVERY**
31 Journey Ste 100, Aliso Viejo (92656-3334)
PHONE..............................949 588-5807
Colleen Lohrman, *Pr*
▲ EMP: 65 EST: 1999
SALES (est): 8.7MM **Privately Held**
Web: www.epicuren.com
SIC: **2835** Enzyme and isoenzyme diagnostic agents

**(P-5751)**
**FREENOME INC**
279 E Grand Ave, South San Francisco (94080-4804)
PHONE..............................650 446-6630
Gabriel Otte, *Pr*
Riley Ennis, *
EMP: 506 EST: 2015
SALES (est): 41.09MM **Privately Held**
Web: www.freenome.com
SIC: **2835** Blood derivative diagnostic agents

**(P-5752)**
**GATE BIOSCIENCE INC**
2000 Sierra Point Pkwy Ste 200, Brisbane (94005-1846)

## 2835 - Diagnostic Substances (P-5753)

PHONE.....................650 241-8057
Jordi Mata-fink, *CEO*
**EMP:** 42 **EST:** 2021
**SALES (est):** 6.85MM **Privately Held**
**SIC: 2835** Microbiology and virology diagnostic products

**(P-5753)**
**GATEWAY GENOMICS LLC**
11436 Sorrento Valley Rd, San Diego (92121-1350)
P.O. Box 99129 (92169-1129)
PHONE.....................858 886-7250
Christopher Jacob, *CEO*
**EMP:** 53 **EST:** 2018
**SALES (est):** 3.67MM **Publicly Held**
Web: www.myriad.com
**SIC: 2835** Microbiology and virology diagnostic products
**PA:** Myriad Genetics, Inc.
322 North 2200 West

**(P-5754)**
**GEN-PROBE INCORPORATED**
10210 Genetic Center Dr, San Diego (92121-4394)
PHONE.....................858 410-8000
**EMP:** 74
**SALES (corp-wide):** 4.03B **Publicly Held**
Web: www.gen-probe.com
**SIC: 2835** In vitro diagnostics
**HQ:** Gen-Probe Incorporated
250 Campus Dr
Marlborough MA 01752
508 263-8937

**(P-5755)**
**HELICA BIOSYSTEMS INC**
3310 W Macarthur Blvd, Santa Ana (92704-6804)
PHONE.....................714 578-7830
Wondu Wolde Mariam, *Pr*
**EMP:** 17 **EST:** 1999
**SQ FT:** 7,500
**SALES (est):** 1.98MM **Privately Held**
Web: www.helica.com
**SIC: 2835** 2836 In vitro diagnostics; Biological products, except diagnostic

**(P-5756)**
**IMMUNOSCIENCE LLC**
6780 Sierra Ct Ste M, Dublin (94568-2630)
P.O. Box 3279 (94526-9479)
PHONE.....................925 400-6055
**EMP:** 57
**SALES (corp-wide):** 2.41MM **Privately Held**
**SIC: 2835** Microbiology and virology diagnostic products
**PA:** Immunoscience, Llc
6780 Sierra Ct Ste M
925 460-8111

**(P-5757)**
**INOVA DIAGNOSTICS INC**
9675 Businesspark Ave, San Diego (92131-1644)
PHONE.....................858 586-9900
Roger Ingles, *Brnch Mgr*
**EMP:** 143
Web: www.werfen.com
**SIC: 2835** Diagnostic substances
**HQ:** Inova Diagnostics, Inc.
9900 Old Grove Rd
San Diego CA 92131
858 586-9900

**(P-5758)**
**JANE NEXTGEN INC**
400 29th St Ste 105, Oakland (94609-3546)

PHONE.....................415 722-2226
Ridhi Tariyal, *Sec*
Ridhi Tariyal, *CEO*
Stephen Gire, *Pr*
Linda Giudice, *Bd of Dir*
William Crowley, *Bd of Dir*
**EMP:** 16 **EST:** 2015
**SALES (est):** 6.34MM **Privately Held**
Web: www.nextgenjane.com
**SIC: 2835** Microbiology and virology diagnostic products

**(P-5759)**
**LEHMAN MILLET INCORPORATED**
Also Called: Leham Millet West
3 Macarthur Pl Ste 700, Santa Ana (92707-6078)
PHONE.....................714 850-7900
Bruce Lehman, *CEO*
**EMP:** 49
**SALES (corp-wide):** 15.2MM **Privately Held**
Web: www.precisioneffect.com
**SIC: 2835** Diagnostic substances
**HQ:** Lehman Millet Incorporated
101 Tremont St Ste 205
Boston MA 02108
617 722-0019

**(P-5760)**
**LIFE TECHNOLOGIES CORPORATION (HQ)**
Also Called: Thermo Fisher Scientific
5781 Van Allen Way, Carlsbad (92008-7321)
P.O. Box 1039 (92018-1039)
PHONE.....................760 603-7200
Seth Hoogasian, *CEO*
Mark P Stevenson, *
John A Cottingham, *CLO*
◆ **EMP:** 140 **EST:** 1997
**SALES (est):** 888.72MM
**SALES (corp-wide):** 42.86B **Publicly Held**
Web: www.thermofisher.com
**SIC: 2835** 2836 Diagnostic substances; Biological products, except diagnostic
**PA:** Thermo Fisher Scientific Inc.
168 3rd Ave
781 622-1000

**(P-5761)**
**LUCIRA HEALTH INC**
Also Called: Lucira Health
1315 63rd St, Emeryville (94608-2103)
PHONE.....................510 350-7162
Erik T Engelson, *Pr*
**EMP:** 57 **EST:** 2013
**SALES (est):** 8.75MM **Privately Held**
Web: www.lucirabypfizer.com
**SIC: 2835** Diagnostic substances

**(P-5762)**
**METRA BIOSYSTEMS INC (DH)**
2981 Copper Rd, Santa Clara (95051-0716)
PHONE.....................408 616-4300
John Tamerius, *Genl Mgr*
Bill Sommer, *
**EMP:** 50 **EST:** 1990
**SQ FT:** 24,000
**SALES (est):** 1.25MM
**SALES (corp-wide):** 3B **Publicly Held**
**SIC: 2835** Diagnostic substances
**HQ:** Quidel Corporation
9975 Summers Ridge Rd
San Diego CA 92121
858 552-1100

**(P-5763)**
**MICROPOINT BIOSCIENCE INC**
3521 Leonard Ct, Santa Clara (95054-2043)
PHONE.....................408 588-1682
Nan Zhang, *CEO*
▲ **EMP:** 30 **EST:** 2007
**SALES (est):** 4.02MM **Privately Held**
Web: www.micropointbio.com
**SIC: 2835** Diagnostic substances
**PA:** Micropoint Biotechnologies,Co.,Ltd.
5f, Building 1, Runheng Dingfeng Industrial Park, Liuxian 2nd Rd

**(P-5764)**
**MINDRAY DS USA INC**
Also Called: Mindray Innvtion Ctr Slcon Vly
2100 Gold St, San Jose (95002-3700)
PHONE.....................650 230-2800
**EMP:** 4025
Web: www.mindray.com
**SIC: 2835** 3841 3845 In vitro diagnostics; Surgical and medical instruments; Patient monitoring apparatus, nec
**HQ:** Mindray Ds Usa, Inc.
800 Macarthur Blvd
Mahwah NJ 07430

**(P-5765)**
**MOLECULAR PROBES INC**
5781 Van Allen Way, Carlsbad (92008-7321)
PHONE.....................760 603-7200
**EMP:** 31
**SALES (corp-wide):** 42.86B **Publicly Held**
**SIC: 2835** Diagnostic substances
**HQ:** Molecular Probes, Inc.
29851 Willow Creek Rd
Eugene OR 97402
760 603-7200

**(P-5766)**
**MONOCENT INC**
Also Called: Monocent
8920 Quartz Ave, Northridge (91324-3339)
PHONE.....................424 310-0777
Shervin Taheri, *CEO*
**EMP:** 18 **EST:** 2019
**SALES (est):** 2.74MM **Privately Held**
Web: www.monocent.com
**SIC: 2835** In vitro diagnostics

**(P-5767)**
**MONOGRAM BIOSCIENCES INC**
345 Oyster Point Blvd, South San Francisco (94080-1913)
PHONE.....................650 635-1100
Floyd S Eberts Iii, *CEO*
Alfred G Merriweather, *
Michael J Dunn, *Chief Business Officer*
Kathy L Hibbs, *
William J Welch, *Chief Commercial Officer*
**EMP:** 382 **EST:** 1995
**SQ FT:** 41,000
**SALES (est):** 20.69MM
**SALES (corp-wide):** 12.18B **Publicly Held**
Web: monogrambio.labcorp.com
**SIC: 2835** Diagnostic substances
**HQ:** Laboratory Corporation Of America Holdings
358 S Main St
Burlington NC 27215

**(P-5768)**
**NAXCOR INC**
320 Logue Ave # 200, Mountain View (94043-4040)
PHONE.....................650 328-9398
Doug Thien, *Pr*
Susan Williams-clark, *VP*

August Moretti, *Sec*
**EMP:** 15 **EST:** 1988
**SQ FT:** 9,000
**SALES (est):** 219.68K **Privately Held**
**SIC: 2835** 2834 Diagnostic substances; Medicines, capsuled or ampuled

**(P-5769)**
**NOVARTIS PHARMACEUTICALS CORP**
Also Called: Novartis Bphrmctcal Oprtons -
2010 Cessna Dr, Vacaville (95688-8712)
PHONE.....................707 452-8081
Chris Busstioneau, *Mgr*
**EMP:** 272
Web: www.novartis.com
**SIC: 2835** 2834 Diagnostic substances; Pharmaceutical preparations
**HQ:** Novartis Pharmaceuticals Corporation
1 Health Plz
East Hanover NJ 07936
862 778-8300

**(P-5770)**
**ONCOCYTE CORPORATION (PA)**
15 Cushing, Irvine (92602)
PHONE.....................949 409-7600
Ronald Andrews, *CEO*
Cavan Redmond, *Ch Bd*
Gisela Paulsen, *Pr*
Douglas Ross, *CSO*
Padma Sundar, *CCO*
**EMP:** 17 **EST:** 2009
**SALES (est):** 1.5MM **Publicly Held**
Web: www.oncocyte.com
**SIC: 2835** Diagnostic substances

**(P-5771)**
**ORTHO-CLINICAL DIAGNOSTICS INC**
1401 Red Hawk Cir Apt E307, Fremont (94538-4747)
PHONE.....................908 704-5910
**EMP:** 32
**SALES (corp-wide):** 3B **Publicly Held**
Web: www.orthoclinicaldiagnostics.com
**SIC: 2835** Blood derivative diagnostic agents
**HQ:** Ortho-Clinical Diagnostics, Inc.
1001 Us Hwy 202
Raritan NJ 08869
908 218-8000

**(P-5772)**
**ORTHO-CLINICAL DIAGNOSTICS INC**
612 W Katella Ave Ste B, Orange (92867-4608)
PHONE.....................714 639-2323
Robert Black, *Brnch Mgr*
**EMP:** 27
**SQ FT:** 2,200
**SALES (corp-wide):** 3B **Publicly Held**
Web: www.orthoclinicaldiagnostics.com
**SIC: 2835** Blood derivative diagnostic agents
**HQ:** Ortho-Clinical Diagnostics, Inc.
1001 Us Hwy 202
Raritan NJ 08869
908 218-8000

**(P-5773)**
**PACIFIC BIOTECH INC**
10165 Mckellar Ct, San Diego (92121-4201)
PHONE.....................858 552-1100
Wayne Kay, *Pr*
**EMP:** 43 **EST:** 1981
**SQ FT:** 70,000
**SALES (est):** 4.87MM
**SALES (corp-wide):** 3B **Publicly Held**

## PRODUCTS & SERVICES SECTION — 2836 - Biological Products, Except Diagnostic (P-5793)

SIC: 2835 Pregnancy test kits
HQ: Quidel Corporation
9975 Summers Ridge Rd
San Diego CA 92121
858 552-1100

**(P-5774)**
**PLASTIKON HEALTHCARE LLC**
688 Sandoval Way, Hayward (94544-7129)
P.O. Box 667 (66044-0667)
PHONE..................................785 330-7100
Fred Soofer, *Managing Member*
John Low, *
EMP: 34 EST: 2010
SQ FT: 45,000
SALES (est): 9.5MM
SALES (corp-wide): 151.6MM **Privately Held**
Web: www.plastikon.com
SIC: 2835 Diagnostic substances
PA: Plastikon Industries
688 Sandoval Way
510 400-1010

**(P-5775)**
**QUANTIMETRIX**
2005 Manhattan Beach Blvd, Redondo Beach (90278-1205)
PHONE..................................310 536-0006
Monty Ban, *Pr*
Edward Cleek, *
Abdee Akhavan, *
EMP: 70 EST: 1974
SQ FT: 86,400
SALES (est): 8.77MM **Privately Held**
Web: www.quantimetrix.com
SIC: 2835 Diagnostic substances

**(P-5776)**
**QUIDEL CORPORATION**
10165 Mckellar Ct, San Diego (92121-4299)
PHONE..................................858 552-1100
EMP: 46
SALES (corp-wide): 3B **Publicly Held**
Web: www.quidelortho.com
SIC: 2835 Diagnostic substances
HQ: Quidel Corporation
9975 Summers Ridge Rd
San Diego CA 92121
858 552-1100

**(P-5777)**
**QUIDEL CORPORATION (HQ)**
9975 Summers Ridge Rd, San Diego (92121-2997)
PHONE..................................858 552-1100
Randall J Steward, *CFO*
Robert J Bujarski, *Senior Vice President Business Development*
Werner Kroll, *Senior Vice President Research & Development*
EMP: 90 EST: 1977
SQ FT: 30,000
SALES (est): 1.7B
SALES (corp-wide): 3B **Publicly Held**
Web: www.quidelortho.com
SIC: 2835 Pregnancy test kits
PA: Quidelortho Corporation
9975 Summers Ridge Rd
858 552-1100

**(P-5778)**
**QUIDELORTHO CORPORATION (PA)**
9975 Summers Ridge Rd, San Diego (92121-2997)
PHONE..................................858 552-1100
Brian J Blaser, *Pr*
Kenneth F Buechler, *Non-Executive Chairman of the Board*
Robert J Bujarski, *Pr*
Joseph M Busky, *CFO*
Michael S Iskra, *CCO*
EMP: 39 EST: 2021
SALES (est): 3B
SALES (corp-wide): 3B **Publicly Held**
Web: www.quidelortho.com
SIC: 2835 Pregnancy test kits

**(P-5779)**
**RESPONSE GENETICS INC**
1640 Marengo St Ste 7, Los Angeles (90033-1057)
PHONE..................................323 224-3900
EMP: 113
Web: www.responsegenetics.com
SIC: 2835 Diagnostic substances

**(P-5780)**
**SYNBIOTICS LLC**
16420 Via Esprillo, San Diego (92127-1702)
PHONE..................................858 451-3771
Keith A Butler, *Brnch Mgr*
EMP: 22
SALES (corp-wide): 8.54B **Publicly Held**
SIC: 2835 Veterinary diagnostic substances
HQ: Synbiotics Llc
12200 Nw Ambssdor Dr Ste
Kansas City MO 64163
816 464-3500

**(P-5781)**
**SYNTRON BIORESEARCH INC**
2774 Loker Ave W, Carlsbad (92010-6610)
PHONE..................................760 930-2200
Charles Yu, *Pr*
▲ EMP: 278 EST: 1986
SALES (est): 18.83MM **Privately Held**
Web: www.syntron.net
SIC: 2835 5122 Diagnostic substances; Biologicals and allied products

**(P-5782)**
**TECO DIAGNOSTICS**
Also Called: Lab Health Medical
1268 N Lakeview Ave, Anaheim (92807-1831)
PHONE..................................714 693-7788
K C Chen, *Pr*
◆ EMP: 70 EST: 1985
SQ FT: 40,000
SALES (est): 9.65MM **Privately Held**
Web: www.tecodiagnostics.com
SIC: 2835 5049 Diagnostic substances; Laboratory equipment, except medical or dental

**(P-5783)**
**TETHYS BIOSCIENCE INC**
5858 Horton St Ste 280, Emeryville (94608-2007)
P.O. Box 4370 (95337-0007)
PHONE..................................888 483-8497
EMP: 103
Web: www.tethysbio.com
SIC: 2835 Diagnostic substances

**(P-5784)**
**VEDABIO INC**
11125 Flintkote Ave Ste A, San Diego (92121-1213)
PHONE..................................858 310-1330
Frederic Sweeney, *Pr*
Maurice Exner, *COO*
Jorge Bernate, *Ex Dir*
EMP: 18 EST: 2021
SALES (est): 2.73MM **Privately Held**
SIC: 2835 Microbiology and virology diagnostic products

**(P-5785)**
**VERGE GENOMICS**
131 Oyster Point Blvd, South San Francisco (94080-2032)
PHONE..................................312 489-7455
Alice Zhang, *CEO*
Jane Rhodes, *Chief Business Officer*
EMP: 59 EST: 2017
SALES (est): 9.1MM **Privately Held**
Web: www.vergegenomics.com
SIC: 2835 Microbiology and virology diagnostic products

## 2836 Biological Products, Except Diagnostic

**(P-5786)**
**ADVERUM BIOTECHNOLOGIES INC (PA)**
Also Called: ADVERUM
100 Cardinal Way, Redwood City (94063-4755)
PHONE..................................650 656-9323
Laurent Fischer, *Pr*
Patrick Machado, *Ch Bd*
Kishor Peter Soparkar, *COO*
Linda Rubinstein, *CFO*
Setareh Seyedkazemi, *CDO*
EMP: 64 EST: 2006
SQ FT: 79,675
SALES (est): 3.6MM
SALES (corp-wide): 3.6MM **Publicly Held**
Web: www.adverum.com
SIC: 2836 8731 Biological products, except diagnostic; Biotechnical research, commercial

**(P-5787)**
**ALIGOS THERAPEUTICS INC (PA)**
Also Called: Aligos Therapeutics
1 Corporate Dr Fl 2, South San Francisco (94080-7043)
PHONE..................................800 466-6059
Lawrence M Blatt, *Ch Bd*
Lesley Ann Calhoun, *Ex VP*
Julian A Symons, *CSO*
Hardean Achneck, *CMO*
EMP: 30 EST: 2018
SQ FT: 51,000
SALES (est): 15.53MM
SALES (corp-wide): 15.53MM **Publicly Held**
Web: www.aligos.com
SIC: 2836 2834 Biological products, except diagnostic; Pharmaceutical preparations

**(P-5788)**
**ALLOGENE THERAPEUTICS INC (PA)**
Also Called: ALLOGENE THERAPEUTICS
210 E Grand Ave, South San Francisco (94080-4811)
PHONE..................................650 457-2700
David Chang, *Pr*
Arie Belldegrun, *Ex Ch Bd*
Geoffrey Parker, *Ex VP*
Timothy Moore, *Ex VP*
Zachary Roberts, *CMO*
EMP: 191 EST: 2017
SQ FT: 68,072
SALES (est): 95K
SALES (corp-wide): 95K **Publicly Held**
Web: www.allogene.com
SIC: 2836 8731 Biological products, except diagnostic; Biological research

**(P-5789)**
**ALPHA TEKNOVA INC (PA)**
2451 Bert Dr, Hollister (95023-2563)
PHONE..................................831 637-1100
Stephen Gunstream, *Pr*
Paul Grossman, *
Matthew Lowell, *CFO*
Damon Terrill, *CCO*
EMP: 54 EST: 1996
SQ FT: 114,000
SALES (est): 36.68MM **Publicly Held**
Web: www.teknova.com
SIC: 2836 Biological products, except diagnostic

**(P-5790)**
**ALUMIS INC**
280 E Grand Ave, South San Francisco (94080-4808)
PHONE..................................650 231-6625
Martin Babler, *Ch Bd*
John Schroer, *CFO*
David M Goldstein, *CSO*
Roy Hardiman, *Business Legal*
Sara Klein, *Corporate Secretary*
EMP: 109 EST: 2021
SQ FT: 55,000
Web: www.alumis.com
SIC: 2836 Biological products, except diagnostic

**(P-5791)**
**AMBRX BIOPHARMA INC**
Also Called: Ambrx
10975 N Torrey Pines Rd, La Jolla (92037-1051)
PHONE..................................858 875-2400
Daniel J Oconnor, *CEO*
EMP: 70 EST: 2015
SQ FT: 36,172
SALES (est): 2.44MM
SALES (corp-wide): 85.16B **Publicly Held**
Web: www.ambrx.com
SIC: 2836 Biological products, except diagnostic
PA: Johnson & Johnson
1 Johnson & Johnson Plz
732 524-0400

**(P-5792)**
**AMERICAN PEPTIDE COMPANY INC**
1271 Avenida Chelsea, Vista (92081-8315)
PHONE..................................408 733-7604
▲ EMP: 86
SIC: 2836 5169 Biological products, except diagnostic; Chemicals and allied products, nec

**(P-5793)**
**AMGEN INC (PA)**
Also Called: Amgen
1 Amgen Center Dr, Thousand Oaks (91320-1799)
PHONE..................................805 447-1000
Robert A Bradway, *Ch Bd*
Esteban Santos, *Operations*
Peter H Griffith, *Ex VP*
Jonathan P Graham, *Ex VP*
David M Reese, *Ex VP*
◆ EMP: 1942 EST: 1980
SALES (est): 28.19B
SALES (corp-wide): 28.19B **Publicly Held**
Web: www.amgen.com
SIC: 2836 Biological products, except diagnostic

## 2836 - Biological Products, Except Diagnostic (P-5794)

**(P-5794)**
**ARCELLX INC**
Also Called: ARCELLX
800 Bridge Pkwy, Redwood City (94065-1156)
PHONE.................................240 327-0630
Rami Elghandour, *Ch Bd*
Michelle Gilson, *CFO*
Christopher Heery, *CMO*
**EMP:** 130 **EST:** 2014
**SQ FT:** 13,571
**SALES (est):** 110.32MM **Privately Held**
**Web:** www.arcellx.com
**SIC: 2836** Biological products, except diagnostic

**(P-5795)**
**ARK ANIMAL HEALTH INC**
4955 Directors Pl, San Diego (92121-3836)
PHONE.................................858 203-4100
**EMP:** 44 **EST:** 2017
**SALES (est):** 810.28K
**SALES (corp-wide):** 62.84MM **Publicly Held**
**Web:** www.arkanimalhealth.com
**SIC: 2836** Biological products, except diagnostic
**PA:** Sorrento Therapeutics, Inc.
4955 Directors Pl
858 203-4100

**(P-5796)**
**ARMATA PHARMACEUTICALS INC (PA)**
Also Called: ARMATA PHARMACEUTICALS
5005 Mcconnell Ave, Los Angeles (90066-6715)
PHONE.................................310 665-2928
Todd R Patrick, *CEO*
Brian Varnum, *CDO*
Steve R Martin, *CFO*
Duane Morris, *VP*
**EMP:** 24 **EST:** 1989
**SQ FT:** 35,500
**SALES (est):** 5.51MM **Publicly Held**
**Web:** www.armatapharma.com
**SIC: 2836** Biological products, except diagnostic

**(P-5797)**
**ARTIVA BIOTHERAPEUTICS INC**
5505 Morehouse Dr Ste 100, San Diego (92121-1720)
PHONE.................................858 267-4467
Fred Aslan, *Pr*
Brian Daniels, *
Neha Krishnamohan, *Ex VP*
Christopher P Horan, *Chief Technician*
Thorsten Graef, *CMO*
**EMP:** 81 **EST:** 2019
**SQ FT:** 51,621
**SALES (est):** 33.49MM **Privately Held**
**Web:** www.artivabio.com
**SIC: 2836** Biological products, except diagnostic

**(P-5798)**
**ASTELLAS GENE THERAPIES INC (DH)**
Also Called: Audentes
480 Forbes Blvd, South San Francisco (94080-2015)
PHONE.................................415 818-1001
Morten Sogaard, *Pr*
**EMP:** 27 **EST:** 2012
**SALES (est):** 100.97MM **Privately Held**
**Web:** www.audentestx.com
**SIC: 2836** Biological products, except diagnostic
**HQ:** Astellas Us Holding, Inc.
1 Astellas Way
Northbrook IL 60062

**(P-5799)**
**ASTELLAS GENE THERAPIES INC**
201 Gateway Blvd, South San Francisco (94080-7019)
PHONE.................................415 818-1001
Jonathan Silverstein, *Ch Bd*
**EMP:** 60
**Web:** www.audentestx.com
**SIC: 2836** Biological products, except diagnostic
**HQ:** Astellas Gene Therapies, Inc.
480 Forbes Blvd
South San Francisco CA 94080
415 818-1001

**(P-5800)**
**ASTELLAS GENE THERAPIES INC**
528 Eccles Ave, South San Francisco (94080-1905)
PHONE.................................910 578-9806
**EMP:** 60
**Web:** www.audentestx.com
**SIC: 2836** Biological products, except diagnostic
**HQ:** Astellas Gene Therapies, Inc.
480 Forbes Blvd
South San Francisco CA 94080
415 818-1001

**(P-5801)**
**ATARA BIOTHERAPEUTICS INC (PA)**
Also Called: ATARA BIO
2380 Conejo Spectrum St Ste 200, Thousand Oaks (91320-1444)
PHONE.................................805 623-4211
Anhco Nguyen, *Pr*
Pascal Touchon, *
Eric Hyllengren, *Ex VP*
Amar Murugan, *CLO*
Jill Henrich, *Ex VP*
**EMP:** 160 **EST:** 2012
**SQ FT:** 13,670
**SALES (est):** 8.57MM
**SALES (corp-wide):** 8.57MM **Publicly Held**
**Web:** www.atarabio.com
**SIC: 2836 8731** Biological products, except diagnostic; Biotechnical research, commercial

**(P-5802)**
**ATRECA INC**
835 Industrial Rd Ste 400, San Carlos (94070-3312)
PHONE.................................650 595-2595
John A Orwin, *Pr*
Brian Atwood, *
Courtney J Phillips, *Corporate Secretary*
Philippe Bishop, *CMO*
**EMP:** 134 **EST:** 2010
**SQ FT:** 99,557
**Web:** www.atreca.com
**SIC: 2836** Biological products, except diagnostic

**(P-5803)**
**ATYR PHARMA INC (PA)**
Also Called: ATYR PHARMA
10240 Sorrento Valley Rd Ste 300, San Diego (92121-1605)
PHONE.................................858 731-8389
Sanjay S Shukla, *Pr*
Timothy P Coughlin, *Ch Bd*
Jill M Broadfoot, *CFO*
Nancy E Denyes, *Corporate Secretary*
Danielle Campbell, *Pers/VP*
**EMP:** 58 **EST:** 2005
**SQ FT:** 23,696
**SALES (est):** 353K **Publicly Held**
**Web:** www.atyrpharma.com
**SIC: 2836 2834** Biological products, except diagnostic; Pharmaceutical preparations

**(P-5804)**
**B-BRIDGE INTERNATIONAL INC**
3350 Scott Blvd Bldg 29, Santa Clara (95054-3105)
PHONE.................................408 252-6200
Hiroyuki Masumoto, *CEO*
▲ **EMP:** 30 **EST:** 2000
**SALES (est):** 2.6MM **Privately Held**
**Web:** www.b-bridge.com
**SIC: 2836** Biological products, except diagnostic

**(P-5805)**
**BACHEM AMERICAS INC (DH)**
Also Called: Bachem California
3132 Kashiwa St, Torrance (90505-4087)
PHONE.................................310 784-4440
Brian Gregg, *CEO*
Michael Brenk, *
Najib Masloub, *
▲ **EMP:** 25 **EST:** 1971
**SQ FT:** 70,000
**SALES (est):** 104.75MM **Privately Held**
**Web:** www.bachem.com
**SIC: 2836 2834** Biological products, except diagnostic; Pharmaceutical preparations
**HQ:** Bachem Holding Ag
Hauptstrasse 144
Bubendorf BL 4416

**(P-5806)**
**BACHEM AMERICAS INC**
3152 Kashiwa St, Torrance (90505-4011)
PHONE.................................310 784-4440
**EMP:** 45
**Web:** www.bachem.com
**SIC: 2836 2834** Biological products, except diagnostic; Pharmaceutical preparations
**HQ:** Bachem Americas, Inc.
3132 Kashiwa St
Torrance CA 90505
310 784-4440

**(P-5807)**
**BACHEM AMERICAS INC**
3031 Fujita St, Torrance (90505-4004)
PHONE.................................310 539-4171
**EMP:** 45
**Web:** www.bachem.com
**SIC: 2836** Biological products, except diagnostic
**HQ:** Bachem Americas, Inc.
3132 Kashiwa St
Torrance CA 90505
310 784-4440

**(P-5808)**
**BACHEM BIOSCIENCE INC**
Also Called: Bachem
3132 Kashiwa St, Torrance (90505-4087)
PHONE.................................310 784-7322
Peter Grogg, *Ch Bd*
Peter Grogg, *Ch*
Rolf Nyfeler, *
Michael Pennington, *
David Floyd, *
▲ **EMP:** 21 **EST:** 1987
**SALES (est):** 2.1MM **Privately Held**
**Web:** www.bachem.com
**SIC: 2836 2899** Biological products, except diagnostic; Chemical preparations, nec
**HQ:** Bachem Holding Ag
Hauptstrasse 144
Bubendorf BL 4416

**(P-5809)**
**BAXTER HEALTHCARE CORPORATION**
Also Called: Baxter Bioscience
21026 Alexander Ct, Hayward (94545-1234)
PHONE.................................510 723-2000
Andrea Darsey, *Mgr*
**EMP:** 51
**SALES (corp-wide):** 14.81B **Publicly Held**
**Web:** www.baxter.com
**SIC: 2836 2835 2834 2833** Biological products, except diagnostic; Blood derivative diagnostic agents; Pharmaceutical preparations; Medicinals and botanicals
**HQ:** Baxter Healthcare Corporation
1 Baxter Pkwy
Deerfield IL 60015
224 948-2000

**(P-5810)**
**BIOATLA INC**
11085 Torreyana Rd, San Diego (92121-1104)
PHONE.................................858 558-0708
Jay M Short, *Ch Bd*
Richard A Waldron, *CFO*
Eric Sievers, *CMO*
Christian Vasquez, *Corporate Controller*
**EMP:** 65 **EST:** 2007
**SQ FT:** 43,377
**Web:** www.bioatla.com
**SIC: 2836** Biological products, except diagnostic

**(P-5811)**
**BIOSEARCH TECHNOLOGIES INC (HQ)**
Also Called: Lgc Biosearch Technologies
2199 S Mcdowell Boulevard Ext, Petaluma (94954-6904)
PHONE.................................415 883-8400
Ronald M Cook, *CEO*
**EMP:** 37 **EST:** 1993
**SQ FT:** 121,000
**SALES (est):** 47.79MM
**SALES (corp-wide):** 611.55K **Privately Held**
**Web:** www.biosearchtech.com
**SIC: 2836 2899 2835 2869** Biological products, except diagnostic; Chemical preparations, nec; In vitro diagnostics; Industrial organic chemicals, nec
**PA:** Lgc Science Group Limited
Queens Road
208 943-7000

**(P-5812)**
**CAMBRIDGE EQUITIES LP**
9922 Jefferson Blvd, Culver City (90232-3506)
PHONE.................................858 350-2300
**EMP:** 46 **EST:** 2011
**SALES (est):** 1.38MM **Privately Held**
**SIC: 2836** Biological products, except diagnostic

**(P-5813)**
**CAPSIDA BIOTHERAPEUTICS INC (PA)**
3075 Townsgate Rd, Westlake Village (91361-3076)

## 2836 - Biological Products, Except Diagnostic (P-5831)

PHONE.................805 410-2673
Robert Cuddihy, *CEO*
Pamela Wapnick, *CFO*
**EMP:** 22 **EST:** 2019
**SALES (est):** 32.54MM
**SALES (corp-wide):** 32.54MM **Privately Held**
**Web:** www.capsida.com
**SIC: 2836** Biological products, except diagnostic

### (P-5814)
### CARGO THERAPEUTICS INC
835 Industrial Rd Ste 400, San Carlos (94070-3331)
PHONE.................650 499-8950
Gina Chapman, *Pr*
John Orwin, *
Anup Radhakrishnan, *CFO*
Ginna Laport, *CMO*
**EMP:** 116 **EST:** 2019
**SQ FT:** 99,557
**Web:** www.syncopationlife.com
**SIC: 2836** Biological products, except diagnostic

### (P-5815)
### CARIBOU BIOSCIENCES INC
Also Called: CARIBOU BIOSCIENCES
2929 7th St Ste 105, Berkeley (94710-2753)
PHONE.................510 982-6030
Rachel E Haurwitz, *Pr*
Andrew Guggenhime, *Non-Executive Chairman of the Board**
Jason V O'byrne, *CFO*
Steven B Kanner, *CSO*
**EMP:** 158 **EST:** 2011
**SQ FT:** 61,735
**SALES (est):** 34.48MM **Privately Held**
**Web:** www.cariboubio.com
**SIC: 2836** Biological products, except diagnostic

### (P-5816)
### CERUS CORPORATION (PA)
1220 Concord Ave Ste 600, Concord (94520-4906)
PHONE.................925 288-6000
William M Greenman, *Pr*
Daniel N Swisher Junior, *Ch Bd*
Kevin D Green, *VP*
Vivek Jayaraman, *COO*
Richard Benjamin, *CMO*
▲ **EMP:** 206 **EST:** 1991
**SQ FT:** 84,631
**SALES (est):** 156.37MM **Publicly Held**
**Web:** www.cerus.com
**SIC: 2836** Biological products, except diagnostic

### (P-5817)
### CG ONCOLOGY INC
Also Called: CG ONCOLOGY
400 Spectrum Center Dr Ste 2040, Irvine (92618-5024)
PHONE.................949 409-3700
Arthur Kuan, *Ch Bd*
Ambaw Bellete, *Pr*
Corleen Roche, *CFO*
Vijay Kasturi, *CMO*
**EMP:** 61 **EST:** 2010
**SQ FT:** 1,249
**SALES (est):** 204K **Privately Held**
**Web:** www.cgoncology.com
**SIC: 2836** Biological products, except diagnostic

### (P-5818)
### CIDARA THERAPEUTICS INC (PA)
Also Called: CIDARA THERAPEUTICS
6310 Nancy Ridge Dr Ste 101, San Diego (92121-3209)
PHONE.................858 752-6170
Jeffrey L Stein, *Pr*
Daniel D Burgess, *Ch Bd*
Preetam Shah, *Chief Business Officer*
Paul Daruwala, *COO*
Taylor Sandison, *CMO*
**EMP:** 51 **EST:** 2012
**SQ FT:** 29,638
**SALES (est):** 63.91MM
**SALES (corp-wide):** 63.91MM **Publicly Held**
**Web:** www.cidara.com
**SIC: 2836** 8731 Biological products, except diagnostic; Biotechnical research, commercial

### (P-5819)
### CLARUS THERAPEUTICS INC
355 S Grand Ave, Los Angeles (90071-1560)
PHONE.................847 562-4300
Robert E Dudley, *Pr*
Kimberly Murphy, *Ch Bd*
Richard Peterson, *CFO*
Frank Jaeger, *CCO*
**EMP:** 16 **EST:** 2003
**SALES (est):** 6.37MM
**SALES (corp-wide):** 13.96MM **Privately Held**
**Web:** www.clarustherapeutics.com
**SIC: 2836** Biological products, except diagnostic
**PA:** Clarus Therapeutics Holdings, Inc.
555 Skokie Blvd Ste 340
847 562-4311

### (P-5820)
### CLINIQA CORPORATION (HQ)
Also Called: Cliniqa
495 Enterprise St, San Marcos (92078-4364)
PHONE.................760 744-1900
Kevin Gould, *Pr*
C Granger Haugh, *
Dean Harriman, *
Shing Kwan, *
Larry Beaty, *
▼ **EMP:** 29 **EST:** 1976
**SQ FT:** 25,000
**SALES (est):** 20.7MM
**SALES (corp-wide):** 1.16B **Publicly Held**
**Web:** www.cliniqa.com
**SIC: 2836** Biological products, except diagnostic
**PA:** Bio-Techne Corporation
614 Mckinley Pl Ne
612 379-8854

### (P-5821)
### CLINIQA CORPORATION
258 La Moree Rd, San Marcos (92078-4381)
PHONE.................760 744-1900
Charles G Haugh, *CEO*
**EMP:** 58
**SALES (corp-wide):** 1.16B **Publicly Held**
**Web:** www.cliniqa.com
**SIC: 2836** Biological products, except diagnostic
**HQ:** Cliniqa Corporation
495 Enterprise St
San Marcos CA 92078
760 744-1900

### (P-5822)
### COHERUS BIOSCIENCES INC (PA)
Also Called: COHERUS BIOSCIENCES
333 Twin Dolphin Dr Ste 600, Redwood City (94065-1442)
PHONE.................650 649-3530
Dennis M Lanfear, *Ch Bd*
Bryan Mcmichael, *Interim Chief Financial Officer*
Paul Reider, *CCO*
**EMP:** 218 **EST:** 2010
**SALES (est):** 257.24MM
**SALES (corp-wide):** 257.24MM **Publicly Held**
**Web:** www.coherus.com
**SIC: 2836** Biological products, except diagnostic

### (P-5823)
### DENALI THERAPEUTICS INC (PA)
Also Called: DENALI THERAPEUTICS
161 Oyster Point Blvd, South San Francisco (94080-2042)
PHONE.................650 866-8548
Ryan J Watts, *Pr*
Vicki Sato, *Non-Executive Chairman of the Board*
Alexander O Schuth, *COO*
Carole Ho, *CMO*
**EMP:** 430 **EST:** 2015
**SQ FT:** 148,020
**SALES (est):** 330.53MM
**SALES (corp-wide):** 330.53MM **Publicly Held**
**Web:** www.denalitherapeutics.com
**SIC: 2836** 2834 Biological products, except diagnostic; Pharmaceutical preparations

### (P-5824)
### DNATRIX INC
2659 State St # 100, Carlsbad (92008-1627)
PHONE.................832 930-2401
Jeffrey Knapp, *CEO*
Imran Alibhai, *Sr VP*
Reenie Mccarthy, *Prin*
Frank Tufaro Ph.d., *Prin*
**EMP:** 20 **EST:** 2005
**SALES (est):** 2.31MM **Privately Held**
**Web:** www.dnatrix.com
**SIC: 2836** Biological products, except diagnostic

### (P-5825)
### DYNAVAX TECHNOLOGIES CORP (PA)
2100 Powell St 7th Fl, Emeryville (94608-1873)
PHONE.................510 848-5100
Ryan Spencer, *CEO*
David F Novack, *Pr*
Kelly Macdonald, *Sr VP*
Robert Janssen, *CMO*
Scott Myers, *
**EMP:** 82 **EST:** 1996
**SQ FT:** 23,976
**SALES (est):** 232.28MM **Publicly Held**
**Web:** www.dynavax.com
**SIC: 2836** 8731 Biological products, except diagnostic; Biological research

### (P-5826)
### EMD MILLIPORE CORPORATION
Also Called: Bioscience Research Reagents
28820 Single Oak Dr, Temecula (92590-3607)
PHONE.................951 676-8080
John Ambroziak, *Mgr*
**EMP:** 69
**SALES (corp-wide):** 22.82B **Privately Held**
**Web:** www.emdmillipore.com
**SIC: 2836** 2835 3826 Biological products, except diagnostic; Diagnostic substances; Liquid testing apparatus
**HQ:** Emd Millipore Corporation
400 Summit Dr
Burlington MA 01803
800 645-5476

### (P-5827)
### EXCELLOS INCORPORATED
1155 Island Ave, San Diego (92101-7230)
PHONE.................619 400-8235
David Wellis, *CEO*
**EMP:** 20 **EST:** 2020
**SALES (est):** 11.13MM **Privately Held**
**Web:** www.excellos.com
**SIC: 2836** Vaccines and other immunizing products

### (P-5828)
### EXELIXIS INC (PA)
Also Called: EXELIXIS
1851 Harbor Bay Pkwy, Alameda (94502-3010)
PHONE.................650 837-7000
Michael M Morrissey, *Pr*
Stelios Papadopoulos, *
Christopher J Senner, *Ex VP*
Amy C Peterson, *CMO*
Dana T Aftab, *CSO*
**EMP:** 57 **EST:** 1994
**SQ FT:** 610,000
**SALES (est):** 1.83B **Publicly Held**
**Web:** www.exelixis.com
**SIC: 2836** Biological products, except diagnostic

### (P-5829)
### EXPRESSION SYSTEMS LLC (PA)
2537 2nd St, Davis (95618-5475)
PHONE.................877 877-7421
**EMP:** 24 **EST:** 1997
**SQ FT:** 27,000
**SALES (est):** 7.21MM
**SALES (corp-wide):** 7.21MM **Privately Held**
**Web:** www.expressionsystems.com
**SIC: 2836** Culture media

### (P-5830)
### FUJIFILM DSYNTH BTCHNLGIES CAL
2430 Conejo Spectrum St, Thousand Oaks (91320-1445)
PHONE.................914 789-8100
Martin Meeson, *Pr*
Gerry Farrell, *COO*
Hideru Sato, *Treas*
Steve Lee, *Sec*
**EMP:** 29
**SALES (est):** 29.15MM **Privately Held**
**Web:** www.fujifilmdiosynth.com
**SIC: 2836** Biological products, except diagnostic
**HQ:** Fujifilm Diosynth Biotechnologies Uk Limited
New Billingham House
Billingham TS23

### (P-5831)
### FUJIFILM DSYNTH BTCHNLGIES USA
2430 Conejo Spectrum St, Thousand Oaks (91320-1445)

# 2836 - Biological Products, Except Diagnostic (P-5832)

PHONE..................805 699-5579
Takatoshi Ishikawa, *Brnch Mgr*
**EMP:** 134
**Web:** www.atarabio.com
**SIC:** **2836** Biological products, except diagnostic
**HQ:** Fujifilm Diosynth Biotechnologies U.S.A., Inc.
101 J Morris Comns Ln
Morrisville NC 27560

### (P-5832)
### FUJIFILM IRVINE SCIENTIFIC INC (DH)
Also Called: Irvine Scientific
1830 E Warner Ave, Santa Ana (92705-5505)
PHONE..................949 261-7800
Yutaka Yamaguchi, *CEO*
Judy Malillo, *
Ryo Iguchi, *
▲ **EMP:** 44 **EST:** 1970
**SQ FT:** 20,000
**SALES (est):** 124.93MM **Privately Held**
**Web:** www.irvinesci.com
**SIC:** **2836** 5047 Blood derivatives; Medical laboratory equipment
**HQ:** Fujifilm Holdings America Corporation
200 Summit Lake Dr
Valhalla NY 10595

### (P-5833)
### GRIFOLS BIOLOGICALS LLC (DH)
5555 Valley Blvd, Los Angeles (90032-3520)
PHONE..................323 225-2221
David Bell, *
Max Debrouwer, *
Willie Zuniga, *
▲ **EMP:** 67 **EST:** 2003
**SALES (est):** 185.52MM **Privately Held**
**Web:** www.grifols.com
**SIC:** **2836** 2834 Plasmas; Pharmaceutical preparations
**HQ:** Grifols Shared Services North America, Inc.
2410 Lillyvale Ave
Los Angeles CA 90032
323 225-2221

### (P-5834)
### GRIFOLS USA LLC
Also Called: Access Biologicals
995 Park Center Dr, Vista (92081-8312)
PHONE..................760 931-8444
**EMP:** 71
**Web:** www.grifols.com
**SIC:** **2836** Biological products, except diagnostic
**HQ:** Grifols Usa, Llc
2410 Grifols Way
Los Angeles CA 90032
323 225-2221

### (P-5835)
### GRITSTONE BIO INC (PA)
Also Called: Gritstone
5959 Horton St Ste 300, Emeryville (94608-2120)
PHONE..................510 871-6100
Andrew Allen, *Pr*
Elaine V Jones, *Ch Bd*
Vassiliki Economides, *Ex VP*
Erin Jones, *COO*
James Cho, *CAO*
**EMP:** 227 **EST:** 2015
**SQ FT:** 34,569
**SALES (est):** 19.95MM
**SALES (corp-wide):** 19.95MM **Publicly Held**
**Web:** www.gritstonebio.com
**SIC:** **2836** Biological products, except diagnostic

### (P-5836)
### HALOZYME THERAPEUTICS INC (PA)
Also Called: HALOZYME
12390 El Camino Real, San Diego (92130-3162)
PHONE..................858 794-8889
Helen I Torley, *Pr*
Jeffrey W Henderson, *Ch Bd*
Nicole Labrosse, *Sr VP*
Mark Snyder, *CCO*
Michael J Labarre, *Sr VP*
**EMP:** 62 **EST:** 1998
**SALES (est):** 829.25MM
**SALES (corp-wide):** 829.25MM **Publicly Held**
**Web:** www.halozyme.com
**SIC:** **2836** 2834 Biological products, except diagnostic; Pharmaceutical preparations

### (P-5837)
### HEMOSTAT LABORATORIES INC (PA)
515 Industrial Way, Dixon (95620-9779)
P.O. Box 790 (95620-0790)
PHONE..................707 678-9594
Jim Mc Elligott, *Pr*
Gordon Murphy, *VP*
**EMP:** 20 **EST:** 1980
**SQ FT:** 9,500
**SALES (est):** 4.87MM
**SALES (corp-wide):** 4.87MM **Privately Held**
**Web:** www.hemostat.com
**SIC:** **2836** 2673 Blood derivatives; Plastic and pliofilm bags

### (P-5838)
### HYGIEIA BIOLOGICAL LABS
1240 Commerce Ave Ste B, Woodland (95776-5923)
PHONE..................530 661-1442
James L Wallis, *Mgr*
**EMP:** 20
**Web:** www.hygieialabs.com
**SIC:** **2836** Biological products, except diagnostic
**PA:** Hygieia Biological Laboratories
1785 E Main St Ste 4

### (P-5839)
### IGM BIOSCIENCES INC
325 E Middlefield Rd, Mountain View (94043-4003)
PHONE..................650 965-7873
Mary Beth Harler, *CEO*
Misbah Tahir, *CFO*
Lisa L Decker, *Chief Business Officer*
**EMP:** 224 **EST:** 1993
**SQ FT:** 114,100
**SALES (est):** 2.13MM **Privately Held**
**Web:** www.igmbio.com
**SIC:** **2836** Biological products, except diagnostic

### (P-5840)
### IMMUNITYBIO INC (PA)
Also Called: IMMUNITYBIO
3530 John Hopkins Ct, San Diego (92121-1121)
PHONE..................844 696-5235
Richard Adcock, *Pr*
Patrick Soon-shiong, *Ex Ch Bd*
David Sachs, *CFO*
Barry J Simon, *CORP AFFAIRS*
**EMP:** 51 **EST:** 2002
**SQ FT:** 44,681
**SALES (est):** 622K **Publicly Held**
**Web:** www.immunitybio.com
**SIC:** **2836** Biological products, except diagnostic

### (P-5841)
### INFRATAB
4347 Raytheon Rd Unit 6, Oxnard (93033-8225)
PHONE..................805 986-8880
Therese E Myers, *Prin*
Stanton Kaye, *Prin*
**EMP:** 20 **EST:** 2004
**SQ FT:** 15,000
**SALES (est):** 1.27MM **Privately Held**
**Web:** www.infratab.com
**SIC:** **2836** Biological products, except diagnostic

### (P-5842)
### INHIBRX INC (HQ)
Also Called: Inhibrx
11025 N Torrey Pines Rd Ste 200, La Jolla (92037-1030)
PHONE..................858 795-4220
Mark P Lappe, *Pr*
Kelly Deck, *CFO*
Klaus W Wagner, *CMO*
Brendan P Eckelman, *CSO*
David Matly, *CCO*
**EMP:** 127 **EST:** 2010
**SQ FT:** 34,000
**SALES (est):** 1.8MM **Publicly Held**
**Web:** www.inhibrx.com
**SIC:** **2836** Biological products, except diagnostic
**PA:** Sanofi
46 Avenue De La Grande Armee

### (P-5843)
### JASPER THERAPEUTICS INC (PA)
2200 Bridge Pkwy Ste 102, Redwood City (94065-1186)
PHONE..................650 549-1400
Ronald Martell, *Pr*
Thomas G Wiggans, *Ch Bd*
Jeet Mahal, *COO*
Herb Cross, *Corporate Secretary*
Edwin J Tucker, *Chief Medical Officer*
**EMP:** 18 **EST:** 2019
**SQ FT:** 13,400
**Web:** www.jaspertherapeutics.com
**SIC:** **2836** Biological products, except diagnostic

### (P-5844)
### KYVERNA THERAPEUTICS INC
5980 Horton St Ste 550, Emeryville (94608-2045)
PHONE..................510 925-2492
Peter Maag, *CEO*
Ian Clark, *
Dominic Borie, *Pr*
Ryan Jones, *CFO*
**EMP:** 96 **EST:** 2018
**SQ FT:** 33,000
**Web:** www.kyvernatx.com
**SIC:** **2836** 8731 Biological products, except diagnostic; Biotechnical research, commercial

### (P-5845)
### LINEAGE CELL THERAPEUTICS INC (PA)
Also Called: LINEAGE
2173 Salk Ave Ste 200, Carlsbad (92008-7354)
PHONE..................510 521-3390
Brian M Culley, *CEO*
Alfred D Kingsley, *Ch Bd*
Gary S Hogge, *Sr VP*
George A Samuel Iii, *Corporate Secretary*
Jill A Howe, *CFO*
**EMP:** 20 **EST:** 1990
**SQ FT:** 8,841
**SALES (est):** 8.95MM **Publicly Held**
**Web:** www.biotimeinc.com
**SIC:** **2836** 8731 Biological products, except diagnostic; Biotechnical research, commercial

### (P-5846)
### LIST BIOLOGICAL LABS INC
Also Called: List Labs
540 Division St, Campbell (95008-6906)
PHONE..................408 866-6363
Karen Crawford, *Pr*
Linda Eaton, *
Debra Booth, *
▼ **EMP:** 25 **EST:** 1978
**SQ FT:** 11,000
**SALES (est):** 5.57MM **Privately Held**
**Web:** www.listlabs.com
**SIC:** **2836** Biological products, except diagnostic

### (P-5847)
### MEDIATECH INC
1215 Commerce Ave, Woodland (95776-5902)
PHONE..................530 666-9825
Tony Tucker, *Brnch Mgr*
**EMP:** 26
**SALES (corp-wide):** 12.59B **Publicly Held**
**Web:** www.corning.com
**SIC:** **2836** Biological products, except diagnostic
**HQ:** Mediatech, Inc.
9345 Discovery Blvd
Manassas VA 20109
978 221-7701

### (P-5848)
### MEDIATECH INC
Also Called: J R Scientific
1242 Commerce Ave, Woodland (95776-5916)
PHONE..................530 666-9868
James Carver, *CEO*
**EMP:** 26
**SALES (corp-wide):** 12.59B **Publicly Held**
**Web:** www.corning.com
**SIC:** **2836** Biological products, except diagnostic
**HQ:** Mediatech, Inc.
9345 Discovery Blvd
Manassas VA 20109
978 221-7701

### (P-5849)
### MINDERA CORP
1221 Liberty Way, Vista (92081-8368)
PHONE..................858 810-6070
Frank Stubbe, *Admn*
Philippe Nore, *
**EMP:** 30 **EST:** 2014
**SALES (est):** 6.43MM **Privately Held**
**Web:** www.minderadx.com
**SIC:** **2836** Biological products, except diagnostic

### (P-5850)
### NEUROCRINE BIOSCIENCES INC (PA)
Also Called: NEUROCRINE
12780 El Camino Real, San Diego (92130-2042)
PHONE..................858 617-7600

## PRODUCTS & SERVICES SECTION
### 2836 - Biological Products, Except Diagnostic (P-5868)

Kevin C Gorman, *Pr*
William H Rastetter, *
Matthew C Abernethy, *CFO*
Julie S Cooke, *Chief Human Resources Officer*
Darin M Lippoldt, *CLO*
**EMP:** 264 **EST:** 1992
**SQ FT:** 141,000
**SALES (est):** 1.89B **Publicly Held**
**Web:** www.neurocrine.com
**SIC: 2836** Biological products, except diagnostic

**(P-5851)**
### NITTOBO AMERICA INC (HQ)
41900 Brown St, Murrieta (92562-9621)
**PHONE**......................951 677-5629
Eva Rafalik, *Pr*
Tatsuo Sakae, *
◆ **EMP:** 15 **EST:** 1986
**SALES (est):** 36.66MM **Privately Held**
**Web:** www.nittobous.com
**SIC: 2836** Biological products, except diagnostic
**PA:** Nitto Boseki Co., Ltd.
2-4-1, Kojimachi

**(P-5852)**
### ORIGIN MATERIALS INC (PA)
Also Called: Origin
930 Riverside Pkwy Ste 10, West Sacramento (95605-1511)
**PHONE**......................916 231-9329
R Tony Tripeny, *Ch Bd*
Matthew Plavan, *CFO*
**EMP:** 25 **EST:** 2008
**SQ FT:** 41,443
**SALES (est):** 28.8MM
**SALES (corp-wide):** 28.8MM **Publicly Held**
**Web:** www.originmaterials.com
**SIC: 2836** Biological products, except diagnostic

**(P-5853)**
### POSEIDA THERAPEUTICS INC (PA)
Also Called: POSEIDA
9390 Towne Centre Dr Ste 200, San Diego (92121-3026)
**PHONE**......................858 779-3100
Kristin Yarema, *Pr*
Mark J Gergen, *Ex Ch Bd*
Harry J Leonhardt, *CCO*
Johanna M Mylet, *CFO*
Syed Rizvi, *CMO*
**EMP:** 329 **EST:** 2014
**SQ FT:** 87,000
**SALES (est):** 64.7MM
**SALES (corp-wide):** 64.7MM **Publicly Held**
**Web:** www.poseida.com
**SIC: 2836 2834** Biological products, except diagnostic; Pharmaceutical preparations

**(P-5854)**
### PROLACTA BIOSCIENCE INC (PA)
757 Baldwin Park Blvd, City Of Industry (91746-1504)
**PHONE**......................626 599-9260
Scott A Elster, *CEO*
Scott A Elster, *CEO*
Joseph Fournell, *VP*
Alan Kofsky, *VP*
Tami D Ciranna, *CFO*
▼ **EMP:** 132 **EST:** 1999
**SQ FT:** 65,000
**SALES (est):** 91.91MM
**SALES (corp-wide):** 91.91MM **Privately Held**
**Web:** www.prolacta.com
**SIC: 2836** Biological products, except diagnostic

**(P-5855)**
### PROLACTA FACILITY LLC
757 Baldwin Park Blvd, City Of Industry (91746-1504)
**PHONE**......................626 599-9260
John Bacich Junior, *Prin*
**EMP:** 15 **EST:** 2012
**SALES (est):** 490.81K **Privately Held**
**Web:** www.prolacta.com
**SIC: 2836** Biological products, except diagnostic

**(P-5856)**
### PROTEUS DIGITAL HEALTH INC (PA)
2600 Bridge Pkwy, Redwood City (94065-6136)
**PHONE**......................650 632-4031
Lawrence Perkins, *Interim Chief Executive Officer*
Mark J Zdeblick, *Prin*
George M Savage, *Prin*
Ben Costello, *VP Opers*
▲ **EMP:** 88 **EST:** 2001
**SALES (est):** 10.13MM
**SALES (corp-wide):** 10.13MM **Privately Held**
**Web:** www.proteus.com
**SIC: 2836** Biological products, except diagnostic

**(P-5857)**
### QUINCE THERAPEUTICS INC (PA)
Also Called: Cortexyme
611 Gateway Blvd Fl 2, South San Francisco (94080-7040)
**PHONE**......................415 910-5717
Dirk Thye, *CMO*
David A Lamond, *Ch Bd*
Charles Ryan, *Pr*
Brendan Hannah, *Chief Business Officer CCO*
**EMP:** 18 **EST:** 2012
**SALES (est):** 5.73MM
**SALES (corp-wide):** 5.73MM **Publicly Held**
**Web:** www.cortexyme.com
**SIC: 2836** Biological products, except diagnostic

**(P-5858)**
### SANGAMO THERAPEUTICS INC (PA)
Also Called: SANGAMO
501 Canal Blvd, Richmond (94804-3559)
**PHONE**......................510 970-6000
Alexander D Macrae, *Pr*
H Stewart Parker, *Ch Bd*
D Mark Mcclung, *Ex VP*
Prathyusha Duraibabu, *Sr VP*
Nathalie Dubois-stringfellow, *CDO*
**EMP:** 425 **EST:** 1995
**SQ FT:** 87,700
**SALES (est):** 176.23MM **Publicly Held**
**Web:** www.sangamo.com
**SIC: 2836** Biological products, except diagnostic

**(P-5859)**
### SCRIPPS LABORATORIES
6838 Flanders Dr, San Diego (92121-2904)
**PHONE**......................858 546-5800
Simon C Khoury, *Pr*
James Scoffin, *Treas*
**EMP:** 20 **EST:** 1984
**SQ FT:** 32,000
**SALES (est):** 5.01MM
**SALES (corp-wide):** 4.06B **Privately Held**
**Web:** www.scrippslabs.com
**SIC: 2836 2835** Biological products, except diagnostic; Diagnostic substances
**PA:** Scripps Health
10140 Cmpus Pt Dr Cpa 415
800 727-4777

**(P-5860)**
### SENTI BIOSCIENCES INC (PA)
Also Called: Senti
2 Corporate Dr Fl 1, South San Francisco (94080-7047)
**PHONE**......................650 239-2030
Timothy Lu, *CEO*
Kanya Rajangam, *Head Research & Development*
Yvonne Li, *CFO*
**EMP:** 27 **EST:** 2016
**SQ FT:** 40,000
**SALES (est):** 2.56MM
**SALES (corp-wide):** 2.56MM **Publicly Held**
**Web:** www.sentibio.com
**SIC: 2836 8731** Biological products, except diagnostic; Biotechnical research, commercial

**(P-5861)**
### SORRENTO THERAPEUTICS INC (PA)
4955 Directors Pl, San Diego (92121-3836)
**PHONE**......................858 203-4100
Henry Ji, *Ch Bd*
**EMP:** 64 **EST:** 2006
**SQ FT:** 30,000
**SALES (est):** 62.84MM
**SALES (corp-wide):** 62.84MM **Publicly Held**
**Web:** www.sorrentotherapeutics.com
**SIC: 2836** Biological products, except diagnostic

**(P-5862)**
### SOUND AGRICULTURE COMPANY
6401 Hollis St Ste 100, Emeryville (94608-1463)
**PHONE**......................512 650-8290
Eric Davidson, *CEO*
**EMP:** 30 **EST:** 2012
**SALES (est):** 9.91MM **Privately Held**
**Web:** www.sound.ag
**SIC: 2836** Biological products, except diagnostic

**(P-5863)**
### SURROZEN INC (PA)
171 Oyster Point Blvd Ste 300, South San Francisco (94080-2013)
**PHONE**......................650 489-9000
Craig Parker, *Pr*
Tim Kutzkey, *Ch Bd*
Charles Williams, *CFO*
Geertrui Vanhove, *CMO*
Wen-chen Yeh, *CSO*
**EMP:** 20 **EST:** 2020
**Web:** www.surrozen.com
**SIC: 2836** Biological products, except diagnostic

**(P-5864)**
### SUTRO BIOPHARMA INC (PA)
Also Called: SUTRO BIOPHARMA
111 Oyster Point Blvd Ste 100, South San Francisco (94080-2038)
**PHONE**......................650 881-6500
William J Newell, *CEO*
Jane Chung, *Pr*
Edward Albini, *CFO*
Anne Borgman, *CMO*
Linda Fitzpatrick, *CPO CCO*
**EMP:** 297 **EST:** 2003
**SQ FT:** 115,466
**SALES (est):** 153.73MM
**SALES (corp-wide):** 153.73MM **Publicly Held**
**Web:** www.sutrobio.com
**SIC: 2836** Biological products, except diagnostic

**(P-5865)**
### TARSUS PHARMACEUTICALS INC
15440 Laguna Canyon Rd Ste 160, Irvine (92618-2143)
**PHONE**......................949 409-9820
Bobak Azamian, *Pr*
Michael Ackermann, *
Jeff Farrow, *CSO*
Seshadri Neervannan, *COO*
Aziz Mottiwala, *CCO*
**EMP:** 244 **EST:** 2016
**SQ FT:** 10,879
**SALES (est):** 17.45MM **Privately Held**
**Web:** www.tarsusrx.com
**SIC: 2836** Biological products, except diagnostic

**(P-5866)**
### TENAYA THERAPEUTICS INC
171 Oyster Point Blvd Ste 500, South San Francisco (94080-2028)
**PHONE**......................760 310-9976
Faraz Ali, *INTERIM PFO CHIEF EXECUTIVE OFFICER*
David Goeddel, *
Timothy Hoey, *CSO*
Whittemore Tingley, *CMO*
Chihiro Saito, *Interim CAO*
**EMP:** 140 **EST:** 2016
**SQ FT:** 32,370
**Web:** www.tenayatherapeutics.com
**SIC: 2836** Biological products, except diagnostic

**(P-5867)**
### VAXCYTE INC (PA)
Also Called: VAXCYTE
825 Industrial Rd Ste 300, San Carlos (94070-3325)
**PHONE**......................650 837-0111
Grant Pickering, *CEO*
Carlos Paya, *Ch Bd*
Andrew Guggenhime, *Pr*
Jim Wassil, *Ex VP*
Mikhail Eydelman, *CCO*
**EMP:** 77 **EST:** 2013
**SQ FT:** 77,498
**Web:** www.vaxcyte.com
**SIC: 2836** Biological products, except diagnostic

**(P-5868)**
### VECTOR LABORATORIES INC (PA)
Also Called: Vector Laboratories
6737 Mowry Ave, Newark (94560-4927)
**PHONE**......................800 227-6666
Lisa Sellers, *CEO*
Vatea Herman, *
Pamela James, *
Kum Ming Woo, *
Kenny Drew, *
◆ **EMP:** 52 **EST:** 1984
**SQ FT:** 65,000
**SALES (est):** 24.37MM

# 2836 - Biological Products, Except Diagnostic (P-5869)

SALES (corp-wide): 24.37MM **Privately Held**
Web: www.vectorlabs.com
SIC: 2836 2899 Biological products, except diagnostic; Chemical preparations, nec

**(P-5869)**
**VIR BIOTECHNOLOGY INC (PA)**
1800 Owens St Fl 11, San Francisco (94158-2388)
PHONE.....................415 906-4324
Marianne De Backer, *CEO*
Saira Ramasastry, *Ch Bd*
Brent Sabatini, *CAO PAO*
Jason O'byrne, *Ex VP*
Jeffrey Calcagno, *Chief Business Officer*
EMP: 374 EST: 2016
SQ FT: 179,566
SALES (est): 86.18MM
SALES (corp-wide): 86.18MM **Publicly Held**
Web: www.vir.bio
SIC: 2836 Biological products, except diagnostic

## 2841 Soap And Other Detergents

**(P-5870)**
**ALL ONE GOD FAITH INC**
Also Called: Dr. Bronners Magic Soaps
1225 Park Center Dr Ste D, Vista (92081-8353)
PHONE.....................760 599-4010
David Bronner, *CEO*
EMP: 70
Web: www.drbronner.com
SIC: 2841 Soap: granulated, liquid, cake, flaked, or chip
PA: All One God Faith, Inc.
1335 Park Ctr Dr

**(P-5871)**
**ALL ONE GOD FAITH INC (PA)**
Also Called: Dr. Bronners Magic Soaps
1335 Park Center Dr, Vista (92081-8357)
P.O. Box 1958 (92085-1958)
PHONE.....................844 937-2551
David Bronner, *CEO*
Michael Bronner, *
Trudy Bronner, *
◆ EMP: 170 EST: 1973
SQ FT: 126,000
SALES (est): 41.33MM **Privately Held**
Web: www.drbronner.com
SIC: 2841 2834 2844 Soap: granulated, liquid, cake, flaked, or chip; Lip balms; Lotions, shaving

**(P-5872)**
**BRADFORD SOAP MEXICO INC**
1778 Zinetta Rd Ste G, Calexico (92231-9510)
PHONE.....................760 768-4539
John Howland, *CEO*
EMP: 493
SALES (corp-wide): 227.55MM **Privately Held**
Web: www.bradfordsoap.com
SIC: 2841 Soap: granulated, liquid, cake, flaked, or chip
HQ: Bradford Soap Mexico, Inc.
200 Providence St
West Warwick RI 02893
401 821-2141

**(P-5873)**
**CHURCH & DWIGHT CO INC**
17486 Nisqualli Rd, Victorville (92395-7740)
PHONE.....................609 613-1551
Laura Syblowski, *Coordtr*
EMP: 19
SALES (corp-wide): 5.87B **Publicly Held**
Web: www.churchdwight.com
SIC: 2841 Soap and other detergents
PA: Church & Dwight Co., Inc.
500 Charles Ewing Blvd
609 806-1200

**(P-5874)**
**GOODWIN AMMONIA COMPANY LLC (PA)**
12361 Monarch St, Garden Grove (92841-2908)
PHONE.....................714 894-0531
Tom Goodwin, *Pr*
Gary Goodwin, *VP*
Janice Fleet, *Sec*
Lois Neesen, *Contrlr*
◆ EMP: 15 EST: 1922
SALES (est): 52.56MM
SALES (corp-wide): 52.56MM **Privately Held**
Web: www.goodwininc.com
SIC: 2841 5169 Soap and other detergents; Chemicals and allied products, nec

**(P-5875)**
**GOODWIN AMMONIA COMPANY LLC**
Also Called: The Goodwin Company
12361 Monarch St, Garden Grove (92841-2908)
PHONE.....................714 894-0531
Tom Goodwin, *Pr*
EMP: 68
SALES (corp-wide): 52.56MM **Privately Held**
Web: www.goodwininc.com
SIC: 2841 Soap and other detergents
PA: The Goodwin Ammonia Company Llc
12361 Monarch St
714 894-0531

**(P-5876)**
**KINGMAN INDUSTRIES INC**
26370 Beckman Ct Ste A, Murrieta (92562-1005)
PHONE.....................951 698-1812
Barbara Mandel, *CEO*
Paul Mandel Junior, *Pr*
Mitch Mayer, *Pr*
▲ EMP: 20 EST: 1974
SQ FT: 23,000
SALES (est): 3.38MM **Privately Held**
Web: www.kingmanlabs.com
SIC: 2841 2869 5169 5122 Soap and other detergents; Industrial organic chemicals, nec; Detergents and soaps, except specialty cleaning; Cosmetics

**(P-5877)**
**METHOD PRODUCTS INC**
Also Called: Method Home Care
631 Howard St Fl 5, San Francisco (94105-3934)
PHONE.....................415 931-3947
▲ EMP: 115 EST: 1992
SALES (est): 23.23MM
SALES (corp-wide): 1.11B **Privately Held**
Web: www.methodproducts.com
SIC: 2841 Soap and other detergents
PA: S. C. Johnson & Son, Inc.
1525 Howe St
262 260-2000

**(P-5878)**
**MISSION KLEENSWEEP PROD INC**
Also Called: Mission Laboratories
13644 Live Oak Ln, Baldwin Park (91706-1317)
PHONE.....................323 223-1405
TOLL FREE: 888
Helen Rosenbaum, *Pr*
EMP: 53 EST: 1936
SQ FT: 75,000
SALES (est): 5MM **Privately Held**
SIC: 2841 2842 Soap and other detergents; Polishes and sanitation goods

**(P-5879)**
**PANROSA ENTERPRISES INC**
550 Monica Cir, Corona (92878-5496)
PHONE.....................951 339-5888
Peter Chengjian Pan, *Pr*
Jingwen Zhao, *
Chenyang Sun, *
▲ EMP: 60 EST: 2003
SALES (est): 5.49MM **Privately Held**
Web: www.panrosa.com
SIC: 2841 Soap and other detergents

**(P-5880)**
**PROCTER & GAMBLE MFG CO**
Also Called: Procter & Gamble
8201 Fruitridge Rd, Sacramento (95826-4716)
PHONE.....................916 383-3800
Bob Randall, *Brnch Mgr*
EMP: 438
SALES (corp-wide): 84.04B **Publicly Held**
Web: us.pg.com
SIC: 2841 Detergents, synthetic organic or inorganic alkaline
HQ: The Procter & Gamble Manufacturing Company
1 Procter And Gamble Plz
Cincinnati OH 45202
513 983-1100

**(P-5881)**
**ROOTS COMMUNITY HEALTH CENTER**
Also Called: Clean 360
9925 International Blvd Ste 5, Oakland (94603-2558)
PHONE.....................510 777-1177
Noha Aboelata Md, *CEO*
EMP: 84 EST: 2008
SALES (est): 12.35MM **Privately Held**
Web: www.rootsclinic.org
SIC: 2841 Soap and other detergents

**(P-5882)**
**SHIFT PACKAGING LLC**
14261 Proctor Ave Ste A, La Puente (91746-2936)
PHONE.....................206 412-4253
Jeffrey Welch, *Pr*
EMP: 15 EST: 2020
SALES (est): 1.25MM **Privately Held**
SIC: 2841 Soap and other detergents

**(P-5883)**
**STAR PACIFIC INC**
27462 Sunrise Farm Rd, Los Altos Hills (94022-3221)
PHONE.....................510 471-6555
John Miller, *Pr*
Lee Price, *Treas*
Ed Kubiak, *VP*
EMP: 20 EST: 1996
SQ FT: 57,000
SALES (est): 3.64MM **Privately Held**
SIC: 2841 Soap and other detergents

**(P-5884)**
**VALUE PRODUCTS INC**
Also Called: Pride Line Products
2128 Industrial Dr, Stockton (95206-4936)
PHONE.....................209 345-3817
Douglas Hall, *Pr*
Erica Hall, *
EMP: 25 EST: 1969
SQ FT: 34,000
SALES (est): 4.5MM **Privately Held**
Web: www.valueproductsinc.com
SIC: 2841 Detergents, synthetic organic or inorganic alkaline

## 2842 Polishes And Sanitation Goods

**(P-5885)**
**2ND GEN PRODUCTIONS INC**
Also Called: Mark V Products
400 El Sobrante Rd, Corona (92879-5755)
PHONE.....................800 877-6282
Mark Marchese, *CEO*
Dora Marchese, *Pr*
Frank Marchese, *VP Mktg*
Robert Marchese, *Sec*
EMP: 15 EST: 1961
SALES (est): 4.21MM **Privately Held**
Web: www.mark-v.com
SIC: 2842 5013 Waxes for wood, leather, and other materials; Automotive supplies

**(P-5886)**
**3D/INTERNATIONAL INC**
20724 Centre Pointe Pkwy Unit 1, Santa Clarita (91350-2980)
PHONE.....................661 250-2020
Tony Goren, *Mgr*
EMP: 142
SALES (corp-wide): 5.44B **Publicly Held**
Web: www.3dproducts.com
SIC: 2842 Automobile polish
HQ: 3d/International, Inc.
2200 West Loop S Ste 200
Houston TX 77027
713 871-7000

**(P-5887)**
**AM WAX INC**
625 The City Dr S Ste 325, Orange (92868-4985)
PHONE.....................714 228-1999
Matthew Peng, *Pr*
EMP: 16 EST: 2008
SALES (est): 1.1MM **Privately Held**
SIC: 2842 Beeswax, processing of

**(P-5888)**
**AMREP INC**
1555 S Cucamonga Ave, Ontario (91761-4512)
PHONE.....................770 422-2071
William Redmond, *Pr*
EMP: 285
SALES (corp-wide): 978.45MM **Privately Held**
Web: www.amrepproducts.com
SIC: 2842 Specialty cleaning
HQ: Amrep, Inc.
600 Galleria Pkwy Se
Atlanta GA 30339
877 428-9937

**(P-5889)**
**AUTO-CHLOR SYSTEM WASH INC**

## 2842 - Polishes And Sanitation Goods (P-5910)

16141 Hart St, Van Nuys (91406-3904)
PHONE..............................818 376-0940
Brian Gate, *Mgr*
**EMP:** 15
**SALES (corp-wide):** 285.79MM **Privately Held**
Web: www.autochlor.com
**SIC: 2842** Laundry cleaning preparations
**PA:** Auto-Chlor System Of Washington, Inc.
450 Ferguson Dr
650 967-3085

### (P-5890)
### AWESOME PRODUCTS INC (PA)
Also Called: La's Totally Awesome
6370 Altura Blvd, Buena Park (90620-1001)
PHONE..............................714 562-8873
Loksarang D Hardas, *CEO*
◆ **EMP:** 125 **EST:** 1983
**SQ FT:** 250,000
**SALES (est):** 80.68MM
**SALES (corp-wide):** 80.68MM **Privately Held**
Web: www.lastotallyawesome.com
**SIC: 2842** Cleaning or polishing preparations, nec

### (P-5891)
### B&D INVESTMENT PARTNERS INC (PA)
20950 Centre Pointe Pkwy, Santa Clarita (91350-2975)
◆ **EMP:** 48 **EST:** 1960
**SQ FT:** 100,000
**SALES (est):** 28.05MM
**SALES (corp-wide):** 28.05MM **Privately Held**
Web: www.bc-labs.com
**SIC: 2842** 2844 Cleaning or polishing preparations, nec; Perfumes, cosmetics and other toilet preparations

### (P-5892)
### BEST SANITIZERS INC
310 Providence Mine Rd Ste 120, Nevada City (95959-2981)
P.O. Box 1360 (95946-1360)
PHONE..............................530 265-1800
Hillard T Witt, *Pr*
Ed Hay, *
Ryan Witt, *
▲ **EMP:** 52 **EST:** 1995
**SQ FT:** 10,000
**SALES (est):** 11.71MM **Privately Held**
Web: www.bestsanitizers.com
**SIC: 2842** Sanitation preparations

### (P-5893)
### BURNS ENVIRONMENTAL SVCS INC
19360 Rinaldi St Ste 381, Northridge (91326-1607)
PHONE..............................800 577-4009
**EMP:** 42 **EST:** 2005
**SALES (est):** 397.67K **Privately Held**
Web: www.burns-enviro.com
**SIC: 2842** Polishes and sanitation goods

### (P-5894)
### CALIFORNIA SCENTS LLC
18850 Von Karman Ave Ste 200, Irvine (92612-1586)
◆ **EMP:** 18 **EST:** 1993
**SQ FT:** 13,000
**SALES (est):** 2.74MM
**SALES (corp-wide):** 2.96B **Publicly Held**
Web: www.californiascents.com
**SIC: 2842** 2844 Polishes and sanitation goods; Perfumes, cosmetics and other toilet preparations

**PA:** Energizer Holdings, Inc.
533 Maryville Univ Dr
314 985-2000

### (P-5895)
### CHEMETALL US INC
Also Called: Chemetall Oakite
46716 Lakeview Blvd, Fremont (94538-6529)
PHONE..............................408 387-5340
Daryl Burnett, *Mgr*
**EMP:** 50
**SALES (corp-wide):** 74.89B **Privately Held**
Web: www.chemetallna.com
**SIC: 2842** Automobile polish
**HQ:** Chemetall U.S., Inc.
675 Central Ave
New Providence NJ 07974

### (P-5896)
### CILAJET LLC
16425 Ishida Ave, Gardena (90248-2924)
PHONE..............................310 320-8000
Jaci Warren, *Pr*
**EMP:** 25 **EST:** 2006
**SALES (est):** 3.49MM **Privately Held**
Web: www.cilajet.com
**SIC: 2842** 7542 Automobile polish; Washing and polishing, automotive

### (P-5897)
### CLOROX COMPANY
Also Called: Clorox
4900 Johnson Dr, Pleasanton (94588-3308)
PHONE..............................925 368-6000
Wayne L Delker, *Pr*
**EMP:** 19
**SALES (corp-wide):** 7.09B **Publicly Held**
Web: www.thecloroxcompany.com
**SIC: 2842** Polishes and sanitation goods
**PA:** The Clorox Company
1221 Broadway
510 271-7000

### (P-5898)
### CLOROX COMPANY (PA)
Also Called: CLOROX
1221 Broadway, Oakland (94612-1871)
PHONE..............................510 271-7000
Linda Rendle, *CEO*
Matthew J Shattock, *
Kevin B Jacobsen, *Ex VP*
Eric Reynolds, *Ex VP*
Angela Hilt, *CLO*
▼ **EMP:** 1232 **EST:** 1913
**SALES (est):** 7.09B
**SALES (corp-wide):** 7.09B **Publicly Held**
Web: www.thecloroxcompany.com
**SIC: 2842** 2673 2035 2844 Laundry cleaning preparations; Food storage and frozen food bags, plastic; Seasonings and sauces, except tomato and dry; Cosmetic preparations

### (P-5899)
### CLOROX MANUFACTURING COMPANY
Also Called: Clorox
2300 W San Bernardino Ave, Redlands (92374-5000)
PHONE..............................909 307-2756
**EMP:** 47
**SALES (corp-wide):** 7.09B **Publicly Held**
Web: www.thecloroxcompany.com
**SIC: 2842** Polishes and sanitation goods
**HQ:** Clorox Manufacturing Company
1221 Broadway
Oakland CA 94612

### (P-5900)
### CLOROX MANUFACTURING COMPANY (HQ)
Also Called: Clorox
1221 Bdwy, Oakland (94612-1837)
PHONE..............................510 271-7000
T E Bailey, *CEO*
Karen M Rose, *
Suzanne Thompson, *
◆ **EMP:** 180 **EST:** 1996
**SALES (est):** 468.32MM
**SALES (corp-wide):** 7.09B **Publicly Held**
Web: www.thecloroxcompany.com
**SIC: 2842** Polishes and sanitation goods
**PA:** The Clorox Company
1221 Broadway
510 271-7000

### (P-5901)
### CLOROX MANUFACTURING COMPANY
Also Called: Clorox
2600 Huntington Dr, Fairfield (94533-9736)
PHONE..............................707 437-1051
Scott Johnston, *Mgr*
**EMP:** 106
**SALES (corp-wide):** 7.09B **Publicly Held**
Web: www.thecloroxcompany.com
**SIC: 2842** Bleaches, household: dry or liquid
**HQ:** Clorox Manufacturing Company
1221 Broadway
Oakland CA 94612

### (P-5902)
### CLOROX SERVICES COMPANY (HQ)
Also Called: Clorox
1221 Broadway, Oakland (94612-1837)
PHONE..............................510 271-7000
Benno Dorer, *Ch*
Kevin Jacobsen, *
**EMP:** 100 **EST:** 1996
**SALES (est):** 201.2MM
**SALES (corp-wide):** 7.09B **Publicly Held**
Web: www.thecloroxcompany.com
**SIC: 2842** 5169 Polishes and sanitation goods; Specialty cleaning and sanitation preparations
**PA:** The Clorox Company
1221 Broadway
510 271-7000

### (P-5903)
### ENVIRNMNTAL CMPLIANCE PROS INC
2701 Del Paso Rd Ste 130-704, Sacramento (95835-2306)
PHONE..............................916 953-9006
Joy Brown, *CEO*
**EMP:** 31 **EST:** 2021
**SALES (est):** 1.8MM **Privately Held**
Web: www.environmentalcomplianceprosinc.com
**SIC: 2842** Sanitation preparations

### (P-5904)
### FLO-KEM INC
19402 S Susana Rd, Compton (90221-5712)
PHONE..............................310 632-7124
**EMP:** 48
Web: www.flo-kem.com
**SIC: 2842** Cleaning or polishing preparations, nec

### (P-5905)
### GEA FARM TECHNOLOGIES INC
Also Called: W S West
2717 S 4th St, Fresno (93725-1938)

PHONE..............................559 497-5074
Warren Dorathy, *Mgr*
**EMP:** 40
**SALES (corp-wide):** 5.84B **Privately Held**
Web: www.gea.com
**SIC: 2842** Polishes and sanitation goods
**HQ:** Gea Farm Technologies, Inc.
1385 N Weber Rd
Romeoville IL 60446
630 369-8100

### (P-5906)
### GEN LABS INC (PA)
5568 Schaefer Ave, Chino (91710-9041)
P.O. Box 1697 (91708-1697)
PHONE..............................909 591-8451
**EMP:** 135 **EST:** 1968
**SALES (est):** 33.04MM
**SALES (corp-wide):** 33.04MM **Privately Held**
Web: www.genlabscorp.com
**SIC: 2842** 2841 5169 7389 Polishes and sanitation goods; Soap and other detergents; Chemicals and allied products, nec; Packaging and labeling services

### (P-5907)
### GPS ASSOCIATES INC
1803 Carnegie Ave, Santa Ana (92705-5502)
PHONE..............................949 408-3162
Joe Parisi, *CEO*
Renee Gaudreau, *
**EMP:** 49 **EST:** 1993
**SALES (est):** 1.85MM
**SALES (corp-wide):** 1.85MM **Publicly Held**
Web: www.guardrxhandsanitizer.com
**SIC: 2842** Sanitation preparations, disinfectants and deodorants
**PA:** Mountain High Acquisitions Corp.
4350 Executive Dr Ste 200
760 402-5105

### (P-5908)
### GRANITE GOLD INC
12780 Danielson Ct Ste A, Poway (92064-8857)
PHONE..............................858 499-8933
Lenny Sciarrino, *CEO*
Scott Martin, *COO*
Leonard Pellegrino, *VP*
**EMP:** 91 **EST:** 2002
**SALES (est):** 4.64MM **Privately Held**
Web: www.granitegold.com
**SIC: 2842** Cleaning or polishing preparations, nec

### (P-5909)
### GRANITIZE PRODUCTS INC
Also Called: Granitize Aviation Intl
11022 Vulcan St, South Gate (90280-7621)
P.O. Box 2306 (90280-9306)
PHONE..............................562 923-5438
Tony Raymondo, *CEO*
Betty Raymondo, *
◆ **EMP:** 75 **EST:** 1930
**SQ FT:** 30,000
**SALES (est):** 19.81MM **Privately Held**
Web: www.granitize.com
**SIC: 2842** Automobile polish

### (P-5910)
### JASON MARKK INC (PA)
15325 Blackburn Ave, Norwalk (90650-6842)
PHONE..............................213 687-7060
Jason M Angsuvarn, *CEO*
▲ **EMP:** 32 **EST:** 2007
**SALES (est):** 4.12MM

## 2842 - Polishes And Sanitation Goods (P-5911)

SALES (corp-wide): 4.12MM **Privately Held**
Web: www.jasonmarkk.com
SIC: **2842** Shoe polish or cleaner

### (P-5911)
### KIK-SOCAL INC
Also Called: Kik
9028 Dice Rd, Santa Fe Springs (90670-2520)
PHONE..................................562 946-6427
Jeffrey M Nodland, *CEO*
Stratis Katsiris, *
William Smith, *
Ben W Kaak, *
**EMP:** 3000 **EST:** 1995
**SQ FT:** 3,000,000
SALES (est): 28.04MM
SALES (corp-wide): 771.06MM **Privately Held**
SIC: **2842** Bleaches, household: dry or liquid
HQ: Kik International Llc
   1725 N Brown Rd
   Lawrenceville GA 30043

### (P-5912)
### LAB CLEAN INC
3627 Briggeman Dr, Los Alamitos (90720-2475)
PHONE..................................714 689-0063
Mark Cunningham, *CEO*
Mark Cunningham, *Managing Member*
Matthew Bays, *
**EMP:** 25 **EST:** 2005
**SQ FT:** 40,000
SALES (est): 2.29MM **Privately Held**
Web: www.lab-clean.com
SIC: **2842** Cleaning or polishing preparations, nec

### (P-5913)
### LMC ENTERPRISES (PA)
Also Called: Chemco Products Company
6401 Alondra Blvd, Paramount (90723-3758)
PHONE..................................562 602-2116
Elaine S Cooper, *CEO*
Janis Utz, *
John D Grimes, *
**EMP:** 70 **EST:** 1962
**SQ FT:** 15,000
SALES (est): 41.67MM
SALES (corp-wide): 41.67MM **Privately Held**
Web: www.chemcoprod.com
SIC: **2842** Cleaning or polishing preparations, nec

### (P-5914)
### LMC ENTERPRISES
Also Called: Flo-Kem
19402 S Susana Rd, Compton (90221-5712)
PHONE..................................310 632-7124
Elaine Cooper, *CEO*
**EMP:** 50
**SQ FT:** 20,000
SALES (corp-wide): 41.67MM **Privately Held**
Web: www.chemcoprod.com
SIC: **2842** Cleaning or polishing preparations, nec
PA: Lmc Enterprises
   6401 E Alondra Blvd
   562 602-2116

### (P-5915)
### MAINTEX INC (PA)
13300 Nelson Ave, City Of Industry (91746-1516)
P.O. Box 7110 (91744-7110)
PHONE..................................800 446-1888
TOLL FREE: 800
▲ **EMP:** 140 **EST:** 1960
SALES (est): 66.69MM
SALES (corp-wide): 66.69MM **Privately Held**
Web: www.maintex.com
SIC: **2842** 5087 Cleaning or polishing preparations, nec; Janitors' supplies

### (P-5916)
### MEGUIARS INC (HQ)
Also Called: Brilliant Solutions
213 Technology Dr, Irvine (92618-2437)
PHONE..................................949 752-8000
Barry J Meguiar, *Pr*
Michael W Meguiar, *
Catherine E Bayless, *
◆ **EMP:** 50 **EST:** 1901
SALES (est): 49.16MM
SALES (corp-wide): 32.68B **Publicly Held**
Web: www.meguiars.com
SIC: **2842** Cleaning or polishing preparations, nec
PA: 3m Company
   3m Center
   651 733-1110

### (P-5917)
### MORGAN GALLACHER INC
Also Called: Custom Chemical Formulators
8707 Millergrove Dr, Santa Fe Springs (90670-2001)
PHONE..................................562 695-1232
Harriet Von Luft, *Ch Bd*
David M Smith, *
Tam Sarmiento, *
▼ **EMP:** 46 **EST:** 1964
**SQ FT:** 100,000
SALES (est): 3.55MM **Privately Held**
Web: www.morgan-gallacher.com
SIC: **2842** 5169 Cleaning or polishing preparations, nec; Industrial chemicals

### (P-5918)
### MPM BUILDING SERVICES INC
Also Called: Mpm & Associates
7011 Hayvenhurst Ave Ste F, Van Nuys (91406-3822)
PHONE..................................818 708-9676
Paul Davis, *Pr*
Mike Danesh, *VP*
**EMP:** 25 **EST:** 1975
**SQ FT:** 35,000
SALES (est): 890.5K **Privately Held**
Web: www.mpmco.com
SIC: **2842** Polishes and sanitation goods

### (P-5919)
### MYSMILE ORAL CARE INC
8238 Mayten Ave, Rancho Cucamonga (91730-3922)
PHONE..................................909 908-4615
Hong Chen, *CEO*
**EMP:** 20 **EST:** 2022
SALES (est): 320.24K **Privately Held**
SIC: **2842** Polishes and sanitation goods

### (P-5920)
### NO PRSSURE PRSSURE WSHG SVCS L
Also Called: No Pressure Landscape Services
41880 Kalmia St Ste 165, Murrieta (92562-8838)
PHONE..................................951 477-1988
Lennix Gibson, *Managing Member*
**EMP:** 20 **EST:** 2015
SALES (est): 3.07MM **Privately Held**
SIC: **2842** 0782 8744 4971 Polishes and sanitation goods; Lawn and garden services; Facilities support services; Irrigation systems

### (P-5921)
### OIL-DRI CORPORATION AMERICA
950 Petroleum Club Rd, Taft (93268-9748)
P.O. Box 1277 (93268-1277)
PHONE..................................661 765-7194
**EMP:** 46
SALES (corp-wide): 437.59MM **Publicly Held**
Web: www.oildri.com
SIC: **2842** Sweeping compounds, oil or water absorbent, clay or sawdust
PA: Oil-Dri Corporation Of America
   410 N Mich Ave Ste 400
   312 321-1515

### (P-5922)
### OLYMPUS WATER HOLDINGS IV LP (PA)
360 N Crescent Dr Bldg S, Beverly Hills (90210-2529)
PHONE..................................310 739-6325
Mary Ann Sigler, *Pr*
**EMP:** 23 **EST:** 2020
SALES (est): 17.33MM
SALES (corp-wide): 17.33MM **Privately Held**
SIC: **2842** Polishes and sanitation goods

### (P-5923)
### PACE INTERNATIONAL LLC
Also Called: Pace
8030 W Doe Ave, Visalia (93291-9721)
PHONE..................................559 651-4877
**EMP:** 15
SALES (corp-wide): 161.94MM **Privately Held**
Web: www.paceint.com
SIC: **2842** 2879 2873 2899 Specialty cleaning; Agricultural chemicals, nec; Plant foods, mixed: from plants making nitrog. fertilizers; Water treating compounds
HQ: Pace International, Llc
   5661 Branch Rd
   Wapato WA 98951
   800 722-2476

### (P-5924)
### PATRIOT POLISHING COMPANY
47260 Wrangler Rd, Aguanga (92536-9518)
PHONE..................................310 903-7409
Raymond Esfandi, *CFO*
**EMP:** 15 **EST:** 2016
SALES (est): 201.24K **Privately Held**
SIC: **2842** Metal polish

### (P-5925)
### PEERLESS MATERIALS COMPANY
4442 E 26th St, Vernon (90058-4318)
P.O. Box 33228 (90033)
PHONE..................................323 266-0313
Louis J Buty, *Pr*
Peter H Pritchard, *
▲ **EMP:** 40 **EST:** 1967
**SQ FT:** 35,000
SALES (est): 7.39MM **Privately Held**
Web: www.americantex.com
SIC: **2842** Sweeping compounds, oil or water absorbent, clay or sawdust

### (P-5926)
### PRESERVE INC
Also Called: Preserve International
1355 Paulson Rd, Turlock (95380-5541)
P.O. Box 3135 (95381-3135)
PHONE..................................800 995-1607
**EMP:** 28
SIC: **2842** Sanitation preparations

### (P-5927)
### QUANTUM GLOBAL TECH LLC (HQ)
Also Called: Quantumclean
26462 Corporate Ave, Hayward (94545-3914)
P.O. Box 1000 (18917-1000)
PHONE..................................215 892-9300
Scott Nicholas, *CEO*
David Zuck, *
Stephen Dirugeris, *
Rahul Naik, *CIO*
▲ **EMP:** 105 **EST:** 2000
SALES (est): 48.58MM
SALES (corp-wide): 1.73B **Publicly Held**
Web: www.uct.com
SIC: **2842** Specialty cleaning
PA: Ultra Clean Holdings, Inc.
   26462 Corporate Ave
   510 576-4400

### (P-5928)
### SOAPTRONIC LLC
19771 Pauling, Foothill Ranch (92610)
PHONE..................................949 465-8955
Horst Binderbauer, *Managing Member*
◆ **EMP:** 25 **EST:** 1998
SALES (est): 4.84MM **Privately Held**
Web: www.germstar.com
SIC: **2842** 2841 Sanitation preparations, disinfectants and deodorants; Soap and other detergents

### (P-5929)
### SUNSHINE MAKERS INC (PA)
Also Called: Simple Green
15922 Pacific Coast Hwy, Huntington Beach (92649-1894)
PHONE..................................562 795-6000
Bruce P Fabrizio, *
Bruce P Fabrizio, *
Rose Concilia, *
Jeffrey Hyder, *
Patrick Sheehan, *
▼ **EMP:** 51 **EST:** 1981
**SQ FT:** 25,000
SALES (est): 25.67MM
SALES (corp-wide): 25.67MM **Privately Held**
Web: www.simplegreen.com
SIC: **2842** Cleaning or polishing preparations, nec

### (P-5930)
### SURTEC INC
Also Called: Surtec System, The
2350 Interlaken Ct, Lodi (95242-9195)
PHONE..................................209 820-3700
William A Fields, *Pr*
Don C Fromm, *
◆ **EMP:** 50 **EST:** 1975
SALES (est): 9.98MM **Privately Held**
Web: www.surtecsystem.com
SIC: **2842** 5087 Specialty cleaning; Floor machinery, maintenance

### (P-5931)
### SUSTAINABLE CARE COMPANY INC ✪
633 W 5th St Fl 28, Los Angeles (90071)

▲ = Import ▼ = Export
◆ = Import/Export

# PRODUCTS & SERVICES SECTION

## 2844 - Toilet Preparations (P-5954)

PHONE.....................310 210-7090
Mark Sorensen, *CEO*
Thomas Riebs, *
**EMP:** 25 **EST:** 2024
**SALES (est):** 825.06K **Privately Held**
**SIC:** 2842 Polishes and sanitation goods

### (P-5932)
### SYNSUS PRVATE LBEL PRTNERS LLC
980 Rancheros Dr, San Marcos (92069-3029)
PHONE.....................713 714-0225
Greg Crawford, *Brnch Mgr*
**EMP:** 59
**SALES (corp-wide):** 49.88MM **Privately Held**
Web: www.synsus.com
**SIC:** 2842 Polishes and sanitation goods
**PA:** Synsus Private Label Partners, Llc
 18211 Katy Fwy Ste 325
 713 714-0225

### (P-5933)
### ULTRA CHEM LABS CORP
1370 Valley Vista Dr, Diamond Bar (91765-3921)
PHONE.....................909 605-1640
Christopher Shieh, *Pr*
Cesar Castro, *Sec*
▲ **EMP:** 15 **EST:** 2014
**SALES (est):** 2.51MM **Privately Held**
Web: www.ultrachemlabs.com
**SIC:** 2842 Floor waxes

### (P-5934)
### US CONTINENTAL MARKETING INC (PA)
Also Called: U.S. Continental
310 Reed Cir, Corona (92879-1349)
PHONE.....................951 808-8888
David Lee Williams, *Pr*
◆ **EMP:** 81 **EST:** 1988
**SQ FT:** 40,000
**SALES (est):** 22.78MM **Privately Held**
Web: www.uscontinental.com
**SIC:** 2842 Leather dressings and finishes

## 2843 Surface Active Agents

### (P-5935)
### CHEMEOR INC
727 Arrow Grand Cir, Covina (91722-2148)
PHONE.....................626 966-3808
Yongchun Tang, *Ch Bd*
Pat Mills, *
Patrick Shuler, *
Carl Aften, *
▲ **EMP:** 40 **EST:** 2005
**SQ FT:** 16,000
**SALES (est):** 9.29MM **Privately Held**
Web: www.chemeor.com
**SIC:** 2843 1389 2911 Surface active agents; Chemically treating wells; Aromatic chemical products

### (P-5936)
### HENKEL US OPERATIONS CORP
21551 Prairie St, Chatsworth (91311-5831)
PHONE.....................818 435-0889
**EMP:** 41
**SALES (corp-wide):** 23.39B **Privately Held**
Web: www.henkel-northamerica.com
**SIC:** 2843 Surface active agents
**HQ:** Henkel Us Operations Corporation
 1 Henkel Way
 Rocky Hill CT 06067
 860 571-5100

### (P-5937)
### HENKEL US OPERATIONS CORP
20021 S Susana Rd, Compton (90221-5721)
PHONE.....................562 297-6840
Tam Nguyen, *Brnch Mgr*
**EMP:** 175
**SALES (corp-wide):** 23.39B **Privately Held**
Web: www.henkel.com
**SIC:** 2843 Surface active agents
**HQ:** Henkel Us Operations Corporation
 1 Henkel Way
 Rocky Hill CT 06067
 860 571-5100

### (P-5938)
### JUSTICE BROS DIST CO INC
Also Called: Justice Bros-J B Car Care Pdts
2734 Huntington Dr, Duarte (91010-2301)
PHONE.....................626 359-9174
Edward R Justice Senior, *Ch Bd*
Edward R Justice Junior, *Pr*
▲ **EMP:** 25 **EST:** 1947
**SQ FT:** 33,000
**SALES (est):** 5.22MM **Privately Held**
Web: www.justicebrothers.com
**SIC:** 2843 2899 Surface active agents; Chemical preparations, nec

## 2844 Toilet Preparations

### (P-5939)
### ADONIS INC
475 N Sheridan St, Corona (92878-4021)
PHONE.....................951 432-3960
Helga Arminak, *CEO*
**EMP:** 42 **EST:** 2020
**SQ FT:** 73,200
**SALES (est):** 9.01MM **Privately Held**
Web: www.adoniscontractmanufacturer.com
**SIC:** 2844 Perfumes, cosmetics and other toilet preparations

### (P-5940)
### ALASTIN SKINCARE INC
5999 Avenida Encinas, Carlsbad (92008-4431)
PHONE.....................844 858-7546
Amber Edwards, *CEO*
Alan Widgerow, *CMO**
John Garruto, *
Tom Christenson, *
Cam Garner, *Ch Bd*
**EMP:** 150 **EST:** 2015
**SALES (est):** 32.27MM **Privately Held**
Web: www.alastin.com
**SIC:** 2844 Perfumes, cosmetics and other toilet preparations

### (P-5941)
### ALL GOOD
1149 Market Ave, Morro Bay (93442-2011)
PHONE.....................877 239-4667
**EMP:** 27 **EST:** 2019
**SALES (est):** 285.78K **Privately Held**
Web: www.allgoodbodycare.com
**SIC:** 2844 Perfumes, cosmetics and other toilet preparations

### (P-5942)
### ALLURE LABS LLC
Also Called: Allure Labs
30901 Wiegman Ct, Hayward (94544-7809)
PHONE.....................510 489-8896
Sam Dhatt, *CEO*
Renu Dhatt, *
▲ **EMP:** 70 **EST:** 1995
**SQ FT:** 50,000
**SALES (est):** 13.53MM **Privately Held**
Web: www.allurelabs.com
**SIC:** 2844 Cosmetic preparations

### (P-5943)
### AMERICAN INTL INDS INC
Also Called: Aii Beauty
2220 Gaspar Ave, Commerce (90040-1516)
PHONE.....................323 728-2999
David Eisenstein, *CEO*
◆ **EMP:** 1100 **EST:** 1998
**SQ FT:** 224,000
**SALES (est):** 9.53MM **Privately Held**
Web: www.aiibeauty.com
**SIC:** 2844 Perfumes, cosmetics and other toilet preparations

### (P-5944)
### ARCHIPELAGO INC
Also Called: Archipelago Botanicals
1548 18th St, Santa Monica (90404-3404)
PHONE.....................213 743-9200
David Klass, *CEO*
Gregory Corzine, *
◆ **EMP:** 110 **EST:** 1994
**SALES (est):** 12.06MM **Privately Held**
Web: www.shoparchipelago.com
**SIC:** 2844 3999 Perfumes, cosmetics and other toilet preparations; Candles

### (P-5945)
### AWARE PRODUCTS LLC
Also Called: Voyant Beauty
9250 Mason Ave, Chatsworth (91311-6005)
PHONE.....................818 206-6700
Richard Mcevoy, *CEO*
Bill Saracco, *
▲ **EMP:** 150 **EST:** 1973
**SQ FT:** 60,000
**SALES (est):** 44.89MM
**SALES (corp-wide):** 771.06MM **Privately Held**
**SIC:** 2844 Hair preparations, including shampoos
**HQ:** Voyant Beauty Holdings, Inc.
 6710 River Rd
 Hodgkins IL 60525
 708 482-8881

### (P-5946)
### AZK INC
1990 San Pablo Ave, Pinole (94564)
PHONE.....................510 724-9999
Ali Z Khan, *CEO*
Wali Zia, *Sls Mgr*
**EMP:** 22 **EST:** 2007
**SALES (est):** 1.27MM **Privately Held**
Web: www.martinniinc.com
**SIC:** 2844 Cosmetic preparations

### (P-5947)
### BBEAUTIFUL LLC
Also Called: Chrislie Formulations
1361 Mountain View Cir, Azusa (91702-1649)
PHONE.....................626 610-2332
◆ **EMP:** 40
**SIC:** 2844 5999 Cosmetic preparations; Cosmetics

### (P-5948)
### BIO CREATIVE ENTERPRISES (PA)
Also Called: Bio Creative Labs
350 Kalmus Dr, Costa Mesa (92626-6013)
PHONE.....................714 352-3600
Jason Freeman, *CEO*
▲ **EMP:** 15 **EST:** 2003
**SALES (est):** 4.06MM **Privately Held**
Web: www.becarelove.com
**SIC:** 2844 Perfumes, cosmetics and other toilet preparations

### (P-5949)
### BLUEFIELD ASSOCIATES INC
5430 Brooks St, Montclair (91763-4520)
PHONE.....................909 476-6027
Iheatu N Obioha, *CEO*
Chimere K Obioha, *
Tembi Sukuta, *
◆ **EMP:** 30 **EST:** 1986
**SQ FT:** 30,000
**SALES (est):** 2.5MM **Privately Held**
Web: www.bluefieldinc.com
**SIC:** 2844 5122 Cosmetic preparations; Cosmetics, perfumes, and hair products

### (P-5950)
### BOTANX LLC
3357 E Miraloma Ave Ste 156, Anaheim (92806-1937)
PHONE.....................714 854-1601
James Mcgee, *Managing Member*
▲ **EMP:** 50 **EST:** 2005
**SALES (est):** 5.21MM **Privately Held**
Web: www.botanx.com
**SIC:** 2844 Cosmetic preparations

### (P-5951)
### BRIGHT INNOVATION LABS
Also Called: Bocchi Laboratories
26421 Ruether Ave, Santa Clarita (91350-2621)
PHONE.....................661 252-3807
Robert J Bocchi, *Managing Member*
**EMP:** 29
**SQ FT:** 86,200
**SALES (corp-wide):** 277.12MM **Privately Held**
Web: www.brightinnovationlabs.com
**SIC:** 2844 Perfumes, cosmetics and other toilet preparations
**HQ:** Shadow Holdings, Llc
 9200 Smiths Mill Rd
 New Albany OH 43054
 614 741-7458

### (P-5952)
### CALI CHEM INC
Also Called: Be Beauty
14271 Corporate Dr Ste B, Garden Grove (92843-5000)
PHONE.....................714 265-3740
Tung Doan, *CEO*
Duc Doan, *
Amy Doan, *
▲ **EMP:** 25 **EST:** 2005
**SQ FT:** 50,000
**SALES (est):** 7.1MM **Privately Held**
Web: www.bebeautyproducts.com
**SIC:** 2844 Face creams or lotions

### (P-5953)
### CALIFORNIA INTERFILL INC
8178 Mar Vista Ct, Riverside (92504-4324)
PHONE.....................951 351-2619
Thomas E Boyes, *Pr*
▲ **EMP:** 15 **EST:** 2000
**SQ FT:** 20,000
**SALES (est):** 2.46MM **Privately Held**
**SIC:** 2844 Cosmetic preparations

### (P-5954)
### CAROLINE CHU INC
288 Evelyn Way, San Francisco (94127-1712)
PHONE.....................415 279-2358
Caroline Chu, *CEO*
◆ **EMP:** 24 **EST:** 2007

---

(PA)=Parent Co (HQ)=Headquarters
✪ = New Business established in last 2 years

## 2844 - Toilet Preparations (P-5955)

**SALES (est):** 1.02MM **Privately Held**
**Web:** www.carolinechu.com
**SIC: 2844** Shampoos, rinses, conditioners: hair

### (P-5955)
### COLONIAL ENTERPRISES INC
690 Knox St Ste 200, Torrance (90502-1323)
**PHONE**.....................909 822-8700
Louis Navarro, *COO*
**EMP:** 40 **EST:** 1977
**SALES (est):** 4.92MM **Privately Held**
**SIC: 2844** 2087 Shampoos, rinses, conditioners: hair; Powders, drink

### (P-5956)
### COLUMBIA COSMETICS MFRS INC (PA)
1661 Timothy Dr, San Leandro (94577-2311)
**PHONE**.....................510 562-5900
Rachel Rendel, *CEO*
▲ **EMP:** 75 **EST:** 1972
**SQ FT:** 31,000
**SALES (est):** 14.13MM
**SALES (corp-wide):** 14.13MM **Privately Held**
**Web:** www.columbiacosmetics.com
**SIC: 2844** Cosmetic preparations

### (P-5957)
### COOLA LLC
Also Called: Coola Suncare
6023 Innovation Way Ste 110, Carlsbad (92009)
**PHONE**.....................760 940-2125
Eric Mccue, *CEO*
Christopher Birchby, *CCO*
Ron Wangerin, *
**EMP:** 56 **EST:** 2004
**SALES (est):** 8.05MM **Privately Held**
**Web:** www.coola.com
**SIC: 2844** 5722 Suntan lotions and oils; Suntanning equipment and supplies

### (P-5958)
### COOLA SUNBLOCK
1726 Ord Way, Oceanside (92056-1501)
**PHONE**.....................760 940-2125
**EMP:** 16 **EST:** 2018
**SALES (est):** 242.5K **Privately Held**
**Web:** www.coola.com
**SIC: 2844** Perfumes, cosmetics and other toilet preparations

### (P-5959)
### COSMETIC ENTERPRISES LTD
12848 Pierce St, Pacoima (91331-2524)
**PHONE**.....................818 896-5355
Richard Saute, *Pr*
Arda Saute, *Treas*
▲ **EMP:** 19 **EST:** 1980
**SQ FT:** 65,000
**SALES (est):** 4.04MM **Privately Held**
**Web:** www.cosmeticent.com
**SIC: 2844** Hair preparations, including shampoos

### (P-5960)
### COSMETIC GROUP USA INC
12708 Branford St, Pacoima (91331-4203)
**PHONE**.....................818 767-2889
Andrea Chuchvara, *CEO*
Judy Zegarelli, *
▼ **EMP:** 180 **EST:** 1984
**SQ FT:** 80,000
**SALES (est):** 18.46MM **Privately Held**
**Web:** www.cosmeticgroupusa.com

**SIC: 2844** Cosmetic preparations

### (P-5961)
### COSMETIC TECHNOLOGIES LLC
2585 Azurite Cir, Newbury Park (91320-1202)
**PHONE**.....................805 376-9960
▲ **EMP:** 60
**Web:** www.cosmetictechnologies.com
**SIC: 2844** Cosmetic preparations

### (P-5962)
### COSMO INTERNATIONAL CORP
Also Called: Cosmo International Fragrances
9200 W Sunset Blvd Ste 401, West Hollywood (90069-3502)
**PHONE**.....................310 271-1100
Axel Van Liempt, *Brnch Mgr*
**EMP:** 63
**SALES (corp-wide):** 49.87MM **Privately Held**
**Web:** www.cosmo-fragrances.com
**SIC: 2844** Perfumes, natural or synthetic
**PA:** Cosmo International Corp
  1341 W Newport Center Dr
  954 798-4500

### (P-5963)
### COSMOBEAUTI LABS & MFG INC
Also Called: Cosmo Beauty Lab & Mfg
480 E Arrow Hwy, San Dimas (91773-3340)
**PHONE**.....................909 971-9832
Barbara Choi, *Pr*
Ko Quach, *Stockholder*
▲ **EMP:** 15 **EST:** 2000
**SQ FT:** 10,000
**SALES (est):** 2.03MM **Privately Held**
**Web:** www.cosmobeautilab.com
**SIC: 2844** Face creams or lotions

### (P-5964)
### COSRICH GROUP INC
12243 Branford St, Sun Valley (91352-1010)
**PHONE**.....................818 686-2500
**EMP:** 35
**SALES (corp-wide):** 1.71B **Privately Held**
**Web:** www.ouchiesonline.com
**SIC: 2844** Perfumes, cosmetics and other toilet preparations
**HQ:** Cosrich Group, Inc.
  51 La France Ave 55
  Bloomfield NJ 07003
  866 771-7473

### (P-5965)
### COSWAY COMPANY INC
14805 S Maple Ave, Gardena (90248-1994)
**PHONE**.....................310 527-9135
Jose Lozano, *Mgr*
**EMP:** 15
**SALES (corp-wide):** 67.33MM **Privately Held**
**Web:** www.cosway.com
**SIC: 2844** 5699 Face creams or lotions; Bathing suits
**PA:** Cosway Company, Inc.
  20633 S Fordyce Ave
  310 900-4100

### (P-5966)
### COSWAY COMPANY INC (PA)
20633 S Fordyce Ave, Carson (90810-1019)
**PHONE**.....................310 900-4100
Richard L Hough, *CEO*
▲ **EMP:** 20 **EST:** 1963
**SALES (est):** 67.33MM

**SALES (corp-wide):** 67.33MM **Privately Held**
**Web:** www.cosway.com
**SIC: 2844** Face creams or lotions

### (P-5967)
### COSWAY COMPANY INC
20488 S Reeves Ave, Carson (90810-1011)
**PHONE**.....................310 609-3352
**EMP:** 15
**SALES (corp-wide):** 67.33MM **Privately Held**
**Web:** www.cosway.com
**SIC: 2844** Face creams or lotions
**PA:** Cosway Company, Inc.
  20633 S Fordyce Ave
  310 900-4100

### (P-5968)
### DAVIDS NATURAL TOOTHPASTE INC
33360 Zeiders Rd Ste 106, Menifee (92584-1408)
**PHONE**.....................949 933-1185
Eric Buss, *CEO*
**EMP:** 20 **EST:** 2015
**SALES (est):** 3.63MM **Privately Held**
**Web:** www.davids-usa.com
**SIC: 2844** Toothpastes or powders, dentifrices

### (P-5969)
### DEN-MAT CORPORATION (DH)
236 S Bdwy, Orcutt (93455-4605)
**PHONE**.....................805 922-8491
Robert L Ibsen, *CEO*
Noreen Freitas, *
▲ **EMP:** 500 **EST:** 1972
**SQ FT:** 2,500
**SALES (est):** 95.51MM
**SALES (corp-wide):** 167.38MM **Privately Held**
**Web:** www.denmat.com
**SIC: 2844** 3843 Toothpastes or powders, dentifrices; Dental materials
**HQ:** Den-Mat Holdings, Llc
  1017 W Central Ave
  Lompoc CA 93436

### (P-5970)
### DEN-MAT CORPORATION
21515 Vanowen St Ste 200, Canoga Park (91303-2715)
**PHONE**.....................800 445-0345
Robert Brennis, *Mgr*
**EMP:** 179
**SALES (corp-wide):** 167.38MM **Privately Held**
**Web:** www.denmat.com
**SIC: 2844** Toothpastes or powders, dentifrices
**HQ:** Den-Mat Corporation
  236 S Broadway St
  Orcutt CA 93455
  805 922-8491

### (P-5971)
### DERMALOGICA LLC (HQ)
Also Called: Dermal Group, The
1535 Beachey Pl, Carson (90746-4005)
**PHONE**.....................310 900-4000
Aurelian Lis, *Pr*
Jane Wurwand, *
◆ **EMP:** 150 **EST:** 1983
**SQ FT:** 52,000
**SALES (est):** 100.72MM
**SALES (corp-wide):** 64.79B **Privately Held**
**Web:** www.dermalogica.com
**SIC: 2844** Cosmetic preparations
**PA:** Unilever Plc
  Unilever House

207 572-1202

### (P-5972)
### DIAMOND WIPES INTL INC
4200 E Mission Blvd, Ontario (91761-2952)
**PHONE**.....................909 230-9888
**EMP:** 135
**SALES (corp-wide):** 51.1MM **Privately Held**
**Web:** www.diamondwipes.com
**SIC: 2844** Towelettes, premoistened
**PA:** Diamond Wipes International, Inc.
  4651 Schaefer Ave
  909 230-9888

### (P-5973)
### DIAMOND WIPES INTL INC
13775 Ramona Ave, Chino (91710-5405)
**PHONE**.....................909 230-9888
**EMP:** 68
**SALES (corp-wide):** 51.1MM **Privately Held**
**Web:** www.diamondwipes.com
**SIC: 2844** Towelettes, premoistened
**PA:** Diamond Wipes International, Inc.
  4651 Schaefer Ave
  909 230-9888

### (P-5974)
### DIAMOND WIPES INTL INC (PA)
Also Called: Diamond Wipes
4651 Schaefer Ave, Chino (91710-5542)
**PHONE**.....................909 230-9888
Steve Gallo, *CEO*
Jessica Chang Lum, *
Vivian Kul, *
Neville Kadimi, *
▲ **EMP:** 100 **EST:** 1994
**SALES (est):** 51.1MM
**SALES (corp-wide):** 51.1MM **Privately Held**
**Web:** www.diamondwipes.com
**SIC: 2844** Towelettes, premoistened

### (P-5975)
### DR SQUATCH LLC
4065 Glencoe Ave Apt 300b, Marina Del Rey (90292-6079)
**PHONE**.....................631 229-7068
Josh Friedman, *Pr*
Daniel Larson, *CFO*
**EMP:** 250 **EST:** 2013
**SALES (est):** 96.12MM **Privately Held**
**Web:** www.drsquatch.com
**SIC: 2844** 7389 Perfumes, cosmetics and other toilet preparations; Business services, nec

### (P-5976)
### EDEN BEAUTY CONCEPTS INC
Also Called: Eufora
5876 Owens Ave Ste 200, Carlsbad (92008)
**PHONE**.....................760 330-9941
Donald Bewley, *CEO*
Don Bewley, *CEO*
▲ **EMP:** 20 **EST:** 1994
**SALES (est):** 3.69MM **Privately Held**
**Web:** www.eufora.net
**SIC: 2844** 5087 Shampoos, rinses, conditioners: hair; Beauty salon and barber shop equipment and supplies

### (P-5977)
### EVERBRANDS INC
11791 Monarch St, Garden Grove (92841-1818)
**PHONE**.....................855 595-2999
Michael Florman, *CEO*
Joshua Wallace, *

# PRODUCTS & SERVICES SECTION

## 2844 - Toilet Preparations (P-5999)

**EMP:** 45 **EST:** 2013
**SQ FT:** 6,000
**SALES (est):** 7.99MM Privately Held
**Web:** www.eversmilewhite.com
**SIC: 2844** Oral preparations

### (P-5978)
### FNC MEDICAL CORPORATION
Also Called: Show Off Time
6000 Leland St, Ventura (93003-7605)
**PHONE**.................805 644-7576
Samuel S Pattillo, *Pr*
Samuel Pattillo, *Pr*
Synora Pattillo, *VP*
**EMP:** 20 **EST:** 1992
**SQ FT:** 36,000
**SALES (est):** 2.53MM Privately Held
**Web:** www.fncmedical.com
**SIC: 2844** Cosmetic preparations

### (P-5979)
### GAR LABORATORIES INC
1844 Massachusetts Ave, Riverside (92507-2662)
**PHONE**.................951 788-0700
▲ **EMP:** 110 **EST:** 1978
**SALES (est):** 22.48MM Privately Held
**Web:** www.garlabs.com
**SIC: 2844** Perfumes, cosmetics and other toilet preparations

### (P-5980)
### GIOVANNI COSMETICS INC
Also Called: Giovanni Hair Care & Cosmetics
2064 E University Dr, Rancho Dominguez (90220-6419)
P.O. Box 6990 (90212-6990)
**PHONE**.................310 952-9960
Giovanni J Guidotti, *CEO*
Arthur Guidotti, *
◆ **EMP:** 56 **EST:** 1979
**SALES (est):** 12.89MM Privately Held
**Web:** www.giovannicosmetics.com
**SIC: 2844** 5122 5999 Cosmetic preparations; Cosmetics, perfumes, and hair products; Cosmetics

### (P-5981)
### GLAM AND GLITS NAIL DESIGN INC
Also Called: Kiara Sky Professional Nails
8700 Swigert Ct Unit 209, Bakersfield (93311-9696)
**PHONE**.................661 393-4800
Khoa Duong, *CEO*
▲ **EMP:** 65 **EST:** 2013
**SALES (est):** 7.35MM Privately Held
**Web:** www.glamandglits.com
**SIC: 2844** Manicure preparations

### (P-5982)
### GRAHAM WEBB INTERNATIONAL INC (HQ)
6109 De Soto Ave, Woodland Hills (91367-3709)
**PHONE**.................760 918-3600
Rick Kornbluth, *Pr*
Thomas P Baumann, *VP*
**EMP:** 70 **EST:** 1989
**SQ FT:** 30,000
**SALES (est):** 2.44MM Publicly Held
**SIC: 2844** Hair preparations, including shampoos
**PA:** Coty Inc.
350 5th Ave

### (P-5983)
### GS COSMECEUTICAL USA INC
131 Pullman St, Livermore (94551-5128)
**PHONE**.................925 371-5000
Gurpreet Sangha, *CEO*
Varinder Sangha, *
▲ **EMP:** 68 **EST:** 1998
**SQ FT:** 60,000
**SALES (est):** 18MM Privately Held
**Web:** www.gscos.com
**SIC: 2844** Face creams or lotions

### (P-5984)
### H2O PLUS LLC (PA)
111 Sutter St Fl 22, San Francisco (94104-4540)
**PHONE**.................800 242-2284
Joy Chen, *Pr*
Robert Seidl, *VP*
◆ **EMP:** 90 **EST:** 1993
**SQ FT:** 82,000
**SALES (est):** 7.17MM Privately Held
**SIC: 2844** 5999 5122 Perfumes, cosmetics and other toilet preparations; Cosmetics; Cosmetics

### (P-5985)
### HAIN CELESTIAL GROUP INC
Also Called: Jason's Natural
5630 Rickenbacker Rd, Bell (90201-6412)
**PHONE**.................323 859-0553
David Vazquez, *Brnch Mgr*
**EMP:** 150
**Web:** www.hain.com
**SIC: 2844** Perfumes, cosmetics and other toilet preparations
**PA:** The Hain Celestial Group Inc
221 River St Ste 12

### (P-5986)
### HENKEL US OPERATIONS CORP
12155 Paine Pl, Poway (92064-7154)
**PHONE**.................203 655-8911
Tracy Henslin, *Brnch Mgr*
**EMP:** 46
**SALES (corp-wide):** 23.39B Privately Held
**Web:** www.henkel.com
**SIC: 2844** Hair preparations, including shampoos
**HQ:** Henkel Us Operations Corporation
1 Henkel Way
Rocky Hill CT 06067
860 571-5100

### (P-5987)
### HENKEL US OPERATIONS CORP
Joico Laboratories Division
5800 Bristol Pkwy, Culver City (90230-6696)
**PHONE**.................626 321-4100
Annie Hu, *Brnch Mgr*
**EMP:** 29
**SALES (corp-wide):** 23.39B Privately Held
**Web:** www.joico.com
**SIC: 2844** Hair preparations, including shampoos
**HQ:** Henkel Us Operations Corporation
1 Henkel Way
Rocky Hill CT 06067
860 571-5100

### (P-5988)
### HIMS INC (HQ)
Also Called: Hims & Hers
2269 Chestnut St # 523, San Francisco (94123-2600)
**PHONE**.................415 851-0195
Andrew Dudum, *CEO*
Spencer Lee, *CFO*
**EMP:** 28 **EST:** 2013
**SALES (est):** 53.04MM
**SALES (corp-wide):** 872MM Publicly Held
**Web:** www.hims.com
**SIC: 2844** 2329 2211 3143 Perfumes, cosmetics and other toilet preparations; Sweaters and sweater jackets, men's and boys'; Corduroys, cotton; Boots, dress or casual: men's
**PA:** Hims & Hers Health, Inc.
2269 Chestnut St # 523
415 851-0195

### (P-5989)
### HUNNIFACE LLC
9350 Wilshire Blvd Ste 203, Beverly Hills (90212-3214)
**PHONE**.................424 966-0281
Teairra Thomas, *CEO*
**EMP:** 15 **EST:** 2020
**SALES (est):** 436.6K Privately Held
**Web:** www.hunniface.com
**SIC: 2844** Cosmetic preparations

### (P-5990)
### HUNTER VAUGHAN LLC
Also Called: H2v By Burke Williams
450 N Oak St, Inglewood (90302)
**PHONE**.................626 534-7050
William K Armour, *CEO*
**EMP:** 250 **EST:** 2001
**SALES (est):** 448.69K Privately Held
**Web:** www.burkewilliams.com
**SIC: 2844** Perfumes, cosmetics and other toilet preparations

### (P-5991)
### IBG HOLDINGS INC
24841 Avenue Tibbitts, Valencia (91355-3405)
**PHONE**.................661 702-8680
Richard Mayne, *Pr*
Marissa Pomerantz, *VP*
▲ **EMP:** 20 **EST:** 2002
**SQ FT:** 5,000
**SALES (est):** 1.77MM Privately Held
**Web:** www.colorevolution.com
**SIC: 2844** Cosmetic preparations

### (P-5992)
### IDA CLASSIC INC (PA)
9530 De Soto Ave, Chatsworth (91311-5010)
**PHONE**.................818 773-9042
Ida Csiszar, *CEO*
Steve Csiszar, *
Frank Csiszar, *
▲ **EMP:** 125 **EST:** 1988
**SQ FT:** 70,000
**SALES (est):** 20.86MM Privately Held
**Web:** www.classiccosmetics.com
**SIC: 2844** Cosmetic preparations

### (P-5993)
### INNOVATIVE BIOSCIENCES CORP
Also Called: Innovative Body Science
1849 Diamond St, San Marcos (92078)
**PHONE**.................760 603-0772
Michelle Barton, *Pr*
▲ **EMP:** 20 **EST:** 1987
**SQ FT:** 16,000
**SALES (est):** 5.47MM Privately Held
**Web:** www.innovativebodyscience.com
**SIC: 2844** 8742 Perfumes, cosmetics and other toilet preparations; Management consulting services

### (P-5994)
### INSPARATION INC
Also Called: Brian Guy Electric Ltg Svcs Co
11950 Hertz Ave, Moorpark* (93021-7145)
**PHONE**.................805 553-0820
Lori Guy, *CEO*
**EMP:** 38 **EST:** 1987
**SALES (est):** 5.18MM Privately Held
**Web:** www.insparation.com
**SIC: 2844** Cosmetic preparations

### (P-5995)
### JOICO LABORATORIES INC
5800 Bristol Pkwy, Culver City (90230-6696)
**PHONE**.................626 321-4100
Sara Jones, *Pr*
Akira Mochizuki, *
Takahiro Iwabuchi, *
▲ **EMP:** 26 **EST:** 1976
**SALES (est):** 2.1MM Privately Held
**Web:** www.joico.com
**SIC: 2844** Hair preparations, including shampoos

### (P-5996)
### KAMSUT INCORPORATED
Also Called: Kama Sutra
5260 Kazuko Ct, Moorpark (93021-1789)
**PHONE**.................805 495-7479
Joseph Bolstad, *Pr*
▲ **EMP:** 20 **EST:** 1968
**SALES (est):** 2.43MM Privately Held
**Web:** www.kamasutra.com
**SIC: 2844** Cosmetic preparations

### (P-5997)
### KDC/ONE CHATSWORTH INC (DH)
20245 Sunburst St, Chatsworth (91311-6219)
**PHONE**.................818 709-1345
Nicholas Whitley, *CEO*
**EMP:** 99 **EST:** 2020
**SALES (est):** 96.64MM
**SALES (corp-wide):** 2.66B Privately Held
**Web:** www.kdc-one.com
**SIC: 2844** Shampoos, rinses, conditioners: hair
**HQ:** Kdc Us Holdings, Inc.
4400 S Hamilton Rd
Groveport OH 43125

### (P-5998)
### KDC/ONE CHATSWORTH INC
Also Called: Cosmetic Laboratories-America
20320 Prairie St, Chatsworth (91311-6026)
**PHONE**.................818 709-1345
Nicholas Whitley, *CEO*
**EMP:** 199
**SALES (corp-wide):** 2.66B Privately Held
**Web:** www.kdc-one.com
**SIC: 2844** Cosmetic preparations
**HQ:** Kdc/One Chatsworth, Inc.
20245 Sunburst St
Chatsworth CA 91311
818 709-1345

### (P-5999)
### KENVUE BRANDS LLC
Also Called: Neutrogena
5760 W 96th St, Los Angeles (90045)
**PHONE**.................310 642-1150
**EMP:** 237
**SALES (corp-wide):** 15.44B Publicly Held
**Web:** www.neutrogena.com
**SIC: 2844** Perfumes, cosmetics and other toilet preparations
**HQ:** Kenvue Brands Llc
1 Kenvue Way
Summit NJ 07901
908 874-1000

## 2844 - Toilet Preparations (P-6000)

**(P-6000)**
**KIM LAUBE & COMPANY INC**
Also Called: Kelco
2221 Statham Blvd, Oxnard (93033)
PHONE..................805 240-1300
Kim E Laube, *Pr*
▲ **EMP:** 40 **EST:** 1982
**SALES (est):** 4.96MM **Privately Held**
Web: www.kimlaubeco.com
**SIC: 2844** 3999 Hair preparations, including shampoos; Hair clippers for human use, hand and electric

**(P-6001)**
**KUM KANG TRADING USA INC**
Also Called: Black N Gold
6433 Alondra Blvd, Paramount (90723-3758)
PHONE..................562 531-6111
Yoon Oh, *Pr*
◆ **EMP:** 25 **EST:** 1987
**SQ FT:** 20,000
**SALES (est):** 994.86K **Privately Held**
**SIC: 2844** Hair preparations, including shampoos

**(P-6002)**
**LEE PHARMACEUTICALS**
1434 Santa Anita Ave, South El Monte (91733-3312)
PHONE..................626 442-3141
Ronald G Lee, *CEO*
Mike Agresti, *
▲ **EMP:** 82 **EST:** 1971
**SALES (est):** 2.33MM **Privately Held**
Web: www.leepharmaceuticals.com
**SIC: 2844** 2834 3843 Manicure preparations; Pharmaceutical preparations; Enamels, dentists'

**(P-6003)**
**LIBBY LABORATORIES INC**
1700 6th St, Berkeley (94710)
PHONE..................510 527-5400
Susan Libby, *Pr*
Gordon Libby, *
**EMP:** 23 **EST:** 1959
**SQ FT:** 25,000
**SALES (est):** 2.91MM **Privately Held**
Web: www.libbylabs.com
**SIC: 2844** 2834 2899 Cosmetic preparations; Pharmaceutical preparations; Chemical preparations, nec

**(P-6004)**
**MASTEY DE PARIS INC**
24841 Avenue Tibbitts, Valencia (91355-1269)
PHONE..................661 257-4814
Stephen Mastey, *Pr*
Lesley Mastey, *
Henri Mastey, *
**EMP:** 50 **EST:** 1976
**SALES (est):** 2.1MM **Privately Held**
Web: www.mastey.com
**SIC: 2844** Hair preparations, including shampoos

**(P-6005)**
**MEGA CREATION INC**
Also Called: Protec
228 Linus Pauling Dr, Hercules (94547-1823)
PHONE..................510 741-9998
Newton Lun, *CEO*
**EMP:** 30 **EST:** 2006
**SALES (est):** 2.73MM **Privately Held**
**SIC: 2844** Cosmetic preparations

**(P-6006)**
**MELISSA TRINIDAD**
Also Called: Paisleyriversoapco
3589 Vine St, Paso Robles (93446-1014)
PHONE..................805 536-0954
Melissa Trinidad, *Owner*
**EMP:** 21 **EST:** 2021
**SALES (est):** 271.56K **Privately Held**
**SIC: 2844** Bath salts

**(P-6007)**
**MERLE NORMAN COSMETICS INC (PA)**
Also Called: Merle Norman Cosmetics
9130 Bellanca Ave, Los Angeles (90045-4772)
PHONE..................310 641-3000
Jack B Nethercutt, *Ch Bd*
Amy Hackbart, *
Michael Cassidy, *
Helen Nethercutt, *
Rick Rosa, *
▲ **EMP:** 345 **EST:** 1974
**SQ FT:** 354,000
**SALES (est):** 39.64MM
**SALES (corp-wide):** 39.64MM **Privately Held**
Web: www.merlenorman.com
**SIC: 2844** 5999 Cosmetic preparations; Cosmetics

**(P-6008)**
**MOEHAIR USA INC**
1061 S Melrose St Ste A, Placentia (92870-7136)
PHONE..................888 663-7032
Imtiaz Rangrez, *CEO*
Jarrah Hala Al, *CEO*
▲ **EMP:** 15 **EST:** 2013
**SALES (est):** 2.08MM **Privately Held**
Web: www.moehair.com
**SIC: 2844** Hair preparations, including shampoos

**(P-6009)**
**NATIVE**
201 California St Ste 450, San Francisco (94111-5032)
PHONE..................562 217-9338
Katie Weltz, *Prin*
**EMP:** 21 **EST:** 2019
**SALES (est):** 2.15MM **Privately Held**
Web: www.nativecos.com
**SIC: 2844** Suntan lotions and oils

**(P-6010)**
**NATURAL THOUGHTS INCORPORATED**
Also Called: Biotone Professional Products
4757 Old Cliffs Rd, San Diego (92120-1134)
PHONE..................619 582-0027
▲ **EMP:** 38 **EST:** 1978
**SALES (est):** 5.02MM **Privately Held**
Web: www.biotone.com
**SIC: 2844** 5122 Cosmetic preparations; Drugs, proprietaries, and sundries

**(P-6011)**
**NEUTRADERM INC**
20660 Nordhoff St, Chatsworth (91311-6114)
PHONE..................818 534-3190
Samuel D Raoof, *CEO*
Toora J Raoof, *
▲ **EMP:** 25 **EST:** 2003
**SALES (est):** 11.54MM **Privately Held**
Web: www.neutraderm.com

**SIC: 2844** Cosmetic preparations

**(P-6012)**
**NYX LOS ANGELES INC**
Also Called: Nyx Cosmetics
588 Crenshaw Blvd, Torrance (90503-1705)
PHONE..................323 869-9420
◆ **EMP:** 140
**SIC: 2844** 5122 Perfumes, cosmetics and other toilet preparations; Cosmetics

**(P-6013)**
**O P I PRODUCTS INC (HQ)**
13034 Saticoy St, North Hollywood (91605-3510)
PHONE..................818 759-8688
Jules Kaufman, *CEO*
John Heffner, *
Susan Weiss-fischmann, *Ex VP*
Eric Schwartz, *
William Halfacre, *Executive Sales & Marketing Vice President*
◆ **EMP:** 500 **EST:** 1981
**SQ FT:** 250,000
**SALES (est):** 22.31MM **Publicly Held**
Web: www.opi.com
**SIC: 2844** Perfumes, cosmetics and other toilet preparations
**PA:** Coty Inc.
350 5th Ave

**(P-6014)**
**ORLY INTERNATIONAL INC (PA)**
Also Called: Sparitual
7710 Haskell Ave, Van Nuys (91406-1905)
PHONE..................818 994-1001
Jeff Pink, *Pr*
◆ **EMP:** 99 **EST:** 1977
**SQ FT:** 65,000
**SALES (est):** 24.85MM
**SALES (corp-wide):** 24.85MM **Privately Held**
Web: www.orlybeauty.com
**SIC: 2844** Cosmetic preparations

**(P-6015)**
**OYEWAN INC**
20501 Earlgate St, Walnut (91789-2909)
PHONE..................909 869-6200
Nick Whitley, *CEO*
▲ **EMP:** 20 **EST:** 2007
**SALES (est):** 2.7MM **Privately Held**
Web: www.vmlcosmetics.com
**SIC: 2844** Cosmetic preparations

**(P-6016)**
**PACIFIC WORLD CORPORATION (PA)**
757 S Alameda St Ste 280, Los Angeles (90021-1674)
PHONE..................949 598-2400
William George, *CEO*
Stuart Noyes, *
Bart Dibie, *
Justin Martini, *
Bob Nabholz, *
◆ **EMP:** 99 **EST:** 1947
**SALES (est):** 30.53MM
**SALES (corp-wide):** 30.53MM **Privately Held**
Web: www.pacificworldcorp.com
**SIC: 2844** 3421 3999 5199 Cosmetic preparations; Clippers, fingernail and toenail; Fingernails, artificial; General merchandise, non-durable

**(P-6017)**
**PANGAEA HOLDINGS INC**
Also Called: Lumin
1968 S Coast Hwy Pmb 3080, Laguna Beach (92651-3681)
PHONE..................402 704-7546
Ingrid Jackel, *CEO*
Richard Hong, *
**EMP:** 24 **EST:** 2018
**SALES (est):** 1.78MM **Privately Held**
Web: www.pmall.shop
**SIC: 2844** Perfumes, cosmetics and other toilet preparations

**(P-6018)**
**PERSON & COVEY INC**
616 Allen Ave, Glendale (91201-2014)
P.O. Box 25018 (91221-5018)
PHONE..................818 937-5000
Lorne Person Junior, *CEO*
Lorne Person Senior, *Ch Bd*
Sue Person, *
**EMP:** 45 **EST:** 1941
**SQ FT:** 36,000
**SALES (est):** 9.42MM **Privately Held**
Web: www.personandcovey.com
**SIC: 2844** 2834 Cosmetic preparations; Dermatologicals

**(P-6019)**
**PETRA-1 LP**
12386 Osborne Pl, Pacoima (91331-2013)
PHONE..................866 334-3702
Benjamin Whitham, *Pt*
**EMP:** 15 **EST:** 2016
**SALES (est):** 1.56MM **Privately Held**
Web: www.petra-1.com
**SIC: 2844** Perfumes, cosmetics and other toilet preparations

**(P-6020)**
**PHILIP B BOTANICALS PRODUCTS**
9053 Nemo St, West Hollywood (90069-5511)
PHONE..................202 759-0650
**EMP:** 16 **EST:** 2008
**SALES (est):** 159.95K **Privately Held**
Web: www.philipb.com
**SIC: 2844** Shampoos, rinses, conditioners: hair

**(P-6021)**
**PHYSICANS FORMULA HOLDINGS INC (HQ)**
Also Called: Physicians Formula
22067 Ferrero, Walnut (91789-5214)
PHONE..................626 334-3395
Ingrid Jackel, *CEO*
Jeffrey P Rogers, *Pr*
Leslie H Keegan, *VP Fin*
Chad Boise, *Ex Sec*
▲ **EMP:** 31 **EST:** 2003
**SQ FT:** 82,000
**SALES (est):** 22.27MM
**SALES (corp-wide):** 270.93MM **Privately Held**
Web: www.physiciansformula.com
**SIC: 2844** 5122 Cosmetic preparations; Drugs, proprietaries, and sundries
**PA:** Markwins Beauty Brands, Inc.
22067 Ferrero Pkwy
909 595-8898

**(P-6022)**
**PHYSICIANS FORMULA INC (DH)**
22067 Ferrero, City Of Industry (91789-5214)
PHONE..................626 334-3395
Ingrid Jackel, *CEO*
Jeff Rogers, *
Rick Kirchhoff, *
Joseph J Jaeger, *

**PRODUCTS & SERVICES SECTION**  **2844 - Toilet Preparations (P-6043)**

Richard John Almeida External Reporting, Mgr
▲ **EMP:** 57 **EST:** 1980
**SQ FT:** 82,800
**SALES (est):** 22.27MM
**SALES (corp-wide):** 270.93MM **Privately Held**
**Web:** www.physiciansformula.com
**SIC: 2844** Cosmetic preparations
**HQ:** Physicians Formula Holdings, Inc.
  22067 Ferrero
  Walnut CA 91789

**(P-6023)**
**PHYSICIANS FORMULA COSMT INC**
22067 Ferrero, City Of Industry (91789-5214)
**PHONE**.................................626 334-3395
Jeffrey P Rogers, Pr
Joseph J Jaeger, CFO
**EMP:** 72 **EST:** 1937
**SALES (est):** 2.47MM
**SALES (corp-wide):** 270.93MM **Privately Held**
**Web:** www.physiciansformula.com
**SIC: 2844** Cosmetic preparations
**HQ:** Physicians Formula, Inc.
  22067 Ferrero
  City Of Industry CA 91789
  626 334-3395

**(P-6024)**
**PLZ CORP**
2321 3rd St, Riverside (92507-3306)
**PHONE**.................................951 683-2912
Ian Sishman, Mgr
**EMP:** 86
**SALES (corp-wide):** 766.3MM **Privately Held**
**Web:** www.plzcorp.com
**SIC: 2844** 5122 5087 Cosmetic preparations; Cosmetics, perfumes, and hair products; Beauty parlor equipment and supplies
**PA:** Plz Corp.
  2651 Wrrnvlle Rd Stre 300 300 Stre
  630 628-3000

**(P-6025)**
**PLZ CORP**
14425 Yorba Ave, Chino (91710-5733)
**PHONE**.................................909 393-9475
Mikel Pruett, Brnch Mgr
**EMP:** 64
**SALES (corp-wide):** 766.3MM **Privately Held**
**Web:** www.plzcorp.com
**SIC: 2844** Cosmetic preparations
**PA:** Plz Corp.
  2651 Wrrnville Rd Ste 300
  630 628-3000

**(P-6026)**
**PLZ CORP**
2375 3rd St, Riverside (92507-3306)
**PHONE**.................................951 683-2912
Marcelo Jimenez, Brnch Mgr
**EMP:** 126
**SALES (corp-wide):** 766.3MM **Privately Held**
**Web:** www.plzcorp.com
**SIC: 2844** Cosmetic preparations
**PA:** Plz Corp.
  2651 Wrrnville Rd Ste 300
  630 628-3000

**(P-6027)**
**PRIMA FLEUR BOTANICALS INC**
84 Galli Dr, Novato (94949-5706)
**PHONE**.................................415 455-0957
Marianne Griffeth, Pr
Ron Griffeth, Sec
▲ **EMP:** 16 **EST:** 1993
**SQ FT:** 5,000
**SALES (est):** 6.16MM **Privately Held**
**Web:** www.primafleur.com
**SIC: 2844** 5169 Suntan lotions and oils; Essential oils

**(P-6028)**
**PROLABS FACTORY INC**
15001 Oxnard St, Van Nuys (91411-2613)
P.O. Box 492419 (90049-8419)
**PHONE**.................................818 646-3677
**EMP:** 26 **EST:** 2020
**SALES (est):** 790.63K **Privately Held**
**SIC: 2844** Cosmetic preparations

**(P-6029)**
**PURA NATURALS INC (HQ)**
Also Called: Advanced Innvtive Rcovery Tech
23615 El Toro Rd Ste X300, Lake Forest (92630-4707)
**PHONE**.................................949 273-8100
Robert Doherty, CEO
Robert Switzer, Sec
Derek Duhame, Pr
**EMP:** 15 **EST:** 2013
**SQ FT:** 4,000
**SALES (est):** 1.3MM
**SALES (corp-wide):** 14.06MM **Privately Held**
**Web:** www.puranaturalsproducts.com
**SIC: 2844** Cosmetic preparations
**PA:** Advanced Innovative Recovery Technologies, Inc.
  23615 El Toro Rd
  949 273-8100

**(P-6030)**
**RADIANCE BEAUTY & WELLNESS INC**
9419 Mason Ave, Chatsworth (91311-5204)
**PHONE**.................................818 812-9740
Debra Q Saavedra, CFO
Hugo Saavedra, CEO
**EMP:** 22 **EST:** 2021
**SALES (est):** 2.08MM **Privately Held**
**SIC: 2844** Perfumes, cosmetics and other toilet preparations

**(P-6031)**
**REVLON INC**
Creative Nail Design
1125 Joshua Way Ste 12, Vista (92081-7840)
**PHONE**.................................619 372-1379
Jim Northstrum, Brnch Mgr
**EMP:** 74
**Web:** www.revlon.com
**SIC: 2844** Cosmetic preparations
**HQ:** Revlon, Inc.
  55 Water St
  New York NY 10041

**(P-6032)**
**RMF SALT HOLDINGS LLC**
Also Called: San Francisco Bath Salt Co
2217 S Shore Ctr # 200, Alameda (94501-8073)
**PHONE**.................................510 477-9600
Lee J Williamson, Pr
◆ **EMP:** 16 **EST:** 2002
**SALES (est):** 2.45MM
**SALES (corp-wide):** 58.14MM **Privately Held**
**Web:** www.sfsalt.com
**SIC: 2844** 5149 Bath salts; Salt, edible
**PA:** Red Monkey Foods, Inc.
  6751 W Kings St
  417 319-7300

**(P-6033)**
**SAMUEL RAOOF**
Also Called: Brandmd Skin Care
20660 Nordhoff St, Chatsworth (91311-6114)
**PHONE**.................................818 534-3180
Samuel Raoof, Owner
**EMP:** 19 **EST:** 2014
**SALES (est):** 670.03K **Privately Held**
**Web:** www.brandmd.com
**SIC: 2844** Deodorants, personal

**(P-6034)**
**SAYDEL INC (PA)**
Also Called: Nina Religion
2475 E Slauson Ave, Huntington Park (90255-2887)
**PHONE**.................................323 585-2800
Santo Gil Orta, Owner
Santo Gil Orta, Pr
Michael Orta, VP
**EMP:** 15 **EST:** 1968
**SQ FT:** 11,000
**SALES (est):** 1.86MM
**SALES (corp-wide):** 1.86MM **Privately Held**
**Web:** www.saydel.com
**SIC: 2844** 5049 5999 Perfumes, natural or synthetic; Religious supplies; Religious goods

**(P-6035)**
**SEPHORA CO LLC (PA)**
6103 Obispo Ave, Long Beach (90805-3799)
**PHONE**.................................760 798-7654
Oscar Sadegi, Managing Member
◆ **EMP:** 20 **EST:** 2003
**SQ FT:** 20,000
**SALES (est):** 2.39MM
**SALES (corp-wide):** 2.39MM **Privately Held**
**Web:** www.sephora.com
**SIC: 2844** Cosmetic preparations

**(P-6036)**
**SHANI DARDEN SKINCARE INC**
1800 Century Park E Ste 400, Los Angeles (90067-1501)
**PHONE**.................................310 745-3150
Jessica Goldin, CEO
**EMP:** 21 **EST:** 2016
**SALES (est):** 2.22MM **Privately Held**
**Web:** www.shanidarden.com
**SIC: 2844** 5122 5961 Perfumes, cosmetics and other toilet preparations; Cosmetics, perfumes, and hair products; Cosmetics and perfumes, mail order

**(P-6037)**
**SHARPMART LLC** ✪
3911 Cleveland Ave, San Diego (92103-3402)
**PHONE**.................................619 278-1473
**EMP:** 25 **EST:** 2023
**SALES (est):** 127.8K **Privately Held**
**SIC: 2844** Perfumes, cosmetics and other toilet preparations

**(P-6038)**
**SMALL WORLD TRADING CO**
Also Called: Eo Products
90 Windward Way, San Rafael (94901-7200)
**PHONE**.................................415 945-1900
Susan Griffin-black, CEO
Brad Black, *
**EMP:** 150 **EST:** 1991
**SQ FT:** 40,000
**SALES (est):** 25.88MM **Privately Held**
**Web:** www.eoproducts.com
**SIC: 2844** Cosmetic preparations

**(P-6039)**
**SOLEVY CO LLC**
Also Called: VI Degrees Collective
28918 Hancock Pkwy, Valencia (91355)
**PHONE**.................................661 622-4880
Solomon Levy, Pr
**EMP:** 60 **EST:** 2017
**SALES (est):** 1.57MM **Privately Held**
**SIC: 2844** Perfumes, cosmetics and other toilet preparations

**(P-6040)**
**SPATZ CORPORATION**
Also Called: Spatz Laboratories
1600 Westar Dr, Oxnard (93033-2423)
**PHONE**.................................805 487-2122
Joel Lynn Nelson, CEO
Laura Nelson, *
George Jefferson, *
John Nelson, *
▲ **EMP:** 145 **EST:** 1954
**SQ FT:** 62,000
**SALES (est):** 44.34MM **Privately Held**
**Web:** www.spatzlabs.com
**SIC: 2844** 3089 Cosmetic preparations; Plastics containers, except foam

**(P-6041)**
**STILA STYLES LLC (HQ)**
Also Called: Stila Cosmetics
801 N Brand Blvd Ste 910, Glendale (91203)
**PHONE**.................................866 784-5201
Lynn Tilton, CEO
Desiree Tordecilla, CMO CCO
Sarah Lucero, OF EDUCATION AND ARTISTRY
▲ **EMP:** 44 **EST:** 2009
**SALES (est):** 19.97MM
**SALES (corp-wide):** 1.17K **Privately Held**
**Web:** www.stilacosmetics.com
**SIC: 2844** Cosmetic preparations
**PA:** Patriarch Partners, Llc
  1 Liberty Plz Rm 3500
  212 825-0550

**(P-6042)**
**SUMMER FRIDAYS LLC**
9180 Wilshire Blvd, Beverly Hills (90212-3414)
**PHONE**.................................612 804-0868
**EMP:** 20 **EST:** 2017
**SALES (est):** 378.48K **Privately Held**
**Web:** www.summerfridays.com
**SIC: 2844** Face creams or lotions

**(P-6043)**
**SUN DEEP INC (PA)**
Also Called: Sun Deep Cosmetics
31285 San Clemente St, Hayward (94544-7814)
P.O. Box 2814 (94526)
**PHONE**.................................510 441-2525
Sundeep Gill, Ex Dir
Jay Gill, CEO
Prabhleen S Gill, Pr
Ravi Gill, Sec
Sundeep Gill, VP
◆ **EMP:** 82 **EST:** 1987
**SQ FT:** 40,000
**SALES (est):** 19.68MM
**SALES (corp-wide):** 19.68MM **Privately Held**
**Web:** www.sundeepinc.com

## 2844 - Toilet Preparations (P-6044)

SIC: **2844** 5122 Cosmetic preparations; Cosmetics, perfumes, and hair products

**(P-6044)**
**SUNEVA MEDICAL INC (PA)**
5870 Pacific Center Blvd, San Diego (92121-4204)
PHONE.....................858 550-9999
Patricia Altavilla, *CEO*
Joseph A Newcomb, *
Stewart M Brown, *
Nicola Selley, *
Brian Pilcher, *CSO*
**EMP:** 42 **EST:** 2009
**SALES (est):** 15.41MM
**SALES (corp-wide):** 15.41MM **Privately Held**
Web: www.sunevamedical.com
SIC: **2844** 3842 Cosmetic preparations; Cosmetic restorations

**(P-6045)**
**TRADEMARK COSMETICS LLC**
545 Columbia Ave, Riverside (92507-2183)
PHONE.....................951 683-2631
Kristopher Dover, *CEO*
Joy Boiani, *
▲ **EMP:** 38 **EST:** 1994
**SQ FT:** 160,000
**SALES (est):** 2.54MM
**SALES (corp-wide):** 25.73MM **Privately Held**
Web: www.trademarkcosmetics.com
SIC: **2844** 7231 5999 5122 Hair preparations, including shampoos; Beauty shops; Cosmetics; Cosmetics
PA: Truarc Partners, Lp
545 Madison Ave
212 508-3300

**(P-6046)**
**TRANS-INDIA PRODUCTS INC**
Also Called: Shikai Products
3330 Coffey Ln Ste A, Santa Rosa (95403-1917)
P.O. Box 2866 (95405-0866)
PHONE.....................707 544-0298
Dennis Sepp, *Pr*
Vasant Telang, *
Carol Sepp, *
Jason Sepp, *
◆ **EMP:** 25 **EST:** 1970
**SQ FT:** 30,000
**SALES (est):** 3.57MM **Privately Held**
Web: www.shikai.com
SIC: **2844** Face creams or lotions

**(P-6047)**
**TRUE BOTANICALS INC**
1 Lovell Ave, Mill Valley (94941-1848)
PHONE.....................415 420-0403
Hillary Peterson, *CEO*
**EMP:** 86 **EST:** 2016
**SALES (est):** 8.25MM **Privately Held**
Web: www.truebotanicals.com
SIC: **2844** 5961 Perfumes, cosmetics and other toilet preparations; Cosmetics and perfumes, mail order

**(P-6048)**
**TU-K INDUSTRIES LLC**
5702 Firestone Pl, South Gate (90280-3714)
PHONE.....................562 927-3365
Arman Cornell, *Prin*
Alpin K Kaler, *
Eleanor Kaler, *
▲ **EMP:** 50 **EST:** 1970
**SQ FT:** 40,000
**SALES (est):** 5.32MM **Privately Held**
Web: www.tukindustries.com
SIC: **2844** Cosmetic preparations

**(P-6049)**
**TWILA TRUE COLLABORATIONS LLC**
Also Called: Trueclass
27156 Burbank, Foothill Ranch (92610-2503)
PHONE.....................949 258-9720
**EMP:** 20 **EST:** 2018
**SALES (est):** 1.51MM **Privately Held**
Web: www.twilatruecollaborations.com
SIC: **2844** 2389 Perfumes, cosmetics and other toilet preparations; Men's miscellaneous accessories

**(P-6050)**
**UNIVERSAL PACKG SYSTEMS INC (PA)**
Also Called: Paklab
14570 Monte Vista Ave, Chino (91710-5743)
PHONE.....................909 517-2442
Jeffery Morlando, *CEO*
Alan Kristel, *
William Wachtel, *
◆ **EMP:** 750 **EST:** 1987
**SALES (est):** 379.38MM
**SALES (corp-wide):** 379.38MM **Privately Held**
Web: www.paklab.com
SIC: **2844** 7389 3565 2671 Cosmetic preparations; Packaging and labeling services; Bottling machinery: filling, capping, labeling; Plastic film, coated or laminated for packaging

**(P-6051)**
**US COTTON LLC**
7100 W Sunnyview Ave, Visalia (93291-9639)
PHONE.....................559 651-3015
Gary S Jordan, *Prin*
**EMP:** 69
**SALES (corp-wide):** 1.44B **Privately Held**
Web: www.uscotton.com
SIC: **2844** Perfumes, cosmetics and other toilet preparations
HQ: U.S. Cotton, Llc
531 Cotton Blossom Cir
Gastonia NC 28054
216 676-6400

**(P-6052)**
**USP INC**
Also Called: Enjoy Haircare
1818 Ord Way, Oceanside (92056-1502)
PHONE.....................760 842-7700
Patrick Dockry, *Prin*
Gordon Fletcher, *
▲ **EMP:** 60 **EST:** 1995
**SQ FT:** 60,000
**SALES (est):** 8.58MM **Privately Held**
Web: www.enjoyhaircare.com
SIC: **2844** Hair preparations, including shampoos

**(P-6053)**
**VEGE - KURL INC**
Also Called: Vege-Tech Company
412 W Cypress St, Glendale (91204-2402)
PHONE.....................818 956-5582
Eric W Huffman, *Pr*
Helen Huffman, *
**EMP:** 60 **EST:** 1959
**SALES (est):** 9.8MM **Privately Held**
Web: www.vegelabs.com

SIC: **2844** 2833 5122 Shampoos, rinses, conditioners: hair; Medicinals and botanicals; Cosmetics, perfumes, and hair products

**(P-6054)**
**VINTNERS DAUGHTER LLC**
38 Keyes Ave, San Francisco (94129-1707)
PHONE.....................415 906-6735
**EMP:** 18 **EST:** 2017
**SALES (est):** 4.04MM **Privately Held**
Web: www.vintnersdaughter.com
SIC: **2844** Perfumes, cosmetics and other toilet preparations

**(P-6055)**
**W3LL PEOPLE INC**
570 10th St # 3, Oakland (94607-4038)
PHONE.....................800 790-1563
Tarang P Amin, *CEO*
▲ **EMP:** 15 **EST:** 2017
**SALES (est):** 636.68K
**SALES (corp-wide):** 1.02B **Publicly Held**
Web: www.wellpeople.com
SIC: **2844** Cosmetic preparations
PA: E.L.F. Beauty, Inc.
570 10th St
510 778-7787

**(P-6056)**
**WELLA CORPORATION (HQ)**
4500 Park Granada # 100, Calabasas (91302)
PHONE.....................800 422-2336
◆ **EMP:** 250 **EST:** 1935
**SALES (est):** 32.47MM **Publicly Held**
Web: us.wella.professionalstore.com
SIC: **2844** Toilet preparations
PA: Kkr & Co. Inc.
30 Hudson Yards

**(P-6057)**
**WESTRIDGE LABORATORIES INC**
1671 E Saint Andrew Pl, Santa Ana (92705-4932)
PHONE.....................714 259-9400
Gregg Richard Haskell, *CEO*
John Speelman, *
▲ **EMP:** 28 **EST:** 1993
**SALES (est):** 5.18MM **Privately Held**
Web: www.idlube.com
SIC: **2844** Cosmetic preparations

**(P-6058)**
**WESTWOOD LABORATORIES LLC**
766 S Ayon Ave, Azusa (91702-5112)
PHONE.....................626 969-3305
Arnel Garcia, *Mgr*
**EMP:** 25
Web: www.westwoodlabs.com
SIC: **2844** Perfumes, cosmetics and other toilet preparations
PA: Westwood Laboratories, Llc
710 S Ayon Ave

**(P-6059)**
**WESTWOOD LABORATORIES LLC (PA)**
710 S Ayon Ave, Azusa (91702)
PHONE.....................626 969-3305
Paul Schirmer, *CEO*
Brian Surpia Ctrl, *Prin*
▲ **EMP:** 25 **EST:** 2004
**SALES (est):** 12.06MM **Privately Held**
Web: www.westwoodlabs.com
SIC: **2844** Perfumes, cosmetics and other toilet preparations

**(P-6060)**
**XAVIER GROUP**
Also Called: Actsyl
707 Wilshire Blvd Ste 4375, Los Angeles (90017-3988)
P.O. Box 3667 (90266-1667)
PHONE.....................844 928-4378
Adam Xavier, *CEO*
**EMP:** 15 **EST:** 2019
**SALES (est):** 993.95K **Privately Held**
Web: www.xaviergroupinc.com
SIC: **2844** Hair preparations, including shampoos

**(P-6061)**
**YES TO INC**
Also Called: Yes To Carrots
3945 Freedom Cir Ste 560, Santa Clara (95054-1269)
PHONE.....................626 365-1976
Ingrid Jackel, *CEO*
Lance Kalish, *Stockholder*
Ido Leffler, *Stockholder*
▲ **EMP:** 40 **EST:** 2009
**SALES (est):** 6.34MM **Privately Held**
Web: www.yesto.com
SIC: **2844** 5122 Face creams or lotions; Cosmetics

**(P-6062)**
**YG LABORATORIES INC**
Also Called: Youthglow
11520 Warner Ave, Fountain Valley (92708-2512)
PHONE.....................714 474-2800
**EMP:** 28 **EST:** 1977
**SALES (est):** 4.05MM **Privately Held**
Web: www.yglabs.com
SIC: **2844** Cosmetic preparations

**(P-6063)**
**YOUTH TO PEOPLE INC**
888 N Douglas St, El Segundo (90245-2839)
PHONE.....................309 648-5500
Joseph Cloyes, *CEO*
Greg Gonzalez, *
**EMP:** 95 **EST:** 2018
**SALES (est):** 12.12MM
**SALES (corp-wide):** 6.5B **Privately Held**
Web: www.youthtothepeople.com
SIC: **2844** Lotions, shaving
PA: L'oreal
14 Rue Royale
140206000

**(P-6064)**
**ZENLEN INC**
Also Called: Native Deodorants
201 California St, San Francisco (94111-5002)
PHONE.....................415 834-8238
Tyler Myhan, *CEO*
Moiz Ali, *
**EMP:** 25 **EST:** 2016
**SALES (est):** 16.77MM
**SALES (corp-wide):** 84.04B **Publicly Held**
Web: www.nativecos.com
SIC: **2844** Deodorants, personal
PA: The Procter & Gamble Company
1 Procter & Gamble Plz
513 983-1100

**(P-6065)**
**ZO SKIN HEALTH INC (DH)**
9685 Research Dr, Irvine (92618-4657)
PHONE.....................949 988-7524
Mark Williams, *CEO*
Kevin Cornett, *
▲ **EMP:** 80 **EST:** 2006

SQ FT: 12,000
SALES (est): 38.31MM
SALES (corp-wide): 8.02B **Publicly Held**
Web: www.zoskinhealth.com
SIC: **2844** Face creams or lotions
HQ: Blackstone Tactical Opportunities
Advisors L.L.C.
345 Park Ave
New York NY 10154
212 583-5000

## 2851 Paints And Allied Products

**(P-6066)**
**AKZO NOBEL COATINGS INC**
2100 Adams Ave, San Leandro (94577-1010)
PHONE..................................510 562-8812
Greg Decker, *Pr*
**EMP:** 18
**SALES (corp-wide):** 11.6B **Privately Held**
SIC: **2851** Paints and allied products
HQ: Akzo Nobel Coatings Inc.
535 Marriott Dr Ste 500
Nashville TN 37214
440 297-5100

**(P-6067)**
**ALLIED COATINGS INC**
795 North Ave Ste D, Vista (92083-2926)
PHONE..................................800 630-2375
Donald J Palazzo, *Prin*
**EMP:** 16 **EST:** 2008
**SALES (est):** 1.46MM **Privately Held**
Web: www.alliedcoatings.com
SIC: **2851** Vinyl coatings, strippable

**(P-6068)**
**BEHR HOLDINGS CORPORATION (HQ)**
3400 W Segerstrom Ave, Santa Ana (92704-6405)
PHONE..................................714 545-7101
Jeff Filley, *Pr*
**EMP:** 26 **EST:** 1997
**SALES (est):** 1.5B
**SALES (corp-wide):** 7.97B **Publicly Held**
Web: www.behr.com
SIC: **2851** Paints and paint additives
PA: Masco Corporation
17450 College Pkwy
313 274-7400

**(P-6069)**
**BEHR PROCESS LLC (DH)**
Also Called: Behr Paint Company
1801 E Saint Andrew Pl, Santa Ana (92705-5044)
PHONE..................................714 545-7101
Megan Selby, *Pr*
Jonathan Sullivan, *
John G Sznewajs, *
Lawrence F Leaman, *
▼ **EMP:** 700 **EST:** 1947
**SQ FT:** 220,000
**SALES (est):** 1.5B
**SALES (corp-wide):** 7.97B **Publicly Held**
Web: www.behr.com
SIC: **2851** Paints and paint additives
HQ: Behr Holdings Corporation
3400 W Segerstrom Ave
Santa Ana CA 92704

**(P-6070)**
**BEHR SALES INC (HQ)**
Also Called: Behr Holdings
3400 W Segerstrom Ave, Santa Ana (92704-6405)
PHONE..................................714 545-7101
Jeffrey D Filley, *CEO*
Jonathan M Sullivan, *
Anthony Demiro, *
**EMP:** 169 **EST:** 1948
**SQ FT:** 54,000
**SALES (est):** 127.41MM
**SALES (corp-wide):** 7.97B **Publicly Held**
Web: www.behr.com
SIC: **2851** Paints and paint additives
PA: Masco Corporation
17450 College Pkwy
313 274-7400

**(P-6071)**
**CARDINAL INDUSTRIAL FINISHES (PA)**
1329 Potrero Ave Ca, South El Monte (91733-3088)
P.O. Box 9296 (91733)
PHONE..................................626 444-9274
Lawrence C Felix, *CEO*
◆ **EMP:** 100 **EST:** 1952
**SQ FT:** 50,000
**SALES (est):** 23.35MM
**SALES (corp-wide):** 23.35MM **Privately Held**
Web: www.cardinalpaint.com
SIC: **2851** Lacquers, varnishes, enamels, and other coatings

**(P-6072)**
**CARDINAL PAINT AND POWDER INC**
15010 Don Julian Rd, City Of Industry (91746-3301)
PHONE..................................626 937-6767
Stanley W Ekstrom, *Brnch Mgr*
**EMP:** 143
**SALES (corp-wide):** 95.19MM **Privately Held**
Web: www.cardinalpaint.com
SIC: **2851** Paints and allied products
PA: Cardinal Paint And Powder, Inc.
1900 Aerojet Way
702 852-2333

**(P-6073)**
**CARDINAL PAINT AND POWDER INC**
890 Commercial St, San Jose (95112-1410)
PHONE..................................408 452-8522
Tom Cross, *Mgr*
**EMP:** 96
**SALES (corp-wide):** 95.19MM **Privately Held**
Web: www.cardinalpaint.com
SIC: **2851** Paints and allied products
PA: Cardinal Paint And Powder, Inc.
1900 Aerojet Way
702 852-2333

**(P-6074)**
**CARDINAL PAINT AND POWDER INC**
1329 Potrero Ave, South El Monte (91733-3012)
PHONE..................................626 444-9274
**EMP:** 98 **EST:** 2016
**SALES (est):** 5.01MM **Privately Held**
Web: www.cardinalpaint.com
SIC: **2851** Paints and allied products

**(P-6075)**
**CHEMCRAFT COATINGS TECHNOLOGY INC**
311 Otterson Dr Ste 60, Chico (95928-8236)
PHONE..................................530 894-3585
**EMP:** 86
SIC: **2851** Paints and allied products

**(P-6076)**
**COMMERCE COATING SERVICES INC**
20725 S Western Ave Ste 144, Torrance (90501-1884)
PHONE..................................310 345-1979
Chris Palicke, *Pr*
Rene Ditton, *
**EMP:** 60 **EST:** 2018
**SALES (est):** 3.99MM **Privately Held**
Web: www.commercecoatingservices.com
SIC: **2851** Paints and allied products

**(P-6077)**
**CONSOLIDATED COLOR CORPORATION**
12316 Carson St, Hawaiian Gardens (90716-1604)
PHONE..................................562 420-7714
Michael J Muldown, *Pr*
Deborah Muldown, *
**EMP:** 25 **EST:** 1993
**SQ FT:** 30,000
**SALES (est):** 2.78MM **Privately Held**
Web: www.consolidatedcolorcorp.com
SIC: **2851** **2865** Paints and paint additives; Cyclic crudes and intermediates

**(P-6078)**
**CONTINENTAL COATINGS INC**
10938 Beech Ave, Fontana (92337-7216)
PHONE..................................909 355-1200
Te-hsiung Chang, *CEO*
Shih-yu Tseng, *Sec*
Ya-ju Chang, *CFO*
Te-hsien Chang, *Dir*
Te-jen Chang, *Dir*
▲ **EMP:** 16 **EST:** 1978
**SQ FT:** 20,000
**SALES (est):** 7.04MM **Privately Held**
Web: www.continentalyca.com
SIC: **2851** Paints and paint additives

**(P-6079)**
**DUCKBACK ACQUISITION CORP**
Also Called: Duckback Products
2644 Hegan Ln, Chico (95928-9572)
P.O. Box 980 (95927-0980)
PHONE..................................530 343-3261
▲ **EMP:** 44
Web: www.superdeck.com
SIC: **2851** Stains: varnish, oil, or wax

**(P-6080)**
**DUNCAN ENTERPRISES (PA)**
Also Called: Ilovetocreate A Duncan Entps
555 E Serena Ave, Fresno (93720-1617)
PHONE..................................559 291-4444
◆ **EMP:** 170 **EST:** 1944
**SALES (est):** 30.18MM
**SALES (corp-wide):** 30.18MM **Privately Held**
Web: www.ilovetocreate.com
SIC: **2851** **3299** **3952** **3944** Colors in oil, except artists'; Ceramic fiber; Lead pencils and art goods; Games, toys, and children's vehicles

**(P-6081)**
**DURA CHEMICALS INC (PA)**
Also Called: Amudan International
1901 Harrison St Ste 1100, Oakland (94612-3648)
PHONE..................................510 658-1987
Raghu Santhanam, *CEO*
◆ **EMP:** 29 **EST:** 1991
**SALES (est):** 9.21MM **Privately Held**
Web: www.durachem.com
SIC: **2851** **2819** Epoxy coatings; Catalysts, chemical

**(P-6082)**
**DURA TECHNOLOGIES INC**
2720 S Willow Ave Ste A, Bloomington (92316-3259)
P.O. Box 333 (92316-0333)
PHONE..................................909 877-8477
Douglas L Dennis, *Pr*
Gina L Dennis, *
▲ **EMP:** 150 **EST:** 1977
**SQ FT:** 14,000
**SALES (est):** 8.35MM **Privately Held**
SIC: **2851** Paints and allied products

**(P-6083)**
**ENNIS TRAFFIC SAFETY SOLUTIONS**
Also Called: Colorama Paints
6624 Stanford Ave, Los Angeles (90001-1538)
P.O. Box 1496 (90001-0496)
PHONE..................................323 758-1147
**EMP:** 48
SIC: **2851** Paints and allied products

**(P-6084)**
**EPMAR CORPORATION**
9930 Painter Ave, Whittier (90605-2759)
PHONE..................................562 946-8781
Peter Weissman, *Pr*
Joe Matrange, *
◆ **EMP:** 38 **EST:** 1980
**SQ FT:** 26,000
**SALES (est):** 1.62MM
**SALES (corp-wide):** 1.95B **Publicly Held**
Web: www.epmar.com
SIC: **2851** **2891** **2821** **3087** Epoxy coatings; Adhesives and sealants; Plastics materials and resins; Custom compound purchased resins
PA: Quaker Chemical Corporation
901 E Hector St
610 832-4000

**(P-6085)**
**FRAZEE INDUSTRIES INC**
Also Called: Frazee Paint & Wallcovering
6625 Miramar Rd, San Diego (92121-2508)
PHONE..................................858 626-3600
**EMP:** 900
Web: www.sherwin-williams.com
SIC: **2851** **5198** **5231** Paints, waterproof; Paints; Paint

**(P-6086)**
**FSI COATING TECHNOLOGIES INC**
45 Parker Ste 100, Irvine (92618-1658)
PHONE..................................949 540-1140
Antonios Grigoriou, *Pr*
Richard Chang, *CFO*
**EMP:** 24 **EST:** 1986
**SALES (est):** 2.6MM **Privately Held**
Web: www.fsicti.com
SIC: **2851** Lacquers, varnishes, enamels, and other coatings
HQ: Sdc Technologies, Inc.
45 Parker Ste 100
Irvine CA 92618
714 939-8300

## 2851 - Paints And Allied Products (P-6087)

**PRODUCTS & SERVICES SECTION**

**(P-6087)**
**INTEGRATED OPTICAL SVCS CORP**
Also Called: Ios Optics
3270 Keller St Ste 102, Santa Clara (95054-2615)
PHONE................408 982-9510
Douglas Fitzpatrick, *Pr*
Elmer Valencia, *
▲ **EMP:** 35 **EST:** 1978
**SALES (est):** 10.06MM **Privately Held**
Web: www.iosoptics.com
**SIC: 2851** 3827  Paints and allied products; Prisms, optical

**(P-6088)**
**JANCO CHEMICAL CORPORATION**
Also Called: Janco Airless Center
1235 5th St, Berkeley (94710-1395)
PHONE................510 527-9770
Kevin Glenn Kjelstrom, *Pr*
Janice S Kjelstrom, *
**EMP:** 33 **EST:** 1962
**SQ FT:** 12,000
**SALES (est):** 2.46MM **Privately Held**
**SIC: 2851** 5198  Wood stains; Paint brushes, rollers, sprayers

**(P-6089)**
**KELLY-MOORE PAINT COMPANY INC (HQ)**
Also Called: Kelly-Moore Paints
1390 El Camino Real Ste 300, San Carlos (94070-5146)
P.O. Box 3016  (94070-1316)
PHONE................650 592-8337
Charles Gassenheimer, *CEO*
Steve Devoe, *CRO*
◆ **EMP:** 250 **EST:** 1946
**SALES (est):** 451.78MM
**SALES (corp-wide):** 482.94MM **Privately Held**
Web: www.kellymoore.com
**SIC: 2851**  Paints: oil or alkyd vehicle or water thinned
**PA:** The Flacks Group
1450 Brickell Ave
305 647-2655

**(P-6090)**
**KELLY-MOORE PAINT COMPANY INC**
Also Called: Kelly-Moore Paints
320 Industrial Rd, San Carlos (94070-6285)
PHONE................650 595-1654
Jasjit Valbiel, *Mgr*
**EMP:** 23
**SALES (corp-wide):** 482.94MM **Privately Held**
Web: www.kellymoore.com
**SIC: 2851** 5231  Vinyl coatings, strippable; Paint
**HQ:** Kelly-Moore Paint Company Inc
1390 El Camino Real Fl 3
San Carlos CA 94070
650 592-8337

**(P-6091)**
**KRETUS INC**
1055 W Struck Ave, Orange (92867-3527)
PHONE................714 694-2061
Ronald Webber, *Pr*
**EMP:** 15 **EST:** 2019
**SALES (est):** 4.61MM **Privately Held**
Web: www.kretus.com
**SIC: 2851**  Paints and paint additives

**(P-6092)**
**LAIRD COATINGS CORPORATION**
Also Called: Coatings Resource
15541 Commerce Ln, Huntington Beach (92649-1601)
PHONE................714 894-5252
Jeff Laird, *CEO*
▲ **EMP:** 51 **EST:** 1976
**SQ FT:** 17,500
**SALES (est):** 1.55MM **Privately Held**
Web: www.coatingsresource.com
**SIC: 2851** 2865  Paints and paint additives; Dyes, synthetic organic

**(P-6093)**
**LIFE PAINT COMPANY (PA)**
Also Called: Life Specialty Coatings
12927 Sunshine Ave, Santa Fe Springs (90670-4732)
P.O. Box P.O. Box 2488  (90670-0488)
PHONE................562 944-6391
Ronald Sibbrel, *Pr*
Mike De La Vega, *
Fred Benson, *
▲ **EMP:** 22 **EST:** 1963
**SQ FT:** 30,000
**SALES (est):** 17.05MM
**SALES (corp-wide):** 17.05MM **Privately Held**
Web: www.lifespecialtycoatings.com
**SIC: 2851** 2899 2821  Paints and allied products; Waterproofing compounds; Thermosetting materials

**(P-6094)**
**MAST TECHNOLOGIES LLC**
8380 Camino Santa Fe Ste 200, San Diego (92121-2657)
PHONE................858 452-1700
Andrew Sundsmo, *Pr*
Mike Vanderby, *Treas*
Steve Burningham, *Sec*
Steven Chevillotte, *VP*
**EMP:** 18 **EST:** 2020
**SQ FT:** 4,995
**SALES (est):** 20.76MM
**SALES (corp-wide):** 150.17MM **Privately Held**
Web: www.masttechnologies.com
**SIC: 2851** 2891  Paints and allied products; Adhesives and sealants
**PA:** Sanders Industries Holdings, Inc.
3701 E Conant St
562 354-2920

**(P-6095)**
**MICROBLEND INC**
Also Called: Microblend Technologies
543 Country Club Dr, Simi Valley (93065-0637)
PHONE................330 998-4602
John E Tyson, *CEO*
Melvin J Sauder, *
Dan Trevino, *
John Bond, *
Jennifer Haslip, *
◆ **EMP:** 46 **EST:** 2014
**SALES (est):** 4.22MM **Privately Held**
Web: www.microblend.com
**SIC: 2851**  Paints and paint additives

**(P-6096)**
**MONOPOLE INC**
4661 Alger St, Los Angeles (90039-1127)
P.O. Box 250534 (91225-0534)
PHONE................818 500-8585
Antoine Abikhalil, *Pr*
▲ **EMP:** 15 **EST:** 1976
**SQ FT:** 40,000
**SALES (est):** 4.4MM **Privately Held**
Web: www.monopoleinc.com
**SIC: 2851**  Paints and allied products

**(P-6097)**
**MULTICOAT PRODUCTS INC**
23331 Antonio Pkwy, Rcho Sta Marg (92688-2664)
PHONE................949 888-7100
Dave Maietta, *Pr*
John Dill, *VP*
**EMP:** 15 **EST:** 1995
**SALES (est):** 2.51MM **Privately Held**
Web: www.multicoat.com
**SIC: 2851** 2899 3299 3479  Paints and paint additives; Waterproofing compounds; Stucco; Painting, coating, and hot dipping

**(P-6098)**
**OLIVE REFINISH**
19014 Pacific Coast Hwy, Malibu (90265-5406)
PHONE................805 273-5072
Albert Banoun, *Owner*
**EMP:** 25 **EST:** 2004
**SALES (est):** 536.84K **Privately Held**
Web: www.oliverefinish.com
**SIC: 2851**  Paints and allied products

**(P-6099)**
**PAINT-CHEM INC**
Also Called: Transchem Coatings
1680 Miller Ave, Los Angeles (90063-1613)
P.O. Box 151014 (90015-8014)
PHONE................213 747-7725
Amir Afshar, *Pr*
Eugene Golling, *VP*
Eddie Andrews, *Sec*
**EMP:** 15 **EST:** 1970
**SQ FT:** 8,000
**SALES (est):** 2.6MM **Privately Held**
Web: www.paint-chem.com
**SIC: 2851** 5198  Coating, air curing; Paints

**(P-6100)**
**PERFORMANCE COATINGS INC**
360 Lake Mendocino Dr, Ukiah (95482-9497)
P.O. Box 1569 (95482-1569)
PHONE................707 462-3023
Barbara Newell, *Ch Bd*
◆ **EMP:** 20 **EST:** 1983
**SQ FT:** 4,300
**SALES (est):** 7.86MM **Privately Held**
Web: www.penofin.com
**SIC: 2851**  Wood stains

**(P-6101)**
**POLY-FIBER INC (PA)**
Also Called: Consolidated Aircraft Coatings
4343 Fort Dr, Riverside (92509-6784)
P.O. Box 3129 (92519-3129)
PHONE................951 684-4280
Jon Goldenbaum, *Pr*
Greg Albarin, *Genl Mgr*
**EMP:** 17 **EST:** 1992
**SQ FT:** 75,000
**SALES (est):** 4.71MM **Privately Held**
Web: www.conaircraft.com
**SIC: 2851**  Undercoatings, paint

**(P-6102)**
**PPG INDUSTRIES INC**
10060 Mission Mill Rd, City Of Industry (90601-1738)
PHONE................562 692-4010
Gerald Roberts, *Mgr*
**EMP:** 17
**SALES (corp-wide):** 17.65B **Publicly Held**
Web: www.ppg.com
**SIC: 2851**  Paints and allied products
**PA:** Ppg Industries, Inc.
1 Ppg Pl
412 434-3131

**(P-6103)**
**PPG INDUSTRIES INC**
Also Called: Industrial Coatings Division
15541 Commerce Ln, Huntington Beach (92649-1601)
PHONE................714 894-5252
Jeff Laird, *Mgr*
**EMP:** 21
**SALES (corp-wide):** 17.65B **Publicly Held**
Web: www.ppg.com
**SIC: 2851**  Paints and allied products
**PA:** Ppg Industries, Inc.
1 Ppg Pl
412 434-3131

**(P-6104)**
**PPG INDUSTRIES INC**
11601 United St, Mojave (93501-7048)
PHONE................661 824-4532
Michelle Brown, *Mgr*
**EMP:** 24
**SALES (corp-wide):** 17.65B **Publicly Held**
Web: www.ppg.com
**SIC: 2851**  Paints and allied products
**PA:** Ppg Industries, Inc.
1 Ppg Pl
412 434-3131

**(P-6105)**
**PPG PAINTS**
12780 San Fernando Rd, Sylmar (91342-3728)
PHONE................818 362-6711
James Romano, *Mgr*
**EMP:** 15 **EST:** 1990
**SALES (est):** 5.23MM **Privately Held**
Web: www.ppg.com
**SIC: 2851**  Paints and allied products

**(P-6106)**
**PRC - DESOTO INTERNATIONAL INC**
Also Called: PPG Aerospace
1608 4th St Ste C2, Berkeley (94710-1749)
PHONE................510 526-1525
Carl Walker, *Brnch Mgr*
**EMP:** 55
**SALES (corp-wide):** 17.65B **Publicly Held**
Web: www.ppgaerospace.com
**SIC: 2851**  Paints and allied products
**HQ:** Prc - Desoto International, Inc.
24811 Ave Rockefeller
Valencia CA 91355
661 678-4209

**(P-6107)**
**PRODUCTS/TECHNIQUES INC**
Also Called: P T I
20282 Opus Dr, Riverside (92507-0154)
PHONE................909 877-3951
Steven Andrews, *Pr*
Barry Boden, *VP*
Ryan Andrews, *Treas*
**EMP:** 16 **EST:** 1947
**SALES (est):** 3.66MM **Privately Held**
Web: www.ptipaint.com
**SIC: 2851**  Coating, air curing

**(P-6108)**
**R & S MANUFACTURING & SUP INC**
16616 Garfield Ave, Paramount (90723-5305)
PHONE................909 622-5881

## PRODUCTS & SERVICES SECTION
### 2869 - Industrial Organic Chemicals, Nec (P-6126)

Ronald Hoffman, *Prin*
Susan Hoffman, *Sec*
**EMP:** 18 **EST:** 1976
**SQ FT:** 20,000
**SALES (est):** 2.8MM **Privately Held**
**Web:** www.rsmfgsupply.com
**SIC: 2851** Colors in oil, except artists'

**(P-6109)**
**R J MCGLENNON COMPANY INC (PA)**
Also Called: Maclac Co
198 Utah St, San Francisco (94103-4826)
**PHONE**.................................415 552-0311
Michael Mcglennon, *Pr*
Michael Mc Glennon, *Pr*
**EMP:** 22 **EST:** 1961
**SQ FT:** 30,000
**SALES (est):** 823.61K
**SALES (corp-wide):** 823.61K **Privately Held**
**Web:** www.maclac.com
**SIC: 2851** Lacquer: bases, dopes, thinner

**(P-6110)**
**RHINO LININGS CORPORATION (PA)**
9747 Businesspark Ave, San Diego (92131-1661)
**PHONE**.................................858 450-0441
Pierre M Gagnon, *CEO*
Russel Lewis, *
Sandra S Roberts, *
◆ **EMP:** 65 **EST:** 1988
**SQ FT:** 20,000
**SALES (est):** 48.17MM
**SALES (corp-wide):** 48.17MM **Privately Held**
**Web:** www.rhinolinings.com
**SIC: 2851** Coating, air curing

**(P-6111)**
**RUPERT GIBBON & SPIDER INC**
Also Called: Jacquard Products
1147 Healdsburg Ave, Healdsburg (95448-3405)
P.O. Box 425 (95448-0425)
**PHONE**.................................800 442-0455
Asher Katz, *Pr*
Devon Scrivner, *
**EMP:** 35 **EST:** 2013
**SQ FT:** 24,570
**SALES (est):** 10.14MM **Privately Held**
**Web:** www.jacquardproducts.com
**SIC: 2851 8742 5169** Paints and allied products; Merchandising consultant; Waxes, except petroleum

**(P-6112)**
**SIERRACIN CORPORATION (HQ)**
12780 San Fernando Rd, Sylmar (91342-3796)
**PHONE**.................................818 741-1656
Barry N Gillespie, *CEO*
David B Navikas, *
Michael H Mcgarry, *Ex VP*
Frank S Sklarsky, *
Viktoras R Sekmakas, *
▲ **EMP:** 550 **EST:** 1952
**SQ FT:** 287,000
**SALES (est):** 60.14MM
**SALES (corp-wide):** 17.65B **Publicly Held**
**Web:** www.ppgaerospace.com
**SIC: 2851** Paints and allied products
**PA:** Ppg Industries, Inc.
  1 Ppg Pl
  412 434-3131

**(P-6113)**
**SIMPSON COATINGS GROUP INC**
401 S Canal St A, South San Francisco (94080-4606)
P.O. Box 2265 (94083-2265)
**PHONE**.................................650 873-5990
**EMP:** 25
**SQ FT:** 35,000
**SALES (est):** 4.6MM
**SALES (corp-wide):** 5.06MM **Privately Held**
**SIC: 2851** Paints and allied products
**PA:** D J Simpson Company
  401 S Canal St A
  650 225-9404

**(P-6114)**
**SPECIALIZED MILLING CORP**
Also Called: Specialty Finishes
10330 Elm Ave, Fontana (92337-7319)
**PHONE**.................................909 357-7890
Jack Neems, *Pr*
Seymour S Neems, *Ch Bd*
Adele Neems, *Treas*
**EMP:** 50 **EST:** 1968
**SQ FT:** 11,000
**SALES (est):** 2.5MM **Privately Held**
**SIC: 2851** Paints and allied products

**(P-6115)**
**TRIANGLE COATINGS INC (PA)**
Also Called: Triangle Paint
4763 Bennett Dr, Livermore (94551-4804)
**PHONE**.................................510 895-8000
▲ **EMP:** 35 **EST:** 1932
**SALES (est):** 5.66MM
**SALES (corp-wide):** 5.66MM **Privately Held**
**Web:** www.tricoat.com
**SIC: 2851 3861** Paints, waterproof; Graphic arts plates, sensitized

**(P-6116)**
**VINYLVISIONS COMPANY LLC**
Also Called: Trim Quick
1233 Enterprise Ct, Corona (92882-7126)
**PHONE**.................................800 321-8746
John P Halle, *Managing Member*
Helen Halle, *Managing Member*
**EMP:** 20 **EST:** 2001
**SQ FT:** 40,000
**SALES (est):** 2.51MM
**SALES (corp-wide):** 6.64MM **Privately Held**
**Web:** www.vinylvisions.com
**SIC: 2851** Vinyl coatings, strippable
**PA:** Halle-Hopper, Llc
  5380 E Larry Caldwell Dr
  951 284-7373

**(P-6117)**
**WALTON INDUSTRIES INC**
Also Called: General Coatings
1220 E North Ave, Fresno (93725-1930)
P.O. Box 11127 (93771-1127)
**PHONE**.................................559 495-4004
Lee Walton, *Pr*
**EMP:** 23 **EST:** 1987
**SQ FT:** 40,000
**SALES (est):** 3.73MM **Privately Held**
**Web:** www.generalcoatings.net
**SIC: 2851 3086** Paints and allied products; Insulation or cushioning material, foamed plastics

### 2861 Gum And Wood Chemicals

**(P-6118)**
**KINGSFORD PRODUCTS COMPANY LLC (HQ)**
Also Called: Kingsford
1221 Broadway Fl 13, Oakland (94612-1837)
**PHONE**.................................510 271-7000
Richard T Conti, *Pr*
A W Biebl, *
Karen Rose, *
B C Blewett, *
L L Hoover, *
▲ **EMP:** 75 **EST:** 1971
**SQ FT:** 506,000
**SALES (est):** 106.96MM
**SALES (corp-wide):** 7.09B **Publicly Held**
**SIC: 2861 2099 2035 2033** Charcoal, except activated; Dressings, salad: dry mixes; Dressings, salad: raw and cooked (except dry mixes); Barbecue sauce: packaged in cans, jars, etc.
**PA:** The Clorox Company
  1221 Broadway
  510 271-7000

### 2865 Cyclic Crudes And Intermediates

**(P-6119)**
**COLOR SCIENCE INC**
Also Called: C S I
1230 E Glenwood Pl, Santa Ana (92707-3000)
**PHONE**.................................714 434-1033
Jocelyn Eubank, *CEO*
Mark Hoffenberg, *
**EMP:** 45 **EST:** 1989
**SQ FT:** 9,000
**SALES (est):** 22.22MM
**SALES (corp-wide):** 24.9MM **Privately Held**
**Web:** www.modifiedplastics.com
**SIC: 2865** Color pigments, organic
**PA:** Modified Plastics, Inc.
  1240 E Glenwood Pl
  714 546-4667

**(P-6120)**
**HAZTECH SYSTEMS INC**
4996 Gold Leaf Dr, Mariposa (95338-8510)
P.O. Box 929 (95338-0929)
**PHONE**.................................209 966-8088
Thomas Archibald, *CEO*
Brenda Archibald, *Sec*
**EMP:** 20 **EST:** 1986
**SALES (est):** 941.86K **Privately Held**
**Web:** www.hazcat.com
**SIC: 2865** Chemical indicators

### 2869 Industrial Organic Chemicals, Nec

**(P-6121)**
**AEMETIS ADVNCED FELS KEYES INC**
4209 Jessup Rd, Ceres (95307-9604)
P.O. Box 879 (95328-0879)
**PHONE**.................................209 632-4511
Eric Mcafee, *CEO*
Todd Waltz, *
Andy Foster, *
**EMP:** 47 **EST:** 2009
**SALES (est):** 25.72MM **Publicly Held**
**Web:** www.aemetis.com
**SIC: 2869** Ethyl alcohol, ethanol
**PA:** Aemetis, Inc.
  20400 Stvens Creek Blvd S

**(P-6122)**
**AEROJET ROCKETDYNE DE INC (DH)**
Also Called: Aerojet Rocketdyne
8900 De Soto Ave, Canoga Park (91304-1967)
P.O. Box 7922 (91309-7922)
**PHONE**.................................818 586-1000
Eileen P Drake, *CEO*
Pete Gleszer, *
Jerry Tucker, *
▲ **EMP:** 417 **EST:** 2005
**SALES (est):** 513.21MM
**SALES (corp-wide):** 19.42B **Publicly Held**
**Web:** www.l3harris.com
**SIC: 2869 3724** Rocket engine fuel, organic; Aircraft engines and engine parts
**HQ:** Aerojet Rocketdyne Holdings, Inc.
  222 N Pcf Cast Hwy Ste 50
  El Segundo CA 90245
  310 252-8100

**(P-6123)**
**AEROJET ROCKETDYNE DE INC**
8495 Carla Ln, West Hills (91304-3201)
**PHONE**.................................818 586-9629
**EMP:** 126
**SALES (corp-wide):** 19.42B **Publicly Held**
**Web:** www.l3harris.com
**SIC: 2869 3724** Rocket engine fuel, organic; Aircraft engines and engine parts
**HQ:** Inc Aerojet Rocketdyne Of De
  8900 De Soto Ave
  Canoga Park CA 91304
  818 586-1000

**(P-6124)**
**AEROJET ROCKETDYNE DE INC**
9001 Lurline Ave, Chatsworth (91311-6122)
P.O. Box 7922 (91309-7922)
**PHONE**.................................818 586-1000
Helen Lubin, *Brnch Mgr*
**EMP:** 115
**SALES (corp-wide):** 19.42B **Publicly Held**
**Web:** www.l3harris.com
**SIC: 2869 3724** Rocket engine fuel, organic; Aircraft engines and engine parts
**HQ:** Inc Aerojet Rocketdyne Of De
  8900 De Soto Ave
  Canoga Park CA 91304
  818 586-1000

**(P-6125)**
**ALLIANCE HOSE & EXTRUSIONS INC**
533 W Collins Ave, Orange (92867-5509)
P.O. Box 1037 (90249-0037)
**PHONE**.................................714 202-8500
Scott H Franklin, *VP*
▲ **EMP:** 15 **EST:** 1999
**SQ FT:** 15,000
**SALES (est):** 2.11MM
**SALES (corp-wide):** 5.74MM **Privately Held**
**Web:** www.ahehose.com
**SIC: 2869** Silicones
**PA:** California Gasket And Rubber Corporation
  533 W Collins Ave
  714 202-8500

**(P-6126)**
**AMYRIS INC (PA)**
Also Called: Amyris
5885 Hollis St Ste 100, Emeryville (94608-2405)

## 2869 - Industrial Organic Chemicals, Nec (P-6127)

PHONE..................................510 450-0761
Kathy L Fortmann, *CEO*
Geoffrey Duyk, *Interim Chairman of the Board*
Han Kieftenbeld, *Interim Chief Executive Officer*
Eduardo Alvarez, *COO*
◆ **EMP:** 258 **EST:** 2003
**SQ FT:** 136,000
**SALES (est):** 269.85MM
**SALES (corp-wide):** 269.85MM **Publicly Held**
Web: www.amyris.com
**SIC: 2869** Industrial organic chemicals, nec

### (P-6127)
### AST ENZYMES
4880 Murietta St, Chino (91710-5100)
PHONE..................................800 608-1688
Luis Girarldy, *Dir*
**EMP:** 17 **EST:** 2011
**SALES (est):** 170.16K **Privately Held**
Web: www.astenzymes.com
**SIC: 2869** Enzymes

### (P-6128)
### AVIENT COLORANTS USA LLC
14355 Ramona Ave, Chino (91710-5740)
PHONE..................................909 606-1325
Mike Urbano, *Brnch Mgr*
**EMP:** 94
Web: www.avient.com
**SIC: 2869** Industrial organic chemicals, nec
HQ: Avient Colorants Usa Llc
    85 Industrial Dr
    Holden MA 01520
    877 546-2885

### (P-6129)
### BASF CORPORATION
138 E Meats Ave, Orange (92865-3310)
PHONE..................................714 921-1430
John Zomer, *Mgr*
**EMP:** 127
**SQ FT:** 10,000
**SALES (corp-wide):** 74.89B **Privately Held**
Web: www.basf.com
**SIC: 2869** 2821 Industrial organic chemicals, nec; Plastics materials and resins
HQ: Basf Corporation
    100 Park Ave
    Florham Park NJ 07932
    800 962-7831

### (P-6130)
### BASF CORPORATION
Also Called: Master Builder Solutions
38403 Cherry St, Newark (94560-4716)
PHONE..................................510 796-9911
Rich Hall, *Mgr*
**EMP:** 55
**SALES (corp-wide):** 74.89B **Privately Held**
Web: www.basf.com
**SIC: 2869** Industrial organic chemicals, nec
HQ: Basf Corporation
    100 Park Ave
    Florham Park NJ 07932
    800 962-7831

### (P-6131)
### BASF CORPORATION
6700 8th St, Buena Park (90620-1097)
PHONE..................................714 521-6085
Tim Stmarseille, *Mgr*
**EMP:** 29
**SALES (corp-wide):** 74.89B **Privately Held**
Web: www.basf.com
**SIC: 2869** Industrial organic chemicals, nec
HQ: Basf Corporation
    100 Park Ave
    Florham Park NJ 07932
    800 962-7831

### (P-6132)
### BASF ENZYMES LLC (DH)
3550 John Hopkins Ct, San Diego (92121-1121)
PHONE..................................858 431-8520
◆ **EMP:** 86 **EST:** 1992
**SALES (est):** 12.07MM
**SALES (corp-wide):** 74.89B **Privately Held**
Web: nutrition.basf.com
**SIC: 2869** Industrial organic chemicals, nec
HQ: Basf Corporation
    100 Park Ave
    Florham Park NJ 07932
    800 962-7831

### (P-6133)
### BASF VENTURE CAPITAL AMER INC
46820 Fremont Blvd, Fremont (94538-6571)
PHONE..................................510 445-6140
Hans Ulrich Engel, *Pr*
**EMP:** 41 **EST:** 2003
**SALES (est):** 5.38MM
**SALES (corp-wide):** 74.89B **Privately Held**
Web: www.basf.com
**SIC: 2869** Industrial organic chemicals, nec
HQ: Basfin Corporation
    100 Park Ave
    Florham Park NJ 07932
    973 245-6000

### (P-6134)
### BEARS FOR HUMANITY INC
Also Called: Futurama
841 Ocean View Ave, San Mateo (94401-3139)
PHONE..................................866 325-1668
Renju Prathap, *Pr*
**EMP:** 50 **EST:** 2016
**SQ FT:** 10,000
**SALES (est):** 4.7MM **Privately Held**
Web: www.bearsforhumanity.com
**SIC: 2869** Industrial organic chemicals, nec

### (P-6135)
### BIOTIX (HQ)
10636 Scripps Summit Ct Ste 130, San Diego (92131-3979)
PHONE..................................858 875-7696
Paul Nowak, *CEO*
Tony Altig, *
Ron Perkins, *
Celia Reyes, *
Mickie Henshall, *
◆ **EMP:** 15 **EST:** 2006
**SALES (est):** 20.77MM **Privately Held**
Web: www.biotix.com
**SIC: 2869** Laboratory chemicals, organic
PA: Biotix Holdings, Inc.
    10636 Scripps Summit Ct

### (P-6136)
### CAL-INDIA FOODS INTERNATIONAL
Also Called: Specilty Enzymes Btechnologies
13591 Yorba Ave, Chino (91710-5071)
PHONE..................................909 613-1660
Vic Rathi, *Pr*
▲ **EMP:** 20 **EST:** 1982
**SQ FT:** 12,000
**SALES (est):** 6.25MM **Privately Held**
Web: www.specialtyenzymes.com
**SIC: 2869** Enzymes

### (P-6137)
### CALERA CORPORATION
Also Called: Chemetry
11500 Dolan Road Moss Landing, Moss Landing (95039)
**EMP:** 40 **EST:** 1985
**SALES (est):** 9.65MM **Privately Held**
Web: www.chemetrycorp.com
**SIC: 2869** Industrial organic chemicals, nec

### (P-6138)
### CALYSTA INC (PA)
1900 Alameda De Las Pulgas Ste 200, San Mateo (94403-1295)
PHONE..................................650 492-6880
Alan Shaw, *CEO*
Craig Barratt, *VP*
Ted Hull, *CFO*
Lynsey Wenger, *CSO*
Keysha Bailey, *CFO*
**EMP:** 19 **EST:** 2011
**SALES (est):** 12.78MM **Privately Held**
Web: www.calysta.com
**SIC: 2869** Industrial organic chemicals, nec

### (P-6139)
### CHEMLOGICS GROUP LLC
Also Called: Envirochem Technologies
7305 Morro Rd Ste 200, Atascadero (93422-4445)
PHONE..................................805 591-3314
**EMP:** 35
**SIC: 2869** Industrial organic chemicals, nec

### (P-6140)
### CIRCLE GREEN INC
Also Called: Beneficial AG Services
8271 Chino Ave, Ontario (91761-9412)
PHONE..................................909 930-0200
Kevin Sutton, *CEO*
**EMP:** 16 **EST:** 2009
**SALES (est):** 4.16MM **Privately Held**
Web: www.compostmulchservices.com
**SIC: 2869** Laboratory chemicals, organic

### (P-6141)
### CLARIANT CORPORATION
3355 Olive Ave, Signal Hill (90755-4619)
PHONE..................................562 322-6647
Devon Bench, *Mgr*
**EMP:** 18
Web: www.clariant.com
**SIC: 2869** Industrial organic chemicals, nec
HQ: Clariant Corporation
    500 E Morehead St Ste 400
    Charlotte NC 28202
    704 331-7000

### (P-6142)
### EDENIQ INC
6910 W Pershing Ct, Visalia (93291-7942)
PHONE..................................559 302-1777
Brian Thome, *CEO*
Cam Cast, *Operations*
Peter Kilner, *OF Business Development*
Dan Michalopoulos, *Technology Vice President*
Scott Janssen, *CFO*
▲ **EMP:** 100 **EST:** 2007
**SALES (est):** 14.68MM **Privately Held**
Web: www.edeniq.com
**SIC: 2869** Fuels

### (P-6143)
### ENTEXS CORPORATION
3720 Trade Way Ste A, Cameron Park (95682-8565)
PHONE..................................888 960-3689
Ali Rashid, *CEO*
Justin Cileo, *CFO*
**EMP:** 15 **EST:** 2019
**SALES (est):** 2.52MM **Privately Held**
Web: www.entexs.com
**SIC: 2869** Laboratory chemicals, organic

### (P-6144)
### ENZYME CORPORATION
340 S Lemon Ave, Walnut (91789-2706)
PHONE..................................415 638-9595
**EMP:** 25 **EST:** 2016
**SALES (est):** 3.48MM **Privately Held**
Web: www.enzyme.com
**SIC: 2869** Enzymes

### (P-6145)
### ES OPERATING CO
Also Called: Esionic
19200 Stevens Creek Blvd Ste 200, Cupertino (95014-2530)
**EMP:** 15 **EST:** 2011
**SALES (est):** 2.24MM **Privately Held**
**SIC: 2869** Accelerators, rubber processing: cyclic or acyclic

### (P-6146)
### FIRMENICH
424 S Atchison St, Anaheim (92805-4045)
PHONE..................................714 535-2871
**EMP:** 89
**SALES (est):** 38.34MM **Privately Held**
Web: www.firmenich.com
**SIC: 2869** Industrial organic chemicals, nec

### (P-6147)
### GFP ETHANOL LLC
Also Called: Calgren Renewable Fuels
11704 Road 120, Pixley (93256-9727)
P.O. Box E (93256-1005)
PHONE..................................559 757-3850
**EMP:** 34 **EST:** 2011
**SALES (est):** 11.33MM
**SALES (corp-wide):** 11.33MM **Privately Held**
Web: www.calgren.com
**SIC: 2869** 2046 Ethyl alcohol, ethanol; Corn oil, crude
PA: Sjv Biodiesel, Llc
    11704 Road 120
    559 757-3850

### (P-6148)
### INTERNATIONAL ACADEMY OF FIN (PA)
Also Called: Cordova Industries
13177 Foothill Blvd, Sylmar (91342-4830)
P.O. Box 922079 (91392-2079)
PHONE..................................818 361-7724
Sam Cordova, *Pr*
Steven M Cordova, *
Rodrick Cordova, *
Sam Scott Cordova, *
Steven Schector, *
**EMP:** 24 **EST:** 1963
**SQ FT:** 6,000
**SALES (est):** 1.69MM **Privately Held**
**SIC: 2869** 3944 2879 Alcohols, industrial: denatured (non-beverage); Video game machines, except coin-operated; Insecticides, agricultural or household

### (P-6149)
### JSR MICRO INC (DH)
Also Called: Materials Innovation
1280 N Mathilda Ave, Sunnyvale (94089-1213)
PHONE..................................408 543-8800
Eric R Johnson, *Pr*
Hitoshi Inoue, *
◆ **EMP:** 140 **EST:** 1990

# PRODUCTS & SERVICES SECTION

## 2873 - Nitrogenous Fertilizers (P-6169)

SQ FT: 12,125
SALES (est): 100.92MM **Privately Held**
Web: www.jsrmicro.com
SIC: **2869** 2899 Industrial organic chemicals, nec; Chemical preparations, nec
HQ: Jsr Corporation
1-9-2, Higashishimbashi
Minato-Ku TKY 105-0

### (P-6150)
### LA SUPPLY COMPANY LLC
15040 Desman Rd, La Mirada (90638-5735)
PHONE.................................310 980-3404
Sung-lip Chun, *Managing Member*
Song-tak Chun, *Managing Member*
◆ EMP: 15 EST: 1989
SQ FT: 24,000
SALES (est): 3.9MM **Privately Held**
Web: www.lasupply.co
SIC: **2869** 2865 Industrial organic chemicals, nec; Dyes and pigments

### (P-6151)
### LAMB FUELS INC
10723 Prospect Ave, Santee (92071-4536)
PHONE.................................619 777-9135
Gregory Scott Lamb, *Pr*
Gregory Scott Lamb, *CEO*
Rochelle Lamb, *Sec*
▼ EMP: 21 EST: 1985
SALES (est): 5.42MM **Privately Held**
Web: www.lambfuels.com
SIC: **2869** Fuels

### (P-6152)
### MERCFUEL LLC (HQ)
Also Called: Mercury Fuels
2780 Skypark Dr Ste 300, Torrance (90505-7518)
PHONE.................................281 442-3000
Eric Beelar, *Pr*
EMP: 18 EST: 2001
SALES (est): 20.32MM
SALES (corp-wide): 208.58MM **Privately Held**
Web: www.mercfuel.com
SIC: **2869** Fuels
PA: Mercury Aviation Companies, Llc
2780 Skypark Dr Ste 300
310 602-3770

### (P-6153)
### MOLECULE LABS INC
524 Stone Rd Ste A, Benicia (94510-1169)
PHONE.................................925 473-8200
Michael Guasch, *CEO*
EMP: 50 EST: 2006
SALES (est): 7.48MM **Privately Held**
Web: www.moleculelabs.com
SIC: **2869** Laboratory chemicals, organic

### (P-6154)
### OAKBIO INC
Also Called: Novonutrients
1292 Anvilwood Ct, Sunnyvale (94089-2200)
PHONE.................................888 591-9413
Rusell J Howard, *CEO*
Brian Sefton, *Pr*
Pierre Pujol, *CFO*
EMP: 17 EST: 2010
SQ FT: 3,000
SALES (est): 7.11MM **Privately Held**
Web: www.oakbio.com
SIC: **2869** 5172 2821 8731 Industrial organic chemicals, nec; Engine fuels and oils; Thermoplastic materials; Biological research

### (P-6155)
### PROPEL FUELS CALIFORNIA INC
1815 19th St, Sacramento (95811-6712)
PHONE.................................916 716-7605
Robert Elam, *CEO*
EMP: 19 EST: 2008
SALES (est): 1.63MM
SALES (corp-wide): 4.9MM **Privately Held**
SIC: **2869** Fuels
PA: Propel Fuels, Inc.
1815 19th Street
800 871-0773

### (P-6156)
### PROVIVI INC
1701 Colorado Ave, Santa Monica (90404-3436)
PHONE.................................310 828-2307
Pedro S L Coelho, *CEO*
Peter Meinhold, *
Eduardo Sein, *
Teri Quinn Gray, *
EMP: 75 EST: 2012
SALES (est): 12.86MM **Privately Held**
Web: www.provivi.com
SIC: **2869** Laboratory chemicals, organic

### (P-6157)
### RENNOVIA INC
3040 Oakmead Village Dr, Santa Clara (95051-0808)
PHONE.................................650 804-7400
Robert Wedinger, *CEO*
Thomas Boussie, *VP*
◆ EMP: 15 EST: 2009
SQ FT: 14,000
SALES (est): 2.47MM **Privately Held**
Web: www.rennovia.com
SIC: **2869** 8731 Industrial organic chemicals, nec; Biotechnical research, commercial

### (P-6158)
### SAINT-GOBAIN CERAMICS PLAS INC
Innovative Organics Division
4905 E Hunter Ave, Anaheim (92807-2058)
PHONE.................................714 701-3900
Robert E Futrell Junior, *Brnch Mgr*
EMP: 209
SALES (corp-wide): 402.18MM **Privately Held**
Web: www.saint-gobain.com
SIC: **2869** 2899 Industrial organic chemicals, nec; Chemical preparations, nec
HQ: Saint-Gobain Ceramics & Plastics, Inc.
20 Moores Rd
Malvern PA 19355

### (P-6159)
### SOLVAY USA INC
7305 Morro Rd Ste 200, Atascadero (93422-4445)
PHONE.................................805 591-3314
EMP: 21
SALES (corp-wide): 11.45MM **Privately Held**
SIC: **2869** Industrial organic chemicals, nec
HQ: Solvay Usa Inc.
504 Carnegie Ctr
Princeton NJ 08540
609 860-4000

### (P-6160)
### SPECILTY ENZYMES BTECHNOLOGIES
Also Called: Seb
13591 Yorba Ave, Chino (91710-5071)
PHONE.................................909 613-1660

Vasant Rathi, *Prin*
EMP: 18 EST: 2011
SALES (est): 7.2MM **Privately Held**
Web: www.specialtyenzymes.com
SIC: **2869** Enzymes

### (P-6161)
### STRATOS RENEWABLES CORPORATION
Also Called: A Development Stage Company
9440 Santa Monica Blvd Ste 401, Beverly Hills (90210-4653)
PHONE.................................310 402-5901
Thomas Snyder, *Pr*
Julio Cesar Alonso, *
Valerie Broadbent, *
Jorge Eduardo Aza, *
Sanjay Pai, *Chief Strategy Officer*
EMP: 28 EST: 2004
SALES (est): 4.01MM **Privately Held**
Web: www.stratosrenewables.com
SIC: **2869** 0133 Ethyl alcohol, ethanol; Sugarcane and sugar beets

### (P-6162)
### SUGAR FOODS LLC (HQ)
Also Called: Sugar Foods
3059 Townsgate Rd Ste 101, Westlake Village (91361-2936)
PHONE.................................805 396-5000
Marty Wilson, *Pr*
Donald G Tober, *
Stephen Odell, *
Jack Vivinetto, *
◆ EMP: 34 EST: 1961
SQ FT: 10,000
SALES (est): 510.8MM
SALES (corp-wide): 677.96MM **Privately Held**
Web: www.sugarfoods.com
SIC: **2869** 2023 2099 2068 Sweeteners, synthetic; Cream substitutes; Sugar; Salted and roasted nuts and seeds
PA: Ppc Investment Partners Lp
110 N Wacker Dr Ste 4400
312 447-6050

### (P-6163)
### TASTEPOINT INC
Also Called: Tastepoint By Iff
790 E Harrison St, Corona (92879-1348)
PHONE.................................951 734-6620
EMP: 188
SALES (corp-wide): 11.48B **Publicly Held**
Web: www.tastepoint.com
SIC: **2869** Flavors or flavoring materials, synthetic
HQ: Tastepoint Inc.
7800 Holstein Ave
Philadelphia PA 19153
215 365-7800

### (P-6164)
### USL PARALLEL PRODUCTS CAL
12281 Arrow Rte, Rancho Cucamonga (91739-9601)
PHONE.................................909 980-1200
Gene Kiesel, *CEO*
Ken Reese, *
Jim Russell, *
Bob Pasma, *
Tim Cusson, *
▲ EMP: 35 EST: 1981
SQ FT: 6,000
SALES (est): 6.1MM
SALES (corp-wide): 87.06MM **Privately Held**
Web: www.parallelproducts.com
SIC: **2869** Alcohols, industrial: denatured (non-beverage)

PA: Parallel Environmental Services Corporation
401 Industry Rd
502 471-2444

### (P-6165)
### UTAK LABORATORIES INC
25020 Avenue Tibbitts, Valencia (91355-3447)
PHONE.................................661 294-3935
James D Plutchak, *CEO*
EMP: 26 EST: 1974
SQ FT: 12,000
SALES (est): 9.82MM **Privately Held**
Web: www.utak.com
SIC: **2869** Industrial organic chemicals, nec

### (P-6166)
### VERENIUM CORPORATION
3550 John Hopkins Ct, San Diego (92121-1121)
P.O. Box 685 (07932-0685)
PHONE.................................858 431-8500
▲ EMP: 111
Web: nutrition.basf.com
SIC: **2869** Industrial organic chemicals, nec

### (P-6167)
### WACKER CHEMICAL CORPORATION
Also Called: Precision Silicones
13910 Oaks Ave, Chino (91710-7010)
PHONE.................................909 590-8822
Sudipta Das, *Brnch Mgr*
EMP: 97
SALES (corp-wide): 6.96B **Privately Held**
Web: www.wacker.com
SIC: **2869** 5169 Silicones; Industrial chemicals
HQ: Wacker Chemical Corporation
3301 Sutton Rd
Adrian MI 49221
517 264-8500

## 2873 Nitrogenous Fertilizers

### (P-6168)
### AGRI TECHNOVATION INC
516 Villa Ave, Clovis (93612-7605)
PHONE.................................559 931-3332
Dirk Cornelis Barnard, *Dir*
EMP: 200 EST: 2018
SALES (est): 5.9MM **Privately Held**
Web: www.agritechnovation.com
SIC: **2873** Plant foods, mixed: from plants making nitrog. fertilizers

### (P-6169)
### AURORA INNOVATIONS LLC
Also Called: Aurora Innovation
2225 Huntington Dr, Fairfield (94533-9732)
PHONE.................................541 359-1580
Bowe Mcginnis, *Pr*
Austin Weiner, *
Irving Weiner, *
Eileen Loritsch, *
▲ EMP: 120 EST: 2005
SALES (est): 17.23MM
SALES (corp-wide): 226.58MM **Publicly Held**
Web: www.aurorainnovations.com
SIC: **2873** 2875 Plant foods, mixed: from plants making nitrog. fertilizers; Compost
PA: Hydrofarm Holdings Group, Inc.
1510 Main St
707 765-9990

## 2873 - Nitrogenous Fertilizers (P-6170)

**(P-6170)**
**BOYER INC**
105 Thompson Rd, Watsonville (95076-8658)
P.O. Box 82 (95077-0082)
PHONE.................831 724-0123
Fred Willoughby, *CEO*
▲ **EMP:** 22 **EST:** 1925
**SALES (est):** 1.47MM
**SALES (corp-wide):** 5.49MM **Privately Held**
Web: www.boyerinc.com
**SIC: 2873** 2874  Nitrogenous fertilizers; Phosphatic fertilizers
**PA:** Willoughby Farms, Inc.
261 Coward Rd
831 722-7763

**(P-6171)**
**DR EARTH INC**
4021 Devon Ct, Vacaville (95688-8730)
P.O. Box 500 (95625)
PHONE.................707 448-4676
Milad Shammas, *CEO*
Ray Sidey, *Pr*
Debra White, *COO*
Tyler Vinyard, *VP Opers*
▲ **EMP:** 15 **EST:** 1992
**SQ FT:** 958,320
**SALES (est):** 9.29MM **Privately Held**
Web: www.drearth.com
**SIC: 2873** 5191  Fertilizers: natural (organic), except compost; Fertilizer and fertilizer materials

**(P-6172)**
**GRO-POWER INC**
15065 Telephone Ave, Chino (91710-9614)
PHONE.................909 393-3744
Brent Holden, *Pr*
▼ **EMP:** 25 **EST:** 1966
**SALES (est):** 4.12MM **Privately Held**
Web: www.gropower.com
**SIC: 2873** 0782 0721  Fertilizers: natural (organic), except compost; Lawn and garden services; Crop planting and protection

**(P-6173)**
**GROW WEST LLC**
7235 Tremont Rd, Dixon (95620-9689)
PHONE.................707 678-5542
**EMP:** 44
**SALES (corp-wide):** 1.57MM **Privately Held**
Web: www.growwest.com
**SIC: 2873**  Fertilizers: natural (organic), except compost
**PA:** Grow West Llc
201 East St
530 662-5442

**(P-6174)**
**HAWTHORNE HYDROPONICS LLC**
2877 Giffen Ave, Santa Rosa (95407-5064)
PHONE.................800 221-1760
Chris Hagedorn, *Managing Member*
**EMP:** 20
**SALES (corp-wide):** 3.55B **Publicly Held**
Web: www.hawthorne-gardening.com
**SIC: 2873**  Fertilizers: natural (organic), except compost
**HQ:** Hawthorne Hydroponics Llc
14111 Scottslawn Rd
Marysville OH 43040
888 478-6544

**(P-6175)**
**HYPONEX CORPORATION**
Also Called: Scotts- Hyponex
12273 Brown Ave, Jurupa Valley (92509-1828)
PHONE.................909 597-2811
Roclund White, *Brnch Mgr*
**EMP:** 184
**SALES (corp-wide):** 3.55B **Publicly Held**
Web: www.suntreksolar.com
**SIC: 2873**  Fertilizers: natural (organic), except compost
**HQ:** Hyponex Corporation
14111 Scottslawn Rd
Marysville OH 43040
937 644-0011

**(P-6176)**
**HYPONEX CORPORATION**
Also Called: Scotts- Hyponex
23390 E Flood Rd, Linden (95236-9488)
P.O. Box 479 (95236-0479)
PHONE.................209 887-3845
Aaron Teach, *Mgr*
**EMP:** 45
**SALES (corp-wide):** 3.55B **Publicly Held**
Web: www.suntreksolar.com
**SIC: 2873**  Plant foods, mixed: from plants making nitrog. fertilizers
**HQ:** Hyponex Corporation
14111 Scottslawn Rd
Marysville OH 43040
937 644-0011

**(P-6177)**
**KELLOGG SUPPLY INC**
Also Called: Kellogg Garden Product
12686 Locke Rd, Lockeford (95237-9701)
PHONE.................209 727-3130
Clayton De Bie, *Prin*
**EMP:** 108
**SALES (corp-wide):** 36.89MM **Privately Held**
Web: www.kellogggarden.com
**SIC: 2873** 5191 2875  Nitrogenous fertilizers; Fertilizer and fertilizer materials; Fertilizers, mixing only
**PA:** Kellogg Supply, Inc.
350 W Sepulveda Blvd
310 830-2200

**(P-6178)**
**NITRICITY INC**
44530 S Grimmer Blvd, Fremont (94538-6386)
PHONE.................303 475-6197
Nicolas Pinkowski, *CEO*
**EMP:** 21 **EST:** 2018
**SALES (est):** 8.81MM **Privately Held**
Web: www.nitricity.co
**SIC: 2873** 7389  Nitrogenous fertilizers; Business Activities at Non-Commercial Site

**(P-6179)**
**NUTRIEN AG SOLUTIONS INC**
2150 Eastman Ave, Oxnard (93030-5168)
P.O. Box 1307 (93032-1307)
PHONE.................805 488-3646
Mike Dinsley, *Mgr*
**EMP:** 16
**SALES (corp-wide):** 29.06B **Privately Held**
Web: www.nutrienagsolutions.com
**SIC: 2873** 5261  Fertilizers: natural (organic), except compost; Fertilizer
**HQ:** Nutrien Ag Solutions, Inc.
3005 Rocky Mountain Ave
Loveland CO 80538
970 685-3300

**(P-6180)**
**OMEX AGRIFLUIDS INC**
Also Called: Omex USA
1675 Dockery Ave, Selma (93662-9785)
PHONE.................559 661-6138
David Featherstone, *Pr*
Inn Listel, *VP*
Alastair Rubie, *Treas*
S A Dekock, *Sec*
▲ **EMP:** 18 **EST:** 1976
**SQ FT:** 10,000
**SALES (est):** 2.86MM **Privately Held**
Web: www.omex.com
**SIC: 2873**  Fertilizers: natural (organic), except compost

**(P-6181)**
**RENTECH NTRGN PASADENA SPA LLC**
10877 Wilshire Blvd Ste 710, Los Angeles (90024-4341)
PHONE.................310 571-9805
**EMP:** 31 **EST:** 1987
**SALES (est):** 853.96K **Publicly Held**
**SIC: 2873**  Nitrogenous fertilizers
**HQ:** Cvr Nitrogen, Lp
10877 Wilshire Blvd Fl 10
Los Angeles CA 90024
310 571-9800

**(P-6182)**
**SCOTTS COMPANY LLC**
742 Industrial Way, Shafter (93263-4018)
PHONE.................661 387-9555
Aaron Leach, *Brnch Mgr*
**EMP:** 23
**SALES (corp-wide):** 3.55B **Publicly Held**
Web: www.scotts.com
**SIC: 2873**  Fertilizers: natural (organic), except compost
**HQ:** The Scotts Company Llc
14111 Scottslawn Rd
Marysville OH 43040
937 644-0011

**(P-6183)**
**UNITED COMPOST & ORGANICS INC**
Also Called: United Compost And Organics, Inc.
1900 Bendixsen St, Samoa (95564-9526)
PHONE.................707 443-4369
**EMP:** 43
Web: www.foxfarm.com
**SIC: 2873**  Nitrogenous fertilizers
**PA:** United Compost And Organics
8601 N Scottsdale Rd # 309

**(P-6184)**
**WHITTIER FERTILIZER COMPANY**
9441 Kruse Rd, Pico Rivera (90660-1492)
PHONE.................562 699-3461
Robert Osborn, *CEO*
Janet Osborn, *
▲ **EMP:** 51 **EST:** 1930
**SQ FT:** 20,000
**SALES (est):** 9.92MM **Privately Held**
Web: www.whittierfertilizer.com
**SIC: 2873** 5261 2875  Fertilizers: natural (organic), except compost; Garden supplies and tools, nec; Fertilizers, mixing only

## 2875 Fertilizers, Mixing Only

**(P-6185)**
**BRANDT CONSOLIDATED INC**
3654 S Willow Ave, Fresno (93725-9036)
PHONE.................559 499-2100
**EMP:** 165
**SALES (corp-wide):** 320.53MM **Privately Held**
Web: www.brandt.co
**SIC: 2875** 5191  Fertilizers, mixing only; Farm supplies
**HQ:** Brandt Consolidated, Inc.
2935 S Koke Mill Rd
Springfield IL 62711
217 547-5800

**(P-6186)**
**COLD CREEK COMPOST INC**
6000 E Side Potter Valley Rd, Ukiah (95482-9260)
PHONE.................707 485-5966
Martin Mileck, *Pr*
Mari Mileck, *Sec*
**EMP:** 18 **EST:** 1983
**SALES (est):** 2.08MM **Privately Held**
Web: www.coldcreekcompost.com
**SIC: 2875** 5261  Compost; Fertilizer

**(P-6187)**
**GENERAL HYDROPONICS INC**
Also Called: General Hydroponics
3789 Vine Hill Rd, Sebastopol (95472-2348)
P.O. Box 1576 (95473-1576)
PHONE.................707 824-9376
▲ **EMP:** 72
Web: www.generalhydroponics.com
**SIC: 2875** 3999 8748  Fertilizers, mixing only; Hydroponic equipment; Business consulting, nec

**(P-6188)**
**JH BIOTECH INC (PA)**
Also Called: Jh Biotech
4951 Olivas Park Dr, Ventura (93003-7667)
P.O. Box 3538 (93006)
PHONE.................805 650-8933
Hsinhung John Hsu, *Pr*
◆ **EMP:** 23 **EST:** 1986
**SQ FT:** 3,000
**SALES (est):** 15.43MM
**SALES (corp-wide):** 15.43MM **Privately Held**
Web: www.jhbiotech.com
**SIC: 2875**  Fertilizers, mixing only

**(P-6189)**
**NUTRIEN AG SOLUTIONS INC**
3348 Claus Rd, Modesto (95355-9725)
PHONE.................209 551-1424
Dan Sardella, *Mgr*
**EMP:** 19
**SQ FT:** 28,395
**SALES (corp-wide):** 29.06B **Privately Held**
Web: www.nutrienagsolutions.com
**SIC: 2875** 5261 5191 5999  Fertilizers, mixing only; Fertilizer; Fertilizer and fertilizer materials; Insecticide
**HQ:** Nutrien Ag Solutions, Inc.
3005 Rocky Mountain Ave
Loveland CO 80538
970 685-3300

**(P-6190)**
**ROYAL GOLD LLC**
600 F St Ste 3, Arcata (95521-6301)
PHONE.................707 822-4653
Franklin C Waters, *Managing Member*

## 2879 - Agricultural Chemicals, Nec (P-6210)

▲ EMP: 19 EST: 2010
SQ FT: 70,000
SALES (est): 10.79MM Privately Held
Web: www.royalgoldcoco.com
SIC: 2875 Potting soil, mixed

### 2879 Agricultural Chemicals, Nec

**(P-6191)**
**AMERICAN VANGUARD CORPORATION (PA)**
Also Called: AVD
4695 Macarthur Ct, Newport Beach (92660-1882)
PHONE..................949 260-1200
Eric G Wintemute, Ch Bd
David T Johnson, VP
◆ EMP: 67 EST: 1969
SQ FT: 19,953
SALES (est): 579.37MM
SALES (corp-wide): 579.37MM Publicly Held
Web: www.american-vanguard.com
SIC: 2879 Pesticides, agricultural or household

**(P-6192)**
**AMVAC CHEMICAL CORPORATION (HQ)**
4695 Macarthur Ct Ste 1200, Newport Beach (92660-8859)
PHONE..................323 264-3910
Eric G Wintemute, Ch
Bob Trogele, *
David T Johnson, *
Glen Johnson, *
Cindy Baker Smith, *
◆ EMP: 36 EST: 1945
SQ FT: 152,000
SALES (est): 95.98MM
SALES (corp-wide): 579.37MM Publicly Held
Web: www.amvac-chemical.com
SIC: 2879 Pesticides, agricultural or household
PA: American Vanguard Corporation
4695 Macarthur Ct
949 260-1200

**(P-6193)**
**BIAGRO WESTERN SALES INC**
35803 Road 132, Visalia (93292-9387)
PHONE..................559 635-4784
▲ EMP: 20
SIC: 2879 Agricultural chemicals, nec

**(P-6194)**
**CELLU-CON INC**
19994 Meredith Dr, Strathmore (93267-9691)
P.O. Box 185 (93267-0185)
PHONE..................559 568-0190
Duane Hilty, Pr
Carol Hilty, *
John Yale, *
EMP: 25 EST: 1979
SQ FT: 15,000
SALES (est): 2.45MM Privately Held
Web: www.americanextracts.com
SIC: 2879 Soil conditioners

**(P-6195)**
**CERTIS USA LLC**
Also Called: Thermo Trilogy
720 5th St, Wasco (93280-1420)
PHONE..................661 758-8471
Michael Hillberry, Prin
EMP: 40
Web: www.certisbio.com
SIC: 2879 5191 Pesticides, agricultural or household; Insecticides
HQ: Certis U.S.A. L.L.C.
9145 Guilford Rd Ste 175
Columbia MD 21046

**(P-6196)**
**CIBUS INC**
Also Called: Cibus
6455 Nancy Ridge Dr, San Diego (92121-2249)
PHONE..................858 450-0008
Rory Riggs, Ch Bd
Gerhard Prante, *
Peter Beetham, *
Cornelis Broos, Interim Chief Financial Officer
Greg Gocal, CSO
◆ EMP: 183 EST: 2010
SQ FT: 53,423
SALES (est): 1.82MM Privately Held
Web: www.calyxt.com
SIC: 2879 8731 0721 Agricultural chemicals, nec; Agricultural research; Crop planting and protection

**(P-6197)**
**CLOROX INTERNATIONAL COMPANY (HQ)**
Also Called: Clorox
1221 Broadway Fl 13, Oakland (94612-1837)
P.O. Box 24305 (94623-1305)
PHONE..................510 271-7000
Benno Dorer, Prin
Larry Peirof, CEO
Warwick Every-burns, Pr
William F Ausfahl, VP
Edward A Cutter, Sec
◆ EMP: 75 EST: 1972
SALES (est): 94.38MM
SALES (corp-wide): 7.09B Publicly Held
Web: www.thecloroxcompany.com
SIC: 2879 2842 Insecticides, agricultural or household; Bleaches, household: dry or liquid
PA: The Clorox Company
1221 Broadway
510 271-7000

**(P-6198)**
**CMR MARKETING AND RES INC**
3594 E Wawona Ave, Fresno (93725-9021)
P.O. Box 35000 (93745-5000)
PHONE..................559 499-2100
John Salmonson, Pr
▲ EMP: 294 EST: 1970
SQ FT: 70,000
SALES (est): 2.37MM
SALES (corp-wide): 320.53MM Privately Held
SIC: 2879 Agricultural chemicals, nec
HQ: Brandt Consolidated, Inc.
2935 S Koke Mill Rd
Springfield IL 62711
217 547-5800

**(P-6199)**
**DECCO US POST-HARVEST INC (HQ)**
1713 S California Ave, Monrovia (91016-4623)
P.O. Box 120 (91016)
PHONE..................800 221-0925
Francois Girin, Pr
◆ EMP: 18 EST: 2009
SALES (est): 4.24MM Privately Held
Web: www.deccopostharvest.com

SIC: 2879 Agricultural chemicals, nec
PA: Upl Limited
Upl House, 610 B/2, Bandra Village,

**(P-6200)**
**ECOSMART TECHNOLOGIES INC**
1585 W Mission Blvd, Pomona (91766-1233)
PHONE..................770 667-0006
EMP: 25
SIC: 2879 Insecticides and pesticides

**(P-6201)**
**GROW MORE INC**
15600 New Century Dr, Gardena (90248-2129)
PHONE..................310 515-1700
John Atwill Ii, CEO
◆ EMP: 62 EST: 1918
SQ FT: 43,560
SALES (est): 1.74MM Privately Held
Web: www.growmore.com
SIC: 2879 2899 2873 2869 Agricultural chemicals, nec; Chemical preparations, nec ; Nitrogenous fertilizers; Industrial organic chemicals, nec

**(P-6202)**
**MONSANTO COMPANY**
Also Called: Monsanto
2700 Camino Del Sol, Oxnard (93030-7967)
PHONE..................805 827-2341
EMP: 23
SALES (corp-wide): 51.78B Privately Held
Web: www.monsanto.com
SIC: 2879 Agricultural chemicals, nec
HQ: Monsanto Technology Llc.
800 N Lindbergh Blvd
Saint Louis MO 63167
314 694-1000

**(P-6203)**
**MONTEREY CHEMICAL COMPANY**
Also Called: Monterey Agresources
3654 S Willow Ave, Fresno (93725-9036)
P.O. Box 35000 (93745-5000)
PHONE..................559 499-2100
▲ EMP: 65
Web: www.montereychemical.com
SIC: 2879 Agricultural chemicals, nec

**(P-6204)**
**NUSEED AMERICAS INC (HQ)**
990 Riverside Pkwy Ste 140, West Sacramento (95605-1533)
PHONE..................800 345-3330
Darryl Matthews, Pr
EMP: 49 EST: 2011
SALES (est): 30.82MM Privately Held
Web: www.nuseed.com
SIC: 2879 Agricultural chemicals, nec
PA: Nufarm Limited
103-105 Pipe Rd

**(P-6205)**
**PRO FARM GROUP INC (PA)**
Also Called: Marrone Bio Innovations
1530 Drew Ave, Davis (95618-6320)
PHONE..................530 750-2800
Kevin Helash, CEO
Robert A Woods, *
Ladon Johnson, Interim Chief Financial Officer
Linda V Moore, CCO
Amit Vasavada, Sr VP
▲ EMP: 116 EST: 2006

SQ FT: 2,291
SALES (est): 44.31MM Privately Held
Web: www.marronebio.com
SIC: 2879 Agricultural chemicals, nec

**(P-6206)**
**SAN GROUP BIOTECH USA INC**
Also Called: Westbridge
1260 Avenida Chelsea, Vista (92081-8315)
PHONE..................760 599-8855
Christine Koenemann, CEO
Tina Koenemann, Pr
Larry Parker, VP
Richard Forsyth, CFO
▲ EMP: 15 EST: 1976
SQ FT: 8,000
SALES (est): 11.93MM
SALES (corp-wide): 11.93MM Privately Held
Web: www.san-agrow.com
SIC: 2879 Agricultural chemicals, nec
PA: Westbridge Research Group
1260 Avenida Chelsea
760 599-8855

**(P-6207)**
**SKELL INC**
Also Called: Bug-A-Salt
2401 Lincoln Blvd Ste C, Santa Monica (90405-3863)
PHONE..................310 392-3288
Lorenzo Maggiore, CEO
▲ EMP: 15 EST: 2009
SQ FT: 2,000
SALES (est): 1.32MM Privately Held
Web: www.bugasalt.com
SIC: 2879 Insecticides and pesticides

**(P-6208)**
**TRICAL INC**
28679 Rd 68, Visalia (93277)
PHONE..................559 651-0736
Dean Storkan, Pr
EMP: 23
SALES (corp-wide): 45.04MM Privately Held
Web: www.trical.com
SIC: 2879 Agricultural chemicals, nec
PA: Trical, Inc.
8100 Arroyo Cir
831 637-0195

**(P-6209)**
**TRICAL INC (PA)**
8100 Arroyo Cir, Gilroy (95020-7305)
P.O. Box 1327 (95024-1327)
PHONE..................831 637-0195
Dean Storkan, CEO
Joanne Vargas, *
Hank Maze, *
▲ EMP: 30 EST: 1961
SQ FT: 6,000
SALES (est): 45.04MM
SALES (corp-wide): 45.04MM Privately Held
Web: www.trical.com
SIC: 2879 Agricultural chemicals, nec

**(P-6210)**
**TRICAL INC**
8770 Hwy 25, Hollister (95023)
PHONE..................831 637-0195
Dean Storkan, CEO
EMP: 22
SALES (corp-wide): 45.04MM Privately Held
Web: www.trical.com
SIC: 2879 Agricultural chemicals, nec
PA: Trical, Inc.
8100 Arroyo Cir

# 2879 - Agricultural Chemicals, Nec (P-6211)

831 637-0195

**(P-6211)**
**TRICAL INC**
1029 Railroad St, Corona (92882-2416)
PHONE...............................951 737-6960
Joanne Vargas, *Mgr*
**EMP:** 22
**SALES (corp-wide):** 45.04MM **Privately Held**
**Web:** www.trical.com
**SIC:** 2879 Agricultural chemicals, nec
**PA:** Trical, Inc.
    8100 Arroyo Cir
    831 637-0195

**(P-6212)**
**TRICAL INC**
1667 Purdy Rd, Mojave (93501-7403)
PHONE...............................661 824-2494
Neil Adkins, *Brnch Mgr*
**EMP:** 22
**SALES (corp-wide):** 45.04MM **Privately Held**
**Web:** www.trical.com
**SIC:** 2879 Agricultural chemicals, nec
**PA:** Trical, Inc.
    8100 Arroyo Cir
    831 637-0195

**(P-6213)**
**VALENT USA LLC (DH)**
Also Called: Valent
4600 Norris Canyon Rd, San Ramon (94583-1320)
P.O. Box 5075 (94583)
PHONE...............................925 256-2700
◆ **EMP:** 80 **EST:** 2017
**SALES (est):** 261.51MM **Privately Held**
**Web:** www.valent.com
**SIC:** 2879 Agricultural chemicals, nec
**HQ:** Valent North America Llc
    4600 Nrris Cyn Rd Ste 100
    San Ramon CA 94583
    925 256-2755

**(P-6214)**
**YASHENG GROUP**
251 Ginko Ter, Sunnyvale (94086-6564)
PHONE...............................650 363-8345
▲ **EMP:** 10000
**Web:** www.yashenggroup.com
**SIC:** 2879 0111 0115 0116 Agricultural chemicals, nec; Wheat; Corn; Soybeans

## 2891 Adhesives And Sealants

**(P-6215)**
**AC PRODUCTS INC**
Also Called: Quaker
9930 Painter Ave, Whittier (90605-2759)
PHONE...............................714 630-7311
Peter Weissman, *Pr*
Joseph Matrange, *
Hugh H Muller, *
Sheldon I Weinstein, *
◆ **EMP:** 35 **EST:** 1972
**SQ FT:** 28,000
**SALES (est):** 11.58MM
**SALES (corp-wide):** 1.95B **Publicly Held**
**Web:** www.acpmaskants.com
**SIC:** 2891 2952 8731 Adhesives and sealants; Coating compounds, tar; Chemical laboratory, except testing
**PA:** Quaker Chemical Corporation
    901 E Hector St
    610 832-4000

**(P-6216)**
**ADVANCED CHEMISTRY & TECHNOLOGY INC**
Also Called: AC Tech
7341 Anaconda Ave, Garden Grove (92841-2921)
PHONE...............................714 373-8118
▲ **EMP:** 70
**Web:** www.actechaero.com
**SIC:** 2891 Sealants

**(P-6217)**
**ADVANTAGE ADHESIVES INC**
1420 S Vintage Ave, Ontario (91761-3646)
PHONE...............................909 204-4990
Greg Lane, *Pr*
▲ **EMP:** 26 **EST:** 1998
**SALES (est):** 8.95MM **Privately Held**
**Web:** www.advantageadhesives.com
**SIC:** 2891 Adhesives

**(P-6218)**
**ARELAC INC**
Also Called: Fortera
100 Great Oaks Blvd Ste 120, San Jose (95119-1462)
PHONE...............................669 267-6400
Ryan Gilliam, *CEO*
**EMP:** 65 **EST:** 2019
**SALES (est):** 13.31MM **Privately Held**
**Web:** www.forteraglobal.com
**SIC:** 2891 2819 Cement, except linoleum and tile; Industrial inorganic chemicals, nec

**(P-6219)**
**AXIOM MATERIALS INC**
2320 Pullman St, Santa Ana (92705-5507)
PHONE...............................949 623-4400
Murat Oguz Arca, *CEO*
Olcay Demirkesen, *
▲ **EMP:** 35 **EST:** 2009
**SQ FT:** 15,000
**SALES (est):** 18.58MM **Privately Held**
**Web:** www.axiommaterials.com
**SIC:** 2891 2295 Epoxy adhesives; Resin or plastic coated fabrics
**HQ:** Kordsa, Inc.
    4501 N Access Rd
    Chattanooga TN 37415
    423 643-8300

**(P-6220)**
**BONDLINE ELCTRNIC ADHSIVE CORP**
777 N Pastoria Ave, Sunnyvale (94085-2918)
PHONE...............................408 830-9200
Erik Olson, *CEO*
Neal Olson, *CEO*
Erik V Olson, *Pr*
**EMP:** 20 **EST:** 1987
**SQ FT:** 12,000
**SALES (est):** 5.77MM **Privately Held**
**Web:** www.bondline.net
**SIC:** 2891 Adhesives

**(P-6221)**
**BOSTIK INC**
27460 Bostik Ct, Temecula (92590-3698)
PHONE...............................951 296-6425
Ed Lui, *Brnch Mgr*
**EMP:** 46
**SALES (corp-wide):** 125.67MM **Privately Held**
**Web:** www.bostik.com
**SIC:** 2891 2899 Adhesives; Chemical preparations, nec
**HQ:** Bostik, Inc.
    11320 W Watertwn Plnk Rd
    Wauwatosa WI 53226
    414 774-2250

**(P-6222)**
**BOYD CORPORATION (HQ)**
5960 Inglewood Dr Ste 125, Pleasanton (94588)
PHONE...............................209 236-1111
Mitchell Aiello, *Pr*
**EMP:** 58 **EST:** 1934
**SALES (est):** 570.87MM **Privately Held**
**Web:** www.boydcorp.com
**SIC:** 2891 Adhesives and sealants
**PA:** Lti Holdings, Inc.
    5960 Inglewood Dr Ste 115

**(P-6223)**
**CTS CEMENT MANUFACTURING CORP**
Also Called: CTS Cement Manufacturing Co
2077 Linda Flora Dr, Los Angeles (90077-1406)
PHONE...............................310 472-4004
Edward K Rice, *Brnch Mgr*
**EMP:** 20
**SALES (corp-wide):** 61.8MM **Privately Held**
**Web:** www.ctscement.com
**SIC:** 2891 Cement, except linoleum and tile
**PA:** Cts Cement Manufacturing Corporation
    12442 Knott St
    714 379-8260

**(P-6224)**
**CUSTOM BUILDING PRODUCTS LLC (DH)**
Also Called: C-Cure
7711 Center Ave Ste 500, Huntington Beach (92647-3076)
PHONE...............................800 272-8786
Don Devine, *CEO*
Thomas Peck Junior, *Pr*
Marc Powell, *
◆ **EMP:** 65 **EST:** 2005
**SQ FT:** 15,000
**SALES (est):** 386.06MM **Privately Held**
**Web:** www.custombuildingproducts.com
**SIC:** 2891 Adhesives and sealants
**HQ:** The Quikrete Companies Llc
    5 Concourse Pkwy Ste 1900
    Atlanta GA 30328
    404 634-9100

**(P-6225)**
**CUSTOM BUILDING PRODUCTS LLC**
6511 Salt Lake Ave, Bell (90201-2126)
PHONE...............................323 582-0846
Tom Milan, *Manager*
**EMP:** 141
**Web:** www.custombuildingproducts.com
**SIC:** 2891 3273 2899 5032 Adhesives and sealants; Ready-mixed concrete; Chemical preparations, nec; Ceramic wall and floor tile, nec
**HQ:** Custom Building Products Llc
    7711 Center Ave Ste 500
    Huntington Beach CA 92647
    800 272-8786

**(P-6226)**
**DESMOND VENTURES INC**
17451 Von Karman Ave, Irvine (92614-6205)
P.O. Box 19507 (92623-9507)
PHONE...............................949 474-0400
▲ **EMP:** 135

SIC: 2891 2851 Adhesives and sealants; Lacquers, varnishes, enamels, and other coatings

**(P-6227)**
**ESSENTRA INTERNATIONAL LLC**
Also Called: Duraco Express
21303 Ferrero, Walnut (91789-5231)
PHONE...............................708 315-7498
**EMP:** 1121
**SALES (corp-wide):** 394.25MM **Privately Held**
**Web:** www.essentra.com
**SIC:** 2891 Adhesives and sealants
**HQ:** Essentra International Llc
    2 Westbrook Corp Ctr
    Westchester IL 60154
    866 800-0775

**(P-6228)**
**FLAMEMASTER CORPORATION**
Also Called: Chemseal
13576 Desmond St, Pacoima (91331-2315)
P.O. Box 4510 (91333-4500)
PHONE...............................818 890-1401
Joshua Mazin, *Pr*
▲ **EMP:** 28 **EST:** 1942
**SALES (est):** 5.72MM **Privately Held**
**Web:** www.flamemaster.com
**SIC:** 2891 Sealants

**(P-6229)**
**GENERAL SEALANTS**
300 Turnbull Canyon Rd, City Of Industry (91745-1009)
P.O. Box 3855 (91744-0855)
PHONE...............................626 961-0211
Bradley Boyle, *Pr*
Patricia Boyle, *
Patrick Boyle, *
◆ **EMP:** 120 **EST:** 1964
**SQ FT:** 96,000
**SALES (est):** 19.45MM **Privately Held**
**Web:** www.generalsealants.com
**SIC:** 2891 Adhesives

**(P-6230)**
**HB FULLER COMPANY**
Also Called: Adhesves Sealants Coatings Div
10500 Industrial Ave, Roseville (95678-6212)
PHONE...............................916 787-6000
Frank Strasser, *Mgr*
**EMP:** 43
**SQ FT:** 5,760
**SALES (corp-wide):** 3.51B **Publicly Held**
**Web:** www.hbfuller.com
**SIC:** 2891 2851 2821 Adhesives; Paints and allied products; Plastics materials and resins
**PA:** H.B. Fuller Company
    1200 Willow Lake Blvd
    651 236-5900

**(P-6231)**
**HENKEL CHEMICAL MANAGEMENT LLC**
Also Called: Henkel Electronic Mtls LLC
14000 Jamboree Rd, Irvine (92606-1730)
PHONE...............................888 943-6535
Benoit Pouliquen, *VP*
Alan P Syzdek, *
Paul R Berry, *
**EMP:** 170 **EST:** 2010
**SQ FT:** 75,000
**SALES (est):** 4.31MM
**SALES (corp-wide):** 23.39B **Privately Held**
**Web:** www.henkel.com
**SIC:** 2891 Adhesives
**PA:** Henkel Ag & Co. Kgaa
    Henkelstr. 67

## 2891 - Adhesives And Sealants (P-6250)

2117970

**(P-6232)**
**HENKEL US OPERATIONS CORP**
Dexter Electronics Mtls Div
15051 Don Julian Rd, City Of Industry (91746-3302)
P.O. Box 1282 (91749-1282)
PHONE..................................626 968-6511
Jim Dehart, *Mgr*
**EMP:** 60
**SALES (corp-wide):** 23.39B **Privately Held**
Web: www.henkel.com
**SIC: 2891** Adhesives
HQ: Henkel Us Operations Corporation
1 Henkel Way
Rocky Hill CT 06067
860 571-5100

**(P-6233)**
**INTERNATIONAL COATINGS CO INC (PA)**
Also Called: International Coatings
13929 166th St, Cerritos (90703-2431)
PHONE..................................562 926-1010
Stephen W Kahane, *CEO*
Herbert A Wells, *
Janet Wells, *
◆ **EMP:** 40 **EST:** 1957
**SQ FT:** 50,000
**SALES (est):** 15.32MM
**SALES (corp-wide):** 15.32MM **Privately Held**
Web: www.iccink.com
**SIC: 2891** 2899 3555 2893 Adhesives; Ink or writing fluids; Printing trades machinery; Printing ink

**(P-6234)**
**IPS CORPORATION (HQ)**
Also Called: Weld-On Adhesives
455 W Victoria St, Compton (90220-6064)
PHONE..................................310 898-3300
Tracy Bilbrough, *CEO*
Will Barton, *
Gary Rosenfield, *
◆ **EMP:** 180 **EST:** 1953
**SQ FT:** 22,000
**SALES (est):** 717.97MM **Privately Held**
Web: www.ipscorp.com
**SIC: 2891** Adhesives, plastic
PA: Centerbridge Partners, L.P.
375 Park Ave Fl 12 C

**(P-6235)**
**KWIK BOND POLYMERS LLC**
923 Teal Dr Ste A, Benicia (94510-1225)
PHONE..................................866 434-1772
Randy Slezak, *Managing Member*
▲ **EMP:** 20 **EST:** 2001
**SALES (est):** 12.29MM **Privately Held**
Web: www.kwikbondpolymers.com
**SIC: 2891** Adhesives
PA: Sika Ag
Zugerstrasse 50

**(P-6236)**
**MASK-OFF COMPANY INC**
345 W Maple Ave, Monrovia (91016-3331)
PHONE..................................626 359-3261
Steven B Sites, *Pr*
Dimitrianne Wood, *Sec*
Jim Sites, *Dir*
▲ **EMP:** 18 **EST:** 1950
**SQ FT:** 28,160
**SALES (est):** 6.08MM **Privately Held**
Web: www.mask-off.com
**SIC: 2891** Adhesives

**(P-6237)**
**MITSUBISHI CHEMICAL CRBN FBR**
Also Called: Mitsubishi Chemical Carbon Fiber and Composites, Inc.
1822 Reynolds Ave, Irvine (92614-5714)
PHONE..................................800 929-5471
Takashi Sasaki, *VP*
**EMP:** 110
Web: www.mccfc.com
**SIC: 2891** 5169 Adhesives; Chemical additives
HQ: Mitsubishi Chemical Carbon Fiber And Composites, Inc
5900 88th St
Sacramento CA 95828

**(P-6238)**
**PACER TECHNOLOGY (HQ)**
Also Called: Super Glue
3281 E Guasti Rd Ste 260, Ontario (91761-7642)
PHONE..................................909 987-0550
E T Gravette, *CEO*
Ronald T Gravette, *
Kristine Wright, *
James Gallagher, *
Marsha Gravette, *
◆ **EMP:** 107 **EST:** 1975
**SQ FT:** 47,700
**SALES (est):** 24.1MM
**SALES (corp-wide):** 24.1MM **Privately Held**
Web: www.supergluecorp.com
**SIC: 2891** 3089 3085 Adhesives and sealants; Plastics containers, except foam; Plastics bottles
PA: Cyan Holding Corporation
9420 Santa Anita Ave
909 987-0550

**(P-6239)**
**PACKAGING SYSTEMS INC**
26435 Summit Cir, Santa Clarita (91350-2991)
PHONE..................................661 253-5700
Raymond J Gray, *CEO*
Steve Gray, *
Patricia Gray, *
▼ **EMP:** 42 **EST:** 1976
**SQ FT:** 25,700
**SALES (est):** 9.52MM **Privately Held**
Web: www.pkgsys.net
**SIC: 2891** Adhesives and sealants

**(P-6240)**
**PRC - DESOTO INTERNATIONAL INC (HQ)**
Also Called: PPG Aerospace
24811 Avenue Rockefeller, Valencia (91355-3468)
PHONE..................................661 678-4209
Michael H Mcgarry, *Pr*
Barry Gillespie, *
David P Morris, *
John Machin, *
Donna Lee Walker, *Tax Administration Vice President*
▲ **EMP:** 320 **EST:** 1945
**SQ FT:** 200,000
**SALES (est):** 138.57MM
**SALES (corp-wide):** 17.65B **Publicly Held**
Web: www.ppgaerospace.com
**SIC: 2891** 3089 Sealing compounds, synthetic rubber or plastic; Plastics containers, except foam
PA: Ppg Industries, Inc.
1 Ppg Pl
412 434-3131

**(P-6241)**
**PRC - DESOTO INTERNATIONAL INC**
Also Called: PPG Aerospace
11601 United St, Mojave (93501-7048)
PHONE..................................661 824-4532
Dave Richardson, *Brnch Mgr*
**EMP:** 130
**SALES (corp-wide):** 17.65B **Publicly Held**
Web: guide13227.guidechem.com
**SIC: 2891** Sealing compounds, synthetic rubber or plastic
HQ: Prc - Desoto International, Inc.
24811 Ave Rockefeller
Valencia CA 91355
661 678-4209

**(P-6242)**
**QSPAC INDUSTRIES INC (PA)**
Also Called: Quality Service Pac Industry
15020 Marquardt Ave, Santa Fe Springs (90670-5704)
PHONE..................................562 407-3868
Jow-lin Tang, *Pr*
Wu-hsiung Chung, *CFO*
Vic Lee, *
◆ **EMP:** 52 **EST:** 2009
**SQ FT:** 96,000
**SALES (est):** 2.18MM **Privately Held**
Web: www.qspac.com
**SIC: 2891** Adhesives

**(P-6243)**
**RELIABLE PACKAGING SYSTEMS INC**
Also Called: Astro Packaging
1300 N Jefferson St, Anaheim (92807-1614)
PHONE..................................714 572-1094
Debra Lynn Dillon, *Pr*
Debra Dillon, *Pr*
**EMP:** 17 **EST:** 1994
**SQ FT:** 5,500
**SALES (est):** 9.17MM **Privately Held**
Web: www.astropackaging.com
**SIC: 2891** 3565 5084 5169 Adhesives and sealants; Packaging machinery; Packaging machinery and equipment; Adhesives and sealants

**(P-6244)**
**RESIN DESIGNS LLC**
39714 Eureka Dr, Newark (94560-4808)
PHONE..................................510 413-0115
**EMP:** 22
Web: www.chasecorp.com
**SIC: 2891** Adhesives
HQ: Resin Designs, Llc
11 State St
Woburn MA 01801
781 935-3133

**(P-6245)**
**SEAL FOR LIFE INDUSTRIES LLC (HQ)**
2290 Enrico Fermi Dr Ste 22, San Diego (92154-7228)
PHONE..................................619 671-0932
Jeffrey Oravitz, *CEO*
Dirk Totte, *Pr*
Mauricio Perini, *CFO*
▲ **EMP:** 44 **EST:** 2012
**SQ FT:** 260,831
**SALES (est):** 51.28MM
**SALES (corp-wide):** 23.39B **Privately Held**
Web: www.sealforlife.com
**SIC: 2891** 2952 Sealing compounds, synthetic rubber or plastic; Coating compounds, tar

PA: Henkel Ag & Co. Kgaa
Henkelstr. 67
2117970

**(P-6246)**
**SIGNATURE FLEXIBLE PACKG LLC (PA)**
Also Called: Dazpak Flexible Packaging
19310 San Jose Ave, City Of Industry (91748-1419)
PHONE..................................909 598-7844
Adrian Backer, *Pr*
Jeff Sewel, *
Kelly Redding, *
▲ **EMP:** 50 **EST:** 1954
**SALES (est):** 30.99MM
**SALES (corp-wide):** 30.99MM **Privately Held**
Web: www.dazpak.com
**SIC: 2891** 2673 Adhesives and sealants; Bags: plastic, laminated, and coated

**(P-6247)**
**SIGNATURE FLEXIBLE PACKG LLC**
Also Called: Dazpak Flexible Packaging
17032 Armstrong Ave, Irvine (92614-5716)
PHONE..................................949 475-2300
**EMP:** 16
**SALES (corp-wide):** 30.99MM **Privately Held**
Web: www.dazpak.com
**SIC: 2891** 2673 Adhesives and sealants; Bags: plastic, laminated, and coated
PA: Signature Flexible Packaging, Llc
19310 San Jose Ave
909 598-7844

**(P-6248)**
**STIC-ADHESIVE PRODUCTS CO INC**
3950 Medford St, Los Angeles (90063-1675)
PHONE..................................323 268-2956
Junho Suh, *Pr*
**EMP:** 150 **EST:** 1975
**SQ FT:** 75,000
**SALES (est):** 9.5MM **Privately Held**
Web: www.milspeccoating.com
**SIC: 2891** 2851 Adhesives; Paints and allied products

**(P-6249)**
**TECHNICOTE INC**
1587 E Bentley Dr Ste 101, Corona (92879)
PHONE..................................951 372-0627
George Parker, *Mgr*
**EMP:** 40
**SALES (corp-wide):** 62.09MM **Privately Held**
Web: www.technicote.com
**SIC: 2891** 2675 Adhesives; Die-cut paper and board
PA: Technicote, Inc.
6206 Wolf Creek Pike
800 358-4448

**(P-6250)**
**THE ADHESIVE PRODUCTS INC (PA)**
520 Cleveland Ave, Albany (94710-1098)
PHONE..................................510 526-7616
◆ **EMP:** 25 **EST:** 1878
**SALES (est):** 5.02MM
**SALES (corp-wide):** 5.02MM **Privately Held**
Web: www.adhesiveproductsinc.com
**SIC: 2891** 2672 Adhesives; Gummed paper: made from purchased materials

## 2892 Explosives

**(P-6251)**
**MP ASSOCIATES INC**
Also Called: M P A
6555 Jackson Valley Rd, Ione (95640-9630)
P.O. Box 546 (95640-0546)
PHONE.................................209 274-4715
Thaine Morris, *Pr*
David Pier, *
▲ EMP: 170 EST: 1981
SQ FT: 3,112
SALES (est): 8.31MM **Privately Held**
Web: www.boehmface.com
SIC: 2892 2899 Explosives; Pyrotechnic ammunition: flares, signals, rockets, etc.

**(P-6252)**
**TELEDYNE REYNOLDS INC**
1001 Knox St, Torrance (90502-1030)
PHONE.................................310 823-5491
EMP: 250
SIC: 2892 3489 3678 3643 Explosives; Ordnance and accessories, nec; Electronic connectors; Current-carrying wiring services

## 2893 Printing Ink

**(P-6253)**
**DIVERSFIED NANO SOLUTIONS CORP**
12140 Community Rd, Poway (92064-6871)
PHONE.................................858 924-1013
EMP: 21
SALES (corp-wide): 10.22MM **Privately Held**
Web: www.diversifiednano.com
SIC: 2893 Printing ink
PA: Diversified Nano Solutions Corporation
2900 S Highland Dr Ste 17
858 924-1005

**(P-6254)**
**GANS INK AND SUPPLY CO INC (PA)**
Also Called: Gans Digital
1441 Boyd St, Los Angeles (90033-3714)
P.O. Box 33806 (90033-0806)
PHONE.................................323 264-2200
Jeffrey Koppelman, *Pr*
◆ EMP: 50 EST: 1950
SQ FT: 28,000
SALES (est): 20.46MM
SALES (corp-wide): 20.46MM **Privately Held**
Web: www.gansink.com
SIC: 2893 Printing ink

**(P-6255)**
**INK SOLUTIONS LLC**
5928 Garfield Ave, Commerce (90040-3607)
PHONE.................................323 726-8100
Ed Foff, *Brnch Mgr*
EMP: 15
SALES (corp-wide): 9.07MM **Privately Held**
Web: www.inksolutions.us
SIC: 2893 Printing ink
PA: Ink Solutions, Llc
800 Estes Ave
847 593-5200

**(P-6256)**
**INK SYSTEMS INC (PA)**
2311 S Eastern Ave, Commerce (90040-1430)
PHONE.................................323 720-4000
▲ EMP: 55 EST: 1985
SALES (est): 24.96MM
SALES (corp-wide): 24.96MM **Privately Held**
Web: www.inksystems.com
SIC: 2893 Printing ink

**(P-6257)**
**INX INTERNATIONAL INK CO**
Also Called: INX INTERNATIONAL INK CO
16700 Valley View Ave Ste 275, La Mirada (90638-5843)
PHONE.................................630 382-1800
Joe Mccabe, *Brnch Mgr*
EMP: 17
Web: www.inxinternational.com
SIC: 2893 Printing ink
HQ: Inx International Ink Co.
150 N Martingale Rd # 700
Schaumburg IL 60173
630 382-1800

**(P-6258)**
**INX INTERNATIONAL INK CO**
Also Called: INX Digital Intl
2125 Williams St, San Leandro (94577-3224)
PHONE.................................510 895-8001
Micol Kranz, *Mgr*
EMP: 23
Web: www.inxinternational.com
SIC: 2893 Printing ink
HQ: Inx International Ink Co.
150 N Mrtngale Rd Ste 700
Schaumburg IL 60173
630 382-1800

**(P-6259)**
**INX INTERNATIONAL INK CO**
1000 Business Park Dr, Dixon (95620-4310)
PHONE.................................707 693-2990
EMP: 16
Web: www.inxinternational.com
SIC: 2893 Printing ink
HQ: Inx International Ink Co.
150 N Martingale Rd # 700
Schaumburg IL 60173
630 382-1800

**(P-6260)**
**PRISM INKS**
Also Called: Graphics One
824 W Ahwanee Ave, Sunnyvale (94085-1409)
PHONE.................................408 744-6710
Amir Ajanee, *Pr*
Graham Dracup, *
Sarah Finlay, *
▲ EMP: 30 EST: 1999
SQ FT: 30,000
SALES (est): 7.26MM **Privately Held**
Web: www.prisminks.com
SIC: 2893 Printing ink

**(P-6261)**
**SUN CHEMICAL CORPORATION**
General Printing Ink Division
12963 Park St, Santa Fe Springs (90670-4083)
PHONE.................................562 946-2327
Paul Stack, *Mgr*
EMP: 27
Web: www.sunchemical.com
SIC: 2893 5084 Printing ink; Printing trades machinery, equipment, and supplies
HQ: Sun Chemical Corporation
35 Waterview Blvd
Parsippany NJ 07054
973 404-6000

**(P-6262)**
**SUN CHEMICAL CORPORATION**
1599 Factor Ave, San Leandro (94577-5630)
PHONE.................................510 618-1302
Tom Philis, *Brnch Mgr*
EMP: 60
Web: www.sunchemical.com
SIC: 2893 Printing ink
HQ: Sun Chemical Corporation
35 Waterview Blvd
Parsippany NJ 07054
973 404-6000

**(P-6263)**
**TW GRAPHICS GROUP COMPANY (PA)**
Also Called: TW Graphics
3323 S Malt Ave, Commerce (90040-3125)
P.O. Box 876 (50263-0876)
PHONE.................................323 721-1400
▲ EMP: 15 EST: 1922
SALES (est): 4.45MM
SALES (corp-wide): 4.45MM **Privately Held**
Web: www.eptanova.com
SIC: 2893 5084 Screen process ink; Printing trades machinery, equipment, and supplies

## 2895 Carbon Black

**(P-6264)**
**ALDILA MATERIALS TECH CORP (DH)**
13450 Stowe Dr, Poway (92064-6860)
PHONE.................................858 486-6970
Pete Matthewson, *Pr*
▼ EMP: 33 EST: 1997
SALES (est): 3.17MM **Privately Held**
Web: www.aldila.com
SIC: 2895 Carbon black
HQ: Aldila, Inc.
1945 Kellogg Ave
Carlsbad CA 92008
858 513-1801

## 2899 Chemical Preparations, Nec

**(P-6265)**
**ACORN ENGINEERING COMPANY (PA)**
Also Called: Morris Group International
15125 Proctor Ave, City Of Industry (91746-3327)
P.O. Box 3527 (91744-0527)
PHONE.................................800 488-8999
Donald E Morris, *CEO*
William D Morris, *
Kristin E Kahle, *
Randal Morris, *
Barrett Morris, *
◆ EMP: 702 EST: 1955
SQ FT: 120,000
SALES (est): 99.75MM
SALES (corp-wide): 99.75MM **Privately Held**
Web: www.acorneng.com
SIC: 2899 3431 Distilled water; Drinking fountains, metal

**(P-6266)**
**ALEDON INC**
Also Called: Employment Screening Resources
655 Irwin St Ste 1015, San Rafael (94901-4071)
PHONE.................................415 898-0044
Lester Rosen, *CEO*
EMP: 30 EST: 1997
SALES (est): 3.91MM **Privately Held**
SIC: 2899 7323 7375 8742 Drug testing kits, blood and urine; Credit reporting services; Information retrieval services; Human resource consulting services

**(P-6267)**
**AMERICAN CONSUMER PRODUCTS LLC**
120 E 8th St Ste 908, Los Angeles (90014-3332)
PHONE.................................323 289-6610
David Molayem, *Pr*
David Molayen, *
Kam Jahanbigloo, *
Daryoosh Molayem, *
◆ EMP: 73 EST: 1999
SALES (est): 1.31MM
SALES (corp-wide): 17.62MM **Privately Held**
Web: www.american-consumer-products.com
SIC: 2899 2844 2834 Chemical preparations, nec; Cosmetic preparations; Pharmaceutical preparations
PA: Tabletops Unlimited, Inc.
23000 Avalon Blvd
310 549-6000

**(P-6268)**
**APOLLOTEK INTERNATIONAL INC**
1702 Mcgaw Ave, Irvine (92614-5732)
PHONE.................................800 787-1244
Jeff Hatamkhani, *CEO*
EMP: 15 EST: 2011
SALES (est): 2.36MM **Privately Held**
Web: www.lefay.com
SIC: 2899 Water treating compounds

**(P-6269)**
**AT APOLLO TECHNOLOGIES LLC**
31441 Santa Margarita Pkwy Ste A219, Rcho Sta Marg (92688-1836)
PHONE.................................949 888-0573
Austin Browning, *Managing Member*
EMP: 23 EST: 1980
SALES (est): 2.25MM **Privately Held**
Web: www.apolloh2o.com
SIC: 2899 Water treating compounds

**(P-6270)**
**AVISTA TECHNOLOGIES INC**
140 Bosstick Blvd, San Marcos (92069-5930)
PHONE.................................760 744-0536
Dave Walker, *Pr*
Greg Leiser, *Ex VP*
Takefumi Shimoda, *Ex VP*
▼ EMP: 19 EST: 1999
SQ FT: 15,500
SALES (est): 1.34MM **Privately Held**
Web: www.avistamembranesolutions.com
SIC: 2899 Chemical supplies for foundries
PA: Kurita Water Industries Ltd.
4-10-1, Nakano

## 2899 - Chemical Preparations, Nec (P-6292)

**(P-6271)**
**CADE CORPORATION**
Also Called: Cade Co
100 Lewis St, San Jose (95112-5853)
PHONE.............................310 539-2508
Norman Angell, Pr
Rozann Stenshoel, *
Michael Stenshoel, Stockholder*
EMP: 61 EST: 1984
SQ FT: 25,000
SALES (est): 8MM Privately Held
Web: www.cadeco.com
SIC: 2899 Waterproofing compounds

**(P-6272)**
**CALIFORNIA RESPIRATORY CARE**
16055 Ventura Blvd # 715, Encino (91436-2601)
PHONE.............................818 379-9999
EMP: 55
SALES (est): 4.18MM Privately Held
SIC: 2899 5047 5169 Chemical preparations, nec; Medical and hospital equipment; Oxygen

**(P-6273)**
**CHEMDIV INC**
Also Called: Chemical Diversity Labs
12730 High Bluff Dr, San Diego (92130-2076)
PHONE.............................858 794-4860
Nikolay P Savchuk, CEO
A Ivachtchenko, Ch
EMP: 40 EST: 1995
SALES (est): 9.74MM Privately Held
Web: www.chemdiv.com
SIC: 2899 Chemical preparations, nec

**(P-6274)**
**CHEMTREAT INC**
Also Called: Trident Technologies
8885 Rehco Rd, San Diego (92121-3261)
PHONE.............................804 935-2000
EMP: 94
SALES (corp-wide): 1.73B Publicly Held
Web: www.chemtreat.com
SIC: 2899 Water treating compounds
HQ: Chemtreat, Inc.
    5640 Cox Rd
    Glen Allen VA 23060
    804 935-2000

**(P-6275)**
**CHEVRON ORONITE COMPANY LLC (DH)**
Also Called: Chevron Oronite
5001 Executive Pkwy, San Ramon (94583-5006)
PHONE.............................713 954-6060
Desmond King, Pr
Rich Conway, CFO
K Endries, Managing Member
B A Claar, Managing Member
◆ EMP: 50 EST: 2000
SALES (est): 499.15MM
SALES (corp-wide): 200.95B Publicly Held
Web: www.oronite.com
SIC: 2899 2869 1311 2821 Chemical preparations, nec; Industrial organic chemicals, nec; Crude petroleum and natural gas; Polystyrene resins
HQ: Chevron U.S.A. Inc.
    5001 Exec Pkwy Ste 200
    San Ramon CA 94583
    925 842-1000

**(P-6276)**
**COATINC UNITED STATES INC**
325 W Washington St Ste 2340, San Diego (92103-1946)
PHONE.............................619 638-7261
Paul Mcsweeney, CEO
EMP: 42 EST: 2014
SALES (est): 166.04K Privately Held
Web: www.coatinc.com
SIC: 2899 Fluxes: brazing, soldering, galvanizing, and welding

**(P-6277)**
**COPPER HARBOR COMPANY INC**
Also Called: Wine Chemicals
2300 Davis St, San Leandro (94577-2206)
PHONE.............................510 639-4670
Daniel Walters, Pr
EMP: 16 EST: 1997
SQ FT: 18,000
SALES (est): 4.73MM Privately Held
Web: ehevk-chdzo.servertrust.com
SIC: 2899 2865 2911 Chemical supplies for foundries; Solvent naphtha; Solvents

**(P-6278)**
**CP KELCO US INC**
2031 E Belt St, San Diego (92113)
PHONE.............................619 652-5326
EMP: 20
SALES (corp-wide): 1.24B Privately Held
Web: www.cpkelco.com
SIC: 2899 Chemical preparations, nec
HQ: Cp Kelco U.S., Inc.
    3100 Cumberland Blvd Se # 600
    Atlanta GA 30339
    678 247-7300

**(P-6279)**
**CUTWATER SPIRITS LLC (HQ)**
9750 Distribution Ave, San Diego (92121-2310)
PHONE.............................858 672-3848
EMP: 79 EST: 2016
SALES (est): 14.42MM
SALES (corp-wide): 1.7B Privately Held
Web: www.cutwaterspirits.com
SIC: 2899 Distilled water
PA: Anheuser-Busch Inbev
    Grand-Place 1
    25049660

**(P-6280)**
**CYANTEK CORPORATION**
3055 Osgood Ct, Fremont (94539-5612)
P.O. Box 1209 (95038-1209)
▲ EMP: 23 EST: 1988
SQ FT: 16,000
SALES (est): 1.56MM Privately Held
Web: www.cyantek.com
SIC: 2899 Chemical preparations, nec
HQ: Cmc Materials Kmg Corporation
    300 Throckmorton St
    Fort Worth TX 76102
    817 761-6100

**(P-6281)**
**CYTEC ENGINEERED MATERIALS INC**
645 N Cypress St, Orange (92867-6603)
PHONE.............................714 630-9400
Ron Martin, Brnch Mgr
EMP: 130
SQ FT: 300,000
SALES (corp-wide): 8.01MM Privately Held
Web: www.syensqo.com
SIC: 2899 Chemical preparations, nec
HQ: Cytec Engineered Materials Inc.
    2085 E Tech Cir Ste 102
    Tempe AZ 85284

**(P-6282)**
**DIAMON FUSION INTL INC**
Also Called: Diamon Fusion
9361 Irvine Blvd, Irvine (92618-1669)
PHONE.............................949 388-8000
Adam Zax, Pr
Russell Slaybaugh, VP
EMP: 16 EST: 1997
SQ FT: 4,500
SALES (est): 3.27MM Privately Held
Web: www.dfisolutions.com
SIC: 2899 6794 Chemical preparations, nec; Patent owners and lessors

**(P-6283)**
**EVONIK CORPORATION**
Also Called: Air Products
3305 E 26th St, Vernon (90058-4101)
PHONE.............................323 264-0311
William Ayacha, Brnch Mgr
EMP: 79
SALES (corp-wide): 16.59B Privately Held
Web: corporate.evonik.com
SIC: 2899 2891 2821 Chemical preparations, nec; Adhesives and sealants; Plastics materials and resins
HQ: Evonik Corporation
    2 Turner Pl
    Piscataway NJ 08854
    732 981-5060

**(P-6284)**
**FIRMENICH INCORPORATED**
10636 Scripps Summit Ct, San Diego (92131-3965)
PHONE.............................858 646-8323
Kym Coleman, Brnch Mgr
EMP: 57
Web: www.firmenich.com
SIC: 2899 Essential oils
HQ: Firmenich Incorporated
    250 Plainsboro Rd
    Plainsboro NJ 08536
    609 452-1000

**(P-6285)**
**FIRMENICH INCORPORATED**
Also Called: Firmenich
424 S Atchison St, Anaheim (92805-4045)
PHONE.............................714 535-2871
EMP: 233
Web: www.firmenich.com
SIC: 2899 2869 Essential oils; Perfumes, flavorings, and food additives
HQ: Firmenich Incorporated
    250 Plainsboro Rd
    Plainsboro NJ 08536
    609 452-1000

**(P-6286)**
**FUJIFILM ULTRA PURE SLTONS INC (DH)**
11225 Commercial Pkwy, Castroville (95012-3205)
PHONE.............................831 632-2120
Christopher Fitzjohn, Pr
Sherman Stever, VP
Bill Robb, VP
Mike Doi, Sec
▲ EMP: 20 EST: 1998
SALES (est): 22.07MM Privately Held
SIC: 2899 Chemical preparations, nec
HQ: Fujifilm Electronic Materials U.S.A., Inc.
    80 Circuit Dr
    North Kingstown RI 02852
    401 522-9499

**(P-6287)**
**GARRATT-CALLAHAN COMPANY (PA)**
50 Ingold Rd, Burlingame (94010-2206)
PHONE.............................650 697-5811
Jeffrey L Garratt, CEO
Matthew Colvin, *
Matthew R Garratt, *
EMP: 64 EST: 1904
SQ FT: 60,000
SALES (est): 46.27MM
SALES (corp-wide): 46.27MM Privately Held
Web: www.garrattcallahan.com
SIC: 2899 2911 Water treating compounds; Oils, lubricating

**(P-6288)**
**GENERAL GRAPHIC CHEM CO INC**
729 Fulton Shipyard Rd Ste A2, Antioch (94509-7566)
P.O. Box 24472 (94623-1472)
PHONE.............................510 879-7010
Andrew Greenberg, Pr
◆ EMP: 17 EST: 1957
SQ FT: 14,000
SALES (est): 1.91MM Privately Held
SIC: 2899 Chemical preparations, nec

**(P-6289)**
**GGTW LLC**
Also Called: South Bay Salt Works
1470 Bay Blvd, Chula Vista (91911-3942)
PHONE.............................619 423-3388
Glenn Warner, Owner
Tracy Strahl, Prin
▼ EMP: 24 EST: 1930
SALES (est): 4.17MM Privately Held
SIC: 2899 Salt

**(P-6290)**
**GUSMER ENTERPRISES INC**
2200 Northpoint Pkwy, Santa Rosa (95407-7398)
PHONE.............................866 213-1131
EMP: 22
SALES (corp-wide): 48.93MM Privately Held
Web: www.gusmerenterprises.com
SIC: 2899 Chemical preparations, nec
PA: Gusmer Enterprises, Inc.
    1165 Globe Ave
    908 301-1811

**(P-6291)**
**HEMOSURE INC**
5358 Irwindale Ave, Baldwin Park (91706-2086)
PHONE.............................888 436-6787
Doctor John Wan, Pr
Sherry Wang, *
EMP: 40 EST: 2003
SALES (est): 3.98MM Privately Held
Web: www.hemosure.com
SIC: 2899 3841 Chemical preparations, nec; Surgical and medical instruments
PA: W.H.P.M. Inc.
    5358 Irwindale Ave

**(P-6292)**
**HOME & BODY COMPANY (PA)**
Also Called: Direct Chemicals
5800 Skylab Rd, Huntington Beach (92647-2054)
PHONE.............................714 842-8000
Hazem H Haddad, Pr
Nadene Haddad, *
▲ EMP: 349 EST: 1997

## 2899 - Chemical Preparations, Nec (P-6293)

SALES (est): 41.68MM
SALES (corp-wide): 41.68MM **Privately Held**
Web: www.homeandbodyco.com
SIC: **2899** 2841 5999 2844  Essential oils; Textile soap; Toiletries, cosmetics, and perfumes; Face creams or lotions

### (P-6293)
### HYDRANAUTICS (DH)
401 Jones Rd, Oceanside (92058-1216)
PHONE...............................760 901-2500
Masaaki Ando, *Pr*
Michael Concannon, *
Randolph Truby, *
Marek Wilf, *
Norio Ikeyama, *
◆ EMP: 400 EST: 1987
SQ FT: 150,000
SALES (est): 106.12MM **Privately Held**
Web: www.membranes.com
SIC: **2899** 3589  Chemical preparations, nec; Water treatment equipment, industrial
HQ: Nitto Americas, Inc.
    400 Frank W Burr Blvd Ste
    Teaneck NJ 07666
    510 445-5400

### (P-6294)
### IL HELTH BUTY NATURAL OILS INC
Also Called: Hbno
2644 Hegan Ln, Chico (95928-9572)
PHONE...............................530 399-3782
Josef Demangeat, *CEO*
EMP: 50 EST: 2013
SALES (est): 9.1MM **Privately Held**
Web: www.essentialnaturaloils.com
SIC: **2899** 2836  Essential oils; Extracts

### (P-6295)
### INDEPENDENT INK INC (PA)
Also Called: Bubbie's Bagel Scooper
13700 Gramercy Pl, Gardena (90249-2455)
PHONE...............................310 523-4657
▲ EMP: 16 EST: 1983
SALES (est): 4.58MM
SALES (corp-wide): 4.58MM **Privately Held**
Web: www.independentink.com
SIC: **2899**  Ink or writing fluids

### (P-6296)
### INDIO PRODUCTS  INC
Cultural Heritage Candle Co
5331 E Slauson Ave, Commerce (90040-2916)
PHONE...............................323 720-9117
Marty Mayer, *Owner*
EMP: 33
SALES (corp-wide): 26.98MM **Privately Held**
Web: www.indioproducts.com
SIC: **2899** 3999 5199 5049  Incense; Candles ; Candles; Religious supplies
PA: Indio Products, Inc.
    12910 Mulberry Dr Unit A
    323 720-1188

### (P-6297)
### INNOVATIVE HEALTHCARE SVCS LLC
2108 N St Ste 8083, Sacramento (95816-5712)
PHONE...............................909 280-0559
EMP: 25 EST: 2015
SALES (est): 2.19MM **Privately Held**
Web: www.innovativehealthcareservices.com

SIC: **2899** 8099 8059 8361  Drug testing kits, blood and urine; Health and allied services, nec; Personal care home, with health care; Rehabilitation center, residential: health care incidental

### (P-6298)
### INSULTECH LLC (PA)
Also Called: Insultech
3530 W Garry Ave, Santa Ana (92704-6423)
PHONE...............................714 384-0506
Ryan Barto, *Managing Member*
◆ EMP: 45 EST: 1994
SQ FT: 30,000
SALES (est): 15.61MM **Privately Held**
Web: www.insultech.com
SIC: **2899**  Insulating compounds

### (P-6299)
### INX INTERNATIONAL INK CO
13821 Marquardt Ave, Santa Fe Springs (90670-5016)
PHONE...............................562 404-5664
Elvis Tran, *Mgr*
EMP: 30
Web: www.inxinternational.com
SIC: **2899** 2893  Ink or writing fluids; Printing ink
HQ: Inx International Ink Co.
    150 N Mrtngale Rd Ste 700
    Schaumburg IL 60173
    630 382-1800

### (P-6300)
### K2 PURE SOLUTIONS NOCAL LP
Also Called: K2 Pure Solutions
950 Loveridge Rd, Pittsburg (94565-2808)
PHONE...............................713 249-8057
Chris Mclean, *Pt*
Rochelle Aquino, *Pt*
Rosemary Aldrich, *Pt*
EMP: 21 EST: 2007
SALES (est): 4.38MM **Privately Held**
Web: www.k2pure.com
SIC: **2899**  Chemical preparations, nec

### (P-6301)
### KEMIRA WATER SOLUTIONS INC
Also Called: Kemiron Pacific
14000 San Bernardino Ave, Fontana (92335-5258)
PHONE...............................909 350-5678
Hailu Mequira, *Mgr*
EMP: 24
SALES (corp-wide): 3.68B **Privately Held**
Web: www.kemira.com
SIC: **2899**  Water treating compounds
HQ: Kemira Water Solutions, Inc.
    200 Gllria Pkwy Se Ste 15
    Atlanta GA 30339

### (P-6302)
### KIK POOL ADDITIVES INC
5160 E Airport Dr, Ontario (91761-7824)
PHONE...............................909 390-9912
John A Christensen, *Pr*
David M Christensen, *VP*
Debra Schonk, *VP*
Brian Patterson, *CFO*
Chet Yoakum, *VP*
▲ EMP: 140 EST: 1958
SALES (est): 16.87MM **Privately Held**
Web: www.kem-tek.com
SIC: **2899** 3089 7389 5169  Chemical preparations, nec; Plastics hardware and building products; Packaging and labeling services; Swimming pool and spa chemicals

### (P-6303)
### L M SCOFIELD COMPANY (DH)
12767 Imperial Hwy, Santa Fe Springs (90670-4711)
PHONE...............................323 720-3000
Phillip J Arnold, *Pr*
◆ EMP: 50 EST: 1915
SQ FT: 36,000
SALES (est): 10.48MM **Privately Held**
Web: usa.sika.com
SIC: **2899**  Concrete curing and hardening compounds
HQ: Sika Corporation
    201 Polito Ave
    Lyndhurst NJ 07071
    201 933-8800

### (P-6304)
### LG NANOH2O  LLC
Also Called: Lg Nanoh2o, Inc.
21250 Hawthorne Blvd Ste 330, Torrance (90503-5506)
PHONE...............................424 218-4000
Jeff Green, *CEO*
Michael Demartino, *VP*
John Markovich, *CFO*
Doug Barnes, *COO*
Cj Kurth, *VP*
▲ EMP: 35 EST: 2005
SQ FT: 2,000
SALES (est): 7.3MM **Privately Held**
SIC: **2899**  Distilled water
PA: Lg Chem, Ltd.
    128 Yeoui-Daero, Yeongdeungpo-Gu

### (P-6305)
### LUBRIZOL GLOBAL MANAGEMENT INC
3115 Propeller Dr, Paso Robles (93446-8524)
PHONE...............................805 239-1550
Daniel Mccornack, *Prin*
EMP: 34
SALES (corp-wide): 364.48B **Publicly Held**
Web: www.lubrizol.com
SIC: **2899**  Chemical preparations, nec
HQ: Lubrizol Global Management, Inc.
    9911 Brecksville Rd
    Cleveland OH 44141
    216 447-5000

### (P-6306)
### MASTER BUILDERS  LLC
Degussa Construction
9060 Haven Ave, Rancho Cucamonga (91730-5405)
PHONE...............................909 987-1758
Dave Lougheed, *Mgr*
EMP: 878
Web: master-builders-solutions.basf.us
SIC: **2899**  Chemical preparations, nec
HQ: Master Builders, Llc
    23700 Chagrin Blvd
    Beachwood OH 44122
    800 228-3318

### (P-6307)
### MATSUI INTERNATIONAL CO INC (HQ)
Also Called: Unimark
1501 W 178th St, Gardena (90248-3203)
PHONE...............................310 767-7812
Masa Matsui, *Pr*
Yoshi Haga, *
◆ EMP: 32 EST: 1987
SQ FT: 30,000
SALES (est): 24.62MM **Privately Held**
Web: www.matsui-color.com

SIC: **2899**  Ink or writing fluids
PA: Matsui Shikiso Chemical Co., Ltd.
    64, Kamikazansakuradani, Yamashina-Ku

### (P-6308)
### MCGRAYEL COMPANY
Also Called: Eascare Products USA
5361 S Villa Ave, Fresno (93725-8903)
P.O. Box 12362 (93777-2362)
PHONE...............................559 299-7660
Marvin J Rezac Junior, *CEO*
Evangelina Serrano, *
Todd Wilson, *
Tiffany Rolofson, *
Rosemarie Arneas, *
EMP: 25 EST: 1978
SQ FT: 10,000
SALES (est): 5.18MM **Privately Held**
Web: www.easycarewater.com
SIC: **2899**  Water treating compounds

### (P-6309)
### MEDICAL CHEMICAL CORPORATION
Also Called: M C C
19250 Van Ness Ave, Torrance (90501-1102)
P.O. Box 6217 (90504-0217)
PHONE...............................310 787-6800
Emmanuel Didier, *Pr*
Patrick Braden, *
Andy Rocha, *
Kris Kontis, *
◆ EMP: 45 EST: 1954
SALES (est): 11.8MM **Privately Held**
Web: www.med-chem.com
SIC: **2899** 2841  Chemical preparations, nec; Soap and other detergents

### (P-6310)
### MOC PRODUCTS COMPANY INC (PA)
Also Called: Auto Edge Solutions
12306 Montague St, Pacoima (91331-2279)
PHONE...............................818 794-3500
Mark Waco, *CEO*
Dave Waco, *
◆ EMP: 75 EST: 1954
SQ FT: 100,000
SALES (est): 52.48MM
SALES (corp-wide): 52.48MM **Privately Held**
Web: www.mocproducts.com
SIC: **2899** 7549 5169  Corrosion preventive lubricant; Automotive maintenance services ; Chemicals and allied products, nec

### (P-6311)
### MORTON SALT  INC
1050 Pier F Ave, Long Beach (90802-6215)
P.O. Box 2289 (90801-2289)
PHONE...............................562 437-0071
Ken Dobson, *Brnch Mgr*
EMP: 86
SALES (corp-wide): 3.82B **Privately Held**
Web: www.mortonsalt.com
SIC: **2899**  Salt
HQ: Morton Salt, Inc.
    444 W Lake St Ste 3000
    Chicago IL 60606

### (P-6312)
### NEO TECH AQUA SOLUTIONS INC
3853 Calle Fortunada, San Diego (92123-1824)
PHONE...............................858 571-6590

## PRODUCTS & SERVICES SECTION
## 2911 - Petroleum Refining (P-6331)

Stephen Dunham, *Pr*
George Diefenthal, *COO*
**EMP:** 15 **EST:** 2002
**SQ FT:** 6,000
**SALES (est):** 2.71MM **Privately Held**
**Web:** www.reflex-uv.com
**SIC:** 2899 Water treating compounds

### (P-6313)
### NUGENERATION TECHNOLOGIES LLC (PA)
Also Called: Nugentec
1155 Park Ave, Emeryville (94608-3631)
P.O. Box 30428 (95213-0428)
**PHONE**.................................415 747-2768
Donato Polignone, *CEO*
Stephen Utschig-samuels, *Prin*
◆ **EMP:** 17 **EST:** 1997
**SQ FT:** 11,000
**SALES (est):** 8.48MM
**SALES (corp-wide):** 8.48MM **Privately Held**
**Web:** www.nugentec.com
**SIC:** 2899 2841 1389 Chemical preparations, nec; Soap and other detergents; Lease tanks, oil field: erecting, cleaning, and repairing

### (P-6314)
### OLDE THOMPSON LLC (DH)
3250 Camino Del Sol, Oxnard (93030-8998)
**PHONE**.................................805 983-0388
David Sugarman, *CEO*
Jeffrey M Shumway, *
◆ **EMP:** 21 **EST:** 1944
**SQ FT:** 88,000
**SALES (est):** 119.93MM
**SALES (corp-wide):** 174.1MM **Privately Held**
**Web:** www.oldethompson.com
**SIC:** 2899 2099 5149 Salt; Seasonings and spices; Spices and seasonings
**HQ:** Olam Food Ingredients Vietnam Pte. Ltd.
7 Straits View
Singapore 01893

### (P-6315)
### OPTIVA INC
384 Oyster Point Blvd Ste 16, South San Francisco (94080-1968)
**PHONE**.................................650 616-7600
Peter Hopper, *CEO*
Pavel I Lazarev, *Chief Technical Officer*
Joan Varrone, *VP Fin*
Rob Harrison, *S&M/VP*
Pete Smith, *VP Opers*
**EMP:** 85 **EST:** 1997
**SQ FT:** 9,400
**SALES (est):** 1.9MM **Privately Held**
**SIC:** 2899 Ink or writing fluids

### (P-6316)
### PACIFIC SCIENTIFIC ENERGETIC (HQ)
Also Called: Pacific Scientific
3601 Union Rd, Hollister (95023-9635)
**PHONE**.................................831 637-3731
Gregory Scaven, *Pr*
John Collins, *CFO*
**EMP:** 300 **EST:** 1945
**SQ FT:** 65,000
**SALES (est):** 198.61MM
**SALES (corp-wide):** 6.07B **Publicly Held**
**Web:** www.psemc.com

**SIC:** 2899 3489 3483 3699 Igniter grains, boron potassium nitrate; Projectors: depth charge, grenade, rocket, etc.; Arming and fusing devices for missiles; High-energy particle physics equipment
**PA:** Fortive Corporation
6920 Seaway Blvd
425 446-5000

### (P-6317)
### PHIBRO ANIMAL HEALTH CORP
Phibro-Tech
8851 Dice Rd, Santa Fe Springs (90670-2515)
**PHONE**.................................562 698-8036
Mark Alling, *Mgr*
**EMP:** 29
**SALES (corp-wide):** 1.02B **Publicly Held**
**Web:** www.pahc.com
**SIC:** 2899 2819 Chemical preparations, nec; Industrial inorganic chemicals, nec
**HQ:** Phibro Animal Health Corporation
300 Frank W Burr Blvd Ste
Teaneck NJ 07666
201 329-7300

### (P-6318)
### PRESTONE PRODUCTS CORPORATION
Also Called: Kik Custom Products
19500 Mariner Ave, Torrance (90503-1644)
**PHONE**.................................424 271-4836
Raymond Yu, *Manager*
**EMP:** 30
**Web:** www.prestone.com
**SIC:** 2899 5531 5169 Antifreeze compounds; Automotive parts; Anti-freeze compounds
**HQ:** Prestone Products Corporation
6250 N River Rd Ste 6000
Rosemont IL 60018

### (P-6319)
### RADIATOR SPECIALTY COMPANY
Also Called: Highway Safety Control
935 Enterprise Way, Napa (94558-6209)
**PHONE**.................................707 252-0122
David Brock, *Mgr*
**EMP:** 64
**SALES (corp-wide):** 45.45MM **Privately Held**
**Web:** www.rscbrands.com
**SIC:** 2899 3993 3561 3669 Antifreeze compounds; Signs and advertising specialties; Pumps and pumping equipment; Transportation signaling devices
**PA:** Radiator Specialty Company Inc
600 Radiator Rd
704 688-2302

### (P-6320)
### RELTON CORPORATION
317 Rolyn Pl, Arcadia (91007-2838)
P.O. Box 60019 (91066-6019)
**PHONE**.................................800 423-1505
William Kinard, *Ch*
Wm Craig Kinard, *
Craig Kinard, *
Kevin Kinard, *
Chris Kinard, *
◆ **EMP:** 65 **EST:** 1946
**SQ FT:** 20,000
**SALES (est):** 9.03MM **Privately Held**
**Web:** www.relton.com
**SIC:** 2899 3423 3546 2992 Chemical preparations, nec; Masons' hand tools; Power-driven handtools; Lubricating oils and greases

### (P-6321)
### RICHARD K GOULD INC
Also Called: Sierra Chemical Company
788 Northport Dr, West Sacramento (95691-2145)
**PHONE**.................................916 371-5943
Robert Gould, *CEO*
Steve Gould, *Pr*
Karen Silva, *Sec*
**EMP:** 25 **EST:** 1978
**SQ FT:** 18,500
**SALES (est):** 4.19MM **Privately Held**
**Web:** www.sierrachemicalcompany.com
**SIC:** 2899 5999 Oils and essential oils; Cleaning equipment and supplies

### (P-6322)
### ROYAL ADHESIVES & SEALANTS LLC
800 E Anaheim St, Wilmington (90744-3637)
**PHONE**.................................310 830-9904
Theodore M Clark, *Managing Member*
▲ **EMP:** 20 **EST:** 2006
**SALES (est):** 4.79MM
**SALES (corp-wide):** 3.51B **Publicly Held**
**Web:** www.hbfuller.com
**SIC:** 2899 3479 Waterproofing compounds; Painting, coating, and hot dipping
**PA:** H.B. Fuller Company
1200 Willow Lake Blvd
651 236-5900

### (P-6323)
### SIGMA-ALDRICH CORPORATION
Also Called: Safc Pharma
6211 El Camino Real, Carlsbad (92009-1604)
**PHONE**.................................760 710-6213
Tim Quinn, *Mgr*
**EMP:** 50
**SALES (corp-wide):** 22.82B **Privately Held**
**Web:** www.sigmaaldrich.com
**SIC:** 2899 Chemical preparations, nec
**HQ:** Sigma-Aldrich Corporation
3050 Spruce St
Saint Louis MO 63103
314 771-5765

### (P-6324)
### SIKA CORPORATION
12767 Imperial Hwy, Santa Fe Springs (90670-4711)
**PHONE**.................................562 941-0231
Jerry Monarch, *Brnch Mgr*
**EMP:** 17
**SQ FT:** 26,186
**Web:** usa.sika.com
**SIC:** 2899 Concrete curing and hardening compounds
**HQ:** Sika Corporation
201 Polito Ave
Lyndhurst NJ 07071
201 933-8800

### (P-6325)
### THE LUBRIZOL CORPORATION
30211 Avenida De Las Bandera, Rancho Santa Margari (92688-2147)
**PHONE**.................................949 212-1863
**EMP:** 19
**SALES (corp-wide):** 364.48B **Publicly Held**
**Web:** www.lubrizol.com
**SIC:** 2899 Chemical preparations, nec
**HQ:** The Lubrizol Corporation
29400 Lakeland Blvd
Wickliffe OH 44092
440 943-4200

### (P-6326)
### TORAY MEMBRANE USA INC (DH)
13435 Danielson St, Poway (92064-6825)
**PHONE**.................................858 218-2360
Steve Cappos, *CEO*
Tak Wakisaka, *
Gabriel Juarez, *
◆ **EMP:** 85 **EST:** 2006
**SQ FT:** 90,000
**SALES (est):** 25.57MM **Privately Held**
**Web:** www.water.toray
**SIC:** 2899 Water treating compounds
**HQ:** Toray Holding (U.S.A.), Inc.
461 5th Ave Fl 9
New York NY 10017
212 697-8150

### (P-6327)
### TUMELO INC
Also Called: Le Petite Fleur
420 Tesconi Cir Ste B, Santa Rosa (95401-4681)
**PHONE**.................................707 523-4411
Scott Maddock, *Prin*
**EMP:** 25 **EST:** 2017
**SALES (est):** 3.2MM **Privately Held**
**Web:** www.sonomalavender.com
**SIC:** 2899 2841 Oils and essential oils; Soap and other detergents

### (P-6328)
### VEOLIA WTS USA INC
Also Called: GE Water & Process Tech
8.5 Miles Nw Avila Beach, Avila Beach (93424)
**PHONE**.................................805 545-3743
**EMP:** 90
**Web:** www.watertechnologies.com
**SIC:** 2899 Water treating compounds
**HQ:** Veolia Wts Usa, Inc.
3600 Horizon Blvd
Trevose PA 19053
866 439-2837

### (P-6329)
### VULPINE INC
Also Called: Shape Products
1127 57th Ave, Oakland (94621-4427)
**PHONE**.................................510 534-1186
Dan Daniel, *Pr*
Tony Weiler, *VP*
▲ **EMP:** 29 **EST:** 1979
**SQ FT:** 22,000
**SALES (est):** 2.37MM **Privately Held**
**Web:** www.shapeproduct.com
**SIC:** 2899 5169 Chemical preparations, nec; Chemicals and allied products, nec

## 2911 Petroleum Refining

### (P-6330)
### ACCU-BLEND CORPORATION
364 Malbert St, Perris (92570-8336)
**PHONE**.................................626 334-7744
Xia Wang, *CEO*
Kenny Wang, *Pr*
▲ **EMP:** 17 **EST:** 2005
**SALES (est):** 2.19MM **Privately Held**
**Web:** www.accu-blend.com
**SIC:** 2911 Paraffin wax

### (P-6331)
### AIR PRODUCTS AND CHEMICALS INC
Also Called: Air Products
3700 W 190th St, Torrance (90504-5733)
**PHONE**.................................310 212-2800

## 2911 - Petroleum Refining (P-6332)

Pete Trelenberg, *Mgr*
**EMP:** 15
**SALES (corp-wide):** 12.6B **Publicly Held**
**Web:** www.pbfenergy.com
**SIC: 2911** 5541 Petroleum refining; Gasoline service stations
**PA:** Air Products And Chemicals, Inc.
1940 Air Products Blvd
610 481-4911

### (P-6332)
### CASTAIC TRUCK STOP INC
31611 Castaic Rd, Castaic (91384-3929)
**PHONE**.................661 295-1374
Sarkis Khrimian, *Pr*
Refe Dimmuck, *
**EMP:** 26 **EST:** 1994
**SQ FT:** 2,000
**SALES (est):** 3.92MM **Privately Held**
**Web:** www.castaictruckstop.com
**SIC: 2911** 7389 5812 Diesel fuels; Flea market; American restaurant

### (P-6333)
### CHEVRON CORPORATION (PA)
Also Called: Chevron
5001 Executive Pkwy Ste 200, San Ramon (94583-5006)
**PHONE**.................925 842-1000
Michael K Wirth, *Ch Bd*
Mark A Nelson, *
Pierre R Breber, *VP*
Rhonda J Morris, *Chief Human Resource Officer*
R Hewitt Pate, *VP*
**EMP:** 1126 **EST:** 1926
**SALES (est):** 200.95B
**SALES (corp-wide):** 200.95B **Publicly Held**
**Web:** www.chevron.com
**SIC: 2911** 1311 1382 1321 Petroleum refining; Crude petroleum production; Oil and gas exploration services; Natural gas liquids

### (P-6334)
### CHEVRON GLOBAL ENERGY INC (HQ)
Also Called: Chevron Global Lubricants
5001 Executive Pkwy, San Ramon (94583-5006)
P.O. Box 6046 (94583-0746)
**PHONE**.................925 842-1000
Jock D Mckenzie, *Ch Bd*
Larry Bennison, *Operations*
Barry A Chafitz, *General*
Malcolm J Mcauley, *Sr VP*
Richard J Guiltinan, *VP*
**EMP:** 100 **EST:** 1936
**SALES (est):** 40.77MM
**SALES (corp-wide):** 200.95B **Publicly Held**
**Web:** www.chevronlubricants.com
**SIC: 2911** 4731 5172 Petroleum refining; Freight transportation arrangement; Petroleum products, nec
**PA:** Chevron Corporation
5001 Exec Pkwy Ste 200
925 842-1000

### (P-6335)
### CHEVRON USA INC
Also Called: Chevron
841 Chevron Way Frnt, Richmond (94801-2007)
P.O. Box 4107 (94804-0107)
**PHONE**.................510 242-3000
Gary Masada, *Brnch Mgr*
**EMP:** 100
**SALES (corp-wide):** 200.95B **Publicly Held**

**Web:** www.chevron.com
**SIC: 2911** Gasoline blending plants
**HQ:** Chevron U.S.A. Inc.
5001 Exec Pkwy Ste 200
San Ramon CA 94583
925 842-1000

### (P-6336)
### DE MENNO-KERDOON TRADING CO (HQ)
2000 N Alameda St, Compton (90222-2799)
**PHONE**.................310 537-7100
Jim Ennis, *COO*
Jay Demel, *
**EMP:** 149 **EST:** 1990
**SQ FT:** 60,000
**SALES (est):** 38.18MM
**SALES (corp-wide):** 128.17MM **Privately Held**
**SIC: 2911** Oils, fuel
**PA:** World Oil Marketing Company
9302 Garfield Ave
562 928-0100

### (P-6337)
### EXXON MBIL - RFNERY DIST PLANT
2619 E 37th St, Vernon (90058-1722)
**PHONE**.................323 586-5329
**EMP:** 15 **EST:** 2017
**SALES (est):** 509.77K **Privately Held**
**SIC: 2911** Petroleum refining

### (P-6338)
### GOLDEN WEST REFINING COMPANY
13116 Imperial Hwy, Santa Fe Springs (90670-4817)
P.O. Box 2128 (90670-0138)
**PHONE**.................562 921-3581
Ted Orden, *Pr*
Moshe Sassover, *Sr VP*
**EMP:** 19 **EST:** 1978
**SQ FT:** 22,000
**SALES (est):** 4.17MM
**SALES (corp-wide):** 9.87MM **Privately Held**
**SIC: 2911** Gas, refinery
**PA:** Thrifty Oil Co.
13116 Imperial Hwy
562 921-3581

### (P-6339)
### INTERNATIONAL GROUP INC
102 Cutting Blvd, Richmond (94804-2126)
**PHONE**.................510 232-8704
**EMP:** 58
**SALES (corp-wide):** 419.36K **Privately Held**
**Web:** www.igiwax.com
**SIC: 2911** Paraffin wax
**HQ:** The International Group Inc
1007 E Spring St
Titusville PA 16354
814 827-4900

### (P-6340)
### KERN OIL & REFINING CO (HQ)
Also Called: Kern Energy
7724 E Panama Ln, Bakersfield (93307-9210)
**PHONE**.................661 845-0761
**EMP:** 125 **EST:** 1971
**SALES (est):** 53.04MM
**SALES (corp-wide):** 100.28MM **Privately Held**
**Web:** www.kernenergy.com

**SIC: 2911** Petroleum refining
**PA:** Casey Company
180 E Ocean Blvd Ste 1010
562 436-9685

### (P-6341)
### MOLECULUM
3128 Red Hill Ave, Costa Mesa (92626-4525)
**PHONE**.................714 619-5139
**EMP:** 18 **EST:** 2015
**SALES (est):** 1.36MM **Privately Held**
**Web:** www.moleculum.com
**SIC: 2911** Aromatic chemical products

### (P-6342)
### MTS SOLUTIONS LLC ◆
7131 Charity Ave, Bakersfield (93308-5870)
**PHONE**.................661 589-5804
**EMP:** 36 **EST:** 2023
**SALES (est):** 5.62MM **Privately Held**
**Web:** www.mts-stim.com
**SIC: 2911** Petroleum refining

### (P-6343)
### NEW LEAF BIOFUEL LLC
2285 Newton Ave, San Diego (92113-3619)
**PHONE**.................619 236-8500
Jennifer Case, *Pt*
Nicole Kennard, *Managing Member*
▲ **EMP:** 35 **EST:** 2006
**SALES (est):** 6.14MM **Privately Held**
**Web:** www.newleafbiofuel.com
**SIC: 2911** 8742 Diesel fuels; Restaurant and food services consultants

### (P-6344)
### PARAMOUNT PETROLEUM CORP (DH)
Also Called: Paramount Asphalt
14700 Downey Ave, Paramount (90723-4526)
**PHONE**.................562 531-2060
W S Lovejoy, *CEO*
◆ **EMP:** 155 **EST:** 1980
**SQ FT:** 6,000
**SALES (est):** 43.14MM
**SALES (corp-wide):** 16.92B **Publicly Held**
**Web:** www.alon.com
**SIC: 2911** Petroleum refining
**HQ:** Alon Usa Energy, Inc.
310 Seven Springs Way # 500
Brentwood TN 37027

### (P-6345)
### PASADENA REFINING SYSTEM INC
6001 Bollinger Canyon Rd, San Ramon (94583-2324)
**PHONE**.................713 920-1874
**EMP:** 325
**SALES (corp-wide):** 200.95B **Publicly Held**
**Web:** pasadena.chevron.com
**SIC: 2911** Petroleum refining
**HQ:** Pasadena Refining System, Inc.
10350 Richmond Ave # 1400
Houston TX 77042
713 920-1874

### (P-6346)
### QUANTEN CONSORTIUM ANGOLA LLC
1161-70 Ringwood Ct, San Jose (95131-1754)
**PHONE**.................408 955-0768
Segun Thomas, *Managing Member*
**EMP:** 20 **EST:** 2021

**SALES (est):** 677.01K **Privately Held**
**Web:** www.quantenangola.com
**SIC: 2911** Petroleum refining

### (P-6347)
### REED & GRAHAM INC (PA)
690 Sunol St, San Jose (95126-3751)
P.O. Box 5940 (95150-5940)
**PHONE**.................408 287-1400
Gerald R Graham Junior, *Pr*
Gerald R Graham Senior, *Ch Bd*
Steven Reed Graham, *
▲ **EMP:** 50 **EST:** 1923
**SQ FT:** 8,000
**SALES (est):** 41.13MM
**SALES (corp-wide):** 41.13MM **Privately Held**
**Web:** www.rginc.com
**SIC: 2911** 2952 8731 5032 Asphalt or asphaltic materials, made in refineries; Coating compounds, tar; Commercial research laboratory; Brick, stone, and related material

### (P-6348)
### REH COMPANY
1703 W Olive Ave, Fresno (93728-2617)
**PHONE**.................559 351-1916
**EMP:** 79
**SALES (corp-wide):** 457.26MM **Privately Held**
**Web:** www.sinclairoil.com
**SIC: 2911** Petroleum refining
**PA:** Reh Company
550 E S Temple
801 524-2700

### (P-6349)
### REH COMPANY
5792 N Palm Ave, Fresno (93704-1844)
**PHONE**.................559 997-3617
**EMP:** 119
**SALES (corp-wide):** 457.26MM **Privately Held**
**Web:** www.sinclairoil.com
**SIC: 2911** Petroleum refining
**PA:** Reh Company
550 E S Temple
801 524-2700

### (P-6350)
### ROCK ENGINEERED MCHY CO INC
Also Called: Remco
1627 Army Ct Ste 1, Stockton (95206-1189)
**PHONE**.................925 447-0805
Kevin Cadwalader, *Pr*
◆ **EMP:** 19 **EST:** 1983
**SALES (est):** 6.75MM **Privately Held**
**Web:** www.remcovsi.com
**SIC: 2911** 5084 Heavy distillates; Crushing machinery and equipment

### (P-6351)
### SACAHN JV
15916 Bernardo Center Dr, San Diego (92127-1828)
**PHONE**.................858 924-1110
**EMP:** 99 **EST:** 2014
**SQ FT:** 3,000
**SALES (est):** 4.22MM **Privately Held**
**SIC: 2911** Oils, fuel

### (P-6352)
### SAN JOAQUIN REFINING CO INC
3500 Shell St, Bakersfield (93388)
P.O. Box 5576 (93388)
**PHONE**.................661 327-4257

▲ = Import ▼ = Export
◆ = Import/Export

## PRODUCTS & SERVICES SECTION
### 2952 - Asphalt Felts And Coatings (P-6373)

Kenneth E Fait, *Ch Bd*
Majid Mojibi, *
Dorothy A Gribben, *
**EMP:** 130 **EST:** 1979
**SQ FT:** 15,000
**SALES (est):** 47.17MM **Privately Held**
**Web:** www.sjr.com
**SIC:** 2911 Oils, fuel

### (P-6353)
### TESORO REFINING & MKTG CO LLC
5905 N Paramount Blvd, Long Beach (90805-3709)
**PHONE**...................562 728-2215
**EMP:** 71
**SIC:** 2911 5541 Petroleum refining; Gasoline service stations
**HQ:** Tesoro Refining & Marketing Company Llc
19100 Ridgewood Pkwy
San Antonio TX 78259
210 626-6000

### (P-6354)
### TORRANCE REFINING COMPANY LLC
3700 W 190th St, Torrance (90504-5733)
**PHONE**...................310 212-2800
Thomas J Nimbley, *CEO*
**EMP:** 600 **EST:** 2015
**SALES (est):** 72.92MM
**SALES (corp-wide):** 46.78B **Privately Held**
**Web:** www.pbfenergy.com
**SIC:** 2911 2992 Petroleum refining; Lubricating oils
**HQ:** Pbf Energy Western Region Llc
3760 Klroy Arprt Way Ste
Long Beach CA 90806
973 455-7500

### (P-6355)
### TRICOR REFINING LLC
1134 Manor St, Bakersfield (93308-3553)
P.O. Box 5877 (93388-5877)
**PHONE**...................661 393-7110
Majid Mojibi, *Managing Member*
Don Brookes, *Managing Member* ✪
Kenneth E Fait, *Managing Member* ✪
**EMP:** 28 **EST:** 2001
**SALES (est):** 9.74MM **Privately Held**
**Web:** www.tricorrefining.com
**SIC:** 2911 Oils, fuel

### (P-6356)
### ULTRAMAR INC
Also Called: Village Center Ultramar
9508 E Palmdale Blvd, Palmdale (93591-2202)
**PHONE**...................661 944-2496
Ken Berglund, *Mgr*
**EMP:** 64
**SALES (corp-wide):** 144.77B **Publicly Held**
**Web:** www.valero.com
**SIC:** 2911 Petroleum refining
**HQ:** Ultramar Inc.
1 Valero Way
San Antonio TX 78249
210 345-2000

### (P-6357)
### VALERO REF COMPANY-CALIFORNIA
Also Called: Valero
2401 E Anaheim St, Wilmington (90744-4009)
**PHONE**...................562 491-6754
Mark Thair, *Mgr*

**EMP:** 1084
**SALES (corp-wide):** 144.77B **Publicly Held**
**Web:** www.valero.com
**SIC:** 2911 Petroleum refining
**HQ:** Valero Refining Company-California
1 Valero Way
San Antonio TX 78249
210 345-2000

### (P-6358)
### WD-40 COMPANY
Also Called: Hdp Holdings
9715 Businesspark Ave, San Diego (92131-1642)
**PHONE**...................619 275-1400
Garry Ridge, *Pr*
**EMP:** 233
**SALES (corp-wide):** 590.56MM **Publicly Held**
**Web:** www.wd40company.com
**SIC:** 2911 Oils, lubricating
**PA:** Wd-40 Company
9715 Businesspark Ave
619 275-1400

## 2951 Asphalt Paving Mixtures And Blocks

### (P-6359)
### ACC CA INC (HQ)
Also Called: Recycled Aggregate Mtls Co Inc
2655 1st St Ste 210, Simi Valley (93065-1578)
**PHONE**...................805 522-1646
Dennis L Newman, *Pr*
**EMP:** 18 **EST:** 2006
**SALES (est):** 6.21MM
**SALES (corp-wide):** 2.31B **Publicly Held**
**Web:** ramco.us.com
**SIC:** 2951 Concrete, asphaltic (not from refineries)
**PA:** Arcosa, Inc.
500 N Akard St Ste 400
972 942-6500

### (P-6360)
### AJW CONSTRUCTION
966 81st Ave, Oakland (94621-2512)
**PHONE**...................510 568-2300
Ed Webster, *Prin*
Juan Quintor, *
Alfonso Quintor, *
**EMP:** 42 **EST:** 1996
**SALES (est):** 5.59MM **Privately Held**
**Web:** www.brooksconsultingservices.com
**SIC:** 2951 Asphalt paving mixtures and blocks

### (P-6361)
### DELTA TRADING LP
Also Called: Crimson Resource Management
17731 Millux Rd, Bakersfield (93311-9714)
**PHONE**...................661 834-5560
Mike Purdy, *Pt*
Rob Mcelroy, *Genl Mgr*
**EMP:** 20 **EST:** 2004
**SALES (est):** 9.83MM **Privately Held**
**Web:** www.deltatradinglp.com
**SIC:** 2951 Asphalt paving mixtures and blocks

### (P-6362)
### DESERT BLOCK CO INC
11374 Tuxford St, Sun Valley (91352-2636)
**PHONE**...................661 824-2624
Bill Fenzel, *Pr*
William Gapastione, *VP*

**EMP:** 22 **EST:** 1991
**SALES (est):** 843.66K **Privately Held**
**Web:** www.angelusblock.com
**SIC:** 2951 3272 Concrete, asphaltic (not from refineries); Concrete products, precast, nec

### (P-6363)
### GOLDSTAR ASPHALT PRODUCTS INC
1354 Jet Way, Perris (92571-7466)
**PHONE**...................951 940-1610
Jeff S Nelson, *Pr*
**EMP:** 32 **EST:** 1997
**SALES (est):** 1.3MM **Privately Held**
**Web:** www.goldstarasphalt.com
**SIC:** 2951 Asphalt paving mixtures and blocks

### (P-6364)
### GRANITE ROCK COMPANY
Also Called: Peninsula Road Materials
365 Blomquist St, Redwood City (94063-2701)
**PHONE**...................650 482-3800
Rich Sacher, *Brnch Mgr*
**EMP:** 60
**SQ FT:** 2,500
**SALES (corp-wide):** 501.14MM **Privately Held**
**Web:** www.graniterock.com
**SIC:** 2951 2992 5032 Asphalt and asphaltic paving mixtures (not from refineries); Lubricating oils and greases; Brick, stone, and related material
**PA:** Granite Rock Company
350 Technology Dr
831 768-2000

### (P-6365)
### MAXIM EQUIPMENT INC
339 Doak Blvd, Ripon (95366-2659)
P.O. Box 630 (95366-0630)
**PHONE**...................209 649-7225
Robert Charles Evans, *Pr*
**EMP:** 19 **EST:** 2008
**SALES (est):** 4.68MM **Privately Held**
**Web:** www.maximequipment.com
**SIC:** 2951 Asphalt paving mixtures and blocks

### (P-6366)
### NPG INC (PA)
Also Called: Goldstar Asphalt Products
1354 Jet Way, Perris (92571-7466)
P.O. Box 1515 (92572-1515)
**PHONE**...................951 940-0200
Jeff Nelson, *Pr*
Sharon Nelson, *
**EMP:** 54 **EST:** 1962
**SQ FT:** 6,900
**SALES (est):** 22.79MM **Privately Held**
**Web:** www.goldstarasphalt.com
**SIC:** 2951 1799 1771 Asphalt and asphaltic paving mixtures (not from refineries); Parking lot maintenance; Driveway, parking lot, and blacktop contractors

### (P-6367)
### PAVEMENT RECYCLING SYSTEMS INC
Also Called: West Coast Milling
48028 90th St W, Lancaster (93536-9366)
**PHONE**...................661 948-5599
Steve Ward, *Mgr*
**EMP:** 60
**Web:** www.pavementrecycling.com
**SIC:** 2951 1611 Asphalt paving mixtures and blocks; Surfacing and paving
**PA:** Pavement Recycling Systems, Inc.
10240 San Sevaine Way

### (P-6368)
### PETROCHEM MANUFACTURING INC
Also Called: PMI
6168 Innovation Way, Carlsbad (92009-1728)
**PHONE**...................760 603-0961
**EMP:** 49 **EST:** 2002
**SALES (est):** 2.25MM **Privately Held**
**Web:** www.pmitechnology.com
**SIC:** 2951 1522 Asphalt paving mixtures and blocks; Residential construction, nec

### (P-6369)
### REED & GRAHAM INC
26 Light Sky Ct, Sacramento (95828-1068)
**PHONE**...................888 381-0800
Bruce Adams, *Brnch Mgr*
**EMP:** 44
**SALES (corp-wide):** 41.13MM **Privately Held**
**Web:** www.rginc.com
**SIC:** 2951 Paving mixtures
**PA:** Reed & Graham, Inc.
690 Sunol St
408 287-1400

### (P-6370)
### SAN RAFAEL ROCK QUARRY INC
Also Called: Dutra Materials
961 Western Dr, Richmond (94801-3756)
**PHONE**...................510 970-7700
Erin Johnson, *Mgr*
**EMP:** 36
**SALES (corp-wide):** 191.66MM **Privately Held**
**Web:** www.dutragroup.com
**SIC:** 2951 Asphalt paving mixtures and blocks
**HQ:** San Rafael Rock Quarry, Inc.
2350 Kerner Blvd Ste 200
San Rafael CA 94901

### (P-6371)
### SURFACE-TECH LLC
888 Prospect St Ste 200, La Jolla (92037-4261)
**PHONE**...................619 880-0265
**EMP:** 17 **EST:** 2013
**SALES (est):** 3.07MM **Privately Held**
**Web:** www.surface-tech.com
**SIC:** 2951 Asphalt paving mixtures and blocks

## 2952 Asphalt Felts And Coatings

### (P-6372)
### ASPHALT DR INC
7440 Downing Ave, Bakersfield (93308-5006)
P.O. Box 9914 (93389-1914)
**PHONE**...................661 437-5995
Jeffrey Marvin White, *Pr*
**EMP:** 20 **EST:** 2014
**SALES (est):** 2.45MM **Privately Held**
**Web:** www.asphaltdoctr.com
**SIC:** 2952 Asphalt felts and coatings

### (P-6373)
### CERTAINTEED LLC
6400 Stevenson Blvd, Fremont (94538-2468)
**PHONE**...................510 490-0890
Ed Foster, *Mgr*
**EMP:** 74
**SQ FT:** 20,000

# 2952 - Asphalt Felts And Coatings (P-6374)

**SALES (corp-wide):** 402.18MM **Privately Held**
**Web:** www.certainteed.com
**SIC: 2952** 2951 Asphalt felts and coatings; Asphalt paving mixtures and blocks
**HQ:** Certainteed Llc
20 Moores Rd
Malvern PA 19355
610 893-5000

### (P-6374)
### FONTANA PAPER MILLS INC
13733 Valley Blvd, Fontana (92335-5291)
P.O. Box 339 (92334-0339)
**PHONE**..................................909 823-4100
George Thagard Iii, *Pr*
Jeff Thagard, *
Ray G Thagard Junior, *Sec*
**EMP:** 56 **EST:** 1967
**SQ FT:** 28,000
**SALES (est):** 9.57MM **Privately Held**
**Web:** www.fontanaroof.com
**SIC: 2952** 2621 Roofing materials; Felts, building

### (P-6375)
### HCO HOLDING II CORPORATION
999 N Pacific Coast Hwy Ste 800, El Segundo (90245-2714)
**PHONE**..................................310 955-9200
Brian C Strauss, *Pr*
**EMP:** 560 **EST:** 2005
**SALES (est):** 3.85MM
**SALES (corp-wide):** 249.72MM **Privately Held**
**SIC: 2952** 2821 2891 Roof cement: asphalt, fibrous, or plastic; Polyurethane resins; Sealants
**HQ:** Hco Holding I Corporation
999 N Splveda Blvd Ste 80
El Segundo CA 90245
323 583-5000

### (P-6376)
### HENRY COMPANY LLC (HQ)
Also Called: Henry Building Products
999 N Pacific Coast Hwy Ste 800, El Segundo (90245-2716)
**PHONE**..................................310 955-9200
Frank Ready, *Pr*
Jason Peel, *
◆ **EMP:** 100 **EST:** 1981
**SALES (est):** 212.61MM
**SALES (corp-wide):** 4.59B **Publicly Held**
**Web:** www.henry.com
**SIC: 2952** 2821 2891 Roof cement: asphalt, fibrous, or plastic; Polyurethane resins; Sealants
**PA:** Carlisle Companies Incorporated
16430 N Scttsdale Rd Ste
480 781-5000

### (P-6377)
### HNC PARENT INC (PA)
999 N Pacific Coast Hwy Ste 800, El Segundo (90245-2716)
**PHONE**..................................310 955-9200
Rob Newbold, *Prin*
**EMP:** 100 **EST:** 2012
**SALES (est):** 249.72MM
**SALES (corp-wide):** 249.72MM **Privately Held**
**SIC: 2952** 2821 2891 Roof cement: asphalt, fibrous, or plastic; Polyurethane resins; Sealants

### (P-6378)
### JAMES HARDIE TRADING CO INC
26300 La Alameda Ste 400, Mission Viejo (92691-8372)
**PHONE**..................................949 582-2378
Bryon G Borgardt, *Pr*
**EMP:** 160 **EST:** 1995
**SALES (est):** 17.15MM **Privately Held**
**Web:** www.jameshardie.com
**SIC: 2952** Siding materials
**HQ:** James Hardie Transition Co., Inc.
26300 La Alameda Ste 400
Mission Viejo CA 92691
949 348-1800

### (P-6379)
### LUNDAY-THAGARD COMPANY
9301 Garfield Ave, South Gate (90280-3804)
P.O. Box 1519 (90280-1519)
**PHONE**..................................562 928-6990
John Todorovich, *VP Opers*
**EMP:** 369
**SALES (corp-wide):** 128.17MM **Privately Held**
**SIC: 2952** 2951 Roofing materials; Asphalt paving mixtures and blocks
**HQ:** Lunday-Thagard Company
9302 Garfield Ave
South Gate CA 90280
562 928-7000

### (P-6380)
### MBTECHNOLOGY
188 S Teilman Ave, Fresno (93706-1334)
**PHONE**..................................559 233-2181
Bahman Behbehani, *Pr*
Rostam Felfeli, *
Khogasteh Behbehani, *
◆ **EMP:** 31 **EST:** 1981
**SQ FT:** 54,000
**SALES (est):** 8.64MM
**SALES (corp-wide):** 4.59B **Publicly Held**
**Web:** www.mbtechnology.com
**SIC: 2952** Roofing materials
**HQ:** Carlisle Construction Materials, Llc
1285 Ritner Hwy
Carlisle PA 17013

### (P-6381)
### NATIONAL COATINGS CORPORATION
1201 Calle Suerte, Camarillo (93012-8087)
**PHONE**..................................805 388-7112
▲ **EMP:** 20 **EST:** 1981
**SALES (est):** 7.35MM
**SALES (corp-wide):** 4.59B **Publicly Held**
**Web:** www.nationalcoatings.com
**SIC: 2952** Roofing felts, cements, or coatings, nec
**HQ:** Henry Company Llc
999 N Pcf Cast Hwy Ste 80
El Segundo CA 90245
310 955-9200

### (P-6382)
### OWENS CORNING SALES LLC
Also Called: Owens Corning
1501 N Tamarind Ave, Compton (90222-4130)
P.O. Box 5665 (90224-5665)
**PHONE**..................................310 631-1062
David Randalph, *Brnch Mgr*
**EMP:** 102
**Web:** www.owenscorning.com
**SIC: 2952** 2951 1761 Roofing felts, cements, or coatings, nec; Asphalt paving mixtures and blocks; Roofing, siding, and sheetmetal work
**HQ:** Owens Corning Sales, Llc
1 Owens Corning Pkwy
Toledo OH 43659
419 248-8000

### (P-6383)
### RGM PRODUCTS INC
Also Called: Ridgeline
3301 Navone Rd, Stockton (95215-9312)
**PHONE**..................................559 499-2222
Clay Crum, *Pr*
Gus Freshwater, *
▲ **EMP:** 426 **EST:** 1993
**SALES (est):** 2.78MM
**SALES (corp-wide):** 6.35B **Privately Held**
**SIC: 2952** Asphalt felts and coatings
**HQ:** Elk Premium Building Products, Inc.
14911 Quorum Dr Ste 600
Dallas TX 75254

### (P-6384)
### SIPLAST INC
Also Called: Ice Splash
1754 Technology Dr Ste 120-E, San Jose (95110-1308)
**PHONE**..................................408 490-4268
**EMP:** 31
**SALES (corp-wide):** 6.35B **Privately Held**
**Web:** www.siplast.com
**SIC: 2952** Asphalt felts and coatings
**HQ:** Siplast, Inc.
14911 Quorum Dr Ste 600
Dallas TX 75254
469 995-2200

### (P-6385)
### TROPICAL ASPHALT LLC (PA)
Also Called: Tropical Roofing Products CA
14435 Macaw St, La Mirada (90638-5210)
**PHONE**..................................714 739-1408
**EMP:** 15 **EST:** 1998
**SQ FT:** 27,000
**SALES (est):** 12.6MM
**SALES (corp-wide):** 12.6MM **Privately Held**
**Web:** www.tropicalroofingproducts.com
**SIC: 2952** Asphalt felts and coatings

## 2992 Lubricating Oils And Greases

### (P-6386)
### AOCLSC INC
Also Called: Aocusa
3365 E Slauson Ave, Vernon (90058-3914)
**PHONE**..................................562 776-4000
Stephen Milam, *CEO*
**EMP:** 30
**SALES (corp-wide):** 50.84MM **Privately Held**
**SIC: 2992** Lubricating oils and greases
**HQ:** Aoclsc, Inc.
1601 Mccloskey Blvd
Tampa FL 33605
813 248-1988

### (P-6387)
### AOCLSC INC
Also Called: Aocusa
8015 Paramount Blvd, Pico Rivera (90660-4811)
**PHONE**..................................813 248-1988
Harry Barkett, *Brnch Mgr*
**EMP:** 150
**SALES (corp-wide):** 50.84MM **Privately Held**
**SIC: 2992** Lubricating oils
**HQ:** Aoclsc, Inc.
1601 Mccloskey Blvd
Tampa FL 33605
813 248-1988

### (P-6388)
### CHEM ARROW CORP
13643 Live Oak Ln, Irwindale (91706-1317)
P.O. Box 2366 (91706-1198)
**PHONE**..................................626 358-2255
Alphonse Spalding, *Ch Bd*
Hemith Mitchello, *
▼ **EMP:** 25 **EST:** 1977
**SQ FT:** 36,000
**SALES (est):** 7.87MM **Privately Held**
**Web:** www.chemarrow.com
**SIC: 2992** 2899 Lubricating oils; Fuel tank or engine cleaning chemicals

### (P-6389)
### CHEMTOOL INCORPORATED
1300 Goodrick Dr, Tehachapi (93561)
**PHONE**..................................661 823-7190
Bill Hart, *Mgr*
**EMP:** 125
**SALES (corp-wide):** 364.48B **Publicly Held**
**Web:** www.chemtool.com
**SIC: 2992** 2899 5172 Oils and greases, blending and compounding; Chemical preparations, nec; Lubricating oils and greases
**HQ:** Chemtool Incorporated
29400 Lakeland Blvd
Wickliffe OH 44092
815 957-4140

### (P-6390)
### DEMENNO/KERDOON HOLDINGS
Also Called: D K Environmental
3650 E 26th St, Vernon (90058-4104)
**PHONE**..................................323 268-3387
Rodney Ananda, *Mgr*
**EMP:** 27
**SALES (corp-wide):** 128.17MM **Privately Held**
**Web:** www.worldoilcorp.com
**SIC: 2992** 4953 Oils and greases, blending and compounding; Refuse systems
**HQ:** Demenno/Kerdoon Holdings
9302 Garfield Ave
South Gate CA 90280
562 231-1550

### (P-6391)
### DEMENNO/KERDOON HOLDINGS (DH)
Also Called: Demenno-Kerdoon
9302 Garfield Ave, South Gate (90280-3805)
**PHONE**..................................562 231-1550
Robert Roth, *Ch Bd*
Bruce Demenno, *
Steve Kerdoon, *
**EMP:** 67 **EST:** 1971
**SQ FT:** 21,000
**SALES (est):** 20.12MM
**SALES (corp-wide):** 128.17MM **Privately Held**
**Web:** www.worldoilcorp.com
**SIC: 2992** 2911 Oils and greases, blending and compounding; Petroleum refining
**HQ:** De Menno-Kerdoon Trading Company
2000 N Alameda Street
Compton CA 90222

### (P-6392)
### EVERGREEN HOLDINGS INC
18952 Macarthur Blvd Ste 410, Irvine (92612-1402)
**PHONE**..................................949 757-7770
▲ **EMP:** 189

SIC: 2992 4953 Re-refining lubricating oils and greases, nec; Liquid waste, collection and disposal

**(P-6393)**
**EVERGREEN OIL INC (HQ)**
Also Called: Evergreen Environmental Svcs
18025 S Broadway, Gardena (90248-3539)
PHONE..............................949 757-7770
Jake Voogd, *CEO*
George Lamont, *Ex VP*
Obert Gwaltney, *VP Opers*
Jesus Romero, *VP*
**EMP:** 23 **EST:** 1983
**SALES (est):** 23.19MM
**SALES (corp-wide):** 5.41B **Publicly Held**
**SIC:** 2992 2911 4953 Lubricating oils and greases; Petroleum refining; Refuse systems
**PA:** Clean Harbors, Inc.
42 Longwater Dr
781 792-5000

**(P-6394)**
**EZ LUBE LLC**
532 W Florida Ave, Hemet (92543-4007)
PHONE..............................951 766-1996
Richie Berling, *Mgr*
**EMP:** 72
**SALES (corp-wide):** 21.83MM **Privately Held**
Web: www.ezlube.com
**SIC:** 2992 Lubricating oils
**PA:** Ez Lube, Llc
3540 Howard Way Ste 200

**(P-6395)**
**INTERNTNAL PTRO PDTS ADDTVES I**
Also Called: Ipac
7600 Dublin Blvd Ste 240, Dublin (94568-2908)
P.O. Box 2100 (94568)
PHONE..............................925 556-5530
Brian J Cereghino, *CEO*
Alan Krock, *CFO*
▲ **EMP:** 17 **EST:** 1999
**SQ FT:** 7,500
**SALES (est):** 12.38MM **Privately Held**
Web: www.ipac-inc.com
**SIC:** 2992 5172 2911 Lubricating oils and greases; Petroleum products, nec; Fuel additives

**(P-6396)**
**IPAC INC**
7600 Dublin Blvd Ste 240, Dublin (94568-2908)
P.O. Box 2100 (94568)
PHONE..............................925 556-5530
Brian Cereghino, *Pr*
**EMP:** 18 **EST:** 2011
**SALES (est):** 2.33MM **Privately Held**
Web: www.ipac-inc.com
**SIC:** 2992 Lubricating oils and greases

**(P-6397)**
**LUBECO INC**
6859 Downey Ave, Long Beach (90805-1967)
PHONE..............................562 602-1791
Steven Rossi, *Pr*
**EMP:** 45 **EST:** 1958
**SQ FT:** 20,000
**SALES (est):** 5.33MM **Privately Held**
Web: www.lubecoinc.com
**SIC:** 2992 2851 Lubricating oils and greases; Paints and allied products

**(P-6398)**
**LUBRICATING SPECIALTIES COMPANY**
Also Called: AOC USA
8015 Paramount Blvd, Pico Rivera (90660-4811)
PHONE..............................562 776-4000
◆ **EMP:** 170
**SIC:** 2992 Lubricating oils

**(P-6399)**
**RED LINE SYNTHETIC OIL CORPORATION**
6100 Egret Ct, Benicia (94510-1269)
PHONE..............................707 745-6100
◆ **EMP:** 17
**SIC:** 2992 Lubricating oils

**(P-6400)**
**SOUTH WEST LUBRICANTS INC**
Also Called: Maxima Racing Oils
9266 Abraham Way, Santee (92071-5611)
PHONE..............................619 449-5000
Daniel J Massie, *CEO*
◆ **EMP:** 54 **EST:** 1979
**SQ FT:** 50,000
**SALES (est):** 2.46MM **Privately Held**
Web: www.maximausa.com
**SIC:** 2992 5172 Lubricating oils and greases; Lubricating oils and greases

**(P-6401)**
**WD-40 COMPANY (PA)**
9715 Businesspark Ave, San Diego (92131-1642)
PHONE..............................619 275-1400
Steven A Brass, *Pr*
Gregory A Sandfort, *
Sara K Hyzer, *VP Fin*
Phenix Q Kiamilev, *Corporate Secretary*
Jeffrey G Lindeman, *Chief Human Resources Officer*
**EMP:** 133 **EST:** 1953
**SALES (est):** 590.56MM
**SALES (corp-wide):** 590.56MM **Publicly Held**
Web: www.wd40company.com
**SIC:** 2992 2851 Lubricating oils; Removers and cleaners

## 2999 Petroleum And Coal Products, Nec

**(P-6402)**
**LUNDAY-THAGARD COMPANY (HQ)**
Also Called: Ltr
9302 Garfield Ave, South Gate (90280-3805)
P.O. Box 1519 (90280-1519)
PHONE..............................562 928-7000
Bernard B Roth, *Ch Bd*
Robert Roth, *
Steve Roth, *
Bert Wootan, *
Peter Stockhausen, *
**EMP:** 106 **EST:** 1937
**SQ FT:** 16,000
**SALES (est):** 17.74MM
**SALES (corp-wide):** 128.17MM **Privately Held**
**SIC:** 2999 2951 2911 Coke; Paving blocks; Gases and liquefied petroleum gases
**PA:** World Oil Marketing Company
9302 Garfield Ave
562 928-0100

**(P-6403)**
**RENTECH INC (PA)**
10880 Wilshire Blvd Ste 1101, Los Angeles (90024-4112)
PHONE..............................310 571-9800
Keith Forman, *Pr*
Halbert S Washburn, *
Keith B Forman, *
Paul M Summers, *
Colin M Morris, *
**EMP:** 50 **EST:** 1981
**SQ FT:** 600
**SALES (est):** 30.98MM
**SALES (corp-wide):** 30.98MM **Privately Held**
Web: www.rentechinc.com
**SIC:** 2999 2873 6794 Waxes, petroleum: not produced in petroleum refineries; Nitrogenous fertilizers; Patent buying, licensing, leasing

## 3011 Tires And Inner Tubes

**(P-6404)**
**AMERICAN GENERAL TOOL GROUP**
929 Poinsettia Ave Ste 101, Vista (92081-8459)
PHONE..............................760 745-7993
Nasreen Godil, *Pr*
**EMP:** 40 **EST:** 2014
**SALES (est):** 4.5MM **Privately Held**
Web: www.americangeneraltools.com
**SIC:** 3011 3492 3535 3822 Pneumatic tires, all types; Control valves, aircraft: hydraulic and pneumatic; Pneumatic tube conveyor systems; Switches, pneumatic positioning remote

**(P-6405)**
**BIG BRAND TIRE & SERVICE**
Also Called: Big Brand Tire & Svc - Menifee
26920 Newport Rd, Menifee (92584-9076)
PHONE..............................951 679-6266
**EMP:** 99 **EST:** 2020
**SALES (est):** 2.65MM **Privately Held**
**SIC:** 3011 Automobile tires, pneumatic

**(P-6406)**
**BRIDGESTONE AMERICAS INC**
Also Called: Firestone Cmplete Auto Care 79
3690 Murphy Canyon Rd, San Diego (92123-4455)
PHONE..............................858 874-3109
**EMP:** 23
Web: www.bridgestoneamericas.com
**SIC:** 3011 Tires and inner tubes
**HQ:** Bridgestone Americas, Inc.
200 4th Ave S Ste 100
Nashville TN 37201
615 937-1000

**(P-6407)**
**CRM OF AMERICA LLC (PA)**
1301 Dove St Ste 940, Newport Beach (92660-2483)
PHONE..............................949 263-9100
Hossein B Takallou, *Managing Member*
H Barry Takalou, *Managing Member*
**EMP:** 17 **EST:** 1993
**SALES (est):** 9.98MM
**SALES (corp-wide):** 9.98MM **Privately Held**
Web: www.crmrubber.com
**SIC:** 3011 Industrial tires, pneumatic

**(P-6408)**
**DESSER TIRE & RUBBER CO LLC (DH)**
Also Called: Desser Tire & Rubber Co
6900 W Acco St, Montebello (90640-5435)
P.O. Box 1028 (90640-1028)
PHONE..............................323 721-4900
◆ **EMP:** 35 **EST:** 1995
**SALES (est):** 22.97MM
**SALES (corp-wide):** 860.49MM **Publicly Held**
Web: www.desser.com
**SIC:** 3011 Airplane tires, pneumatic
**HQ:** Desser Holding Company, Llc
6900 W Acco St
Montebello CA 90640
323 721-4900

**(P-6409)**
**EAST BAY TIRE CO**
4961 Park Rd, Benicia (94510-1190)
PHONE..............................707 747-5613
Neil Larimer, *Brnch Mgr*
**EMP:** 19
**SALES (corp-wide):** 99.41MM **Privately Held**
Web: www.eastbaytire.com
**SIC:** 3011 5014 Tires and inner tubes; Tires and tubes
**PA:** East Bay Tire Co.
2200 Huntington Dr Unit C
707 437-4700

**(P-6410)**
**EUHOMY LLC**
1230 Santa Anita Ave, South El Monte (91733-3861)
PHONE..............................213 265-5081
**EMP:** 20
**SALES (est):** 788.43K **Privately Held**
**SIC:** 3011 Tires and inner tubes

**(P-6411)**
**HSB HOLDINGS INC**
14050 Day St, Moreno Valley (92553-9106)
PHONE..............................951 214-6590
Ohannes Beudjekian, *Ch Bd*
Sarkis Beudjeaian, *
▲ **EMP:** 40 **EST:** 1989
**SQ FT:** 80,000
**SALES (est):** 5.25MM **Privately Held**
Web: www.basrecycling.com
**SIC:** 3011 Tires, cushion or solid rubber

**(P-6412)**
**SKAT-TRAK**
654 Avenue K, Calimesa (92320-1115)
P.O. Box 518 (92320-0518)
PHONE..............................909 795-2505
Ken Stuart, *Pr*
Diane Stuart, *
**EMP:** 15 **EST:** 1952
**SQ FT:** 3,000
**SALES (est):** 2.8MM **Privately Held**
Web: www.skat-trak.com
**SIC:** 3011 3599 3366 Tires and inner tubes; Propellers, ship and boat: machined; Copper foundries

**(P-6413)**
**TOYO TIRE HLDINGS AMERICAS INC (HQ)**
3565 Harbor Blvd, Costa Mesa (92626-1405)
PHONE..............................714 229-6100
Tomoshige Mizutani, *CEO*
▲ **EMP:** 20 **EST:** 1988
**SALES (est):** 1.03B **Privately Held**
Web: www.toyotires.com

# 3011 - Tires And Inner Tubes (P-6414)

## PRODUCTS & SERVICES SECTION

SIC: 3011 Automobile inner tubes
PA: Toyo Tire Corporation
2-2-13, Fujinoki

### (P-6414)
### YOKOHAMA CORP NORTH AMERICA (HQ)
Also Called: Yokohama Tire
1 Macarthur Pl, Santa Ana (92707-5927)
PHONE..................540 389-5426
Yasuo Tominaga, CEO
Takaharu Fushimi, *
◆ EMP: 250 EST: 1917
SALES (est): 792.7MM Privately Held
Web: www.yokohamatire.com
SIC: 3011 5014 Tires and inner tubes; Tires and tubes
PA: Yokohama Rubber Company, Limited, The
2-1, Oiwake

## 3021 Rubber And Plastics Footwear

### (P-6415)
### IMPLUS LLC
1610 Dell Ave Ste S, Campbell (95008-6914)
PHONE..................408 796-7739
EMP: 22
SALES (corp-wide): 300MM Privately Held
Web: www.implus.com
SIC: 3021 Rubber and plastics footwear
HQ: Implus, Llc
2001 Tw Alexander Dr
Durham NC 27709
919 544-7900

### (P-6416)
### K-SWISS INC (DH)
Also Called: K-Swiss
101 N Brand Blvd Ste 1700, Glendale (91203-2628)
PHONE..................323 675-2700
Holly Li, CEO
Barney Waters, CMO*
◆ EMP: 30 EST: 1990
SALES (est): 35.56MM Privately Held
Web: www.kswiss.com
SIC: 3021 5661 Rubber and plastics footwear; Children's shoes
HQ: Xtep International Holdings Limited
Rm A 27/F Billion Ctr Twr A
Kowloon Bay KLN

### (P-6417)
### K-SWISS INC
12450 Philadelphia Ave, Eastvale (91752-3230)
PHONE..................951 361-7501
EMP: 41
Web: www.kswiss.com
SIC: 3021 Rubber and plastics footwear
HQ: K-Swiss Inc.
101 N Brand Blvd
Glendale CA 91203
323 675-2700

### (P-6418)
### K-SWISS SALES CORP
101 N Brand Blvd, Glendale (91203-2639)
PHONE..................323 675-2700
Cheryl Kuchinka, Pr
EMP: 143 EST: 1999
SALES (est): 1.95MM Privately Held
Web: www.kswiss.com
SIC: 3021 Rubber and plastics footwear
HQ: K-Swiss Inc.
101 N Brand Blvd

Glendale CA 91203
323 675-2700

### (P-6419)
### PLS DIABETIC SHOE COMPANY INC
21500 Osborne St, Canoga Park (91304-1522)
PHONE..................818 734-7080
Ambartsum Kumuryan, Pr
Konstandin Kumuryan, *
▲ EMP: 32 EST: 2004
SQ FT: 24,031
SALES (est): 1.66MM Privately Held
Web: www.pedorthiclab.com
SIC: 3021 Shoes, rubber or plastic molded to fabric

### (P-6420)
### PRINCIPLE PLASTICS
1136 W 135th St, Gardena (90247-1919)
P.O. Box 2408 (90247-0408)
PHONE..................310 532-3411
David Hoyt, Pr
Robert Hoyt, *
▲ EMP: 27 EST: 1948
SQ FT: 28,000
SALES (est): 5.18MM Privately Held
Web: www.sloggers.com
SIC: 3021 3949 2519 Galoshes, plastic; Golf equipment; Lawn and garden furniture, except wood and metal

### (P-6421)
### SKECHERS COLLECTION LLC
Also Called: SKECHERS
228 Manhattan Beach Blvd, Manhattan Beach (90266-5347)
PHONE..................310 318-3100
Robert Greenberg, Managing Member
◆ EMP: 20 EST: 1999
SALES (est): 173.77K Publicly Held
Web: www.skechers.com
SIC: 3021 5661 Shoes, rubber or plastic molded to fabric; Shoe stores
PA: Skechers U.S.A., Inc.
228 Manhattan Beach Blvd

### (P-6422)
### SUMMER RIO CORP (PA)
17501 Rowland St, City Of Industry (91748-1115)
PHONE..................626 854-1498
Qing Li, Pr
◆ EMP: 15 EST: 2000
SALES (est): 2.04MM
SALES (corp-wide): 2.04MM Privately Held
Web: www.summerrio.com
SIC: 3021 Canvas shoes, rubber soled

### (P-6423)
### VANS INC (DH)
Also Called: Vans Shoes
1588 S Coast Dr, Costa Mesa (92626-1533)
PHONE..................714 755-4000
Arthur I Carver, Senior Vice President Global Operations
Robert L Nagel, *
Craig E Gosselin, *
Scott J Blechman, *
Marissa Pardini, PRODUCT Merchandising*
▲ EMP: 279 EST: 1987
SQ FT: 185,000
SALES (est): 495.69MM
SALES (corp-wide): 10.45B Publicly Held
Web: www.vans.com

SIC: 3021 2321 2329 2325 Canvas shoes, rubber soled; Men's and boys' sports and polo shirts; Men's and boys' sportswear and athletic clothing; Slacks, dress: men's, youths', and boys'
HQ: Vf Outdoor, Llc
1551 Wewatta St
Denver CO 80202
855 500-8639

## 3052 Rubber And Plastics Hose And Beltings

### (P-6424)
### AMFLEX PLASTICS INCORPORATED
Also Called: Nationwide and International
4039 Calle Platino Ste G, Oceanside (92056-5827)
PHONE..................760 643-1756
Raul Castro, CEO
Raul A Castro, Pr
Ana Maria Castro, CFO
EMP: 21 EST: 1996
SQ FT: 18,000
SALES (est): 1.97MM Privately Held
Web: www.amflex.com
SIC: 3052 3089 Rubber and plastics hose and beltings; Extruded finished plastics products, nec

### (P-6425)
### JAIN IRRIGATION INC
7545 Carroll Rd, San Diego (92121-2401)
PHONE..................315 782-1170
Aric Olson, Brnch Mgr
EMP: 15
Web: www.jainsusa.com
SIC: 3052 3523 Plastic hose; Fertilizing, spraying, dusting, and irrigation machinery
HQ: Jain Irrigation, Inc.
5965 S 900 E Ste 450
Murray UT 84121
909 395-5200

### (P-6426)
### NORTH AMERICAN FIRE HOSE CORP
Also Called: Nafhc
910 Noble Way, Santa Maria (93454-1506)
P.O. Box 1968 (93456-1968)
PHONE..................805 922-7076
Michael S Aubuchon, CEO
Virginia Aubuchon, *
▲ EMP: 55 EST: 1980
SQ FT: 43,000
SALES (est): 6.4MM Privately Held
Web: www.nafhc.com
SIC: 3052 Fire hose, rubber

### (P-6427)
### PARKER-HANNIFIN CORPORATION
Also Called: Parker Service Center
8460 Kass Dr, Buena Park (90621-3808)
PHONE..................714 522-8840
Chris Wright, Brnch Mgr
EMP: 69
SALES (corp-wide): 19.93B Publicly Held
Web: www.parker.com
SIC: 3052 3429 Rubber and plastics hose and beltings; Hardware, nec
PA: Parker-Hannifin Corporation
6035 Parkland Blvd
216 896-3000

### (P-6428)
### RAINMAKER SOLUTIONS INC
Also Called: Fluidlogic
121 Sierra St, El Segundo (90245-4118)
PHONE..................855 463-5843
Sara Blackmer, CEO
Valbona Watkins, CFO
EMP: 16 EST: 2015
SALES (est): 629.49K Privately Held
Web: www.fluidlogic.com
SIC: 3052 3594 Air line or air brake hose, rubber or rubberized fabric; Motors: hydraulic, fluid power, or air

### (P-6429)
### SANISURE INC (HQ)
Also Called: Sani-Tech West, Inc.
1020 Flynn Rd, Camarillo (93012-8705)
PHONE..................805 389-0400
Richard J Shor, Pr
Sherry Maxson, *
EMP: 61 EST: 1991
SQ FT: 27,000
SALES (est): 59.92MM
SALES (corp-wide): 5.01B Privately Held
Web: www.sani-techwest.com
SIC: 3052 3053 Rubber hose; Gasket materials
PA: 3i Group Plc
16 Palace Street

### (P-6430)
### SPECIALTY HOSE XPRESS LLC
Also Called: Specialty Hose Xpress
7515 Lander Ave, Hilmar (95324-9790)
P.O. Box 3574 (95381)
PHONE..................209 226-1031
Eric Plagenza, Managing Member
EMP: 20 EST: 2016
SQ FT: 1,600
SALES (est): 6.83MM Privately Held
Web: www.specialtyhosexpress.com
SIC: 3052 Air line or air brake hose, rubber or rubberized fabric

### (P-6431)
### SUTTER BUTTES RUBBER CO LLC (PA)
286 W Evans Reimer Rd, Gridley (95948-9536)
PHONE..................530 846-9533
Jack Kirby, Managing Member
EMP: 15 EST: 2018
SQ FT: 4,000
SALES (est): 6.22MM
SALES (corp-wide): 6.22MM Privately Held
Web: www.tuffboyequip.com
SIC: 3052 3053 Rubber and plastics hose and beltings; Gaskets; packing and sealing devices

### (P-6432)
### TECHNICAL HEATERS INC
Also Called: Thermolab
10959 Tuxford St, Sun Valley (91352-2626)
PHONE..................818 361-7185
Bruce W Jones, Pr
EMP: 18 EST: 1969
SQ FT: 35,000
SALES (est): 3.02MM Privately Held
Web: www.techheat.com
SIC: 3052 Plastic hose

### (P-6433)
### TK PAX INC
Also Called: P A X Industries
1545 Macarthur Blvd, Costa Mesa (92626-1407)
PHONE..................714 850-1330

Tom Kawaguchi, Pr
Randy Tamura, *
▲ EMP: 30 EST: 1985
SALES (est): 4.62MM **Privately Held**
Web: www.paxindustries.com
SIC: **3052** 3053 Rubber hose; Gaskets, all materials

**(P-6434)**
**TTI FLOOR CARE NORTH AMER INC**
13055 Valley Blvd, Fontana (92335-2603)
PHONE.................................440 996-2802
Ross Verrocchi, Mgr
EMP: 100
Web: www.ttifloorcare.com
SIC: **3052** 5722 Vacuum cleaner hose, plastic; Vacuum cleaners
HQ: Tti Floor Care North America, Inc.
  8405 Ibm Dr
  Charlotte NC 28262

**(P-6435)**
**WESTFLEX INC (PA)**
Also Called: Western Hose & Gasket
325 W 30th St, National City (91950-7205)
P.O. Box 506 (91951)
PHONE.................................619 474-7400
Dixon G Legros, Pr
Paula Legros, CFO
◆ EMP: 22 EST: 1981
SQ FT: 56,000
SALES (est): 8.06MM
SALES (corp-wide): 8.06MM **Privately Held**
Web: www.westflex.com
SIC: **3052** 3053 5085 Rubber and plastics hose and beltings; Gaskets; packing and sealing devices; Hose, belting, and packing

## 3053 Gaskets; Packing And Sealing Devices

**(P-6436)**
**A & D RUBBER PRODUCTS CO INC (PA)**
1438 Bourbon St, Stockton (95204-2404)
PHONE.................................209 941-0100
Dale W Wolford, Pr
Ann Wolford, *
▲ EMP: 18 EST: 1991
SQ FT: 20,000
SALES (est): 3.22MM **Privately Held**
Web: www.adrubber.com
SIC: **3053** 5085 2822 5169 Gaskets; packing and sealing devices; Industrial supplies; Synthetic rubber; Synthetic resins, rubber, and plastic materials

**(P-6437)**
**ABLE INDUSTRIAL PRODUCTS INC (PA)**
2006 S Baker Ave, Ontario (91761-7709)
PHONE.................................909 930-1585
Gilbert J Martinez, CEO
Debbie Viramontes, *
Gloria Martinez, CTRL*
▲ EMP: 30 EST: 1974
SQ FT: 21,120
SALES (est): 16.99MM
SALES (corp-wide): 16.99MM **Privately Held**
Web: www.able123.com
SIC: **3053** 3069 5085 Gaskets, all materials; Weather strip, sponge rubber; Industrial supplies

**(P-6438)**
**BRYANT RUBBER CORP (PA)**
1580 W Carson St, Long Beach (90810-1455)
PHONE.................................310 530-2530
Steven Bryant, Prin
Steven Bryant, Prin
Robert Tracewell, Prin
Brogan Bryant, Prin
Tracy Hunter, *
▲ EMP: 37 EST: 1971
SALES (est): 24.17MM
SALES (corp-wide): 24.17MM **Privately Held**
Web: www.bryantrubber.com
SIC: **3053** Gaskets; packing and sealing devices

**(P-6439)**
**BRYANT RUBBER CORP**
Also Called: Ingla Rubber Products
1083 W 251st St., Bellflower (90706)
PHONE.................................310 530-2530
Jack Klimek, Brnch Mgr
EMP: 113
SALES (corp-wide): 24.17MM **Privately Held**
Web: www.bryantrubber.com
SIC: **3053** 3061 Gaskets; packing and sealing devices; Mechanical rubber goods
PA: Bryant Rubber Corp.
  1580 W Carson St
  310 530-2530

**(P-6440)**
**CANNON GASKET INC**
7784 Edison Ave, Fontana (92336-3635)
PHONE.................................909 355-1547
Billy Cannon, Pr
Billy Jr P Cannon, *
Candy Houle, *
▲ EMP: 27 EST: 1971
SQ FT: 10,000
SALES (est): 2.39MM **Privately Held**
Web: www.cannongasket.com
SIC: **3053** Gaskets, all materials

**(P-6441)**
**CHAVERS GASKET CORPORATION**
23325 Del Lago Dr, Laguna Hills (92653-1309)
PHONE.................................949 472-8118
Riley Cole, CEO
Christopher Cole, *
▲ EMP: 25 EST: 1986
SQ FT: 13,000
SALES (est): 4.47MM **Privately Held**
Web: www.chaversgasket.com
SIC: **3053** Gaskets, all materials

**(P-6442)**
**CIASONS INDUSTRIAL INC**
1615 Boyd St, Santa Ana (92705-5103)
PHONE.................................714 259-0838
Paul Hsieh, Pr
Grace S P Hsieh, *
Samuel Hsieh, *
▲ EMP: 30 EST: 1985
SQ FT: 25,000
SALES (est): 2MM **Privately Held**
Web: www.ciasons.com
SIC: **3053** 3563 Packing: steam engines, pipe joints, air compressors, etc.; Air and gas compressors

**(P-6443)**
**D W MACK CO INC**
900 W 8th St, Azusa (91702-2216)
P.O. Box 1247 (91017-1247)
PHONE.................................626 969-1817
Danny J Mack, Pr
Joseph Demarco, *
Dennis S Mack, *
▲ EMP: 40 EST: 1979
SALES (est): 4.71MM **Privately Held**
Web: www.dwmack.com
SIC: **3053** Gaskets, all materials

**(P-6444)**
**DAN-LOC GROUP LLC**
Also Called: Dan-Loc Bolt & Gasket
20444 Tillman Ave, Carson (90746-3516)
PHONE.................................310 538-2822
Rudy Estrada, Brnch Mgr
EMP: 66
SALES (corp-wide): 23.23MM **Privately Held**
Web: www.danlocgroup.com
SIC: **3053** 3452 Gaskets and sealing devices; Bolts, nuts, rivets, and washers
PA: Dan-Loc Group, Llc
  725 N Drennan St
  713 356-3500

**(P-6445)**
**DAR-KEN INC**
Also Called: K & S Enterprises
10515 Rancho Rd, Adelanto (92301-3414)
PHONE.................................760 246-4010
Ken Mc Gilp, Pt
Darla Mc Gilp, *
EMP: 32 EST: 1965
SQ FT: 10,000
SALES (est): 2.33MM **Privately Held**
Web: www.ksentusa.com
SIC: **3053** 3728 Gaskets; packing and sealing devices; Aircraft parts and equipment, nec

**(P-6446)**
**FREUDENBERG-NOK GENERAL PARTNR**
Also Called: International Seal Company
2041 E Wilshire Ave, Santa Ana (92705-4726)
PHONE.................................714 834-0602
John Hudspeth, Mgr
EMP: 150
SQ FT: 28,928
SALES (corp-wide): 12.96B **Privately Held**
Web: www.fst.com
SIC: **3053** Gaskets and sealing devices
HQ: Freudenberg-Nok General Partnership
  47774 W Anchor Ct
  Plymouth MI 48170
  734 451-0020

**(P-6447)**
**G F COLE CORPORATION (PA)**
21735 S Western Ave, Torrance (90501-3718)
PHONE.................................310 320-0601
Fritz Cole, Pr
Cathy Cole, *
▼ EMP: 18 EST: 1982
SQ FT: 26,000
SALES (est): 4.45MM
SALES (corp-wide): 4.45MM **Privately Held**
Web: www.gfcole.com
SIC: **3053** 3069 Gaskets, all materials; Hard rubber and molded rubber products

**(P-6448)**
**GASKET ASSOCIATES LP (PA)**
10816 Kurt St, Sylmar (91342-6844)
PHONE.................................310 217-5600
Dewain R Butler, Pt
Edward R Hare, Pt
David L Price, Pt
Mureen Lador, Owner
EMP: 17 EST: 1991
SALES (est): 5.69MM **Privately Held**
SIC: **3053** Gaskets, all materials

**(P-6449)**
**GASKET MANUFACTURING CO**
8427 Secura Way, Santa Fe Springs (90670-2215)
PHONE.................................310 217-5600
TOLL FREE: 800
Maureen E Labor, CEO
Dewain R Butler, *
Maureen E Labor, Pr
Vince Labor, *
EMP: 33 EST: 1937
SALES (est): 5.69MM **Privately Held**
Web: www.gasketmfg.com
SIC: **3053** Gaskets, all materials
PA: Gasket Associates Lp
  10816 Kurt St

**(P-6450)**
**GASKET SPECIALTIES INC (PA)**
1143 Marina Way S, Richmond (94804-3742)
PHONE.................................510 547-7955
▲ EMP: 20 EST: 1971
SALES (est): 9.86MM
SALES (corp-wide): 9.86MM **Privately Held**
Web: www.gasketspecialties.com
SIC: **3053** 5085 Gaskets, all materials; Gaskets

**(P-6451)**
**HDZ BROTHERS INC**
1924 E Mcfadden Ave, Santa Ana (92705-4705)
PHONE.................................714 953-4010
Zeferino Hernandez, Pr
EMP: 23 EST: 2007
SALES (est): 532.57K **Privately Held**
SIC: **3053** Gaskets; packing and sealing devices

**(P-6452)**
**HUTCHINSON SEAL CORPORATION (DH)**
Also Called: National O Rings
11634 Patton Rd, Downey (90241-5212)
PHONE.................................248 375-4190
Christian Groche, Pr
▲ EMP: 120 EST: 1996
SQ FT: 125,000
SALES (est): 6.37MM
SALES (corp-wide): 5.46B **Privately Held**
Web: www.hutchinson-seal.com
SIC: **3053** Gaskets and sealing devices
HQ: Hutchinson Corporation
  460 Fuller Ave Ne
  Grand Rapids MI 49503
  616 459-4541

**(P-6453)**
**INDUSTRIAL GASKET AND SUP CO**
Also Called: Gasketfab Division
2702 Dashwood St, Lakewood (90712-2136)
P.O. Box 4138 (90510-4138)
PHONE.................................310 530-1771
William P Hynes, Pr
Kevin P Treacy, VP
Theresa Holmes, Sec
EMP: 23 EST: 1970
SALES (est): 2.41MM **Privately Held**
SIC: **3053** 5085 Gaskets, all materials; Gaskets

## 3053 - Gaskets; Packing And Sealing Devices (P-6454)

**(P-6454)**
**INERTECH SUPPLY INC**
Also Called: Inertech
641 Monterey Pass Rd, Monterey Park (91754-2418)
PHONE..................626 282-2000
James Huang, *Pr*
Charlie C Miskell, *
Bruce Wang, *
Walter Lee, *
▲ **EMP:** 75 **EST:** 1991
**SQ FT:** 14,000
**SALES (est):** 4.6MM **Privately Held**
Web: www.inertech.com
SIC: 3053 5085 2891 Gasket materials; Gaskets; Adhesives and sealants

**(P-6455)**
**J MILLER CO INC**
Also Called: Miller Gasket Co
11537 Bradley Ave, San Fernando (91340-2519)
PHONE..................818 837-0181
**TOLL FREE:** 800
Dennis D Miller, *Pr*
Elaine Miller, *
▲ **EMP:** 35 **EST:** 1961
**SQ FT:** 20,000
**SALES (est):** 2.41MM **Privately Held**
Web: www.millergasket.com
SIC: 3053 Gaskets, all materials

**(P-6456)**
**KIRKHILL INC**
Also Called: Haskon, Div of
300 E Cypress St, Brea (92821-4007)
PHONE..................714 529-4901
Michael Harden, *Brnch Mgr*
**EMP:** 700
**SALES (corp-wide):** 7.94B **Publicly Held**
Web: www.kirkhill.com
SIC: 3053 3728 2822 Gaskets; packing and sealing devices; Aircraft parts and equipment, nec; Synthetic rubber
HQ: Kirkhill Inc.
300 E Cypress St
Brea CA 92821
714 529-4901

**(P-6457)**
**LGG INDUSTRIAL INC**
15500 Blackburn Ave, Norwalk (90650-6845)
PHONE..................562 802-7782
**EMP:** 74
**SALES (corp-wide):** 437.91MM **Privately Held**
Web: www.lggindustrial.com
SIC: 3053 3965 3052 2992 Gaskets, all materials; Fasteners; Heater hose, rubber; Lubricating oils
PA: Lgg Industrial, Inc.
650 Washington Rd Ste 500
800 937-9070

**(P-6458)**
**PACIFIC DIE CUT INDUSTRIES**
3399 Arden Rd, Hayward (94545-3924)
PHONE..................510 732-8103
Mohammed M Behnam, *CEO*
Vanessa Hanamoto, *Prin*
Elsa Heredia, *Prin*
Guy Mendez, *Prin*
▲ **EMP:** 73 **EST:** 1989
**SQ FT:** 30,000
**SALES (est):** 16.27MM **Privately Held**
Web: www.pacificdiecut.com
SIC: 3053 Gaskets, all materials

**(P-6459)**
**PACIFIC STATES FELT MFG CO INC**
23850 Clawiter Rd Ste 20, Hayward (94545-1719)
P.O. Box 5024 (94540-5024)
PHONE..................510 783-2357
**TOLL FREE:** 800
Walter L Perscheid Junior, *CEO*
**EMP:** 16 **EST:** 1920
**SQ FT:** 23,000
**SALES (est):** 2.18MM **Privately Held**
Web: www.pacificstatesfelt.net
SIC: 3053 5085 Gaskets, all materials; Industrial supplies

**(P-6460)**
**PARCO LLC (DH)**
1801 S Archibald Ave, Ontario (91761-7677)
PHONE..................909 947-2200
Adam Morrison Burgener, *CEO*
Angie Garcia, *VP*
▲ **EMP:** 113 **EST:** 1989
**SALES (est):** 54.03MM **Privately Held**
Web: www.parcoinc.com
SIC: 3053 Gaskets; packing and sealing devices
HQ: Datwyler Schweiz Ag
Militarstrasse 7
Schattdorf UR 6467

**(P-6461)**
**PREMIUM SEALS LLC (PA)**
19270 Tenaja Rd, Murrieta (92562-7163)
PHONE..................619 207-7603
Alejandro Borboa, *Genl Mgr*
Alejandro Borboa, *Prin*
**EMP:** 110 **EST:** 2005
**SALES (est):** 422.3K **Privately Held**
SIC: 3053 Gaskets; packing and sealing devices

**(P-6462)**
**REAL SEAL CO INC**
Also Called: Real Seal
1971 Don Lee Pl, Escondido (92029-1141)
PHONE..................760 743-7263
Patrick Thomas Tobin, *CEO*
Rose Ann Tobin, *
◆ **EMP:** 25 **EST:** 1970
**SQ FT:** 22,000
**SALES (est):** 2.59MM **Privately Held**
Web: www.real-seal.com
SIC: 3053 5085 Oil seals, rubber; Industrial supplies

**(P-6463)**
**ROCKYS GASKET SHOP INC**
Also Called: Rgs Industries
445 Laurelwood Rd, Santa Clara (95054-2416)
PHONE..................408 980-9190
Heraclio Caballero, *Pr*
Lisa Southard, *Sec*
**EMP:** 18 **EST:** 1980
**SALES (est):** 3.18MM **Privately Held**
Web: www.rgsindustries.com
SIC: 3053 Gaskets, all materials

**(P-6464)**
**ROETTELE INDUSTRIES**
15485 Dupont Ave, Chino (91710-7605)
PHONE..................909 606-8252
Mark Roettele, *Pr*
Maurice Roettele, *Ch Bd*
Lon Roettele, *VP*
Randal Roettele, *Treas*
▲ **EMP:** 19 **EST:** 1979
**SQ FT:** 15,000
**SALES (est):** 2.33MM **Privately Held**
Web: www.roetteleindustries.com
SIC: 3053 5085 Gaskets, all materials; Industrial supplies

**(P-6465)**
**RPM PRODUCTS INC (PA)**
Also Called: Rubber Plastic & Metal Pdts
23201 Antonio Pkwy, Rancho Santa Margari (92688-2653)
PHONE..................949 888-8543
Mark Paolella, *Pr*
Suzanne Paolella, *
▲ **EMP:** 35 **EST:** 1994
**SALES (est):** 3.92MM **Privately Held**
Web: www.rpmproducts.com
SIC: 3053 3089 5085 Gaskets and sealing devices; Injection molding of plastics; Gaskets and seals

**(P-6466)**
**SEAL SCIENCE INC (HQ)**
Also Called: S S I
3701 E Conant St, Long Beach (90808-1783)
PHONE..................949 253-3130
Frederick E Tuliper, *CEO*
Patricia Tuliper, *
▲ **EMP:** 68 **EST:** 1985
**SALES (est):** 16.33MM
**SALES (corp-wide):** 137.12MM **Privately Held**
Web: www.sealscience.com
SIC: 3053 3089 3061 Gaskets, all materials; Injection molding of plastics; Mechanical rubber goods
PA: Sanders Industries Holdings, Inc.
3701 E Conant St
562 354-2920

**(P-6467)**
**SEWING COLLECTION INC (PA)**
3113 E 26th St, Vernon (90058-8006)
PHONE..................323 264-2223
Touraj Tour, *Pr*
Houshang Tour, *VP*
◆ **EMP:** 100 **EST:** 1991
**SQ FT:** 135,000
**SALES (est):** 24.36MM
**SALES (corp-wide):** 24.36MM **Privately Held**
Web: www.sewingcollection.com
SIC: 3053 5199 4953 Packing materials; Packaging materials; Recycling, waste materials

**(P-6468)**
**SPIRA MANUFACTURING CORP**
650 Jessie St, San Fernando (91340-2233)
PHONE..................818 764-8222
George M Kunkel, *Pr*
Bonnie Paul, *
Michael Kunkel, *
Wendy Kunkel, *
**EMP:** 30 **EST:** 1972
**SQ FT:** 15,000
**SALES (est):** 5.34MM **Privately Held**
Web: www.spira-emi.com
SIC: 3053 Gaskets, all materials

**(P-6469)**
**SWABPLUS INC**
9669 Hermosa Ave, Rancho Cucamonga (91730-5813)
PHONE..................909 987-7898
Tom Y Lee, *CEO*
Garry Tsaur, *
Eddy C Wan, *
▲ **EMP:** 41 **EST:** 1998
**SALES (est):** 1.12MM **Privately Held**

SIC: 3053 Packing materials

**(P-6470)**
**TILLEY MANUFACTURING CO INC (PA)**
Also Called: Precision Graphics
2734 Spring St, Redwood City (94063-3524)
P.O. Box 5766 (94063-0766)
PHONE..................650 365-3598
Owen Conley, *Pr*
▲ **EMP:** 78 **EST:** 1958
**SQ FT:** 35,000
**SALES (est):** 2.16MM
**SALES (corp-wide):** 2.16MM **Privately Held**
Web: www.tilleymfg.com
SIC: 3053 3411 3634 3312 Gaskets, all materials; Food containers, metal; Urns, electric: household; Tool and die steel and alloys

**(P-6471)**
**WEST COAST GASKET CO**
300 Ranger Ave, Brea (92821-6217)
PHONE..................714 869-0123
Louis Russell, *Prin*
Jean Grey, *
**EMP:** 75 **EST:** 1979
**SQ FT:** 50,000
**SALES (est):** 9.43MM **Privately Held**
Web: www.westcoastgasket.com
SIC: 3053 3061 3469 5085 Gaskets, all materials; Mechanical rubber goods; Metal stampings, nec; Industrial supplies

## 3061 Mechanical Rubber Goods

**(P-6472)**
**CRM CO LLC (PA)**
Also Called: C R M
1301 Dove St Ste 940, Newport Beach (92660-2483)
PHONE..................949 263-9100
H Barry Takallou, *CEO*
▲ **EMP:** 18 **EST:** 1998
**SALES (est):** 10.25MM
**SALES (corp-wide):** 10.25MM **Privately Held**
Web: www.crmrubber.com
SIC: 3061 Mechanical rubber goods

**(P-6473)**
**DYNATECT RO-LAB INC**
8830 W Linne Rd, Tracy (95304-9109)
P.O. Box 450 (95378-0450)
PHONE..................262 786-1500
Henry Wright, *Genl Mgr*
John Dodge, *
Marina Wright, *
▲ **EMP:** 50 **EST:** 1971
**SQ FT:** 65,000
**SALES (est):** 16.71MM
**SALES (corp-wide):** 2.8B **Privately Held**
Web: www.dynatect.com
SIC: 3061 3052 3069 3089 Mechanical rubber goods; Rubber and plastics hose and beltings; Hard rubber and molded rubber products; Plastics hardware and building products
HQ: Dynatect Manufacturing, Inc.
2300 S Calhoun Rd
New Berlin WI 53151
262 786-1500

## 3069 - Fabricated Rubber Products, Nec (P-6494)

**(P-6474)**
**OMNI SEALS INC**
11031 Jersey Blvd Ste A, Rancho Cucamonga (91730-5150)
PHONE.................909 946-0181
EMP: 68
SIC: 3061 Mechanical rubber goods

**(P-6475)**
**PERFORMANCE POLYMER TECH LLC**
8801 Washington Blvd Ste 109, Roseville (95678-6200)
PHONE.................916 677-1414
Ian Macauley, *
Martha Wimberly, *
EMP: 35 EST: 1995
SQ FT: 37,000
SALES (est): 3.97MM Privately Held
Web: www.pptech.com
SIC: 3061 3069 Mechanical rubber goods; Molded rubber products

**(P-6476)**
**R D RUBBER TECHNOLOGY CORP**
12870 Florence Ave, Santa Fe Springs (90670-4540)
PHONE.................562 941-4800
Walter V Hopkins Junior, Pr
Rosanne Dukowitz, *
EMP: 27 EST: 1986
SQ FT: 15,600
SALES (est): 3.7MM Privately Held
Web: www.rdrubber.com
SIC: 3061 Mechanical rubber goods

**(P-6477)**
**RUBBERCRAFT CORP CAL LTD (HQ)**
Also Called: Rubber Teck Division
3701 E Conant St, Long Beach (90808-1783)
PHONE.................562 354-2800
Marc Sanders, CEO
Eric Sanders, *
EMP: 238 EST: 1984
SQ FT: 40,000
SALES (est): 48.96MM
SALES (corp-wide): 150.17MM Privately Held
Web: www.rubbercraft.com
SIC: 3061 Appliance rubber goods (mechanical)
PA: Sanders Industries Holdings, Inc.
3701 E Conant St
562 354-2920

**(P-6478)**
**WESTLAND TECHNOLOGIES INC**
107 S Riverside Dr, Modesto (95354-4004)
PHONE.................800 877-7734
John Grizzard, Pr
EMP: 60 EST: 1991
SQ FT: 117,000
SALES (est): 21.73MM Publicly Held
Web: westland.globecomposite.com
SIC: 3061 3069 Mechanical rubber goods; Flooring, rubber: tile or sheet
PA: Esco Technologies Inc.
9900 A Clayton Rd

## 3069 Fabricated Rubber Products, Nec

**(P-6479)**
**3M COMPANY**
Also Called: 3M
1601 S Shamrock Ave, Monrovia (91016-4248)
PHONE.................626 358-0136
Bob Palmer, Mgr
EMP: 46
SALES (corp-wide): 32.68B Publicly Held
Web: www.3m.com
SIC: 3069 Rubber coated fabrics and clothing
PA: 3m Company
3m Center
651 733-1110

**(P-6480)**
**A B BOYD CO (PA)**
Also Called: Boyd
5960 Inglewood Dr Ste 115, Pleasanton (94588-8611)
PHONE.................888 244-6931
Douglas Britt, Pr
Eric Struik, *
▲ EMP: 45 EST: 1949
SALES (est): 12.12MM
SALES (corp-wide): 12.12MM Privately Held
Web: www.boydcorp.com
SIC: 3069 2822 Hard rubber and molded rubber products; Synthetic rubber

**(P-6481)**
**ABBA ROLLER LLC (DH)**
1351 E Philadelphia St, Ontario (91761-5719)
PHONE.................909 947-1244
▲ EMP: 19 EST: 2010
SQ FT: 4,000
SALES (est): 5.62MM Privately Held
Web: www.abbaroller.com
SIC: 3069 Roll coverings, rubber
HQ: Electro-Coatings, Inc.
216 Baywood St
Houston TX 77011
713 923-5935

**(P-6482)**
**ADVANCE FABRICATION INC**
Also Called: Advance Fabrication
370 Tomkins Ct Ste A, Gilroy (95020-3698)
PHONE.................408 779-5424
Mary Barger, Pr
Michael Barger, Pr
Mary S Barger, Sec
EMP: 20 EST: 1988
SQ FT: 11,000
SALES (est): 1.4MM Privately Held
Web: www.advancefabrication.com
SIC: 3069 3842 Orthopedic sundries, molded rubber; Braces, orthopedic

**(P-6483)**
**ALPHA GROUP US LLC**
2100 E Grand Ave 5th Fl, El Segundo (90245-5024)
PHONE.................844 303-8936
Yongqiang Cao, Managing Member
EMP: 22 EST: 2016
SALES (est): 1.75MM Privately Held
Web: www.alphatoys.com
SIC: 3069 Toys, rubber
PA: Alpha Group
Floor 37, Qiaoxin International Finance Center, No.62, Jinsui Ro

**(P-6484)**
**AMES RUBBER MFG CO INC**
Also Called: Ames Industrial
4516 Brazil St, Los Angeles (90039-1002)
PHONE.................818 240-9313
TOLL FREE: 800
Timothy L Brown, CEO
Pat Brown, *
▲ EMP: 30 EST: 1954
SQ FT: 20,000
SALES (est): 4.59MM Privately Held
Web: www.amesrubberonline.com
SIC: 3069 3061 Medical and laboratory rubber sundries and related products; Mechanical rubber goods

**(P-6485)**
**BURKE INDUSTRIES DELAWARE INC (HQ)**
2250 S 10th St, San Jose (95112-4197)
PHONE.................408 297-3500
Robert Pitman, Pr
Edward Reginelli, *
◆ EMP: 116 EST: 1976
SQ FT: 115,930
SALES (est): 8.41MM
SALES (corp-wide): 686.34MM Privately Held
Web: dtfd3lamy9hb1.cloudfront.net
SIC: 3069 2822 2821 3061 Flooring, rubber: tile or sheet; Polyethylene, chlorosulfonated, hypalon; Plastics materials and resins; Mechanical rubber goods
PA: Mannington Mills Inc.
75 Mannington Mills Rd
800 356-6787

**(P-6486)**
**CALIFORNIA GASKET AND RBR CORP (PA)**
533 W Collins Ave, Orange (92867-5509)
PHONE.................714 202-8500
Scott H Franklin, VP
Armando Rodriguez, *
EMP: 25 EST: 1942
SQ FT: 51,000
SALES (est): 5.74MM
SALES (corp-wide): 5.74MM Privately Held
Web: www.californiagasket.com
SIC: 3069 3053 3469 3061 Molded rubber products; Gaskets; packing and sealing devices; Metal stampings, nec; Appliance rubber goods (mechanical)

**(P-6487)**
**COI RUBBER PRODUCTS INC**
19255 San Jose Ave Unit D-1, City Of Industry (91748-1418)
PHONE.................626 965-9966
David Chao, CEO
EMP: 450 EST: 2013
SQ FT: 2,500
SALES (est): 2.39MM Privately Held
Web: www.coirubber.com
SIC: 3069 Medical and laboratory rubber sundries and related products

**(P-6488)**
**CRICKET COMPANY LLC**
68 Leveroni Ct Ste 200, Novato (94949-5769)
PHONE.................415 475-4150
Wayne Clark, Managing Member
▲ EMP: 25 EST: 2003
SALES (est): 2.65MM Privately Held
Web: www.cricketco.com
SIC: 3069 Capes, vulcanized rubber or rubberized fabric

**(P-6489)**
**DURO ROLLER COMPANY INC**
Also Called: Cal State Rubber
13006 Park St, Santa Fe Springs (90670-4098)
PHONE.................562 944-8856
Maureen Wayda, Pr
Julie Wayda, VP
▲ EMP: 16 EST: 1973
SQ FT: 8,100
SALES (est): 2.31MM Privately Held
Web: www.duroroller.com
SIC: 3069 3599 Molded rubber products; Machine and other job shop work

**(P-6490)**
**DURO-FLEX RUBBER PRODUCTS INC**
13215 Lakeland Rd, Santa Fe Springs (90670-4522)
PHONE.................562 946-5533
John A Lozano, Pr
EMP: 21 EST: 1967
SQ FT: 6,000
SALES (est): 495.07K Privately Held
Web: www.duroflexrubber.com
SIC: 3069 Molded rubber products

**(P-6491)**
**ENVIRNMNTAL MLDING CNCPTS LLC**
Also Called: E M C
14050 Day St, Moreno Valley (92553-9106)
PHONE.................951 214-6596
Sarkis Beudjekian, Managing Member
◆ EMP: 15 EST: 1997
SQ FT: 15,000
SALES (est): 1.02MM Privately Held
Web: www.emcmolding.com
SIC: 3069 Reclaimed rubber and specialty rubber compounds

**(P-6492)**
**EXROX INC**
535 Ceres Ave, Los Angeles (90013-1716)
PHONE.................213 536-5290
Alex Echeverry, Brnch Mgr
EMP: 21
SALES (corp-wide): 32MM Privately Held
SIC: 3069 Rubber coated fabrics and clothing
PA: Exrox Inc.
323 S Clarence St
213 536-5290

**(P-6493)**
**FALCON WATERFREE TECH LLC (HQ)**
2255 Barry Ave, Los Angeles (90064-1401)
PHONE.................310 209-7250
◆ EMP: 20 EST: 2000
SALES (est): 4.41MM
SALES (corp-wide): 28.74MM Privately Held
Web: www.falconwatertech.com
SIC: 3069 Pump sleeves, rubber
PA: Management Kingsley Llc Mapleton
9952 Santa Monica Blvd
310 282-0780

**(P-6494)**
**FLEX COMPANY**
318 Lincoln Blvd Ste 204, Venice (90291)
PHONE.................424 209-2711
Lauren Schulte, CEO
Brian Wang, *
EMP: 30 EST: 2015
SQ FT: 4,500
SALES (est): 7.2MM Privately Held
Web: www.flexfits.com

## 3069 - Fabricated Rubber Products, Nec (P-6495)

SIC: **3069** 5999 5122 Birth control devices, rubber; Toiletries, cosmetics, and perfumes; Drugs, proprietaries, and sundries

**(P-6495)**
### FUEL TOTAL SYSTEMS CALIFORNIA CORPORATION
18231 Murphy Pkwy, Lathrop (95330-8754)
▲ **EMP:** 30
SIC: **3069** Fuel tanks, collapsible: rubberized fabric

**(P-6496)**
### GIBBS PLASTIC & RUBBER LLC
Also Called: Mint Grips
3959 Teal Ct, Benicia (94510-1212)
PHONE..............................707 746-7300
TOLL FREE: 800
Lee Michels, *Pt*
**EMP:** 15 **EST:** 1926
**SQ FT:** 14,000
**SALES (est):** 2.37MM **Privately Held**
Web: www.mintgrip.com
SIC: **3069** 3061 Molded rubber products; Mechanical rubber goods

**(P-6497)**
### GOOD-WEST RUBBER CORP (PA)
Also Called: Goodyear Rbr Co Southern Cal
9615 Feron Blvd, Rancho Cucamonga (91730-4503)
PHONE..............................909 987-1774
Christian Groche, *Pr*
Harold W Sears, *
Patrick Sears, *
Fred Ledesma, *
▲ **EMP:** 145 **EST:** 1961
**SQ FT:** 56,000
**SALES (est):** 19.69MM
**SALES (corp-wide):** 19.69MM **Privately Held**
Web: www.goodyearrubber.com
SIC: **3069** 3061 5531 Molded rubber products; Mechanical rubber goods; Automotive tires

**(P-6498)**
### GOODWEST RUBBER LININGS INC
Also Called: Goodwest Linings & Coatings
8814 Industrial Ln, Rancho Cucamonga (91730-4528)
PHONE..............................888 499-0085
Ryan Sears, *Pr*
Larry Sears, *Sec*
Patrick Sears, *VP*
Fred Ledesma, *VP*
**EMP:** 20 **EST:** 1995
**SQ FT:** 300,000
**SALES (est):** 4.83MM **Privately Held**
Web: www.uia.net
SIC: **3069** Linings, vulcanizable rubber

**(P-6499)**
### HEXPOL COMPOUNDING CA INC (DH)
Also Called: Valley Processing
2500 E Thompson St, Long Beach (90805-1836)
PHONE..............................626 961-0311
Tracy Garrison, *Pr*
Ernie Ulmer, *CFO*
**EMP:** 93 **EST:** 2011
**SALES (est):** 38MM
**SALES (corp-wide):** 6.47MM **Privately Held**
Web: www.hexpol.com

SIC: **3069** Custom compounding of rubber materials
HQ: Hexpol Holding Inc.
14330 Kinsman Rd
Burton OH 44021
440 834-4644

**(P-6500)**
### HITT COMPANIES
Also Called: Hitt Marking Devices I D Tech
3231 W Macarthur Blvd, Santa Ana (92704-6801)
PHONE..............................714 979-1405
Harold G Hitt, *Pr*
Ken Hitt, *
Heidi Hitt, *
▲ **EMP:** 24 **EST:** 1987
**SQ FT:** 10,000
**SALES (est):** 4.4MM **Privately Held**
Web: www.thehittcompanies.com
SIC: **3069** 3993 5199 Stationer's rubber sundries; Signs and advertising specialties; Badges

**(P-6501)**
### HOLZ RUBBER COMPANY INC
Also Called: Hr
1129 S Sacramento St, Lodi (95240-5701)
PHONE..............................209 368-7171
James R Dryburgh, *Pr*
David Smith, *
▲ **EMP:** 120 **EST:** 1935
**SQ FT:** 144,000
**SALES (est):** 9.94MM **Privately Held**
Web: www.holzrubber.com
SIC: **3069** 3441 3061 Molded rubber products; Fabricated structural metal; Mechanical rubber goods

**(P-6502)**
### HUTCHINSON AROSPC & INDUST INC
Also Called: Barry Controls Aerospace
4510 W Vanowen St, Burbank (91505-1135)
P.O. Box 7710 (91510-7710)
PHONE..............................818 843-1000
Grant Hintze, *CEO*
**EMP:** 156
**SALES (corp-wide):** 5.46B **Privately Held**
Web: www.hutchinsonai.com
SIC: **3069** Molded rubber products
HQ: Hutchinson Aerospace & Industry, Inc.
82 South St
Hopkinton MA 01748
508 417-7000

**(P-6503)**
### INNOCOR WEST LLC
300 S Tippecanoe Ave 310, San Bernardino (92408-2605)
PHONE..............................909 307-3737
Carol S Eicher, *CEO*
Doug Vaughan, *CFO*
▲ **EMP:** 556 **EST:** 2003
**SQ FT:** 150,000
**SALES (est):** 2.08MM **Privately Held**
SIC: **3069** 5021 Pillows, sponge rubber; Mattresses
HQ: Innocor, Inc.
200 Schulz Dr Ste 2
Red Bank NJ 07701

**(P-6504)**
### INTERNATIONAL RUBBER PDTS INC (HQ)
Also Called: Irp
1035 Calle Amanecer, San Clemente (92673-6260)
PHONE..............................909 947-1244

Rich Mcmanus, *CEO*
▲ **EMP:** 58 **EST:** 2003
**SQ FT:** 45,000
**SALES (est):** 29.52MM
**SALES (corp-wide):** 150.17MM **Privately Held**
Web: www.irpi.com
SIC: **3069** Medical and laboratory rubber sundries and related products
PA: Sanders Industries Holdings, Inc.
3701 E Conant St
562 354-2920

**(P-6505)**
### JJ ACQUISITIONS LLC
8501 Fallbrook Ave Ste 370, West Hills (91304-3242)
PHONE..............................818 772-0100
Matthew Matsudaira, *Managing Member*
**EMP:** 41 **EST:** 2014
**SALES (est):** 7MM **Privately Held**
SIC: **3069** Toys, rubber

**(P-6506)**
### JOHNSON DOC ENTERPRISES
11933 Vose St, North Hollywood (91605)
PHONE..............................818 764-1543
Ronald Braverman, *Pr*
Chad Braverman, *Dir*
◆ **EMP:** 24 **EST:** 1987
**SALES (est):** 4.52MM **Privately Held**
Web: www.docjohnson.com
SIC: **3069** Toys, rubber

**(P-6507)**
### KIRKHILL INC
1451 S Carlos Ave, Ontario (91761-7676)
P.O. Box 7012 (90242-7012)
PHONE..............................562 803-1117
Robert L Harold, *Ch*
Bruce Mekjian, *
Arlene Hite, *
Gary Riopelle, *
**EMP:** 95 **EST:** 1941
**SALES (est):** 1.9MM **Privately Held**
Web: www.kirkhill.com
SIC: **3069** Acid bottles, rubber

**(P-6508)**
### KIRKHILL RUBBER COMPANY
2500 E Thompson St, Long Beach (90805-1836)
PHONE..............................562 803-1117
David Schlothauer, *Pr*
Edward Reker, *
**EMP:** 99 **EST:** 2018
**SALES (est):** 19.97MM
**SALES (corp-wide):** 6.47MM **Privately Held**
Web: www.kirkhill.com
SIC: **3069** Medical and laboratory rubber sundries and related products
HQ: Hexpol Holding Inc.
14330 Kinsman Rd
Burton OH 44021
440 834-4644

**(P-6509)**
### KMC ACQUISITION LLC (PA)
Also Called: Kirkhill Manufacturing Company
1451 S Carlos Ave, Ontario (91761-7676)
PHONE..............................562 396-0121
▲ **EMP:** 49 **EST:** 1996
**SALES (est):** 24.5MM **Privately Held**
Web: www.rubbersales.com
SIC: **3069** Molded rubber products

**(P-6510)**
### LEONARDS MOLDED PRODUCTS INC
25031 Anza Dr, Valencia (91355-3414)
PHONE..............................661 253-2227
Randy Smith, *Pr*
Randy Smith, *Pr*
Frank Smith, *
▲ **EMP:** 25 **EST:** 1984
**SQ FT:** 5,000
**SALES (est):** 2.43MM **Privately Held**
Web: www.lmprubber.com
SIC: **3069** Molded rubber products

**(P-6511)**
### MATZ RUBBER COMPANY INC
1209 Chestnut St, Burbank (91506-1626)
PHONE..............................323 849-5170
Carmela B San Diego, *CEO*
Jan Jensen, *Sec*
**EMP:** 20 **EST:** 1954
**SQ FT:** 12,000
**SALES (est):** 2.42MM **Privately Held**
Web: www.matzabrasive.com
SIC: **3069** 3541 3291 Rubber covered motor mounting rings (rubber bonded); Machine tools, metal cutting type; Abrasive products

**(P-6512)**
### MCP INDUSTRIES INC (PA)
Also Called: Mission Rubber Co
708 S Temescal St Ste 101, Corona (92879-2096)
P.O. Box 1839 (92878-1839)
PHONE..............................951 736-1881
Walter N Garrett, *CEO*
Owen Garrett, *VP*
Charlotte Garrett, *Sec*
▲ **EMP:** 15 **EST:** 1950
**SQ FT:** 100,000
**SALES (est):** 66.6MM
**SALES (corp-wide):** 66.6MM **Privately Held**
Web: www.missionclay.com
SIC: **3069** 3259 3089 Molded rubber products; Sewer pipe or fittings, clay; Injection molding of plastics

**(P-6513)**
### MITCHELL PROCESSING LLC
2778 Pomona Blvd, Pomona (91768-3222)
PHONE..............................909 519-5759
**EMP:** 20 **EST:** 2012
**SQ FT:** 100,000
**SALES (est):** 1.6MM **Privately Held**
Web: www.mitchellkidcover.com
SIC: **3069** Custom compounding of rubber materials

**(P-6514)**
### MITCHELL RUBBER PRODUCTS LLC (PA)
1880 Iowa Ave Ste 400, Riverside (92507-7405)
P.O. Box 7577 (92658-7577)
PHONE..............................951 681-5655
Theodore Ballou, *CEO*
Mark Mitchell, *Corporate Secretary* *
◆ **EMP:** 120 **EST:** 1967
**SALES (est):** 9.86MM
**SALES (corp-wide):** 9.86MM **Privately Held**
Web: www.mitchellrubber.com
SIC: **3069** 2891 2822 Mats or matting, rubber, nec; Adhesives and sealants; Synthetic rubber

**(P-6515)**
### MODUS ADVANCED INC
2772 Loker Ave W, Carlsbad (92010-6610)
PHONE..............................925 960-8700
Richard Mackirdy Junior, *CEO*
Don E Ulery, *

## PRODUCTS & SERVICES SECTION
## 3069 - Fabricated Rubber Products, Nec (P-6537)

Natalia Spruiell, *
▲ EMP: 53 EST: 1976
SALES (est): 14.66MM Privately Held
Web: www.modusadvanced.com
SIC: 3069 3599 3053 Molded rubber products; Machine and other job shop work; Gaskets; packing and sealing devices

### (P-6516)
### MOMENTUM MANAGEMENT LLC
Also Called: Bushman Products
1206 W Jon St, Torrance (90502-1208)
PHONE...................310 329-2599
Aumann Conde, Prin
Keith Caggiano, Prin
▲ EMP: 15 EST: 2003
SALES (est): 2.83MM Privately Held
Web: www.screamingo.com
SIC: 3069 Toys, rubber

### (P-6517)
### NEWBY RUBBER INC
320 Industrial St, Bakersfield (93307-2706)
PHONE...................661 327-5137
TOLL FREE: 800
Kelly Newby, Pr
Lori Newby, *
▼ EMP: 25 EST: 1958
SQ FT: 80,000
SALES (est): 4.39MM Privately Held
Web: www.newbyrubber.com
SIC: 3069 Molded rubber products

### (P-6518)
### NUSIL TECHNOLOGY LLC (DH)
Also Called: Nusil
1050 Cindy Ln, Carpinteria (93013-2906)
PHONE...................805 684-8780
◆ EMP: 400 EST: 1980
SALES (est): 131.69MM
SALES (corp-wide): 6.97B Publicly Held
Web: nusil.avantorsciences.com
SIC: 3069 Medical and laboratory rubber sundries and related products
HQ: Avantor Performance Materials, Llc
100 Mtsnford Rd Bldg 1 St
Radnor PA 19087
610 573-2600

### (P-6519)
### ONEILL WETSUITS LLC (PA)
Also Called: O'Neill Wetsuits
1071 41st Ave, Santa Cruz (95062-4400)
P.O. Box 6300 (95063-6300)
PHONE...................831 475-7500
Pat O'neill, Managing Member
◆ EMP: 70 EST: 1952
SQ FT: 14,000
SALES (est): 24.04MM Privately Held
Web: us.oneill.com
SIC: 3069 5091 Wet suits, rubber; Watersports equipment and supplies

### (P-6520)
### OXYSTRAP INTERNATIONAL INC
8705 Complex Dr, San Diego (92123-1401)
PHONE...................800 699-6901
Bruce L Gertsch, CEO
EMP: 28 EST: 2015
SALES (est): 588.5K Privately Held
Web: www.oxystrap.com
SIC: 3069 2326 3949 Medical and laboratory rubber sundries and related products; Medical and hospital uniforms, men's; Team sports equipment

### (P-6521)
### PATTEN CO INC
Also Called: Patten Group
3701 Mt Diablo Blvd, Lafayette (94549-3514)
PHONE...................707 826-2887
Fred Kaplan, Pr
EMP: 38 EST: 1974
SALES (est): 4.83MM
SALES (corp-wide): 34.18MM Privately Held
Web: www.pattencompany.com
SIC: 3069 Life rafts, rubber
HQ: Wing Inflatables, Inc.
1220 5th St
Arcata CA 95521

### (P-6522)
### PLAYMAX SURFACING INC
Also Called: Califrnia Rcrtion Instllations
1950 Compton Ave Ste 111, Corona (92881-6471)
P.O. Box 77372 (92877-0112)
PHONE...................951 250-6039
Chris Wolf, Pr
EMP: 19 EST: 2014
SQ FT: 3,500
SALES (est): 2.14MM Privately Held
Web: www.playmaxsurfacing.com
SIC: 3069 5091 1752 1771 Flooring, rubber: tile or sheet; Sporting and recreation goods; Floor laying and floor work, nec; Flooring contractor

### (P-6523)
### PMR PRECISION MFG & RBR CO INC
1330 Etiwanda Ave, Ontario (91761-8605)
PHONE...................909 605-7525
Samuel Surh, Pr
George Surh, *
EMP: 30 EST: 1996
SQ FT: 36,800
SALES (est): 2.2MM Privately Held
Web: www.pmrubbertech.com
SIC: 3069 2295 Rubberized fabrics; Coated fabrics, not rubberized

### (P-6524)
### POLY-SEAL INDUSTRIES
725 Channing Way, Berkeley (94710-2494)
PHONE...................510 843-9722
Daniel K Baker, Pr
▼ EMP: 15 EST: 1974
SQ FT: 6,250
SALES (est): 2.12MM Privately Held
Web: www.polysealind.com
SIC: 3069 Molded rubber products

### (P-6525)
### POLYMERIC TECHNOLOGY INC
1900 Marina Blvd, San Leandro (94577-3207)
PHONE...................510 895-6001
Patrick Tool, CEO
▲ EMP: 50 EST: 1963
SQ FT: 90,000
SALES (est): 8.08MM Privately Held
Web: www.poly-tek.com
SIC: 3069 2821 8731 3061 Molded rubber products; Plastics materials and resins; Commercial physical research; Mechanical rubber goods

### (P-6526)
### PRO LAB ORTHOTICS INC
Also Called: Prolab
575 Airpark Rd, Napa (94558-7514)
PHONE...................707 257-4400
Paul Scherer, CEO

Aaron Meltzer, *
EMP: 42 EST: 1976
SQ FT: 8,200
SALES (est): 4.54MM Privately Held
Web: www.prolaborthotics.com
SIC: 3069 3842 Medical and laboratory rubber sundries and related products; Surgical appliances and supplies

### (P-6527)
### PROCO PRODUCTS INC (PA)
2431 Wigwam Dr, Stockton (95205-2430)
P.O. Box 590 (95201-0590)
PHONE...................209 943-6088
Edward Marchese, Pr
Mike Lassas, *
Jerry Oprondek, *
Robert Coffee, *
Scott Wallace, *
◆ EMP: 26 EST: 1984
SQ FT: 22,000
SALES (est): 9.43MM
SALES (corp-wide): 9.43MM Privately Held
Web: www.procoproducts.com
SIC: 3069 2821 3443 3441 Molded rubber products; Polytetrafluoroethylene resins, teflon; Pipe, standpipe, and culverts; Fabricated structural metal

### (P-6528)
### PROMOTONAL DESIGN CONCEPTS INC
Also Called: Creative Inflatables
9872 Rush St, South El Monte (91733-2635)
PHONE...................626 579-4454
Adam Melendez, CEO
◆ EMP: 71 EST: 1984
SALES (est): 2MM Privately Held
Web: www.promotionaldesigngroup.com
SIC: 3069 7389 5092 2394 Balloons, advertising and toy: rubber; Balloons, novelty and toy; Toy novelties and amusements; Canvas and related products

### (P-6529)
### PURUS INTERNATIONAL INC
82860 Avenue 45, Indio (92201-2396)
PHONE...................760 775-4500
Dennis Baldwin, Pr
Jessica Baldwin, CFO
◆ EMP: 19 EST: 2002
SQ FT: 3,000
SALES (est): 3.4MM Privately Held
Web: www.purusint.com
SIC: 3069 2381 Mats or matting, rubber, nec; Glove linings, except fur

### (P-6530)
### QUALITY RUBBER SOURCING INC
3988 Short St Ste 110, San Luis Obispo (93401-7574)
P.O. Box 796 (93453-0796)
PHONE...................805 544-7770
Brian Hotovec, Prin
▲ EMP: 16 EST: 2008
SALES (est): 831.98K Privately Held
Web: www.qualityrubbersourcing.com
SIC: 3069 Fabricated rubber products, nec

### (P-6531)
### R & R RUBBER MOLDING INC
2444 Loma Ave, South El Monte (91733-1416)
P.O. Box 3533 (91733-0533)
PHONE...................626 575-8105
Richard P Norman, Pr
EMP: 35 EST: 1977

SQ FT: 6,100
SALES (est): 1.86MM Privately Held
Web: www.rrrubber.com
SIC: 3069 Molded rubber products

### (P-6532)
### R & R SERVICES CORPORATION
Also Called: Geolabs Westlake Village
3595 Old Conejo Rd, Newbury Park (91320-2122)
PHONE...................818 889-2562
Ronald Z Shmerling, Pr
EMP: 16 EST: 1983
SALES (est): 2.82MM Privately Held
SIC: 3069 8999 8711 Laboratory sundries: cases, covers, funnels, cups, etc.; Geological consultant; Engineering services

### (P-6533)
### R & S PROCESSING CO INC
15712 Illinois Ave, Paramount (90723-4113)
P.O. Box 2037 (90723-8037)
PHONE...................562 531-0738
Karen A Kelly, Pr
Linda M Inga, *
Anthony J Inga, *
EMP: 73 EST: 1959
SQ FT: 53,000
SALES (est): 5.2MM Privately Held
Web: www.rsprocessing.com
SIC: 3069 Reclaimed rubber (reworked by manufacturing processes)

### (P-6534)
### ROGERS CORPORATION
Also Called: Diversified Silicone
13937 Rosecrans Ave, Santa Fe Springs (90670-5209)
PHONE...................562 404-8942
Brian Lindey, Genl Mgr
EMP: 60
SALES (corp-wide): 908.4MM Publicly Held
Web: www.rogerscorp.com
SIC: 3069 Bags, rubber or rubberized fabric
PA: Rogers Corporation
2225 W Chandler Blvd
480 917-6000

### (P-6535)
### RUBBER-CAL INC
18424 Mount Langley St, Fountain Valley (92708-6905)
PHONE...................714 772-3000
EMP: 76 EST: 2019
SALES (est): 3.63MM Privately Held
Web: www.rubbercal.com
SIC: 3069 Fabricated rubber products, nec

### (P-6536)
### S & H RUBBER CO
1141 E Elm Ave, Fullerton (92831-5023)
PHONE...................714 525-0277
Stephen Haney, Pr
Mike Haney, Mgr
EMP: 28 EST: 1967
SQ FT: 5,406
SALES (est): 3.14MM Privately Held
Web: www.shrubber.com
SIC: 3069 Washers, rubber

### (P-6537)
### SFRLC INC
12306 Washington Blvd, Whittier (90606)
PHONE...................562 693-2776
William Krames, Pr
Mike Peterman, *
EMP: 50 EST: 1966
SQ FT: 30,000

## 3069 - Fabricated Rubber Products, Nec (P-6538)

SALES (est): 2.16MM **Privately Held**
Web: www.santaferubber.com
SIC: **3069** Molded rubber products

### (P-6538)
### SHERCON LLC
Also Called: Shercon, Inc.
18704 S Ferris Pl, Rancho Dominguez
(90220-6400)
▲ **EMP:** 60 **EST:** 1966
**SQ FT:** 50,000
**SALES (est):** 1.5MM
**SALES (corp-wide):** 2.26B **Privately Held**
Web: www.caplugs.com
SIC: **3069** 3089 2672 Tape, pressure sensitive: rubber; Injection molded finished plastics products, nec; Paper; coated and laminated, nec
HQ: Caplugs, Inc.
   2150 Elmwood Ave
   Buffalo NY 14207
   716 876-9855

### (P-6539)
### SPANGLER INDUSTRIES INC
Also Called: A S I American
1711 N Delilah St, Corona (92879-1865)
P.O. Box 1445 (92878-1445)
PHONE..............................951 735-5000
Bernard D Spangler, *Pr*
Greg Spangler, *
**EMP:** 165 **EST:** 1970
**SQ FT:** 37,897
**SALES (est):** 8.53MM **Privately Held**
SIC: **3069** Rubber bands

### (P-6540)
### STOCKTON RUBBER MFGCOINC
Also Called: SRC
5023 N Flood Rd, Linden (95236-9455)
P.O. Box 639 (95236-0639)
PHONE..............................209 887-1172
Earl D Wilson, *CEO*
Ursula Wilson, *
**EMP:** 28 **EST:** 1987
**SQ FT:** 7,500
**SALES (est):** 5.81MM **Privately Held**
Web: www.stocktonrubber.com
SIC: **3069** Medical and laboratory rubber sundries and related products

### (P-6541)
### TA AEROSPACE CO (DH)
28065 Franklin Pkwy, Valencia
(91355-4117)
PHONE..............................661 775-1100
Carol Marinello, *Pr*
▲ **EMP:** 250 **EST:** 1919
**SQ FT:** 100,000
**SALES (est):** 193.2MM
**SALES (corp-wide):** 7.94B **Publicly Held**
Web: www.taaerospace.com
SIC: **3069** Reclaimed rubber and specialty rubber compounds
HQ: Esterline Technologies Corp
   1350 Euclid Ave Ste 1600
   Cleveland OH 44114
   216 706-2960

### (P-6542)
### TALCO FOAM INC (PA)
Also Called: Talco Foam Products
1631 Enterprise Blvd Ste 30, West Sacramento (95691-5046)
PHONE..............................916 492-8840
Dave Talbot, *Prin*
▲ **EMP:** 15 **EST:** 1990
**SQ FT:** 30,000
**SALES (est):** 1.11MM **Privately Held**
SIC: **3069** Foam rubber

### (P-6543)
### TANGLE INC
Also Called: Tangle Creations
310 Littlefield Ave, South San Francisco
(94080-6103)
PHONE..............................650 616-7900
Nicholas Zawitz, *Pr*
Richard Zawitz, *
Nicholas Zawitz, *Treas*
▲ **EMP:** 26 **EST:** 1982
**SQ FT:** 5,000
**SALES (est):** 2.63MM **Privately Held**
Web: www.tanglecreations.com
SIC: **3069** Toys, rubber

### (P-6544)
### TIMEMED LABELING SYSTEMS INC (DH)
27770 Entertainment Dr Ste 200, Valencia
(91355-1094)
PHONE..............................818 897-1111
Cecil Kost, *CEO*
Mark Segal, *
Tracey Carpentier, *
**EMP:** 100 **EST:** 1953
**SQ FT:** 75,000
**SALES (est):** 6.13MM
**SALES (corp-wide):** 1.34B **Publicly Held**
Web: www.pdchealthcare.com
SIC: **3069** Tape, pressure sensitive: rubber
HQ: Precision Dynamics Corporation
   25124 Sprngfeld Ct Ste 20
   Valencia CA 91355
   818 897-1111

### (P-6545)
### UROCARE PRODUCTS INC
2735 Melbourne Ave, Pomona
(91767-1931)
PHONE..............................909 621-6013
Friedhelm Franke, *CEO*
Raymond Halsey-franke, *Pr*
Glenn Franke, *Sec*
Sylvia Bender, *CFO*
▲ **EMP:** 16 **EST:** 1975
**SQ FT:** 30,000
**SALES (est):** 1.53MM **Privately Held**
Web: www.urocare.com
SIC: **3069** 3089 Medical and laboratory rubber sundries and related products; Injection molded finished plastics products, nec

### (P-6546)
### US RUBBER RECYCLING INC
1231 Lincoln St, Colton (92324-3533)
PHONE..............................909 825-1200
Rick Snyder, *Pr*
▲ **EMP:** 22 **EST:** 1996
**SQ FT:** 30,000
**SALES (est):** 4.05MM **Privately Held**
Web: www.usrubber.com
SIC: **3069** Acid bottles, rubber

### (P-6547)
### VIKING RUBBER PRODUCTS INC
2600 Homestead Pl, Compton
(90220-5610)
PHONE..............................310 868-5200
Rod Trujillo, *CEO*
Leigh Munsell, *Pr*
Ricardo Ordonez, *CFO*
**EMP:** 17 **EST:** 1981
**SALES (est):** 3.37MM
**SALES (corp-wide):** 137.12MM **Privately Held**
Web: www.irpi.com

SIC: **3069** 3061 Custom compounding of rubber materials; Mechanical rubber goods
HQ: International Rubber Products, Inc.
   1035 Calle Amanecer
   San Clemente CA 92673

### (P-6548)
### VIP RUBBER COMPANY INC (PA)
540 S Cypress St, La Habra (90631-6127)
PHONE..............................562 905-3456
Bernardyne Louise Campana, *Pr*
Howard Vipperman, *
Deena Campana, *
Kathy Leclair, *
Thomas Leclair, *
▲ **EMP:** 107 **EST:** 1970
**SQ FT:** 58,000
**SALES (est):** 23.69MM
**SALES (corp-wide):** 23.69MM **Privately Held**
Web: www.viprubber.com
SIC: **3069** 3089 3061 Rubber hardware; Plastics hardware and building products; Mechanical rubber goods

### (P-6549)
### WEST AMERICAN RUBBER CO LLC (PA)
Also Called: Warco
1337 W Braden Ct, Orange (92868-1123)
P.O. Box 6146 (92863-6146)
PHONE..............................714 532-3355
Tim Hemstreet, *Managing Member*
▲ **EMP:** 124 **EST:** 1910
**SQ FT:** 12,500
**SALES (est):** 48.04MM
**SALES (corp-wide):** 48.04MM **Privately Held**
Web: www.warco.com
SIC: **3069** 3061 3053 Sheets, hard rubber; Mechanical rubber goods; Gaskets, all materials

### (P-6550)
### WEST AMERICAN RUBBER CO LLC
Also Called: Warco
750 N Main St, Orange (92868-1106)
P.O. Box 6146 (92863-6146)
PHONE..............................714 532-3355
Renan Mendez, *Com Operations Vice President*
**EMP:** 165
**SALES (est):** 48.04MM **Privately Held**
Web: www.warco.com
SIC: **3069** Sheets, hard rubber
PA: West American Rubber Company Llc
   1337 Braden Ct
   714 532-3355

## 3081 Unsupported Plastics Film And Sheet

### (P-6551)
### ARLON GRAPHICS LLC
200 Boysenberry Ln, Placentia
(92870-6413)
PHONE..............................714 985-6300
Andrew Mcneill, *Pr*
Andrew Huddlestone, *Area President**
Rich Trombino, *
Chad Russell, *
◆ **EMP:** 150 **EST:** 2011
**SALES (est):** 56.17MM
**SALES (corp-wide):** 314.36MM **Privately Held**
Web: www.arlon.com

SIC: **3081** Vinyl film and sheet
PA: Flexcon Company, Inc.
   1 Flexcon Industrial Park
   508 885-8200

### (P-6552)
### ARVINYL LAMINATES LP
233 N Sherman Ave, Corona (92882-1844)
PHONE..............................951 371-7800
Andy Peters, *Pt*
**EMP:** 51 **EST:** 2011
**SALES (est):** 10.64MM **Privately Held**
Web: www.arvinyl.com
SIC: **3081** Vinyl film and sheet

### (P-6553)
### BERRY GLOBAL FILMS LLC
14000 Monte Vista Ave, Chino
(91710-5537)
PHONE..............................909 517-2872
J Brendan Barba, *Pr*
**EMP:** 149
**SQ FT:** 63,480
Web: www.berryglobal.com
SIC: **3081** 2673 Polyethylene film; Bags: plastic, laminated, and coated
HQ: Berry Global Films, Llc
   95 Chestnut Ridge Rd
   Montvale NJ 07645
   201 641-6600

### (P-6554)
### COMPASS INNOVATIONS INC
Also Called: Careray USA
2352 Walsh Ave, Santa Clara (95051-1301)
PHONE..............................408 418-3985
Jianqiang Liu, *CEO*
**EMP:** 120 **EST:** 2017
**SALES (est):** 6.87MM
**SALES (corp-wide):** 38.28MM **Privately Held**
Web: www.careray.com
SIC: **3081** 5047 Photographic and X-ray film and sheet; X-ray film and supplies
PA: Jiangsu Kangzhong Digital Medical Technology Co., Ltd.
   Room 501, Floor ,B3, Floor A2,
   Shengwu Nami Park, No.218, Xinghu
   51286860288

### (P-6555)
### CREATIVE IMPRESSIONS INC
7697 9th St, Buena Park (90621-2898)
PHONE..............................714 521-4441
Marc D Abbott, *Pr*
▲ **EMP:** 17 **EST:** 1991
**SQ FT:** 8,000
**SALES (est):** 1.22MM **Privately Held**
Web: www.emenucovers.com
SIC: **3081** Plastics film and sheet

### (P-6556)
### DELSTAR HOLDING CORP
9225 Isaac St, Santee (92071-5615)
PHONE..............................619 258-1503
Scott Anglin, *Brnch Mgr*
▲ **EMP:** 26
Web: www.swmintl.com
SIC: **3081** Polypropylene film and sheet
HQ: Delstar Holding Corp.
   100 N Point Ctr E Ste 600
   Alpharetta GA 30022
   800 514-0186

### (P-6557)
### DELSTAR TECHNOLOGIES INC
Also Called: Swm
1306 Fayette St, El Cajon (92020-1513)
PHONE..............................619 258-1503
Mark Laughlin, *Mgr*

## PRODUCTS & SERVICES SECTION

### 3082 - Unsupported Plastics Profile Shapes (P-6577)

**EMP:** 50
**Web:** www.delstarinc.com
**SIC:** 3081 Polypropylene film and sheet
**HQ:** Delstar Technologies, Inc.
  601 Industrial Dr
  Middletown DE 19709
  302 378-8888

**(P-6558)**
**DINSMORE & ASSOCIATES LLC**
1681 Kettering, Irvine (92614-5613)
**PHONE**............................714 641-7111
Jason Dinsmore, CEO
▲ **EMP:** 15 **EST:** 2001
**SALES (est):** 5.16MM
**SALES (corp-wide):** 23MM **Privately Held**
**Web:** www.dinsmoreinc.com
**SIC:** 3081 8711 Film base, cellulose acetate or nitrocellulose plastics; Machine tool design
**PA:** Addman Engineering Llc
  16340 Innovation Ln
  502 553-5602

**(P-6559)**
**FLEXCON COMPANY INC**
12840 Reservoir St, Chino (91710-2944)
**PHONE**............................909 465-0408
David R Trujillo, Mgr
**EMP:** 40
**SALES (corp-wide):** 314.36MM **Privately Held**
**Web:** www.flexcon.com
**SIC:** 3081 2679 Plastics film and sheet; Labels, paper: made from purchased material
**PA:** Flexcon Company, Inc.
  1 Flexcon Industrial Park
  508 885-8200

**(P-6560)**
**GLAD PRODUCTS COMPANY (HQ)**
Also Called: Glad
1221 Broadway Ste A, Oakland (94612-1837)
**PHONE**............................510 271-7000
William V Stephenson, Ch Bd
Thomas H Rowland, *
Donald A De Santis, *
Joseph B Furey, *
◆ **EMP:** 150 **EST:** 1986
**SQ FT:** 40,000
**SALES (est):** 487.15MM
**SALES (corp-wide):** 7.09B **Publicly Held**
**Web:** www.thecloroxcompany.com
**SIC:** 3081 2673 2842 3295 Plastics film and sheet; Plastic bags: made from purchased materials; Automobile polish; Cat box filler
**PA:** The Clorox Company
  1221 Broadway
  510 271-7000

**(P-6561)**
**GRAFFITI SHIELD INC**
2940 E La Palma Ave Ste D, Anaheim (92806-2619)
**PHONE**............................714 575-1100
Jeffrey Green, CEO
**EMP:** 24 **EST:** 2013
**SALES (est):** 6.11MM **Privately Held**
**Web:** www.graffiti-shield.com
**SIC:** 3081 Floor or wall covering, unsupported plastics

**(P-6562)**
**MERCURY PLASTICS INC**
Poly Pak Packaging Division
2939 E Washington Blvd, Los Angeles (90023-4218)

**PHONE**............................323 264-2400
Benjamin Deutsch, Brnch Mgr
**EMP:** 95
**Web:** www.polypak.com
**SIC:** 3081 2677 Polyethylene film; Envelopes
**HQ:** Mercury Plastics, Inc.
  14825 Salt Lake Ave
  City Of Industry CA 91746
  626 961-0165

**(P-6563)**
**MERRILLS PACKAGING INC**
Also Called: Merrill's Packaging Supply
1529 Rollins Rd, Burlingame (94010-2305)
**PHONE**............................650 259-5959
Susan Merrill, CEO
Rick Schulz, *
Leslie Jane Lopez, *
Jon Eide, *
Kehn Merrill, *
◆ **EMP:** 80 **EST:** 1961
**SQ FT:** 60,000
**SALES (est):** 18.01MM **Privately Held**
**Web:** www.merrills.com
**SIC:** 3081 Unsupported plastics film and sheet

**(P-6564)**
**MONTEBELLO PLASTICS LLC**
601 W Olympic Blvd, Montebello (90640-5229)
P.O. Box 789 (90640-0789)
**PHONE**............................323 728-6814
**EMP:** 50 **EST:** 1982
**SQ FT:** 25,000
**SALES (est):** 3.46MM **Privately Held**
**Web:** www.montebelloplastics.com
**SIC:** 3081 2673 3089 Packing materials, plastics sheet; Trash bags (plastic film): made from purchased materials; Extruded finished plastics products, nec

**(P-6565)**
**OCEANIA INC**
14209 Gannet St, La Mirada (90638-5220)
**PHONE**............................562 926-8886
Tai Leong, CEO
Angela Leung, *
▲ **EMP:** 30 **EST:** 2014
**SALES (est):** 1.79MM **Privately Held**
**SIC:** 3081 Plastics film and sheet

**(P-6566)**
**PLASTICS FAMILY HOLDINGS INC**
Also Called: Eplastics
5535 Ruffin Rd, San Diego (92123-1314)
**PHONE**............................858 560-1551
Nate Gardner, Brnch Mgr
**EMP:** 58
**Web:** www.lairdplastics.com
**SIC:** 3081 3082 5162 2541 Unsupported plastics film and sheet; Unsupported plastics profile shapes; Plastics materials and basic shapes; Wood partitions and fixtures
**HQ:** Plastics Family Holdings, Inc.
  5800 Cmpus Cir Dr E Ste 1
  Irving TX 75063
  469 299-7000

**(P-6567)**
**POLY PAK AMERICA INC**
2939 E Washington Blvd, Los Angeles (90023-4277)
**PHONE**............................323 264-2400
**TOLL FREE:** 800
**EMP:** 95
**Web:** www.polypak.com

**SIC:** 3081 2677 Polyethylene film; Envelopes

**(P-6568)**
**PROVIDIEN THERMOFORMING LLC**
Also Called: Providien Thermoforming, Inc.
6740 Nancy Ridge Dr, San Diego (92121)
**PHONE**............................858 850-1591
Jeffrey S Goble, CEO
Jenny Ames, *
Frank Ames Junior, Sec
Paul Jazwin, *
▲ **EMP:** 48 **EST:** 1982
**SQ FT:** 25,500
**SALES (est):** 20.42MM
**SALES (corp-wide):** 4.59B **Publicly Held**
**Web:** www.providienmedical.com
**SIC:** 3081 Unsupported plastics film and sheet
**HQ:** Providien, Llc
  6740 Nancy Ridge Dr
  San Diego CA 92121

**(P-6569)**
**SAINT-GOBAIN SOLAR GARD LLC (DH)**
Also Called: Saint-Gobain Performance Plas
4540 Viewridge Ave, San Diego (92123)
P.O. Box 2864 (52733)
**PHONE**............................866 300-2674
M Shawn Puccio, *
◆ **EMP:** 88 **EST:** 2001
**SQ FT:** 65,000
**SALES (est):** 48.04MM
**SALES (corp-wide):** 402.18MM **Privately Held**
**Web:** www.solargard.com
**SIC:** 3081 5162 3479 Plastics film and sheet; Plastics film; Coating of metals and formed products
**HQ:** Saint-Gobain Performance Plastics Corporation
  20 Moores Rd
  Malvern PA 19355
  440 836-6900

**(P-6570)**
**SCIENTIFIC SPECIALTIES INC**
Also Called: Ssi
1310 Thurman St, Lodi (95240-3145)
**PHONE**............................209 333-2120
Kenneth Hovatter, Prin
◆ **EMP:** 100 **EST:** 1989
**SALES (est):** 20.95MM **Privately Held**
**Web:** www.scientificspecialties.com
**SIC:** 3081 Unsupported plastics film and sheet

**(P-6571)**
**SOLVAY DRAKA INC (DH)**
6900 Elm St, Commerce (90040-2625)
**PHONE**............................323 725-7010
▲ **EMP:** 120 **EST:** 1986
**SALES (est):** 40.32MM
**SALES (corp-wide):** 2.67MM **Privately Held**
**Web:** www.renolit.com
**SIC:** 3081 3087 Vinyl film and sheet; Custom compound purchased resins
**HQ:** Renolit Se
  Horchheimer Str. 50
  Worms RP 67547
  62413030

**(P-6572)**
**TRAFFIC WORKS INC**
5720 Soto St, Huntington Park (90255-2631)
**PHONE**............................323 582-0616
Steve Josephson, Owner

▲ **EMP:** 20 **EST:** 1983
**SQ FT:** 20,000
**SALES (est):** 2.47MM **Privately Held**
**Web:** www.trafficworksinc.com
**SIC:** 3081 2678 Packing materials, plastics sheet; Stationery: made from purchased materials

**(P-6573)**
**TRM MANUFACTURING INC**
375 Trm Cir, Corona (92879)
P.O. Box 77520 (92877)
**PHONE**............................951 256-8550
Ted Moore, Pr
Anaisa Moore, *
▲ **EMP:** 200 **EST:** 1978
**SQ FT:** 200,000
**SALES (est):** 83.74MM **Privately Held**
**Web:** www.trmmfg.com
**SIC:** 3081 Polyethylene film

**(P-6574)**
**UNI-PIXEL INC**
Also Called: UNI-Pixel
4699 Old Ironsides Dr Ste 300, Santa Clara (95054-1824)
**PHONE**............................281 825-4500
Jeff A Hawthorne, Pr
Malcolm J Thompson, *
Anthony J Levecchio, *
Christine A Russell, CFO
**EMP:** 93 **EST:** 1998
**SQ FT:** 4,478
**SALES (est):** 6.01MM **Privately Held**
**Web:** www.oakpartners.co
**SIC:** 3081 Unsupported plastics film and sheet

**(P-6575)**
**UNION CHEMICAR AMERICA INC**
3151 Airway Ave, Costa Mesa (92626-4607)
**PHONE**............................949 770-7072
▲ **EMP:** 16 **EST:** 1992
**SALES (est):** 408.87K **Privately Held**
**Web:** www.unionchemicar.com
**SIC:** 3081 Unsupported plastics film and sheet

**(P-6576)**
**W PLASTICS INC**
Also Called: Western Plastics Temecula
41573 Dendy Pkwy Ste 2543, Temecula (92590-3757)
**PHONE**............................800 442-9727
Michael T F Cunningham, Pr
Patrick Cunningham, VP
Thomas C Cunningham, Treas
◆ **EMP:** 35 **EST:** 1991
**SQ FT:** 65,000
**SALES (est):** 5.05MM **Privately Held**
**Web:** www.wplastics.com
**SIC:** 3081 1799 Plastics film and sheet; Food service equipment installation

### 3082 Unsupported Plastics Profile Shapes

**(P-6577)**
**BIRD B GONE LLC**
1921 E Edinger Ave, Santa Ana (92705-4720)
**PHONE**............................949 472-3122
Bruce Alan Donoho, CEO
Julianne Donoho, *
David Smith, *
◆ **EMP:** 86 **EST:** 1992
**SQ FT:** 7,100
**SALES (est):** 15.9MM **Privately Held**

# 3082 - Unsupported Plastics Profile Shapes (P-6578)

Web: www.birdbgone.com
SIC: 3082 Unsupported plastics profile shapes
HQ: Pelsis Limited
Sterling House
Knaresborough HG5 8
800 988-5359

### (P-6578)
### C&M MANUFACTURING COMPANY INC (PA)
Also Called: C & M Manufacturing
9640b Mission Gorge Rd Ste 165, Santee (92071-3854)
PHONE.................................619 449-7200
Curt Moore, Pr
Lori Moore, VP
EMP: 20 EST: 1986
SALES (est): 6.32MM Privately Held
Web: www.centralizers.com
SIC: 3082 Unsupported plastics profile shapes

### (P-6579)
### JSN PACKAGING PRODUCTS INC
9700 Jeronimo Rd, Irvine (92618-2019)
PHONE.................................949 458-0050
Jim Nagel, Pr
Sandra Nagel, *
James H Nagel Junior, CEO
EMP: 65 EST: 1985
SALES (est): 9.57MM Privately Held
Web: www.jsn.com
SIC: 3082 3089 Tubes, unsupported plastics; Caps, plastics

## 3083 Laminated Plastics Plate And Sheet

### (P-6580)
### ABC PLASTICS INC
Also Called: A B C Plastic Fabrication,
9132 De Soto Ave, Chatsworth (91311-4907)
PHONE.................................818 775-0065
Mark Walters, Pr
Ivan Jackovich, VP
▲ EMP: 15 EST: 1981
SQ FT: 8,000
SALES (est): 1.92MM Privately Held
Web: www.abcplasticfab.com
SIC: 3083 7319 5046 3089 Plastics finished products, laminated; Display advertising service; Store fixtures; Plastics processing

### (P-6581)
### ALCHEM PLASTICS INC
Also Called: Spartech Plastics
14263 Gannet St, La Mirada (90638-5220)
PHONE.................................714 523-2260
▲ EMP: 130
SIC: 3083 Thermoplastics laminates: rods, tubes, plates, and sheet

### (P-6582)
### DAZ INC
Also Called: Duramar Interior Surfaces
2500 White Rd Ste B, Irvine (92614-6276)
PHONE.................................949 724-8800
Nikkisa Abdollahi, CEO
Farhad Abdollahi, Sec
▲ EMP: 15 EST: 2007
SQ FT: 60,000
SALES (est): 2.62MM Privately Held
SIC: 3083 Laminated plastics plate and sheet

### (P-6583)
### JOHNSON LAMINATING COATING INC
20631 Annalee Ave, Carson (90746-3502)
PHONE.................................310 635-4929
Scott Davidson, Pr
▲ EMP: 75 EST: 1960
SQ FT: 50,000
SALES (est): 9.52MM Privately Held
Web: www.johnsonlaminating.com
SIC: 3083 3081 2891 1541 Laminated plastics sheets; Unsupported plastics film and sheet; Adhesives and sealants; Food products manufacturing or packing plant construction

### (P-6584)
### LINDSEY DOORS INC
Also Called: Lindsey Mfg
81101 Indio Blvd Ste D16, Indio (92201-1920)
PHONE.................................760 775-1959
Pierre Letellier, Pr
Katherine Letellier, Sec
EMP: 22 EST: 1996
SALES (est): 4.05MM Privately Held
Web: www.lindseydoors.com
SIC: 3083 1521 Thermoplastics laminates: rods, tubes, plates, and sheet; Single-family housing construction

### (P-6585)
### LITE EXTRUSIONS MFG INC
Also Called: Lite Extrusions
15025 S Main St, Gardena (90248-1922)
PHONE.................................323 770-4298
Paul Puga, Pr
William Puga, *
Barbara Puga, *
EMP: 30 EST: 1973
SQ FT: 23,500
SALES (est): 2.2MM Privately Held
Web: www.liteextrusions.com
SIC: 3083 Thermoplastics laminates: rods, tubes, plates, and sheet

### (P-6586)
### NELCO PRODUCTS INC
1100 E Kimberly Ave, Anaheim (92801-1101)
PHONE.................................714 879-4293
▲ EMP: 135
Web: www.nelcoproducts.com
SIC: 3083 Laminated plastics plate and sheet

### (P-6587)
### PLASTICS RESEARCH CORPORATION
Also Called: PRC
1400 S Campus Ave, Ontario (91761-4330)
PHONE.................................909 391-9050
Gene Gregory, CEO
Robert Black, *
Michael Maedel, *
▲ EMP: 100 EST: 1972
SQ FT: 105,000
SALES (est): 9.79MM Privately Held
Web: www.prccal.com
SIC: 3083 Laminated plastics plate and sheet

### (P-6588)
### PLASTIFAB INC
Also Called: Plastifab/Leed Plastics
1425 Palomares St, La Verne (91750-5294)
PHONE.................................909 596-1927
Rick Donnelly, Pr
EMP: 30 EST: 1977
SQ FT: 15,000
SALES (est): 4.62MM Privately Held

Web: www.plastifabonline.com
SIC: 3083 5162 3089 Laminated plastics sheets; Plastics sheets and rods; Plastics processing

### (P-6589)
### PTM & W INDUSTRIES INC
10640 Painter Ave, Santa Fe Springs (90670-4092)
PHONE.................................562 946-4511
Charles E Owen, CEO
William Ryan, *
▲ EMP: 25 EST: 1959
SQ FT: 25,000
SALES (est): 4.76MM Privately Held
Web: www.ptm-w.com
SIC: 3083 2992 2891 2851 Plastics finished products, laminated; Lubricating oils and greases; Adhesives and sealants; Paints and allied products

### (P-6590)
### REPET INC
14207 Monte Vista Ave, Chino (91710-5724)
PHONE.................................909 594-5333
Shubin Zhao, Pr
▲ EMP: 145 EST: 2009
SALES (est): 6.44MM Privately Held
Web: www.repetinc.com
SIC: 3083 Plastics finished products, laminated

### (P-6591)
### REPSCO INC
5300 Claus Rd Ste 2, Riverbank (95367)
P.O. Box 5300 Claus Rd (95367)
PHONE.................................888 727-7261
Paul Bennett Junior, Pr
Drusilla Harvey, CFO
David Jara, Sec
♦ EMP: 20 EST: 1971
SQ FT: 55,000
SALES (est): 8.5MM Privately Held
Web: www.repsco.com
SIC: 3083 Laminated plastics plate and sheet

### (P-6592)
### SIMMONS FAMILY CORPORATION
Also Called: Teklam
350 W Rincon St, Corona (92880-2004)
PHONE.................................951 278-4563
▲ EMP: 80
SIC: 3083 Laminated plastics plate and sheet

### (P-6593)
### VANDERVEER INDUSTRIAL PLAS LLC
Also Called: Vanderveer Industrial Plastics
515 S Melrose St, Placentia (92870-6337)
PHONE.................................714 579-7700
Greg Geiss, Managing Member
EMP: 46 EST: 2012
SQ FT: 29,000
SALES (est): 6.51MM
SALES (corp-wide): 55.91MM Privately Held
Web: www.vanderveerplastics.com
SIC: 3083 Laminated plastics plate and sheet
PA: The Gund Company Inc
9333 Dielman Indus Dr
314 423-5200

### (P-6594)
### VCLAD LAMINATES INC
2103 Seaman Ave, South El Monte (91733-2628)
PHONE.................................626 442-2100

David Thomson, Pr
▲ EMP: 20 EST: 2002
SALES (est): 3.79MM Privately Held
Web: www.vclad.com
SIC: 3083 2434 Laminated plastics sheets; Wood kitchen cabinets

## 3084 Plastics Pipe

### (P-6595)
### ADVANCED DRAINAGE SYSTEMS INC
1025 Commerce Dr, Madera (93637-5201)
P.O. Box 1117 (93639-1117)
PHONE.................................559 674-4989
Richard Tartaglia, Brnch Mgr
EMP: 81
SQ FT: 16,000
SALES (corp-wide): 2.87B Publicly Held
Web: www.adspipe.com
SIC: 3084 Plastics pipe
PA: Advanced Drainage Systems, Inc.
4640 Trueman Blvd
614 658-0050

### (P-6596)
### EXCALIBUR EXTRUSION INC
110 E Crowther Ave, Placentia (92870-5637)
PHONE.................................714 528-8834
EMP: 50
Web: www.viprubber.com
SIC: 3084 3089 Plastics pipe; Fittings for pipe, plastics

### (P-6597)
### HANCOR INC
140 Vineland Rd, Bakersfield (93307-9515)
PHONE.................................661 366-1520
James Tingle, Mgr
EMP: 52
SALES (corp-wide): 2.87B Publicly Held
Web: www.adspipe.com
SIC: 3084 5051 Plastics pipe; Pipe and tubing, steel
HQ: Hancor, Inc.
4640 Trueman Blvd
Hilliard OH 43026
614 658-0050

### (P-6598)
### J-M MANUFACTURING COMPANY INC (PA)
Also Called: JM Eagle
5200 W Century Blvd, Los Angeles (90045-5928)
PHONE.................................310 693-8200
Walter Wang, Ch
Shirley Wang, *
♦ EMP: 150 EST: 1982
SQ FT: 24,000
SALES (est): 304.63MM
SALES (corp-wide): 304.63MM Privately Held
Web: www.jmeagle.com
SIC: 3084 2821 3082 Plastics pipe; Polyvinyl chloride resins, PVC; Unsupported plastics profile shapes

### (P-6599)
### KAKUICHI AMERICA INC
23540 Telo Ave, Torrance (90505-4013)
PHONE.................................310 539-1590
Yasuo Ogami, CEO
Kenichi Tanaka, *
▲ EMP: 100 EST: 1973
SQ FT: 110,000
SALES (est): 10.25MM Privately Held
Web: www.pacificecho.com

# PRODUCTS & SERVICES SECTION

## 3086 - Plastics Foam Products (P-6621)

SIC: 3084 Plastics pipe
HQ: Kakuichi Co., Ltd.
1415, Midoricho, Tsuruga
Nagano NAG 380-0

**(P-6600)**
**PACIFIC PLASTICS INC**
111 S Berry St, Brea (92821-4827)
PHONE..................714 990-9050
Anayat Raminfar, *Pr*
Farhad Bahremand, *
Rahim Arian, *
John Ramin, *
Ata Ramin, *
▲ **EMP:** 71 **EST:** 1980
**SQ FT:** 32,000
**SALES (est):** 11.9MM **Privately Held**
Web: www.pacificplastics.us
SIC: 3084 Plastics pipe

**(P-6601)**
**PW EAGLE INC**
Also Called: JM Eagle
5200 W Century Blvd, Los Angeles (90045-5928)
PHONE..................800 621-4404
▼ **EMP:** 1087
SIC: 3084 Plastics pipe

**(P-6602)**
**SPEARS MANUFACTURING CO**
15860 Olden St, Rancho Cascades (91342-1241)
PHONE..................818 364-1611
**EMP:** 26
**SALES (corp-wide):** 1.37B **Privately Held**
Web: www.spearsmfg.net
SIC: 3084 Plastics pipe
PA: Spears Manufacturing Co.
15853 Olden St
818 364-1611

**(P-6603)**
**TRENCHLESS PIPE COMPANY INC**
3410 Bronze Ct, Shasta Lake (96019-9133)
PHONE..................530 275-9400
**EMP:** 20
Web: www.trenchlesspipecompany.com
SIC: 3084 Plastics pipe

**(P-6604)**
**US PIPE FABRICATION LLC**
Also Called: Water Works Manufacturing
3387 Plumas Arboga Rd, Marysville (95901)
P.O. Box 2480 (95901-0089)
PHONE..................530 742-5171
Tom Nascimento, *VP*
**EMP:** 33
Web: www.uspipe.com
SIC: 3084 3088 3494 Plastics pipe; Plastics plumbing fixtures; Valves and pipe fittings, nec
HQ: Us Pipe Fabrication, Llc
2 Chase Corp Dr Ste 200
Birmingham AL 35244

**(P-6605)**
**VALENCIA PIPE COMPANY**
Also Called: Home-Flex
28305 Livingston Ave, Valencia (91355-4164)
PHONE..................661 257-3923
Andrew Dervin, *CEO*
Curt Meyer, *
Peter Dervin, *
Uriel Sandoval, *
▲ **EMP:** 28 **EST:** 2007
**SALES (est):** 15.19MM **Privately Held**
Web: www.valenciapipe.com
SIC: 3084 5074 3479 3312 Plastics pipe; Pipes and fittings, plastic; Coating or wrapping steel pipe; Galvanized pipes, plates, sheets, etc.; iron and steel

## 3085 Plastics Bottles

**(P-6606)**
**ALTIUM PACKAGING LLC**
Mayfair Plastics
1500 E 223rd St, Carson (90745-4316)
PHONE..................310 952-8736
Larry Lindsey, *Mgr*
**EMP:** 86
**SALES (corp-wide):** 15.9B **Publicly Held**
Web: www.altiumpkg.com
SIC: 3085 2656 Plastics bottles; Sanitary food containers
HQ: Altium Packaging Llc
2500 Windy Ridge Pkwy Se # 1400
Atlanta GA 30339
678 742-4600

**(P-6607)**
**ALTIUM PACKAGING LLC**
1620 Gobel Way, Modesto (95358-5745)
PHONE..................209 531-9180
Michael Foley, *Prin*
**EMP:** 20
**SALES (corp-wide):** 15.9B **Publicly Held**
Web: www.altiumpkg.com
SIC: 3085 2821 3089 Plastics bottles; Polycarbonate resins; Plastics containers, except foam
HQ: Altium Packaging Llc
2500 Windy Ridge Pkwy Se # 1400
Atlanta GA 30339
678 742-4600

**(P-6608)**
**CLASSIC CONTAINERS INC**
1700 S Hellman Ave, Ontario (91761-7638)
PHONE..................909 930-3610
Manny G Hernandez Senior, *CEO*
Ernie Hernandez, *
Maria Hernandez, *
Manny Hernandez Junior, *Treas*
**EMP:** 280 **EST:** 1988
**SQ FT:** 60,000
**SALES (est):** 22.4MM **Privately Held**
Web: www.classiccontainers.com
SIC: 3085 3089 5085 Plastics bottles; Plastics containers, except foam; Industrial supplies

**(P-6609)**
**MUNCHKIN INC**
27334 San Bernardino Ave, Redlands (92374-5051)
PHONE..................818 893-5000
Steven Dunn, *Brnch Mgr*
**EMP:** 36
Web: www.munchkin.com
SIC: 3085 Plastics bottles
PA: Munchkin, Inc.
7835 Gloria Ave

**(P-6610)**
**MUNCHKIN INC (PA)**
Also Called: Curio Home Goods
7835 Gloria Ave, Van Nuys (91406-1822)
PHONE..................800 344-2229
Steven Dunn, *CEO*
Andrew Keimach, *
David Dunn, *
Gary Rolfes, *
Jeff Hale, *
◆ **EMP:** 123 **EST:** 1991
**SQ FT:** 63,000
**SALES (est):** 48.13MM **Privately Held**
Web: www.munchkin.com
SIC: 3085 3069 5999 Plastics bottles; Teething rings, rubber; Infant furnishings and equipment

**(P-6611)**
**NARAYAN CORPORATION**
Also Called: Plastic Processing Co
13432 Estrella Ave, Gardena (90248-1513)
PHONE..................310 719-7330
Harshad Desai, *Pr*
▲ **EMP:** 37 **EST:** 2002
**SALES (est):** 1.67MM **Privately Held**
Web: www.plasticprocessing.net
SIC: 3085 3089 Plastics bottles; Bottle caps, molded plastics

**(P-6612)**
**PLASCOR INC**
972 Columbia Ave, Riverside (92507-2140)
PHONE..................951 328-1010
David Harrigan, *Pr*
▼ **EMP:** 135 **EST:** 1993
**SQ FT:** 50,000
**SALES (est):** 8.73MM **Privately Held**
Web: www.plascorinc.net
SIC: 3085 Plastics bottles

**(P-6613)**
**PLAXICON HOLDING CORPORATION**
Also Called: Plaxicon Co
10660 Acacia St, Rancho Cucamonga (91730-5409)
PHONE..................909 944-6868
Bill Williams, *CEO*
**EMP:** 270 **EST:** 1983
**SQ FT:** 150,000
**SALES (est):** 1.99MM **Privately Held**
SIC: 3085 3089 Plastics bottles; Plastics containers, except foam
PA: Graham Packaging Company Europe Llc
700 Indian Springs Dr # 100

**(P-6614)**
**POLY-TAINER INC (PA)**
Also Called: Custom Molded Devices
450 W Los Angeles Ave, Simi Valley (93065-1646)
PHONE..................805 526-3424
TOLL FREE: 800
Julie Williams, *CEO*
Paul Strong, *Pr*
Stephanie Strong, *VP*
Tim Williams, *CFO*
▲ **EMP:** 120 **EST:** 1970
**SQ FT:** 95,000
**SALES (est):** 47.83MM
**SALES (corp-wide):** 47.83MM **Privately Held**
Web: www.polytainer.com
SIC: 3085 Plastics bottles

**(P-6615)**
**POLYCYCLE SOLUTIONS LLC**
4516 Azusa Canyon Rd, Irwindale (91706-2742)
PHONE..................626 856-2100
▲ **EMP:** 60
SIC: 3085 Plastics bottles

**(P-6616)**
**RING CONTAINER TECH LLC**
3643 Finch Rd, Modesto (95357-4143)
PHONE..................209 238-3426
Joel Mcdonald, *Mgr*
**EMP:** 55
**SALES (corp-wide):** 1.37B **Privately Held**
Web: www.ringcontainer.com
SIC: 3085 3411 Plastics bottles; Food containers, metal
HQ: Ring Container Technologies, Llc.
1 Industrial Park
Oakland TN 38060
800 280-7464

**(P-6617)**
**RING CONTAINER TECH LLC**
8275 Almeria Ave, Fontana (92335-3280)
PHONE..................909 350-8416
Fred Miller, *Brnch Mgr*
**EMP:** 56
**SQ FT:** 60,800
**SALES (corp-wide):** 1.37B **Privately Held**
Web: www.ringcontainer.com
SIC: 3085 3411 3089 Plastics bottles; Food containers, metal; Blow molded finished plastics products, nec
HQ: Ring Container Technologies, Llc.
1 Industrial Park
Oakland TN 38060
800 280-7464

## 3086 Plastics Foam Products

**(P-6618)**
**ABAD FOAM INC**
6560 Caballero Blvd, Buena Park (90620-1130)
PHONE..................714 994-2223
Cesar Chavez, *CEO*
▲ **EMP:** 50 **EST:** 1974
**SALES (est):** 10.19MM **Privately Held**
Web: www.ibscomfort.com
SIC: 3086 Plastics foam products

**(P-6619)**
**ALTIUM PACKAGING LP**
Also Called: A Division Continental Can Co
1217 E Saint Gertrude Pl, Santa Ana (92707-3029)
PHONE..................714 241-6640
Cesare Calabrese, *Brnch Mgr*
**EMP:** 37
**SALES (corp-wide):** 15.9B **Publicly Held**
Web: www.altiumpkg.com
SIC: 3086 3085 Plastics foam products; Plastics bottles
HQ: Altium Packaging Lp
3101 Towercreek Pkwy
Atlanta GA 30339
678 742-4600

**(P-6620)**
**AMERICAN POLY-FOAM COMPANY INC**
1455 Crocker Ave, Hayward (94544-7032)
P.O. Box 3307 (94540-3307)
PHONE..................510 786-3626
Steven T Alexakos, *Pr*
▲ **EMP:** 25 **EST:** 1978
**SALES (est):** 5.65MM
**SALES (corp-wide):** 495.02MM **Privately Held**
Web: www.americanpolyfoam.com
SIC: 3086 Packaging and shipping materials, foamed plastics
PA: Future Foam, Inc.
1610 Ave N
712 323-9122

**(P-6621)**
**AMFOAM INC (PA)**
Also Called: American Foam & Packaging
15110 S Broadway, Gardena (90248-1822)
PHONE..................310 327-4003

# 3086 - Plastics Foam Products (P-6622)

## PRODUCTS & SERVICES SECTION

Brian Leecing, *Pr*
Alex Gelbard, *
▲ **EMP:** 45 **EST:** 1993
**SQ FT:** 42,000
**SALES (est):** 1.6MM **Privately Held**
**Web:** www.amfoaminc.com
**SIC: 3086** 5199 Packaging and shipping materials, foamed plastics; Foam rubber

### (P-6622)
### ATLAS FOAM PRODUCTS
12836 Arroyo St, Sylmar (91342-5304)
**PHONE**.................818 837-3626
Sal Damji, *Pr*
Jeff Naples, *Pr*
Sandra Naples, *Sec*
**EMP:** 20 **EST:** 1987
**SQ FT:** 28,000
**SALES (est):** 2.41MM **Privately Held**
**Web:** www.atlasfoam.com
**SIC: 3086** Plastics foam products

### (P-6623)
### ATLAS ROOFING CORPORATION
2335 Roll Dr Ste 4121, San Diego (92154-7298)
**PHONE**.................626 334-5358
Edith Villegas, *Mgr*
**EMP:** 26
**Web:** www.achfoam.com
**SIC: 3086** Insulation or cushioning material, foamed plastics
**HQ:** Atlas Roofing Corporation
2100 Riveredge Pkwy
Atlanta GA 30328
800 388-6134

### (P-6624)
### BACK SUPPORT SYSTEMS INC
1064 N E St, San Bernardino (92410-3506)
P.O. Box 961 (92240)
**PHONE**.................760 329-1472
Jeffrey A Kalatsky, *Pr*
▲ **EMP:** 17 **EST:** 1989
**SQ FT:** 9,800
**SALES (est):** 2.49MM **Privately Held**
**Web:** www.backsupportsystems.com
**SIC: 3086** 5047 Plastics foam products; Therapy equipment

### (P-6625)
### CALIFORNIA PERFORMANCE PACKG
Also Called: Pacific Tech Products Ontario
33200 Lewis St, Union City (94587-2202)
**PHONE**.................909 390-4422
Randall Lake, *Pr*
**EMP:** 99 **EST:** 1999
**SALES (est):** 1.4MM
**SALES (corp-wide):** 33.99MM **Privately Held**
**SIC: 3086** Packaging and shipping materials, foamed plastics
**HQ:** Great American Industries Inc
300 Plaza Dr
Vestal NY 13850
607 729-9331

### (P-6626)
### CARPENTER CO
Also Called: Carpenter E R Co
7809 Lincoln Ave, Riverside (92504-4442)
P.O. Box 7788 (92513-7788)
**PHONE**.................951 354-7550
Jim Nanfeldt, *Mgr*
**EMP:** 45
**SALES (corp-wide):** 506.96MM **Privately Held**
**Web:** www.carpenter.com

**SIC: 3086** 2821 7389 5033 Insulation or cushioning material, foamed plastics; Plastics materials and resins; Furniture finishing; Insulation materials
**PA:** Carpenter Co.
5016 Monument Ave
804 359-0800

### (P-6627)
### CARPENTER CO
17100 S Harlan Rd, Lathrop (95330-9786)
P.O. Box 27205 (23261-7205)
**PHONE**.................209 982-4800
Stan Pauley, *Pr*
**EMP:** 85
**SQ FT:** 40,000
**SALES (corp-wide):** 506.96MM **Privately Held**
**Web:** www.carpenter.com
**SIC: 3086** 2273 Insulation or cushioning material, foamed plastics; Carpets and rugs
**PA:** Carpenter Co.
5016 Monument Ave
804 359-0800

### (P-6628)
### CLEAN CUT TECHNOLOGIES LLC
1145 N Ocean Cir, Anaheim (92806-1939)
**PHONE**.................714 864-3500
**EMP:** 100
**Web:** www.oliverhcp.com
**SIC: 3086** Packaging and shipping materials, foamed plastics

### (P-6629)
### DART CONTAINER CORP CALIFORNIA (PA)
Also Called: Dtx
150 S Maple Center, Corona (92880)
**PHONE**.................951 735-8115
Keith Clark, *CEO*
Sujith Chandran, *
▲ **EMP:** 300 **EST:** 1937
**SQ FT:** 50,000
**SALES (est):** 34.69MM
**SALES (corp-wide):** 34.69MM **Privately Held**
**SIC: 3086** Cups and plates, foamed plastics

### (P-6630)
### DART CONTAINER CORP CALIFORNIA
Also Called: Dart Container Corp Calif
1400 E Victor Rd, Lodi (95240)
**PHONE**.................209 333-8088
John Brice, *Mgr*
**EMP:** 55
**SALES (corp-wide):** 34.69MM **Privately Held**
**SIC: 3086** Cups and plates, foamed plastics
**PA:** Dart Container Corporation Of California
150 S Maple Center
951 735-8115

### (P-6631)
### DIAB HOLDINGS INC
830 Stewart Dr, Sunnyvale (94085-4513)
**PHONE**.................408 598-2241
Charles Previte, *VP*
**EMP:** 32
**SALES (corp-wide):** 2.85B **Privately Held**
**Web:** www.diabgroup.com
**SIC: 3086** Plastics foam products
**HQ:** Diab Holdings Inc.
220 E Danieldale Rd
Desoto TX 75115
972 228-7600

### (P-6632)
### EPE INDUSTRIES USA INC (HQ)
Also Called: Epe USA
17835 Newhope St Ste G, Fountain Valley (92708)
**PHONE**.................800 315-0336
Troy Merrell, *CEO*
Toshio Yanagi, *CFO*
**EMP:** 18 **EST:** 2010
**SALES (est):** 61.22MM **Privately Held**
**Web:** www.epeusa.com
**SIC: 3086** Ice chests or coolers (portable), foamed plastics
**PA:** Epe Corporation
2-57-5, Nishinippori

### (P-6633)
### FIVE STAR FOOD CONTAINERS INC
250 Eastgate Rd, Barstow (92311-3224)
**PHONE**.................626 437-6219
Larry Luc, *Pr*
▲ **EMP:** 60 **EST:** 2016
**SALES (est):** 2.32MM **Privately Held**
**SIC: 3086** Plastics foam products

### (P-6634)
### FOAM CONCEPTS INC
4729 E Wesley Dr, Anaheim (92807-1941)
**PHONE**.................714 693-1037
Stephen C Ross, *Owner*
▲ **EMP:** 20 **EST:** 1995
**SQ FT:** 9,000
**SALES (est):** 4.01MM **Privately Held**
**Web:** www.foamconcepts.net
**SIC: 3086** Packaging and shipping materials, foamed plastics

### (P-6635)
### FOAM FACTORY INC
17515 S Santa Fe Ave, Compton (90221-5400)
**PHONE**.................310 603-9808
Felipe Alcazar, *Pr*
▼ **EMP:** 45 **EST:** 1989
**SQ FT:** 40,000
**SALES (est):** 4.97MM **Privately Held**
**SIC: 3086** 3069 5199 5087 Insulation or cushioning material, foamed plastics; Foam rubber; Foams and rubber; Upholsterers' equipment and supplies

### (P-6636)
### FOAM MOLDERS AND SPECIALTIES (PA)
Also Called: Foam Specialties
11110 Business Cir, Cerritos (90703-5523)
**PHONE**.................562 924-7757
Daniel M Doke, *Pr*
Dan Doke, *
Rory Strammer, *
Roberta J Doke, *
Norman Himel, *
▲ **EMP:** 50 **EST:** 1973
**SQ FT:** 35,600
**SALES (est):** 15.38MM
**SALES (corp-wide):** 15.38MM **Privately Held**
**Web:** www.foammolders.com
**SIC: 3086** 3089 Plastics foam products; Thermoformed finished plastics products, nec

### (P-6637)
### FOAM MOLDERS AND SPECIALTIES
20004 State Rd, Cerritos (90703-6495)
**PHONE**.................562 924-7757
**EMP:** 50

**SALES (corp-wide):** 15.38MM **Privately Held**
**Web:** www.foammolders.com
**SIC: 3086** Packaging and shipping materials, foamed plastics
**PA:** Foam Molders And Specialties
11110 Business Cir
562 924-7757

### (P-6638)
### FOAM PLASTICS & RBR PDTS CORP
Also Called: Case Club
4765 E Bryson St, Anaheim (92807-1901)
**PHONE**.................714 779-0990
Kirk Plehn, *Pr*
**EMP:** 15 **EST:** 1990
**SQ FT:** 10,000
**SALES (est):** 2.66MM **Privately Held**
**Web:** www.caseclub.com
**SIC: 3086** 5099 Plastics foam products; Carrying cases

### (P-6639)
### FOAM-CRAFT INC
2441 Cypress Way, Fullerton (92831-5103)
**PHONE**.................714 459-9971
Bruce Schneider, *Pr*
Michael Blatt, *
▲ **EMP:** 165 **EST:** 1965
**SQ FT:** 110,000
**SALES (est):** 3.87MM
**SALES (corp-wide):** 495.02MM **Privately Held**
**SIC: 3086** Plastics foam products
**PA:** Future Foam, Inc.
1610 Ave N
712 323-9122

### (P-6640)
### FOAMEX LP
Also Called: Foamex
1400 E Victoria Ave, San Bernardino (92408-2924)
**PHONE**.................909 824-8981
Ron Paez, *Mgr*
**EMP:** 24
**Web:** www.fxi.com
**SIC: 3086** Carpet and rug cushions, foamed plastics
**PA:** Foamex L.P.
100 W Matsonford Rd # 5

### (P-6641)
### FUTURE FOAM INC
Also Called: Future Foam
2441 Cypress Way, Fullerton (92831-5103)
**PHONE**.................714 459-9971
**EMP:** 165
**SALES (corp-wide):** 495.02MM **Privately Held**
**Web:** www.futurefoam.com
**SIC: 3086** Plastics foam products
**PA:** Future Foam, Inc.
1610 Ave N
712 323-9122

### (P-6642)
### FUTURE FOAM INC
1050 E Grant Line Rd Ste 100, Tracy (95304-2841)
**PHONE**.................209 832-1886
Michael Walsh, *Brnch Mgr*
**EMP:** 15
**SALES (corp-wide):** 495.02MM **Privately Held**
**Web:** www.futurefoam.com
**SIC: 3086** Carpet and rug cushions, foamed plastics
**PA:** Future Foam, Inc.
1610 Ave N

# PRODUCTS & SERVICES SECTION

## 3086 - Plastics Foam Products (P-6663)

712 323-9122

**(P-6643)**
**FUTURE FOAM INC**
2451 Cypress Way, Fullerton (92831-5103)
PHONE..................................714 871-2344
Randall Lake, *Mgr*
**EMP:** 30
**SALES (corp-wide):** 495.02MM **Privately Held**
Web: www.futurefoam.com
**SIC: 3086** Insulation or cushioning material, foamed plastics
PA: Future Foam, Inc.
1610 Ave N
712 323-9122

**(P-6644)**
**GLORIANN FARMS INC**
11104 W Tracy Blvd, Tracy (95304-9434)
P.O. Box 571 (95378-0571)
PHONE..................................209 221-7121
Mark Bacchetti, *Brnch Mgr*
**EMP:** 203
**SALES (corp-wide):** 18.53MM **Privately Held**
Web: www.gloriannfarms.com
**SIC: 3086** Plastics foam products
PA: Gloriann Farms, Inc.
3590 W Lehman Rd
209 834-0010

**(P-6645)**
**GREEN RUBBER-KENNEDY AG LP (PA)**
1310 Dayton St, Salinas (93901-4416)
P.O. Box 7488 (93962-7488)
PHONE..................................831 753-6100
John H Green, *Pt*
Patricia Green, *Pt*
Mark D Kennedy, *Pt*
John T Green, *Pt*
◆ **EMP:** 40 **EST:** 1990
**SQ FT:** 13,500
**SALES (est):** 26.18MM **Privately Held**
Web: www.greenrubber.com
**SIC: 3086** 3535 5083 5085 Plastics foam products; Belt conveyor systems, general industrial use; Agricultural machinery and equipment; Industrial supplies

**(P-6646)**
**HUHTAMAKI INC**
4209 Noakes St, Commerce (90023-4024)
PHONE..................................323 269-0151
Mark Pettigrew, *Brnch Mgr*
**EMP:** 110
**SALES (corp-wide):** 4.53B **Privately Held**
Web: www.huhtamaki.com
**SIC: 3086** 3089 2657 2656 Cups and plates, foamed plastics; Plastics containers, except foam; Folding paperboard boxes; Sanitary food containers
HQ: Huhtamaki, Inc.
9201 Packaging Dr
De Soto KS 66018
913 583-3025

**(P-6647)**
**MARKO FOAM PRODUCTS INC (PA)**
Also Called: Marko Foam Products
17592 Metzler Ln, Huntington Beach (92647-6241)
PHONE..................................949 417-3307
Donald J Peterson, *Ch Bd*
Tyson Peterson, *
▲ **EMP:** 30 **EST:** 1962
**SQ FT:** 114,000
**SALES (est):** 22.66MM

**SALES (corp-wide):** 22.66MM **Privately Held**
Web: www.markofoam.com
**SIC: 3086** 5999 Packaging and shipping materials, foamed plastics; Packaging materials: boxes, padding, etc.

**(P-6648)**
**MONSTER CITY STUDIOS**
411 S West Ave, Fresno (93706-1320)
PHONE..................................559 498-0540
Dennis Keiser, *Ch Bd*
Randal Keiser, *V Ch Bd*
Kathy Keiser, *Sec*
Gyl Keiser, *Dir*
**EMP:** 22 **EST:** 2011
**SALES (est):** 2.87MM **Privately Held**
Web: www.monstercitystudios.com
**SIC: 3086** Plastics foam products

**(P-6649)**
**MULTI-LINK INTERNATIONAL CORP**
933 Montecito Dr, San Gabriel (91776-2336)
PHONE..................................562 941-5380
Sai Hung Chan, *Pr*
◆ **EMP:** 20 **EST:** 1993
**SALES (est):** 2.36MM **Privately Held**
Web: www.multilinkintl.com
**SIC: 3086** Plastics foam products

**(P-6650)**
**NORTH AMRCN FOAM PPR CNVERTERS**
11835 Wicks St, Sun Valley (91352-1906)
PHONE..................................818 255-3383
Bijan Toobian, *CEO*
Haydeh Toobian, *
▲ **EMP:** 25 **EST:** 1998
**SQ FT:** 30,000
**SALES (est):** 4.87MM **Privately Held**
**SIC: 3086** 2672 5087 Plastics foam products; Paper; coated and laminated, nec; Laundry equipment and supplies

**(P-6651)**
**PLASTIC SERVICES AND PRODUCTS**
Also Called: General Plastics
12243 Branford St, Sun Valley (91352-1010)
P.O. Box 1367 (91353-1367)
PHONE..................................818 896-1101
◆ **EMP:** 3000
**SIC: 3086** 3674 2865 2816 Plastics foam products; Semiconductors and related devices; Food dyes or colors, synthetic; Color pigments

**(P-6652)**
**PMC INC**
345 Saratoga Ave, Santa Clara (95050-7002)
PHONE..................................562 905-3101
**EMP:** 123
**SALES (corp-wide):** 1.71B **Privately Held**
Web: www.pmcglobalinc.com
**SIC: 3086** Plastics foam products
HQ: Pmc, Inc.
12243 Branford St
Sun Valley CA 91352
818 896-1101

**(P-6653)**
**PMC GLOBAL INC (PA)**
12243 Branford St, Sun Valley (91352-1010)
PHONE..................................818 896-1101

Philip Kamins, *CEO*
Gary Kamins, *
Thian Cheong, *
Steven Cohen, *
◆ **EMP:** 75 **EST:** 1996
**SALES (est):** 1.71B
**SALES (corp-wide):** 1.71B **Privately Held**
Web: www.pmcglobalinc.com
**SIC: 3086** 3674 2865 2816 Plastics foam products; Semiconductors and related devices; Food dyes or colors, synthetic; Color pigments

**(P-6654)**
**PMC LEADERS IN CHEMICALS INC (HQ)**
12243 Branford St, Sun Valley (91352-1010)
PHONE..................................818 896-1101
Gary Kamins, *Pr*
**EMP:** 200 **EST:** 1992
**SQ FT:** 180,000
**SALES (est):** 95.64MM
**SALES (corp-wide):** 1.71B **Privately Held**
Web: www.pmcglobalinc.com
**SIC: 3086** 5169 Plastics foam products; Chemicals and allied products, nec
PA: Pmc Global, Inc.
12243 Branford St
818 896-1101

**(P-6655)**
**POMONA QUALITY FOAM LLC**
1279 Philadelphia St, Pomona (91766-5536)
PHONE..................................909 628-7844
**EMP:** 67 **EST:** 2015
**SQ FT:** 70,000
**SALES (est):** 5.77MM **Privately Held**
Web: www.pomonaqualityfoam.com
**SIC: 3086** Plastics foam products

**(P-6656)**
**PREMIER PACKAGING LLC**
10700 Business Dr Ste 100, Fontana (92337-8201)
PHONE..................................909 749-5123
**EMP:** 38
Web: www.prempack.com
**SIC: 3086** 5085 5113 Packaging and shipping materials, foamed plastics; Packing, industrial; Corrugated and solid fiber boxes
PA: Premier Packaging, Llc
3900 Produce Rd

**(P-6657)**
**PREZERO US PACKAGING LLC**
3155 S 5th Ave, Oroville (95965-5858)
PHONE..................................800 767-5278
**EMP:** 68 **EST:** 2021
**SALES (est):** 5.02MM
**SALES (corp-wide):** 3.49B **Privately Held**
Web: www.prezero.us
**SIC: 3086** Packaging and shipping materials, foamed plastics
HQ: Prezero Us, Inc.
4388 Serrano Dr
Jurupa Valley CA 91752
858 677-0884

**(P-6658)**
**QUALITY FOAM PACKAGING INC**
31855 Corydon St, Lake Elsinore (92530-8501)
PHONE..................................951 245-4429
Noel A Castellon, *Pr*
Ruth Castellon, *Sec*
James Barrett, *VP*

▲ **EMP:** 25 **EST:** 1973
**SQ FT:** 56,000
**SALES (est):** 16.08MM **Privately Held**
Web: www.qualityfoam.com
**SIC: 3086** Packaging and shipping materials, foamed plastics

**(P-6659)**
**SEALED AIR CORPORATION**
Packaging Products Div
1835 W Almond Ave, Madera (93637-5209)
PHONE..................................559 675-0152
Arnold Sierra, *Mgr*
**EMP:** 237
**SQ FT:** 118,000
**SALES (corp-wide):** 5.49B **Publicly Held**
Web: www.sealedair.com
**SIC: 3086** Packaging and shipping materials, foamed plastics
PA: Sealed Air Corporation
2415 Cascade Pointe Blvd
980 221-3235

**(P-6660)**
**SEALED AIR CORPORATION**
Packaging Products Div
19440 Arenth Ave, City Of Industry (91748-1424)
PHONE..................................909 594-1791
**EMP:** 126
**SALES (corp-wide):** 5.49B **Publicly Held**
Web: www.sealedair.com
**SIC: 3086** Packaging and shipping materials, foamed plastics
PA: Sealed Air Corporation
2415 Cascade Pointe Blvd
980 221-3235

**(P-6661)**
**SEALED AIR CORPORATION**
Also Called: Special Products Group
2311 Boswell Rd Ste 8, Chula Vista (91914-3512)
PHONE..................................619 421-9003
David Rader, *Mgr*
**EMP:** 34
**SALES (corp-wide):** 5.49B **Publicly Held**
Web: www.sealedair.com
**SIC: 3086** Packaging and shipping materials, foamed plastics
PA: Sealed Air Corporation
2415 Cascade Pointe Blvd
980 221-3235

**(P-6662)**
**SLEEPCOMP WEST LLC**
Also Called: Latexco West
10006 Santa Fe Springs Rd, Santa Fe Springs (90670-2922)
PHONE..................................562 946-3222
Roger Coffey, *Pr*
▲ **EMP:** 40 **EST:** 2002
**SQ FT:** 53,000
**SALES (est):** 2.04MM **Privately Held**
Web: www.novaya-comfort.com
**SIC: 3086** Plastics foam products

**(P-6663)**
**SPECIALTY ENTERPRISES CO**
Also Called: Seco Industries
6858 E Acco St, Commerce (90040-1902)
PHONE..................................323 726-9721
Charles De Heras, *Pr*
▲ **EMP:** 100 **EST:** 1983
**SQ FT:** 60,000
**SALES (est):** 23.69MM **Privately Held**
Web: www.specialtyenterprises.com
**SIC: 3086** 3565 Plastics foam products; Packaging machinery
HQ: Cnh Industrial America Llc
711 Jorie Blvd

# 3086 - Plastics Foam Products (P-6664)

Oak Brook IL 60523
630 887-2233

**(P-6664)**
**SPORTS VENUE PADDING INC**
Also Called: Artistic Coverings
14135 Artesia Blvd, Cerritos (90703-7025)
PHONE.....................562 404-9343
Troy Robinson, *CEO*
Michelle Robinson, *
Ken Robinson, *
▲ **EMP:** 30 **EST:** 2000
**SALES (est):** 5.1MM **Privately Held**
Web: www.sportsvenuepadding.com
**SIC: 3086** 3949 2759 7941 Padding, foamed plastics; Track and field athletic equipment; Commercial printing, nec; Sports field or stadium operator, promoting sports events

**(P-6665)**
**STYROTEK INC**
345 Road 176, Delano (93215-9471)
P.O. Box 2870 (93303-2870)
PHONE.....................661 725-4957
Martin Caratan, *Pr*
Dale Arthur, *
▲ **EMP:** 110 **EST:** 1973
**SQ FT:** 18,500
**SALES (est):** 8.7MM **Privately Held**
Web: www.styrotek.com
**SIC: 3086** Packaging and shipping materials, foamed plastics

**(P-6666)**
**TEMPO PLASTIC CO**
1227 N Miller Park Ct, Visalia (93291-9343)
P.O. Box 44 (93443-0044)
PHONE.....................559 651-7711
Douglas B Rogers, *Pr*
▲ **EMP:** 15 **EST:** 1960
**SQ FT:** 26,000
**SALES (est):** 2.23MM **Privately Held**
Web: www.tempogloss.com
**SIC: 3086** Packaging and shipping materials, foamed plastics

**(P-6667)**
**UFP TECHNOLOGIES INC**
20211 S Susana Rd, Compton (90221-5725)
PHONE.....................714 662-0277
Richard Tunila, *Brnch Mgr*
**EMP:** 50
**SALES (corp-wide):** 400.07MM **Publicly Held**
Web: www.ufpt.com
**SIC: 3086** Packaging and shipping materials, foamed plastics
**PA:** Ufp Technologies, Inc.
100 Hale St
978 352-2200

**(P-6668)**
**URETHANE MASTERS INC**
455 54th St Ste 102, San Diego (92114-2220)
PHONE.....................651 829-1032
Gayle Mcenroe, *Managing Member*
**EMP:** 15 **EST:** 2019
**SALES (est):** 2.85MM **Privately Held**
Web: www.urethanemasters.com
**SIC: 3086** Plastics foam products

**(P-6669)**
**VEFO INC**
3202 Factory Dr, Pomona (91768-3903)
PHONE.....................909 598-3856
Roger Voss, *Pr*
Pat Voss, *Sec*
**EMP:** 20 **EST:** 1970
**SQ FT:** 11,000
**SALES (est):** 3.37MM **Privately Held**
Web: www.vefoinc.com
**SIC: 3086** Plastics foam products

**(P-6670)**
**WALTER N COFFMAN INC**
5180 Naranja St, San Diego (92114-3515)
PHONE.....................619 266-2642
Walter N Coffman, *CEO*
**EMP:** 70 **EST:** 2000
**SALES (est):** 5.38MM **Privately Held**
Web: www.wncfoam.com
**SIC: 3086** Cups and plates, foamed plastics

**(P-6671)**
**WARDLEY INDUSTRIAL INC**
907 Stokes Ave, Stockton (95210)
P.O. Box 55323 (95205-8823)
PHONE.....................209 932-1088
Jackey Wong, *Pr*
Margaret Wong, *
Ambrose Tam, *
▲ **EMP:** 43 **EST:** 1992
**SQ FT:** 165,000
**SALES (est):** 9.19MM **Privately Held**
Web: www.wardleyfilm.com
**SIC: 3086** 5084 Packaging and shipping materials, foamed plastics; Industrial machinery and equipment

## 3087 Custom Compound Purchased Resins

**(P-6672)**
**AUBIN INDUSTRIES INC**
23833 S Chrisman Rd, Tracy (95304-8003)
PHONE.....................800 324-0051
Philip Aubin, *Pr*
Linda Aubin, *Sec*
**EMP:** 15 **EST:** 1994
**SQ FT:** 13,000
**SALES (est):** 4.58MM **Privately Held**
Web: www.aubinindustries.com
**SIC: 3087** Custom compound purchased resins

## 3088 Plastics Plumbing Fixtures

**(P-6673)**
**AQUATIC CO**
1700 N Delilah St, Corona (92879-1893)
PHONE.....................714 993-1220
Gary Anderson, *Pr*
**EMP:** 214
**SALES (corp-wide):** 594.73MM **Privately Held**
Web: www.aquaticbath.com
**SIC: 3088** Plastics plumbing fixtures
**HQ:** Aquatic Co.
665 Industrial Rd
Savannah TN 38372

**(P-6674)**
**AQUATIC CO**
Lasco Bathware
8101 E Kaiser Blvd Ste 200, Anaheim (92808-2287)
PHONE.....................714 993-1220
Scott Hartman, *Mgr*
**EMP:** 110
**SQ FT:** 5,000
**SALES (corp-wide):** 594.73MM **Privately Held**
Web: www.aquaticbath.com

**SIC: 3088** 1711 5211 Shower stalls, fiberglass and plastics; Plumbing, heating, air-conditioning; Bathroom fixtures, equipment and supplies
**HQ:** Aquatic Co.
665 Industrial Rd
Savannah TN 38372

**(P-6675)**
**EDGE THEORY LABS INC**
Also Called: Edge Theory Labs
5825 Avenida Encinas Ste 109, Carlsbad (92008-4401)
PHONE.....................858 358-5386
Joshua Church, *CEO*
Robert Church, *CFO*
**EMP:** 15 **EST:** 2021
**SALES (est):** 3.21MM **Privately Held**
**SIC: 3088** Hot tubs, plastics or fiberglass

**(P-6676)**
**ELMCO & ASSOC (HQ)**
11225 Trade Center Dr Ste 100, Rancho Cordova (95742-6248)
PHONE.....................916 383-0110
Kirk Kleinen, *VP*
**EMP:** 17 **EST:** 2006
**SALES (est):** 6.17MM
**SALES (corp-wide):** 92.66MM **Privately Held**
Web: www.elmcoassoc.com
**SIC: 3088** Plastics plumbing fixtures
**PA:** Morris Group International
15125 Proctor Ave
626 336-4561

**(P-6677)**
**EUROTECH SHOWERS INC**
Also Called: Eurotech Luxury Shower Doors
23552 Commerce Center Dr Ste B, Laguna Hills (92653-1514)
PHONE.....................949 716-4099
James Simmons, *Pr*
**EMP:** 25 **EST:** 2006
**SQ FT:** 2,800
**SALES (est):** 2.21MM **Privately Held**
Web: www.eurotechshowers.com
**SIC: 3088** Shower stalls, fiberglass and plastics

**(P-6678)**
**FIBER CARE BATHS INC**
9832 Yucca Rd Ste A, Adelanto (92301-2471)
PHONE.....................760 246-0019
Harry R Kilpatrick, *CEO*
Kaye Allen, *
**EMP:** 275 **EST:** 1996
**SQ FT:** 6,000
**SALES (est):** 48.99MM **Privately Held**
Web: www.fibercarebaths.com
**SIC: 3088** Shower stalls, fiberglass and plastics

**(P-6679)**
**FLORES FAMILY DEVELOPMENT (HQ)**
2851 Falcon Dr, Madera (93637-9287)
PHONE.....................559 661-4171
Rick Stonecipher, *CEO*
▲ **EMP:** 37 **EST:** 1947
**SQ FT:** 190,000
**SALES (est):** 9.52MM
**SALES (corp-wide):** 594.73MM **Privately Held**
Web: www.florestone.com
**SIC: 3088** Shower stalls, fiberglass and plastics
**PA:** American Bath Group, Llc
500 E Border St
731 925-7656

**(P-6680)**
**JACUZZI PRODUCTS CO (DH)**
13925 City Center Dr Ste 200, Chino Hills (91709-5438)
PHONE.....................909 606-1416
Thomas D Koos, *CEO*
Philip Weeks, *
▲ **EMP:** 120 **EST:** 1959
**SALES (est):** 65.57MM
**SALES (corp-wide):** 440.01K **Privately Held**
Web: www.jacuzzi.com
**SIC: 3088** Tubs (bath, shower, and laundry), plastics
**HQ:** Jacuzzi Inc.
17872 Gllette Ave Ste 300
Irvine CA 92614
909 606-7733

**(P-6681)**
**JACUZZI PRODUCTS CO**
14525 Monte Vista Ave, Chino (91710-5721)
PHONE.....................909 548-7732
Jim Barry, *Mgr*
**EMP:** 340
**SALES (corp-wide):** 440.01K **Privately Held**
Web: www.jacuzzi.com
**SIC: 3088** 5091 Tubs (bath, shower, and laundry), plastics; Fitness equipment and supplies
**HQ:** Jacuzzi Products Co.
13925 City Center Dr # 200
Chino Hills CA 91709
909 606-1416

**(P-6682)**
**KING BROS ENTERPRISES LLC**
29101 The Old Rd, Valencia (91355-1014)
P.O. Box 9203 (91392-9203)
PHONE.....................661 257-3262
▲ **EMP:** 125
**SIC: 3088** 5169 Plastics plumbing fixtures; Synthetic resins, rubber, and plastic materials

**(P-6683)**
**LE ELEGANT BATH INC**
Also Called: American Bath Factory
13405 Estelle St, Corona (92879-1877)
P.O. Box 127 (92878-0127)
PHONE.....................951 734-0238
Richard Wheeler, *Pr*
Debbie Wheeler, *
◆ **EMP:** 120 **EST:** 1984
**SQ FT:** 18,000
**SALES (est):** 9.33MM **Privately Held**
Web: www.americanbathfactory.com
**SIC: 3088** Tubs (bath, shower, and laundry), plastics

**(P-6684)**
**PEGGY S LANE INC**
Also Called: C M P
2701 Merced St, San Leandro (94577-5601)
PHONE.....................510 483-1202
**TOLL FREE:** 800
Matt Clementz, *Pr*
**EMP:** 100 **EST:** 1979
**SQ FT:** 35,000
**SALES (est):** 9.03MM **Privately Held**
Web: www.marbleproducts.com

# PRODUCTS & SERVICES SECTION

## 3089 - Plastics Products, Nec (P-6704)

SIC: 3088 3281 1752 1743 Tubs (bath, shower, and laundry), plastics; Cut stone and stone products; Floor laying and floor work, nec; Terrazzo, tile, marble and mosaic work

### (P-6685)
### REBOOT LABS LLC
Also Called: Plunge
1721 Aviation Blvd Ste 100, Lincoln (95648-9676)
PHONE.....................916 926-1716
Michael Garrett, CEO
Eric Clifford, *
Rey Luna, *
EMP: 54 EST: 2020
SALES (est): 17.22MM **Privately Held**
Web: www.plunge.com
SIC: 3088 Plastics plumbing fixtures

### (P-6686)
### SMITHS ACTION PLASTICS INC (PA)
Also Called: Action Plastics
645 S Santa Fe St, Santa Ana (92705-4143)
PHONE.....................714 836-4141
James A Smith, Pr
EMP: 15 EST: 1975
SQ FT: 5,000
SALES (est): 3.39MM
SALES (corp-wide): 3.39MM **Privately Held**
Web: www.action-plastics.com
SIC: 3088 5063 3089 Plastics plumbing fixtures; Electrical fittings and construction materials; Plastics processing

### (P-6687)
### VANTAGE ASSOCIATES INC
Glassform
1565 Macarthur Blvd, Costa Mesa (92626-1407)
PHONE.....................800 995-8322
Paul Roy, CEO
EMP: 25
SALES (corp-wide): 24.86MM **Privately Held**
Web: www.vantageassoc.com
SIC: 3088 2519 Plastics plumbing fixtures; Fiberglass and plastic furniture
PA: Vantage Associates Inc.
1565 Macarthur Blvd
619 477-6940

### (P-6688)
### WATKINS MANUFACTURING CORP
1325 Hot Springs Way, Vista (92081-8360)
PHONE.....................760 598-6464
EMP: 289
SALES (corp-wide): 7.97B **Publicly Held**
Web: www.hotspring.com
SIC: 3088 Hot tubs, plastics or fiberglass
HQ: Watkins Manufacturing Corporation
1280 Park Center Dr
Vista CA 92081
760 598-6464

## 3089 Plastics Products, Nec

### (P-6689)
### 10 DAY PARTS INC
Also Called: Westfall Technik
20109 Paseo Del Prado, Walnut (91789-2665)
PHONE.....................951 279-4810
Brian Laibach, Dir Opers
EMP: 35 EST: 2018
SALES (est): 9.93MM
SALES (corp-wide): 500.49MM **Privately Held**
Web: www.westfalltechnik.com
SIC: 3089 Injection molding of plastics
PA: Westfall Technik, Llc
9280 S Kyrene Rd
702 659-9898

### (P-6690)
### 3D CAM INC
Also Called: 3 D CAM
9801 Variel Ave, Chatsworth (91311-4317)
PHONE.....................818 773-8777
Gary Vassighi, CEO
EMP: 21 EST: 1990
SQ FT: 16,000
SALES (est): 2.61MM **Privately Held**
Web: www.3d-cam.com
SIC: 3089 8711 3369 3544 Injection molded finished plastics products, nec; Machine tool design; Nonferrous foundries, nec; Special dies, tools, jigs, and fixtures

### (P-6691)
### A & S MOLD AND DIE CORP
9705 Eton Ave, Chatsworth (91311-4306)
PHONE.....................818 341-5393
Arno Adlhoch, CEO
Karen Adlhoch, *
▲ EMP: 90 EST: 1969
SQ FT: 35,000
SALES (est): 4.49MM **Privately Held**
Web: www.aandsmold.com
SIC: 3089 3544 Injection molding of plastics; Special dies, tools, jigs, and fixtures

### (P-6692)
### A&A GLOBAL IMPORTS LLC (PA)
Also Called: A&A Fulfillment Center
1801 E 41st St, Vernon (90058-1533)
PHONE.....................888 315-2453
David Aryan, Pr
Brian Anowns, *
James Bunting, *
Adam Wolf, *
▲ EMP: 59 EST: 2011
SALES (est): 9.76MM
SALES (corp-wide): 9.76MM **Privately Held**
Web: www.aaglobalimports.com
SIC: 3089 3999 Injection molded finished plastics products, nec

### (P-6693)
### ACE COMPOSITES INC
Also Called: Custom Cmpstes Fbrgls Fbrction
1394 Sky Harbor Dr, Olivehurst (95961-7416)
P.O. Box 59 (95961-0059)
PHONE.....................530 743-1885
Todd Hambrook, Pr
Noe Lopez, *
John Pimentel, *
Mark Phelps, *
EMP: 35 EST: 2004
SQ FT: 40,000
SALES (est): 4.47MM **Privately Held**
Web: www.acecomposites.net
SIC: 3089 Plastics and fiberglass tanks

### (P-6694)
### ACORN-GENCON PLASTICS LLC
13818 Oaks Ave, Chino (91710-7008)
PHONE.....................909 591-8461
Donald E Morris, Managing Member
▲ EMP: 68 EST: 2001
SQ FT: 94,000
SALES (est): 4.3MM
SALES (corp-wide): 99.75MM **Privately Held**
Web: www.acorn-gencon.com
SIC: 3089 3088 3821 3082 Injection molded finished plastics products, nec; Plastics plumbing fixtures; Laboratory apparatus and furniture; Unsupported plastics profile shapes
HQ: Acorn Plastics, Inc.
13818 Oaks Ave
Chino CA 91710
909 591-8461

### (P-6695)
### ACUANTIA INC
Also Called: Tank Depot
13375 11th Ave, Hanford (93230-9591)
PHONE.....................559 648-8235
EMP: 24
Web: www.plastic-mart.com
SIC: 3089 Septic tanks, plastics
HQ: Acuantia Inc
1121 Riverside Dr
Fort Worth TX 76111

### (P-6696)
### ADVANCED CMPSITE PDTS TECH INC
Also Called: Acpt
15602 Chemical Ln, Huntington Beach (92649-1507)
PHONE.....................714 895-5544
James C Leslie Ii, Pr
EMP: 45 EST: 1984
SQ FT: 25,300
SALES (est): 8.77MM **Privately Held**
Web: www.acpt.com
SIC: 3089 8748 Hardware, plastics; Business consulting, nec

### (P-6697)
### ADVANCED ENGRG MLDING TECH INC
6510 Box Springs Blvd Ste B, Riverside (92507-0740)
P.O. Box 5620 (92517-5620)
PHONE.....................888 264-0392
Donald Furness, Pr
Helen Furness, VP
▲ EMP: 20 EST: 1968
SQ FT: 12,000
SALES (est): 2.9MM **Privately Held**
Web: www.aemt.com
SIC: 3089 Molding primary plastics

### (P-6698)
### ADVANCED MATERIALS INC (HQ)
20211 S Susana Rd, Compton (90221-5725)
PHONE.....................310 537-5444
Steve Scott, Pr
◆ EMP: 29 EST: 1959
SQ FT: 56,000
SALES (est): 5.09MM
SALES (corp-wide): 400.07MM **Publicly Held**
SIC: 3089 Injection molding of plastics
PA: Ufp Technologies, Inc.
100 Hale St
978 352-2200

### (P-6699)
### ADVANCED POLYMER TECHNOLOGIES LLC
3837 Imperial Way, Stockton (95215-9691)
PHONE.....................209 464-2701
◆ EMP: 22
Web: www.mcam.com
SIC: 3089 Injection molding of plastics

### (P-6700)
### AJAX - UNTD PTTRNS & MOLDS INC
Also Called: Ajax Custom Manufacturing
34585 7th St, Union City (94587-3673)
PHONE.....................510 476-8000
Dana Waldman, CEO
▲ EMP: 140 EST: 1945
SQ FT: 85,000
SALES (est): 4.26MM
SALES (corp-wide): 811.12MM **Publicly Held**
SIC: 3089 3599 3543 Plastics processing; Machine shop, jobbing and repair; Foundry patternmaking
PA: Ichor Holdings, Ltd.
3185 Laurelview Ct
510 897-5200

### (P-6701)
### AKRA PLASTIC PRODUCTS INC
1504 E Cedar St, Ontario (91761-5761)
PHONE.....................909 930-1999
Alexander Semeczko, CEO
R Wayne Callaway, *
Bentley Callaway, *
Alex Semeczko, *
EMP: 37 EST: 1972
SQ FT: 36,000
SALES (est): 7.82MM **Privately Held**
Web: www.akraplastics.com
SIC: 3089 2821 2542 5063 Plastics processing; Plastics materials and resins; Office and store showcases and display fixtures; Lighting fixtures, commercial and industrial

### (P-6702)
### ALLEN MOLD INC
1100 W Katella Ave Ste N, Orange (92867-3515)
PHONE.....................714 538-6517
Clayton Allen, Pr
EMP: 18 EST: 1997
SQ FT: 5,800
SALES (est): 2.46MM **Privately Held**
Web: www.allenmold.com
SIC: 3089 Injection molding of plastics

### (P-6703)
### ALLSTATE PLASTICS LLC
1763 Sabre St, Hayward (94545-1015)
PHONE.....................510 783-9600
Angela Leung, Managing Member
◆ EMP: 17 EST: 2007
SQ FT: 26,538
SALES (est): 3.42MM **Privately Held**
Web: www.allstate-plastics.com
SIC: 3089 Injection molding of plastics

### (P-6704)
### ALLTEC INTEGRATED MFG INC
Also Called: New Age Enclosures
2240 S Thornburg St, Santa Maria (93455-1248)
PHONE.....................805 595-3500
Randall Dennis, CEO
◆ EMP: 40 EST: 2002
SQ FT: 13,500
SALES (est): 9.89MM **Privately Held**
Web: www.alltecmfg.com
SIC: 3089 2821 Injection molding of plastics; Plastics materials and resins

## 3089 - Plastics Products, Nec (P-6705)

**(P-6705)**
**ALPHAGEM BIO INC**
4201 Business Center Dr, Fremont (94538-6357)
PHONE..................510 999-1153
Dale Taunk, *CEO*
▲ EMP: 30 EST: 2012
SALES (est): 3.84MM **Privately Held**
Web: www.alphagembio.com
SIC: 3089 Injection molding of plastics

**(P-6706)**
**ALTIUM HOLDINGS LLC**
Also Called: California Plastics
12165 Madera Way, Riverside (92503-4849)
PHONE..................951 340-9390
Steve Thompson, *Mgr*
EMP: 1183
SALES (corp-wide): 77.81MM **Privately Held**
Web: www.altiumpkg.com
SIC: 3089 Plastics containers, except foam
PA: Altium Holdings Llc
   2500 Wndy Rdge Pkwy Ste 1
   678 742-4600

**(P-6707)**
**ALTIUM PACKAGING**
Also Called: ALTIUM PACKAGING
4516 Azusa Canyon Rd, Irwindale (91706-2742)
PHONE..................626 856-2100
EMP: 60
SALES (corp-wide): 15.9B **Publicly Held**
Web: www.altiumpkg.com
SIC: 3089 Plastics containers, except foam
HQ: Altium Packaging Lp
   2500 Windy Ridge Pkwy Se # 1400
   Atlanta GA 30339
   678 742-4600

**(P-6708)**
**ALTIUM PACKAGING LLC**
Also Called: Reid Plastics Customer Svcs
1070 Samuelson St, City Of Industry (91748-1219)
PHONE..................888 425-7343
Fred Braham, *Prin*
EMP: 72
SALES (corp-wide): 15.9B **Publicly Held**
Web: www.altiumpkg.com
SIC: 3089 3085 Plastics containers, except foam; Plastics bottles
HQ: Altium Packaging Llc
   2500 Windy Ridge Pkwy Se # 1400
   Atlanta GA 30339
   678 742-4600

**(P-6709)**
**ALTIUM PACKAGING LLC**
Also Called: Stewart/Walker Company
75 W Valpico Rd, Tracy (95376-9129)
PHONE..................209 820-1700
Fred Branham, *Mgr*
EMP: 74
SALES (corp-wide): 15.9B **Publicly Held**
Web: www.tracyplasticpackaging.com
SIC: 3089 3085 Pallets, plastics; Plastics bottles
HQ: Altium Packaging Llc
   2500 Windy Ridge Pkwy Se # 1400
   Atlanta GA 30339
   678 742-4600

**(P-6710)**
**ALTIUM PACKAGING LP**
Envision Plastics
14312 Central Ave, Chino (91710-5752)
PHONE..................909 590-7334
EMP: 50
SALES (corp-wide): 15.9B **Publicly Held**
Web: www.altiumpkg.com
SIC: 3089 Plastics containers, except foam
HQ: Altium Packaging Lp
   3101 Towercreek Pkwy
   Atlanta GA 30339
   678 742-4600

**(P-6711)**
**AMA PLASTICS**
1100 Citrus St, Riverside (92507-1731)
PHONE..................951 734-5600
Mark Atchinson, *CEO*
Gary Atchinson, *
◆ EMP: 393 EST: 1971
SQ FT: 92,000
SALES (est): 49.55MM
SALES (corp-wide): 500.49MM **Privately Held**
Web: www.westfalltechnik.com
SIC: 3089 3544 Molding primary plastics; Forms (molds), for foundry and plastics working machinery
PA: Westfall Technik, Llc
   9280 S Kyrene Rd
   702 659-9898

**(P-6712)**
**AMERICAN DESIGN INC**
1672 Industrial Blvd, Chula Vista (91911-3920)
PHONE..................619 429-1995
Bruce R Jamieson, *Pr*
Catherine Jamieson, *Sec*
EMP: 16 EST: 1976
SQ FT: 20,000
SALES (est): 2.39MM **Privately Held**
Web: www.ediplastics.com
SIC: 3089 Injection molding of plastics

**(P-6713)**
**AMERICAN INTEGRITY CORP**
13510 Central Rd, Apple Valley (92308-6561)
P.O. Box 999 (92307-0017)
PHONE..................760 247-1082
EMP: 50
Web: www.americanintegrity.com
SIC: 3089 5211 Window frames and sash, plastics; Lumber and other building materials

**(P-6714)**
**AMERICAN LAMINATES INC**
3142 Talbot Ave, Riverbank (95367-2842)
P.O. Box 778 (95367-0778)
PHONE..................209 869-2536
EMP: 30 EST: 1999
SALES (est): 22.78MM **Privately Held**
Web: www.americanlaminates.com
SIC: 3089 Thermoformed finished plastics products, nec

**(P-6715)**
**AMERIMADE TECHNOLOGY INC**
449 Mountain Vista Pkwy, Livermore (94551-8212)
PHONE..................925 243-9090
Todd Thomas, *Pr*
EMP: 50 EST: 1994
SQ FT: 65,000
SALES (est): 9.55MM **Privately Held**
Web: www.amerimade.com
SIC: 3089 3674 Injection molding of plastics; Semiconductors and related devices

**(P-6716)**
**AMS PLASTICS INC (PA)**
Also Called: Westfall Technik
20109 Paseo Del Prado, Walnut (91789)
PHONE..................619 713-2000
Adolfo Arellano, *CEO*
Diane L Plein, *Sec*
▲ EMP: 43 EST: 1983
SALES (est): 9.68MM **Privately Held**
Web: www.westfalltechnik.com
SIC: 3089 Injection molding of plastics

**(P-6717)**
**AMS PLASTICS INC**
Also Called: Westfall Technik
1100 Citrus St, Riverside (92507-1731)
PHONE..................951 734-5600
Jim Henke, *Brnch Mgr*
EMP: 393
Web: www.westfalltechnik.com
SIC: 3089 Molding primary plastics
PA: Ams Plastics, Inc.
   20109 Paseo Del Prado

**(P-6718)**
**ANAHEIM CUSTOM EXTRUDERS INC**
Also Called: Ace
1360 N Mccan St, Anaheim (92806-1316)
PHONE..................714 693-8508
TOLL FREE: 800
William A Czapar, *Ch Bd*
Chrintina Smith, *
EMP: 48 EST: 1977
SALES (est): 7.46MM **Privately Held**
Web: www.acextrusions.com
SIC: 3089 3082 Extruded finished plastics products, nec; Unsupported plastics profile shapes

**(P-6719)**
**ANDERSON MOULDS INCORPORATED**
3131 E Anita St, Stockton (95205-3904)
PHONE..................209 943-1145
Garry W Anderson, *Pr*
Victoria Anderson, *Sec*
▲ EMP: 15 EST: 1975
SQ FT: 48,000
SALES (est): 2.5MM **Privately Held**
Web: www.andersonmoulds.com
SIC: 3089 Injection molding of plastics

**(P-6720)**
**APON INDUSTRIES CORP**
10005 Marconi Dr Ste 2, San Diego (92154-5208)
▲ EMP: 200 EST: 1998
SALES (est): 2.05MM **Privately Held**
Web: www.aponindustries.com
SIC: 3089 Injection molding of plastics

**(P-6721)**
**ARC PLASTICS INC**
14010 Shoemaker Ave, Norwalk (90650-4536)
PHONE..................562 802-3299
Richard Renaudo, *Pr*
Olga Peralta, *VP*
EMP: 20 EST: 2002
SQ FT: 1,600
SALES (est): 3.23MM **Privately Held**
Web: arcplastics.tripod.com
SIC: 3089 Injection molded finished plastics products, nec

**(P-6722)**
**ARCHITECTURAL PLASTICS INC**
1299 N Mcdowell Blvd, Petaluma (94954-1133)
PHONE..................707 765-9898

Pierre Miremont, *Pr*
Mark Lindlow, *
▼ EMP: 32 EST: 1974
SQ FT: 16,000
SALES (est): 4.97MM **Privately Held**
Web: www.archplastics.com
SIC: 3089 Injection molding of plastics

**(P-6723)**
**ARGEE MFG CO SAN DIEGO INC**
Also Called: Argee
9550 Pathway St, Santee (92071-4169)
PHONE..................619 449-5050
Robert Goldman, *Pr*
Ruth Goldman, *
▲ EMP: 75 EST: 1961
SQ FT: 65,000
SALES (est): 4.99MM **Privately Held**
Web: www.argeecorp.com
SIC: 3089 Plastics hardware and building products

**(P-6724)**
**ARLON LLC**
Arlon Adhesives-Films Division
2811 S Harbor Blvd, Santa Ana (92704-5805)
P.O. Box 5260 (92704-0260)
PHONE..................714 540-2811
Elmer Pruim, *Pr*
EMP: 150
SQ FT: 124,478
SALES (corp-wide): 908.4MM **Publicly Held**
Web: www.arlonecp.com
SIC: 3089 3081 2672 Plastics hardware and building products; Unsupported plastics film and sheet; Paper; coated and laminated, nec
HQ: Arlon Llc
   1100 Governor Lea Rd
   Bear DE 19701

**(P-6725)**
**ARMORCAST PRODUCTS COMPANY INC**
500 S Dupont Ave, Ontario (91761-1508)
PHONE..................909 390-1365
Paul Boghossian, *Brnch Mgr*
EMP: 40
SALES (corp-wide): 5.37B **Publicly Held**
Web: www.armorcastprod.com
SIC: 3089 5092 Plastics processing; Toys, nec
HQ: Armorcast Products Company, Inc.
   9140 Lurline Ave
   Chatsworth CA 91311
   818 982-3600

**(P-6726)**
**ARTHURMADE PLASTICS INC**
Also Called: Kirk Containers
2131 Garfield Ave, City Of Commerce (90040)
PHONE..................323 721-7325
Kirk Marounian, *Pr*
Silva Marounian, *
Arthur Marounian, *
EMP: 75 EST: 1984
SQ FT: 20,000
SALES (est): 1.4MM **Privately Held**
SIC: 3089 Injection molding of plastics

**(P-6727)**
**ASSOCIATED MATERIALS INC**
1 Maritime Plz 12th Fl, San Francisco (94111-3404)
PHONE..................415 788-5111
Erik D Ragatz, *Pr*
EMP: 3000 EST: 2010

SALES (est): 392.4MM **Privately Held**
**Web**: www.associatedmaterials.com
**SIC: 3089** 5033 5031 3442 Plastics hardware and building products; Roofing and siding materials; Windows; Metal doors, sash, and trim
**PA**: Associated Materials Group, Inc.
  3773 State Rd

**(P-6728)**
**ATS PRODUCTS INC (PA)**
Also Called: Manufacturing
2785 Goodrick Ave, Richmond (94801-1109)
**PHONE**..................510 234-3173
John Jeffrey Shea, *Pr*
▲ **EMP**: 46 **EST**: 1978
**SQ FT**: 35,000
**SALES (est)**: 12.93MM
**SALES (corp-wide)**: 12.93MM **Privately Held**
**Web**: www.atsduct.com
**SIC: 3089** Plastics hardware and building products

**(P-6729)**
**AXIUM PACKAGING LLC**
5701 Clark St, Ontario (91761-3640)
**PHONE**..................909 969-0766
Kulwinder Singh, *Mgr*
**EMP**: 578
**Web**: www.axiumpackaging.com
**SIC: 3089** Plastics containers, except foam
**PA**: Axium Packaging Llc
  9005 Smiths Mill Rd

**(P-6730)**
**B & S PLASTICS INC**
Also Called: Waterway Plastics
2200 Sturgis Rd, Oxnard (93030-8978)
**PHONE**..................805 981-0262
Bill Spears, *CEO*
Sandy Spears, *
◆ **EMP**: 105 **EST**: 1973
**SQ FT**: 240,000
**SALES (est)**: 43.56MM **Privately Held**
**Web**: www.waterwayplastics.com
**SIC: 3089** Injection molding of plastics

**(P-6731)**
**B AND P PLASTICS INC**
Also Called: Advance Plastics
225 W 30th St, National City (91950-7203)
**PHONE**..................619 477-1893
Bruce Browne, *Pr*
Patricia Browne, *
▲ **EMP**: 35 **EST**: 1974
**SQ FT**: 10,000
**SALES (est)**: 12.34MM **Privately Held**
**Web**: www.advanceplastics.com
**SIC: 3089** 3061 Molding primary plastics; Mechanical rubber goods

**(P-6732)**
**BACE MANUFACTURING INC (HQ)**
Also Called: Spm
3125 E Coronado St, Anaheim (92806-1915)
**PHONE**..................714 630-6002
Richard R Harris, *Pr*
Shannon White, *
**EMP**: 700 **EST**: 1989
**SQ FT**: 200,000
**SALES (est)**: 11.78MM
**SALES (corp-wide)**: 28.39MM **Privately Held**
**SIC: 3089** Injection molding of plastics
**PA**: Medplast Group, Inc.
  7865 Northcourt Rd # 100
  480 553-6400

**(P-6733)**
**BACE MANUFACTURING INC**
Spm/Fremont, CA
45581 Northport Loop W, Fremont (94538-6462)
**PHONE**..................510 657-5800
James W Collins, *Mgr*
**EMP**: 75
**SALES (corp-wide)**: 28.39MM **Privately Held**
**SIC: 3089** 3544 Molding primary plastics; Special dies, tools, jigs, and fixtures
**HQ**: Bace Manufacturing, Inc.
  3125 E Coronado St
  Anaheim CA 92806
  714 630-6002

**(P-6734)**
**BANDLOCK CORPORATION**
1734 S Vineyard Ave, Ontario (91761-7746)
**PHONE**..................909 947-7500
**EMP**: 68
**SIC: 3089** 3492 3082 Extruded finished plastics products, nec; Hose and tube couplings, hydraulic/pneumatic; Unsupported plastics profile shapes

**(P-6735)**
**BARBER-WEBB COMPANY INC (PA)**
12912 Lakeland Rd, Santa Fe Springs (90670-4517)
**PHONE**..................541 488-4821
**TOLL FREE**: 800
Donald B Barber Junior, *Pr*
Brian Barber, *
James Barber, *
Wr Greenbecker, *
▼ **EMP**: 30 **EST**: 1945
**SALES (est)**: 4.55MM
**SALES (corp-wide)**: 4.55MM **Privately Held**
**Web**: www.barber-webb.com
**SIC: 3089** Plastics processing

**(P-6736)**
**BARNES PLASTICS INC**
Also Called: Barnes Plastics
18903 Anelo Ave, Gardena (90248-4598)
**PHONE**..................310 329-6301
Charles Walker, *CEO*
Scott Piepmeyer, *
▲ **EMP**: 30 **EST**: 1930
**SQ FT**: 30,000
**SALES (est)**: 4.46MM **Privately Held**
**Web**: www.barnesplastics.com
**SIC: 3089** Injection molding of plastics

**(P-6737)**
**BAYVIEW PLASTIC SOLUTIONS INC**
43651 S Grimmer Blvd, Fremont (94538-6347)
**PHONE**..................510 360-0001
Martin Hernandez, *Pr*
**EMP**: 26 **EST**: 2007
**SALES (est)**: 3.43MM **Privately Held**
**Web**: www.bayviewplasticsolutions.com
**SIC: 3089** Injection molding of plastics

**(P-6738)**
**BEEMAK PLASTICS LLC**
Also Called: Beemak-Idl Display Products
1515 S Harris Ct, Anaheim (92806-5932)
**PHONE**..................800 421-4393
John Davis, *Managing Member*
Fred Garcy, *
Winfred Ross, *
▲ **EMP**: 100 **EST**: 1951
**SALES (est)**: 25MM
**SALES (corp-wide)**: 475.79MM **Privately Held**
**Web**: www.beemak.com
**SIC: 3089** Injection molding of plastics
**HQ**: Deflecto, Llc
  7035 E 86th St
  Indianapolis IN 46250
  317 849-9555

**(P-6739)**
**BENT MANUFACTURING CO INC**
Also Called: Bent Manufacturing Company
17311 Nichols Ln, Huntington Beach (92647-5721)
**PHONE**..................714 842-0600
**EMP**: 85
**Web**: www.bentmfg.com
**SIC: 3089** 3069 Blow molded finished plastics products, nec; Hard rubber and molded rubber products

**(P-6740)**
**BERICAP LLC**
Also Called: Bericap
1671 Champagne Ave Ste B, Ontario (91761-3650)
**PHONE**..................909 390-5518
Steve Buckley, *Pr*
Steve Buckley, *Managing Member*
David Andison, *
▲ **EMP**: 67 **EST**: 2001
**SALES (est)**: 4.98MM
**SALES (corp-wide)**: 2.67MM **Privately Held**
**Web**: www.bericap.com
**SIC: 3089** Injection molding of plastics
**HQ**: Bericap Holding Gmbh
  Kirchstr. 5
  Budenheim RP 55257
  613929020

**(P-6741)**
**BERRY GLOBAL INC**
4875 E Hunter Ave, Anaheim (92807-2005)
**PHONE**..................714 777-5200
Don Parodi, *Mgr*
**EMP**: 57
**Web**: www.berryglobal.com
**SIC: 3089** 3081 Bottle caps, molded plastics; Unsupported plastics film and sheet
**HQ**: Berry Global, Inc.
  101 Oakley St
  Evansville IN 47710

**(P-6742)**
**BERRY GLOBAL INC**
14000 Monte Vista Ave, Chino (91710-5537)
**PHONE**..................909 465-9055
Salama Elsayed, *Brnch Mgr*
**EMP**: 200
**Web**: www.berryglobal.com
**SIC: 3089** 3081 Bottle caps, molded plastics; Unsupported plastics film and sheet
**HQ**: Berry Global, Inc.
  101 Oakley St
  Evansville IN 47710

**(P-6743)**
**BH-TECH INC**
5425 Oberlin Dr Ste 207, San Diego (92121-1843)
**PHONE**..................858 694-0900
Seung Hoon Han, *CEO*
Woo Hyuk Choi, *CFO*
**EMP**: 700 **EST**: 2018

**SALES (est)**: 6.47MM **Privately Held**
**SIC: 3089** Injection molding of plastics

**(P-6744)**
**BIOMERICS IMP INDUS HLDNGS LLC**
Also Called: Biomerics Imp
4900 Fulton Dr, Fairfield (94534-1641)
**PHONE**..................707 863-4900
**EMP**: 66
**SALES (corp-wide)**: 13.67MM **Privately Held**
**SIC: 3089** Injection molding of plastics
**PA**: Biomerics Imp Industrial Holdings, Llc
  595 S 80 E Ste 400
  801 355-2705

**(P-6745)**
**BLOW MOLDED PRODUCTS INC**
Also Called: Bmp
4720 Felspar St, Riverside (92509-3068)
**PHONE**..................951 360-6055
**EMP**: 40
**Web**: www.blowmoldedproducts.com
**SIC: 3089** Injection molding of plastics

**(P-6746)**
**BM EXTRUSION INC**
1575 Omaha Ct, Riverside (92507-2444)
**PHONE**..................951 782-9020
Bacilio Mejia, *Pr*
**EMP**: 24 **EST**: 2006
**SALES (est)**: 1.75MM **Privately Held**
**SIC: 3089** Plastics containers, except foam

**(P-6747)**
**BOLERO INDS INC A CAL CORP**
Also Called: Bolero Plastics
11850 Burke St, Santa Fe Springs (90670-2536)
**PHONE**..................562 693-3000
Daniel Imasdounian, *CEO*
Daniel Imasdounian, *Pr*
Annie Imasdounian, *TRAE*
Vasken Imasdounian, *VP*
**EMP**: 20 **EST**: 1975
**SQ FT**: 19,500
**SALES (est)**: 3.49MM **Privately Held**
**Web**: www.boleroplastics.com
**SIC: 3089** Injection molding of plastics

**(P-6748)**
**BOMATIC INC (DH)**
Also Called: Bmi
43225 Business Park Dr, Temecula (92590-3648)
**PHONE**..................909 947-3900
Kjeld R Hestehave, *Pr*
Borge Hestehave, *
Mary Ann, *
Kirk Franks, *
Kresten Hestehave, *
▲ **EMP**: 40 **EST**: 1969
**SQ FT**: 35,000
**SALES (est)**: 21.72MM **Privately Held**
**Web**: www.bomatic.com
**SIC: 3089** Plastics containers, except foam
**HQ**: Universal Packaging West, Inc.
  43225 Business Park Dr
  Temecula CA 92590
  909 947-3900

**(P-6749)**
**BOMATIC INC**
2181 E Francis St, Ontario (91761-7723)
**PHONE**..................909 947-3900
Back Melon, *Mgr*
**EMP**: 60
**Web**: www.bomatic.com

# 3089 - Plastics Products, Nec (P-6750)

**SIC: 3089** Plastics containers, except foam
**HQ:** Bomatic, Inc.
43225 Business Park Dr
Temecula CA 92590
909 947-3900

### (P-6750)
### BOTTLEMATE INC (PA)
2095 Leo Ave, Commerce (90040-1626)
PHONE...................................323 887-9009
Kai-win Chuang, CEO
Anderson Chuang, *
Mei-li Chang, Sec
▲ **EMP:** 23 **EST:** 1982
**SQ FT:** 25,000
**SALES (est):** 2.7MM **Privately Held**
Web: www.bottlemate.com
**SIC: 3089** 5162 Blow molded finished plastics products, nec; Plastics products, nec

### (P-6751)
### BRADLEY MANUFACTURING CO INC
Also Called: Bradley's Plastic Bag Co
9368 Stewart And Gray Rd, Downey (90241-5316)
PHONE...................................562 923-5556
Keith Smith, Pr
Richard Lane, *
**EMP:** 28 **EST:** 1933
**SALES (est):** 2.36MM **Privately Held**
Web: www.bradleypackaging.com
**SIC: 3089** 3069 3083 2673 Plastics processing; Tubing, rubber; Laminated plastics plate and sheet; Bags: plastic, laminated, and coated

### (P-6752)
### C & G PLASTICS
Also Called: C & G Mercury Plastics
12729 Foothill Blvd, Sylmar (91342-5314)
PHONE...................................818 837-3773
Greg Leighton, Pr
▲ **EMP:** 25 **EST:** 1963
**SQ FT:** 6,000
**SALES (est):** 4.5MM **Privately Held**
Web: www.cgplastics.net
**SIC: 3089** Injection molding of plastics

### (P-6753)
### C & R MOLDS INC
2737 Palma Dr, Ventura (93003-7651)
P.O. Box 5644 (93005-0644)
PHONE...................................805 658-7098
Randall Ohnemus, Pr
Marla Ohnemus, *
▲ **EMP:** 24 **EST:** 1984
**SQ FT:** 12,000
**SALES (est):** 5.11MM **Privately Held**
Web: www.crmolds.com
**SIC: 3089** 3544 Injection molding of plastics; Special dies, tools, jigs, and fixtures

### (P-6754)
### C & S PLASTICS
18209 Chatsworth St, Porter Ranch (91326-3207)
PHONE...................................818 896-2489
Charles E Spears, Pr
Karen Spears, Sec
**EMP:** 15 **EST:** 1979
**SALES (est):** 1MM **Privately Held**
Web: www.cnsplastics.com
**SIC: 3089** Injection molding of plastics

### (P-6755)
### C-PAK INDUSTRIES INC
4925 Hallmark Pkwy, San Bernardino (92407-1870)
PHONE...................................909 880-6017
Arch Young, Pr
**EMP:** 28 **EST:** 1999
**SQ FT:** 25,000
**SALES (est):** 5.01MM **Privately Held**
Web: www.c-pak.net
**SIC: 3089** Injection molding of plastics

### (P-6756)
### CAL-MIL PLASTIC PRODUCTS INC (PA)
Also Called: Cal-Mil
4079 Calle Platino, Oceanside (92056-5803)
PHONE...................................800 321-9069
Johnny Callahan, CEO
Barney Callahan, *
◆ **EMP:** 20 **EST:** 1965
**SQ FT:** 60,000
**SALES (est):** 5.06MM
**SALES (corp-wide):** 5.06MM **Privately Held**
Web: www.calmil.com
**SIC: 3089** Plastics containers, except foam

### (P-6757)
### CAL-TRON CORPORATION
2290 Dixon Ln, Bishop (93514-8094)
PHONE...................................760 873-8491
Dan J Pool, Pr
Colleen Poo, Sec
**EMP:** 22 **EST:** 1963
**SQ FT:** 24,000
**SALES (est):** 975.28K **Privately Held**
Web: www.caltroncorp.com
**SIC: 3089** Injection molded finished plastics products, nec

### (P-6758)
### CALIFORNIA QUALITY PLAS INC
Also Called: Bel-Air Cases
2104 S Cucamonga Ave, Ontario (91761-5609)
PHONE...................................909 930-5667
Erik Calcott, Brnch Mgr
**EMP:** 20
**SALES (corp-wide):** 10.64MM **Privately Held**
Web: www.calplastics.com
**SIC: 3089** Plastics containers, except foam
**PA:** California Quality Plastics, Inc.
2226 S Castle Harbour Pl
909 930-5535

### (P-6759)
### CAMBRO MANUFACTURING COMPANY
7601 Clay Ave, Huntington Beach (92648-2219)
PHONE...................................714 848-1555
David Capestro, Mgr
**EMP:** 275
**SALES (corp-wide):** 307.89MM **Privately Held**
Web: www.cambro.com
**SIC: 3089** Plastics containers, except foam
**PA:** Cambro Manufacturing Company Inc
5801 Skylab Rd
714 848-1555

### (P-6760)
### CAMBRO MANUFACTURING COMPANY (PA)
Also Called: Cambro
5801 Skylab Rd, Huntington Beach (92647-2051)
P.O. Box 2000 (92647-2000)
PHONE...................................714 848-1555
Argyle Campbell, CEO
◆ **EMP:** 500 **EST:** 1951
**SQ FT:** 300,000
**SALES (est):** 307.89MM
**SALES (corp-wide):** 307.89MM **Privately Held**
Web: www.cambro.com
**SIC: 3089** Trays, plastics

### (P-6761)
### CAMBRO MANUFACTURING COMPANY
Also Called: Cambro Manufacturing
5801 Skylab Rd, Huntington Beach (92647-2051)
PHONE...................................714 848-1555
Argyle Campbell, Pr
**EMP:** 69
**SALES (corp-wide):** 307.89MM **Privately Held**
Web: www.cambro.com
**SIC: 3089** Trays, plastics
**PA:** Cambro Manufacturing Company Inc
5801 Skylab Rd
714 848-1555

### (P-6762)
### CANYON PLASTICS LLC
28455 Livingston Ave, Valencia (91355-4173)
PHONE...................................800 350-6325
**TOLL FREE:** 800
Karshan A Gajera, CEO
▲ **EMP:** 78 **EST:** 1982
**SQ FT:** 110,950
**SALES (est):** 17.37MM **Privately Held**
Web: www.canyonplastics.com
**SIC: 3089** 3544 Plastics containers, except foam; Forms (molds), for foundry and plastics working machinery

### (P-6763)
### CAPLUGS INC
18704 S Ferris Pl, Rancho Dominguez (90220-6400)
PHONE...................................310 537-2300
Fred Karam, Brnch Mgr
**EMP:** 60
**SALES (corp-wide):** 2.26B **Privately Held**
Web: www.caplugs.com
**SIC: 3089** Injection molding of plastics
**HQ:** Caplugs, Inc.
2150 Elmwood Ave
Buffalo NY 14207
716 876-9855

### (P-6764)
### CAPTIVE PLASTICS LLC
601 Nestle Way Ste A, Lathrop (95330-9263)
PHONE...................................209 858-9188
Jim Campbell, Brnch Mgr
**EMP:** 82
Web: www.berryglobal.com
**SIC: 3089** Plastics containers, except foam
**HQ:** Captive Plastics, Llc
101 Oakley St
Evansville IN 47710
812 424-2904

### (P-6765)
### CARR MANAGEMENT INC
22324 Temescal Canyon Rd, Corona (92883-4622)
PHONE...................................951 277-4800
Nick Rende, Brnch Mgr
**EMP:** 70
Web: www.carrmanagement.com
**SIC: 3089** Plastics containers, except foam
**PA:** Carr Management, Inc.
1 Tara Blvd Ste 303

### (P-6766)
### CARSON INDUSTRIES LLC
Also Called: Oldcastle Prcast Enclsure Slto
2434 Rubidoux Blvd, Riverside (92509-2144)
P.O. Box 99697 (60696-7497)
PHONE...................................951 788-9720
◆ **EMP:** 3000
**SIC: 3089** Boxes, plastics

### (P-6767)
### CCI INDUSTRIES INC (PA)
Also Called: Cool Curtain CCI
350 Fischer Ave Ste A, Costa Mesa (92626-4508)
PHONE...................................714 662-3879
Michael Robinson, Pr
▲ **EMP:** 27 **EST:** 1976
**SQ FT:** 15,000
**SALES (est):** 2.75MM
**SALES (corp-wide):** 2.75MM **Privately Held**
Web: www.coolcurtain.com
**SIC: 3089** 3564 3496 Doors, folding: plastics or plastics coated fabric; Aircurtains (blower); Grilles and grillework, woven wire

### (P-6768)
### CCL TUBE INC (HQ)
2250 E 220th St, Carson (90810-1638)
PHONE...................................310 635-4444
Andreas Iseli, CEO
◆ **EMP:** 98 **EST:** 1984
**SQ FT:** 300,000
**SALES (est):** 44.41MM
**SALES (corp-wide):** 4.84B **Privately Held**
Web: www.ccltube.com
**SIC: 3089** Injection molded finished plastics products, nec
**PA:** Ccl Industries Inc.
111 Gordon Baker Rd Suite 801
416 756-8500

### (P-6769)
### CENTRAL CALIFORNIA CONT MFG
Also Called: Synder California Container
800 Commerce Dr, Chowchilla (93610-9395)
P.O. Box 848 (93610-0848)
PHONE...................................559 665-7611
Tom O'connell, CEO
**EMP:** 24 **EST:** 1989
**SQ FT:** 2,500
**SALES (est):** 984.71K **Privately Held**
Web: www.cencaltanks.com
**SIC: 3089** Plastics containers, except foam

### (P-6770)
### CERTIFIED THERMOPLASTICS INC
Also Called: Certified Thermoplastics LLC
26381 Ferry Ct, Santa Clarita (91350-2998)
PHONE...................................661 222-3006
Robert Duncan, Pr
▲ **EMP:** 35 **EST:** 1978
**SQ FT:** 30,000
**SALES (est):** 10.6MM
**SALES (corp-wide):** 756.99MM **Publicly Held**
Web: www.ctplastics.com
**SIC: 3089** Injection molding of plastics
**HQ:** Ducommun Labarge Technologies, Inc.
1601 E Broadway Rd
Phoenix AZ 85040
480 998-0733

## 3089 - Plastics Products, Nec (P-6791)

**(P-6771)**
**CHARMAINE PLASTICS INC**
Also Called: Crafttech
2941 E La Jolla St, Anaheim (92806-1306)
PHONE..................714 630-8117
John Butler, Pr
Alfredo Bonetto, *
John Ayers, *
Douglas Barker, Product Vice President*
Steven Lawson, *
▲ **EMP:** 88 **EST:** 1979
**SQ FT:** 35,000
**SALES (est):** 20.54MM
**SALES (corp-wide):** 43.66MM **Privately Held**
Web: www.craftechcorp.com
**SIC: 3089** 3559 Injection molding of plastics; Plastics working machinery
**PA:** Sage Park Acq. Ct Llc
725 Cool Sprng Blvd Ste 2
615 637-8030

**(P-6772)**
**CHAWK TECHNOLOGY INTL INC (PA)**
31033 Huntwood Ave, Hayward (94544)
PHONE..................510 330-5299
Chase Zunino, CEO
▲ **EMP:** 56 **EST:** 2006
**SALES (est):** 39.58MM **Privately Held**
Web: www.chawktechnology.com
**SIC: 3089** Injection molding of plastics

**(P-6773)**
**CHEMICAL SAFETY TECHNOLOGY INC**
Also Called: C S T I
2461 Autumnvale Dr, San Jose (95131-1802)
PHONE..................408 263-0984
Lincoln Bejan, Pr
Jackie Bejan, *
**EMP:** 26 **EST:** 1986
**SQ FT:** 14,000
**SALES (est):** 4.98MM **Privately Held**
Web: www.kemsafe.com
**SIC: 3089** Injection molding of plastics

**(P-6774)**
**CHINA CUSTOM MANUFACTURING LTD**
Also Called: Pacific Solartech
44843 Fremont Blvd, Fremont (94538-6318)
PHONE..................510 979-1920
George Huang, Pr
Robin Lee, *
◆ **EMP:** 860 **EST:** 2002
**SALES (est):** 2.62MM **Privately Held**
Web: www.pacificbusinessco.com
**SIC: 3089** Injection molded finished plastics products, nec

**(P-6775)**
**CHUBBY GORILLA INC (PA)**
4320 N Harbor Blvd, Fullerton (92835-1091)
PHONE..................844 365-5218
Ibraheim Hamsa Aboabdo, CEO
Eyad Aboabdo, *
**EMP:** 27 **EST:** 2015
**SALES (est):** 7.49MM
**SALES (corp-wide):** 7.49MM **Privately Held**
Web: www.chubbygorilla.com
**SIC: 3089** Closures, plastics

**(P-6776)**
**CLEAR-AD INC**
Also Called: Brochure Holders 4u
2410 W 3rd St, Santa Ana (92703-3519)
PHONE..................866 627-9718
Juan Diaz, CEO
John Diaz, Prin
Bruce Kelly, *
**EMP:** 30 **EST:** 1972
**SQ FT:** 17,006
**SALES (est):** 4.71MM **Privately Held**
Web: www.brochureholders4u.com
**SIC: 3089** 3544 3993 3061 Injection molded finished plastics products, nec; Forms (molds), for foundry and plastics working machinery; Displays and cutouts, window and lobby; Medical and surgical rubber tubing (extruded and lathe-cut)

**(P-6777)**
**CODAN US CORPORATION**
Also Called: Codan US
3501 W Sunflower Ave, Santa Ana (92704-6923)
PHONE..................714 545-2111
Mike Thompson, Pr
▲ **EMP:** 100 **EST:** 1971
**SALES (est):** 21.28MM
**SALES (corp-wide):** 64.2K **Privately Held**
Web: www.codanusa.com
**SIC: 3089** Molding primary plastics
**PA:** Codan Holding Gmbh & Co. Kg
Stig Husted-Andersen Str. 11
43635111

**(P-6778)**
**COLVIN-FRIEDMAN LLC**
Also Called: Colvin-Friedman
1311 Commerce St, Petaluma (94954-1426)
PHONE..................707 769-4488
Mitchell Friedman, Pr
**EMP:** 25 **EST:** 1949
**SQ FT:** 10,000
**SALES (est):** 1.66MM **Privately Held**
Web: www.colvin-friedman.com
**SIC: 3089** 5162 3544 Injection molding of plastics; Plastics materials, nec; Dies, plastics forming

**(P-6779)**
**CONTAINER OPTIONS**
1493 E San Bernardino Ave, San Bernardino (92408-2927)
PHONE..................909 478-0045
Patricia Shockey, CEO
**EMP:** 18 **EST:** 1995
**SQ FT:** 43,000
**SALES (est):** 1.33MM **Privately Held**
**SIC: 3089** Plastics containers, except foam

**(P-6780)**
**COOL-PAK LLC**
Also Called: Bunzl Agrclture Group Chstrfel
401 N Rice Ave, Oxnard (93030-7936)
PHONE..................805 981-2434
Nick Weber, *
Jim Borchard, *
Derek Goodin, *
Patrick Larmon, *
▲ **EMP:** 85 **EST:** 2001
**SQ FT:** 124,000
**SALES (est):** 22.08MM
**SALES (corp-wide):** 14.7B **Privately Held**
Web: www.cool-pak.com
**SIC: 3089** Plastics containers, except foam
**HQ:** Bunzl Distribution Usa, Llc
1 Cityplace Dr Ste 200
Saint Louis MO 63141

**(P-6781)**
**CORNUCOPIA TOOL & PLASTICS INC**
448 Sherwood Rd, Paso Robles (93446-3554)
P.O. Box 1915 (93447-1915)
PHONE..................805 238-7660
Larry Horn, Pr
Art Horn, *
**EMP:** 47 **EST:** 1969
**SQ FT:** 20,000
**SALES (est):** 9.21MM **Privately Held**
Web: www.cornucopiaplastics.com
**SIC: 3089** 3544 Injection molding of plastics; Industrial molds

**(P-6782)**
**COUNTRY PLASTICS INC**
32501 Road 228, Woodlake (93286-9705)
PHONE..................559 597-2556
Jay D Ayres, CEO
Jenny Ayres, Sec
▲ **EMP:** 17 **EST:** 1975
**SQ FT:** 3,000
**SALES (est):** 5.69MM **Privately Held**
Web: www.countryplastics.net
**SIC: 3089** Injection molding of plastics

**(P-6783)**
**COUNTY PLASTICS CORP**
Also Called: Chemtainer Industries
135 E Stanley St, Compton (90220-5604)
PHONE..................310 635-5400
George Karathanas, Mgr
**EMP:** 26
**SALES (corp-wide):** 43.32MM **Privately Held**
Web: www.chemtainer.com
**SIC: 3089** 2821 Plastics and fiberglass tanks; Plastics materials and resins
**PA:** County Plastics Corp.
361 Neptune Ave
631 422-8300

**(P-6784)**
**CPD INDUSTRIES**
Also Called: Custom Packaging Design
4665 State St, Montclair (91763-6130)
PHONE..................909 465-5596
Carlos Hurtado, Pr
Sergio Briceno, *
**EMP:** 29 **EST:** 1985
**SQ FT:** 22,000
**SALES (est):** 4.49MM **Privately Held**
Web: www.cpdindustries.com
**SIC: 3089** Plastics containers, except foam

**(P-6785)**
**CRETEX MED CMPNENT DVC TECH IN**
2840 Research Park Dr Ste 160, Soquel (95073-2076)
PHONE..................831 462-1141
Jeff Wollerman, Mgr
**EMP:** 150
**SALES (corp-wide):** 419.13MM **Privately Held**
Web: www.junopacific.com
**SIC: 3089** Injection molding of plastics
**HQ:** Cretex Medical Component And Device Technologies, Inc.
8701 95th Ave
Minneapolis MN 55445
763 703-5000

**(P-6786)**
**CREU LLC**
12750 Baltic Ct, Rancho Cucamonga (91739-8957)
PHONE..................909 483-4888
Anthony Quezada, CEO
**EMP:** 25 **EST:** 2014
**SALES (est):** 2.1MM **Privately Held**
**SIC: 3089** 5063 Automotive parts, plastic; Lighting fixtures

**(P-6787)**
**CROWN MFG CO INC**
37625 Sycamore St, Newark (94560-3946)
PHONE..................510 742-8800
Aziz Shariat, CEO
▲ **EMP:** 40 **EST:** 1959
**SQ FT:** 60,000
**SALES (est):** 3.6MM **Privately Held**
Web: www.crown-plastics.com
**SIC: 3089** Injection molding of plastics

**(P-6788)**
**CTR AMERICA**
530 Technology Dr Ste 100, Irvine (92618-1350)
PHONE..................323 332-1417
Joohyung Kim, Pr
Joohyung Kim, CEO
Sangheon Ji, Pr
**EMP:** 15 **EST:** 2019
**SALES (est):** 2.59MM **Privately Held**
**SIC: 3089** Automotive parts, plastic
**PA:** Ctr Co.,Ltd.
551 Gongdan-Ro, Seongsan-Gu

**(P-6789)**
**CUSTOM ENGINEERING PLASTICS LP**
Also Called: Custom Engineering Plastics
8558 Miramar Pl, San Diego (92121-2530)
PHONE..................858 452-0961
Sylvia Hammond, Mng Pt
Jack Hammond, Pt
▲ **EMP:** 18 **EST:** 1987
**SQ FT:** 11,400
**SALES (est):** 2.69MM **Privately Held**
Web: www.cepi.com
**SIC: 3089** 3544 Injection molding of plastics; Forms (molds), for foundry and plastics working machinery

**(P-6790)**
**D & T FIBERGLASS INC**
8900 Osage Ave, Sacramento (95828-1124)
P.O. Box 293330 (95829-3330)
PHONE..................916 383-9012
Donald R Stommel, CEO
**EMP:** 37 **EST:** 1987
**SQ FT:** 35,000
**SALES (est):** 5.62MM **Privately Held**
Web: www.dtfiberglass.com
**SIC: 3089** Plastics and fiberglass tanks

**(P-6791)**
**DACHA ENTERPRISES INC (HQ)**
Also Called: Accent Plastics
13948 Mountain Ave, Chino (91710-9018)
PHONE..................951 273-7777
Thomas A Pridonoff, CEO
Bonnie Pridonoff, *
Denise Parks, *
◆ **EMP:** 21 **EST:** 1965
**SALES (est):** 10.01MM
**SALES (corp-wide):** 36.4MM **Privately Held**
Web: www.accentplastics.com
**SIC: 3089** Injection molding of plastics
**PA:** Syntech Development And Manufacturing, Inc.
13948 Mountain Ave
909 465-5554

## 3089 - Plastics Products, Nec (P-6792)

**(P-6792)**
**DACHA ENTERPRISES INC**
1915 Elise Cir, Corona (92879-1882)
PHONE...............................951 273-7777
EMP: 77
SALES (corp-wide): 36.4MM Privately Held
Web: www.accentplastics.com
SIC: 3089 Injection molding of plastics
HQ: Dacha Enterprises, Inc.
13948 Mountain Ave
Chino CA 91710
951 273-7777

**(P-6793)**
**DAMAR PLASTICS MANUFACTURING INC**
Also Called: Damar Plastics
1035 Pioneer Way Ste 160, El Cajon (92020-1978)
PHONE...............................619 283-2300
EMP: 45 EST: 2013
SALES (est): 5.01MM Privately Held
Web: www.damarplastics.com
SIC: 3089 Plastics processing

**(P-6794)**
**DAVID SCHNUR ASSOC**
1755 E Bayshore Rd Ste 8b, Redwood City (94063-4142)
PHONE...............................650 363-8797
Barry Schnur, VP
EMP: 30 EST: 2010
SALES (est): 1.2MM Privately Held
Web: www.dschnur.
SIC: 3089 Injection molding of plastics

**(P-6795)**
**DELAMO MANUFACTURING INC**
7171 Telegraph Rd, Montebello (90640-6511)
PHONE...............................323 936-3566
Fred Morad, CEO
EMP: 80 EST: 2008
SQ FT: 120,000
SALES (est): 2.86MM Privately Held
Web: www.delamo-mfg.com
SIC: 3089 Plastics kitchenware, tableware, and houseware

**(P-6796)**
**DELFIN DESIGN & MFG INC**
15672 Producer Ln, Huntington Beach (92649-1310)
PHONE...............................949 888-4644
John M Rief, Pr
Paul Iverson, *
Rita Williams, *
▲ EMP: 28 EST: 1991
SALES (est): 8.62MM
SALES (corp-wide): 1.19MM Privately Held
Web: www.delfinfs.com
SIC: 3089 3083 Thermoformed finished plastics products, nec; Plastics finished products, laminated
HQ: Steelite International U.S.A. Inc.
154 Keystone Dr
New Castle PA 16105

**(P-6797)**
**DELPHON INDUSTRIES LLC (PA)**
Also Called: Quik-Pak
31398 Huntwood Ave, Hayward (94544-7818)
PHONE...............................510 576-2220
Jeanne Beacham, Managing Member
Diana Morgan, *
▲ EMP: 123 EST: 1972
SQ FT: 40,000
SALES (est): 20.81MM
SALES (corp-wide): 20.81MM Privately Held
Web: www.delphon.com
SIC: 3089 Injection molding of plastics

**(P-6798)**
**DELTA YIMIN TECHNOLOGIES INC**
Also Called: Delta Pacific Products
33170 Central Ave, Union City (94587-2042)
PHONE...............................510 487-4411
Edgar Ferreira, Pr
◆ EMP: 48 EST: 1988
SQ FT: 34,000
SALES (est): 24.92MM
SALES (corp-wide): 500.49MM Privately Held
Web: www.westfalltechnik.com
SIC: 3089 Injection molded finished plastics products, nec
PA: Westfall Technik, Llc
9280 S Kyrene Rd
702 659-9898

**(P-6799)**
**DEMTECH SERVICES INC**
6414 Capitol Ave, Diamond Springs (95619-9393)
PHONE...............................530 621-3200
Dave Mclaury, Pr
▲ EMP: 24 EST: 1999
SQ FT: 8,000
SALES (est): 5.3MM Privately Held
Web: www.demtech.com
SIC: 3089 Thermoformed finished plastics products, nec

**(P-6800)**
**DESIGN OCTAVES**
2701 Research Park Dr, Soquel (95073-2090)
PHONE...............................831 464-8500
Norman Weiss, CEO
Dan Mccabe, VP
EMP: 30 EST: 1979
SQ FT: 21,000
SALES (est): 6.26MM Privately Held
Web: www.designoctaves.com
SIC: 3089 3469 Cases, plastics; Metal stampings, nec

**(P-6801)**
**DESIGN WEST TECHNOLOGIES INC**
2701 Dow Ave, Tustin (92780-7209)
PHONE...............................714 731-0201
Ryan Hur, Pr
▲ EMP: 65 EST: 1994
SQ FT: 60,000
SALES (est): 16.26MM Privately Held
Web: www.dwtusa.com
SIC: 3089 8711 Injection molded finished plastics products, nec; Electrical or electronic engineering

**(P-6802)**
**DIAL INDUSTRIES INC**
Also Called: All-Power Plastcs Div Dial
3616 Noakes St, Los Angeles (90023-3200)
PHONE...............................323 263-6878
Richard Oxford, Pr
EMP: 100
SALES (corp-wide): 10.12MM Privately Held
Web: www.dialind.com
SIC: 3089 3354 Plastics kitchenware, tableware, and houseware; Aluminum extruded products
PA: Dial Industries, Inc.
3628 Noakes St
323 263-6878

**(P-6803)**
**DIAL INDUSTRIES INC (PA)**
3628 Noakes St, Los Angeles (90023-3222)
PHONE...............................323 263-6878
▲ EMP: 80 EST: 1968
SALES (est): 9.14MM
SALES (corp-wide): 9.14MM Privately Held
Web: www.dialind.com
SIC: 3089 Plastics kitchenware, tableware, and houseware

**(P-6804)**
**DISPENSING DYNAMICS INTL INC (PA)**
Also Called: Perrin Craft
1940 Diamond St, San Marcos (92078-5120)
PHONE...............................626 961-3691
Dean Debuhr, Ch
Larry Maccormack, *
Scott Strachan, *
Michael Severyn, *
Rocky Wilske, *
◆ EMP: 99 EST: 1932
SALES (est): 23.51MM
SALES (corp-wide): 23.51MM Privately Held
Web: www.dispensingdynamics.com
SIC: 3089 3993 Injection molding of plastics; Signs and advertising specialties

**(P-6805)**
**DISTINCTIVE PLASTICS INC**
1385 Decision St, Vista (92081)
PHONE...............................760 599-9100
Timothy Curnutt, Pr
Violeta Curnutt, *
▲ EMP: 62 EST: 1982
SQ FT: 44,500
SALES (est): 8.68MM Privately Held
Web: www.dpi-tech.com
SIC: 3089 3312 Injection molding of plastics; Tool and die steel

**(P-6806)**
**DIVERSE OPTICS INC**
10339 Dorset St, Rancho Cucamonga (91730-3067)
PHONE...............................909 593-9330
Erik Fleming, Pr
EMP: 20 EST: 1987
SALES (est): 6.28MM Privately Held
Web: www.diverseoptics.com
SIC: 3089 3827 Injection molding of plastics; Lenses, optical: all types except ophthalmic

**(P-6807)**
**DIVERSIFIED PLASTICS INC**
Also Called: Pacific Plas Injection Molding
1333 Keystone Way, Vista (92081-8311)
PHONE...............................760 598-5333
Rob Gilman, Genl Mgr
EMP: 30
SALES (corp-wide): 11.23MM Privately Held
Web: www.divplast.com
SIC: 3089 3544 Injection molding of plastics; Industrial molds
PA: Diversified Plastics, Inc.
8617 Xylon Ct
763 424-2525

**(P-6808)**
**DOMINO PLASTICS MFG INC**
601 Gateway Ct, Bakersfield (93307-6827)
P.O. Box 71210 (93387)
PHONE...............................661 396-3744
W Thomas Bathe Iii, CEO
Neil Conway, Pr
EMP: 21 EST: 1971
SQ FT: 16,000
SALES (est): 3.12MM Privately Held
Web: www.dominoplastics.com
SIC: 3089 Billfold inserts, plastics

**(P-6809)**
**DOREL JUVENILE GROUP INC**
9950 Calabash Ave, Fontana (92335-5210)
PHONE...............................909 428-0295
Carrisa John, Prin
EMP: 105
SALES (corp-wide): 1.39B Privately Held
Web: na.doreljuvenile.com
SIC: 3089 Plastics kitchenware, tableware, and houseware
HQ: Dorel Juvenile Group, Inc.
2525 State St
Columbus IN 47201
800 457-5276

**(P-6810)**
**DOREL JUVENILE GROUP INC**
Also Called: Cosco Home & Office Products
5400 Shea Center Dr, Ontario (91761-7892)
PHONE...............................909 390-5705
Rick Mc Cook, Mgr
EMP: 157
SALES (corp-wide): 1.39B Privately Held
Web: www.dorel.com
SIC: 3089 Plastics kitchenware, tableware, and houseware
HQ: Dorel Juvenile Group, Inc.
2525 State St
Columbus IN 47201
800 457-5276

**(P-6811)**
**DPP 2020 INC (DH)**
533 E Third St, Beaumont (92223-2715)
P.O. Box 2097 (92223-0997)
PHONE...............................951 845-3161
Kevin Rost, CEO
Monica Rost, *
◆ EMP: 31 EST: 1974
SQ FT: 150,000
SALES (est): 19.81MM Privately Held
Web: www.duraplastics.com
SIC: 3089 Fittings for pipe, plastics
HQ: Tigre Sa Participacoes
Rua Xavantes 54
Joinvile SC 89203

**(P-6812)**
**DURAPLEX INC**
1005 W Hoover Ave, Orange (92867-3513)
PHONE...............................714 538-1335
Gloria J Dunne, Sec
Jeffery W Dunne, Pr
EMP: 15 EST: 1985
SQ FT: 10,000
SALES (est): 605.61K Privately Held
SIC: 3089 Extruded finished plastics products, nec

**(P-6813)**
**E & F PLASTICS INC**
Also Called: E & F Plas Fbrction Spcialists
2742 Aiello Dr, San Jose (95111-2134)
PHONE...............................408 226-6672
EMP: 22 EST: 1980
SALES (est): 2.18MM Privately Held

# PRODUCTS & SERVICES SECTION
## 3089 - Plastics Products, Nec (P-6835)

Web: www.enfplastics.com
SIC: 3089 Thermoformed finished plastics products, nec

### (P-6814)
### EAGLE MOLD TECHNOLOGIES INC
12330 Crosthwaite Cir, Poway (92064-6823)
PHONE..................858 530-0888
Ulrich Bark, *Pr*
Gregory Bark, *VP*
David Bark, *VP*
Ronald Bark, *VP*
Rosemary Bark, *Treas*
EMP: 20 EST: 1969
SQ FT: 10,500
SALES (est): 2.55MM **Privately Held**
Web: www.eaglemold.com
SIC: 3089 3544 Injection molded finished plastics products, nec; Special dies, tools, jigs, and fixtures

### (P-6815)
### EDCO PLASTICS INC
2110 E Winston Rd, Anaheim (92806-5534)
PHONE..................714 772-1986
Edward A Contreras, *Pr*
Maria Contreras, *
▲ EMP: 49 EST: 1984
SQ FT: 25,000
SALES (est): 4.93MM **Privately Held**
Web: www.edcoplastics.com
SIC: 3089 Molding primary plastics

### (P-6816)
### EDRIS PLASTICS MFG INC
4560 Pacific Blvd, Vernon (90058-2208)
PHONE..................323 581-7000
Hovanes Hovik Issagholian, *CEO*
▲ EMP: 26 EST: 1991
SQ FT: 27,000
SALES (est): 4.82MM **Privately Held**
Web: www.edrisplastics.com
SIC: 3089 Injection molding of plastics

### (P-6817)
### EL DORADO MOLDS LLC
2691 Mercantile Dr, Rancho Cordova (95742-6521)
PHONE..................916 635-4558
EMP: 18 EST: 1989
SALES (est): 1.73MM
SALES (corp-wide): 50MM **Privately Held**
Web: www.springboardmfg.com
SIC: 3089 Plastics processing
PA: Kruger Plastic Products Llc
2691 Mercantile Dr
916 853-0717

### (P-6818)
### EMPIRE WEST INC
Also Called: Empire West Plastics
9270 Redwood Rd, Graton (95444-9375)
P.O. Box 511 (95444-0511)
PHONE..................707 823-1190
TOLL FREE: 800
Richard F Yonash, *CEO*
Edward J Davis, *
Donna Yonash, *
EMP: 28 EST: 1973
SQ FT: 30,000
SALES (est): 5.21MM **Privately Held**
Web: www.empirewest.com
SIC: 3089 Injection molding of plastics

### (P-6819)
### ENDUREQUEST CORPORATION
1813 Thunderbolt Dr, Porterville (93257-9300)
PHONE..................559 783-9220
Kenneth Dewing, *Pr*
Russell Sarno, *
▲ EMP: 25 EST: 1991
SQ FT: 10,000
SALES (est): 2.08MM **Privately Held**
Web: www.endurequest.com
SIC: 3089 Plastics hardware and building products

### (P-6820)
### ENGINEERING MODEL ASSOC INC (PA)
Also Called: Ema
1020 Wallace Way, City Of Industry (91748-1027)
PHONE..................626 912-7011
John Jay Wanderman, *Pr*
John Jay Wanderman, *Pr*
Leon Katz, *
EMP: 25 EST: 1955
SQ FT: 28,000
SALES (est): 9.43MM
SALES (corp-wide): 9.43MM **Privately Held**
SIC: 3089 5162 Plastics processing; Plastics products, nec

### (P-6821)
### ENVIRONMENTAL SAMPLING SUP INC
640 143rd Ave, San Leandro (94578-3304)
PHONE..................510 465-4988
William Levey, *Brnch Mgr*
EMP: 91
SALES (corp-wide): 336.21K **Privately Held**
Web: www.essvial.com
SIC: 3089 3231 Plastics containers, except foam; Products of purchased glass
HQ: Environmental Sampling Supply, Inc.
4101 Shuffel St Nw
North Canton OH 44720
330 497-9396

### (P-6822)
### ENVISION PLASTICS INDUSTRIES LLC
Also Called: Envision Plastics
14312 Central Ave, Chino (91710-5752)
PHONE..................909 590-7334
EMP: 50
SIC: 3089 Lamp bases and shades, plastics

### (P-6823)
### EXPANDED RUBBER & PLASTICS CORP
Also Called: Erp
19200 S Laurel Park Rd, Rancho Dominguez (90220-6008)
PHONE..................310 324-6692
EMP: 37 EST: 1957
SALES (est): 5.91MM **Privately Held**
Web: www.expandedrubber.com
SIC: 3089 3086 5088 Molding primary plastics; Plastics foam products; Aircraft and space vehicle supplies and parts

### (P-6824)
### EXTRUMED INC (DH)
Also Called: Vesta
547 Trm Cir, Corona (92879-1768)
PHONE..................951 547-7400
Phil Estes, *Pr*
Chris Guglielmi, *
Eric R Schnur, *
EMP: 25 EST: 1990
SQ FT: 53,000
SALES (est): 19.27MM
SALES (corp-wide): 364.48B **Publicly Held**
SIC: 3089 Injection molding of plastics
HQ: Vesta Intermediate Funding, Inc.
9900 S 57th St
Franklin WI 53132
414 423-0550

### (P-6825)
### FABRICATED EXTRUSION CO LLC (PA)
2331 Hoover Ave, Modesto (95354-3907)
PHONE..................209 529-9200
Jeffrey S Aichele, *Managing Member*
Thomas E Peot, *
EMP: 31 EST: 1988
SQ FT: 36,000
SALES (est): 10.29MM
SALES (corp-wide): 10.29MM **Privately Held**
Web: www.fabexco.com
SIC: 3089 Injection molding of plastics

### (P-6826)
### FISCHER MOLD INCORPORATED
393 Meyer Cir, Corona (92879-1078)
PHONE..................951 279-1140
Robert Fischer, *Pr*
Eleanor Fischer, *
▲ EMP: 60 EST: 1969
SQ FT: 32,000
SALES (est): 9.19MM **Privately Held**
Web: www.fischermold.com
SIC: 3089 3544 Injection molding of plastics; Special dies, tools, jigs, and fixtures

### (P-6827)
### FIT-LINE INC
Also Called: Fit-Line Global
2901 S Tech Center Dr, Santa Ana (92705-5657)
PHONE..................714 549-9091
Ronni Levinson, *CEO*
▼ EMP: 50 EST: 1993
SQ FT: 4,500
SALES (est): 5.53MM **Privately Held**
Web: www.fit-lineglobal.com
SIC: 3089 Fittings for pipe, plastics

### (P-6828)
### FLUIDMASTER INC (PA)
30800 Rancho Viejo Rd, San Juan Capistrano (92675)
PHONE..................949 728-2000
Robert Anderson Schoepe, *CEO*
Michael Draves, *
Robert Connell, *
Derek Baker, *
◆ EMP: 98 EST: 1957
SALES (est): 42.94MM
SALES (corp-wide): 42.94MM **Privately Held**
Web: www.fluidmaster.com
SIC: 3089 3432 1711 Injection molding of plastics; Plumbing fixture fittings and trim; Plumbing contractors

### (P-6829)
### FORMULA PLASTICS INC
451 Tecate Rd Ste 2b, Tecate (91980)
PHONE..................866 307-1362
Alexander Mora, *CEO*
Elias Mora, *
Joe Mora, *
Monica Mora, *
▲ EMP: 500 EST: 1984
SQ FT: 20,000
SALES (est): 1.75MM **Privately Held**
Web: www.formulaplastics.com

SIC: 3089 Injection molding of plastics

### (P-6830)
### FORTUNE BRANDS WINDOWS INC
Also Called: Simonton Windows
2019 E Monte Vista Ave, Vacaville (95688-3100)
PHONE..................707 446-7600
Tom Riseili, *Genl Mgr*
EMP: 215
SALES (corp-wide): 5.58B **Privately Held**
Web: www.simonton.com
SIC: 3089 3442 Window frames and sash, plastics; Sash, door or window: metal
HQ: Fortune Brands Windows, Inc
3948 Twnsfair Way Ste 200
Columbus OH 43219
614 532-3500

### (P-6831)
### FOXCONN ELECTRONICS INC
105 S Puente St, Brea (92821-3844)
PHONE..................714 988-9230
EMP: 20 EST: 2019
SALES (est): 827.21K **Privately Held**
Web: www.foxconnchannel.com
SIC: 3089 Plastics products, nec

### (P-6832)
### FREETECH PLASTICS INC
2211 Warm Springs Ct, Fremont (94539-6773)
PHONE..................510 651-9996
EMP: 27 EST: 1976
SALES (est): 4.42MM **Privately Held**
Web: www.freetechplastics.com
SIC: 3089 Thermoformed finished plastics products, nec

### (P-6833)
### FRESNO PRECISION PLASTICS INC
Also Called: Precision Plastics
8456 Carbide Ct, Sacramento (95828-5609)
PHONE..................916 689-5284
David Frericks, *Mgr*
EMP: 58
SALES (corp-wide): 9.33MM **Privately Held**
Web: www.precisionplasticsinc.com
SIC: 3089 Injection molding of plastics
PA: Fresno Precision Plastics, Inc.
998 N Temperance Ave
559 323-9595

### (P-6834)
### FRUTH CUSTOM PLASTICS INC
Also Called: Cal-AZ Sales & Marketing
701 Richfield Rd, Placentia (92870-6729)
P.O. Box 807 (92811-0807)
PHONE..................714 993-9955
EMP: 80 EST: 1980
SALES (est): 8.76MM **Privately Held**
Web: www.fruth.com
SIC: 3089 3081 2673 Plastics containers, except foam; Plastics film and sheet; Plastic bags: made from purchased materials
HQ: C. P. Converters, Inc.
15 Grumbacher Rd
York PA 17406
717 764-1193

### (P-6835)
### G B REMANUFACTURING INC
2040 E Cherry Industrial Cir, Long Beach (90805)

## 3089 - Plastics Products, Nec (P-6836)

PHONE...............................562 272-7333
Michael J Kitching, *CEO*
F William Kitching, *
Patricia Kitching, *
▲ **EMP:** 70 **EST:** 1986
**SQ FT:** 26,400
**SALES (est):** 13.74MM **Privately Held**
Web: www.gbreman.com
**SIC: 3089** Injection molded finished plastics products, nec

### (P-6836)
### GARY MANUFACTURING INC
2626 Southport Way Ste E, National City (91950-8754)
PHONE...............................619 429-4479
Brian Smith, *Pr*
Helen Smith, *
▲ **EMP:** 35 **EST:** 1958
**SQ FT:** 10,000
**SALES (est):** 4.89MM **Privately Held**
Web: www.garymanufacturing.com
**SIC: 3089** 2392 5162 2673 Plastics containers, except foam; Napkins, fabric and nonwoven: made from purchased materials; Plastics materials and basic shapes; Bags: plastic, laminated, and coated

### (P-6837)
### GEIGER PLASTICS INC
16150 S Maple Ave # A, Gardena (90248-2837)
PHONE...............................310 327-9926
Charlotte May, *Pr*
Vangie Ramirez, *Sec*
**EMP:** 20 **EST:** 1964
**SQ FT:** 10,000
**SALES (est):** 3.19MM **Privately Held**
Web: www.geigerplastics.com
**SIC: 3089** 3559 Injection molding of plastics; Plastics working machinery

### (P-6838)
### GEMINI FILM & BAG INC (PA)
Also Called: Gemini Plastics
3574 Fruitland Ave, Maywood (90270-2008)
P.O. Box 806 (92811-0806)
PHONE...............................323 582-0901
James Fruth, *Pr*
Brian Kunisch, *
**EMP:** 25 **EST:** 1966
**SQ FT:** 12,000
**SALES (est):** 2.31MM
**SALES (corp-wide):** 2.31MM **Privately Held**
**SIC: 3089** 8742 Extruded finished plastics products, nec; Manufacturing management consultant

### (P-6839)
### GENERAL WINDOW CORPORATION
Also Called: Interntnal Window-Northern Cal
30526 San Antonio St, Hayward (94544-7102)
P.O. Box 5025 (94540-5000)
PHONE...............................510 487-1122
**EMP:** 180
Web: www.intlwindow.com
**SIC: 3089** 3442 Window frames and sash, plastics; Casements, aluminum

### (P-6840)
### GEO PLASTICS
2200 E 52nd St, Vernon (90058-3446)
PHONE...............................323 277-8106
Michael Abraham Morris, *CEO*
Justin Hunt, *

▲ **EMP:** 27 **EST:** 1992
**SALES (est):** 4.91MM **Privately Held**
Web: www.geoplastics.com
**SIC: 3089** Extruded finished plastics products, nec

### (P-6841)
### GETPART LA INC
Also Called: Fitparts
13705 Cimarron Ave, Gardena (90249-2463)
PHONE...............................424 331-9599
Ilya S Shchelokov, *CEO*
**EMP:** 23 **EST:** 2016
**SALES (est):** 3.53MM **Privately Held**
Web: www.fitparts.com
**SIC: 3089** Automotive parts, plastic

### (P-6842)
### GIBRALTAR PLASTIC PDTS CORP
12885 Foothill Blvd, Sylmar (91342-5317)
PHONE...............................818 365-9318
Harvey J Jacobs, *Pr*
**EMP:** 25 **EST:** 1964
**SQ FT:** 30,000
**SALES (est):** 5.84MM **Privately Held**
Web: www.gibraltarplastic.com
**SIC: 3089** Injection molded finished plastics products, nec

### (P-6843)
### GILL CORPORATION (PA)
4056 Easy St, El Monte (91731)
PHONE...............................626 443-6094
Stephen E Gill, *Ch*
William Heinze, *
Irv Freund, *Business Development**
Don Clark, *
◆ **EMP:** 236 **EST:** 1945
**SQ FT:** 390,000
**SALES (est):** 225.82MM
**SALES (corp-wide):** 225.82MM **Privately Held**
Web: www.mcgillcorp.com
**SIC: 3089** 3469 3272 2448 Laminating of plastics; Honeycombed metal; Panels and sections, prefabricated concrete; Cargo containers, wood and metal combination

### (P-6844)
### GKN ARSPACE TRNSPRNCY SYSTEMS
12122 Western Ave, Garden Grove (92841)
PHONE...............................714 893-7531
John Danley, *CEO*
Mike Mccann Ceo Aeostructures N America, *Prin*
Joakim Anderson, *Chief Executive Officer Engine Systems**
Gavin Wesson, *
Russ Dunn, *Technology**
▲ **EMP:** 360 **EST:** 1946
**SQ FT:** 324,000
**SALES (est):** 26.21MM
**SALES (corp-wide):** 6.06B **Privately Held**
Web: www.gknaerospace.com
**SIC: 3089** 3231 3827 3728 Windows, plastics; Mirrors, truck and automobile: made from purchased glass; Optical instruments and lenses; Aircraft parts and equipment, nec
HQ: Gkn America Corp.
1180 Pchtree St Ne Ste 24
Atlanta GA 30309
630 972-9300

### (P-6845)
### GOLDEN PLASTICS CORPORATION

8465 Baldwin St, Oakland (94621-1924)
PHONE...............................510 569-6465
Ron Pardee, *Pr*
Stewart Pardee, *Pr*
Daniel K Pardee, *VP*
Ronald S Pardee, *VP*
Ruth Pardee, *Sec*
▲ **EMP:** 15 **EST:** 1945
**SQ FT:** 9,500
**SALES (est):** 1.48MM **Privately Held**
Web: www.goldenplasticscorp.com
**SIC: 3089** Injection molding of plastics

### (P-6846)
### GREENWASTE RECOVERY LLC
610 E Gish Rd, San Jose (95112-2707)
PHONE...............................408 283-4800
Richard Anthony Cristina, *Brnch Mgr*
**EMP:** 39
Web: www.greenwaste.com
**SIC: 3089** Garbage containers, plastics
PA: Greenwaste Recovery, Llc
1500 Berger Dr

### (P-6847)
### GRIFF INDUSTRIES INC
4515 Runway Dr, Lancaster (93536-8530)
PHONE...............................661 728-0111
Michael Griffin, *Pr*
◆ **EMP:** 19 **EST:** 1999
**SQ FT:** 8,400
**SALES (est):** 3.77MM **Privately Held**
Web: www.griffindustries.com
**SIC: 3089** Injection molding of plastics

### (P-6848)
### GT STYLING CORP
2830 E Via Martens, Anaheim (92806-1751)
PHONE...............................714 644-9214
Gregory Allen Knox, *CEO*
Jodee Jensen Smith, *Ex VP*
**EMP:** 27 **EST:** 2001
**SALES (est):** 1.68MM **Privately Held**
Web: www.gtsstyling.com
**SIC: 3089** Molding primary plastics

### (P-6849)
### HARKNESS ENTERPRISES INC
Also Called: Pacific Plastics & Engineering
2840 Research Park Dr Ste 160, Soquel (95073-2076)
PHONE...............................831 462-1141
▲ **EMP:** 100
**SIC: 3089** Plastics processing

### (P-6850)
### HEE ENVIRONMENTAL ENGINEERING LLC
16605 Koala Rd, Adelanto (92301-3925)
PHONE...............................760 530-1409
**EMP:** 38
**SIC: 3089** Plastics and fiberglass tanks

### (P-6851)
### HERMAN ENGINEERING & MFG INC
4501 E Airport Dr Ste B, Ontario (91761-7877)
P.O. Box 418 (43449-0418)
PHONE...............................909 483-1631
Donald B Donisthorpe, *Pr*
▲ **EMP:** 15 **EST:** 1979
**SQ FT:** 30,000
**SALES (est):** 998.09K **Privately Held**
**SIC: 3089** Plastics containers, except foam

### (P-6852)
### HI-REL PLASTICS & MOLDING CORP
7575 Jurupa Ave, Riverside (92504-1012)
PHONE...............................951 354-0258
Rakesh Bajaria, *CEO*
Rick Bajria, *
Harry Thummer, *
Dennis Sovalia, *
▲ **EMP:** 50 **EST:** 1984
**SQ FT:** 15,000
**SALES (est):** 4.54MM **Privately Held**
Web: www.hirelplastics.com
**SIC: 3089** 3549 3599 Injection molded finished plastics products, nec; Assembly machines, including robotic; Machine shop, jobbing and repair

### (P-6853)
### HIGHLAND PLASTICS INC
Also Called: Hi-Plas
3650 Dulles Dr, Mira Loma (91752-3260)
PHONE...............................951 360-9587
James L Nelson, *Prin*
William B Warren, *
◆ **EMP:** 130 **EST:** 1974
**SQ FT:** 150,000
**SALES (est):** 11.51MM **Privately Held**
**SIC: 3089** Injection molding of plastics

### (P-6854)
### HILLCOR DISTRIBUTION INC
5100 Commerce Dr, Baldwin Park (91706-1450)
PHONE...............................626 960-8789
Harry O Hill Iii, *Pr*
▲ **EMP:** 18 **EST:** 1962
**SQ FT:** 18,000
**SALES (est):** 1.85MM **Privately Held**
Web: www.hillcorplastics.com
**SIC: 3089** Injection molding of plastics

### (P-6855)
### HOME CONCEPTS PRODUCTS INC
4199 Bandini Blvd, Vernon (90058-4208)
PHONE...............................866 981-0500
Michael Moghavem, *Pr*
Ata Moghavem, *VP*
Perry Rahban, *VP*
Charles Rahban, *Sec*
▲ **EMP:** 23 **EST:** 2004
**SALES (est):** 444.45K **Privately Held**
**SIC: 3089** 5023 Kitchenware, plastics; Kitchenware

### (P-6856)
### HOOD MANUFACTURING INC
Also Called: Thermobile
2621 S Birch St, Santa Ana (92707-3410)
PHONE...............................714 979-7681
Michael Hood, *Pr*
Patrica Hood, *
Michele Rauschenbach, *CIO**
**EMP:** 60 **EST:** 1948
**SQ FT:** 24,000
**SALES (est):** 7.28MM **Privately Held**
Web: www.hoodmfg.com
**SIC: 3089** 3585 Injection molded finished plastics products, nec; Refrigeration and heating equipment

### (P-6857)
### HOOSIER INC
1152 California Ave, Corona (92881-3324)
P.O. Box 78926 (92877)
PHONE...............................951 272-3070
Robert G Simms, *CEO*
**EMP:** 80 **EST:** 1979

# PRODUCTS & SERVICES SECTION
## 3089 - Plastics Products, Nec (P-6880)

SQ FT: 45,000
SALES (est): 9.78MM Privately Held
Web: www.hoosierinc.com
SIC: 3089 Injection molding of plastics

### (P-6858)
### HOPE PLASTICS CO INC
5353 Strohm Ave, North Hollywood (91601-3526)
PHONE..................818 769-5560
Steven Borden, Pr
Bill Borden, VP
Hope Borden, Sec
▲ EMP: 20 EST: 1964
SQ FT: 17,000
SALES (est): 2.22MM Privately Held
Web: www.hopeplastics.com
SIC: 3089 Injection molding of plastics

### (P-6859)
### HOUSEWARES INTERNATIONAL INC
Also Called American Household Company
1933 S Broadway Ste 867, Los Angeles (90007-4523)
PHONE..................323 581-3000
Kamyar Solouki, CEO
Sean Solouki, *
◆ EMP: 35 EST: 1988
SALES (est): 5.33MM Privately Held
Web: www.housewaresintl.com
SIC: 3089 5023 Kitchenware, plastics; Kitchenware

### (P-6860)
### HUSKY INJCTION MLDING SYSTEMS
5245 Maureen Ln, Moorpark (93021-7125)
PHONE..................805 523-9593
EMP: 50
Web: www.husky.co
SIC: 3089 Injection molding of plastics
HQ: Husky Injection Molding Systems, Inc.
288 North Rd
Milton VT 05468
802 859-8000

### (P-6861)
### HUSKY INJCTION MLDING SYSTEMS
3505 Cadillac Ave Ste N4, Costa Mesa (92626-1433)
PHONE..................714 545-8200
Michael Smith, Mgr
EMP: 75
SQ FT: 6,501
Web: www.husky.co
SIC: 3089 Injection molding of plastics
HQ: Husky Injection Molding Systems, Inc.
288 North Rd
Milton VT 05468
802 859-8000

### (P-6862)
### IDEMIA AMERICA CORP
3150 E Ana St, Compton (90221-5607)
PHONE..................310 884-7900
Eric Dariele, Dir
EMP: 161
SALES (corp-wide): 4.59B Privately Held
Web: www.idemia.com
SIC: 3089 3083 Identification cards, plastics; Plastics finished products, laminated
HQ: Idemia America Corp.
11951 Freedom Dr Ste 1800
Reston VA 20190
703 775-7800

### (P-6863)
### INLINE PLASTICS INC
1950 S Baker Ave, Ontario (91761-7755)
PHONE..................909 923-1033
Kelly Orr, CEO
Alfredo Perez, *
EMP: 25 EST: 1996
SQ FT: 21,000
SALES (est): 5.16MM Privately Held
Web: www.inlineplasticsinc.com
SIC: 3089 Injection molding of plastics

### (P-6864)
### INNOVTIVE RTTIONAL MOLDING INC
Also Called: IRM
2300 W Pecan Ave, Madera (93637-5056)
PHONE..................559 673-4764
Daniel Humphries, Pr
Shellie Humphries, *
EMP: 35 EST: 2007
SALES (est): 5.3MM Privately Held
Web: www.irm-corp.com
SIC: 3089 Injection molding of plastics

### (P-6865)
### INTERTRADE INDUSTRIES LTD
14600 Hoover St, Westminster (92683-5346)
PHONE..................714 894-5566
EMP: 56 EST: 1975
SALES (est): 3.07MM Privately Held
SIC: 3089 Plastics boats and other marine equipment
PA: American Innotek, Inc.
2655 Vista Pacific Dr

### (P-6866)
### IPS INDUSTRIES INC
Also Called: Spectrum Bags
12641 166th St, Cerritos (90703-2101)
PHONE..................562 623-2555
Frank Su, CEO
Peter Hii, *
David Silva, *
Ben Tran, *
Betty Green, *
◆ EMP: 80 EST: 1990
SQ FT: 150,000
SALES (est): 21.08MM Privately Held
Web: www.ipspi.com
SIC: 3089 3629 Battery cases, plastics or plastics combination; Battery chargers, rectifying or nonrotating

### (P-6867)
### ITOUCHLESS HOUSEWARES PDTS INC
777 Mariners Island Blvd Ste 125, San Mateo (94404-5008)
PHONE..................650 578-0578
Fong Chan, Pr
◆ EMP: 50 EST: 1994
SALES (est): 4.09MM Privately Held
Web: www.itouchless.com
SIC: 3089 Plastics kitchenware, tableware, and houseware

### (P-6868)
### J & L CSTM PLSTIC EXTRSONS INC
850 Lawson St, City Of Industry (91748-1103)
PHONE..................626 442-0711
Edwin Woo, CEO
Louis Salmon, *
Jaime Lizarraga, *
EMP: 30 EST: 1974
SALES (est): 3.11MM Privately Held

Web: www.jlplastic.com
SIC: 3089 Plastics hardware and building products

### (P-6869)
### J A ENGLISH II INC
Also Called: Pacific Plstcs-Njction Molding
1333 Keystone Way, Vista (92081-8311)
PHONE..................760 598-5333
▲ EMP: 25
Web: www.divplast.com
SIC: 3089 3544 Injection molding of plastics; Industrial molds

### (P-6870)
### JACOBSON PLASTICS INC
1401 Freeman Ave, Long Beach (90804-2518)
PHONE..................562 433-4911
Jeff Jacobson, Pr
▲ EMP: 75 EST: 1962
SQ FT: 25,000
SALES (est): 3.13MM Privately Held
Web: www.jacobsonplastics.com
SIC: 3089 3544 Injection molding of plastics; Special dies, tools, jigs, and fixtures

### (P-6871)
### JADRA INC
Also Called: Plastic Package
4600 Beloit Dr, Sacramento (95838-2426)
PHONE..................916 921-3399
▲ EMP: 85
Web: www.plasticpack.com
SIC: 3089 Plastics containers, except foam

### (P-6872)
### JASON TOOL AND ENGINEERING INC
7101 Honold Cir, Garden Grove (92841-1424)
PHONE..................714 895-5067
Jack Winterswyk, Pr
Curtis H Thompson, *
▲ EMP: 30 EST: 1979
SQ FT: 30,000
SALES (est): 4.47MM Privately Held
Web: www.jasontool.com
SIC: 3089 3544 Injection molding of plastics; Dies, plastics forming

### (P-6873)
### JB BRANANNE INC
6 Orchard, Lake Forest (92630-8335)
PHONE..................949 215-7704
Jay Kim, CEO
EMP: 20 EST: 1993
SALES (est): 50MM Privately Held
Web: www.jbbrananne.com
SIC: 3089 Automotive parts, plastic

### (P-6874)
### JB PLASTICS INC
1921 E Edinger Ave, Santa Ana (92705-4720)
PHONE..................714 541-8500
Joseph N Chiodo, Pr
Bruce Donoho, *
EMP: 45 EST: 2000
SQ FT: 30,000
SALES (est): 7.95MM Privately Held
Web: www.jb-plastics.com
SIC: 3089 Injection molding of plastics

### (P-6875)
### JEM-HD CO INC
10030 Via De La Amistad Ste F, San Diego (92154-7275)
PHONE..................619 710-1443

Jae Man Lee, CEO
EMP: 22 EST: 2005
SALES (est): 444.8K Privately Held
SIC: 3089 Injection molding of plastics

### (P-6876)
### JET PLASTICS (PA)
941 N Eastern Ave, Los Angeles (90063-1307)
PHONE..................323 268-6706
TOLL FREE: 800
Lee R Johnson, Pr
Lee Johnson, *
Lon Johnson, *
Lowel Johnson, *
◆ EMP: 50 EST: 1948
SQ FT: 30,000
SALES (est): 8.69MM
SALES (corp-wide): 8.69MM Privately Held
Web: www.jetplastics.com
SIC: 3089 Injection molding of plastics

### (P-6877)
### JG PLASTICS GROUP LLC
335 Fischer Ave, Costa Mesa (92626-4522)
PHONE..................714 751-4266
◆ EMP: 50 EST: 1975
SQ FT: 32,000
SALES (est): 9.99MM Privately Held
Web: www.jgplastics.com
SIC: 3089 3544 Injection molding of plastics; Special dies, tools, jigs, and fixtures

### (P-6878)
### JSN INDUSTRIES INC
9700 Jeronimo Rd, Irvine (92618-2019)
PHONE..................949 458-0050
James H Nagel Junior, CEO
Sandra Nagel, *
EMP: 70 EST: 1984
SQ FT: 65,000
SALES (est): 8.37MM Privately Held
Web: www.jsn.com
SIC: 3089 Injection molding of plastics

### (P-6879)
### K&R PRODUCTS INC
Also Called: Economy Plastics
370 Encinal St Ste 200, Santa Cruz (95060-2173)
P.O. Box 1178 (95001-1178)
PHONE..................208 935-8824
Fred Vairetta, CEO
Barbara Lopez, *
EMP: 50 EST: 1960
SQ FT: 4,000
SALES (est): 1.75MM Privately Held
SIC: 3089 3429 Plastics processing; Hardware, nec

### (P-6880)
### KARAT PACKAGING INC (PA)
Also Called: KARAT
6185 Kimball Ave, Chino (91708-9126)
PHONE..................626 965-8882
Alan Yu, Ch Bd
Jian Guo, CFO
Marvin Cheng, VP Mfg
Daniel Quire, CRO
EMP: 26 EST: 2000
SALES (est): 405.65MM
SALES (corp-wide): 405.65MM Publicly Held
Web: www.irkarat.com
SIC: 3089 5113 Plastics containers, except foam; Disposable plates, cups, napkins, and eating utensils

## 3089 - Plastics Products, Nec (P-6881)

**(P-6881)**
**KAS ENGINEERING INC (PA)**
1714 14th St, Santa Monica (90404-4341)
PHONE..................................310 450-8925
EMP: 24 EST: 1958
SALES (est): 5.17MM
SALES (corp-wide): 5.17MM Privately Held
Web: www.kasengineering.com
SIC: 3089 3541 Injection molding of plastics; Machine tools, metal cutting type

**(P-6882)**
**KELCOURT PLASTICS INC (DH)**
Also Called: Kelpac Medical
1000 Calle Recodo, San Clemente (92673-6225)
PHONE..................................949 361-0774
John Wolf, CEO
Rob Bonatakis, *
▲ EMP: 80 EST: 1982
SQ FT: 20,000
SALES (est): 20.23MM
SALES (corp-wide): 2.93B Publicly Held
Web: www.spectrumplastics.com
SIC: 3089 Injection molding of plastics
HQ: Ppc Industries Inc
  10101 78th Ave
  Pleasant Prairie WI 53158
  262 947-0900

**(P-6883)**
**KENNERLEY-SPRATLING INC (PA)**
2116 Farallon Dr, San Leandro (94577)
PHONE..................................510 351-8230
Richard Spratling, CEO
Jeffrey Cranor, *
Bill Roure, *
Paul Hoefler, *
▲ EMP: 250 EST: 1982
SQ FT: 60,000
SALES (est): 89.86MM
SALES (corp-wide): 89.86MM Privately Held
Web: www.ksplastic.com
SIC: 3089 3082 Injection molding of plastics; Unsupported plastics profile shapes

**(P-6884)**
**KENNERLEY-SPRATLING INC**
Also Called: M O S Plastics
2308 Zanker Rd, San Jose (95131-1115)
PHONE..................................408 944-9407
Douglas Cullum, Prin
EMP: 134
SALES (corp-wide): 89.86MM Privately Held
Web: www.ksplastic.com
SIC: 3089 Injection molding of plastics
PA: Kennerley-Spratling, Inc.
  2116 Farallon Dr
  510 351-8230

**(P-6885)**
**KEPNER PLAS FABRICATORS INC**
3131 Lomita Blvd, Torrance (90505-5158)
PHONE..................................562 543-4472
James Garrett Iii, CEO
James Garrett, CEO
Frank Meyers, *
Meryl Bayley, *
▲ EMP: 26 EST: 1960
SQ FT: 50,000
SALES (est): 3.29MM Privately Held
Web: www.elastec.com
SIC: 3089 Injection molding of plastics

**(P-6886)**
**KING BROS INDUSTRIES**
29101 The Old Rd, Valencia (91355-1014)
◆ EMP: 170
Web: www.kbico.com
SIC: 3089 Plastics hardware and building products

**(P-6887)**
**KING PLASTICS INC**
840 N Elm St, Orange (92867-7908)
P.O. Box 6229 (92863-6229)
PHONE..................................714 997-7540
Larry E Lathrum, CEO
◆ EMP: 96 EST: 1962
SQ FT: 100,000
SALES (est): 15.01MM Privately Held
Web: www.kingplastics.com
SIC: 3089 Plastics kitchenware, tableware, and houseware

**(P-6888)**
**KINGSEAL CORPORATION**
12681 Corral Pl, Santa Fe Springs (90670-4748)
PHONE..................................562 944-3100
John Song, Pr
▲ EMP: 16 EST: 1981
SQ FT: 21,000
SALES (est): 2.37MM Privately Held
Web: www.kingseal.com
SIC: 3089 3842 2499 Work gloves, plastics; Gloves, safety; Skewers, wood

**(P-6889)**
**KNIGHTSBRIDGE PLASTICS INC**
Also Called: K P I
3075 Osgood Ct, Fremont (94539)
PHONE..................................510 440-8444
Jean Adell Nagra, CEO
Dave Platt, *
Dave Terry, *
Sean Tregear, *
▲ EMP: 58 EST: 1995
SQ FT: 19,000
SALES (est): 12.3MM Privately Held
Web: www.kpi.net
SIC: 3089 3423 Injection molding of plastics; Hand and edge tools, nec

**(P-6890)**
**KONARK SILICONE TECH INC**
Also Called: Contract Manufacturing
4725 E Bryson St, Anaheim (92807)
PHONE..................................562 372-5415
Sasikanth Kuchibhotla, CEO
Sasikanth Kutchibhotla, Owner
▲ EMP: 15 EST: 2015
SALES (est): 1.11MM Privately Held
Web: www.konarksilicones.com
SIC: 3089 2822 Injection molding of plastics; Silicone rubbers

**(P-6891)**
**KUI CO INC**
266 Calle Pintoresco, San Clemente (92672-7504)
PHONE..................................949 369-7949
Terry Daum, Pr
Sandy Daum, *
EMP: 40 EST: 1996
SQ FT: 14,800
SALES (est): 4.44MM Privately Held
Web: www.kuicoinc.com
SIC: 3089 Plastics processing

**(P-6892)**
**L & H MOLD & ENGINEERING INC (PA)**
Also Called: L & H Molds
140 Atlantic St, Pomona (91768-3285)
PHONE..................................909 930-1547
Stan Hillary, CEO
Steve Hillary, Pr
Brenda Bishop, Sec
EMP: 23 EST: 1974
SQ FT: 6,000
SALES (est): 2.52MM
SALES (corp-wide): 2.52MM Privately Held
SIC: 3089 Injection molding of plastics

**(P-6893)**
**LAMSCO WEST INC**
29101 The Old Rd, Santa Clarita (91355-1014)
PHONE..................................661 295-8620
Steve Griffith, Pr
Scott Wilkinson, *
Rick Casillas, *
EMP: 99 EST: 1993
SQ FT: 31,280
SALES (est): 22.68MM
SALES (corp-wide): 123.82MM Privately Held
Web: www.lamscowest.com
SIC: 3089 Injection molding of plastics
HQ: Avantus Aerospace, Inc.
  29101 The Old Rd
  Valencia CA 91355
  661 295-8620

**(P-6894)**
**LEADING INDUSTRY INC**
Also Called: Pinnacle Plastic Containers
1151 Pacific Ave, Oxnard (93033-2472)
PHONE..................................805 385-4100
◆ EMP: 100
Web: www.perfectdomain.com
SIC: 3089 Plastics processing

**(P-6895)**
**LEHRER BRLLNPRFKTION WERKS INC**
Also Called: Lbi - USA
20801 Nordhoff St, Chatsworth (91311-5925)
P.O. Box 3519 (91313-3519)
PHONE..................................818 407-1890
Keith Lehrer, Pr
Chett Lehrer, *
▲ EMP: 65 EST: 1949
SQ FT: 38,000
SALES (est): 3.01MM Privately Held
SIC: 3089 Cases, plastics

**(P-6896)**
**LINER TECHNOLOGIES INC**
Also Called: Flexi-Liner
4821 Chino Ave, Chino (91710-5132)
PHONE..................................909 594-6610
Tait Eyre, Pr
Angela Eyre, Sec
▼ EMP: 20 EST: 1953
SQ FT: 20,000
SALES (est): 4.11MM Privately Held
Web: www.flexi-liner.com
SIC: 3089 Plastics containers, except foam

**(P-6897)**
**LIQUI-BOX CORPORATION**
Northern CA Operations
5000 Warehouse Way, Sacramento (95826-4914)
PHONE..................................916 381-7054
Scott Falwell, Mgr
EMP: 24
SALES (corp-wide): 5.49B Publicly Held
Web: www.liquibox.com
SIC: 3089 2671 Plastics processing; Paper; coated and laminated packaging
HQ: Liqui-Box Corporation
  2415 Cascade Pointe Blvd
  Charlotte NC 28208
  804 325-1400

**(P-6898)**
**LLC WALKER WEST**
1555 S Vintage Ave, Ontario (91761-3655)
PHONE..................................909 390-4300
Frank San Roman, CEO
Frank San Roman, Managing Member
EMP: 175 EST: 1954
SALES (est): 3.02MM Privately Held
SIC: 3089 Automotive parts, plastic

**(P-6899)**
**MACRO PLASTICS INC (DH)**
2250 Huntington Dr, Fairfield (94533-9732)
PHONE..................................707 437-1200
Alan Walsh, CEO
Aileen Joyce, *
Patrick James Browne, *
▲ EMP: 40 EST: 1991
SQ FT: 28,000
SALES (est): 37.43MM
SALES (corp-wide): 816.52K Privately Held
Web: www.macroplastics.com
SIC: 3089 Injection molding of plastics
HQ: Plastiques Ipl Inc
  1155 Boul Rene-Levesque O Bureau 4100
  Montreal QC H3B 3
  418 789-2880

**(P-6900)**
**MAGIC PLASTICS INC (PA)**
25215 Avenue Stanford, Santa Clarita (91355-3923)
PHONE..................................800 369-0303
John Sarno, CEO
Patrick Madormo, *
Tony Madormo, *
Nan Sarno, *
▲ EMP: 22 EST: 1985
SQ FT: 75,000
SALES (est): 11.77MM
SALES (corp-wide): 11.77MM Privately Held
Web: www.magicplastics.com
SIC: 3089 Injection molding of plastics

**(P-6901)**
**MAKABI 26 INC**
Also Called: Best Buy Imports
2850 E 44th St, Vernon (90058-2402)
PHONE..................................323 588-7666
Benham Makabi, CEO
EMP: 19 EST: 1998
SQ FT: 12,000
SALES (est): 629.36K Privately Held
SIC: 3089 Plastics kitchenware, tableware, and houseware

**(P-6902)**
**MARINE FENDERS INTL INC**
452 W Valley Blvd, Rialto (92376-7718)
PHONE..................................310 834-7037
Gerald Thermos, CEO
Gerald Thermos, Pr
◆ EMP: 35 EST: 2004
SALES (est): 1.6MM Privately Held
Web: www.marinefendersintl.com
SIC: 3089 Plastics boats and other marine equipment

# PRODUCTS & SERVICES SECTION
## 3089 - Plastics Products, Nec (P-6923)

### (P-6903)
**MARTIN CHANCEY CORPORATION**
Also Called: Taral Plastics
525 Malloy Ct, Corona  (92878-4045)
**PHONE**.................510 972-6300
Chancey Price Martin, *CEO*
Emily Martin, *
▲ **EMP:** 25 **EST:** 2003
**SALES (est):** 5.5MM **Privately Held**
Web: www.taralplastics.com
**SIC: 3089** 5085  Jars, plastics; Plastic bottles

### (P-6904)
**MASTER PLASTICS CALIFORNIA INC**
Also Called: Master Plastics
820 Eubanks Dr, Vacaville  (95688-8836)
**PHONE**.................707 451-3168
Steven Tool, *CEO*
**EMP:** 33 **EST:** 2022
**SALES (est):** 5.45MM **Privately Held**
Web: www.masterplastics.com
**SIC: 3089**  Injection molding of plastics

### (P-6905)
**MCNEAL ENTERPRISES INC**
2031 Ringwood Ave, San Jose (95131-1703)
**PHONE**.................408 922-7290
De Anna Mcneal-mirzadegan, *CEO*
Robert Mcneal, *Sec*
**EMP:** 100 **EST:** 1976
**SQ FT:** 62,000
**SALES (est):** 15.81MM **Privately Held**
Web: www.mcneal.com
**SIC: 3089** 3498 3559  Injection molding of plastics; Tube fabricating (contract bending and shaping); Semiconductor manufacturing machinery

### (P-6906)
**MEDEGEN LLC (DH)**
4501 E Wall St, Ontario  (91761-8143)
P.O. Box 515111  (90051-5111)
**PHONE**.................909 390-9080
Michael E Stanley, *
W Mark Dorris, *
Paul M Ellis, *
Jeffrey S Goble, *
▲ **EMP:** 50 **EST:** 2001
**SQ FT:** 3,000
**SALES (est):** 29.64MM
**SALES (corp-wide):** 19.37B **Publicly Held**
Web: www.medegenmed.com
**SIC: 3089**  Injection molded finished plastics products, nec
**HQ:** Carefusion Corporation
3750 Torrey View Ct
San Diego CA 92130

### (P-6907)
**MEDEGEN INC**
930 S Wanamaker Ave, Ontario (91761-8151)
**PHONE**.................909 390-9080
▲ **EMP:** 180
**SIC: 3089** 3544  Injection molded finished plastics products, nec; Special dies, tools, jigs, and fixtures

### (P-6908)
**MEDICAL EXTRUSION TECH INC (PA)**
Also Called: M E T
26608 Pierce Cir Ste A, Murrieta (92562-1008)
**PHONE**.................951 698-4346
Tom E Bauer, *CEO*
I Rikki Bauer, *VP*
**EMP:** 20 **EST:** 1990
**SQ FT:** 16,645
**SALES (est):** 12.8MM **Privately Held**
Web: www.medicalextrusion.com
**SIC: 3089**  Injection molding of plastics

### (P-6909)
**MEDPLAST GROUP INC**
45581 Northport Loop W, Fremont (94538-6462)
**PHONE**.................510 657-5800
Linda Amaral, *Brnch Mgr*
**EMP:** 537
**SALES (corp-wide):** 28.39MM **Privately Held**
Web: www.viantmedical.com
**SIC: 3089**  Injection molding of plastics
**PA:** Medplast Group, Inc.
7865 Northcourt Rd # 100
480 553-6400

### (P-6910)
**MEDWAY PLASTICS CORPORATION**
2250 E Cherry Industrial Cir, Long Beach (90805-4414)
**PHONE**.................562 630-1175
Thomas Hutchinson Junior, *CEO*
Mary Hutchinson, *
Gerry Hutchinson, *
Rick Hutchinson, *
Sheryl Mcdaniel, *VP*
◆ **EMP:** 141 **EST:** 1974
**SALES (est):** 23.1MM **Privately Held**
Web: www.medwayplastics.com
**SIC: 3089**  Injection molding of plastics

### (P-6911)
**MERGER SUB GOTHAM 2 LLC**
6261 Katella Ave Ste 250, Cypress (90630-5200)
**PHONE**.................714 462-4603
Nicholas Kovacevich, *CEO*
**EMP:** 109 **EST:** 2021
**SALES (est):** 2.16MM
**SALES (corp-wide):** 65.37MM **Publicly Held**
**SIC: 3089** 5085  Plastics containers, except foam; Industrial supplies
**PA:** Greenlane Holdings, Inc.
1095 Brken Sund Pkwy Ste
877 292-7660

### (P-6912)
**MERRICK ENGINEERING INC (PA)**
1275 Quarry St, Corona  (92879-1707)
**PHONE**.................951 737-6040
Abraham M Abdi, *Pr*
Katina Brown, *
Mina Abdi, *
◆ **EMP:** 250 **EST:** 1971
**SQ FT:** 150,000
**SALES (est):** 39.41MM
**SALES (corp-wide):** 39.41MM **Privately Held**
Web: www.merrickengineering.com
**SIC: 3089**  Injection molding of plastics

### (P-6913)
**MI TECHNOLOGIES INC**
Also Called: Lutema
2215 Paseo De Las Americas Ste 30, San Diego  (92154-7908)
**PHONE**.................619 710-2637
Amir Tafreshi, *CEO*
John Celms, *
Ali Irani-tehrani, *Prin*
▲ **EMP:** 700 **EST:** 2004
**SQ FT:** 8,000
**SALES (est):** 15.93MM **Privately Held**
Web: www.discount-merchant.com
**SIC: 3089** 3672 5731 3999  Injection molding of plastics; Printed circuit boards; Consumer electronic equipment, nec; Barber and beauty shop equipment

### (P-6914)
**MICROMOLD INC**
2100 Iowa Ave, Riverside  (92507-2413)
P.O. Box 51118  (92517-2118)
**PHONE**.................951 684-7130
Robert Aust, *Pr*
Ron Peterson, *VP*
**EMP:** 15 **EST:** 1979
**SQ FT:** 11,000
**SALES (est):** 2.31MM **Privately Held**
Web: www.micromoldinc.com
**SIC: 3089**  Molding primary plastics

### (P-6915)
**MILGARD MANUFACTURING LLC**
Also Called: Milgard Windows
26879 Diaz Rd, Temecula  (92590-3470)
**PHONE**.................480 763-6000
Cory Hall, *Brnch Mgr*
**EMP:** 280
**SALES (corp-wide):** 822.1MM **Privately Held**
Web: www.milgard.com
**SIC: 3089** 3442 5211 3231  Windows, plastics ; Sash, door or window: metal; Door and window products; Products of purchased glass
**HQ:** Milgard Manufacturing Llc
1498 Pacific Ave Fl 4
Tacoma WA 98402
253 922-4343

### (P-6916)
**MISSION PLASTICS INC**
1930 S Parco Ave, Ontario  (91761-8312)
**PHONE**.................909 947-7287
Patrick Dauphinee, *CEO*
Charles Montes, *
▲ **EMP:** 120 **EST:** 1982
**SQ FT:** 20,000
**SALES (est):** 1.41MM **Privately Held**
Web: www.missionplastics.com
**SIC: 3089**  Injection molding of plastics

### (P-6917)
**MODERN CONCEPTS INC**
3121 E Ana St, E Rncho Dmngz (90221-5606)
**PHONE**.................310 637-0013
Richard J Warpack, *Pr*
◆ **EMP:** 60 **EST:** 1983
**SQ FT:** 42,000
**SALES (est):** 7.25MM **Privately Held**
**SIC: 3089** 3087  Coloring and finishing of plastics products; Custom compound purchased resins

### (P-6918)
**MODIFIED PLASTICS INC (PA)**
1240 E Glenwood Pl, Santa Ana (92707-3000)
**PHONE**.................714 546-4667
Robert Estep, *CEO*
Jocelyn Eubank, *
▲ **EMP:** 27 **EST:** 1976
**SQ FT:** 18,000
**SALES (est):** 22.22MM
**SALES (corp-wide):** 22.22MM **Privately Held**
Web: www.modifiedplastics.com

### (P-6919)
**MOLDED FIBER GL COMPANIES - W**
Also Called: M F G West
9400 Holly Rd, Adelanto  (92301-3900)
P.O. Box 675  (44005-0675)
**PHONE**.................760 246-4042
Richard Morrison, *CEO*
Dave Denny, *
Jim Sommer, *
▲ **EMP:** 100 **EST:** 1958
**SQ FT:** 66,000
**SALES (est):** 8.76MM
**SALES (corp-wide):** 360.86MM **Privately Held**
Web: www.moldedfiberglass.com
**SIC: 3089**  Air mattresses, plastics
**PA:** Molded Fiber Glass Companies
2925 Mfg Pl
440 997-5851

### (P-6920)
**MOLDING CORPORATION AMERICA**
10349 Norris Ave, Pacoima  (91331-2220)
**PHONE**.................818 890-7877
Mark Hurley, *CEO*
Sandra Rinder, *VP*
▲ **EMP:** 50 **EST:** 1967
**SQ FT:** 59,000
**SALES (est):** 5.62MM **Privately Held**
Web: www.moldingcorp.com
**SIC: 3089**  Injection molding of plastics

### (P-6921)
**MOLDING SOLUTIONS INC**
3225 Regional Pkwy, Santa Rosa (95403-8214)
**PHONE**.................707 575-1218
Barbara F Roberts, *Pr*
**EMP:** 61 **EST:** 1970
**SQ FT:** 22,000
**SALES (est):** 5.03MM **Privately Held**
**SIC: 3089**  Plastics hardware and building products

### (P-6922)
**MONCO PRODUCTS INC**
7562 Acacia Ave, Garden Grove (92841-4057)
**PHONE**.................714 891-2788
Tom Monson, *Pr*
Jerry Monson, *
▲ **EMP:** 20 **EST:** 1979
**SQ FT:** 15,000
**SALES (est):** 2.09MM **Privately Held**
Web: www.moncoproducts.com
**SIC: 3089**  Injection molding of plastics

### (P-6923)
**MOSPLASTICS INC**
2308 Zanker Rd, San Jose  (95131-1115)
**PHONE**.................408 944-9407
Douglas Cullum, *CEO*
Werner Schultz, *Pr*
Tom Howard, *Stockholder*
Dan Flamen, *Stockholder*
**EMP:** 15 **EST:** 1977
**SQ FT:** 60,000
**SALES (est):** 5.29MM
**SALES (corp-wide):** 89.86MM **Privately Held**
Web: www.ksplastic.com
**SIC: 3089**  Injection molding of plastics
**PA:** Kennerley-Spratling, Inc.
2116 Farallon Dr
510 351-8230

## 3089 - Plastics Products, Nec (P-6924)

**(P-6924)**
**MOTHER LODE PLAS MOLDING INC**
Also Called: Central Plastics and Mfg
1480 E Pescadero Ave, Tracy (95304-8523)
PHONE..................................209 532-5146
TOLL FREE: 800
Chand Shyani, *CEO*
Hiren Patel, *
▲ EMP: 52 EST: 2013
SALES (est): 10.34MM Privately Held
Web: www.centplasticmfg.com
SIC: 3089 2671 Injection molding of plastics; Thermoplastic coated paper for packaging

**(P-6925)**
**MTECH INC**
Also Called: Blackline Manufacturing
1072 Marauder St Ste 210, Chico (95973-9001)
PHONE..................................530 894-5091
Jason Black, *Pr*
Thomas E Black Senior, *VP*
Bernadette Black, *CFO*
EMP: 19 EST: 1996
SQ FT: 3,000
SALES (est): 6.09MM Privately Held
Web: www.mtechincorporated.com
SIC: 3089 3569 3552 3523 Injection molding of plastics; Firefighting apparatus; Printing machinery, textile; Sprayers and spraying machines, agricultural

**(P-6926)**
**NATIONAL DIVERSIFIED SALES INC (HQ)**
Also Called: Nds
21300 Victory Blvd Ste 215, Woodland Hills (91367-7721)
P.O. Box 339 (93247-0339)
PHONE..................................559 562-9888
Michael Gummeson, *Pr*
Randall Stott, *
Josie Malonado, *
♦ EMP: 200 EST: 1978
SQ FT: 5,000
SALES (est): 210.51MM Privately Held
Web: www.ndspro.com
SIC: 3089 Plastics hardware and building products
PA: Norma Group Se
    Edisonstr. 4

**(P-6927)**
**NEOPACIFIC HOLDINGS INC**
Also Called: Pro-Action Products
14940 Calvert St, Van Nuys (91411-2603)
PHONE..................................818 786-2900
Steve Chan, *Pr*
▲ EMP: 48 EST: 1981
SQ FT: 24,000
SALES (est): 8.04MM Privately Held
Web: www.proactionproducts.com
SIC: 3089 Injection molding of plastics

**(P-6928)**
**NEW WEST PRODUCTS INC**
Also Called: ITW Space Bag
7520 Airway Rd Ste 1, San Diego (92154-8304)
PHONE..................................619 671-9022
♦ EMP: 46
Web: www.ziploc.com
SIC: 3089 2673 Plastics containers, except foam; Bags: plastic, laminated, and coated

**(P-6929)**
**NEWELL BRANDS INC**
17182 Nevada St, Victorville (92394-7806)
PHONE..................................760 246-2700
EMP: 41
SALES (corp-wide): 8.13B Publicly Held
Web: www.newellbrands.com
SIC: 3089 Plastics kitchenware, tableware, and houseware
PA: Newell Brands Inc.
    6655 Pachtree Dunwoody Rd
    770 418-7000

**(P-6930)**
**NEWLIGHT TECHNOLOGIES INC**
Also Called: Aircarbon
14382 Astronautics Ln, Huntington Beach (92647-2081)
PHONE..................................714 556-4500
Mark Herrema, *CEO*
Kenton Kimmel, *
Evan Creelman, *
EMP: 29 EST: 2007
SALES (est): 11.62MM Privately Held
Web: www.newlight.com
SIC: 3089 Plastics processing

**(P-6931)**
**NEWPORT LAMINATES INC**
3121 W Central Ave, Santa Ana (92704-5302)
PHONE..................................714 545-8335
Brad A Bollman, *Pr*
Wendy Bollman, *
EMP: 40 EST: 1974
SQ FT: 24,000
SALES (est): 4.26MM Privately Held
Web: www.newportlaminates.com
SIC: 3089 Fiber, vulcanized

**(P-6932)**
**NEWPORT PLASTICS LLC (PA)**
3200 E Birch St Ste B, Brea (92821-6287)
PHONE..................................800 854-8402
Brand Caso, *Pr*
EMP: 16 EST: 1965
SALES (est): 4.8MM
SALES (corp-wide): 4.8MM Privately Held
Web: www.newportplastics.com
SIC: 3089 3599 7389 Injection molding of plastics; Machine shop, jobbing and repair; Business services, nec

**(P-6933)**
**NORCO INJECTION MOLDING INC**
Also Called: Norco Plastics
14325 Monte Vista Ave, Chino (91710-5726)
P.O. Box 2528 (91708-2528)
PHONE..................................909 393-4000
Jack Williams, *Pr*
John Williams, *CFO*
▲ EMP: 100 EST: 1974
SQ FT: 45,000
SALES (est): 2.81MM Privately Held
Web: www.niminc.com
SIC: 3089 3544 Injection molding of plastics; Special dies, tools, jigs, and fixtures

**(P-6934)**
**NORCO PLASTICS INC**
14325 Monte Vista Ave, Chino (91710-5726)
P.O. Box 2528 (91708-2528)
PHONE..................................909 393-4000
John Williams, *CEO*
▲ EMP: 90 EST: 2010
SALES (est): 9.33MM Privately Held
Web: www.norcoplastics.com
SIC: 3089 Plastics containers, except foam

**(P-6935)**
**NORTHERN CALIFORNIA INJECTION MOLDING LLC**
Also Called: Ncim
2691 Mercantile Dr, Rancho Cordova (95742-6521)
PHONE..................................916 853-0717
EMP: 15 EST: 1997
SALES (est): 9.65MM
SALES (corp-wide): 50MM Privately Held
Web: www.springboardmfg.com
SIC: 3089 Injection molded finished plastics products, nec
PA: Kruger Plastic Products Llc
    2691 Mercantile Dr
    916 853-0717

**(P-6936)**
**NORTON PACKAGING INC (PA)**
Also Called: Norpak
20670 Corsair Blvd, Hayward (94545-1008)
PHONE..................................510 786-1922
Greg Norton, *
Mark Norton, *
♦ EMP: 60 EST: 1901
SQ FT: 7,200
SALES (est): 32.65MM
SALES (corp-wide): 32.65MM Privately Held
Web: www.nortonpackaging.com
SIC: 3089 Plastics containers, except foam

**(P-6937)**
**NORTON PACKAGING INC**
5800 S Boyle Ave, Vernon (90058-3927)
PHONE..................................323 588-6167
Joe Schrick, *Brnch Mgr*
EMP: 25
SALES (corp-wide): 56.46MM Privately Held
Web: www.nortonpackaging.com
SIC: 3089 5162 Plastics containers, except foam; Resins
PA: Norton Packaging, Inc.
    20670 Corsair Blvd
    510 786-1922

**(P-6938)**
**NORTON PACKAGING INC**
Norton Containers/ Norpack
2868 W Winton Ave, Hayward (94545-1122)
PHONE..................................510 786-1922
Joe Schrick, *Brnch Mgr*
EMP: 26
SALES (corp-wide): 32.65MM Privately Held
Web: www.nortonpackaging.com
SIC: 3089 3411 3412 Pails, plastics; Metal cans; Metal barrels, drums, and pails
PA: Norton Packaging, Inc.
    20670 Corsair Blvd
    510 786-1922

**(P-6939)**
**NSA HOLDINGS INC**
Also Called: Amerex Company
888 Marlborough Ave, Riverside (92507-2117)
PHONE..................................951 686-1400
Donald H Circosta, *Pr*
EMP: 22 EST: 1972
SQ FT: 15,500
SALES (est): 385.69K Privately Held
SIC: 3089 Injection molding of plastics

**(P-6940)**
**NUBS PLASTICS INC**
991 Park Center Dr, Vista (92081-8312)
PHONE..................................760 598-2525
Niyogi Ramolia, *Pr*
▼ EMP: 30 EST: 1993
SQ FT: 13,000
SALES (est): 4.84MM Privately Held
Web: www.nubsplasticsinc.com
SIC: 3089 Injection molding of plastics

**(P-6941)**
**NUCONIC PACKAGING LLC**
4889 Loma Vista Ave, Vernon (90058-3216)
PHONE..................................323 588-9033
Alan Franz, *CEO*
Christopher Winkler, *
Skip Farber, *
Jason Farber, *
▲ EMP: 31 EST: 2008
SQ FT: 30,000
SALES (est): 4.6MM Privately Held
Web: www.easypak.com
SIC: 3089 4783 Plastics containers, except foam; Packing and crating

**(P-6942)**
**NYPRO INC**
Also Called: Nypro Healthcare Baja
505 Main St Rm 107, Chula Vista (91911-6059)
PHONE..................................619 498-9250
Gregg Lambert, *Genl Mgr*
EMP: 75
SALES (corp-wide): 28.88B Publicly Held
Web: www.nypromold.com
SIC: 3089 3559 Injection molding of plastics; Robots, molding and forming plastics
HQ: Nypro Inc.
    101 Union St
    Clinton MA 01510
    978 365-9721

**(P-6943)**
**NYPRO SAN DIEGO INC**
505 Main St, Chula Vista (91911-6075)
PHONE..................................619 482-7033
Gordon Lankton, *Sec*
Ernie Rice, *
▼ EMP: 80 EST: 1988
SQ FT: 66,000
SALES (est): 5.04MM
SALES (corp-wide): 28.88B Publicly Held
SIC: 3089 Injection molding of plastics
HQ: Nypro Inc.
    101 Union St
    Clinton MA 01510
    978 365-9721

**(P-6944)**
**ODI MANUFACTURING LLC ✪**
708 S Temescal St Ste 101, Corona (92879-2096)
P.O. Box 1839 (92878-1839)
PHONE..................................951 786-4750
EMP: 129 EST: 2023
SALES (est): 110.82K
SALES (corp-wide): 66.6MM Privately Held
SIC: 3089 Injection molding of plastics
HQ: Mission Rubber Company Llc
    1660 Leeson Ln
    Corona CA 92879
    951 736-1313

**(P-6945)**
**OMNI RESOURCE RECOVERY INC**
1495 N 8th St Ste 150, Colton (92324-1451)

▲ = Import ▼ = Export
♦ = Import/Export

# PRODUCTS & SERVICES SECTION
## 3089 - Plastics Products, Nec (P-6968)

PHONE..............................909 327-2900
**EMP:** 250
**Web:** www.omnirecovery.com
**SIC: 3089** Extruded finished plastics products, nec

### (P-6946)
### ORBIS WHEELS INC
Also Called: Orbis Bioaid
789 Lombardi Ct Ste 204, Santa Rosa (95407-5435)
PHONE..............................415 548-4160
Marcus Hays, *CEO*
**EMP:** 19 **EST:** 2014
**SALES (est):** 4.15MM **Privately Held**
**Web:** www.orbiselectric.com
**SIC: 3089** Automotive parts, plastic

### (P-6947)
### PACTIV LLC
2024 Norris Rd, Bakersfield (93308-2238)
PHONE..............................661 392-4000
Steve Stewart, *Mgr*
**EMP:** 103
**Web:** www.pactivevergreen.com
**SIC: 3089** 3086 Kitchenware, plastics; Plastics foam products
**HQ:** Pactiv Llc
1900 W Field Ct
Lake Forest IL 60045
847 482-2000

### (P-6948)
### PAN PACIFIC PLASTICS MFG INC (PA)
26551 Danti Ct, Hayward (94545-3917)
PHONE..............................510 785-6888
Ying Wang, *Pr*
Mike Tan, *
Maurice Wang, *
Robert Lin, *
◆ **EMP:** 26 **EST:** 1981
**SQ FT:** 46,080
**SALES (est):** 5.42MM
**SALES (corp-wide):** 5.42MM **Privately Held**
**Web:** www.pppmi.com
**SIC: 3089** 2673 Plastics processing; Bags: plastic, laminated, and coated

### (P-6949)
### PARADIGM PACKAGING EAST LLC
Also Called: Paradigm Packaging West
9595 Utica Ave, Rancho Cucamonga (91730-5921)
P.O. Box 10 (91785-0010)
PHONE..............................909 985-2750
Steve Costecki, *Mgr*
**EMP:** 27
**SALES (corp-wide):** 112.7MM **Privately Held**
**SIC: 3089** Plastics containers, except foam
**HQ:** Paradigm Packaging East Llc
141 5th St
Saddle Brook NJ 07663
201 909-3400

### (P-6950)
### PARAMOUNT PANELS INC (PA)
Also Called: California Plasteck
1531 E Cedar St, Ontario (91761-5762)
PHONE..............................909 947-8008
Arthur G Thorne, *Pr*
John G Thorne, *
**EMP:** 32 **EST:** 1962
**SQ FT:** 12,000
**SALES (est):** 3.77MM
**SALES (corp-wide):** 3.77MM **Privately Held**

**Web:** www.paramountpanels.com
**SIC: 3089** 3812 3728 Plastics processing; Search and navigation equipment; Aircraft parts and equipment, nec

### (P-6951)
### PAULEY PLASTIC LLC
17177 Navajo Rd, Apple Valley (92307-1046)
PHONE..............................760 240-3737
**EMP:** 15 **EST:** 2020
**SALES (est):** 3.02MM **Privately Held**
**Web:** www.pauleyplastic.com
**SIC: 3089** Injection molding of plastics

### (P-6952)
### PC VAUGHAN MFG CORP
Also Called: Rostar Filters
1278 Mercantile St, Oxnard (93030-7522)
PHONE..............................805 278-2555
Jeff Starin, *CEO*
Jeff Starin, *Pr*
**EMP:** 65 **EST:** 1979
**SQ FT:** 40,000
**SALES (est):** 4.94MM **Privately Held**
**Web:** www.rostarfilters.com
**SIC: 3089** 3569 3714 5085 Automotive parts, plastic; Filters; Filters: oil, fuel, and air, motor vehicle; Filters, industrial

### (P-6953)
### PEERLESS INJECTION MOLDING LLC
Also Called: Proplas Technologies
14321 Corp Dr, Garden Grove (92843)
PHONE..............................714 689-1920
Scott Taylor, *Pr*
▲ **EMP:** 50 **EST:** 1977
**SQ FT:** 51,112
**SALES (est):** 9.65MM
**SALES (corp-wide):** 39.28MM **Privately Held**
**SIC: 3089** Injection molding of plastics
**PA:** Comar, Inc.
201 Laurel Rd Fl 2
856 692-6100

### (P-6954)
### PERFORMNCE ENGINEERED PDTS INC
Also Called: Honor Plastics
3270 Pomona Blvd, Pomona (91768-3282)
PHONE..............................909 594-7487
Dinesh Savalia, *CEO*
**EMP:** 48 **EST:** 2016
**SQ FT:** 42,000
**SALES (est):** 9MM **Privately Held**
**Web:** www.honorplastics.com
**SIC: 3089** Injection molding of plastics

### (P-6955)
### PINNPACK CAPITAL HOLDINGS LLC
Also Called: Pinnpack Packaging
1151 Pacific Ave, Oxnard (93033-2472)
PHONE..............................805 385-4100
Iraj Maroofian, *CEO*
Irage Barkohanai, *
Sriram Kailasam, *
**EMP:** 205 **EST:** 2021
**SALES (est):** 26.61MM **Privately Held**
**Web:** www.pinnpack.com
**SIC: 3089** Plastics containers, except foam

### (P-6956)
### PLAINFIELD MOLDING INC
Also Called: Plainfield Companies
135 S State College Blvd # 200, Brea (92821-5823)

PHONE..............................815 436-7806
**EMP:** 69
**SIC: 3089** Molding primary plastics

### (P-6957)
### PLAINFIELD TOOL AND ENGINEERING INC
Also Called: Plainfield Stamping-Illinois
135 South College Blvd Ste 200, Brea (92821)
PHONE..............................815 436-5671
▲ **EMP:** 305
**SIC: 3089** 3469 Injection molding of plastics; Metal stampings, nec

### (P-6958)
### PLASIDYNE ENGINEERING & MFG
3230 E 59th St, Long Beach (90805-4502)
P.O. Box 5578 (90805-0578)
PHONE..............................562 531-0510
Dean C Sutherland, *Pr*
**EMP:** 22 **EST:** 1969
**SQ FT:** 15,000
**SALES (est):** 3.32MM **Privately Held**
**Web:** www.plasidyne.com
**SIC: 3089** Injection molding of plastics

### (P-6959)
### PLASTIC AND METAL CENTER INC
23162 La Cadena Dr, Laguna Hills (92653-1405)
PHONE..............................949 770-0610
Faramarz Khaladj, *Pr*
Fred Carr, *
Denise Khaladj, *
**EMP:** 25 **EST:** 1993
**SQ FT:** 20,000
**SALES (est):** 4.42MM **Privately Held**
**Web:** www.plastic-metal.com
**SIC: 3089** Injection molding of plastics

### (P-6960)
### PLASTIC ENGINEERING TECH LLC
4502 Brickell Privado St, Ontario (91761-7827)
PHONE..............................909 390-1323
▲ **EMP:** 16 **EST:** 2005
**SALES (est):** 931.64K **Privately Held**
**SIC: 3089** Plastics hardware and building products

### (P-6961)
### PLASTIC MOLDED COMPONENTS INC
Also Called: P M C
5920 Lakeshore Dr, Cypress (90630-3371)
PHONE..............................714 229-0133
**EMP:** 40 **EST:** 1979
**SALES (est):** 1.22MM **Privately Held**
**Web:** www.moldedplasticcomponents.com
**SIC: 3089** Molding primary plastics

### (P-6962)
### PLASTIC PROCESSING CORP
13432 Estrella Ave, Gardena (90248-1513)
PHONE..............................310 719-7330
Dagmer Schulte-derne, *Ch Bd*
Steve Rockenbach, *
▲ **EMP:** 16 **EST:** 1988
**SQ FT:** 20,000
**SALES (est):** 223.72K **Privately Held**
**Web:** www.plasticprocessing.net
**SIC: 3089** Blow molded finished plastics products, nec

### (P-6963)
### PLASTIC TECHNOLOGIES INC
Also Called: Blow Molded Products
4720 Felspar St, Riverside (92509-3068)
PHONE..............................951 360-6055
Meir Ben-david, *Pr*
Diane Ben-david, *VP*
**EMP:** 50 **EST:** 2018
**SALES (est):** 5.02MM **Privately Held**
**Web:** www.blowmoldedproducts.com
**SIC: 3089** Injection molding of plastics

### (P-6964)
### PLASTICS DEVELOPMENT CORP
960 Calle Negocio, San Clemente (92673-6201)
PHONE..............................949 492-0217
Inder Jain, *Pr*
Sanie Jain, *
Vijay Jain, *
▲ **EMP:** 23 **EST:** 1969
**SQ FT:** 7,000
**SALES (est):** 3.59MM **Privately Held**
**Web:** www.plasticsdev.com
**SIC: 3089** Injection molding of plastics

### (P-6965)
### PLASTICS FAMILY HOLDINGS INC
Also Called: Calsak Plastics
19801 S Rancho Way Unit B, Rancho Dominguez (90220-6316)
PHONE..............................310 928-4100
Sean O'leary, *Brnch Mgr*
**EMP:** 17
**Web:** www.calsakplastics.com
**SIC: 3089** Injection molding of plastics
**HQ:** Plastics Family Holdings, Inc.
5800 Cmpus Cir Dr E Ste 1
Irving TX 75063
469 299-7000

### (P-6966)
### PLASTICS PLUS TECHNOLOGY INC
1495 Research Dr, Redlands (92374-4584)
PHONE..............................909 747-0555
Kathy Bodor, *CEO*
**EMP:** 33 **EST:** 1980
**SQ FT:** 35,000
**SALES (est):** 4.1MM **Privately Held**
**Web:** www.plasticsplus.com
**SIC: 3089** 3544 Injection molding of plastics; Forms (molds), for foundry and plastics working machinery

### (P-6967)
### PLASTIKON INDUSTRIES (PA)
Also Called: Plastikon Automotive
688 Sandoval Way, Hayward (94544-7129)
PHONE..............................510 400-1010
Pete Petri, *CEO*
Fred Soofer, *
Rae R Pourian, *
▲ **EMP:** 156 **EST:** 1979
**SQ FT:** 90,000
**SALES (est):** 151.6MM
**SALES (corp-wide):** 151.6MM **Privately Held**
**Web:** www.plastikon.com
**SIC: 3089** Injection molded finished plastics products, nec

### (P-6968)
### PLASTIKON INDUSTRIES INC
Also Called: PLASTIKON INDUSTRIES, INC.
30260 Santucci Ct, Hayward (94544-7100)
PHONE..............................510 487-1010

## 3089 - Plastics Products, Nec (P-6969)

Fereydoon Soofer, *Brnch Mgr*
**EMP:** 199
**SALES (corp-wide):** 151.6MM **Privately Held**
**Web:** www.plastikon.com
**SIC: 3089** Injection molding of plastics
**PA:** Plastikon Industries
 688 Sandoval Way
 510 400-1010

### (P-6969)
### PLASTIQUE UNIQUE INC
3383 Livonia Ave, Los Angeles (90034-3127)
**PHONE**...................................310 839-3968
Christine Galonska, *Pr*
Lionel Funes, *
Silvia Totado, *
**EMP:** 17 **EST:** 1970
**SQ FT:** 5,000
**SALES (est):** 900.06K **Privately Held**
**Web:** www.plastiqueuniqueinc.com
**SIC: 3089** Injection molding of plastics

### (P-6970)
### PLASTOKER INC
Also Called: Mj-Pak
12 Morgan, Irvine (92618-2003)
**PHONE**...................................714 598-5920
David Greenberg, *CEO*
Michael Boggs, *Pr*
Jason Greenberg, *CFO*
**EMP:** 16 **EST:** 2018
**SALES (est):** 3.57MM **Privately Held**
**SIC: 3089** Tumblers, plastics

### (P-6971)
### PLASTPRO 2000 INC (PA)
Also Called: Plastpro Doors
5200 W Century Blvd, Los Angeles (90045-5928)
**PHONE**...................................310 693-8600
Shirley Wang, *CEO*
Shirley Wang, *Pr*
Johnny Mai, *CFO*
◆ **EMP:** 126 **EST:** 1994
**SALES (est):** 31.01MM **Privately Held**
**Web:** www.plastproinc.com
**SIC: 3089** Fiberglass doors

### (P-6972)
### POLYMER LOGISTICS INC
1725 Sierra Ridge Dr, Riverside (92507-7133)
**PHONE**...................................951 567-2900
Albert Terrazas, *Brnch Mgr*
**EMP:** 57
**SALES (corp-wide):** 217.91MM **Privately Held**
**Web:** www.toscaltd.com
**SIC: 3089** 5085 5162 Pallets, plastics; Boxes, crates, etc., other than paper; Plastics materials and basic shapes
**HQ:** Polymer Logistics, Inc.
 1175 Peachtree St Ne # 1900
 Atlanta GA 30261

### (P-6973)
### POLYMERPAK LLC
6941 W Goshen Ave, Visalia (93291)
**PHONE**...................................559 651-1965
Michael Leraris, *Managing Member*
Jon Charles Buff, *
**EMP:** 130 **EST:** 2015
**SALES (est):** 1.7MM **Privately Held**
**Web:** www.replanetpackaging.com
**SIC: 3089** Plastics containers, except foam

### (P-6974)
### PPP LLC
601 W Olympic Blvd, Montebello (90640-5229)
P.O. Box 789 (90640-0789)
**PHONE**...................................323 832-9627
Evelyn Garcia, *Managing Member*
**EMP:** 17 **EST:** 2001
**SALES (est):** 965.2K **Privately Held**
**SIC: 3089** Injection molding of plastics

### (P-6975)
### PRC COMPOSITES LLC
Also Called: Globe Plastics
13477 12th St, Chino (91710-5206)
**PHONE**...................................909 464-1520
John Upsher, *Brnch Mgr*
**EMP:** 20
**SALES (corp-wide):** 18.14MM **Privately Held**
**Web:** www.prccal.com
**SIC: 3089** 3544 Injection molding of plastics; Special dies, tools, jigs, and fixtures
**PA:** Prc Composites, Llc
 1400 S Campus Ave
 909 391-2006

### (P-6976)
### PRC COMPOSITES LLC (PA)
1400 S Campus Ave, Ontario (91761-4330)
**PHONE**...................................909 391-2006
John Upsher, *Managing Member*
Gene Gregory, *
**EMP:** 79 **EST:** 2014
**SALES (est):** 18.14MM
**SALES (corp-wide):** 18.14MM **Privately Held**
**Web:** www.prccal.com
**SIC: 3089** Plastics containers, except foam

### (P-6977)
### PRE/PLASTICS INC
Also Called: Preplastics
12600 Locksley Ln Ste 100, Auburn (95602-2070)
**PHONE**...................................530 823-1820
Richard L Miller, *CEO*
Linda Miller, *
Brian Miller, *
▲ **EMP:** 30 **EST:** 1986
**SQ FT:** 20,000
**SALES (est):** 9.46MM **Privately Held**
**Web:** www.preplastics.com
**SIC: 3089** Injection molding of plastics

### (P-6978)
### PRECISE AEROSPACE MFG LLC
Also Called: Precise Plastic Products
22951 La Palma Ave, Yorba Linda (92887-6701)
**PHONE**...................................951 898-0500
Ronnie E Harwood, *CEO*
Roxanne Abdi, *
▲ **EMP:** 42 **EST:** 1965
**SQ FT:** 39,000
**SALES (est):** 11.32MM **Privately Held**
**Web:** www.precisemfg.com
**SIC: 3089** 3544 Molding primary plastics; Industrial molds

### (P-6979)
### PREDATOR MOTORSPORTS INC
1250 Distribution Way, Vista (92081-8816)
**PHONE**...................................760 734-1749
Ryan Wilson, *Pr*
Dan Wilson, *VP*
▲ **EMP:** 15 **EST:** 1998
**SQ FT:** 15,000
**SALES (est):** 2.65MM **Privately Held**
**Web:** www.predatorinc.com
**SIC: 3089** 3465 Automotive parts, plastic; Body parts, automobile: stamped metal

### (P-6980)
### PREPRODUCTION PLASTICS INC
Also Called: P P I
210 Teller St, Corona (92879-1886)
**PHONE**...................................951 340-9680
Koby Loosen, *Pr*
Ron Loosen, *
Barbara Loosen, *
▲ **EMP:** 50 **EST:** 1978
**SQ FT:** 45,000
**SALES (est):** 8.44MM **Privately Held**
**Web:** www.ppiplastics.com
**SIC: 3089** 3544 Molding primary plastics; Forms (molds), for foundry and plastics working machinery

### (P-6981)
### PRES-TEK PLASTICS INC (PA)
10700 7th St, Rancho Cucamonga (91730-5404)
**PHONE**...................................909 360-1600
Donna C Pursell, *CEO*
**EMP:** 27 **EST:** 2005
**SALES (est):** 23.72MM
**SALES (corp-wide):** 23.72MM **Privately Held**
**Web:** www.prestekplastics.com
**SIC: 3089** Injection molding of plastics

### (P-6982)
### PRIME PLASTIC PRODUCTS INC
1351 Distribution Way Ste 8, Vista (92081-8832)
**PHONE**...................................760 734-3900
**EMP:** 18 **EST:** 1993
**SALES (est):** 4.87MM **Privately Held**
**Web:** www.primeplastic.com
**SIC: 3089** Plastics processing

### (P-6983)
### PRINCE LIONHEART INC (PA)
2421 Westgate Rd, Santa Maria (93455-1075)
**PHONE**...................................805 922-2250
Kelly Griffiths, *CEO*
Debbie Di Nardi, *
▲ **EMP:** 40 **EST:** 1973
**SQ FT:** 80,000
**SALES (est):** 12.1MM
**SALES (corp-wide):** 12.1MM **Privately Held**
**Web:** www.princelionheart.com
**SIC: 3089** Injection molding of plastics

### (P-6984)
### PRINCETON CASE-WEST INC
1444 W Mccoy Ln, Santa Maria (93455-1005)
**PHONE**...................................805 928-8840
Douglas Laggrenm, *Pr*
**EMP:** 20 **EST:** 1964
**SQ FT:** 22,000
**SALES (est):** 1.8MM **Privately Held**
**Web:** www.princetoncasewest.com
**SIC: 3089** 3161 Cases, plastics; Luggage

### (P-6985)
### PRO DESIGN GROUP INC
438 E Alondra Blvd, Gardena (90248-2902)
**PHONE**...................................310 767-1032
Chris Raab, *Pr*
Christopher Allen Raab, *
Maria Chanlder, *
▲ **EMP:** 35 **EST:** 1990
**SQ FT:** 50,000
**SALES (est):** 4.55MM **Privately Held**
**Web:** www.theprodesigngroup.com
**SIC: 3089** Plastics kitchenware, tableware, and houseware

### (P-6986)
### PRODUCTIVITY CALIFORNIA INC
Also Called: Pro Cal
10533 Sessler St, South Gate (90280-7251)
**PHONE**...................................562 923-3100
Gary Vollers, *Pr*
Don Uchiyama, *
**EMP:** 17 **EST:** 1983
**SQ FT:** 100,000
**SALES (est):** 3.53MM
**SALES (corp-wide):** 813.07MM **Publicly Held**
**Web:** www.myersindustries.com
**SIC: 3089** Injection molding of plastics
**PA:** Myers Industries, Inc.
 1293 S Main St
 330 253-5592

### (P-6987)
### PROULX MANUFACTURING INC
Also Called: Universal Products
11433 6th St, Rancho Cucamonga (91730)
**PHONE**...................................909 980-0662
Richard Proulx, *Pr*
Lorraine Proulx, *
Raymond E Proulx, *
◆ **EMP:** 45 **EST:** 1970
**SALES (est):** 6.5MM **Privately Held**
**Web:** www.proulxmfg.com
**SIC: 3089** Plastics hardware and building products

### (P-6988)
### PROVIDIEN INJCTION MOLDING INC
Also Called: Pedi
6740 Nancy Ridge Dr, San Diego (92121-2230)
**PHONE**...................................760 931-1844
Jeffrey S Goble, *CEO*
Richard D Witchey Junior, *Pr*
Louise Witchey, *
Paul Jazwin, *
◆ **EMP:** 74 **EST:** 1985
**SALES (est):** 11.87MM
**SALES (corp-wide):** 4.59B **Publicly Held**
**Web:** www.providienmedical.com
**SIC: 3089** Injection molded finished plastics products, nec
**HQ:** Witco Industries, Inc.
 2731 Loker Ave W
 Carlsbad CA 92010

### (P-6989)
### QUASHNICK TOOL CORPORATION
225 N Guild Ave, Lodi (95240-0844)
**PHONE**...................................209 334-5283
**EMP:** 45
**Web:** www.quashnick.com
**SIC: 3089** 3544 Injection molding of plastics; Industrial molds

### (P-6990)
### R V BEST INC
Also Called: Shademaster Products
9335 Stevens Rd, Santee (92071-2809)
**PHONE**...................................619 448-7300
Steven Smoot, *Pr*
Mike Scheller, *
Dan Smoot, *
**EMP:** 45 **EST:** 1983
**SQ FT:** 15,000

# PRODUCTS & SERVICES SECTION
## 3089 - Plastics Products, Nec (P-7012)

SALES (est): 1.53MM **Privately Held**
SIC: **3089** 5999 Awnings, fiberglass and plastics combination; Awnings

### (P-6991)
### RAKAR INCORPORATED
1680 Universe Cir, Oxnard (93033-2441)
PHONE..............................805 487-2721
Theresa Padilla, *CEO*
EMP: 48 EST: 1951
SALES (est): 9.05MM **Privately Held**
Web: www.rakarinc.com
SIC: **3089** 3544 Injection molding of plastics; Forms (molds), for foundry and plastics working machinery

### (P-6992)
### RAMKO INJECTION INC
3551 Tanya Ave, Hemet (92545-9447)
PHONE..............................951 929-0360
Robert G Andrei, *Pr*
EMP: 100 EST: 2007
SALES (est): 9.49MM **Privately Held**
Web: www.ramko-inj.com
SIC: **3089** 3364 Blow molded finished plastics products, nec; Nonferrous die-castings except aluminum

### (P-6993)
### RAMTEC ASSOCIATES INC
Also Called: Con-Tech Plastics
3200 E Birch St Ste B, Brea (92821-6287)
PHONE..............................714 996-7477
Ralph Riehl, *Pr*
Vernon Meurer, *
▲ EMP: 28 EST: 1984
SQ FT: 35,000
SALES (est): 4.61MM **Privately Held**
SIC: **3089** Molding primary plastics

### (P-6994)
### RAPID ACCU-FORM INC
3825 Sprig Dr, Benicia (94510-1248)
P.O. Box 699 (94510-0699)
PHONE..............................707 745-1879
George L Brown, *Pr*
Linda Brown, *VP*
EMP: 15 EST: 1976
SQ FT: 29,000
SALES (est): 2.12MM **Privately Held**
Web: www.rapidaccuform.com
SIC: **3089** 3545 Plastics processing; Tools and accessories for machine tools

### (P-6995)
### RATERMANN MANUFACTURING INC (PA)
Also Called: Rmi
275 S K St, Livermore (94550-4512)
PHONE..............................800 264-7793
George Ratermann, *Pr*
◆ EMP: 31 EST: 1995
SALES (est): 10.09MM **Privately Held**
Web: www.rmiorder.com
SIC: **3089** 3081 3679 Plastics processing; Packing materials, plastics sheet; Cryogenic cooling devices for infrared detectors, masers

### (P-6996)
### RAY PRODUCTS COMPANY INC
1700 Chablis Ave, Ontario (91761-3610)
PHONE..............................888 776-9014
EMP: 50 EST: 1949
SALES (est): 8.17MM **Privately Held**
Web: www.rayplastics.com
SIC: **3089** Thermoformed finished plastics products, nec

### (P-6997)
### REEVES EXTRUDED PRODUCTS INC
1032 Stockton Ave, Arvin (93203-2330)
PHONE..............................661 854-5970
Matthew Cobbs, *CEO*
Steve Reeves, *
Beverly Palmer, *
Sandy Shelton, *
EMP: 75 EST: 1967
SQ FT: 45,000
SALES (est): 4.66MM **Privately Held**
Web: www.reevesextruded.com
SIC: **3089** Injection molding of plastics

### (P-6998)
### REHAU CONSTRUCTION LLC
1250 Corona Pointe Ct Ste 301, Corona (92879-2099)
PHONE..............................951 549-9017
Joe Lepire, *Mgr*
EMP: 67
Web: www.rehau.com
SIC: **3089** Plastics processing
HQ: Rehau Construction Llc
    1501 Edwards Ferry Rd Ne
    Leesburg VA 20176

### (P-6999)
### REHRIG PACIFIC COMPANY (HQ)
4010 E 26th St, Los Angeles (90058-4477)
PHONE..............................323 262-5145
William J Rehrig, *Pr*
Michael J Doka, *
James L Drew, *
Rajesh Luhar, *
◆ EMP: 150 EST: 1997
SQ FT: 200,000
SALES (est): 402.13MM **Privately Held**
Web: www.rehrigpacific.com
SIC: **3089** 2821 Cases, plastics; Plasticizer/additive based plastic materials
PA: Rehrig Pacific Holdings, Inc.
    900 Corporate Center Dr

### (P-7000)
### REHRIG PACIFIC HOLDINGS INC (PA)
900 Corporate Center Dr, Monterey Park (91754-7620)
PHONE..............................323 262-5145
William J Rehrig, *CEO*
Michael J Doka, *
William Widmann, *VP*
James L Drew, *CFO*
Muriel Kiser, *Sec*
EMP: 99 EST: 1998
SALES (est): 438.07MM **Privately Held**
Web: www.rehrigpacific.com
SIC: **3089** 2821 Cases, plastics; Plasticizer/additive based plastic materials

### (P-7001)
### REINHOLD INDUSTRIES INC (DH)
12827 Imperial Hwy, Santa Fe Springs (90670-4761)
PHONE..............................562 944-3281
Clarence Hightower, *CEO*
Carl Walker, *
▲ EMP: 145 EST: 1984
SQ FT: 130,000
SALES (est): 22.37MM **Publicly Held**
Web: www.reinhold-ind.com
SIC: **3089** 3764 2531 Molding primary plastics; Space propulsion units and parts; Seats, aircraft
HQ: Reinhold Holdings, Inc.
    12827 E Imperial Hwy
    Santa Fe Springs CA 90670

### (P-7002)
### RENY & CO INC
Also Called: Renymed
4505 Littlejohn St, Baldwin Park (91706-2239)
PHONE..............................626 962-3078
EMP: 18 EST: 1985
SALES (est): 4.81MM **Privately Held**
Web: www.renymed.com
SIC: **3089** Plastics hardware and building products

### (P-7003)
### RESINART CORPORATION
Also Called: Resinart Plastics
1621 Placentia Ave, Costa Mesa (92627-4311)
PHONE..............................949 642-3665
Gary Uecker, *Pr*
Gene Chandler, *
Frank Uecker, *
EMP: 40 EST: 1969
SQ FT: 15,000
SALES (est): 3.45MM **Privately Held**
Web: www.resinart.com
SIC: **3089** Molding primary plastics

### (P-7004)
### REYRICH PLASTICS INC
1704 S Vineyard Ave, Ontario (91761-7746)
PHONE..............................909 484-8444
Tina Richter, *Pr*
Sandy Reyes, *Pr*
Tina Richter, *CFO*
EMP: 21 EST: 2012
SALES (est): 2.44MM **Privately Held**
Web: www.reyrichplastics.com
SIC: **3089** Injection molding of plastics

### (P-7005)
### RIMNETICS INC
Also Called: R I M
3141 Swetzer Rd, Loomis (95650-9579)
PHONE..............................916 652-5555
David L Chew, *Pr*
Marjorie Chew, *Sec*
Gary Quigley, *Prin*
EMP: 17 EST: 1985
SQ FT: 20,000
SALES (est): 4.03MM
SALES (corp-wide): 10.84MM **Privately Held**
Web: www.rimnetics.com
SIC: **3089** Injection molding of plastics
PA: Minimatics, Inc.
    15500 Concord Cir
    650 969-5630

### (P-7006)
### ROLENN MANUFACTURING INC (PA)
2065 Roberta St, Riverside (92507-2644)
PHONE..............................951 682-1185
Thomas J Accatino, *Pr*
Christie Accatino, *Sec*
EMP: 20 EST: 1965
SQ FT: 9,000
SALES (est): 9.65MM
SALES (corp-wide): 9.65MM **Privately Held**
Web: www.rolenn.com
SIC: **3089** 3599 Injection molding of plastics; Machine and other job shop work

### (P-7007)
### RONCO PLASTICS INC
Also Called: Ronco Plastics
15022 Parkway Loop Ste B, Tustin (92780-6518)
PHONE..............................714 259-1385
Raul L Barajas, *Pr*
Ronald L Pearson, *
EMP: 28 EST: 1976
SQ FT: 28,000
SALES (est): 4.84MM **Privately Held**
Web: www.ronco-plastics.com
SIC: **3089** Plastics containers, except foam

### (P-7008)
### RONFORD PRODUCTS INC
1116 E 2nd St, Pomona (91766-2114)
PHONE..............................909 622-7446
Carl Higgins, *Mgr*
EMP: 28
SALES (corp-wide): 2.13MM **Privately Held**
SIC: **3089** 5093 Injection molding of plastics; Plastics scrap
PA: Ronford Products, Inc.
    16616 Garfield Ave
    562 408-1081

### (P-7009)
### ROTATIONAL MOLDING INC
Also Called: R M I
17038 S Figueroa St, Gardena (90248-3089)
PHONE..............................310 327-5401
Mario Poma, *CEO*
Douglas Russell, *
EMP: 80 EST: 2010
SALES (est): 4.21MM **Privately Held**
Web: www.rotationalmoldinginc.com
SIC: **3089** Plastics containers, except foam
PA: Tank Holding Corp.
    6400 N 60th St

### (P-7010)
### ROTO DYNAMICS INC
1925 N Lime St, Orange (92865-4123)
PHONE..............................714 685-0183
Rishi Saran, *Pr*
Yogindra Saran, *
Rishi Saran, *VP*
EMP: 24 EST: 2005
SALES (est): 2.9MM **Privately Held**
Web: www.rotodynamics.com
SIC: **3089** 3949 Plastics containers, except foam; Cases, gun and rod (sporting equipment)

### (P-7011)
### ROTO POWER INC
191 Granite St Ste A, Corona (92879-1286)
PHONE..............................951 751-9850
David Howey, *Operations Officer*
EMP: 16 EST: 2016
SALES (est): 2.43MM **Privately Held**
Web: www.roto-power.com
SIC: **3089** Injection molding of plastics

### (P-7012)
### ROTO-LITE INC
84701 Avenue 48, Coachella (92236-1201)
PHONE..............................909 923-4353
Sandy Canzone, *Pr*
John Hammond, *Sec*
Dan Hammond, *VP*
EMP: 17 EST: 2003
SALES (est): 3.25MM **Privately Held**
Web: www.rotoliteinc.com
SIC: **3089** Plastics containers, except foam

# 3089 - Plastics Products, Nec (P-7013)

**(P-7013)**
**ROYAL INTERPACK NORTH AMER INC**
475 Palmyrita Ave, Riverside (92507-1812)
PHONE...............................951 787-6925
Radhika Shah, *CEO*
Tee Komsan, *
Visnau Chawla, *
Kunal Sidhpura, *
Abu Hossain, *
▲ EMP: 45 EST: 2011
SALES (est): 7.47MM **Privately Held**
Web: www.royalinterpack.com
SIC: 3089 Thermoformed finished plastics products, nec

**(P-7014)**
**RPLANET ERTH LOS ANGLES HLDNGS**
5300 S Boyle Ave, Vernon (90058-3921)
PHONE...............................833 775-2638
EMP: 51 EST: 2015
SALES (est): 14.16MM **Privately Held**
Web: www.rplanetearth.com
SIC: 3089 Injection molding of plastics

**(P-7015)**
**RPM PLASTIC MOLDING INC**
2821 E Miraloma Ave, Anaheim (92806-1804)
PHONE...............................714 630-9300
Michael Ferik, *CEO*
Phil Hothan, *
▲ EMP: 25 EST: 1995
SALES (est): 4.66MM **Privately Held**
Web: www.rpmselect.com
SIC: 3089 Injection molding of plastics

**(P-7016)**
**RSK TOOL INCORPORATED**
410 W Carob St, Compton (90220-5213)
PHONE...............................310 537-3302
Ronald Kohagura, *Pr*
Virginia Kohagura, *
Mark Kohagura, *
EMP: 35 EST: 1974
SQ FT: 27,000
SALES (est): 2.48MM **Privately Held**
Web: www.rsktool.com
SIC: 3089 Injection molding of plastics

**(P-7017)**
**S&B INDUSTRY INC**
Also Called: Fxp Technologies
105 S Puente St, Brea (92821-3844)
PHONE...............................909 569-4155
Paul H Shiung, *Pr*
EMP: 39
SIC: 3089 Injection molded finished plastics products, nec
HQ: S&B Industry, Inc.
13301 Pk Vsta Blvd Ste 10
Fort Worth TX 76177

**(P-7018)**
**S-CURVE TECHNOLOGIES INC**
601 Valley Blvd Unit C, Big Bear City (92314-9021)
P.O. Box 1989 (92315-1989)
PHONE...............................909 584-8898
Jim Mullin, *Pr*
▼ EMP: 20 EST: 1992
SALES (est): 605.42K **Privately Held**
Web: www.s-curve.com
SIC: 3089 Injection molding of plastics

**(P-7019)**
**SAGE PLASTICS LONG BEACH CORP**
2210 E Artesia Blvd, Long Beach (90805-1739)
PHONE...............................562 423-3900
Jeff Vice, *Pr*
Miguel Garcia, *Sec*
EMP: 80 EST: 2003
SQ FT: 20,000
SALES (est): 1.45MM **Privately Held**
Web: california-plastic-containers-inc.hub.biz
SIC: 3089 Injection molding of plastics

**(P-7020)**
**SAN DIEGO ACE INC**
5363 Sweetwater Trl, San Diego (92130-5040)
P.O. Box 486 (91980-0486)
PHONE...............................619 206-7339
Kyung Min Kim, *CEO*
▲ EMP: 200 EST: 1992
SALES (est): 16.51MM **Privately Held**
Web: www.sandiegoace.com
SIC: 3089 Molding primary plastics

**(P-7021)**
**SANDEE PLASTIC EXTRUSIONS**
14932 Gwenchris Ct, Paramount (90723-3423)
PHONE...............................323 979-4020
Thomas Kunkel, *Pr*
EMP: 22 EST: 1982
SQ FT: 14,000
SALES (est): 6.64MM
SALES (corp-wide): 12.69MM **Privately Held**
Web: www.sandeeplastics.com
SIC: 3089 Injection molding of plastics
PA: Sandee Manufacturing Co.
10520 Waveland Ave
847 671-1335

**(P-7022)**
**SANDIA PLASTICS INC**
Also Called: Ultimate Solutions
15571 Container Ln, Huntington Beach (92649-1530)
PHONE...............................714 901-8400
William Allan, *CEO*
Bisson Monty, *
Tim Petersen, *
Christina Limon, *
▲ EMP: 31 EST: 1996
SQ FT: 2,500
SALES (est): 6.86MM **Privately Held**
Web: www.sandiaplastics.com
SIC: 3089 Injection molded finished plastics products, nec

**(P-7023)**
**SCHOLLE IPN PACKAGING INC**
Also Called: SCHOLLE IPN PACKAGING, INC.
2500 Cooper Ave, Merced (95348-4312)
PHONE...............................209 384-3100
EMP: 101
Web: www.scholleipn.com
SIC: 3089 Plastics processing
HQ: Sig Packaging Llc
200 W N Ave
Northlake IL 60164

**(P-7024)**
**SCRIBNER PLASTICS**
11455 Hydraulics Dr, Rancho Cordova (95742-6870)
PHONE...............................916 638-1515
Rick Scribner, *Owner*
EMP: 15 EST: 2001
SALES (est): 834.59K **Privately Held**
Web: www.scribnerplastics.com
SIC: 3089 Molding primary plastics

**(P-7025)**
**SERCO MOLD INC (PA)**
Also Called: Serpac Electronic Enclosures
2009 Wright Ave, La Verne (91750-5812)
PHONE...............................626 331-0517
Patricia Ann Serio, *CEO*
Don Serio Junior, *VP*
▲ EMP: 38 EST: 1978
SQ FT: 85,000
SALES (est): 7.85MM
SALES (corp-wide): 7.85MM **Privately Held**
Web: www.serpac.com
SIC: 3089 3544 5999 Injection molding of plastics; Industrial molds; Electronic parts and equipment

**(P-7026)**
**SETCO LLC**
4875 E Hunter Ave, Anaheim (92807-2005)
PHONE...............................812 424-2904
Patty Harper, *Brnch Mgr*
EMP: 150
Web: www.berryglobal.com
SIC: 3089 Plastics containers, except foam
HQ: Setco, Llc
101 Oakley St
Evansville IN 47710
812 424-2904

**(P-7027)**
**SIERRACIN/SYLMAR CORPORATION**
Also Called: PPG Aerospace
12780 San Fernando Rd, Sylmar (91342-3728)
PHONE...............................818 362-6711
Barry Gillespie, *CEO*
◆ EMP: 600 EST: 1952
SQ FT: 300,000
SALES (est): 62.73MM
SALES (corp-wide): 17.65B **Publicly Held**
Web: www.ppgaerospace.com
SIC: 3089 3812 3621 3231 Windshields, plastics; Search and navigation equipment; Motors and generators; Products of purchased glass
PA: Ppg Industries, Inc.
1 Ppg Pl
412 434-3131

**(P-7028)**
**SISTEMA US INC**
775 Southpoint Blvd, Petaluma (94954-6870)
P.O. Box 5068 (94948-5068)
PHONE...............................707 773-2200
Simon Kirby, *Pr*
Peter Carter, *
▲ EMP: 30 EST: 2007
SQ FT: 42,500
SALES (est): 5.65MM **Privately Held**
SIC: 3089 Plastics kitchenware, tableware, and houseware

**(P-7029)**
**SKB CORPORATION (PA)**
434 W Levers Pl, Orange (92867-3605)
PHONE...............................714 637-1252
Steven A Kottman, *CEO*
David Sanderson, *
Don Weber, *
◆ EMP: 350 EST: 1975
SALES (est): 46.72MM
SALES (corp-wide): 46.72MM **Privately Held**
Web: www.skbcases.com
SIC: 3089 3161 Cases, plastics; Luggage

**(P-7030)**
**SMART LLC**
Also Called: Chemical Guys
3501 Sepulveda Blvd, Torrance (90505-2537)
PHONE...............................866 822-3670
David Knotek, *CEO*
Paul Schneider, *
▼ EMP: 40 EST: 2003
SALES (est): 27.68MM **Privately Held**
Web: www.chemicalguys.com
SIC: 3089 5013 Automotive parts, plastic; Automotive supplies and parts

**(P-7031)**
**SNAPWARE CORPORATION**
Also Called: Corningware Corelle & More
2325 Cottonwood Ave, Riverside (92508-2309)
PHONE...............................951 361-3100
Kris Malkoski, *CEO*
Ken Tran, *
Grant Hartman, *
◆ EMP: 180 EST: 1991
SALES (est): 55.17MM
SALES (corp-wide): 995.87MM **Privately Held**
Web: www.snapware.com
SIC: 3089 Plastics kitchenware, tableware, and houseware
HQ: Instant Brands Llc
3025 Hghland Pkwy Ste 700
Downers Grove IL 60515
847 233-8600

**(P-7032)**
**SNYDER INDUSTRIES LLC**
800 Commerce Dr, Chowchilla (93610-9395)
P.O. Box 848 (93610-0848)
PHONE...............................559 665-7611
Reyes Morales, *CEO*
EMP: 22
Web: www.snydernet.com
SIC: 3089 Pallets, plastics
HQ: Snyder Industries, Llc
6940 O St Ste 100
Lincoln NE 68510
402 467-5221

**(P-7033)**
**SOL-PAK THERMOFORMING INC**
3388 Fruitland Ave, Vernon (90058-3714)
PHONE...............................323 582-3333
Moussa Soleimani-kashi, *Pr*
Joseph Soleimani, *VP*
Joubin Soleimani-kashi, *CFO*
▲ EMP: 23 EST: 2004
SALES (est): 4.62MM **Privately Held**
Web: www.solpak.com
SIC: 3089 Plastics containers, except foam

**(P-7034)**
**SONFARREL**
3000 E La Jolla St, Anaheim (92806-1310)
PHONE...............................714 630-7280
EMP: 25 EST: 1955
SALES (est): 4.5MM **Privately Held**
Web: www.sonfarrel.com
SIC: 3089 Injection molding of plastics

**(P-7035)**
**SOUTHERN CALIFORNIA PLAS INC**
3122 Maple St, Santa Ana (92707-4408)
PHONE...............................714 751-7084

# PRODUCTS & SERVICES SECTION
## 3089 - Plastics Products, Nec (P-7058)

Anthony Codet, *Pr*
▲ **EMP:** 54 **EST:** 1995
**SQ FT:** 240,000
**SALES (est):** 7.9MM **Privately Held**
**SIC:** 3089 Injection molding of plastics

**(P-7036)**
### SP CRAFTECH I LLC
Also Called: Craftech
2941 E La Jolla St, Anaheim (92806-1306)
**PHONE**..................................714 630-8117
Thomas Stenglein, *Prin*
Allen Webb, *Prin*
Robert Joubran, *Prin*
**EMP:** 38 **EST:** 2021
**SALES (est):** 9.79MM **Privately Held**
**Web:** www.craftechcorp.com
**SIC:** 3089 Injection molding of plastics

**(P-7037)**
### SPECIALTY TOOLS INC
11912 Sheldon St, Sun Valley (91352-1509)
**PHONE**..................................818 827-8138
Ron Ortiz, *CEO*
**EMP:** 16 **EST:** 2007
**SALES (est):** 93.65K **Privately Held**
**Web:** www.saundersmidwest.com
**SIC:** 3089 3423 Handles, brush or tool: plastics; Hand and edge tools, nec

**(P-7038)**
### SPIN PRODUCTS INC
13878 Yorba Ave, Chino (91710-5518)
**PHONE**..................................909 590-7000
Paul Burlingham, *Pr*
William Burlingham, *
▲ **EMP:** 24 **EST:** 1996
**SQ FT:** 96,000
**SALES (est):** 4.87MM **Privately Held**
**Web:** www.spinproducts.com
**SIC:** 3089 Plastics containers, except foam

**(P-7039)**
### SR PLASTICS COMPANY LLC
692 Parkridge Ave, Norco (92860-3124)
**PHONE**..................................951 479-5394
**EMP:** 21
**SALES (corp-wide):** 6.06MM **Privately Held**
**Web:** www.srplasticsmolding.com
**SIC:** 3089 Injection molding of plastics
**PA:** Sr Plastics Company, Llc
   640 Parkridge Ave
   951 520-9486

**(P-7040)**
### STACK PLASTICS INC
3525 Haven Ave, Menlo Park (94025-1009)
**PHONE**..................................650 361-8600
Mark Rackley, *Pr*
Michael Mendonca, *
▲ **EMP:** 30 **EST:** 1995
**SQ FT:** 9,000
**SALES (est):** 4.72MM **Privately Held**
**Web:** www.springboardmfg.com
**SIC:** 3089 Injection molding of plastics

**(P-7041)**
### STAR PLASTIC DESIGN
25914 President Ave, Harbor City (90710-3333)
**PHONE**..................................310 530-7119
Dana Maltun, *Pr*
▲ **EMP:** 60 **EST:** 1980
**SQ FT:** 25,000
**SALES (est):** 2.43MM **Privately Held**
**Web:** www.starplastic.com
**SIC:** 3089 Injection molding of plastics

**(P-7042)**
### STAR SANITATION SERVICES
4 Harris Rd, Salinas (93901-4594)
**PHONE**..................................831 754-6794
Bartley Walker, *Managing Member*
**EMP:** 20 **EST:** 2009
**SALES (est):** 5.83MM **Privately Held**
**Web:** www.starsanitation.com
**SIC:** 3089 1799 Toilets, portable chemical: plastics; Fence construction

**(P-7043)**
### STAR SHIELD SOLUTIONS LLC
4315 Santa Ana St, Ontario (91761)
P.O. Box 968 (91743)
**PHONE**..................................866 662-4477
Gil Stanfill, *Managing Member*
**EMP:** 60 **EST:** 2007
**SALES (est):** 5.88MM **Privately Held**
**Web:** www.starshieldsolutions.com
**SIC:** 3089 7389 Automotive parts, plastic; Financial services

**(P-7044)**
### STEWARD PLASTICS INC
Also Called: Smooth-Bor Plastics
23322 Del Lago Dr, Laguna Hills (92653-1310)
**PHONE**..................................949 581-9530
▼ **EMP:** 75 **EST:** 1971
**SALES (est):** 9.57MM **Privately Held**
**Web:** www.smoothborplastics.com
**SIC:** 3089 Plastics processing

**(P-7045)**
### STONE CANYON INDUSTRIES LLC
1875 Century Park E Ste 320, Los Angeles (90067-2539)
**PHONE**..................................310 570-4869
James H Fordyce, *CEO*
Adam Cohn, *
Michael Neumann, *
Sascha Kaeser, *
Shawn Malleck, *
**EMP:** 2708 **EST:** 2014
**SALES (est):** 25.86MM **Privately Held**
**Web:** www.scihinc.com
**SIC:** 3089 3411 Plastics containers, except foam; Metal cans

**(P-7046)**
### STRAND ART COMPANY INC
4700 E Hunter Ave, Anaheim (92807-1919)
**PHONE**..................................714 777-0444
Kevin Strand, *Pr*
Vicky Strand, *
▲ **EMP:** 50 **EST:** 1974
**SQ FT:** 10,480
**SALES (est):** 2.1MM **Privately Held**
**Web:** www.strandart.com
**SIC:** 3089 Injection molded finished plastics products, nec

**(P-7047)**
### SUPERIOR MOLD CO
1927 E Francis St, Ontario (91761-7719)
**PHONE**..................................909 947-7028
Anthony Codet, *CEO*
**EMP:** 21 **EST:** 1972
**SALES (est):** 2.39MM **Privately Held**
**Web:** www.superior-mold.com
**SIC:** 3089 Injection molding of plastics

**(P-7048)**
### SYNTECH DEVELOPMENT & MFG INC (PA)
Also Called: S D M
13948 Mountain Ave, Chino (91710-9018)
**PHONE**..................................909 465-5554
Harry N Herbert, *CEO*
Bob Hobbs, *
Eddie Montelongo, *
**EMP:** 23 **EST:** 1998
**SQ FT:** 11,000
**SALES (est):** 36.4MM
**SALES (corp-wide):** 36.4MM **Privately Held**
**Web:** www.sdmplastics.com
**SIC:** 3089 Injection molding of plastics

**(P-7049)**
### TALCO PLASTICS INC
3270 E 70th St, Long Beach (90805-1821)
**PHONE**..................................562 630-1224
Ajit Ferera, *Mgr*
**EMP:** 64
**SALES (corp-wide):** 22.23MM **Privately Held**
**Web:** www.talcoplastics.com
**SIC:** 3089 4953 Extruded finished plastics products, nec; Recycling, waste materials
**PA:** Talco Plastics, Inc.
   1000 W Rincon St
   951 531-2000

**(P-7050)**
### TAMSHELL CORP
Also Called: Tamshell
545 Monica Cir, Corona (92878-5447)
**PHONE**..................................951 272-9395
John Hernandez, *Pr*
Art Pierce, *
**EMP:** 95 **EST:** 1979
**SALES (est):** 20.25MM **Privately Held**
**Web:** www.tamshell.com
**SIC:** 3089 Caps, plastics

**(P-7051)**
### TENMA AMERICA CORPORATION
333 H St Ste 5000, Chula Vista (91910-5561)
**PHONE**..................................619 754-2250
Kan Kaneko, *CEO*
Takayoshi Hirayama, *Pr*
Hitoshi Nakamura, *VP*
Minoru Watanaba, *Sec*
▲ **EMP:** 168 **EST:** 1996
**SALES (est):** 27.45MM **Privately Held**
**Web:** www.nket.net
**SIC:** 3089 Molding primary plastics
**PA:** Tenma Corporation
   1-63-6, Akabane

**(P-7052)**
### THERMODYNE INTERNATIONAL LTD
1841 S Business Pkwy, Ontario (91761-8537)
**PHONE**..................................909 923-9945
Gary S Ackerman, *Ch Bd*
Scott Ackerman, *
◆ **EMP:** 110 **EST:** 1967
**SQ FT:** 57,500
**SALES (est):** 8.74MM **Privately Held**
**Web:** www.thermodyne.com
**SIC:** 3089 3694 Plastics containers, except foam; Engine electrical equipment

**(P-7053)**
### THREE-D PLASTICS INC (PA)
Also Called: Three-D Traffics Works
430 N Varney St, Burbank (91502-1732)
**PHONE**..................................323 849-1316
Frank J Dvoracek, *CEO*
Joseph Dvoracek, *
Kathleen D Trumbo, *
**EMP:** 35 **EST:** 1968
**SQ FT:** 40,000
**SALES (est):** 4.68MM
**SALES (corp-wide):** 4.68MM **Privately Held**
**Web:** www.3dplastics.com
**SIC:** 3089 Injection molding of plastics

**(P-7054)**
### TNT PLASTIC MOLDING INC (PA)
725 E Harrison St, Corona (92879-1350)
**PHONE**..................................951 808-9700
Diane Mixson, *Pr*
John Chadwick, *
Lynn Chadwick, *
Doug Chadwick, *
Dennis Chadwick, *
▲ **EMP:** 80 **EST:** 1979
**SQ FT:** 30,000
**SALES (est):** 24.69MM
**SALES (corp-wide):** 24.69MM **Privately Held**
**Web:** www.tntplasticmolding.com
**SIC:** 3089 Injection molding of plastics

**(P-7055)**
### TOM YORK ENTERPRISES INC
Also Called: Kal Plastics
2050 E 48th St, Vernon (90058-2022)
**PHONE**..................................323 581-6194
Tom York, *CEO*
**EMP:** 20 **EST:** 1958
**SQ FT:** 45,000
**SALES (est):** 2.85MM **Privately Held**
**Web:** www.kal-plastics.com
**SIC:** 3089 3993 Boxes, plastics; Signs and advertising specialties

**(P-7056)**
### TOTEX MANUFACTURING INC
3050 Lomita Blvd, Torrance (90505-5103)
**PHONE**..................................310 326-2028
Tommy Tong, *Pr*
▲ **EMP:** 70 **EST:** 1998
**SALES (est):** 11.17MM **Privately Held**
**Web:** www.totexmfg.com
**SIC:** 3089 5063 Battery cases, plastics or plastics combination; Batteries, dry cell

**(P-7057)**
### TRELLBORG SLING SLTIONS US INC
3077 Rollie Gates Dr, Paso Robles (93446-9500)
**PHONE**..................................805 239-4284
**EMP:** 34
**SALES (corp-wide):** 45.02B **Privately Held**
**Web:** www.trelleborg.com
**SIC:** 3089 Plastics processing
**HQ:** Trelleborg Sealing Solutions Us, Inc.
   2531 Bremer Rd
   Fort Wayne IN 46803
   260 749-9631

**(P-7058)**
### TRIFORMIX INC
487 Aviation Blvd Ste 100, Santa Rosa (95403-1069)
P.O. Box 2865 (95405-0865)
**PHONE**..................................707 545-7645
Joseph Michael Adam, *CEO*
Dave Whitney, *
▲ **EMP:** 19 **EST:** 2000
**SQ FT:** 15,000
**SALES (est):** 3.06MM **Privately Held**
**SIC:** 3089 Injection molding of plastics

# 3089 - Plastics Products, Nec (P-7059)

**(P-7059)**
**TRIM-LOK INC (PA)**
6855 Hermosa Cir, Buena Park
(90620-1151)
P.O. Box 6180 (90622-6180)
PHONE.................................714 562-0500
Gary Whitener, *Pr*
◆ **EMP:** 178 **EST:** 1971
**SQ FT:** 57,000
**SALES (est):** 51.5MM
**SALES (corp-wide):** 51.5MM **Privately Held**
Web: www.trimlok.com
**SIC: 3089** Molding primary plastics

**(P-7060)**
**TRINITY INTERNATIONAL INDS LLC**
1041 E 230th St, Carson (90745-5007)
PHONE.................................800 985-5506
Cze Chao Tam, *CEO*
▲ **EMP:** 33 **EST:** 2007
**SQ FT:** 35,000
**SALES (est):** 11.14MM **Privately Held**
Web: www.trinityii.com
**SIC: 3089** 2511 2542 Organizers for closets, drawers, etc.: plastics; Storage chests, household: wood; Racks, merchandise display or storage: except wood

**(P-7061)**
**TRU-FORM PLASTICS INC**
14600 Hoover St, Westminster (92683-5346)
PHONE.................................310 327-9444
Douglas W Sahm Senior, *CEO*
John D Evans, *
Anita Lorber, *
Clauve Hurwicz, *
▲ **EMP:** 35 **EST:** 1956
**SQ FT:** 1,000
**SALES (est):** 5.19MM **Privately Held**
Web: www.tru-formplastics.com
**SIC: 3089** Plastics processing

**(P-7062)**
**TST MOLDING LLC**
Also Called: All Amrcan Injction Mlding Svc
42322 Avenida Alvarado, Temecula (92590-3445)
PHONE.................................951 296-6200
Terry Voss, *Managing Member*
**EMP:** 27 **EST:** 2009
**SALES (est):** 4.54MM **Privately Held**
Web: www.tstmolding.com
**SIC: 3089** Injection molding of plastics

**(P-7063)**
**UFO DESIGNS (PA)**
5812 Machine Dr, Huntington Beach (92649-1101)
PHONE.................................714 892-4420
Jitendra Patel, *Pr*
Alfie Patel, *VP*
**EMP:** 16 **EST:** 1976
**SQ FT:** 35,000
**SALES (est):** 1.45MM
**SALES (corp-wide):** 1.45MM **Privately Held**
Web: www.ufodesign.com
**SIC: 3089** Injection molding of plastics

**(P-7064)**
**UFO INC**
2110 Belgrave Ave, Huntington Park (90255-2713)
P.O. Box 58192 (90058-0192)
PHONE.................................323 588-5450
Efi Youavian, *Pr*
Efraim Youavian, *

▲ **EMP:** 50 **EST:** 1982
**SQ FT:** 65,000
**SALES (est):** 9.19MM **Privately Held**
Web: www.ufobrand.com
**SIC: 3089** 2842 5199 Sponges, plastics; Polishes and sanitation goods; Foams and rubber

**(P-7065)**
**URBAN ARMOR GEAR LLC (HQ)**
1601 Alton Pkwy, Irvine (92606-4842)
PHONE.................................949 329-0500
Scott W Hardy, *CEO*
▲ **EMP:** 20 **EST:** 2011
**SALES (est):** 9.77MM
**SALES (corp-wide):** 20.44MM **Privately Held**
Web: www.urbanarmorgear.com
**SIC: 3089** Cases, plastics
PA: Urban Armor Gear Holdings, Inc.
28202 Cabot Rd Ste 300
949 329-0500

**(P-7066)**
**US POLYMERS INC (PA)**
Also Called: Duramax Building Products
1057 S Vail Ave, Montebello (90640-6019)
PHONE.................................323 728-3023
Viken Ohanesian, *CEO*
Jacques Ohanesian, *
Vram Ohanesian, *
Haigan Ohanesian, *
◆ **EMP:** 100 **EST:** 1983
**SQ FT:** 70,000
**SALES (est):** 28.74MM
**SALES (corp-wide):** 28.74MM **Privately Held**
Web: www.uspolymersinc.com
**SIC: 3089** 3084 Shutters, plastics; Plastics pipe

**(P-7067)**
**USA EXTRUDED PLASTICS INC**
965 E Discovery Ln, Anaheim (92801-1147)
PHONE.................................714 991-6061
Joseph Florimonte, *Pr*
Vida Aiona, *VP*
Linda Florimonte, *Sec*
**EMP:** 16 **EST:** 1993
**SQ FT:** 11,000
**SALES (est):** 2.4MM **Privately Held**
Web: www.usaextrudedplastics.com
**SIC: 3089** Extruded finished plastics products, nec

**(P-7068)**
**V-T INDUSTRIES INC**
9818 Firestone Blvd, Downey (90241-5595)
PHONE.................................714 521-2008
**EMP:** 69
**SALES (corp-wide):** 434.93MM **Privately Held**
Web: www.vtindustries.com
**SIC: 3089** 3083 4213 2435 Plastics hardware and building products; Plastics finished products, laminated; Trucking, except local; Hardwood veneer and plywood
PA: V-T Industries Inc.
1000 Industrial Park Rd
712 368-4381

**(P-7069)**
**VALENCIA PLASTICS INC**
Also Called: Valencia Mold
25611 Hercules St, Valencia (91355-5051)
PHONE.................................661 257-0066
Luis Ruiz, *Pr*
**EMP:** 16 **EST:** 2009
**SQ FT:** 11,000
**SALES (est):** 2.73MM **Privately Held**

Web: www.valenciaplastics.com
**SIC: 3089** Injection molding of plastics

**(P-7070)**
**VANTAGE ASSOCIATES INC**
12333 Los Nietos Rd, Santa Fe Springs (90670-2911)
PHONE.................................562 968-1400
Paul Roy, *CEO*
**EMP:** 65
**SQ FT:** 20,000
**SALES (corp-wide):** 24.86MM **Privately Held**
Web: www.vantageassoc.com
**SIC: 3089** 2499 5085 3621 Plastics processing; Spools, reels, and pulleys: wood; Industrial supplies; Motors and generators
PA: Vantage Associates Inc.
1565 Macarthur Blvd
619 477-6940

**(P-7071)**
**VIANT MEDICAL LLC**
45581 Northport Loop W, Fremont (94538-6462)
PHONE.................................510 657-5800
Bill Tarajos, *Brnch Mgr*
**EMP:** 117
**SALES (corp-wide):** 466.54MM **Privately Held**
Web: www.viantmedical.com
**SIC: 3089** Injection molding of plastics
HQ: Viant Medical, Llc
2 Hampshire St
Foxborough MA 02035

**(P-7072)**
**VINVENTIONS USA LLC (PA)**
888 Prospect St, La Jolla (92037-4260)
PHONE.................................919 460-2200
Lars Von Kantzow, *Managing Member*
Peter A Schmitt, *Managing Member*
◆ **EMP:** 230 **EST:** 1998
**SALES (est):** 23.47MM
**SALES (corp-wide):** 23.47MM **Privately Held**
Web: us.vinventions.com
**SIC: 3089** Caps, plastics

**(P-7073)**
**VOLEX INC**
Also Called: Volex De Mexico
511 E San Ysidro Blvd 509, San Ysidro (92173-3150)
PHONE.................................619 205-4900
Christoph Eisenhardt, *Brnch Mgr*
**EMP:** 28
**SALES (corp-wide):** 912.8MM **Privately Held**
Web: www.volex.com
**SIC: 3089** Injection molded finished plastics products, nec
HQ: Volex Inc.
511 E San Ysdro Blvd Ste
San Ysidro CA 92173
669 444-1740

**(P-7074)**
**VPET USA LLC**
12925b Marlay Ave, Fontana (92337-6939)
PHONE.................................909 605-1668
Jeffrey Kellar, *CEO*
Steven Saull, *
**EMP:** 96 **EST:** 2019
**SALES (est):** 13.46MM **Privately Held**
Web: www.vpetusa.com
**SIC: 3089** Plastics containers, except foam

**(P-7075)**
**WADDINGTON NORTH AMERICA INC**
Also Called: Wna City of Industry
1135 Samuelson St, City Of Industry (91748-1222)
PHONE.................................626 913-4022
Mike Evans, *Pr*
**EMP:** 112
**SALES (corp-wide):** 32.64B **Publicly Held**
Web: www.novolex.com
**SIC: 3089** Plastics kitchenware, tableware, and houseware
HQ: Waddington North America, Inc.
3436 Tringdon Way Ste 100
Charlotte NC 28277

**(P-7076)**
**WCP WEST COAST GLASS LLC**
Also Called: West Coast Vinyl Windows
17730 Crusader Ave, Cerritos (90703-2629)
PHONE.................................562 653-9797
Charles Neubauer, *Pr*
▲ **EMP:** 95 **EST:** 1988
**SQ FT:** 50,000
**SALES (est):** 7.29MM
**SALES (corp-wide):** 11.29MM **Privately Held**
Web: www.westcoastglass.com
**SIC: 3089** 3211 Windows, plastics; Insulating glass, sealed units
HQ: Agnora Ltd
200 Mountain Rd
Collingwood ON L9Y 4
705 444-6654

**(P-7077)**
**WEST-BAG INC**
1161 Monterey Pass Rd, Monterey Park (91754-3614)
PHONE.................................323 264-0750
Luis Michel, *Pr*
Sixto Michel, *
**EMP:** 30 **EST:** 1977
**SQ FT:** 12,000
**SALES (est):** 2.47MM **Privately Held**
Web: www.west-bag.com
**SIC: 3089** 5149 Food casings, plastics; Sausage casings

**(P-7078)**
**WESTEC PLASTICS CORPORATION**
6757 Las Positas Rd Ste A, Livermore (94551-5114)
PHONE.................................925 454-3400
▲ **EMP:** 72 **EST:** 1969
**SALES (est):** 9.92MM **Privately Held**
Web: www.westecplastics.com
**SIC: 3089** 3544 Injection molding of plastics; Industrial molds

**(P-7079)**
**WESTERN CASE INCORPORATED**
231 E Alessandro Blvd, Riverside (92508-5084)
PHONE.................................951 214-6380
**TOLL FREE:** 877
Paul F Queyrel, *CEO*
Mario Robles, *Prin*
▲ **EMP:** 60 **EST:** 1981
**SALES (est):** 13.47MM **Privately Held**
Web: www.westerncase.com
**SIC: 3089** 3544 3444 Cases, plastics; Special dies, tools, jigs, and fixtures; Sheet metalwork

# PRODUCTS & SERVICES SECTION
## 3143 - Men's Footwear, Except Athletic (P-7100)

**(P-7080)**
**WHITE BOTTLE INC**
10579 Dale Ave, Stanton (90680-2641)
PHONE.................................949 788-1998
Arash Anvaripour, *Prin*
Robert W Thompson, *Prin*
▲ **EMP:** 20 **EST:** 2009
**SALES (est):** 6.57MM **Privately Held**
**Web:** www.whitebottle.com
**SIC: 3089** Plastics containers, except foam

**(P-7081)**
**WILLIAM KREYSLER & ASSOC INC**
Also Called: Kreysler & Associates
501 Green Island Rd, American Canyon (94503-9649)
PHONE.................................707 552-3500
William Bartley Kreysler, *CEO*
▼ **EMP:** 26 **EST:** 1982
**SALES (est):** 5.29MM **Privately Held**
**Web:** www.kreysler.com
**SIC: 3089** Panels, building: plastics, nec

**(P-7082)**
**WING INFLATABLES INC (HQ)**
Also Called: MTI Adventurewear
1220 5th St, Arcata (95521-6155)
P.O. Box 279 (95518-0279)
PHONE.................................707 826-2887
Andrew Branagh, *CEO*
Michael Dunaway, *
Mark French, *
◆ **EMP:** 26 **EST:** 1990
**SQ FT:** 80,000
**SALES (est):** 25.66MM
**SALES (corp-wide):** 34.18MM **Privately Held**
**Web:** www.inflatablesolutions.com
**SIC: 3089** Plastics boats and other marine equipment
**PA:** Armada Acquisition Group, Llc
3701 Mt Diablo Blvd # 200

**(P-7083)**
**WREX PRODUCTS INC CHICO**
Also Called: Wrex Products
25 Wrex Ct, Chico (95928-7176)
PHONE.................................530 895-3838
**TOLL FREE:** 800
Wrex A Howard, *Ch Bd*
Jim Barnett, *
James Barnett, *
Paul Rye, *
▲ **EMP:** 66 **EST:** 1961
**SQ FT:** 70,000
**SALES (est):** 4.08MM **Privately Held**
**Web:** www.wrexproducts.com
**SIC: 3089** 3363 3544 3599 Injection molding of plastics; Aluminum die-castings; Special dies, tools, jigs, and fixtures; Machine and other job shop work

**(P-7084)**
**WUNDER-MOLD INC**
790 Eubanks Dr, Vacaville (95688-9470)
PHONE.................................707 448-2349
Richard A Martindale, *CEO*
William Martindale, *Prin*
▲ **EMP:** 22 **EST:** 1996
**SQ FT:** 56,000
**SALES (est):** 4.48MM **Privately Held**
**Web:** www.wundermold.com
**SIC: 3089** Injection molding of plastics

## 3111 Leather Tanning And Finishing

**(P-7085)**
**ANDREW ALEXANDER INC**
Also Called: Falltech
1306 S Alameda St, Compton (90221-4803)
PHONE.................................323 752-0066
Michael Dancyger, *Pr*
Jeff Crosson, *
◆ **EMP:** 100 **EST:** 1992
**SQ FT:** 100,000
**SALES (est):** 24.92MM **Privately Held**
**Web:** www.falltech.com
**SIC: 3111** Harness leather

**(P-7086)**
**CUSTOMFAB INC**
7345 Orangewood Ave, Garden Grove (92841-1411)
PHONE.................................714 891-9119
Donald Alhanati, *Pr*
▲ **EMP:** 250 **EST:** 1991
**SQ FT:** 47,000
**SALES (est):** 14.47MM **Privately Held**
**Web:** www.customfabusa.com
**SIC: 3111** 3842 Accessory products, leather; Surgical appliances and supplies

**(P-7087)**
**HERITAGE LEATHER COMPANY INC**
4011 E 52nd St, Maywood (90270-2205)
PHONE.................................323 983-0420
Jose C Munoz, *CEO*
Gustavo Gonzalez, *
▲ **EMP:** 30 **EST:** 2000
**SQ FT:** 5,000
**SALES (est):** 546.15K **Privately Held**
**Web:** www.heritageleather.com
**SIC: 3111** Belting leather

**(P-7088)**
**LA LA LAND PRODUCTION & DESIGN**
1701 S Santa Fe Ave, Los Angeles (90021-2904)
PHONE.................................323 406-9223
Alexander M Zar, *CEO*
**EMP:** 45 **EST:** 2006
**SQ FT:** 30,000
**SALES (est):** 4.7MM **Privately Held**
**Web:** www.lalaland-design.com
**SIC: 3111** Accessory products, leather

**(P-7089)**
**LINEA PELLE INC (PA)**
Also Called: Linea Pelle
7107 Valjean Ave, Van Nuys (91406-3917)
PHONE.................................310 231-9950
Meira Katz, *CEO*
Wynn Katz, *Prin*
▲ **EMP:** 17 **EST:** 1986
**SQ FT:** 5,000
**SALES (est):** 2.67MM
**SALES (corp-wide):** 2.67MM **Privately Held**
**Web:** www.lineapelle.com
**SIC: 3111** 5621 Accessory products, leather; Dress shops

## 3131 Footwear Cut Stock

**(P-7090)**
**1919 INVESTMENT COUNSEL LLC**
49 Stevenson St Ste 1075, San Francisco (94105-2945)
PHONE.................................415 500-6707
**EMP:** 15
**SALES (corp-wide):** 4.35B **Publicly Held**
**Web:** www.1919ic.com
**SIC: 3131** Rands
**HQ:** 1919 Investment Counsel, Llc
1 South St Ste 2500
Baltimore MD 21202

**(P-7091)**
**COUNTER SANTANA ROW LP**
3055 Olin Ave, San Jose (95128-2067)
PHONE.................................408 610-1362
Peter E Katz, *Prin*
**EMP:** 29 **EST:** 2008
**SALES (est):** 881.81K **Privately Held**
**Web:** www.santanarow.com
**SIC: 3131** Counters

**(P-7092)**
**CYDWOQ INC**
2102 Kenmere Ave, Burbank (91504-3413)
PHONE.................................818 848-8307
Rafi Balouzian, *Pr*
Richard Delamarter, *Stockholder*
◆ **EMP:** 28 **EST:** 1996
**SQ FT:** 15,000
**SALES (est):** 1.82MM **Privately Held**
**Web:** www.cydwoq.com
**SIC: 3131** 3199 Laces, shoe and boot: leather; Leather belting and strapping

**(P-7093)**
**SOLE SOCIETY GROUP INC**
11248 Playa Ct # B, Culver City (90230-6127)
P.O. Box 5206 (90231)
PHONE.................................310 220-0808
Andy Solomon, *Managing Member*
Talitha Peters, *
▲ **EMP:** 200 **EST:** 2011
**SALES (est):** 1.66MM
**SALES (corp-wide):** 3.07B **Publicly Held**
**Web:** www.solesociety.com
**SIC: 3131** 5661 5621 Boot and shoe accessories; Men's boots; Ready-to-wear apparel, women's
**HQ:** Vcs Group Llc
1370 Ave Of The Americas
New York NY 10019
646 898-1050

## 3143 Men's Footwear, Except Athletic

**(P-7094)**
**ALLBIRDS INC**
57 Hotaling Pl, San Francisco (94111-2202)
PHONE.................................415 469-1455
**EMP:** 19
**SALES (corp-wide):** 254.06MM **Publicly Held**
**Web:** www.allbirds.com
**SIC: 3143** Men's footwear, except athletic
**PA:** Allbirds Inc.
730 Montgomery St
628 225-4848

**(P-7095)**
**ALLBIRDS INC**
1923 Calle Barcelona Ste 136, Carlsbad (92009-8457)
PHONE.................................442 273-5519
**EMP:** 18
**SALES (corp-wide):** 254.06MM **Publicly Held**
**Web:** www.allbirds.com
**SIC: 3143** Men's footwear, except athletic
**PA:** Allbirds Inc.
730 Montgomery St
628 225-4848

**(P-7096)**
**ALLBIRDS INC**
1636 Redwood Hwy, Corte Madera (94925-1248)
PHONE.................................628 266-0533
**EMP:** 18
**SALES (corp-wide):** 254.06MM **Publicly Held**
**Web:** www.allbirds.com
**SIC: 3143** Men's footwear, except athletic
**PA:** Allbirds Inc.
730 Montgomery St
628 225-4848

**(P-7097)**
**ALLBIRDS INC**
860 S Pacific Coast Hwy, El Segundo (90245-4838)
PHONE.................................424 502-2383
**EMP:** 18
**SALES (corp-wide):** 254.06MM **Publicly Held**
**Web:** www.allbirds.com
**SIC: 3143** Men's footwear, except athletic
**PA:** Allbirds Inc.
730 Montgomery St
628 225-4848

**(P-7098)**
**ALLBIRDS INC**
77 W Colorado Blvd, Pasadena (91105-1927)
PHONE.................................626 344-2622
**EMP:** 18
**SALES (corp-wide):** 254.06MM **Publicly Held**
**Web:** www.allbirds.com
**SIC: 3143** Men's footwear, except athletic
**PA:** Allbirds Inc.
730 Montgomery St
628 225-4848

**(P-7099)**
**ALLBIRDS INC**
1125 Newport Center Dr, Newport Beach (92660-6950)
PHONE.................................949 942-1233
**EMP:** 17
**SALES (corp-wide):** 254.06MM **Publicly Held**
**Web:** www.allbirds.com
**SIC: 3143** Men's footwear, except athletic
**PA:** Allbirds Inc.
730 Montgomery St
628 225-4848

**(P-7100)**
**ALLBIRDS INC**
425 Hayes St, San Francisco (94102-4380)
PHONE.................................415 802-2800
**EMP:** 17
**SALES (corp-wide):** 254.06MM **Publicly Held**
**Web:** www.allbirds.com
**SIC: 3143** Men's footwear, except athletic
**PA:** Allbirds Inc.
730 Montgomery St

## 3143 - Men's Footwear, Except Athletic (P-7101)

**(P-7101)**
**ALLBIRDS INC**
660 Stanford Shopping Ctr, Palo Alto (94304-1400)
PHONE..................650 460-8040
EMP: 18
SALES (corp-wide): 254.06MM **Publicly Held**
Web: www.allbirds.com
SIC: 3143  Men's footwear, except athletic
PA:  Allbirds Inc.
     730 Montgomery St
     628 225-4848

**(P-7102)**
**ALLBIRDS INC**
3228 Livermore Outlets Dr Ste 675, Livermore (94551-4203)
PHONE..................925 800-3331
EMP: 18
SALES (corp-wide): 254.06MM **Publicly Held**
Web: www.allbirds.com
SIC: 3143  Men's footwear, except athletic
PA:  Allbirds Inc.
     730 Montgomery St
     628 225-4848

**(P-7103)**
**ALLBIRDS INC**
4301 La Jolla Village Dr Ste 2010, San Diego (92122-1352)
PHONE..................858 987-9533
EMP: 17
SALES (corp-wide): 254.06MM **Publicly Held**
Web: www.allbirds.com
SIC: 3143  Men's footwear, except athletic
PA:  Allbirds Inc.
     730 Montgomery St
     628 225-4848

**(P-7104)**
**ALLBIRDS INC**
10250 Santa Monica Blvd Ste 1985, Los Angeles (90067-6559)
PHONE..................213 374-2354
EMP: 17
SALES (corp-wide): 254.06MM **Publicly Held**
Web: www.allbirds.com
SIC: 3143  Men's footwear, except athletic
PA:  Allbirds Inc.
     730 Montgomery St
     628 225-4848

**(P-7105)**
**ALLBIRDS INC**
12833 Ventura Blvd, Studio City (91604-2368)
PHONE..................213 374-3533
EMP: 18
SALES (corp-wide): 254.06MM **Publicly Held**
Web: www.allbirds.com
SIC: 3143  Men's footwear, except athletic
PA:  Allbirds Inc.
     730 Montgomery St
     628 225-4848

**(P-7106)**
**ALLBIRDS INC**
1335 Abbot Kinney Blvd, Venice (90291-3739)
PHONE..................424 295-9968
EMP: 18
SALES (corp-wide): 254.06MM **Publicly Held**
Web: www.allbirds.com
SIC: 3143  Men's footwear, except athletic
PA:  Allbirds Inc.
     730 Montgomery St
     628 225-4848

**(P-7107)**
**CAREISMATIC BRANDS LLC (DH)**
Also Called: Cherokee Uniform
15301 Ventura Blvd, Sherman Oaks (91403-3102)
PHONE..................818 671-2128
Sidharth Lakhani, CEO
Robert Pierpoint, *
Kent Percy, CRO*
◆ EMP: 203 EST: 1995
SQ FT: 140,000
SALES (est): 189.35MM
SALES (corp-wide): 609.92MM **Privately Held**
Web: www.careismatic.com
SIC: 3143 3144 5139 2339  Men's footwear, except athletic; Women's footwear, except athletic; Shoes; Women's and misses' outerwear, nec
HQ: Careismatic Group Ii, Inc.
    1119 Colorado Ave
    Santa Monica CA 90401
    818 671-2100

**(P-7108)**
**CAREISMATIC GROUP II INC (HQ)**
1119 Colorado Ave, Santa Monica (90401-3009)
PHONE..................818 671-2100
Kent Percy, CRO
EMP: 18 EST: 2022
SALES (est): 204.35MM
SALES (corp-wide): 609.92MM **Privately Held**
SIC: 3143 3144 5139 2339  Men's footwear, except athletic; Women's footwear, except athletic; Shoes; Women's and misses' outerwear, nec
PA:  Careismatic Group Inc.
     15301 Ventura Blvd
     818 671-2100

**(P-7109)**
**CAREISMATIC GROUP INC (PA)**
15301 Ventura Blvd, Sherman Oaks (91403-3102)
PHONE..................818 671-2100
Kent Percy, CRO
EMP: 19 EST: 2022
SALES (est): 609.92MM
SALES (corp-wide): 609.92MM **Privately Held**
SIC: 3143 3144 5139 2339  Men's footwear, except athletic; Women's footwear, except athletic; Shoes; Women's and misses' outerwear, nec

**(P-7110)**
**LANE INTERNATIONAL TRADING INC**
33155 Transit Ave, Union City (94587-2091)
P.O. Box 2223 (94587-7223)
PHONE..................510 489-7364
Lane Shay, Pr
▲ EMP: 105 EST: 1987
SQ FT: 2,500
SALES (est): 1.86MM **Privately Held**
SIC: 3143 3144  Men's footwear, except athletic; Women's footwear, except athletic

**(P-7111)**
**PHOENIX FOOTWEAR GROUP INC (PA)**
2236 Rutherford Rd Ste 113, Carlsbad (92008-8836)
PHONE..................760 602-9688
James R Riedman, Pr
Dennis Nelson, CFO
◆ EMP: 17 EST: 2002
SQ FT: 21,700
SALES (est): 27.78MM
SALES (corp-wide): 27.78MM **Publicly Held**
Web: www.phoenixfootwear.com
SIC: 3143 3144 2329 2339  Men's footwear, except athletic; Women's footwear, except athletic; Men's and boys' sportswear and athletic clothing; Sportswear, women's

**(P-7112)**
**VIONIC GROUP LLC**
Also Called: Orthaheel
4040 Civic Center Dr Ste 430, San Rafael (94903-4150)
PHONE..................415 526-6932
Chris Gallagher, CEO
Connie X Rishwain, *
Bruce Campbell, *
Steve Furtado, *
Lisa Bazinet, *
▲ EMP: 84 EST: 2006
SQ FT: 16,000
SALES (est): 22.24MM
SALES (corp-wide): 2.82B **Publicly Held**
Web: www.vioniogroup.com
SIC: 3143 3144 3149  Orthopedic shoes, men's; Orthopedic shoes, women's; Orthopedic shoes, children's
PA:  Caleres, Inc.
     8300 Maryland Ave
     314 854-4000

## 3144 Women's Footwear, Except Athletic

**(P-7113)**
**ALPARGATAS USA INC**
Also Called: Havaianas
513 Boccaccio Ave, Venice (90291-4806)
PHONE..................646 277-7171
Marcio Moura, CEO
Afonso Fugiyama, *
◆ EMP: 30 EST: 2006
SALES (est): 7.8MM **Privately Held**
SIC: 3144  Women's footwear, except athletic
PA:  Alpargatas Sa
     Av. Das Nacoes Unidas 14261

**(P-7114)**
**BRYR LLC**
Also Called: Bryr Studio
2331 3rd St, San Francisco (94107-3108)
PHONE..................415 374-7323
Isobel Schofield, Managing Member
EMP: 18 EST: 2015
SALES (est): 1.52MM **Privately Held**
Web: www.bryrstudio.com
SIC: 3144  Women's footwear, except athletic

**(P-7115)**
**EVOLUTION DESIGN LAB INC**
Also Called: Jellypop
144 W Colorado Blvd, Pasadena (91105-1953)
PHONE..................626 960-8388
Jennet Chow, CEO
▲ EMP: 25 EST: 2009
SALES (est): 2.13MM **Privately Held**
Web: www.jellypop-shoes.com
SIC: 3144 5139  Women's footwear, except athletic; Shoes

**(P-7116)**
**IMPO INTERNATIONAL LLC**
Also Called: Chili's
3510 Black Rd, Santa Maria (93455-5927)
P.O. Box 639 (93456-0639)
PHONE..................805 922-7753
Laura Ann Hopkins, Managing Member
◆ EMP: 24 EST: 1968
SQ FT: 30,000
SALES (est): 4.78MM **Privately Held**
Web: www.impo.com
SIC: 3144  Boots, canvas or leather: women's

**(P-7117)**
**MILLENNIAL BRANDS LLC**
126 W 9th St, Los Angeles (90015-1500)
PHONE..................925 230-0617
Catalin Gaitanaru, Prin
EMP: 27
SIC: 3144  Women's footwear, except athletic
PA:  Millennial Brands Llc
     2002 Diablo Rd

**(P-7118)**
**SURGEON WORLDWIDE INC**
3855 S Hill St, Los Angeles (90037-1415)
PHONE..................707 501-7962
Mariko Chambrone, VP
EMP: 27 EST: 2018
SALES (est): 1.83MM **Privately Held**
SIC: 3144 3143  Women's footwear, except athletic; Men's footwear, except athletic

## 3149 Footwear, Except Rubber, Nec

**(P-7119)**
**LUSSO CLOUD INC**
2431 W Coast Hwy Ste 201, Newport Beach (92663-4759)
PHONE..................714 307-4414
EMP: 15
SALES (est): 2.2MM **Privately Held**
Web: www.lussocloud.com
SIC: 3149  Footwear, except rubber, nec

**(P-7120)**
**NELSON SPORTS INC (PA)**
12810 Florence Ave, Santa Fe Springs (90670-4540)
PHONE..................562 944-8081
Young Chu, Pr
Sook Hee Chu, *
▲ EMP: 22 EST: 1986
SALES (est): 4.52MM **Privately Held**
Web: www.madrock.com
SIC: 3149 3021  Athletic shoes, except rubber or plastic; Rubber and plastics footwear

**(P-7121)**
**SANTA FE FOOTWEAR CORPORATION**
9988 Santa Fe Springs Rd, Santa Fe Springs (90670-2946)
PHONE..................562 941-9689
Joel Tan, Pr
Joel O Tan, Pr
Debby Tio, CFO
▲ EMP: 15 EST: 1985
SQ FT: 30,000
SALES (est): 2MM **Privately Held**
SIC: 3149 3144 5139  Children's footwear, except athletic; Women's footwear, except athletic; Footwear

# PRODUCTS & SERVICES SECTION
## 3161 - Luggage (P-7143)

**(P-7122)**
**SKECHERS USA INC (PA)**
Also Called: SKECHERS
228 Manhattan Beach Blvd Ste 200,
Manhattan Beach (90266-5356)
PHONE..............................310 318-3100
Robert Greenberg, *Ch Bd*
Michael Greenberg, *
John Vandemore, *CFO*
David Weinberg, *
Philip Paccione, *Corporate Secretary*
▲ **EMP:** 80 **EST:** 1992
**SQ FT:** 213,000
**SALES (est):** 8B **Publicly Held**
Web: www.skechers.com
SIC: **3149** 3021 Athletic shoes, except rubber or plastic; Shoes, rubber or plastic molded to fabric

**(P-7123)**
**SOLE TECHNOLOGY INC (PA)**
Also Called: Etnies
26921 Fuerte, Lake Forest (92630-8149)
PHONE..............................949 460-2020
Pierre Senizergues, *Pr*
Paul Migaki, *COO*
◆ **EMP:** 95 **EST:** 1996
**SALES (est):** 38.68MM **Privately Held**
Web: www.soletechnology.com
SIC: **3149** 5139 Athletic shoes, except rubber or plastic; Footwear

## 3161 Luggage

**(P-7124)**
**ACE PRODUCTS ENTERPRISES INC**
Also Called: Ace Products Group
625 2nd St, Petaluma (94952-5120)
PHONE..............................707 765-1500
Allen R Poster, *Pr*
◆ **EMP:** 30 **EST:** 1984
**SALES (est):** 2.09MM **Privately Held**
Web: www.aceproducts.com
SIC: **3161** 3931 Musical instrument cases; Drums, parts, and accessories (musical instruments)

**(P-7125)**
**AMERICAN TRAVELER INC**
9509 Feron Blvd, Rancho Cucamonga (91730-4541)
PHONE..............................909 466-4000
Scott Oh, *CEO*
June Yi, *
**EMP:** 25 **EST:** 2009
**SALES (est):** 2.58MM **Privately Held**
Web: www.americantravelerinc.com
SIC: **3161** Luggage

**(P-7126)**
**ANVIL CASES INC**
1242 E Edna Pl Unit B, Covina (91724-2540)
PHONE..............................626 968-4100
Joseph Calzone, *Pr*
Vincent Calzone, *
▲ **EMP:** 125 **EST:** 1952
**SALES (est):** 5.27MM
**SALES (corp-wide):** 20.3MM **Privately Held**
Web: www.calzoneandanvil.com
SIC: **3161** Musical instrument cases
PA: Calzone, Ltd.
225 Black Rock Ave
203 367-5766

**(P-7127)**
**BABYFITS LLC**
3341 Mono Way, Antelope (95843-2032)
PHONE..............................916 544-7018
**EMP:** 23 **EST:** 2020
**SALES (est):** 1.06MM **Privately Held**
SIC: **3161** 7389 Clothing and apparel carrying cases; Business Activities at Non-Commercial Site

**(P-7128)**
**BLOOM DESIGNS CORP**
3347 Michelson Dr Ste 100, Irvine (92612-0661)
PHONE..............................949 250-4929
**EMP:** 18
**SALES (corp-wide):** 32.46MM **Privately Held**
Web: www.incase.com
SIC: **3161** Luggage
HQ: Bloom Designs Corp.
6001 Oak Canyon
Irvine CA 92618

**(P-7129)**
**ENCORE CASES INC**
8600 Tamarack Ave, Sun Valley (91352-2504)
PHONE..............................818 768-8803
Gary A Peterson, *Pr*
▲ **EMP:** 27 **EST:** 1988
**SALES (est):** 2.35MM **Privately Held**
Web: www.encorecases.com
SIC: **3161** Cases, carrying, nec

**(P-7130)**
**G & G QUALITY CASE CO INC**
2025 E 25th St, Vernon (90058-1127)
P.O. Box 58541 (90058-0541)
PHONE..............................323 233-2482
Efren Guzman, *Pr*
Ben Germain, *
Maria Germain, *
▲ **EMP:** 70 **EST:** 1978
**SQ FT:** 13,500
**SALES (est):** 2.13MM **Privately Held**
Web: www.ggqualitycase.com
SIC: **3161** Musical instrument cases

**(P-7131)**
**GOYARD MIAMI LLC**
Also Called: Maison Goyard
345 Powell St, San Francisco (94102-1804)
PHONE..............................415 398-1110
Rogelio Ortega, *Brnch Mgr*
**EMP:** 117
**SALES (corp-wide):** 217.61MM **Privately Held**
Web: www.goyard.com
SIC: **3161** Wardrobe bags (luggage)
HQ: Goyard Miami, Llc
20 E 63rd St
New York NY 10065
212 813-0005

**(P-7132)**
**HAMMITT INC**
2101 Pacific Coast Hwy, Hermosa Beach (90254-2796)
PHONE..............................310 292-5200
Anthony Drockton, *Ch*
Andrew Forbes, *
▲ **EMP:** 51 **EST:** 2008
**SQ FT:** 3,600
**SALES (est):** 26.5MM **Privately Held**
Web: www.hammitt.com
SIC: **3161** 3171 Traveling bags; Women's handbags and purses

**(P-7133)**
**HSIAO & MONTANO INC**
Also Called: Odyssey Innovative Designs
809 W Santa Anita Ave, San Gabriel (91776-1016)
PHONE..............................626 588-2528
Mario Montano, *CEO*
John Hsiao, *
▲ **EMP:** 50 **EST:** 1995
**SALES (est):** 1.64MM **Privately Held**
Web: www.odysseygear.com
SIC: **3161** 3648 5084 1751 Musical instrument cases; Lighting equipment, nec; Woodworking machinery; Cabinet and finish carpentry

**(P-7134)**
**INTERNATIONAL CASES & MFG INC (PA)**
Also Called: Silton Cases
2541 N Fowler Ave, Fresno (93727-8618)
P.O. Box 476 (93626-0476)
PHONE..............................559 253-4111
**EMP:** 25
**SQ FT:** 6,000
**SALES (est):** 2.93MM
**SALES (corp-wide):** 2.93MM **Privately Held**
SIC: **3161** Cases, carrying, nec

**(P-7135)**
**JAN-AL INNERPRIZES INC**
Also Called: Jan-Al Cases
3339 Union Pacific Ave, Los Angeles (90023-3812)
P.O. Box 23337 (90023-0337)
PHONE..............................323 260-7212
Miriam Alejandro, *Pr*
Jan Michael Alejandro, *
**EMP:** 30 **EST:** 1983
**SQ FT:** 16,000
**SALES (est):** 2.56MM **Privately Held**
Web: www.janalcase.com
SIC: **3161** Luggage

**(P-7136)**
**NATUS INC**
38 W Sierra Madre Blvd, Los Alamitos (90720-2624)
PHONE..............................626 355-3746
Jimmy Chen, *Pr*
◆ **EMP:** 90 **EST:** 2009
**SALES (est):** 3.51MM **Privately Held**
SIC: **3161** Suitcases

**(P-7137)**
**OGIO INTERNATIONAL INC**
Also Called: Ogio Powersports
508 Constitution Ave, Camarillo (93012-8510)
PHONE..............................800 326-6325
**EMP:** 77
**SALES (corp-wide):** 4.28B **Publicly Held**
Web: www.ogio.com
SIC: **3161** Luggage
HQ: Ogio International, Inc.
2180 Rutherford Rd
Carlsbad CA 92008
801 619-4100

**(P-7138)**
**OGIO INTERNATIONAL INC (HQ)**
Also Called: Ogio
2180 Rutherford Rd, Carlsbad (92008-7328)
PHONE..............................801 619-4100
Anthony Palma, *CEO*
Michael Pratt, *
▲ **EMP:** 23 **EST:** 1989
**SQ FT:** 70,000
**SALES (est):** 1.25MM
**SALES (corp-wide):** 4.28B **Publicly Held**
Web: www.ogio.com
SIC: **3161** 2393 Traveling bags; Textile bags
PA: Topgolf Callaway Brands Corp.
2180 Rutherford Rd
760 931-1771

**(P-7139)**
**SANDPIPER OF CALIFORNIA INC**
687 Anita St Ste A, Chula Vista (91911-4693)
P.O. Box 489 (91908-0489)
PHONE..............................619 424-2222
**EMP:** 54
SIC: **3161** Luggage

**(P-7140)**
**SLY TRUNK LLC**
481 N Santa Cruz Ave # 120, Los Gatos (95030-5300)
PHONE..............................408 540-6411
Shawn Robinson, *Prin*
Lukasz Wojewoda, *Prin*
**EMP:** 48 **EST:** 2010
**SALES (est):** 326.93K **Privately Held**
SIC: **3161** Trunks

**(P-7141)**
**SPECULATIVE PRODUCT DESIGN LLC (HQ)**
Also Called: Speck Products
400 S El Camino Real Ste 1200, San Mateo (94402-1703)
PHONE..............................650 462-2040
Irene Baran, *CEO*
Donald Walden, *
▲ **EMP:** 28 **EST:** 1996
**SALES (est):** 4.47MM
**SALES (corp-wide):** 49.49MM **Privately Held**
Web: www.speckproducts.com
SIC: **3161** 5999 Cases, carrying, nec; Electronic parts and equipment
PA: Telementum Global, Llc
2140 S Dupont Hwy

**(P-7142)**
**TARGUS US LLC**
1211 N Miller St, Anaheim (92806-1933)
PHONE..............................714 765-5555
Mikel Williams, *CEO*
Victor Streufert, *CFO*
**EMP:** 50 **EST:** 2015
**SQ FT:** 200,656
**SALES (est):** 2.44MM **Publicly Held**
Web: us.targus.com
SIC: **3161** Cases, carrying, nec
HQ: B. Riley Principal Investments, Llc
11100 Santa Monica Blvd
Los Angeles CA 90025
310 966-1444

**(P-7143)**
**TRAVELERS CHOICE TRAVELWARE**
Also Called: Golden Pacific
2805 S Reservoir St, Pomona (91766-6526)
PHONE..............................909 529-7688
Roger Yang, *CEO*
Annie Yang, *CFO*
▲ **EMP:** 55 **EST:** 1993
**SQ FT:** 12,000
**SALES (est):** 3.44MM **Privately Held**
Web: www.travelerchoice.com
SIC: **3161** 5948 Luggage; Luggage and leather goods stores

# 3161 - Luggage (P-7144)

**(P-7144)**
**ZUCA INC**
320 S Milpitas Blvd, Milpitas (95035-5421)
PHONE..............................408 377-9822
Bruce Kinnee, *Pr*
◆ **EMP:** 20 **EST:** 2003
**SALES (est):** 2.31MM **Privately Held**
**Web:** www.zuca.com
**SIC: 3161** 5099 Luggage; Luggage

## 3171 Women's Handbags And Purses

**(P-7145)**
**ISABELLE HANDBAG INC**
3155 Bandini Blvd Unit A, Vernon (90058-4134)
PHONE..............................323 277-9888
Roye Xu, *Pr*
James Li, *VP*
▲ **EMP:** 35 **EST:** 2011
**SQ FT:** 2,000
**SALES (est):** 354.41K **Privately Held**
**Web:** www.emperiahandbags.com
**SIC: 3171** 5632 Handbags, women's; Handbags

**(P-7146)**
**SBNW LLC (PA)**
5600 W Adams Blvd, Los Angeles (90016-2563)
PHONE..............................213 234-5122
Jason Rimokh, *
**EMP:** 110 **EST:** 2018
**SALES (est):** 992.61K
**SALES (corp-wide):** 992.61K **Privately Held**
**SIC: 3171** Handbags, women's

**(P-7147)**
**URBAN EXPRESSIONS INC**
5500 Union Pacific Ave, Commerce (90022-5139)
PHONE..............................310 593-4574
Farbod Shakouri, *CEO*
Arash Vojdani, *Pr*
▲ **EMP:** 20 **EST:** 2005
**SALES (est):** 3.91MM **Privately Held**
**Web:** www.urbanexpressions.net
**SIC: 3171** 5137 Handbags, women's; Handbags

## 3172 Personal Leather Goods, Nec

**(P-7148)**
**KOLTOV INC (PA)**
300 S Lewis Rd Ste A, Camarillo (93012-6620)
P.O. Box 2922 (93011-2922)
PHONE..............................805 764-0280
Joe Covrigaru, *CEO*
Brett Stone, *Pr*
Phillip Shieh, *Prin*
▲ **EMP:** 20 **EST:** 1983
**SALES (est):** 306.41K
**SALES (corp-wide):** 306.41K **Privately Held**
**SIC: 3172** 5199 Personal leather goods, nec; Leather, leather goods, and furs

**(P-7149)**
**LEATHER PRO INC**
Also Called: Turtleback Case
12900 Bradley Ave, Sylmar (91342-3829)
PHONE..............................818 833-8822
Brian Eremita, *Pr*

Al Eremita, *
▲ **EMP:** 24 **EST:** 2001
**SQ FT:** 13,000
**SALES (est):** 2.19MM **Privately Held**
**Web:** www.turtlebackcase.com
**SIC: 3172** Personal leather goods, nec

**(P-7150)**
**MALIBU LEATHER INC**
510 W 6th St Ste 1002, Los Angeles (90014-1311)
PHONE..............................310 985-0707
Allen Cinoglu, *Pr*
**EMP:** 125 **EST:** 2009
**SQ FT:** 12,000
**SALES (est):** 6.8MM **Privately Held**
**SIC: 3172** 5199 5948 Personal leather goods, nec; Leather, leather goods, and furs; Luggage and leather goods stores

**(P-7151)**
**RIDGE WALLET LLC**
Also Called: Ridge Wallet, The
2448 Main St, Santa Monica (90405-3516)
PHONE..............................818 636-2832
Daniel Kane, *Managing Member*
**EMP:** 25 **EST:** 2016
**SALES (est):** 4.78MM **Privately Held**
**Web:** www.ridge.com
**SIC: 3172** Wallets

## 3199 Leather Goods, Nec

**(P-7152)**
**AKER INTERNATIONAL INC**
Also Called: Aker Leather Products
2248 Main St Ste 4, Chula Vista (91911-3932)
PHONE..............................619 423-5182
Kamuran Aker, *CEO*
Laurie Aker, *
Levent Aker, *
▲ **EMP:** 30 **EST:** 1981
**SQ FT:** 10,000
**SALES (est):** 3.44MM **Privately Held**
**Web:** www.akerleather.com
**SIC: 3199** Holsters, leather

**(P-7153)**
**ARIAT INTERNATIONAL INC (HQ)**
Also Called: Stages West
1500 Alvarado St Ste 100, San Leandro (94577-2635)
PHONE..............................510 477-7000
Elizabeth Cross, *CEO*
Pankaj Gupta, *
Todd Levy, *
◆ **EMP:** 922 **EST:** 1991
**SALES (est):** 479.85MM
**SALES (corp-wide):** 479.85MM **Privately Held**
**Web:** www.ariat.com
**SIC: 3199** 5139 5137 5136 Equestrian related leather articles; Footwear; Women's and children's clothing; Men's and boy's clothing
**PA:** Lipzzaner, Inc.
1500 Alvarado St Ste 100
510 477-7000

**(P-7154)**
**CUSTOM LEATHERCRAFT MFG LLC**
Also Called: CLC Work Gear
5701 S Eastern Ave, Commerce (90040-2973)
◆ **EMP:** 73 **EST:** 1983
**SALES (est):** 24.98MM **Privately Held**

**Web:** www.goclc.com
**SIC: 3199** 2394 3111 Leather belting and strapping; Canvas and related products; Glove leather
**HQ:** Hultafors Group Ab
J A Wettergrens Gata 7, Inga
VAstra Frolunda 421 3
337237400

**(P-7155)**
**ELEANOR RIGBY LEATHER CO**
Also Called: Coda Mexico
4660 La Jolla Village Dr Ste 500 Pmb 50054, San Diego (92122-4604)
PHONE..............................619 356-5590
Peter Robinson, *CEO*
▲ **EMP:** 70 **EST:** 2011
**SQ FT:** 2,000
**SALES (est):** 4.74MM **Privately Held**
**Web:** www.eleanorrigbyhome.com
**SIC: 3199** Leather garments

**(P-7156)**
**FOGGY DOG LLC**
3360 20th St Ste A, San Francisco (94110-2655)
PHONE..............................415 993-1130
**EMP:** 15 **EST:** 2016
**SALES (est):** 1.38MM **Privately Held**
**Web:** www.thefoggydog.com
**SIC: 3199** Dog furnishings: collars, leashes, muzzles, etc.: leather

**(P-7157)**
**MASCORRO LEATHER INC**
5921 Sheila St, Commerce (90040-2402)
PHONE..............................323 724-6759
Yolanda Mascorro, *Pr*
Antonio Mascorro, *Pr*
Yolanda Mascorro, *Sec*
▲ **EMP:** 21 **EST:** 1977
**SALES (est):** 753.06K **Privately Held**
**Web:** www.mascorroleather.com
**SIC: 3199** Equestrian related leather articles

**(P-7158)**
**OCCIDENTAL MANUFACTURING LLC**
Also Called: Occidental Leather
3500 N Laughlin Rd Ste 100, Santa Rosa (95403-9098)
PHONE..............................707 824-2560
Peter Rosenquist, *CEO*
**EMP:** 121 **EST:** 1980
**SALES (est):** 2.78MM
**SALES (corp-wide):** 426.63MM **Privately Held**
**SIC: 3199** Leather garments
**PA:** R.A.F. Industries, Inc.
50 Monument Rd Ste 303
215 572-0738

**(P-7159)**
**OMAR LEATHER CO**
4557 Valley Blvd, Los Angeles (90032-3754)
PHONE..............................323 227-5220
Maria M Rojas, *Owner*
**EMP:** 16 **EST:** 1972
**SQ FT:** 5,000
**SALES (est):** 128.71K **Privately Held**
**SIC: 3199** Leather belting and strapping

**(P-7160)**
**OXBASE INC**
3500 N Laughlin Rd 100, Santa Rosa (95403-9098)
PHONE..............................707 824-2560
Darryl G Thurner, *Pr*
**EMP:** 48 **EST:** 1980

**SALES (est):** 4.51MM **Privately Held**
**SIC: 3199** Leather garments

**(P-7161)**
**ROO-HIDE SADDLERY LLC**
341 Crown Ct Bldg C, Imperial (92251-9421)
PHONE..............................877 766-4433
John Burgun, *CEO*
**EMP:** 15 **EST:** 1988
**SQ FT:** 435,600
**SALES (est):** 614.45K **Privately Held**
**Web:** www.roohide.net
**SIC: 3199** 5091 5941 Saddles or parts; Sporting and recreation goods; Saddlery and equestrian equipment

**(P-7162)**
**US DUTY GEAR INC**
1946 S Grove Ave, Ontario (91761-5615)
PHONE..............................909 391-8800
Jose Flores, *CEO*
Jose Flores, *Pr*
Estela Flores, *VP*
**EMP:** 17 **EST:** 2015
**SALES (est):** 769.05K **Privately Held**
**Web:** www.usdutygear.com
**SIC: 3199** Aprons: welders', blacksmiths', etc.: leather

**(P-7163)**
**YATES GEAR INC**
330 N Brand Blvd Ste 700, Glendale (91203-2336)
PHONE..............................530 222-4606
Jeffrey Morris, *CEO*
Kyle E Renninger, *CFO*
Thomas A Burger Junior, *Sec*
▲ **EMP:** 55 **EST:** 1988
**SALES (est):** 4.86MM
**SALES (corp-wide):** 136.41MM **Privately Held**
**Web:** www.yatesgear.com
**SIC: 3199** 3842 Safety belts, leather; Personal safety equipment
**HQ:** Sherrill, Inc.
496 Gllimore Dar Rd Ste D
Greensboro NC 27409
336 378-0444

## 3211 Flat Glass

**(P-7164)**
**BUDGET ENTERPRISES LLC**
Also Called: Solar Art
23042 Mill Creek Dr, Laguna Hills (92653-1214)
PHONE..............................949 697-9544
Matthew Darienzo, *CEO*
**EMP:** 25 **EST:** 2014
**SALES (est):** 5.22MM **Privately Held**
**Web:** www.solarart.com
**SIC: 3211** Construction glass

**(P-7165)**
**CARDINAL GLASS INDUSTRIES INC**
Also Called: Cardinal C G
24100 Cardinal Ave, Moreno Valley (92551-9545)
PHONE..............................951 485-9007
Scott Paisley, *Brnch Mgr*
**EMP:** 159
**SALES (corp-wide):** 1B **Privately Held**
**Web:** www.cardinalcorp.com
**SIC: 3211** 5039 3229 Flat glass; Glass construction materials; Pressed and blown glass, nec
**PA:** Cardinal Glass Industries Inc
775 Pririe Ctr Dr Ste 200

952 229-2600

**(P-7166)**
**CARDINAL GLASS INDUSTRIES INC**
Also Called: Cardinal Cg Company
680 Industrial Dr, Galt  (95632-1598)
PHONE..................................209 744-8940
Michael Potter, *Mgr*
**EMP:** 150
**SALES (corp-wide):** 1B **Privately Held**
Web: www.cardinalcorp.com
**SIC: 3211**  Flat glass
PA: Cardinal Glass Industries Inc
    775 Pririe Ctr Dr Ste 200
    952 229-2600

**(P-7167)**
**CEVIANS LLC (PA)**
3193 Red Hill Ave, Costa Mesa  (92626-3432)
PHONE..................................714 619-5135
Eric Lemay, *Pr*
**EMP:** 84 **EST:** 2014
**SALES (est):** 15.21MM
**SALES (corp-wide):** 15.21MM **Privately Held**
Web: www.cevians.com
**SIC: 3211**  Flat glass

**(P-7168)**
**CL SOLUTIONS  LLC**
1900 S Susan St, Santa Ana  (92704-3924)
PHONE..................................714 597-6499
Corre Marie Myer, *CEO*
**EMP:** 57 **EST:** 2011
**SALES (est):** 3.43MM **Privately Held**
Web: www.transparentarmorsolutions.com
**SIC: 3211**  Flat glass

**(P-7169)**
**GLASSFAB TEMPERING SVCS INC (PA)**
Also Called: Glass Fab Tempering Sv
8690 W Linne Rd, Tracy  (95304-9109)
PHONE..................................209 229-1060
Jagmohan Singh, *CEO*
Surinderpal Bains, *
Usha Mhay, *
**EMP:** 59 **EST:** 2005
**SQ FT:** 60,000
**SALES (est):** 11.55MM **Privately Held**
Web: www.glassfabtempering.com
**SIC: 3211**  Tempered glass

**(P-7170)**
**GUARDIAN INDUSTRIES  LLC**
Also Called: Guardian-Kingsburg
11535 E Mountain View Ave, Kingsburg  (93631-9233)
PHONE..................................559 891-8867
Jeffery Booey, *Mgr*
**EMP:** 275
**SQ FT:** 486,000
**SALES (corp-wide):** 64.37B **Privately Held**
Web: www.guardian.com
**SIC: 3211** 3231  Sheet glass; Products of purchased glass
HQ: Guardian Industries, Llc
    2300 Harmon Rd
    Auburn Hills MI 48326
    248 340-1800

**(P-7171)**
**GWLA ACQUISITION CORP (PA)**
8600 Rheem Ave, South Gate  (90280-3333)
PHONE..................................323 789-7800

Randy Steinberg, *Pr*
▲ **EMP:** 17 **EST:** 2002
**SALES (est):** 48.19MM **Privately Held**
Web: www.glasswerks.com
**SIC: 3211** 3231 6719  Tempered glass; Mirrored glass; Investment holding companies, except banks

**(P-7172)**
**HELIOTROPE TECHNOLOGIES INC**
850 Marina Village Pkwy Ste 102, Alameda  (94501-1007)
PHONE..................................510 871-3980
Peter Green, *CEO*
**EMP:** 18 **EST:** 2013
**SALES (est):** 5.1MM **Privately Held**
**SIC: 3211**  Insulating glass, sealed units

**(P-7173)**
**I G S INC**
Also Called: Industrial Glass Service
916 E California Ave, Sunnyvale  (94085-4505)
PHONE..................................408 733-4621
John R Gracia, *Pr*
▲ **EMP:** 18 **EST:** 1976
**SQ FT:** 15,000
**SALES (est):** 944.64K **Privately Held**
Web: www.igsglass.com
**SIC: 3211**  Optical glass, flat

**(P-7174)**
**INTERNATIONAL SKYLIGHTS**
Also Called: Acralight International
1831 Ritchey St, Santa Ana  (92705-5138)
PHONE..................................800 325-4355
**EMP:** 110
Web: www.acralightsolar.com
**SIC: 3211**  Skylight glass

**(P-7175)**
**LINOLEUM SALES CO  INC (PA)**
Also Called: Anderson's Carpet & Linoleum
1000 W Grand Ave, Oakland  (94607-2933)
PHONE..................................510 652-1032
Don Christophe, *CEO*
Tom Christophe, *
Andrei Wallace, *
Vince Lopez, *
Bob Mullarkey, *
**EMP:** 93 **EST:** 1954
**SQ FT:** 3,500
**SALES (est):** 22.61MM
**SALES (corp-wide):** 22.61MM **Privately Held**
Web: www.andersoncf.com
**SIC: 3211** 5713  Flat glass; Floor covering stores

**(P-7176)**
**MEDILAND CORPORATION**
Also Called: Premium Windows
15 Longitude Way, Corona  (92881-4911)
PHONE..................................562 630-9696
Carlos Landazuri, *CEO*
Jose Medina, *Corporate Secretary*
▲ **EMP:** 79 **EST:** 2005
**SALES (est):** 8.46MM **Privately Held**
Web: www.premiumwindows.com
**SIC: 3211** 3645  Window glass, clear and colored; Garden, patio, walkway and yard lighting fixtures: electric

**(P-7177)**
**SGC INTERNATIONAL  INC**
6489 Corvette St, Commerce  (90040-1702)
PHONE..................................323 318-2998
Xinbo Huang, *CEO*
Rita Huang, *Dir*

▲ **EMP:** 15 **EST:** 2000
**SALES (est):** 7.38MM **Privately Held**
Web: www.sgc-usa.com
**SIC: 3211** 5023 5039  Flat glass; Frames and framing, picture and mirror; Exterior flat glass: plate or window

**(P-7178)**
**SUNDOWN LIQUIDATING CORP (PA)**
Also Called: Bristolite
401 Goetz Ave, Santa Ana  (92707-3709)
PHONE..................................714 540-8950
Randolph Heartfield, *CEO*
Rick Beets, *
◆ **EMP:** 92 **EST:** 1970
**SQ FT:** 100,000
**SALES (est):** 9.29MM
**SALES (corp-wide):** 9.29MM **Privately Held**
**SIC: 3211**  Skylight glass

**(P-7179)**
**US HORIZON MANUFACTURING INC**
Also Called: U.S. Horizon Mfg
28539 Industry Dr, Valencia  (91355-5424)
PHONE..................................661 775-1675
Donald E Friest, *CEO*
Garrett A Russell, *
▲ **EMP:** 39 **EST:** 1998
**SQ FT:** 44,000
**SALES (est):** 5.33MM
**SALES (corp-wide):** 34.95B **Privately Held**
Web: www.ushorizon.com
**SIC: 3211** 3429  Plate and sheet glass; Hardware, nec
HQ: C. R. Laurence Co., Inc.
    2503 E Vernon Ave
    Los Angeles CA 90058
    323 588-1281

**(P-7180)**
**VITRO FLAT GLASS LLC**
Also Called: Fresno Glass Plant
3333 S Peach Ave, Fresno  (93725-9220)
P.O. Box 2748  (93745-2748)
PHONE..................................559 485-4660
Henry Good, *Mgr*
**EMP:** 140
Web: www.vitroglazings.com
**SIC: 3211**  Window glass, clear and colored
HQ: Vitro Flat Glass Llc
    400 Guys Run Rd
    Cheswick PA 15024
    855 887-6457

---

## 3221 Glass Containers

**(P-7181)**
**ACME VIAL & GLASS CO**
Also Called: Acme Vial
1601 Commerce Way, Paso Robles  (93446-3626)
PHONE..................................805 239-2666
Debra C Knowles, *Pr*
Kay Anderson, *
▲ **EMP:** 25 **EST:** 1942
**SALES (est):** 4.54MM **Privately Held**
Web: acmevialglassa.openfos.com
**SIC: 3221** 3231 5113  Vials, glass; Products of purchased glass; Industrial and personal service paper

**(P-7182)**
**GALLO GLASS COMPANY (HQ)**
605 S Santa Cruz Ave, Modesto  (95354-4254)
P.O. Box 1230  (95353-1230)

PHONE..................................209 341-3710
Robert J Gallo, *Pr*
▲ **EMP:** 1000 **EST:** 1957
**SALES (est):** 223.96MM
**SALES (corp-wide):** 2.11B **Privately Held**
Web: www.galloglass.com
**SIC: 3221**  Glass containers
PA: E. & J. Gallo Winery
    600 Yosemite Blvd
    209 341-3111

**(P-7183)**
**LIFEFACTORY INC**
3 Harbor Dr Ste 200, Sausalito  (94965-1491)
PHONE..................................415 729-9820
▲ **EMP:** 30
Web: www.lifefactory.com
**SIC: 3221**  Bottles for packing, bottling, and canning: glass

**(P-7184)**
**OWENS-BROCKWAY GLASS CONT INC**
Also Called: OWENS-BROCKWAY GLASS CONTAINER, INC.
3600 Alameda Ave, Oakland  (94601-3329)
PHONE..................................510 436-2000
Rod Detmear, *Mgr*
**EMP:** 21
**SALES (corp-wide):** 7.11B **Publicly Held**
Web: www.owens-brockway.com
**SIC: 3221**  Glass containers
HQ: Owens-Brockway Glass Container Inc.
    One Michael Owens Way
    Perrysburg OH 43551

**(P-7185)**
**PACIFIC VIAL MFG INC**
2738 Supply Ave, Commerce  (90040-2704)
PHONE..................................323 721-7004
Steven Oh, *Prin*
▲ **EMP:** 40 **EST:** 2001
**SQ FT:** 30,000
**SALES (est):** 12.89MM **Privately Held**
Web: www.pacificvial.com
**SIC: 3221**  Vials, glass

**(P-7186)**
**PACKLINE USA LLC**
9555 Hyssop Dr, Rancho Cucamonga  (91730-6124)
PHONE..................................909 392-8000
Amir Tamshe, *Managing Member*
**EMP:** 26 **EST:** 2018
**SALES (est):** 6.58MM **Privately Held**
Web: www.packlineusa.com
**SIC: 3221** 3089  Bottles for packing, bottling, and canning: glass; Plastics containers, except foam

**(P-7187)**
**WELL ABOVE BOTTLING & CANNING** ✪
8250 Industrial Ave, Roseville  (95678-5900)
PHONE..................................916 918-1946
**EMP:** 30 **EST:** 2023
**SALES (est):** 5.99MM **Privately Held**
**SIC: 3221**  Bottles for packing, bottling, and canning: glass

---

## 3229 Pressed And Blown Glass, Nec

**(P-7188)**
**ALLIANCE FIBER OPTIC PDTS INC**

## 3229 - Pressed And Blown Glass, Nec (P-7189)

840 N Mccarthy Blvd, Milpitas (95035-5114)
PHONE..................408 736-6900
Kevin B Parker, *CEO*
Christy C Lilley, *
▲ **EMP:** 1576 **EST:** 1995
**SALES (est):** 31.31MM
**SALES (corp-wide):** 12.59B **Publicly Held**
**SIC: 3229** 3661 Fiber optics strands; Fiber optics communications equipment
**PA:** Corning Incorporated
 1 Riverfront Plz
 607 974-9000

### (P-7189)
### ANNIEGLASS INC (PA)
310 Harvest Dr, Watsonville (95076-5103)
P.O. Box 2610 (95077-2610)
PHONE..................831 761-2041
Annie Morhauser, *Pr*
**EMP:** 19 **EST:** 1982
**SQ FT:** 16,000
**SALES (est):** 3.51MM
**SALES (corp-wide):** 3.51MM **Privately Held**
**Web:** www.annieglass.com
**SIC: 3229** Tableware, glass or glass ceramic

### (P-7190)
### APUTURE IMAGING INDUSTRIES
1715 N Gower St, Los Angeles (90028-5405)
PHONE..................626 295-6133
Bob Meesterman, *Sls Dir*
**EMP:** 25 **EST:** 2015
**SALES (est):** 773.66K **Privately Held**
**Web:** www.aputure.com
**SIC: 3229** Glass lighting equipment parts

### (P-7191)
### AURORA NETWORKS INC
2450 Walsh Ave, Santa Clara (95051-1303)
PHONE..................408 428-9500
◆ **EMP:** 183
**SIC: 3229** Fiber optics strands

### (P-7192)
### CARLEY (PA)
1502 W 228th St, Torrance (90501-5105)
PHONE..................310 325-8474
James A Carley, *Pr*
▲ **EMP:** 225 **EST:** 1974
**SQ FT:** 14,000
**SALES (est):** 7.82MM
**SALES (corp-wide):** 7.82MM **Privately Held**
**Web:** www.carleylamps.com
**SIC: 3229** 3646 3641 Lamp parts and shades, glass; Commercial lighting fixtures; Electric lamps

### (P-7193)
### CLEAREDGE SOLUTIONS INC
1020 Rock Ave, San Jose (95131-1610)
PHONE..................408 434-5984
Jack Cho, *Pr*
**EMP:** 30 **EST:** 2018
**SALES (est):** 2.53MM **Privately Held**
**SIC: 3229** Fiber optics strands

### (P-7194)
### DONOCO INDUSTRIES INC
Also Called: Encore Plastics
5642 Research Dr Ste B, Huntington Beach (92649-1634)
P.O. Box 3208 (92605-3208)
PHONE..................714 893-7889
Richard Harvey, *CEO*
Donald Okada, *
George West, *
**EMP:** 25 **EST:** 1993
**SQ FT:** 12,000
**SALES (est):** 1.91MM **Privately Held**
**Web:** www.encoreplastics.com
**SIC: 3229** Tableware, glass or glass ceramic

### (P-7195)
### GLAS WERK INC
29710 Avenida De Las Bandera, Rancho Santa Margari (92688-2614)
PHONE..................949 766-1296
Maik Mike Bollhorn, *Pr*
▲ **EMP:** 26 **EST:** 1987
**SQ FT:** 6,000
**SALES (est):** 2.55MM **Privately Held**
**Web:** www.glaswerk.com
**SIC: 3229** Scientific glassware

### (P-7196)
### IFIBER OPTIX INC
14450 Chambers Rd, Tustin (92780-6914)
PHONE..................714 665-9796
Sanjeev Jaiswal, *Pr*
▲ **EMP:** 25 **EST:** 2000
**SQ FT:** 5,731
**SALES (est):** 2.86MM **Privately Held**
**Web:** www.ifiberoptix.com
**SIC: 3229** Fiber optics strands

### (P-7197)
### INTEGRITY BOTTLES LLC
9225 Carlton Hills Blvd Ste 2, Santee (92071-2980)
PHONE..................847 922-0920
Zachary Lewis, *Prin*
**EMP:** 15 **EST:** 2018
**SALES (est):** 4.7MM **Privately Held**
**Web:** www.integritybottles.com
**SIC: 3229** Glassware, art or decorative

### (P-7198)
### MODERN CERAMICS MFG INC
2240 Lundy Ave, San Jose (95131-1816)
PHONE..................408 383-0554
Christina Hoang, *CEO*
▲ **EMP:** 20 **EST:** 1999
**SQ FT:** 3,087
**SALES (est):** 2.52MM **Privately Held**
**Web:** www.modernceramics.com
**SIC: 3229** Tableware, glass or glass ceramic

### (P-7199)
### OKEEFFES INC
Also Called: Safti First
2001 Grogan Ave, Merced (95341-6440)
PHONE..................209 386-1645
**EMP:** 67
**SALES (corp-wide):** 26.33MM **Privately Held**
**Web:** www.safti.com
**SIC: 3229** Glassware, industrial
**PA:** O'keeffe's, Inc.
 100 N Hill Dr Ste 12
 415 822-4222

### (P-7200)
### OPTIWORKS INC (PA)
47211 Bayside Pkwy, Fremont (94538-6517)
PHONE..................510 438-4560
Roger Liang, *CEO*
Annie Kuo, *
Steve Kuo, *
**EMP:** 65 **EST:** 2000
**SALES (est):** 6.88MM
**SALES (corp-wide):** 6.88MM **Privately Held**
**Web:** www.optiworks.com
**SIC: 3229** Fiber optics strands

### (P-7201)
### PERFORMANCE COMPOSITES INC
1418 S Alameda St, Compton (90221-4802)
PHONE..................310 328-6661
Francis Hu, *CEO*
**EMP:** 106 **EST:** 1994
**SQ FT:** 46,000
**SALES (est):** 22.36MM **Privately Held**
**Web:** www.performancecomposites.com
**SIC: 3229** 3624 3544 Glass fiber products; Carbon and graphite products; Special dies, tools, jigs, and fixtures

### (P-7202)
### PLEXUS OPTIX INC
3333 Quality Dr, Rancho Cordova (95670-7985)
PHONE..................800 852-7600
Don Oakley, *Pr*
**EMP:** 40 **EST:** 2009
**SALES (est):** 1.9MM
**SALES (corp-wide):** 53.15MM **Privately Held**
**Web:** www.unitycontactlenses.com
**SIC: 3229** Optical glass
**PA:** Vsp Optical Group, Inc.
 3333 Quality Dr
 916 851-4682

### (P-7203)
### SHAMIR INSIGHT INC
Also Called: Shamir
9938 Via Pasar, San Diego (92126-4559)
PHONE..................858 514-8330
Raanan Naftalovich, *CEO*
Richard Dailey, *
Joyce Hornaday, *
▲ **EMP:** 77 **EST:** 1997
**SALES (est):** 19.3MM
**SALES (corp-wide):** 2.55MM **Privately Held**
**Web:** www.rcpvrewards.com
**SIC: 3229** Optical glass
**HQ:** Shamir Optical Industry Ltd
 Kibbutz
 Shamir 12135

### (P-7204)
### SIMPLY STRAWS LLC
515 Bay Hill Dr, Newport Beach (92660-5245)
PHONE..................855 787-2974
▲ **EMP:** 20 **EST:** 2011
**SALES (est):** 1.63MM **Privately Held**
**Web:** www.simplystraws.com
**SIC: 3229** Straws, glass

### (P-7205)
### SPOTLITE AMERICA CORPORATION (PA)
9937 Jefferson Blvd Ste 110, Culver City (90232-3528)
PHONE..................310 829-0200
Halston Mikail, *CEO*
▲ **EMP:** 20 **EST:** 2014
**SQ FT:** 17,000
**SALES (est):** 2.17MM
**SALES (corp-wide):** 2.17MM **Privately Held**
**Web:** www.spotlite-usa.com
**SIC: 3229** 3699 Bulbs for electric lights; Electrical equipment and supplies, nec

### (P-7206)
### TE CONNECTIVITY MOG INC (PA)
501 Oakside Ave, Redwood City (94063-3800)
PHONE..................650 361-5292
Craig Newell, *Prin*
**EMP:** 16 **EST:** 2014
**SALES (est):** 74.18MM
**SALES (corp-wide):** 74.18MM **Privately Held**
**SIC: 3229** Fiber optics strands

### (P-7207)
### WEST COAST QUARTZ CORPORATION (HQ)
Also Called: W C Q
1000 Corporate Way, Fremont (94539-6105)
PHONE..................510 249-2160
Johng Bae, *CEO*
Dave Lopes, *
Howard Cho, *
Jun Hyung Kim, *
▲ **EMP:** 97 **EST:** 1981
**SQ FT:** 60,000
**SALES (est):** 22.99MM **Privately Held**
**Web:** www.wcq.com
**SIC: 3229** 3679 3674 5065 Glassware, industrial; Quartz crystals, for electronic application; Semiconductors and related devices; Semiconductor devices
**PA:** Worldex Industry & Trading Co.,Ltd
 53-77 4gongdan-Ro 7-Gil

### (P-7208)
### WESTERN FIBERGLASS INC (PA)
1555 Copperhill Pkwy, Santa Rosa (95403-8200)
PHONE..................707 523-2050
◆ **EMP:** 30 **EST:** 1983
**SALES (est):** 2.72MM
**SALES (corp-wide):** 2.72MM **Privately Held**
**Web:** www.westernfg.com
**SIC: 3229** Glass fiber products

### (P-7209)
### ZEONS INC
291 S La Cienega Blvd Ste 102, Beverly Hills (90211-3308)
PHONE..................323 302-8299
Naved Jafry, *Pr*
**EMP:** 312 **EST:** 2014
**SQ FT:** 3,500
**SALES (est):** 3.45MM **Privately Held**
**SIC: 3229** 1629 6211 Insulators, electrical: glass; Power plant construction; Investment certificate sales

## 3231 Products Of Purchased Glass

### (P-7210)
### ALAN LEM & CO INC
Also Called: Advance Aqua Tanks
515 W 130th St, Los Angeles (90061-1180)
PHONE..................310 538-4282
Alan Y Lem, *Pr*
**EMP:** 17 **EST:** 1986
**SQ FT:** 11,000
**SALES (est):** 3.69MM **Privately Held**
**Web:** www.advanceaquatanks.com
**SIC: 3231** Aquariums and reflectors, glass

### (P-7211)
### ATLAS SPECIALTIES CORPORATION (PA)
Also Called: Custom Line Shower Door Co
4337 Astoria St, Sacramento (95838-3001)
PHONE..................503 636-8182
Edwin A Lindquist, *Pr*
Roger Lindquist, *

## PRODUCTS & SERVICES SECTION
### 3231 - Products Of Purchased Glass (P-7232)

Fred Ferri, *
EMP: 28 EST: 1955
SQ FT: 5,000
SALES (est): 4.24MM
SALES (corp-wide): 4.24MM Privately Held
Web: www.atlasshowerdoor.com
SIC: 3231 5039 Doors, glass: made from purchased glass; Glass construction materials

### (P-7212)
### AVALON GLASS & MIRROR COMPANY
Also Called: Avalon Glass & Mirror
642 Alondra Blvd, Carson (90746-1049)
PHONE..................323 321-8806
Salvador G Gomez, Pr
Randy Seeinberg, *
Ed Rosengrant, *
▲ EMP: 19 EST: 1950
SQ FT: 100,000
SALES (est): 4.48MM Privately Held
Web: www.avalonmirrorglass.com
SIC: 3231 5023 5231 3211 Mirrored glass; Glassware; Glass; Flat glass

### (P-7213)
### BEVELED EDGE INC
Also Called: Original Glass Design
1740 Junction Ave Ste D, San Jose (95112-1035)
PHONE..................408 467-9900
Mark Idzal, Pr
▲ EMP: 16 EST: 1988
SQ FT: 8,500
SALES (est): 3.23MM Privately Held
Web: www.originalglassdesigns.com
SIC: 3231 Products of purchased glass

### (P-7214)
### CARDINAL GLASS INDUSTRIES INC
Also Called: Cardinal CT Company
1320 Business Park Dr, Dixon (95620-9765)
PHONE..................323 319-0070
EMP: 147
SALES (corp-wide): 1B Privately Held
Web: www.cardinalcorp.com
SIC: 3231 Products of purchased glass
PA: Cardinal Glass Industries Inc
  775 Pririe Ctr Dr Ste 200
  952 229-2600

### (P-7215)
### CHAM-CAL ENGINEERING CO
12722 Western Ave, Garden Grove (92841-4017)
PHONE..................714 898-9721
▲ EMP: 85 EST: 1970
SALES (est): 9.17MM Privately Held
Web: www.chamcal.com
SIC: 3231 8711 Mirrors, truck and automobile: made from purchased glass; Engineering services

### (P-7216)
### COMMONPATH LLC
Also Called: Ozeri
5963 Olivas Park Dr Ste F, Ventura (93003-7936)
PHONE..................858 922-8116
William Huckestein, Managing Member
Scott Kim, Managing Member
▲ EMP: 17 EST: 2009
SALES (est): 2.62MM Privately Held
Web: www.ozeri.com

SIC: 3231 3365 3596 3829 Decorated glassware: chipped, engraved, etched, etc.; Cooking/kitchen utensils, cast aluminum; Scales and balances, except laboratory; Measuring and controlling devices, nec

### (P-7217)
### CUSTOM INDUSTRIES INC
1371 N Miller St, Anaheim (92806-1412)
PHONE..................714 779-9101
Thomas Mcafee, Pr
▲ EMP: 21 EST: 1992
SALES (est): 6.85MM Privately Held
Web: www.bentcustomglass.net
SIC: 3231 Doors, glass: made from purchased glass

### (P-7218)
### DENNIS DIGIORGIO
Also Called: Oc Direct Shower Door
333 City Blvd W Ste 1700, Orange (92868-5905)
PHONE..................714 408-7527
Dennis Digiorgio, Owner
EMP: 43 EST: 2010
SALES (est): 1MM Privately Held
Web: www.ocframeless.com
SIC: 3231 Products of purchased glass

### (P-7219)
### EMPIRE SHOWER DOORS INC
1217 N Mcdowell Blvd, Petaluma (94954-1112)
PHONE..................707 773-2898
Roy German, Pr
Marylou German, Sec
EMP: 20 EST: 1989
SQ FT: 5,000
SALES (est): 478.31K Privately Held
Web: www.empireshowerdoors.com
SIC: 3231 5031 1793 Doors, glass: made from purchased glass; Doors, nec; Glass and glazing work

### (P-7220)
### FABRICATED GLASS SPC INC
2350 S Watney Way Ste E, Fairfield (94533-6738)
PHONE..................707 429-6160
Harvey Holtz, Pr
EMP: 32
SALES (corp-wide): 3.74MM Privately Held
SIC: 3231 Mirrored glass
PA: Fabricated Glass Specialties, Inc.
  101 E Rapp Rd
  541 535-1582

### (P-7221)
### FLYLEAF WINDOWS INC
11040 Bollinger Canyon Rd E-407, San Ramon (94582-4969)
PHONE..................925 344-1181
Billy Alcantara, Pr
EMP: 40 EST: 2018
SALES (est): 893.46K Privately Held
SIC: 3231 3211 Doors, glass: made from purchased glass; Window glass, clear and colored

### (P-7222)
### GAFFOGLIO FMLY MTLCRAFTERS INC (PA)
Also Called: Camera Ready Cars
11161 Slater Ave, Fountain Valley (92708-4921)
PHONE..................714 444-2000
George Gaffoglio, CEO
Ruben Gaffoglio, *
Mike Alexander, *

EMP: 103 EST: 1979
SQ FT: 94,000
SALES (est): 11.42MM
SALES (corp-wide): 11.42MM Privately Held
Web: www.metalcrafters.com
SIC: 3231 3711 3365 Mirrors, truck and automobile: made from purchased glass; Automobile assembly, including specialty automobiles; Aerospace castings, aluminum

### (P-7223)
### GLASSPLAX
26605 Madison Ave, Murrieta (92562-8909)
PHONE..................951 677-4800
Steve Tortomasi, CEO
Michael Rosato, Sec
▲ EMP: 16 EST: 1984
SALES (est): 484.1K Privately Held
Web: www.glassplax.com
SIC: 3231 5094 Ornamental glass: cut, engraved or otherwise decorated; Trophies

### (P-7224)
### GLASSWERKS LA INC (HQ)
Also Called: Glasswerks Group
8600 Rheem Ave, South Gate (90280)
PHONE..................888 789-7810
Randy Steinberg, CEO
Ruben Huerta, Sec
Edwin Rosengrant, VP Sls
Michael Torres, CFO
▲ EMP: 280 EST: 1949
SQ FT: 100,000
SALES (est): 41.8MM Privately Held
Web: www.glasswerks.com
SIC: 3231 3211 Mirrored glass; Flat glass
PA: Gwla Acquisition Corp.
  8600 Rheem Ave

### (P-7225)
### GP MERGER SUB INC
Also Called: Glaspro
9401 Ann St, Santa Fe Springs (90670-2613)
PHONE..................562 946-7722
Joseph Green, Pr
Jim Martineau, *
Jeff Brown, *
◆ EMP: 85 EST: 1986
SQ FT: 75,000
SALES (est): 11.84MM Privately Held
Web: www.glas-pro.com
SIC: 3231 Laminated glass: made from purchased glass

### (P-7226)
### HALIO INC (PA)
3945 Freedom Cir, Santa Clara (95054-1223)
PHONE..................650 416-5200
Bruce Sohn, CEO
Alok Gupta, *
▲ EMP: 79 EST: 2010
SALES (est): 30.59MM
SALES (corp-wide): 30.59MM Privately Held
Web: www.halioinc.com
SIC: 3231 Products of purchased glass

### (P-7227)
### INDUSTRIAL GLASS PRODUCTS INC
4229 Union Pacific Ave, Los Angeles (90023-4016)
PHONE..................323 526-7125
Esther Ramirez, Pr
▲ EMP: 15 EST: 1990
SQ FT: 10,000
SALES (est): 1.73MM Privately Held

Web: www.iglassprod.com
SIC: 3231 5039 Products of purchased glass ; Glass construction materials

### (P-7228)
### INVENIOS LLC
320 N Nopal St, Santa Barbara (93103-3225)
PHONE..................805 962-3333
Paul Then, Pr
EMP: 83 EST: 2017
SALES (est): 10.65MM
SALES (corp-wide): 12.59B Publicly Held
Web: www.invenios.com
SIC: 3231 Products of purchased glass
PA: Corning Incorporated
  1 Riverfront Plz
  607 974-9000

### (P-7229)
### JUDSON STUDIOS INC
200 S Avenue 66, Los Angeles (90042-3632)
PHONE..................323 255-0131
David Judson, Pr
EMP: 27 EST: 1897
SQ FT: 10,000
SALES (est): 2.27MM Privately Held
Web: www.judsonstudios.com
SIC: 3231 Stained glass: made from purchased glass

### (P-7230)
### LARRY MTHVIN INSTALLATIONS INC (HQ)
Also Called: L M I
501 Kettering Dr, Ontario (91761-8150)
PHONE..................909 563-1700
Larry Methvin, CEO
▲ EMP: 200 EST: 1975
SQ FT: 28,000
SALES (est): 22.86MM
SALES (corp-wide): 3.47B Publicly Held
Web: www.larrymethvin.com
SIC: 3231 3431 1751 Doors, glass: made from purchased glass; Shower stalls, metal; Carpentry work
PA: Patrick Industries, Inc.
  107 W Franklin St
  574 294-7511

### (P-7231)
### LARRY MTHVIN INSTALLATIONS INC
Also Called: LMI
128 N Cluff Ave, Lodi (95240-3104)
PHONE..................209 368-2105
Christy Puerta, VP
EMP: 87
SALES (corp-wide): 3.47B Publicly Held
Web: www.larrymethvin.com
SIC: 3231 3088 Framed mirrors; Shower stalls, fiberglass and plastics
HQ: Larry Methvin Installations, Inc.
  501 Kettering Dr
  Ontario CA 91761
  909 563-1700

### (P-7232)
### LIPPERT COMPONENTS MFG INC
Hehr Glass Co
1021 Walnut Ave, Pomona (91766-6528)
PHONE..................909 628-5557
Pete Adams, Mgr
EMP: 50
SALES (corp-wide): 3.78B Publicly Held
Web: corporate.lippert.com

## 3231 - Products Of Purchased Glass (P-7233)

SIC: 3231 5231 Doors, glass: made from purchased glass; Glass
HQ: Lippert Components Manufacturing, Inc.
3501 County Rd 6 E
Elkhart IN 46514
574 535-1125

**(P-7233)**
**MAC THIN FILMS INC**
2721 Giffen Ave, Santa Rosa (95407-5063)
PHONE.................................707 791-1656
Mark Madigan, CEO
Julie Leonhard, *
▲ EMP: 50 EST: 2014
SALES (est): 5.79MM Privately Held
Web: www.macthinfilms.com
SIC: 3231 Products of purchased glass

**(P-7234)**
**MILGARD MANUFACTURING LLC**
Also Called: Milgard-Simi Valley
355 E Easy St, Simi Valley (93065-1801)
PHONE.................................805 581-6325
Wayne Ramay, Brnch Mgr
EMP: 106
SALES (corp-wide): 822.1MM Privately Held
Web: www.milgard.com
SIC: 3231 Products of purchased glass
HQ: Milgard Manufacturing Llc
1498 Pacific Ave Fl 4
Tacoma WA 98402
253 922-4343

**(P-7235)**
**MIR GROUP INC**
Also Called: Mir Mosaic
2200 Zanker Rd Ste B, San Jose (95131-1112)
PHONE.................................408 432-1000
Emin Mazanov, CEO
▲ EMP: 48 EST: 2012
SALES (est): 6.11MM Privately Held
Web: www.mir-mosaic.com
SIC: 3231 Mosaics, glass: made from purchased glass

**(P-7236)**
**NEW GLASPRO INC**
9401 Ann St, Santa Fe Springs (90670-2613)
PHONE.................................800 776-2368
Joseph Green, Pr
EMP: 23 EST: 2005
SALES (est): 1.19MM Privately Held
Web: www.glas-pro.com
SIC: 3231 Products of purchased glass

**(P-7237)**
**OKEEFFES INC (PA)**
Also Called: Safti First
100 N Hill Dr Ste 12, Brisbane (94005-1010)
PHONE.................................415 822-4222
▲ EMP: 24 EST: 1946
SALES (est): 26.33MM
SALES (corp-wide): 26.33MM Privately Held
Web: www.okeeffes.com
SIC: 3231 3446 Products of purchased glass; Architectural metalwork

**(P-7238)**
**PACIFIC ARTGLASS CORPORATION**
Also Called: Pacific Glass
125 W 157th St, Gardena (90248-2225)
PHONE.................................310 516-7828
John Williams, Pr
▲ EMP: 23 EST: 1976
SQ FT: 18,000
SALES (est): 2.37MM Privately Held
Web: www.pacificartglass.com
SIC: 3231 5231 Products of purchased glass; Glass, leaded or stained

**(P-7239)**
**PRL GLASS SYSTEMS INC**
14760 Don Julian Rd, City Of Industry (91746-3107)
PHONE.................................877 775-2586
EMP: 74
Web: www.prlglass.com
SIC: 3231 Products of purchased glass
PA: Prl Glass Systems, Inc.
13644 Nelson Ave

**(P-7240)**
**PRL GLASS SYSTEMS INC (PA)**
Also Called: P R L
13644 Nelson Ave, City Of Industry (91746-2336)
PHONE.................................626 961-5890
◆ EMP: 200 EST: 1989
SALES (est): 51.31MM Privately Held
Web: www.prlglass.com
SIC: 3231 3354 Products of purchased glass; Aluminum extruded products

**(P-7241)**
**RAYOTEK SCIENTIFIC LLC**
Also Called: Rayotek Scientific
8845 Rehco Rd, San Diego (92121-3261)
PHONE.................................858 558-3671
William Raggio, Pr
Jessica Yadley, *
EMP: 30 EST: 1996
SQ FT: 30,000
SALES (est): 8.35MM
SALES (corp-wide): 10.31MM Privately Held
Web: www.rayotek.com
SIC: 3231 8748 Products of purchased glass; Business consulting, nec
PA: Mcdanel Advanced Ceramic Technologies, Llc
510 9th Ave
724 843-8300

**(P-7242)**
**SREAM INC**
12869 Temescal Canyon Rd Ste A, Corona (92883-4021)
PHONE.................................951 245-6999
Jarir Farraj, CEO
Steve Rodriguez, *
EMP: 34 EST: 2013
SALES (est): 2.5MM Privately Held
Web: www.liquidsciglass.com
SIC: 3231 5231 Products of purchased glass; Glass

**(P-7243)**
**TOTAL MONT LLC**
Also Called: Western States Glass
790 W 12th St, Long Beach (90813-2810)
PHONE.................................562 983-1374
EMP: 44 EST: 2020
SALES (est): 7.37MM Privately Held
SIC: 3231 3211 Insulating glass: made from purchased glass; Tempered glass

**(P-7244)**
**TRIVIEW GLASS INDUSTRIES LLC**
Also Called: Triview
279 Shawnan Ln, La Habra (90631-8087)
PHONE.................................626 363-7980
Alexander A Kastaniuk, CEO
▲ EMP: 99 EST: 2008
SALES (est): 10.82MM Privately Held
Web: triview-glass.squarespace.com
SIC: 3231 Products of purchased glass

**(P-7245)**
**TWED-DELLS INC**
Also Called: California Glass & Mirror Div
1900 S Susan St, Santa Ana (92704-3924)
PHONE.................................714 754-6900
Corey M Myer Junior, Pr
Gayle Myer, *
▲ EMP: 38 EST: 1980
SQ FT: 45,000
SALES (est): 5.6MM Privately Held
Web: www.tbmglass.com
SIC: 3231 Mirrored glass

**(P-7246)**
**ULTRA GLASS**
4001 Vista Park Ct Ste 1, Sacramento (95834-2975)
PHONE.................................916 338-3911
Kurtis Ryder, Pr
EMP: 15 EST: 1990
SQ FT: 10,000
SALES (est): 2.33MM Privately Held
SIC: 3231 Doors, glass: made from purchased glass

**(P-7247)**
**ZADRO INC**
14462 Astronautics Ln Ste 101, Huntington Beach (92647-2077)
PHONE.................................714 892-9200
Zlatko Zadro, CEO
Elizabeth Zadro, Sec
Rebecca Zadro, CFO
Alexander Zadro, Dir
EMP: 20 EST: 2007
SALES (est): 3.49MM Privately Held
Web: www.zadrohs.com
SIC: 3231 Mirrored glass

**(P-7248)**
**ZADRO PRODUCTS INC**
14462 Astronautics Ln Ste 101, Huntington Beach (92647-2077)
PHONE.................................714 892-9200
Zlatko Zadro, Pr
Becky Zadro, *
◆ EMP: 35 EST: 1986
SQ FT: 22,000
SALES (est): 7.51MM Privately Held
Web: www.zadroinc.com
SIC: 3231 3641 Mirrored glass; Electric lamps

## 3241 Cement, Hydraulic

**(P-7249)**
**CALPORTLAND COMPANY**
Also Called: California Portland Cement
9350 Oak Creek Rd, Mojave (93501-7738)
PHONE.................................661 824-2401
Bruce Shaffer, Brnch Mgr
EMP: 130
Web: www.calportland.com
SIC: 3241 5032 5211 Masonry cement; Brick, stone, and related material; Cement
HQ: Calportland Company
2025 E Financial Way
Glendora CA 91741

**(P-7250)**
**CALPORTLAND COMPANY**
Also Called: Oro Grande Cement Plant
19409 National Trails Hwy, Oro Grande (92368-9705)
PHONE.................................760 245-5321
EMP: 58
Web: www.calportland.com
SIC: 3241 3273 5032 Portland cement; Ready-mixed concrete; Brick, stone, and related material
HQ: Calportland Company
2025 E Financial Way
Glendora CA 91741

**(P-7251)**
**CALPORTLAND COMPANY**
2201 W Washington St Ste 6, Stockton (95203-2942)
PHONE.................................209 469-0109
Warren Burchett, Mgr
EMP: 20
Web: www.calportland.com
SIC: 3241 3273 Portland cement; Ready-mixed concrete
HQ: Calportland Company
2025 E Financial Way
Glendora CA 91741

**(P-7252)**
**CALPORTLAND COMPANY (DH)**
Also Called: Arizona Portland Cement
2025 E Financial Way, Glendora (91741-4692)
P.O. Box 371534 (89137-1534)
PHONE.................................626 852-6200
Michio Kimura, Ch Bd
Allen Hamblen, *
James A Repman, *
James A Wendoll, *
John Renninger, *
▲ EMP: 77 EST: 1891
SQ FT: 28,000
SALES (est): 864.13MM Privately Held
Web: www.calportland.com
SIC: 3241 3273 5032 Portland cement; Ready-mixed concrete; Brick, stone, and related material
HQ: Taiheiyo Cement U.S.A., Inc.
2025 E Fincl Way Ste 200
Glendora CA 91741
626 852-6200

**(P-7253)**
**CEMEX CALIFORNIA CEMENT LLC**
5050 83rd St, Sacramento (95826-4723)
PHONE.................................760 381-7616
▲ EMP: 260 EST: 1998
SALES (est): 3.73MM Privately Held
SIC: 3241 Portland cement
HQ: Cemex, Inc.
10100 Katy Fwy Ste 300
Houston TX 77043
713 650-6200

**(P-7254)**
**CEMEX CNSTR MTLS PCF LLC**
Also Called: Aggregate - Lapis Ind Sand/Mar
100 Lapis Rd, Marina (93933)
PHONE.................................831 883-3701
Fred Tresler, Brnch Mgr
EMP: 22
SIC: 3241 Cement, hydraulic
HQ: Cemex Construction Materials Pacific, Llc
1501 Belvedere Rd
West Palm Beach FL 33406
561 833-5555

**(P-7255)**
**CTS CEMENT MANUFACTURING CORP (PA)**

12442 Knott St, Garden Grove (92841-2832)
PHONE.....................714 379-8260
Walter J Hoyle, CEO
▼ EMP: 45 EST: 1978
SQ FT: 14,000
SALES (est): 35.68MM
SALES (corp-wide): 35.68MM **Privately Held**
Web: www.ctscement.com
SIC: 3241 Cement, hydraulic

**(P-7256)**
**JAMES HARDIE BUILDING PDTS INC**
26300 La Alameda Ste 400, Mission Viejo (92691-8372)
PHONE.....................949 348-1800
Louis Gries, Pr
EMP: 86
SQ FT: 97,250
Web: www.jameshardie.com
SIC: 3241 Natural cement
HQ: James Hardie Building Products Inc.
   303 E Wacker Dr
   Chicago IL 60601
   312 291-5072

**(P-7257)**
**LEHIGH SOUTHWEST CEMENT CO**
24001 Stevens Creek Blvd, Cupertino (95014-5659)
PHONE.....................408 996-4271
W Lee, Brnch Mgr
EMP: 15
Web: www.heidelbergmaterials.us
SIC: 3241 2891 5032 5211 Portland cement; Cement, except linoleum and tile; Cement; Cement
HQ: Lehigh Southwest Cement Company
   2300 Clayton Rd Ste 300
   Concord CA 94520
   972 653-5500

**(P-7258)**
**LEHIGH SOUTHWEST CEMENT CO (DH)**
2300 Clayton Rd Ste 300, Concord (94520-2175)
PHONE.....................972 653-5500
Dan Harrington, CEO
▲ EMP: 15 EST: 1925
SQ FT: 10,000
SALES (est): 29.43MM **Privately Held**
Web: www.heidelbergmaterials.us
SIC: 3241 2891 5032 5211 Portland cement; Cement, except linoleum and tile; Cement; Cement
HQ: Calportland Company
   2025 E Financial Way
   Glendora CA 91741

**(P-7259)**
**MITSUBISHI CEMENT CORPORATION**
1150 Pier F Ave, Long Beach (90802-6252)
PHONE.....................562 495-0600
Marty Marcum, Mgr
EMP: 428
Web: www.mitsubishicement.com
HQ: Mitsubishi Cement Corporation
   151 Cassia Way
   Henderson NV 89014
   702 932-3900

**(P-7260)**
**MITSUBISHI CEMENT CORPORATION**
5808 State Highway 18, Lucerne Valley (92356-8179)
PHONE.....................760 248-7373
Jim Russell, Brnch Mgr
EMP: 175
Web: www.mitsubishicement.com
SIC: 3241 Portland cement
HQ: Mitsubishi Cement Corporation
   151 Cassia Way
   Henderson NV 89014
   702 932-3900

**(P-7261)**
**NATIONAL CEMENT COMPANY INC (HQ)**
15821 Ventura Blvd Ste 475, Encino (91436-2935)
PHONE.....................818 728-5200
James E Rotch, Ch Bd
▲ EMP: 38 EST: 1920
SQ FT: 11,446
SALES (est): 452.77MM
SALES (corp-wide): 632.96MM **Privately Held**
Web: www.nationalcement.com
SIC: 3241 3273 Portland cement; Ready-mixed concrete
PA: Vicat
   Les Trois Vallons
   474275900

**(P-7262)**
**RIVERSIDE CEMENT HOLDINGS COMPANY**
Also Called: Txi Riverside Cement
1500 Rubidoux Blvd, Riverside (92509-1840)
P.O. Box 832 (92502-0832)
PHONE.....................951 774-2500
▲ EMP: 380
SIC: 3241 3272 Natural cement; Concrete products, nec

**(P-7263)**
**RMC PACIFIC MATERIALS LLC (PA)**
Also Called: Cemex
6601 Koll Center Pkwy Ste 300, Pleasanton (94566-3112)
P.O. Box 5252 (94566-0252)
◆ EMP: 200 EST: 1998
SQ FT: 30,000
SALES (est): 6.26MM
SALES (corp-wide): 6.26MM **Privately Held**
SIC: 3241 3273 3531 1442 Cement, hydraulic; Ready-mixed concrete; Asphalt plant, including gravel-mix type; Sand mining

## 3251 Brick And Structural Clay Tile

**(P-7264)**
**ARTO BRICK / CALIFORNIA PAVERS**
Also Called: Arto Brick and Cal Pavers
15209 S Broadway, Gardena (90248-1823)
PHONE.....................310 768-8500
Arto Alajian, CEO
EMP: 40 EST: 1966
SQ FT: 18,000
SALES (est): 4.74MM **Privately Held**
Web: www.arto.com

SIC: 3251 Brick and structural clay tile

**(P-7265)**
**BASALITE BUILDING PRODUCTS LLC**
Also Called: Gladding McBean
601 7th St, Lincoln (95648-1828)
PHONE.....................916 645-3341
Bill Padavona, Brnch Mgr
EMP: 250
SALES (corp-wide): 1.21B **Privately Held**
Web: www.gladdingmcbean.com
SIC: 3251 3253 3259 3269 Ceramic glazed brick, clay; Ceramic wall and floor tile; Clay sewer and drainage pipe and tile; Vases, pottery
HQ: Basalite Building Products, Llc
   2150 Douglas Blvd Ste 260
   Roseville CA 95661
   707 678-1901

**(P-7266)**
**MORGAN ADVANCED CERAMICS INC (HQ)**
2425 Whipple Rd, Hayward (94544-7807)
PHONE.....................510 491-1100
▲ EMP: 175 EST: 1927
SALES (est): 106.49MM
SALES (corp-wide): 1.39B **Privately Held**
Web: www.morgantechnicalceramics.com
SIC: 3251 2899 3264 Brick and structural clay tile; Fluxes: brazing, soldering, galvanizing, and welding; Porcelain electrical supplies
PA: Morgan Advanced Materials Plc
   York House
   175 383-7000

## 3253 Ceramic Wall And Floor Tile

**(P-7267)**
**ELYSIUM TILES INC**
Also Called: Elysium
1180 N Anaheim Blvd, Anaheim (92801-2502)
PHONE.....................714 991-7885
Yue Zhou, CEO
▲ EMP: 17 EST: 2009
SALES (est): 5.64MM **Privately Held**
Web: www.elysiumtiles.com
SIC: 3253 Mosaic tile, glazed and unglazed: ceramic

**(P-7268)**
**HEATH CERAMICS LTD (PA)**
400 Gate 5 Rd, Sausalito (94965-2807)
PHONE.....................415 332-3732
EMP: 100 EST: 1948
SALES (est): 15.26MM
SALES (corp-wide): 15.26MM **Privately Held**
Web: www.heathceramics.com
SIC: 3253 3269 Wall tile, ceramic; Stoneware pottery products

**(P-7269)**
**MORGAN ADVANCED MATERIALS INC**
13079 Earhart Ave, Auburn (95602-9536)
PHONE.....................530 823-3401
EMP: 15 EST: 2013
SALES (est): 313.94K **Privately Held**
Web: www.morganadvancedmaterials.com
SIC: 3253 Floor tile, ceramic

**(P-7270)**
**OCEANSIDE GLASSTILE COMPANY (PA)**
Also Called: Mandala
2445 Grand Ave, Vista (92081-7806)
PHONE.....................760 929-4000
Sean M Gildea, CEO
Jim Jensen, *
John Marckx, *
Rick Blacklock, *
Jeff Nibler, *
◆ EMP: 375 EST: 1992
SQ FT: 48,000
SALES (est): 33.6MM **Privately Held**
Web: www.glasstile.com
SIC: 3253 5032 Mosaic tile, glazed and unglazed: ceramic; Tile, clay or other ceramic, excluding refractory

**(P-7271)**
**PACIFIC CERAMICS INC**
3524 Bassett St, Santa Clara (95054-2704)
PHONE.....................408 747-4600
Dennis J Fleming, CEO
EMP: 37 EST: 1994
SALES (est): 4.48MM **Privately Held**
Web: www.pceramics.com
SIC: 3253 Ceramic wall and floor tile

**(P-7272)**
**PROGRESSIVE TECHNOLOGY**
4130 Citrus Ave Ste 17, Rocklin (95677-4006)
PHONE.....................916 632-6715
Shannon Rogers, Pr
Carol Rogers, *
EMP: 17 EST: 1989
SQ FT: 23,000
SALES (est): 937.74K **Privately Held**
Web: www.prgtech.com
SIC: 3253 Ceramic wall and floor tile

## 3259 Structural Clay Products, Nec

**(P-7273)**
**EAGLE ROOFING PRODUCTS FLA LLC**
3546 N Riverside Ave, Rialto (92377-3802)
PHONE.....................909 822-6000
Robert C Burlingame, Managing Member
Seamus P Burlingame, *
Kevin C Burlingame, *
EMP: 18 EST: 2006
SALES (est): 2.69MM **Privately Held**
Web: www.eagleroofing.com
SIC: 3259 Roofing tile, clay

**(P-7274)**
**MARUHACHI CERAMICS AMERICA INC**
1985 Sampson Ave, Corona (92879-6006)
PHONE.....................800 736-6221
Yoshihiro Suzuki, Pr
▲ EMP: 22 EST: 1983
SQ FT: 83,250
SALES (est): 6.9MM **Privately Held**
Web: www.mca-tile.com
SIC: 3259 Roofing tile, clay

**(P-7275)**
**PABCO BUILDING PRODUCTS LLC**
Also Called: Gladding McBean
601 7th St, Lincoln (95648-1828)
P.O. Box 97 (95648-0097)
PHONE.....................916 645-3341

# 3259 - Structural Clay Products, Nec (P-7276)

Erik Absalon, *Genl Mgr*
**EMP:** 72
**SQ FT:** 952
**SALES (corp-wide):** 1.21B **Privately Held**
**Web:** www.pabcogypsum.com
**SIC: 3259** Architectural terra cotta
**HQ:** Pabco Building Products, Llc
  10811 International Dr
  Rancho Cordova CA 95670
  510 792-1577

**(P-7276)**
**UNITED STATES TILE CO**
909 Railroad St, Corona (92882-1906)
**PHONE**.................................951 739-4613
◆ **EMP:** 125
**SIC: 3259** Roofing tile, clay

## 3261 Vitreous Plumbing Fixtures

**(P-7277)**
**LOTUS HYGIENE SYSTEMS INC**
1621 E Saint Andrew Pl, Santa Ana (92705-4932)
**PHONE**.................................714 259-8805
Xiang Liu, *Pr*
▲ **EMP:** 20 **EST:** 2005
**SQ FT:** 10,000
**SALES (est):** 2.03MM **Privately Held**
**Web:** www.lotusseats.com
**SIC: 3261** Vitreous plumbing fixtures

**(P-7278)**
**MICROPHOR INC**
452 E Hill Rd, Willits (95490-9721)
**PHONE**.................................707 459-5563
**TOLL FREE:** 800
▲ **EMP:** 35
**SIC: 3261** 3589 3829 3632  Vitreous plumbing fixtures; Sewage treatment equipment; Oil pressure gauges, motor vehicle; Refrigerators, mechanical and absorption: household

**(P-7279)**
**PULSE SHOWER SPAS INC**
297 Anna St, Watsonville (95076-2436)
**PHONE**.................................831 724-7300
Brian Edwards, *CEO*
Francis Herzog, *COO*
◆ **EMP:** 16 **EST:** 2005
**SQ FT:** 4,500
**SALES (est):** 2.29MM **Privately Held**
**Web:** www.pulseshowerspas.com
**SIC: 3261** Bathroom accessories/fittings, vitreous china or earthenware

**(P-7280)**
**TUBULAR SPECIALTIES MFG INC**
Also Called: T S M
13011 S Spring St, Los Angeles (90061-1685)
**PHONE**.................................310 515-4801
Marcia Lynn Hemphill, *CEO*
L C Huntley, *
Arif Mansuri, *
▲ **EMP:** 62 **EST:** 1966
**SQ FT:** 38,000
**SALES (est):** 4.11MM **Privately Held**
**Web:** www.calltsm.com
**SIC: 3261** 2656 3446  Bathroom accessories/fittings, vitreous china or earthenware; Sanitary food containers; Railings, prefabricated metal

**(P-7281)**
**WESTINGHOUSE A BRAKE TECH CORP**
Microphor
452 E Hill Rd, Willits (95490-9721)
**PHONE**.................................707 459-5563
**EMP:** 35
**Web:** www.wabteccorp.com
**SIC: 3261** 3589  Toilet fixtures, vitreous china ; Sewage treatment equipment
**PA:** Westinghouse Air Brake Technologies Corporation
  30 Isabella St

## 3262 Vitreous China Table And Kitchenware

**(P-7282)**
**SKY ONE INC**
Also Called: Vertex China
1793 W 2nd St, Pomona (91766-1253)
**PHONE**.................................909 622-3333
Hoi Shum, *Pr*
Ken Joyce, *VP*
Gary Dallas, *VP*
▲ **EMP:** 19 **EST:** 1976
**SQ FT:** 14,000
**SALES (est):** 3.8MM **Privately Held**
**Web:** www.vertexchina.com
**SIC: 3262**  Dishes, commercial or household: vitreous china

## 3263 Semivitreous Table And Kitchenware

**(P-7283)**
**MASTERS IN METAL INC**
131 Lombard St, Oxnard (93030-5161)
**PHONE**.................................805 988-1992
Wayne R Haddox, *Pr*
Dennis Haddox, *
▲ **EMP:** 16 **EST:** 1996
**SQ FT:** 11,000
**SALES (est):** 1.42MM **Privately Held**
**Web:** www.mastersinmetal.com
**SIC: 3263** 3952  Commercial tableware or kitchen articles, fine earthenware; Sizes, gold and bronze: artists'

## 3264 Porcelain Electrical Supplies

**(P-7284)**
**MAGNET SALES & MFG CO INC (HQ)**
Also Called: Integrated Magnetics
11250 Playa Ct, Culver City (90230-6127)
**PHONE**.................................310 391-7213
**TOLL FREE:** 800
Anil Nanji, *Pr*
Anil Nanji, *Pr*
Gary Hooper, *
▲ **EMP:** 75 **EST:** 1936
**SQ FT:** 45,000
**SALES (est):** 18.77MM
**SALES (corp-wide):** 46.01MM **Privately Held**
**Web:** www.intemag.com
**SIC: 3264** 3621  Porcelain electrical supplies; Servomotors, electric
**PA:** Integrated Technologies Group, Inc.
  11250 Playa Ct
  310 391-7213

**(P-7285)**
**PRECISION FRRITES CERAMICS INC**
5432 Production Dr, Huntington Beach (92649-1525)
**PHONE**.................................714 901-7622
Frank Hong, *CEO*
Myung Sook Hong, *
Sung Mo Hong, *Pr*
Ji Soo Lee, *General Vice President*
**EMP:** 99 **EST:** 1975
**SQ FT:** 23,811
**SALES (est):** 5.19MM **Privately Held**
**Web:** www.semiceramic.com
**SIC: 3264** 3674 3599  Porcelain electrical supplies; Semiconductors and related devices; Machine shop, jobbing and repair

## 3269 Pottery Products, Nec

**(P-7286)**
**BERNEY-KARP INC**
3350 E 26th St, Vernon (90058-4145)
**PHONE**.................................323 260-7122
Morry Karp, *Pr*
Anna Ramos, *
▲ **EMP:** 74 **EST:** 1970
**SQ FT:** 80,000
**SALES (est):** 4.8MM **Privately Held**
**Web:** berneykarp.openfos.com
**SIC: 3269**  Pottery cooking and kitchen articles

**(P-7287)**
**HAGEN-RENAKER INC (PA)**
914 W Cienega Ave, San Dimas (91773-2415)
P.O. Box 41324 (90853-1324)
**PHONE**.................................909 599-2341
Susan Renaker Nikas, *Pr*
Mary Lou Salas, *
**EMP:** 80 **EST:** 1946
**SQ FT:** 88,964
**SALES (est):** 5.32MM
**SALES (corp-wide):** 5.32MM **Privately Held**
**Web:** www.hagenrenaker.com
**SIC: 3269** 0181  Figures: pottery, china, earthenware, and stoneware; Nursery stock, growing of

**(P-7288)**
**HEATH CERAMICS LTD**
2900 18th St, San Francisco (94110-2005)
**PHONE**.................................415 361-5552
Robin Petravic, *Mgr*
**EMP:** 35
**SALES (corp-wide):** 15.26MM **Privately Held**
**Web:** www.heathceramics.com
**SIC: 3269**  Stoneware pottery products
**PA:** Heath Ceramics, Ltd.
  400 Gate 5 Rd
  415 332-3732

**(P-7289)**
**RBD ONLINE INC**
Also Called: Geoplanter
1800 Lombardi Ln, Santa Rosa (95407-6537)
**PHONE**.................................800 681-1757
Khanhvi Dang, *CEO*
Dennis Franklin Hunter, *CEO*
▲ **EMP:** 20 **EST:** 2010
**SALES (est):** 2.93MM **Privately Held**
**Web:** www.leftcoastwholesale.com
**SIC: 3269**  Flower pots, red earthenware

**(P-7290)**
**SANTA BARBARA DESIGN STUDIO (PA)**
1600 Pacific Ave, Oxnard (93033-2746)
P.O. Box 6087 (93160-6087)
**PHONE**.................................805 966-3883
Raymond Markow, *CEO*
◆ **EMP:** 53 **EST:** 1972
**SQ FT:** 2,400
**SALES (est):** 3.38MM
**SALES (corp-wide):** 3.38MM **Privately Held**
**Web:** www.sb-designstudio.com
**SIC: 3269** 5719  Art and ornamental ware, pottery; Pottery

## 3271 Concrete Block And Brick

**(P-7291)**
**AIR-VOL BLOCK INC**
1 Suburban Rd, San Luis Obispo (93401-7523)
P.O. Box 931 (93406-0931)
**PHONE**.................................805 543-1314
Robert J Miller, *Pr*
Richard Ayres, *
**EMP:** 40 **EST:** 1962
**SQ FT:** 1,400
**SALES (est):** 5.87MM **Privately Held**
**Web:** www.airvolblock.com
**SIC: 3271**  Blocks, concrete or cinder: standard

**(P-7292)**
**ANGELUS BLOCK CO INC (PA)**
11374 Tuxford St, Sun Valley (91352-2678)
**PHONE**.................................714 637-8594
Mario Antonini, *Pr*
Edward Antonini, *
▲ **EMP:** 50 **EST:** 1946
**SQ FT:** 2,000
**SALES (est):** 25.37MM
**SALES (corp-wide):** 25.37MM **Privately Held**
**Web:** www.angelusblock.com
**SIC: 3271**  Concrete block and brick

**(P-7293)**
**BASALITE BUILDING PRODUCTS LLC**
Also Called: Basalite-Tracy
11888 W Linne Rd, Tracy (95377-8102)
**PHONE**.................................209 833-3670
Bryan Langland, *Mgr*
**EMP:** 25
**SQ FT:** 20,000
**SALES (corp-wide):** 1.21B **Privately Held**
**Web:** www.basalite.com
**SIC: 3271** 1741  Blocks, concrete or cinder: standard; Masonry and other stonework
**HQ:** Basalite Building Products, Llc
  2150 Douglas Blvd Ste 260
  Roseville CA 95661
  707 678-1901

**(P-7294)**
**CASTLELITE BLOCK LLC (PA)**
8615 Robben Rd, Dixon (95620)
**PHONE**.................................707 678-3465
**EMP:** 15 **EST:** 2006
**SALES (est):** 5.87MM **Privately Held**
**Web:** www.castleliteblock.com
**SIC: 3271**  Blocks, concrete or cinder: standard

# PRODUCTS & SERVICES SECTION
## 3272 - Concrete Products, Nec (P-7314)

### (P-7295)
**L P MCNEAR BRICK CO INC**
Also Called: McNear Brick & Block
1 Mcnear Brickyard Rd, San Rafael
(94901-8310)
P.O. Box 151380 (94915-1380)
PHONE.............................415 453-7702
John E Mcnear, *CEO*
Jeffrey Mcnear, *Pr*
Daniel Mcnear, *CFO*
◆ **EMP:** 70 **EST:** 1868
**SALES (est):** 10.03MM **Privately Held**
Web: www.mcnear.com
**SIC:** 3271 3251 Brick, concrete; Brick clay: common face, glazed, vitrified, or hollow

### (P-7296)
**ORCO BLOCK & HARDSCAPE (PA)**
11100 Beach Blvd, Stanton (90680-3219)
PHONE.............................714 527-2239
Richard J Muth, *CEO*
Mary M Muth, *
**EMP:** 60 **EST:** 1946
**SQ FT:** 5,000
**SALES (est):** 23.6MM
**SALES (corp-wide):** 23.6MM **Privately Held**
Web: www.orco.com
**SIC:** 3271 Architectural concrete: block, split, fluted, screen, etc.

### (P-7297)
**QUINN DEVELOPMENT CO**
Also Called: Mission Concrete Products
5787 Obata Way, Gilroy (95020-7018)
**EMP:** 15 **EST:** 1963
**SQ FT:** 36,000
**SALES (est):** 1.1MM **Privately Held**
**SIC:** 3271 Blocks, concrete: landscape or retaining wall

### (P-7298)
**RCP BLOCK & BRICK INC (PA)**
8240 Broadway, Lemon Grove (91945-2004)
P.O. Box 579 (91946-0579)
PHONE.............................619 460-9101
Michael Finch, *CEO*
Charles T Finch, *
Eugene M Chubb, *
**EMP:** 57 **EST:** 1947
**SQ FT:** 4,000
**SALES (est):** 27.36MM
**SALES (corp-wide):** 27.36MM **Privately Held**
Web: www.rcpblock.com
**SIC:** 3271 5211 5032 Blocks, concrete or cinder: standard; Masonry materials and supplies; Concrete building products

### (P-7299)
**RCP BLOCK & BRICK INC**
8755 N Magnolia Ave, Santee (92071-4594)
PHONE.............................619 448-2240
Randy Scott, *Brnch Mgr*
**EMP:** 40
**SALES (corp-wide):** 27.36MM **Privately Held**
Web: www.rcpblock.com
**SIC:** 3271 5032 5211 Blocks, concrete or cinder: standard; Concrete and cinder block; Lumber and other building materials
**PA:** Rcp Block & Brick, Inc.
8240 Broadway
619 460-9101

### (P-7300)
**RCP BLOCK & BRICK INC**
75 N 4th Ave, Chula Vista (91910-1007)
PHONE.............................619 474-1516
Tim Ostrom, *Mgr*
**EMP:** 41
**SALES (corp-wide):** 23.81MM **Privately Held**
Web: www.rcpblock.com
**SIC:** 3271 5032 5211 Blocks, concrete or cinder: standard; Concrete and cinder block; Concrete and cinder block
**PA:** Rcp Block & Brick, Inc.
8240 Broadway
619 460-9101

### (P-7301)
**RCP BLOCK & BRICK INC**
577 N Vulcan Ave, Encinitas (92024-2120)
PHONE.............................760 753-1164
Chico Savage, *Mgr*
**EMP:** 41
**SALES (corp-wide):** 27.36MM **Privately Held**
Web: www.rcpblock.com
**SIC:** 3271 5211 Blocks, concrete or cinder: standard; Lumber and other building materials
**PA:** Rcp Block & Brick, Inc.
8240 Broadway
619 460-9101

### (P-7302)
**UV LANDSCAPING LLC**
Also Called: Landscape Contractor
477 Old Natividad Rd, Salinas (93906-1407)
P.O. Box 4022 (93912-4022)
PHONE.............................831 275-5296
**EMP:** 18 **EST:** 2016
**SALES (est):** 3.59MM **Privately Held**
Web: www.uvlandscaping.com
**SIC:** 3271 0782 4971 Blocks, concrete: landscape or retaining wall; Fertilizing services, lawn; Water distribution or supply systems for irrigation

### (P-7303)
**VALLEY ROCK LNDSCPE MATERIAL**
4018 Taylor Rd, Loomis (95650-9004)
PHONE.............................916 652-7209
Kurtis D Nixon, *Pr*
Kelly Nixon, *VP*
Don Clark, *CFO*
**EMP:** 20 **EST:** 1990
**SQ FT:** 300
**SALES (est):** 2.62MM **Privately Held**
Web: www.valleyrock.com
**SIC:** 3271 5261 Blocks, concrete: landscape or retaining wall; Retail nurseries and garden stores

### (P-7304)
**WESTERN STATES WHOLESALE INC (PA)**
Also Called: C-Cure
1420 S Bon View Ave, Ontario (91761-4405)
P.O. Box 3340 (91761-0934)
PHONE.............................909 947-0028
Randall Humphreys, *CEO*
Robert Humphreys, *
Donna Humphreys, *
▲ **EMP:** 70 **EST:** 1995
**SQ FT:** 60,000
**SALES (est):** 29.54MM **Privately Held**
Web: www.wswcorp.com
**SIC:** 3271 5072 5032 5211 Concrete block and brick; Bolts; Drywall materials; Lumber products

### (P-7305)
**WESTERN STATES WHOLESALE INC**
Also Called: Patio Industries
1600 E Francis St, Ontario (91761-5720)
P.O. Box 3340 (91761-0934)
PHONE.............................909 947-0028
Randy Humphries, *Pr*
**EMP:** 145
Web: www.wswcorp.com
**SIC:** 3271 Blocks, concrete or cinder: standard
**PA:** Western States Wholesale, Inc.
1420 S Bon View Ave

---

## 3272 Concrete Products, Nec

### (P-7306)
**ACKER STONE INDUSTRIES INC (DH)**
13296 Temescal Canyon Rd, Corona (92883-5299)
PHONE.............................951 674-0047
Giora Ackerstein, *Ch Bd*
▲ **EMP:** 50 **EST:** 1987
**SQ FT:** 14,000
**SALES (est):** 22.42MM **Privately Held**
Web: www.ackerstone.com
**SIC:** 3272 3271 Concrete products, precast, nec; Paving blocks, concrete
**HQ:** Ackerstein Zvi Ltd.
103 Medinat Hayehudim
Herzliya 46766

### (P-7307)
**AMERON INTERNATIONAL CORP**
Ameron Pole Products & Systems
1020 B St, Fillmore (93015-1024)
PHONE.............................805 524-0223
West Allison, *Mgr*
**EMP:** 100
**SALES (corp-wide):** 8.58B **Publicly Held**
**SIC:** 3272 3648 3646 3441 Concrete products, precast, nec; Lighting equipment, nec; Commercial lighting fixtures; Fabricated structural metal
**HQ:** Ameron International Corporation
7909 Parkwood Circle Dr
Houston TX 77036
713 375-3700

### (P-7308)
**AMERON INTERNATIONAL CORP**
Also Called: Ameron Protective Coatings
1020 B St, Fillmore (93015-1024)
PHONE.............................425 258-2616
William Miner, *Brnch Mgr*
**EMP:** 115
**SALES (corp-wide):** 8.58B **Publicly Held**
**SIC:** 3272 Cylinder pipe, prestressed or pretensioned concrete
**HQ:** Ameron International Corporation
7909 Parkwood Circle Dr
Houston TX 77036
713 375-3700

### (P-7309)
**ARCHITCTRAL FCDES UNLMTD INC**
1346 The Alameda, San Jose (95126-2699)
PHONE.............................408 846-5350
Mary Alice Kinzler Bracken, *CEO*
Francis X Bracken, *
**EMP:** 75 **EST:** 1986

SALES (est): 6.02MM **Privately Held**
Web: www.afuinc.com
**SIC:** 3272 Concrete products, precast, nec

### (P-7310)
**ARCHITECTURAL VENEER SYSTEMS**
Also Called: Veristone Products
2215 Via Cerro, Jurupa Valley (92509-2412)
P.O. Box 1488 (93406-1488)
PHONE.............................951 824-1079
Steffen Weeks, *Pr*
Jacqui Weeks, *VP*
▲ **EMP:** 15 **EST:** 2006
**SQ FT:** 20,000
**SALES (est):** 932.31K **Privately Held**
Web: www.veristone.com
**SIC:** 3272 Concrete products, nec

### (P-7311)
**ASSOCIATED CNSTR & ENGRG INC (PA)**
23232 Peralta Dr Ste 206, Laguna Hills (92653-1437)
PHONE.............................949 455-2682
Lawrence Gene Wombles, *CEO*
Bryan M Wombles, *Sec*
Shawn P Owens, *Dir*
**EMP:** 20 **EST:** 2011
**SALES (est):** 61.08MM
**SALES (corp-wide):** 61.08MM **Privately Held**
Web: www.a-c-e-inc.com
**SIC:** 3272 Tanks, concrete

### (P-7312)
**AVILAS GARDEN ART (PA)**
14608 Merrill Ave, Fontana (92335-4219)
PHONE.............................909 350-4546
Ralph G Avila, *Owner*
**EMP:** 60 **EST:** 1981
**SQ FT:** 7,000
**SALES (est):** 519.27K
**SALES (corp-wide):** 519.27K **Privately Held**
Web: www.avilasgardenart.com
**SIC:** 3272 5261 5211 5199 Precast terrazzo or concrete products; Lawn ornaments; Masonry materials and supplies; Statuary

### (P-7313)
**BASALITE BUILDING PRODUCTS LLC (HQ)**
Also Called: Epic Plastics
2150 Douglas Blvd Ste 260, Roseville (95661-3873)
PHONE.............................707 678-1901
Erik Absalon, *Pr*
Dallas Barrett, *CFO*
Richard Blickensderfer, *Bd of Dir*
Alfred Mueller, *Bd of Dir*
Fredrick Nelson, *Bd of Dir*
◆ **EMP:** 37 **EST:** 1979
**SALES (est):** 185.31MM
**SALES (corp-wide):** 1.21B **Privately Held**
Web: www.basalite.com
**SIC:** 3272 Concrete products, precast, nec
**PA:** Pacific Coast Building Products, Inc.
10811 International Dr
916 631-6500

### (P-7314)
**BOND MANUFACTURING CO INC (PA)**
2516 Verne Roberts Cir Ste H3, Antioch (94509-7904)
PHONE.............................866 771-2663
Daryl Merritt, *CEO*

## 3272 - Concrete Products, Nec (P-7315)

Ronald Merritt, *
Cameron Jenkins, *
◆ **EMP:** 97 **EST:** 1946
**SQ FT:** 250,000
**SALES (est):** 22.21MM
**SALES (corp-wide):** 22.21MM **Privately Held**
Web: www.bondmfg.com
**SIC: 3272** 5083 Fireplaces, concrete; Lawn and garden machinery and equipment

**(P-7315)**
### CALIFRNIA PRCAST STONE MFG INC
1796 Karen Ct, Hemet (92545-1644)
P.O. Box 40 (92546-0040)
**PHONE**..................951 657-7913
Quint Mumford, *Pr*
John Mumford, *VP*
**EMP:** 16 **EST:** 1998
**SQ FT:** 7,700
**SALES (est):** 372.05K **Privately Held**
**SIC: 3272** Concrete products, precast, nec

**(P-7316)**
### CEMEX CNSTR MTLS PCF LLC
Also Called: Readymix - Cordelia R/M
4132 Cordelia Rd, Suisun City (94585)
**PHONE**..................800 992-3639
**EMP:** 23
**SIC: 3272** Concrete products, nec
**HQ:** Cemex Construction Materials Pacific, Llc
1501 Belvedere Rd
West Palm Beach FL 33406
561 833-5555

**(P-7317)**
### CENTRAL PRECAST CONCRETE INC
Also Called: Western Concrete Products
3500 Boulder St, Pleasanton (94566-4700)
P.O. Box 727 (94566-0868)
**PHONE**..................925 417-6854
Don Hmphreys, *Pr*
Vince Bormolini, *
Charles Bormolini, *
**EMP:** 36 **EST:** 1979
**SQ FT:** 3,000
**SALES (est):** 1.02MM **Publicly Held**
**SIC: 3272** 1442 Manhole covers or frames, concrete; Construction sand and gravel
**HQ:** U.S. Concrete, Inc.
331 N Main St
Euless TX 76039
817 835-4105

**(P-7318)**
### CHRISTY VAULT COMPANY (PA)
1000 Collins Ave, Colma (94014-3299)
**PHONE**..................650 994-1378
Robert B Christensen, *Ch Bd*
Gregg Christensen, *
Albert Christensen Stckhdr, *Prin*
**EMP:** 28 **EST:** 1930
**SQ FT:** 16,500
**SALES (est):** 6.27MM
**SALES (corp-wide):** 6.27MM **Privately Held**
Web: www.christyvault.com
**SIC: 3272** Burial vaults, concrete or precast terrazzo

**(P-7319)**
### CLARK - PACIFIC CORPORATION
9367 Holly Rd, Adelanto (92301-3910)
**PHONE**..................626 962-8755
**EMP:** 36

**SALES (corp-wide):** 243.72MM **Privately Held**
Web: www.clarkpacific.com
**SIC: 3272** 5032 Concrete products, precast, nec; Brick, stone, and related material
**PA:** Clark - Pacific Corporation
710 Riverpoint Ct # 100
916 371-0305

**(P-7320)**
### CLARK - PACIFIC CORPORATION
Also Called: Tecon Pacific
4684 Ontario Mills Pkwy Ste 200, Ontario (91764-5151)
**PHONE**..................909 823-1433
Donald Clark, *Owner*
**EMP:** 49
**SALES (corp-wide):** 243.72MM **Privately Held**
Web: www.clarkpacific.com
**SIC: 3272** 5211 Concrete products, precast, nec; Masonry materials and supplies
**PA:** Clark - Pacific Corporation
710 Riverpoint Ct # 100
916 371-0305

**(P-7321)**
### CON-FAB CALIFORNIA CORPORATION (PA)
Also Called: Confab
1910 Lathrop Rd, Lathrop (95330-9708)
**PHONE**..................209 249-4700
Philip French, *Pr*
Miaja French, *Stockholder**
**EMP:** 85 **EST:** 1977
**SQ FT:** 2,400
**SALES (est):** 14.86MM
**SALES (corp-wide):** 14.86MM **Privately Held**
Web: www.confabca.com
**SIC: 3272** Concrete products, precast, nec

**(P-7322)**
### COOK CONCRETE PRODUCTS INC
5461 Eastside Rd, Redding (96001-4533)
P.O. Box 720280 (96099-7280)
**PHONE**..................530 243-2562
L Edward Shaw, *Pr*
**EMP:** 35 **EST:** 1956
**SQ FT:** 1,000
**SALES (est):** 4MM **Privately Held**
Web: www.cookconcreteproducts.com
**SIC: 3272** Concrete products, precast, nec

**(P-7323)**
### CORESLAB STRUCTURES LA INC
150 W Placentia Ave, Perris (92571-3200)
**PHONE**..................951 943-9119
Mario Franciosa, *CEO*
Lou Franciosa, *
Robert H Konoske, *General Vice President**
Jorgen Clausen, *
**EMP:** 200 **EST:** 1955
**SQ FT:** 25,000
**SALES (est):** 30.66MM
**SALES (corp-wide):** 27.34MM **Privately Held**
Web: www.coreslab.com
**SIC: 3272** Concrete products, precast, nec
**HQ:** Coreslab Holdings U S Inc
1-332 Jones Rd
Stoney Creek ON L8E 5
905 643-0220

**(P-7324)**
### CREATIVE STONE MFG INC (PA)
Also Called: Coronado Stone Products
342 W Perry St, Perris (92571-9723)
**PHONE**..................800 847-8663
Melton Bacon, *Pr*
Scott Ebersole, *VP*
Bob Ratkovic, *Mgr*
◆ **EMP:** 180 **EST:** 1962
**SALES (est):** 29.14MM
**SALES (corp-wide):** 29.14MM **Privately Held**
Web: www.coronado.com
**SIC: 3272** Siding, precast stone

**(P-7325)**
### CULTURED STONE CORPORATION (PA)
Hwy 29 & Tower Rd, Napa (94559)
**PHONE**..................707 255-1727
Stephen Nowak, *CEO*
▼ **EMP:** 739 **EST:** 1967
**SQ FT:** 17,000
**SALES (est):** 1.37MM
**SALES (corp-wide):** 1.37MM **Privately Held**
**SIC: 3272** 3281 Cast stone, concrete; Cut stone and stone products

**(P-7326)**
### DCC GENERAL ENGRG CONTRS INC
2180 Meyers Ave, Escondido (92029-1001)
**PHONE**..................760 480-7400
Frank D'agostini, *Pr*
Scott Woods, *
**EMP:** 75 **EST:** 1982
**SQ FT:** 2,100
**SALES (est):** 9.89MM **Privately Held**
Web: www.dccengineering.com
**SIC: 3272** 1771 3531 Concrete products, nec ; Curb and sidewalk contractors; Asphalt plant, including gravel-mix type

**(P-7327)**
### EISEL ENTERPRISES INC
714 Fee Ana St, Placentia (92870-6705)
**PHONE**..................714 993-1706
Lyle Eisel *Pr*
Kim Webster, *
Janis Eisel, *
**EMP:** 25 **EST:** 1970
**SQ FT:** 4,000
**SALES (est):** 2.42MM **Privately Held**
Web: www.eiselenterprises.com
**SIC: 3272** Meter boxes, concrete

**(P-7328)**
### ELDORADO STONE LLC (DH)
3817 Ocean Ranch Blvd, Oceanside (92056-8607)
P.O. Box 2289 (92079-2289)
**PHONE**..................800 925-1491
Donald P Newman, *Managing Member*
◆ **EMP:** 50 **EST:** 2000
**SALES (est):** 63.06MM **Privately Held**
Web: www.eldoradostone.com
**SIC: 3272** Concrete products, precast, nec
**HQ:** Headwaters Incorporated
10701 S Rver Front Pkwy
South Jordan UT 84095

**(P-7329)**
### ELK CORPORATION OF TEXAS
Also Called: Elk
6200 Zerker Rd, Shafter (93263-9612)
**PHONE**..................661 391-3900
Gus Freshwater, *Brnch Mgr*
**EMP:** 147

**SALES (corp-wide):** 6.35B **Privately Held**
**SIC: 3272** 2952 Precast terrazzo or concrete products; Asphalt felts and coatings
**HQ:** Elk Corporation Of Texas
14911 Quorum Dr Ste 600
Dallas TX 75254

**(P-7330)**
### FARLEY PAVING STONE CO INC
Also Called: Farley Interlocking Pav Stones
39301 Badger St, Palm Desert (92211-1162)
P.O. Box 10946 (92255-0946)
**PHONE**..................760 773-3960
Shon Farley, *VP*
Charissa Farley, *
Hector Gonzalez, *
**EMP:** 70 **EST:** 1985
**SALES (est):** 4.07MM **Privately Held**
Web: www.farleypavers.com
**SIC: 3272** 3531 3281 Paving materials, prefabricated concrete; Pavers; Curbing, paving, and walkway stone

**(P-7331)**
### FIORE STONE INC
1814 Commercenter W Ste E, San Bernardino (92408-3332)
**PHONE**..................909 424-0221
Bruce Raabe, *Pr*
**EMP:** 45 **EST:** 2009
**SALES (est):** 4.95MM **Privately Held**
Web: www.fiorestone.com
**SIC: 3272** Concrete products, precast, nec

**(P-7332)**
### FLORENCE & NEW ITLN ART CO INC
27735 Industrial Blvd, Hayward (94545-4045)
**PHONE**..................510 785-9674
Mariano Fontana, *CEO*
Gerard Fontana, *
Marc Fontana, *
▲ **EMP:** 40 **EST:** 1914
**SQ FT:** 30,000
**SALES (est):** 4.36MM **Privately Held**
Web: www.florenceartcompany.com
**SIC: 3272** Concrete products, nec

**(P-7333)**
### FORMS AND SURFACES COMPANY LLC
Also Called: Lightform
6395 Cindy Ln, Carpinteria (93013-2909)
**PHONE**..................805 684-8626
**EMP:** 150 **EST:** 1975
**SQ FT:** 63,000
**SALES (est):** 9.86MM **Privately Held**
Web: www.forms-surfaces.com
**SIC: 3272** 3531 3446 3429 Building materials, except block or brick: concrete; Construction machinery; Architectural metalwork; Hardware, nec

**(P-7334)**
### FORTERRA INC
8050 N Palm Ave Ste 300, Fresno (93711-5510)
**PHONE**..................559 221-2070
Mitchell Gearhart, *Pr*
**EMP:** 17 **EST:** 2001
**SALES (est):** 249.7K **Privately Held**
Web: www.mortgagesolution.net
**SIC: 3272** Concrete products, nec

**(P-7335)**
### FORTERRA PIPE & PRECAST LLC

# PRODUCTS & SERVICES SECTION
## 3272 - Concrete Products, Nec (P-7357)

26380 Palomar Rd, Sun City  (92585-9811)
PHONE......................951 523-7039
EMP: 42
Web: www.rinkerpipe.com
SIC: 3272  Concrete products, nec
HQ: Forterra Pipe & Precast, Llc
    511 E John Crptr Fwy Ste
    Irving TX 75062
    469 458-7973

### (P-7336)
### FORTERRA PIPE & PRECAST LLC
Also Called: South Coast Materials Co
9229 Harris Plant Rd, San Diego  (92145-0001)
P.O. Box 639069  (92163-9069)
PHONE......................858 715-5600
Carol Hartwig, Brnch Mgr
EMP: 40
Web: www.forterrabp.com
SIC: 3272  Concrete products, nec
HQ: Forterra Pipe & Precast, Llc
    511 E John Crptr Fwy Ste
    Irving TX 75062
    469 458-7973

### (P-7337)
### FORTERRA PIPE & PRECAST LLC
7020 Tokay Ave, Sacramento  (95828-2418)
PHONE......................916 379-9695
Drew Black, Mgr
EMP: 80
Web: www.forterrabp.com
SIC: 3272  Pipe, concrete or lined with concrete
HQ: Forterra Pipe & Precast, Llc
    511 E John Crptr Fwy Ste
    Irving TX 75062
    469 458-7973

### (P-7338)
### GIANNINI GARDEN ORNAMENTS INC
225 Shaw Rd, South San Francisco  (94080-6605)
PHONE......................650 873-4493
Piera Giannini, Pr
▲ EMP: 30 EST: 1993
SALES (est): 4.68MM Privately Held
Web: www.gianninigarden.com
SIC: 3272  Concrete products, nec

### (P-7339)
### GOLDEN EMPIRE CON PDTS INC
Also Called: Structurecast
8261 Mccutchen Rd, Bakersfield  (93311-9407)
PHONE......................661 833-4490
Brent Dezember, Pr
Ann Dzember, *
EMP: 65 EST: 1997
SQ FT: 10,000
SALES (est): 10.04MM Privately Held
Web: www.structurecast.com
SIC: 3272  1791  Precast terrazzo or concrete products; Precast concrete structural framing or panels, placing of

### (P-7340)
### GUARDIAN PHRM SOUTHERN CAL LLC
Also Called: Ron's Pharmacy Services
10121 Carroll Canyon Rd, San Diego  (92131-1109)
PHONE......................858 652-6900
Ron Belville, Pr
EMP: 18 EST: 2015
SALES (est): 1.14MM Privately Held
Web: www.ronspharmacyservices.com
SIC: 3272  Building materials, except block or brick: concrete

### (P-7341)
### HANSON ROOF TILE INC
10651 Elm Ave, Fontana  (92337-7324)
P.O. Box 660225  (75266-0225)
PHONE......................888 509-4787
▲ EMP: 422
SIC: 3272  Roofing tile and slabs, concrete

### (P-7342)
### HEADWATERS INCORPORATED
1345 Philadelphia St, Pomona  (91766-5564)
PHONE......................909 627-9066
Jim Johnson, Mgr
EMP: 26
Web: www.ecomaterial.com
SIC: 3272  Concrete products, nec
HQ: Headwaters Incorporated
    10701 S Rver Front Pkwy
    South Jordan UT 84095

### (P-7343)
### HILFIKER PIPE CO
Also Called: Hilfiker Retaining Walls
1902 Hilfiker Ln, Eureka  (95503-5711)
PHONE......................707 443-5091
Harold Hilfiker, Pr
William K Hilfiker, *
Brian Stringer, *
Suzanne Blackburn, *
Brenda Peterson, *
EMP: 30 EST: 1900
SQ FT: 14,400
SALES (est): 4.05MM Privately Held
Web: www.hilfiker.com
SIC: 3272  3315 5051 5074  Concrete products, precast, nec; Welded steel wire fabric; Pipe and tubing, steel; Pipes and fittings, plastic

### (P-7344)
### HINTEX
1230 S Glendale Ave, Glendale  (91205-3205)
PHONE......................320 400-0009
EMP: 18 EST: 2018
SALES (est): 186.73K Privately Held
Web: www.hintex.com
SIC: 3272  3431  Liquid catch basins, tanks, and covers: concrete; Bathtubs: enameled iron, cast iron, or pressed metal

### (P-7345)
### INDEPNDENT FLR TSTG INSPTN INC
1390 Willow Pass Rd Ste 1010, Concord  (94520-5200)
PHONE......................925 676-7682
Lee Eliseian, Pr
EMP: 16 EST: 1997
SALES (est): 2.25MM Privately Held
Web: www.ifti.com
SIC: 3272  8611  Floor slabs and tiles, precast concrete; Business associations

### (P-7346)
### J & R CONCRETE PRODUCTS INC
440 W Markham St, Perris  (92571-8138)
PHONE......................951 943-5855
Raul Ramirez, Pr
EMP: 42 EST: 1981
SQ FT: 40,000
SALES (est): 4.7MM Privately Held
Web: www.jrconcreteproducts.com
SIC: 3272  Meter boxes, concrete

### (P-7347)
### JENSEN ENTERPRISES INC
14221 San Bernardino Ave, Fontana  (92335-5232)
PHONE......................909 357-7264
TOLL FREE: 800
Carol Kohanle, Mgr
EMP: 300
SALES (corp-wide): 237.25MM Privately Held
Web: www.jensenprecast.com
SIC: 3272  7699 5211 5039  Concrete products, precast, nec; Waste cleaning services; Masonry materials and supplies; Septic tanks
PA: Jensen Enterprises, Inc.
    9895 Double R Blvd
    775 352-2700

### (P-7348)
### JENSEN ENTERPRISES INC
7210 State Highway 32, Orland  (95963-9790)
PHONE......................530 865-4277
Don Jensen, Brnch Mgr
EMP: 28
SALES (corp-wide): 237.25MM Privately Held
Web: www.jensenprecast.com
SIC: 3272  5039  Concrete products, precast, nec; Septic tanks
PA: Jensen Enterprises, Inc.
    9895 Double R Blvd
    775 352-2700

### (P-7349)
### JHC MATERIALS INC
601 7th St, Lincoln  (95648-1828)
PHONE......................916 645-3870
John Coburn, Pr
Michael Coburn, *
EMP: 43 EST: 2003
SQ FT: 4,000
SALES (est): 4.76MM Privately Held
Web: www.gcproductsinc.com
SIC: 3272  Concrete products, nec

### (P-7350)
### KIE-CON INC
3551 Wilbur Ave, Antioch  (94509-8530)
PHONE......................925 754-9494
Eric Scott, Pr
EMP: 90 EST: 2010
SALES (est): 13.31MM
SALES (corp-wide): 10.41B Privately Held
Web: www.kiecon.com
SIC: 3272  Concrete products, nec
HQ: Kiewit Corporation
    1550 Mike Fahey St
    Omaha NE 68102
    402 342-2052

### (P-7351)
### KRI STAR ENTERPRISES INC
360 Sutton Pl, Santa Rosa  (95407-8121)
PHONE......................800 579-8819
▲ EMP: 36 EST: 1993
SALES (est): 5.56MM Privately Held
SIC: 3272  Liquid catch basins, tanks, and covers: concrete

### (P-7352)
### KRISTICH-MONTEREY PIPE COMPANY
225 Salinas Rd Ste B, Royal Oaks  (95076-5253)
P.O. Box 606  (95077-0606)
PHONE......................831 724-4186
Chris Kristich, Pr
EMP: 15 EST: 1966
SQ FT: 2,000
SALES (est): 4.03MM Privately Held
SIC: 3272  Pipe, concrete or lined with concrete

### (P-7353)
### KTI INCORPORATED
Also Called: Rialto Concrete Products
3011 N Laurel Ave, Rialto  (92377-3725)
PHONE......................909 434-1888
Kenneth D Thompson, CEO
Daniel J Deming, *
Jerry Cowden, *
EMP: 100 EST: 1987
SQ FT: 400
SALES (est): 11.03MM Privately Held
Web: www.thompsonpipegroup.com
SIC: 3272  Concrete products, precast, nec

### (P-7354)
### MCFIEBOW INC (PA)
17025 S Main St, Gardena  (90248)
PHONE......................310 327-7474
Gordon S Mcwilliams, CEO
Paul Mitchell, *
EMP: 50 EST: 1963
SQ FT: 15,000
SALES (est): 1.44MM
SALES (corp-wide): 1.44MM Privately Held
Web: www.stepstoneinc.com
SIC: 3272  Concrete products, precast, nec

### (P-7355)
### MCFIEBOW INC
13238 S Figueroa St, Los Angeles  (90061)
PHONE......................310 327-7474
Kelsy Carrington, Brnch Mgr
EMP: 25
SALES (corp-wide): 1.44MM Privately Held
Web: www.stepstoneinc.com
SIC: 3272  Concrete products, precast, nec
PA: Mcfiebow Inc.
    17025 S Main St
    310 327-7474

### (P-7356)
### MID-STATE CONCRETE PDTS INC
1625 E Donovan Rd Ste C, Santa Maria  (93454-2519)
P.O. Box 219  (93456-0219)
PHONE......................805 928-2855
TOLL FREE: 800
Ralph Vander Veen, Pr
Pat Vander Veen, VP
EMP: 23 EST: 1975
SQ FT: 2,000
SALES (est): 4.91MM Privately Held
Web: www.midstateconcrete.com
SIC: 3272  Concrete products, precast, nec

### (P-7357)
### N V CAST STONE LLC
Also Called: NAPA Valley Cast Stone
2003 Seville Dr, Napa  (94559-4318)
PHONE......................707 261-6615
Mark Akey, Managing Member
Bill Tough, *
Tom Brown, *
Jeff Latreille, *
EMP: 22 EST: 1991
SALES (est): 941.41K Privately Held
Web: www.californiastonecraft.com

## 3272 - Concrete Products, Nec (P-7358)

SIC: 3272 3281 Concrete products, precast, nec; Cut stone and stone products

**(P-7358)**
**NEWBASIS LLC**
2626 Kansas Ave, Riverside (92507-2600)
PHONE.................................951 787-0600
EMP: 150 EST: 2020
SALES (est): 31.04MM
SALES (corp-wide): 31.04MM **Privately Held**
Web: www.newbasis.com
SIC: 3272 Concrete products, nec
PA: Capital Precast Holdings, Llc
  250 W Nottingham Dr # 120

**(P-7359)**
**NEWBASIS WEST LLC**
2626 Kansas Ave, Riverside (92507-2600)
PHONE.................................951 787-0600
Jennifer Ewing, *
Kim Ruiz, *
◆ EMP: 115 EST: 1989
SALES (est): 24.81MM
SALES (corp-wide): 24.81MM **Privately Held**
Web: www.newbasis.com
SIC: 3272 Manhole covers or frames, concrete
PA: Echo Rock Ventures, Inc.
  370 Hammond Dr
  530 823-9600

**(P-7360)**
**NEWMAN AND SONS INC (PA)**
2655 1st St Ste 210, Simi Valley (93065-1578)
PHONE.................................805 522-1646
Dennis L Newman, Pr
EMP: 40 EST: 1938
SQ FT: 12,500
SALES (est): 809.56K
SALES (corp-wide): 809.56K **Privately Held**
Web: www.newmanandsons.com
SIC: 3272 Paving materials, prefabricated concrete

**(P-7361)**
**NEXT CHAPTER INC**
Also Called: Piranha Pipe & Precast
16000 Avenue 25, Chowchilla (93610-9353)
P.O. Box 820 (93610)
PHONE.................................559 665-7473
Anita Simpson, Pr
▲ EMP: 28 EST: 2000
SALES (est): 5.12MM **Privately Held**
Web: www.piranhapipe.com
SIC: 3272 Precast terrazzo or concrete products

**(P-7362)**
**OLDCAST PRECAST (DH)**
Also Called: Riverside Foundary
2434 Rubidoux Blvd, Riverside (92509-2144)
PHONE.................................951 788-9720
Thomas D Lynch, Ch Bd
John R Waren, *
EMP: 35 EST: 1966
SQ FT: 7,000
SALES (est): 2.05MM
SALES (corp-wide): 34.95B **Privately Held**
Web: www.inland-concrete.com
SIC: 3272 3271 Concrete products, precast, nec; Concrete block and brick
HQ: Oldcastle Infrastructure, Inc.
  7000 Central Pkwy Ste 800
  Atlanta GA 30328
  770 270-5000

**(P-7363)**
**OLDCASTLE INFRASTRUCTURE INC**
Also Called: Old Castle Inclosure Solution
801 S Pine St, Madera (93637-5219)
PHONE.................................559 675-1813
Greg Barner, Mgr
EMP: 20
SALES (corp-wide): 34.95B **Privately Held**
Web: locator.oldcastleinfrastructure.com
SIC: 3272 Concrete products, nec
HQ: Oldcastle Infrastructure, Inc.
  7000 Central Pkwy Ste 800
  Atlanta GA 30328
  770 270-5000

**(P-7364)**
**OLDCASTLE INFRASTRUCTURE INC**
Also Called: Utility Vault
10650 Hemlock Ave, Fontana (92337-7296)
P.O. Box 310039 (92331-0039)
PHONE.................................909 428-3700
Glenn Scheaffer, Mgr
EMP: 49
SALES (corp-wide): 34.95B **Privately Held**
Web: locator.oldcastleinfrastructure.com
SIC: 3272 Concrete products, precast, nec
HQ: Oldcastle Infrastructure, Inc.
  7000 Central Pkwy Ste 800
  Atlanta GA 30328
  770 270-5000

**(P-7365)**
**OLDCASTLE INFRASTRUCTURE INC**
Also Called: Utility Vault
3786 Valley Ave, Pleasanton (94566-4766)
P.O. Box 727 (94566-0868)
PHONE.................................925 846-8183
Miles Bennett, Genl Mgr
EMP: 35
SQ FT: 36,000
SALES (corp-wide): 34.95B **Privately Held**
Web: locator.oldcastleinfrastructure.com
SIC: 3272 5211 Concrete products, precast, nec; Masonry materials and supplies
HQ: Oldcastle Infrastructure, Inc.
  7000 Central Pkwy Ste 800
  Atlanta GA 30328
  770 270-5000

**(P-7366)**
**OLDCASTLE INFRASTRUCTURE INC**
Also Called: Utility Vault
2512 Harmony Grove Rd, Escondido (92029-2800)
PHONE.................................951 683-8200
EMP: 50
SALES (corp-wide): 29.71B **Privately Held**
SIC: 3272 3446 Concrete products, precast, nec; Open flooring and grating for construction
HQ: Oldcastle Infrastructure, Inc.
  7000 Cntl Prkaway Ste 800
  Atlanta GA 30328
  470 602-2000

**(P-7367)**
**OLDCASTLE INFRASTRUCTURE INC**
2960 S Highway 99, Stockton (95215-8047)
P.O. Box 30610 (95213-0610)
PHONE.................................209 235-1173
Cy Thomson, Mgr
EMP: 21
SALES (corp-wide): 34.95B **Privately Held**
Web: www.oldcastleinfrastructure.com
SIC: 3272 Pipe, concrete or lined with concrete
HQ: Oldcastle Infrastructure, Inc.
  7000 Central Pkwy Ste 800
  Atlanta GA 30328
  770 270-5000

**(P-7368)**
**OLDCASTLE INFRASTRUCTURE INC**
19940 Hansen Ave, Nuevo (92567-9649)
PHONE.................................951 928-8713
EMP: 30
SALES (corp-wide): 34.95B **Privately Held**
Web: www.oldcastleinfrastructure.com
SIC: 3272 Concrete products, nec
HQ: Oldcastle Infrastructure, Inc.
  7000 Central Pkwy Ste 800
  Atlanta GA 30328
  770 270-5000

**(P-7369)**
**PACIFIC CORRUGATED PIPE CO LLC**
5999 Power Inn Rd, Sacramento (95824-2318)
PHONE.................................916 383-4891
TOLL FREE: 800
Rob Roles, Brnch Mgr
EMP: 31
SALES (corp-wide): 13.96MM **Privately Held**
Web: www.pcpipe.com
SIC: 3272 Culvert pipe, concrete
HQ: Pacific Corrugated Pipe Company, Llc
  19800 Mcrthur Blvd Ste 51
  Irvine CA 92612
  949 650-4555

**(P-7370)**
**PACIFIC STONE DESIGN INC**
1201 E Wakeham Ave, Santa Ana (92705-4145)
PHONE.................................714 836-5757
Scott Sterling, Pr
Kathy Sterling, *
EMP: 45 EST: 1996
SQ FT: 40,000
SALES (est): 4.33MM **Privately Held**
Web: www.pacificstone.net
SIC: 3272 Concrete products, precast, nec

**(P-7371)**
**PARAGON BUILDING PRODUCTS INC (PA)**
2191 5th St Ste 111, Norco (92860-1966)
P.O. Box 99 (92860-0099)
PHONE.................................951 549-1155
Jeffrey M Goodman, Pr
Jack Goodman, *
Richard Goodman, *
▲ EMP: 25 EST: 1984
SQ FT: 16,500
SALES (est): 24.85MM
SALES (corp-wide): 24.85MM **Privately Held**
Web: www.paragonbp.us
SIC: 3272 3271 5032 Dry mixture concrete; Concrete block and brick; Brick, stone, and related material

**(P-7372)**
**PRE-CON PRODUCTS**
240 W Los Angeles Ave, Simi Valley (93065-1695)
P.O. Box 940669 (93094-0669)
PHONE.................................805 527-0841
EMP: 70 EST: 1964
SALES (est): 5.66MM **Privately Held**
Web: www.preconproducts.com
SIC: 3272 Pipe, concrete or lined with concrete

**(P-7373)**
**PRECAST CON TECH UNLIMITED LLC**
Also Called: Ctu Precast
1260 Furneaux Rd, Olivehurst (95961-7415)
PHONE.................................530 749-6501
EMP: 80 EST: 2008
SQ FT: 160,000
SALES (est): 12.57MM **Privately Held**
Web: www.ctuprecast.com
SIC: 3272 Concrete products, precast, nec

**(P-7374)**
**PRECAST INNOVATIONS INC**
1670 N Main St, Orange (92867-3405)
PHONE.................................714 921-4060
Chester Valdovinos, Pr
EMP: 28 EST: 2011
SQ FT: 20,000
SALES (est): 4.01MM **Privately Held**
Web: www.precastinnovations.com
SIC: 3272 1791 Concrete products, precast, nec; Precast concrete structural framing or panels, placing of

**(P-7375)**
**PRIME FORMING & CNSTR SUPS INC**
Also Called: Fitzgerald Formliners
1500a E Chestnut Ave, Santa Ana (92701-6321)
PHONE.................................714 547-6710
Edward Fitzgerald, Pr
EMP: 46 EST: 1988
SQ FT: 30,000
SALES (est): 8.76MM **Privately Held**
Web: www.formliners.com
SIC: 3272 Concrete products, nec

**(P-7376)**
**PRO-CAST PRODUCTS INC (PA)**
27417 3rd St, Highland (92346-4258)
P.O. Box 602 (92346-0602)
PHONE.................................909 793-7602
TOLL FREE: 800
EMP: 49 EST: 1987
SALES (est): 7.24MM
SALES (corp-wide): 7.24MM **Privately Held**
Web: www.procastproducts.com
SIC: 3272 Concrete products, nec

**(P-7377)**
**QUICK CRETE PRODUCTS CORP**
731 Parkridge Ave, Norco (92860-3149)
P.O. Box 639 (92860-0639)
PHONE.................................951 737-6240
EMP: 180 EST: 1976
SALES (est): 24.38MM **Privately Held**
Web: www.quickcrete.com
SIC: 3272 Concrete products, precast, nec

**(P-7378)**
**QUIKRETE CALIFORNIA LLC (DH)**
Also Called: Quickrete
3940 Temescal Canyon Rd, Corona (92883-5618)
PHONE.................................951 277-3155
John O Winshester, Managing Member
EMP: 43 EST: 2004
SALES (est): 27.68MM **Privately Held**

## PRODUCTS & SERVICES SECTION
### 3273 - Ready-mixed Concrete (P-7399)

SIC: 3272 Concrete products, nec
HQ: The Quikrete Companies Llc
5 Concourse Pkwy Ste 1900
Atlanta GA 30328
404 634-9100

**(P-7379)**
**QUIKRETE CALIFORNIA LLC**
6950 Stevenson Blvd, Fremont (94538-2400)
PHONE..................510 490-4670
EMP: 44
SIC: 3272 Concrete products, nec
HQ: Quikrete California, Llc
3940 Temescal Canyon Rd
Corona CA 92883
951 277-3155

**(P-7380)**
**QUIKRETE CALIFORNIA LLC**
7705 Wilbur Way, Sacramento (95828-4929)
PHONE..................916 689-8840
David Vasquez, *Brnch Mgr*
EMP: 44
SIC: 3272 Concrete products, nec
HQ: Quikrete California, Llc
3940 Temescal Canyon Rd
Corona CA 92883
951 277-3155

**(P-7381)**
**QUIKRETE COMPANIES LLC**
Also Called: Quikrete Northern California
14200 Road 284, Porterville (93257-9374)
PHONE..................559 781-1949
Ron Santiago, *Genl Mgr*
EMP: 29
Web: www.quikrete.com
SIC: 3272 Concrete products, nec
HQ: The Quikrete Companies Llc
5 Concourse Pkwy Ste 1900
Atlanta GA 30328
404 634-9100

**(P-7382)**
**QUIKRETE COMPANIES LLC**
Also Called: Quikrete of Atlanta
6950 Stevenson Blvd, Fremont (94538-2400)
PHONE..................510 490-4670
EMP: 42
Web: www.quikrete.com
SIC: 3272 5032 Concrete products, precast, nec; Cement
HQ: The Quikrete Companies Llc
5 Concourse Pkwy Ste 1900
Atlanta GA 30328
404 634-9100

**(P-7383)**
**QUIKRETE COMPANIES LLC**
Also Called: True Cast Concrete Products
11145 Tuxford St, Sun Valley (91352-2632)
PHONE..................323 875-1367
Greg Gibhel, *Principal B*
EMP: 34
Web: www.quikrete.com
SIC: 3272 3271 5211 Steps, prefabricated concrete; Concrete block and brick; Masonry materials and supplies
HQ: The Quikrete Companies Llc
5 Concourse Pkwy Ste 1900
Atlanta GA 30328
404 634-9100

**(P-7384)**
**QUIKRETE COMPANIES LLC**
7705 Wilbur Way, Sacramento (95828-4929)

PHONE..................510 490-4670
Dennis Mcgovern, *Brnch Mgr*
EMP: 41
Web: www.quikrete.com
SIC: 3272 Dry mixture concrete
HQ: The Quikrete Companies Llc
5 Concourse Pkwy Ste 1900
Atlanta GA 30328
404 634-9100

**(P-7385)**
**RMR PRODUCTS INC (PA)**
11011 Glenoaks Blvd Ste 1, Pacoima (91331-1634)
PHONE..................818 890-0896
David Mckendrick, *CEO*
Jim Mckendrick, *Pr*
EMP: 25 EST: 1984
SQ FT: 3,200
SALES (est): 726.24K
SALES (corp-wide): 726.24K Privately Held
Web: www.chimneyproductsinc.com
SIC: 3272 Chimney caps, concrete

**(P-7386)**
**ROYAL WESTLAKE ROOFING LLC**
Also Called: Monier Lifetile
3511 N Riverside Ave, Rialto (92377-3803)
PHONE..................909 822-4407
Kevin O Neil, *Mgr*
EMP: 29
Web: www.westlakeroyalroofing.com
SIC: 3272 3251 5032 2952 Roofing tile and slabs, concrete; Brick clay: common face, glazed, vitrified, or hollow; Cinders; Asphalt felts and coatings
HQ: Royal Westlake Roofing Llc
2801 Post Oak Blvd # 600
Houston TX 77056
800 658-8004

**(P-7387)**
**ROYAL WESTLAKE ROOFING LLC**
9508 S Harlan Rd, French Camp (95231-9625)
PHONE..................209 982-1473
EMP: 17
Web: www.westlakeroyalroofing.com
SIC: 3272 Concrete products, nec
HQ: Royal Westlake Roofing Llc
2801 Post Oak Blvd # 600
Houston TX 77056
800 658-8004

**(P-7388)**
**SAN BENITO SUPPLY (PA)**
1060 Nash Rd, Hollister (95023-5303)
PHONE..................831 637-5526
Mark Schipper, *Pr*
Ted Schipper, *
EMP: 129 EST: 1978
SQ FT: 1,870
SALES (est): 19.59MM
SALES (corp-wide): 19.59MM Privately Held
Web: www.sbs-cas.com
SIC: 3272 5032 Concrete products, nec; Brick, stone, and related material

**(P-7389)**
**SAN DIEGO PRECAST CONCRETE INC (DH)**
Also Called: US Concrete Precast
2735 Cactus Rd, San Diego (92154-8024)
PHONE..................619 240-8000
Douglas Mclaughlin, *Pr*

EMP: 28 EST: 1999
SQ FT: 1,600
SALES (est): 3.62MM Publicly Held
Web: www.sandiego.gov
SIC: 3272 3281 Meter boxes, concrete; Urns, cut stone
HQ: U.S. Concrete, Inc.
331 N Main St
Euless TX 76039
817 835-4105

**(P-7390)**
**SANDMAN INC (PA)**
Also Called: Star Concrete
1404 S 7th St, San Jose (95112-5927)
PHONE..................408 947-0669
Gerald Ray Blatt, *CEO*
Nicole Candelaria, *
EMP: 89 EST: 1969
SQ FT: 14,000
SALES (est): 19.54MM
SALES (corp-wide): 19.54MM Privately Held
Web: www.starqualityconcrete.com
SIC: 3272 3273 Dry mixture concrete; Ready-mixed concrete

**(P-7391)**
**SISSELL BROS**
4322 E 3rd St, Los Angeles (90022-1501)
PHONE..................323 261-0106
John F Foote, *Pr*
Dorothy Sissell, *VP*
Joan M Foote, *Sec*
EMP: 23 EST: 1930
SQ FT: 7,000
SALES (est): 979.02K Privately Held
SIC: 3272 Burial vaults, concrete or precast terrazzo

**(P-7392)**
**SOUTHWEST CONCRETE PRODUCTS**
519 S Benson Ave, Ontario (91762-4002)
PHONE..................909 983-9789
Bob Dzajkich, *Pr*
Eileen Dzajkich, *
Natalie Dzajkich, *
▲ EMP: 27 EST: 1966
SQ FT: 25,000
SALES (est): 4.08MM Privately Held
SIC: 3272 5032 Manhole covers or frames, concrete; Brick, stone, and related material

**(P-7393)**
**SPEC FORMLINERS INC**
1038 E 4th St, Santa Ana (92701-4751)
P.O. Box 10277 (92711-0277)
PHONE..................714 429-9500
Stephen A Deering, *CEO*
Anthony Zaha, *
EMP: 26 EST: 1996
SQ FT: 23,000
SALES (est): 1.04MM Privately Held
Web: www.specformliners.com
SIC: 3272 Concrete products, nec

**(P-7394)**
**VAULT PREP INC**
2500 Broadway Ste F125, Santa Monica (90404-3080)
PHONE..................310 971-9091
John Duda, *CEO*
EMP: 20 EST: 2012
SALES (est): 2.4MM Privately Held
Web: www.vault-prep.com
SIC: 3272 8748 Burial vaults, concrete or precast terrazzo; Testing service, educational or personnel

**(P-7395)**
**W R MEADOWS INC**
Also Called: W. R. Meadows Southern Cal
2300 Valley Blvd, Pomona (91768-1168)
P.O. Box 667 (91788-0667)
PHONE..................909 469-2606
Michael Knapp, *Brnch Mgr*
EMP: 27
SALES (corp-wide): 26.89K Privately Held
Web: www.wrmeadows.com
SIC: 3272 3444 2899 2891 Concrete products, nec; Concrete forms, sheet metal; Chemical preparations, nec; Adhesives and sealants
PA: W. R. Meadows, Inc.
300 Industrial Dr
800 342-5976

**(P-7396)**
**WALTERS & WOLF GLASS COMPANY**
41450 Cowbell Rd, Fremont (94538)
PHONE..................510 226-9800
Jody Vegas, *Brnch Mgr*
EMP: 55
SALES (corp-wide): 86.87MM Privately Held
Web: www.waltersandwolf.com
SIC: 3272 Precast terrazzo or concrete products
PA: Walters & Wolf Glass Company
41450 Boscell Rd
510 490-1115

**(P-7397)**
**WALTERS & WOLF PRECAST**
41450 Boscell Rd, Fremont (94538-3103)
PHONE..................510 226-9800
Randy A Wolf, *Pr*
Doug Frost, *
Ed Knowles, *
Juliusz Knuzynkski, *
Jeff B Belzer, *
▲ EMP: 160 EST: 1996
SALES (est): 19.63MM Privately Held
Web: www.waltersandwolf.com
SIC: 3272 Concrete products, precast, nec

**(P-7398)**
**WILLIS CONSTRUCTION CO INC**
2261 San Juan Hwy, San Juan Bautista (95045-9565)
PHONE..................831 623-2900
Lawrence M Willis, *CEO*
Mark Hildebrand, *
Tom Yezek, *
Roger Ely, *
◆ EMP: 120 EST: 1976
SQ FT: 4,000
SALES (est): 24.07MM Privately Held
Web: www.willisconstruction.com
SIC: 3272 1791 Concrete products, precast, nec; Precast concrete structural framing or panels, placing of

### 3273 Ready-mixed Concrete

**(P-7399)**
**A & A READY MIXED CONCRETE INC (PA)**
Also Called: A&A Concrete Supply
4621 Teller Ave Ste 130, Newport Beach (92660-2165)
PHONE..................949 253-2800
Kurt Caillier, *Pr*
Randy Caillier, *
▲ EMP: 45 EST: 1956
SQ FT: 8,000
SALES (est): 49.53MM

# 3273 - Ready-mixed Concrete (P-7400)

SALES (corp-wide): 49.53MM **Privately Held**
Web: www.aareadymix.com
SIC: **3273**  Ready-mixed concrete

## (P-7400)
### ALLIANCE READY MIX INC
310 James Way Ste 210, Pismo Beach (93449-2877)
P.O. Box 1163 (93421-1163)
PHONE.....................805 556-3015
Brandt Robertson, *Brnch Mgr*
EMP: 27
SIC: **3273**  Ready-mixed concrete
PA: Alliance Ready Mix, Inc.
    915 Sheridan Rd

## (P-7401)
### ALLIED CONCRETE AND SUPPLY CO
440 Mitchell Rd Ste B, Modesto (95354-3915)
P.O. Box 66001 (95206-0901)
PHONE.....................209 524-3177
Michael G Ruddy, *Pr*
Michael G Ruddy Senior, *Pr*
Martin Ruddy Junior, *VP*
Sally Ruddy, *VP*
James M Ruddy, *VP*
EMP: 20 EST: 1952
SQ FT: 3,500
SALES (est): 2.64MM **Privately Held**
Web: www.allied-concrete-supply.com
SIC: **3273**  Ready-mixed concrete

## (P-7402)
### ALPHA MATERIALS INC
6170 20th St, Riverside (92509-2031)
PHONE.....................951 788-5150
Brian Oaks, *Pr*
EMP: 36 EST: 2002
SQ FT: 1,200
SALES (est): 11.18MM **Privately Held**
Web: www.alpha-materials-inc.com
SIC: **3273**  Ready-mixed concrete

## (P-7403)
### AMERICAN READY MIX INC
1141 W Graaf Ave, Ridgecrest (93555-2307)
P.O. Box 1138 (93556-1138)
PHONE.....................760 446-4556
Leroy Ladd, *Pr*
Donna Ladd, *VP*
EMP: 15 EST: 1977
SQ FT: 500
SALES (est): 571.58K **Privately Held**
Web: www.americanreadymix.net
SIC: **3273**  Ready-mixed concrete

## (P-7404)
### ARROW TRANSIT MIX
507 E Avenue L12, Lancaster (93535-5417)
P.O. Box 6677 (93539-6677)
PHONE.....................661 945-7600
H D Follendore, *Pr*
Christine Follendore, *
EMP: 35 EST: 1998
SQ FT: 7,200
SALES (est): 5.96MM **Privately Held**
Web: www.arrowtransitmix.com
SIC: **3273**  Ready-mixed concrete

## (P-7405)
### ASSOCIATED READY MIX CON INC
Also Called: ASSOCIATED READY MIX CONCRETE, INC.
8946 Bradley Ave, Sun Valley (91352-2601)
PHONE.....................818 504-3100
Tim Sullivan, *Mgr*
EMP: 77
Web: www.aareadymix.com
SIC: **3273**  Ready-mixed concrete
PA: Associated Ready Mixed Concrete, Inc.
    4621 Teller Ave Ste 130

## (P-7406)
### ASSOCIATED READY MIXED CON INC (PA)
4621 Teller Ave Ste 130, Newport Beach (92660-2165)
PHONE.....................949 253-2800
Kurt Caillier, *Pr*
Randy Caillier, *
Chris Pizano, *
EMP: 40 EST: 1996
SALES (est): 17.83MM **Privately Held**
Web: www.assocrmc.com
SIC: **3273**  Ready-mixed concrete

## (P-7407)
### BENDER READY MIX INC
Also Called: Bender Ready Mix Concrete
516 S Santa Fe St, Santa Ana (92705-4142)
PHONE.....................714 560-0744
Sarah Bender, *CEO*
Greg Bender, *Pr*
EMP: 25 EST: 2007
SALES (est): 6.24MM **Privately Held**
Web: www.benderreadymix.com
SIC: **3273**  Ready-mixed concrete

## (P-7408)
### BUILDERS CONCRETE INC (DH)
3664 W Ashlan Ave, Fresno (93722-4499)
P.O. Box 9129 (93790-9129)
PHONE.....................559 225-3667
Charlie Wensley, *CEO*
Don Unmacht, *
Dominique Bidet, *
EMP: 50 EST: 1953
SQ FT: 2,500
SALES (est): 10.13MM
SALES (corp-wide): 632.96MM **Privately Held**
Web: www.nationalcement.com
SIC: **3273**  Ready-mixed concrete
HQ: National Cement Company Of California, Inc.
    15821 Vntura Blvd Ste 475
    Encino CA 91436
    818 728-5200

## (P-7409)
### CALAVERAS MATERIALS INC
1301 Fulkerth Rd, Turlock (95380-2206)
PHONE.....................209 634-4931
Jess Blaker, *Pr*
EMP: 20
SIC: **3273**  Ready-mixed concrete
HQ: Calaveras Materials Inc.
    1100 Lowe Rd
    Hughson CA 95326
    209 883-0448

## (P-7410)
### CALAVERAS MATERIALS INC (HQ)
Also Called: CMI
1100 Lowe Rd, Hughson (95326-9178)
P.O. Box 26540 (93729-6240)
PHONE.....................209 883-0448
David Vickers, *Pr*
EMP: 20 EST: 1984
SQ FT: 8,000
SALES (est): 24.06MM **Publicly Held**
SIC: **3273** 5032 3272 2951  Ready-mixed concrete; Sand, construction; Concrete products, nec; Asphalt paving mixtures and blocks
PA: Martin Marietta Materials Inc
    4123 Parklake Ave

## (P-7411)
### CALIFORNIA COMMERCIAL ASP LLC
4211 Ponderosa Ave Ste C, San Diego (92123-1665)
PHONE.....................858 513-0611
Donald Daley Junior, *Pr*
EMP: 19 EST: 2005
SALES (est): 320.24K **Privately Held**
Web: www.ccallc.com
SIC: **3273**  Ready-mixed concrete

## (P-7412)
### CALPORTLAND
2025 E Financial Way, Glendora (91741-4692)
P.O. Box 371534 (89137-1534)
PHONE.....................760 343-3403
Terri Stelter, *Pr*
Diane Sarauer, *VP*
Debra Rubenzer, *Sec*
EMP: 59 EST: 1973
SQ FT: 480
SALES (est): 2.3MM **Privately Held**
Web: www.calportland.com
SIC: **3273**  Ready-mixed concrete

## (P-7413)
### CALPORTLAND COMPANY
Also Called: Califrnia Prtland Cem Dispatch
1862 E 27th St, Vernon (90058-1120)
PHONE.....................800 272-1891
Basil Ortiz, *Brnch Mgr*
EMP: 19
Web: www.calportland.com
SIC: **3273**  Ready-mixed concrete
HQ: Calportland Company
    2025 E Financial Way
    Glendora CA 91741

## (P-7414)
### CALPORTLAND COMPANY
Also Called: Catalina Pacific Concrete
1030 W Gladstone St, Azusa (91702-4207)
PHONE.....................626 334-3226
Bill Klawatter, *Mgr*
EMP: 15
Web: www.calportland.com
SIC: **3273**  Ready-mixed concrete
HQ: Calportland Company
    2025 E Financial Way
    Glendora CA 91741

## (P-7415)
### CAPITAL READY MIX INC
11311 Pendleton St, Sun Valley (91352-1530)
PHONE.....................818 771-1122
Tigran Aneian, *CEO*
EMP: 32 EST: 2014
SALES (est): 6.29MM **Privately Held**
SIC: **3273**  Ready-mixed concrete

## (P-7416)
### CATALINA PACIFIC CONCRETE
19030 Normandie Ave, Torrance (90502-1009)
PHONE.....................310 532-4600
Patrick E Greene, *Pr*
EMP: 22 EST: 1969
SQ FT: 1,500
SALES (est): 186.46K **Privately Held**
SIC: **3273**  Ready-mixed concrete

## (P-7417)
### CEMEX
5180 Golden Foothill Pkwy Ste 200, El Dorado Hills (95762-9345)
PHONE.....................916 941-2800
EMP: 98
SIC: **3273**  Ready-mixed concrete

## (P-7418)
### CEMEX INC
2365 Iron Point Rd, Folsom (95630-8711)
PHONE.....................916 941-2999
EMP: 51
Web: www.cemex.com
SIC: **3273** 3272 5032  Ready-mixed concrete; Concrete products, nec; Cement
HQ: Cemex, Inc.
    10100 Katy Fwy Ste 300
    Houston TX 77043
    713 650-6200

## (P-7419)
### CEMEX CEMENT INC
25220 Black Mountain Quarry Rd, Apple Valley (92307-9341)
PHONE.....................760 381-7616
Luis Lopez, *Brnch Mgr*
EMP: 200
SIC: **3273**  Ready-mixed concrete
HQ: Cemex Cement, Inc.
    10100 Katy Fwy Ste 300
    Houston TX 77043
    713 650-6200

## (P-7420)
### CEMEX CNSTR MTLS PCF LLC
Also Called: Aggregate -Eliot Quarry
1544 Stanley Blvd, Pleasanton (94566-6308)
P.O. Box 697 (94566-0866)
PHONE.....................925 846-2824
Gordon Brown, *Brnch Mgr*
EMP: 45
Web: www.cemexusa.com
SIC: **3273**  Ready-mixed concrete
HQ: Cemex Construction Materials Pacific, Llc
    1501 Belvedere Rd
    West Palm Beach FL 33406
    561 833-5555

## (P-7421)
### CEMEX CNSTR MTLS PCF LLC
Also Called: Shop -Ncal Rmx Fixed Maint Sho
1601 Cement Hill Rd, Fairfield (94533-2659)
PHONE.....................707 422-2520
Graham Dubois, *Brnch Mgr*
EMP: 33
SIC: **3273**  Ready-mixed concrete
HQ: Cemex Construction Materials Pacific, Llc
    1501 Belvedere Rd
    West Palm Beach FL 33406
    561 833-5555

## (P-7422)
### CEMEX CNSTR MTLS PCF LLC
Also Called: Readymix -Redlands Rm Dual
8203 Alabama Ave, Highland (92346-4255)
PHONE.....................909 335-3105
Erick Garcia, *Brnch Mgr*
EMP: 17
SIC: **3273**  Ready-mixed concrete
HQ: Cemex Construction Materials Pacific, Llc
    1501 Belvedere Rd
    West Palm Beach FL 33406
    561 833-5555

## PRODUCTS & SERVICES SECTION
## 3273 - Ready-mixed Concrete (P-7444)

**(P-7423)**
**CEMEX CNSTR MTLS PCF LLC**
Also Called: Readymix - Union City Rm
900 Whipple Rd, Union City (94587-1347)
PHONE..................................855 292-8453
EMP: 23
SIC: 3273 Ready-mixed concrete
HQ: Cemex Construction Materials Pacific, Llc
    1501 Belvedere Rd
    West Palm Beach FL 33406
    561 833-5555

**(P-7424)**
**CEMEX CNSTR MTLS PCF LLC**
Also Called: Readymix- Lodi Rm
1290 E Turner Rd, Lodi (95240-0749)
PHONE..................................855 292-8453
EMP: 23
SIC: 3273 Ready-mixed concrete
HQ: Cemex Construction Materials Pacific, Llc
    1501 Belvedere Rd
    West Palm Beach FL 33406
    561 833-5555

**(P-7425)**
**CEMEX MATERIALS LLC**
100 Lapis Rd, Marina (93933)
P.O. Box 337 (93933-0337)
PHONE..................................831 883-3700
EMP: 108
SIC: 3273 Ready-mixed concrete
HQ: Cemex Materials Llc
    1720 Cntrpark Dr E Ste 10
    West Palm Beach FL 33401
    561 833-5555

**(P-7426)**
**CEMEX MATERIALS LLC**
7059 Tremont Rd, Dixon (95620-9609)
PHONE..................................707 678-4311
Ed Ozbun, *Brnch Mgr*
EMP: 54
SIC: 3273 Ready-mixed concrete
HQ: Cemex Materials Llc
    1720 Cntrpark Dr E Ste 10
    West Palm Beach FL 33401
    561 833-5555

**(P-7427)**
**CEMEX MATERIALS LLC**
1645 Stanley Blvd, Pleasanton (94566-6309)
PHONE..................................855 292-8453
Joe Sostaric, *Brnch Mgr*
EMP: 38
SIC: 3273 Ready-mixed concrete
HQ: Cemex Materials Llc
    1720 Cntrpark Dr E Ste 10
    West Palm Beach FL 33401
    561 833-5555

**(P-7428)**
**CEMEX MATERIALS LLC**
401 Wright Ave, Richmond (94804-3508)
PHONE..................................510 234-3616
Karl H Watson Junior, *Brnch Mgr*
EMP: 163
SIC: 3273 Ready-mixed concrete
HQ: Cemex Materials Llc
    1720 Cntrpark Dr E Ste 10
    West Palm Beach FL 33401
    561 833-5555

**(P-7429)**
**CEMEX MATERIALS LLC**
385 Tower Rd, Napa (94558)
P.O. Box 3508 (94558-0553)
PHONE..................................707 255-3035
George Kerr, *Mgr*
EMP: 117
SQ FT: 30,000
SIC: 3273 Ready-mixed concrete
HQ: Cemex Materials Llc
    1720 Cntrpark Dr E Ste 10
    West Palm Beach FL 33401
    561 833-5555

**(P-7430)**
**CEMEX MATERIALS LLC**
Also Called: Cemex
4150 N Brawley Ave, Fresno (93722-3914)
PHONE..................................559 275-2241
EMP: 96
SIC: 3273 Ready-mixed concrete
HQ: Cemex Materials Llc
    1720 Cntrpark Dr E Ste 10
    West Palm Beach FL 33401
    561 833-5555

**(P-7431)**
**CEMEX MATERIALS LLC**
1205 S Rancho Ave, Colton (92324-3343)
PHONE..................................909 825-1500
Lindsey Hank, *Mgr*
EMP: 88
SIC: 3273 Ready-mixed concrete
HQ: Cemex Materials Llc
    1720 Cntrpark Dr E Ste 10
    West Palm Beach FL 33401
    561 833-5555

**(P-7432)**
**CEMEX USA INC**
4120 Jurupa St Ste 202, Ontario (91761-1423)
PHONE..................................909 974-5500
Mike Bauder, *Prin*
EMP: 18 EST: 2010
SALES (est): 1.08MM **Privately Held**
SIC: 3273 Ready-mixed concrete

**(P-7433)**
**CENTRAL CONCRETE SUPPLY CO INC (DH)**
Also Called: Westside Building Materials
755 Stockton Ave, San Jose (95126-1839)
PHONE..................................408 293-6272
William T Albanese, *CEO*
David Perry, *
Scott Perrine, *SUSTAINBLTY**
Jeff Davis, *
Laurie Cerrito, *
EMP: 80 EST: 1951
SQ FT: 2,000
SALES (est): 48MM **Publicly Held**
Web: www.centralconcrete.com
SIC: 3273 Ready-mixed concrete
HQ: U.S. Concrete, Inc.
    331 N Main St
    Euless TX 76039
    817 835-4105

**(P-7434)**
**CONCRETE INC (DH)**
400 S Lincoln St, Stockton (95203-3312)
P.O. Box 66001 (95206-0901)
PHONE..................................209 933-6999
David C Barney, *CEO*
Terry D Hildestad, *
Mary Ann Johnson, *
Larry Hansen, *
Lester H Loble Ii, *Sec*
EMP: 55 EST: 1986
SALES (est): 24.41MM
SALES (corp-wide): 2.83B **Publicly Held**
Web: www.con-inc.com

SIC: 3273 5032 Ready-mixed concrete; Brick, stone, and related material
HQ: Krc Materials, Inc.
    1150 W Century Ave
    Bismarck ND 58506
    701 530-1400

**(P-7435)**
**CONCRETE HOLDING CO CAL INC**
15821 Ventura Blvd Ste 475, Encino (91436-2915)
PHONE..................................818 788-4228
Don Unmacht, *Pr*
Dominique Bidet, *
EMP: 702 EST: 1988
SQ FT: 4,000
SALES (est): 1.41MM
SALES (corp-wide): 632.96MM **Privately Held**
Web: www.nationalcement.com
SIC: 3273 Ready-mixed concrete
HQ: National Cement Company, Inc.
    15821 Ventura Blvd # 475
    Encino CA 91436
    818 728-5200

**(P-7436)**
**CONCRETE READY MIX INC**
33 Hillsdale Ave, San Jose (95136-1308)
P.O. Box 5006 (95150-5006)
PHONE..................................408 224-2452
Ron Minnis, *Pr*
EMP: 35 EST: 1983
SALES (est): 9.12MM **Privately Held**
Web: www.concretecrm.com
SIC: 3273 Ready-mixed concrete

**(P-7437)**
**CORONET CONCRETE PRODUCTS INC (PA)**
Also Called: Desert Redi Mix
83801 Avenue 45, Indio (92201-3311)
PHONE..................................760 398-2441
James Richert, *CEO*
EMP: 22 EST: 1982
SQ FT: 2,000
SALES (est): 8.32MM
SALES (corp-wide): 8.32MM **Privately Held**
SIC: 3273 3272 Ready-mixed concrete; Concrete products, nec

**(P-7438)**
**DIVERSIFIED MINERALS INC**
Also Called: Dmi Ready Mix
1100 Mountain View Ave Ste F, Oxnard (93030-7213)
PHONE..................................805 247-1069
James W Price, *Pr*
Sharron Price, *
▲ EMP: 44 EST: 1990
SQ FT: 44,482
SALES (est): 10.89MM **Privately Held**
Web: www.dmicement.com
SIC: 3273 4013 3531 3241 Ready-mixed concrete; Railroad terminals; Bituminous, cement and concrete related products and equip.; Pozzolana cement

**(P-7439)**
**E-Z HAUL READY MIX INC**
Also Called: Star Building Products
1538 N Blackstone Ave, Fresno (93703-3612)
PHONE..................................559 233-6603
Calvin Coley, *Pr*
Donald Crawford, *
Pat Coley, *
EMP: 30 EST: 1969

SQ FT: 1,500
SALES (est): 2.1MM **Privately Held**
Web: www.starbuildingsupplies.com
SIC: 3273 5211 Ready-mixed concrete; Cement

**(P-7440)**
**E-Z MIX INC (PA)**
11450 Tuxford St, Sun Valley (91352-2638)
PHONE..................................818 768-0568
William Frenzel, *CEO*
Sunjiv Parekh, *
EMP: 33 EST: 1992
SQ FT: 50,000
SALES (est): 9.21MM **Privately Held**
Web: www.ezmixinc.com
SIC: 3273 Ready-mixed concrete

**(P-7441)**
**EBAC INVESTMENTS INC (PA)**
181 Lynch Creek Way, Petaluma (94954-2372)
P.O. Box 751300 (94975-1300)
PHONE..................................707 781-9000
Eugene B Ceccotti, *CEO*
Robert Bowen, *
▲ EMP: 25 EST: 1945
SQ FT: 5,000
SALES (est): 15.34MM
SALES (corp-wide): 15.34MM **Privately Held**
Web: www.shamrockmaterials.com
SIC: 3273 5211 Ready-mixed concrete; Lumber and other building materials

**(P-7442)**
**EBAC INVESTMENTS INC**
Also Called: Cloverdale Ready Mix
Levee Rd, Cloverdale (95425)
PHONE..................................707 894-4425
Dave Ripple, *Mgr*
EMP: 18
SALES (corp-wide): 15.34MM **Privately Held**
Web: www.shamrockmaterials.com
SIC: 3273 1442 Ready-mixed concrete; Sand mining
PA: Ebac Investments, Inc.
    181 Lynch Creek Way
    707 781-9000

**(P-7443)**
**EBAC INVESTMENTS INC**
Also Called: Shamrock Materials of Cotati
8150 Gravenstein Hwy, Cotati (94931-4127)
PHONE..................................707 792-4695
Jorge Barjas, *Mgr*
EMP: 27
SALES (corp-wide): 15.34MM **Privately Held**
Web: www.shamrockmaterials.com
SIC: 3273 Ready-mixed concrete
PA: Ebac Investments, Inc.
    181 Lynch Creek Way
    707 781-9000

**(P-7444)**
**EBAC INVESTMENTS INC**
Also Called: Shamrock Fireplace
548 Du Bois St, San Rafael (94901-3964)
P.O. Box 751300 (94975-1300)
PHONE..................................415 455-1575
Mike Isetta, *Mgr*
EMP: 43
SALES (corp-wide): 15.34MM **Privately Held**
Web: www.blazefireplaces.com
SIC: 3273 Ready-mixed concrete
PA: Ebac Investments, Inc.
    181 Lynch Creek Way

## 3273 - Ready-mixed Concrete (P-7445)

707 781-9000

**(P-7445)**
**ELITE READY-MIX LLC**
6790 Bradshaw Rd, Sacramento (95829-9303)
PHONE..................916 366-4627
Billie Sposeto, *
EMP: 35 EST: 2008
SALES (est): 6.04MM Privately Held
Web: www.elitereadymix.net
SIC: 3273 Ready-mixed concrete

**(P-7446)**
**FOLSOM READY MIX INC (HQ)**
3401 Fitzgerald Rd, Rancho Cordova (95742-6815)
PHONE..................916 851-8300
Scott Silva, CEO
Scott Silva, Pr
Randy Barnes, *
EMP: 16 EST: 1999
SALES (est): 10.04MM
SALES (corp-wide): 98.19MM Privately Held
Web: www.folsomreadymix.com
SIC: 3273 Ready-mixed concrete
PA: Farmer Holding Company, Inc.
221 Bolivar St Ste 401
573 635-2255

**(P-7447)**
**GARY BALE REDI-MIX CON INC**
16131 Construction Cir W, Irvine (92606-4410)
PHONE..................949 786-9441
Kyle Goerlitz, CEO
EMP: 80 EST: 1968
SALES (est): 4.37MM Privately Held
Web: www.garybaleredimix.com
SIC: 3273 Ready-mixed concrete

**(P-7448)**
**GIBSON & SCHAEFER INC (PA)**
1126 Rock Wood Rd, Heber (92249)
P.O. Box 1539 (92249-1539)
PHONE..................619 352-3535
Don Gibson, Pr
P M Schaefer, *
Maria Schaefer, *
Rhoberta Gibson, *
EMP: 50 EST: 1989
SQ FT: 1,440
SALES (est): 10.1MM Privately Held
Web: www.gibsonandschaeferinc.com
SIC: 3273 5032 Ready-mixed concrete; Gravel

**(P-7449)**
**GRANITE ROCK CO**
Also Called: Pavex Construction Co
1755 Del Monte Blvd, Seaside (93955-3603)
PHONE..................831 392-3700
Mike Chernetsky, Mgr
EMP: 60
SALES (corp-wide): 501.14MM Privately Held
Web: www.graniterock.com
SIC: 3273 5032 Ready-mixed concrete; Brick, stone, and related material
PA: Granite Rock Company
350 Technology Dr
831 768-2000

**(P-7450)**
**HANFORD READY-MIX INC**
9800 Kent St, Elk Grove (95624-9483)
PHONE..................916 405-1918
Preston Hanford Junior, CEO
Diane Hanford-butz, VP
Preston Hanford Iii, Prin
EMP: 20 EST: 1981
SQ FT: 3,500
SALES (est): 2.74MM Privately Held
Web: www.hanfordsandandgravel.com
SIC: 3273 Ready-mixed concrete

**(P-7451)**
**HANSON AGGRGTES MD-PACIFIC INC**
7999 Athenour Way, Sunol (94586-9454)
PHONE..................925 862-2236
EMP: 18
SALES (corp-wide): 21.19B Privately Held
SIC: 3273 Ready-mixed concrete
HQ: Hanson Aggregates Mid-Pacific, Inc.
12667 Alcosta Blvd # 400
San Ramon CA

**(P-7452)**
**HANSON AGGRGTES MD-PACIFIC INC**
699 Virginia St, Berkeley (94710-1727)
PHONE..................510 526-1611
EMP: 18
SALES (corp-wide): 21.19B Privately Held
SIC: 3273 Ready-mixed concrete
HQ: Hanson Aggregates Mid-Pacific, Inc.
12667 Alcosta Blvd # 400
San Ramon CA

**(P-7453)**
**HEIDELBERG MTLS STHWEST AGG LL**
Also Called: HEIDELBERG MATERIALS SOUTHWEST AGG LLC
5330 Main St, Chula Vista (91911)
PHONE..................619 425-0290
Gary Mc Claus, Brnch Mgr
EMP: 15
SALES (corp-wide): 23.02B Privately Held
Web: www.heidelbergmaterials.us
SIC: 3273 Ready-mixed concrete
HQ: Hanson Aggregates Llc
8505 Freport Pkwy Ste 500
Irving TX 75063
469 417-1200

**(P-7454)**
**HEIDELBERG MTLS STHWEST AGG LL**
Also Called: HEIDELBERG MATERIALS SOUTHWEST AGG LLC
10331 Highway 76, Pala (92059-2304)
PHONE..................877 642-6766
EMP: 15
SALES (corp-wide): 23.02B Privately Held
Web: www.heidelbergmaterials.us
SIC: 3273 Ready-mixed concrete
HQ: Hanson Aggregates Llc
8505 Freport Pkwy Ste 500
Irving TX 75063
469 417-1200

**(P-7455)**
**HI-GRADE MATERIALS CO**
6500 E Avenue T, Littlerock (93543-1722)
P.O. Box 1050 (93543-1050)
PHONE..................661 533-3100
Rod Elderton, Mgr
EMP: 88
SALES (corp-wide): 49.72MM Privately Held
Web: www.robar.com
SIC: 3273 Ready-mixed concrete
HQ: Hi-Grade Materials Co.
17671 Bear Valley Rd
Hesperia CA
760 244-9325

**(P-7456)**
**HOLLIDAY TRUCKING INC (PA)**
1401 N Benson Ave, Upland (91786-2166)
PHONE..................909 982-1553
Frederick N Holliday, Pr
Penny Holliday, *
John Holliday, *
Ronald Chambers, *
EMP: 60 EST: 1964
SQ FT: 2,000
SALES (est): 5.1MM
SALES (corp-wide): 5.1MM Privately Held
Web: www.hollidayrock.com
SIC: 3273 4212 Ready-mixed concrete; Local trucking, without storage

**(P-7457)**
**HOLLIDAY TRUCKING INC**
2300 W Base Line St, San Bernardino (92410-1002)
PHONE..................888 273-2200
Frederick N Holliday, Brnch Mgr
EMP: 60
SALES (corp-wide): 3.96MM Privately Held
Web: www.hollidayrock.com
SIC: 3273 Ready-mixed concrete
PA: Holliday Trucking Inc.
1401 N Benson Ave
909 982-1553

**(P-7458)**
**HOLLISTER LANDSCAPE SUPPLY INC**
2410 San Juan Rd, Hollister (95023-9107)
PHONE..................831 636-8750
Barabara A Chaplin, Pr
EMP: 55
Web: www.hollisterlandscapesupply.com
SIC: 3273 Ready-mixed concrete
HQ: Hollister Landscape Supply, Inc.
520 Crazy Horse Canyon Rd A
Salinas CA 93907
831 443-8644

**(P-7459)**
**JP GUNITE INC**
9458 New Colt Ct, El Cajon (92021-2323)
PHONE..................619 938-0228
Juan Padilla, Pr
EMP: 20 EST: 1990
SALES (est): 2.57MM Privately Held
Web: www.jpgunite.com
SIC: 3273 Ready-mixed concrete

**(P-7460)**
**L K LEHMAN TRUCKING**
Also Called: A & L Ready Mix
19333 Industrial Dr, Sonora (95370-9232)
P.O. Box 9 (95373-0009)
PHONE..................209 532-5586
Lowell K Lehman, Pr
Darlene Lehman, *
EMP: 35 EST: 1976
SQ FT: 1,500
SALES (est): 4.85MM Privately Held
Web: www.lklehmantrucking.com
SIC: 3273 4214 Ready-mixed concrete; Local trucking with storage

**(P-7461)**
**LAS ANIMAS CON & BLDG SUP INC**
Also Called: Las Animas Concrete
146 Encinal St, Santa Cruz (95060-2111)
P.O. Box 507 (95061-0507)
PHONE..................831 425-4084
Scott French, Pr
EMP: 20 EST: 1965
SALES (est): 4.97MM Privately Held
Web: www.lasanimasconcrete.com
SIC: 3273 Ready-mixed concrete

**(P-7462)**
**LEBATA INC**
Also Called: A & A Ready Mix Concrete
4621 Teller Ave Ste 130, Newport Beach (92660-2165)
PHONE..................949 253-2800
Kurt Caillier, Pr
EMP: 30 EST: 1987
SALES (est): 5.1MM Privately Held
SIC: 3273 Ready-mixed concrete

**(P-7463)**
**LEES CONCRETE MATERIALS INC**
200 S Pine St, Madera (93637-5206)
P.O. Box 509 (93639-0509)
PHONE..................559 486-2440
Tom Da Silva, Pr
Deidre Da Silva, Treas
EMP: 18 EST: 1963
SQ FT: 7,000
SALES (est): 3.36MM Privately Held
SIC: 3273 Ready-mixed concrete

**(P-7464)**
**LEGACY VULCAN LLC**
11599 Old Friant Rd, Fresno (93730-1214)
PHONE..................559 434-1202
Frank Costa, Brnch Mgr
EMP: 25
Web: www.vulcanmaterials.com
SIC: 3273 Ready-mixed concrete
HQ: Legacy Vulcan, Llc
1200 Urban Center Dr
Birmingham AL 35242
205 298-3000

**(P-7465)**
**LIVINGSTONS CONCRETE SVC INC (PA)**
Also Called: Livingston's
5416 Roseville Rd, North Highlands (95660-5097)
PHONE..................916 334-4313
Patricia Henley, Pr
Edith Livingston, *
Michael Livingston, *
Richard G Livingston, *
Larry Livingston, *
EMP: 24 EST: 1946
SALES (est): 15MM
SALES (corp-wide): 15MM Privately Held
Web: www.livingstonsconcrete.com
SIC: 3273 Ready-mixed concrete

**(P-7466)**
**LIVINGSTONS CONCRETE SVC INC**
Also Called: Plant 1
5416 Roseville Rd, North Highlands (95660-5097)
PHONE..................916 334-4313
Terry Regan, Brnch Mgr
EMP: 25
SALES (corp-wide): 15MM Privately Held
Web: www.livingstonsconcrete.com
SIC: 3273 Ready-mixed concrete
PA: Livingston's Concrete Service, Inc.
5416 Roseville Rd
916 334-4313

**(P-7467)**
**LIVINGSTONS CONCRETE SVC INC** ◆
Also Called: Plant 3

## PRODUCTS & SERVICES SECTION
## 3273 - Ready-mixed Concrete (P-7486)

2915 Lesvos Ct, Lincoln  (95648-9341)
PHONE..................................916 334-4313
Bill Redden, *Brnch Mgr*
**EMP:** 25
**SALES (corp-wide):** 15MM **Privately Held**
**Web:** www.livingstonsconcrete.com
**SIC: 3273** Ready-mixed concrete
**PA:** Livingston's Concrete Service, Inc.
  5416 Roseville Rd
  916 334-4313

**(P-7468)**
**LYNCH READY MIX CONCRETE CO**
Also Called: Mission Ready Mix
11011 Azahar St Ste 4, Ventura
  (93004-1944)
PHONE..................................805 647-2817
Robert A Lynch, *Pr*
Laverne Lynch, *VP*
**EMP:** 15 **EST:** 1989
**SQ FT:** 500
**SALES (est):** 2.71MM **Privately Held**
**Web:** www.statereadymix.com
**SIC: 3273** Ready-mixed concrete

**(P-7469)**
**MATHEWS READY MIX LLC**
1619 Skyway, Chico  (95928-8833)
PHONE..................................530 893-8856
Chad Christee, *Brnch Mgr*
**EMP:** 20
**SQ FT:** 4,780
**SALES (corp-wide):** 2.15B **Publicly Held**
**Web:** www.mathewsreadymixllc.com
**SIC: 3273** Ready-mixed concrete
**HQ:** Mathews Ready Mix Llc
  4711 Hammonton Rd
  Marysville CA 95901
  530 749-6525

**(P-7470)**
**MATHEWS READY MIX LLC**
Also Called: Mathews Readymix
249 Lamon St, Yuba City  (95991-4200)
P.O. Box 749 (95901-0020)
PHONE..................................530 671-2400
Lee Cooper, *Mgr*
**EMP:** 23
**SALES (corp-wide):** 2.15B **Publicly Held**
**Web:** www.mathewsreadymixllc.com
**SIC: 3273** Ready-mixed concrete
**HQ:** Mathews Ready Mix Llc
  4711 Hammonton Rd
  Marysville CA 95901
  530 749-6525

**(P-7471)**
**MOUNTAIN MATERIALS INC**
1117 Tavern Rd, Alpine  (91901-3817)
PHONE..................................619 445-4150
Daniel Shea, *Pr*
Michele Bracco, *CFO*
Steve Finch, *VP*
**EMP:** 21 **EST:** 1998
**SALES (est):** 3.96MM **Privately Held**
**Web:** www.mountainmaterialsinc.com
**SIC: 3273** Ready-mixed concrete

**(P-7472)**
**NATIONAL CEMENT CO CAL INC (DH)**
15821 Ventura Blvd Ste 475, Encino
  (91436-2935)
PHONE..................................818 728-5200
Steven Weiss, *Pr*
Pragati Kapoor, *CFO*
Dominique Bidet, *VP*
▲ **EMP:** 37 **EST:** 1987
**SQ FT:** 12,000
**SALES (est):** 61.15MM
**SALES (corp-wide):** 632.96MM **Privately Held**
**Web:** www.nationalcement.com
**SIC: 3273** Ready-mixed concrete
**HQ:** National Cement Company, Inc.
  15821 Ventura Blvd # 475
  Encino CA 91436
  818 728-5200

**(P-7473)**
**NATIONAL CEMENT COMPANY INC**
2626 E 26th St, Vernon  (90058-1218)
PHONE..................................323 923-4466
**EMP:** 78
**SALES (corp-wide):** 632.96MM **Privately Held**
**Web:** www.nationalcement.com
**SIC: 3273** Ready-mixed concrete
**HQ:** National Cement Company, Inc.
  15821 Ventura Blvd # 475
  Encino CA 91436
  818 728-5200

**(P-7474)**
**NATIONAL READY MIXED CON CO**
9010 Norris Ave, Sun Valley  (91352-2617)
PHONE..................................818 768-0050
Mike Randolf, *Mgr*
**EMP:** 15
**SALES (corp-wide):** 632.96MM **Privately Held**
**Web:** www.nrmcc.com
**SIC: 3273** Ready-mixed concrete
**HQ:** National Ready Mixed Concrete Co
  15821 Vntura Blvd Ste 475
  Encino CA 91436
  818 728-5200

**(P-7475)**
**NATIONAL READY MIXED CON CO**
4549 Brazil St, Los Angeles  (90039-1001)
PHONE..................................323 245-5539
Bob Mcfarlane, *Brnch Mgr*
**EMP:** 15
**SALES (corp-wide):** 632.96MM **Privately Held**
**Web:** www.nationalcement.com
**SIC: 3273** Ready-mixed concrete
**HQ:** National Ready Mixed Concrete Co
  15821 Vntura Blvd Ste 475
  Encino CA 91436
  818 728-5200

**(P-7476)**
**NATIONAL READY MIXED CON CO**
6969 Deering Ave, Canoga Park
  (91303-2171)
PHONE..................................818 884-0893
Mike Randolph, *Mgr*
**EMP:** 15
**SALES (corp-wide):** 632.96MM **Privately Held**
**Web:** www.nationalcement.com
**SIC: 3273** Ready-mixed concrete
**HQ:** National Ready Mixed Concrete Co
  15821 Vntura Blvd Ste 475
  Encino CA 91436
  818 728-5200

**(P-7477)**
**NATIONAL READY MIXED CON CO (DH)**
Also Called: National Cement Ready Mix
15821 Ventura Blvd Ste 475, Encino
  (91436-2935)
PHONE..................................818 728-5200
Tim Toland, *CEO*
Don Unmacht, *VP*
▲ **EMP:** 20 **EST:** 1946
**SQ FT:** 40,000
**SALES (est):** 25.25MM
**SALES (corp-wide):** 632.96MM **Privately Held**
**Web:** www.nrmcc.com
**SIC: 3273** Ready-mixed concrete
**HQ:** National Cement Company Of California, Inc.
  15821 Vntura Blvd Ste 475
  Encino CA 91436
  818 728-5200

**(P-7478)**
**NATIONAL READY MIXED CON CO**
11725 Artesia Blvd, Artesia  (90701-3850)
PHONE..................................562 865-6211
Sher Cowan, *Brnch Mgr*
**EMP:** 15
**SALES (corp-wide):** 632.96MM **Privately Held**
**Web:** www.nrmcc.com
**SIC: 3273** Ready-mixed concrete
**HQ:** National Ready Mixed Concrete Co
  15821 Vntura Blvd Ste 475
  Encino CA 91436
  818 728-5200

**(P-7479)**
**NATIONAL READY MIXED CON CO**
27050 Ruether Ave, Canyon Country
  (91351-6643)
PHONE..................................661 252-8181
Allen Ellis, *Prin*
**EMP:** 15
**SALES (corp-wide):** 632.96MM **Privately Held**
**Web:** www.nationalcement.com
**SIC: 3273** Ready-mixed concrete
**HQ:** National Ready Mixed Concrete Co
  15821 Vntura Blvd Ste 475
  Encino CA 91436
  818 728-5200

**(P-7480)**
**NATIONAL READY MIXED CON CO**
16282 Construction Cir E, Irvine
  (92606-4405)
PHONE..................................949 552-5566
Sam Hill, *Brnch Mgr*
**EMP:** 15
**SALES (corp-wide):** 632.96MM **Privately Held**
**Web:** www.nrmcc.com
**SIC: 3273** 5211 Ready-mixed concrete; Cement
**HQ:** National Ready Mixed Concrete Co
  15821 Vntura Blvd Ste 475
  Encino CA 91436
  818 728-5200

**(P-7481)**
**NORCAL MATERIALS INC**
Also Called: Harbor Ready Mix
941 Bransten Rd, San Carlos  (94070-4021)
PHONE..................................650 365-4811
**EMP:** 20
**Web:** www.harborreadymix.com
**SIC: 3273** Ready-mixed concrete
**HQ:** Norcal Materials, Inc.
  331 N Main St
  Euless TX 76039
  817 835-4105

**(P-7482)**
**OUTBACK INC (PA)**
Also Called: Outback Materials
4201 W Shaw Ave Ste 106, Fresno
  (93722-6216)
PHONE..................................559 293-3880
**EMP:** 30 **EST:** 1968
**SALES (est):** 15.79MM
**SALES (corp-wide):** 15.79MM **Privately Held**
**Web:** www.outbackmaterials.com
**SIC: 3273** 3272 Ready-mixed concrete; Concrete products, nec

**(P-7483)**
**P & L CONCRETE PRODUCTS INC**
1900 Roosevelt Ave, Escalon  (95320-1763)
PHONE..................................209 838-1448
**TOLL FREE:** 800
Jeff Francis, *Pr*
Arlene Francis, *VP*
**EMP:** 22 **EST:** 1972
**SQ FT:** 1,500
**SALES (est):** 3.71MM **Privately Held**
**Web:** www.plconcrete.net
**SIC: 3273** Ready-mixed concrete

**(P-7484)**
**PACIFIC AGGREGATES INC**
28251 Lake St, Lake Elsinore  (92530-1635)
PHONE..................................951 245-2460
Kai Chin, *CEO*
Dale Kline, *
▲ **EMP:** 75 **EST:** 2002
**SQ FT:** 1,000
**SALES (est):** 11.57MM
**SALES (corp-wide):** 372.87MM **Privately Held**
**Web:** www.pacificaggregates.com
**SIC: 3273** Ready-mixed concrete
**PA:** Castle & Cooke, Inc.
  10000 Stockdale Hwy # 300
  818 879-6700

**(P-7485)**
**PLEASANTON READY MIX CON INC**
Also Called: Pleasanton Readymix Concrete
3400 Boulder St, Pleasanton  (94566-4769)
P.O. Box 879 (94566-0874)
PHONE..................................925 846-3226
Albert Riebli, *Pr*
John Santos, *Treas*
**EMP:** 15 **EST:** 1966
**SQ FT:** 1,000
**SALES (est):** 2.59MM **Privately Held**
**Web:** www.pleasantonreadymix.com
**SIC: 3273** Ready-mixed concrete

**(P-7486)**
**PUENTE READY MIX SERVICES INC (PA)**
209 N California Ave, City Of Industry
  (91744-4324)
P.O. Box 3345 (91744-0345)
PHONE..................................626 968-0711
**TOLL FREE:** 800
Mark Keuning, *Ch Bd*
Ronald A Biang, *
Kevin Keuning, *
Marcia Biang, *
**EMP:** 22 **EST:** 1949
**SQ FT:** 5,000
**SALES (est):** 5.96MM
**SALES (corp-wide):** 5.96MM **Privately Held**
**Web:** www.puentereadymix.com

# 3273 - Ready-mixed Concrete (P-7487)

SIC: 3273 Ready-mixed concrete

**(P-7487)**
**RC READYMIX CO INC**
1227 Greenville Rd, Livermore
(94550-9299)
PHONE..................................925 449-7785
Rob Costa, *Pr*
Rob C0sta, *
EMP: 24 EST: 1998
SALES (est): 4.46MM **Privately Held**
Web: www.rcreadymixco.com
SIC: 3273 Ready-mixed concrete

**(P-7488)**
**ROBAR ENTERPRISES INC (PA)**
17671 Bear Valley Rd, Hesperia
(92345-4902)
PHONE..................................760 244-5456
Jonathan D Hove, *CEO*
Robert E Hove, *
Al Calvanico, *
EMP: 150 EST: 1981
SQ FT: 26,000
SALES (est): 49.72MM
SALES (corp-wide): 49.72MM **Privately Held**
Web: www.robarenterprises.com
SIC: 3273 5051 3441 Ready-mixed concrete
; Steel; Building components, structural steel

**(P-7489)**
**ROBERTSONS RDYMX LTD A CAL LTD (PA)**
Also Called: Robertson's
200 S Main St Ste 200, Corona
(92882-2212)
P.O. Box 3600 (92878-3600)
PHONE..................................951 493-6500
TOLL FREE: 800
Jon Troesh, *Pt*
▲ EMP: 85 EST: 1991
SQ FT: 22,008
SALES (est): 458.49MM
SALES (corp-wide): 458.49MM **Privately Held**
Web: www.rrmca.com
SIC: 3273 3531 5032 2951 Ready-mixed concrete; Bituminous, cement and concrete related products and equip.; Asphalt mixture; Asphalt paving mixtures and blocks

**(P-7490)**
**ROBERTSONS RDYMX LTD A CAL LTD**
27401 3rd St, Highland (92346-4242)
PHONE..................................909 425-2930
Dennis Troesh, *Pr*
EMP: 154
SALES (corp-wide): 458.49MM **Privately Held**
Web: www.rrmca.com
SIC: 3273 Ready-mixed concrete
PA: Robertson's Ready Mix, Ltd., A California Limited Partnership
200 S Main St Ste 200
951 493-6500

**(P-7491)**
**ROBERTSONS READY MIX LTD**
9635 C Ave, Hesperia (92345-6047)
PHONE..................................760 244-7239
EMP: 61
SALES (corp-wide): 458.49MM **Privately Held**
Web: www.rrmca.com
SIC: 3273 Ready-mixed concrete
PA: Robertson's Ready Mix, Ltd., A California Limited Partnership
200 S Main St Ste 200
951 493-6500

**(P-7492)**
**ROBERTSONS READY MIX LTD**
Also Called: Miramar Plant 33
5692 Eastgate Dr, San Diego (92121-2816)
PHONE..................................800 834-7557
EMP: 92
SALES (corp-wide): 458.49MM **Privately Held**
Web: www.rrmca.com
SIC: 3273 Ready-mixed concrete
PA: Robertson's Ready Mix, Ltd., A California Limited Partnership
200 S Main St Ste 200
951 493-6500

**(P-7493)**
**ROBERTSONS READY MIX LTD**
7900 Moss Ave, California City
(93505-4311)
PHONE..................................760 373-4815
EMP: 92
SALES (corp-wide): 458.49MM **Privately Held**
Web: www.rrmca.com
SIC: 3273 Ready-mixed concrete
PA: Robertson's Ready Mix, Ltd., A California Limited Partnership
200 S Main St Ste 200
951 493-6500

**(P-7494)**
**ROBERTSONS READY MIX LTD**
1310 Simpson Way, Escondido
(92029-1377)
PHONE..................................951 685-4600
EMP: 62
SALES (corp-wide): 458.49MM **Privately Held**
Web: www.rrmca.com
SIC: 3273 Ready-mixed concrete
PA: Robertson's Ready Mix, Ltd., A California Limited Partnership
200 S Main St Ste 200
951 493-6500

**(P-7495)**
**RWH INC**
Also Called: Holiday Transportation
15115 Oxnard St, Van Nuys (91411-2615)
PHONE..................................818 782-2350
TOLL FREE: 800
EMP: 30 EST: 1964
SALES (est): 4.3MM **Privately Held**
Web: www.bonanzaconcrete.com
SIC: 3273 4212 Ready-mixed concrete; Local trucking, without storage

**(P-7496)**
**SHORT LOAD CONCRETE INC**
605 E Commercial St, Anaheim
(92801-2511)
PHONE..................................714 524-7013
Ryan Van Derhook, *Pr*
EMP: 20 EST: 1996
SALES (est): 3.85MM **Privately Held**
Web: www.shortloadconcrete.com
SIC: 3273 Ready-mixed concrete

**(P-7497)**
**SIERRA-TAHOE READY MIX INC**
1526 Emerald Bay Rd, South Lake Tahoe
(96150-6112)
PHONE..................................530 541-1877
Donald Wallace, *Pr*
EMP: 22 EST: 1970
SQ FT: 2,000
SALES (est): 2.89MM **Privately Held**
SIC: 3273 Ready-mixed concrete

**(P-7498)**
**SOUTH VALLEY MATERIALS INC**
1132 N Belmont Rd, Exeter (93221-9669)
PHONE..................................559 594-4142
EMP: 17
SIC: 3273 Ready-mixed concrete
HQ: South Valley Materials, Inc.
114 E Shaw Ave Ste 100
Fresno CA 93710
559 277-7060

**(P-7499)**
**SOUTH VALLEY MATERIALS INC (HQ)**
114 E Shaw Ave Ste 100, Fresno
(93710-7621)
P.O. Box 26240 (93729-6240)
PHONE..................................559 277-7060
James G Brown, *Pr*
EMP: 60 EST: 1996
SQ FT: 6,000
SALES (est): 4.99MM **Publicly Held**
SIC: 3273 Ready-mixed concrete
PA: Martin Marietta Materials Inc
4123 Parklake Ave

**(P-7500)**
**SOUTH VALLEY MATERIALS INC**
7761 Hanford Armona Rd, Hanford
(93230-9343)
P.O. Box 26240 (93729-6240)
PHONE..................................559 582-0532
David Vickers, *Brnch Mgr*
EMP: 17
SIC: 3273 Ready-mixed concrete
HQ: South Valley Materials, Inc.
114 E Shaw Ave Ste 100
Fresno CA 93710
559 277-7060

**(P-7501)**
**SPRAGUES ROCK AND SAND COMPANY (PA)**
Also Called: Spragues Ready Mix
230 Longden Ave, Irwindale (91706-1328)
PHONE..................................626 445-2125
Carole Cotter, *Ch Bd*
Michael Toland, *Pr*
Steven Toland, *VP*
Juli Paez, *Sec*
EMP: 22 EST: 1953
SQ FT: 2,100
SALES (est): 10.63MM
SALES (corp-wide): 10.63MM **Privately Held**
Web: www.srmconcrete.com
SIC: 3273 Ready-mixed concrete

**(P-7502)**
**STANDARD CONCRETE PRODUCTS INC (HQ)**
Also Called: Associated Ready Mix Concrete
13550 Live Oak Ln, Baldwin Park
(91706-1318)
P.O. Box 15326 (92735-0326)
PHONE..................................310 829-4537
David Hummel, *Pr*
Brian Serra, *VP*
EMP: 20 EST: 1986
SQ FT: 2,400
SALES (est): 2.71MM
SALES (corp-wide): 49.53MM **Privately Held**
Web: www.nationalcement.com

SIC: 3273 Ready-mixed concrete
PA: A & A Ready Mixed Concrete, Inc.
4621 Teller Ave Ste 130
949 253-2800

**(P-7503)**
**STATE READY MIX INC**
3127 Los Angeles Ave, Oxnard
(93036-1010)
PHONE..................................805 647-2817
Robert Lynch, *Pr*
EMP: 19
SALES (corp-wide): 5.63MM **Privately Held**
Web: www.statereadymix.com
SIC: 3273 Ready-mixed concrete
PA: State Ready Mix, Inc.
1011 Azahar St Ste 1
805 647-2817

**(P-7504)**
**STATE READY MIX INC (PA)**
1011 Azahar St Ste 1, Ventura (93004)
PHONE..................................805 647-2817
Russell Cochran, *CEO*
Robert A Lynch, *
EMP: 21 EST: 1988
SALES (est): 5.63MM
SALES (corp-wide): 5.63MM **Privately Held**
Web: www.statereadymix.com
SIC: 3273 Ready-mixed concrete

**(P-7505)**
**SUPERIOR READY MIX CONCRETE LP**
Also Called: Srm Contracting & Paving
7192 Mission Gorge Rd, San Diego
(92120-1131)
PHONE..................................619 265-0955
Brent Cooper, *Brnch Mgr*
EMP: 70
SALES (corp-wide): 205.26MM **Privately Held**
Web: www.superiorrm.com
SIC: 3273 Ready-mixed concrete
PA: Superior Ready Mix Concrete L.P.
1564 Mission Rd
760 745-0556

**(P-7506)**
**SUPERIOR READY MIX CONCRETE LP**
Also Called: Canyon Rock & Asphalt
7500 Mission Gorge Rd, San Diego
(92120-1304)
PHONE..................................619 265-0296
Tracy Mall, *Mgr*
EMP: 70
SALES (corp-wide): 205.26MM **Privately Held**
Web: www.superiorrm.com
SIC: 3273 Ready-mixed concrete
PA: Superior Ready Mix Concrete L.P.
1564 Mission Rd
760 745-0556

**(P-7507)**
**SUPERIOR READY MIX CONCRETE LP**
802 E Main St, El Centro (92243-9474)
P.O. Box 400 (92244-0400)
PHONE..................................760 352-4341
Donald Lee, *Brnch Mgr*
EMP: 70
SALES (corp-wide): 205.26MM **Privately Held**
Web: www.superiorrm.com

## PRODUCTS & SERVICES SECTION
### 3275 - Gypsum Products (P-7527)

SIC: **3273** Ready-mixed concrete
PA: Superior Ready Mix Concrete L.P.
1564 Mission Rd
760 745-0556

### (P-7508)
### SUPERIOR READY MIX CONCRETE LP
Also Called: American Ready Mix
1564 Mission Rd, Escondido (92029-1194)
PHONE.................760 728-1128
Greg Sage, *Mgr*
EMP: 71
SALES (corp-wide): 205.26MM **Privately Held**
Web: www.superiorrm.com
SIC: **3273** 1442 Ready-mixed concrete; Construction sand and gravel
PA: Superior Ready Mix Concrete L.P.
1564 Mission Rd
760 745-0556

### (P-7509)
### SUPERIOR READY MIX CONCRETE LP
Also Called: Superior Ready Mix Concrete
24635 Temescal Canyon Rd, Corona (92883-5422)
PHONE.................951 277-3553
Justine Moss, *Brnch Mgr*
EMP: 71
SALES (corp-wide): 205.26MM **Privately Held**
Web: www.superiorrm.com
SIC: **3273** Ready-mixed concrete
PA: Superior Ready Mix Concrete L.P.
1564 Mission Rd
760 745-0556

### (P-7510)
### SUPERIOR READY MIX CONCRETE LP (PA)
Also Called: Southland Ready Mix Concrete
1564 Mission Rd, Escondido (92029-1194)
PHONE.................760 745-0556
Donald Lee, *Pr*
EMP: 50 EST: 1957
SALES (est): 205.26MM
SALES (corp-wide): 205.26MM **Privately Held**
Web: www.superiorrm.com
SIC: **3273** 1611 5032 Ready-mixed concrete; Surfacing and paving; Gravel

### (P-7511)
### SUPERIOR READY MIX CONCRETE LP
Also Called: Hemet Ready Mix
1130 N State St, Hemet (92543-1510)
PHONE.................951 658-9225
Wayne Heckerman, *Prin*
EMP: 71
SALES (corp-wide): 205.26MM **Privately Held**
Web: www.superiorrm.com
SIC: **3273** 5211 Ready-mixed concrete; Masonry materials and supplies
PA: Superior Ready Mix Concrete L.P.
1564 Mission Rd
760 745-0556

### (P-7512)
### SUPERIOR READY MIX CONCRETE LP
Also Called: TTT Concrete
12494 Highway 67, Lakeside (92040-1133)
PHONE.................619 443-7510
Jerry Anderson, *Mgr*
EMP: 71

SQ FT: 3,200
SALES (corp-wide): 205.26MM **Privately Held**
Web: www.superiorrm.com
SIC: **3273** Ready-mixed concrete
PA: Superior Ready Mix Concrete L.P.
1564 Mission Rd
760 745-0556

### (P-7513)
### SUPERIOR READY MIX CONCRETE LP
Also Called: Superior Ready Mix Concrete
72270 Varner Rd, Thousand Palms (92276-3341)
PHONE.................760 343-3418
Mark Higgins, *Mgr*
EMP: 71
SALES (corp-wide): 205.26MM **Privately Held**
Web: www.superiorrm.com
SIC: **3273** Ready-mixed concrete
PA: Superior Ready Mix Concrete L.P.
1564 Mission Rd
760 745-0556

### (P-7514)
### SYAR INDUSTRIES INC
Also Called: Syar Industries
13666 Healdsburg Ave, Healdsburg (95448-9234)
P.O. Box 325 (95448-0325)
PHONE.................707 433-3366
Dick Love, *Mgr*
EMP: 15
Web: www.syarindustriesinc.com
SIC: **3273** Ready-mixed concrete
HQ: Syar Industries, Llc
2301 Napa Vallejo Hwy
Napa CA 94558
707 252-8711

### (P-7515)
### TEICHERT INC (PA)
5200 Franklin Dr Ste 115, Pleasanton (94588-3363)
P.O. Box 15002 (95851-0002)
PHONE.................916 484-3011
Judson T Riggs, *Pr*
Louis V Riggs, *
Narendra M Pathipati, *
Anne S Haslam, *
▲ EMP: 161 EST: 1887
SALES (est): 827.08MM
SALES (corp-wide): 827.08MM **Privately Held**
Web: www.teichert.com
SIC: **3273** 5032 1611 1442 Ready-mixed concrete; Brick, stone, and related material; Highway and street construction; Construction sand and gravel

### (P-7516)
### TEICHERT INC
Also Called: Teichert Readymix
8609 Jackson Rd, Sacramento (95826-9731)
PHONE.................916 386-6974
Dave Bearden, *Div Mgr*
EMP: 57
SALES (corp-wide): 827.08MM **Privately Held**
Web: www.teichert.com
SIC: **3273** Ready-mixed concrete
HQ: A. Teichert & Son, Inc.
3500 American River Dr
Sacramento CA 95864

### (P-7517)
### TEICHERT INC
Also Called: Teichert Readymix
721 Berry St, Roseville (95678-1307)
PHONE.................916 783-7132
Dave Bearden, *Div Mgr*
EMP: 30
SALES (corp-wide): 827.08MM **Privately Held**
Web: www.teichert.com
SIC: **3273** Ready-mixed concrete
HQ: A. Teichert & Son, Inc.
3500 American River Dr
Sacramento CA 95864

### (P-7518)
### VULCAN CONSTRUCTION MTLS LLC
346 Mathew St, Santa Clara (95050-3114)
PHONE.................408 213-4270
EMP: 20
Web: www.vulcanmaterials.com
SIC: **3273** Ready-mixed concrete
HQ: Vulcan Construction Materials, Llc
1200 Urban Ctr Dr
Birmingham AL 35242
205 298-3000

### (P-7519)
### VULCAN CONSTRUCTION MTLS LLC
35800 146th St E, Pearblossom (93553)
PHONE.................661 810-2285
James Mcconnell, *Brnch Mgr*
EMP: 20
Web: www.vulcanmaterials.com
SIC: **3273** Ready-mixed concrete
HQ: Vulcan Construction Materials, Llc
1200 Urban Ctr Dr
Birmingham AL 35242
205 298-3000

### (P-7520)
### VULCAN MATERIALS CO
849 W Washington Ave, Escondido (92025-1634)
PHONE.................760 737-3486
TOLL FREE: 800
A F Gerstell, *Pr*
EMP: 210 EST: 1957
SALES (est): 531.78K **Publicly Held**
SIC: **3273** Ready-mixed concrete
HQ: Calmat Co.
1200 Urban Center Dr
Birmingham AL 35242
818 553-8821

### (P-7521)
### WERNER CORPORATION
Also Called: Foster Sand & Gravel
25050 Maitri Rd, Corona (92883-5105)
P.O. Box 77850 (92877-0128)
PHONE.................951 277-4586
Mark Miller, *Mgr*
EMP: 20
SALES (corp-wide): 9.43MM **Privately Held**
Web: www.wernercorp.net
SIC: **3273** Ready-mixed concrete
PA: Werner Corporation
25555 Maitri Rd
951 277-3900

### (P-7522)
### WESTWOOD BUILDING MATERIALS CO
15708 Inglewood Ave, Lawndale (90260-2544)
PHONE.................310 643-9158

Craig St John, *Pr*
Liza Peitzmeier, *
EMP: 36 EST: 1941
SQ FT: 23,500
SALES (est): 10.06MM **Privately Held**
Web: www.westwoodbm.com
SIC: **3273** Ready-mixed concrete

## 3274 Lime

### (P-7523)
### LIME LIGHT CRM INC
89 De Boom St, San Francisco (94107-1425)
PHONE.................800 455-9645
Brian A Bogosian, *Pr*
EMP: 18 EST: 2015
SALES (est): 540.65K **Privately Held**
Web: www.sticky.io
SIC: **3274** Lime

## 3275 Gypsum Products

### (P-7524)
### GEORGIA-PACIFIC LLC
Also Called: Georgia-Pacific
801 Minaker Dr, Antioch (94509-2134)
P.O. Box 460 (94509-0511)
PHONE.................925 757-2870
Kurt Betty, *Mgr*
EMP: 90
SALES (corp-wide): 64.37B **Privately Held**
Web: www.gp.com
SIC: **3275** Wallboard, gypsum
HQ: Georgia-Pacific Llc
133 Peachtree St Nw
Atlanta GA 30303
404 652-4000

### (P-7525)
### PABCO BUILDING PRODUCTS LLC
Also Called: Pabco Gypsum
37851 Cherry St, Newark (94560-4348)
P.O. Box 405 (94560-0405)
PHONE.................510 792-9555
Phil Bonnell, *Pr*
EMP: 114
SALES (corp-wide): 1.21B **Privately Held**
Web: www.pabcogypsum.com
SIC: **3275** Gypsum products
HQ: Pabco Building Products, Llc
10811 International Dr
Rancho Cordova CA 95670
510 792-1577

### (P-7526)
### PABCO BUILDING PRODUCTS LLC
37849 Cherry St, Newark (94560-4348)
PHONE.................510 792-1577
Ryan Lucchetti, *Pr*
EMP: 31
SALES (corp-wide): 1.21B **Privately Held**
Web: www.pabcogypsum.com
SIC: **3275** 3251 3259 Gypsum products; Brick clay: common face, glazed, vitrified, or hollow; Architectural terra cotta
HQ: Pabco Building Products, Llc
10811 International Dr
Rancho Cordova CA 95670
510 792-1577

### (P-7527)
### PABCO BUILDING PRODUCTS LLC (HQ)
Also Called: Quietrock
10811 International Dr, Rancho Cordova (95670-7319)

# 3275 - Gypsum Products (P-7528)

## PRODUCTS & SERVICES SECTION

P.O. Box 419074 (95741-9074)
PHONE..............................510 792-1577
Phil Bonnell, *Pr*
Emil Kopilovich, *VP Mfg*
Brian Hobdy, *CFO*
Michael Willoughby, *Quality Vice President*
John Corbett, *ROOFING Operations*
▲ **EMP:** 20 **EST:** 1976
**SALES (est):** 171.4MM
**SALES (corp-wide):** 1.21B **Privately Held**
Web: www.pabcogypsum.com
**SIC: 3275** 3251 3259 Gypsum products; Brick clay: common face, glazed, vitrified, or hollow; Architectural terra cotta
**PA:** Pacific Coast Building Products, Inc.
  10811 International Dr
  916 631-6500

### (P-7528)
### PABCO BUILDING PRODUCTS LLC
Also Called: Pabco Paper
4460 Pacific Blvd, Vernon (90058-2206)
PHONE..............................323 581-6113
Phil Bonnell, *Pr*
**EMP:** 134
**SALES (corp-wide):** 1.21B **Privately Held**
Web: www.pabcogypsum.com
**SIC: 3275** Gypsum products
**HQ:** Pabco Building Products, Llc
  10811 International Dr
  Rancho Cordova CA 95670
  510 792-1577

### (P-7529)
### PACIFIC COAST BUILDING PRODUCTS INC (PA)
10811 International Dr, Rancho Cordova (95670-7319)
P.O. Box 419074 (95741)
PHONE..............................916 631-6500
◆ **EMP:** 120 **EST:** 1953
**SALES (est):** 1.21B
**SALES (corp-wide):** 1.21B **Privately Held**
Web: www.paccoast.com
**SIC: 3275** 3271 5031 1761 Wallboard, gypsum; Concrete block and brick; Lumber, plywood, and millwork; Roofing contractor

### (P-7530)
### PACIFIC COAST SUPPLY LLC
Also Called: Pacific Supply
30158 Road 68, Visalia (93291-9586)
P.O. Box 1429 (93279-1429)
PHONE..............................559 651-2185
Kevin Viera, *Brnch Mgr*
**EMP:** 30
**SALES (corp-wide):** 1.21B **Privately Held**
Web: www.paccoastsupply.com
**SIC: 3275** 3272 2952 5211 Wallboard, gypsum; Concrete products, nec; Asphalt felts and coatings; Lumber and other building materials
**HQ:** Pacific Coast Supply, Llc
  4290 Roseville Rd
  North Highlands CA 95660
  916 971-2301

### (P-7531)
### PROFORM FINISHING PRODUCTS LLC
1850 Pier B St, Long Beach (90813-2604)
P.O. Box 1888 (90801-1888)
PHONE..............................562 435-4465
Tim Fout, *Mgr*
**EMP:** 39
**SALES (corp-wide):** 795.88MM **Privately Held**
Web: www.nationalgypsum.com
**SIC: 3275** Gypsum products
**HQ:** Proform Finishing Products, Llc
  2001 Rexford Rd
  Charlotte NC 28211

### (P-7532)
### UNITED STATES GYPSUM COMPANY
401 Van Ness Ave, Torrance (90501-1422)
PHONE..............................908 232-8900
Matt Craig, *Mgr*
**EMP:** 100
**SQ FT:** 71,800
**SALES (corp-wide):** 16B **Privately Held**
Web: www.usg.com
**SIC: 3275** Gypsum products
**HQ:** United States Gypsum Company
  550 W Adams St
  Chicago IL 60661
  312 606-4000

### (P-7533)
### UNITED STATES GYPSUM COMPANY
3810 Evan Hewes Hwy, Imperial (92251-9529)
P.O. Box 2450 (92244-2450)
PHONE..............................760 358-3200
George Keelan, *Dir Fin*
**EMP:** 102
**SALES (corp-wide):** 16B **Privately Held**
Web: www.usg.com
**SIC: 3275** Gypsum products
**HQ:** United States Gypsum Company
  550 W Adams St
  Chicago IL 60661
  312 606-4000

## 3281 Cut Stone And Stone Products

### (P-7534)
### BEST-WAY MARBLE & TILE CO INC
Also Called: Best Way Marble
5037 Telegraph Rd, Los Angeles (90022-4922)
PHONE..............................323 266-6794
Shelley Herrera, *Pr*
◆ **EMP:** 28 **EST:** 1981
**SQ FT:** 16,000
**SALES (est):** 2.45MM **Privately Held**
Web: www.bestwaymarble.com
**SIC: 3281** 1743 Table tops, marble; Marble installation, interior

### (P-7535)
### CARNEVALE & LOHR INC
6521 Clara St, Bell Gardens (90201-5634)
PHONE..............................562 927-8311
Louie Carnevale, *CEO*
Edmund B Lohr Iv, *Prin*
David Carnevale, *
Michael Carnevale, *
▲ **EMP:** 33 **EST:** 1958
**SALES (est):** 4.01MM **Privately Held**
Web: www.carnevaleandlohr.com
**SIC: 3281** 1741 Cut stone and stone products; Marble masonry, exterior construction

### (P-7536)
### COAST FLAGSTONE CO
1810 Colorado Ave, Santa Monica (90404-3412)
PHONE..............................310 829-4010
Timothy Wang, *Owner*
**EMP:** 70 **EST:** 2010

**SALES (est):** 986.4K **Privately Held**
Web: www.bourgetbros.com
**SIC: 3281** Flagstones

### (P-7537)
### GGF MARBLE & SUPPLY INC
1375 Franquette Ave Ste F, Concord (94520-7932)
PHONE..............................925 676-8385
Gaspare G Fundaro, *Pr*
◆ **EMP:** 23 **EST:** 1986
**SQ FT:** 2,500
**SALES (est):** 234.36K **Privately Held**
Web: www.gmmarbleandgranite.net
**SIC: 3281** Furniture, cut stone

### (P-7538)
### GREAT WALL INTERNATIONAL CORP
Also Called: Gw Stone
617 S Raymond Ave, Alhambra (91803-1534)
PHONE..............................626 457-1022
Mandy Li, *Pr*
◆ **EMP:** 15 **EST:** 1998
**SALES (est):** 1.94MM **Privately Held**
Web: www.mandylicollection.com
**SIC: 3281** Cut stone and stone products

### (P-7539)
### HALABI INC (PA)
Also Called: Duracite
4447 Green Valley Rd, Fairfield (94534-1365)
PHONE..............................707 402-1600
**TOLL FREE:** 800
Fadi M Halabi, *CEO*
George Marino, *
◆ **EMP:** 137 **EST:** 1995
**SALES (est):** 8.26MM
**SALES (corp-wide):** 8.26MM **Privately Held**
Web: www.duracite.com
**SIC: 3281** 1799 Cut stone and stone products; Counter top installation

### (P-7540)
### KAMMERER ENTERPRISES INC
Also Called: American Marble
1280 N Melrose Dr, Vista (92083-3469)
PHONE..............................760 560-0550
William S Kammerer, *CEO*
Bill Kammerer, *
Karl Miethke, *
▲ **EMP:** 100 **EST:** 1985
**SALES (est):** 15.21MM **Privately Held**
Web: www.amarble.com
**SIC: 3281** Curbing, granite or stone

### (P-7541)
### L&S STONE LLC (DH)
Also Called: L & S Stone and Fireplace Shop
1370 Grand Ave Ste B, San Marcos (92078-2404)
PHONE..............................760 736-3232
◆ **EMP:** 50 **EST:** 1970
**SQ FT:** 35,000
**SALES (est):** 15.99MM **Privately Held**
Web: www.eldoradostone.com
**SIC: 3281** Cut stone and stone products
**HQ:** Eldorado Stone Llc
  3817 Ocean Ranch Blvd # 114
  Oceanside CA 92056
  800 925-1491

### (P-7542)
### MANTELS & MORE CORP
2909 Tanager Ave, Commerce (90040-2723)
PHONE..............................323 869-9764

**EMP:** 16
**SALES (est):** 918.16K **Privately Held**
**SIC: 3281** Stone, quarrying and processing of own stone products

### (P-7543)
### PAVESTONE LLC
27600 County Road 90, Winters (95694-9003)
PHONE..............................530 795-4400
Wes May, *Mgr*
**EMP:** 49
Web: www.pavestone.com
**SIC: 3281** Paving blocks, cut stone
**HQ:** Pavestone, Llc
  5 Concourse Pkwy Ste 1900
  Atlanta GA 30328
  404 926-3167

### (P-7544)
### RUGGERI MARBLE AND GRANITE INC
25028 Vermont Ave, Harbor City (90710-3116)
PHONE..............................310 513-2155
Andre Ruggeri, *Pr*
Robert Ruggeri, *
◆ **EMP:** 80 **EST:** 1991
**SALES (est):** 4.6MM **Privately Held**
Web: www.ruggerimarble.com
**SIC: 3281** 5032 Marble, building: cut and shaped; Ceramic wall and floor tile, nec

### (P-7545)
### SAMPLE TILE AND STONE INC
1410 Richardson St, San Bernardino (92408-2962)
PHONE..............................951 776-8562
Curtis Sample, *CEO*
**EMP:** 45 **EST:** 2011
**SQ FT:** 13,500
**SALES (est):** 6.07MM **Privately Held**
Web: www.sampletileandstone.com
**SIC: 3281** 5032 1411 1743 Cut stone and stone products; Limestone; Limestone and marble dimension stone; Terrazzo, tile, marble and mosaic work

### (P-7546)
### SINOSOURCE INTL CO INC
282 Harbor Way, South San Francisco (94080-6816)
PHONE..............................650 697-6668
Ken Jiang, *Pr*
◆ **EMP:** 15 **EST:** 1999
**SALES (est):** 2.6MM **Privately Held**
Web: www.sinosource.biz
**SIC: 3281** Urns, cut stone

### (P-7547)
### SOUTH BAY MARBLE INC
797 Industrial Rd, San Carlos (94070-3310)
PHONE..............................650 592-7416
Mike Sutton, *of Mfng Operations*
**EMP:** 15
**SALES (corp-wide):** 755.86K **Privately Held**
Web: www.southbaymarble.com
**SIC: 3281** Marble, building: cut and shaped
**PA:** South Bay Marble, Inc.
  7633 Arya Ct
  650 594-4251

### (P-7548)
### STANDRIDGE GRANITE CORPORATION
9437 Santa Fe Springs Rd, Santa Fe Springs (90670-2684)
PHONE..............................562 946-6334

# PRODUCTS & SERVICES SECTION

## 3295 - Minerals, Ground Or Treated (P-7569)

Deborah Deleon, *Pr*
**EMP:** 30 **EST:** 1965
**SQ FT:** 24,000
**SALES (est):** 5.41MM **Privately Held**
Web: www.standridgegranite.com
**SIC: 3281** 1411 Granite, cut and shaped; Dimension stone

### (P-7549)
### SULLIVANS STONE FACTORY INC
83778 Avenue 45, Indio (92201-3310)
**PHONE**...................760 347-5535
Robert J Sullivan, *Pr*
▲ **EMP:** 25 **EST:** 2004
**SALES (est):** 2.41MM **Privately Held**
Web: www.sullivansstonefactory.com
**SIC: 3281** Granite, cut and shaped

### (P-7550)
### WESTLAKE ROYAL STONE LLC
3817 Ocean Ranch Blvd, Oceanside (92056-8607)
**PHONE**...................800 255-1727
Michael Mildenhall, *Managing Member*
**EMP:** 63 **EST:** 2006
**SALES (est):** 4.56MM **Publicly Held**
Web: www.elevatewithstone.com
**SIC: 3281** Building stone products
**HQ:** Westlake Pipe & Fittings Corporation
2801 Post Oak Blvd Ste 60
Houston TX 77056

## 3291 Abrasive Products

### (P-7551)
### BUFF AND SHINE MFG INC
2139 E Del Amo Blvd, Rancho Dominguez (90220-6301)
**PHONE**...................310 886-5111
Richard Umbrell, *Pr*
Elizabeth Umbrell, *
◆ **EMP:** 40 **EST:** 1987
**SQ FT:** 25,792
**SALES (est):** 4.22MM **Privately Held**
Web: www.buffandshine.com
**SIC: 3291** Buffing or polishing wheels, abrasive or nonabrasive

### (P-7552)
### CRATEX MANUFACTURING CO INC
Also Called: Cratex
328 Encinitas Blvd Ste 200, Encinitas (92024-3723)
**PHONE**...................760 942-2877
Allen R Mccasland, *CEO*
Barbara Mccasland, *Sec*
▲ **EMP:** 75 **EST:** 1946
**SALES (est):** 5.06MM **Privately Held**
Web: www.cratex.com
**SIC: 3291** Wheels, grinding: artificial

### (P-7553)
### HONE MAXWELL LLP
3465 Camino Del Rio S Ste 400, San Diego (92108-3909)
**PHONE**...................415 765-1754
Aubrey Hone, *Prin*
**EMP:** 15 **EST:** 2013
**SALES (est):** 1.63MM **Privately Held**
Web: www.honemaxwell.com
**SIC: 3291** Hones

### (P-7554)
### JASON INCORPORATED
Jackson Lea Division
13006 Philadelphia St Ste 305, Whittier (90601-4210)

**PHONE**...................562 921-9821
Ron Locher, *Brnch Mgr*
**EMP:** 25
**SQ FT:** 30,000
**SALES (corp-wide):** 173.28MM **Privately Held**
Web: www.osborn.com
**SIC: 3291** 2273 3599 Buffing or polishing wheels, abrasive or nonabrasive; Automobile floor coverings, except rubber or plastic; Custom machinery
**PA:** Jason Incorporated
833 E Michigan St Ste 900

### (P-7555)
### MAVERICK ABRASIVES CORPORATION
4340 E Miraloma Ave, Anaheim (92807-1886)
**PHONE**...................714 854-9531
Rami Aryan, *Pr*
◆ **EMP:** 60 **EST:** 1997
**SQ FT:** 15,000
**SALES (est):** 9.83MM **Privately Held**
Web: www.maverickabrasives.com
**SIC: 3291** Abrasive products

### (P-7556)
### MIPOX INTERNATIONAL CORP
1065 E Hillsdale Blvd Ste 401, Foster City (94404-1613)
**PHONE**...................650 638-9830
Tetsujiro Tada, *Pr*
◆ **EMP:** 26 **EST:** 1989
**SQ FT:** 14,000
**SALES (est):** 1.3MM **Privately Held**
Web: www.mipox.co.jp
**SIC: 3291** Abrasive products
**PA:** Mipox Corporation
18, Satsukicho

### (P-7557)
### SIMPSON MANUFACTURING CO INC
5151 S Airport Way, Stockton (95206-3991)
**PHONE**...................209 234-7775
David Mcdonald, *Mgr*
**EMP:** 30
**SALES (corp-wide):** 2.21B **Publicly Held**
Web: www.simpsonmfg.com
**SIC: 3291** Metallic abrasive
**PA:** Simpson Manufacturing Co., Inc.
5956 W Las Positas Blvd
925 560-9000

### (P-7558)
### TECHNIFEX PRODUCTS LLC
25261 Rye Canyon Rd, Valencia (91355-1203)
**PHONE**...................661 294-3800
Joe Ortiz, *VP*
▲ **EMP:** 25 **EST:** 1999
**SALES (est):** 4.87MM **Privately Held**
Web: www.technifex.com
**SIC: 3291** Steel wool

### (P-7559)
### VIBRA FINISH CO (PA)
Also Called: Vibrahone
2220 Shasta Way, Simi Valley (93065-1831)
**PHONE**...................805 578-0033
Haskel Hall, *Pr*
Jerry Rindal, *VP*
▲ **EMP:** 20 **EST:** 1924
**SQ FT:** 41,000
**SALES (est):** 5.2MM
**SALES (corp-wide):** 5.2MM **Privately Held**
Web: www.vibrafinish.com

**SIC: 3291** Abrasive products

### (P-7560)
### YEAGER ENTERPRISES CORP
Also Called: Pasco
7100 Village Dr, Buena Park (90621-2261)
**PHONE**...................714 994-2040
Joseph O'mera, *CEO*
David M Yeager, *
Joan F Yeager, *
▲ **EMP:** 81 **EST:** 1920
**SQ FT:** 55,000
**SALES (est):** 1.34MM **Privately Held**
**SIC: 3291** Abrasive products

## 3292 Asbestos Products

### (P-7561)
### HHB HOLDINGS INC
2600 Central Ave Ste E, Union City (94587-3126)
P.O. Box 2936 (31534-2936)
**PHONE**...................510 489-8100
▲ **EMP:** 110
**SIC: 3292** 3559 Blankets, insulating for aircraft asbestos; Bag seaming and closing machines (sewing machinery)

### (P-7562)
### LAMART CORPORATION
Also Called: Orcon Aerospace
2600 Central Ave Ste E, Union City (94587-3126)
P.O. Box 487 (94914-0487)
**PHONE**...................510 489-8100
**EMP:** 110
**SALES (corp-wide):** 28.22MM **Privately Held**
Web: www.lamartcorp.com
**SIC: 3292** 3559 Blankets, insulating for aircraft asbestos; Bag seaming and closing machines (sewing machinery)
**PA:** Lamart Corporation
16 Richmond St
973 772-6262

## 3295 Minerals, Ground Or Treated

### (P-7563)
### 3M COMPANY
Also Called: 3M
18750 Minnesota Rd, Corona (92881-4313)
**PHONE**...................951 737-3441
Flees Peter, *Brnch Mgr*
**EMP:** 47
**SALES (corp-wide):** 32.68B **Publicly Held**
Web: www.3m.com
**SIC: 3295** 2952 Roofing granules; Asphalt felts and coatings
**PA:** 3m Company
3m Center
651 733-1110

### (P-7564)
### AZTEC PERLITE COMPANY INC
1518 Simpson Way, Escondido (92029-1205)
**PHONE**...................760 741-1733
Domenic Di Nardo, *Pr*
Anna Di Nardo, *Owner*
**EMP:** 15 **EST:** 1976
**SQ FT:** 5,000
**SALES (est):** 917K **Privately Held**
Web: www.aztecperlite.com
**SIC: 3295** Perlite, aggregate or expanded

### (P-7565)
### DICALITE MINERALS LLC (HQ)
Also Called: Dicalite
36994 Summit Lake Rd, Burney (96013-9636)
**PHONE**...................530 335-5451
Raymond Perlman, *Pr*
◆ **EMP:** 24 **EST:** 1995
**SQ FT:** 3,000
**SALES (est):** 2.98MM
**SALES (corp-wide):** 111.67MM **Privately Held**
Web: www.dicalite.com
**SIC: 3295** Minerals, ground or treated
**PA:** Dicalite Management Group, Llc
1001 Cnshohckn State Rd 2-201
610 660-8808

### (P-7566)
### IMERYS FILTRATION MINERALS INC (DH)
1732 N 1st St Ste 450, San Jose (95112-4579)
**PHONE**...................805 562-0200
Douglas A Smith, *CEO*
John Oskan, *
Paul Woodberry, *
Fred Weber, *
◆ **EMP:** 50 **EST:** 1992
**SQ FT:** 11,600
**SALES (est):** 101.4MM
**SALES (corp-wide):** 5.36MM **Privately Held**
Web: www.imerys.com
**SIC: 3295** Minerals, ground or treated
**HQ:** Imerys Usa, Inc.
100 Mansell Ct E Ste 300
Roswell GA 30076
770 645-3300

### (P-7567)
### IMERYS TALC AMERICA INC (DH)
1732 N 1st St Ste 450, San Jose (95112-4579)
◆ **EMP:** 277 **EST:** 1992
**SALES (est):** 46.36MM
**SALES (corp-wide):** 5.36MM **Privately Held**
**SIC: 3295** 1499 Talc, ground or otherwise treated; Talc mining
**HQ:** Imerys
43 Quai De Grenelle
Paris 15 IDF 75015
142229512

### (P-7568)
### ISP GRANULE PRODUCTS INC
1900 Hwy 104, Ione (95640)
**PHONE**...................209 274-2930
Sunil Kumar, *Pr*
**EMP:** 195 **EST:** 2002
**SALES (est):** 689.98K
**SALES (corp-wide):** 6.35B **Privately Held**
**SIC: 3295** Roofing granules
**HQ:** Isp Minerals Llc
34 Charles St
Hagerstown MD 21740

### (P-7569)
### JOHN CRANE INC
Also Called: Crane, John
12760 Florence Ave, Santa Fe Springs (90670-3906)
**PHONE**...................562 802-2555
Dave Bretfch, *Genl Mgr*
**EMP:** 15
**SALES (corp-wide):** 3.97B **Privately Held**
Web: www.johncrane.com

## 3295 - Minerals, Ground Or Treated (P-7570)

SIC: **3295** 3541 3053 Minerals, ground or treated; Lapping machines; Gaskets; packing and sealing devices
HQ: John Crane Inc.
6400 Oakton St
Morton Grove IL 60053
312 605-7800

**(P-7570)**
**JON BROOKS INC (PA)**
Also Called: Laguna Clay Company
14400 Lomitas Ave, City Of Industry (91746-3018)
PHONE.................626 330-0631
Jon Brooks, *Pr*
Laurie Brooks, *
◆ **EMP:** 100 **EST:** 1981
**SQ FT:** 117,000
**SALES (est):** 20.91MM
**SALES (corp-wide):** 20.91MM **Privately Held**
Web: www.lagunaclay.com
SIC: **3295** 5085 Clay, ground or otherwise treated; Refractory material

**(P-7571)**
**SGL TECHNIC LLC (DH)**
Also Called: Inc Polycarbon
28176 Avenue Stanford, Valencia (91355-1119)
PHONE.................661 257-0500
Ken Mamon, *Pr*
Brian Green, *VP*
▲ **EMP:** 48 **EST:** 1967
**SQ FT:** 130,000
**SALES (est):** 13.74MM
**SALES (corp-wide):** 1.18B **Privately Held**
Web: www.sglcarbon.com
SIC: **3295** 3624 Graphite, natural: ground, pulverized, refined, or blended; Carbon and graphite products
HQ: Sgl Carbon, Llc
10715 Dvid Tylor Dr Ste 4
Charlotte NC 28262
704 593-5100

**(P-7572)**
**SPECIALTY GRANULES LLC**
1900 State Hwy 104, Ione (95640)
P.O. Box 400 (95640-0400)
PHONE.................209 274-5323
George Dias, *Manager*
**EMP:** 50
**SALES (corp-wide):** 6.35B **Privately Held**
Web: www.specialtygranules.com
SIC: **3295** Roofing granules
HQ: Specialty Granules Llc
13424 Pa Ave Ste 303
Hagerstown MD 21742
301 733-4000

### 3296 Mineral Wool

**(P-7573)**
**C A SCHROEDER INC (PA)**
Also Called: Casco Mfg
1318 1st St, San Fernando (91340-2804)
PHONE.................818 365-9561
Susan A Knudsen, *CEO*
Clifford A Schroeder, *
**EMP:** 42 **EST:** 1969
**SQ FT:** 18,500
**SALES (est):** 7.17MM
**SALES (corp-wide):** 7.17MM **Privately Held**
Web: www.casco-flex.com
SIC: **3296** 3585 3444 3433 Fiberglass insulation; Refrigeration and heating equipment; Sheet metalwork; Heating equipment, except electric

**(P-7574)**
**CERTAINTEED LLC**
17775 Avenue 23 1/2, Chowchilla (93610-9551)
PHONE.................559 665-4831
James Vicary, *Mgr*
**EMP:** 57
**SALES (corp-wide):** 402.18MM **Privately Held**
Web: www.certainteed.com
SIC: **3296** 5033 Fiberglass insulation; Insulation materials
HQ: Certainteed Llc
20 Moores Rd
Malvern PA 19355
610 893-5000

**(P-7575)**
**CONSOLIDATED FIBRGLS PDTS CO**
Also Called: Conglas
3801 Standard St, Bakersfield (93308-5230)
PHONE.................661 323-6026
Daron J Thomas, *CEO*
Jack Pfeffer, *
**EMP:** 60 **EST:** 1972
**SQ FT:** 20,000
**SALES (est):** 7.81MM **Privately Held**
SIC: **3296** Fiberglass insulation

**(P-7576)**
**JOHNS MANVILLE CORPORATION**
4301 Firestone Blvd, South Gate (90280-3318)
PHONE.................323 568-2220
Rudi Bianchi, *Mgr*
**EMP:** 54
**SALES (corp-wide):** 364.48B **Publicly Held**
Web: www.jm.com
SIC: **3296** Mineral wool
HQ: Johns Manville Corporation
717 17th St
Denver CO 80202
303 978-2000

**(P-7577)**
**JOHNS MANVILLE CORPORATION**
5916 County Road 49, Willows (95988-9703)
PHONE.................530 934-6243
Tom Lowe, *Brnch Mgr*
**EMP:** 58
**SALES (corp-wide):** 364.48B **Publicly Held**
Web: www.jm.com
SIC: **3296** Fiberglass insulation
HQ: Johns Manville Corporation
717 17th St
Denver CO 80202
303 978-2000

**(P-7578)**
**KAINALU BLUE INC**
4675 North Ave, Oceanside (92056-3511)
PHONE.................760 806-6400
Robin Gray, *Pr*
**EMP:** 30 **EST:** 1965
**SQ FT:** 30,000
**SALES (est):** 4.62MM **Privately Held**
Web: www.lamvin.com
SIC: **3296** 3275 Acoustical board and tile, mineral wool; Gypsum products

**(P-7579)**
**KNAUF INSULATION INC**
Also Called: Knauf Insulation
3100 Ashby Rd, Shasta Lake (96019-9136)
PHONE.................530 275-9665
Bill Taylor, *Brnch Mgr*
**EMP:** 592
**SALES (corp-wide):** 16B **Privately Held**
Web: www.knaufnorthamerica.com
SIC: **3296** Fiberglass insulation
HQ: Knauf Insulation, Inc.
1 Knauf Dr
Shelbyville IN 46176
317 398-4434

**(P-7580)**
**LAMART CALIFORNIA INC**
7560 Bristow Ct Ste C, San Diego (92154-7428)
P.O. Box 1648 (07015-1648)
PHONE.................973 772-6262
Steven Hirsh, *Pr*
Graeme Silbert, *CFO*
**EMP:** 20 **EST:** 2016
**SALES (est):** 3.81MM
**SALES (corp-wide):** 28.22MM **Privately Held**
Web: www.lamartcorp.com
SIC: **3296** Fiberglass insulation
PA: Lamart Corporation
16 Richmond St
973 772-6262

**(P-7581)**
**ROCK STRUCTURES-RIP RAP**
11126 Silverton Ct, Corona (92881-5626)
PHONE.................951 371-1112
Antonio Paredes, *Owner*
**EMP:** 30 **EST:** 2003
**SQ FT:** 3,500
**SALES (est):** 2.34MM **Privately Held**
SIC: **3296** Insulation: rock wool, slag, and silica minerals

**(P-7582)**
**SOUND SEAL INC**
Lamvin
4675 North Ave, Oceanside (92056-3511)
PHONE.................760 806-6400
Robin Gray, *Mgr*
**EMP:** 25
Web: www.soundseal.com
SIC: **3296** 3275 Acoustical board and tile, mineral wool; Gypsum products
HQ: Sound Seal, Inc.
50 Hp Almgren Dr
Agawam MA 01001
413 789-1770

**(P-7583)**
**USMPC BUYER INC**
Also Called: Isolatek International
4062 Georgia Blvd, San Bernardino (92407-1847)
PHONE.................909 473-3027
Adrienne Bowen, *Brnch Mgr*
**EMP:** 41
**SALES (corp-wide):** 28.2MM **Privately Held**
Web: www.isolatek.com
SIC: **3296** Mineral wool insulation products
PA: Usmpc Buyer Inc.
41 Furnace St
973 347-1200

### 3299 Nonmetallic Mineral Products,

**(P-7584)**
**3M TECHNICAL CERAMICS INC (HQ)**
1922 Barranca Pkwy, Irvine (92606-4826)
PHONE.................949 862-9600
Joel P Moskowitz, *CEO*
Jerrold J Pellizzon, *Corporate Secretary**
Thomas A Cole, *
Terry M Hart, *
David P Reed, *Assistant Corporate Secretary**
◆ **EMP:** 78 **EST:** 1987
**SQ FT:** 99,000
**SALES (est):** 284.05MM
**SALES (corp-wide):** 32.68B **Publicly Held**
Web: www.ceradyne.com
SIC: **3299** 3671 Ceramic fiber; Cathode ray tubes, including rebuilt
PA: 3m Company
3m Center
651 733-1110

**(P-7585)**
**3M TECHNICAL CERAMICS INC**
17466 Daimler St, Irvine (92614-5514)
PHONE.................949 756-0642
Joel Moskowitz, *Brnch Mgr*
**EMP:** 25
**SQ FT:** 33,965
**SALES (corp-wide):** 32.68B **Publicly Held**
Web: www.ceradyne.com
SIC: **3299** 3264 Ceramic fiber; Porcelain electrical supplies
HQ: 3m Technical Ceramics, Inc.
1922 Barranca Pkwy
Irvine CA 92606
949 862-9600

**(P-7586)**
**ALS GARDEN ART INC (PA)**
311 W Citrus St, Colton (92324-1412)
PHONE.................909 424-0221
Donald Bracci, *Pr*
**EMP:** 290 **EST:** 1949
**SQ FT:** 305,000
**SALES (est):** 1.21MM
**SALES (corp-wide):** 1.21MM **Privately Held**
Web: www.alsgardenart.com
SIC: **3299** 3272 Statuary: gypsum, clay, papier mache, metal, etc.; Concrete products, nec

**(P-7587)**
**BRANDELLI ARTS INC**
1250 Shaws Flat Rd, Sonora (95370-5433)
PHONE.................714 537-0969
Robert Brandelli, *Pr*
Aurora Brandelli, *
**EMP:** 46 **EST:** 1969
**SALES (est):** 308.41K **Privately Held**
Web: www.brandelliarts.com
SIC: **3299** 3272 Statuary: gypsum, clay, papier mache, metal, etc.; Concrete products, nec

**(P-7588)**
**BURLINGAME INDUSTRIES INC**
Also Called: Eagle Roofing Products Co
2352 N Locust Ave, Rialto (92377-5000)
PHONE.................909 355-7000
Robert Burlingame, *Pr*
**EMP:** 109
**SQ FT:** 76,704
**SALES (corp-wide):** 54.45MM **Privately Held**

Web: www.eagleroofing.com
SIC: 3299 3272 2952 Tile, sand lime; Concrete products, nec; Asphalt felts and coatings
PA: Burlingame Industries, Incorporated
3546 N Riverside Ave
909 355-7000

### (P-7589)
### CERADYNE ESK LLC
3169 Red Hill Ave M, Costa Mesa (92626-3419)
PHONE..................714 549-0421
Joel P Moskowitz, CEO
Jason Smith, CFO
EMP: 27 EST: 2004
SALES (est): 9.43MM
SALES (corp-wide): 32.68B Publicly Held
SIC: 3299 Ceramic fiber
HQ: 3m Technical Ceramics, Inc.
1922 Barranca Pkwy
Irvine CA 92606
949 862-9600

### (P-7590)
### FOUNDRY SERVICE & SUPPLIES INC
2029 S Parco Ave, Ontario (91761-5700)
PHONE..................909 284-5000
Curt Parnell, CEO
Joel Leathers, *
◆ EMP: 24 EST: 1962
SQ FT: 40,000
SALES (est): 2.72MM Privately Held
Web: www.foundryservice.com
SIC: 3299 Art goods: plaster of paris, papier mache, and scagliola

### (P-7591)
### HARRINGTON & SONS INC
Also Called: Storyland Studios
590 Crane St, Lake Elsinore (92530-2737)
PHONE..................951 674-0998
EMP: 20 EST: 1979
SALES (est): 2.2MM Privately Held
SIC: 3299 Ornamental and architectural plaster work

### (P-7592)
### INTEXFORMS INC
9293 Beatty Dr, Sacramento (95826-9733)
PHONE..................916 388-9933
Brian Jiles, Pr
John Ramirez, *
James Byerly, *
EMP: 55 EST: 1994
SQ FT: 41,400
SALES (est): 2.2MM Privately Held
Web: www.intexforms.com
SIC: 3299 2899 Ornamental and architectural plaster work; Chemical preparations, nec

### (P-7593)
### LOMELIS STATUARY INC (PA)
Also Called: Lomeli's Gardens
11921 E Brandt Rd, Lockeford (95237-9708)
P.O. Box 1356 (95237-1356)
PHONE..................209 367-1131
Doris Lomeli, Pr
Elsa Lomeli, *
Adriana Lomeli, *
Carlos Lomeli, *
EMP: 25 EST: 1971
SQ FT: 28,000
SALES (est): 2.39MM
SALES (corp-wide): 2.39MM Privately Held

SIC: 3299 5021 5261 Statuary: gypsum, clay, papier mache, metal, etc.; Outdoor and lawn furniture, nec; Retail nurseries and garden stores

### (P-7594)
### MORGAN TECHNICAL CERAMICS INC
2425 Whipple Rd, Hayward (94544-7807)
PHONE..................510 491-1100
Mark Robertshaw, CEO
Andrew Shilston, Ch
Andrew Hosty, COO
Kevin Dangerfield, CFO
EMP: 99 EST: 1991
SALES (est): 1.8MM Privately Held
SIC: 3299 Ceramic fiber

### (P-7595)
### OMEGA PRODUCTS CORP (HQ)
Also Called: Omega Products International
1681 California Ave, Corona (92881-3375)
P.O. Box 77220 (92877-0107)
PHONE..................951 737-7447
Michael G Dawe, CEO
Todd Martin, *
▲ EMP: 60 EST: 1973
SQ FT: 11,000
SALES (est): 47.21MM
SALES (corp-wide): 91.19MM Privately Held
Web: www.omega-products.com
SIC: 3299 2899 Stucco; Chemical preparations, nec
PA: Opal Service, Inc.
282 S Anita Dr
714 935-0900

### (P-7596)
### OMEGA PRODUCTS CORP
8111 Fruitridge Rd, Sacramento (95826-4759)
PHONE..................916 635-3335
EMP: 26
SALES (corp-wide): 76.01MM Privately Held
Web: www.omega-products.com
SIC: 3299 2899 Stucco; Chemical preparations, nec
HQ: Omega Products Corp.
1681 California Ave
Corona CA 92881
951 737-7447

### (P-7597)
### OMEGA PRODUCTS CORP
282 S Anita Dr 3rd Fl, Orange (92868-3308)
P.O. Box 1149 (92856-0149)
PHONE..................714 935-0900
Todd Martin, Mgr
EMP: 26
SALES (corp-wide): 91.19MM Privately Held
Web: www.omega-products.com
SIC: 3299 Stucco
HQ: Omega Products Corp.
1681 California Ave
Corona CA 92881
951 737-7447

### (P-7598)
### OPAL SERVICE INC (PA)
282 S Anita Dr, Orange (92868-3308)
P.O. Box 1149 (92856-0149)
PHONE..................714 935-0900
Kenneth R Thompson, CEO
▲ EMP: 30 EST: 1962
SQ FT: 1,200
SALES (est): 76.01MM

SALES (corp-wide): 76.01MM Privately Held
SIC: 3299 5031 5211 Stucco; Doors and windows; Lumber and other building materials

### (P-7599)
### PAREX USA INC (DH)
2150 Eastridge Ave, Riverside (92507-0720)
PHONE..................714 778-2266
Rodrigo Lacerda, Pr
◆ EMP: 30 EST: 1926
SALES (est): 118.03MM Privately Held
Web: www.parexusa.com
SIC: 3299 5031 Stucco; Building materials, interior
HQ: Sika France
84 Rue Edouard Vaillant
Le Bourget IDF 93350
149928000

### (P-7600)
### ROLLS-ROYCE HIGH TEMPERATURE COMPOSITES INC
Also Called: Rolls-Royce Htc
5730 Katella Ave, Cypress (90630-5005)
PHONE..................714 375-4085
EMP: 50 EST: 1992
SALES (est): 15.85MM
SALES (corp-wide): 20.55B Privately Held
SIC: 3299 Mica products
HQ: Rolls-Royce North America (Usa) Holdings Co.
1900 Rston Mtro Plz Ste 4
Reston VA 20190
703 834-1700

### (P-7601)
### YLA INC
Also Called: CCS Composites
2450 Cordelia Rd, Fairfield (94534-1651)
PHONE..................707 359-3400
EMP: 87
SIC: 3299 Ceramic fiber

---

## 3312 Blast Furnaces And Steel Mills

### (P-7602)
### 2ND SOURCE WIRE & CABLE INC
Also Called: 2nd Source Wire & Cable
20445 E Walnut Dr N, Walnut (91789-2918)
PHONE..................714 482-2866
Donna Silvers, Pr
Danny Chargualaf, *
Cathy Moorhead, *
Lois Ginn, *
EMP: 65 EST: 1989
SALES (est): 4.63MM
SALES (corp-wide): 1.89B Privately Held
Web: www.alignprecision.com
SIC: 3312 3399 Pipes and tubes; Brads: aluminum, brass, or other nonferrous metal or wire
HQ: Align Precision - Anaheim, Inc.
7100 Belgrave Ave
Garden Grove CA 92841

### (P-7603)
### AMERICAN PLANT SERVICES INC (PA)
6242 N Paramount Blvd, Long Beach (90805-3714)
P.O. Box 727 (90801-0727)
PHONE..................562 630-1773

George M Bragg, Pr
Mary-ann Pool, Sec
EMP: 24 EST: 1981
SALES (est): 1.25MM
SALES (corp-wide): 1.25MM Privately Held
SIC: 3312 Blast furnaces and steel mills

### (P-7604)
### ARTSONS MANUFACTURING COMPANY
11121 Garfield Ave, South Gate (90280-7505)
PHONE..................323 773-3469
Jeffery A Winders, CEO
Jeffrey A Winders, *
Steve Winders, *
Art L Winders, *
▲ EMP: 28 EST: 1958
SALES (est): 1.59MM Privately Held
Web: www.artsonswire.com
SIC: 3312 Wire products, steel or iron

### (P-7605)
### BAMBACIGNO STEEL COMPANY
4930 Mchenry Ave, Modesto (95356-9523)
PHONE..................209 524-9681
Mary Bambacigno, CEO
Loretta Bambacigno, Prin
Bill Boughton, *
Sheila Arnold, *
Nicole Kochman, *
EMP: 48 EST: 1955
SQ FT: 51,440
SALES (est): 9.35MM Privately Held
Web: www.bambacigno.com
SIC: 3312 Structural shapes and pilings, steel

### (P-7606)
### BORRMANN METAL CENTER
12790 Holly St, Riverside (92509-2364)
PHONE..................951 367-1510
EMP: 20
SALES (corp-wide): 531.51MM Privately Held
Web: www.borrmannmetals.com
SIC: 3312 Iron and steel products, hot-rolled
HQ: Borrmann Metal Center
110 W Olive Ave
Burbank CA 91502
818 846-7171

### (P-7607)
### BROWN-PACIFIC INC
Also Called: B P W
13639 Bora Dr, Santa Fe Springs (90670-5010)
PHONE..................562 921-3471
Ron R Nagele, CEO
Claudia Nagele, *
Kenneth Brown, *
EMP: 32 EST: 1967
SQ FT: 35,000
SALES (est): 4.53MM Privately Held
Web: www.brownpacific.com
SIC: 3312 3355 3357 3356 Bar, rod, and wire products; Wire, aluminum: made in rolling mills; Nonferrous wiredrawing and insulating; Nonferrous rolling and drawing, nec

### (P-7608)
### CALIFORNIA AMFORGE CORPORATION
Also Called: California Amforge
750 N Vernon Ave, Azusa (91702-2231)
PHONE..................626 334-4931
William Taylor, Brnch Mgr
EMP: 102

## 3312 - Blast Furnaces And Steel Mills (P-7609)

SQ FT: 20,000
SALES (corp-wide): 23.95MM **Privately Held**
Web: www.cal-amforge.com
SIC: **3312** 3462 Forgings, iron and steel; Iron and steel forgings
PA: California Amforge Corporation
750 N Vernon Ave
626 334-4931

**(P-7609)**
**CALIFORNIA STEEL INDS INC (HQ)**
Also Called: Si
14000 San Bernardino Ave, Fontana (92335-5259)
P.O. Box 5080 (92334-5080)
PHONE..................................909 350-6300
Marcelo Botelho, *Pr*
Ricardo Bernardes, *Executive Commercial Vice President\**
Brett Guge, *Executive Vice President Finance & Administration\**
▲ EMP: 238 EST: 1983
SALES (est): 439.17MM
SALES (corp-wide): 34.71B **Publicly Held**
Web: www.californiasteel.com
SIC: **3312** 3317 Slabs, steel; Pipes, wrought: welded, lock joint, or heavy riveted
PA: Nucor Corporation
1915 Rexford Rd
704 366-7000

**(P-7610)**
**CALPIPE INDUSTRIES LLC**
923 Calpipe Rd, Santa Paula (93060-9155)
PHONE..................................562 803-4388
Francisco Hernandez, *Prin*
EMP: 38
Web: www.atkore.com
SIC: **3312** Pipes and tubes
HQ: Calpipe Industries, Llc
16100 Lathrop Ave
Harvey IL 60426

**(P-7611)**
**EASYFLEX INC**
Also Called: Easyflex
2700 N Main St Ste 800, Santa Ana (92705)
PHONE..................................888 577-8999
Mary Sunmin Kim, *Pr*
◆ EMP: 25 EST: 2005
SALES (est): 2.49MM **Privately Held**
Web: www.easyflexusa.com
SIC: **3312** Stainless steel

**(P-7612)**
**ENGENSE INC**
Also Called: Dfndr Armor
2255 Pleasant Valley Rd Ste G, Camarillo (93012-8569)
PHONE..................................805 484-8317
David Fernandez, *Pr*
EMP: 17 EST: 2013
SALES (est): 3.27MM **Privately Held**
Web: www.engense.com
SIC: **3312** Armor plate

**(P-7613)**
**FLOW DYNAMICS INC**
1215 E Acacia St Ste 104, Ontario (91761-4003)
PHONE..................................909 930-5522
John Mccarthy, *Pr*
Philip Espinoza, *VP*
EMP: 16 EST: 2004
SQ FT: 2,222
SALES (est): 3.91MM **Privately Held**
Web: www.flowdynamicsonline.com

SIC: **3312** Stainless steel

**(P-7614)**
**HARDY FRAMES INC**
Also Called: My Tech USA
250 Klug Cir, Corona (92878-5409)
PHONE..................................951 245-9525
Clifford Grant, *Brnch Mgr*
EMP: 100
SALES (corp-wide): 3.9MM **Privately Held**
Web: www.hardyframe.com
SIC: **3312** Stainless steel
PA: Hardy Frames, Inc.
555 S Promenade Ave # 104
805 477-0793

**(P-7615)**
**HOLT TOOL & MACHINE INC**
2909 Middlefield Rd, Redwood City (94063-3328)
PHONE..................................650 364-2547
Leo Hoenighausen, *Pr*
Ulrich Hoenighausen, *CFO*
EMP: 21 EST: 1933
SQ FT: 12,000
SALES (est): 3.31MM **Privately Held**
Web: www.holttool.com
SIC: **3312** 3469 7692 3544 Tool and die steel and alloys; Metal stampings, nec; Welding repair; Special dies, tools, jigs, and fixtures

**(P-7616)**
**INTERNATIONAL MFG TECH INC (DH)**
Also Called: Nassco
2798 Harbor Dr, San Diego (92113-3650)
PHONE..................................619 544-7741
Willam J Cuddy, *CEO*
James C Scott, *\**
▲ EMP: 57 EST: 1990
SALES (est): 47.05MM
SALES (corp-wide): 42.27B **Publicly Held**
SIC: **3312** 3731 Structural and rail mill products; Shipbuilding and repairing
HQ: Nassco Holdings Incorporated
2798 East Harbor Dr
San Diego CA 92106

**(P-7617)**
**INTERSTATE STEEL CENTER CO INC**
7001 S Alameda St, Los Angeles (90001-2204)
PHONE..................................323 583-0855
Leon Banks, *Pr*
William Korth, *\**
EMP: 50 EST: 1972
SQ FT: 53,000
SALES (est): 7.4MM **Privately Held**
Web: www.interstateleveling.com
SIC: **3312** 5051 Blast furnaces and steel mills; Iron and steel (ferrous) products

**(P-7618)**
**LAMAR TOOL & DIE CASTING INC**
4230 Technology Dr, Modesto (95356)
PHONE..................................209 545-5525
Larry Snoreen, *Pr*
Margie Snoreen, *\**
Brian Kolsters, *\**
▲ EMP: 75 EST: 1982
SQ FT: 20,000
SALES (est): 8.9MM **Privately Held**
Web: www.lamartoolanddie.com
SIC: **3312** 3463 3364 Tool and die steel and alloys; Nonferrous forgings; Nonferrous die-castings except aluminum

**(P-7619)**
**LEXANI WHEEL CORPORATION**
Also Called: Lexani
1121 Olympic Dr, Corona (92881-3391)
PHONE..................................951 808-4220
Frank J Hodges, *CEO*
◆ EMP: 33 EST: 1996
SQ FT: 35,000
SALES (est): 6.52MM **Privately Held**
Web: www.lexani.com
SIC: **3312** Wheels

**(P-7620)**
**NUCOR BLDG SYSTEMS UTAH LLC**
1100 Pinot Noir Dr, Lodi (95240-7410)
PHONE..................................209 608-7701
EMP: 86
SALES (corp-wide): 34.71B **Publicly Held**
Web: www.nucorbuildingsystems.com
SIC: **3312** Blast furnaces and steel mills
HQ: Nucor Building Systems Utah Llc
1050 N Watery Ln
Brigham City UT 84302

**(P-7621)**
**PASO ROBLES TANK INC (HQ)**
825 26th St, Paso Robles (93446-1242)
P.O. Box 3229 (93447-3229)
PHONE..................................805 227-1641
Shawn P Owens, *CEO*
Shane P Wombles, *\**
Eduardo Peralta, *\**
▲ EMP: 63 EST: 2000
SALES (est): 46.24MM
SALES (corp-wide): 61.08MM **Privately Held**
Web: www.pasoroblestank.com
SIC: **3312** 3443 Blast furnaces and steel mills; Tanks, standard or custom fabricated: metal plate
PA: Associated Construction And Engineering, Inc.
23232 Peralta Dr Ste 206
949 455-2682

**(P-7622)**
**PRICE INDUSTRIES INC**
Also Called: International Iron Products
10883 Thornmint Rd, San Diego (92127-2403)
PHONE..................................858 673-4451
Kenneth Alan Price, *Pr*
Barbara Price, *\**
EMP: 75 EST: 1968
SQ FT: 4,000
SALES (est): 8.73MM **Privately Held**
Web: www.priceindustries.com
SIC: **3312** 3441 1791 5072 Structural and rail mill products; Fabricated structural metal; Structural steel erection; Bolts, nuts, and screws

**(P-7623)**
**RSR STEEL FABRICATION INC**
11040 I Ave, Hesperia (92345-5214)
PHONE..................................760 244-2210
Hector Grijalva, *Pr*
Ruth Grijalva, *VP*
EMP: 24 EST: 1993
SQ FT: 12,000
SALES (est): 2.27MM **Privately Held**
SIC: **3312** Structural shapes and pilings, steel

**(P-7624)**
**RTM PRODUCTS INC**
13120 Arctic Cir, Santa Fe Springs (90670-5508)
PHONE..................................562 926-2400

Robert M Thierjung, *Prin*
EMP: 23 EST: 2007
SALES (est): 2.5MM **Privately Held**
Web: www.rtmproducts.com
SIC: **3312** Tool and die steel and alloys

**(P-7625)**
**SAN DEGO PRCSION MACHINING INC**
9375 Ruffin Ct, San Diego (92123-5304)
PHONE..................................858 499-0379
William Matteson, *CEO*
EMP: 40 EST: 1971
SQ FT: 23,000
SALES (est): 4.34MM **Privately Held**
Web: www.sdpm.com
SIC: **3312** 3599 Stainless steel; Machine shop, jobbing and repair

**(P-7626)**
**SEARING INDUSTRIES INC**
Also Called: Searing Industries
8901 Arrow Rte, Rancho Cucamonga (91730)
P.O. Box 3059 (91729)
PHONE..................................909 948-3030
Lee Searing, *CEO*
Jim Searing, *\**
Mmargaret Cantu, *\**
◆ EMP: 120 EST: 1985
SQ FT: 265,000
SALES (est): 23.05MM **Privately Held**
Web: www.searingindustries.com
SIC: **3312** 3317 Tubes, steel and iron; Steel pipe and tubes

**(P-7627)**
**SIMEC USA CORPORATION**
Also Called: Pacific Steel
333 H St Ste 5000, Chula Vista (91910-5561)
PHONE..................................619 474-7081
Sergio Vigil Gonzalez, *CEO*
Mario Moreno Cortez, *CFO*
Van Haynie, *Sec*
EMP: 20 EST: 2009
SALES (est): 12.39MM **Privately Held**
Web: www.gsimec.com.mx
SIC: **3312** Bars, iron: made in steel mills
HQ: Simec International 6, S.A. De C.V.
Av. Lazaro Cardenas No. 601 Edif. A-3, Piso 4
Guadalajara JAL 44470

**(P-7628)**
**STAR STAINLESS SCREW CO**
30150 Ahern Ave, Union City (94587-1202)
PHONE..................................510 489-6569
Tim Roberto, *Mgr*
EMP: 27
SALES (corp-wide): 54.04MM **Privately Held**
Web: www.starstainless.com
SIC: **3312** 5072 Stainless steel; Hardware
PA: Star Stainless Screw Co.
30 W End Rd
973 256-2300

**(P-7629)**
**STATE PIPE & SUPPLY INC**
Westcoast Pipe Lining Division
2180 N Locust Ave, Rialto (92377-4166)
PHONE..................................909 356-5670
Kenneth Walker, *Mgr*
EMP: 50
Web: www.statepipe.com
SIC: **3312** Blast furnaces and steel mills
HQ: State Pipe & Supply, Inc.
183 S Cedar Ave
Rialto CA 92376
909 877-9999

## PRODUCTS & SERVICES SECTION
## 3315 - Steel Wire And Related Products (P-7649)

**(P-7630)**
**TAMCO (HQ)**
Also Called: CMC Steel California
5425 Industrial Pkwy, San Bernardino (92407-1803)
PHONE..............................909 899-0660
Chia Yuan Wang, *CEO*
Harley Scardoelli, *
Vilmar Babot, *
◆ **EMP:** 50 **EST:** 1974
**SALES (est):** 35.89MM
**SALES (corp-wide):** 7.93B **Publicly Held**
Web: www.asgsales.com
SIC: 3312 Blast furnaces and steel mills
PA: Commercial Metals Company
 6565 N Mcrthur Blvd Ste 8
 214 689-4300

**(P-7631)**
**TRUSTEEL LLC**
416 Crown Point Cir Ste 1, Grass Valley (95945-9558)
PHONE..............................530 802-0420
**EMP:** 15 **EST:** 2017
**SALES (est):** 3.2MM **Privately Held**
Web: www.trusteel.com
SIC: 3312 Rails, steel or iron

**(P-7632)**
**WAYNE TOOL & DIE CO**
15853 Olden St, Sylmar (91342-1249)
PHONE..............................818 364-1611
Kenneth E Ruggles, *Pr*
**EMP:** 20 **EST:** 1978
**SQ FT:** 1,200
**SALES (est):** 275.58K **Privately Held**
SIC: 3312 Tool and die steel

**(P-7633)**
**WEST CAST STL PROC HLDINGS LLC (PA)**
13568 Vintage Pl, Chino (91710-5243)
PHONE..............................909 393-8405
Erik Gamm, *CEO*
Ron Searcy, *Pr*
**EMP:** 25 **EST:** 2021
**SALES (est):** 59.06MM
**SALES (corp-wide):** 59.06MM **Privately Held**
Web: www.steelcousa.com
SIC: 3312 6719 3444 5075 Stainless steel; Investment holding companies, except banks; Elbows, for air ducts, stovepipes, etc.: sheet metal; Warm air heating and air conditioning

**(P-7634)**
**WHEEL AND TIRE CLUB INC**
Also Called: Discounted Wheel Warehouse
1909 S Susan St Ste D, Santa Ana (92704-3901)
PHONE..............................800 901-6003
Naeem Niamat, *CEO*
◆ **EMP:** 35 **EST:** 2013
**SQ FT:** 42,000
**SALES (est):** 3.95MM **Privately Held**
Web: www.discountedwheelwarehouse.com
SIC: 3312 5013 5014 Locomotive wheels, rolled; Wheels, motor vehicle; Tires and tubes

## 3313 Electrometallurgical Products

**(P-7635)**
**NIKON AM SYNERGY INC**
3550 E Carson St, Long Beach (90808-2330)
PHONE..............................310 607-0188
Thomas David Mckee, *CEO*
Gary Handley, *
**EMP:** 30 **EST:** 2013
**SALES (est):** 16.58MM **Privately Held**
Web: www.morf3d.com
SIC: 3313 3499 Alloys, additive, except copper: not made in blast furnaces; Fire- or burglary-resistive products
PA: Nikon Corporation
 1-5-20, Nishioi

**(P-7636)**
**R D MATHIS COMPANY**
2840 Gundry Ave, Signal Hill (90755-1813)
P.O. Box 92916 (90809-2916)
PHONE..............................562 426-7049
Robert Lumley, *Pr*
Kirk Bennett, *
Barbara Bennett, *
**EMP:** 25 **EST:** 1963
**SQ FT:** 10,000
**SALES (est):** 2.7MM **Privately Held**
Web: www.rdmathis.com
SIC: 3313 8711 3567 3443 Molybdenum silicon, not made in blast furnaces; Engineering services; Industrial furnaces and ovens; Fabricated plate work (boiler shop)

## 3315 Steel Wire And Related Products

**(P-7637)**
**BARRETTE OUTDOOR LIVING INC**
1151 Palmyrita Ave, Riverside (92507-1703)
PHONE..............................800 336-2383
Rick Paulson, *Mgr*
**EMP:** 25
**SALES (corp-wide):** 34.95B **Privately Held**
Web: www.barretteoutdoorliving.com
SIC: 3315 Fence gates, posts, and fittings: steel
HQ: Barrette Outdoor Living, Inc.
 7830 Freeway Cir
 Middleburg Heights OH 44130
 440 891-0790

**(P-7638)**
**CAL STATE SITE SERVICES**
4518 Industrial St, Simi Valley (93063-3411)
PHONE..............................800 499-5757
**EMP:** 20 **EST:** 2014
**SALES (est):** 2.28MM **Privately Held**
Web: www.rentfenceandtoilets.com
SIC: 3315 5099 3431 Fencing made in wiredrawing plants; Toilets, portable; Bathroom fixtures, including sinks

**(P-7639)**
**DAVIS WIRE CORPORATION (HQ)**
5555 Irwindale Ave, Irwindale (91706-2046)
PHONE..............................626 969-7651
Jim Baske, *Pr*
Emily Heisley, *
▲ **EMP:** 150 **EST:** 1927
**SQ FT:** 265,000
**SALES (est):** 36.65MM **Privately Held**
Web: www.daviswire.com
SIC: 3315 Wire, ferrous/iron
PA: The Heico Companies L L C
 70 W Madison Ste 5600

**(P-7640)**
**DAYTON SUPERIOR CORPORATION**
6001 20th St, Riverside (92509-2030)
PHONE..............................951 782-9517
Jeffrey Bokn, *Brnch Mgr*
**EMP:** 21
**SALES (corp-wide):** 7.35B **Privately Held**
Web: www.daytonsuperior.com
SIC: 3315 Steel wire and related products
HQ: Dayton Superior Corporation
 1125 Byers Rd
 Miamisburg OH 45342
 937 866-0711

**(P-7641)**
**HALSTEEL INC (DH)**
4190 Santa Ana St Ste A, Ontario (91761-1527)
P.O. Box 90100 (92427-1100)
PHONE..............................909 937-1001
Rebecca Kalis, *Pr*
Ed Halstead, *VP*
Donald Halstead, *Treas*
**EMP:** 21 **EST:** 1996
**SQ FT:** 100,000
**SALES (est):** 1.99MM
**SALES (corp-wide):** 185.25MM **Privately Held**
Web: www.treeisland.com
SIC: 3315 5051 Nails, steel: wire or cut; Nails
HQ: Tree Island Industries Ltd
 3933 Boundary Rd
 Richmond BC
 604 524-3744

**(P-7642)**
**HAMROCK INC**
3019 Wilshire Blvd, Santa Monica (90403-2301)
PHONE..............................562 944-0255
Stephen R Hamrock, *Prin*
Michael E Hamrock, *Prin*
▲ **EMP:** 250 **EST:** 1976
**SALES (est):** 2.97MM **Privately Held**
Web: www.hamrockmusic.com
SIC: 3315 2542 3496 3317 Wire and fabricated wire products; Racks, merchandise display or storage: except wood; Miscellaneous fabricated wire products; Steel pipe and tubes

**(P-7643)**
**HOGAN CO INC**
2741 S Lilac Ave, Bloomington (92316-3213)
PHONE..............................909 421-0245
Kraig B Hogan, *Pr*
◆ **EMP:** 20 **EST:** 1939
**SQ FT:** 9,150
**SALES (est):** 5.6MM **Privately Held**
Web: www.hoganco.com
SIC: 3315 3531 Spikes, steel: wire or cut; Bituminous, cement and concrete related products and equip.

**(P-7644)**
**INWESCO INCORPORATED (HQ)**
746 N Coney Ave, Azusa (91702-2239)
PHONE..............................626 334-7115
David L Morris, *CEO*
**EMP:** 65 **EST:** 1967
**SQ FT:** 30,000
**SALES (est):** 25MM
**SALES (corp-wide):** 34.95B **Privately Held**
Web: www.inwesco.com
SIC: 3315 Steel wire and related products
PA: Crh Public Limited Company
 Stonemason S Way
 14041000

**(P-7645)**
**MASTER-HALCO INC**
27474 5th St, Highland (92346-4217)
PHONE..............................909 350-4740
Paul Stites, *Brnch Mgr*
**EMP:** 15
Web: www.masterhalco.com
SIC: 3315 4226 7692 3496 Fence gates, posts, and fittings: steel; Special warehousing and storage, nec; Welding repair; Miscellaneous fabricated wire products
HQ: Master-Halco, Inc.
 3010 Lyndon B Jhnson Fwy
 Dallas TX 75234
 972 714-7300

**(P-7646)**
**MERCHANTS METALS LLC**
Also Called: Merchants Metals
6466 Mission Blvd, Riverside (92509-4128)
PHONE..............................951 686-1888
Rob Sisco, *Mgr*
**EMP:** 108
**SQ FT:** 8,750
**SALES (corp-wide):** 1.09B **Privately Held**
Web: www.merchantsmetals.com
SIC: 3315 3496 Fence gates, posts, and fittings: steel; Miscellaneous fabricated wire products
HQ: Merchants Metals Llc
 3 Ravinia Dr Ste 1750
 Atlanta GA 30346
 770 741-0300

**(P-7647)**
**MK MAGNETICS INC**
17030 Muskrat Ave, Adelanto (92301-2258)
PHONE..............................760 246-6373
Lill Runge, *Pr*
Magne Stangenes, *
John Stangenes, *
Jay Runge, *Corporate Secretary*
Karen Warren, *
▲ **EMP:** 53 **EST:** 2003
**SQ FT:** 45,000
**SALES (est):** 4.15MM
**SALES (corp-wide):** 23.07MM **Privately Held**
Web: www.mkmagnetics.com
SIC: 3315 Steel wire and related products
PA: Stangenes Industries, Inc.
 1052 E Meadow Cir
 650 855-9926

**(P-7648)**
**NATIONAL WIRE AND CABLE CORPORATION**
Also Called: National Wire and Cable
136 N San Fernando Rd, Los Angeles (90031-1780)
P.O. Box 31307 (90031-0307)
PHONE..............................323 225-5611
**EMP:** 170 **EST:** 1952
**SALES (est):** 22.05MM **Privately Held**
Web: www.nationalwire.com
SIC: 3315 5031 Cable, steel: insulated or armored; Molding, all materials

**(P-7649)**
**NEW PRDUCT INTGRTION SLTONS IN (HQ)**
Also Called: Npi Solutions
685 Jarvis Dr Ste A, Morgan Hill (95037-2813)
PHONE..............................408 944-9178
Kevin R Andersen, *Pr*
▲ **EMP:** 48 **EST:** 2000
**SQ FT:** 15,000
**SALES (est):** 23.59MM

## 3315 - Steel Wire And Related Products (P-7650)

SALES (corp-wide): 12.55B **Publicly Held**
Web: www.npisolutions.com
SIC: 3315 Cable, steel: insulated or armored
PA: Amphenol Corporation
358 Hall Ave
203 265-8900

**(P-7650)**
**PRO DETENTION INC**
Also Called: Viking Products
2238 N Glassell St Ste E, Orange (92865-2742)
PHONE...............................714 881-3680
Mike Peterson, *CEO*
▲ **EMP:** 70 **EST:** 2012
**SALES (est):** 9.11MM **Privately Held**
SIC: 3315 Wire and fabricated wire products

**(P-7651)**
**SOUTH BAY WIRE & CABLE CO LLC (PA)**
54125 Maranatha Dr, Idyllwild (92549-0075)
P.O. Box 67 (92549-0067)
PHONE...............................951 659-2183
**EMP:** 80 **EST:** 2021
**SALES (est):** 10.04MM
**SALES (corp-wide):** 10.04MM **Privately Held**
Web: www.southbaycable.com
SIC: 3315 Wire and fabricated wire products

**(P-7652)**
**SOUTHWESTERN WIRE INC**
4318 Dudley Blvd, Mcclellan (95652-2515)
PHONE...............................916 333-5289
Kathlyn Moore, *Prin*
**EMP:** 18
Web: www.southwesternwire.com
SIC: 3315 Wire and fabricated wire products
PA: Southwestern Wire, Inc.
3505 N Interstate Dr

**(P-7653)**
**SUN POWER SECURITY GATES INC**
438 Tyler Rd, Merced (95341-8807)
P.O. Box 2044 (95344-0044)
PHONE...............................209 722-3990
Robert Osborn, *Pr*
Gene Felling, *VP*
Dusty Major, *Genl Mgr*
**EMP:** 17 **EST:** 1990
**SQ FT:** 3,500
**SALES (est):** 2.19MM **Privately Held**
SIC: 3315 3677 Fence gates, posts, and fittings: steel; Transformers power supply, electronic type

**(P-7654)**
**TREE ISLAND WIRE (USA) INC**
Industrial Alloys
13470 Philadelphia Ave, Fontana (92337-7700)
PHONE...............................909 594-7511
Rebecca Kalis, *Brnch Mgr*
**EMP:** 115
**SALES (corp-wide):** 185.25MM **Privately Held**
Web: www.treeisland.com
SIC: 3315 Wire, steel: insulated or armored
HQ: Tree Island Wire (Usa), Inc.
3880 Valley Blvd
Walnut CA 91789

**(P-7655)**
**TREE ISLAND WIRE (USA) INC**
K-Lath
3880 W Valley Blvd, Pomona (91769)

PHONE...............................909 595-6617
Ken Stufford, *Mgr*
**EMP:** 115
**SALES (corp-wide):** 185.25MM **Privately Held**
Web: www.treeisland.com
SIC: 3315 Wire, steel: insulated or armored
HQ: Tree Island Wire (Usa), Inc.
3880 Valley Blvd
Walnut CA 91789

**(P-7656)**
**TREE ISLAND WIRE (USA) INC (DH)**
Also Called: TI Wire
3880 Valley Blvd, Walnut (91789-1515)
P.O. Box 90100 (92427-1100)
PHONE...............................909 594-7511
Amar S Doman, *Ch Bd*
Nancy Davies, *CEO*
Brian Liu, *CFO*
Stephen Ogden, *VP*
▲ **EMP:** 250 **EST:** 1980
**SALES (est):** 24MM
**SALES (corp-wide):** 185.25MM **Privately Held**
Web: www.treeisland.com
SIC: 3315 Steel wire and related products
HQ: Tree Island Industries Ltd
3933 Boundary Rd
Richmond BC
604 524-3744

**(P-7657)**
**US HANGER COMPANY LLC**
17501 S Denver Ave, Gardena (90248-3410)
PHONE...............................310 323-8030
Gene Livshin, *Managing Member*
▲ **EMP:** 47 **EST:** 2008
**SALES (est):** 3.69MM **Privately Held**
SIC: 3315 5199 Hangers (garment), wire; Clothes hangers

**(P-7658)**
**WIRETECH INC (PA)**
6440 Canning St, Commerce (90040-3122)
PHONE...............................323 722-4933
William Hillpot, *CEO*
Irene Sanchez, *
Garry Goodson, *
Simon Correa, *
▲ **EMP:** 87 **EST:** 2001
**SALES (est):** 22.2MM
**SALES (corp-wide):** 22.2MM **Privately Held**
Web: wiretechincorporated.wordpress.com
SIC: 3315 Steel wire and related products

## 3316 Cold Finishing Of Steel Shapes

**(P-7659)**
**NEXCOIL STEEL LLC**
1265 Shaw Rd, Stockton (95215-4020)
PHONE...............................209 900-1919
Gary Stein, *Prin*
Robert Elkington, *Prin*
Fred Morrison, *Prin*
**EMP:** 17 **EST:** 2012
**SALES (est):** 2.01MM **Privately Held**
SIC: 3316 Bars, steel, cold finished, from purchased hot-rolled

**(P-7660)**
**ONETO METAL PRODUCTS CORP**

7485 Reese Rd, Sacramento (95828-3721)
P.O. Box 293239 (95829-3239)
PHONE...............................916 681-6555
**EMP:** 24 **EST:** 1980
**SALES (est):** 4.08MM **Privately Held**
Web: www.onetometal.com
SIC: 3316 Sheet, steel, cold-rolled, nec: from purchased hot-rolled

## 3317 Steel Pipe And Tubes

**(P-7661)**
**CALIFORNIA STEEL INDS INC**
1 California Steel Way, Fontana (92335)
PHONE...............................909 350-6300
Kyle Schulty, *Brnch Mgr*
**EMP:** 429
**SALES (corp-wide):** 34.71B **Publicly Held**
Web: www.californiasteel.com
SIC: 3317 5051 Pipes, wrought: welded, lock joint, or heavy riveted; Iron and steel (ferrous) products
HQ: California Steel Industries, Inc.
14000 San Bernardino Ave
Fontana CA 92335
909 350-6300

**(P-7662)**
**CHARMAN MANUFACTURING INC**
5681 S Downey Rd, Vernon (90058-3719)
PHONE...............................213 489-7000
Shahab Namvar, *Pr*
Shawn Namvar, *Pr*
Ezra Namvar, *VP*
▲ **EMP:** 16 **EST:** 2006
**SALES (est):** 3.51MM **Privately Held**
Web: www.charmaninc.com
SIC: 3317 Steel pipe and tubes

**(P-7663)**
**IMPERIAL PIPE SERVICES LLC**
1666 20th St, Santa Monica (90404-3827)
PHONE...............................951 682-3307
**EMP:** 21 **EST:** 2002
**SALES (est):** 10.09MM
**SALES (corp-wide):** 134.62MM **Privately Held**
Web: www.imperialpipe.com
SIC: 3317 Steel pipe and tubes
PA: Shapco Inc.
1666 20th St Ste 100
310 264-1666

**(P-7664)**
**INTERNATIONAL CONSULTING UNLTD**
Also Called: Kns Industrial Supply
13045 Park St, Santa Fe Springs (90670-4005)
PHONE...............................714 449-3318
Karen Scott, *CEO*
**EMP:** 25 **EST:** 2016
**SALES (est):** 6.54MM **Privately Held**
Web: www.knsindustrialsupplies.com
SIC: 3317 Steel pipe and tubes

**(P-7665)**
**K-TUBE CORPORATION**
Also Called: K Tube Technologies
13400 Kirkham Way Frnt, Poway (92064-7167)
PHONE...............................858 513-9229
Greg May, *CEO*
**EMP:** 100 **EST:** 1982
**SQ FT:** 75,000
**SALES (est):** 23.54MM
**SALES (corp-wide):** 1.61B **Privately Held**
Web: www.k-tube.com

SIC: 3317 Tubing, mechanical or hypodermic sizes: cold drawn stainless
PA: Cook Group Incorporated
750 Daniels Way
812 339-2235

**(P-7666)**
**MARUICHI AMERICAN CORPORATION**
11529 Greenstone Ave, Santa Fe Springs (90670-4697)
PHONE...............................562 903-8600
Wataru Morita, *Pr*
Teruo Horikawa, *
Takehiko Katsumata, *
Makoto Ishikawa, *
Takuhiro Ishihara, *
▲ **EMP:** 96 **EST:** 1978
**SQ FT:** 240,000
**SALES (est):** 21.97MM **Privately Held**
Web: www.macsfs.com
SIC: 3317 Pipes, seamless steel
PA: Maruichi Steel Tube Ltd.
5-1-60, Namba, Chuo-Ku

**(P-7667)**
**NORTHWEST PIPE COMPANY**
12351 Rancho Rd, Adelanto (92301-2711)
PHONE...............................760 246-3191
Charles Koenig, *VP*
**EMP:** 154
**SALES (corp-wide):** 444.36MM **Publicly Held**
Web: www.nwpipe.com
SIC: 3317 3321 Pipes, wrought: welded, lock joint, or heavy riveted; Gray and ductile iron foundries
PA: Northwest Pipe Company
201 Ne Pk Plz Dr Ste 100
360 397-6250

**(P-7668)**
**NUCOR WAREHOUSE SYSTEMS INC (HQ)**
3851 S Santa Fe Ave, Vernon (90058-1712)
PHONE...............................323 588-4261
**TOLL FREE:** 800
Dave Olmstead, *Pr*
Steve Rogers, *VP*
Sturgeon Baker, *Contrlr*
Matthew Devries, *Supply Chain Manager*
◆ **EMP:** 177 **EST:** 1985
**SQ FT:** 285,000
**SALES (est):** 158.73MM
**SALES (corp-wide):** 34.71B **Publicly Held**
Web: www.nucorwarehousesystems.com
SIC: 3317 Tubes, seamless steel
PA: Nucor Corporation
1915 Rexford Rd
704 366-7000

**(P-7669)**
**PRIMUS PIPE AND TUBE INC (DH)**
5855 Obispo Ave, Long Beach (90805-3715)
PHONE...............................562 808-8000
Tommy Grahn, *Pr*
Chris Podsaid, *VP*
Karl Almond, *VP Fin*
Roy Harrison, *VP Opers*
Scott Templeton, *Ex VP*
▲ **EMP:** 51 **EST:** 1967
**SQ FT:** 120,000
**SALES (est):** 24.51MM **Privately Held**
Web: www.primuspipeandtube.com
SIC: 3317 Steel pipe and tubes
HQ: Ta Chen International, Inc.
5860 N Paramount Blvd

# PRODUCTS & SERVICES SECTION

## 3324 - Steel Investment Foundries (P-7689)

Long Beach CA 90805
562 808-8000

**(P-7670)**
**ROSCOE MOSS MANUFACTURING CO (PA)**
Also Called: Roscoe Moss Company
4360 Worth St, Los Angeles (90063-2536)
P.O. Box 31064 (90031-0064)
PHONE.................................323 261-4185
Roscoe Moss Junior, *Ch Bd*
George E Moss, *
Robert A Vanvaler, *
Tony Creque, *
Regis Coyle, *Corporate Secretary*
◆ **EMP:** 90 **EST:** 1913
**SQ FT:** 20,000
**SALES (est):** 21.74MM
**SALES (corp-wide):** 21.74MM **Privately Held**
Web: www.roscoemoss.com
**SIC: 3317** Well casing, wrought: welded, lock joint, or heavy riveted

**(P-7671)**
**TUBE ONE INDUSTRIES INC**
Also Called: Tube One
4055 Garner Rd, Riverside (92501-1043)
PHONE.................................951 300-2998
Kimber Liu, *CEO*
Chun Ling Lai Liu, *CFO*
▲ **EMP:** 15 **EST:** 1991
**SQ FT:** 46,000
**SALES (est):** 4.1MM **Privately Held**
Web: www.tube-one.com
**SIC: 3317** Steel pipe and tubes

**(P-7672)**
**UNITED SPIRAL PIPE LLC**
Also Called: United Spiral Pipe
900 E 3rd St, Pittsburg (94565-2103)
PHONE.................................925 526-3100
▲ **EMP:** 106
**SIC: 3317** Steel pipe and tubes

**(P-7673)**
**VALLEY METALS LLC**
Also Called: Leggett & Platt 0768
13125 Gregg St, Poway (92064-7122)
P.O. Box 85402 (92186-5402)
PHONE.................................858 513-1300
Kirk Nelson, *Managing Member*
**EMP:** 40 **EST:** 1946
**SQ FT:** 47,700
**SALES (est):** 15.13MM
**SALES (corp-wide):** 5.15B **Publicly Held**
Web: www.leggettaerospace.com
**SIC: 3317** Tubes, wrought: welded or lock joint
HQ: Western Pneumatic Tube Company, Llc
835 6th St S
Kirkland WA 98033
425 822-8271

## 3321 Gray And Ductile Iron Foundries

**(P-7674)**
**ALHAMBRA FOUNDRY COMPANY LTD**
Also Called: Afco
1147 S Meridian Ave, Alhambra (91803-1218)
P.O. Box 469 (91802-0469)
PHONE.................................626 289-4294
Arzhang Baghkhanian, *CEO*
James Wright, *
Mike Smalski, *

▲ **EMP:** 46 **EST:** 1984
**SQ FT:** 48,370
**SALES (est):** 885 **Privately Held**
Web: www.ejco.com
**SIC: 3321** 3312 5051 Gray iron castings, nec; Structural shapes and pilings, steel; Iron and steel (ferrous) products

**(P-7675)**
**GLOBE IRON FOUNDRY INC**
5649 Randolph St, Commerce (90040-3404)
PHONE.................................323 723-8983
John M Pratto, *Pr*
Othon Garcia, *
John Pratto Junior, *VP Prd*
Jeff Pratto, *
**EMP:** 70 **EST:** 1929
**SQ FT:** 58,000
**SALES (est):** 8.59MM **Privately Held**
Web: www.globeiron.com
**SIC: 3321** 3543 3369 Gray iron castings, nec; Industrial patterns; Nonferrous foundries, nec

**(P-7676)**
**JDH PACIFIC INC (PA)**
1818 E Orangethorpe Ave, Fullerton (92831-5324)
PHONE.................................562 926-8088
Donald Hu, *CEO*
▲ **EMP:** 30 **EST:** 1989
**SALES (est):** 24.88MM **Privately Held**
Web: www.jdhpacific.com
**SIC: 3321** 3324 3599 3462 Gray iron castings, nec; Commercial investment castings, ferrous; Crankshafts and camshafts, machining; Iron and steel forgings

**(P-7677)**
**LODI IRON WORKS INC (PA)**
Also Called: Galt Steel Foundry
820 S Sacramento St, Lodi (95240-4710)
P.O. Box 1150 (95241-1150)
PHONE.................................209 368-5395
Kevin Van Steenberge, *Pr*
Michael Van Steenberge, *
**EMP:** 37 **EST:** 1943
**SQ FT:** 11,000
**SALES (est):** 9.88MM
**SALES (corp-wide):** 9.88MM **Privately Held**
Web: www.lodiiron.com
**SIC: 3321** 3312 Gray iron castings, nec; Stainless steel

**(P-7678)**
**MCWANE INC**
Also Called: A B & I
2581 S Golden State Blvd Apt A, Fowler (93625-2681)
PHONE.................................559 834-4630
Kirt Winter, *Brnch Mgr*
**EMP:** 15
**SALES (corp-wide):** 970.37MM **Privately Held**
Web: www.abifoundry.com
**SIC: 3321** Soil pipe and fittings: cast iron
PA: Mcwane, Inc.
2900 Hwy 280 S Ste 300
205 414-3100

**(P-7679)**
**PACIFIC ALLOY CASTING COMPANY INC**
5900 Firestone Blvd Fl 1, South Gate (90280-3708)
PHONE.................................562 928-1387
**EMP:** 120 **EST:** 1937

**SALES (est):** 17.06MM **Privately Held**
Web: www.pacificalloy.com
**SIC: 3321** Gray and ductile iron foundries

**(P-7680)**
**PACIFIC SEWER MAINTENANCE CORP**
Also Called: PSM
4008 Via Rio Ave, Oceanside (92057-6439)
PHONE.................................800 292-9927
Richard Gayman, *Pr*
Brett Gayman, *VP*
Scott Gayman, *VP*
Todd Gayman, *VP*
Mary Gayman, *Sec*
**EMP:** 19 **EST:** 1977
**SQ FT:** 1,400
**SALES (est):** 2.17MM **Privately Held**
Web: www.pacificsewer.net
**SIC: 3321** 1623 Sewer pipe, cast iron; Water and sewer line construction

**(P-7681)**
**THOMPSON GUNDRILLING INC**
13840 Saticoy St, Van Nuys (91402-6582)
PHONE.................................323 873-4045
Michael Thompson, *Pr*
Robert Thompson, *
**EMP:** 39 **EST:** 1973
**SQ FT:** 32,000
**SALES (est):** 2.81MM **Privately Held**
Web: www.thompsongundrilling.com
**SIC: 3321** Gray and ductile iron foundries

## 3322 Malleable Iron Foundries

**(P-7682)**
**STEVEN HANDELMAN STUDIOS INC (PA)**
716 N Milpas St, Santa Barbara (93103-3029)
PHONE.................................805 884-9070
Steven Handelman, *Owner*
**EMP:** 41 **EST:** 1973
**SALES (est):** 2.28MM
**SALES (corp-wide):** 2.28MM **Privately Held**
Web: www.lightingshs.com
**SIC: 3322** Malleable iron foundries

## 3324 Steel Investment Foundries

**(P-7683)**
**CAST PARTS INC (HQ)**
Also Called: Cpp-Pomona
4200 Valley Blvd, Walnut (91789-1408)
PHONE.................................909 595-2252
James Stewart, *CEO*
Steve Clodfelter, *
Ali Ghavami, *
Anthony Klemenc, *
**EMP:** 185 **EST:** 2000
**SQ FT:** 300,000
**SALES (est):** 37.66MM
**SALES (corp-wide):** 957.88MM **Privately Held**
**SIC: 3324** 3365 Steel investment foundries; Aluminum foundries
PA: Consolidated Precision Products Corp.
1621 Euclid Ave Ste 1850
216 453-4800

**(P-7684)**
**CAST PARTS INC**
Also Called: Cpp-City of Industry
16800 Chestnut St, City Of Industry (91748-1017)

PHONE.................................626 937-3444
David Atwood, *Brnch Mgr*
**EMP:** 231
**SALES (corp-wide):** 957.88MM **Privately Held**
Web: www.cppcorp.com
**SIC: 3324** Aerospace investment castings, ferrous
HQ: Cast Parts, Inc.
4200 Valley Blvd
Walnut CA 91789
909 595-2252

**(P-7685)**
**CFI HOLDINGS CORP**
Also Called: Consolidated Foundries
4200 Valley Blvd, Pomona (91765)
PHONE.................................909 595-2252
Debbie Comstock, *Prin*
**EMP:** 19 **EST:** 1979
**SALES (est):** 2.76MM **Privately Held**
**SIC: 3324** 3365 Steel investment foundries; Aluminum foundries

**(P-7686)**
**HOWMET CORPORATION**
900 E Watson Center Rd, Carson (90745-4201)
PHONE.................................310 847-8152
**EMP:** 1121
**SALES (corp-wide):** 6.64B **Publicly Held**
Web: www.howmet.com
**SIC: 3324** Commercial investment castings, ferrous
HQ: Howmet Corporation
3850 White Lake Dr
Whitehall MI 49461
231 894-5686

**(P-7687)**
**HOWMET GLOBL FSTNING SYSTEMS I**
Rosan / Eagle Products
800 S State College Blvd, Fullerton (92831-5334)
PHONE.................................714 871-1550
Craig Brown, *Mgr*
**EMP:** 100
**SALES (corp-wide):** 6.64B **Publicly Held**
**SIC: 3324** 3365 Aerospace investment castings, ferrous; Aerospace castings, aluminum
HQ: Howmet Global Fastening Systems Inc.
3990a Heritage Oak Ct
Simi Valley CA 93063
805 426-2270

**(P-7688)**
**INITIUM AEROSPACE LLC**
4255 Ruffin Rd Ste 100, San Diego (92123-1247)
PHONE.................................818 324-3684
Etienne Boisseau, *CEO*
**EMP:** 17 **EST:** 2018
**SQ FT:** 2,500
**SALES (est):** 772.87K **Privately Held**
**SIC: 3324** 3369 3365 3812 Aerospace investment castings, ferrous; Aerospace castings, nonferrous: except aluminum; Aerospace castings, aluminum; Aircraft/aerospace flight instruments and guidance systems

**(P-7689)**
**LISI AEROSPACE NORTH AMER INC**
2602 Skypark Dr, Torrance (90505-5314)
PHONE.................................310 326-8110
Christian Darville, *CEO*
◆ **EMP:** 900 **EST:** 2009

# 3324 - Steel Investment Foundries (P-7690)

SALES (est): 29.28MM
SALES (corp-wide): 2.67MM **Privately Held**
Web: www.lisi-aerospace.com
SIC: **3324** Aerospace investment castings, ferrous
HQ: Lisi Aerospace
    42 A 52
    Paris 12 IDF 75012
    140198200

### (P-7690)
### MCDANIEL INC
10807 Monte Vista Ave, Montclair (91763-6113)
PHONE.............................909 591-8353
Timothy Mcdaniel, *Pr*
Shelly Mcdaniel, *VP*
EMP: 16 EST: 1997
SALES (est): 4.87MM **Privately Held**
Web: www.mcdanielinc.net
SIC: **3324** Steel investment foundries

### (P-7691)
### MILLER CASTINGS INC (PA)
2503 Pacific Park Dr, Whittier (90601-1680)
PHONE.............................562 695-0461
Hadi Khandehroo, *Pr*
Ralph Miller, *
Hadi Khandehroo, *CEO*
▲ EMP: 328 EST: 1973
SQ FT: 40,000
SALES (est): 49.35MM
SALES (corp-wide): 49.35MM **Privately Held**
Web: www.millercastings.com
SIC: **3324** Steel investment foundries

### (P-7692)
### NET SHAPES INC (PA)
1336 E Francis St Ste B, Ontario (91761-5723)
PHONE.............................909 947-3231
Joseph S Cannone, *Pr*
James Cannone, *VP*
EMP: 63 EST: 1986
SQ FT: 43,500
SALES (est): 8.89MM
SALES (corp-wide): 8.89MM **Privately Held**
Web: www.netshapes.com
SIC: **3324** Steel investment foundries

### (P-7693)
### PAC-RANCHO INC (HQ)
Also Called: Cpp Rancho Cucamonga
11000 Jersey Blvd, Rancho Cucamonga (91730-5103)
PHONE.............................909 987-4721
James Stewart, *CEO*
EMP: 102 EST: 1984
SQ FT: 55,000
SALES (est): 23.85MM
SALES (corp-wide): 957.88MM **Privately Held**
SIC: **3324** 3354 3369 Commercial investment castings, ferrous; Aluminum extruded products; Nonferrous foundries, nec
PA: Consolidated Precision Products Corp.
    1621 Euclid Ave Ste 1850
    216 453-4800

### (P-7694)
### PRECISION CASTPARTS CORP
Also Called: PCC Fluid Fittings
14800 S Figueroa St, Gardena (90248-1719)
PHONE.............................310 323-6200
EMP: 18
SALES (corp-wide): 364.48B **Publicly Held**
Web: www.precast.com
SIC: **3324** 3369 3724 3511 Aerospace investment castings, ferrous; Nonferrous foundries, nec; Aircraft engines and engine parts; Turbines and turbine generator sets and parts
HQ: Precision Castparts Corp.
    5885 Meadows Rd Ste 620
    Lake Oswego OR 97035
    503 946-4800

### (P-7695)
### REED MANUFACTURING INC
Also Called: American Casting Co
205 Apollo Way Ste A, Hollister (95023-2507)
PHONE.............................831 637-5641
John Reed, *Pr*
Simeon Bauer, *
Chris St John, *
EMP: 35 EST: 1977
SQ FT: 7,200
SALES (est): 5.6MM **Privately Held**
Web: www.americancastingco.com
SIC: **3324** Commercial investment castings, ferrous

### (P-7696)
### SIERRA TECHNICAL SERVICES INC
Also Called: STS
101 Commercial Way Unit D, Tehachapi (93561-1427)
PHONE.............................661 823-1092
Roger Hayes, *Pr*
Debra Hayes, *VP*
EMP: 15 EST: 2006
SQ FT: 7,000
SALES (est): 3.8MM **Publicly Held**
Web: www.sierratechnicalservices.com
SIC: **3324** 8711 Aerospace investment castings, ferrous; Engineering services
PA: Kratos Defense & Security Solutions, Inc.
    10680 Treena St Ste 600

# 3325 Steel Foundries, Nec

### (P-7697)
### CWI STEEL TECHNOLOGIES CORPORATION
2415 Campus Dr Ste 100, Irvine (92612-8529)
PHONE.............................949 476-7600
EMP: 48
SIC: **3325** Steel foundries, nec

### (P-7698)
### DAMERON ALLOY FOUNDRIES (PA)
6330 Gateway Dr Ste B, Cypress (90630-4836)
PHONE.............................310 631-5165
John W Dameron, *Pr*
Augustin Huerta, *
▲ EMP: 100 EST: 1946
SQ FT: 5,000
SALES (est): 23.95MM
SALES (corp-wide): 23.95MM **Privately Held**
Web: www.dameron.net
SIC: **3325** 3324 Steel foundries, nec; Commercial investment castings, ferrous

### (P-7699)
### SECOND STREET PROPERTIES
1333 2nd St, Berkeley (94710-1317)
◆ EMP: 550
SIC: **3325** 3369 Alloy steel castings, except investment; Nonferrous foundries, nec

### (P-7700)
### WCS EQUIPMENT HOLDINGS LLC
Also Called: Deluxe Building Products
1350 E Lexington Ave, Pomona (91766-5521)
PHONE.............................909 993-5700
EMP: 59
SALES (corp-wide): 59.06MM **Privately Held**
Web: www.deluxebuildingproducts.com
SIC: **3325** Steel foundries, nec
HQ: Wcs Equipment Holdings, Llc
    13568 Vintage Pl
    Chino CA 91710

### (P-7701)
### WCS EQUIPMENT HOLDINGS LLC (HQ)
Also Called: Steelco USA
13568 Vintage Pl, Chino (91710-5243)
PHONE.............................909 393-8405
Erik Gamm, *CEO*
EMP: 36 EST: 2006
SALES (est): 49.58MM
SALES (corp-wide): 59.06MM **Privately Held**
Web: www.steelcousa.com
SIC: **3325** Steel foundries, nec
PA: West Coast Steel & Processing Holdings, Llc
    13568 Vintage Pl
    909 393-8405

### (P-7702)
### WEST COAST FOUNDRY LLC (HQ)
2450 E 53rd St, Huntington Park (90255)
PHONE.............................323 583-1421
Michael Bargani, *Pr*
John Heine, *CFO*
▲ EMP: 20 EST: 1972
SQ FT: 18,000
SALES (est): 10.13MM
SALES (corp-wide): 85.77MM **Privately Held**
Web: www.westcoastfoundry.com
SIC: **3325** Alloy steel castings, except investment
PA: Speyside Equity Fund I Lp
    430 E 86th St
    212 994-0308

# 3331 Primary Copper

### (P-7703)
### CORRPRO COMPANIES INC
23309 La Palma Ave, Yorba Linda (92887-4773)
PHONE.............................562 944-1636
Randy Galinski, *Prin*
EMP: 23
SALES (corp-wide): 1.48B **Privately Held**
Web: www.corrpro.com
SIC: **3331** 1799 Cathodes (primary), copper; Corrosion control installation
HQ: Corrpro Companies, Inc.
    580 Goddard Ave
    Chesterfield MO 63005
    636 530-8000

# 3334 Primary Aluminum

### (P-7704)
### ADVANCED PATTERN & MOLD INC
1720 S Balboa Ave, Ontario (91761-7773)
PHONE.............................909 930-3444
Dan Hilger, *Pt*
Chris Vanderhagen, *Pt*
EMP: 15 EST: 1996
SQ FT: 10,400
SALES (est): 2.61MM **Privately Held**
SIC: **3334** Primary aluminum

### (P-7705)
### ALUMINUM PRECISION PDTS INC (PA)
3333 W Warner Ave, Santa Ana (92704-5316)
PHONE.............................714 546-8125
Gregory S Keeler, *Pr*
Roark Keeler, *VP*
Simona Manoiu, *CFO*
◆ EMP: 550 EST: 1965
SALES (est): 37.3MM
SALES (corp-wide): 37.3MM **Privately Held**
Web: www.aluminumprecision.com
SIC: **3334** Primary aluminum

### (P-7706)
### HOWMET AEROSPACE INC
3016 Lomita Blvd, Torrance (90505-5103)
PHONE.............................212 836-2674
EMP: 356
SALES (corp-wide): 6.64B **Publicly Held**
Web: www.howmet.com
SIC: **3334** Primary aluminum
PA: Howmet Aerospace Inc.
    201 Isabella St Ste 200
    412 553-1950

### (P-7707)
### INOVATIV INC
1500 W Mckinley St, Azusa (91702-3218)
PHONE.............................626 969-5300
Patrick Blewett, *CEO*
Tracy Barbosa, *
EMP: 40 EST: 2013
SALES (est): 6.22MM **Privately Held**
Web: www.inovativ.com
SIC: **3334** Primary aluminum

### (P-7708)
### KAISER ALUMINUM INTL CORP
6177 Sunal Blvd, Pleasanton (94566)
PHONE.............................949 614-1740
Jack A Hockema, *Pr*
EMP: 76 EST: 1957
SALES (est): 10.18MM **Privately Held**
SIC: **3334** 3353 3354 3355 Primary aluminum; Aluminum sheet, plate, and foil; Aluminum extruded products; Aluminum rolling and drawing, nec

### (P-7709)
### MAURICE & MAURICE ENGRG INC
17579 Mesa St Ste B4, Hesperia (92345-8308)
P.O. Box 403682 (92340-3682)
PHONE.............................760 949-5151
Jennifer Thomas, *CEO*
Aron Maurice, *
Jennifer Maurice, *
EMP: 27 EST: 1973
SQ FT: 22,000
SALES (est): 2.39MM **Privately Held**

**PRODUCTS & SERVICES SECTION**  **3353 - Aluminum Sheet, Plate, And Foil (P-7727)**

SIC: 3334 Primary aluminum

## 3339 Primary Nonferrous Metals, Nec

**(P-7710)**
**ARGEN CORPORATION (PA)**
Also Called: Jelenko
8515 Miralani Dr, San Diego (92126-4352)
PHONE.................................858 455-7900
Anton Woolf, CEO
Jackie Woolf, *
Paul Cascone, *
Joel Freedman, *
Andrea Ravid, *
▲ EMP: 203 EST: 1963
SQ FT: 39,609
SALES (est): 75.94MM
SALES (corp-wide): 75.94MM Privately Held
Web: www.argen.com
SIC: 3339 3843 Precious metals; Dental equipment and supplies

**(P-7711)**
**COMMODITY RESOURCE ENVMTL INC**
Also Called: Commodity Rsource Enviromental
11847 United St, Mojave (93501-7047)
PHONE.................................661 824-2416
Mike Kelsey, Mgr
EMP: 40
SALES (corp-wide): 10.85MM Privately Held
Web: www.creweb.com
SIC: 3339 3341 Precious metals; Secondary nonferrous metals
PA: Commodity Resource & Environmental, Inc.
116 E Prospect Ave
818 843-2811

**(P-7712)**
**PCC ROLLMET INC**
1822 Deere Ave, Irvine (92606-4817)
PHONE.................................949 221-5333
Ken Buck, Pr
Mark Donegan, Ch Bd
Emi Donis, VP
Shawn Hagel, CFO
EMP: 70 EST: 2011
SALES (est): 22.38MM
SALES (corp-wide): 364.48B Publicly Held
Web: www.rollmetusa.com
SIC: 3339 Nickel refining (primary)
HQ: Precision Castparts Corp.
5885 Meadows Rd Ste 620
Lake Oswego OR 97035
503 946-4800

**(P-7713)**
**SUPERIOR QUARTZ INC**
Also Called: Silica Engineering Group
1126 Yosemite Dr, Milpitas (95035-5404)
PHONE.................................408 844-9663
Nermin Aganbegovic, Pr
EMP: 15 EST: 1999
SALES (est): 2.64MM Privately Held
Web: www.silicaeng.com
SIC: 3339 3679 3264 Silicon, pure; Quartz crystals, for electronic application; Magnets, permanent: ceramic or ferrite

**(P-7714)**
**WESTERN MESQUITE MINES INC**
6502 E Us Highway 78, Brawley (92227-9306)
PHONE.................................928 341-4653
Randall Oliphant, Ch
Robert Gallagher, CEO
Cory Atiyeh, Pr
W Hanson P Geo, VP
Penny Brian, Sec
EMP: 20 EST: 1985
SALES (est): 22.91MM
SALES (corp-wide): 1.09B Privately Held
SIC: 3339 Gold refining (primary)
PA: Equinox Gold Corp
1501-700 W Pender St
604 558-0560

## 3341 Secondary Nonferrous Metals

**(P-7715)**
**ALL METALS INC (PA)**
Also Called: Ecs Refining
705 Reed St, Santa Clara (95050-3942)
PHONE.................................408 200-7000
James L Taggart, Pr
Kenneth Taggart, VP Fin
▲ EMP: 20 EST: 1980
SQ FT: 24,000
SALES (est): 10.36MM
SALES (corp-wide): 10.36MM Privately Held
Web: www.ecsrefining.com
SIC: 3341 4953 3339 Secondary precious metals; Refuse systems; Primary nonferrous metals, nec

**(P-7716)**
**CERTIFIED ALLOY PRODUCTS INC**
3245 Cherry Ave, Long Beach (90807-5213)
P.O. Box 90 (90801-0090)
PHONE.................................562 595-6621
▲ EMP: 110 EST: 1943
SALES (est): 34.84MM
SALES (corp-wide): 388.18K Privately Held
Web: www.doncasters.com
SIC: 3341 3313 3325 3312 Nickel smelting and refining (secondary); Ferroalloys; Steel foundries, nec; Blast furnaces and steel mills
HQ: Doncasters Limited
1 Park Row
Leeds LS1 5
133 286-4900

**(P-7717)**
**CUSTOM ALLOY SALES INC (PA)**
Also Called: Custom Alloy Light Metals
13181 Crossroads Pkwy N Ste 440, City Of Industry (91746-3499)
PHONE.................................626 369-3641
Brandon Cox, CEO
Kenneth J Cox, Ch
Nicholas Drakos, VP
Brett Jordan, VP
Tim Chisum, CFO
◆ EMP: 15 EST: 1969
SALES (est): 24.69MM
SALES (corp-wide): 24.69MM Privately Held
Web: www.customalloysales.com
SIC: 3341 5051 Aluminum smelting and refining (secondary); Zinc

**(P-7718)**
**DAVID H FELL & CO INC (PA)**
6009 Bandini Blvd, Los Angeles (90040-2967)
PHONE.................................323 722-9992
TOLL FREE: 800
Larry Fell, Ch
Lawrence Fell, *
Sondra Fell, *
▼ EMP: 24 EST: 1973
SQ FT: 18,000
SALES (est): 5.38MM
SALES (corp-wide): 5.38MM Privately Held
Web: www.dhfco.com
SIC: 3341 5094 Secondary precious metals; Bullion, precious metals

**(P-7719)**
**GEMINI INDUSTRIES INC**
2311 Pullman St, Santa Ana (92705-5506)
PHONE.................................949 250-4011
M Elguindy, CEO
Diana Keiffer, *
▲ EMP: 75 EST: 1973
SALES (est): 9.08MM Privately Held
Web: www.gemini-catalyst.com
SIC: 3341 Secondary precious metals

**(P-7720)**
**HERAEUS PRCOUS MTLS N AMER LLC (DH)**
15524 Carmenita Rd, Santa Fe Springs (90670-5610)
PHONE.................................562 921-7464
Andre Christl, Managing Member
Uve Kupka, *
◆ EMP: 200 EST: 1970
SQ FT: 71,000
SALES (est): 32.26MM
SALES (corp-wide): 2.67MM Privately Held
Web: www.heraeus-hpmn.com
SIC: 3341 2899 Gold smelting and refining (secondary); Chemical preparations, nec
HQ: Heraeus Holding Gesellschaft Mit Beschrankter Haftung
Heraeusstr. 12-14
Hanau HE 63450
6181350

**(P-7721)**
**JOHNSON MATTHEY INC**
Also Called: Noble Metals
12205 World Trade Dr, San Diego (92128-3766)
P.O. Box Orld Trade (92128)
PHONE.................................858 716-2400
Steve Hill, Brnch Mgr
EMP: 204
SALES (corp-wide): 16.3B Privately Held
Web: www.matthey.com
SIC: 3341 Secondary nonferrous metals
HQ: Johnson Matthey Inc.
435 Devon Park Dr Ste 600
Wayne PA 19087
610 971-3000

**(P-7722)**
**QUEMETCO WEST LLC**
720 S 7th Ave, City Of Industry (91746-3124)
PHONE.................................626 330-2294
Robert E Finn, Managing Member
▲ EMP: 20 EST: 2000
SALES (est): 10.91MM
SALES (corp-wide): 68.61MM Privately Held
Web: www.quemetco.com
SIC: 3341 Lead smelting and refining (secondary)
HQ: Eco-Bat Technologies Limited
Cowley Lodge
Matlock DE4 2

**(P-7723)**
**TEXAS TST INC**
13428 Benson Ave, Chino (91710-5258)
PHONE.................................951 685-2155
◆ EMP: 50
Web: www.tst-inc.com
SIC: 3341 Aluminum smelting and refining (secondary)

**(P-7724)**
**TST INC (PA)**
Also Called: Alpase
13428 Benson Ave, Chino (91710-5258)
PHONE.................................951 685-2155
Andrew G Stein, CEO
Robert A Stein, *
Greg Levine, *
James Davidson, *
◆ EMP: 260 EST: 1961
SQ FT: 123,000
SALES (est): 36.95MM
SALES (corp-wide): 36.95MM Privately Held
Web: www.tst-inc.com
SIC: 3341 5093 Aluminum smelting and refining (secondary); Metal scrap and waste materials

## 3351 Copper Rolling And Drawing

**(P-7725)**
**C F W RESEARCH & DEV CO**
Also Called: Cfw Precision Metal Components
338 S 4th St, Grover Beach (93433-1999)
P.O. Box 446 (93483-0446)
PHONE.................................805 489-8750
Michael A Greenelsh, Pr
Harlan Silva, VP
Kathryn Greenelsh, Sec
EMP: 16 EST: 1976
SQ FT: 10,000
SALES (est): 3.47MM
SALES (corp-wide): 10.4MM Privately Held
Web: www.cfwpmc.com
SIC: 3351 Wire, copper and copper alloy
PA: California Fine Wire Co.
338 S 4th St
805 489-5144

## 3353 Aluminum Sheet, Plate, And Foil

**(P-7726)**
**ALUM-A-FOLD PACIFIC INC**
Also Called: AFP
3730 Capitol Ave, City Of Industry (90601-1731)
PHONE.................................562 699-4550
▲ EMP: 45
Web: www.perfectdomain.com
SIC: 3353 Aluminum sheet, plate, and foil

**(P-7727)**
**GOLDEN STATE ASSEMBLY INC**
18220 Butterfield Blvd, Morgan Hill (95037-2824)
PHONE.................................510 226-8155
EMP: 120
Web: www.gsassembly.com

# 3353 - Aluminum Sheet, Plate, And Foil (P-7728)

**SIC: 3353** 3569 Aluminum sheet and strip; Assembly machines, non-metalworking
**PA:** Golden State Assembly, Inc.
47823 Westinghouse Dr

### (P-7728)
### GOLDEN STATE ASSEMBLY INC (PA)
47823 Westinghouse Dr, Fremont (94539-7437)
P.O. Box 611913 (95161)
**PHONE**..................510 226-8155
Cesar Madrueno, *CEO*
Maarten Oostendorp, *
**EMP:** 176 **EST:** 2009
**SALES (est):** 49.95MM **Privately Held**
**Web:** www.gsassembly.com
**SIC: 3353** 3569 3312 3679 Aluminum sheet and strip; Assembly machines, non-metalworking; Wire products, steel or iron; Harness assemblies, for electronic use: wire or cable

### (P-7729)
### HOWMET AEROSPACE INC
Also Called: Howmet Aerospace Inc
1550 Gage Rd, Montebello (90640-6614)
**PHONE**..................323 728-3901
**EMP:** 135
**SALES (corp-wide):** 6.64B **Publicly Held**
**Web:** www.howmet.com
**SIC: 3353** Aluminum sheet and strip
**PA:** Howmet Aerospace Inc.
201 Isabella St Ste 200
412 553-1950

### (P-7730)
### MATERIAL SCIENCES CORPORATION
Also Called: MSC-La
3730 Capitol Ave, City Of Industry (90601-1731)
**PHONE**..................562 699-4550
Patrick Murley, *CEO*
**EMP:** 45
**SALES (corp-wide):** 120.84MM **Privately Held**
**Web:** www.materialsciencescorp.com
**SIC: 3353** Aluminum sheet, plate, and foil
**PA:** Material Sciences Corporation
6855 Commerce Blvd
734 207-4444

### (P-7731)
### SOUTHWIRE COMPANY LLC
Southwire Master Service Ctr
9199 Cleveland Ave Ste 100, Rancho Cucamonga (91730-8559)
**PHONE**..................909 989-2888
David Jordan, *Brnch Mgr*
**EMP:** 95
**SALES (corp-wide):** 1.7B **Privately Held**
**Web:** www.southwire.com
**SIC: 3353** Aluminum sheet and strip
**PA:** Southwire Company, Llc
One Southwire Dr
770 832-4529

### (P-7732)
### SOUTHWIRE INC
Also Called: Alflex
20250 S Alameda St, Compton (90221-6207)
**PHONE**..................310 886-8300
Jorge Eulloqui, *Mgr*
**EMP:** 500
**SALES (corp-wide):** 1.7B **Privately Held**
**Web:** www.southwire.com
**SIC: 3353** 3644 3315 Coils, sheet aluminum; Electric conduits and fittings; Cable, steel: insulated or armored
**HQ:** Southwire Inc
11695 Pacific Ave
Fontana CA 92337
310 884-8500

### (P-7733)
### SOUTHWIRE INC (HQ)
Also Called: Electrical Products Division
11695 Pacific Ave, Fontana (92337-8225)
**PHONE**..................310 884-8500
Mark Kaminski, *COO*
John Wasz, *Pr*
Guyton Cochran, *Prin*
**EMP:** 15 **EST:** 1984
**SQ FT:** 210,000
**SALES (est):** 43.09MM
**SALES (corp-wide):** 1.7B **Privately Held**
**Web:** www.southwire.com
**SIC: 3353** 3644 3315 Coils, sheet aluminum; Electric conduits and fittings; Cable, steel: insulated or armored
**PA:** Southwire Company, Llc
One Southwire Dr
770 832-4529

### (P-7734)
### TCI TEXARKANA INC
Also Called: Texarkana Aluminum
5855 Obispo Ave, Long Beach (90805)
**PHONE**..................562 808-8000
Johnny Hsieh, *CEO*
James Chang, *VP*
Andrew Chang, *Contrlr*
**EMP:** 100 **EST:** 2018
**SALES (est):** 2.54MM **Privately Held**
**SIC: 3353** Coils, sheet aluminum
**HQ:** Ta Chen International, Inc.
5860 N Paramount Blvd
Long Beach CA 90805
562 808-8000

---

## 3354 Aluminum Extruded Products

### (P-7735)
### ANAHEIM EXTRUSION CO INC
1330 N Kraemer Blvd, Anaheim (92806-1401)
P.O. Box 6380 (92816-0380)
**PHONE**..................714 630-3111
**EMP:** 80 **EST:** 1974
**SALES (est):** 14.35MM **Privately Held**
**Web:** www.anaheimextrude.com
**SIC: 3354** Aluminum extruded products
**HQ:** Universal Molding Company
9151 Imperial Hwy
Downey CA 90242
310 886-1750

### (P-7736)
### DARFIELD INDUSTRIES INC (PA)
4626 Sperry St, Los Angeles (90039-1018)
**PHONE**..................818 247-8350
Rosanne M Kusar, *Ch Bd*
Jennifer K Hillman, *Pr*
Rosanne M Kusar, *Corporate Secretary*
Angelica K Clark, *Treas*
**EMP:** 16 **EST:** 1957
**SQ FT:** 64,980
**SALES (est):** 8.63MM
**SALES (corp-wide):** 8.63MM **Privately Held**
**Web:** www.sunvalleyextrusion.com
**SIC: 3354** Aluminum extruded products

### (P-7737)
### DWA COMPOSITE SPECIALTIES INC
Also Called: Dwa Aluminum Composites
21100 Superior St, Chatsworth (91311-4308)
**PHONE**..................818 885-8654
**EMP:** 19
**SIC: 3354** Aluminum extruded products

### (P-7738)
### FRY REGLET CORPORATION (PA)
14013 Marquardt Ave, Santa Fe Springs (90670-5018)
P.O. Box 665 (90637-0665)
**PHONE**..................800 237-9773
Stephen Reed, *CEO*
Avon M Hall, *
James Tuttle, *
**EMP:** 75 **EST:** 1945
**SQ FT:** 20,000
**SALES (est):** 35.64MM
**SALES (corp-wide):** 35.64MM **Privately Held**
**Web:** www.fryreglet.com
**SIC: 3354** Aluminum extruded products

### (P-7739)
### GLOBAL TRUSS AMERICA LLC
Also Called: Global Truss
4295 Charter St, Vernon (90058-2520)
**PHONE**..................323 415-6225
Charles Davies, *Managing Member*
Kenneth Kahn, *
◆ **EMP:** 55 **EST:** 2004
**SQ FT:** 60,000
**SALES (est):** 6.98MM **Privately Held**
**Web:** www.globaltruss.com
**SIC: 3354** Aluminum extruded products

### (P-7740)
### HYDRO EXTRUSION USA LLC
18111 Railroad St, City Of Industry (91748-1216)
**PHONE**..................626 964-3411
Matt Zundel, *Sls Dir*
**EMP:** 300
**Web:** www.hydro.com
**SIC: 3354** Aluminum extruded products
**HQ:** Hydro Extrusion Usa, Llc
6250 N River Rd Ste 5000
Rosemont IL 60018

### (P-7741)
### KAISER ALUMINUM CORPORATION
6250 Bandini Blvd, Commerce (90040-3168)
**PHONE**..................323 726-8011
**EMP:** 74
**SALES (corp-wide):** 3.09B **Publicly Held**
**Web:** www.kaiseraluminum.com
**SIC: 3354** Aluminum extruded products
**PA:** Kaiser Aluminum Corporation
1550 W Mcewen Dr Ste 500
629 252-7040

### (P-7742)
### LUXFER INC
1995 3rd St, Riverside (92507-3483)
**PHONE**..................951 684-5110
Brian Mcguire, *Mgr*
**EMP:** 31
**SALES (corp-wide):** 405MM **Privately Held**
**Web:** www.luxfercylinders.com

**SIC: 3354** 3728 Aluminum extruded products; Aircraft parts and equipment, nec
**HQ:** Luxfer Inc.
3016 Kansas Ave Bldg 1
Riverside CA 92507
951 684-5110

### (P-7743)
### MERIT ALUMINUM INC (PA)
2480 Railroad St, Corona (92880)
**PHONE**..................951 735-1770
Michael Rapport, *CEO*
Evan Rapport, *
▲ **EMP:** 122 **EST:** 1990
**SQ FT:** 58,000
**SALES (est):** 39.33MM **Privately Held**
**Web:** www.meritaluminum.com
**SIC: 3354** Aluminum extruded products

### (P-7744)
### NEAL FEAY COMPANY
Also Called: Troy Metal Products
133 S La Patera Ln, Goleta (93117-3291)
**PHONE**..................805 967-4521
Neal C Rasmussen, *CEO*
N J Rasmussen, *
Alex Rasmussen, *
**EMP:** 60 **EST:** 1944
**SQ FT:** 50,000
**SALES (est):** 3.9MM **Privately Held**
**Web:** www.nealfeay.com
**SIC: 3354** 3469 Tube, extruded or drawn, aluminum; Electronic enclosures, stamped or pressed metal

### (P-7745)
### PENGCHENG ALUMINUM ENTERPRISE INC USA
Also Called: Zhong W Ang Group
19605 E Walnut Dr N, Walnut (91789-2815)
**PHONE**..................909 598-7933
▲ **EMP:** 30
**Web:** www.pcaus.com
**SIC: 3354** Aluminum extruded products

### (P-7746)
### PRL ALUMINUM INC
14760 Don Julian Rd, City Of Industry (91746-3107)
**PHONE**..................626 968-7507
Roberto Landeros, *CEO*
**EMP:** 100 **EST:** 2004
**SALES (est):** 8.07MM **Privately Held**
**Web:** www.architecturalglassandmetal.com
**SIC: 3354** Aluminum extruded products
**PA:** Prl Glass Systems, Inc.
13644 Nelson Ave

### (P-7747)
### SAMUEL SON & CO (USA) INC
Also Called: Sierra Aluminum
2345 Fleetwood Dr, Riverside (92509-2410)
**PHONE**..................951 781-7800
**EMP:** 24
**SALES (corp-wide):** 1.54B **Privately Held**
**Web:** www.samuel.com
**SIC: 3354** Aluminum extruded products
**HQ:** Samuel, Son & Co. (Usa) Inc.
1401 Davey Rd Ste 300
Woodridge IL 60517
800 323-4424

### (P-7748)
### SIERRA ALUMINUM COMPANY
2345 Fleetwood Dr, Riverside (92509-2426)
**PHONE**..................951 781-7800
▲ **EMP:** 24
**Web:** www.samuel.com

SIC: 3354  Aluminum extruded products

**(P-7749)**
**SUN VALLEY PRODUCTS  INC**
Also Called: Sun Valley Extrusion
4640 Sperry St, Los Angeles  (90039-1018)
PHONE..............................818 247-8350
Kerry Dodge, *Brnch Mgr*
EMP: 20
SALES (corp-wide): 8.63MM **Privately Held**
Web: www.sunvalleyextrusion.com
SIC: 3354  Aluminum extruded products
HQ: Sun Valley Products, Inc.
 4626 Sperry St
 Los Angeles CA 90039
 818 247-8350

**(P-7750)**
**SUN VALLEY PRODUCTS  INC (HQ)**
4626 Sperry St, Los Angeles  (90039-1018)
PHONE..............................818 247-8350
Jennifer K Hillman, *Pr*
Rosanne M Kusar,
Angelica K Clark, *
EMP: 40 EST: 1960
SQ FT: 64,980
SALES (est): 8.63MM
SALES (corp-wide): 8.63MM **Privately Held**
Web: www.sunvalleyextrusion.com
SIC: 3354  Aluminum extruded products
PA: Darfield Industries, Inc.
 4626 Sperry St
 818 247-8350

**(P-7751)**
**SUPERIOR METAL SHAPES  INC**
4730 Eucalyptus Ave, Chino  (91710-9255)
PHONE..............................909 947-3455
David A Stockton, *Pr*
EMP: 40 EST: 1983
SQ FT: 64,000
SALES (est): 4.68MM **Privately Held**
Web: www.superiormetalshapes.net
SIC: 3354  Shapes, extruded aluminum, nec

**(P-7752)**
**TRULITE GL ALUM SOLUTIONS LLC**
19430 San Jose Ave, City Of Industry  (91748-1421)
PHONE..............................800 877-8439
Elizabeth Hemsing, *Mgr*
EMP: 72
Web: www.trulite.com
SIC: 3354  Aluminum extruded products
PA: Trulite Glass & Aluminum Solutions, Llc
 1750 Funders Pkwy Ste 154

**(P-7753)**
**US POLYMERS  INC**
5910 Bandini Blvd, Commerce  (90040-2963)
PHONE..............................323 727-6888
Vram Ohanesiam, *Mgr*
EMP: 100
SALES (corp-wide): 28.74MM **Privately Held**
Web: www.uspolymersinc.com
SIC: 3354 5719  Aluminum extruded products ; Window furnishings
PA: U.S. Polymers, Inc.
 1057 S Vail Ave
 323 728-3023

**(P-7754)**
**VISION SYSTEMS  INC**
11322 Woodside Ave N, Santee  (92071-4728)
PHONE..............................619 258-7300
Fred W Witte, *Pr*
James Schlereth, *
▲ EMP: 60 EST: 1984
SQ FT: 32,000
SALES (est): 19.28MM **Privately Held**
Web: www.visionsystems.com
SIC: 3354 3442  Aluminum extruded products ; Window and door frames

**(P-7755)**
**VISTA METALS CORP (PA)**
13425 Whittram Ave, Fontana  (92335-2999)
PHONE..............................909 823-4278
Andrew Primack, *CEO*
Raymond Alpert, *
Steve Chevlin, *
Robert Praefke, *
◆ EMP: 235 EST: 1968
SQ FT: 17,000
SALES (est): 30.25MM
SALES (corp-wide): 30.25MM **Privately Held**
Web: www.vistametals.com
SIC: 3354 3341  Aluminum extruded products ; Aluminum smelting and refining (secondary)

## 3355 Aluminum Rolling And Drawing, Nec

**(P-7756)**
**ARCADIA INC**
Also Called: ARCADIA INC.
2324 Del Monte St, West Sacramento  (95691-3807)
PHONE..............................916 375-1478
Eddy Sala, *Brnch Mgr*
EMP: 22
SALES (corp-wide): 719.19MM **Publicly Held**
Web: www.arcadiainc.com
SIC: 3355  Extrusion ingot, aluminum: made in rolling mills
HQ: Arcadia Products, Llc
 2301 E Vernon Ave
 Los Angeles CA 90023
 323 771-9819

**(P-7757)**
**ARCADIA PRODUCTS  LLC (HQ)**
Also Called: Arcadia Norcal
2301 E Vernon Ave, Los Angeles  (90023)
PHONE..............................323 771-9819
James Schladen, *CEO*
Khan Chow, *CFO*
▲ EMP: 250 EST: 1985
SQ FT: 50,000
SALES (est): 71.39MM
SALES (corp-wide): 719.19MM **Publicly Held**
Web: www.arcadiainc.com
SIC: 3355  Extrusion ingot, aluminum: made in rolling mills
PA: Dmc Global Inc.
 11800 Ridge Pkwy Ste 300
 303 665-5700

**(P-7758)**
**DURALUM PRODUCTS  INC**
Also Called: Duralum
551 N Loop Dr, Ontario  (91761-8629)
PHONE..............................951 736-4500
Ron Cull, *Mgr*
EMP: 15
SALES (corp-wide): 13.17MM **Privately Held**
Web: www.duralum.com
SIC: 3355  Aluminum rolling and drawing, nec
PA: Duralum Products, Inc.
 2485 Railroad St
 916 452-7021

**(P-7759)**
**METALS USA BUILDING PDTS LP (DH)**
Also Called: Metals USA
955 Columbia St, Brea  (92821-2923)
PHONE..............................713 946-9000
Charles Canning, *Pt*
Robert Mcpherson, *Pt*
▲ EMP: 700 EST: 1960
SQ FT: 60,000
SALES (est): 31.78MM
SALES (corp-wide): 14.81B **Publicly Held**
Web: www.metalsusa.com
SIC: 3355 5031 1542  Structural shapes, rolled, aluminum; Building materials, exterior ; Commercial and office buildings, renovation and repair
HQ: Metals Usa, Inc.
 800 W Cypress Creed Rd St
 Fort Lauderdale FL 33309
 215 673-3595

**(P-7760)**
**METALS USA BUILDING PDTS LP**
1951 S Parco Ave Ste C, Ontario  (91761-8315)
PHONE..............................800 325-1305
Steve Brang, *Mgr*
EMP: 90
SALES (corp-wide): 14.81B **Publicly Held**
Web: www.metalsusa.com
SIC: 3355  Structural shapes, rolled, aluminum
HQ: Metals Usa Building Products Lp
 955 Columbia St
 Brea CA 92821
 713 946-9000

**(P-7761)**
**SOUTHERN ALUM FINSHG CO INC**
Also Called: Saf West
4356 Caterpillar Rd, Redding  (96003-1422)
PHONE..............................530 244-7518
Sam Heier, *Brnch Mgr*
EMP: 90
SALES (corp-wide): 49.04MM **Privately Held**
Web: www.saf.com
SIC: 3355  Structural shapes, rolled, aluminum
PA: Southern Aluminum Finishing Company, Inc.
 1581 Huber St Nw
 404 355-1560

## 3356 Nonferrous Rolling And Drawing, Nec

**(P-7762)**
**DYNAMET INCORPORATED**
16052 Beach Blvd Ste 221, Huntington Beach  (92647-3855)
PHONE..............................714 375-3150
Tom Proteau, *Mgr*
EMP: 32
SALES (corp-wide): 2.76B **Publicly Held**
Web: www.carpentertechnology.com
SIC: 3356  Titanium and titanium alloy bars, sheets, strip, etc.
HQ: Dynamet Incorporated
 195 Museum Rd
 Washington PA 15301
 724 228-1000

**(P-7763)**
**INTERSPACE BATTERY  INC (PA)**
2009 W San Bernardino Rd, West Covina  (91790-1006)
PHONE..............................626 813-1234
Paul Godber, *Ch Bd*
Donald W Godber, *Pr*
EMP: 23 EST: 1970
SQ FT: 36,000
SALES (est): 3.57MM
SALES (corp-wide): 3.57MM **Privately Held**
Web: www.concordebattery.com
SIC: 3356 3691  Battery metal; Storage batteries

**(P-7764)**
**NEW CNTURY MTALS SOUTHEAST INC**
Also Called: Rti Los Angeles
15723 Shoemaker Ave, Norwalk  (90650-6863)
PHONE..............................562 356-6804
Jeremy S Halford, *CEO*
Marie T Batz, *
EMP: 224 EST: 1998
SALES (est): 2.18MM
SALES (corp-wide): 6.64B **Publicly Held**
SIC: 3356  Titanium
HQ: Rmi Titanium Company, Llc
 1000 Warren Ave
 Niles OH 44446
 330 652-9952

**(P-7765)**
**OCEANIA INTERNATIONAL  LLC**
Also Called: Stanford Advanced Materials
23661 Birtcher Dr, Lake Forest  (92630-1770)
PHONE..............................949 407-8904
Alexander Chen, *Managing Member*
▲ EMP: 40 EST: 2012
SALES (est): 3.69MM **Privately Held**
Web: www.samaterials.com
SIC: 3356 3313  Titanium and titanium alloy bars, sheets, strip, etc.; Ferromolybdenum

**(P-7766)**
**P KAY METAL  INC (PA)**
Also Called: P K Metal
2448 E 25th St, Los Angeles  (90058-1209)
PHONE..............................323 585-5058
Larry Kay, *Pr*
Sharon Kay, *
Cindy Flame, *
▲ EMP: 44 EST: 1977
SALES (est): 10.77MM
SALES (corp-wide): 10.77MM **Privately Held**
Web: www.pkaymetal.com
SIC: 3356  Lead and lead alloy bars, pipe, plates, shapes, etc.

**(P-7767)**
**SEMCO ENTERPRISES INC**
475 Wilson Way, City Of Industry  (91744-3935)
PHONE..............................626 333-2237
EMP: 16 EST: 1973
SALES (est): 2.3MM **Privately Held**
Web: www.semcozinc.com
SIC: 3356  Zinc and zinc alloy: rolling, drawing, or extruding

# 3356 - Nonferrous Rolling And Drawing, Nec (P-7768)

## (P-7768)
### UMC ACQUISITION CORP (PA)
Also Called: Universal Molding Company
9151 Imperial Hwy, Downey (90242-2808)
PHONE.................................562 940-0300
Dominick L Baione, *Ch Bd*
Edward L Koch Iii, *Pr*
**EMP:** 50 **EST:** 1998
**SALES (est):** 100.77MM **Privately Held**
Web: www.universalmold.com
**SIC: 3356** 3354 3471 3479 Nonferrous rolling and drawing, nec; Aluminum extruded products; Anodizing (plating) of metals or formed products; Aluminum coating of metal products

## (P-7769)
### UNIVERSAL MOLDING COMPANY (HQ)
9151 Imperial Hwy, Downey (90242-2808)
PHONE.................................310 886-1750
Dominick L Baione, *Ch Bd*
**EMP:** 160 **EST:** 1952
**SQ FT:** 62,000
**SALES (est):** 97.2MM **Privately Held**
Web: www.universalmold.com
**SIC: 3356** 3354 3448 3471 Nonferrous rolling and drawing, nec; Aluminum extruded products; Screen enclosures; Anodizing (plating) of metals or formed products
PA: Umc Acquisition Corp.
9151 E Imperial Hwy

## (P-7770)
### VSMPO-TIRUS US INC
Also Called: West Coast Service Center
2850 E Cedar St, Ontario (91761-8514)
PHONE.................................909 230-9020
Dave Richardson, *Mgr*
**EMP:** 61
Web: www.vsmpo-tirus.com
**SIC: 3356** Titanium
HQ: Vsmpo-Tirus, U.S., Inc.
401 Riverport Dr
Leetsdale PA 15056
720 746-1023

## 3357 Nonferrous Wiredrawing And Insulating

## (P-7771)
### ARIA TECHNOLOGIES INC
102 Wright Brothers Ave, Livermore (94551-9240)
PHONE.................................925 447-7500
Matthew Mccormick, *CEO*
Joe Mcguinness, *Pr*
Dave Dickens, *
▲ **EMP:** 144 **EST:** 1991
**SQ FT:** 15,000
**SALES (est):** 23.6MM
**SALES (corp-wide):** 12.55B **Publicly Held**
Web: www.ariatech.com
**SIC: 3357** Communication wire
PA: Amphenol Corporation
358 Hall Ave
203 265-8900

## (P-7772)
### BEE WIRE & CABLE INC
2850 E Spruce St, Ontario (91761-8550)
PHONE.................................909 923-5800
Arjan Bera, *Pr*
Kiran Kaneria, *
Nalin Kaneria, *
▲ **EMP:** 26 **EST:** 1979
**SQ FT:** 34,400
**SALES (est):** 3.56MM **Privately Held**
Web: www.beeflex.com
**SIC: 3357** Building wire and cable, nonferrous

## (P-7773)
### BELDEN INC
Also Called: Coast Custom Cable
1048 E Burgrove St, Carson (90746-3514)
PHONE.................................310 639-9473
Michael Dugar, *Bmch Mgr*
**EMP:** 750
**SALES (corp-wide):** 2.51B **Publicly Held**
Web: www.alphawire.com
**SIC: 3357** 3699 Coaxial cable, nonferrous; Electrical equipment and supplies, nec
PA: Belden Inc.
1 N Brentwood Blvd Fl 15
314 854-8000

## (P-7774)
### BRIDGEWAVE COMMUNICATIONS INC
17034 Camino San Bernardo, San Diego (92127-5708)
PHONE.................................408 567-6900
Amir Makleff, *Pr*
John Keating, *
▲ **EMP:** 25 **EST:** 1998
**SALES (est):** 4.29MM **Privately Held**
Web: www.bridgewave.com
**SIC: 3357** 3229 Communication wire; Pressed and blown glass, nec

## (P-7775)
### BROADATA COMMUNICATIONS INC
2545 W 237th St Ste K, Torrance (90505-5229)
PHONE.................................310 530-1416
David Faulkner, *CEO*
Freddie Lin, *
Patty Shaw, *
German Lopez, *
◆ **EMP:** 40 **EST:** 2000
**SQ FT:** 10,000
**SALES (est):** 12.08MM **Privately Held**
Web: www.broadatacom.com
**SIC: 3357** 3663 Fiber optic cable (insulated); Television broadcasting and communications equipment

## (P-7776)
### CABLESYS LLC
1270 N Hancock St, Anaheim (92807-1922)
PHONE.................................562 356-3222
Mike Lin, *Managing Member*
▲ **EMP:** 20 **EST:** 1997
**SQ FT:** 10,000
**SALES (est):** 2.49MM **Privately Held**
Web: www.cablesys.com
**SIC: 3357** Communication wire

## (P-7777)
### CALIFORNIA FINE WIRE CO (PA)
338 S 4th St, Grover Beach (93433-1999)
P.O. Box 446 (93483-0446)
PHONE.................................805 489-5144
**EMP:** 36 **EST:** 1961
**SALES (est):** 10.4MM
**SALES (corp-wide):** 10.4MM **Privately Held**
Web: www.calfinewire.com
**SIC: 3357** 3315 3466 3341 Nonferrous wiredrawing and insulating; Wire, ferrous/iron; Closures, stamped metal; Secondary nonferrous metals

## (P-7778)
### CALIFORNIA INSULATED WIRE &
3050 N California St, Burbank (91504-2004)
PHONE.................................818 569-4930
Bill Boyd, *Pr*
Micheal Boyd, *
Bruce Boyd, *
Lois Boyd, *
**EMP:** 60 **EST:** 1978
**SQ FT:** 26,000
**SALES (est):** 8.72MM **Privately Held**
Web: www.ciwinc.com
**SIC: 3357** Communication wire

## (P-7779)
### CALMONT ENGRG & ELEC CORP (PA)
Also Called: Calmont Wire & Cable
420 E Alton Ave, Santa Ana (92707-4242)
PHONE.................................714 549-0336
Barbara Monteleone, *Pr*
Blanche F Chilcote, *
**EMP:** 36 **EST:** 1970
**SQ FT:** 24,000
**SALES (est):** 5.41MM
**SALES (corp-wide):** 5.41MM **Privately Held**
Web: www.calmont.com
**SIC: 3357** 3061 Nonferrous wiredrawing and insulating; Medical and surgical rubber tubing (extruded and lathe-cut)

## (P-7780)
### CENTURUM INFORMATION TECH INC
4250 Pacific Hwy Ste 105, San Diego (92110-3219)
PHONE.................................619 224-1100
Brad Geiger, *Mgr*
**EMP:** 26
**SALES (corp-wide):** 43.66MM **Privately Held**
Web: www.centurum.com
**SIC: 3357** Shipboard cable, nonferrous
HQ: Centurum Information Technology, Inc.
651 Route 73 N Ste 107
Marlton NJ 08053
856 751-1111

## (P-7781)
### CENTURY WIRE & CABLE INC
5701 S Eastern Ave, Commerce (90040-2973)
PHONE.................................800 999-5566
David Lifschitz, *CEO*
Carl Tom, *
Rowdy Oxford, *
William Suddarth, *
**EMP:** 100 **EST:** 1982
**SALES (est):** 8.88MM
**SALES (corp-wide):** 127.37MM **Privately Held**
Web: www.centurywire.com
**SIC: 3357** 5063 Nonferrous wiredrawing and insulating; Electrical apparatus and equipment
HQ: Gehr Industries, Inc.
5701 S Eastern Ave
Commerce CA 90040
323 728-5558

## (P-7782)
### CFKBA INC
508 2nd Ave, Redwood City (94063-3848)
PHONE.................................650 302-6331
**EMP:** 37
**SALES (corp-wide):** 5.84MM **Privately Held**
**SIC: 3357** Nonferrous wiredrawing and insulating
PA: Cfkba Inc.
150 Jefferson Dr
650 847-3900

## (P-7783)
### CFKBA INC (PA)
150 Jefferson Dr, Menlo Park (94025-1115)
PHONE.................................650 847-3900
Richard Johns, *Ch Bd*
Wendell Jesseman, *
Laurent Mayer, *
◆ **EMP:** 27 **EST:** 1962
**SQ FT:** 43,000
**SALES (est):** 2.85MM
**SALES (corp-wide):** 2.85MM **Privately Held**
**SIC: 3357** 5063 Nonferrous wiredrawing and insulating; Wire and cable

## (P-7784)
### DICAR INC
1285 Alma Ct, San Jose (95112-5943)
P.O. Box 1653 (95038-1653)
PHONE.................................408 295-1106
Edward Garcia, *CEO*
Ed Garcia, *
Carol Garcia, *
Diana M Garcia, *
**EMP:** 26 **EST:** 1980
**SQ FT:** 9,900
**SALES (est):** 1.17MM **Privately Held**
Web: www.dicar.com
**SIC: 3357** 3599 3089 3679 Coaxial cable, nonferrous; Machine and other job shop work; Blow molded finished plastics products, nec; Harness assemblies, for electronic use: wire or cable

## (P-7785)
### FIBEROPTIC SYSTEMS INC
60 Moreland Rd Ste A, Simi Valley (93065-1643)
PHONE.................................805 579-6600
Sanford S Stark, *Pr*
Kathy Hanau, *
**EMP:** 29 **EST:** 1982
**SQ FT:** 14,000
**SALES (est):** 6.21MM **Privately Held**
Web: www.fiberopticsystems.com
**SIC: 3357** 3229 Fiber optic cable (insulated); Fiber optics strands

## (P-7786)
### GEHR INDUSTRIES INC (HQ)
Also Called: Gehr Group
5701 S Eastern Ave, Commerce (90040-2973)
PHONE.................................323 728-5558
David Lifschitz, *CEO*
Carlton Tom, *
Mark Goldman, *
William Suddarth, *
Maximilian Paetzold, *
▲ **EMP:** 140 **EST:** 1966
**SALES (est):** 57.64MM
**SALES (corp-wide):** 127.37MM **Privately Held**
Web: www.gehrindustries.com
**SIC: 3357** 5063 5072 5085 Nonferrous wiredrawing and insulating; Electrical apparatus and equipment; Hardware; Industrial supplies
PA: The Gehr Group Inc
5701 S Eastern Ave
323 728-5558

# PRODUCTS & SERVICES SECTION

## 3363 - Aluminum Die-castings (P-7807)

**(P-7787)**
**HELISTRAND INC**
707 E Yanonali St, Santa Barbara (93103-3273)
PHONE..................805 963-4518
EMP: 20 EST: 1972
SALES (est): 600K Privately Held
Web: www.helistrand.com
SIC: 3357 Aircraft wire and cable, nonferrous

**(P-7788)**
**JEB HOLDINGS CORP**
42033 Rio Nedo, Temecula (92590-3705)
P.O. Box 67 (92549-0067)
PHONE..................951 296-9900
Gordon Brown, Pr
EMP: 23
SALES (corp-wide): 8.59MM Privately Held
Web: www.southbaycable.com
SIC: 3357 Nonferrous wiredrawing and insulating
PA: Jeb Holdings Corp.
54125 Maranatha Dr
951 659-2183

**(P-7789)**
**NEPTEC OS INC**
Also Called: Neptec Optical Solutions
454 Kato Ter, Fremont (94539-8332)
PHONE..................510 687-1101
David Cheng, Pr
Chaoyu Yue, *
EMP: 25 EST: 2008
SALES (est): 5.39MM Privately Held
Web: www.neptecos.com
SIC: 3357 Fiber optic cable (insulated)

**(P-7790)**
**OKONITE COMPANY INC**
2900 Skyway Dr, Santa Maria (93455-1897)
PHONE..................805 922-6682
Rick Flory, Brnch Mgr
EMP: 132
SQ FT: 10,000
SALES (corp-wide): 55.09MM Privately Held
Web: www.okonite.com
SIC: 3357 Nonferrous wiredrawing and insulating
PA: The Okonite Company Inc
102 Hilltop Rd
201 825-0300

**(P-7791)**
**PHILATRON INTERNATIONAL**
15645 Clanton Cir, Santa Fe Springs (90670-5613)
PHONE..................562 802-2570
EMP: 20
SALES (corp-wide): 24.17MM Privately Held
Web: www.philatron.com
SIC: 3357 Nonferrous wiredrawing and insulating
PA: Philatron International
15315 Cornet Ave
562 802-0452

**(P-7792)**
**PRECISION FIBER PRODUCTS INC**
Also Called: Pfp
642 Palomar St, Chula Vista (91911-2626)
PHONE..................408 946-4040
Ray Pierce, Pr
◆ EMP: 30 EST: 2003
SALES (est): 3.47MM Privately Held
Web: www.precisionfiberproducts.com

SIC: 3357 Fiber optic cable (insulated)

**(P-7793)**
**PRIME WIRE & CABLE INC (HQ)**
Also Called: Clear Power Innovations Co
1330 Valley Vista Dr, Diamond Bar (91765-3910)
PHONE..................888 445-9955
Juhng-shyu Shieh, CEO
▲ EMP: 21 EST: 1981
SQ FT: 150,000
SALES (est): 122.32MM Privately Held
Web: www.primewirecable.com
SIC: 3357 5063 Building wire and cable, nonferrous; Wire and cable
PA: Yfc-Boneagle Electric Co., Ltd.
No. 12-9, Lane 130, Zhongshan E. Rd., Sec. 2

**(P-7794)**
**PRIME WIRE & CABLE INC**
11701 6th St, Rancho Cucamonga (91730-6030)
PHONE..................323 266-2010
EMP: 85
Web: www.primewirecable.com
SIC: 3357 Nonferrous wiredrawing and insulating
HQ: Prime Wire & Cable, Inc.
1330 Valley Vista Dr
Diamond Bar CA 91765
888 445-9955

**(P-7795)**
**QPC FIBER OPTIC LLC**
27612 El Lazo, Laguna Niguel (92677-3913)
PHONE..................949 361-8855
Steven J Wilkes, Pr
David Olsen, *
EMP: 30 EST: 1999
SQ FT: 1,400
SALES (est): 9.54MM Privately Held
Web: www.qpcfiber.com
SIC: 3357 Fiber optic cable (insulated)

**(P-7796)**
**STANDARD WIRE & CABLE CO (PA)**
Also Called: American Wire Sales
2050 E Vista Bella Way, Rancho Dominguez (90220-6109)
PHONE..................310 609-1811
Russell J Skrable, Pr
Dick Hampikian, Ch Bd
◆ EMP: 22 EST: 1947
SQ FT: 45,500
SALES (est): 10.86MM
SALES (corp-wide): 10.86MM Privately Held
Web: www.standard-wire.com
SIC: 3357 5063 Coaxial cable, nonferrous; Wire and cable

**(P-7797)**
**SUPERIOR ESSEX INC**
5250 Ontario Mills Pkwy Ste 300, Ontario (91764-5131)
PHONE..................909 481-4804
Victor Alegria, Brnch Mgr
EMP: 103
Web: www.superioressex.com
SIC: 3357 Nonferrous wiredrawing and insulating
HQ: Superior Essex Inc.
5770 Pwers Frry Rd Nw Ste
Atlanta GA 30327
770 657-6000

**(P-7798)**
**VICTOR WIRE & CABLE INC**
12915 S Spring St, Los Angeles (90061-1631)
PHONE..................310 842-9933
Joe Benson, CEO
Mark Daniels, CFO
EMP: 15 EST: 2021
SALES (est): 652.4K Privately Held
Web: www.victorwire.com
SIC: 3357 5051 Building wire and cable, nonferrous; Cable, wire

**(P-7799)**
**WAVENET INC (PA)**
707 E Sepulveda Blvd, Carson (90745-6032)
PHONE..................310 885-4200
Yl Hong Jang, CEO
Kevin Chang, COO
Keun Hee Chang, Sec
▲ EMP: 18 EST: 1990
SQ FT: 29,000
SALES (est): 6.29MM Privately Held
Web: www.wavenetcable.com
SIC: 3357 Fiber optic cable (insulated)

**(P-7800)**
**WINCHSTER INTRCNNECT CM CA INC**
Also Called: C B S
1810 Diamond St, San Marcos (92078-5100)
PHONE..................800 848-4257
Lewis Brian Falk, CEO
Donald Falk, *
Shannon Baroni, *
▲ EMP: 175 EST: 1965
SQ FT: 40,000
SALES (est): 46.8MM Privately Held
Web: www.falmat.com
SIC: 3357 5063 Nonferrous wiredrawing and insulating; Wire and cable
HQ: Aptiv Corporation
5725 Innovation Dr
Troy MI 48098

**(P-7801)**
**WINSTRONICES INTERNATIONAL INC**
Also Called: Winstronics
3817 Spinnaker Ct, Fremont (94538-6537)
PHONE..................510 226-7588
Ben Yueh, Pr
▲ EMP: 25 EST: 1992
SQ FT: 12,000
SALES (est): 7.44MM Privately Held
Web: www.winstronics.com
SIC: 3357 Communication wire

**(P-7802)**
**WIRE TECHNOLOGY CORPORATION**
9527 Laurel St, Los Angeles (90002-2653)
P.O. Box 1608 (90280-1608)
PHONE..................310 635-6935
Rachel Mendoza, Pr
Darlene Delange, *
Robert Mendoza, *
EMP: 25 EST: 1970
SQ FT: 4,000
SALES (est): 3.02MM Privately Held
Web: www.wiretechnologycorp.com
SIC: 3357 Nonferrous wiredrawing and insulating

## 3363 Aluminum Die-castings

**(P-7803)**
**A & B DIE CASTING COMPANY INC**
900 Alfred Nobel Dr, Hercules (94547-1814)
PHONE..................877 708-0009
Bernard E Dathe, Pr
Alex Hantke, *
Robert Dathe, *
EMP: 17 EST: 1951
SQ FT: 19,000
SALES (est): 1.41MM Privately Held
Web: www.abdiecasting.com
SIC: 3363 3364 Aluminum die-castings; Zinc and zinc-base alloy die-castings

**(P-7804)**
**AEROTEC ALLOYS INC**
10632 Alondra Blvd, Norwalk (90650-5301)
PHONE..................562 809-1378
Robert W Franklin, CEO
Mitchell Frahm, *
EMP: 50 EST: 1986
SQ FT: 18,000
SALES (est): 7.11MM Privately Held
Web: www.aerotecalloys.com
SIC: 3363 3312 3365 3325 Aluminum die-castings; Blast furnaces and steel mills; Aluminum foundries; Steel foundries, nec

**(P-7805)**
**ALLOY DIE CASTING CO (PA)**
Also Called: ADC Aerospace
6550 Caballero Blvd, Buena Park (90620-1130)
PHONE..................714 521-9800
Rick Simpson, CEO
Eric Sanders, Pr
Wim Huijs, VP
Maeli Garcia, Dir
EMP: 135 EST: 1939
SQ FT: 55,000
SALES (est): 23.12MM
SALES (corp-wide): 23.12MM Privately Held
Web: www.adc-aerospace.com
SIC: 3363 Aluminum die-castings

**(P-7806)**
**ALUMINUM DIE CASTING CO INC**
10775 San Sevaine Way, Jurupa Valley (91752-1146)
PHONE..................951 681-3900
Steve Bennett, CEO
Rudy Bennett, *
James Bennett, Stockholder*
EMP: 65 EST: 1950
SQ FT: 31,000
SALES (est): 3.39MM Privately Held
Web: www.adc3900.com
SIC: 3363 3364 Aluminum die-castings; Nonferrous die-castings except aluminum

**(P-7807)**
**COOLING SOURCE INC**
2021 Las Positas Ct Ste 101, Livermore (94551-7304)
PHONE..................925 292-1293
Michel Gelinas, Pr
▲ EMP: 118 EST: 2009
SQ FT: 4,000
SALES (est): 8.8MM Privately Held
Web: www.coolingsource.com
SIC: 3363 3354 3325 3469 Aluminum die-castings; Shapes, extruded aluminum, nec; Alloy steel castings, except investment; Metal stampings, nec

# 3363 - Aluminum Die-castings (P-7808)

**(P-7808)**
**EDELBROCK FOUNDRY CORP**
1320 S Buena Vista St, San Jacinto (92583-4665)
PHONE.................................951 654-6677
Otis Victor Edelbrock, *Pr*
Ronald L Webb, *
Nancy Edelbrock, *
Aristedes Seles, *
Camme Edelbrock, *
**EMP:** 29 **EST:** 1938
**SQ FT:** 75,000
**SALES (est):** 4.34MM **Privately Held**
Web: www.edelbrockfoundry.com
**SIC: 3363** 3365 3325  Aluminum die-castings; Aluminum foundries; Steel foundries, nec
HQ: Edelbrock, Llc
  8649 Hacks Cross Rd
  Olive Branch MS 38654
  310 781-2222

**(P-7809)**
**HYATT DIE CAST AND ENGINEERING CORPORATION - SOUTH (PA)**
4656 Lincoln Ave, Cypress (90630-2650)
P.O. Box 728 (90630-0728)
PHONE.................................714 826-7550
**EMP:** 80 **EST:** 1956
**SALES (est):** 24.28MM
**SALES (corp-wide):** 24.28MM **Privately Held**
Web: www.hyattdiecast.com
**SIC: 3363**  Aluminum die-castings

**(P-7810)**
**HYATT DIE CAST ENGRG CORP - S**
12250 Industry St, Garden Grove (92841-2816)
PHONE.................................714 622-2131
Mike Senter, *Brnch Mgr*
**EMP:** 35
**SALES (corp-wide):** 24.28MM **Privately Held**
Web: www.hyattdiecast.com
**SIC: 3363**  Aluminum die-castings
PA: Hyatt Die Cast And Engineering Corporation - South
  4656 Lincoln Ave
  714 826-7550

**(P-7811)**
**HYATT DIE CAST ENGRG CORP - S**
Also Called: Hyatt Die Casting
1250 Kifer Rd, Sunnyvale (94086-5304)
PHONE.................................408 523-7000
Kul Dhanota, *Brnch Mgr*
**EMP:** 42
**SALES (corp-wide):** 24.28MM **Privately Held**
Web: www.hyattdiecast.com
**SIC: 3363**  Aluminum die-castings
PA: Hyatt Die Cast And Engineering Corporation - South
  4656 Lincoln Ave
  714 826-7550

**(P-7812)**
**KEARNEYS ALUMINUM FOUNDRY INC (PA)**
2660 S Dearing Ave, Fresno (93725-2104)
P.O. Box 2926 (93745-2926)
PHONE.................................559 233-2591
Victor T Kearney Senior, *CEO*
Gary A Kearney, *Pr*
William Kearney, *Pr*
Michael Kearney, *Pr*
Robert Kearney Junior, *VP*
▲ **EMP:** 20 **EST:** 1944
**SQ FT:** 80,000
**SALES (est):** 3.55MM
**SALES (corp-wide):** 3.55MM **Privately Held**
**SIC: 3363**  Aluminum die-castings

**(P-7813)**
**KENWALT DIE CASTING CORP**
Also Called: Kenwait Die Casting Company
8719 Bradley Ave, Sun Valley (91352-2799)
PHONE.................................818 768-5800
TOLL FREE: 800
Ken Zaucha Senior, *Pr*
Rose Zaucha, *Stockholder**
▼ **EMP:** 25 **EST:** 1974
**SQ FT:** 20,000
**SALES (est):** 3.55MM **Privately Held**
Web: www.kenwalt.com
**SIC: 3363**  Aluminum die-castings

**(P-7814)**
**MAGNESIUM ALLOY PDTS CO INC**
2420 N Alameda St, Compton (90222-2895)
P.O. Box 4668 (90224-4668)
PHONE.................................310 605-1440
J W Long, *Pr*
M B Long, *
**EMP:** 46 **EST:** 1945
**SQ FT:** 90,000
**SALES (est):** 4.39MM **Privately Held**
Web: www.magnesiumalloy.com
**SIC: 3363**  Aluminum die-castings

**(P-7815)**
**MAGNESIUM ALLOY PRODUCTS CO LP**
2420 N Alameda St, Compton (90222-2895)
PHONE.................................323 636-2276
Richard Killen, *Pt*
James Long, *Pt*
**EMP:** 50 **EST:** 1956
**SALES (est):** 2.29MM **Privately Held**
Web: www.magnesiumalloy.com
**SIC: 3363**  Aluminum die-castings

**(P-7816)**
**PACIFIC DIE CASTING CORP**
6155 S Eastern Ave, Commerce (90040-3401)
PHONE.................................323 725-1308
Jeff Orlandini, *VP*
Sonny Yun, *Stockholder**
▲ **EMP:** 150 **EST:** 1954
**SQ FT:** 8,000
**SALES (est):** 6.65MM **Privately Held**
Web: www.pacdiecast.com
**SIC: 3363**  Aluminum die-castings

**(P-7817)**
**PERFORMANCE ALUMINUM PRODUCTS**
Also Called: Performance Aluminum
520 S Palmetto Ave, Ontario (91762-4121)
PHONE.................................909 391-4131
John Reed, *Pr*
▲ **EMP:** 20 **EST:** 1985
**SALES (est):** 2.59MM **Privately Held**
Web: www.perfalum.com
**SIC: 3363**  Aluminum die-castings

**(P-7818)**
**PIONEER DIECASTERS INC**
4209 Chevy Chase Dr, Los Angeles (90039-1274)
P.O. Box 406 (91012-0406)
PHONE.................................323 245-6561
Carl H Spahr, *Pr*
Gretchen Perry, *Sec*
**EMP:** 17 **EST:** 1949
**SQ FT:** 18,000
**SALES (est):** 2.55MM **Privately Held**
**SIC: 3363** 3364 5051  Aluminum die-castings; Zinc and zinc-base alloy die-castings; Aluminum bars, rods, ingots, sheets, pipes, plates, etc.

**(P-7819)**
**RANGERS DIE CASTING CO**
10828 Alameda St, Lynwood (90262-1721)
P.O. Box 127 (90262-0127)
PHONE.................................310 764-1800
**EMP:** 40
Web: www.rangersdiecasting.com
**SIC: 3363** 3544 3599  Aluminum die-castings; Special dies, tools, jigs, and fixtures; Machine and other job shop work

**(P-7820)**
**SAN JOSE DIE CASTING CORP**
600 Business Park Dr Ste 100, Lincoln (95648-9364)
PHONE.................................408 262-6500
Everett Callaghan, *Pr*
▲ **EMP:** 27 **EST:** 1955
**SALES (est):** 2.4MM **Privately Held**
Web: www.sjdiecasting.com
**SIC: 3363** 3364 3599 3441  Aluminum die-castings; Zinc and zinc-base alloy die-castings; Machine shop, jobbing and repair; Fabricated structural metal

**(P-7821)**
**SEA SHIELD MARINE PRODUCTS INC**
Also Called: American Zinc Enterprises
20832 Currier Rd, Walnut (91789-3017)
PHONE.................................909 594-2507
Wendell Walter Godwin, *CEO*
Shelley Lopez, *
Alicia Vongoeben, *
▲ **EMP:** 45 **EST:** 1971
**SQ FT:** 25,000
**SALES (est):** 4.36MM **Privately Held**
Web: www.seashieldmarine.com
**SIC: 3363** 3364  Aluminum die-castings; Magnesium and magnesium-base alloy die-castings

**(P-7822)**
**SKS DIE CAST & MACHINING INC (PA)**
1849 Oak St, Alameda (94501)
PHONE.................................510 523-2541
Sean Keating, *CEO*
Jerome W Keating, *
Menelos J Moore, *
Leonore Keating, *
Jesusa Fusade, *
▲ **EMP:** 35 **EST:** 1947
**SQ FT:** 50,000
**SALES (est):** 4.36MM
**SALES (corp-wide):** 4.36MM **Privately Held**
Web: www.sksdiecasting.com
**SIC: 3363** 3845  Aluminum die-castings; Electromedical equipment

**(P-7823)**
**VENUS ALLOYS INC (PA)**
1415 S Allec St, Anaheim (92805-6306)
PHONE.................................714 635-8800
E K Venugopal, *Pr*
Kousalya Venugopal, *
**EMP:** 24 **EST:** 1989
**SQ FT:** 20,000
**SALES (est):** 4.58MM **Privately Held**
**SIC: 3363** 3364  Aluminum die-castings; Brass and bronze die-castings

## 3364 Nonferrous Die-castings Except Aluminum

**(P-7824)**
**ALCAST MFG INC**
2910 Fisk Ln, Redondo Beach (90278-5437)
PHONE.................................310 542-3581
**EMP:** 30
**SALES (corp-wide):** 9.6MM **Privately Held**
Web: www.alcast-foundry.com
**SIC: 3364** 3363  Brass and bronze die-castings; Aluminum die-castings
PA: Alcast Mfg, Inc.
  7355 E Slauson Ave
  310 542-3581

**(P-7825)**
**AMERICAN DIE CASTING INC**
14576 Fontlee Ln, Fontana (92335-2599)
PHONE.................................909 356-7768
TOLL FREE: 800
Walter Mueller, *Pr*
Jeffrey Mueller, *
Marjorie Mueller, *
**EMP:** 50 **EST:** 1992
**SQ FT:** 20,000
**SALES (est):** 4.67MM **Privately Held**
Web: www.americandiecasting.com
**SIC: 3364** 3363  Zinc and zinc-base alloy die-castings; Aluminum die-castings

**(P-7826)**
**CALIFORNIA DIE CASTING INC**
1820 S Grove Ave, Ontario (91761-5613)
PHONE.................................909 947-9947
Dan C Lane, *Pr*
Jerry C Holland, *
Roy Herring, *
**EMP:** 49 **EST:** 1996
**SQ FT:** 3,000
**SALES (est):** 8.52MM **Privately Held**
Web: www.caldiecast.com
**SIC: 3364** 3363  Nonferrous die-castings except aluminum; Aluminum die-castings

**(P-7827)**
**DEL MAR INDUSTRIES (PA)**
Also Called: Del Mar Die Casting Co
12901 S Western Ave, Gardena (90249-1917)
P.O. Box 881 (90294-0881)
PHONE.................................323 321-0600
Doctor Taylor, *CEO*
Louis A Cuhrt, *
Judith Taylor, *
Susan Davis, *Stockholder**
**EMP:** 100 **EST:** 1968
**SQ FT:** 68,000
**SALES (est):** 2.05MM
**SALES (corp-wide):** 2.05MM **Privately Held**
Web: www.delmarindustries.com
**SIC: 3364**  Zinc and zinc-base alloy die-castings

**(P-7828)**
**DYNACAST LLC**
Also Called: Dynacast, LLC
25952 Commercentre Dr, Lake Forest (92630-8815)
PHONE.................................949 707-1211
John Hess, *Brnch Mgr*
**EMP:** 140

## PRODUCTS & SERVICES SECTION
### 3365 - Aluminum Foundries (P-7848)

SALES (corp-wide): 1.08B **Privately Held**
Web: www.dynacast.com
SIC: **3364** Nonferrous die-castings except aluminum
HQ: Dynacast Us Holdings, Inc.
14045 Balntyn Corp Pl
Charlotte NC 28277
704 927-2790

**(P-7829)**
**FTG AEROSPACE INC (DH)**
20740 Marilla St, Chatsworth (91311-4407)
PHONE.................................818 407-4024
Michael Labrador, *Pr*
▼ **EMP**: 42 **EST**: 2011
**SQ FT**: 13,000
**SALES (est)**: 24.49MM
**SALES (corp-wide)**: 98.06MM **Privately Held**
Web: www.ftgcorp.com
SIC: **3364** Nonferrous die-castings except aluminum
HQ: Firan Technology Group (Usa) Corporation
20750 Marilla St
Chatsworth CA 91311
818 407-4024

**(P-7830)**
**PROTECH MATERIALS INC**
Also Called: Protech Materials
20919 Cabot Blvd, Hayward (94545-1155)
PHONE.................................510 887-5870
Mei Zhang, *Pr*
Larry Liu, *VP*
▲ **EMP**: 16 **EST**: 2006
**SQ FT**: 7,100
**SALES (est)**: 3.04MM **Privately Held**
Web: www.protechmaterials.net
SIC: **3364** 3443 Nonferrous die-castings except aluminum; High vacuum coaters, metal plate

**(P-7831)**
**VERTECHS ENTERPRISES INC (PA)**
1071 Industrial Pl, El Cajon (92020-3107)
PHONE.................................858 578-3900
Geosef Straza, *CEO*
George C Straza, *
▲ **EMP**: 46 **EST**: 2007
**SALES (est)**: 8.7MM **Privately Held**
Web: www.vertechsusa.com
SIC: **3364** 3724 3544 Copper and copper alloy die-castings; Aircraft engines and engine parts; Die sets for metal stamping (presses)

**(P-7832)**
**WHITEFOX DEFENSE TECH INC**
854 Monterey St, San Luis Obispo (93401-3225)
PHONE.................................805 225-4506
Mark Kulam, *Pr*
**EMP**: 54 **EST**: 2016
**SALES (est)**: 5.81MM **Privately Held**
Web: www.whitefoxdefense.com
SIC: **3364** Nonferrous die-castings except aluminum

### 3365 Aluminum Foundries

**(P-7833)**
**AEROL CO INC**
Also Called: Aerol Co
19560 S Rancho Way, Rancho Dominguez (90220-6038)
PHONE.................................310 762-2660
▲ **EMP**: 36

Web: www.aerol.com
SIC: **3365** 2821 3714 3728 Aluminum foundries; Plastics materials and resins; Motor vehicle parts and accessories; Wheels, aircraft

**(P-7834)**
**ALCAST MFG INC (PA)**
7355 E Slauson Ave, Commerce (90040-3626)
PHONE.................................310 542-3581
Kiwon Ban, *CEO*
Soo Ban, *Treas*
Lily Martinez, *
▲ **EMP**: 25 **EST**: 1986
**SALES (est)**: 9.6MM
**SALES (corp-wide)**: 9.6MM **Privately Held**
Web: www.alcast-foundry.com
SIC: **3365** 3366 3544 3369 Aluminum and aluminum-based alloy castings; Brass foundry, nec; Special dies, tools, jigs, and fixtures; Nonferrous foundries, nec

**(P-7835)**
**ALUMISTAR INC**
Also Called: Pacific Cast Products
520 S Palmetto Ave, Ontario (91762-4121)
PHONE.................................562 633-6673
Peter Lake, *Pr*
▲ **EMP**: 26 **EST**: 1982
**SALES (est)**: 2.54MM **Privately Held**
Web: www.pacificcastproducts.com
SIC: **3365** Aluminum and aluminum-based alloy castings

**(P-7836)**
**BUDDY BAR CASTING LLC**
10801 Sessler St, South Gate (90280-7222)
PHONE.................................562 861-9664
Ky Fell, *CEO*
Edward W Barksdale Senior, *Prin*
Bill Fell, *
Mike Mckeen, *VP*
John Fell, *
▲ **EMP**: 130 **EST**: 1953
**SQ FT**: 25,000
**SALES (est)**: 8.43MM **Privately Held**
Web: www.buddybarcasting.com
SIC: **3365** Aluminum foundries

**(P-7837)**
**CALIDAD INC**
1730 S Balboa Ave, Ontario (91761-7773)
PHONE.................................909 947-3937
Don Cornell, *Pr*
Daniel Garcia, *
**EMP**: 30 **EST**: 1986
**SQ FT**: 10,000
**SALES (est)**: 2.67MM **Privately Held**
Web: www.calidadinc.com
SIC: **3365** 3324 Aluminum foundries; Steel investment foundries

**(P-7838)**
**CONSOLDTED PRECISION PDTS CORP**
705 Industrial Way, Port Hueneme (93041-3505)
PHONE.................................805 488-6451
**EMP**: 88
**SALES (corp-wide)**: 957.88MM **Privately Held**
Web: www.cppcorp.com
SIC: **3365** Aluminum foundries
PA: Consolidated Precision Products Corp.
1621 Euclid Ave Ste 1850
216 453-4800

**(P-7839)**
**CONSOLDTED PRECISION PDTS CORP**
Also Called: Cpp - Pomona
4200 West Valley Blvd, Pomona (91769)
PHONE.................................909 595-2252
James Stewart, *CEO*
**EMP**: 93
**SALES (corp-wide)**: 957.88MM **Privately Held**
Web: www.cppcorp.com
SIC: **3365** 3324 Aluminum foundries; Steel investment foundries
PA: Consolidated Precision Products Corp.
1621 Euclid Ave Ste 1850
216 453-4800

**(P-7840)**
**CONSOLIDATED FOUNDRIES INC**
Also Called: Cpp Cudahy
8333 Wilcox Ave, Cudahy (90201-5919)
P.O. Box 1099 (90201)
PHONE.................................323 773-2363
Steve Gallardo, *Brnch Mgr*
**EMP**: 121
**SALES (corp-wide)**: 957.88MM **Privately Held**
Web: www.cppcorp.com
SIC: **3365** 3324 Aluminum foundries; Steel investment foundries
HQ: Consolidated Foundries, Inc.
1621 Euclid Ave Ste 1850
Cleveland OH 44115

**(P-7841)**
**CYTEC ENGINEERED MATERIALS INC**
Also Called: Solvay Composite Materials
1440 N Kraemer Blvd, Anaheim (92806-1404)
PHONE.................................714 632-1174
Ron Martin, *Brnch Mgr*
**EMP**: 125
**SQ FT**: 135,055
**SALES (corp-wide)**: 8.01MM **Privately Held**
Web: www.syensqo.com
SIC: **3365** 2891 2851 2823 Aerospace castings, aluminum; Adhesives and sealants; Paints and allied products; Cellulosic manmade fibers
HQ: Cytec Engineered Materials Inc.
2085 E Tech Cir Ste 102
Tempe AZ 85284

**(P-7842)**
**DC PARTNERS INC (PA)**
Also Called: Soligen 2006
1356 N Santiago St, Santa Ana (92701-2515)
PHONE.................................714 558-9444
Yehoram Uziel, *Pr*
Alecia Wagner, *
**EMP**: 32 **EST**: 2005
**SALES (est)**: 4.07MM **Privately Held**
Web: www.soligen2006.com
SIC: **3365** 3599 Aluminum foundries; Machine and other job shop work

**(P-7843)**
**DWA ALMINUM COMPOSITES USA INC**
21100 Superior St, Chatsworth (91311-4308)
PHONE.................................818 998-1504
Mark R Van Den Bergh, *CEO*
J J Shah, *CFO*
Gary Wolfe, *COO*

**EMP**: 20 **EST**: 2013
**SQ FT**: 40,000
**SALES (est)**: 5MM **Privately Held**
Web: www.dwa-usa.com
SIC: **3365** Aluminum and aluminum-based alloy castings

**(P-7844)**
**EMPLOYEE OWNED PCF CAST PDTS I**
Also Called: Aluminum Casting Company
520 S Palmetto Ave, Ontario (91762-4121)
PHONE.................................562 633-6673
Alex B Hall, *Pr*
**EMP**: 24 **EST**: 2000
**SALES (est)**: 983.13K **Privately Held**
SIC: **3365** Aluminum and aluminum-based alloy castings

**(P-7845)**
**GC INTERNATIONAL INC (PA)**
Also Called: Alj
4671 Calle Carga, Camarillo (93012-8560)
PHONE.................................805 389-4631
Mark Griffith, *Pr*
Richard R Carlson, *Pr*
Mark R Griffith, *VP*
Terry Carlson, *VP*
F Willard Griffith, *CEO*
▼ **EMP**: 43 **EST**: 1975
**SQ FT**: 45,000
**SALES (est)**: 10.1MM
**SALES (corp-wide)**: 10.1MM **Privately Held**
Web: www.aljcast.com
SIC: **3365** 3695 3369 3061 Aluminum and aluminum-based alloy castings; Magnetic disks and drums; Lead, zinc, and white metal; Appliance rubber goods (mechanical)

**(P-7846)**
**GENERAL FOUNDRY SERVICE CORP**
1390 Business Center Pl, San Leandro (94577-2212)
PHONE.................................510 297-5040
Edward J Ritelli Junior, *CEO*
Edward J Ritelli Senior, *Pr*
**EMP**: 70 **EST**: 1946
**SQ FT**: 15,200
**SALES (est)**: 9.17MM **Privately Held**
Web: www.genfoundry.com
SIC: **3365** 3543 3369 3324 Aluminum and aluminum-based alloy castings; Industrial patterns; Nonferrous foundries, nec; Steel investment foundries

**(P-7847)**
**GRISWOLD INDUSTRIES (PA)**
Also Called: Cla-Val Co
1701 Placentia Ave, Costa Mesa (92627-4416)
P.O. Box 1325 (92659-0325)
PHONE.................................949 722-4800
◆ **EMP**: 420 **EST**: 1936
**SALES (est)**: 103.11MM
**SALES (corp-wide)**: 103.11MM **Privately Held**
Web: www.cla-val.com
SIC: **3365** 3366 3492 3325 Aluminum foundries; Brass foundry, nec; Control valves, fluid power: hydraulic and pneumatic; Steel foundries, nec

**(P-7848)**
**MAGPARTS (HQ)**
Also Called: Cpp-Azusa
1545 W Roosevelt St, Azusa (91702-3281)
P.O. Box 1099 (90201-7099)
PHONE.................................626 334-7897

## 3365 - Aluminum Foundries (P-7849)

Richard H Emerson, Pr
L Scott Donald Mac, VP
Ellen E Skatvold, *
**EMP:** 108 **EST:** 1958
**SQ FT:** 100,000
**SALES (est):** 19.03MM
**SALES (corp-wide):** 957.88MM **Privately Held**
Web: www.perfectdomain.com
**SIC: 3365** 3369 Aluminum and aluminum-based alloy castings; Magnesium and magnes.-base alloy castings, exc. die-casting
**PA:** Consolidated Precision Products Corp.
1621 Euclid Ave Ste 1850
216 453-4800

### (P-7849)
### SONFARREL AEROSPACE LLC
3010 E La Jolla St, Anaheim (92806-1310)
**PHONE**................714 630-7280
Jeffrey Greer, CEO
Ken Anderson, *
**EMP:** 96 **EST:** 2018
**SALES (est):** 10.43MM **Privately Held**
Web: www.son-aero.com
**SIC: 3365** Aerospace castings, aluminum

### (P-7850)
### SUPERNAL LLC
15555 Laguna Canyon Rd, Irvine (92618-7722)
**PHONE**................202 422-3275
Jaiwon Shin, Brnch Mgr
**EMP:** 101
Web: www.supernal.aero
**SIC: 3365** Aerospace castings, aluminum
**HQ:** Supernal, Llc
1101 16th St Nw
Washington DC 20036
202 422-3175

### (P-7851)
### TRILORE TECHNOLOGIES INC
3000 Danville Blvd Ste F # 525, Alamo (94507-1538)
**PHONE**................925 295-0734
**EMP:** 30
**SIC: 3365** Aluminum foundries

## 3366 Copper Foundries

### (P-7852)
### FLEETWOOD CONTINENTAL INC
19451 S Susana Rd, Compton (90221-5713)
**PHONE**................310 609-1477
David J Forster, Pr
▲ **EMP:** 75 **EST:** 1965
**SQ FT:** 5,000
**SALES (est):** 9.65MM **Privately Held**
Web: www.fleetcon.com
**SIC: 3366** 3823 3561 3523 Castings (except die), nec, bronze; Turbine flow meters, industrial process type; Pumps and pumping equipment; Farm machinery and equipment

### (P-7853)
### GALAXY DIE AND ENGINEERING INC
Also Called: Galaxy Bearing Company
24910 Avenue Tibbitts, Valencia (91355-3426)
**PHONE**................661 775-9301
Jawahar Saini, Pr
Hamid Baig, *
Sooltan Ali Bhoy, *

Malkiat Saini, Stockholder*
**EMP:** 40 **EST:** 1958
**SQ FT:** 30,000
**SALES (est):** 5.75MM **Privately Held**
Web: www.galaxybearing.com
**SIC: 3366** 3575 Bushings and bearings; Computer terminals

### (P-7854)
### HILLER COMPANIES LLC
Also Called: Hiller Marine
7070 Convoy Ct, San Diego (92111-1017)
**PHONE**................858 899-5008
**EMP:** 27
**SALES (corp-wide):** 179.36MM **Privately Held**
**SIC: 3366** Propellers
**PA:** The Hiller Companies, Llc
3751 Joy Springs Dr
251 661-1275

### (P-7855)
### MONTCLAIR BRONZE INC
2535 E 57th St, Huntington Park (90255-2520)
P.O. Box 2009 (91763-0509)
**PHONE**................909 986-2664
Dan Griffiths, *
Wayne Freeberg, *
Thomas Freeberg, *
**EMP:** 30 **EST:** 1963
**SALES (est):** 5.21MM **Privately Held**
Web: www.montclairbronze.com
**SIC: 3366** 3599 Bronze foundry, nec; Machine shop, jobbing and repair

### (P-7856)
### PAC FOUNDRIES INC
Also Called: Cpp-Port Hueneme
705 Industrial Way, Port Hueneme (93041-3505)
**PHONE**................805 986-1308
James Stewart, CEO
**EMP:** 176 **EST:** 1978
**SALES (est):** 10.35MM
**SALES (corp-wide):** 957.88MM **Privately Held**
Web: www.cppcorp.com
**SIC: 3366** Copper foundries
**PA:** Consolidated Precision Products Corp.
1621 Euclid Ave Ste 1850
216 453-4800

## 3369 Nonferrous Foundries, Nec

### (P-7857)
### ALLIEDSIGNAL AROSPC SVC CORP (HQ)
Also Called: Allied Signal Aerospace
2525 W 190th St, Torrance (90504-6002)
**PHONE**................310 323-9500
Bernd F Kessler, Pr
Mary Beth Orson, *
James V Gelly, *
**EMP:** 53 **EST:** 2003
**SALES (est):** 14.93MM
**SALES (corp-wide):** 36.66B **Publicly Held**
**SIC: 3369** 3822 3812 3769 Nonferrous foundries, nec; Environmental controls; Search and navigation equipment; Space vehicle equipment, nec
**PA:** Honeywell International Inc.
855 S Mint St
704 627-6200

### (P-7858)
### CAST PARTNER INC
4658 W Washington Blvd, Los Angeles (90016-1743)
**PHONE**................323 876-9000
Fridlizius Theo, Pr
**EMP:** 28 **EST:** 2013
**SALES (est):** 2.32MM **Privately Held**
Web: www.castpartner.com
**SIC: 3369** Nonferrous foundries, nec

### (P-7859)
### CAST-RITE INTERNATIONAL INC (PA)
515 E Airline Way, Gardena (90248-2501)
**PHONE**................310 532-2080
Donald E Dehaan, CEO
Wynn Chapman, *
Howard Watkins, *
◆ **EMP:** 90 **EST:** 1961
**SQ FT:** 59,330
**SALES (est):** 24.75MM
**SALES (corp-wide):** 24.75MM **Privately Held**
Web: www.cast-rite.com
**SIC: 3369** Zinc and zinc-base alloy castings, except die-castings

### (P-7860)
### DECCO CASTINGS INC (PA)
1596 Pioneer Way, El Cajon (92020-1673)
**PHONE**................619 444-9437
Colm Plunkett, CEO
Randy Eder, CMO
**EMP:** 15 **EST:** 1974
**SQ FT:** 20,000
**SALES (est):** 11.3MM
**SALES (corp-wide):** 11.3MM **Privately Held**
Web: www.deccocastings.com
**SIC: 3369** 3365 3325 Nonferrous foundries, nec; Aluminum foundries; Steel foundries, nec

### (P-7861)
### DECCO CASTINGS INC
1410 Hill St, El Cajon (92020-5749)
**PHONE**................818 416-0068
Colm Plunkett, Brnch Mgr
**EMP:** 30
**SALES (corp-wide):** 11.3MM **Privately Held**
Web: www.deccocastings.com
**SIC: 3369** Nonferrous foundries, nec
**PA:** Decco Castings, Inc.
1596 Pioneer Way
619 444-9437

### (P-7862)
### DELT INDUSTRIES INC
90 W Easy St Ste 2, Simi Valley (93065-6206)
P.O. Box 940067 (93094-0067)
**PHONE**................805 579-0213
Estelle Lee, Pr
Debra Schultz, Sec
Jerry Martin, VP
**EMP:** 18 **EST:** 1994
**SQ FT:** 10,000
**SALES (est):** 2.46MM **Privately Held**
Web: www.deltindustries.com
**SIC: 3369** 5088 Nonferrous foundries, nec; Transportation equipment and supplies

### (P-7863)
### FENICO PRECISION CASTINGS INC
7805 Madison St, Paramount (90723-4220)
**PHONE**................562 634-5000

Don Tomeo, Pr
Sherry Tomeo, *
▲ **EMP:** 75 **EST:** 1987
**SQ FT:** 20,000
**SALES (est):** 4.83MM **Privately Held**
Web: www.fenicocastings.com
**SIC: 3369** 3366 3324 3322 Machinery castings, exc. die, nonferrous, exc. alum. copper; Copper foundries; Steel investment foundries; Malleable iron foundries

### (P-7864)
### FS - PRECISION TECH CO LLC
3025 E Victoria St, Compton (90221-5616)
**PHONE**................310 638-0595
Israel M Sanchez, *
▲ **EMP:** 100 **EST:** 2004
**SALES (est):** 24.83MM **Privately Held**
Web: www.fs-precision.com
**SIC: 3369** Titanium castings, except die-casting
**PA:** Fs-Elliott Company, Inc.
5710 Mellon Rd

### (P-7865)
### INTERNATIONAL DIE CASTING INC
515 E Airline Way, Gardena (90248-2501)
**PHONE**................310 324-2278
▲ **EMP:** 38 **EST:** 1977
**SALES (est):** 3.25MM
**SALES (corp-wide):** 7.59MM **Privately Held**
Web: www.internationaldiecasting.com
**SIC: 3369** 2842 3364 Zinc and zinc-base alloy castings, except die-castings; Metal polish; Nonferrous die-castings except aluminum
**PA:** Cast-Rite International, Inc.
515 E Airline Way
310 532-2080

### (P-7866)
### INTRICAST COMPANY INCORPORATED
2160 Walsh Ave, Santa Clara (95050-2512)
**PHONE**................408 988-6200
▲ **EMP:** 47
Web: www.intricast.com
**SIC: 3369** 3544 3324 Castings, except die-castings, precision; Special dies, tools, jigs, and fixtures; Steel investment foundries

### (P-7867)
### ORLANDINI ENTPS PCF DIE CAST
Also Called: Pacific Die Casting
6155 S Eastern Ave, Commerce (90040-3401)
**PHONE**................323 725-1332
Jeff Orlandini, *
Vincent Orlandini, *
▲ **EMP:** 125 **EST:** 1955
**SQ FT:** 45,000
**SALES (est):** 2.17MM **Privately Held**
Web: www.pacdiecast.com
**SIC: 3369** 3363 Machinery castings, exc. die, nonferrous, exc. alum. copper; Aluminum die-castings

### (P-7868)
### PANKL AEROSPACE SYSTEMS
16615 Edwards Rd, Cerritos (90703-2437)
**PHONE**................562 207-6300
Horst Rieger, CEO
Barry Calvert, *
Wolfgang Plasser, *
Harry Glieder, *
**EMP:** 75 **EST:** 2000

# PRODUCTS & SERVICES SECTION

## 3398 - Metal Heat Treating (P-7888)

SQ FT: 63,040
SALES (est): 21.15MM
SALES (corp-wide): 3.83B **Privately Held**
Web: www.pankl.com
SIC: **3369** 3724  Aerospace castings, nonferrous: except aluminum; Aircraft engines and engine parts
HQ: Pankl Holdings, Inc.
  1902 Mcgaw Ave
  Irvine CA 92614

### (P-7869)
### PCC STRUCTURALS INC
Also Called: PCC Structurals-San Leandro
414 Hester St, San Leandro (94577-1024)
PHONE..............................510 568-6400
Craig Milton, *Brnch Mgr*
EMP: 180
SALES (corp-wide): 364.48B **Publicly Held**
Web: www.pccstructurals.com
SIC: **3369**  Nonferrous foundries, nec
HQ: Pcc Structurals, Inc.
  4600 Se Harney Dr
  Portland OR 97206
  503 777-3881

### (P-7870)
### RADIAN THERMAL PRODUCTS INC
Also Called: Radian Heat Sinks
2160 Walsh Ave, Santa Clara (95050)
PHONE..............................408 988-6200
Gerald L Mcintyre, *Ch*
Mong Hu, *
▲ EMP: 54 EST: 1984
SQ FT: 26,500
SALES (est): 4.95MM **Privately Held**
Web: www.radianheatsinks.com
SIC: **3369**  Castings, except die-castings, precision

### (P-7871)
### SYNERTECH PM INC
11711 Monarch St, Garden Grove (92841-1830)
PHONE..............................714 898-9151
Charles Barre, *CEO*
Kristen Barre, *Pr*
Victor Samarov, *VP*
◆ EMP: 17 EST: 2000
SQ FT: 20,000
SALES (est): 2.5MM **Privately Held**
Web: www.synertechpm.com
SIC: **3369**  Aerospace castings, nonferrous: except aluminum

### (P-7872)
### TECHNI-CAST CORP
Also Called: Techni Cast Corp
11220 Garfield Ave, South Gate (90280-7586)
PHONE..............................562 923-4585
Bryn Jhan Van Hiel Ii, *Pr*
Donald Van Hiel, *
Lynne Van Hiel, *
Elaine M Kay, *
▲ EMP: 80 EST: 1954
SQ FT: 60,000
SALES (est): 9.88MM **Privately Held**
Web: www.techni-cast.com
SIC: **3369** 3599 3364 3325  Lead, zinc, and white metal; Machine shop, jobbing and repair; Nonferrous die-castings except aluminum; Steel foundries, nec

## 3398 Metal Heat Treating

### (P-7873)
### ACCURATE STEEL TREATING INC
10008 Miller Way, South Gate (90280-5496)
PHONE..............................562 927-6528
Ronald Loyns, *Pr*
Mike Bastin, *
EMP: 38 EST: 1962
SQ FT: 10,000
SALES (est): 4.59MM **Privately Held**
Web: www.accuratesteeltreating.com
SIC: **3398**  Metal heat treating

### (P-7874)
### AEROCRAFT HEAT TREATING CO INC
15701 Minnesota Ave, Paramount (90723-4120)
PHONE..............................562 674-2400
David W Dickson, *CEO*
Robert Lyddon, *
EMP: 57 EST: 1957
SQ FT: 18,000
SALES (est): 9.8MM
SALES (corp-wide): 364.48B **Publicly Held**
Web: www.aerocraft-ht.com
SIC: **3398**  Metal heat treating
HQ: Precision Castparts Corp.
  5885 Meadows Rd Ste 620
  Lake Oswego OR 97035
  503 946-4800

### (P-7875)
### AREMAC HEAT TREATING INC
330 S 9th Ave, City Of Industry (91746-3311)
P.O. Box 90068 (91715-0068)
PHONE..............................626 333-3898
B E Kopaskie, *Pr*
Bernard E Kopaskie, *
Doctor Butler, *VP*
Jan Kopaskie, *
EMP: 38 EST: 1967
SQ FT: 14,000
SALES (est): 1.27MM **Privately Held**
Web: www.aremac.com
SIC: **3398**  Metal heat treating

### (P-7876)
### ASTRO ALUMINUM TREATING CO
11040 Palmer Ave, South Gate (90280-7497)
PHONE..............................562 923-4344
Mark R Dickson, *Pr*
Mike Burns, *
EMP: 90 EST: 1977
SQ FT: 4,800
SALES (est): 19.09MM **Privately Held**
Web: www.astroaluminum.com
SIC: **3398**  Metal heat treating

### (P-7877)
### BODYCOTE THERMAL PROC INC
515 W Apra St Ste A, Rancho Dominguez (90220-5523)
PHONE..............................310 604-8000
Jose Catano, *Brnch Mgr*
EMP: 21
SALES (corp-wide): 1B **Privately Held**
Web: www.bodycote.com
SIC: **3398**  Metal heat treating
HQ: Bodycote Thermal Processing, Inc.
  12750 Merit Dr Ste 1400
  Dallas TX 75251
  214 904-2420

### (P-7878)
### BODYCOTE THERMAL PROC INC
7474 Garden Grove Blvd, Westminster (92683-2227)
PHONE..............................714 893-6561
Manuel Granillo, *Brnch Mgr*
EMP: 34
SQ FT: 7,369
SALES (corp-wide): 1B **Privately Held**
Web: www.bodycote.com
SIC: **3398**  Metal heat treating
HQ: Bodycote Thermal Processing, Inc.
  12750 Merit Dr Ste 1400
  Dallas TX 75251
  214 904-2420

### (P-7879)
### BODYCOTE THERMAL PROC INC
4240 Technology Dr, Fremont (94538-6337)
PHONE..............................510 492-4200
Paul Dymond, *Mgr*
EMP: 48
SALES (corp-wide): 1B **Privately Held**
Web: www.bodycote.com
SIC: **3398** 3443  Metal heat treating; Boiler and boiler shop work
HQ: Bodycote Thermal Processing, Inc.
  12750 Merit Dr Ste 1400
  Dallas TX 75251
  214 904-2420

### (P-7880)
### BODYCOTE THERMAL PROC INC
9921 Romandel Ave, Santa Fe Springs (90670-3441)
PHONE..............................562 946-1717
Manuel Granillo, *Prin*
EMP: 48
SALES (corp-wide): 1B **Privately Held**
Web: www.bodycote.com
SIC: **3398**  Metal heat treating
HQ: Bodycote Thermal Processing, Inc.
  12750 Merit Dr Ste 1400
  Dallas TX 75251
  214 904-2420

### (P-7881)
### BODYCOTE USA INC
2900 S Sunol Dr, Vernon (90058-4315)
PHONE..............................323 264-0111
EMP: 2260
SQ FT: 31,717
SALES (corp-wide): 1B **Privately Held**
Web: www.bodycote.com
SIC: **3398**  Metal heat treating
HQ: Bodycote Usa, Inc.
  12750 Merit Dr Ste 1400
  Dallas TX 75251
  214 904-2420

### (P-7882)
### BURBANK STEEL TREATING INC
415 S Varney St, Burbank (91502-2194)
PHONE..............................818 842-0975
Mildred Bennett, *Ch Bd*
Larry Bennett, *
Kenneth Bennett, *
EMP: 45 EST: 1969
SQ FT: 16,000
SALES (est): 5.16MM **Privately Held**
Web: www.burbanksteel.com
SIC: **3398**  Metal heat treating

### (P-7883)
### CONTINENTAL HEAT TREATING INC
10643 Norwalk Blvd, Santa Fe Springs (90670-3821)
PHONE..............................562 944-8808
James Stull, *Pr*
Shaun Radford, *
Laura Rubio, *
Don Lowman, *
Dennis Hugie, *
EMP: 62 EST: 1957
SQ FT: 20,000
SALES (est): 9.92MM **Privately Held**
Web: www.continentalht.com
SIC: **3398**  Metal heat treating

### (P-7884)
### COOK INDUCTION HEATING CO INC
Also Called: Cook Induction Heating Co.
4925 Slauson Ave, Maywood (90270-3094)
P.O. Box 430 (90270-0430)
PHONE..............................323 560-1327
Keith Doolittle, *CEO*
Richard Egkan, *VP Sls*
EMP: 21 EST: 1945
SQ FT: 24,500
SALES (est): 2.8MM **Privately Held**
Web: www.cookinduction.com
SIC: **3398** 3728  Metal heat treating; Aircraft assemblies, subassemblies, and parts, nec

### (P-7885)
### CURTISS-WRIGHT SURFC TECH LLC
2151 S Hathaway St, Santa Ana (92705-5247)
PHONE..............................714 546-4160
EMP: 17
SALES (corp-wide): 2.85B **Publicly Held**
Web: www.cwst.com
SIC: **3398**  Metal heat treating
HQ: Curtiss-Wright Surface Technologies Llc
  80 E Rte 4 Ste 310
  Paramus NJ 07652
  201 843-7800

### (P-7886)
### INTERNTNAL MTLLRGICAL SVCS LLC
Also Called: Scarrott Metallurgical Co
6371 Arizona Cir, Los Angeles (90045-1201)
PHONE..............................310 645-7300
Brent Daldo, *CEO*
Dave Scarrott, *Pr*
Ralph Jones, *VP*
Shannon Hemmersbach, *Prin*
EMP: 19 EST: 1977
SQ FT: 8,000
SALES (est): 4.79MM **Privately Held**
Web: www.scarrott.com
SIC: **3398**  Brazing (hardening) of metal

### (P-7887)
### KITTYHAWK INC (PA)
11651 Monarch St, Garden Grove (92841-1816)
PHONE..............................714 895-5024
Brandon Creason, *Pr*
Daniel Bednar, *
EMP: 50 EST: 1995
SALES (est): 4.75MM
SALES (corp-wide): 4.75MM **Privately Held**
Web: www.kittyhawkinc.com
SIC: **3398**  Metal heat treating

### (P-7888)
### KITTYHAWK PRODUCTS CA LLC
11651 Monarch St, Garden Grove (92841-1816)

# 3398 - Metal Heat Treating (P-7889)

PHONE..................................714 895-5024
Brandon Creason, *Prin*
Kimberly Dickerson, *Prin*
Daniel Bednar, *Prin*
**EMP:** 25 **EST:** 2019
**SALES (est):** 345.5K **Privately Held**
**Web:** www.kittyhawkinc.com
**SIC:** 3398 Metal heat treating

### (P-7889)
### KPI SERVICES INC
Also Called: Kittyhawk Products
11651 Monarch St, Garden Grove
(92841-1816)
PHONE..................................714 895-5024
Charles Barre, *CEO*
Dennis Poor, *
Steve Belloise, *
Dee Dee Poor, *
Lois Barre, *
▲ **EMP:** 35 **EST:** 1995
**SQ FT:** 12,500
**SALES (est):** 7.33MM **Privately Held**
**Web:** www.kittyhawkinc.com
**SIC:** 3398 Metal heat treating

### (P-7890)
### METAL IMPROVEMENT COMPANY LLC
2588 Industry Way Ste A, Lynwood
(90262-4015)
PHONE..................................323 585-2168
Amando Yanez, *Mgr*
**EMP:** 103
**SQ FT:** 28,260
**SALES (corp-wide):** 2.85B **Publicly Held**
**Web:** www.imrtest.com
**SIC:** 3398 Shot peening (treating steel to reduce fatigue)
**HQ:** Metal Improvement Company, Llc
80 Route 4 E Ste 310
Paramus NJ 07652
201 843-7800

### (P-7891)
### METAL IMPROVEMENT COMPANY LLC
E/M Coatings Solutions
6940 Farmdale Ave, North Hollywood
(91605-6210)
PHONE..................................818 983-1952
Brent Taylor, *Brnch Mgr*
**EMP:** 85
**SALES (corp-wide):** 2.85B **Publicly Held**
**Web:** www.imrtest.com
**SIC:** 3398 Shot peening (treating steel to reduce fatigue)
**HQ:** Metal Improvement Company, Llc
80 Route 4 E Ste 310
Paramus NJ 07652
201 843-7800

### (P-7892)
### METAL IMPROVEMENT COMPANY LLC
Also Called: Para Tech Coating
35 Argonaut Ste A1, Laguna Hills
(92656-4151)
PHONE..................................949 855-8010
Bill Gleason, *Mgr*
**EMP:** 30
**SALES (corp-wide):** 2.85B **Publicly Held**
**Web:** www.imrtest.com
**SIC:** 3398 Shot peening (treating steel to reduce fatigue)
**HQ:** Metal Improvement Company, Llc
80 Route 4 E Ste 310
Paramus NJ 07652
201 843-7800

### (P-7893)
### METAL IMPROVEMENT COMPANY LLC
E/M Coatings Services
20751 Superior St, Chatsworth
(91311-4416)
PHONE..................................818 407-6280
Brent Taylor, *Brnch Mgr*
**EMP:** 96
**SALES (corp-wide):** 2.85B **Publicly Held**
**Web:** www.imrtest.com
**SIC:** 3398 Shot peening (treating steel to reduce fatigue)
**HQ:** Metal Improvement Company, Llc
80 Route 4 E Ste 310
Paramus NJ 07652
201 843-7800

### (P-7894)
### METAL IMPROVEMENT COMPANY LLC
7655 Longard Rd Bldg A, Livermore
(94551-8208)
PHONE..................................925 960-1090
Jim Mcmanus, *Mgr*
**EMP:** 40
**SALES (corp-wide):** 2.85B **Publicly Held**
**Web:** www.imrtest.com
**SIC:** 3398 Shot peening (treating steel to reduce fatigue)
**HQ:** Metal Improvement Company, Llc
80 Route 4 E Ste 310
Paramus NJ 07652
201 843-7800

### (P-7895)
### METAL IMPROVEMENT COMPANY LLC
2151 S Hathaway St, Santa Ana
(92705-5247)
PHONE..................................714 546-4160
Joe Wheaton, *Mgr*
**EMP:** 21
**SALES (corp-wide):** 2.85B **Publicly Held**
**Web:** www.imrtest.com
**SIC:** 3398 Shot peening (treating steel to reduce fatigue)
**HQ:** Metal Improvement Company, Llc
80 Route 4 E Ste 310
Paramus NJ 07652
201 843-7800

### (P-7896)
### NEWTON HEAT TREATING CO INC
19235 E Walnut Dr N, City Of Industry
(91748-1494)
P.O. Box 8010 (91748-0010)
PHONE..................................626 964-6528
Greg Newton, *Pr*
Linda Malcor, *
**EMP:** 71 **EST:** 1968
**SQ FT:** 1,900
**SALES (est):** 8.67MM **Privately Held**
**Web:** www.newtonheattreating.com
**SIC:** 3398 8734 3444 Metal heat treating; X-ray inspection service, industrial; Sheet metalwork

### (P-7897)
### PRO TECH THERMAL SERVICES
1954 Tandem, Norco (92860-3607)
PHONE..................................951 272-5808
Brian Grier, *Pr*
Nathan Smith, *
Carolyn Dearborn, *
**EMP:** 33 **EST:** 1997
**SQ FT:** 4,000
**SALES (est):** 6.97MM **Privately Held**
**Web:** www.protechthermal.com
**SIC:** 3398 Metal heat treating

### (P-7898)
### QUALITY HEAT TREATING INC
3305 Burton Ave, Burbank (91504-3199)
PHONE..................................818 840-8212
James G Stull, *Pr*
**EMP:** 34 **EST:** 1945
**SQ FT:** 20,000
**SALES (est):** 7.42MM **Privately Held**
**Web:** www.qualityht.com
**SIC:** 3398 3471 Metal heat treating; Sand blasting of metal parts

### (P-7899)
### SOLAR ATMOSPHERES INC
8606 Live Oak Ave, Fontana (92335-3172)
PHONE..................................909 217-7400
**EMP:** 24
**Web:** www.solaratm.com
**SIC:** 3398 Annealing of metal
**PA:** Solar Atmospheres, Inc.
1969 Clearview Rd

### (P-7900)
### SUPERHEAT FGH SERVICES INC
1940 Olivera Rd Ste C, Concord
(94520-5484)
PHONE..................................925 808-6711
Brad Hennig, *Brnch Mgr*
**EMP:** 18
**SALES (corp-wide):** 70.07MM **Privately Held**
**Web:** www.superheat.com
**SIC:** 3398 Metal heat treating
**PA:** Superheat Fgh Services, Inc.
313 Garnet Dr
708 478-0205

### (P-7901)
### TEAM INC
Also Called: Team Industrial Services
1515 240th St, Harbor City (90710-1308)
PHONE..................................310 514-2312
Bill Pigeon, *Mgr*
**EMP:** 23
**SALES (corp-wide):** 862.62MM **Publicly Held**
**Web:** www.teaminc.com
**SIC:** 3398 3567 Metal heat treating; Heating units and devices, industrial: electric
**HQ:** Team, Inc.
5095 Paris St
Denver CO 80239

### (P-7902)
### THERMAL-VAC TECHNOLOGY INC
Also Called: City Steel Heat Treating
1221 W Struck Ave, Orange (92867-3531)
PHONE..................................714 997-2601
Steve Driscol, *CEO*
Aaron Anderson, *
Jennider Kovatch, *
**EMP:** 41 **EST:** 1985
**SQ FT:** 26,800
**SALES (est):** 8.71MM **Privately Held**
**Web:** www.thermalvac.com
**SIC:** 3398 Brazing (hardening) of metal

### (P-7903)
### THERMO-FUSION INC
2342 American Ave, Hayward
(94545-1808)
PHONE..................................510 782-7755
**EMP:** 26 **EST:** 1968
**SALES (est):** 4.23MM **Privately Held**
**Web:** www.thermo-fusion.com
**SIC:** 3398 7692 Metal heat treating; Brazing

### (P-7904)
### TRI-J METAL HEAT TREATING CO (PA)
327 E Commercial St, Pomona
(91767-5505)
PHONE..................................909 622-9999
Debra Cramer, *Sec*
Albert W James Junior, *Pr*
Robert L James, *VP Fin*
Lena James, *Sec*
▲ **EMP:** 19 **EST:** 1976
**SQ FT:** 17,500
**SALES (est):** 2.75MM
**SALES (corp-wide):** 2.75MM **Privately Held**
**Web:** www.trijonline.com
**SIC:** 3398 Annealing of metal

### (P-7905)
### TRIW1969 INC
877 Vernon Way, El Cajon (92020-1940)
PHONE..................................619 593-3636
Derick Dennis, *Pr*
Chris Constable, *
**EMP:** 33 **EST:** 1969
**SQ FT:** 29,500
**SALES (est):** 4.32MM **Privately Held**
**Web:** www.certifiedmetalcraft.com
**SIC:** 3398 Brazing (hardening) of metal
**PA:** Solar Atmospheres, Inc.
1969 Clearview Rd

### (P-7906)
### VALLEY METAL TREATING INC
355 Se End Ave, Pomona (91766-2312)
PHONE..................................909 623-6316
James G Stull, *Pr*
**EMP:** 38 **EST:** 1986
**SQ FT:** 8,000
**SALES (est):** 2.55MM **Privately Held**
**Web:** www.valleymt.net
**SIC:** 3398 Metal heat treating

## 3399 Primary Metal Products

### (P-7907)
### CELLMOBILITY INC
808 Gilman St, Berkeley (94710-1422)
PHONE..................................510 549-3300
Heeman Choe, *CEO*
**EMP:** 30 **EST:** 2017
**SALES (est):** 644.29K **Privately Held**
**Web:** www.cellmoinc.com
**SIC:** 3399 Metal powders, pastes, and flakes

### (P-7908)
### MICRO SURFACE ENGR INC (PA)
Also Called: Ball TEC
1550 E Slauson Ave, Los Angeles
(90011-5099)
P.O. Box 58611 (90011)
PHONE..................................323 582-7348
**TOLL FREE:** 800
Eugene A Gleason Junior, *Pr*
Helen Gleason, *
Eugene A Gleason Iii, *Sec*
**EMP:** 35 **EST:** 1952
**SQ FT:** 46,000
**SALES (est):** 9.4MM
**SALES (corp-wide):** 9.4MM **Privately Held**
**Web:** www.precisionballs.com
**SIC:** 3399 Steel balls

## 3411 - Metal Cans (P-7930)

**(P-7909)**
**PARMATECH CORPORATION**
2221 Pine View Way, Petaluma (94954-5688)
PHONE.................................707 778-2266
Peter Frost, *CEO*
Caryn E Mitchell, *
▲ **EMP:** 75 **EST:** 1973
**SQ FT:** 22,000
**SALES (est):** 22.64MM
**SALES (corp-wide):** 55.07MM **Privately Held**
**Web:** www.atwcompanies.com
**SIC:** 3399 Powder, metal
**PA:** Atw Companies, Inc.
55 Service Ave
401 739-0740

**(P-7910)**
**PRECISION PWDRED MET PARTS INC**
145 Atlantic St, Pomona (91768-3286)
PHONE.................................909 595-5656
Maurice Bridgman, *Pr*
David Connelly, *
▲ **EMP:** 48 **EST:** 1978
**SQ FT:** 25,000
**SALES (est):** 2.84MM **Privately Held**
**Web:** www.precisionpm.com
**SIC:** 3399 Powder, metal

**(P-7911)**
**QUANTUMSPHERE INC**
28981 Modjeska Peak Ln, Trabuco Canyon (92679-1025)
PHONE.................................714 545-6266
Kevin D Maloney, *Pr*
Stephen Gillings, *CFO*
Stephanie Hargis Administrative, *Prin*
**EMP:** 18 **EST:** 2003
**SQ FT:** 6,000
**SALES (est):** 2.53MM **Privately Held**
**Web:** www.qsinano.com
**SIC:** 3399 5169 2819 Metal powders, pastes, and flakes; Ammonia; Catalysts, chemical

**(P-7912)**
**RONMAN PRODUCTS INC**
8440 Kass Dr, Buena Park (90621-3822)
PHONE.................................714 994-3700
Robert J Wilkinson, *CEO*
Carmen Wilkinson, *Pr*
▲ **EMP:** 15 **EST:** 1962
**SQ FT:** 22,000
**SALES (est):** 2.38MM **Privately Held**
**Web:** www.ronman.com
**SIC:** 3399 Metal fasteners

**(P-7913)**
**SCAFCO CORPORATION**
2443 Foundry Park Ave, Fresno (93706-4531)
PHONE.................................559 256-9911
Larry Stone, *Pr*
**EMP:** 22
**SALES (corp-wide):** 29.47MM **Privately Held**
**Web:** www.scafco.com
**SIC:** 3399 Iron ore recovery from open hearth slag
**PA:** Scafco Corporation
2800 E Main Ave
509 343-9000

**(P-7914)**
**SENJU COMTEK CORP**
1171 N 4th St Ste 80, San Jose (95112-4968)
PHONE.................................408 792-3830
Ryoichi Suzuki, *Brnch Mgr*
**EMP:** 16
**Web:** www.senju.com
**SIC:** 3399 Paste, metal
**HQ:** Senju Comtek Corp.
2989 San Ysidro Way
Santa Clara CA 95051

**(P-7915)**
**SIMPSON MANUFACTURING CO INC (PA)**
5956 W Las Positas Blvd, Pleasanton (94588-8540)
PHONE.................................925 560-9000
Michael Olosky, *Pr*
James Andrasick, *
Brian Magstadt, *CFO*
Cassandra Payton, *Ex VP*
**EMP:** 150 **EST:** 1956
**SALES (est):** 2.21B
**SALES (corp-wide):** 2.21B **Publicly Held**
**Web:** www.simpsonmfg.com
**SIC:** 3399 3441 Metal fasteners; Building components, structural steel

**(P-7916)**
**USA TOLERANCE RINGS**
831 Sir Francis Drake Blvd, San Anselmo (94960-1944)
P.O. Box 658 (94978-0658)
PHONE.................................415 457-6711
Al Dedliso, *CEO*
**EMP:** 25 **EST:** 1973
**SALES (est):** 345.44K **Privately Held**
**Web:** www.usatolerancerings.com
**SIC:** 3399 Metal fasteners

**(P-7917)**
**VALIMET INC (PA)**
431 Sperry Rd, Stockton (95206-3907)
P.O. Box 31690 (95213-1690)
PHONE.................................209 444-1600
Kurt F Leopold, *CEO*
George Campbell, *Pr*
Michaela Leopold, *Sec*
**EMP:** 55 **EST:** 1957
**SQ FT:** 200,000
**SALES (est):** 13.48MM
**SALES (corp-wide):** 13.48MM **Privately Held**
**Web:** www.valimet.com
**SIC:** 3399 Powder, metal

---

### 3411 Metal Cans

**(P-7918)**
**BALL CORPORATION**
Also Called: Metal Fd Hhld Pdts Pckging Div
300 Greger St, Oakdale (95361-8613)
PHONE.................................209 848-6500
Michael Wright, *Brnch Mgr*
**EMP:** 260
**SALES (corp-wide):** 14.03B **Publicly Held**
**Web:** www.ball.com
**SIC:** 3411 Metal cans
**PA:** Ball Corporation
9200 W 108th Cir
303 469-3131

**(P-7919)**
**BALL METAL BEVERAGE CONT CORP**
Ball Metal Beverage Cont Div
2400 Huntington Dr, Fairfield (94533-9734)
PHONE.................................707 437-7516
David R Trujillo, *Brnch Mgr*
**EMP:** 172
**SQ FT:** 115,000
**SALES (corp-wide):** 14.03B **Publicly Held**
**Web:** www.ball.com
**SIC:** 3411 Metal cans
**HQ:** Ball Metal Beverage Container Corp.
9300 W 108th Cir
Westminster CO 80021

**(P-7920)**
**CONTAINER SUPPLY COMPANY INCORPORATED**
Also Called: C S C
12571 Western Ave, Garden Grove (92841-4012)
P.O. Box 5367 (92846-0367)
PHONE.................................714 892-8321
▲ **EMP:** 105 **EST:** 1947
**SALES (est):** 21.09MM **Privately Held**
**Web:** www.containersupplycompany.com
**SIC:** 3411 2656 Food and beverage containers; Sanitary food containers

**(P-7921)**
**JOSEPH COMPANY INTL INC**
1711 Langley Ave, Irvine (92614-5679)
▲ **EMP:** 20 **EST:** 2010
**SQ FT:** 18,000
**SALES (est):** 3.95MM **Privately Held**
**Web:** www.chillcan.com
**SIC:** 3411 Food and beverage containers

**(P-7922)**
**KLEAN KANTEEN INC**
3960 Morrow Ln, Chico (95928-8912)
PHONE.................................530 592-4552
Gordon Smith, *CEO*
Michelle Kalberer, *
Jeffrey Cresswell, *
▲ **EMP:** 52 **EST:** 1978
**SQ FT:** 5,000
**SALES (est):** 9.94MM **Privately Held**
**Web:** www.kleankanteen.com
**SIC:** 3411 Food containers, metal

**(P-7923)**
**METAL CONTAINER CORPORATION**
10980 Inland Ave, Jurupa Valley (91752-1127)
PHONE.................................951 360-4500
Otto Sosapavon, *Prin*
**EMP:** 158
**SALES (corp-wide):** 1.7B **Privately Held**
**Web:** www.metal-containers.com
**SIC:** 3411 Aluminum cans
**HQ:** Metal Container Corporation
3636 S Geyer Rd Ste 100
Saint Louis MO 63127
314 577-2000

**(P-7924)**
**METAL CONTAINER CORPORATION**
7155 Central Ave, Riverside (92504-1400)
PHONE.................................951 354-0444
Bob Parker, *Brnch Mgr*
**EMP:** 158
**SALES (corp-wide):** 1.7B **Privately Held**
**Web:** www.metal-containers.com
**SIC:** 3411 Can lids and ends, metal
**HQ:** Metal Container Corporation
3636 S Geyer Rd Ste 100
Saint Louis MO 63127
314 577-2000

**(P-7925)**
**SILGAN CAN COMPANY**
Also Called: Silgan
21600 Oxnard St Ste 1600, Woodland Hills (91367-5082)
PHONE.................................818 348-3700
**EMP:** 166
**SIC:** 3411 2032 Metal cans; Canned specialties

**(P-7926)**
**SILGAN CONTAINERS CORPORATION (DH)**
Also Called: Silgan
21600 Oxnard St Ste 1600, Woodland Hills (91367-3609)
PHONE.................................818 710-3700
Anthony J Allott, *CEO*
Thomas J Snyder, *Ch Bd*
R Phillip Silver, *V Ch Bd*
James D Beam, *Pr*
Joseph Heaney, *VP*
◆ **EMP:** 100 **EST:** 1987
**SALES (est):** 478.49MM **Publicly Held**
**Web:** www.silgancontainers.com
**SIC:** 3411 Food containers, metal
**HQ:** Silgan Containers Llc
21600 Oxnard St Ste 1600
Woodland Hills CA 91367
818 710-3700

**(P-7927)**
**SILGAN CONTAINERS LLC (HQ)**
21600 Oxnard St Ste 1600, Woodland Hills (91367-3609)
PHONE.................................818 710-3700
Thomas Snyder, *Pr*
Joseph Heaney, *
Anthony Cost, *
Richard Brewer, *
Michael Beninato, *Supply Chain Management Vice-President*
◆ **EMP:** 100 **EST:** 1997
**SALES (est):** 1.63B **Publicly Held**
**Web:** www.silgancontainers.com
**SIC:** 3411 Food containers, metal
**PA:** Silgan Holdings Inc.
4 Landmark Sq Ste 400

**(P-7928)**
**SILGAN CONTAINERS MFG CORP**
Also Called: Silgan
4000 Yosemite Blvd, Modesto (95357-1580)
PHONE.................................209 521-6469
**EMP:** 32
**Web:** www.silgancontainers.com
**SIC:** 3411 Metal cans
**HQ:** Silgan Containers Manufacturing Corporation
21600 Oxnard St Ste 1600
Woodland Hills CA 91367

**(P-7929)**
**SILGAN CONTAINERS MFG CORP**
Also Called: Silgan
2200 Wilbur Ave, Antioch (94509)
PHONE.................................925 778-8000
Arnold Naimark, *Brnch Mgr*
**EMP:** 31
**Web:** www.silgancontainers.com
**SIC:** 3411 Metal cans
**HQ:** Silgan Containers Manufacturing Corporation
21600 Oxnard St Ste 1600
Woodland Hills CA 91367

**(P-7930)**
**SILGAN CONTAINERS MFG CORP**
Also Called: Silgan
3250 Patterson Rd, Riverbank (95367-2938)

## 3411 - Metal Cans (P-7931)

**PHONE**.....................209 869-3601
Gary Miller, *Brnch Mgr*
**EMP:** 38
**SQ FT:** 200,000
**Web:** www.silgancontainers.com
**SIC:** 3411   Metal cans
**HQ:** Silgan Containers Manufacturing
Corporation
21600 Oxnard St Ste 1600
Woodland Hills CA 91367

### (P-7931)
### SILGAN CONTAINERS MFG CORP (DH)
Also Called: Silgan
21600 Oxnard St Ste 1600, Woodland Hills (91367-5082)
**PHONE**.....................818 710-3700
Thomas Snyder, *Prin*
**EMP:** 134   **EST:** 1997
**SALES (est):** 481.14MM **Publicly Held**
**Web:** www.silgancontainers.com
**SIC:** 3411   Metal cans
**HQ:** Silgan Containers Llc
21600 Oxnard St Ste 1600
Woodland Hills CA 91367
818 710-3700

### (P-7932)
### VAN CAN COMPANY
13230 Evening Creek Dr S Ste 212, San Diego  (92128-4104)
**PHONE**.....................858 391-8084
▲ **EMP:** 200
**Web:** www.vancan.com
**SIC:** 3411   Tin cans

---

## 3412 Metal Barrels, Drums, And Pails

### (P-7933)
### B STEPHEN COOPERAGE  INC
10746 Vernon Ave, Ontario  (91762-4039)
P.O. Box 9537  (91762-9537)
**PHONE**.....................909 591-2929
**TOLL FREE:** 877
Mike Stephen, *CEO*
Ben Stephen, *Pr*
**EMP:** 15   **EST:** 1952
**SQ FT:** 174,240
**SALES (est):** 2.85MM **Privately Held**
**Web:** www.bstephencooperage.com
**SIC:** 3412   Metal barrels, drums, and pails

### (P-7934)
### GREIF  INC
8250 Almeria Ave, Fontana  (92335-3279)
**PHONE**.....................909 350-2112
Andy Wade, *Mgr*
**EMP:** 54
**SQ FT:** 73,320
**SALES (corp-wide):** 5.22B **Publicly Held**
**Web:** www.greif.com
**SIC:** 3412 2674 2655 2449   Drums, shipping: metal; Bags: uncoated paper and multiwall; Fiber cans, drums, and similar products; Wood containers, nec
**PA:** Greif, Inc.
425 Winter Rd
740 549-6000

---

## 3421 Cutlery

### (P-7935)
### ARCH FOODS INC
610 85th Ave, Oakland  (94621-1223)
**PHONE**.....................510 868-6000
**EMP:** 23

**Web:** www.archfoods.com
**SIC:** 3421 5149   Cutlery; Dried or canned foods
**PA:** Arch Foods Inc
25817 Clawiter Rd

### (P-7936)
### ARCH FOODS INC (PA)
25817 Clawiter Rd, Hayward  (94545-3217)
P.O. Box 2355  (93613-2355)
**PHONE**.....................510 331-8352
Jeff Lim, *CEO*
▼ **EMP:** 17   **EST:** 2009
**SQ FT:** 2,000
**SALES (est):** 4.86MM **Privately Held**
**Web:** www.archfoods.com
**SIC:** 3421 5149   Cutlery; Dried or canned foods

### (P-7937)
### KAI USA  LTD
6031 Malburg Way, Vernon  (90058-3947)
**PHONE**.....................323 589-2600
**EMP:** 28
**Web:** zt.kaiusa.com
**SIC:** 3421   Carving sets
**HQ:** Kai U.S.A., Ltd.
18600 Sw Teton Ave
Tualatin OR 97062
503 682-1966

### (P-7938)
### NADOLIFE  INC
1025 Orange Ave, Coronado  (92118-3405)
**PHONE**.....................619 522-0077
**EMP:** 28
**SALES (corp-wide):** 2.89MM **Privately Held**
**SIC:** 3421   Table and food cutlery, including butchers'
**PA:** Nadolife, Inc.
2709 Newton Ave
619 522-6890

### (P-7939)
### PACIUGO
122 Main St Ste 122, Huntington Beach  (92648-5126)
**PHONE**.....................714 536-5388
**EMP:** 25   **EST:** 2009
**SALES (est):** 1.45MM **Privately Held**
**SIC:** 3421   Table and food cutlery, including butchers'

### (P-7940)
### PHC SHARP HOLDINGS  INC (HQ)
17819 Gillette Ave, Irvine  (92614-6501)
**PHONE**.....................714 662-1033
Mark Marinovich, *CEO*
Joe Garavaglia, *CFO*
**EMP:** 23   **EST:** 2006
**SQ FT:** 27,000
**SALES (est):** 9.99MM
**SALES (corp-wide):** 25.23MM **Privately Held**
**SIC:** 3421   Cutlery
**PA:** Levine Leichtman Capital Partners, Llc
345 N Maple Dr Ste 300
310 275-5335

### (P-7941)
### SCHNOOGS
19051 Standard Rd, Sonora  (95370-7542)
**PHONE**.....................209 532-5279
Michael Arnold, *Brnch Mgr*
**EMP:** 59
**SALES (corp-wide):** 731.3K **Privately Held**
**Web:** www.schnoogs.com

**SIC:** 3421   Table and food cutlery, including butchers'
**PA:** Schnoog's
1005 Mono Way
209 533-2486

---

## 3423 Hand And Edge Tools, Nec

### (P-7942)
### ADVANCED CUTTING TOOLS INC
17741 Metzler Ln, Huntington Beach  (92647-6246)
**PHONE**.....................714 842-9376
Stjepan Herceg, *Pr*
**EMP:** 30   **EST:** 1987
**SQ FT:** 10,200
**SALES (est):** 2.64MM **Privately Held**
**Web:** www.actincorporated.com
**SIC:** 3423 3545 5251   Hand and edge tools, nec; Machine tool accessories; Tools

### (P-7943)
### ALLEGION ACCESS TECH LLC
8380 Camino Santa Fe Ste 100, San Diego  (92121-2657)
**PHONE**.....................858 431-5940
Michael Hecker, *Brnch Mgr*
**EMP:** 32
**Web:** www.stanleyaccess.com
**SIC:** 3423   Hand and edge tools, nec
**HQ:** Allegion Access Technologies Llc
65 Scott Swamp Rd
Farmington CT 06032

### (P-7944)
### ALLEGION ACCESS TECH LLC
15750 Jurupa Ave, Fontana  (92337-7329)
**PHONE**.....................909 628-9272
John Rapisarda, *Mgr*
**EMP:** 32
**Web:** www.stanleyaccess.com
**SIC:** 3423   Hand and edge tools, nec
**HQ:** Allegion Access Technologies Llc
65 Scott Swamp Rd
Farmington CT 06032

### (P-7945)
### ALLEGION ACCESS TECH LLC
1312 Dupont Ct, Manteca  (95336-6004)
**PHONE**.....................209 221-4066
Brian Sheppard, *Mgr*
**EMP:** 32
**Web:** www.stanleyaccess.com
**SIC:** 3423   Hand and edge tools, nec
**HQ:** Allegion Access Technologies Llc
65 Scott Swamp Rd
Farmington CT 06032

### (P-7946)
### ASSEMBLY SYSTEMS (PA)
16595 Englewood Ave, Los Gatos  (95032-5622)
**PHONE**.....................408 395-5313
Malcolm Macdonald, *Pr*
**EMP:** 20   **EST:** 1977
**SQ FT:** 10,000
**SALES (est):** 658.49K
**SALES (corp-wide):** 658.49K **Privately Held**
**Web:** www.assemblysystems.net
**SIC:** 3423   Hand and edge tools, nec

### (P-7947)
### AUGERSCOPE INC
Also Called: Marco Products
10375 Wilshire Blvd Apt 1b, Los Angeles  (90024-4728)

▲ **EMP:** 45   **EST:** 1924
**SALES (est):** 1.07MM **Privately Held**
**SIC:** 3423   Plumbers' hand tools

### (P-7948)
### CALIFORNIA FLEXRAKE CORP
Also Called: Flexrake
9620 Gidley St, Temple City  (91780-4215)
P.O. Box 1289  (91780-1289)
**PHONE**.....................626 443-4026
John P Mcguire, *Pr*
▲ **EMP:** 25   **EST:** 1946
**SALES (est):** 2.82MM **Privately Held**
**Web:** www.flexrake.com
**SIC:** 3423   Garden and farm tools, including shovels

### (P-7949)
### CRAFTSMAN CUTTING DIES INC (PA)
Also Called: Ccd
1992 Rockefeller Dr, Ceres  (95307-7274)
**PHONE**.....................714 776-8995
Thomas Hughes, *Pr*
Ronald Ong, *
Cathy Ong-chan, *Sec*
▲ **EMP:** 22   **EST:** 1986
**SALES (est):** 5.56MM
**SALES (corp-wide):** 5.56MM **Privately Held**
**Web:** www.craftsmancuttingdies.com
**SIC:** 3423 3544   Cutting dies, except metal cutting; Special dies, tools, jigs, and fixtures

### (P-7950)
### CRAFTSMAN UNITY  LLC
2273 E Via Burton, Anaheim  (92806-1222)
**PHONE**.....................714 776-8995
Justin Hennings, *Managing Member*
**EMP:** 175   **EST:** 1986
**SALES (est):** 9.66MM **Privately Held**
**Web:** www.craftsmancuttingdies.com
**SIC:** 3423   Cutting dies, except metal cutting

### (P-7951)
### DURSTON MANUFACTURING COMPANY
Also Called: Vim Tools
1395 Palomares St, La Verne  (91750-5241)
P.O. Box 340  (91750-0340)
**PHONE**.....................909 593-1506
Donovan Norton, *CEO*
Mary Dills, *Acctg Mgr*
Donovan Norton, *Sec*
James Maloney, *Treas*
▲ **EMP:** 18   **EST:** 1946
**SQ FT:** 29,000
**SALES (est):** 2.24MM **Privately Held**
**Web:** www.vimtools.com
**SIC:** 3423   Mechanics' hand tools

### (P-7952)
### EVEREST GROUP USA INC
2030 S Carlos Ave, Ontario  (91761-8032)
**PHONE**.....................909 923-1818
Niko Peng, *CEO*
◆ **EMP:** 20   **EST:** 2008
**SALES (est):** 3.42MM **Privately Held**
**Web:** www.everestgroupusa.com
**SIC:** 3423 2298   Jacks: lifting, screw, or ratchet (hand tools); Ropes and fiber cables

### (P-7953)
### FUN PROPERTIES INC
Also Called: PEC Tool
2645 Maricopa St, Torrance  (90503-5144)
**PHONE**.....................310 787-4500
Richard A Lubovski, *CEO*
Sandy Luboviski, *

Bernard Brooks, *
◆ EMP: 60 EST: 1960
SQ FT: 68,000
SALES (est): 5.02MM **Privately Held**
Web: www.pec.tools
SIC: 3423 Hand and edge tools, nec

**(P-7954)**
**GARDEN PALS INC**
3632 E Moonlight St Unit 91, Ontario (91761-2794)
PHONE..................................909 605-0200
Wei Chun Hsu, *CEO*
Robert Deal, *COO*
◆ EMP: 20 EST: 1990
SALES (est): 2.53MM **Privately Held**
Web: www.gardenpals.com
SIC: 3423 Garden and farm tools, including shovels

**(P-7955)**
**HALEX CORPORATION (DH)**
4200 Santa Ana St Ste A, Ontario (91761-1539)
PHONE..................................909 629-6219
Mark Chichak, *Pr*
◆ EMP: 43 EST: 2002
SALES (est): 4.61MM
SALES (corp-wide): 402.18MM **Privately Held**
Web: www.traxxcorp.com
SIC: 3423 Carpet layers' hand tools
HQ: Gcp Applied Technologies Inc.
2325 Lkeview Pkwy Ste 400
Alpharetta GA 30009
617 876-1400

**(P-7956)**
**KAL-CAMERON MANUFACTURING CORP (HQ)**
Also Called: Pro American Premium Tools
4265 Puente Ave, Baldwin Park (91706-3420)
PHONE..................................626 338-7308
John Toshima, *Ch Bd*
EMP: 100 EST: 1983
SQ FT: 32,000
SALES (est): 3.98MM
SALES (corp-wide): 8.76MM **Privately Held**
SIC: 3423 Mechanics' hand tools
PA: American Kal Enterprises, Inc.
4265 Puente Ave
626 338-7308

**(P-7957)**
**KEMPER ENTERPRISES INC**
13595 12th St, Chino (91710-5208)
P.O. Box 696 (91708-0696)
PHONE..................................909 627-6191
Herbert H Stampfl, *Pr*
Librado Cortez, *
▲ EMP: 15 EST: 1947
SQ FT: 30,000
SALES (est): 1.43MM **Privately Held**
Web: www.kempertools.com
SIC: 3423 Hand and edge tools, nec

**(P-7958)**
**LARIN CORP**
5651 Schaefer Ave, Chino (91710-9048)
PHONE..................................909 464-0605
Shouyun Zhang, *Pr*
▲ EMP: 20 EST: 1989
SQ FT: 50,000
SALES (est): 2.14MM **Privately Held**
Web: www.larincorp.com
SIC: 3423 Jacks: lifting, screw, or ratchet (hand tools)

**(P-7959)**
**LEVINE ARTHUR LANSKY & ASSOC (PA)**
Also Called: Lansky Sharpeners
3914 Delmont Ave, Oakland (94605-2233)
PHONE..................................415 234-6020
Arthur Lansky Levine, *Pr*
EMP: 16 EST: 1974
SQ FT: 68,000
SALES (est): 1.74MM
SALES (corp-wide): 1.74MM **Privately Held**
Web: www.waterfordlexington.com
SIC: 3423 Hand and edge tools, nec

**(P-7960)**
**MONSTER TOOL LLC**
2470 Ash St U 2, Vista (92081-8461)
PHONE..................................760 477-1000
Richard Mcintyre, *Pr*
Kevin Zimmerman, *CFO*
EMP: 150 EST: 2021
SQ FT:
SALES (est): 5.82MM
SALES (corp-wide): 12.03B **Privately Held**
Web: www.monstertool.com
SIC: 3423 Hand and edge tools, nec
PA: Sandvik Ab
Spangvagen 10
26260000

**(P-7961)**
**MORGAN MANUFACTURING INC**
521 2nd St, Petaluma (94952-5121)
P.O. Box 737 (94953-0737)
PHONE..................................707 763-6848
Carl T Palmgren, *Pr*
Lillian Raposo, *VP*
EMP: 15 EST: 1954
SALES (est): 3.15MM **Privately Held**
Web: www.morganmfg.com
SIC: 3423 3499 Hand and edge tools, nec; Stabilizing bars (cargo), metal

**(P-7962)**
**PACIFIC HANDY CUTTER INC (DH)**
Also Called: PHC
170 Technology Dr, Irvine (92618-2401)
PHONE..................................714 662-1033
Mark Marinovich, *CEO*
▲ EMP: 34 EST: 1960
SALES (est): 9.99MM
SALES (corp-wide): 25.23MM **Privately Held**
Web: www.phcsafety.com
SIC: 3423 3421 Hand and edge tools, nec; Cutlery
HQ: Phc Sharp Holdings, Inc.
17819 Gillette Ave
Irvine CA 92614
714 662-1033

**(P-7963)**
**PHC MERGER INC**
Also Called: PHC
17819 Gillette Ave, Irvine (92614-6501)
PHONE..................................714 662-1033
▲ EMP: 50
Web: www.phcsafety.com
SIC: 3423 3421 Hand and edge tools, nec; Cutlery

**(P-7964)**
**PRODUCTS ENGINEERING CORP**
Also Called: PEC
2645 Maricopa St, Torrance (90503-5144)
PHONE..................................310 787-4500
Hongguang Ren, *Pr*

Jianhua Ren, *
EMP: 49 EST: 1961
SALES (est): 4.35MM **Privately Held**
Web: www.pec.tools
SIC: 3423 3596 4731 Hand and edge tools, nec; Scales and balances, except laboratory; Freight transportation arrangement

**(P-7965)**
**PURITY POOL INC**
Also Called: Manufacturer
9533 Crossroads Dr, Redding (96003-6814)
P.O. Box 160 (96096-0160)
PHONE..................................800 527-1961
Richard Gross, *Pr*
Julia Gross, *
Richard S Gross, *
Jason Gross, *Stockholder*
EMP: 25 EST: 1961
SQ FT: 3,600
SALES (est): 1.74MM **Privately Held**
Web: www.puritypool.com
SIC: 3423 Leaf skimmers or swimming pool rakes

**(P-7966)**
**SUPERCLOSET**
Also Called: Kind Led Grow Lights
2321 Circadian Way, Santa Rosa (95407-5416)
P.O. Box 6105 (95406)
PHONE..................................831 588-7829
Kip Lewis Andersen, *CEO*
Nicholas Schweitzer, *COO*
Rory Kagan, *CEO*
◆ EMP: 20 EST: 2002
SALES (est): 2.21MM **Privately Held**
Web: www.supercloset.com
SIC: 3423 5261 Garden and farm tools, including shovels; Lawn and garden equipment

**(P-7967)**
**TOUGHBUILT INDUSTRIES INC (PA)**
Also Called: Toughbuilt
8669 Research Dr, Irvine (92618-4204)
PHONE..................................949 528-3100
Michael Panosian, *Ch Bd*
Martin Galstyan, *CFO*
Joshua Keeler, *CDO*
Zareh Khachatoorian, *COO*
EMP: 255 EST: 2012
SQ FT: 15,500
SALES (est): 95.25MM
SALES (corp-wide): 95.25MM **Publicly Held**
Web: www.toughbuilt.com
SIC: 3423 3429 3069 Hand and edge tools, nec; Hardware, nec; Kneeling pads, rubber

**(P-7968)**
**TRONEX TECHNOLOGY INCORPORATED**
2860 Cordelia Rd Ste 230, Fairfield (94534-1808)
PHONE..................................707 426-2550
Arne Salvesen, *Pr*
Karin Salvesen, *VP*
EMP: 20 EST: 1982
SQ FT: 4,000
SALES (est): 1.59MM **Privately Held**
Web: tronex.descoindustries.com
SIC: 3423 5049 Screw drivers, pliers, chisels, etc. (hand tools); Precision tools

### 3425 Saw Blades And Handsaws

**(P-7969)**
**HILTI US MANUFACTURING INC**
Also Called: Dbi
6601 Darin Way, Cypress (90630-5130)
P.O. Box 21148 (74121-1148)
PHONE..................................714 230-7410
EMP: 30 EST: 1984
SALES (est): 3.48MM **Privately Held**
SIC: 3425 Saw blades and handsaws
HQ: Hilti, Inc.
5400 S 122nd East Ave
Tulsa OK 74146
800 879-8000

**(P-7970)**
**KUZ & KIRB**
Also Called: K 2 Diamond
23911 Garnier St Ste C, Torrance (90505)
P.O. Box 346 (90508)
PHONE..................................310 539-6116
Les Kuzmick, *Ch Bd*
Richard Kirby, *Pr*
EMP: 21 EST: 1993
SQ FT: 7,600
SALES (est): 2.86MM **Privately Held**
Web: www.k2diamond.com
SIC: 3425 3531 5082 Saw blades and handsaws; Construction machinery; Concrete processing equipment

**(P-7971)**
**WESTERN SAW MANUFACTURERS INC**
Also Called: Western Saw
3200 Camino Del Sol, Oxnard (93030-8998)
PHONE..................................805 981-0999
Kevin Baron, *CEO*
Frank Baron, *
Kraig Baron, *
Nancy Pounds, *
◆ EMP: 50 EST: 1930
SQ FT: 70,000
SALES (est): 9.67MM **Privately Held**
Web: www.westernsaw.com
SIC: 3425 3546 Saw blades and handsaws; Power-driven handtools

### 3429 Hardware, Nec

**(P-7972)**
**ACCURIDE INTERNATIONAL INC (PA)**
12311 Shoemaker Ave, Santa Fe Springs (90670-4721)
PHONE..................................562 903-0200
Scott E Jordan, *CEO*
Jeffrey A Dunlap, *
Jerome Barr, *
Kent A Jordan, *
▲ EMP: 47 EST: 1966
SALES (est): 69.27MM
SALES (corp-wide): 69.27MM **Privately Held**
Web: www.accuride.com
SIC: 3429 Cabinet hardware

**(P-7973)**
**ACTRON MANUFACTURING INC**
1841 Railroad St, Corona (92878-5012)
PHONE..................................951 371-0885
Frank Rechberg, *CEO*
Dow Rechberg, *
EMP: 93 EST: 1971

## 3429 - Hardware, Nec (P-7974)

SQ FT: 30,000
SALES (est): 16.66MM **Privately Held**
Web: www.actronmfginc.com
SIC: 3429 Aircraft hardware

**(P-7974)**
**ALARIN AIRCRAFT HINGE INC**
Also Called: Commerce
6231 Randolph St, Commerce (90040-3514)
PHONE.................................323 725-1666
Gregory A Sanders, *Pr*
EMP: 25 EST: 1988
SQ FT: 11,000
SALES (est): 6.73MM **Privately Held**
Web: www.alarin.com
SIC: 3429 3728 Aircraft hardware; Aircraft parts and equipment, nec

**(P-7975)**
**ASCO SINTERING CO**
2750 Garfield Ave, Commerce (90040-2610)
P.O. Box 911157 (90091-1157)
PHONE.................................323 725-3550
Neil Moore, *CEO*
Robert Lebrun, *VP*
▲ EMP: 33 EST: 1971
SQ FT: 69,000
SALES (est): 4.6MM **Privately Held**
Web: www.ascosintering.com
SIC: 3429 3714 Hardware, nec; Motor vehicle parts and accessories

**(P-7976)**
**ASSA ABLOY ACC DOOR CNTRLS GRO**
Also Called: Markar & Pemko Products
4226 Transport St, Ventura (93003-5627)
PHONE.................................805 642-2600
EMP: 69
SIC: 3429 3466 Locks or lock sets; Crowns and closures
HQ: Assa Abloy Accessories And Door Controls Group, Inc.
    1902 Airport Rd
    Monroe NC 28110
    877 974-2255

**(P-7977)**
**AUTOMOTIVE RACING PRODUCTS INC (PA)**
Also Called: A R P
1863 Eastman Ave, Ventura (93003-8084)
PHONE.................................805 339-2200
Gary Holzapfel, *CEO*
Mike Holzapfel, *
Robert Flourin, *
Kelly Schau, *
▲ EMP: 65 EST: 1975
SQ FT: 10,000
SALES (est): 59.57K
SALES (corp-wide): 59.57K **Privately Held**
Web: www.arp-bolts.com
SIC: 3429 3714 3452 Hardware, nec; Motor vehicle parts and accessories; Bolts, nuts, rivets, and washers

**(P-7978)**
**AUTOMOTIVE RACING PRODUCTS INC**
Also Called: A R P
1760 E Lemonwood Dr, Santa Paula (93060-9510)
PHONE.................................805 525-1497
Michael Holzapsel, *Brnch Mgr*
EMP: 87
SALES (corp-wide): 59.57K **Privately Held**
Web: www.arp-bolts.com

SIC: 3429 Hardware, nec
PA: Automotive Racing Products, Inc.
    1863 Eastman Ave
    805 339-2200

**(P-7979)**
**AVANTUS AEROSPACE INC**
14957 Gwenchris Ct, Paramount (90723-3423)
PHONE.................................562 633-6626
Brian Williams, *Brnch Mgr*
EMP: 50
SALES (corp-wide): 123.82MM **Privately Held**
Web: www.calscrew.net
SIC: 3429 3452 Metal fasteners; Bolts, nuts, rivets, and washers
HQ: Avantus Aerospace, Inc.
    29101 The Old Rd
    Valencia CA 91355
    661 295-8620

**(P-7980)**
**AVIBANK MFG INC**
Avk Industrial Products
25323 Rye Canyon Rd, Valencia (91355-1205)
PHONE.................................661 257-2329
James M Wolpert, *Genl Mgr*
EMP: 85
SQ FT: 23,000
SALES (corp-wide): 364.48B **Publicly Held**
Web: www.avibank.com
SIC: 3429 3541 3452 Hardware, nec; Machine tools, metal cutting type; Bolts, nuts, rivets, and washers
HQ: Avibank Mfg., Inc.
    11500 Sherman Way
    North Hollywood CA 91605
    818 392-2100

**(P-7981)**
**B & B SPECIALTIES INC (PA)**
4321 E La Palma Ave, Anaheim (92807-1887)
PHONE.................................714 985-3000
Bruce Borchardt, *Pr*
▲ EMP: 90 EST: 1971
SQ FT: 40,000
SALES (est): 22.69MM
SALES (corp-wide): 22.69MM **Privately Held**
Web: www.bbspecialties.com
SIC: 3429 3452 Metal fasteners; Bolts, nuts, rivets, and washers

**(P-7982)**
**BAIER MARINE COMPANY INC**
2920 Airway Ave, Costa Mesa (92626-6008)
PHONE.................................800 455-3917
Mark Smith, *Pr*
Felice Lineberry, *Mgr*
◆ EMP: 20 EST: 2007
SALES (est): 826.25K **Privately Held**
Web: www.baiermarine.com
SIC: 3429 Hardware, nec

**(P-7983)**
**BALDWIN HARDWARE CORPORATION (DH)**
Also Called: Baldwin Brass
19701 Da Vinci, Lake Forest (92610-2622)
PHONE.................................949 672-4000
David R Lumley, *CEO*
◆ EMP: 816 EST: 1944
SQ FT: 300,000
SALES (est): 11.25MM
SALES (corp-wide): 2.92B **Publicly Held**

Web: www.baldwinhardware.com
SIC: 3429 Builders' hardware
HQ: Spectrum Brands, Inc.
    3001 Deming Way
    Middleton WI 53562
    608 275-3340

**(P-7984)**
**BIRMINGHAM FASTENER & SUP INC**
Also Called: Pacific Coast Bolt
12748 Florence Ave, Santa Fe Springs (90670-3906)
PHONE.................................562 944-9549
Brad Tinney, *Brnch Mgr*
EMP: 38
SALES (corp-wide): 193.68MM **Privately Held**
Web: www.bhamfast.com
SIC: 3429 Hardware, nec
PA: Birmingham Fastener & Supply, Inc.
    931 Ave W
    205 595-3511

**(P-7985)**
**CAESAR HARDWARE INTL LTD**
4985 Hallmark Pkwy, San Bernardino (92407-1870)
PHONE.................................800 306-3829
Chao Xu, *CEO*
EMP: 20 EST: 2012
SALES (est): 4.64MM **Privately Held**
Web: www.caesarfireplace.com
SIC: 3429 3999 5021 Fireplace equipment, hardware: andirons, grates, screens; Atomizers, toiletry; Outdoor and lawn furniture, nec
PA: Yuyao Super Wing Foreign Trade Co., Ltd
    Room 1401, Yangguang International Mansion, No.55, Yuli Road

**(P-7986)**
**CAL-JUNE INC (PA)**
Also Called: Jim-Buoy
5238 Vineland Ave, North Hollywood (91601-3221)
P.O. Box 9551 (91609-1551)
PHONE.................................323 877-4164
James H Robertson, *Pr*
Jennifer D Jacobson, *
Melini Robertson, *
Andrea Robertson, *
◆ EMP: 30 EST: 1966
SQ FT: 3,000
SALES (est): 5.42MM
SALES (corp-wide): 5.42MM **Privately Held**
Web: www.jimbuoy.com
SIC: 3429 Marine hardware

**(P-7987)**
**CALIFORNIA SCREW PRODUCTS CORP**
14950 Gwenchris Ct, Paramount (90723-3423)
P.O. Box 228 (90723-0228)
PHONE.................................562 633-6626
Dan Strangio, *CEO*
Dennis Suedkamp, *
EMP: 75 EST: 1966
SQ FT: 20,000
SALES (est): 9.37MM **Privately Held**
Web: www.calscrew.net
SIC: 3429 3452 Metal fasteners; Bolts, nuts, rivets, and washers

**(P-7988)**
**CALMEX FIREPLACE EQP MFG INC**
Also Called: Calmex Fireplace Equip Mfg
13629 Talc St, Santa Fe Springs (90670-5113)
PHONE.................................716 645-2901
Maria Hirshal, *Pr*
Rosa Franco, *VP*
EMP: 23 EST: 1964
SQ FT: 15,000
SALES (est): 736.77K **Privately Held**
SIC: 3429 Fireplace equipment, hardware: andirons, grates, screens

**(P-7989)**
**CONSOLIDATED AEROSPACE MFG LLC**
630 E Lambert Rd, Brea (92821-4119)
PHONE.................................714 989-2802
EMP: 82 EST: 2014
SALES (est): 5.1MM **Privately Held**
Web: www.camaerospace.com
SIC: 3429 Metal fasteners

**(P-7990)**
**CRAIN CUTTER COMPANY INC**
1155 Wrigley Way, Milpitas (95035-5426)
PHONE.................................408 946-6100
Millard Crain Junior, *CEO*
Lance Crain, *Stockholder**
Jennifer Crain, *Stockholder**
▲ EMP: 87 EST: 1956
SQ FT: 110,000
SALES (est): 4.3MM **Privately Held**
Web: www.craintools.com
SIC: 3429 3545 Hardware, nec; Machine tool accessories

**(P-7991)**
**CRD MFG INC**
615 Fee Ana St, Placentia (92870-6704)
PHONE.................................714 871-3300
Timothy Carroll, *CEO*
EMP: 25 EST: 2011
SALES (est): 2.49MM **Privately Held**
Web: www.crdmfg.com
SIC: 3429 3699 Motor vehicle hardware; Welding machines and equipment, ultrasonic

**(P-7992)**
**DARNELL-ROSE INC**
1205 Via Roma, Colton (92324-3909)
PHONE.................................626 912-1688
Brent Bargar, *Pr*
John Posen, *
Robbie Mccullah, *VP Opers*
EMP: 40 EST: 1984
SALES (est): 2.73MM **Privately Held**
Web: www.casters.com
SIC: 3429 Aircraft & marine hardware, inc. pulleys & similar items

**(P-7993)**
**DIVERSIFIED TRADING CORP**
1640 E Miraloma Ave, Placentia (92870-6622)
P.O. Box 17904 (92817-7904)
PHONE.................................714 237-9995
Robert Carrillo, *Pr*
Linda Carrillo, *VP*
▲ EMP: 17 EST: 1986
SALES (est): 1.67MM **Privately Held**
SIC: 3429 7032 Hardware, nec; Sporting and recreational camps

## PRODUCTS & SERVICES SECTION

## 3429 - Hardware, Nec (P-8016)

**(P-7994)**
**DOVAL INDUSTRIES INC**
Also Called: Doval Industries Co
3961 N Mission Rd, Los Angeles
(90031-2931)
PHONE.................................323 226-0335
Cruz Sandoval, *CEO*
▲ **EMP:** 65 **EST:** 1985
**SALES (est):** 1.86MM **Privately Held**
Web: www.doval.com
**SIC:** 3429 5072 2759 Keys, locks, and related hardware; Hardware; Screen printing

**(P-7995)**
**FORESPAR PRODUCTS CORP**
Also Called: Tea Tree Essentials
22322 Gilberto, Rancho Santa Margari (92688-2110)
PHONE.................................949 858-8820
◆ **EMP:** 60 **EST:** 1964
**SALES (est):** 3.36MM **Privately Held**
Web: www.forespar.com
**SIC:** 3429 Marine hardware

**(P-7996)**
**FRAMELESS HARDWARE COMPANY LLC**
Also Called: Fhc
4361 Firestone Blvd, South Gate (90280-3340)
PHONE.................................888 295-4531
Donald Friese Junior, *Managing Member*
**EMP:** 46 **EST:** 2020
**SALES (est):** 1.4MM **Privately Held**
Web: www.fhc-usa.com
**SIC:** 3429 1793 2591 Builders' hardware; Glass and glazing work; Drapery hardware and window blinds and shades

**(P-7997)**
**FXC CORPORATION (PA)**
3050 Red Hill Ave, Costa Mesa (92626-4524)
PHONE.................................714 556-7400
Irene Chevrier, *CEO*
**EMP:** 21 **EST:** 1973
**SQ FT:** 26,000
**SALES (est):** 9.75MM
**SALES (corp-wide):** 9.75MM **Privately Held**
Web: www.fxcguardian.com
**SIC:** 3429 2399 Parachute hardware; Parachutes

**(P-7998)**
**GARDNER FAMILY LTD PARTNERSHIP**
Also Called: HMC Display
300 Commerce Dr, Madera (93637-5215)
PHONE.................................559 675-8149
▲ **EMP:** 25 **EST:** 1967
**SQ FT:** 45,000
**SALES (est):** 4.85MM **Privately Held**
Web: www.hmcdisplay.com
**SIC:** 3429 Hardware, nec

**(P-7999)**
**GCX CORPORATION (DH)**
3875 Cypress Dr, Petaluma (94954-5635)
PHONE.................................707 773-1100
◆ **EMP:** 62 **EST:** 1971
**SALES (est):** 60.66MM
**SALES (corp-wide):** 2.8B **Privately Held**
Web: www.gcx.com
**SIC:** 3429 Hardware, nec
**HQ:** Audax Private Equity Fund Ii, L.P.
101 Huntington Ave
Boston MA 02199

**(P-8000)**
**HAMPTON PRODUCTS INTL CORP (PA)**
50 Icon, Foothill Ranch (92610-3000)
PHONE.................................800 562-5625
Gregory J Gluchowski, *Pr*
▲ **EMP:** 175 **EST:** 1973
**SQ FT:** 160,000
**SALES (est):** 32.34MM
**SALES (corp-wide):** 32.34MM **Privately Held**
Web: www.hamptonproducts.com
**SIC:** 3429 Padlocks

**(P-8001)**
**HARTWELL CORPORATION (DH)**
Also Called: Hasco
900 Richfield Rd, Placentia (92870-6788)
PHONE.................................714 993-4200
Dain Miller, *Pr*
▲ **EMP:** 200 **EST:** 1957
**SQ FT:** 134,000
**SALES (est):** 68.68MM
**SALES (corp-wide):** 7.94B **Publicly Held**
Web: www.hartwellcorp.com
**SIC:** 3429 Aircraft hardware
**HQ:** Mckechnie Aerospace Investments, Inc.
20 Pacifica Ste 200
Irvine CA

**(P-8002)**
**HODGE PRODUCTS INC**
Also Called: Lock People, The
7365 Mission Gorge Rd Ste F, San Diego (92120)
P.O. Box 1326 (92022)
PHONE.................................800 778-2217
Anthony A Hodge, *CEO*
Allan Hodge, *
▲ **EMP:** 25 **EST:** 1971
**SALES (est):** 5.34MM **Privately Held**
Web: www.hpionline.com
**SIC:** 3429 5099 Locks or lock sets; Locks and lock sets

**(P-8003)**
**HOLLYWOOD BED SPRING MFG INC (PA)**
Also Called: Hollywood Bed & Spring Mfg
5959 Corvette St, Commerce (90040-1601)
PHONE.................................323 887-9500
Larry Harrow, *CEO*
Jason Harrow, *
Andrea Harrow, *
◆ **EMP:** 78 **EST:** 1945
**SQ FT:** 55,000
**SALES (est):** 17.5MM
**SALES (corp-wide):** 17.5MM **Privately Held**
Web: www.hollywoodbed.com
**SIC:** 3429 2515 2511 2514 Hardware, nec; Mattresses and bedsprings; Wood household furniture; Frames for box springs or bedsprings: metal

**(P-8004)**
**INSPIRED FLIGHT TECH INC**
Also Called: Inspired Flight
225 Suburban Rd Ste A, San Luis Obispo (93401-7547)
PHONE.................................805 776-3640
Richard Stollmeyer, *CEO*
Marcus Stollmeyer, *
**EMP:** 34 **EST:** 2017
**SALES (est):** 3.63MM **Privately Held**
Web: www.inspiredflight.com
**SIC:** 3429 Aircraft hardware

**(P-8005)**
**INTELLIGENT ENERGY INC**
1731 Technology Dr Ste 755, San Jose (95110-1325)
PHONE.................................562 997-3600
Henri Winand, *Pr*
Hazen Burford, *
Larry Frost, *
**EMP:** 23 **EST:** 2002
**SQ FT:** 9,600
**SALES (est):** 2.61MM
**SALES (corp-wide):** 11.28MM **Privately Held**
Web: www.intelligent-energy.com
**SIC:** 3429 3694 Bicycle racks, automotive; Alternators, automotive
**PA:** Intelligent Energy Limited
Charnwood Building Holywell Park
150 927-1271

**(P-8006)**
**J & M PRODUCTS INC**
1647 Truman St, San Fernando (91340-3119)
PHONE.................................818 837-0205
**EMP:** 97 **EST:** 1995
**SALES (est):** 16.69MM **Privately Held**
Web: www.jmproducts.com
**SIC:** 3429 3679 Hardware, nec; Harness assemblies, for electronic use: wire or cable

**(P-8007)**
**JONATHAN ENGNRED SLUTIONS CORP (HQ)**
250 Commerce Ste 100, Irvine (92602-1318)
PHONE.................................714 665-4400
Jack Frickel, *Pr*
Jason Ciancarulo, *
▲ **EMP:** 44 **EST:** 1954
**SQ FT:** 120,000
**SALES (est):** 99.21MM
**SALES (corp-wide):** 397.46MM **Privately Held**
Web: www.jonathanengr.com
**SIC:** 3429 3562 Hardware, nec; Ball bearings and parts
**PA:** Jll Partners, Llc
300 Park Ave 18th Fl
212 286-8600

**(P-8008)**
**KARCHER DESIGN**
Also Called: Izabel Karcher, Owner
235 W Paul Ave, Clovis (93612-0250)
PHONE.................................253 220-8244
Jan Karcher, *Owner*
▲ **EMP:** 80 **EST:** 2015
**SALES (est):** 4.14MM **Privately Held**
Web: www.karcher-design.com
**SIC:** 3429 Builders' hardware

**(P-8009)**
**KWIKSET CORPORATION**
Also Called: Spectrum Brands Hdwr HM Imprv
19701 Da Vinci, Foothill Ranch (92610-2622)
P.O. Box 620992 (53562-0992)
PHONE.................................949 672-4000
▲ **EMP:** 3200
Web: www.kwikset.com
**SIC:** 3429 Keys, locks, and related hardware

**(P-8010)**
**LIGHT COMPOSITE CORPORATION**
Also Called: Forespar
22322 Gilberto, Rcho Sta Marg (92688-2102)
PHONE.................................949 858-8820
Robert R Foresman, *Pr*
Juin Foresman, *
Marilyn Holst, *Sec*
▼ **EMP:** 24 **EST:** 1991
**SALES (est):** 1.11MM **Privately Held**
Web: www.forespar.com
**SIC:** 3429 Marine hardware

**(P-8011)**
**LOCK AMERICA INC**
Also Called: Mr Lock
9168 Stellar Ct, Corona (92883-4923)
PHONE.................................951 277-5180
Ming Shiao, *Pr*
Frank Minnella, *CEO*
Watson Visuwan, *VP*
◆ **EMP:** 19 **EST:** 1989
**SQ FT:** 11,500
**SALES (est):** 2.42MM **Privately Held**
Web: www.laigroup.com
**SIC:** 3429 5099 Keys, locks, and related hardware; Locks and lock sets

**(P-8012)**
**LUCKY LINE PRODUCTS INC**
7890 Dunbrook Rd, San Diego (92126-4369)
PHONE.................................858 549-6699
◆ **EMP:** 26 **EST:** 1948
**SALES (est):** 6.51MM **Privately Held**
Web: www.luckyline.com
**SIC:** 3429 3993 Keys, locks, and related hardware; Signs and advertising specialties

**(P-8013)**
**M A G ENGINEERING MFG CO**
Also Called: M.A.g Engineering & Mfg
17305 Demler St, Irvine (92614)
▲ **EMP:** 40 **EST:** 1968
**SALES (est):** 3.7MM **Privately Held**
**SIC:** 3429 Locks or lock sets

**(P-8014)**
**MCDANIEL MANUFACTURING INC**
6180 Enterprise Dr Ste D, Diamond Springs (95619-9471)
PHONE.................................530 626-6336
John Mcdaniel, *Pr*
Nora Mcdaniel, *Sec*
**EMP:** 15 **EST:** 1992
**SALES (est):** 2.37MM **Privately Held**
Web: www.mcdanielmfg.com
**SIC:** 3429 3443 3089 Hardware, nec; Stills, pressure: metal plate; Hardware, plastics

**(P-8015)**
**MCMAHON STEEL COMPANY INC**
1880 Nirvana Ave, Chula Vista (91911-6118)
PHONE.................................619 671-9700
Derek J Mcmahon, *Pr*
Kevin Mcmahon, *VP*
**EMP:** 120 **EST:** 1970
**SQ FT:** 14,300
**SALES (est):** 23.18MM **Privately Held**
Web: www.mcmahonsteel.com
**SIC:** 3429 1791 3441 Hardware, nec; Structural steel erection; Fabricated structural metal

**(P-8016)**
**MID-WEST WHOLESALE HARDWARE CO**
Also Called: Banner Solutions
1641 S Sunkist St, Anaheim (92806-5813)
PHONE.................................714 630-4751

## 3429 - Hardware, Nec (P-8017)

Terry Olson, *Brnch Mgr*
**EMP:** 22
**SALES (corp-wide):** 45.65MM **Privately Held**
**Web:** www.bannersolutions.com
**SIC: 3429** 5072 Hardware, nec; Hardware
**PA:** Mid-West Wholesale Hardware Co Inc
1000 Century Ave
816 245-1142

### (P-8017)
### MOELLER MFG & SUP LLC
630 E Lambert Rd, Brea (92821-4119)
**PHONE**.................................714 999-5551
Stevens Chevillotte, *Pr*
Peter George, *
**EMP:** 45 **EST:** 1978
**SALES (est):** 14MM
**SALES (corp-wide):** 15.78B **Publicly Held**
**SIC: 3429** 3452 Aircraft hardware; Washers, metal
**HQ:** Consolidated Aerospace
Manufacturing, Llc
1425 S Acacia Ave
Fullerton CA 92831
714 989-2797

### (P-8018)
### MONADNOCK COMPANY
Also Called: Lisi Aerospace
16728 Gale Ave, City Of Industry (91745-1803)
**PHONE**.................................626 964-6581
Christian Darville, *CEO*
Michael Reyes, *
▼ **EMP:** 190 **EST:** 1987
**SQ FT:** 90,000
**SALES (est):** 25.82MM
**SALES (corp-wide):** 2.67MM **Privately Held**
**SIC: 3429** Aircraft hardware
**HQ:** Lisi Aerospace
42 A 52
Paris 12 IDF 75012
140198200

### (P-8019)
### MONOGRAM AEROSPACE FAS INC
3423 Garfield Ave, Commerce (90040-3103)
**PHONE**.................................323 722-4760
John P Schaefer, *CEO*
David Adler, *
▲ **EMP:** 250 **EST:** 1990
**SQ FT:** 97,500
**SALES (est):** 36.42MM
**SALES (corp-wide):** 893.55MM **Publicly Held**
**Web:** www.trsaero.com
**SIC: 3429** 3452 Hardware, nec; Bolts, metal
**PA:** Trimas Corporation
38505 Wodward Ave Ste 200
248 631-5450

### (P-8020)
### NATIONAL MANUFACTURING CO
Also Called: Stanley National Hardware
19701 Da Vinci, Lake Forest (92610-2622)
**PHONE**.................................800 346-9445
◆ **EMP:** 1660 **EST:** 1901
**SALES (est):** 3.94MM
**SALES (corp-wide):** 15.78B **Publicly Held**
**SIC: 3429** Builders' hardware
**PA:** Stanley Black & Decker, Inc.
1000 Stanley Dr
860 225-5111

### (P-8021)
### NUSET INC
2432 Peck Rd, City Of Industry (90601-1604)
**PHONE**.................................626 246-1668
Caron Ng, *CEO*
**EMP:** 20 **EST:** 2017
**SALES (est):** 2.53MM **Privately Held**
**Web:** www.nusetlock.com
**SIC: 3429** Keys, locks, and related hardware

### (P-8022)
### ORION ORNAMENTAL IRON INC
6918 Tujunga Ave, North Hollywood (91605-6212)
**PHONE**.................................818 752-0688
Sunil Patel, *CEO*
Atul Patel, *
▲ **EMP:** 40 **EST:** 1983
**SQ FT:** 30,000
**SALES (est):** 5.41MM **Privately Held**
**Web:** www.ironartbyorion.com
**SIC: 3429** Builders' hardware

### (P-8023)
### PACIFIC LOCK COMPANY (PA)
25605 Hercules St, Valencia (91355-5051)
**PHONE**.................................661 294-3707
Gregory B Waugh, *Pr*
Joshua Fleagane, *
Patty Yang, *
▲ **EMP:** 29 **EST:** 1998
**SQ FT:** 18,000
**SALES (est):** 3.2MM **Privately Held**
**Web:** www.paclock.com
**SIC: 3429** 3699 5099 Keys and key blanks; Security devices; Locks and lock sets

### (P-8024)
### RPC LEGACY INC
Also Called: Terry Hinge & Hardware
14600 Arminta St, Van Nuys (91402-5902)
**PHONE**.................................818 787-9000
Authur William, *Brnch Mgr*
**EMP:** 20
**SALES (corp-wide):** 9.58MM **Privately Held**
**SIC: 3429** Hardware, nec
**PA:** Rpc Legacy, Inc.
2020 7th St
815 966-2000

### (P-8025)
### SATURN FASTENERS INC
425 S Varney St, Burbank (91502-2193)
**PHONE**.................................818 973-1807
Raymond David Barker Junior, *C*
Laura Elaine Barker, *
Raymond D Barker Junior, *Pr*
▼ **EMP:** 112 **EST:** 1989
**SQ FT:** 38,000
**SALES (est):** 12.38MM **Privately Held**
**Web:** www.saturnfasteners.com
**SIC: 3429** 5085 5072 3452 Metal fasteners; Industrial supplies; Bolts, nuts, and screws; Bolts, nuts, rivets, and washers
**HQ:** Acument Global Technologies, Inc.
6125 18 Mile Rd
Sterling Heights MI 48314
586 997-5600

### (P-8026)
### SNAPNRACK INC
775 Fiero Ln Ste 200, San Luis Obispo (93401-7904)
**PHONE**.................................877 732-2860
Lyn Cowgill, *Off Mgr*
**EMP:** 26 **EST:** 2014
**SALES (est):** 977.53K **Privately Held**
**Web:** www.snapnrack.com
**SIC: 3429** Clamps, couplings, nozzles, and other metal hose fittings

### (P-8027)
### SOLID-SCOPE MACHINING CO INC
Also Called: Solid-Scope
17925 Adria Maru Ln, Carson (90746-1401)
**PHONE**.................................310 523-2366
Patsy Rhinehart, *Pr*
Robert Rhinehart, *VP*
**EMP:** 16 **EST:** 1979
**SQ FT:** 6,000
**SALES (est):** 2.76MM **Privately Held**
**Web:** www.solid-scope.com
**SIC: 3429** 3728 Aircraft hardware; Aircraft parts and equipment, nec

### (P-8028)
### SPEP ACQUISITION CORP (PA)
Also Called: Sierra Pacific Engrg & Pdts
4041 Via Oro Ave, Long Beach (90810-1458)
P.O. Box 5246 (90749-5246)
**PHONE**.................................310 608-0693
Barry Stein, *Pr*
Larry Mirick, *
◆ **EMP:** 70 **EST:** 1986
**SQ FT:** 48,300
**SALES (est):** 20.69MM
**SALES (corp-wide):** 20.69MM **Privately Held**
**Web:** www.spep.com
**SIC: 3429** 8711 5072 Hardware, nec; Engineering services; Hardware

### (P-8029)
### STAR DIE CASTING INC
12209 Slauson Ave, Santa Fe Springs (90670-2605)
**PHONE**.................................562 698-0627
Jer Ming Yu, *Pr*
Mei H Yu, *VP*
▲ **EMP:** 80 **EST:** 1980
**SQ FT:** 13,290
**SALES (est):** 1.43MM **Privately Held**
**Web:** www.stargroupglobal.com
**SIC: 3429** 3364 3544 Builders' hardware; Nonferrous die-castings except aluminum; Special dies and tools

### (P-8030)
### T G SCHMEISER CO INC
Also Called: Schmeiser Farm Equipment
3160 E California Ave, Fresno (93702-4108)
P.O. Box 1047 (93714-1047)
**PHONE**.................................559 486-4569
Andrew W Cummings, *CEO*
Shirley Cummings, *
▼ **EMP:** 35 **EST:** 1929
**SQ FT:** 36,000
**SALES (est):** 5.06MM **Privately Held**
**Web:** www.tgschmeiser.com
**SIC: 3429** 3523 Hardware, nec; Soil preparation machinery, except turf and grounds

### (P-8031)
### TOP LINE MFG INC
Also Called: Sroodtuo
7032 Alondra Blvd, Paramount (90723-3926)
P.O. Box 739 (90723-0739)
**PHONE**.................................562 633-0605
Anne Graffy, *CEO*
▲ **EMP:** 29 **EST:** 1982
**SQ FT:** 20,000
**SALES (est):** 7.11MM **Privately Held**
**Web:** www.toplinemfg.com
**SIC: 3429** Motor vehicle hardware

### (P-8032)
### TOWNSTEEL INC
17901 Railroad St, City Of Industry (91748-1113)
**PHONE**.................................626 965-8917
Lydia Meng, *Pr*
Shien Cheng Meng, *VP*
◆ **EMP:** 100 **EST:** 2001
**SQ FT:** 10,000
**SALES (est):** 9.12MM **Privately Held**
**Web:** www.townsteel.com
**SIC: 3429** Door locks, bolts, and checks

### (P-8033)
### UMPCO INC
7100 Lampson Ave, Garden Grove (92841-3914)
P.O. Box 5158 (92846-0158)
**PHONE**.................................714 897-3531
Dan Miller, *CEO*
**EMP:** 75 **EST:** 1963
**SQ FT:** 60,000
**SALES (est):** 9.27MM **Privately Held**
**Web:** www.umpco.com
**SIC: 3429** Clamps, metal

### (P-8034)
### VIT PRODUCTS INC
2063 Wineridge Pl, Escondido (92029-1931)
**PHONE**.................................760 480-6702
Don Pagano, *Pr*
Arthur Arns, *
**EMP:** 36 **EST:** 1972
**SQ FT:** 24,000
**SALES (est):** 4.06MM **Privately Held**
**Web:** www.vitproducts.com
**SIC: 3429** 2295 Clamps, couplings, nozzles, and other metal hose fittings; Coated fabrics, not rubberized

### (P-8035)
### W & F MFG INC
10635 Keswick St, Sun Valley (91352-4610)
P.O. Box 1219 (91353-1219)
**PHONE**.................................818 394-6060
▲ **EMP:** 50
**SIC: 3429** Door opening and closing devices, except electrical

### (P-8036)
### WEISER LOCK CORPORATION
19701 Da Vinci, Foothill Ranch (92610-2622)
P.O. Box 620992 (53562-0992)
**PHONE**.................................949 672-4000
◆ **EMP:** 18
**Web:** ca.weiserlock.com
**SIC: 3429** Door locks, bolts, and checks

### (P-8037)
### WESTERN HARDWARE COMPANY
161 Commerce Way, Walnut (91789-2719)
**PHONE**.................................909 595-6201
Gayle E Pacheco, *Pr*
▲ **EMP:** 19 **EST:** 1968
**SALES (est):** 862.83K **Privately Held**
**Web:** www.westernhardware.com
**SIC: 3429** Hardware, nec

### (P-8038)
### WINFIELD LOCKS INC
Also Called: Computerized Security Systems
1721 Whittier Ave, Costa Mesa (92627-4580)

PHONE..................949 722-5400
John Kimes, Pr
EMP: 5006 EST: 1977
SQ FT: 30,000
SALES (est): 2.14MM
SALES (corp-wide): 7.97B Publicly Held
Web: www.zeusbeard.com
SIC: 3429 Locks or lock sets
HQ: Masco Building Products Corp.
17450 College Pkwy
Livonia MI 48152
313 274-7400

### (P-8039)
### YOUNG ENGINEERS INC
25841 Commercentre Dr, Lake Forest (92630-8812)
P.O. Box 278 (92609-0278)
PHONE..................949 581-9411
Pat Wells, Pr
EMP: 64 EST: 1963
SQ FT: 26,000
SALES (est): 9.37MM
SALES (corp-wide): 218.18MM Privately Held
Web: www.youngengineers.com
SIC: 3429 Aircraft hardware
PA: Novaria Group, L.L.C.
6685 Iron Horse Blvd
214 707-8980

## 3431 Metal Sanitary Ware

### (P-8040)
### EMC WATER LLC
4114 S Airport Way, Stockton (95206-4400)
PHONE..................209 616-6963
EMP: 67
Web: www.zurnelkay.com
SIC: 3431 Metal sanitary ware
HQ: Emc Water Llc
1333 Bttrfield Rd Ste 200
Downers Grove IL 60515
630 574-8484

### (P-8041)
### HYDRO SYSTEMS INC (PA)
29132 Avenue Paine, Valencia (91355-5402)
PHONE..................661 775-0686
Scott G Steinhardt, Pr
Dave Ortwein, *
Larry Burroughs, *
EMP: 95 EST: 1979
SQ FT: 90,000
SALES (est): 18.92MM
SALES (corp-wide): 18.92MM Privately Held
Web: www.hydrosystem.com
SIC: 3431 3432 3088 Bathtubs: enameled iron, cast iron, or pressed metal; Plumbing fixture fittings and trim; Plastics plumbing fixtures

### (P-8042)
### MAG AEROSPACE INDUSTRIES LLC
Also Called: Monogram Systems
1500 Glenn Curtiss St, Carson (90746-4012)
P.O. Box 11189 (90749)
PHONE..................801 400-7944
Sebastien Weber, Pr
Mark Scott, *
David Conrad, *
Mike Nieves, SUPPLY CHAIN*
Tim Birbeck, *
◆ EMP: 350 EST: 1989
SQ FT: 150,000
SALES (est): 99.67MM

SALES (corp-wide): 940.23MM Privately Held
SIC: 3431 3728 Plumbing fixtures: enameled iron, cast iron,or pressed metal; Aircraft parts and equipment, nec
PA: Safran
2 Boulevard Du General Martial Valin

### (P-8043)
### OZIG LLC
490 43rd St Ste 206, Oakland (94609-2138)
PHONE..................510 588-7952
Guanglin Duan, Managing Member
EMP: 50 EST: 2021
SALES (est): 901.95K Privately Held
SIC: 3431 5084 Sinks: enameled iron, cast iron, or pressed metal; Countersinks

### (P-8044)
### SEACHROME CORPORATION
Also Called: Seachrome
1906 E Dominguez St, Long Beach (90810-1002)
PHONE..................310 427-8010
Sam C Longo Junior, CEO
▲ EMP: 112 EST: 1983
SQ FT: 50,000
SALES (est): 22.1MM Privately Held
Web: www.seachrome.com
SIC: 3431 5072 3842 3429 Bathroom fixtures, including sinks; Builders' hardware, nec; Surgical appliances and supplies; Hardware, nec

## 3432 Plumbing Fixture Fittings And Trim

### (P-8045)
### ACORNVAC INC
Also Called: Acorn Vac
13818 Oaks Ave, Chino (91710-7008)
PHONE..................909 902-1141
Donald E Morris, CEO
EMP: 20 EST: 2000
SALES (est): 12.74MM
SALES (corp-wide): 99.75MM Privately Held
Web: www.acornvac.com
SIC: 3432 Plastic plumbing fixture fittings, assembly
PA: Acorn Engineering Company
15125 E Proctor Ave
800 488-8999

### (P-8046)
### BRASSTECH INC
1301 E Wilshire Ave, Santa Ana (92705-4420)
PHONE..................714 796-9278
EMP: 239
SALES (corp-wide): 7.97B Publicly Held
Web: www.brasstech.com
SIC: 3432 Plumbing fixture fittings and trim
HQ: Brasstech, Inc.
2001 Carnegie Ave
Santa Ana CA 92705
949 417-5207

### (P-8047)
### BRASSTECH INC (HQ)
Also Called: Newport Brass
2001 Carnegie Ave, Santa Ana (92705-5531)
PHONE..................949 417-5207
Jonathan Wood, CEO
John G Sznewajs, *
Kenneth G Cole, *
Kathleen S Rodes, *

◆ EMP: 101 EST: 1987
SQ FT: 70,000
SALES (est): 82.87MM
SALES (corp-wide): 7.97B Publicly Held
Web: www.brasstech.com
SIC: 3432 Plumbing fixture fittings and trim
PA: Masco Corporation
17450 College Pkwy
313 274-7400

### (P-8048)
### CALIFORNIA FAUCETS INC
5231 Argosy Ave, Huntington Beach (92649-1015)
PHONE..................657 400-1639
Blas Ramierez, Brnch Mgr
EMP: 39
Web: www.calfaucets.com
SIC: 3432 Faucets and spigots, metal and plastic
PA: California Faucets, Inc.
5271 Argosy Dr

### (P-8049)
### CALIFORNIA FAUCETS INC (PA)
Also Called: Pvd Coatings
5271 Argosy Ave, Huntington Beach (92649-1015)
PHONE..................800 822-8855
Jeffrey Howard Silverstein, CEO
Sonia Silverstein, *
◆ EMP: 36 EST: 1988
SALES (est): 23.27MM Privately Held
Web: www.calfaucets.com
SIC: 3432 Faucets and spigots, metal and plastic

### (P-8050)
### CENTRAL VLY ASSEMBLY PACKG INC
5515 E Lamona Ave # 103, Fresno (93727-2367)
PHONE..................559 486-4260
Nate Perry, CEO
John Perry, *
EMP: 24 EST: 2003
SALES (est): 2.43MM Privately Held
Web: www.centralvalleyassembly.com
SIC: 3432 3565 3089 3824 Plastic plumbing fixture fittings, assembly; Bag opening, filling, and closing machines; Blister or bubble formed packaging, plastics; Linear counters

### (P-8051)
### COLLICUTT ENERGY SERVICES INC
12349 Hawkins St, Santa Fe Springs (90670-3366)
PHONE..................562 944-4413
TOLL FREE: 866
Tim Rahman, Brnch Mgr
EMP: 21
SQ FT: 77,000
SALES (corp-wide): 33.54MM Privately Held
Web: www.collicutt.com
SIC: 3432 Plumbing fixture fittings and trim
HQ: Collicutt Energy Services Inc.
840 Riverside Pkwy
West Sacramento CA 95605

### (P-8052)
### COLUMBIA SANITARY PRODUCTS INC
Also Called: Columbia Products Co
1622 Browning, Irvine (92606-4809)
PHONE..................949 474-0777
Dorothy Lazier, CEO

Paul Escalera, Pr
▲ EMP: 20 EST: 1949
SQ FT: 20,000
SALES (est): 3.63MM Privately Held
Web: www.columbiasinks.com
SIC: 3432 Plumbing fixture fittings and trim

### (P-8053)
### G T WATER PRODUCTS INC
5239 N Commerce Ave, Moorpark (93021-1763)
PHONE..................805 529-2900
George Tash, Pr
Debra Tash, VP
Russell Reasner, VP
Steve Schmitt, VP
Julie Shipley, VP
▲ EMP: 17 EST: 1971
SQ FT: 20,000
SALES (est): 4.05MM Privately Held
Web: www.gtwaterproducts.com
SIC: 3432 Plumbing fixture fittings and trim

### (P-8054)
### PRICE PFISTER INC
Also Called: Price Pfister Brass Mfg
19701 Da Vinci, Lake Forest (92610-2622)
P.O. Box 620992 (53562-0992)
PHONE..................949 672-4000
▲ EMP: 2300
SALES (est): 128.86MM Privately Held
Web: www.pfisterfaucets.com
SIC: 3432 Faucets and spigots, metal and plastic

### (P-8055)
### RAIN BIRD CORPORATION
Also Called: Rain Bird Golf Division
970 W Sierra Madre Ave, Azusa (91702-1873)
PHONE..................626 812-3400
Matt Circle, Mgr
EMP: 52
SALES (corp-wide): 433.78MM Privately Held
Web: www.rainbird.com
SIC: 3432 3494 3433 Plumbing fixture fittings and trim; Valves and pipe fittings, nec; Heating equipment, except electric
PA: Rain Bird Corporation
970 W Sierra Madre Ave
626 812-3400

### (P-8056)
### SANTEC INC
3501 Challenger St Fl 2, Torrance (90503-1697)
PHONE..................310 542-0063
Nicolas Chen, CEO
James S Chen, *
▲ EMP: 50 EST: 1981
SQ FT: 32,000
SALES (est): 5.51MM Privately Held
Web: www.santecfaucet.com
SIC: 3432 Faucets and spigots, metal and plastic

### (P-8057)
### TBS IRRIGATION PRODUCTS INC
Also Called: T.B.S. Irrigation
8787 Olive Ln Bldg 3, Santee (92071-4137)
PHONE..................619 579-0520
Michael J Folkman, Pr
William Butson, VP
Neil Faulkman, Sec
EMP: 20 EST: 1997
SQ FT: 25,000
SALES (est): 3.4MM Privately Held
Web: www.tbsirrigation.com

# 3433 - Heating Equipment, Except Electric (P-8058)

SIC: 3432 3523 3088 Lawn hose nozzles and sprinklers; Farm machinery and equipment; Plastics plumbing fixtures

## 3433 Heating Equipment, Except Electric

**(P-8058)**
**ADVANCED CNSRVTION TECH DIST I**
Also Called: Act Inc Dmand Kontrols Systems
3176 Pullman St Ste 119, Costa Mesa (92626)
PHONE..................714 668-1200
Larry Acker, *CEO*
Donna-marie Acker, *Pr*
Kristine Parker, *Interim Vice President*
EMP: 16 EST: 1990
SQ FT: 7,000
SALES (est): 847.8K **Privately Held**
Web: www.gothotwater.com
SIC: 3433 Boilers, low-pressure heating: steam or hot water

**(P-8059)**
**AMERICAN SOLAR LLC**
8484 Wilshire Blvd Ste 630, Beverly Hills (90211-3227)
PHONE..................323 250-1307
Meir Yaniv, *CEO*
EMP: 30 EST: 2020
SALES (est): 916.76K **Privately Held**
Web: www.americansolar.net
SIC: 3433 Solar heaters and collectors

**(P-8060)**
**BENCHMARK THERMAL CORPORATION**
13185 Nevada City Ave, Grass Valley (95945-9568)
PHONE..................530 477-5011
Vincent Palmieri, *CEO*
Gil Mathew, *
Laralee Hannah, *
EMP: 52 EST: 1984
SQ FT: 20,000
SALES (est): 4.62MM **Privately Held**
Web: www.benchmarkthermal.com
SIC: 3433 Heating equipment, except electric

**(P-8061)**
**BIOTHERM HYDRONIC INC**
Also Called: True Leaf Technologies
476 Primero Ct, Cotati (94931-3014)
P.O. Box 750967 (94975-0967)
PHONE..................707 794-9660
Jim K Rearden, *CEO*
Michael G Muchow, *VP*
▲ EMP: 15 EST: 1989
SQ FT: 10,000
SALES (est): 924.27K **Privately Held**
Web: www.biothermsolutions.com
SIC: 3433 Heating equipment, except electric

**(P-8062)**
**CANDELA RENEWABLES LLC**
500 Sansome St Ste 500, San Francisco (94111-3211)
PHONE..................415 515-9627
EMP: 22 EST: 2017
SALES (est): 2.15MM **Privately Held**
Web: www.candelarenewables.com
SIC: 3433 Heating equipment, except electric

**(P-8063)**
**CAPITAL COOKING EQUIPMENT INC**
Also Called: Capital Cooking
1025 E Bedmar St, Carson (90746-3601)
PHONE..................562 903-1168
Roberto Bernal, *
Alejandro Bernal, *
Porfiro Guzman, *
Rafael Romero, *
▲ EMP: 47 EST: 2001
SALES (est): 4.66MM **Privately Held**
Web: www.capital-cooking.com
SIC: 3433 3631 Stoves, wood and coal burning; Gas ranges, domestic

**(P-8064)**
**COEN COMPANY INC (DH)**
951 Mariners Island Blvd, San Mateo (94404-1558)
PHONE..................650 522-2100
Earl W Schnell, *Pr*
◆ EMP: 40 EST: 1912
SALES (est): 5.09MM
SALES (corp-wide): 64.37B **Privately Held**
Web: www.johnzinkhamworthy.com
SIC: 3433 3823 Burners, furnaces, boilers, and stokers; Combustion control instruments
HQ: Koch Engineered Solutions, Llc
4111 E 37th St N
Wichita KS 67220
316 828-5110

**(P-8065)**
**EMPIRE PRODUCTS INC**
5061 Brooks St, Montclair (91763-4835)
PHONE..................909 399-3355
Robert Beck, *Ch Bd*
EMP: 57 EST: 1982
SQ FT: 6,000
SALES (est): 476.13K **Privately Held**
SIC: 3433 3429 3631 Logs, gas fireplace; Fireplace equipment, hardware: andirons, grates, screens; Household cooking equipment

**(P-8066)**
**FAFCO INC (PA)**
435 Otterson Dr, Chico (95928-8207)
PHONE..................530 332-2100
Freeman A Ford, *Ch Bd*
Nancy I Garvin, *
Robert C Leckinger, *
◆ EMP: 46 EST: 1969
SQ FT: 57,500
SALES (est): 10.89MM
SALES (corp-wide): 10.89MM **Privately Held**
Web: www.fafco.com
SIC: 3433 Heaters, swimming pool: oil or gas

**(P-8067)**
**GEMTECH SALES CORP**
Also Called: Free Hot Water
2146 Bering Dr, San Jose (95131-2013)
P.O. Box 112045 (95011-2045)
PHONE..................408 432-9900
Gal Moyal, *Pr*
EMP: 20 EST: 1999
SQ FT: 9,000
SALES (est): 520.87K **Privately Held**
Web: www.freehotwater.com
SIC: 3433 Solar heaters and collectors

**(P-8068)**
**GREENVOLTS INC**
19200 Stevens Creek Blvd Ste 200, Cupertino (95014-2530)
PHONE..................415 963-4030
EMP: 90 EST: 2005
SALES (est): 2.44MM **Privately Held**
Web: www.greenvolts.com
SIC: 3433 Solar heaters and collectors

**(P-8069)**
**INDEPENDENT ENERGY SOLUTIONS INC**
663 S Rancho Santa Fe Rd Ste 682, San Marcos (92078-3973)
PHONE..................760 752-9706
▲ EMP: 42
Web: www.indenergysolutions.com
SIC: 3433 Heating equipment, except electric

**(P-8070)**
**INFRARED DYNAMICS INC**
3830 Prospect Ave, Yorba Linda (92886-1742)
PHONE..................714 572-4050
Robert Cowan, *Pr*
▲ EMP: 22 EST: 1959
SQ FT: 23,500
SALES (est): 2.96MM **Privately Held**
Web: www.infradyne.com
SIC: 3433 5075 Heating equipment, except electric; Warm air heating equipment and supplies

**(P-8071)**
**MANUFACTURERS COML FIN LLC**
Also Called: Benchmark Thermal
13185 Nevada City Ave, Grass Valley (95945-9568)
PHONE..................530 477-5011
Michael Kayman, *Pr*
Roger Ruttenberg, *VP*
Eric Doan, *Acctnt*
EMP: 40
SQ FT: 8,000
SALES (est): 412.82K **Privately Held**
Web: www.benchmarkthermal.com
SIC: 3433 Room and wall heaters, including radiators

**(P-8072)**
**OMC-THC LIQUIDATING INC**
12131 Community Rd, Poway (92064-8893)
PHONE..................858 486-8846
Frank Polese, *Prin*
EMP: 23 EST: 2005
SALES (est): 962.37K **Privately Held**
Web: www.fralock.com
SIC: 3433 Heating equipment, except electric

**(P-8073)**
**PLANTED SOLAR INC**
1901 Poplar St, Oakland (94607-2310)
PHONE..................650 861-1455
Eric Brown, *CEO*
Keith Steel, *CFO*
EMP: 20 EST: 2020
SALES (est): 3.45MM **Privately Held**
SIC: 3433 Solar heaters and collectors

**(P-8074)**
**PREMIER POWER RENEWABLE ENERGY INC**
4961 Windplay Dr Ste 100, El Dorado Hills (95762-9366)
PHONE..................916 939-0400
▲ EMP: 48
Web: www.premierpower.com
SIC: 3433 7389 8711 Heating equipment, except electric; Design, commercial and industrial; Engineering services

**(P-8075)**
**RASMUSSEN IRON WORKS INC**
12028 Philadelphia St, Whittier (90601-3925)
PHONE..................562 696-8718
Theodore Rasmussen, *Pr*
T E Rasmussen, *
▲ EMP: 62 EST: 1907
SQ FT: 40,000
SALES (est): 4.81MM **Privately Held**
Web: www.radiantpatioheater.com
SIC: 3433 Logs, gas fireplace

**(P-8076)**
**RAYPAK INC (DH)**
2151 Eastman Ave, Oxnard (93030-5194)
PHONE..................805 278-5300
Kevin Mcdonald, *VP*
◆ EMP: 320 EST: 1949
SQ FT: 250,000
SALES (est): 48.03MM **Privately Held**
Web: www.raypak.com
SIC: 3433 Heaters, swimming pool: oil or gas
HQ: Rheem Manufacturing Company Inc
1100 Abrnathy Rd Ste 1700
Atlanta GA 30328
770 351-3000

**(P-8077)**
**RE TRANQUILLITY 8 LLC**
300 California St Fl 7, San Francisco (94104-1415)
PHONE..................415 675-1500
Yumin Liu, *Pr*
Helen Kang Shin, *
EMP: 64 EST: 2013
SALES (est): 486.27K
SALES (corp-wide): 1.97B **Privately Held**
SIC: 3433 Solar heaters and collectors
HQ: Recurrent Energy Development Holdings, Llc
3000 Oak Rd Ste 300
Walnut Creek CA 94597
415 675-1501

**(P-8078)**
**RETECH SYSTEMS LLC**
168 Washington Ave Ste B, Ukiah (95482-8324)
PHONE..................707 462-6522
EMP: 62 EST: 2001
SALES (est): 2.52MM **Privately Held**
Web: www.retechsystemsllc.com
SIC: 3433 Heating equipment, except electric

**(P-8079)**
**SCHEU MANUFACTURING COMPANY (PA)**
297 Stowell St, Upland (91786-6624)
P.O. Box 250 (91785-0250)
PHONE..................909 982-8933
Leland C Scheu, *Ch Bd*
Allyn Scheu, *Pr*
Daniel N League Junior, *Stockholder*
▲ EMP: 15 EST: 1930
SQ FT: 7,000
SALES (est): 2.29MM
SALES (corp-wide): 2.29MM **Privately Held**
SIC: 3433 Space heaters, except electric

**(P-8080)**
**SOLARRESERVE LLC (PA)**
520 Broadway 6th Fl, Santa Monica (90401-2420)
PHONE..................310 315-2200
Tom Georgis, *CEO*
Kevin Smith, *CEO*
Tim Rosenzweig, *CFO*
Alistair Jessop, *Sr VP*

## PRODUCTS & SERVICES SECTION
### 3441 - Fabricated Structural Metal (P-8103)

Stephen Mullennix, *Sr VP*
**EMP:** 19 **EST:** 2007
**SALES (est):** 5.25MM **Privately Held**
**Web:** www.solarreserve.com
**SIC: 3433** 1711 4911  Solar heaters and collectors; Solar energy contractor; Electric services

**(P-8081)**
### SOLON CORPORATION
44 Montgomery St Ste 2040, San Francisco (94104-4707)
**PHONE**.................................520 807-1300
Olaf Koester, *Pr*
**EMP:** 18
**Web:** www.solonamerica.com
**SIC: 3433**  Solar heaters and collectors
**HQ:** Solon Corporation
2155 N Frbes Blvd Ste 101
Tucson AZ 85745

**(P-8082)**
### SPI SOLAR INC (PA)
4803 Urbani Ave, Mcclellan (95652-2000)
**PHONE**.................................408 919-8000
Xiaofeng Peng, *CEO*
**EMP:** 451 **EST:** 2006
**SALES (est):** 177.52MM **Publicly Held**
**Web:** www.spigroups.com
**SIC: 3433**  Solar heaters and collectors

**(P-8083)**
### SUNRUN SOLAR ✪
775 Fiero Ln Ste 200, San Luis Obispo (93401-7904)
**PHONE**.................................833 324-5886
**EMP:** 17 **EST:** 2023
**SALES (est):** 6.09MM **Privately Held**
**SIC: 3433**  Heating equipment, except electric

## 3441 Fabricated Structural Metal

**(P-8084)**
### A & A FABRICATION & POLSG CORP
610 S Vail Ave, Montebello (90640-4952)
**PHONE**.................................562 696-0441
Kimberlina Gutierrez, *CEO*
Edward Henderson, *VP*
**EMP:** 16 **EST:** 1999
**SQ FT:** 14,000
**SALES (est):** 2.2MM **Privately Held**
**Web:** www.aafabpolishing.com
**SIC: 3441**  Fabricated structural metal

**(P-8085)**
### A AND M WELDING INC
16935 S Broadway, Gardena (90248-3111)
**PHONE**.................................310 329-2700
Tom A Jorgenson, *Pr*
Linda Jorgenson, *VP*
**EMP:** 15 **EST:** 1952
**SQ FT:** 25,000
**SALES (est):** 2.8MM **Privately Held**
**Web:** www.ammetalforming.com
**SIC: 3441**  Fabricated structural metal

**(P-8086)**
### ABLE IRON WORKS
222 Hershey St, Pomona (91767-5810)
**PHONE**.................................909 397-5300
Stephen Holmes, *CEO*
**EMP:** 20 **EST:** 1993
**SQ FT:** 12,000
**SALES (est):** 5.03MM **Privately Held**
**Web:** www.ableironwork.com

**SIC: 3441**  Fabricated structural metal

**(P-8087)**
### ACCURATE METAL PRODUCTS INC
4276 Campbell St, Riverside (92509-2617)
**PHONE**.................................951 360-3594
Elanor Quintero, *Pr*
Tony Schmidt, *Sec*
**EMP:** 15 **EST:** 1997
**SALES (est):** 1.45MM **Privately Held**
**Web:** www.accuratemetalinc.com
**SIC: 3441**  Fabricated structural metal

**(P-8088)**
### ADTEK INC
1460 Ellerd Dr, Turlock (95380-5749)
**PHONE**.................................209 634-0300
Bob Zinzenoul, *Prin*
**EMP:** 30 **EST:** 2003
**SALES (est):** 2.62MM **Privately Held**
**Web:** www.adtekusa.com
**SIC: 3441**  Building components, structural steel

**(P-8089)**
### AEC - ABLE ENGINEERING COMPANY INC
600 Pine Ave, Goleta (93117-3803)
**PHONE**.................................805 685-2262
**EMP:** 120
**SIC: 3441** 3769  Fabricated structural metal; Space vehicle equipment, nec

**(P-8090)**
### AEROFAB CORPORATION
4001 E Leaverton Ct, Anaheim (92807-1610)
**PHONE**.................................714 635-0902
Matthew Owen, *Pr*
George Robinson, *VP*
**EMP:** 17 **EST:** 2007
**SQ FT:** 10,000
**SALES (est):** 3.83MM **Privately Held**
**Web:** www.aerofab-corp.com
**SIC: 3441**  Fabricated structural metal

**(P-8091)**
### AG MACHINING INC
2401 W Almond Ave, Madera (93637-4807)
**PHONE**.................................805 531-9555
Angel Garcia, *Pr*
Eddie Garcia, *
Bryan Garcia, *
▲ **EMP:** 85 **EST:** 1986
**SALES (est):** 15.8MM **Privately Held**
**Web:** agm.us.com
**SIC: 3441** 3444  Fabricated structural metal; Sheet metalwork

**(P-8092)**
### AHLBORN STRUCTURAL STEEL INC
1230 Century Ct, Santa Rosa (95403-1042)
**PHONE**.................................707 573-0742
Thomas Ahlborn, *CEO*
Lance Ballenger, *
Cathy Ahlborn, *
**EMP:** 34 **EST:** 2004
**SALES (est):** 5.01MM **Privately Held**
**Web:** www.ahlbornstructural.com
**SIC: 3441**  Fabricated structural metal

**(P-8093)**
### AMAZING STEEL COMPANY
Also Called: Mitchellamazing
4564 Mission Blvd, Montclair (91763-6106)
**PHONE**.................................909 590-0393

**EMP:** 20 **EST:** 1985
**SQ FT:** 25,000
**SALES (est):** 1.84MM **Privately Held**
**Web:** www.mitchellamazing.com
**SIC: 3441** 7692 7699  Fabricated structural metal; Welding repair; Hydraulic equipment repair

**(P-8094)**
### AMERICAN MECHANICAL & MFG INC
Also Called: American Mechanical & Mfg.
10096 6th St Ste B, Rancho Cucamonga (91730-5750)
**PHONE**.................................909 466-4713
James Henderson, *Pr*
Madeline Henderson, *Sec*
**EMP:** 16 **EST:** 2018
**SALES (est):** 661.14K **Privately Held**
**Web:** www.americanmechanicalmfg.com
**SIC: 3441**  Fabricated structural metal

**(P-8095)**
### AMT METAL FABRICATORS INC
211 Parr Blvd, Richmond (94801-1119)
P.O. Box 962 (95693-0962)
**PHONE**.................................510 236-1414
Michael R Turpen, *Pr*
Cheryl Turpen, *Sec*
**EMP:** 20 **EST:** 1950
**SQ FT:** 12,000
**SALES (est):** 4.91MM **Privately Held**
**Web:** www.amtmetals.com
**SIC: 3441**  Building components, structural steel

**(P-8096)**
### ANDERSON CHRNESKY STRL STL INC
Also Called: Acss
353 Risco Cir, Beaumont (92223-2676)
**PHONE**.................................951 769-5700
Kevin Charneskey, *Pr*
Kevin Charnesky, *
**EMP:** 85 **EST:** 1984
**SQ FT:** 6,600
**SALES (est):** 36.73MM **Privately Held**
**Web:** www.acssteelinc.com
**SIC: 3441**  Fabricated structural metal

**(P-8097)**
### ASSOCIATED REBAR INC
1095 Madison Ln, Salinas (93907-1815)
P.O. Box 10212 (93912-7212)
**PHONE**.................................831 758-1820
Chris Bartlebaugh, *Pr*
Alfredo Garcia, *Sec*
**EMP:** 20 **EST:** 1988
**SQ FT:** 1,500
**SALES (est):** 2.82MM **Privately Held**
**Web:** www.associatedrebar.com
**SIC: 3441**  Fabricated structural metal

**(P-8098)**
### AZTEC TECHNOLOGY CORPORATION (PA)
Also Called: Aztec Container
2550 S Santa Fe Ave, Vista (92084-8005)
**PHONE**.................................760 727-2300
Brian Hyndman, *CEO*
Catherine Hyndman, *VP*
Michael Hyndman, *Treas*
Steven Hyndman, *Sec*
Teresa Gualtieri, *Contrlr*
**EMP:** 20 **EST:** 1969
**SQ FT:** 3,000
**SALES (est):** 7.03MM
**SALES (corp-wide):** 7.03MM **Privately Held**

**Web:** www.azteccontainer.com
**SIC: 3441**  Fabricated structural metal

**(P-8099)**
### B METAL FABRICATION INC
318 S Maple Ave, South San Francisco (94080-6306)
**PHONE**.................................650 615-7705
Robert Steinebel, *CEO*
Berthold Steinebel, *
Barbara Blundell, *
Brigitte Steinebel, *
**EMP:** 30 **EST:** 1987
**SQ FT:** 14,000
**SALES (est):** 6.92MM **Privately Held**
**Web:** www.bmetalfabrication.com
**SIC: 3441**  Fabricated structural metal

**(P-8100)**
### BAY CITY MARINE INC (PA)
1625 Cleveland Ave, National City (91950-4212)
**PHONE**.................................619 477-3991
Paul Ralph, *CEO*
Michelle Ralph, *
Timothy Dernbach, *
Steve Johnston, *
**EMP:** 24 **EST:** 1971
**SQ FT:** 11,000
**SALES (est):** 4.72MM
**SALES (corp-wide):** 4.72MM **Privately Held**
**Web:** www.baycmarine.com
**SIC: 3441** 3731 7699  Fabricated structural metal; Military ships, building and repairing; Boat repair

**(P-8101)**
### BELL BROS STEEL INC
1510 Palmyrita Ave, Riverside (92507-1629)
**PHONE**.................................951 784-0903
James Bell, *Pr*
**EMP:** 17 **EST:** 2001
**SQ FT:** 1,400
**SALES (est):** 3.05MM **Privately Held**
**Web:** www.bellbrossteel.com
**SIC: 3441**  Fabricated structural metal

**(P-8102)**
### BELLOWS MFG & RES INC
864 Arroyo St, San Fernando (91340-1832)
**PHONE**.................................818 838-1333
Arteom Art Bulgadarian, *CEO*
Kent L Fortin, *
**EMP:** 30 **EST:** 2005
**SQ FT:** 28,000
**SALES (est):** 8.68MM **Privately Held**
**Web:** www.bellowsmfg.com
**SIC: 3441** 3724 3764  Fabricated structural metal; Aircraft engines and engine parts; Propulsion units for guided missiles and space vehicles

**(P-8103)**
### BERGER STEEL CORPORATION
4728 Kilzer Ave # 692, Mcclellan (95652-2300)
**PHONE**.................................916 640-8778
Jason Michael Berger, *Pr*
Jason Michael Berger, *Pr*
Cody Berger, *
Phil Berger, *
**EMP:** 27 **EST:** 2012
**SALES (est):** 8.4MM **Privately Held**
**Web:** www.bergersteel.com
**SIC: 3441** 5051  Fabricated structural metal; Structural shapes, iron or steel

## 3441 - Fabricated Structural Metal (P-8104)

**(P-8104)**
**BLUE STAR STEEL INC**
12122 Industry Rd, Lakeside (92040)
PHONE....................................619 448-5520
Rodney Walker, *Pr*
**EMP:** 45 **EST:** 1962
**SALES (est):** 3.54MM **Privately Held**
Web: www.bluestarsteelinc.com
**SIC: 3441** Fabricated structural metal

**(P-8105)**
**BOK MODERN LLC**
912 Irwin St, San Rafael (94901-3318)
PHONE....................................415 749-6500
Vic Grizzle, *Pr*
**EMP:** 31 **EST:** 2010
**SALES (est):** 4.34MM
**SALES (corp-wide):** 1.3B **Publicly Held**
Web: www.bokmodern.com
**SIC: 3441** Fabricated structural metal
**PA:** Armstrong World Industries, Inc.
2500 Columbia Ave
717 397-0611

**(P-8106)**
**BOYD CORPORATION (PA)**
Also Called: Boyd Construction
5832 Ohio St, Yorba Linda (92886-5323)
P.O. Box 6012 (92816-0012)
PHONE....................................714 533-2375
Mitch Aiello, *Pr*
**EMP:** 29 **EST:** 1980
**SALES (est):** 9.77MM
**SALES (corp-wide):** 9.77MM **Privately Held**
Web: www.boydcorp.com
**SIC: 3441** 2891 Fabricated structural metal; Adhesives

**(P-8107)**
**BRUNTON ENTERPRISES INC**
Also Called: Plas-Tal Manufacturing Co
8815 Sorensen Ave, Santa Fe Springs (90670-2636)
PHONE....................................562 945-0013
Sean P Brunton, *CEO*
John W Brunton Junior, *Pr*
**EMP:** 125 **EST:** 1947
**SQ FT:** 45,000
**SALES (est):** 10.78MM **Privately Held**
Web: www.plas-tal.com
**SIC: 3441** Fabricated structural metal

**(P-8108)**
**BUTTE STEEL & FABRICATION INC**
13290 Contractors Dr, Chico (95973-8837)
**EMP:** 45
**SIC: 3441** Fabricated structural metal

**(P-8109)**
**C A BUCHEN CORP**
9231 Glenoaks Blvd, Sun Valley (91352-2688)
PHONE....................................818 767-5408
John Oster, *CEO*
Ryan Chapman, *
**EMP:** 25 **EST:** 1962
**SQ FT:** 22,500
**SALES (est):** 2.53MM **Privately Held**
Web: www.cabuchen.com
**SIC: 3441** 1791 3312 Fabricated structural metal; Structural steel erection; Galvanized pipes, plates, sheets, etc.: iron and steel

**(P-8110)**
**CAD WORKS INC**
16366 E Valley Blvd, La Puente (91744-5546)
PHONE....................................626 336-5491
David Paquini, *Pr*
Avrahan Garcia, *VP*
Cecilia Chavez, *CFO*
**EMP:** 20 **EST:** 2004
**SQ FT:** 10,000
**SALES (est):** 1.6MM **Privately Held**
Web: www.cadworks.us
**SIC: 3441** Fabricated structural metal

**(P-8111)**
**CALCRAFT CORPORATION**
Also Called: Calcraft Company
1426 S Willow Ave, Rialto (92376-7720)
PHONE....................................909 879-2900
Daniel Steven Ensman, *Pr*
Gloria Ensman, *Sec*
**EMP:** 15 **EST:** 2004
**SQ FT:** 30,000
**SALES (est):** 2.49MM **Privately Held**
Web: www.calcraft.com
**SIC: 3441** Fabricated structural metal

**(P-8112)**
**CALIFORNIA STL FABRICATORS INC**
1120 Reno Ave, Modesto (95351-1128)
PHONE....................................209 566-0629
Paul R Osborne, *CEO*
**EMP:** 16 **EST:** 2013
**SALES (est):** 4.38MM **Privately Held**
Web: www.calsteelfab.com
**SIC: 3441** Fabricated structural metal

**(P-8113)**
**CAMPBELL CERTIFIED INC**
1629 Ord Way, Oceanside (92056-3599)
PHONE....................................760 722-9353
Mark Anthony Campbell, *CEO*
Linzie Walker, *
**EMP:** 30 **EST:** 1991
**SQ FT:** 45,000
**SALES (est):** 3.72MM **Privately Held**
Web: www.campbellcertified.com
**SIC: 3441** Fabricated structural metal

**(P-8114)**
**CANYON STEEL FABRICATORS INC**
4280 Patterson Ave, Perris (92571-9714)
PHONE....................................951 683-2352
Thomas J Baggett, *Pr*
Ray Magnon, *VP*
Doug Magnon, *Sec*
**EMP:** 22 **EST:** 2007
**SALES (est):** 5.29MM **Privately Held**
Web: www.canyonsteelfab.com
**SIC: 3441** Fabricated structural metal

**(P-8115)**
**CAPITOL IRON WORKS INC**
7009 Power Inn Rd, Sacramento (95828-2498)
PHONE....................................916 381-1554
Daniel D Howard, *Pr*
Diana Howard, *Sec*
Steve Hartzell, *Pr*
**EMP:** 20 **EST:** 1962
**SQ FT:** 3,000
**SALES (est):** 2.01MM **Privately Held**
Web: www.capitolironworks.com
**SIC: 3441** Fabricated structural metal

**(P-8116)**
**CAPITOL STEEL FABRICATORS INC**
3522 Greenwood Ave, Commerce (90040-3319)
P.O. Box 640 (91017-0640)
PHONE....................................323 721-5460
James Moreland, *Pr*
Janice Moreland, *
Eric Jonkey, *Stockholder**
**EMP:** 25 **EST:** 1984
**SALES (est):** 8.77MM **Privately Held**
Web: www.capitolsteel.com
**SIC: 3441** Fabricated structural metal

**(P-8117)**
**CAPITOL STEEL PRODUCTS**
Also Called: Ruben Ortiz
6331 Power Inn Rd Ste B, Sacramento (95824-2353)
PHONE....................................916 383-3368
Ruben Ortiz, *Genl Mgr*
Bud Lindau, *Owner*
**EMP:** 24 **EST:** 2005
**SALES (est):** 3.62MM **Privately Held**
Web: www.capitolsteelcompany.com
**SIC: 3441** Fabricated structural metal

**(P-8118)**
**CARROLL METAL WORKS INC**
740 W 16th St, National City (91950-4205)
PHONE....................................619 477-9125
Pat Carroll, *Pr*
**EMP:** 95 **EST:** 1984
**SQ FT:** 11,500
**SALES (est):** 4.82MM **Privately Held**
Web: www.carrollmetalworks.com
**SIC: 3441** Fabricated structural metal

**(P-8119)**
**CARTER GROUP (PA)**
Also Called: Alling Iron Works
3709 Seaport Blvd, West Sacramento (95691-3558)
PHONE....................................916 373-0148
Joe Neal Carter, *Pr*
Renee Mason, *Sec*
**EMP:** 20 **EST:** 1920
**SALES (est):** 5.27MM
**SALES (corp-wide):** 5.27MM **Privately Held**
Web: www.farallonboats.com
**SIC: 3441** 5551 Fabricated structural metal; Boat dealers

**(P-8120)**
**COLUMBIA ALUMINUM PRODUCTS LLC**
1150 W Rincon St, Corona (92878-9601)
PHONE....................................323 728-7361
Drew D Mumford, *Managing Member*
Grant Palenske, *
▲ **EMP:** 70 **EST:** 1989
**SALES (est):** 8.61MM **Privately Held**
Web: www.columbiaaluminumproductsllc.com
**SIC: 3441** Fabricated structural metal

**(P-8121)**
**COLUMBIA STEEL INC**
2175 N Linden Ave, Rialto (92377-4445)
PHONE....................................909 874-8840
Gustavo Waldemar Theisen, *CEO*
William Young, *
Luis Theisen, *
Charmaine Helenihi, *
**EMP:** 75 **EST:** 1975
**SQ FT:** 63,384
**SALES (est):** 25.8MM **Privately Held**
Web: www.csirialto.com
**SIC: 3441** Building components, structural steel

**(P-8122)**
**COMMERCIAL SHTMTL WORKS INC**
Also Called: CSM Metal Fabricating & Engrg
1800 S San Pedro St, Los Angeles (90015-3711)
PHONE....................................213 748-7321
Jack L Gardener, *CEO*
▲ **EMP:** 27 **EST:** 1916
**SQ FT:** 22,000
**SALES (est):** 5.58MM **Privately Held**
Web: www.csmworks.com
**SIC: 3441** Fabricated structural metal

**(P-8123)**
**CONCORD IRON WORKS INC**
Also Called: C I W
1 Leslie Dr, Pittsburg (94565-2654)
PHONE....................................925 432-0136
Jill Lee, *Pr*
Rita Gonsalves, *
David Maggi, *
**EMP:** 50 **EST:** 1975
**SALES (est):** 8.73MM **Privately Held**
Web: www.concordiron.com
**SIC: 3441** Fabricated structural metal

**(P-8124)**
**CONXTECH INC**
6600 Koll Center Pkwy Ste 210, Pleasanton (94566-3167)
PHONE....................................510 264-9111
Robert J Simmons, *Pr*
Raymond G Kitasoe, *
◆ **EMP:** 150 **EST:** 2004
**SQ FT:** 100,000
**SALES (est):** 44.01MM **Privately Held**
Web: www.conxtech.com
**SIC: 3441** Building components, structural steel

**(P-8125)**
**CRAFTECH METAL FORMING INC**
24100 Water Ave Ste B, Perris (92570-6738)
PHONE....................................951 940-6444
Richard L Shaw, *Pr*
**EMP:** 40 **EST:** 1996
**SQ FT:** 26,000
**SALES (est):** 4.66MM **Privately Held**
Web: www.craftechmetal.com
**SIC: 3441** 3499 3444 Fabricated structural metal; Fire- or burglary-resistive products; Sheet metalwork

**(P-8126)**
**CROSNO CONSTRUCTION INC**
819 Sheridan Rd, Arroyo Grande (93420-5833)
PHONE....................................805 343-7437
Wade Crosno, *Pr*
Wade Crosno, *Pr*
Jaime Crosno, *
**EMP:** 48 **EST:** 2004
**SQ FT:** 5,000
**SALES (est):** 8.64MM **Privately Held**
Web: www.crosnoconstruction.com
**SIC: 3441** Fabricated structural metal

**(P-8127)**
**CUSTOM IRON CORPORATION**
26895 Aliso Creek Rd Ste B787, Aliso Viejo (92656-5301)
PHONE....................................949 939-4379
Michael Knee, *Pr*
**EMP:** 15 **EST:** 2013
**SALES (est):** 8.1MM **Privately Held**
Web: www.customironcorp.com

▲ = Import ▼ = Export
◆ = Import/Export

# PRODUCTS & SERVICES SECTION
## 3441 - Fabricated Structural Metal (P-8149)

SIC: 3441 Fabricated structural metal

**(P-8128)**
**CUSTOM STEEL FABRICATION INC**
Also Called: C & J Industries
11966 Rivera Rd, Santa Fe Springs (90670-2232)
PHONE.................................562 907-2777
John Toscano, *Pr*
Carole Toscano, *CEO*
EMP: 17 EST: 2006
SQ FT: 3,400
SALES (est): 2.87MM **Privately Held**
Web: www.cnjindustries.com
SIC: 3441 Fabricated structural metal

**(P-8129)**
**D & M STEEL INC**
13020 Pierce St, Pacoima (91331-2528)
PHONE.................................818 896-2070
Michael Atia, *Pr*
David Dagni, *
EMP: 37 EST: 1980
SQ FT: 16,500
SALES (est): 6.19MM **Privately Held**
Web: www.d-msteel.com
SIC: 3441 Fabricated structural metal

**(P-8130)**
**D D WIRE CO INC (PA)**
4335 Temple City Blvd, Temple City (91780-4229)
PHONE.................................626 442-0459
Wes Berry, *Pr*
David Berry, *CFO*
Elizabeth D Berry, *Sec*
James Howe, *COO*
Dorsey Wire, *Prin*
EMP: 22 EST: 1963
SQ FT: 24,000
SALES (est): 5.48MM
SALES (corp-wide): 5.48MM **Privately Held**
Web: www.ddwire.com
SIC: 3441 3469 Fabricated structural metal; Stamping metal for the trade

**(P-8131)**
**D&A METAL FABRICATION INC**
16129 Runnymede St, Van Nuys (91406-2913)
PHONE.................................818 780-8231
Jenny Anastasiu, *Off Mgr*
EMP: 16 EST: 2014
SALES (est): 1.33MM **Privately Held**
Web: www.dametalfabrication.com
SIC: 3441 Fabricated structural metal

**(P-8132)**
**DAVISON IRON WORKS INC**
8845 Elder Creek Rd Ste A, Sacramento (95828-1813)
PHONE.................................916 381-2121
Andrew Peszynski, *Pr*
Candy Holland, *
EMP: 50 EST: 1959
SQ FT: 3,500
SALES (est): 889.77K **Privately Held**
Web: www.davisoniron.com
SIC: 3441 Fabricated structural metal

**(P-8133)**
**EAST CAST REPR FABRICATION LLC**
Also Called: West Coast Operations
280 Trousdale Dr Ste E, Chula Vista (91910-1079)
PHONE.................................619 591-9577
Brett Baker, *Prin*
EMP: 29
SALES (corp-wide): 27.35MM **Privately Held**
Web: www.ecrfab.com
SIC: 3441 Fabricated structural metal
PA: East Coast Repair & Fabrication, L.L.C.
1201 Terminal Ave
757 455-9600

**(P-8134)**
**ELIGIUS MANUFACTURING INC**
Also Called: Eligius Manufacturing & Cnstr
1177 N 15th St, San Jose (95112-1422)
PHONE.................................408 437-0337
Leon Schaper, *Pr*
Jina Duncan, *Executive Administrator**
EMP: 30 EST: 2017
SALES (est): 4.08MM **Privately Held**
Web: www.eligiusmfg.com
SIC: 3441 Fabricated structural metal

**(P-8135)**
**EW CORPRTION INDUS FABRICATORS (PA)**
1002 E Main St, El Centro (92243)
P.O. Box 2189 (92244-2189)
PHONE.................................760 337-0020
Tiberio R Esparza, *Pr*
◆ EMP: 69 EST: 1973
SQ FT: 100,000
SALES (est): 4.98MM
SALES (corp-wide): 4.98MM **Privately Held**
Web: www.ewcorporation.com
SIC: 3441 Fabricated structural metal

**(P-8136)**
**EXCELSIOR METALS LLC**
Also Called: Excelsior Construction
795 E Levin Ave, Tulare (93274)
PHONE.................................559 346-0932
Raymond R Roush Iii, *Pr*
EMP: 27 EST: 1996
SALES (est): 10.42MM **Privately Held**
Web: www.excelsiormetals.com
SIC: 3441 Fabricated structural metal

**(P-8137)**
**FABCO STEEL FABRICATION INC**
14688 San Bernardino Ave, Fontana (92335-5319)
P.O. Box 8636 (91701-0636)
PHONE.................................909 350-1535
John E Schick, *Pr*
Rich Schick, *
EMP: 35 EST: 1979
SQ FT: 30,000
SALES (est): 1.27MM **Privately Held**
Web: www.fabcosteel.com
SIC: 3441 Fabricated structural metal

**(P-8138)**
**FABRICATION TECH INDS INC**
2200 Haffley Ave, National City (91950-6418)
P.O. Box 1447 (91951-1447)
PHONE.................................619 477-4141
Joey Houshar, *Ch Bd*
Martha Houshar, *
▲ EMP: 75 EST: 1994
SQ FT: 50,000
SALES (est): 9.11MM **Privately Held**
Web: www.ftisd.com
SIC: 3441 Fabricated structural metal

**(P-8139)**
**FERROSAUR INC**
Also Called: Industrial Welding
4821 Mountain Lakes Blvd, Redding (96003-1454)
PHONE.................................530 246-7843
Thomas Largent, *VP*
Thomas R Largent, *CEO*
EMP: 41 EST: 1993
SQ FT: 33,000
SALES (est): 3.05MM **Privately Held**
SIC: 3441 7692 2298 5932 Fabricated structural metal; Welding repair; Rope, except asbestos and wire; Building materials, secondhand

**(P-8140)**
**FIFE METAL FABRICATING INC**
2305 Radio Ln, Redding (96001-3884)
PHONE.................................530 243-4696
Doyle Fife Junior, *Pr*
Joanne Fife, *Sec*
EMP: 15 EST: 1965
SALES (est): 3.17MM **Privately Held**
SIC: 3441 3446 Building components, structural steel; Architectural metalwork

**(P-8141)**
**FLORIAN INDUSTRIES INC**
151 Industrial Way, Brisbane (94005-1003)
PHONE.................................415 330-9000
Chuck Lutz, *Pr*
EMP: 15 EST: 2007
SQ FT: 2,000
SALES (est): 5.42MM **Privately Held**
Web: www.florianindustries.com
SIC: 3441 Fabricated structural metal

**(P-8142)**
**FOSS MARITIME COMPANY**
Also Called: FOSS MARITIME COMPANY
49 W Pier D St, Long Beach (90802-1020)
PHONE.................................562 437-6098
Wendall Koi, *Prin*
EMP: 15
SALES (corp-wide): 2.75B **Privately Held**
Web: www.foss.com
SIC: 3441 Boat and barge sections, prefabricated metal
HQ: Foss Maritime Company, Llc.
450 Alaskan Way S Ste 706
Seattle WA 98104
206 281-3800

**(P-8143)**
**FREEBERG INDUS FBRICATION CORP**
Also Called: Freeberg Industrial
2874 Progress Pl, Escondido (92029-1516)
PHONE.................................760 737-7614
Marc Brown, *Pr*
James R St John, *
EMP: 85 EST: 1992
SQ FT: 128,000
SALES (est): 23.39MM **Privately Held**
Web: www.freeberg.com
SIC: 3441 3444 Fabricated structural metal; Sheet metalwork

**(P-8144)**
**FRESNO FAB-TECH INC**
1035 K St, Sanger (93657-3383)
PHONE.................................559 875-9800
Chris Kisling, *Pr*
EMP: 40 EST: 1988
SQ FT: 35,000
SALES (est): 6.55MM **Privately Held**
Web: www.fresnofabtech.com

SIC: 3441 Fabricated structural metal

**(P-8145)**
**GERLINGER FNDRY MCH WORKS INC (PA)**
Also Called: Gerlinger Steel & Supply Co.
1527 Sacramento St, Redding (96001-1914)
P.O. Box 992195 (96099-2195)
PHONE.................................530 243-1053
TOLL FREE: 800
Fred Gerlinger, *CEO*
Tim Gerlinger, *
Jo Gerlinger, *
EMP: 37 EST: 1929
SQ FT: 45,000
SALES (est): 12.06MM
SALES (corp-wide): 12.06MM **Privately Held**
Web: www.gerlinger.com
SIC: 3441 3494 7692 5051 Fabricated structural metal; Valves and pipe fittings, nec; Welding repair; Steel

**(P-8146)**
**GLAZIER STEEL INC**
Also Called: Glazier Steel
650 Sandoval Way, Hayward (94544-7129)
PHONE.................................510 471-5300
Craig Glazier, *CEO*
Harold Glazier, *
EMP: 75 EST: 1982
SQ FT: 26,897
SALES (est): 21.09MM **Privately Held**
Web: www.glaziersteel.com
SIC: 3441 Fabricated structural metal

**(P-8147)**
**GOLDEN GATE STEEL INC**
19826 S Alameda St, Compton (90221-6211)
PHONE.................................310 638-0855
Yohann Chang, *Pr*
EMP: 15 EST: 1990
SALES (est): 1.41MM **Privately Held**
SIC: 3441 Building components, structural steel

**(P-8148)**
**GRATING PACIFIC INC (PA)**
3651 Sausalito St, Los Alamitos (90720-2436)
PHONE.................................562 598-4314
TOLL FREE: 800
Ronald S Robertson, *Pr*
Jeffrey Robertson, *VP*
▲ EMP: 20 EST: 1971
SQ FT: 40,000
SALES (est): 23.57MM
SALES (corp-wide): 23.57MM **Privately Held**
Web: www.gratingpacific.com
SIC: 3441 3446 Fabricated structural metal; Architectural metalwork

**(P-8149)**
**HALLSTEN CORPORATION**
6944 34th St, North Highlands (95660-3107)
P.O. Box 41036 (95841-0036)
PHONE.................................916 331-7211
EMP: 40 EST: 1966
SALES (est): 6MM **Privately Held**
Web: www.hallsten.com
SIC: 3441 3448 Fabricated structural metal; Prefabricated metal buildings and components

## 3441 - Fabricated Structural Metal (P-8150)

**(P-8150)**
**HERRICK CORPORATION (PA)**
Also Called: San Bernardina Steel
3003 E Hammer Ln, Stockton (95212-2801)
P.O. Box 8429 (95208-0429)
PHONE..................................209 956-4751
David H Dornsife, *CEO*
Roger Schwab, *Vice Chairman**
Doug Griffin, *
Peter Abila, *
▲ **EMP:** 50 **EST:** 1921
**SALES (est):** 221.85MM
**SALES (corp-wide):** 221.85MM **Privately Held**
Web: www.herricksteel.com
SIC: **3441** Fabricated structural metal

**(P-8151)**
**HITECH METAL FABRICATION CORP**
Also Called: H M F
1705 S Claudina Way, Anaheim (92805-6544)
PHONE..................................714 635-3505
Ba V Nguyen, *Pr*
Matthew Vu, *
**EMP:** 60 **EST:** 1989
**SQ FT:** 42,850
**SALES (est):** 7.6MM **Privately Held**
Web: www.hmfcorp.com
SIC: **3441** Fabricated structural metal

**(P-8152)**
**HOMESTEAD SHEET METAL**
9031 Memory Ln, Spring Valley (91977-2152)
PHONE..................................619 469-4373
George Tomlanovich, *Pr*
Chuck Highfill, *Sec*
**EMP:** 27 **EST:** 1996
**SQ FT:** 5,625
**SALES (est):** 4.01MM **Privately Held**
Web: www.homesteadsheetmetal.com
SIC: **3441** Fabricated structural metal

**(P-8153)**
**INTAKE SCREENS INC**
8417 River Rd, Sacramento (95832-9710)
PHONE..................................916 665-2727
Russell Berry Iv, *Pr*
Russell M Berry Iii, *VP*
Ronaele Berry, *Sec*
**EMP:** 15 **EST:** 1996
**SQ FT:** 3,300
**SALES (est):** 5.22MM **Privately Held**
Web: www.isi-screens.com
SIC: **3441** Fabricated structural metal

**(P-8154)**
**IRON DOG FABRICATION INC**
3450 Regional Pkwy Ste E, Santa Rosa (95403-8247)
PHONE..................................707 579-7831
Duncan Woods, *Pr*
Cynthia Woods, *Sec*
**EMP:** 17 **EST:** 1994
**SQ FT:** 18,000
**SALES (est):** 2.31MM **Privately Held**
Web: www.irondogfab.com
SIC: **3441** 7692 1791 Building components, structural steel; Welding repair; Structural steel erection

**(P-8155)**
**J L M C INC**
1944 S Bon View Ave, Ontario (91761-5503)
P.O. Box 3817 (91761-0979)
PHONE..................................909 947-2980
**EMP:** 35 **EST:** 1984
**SALES (est):** 2.04MM **Privately Held**
Web: www.jlmc.com
SIC: **3441** Fabricated structural metal

**(P-8156)**
**JC METAL SPECIALISTS INC**
2708 Ingalls St, San Francisco (94124-3644)
PHONE..................................415 822-3878
Jeffrey Chan, *Pr*
**EMP:** 38
Web: www.jcmetals.com
SIC: **3441** Fabricated structural metal
PA: J.C. Metal Specialists, Inc.
238 Michelle Ct

**(P-8157)**
**JC METAL SPECIALISTS INC (PA)**
238 Michelle Ct, South San Francisco (94080-6201)
PHONE..................................650 827-1618
Judy Chan, *Pr*
Jeffrey Chan, *CFO*
**EMP:** 21 **EST:** 1979
**SQ FT:** 7,500
**SALES (est):** 4.97MM **Privately Held**
Web: www.jcmetals.com
SIC: **3441** Building components, structural steel

**(P-8158)**
**JCI METAL PRODUCTS (PA)**
6540 Federal Blvd, Lemon Grove (91945-1311)
PHONE..................................619 229-8206
Marcel Becker, *CEO*
Mark Withers, *
Rich Bartlett, *
Lorey Topham, *
**EMP:** 57 **EST:** 1984
**SQ FT:** 21,000
**SALES (est):** 8.68MM **Privately Held**
SIC: **3441** 1761 Fabricated structural metal for ships; Architectural sheet metal work

**(P-8159)**
**JOHASEE REBAR INC**
Also Called: Johasee Rebar
26365 Earthmover Cir, Corona (92883-5270)
PHONE..................................661 589-0972
Mike Hill Senior, *CEO*
Tamara L Chapman, *
Michael Hill Junior, *COO*
**EMP:** 47 **EST:** 1979
**SALES (est):** 3.96MM
**SALES (corp-wide):** 3.49MM **Privately Held**
SIC: **3441** 1791 Fabricated structural metal; Concrete reinforcement, placing of
PA: Lms Holdings (Ab) Ltd
7452 132 St
604 598-9930

**(P-8160)**
**JUNIOR STEEL CO**
134 W 168th St, Gardena (90248-2729)
PHONE..................................310 856-6868
**EMP:** 34 **EST:** 2018
**SALES (est):** 4.99MM **Privately Held**
Web: www.anvilsteel.com
SIC: **3441** Fabricated structural metal

**(P-8161)**
**JUSTIFIED PERFORMANCE LLC**
1111 W Sunset Blvd, Rocklin (95765-1304)
PHONE..................................916 771-8994
Thomas Williams, *Pr*
**EMP:** 16 **EST:** 2017

**SALES (est):** 5.5MM **Privately Held**
Web: www.justified-performance.com
SIC: **3441** 3499 3353 3444 Fabricated structural metal; Fabricated metal products, nec; Aluminum sheet, plate, and foil; Sheet metalwork

**(P-8162)**
**KASCO FAB INC**
4529 S Chestnut Ave Lowr, Fresno (93725-9244)
PHONE..................................559 442-1018
Hidemi Kimura, *CEO*
Ken Kimura, *
**EMP:** 75 **EST:** 1980
**SQ FT:** 200,000
**SALES (est):** 9.52MM **Privately Held**
Web: www.kascofab.com
SIC: **3441** 3449 Building components, structural steel; Miscellaneous metalwork

**(P-8163)**
**KATCH INC**
520 Hofgaarden St, City Of Industry (91744)
PHONE..................................626 369-0958
John Zheng, *CEO*
Son T Nguyen, *
**EMP:** 25 **EST:** 2003
**SQ FT:** 20,000
**SALES (est):** 4.09MM **Privately Held**
Web: www.integralfab.com
SIC: **3441** Fabricated structural metal

**(P-8164)**
**KERN STEEL FABRICATION INC (PA)**
627 Williams St, Bakersfield (93305-5445)
PHONE..................................661 327-9588
Tom Champness, *CEO*
Ali E Champness, *
Samuel E Champness, *
◆ **EMP:** 54 **EST:** 1959
**SQ FT:** 50,000
**SALES (est):** 22.92MM
**SALES (corp-wide):** 22.92MM **Privately Held**
Web: www.kernsteel.com
SIC: **3441** 3728 4581 3412 Fabricated structural metal; Aircraft parts and equipment, nec; Aircraft maintenance and repair services; Metal barrels, drums, and pails

**(P-8165)**
**KSU CORPORATION**
3 Emmy Ln, Ladera Ranch (92694-1521)
P.O. Box 3103 (92690-1103)
PHONE..................................951 409-7055
Luz Marina Agreda, *CEO*
**EMP:** 15 **EST:** 2015
**SALES (est):** 1.19MM **Privately Held**
SIC: **3441** Building components, structural steel

**(P-8166)**
**KUMAR INDUSTRIES**
4775 Chino Ave, Chino (91710-5130)
PHONE..................................909 591-0722
**EMP:** 23 **EST:** 1980
**SALES (est):** 11.01MM **Privately Held**
Web: www.kumarindustries.net
SIC: **3441** Building components, structural steel

**(P-8167)**
**LEES IMPERIAL WELDING INC**
3300 Edison Way, Fremont (94538-6150)
PHONE..................................510 657-4900
Gary Lee, *CEO*

Keith Lee, *
**EMP:** 150 **EST:** 1958
**SQ FT:** 59,000
**SALES (est):** 9.18MM **Privately Held**
Web: www.leeiw.com
SIC: **3441** Fabricated structural metal

**(P-8168)**
**LEHMANS MANUFACTURING CO INC**
4960 E Jensen Ave, Fresno (93725-1897)
PHONE..................................559 486-1700
Adam Lehman Junior, *Ch Bd*
Kenneth Lehman, *Pr*
Joyce Lehman, *Sec*
**EMP:** 15 **EST:** 1946
**SQ FT:** 36,000
**SALES (est):** 2.9MM **Privately Held**
Web: www.lehmansmfg.com
SIC: **3441** Fabricated structural metal

**(P-8169)**
**LEXINGTON ACQUISITION INC**
Also Called: Lexington
11125 Vanowen St, North Hollywood (91605-6316)
PHONE..................................818 768-5768
**EMP:** 145
SIC: **3441** Fabricated structural metal

**(P-8170)**
**LIGHTCAP INDUSTRIES INC**
Also Called: JC Supply & Manufacturing
1612 S Cucamonga Ave, Ontario (91761-4513)
PHONE..................................909 930-3772
**EMP:** 50
SIC: **3441** 3479 Building components, structural steel; Painting, coating, and hot dipping

**(P-8171)**
**LINDBLADE METALWORKS INC**
Also Called: Lindblade Metal Works
14355 Macaw St, La Mirada (90638-5208)
PHONE..................................714 670-7172
Vernon Lindblade, *CEO*
Marilyn Lindblade, *VP*
**EMP:** 20 **EST:** 1973
**SQ FT:** 16,250
**SALES (est):** 2.42MM **Privately Held**
Web: www.lindblademetalworks.com
SIC: **3441** Fabricated structural metal

**(P-8172)**
**M AND M STAMPING CORP**
13821 Oaks Ave, Chino (91710-7009)
PHONE..................................909 590-2704
Juan Uribe Senior, *Pr*
Juan Uribe Junior, *VP*
**EMP:** 15 **EST:** 2015
**SQ FT:** 8,000
**SALES (est):** 3.2MM **Privately Held**
Web: www.mandmstamping.com
SIC: **3441** 3444 Fabricated structural metal; Sheet metalwork

**(P-8173)**
**M W REID WELDING INC**
Also Called: South Bay Welding
781 Oconner St, El Cajon (92020-1644)
PHONE..................................619 401-5880
Bruce A Reid, *Pr*
Timothy Hill, *
Timothy Fair, *
Susan Reid, *
**EMP:** 78 **EST:** 1965
**SQ FT:** 25,000
**SALES (est):** 8.44MM **Privately Held**
Web: www.southbaywelding.com

# PRODUCTS & SERVICES SECTION

## 3441 - Fabricated Structural Metal (P-8195)

SIC: **3441** Fabricated structural metal

### (P-8174)
**MADISON INC OF OKLAHOMA**
18000 Studebaker Rd, Cerritos (90703-2679)
PHONE..................................918 224-6990
John Samuel Frey, *Pr*
Robert E Hansen, *
Barbara Cruncleton, *
**EMP:** 67 **EST:** 1946
**SALES (est):** 9.15MM
**SALES (corp-wide):** 44.99MM **Privately Held**
**SIC: 3441** 1541 3448 3444 Fabricated structural metal; Prefabricated building erection, industrial; Prefabricated metal buildings and components; Sheet metalwork
**PA:** John S. Frey Enterprises
1900 E 64th St
323 583-4061

### (P-8175)
**MADRUGA IRON WORKS INC**
305 Gandy Dancer Dr, Tracy (95377-9083)
PHONE..................................209 832-7003
Joseph Raymond Madruga, *CEO*
Elizabeth Betsy Madruga, *
Raymond M Madruga, *
**EMP:** 45 **EST:** 1914
**SQ FT:** 50,000
**SALES (est):** 4.91MM **Privately Held**
Web: www.madrugaironworks.com
**SIC: 3441** 3599 Fabricated structural metal; Machine shop, jobbing and repair

### (P-8176)
**MAXIMUM QUALITY METAL PDTS INC**
Also Called: Max Q
1017 E Acacia St, Ontario (91761-4554)
PHONE..................................909 902-5018
John Kim, *Pr*
Paul Kim, *Sec*
John Kim, *Pr*
**EMP:** 20 **EST:** 1998
**SQ FT:** 10,000
**SALES (est):** 2.68MM **Privately Held**
Web: www.maxqmetalproducts.com
**SIC: 3441** Fabricated structural metal

### (P-8177)
**MAYA STEEL FABRICATIONS INC**
301 E Compton Blvd, Gardena (90248-2015)
PHONE..................................310 532-8830
Meir Amsalam, *CEO*
Yechiel Yogev, *
Sara Haddad, *
**EMP:** 64 **EST:** 1982
**SQ FT:** 65,000
**SALES (est):** 8.81MM **Privately Held**
Web: www.mayasteel.com
**SIC: 3441** Building components, structural steel

### (P-8178)
**MCCAIN MANUFACTURING INC**
2633 Progress St, Vista (92081-8402)
P.O. Box 2307 (92067)
PHONE..................................760 295-9290
Jeffrey Lynn Mccain, *CEO*
**EMP:** 61 **EST:** 2016
**SALES (est):** 4.46MM **Privately Held**
**SIC: 3441** Fabricated structural metal

### (P-8179)
**MCM FABRICATORS INC**
Also Called: Global Fabricators
720 Commerce Way, Shafter (93263-9530)
P.O. Box 80247 (93380-0247)
PHONE..................................661 589-2774
Jim L Moses, *Pr*
Gary E Moses, *
Bill Chaney, *
**EMP:** 140 **EST:** 1982
**SQ FT:** 12,000
**SALES (est):** 6.1MM **Privately Held**
**SIC: 3441** Fabricated structural metal

### (P-8180)
**MCWHIRTER STEEL INC**
42211 7th St E, Lancaster (93535-5400)
PHONE..................................661 951-8998
David Mcwhirter, *Pr*
Angela Mcwhirter, *CFO*
Nathan Mcwhirter, *Dir*
**EMP:** 95 **EST:** 1992
**SQ FT:** 21,000
**SALES (est):** 14.14MM **Privately Held**
Web: www.mcwhirtersteel.com
**SIC: 3441** 1791 Fabricated structural metal; Structural steel erection

### (P-8181)
**MEDSCO FABRICATION & DIST INC**
938 N Eastern Ave, Los Angeles (90063-1308)
PHONE..................................323 263-0511
Michael Nevarez, *Ch Bd*
Brian Powell, *Pr*
Jim Stock, *CFO*
John Millan, *COO*
Laura Nevarez, *Sec*
**EMP:** 56 **EST:** 2001
**SALES (est):** 4.93MM **Privately Held**
Web: www.medscofabrication.com
**SIC: 3441** Fabricated structural metal

### (P-8182)
**MERRIMANS INCORPORATED**
32195 Dunlap Blvd, Yucaipa (92399-1728)
P.O. Box 547 (92320-0547)
PHONE..................................909 795-5301
**TOLL FREE:** 800
Tod Merriman, *Pr*
Janice Merriman, *
Lisa Merriman, *
Elaine Onken, *
**EMP:** 30 **EST:** 1965
**SQ FT:** 5,000
**SALES (est):** 4.38MM **Privately Held**
Web: www.merrimansinc.com
**SIC: 3441** 5271 1521 Building components, structural steel; Mobile home parts and accessories; General remodeling, single-family houses

### (P-8183)
**METAL SUPPLY LLC**
11810 Center St, South Gate (90280-7832)
PHONE..................................562 634-9940
**TOLL FREE:** 800
Dion Genchi, *Pr*
Bruce E Hubert, *
▼ **EMP:** 63 **EST:** 1961
**SQ FT:** 50,000
**SALES (est):** 3.74MM **Privately Held**
Web: www.metalsupply.com
**SIC: 3441** 5051 Fabricated structural metal; Iron and steel (ferrous) products

### (P-8184)
**METAL TEK COMPANY**
3801 S H St, Bakersfield (93304-6502)
PHONE..................................661 832-6011
**EMP:** 20 **EST:** 1979
**SALES (est):** 3.32MM **Privately Held**
Web: www.metaltekonline.com
**SIC: 3441** Fabricated structural metal

### (P-8185)
**METALS USA BUILDING PDTS LP**
6450 Caballero Blvd Ste A, Buena Park (90620-1007)
PHONE..................................714 522-7852
Tom Bush, *Brnch Mgr*
**EMP:** 120
**SALES (corp-wide):** 14.81B **Publicly Held**
Web: www.metalsusa.com
**SIC: 3441** 3444 Fabricated structural metal; Sheet metalwork
**HQ:** Metals Usa Building Products Lp
955 Columbia St
Brea CA 92821
713 946-9000

### (P-8186)
**METALSET INC**
1200 Hensley St, Richmond (94801-1900)
PHONE..................................510 233-9998
Wesley Sillineri, *Pr*
**EMP:** 22 **EST:** 1995
**SALES (est):** 6.8MM **Privately Held**
Web: www.metalsetinc.com
**SIC: 3441** Fabricated structural metal

### (P-8187)
**MIKES METAL WORKS INC**
3552 Fowler Canyon Rd, Jamul (91935-1602)
PHONE..................................619 440-8804
Mike Hancock, *Pr*
**EMP:** 18 **EST:** 1984
**SQ FT:** 6,000
**SALES (est):** 4.54MM **Privately Held**
Web: www.mikesmetalworks.net
**SIC: 3441** Fabricated structural metal

### (P-8188)
**MILLERS FAB & WELD CORP**
6100 Industrial Ave, Riverside (92504-1120)
PHONE..................................951 359-3100
James Miller, *CEO*
**EMP:** 21 **EST:** 1964
**SQ FT:** 2,100
**SALES (est):** 2.28MM **Privately Held**
Web: www.millersfab.net
**SIC: 3441** Fabricated structural metal

### (P-8189)
**MITCHELL FABRICATION**
Also Called: Amazing Steel
4564 Mission Blvd, Montclair (91763-6106)
PHONE..................................909 590-0393
Jim Mitchell, *Pr*
▲ **EMP:** 30 **EST:** 1985
**SQ FT:** 35,000
**SALES (est):** 3.9MM **Privately Held**
Web: www.mitchellamazing.com
**SIC: 3441** Fabricated structural metal

### (P-8190)
**MODERN WELDING COMPANY OF CALIFORNIA INC**
4141 N Brawley Ave, Fresno (93722-3915)
PHONE..................................559 275-9353
**EMP:** 24 **EST:** 1993
**SALES (est):** 11.86MM
**SALES (corp-wide):** 136.77MM **Privately Held**
Web: www.modweldco.com
**SIC: 3441** Fabricated structural metal
**PA:** Modern Welding Company, Inc.
2880 New Hartford Rd
270 685-4400

### (P-8191)
**MONTEREY STRUCTURAL STEEL INC**
404 W Beach St, Watsonville (95076-4533)
PHONE..................................831 768-1277
Kenneth J Bachini, *Pr*
**EMP:** 15 **EST:** 2000
**SALES (est):** 2.29MM **Privately Held**
Web: montereystructuralsteel.thebluebook.com
**SIC: 3441** Fabricated structural metal

### (P-8192)
**MUHLHAUSER ENTERPRISES INC (PA)**
Also Called: Muhlhauser Steel
25825 Adams Ave, Murrieta (92562-0601)
P.O. Box 159 (92316-0159)
PHONE..................................909 877-2792
William C Muhlhauser, *Pr*
Gisela Muhlhauser, *
**EMP:** 19 **EST:** 1961
**SALES (est):** 1.24MM
**SALES (corp-wide):** 1.24MM **Privately Held**
Web: www.msisteel.com
**SIC: 3441** 1791 Building components, structural steel; Structural steel erection

### (P-8193)
**MUHLHAUSER STEEL INC**
25825 Adams Ave, Murrieta (92562-0601)
P.O. Box 159 (92316-0159)
PHONE..................................909 877-2792
William Muhlhauser, *Pr*
Zigfried Muhlhauser, *Sr VP*
**EMP:** 20 **EST:** 1988
**SALES (est):** 7.8MM
**SALES (corp-wide):** 8.89MM **Privately Held**
Web: www.msisteel.com
**SIC: 3441** 1791 Building components, structural steel; Structural steel erection
**PA:** Muhlhauser Enterprises, Inc.
25825 Adams Ave
909 877-2792

### (P-8194)
**MYWI FABRICATORS INC**
2115 Edwards Ave 2119, South El Monte (91733-2037)
PHONE..................................626 279-6994
Henry Yue, *Pr*
Jeanne Yue, *Sec*
**EMP:** 18 **EST:** 1993
**SQ FT:** 5,000
**SALES (est):** 3.68MM **Privately Held**
Web: www.mywifabricators.com
**SIC: 3441** Fabricated structural metal

### (P-8195)
**NORTHLAND PROCESS PIPING INC**
400 E St, Lemoore (93245-2616)
PHONE..................................559 925-9724
Cal Bredek, *Supervisor*
**EMP:** 20
Web: www.nppmn.com
**SIC: 3441** Fabricated structural metal
**PA:** Northland Process Piping, Inc.
1662 320th Ave

## 3441 - Fabricated Structural Metal (P-8196)

**(P-8196)**
**OLSON AND CO STEEL**
3488 W Ashlan Ave, Fresno (93722-4443)
PHONE......................559 224-7811
Del Stephens, Brnch Mgr
EMP: 125
SALES (corp-wide): 49.79MM **Privately Held**
Web: www.olsonsteel.com
SIC: 3441 3446 Building components, structural steel; Architectural metalwork
PA: Olson And Co. Steel
1941 Davis St
510 567-2200

**(P-8197)**
**PACIFIC MARITIME INDS CORP**
Also Called: P M I
1790 Dornoch Ct, San Diego (92154-7206)
PHONE......................619 575-8141
John Atkinson, CEO
▲ EMP: 110 EST: 1995
SQ FT: 38,000
SALES (est): 20.11MM **Privately Held**
Web: pacificmaritimeindm.openfos.com
SIC: 3441 Fabricated structural metal

**(P-8198)**
**PARCELL STEEL CORP**
Also Called: Parcell Steel
26365 Earthmover Cir, Corona (92883-5270)
PHONE......................951 471-3200
EMP: 140
Web: www.parcellsteel.com
SIC: 3441 Fabricated structural metal

**(P-8199)**
**PARK STEEL CO INC**
515 E Pine St, Compton (90222-2817)
P.O. Box 4787 (90224-4787)
PHONE......................310 638-6101
Gregory M Park, Pr
Sally O Park, Treas
Randy Park, Sec
EMP: 18 EST: 1980
SQ FT: 70,000
SALES (est): 2.11MM **Privately Held**
Web: www.parksteel.net
SIC: 3441 1791 Bridge sections, prefabricated, highway; Concrete reinforcement, placing of

**(P-8200)**
**PLACER WATERWORKS INC**
1325 Furneaux Rd, Plumas Lake (95961-7485)
PHONE......................530 742-9675
Karl Kern, Pr
Sheila Kern, VP
EMP: 20 EST: 1993
SQ FT: 10,500
SALES (est): 3.8MM **Privately Held**
Web: www.placerwaterworks.com
SIC: 3441 Fabricated structural metal

**(P-8201)**
**PRECISION METAL CRAFTS INC**
11965 Rivera Rd, Santa Fe Springs (90670-2209)
PHONE......................562 468-7080
Coleman Conrad Iii, CEO
Rosemary Coleman, Sec
Coleman Conrad Junior, CFO
EMP: 20 EST: 2006
SALES (est): 825.9K **Privately Held**
Web: www.precisionmetalcrafts.com
SIC: 3441 Fabricated structural metal

**(P-8202)**
**PRECISION WELDING INC**
241 Enterprise Pkwy, Lancaster (93534-7201)
PHONE......................661 729-3436
David R Jones, Pr
David Jones, Pr
EMP: 23 EST: 1995
SQ FT: 10,000
SALES (est): 3.96MM **Privately Held**
Web: www.precisionweldingla.com
SIC: 3441 1799 Fabricated structural metal; Welding on site

**(P-8203)**
**PREMIER STEEL STRUCTURES INC**
13345 Estelle St, Corona (92879-1881)
PHONE......................951 356-6655
Armando Rodarte, Pr
EMP: 30 EST: 2016
SALES (est): 5.71MM **Privately Held**
Web: www.psspremiersteelstructures.com
SIC: 3441 Fabricated structural metal

**(P-8204)**
**PROGRESSIVE FRAME & FABG CO**
5050 Everett Ct, Vernon (90058-3141)
PHONE......................323 589-9933
EMP: 15
SQ FT: 15,500
SALES (est): 3.62MM **Privately Held**
SIC: 3441 Building components, structural steel

**(P-8205)**
**PROGRSSIVE STL FABRICATORS INC**
9188 Harness St, Spring Valley (91977-3947)
PHONE......................619 460-7150
Wayne Ritter, Pr
Curtis Mayfield, VP
Susan Ritter, Sec
Susanna Mayfield, Treas
EMP: 15 EST: 1968
SQ FT: 1,450
SALES (est): 2.2MM **Privately Held**
SIC: 3441 Fabricated structural metal

**(P-8206)**
**PROLINE METAL FABRICATORS INC**
42650 Osgood Rd, Fremont (94539-5603)
PHONE......................510 438-0300
Mark Martinek, CEO
▲ EMP: 30 EST: 1963
SQ FT: 38,760
SALES (est): 467.07K **Privately Held**
Web: www.gotopmf.com
SIC: 3441 Fabricated structural metal

**(P-8207)**
**R & D STEEL INC**
7930 E Tarma St, Long Beach (90808-3140)
PHONE......................310 631-6183
Joie A Dunyon, Pr
Jim Dunyon, *
▲ EMP: 30 EST: 1979
SQ FT: 8,000
SALES (est): 2.52MM **Privately Held**
Web: www.rdsteelinc.com
SIC: 3441 Fabricated structural metal

**(P-8208)**
**R & I INDUSTRIES INC**
Also Called: R & I
1876 S Taylor Ave, Ontario (91761-5556)
PHONE......................909 923-7747
William Franklin Rowan Senior, CEO
William Franklin Rowan Junior, VP
Ardith Rowan, *
EMP: 40 EST: 1978
SQ FT: 12,000
SALES (est): 6.76MM **Privately Held**
Web: www.rimetal.com
SIC: 3441 Building components, structural steel

**(P-8209)**
**RICHARDSON STEEL INC**
9102 Harness St Ste A, Spring Valley (91977-3924)
PHONE......................619 697-5892
John Richardson, Pr
Lance Richardson, *
Natalie N Lautner, *
EMP: 32 EST: 1993
SQ FT: 5,000
SALES (est): 4.62MM **Privately Held**
Web: www.richardsonsteelinc.com
SIC: 3441 Fabricated structural metal

**(P-8210)**
**RND CONTRACTORS INC**
14796 Jurupa Ave Ste A, Fontana (92337-7232)
PHONE......................909 429-8500
Nancy Sauter, Pr
EMP: 40 EST: 2007
SALES (est): 9.62MM **Privately Held**
Web: www.uia.net
SIC: 3441 Fabricated structural metal

**(P-8211)**
**ROBECKS WLDG & FABRICATION INC**
1150 Mabury Rd Ste 1, San Jose (95133-1031)
PHONE......................408 287-0202
Armon Robeck, Pr
Ronald Robeck, VP
Laurie Morado, Sec
EMP: 22 EST: 1993
SQ FT: 6,000
SALES (est): 2.21MM **Privately Held**
Web: www.robecks.com
SIC: 3441 7692 Fabricated structural metal; Welding repair

**(P-8212)**
**ROBERT J ALANDT & SONS**
Also Called: Central Cal Metals
4692 N Brawley Ave, Fresno (93722-3921)
PHONE......................559 275-1391
Frank Alandt, Pr
Robert Alandt, *
Joseph Alandt, *
EMP: 45 EST: 1950
SQ FT: 50,000
SALES (est): 7.07MM **Privately Held**
Web: www.cencalmetals.com
SIC: 3441 Fabricated structural metal

**(P-8213)**
**S & R ARCHITECTURAL METALS INC**
2609 W Woodland Dr, Anaheim (92801-2627)
PHONE......................714 226-0108
EMP: 45
SIC: 3441 Fabricated structural metal

**(P-8214)**
**SCHROEDER IRON CORPORATION**
8417 Beech Ave, Fontana (92335-1200)
PHONE......................909 428-6471
Linda Schroeder, Pr
EMP: 30 EST: 1993
SQ FT: 23,000
SALES (est): 9.75MM **Privately Held**
Web: www.schroederiron.com
SIC: 3441 Building components, structural steel

**(P-8215)**
**SIERRA METAL FABRICATORS INC**
Also Called: Sierra Metalk Fabricators
529 Searls Ave, Nevada City (95959-3003)
P.O. Box 1359 (95959-1359)
PHONE......................530 265-4591
Jason White, Pr
EMP: 30 EST: 1974
SQ FT: 30,000
SALES (est): 2.51MM **Privately Held**
Web: www.sierrametal.com
SIC: 3441 Fabricated structural metal

**(P-8216)**
**SIMPLEX SUPPLIES INC**
Also Called: JC Supply & Manufacturing
1370 Valley Vista Dr Ste 200, Diamond Bar (91765-3911)
PHONE......................618 594-6450
Neysa Schwend, Brnch Mgr
EMP: 15
SALES (corp-wide): 18.99MM **Privately Held**
SIC: 3441 3479 Building components, structural steel; Painting, coating, and hot dipping
PA: Simplex Supplies, Inc.
9020 W 35 W Service Dr
763 398-0040

**(P-8217)**
**SMB INDUSTRIES INC**
Also Called: Metal Works Supply
558 Georgia Pacific Way, Oroville (95965-9638)
PHONE......................530 538-0101
EMP: 25
SALES (corp-wide): 20.87MM **Privately Held**
Web: www.mtlwks.com
SIC: 3441 Fabricated structural metal
PA: Smb Industries, Inc.
550 Georgia Pacific Way
530 534-6266

**(P-8218)**
**SMB INDUSTRIES INC (PA)**
Also Called: Metal Works Supply
550 Georgia Pacific Way, Oroville (95965-9638)
PHONE......................530 534-6266
Sean Pierce, Pr
Mike Phulps, *
EMP: 50 EST: 1988
SQ FT: 45,000
SALES (est): 20.87MM
SALES (corp-wide): 20.87MM **Privately Held**
Web: www.mtlwks.com
SIC: 3441 Expansion joints (structural shapes), iron or steel

**(P-8219)**
**SO-CAL STRL STL FBRICATION INC**

## PRODUCTS & SERVICES SECTION
## 3441 - Fabricated Structural Metal (P-8240)

130 S Spruce Ave, Rialto (92376-9005)
PHONE.............................909 877-1299
Craig B Yates, *CEO*
Kim Yates, *
**EMP:** 50 **EST:** 1995
**SQ FT:** 40,000
**SALES (est):** 9.26MM **Privately Held**
**SIC: 3441** Fabricated structural metal

*(P-8220)*
### SOUTH BAY FOUNDRY INC (HQ)
895 Inland Center Dr, San Bernardino (92408-1828)
PHONE.............................909 383-1823
Bill Rogers, *Pr*
Russell Goodsell, *
▲ **EMP:** 35 **EST:** 1990
**SQ FT:** 12,002
**SALES (est):** 23.55MM
**SALES (corp-wide):** 46.84MM **Privately Held**
Web: www.southbayfoundry.com
**SIC: 3441** 3322 Fabricated structural metal; Malleable iron foundries
**PA:** Olympic Foundry Inc.
5200 Airport Way S
206 764-6200

*(P-8221)*
### SPARTAN INC
3030 M St, Bakersfield (93301-2137)
PHONE.............................661 327-1205
John Wood, *Pr*
Louis Stern, *
John D Clemmey, *
Teresa Wood, *
▼ **EMP:** 65 **EST:** 2002
**SQ FT:** 125,000
**SALES (est):** 9.49MM **Privately Held**
Web: www.spartaninc.net
**SIC: 3441** 8711 Fabricated structural metal; Engineering services

*(P-8222)*
### STEEL-TECH INDUSTRIAL CORP
1268 Sherborn St, Corona (92879-2090)
PHONE.............................951 270-0144
Michael R Black, *Pr*
Braebon Black, *
Linda Black, *
Elise Roberts, *
**EMP:** 47 **EST:** 1984
**SQ FT:** 15,000
**SALES (est):** 8.96MM **Privately Held**
Web: www.steeltech.org
**SIC: 3441** Fabricated structural metal

*(P-8223)*
### STRUCTURAL STL FABRICATORS INC
10641 Sycamore Ave, Stanton (90680-2639)
P.O. Box 707 (90680-0707)
PHONE.............................714 761-1695
Rex Shaw, *Pr*
Maureen Shaw, *
**EMP:** 25 **EST:** 1983
**SQ FT:** 3,600
**SALES (est):** 5.53MM **Privately Held**
**SIC: 3441** Fabricated structural metal

*(P-8224)*
### SUBURBAN STEEL INC (PA)
706 W California Ave, Fresno (93706-3599)
PHONE.............................559 268-6281
Stan J Cavalla, *Pr*
Ron Cavalla, *
**EMP:** 22 **EST:** 1945
**SQ FT:** 12,000
**SALES (est):** 5.54MM
**SALES (corp-wide):** 5.54MM **Privately Held**
**SIC: 3441** 3446 Building components, structural steel; Railings, banisters, guards, etc: made from metal pipe

*(P-8225)*
### SUMMIT STEEL WORKS CORPORATION
850 Faulstich Ct, San Jose (95112-1361)
PHONE.............................408 510-5880
Peter Kockelman, *Pr*
Ian Gravina, *
Nicola Kockelman, *
**EMP:** 30 **EST:** 1988
**SQ FT:** 4,500
**SALES (est):** 5.61MM **Privately Held**
Web: www.summitsteelworks.com
**SIC: 3441** Fabricated structural metal

*(P-8226)*
### T&S MANUFACTURING TECH LLC
Also Called: Atech Manufacturing
1530 Oakland Rd Ste 120, San Jose (95112-1241)
PHONE.............................408 441-0285
**EMP:** 16 **EST:** 2008
**SQ FT:** 6,000
**SALES (est):** 3.41MM **Privately Held**
Web: www.atechmanufacturing.com
**SIC: 3441** 3999 Fabricated structural metal; Atomizers, toiletry

*(P-8227)*
### TERMINAL MANUFACTURING CO LLC
Also Called: T M C
707 Gilman St, Berkeley (94710-1312)
PHONE.............................510 526-3071
Steve Millinger, *Managing Member*
Richard Robison, *
**EMP:** 30 **EST:** 1918
**SQ FT:** 30,000
**SALES (est):** 6.91MM **Privately Held**
Web: www.terminalem.com
**SIC: 3441** Fabricated structural metal

*(P-8228)*
### TITAN METAL FABRICATORS INC (PA)
Also Called: Titan
352 Balboa Cir, Camarillo (93012-8644)
PHONE.............................805 487-5050
Steve Muscarella, *Pr*
Tom Muscarella, *
▲ **EMP:** 69 **EST:** 1998
**SQ FT:** 15,000
**SALES (est):** 20.85MM
**SALES (corp-wide):** 20.85MM **Privately Held**
Web: www.titanmf.com
**SIC: 3441** Fabricated structural metal

*(P-8229)*
### TOBIN STEEL COMPANY INC
817 E Santa Ana Blvd, Santa Ana (92701-3909)
P.O. Box 717 (92702-0717)
PHONE.............................714 541-2268
Linda A Robin, *CEO*
Carl Tobin, *
Steve Tobin, *
Jim Tobin, *
**EMP:** 65 **EST:** 1978
**SQ FT:** 20,000
**SALES (est):** 9.44MM **Privately Held**
Web: www.tobinsteel.com

SIC: 3441 Building components, structural steel

*(P-8230)*
### TOLAR MANUFACTURING CO INC
258 Mariah Cir, Corona (92879-1751)
PHONE.............................951 808-0081
Gary Tolar, *Pr*
Rhonda Tolar, *
▲ **EMP:** 40 **EST:** 1991
**SQ FT:** 22,000
**SALES (est):** 8.58MM **Privately Held**
Web: www.tolarmfg.com
**SIC: 3441** 3599 3448 Fabricated structural metal; Machine shop, jobbing and repair; Prefabricated metal buildings and components

*(P-8231)*
### TOMS METAL SPECIALISTS INC
Also Called: Toms Welding & Fabrication
1416 Wallace Ave, San Francisco (94124-3318)
P.O. Box 24385 (94124-0385)
PHONE.............................415 822-7971
Tom Chang, *CEO*
**EMP:** 33 **EST:** 2002
**SQ FT:** 4,000
**SALES (est):** 4.69MM **Privately Held**
Web: www.tomsmetal.com
**SIC: 3441** Fabricated structural metal

*(P-8232)*
### TRANS BAY STEEL CORPORATION (PA)
536 Cleveland Ave, Berkeley (94710-1007)
PHONE.............................510 277-3756
William Kavicky, *Pr*
William Kavicky, *Pr*
William H Kroplin, *
**EMP:** 35 **EST:** 1987
**SALES (est):** 1.57MM
**SALES (corp-wide):** 1.57MM **Privately Held**
Web: www.transbaysteel.com
**SIC: 3441** Fabricated structural metal

*(P-8233)*
### TRUSSWORKS INTERNATIONAL INC
1275 E Franklin Ave, Pomona (91766-5450)
PHONE.............................714 630-2772
Michael Farrell, *Pr*
Ali Shantyaei, *
**EMP:** 60 **EST:** 2007
**SALES (est):** 9.21MM **Privately Held**
Web: www.twifab.com
**SIC: 3441** 3446 1791 Fabricated structural metal; Architectural metalwork; Building front installation, metal

*(P-8234)*
### UNION MINE IRON
12525 Quicksilver Dr, Rancho Cordova (95742-6905)
PHONE.............................916 985-0332
Richard Allen, *VP*
**EMP:** 30 **EST:** 2013
**SALES (est):** 2.25MM **Privately Held**
**SIC: 3441** Fabricated structural metal

*(P-8235)*
### UNITED MISC & ORNA STL INC
Also Called: Umo Steel
4700 Horner St, Union City (94587-2531)
PHONE.............................510 429-8755
Juan M Romero, *Pr*

Jose Barrera, *
Jose G Romero, *
**EMP:** 48 **EST:** 2004
**SALES (est):** 9.29MM **Privately Held**
**SIC: 3441** Fabricated structural metal

*(P-8236)*
### UNITED PIPE & STL FABRICATION
100 Quantico Ave, Bakersfield (93307-2839)
PHONE.............................661 489-4100
**EMP:** 26 **EST:** 2019
**SALES (est):** 5.69MM **Privately Held**
Web: www.upsfab.com
**SIC: 3441** Fabricated structural metal

*(P-8237)*
### UNIVERSAL STEEL SERVICES INC
5034 Heintz St, Baldwin Park (91706-1816)
P.O. Box 2428 (91706-1232)
PHONE.............................626 960-1455
Ramon T Lopez, *CEO*
**EMP:** 21 **EST:** 2001
**SALES (est):** 2.65MM **Privately Held**
Web: www.universalsteelservices.com
**SIC: 3441** Building components, structural steel

*(P-8238)*
### US TOWER CORP (PA)
Also Called: US Tower
1099 W Ropes Ave, Woodlake (93286-1806)
P.O. Box 285 (67455-0285)
PHONE.............................785 524-9966
Bruce Kopitar, *Pr*
Chuck Diehl, *
▲ **EMP:** 30 **EST:** 1985
**SALES (est):** 10.42MM
**SALES (corp-wide):** 10.42MM **Privately Held**
Web: www.ustower.com
**SIC: 3441** Tower sections, radio and television transmission

*(P-8239)*
### V & F FABRICATION COMPANY INC
13902 Seaboard Cir, Garden Grove (92843-3910)
PHONE.............................714 265-0630
Vinh Nguyen, *Pr*
Vinh Van Nguyen, *
Senator Truong, *Sec*
▲ **EMP:** 35 **EST:** 1989
**SALES (est):** 4.71MM **Privately Held**
**SIC: 3441** 3599 3769 3444 Fabricated structural metal; Machine shop, jobbing and repair; Space vehicle equipment, nec; Sheet metalwork

*(P-8240)*
### VALENCE SURFACE TECH LLC
7718 Adams St, Paramount (90723-4202)
PHONE.............................562 531-7666
Chris Celtruda, *Brnch Mgr*
**EMP:** 18
**SALES (corp-wide):** 138.9MM **Privately Held**
Web: www.valencesurfacetech.com
**SIC: 3441** Fabricated structural metal
**PA:** Valence Surface Technologies Llc
300 Cntnntal Blvd Ste 600
888 540-0878

# 3441 - Fabricated Structural Metal (P-8241)

## (P-8241)
**VIRGIL WALKER INC**
Also Called: Auton Motorized Systems
24856 Avenue Rockefeller, Valencia
(91355-3467)
P.O. Box 801960 (91380-1960)
PHONE..................................661 797-4101
Arthur Walker, *CEO*
**EMP:** 15 **EST:** 2010
**SALES (est):** 4.01MM **Privately Held**
**Web:** www.auton.com
**SIC:** 3441 Fabricated structural metal

## (P-8242)
**VISTA STEEL COMPANY (PA)**
6100 Francis Botello Rd Ste C, Goleta
(93117-3264)
PHONE..................................805 964-4732
Maria Di Maggio, *Pr*
**EMP:** 50 **EST:** 1969
**SQ FT:** 600
**SALES (est):** 1.87MM
**SALES (corp-wide):** 1.87MM **Privately Held**
**Web:** www.vistasteelco.com
**SIC:** 3441 Fabricated structural metal

## (P-8243)
**WADCO INDUSTRIES INC**
Also Called: Wadco Steel Sales
2625 S Willow Ave, Bloomington
(92316-3258)
PHONE..................................909 874-7800
David D Scheibel, *CEO*
Salvador Arratia, *
Anthony Salazar, *
Scott Brown, *
**EMP:** 47 **EST:** 1979
**SQ FT:** 50,000
**SALES (est):** 1.71MM **Privately Held**
**Web:** www.wadcoindustries.com
**SIC:** 3441 5051 Building components, structural steel; Steel

## (P-8244)
**WELDWAY INC**
521 Hi Tech Pkwy, Oakdale (95361-9395)
PHONE..................................209 847-8083
Mike Sala, *Pr*
Steve Brooks, *
**EMP:** 35 **EST:** 1983
**SQ FT:** 4,500
**SALES (est):** 7.11MM **Privately Held**
**Web:** www.weldwayinc.com
**SIC:** 3441 Fabricated structural metal

## (P-8245)
**WESTCO INDUSTRIES INC**
Also Called: Corbell Products
2625 S Willow Ave, Bloomington
(92316-3258)
PHONE..................................909 874-8700
David Schibel, *Pr*
▲ **EMP:** 25 **EST:** 2005
**SQ FT:** 25,000
**SALES (est):** 1.6MM **Privately Held**
**Web:** www.westcoind.com
**SIC:** 3441 Fabricated structural metal

## (P-8246)
**WESTCO IRON WORKS INC (PA)**
Also Called: Westco
1080 Concannon Blvd Ste 110, Livermore
(94550-6576)
PHONE..................................925 961-9152
Mark Shoermsser, *Pr*
Brad Thompson, *
John Winger, *
Scott Hofstede, *
**EMP:** 70 **EST:** 2005
**SALES (est):** 18.49MM **Privately Held**
**Web:** www.westcoironworks.com
**SIC:** 3441 Fabricated structural metal

## (P-8247)
**WESTEEL BUILDERS**
287 Vernon Way, El Cajon (92020-1928)
PHONE..................................858 524-4353
Ali Seif, *CEO*
**EMP:** 15 **EST:** 2016
**SQ FT:** 1,100
**SALES (est):** 1.01MM **Privately Held**
**Web:** www.westeelbuilders.com
**SIC:** 3441 Fabricated structural metal

## (P-8248)
**WESTERN BAY SHEET METAL INC**
1410 Hill St, El Cajon (92020-5749)
PHONE..................................619 233-1753
James Lozano, *Pr*
Roy Lozano, *
Helena Lopez, *
▲ **EMP:** 45 **EST:** 1981
**SQ FT:** 9,800
**SALES (est):** 8.92MM **Privately Held**
**Web:** www.westernbay.net
**SIC:** 3441 3444 Fabricated structural metal; Sheet metalwork

## (P-8249)
**ZIA AAMIR**
Also Called: Bridge Metals
2043 Imperial St, Los Angeles
(90021-3203)
PHONE..................................714 337-7861
Aamir Zia, *Owner*
**EMP:** 25 **EST:** 2017
**SALES (est):** 1.53MM **Privately Held**
**Web:** www.bridgemetals.com
**SIC:** 3441 Fabricated structural metal

---

## 3442 Metal Doors, Sash, And Trim

## (P-8250)
**ACCENT INDUSTRIES INC (PA)**
Also Called: Accent Awnings
1600 E Saint Gertrude Pl, Santa Ana
(92705-5312)
PHONE..................................714 708-1389
**TOLL FREE:** 800
Karl Desmarais, *CEO*
▲ **EMP:** 17 **EST:** 1993
**SQ FT:** 26,000
**SALES (est):** 3.16MM **Privately Held**
**Web:** www.accentawnings.com
**SIC:** 3442 3444 2394 5999 Shutters, door or window: metal; Awnings and canopies; Canvas and related products; Awnings

## (P-8251)
**ACTIVE WINDOW PRODUCTS**
Also Called: Z Industries
5431 W San Fernando Rd, Los Angeles
(90039-1088)
P.O. Box 39125 (90039-0125)
PHONE..................................323 245-5185
**TOLL FREE:** 800
Michael Schoenfeld, *Pr*
Rosa Castro, *
▲ **EMP:** 53 **EST:** 1952
**SQ FT:** 96,000
**SALES (est):** 7.45MM **Privately Held**
**Web:** www.activewindowproducts.com
**SIC:** 3442 Storm doors or windows, metal

## (P-8252)
**AIR LOUVERS INC**
6285 Randolph St, Commerce
(90040-3514)
PHONE..................................800 554-6077
**EMP:** 50
**SALES (corp-wide):** 142.69MM **Privately Held**
**Web:** www.activarcpg.com
**SIC:** 3442 Metal doors, sash, and trim
**HQ:** Air Louvers, Inc.
9702 Newton Ave S
Bloomington MN 55431
800 554-6077

## (P-8253)
**ANLIN WINDOWS & DOORS**
1665 Tollhouse Rd, Clovis (93611-0523)
PHONE..................................800 287-7996
**EMP:** 432 **EST:** 2021
**SALES (est):** 18.35MM
**SALES (corp-wide):** 1.66B **Privately Held**
**Web:** www.anlin.com
**SIC:** 3442 Metal doors, sash, and trim
**HQ:** Pgt Innovations, Inc.
1070 Technology Dr
North Venice FL 34275
941 480-1600

## (P-8254)
**ARCHITECTURAL BLOMBERG LLC**
Also Called: Blomberg Window Systems
1453 Blair Ave, Sacramento (95822-3410)
P.O. Box 22485 (95822-0485)
PHONE..................................916 428-8060
Jeremy Drucker, *Managing Member*
**EMP:** 32 **EST:** 2014
**SALES (est):** 7.16MM **Privately Held**
**Web:** www.blombergwindows.com
**SIC:** 3442 Window and door frames

## (P-8255)
**BAYFAB METALS INC**
870 Doolittle Dr, San Leandro (94577-1079)
PHONE..................................510 568-8950
Susan Miranda, *Pr*
**EMP:** 20 **EST:** 1969
**SQ FT:** 21,000
**SALES (est):** 2.87MM **Privately Held**
**Web:** www.bayfabmetals.com
**SIC:** 3442 3444 3446 3499 Metal doors, sash, and trim; Metal housings, enclosures, casings, and other containers; Louvers, ventilating; Shims, metal

## (P-8256)
**BELCO CABINETS INC**
1109 Black Diamond Way, Lodi
(95240-0746)
PHONE..................................209 334-5437
Roy Belanger, *Pr*
**EMP:** 15 **EST:** 1978
**SQ FT:** 21,000
**SALES (est):** 2.3MM **Privately Held**
**Web:** www.belcocabinetsinc.com
**SIC:** 3442 2434 Metal doors; Wood kitchen cabinets

## (P-8257)
**BEST ROLL-UP DOOR INC**
13202 Arctic Cir, Santa Fe Springs
(90670-5510)
PHONE..................................562 802-2233
Edward Choi, *Pr*
▲ **EMP:** 20 **EST:** 1978
**SQ FT:** 15,000
**SALES (est):** 2.34MM **Privately Held**
**Web:** www.bestrollup.com
**SIC:** 3442 Rolling doors for industrial buildings or warehouses; metal

## (P-8258)
**BLOMBERG BUILDING MATERIALS (PA)**
Also Called: Blomberg Window Systems
1453 Blair Ave, Sacramento (95822-3410)
PHONE..................................916 428-8060
**TOLL FREE:** 800
Philip Collier, *CEO*
**EMP:** 98 **EST:** 1956
**SALES (est):** 3.93MM
**SALES (corp-wide):** 3.93MM **Privately Held**
**Web:** www.blombergwindows.com
**SIC:** 3442 Metal doors, sash, and trim

## (P-8259)
**BLUM CONSTRUCTION CO INC**
Also Called: European Rolling Shutters
404 Umbarger Rd Ste A, San Jose
(95111-2087)
PHONE..................................408 629-3740
**TOLL FREE:** 800
Helmut Blum, *Pr*
Renate Blum, *VP*
▲ **EMP:** 15 **EST:** 1984
**SQ FT:** 10,500
**SALES (est):** 2.48MM **Privately Held**
**Web:** www.ersshading.com
**SIC:** 3442 3444 1751 1799 Shutters, door or window: metal; Awnings and canopies; Window and door installation and erection; Awning installation

## (P-8260)
**CLEAR VIEW LLC**
1650 Las Plumas Ave Ste A, San Jose
(95133-1657)
PHONE..................................408 271-2734
Andrew Lezotte, *Managing Member*
**EMP:** 15 **EST:** 2015
**SALES (est):** 1.01MM **Privately Held**
**SIC:** 3442 5084 Screen doors, metal; Industrial machinery and equipment

## (P-8261)
**CRYSTAL PCF WIN & DOOR SYS LLC**
Also Called: Crystal
1850 Atlanta Ave, Riverside (92507-2476)
PHONE..................................951 779-9300
Thomas C Chen, *Managing Member*
**EMP:** 102 **EST:** 2010
**SALES (est):** 23.79MM **Privately Held**
**Web:** www.cpwds.com
**SIC:** 3442 Window and door frames

## (P-8262)
**DOOR COMPONENTS INC**
Also Called: DCI Hollow Metal On Demand
7980 Redwood Ave, Fontana (92336-1638)
PHONE..................................909 770-5700
Robert Briggs, *Pr*
Ronald Green, *
**EMP:** 200 **EST:** 1981
**SQ FT:** 45,000
**SALES (est):** 28.07MM **Privately Held**
**Web:** www.doorcomponents.com
**SIC:** 3442 Metal doors

## (P-8263)
**ELITE SHUTTERS & SHADINGS INC**
2343 W Yosemite Ave, Manteca
(95337-8332)
PHONE..................................209 825-1400
Javier Campos, *CEO*

# PRODUCTS & SERVICES SECTION
## 3442 - Metal Doors, Sash, And Trim (P-8285)

**EMP:** 16 **EST:** 2016
**SALES (est):** 771.08K **Privately Held**
**Web:** www.eliteshadings.com
**SIC: 3442** 1771 Shutters, door or window: metal; Flooring contractor

### (P-8264)
### ELIZABETH SHUTTERS INC
Also Called: Elizabeth Shutters
525 S Rancho Ave, Colton (92324-3240)
P.O. Box 1345 (92324)
**PHONE**..................909 825-1531
Dean Frost, *CEO*
Maren Frost, *
Maggie Castaneda, *Accounts Payable*
**EMP:** 45 **EST:** 1996
**SQ FT:** 51,000
**SALES (est):** 4.86MM **Privately Held**
**Web:** www.elizabethshutters.com
**SIC: 3442** 5023 5211 2431 Shutters, door or window: metal; Window furnishings; Door and window products; Millwork

### (P-8265)
### EUROLINE STEEL WINDOWS
Also Called: Euroline Steel Windows & Doors
22600 Savi Ranch Pkwy Ste E, Yorba Linda (92887-4646)
**PHONE**..................877 590-2741
Elyas Balta, *CEO*
▲ **EMP:** 54 **EST:** 2013
**SALES (est):** 7.54MM **Privately Held**
**Web:** www.eurolinesteelwindows.com
**SIC: 3442** Window and door frames

### (P-8266)
### FANBOYS WINDOW FACTORY INC (PA)
1250 S Johnson Dr, City Of Industry (91745-2408)
**PHONE**..................626 280-8787
Lili Bell, *CEO*
Jeff Bell, *COO*
**EMP:** 21 **EST:** 2015
**SALES (est):** 2.33MM
**SALES (corp-wide):** 2.33MM **Privately Held**
**SIC: 3442** Window and door frames

### (P-8267)
### GILWIN COMPANY
2354 Lapham Dr, Modesto (95354-3912)
**PHONE**..................209 522-9775
Donald P Miller, *Pr*
**EMP:** 23 **EST:** 1990
**SQ FT:** 27,000
**SALES (est):** 2.19MM **Privately Held**
**Web:** www.gilwin.com
**SIC: 3442** Window and door frames

### (P-8268)
### HEHR INTERNATIONAL INC
Also Called: Hehr International Polymers
P.O. Box 39160 (90039-0160)
**PHONE**..................323 663-1261
▲ **EMP:** 199
**Web:** www.hehr-international.com
**SIC: 3442** Window and door frames

### (P-8269)
### J T WALKER INDUSTRIES INC
Also Called: Rite Screen
9322 Hyssop Dr, Rancho Cucamonga (91730-6103)
**PHONE**..................909 481-1909
Dan Harvey, *Pr*
**EMP:** 4194
**SQ FT:** 36,929
**SALES (corp-wide):** 26.58MM **Privately Held**

**SIC: 3442** Screen and storm doors and windows
**PA:** J. T. Walker Industries, Inc.
1310 N Hercules Ave
727 461-0501

### (P-8270)
### JANUS INTERNATIONAL GROUP LLC
2535 W La Palma Ave, Anaheim (92801-2612)
**PHONE**..................714 503-6120
David Curtis, *Prin*
**EMP:** 16
**SALES (corp-wide):** 1.07B **Publicly Held**
**Web:** www.janusintl.com
**SIC: 3442** Metal doors
**HQ:** Janus International Group, Llc
135 Janus Intl Blvd
Temple GA 30179
770 562-2850

### (P-8271)
### KAWNEER COMPANY INC
925 Marlborough Ave, Riverside (92507-2138)
**PHONE**..................951 410-4779
**EMP:** 91
**SALES (corp-wide):** 8.96B **Privately Held**
**Web:** www.kawneer.us
**SIC: 3442** Metal doors, sash, and trim
**HQ:** Kawneer Company, Inc.
555 Guthridge Ct
Norcross GA 30092
770 449-5555

### (P-8272)
### KRIEGER SPECIALITY PDTS LLC (DH)
Also Called: Krieger Steel Products
4880 Gregg Rd, Pico Rivera (90660-2107)
**PHONE**..................562 695-0645
Robert J Mccluney, *Pr*
A W Mc Cluney, *Ch Bd*
William Mc Cluney, *Ex VP*
James Mc Cluney, *Stockholder*
Charles Mc Cluney, *Stockholder*
**EMP:** 58 **EST:** 1974
**SQ FT:** 39,000
**SALES (est):** 9.41MM **Privately Held**
**Web:** www.kriegerproducts.com
**SIC: 3442** 1751 Metal doors; Window and door (prefabricated) installation
**HQ:** Schlage Lock Company Llc
11819 N Pennsylvania St
Carmel IN 46032
317 810-3700

### (P-8273)
### LAWRENCE ROLL UP DOORS INC (PA)
4525 Littlejohn St, Baldwin Park (91706-2239)
**PHONE**..................626 962-4163
**TOLL FREE:** 800
Paul Weston Freberg, *CEO*
◆ **EMP:** 35 **EST:** 1925
**SQ FT:** 35,000
**SALES (est):** 17.42MM
**SALES (corp-wide):** 17.42MM **Privately Held**
**Web:** www.lawrencedoors.com
**SIC: 3442** 3446 Rolling doors for industrial buildings or warehouses, metal; Architectural metalwork

### (P-8274)
### LINDSAY WINDOWS CALIFORNIA LLC
13510 Central Rd, Apple Valley (92308-6561)
P.O. Box 999 (92307-0017)
**PHONE**..................760 247-1082
Geoff Roise, *Mng Pt*
**EMP:** 15 **EST:** 2016
**SALES (est):** 1.14MM **Privately Held**
**Web:** www.lindsaywindows.com
**SIC: 3442** Metal doors, sash, and trim

### (P-8275)
### MAZONA INC
1885 Kinser Rd, Ceres (95307-4606)
**PHONE**..................209 538-3667
David Stiles, *Pr*
Steve Stiles, *
Jim Ludlow, *
**EMP:** 87 **EST:** 1973
**SQ FT:** 56,000
**SALES (est):** 10.24MM **Privately Held**
**Web:** www.stilesdoors.com
**SIC: 3442** Metal doors

### (P-8276)
### METAL MANUFACTURING CO INC
2240 Evergreen St, Sacramento (95815-3281)
**PHONE**..................916 922-3484
Jerry Guest, *Pr*
Troy Smith, *Treas*
Henry Baum, *Sec*
**EMP:** 20 **EST:** 1972
**SQ FT:** 19,000
**SALES (est):** 1.07MM **Privately Held**
**Web:** www.metalmfgco.com
**SIC: 3442** Metal doors

### (P-8277)
### MILLWORKS ETC INC
Also Called: Steel Works Etc
2230 Statham Blvd Ste 100, Oxnard (93033-3909)
**PHONE**..................805 499-3400
Robin W Shattuck, *CEO*
◆ **EMP:** 25 **EST:** 1985
**SALES (est):** 5.98MM **Privately Held**
**Web:** www.millworksetc.com
**SIC: 3442** Window and door frames

### (P-8278)
### MNM MANUFACTURING INC
3019 E Harcourt St, Compton (90221-5503)
**PHONE**..................310 898-1099
Matt Klein, *Pr*
Elizabeth Klein, *
Marlene Klein, *
**EMP:** 60 **EST:** 1980
**SQ FT:** 24,000
**SALES (est):** 4.53MM **Privately Held**
**Web:** www.mnmmfg.com
**SIC: 3442** Sash, door or window: metal

### (P-8279)
### MULHOLLAND SECURITY CTRS LLC
Also Called: Mulholland Brand
21260 Deering Ct, Canoga Park (91304-5015)
**PHONE**..................800 562-5770
Avi Ben David, *CEO*
Henry Zimmerman, *Pr*
Eyal Sibrower, *COO*
Avi 'coby' Jacoby, *CFO*
**EMP:** 65 **EST:** 2018
**SALES (est):** 7.6MM **Privately Held**
**Web:** www.mulhollandbrand.com
**SIC: 3442** 7699 Garage doors, overhead: metal; Locksmith shop

### (P-8280)
### NANA WALL SYSTEMS INC
Also Called: Nana Wall Systems
100 Meadowcreek Dr Ste 250, Corte Madera (94925-2500)
**PHONE**..................415 383-3148
Ebrahim M Nana, *Pr*
Ozair Nana, *
Ahmad M Nana, *
Ilyas Nana, *
◆ **EMP:** 47 **EST:** 1989
**SQ FT:** 10,000
**SALES (est):** 7.98MM **Privately Held**
**Web:** www.nanawall.com
**SIC: 3442** Metal doors

### (P-8281)
### OMNIMAX INTERNATIONAL LLC
Also Called: Alumax Building Products
28921 Us Highway 74, Sun City (92585-9675)
**PHONE**..................951 928-1000
Mitchell B Lewis, *CEO*
**EMP:** 60
**Web:** www.omnimax.com
**SIC: 3442** 3444 5999 Casements, aluminum ; Sheet metalwork; Awnings
**HQ:** Omnimax International, Llc
30 Technlogy Pkwy S Ste 4
Peachtree Corners GA 30092
770 449-7066

### (P-8282)
### P I INC
Also Called: Pacific Industries
3511 Finch Rd, Modesto (95357-4143)
**PHONE**..................209 527-8020
T G Myers, *Pr*
Donna Myers, *
Horace Ladeoux, *
**EMP:** 80 **EST:** 1960
**SQ FT:** 67,000
**SALES (est):** 682.46K **Privately Held**
**SIC: 3442** Window and door frames

### (P-8283)
### PEMKO MANUFACTURING CO
4226 Transport St, Ventura (93003-5627)
P.O. Box 3780 (93006-3780)
**PHONE**..................800 283-9988
◆ **EMP:** 250
**SIC: 3442** Weather strip, metal

### (P-8284)
### PRECISE IRON DOORS INC
12331 Foothill Blvd, Sylmar (91342-6003)
**PHONE**..................818 338-6269
Haik Pambuckchyan, *CEO*
**EMP:** 20 **EST:** 2015
**SALES (est):** 2.62MM **Privately Held**
**Web:** www.preciseirondoors.com
**SIC: 3442** 5031 5999 Metal doors; Metal doors, sash and trim; Miscellaneous retail stores, nec

### (P-8285)
### R & S AUTOMATION INC
283 W Bonita Ave, Pomona (91767-1848)
**PHONE**..................800 962-3111
Jerry Bradfield, *Mgr*
**EMP:** 27
**SALES (corp-wide):** 5.23MM **Privately Held**
**Web:** www.rsoperators.com
**SIC: 3442** 3446 5031 5063 Metal doors; Grillwork, ornamental metal; Doors, nec; Motor controls, starters and relays: electric
**PA:** R & S Automation, Inc.
2041 W Avenue 140th
510 357-4110

## 3442 - Metal Doors, Sash, And Trim (P-8286)

**(P-8286)**
**R & S MANUFACTURING INC (HQ)**
Also Called: R & S Rolling Door Products
33955 7th St, Union City (94587-3521)
P.O. Box 2737 (94587-7737)
PHONE.................510 429-1788
Gordon J Ong, Pr
Ray Zarodney, *
James Greaves, *
Robert R Smith, *
▲ EMP: 25 EST: 1979
SQ FT: 36,136
SALES (est): 10.78MM
SALES (corp-wide): 10.78MM Privately Held
Web: www.rsdoorproducts.com
SIC: 3442 3231 Rolling doors for industrial buildings or warehouses, metal; Products of purchased glass
PA: R & S Erection, Incorporated
2057 W Avenue 140th
510 483-3710

**(P-8287)**
**R LANG COMPANY**
Also Called: Truframe
8240 W Doe Ave, Visalia (93291-9263)
P.O. Box 7960 (93290-7960)
PHONE.................559 651-0701
Richard A Lang, Pr
Judith D Lang, *
◆ EMP: 75 EST: 1967
SALES (est): 4.02MM Privately Held
Web: www.rollaway.com
SIC: 3442 3444 3211 5031 Screen doors, metal; Skylights, sheet metal; Flat glass; Windows

**(P-8288)**
**S E - G I PRODUCTS INC**
20521 Teresita Way, Lake Forest (92630-8142)
PHONE.................949 297-8530
EMP: 180 EST: 1976
SALES (est): 10.81MM
SALES (corp-wide): 1.62B Privately Held
SIC: 3442 Sash, door or window: metal
HQ: Truck Accessories Group, Llc
28858 Ventura Dr
Elkhart IN 46517
574 522-5337

**(P-8289)**
**SAN JOAQUIN WINDOW INC**
Also Called: ATI Windows
1455 Columbia Ave, Riverside (92507-2013)
PHONE.................909 946-3697
Stephen Schwartz, CEO
Daniel Schwartz, *
EMP: 120 EST: 1992
SQ FT: 190,000
SALES (est): 15.14MM Privately Held
SIC: 3442 5211 Metal doors, sash, and trim; Door and window products

**(P-8290)**
**SDS INDUSTRIES INC**
Also Called: Timely Prefinished Steel
10241 Norris Ave, Pacoima (91331-2292)
PHONE.................818 492-3500
EMP: 130 EST: 1973
SALES (est): 21.7MM Privately Held
Web: www.timelyframes.com
SIC: 3442 Window and door frames

**(P-8291)**
**SOLATUBE INTERNATIONAL INC (DH)**
Also Called: Solatube
2210 Oak Ridge Way, Vista (92081-8341)
PHONE.................888 765-2882
Robert E Westfall Junior, CEO
Francisco Lopez, *
▲ EMP: 100 EST: 1995
SQ FT: 105,000
SALES (est): 38.22MM Privately Held
Web: www.solatube.com
SIC: 3442 Metal doors, sash, and trim
HQ: Kingspan Light & Air Llc
28662 N Ballard Dr
Lake Forest IL 60045
847 816-1060

**(P-8292)**
**STEELWORKS ETC INC**
Also Called: Shattuck Group, The
2230 Statham Blvd Ste 100, Oxnard (93033-3914)
PHONE.................805 487-3000
Rob Shattuck, Pr
EMP: 15 EST: 2010
SALES (est): 6.33MM Privately Held
Web: www.steelworksetc.com
SIC: 3442 Metal doors, sash, and trim

**(P-8293)**
**TORRANCE STEEL WINDOW CO INC**
1819 Abalone Ave, Torrance (90501-3704)
PHONE.................310 328-9181
Dong K Lim, Pr
▲ EMP: 30 EST: 1964
SQ FT: 32,000
SALES (est): 3.68MM Privately Held
Web: www.torrancesteelwindow.com
SIC: 3442 Window and door frames

**(P-8294)**
**WINDOW ENTERPRISES INC**
Also Called: Torrence Aluminum Window
430 Nevada St, Redlands (92373-4244)
PHONE.................951 943-4894
▲ EMP: 30 EST: 1970
SALES (est): 3.14MM Privately Held
SIC: 3442 Storm doors or windows, metal

## 3443 Fabricated Plate Work (boiler Shop)

**(P-8295)**
**AAR MANUFACTURING INC**
Also Called: Telair International
2220 E Cerritos Ave, Anaheim (92806-5709)
PHONE.................714 634-8807
EMP: 150
SALES (corp-wide): 1.77B Publicly Held
SIC: 3443 Containers, shipping (bombs, etc.): metal plate
HQ: Aar Manufacturing, Inc.
1100 N Wood Dale Rd
Wood Dale IL 60191
630 227-2000

**(P-8296)**
**ACD LLC (DH)**
Also Called: Nikkiso Acd
2321 Pullman St, Santa Ana (92705-5512)
PHONE.................949 261-7533
Peter Wagner, CEO
James Estes, *
◆ EMP: 49 EST: 1978
SQ FT: 52,000
SALES (est): 47.65MM Privately Held
Web: www.nikkisoceig.com
SIC: 3443 3559 Cryogenic tanks, for liquids and gases; Cryogenic machinery, industrial
HQ: Cryogenic Industries, Inc.
27710 Jffrson Ave Ste 301
Temecula CA 92590
951 677-2081

**(P-8297)**
**AERO-CLSSICS HEAT TRNSF PDTS I**
1677 Curtiss Ct, La Verne (91750-5848)
PHONE.................909 596-1630
Paul Saurenman, CEO
EMP: 15 EST: 2007
SALES (est): 2.59MM Privately Held
Web: www.aero-classics.com
SIC: 3443 Heat exchangers: coolers (after, inter), condensers, etc.

**(P-8298)**
**AJAX BOILER INC**
Also Called: Ace Boiler
2701 S Harbor Blvd, Santa Ana (92704-5838)
PHONE.................714 437-9050
▼ EMP: 68
Web: www.aceheaters.com
SIC: 3443 Fabricated plate work (boiler shop)

**(P-8299)**
**ATCO RUBBER PRODUCTS INC**
3080 12th St, Riverside (92507-4903)
PHONE.................951 788-4345
Bertha Almanza, Brnch Mgr
EMP: 18
Web: www.atcoflex.com
SIC: 3443 Fabricated plate work (boiler shop)
HQ: Atco Rubber Products, Inc.
7101 Atco Dr
Fort Worth TX 76118
817 595-2894

**(P-8300)**
**BA HOLDINGS INC (DH)**
3016 Kansas Ave Bldg 1, Riverside (92507-3445)
PHONE.................951 684-5110
John S Rhodes, CEO
EMP: 30 EST: 1996
SALES (est): 115.7MM
SALES (corp-wide): 405MM Privately Held
Web: www.mediluxcylinders.com
SIC: 3443 3728 Cylinders, pressure: metal plate; Aircraft parts and equipment, nec
HQ: Luxfer Overseas Holdings Limited
Anchorage Gateway, 5 Anchorage Quay
Salford LANCS M50 3

**(P-8301)**
**BASIC INDUSTRIES INTL INC (PA)**
Also Called: Pacific Metal Products
10850 Wilshire Blvd Ste 760, Los Angeles (90024-4305)
PHONE.................951 226-1500
John Wallace, Pr
Steven W Burge, *
EMP: 50 EST: 2000
SALES (est): 3.01MM
SALES (corp-wide): 3.01MM Privately Held
Web: www.biidemexico.com
SIC: 3443 3446 Fabricated plate work (boiler shop); Architectural metalwork

**(P-8302)**
**BENICIA FABRICATION & MCH INC**
101 E Channel Rd, Benicia (94510-1155)
PHONE.................707 745-8111
Thomas D Cepernich, CEO
Steven Rose, *
Dennis Michael Rose, *
EMP: 150 EST: 1983
SQ FT: 80,000
SALES (est): 22.46MM Privately Held
Web: www.beniciafab.com
SIC: 3443 3599 Fabricated plate work (boiler shop); Machine shop, jobbing and repair

**(P-8303)**
**CALIFORNIA METAL & SUPPLY INC**
Also Called: California Metal
14020 Bolsa Ln, Cerritos (90703-7026)
PHONE.................800 707-6061
Kenneth M Lee, CEO
◆ EMP: 16 EST: 1984
SALES (est): 2.53MM Privately Held
Web: www.californiametal.com
SIC: 3443 3469 3599 5051 Metal parts; Machine parts, stamped or pressed metal; Machine shop, jobbing and repair; Metals service centers and offices

**(P-8304)**
**CENTRAL VALLEY TANK OF CAL**
Also Called: Used Tank Sales of California
4752 E Carmen Ave, Fresno (93703-4501)
PHONE.................559 456-3500
Kathy Tackett, Pr
EMP: 16 EST: 2008
SALES (est): 4.8MM Privately Held
Web: www.centralvalleytank.com
SIC: 3443 Boiler shop products: boilers, smokestacks, steel tanks

**(P-8305)**
**CERTIFIED STAINLESS SVC INC**
Also Called: Westmark
441 Business Park Way, Atwater (95301-9499)
PHONE.................209 356-3300
Chris Portmann, Brnch Mgr
EMP: 76
SALES (corp-wide): 29.85MM Privately Held
Web: www.west-mark.com
SIC: 3443 3569 Tanks for tank trucks, metal plate; Firefighting and related equipment
PA: Certified Stainless Service Inc.
2704 Railroad Ave
209 537-4747

**(P-8306)**
**CERTIFIED STAINLESS SVC INC (PA)**
Also Called: West-Mark
2704 Railroad Ave, Ceres (95307-4600)
P.O. Box 100 (95307-0100)
PHONE.................209 537-4747
Scott Vincent, CEO
Grant Smith, *
Scott Vincent, Sec
Jack Smith, Stockholder*
Todd Vincent, *
▲ EMP: 40 EST: 1967
SQ FT: 64,000
SALES (est): 29.85MM
SALES (corp-wide): 29.85MM Privately Held
Web: www.west-mark.com

# PRODUCTS & SERVICES SECTION
## 3443 - Fabricated Plate Work (boiler Shop)

SIC: 3443 3715 7538  Tanks for tank trucks, metal plate; Truck trailers; General truck repair

### (P-8307) CERTIFIED STAINLESS SVC INC
Also Called: West-Mark
581 Industry Way, Atwater  (95301-9457)
P.O. Box 100  (95307-0100)
PHONE..............................209 537-4747
Grant Smith, *Brnch Mgr*
EMP: 87
SALES (corp-wide): 29.85MM **Privately Held**
Web: www.west-mark.com
SIC: 3443 3569  Tanks for tank trucks, metal plate; Firefighting and related equipment
PA: Certified Stainless Service Inc.
    2704 Railroad Ave
    209 537-4747

### (P-8308) CJI PROCESS SYSTEMS INC
Also Called: Lee Ray Sandblasting
12000 Clark St, Santa Fe Springs (90670-3709)
PHONE..............................562 777-0614
Archie Cholakian, *Pr*
John Cholakian, *
▼ EMP: 70 EST: 1982
SQ FT: 35,000
SALES (est): 8.88MM **Privately Held**
Web: www.cjiprocesssystems.com
SIC: 3443 3441 3444  Tanks, lined: metal plate; Fabricated structural metal; Sheet metalwork

### (P-8309) CMT SHEET METAL
22732 Granite Way Ste C, Laguna Hills (92653-1263)
PHONE..............................949 679-9868
Wes Hinze, *CEO*
Wes Hinze Junior, *Pr*
Gayle Hinze, *Sec*
EMP: 15 EST: 2000
SALES (est): 2.92MM **Privately Held**
SIC: 3443  Boiler and boiler shop work

### (P-8310) COMMERCIAL METAL FORMING INC
Also Called: Commercial Metal Forming
341 W Collins Ave, Orange  (92867-5505)
PHONE..............................714 532-6321
William Kowal, *Pr*
Donald E Washdewicz, *VP*
▲ EMP: 25 EST: 2003
SALES (est): 4.45MM **Privately Held**
Web: www.cmforming.com
SIC: 3443  Fabricated plate work (boiler shop)

### (P-8311) CONSOLIDATED FABRICATORS CORP (PA)
Also Called: Confab
14620 Arminta St, Van Nuys  (91402-5993)
PHONE..............................800 635-8335
Michael J Melideo, *CEO*
Jeff Lombardi, *
▲ EMP: 110 EST: 1974
SQ FT: 150,000
SALES (est): 26.61MM
SALES (corp-wide): 26.61MM **Privately Held**
Web: www.con-fab.com
SIC: 3443 5051 3444  Dumpsters, garbage; Steel; Studs and joists, sheet metal

### (P-8312) CONTAINMENT CONSULTANTS INC
Also Called: Ideal Envmtl Pdts & Svcs
110 Old Gilroy St, Gilroy  (95020-6948)
P.O. Box 307  (95021-0307)
PHONE..............................408 848-6998
Anne Anderson, *Pr*
EMP: 16 EST: 1992
SQ FT: 14,000
SALES (est): 2.4MM **Privately Held**
Web: www.chem-stor.com
SIC: 3443 8748  Tanks, standard or custom fabricated: metal plate; Environmental consultant

### (P-8313) COOK AND COOK INCORPORATED
Also Called: Royal Welding & Fabricating
1000 E Elm Ave, Fullerton  (92831-5022)
PHONE..............................714 680-6669
Wallace F Cook, *Pr*
Patricia Cook, *
EMP: 30 EST: 1967
SQ FT: 30,000
SALES (est): 4.74MM **Privately Held**
Web: www.royalwelding.com
SIC: 3443 3599 3444  Industrial vessels, tanks, and containers; Amusement park equipment; Sheet metalwork

### (P-8314) CRYOWEST INC
25 Hangar Way, Watsonville  (95076-2403)
PHONE..............................831 786-9721
John Wolfe, *Pr*
Rita Wolfe, *Prin*
◆ EMP: 30 EST: 2011
SALES (est): 2.5MM **Privately Held**
Web: www.cryowest.com
SIC: 3443  Cryogenic tanks, for liquids and gases

### (P-8315) DESOTEC US LLC
11711 Reading Rd, Red Bluff  (96080-9745)
PHONE..............................530 527-2664
Bryan Blackwell, *Brnch Mgr*
EMP: 30
SALES (corp-wide): 2.67MM **Privately Held**
Web: www.evoqua.com
SIC: 3443  Reactor containment vessels, metal plate
HQ: Desotec Us Llc
    118 Park Rd
    Darlington PA 16115
    724 827-8181

### (P-8316) ELITE ENGINEERING AND MFG LLC ✪
340 Martin Ave, Santa Clara  (95050-3112)
PHONE..............................408 988-3505
Dean Pettinga, *CFO*
Dean Pettinga, *Secretary General*
EMP: 30 EST: 2023
SALES (est): 2.57MM **Privately Held**
SIC: 3443 3559  Metal parts; Plastics working machinery

### (P-8317) HYUNDAI TRANSLEAD (HQ)
8880 Rio San Diego Dr Ste 600, San Diego (92108-1640)
PHONE..............................619 574-1500
Sean Kenney, *CEO*
Glen Harney, *
Jangsoo Choi, *
Hae Sung Park, *
▲ EMP: 87 EST: 1989
SALES (est): 440.44MM **Privately Held**
Web: www.translead.com
SIC: 3443 3715 3412  Industrial vessels, tanks, and containers; Semitrailers for truck tractors; Metal barrels, drums, and pails
PA: Hyundai Motor Company
    12 Heolleung-Ro, Seocho-Gu

### (P-8318) ITW BLDING CMPONENTS GROUP INC
Also Called: ITW Alpine
8801 Folsom Blvd Ste 107, Sacramento (95826-3249)
PHONE..............................916 387-0116
Sally Thomas, *Off Mgr*
EMP: 26
SALES (corp-wide): 16.11B **Publicly Held**
Web: www.itw.com
SIC: 3443 3469  Truss plates, metal; Stamping metal for the trade
HQ: Itw Building Components Group, Inc.
    13389 Lakefront Dr
    Earth City MO 63045
    314 344-9121

### (P-8319) JONNA CORPORATION INC
Also Called: Premiere Recycle
348 Phelan Ave, San Jose  (95112-4103)
PHONE..............................408 297-7910
Robert Hill, *Pr*
EMP: 50 EST: 1998
SALES (est): 5.02MM **Privately Held**
Web: www.premierrecycle.com
SIC: 3443 4953 4212  Dumpsters, garbage; Garbage: collecting, destroying, and processing; Local trucking, without storage

### (P-8320) MELCO STEEL INC
1100 W Foothill Blvd, Azusa  (91702-2818)
PHONE..............................626 334-7875
Michel Kashou, *Pr*
Mazin Kashou, *
Joann Reese, *
▲ EMP: 30 EST: 1971
SQ FT: 25,500
SALES (est): 4.43MM **Privately Held**
Web: www.melcosteel.com
SIC: 3443  Vessels, process or storage (from boiler shops): metal plate

### (P-8321) MODERN CUSTOM FABRICATION INC
4922 E Jensen Ave, Fresno  (93725-1806)
P.O. Box 11925  (93775-1925)
PHONE..............................559 264-4741
James E Jones, *CEO*
James W Gray, *
John W Jones, *
EMP: 35 EST: 2001
SALES (est): 12.72MM
SALES (corp-wide): 136.77MM **Privately Held**
Web: www.modweldco.com
SIC: 3443  Fabricated plate work (boiler shop)
PA: Modern Welding Company, Inc.
    2880 New Hartford Rd
    270 685-4400

### (P-8322) NATIONWIDE BOILER INCORPORATED (PA)
42400 Christy St, Fremont  (94538-3141)
PHONE..............................510 490-7100
Larry Day, *Pr*
James Hermerding, *
Michele Tomas, *Finance*
◆ EMP: 47 EST: 1967
SQ FT: 35,000
SALES (est): 20.1MM
SALES (corp-wide): 20.1MM **Privately Held**
Web: www.nationwideboiler.com
SIC: 3443  Fabricated plate work (boiler shop)

### (P-8323) NWPC LLC
Also Called: Northwest Pipe Company
10100 W Linne Rd, Tracy  (95377-9128)
PHONE..............................209 836-5050
Scott Montross, *CEO*
EMP: 75 EST: 2019
SALES (est): 39MM
SALES (corp-wide): 444.36MM **Publicly Held**
Web: www.nwpipe.com
SIC: 3443 3317  Fabricated plate work (boiler shop); Steel pipe and tubes
PA: Northwest Pipe Company
    201 Ne Pk Plz Dr Ste 100
    360 397-6250

### (P-8324) OMEGA II INC
Also Called: Omega Industrial Marine
3525 Main St, Chula Vista  (91911-5830)
PHONE..............................619 920-6650
Greg Lewis, *CEO*
Nicholas Ruiz, *MNG*
EMP: 39 EST: 1986
SALES (est): 3.82MM **Privately Held**
Web: www.omegaindustrial.net
SIC: 3443 1542 1629 1541  Air coolers, metal plate; Nonresidential construction, nec; Marine construction; Industrial buildings and warehouses

### (P-8325) PACIFIC STEAM EQUIPMENT INC
Also Called: P S E Boilers
11748 Slauson Ave, Santa Fe Springs (90670-2227)
PHONE..............................562 906-9292
William S M Shanahan Md, *Pr*
Shin Duk David Kang, *VP*
▲ EMP: 25 EST: 1954
SQ FT: 22,500
SALES (est): 3.67MM **Privately Held**
Web: www.pacificsteam.com
SIC: 3443 5074 3582 2841  Tanks, standard or custom fabricated: metal plate; Plumbing and hydronic heating supplies; Commercial laundry equipment; Soap and other detergents

### (P-8326) PACIFIC TANK & CNSTR INC
17995 E Highway 46, Shandon (93461-9636)
PHONE..............................805 237-2929
Tom Yanaga, *Mgr*
EMP: 30
Web: www.pacifictank.net
SIC: 3443  Fabricated plate work (boiler shop)
PA: Pacific Tank & Construction, Inc.
    31551 Avnida Los Cerritos

### (P-8327) PARKER-HANNIFIN CORPORATION
Hydraulic Accumulator Division
14087 Borate St, Santa Fe Springs (90670-5336)

## 3443 - Fabricated Plate Work (boiler Shop) (P-8328)

PHONE..................562 404-1938
Mark Gagnon, *Brnch Mgr*
**EMP:** 53
**SALES (corp-wide):** 19.93B **Publicly Held**
Web: www.parker.com
**SIC: 3443** 3052 2822 Fabricated plate work (boiler shop); Rubber and plastics hose and beltings; Synthetic rubber
**PA:** Parker-Hannifin Corporation
6035 Parkland Blvd
216 896-3000

### (P-8328)
### PLUCKYS DUMP RENTAL LLC
10136 Bowman Ave, South Gate (90280-6233)
PHONE..................323 540-3510
**EMP:** 45 **EST:** 2021
**SALES (est):** 1.08MM **Privately Held**
**SIC: 3443** Dumpsters, garbage

### (P-8329)
### PROTEC ARISAWA AMERICA INC
2455 Ash St, Vista (92081-8424)
PHONE..................760 599-4800
Lee Hancock, *Pr*
◆ **EMP:** 50 **EST:** 2005
**SALES (est):** 9.35MM **Privately Held**
Web: www.protec-arisawa.com
**SIC: 3443** Process vessels, industrial: metal plate

### (P-8330)
### RITE ENGINEERING & MANUFACTURING CORPORATION
5832 Garfield Ave, Commerce (90040-3605)
PHONE..................562 862-2135
**EMP:** 25 **EST:** 1952
**SALES (est):** 5.96MM **Privately Held**
Web: www.riteboiler.com
**SIC: 3443** Boilers: industrial, power, or marine

### (P-8331)
### ROY E HANSON JR MFG (PA)
Also Called: Hanson Tank
1600 E Washington Blvd, Los Angeles (90021-3123)
P.O. Box 30507 (90030-0507)
PHONE..................213 747-7514
Jonathan Goss, *CEO*
Johnathan Goss, *
Cliff Jones, *
Thys Dorenbosch, *
Dorothy Griffen, *
▼ **EMP:** 80 **EST:** 1932
**SQ FT:** 55,000
**SALES (est):** 10.18MM
**SALES (corp-wide):** 10.18MM **Privately Held**
Web: www.hansontank.com
**SIC: 3443** Fuel tanks (oil, gas, etc.), metal plate

### (P-8332)
### S & H WELDING INC
8604 Elder Creek Rd, Sacramento (95828-1803)
PHONE..................916 386-8921
John Jones, *Pr*
**EMP:** 15 **EST:** 1990
**SQ FT:** 10,000
**SALES (est):** 2.49MM **Privately Held**
**SIC: 3443** Fabricated plate work (boiler shop)

### (P-8333)
### S BRAVO SYSTEMS INC
Also Called: Bravo Support
2929 Vail Ave, Los Angeles (90040-2615)
PHONE..................323 888-4133
Paola Bravo Recendez, *CEO*
▲ **EMP:** 26 **EST:** 1986
**SQ FT:** 40,000
**SALES (est):** 10MM **Privately Held**
Web: www.sbravo.com
**SIC: 3443** Containers, shipping (bombs, etc.): metal plate

### (P-8334)
### SAN-I-PAK PACIFIC INC
23535 S Bird Rd, Tracy (95304)
P.O. Box 1183 (95378)
PHONE..................209 836-2310
Roman Flores, *Pr*
John L Hall, *
Wilburn Hall, *
**EMP:** 69 **EST:** 1982
**SQ FT:** 25,000
**SALES (est):** 9.44MM **Privately Held**
Web: www.sanipak.com
**SIC: 3443** 3821 Sterilizing chambers, metal plate; Sterilizers

### (P-8335)
### SID E PARKER BOILER MFG CO INC
Also Called: Parker Boiler Co
5930 Bandini Blvd, Commerce (90040-2903)
PHONE..................323 727-9800
Sid D Danenhauer, *Ch Bd*
Greg G Danenhauer, *
Ed Marchak, *
◆ **EMP:** 66 **EST:** 1939
**SQ FT:** 80,000
**SALES (est):** 9.23MM **Privately Held**
Web: www.parkerboiler.com
**SIC: 3443** 3433 Boilers: industrial, power, or marine; Heating equipment, except electric

### (P-8336)
### SONOMA STAINLESS INC
Also Called: Fabricator
170 Todd Rd, Santa Rosa (95407-8155)
PHONE..................707 546-3945
Vincent Frere, *Pr*
Andre Frere, *Pr*
**EMP:** 15 **EST:** 2013
**SALES (est):** 3.36MM **Privately Held**
Web: www.sonomastainless.com
**SIC: 3443** Fabricated plate work (boiler shop)

### (P-8337)
### SOUTH GATE ENGINEERING LLC
13477 Yorba Ave, Chino (91710-5055)
PHONE..................909 628-2779
William Paolino, *Managing Member*
**EMP:** 115 **EST:** 1947
**SALES (est):** 22.09MM **Privately Held**
Web: www.southgateengineering.com
**SIC: 3443** Vessels, process or storage (from boiler shops): metal plate

### (P-8338)
### SPX COOLING TECH LLC
Also Called: Recold
550 Mercury Ln, Brea (92821-4830)
PHONE..................714 529-6080
Doug Vickers, *Brnch Mgr*
**EMP:** 18
**SALES (corp-wide):** 1.83B **Privately Held**
Web: www.spxcooling.com
**SIC: 3443** Fabricated plate work (boiler shop)
**HQ:** Canvas Ct, Llc
7401 W 129th St
Overland Park KS 66213
913 664-7400

### (P-8339)
### SPX FLOW US LLC
Also Called: A P V Crepaco
26561 Rancho Pkwy S, Lake Forest (92630-8301)
PHONE..................949 455-8150
Brian Ahern, *Mgr*
**EMP:** 39
**SALES (corp-wide):** 1.78B **Privately Held**
**SIC: 3443** Fabricated plate work (boiler shop)
**HQ:** Spx Flow Us, Llc
135 Mt Read Blvd
Rochester NY 14611
585 436-5550

### (P-8340)
### STEEL STRUCTURES INC
28777 Avenue 15 1/2, Madera (93638-2316)
PHONE..................559 673-8021
Daniel Riley, *Pr*
Tracy Riley, *VP*
**EMP:** 22 **EST:** 1953
**SQ FT:** 44,000
**SALES (est):** 3.83MM **Privately Held**
Web: www.steelstructuresinc.com
**SIC: 3443** Tanks, standard or custom fabricated: metal plate

### (P-8341)
### STRUCTURAL COMPOSITES INDS LLC (DH)
Also Called: SCI
336 Enterprise Pl, Pomona (91768-3244)
PHONE..................909 594-7777
Ken Miller, *Managing Member*
◆ **EMP:** 49 **EST:** 2007
**SALES (est):** 33.29MM
**SALES (corp-wide):** 405MM **Privately Held**
**SIC: 3443** Tanks, lined: metal plate
**HQ:** Luxfer Inc.
3016 Kansas Ave Bldg 1
Riverside CA 92507
951 684-5110

### (P-8342)
### SUPERIOR STORAGE TANK INC
Also Called: Superior
14700 Industry Cir, La Mirada (90638-5817)
PHONE..................714 226-1914
Griff Williams, *CEO*
Rob Henderson, *COO*
**EMP:** 15 **EST:** 2010
**SALES (est):** 2.99MM **Privately Held**
Web: www.superior-tanks.com
**SIC: 3443** 7692 Fuel tanks (oil, gas, etc.), metal plate; Welding repair

### (P-8343)
### SUPERIOR TANK CO INC (PA)
Also Called: Stci
9500 Lucas Ranch Rd, Rancho Cucamonga (91730-5724)
PHONE..................909 912-0580
Jesus Eric Marquez, *Pr*
George Marquez, *
Lewis A Marquez, *
◆ **EMP:** 50 **EST:** 1984
**SQ FT:** 53,392
**SALES (est):** 44.83MM
**SALES (corp-wide):** 44.83MM **Privately Held**
Web: www.superiortank.com
**SIC: 3443** 3494 1791 1794 Fuel tanks (oil, gas, etc.), metal plate; Valves and pipe fittings, nec; Structural steel erection; Excavation work

### (P-8344)
### TAIT & ASSOCIATES INC
2131 S Dupont Dr, Anaheim (92806-6102)
PHONE..................714 560-8222
Jim Streipz, *Brnch Mgr*
**EMP:** 49
**SALES (corp-wide):** 23.79MM **Privately Held**
Web: www.tait.com
**SIC: 3443** Fuel tanks (oil, gas, etc.), metal plate
**PA:** Tait & Associates, Inc.
701 N Park Center Dr
866 584-0283

### (P-8345)
### TARICCO CORP
1500 W 16th St, Long Beach (90813-1211)
PHONE..................562 437-5433
**EMP:** 16 **EST:** 1987
**SALES (est):** 4.6MM **Privately Held**
Web: www.taricco.com
**SIC: 3443** 3491 Autoclaves, industrial; Process control regulator valves

### (P-8346)
### THERMLLY ENGNRED MNFCTRED PDTS
Also Called: T E M P
543 W 135th St, Gardena (90248-1505)
PHONE..................310 523-9934
Robert Greenwood, *Pr*
Binh Vinh, *
▲ **EMP:** 27 **EST:** 1994
**SQ FT:** 50,000
**SALES (est):** 5.08MM **Privately Held**
Web: www.tempinc.com
**SIC: 3443** Heat exchangers, condensers, and components

### (P-8347)
### THOMPSON TANK INC
8029 Phlox St, Downey (90241-4816)
P.O. Box 790 (90714-0790)
PHONE..................562 869-7711
David B Thompson, *Pr*
Robert I Grue, *Treas*
**EMP:** 19 **EST:** 1993
**SQ FT:** 225,000
**SALES (est):** 4.57MM **Privately Held**
Web: www.thompsontank.com
**SIC: 3443** 7699 3715 3713 Tanks, standard or custom fabricated: metal plate; Tank repair and cleaning services; Truck trailers; Truck and bus bodies

### (P-8348)
### TODD STREET INC
Also Called: Schweitzers Metal Fabricators
770 N Todd Ave, Azusa (91702-2227)
P.O. Box 963 (91702-0963)
PHONE..................626 815-1175
Jerry Childress, *Pr*
Frank Lewis, *Sec*
**EMP:** 20 **EST:** 1939
**SALES (est):** 5.11MM **Privately Held**
Web: www.toddstreetinc.com
**SIC: 3443** Tanks, standard or custom fabricated: metal plate

### (P-8349)
### UNIVERSAL DEFENSE
412 Cucamonga Ave, Claremont (91711-5019)
P.O. Box 1372 (91711-1372)

# PRODUCTS & SERVICES SECTION
## 3444 - Sheet Metalwork (P-8371)

**PHONE**.................909 626-4178
**EMP:** 20
**SALES (est):** 1.72MM **Privately Held**
**SIC: 3443** Fabricated plate work (boiler shop)

### (P-8350)
### UTTAM COMPOSITES LLC
11700 Monarch St, Garden Grove (92841-1819)
**PHONE**.................714 894-5300
Mary Leonard, *Brnch Mgr*
**EMP:** 16
**Web:** www.uttam.com
**SIC: 3443** Cylinders, pressure: metal plate
**HQ:** Uttam Composites, Llc
  1409 Post Oak Blvd
  Houston TX 77056
  202 644-3222

### (P-8351)
### WAGNER PLATE WORKS WEST INC (PA)
Also Called: P V T Supply
28100 Shady Meadow Ln, Yorba Linda (92887-5828)
**PHONE**.................562 531-6050
Jack Brian Purtell, *Pr*
**EMP:** 21 **EST:** 1994
**SALES (est):** 4.6MM **Privately Held**
**SIC: 3443** 5051 Tanks, lined: metal plate; Pipe and tubing, steel

### (P-8352)
### WATERCREST INC
4850 E Airport Dr, Ontario (91761-7818)
**PHONE**.................909 390-3944
Jeremiah B Robins, *CEO*
Gary F Johnson, *Pr*
▲ **EMP:** 28 **EST:** 1996
**SQ FT:** 29,000
**SALES (est):** 3.26MM **Privately Held**
**Web:** www.yinluntdi.com
**SIC: 3443** Heat exchangers, condensers, and components

### (P-8353)
### WELLS STRUTHERS CORPORATION
Also Called: Tei Struthers Wells
10375 Slusher Dr, Santa Fe Springs (90670-3748)
**PHONE**.................814 726-1000
John C Wallace, *Pr*
John M Carey, *
Burton M Abrams, *
**EMP:** 30 **EST:** 1937
**SQ FT:** 30,000
**SALES (est):** 597.46K **Privately Held**
**SIC: 3443** Heat exchangers, plate type

### (P-8354)
### WORTHINGTON CYLINDER CORP
336 Enterprise Pl, Pomona (91768-3244)
**PHONE**.................909 594-7777
**EMP:** 154
**SALES (corp-wide):** 1.25B **Publicly Held**
**Web:** www.worthingtonenterprises.com
**SIC: 3443** Cylinders, pressure: metal plate
**HQ:** Worthington Cylinder Corporation
  200 W Old Wilson Bridge Rd
  Worthington OH 43085
  614 840-3210

### (P-8355)
### XCHANGER MANUFACTURING CORP
Also Called: Wiegmann & Rose
849 Jackson St, Benicia (94510-2907)
P.O. Box 4187 (94614-4187)
**PHONE**.................510 632-8828
Scott E Logan, *Pr*
**EMP:** 21 **EST:** 1950
**SALES (est):** 2.66MM **Privately Held**
**Web:** www.wiegmannandrose.com
**SIC: 3443** Heat exchangers: coolers (after, inter), condensers, etc.

### (P-8356)
### XKT ENGINEERING INC
Also Called: Nesco Fabricators
390 Railroad Ave, Vallejo (94592-1002)
P.O. Box 152 (94590-0015)
**PHONE**.................707 562-2500
**EMP:** 85 **EST:** 1986
**SALES (est):** 1.3MM **Privately Held**
**Web:** www.xktengineering.com
**SIC: 3443** Fabricated plate work (boiler shop)

## 3444 Sheet Metalwork

### (P-8357)
### A & J PRECISION SHEETMETAL INC
2233 Paragon Dr Ste A, San Jose (95131-1339)
**PHONE**.................408 885-9134
Amrik Atwal, *CEO*
Amrik Atwal, *Pr*
Jagtar Atwal, *
Suki Atwal, *
▲ **EMP:** 52 **EST:** 1994
**SALES (est):** 4.41MM **Privately Held**
**Web:** www.ajsheetmetal.com
**SIC: 3444** Sheet metalwork

### (P-8358)
### A-1 METAL PRODUCTS INC
2707 Supply Ave, Commerce (90040-2703)
**PHONE**.................323 721-3334
Jerry Calsbeek, *Pr*
Patricia Calsbeek, *
**EMP:** 24 **EST:** 1952
**SQ FT:** 40,000
**SALES (est):** 3.11MM **Privately Held**
**Web:** www.a1metalproducts.com
**SIC: 3444** Sheet metal specialties, not stamped

### (P-8359)
### ABLE SHEET METAL INC (PA)
614 N Ford Blvd, Los Angeles (90022-1195)
**PHONE**.................323 269-2181
Dmitri Triphon, *CEO*
Gurgen Tovmasyan, *General Vice President*
◆ **EMP:** 40 **EST:** 2001
**SQ FT:** 25,000
**SALES (est):** 7.98MM
**SALES (corp-wide):** 7.98MM **Privately Held**
**Web:** www.ablemetal.com
**SIC: 3444** Sheet metal specialties, not stamped

### (P-8360)
### ACCURATE HEATING & COOLING INC
Also Called: Tru-Fit Manufacturing
3515 Yosemite Ave, Lathrop (95330-9748)
**PHONE**.................209 858-4125
**TOLL FREE:** 800
Joan Kauffman, *Pr*
Jill Brandenburg, *
Melvin Kauffman, *Stockholder*
**EMP:** 23 **EST:** 1954
**SQ FT:** 30,000
**SALES (est):** 2.53MM **Privately Held**
**Web:** www.deltaac.com
**SIC: 3444** Ducts, sheet metal

### (P-8361)
### ADAMS-CAMPBELL COMPANY LTD (PA)
Also Called: Accent Ceilings
15343 Proctor Ave, City Of Industry (91745-1022)
P.O. Box 3867 (91744-0867)
**PHONE**.................626 330-3425
**EMP:** 74 **EST:** 1909
**SALES (est):** 12MM
**SALES (corp-wide):** 12MM **Privately Held**
**Web:** www.adamscampbell.com
**SIC: 3444** 3469 3431 Sheet metalwork; Metal stampings, nec; Metal sanitary ware

### (P-8362)
### ADVANCED METAL MFG INC
49 Strathearn Pl, Simi Valley (93065-1653)
**PHONE**.................805 322-4161
Scott Stewart, *CEO*
Gina Stewart Ctrl, *Prin*
▲ **EMP:** 30 **EST:** 2010
**SALES (est):** 4.13MM **Privately Held**
**Web:** www.advancedmetalmfg.com
**SIC: 3444** Sheet metalwork

### (P-8363)
### ADVANCED MFG & DEV INC
Also Called: Metalfx
200 N Lenore Ave, Willits (95490-3209)
**PHONE**.................707 459-9451
Henry Moss, *Pr*
▲ **EMP:** 205 **EST:** 1976
**SQ FT:** 65,000
**SALES (est):** 18.68MM **Privately Held**
**Web:** www.metalfx.com
**SIC: 3444** 2541 3469 3567 Housings for business machines, sheet metal; Cabinets, except refrigerated: show, display, etc.: wood; Metal stampings, nec; Industrial furnaces and ovens
**PA:** Montage Partners, Llc
  6720 N Scttsdale Rd Ste 3

### (P-8364)
### ADVANTAGE METAL PRODUCTS INC
Also Called: Segundo Metal Products, Inc.
7855 Southfront Rd, Livermore (94551)
**PHONE**.................925 667-2009
Mike Segundo, *Pr*
Phil Segundo, *
▲ **EMP:** 80 **EST:** 1988
**SQ FT:** 60,000
**SALES (est):** 18.88MM
**SALES (corp-wide):** 2.37B **Privately Held**
**Web:** www.advantagemetal.com
**SIC: 3444** Sheet metalwork
**PA:** Middleground Management, Lp
  1500 Aristides Blvd

### (P-8365)
### AERO ARC
16634 S Figueroa St, Gardena (90248-2627)
**PHONE**.................310 324-3400
**EMP:** 38 **EST:** 1984
**SALES (est):** 10.47MM **Privately Held**
**Web:** www.aeroarc.com
**SIC: 3444** 3498 Sheet metalwork; Fabricated pipe and fittings

### (P-8366)
### AERO BENDING COMPANY
560 Auto Center Dr Ste A, Palmdale (93551-4485)
**PHONE**.................661 948-2363
Robert Burns, *Pr*
**EMP:** 80 **EST:** 1944
**SQ FT:** 26,000
**SALES (est):** 1.45MM **Privately Held**
**Web:** www.aerobendingco.com
**SIC: 3444** 5088 Sheet metalwork; Aircraft engines and engine parts

### (P-8367)
### AERO PRECISION ENGINEERING
11300 Hindry Ave, Los Angeles (90045-6228)
**PHONE**.................310 642-9747
Sherry L Martinez, *Pr*
Tom Segotta, *
**EMP:** 45 **EST:** 1984
**SQ FT:** 55,000
**SALES (est):** 10.27MM **Privately Held**
**Web:** www.aeroprecisioneng.com
**SIC: 3444** 3599 Sheet metal specialties, not stamped; Machine shop, jobbing and repair

### (P-8368)
### AIRTRONICS METAL PRODUCTS INC (PA)
140 San Pedro Ave, Morgan Hill (95037-5123)
**PHONE**.................408 977-7800
Jeff Burke, *CEO*
John Richardson, *
Fermin Rodriguez, *
James Ellis, *
▲ **EMP:** 211 **EST:** 1962
**SQ FT:** 55,000
**SALES (est):** 22.35MM
**SALES (corp-wide):** 22.35MM **Privately Held**
**Web:** www.airtronics.com
**SIC: 3444** 3479 Sheet metalwork; Painting, coating, and hot dipping

### (P-8369)
### ALL-WAYS METAL INC
401 E Alondra Blvd, Gardena (90248-2901)
**PHONE**.................310 217-1177
Shirley Pickens, *Pr*
Scott Pickens, *
**EMP:** 30 **EST:** 1983
**SQ FT:** 29,000
**SALES (est):** 2.6MM **Privately Held**
**Web:** www.allwaysmetal.com
**SIC: 3444** Sheet metal specialties, not stamped

### (P-8370)
### ALLIANCE METAL PRODUCTS INC
20844 Plummer St, Chatsworth (91311-5004)
**PHONE**.................818 709-1204
Dan L Rowlett Junior, *CEO*
**EMP:** 212 **EST:** 2002
**SQ FT:** 2,000
**SALES (est):** 3.44MM **Privately Held**
**Web:** www.alliancemp.com
**SIC: 3444** Sheet metal specialties, not stamped

### (P-8371)
### AMD INTERNATIONAL TECH LLC
Also Called: International Rite-Way Pdts
1725 S Campus Ave, Ontario (91761-4346)
**PHONE**.................909 985-8300
**EMP:** 25 **EST:** 1994
**SQ FT:** 17,000
**SALES (est):** 3.67MM **Privately Held**
**Web:** www.intlrwp.com
**SIC: 3444** 1761 Sheet metal specialties, not stamped; Sheet metal work, nec

## 3444 - Sheet Metalwork (P-8372)

**(P-8372)**
**AMERICAN AIRCRAFT PRODUCTS INC**
Also Called: A A P
15411 S Broadway, Gardena (90248-2207)
PHONE..................310 532-7434
Gerald R Tupper, Pr
EMP: 67 EST: 1975
SQ FT: 54,000
SALES (est): 9.77MM Privately Held
Web: www.americanaircraft.com
SIC: 3444 3599 Sheet metalwork; Machine shop, jobbing and repair

**(P-8373)**
**AMERICAN RANGE CORPORATION**
13592 Desmond St, Pacoima (91331-2315)
PHONE..................818 897-0808
Lorne G Deacon, Pr
Cindy M Cervantes, *
▲ EMP: 120 EST: 1989
SQ FT: 125,000
SALES (est): 22.74MM
SALES (corp-wide): 48.03MM Privately Held
Web: www.americanrange.com
SIC: 3444 3631 Hoods, range: sheet metal; Household cooking equipment
PA: Hatco Corporation
635 S 28th St
414 671-6350

**(P-8374)**
**AMF ANAHEIM LLC**
2100 E Orangewood Ave, Anaheim (92806-6108)
PHONE..................714 363-9206
▲ EMP: 120
SIC: 3444 Sheet metalwork

**(P-8375)**
**ANDRUS SHEET METAL INC**
Also Called: Seaport Stainless
5021 Seaport Ave, Richmond (94804-4638)
PHONE..................510 232-8687
Ray Doving, Pr
Linda Doving, *
EMP: 30 EST: 1977
SQ FT: 14,000
SALES (est): 4.64MM Privately Held
Web: www.seaportstainless.com
SIC: 3444 Restaurant sheet metalwork

**(P-8376)**
**ANOROC PRECISION SHTMTL INC**
Also Called: Anoroc
19122 S Santa Fe Ave, Compton (90221-5910)
PHONE..................310 515-6015
Roxanne Zavala, CEO
Pete Corona, Lending Vice President*
EMP: 25 EST: 1978
SQ FT: 15,000
SALES (est): 2.06MM Privately Held
Web: www.anoroc.com
SIC: 3444 Sheet metal specialties, not stamped

**(P-8377)**
**AP PRECISION METALS INC**
1185 Park Center Dr, Vista (92081)
PHONE..................619 628-0003
Lane A Litke, CEO
Victor B Miller, *
Susan D Miller, *
EMP: 35 EST: 2000
SALES (est): 13.43MM Privately Held

Web: www.apprecision.com
SIC: 3444 Sheet metalwork

**(P-8378)**
**ARMORCAST PRODUCTS COMPANY INC (DH)**
9140 Lurline Ave, Chatsworth (91311-5923)
PHONE..................818 982-3600
▲ EMP: 220 EST: 1972
SALES (est): 42.41MM
SALES (corp-wide): 5.37B Publicly Held
Web: www.armorcastprod.com
SIC: 3444 3089 Sheet metalwork; Plastics processing
HQ: Hubbell Lenoir City, Inc.
3621 Industrial Park Dr
Lenoir City TN 37771
865 986-9726

**(P-8379)**
**ARRK NORTH AMERICA INC**
4660 La Jolla Village Dr Ste 100, San Diego (92122-4604)
PHONE..................858 552-1587
Carlos Herrera, Pr
Koji Tsujino, *
Takuya Kasai, *
▲ EMP: 145 EST: 1984
SALES (est): 17.46MM Privately Held
Web: www.arrk.com
SIC: 3444 Sheet metalwork
HQ: Arrk Corporation
2-2-9, Minamihonmachi, Chuo-Ku
Osaka OSK 541-0

**(P-8380)**
**ARROYO HOLDINGS INC (PA)**
898 N Fair Oaks Ave, Pasadena (91103-3068)
PHONE..................626 765-9340
Michael C Doyle, Pr
EMP: 15 EST: 1985
SALES (est): 2.43MM
SALES (corp-wide): 2.43MM Privately Held
SIC: 3444 3669 8111 Sheet metalwork; Pedestrian traffic control equipment; Will, estate and trust law

**(P-8381)**
**ARTISTIC WELDING**
Also Called: Precision Sheet Metal
505 E Gardena Blvd, Gardena (90248-2915)
PHONE..................310 515-4922
George R Sandoval, Pr
Mary Sandoval, *
EMP: 65 EST: 1974
SQ FT: 85,000
SALES (est): 5.97MM Privately Held
Web: www.artistic-welding.com
SIC: 3444 Sheet metalwork

**(P-8382)**
**ARTS SHEET METAL MFG INC**
16075 Caputo Dr, Morgan Hill (95037-5533)
PHONE..................408 778-0606
EMP: 55 EST: 1989
SALES (est): 7.4MM Privately Held
SIC: 3444 Sheet metalwork

**(P-8383)**
**ASM CONSTRUCTION INC**
Also Called: American Sheet Metal
1947 John Towers Ave, El Cajon (92020-1117)
PHONE..................619 449-1966
Robert Burner, Pr
Ron Burner Junior, CFO

EMP: 41 EST: 1993
SQ FT: 9,000
SALES (est): 2.37MM Privately Held
SIC: 3444 Sheet metalwork

**(P-8384)**
**ASM PRECISION INC**
613 Martin Ave Ste 106, Rohnert Park (94928-2050)
PHONE..................707 584-7950
Mario R Felciano, Pr
Jay Sandoval, VP
EMP: 15 EST: 2007
SQ FT: 9,000
SALES (est): 3.86MM Privately Held
Web: www.asmprecision.com
SIC: 3444 Sheet metal specialties, not stamped

**(P-8385)**
**ATCO RUBBER PRODUCTS INC**
1701 Diesel Dr, Sacramento (95838-2435)
PHONE..................916 649-8690
Marcia Kitchell, Mgr
EMP: 71
Web: www.atcoflex.com
SIC: 3444 Sheet metal specialties, not stamped
HQ: Atco Rubber Products, Inc.
7101 Atco Dr
Fort Worth TX 76118
817 595-2894

**(P-8386)**
**ATLAS SHEET METAL INC**
11614 Martens River Cir, Fountain Valley (92708-4204)
PHONE..................949 600-8787
James M Odlum, Pr
EMP: 17 EST: 1998
SALES (est): 5.08MM Privately Held
Web: www.atlassheetmetal.com
SIC: 3444 Sheet metalwork

**(P-8387)**
**BARZILLAI MANUFACTURING CO INC**
1889 N Omalley Way, Upland (91784-8712)
PHONE..................909 947-4200
Ray Richmond, Pr
Garrett Zopf, Treas
EMP: 17 EST: 2003
SALES (est): 1.99MM Privately Held
SIC: 3444 Sheet metalwork

**(P-8388)**
**BASMAT INC (PA)**
Also Called: McStarlite
1531 240th St, Harbor City (90710-1308)
PHONE..................310 325-2063
John W Basso, CEO
John Allen Basso, *
Sharon Stelter, *
▲ EMP: 100 EST: 1952
SQ FT: 42,000
SALES (est): 19.67MM
SALES (corp-wide): 19.67MM Privately Held
Web: www.mcstarlite.com
SIC: 3444 Sheet metalwork

**(P-8389)**
**BAY CITIES TIN SHOP INC**
Also Called: Bay Cities Metal Products
301 E Alondra Blvd, Gardena (90248-2809)
PHONE..................310 660-0351
Majid Abai, CEO
Henry Kamberg, *
Gary Mugford, *
Debra Childress, *

EMP: 170 EST: 1958
SALES (est): 17.53MM Privately Held
Web: www.bcmet.com
SIC: 3444 Sheet metal specialties, not stamped

**(P-8390)**
**BAY SHEET METAL INC**
9343 Bond Ave Ste C, El Cajon (92021-2839)
PHONE..................619 401-9270
Michael Hayes, Pr
EMP: 28 EST: 2000
SALES (est): 3.49MM Privately Held
Web: www.westernbay.net
SIC: 3444 Sheet metalwork

**(P-8391)**
**BEND-TEK INC (PA)**
2205 S Yale St, Santa Ana (92704-4426)
PHONE..................714 210-8966
Melinda Nguyen, CEO
Mac Le, Ofcr
Eric Tran, CFO
EMP: 46 EST: 1999
SQ FT: 7,000
SALES (est): 7.72MM
SALES (corp-wide): 7.72MM Privately Held
Web: www.bendtekinc.com
SIC: 3444 Pipe, sheet metal

**(P-8392)**
**BMB METAL PRODUCTS CORPORATION**
Also Called: B M B
11460 Elks Cir, Rancho Cordova (95742-7332)
PHONE..................916 631-9120
Jerry Mc Donald, Pr
EMP: 24 EST: 1966
SQ FT: 23,000
SALES (est): 3.24MM Privately Held
Web: bmbmetalproductsc.openfos.com
SIC: 3444 Sheet metalwork

**(P-8393)**
**BOOZAK INC**
Also Called: K Squared Metals
508 Chaney St Ste A, Lake Elsinore (92530-2797)
PHONE..................951 245-6045
Kevin Kluzak, Pr
Kevin Booth, *
EMP: 45 EST: 2004
SALES (est): 2.35MM Privately Held
SIC: 3444 Sheet metal specialties, not stamped

**(P-8394)**
**BROADWAY AC HTG & SHTMTL**
Also Called: Broadway Sheet Metal
7855 Burnet Ave, Van Nuys (91405-1010)
PHONE..................818 781-1477
Alexander Merzel, Pr
Vince Lombardo, *
Anna Merzel, *
EMP: 35 EST: 1926
SQ FT: 7,000
SALES (est): 2.08MM Privately Held
Web: www.broadwaysm.com
SIC: 3444 Sheet metalwork

**(P-8395)**
**BRYDENSCOT METAL PRODUCTS INC**
1299 Riverview Dr, San Bernardino (92408-2955)
PHONE..................909 799-0088

## PRODUCTS & SERVICES SECTION
### 3444 - Sheet Metalwork (P-8417)

EMP: 18 EST: 1983
SALES (est): 3.2MM **Privately Held**
Web: www.brydenscot.com
SIC: **3444** Sheet metalwork

**(P-8396)**
**BUXCON SHEETMETAL INC**
11222 Woodside Ave N, Santee (92071-4716)
PHONE..................................619 937-0001
Richard Buxton, *Pr*
Thomas Buxton, *CFO*
Larry Henry, *Sec*
EMP: 15 EST: 2000
SQ FT: 18,138
SALES (est): 4.46MM **Privately Held**
Web: www.buxconsheetmetal.com
SIC: **3444** Sheet metalwork

**(P-8397)**
**C & K JOHNSON INDUSTRIES INC**
Also Called: Johnson Industries
1061 Samoa Blvd, Arcata (95521-6605)
PHONE..................................707 822-7687
EMP: 20 EST: 1982
SALES (est): 6.5MM **Privately Held**
Web: www.ckjohnsonind.com
SIC: **3444** Pipe, sheet metal

**(P-8398)**
**C&O MANUFACTURING COMPANY INC**
9640 Beverly Rd, Pico Rivera (90660-2137)
PHONE..................................562 692-7525
Cesar Gonzalez, *Pr*
Oscar Valdez, *
EMP: 67 EST: 1995
SQ FT: 22,000
SALES (est): 9.27MM **Privately Held**
Web: www.cnomfg.com
SIC: **3444** Sheet metal specialties, not stamped

**(P-8399)**
**CAL PAC SHEET METAL INC**
Also Called: Cal Pac Sheet Metal
2720 S Main St Ste B, Santa Ana (92707-3404)
PHONE..................................714 979-2733
Marushkah Kurtz, *CEO*
Bob Catalano, *
Carolyn Miller, *
EMP: 40 EST: 1977
SQ FT: 5,000
SALES (est): 4.53MM **Privately Held**
Web: www.calpacsheetmetal.com
SIC: **3444** Sheet metal specialties, not stamped

**(P-8400)**
**CAL-COAST MANUFACTURING INC**
424 S Tegner Rd, Turlock (95380-9406)
P.O. Box 1864 (95381-1864)
PHONE..................................209 634-9026
Lewis E Baptista, *Pr*
Larry Baptista, *VP*
Dolores Baptista, *Sec*
EMP: 15 EST: 1970
SALES (est): 3.27MM **Privately Held**
Web: www.calcoastinc.com
SIC: **3444** 1542 Sheet metalwork; Agricultural building contractors

**(P-8401)**
**CALIFORNIA CHASSIS INC**
3356 E La Palma Ave, Anaheim (92806-2814)
PHONE..................................714 666-8511
EMP: 110 EST: 1947
SALES (est): 1.7MM
SALES (corp-wide): 2.43MM **Privately Held**
SIC: **3444** 2522 Metal housings, enclosures, casings, and other containers; Office furniture, except wood
PA: Arroyo Holdings Inc
898 N Fair Oaks Ave
626 765-9340

**(P-8402)**
**CALIFORNIA HYDROFORMING CO INC**
850 Lawson St, City Of Industry (91748-1103)
PHONE..................................626 912-0036
David Bonafede, *Pr*
David Wickey, *VP*
EMP: 15 EST: 1956
SQ FT: 17,500
SALES (est): 2.15MM **Privately Held**
Web: www.californiahydroforming.com
SIC: **3444** 3469 Sheet metalwork; Stamping metal for the trade

**(P-8403)**
**CAPTIVE-AIRE SYSTEMS INC**
1123 Washington Ave, Santa Monica (90403-4159)
PHONE..................................310 876-8505
EMP: 23
SALES (corp-wide): 485.13MM **Privately Held**
Web: www.captiveaire.com
SIC: **3444** Sheet metalwork
PA: Captive-Aire Systems, Inc.
4641 Pragon Pk Rd Ste 104
919 882-2410

**(P-8404)**
**CAPTIVE-AIRE SYSTEMS INC**
6856 Lockheed Dr, Redding (96002-9769)
PHONE..................................530 351-7150
Csaba Sikur, *Brnch Mgr*
EMP: 140
SALES (corp-wide): 485.13MM **Privately Held**
Web: www.captiveair.com
SIC: **3444** Metal ventilating equipment
PA: Captive-Aire Systems, Inc.
4641 Pragon Pk Rd Ste 104
919 882-2410

**(P-8405)**
**CARLA SENTER**
Also Called: Swift Fab
515 E Alondra Blvd, Gardena (90248-2903)
PHONE..................................310 366-7295
Carla Senter, *Owner*
Robert Senter, *Owner*
EMP: 18 EST: 1988
SQ FT: 6,000
SALES (est): 2.65MM **Privately Held**
Web: www.swiftfab.com
SIC: **3444** Sheet metal specialties, not stamped

**(P-8406)**
**CARTEL INDUSTRIES LLC**
Also Called: Cartel Industries
17152 Armstrong Ave, Irvine (92614-5718)
PHONE..................................949 474-3200
Gant Penick, *
▲ EMP: 49 EST: 1971
SQ FT: 30,000
SALES (est): 9.68MM **Privately Held**
Web: www.cartelind.com

SIC: **3444** Sheet metal specialties, not stamped

**(P-8407)**
**CASTLE INDUSTRIES INC OF CALIFORNIA**
Also Called: M.C. Gill
4056 Easy St, El Monte (91731-1054)
PHONE..................................909 390-0899
EMP: 48
SIC: **3444** Sheet metalwork

**(P-8408)**
**CELESTICA INC**
40725 Encyclopedia Cir, Fremont (94538-2451)
PHONE..................................408 727-0880
Robert A Mionis, *Brnch Mgr*
EMP: 59
SALES (corp-wide): 7.96B **Privately Held**
Web: www.celestica.com
SIC: **3444** Sheet metalwork
PA: Celestica Inc
1900-5140 Yonge St
416 448-5800

**(P-8409)**
**CEMCO LLC (DH)**
Also Called: Cemco Steel
13191 Crossroads Pkwy N Ste 325, City Of Industry (91746-3438)
PHONE..................................800 775-2362
Tom Porter, *Pr*
Toshihiko Iizuka, *
◆ EMP: 68 EST: 1973
SQ FT: 40,000
SALES (est): 78.14MM **Privately Held**
Web: www.cemcosteel.com
SIC: **3444** Sheet metalwork
HQ: Shoji Jfe America Holdings Inc
301 E Ocean Blvd Ste 1750
Long Beach CA 90802
562 637-3500

**(P-8410)**
**CLARKWESTERN DIETRICH BUILDING**
Also Called: Clarkdietrich Building Systems
6510 General Rd, Riverside (92509-0103)
PHONE..................................951 360-3500
Clark Dietrich, *Owner*
EMP: 42
SALES (corp-wide): 1.25B **Publicly Held**
Web: www.clarkdietrich.com
SIC: **3444** 8711 3081 Studs and joists, sheet metal; Engineering services; Vinyl film and sheet
HQ: Clarkwestern Dietrich Building Systems Llc
9050 Cntre Pnte Dr Ste 40
West Chester OH 45069

**(P-8411)**
**COAST SHEET METAL INC**
990 W 17th St, Costa Mesa (92627-4403)
PHONE..................................949 645-2224
Wayne Chambers, *Pr*
Marna Chambers, *
EMP: 35 EST: 1960
SQ FT: 3,800
SALES (est): 2.65MM **Privately Held**
Web: www.coastsheetmetal.com
SIC: **3444** Sheet metalwork

**(P-8412)**
**COMPACTOR MANAGEMENT CO LLC**
Also Called: Compactor Management Company
32420 Central Ave, Union City (94587-2007)
PHONE..................................510 623-2323
David Lucio, *CEO*
Sandra Garcia, *
Emilio Lucio, *
EMP: 26 EST: 2006
SALES (est): 4.87MM **Privately Held**
Web: www.compactormc.com
SIC: **3444** 4953 Bins, prefabricated sheet metal; Recycling, waste materials

**(P-8413)**
**COMPUMERIC ENGINEERING INC**
Also Called: Bearsaver
1390 S Milliken Ave, Ontario (91761-1585)
PHONE..................................909 605-7666
Jeannie Hankins, *CEO*
EMP: 45 EST: 1989
SQ FT: 30,000
SALES (est): 4.73MM **Privately Held**
Web: www.compumeric.com
SIC: **3444** Sheet metalwork

**(P-8414)**
**COMPUTER METAL PRODUCTS CORP**
Also Called: Vline Industries
370 E Easy St, Simi Valley (93065-1802)
PHONE..................................805 520-6966
Jim Visage, *Pr*
Karen Bender, *
EMP: 90 EST: 1971
SQ FT: 25,000
SALES (est): 5.31MM **Privately Held**
Web: www.computermetal.com
SIC: **3444** Sheet metalwork

**(P-8415)**
**CONCISE FABRICATORS INC**
Also Called: Concise Fabricators
7550 Panasonic Way, San Diego (92154-8207)
PHONE..................................520 746-3226
James Dean Johnson, *Pr*
Bill Maples, *
▼ EMP: 50 EST: 1981
SQ FT: 120,000
SALES (est): 14.43MM **Privately Held**
SIC: **3444** Sheet metalwork
PA: Blackbird Management Group, Llc
240 E Illinois St # 2004

**(P-8416)**
**CONTRACT METAL PRODUCTS INC**
6451 W Schulte Rd Ste 110, Tracy (95377-8131)
PHONE..................................510 979-0000
John Young, *Pr*
EMP: 30 EST: 1974
SALES (est): 4.86MM **Privately Held**
Web: www.contractmetalproducts.com
SIC: **3444** 3599 7692 Sheet metal specialties, not stamped; Machine shop, jobbing and repair; Welding repair

**(P-8417)**
**CORTEC PRECISION SHTMTL INC (PA)**
2231 Will Wool Dr, San Jose (95112)
PHONE..................................408 278-8540
Anthony Corrales, *Pr*
Mike Corrales, *
John Corrales, *
Richard Corrales, *
EMP: 153 EST: 1989
SQ FT: 78,000

## 3444 - Sheet Metalwork (P-8418)

SALES (est): 43.78MM **Privately Held**
Web: www.cortecprecision.com
SIC: **3444** Sheet metal specialties, not stamped

### (P-8418)
### COWELCO
Also Called: Cowelco Steel Contractors
1634 W 14th St, Long Beach (90813-1205)
PHONE.................................562 432-5766
EMP: 50 EST: 1947
SALES (est): 4.68MM **Privately Held**
Web: www.cowelco.com
SIC: **3444** 3441 3443 1791 Sheet metalwork; Fabricated structural metal; Fabricated plate work (boiler shop); Structural steel erection

### (P-8419)
### COY INDUSTRIES INC
Also Called: E R C Company
2970 E Maria St, E Rncho Dmngz (90221-5802)
PHONE.................................310 603-2970
Michael Coy, *Pr*
James Patrick Coy, *
EMP: 95 EST: 1972
SQ FT: 50,000
SALES (est): 10.36MM **Privately Held**
Web: www.ercco.com
SIC: **3444** 3469 Sheet metal specialties, not stamped; Metal stampings, nec

### (P-8420)
### CPC FABRICATION INC
2904 Oak St, Santa Ana (92707-3723)
PHONE.................................714 549-2426
Thomas Baker, *CEO*
Lyn Baker, *
EMP: 16 EST: 1980
SQ FT: 15,000
SALES (est): 3.66MM **Privately Held**
SIC: **3444** Sheet metal specialties, not stamped

### (P-8421)
### CREATIVE MFG SOLUTIONS INC
18400 Sutter Blvd, Morgan Hill (95037-2819)
PHONE.................................408 327-0600
Tim Patrick Herlihy, *Pr*
Tammy Herlihy, *CFO*
EMP: 22 EST: 2006
SQ FT: 12,000
SALES (est): 4.91MM **Privately Held**
Web: www.creativemanufacturingsolutions.com
SIC: **3444** Sheet metal specialties, not stamped

### (P-8422)
### CROWN PRODUCTS INC
Also Called: Crown Steel
177 Newport Dr Ste A, San Marcos (92069-1470)
PHONE.................................760 471-1188
David J Carr, *Pr*
EMP: 22 EST: 1969
SQ FT: 20,000
SALES (est): 2.29MM **Privately Held**
Web: www.crownsteelmfg.net
SIC: **3444** 3589 Sheet metalwork; Commercial cooking and foodwarming equipment

### (P-8423)
### DALE BRISCO INC
2132 S Temperance Ave, Fowler (93625-9760)
PHONE.................................559 834-5926
Jamie Brisco, *Pr*
EMP: 17 EST: 1967
SQ FT: 50,000
SALES (est): 2.55MM **Privately Held**
Web: www.dalebriscoinc.com
SIC: **3444** Pipe, sheet metal

### (P-8424)
### DANRICH WELDING CO INC
155 N Eucla Ave, San Dimas (91773-2587)
PHONE.................................562 634-4811
Richard Schenk, *Pr*
EMP: 26 EST: 1970
SALES (est): 1.26MM **Privately Held**
Web: www.danrichwelding.com
SIC: **3444** 7692 Sheet metalwork; Welding repair

### (P-8425)
### DAVE WHIPPLE SHEET METAL INC
1077 N Cuyamaca St, El Cajon (92020-1803)
PHONE.................................619 562-6962
Dave Whipple Senior, *Pr*
Carol Whipple, *
EMP: 34 EST: 1993
SQ FT: 9,000
SALES (est): 4.94MM **Privately Held**
Web: www.whipplesm.com
SIC: **3444** Sheet metalwork

### (P-8426)
### DAVIS CALIFORNIA INDUSTRIES LTD
Also Called: Davis California Industries
11323 Hartland St, North Hollywood (91605-6310)
PHONE.................................818 980-6178
EMP: 20
Web: www.dimfg.com
SIC: **3444** 3599 Sheet metal specialties, not stamped; Machine shop, jobbing and repair

### (P-8427)
### DECK WEST INC
1900 Sanguinetti Ln, Stockton (95205-3403)
PHONE.................................209 939-9700
Patty Shipman, *CEO*
EMP: 20 EST: 1995
SQ FT: 26,000
SALES (est): 411.37K **Privately Held**
Web: www.deckwest.com
SIC: **3444** Metal roofing and roof drainage equipment

### (P-8428)
### DECRA ROOFING SYSTEMS INC (DH)
Also Called: Decra
1230 Railroad St, Corona (92882-1837)
PHONE.................................951 272-8180
Willard C Hudson Junior, *Pr*
◆ EMP: 70 EST: 1998
SQ FT: 60,000
SALES (est): 22.45MM **Privately Held**
Web: www.decra.com
SIC: **3444** Metal roofing and roof drainage equipment
HQ: Fletcher Building Holdings Usa, Inc.
1230 Railroad St
Corona CA 92882
951 272-8180

### (P-8429)
### DELAFOIL HOLDINGS INC (PA)
18500 Von Karman Ave Ste 450, Irvine (92612-0504)
PHONE.................................949 752-4580
Drew Adams, *Dir*
EMP: 230 EST: 1999
SALES (est): 1.67MM
SALES (corp-wide): 1.67MM **Privately Held**
SIC: **3444** Radiator shields or enclosures, sheet metal

### (P-8430)
### DEPENDABLE PRECISION MFG INC
1111 S Stockton St Ste A, Lodi (95240-5933)
PHONE.................................209 369-1055
Clifford L Mcbride, *Pr*
EMP: 17 EST: 1978
SQ FT: 30,000
SALES (est): 3.12MM **Privately Held**
Web: www.dependableprecision.com
SIC: **3444** Sheet metal specialties, not stamped

### (P-8431)
### DEROSA ENTERPRISES INC
Also Called: PSI
15935 Spring Oaks Rd Spc 1, El Cajon (92021-2648)
PHONE.................................760 743-5500
EMP: 15 EST: 1974
SQ FT: 13,000
SALES (est): 375.44K **Privately Held**
SIC: **3444** Sheet metal specialties, not stamped

### (P-8432)
### DEVINCENZI METAL PRODUCTS INC
1809 Castenada Dr, Burlingame (94010-5716)
PHONE.................................650 692-5800
Robert C Devincenzi, *CEO*
Steven Devincenzi, *
Janice Samuelson, *
▲ EMP: 75 EST: 1978
SQ FT: 90,000
SALES (est): 3.56MM **Privately Held**
Web: www.devincenziarch.com
SIC: **3444** Sheet metal specialties, not stamped

### (P-8433)
### DIMIC STEEL TECH INC
145 N 8th Ave, Upland (91786-5402)
PHONE.................................909 946-6767
Miles Dimic, *Pr*
Anna Dimic, *
▲ EMP: 24 EST: 1973
SQ FT: 45,000
SALES (est): 6.21MM **Privately Held**
Web: www.dimicsteeltech.com
SIC: **3444** Sheet metal specialties, not stamped

### (P-8434)
### DOKA USA LTD
Also Called: Conesco Industries
6901 Central Ave, Riverside (92504-1407)
PHONE.................................951 509-0023
Peter Franceschina, *Prin*
EMP: 21
SALES (corp-wide): 2.01B **Privately Held**
Web: www.doka.com
SIC: **3444** Concrete forms, sheet metal
HQ: Doka Usa Ltd.
251 Monroe Ave
Kenilworth NJ 07033
201 641-6500

### (P-8435)
### DUR-RED PRODUCTS
5634 Costa Dr, Chino Hills (91709-3996)
PHONE.................................323 771-9000
Russell Smith, *Pr*
Linda Harrison, *
EMP: 50 EST: 1961
SALES (est): 1.73MM **Privately Held**
Web: www.activarcpg.com
SIC: **3444** 3446 Sheet metalwork; Architectural metalwork

### (P-8436)
### DYNAMO AVIATION INC
9601 Mason Ave # A, Chatsworth (91311-5207)
P.O. Box 14040 (91409)
PHONE.................................818 785-9561
Masoud S Rabadi, *CEO*
Robin C Scott, *
Lary Hockens, *CAO**
Christopher Rabadi, *
Riley Drake, *Finance**
EMP: 86 EST: 1986
SQ FT: 27,000
SALES (est): 18.54MM **Privately Held**
Web: www.dynamoaviation.com
SIC: **3444** Sheet metalwork

### (P-8437)
### E-M MANUFACTURING INC
1290 Dupont Ct, Manteca (95336-6003)
P.O. Box 397 (94019-0397)
PHONE.................................209 825-1800
Jody Elliot, *Pr*
Mike Elliot, *Sec*
EMP: 19 EST: 2009
SQ FT: 15,500
SALES (est): 2.78MM **Privately Held**
Web: www.emmanufacturing.com
SIC: **3444** Sheet metal specialties, not stamped

### (P-8438)
### ECB CORP
Also Called: Omni Duct Systems
1650 Parkway Blvd, West Sacramento (95691-5020)
PHONE.................................916 492-8900
Lou Yuhas, *Brnch Mgr*
EMP: 25
SALES (corp-wide): 26.22MM **Privately Held**
Web: www.omniduct.com
SIC: **3444** Ducts, sheet metal
PA: Ecb Corp.
6400 Artesia Blvd
714 385-8900

### (P-8439)
### ECLIPSE METAL FABRICATION INC
17700 Shideler Pkwy, Lathrop (95330-9356)
PHONE.................................650 298-8731
Joe Anaya, *Pr*
Eduardo Melina, *
EMP: 50 EST: 1999
SALES (est): 4.47MM **Privately Held**
Web: www.eclipsemf.com
SIC: **3444** Sheet metalwork

### (P-8440)
### ELITE E/M INC
340 Martin Ave, Santa Clara (95050-3112)
PHONE.................................408 988-3505
Igor Brovarny, *Pr*
EMP: 32 EST: 1988
SQ FT: 12,300
SALES (est): 5.85MM **Privately Held**

# PRODUCTS & SERVICES SECTION
## 3444 - Sheet Metalwork (P-8462)

Web: www.eliteem.com
SIC: **3444** 3559 3599 3542 Forming machine work, sheet metal; Semiconductor manufacturing machinery; Machine and other job shop work; Presses: forming, stamping, punching, sizing (machine tools)

**(P-8441)**
**EMPIRE SHEET METAL INC**
1215 S Bon View Ave, Ontario (91761-4402)
PHONE..............................909 923-2927
Martin Layman, *Pr*
**EMP:** 16 **EST:** 1999
**SALES (est):** 2.13MM **Privately Held**
Web: www.empiresheetmetal.com
SIC: **3444** Sheet metalwork

**(P-8442)**
**EMTEC ENGINEERING**
16840 Joleen Way Ste F1, Morgan Hill (95037-4606)
PHONE..............................408 779-5800
Edward R Ruminski, *Pr*
**EMP:** 15 **EST:** 1986
**SQ FT:** 16,000
**SALES (est):** 3.7MM **Privately Held**
Web: www.emtec.cc
SIC: **3444** 3599 3469 Sheet metalwork; Machine shop, jobbing and repair; Metal stampings, nec

**(P-8443)**
**ENCORE INDUSTRIES**
597 Brennan St, San Jose (95131-1202)
PHONE..............................408 416-0501
Gary Vogel, *CEO*
Gordon Tigue, *
Tom Fitzgerald, *
▲ **EMP:** 50 **EST:** 1997
**SALES (est):** 9.22MM **Privately Held**
Web: www.encoreindustries.com
SIC: **3444** 3441 Sheet metalwork; Fabricated structural metal

**(P-8444)**
**EPIC SHEET METAL INC**
1720 Industrial Ave, Norco (92860-2949)
PHONE..............................714 679-5917
Raymond Kyle Auslander, *CFO*
**EMP:** 16 **EST:** 2018
**SALES (est):** 5.69MM **Privately Held**
SIC: **3444** Sheet metalwork

**(P-8445)**
**EQUIPMENT DESIGN & MFG INC**
119 Explorer St, Pomona (91768-3278)
PHONE..............................909 594-2229
Rick Clewett, *CEO*
Steve Clewett, *
Ryan Clewett, *
**EMP:** 55 **EST:** 1976
**SQ FT:** 27,400
**SALES (est):** 6.43MM **Privately Held**
Web: www.equipmentdesign.net
SIC: **3444** Sheet metalwork

**(P-8446)**
**ESM AEROSPACE INC**
1203 W Isabel St, Burbank (91506-1407)
PHONE..............................818 841-3653
Jerome Flament, *Pr*
Rina Flament, *
**EMP:** 25 **EST:** 2005
**SQ FT:** 8,900
**SALES (est):** 2.96MM **Privately Held**
Web: www.esmaerospace.com
SIC: **3444** Casings, sheet metal

**(P-8447)**
**EXCEL SHEET METAL INC (PA)**
Also Called: Excel Bridge Manufacturing Co.
12001 Shoemaker Ave, Santa Fe Springs (90670-4718)
PHONE..............................562 944-0701
Craig E Vasquez, *CEO*
Jeffrey Vasquez, *
▼ **EMP:** 53 **EST:** 1952
**SQ FT:** 16,000
**SALES (est):** 2.7MM
**SALES (corp-wide):** 2.7MM **Privately Held**
Web: www.excelsheetmetal.com
SIC: **3444** 1622 Sheet metalwork; Bridge construction

**(P-8448)**
**EXHAUST CENTER INC**
Also Called: Eci Fuel Systems
1794 W 11th St, Upland (91786-3504)
PHONE..............................951 685-8602
Greg S Mitchell, *CEO*
Robert Mitchell, *CFO*
**EMP:** 15 **EST:** 1977
**SQ FT:** 15,000
**SALES (est):** 4.75MM **Privately Held**
Web: www.vectorperformance.com
SIC: **3444** Sheet metalwork

**(P-8449)**
**F T B & SON INC**
11551 Markon Dr, Garden Grove (92841-1808)
PHONE..............................714 891-8003
Frank Taylor Brown, *CEO*
Kathy M Ayers, *CFO*
**EMP:** 44 **EST:** 1972
**SQ FT:** 37,000
**SALES (est):** 592.46K **Privately Held**
Web: www.ftbson.com
SIC: **3444** Ducts, sheet metal

**(P-8450)**
**FABRICATION CONCEPTS CORPORATION**
Also Called: Fabcon
1800 E Saint Andrew Pl, Santa Ana (92705-5043)
PHONE..............................714 881-2000
◆ **EMP:** 180
Web: www.fabcon.com
SIC: **3444** Sheet metalwork

**(P-8451)**
**FABRICATION NETWORK INC**
Also Called: Fabnet
5410 E La Palma Ave, Anaheim (92807-2023)
PHONE..............................714 393-5282
**EMP:** 16 **EST:** 1990
**SQ FT:** 45,000
**SALES (est):** 373.94K **Privately Held**
Web: www.thefabnet.com
SIC: **3444** 3599 Metal housings, enclosures, casings, and other containers; Machine shop, jobbing and repair

**(P-8452)**
**FABTRONICS INC**
5026 Calmview Ave, Baldwin Park (91706-1899)
PHONE..............................626 962-3293
Carlos Duarte, *Pr*
David Thompson, *VP*
▼ **EMP:** 20 **EST:** 1976
**SQ FT:** 26,000
**SALES (est):** 2.57MM **Privately Held**
Web: www.fabtronics.com

SIC: **3444** 3829 Sheet metal specialties, not stamped; Fare registers, for street cars, buses, etc.

**(P-8453)**
**FACILITY MAKERS INC**
345 W Freedom Ave, Orange (92865-2647)
P.O. Box 60066 (92602-6002)
PHONE..............................714 544-1702
Cameron Kazemi, *CEO*
**EMP:** 20 **EST:** 2009
**SALES (est):** 7.19MM **Privately Held**
Web: www.facilitymakers.com
SIC: **3444** 1542 3446 Sheet metal specialties, not stamped; Commercial and office building, new construction; Architectural metalwork

**(P-8454)**
**FLETCHER BLDG HOLDINGS USA INC (DH)**
1230 Railroad St, Corona (92882-1837)
PHONE..............................951 272-8180
Willard Hudson, *Pr*
John Miller, *
Steve Jones, *
◆ **EMP:** 70 **EST:** 1998
**SQ FT:** 60,000
**SALES (est):** 40.43MM **Privately Held**
Web: www.decra.com
SIC: **3444** Metal roofing and roof drainage equipment
HQ: Fletcher Building (Australia) Pty Ltd
1035 Nudgee Road
Banyo QLD 4014

**(P-8455)**
**GAINES MANUFACTURING INC**
12200 Kirkham Rd, Poway (92064-6806)
PHONE..............................858 486-7100
Ted Gaines, *Prin*
**EMP:** 40 **EST:** 1989
**SQ FT:** 23,000
**SALES (est):** 2.15MM **Privately Held**
Web: www.gainesmfg.com
SIC: **3444** Mail (post office) collection or storage boxes, sheet metal

**(P-8456)**
**GARD INC**
Also Called: Reliable Sheet Metal Works
524 E Walnut Ave, Fullerton (92832-2540)
PHONE..............................714 738-5891
Arthur Schade, *Pr*
Arthur Schade Junior, *VP*
Dan Schade, *Sec*
**EMP:** 20 **EST:** 1956
**SQ FT:** 12,000
**SALES (est):** 2.48MM **Privately Held**
Web: www.reliablesheetmetal.com
SIC: **3444** Sheet metal specialties, not stamped

**(P-8457)**
**GCM MEDICAL & OEM INC (PA)**
Also Called: Global Contract Manufacturing
1350 Atlantic St, Union City (94587-2004)
PHONE..............................510 475-0404
Seanus Meaghr, *Pr*
◆ **EMP:** 77 **EST:** 1983
**SQ FT:** 80,000
**SALES (est):** 41.64MM
**SALES (corp-wide):** 41.64MM **Privately Held**
Web: www.gogcm.com
SIC: **3444** 3541 Sheet metalwork; Machine tools, metal cutting type

**(P-8458)**
**GKN AEROSPACE CAMARILLO INC**
3030 Redhll Ave, Santa Ana (92705-5823)
PHONE..............................805 383-6684
Richard Oldfield, *CEO*
David Lind, *Pr*
Bernd Hermann, *CFO*
▲ **EMP:** 19 **EST:** 2009
**SALES (est):** 4.15MM
**SALES (corp-wide):** 4.18B **Privately Held**
Web: www.gknaerospace.com
SIC: **3444** Sheet metalwork
HQ: Gkn Limited
11th Floor, The Colmore Building
Birmingham W MIDLANDS B4 6A
121 210-9800

**(P-8459)**
**GRAYD-A PRCSION MET FBRICATORS**
13233 Florence Ave, Santa Fe Springs (90670-4509)
PHONE..............................562 944-8951
William Gray Junior, *Pr*
William Gray Iii, *VP*
Jo Dell Gray, *Sec*
**EMP:** 20 **EST:** 1964
**SQ FT:** 17,500
**SALES (est):** 2.37MM **Privately Held**
Web: www.grayd-a.com
SIC: **3444** Sheet metal specialties, not stamped

**(P-8460)**
**GRAYSIX COMPANY**
2427 4th St, Berkeley (94710-2488)
PHONE..............................510 845-5936
Robert Gray, *Pr*
**EMP:** 24 **EST:** 1946
**SQ FT:** 16,000
**SALES (est):** 2.15MM **Privately Held**
SIC: **3444** 3469 Housings for business machines, sheet metal; Metal stampings, nec

**(P-8461)**
**GREAT PACIFIC ELBOW LLC**
Also Called: Great Pacific Elbow Company
13900 Sycamore Way, Chino (91710-7016)
PHONE..............................909 606-5551
Erik Gamm, *CEO*
Ron Searcy, *Pr*
**EMP:** 25 **EST:** 2021
**SALES (est):** 4.94MM
**SALES (corp-wide):** 59.06MM **Privately Held**
Web: www.greatpacificelbow.com
SIC: **3444** 3827 Elbows, for air ducts, stovepipes, etc.: sheet metal; Telescopes: elbow, panoramic, sighting, fire control, etc.
PA: West Coast Steel & Processing Holdings, Llc
13568 Vintage Pl
909 393-8405

**(P-8462)**
**GROUP MANUFACTURING SVCS INC (PA)**
1928 Hartog Dr, San Jose (95131)
PHONE..............................408 436-1040
Curtis Molyneaux, *Pr*
Patti Thatcher, *
**EMP:** 80 **EST:** 1983
**SQ FT:** 30,000
**SALES (est):** 14.77MM
**SALES (corp-wide):** 14.77MM **Privately Held**
Web: www.groupmanufacturing.com

## 3444 - Sheet Metalwork (P-8463)

**(P-8463)**
**GROUP MANUFACTURING SVCS INC**
2751 Mercantile Dr Ste 900, Rancho Cordova (95742-7516)
PHONE..............................916 858-3270
Jerry Myrick, *Mgr*
**EMP:** 18
**SALES (corp-wide):** 14.77MM **Privately Held**
**Web:** www.groupmanufacturing.com
**SIC: 3444** Sheet metal specialties, not stamped
**PA:** Group Manufacturing Services, Inc.
1928 Hartog Dr
408 436-1040

**(P-8464)**
**HALLMARK METALS INC**
600 W Foothill Blvd, Glendora (91741-2403)
PHONE..............................626 335-1263
Scott Schoenick, *Pr*
Joseph Allen Zerucha, *
David Peifer, *
Candice Schoenick, *
Marina Carmona, *
**EMP:** 28 **EST:** 1959
**SQ FT:** 23,000
**SALES (est):** 4.42MM **Privately Held**
**Web:** www.hallmarkmetals.com
**SIC: 3444** 3469 Sheet metalwork; Machine parts, stamped or pressed metal

**(P-8465)**
**HAMILTON METALCRAFT INC**
848 N Fair Oaks Ave, Pasadena (91103-3046)
PHONE..............................626 795-4811
Sandra Stahler, *Pr*
**EMP:** 25 **EST:** 1966
**SQ FT:** 10,000
**SALES (est):** 2.15MM **Privately Held**
**Web:** www.hmetal.com
**SIC: 3444** Casings, sheet metal

**(P-8466)**
**HARDCRAFT INDUSTRIES INC**
Also Called: Peninsula Metal Fabrication
2221 Ringwood Ave, San Jose (95131-1736)
PHONE..............................408 432-8340
Andrew Brandt Kwiram, *Pr*
**EMP:** 52 **EST:** 2016
**SALES (est):** 11.3MM **Privately Held**
**Web:** www.hardcraft.com
**SIC: 3444** Forming machine work, sheet metal

**(P-8467)**
**HAUSLANE INC**
222 Harris Ct, South San Francisco (94080-6004)
PHONE..............................800 929-0168
Jiaxing Ruan, *CEO*
**EMP:** 19 **EST:** 2018
**SALES (est):** 7.23MM **Privately Held**
**Web:** www.hauslane.com
**SIC: 3444** 5722 Hoods, range: sheet metal; Household appliance stores

**(P-8468)**
**HI-CRAFT METAL PRODUCTS**
606 W 184th St, Gardena (90248-4282)
PHONE..............................310 323-6949
Bill Gerich, *CEO*
Edward P Gerich, *VP*
Liz Gallagher, *Sec*
Ted Gerich, *Stockholder*
Jennifer Gerich, *Stockholder*
**EMP:** 20 **EST:** 1948
**SQ FT:** 11,000
**SALES (est):** 2.3MM **Privately Held**
**Web:** www.hicraftmetal.com
**SIC: 3444** 3469 Sheet metal specialties, not stamped; Metal stampings, nec

**(P-8469)**
**HILL MANUFACTURING COMPANY LLC**
3363 Edward Ave, Santa Clara (95054-2334)
PHONE..............................408 988-4744
**EMP:** 46 **EST:** 1971
**SQ FT:** 24,500
**SALES (est):** 4.22MM **Privately Held**
**Web:** www.hill-mfg.com
**SIC: 3444** Sheet metal specialties, not stamped

**(P-8470)**
**HSI MECHANICAL INC**
1013 N Emerald Ave, Modesto (95351-2851)
PHONE..............................209 408-0183
Tim Scott, *Prin*
Brent Holloway, *VP*
Preston Stephens, *Pr*
Tim Scott, *Sec*
**EMP:** 21 **EST:** 2015
**SQ FT:** 4,000
**SALES (est):** 4.73MM **Privately Held**
**Web:** www.hsimechanicalinc.com
**SIC: 3444** Sheet metalwork

**(P-8471)**
**I & A INC**
Also Called: Peninsula Metal Fabrication
2221 Ringwood Ave, San Jose (95131-1736)
PHONE..............................408 432-8340
Anthony Davis, *Pr*
Ishbel Davis, *
Heather Jevens, *
Ian Davis, *
**EMP:** 41 **EST:** 2002
**SQ FT:** 48,000
**SALES (est):** 6.8MM **Privately Held**
**Web:** www.pmf.com
**SIC: 3444** Sheet metal specialties, not stamped

**(P-8472)**
**INFINITY KITCHEN PRODUCTS INC**
Also Called: Infinity Stainless Products
7750 Scout Ave, Bell Gardens (90201-4942)
PHONE..............................562 806-5771
Serafin Valdez, *Pr*
▲ **EMP:** 15 **EST:** 1999
**SQ FT:** 25,000
**SALES (est):** 1.77MM **Privately Held**
**Web:** www.infinitystainless.com
**SIC: 3444** Restaurant sheet metalwork

**(P-8473)**
**INLAND MARINE INDUSTRIES INC (PA)**
Also Called: Inland Metal Technologies
3245 Depot Rd, Hayward (94545-2709)
PHONE..............................510 785-8555
Jennifer Sutton, *Pr*
◆ **EMP:** 180 **EST:** 1962
**SALES (est):** 41MM
**SALES (corp-wide):** 41MM **Privately Held**
**Web:** www.inlandmetal.com

**(P-8474)**
**INNOVATIVE METAL PRODUCTS INC**
2443 Cades Way Ste 200, Vista (92081-7885)
PHONE..............................760 734-1010
Scott Whitney, *CEO*
**EMP:** 15 **EST:** 2006
**SALES (est):** 1.83MM **Privately Held**
**SIC: 3444** 3542 Sheet metalwork; Sheet metalworking machines

**(P-8475)**
**INNOVTIVE DSIGN SHTMTL PDTS IN**
Also Called: Innovative Emergency Equipment
616 Marlborough Ave Unit S-1, Riverside (92507)
PHONE..............................951 222-2270
Sheri Kelley, *CEO*
**EMP:** 16 **EST:** 2015
**SALES (est):** 2.34MM **Privately Held**
**Web:** www.idsmp.com
**SIC: 3444** 3699 3647 3641 Forming machine work, sheet metal; Trouble lights; Dome lights, automotive; Pilot lights, radio

**(P-8476)**
**INTERNATIONAL WEST INC**
Also Called: Continental Industries
1025 N Armando St, Anaheim (92806-2606)
PHONE..............................714 632-9190
Jeffery Aaron Hayden, *Pr*
Tami Hayden, *
**EMP:** 31 **EST:** 1985
**SQ FT:** 8,500
**SALES (est):** 5.56MM **Privately Held**
**Web:** www.continental-ind.com
**SIC: 3444** Sheet metalwork

**(P-8477)**
**JBW PRECISION INC**
2650 Lavery Ct, Newbury Park (91320-1581)
PHONE..............................805 499-1973
David Ogden, *Pr*
Jack Ogden, *
Dawn Spalding, *
**EMP:** 23 **EST:** 1969
**SQ FT:** 2,500
**SALES (est):** 4.18MM **Privately Held**
**Web:** www.jbwprecision.com
**SIC: 3444** Sheet metal specialties, not stamped

**(P-8478)**
**JEFFREY FABRICATION LLC**
Also Called: C & J Metal Prducts
6323 Alondra Blvd, Paramount (90723-3750)
PHONE..............................562 634-3101
Lilly Chang, *Managing Member*
**EMP:** 50 **EST:** 2011
**SALES (est):** 2.46MM **Privately Held**
**Web:** www.cjmetals.com
**SIC: 3444** Sheet metalwork

**(P-8479)**
**JORDAHL USA INC**
34420 Gateway Dr, Palm Desert (92211-0843)
PHONE..............................866 332-6687
Frank Metelmann, *CEO*
**EMP:** 20 **EST:** 2019
**SALES (est):** 2.36MM **Privately Held**
**Web:** www.jordahlusa.com
**SIC: 3444** Sheet metalwork

**(P-8480)**
**KARGO MASTER INC**
11261 Trade Center Dr, Rancho Cordova (95742-6223)
PHONE..............................916 638-8703
John Hancock, *Pr*
David Lewis, *
**EMP:** 40 **EST:** 1983
**SALES (est):** 4.18MM **Privately Held**
**Web:** www.holman.com
**SIC: 3444** Sheet metalwork

**(P-8481)**
**KB SHEETMETAL FABRICATION INC**
17371 Mount Wynne Cir # B, Fountain Valley (92708-4107)
PHONE..............................714 979-1780
Cong Nguyen, *Pr*
**EMP:** 25 **EST:** 2001
**SQ FT:** 12,000
**SALES (est):** 4.81MM **Privately Held**
**Web:** www.kb-sheetmetal.com
**SIC: 3444** 3441 Sheet metalwork; Fabricated structural metal

**(P-8482)**
**KEITH E ARCHAMBEAU SR INC**
Also Called: American Precision Sheet Metal
20615 Plummer St, Chatsworth (91311-5112)
PHONE..............................818 718-6110
Keith Archambeau Junior, *Pr*
John Wetlsch, *VP*
**EMP:** 20 **EST:** 1986
**SQ FT:** 10,000
**SALES (est):** 3.1MM **Privately Held**
**Web:** www.americanprecision.net
**SIC: 3444** Sheet metal specialties, not stamped

**(P-8483)**
**L & T PRECISION LLC**
12105 Kirkham Rd, Poway (92064-6870)
PHONE..............................858 513-7874
Loc Nguyen, *Pr*
Loc Nguyen, *Pr*
Tho Nguyen, *
Tien D Nguyen, *
**EMP:** 110 **EST:** 1984
**SQ FT:** 48,000
**SALES (est):** 18.78MM **Privately Held**
**Web:** www.ltprecision.com
**SIC: 3444** 3599 Sheet metal specialties, not stamped; Machine and other job shop work

**(P-8484)**
**LAPTALO ENTERPRISES INC (PA)**
Also Called: J L Precision Sheet Metal
2360 Zanker Rd, San Jose (95131-1115)
PHONE..............................408 727-6633
Jakov Laptalo, *CEO*
Michael Laptalo, *Pr*
Slavko Laptalo, *Sec*
**EMP:** 100 **EST:** 1984
**SQ FT:** 60,000
**SALES (est):** 17.27MM
**SALES (corp-wide):** 17.27MM **Privately Held**
**Web:** www.jlprecision.com
**SIC: 3444** Sheet metal specialties, not stamped

PRODUCTS & SERVICES SECTION                    3444 - Sheet Metalwork (P-8507)

**(P-8485)**
**LARA MANUFACTURING INC**
Also Called: M & J Precision
16235 Vineyard Blvd, Morgan Hill (95037-7123)
PHONE.............................408 778-0811
EMP: 20
SIC: 3444  Sheet metalwork

**(P-8486)**
**LEVMAR INC**
Also Called: Concord Sheet Metal
1666 Willow Pass Rd, Pittsburg (94565-1702)
PHONE.............................925 680-8723
Mark Riley, *Pr*
EMP: 15 EST: 2011
SALES (est): 1.84MM Privately Held
Web: www.concordsheetmetal.com
SIC: 3444  Sheet metalwork

**(P-8487)**
**LLC WALKER WEST**
Impac International
11445 Pacific Ave, Fontana (92337-8227)
PHONE.............................951 685-9660
Kory Lavoy, *Div Mgr*
EMP: 52
Web: www.impac-international.com
SIC: 3444  3315  Housings for business machines, sheet metal; Steel wire and related products
PA: Walker West, Llc
    1555 S Vintage Ave

**(P-8488)**
**LOR-VAN MANUFACTURING LLC**
3307 Edward Ave, Santa Clara (95054-2341)
PHONE.............................408 980-1045
EMP: 24 EST: 2005
SQ FT: 6,400
SALES (est): 6.29MM Privately Held
Web: www.lor-vanmfg.com
SIC: 3444  3699  Sheet metal specialties, not stamped; Laser welding, drilling, and cutting equipment

**(P-8489)**
**LUNAS SHEET METAL INC**
3125 Molinaro St Ste 102, Santa Clara (95054-2433)
PHONE.............................408 492-1260
Antonio Luna, *Pr*
Maria Luna, *CFO*
EMP: 15 EST: 1989
SQ FT: 10,000
SALES (est): 2.29MM Privately Held
Web: www.lunasheetmetal.com
SIC: 3444  Sheet metalwork

**(P-8490)**
**LYNAM INDUSTRIES INC (PA)**
11027 Jasmine St, Fontana (92337-6955)
PHONE.............................951 360-1919
Troy Lindstrom, *Pr*
Greg Traeger Pe, *Dir*
▲ EMP: 85 EST: 1989
SQ FT: 39,000
SALES (est): 14.35MM Privately Held
Web: www.lynaminc.com
SIC: 3444  Sheet metal specialties, not stamped

**(P-8491)**
**LYNX ENTERPRISES INC**
724 E Grant Line Rd Ste B, Tracy (95304-2800)
PHONE.............................209 833-3400
Vance R Anderson, *CEO*
Vance R Anderson, *Pr*
Keith J Anderson, *
▲ EMP: 140 EST: 1993
SQ FT: 52,000
SALES (est): 13.57MM Privately Held
Web: www.lynxenterprises.com
SIC: 3444  3446  3443  3441  Sheet metalwork ; Architectural metalwork; Fabricated plate work (boiler shop); Fabricated structural metal

**(P-8492)**
**M C I MANUFACTURING INC (PA)**
1020 Rock Ave, San Jose (95131-1610)
PHONE.............................408 456-2700
Henry Li, *Pr*
EMP: 45 EST: 1992
SQ FT: 22,000
SALES (est): 2.83MM Privately Held
Web: www.mcimfg.com
SIC: 3444  Metal housings, enclosures, casings, and other containers

**(P-8493)**
**M-5 STEEL MFG INC (PA)**
1353 Philadelphia St, Pomona (91766-5554)
PHONE.............................323 263-9383
Douglas Linkon, *CEO*
▲ EMP: 46 EST: 1970
SALES (est): 5.43MM
SALES (corp-wide): 5.43MM Privately Held
Web: www.m5steel.com
SIC: 3444  3443  Gutters, sheet metal; Fabricated plate work (boiler shop)

**(P-8494)**
**MAC CAL COMPANY**
Also Called: Mac Cal Manufacturing
2520 Zanker Rd, San Jose (95131-1127)
PHONE.............................408 441-1435
Michael Hall, *Pr*
Renee Hall, *
Cathy Mcdonald, *CFO*
EMP: 80 EST: 1960
SALES (est): 24.64MM Privately Held
Web: www.maccal.com
SIC: 3444  3479  7336  Sheet metal specialties, not stamped; Name plates: engraved, etched, etc.; Silk screen design

**(P-8495)**
**MAJESTIC STEEL USA INC**
620 Clark Ave, Pittsburg (94565-5000)
PHONE.............................800 445-6374
EMP: 25
SALES (corp-wide): 473.49MM Privately Held
Web: www.majesticsteel.com
SIC: 3444  5051  Sheet metalwork; Sheets, metal
PA: Majestic Steel Usa, Inc.
    31099 Chgrin Blvd Ste 150
    440 786-2666

**(P-8496)**
**MARATHON FINISHING SYSTEMS INC**
Also Called: Manufacturing
42355 Rio Nedo, Temecula (92590-3701)
PHONE.............................310 791-5601
Christian Rerucha, *Pr*
▲ EMP: 25 EST: 2004
SALES (est): 2.59MM Privately Held
Web: www.marathonspraybooths.com
SIC: 3444  Booths, spray: prefabricated sheet metal

**(P-8497)**
**MARINE & REST FABRICATORS INC**
3768 Dalbergia St, San Diego (92113-3815)
PHONE.............................619 232-7267
Carlos Velazquez, *Pr*
EMP: 44 EST: 1986
SQ FT: 7,600
SALES (est): 4.44MM Privately Held
Web: www.mrf.bz
SIC: 3444  3731  Restaurant sheet metalwork ; Military ships, building and repairing

**(P-8498)**
**MASS PRECISION INC**
46555 Landing Pkwy, Fremont (94538-6421)
PHONE.............................408 954-0200
Greg Kraus, *Mgr*
EMP: 125
SALES (corp-wide): 38.7MM Privately Held
Web: www.massprecision.com
SIC: 3444  3599  Sheet metalwork; Machine shop, jobbing and repair
PA: Mass Precision, Inc.
    2110 Oakland Rd
    408 954-0200

**(P-8499)**
**MASS PRECISION INC (PA)**
Also Called: Machining and Frame Division
2110 Oakland Rd, San Jose (95131-1565)
PHONE.............................408 954-0200
Al Stucky Junior, *Pr*
W Ray Allen, *CFO*
▲ EMP: 200 EST: 1984
SQ FT: 200,000
SALES (est): 38.7MM
SALES (corp-wide): 38.7MM Privately Held
Web: www.massprecision.com
SIC: 3444  3599  Sheet metal specialties, not stamped; Machine shop, jobbing and repair

**(P-8500)**
**MASTER ENTERPRISES INC**
Also Called: A B C Restaurant Equipment Co
2025 Lee Ave, South El Monte (91733-2505)
PHONE.............................626 442-1821
Brian Kim Lien, *CEO*
Wen Lin, *VP*
Thanh Quach, *Sec*
EMP: 20 EST: 1988
SQ FT: 20,000
SALES (est): 3.09MM Privately Held
Web: www.chineserange.com
SIC: 3444  5087  Restaurant sheet metalwork ; Restaurant supplies

**(P-8501)**
**MAYONI ENTERPRISES**
10320 Glenoaks Blvd, Pacoima (91331-1699)
PHONE.............................818 896-0026
Isaac Benyehuda, *CEO*
Isaac Glazer, *
EMP: 60 EST: 1984
SQ FT: 17,000
SALES (est): 3.89MM Privately Held
Web: www.mayoni.com
SIC: 3444  3581  Sheet metal specialties, not stamped; Automatic vending machines

**(P-8502)**
**MEADOWS SHEET METAL AND AC INC**
Also Called: Meadows Mechanical
333 Crown Vista Dr, Gardena (90248-1705)
PHONE.............................310 615-1125
Madonna Rose, *CEO*
Thomas Nolan, *
Dennis Johnson, *
EMP: 50 EST: 1949
SQ FT: 5,000
SALES (est): 10.13MM Privately Held
SIC: 3444  1711  Sheet metalwork; Heating and air conditioning contractors

**(P-8503)**
**METAL ENGINEERING INC**
1642 S Sacramento Ave, Ontario (91761-8052)
PHONE.............................626 334-1819
Arthur A Valenzuela, *Pr*
EMP: 23 EST: 2002
SQ FT: 14,000
SALES (est): 933.88K Privately Held
Web: www.metaleng.com
SIC: 3444  1761  Awnings and canopies; Sheet metal work, nec

**(P-8504)**
**METAL MASTER INC**
4611 Overland Ave, San Diego (92123-1233)
PHONE.............................858 292-8880
Benito Garrido, *Pr*
Donald Wagner, *
Dianne Yeaman, *
EMP: 41 EST: 1987
SQ FT: 30,000
SALES (est): 4.36MM Privately Held
Web: www.metalmasterinc.com
SIC: 3444  3541  Sheet metalwork; Milling machines

**(P-8505)**
**METAL SALES MANUFACTURING CORP**
Also Called: Metal Sales
1326 Paddock Pl, Woodland (95776-5919)
PHONE.............................707 826-2653
Ray Kirchner, *Mgr*
EMP: 32
SALES (corp-wide): 484.26MM Privately Held
Web: metalsales.us.com
SIC: 3444  3448  Roof deck, sheet metal; Prefabricated metal buildings and components
HQ: Metal Sales Manufacturing Corporation
    545 S 3rd St Ste 200
    Louisville KY 40202
    502 855-4300

**(P-8506)**
**METAL-FAB SERVICES INDUST INC**
2500 E Miraloma Way, Anaheim (92806-1608)
PHONE.............................714 630-7771
Carlos Mondragon, *Pr*
▲ EMP: 34 EST: 2003
SQ FT: 28,000
SALES (est): 5.96MM Privately Held
Web: www.metalfabsi.com
SIC: 3444  Sheet metal specialties, not stamped

**(P-8507)**
**METALS DIRECT INC**
Also Called: Mdi General Contracting

## 3444 - Sheet Metalwork (P-8508)

6771 Eastside Rd, Redding (96001-5059)
PHONE..................530 605-1931
Dale Williams, *Pr*
Terry Williams, *
**EMP:** 29 **EST:** 2009
**SALES (est):** 4.61MM **Privately Held**
**Web:** www.metalsdirect.com
**SIC: 3444** 5082 1761 5039 Siding, sheet metal; Contractor's materials; Roofing, siding, and sheetmetal work; Metal buildings

### (P-8508)
### MICROFAB MANUFACTURING INC
Also Called: Microfab Mfg Shtmtl Pdts
220 Distribution St, San Marcos (92078-4358)
PHONE..................760 744-7240
Scott Dillard, *Pr*
Nancy Dillard, *VP*
**EMP:** 16 **EST:** 1982
**SQ FT:** 10,252
**SALES (est):** 914.71K **Privately Held**
**Web:** www.microfabmfg.com
**SIC: 3444** Sheet metal specialties, not stamped

### (P-8509)
### MICROFORM PRECISION LLC
4244 S Market Ct Ste A, Sacramento (95834-1243)
PHONE..................916 419-0580
Timothy E Rice, *Managing Member*
▲ **EMP:** 55 **EST:** 1981
**SQ FT:** 42,000
**SALES (est):** 9.66MM **Privately Held**
**Web:** www.mform.com
**SIC: 3444** Sheet metal specialties, not stamped

### (P-8510)
### MIKES SHEET METAL PDTS INC
Also Called: Uniproducts
3315 Elkhorn Blvd, North Highlands (95660-3112)
PHONE..................916 348-3800
Michael R Meredith, *Pr*
Ginny Meredith, *
**EMP:** 25 **EST:** 1978
**SQ FT:** 10,000
**SALES (est):** 2.45MM **Privately Held**
**SIC: 3444** Ducts, sheet metal

### (P-8511)
### MILLENNIUM METALCRAFT INC
3201 Osgood Cmn, Fremont (94539-5029)
PHONE..................510 657-4700
Kenneth Watson, *Pr*
Gwendolyn Watson, *CFO*
**EMP:** 22 **EST:** 1994
**SQ FT:** 8,100
**SALES (est):** 5.52MM **Privately Held**
**Web:** www.mmcraft.com
**SIC: 3444** Sheet metal specialties, not stamped

### (P-8512)
### MILLS ACQUISITION CORPORATION
Also Called: Advanced Components Technology
1035 22nd Ave, Oakland (94606-5253)
▲ **EMP:** 20 **EST:** 1971
**SALES (est):** 958.49K **Privately Held**
**SIC: 3444** Sheet metalwork

### (P-8513)
### MMP SHEET METAL INC
501 Commercial Way, La Habra (90631-6170)
PHONE..................562 691-1055
Frank Varanelli, *Pr*
**EMP:** 30 **EST:** 1977
**SQ FT:** 8,500
**SALES (est):** 2.29MM **Privately Held**
**Web:** www.mmp-sheetmetal.com
**SIC: 3444** Sheet metal specialties, not stamped

### (P-8514)
### MODERN-AIRE VENTILATING INC
Also Called: Modern Aire Ventilating
7319 Lankershim Blvd, North Hollywood (91605-3895)
PHONE..................818 765-9870
Steven Herman, *Pr*
**EMP:** 20 **EST:** 1956
**SQ FT:** 20,000
**SALES (est):** 2.12MM **Privately Held**
**Web:** www.modernaire.com
**SIC: 3444** 3645 Hoods, range: sheet metal; Residential lighting fixtures

### (P-8515)
### MODULAR METAL FABRICATORS INC
24600 Nandina Ave, Moreno Valley (92551-9518)
PHONE..................951 242-3154
E E Gearing, *CEO*
Don Gearing, *
Mike Beam, *
John Wingate, *
Pat Geary, *
▲ **EMP:** 130 **EST:** 1970
**SQ FT:** 200,000
**SALES (est):** 21.24MM **Privately Held**
**SIC: 3444** Pipe, sheet metal

### (P-8516)
### MS INDUSTRIAL SHTMTL INC
Also Called: Baghouse and Indus Shtmtl Svcs
1731 Pomona Rd, Corona (92878-4363)
PHONE..................951 272-6610
Nancy Nicola, *CEO*
Warren Lampkin, *
Dan Suffel, *
**EMP:** 130 **EST:** 1985
**SQ FT:** 35,000
**SALES (est):** 24MM **Privately Held**
**Web:** www.1888baghouse.com
**SIC: 3444** Sheet metalwork

### (P-8517)
### NEW CAL METALS INC
3495 Swetzer Rd, Loomis (95650-9581)
P.O. Box 1126 (95650-1126)
PHONE..................916 652-7424
Chris Tatasciore, *CEO*
Larry Dumm, *
Chris Tataschiore, *
Slate Bryer, *Stockholder*
▲ **EMP:** 50 **EST:** 2008
**SQ FT:** 15,000
**SALES (est):** 6.22MM **Privately Held**
**Web:** www.vulcanvents.com
**SIC: 3444** Metal ventilating equipment

### (P-8518)
### NOLL/NORWESCO LLC
1320 Performance Dr, Stockton (95206-4925)
PHONE..................209 234-1600
Gary Henry, *Managing Member*
**EMP:** 130 **EST:** 2007
**SALES (est):** 7.08MM
**SALES (corp-wide):** 1.38B **Publicly Held**
**SIC: 3444** Sheet metalwork
**PA:** Gibraltar Industries, Inc.
3556 Lake Shore Rd

716 826-6500

### (P-8519)
### OC METALS INC
Also Called: Oc Metals
2720 S Main St Ste B, Santa Ana (92707-3404)
PHONE..................714 668-0783
Marushkah Kurtz, *CEO*
Mari Kurtz, *Pr*
**EMP:** 20 **EST:** 2000
**SQ FT:** 23,000
**SALES (est):** 4.68MM **Privately Held**
**Web:** www.ocmetals.com
**SIC: 3444** Sheet metalwork

### (P-8520)
### OMNIMAX INTERNATIONAL LLC
Amerimax Building Products
28921 Us Highway 74, Sun City (92585-9675)
PHONE..................951 928-1000
Mitchell B Lewis, *CEO*
**EMP:** 18
**Web:** www.omnimax.com
**SIC: 3444** Sheet metalwork
**HQ:** Omnimax International, Llc
30 Technlogy Pkwy S Ste 4
Peachtree Corners GA 30092
770 449-7066

### (P-8521)
### ORECO DUCT SYSTEMS INC
5119 Azusa Canyon Rd, Baldwin Park (91706-1833)
P.O. Box 1460 (91706-7460)
PHONE..................626 337-8832
Robert I Havai, *Pr*
**EMP:** 110 **EST:** 1985
**SQ FT:** 57,600
**SALES (est):** 852.25K **Privately Held**
**Web:** www.orecoduct.com
**SIC: 3444** Sheet metalwork

### (P-8522)
### OXNARD PRCSION FABRICATION INC
Also Called: O P F
2200 Teal Club Rd, Oxnard (93030-8640)
PHONE..................805 985-0447
David Garza, *Pr*
David Garza, *Pr*
Robert Valles, *
**EMP:** 30 **EST:** 1987
**SQ FT:** 107,000
**SALES (est):** 3.87MM **Privately Held**
**Web:** www.opfmfg.com
**SIC: 3444** 3469 3443 Sheet metal specialties, not stamped; Metal stampings, nec; Fabricated plate work (boiler shop)

### (P-8523)
### P A S U INC
1891 Nirvana Ave, Chula Vista (91911-6117)
PHONE..................619 421-1151
Donald R Palumbo, *Pr*
▲ **EMP:** 36 **EST:** 1979
**SQ FT:** 100,000
**SALES (est):** 665.05K **Privately Held**
**SIC: 3444** 3825 Sheet metalwork; Test equipment for electronic and electrical circuits

### (P-8524)
### P T INDUSTRIES INC
3220 Industry Dr, Signal Hill (90755-4014)
PHONE..................562 961-3431
Kim Nguyen, *Pr*
Thuy Nguyen, *Sec*
**EMP:** 19 **EST:** 1999
**SQ FT:** 19,000
**SALES (est):** 3.05MM **Privately Held**
**Web:** www.ptindustriesinc.com
**SIC: 3444** Sheet metal specialties, not stamped

### (P-8525)
### PACIFIC AWARD METALS INC (HQ)
Also Called: Award Metals
1450 Virginia Ave, Baldwin Park (91706-5819)
PHONE..................626 814-4410
Brian J Lipke, *CEO*
W Brent Taylor, *
Frank Fulford, *
**EMP:** 100 **EST:** 2001
**SQ FT:** 110,000
**SALES (est):** 48.48MM
**SALES (corp-wide):** 1.38B **Publicly Held**
**Web:** www.gibraltarbuildingproducts.com
**SIC: 3444** 3312 Sheet metalwork; Blast furnaces and steel mills
**PA:** Gibraltar Industries, Inc.
3556 Lake Shore Rd
716 826-6500

### (P-8526)
### PACIFIC AWARD METALS INC
Also Called: Award Metals
10302 Birtcher Dr, Jurupa Valley (91752-1829)
PHONE..................360 694-9530
Mark Shaff, *Mgr*
**EMP:** 40
**SALES (corp-wide):** 1.38B **Publicly Held**
**Web:** www.gibraltarbuildingproducts.com
**SIC: 3444** 3443 Concrete forms, sheet metal ; Fabricated plate work (boiler shop)
**HQ:** Pacific Award Metals, Inc.
1450 Virginia Ave
Baldwin Park CA 91706
626 814-4410

### (P-8527)
### PACIFIC DUCT INC
5499 Brooks St, Montclair (91763-4563)
PHONE..................909 635-1335
Riad M Wahid, *Pr*
▲ **EMP:** 18 **EST:** 1996
**SQ FT:** 15,000
**SALES (est):** 4.93MM **Privately Held**
**Web:** www.pacificduct.com
**SIC: 3444** 5075 5039 Metal ventilating equipment; Warm air heating and air conditioning; Air ducts, sheet metal

### (P-8528)
### PACIFIC MARINE SHEET METAL CORPORATION
Also Called: Southwest Manufacturing Svcs
2650 Jamacha Rd Ste 147 Pmb, El Cajon (92019-6316)
PHONE..................858 869-8900
◆ **EMP:** 200
**SIC: 3444** Sheet metalwork

### (P-8529)
### PACIFIC MODERN HOMES INC
9723 Railroad St, Elk Grove (95624-2456)
P.O. Box 670 (95759-0670)
PHONE..................916 685-9514
**TOLL FREE:** 800
Anthony Colbert, *Pr*
Anthony B Colbert, *Pr*
Chris J Fellersen, *Sr VP*
Kenneth S Rader, *VP*

## PRODUCTS & SERVICES SECTION
### 3444 - Sheet Metalwork (P-8552)

▼ **EMP:** 20 **EST:** 1968
**SQ FT:** 3,800
**SALES (est):** 2.86MM **Privately Held**
**Web:** www.pmhi.com
**SIC: 3444** 5031  Metal roofing and roof drainage equipment; Building materials, exterior

**(P-8530)**
### PARIS PRECISION LLC
1650 Ramada Dr, Paso Robles (93446-5976)
**PHONE**................805 239-2500
**EMP:** 150
**SIC: 3444**  Sheet metalwork

**(P-8531)**
### PCH SHEET METAL & AC INC
118 Calle De Los Molinos, San Clemente (92672-3831)
**PHONE**................949 361-9905
Kathy Mcgarry, *Pr*
Delma Mcgarry, *Sec*
**EMP:** 18 **EST:** 2002
**SQ FT:** 6,000
**SALES (est):** 4.94MM **Privately Held**
**Web:** www.pchsheetmetal.com
**SIC: 3444**  Sheet metalwork

**(P-8532)**
### PCI INDUSTRIES INC
Pottorff
700 S Vail Ave, Montebello (90640-4954)
**PHONE**................323 889-6770
**EMP:** 28
**SALES (corp-wide):** 45.1MM **Privately Held**
**Web:** www.pottorff.com
**SIC: 3444**  Sheet metalwork
**PA:** Pci Industries, Inc.
5101 Blue Mound Rd
817 509-2300

**(P-8533)**
### PCI INDUSTRIES INC
6501 Potello St, Commerce (90040)
**PHONE**................323 728-0004
Greg Skilley, *VP*
**EMP:** 28
**SALES (corp-wide):** 45.1MM **Privately Held**
**Web:** www.pottorff.com
**SIC: 3444** 3564  Metal ventilating equipment; Filters, air: furnaces, air conditioning equipment, etc.
**PA:** Pci Industries, Inc.
5101 Blue Mound Rd
817 509-2300

**(P-8534)**
### PEGA PRECISION INC
18800 Adams Ct, Morgan Hill (95037-2816)
**PHONE**................408 776-3700
Lewis H Fast, *Pr*
Aaron Fast, *VP*
**EMP:** 20 **EST:** 1988
**SQ FT:** 30,000
**SALES (est):** 2.46MM **Privately Held**
**Web:** www.pegaprecision.com
**SIC: 3444** 3599  Housings for business machines, sheet metal; Machine shop, jobbing and repair

**(P-8535)**
### PENFIELD PRODUCTS INC
Also Called: Custom Home Accessories
11300 Trade Center Dr Ste A, Rancho Cordova (95742-6330)
**PHONE**................916 635-0231
Jeffrey Feldman, *CEO*

**EMP:** 22 **EST:** 2013
**SQ FT:** 18,000
**SALES (est):** 2.26MM **Privately Held**
**Web:** store.mailboxes.info
**SIC: 3444** 5999  Mail (post office) collection or storage boxes, sheet metal; Trophies and plaques

**(P-8536)**
### PICO METAL PRODUCTS INC
Also Called: Pico Metal Products Since 1919
10640 Springdale Ave, Santa Fe Springs (90670-3843)
**PHONE**................562 944-0626
▲ **EMP:** 20
**Web:** www.picometal.com
**SIC: 3444**  Sheet metalwork

**(P-8537)**
### PINNACLE MANUFACTURING CORP
17680 Butterfield Blvd Ste 100, Morgan Hill (95037-3173)
**PHONE**................408 778-6100
Philip Stolzman, *Pr*
▲ **EMP:** 35 **EST:** 2002
**SALES (est):** 10.56MM **Privately Held**
**Web:** www.team-pinnacle.com
**SIC: 3444**  Sheet metalwork

**(P-8538)**
### PINNACLE PRECISION SHTMTL CORP (HQ)
5410 E La Palma Ave, Anaheim (92807-2023)
**PHONE**................714 777-3129
David Oddo, *Pr*
Brian Mclaughlin, *VP*
Paul Oddo, *Stockholder**
**EMP:** 61 **EST:** 1973
**SALES (est):** 27.14MM
**SALES (corp-wide):** 48.83MM **Privately Held**
**Web:** www.pinnaclemetal.com
**SIC: 3444**  Sheet metalwork
**PA:** The Partner Companies Llc
155 N Wacker Dr Ste 4670
312 883-7266

**(P-8539)**
### PINNACLE PRECISION SHTMTL CORP
Fabnet
5410 E La Palma Ave, Anaheim (92807-2023)
**PHONE**................714 777-3129
Robert F Denham, *Brnch Mgr*
**EMP:** 88
**SALES (corp-wide):** 48.83MM **Privately Held**
**Web:** www.pinnaclemetal.com
**SIC: 3444** 3599  Metal housings, enclosures, casings, and other containers; Machine shop, jobbing and repair
**HQ:** Pinnacle Precision Sheet Metal Corporation
5410 E La Palma Ave
Anaheim CA 92807
714 777-3129

**(P-8540)**
### PLENUMS PLUS LLC
67 Brisbane St, Chula Vista (91910-1065)
**PHONE**................619 422-5515
**EMP:** 75 **EST:** 1986
**SALES (est):** 5.39MM **Privately Held**
**Web:** www.plenumsplus.com
**SIC: 3444**  Sheet metalwork

**(P-8541)**
### PNA CONSTRUCTION TECH INC
301 Espee St Ste E, Bakersfield (93301-2659)
**PHONE**................661 326-1700
Matt Wilen, *Prin*
**EMP:** 33
**SALES (corp-wide):** 5.83MM **Privately Held**
**Web:** www.pna-inc.com
**SIC: 3444**  Concrete forms, sheet metal
**PA:** P.N.A. Construction Technologies, Inc.
1349 W Bryn Mawr Ave
770 668-9500

**(P-8542)**
### PRECISE INDUSTRIES INC
610 Neptune Ave, Brea (92821-2909)
**PHONE**................714 482-2333
Terry D Wells, *Pr*
Robert L Wells, **
▲ **EMP:** 120 **EST:** 2004
**SQ FT:** 78,000
**SALES (est):** 12.13MM **Privately Held**
**Web:** www.preciseind.com
**SIC: 3444** 3679 3599  Sheet metalwork; Electronic circuits; Machine and other job shop work

**(P-8543)**
### PRECISION STEEL PRODUCTS INC
Also Called: Steel Products International
13124 Avalon Blvd, Los Angeles (90061-2738)
**PHONE**................310 523-2002
Raul De Latorre, *Pr*
Deborah De Latorre, *Sec*
**EMP:** 22 **EST:** 1994
**SQ FT:** 24,000
**SALES (est):** 3.75MM **Privately Held**
**Web:** www.steelproducts.biz
**SIC: 3444** 3441  Sheet metalwork; Fabricated structural metal

**(P-8544)**
### PRISM AEROSPACE
3087 12th St, Riverside (92507-4904)
**PHONE**................951 582-2850
Eng Tan, *CEO*
Peng Tan, **
**EMP:** 50 **EST:** 2014
**SQ FT:** 100,000
**SALES (est):** 8.17MM **Privately Held**
**Web:** www.prismaerospace.com
**SIC: 3444** 3812  Forming machine work, sheet metal; Aircraft/aerospace flight instruments and guidance systems

**(P-8545)**
### PRO-TEK MANUFACTURING INC
Also Called: Pro-Tek Manufacturing
4849 Southfront Rd, Livermore (94551-9482)
**PHONE**................925 454-8100
Steven M Krider, *Pr*
Sargon Alkurge, **
Daniel Mckenzie, *VP*
▲ **EMP:** 49 **EST:** 1980
**SQ FT:** 35,240
**SALES (est):** 9.85MM **Privately Held**
**Web:** www.protekmfg.com
**SIC: 3444** 3449  Sheet metalwork; Miscellaneous metalwork

**(P-8546)**
### PROMPT PRECISION METALS INC
1649 E Whitmore Ave, Ceres (95307-7203)

**PHONE**................209 531-1210
Don Widdifield, *Pr*
Joan Widdifield, **
**EMP:** 25 **EST:** 1988
**SQ FT:** 70,000
**SALES (est):** 4.23MM **Privately Held**
**Web:** www.promptprecision.com
**SIC: 3444**  Sheet metal specialties, not stamped

**(P-8547)**
### PROTOTEK HOLDINGS LLC (PA)
215 Devcon Dr, San Jose (95112-4211)
**PHONE**................800 403-9777
Bill Bonadio, *CEO*
**EMP:** 23 **EST:** 2017
**SALES (est):** 10.02MM
**SALES (corp-wide):** 10.02MM **Privately Held**
**Web:** www.prototek.com
**SIC: 3444** 3443  Sheet metalwork; Metal parts

**(P-8548)**
### QUALITY FABRICATION INC (PA)
4020 Garner Rd, Riverside (92501-1006)
**PHONE**................818 407-5015
Pradeep Kumar, *CEO*
▲ **EMP:** 99 **EST:** 1980
**SALES (est):** 14.95MM
**SALES (corp-wide):** 14.95MM **Privately Held**
**Web:** www.quality-fab.com
**SIC: 3444**  Sheet metal specialties, not stamped

**(P-8549)**
### QUALITY METAL FABRICATION LLC
2350 Wilbur Way, Auburn (95602-9500)
**PHONE**................530 887-7388
Thomas Neithercutt, *Managing Member*
**EMP:** 27 **EST:** 1996
**SQ FT:** 12,000
**SALES (est):** 5.17MM **Privately Held**
**Web:** www.qualitymetalfabrication.com
**SIC: 3444** 1799  Sheet metalwork; Welding on site

**(P-8550)**
### R & D METAL FABRICATORS INC
Also Called: R&D Metal
5250 Rancho Rd, Huntington Beach (92647-2052)
**PHONE**................714 891-4878
**EMP:** 36 **EST:** 1971
**SALES (est):** 5.78MM **Privately Held**
**Web:** www.rdmetal.com
**SIC: 3444**  Sheet metalwork

**(P-8551)**
### R & R DUCTWORK LLC
Also Called: R & R Ductwork
12820 Lakeland Rd, Santa Fe Springs (90670-4515)
**PHONE**................562 944-9660
Brian Klebowski, *Managing Member*
**EMP:** 18 **EST:** 1997
**SQ FT:** 14,000
**SALES (est):** 2.56MM **Privately Held**
**Web:** www.rrductwork.com
**SIC: 3444**  Ducts, sheet metal

**(P-8552)**
### RADIATION PROTECTION & SPC INC
Also Called: RPS
5991 Short St, Yorba Linda (92886-5370)
**PHONE**................714 771-7702
John Jory, *Pr*

## 3444 - Sheet Metalwork (P-8553)

**EMP:** 15 **EST:** 2008
**SALES (est):** 2.44MM Privately Held
**SIC: 3444** Radiator shields or enclosures, sheet metal

### (P-8553)
### RAH INDUSTRIES INC (PA)
24800 Avenue Rockefeller, Valencia (91355)
**PHONE**.................661 295-5190
**EMP:** 185 **EST:** 1971
**SALES (est):** 21.83MM
**SALES (corp-wide):** 21.83MM Privately Held
**Web:** www.rah-ind.com
**SIC: 3444** 3599 Sheet metalwork; Machine shop, jobbing and repair

### (P-8554)
### RAMDA METAL SPECIALTIES INC
Also Called: Ramda Metal Specialties
13012 Crenshaw Blvd, Gardena (90249-1544)
**PHONE**.................310 538-2136
Daniel Guevara, CEO
**EMP:** 25 **EST:** 1985
**SQ FT:** 25,000
**SALES (est):** 4.12MM Privately Held
**Web:** www.ramda.com
**SIC: 3444** Metal housings, enclosures, casings, and other containers

### (P-8555)
### RDFABRICATORS INC
11880 Western Ave, Stanton (90680-3438)
**PHONE**.................714 634-2078
Raymond D Foye, Pr
**EMP:** 18 **EST:** 1979
**SQ FT:** 12,000
**SALES (est):** 974.72K Privately Held
**SIC: 3444** Sheet metal specialties, not stamped

### (P-8556)
### RECOATING-WEST INC (PA)
Also Called: Rwi
4170 Douglas Blvd Ste 120, Granite Bay (95746-9703)
**PHONE**.................916 652-8290
Brian Hope, Pr
Ian Cameron, *
▲ **EMP:** 35 **EST:** 1982
**SQ FT:** 41,000
**SALES (est):** 3.96MM Privately Held
**Web:** www.recoatingwest.com
**SIC: 3444** Sheet metalwork

### (P-8557)
### RESPONSIBLE METAL FAB INC
1256 Lawrence Station Rd, Sunnyvale (94089-2218)
**PHONE**.................408 734-0713
Peter Goglia, Pr
**EMP:** 45 **EST:** 1979
**SALES (est):** 5.21MM Privately Held
**Web:** www.responsiblemetal.com
**SIC: 3444** Sheet metalwork

### (P-8558)
### RIGOS EQUIPMENT MFG LLC
Also Called: Rigos Sheet Metal
14501 Joanbridge St, Baldwin Park (91706-1749)
**PHONE**.................626 813-6621
**EMP:** 23 **EST:** 1977
**SQ FT:** 3,600
**SALES (est):** 4.91MM Privately Held
**Web:** www.rigosequipment.com
**SIC: 3444** Sheet metalwork

### (P-8559)
### ROBERT F CHAPMAN INC
43100 Exchange Pl, Lancaster (93535-4524)
**PHONE**.................661 940-9482
Tim Mitchell, CEO
John H Mitchell, *
Paulette Mitchell, *
**EMP:** 53 **EST:** 1959
**SQ FT:** 62,000
**SALES (est):** 4.92MM Privately Held
**Web:** www.robertfchapman.com
**SIC: 3444** 3549 Sheet metalwork; Metalworking machinery, nec

### (P-8560)
### ROMLA CO
Also Called: Romla Ventilator Co
9668 Heinrich Hertz Dr Ste D, San Diego (92154-7917)
**PHONE**.................619 946-1224
Ronald W Haneline, CEO
Robert Haneline, *
Bob Haneline, *
▲ **EMP:** 33 **EST:** 1945
**SQ FT:** 18,000
**SALES (est):** 6.52MM Privately Held
**Web:** www.romlair.com
**SIC: 3444** Metal ventilating equipment

### (P-8561)
### ROSEVILLE PRECISION INC
1180 Tara Ct, Rocklin (95765-1212)
**PHONE**.................916 645-1628
**EMP:** 22 **EST:** 1988
**SALES (est):** 2.51MM Privately Held
**Web:** www.gotorpi.com
**SIC: 3444** Sheet metalwork

### (P-8562)
### RUSS INTERNATIONAL INC
1658 W 132nd St, Gardena (90249-2006)
**PHONE**.................310 329-7121
Randy Carter, CEO
Edmond Russ, Ch
▲ **EMP:** 22 **EST:** 1952
**SQ FT:** 20,000
**SALES (est):** 2.21MM Privately Held
**Web:** www.russ-international.com
**SIC: 3444** Sheet metal specialties, not stamped

### (P-8563)
### SA SERVING LINES INC
Also Called: G A Systems
226 W Carleton Ave, Orange (92867-3608)
**PHONE**.................714 848-7529
Steve Aderson, CEO
Pat Devalle, CFO
Virginia Anderson, Sec
**EMP:** 29 **EST:** 2011
**SALES (est):** 1.66MM Privately Held
**Web:** www.gasystemsmfg.com
**SIC: 3444** Metal housings, enclosures, casings, and other containers

### (P-8564)
### SAE ENGINEERING INC
15500 Concord Cir # 150, Morgan Hill (95037-7109)
P.O. Box 396 (95052-0396)
**PHONE**.................408 492-1784
▲ **EMP:** 40
**Web:** www.saeeng.com
**SIC: 3444** 3599 Sheet metalwork; Machine shop, jobbing and repair

### (P-8565)
### SAL J ACSTA SHEETMETAL MFG INC
Also Called: Acosta Sheet Metal Mfg Co
930 Remillard Ct, San Jose (95122-2625)
**PHONE**.................408 275-6370
Sal J Acosta, CEO
Sandi Acosta, *
Randy Acosta, *
Michelle Acosta, *
Anthony Morales, *
▲ **EMP:** 65 **EST:** 1974
**SQ FT:** 118,000
**SALES (est):** 9.61MM Privately Held
**Web:** www.acostamfg.com
**SIC: 3444** Sheet metal specialties, not stamped

### (P-8566)
### SANMINA CORPORATION
427535 Christy St, Fremont (94538)
**PHONE**.................510 897-2000
**EMP:** 99
**Web:** www.sanmina.com
**SIC: 3444** Sheet metalwork
**PA:** Sanmina Corporation
2700 N 1st St

### (P-8567)
### SCOTT A HUMPHREYS INC (PA)
4600 Industrial St, Simi Valley (93063-3413)
**PHONE**.................805 581-2971
**EMP:** 21 **EST:** 1975
**SALES (est):** 2.42MM
**SALES (corp-wide):** 2.42MM Privately Held
**Web:** scottahumphreys.mfgpages.com
**SIC: 3444** Sheet metalwork

### (P-8568)
### SCREEN TECH INC
4754 Bennett Dr, Livermore (94551-4877)
P.O. Box 23484 (95153-3484)
**PHONE**.................408 885-9750
Stevan S Robertson, Prin
Marsha Robertson, *
▲ **EMP:** 60 **EST:** 1964
**SQ FT:** 52,000
**SALES (est):** 2.88MM Privately Held
**Web:** www.screentechinc.com
**SIC: 3444** Sheet metal specialties, not stamped

### (P-8569)
### SHADE STRUCTURES INC
Also Called: Fabritec Structures
115 E 2nd St Ste 101, Tustin (92780-3684)
**PHONE**.................714 427-6980
Cathy Wanamaker, Brnch Mgr
**EMP:** 22
**Web:** www.usa-shade.com
**SIC: 3444** 1799 2394 Sheet metalwork; Welding on site; Canvas and related products
**HQ:** Shade Structures, Inc.
2580 Esters Blvd 100
Dfw Airport TX 75261
214 905-9500

### (P-8570)
### SHEET METAL ENGINEERING
1780 Voyager Ave, Simi Valley (93063-3301)
**PHONE**.................805 306-0390
Kenneth Chamberlain, Pr
Kenneth Chamberlain, Pr
David Reed, *
Kathy Chou, *
**EMP:** 25 **EST:** 1983

**SQ FT:** 21,000
**SALES (est):** 2.4MM Privately Held
**Web:** www.sheetmetaleng.com
**SIC: 3444** 1799 Sheet metal specialties, not stamped; Welding on site

### (P-8571)
### SHEET METAL SERVICE
2310 E Orangethorpe Ave, Anaheim (92806-1231)
**PHONE**.................714 446-0196
Miguel Nunez, Pr
**EMP:** 18 **EST:** 1991
**SQ FT:** 10,000
**SALES (est):** 2.35MM Privately Held
**Web:** www.smsfab.com
**SIC: 3444** Sheet metalwork

### (P-8572)
### SHOWERDOORDIRECT LLC
20100 Normandie Ave, Torrance (90502-1211)
**PHONE**.................310 327-8060
▲ **EMP:** 17 **EST:** 2010
**SALES (est):** 1.34MM
**SALES (corp-wide):** 3.83MM Privately Held
**Web:** www.showerdoordirect.com
**SIC: 3444** Bins, prefabricated sheet metal
**PA:** Century Shower Door Co., Inc.
20100 Normandie Ave
310 327-8060

### (P-8573)
### SIENNA CORPORATION
41350 Christy St, Fremont (94538-3115)
**PHONE**.................510 440-0200
Eldon R Hugie, CEO
**EMP:** 198 **EST:** 1982
**SALES (est):** 8.63MM Privately Held
**Web:** www.avalonsienna.com
**SIC: 3444** Sheet metalwork

### (P-8574)
### SMS FABRICATIONS INC
11698 Warm Springs Rd, Riverside (92505-5862)
**PHONE**.................951 351-6828
Michael A Uranga, CEO
Sandy Sligar, *
Scott Sligar, *
**EMP:** 36 **EST:** 2003
**SALES (est):** 3.54MM Privately Held
**Web:** www.sheetmetalspecialists.com
**SIC: 3444** Sheet metalwork

### (P-8575)
### SOUTH BAY DIVERSFD SYSTEMS INC
Also Called: U S Fabrications
1841 National Ave, Hayward (94545-1707)
**PHONE**.................510 784-3094
Thomas S Waller, Pr
▲ **EMP:** 15 **EST:** 1981
**SALES (est):** 3.45MM Privately Held
**Web:** www.usfabrications.com
**SIC: 3444** Sheet metalwork

### (P-8576)
### SPACESONICS INCORPORATED
Also Called: Paysonic
30300 Union City Blvd, Union City (94587-1514)
**PHONE**.................650 610-0999
Ignacio C Palomarez, Pr
Hortencia Villanuedo, *
Elizabeth Palomarez, *
▲ **EMP:** 90 **EST:** 1967
**SQ FT:** 55,000
**SALES (est):** 4.63MM Privately Held

## PRODUCTS & SERVICES SECTION
### 3444 - Sheet Metalwork (P-8598)

Web: www.spacesonic.com
SIC: **3444** Metal housings, enclosures, casings, and other containers

**(P-8577)**
**SPAN-O-MATIC INC**
825 Columbia St, Brea (92821-2917)
PHONE.............................714 256-4700
Wolfgang Arnold, *Pr*
Lynda Arnold, *
Erik A Arnold, *
Carl Arnold, *
**EMP:** 40 **EST:** 1972
**SQ FT:** 50,000
**SALES (est):** 4.39MM **Privately Held**
Web: www.spanomatic.com
SIC: **3444** Sheet metalwork

**(P-8578)**
**SPEC-BUILT SYSTEMS INC**
2150 Michael Faraday Dr, San Diego (92154-7903)
P.O. Box 531581 (92153)
PHONE.............................619 661-8100
Randy Eifler, *Pr*
**EMP:** 75 **EST:** 1986
**SQ FT:** 25,000
**SALES (est):** 19.94MM **Privately Held**
Web: www.specbuilt.com
SIC: **3444** Sheet metalwork

**(P-8579)**
**SPECIALTY FABRICATIONS INC**
2674 Westhills Ct, Simi Valley (93065-6234)
PHONE.............................805 579-9730
Mark Zimmerman, *Pr*
Randy Zimmerman, *
**EMP:** 49 **EST:** 1978
**SQ FT:** 80,000
**SALES (est):** 2.15MM **Privately Held**
Web: www.specfabinc.com
SIC: **3444** 3599 Sheet metalwork; Machine and other job shop work

**(P-8580)**
**SPRAY ENCLOSURE TECH INC**
Also Called: Spray Tech
1427 N Linden Ave, Rialto (92376-8601)
PHONE.............................909 419-7011
Tyler Rand, *Pr*
▲ **EMP:** 30 **EST:** 1994
**SQ FT:** 59,000
**SALES (est):** 10.31MM **Privately Held**
Web: www.spraytech.com
SIC: **3444** Booths, spray: prefabricated sheet metal

**(P-8581)**
**STAR STAR**
621 W Rosecrans Ave Ste 1, Gardena (90248-1516)
PHONE.............................310 901-1079
**EMP:** 22 **EST:** 2018
**SALES (est):** 755.4K **Privately Held**
SIC: **3444** Sheet metalwork

**(P-8582)**
**STEELDYNE INDUSTRIES**
Also Called: ABC Sheet Metal
2871 E La Cresta Ave, Anaheim (92806-1817)
PHONE.............................714 630-6200
Jeff Duveneck, *Pr*
Richard Duveneck, *
**EMP:** 40 **EST:** 1995
**SQ FT:** 20,000
**SALES (est):** 10.17MM **Privately Held**
Web: www.abcsheetmetal.com

SIC: **3444** Sheet metal specialties, not stamped

**(P-8583)**
**STEIN INDUSTRIES INC (PA)**
4005 Artesia Ave, Fullerton (92833-2519)
PHONE.............................714 522-4560
Rudi Steinhilber, *CEO*
Theodore Steinhilber, *
Dave Spivy, *
**EMP:** 30 **EST:** 1982
**SQ FT:** 30,800
**SALES (est):** 4.3MM
**SALES (corp-wide):** 4.3MM **Privately Held**
Web: www.stein-industries.com
SIC: **3444** 2599 Sheet metalwork; Work benches, factory

**(P-8584)**
**STOLL METALCRAFT INC**
24808 Anza Dr, Valencia (91355-1258)
PHONE.............................661 295-0401
Gunter Stoll, *Pr*
**EMP:** 105 **EST:** 1973
**SQ FT:** 45,000
**SALES (est):** 24.7MM **Privately Held**
Web: www.stoll-metalcraft.com
SIC: **3444** Sheet metal specialties, not stamped

**(P-8585)**
**STRETCH FORMING CORPORATION**
Also Called: Sfc
804 S Redlands Ave, Perris (92570-2478)
PHONE.............................951 443-0911
Brian D Geary, *Owner*
Brian D Geary, *CEO*
▲ **EMP:** 85 **EST:** 2009
**SQ FT:** 97,000
**SALES (est):** 14.27MM **Privately Held**
Web: www.stretchformingcorp.com
SIC: **3444** Sheet metalwork

**(P-8586)**
**SUN SHEETMETAL SOLUTIONS INC**
Also Called: Sun Manufacturing Solutions
3565 Charter Park Dr, San Jose (95136-1346)
P.O. Box 731244 (95173-1244)
PHONE.............................408 445-8047
Chau Nguyen, *Pr*
Tom Nguyen, *VP*
Rebecca Trinhle, *CFO*
**EMP:** 20 **EST:** 2000
**SQ FT:** 10,000
**SALES (est):** 2.41MM **Privately Held**
Web: www.sunmfgsolutions.com
SIC: **3444** 3552 Sheet metal specialties, not stamped; Fabric forming machinery and equipment

**(P-8587)**
**SUPERIOR DUCT FABRICATION INC**
1683 Mount Vernon Ave, Pomona (91768)
PHONE.............................909 620-8565
Mike Hilgert, *CEO*
Kerry Bootke, *
◆ **EMP:** 107 **EST:** 2002
**SQ FT:** 3,900
**SALES (est):** 19.01MM **Privately Held**
Web: www.sdfab.com
SIC: **3444** Ducts, sheet metal

**(P-8588)**
**SUPERIOR METALS INC**
838 Jury Ct Ste B, San Jose (95112-2815)

PHONE.............................408 938-3488
Hugo Navarez, *Pr*
**EMP:** 15 **EST:** 1999
**SQ FT:** 7,000
**SALES (est):** 2.53MM **Privately Held**
Web: www.smiprecision.com
SIC: **3444** Sheet metalwork

**(P-8589)**
**T & F SHEET MTLS FAB MCHNING I**
15607 New Century Dr, Gardena (90248-2128)
PHONE.............................310 516-8548
Thomas Medina, *Pr*
Hector Medina, *
**EMP:** 32 **EST:** 2005
**SQ FT:** 9,800
**SALES (est):** 3.55MM **Privately Held**
Web: tandfinc.eazy-ecpt.com
SIC: **3444** Sheet metalwork

**(P-8590)**
**TAYLOR WINGS INC**
11496 Refinement Rd Ste A, Rancho Cordova (95742-7373)
PHONE.............................916 851-9464
Brad Durga, *Pr*
**EMP:** 25 **EST:** 1979
**SALES (est):** 2.5MM **Privately Held**
Web: www.taylorwings.com
SIC: **3444** Sheet metalwork

**(P-8591)**
**TEE -N -JAY MANUFACTURING INC**
9145 Glenoaks Blvd, Sun Valley (91352-2612)
PHONE.............................818 504-2961
Jeff Berns, *Pr*
Tamara Berns, *Sec*
**EMP:** 20 **EST:** 1973
**SQ FT:** 10,187
**SALES (est):** 2.39MM **Privately Held**
Web: www.tee-n-jay.com
SIC: **3444** Sheet metalwork

**(P-8592)**
**TFC MANUFACTURING INC**
4001 Watson Plaza Dr, Lakewood (90712-4034)
PHONE.............................562 426-9559
Majid Shahbazi, *Pr*
Hamid Sharifat, *
**EMP:** 81 **EST:** 1999
**SQ FT:** 28,500
**SALES (est):** 10.07MM **Privately Held**
Web: www.tfcmfg.com
SIC: **3444** Sheet metalwork

**(P-8593)**
**THERMA LLC**
1601 Las Plumas Ave, San Jose (95133-1613)
PHONE.............................408 347-3400
Joseph Parisi, *CEO*
Nicki Parisi, *
▲ **EMP:** 1200 **EST:** 1967
**SALES (est):** 28.16MM
**SALES (corp-wide):** 700MM **Privately Held**
Web: www.therma.com
SIC: **3444** 3448 Sheet metalwork; Prefabricated metal components
HQ: Therma Holdings Llc
1601 Las Plumas Ave
San Jose CA 95133
408 347-3400

**(P-8594)**
**TIDE ROCK HOLDINGS LLC (PA)**
343 S Highway 101 Ste 200, Solana Beach (92075-1879)
PHONE.............................858 204-7438
Ryan Peddycord, *CEO*
**EMP:** 28 **EST:** 2013
**SALES (est):** 68.36MM
**SALES (corp-wide):** 68.36MM **Privately Held**
Web: www.tiderock.com
SIC: **3444** Sheet metalwork

**(P-8595)**
**TN SHEET METAL INC**
18385 Bandilier Cir, Fountain Valley (92708-7001)
PHONE.............................714 593-0100
Thony Quang Nguyen, *CEO*
Christine Lee, *Contrlr*
Thony Quang Nguyen, *Pr*
▲ **EMP:** 19 **EST:** 2001
**SQ FT:** 12,035
**SALES (est):** 2.11MM **Privately Held**
Web: www.tnsheetmetal.com
SIC: **3444** Ducts, sheet metal

**(P-8596)**
**TOBAR INDUSTRIES INC**
875 Jarvis Dr Ste 120, Morgan Hill (95037-2887)
PHONE.............................408 778-3901
Vinai Kumar, *Pr*
Farid Ghantous, *COO*
**EMP:** 20 **EST:** 1983
**SQ FT:** 30,000
**SALES (est):** 2.48MM **Privately Held**
Web: www.tobarind.com
SIC: **3444** Sheet metal specialties, not stamped

**(P-8597)**
**TREND TECHNOLOGIES LLC (DH)**
Also Called: Trend Technologies
4626 Eucalyptus Ave, Chino (91710-9215)
P.O. Box 51 5001 (90051-5001)
PHONE.............................909 597-7861
Earl Payton, *Managing Member*
▲ **EMP:** 220 **EST:** 2002
**SQ FT:** 125,000
**SALES (est):** 145.24MM **Privately Held**
Web: www.trendtechnologies.com
SIC: **3444** 3469 3499 3089 Metal housings, enclosures, casings, and other containers; Electronic enclosures, stamped or pressed metal; Aquarium accessories, metal; Injection molding of plastics
HQ: Ttl Holdings, Llc
4626 Eucalyptus Ave
Chino CA 91710
909 597-7861

**(P-8598)**
**TRI FAB ASSOCIATES INC**
48351 Lakeview Blvd, Fremont (94538-6533)
PHONE.............................510 651-7628
Ronald A Brochu, *Pr*
Joseph R Santosuosso, *
**EMP:** 90 **EST:** 1989
**SQ FT:** 35,000
**SALES (est):** 9.62MM **Privately Held**
Web: www.trifabusa.com
SIC: **3444** Sheet metal specialties, not stamped

## 3444 - Sheet Metalwork (P-8599)

**(P-8599)**
**TRI PRECISION SHEETMETAL INC**
1104 N Armando St, Anaheim (92806-2609)
PHONE...............................714 632-8838
Leonardo Cortes, CEO
Ross Morrow, *
Rob Morrow, *
EMP: 40 EST: 1988
SALES (est): 4.93MM Privately Held
Web: www.triprecision.com
SIC: 3444 3542 Sheet metalwork; Sheet metalworking machines

**(P-8600)**
**TRIO METAL STAMPING INC**
Also Called: Trio Metal Stamping
15318 Proctor Ave, City Of Industry (91745-1023)
PHONE...............................626 336-1228
Damian Rickard, CEO
Georgia Boris, *
EMP: 53 EST: 1947
SQ FT: 75,000
SALES (est): 4.92MM Privately Held
Web: www.triometalstamping.com
SIC: 3444 3469 Sheet metalwork; Stamping metal for the trade

**(P-8601)**
**TRU-DUCT INC**
2515 Industry St, Oceanside (92054-4807)
PHONE...............................619 660-3858
Drew E Miles, CEO
EMP: 45 EST: 1991
SALES (est): 9.76MM Privately Held
Web: www.tru-duct.com
SIC: 3444 Ducts, sheet metal

**(P-8602)**
**UNITED DURALUME PRODUCTS INC**
350 S Raymond Ave, Fullerton (92831-4689)
PHONE...............................714 773-4011
Mike Winston Adams, CEO
EMP: 15 EST: 1970
SQ FT: 128,600
SALES (est): 1.88MM Privately Held
SIC: 3444 1521 Awnings and canopies; Patio and deck construction and repair

**(P-8603)**
**UNITED MECH MET FBRICATORS INC**
Also Called: Umec
33353 Lewis St, Union City (94587-2205)
PHONE...............................510 537-4744
Gina Wang, CEO
Barry Brescia, *
EMP: 50 EST: 1982
SALES (est): 11.04MM Privately Held
Web: www.umec.net
SIC: 3444 3443 3841 Sheet metalwork; Fabricated plate work (boiler shop); Surgical and medical instruments

**(P-8604)**
**US PRECISION SHEET METAL INC**
Also Called: U S Precision Manufacturing
4020 Garner Rd, Riverside (92501-1006)
PHONE...............................951 276-2611
Amanda Hawkins, CEO
Ray Mayo, *
Sal Giulano, *
EMP: 68 EST: 1981
SQ FT: 25,000
SALES (est): 7.31MM Privately Held
Web: www.usprecision.net
SIC: 3444 Sheet metal specialties, not stamped

**(P-8605)**
**USK MANUFACTURING INC**
720 Zwissig Way, Union City (94587-3602)
PHONE...............................510 471-7555
Moon Do Kim, CEO
Jina Kim, *
Cindy Fong, *
▲ EMP: 45 EST: 1987
SQ FT: 85,000
SALES (est): 5MM Privately Held
Web: www.uskmfg.com
SIC: 3444 Sheet metalwork

**(P-8606)**
**VALLEY PRECISION MET PDTS INC**
Also Called: Valley Precision Metal Pdts
27771 Avenue Hopkins, Valencia (91355-1223)
PHONE...............................661 607-0100
Howard Vermillion Junior, Pr
Jon Cantor, *
EMP: 30 EST: 1948
SQ FT: 5,800
SALES (est): 4.69MM Privately Held
Web: www.veiaerospace.com
SIC: 3444 Sheet metalwork

**(P-8607)**
**VERSAFAB CORP (PA)**
15919 S Broadway, Gardena (90248-2489)
PHONE...............................800 421-1822
Edward Penfold Junior, Ch Bd
Joe Flynn, Pr
EMP: 40 EST: 1982
SQ FT: 35,000
SALES (est): 5.05MM
SALES (corp-wide): 5.05MM Privately Held
Web: www.versafabcorp.com
SIC: 3444 3465 3496 3469 Sheet metalwork ; Moldings or trim, automobile: stamped metal; Miscellaneous fabricated wire products; Metal stampings, nec

**(P-8608)**
**VERSAFORM CORPORATION**
Also Called: Sonaca North America
1377 Specialty Dr, Vista (92081-8521)
PHONE...............................760 599-4477
Ronals S Saks, Pr
EMP: 73 EST: 1974
SQ FT: 24,000
SALES (est): 3.69MM Privately Held
Web: www.lmiaerospace.com
SIC: 3444 3549 3398 Forming machine work, sheet metal; Metalworking machinery, nec; Metal heat treating
HQ: Lmi Aerospace, Inc.
3600 Mueller Rd
Saint Charles MO 63301
636 946-6525

**(P-8609)**
**VTS SHEETMETAL SPECIALIST CO**
13831 Seaboard Cir, Garden Grove (92843-3908)
PHONE...............................714 237-1420
Thomas Bonnett, Pr
Tom Bonnett, *
Sa H Vo, Sec
EMP: 31 EST: 1986
SQ FT: 21,300
SALES (est): 4.86MM Privately Held
Web: www.vtsfab.com
SIC: 3444 Metal housings, enclosures, casings, and other containers

**(P-8610)**
**WCS EQUIPMENT HOLDINGS LLC**
Also Called: Steelco USA
13066 14th St, Chino (91710-4365)
PHONE...............................909 393-8405
Erik Gamm, Prin
EMP: 59
SALES (corp-wide): 59.06MM Privately Held
Web: www.steelcousa.com
SIC: 3444 Sheet metalwork
HQ: Wcs Equipment Holdings, Llc
13568 Vintage Pl
Chino CA 91710

**(P-8611)**
**WEST COAST FAB INC**
700 S 32nd St, Richmond (94804-4106)
PHONE...............................510 529-0177
Thomas Nelson, Pr
EMP: 15 EST: 1973
SQ FT: 18,000
SALES (est): 2.67MM Privately Held
Web: www.westcoastfab.com
SIC: 3444 Sheet metal specialties, not stamped

**(P-8612)**
**WESTFAB MANUFACTURING INC**
3370 Keller St, Santa Clara (95054-2612)
PHONE...............................408 727-0550
Akbar Soleimanieh, Pr
Homeira Lotfi, *
EMP: 45 EST: 1987
SQ FT: 22,000
SALES (est): 4.88MM Privately Held
Web: www.westfab.com
SIC: 3444 Sheet metalwork

**(P-8613)**
**WILL-MANN INC**
225 E Santa Fe Ave, Fullerton (92832-1917)
P.O. Box 976 (92836-0976)
PHONE...............................714 870-0350
Manfred Frischmuth, Pr
Lore Frischmuth, *
Sabina Andrassy, *
EMP: 40 EST: 1968
SQ FT: 30,000
SALES (est): 4.56MM Privately Held
Web: www.will-mann.com
SIC: 3444 7692 3471 Sheet metal specialties, not stamped; Welding repair; Plating and polishing

## 3446 Architectural Metalwork

**(P-8614)**
**ACCESS PROFESSIONAL INC**
Also Called: Access Professional Systems
10225 Prospect Ave Ste A, Santee (92071-4473)
PHONE...............................858 571-4444
Russell Scheppmann, Pr
EMP: 18 EST: 1994
SALES (est): 3.07MM Privately Held
Web: www.accessprofessionals.com
SIC: 3446 7521 1731 Fences, gates, posts, and flagpoles; Automobile parking; Voice, data, and video wiring contractor

**(P-8615)**
**ADF INCORPORATED**
Also Called: Able Design and Fabrication
1550 W Mahalo Pl, Rancho Dominguez (90220-5422)
PHONE...............................310 669-9700
Lou Mannick, Pr
EMP: 30 EST: 1993
SQ FT: 23,000
SALES (est): 3.81MM
SALES (corp-wide): 46.29MM Privately Held
Web: www.adfvisual.com
SIC: 3446 Partitions and supports/studs, including acoustical systems
PA: Peerless Industries, Inc.
2300 White Oak Cir
630 375-5100

**(P-8616)**
**ALABAMA METAL INDUSTRIES CORP**
Also Called: Amico Fontana
11093 Beech Ave, Fontana (92337-7268)
P.O. Box 310353 (92331-0353)
PHONE...............................909 350-9280
Lilly Mc Donalds, Brnch Mgr
EMP: 25
SALES (corp-wide): 92.55MM Privately Held
Web: www.amicoglobal.com
SIC: 3446 Open flooring and grating for construction
PA: Alabama Metal Industries Corporation
3245 Fayette Ave
205 787-2611

**(P-8617)**
**AMERICAN STEEL & STAIRWAYS INC**
8525 Forest St Ste A, Gilroy (95020-3645)
PHONE...............................408 848-2992
Martin Vollrath, Pr
Margit Vollrath, *
EMP: 33 EST: 1975
SQ FT: 18,000
SALES (est): 5.33MM Privately Held
Web: www.americansteelandstairways.com
SIC: 3446 3441 Ornamental metalwork; Fabricated structural metal

**(P-8618)**
**ARBOR FENCE INC**
22660 Broadway, Sonoma (95476-8217)
PHONE...............................707 938-3133
Ronald Wooden, Pr
EMP: 22 EST: 1990
SALES (est): 2.41MM Privately Held
Web: www.arborfenceinc.com
SIC: 3446 3315 2499 5211 Fences, gates, posts, and flagpoles; Chain link fencing; Fencing, wood; Fencing

**(P-8619)**
**ATR TECHNOLOGIES INCORPORATED**
Also Called: Aluminum Tube Railings
805 Towne Center Dr, Pomona (91767-5901)
PHONE...............................909 399-9724
Donald Terry, Pr
Dave C Terry, VP
Debra L Terry, Sec
▼ EMP: 15 EST: 1963
SQ FT: 15,800
SALES (est): 2.39MM Privately Held
Web: www.atr-technologies.com

## PRODUCTS & SERVICES SECTION
### 3446 - Architectural Metalwork (P-8641)

SIC: 3446 Architectural metalwork

**(P-8620)**
**CANTERBURY DESIGNS INC**
Also Called: Canterbury International
6195 Maywood Ave, Huntington Park (90255-3213)
PHONE.............................323 936-7111
Larry Snyder, *Pr*
Laura Snyder, *VP*
▲ **EMP:** 20 **EST:** 1964
**SALES (est):** 2.29MM **Privately Held**
Web: www.canterbury-designs.com
SIC: 3446 3873 Architectural metalwork; Clocks, assembly of

**(P-8621)**
**CLARK STEEL FABRICATORS INC**
12610 Vigilante Rd, Lakeside (92040-1113)
P.O. Box 1370 (92040-0910)
PHONE.............................619 390-1502
Kimberley L Clark, *Pr*
Kevin B Clark, *
**EMP:** 45 **EST:** 1977
**SQ FT:** 12,500
**SALES (est):** 7.68MM **Privately Held**
Web: www.clarksteelfab.com
SIC: 3446 3441 Architectural metalwork; Fabricated structural metal

**(P-8622)**
**CURRAN ENGINEERING COMPANY I**
Also Called: Manufacturing
28727 Industry Dr, Valencia (91355-5414)
P.O. Box 26 (91310-0026)
PHONE.............................800 643-6353
Patrick Curran, *CEO*
Douglas M Curran, *CEO*
Patrick Curran, *Pr*
**EMP:** 20 **EST:** 1947
**SQ FT:** 20,000
**SALES (est):** 2.75MM **Privately Held**
Web: www.curranengineering.com
SIC: 3446 Architectural metalwork

**(P-8623)**
**DELTA IRONWORKS INC**
Also Called: Delta Ironworks
15420 Meridian Rd, Salinas (93907-8788)
P.O. Box 10580 (93907)
PHONE.............................831 663-1190
Salomon M Dominguez, *CEO*
**EMP:** 15 **EST:** 1994
**SQ FT:** 9,000
**SALES (est):** 3.71MM **Privately Held**
Web: www.deltaironworks.com
SIC: 3446 3441 Architectural metalwork; Fabricated structural metal

**(P-8624)**
**DENNISON INC**
Also Called: Maxxon Company
17901 Railroad St, City Of Industry (91748-1113)
PHONE.............................626 965-8917
Dennis Ma, *CEO*
◆ **EMP:** 47 **EST:** 1990
**SQ FT:** 26,000
**SALES (est):** 4.7MM **Privately Held**
SIC: 3446 Architectural metalwork

**(P-8625)**
**EUROCRAFT ARCHTECTURAL MET INC**
5619 Watcher St, Bell Gardens (90201-1632)
PHONE.............................323 771-1323
John Fechter, *Pr*
**EMP:** 30 **EST:** 1976
**SQ FT:** 30,000
**SALES (est):** 4.36MM **Privately Held**
Web: www.eurocraftmetal.com
SIC: 3446 Architectural metalwork

**(P-8626)**
**FORMS AND SURFACES INC**
6395 Cindy Ln, Carpinteria (93013-2909)
PHONE.............................805 684-8626
George Hickmann, *Brnch Mgr*
**EMP:** 80
**SALES (corp-wide):** 94.26MM **Privately Held**
Web: www.forms-surfaces.com
SIC: 3446 Architectural metalwork
PA: Forms And Surfaces, Inc.
30 Pine St
412 781-9003

**(P-8627)**
**GREGORY PATTERSON**
Also Called: Ccoi Gate & Fence
2960 San Juan Rd, Aromas (95004-9752)
P.O. Box 669 (95004-0669)
PHONE.............................831 636-1015
Gregory Patterson, *Owner*
Kate Deegan Sales, *Prin*
**EMP:** 20 **EST:** 1989
**SQ FT:** 3,000
**SALES (est):** 2.41MM **Privately Held**
Web: www.ccoigateandfence.com
SIC: 3446 Fences or posts, ornamental iron or steel

**(P-8628)**
**HART & COOLEY INC**
Also Called: HART & COOLEY, INC.
10855 Philadelphia Ave Ste B, Jurupa Valley (91752-3289)
PHONE.............................951 332-5132
**EMP:** 44
Web: www.hartandcooley.com
SIC: 3446 Architectural metalwork
HQ: Hart & Cooley Llc
4460 44th St Se Ste F
Grand Rapids MI 49512
800 433-6341

**(P-8629)**
**J TALLEY CORPORATION (PA)**
Also Called: Talley Metal Fabrication
989 W 7th St, San Jacinto (92582-3813)
P.O. Box 850 (92581-0850)
PHONE.............................951 654-2123
Joe Brown Talley, *CEO*
**EMP:** 86 **EST:** 1963
**SQ FT:** 13,400
**SALES (est):** 984.4K
**SALES (corp-wide):** 984.4K **Privately Held**
Web: www.talleymetalfabrication.com
SIC: 3446 3444 Railings, prefabricated metal; Culverts, flumes, and pipes

**(P-8630)**
**JANSEN ORNAMENTAL SUPPLY CO**
10926 Schmidt Rd, El Monte (91733-2708)
PHONE.............................626 442-0271
Mike Jansen, *CEO*
Harry Jansen, *
John Jansen, *
▲ **EMP:** 30 **EST:** 1960
**SQ FT:** 22,000
**SALES (est):** 2.51MM **Privately Held**
Web: www.jansensupply.com
SIC: 3446 Architectural metalwork

**(P-8631)**
**K & J WIRE PRODUCTS CORP**
1220 N Lance Ln, Anaheim (92806-1812)
PHONE.............................714 816-0360
Klaus Borutzki, *Pr*
Barbara Borutzki, *
**EMP:** 25 **EST:** 1989
**SQ FT:** 21,000
**SALES (est):** 952.89K **Privately Held**
Web: www.kjwire.com
SIC: 3446 3496 5046 3315 Architectural metalwork; Miscellaneous fabricated wire products; Store fixtures and display equipment; Wire and fabricated wire products

**(P-8632)**
**KAWNEER COMPANY INC**
Also Called: Brite Vue Div
7200 W Doe Ave, Visalia (93291-9296)
PHONE.............................559 651-4000
Norris Mcelroy, *Brnch Mgr*
**EMP:** 129
**SQ FT:** 200,000
**SALES (corp-wide):** 8.96B **Privately Held**
Web: www.kawneer.us
SIC: 3446 Architectural metalwork
HQ: Kawneer Company, Inc.
555 Guthridge Ct
Norcross GA 30092
770 449-5555

**(P-8633)**
**KIMCO IRON INC**
8235 Inverness Grn, Buena Park (90621-1336)
PHONE.............................714 293-6442
Hak Kim, *CEO*
Kyung Moon Jung, *Sec*
**EMP:** 18 **EST:** 2018
**SALES (est):** 1.19MM **Privately Held**
Web: www.kimco.com
SIC: 3446 Architectural metalwork

**(P-8634)**
**LAVI INDUSTRIES LLC (PA)**
27810 Avenue Hopkins, Valencia (91355-3409)
PHONE.............................877 275-5284
Gavriel Lavi, *Pr*
Susan Lavi, *
◆ **EMP:** 80 **EST:** 1979
**SQ FT:** 80,000
**SALES (est):** 19.06MM
**SALES (corp-wide):** 19.06MM **Privately Held**
Web: www.lavi.com
SIC: 3446 Railings, banisters, guards, etc: made from metal pipe

**(P-8635)**
**LNI CUSTOM MANUFACTURING INC**
15542 Broadway Center St, Gardena (90248-2137)
PHONE.............................310 978-2000
Scott Blakely, *CEO*
**EMP:** 50 **EST:** 1995
**SALES (est):** 9.48MM **Privately Held**
Web: www.lnisigns.com
SIC: 3446 5046 Architectural metalwork; Neon signs

**(P-8636)**
**LUR INC**
Also Called: Lumar Metals
9936 Albany Ave, Rancho Cucamonga (91701-5919)
PHONE.............................909 623-4999
Marlene Racca, *Pr*
**EMP:** 15 **EST:** 1986
**SALES (est):** 941.05K **Privately Held**
SIC: 3446 Architectural metalwork

**(P-8637)**
**MC METAL INC**
1347 Donner Ave, San Francisco (94124-3612)
PHONE.............................415 822-2288
Jeffrey Mark, *Pr*
**EMP:** 17 **EST:** 1997
**SALES (est):** 2.21MM **Privately Held**
Web: www.mcmetalinc.com
SIC: 3446 Architectural metalwork

**(P-8638)**
**NGO METALS INC**
Also Called: Moz Designs
711 Kevin Ct, Oakland (94621-4039)
PHONE.............................510 632-0853
Murry Sandford, *CEO*
Herbert M Sandford Iii, *VP*
Tripp Sanford, *
◆ **EMP:** 25 **EST:** 1990
**SQ FT:** 10,000
**SALES (est):** 10.39MM
**SALES (corp-wide):** 1.3B **Publicly Held**
Web: www.mozdesigns.com
SIC: 3446 Architectural metalwork
PA: Armstrong World Industries, Inc.
2500 Columbia Ave
717 397-0611

**(P-8639)**
**OLSON AND CO STEEL (PA)**
1941 Davis St, San Leandro (94577-1262)
PHONE.............................510 567-2200
David Olson, *CEO*
Dylan Olson, *
Thomas Fluehr, *Prin*
Kevin Cullen, *Prin*
▲ **EMP:** 225 **EST:** 1960
**SQ FT:** 130,000
**SALES (est):** 49.79MM
**SALES (corp-wide):** 49.79MM **Privately Held**
Web: www.olsonsteel.com
SIC: 3446 3441 Architectural metalwork; Fabricated structural metal

**(P-8640)**
**PARAMOUNT METAL & SUPPLY INC**
8140 Rosecrans Ave, Paramount (90723-2754)
PHONE.............................562 634-8180
Vincent Jue, *CEO*
George Jue, *
Helen Jue, *
**EMP:** 25 **EST:** 1955
**SQ FT:** 80,000
**SALES (est):** 2.39MM **Privately Held**
Web: www.paramountmetals.com
SIC: 3446 Architectural metalwork

**(P-8641)**
**RAMI DESIGNS INC**
24 Hammond Ste E, Irvine (92618-1680)
PHONE.............................949 588-8288
Ron Taybi, *Pr*
**EMP:** 19 **EST:** 1982
**SQ FT:** 6,000
**SALES (est):** 3.33MM **Privately Held**
Web: www.ramidesigns.com
SIC: 3446 3299 3229 Architectural metalwork; Architectural sculptures: gypsum, clay, papier mache, etc.; Glass furnishings and accessories

## 3446 - Architectural Metalwork (P-8642)

**(P-8642)**
**RINCON IRON INC**
Also Called: Rincon Ironworks
531 Montgomery Ave, Oxnard (93036-1066)
PHONE..................805 455-2904
Rick Sanchez, *CEO*
▲ EMP: 15 EST: 2001
SQ FT: 5,000
SALES (est): 1.28MM **Privately Held**
Web: www.rinconiron.com
SIC: 3446 Architectural metalwork

**(P-8643)**
**SANIE MANUFACTURING COMPANY**
320 E Alton Ave, Santa Ana (92707-4419)
PHONE..................714 751-7700
Mendi Haidarali, *Pr*
Mohammad Haidari, *VP*
EMP: 18 EST: 1981
SALES (est): 4.56MM **Privately Held**
Web: www.saniemfg.com
SIC: 3446 Fences or posts, ornamental iron or steel

**(P-8644)**
**SAPPHIRE MANUFACTURING INC**
505 Porter Way, Placentia (92870-6454)
PHONE..................714 401-3117
Hector Garibay, *CEO*
EMP: 20 EST: 2015
SQ FT: 25,000
SALES (est): 3.52MM **Privately Held**
Web: www.sapphiremfg.com
SIC: 3446 7371 Fences or posts, ornamental iron or steel; Computer software development and applications

**(P-8645)**
**SECURUS INC**
Also Called: Holdrite
14284 Danielson St, Poway (92064-8885)
◆ EMP: 50 EST: 1983
SQ FT: 46,000
SALES (est): 2.73MM **Privately Held**
SIC: 3446 3351 3431 5162 Acoustical suspension systems, metal; Tubing, copper and copper alloy; Plumbing fixtures: enameled iron, cast iron,or pressed metal; Plastics materials and basic shapes
PA: Reliance Worldwide Corporation Limited
 Level 32 140 William Street

**(P-8646)**
**TJS METAL MANUFACTURING INC**
10847 Drury Ln, Lynwood (90262-1833)
PHONE..................310 604-1545
Jose Antonio Gallegos, *CEO*
EMP: 26 EST: 1999
SQ FT: 30,000
SALES (est): 4.23MM **Privately Held**
Web: www.tjsmetal.com
SIC: 3446 Architectural metalwork

**(P-8647)**
**TRI-STATE STAIRWAY CORP**
706 W California Ave, Fresno (93706-3502)
PHONE..................559 268-0875
Ron Cavella, *Pr*
Stan Cavella, *VP*
Sharry Cavella, *Sec*
EMP: 18 EST: 1949
SQ FT: 1,000
SALES (est): 2.07MM
SALES (corp-wide): 5.54MM **Privately Held**

SIC: 3446 3272 Railings, banisters, guards, etc: made from metal pipe; Concrete products, precast, nec
PA: Suburban Steel, Inc.
 706 W California Ave
 559 268-6281

**(P-8648)**
**VALLEY STAIRWAY INC**
5684 E Shields Ave, Fresno (93727-7818)
P.O. Box 245 (93613-0245)
PHONE..................559 299-0151
Jerry De George, *Pr*
Anthony De George Junior, *Sec*
EMP: 16 EST: 1957
SQ FT: 29,464
SALES (est): 1.77MM **Privately Held**
Web: www.valleystairwayinc.com
SIC: 3446 Stairs, staircases, stair treads: prefabricated metal

**(P-8649)**
**WASHINGTON ORNA IR WORKS INC**
Production Steel
17913 S Main St, Gardena (90248-3520)
PHONE..................310 327-8660
Luke Welsh, *Mgr*
EMP: 23
SALES (corp-wide): 25.46MM **Privately Held**
SIC: 3446 1542 Architectural metalwork; Nonresidential construction, nec
PA: Washington Ornamental Iron Works Inc.
 17926 S Broadway St
 310 327-8660

**(P-8650)**
**WESTERN SQUARE INDUSTRIES INC**
1621 N Brdwy, Stockton (95205)
PHONE..................209 944-0921
David Bowyer, *CEO*
Trygue Mikkelsen, *
◆ EMP: 40 EST: 1978
SQ FT: 44,000
SALES (est): 4.26MM **Privately Held**
Web: www.westernsquare.com
SIC: 3446 2542 2514 3441 Fences or posts, ornamental iron or steel; Racks, merchandise display or storage: except wood; Tables, household: metal; Fabricated structural metal

---

## 3448 Prefabricated Metal Buildings

**(P-8651)**
**AGRA TECH INC**
2131 Piedmont Way, Pittsburg (94565-5071)
PHONE..................925 432-3399
◆ EMP: 15 EST: 1973
SALES (est): 2.47MM **Privately Held**
Web: www.agratech.com
SIC: 3448 Greenhouses, prefabricated metal

**(P-8652)**
**ALLIED CONTAINER SYSTEMS INC**
Also Called: ACS
511 Wilbur Ave Ste B4, Antioch (94509-7563)
PHONE..................925 944-7600
Brian Horsfall, *Ch Bd*
Susan Horsfall, *
◆ EMP: 140 EST: 1992

SQ FT: 20,000
SALES (est): 19.65MM **Privately Held**
SIC: 3448 8748 3559 Prefabricated metal buildings and components; Environmental consultant; Chemical machinery and equipment

**(P-8653)**
**ALLIED MDULAR BLDG SYSTEMS INC (PA)**
642 W Nicolas Ave, Orange (92868-1316)
PHONE..................714 516-1188
Kevin Peithman, *CEO*
Raj Singh, *
Cathy Peithman, *
Richard Navarro, *
EMP: 38 EST: 1996
SQ FT: 35,000
SALES (est): 14.08MM **Privately Held**
Web: www.alliedmodular.com
SIC: 3448 Prefabricated metal buildings

**(P-8654)**
**ALUMAWALL INC**
1701 S 7th St Ste 9, San Jose (95112-6000)
PHONE..................408 275-7165
David M Warda, *Pr*
Lori Warda, *
EMP: 65 EST: 1984
SQ FT: 50,000
SALES (est): 9.47MM **Privately Held**
Web: www.alumawall.com
SIC: 3448 Prefabricated metal components

**(P-8655)**
**BIG ENTERPRISES**
9702 Rush St, El Monte (91733-1731)
PHONE..................626 448-1449
EMP: 49 EST: 1971
SALES (est): 8.5MM **Privately Held**
Web: www.bigbooth.com
SIC: 3448 Buildings, portable: prefabricated metal

**(P-8656)**
**BLUESCOPE BUILDINGS N AMER INC**
Also Called: Butler Manufacturing
7440 W Doe Ave, Visalia (93291-9296)
P.O. Box 1590 (93279-1590)
PHONE..................559 651-5300
Juan Carlos Garcia, *Brnch Mgr*
EMP: 200
Web: www.bluescopeconstruction.com
SIC: 3448 Prefabricated metal buildings and components
HQ: Bluescope Buildings North America, Inc.
 1540 Genessee St
 Kansas City MO 64102

**(P-8657)**
**BORGA INC**
Also Called: Metal Buildings & Components
300 W Peach St, Fowler (93625-2530)
P.O. Box 35 (93625-0035)
PHONE..................559 834-5375
▲ EMP: 31
Web: www.borgasteel.com
SIC: 3448 Prefabricated metal components

**(P-8658)**
**BORGA STL BLDNGS CMPONENTS INC**
Also Called: Borga
300 W Peach St, Fowler (93625-2530)
P.O. Box 35 (93625-0035)
PHONE..................559 834-5375

Ronald Heskett, *CEO*
EMP: 62 EST: 2013
SQ FT: 90,000
SALES (est): 10.33MM **Privately Held**
Web: www.borgasteel.com
SIC: 3448 Prefabricated metal buildings and components

**(P-8659)**
**CBC STEEL BUILDINGS LLC**
1700 E Louise Ave, Lathrop (95330-9795)
P.O. Box 1009 (95330-1009)
PHONE..................209 858-2425
EMP: 120 EST: 2007
SQ FT: 105,000
SALES (est): 26.87MM
SALES (corp-wide): 34.71B **Publicly Held**
Web: www.cbcsteelbuildings.com
SIC: 3448 Prefabricated metal buildings
PA: Nucor Corporation
 1915 Rexford Rd
 704 366-7000

**(P-8660)**
**CEMCO LLC**
Also Called: Cemco
1001a Pittsburg Antioch Hwy, Pittsburg (94565-4123)
PHONE..................925 473-9340
Ned Martin, *Mgr*
EMP: 70
Web: www.cemcosteel.com
SIC: 3448 3449 3444 3441 Prefabricated metal buildings and components; Miscellaneous metalwork; Sheet metalwork; Fabricated structural metal
HQ: Cemco, Llc
 13191 Crssrads Pkwy N Ste
 City Of Industry CA 91746
 800 775-2362

**(P-8661)**
**CLAMSHELL STRUCTURES INC**
Also Called: Clamshell Buildings
300 Graves Ave Ste B, Oxnard (93030-8938)
PHONE..................805 988-1340
Gregory J Mangan, *CEO*
EMP: 15 EST: 1982
SQ FT: 46,000
SALES (est): 4.2MM
SALES (corp-wide): 4.85MM **Privately Held**
Web: www.clamshell.com
SIC: 3448 Prefabricated metal buildings
PA: Clamshell Holdings, Inc.
 300 Graves Ave Ste B
 805 988-1340

**(P-8662)**
**CRATE MODULAR INC**
3025 E Dominguez St, Carson (90810-1437)
PHONE..................310 405-0829
Rich Rozycki, *CEO*
Natasaha Deski, *
Moises Bada, *
EMP: 99 EST: 2018
SALES (est): 17.29MM **Privately Held**
Web: www.cratemodular.com
SIC: 3448 Prefabricated metal buildings and components

**(P-8663)**
**DURACOLD REFRIGERATION MFG LLC**
1551 S Primrose Ave, Monrovia (91016-4542)
PHONE..................626 358-1710
Harold Monsher, *Genl Pt*

## PRODUCTS & SERVICES SECTION
### 3448 - Prefabricated Metal Buildings (P-8682)

Ben Monsher, *Pt*
**EMP:** 22 **EST:** 1996
**SQ FT:** 25,000
**SALES (est):** 1.17MM **Privately Held**
**Web:** www.arcticwalkins.com
**SIC: 3448** 3585 Prefabricated metal components; Refrigeration and heating equipment

### (P-8664)
### EMERALD KINGDOM GREENHOUSE LLC
1593 Beltline Rd, Redding (96003-1407)
**PHONE**.................................530 241-5670
**EMP:** 17
**SALES (corp-wide):** 6.13MM **Privately Held**
**Web:** www.emeraldkingdomgreenhouse.com
**SIC: 3448** Greenhouses, prefabricated metal
**PA:** Emerald Kingdom Greenhouse Llc
  104 Masonic Ln
  530 215-5670

### (P-8665)
### ENVIROPLEX INC
4777 Carpenter Rd, Stockton (95215-8106)
**PHONE**.................................209 466-8000
Glenn Owens, *Pr*
**EMP:** 60 **EST:** 1991
**SQ FT:** 102,000
**SALES (est):** 10.11MM
**SALES (corp-wide):** 831.84MM **Publicly Held**
**Web:** www.enviroplex.com
**SIC: 3448** Buildings, portable: prefabricated metal
**PA:** Mcgrath Rentcorp
  5700 Las Positas Rd
  925 606-9200

### (P-8666)
### FCP INC (PA)
23100 Wildomar Trl, Wildomar (92595-9699)
P.O. Box 1555 (92595-1555)
**PHONE**.................................951 678-4571
Russell J Greer, *CEO*
Barret Hilzer, *
**EMP:** 84 **EST:** 1982
**SQ FT:** 200,000
**SALES (est):** 6.5MM
**SALES (corp-wide):** 6.5MM **Privately Held**
**Web:** www.fcpbarns.com
**SIC: 3448** 1541 Prefabricated metal components; Steel building construction

### (P-8667)
### FCP INC
4125 Market St Ste 14, Ventura (93003-5643)
P.O. Box 1217 (93014-1217)
**PHONE**.................................805 684-1117
Barryet Hilzer, *Pr*
**EMP:** 16
**SALES (corp-wide):** 6.5MM **Privately Held**
**Web:** www.fcpbarns.com
**SIC: 3448** 1541 Prefabricated metal components; Steel building construction
**PA:** Fcp, Inc.
  23100 Baxter Rd
  951 678-4571

### (P-8668)
### GCN SUPPLY LLC
9070 Bridgeport Pl, Rancho Cucamonga (91730-5530)
**PHONE**.................................909 643-4603
Gustavo Chona Senior, *Managing Member*
**EMP:** 50 **EST:** 2015
**SALES (est):** 1.4MM **Privately Held**
**Web:** www.gcnsupply.com
**SIC: 3448** 2671 Prefabricated metal buildings and components; Plastic film, coated or laminated for packaging

### (P-8669)
### GLOBAL MODULAR INC (HQ)
450 Commerce Ave, Atwater (95301-9412)
P.O. Box 369 (93610)
**PHONE**.................................209 676-8029
Adam Debard, *Pr*
Adam De Bard, *Pr*
Milo King, *Sec*
**EMP:** 20 **EST:** 2001
**SALES (est):** 16.97MM
**SALES (corp-wide):** 16.97MM **Privately Held**
**Web:** www.gdvi.net
**SIC: 3448** Prefabricated metal buildings and components
**PA:** Global Diversified Industries, Inc.
  450 Commerce Ave
  559 665-5800

### (P-8670)
### H ROBERTS CONSTRUCTION
2165 W Gaylord St, Long Beach (90813-1033)
**PHONE**.................................562 590-4825
Kathleen F Roberts, *Pr*
**EMP:** 51 **EST:** 1988
**SQ FT:** 1,100
**SALES (est):** 1.93MM **Privately Held**
**Web:** www.robertsconstructionllc.net
**SIC: 3448** Buildings, portable: prefabricated metal

### (P-8671)
### JOHN L CONLEY INC
Also Called: Conleys Greenhouse Mfg & Sales
4344 Mission Blvd, Montclair (91763-6017)
**PHONE**.................................909 627-0981
John L Conley, *CEO*
Tom Conley, *
Dean Conley, *
Howard Davis, *
◆ **EMP:** 75 **EST:** 1946
**SALES (est):** 8.75MM **Privately Held**
**Web:** www.conleys.com
**SIC: 3448** 3441 Greenhouses, prefabricated metal; Fabricated structural metal

### (P-8672)
### JTS MODULAR INC
7001 Mcdivitt Dr Ste B, Bakersfield (93313-2006)
P.O. Box 41765 (93384-1765)
**PHONE**.................................661 835-9270
Dene Hurlbert, *Pr*
John Hurlbert, *
Lee Hawkins, *
Phillip Engler, *
**EMP:** 50 **EST:** 2000
**SQ FT:** 4,000
**SALES (est):** 8.5MM **Privately Held**
**Web:** www.jtsmodular.com
**SIC: 3448** Prefabricated metal buildings and components

### (P-8673)
### KINGSPAN INSULATED PANELS INC
Kingspan API
2000 Morgan Rd, Modesto (95358-9407)
**PHONE**.................................209 531-9091
Russell Shiels, *Pr*
**EMP:** 203
**Web:** www.kingspan.com
**SIC: 3448** Prefabricated metal buildings and components
**HQ:** Kingspan Insulated Panels Inc.
  726 Summerhill Dr
  Deland FL 32724
  386 626-6789

### (P-8674)
### MADISON INDUSTRIES (HQ)
17201 Darwin Ave, Hesperia (92345-5178)
**PHONE**.................................562 484-5099
John Frey Junior, *Pr*
John Samuel Frey, *
Grace Lee, *Corporate Controller**
**EMP:** 28 **EST:** 1974
**SALES (est):** 11.51MM
**SALES (corp-wide):** 44.99MM **Privately Held**
**Web:** www.madisonind.com
**SIC: 3448** 3441 1542 Prefabricated metal buildings and components; Fabricated structural metal; Nonresidential construction, nec
**PA:** John S. Frey Enterprises
  1900 E 64th St
  323 583-4061

### (P-8675)
### MCELROY METAL MILL INC
Also Called: McElroy Metal
17031 Koala Rd, Adelanto (92301-2246)
**PHONE**.................................760 246-5545
Pete Nadler, *Mgr*
**EMP:** 37
**SQ FT:** 37,700
**SALES (corp-wide):** 104.96MM **Privately Held**
**Web:** www.mcelroymetal.com
**SIC: 3448** Prefabricated metal components
**PA:** Mcelroy Metal Mill, Inc.
  1500 Hamilton Rd
  318 747-8000

### (P-8676)
### MOBILE MODULAR MANAGEMENT CORP
Also Called: Trs Rentelco
11450 Mission Blvd, Jurupa Valley (91752-1015)
**PHONE**.................................800 819-1084
Thomas Sanders, *Mgr*
**EMP:** 112
**SALES (corp-wide):** 831.84MM **Publicly Held**
**Web:** www.mgrc.com
**SIC: 3448** 7519 Prefabricated metal buildings and components; Trailer rental
**HQ:** Mobile Modular Management Corporation
  5700 Las Positas Rd
  Livermore CA 94551
  925 443-8052

### (P-8677)
### MORIN CORPORATION
Also Called: Morin West
10707 Commerce Way, Fontana (92337-8216)
**PHONE**.................................909 428-3747
Ilhan Eser, *VP*
**EMP:** 40
**Web:** www.morincorp.com
**SIC: 3448** Prefabricated metal buildings and components
**HQ:** Morin Corporation
  685 Middle St Ste 1
  Bristol CT 06010

### (P-8678)
### NCI GROUP INC
Also Called: Metal Coaters
9123 Center Ave, Rancho Cucamonga (91730-5312)
**PHONE**.................................909 987-4681
Colin Lally, *Brnch Mgr*
**EMP:** 22
**SALES (corp-wide):** 5.58B **Privately Held**
**Web:** www.bluescopecoatedproducts.com
**SIC: 3448** 3446 Prefabricated metal buildings; Architectural metalwork
**HQ:** Nci Group, Inc.
  13105 Nw Fwy Ste 500
  Houston TX 77040
  281 897-7788

### (P-8679)
### ORANGE COUNTY ERECTORS INC
517 E La Palma Ave, Anaheim (92801-2536)
**PHONE**.................................714 502-8455
Richard Lewis, *CEO*
Sandra Lewis, *
**EMP:** 50 **EST:** 1975
**SQ FT:** 80,000
**SALES (est):** 10.04MM **Privately Held**
**Web:** www.ocerectors.com
**SIC: 3448** 3441 1791 Buildings, portable: prefabricated metal; Fabricated structural metal; Structural steel erection

### (P-8680)
### PRE-INSULATED METAL TECH INC (HQ)
Also Called: All Weather Insulated Panels
929 Aldridge Rd, Vacaville (95688-9282)
**PHONE**.................................707 359-2280
William H Lowery, *Pr*
Michael T Lowery, *VP*
◆ **EMP:** 23 **EST:** 2010
**SQ FT:** 96,000
**SALES (est):** 31.15MM **Privately Held**
**Web:** www.awipanels.com
**SIC: 3448** Panels for prefabricated metal buildings
**PA:** Kingspan Group Public Limited Company
  Dublin Road

### (P-8681)
### PROGRESSIVE MARKETING PDTS INC
Also Called: Progressive Marketing
4571 Avenida Del Este, Yorba Linda (92886-3002)
**PHONE**.................................714 888-1700
Leonard Dozier, *CEO*
Scott Hillstrom, *Dir*
Sam Malik, *Ex VP*
Tiffany Dozier, *Ex VP*
◆ **EMP:** 80 **EST:** 1977
**SALES (est):** 4.61MM **Privately Held**
**Web:** www.premiermounts.com
**SIC: 3448** Prefabricated metal buildings and components

### (P-8682)
### ROBERTSON-CECO II CORPORATION
Also Called: Star Building Systems
12101 E Brandt Rd, Lockeford (95237-9550)
**PHONE**.................................209 727-5504
Greg Lewis, *Mgr*
**EMP:** 60
**SQ FT:** 7,000

## 3448 - Prefabricated Metal Buildings (P-8683)

SALES (corp-wide): 5.58B **Privately Held**
Web: robertson-cecoii.mfgpages.com
SIC: **3448** Buildings, portable: prefabricated metal
HQ: Robertson-Ceco Ii Corporation
10943 N Sam Huston Pkwy W
Houston TX 77064

### (P-8683)
### ROOFSCREEN MFG INC
347 Coral St, Santa Cruz (95060-2106)
PHONE.................................831 421-9230
Ryan W Bruce, *Pr*
David Wallace, *
EMP: 31 EST: 2002
SALES (est): 12MM **Privately Held**
Web: www.roofscreen.com
SIC: **3448** Screen enclosures

### (P-8684)
### SARAMARK INC
15660 Mckinley Ave, Lathrop (95330-8525)
P.O. Box 1369 (95330-1369)
PHONE.................................408 971-3881
Mark A Collishaw, *CEO*
EMP: 50 EST: 1900
SALES (est): 1.6MM **Privately Held**
Web: www.saramark.com
SIC: **3448** Prefabricated metal buildings and components

### (P-8685)
### SHADE STRUCTURES INC
Also Called: Shade Structures
1085 N Main St Ste C, Orange (92867-5458)
PHONE.................................714 427-6980
Christina Bennett, *Brnch Mgr*
EMP: 22
Web: www.usa-shade.com
SIC: **3448** Prefabricated metal components
HQ: Shade Structures, Inc.
2580 Esters Blvd 100
Dfw Airport TX 75261
214 905-9500

### (P-8686)
### STELL INDUSTRIES INC
Also Called: C-Thru Sunrooms
1951 S Parco Ave Ste B, Ontario (91761-8315)
PHONE.................................951 369-8777
Gary P Stell Junior, *CEO*
Jason S Albany, *
Mike Leigh, *
EMP: 50 EST: 1947
SALES (est): 2.77MM **Privately Held**
SIC: **3448** Sunrooms, prefabricated metal

### (P-8687)
### T M P SERVICES INC (PA)
2929 Kansas Ave, Riverside (92507-2639)
PHONE.................................951 213-3900
Prentiss Tarver Junior, *Stockholder*
Shari Taylor, *
EMP: 21 EST: 1993
SQ FT: 32,000
SALES (est): 4.74MM **Privately Held**
Web: www.tmpservices.com
SIC: **3448** Ramps, prefabricated metal

### (P-8688)
### UNITED CARPORTS LLC
7280 Sycamore Canyon Blvd Ste 1, Riverside (92508-2333)
PHONE.................................800 757-6742
Ryan Spates, *Pr*
Ryan Spates, *Managing Member*
Garrett Spates, *
EMP: 28 EST: 2011
SQ FT: 5,000
SALES (est): 6.64MM **Privately Held**
Web: www.unitedcarports.com
SIC: **3448** Prefabricated metal buildings and components

### (P-8689)
### WESTERN METAL SUPPLY CO INC
530 State Pl, Escondido (92029-1326)
PHONE.................................760 233-7800
Abel Caballero, *Pr*
Scott Tanner, *Sec*
EMP: 15 EST: 2004
SALES (est): 2.19MM **Privately Held**
Web: www.westernmetalsupplyco.com
SIC: **3448** Prefabricated metal buildings and components

---

## 3449 Miscellaneous Metalwork

### (P-8690)
### 3G REBAR INC
6400 Price Way, Bakersfield (93308-5119)
PHONE.................................661 588-0294
John Michael Dean, *Pr*
EMP: 15 EST: 2011
SQ FT: 5,600
SALES (est): 3.04MM **Privately Held**
SIC: **3449** Bars, concrete reinforcing: fabricated steel

### (P-8691)
### AMC MACHINING INC
1540 Commerce Way, Paso Robles (93446-3524)
P.O. Box 665 (93447-0665)
PHONE.................................805 238-5452
Alex Camp, *Pr*
EMP: 35 EST: 2007
SQ FT: 10,000
SALES (est): 6.07MM **Privately Held**
Web: www.amcmachining.com
SIC: **3449** Miscellaneous metalwork

### (P-8692)
### ARCHITECTURAL ENTERPRISES INC
Also Called: Hi-Tech Iron Works
5821 Randolph St, Commerce (90040-3415)
PHONE.................................323 268-4000
Kevin Drake, *Pr*
John S Lee, *
Alma Gutierrez, *
EMP: 40 EST: 1984
SQ FT: 20,000
SALES (est): 6.19MM **Privately Held**
SIC: **3449** Miscellaneous metalwork

### (P-8693)
### C&K FORM FABRICATION INC
370 N 9th St, Colton (92324-2909)
P.O. Box 431 (92324-0431)
PHONE.................................909 825-1882
Kyle A Paxson, *CEO*
EMP: 43 EST: 2016
SALES (est): 2.76MM
SALES (corp-wide): 25.12MM **Privately Held**
SIC: **3449** Miscellaneous metalwork
PA: Squires Lumber Company
370 N 9th St
909 825-1882

### (P-8694)
### CAMBLIN STEEL SERVICE INC
548 Gibson Dr Ste 150, Roseville (95678-5501)
PHONE.................................916 644-1300
▲ EMP: 60 EST: 1954
SALES (est): 11.11MM **Privately Held**
Web: www.camblinsteel.com
SIC: **3449** Miscellaneous metalwork

### (P-8695)
### CMC STEEL US LLC
Also Called: Gerdau Ameristeel
5425 Industrial Pkwy, San Bernardino (92407-1803)
PHONE.................................909 646-7827
EMP: 43
SALES (corp-wide): 7.93B **Publicly Held**
Web: www.cmc.com
SIC: **3449** Bars, concrete reinforcing: fabricated steel
HQ: Cmc Steel Us, Llc
6565 N Mcrthur Blvd Ste 8
Irving TX 75039
214 689-4300

### (P-8696)
### DB BUILDING FASTENERS INC (PA)
Also Called: Db Building Fasteners
5555 E Gibralter, Ontario (91764-5121)
P.O. Box 4407 (91729-4407)
PHONE.................................909 581-6740
Brent Dooley, *Owner*
Brent Dooley, *Pr*
John Dooley Iii, *VP*
Andrew Cohn, *Sec*
▲ EMP: 18 EST: 1992
SALES (est): 5.55MM
SALES (corp-wide): 5.55MM **Privately Held**
Web: www.selfdrillers.com
SIC: **3449** Miscellaneous metalwork

### (P-8697)
### FAB SERVICES WEST INC
10007 Elm Ave, Fontana (92335-6318)
PHONE.................................909 350-7500
EMP: 77 EST: 2011
SALES (est): 4.79MM **Privately Held**
SIC: **3449** Miscellaneous metalwork
HQ: Fab Holding Llc
3335 Susan St
Costa Mesa CA 92626
949 236-5520

### (P-8698)
### H WAYNE LEWIS INC
Also Called: Amber Steel Co.
312 S Willow Ave, Rialto (92376-6313)
P.O. Box 900 (92377-0900)
PHONE.................................909 874-2213
H Wayne Lewis, *CEO*
Dan Bergen, *
Janet Lewis, *
Kriss Lewis, *
EMP: 40 EST: 1983
SQ FT: 8,100
SALES (est): 4.55MM **Privately Held**
Web: www.ambersteelco.com
SIC: **3449** Bars, concrete reinforcing: fabricated steel

### (P-8699)
### INNOVATIVE METAL INDS INC
Also Called: Southwest Data Products
1330 Riverview Dr, San Bernardino (92408-2944)
PHONE.................................909 796-6200
Kelly Brodhagan, *CEO*
▲ EMP: 100 EST: 2006
SQ FT: 150,000
SALES (est): 23.97MM
SALES (corp-wide): 34.71B **Publicly Held**
Web: www.imiac.com
SIC: **3449** Curtain wall, metal
PA: Nucor Corporation
1915 Rexford Rd
704 366-7000

### (P-8700)
### JLJ REBAR EXTREME INC
1532 Wall Ave, San Bernardino (92404-5018)
PHONE.................................909 381-9177
Jose Luis Jaime, *CEO*
EMP: 50 EST: 2019
SALES (est): 3.74MM **Privately Held**
SIC: **3449** Bars, concrete reinforcing: fabricated steel

### (P-8701)
### JR DANIELS COMMERCIAL BLDRS
Also Called: Innovative Steel Structures
907 Maze Blvd, Modesto (95351-1851)
PHONE.................................209 545-6040
James R Daniels, *Pr*
EMP: 15 EST: 1991
SQ FT: 1,900
SALES (est): 588.72K **Privately Held**
SIC: **3449** Bars, concrete reinforcing: fabricated steel

### (P-8702)
### KING WIRE PARTITIONS INC
Also Called: A A A Partitions
6044 N Figueroa St, Los Angeles (90042-4232)
PHONE.................................323 256-4848
Max Behshid, *Pr*
Millie Behshid, *
Farid Behshid, *
▲ EMP: 30 EST: 1978
SQ FT: 24,000
SALES (est): 938K **Privately Held**
Web: www.kingwireusa.com
SIC: **3449** 5046 3496 Miscellaneous metalwork; Partitions; Miscellaneous fabricated wire products

### (P-8703)
### LMS REINFORCING STEEL USA LP (HQ)
Also Called: LMS Reinforcing Steel Group
26365 Earthmover Cir, Corona (92883)
PHONE.................................951 307-0972
Norm Streu, *Pr*
Janice Comeau, *CFO*
Mike Schutz, *VP Fin*
EMP: 15 EST: 2016
SALES (est): 6.48MM
SALES (corp-wide): 3.49MM **Privately Held**
SIC: **3449** Bars, concrete reinforcing: fabricated steel
PA: Lms Holdings (Ab) Ltd
7452 132 St
604 598-9930

### (P-8704)
### NORTH STAR ACQUISITION INC
Also Called: North Star Company
14912 S Broadway, Gardena (90248-1818)
PHONE.................................310 515-2200
EMP: 63 EST: 1950
SALES (est): 4.09MM **Privately Held**
Web: www.northstarcompany.com

SIC: 3449 3444 3321 3316 Custom roll formed products; Sheet metalwork; Gray and ductile iron foundries; Cold finishing of steel shapes

**(P-8705)**
**PACIFIC STEEL GROUP**
Also Called: Pacific Steel Group
2301 Napa Vallejo Hwy, Napa (94558-6242)
PHONE..............................707 669-3136
Alfredo Gonzalez, *Brnch Mgr*
EMP: 21
SALES (corp-wide): 123.74MM **Privately Held**
Web: www.pacificsteelgroup.com
SIC: 3449 Bars, concrete reinforcing; fabricated steel
PA: Pacific Steel Group, Llc
4805 Murphy Canyon Rd
858 251-1100

**(P-8706)**
**PACIFIC STEEL GROUP LLC (PA)**
Also Called: Psg
4805 Murphy Canyon Rd, San Diego (92123-4324)
PHONE..............................858 251-1100
Eric Benson, *Prin*
Eric Benson, *CEO*
John Scurlock, *
Monica Kamoss, *
EMP: 114 EST: 2014
SQ FT: 26,000
SALES (est): 123.74MM
SALES (corp-wide): 123.74MM **Privately Held**
Web: www.pacificsteelgroup.com
SIC: 3449 Bars, concrete reinforcing; fabricated steel

**(P-8707)**
**PACIFIC WEST FOREST PRODUCTS**
13434 Browns Valley Dr, Chico (95973-9322)
P.O. Box 2082 (95927-2082)
PHONE..............................530 899-7313
Keith Lindquist, *Pr*
Kevin Linquist, *VP*
▲ EMP: 16 EST: 1997
SQ FT: 37,000
SALES (est): 2.36MM **Privately Held**
Web: www.pacificwestforest.com
SIC: 3449 5031 Custom roll formed products ; Lumber: rough, dressed, and finished

**(P-8708)**
**QUALITY STEEL FABRICATORS INC**
13275 Gregg St, Poway (92064-7120)
PHONE..............................858 748-8400
Bryan J Miller, *Pr*
Cheryl Wolf, *Contrlr*
EMP: 22 EST: 1997
SALES (est): 1.57MM **Privately Held**
Web: www.qualityreinforcing.com
SIC: 3449 Bars, concrete reinforcing; fabricated steel

**(P-8709)**
**SIMPSON STRONG-TIE COMPANY INC (HQ)**
5956 W Las Positas Blvd, Pleasanton (94588-8540)
P.O. Box 10789 (94588)
PHONE..............................925 560-9000
Michael Olosky, *Pr*

Bryan Magstaet, *CFO*
◆ EMP: 150 EST: 1914
SQ FT: 89,000
SALES (est): 502.51MM
SALES (corp-wide): 2.21B **Publicly Held**
Web: www.strongtie.com
SIC: 3449 2891 Joists, fabricated bar; Adhesives
PA: Simpson Manufacturing Co., Inc.
5956 W Las Positas Blvd
925 560-9000

**(P-8710)**
**SIMPSON STRONG-TIE COMPANY INC**
5151 S Airport Way, Stockton (95206-3991)
PHONE..............................209 234-7775
Bruce Lewis, *Brnch Mgr*
EMP: 100
SALES (corp-wide): 2.21B **Publicly Held**
Web: www.strongtie.com
SIC: 3449 3444 3441 Joists, fabricated bar; Sheet metalwork; Fabricated structural metal
HQ: Simpson Strong-Tie Company Inc.
5956 W Las Positas Blvd
Pleasanton CA 94588
925 560-9000

**(P-8711)**
**SIMPSON STRONG-TIE INTL INC (DH)**
5956 W Las Positas Blvd, Pleasanton (94588-8540)
P.O. Box 10789 (94588-0789)
PHONE..............................925 560-9000
Mike Olosky, *CEO*
▲ EMP: 100 EST: 1993
SQ FT: 89,000
SALES (est): 7.52MM
SALES (corp-wide): 2.21B **Publicly Held**
Web: www.strongtie.com
SIC: 3449 Joists, fabricated bar
HQ: Simpson Strong-Tie Company Inc.
5956 W Las Positas Blvd
Pleasanton CA 94588
925 560-9000

**(P-8712)**
**TAMCO**
Also Called: Gerdau Rancho Cucamonga
1000 Quail St Ste 260, Newport Beach (92660-2784)
P.O. Box 13158 (92658-5087)
PHONE..............................949 552-9714
EMP: 300
SALES (corp-wide): 7.93B **Publicly Held**
Web: www.asgsales.com
SIC: 3449 Bars, concrete reinforcing; fabricated steel
HQ: Tamco
5425 Industrial Pkwy
San Bernardino CA 92407
909 899-0660

## 3451 Screw Machine Products

**(P-8713)**
**ABEL AUTOMATICS LLC**
Also Called: Abel Reels
165 N Aviador St, Camarillo (93010-8314)
PHONE..............................805 388-3721
David Dragoo, *Ch Bd*
◆ EMP: 30 EST: 1980
SQ FT: 16,000
SALES (est): 2.44MM **Privately Held**
Web: www.abelreels.com
SIC: 3451 3949 Screw machine products; Reels, fishing

**(P-8714)**
**ACCU-SWISS INC (PA)**
544 Armstrong Way, Oakdale (95361-9567)
PHONE..............................209 847-1016
TOLL FREE: 800
Sohel Sareshwala, *Pr*
Asfiya Sareshwala, *Sec*
EMP: 17 EST: 1977
SQ FT: 10,000
SALES (est): 3.38MM
SALES (corp-wide): 3.38MM **Privately Held**
Web: www.accuswissinc.com
SIC: 3451 8711 Screw machine products; Engineering services

**(P-8715)**
**ALGER PRECISION MACHINING LLC**
724 S Bon View Ave, Ontario (91761-1913)
PHONE..............................909 986-4591
Duane Femrite, *Prin*
Jim Hemingway, *Prin*
Danny Hankla, *Prin*
▲ EMP: 160 EST: 1986
SQ FT: 35,000
SALES (est): 23.2MM **Privately Held**
Web: www.algerprecision.com
SIC: 3451 Screw machine products

**(P-8716)**
**ALPHA OMEGA SWISS INC**
23305 La Palma Ave, Yorba Linda (92887-4773)
PHONE..............................714 692-8009
Dale La Rock, *Pr*
Randy L Jones, *
EMP: 20 EST: 1980
SQ FT: 15,500
SALES (est): 713.2K **Privately Held**
Web: www.alphaomegaswiss.com
SIC: 3451 3599 Screw machine products; Machine shop, jobbing and repair

**(P-8717)**
**ASSOCIATED SCREW MACHINE PDTS**
Also Called: A S M P
23978 Connecticut St Ste A, Hayward (94545-1637)
PHONE..............................510 783-3831
Mike Schenkhuizen, *Pr*
EMP: 25 EST: 1959
SQ FT: 12,000
SALES (est): 2.17MM **Privately Held**
Web: www.asmpinc.net
SIC: 3451 Screw machine products

**(P-8718)**
**ATHANOR GROUP INC**
921 E California St, Ontario (91761-1918)
PHONE..............................909 467-1205
Duane L Femrite, *Pr*
Richard Krause, *VP*
EMP: 22 EST: 1958
SQ FT: 35,600
SALES (est): 180.28K **Privately Held**
SIC: 3451 Screw machine products

**(P-8719)**
**BALDA HK PLASTICS INC**
Also Called: H K Prcision Turning Machining
3229 Roymar Rd, Oceanside (92058-1311)
PHONE..............................760 757-1100
Dan Wannigen, *Mgr*
EMP: 40
SQ FT: 9,808
SALES (corp-wide): 2.67MM **Privately Held**

SIC: 3451 3544 3089 Screw machine products; Special dies and tools; Injection molded finished plastics products, nec
HQ: Balda Precision, Inc.
3233 Roymar Rd
Oceanside CA 92058
760 757-1100

**(P-8720)**
**BALDA PRECISION INC (DH)**
Also Called: HK Precision Turning Machining
3233 Roymar Rd, Oceanside (92058-1311)
PHONE..............................760 757-1100
EMP: 80 EST: 1974
SALES (est): 18.8MM
SALES (corp-wide): 2.67MM **Privately Held**
SIC: 3451 3544 3089 Screw machine products; Special dies and tools; Injection molded finished plastics products, nec
HQ: Clere Ag
Schluterstr. 45
Berlin BE 10707
302 130-0430

**(P-8721)**
**DESIGNED METAL CONNECTIONS INC**
Also Called: DMC
623 E Artesia Blvd, Carson (90746-1201)
PHONE..............................310 323-6200
EMP: 25
SALES (corp-wide): 364.48B **Publicly Held**
Web: www.pccfluidfittings.com
SIC: 3451 Screw machine products
HQ: Designed Metal Connections, Inc.
14800 S Figueroa St
Gardena CA 90248
310 323-6200

**(P-8722)**
**FASTENER INNOVATION TECH INC**
Also Called: F I T
19300 S Susana Rd, Compton (90221-5711)
PHONE..............................310 538-1111
Larry Valeriano, *Pr*
EMP: 99 EST: 1979
SQ FT: 65,000
SALES (est): 15.95MM
SALES (corp-wide): 123.82MM **Privately Held**
Web: www.fitfastener.com
SIC: 3451 3728 3452 3429 Screw machine products; Aircraft parts and equipment, nec; Bolts, nuts, rivets, and washers; Hardware, nec
HQ: Avantus Aerospace, Inc.
29101 The Old Rd
Valencia CA 91355
661 295-8620

**(P-8723)**
**GALGON INDUSTRIES INC**
37399 Centralmont Pl, Fremont (94536-6549)
PHONE..............................510 792-8211
▲ EMP: 39
SIC: 3451 3444 Screw machine products; Sheet metalwork

**(P-8724)**
**GT PRECISION INC**
Also Called: Alard Machine Products
1629 W 132nd St, Gardena (90249-2005)
PHONE..............................310 323-4374
Gregg Thompson, *CEO*
▲ EMP: 107 EST: 1967

# 3451 - Screw Machine Products (P-8725)

SQ FT: 11,700
SALES (est): 23.08MM **Privately Held**
Web: www.alardmachine.com
SIC: **3451** Screw machine products

**(P-8725)**
**M & R ENGINEERING CO**
227 E Meats Ave, Orange (92865-3311)
PHONE..................................714 991-8480
Natalia Sephton, *Pr*
EMP: 15 EST: 1973
SQ FT: 32,000
SALES (est): 2.37MM **Privately Held**
Web: www.m-reng.com
SIC: **3451** 3541 Screw machine products; Lathes

**(P-8726)**
**MERCED SCREW PRODUCTS INC**
1861 Grogan Ave, Merced (95341-6432)
PHONE..................................209 723-7706
Steve Centivich, *Pr*
EMP: 40 EST: 1980
SQ FT: 17,000
SALES (est): 848.19K **Privately Held**
Web: www.mercedscrewproducts.com
SIC: **3451** Screw machine products

**(P-8727)**
**ONYX INDUSTRIES INC (PA)**
Also Called: Quad R Tech
1227 254th St, Harbor City (90710-2912)
PHONE..................................310 539-8830
Vladimir Reil, *CEO*
▲ EMP: 100 EST: 1978
SQ FT: 30,000
SALES (est): 18.41MM
SALES (corp-wide): 18.41MM **Privately Held**
Web: www.onyxindustries.com
SIC: **3451** Screw machine products

**(P-8728)**
**ONYX INDUSTRIES INC**
521 W Rosecrans Ave, Gardena (90248-1514)
PHONE..................................310 851-6161
Siamak Maghoul, *Brnch Mgr*
EMP: 100
SALES (corp-wide): 18.41MM **Privately Held**
Web: www.studex.com
SIC: **3451** Screw machine products
PA: Onyx Industries Inc.
1227 254th St
310 539-8830

**(P-8729)**
**PACIFIC PRECISION INC**
1318 Palomares St, La Verne (91750-5232)
PHONE..................................909 392-5610
EMP: 40 EST: 1981
SALES (est): 9.38MM **Privately Held**
Web: www.pacificprecisioninc.com
SIC: **3451** Screw machine products

**(P-8730)**
**PRICE MANUFACTURING CO INC**
372 N Smith Ave, Corona (92878-4371)
P.O. Box 1209 (92878-1209)
PHONE..................................951 371-5660
Robert P Schiffmacher, *CEO*
Ively Schiffmacher, *
EMP: 32 EST: 1979
SQ FT: 15,600
SALES (est): 5.55MM **Privately Held**
Web: www.pricemfg.com

SIC: **3451** Screw machine products

**(P-8731)**
**SORENSON ENGINEERING INC (PA)**
32032 Dunlap Blvd, Yucaipa (92399-1706)
PHONE..................................909 795-2434
David L Sorenson, *Pr*
Paul Sewell, *
◆ EMP: 161 EST: 1956
SQ FT: 61,000
SALES (est): 46.64MM
SALES (corp-wide): 46.64MM **Privately Held**
Web: www.sorensoneng.com
SIC: **3451** Screw machine products

**(P-8732)**
**SWISS-MICRON INC**
22361 Gilberto Ste A, Rcho Sta Marg (92688-2103)
PHONE..................................949 589-0430
Kurt Sollberger, *CEO*
Beverley Sollberger, *
EMP: 53 EST: 1984
SQ FT: 16,000
SALES (est): 4.78MM **Privately Held**
Web: www.swissmicron.com
SIC: **3451** Screw machine products

**(P-8733)**
**SWISS-TECH MACHINING LLC**
Also Called: Manufacturer
10564 Industrial Ave, Roseville (95678-6224)
PHONE..................................916 797-6010
EMP: 25 EST: 1994
SQ FT: 20,000
SALES (est): 4.11MM **Privately Held**
Web: www.stmachining.com
SIC: **3451** Screw machine products

**(P-8734)**
**TL MACHINE INC**
14272 Commerce Dr, Garden Grove (92843-4942)
PHONE..................................714 554-4154
Thanh X Ly, *Pr*
Thanh Ly, *
Tuyen Ly, *
Quang Ly, *
▲ EMP: 90 EST: 2001
SQ FT: 39,126
SALES (est): 14.53MM **Privately Held**
Web: www.tlmachine.com
SIC: **3451** 3561 3593 3728 Screw machine products; Pumps and pumping equipment; Fluid power cylinders and actuators; Aircraft parts and equipment, nec

**(P-8735)**
**TRIUMPH PRECISION PRODUCTS**
Also Called: TP Products
13636 Vaughn St Ste A, San Fernando (91340-3052)
PHONE..................................818 897-4700
Victor Linares, *Pr*
Javier Cervantes, *VP*
Jesus Cervantes, *Sec*
EMP: 17 EST: 1967
SQ FT: 19,500
SALES (est): 474.32K **Privately Held**
SIC: **3451** Screw machine products

**(P-8736)**
**UNIVERSAL SCREW PRODUCTS**
20421 Earl St, Torrance (90503-2414)
P.O. Box 14241 (90503-8241)

PHONE..................................310 371-1170
Ken Shank, *Pr*
Michael Flannigan, *Sec*
EMP: 15 EST: 1970
SQ FT: 6,000
SALES (est): 231.56K **Privately Held**
SIC: **3451** Screw machine products

**(P-8737)**
**V M P INC**
24830 Avenue Tibbitts, Valencia (91355-3404)
PHONE..................................661 294-9934
Betty Schreiner, *Pr*
Robert Schreiner Junior, *VP*
Suzanne St George, *Sec*
Steve Schreiner, *Treas*
▲ EMP: 16 EST: 1960
SQ FT: 25,000
SALES (est): 2.46MM **Privately Held**
Web: www.vmpinc.com
SIC: **3451** Screw machine products

**(P-8738)**
**WYATT PRECISION MACHINE INC**
3301 E 59th St, Long Beach (90805-4503)
PHONE..................................562 634-0524
Dennis Allison, *Pr*
Paul Layton, *
Allen Harmon, *
EMP: 47 EST: 1952
SQ FT: 14,000
SALES (est): 5.29MM **Privately Held**
Web: www.wyattprecisionmachine.com
SIC: **3451** Screw machine products

**(P-8739)**
**ZENITH SCREW PRODUCTS INC**
10910 Painter Ave, Santa Fe Springs (90670-4552)
P.O. Box 2747 (90670-0747)
PHONE..................................562 941-0281
Kenneth Miller, *Pr*
Donald S Miller, *Ch Bd*
Keith L Miller, *VP*
Connie Miller, *Sec*
EMP: 20 EST: 1953
SQ FT: 7,000
SALES (est): 2.48MM **Privately Held**
Web: www.zspinc.com
SIC: **3451** Screw machine products

## 3452 Bolts, Nuts, Rivets, And Washers

**(P-8740)**
**3-V FASTENER CO INC**
630 E Lambert Rd, Brea (92821-4119)
PHONE..................................949 888-7700
Peter George, *CEO*
EMP: 56 EST: 1982
SQ FT: 18,500
SALES (est): 23.26MM
SALES (corp-wide): 15.78B **Publicly Held**
SIC: **3452** Bolts, metal
HQ: Consolidated Aerospace Manufacturing, Llc
1425 S Acacia Ave
Fullerton CA 92831
714 989-2797

**(P-8741)**
**A J FASTENERS INC**
Also Called: Pacific Hardware Sales
2800 E Miraloma Ave, Anaheim (92806-1803)
PHONE..................................714 630-1556
Lawrence Roa, *Pr*

▲ EMP: 20 EST: 1975
SQ FT: 15,000
SALES (est): 2.49MM **Privately Held**
Web: www.ajfasteners.com
SIC: **3452** 5072 3469 Screws, metal; Screws; Metal stampings, nec

**(P-8742)**
**ANILLO INDUSTRIES LLC**
Also Called: Anillo Industries
2090 N Glassell St, Orange (92865-3306)
P.O. Box 5586 (92863-5586)
PHONE..................................714 637-7000
Kurt Hilton Koch, *Pr*
Mark Koch, *VP*
EMP: 28 EST: 1957
SQ FT: 80,000
SALES (est): 5.63MM
SALES (corp-wide): 40.07MM **Privately Held**
Web: www.anilloinc.com
SIC: **3452** 3325 3499 3429 Washers; Bushings, cast steel: except investment; Shims, metal; Hardware, nec
PA: Novaria Holdings, Llc
809 W Vickery Blvd
817 381-3810

**(P-8743)**
**AZTEC MANUFACTURING INC (PA)**
Also Called: Aztec Washer Company
13821 Danielson St, Poway (92064-6891)
PHONE..................................858 513-4350
▲ EMP: 25 EST: 1970
SALES (est): 24.82MM
SALES (corp-wide): 24.82MM **Privately Held**
Web: www.aztecwasher.com
SIC: **3452** Washers

**(P-8744)**
**BAY STANDARD MANUFACTURING INC (PA)**
Also Called: Bsmi
24485 Marsh Creek Rd, Brentwood (94513-4319)
P.O. Box 801 (94513-0801)
PHONE..................................925 634-1181
Gary W Landgraf, *CEO*
Gregory Iverson, *Pr*
Karen Landgraf, *VP*
◆ EMP: 50 EST: 1959
SQ FT: 25,000
SALES (est): 9.68MM
SALES (corp-wide): 9.68MM **Privately Held**
Web: www.baystandard.com
SIC: **3452** 5072 Bolts, metal; Bolts

**(P-8745)**
**BLUE CIRCLE CORP**
7520 Monroe St, Paramount (90723-4922)
PHONE..................................562 531-2711
Ronald E Anderson, *Pr*
Chris Anderson, *VP*
Jeffrey Anderson, *VP*
Walda Anderson, *Sec*
EMP: 15 EST: 1971
SQ FT: 13,000
SALES (est): 1.41MM **Privately Held**
SIC: **3452** 3365 Bolts, metal; Aluminum and aluminum-based alloy castings

**(P-8746)**
**BRILES AEROSPACE LLC**
1559 W 135th St, Gardena (90249-2219)
PHONE..................................424 320-3817
Richard Alessi, *Managing Member*
Daniel Yoon, *Dir*

## PRODUCTS & SERVICES SECTION
### 3452 - Bolts, Nuts, Rivets, And Washers (P-8770)

EMP: 52 EST: 2012
SQ FT: 22,000
SALES (est): 900K **Privately Held**
Web: www.brilesaerospace.com
SIC: 3452  Bolts, nuts, rivets, and washers

### (P-8747)
### BRISTOL INDUSTRIES LLC
630 E Lambert Rd, Brea (92821-4119)
PHONE.....................714 990-4121
EMP: 152 EST: 1973
SALES (est): 47.7MM
SALES (corp-wide): 15.78B **Publicly Held**
Web: www.bristolindustries.com
SIC: 3452  Bolts, nuts, rivets, and washers
HQ: Consolidated Aerospace
Manufacturing, Llc
1425 S Acacia Ave
Fullerton CA 92831
714 989-2797

### (P-8748)
### BUTLER INC
2140 S Dupont Dr, Anaheim (92806-6101)
PHONE.....................310 323-3114
John Hollern, Pr
Cynthia Hollern, VP
EMP: 19 EST: 1974
SALES (est): 515.1K **Privately Held**
Web: www.butlerbolt.com
SIC: 3452  Bolts, metal

### (P-8749)
### CBS FASTENERS LLC
1345 N Brasher St, Anaheim (92807-2046)
PHONE.....................714 779-6368
Vic Luna, Pr
Gerald Bozarth, *
EMP: 49 EST: 1978
SQ FT: 10,400
SALES (est): 9.12MM **Privately Held**
Web: www.cbsfasteners.com
SIC: 3452  Bolts, metal

### (P-8750)
### CONKLIN & CONKLIN INCORPORATED
34201 7th St, Union City (94587-3655)
PHONE.....................510 489-5500
James Edward Conklin, Pr
Barbara Conklin, *
▲ EMP: 30 EST: 1969
SQ FT: 23,000
SALES (est): 5.77MM **Privately Held**
SIC: 3452  Bolts, nuts, rivets, and washers

### (P-8751)
### DGL HOLDINGS INC
3850 E Miraloma Ave, Anaheim (92806-2108)
PHONE.....................714 630-7840
George Hennes, Pr
David Boehm, *
EMP: 50 EST: 1969
SQ FT: 35,500
SALES (est): 9.61MM **Privately Held**
Web: www.mwcomponents.com
SIC: 3452  Bolts, nuts, rivets, and washers

### (P-8752)
### DOUBLECO INCORPORATED
Also Called: R & D Fasteners
9444 9th St, Rancho Cucamonga (91730-4509)
P.O. Box 250 (91785-0250)
PHONE.....................909 481-0799
Craig Scheu, Pr
EMP: 100 EST: 1986
SQ FT: 30,000
SALES (est): 23.62MM **Privately Held**

Web: www.rdfast.com
SIC: 3452  5072  Bolts, metal; Bolts

### (P-8753)
### DUNCAN BOLT CO
5555 E Gibralter, Ontario (91764-5121)
PHONE.....................909 581-6740
Brent Dooley, Mgr
EMP: 19
SALES (corp-wide): 29.58MM **Privately Held**
Web: www.duncanbolt.com
SIC: 3452  Bolts, nuts, rivets, and washers
PA: Duncan Bolt Co.
8535 Dice Rd
562 698-8800

### (P-8754)
### DUPREE INC
Also Called: Stake Fastener
14395 Ramona Ave, Chino (91710-5740)
P.O. Box 1797 (91708-1797)
PHONE.....................909 597-4889
Jim Pon, Pr
James D Dupree, *
▲ EMP: 31 EST: 1958
SQ FT: 60,000
SALES (est): 4.57MM **Privately Held**
Web: www.dupreeinc.com
SIC: 3452  6512  Bolts, metal; Commercial and industrial building operation

### (P-8755)
### FEDERAL MANUFACTURING CORP
9825 De Soto Ave, Chatsworth (91311-4412)
PHONE.....................818 341-9825
Helen Rainey, Pr
Arthur Rainey, *
Paul Rainey, *
EMP: 42 EST: 1951
SQ FT: 36,000
SALES (est): 6.51MM **Privately Held**
Web: www.federalmanufacturing.com
SIC: 3452  3812  3462  3429  Bolts, metal; Search and navigation equipment; Iron and steel forgings; Hardware, nec

### (P-8756)
### GOLDEN BOLT LLC
9361 Canoga Ave, Chatsworth (91311-5879)
PHONE.....................818 626-8261
EMP: 42 EST: 2016
SALES (est): 5.14MM **Privately Held**
Web: www.goldenboltllc.com
SIC: 3452  Bolts, metal

### (P-8757)
### HI-SHEAR CORPORATION (DH)
2600 Skypark Dr, Torrance (90505-5373)
PHONE.....................310 326-8110
Christian Darville, CEO
▲ EMP: 600 EST: 1943
SQ FT: 180,000
SALES (est): 128.01MM
SALES (corp-wide): 2.67MM **Privately Held**
Web: www.hi-shear.com
SIC: 3452  3429  Bolts, nuts, rivets, and washers; Aircraft hardware
HQ: Lisi Aerospace
42 A 52
Paris 12 IDF 75012
140198200

### (P-8758)
### HUCK INTERNATIONAL INC
Also Called: Arconic Fastening Systems
900 E Watson Center Rd, Carson (90745-4201)
PHONE.....................310 830-8200
Jim Dawn, Mgr
EMP: 203
SALES (corp-wide): 6.64B **Publicly Held**
Web: www.howmet.com
SIC: 3452  Nuts, metal
HQ: Huck International, Inc.
3724 E Columbia St
Tucson AZ 85714
520 519-7400

### (P-8759)
### INSTRUMENT BEARING FACTORY USA
19360 Rinaldi St, Northridge (91326-1607)
PHONE.....................818 989-5052
EMP: 50
SQ FT: 30,000
SALES (est): 2.67MM **Privately Held**
SIC: 3452  5085  Bolts, metal; Industrial supplies

### (P-8760)
### KING HOLDING CORPORATION
360 N Crescent Dr, Beverly Hills (90210-4874)
PHONE.....................586 254-3900
EMP: 7970
SIC: 3452  3465  3469  3089  Bolts, nuts, rivets, and washers; Automotive stampings; Metal stampings, nec; Injection molded finished plastics products, nec

### (P-8761)
### KINGFA GLOBAL INC
1455 S Archibald Ave, Ontario (91761-7626)
PHONE.....................909 212-5413
Xiaojun Gao, CEO
EMP: 15 EST: 2015
SALES (est): 3.99MM **Privately Held**
Web: www.litagrass.com
SIC: 3452  5961  Bolts, nuts, rivets, and washers; Tools and hardware, mail order
PA: Wuxi Zhuocheng Mechanical Components Co., Ltd.
No.155-1, Xihu W. Road, Liangxi District

### (P-8762)
### MS AEROSPACE INC
13928 Balboa Blvd, Sylmar (91342)
PHONE.....................818 833-9095
Michel Szostak, CEO
Jerome Taieb, *
Jim Cole, General Vice President*
EMP: 302 EST: 1992
SALES (est): 48.59MM **Privately Held**
Web: www.msaerospace.com
SIC: 3452  3728  Bolts, nuts, rivets, and washers; Aircraft parts and equipment, nec

### (P-8763)
### NYLOK LLC
Also Called: Nylok Western Fastener
313 N Euclid Way, Anaheim (92801-6738)
PHONE.....................714 635-3993
Scott Plantiga, Mgr
EMP: 45
SALES (corp-wide): 32.23MM **Privately Held**
Web: www.nylok.com
SIC: 3452  Bolts, nuts, rivets, and washers
PA: Nylok, Llc
15260 Hallmark Ct

586 786-0100

### (P-8764)
### PAUL R BRILES INC
Also Called: Pb Fasteners
1700 W 132nd St, Gardena (90249-2008)
PHONE.....................310 323-6222
▲ EMP: 1262
Web: www.pccfasteners.com
SIC: 3452  Bolts, nuts, rivets, and washers

### (P-8765)
### POWER FASTENERS INC
650 E 60th St, Los Angeles (90001-1012)
P.O. Box 512056 (90051-0056)
PHONE.....................323 232-4362
Patrick Harrington, Pr
▲ EMP: 30 EST: 1991
SQ FT: 35,000
SALES (est): 831.13K **Privately Held**
Web: 041d6c8.netsolhost.com
SIC: 3452  3448  Bolts, nuts, rivets, and washers; Prefabricated metal components

### (P-8766)
### RISCO INC
390 Risco Cir, Beaumont (92223-2676)
PHONE.....................951 769-2899
Joseph A Frainee Ii, CEO
Cynthia R Frainee, *
EMP: 30 EST: 1964
SQ FT: 30,000
SALES (est): 3.93MM **Privately Held**
Web: www.risco-fasteners.com
SIC: 3452  Bolts, metal

### (P-8767)
### SUNLAND AEROSPACE FASTENERS
12920 Pierce St, Pacoima (91331-2526)
PHONE.....................818 485-8929
Anik Khochou, Admn
Jack Wilson, *
EMP: 80 EST: 2012
SQ FT: 11,000
SALES (est): 1.79MM **Privately Held**
Web: www.sunlandaerospace.com
SIC: 3452  Bolts, nuts, rivets, and washers

### (P-8768)
### TWIST TITE MFG INC
13344 Cambridge St, Santa Fe Springs (90670-4904)
PHONE.....................562 229-0990
Spiro Aykias, CEO
Martha Leonard, *
EMP: 32 EST: 1994
SQ FT: 18,200
SALES (est): 1.77MM **Privately Held**
Web: www.twisttite.com
SIC: 3452  Bolts, nuts, rivets, and washers

### (P-8769)
### U-C COMPONENTS INC (PA)
18700 Adams Ct, Morgan Hill (95037-2804)
P.O. Box 430 (95038-0430)
PHONE.....................408 782-1929
Nancy Anderson, Pr
EMP: 23 EST: 1974
SQ FT: 16,000
SALES (est): 6.45MM
SALES (corp-wide): 6.45MM **Privately Held**
Web: www.uccomponents.com
SIC: 3452  Screws, metal

### (P-8770)
### VALLEY-TODECO INC
Also Called: Arconic Fastening Systems

# 3462 - Iron And Steel Forgings (P-8771)

135 N Unruh Ave, City Of Industry (91744-4427)
PHONE.................................800 992-4444
Jim Cotello, Pr
▲ EMP: 130 EST: 1995
SALES (est): 12.07MM
SALES (corp-wide): 6.64B Publicly Held
SIC: 3452 5085 Bolts, nuts, rivets, and washers; Fasteners, industrial: nuts, bolts, screws, etc.
HQ: Howmet Global Fastening Systems Inc.
  3990a Heritage Oak Ct
  Simi Valley CA 93063
  805 426-2270

## 3462 Iron And Steel Forgings

**(P-8771)**
**ADVANCED STRUCTURAL TECH INC**
Also Called: Asa
950 Richmond Ave, Oxnard (93030-7212)
PHONE.................................805 204-9133
Robert Melsness, Pr
Douglas Jones, *
▼ EMP: 135 EST: 2009
SALES (est): 23.97MM Privately Held
Web: www.astforgetech.com
SIC: 3462 Aircraft forgings, ferrous

**(P-8772)**
**AJAX FORGE COMPANY (PA)**
1956 E 48th St, Vernon (90058-2006)
PHONE.................................323 582-6307
TOLL FREE: 800
Fred Goble, Pr
Steve Mc Elrath, Stockholder
EMP: 19 EST: 1939
SQ FT: 10,000
SALES (est): 3.93MM
SALES (corp-wide): 3.93MM Privately Held
Web: www.ajaxforge.com
SIC: 3462 Iron and steel forgings

**(P-8773)**
**BIERWITH FORGE & TOOL INC**
Also Called: Berkeley Forge & Tool
1331 Eastshore Hwy, Berkeley (94710-1320)
P.O. Box 8008 (94662-0901)
PHONE.................................510 526-5034
Peter Bierwith, Pr
Robert Bierwith, *
Ed Hinckley, *
Paul Bierwith, Stockholder*
▲ EMP: 88 EST: 1948
SQ FT: 50,000
SALES (est): 9.1MM Privately Held
Web: www.berkforge.com
SIC: 3462 Construction or mining equipment forgings, ferrous

**(P-8774)**
**COULTER FORGE TECHNOLOGY INC**
Also Called: Coulter Steel and Forge
1494 67th St, Emeryville (94608-1016)
P.O. Box 8008 (94662-0901)
PHONE.................................510 420-3500
Peter Bierwith, Pr
Robert Bierwith, VP
▲ EMP: 18 EST: 2002
SQ FT: 20,000
SALES (est): 4.16MM Privately Held
Web: www.coulter-forge.com
SIC: 3462 Iron and steel forgings

**(P-8775)**
**ESCO INDUSTRIES INC**
1755 Iowa Ave Bldg A, Riverside (92507-0525)
P.O. Box 52568 (92517-3568)
PHONE.................................951 782-2130
Chung Li Lin, Pr
▲ EMP: 15 EST: 1990
SALES (est): 2.37MM Privately Held
Web: www.escousa.com
SIC: 3462 Automotive and internal combustion engine forgings

**(P-8776)**
**FORGED METALS INC**
10685 Beech Ave, Fontana (92337-7212)
PHONE.................................909 350-9260
Torben Kaese, CEO
◆ EMP: 200 EST: 1982
SQ FT: 4,800
SALES (est): 24.06MM
SALES (corp-wide): 6.64B Publicly Held
SIC: 3462 Iron and steel forgings
PA: Howmet Aerospace Inc.
  201 Isabella St Ste 200
  412 553-1950

**(P-8777)**
**INDEPENDENT FORGE COMPANY**
692 N Batavia St, Orange (92868-1221)
PHONE.................................714 997-7337
Rosemary Ruiz, Pr
Joe Ramirez, *
Gloria Lopez, *
▲ EMP: 40 EST: 1975
SQ FT: 11,900
SALES (est): 4.62MM Privately Held
Web: www.independentforge.com
SIC: 3462 Iron and steel forgings

**(P-8778)**
**IRONWOOD FABRICATION INC**
Also Called: South Coast Iron
761 Monroe Way, Placentia (92870-6309)
PHONE.................................714 576-7320
Sean Michael, Pr
Sean D Michael, Prin
EMP: 18 EST: 2018
SALES (est): 2.51MM Privately Held
Web: www.southcoastiron.com
SIC: 3462 1791 Iron and steel forgings; Structural steel erection

**(P-8779)**
**JMMCA INC (PA)**
Also Called: Pmp Forge
850 W Bradley Ave, El Cajon (92020-1218)
PHONE.................................619 448-2711
James Matarese, CEO
Betty Matarese, *
▲ EMP: 83 EST: 1963
SQ FT: 92,000
SALES (est): 18.37MM
SALES (corp-wide): 18.37MM Privately Held
Web: www.pmpforge.com
SIC: 3462 Iron and steel forgings

**(P-8780)**
**MAINSPRING ENERGY INC**
Also Called: Etagen
3601 Haven Ave, Menlo Park (94025-1064)
PHONE.................................408 529-5651
EMP: 300
Web: www.mainspringenergy.com
SIC: 3462 Automotive forgings, ferrous: crankshaft, engine, axle, etc.
PA: Mainspring Energy, Inc.
  3601 Haven Ave

**(P-8781)**
**MATTCO FORGE INC (HQ)**
16443 Minnesota Ave, Paramount (90723-4985)
PHONE.................................562 634-8635
Robert Lewis, Pr
Andrew Fite, *
▲ EMP: 19 EST: 1998
SQ FT: 150,000
SALES (est): 23.82MM
SALES (corp-wide): 40.39MM Privately Held
Web: www.mattcoforge.com
SIC: 3462 Iron and steel forgings
PA: Mattco Forge Holdings, Llc
  16443 Minnesota Ave
  562 634-8635

**(P-8782)**
**MATTCO FORGE INC**
7530 Jackson St, Paramount (90723-4910)
PHONE.................................562 634-8635
Denis B Brady, CEO
EMP: 34
SALES (corp-wide): 40.39MM Privately Held
Web: www.mattcoforge.com
SIC: 3462 Iron and steel forgings
HQ: Mattco Forge, Inc.
  16443 Minnesota Ave
  Paramount CA 90723
  562 634-8635

**(P-8783)**
**PACIFIC FORGE INC**
10641 Etiwanda Ave, Fontana (92337-6991)
PHONE.................................909 390-0701
Ronald D Browne, Pr
Jacqueline Dyer, *
EMP: 55 EST: 1955
SQ FT: 34,816
SALES (est): 1.9MM
SALES (corp-wide): 474.53MM Privately Held
Web: www.pacificforge.com
SIC: 3462 3463 Iron and steel forgings; Nonferrous forgings
PA: Avis Industrial Corporation
  1909 S Main St
  765 998-8100

**(P-8784)**
**PARAMOUNT FORGE INC**
1721 E Colon St, Wilmington (90744-2210)
P.O. Box 205 (90748-0205)
PHONE.................................323 775-6803
Donald Ferguson, Pr
EMP: 20 EST: 1962
SALES (est): 1.64MM Privately Held
SIC: 3462 Iron and steel forgings

**(P-8785)**
**PERFORMANCE FORGE INC**
7401 Telegraph Rd, Montebello (90640-6500)
PHONE.................................323 722-3460
Wayne Ramay, Pr
EMP: 30 EST: 2012
SALES (est): 5.5MM Privately Held
Web: www.performance-forge.com
SIC: 3462 Iron and steel forgings

**(P-8786)**
**PREMIER GEAR & MACHINING INC**
2360 Pomona Rd, Corona (92880)
P.O. Box 2799 (92878-2799)
PHONE.................................951 278-5505
Steve Golden, Pr
Huy Nguyen, *
EMP: 25 EST: 1986
SQ FT: 21,000
SALES (est): 7.5MM Privately Held
Web: www.premiergearinc.com
SIC: 3462 3599 Iron and steel forgings; Machine shop, jobbing and repair

**(P-8787)**
**PRESS FORGE COMPANY**
7700 Jackson St, Paramount (90723-5029)
P.O. Box 1432 (90723-1432)
PHONE.................................562 531-4962
Jeffrey M Carlton, CEO
Michael Buxton, *
Mike Buxton, *
▲ EMP: 80 EST: 1978
SQ FT: 32,726
SALES (est): 21.04MM
SALES (corp-wide): 364.48B Publicly Held
Web: www.pressforge.com
SIC: 3462 Iron and steel forgings
HQ: Precision Castparts Corp.
  5885 Meadows Rd Ste 620
  Lake Oswego OR 97035
  503 946-4800

**(P-8788)**
**RUBICON GEAR INC**
Also Called: Rubicon Gear
225 Citation Cir, Corona (92878-5023)
PHONE.................................951 356-3800
Cheryl A Edwards, Ch Bd
Ryan B Edwards, *
Frank Salazar, *
EMP: 68 EST: 1970
SQ FT: 25,000
SALES (est): 8.34MM Privately Held
Web: www.rubicon-gear.com
SIC: 3462 Gears, forged steel

**(P-8789)**
**TIMKEN GEARS & SERVICES INC**
Also Called: Philadelphia Gear
12935 Imperial Hwy, Santa Fe Springs (90670-4715)
PHONE.................................310 605-2600
Tony Tartaglio, Brnch Mgr
EMP: 23
SALES (corp-wide): 4.77B Publicly Held
Web: www.philagear.com
SIC: 3462 Gear and chain forgings
HQ: Timken Gears & Services Inc.
  935 1st Ave Ste 200
  King Of Prussia PA 19406

**(P-8790)**
**TURBO INTL PARTNERS LLC**
2151 Las Palmas Dr Ste E, Carlsbad (92011-1525)
PHONE.................................760 476-1444
Seth Carks, CEO
▲ EMP: 25 EST: 1989
SALES (est): 1.83MM Privately Held
Web: www.turbointernational.com
SIC: 3462 Automotive forgings, ferrous: crankshaft, engine, axle, etc.

**(P-8791)**
**VALLEY FORGE ACQUISITION CORP**
Also Called: Valley Forge
444 S Motor Ave, Azusa (91702-3231)
PHONE.................................626 969-8701
Michael K Holmes, Pr
Michael Holmes, Pr
EMP: 15 EST: 1955
SQ FT: 37,000
SALES (est): 10.44MM

**PRODUCTS & SERVICES SECTION**   **3465 - Automotive Stampings (P-8811)**

SALES (corp-wide): 34.31MM **Privately Held**
Web: www.valleyforgeproducts.com
SIC: **3462** Iron and steel forgings
PA: Tuffli Company Incorporated
2245 W 190th St
310 326-4747

**(P-8792)**
**VI-STAR GEAR CO INC**
7312 Jefferson St, Paramount (90723-4094)
PHONE..................................323 774-3750
Thomas R Redfield, *Pr*
Chris Redfield, *
**EMP:** 30 **EST:** 1960
**SQ FT:** 12,000
**SALES (est):** 5.71MM **Privately Held**
Web: www.vistargear.com
SIC: **3462** 3728 Iron and steel forgings; Gears, aircraft power transmission

**(P-8793)**
**VOSSLOH SIGNALING USA INC**
Also Called: J Manufacturing
12799 Loma Rica Dr, Grass Valley (95945-9552)
P.O. Box 600 (95945-0600)
PHONE..................................530 272-8194
▲ **EMP:** 24
Web: www.jmirail.com
SIC: **3462** Railroad wheels, axles, frogs, or other equipment: forged

---

### 3463 Nonferrous Forgings

**(P-8794)**
**ALUM-ALLOY CO INC**
603 S Hope Ave, Ontario (91761-1824)
PHONE..................................909 986-0410
David Howell, *CEO*
Marilyn Howell, *
Clark Howell, *
**EMP:** 40 **EST:** 1961
**SQ FT:** 20,000
**SALES (est):** 3.01MM **Privately Held**
Web: www.lynwoodpattern.com
SIC: **3463** 3365 Aluminum forgings; Aluminum foundries

**(P-8795)**
**CARLTON FORGE WORKS LLC**
Also Called: Carlton Forge Works
7743 Adams St, Paramount (90723)
PHONE..................................562 633-1131
◆ **EMP:** 300 **EST:** 1929
**SALES (est):** 50.31MM
**SALES (corp-wide):** 364.48B **Publicly Held**
Web: www.cfworks.com
SIC: **3463** 3462 Nonferrous forgings; Iron and steel forgings
HQ: Precision Castparts Corp.
5885 Meadows Rd Ste 620
Lake Oswego OR 97035
503 946-4800

**(P-8796)**
**CONTINENTAL FORGE COMPANY LLC**
412 E El Segundo Blvd, Compton (90222-2317)
PHONE..................................310 603-1014
Olivier Jarrault, *CEO*
Peter Manos, *
**EMP:** 90 **EST:** 1968
**SQ FT:** 27,000
**SALES (est):** 10.65MM
**SALES (corp-wide):** 170.38MM **Privately Held**

Web: www.cforge.com
SIC: **3463** Aluminum forgings
HQ: Forged Solutions Group Limited
Dale Road North
Matlock DE4 2
792 065-5762

**(P-8797)**
**GEL INDUSTRIES INC**
Also Called: Quality Aluminum Forge Div
810 N Lemon St, Orange (92867-6616)
PHONE..................................714 639-8191
**EMP:** 150
SIC: **3463** Aluminum forgings

**(P-8798)**
**LINDSEY MANUFACTURING CO**
Also Called: Lindsey Systems
760 N Georgia Ave, Azusa (91702-2249)
P.O. Box 877 (91702-0877)
PHONE..................................626 969-3471
Keith E Lindsey, *Pr*
Frederick Findley, *
Lela Lindsey, *
▲ **EMP:** 110 **EST:** 1947
**SQ FT:** 60,000
**SALES (est):** 15.17MM **Privately Held**
Web: www.lindsey-usa.com
SIC: **3463** 3644 Pole line hardware forgings, nonferrous; Noncurrent-carrying wiring devices

**(P-8799)**
**LUXFER INC**
Superform USA
6825 Jurupa Ave, Riverside (92504-1039)
PHONE..................................951 351-4100
Michael Reynolds, *VP*
**EMP:** 38
**SALES (corp-wide):** 405MM **Privately Held**
Web: www.luxfercylinders.com
SIC: **3463** Aluminum forgings
HQ: Luxfer Inc.
3016 Kansas Ave Bldg 1
Riverside CA 92507
951 684-5110

**(P-8800)**
**QUALITY ALUMINUM FORGE LLC (HQ)**
793 N Cypress St, Orange (92867-6605)
PHONE..................................714 639-8191
**EMP:** 44 **EST:** 2011
**SALES (est):** 40.36MM
**SALES (corp-wide):** 87.02MM **Publicly Held**
Web: www.sifco.com
SIC: **3463** Aluminum forgings
PA: Sifco Industries, Inc.
970 E 64th St
216 881-8600

**(P-8801)**
**QUALITY ALUMINUM FORGE LLC**
794 N Cypress St, Orange (92867-6606)
PHONE..................................714 639-8191
**EMP:** 186
**SALES (corp-wide):** 87.02MM **Publicly Held**
Web: www.sifco.com
SIC: **3463** Aluminum forgings
HQ: Quality Aluminum Forge, Llc
793 N Cypress St
Orange CA 92867
714 639-8191

**(P-8802)**
**SHULTZ STEEL COMPANY LLC**
Also Called: S S
5321 Firestone Blvd, South Gate (90280-3629)
PHONE..................................323 357-3200
◆ **EMP:** 490 **EST:** 1956
**SALES (est):** 74.94MM
**SALES (corp-wide):** 364.48B **Publicly Held**
Web: www.shultzsteel.com
SIC: **3463** 3462 Aircraft forgings, nonferrous; Aircraft forgings, ferrous
HQ: Precision Castparts Corp.
5885 Meadows Rd Ste 620
Lake Oswego OR 97035
503 946-4800

**(P-8803)**
**STS METALS INC**
Also Called: Sierra Alloys Company
5467 Ayon Ave, Irwindale (91706-2044)
PHONE..................................626 969-6711
Craig Culaciati, *CEO*
Ed Brennan, *VP*
Jeff Augustyn, *Ex VP*
▲ **EMP:** 52 **EST:** 1974
**SQ FT:** 75,000
**SALES (est):** 17.23MM **Privately Held**
Web: www.sierraalloys.com
SIC: **3463** 3494 3312 Nonferrous forgings; Valves and pipe fittings, nec; Blast furnaces and steel mills

**(P-8804)**
**WEBER METALS INC (HQ)**
16706 Garfield Ave, Paramount (90723-5307)
PHONE..................................562 602-0260
John R Creed, *CEO*
Paul Dennis, *
◆ **EMP:** 39 **EST:** 1962
**SQ FT:** 270,000
**SALES (est):** 66.09MM
**SALES (corp-wide):** 2.94B **Privately Held**
Web: www.webermetals.com
SIC: **3463** Aluminum forgings
PA: Otto Fuchs Beteiligungen Kg
Derschlager Str. 26
2354730

**(P-8805)**
**WEBER METALS INC**
233 E Manville St, Compton (90220-5602)
PHONE..................................562 543-3316
**EMP:** 461
**SALES (corp-wide):** 2.94B **Privately Held**
Web: www.webermetals.com
SIC: **3463** Aluminum forgings
HQ: Weber Metals, Inc.
16706 Garfield Ave
Paramount CA 90723
562 602-0260

**(P-8806)**
**WJB BEARINGS INC**
535 Brea Canyon Rd, City Of Industry (91789-3001)
PHONE..................................909 598-6238
John Jun Jiang, *CEO*
▲ **EMP:** 25 **EST:** 1992
**SQ FT:** 30,000
**SALES (est):** 4.87MM **Privately Held**
Web: www.wjbgroup.us
SIC: **3463** 5085 Bearing and bearing race forgings, nonferrous; Bearings

---

### 3465 Automotive Stampings

**(P-8807)**
**APOLLO METAL SPINNING CO INC**
15315 Illinois Ave, Paramount (90723-4108)
PHONE..................................562 634-5141
George Di Matteo, *Pr*
Josephine Di Matteo, *Sec*
**EMP:** 15 **EST:** 1968
**SQ FT:** 4,650
**SALES (est):** 978.31K **Privately Held**
Web: www.apollometalspinning.com
SIC: **3465** 3469 5015 Hub caps, automobile: stamped metal; Spinning metal for the trade ; Automotive parts and supplies, used

**(P-8808)**
**SALEEN AUTOMOTIVE INC (PA)**
2735 Wardlow Rd, Corona (92882-2869)
PHONE..................................800 888-8945
Steve Saleen, *Ch Bd*
David Fiene, *CFO*
Amy Boylan, *Pr*
**EMP:** 21 **EST:** 2011
**SALES (est):** 3.84MM **Privately Held**
Web: www.saleen.com
SIC: **3465** 3711 Body parts, automobile: stamped metal; Automobile assembly, including specialty automobiles

**(P-8809)**
**STEELCRAFT LLC**
2120 California Ave, Corona (92881-3301)
P.O. Box 77370 (92877-0112)
PHONE..................................888 261-4537
▲ **EMP:** 16 **EST:** 1998
**SQ FT:** 6,000
**SALES (est):** 2.24MM **Privately Held**
Web: www.steelcraftautomotive.com
SIC: **3465** Body parts, automobile: stamped metal

**(P-8810)**
**T-REX TRUCK PRODUCTS INC**
Also Called: T-Rex Grilles
2365 Railroad St, Corona (92878-5411)
PHONE..................................800 287-5900
Behrouz Mizban, *Pr*
▼ **EMP:** 55 **EST:** 1995
**SQ FT:** 45,000
**SALES (est):** 3.63MM **Privately Held**
Web: www.trexbillet.com
SIC: **3465** Automotive stampings

**(P-8811)**
**TROY SHEET METAL WORKS INC (PA)**
Also Called: Troy Products
1024 S Vail Ave, Montebello (90640-6020)
PHONE..................................323 720-4100
Carl Moses Kahalewai, *CEO*
Paul Alvarado, *Stockholder**
Carol Stewart, *Stockholder**
Marci Norkin, *Stockholder**
Rigo Guadiana, *
**EMP:** 73 **EST:** 1930
**SQ FT:** 16,000
**SALES (est):** 10.81MM
**SALES (corp-wide):** 10.81MM **Privately Held**
Web: www.troyproducts.com
SIC: **3465** 3444 3714 3564 Automotive stampings; Sheet metalwork; Motor vehicle parts and accessories; Blowers and fans

## 3466 Crowns And Closures

**(P-8812)**
**RIEKE LLC**
1200 Valley House Dr Ste 100, Rohnert Park (94928-4934)
PHONE..............................707 238-9250
EMP: 180
SALES (corp-wide): 893.55MM **Publicly Held**
Web: www.riekepackaging.com
SIC: **3466** 3089 Closures, stamped metal; Injection molding of plastics
HQ: Rieke Llc
500 W 7th St
Auburn IN 46706
260 925-3700

## 3469 Metal Stampings, Nec

**(P-8813)**
**A & J MANUFACTURING COMPANY**
70 Icon, Foothill Ranch (92610-3000)
PHONE..............................714 544-9570
Barry Lyerly, *CEO*
Janice Lyerly, *
EMP: 32 EST: 1954
SQ FT: 40,000
SALES (est): 4.14MM **Privately Held**
Web: www.aj-racks.com
SIC: **3469** Electronic enclosures, stamped or pressed metal

**(P-8814)**
**A-W ENGINEERING COMPANY INC**
8528 Dice Rd, Santa Fe Springs (90670-2590)
PHONE..............................562 945-1041
Guy Hansen, *Pr*
Anthony Giangrande, *
EMP: 36 EST: 1965
SQ FT: 38,000
SALES (est): 5.14MM **Privately Held**
Web: www.aw-eng.com
SIC: **3469** 3544 Stamping metal for the trade ; Special dies and tools

**(P-8815)**
**ACRONTOS MANUFACTURING INC**
Also Called: Al Industries
1641 E Saint Gertrude Pl, Santa Ana (92705-5311)
PHONE..............................714 850-9133
Ngoc V Hoang, *Pr*
EMP: 30 EST: 1991
SQ FT: 22,000
SALES (est): 2MM **Privately Held**
SIC: **3469** 3599 3441 Stamping metal for the trade; Machine and other job shop work; Fabricated structural metal

**(P-8816)**
**ACTION STAMPING INC**
119 Explorer St, Pomona (91768-3278)
P.O. Box 778 (91740-0778)
PHONE..............................626 914-7466
Henry Reynolds, *CEO*
Terry Reynolds, *
▲ EMP: 42 EST: 1982
SALES (est): 4.54MM **Privately Held**
Web: www.actionstamping.com
SIC: **3469** Stamping metal for the trade

**(P-8817)**
**ALL NEW STAMPING CO**
10801 Lower Azusa Rd, El Monte (91731-1307)
P.O. Box 5948 (91734-1948)
PHONE..............................626 443-8813
TOLL FREE: 800
Donald Schuil, *Pr*
Robert Larson, *
EMP: 150 EST: 1962
SQ FT: 40,000
SALES (est): 12.33MM **Privately Held**
Web: www.allnewstamping.com
SIC: **3469** 3441 3444 Stamping metal for the trade; Fabricated structural metal; Sheet metal specialties, not stamped

**(P-8818)**
**APT METAL FABRICATORS INC**
11164 Bradley Ave, Pacoima (91331-2405)
PHONE..............................818 896-7478
Dennis M Vigo, *Pr*
Susan Vigo, *
▼ EMP: 26 EST: 1975
SQ FT: 18,000
SALES (est): 2.75MM **Privately Held**
Web: www.aptmetal.com
SIC: **3469** Stamping metal for the trade

**(P-8819)**
**ASCENT MANUFACTURING LLC**
2545 W Via Palma, Anaheim (92801-2624)
PHONE..............................714 540-6414
Travis Mullen, *CEO*
David Kramer, *
EMP: 34 EST: 2001
SQ FT: 17,000
SALES (est): 2.92MM **Privately Held**
Web: www.ascentmfg.com
SIC: **3469** 1796 Machine parts, stamped or pressed metal; Machinery installation

**(P-8820)**
**BANDEL MFG INC**
4459 Alger St, Los Angeles (90039-1292)
PHONE..............................818 246-7493
Jeannie Finley, *Pr*
Ed Finley, *
Chester Carlson, *
EMP: 23 EST: 1947
SQ FT: 15,000
SALES (est): 2.74MM **Privately Held**
Web: www.bandel.com
SIC: **3469** Stamping metal for the trade

**(P-8821)**
**BINDER METAL PRODUCTS INC**
14909 S Broadway, Gardena (90248-1817)
P.O. Box 2306 (90247-0306)
PHONE..............................800 233-0896
Steve Binder, *Pr*
Adam Binder, *
Ana Weber, *
▲ EMP: 75 EST: 1925
SQ FT: 35,000
SALES (est): 9.25MM **Privately Held**
Web: www.bindermetal.com
SIC: **3469** Stamping metal for the trade

**(P-8822)**
**BLOOMERS METAL STAMPINGS INC**
28615 Braxton Ave, Valencia (91355-4112)
PHONE..............................661 257-2955
Matt Holland, *CEO*
Perry Bloomer, *
Ella H Bloomer, *
EMP: 30 EST: 1976
SQ FT: 25,000
SALES (est): 3.93MM **Privately Held**
Web: www.bloomersmetal.com
SIC: **3469** Stamping metal for the trade

**(P-8823)**
**BRAXTON CARIBBEAN MFG CO INC**
2641 Walnut Ave, Tustin (92780-7005)
P.O. Box 425 (92781-0425)
PHONE..............................714 508-3570
Thomas Ordway, *Pr*
Robert Dionne, *
Joesph Triano, *
EMP: 62 EST: 1972
SALES (est): 5MM **Privately Held**
Web: www.braxtonmfg.com
SIC: **3469** Stamping metal for the trade

**(P-8824)**
**BRICE TOOL & STAMPING INC**
1170 N Van Horne Way, Anaheim (92806-2506)
PHONE..............................714 630-6400
Russel Brice, *Pr*
EMP: 15 EST: 1956
SQ FT: 10,000
SALES (est): 1.61MM **Privately Held**
Web: www.bricetool.com
SIC: **3469** 3544 Stamping metal for the trade ; Dies, steel rule

**(P-8825)**
**C WOLFE INDUSTRIES INC**
Also Called: Wolfe Industries
14420 Marquardt Ave, Santa Fe Springs (90670-5119)
PHONE..............................626 443-7185
EMP: 21 EST: 1991
SALES (est): 5.86MM **Privately Held**
Web: www.wolfeindustries.net
SIC: **3469** Metal stampings, nec

**(P-8826)**
**CABRAC INC**
13250 Paxton St, Pacoima (91331-2356)
PHONE..............................818 834-0177
Hans Kaufmann, *Pr*
EMP: 20 EST: 1973
SQ FT: 20,000
SALES (est): 2.96MM **Privately Held**
Web: www.cabrac.com
SIC: **3469** Electronic enclosures, stamped or pressed metal

**(P-8827)**
**CAMISASCA AUTOMOTIVE MFG INC**
20341 Hermana Cir, Lake Forest (92630-8701)
PHONE..............................949 452-0195
Henry Camisasca, *CEO*
EMP: 20
SALES (corp-wide): 6.5MM **Privately Held**
Web: www.camincusa.com
SIC: **3469** Automobile license tags, stamped metal
PA: Camisasca Automotive Manufacturing, Inc.
20352 Hermana Cir
949 452-0195

**(P-8828)**
**CAMISASCA AUTOMOTIVE MFG INC (PA)**
20352 Hermana Cir, Lake Forest (92630-8701)
PHONE..............................949 452-0195
Colin Camisasca, *Pr*
Georgann Camisasca, *Sec*
▲ EMP: 20 EST: 1982
SQ FT: 16,000
SALES (est): 6.5MM
SALES (corp-wide): 6.5MM **Privately Held**
Web: www.camincusa.com
SIC: **3469** 5013 3465 2399 Automobile license tags, stamped metal; Automotive trim; Automotive stampings; Emblems, badges, and insignia

**(P-8829)**
**CARAN PRECISION ENGINEERING & MANUFACTURING CORP (PA)**
2830 Orbiter St, Brea (92821-6224)
PHONE..............................714 447-5400
▲ EMP: 98 EST: 1964
SALES (est): 23.83MM
SALES (corp-wide): 23.83MM **Privately Held**
Web: www.caranprecision.com
SIC: **3469** Metal stampings, nec

**(P-8830)**
**CARSONS COATINGS INC**
Also Called: Carson's Coatings
550 Industrial Dr Ste 200, Galt (95632-1647)
PHONE..............................209 745-2387
Duane Carson, *Pr*
Terry Carson, *VP*
▲ EMP: 20 EST: 1991
SQ FT: 53,000
SALES (est): 2.16MM **Privately Held**
Web: www.carsonscoatings.com
SIC: **3469** Architectural panels or parts, porcelain enameled

**(P-8831)**
**CONTEXT ENGINEERING CO**
Also Called: Sidco Labelling Systems
6805 Silacci Way, Gilroy (95020-7095)
PHONE..............................408 748-9112
David Clemson, *Pr*
Martin Clemson, *
Mary Clemson, *
▲ EMP: 25 EST: 1983
SALES (est): 3.86MM **Privately Held**
Web: www.sidcolabeling.com
SIC: **3469** 5131 5084 Electronic enclosures, stamped or pressed metal; Labels; Industrial machinery and equipment

**(P-8832)**
**CUDOQUANTA PHOTONICS INC**
Also Called: Cudoform Inc.
802 Calle Plano, Camarillo (93012-8557)
PHONE..............................805 617-0818
Ryan Vallance, *CEO*
Elizabeth Lee, *CFO*
EMP: 15 EST: 2019
SALES (est): 4.15MM **Privately Held**
Web: www.cudoform.com
SIC: **3469** Machine parts, stamped or pressed metal
HQ: Senko Advanced Components, Inc.
2 Cabot Rd Ste 103
Hudson MA 01749
508 481-9999

**(P-8833)**
**CYGNET STAMPNG & FABRICTNG INC (PA)**
613 Justin Ave, Glendale (91201-2326)
PHONE..............................818 240-7574
Marko Swan, *Pr*
E Michael Swan, *
John Swan, *
EMP: 29 EST: 1976
SQ FT: 28,000

PRODUCTS & SERVICES SECTION  3469 - Metal Stampings, Nec (P-8857)

SALES (est): 5.11MM
SALES (corp-wide): 5.11MM **Privately Held**
Web: www.cygnetstamping.com
SIC: **3469** Stamping metal for the trade

### (P-8834)
### DAVID ENGINEERING & MFG INC
Also Called: David Engineering & Mfg
1230 Quarry St, Corona (92879-1708)
P.O. Box 77035 (92877-0101)
PHONE..................................951 735-5200
Mike David, *CEO*
Michael David, *
EMP: 30 EST: 2003
SALES (est): 6.49MM **Privately Held**
Web: www.davidengineering.com
SIC: **3469** 3544 Stamping metal for the trade; Special dies and tools

### (P-8835)
### DAYTON ROGERS OF CALIFORNIA INC
13630 Saticoy St, Van Nuys (91402-6302)
PHONE..................................763 784-7714
EMP: 158
SIC: **3469** Stamping metal for the trade

### (P-8836)
### DIE AND TOOL PRODUCTS INC
1842 Sabre St, Hayward (94545-1024)
PHONE..................................415 822-2888
Victor Tschirky, *Pr*
Mariette Tschirky, *Sec*
EMP: 16 EST: 1948
SALES (est): 4.03MM **Privately Held**
SIC: **3469** Stamping metal for the trade

### (P-8837)
### DIVERSIFIED TOOL & DIE
2585 Birch St, Vista (92081-8433)
PHONE..................................760 598-9100
Ernst Wilms, *CEO*
Rosa Wilms, *
EMP: 30 EST: 1972
SQ FT: 33,000
SALES (est): 4.64MM **Privately Held**
Web: www.stamping.com
SIC: **3469** 3544 Stamping metal for the trade; Special dies and tools

### (P-8838)
### E2E MFG LLC
3500 Yale Way, Fremont (94538-6180)
PHONE..................................925 862-2057
Gioni Bianchini, *
▲ EMP: 46 EST: 2000
SALES (est): 9.45MM **Privately Held**
Web: www.e2emfg.com
SIC: **3469** Metal stampings, nec

### (P-8839)
### EAGLEWARE MANUFACTURING CO INC
12683 Corral Pl, Santa Fe Springs (90670-4748)
PHONE..................................562 320-3100
Brett L Gross, *Pr*
Eric Gross, *
▲ EMP: 32 EST: 1963
SQ FT: 130,000
SALES (est): 2.29MM **Privately Held**
SIC: **3469** 3421 Stamping metal for the trade; Cutlery

### (P-8840)
### ELIXIR INDUSTRIES
24800 Chrisanta Dr Ste 210, Mission Viejo (92691-4833)
PHONE..................................949 860-5000
◆ EMP: 64
Web: www.elixirind.com
SIC: **3469** Metal stampings, nec

### (P-8841)
### ENTERPRISES INDUSTRIES INC
7500 Tyrone Ave, Van Nuys (91405-1447)
PHONE..................................818 989-6103
Tony Magnome, *Pr*
Rolando Loera, *
Livino D Ribaya Junior, *VP Mfg*
Frank Ramirez Iii, *VP Engg*
Charles E Shaw, *
EMP: 130 EST: 1971
SALES (est): 1.13MM **Privately Held**
SIC: **3469** Stamping metal for the trade

### (P-8842)
### FALLBROOK INDUSTRIES INC
Also Called: Standish Precision Products
323 Industrial Way Ste 1, Fallbrook (92028-2357)
PHONE..................................760 728-7229
Michael Standish, *Pr*
Dennis Standish, *VP*
▲ EMP: 28 EST: 1973
SQ FT: 15,000
SALES (est): 3.6MM **Privately Held**
Web: www.standishproducts.com
SIC: **3469** Stamping metal for the trade

### (P-8843)
### FORM & FUSION MFG INC (PA)
Also Called: Urgent Upfits
11261 Trade Center Dr, Rancho Cordova (95742-6223)
PHONE..................................916 638-8576
John Hancock, *Pr*
Dave Lewis, *Stockholder*
EMP: 27 EST: 1971
SQ FT: 40,000
SALES (est): 4.13MM
SALES (corp-wide): 4.13MM **Privately Held**
Web: www.form-fusion.com
SIC: **3469** 3465 Metal stampings, nec; Automotive stampings

### (P-8844)
### FRED R RIPPY INC
12450 Whittier Blvd, Whittier (90602-1017)
PHONE..................................562 698-9801
▼ EMP: 35 EST: 1950
SALES (est): 7.08MM **Privately Held**
Web: www.frrippy.com
SIC: **3469** Metal stampings, nec

### (P-8845)
### FTR ASSOCIATES INC
11862 Burke St, Santa Fe Springs (90670-2536)
PHONE..................................562 945-7504
EMP: 32 EST: 1986
SALES (est): 4.75MM **Privately Held**
Web: www.ftrmetalproducts.com
SIC: **3469** Metal stampings, nec

### (P-8846)
### GASKET MANUFACTURING ENGRG INC
8427 Secura Way, Santa Fe Springs (90670-2215)
PHONE..................................310 217-5600
Ramon Cardenas, *CEO*
Maureen Labor, *Dir Opers*
Juan Ramirez, *Prin*
EMP: 16 EST: 2020
SALES (est): 1.65MM **Privately Held**
Web: www.gasketmanufacturers.org
SIC: **3469** Metal stampings, nec

### (P-8847)
### GLOBAL PCCI (GPC) (PA)
Also Called: Gpc
2465 Campus Dr Ste 100, Irvine (92612-1502)
PHONE..................................757 637-9000
Sherri Bovino, *Pt*
EMP: 120 EST: 1989
SQ FT: 10,000
SALES (est): 17.65MM **Privately Held**
SIC: **3469** 4499 Metal stampings, nec; Salvaging, distressed vessels and cargoes

### (P-8848)
### HANMAR LLC (PA)
Also Called: Metalite Manufacturing
11441 Bradley Ave, Pacoima (91331-2304)
PHONE..................................818 890-2802
John Schachtner, *CEO*
Hannes Michael Schachtner, *
EMP: 49 EST: 1969
SQ FT: 25,000
SALES (est): 17MM
SALES (corp-wide): 17MM **Privately Held**
Web: www.metalite.net
SIC: **3469** Spinning metal for the trade

### (P-8849)
### HI TECH HONEYCOMB INC
9355 Ruffin Ct, San Diego (92123-5304)
PHONE..................................858 974-1600
Joao J Costa, *CEO*
John J Costa, *
Selma Costa, *
John Costa, *
EMP: 136 EST: 1989
SQ FT: 20,000
SALES (est): 20.93MM **Privately Held**
Web: www.hitechhoneycomb.com
SIC: **3469** Honeycombed metal

### (P-8850)
### HOUSTON BAZZ CO
Also Called: Bazz Houston Co
12700 Western Ave, Garden Grove (92841-4017)
PHONE..................................714 898-2666
Javier Castro, *Pr*
Chester O Houston, *
▲ EMP: 85 EST: 1957
SQ FT: 50,000
SALES (est): 23.33MM **Privately Held**
Web: www.bhisolutions.com
SIC: **3469** 3495 3493 Machine parts, stamped or pressed metal; Mechanical springs, precision; Steel springs, except wire

### (P-8851)
### IMPERIAL CAL PRODUCTS INC
425 Apollo St, Brea (92821-3110)
PHONE..................................714 990-9100
Shari Bittel, *Pr*
Kathy Flentye, *
▲ EMP: 35 EST: 1961
SQ FT: 35,000
SALES (est): 3.8MM **Privately Held**
Web: www.imperialhoods.com
SIC: **3469** Kitchen fixtures and equipment: metal, except cast aluminum

### (P-8852)
### INNOVATIVE STAMPING INC
Also Called: Innovative Systems
2068 E Gladwick St, Compton (90220-6202)
P.O. Box 5327 (90224-5327)
PHONE..................................310 537-6996
Gerald L Czaban, *Pr*
Kim Stevenson, *
▼ EMP: 32 EST: 1976
SQ FT: 128,000
SALES (est): 4.7MM **Privately Held**
Web: www.innovative-sys.com
SIC: **3469** Stamping metal for the trade

### (P-8853)
### IPT HOLDING INC (PA)
751 S Kellogg Ave, Goleta (93117-3806)
PHONE..................................805 683-3414
Stephen Braunheim, *Pr*
Ron Williams, *CFO*
EMP: 18 EST: 2002
SALES (est): 21.69MM
SALES (corp-wide): 21.69MM **Privately Held**
Web: www.intriplex.com
SIC: **3469** Stamping metal for the trade

### (P-8854)
### J-MARK MANUFACTURING INC
Also Called: J-Mark Company
2480 Coral St, Vista (92081-8430)
PHONE..................................760 727-6956
Mark Baker, *
Mark Baker, *Pr*
Dale Jackson, *VP*
Debbie Baker, *Treas*
Carol Jackson, *
EMP: 22 EST: 1988
SQ FT: 24,000
SALES (est): 4.98MM **Privately Held**
Web: www.j-markmfg.com
SIC: **3469** 3599 Electronic enclosures, stamped or pressed metal; Machine shop, jobbing and repair

### (P-8855)
### KAGA (USA) INC
2620 S Susan St, Santa Ana (92704-5816)
PHONE..................................714 540-2697
Masaaki Nozaki, *Pr*
Takashi Nozaki, *
Nobuharu Nozaki, *
Fumio Shiina, *
▲ EMP: 30 EST: 1981
SQ FT: 38,400
SALES (est): 5.82MM **Privately Held**
Web: www.kagainc.com
SIC: **3469** Stamping metal for the trade
PA: Kaga,Inc.
140, Ni, Ota, Tsubatamachi

### (P-8856)
### KB DELTA INC
Also Called: KB Delta Comprsr Valve Parts
3155 Fujita St, Torrance (90505-4006)
PHONE..................................310 530-1539
Boris Giourof, *CEO*
Katarina Giourof, *
◆ EMP: 37 EST: 1982
SALES (est): 5.57MM **Privately Held**
Web: www.kbdelta.com
SIC: **3469** 5085 7699 Machine parts, stamped or pressed metal; Industrial supplies; Compressor repair

### (P-8857)
### KITCOR CORPORATION
9959 Glencoaks Blvd, Sun Valley (91352-1085)
PHONE..................................323 875-2820
Kent Kitchen, *Prin*
Kent Kitchen, *Pr*
Alice Kitchen, *
Jim Kitchen, *
Bob Kitchen, *
EMP: 35 EST: 1943

# 3469 - Metal Stampings, Nec (P-8858)

SQ FT: 42,000
SALES (est): 8.24MM **Privately Held**
Web: www.kitcor.com
SIC: 3469 Kitchen fixtures and equipment: metal, except cast aluminum

**(P-8858)**
**KOPYKAKE ENTERPRISES INC (PA)**
Also Called: Mayer Baking Co
3699 W 240th St, Torrance (90505-6002)
PHONE..................310 373-8906
Gerald G Mayer, Pr
Greg Mayer, VP
Rick Mayer, VP
▲ EMP: 19 EST: 1970
SQ FT: 22,000
SALES (est): 4.92MM
SALES (corp-wide): 4.92MM **Privately Held**
Web: www.kopykake.com
SIC: 3469 2051 Kitchen fixtures and equipment: metal, except cast aluminum; Bakery: wholesale or wholesale/retail combined

**(P-8859)**
**LARRY SPUN PRODUCTS INC**
1533 S Downey Rd, Los Angeles (90023-4042)
PHONE..................323 881-6300
Hilario F Hurtado, CEO
EMP: 49 EST: 1958
SQ FT: 6,000
SALES (est): 4.95MM **Privately Held**
Web: www.larryspunproducts.com
SIC: 3469 Stamping metal for the trade

**(P-8860)**
**LOCK-RIDGE TOOL COMPANY INC**
145 N 8th Ave, Upland (91786-5402)
PHONE..................909 865-8309
Keith Clark, Pr
Ashford Clark, *
Penney Clark, *
▲ EMP: 52 EST: 1962
SALES (est): 8.97MM **Privately Held**
Web: www.lockridgetool.com
SIC: 3469 Stamping metal for the trade

**(P-8861)**
**LUPPEN HOLDINGS INC (PA)**
Also Called: Metal Products Engineering
3050 Leonis Blvd, Vernon (90058-2914)
PHONE..................323 581-8121
TOLL FREE: 800
Luppe R Luppen, Ch Bd
Paula Luppen, *
Ray Woodmansee, *
▲ EMP: 23 EST: 1940
SQ FT: 40,000
SALES (est): 688.31K
SALES (corp-wide): 688.31K **Privately Held**
Web: www.metalproductseng.com
SIC: 3469 3578 3596 Stamping metal for the trade; Change making machines; Scales and balances, except laboratory

**(P-8862)**
**MASTER FAB INC**
2279 Eagle Glen Pkwy Ste 112, Corona (92883-0790)
PHONE..................951 277-4772
Kenneth Scheel, Pr
Troy Jackson, Sec
EMP: 16 EST: 1980
SALES (est): 2.34MM **Privately Held**
Web: www.masterfabca.com
SIC: 3469 Stamping metal for the trade

**(P-8863)**
**MC WILLIAM & SON INC**
Also Called: California Tool & Die
421 S Irwindale Ave, Azusa (91702-3217)
PHONE..................626 969-1821
Dan Mcwilliam, Pr
Dana Matejka, Sec
EMP: 19 EST: 1967
SQ FT: 26,000
SALES (est): 2.88MM **Privately Held**
Web: www.californiatool-die.com
SIC: 3469 3544 Stamping metal for the trade; Special dies, tools, jigs, and fixtures

**(P-8864)**
**METALITE MANUFACTURING COMPANY**
Also Called: Metalite Mfg Companys
11441 Bradley Ave, Pacoima (91331-2304)
PHONE..................818 890-2802
Hanness Schachtner, CEO
Jan Schacatner, *
EMP: 41 EST: 1923
SQ FT: 58,000
SALES (est): 2.74MM
SALES (corp-wide): 17MM **Privately Held**
Web: www.metalite.net
SIC: 3469 Stamping metal for the trade
PA: Hanmar, Llc
11441 Bradley Ave
818 890-2802

**(P-8865)**
**METCO MANUFACTURING INC**
Also Called: Metco Fourslide Manufacturing
17540 S Denver Ave, Gardena (90248-3411)
PHONE..................310 516-6547
Jack Bishop, Pr
Darryl Scholl, *
Shirley Bishop, *
Dana Beisel, *
EMP: 29 EST: 1980
SQ FT: 11,200
SALES (est): 4.83MM **Privately Held**
Web: www.metcofourslide.com
SIC: 3469 Stamping metal for the trade

**(P-8866)**
**MEYER COOKWARE INDUSTRIES INC**
1 Meyer Plz, Vallejo (94590-5925)
PHONE..................707 551-2800
Stanley Cheng, Ch Bd
EMP: 38 EST: 1992
SALES (est): 3.04MM **Privately Held**
SIC: 3469 Cooking ware, except porcelain enameled
HQ: Meyer Corporation, U.S.
1 Meyer Plz
Vallejo CA 94590
707 551-2800

**(P-8867)**
**MEYER CORPORATION US (HQ)**
Also Called: Meyer Wines
1 Meyer Plz, Vallejo (94590-5925)
PHONE..................707 551-2800
Stanley Kin Sui Cheng, CEO
Ed Blackman, *
Christopher Banning, *
◆ EMP: 80 EST: 1980
SQ FT: 180,000
SALES (est): 89.59MM **Privately Held**
Web: www.meyerus.com
SIC: 3469 3631 5023 Cooking ware, except porcelain enameled; Household cooking equipment; Kitchenware
PA: Meyer International Holdings Limited
C/O Vistra (Bvi) Limited

**(P-8868)**
**MICRO MATRIX SYSTEMS**
Also Called: M M S
1899 Salem Ct, Claremont (91711-2638)
PHONE..................909 626-8544
Grant P Zarbock, CEO
Kerry Zarbock, *
▲ EMP: 25 EST: 1968
SALES (est): 2.49MM **Privately Held**
Web: www.mmsys.biz
SIC: 3469 Stamping metal for the trade

**(P-8869)**
**NANOPRECISION PRODUCTS INC**
802 Calle Plano, Camarillo (93012-8557)
PHONE..................310 597-4991
Michael K Barnoski, CEO
EMP: 25 EST: 2002
SALES (est): 2.22MM **Privately Held**
Web: www.nanoprecision.com
SIC: 3469 3721 Stamping metal for the trade; Research and development on aircraft by the manufacturer

**(P-8870)**
**NATIONAL METAL STAMPINGS INC**
42110 8th St E, Lancaster (93535-5444)
PHONE..................661 945-1157
William T Bloomer, Pr
Madeleine J Bloomer, *
▲ EMP: 70 EST: 1979
SQ FT: 20,000
SALES (est): 9.91MM **Privately Held**
Web: www.nationalmetal.com
SIC: 3469 Stamping metal for the trade

**(P-8871)**
**NELLXO LLC**
5990 Bald Eagle Dr, Fontana (92336-4573)
PHONE..................909 320-8501
EMP: 37 EST: 2021
SALES (est): 606.86K **Privately Held**
SIC: 3469 7389 Household cooking and kitchen utensils, metal; Business services, nec

**(P-8872)**
**NEW GORDON INDUSTRIES LLC**
Also Called: New Gordon Industries
13750 Rosecrans Ave, Santa Fe Springs (90670-5027)
P.O. Box 599 (90633-0599)
PHONE..................562 483-7378
EMP: 22
SIC: 3469 Stamping metal for the trade

**(P-8873)**
**PACIFIC METAL STAMPINGS INC**
28415 Witherspoon Pkwy, Valencia (91355-4174)
PHONE..................661 257-7656
Brian Schlotfelt, CEO
Scott Schlotfelt, *
▲ EMP: 30 EST: 1954
SQ FT: 21,000
SALES (est): 6.76MM **Privately Held**
Web: www.pacificmetalstampings.com
SIC: 3469 Stamping metal for the trade

**(P-8874)**
**PACIFIC PRECISION METALS INC**
Also Called: Tubing Seal Cap Co
1100 E Orangethorpe Ave Ste 253, Anaheim (92801-1164)
P.O. Box 51481 (91761)
PHONE..................951 226-1500
Ajay N Thakkar, Pr
EMP: 200 EST: 1987
SQ FT: 2,063
SALES (est): 20.05MM **Privately Held**
Web: www.pacificprecisioninc.com
SIC: 3469 3429 2599 8711 Stamping metal for the trade; Door locks, bolts, and checks; Cabinets, factory; Machine tool design
PA: Triyar Sv, Llc
10850 Wilshire Blvd

**(P-8875)**
**PERIDOT CORPORATION**
1072 Serpentine Ln, Pleasanton (94566-4731)
PHONE..................925 461-8830
Patrick Pickerell, Pr
Debra Vansickle, *
EMP: 60 EST: 1996
SQ FT: 30,000
SALES (est): 15.3MM **Privately Held**
Web: www.peridotcorp.com
SIC: 3469 Metal stampings, nec
PA: Seisa Medical, Inc.
9005 Montana Ave

**(P-8876)**
**PRECISION RESOURCE INC**
Also Called: Precision Resource Cal Div
5803 Engineer Dr, Huntington Beach (92649-1127)
PHONE..................714 891-4439
Robert Fitzgerald, Prin
EMP: 104
SQ FT: 27,000
SALES (corp-wide): 147.25MM **Privately Held**
Web: www.precisionresource.com
SIC: 3469 3544 Stamping metal for the trade; Special dies, tools, jigs, and fixtures
PA: Precision Resource, Inc.
25 Forest Pkwy
203 925-0012

**(P-8877)**
**PROFESSNL FNSHG SYSTEMS SUPS**
Also Called: Pfs
12341 Gladstone Ave, Sylmar (91342-5319)
PHONE..................818 365-8888
Vern Coley, CEO
Pat Ramnarine, VP
EMP: 17 EST: 1980
SQ FT: 14,000
SALES (est): 3.04MM **Privately Held**
Web: www.profinishing.com
SIC: 3469 5084 3471 Machine parts, stamped or pressed metal; Machine tools and metalworking machinery; Plating and polishing

**(P-8878)**
**PROFORMANCE MANUFACTURING INC**
1922 Elise Cir, Corona (92879-1882)
PHONE..................951 279-1230
Robert Morales, Pr
EMP: 20 EST: 1987
SQ FT: 21,000
SALES (est): 2.9MM **Privately Held**
Web: www.proformancemfg.com
SIC: 3469 3599 3451 3312 Machine parts, stamped or pressed metal; Machine and other job shop work; Screw machine products; Blast furnaces and steel mills

# PRODUCTS & SERVICES SECTION
## 3469 - Metal Stampings, Nec (P-8899)

**(P-8879)**
**PROTOTYPE & SHORT-RUN SVCS INC**
Also Called: Pass
1310 W Collins Ave, Orange (92867-5415)
PHONE....................714 449-9661
Jack Mc Devitt, *Pr*
**EMP:** 25 **EST:** 1989
**SQ FT:** 6,700
**SALES (est):** 6.02MM
**SALES (corp-wide):** 10.6MM **Privately Held**
Web: www.prototype-shortrun.com
**SIC: 3469** Stamping metal for the trade
**PA:** Apl Manufacturing Inc
1310 W Collins Ave
714 542-1942

**(P-8880)**
**QUALITY MTAL SPNNING MCHNING I**
Also Called: Quality Metal Spinning
4047 Transport St, Palo Alto (94303-4914)
PHONE....................650 858-2491
Joseph Czisch Junior, *Pr*
Xenia Czisch, *
**EMP:** 30 **EST:** 1967
**SQ FT:** 34,000
**SALES (est):** 6.2MM **Privately Held**
Web: www.qualitymetalspinning.us
**SIC: 3469** 3599 Stamping metal for the trade; Machine shop, jobbing and repair

**(P-8881)**
**QUICK DRAW AND MACHINING INC**
4869 Mcgrath St Ste130, Ventura (93003-7767)
PHONE....................805 644-7882
**EMP:** 18 **EST:** 1953
**SALES (est):** 3.2MM **Privately Held**
Web: www.quickdraw.com
**SIC: 3469** Metal stampings, nec

**(P-8882)**
**R ZAMORA INC**
Also Called: Tecxel
4645 North Ave Ste 102, Oceanside (92056-3593)
PHONE....................760 597-1130
Reggie Zamora, *Pr*
**EMP:** 21 **EST:** 2001
**SQ FT:** 10,000
**SALES (est):** 2.52MM **Privately Held**
Web: www.tecxel.com
**SIC: 3469** Machine parts, stamped or pressed metal

**(P-8883)**
**RAGO & SON INC**
1029 51st Ave, Oakland (94601-5653)
P.O. Box 7309 (94601-0309)
PHONE....................510 536-5700
Dominic Anthony Rago, *CEO*
Dominic Nic Rago, *Pr*
Gerald Accardo Senior, *VP*
Joseph E Rago, *
Edward Rago, *
**EMP:** 80 **EST:** 1969
**SQ FT:** 38,000
**SALES (est):** 8.07MM **Privately Held**
Web: www.rago-son.com
**SIC: 3469** Stamping metal for the trade

**(P-8884)**
**RESEARCH TOOL & DIE WORKS LLC**
Also Called: RT&d
17124 Keegan Ave, Carson (90746-1379)
PHONE....................310 639-5722
**EMP:** 66 **EST:** 1952
**SALES (est):** 7.73MM
**SALES (corp-wide):** 653.43MM **Privately Held**
Web: www.fairbanksmorsedefense.com
**SIC: 3469** Metal stampings, nec
**HQ:** Fairbanks Morse, Llc
701 White Ave
Beloit WI 53511
800 356-6955

**(P-8885)**
**SCANDIC SPRINGS INC**
700 Montague St, San Leandro (94577-4326)
P.O. Box 2196 (94577-0269)
PHONE....................510 352-3700
**EMP:** 36 **EST:** 1969
**SALES (est):** 8.53MM **Privately Held**
Web: www.scandic.com
**SIC: 3469** 3495 3496 Stamping metal for the trade; Mechanical springs, precision; Miscellaneous fabricated wire products

**(P-8886)**
**SCHUBERTH NORTH AMERICA LLC**
12707 High Bluff Dr Ste 200, San Diego (92130-2223)
PHONE....................949 215-0893
**EMP:** 15 **EST:** 2010
**SALES (est):** 4.85MM
**SALES (corp-wide):** 183.75K **Privately Held**
Web: www.schuberth.com
**SIC: 3469** Helmets, steel
**HQ:** Schubert Gmbh
Stegelitzer Str. 12
Magdeburg ST 39126
39181060

**(P-8887)**
**SERRA MANUFACTURING CORP (PA)**
3039 E Las Hermanas St, Compton (90221-5575)
PHONE....................310 537-4560
Sylvia G Hernandez, *Ch Bd*
John B Hernandez, *
Kris Hernandez, *
**EMP:** 53 **EST:** 1959
**SQ FT:** 23,916
**SALES (est):** 8.52MM
**SALES (corp-wide):** 8.52MM **Privately Held**
Web: www.serramfg.com
**SIC: 3469** Stamping metal for the trade

**(P-8888)**
**SLIDE SYSTEMS INC**
1448 240th St, Harbor City (90710-1307)
P.O. Box 304 (90277-0304)
PHONE....................310 539-3416
Myra Beisel, *Pr*
Marla Smith, *VP*
**EMP:** 19 **EST:** 1969
**SQ FT:** 10,000
**SALES (est):** 818.72K **Privately Held**
Web: www.slidesys.com
**SIC: 3469** Stamping metal for the trade

**(P-8889)**
**SOUTHWEST GREENE INTL INC**
Also Called: Greene Group Industries
4055b Calle Platino, Oceanside (92056-5805)
PHONE....................760 639-4960
Alexis Willingham, *Pr*
▲ **EMP:** 100 **EST:** 1997
**SQ FT:** 80,000
**SALES (est):** 18.38MM **Privately Held**
Web: www.greenegroup.com
**SIC: 3469** Metal stampings, nec

**(P-8890)**
**SPOTTER GLOBAL INC**
1204 N Miller St Unit A, Anaheim (92806-1958)
PHONE....................515 817-3726
Luke Zhao, *CEO*
**EMP:** 140 **EST:** 2021
**SALES (est):** 2MM **Privately Held**
**SIC: 3469** 5064 Household cooking and kitchen utensils, metal; Electric household appliances, nec

**(P-8891)**
**SPRING R&D & STAMP INC**
5757 Chino Ave, Chino (91710-5226)
P.O. Box 2875 (91708-2875)
PHONE....................909 465-5166
**EMP:** 18 **EST:** 1982
**SALES (est):** 961.97K **Privately Held**
Web: www.rdspring.com
**SIC: 3469** 3493 Metal stampings, nec; Steel springs, except wire

**(P-8892)**
**STEICO INDUSTRIES INC**
Also Called: Steico
1814 Ord Way, Oceanside (92056-1502)
PHONE....................760 438-8015
Troy Steiner, *CEO*
▲ **EMP:** 230 **EST:** 2001
**SQ FT:** 52,000
**SALES (est):** 51.17MM
**SALES (corp-wide):** 1.2B **Privately Held**
Web: www.steicoindustries.com
**SIC: 3469** 5051 Metal stampings, nec; Metals service centers and offices
**HQ:** Senior Operations Llc
300 E Devon Ave
Bartlett IL 60103
630 372-3500

**(P-8893)**
**SUNSTONE COMPONENTS GROUP INC (HQ)**
Also Called: Sun Stone Sales
42136 Avenida Alvarado, Temecula (92590-3400)
PHONE....................951 296-5010
Bradway B Adams, *CEO*
David Bernard, *
**EMP:** 41 **EST:** 1990
**SALES (est):** 9.89MM
**SALES (corp-wide):** 27.84MM **Privately Held**
Web: www.4scg.com
**SIC: 3469** Metal stampings, nec
**PA:** Pancon Corporation
350 Revolutionary Dr
781 297-6000

**(P-8894)**
**TEAM MANUFACTURING INC**
2625 Homestead Pl, Rancho Dominguez (90220-5610)
PHONE....................310 639-0251
Ed Ellis, *CEO*
James Cheatham, *
▲ **EMP:** 50 **EST:** 1975
**SQ FT:** 34,000
**SALES (est):** 4.86MM **Privately Held**
Web: www.teammfg.com
**SIC: 3469** 3544 Stamping metal for the trade; Die sets for metal stamping (presses)

**(P-8895)**
**TRU-FORM INDUSTRIES INC (PA)**
Also Called: Tru Form Industries
14511 Anson Ave, Santa Fe Springs (90670-5393)
PHONE....................562 802-2041
Vernon M Hildebrandt, *CEO*
▲ **EMP:** 69 **EST:** 1974
**SQ FT:** 50,000
**SALES (est):** 9.75MM
**SALES (corp-wide):** 9.75MM **Privately Held**
Web: www.tru-form.com
**SIC: 3469** 3496 3429 Metal stampings, nec; Clips and fasteners, made from purchased wire; Hardware, nec

**(P-8896)**
**USG CEILINGS PLUS LLC**
6711 E Washington Blvd, Commerce (90040-1801)
PHONE....................323 724-8166
Nancy Mercolino, *Pr*
**EMP:** 24 **EST:** 2017
**SALES (est):** 10.1MM
**SALES (corp-wide):** 16B **Privately Held**
Web: www.usg.com
**SIC: 3469** Architectural panels or parts, porcelain enameled
**HQ:** Usg Corporation
550 W Adams St
Chicago IL 60661
312 436-4000

**(P-8897)**
**VANGUARD TOOL & MFG CO INC**
Also Called: Vanguard Tool & Manufacturing
8388 Utica Ave, Rancho Cucamonga (91730-3849)
PHONE....................909 980-9392
Robert A Scudder, *Pr*
Connie Scudder, *
**EMP:** 49 **EST:** 1970
**SQ FT:** 47,000
**SALES (est):** 8.86MM **Privately Held**
Web: www.vanguardtoolmfg.net
**SIC: 3469** Stamping metal for the trade

**(P-8898)**
**VERDUGO TOOL & ENGRG CO INC**
20600 Superior St, Chatsworth (91311-4414)
PHONE....................818 998-1101
Kevin Gresiak, *Pr*
**EMP:** 19 **EST:** 1957
**SQ FT:** 15,000
**SALES (est):** 3.14MM **Privately Held**
Web: www.verdugotool.com
**SIC: 3469** 3544 Stamping metal for the trade; Special dies and tools

**(P-8899)**
**WALKER SPRING & STAMPING CORP**
Also Called: Walker
1555 S Vintage Ave, Ontario (91761-3655)
PHONE....................909 390-4300
Lang Walker, *Ch Bd*
Bruce Walker, *Pr*
James D Walker Junior, *VP Mfg*
Randy Walker, *VP Sls*
Carmen Prieto, *Sec*
▲ **EMP:** 110 **EST:** 1954
**SQ FT:** 108,000
**SALES (est):** 19.83MM **Privately Held**

## 3469 - Metal Stampings, Nec (P-8900)

SIC: 3469 3495 Stamping metal for the trade ; Precision springs

**(P-8900)**
**WEST COAST MANUFACTURING INC**
Also Called: West Coast Manufacturing
11822 Western Ave, Stanton (90680-3438)
PHONE..................714 897-4221
Patrick Hundley, Pr
Minerva Hundley, *
▲ EMP: 26 EST: 1993
SQ FT: 8,000
SALES (est): 4.91MM Privately Held
Web: www.westcoastmfg.com
SIC: 3469 Machine parts, stamped or pressed metal

**(P-8901)**
**WEST COAST METAL STAMPING INCORPORATED**
550 W Crowther Ave, Placentia (92870-6312)
PHONE..................714 792-0322
EMP: 32 EST: 1966
SALES (est): 6.71MM Privately Held
Web: www.wcmetalstamping.com
SIC: 3469 Stamping metal for the trade

**(P-8902)**
**WEST VALLEY PRECISION INC**
2055 Otoole Ave, San Jose (95131-1303)
PHONE..................408 519-5959
EMP: 45 EST: 1987
SALES (est): 4.2MM Privately Held
Web: www.wvpi.org
SIC: 3469 Machine parts, stamped or pressed metal

---

## 3471 Plating And Polishing

**(P-8903)**
**A & E ANODIZING**
652 Charles St Ste A, San Jose (95112-1433)
PHONE..................408 297-5910
Edwardo Ibanez, Pr
Angelica Ibanez, CFO
EMP: 15 EST: 1988
SALES (est): 2.29MM Privately Held
Web: www.aeanodizing.com
SIC: 3471 Electroplating of metals or formed products

**(P-8904)**
**A&A METAL FINISHING ENTPS LLC**
8290 Alpine Ave, Sacramento (95826-4748)
PHONE..................916 442-1063
EMP: 20 EST: 2008
SALES (est): 1.93MM Privately Held
Web: www.metalfinishinggroupllc.com
SIC: 3471 Electroplating of metals or formed products

**(P-8905)**
**AAA PLATING & INSPECTION INC**
424 E Dixon St, Compton (90222-1420)
PHONE..................323 979-8930
Gerald Wahlin, CEO
Charles Schwan, *
EMP: 95 EST: 1958
SQ FT: 50,000
SALES (est): 8.7MM Privately Held
Web: www.aaaplating.com

SIC: 3471 8734 Anodizing (plating) of metals or formed products; Metallurgical testing laboratory

**(P-8906)**
**ACCURATE PLATING COMPANY**
2811 Alcazar St, Los Angeles (90033-1108)
P.O. Box 33348 (90033-0348)
PHONE..................323 268-8567
Dennis Orr, Pr
Rigo Rodriguez, *
EMP: 30 EST: 1949
SQ FT: 18,000
SALES (est): 3.47MM Privately Held
Web: www.accurateplatingco.com
SIC: 3471 Electroplating of metals or formed products

**(P-8907)**
**ADVANCE-TECH PLATING INC**
1061 N Grove St, Anaheim (92806-2015)
PHONE..................714 630-7093
Meliton Gomez, Pr
EMP: 16 EST: 2001
SALES (est): 2.74MM Privately Held
SIC: 3471 Electroplating of metals or formed products

**(P-8908)**
**ADVANCED METAL FINISHING LLC**
Also Called: AMF
2130 March Rd, Roseville (95747-9308)
PHONE..................530 888-7772
EMP: 20 EST: 2000
SQ FT: 4,500
SALES (est): 5.4MM Privately Held
Web: www.amfservices.net
SIC: 3471 Electroplating of metals or formed products

**(P-8909)**
**AI INDUSTRIES INC (PA)**
Also Called: Ai Industries
1725 E Bayshore Rd Ste 101, Redwood City (94063-4145)
PHONE..................650 366-4099
Danny Pham, Prin
EMP: 95 EST: 1977
SQ FT: 27,000
SALES (est): 20.18MM
SALES (corp-wide): 20.18MM Privately Held
Web: www.ai-industries.com
SIC: 3471 3479 Anodizing (plating) of metals or formed products; Coating of metals and formed products

**(P-8910)**
**ALCO PLATING CORP (PA)**
Also Called: Modern Plating
1400 Long Beach Ave, Los Angeles (90021-2794)
PHONE..................213 749-7561
E Edward Chuck Manzetti, Pr
Emil Edward Chuck Manzetti, Pr
David Manzetti, *
▲ EMP: 50 EST: 1929
SQ FT: 65,000
SALES (est): 3.17MM
SALES (corp-wide): 3.17MM Privately Held
Web: www.alconickelchrome.com
SIC: 3471 Electroplating of metals or formed products

**(P-8911)**
**ALERT PLATING COMPANY**
Also Called: Alert Plating
9939 Glenoaks Blvd, Sun Valley (91352-1023)
PHONE..................818 771-9304
David La Liberte, Pr
Maurice La Liberte, *
Shirley La Liberte, *
Ed Lee, *
EMP: 45 EST: 1968
SQ FT: 22,000
SALES (est): 4.37MM Privately Held
SIC: 3471 Finishing, metals or formed products

**(P-8912)**
**ALL METALS PROCESSING OF SAN DIEGO INC**
Also Called: AMC
8401 Standustrial St, Stanton (90680-2619)
PHONE..................714 828-8238
EMP: 120
Web: www.allmetalsprocessing.com
SIC: 3471 3479 8734 Electroplating of metals or formed products; Enameling, including porcelain, of metal products; X-ray inspection service, industrial

**(P-8913)**
**ALL MTALS PROC ORANGE CNTY LLC**
8401 Standustrial St, Stanton (90680-2688)
PHONE..................714 828-8238
Scott Christman, CFO
Bob Wolfsberger, *
Rose Blikian, *
Michael Coburn, *
Derek Watson, *
EMP: 125 EST: 2015
SALES (est): 19.36MM Privately Held
Web: www.allmetalsprocessing.com
SIC: 3471 3479 8734 Electroplating of metals or formed products; Enameling, including porcelain, of metal products; X-ray inspection service, industrial

**(P-8914)**
**ALLBLACK CO INC**
8155 Byron Rd, Whittier (90606-2615)
PHONE..................562 946-2955
Juan F Guerrero, Pr
Lorena Guerrero, *
▲ EMP: 39 EST: 1992
SQ FT: 12,000
SALES (est): 4.63MM Privately Held
Web: www.allblackco-inc.com
SIC: 3471 Electroplating of metals or formed products

**(P-8915)**
**ALLIANCE CHEMICAL & ENVMTL**
Also Called: Alliance Finishing and Mfg
1721 Ives Ave, Oxnard (93033-1866)
PHONE..................805 385-3330
Mark Hyman, Pr
Heather Hyman, VP
EMP: 16 EST: 1991
SQ FT: 15,600
SALES (est): 2.6MM Privately Held
Web: www.alliance-finishing.com
SIC: 3471 Electroplating of metals or formed products

**(P-8916)**
**ALPHA POLISHING CORPORATION (PA)**
Also Called: General Plating
1313 Mirasol St, Los Angeles (90023-3108)
PHONE..................323 263-7593
TOLL FREE: 800
Alan Olick, Pr
Alan Olick, Pr
Trinidad Gonzales, *
EMP: 60 EST: 1940
SQ FT: 7,500
SALES (est): 2.45MM
SALES (corp-wide): 2.45MM Privately Held
Web: www.generalplatingco.net
SIC: 3471 3911 Plating of metals or formed products; Pins (jewelry), precious metal

**(P-8917)**
**ALUMINUM COATING TECH INC**
Also Called: A.C.T.
8290 Alpine Ave, Sacramento (95826-4748)
PHONE..................916 442-1063
Steven S Hickey, CEO
EMP: 20 EST: 1991
SALES (est): 2.34MM Privately Held
SIC: 3471 Electroplating of metals or formed products

**(P-8918)**
**AMEX PLATING INCORPORATED**
3333 Woodward Ave, Santa Clara (95054-2628)
PHONE..................408 986-8222
Jose Rodriguez, Pr
Sylvia D Rodriguez, *
Rebeca Rodriguez, *
EMP: 30 EST: 1983
SQ FT: 10,850
SALES (est): 2.07MM Privately Held
Web: www.amexplating.com
SIC: 3471 Finishing, metals or formed products

**(P-8919)**
**ANAPLEX CORPORATION**
15547 Garfield Ave, Paramount (90723-4033)
PHONE..................714 522-4481
Carmen Campbell, CEO
Bernie Kerper, *
EMP: 48 EST: 1962
SQ FT: 38,000
SALES (est): 4.34MM Privately Held
Web: www.anaplexcorp.com
SIC: 3471 Electroplating of metals or formed products

**(P-8920)**
**ANODIZING INDUSTRIES INC**
5222 Alhambra Ave, Los Angeles (90032-3403)
P.O. Box 32459 (90032-0459)
PHONE..................323 227-4916
Eugene J Golling, Pr
Amir Afshar, *
▲ EMP: 30 EST: 1980
SQ FT: 8,000
SALES (est): 3.01MM Privately Held
Web: www.anodizingindustries.com
SIC: 3471 3479 2396 Anodizing (plating) of metals or formed products; Painting of metal products; Automotive and apparel trimmings

**(P-8921)**
**ANODYNE INC**
2230 S Susan St, Santa Ana (92704-4493)
PHONE..................714 549-3321
Ralph Adams, Pr
Patti Kientz, *
EMP: 49 EST: 1960

# PRODUCTS & SERVICES SECTION

## 3471 - Plating And Polishing (P-8943)

SQ FT: 30,000
SALES (est): 3.71MM **Privately Held**
Web: www.anodyne.aero
SIC: **3471** 8734 Anodizing (plating) of metals or formed products; Testing laboratories

### (P-8922)
### APPLIED ANODIZE INC
622 Charcot Ave Ste D, San Jose (95131-2205)
PHONE.............................408 435-9191
Jose Muguerza, *Pr*
EMP: 17 EST: 1978
SQ FT: 14,000
SALES (est): 2.67MM **Privately Held**
Web: www.appliedanodize.com
SIC: **3471** Electroplating of metals or formed products

### (P-8923)
### AQUARIAN COATINGS CORP
600 N Batavia St, Orange (92868-1221)
PHONE.............................714 632-0230
Ronald Marquez, *Pr*
Rose Marquez, *
EMP: 15 EST: 1974
SALES (est): 767.74K **Privately Held**
Web: aquariancoatings.openfos.com
SIC: **3471** Electroplating of metals or formed products

### (P-8924)
### ARNOLDS METAL FINISHING INC
805 Aldo Ave Ste 104, Santa Clara (95054-2200)
PHONE.............................408 588-0079
Arnold Sanchez, *Pr*
EMP: 54 EST: 2008
SALES (est): 5.91MM **Privately Held**
Web: www.arnoldmetalfinishing.com
SIC: **3471** Finishing, metals or formed products

### (P-8925)
### ARTISTIC PLTG & MET FINSHG INC
2801 E Miraloma Ave, Anaheim (92806-1804)
PHONE.............................619 661-1691
Kipton Kahler, *Pr*
EMP: 50 EST: 1992
SQ FT: 44,573
SALES (est): 988.12K **Privately Held**
SIC: **3471** Chromium plating of metals or formed products

### (P-8926)
### ASSOCIATED PLATING COMPANY
9636 Ann St, Santa Fe Springs (90670-2902)
PHONE.............................562 946-5525
Michael Evans, *Pr*
Jon Shulkin, *Stockholder**
▲ EMP: 26 EST: 1952
SQ FT: 18,000
SALES (est): 2.56MM **Privately Held**
Web: www.associatedplating.com
SIC: **3471** Finishing, metals or formed products

### (P-8927)
### ATMF INC
Also Called: Ano-Tech Metal Finishing
807 Lincoln Ave, Clovis (93612-2245)
PHONE.............................559 299-6836
Carol Downs, *CEO*
Kelly S Downs, *

Gregory Ott, *
EMP: 30 EST: 1981
SQ FT: 8,000
SALES (est): 5.19MM **Privately Held**
Web: www.atmfinc.com
SIC: **3471** Anodizing (plating) of metals or formed products

### (P-8928)
### AUTOMATION PLATING CORPORATION
927 Thompson Ave, Glendale (91201-2011)
PHONE.............................323 245-4951
Peter K Wiggins, *
Edward Lee, *
Pat Kinzy, *
Marcia Mitchell, *
EMP: 40 EST: 1941
SQ FT: 65,000
SALES (est): 5.06MM **Privately Held**
Web: www.apczinc.com
SIC: **3471** Plating of metals or formed products

### (P-8929)
### BARRY AVENUE PLATING CO INC
2210 Barry Ave, Los Angeles (90064-1488)
PHONE.............................310 478-0078
Chuck Kearsley, *Pr*
Charles B Kearsley Iv, *Pr*
Kenneth F Kearsley, *
▼ EMP: 88 EST: 1951
SQ FT: 26,000
SALES (est): 10.36MM **Privately Held**
Web: www.barryavenueplating.com
SIC: **3471** Electroplating of metals or formed products

### (P-8930)
### BHC INDUSTRIES INC
239 E Greenleaf Blvd, Compton (90220-4913)
PHONE.............................310 632-2000
Gary Barken, *Pr*
EMP: 25 EST: 2000
SQ FT: 20,000
SALES (est): 719.37K **Privately Held**
Web: www.barkenshardchrome.com
SIC: **3471** Electroplating of metals or formed products

### (P-8931)
### BLACK OXIDE INDUSTRIES INC
Also Called: Black Oxide
1745 N Orangethorpe Park Ste A, Anaheim (92801-1139)
PHONE.............................714 870-9610
Pete Mata, *Pr*
Edward Mata, *
Evelyn Mata, *
EMP: 35 EST: 1974
SALES (est): 3.74MM **Privately Held**
Web: www.blackoxideindustries.com
SIC: **3471** 3479 Electroplating of metals or formed products; Coating of metals and formed products

### (P-8932)
### BODYCOTE THERMAL PROC INC
3370 Benedict Way, Huntington Park (90255-4517)
PHONE.............................323 583-1231
Chris Hall, *Brnch Mgr*
EMP: 87
SQ FT: 16,694
SALES (corp-wide): 1B **Privately Held**
Web: www.bodycote.com

SIC: **3471** 3398 Plating and polishing; Metal heat treating
HQ: Bodycote Thermal Processing, Inc.
12750 Merit Dr Ste 1400
Dallas TX 75251
214 904-2420

### (P-8933)
### BOWMAN PLATING CO INC
2631 E 126th St, Compton (90222-1599)
P.O. Box 5205 (90224-5205)
PHONE.............................310 639-4343
Mac Esfandi, *Pr*
Rashel Esfandi, *
John Esfandi, *Stockholder**
Cyrus Gipoor, *Stockholder**
EMP: 150 EST: 1952
SALES (est): 8.51MM **Privately Held**
Web: www.bowmanplating.com
SIC: **3471** Electroplating of metals or formed products

### (P-8934)
### BOWMAN-FIELD INC
Also Called: Chrome Nickel Plating
2800 Martin Luther King Jr Blvd, Lynwood (90262-1829)
PHONE.............................310 638-8519
Hector Flores, *Pr*
Ron Storer, *
▲ EMP: 60 EST: 1946
SQ FT: 20,000
SALES (est): 1.03MM **Privately Held**
Web: www.chrome1.com
SIC: **3471** 3714 Chromium plating of metals or formed products; Motor vehicle parts and accessories

### (P-8935)
### BRONZE-WAY PLATING CORPORATION (PA)
3301 E 14th St, Los Angeles (90023-3893)
PHONE.............................323 266-6933
Sarkis Mikhael-fard, *Pr*
Benjamin Mikhael-fard, *VP*
Fiyodor Mikhael-fard, *VP*
Fred Mikhael-fard, *VP*
EMP: 44 EST: 1956
SQ FT: 27,000
SALES (est): 549.68K
SALES (corp-wide): 549.68K **Privately Held**
Web: www.generalplatingco.net
SIC: **3471** Electroplating of metals or formed products

### (P-8936)
### CAL ELECTRO-COATINGS INC
893 Carleton St, Berkeley (94710-2609)
PHONE.............................510 849-4075
Jeff Garvens, *Pr*
EMP: 20 EST: 1994
SQ FT: 19,397
SALES (est): 3.85MM **Privately Held**
Web: www.electro-coatings.com
SIC: **3471** Electroplating of metals or formed products

### (P-8937)
### CAL-AURUM INDUSTRIES
Also Called: Cal-Aurum
15632 Container Ln, Huntington Beach (92649-1533)
PHONE.............................714 898-0996
Paul A Ginder, *Pr*
Chuck Tygard, *
EMP: 35 EST: 1971
SQ FT: 25,000
SALES (est): 5.05MM **Privately Held**
Web: www.cal-aurum.com

SIC: **3471** Electroplating of metals or formed products

### (P-8938)
### CAL-TRON PLATING INC
11919 Rivera Rd, Santa Fe Springs (90670-2209)
PHONE.............................562 945-1181
Carl Troncale Junior, *CEO*
Carl Troncale Senior, *Ch Bd*
EMP: 45 EST: 1961
SQ FT: 15,000
SALES (est): 1.53MM **Privately Held**
Web: www.cal-tronplating.com
SIC: **3471** Electroplating of metals or formed products

### (P-8939)
### CERTIFIED STEEL TREATING CORP
2454 E 58th St, Vernon (90058-3592)
PHONE.............................323 583-8711
Janice Davis, *Pr*
Pauline Nicolls, *Stockholder**
Jeff Davis, *
EMP: 42 EST: 1947
SQ FT: 30,000
SALES (est): 7.5MM **Privately Held**
SIC: **3471** 3398 Sand blasting of metal parts; Annealing of metal

### (P-8940)
### CHROMAL PLATING COMPANY
Also Called: Chromal Plating & Grinding
1748 Workman St, Los Angeles (90031-3395)
PHONE.............................323 222-0119
Ethel Bokelman, *Pr*
Ray F Bokelman Junior, *VP*
Diane L Remilinger, *
Robin Bokelman, *
Robin Ospoin, *
EMP: 28 EST: 1946
SQ FT: 20,625
SALES (est): 2.51MM **Privately Held**
Web: www.chromal.com
SIC: **3471** 3999 Electroplating of metals or formed products; Grinding and pulverizing of materials, nec

### (P-8941)
### CHROME TECH INC
2310 Cape Cod Way, Santa Ana (92703-3562)
PHONE.............................714 543-4092
EMP: 107
Web: www.chrometechwheels.com
SIC: **3471** Plating and polishing

### (P-8942)
### COAST PLATING INC (PA)
Also Called: Valence Los Angeles
128 W 154th St, Gardena (90248-2202)
PHONE.............................323 770-0240
EMP: 50 EST: 1965
SALES (est): 9.44MM
SALES (corp-wide): 9.44MM **Privately Held**
Web: www.coastplating.com
SIC: **3471** Plating of metals or formed products

### (P-8943)
### COAST TO COAST MET FINSHG CORP
401 S Raymond Ave, Alhambra (91803-1532)
PHONE.............................626 282-2122
Gildardo Bernal, *Pr*

# 3471 - Plating And Polishing (P-8944)

David Bernal, *
**EMP:** 25 **EST:** 1978
**SQ FT:** 20,000
**SALES (est):** 2.08MM **Privately Held**
**Web:** www.ctclightingmfg.com
**SIC: 3471** 3646 3645 Finishing, metals or formed products; Commercial lighting fixtures; Residential lighting fixtures

## (P-8944)
### COASTLINE METAL FINISHING CORP
7061 Patterson Dr, Garden Grove (92841-1414)
**PHONE**................................714 895-9099
Tracy Glende, *CEO*
Jamie Mitchell, *
Matthew Alty, *
**EMP:** 83 **EST:** 1987
**SQ FT:** 18,600
**SALES (est):** 8.26MM **Privately Held**
**Web:** www.valencesurfacetech.com
**SIC: 3471** Finishing, metals or formed products

## (P-8945)
### COMPONENT SURFACES INC
11880 Community Rd Ste 380, Poway (92064-8877)
**PHONE**................................858 513-3656
David Sheilds, *Pr*
**EMP:** 15 **EST:** 2004
**SQ FT:** 1,000
**SALES (est):** 5.33MM **Privately Held**
**Web:** www.componentsurfaces.com
**SIC: 3471** Electroplating of metals or formed products

## (P-8946)
### CONNELL PROCESSING INC (PA)
3094 N Avon St, Burbank (91504-2003)
**PHONE**................................818 845-7661
Stephen Lee, *Pr*
David Augustine, *
**EMP:** 27 **EST:** 1946
**SQ FT:** 25,000
**SALES (est):** 2.81MM
**SALES (corp-wide):** 2.81MM **Privately Held**
**Web:** www.connellprocessing.com
**SIC: 3471** Electroplating of metals or formed products

## (P-8947)
### DAE-IL USA INC
5712 Cherry Ave, Long Beach (90805-4404)
**PHONE**................................562 422-4046
Joe Reyes, *Brnch Mgr*
**EMP:** 19
**SIC: 3471** Polishing, metals or formed products
**HQ:** Dae-Il Usa, Inc.
112 Robert Young Blvd
Murray KY 42071

## (P-8948)
### DANCO ANODIZING INC
Also Called: Danco
1750 E Monticello Ct, Ontario (91761-7740)
**PHONE**................................909 923-0562
Joe Galvan, *Mgr*
**EMP:** 102
**SALES (corp-wide):** 15.68MM **Privately Held**
**Web:** www.danco.net
**SIC: 3471** Anodizing (plating) of metals or formed products
**PA:** Danco Anodizing, Inc.
44 La Porte St
626 445-3303

## (P-8949)
### DANCO ANODIZING INC (PA)
Also Called: Danco Metal Surfacing
44 La Porte St, Arcadia (91006-2827)
P.O. Box 660727 (91066-0727)
**PHONE**................................626 445-3303
Sherri Vivian Scherer, *Pr*
David Tatge, *
**EMP:** 40 **EST:** 1971
**SQ FT:** 10,000
**SALES (est):** 15.68MM
**SALES (corp-wide):** 15.68MM **Privately Held**
**Web:** www.danco.net
**SIC: 3471** Electroplating of metals or formed products

## (P-8950)
### E M E INC
Also Called: Electro Machine & Engrg Co
500 E Pine St, Compton (90222-2818)
P.O. Box 4998 (90224-4998)
**PHONE**................................310 639-1621
Wesley Turnbow, *CEO*
Randy Turnbow, *
Steven Turnbow, *
**EMP:** 125 **EST:** 1962
**SQ FT:** 65,000
**SALES (est):** 10.97MM **Privately Held**
**Web:** www.emeplating.com
**SIC: 3471** 2899 Anodizing (plating) of metals or formed products; Chemical preparations, nec

## (P-8951)
### ELECTRO-PLATING SPC INC
2436 American Ave, Hayward (94545-1810)
**PHONE**................................510 786-1881
Mary L Hall, *Pr*
**EMP:** 32 **EST:** 1973
**SQ FT:** 10,000
**SALES (est):** 3.39MM **Privately Held**
**Web:** www.eps-plating.com
**SIC: 3471** Electroplating of metals or formed products

## (P-8952)
### ELECTROCHEM SOLUTIONS LLC
Also Called: Pioneer Metal Finishing
32500 Central Ave, Union City (94587-2032)
**PHONE**................................510 476-1840
**EMP:** 22 **EST:** 2003
**SQ FT:** 21,315
**SALES (est):** 1.45MM **Privately Held**
**Web:** www.pioneermetal.com
**SIC: 3471** Electroplating of metals or formed products

## (P-8953)
### ELECTRODE TECHNOLOGIES INC
Also Called: Reid Metal Finishing
3110 W Harvard St Ste 14, Santa Ana (92704-3940)
**PHONE**................................714 549-3771
Tim A Grandcolas, *Pr*
Ivan Padron, *
▲ **EMP:** 40 **EST:** 1978
**SQ FT:** 10,000
**SALES (est):** 7.43MM **Privately Held**
**Web:** www.rmfusa.com
**SIC: 3471** Finishing, metals or formed products

## (P-8954)
### ELECTROLIZING INC
1947 Hooper Ave, Los Angeles (90011-1354)
P.O. Box 11900 (90011-0900)
**PHONE**................................213 749-7876
Susan B Grant, *Pr*
Jack Morgan, *
**EMP:** 26 **EST:** 1947
**SQ FT:** 10,000
**SALES (est):** 2.68MM **Privately Held**
**Web:** www.electrolizingofla.com
**SIC: 3471** Electroplating of metals or formed products

## (P-8955)
### ELECTROLURGY INC
1121 Duryea Ave, Irvine (92614-5519)
**PHONE**................................949 250-4494
Eron G Eklund, *Pr*
June Eklund, *
Sean Eklund, *
Stefni Gritten, *
**EMP:** 68 **EST:** 1969
**SQ FT:** 25,000
**SALES (est):** 8.3MM **Privately Held**
**Web:** www.electrolurgy.com
**SIC: 3471** 3429 Electroplating of metals or formed products; Marine hardware

## (P-8956)
### ELECTROMATIC
14025 Stage Rd, Santa Fe Springs (90670-5225)
**PHONE**................................562 623-9993
Diego Alvizo, *Mgr*
**EMP:** 15
**SALES (corp-wide):** 3.77MM **Privately Held**
**Web:** www.electromatic.com
**SIC: 3471** Electroplating of metals or formed products
**PA:** Electromatic
75 Aero Camino Ste 204
805 964-9880

## (P-8957)
### ELECTRONIC CHROME GRINDING INC
9128 Dice Rd, Santa Fe Springs (90670-2545)
**PHONE**................................562 946-6671
Philip Reed, *Pr*
Mike Reed, *VP*
Dale Reed, *VP*
Jeannette Goble, *Sec*
**EMP:** 22 **EST:** 1956
**SQ FT:** 55,000
**SALES (est):** 2.26MM **Privately Held**
**Web:** www.ecgrinding.com
**SIC: 3471** 3599 Electroplating of metals or formed products; Machine shop, jobbing and repair

## (P-8958)
### ELECTRONIC PRECISION SPC INC
545 Mercury Ln, Brea (92821-4831)
**PHONE**................................714 256-8950
Thomas Olszewski, *CEO*
Henry Brown, *
**EMP:** 34 **EST:** 1980
**SQ FT:** 4,000
**SALES (est):** 5.14MM **Privately Held**
**Web:** www.elecprec.com
**SIC: 3471** Electroplating of metals or formed products

## (P-8959)
### ELITE METAL FINISHING LLC (PA)
Also Called: Metal Finishing Pntg Lab Tstg
540 Spectrum Cir, Oxnard (93030-8988)
**PHONE**................................805 983-4320
Joel Clemons, *Pt*
Joe Hansen, *
George Hansen, *
**EMP:** 109 **EST:** 2001
**SQ FT:** 55,000
**SALES (est):** 20.1MM
**SALES (corp-wide):** 20.1MM **Privately Held**
**Web:** www.elitemetalfinishing.com
**SIC: 3471** 8734 Plating of metals or formed products; Testing laboratories

## (P-8960)
### FINE QUALITY METAL FINSHG INC
Also Called: Fine Quality Metal
1640 Daisy Ave, Long Beach (90813-1525)
**PHONE**................................562 983-7425
Edna Bolour, *Pr*
Manoucher Esfandi, *Treas*
Cy Gipoor, *Stockholder*
**EMP:** 15 **EST:** 1981
**SQ FT:** 6,000
**SALES (est):** 2.82MM **Privately Held**
**Web:** www.finequalitymetalfinishing.com
**SIC: 3471** Electroplating of metals or formed products

## (P-8961)
### FLARE GROUP
1571 Macarthur Blvd, Costa Mesa (92626-1407)
**PHONE**................................714 549-0202
**EMP:** 25
**SALES (est):** 1.04MM **Privately Held**
**SIC: 3471** Plating and polishing

## (P-8962)
### FOUR D METAL FINISHING
1065 Memorex Dr, Santa Clara (95050-2809)
**PHONE**................................408 730-5722
Peter Deguara, *Pr*
**EMP:** 30 **EST:** 1973
**SQ FT:** 11,000
**SALES (est):** 2.16MM **Privately Held**
**Web:** www.fourdmetal.com
**SIC: 3471** Electroplating of metals or formed products

## (P-8963)
### GENES PLATING WORKS INC (PA)
3498 E 14th St, Los Angeles (90023-3819)
**PHONE**................................323 269-8748
Harry W Levy, *Pr*
John F Whitney, *VP*
**EMP:** 30 **EST:** 2002
**SQ FT:** 13,000
**SALES (est):** 1.31MM
**SALES (corp-wide):** 1.31MM **Privately Held**
**Web:** www.lombardtechnologies.com
**SIC: 3471** Plating of metals or formed products

## (P-8964)
### GEORGE INDUSTRIES (HQ)
4116 Whiteside St, Los Angeles (90063-1619)
**PHONE**................................323 264-6660
Jeff Briggs, *Pr*
**EMP:** 40 **EST:** 1953

## PRODUCTS & SERVICES SECTION
### 3471 - Plating And Polishing (P-8986)

SQ FT: 38,200
SALES (est): 5.46MM
SALES (corp-wide): 4.17B **Publicly Held**
Web: www.valmontcoatings.com
SIC: **3471** 3479 Anodizing (plating) of metals or formed products; Aluminum coating of metal products
PA: Valmont Industries, Inc.
 15000 Valmont Plz
 402 963-1000

**(P-8965)**
**GLOBAL METAL SOLUTIONS INC**
2150 Mcgaw Ave, Irvine (92614-0912)
PHONE..............................949 872-2995
Mario Robles, *Pr*
Mario Robles, *Pr*
Thomas Linovitz, *
EMP: 35 EST: 2016
SALES (est): 8.41MM **Privately Held**
Web: www.gms1.net
SIC: **3471** Polishing, metals or formed products

**(P-8966)**
**GLOBAL PLATING INC**
44620 S Grimmer Blvd, Fremont (94538-6386)
PHONE..............................510 659-8764
Douglas Brothers, *Pr*
EMP: 35 EST: 1985
SQ FT: 23,000
SALES (est): 2.5MM **Privately Held**
Web: www.globalplating.com
SIC: **3471** Plating of metals or formed products

**(P-8967)**
**GSP METAL FINISHING INC**
16520 S Figueroa St, Gardena (90248-2625)
PHONE..............................818 744-1328
Mike Palatas, *VP*
EMP: 35 EST: 2019
SALES (est): 2.46MM **Privately Held**
Web: www.gspmf.com
SIC: **3471** Electroplating of metals or formed products

**(P-8968)**
**HAMMON PLATING CORPORATION**
890 Commercial St, Palo Alto (94303-4905)
PHONE..............................650 494-2691
Tom Wooten, *Pr*
Glen Phinney, *
EMP: 35 EST: 1960
SQ FT: 5,000
SALES (est): 5.9MM **Privately Held**
Web: www.hammonplating.com
SIC: **3471** Electroplating of metals or formed products

**(P-8969)**
**HANE AND HANE INC**
Also Called: University Plating Co
303 Piercy Rd, San Jose (95138-1403)
PHONE..............................408 292-2140
Carter Hane, *Pr*
EMP: 20 EST: 1958
SALES (est): 508.5K **Privately Held**
SIC: **3471** Electroplating of metals or formed products

**(P-8970)**
**HIGHTOWER PLATING & MFG CO LLC**
Also Called: Anillo Industries

2090 N Glassell St, Orange (92865-3306)
P.O. Box 5586 (92863-5586)
PHONE..............................714 637-9110
Kurt Koch, *Pr*
Mark Koch, *
EMP: 50 EST: 1957
SQ FT: 8,000
SALES (est): 2.06MM **Privately Held**
SIC: **3471** Plating of metals or formed products

**(P-8971)**
**HIXSON METAL FINISHING**
829 Production Pl, Newport Beach (92663-2809)
PHONE..............................800 900-9798
Carl Blazik, *Prin*
Douglas Greene, *
EMP: 69 EST: 1960
SQ FT: 38,000
SALES (est): 5.76MM **Privately Held**
Web: www.hmfgroup.com
SIC: **3471** Finishing, metals or formed products

**(P-8972)**
**INDUSTRIAL METAL FINISHING INC**
1941 Petra Ln, Placentia (92870-6749)
PHONE..............................714 628-8808
Robert E Hayden, *Pr*
EMP: 19 EST: 1991
SQ FT: 12,000
SALES (est): 1.55MM **Privately Held**
Web: www.indmetfin.com
SIC: **3471** 3398 Finishing, metals or formed products; Shot peening (treating steel to reduce fatigue)

**(P-8973)**
**INTERNATIONAL PLATING SVC LLC (PA)**
4045 Bonita Rd Ste 309, Bonita (91902-1337)
P.O. Box 210310 (91921-0310)
PHONE..............................619 454-2135
Guillermo A Fernandez, *Managing Member*
Jeffrey Robert Adams, *
EMP: 34 EST: 1996
SQ FT: 500
SALES (est): 2.33MM
SALES (corp-wide): 2.33MM **Privately Held**
Web: www.platinadorabaja.com
SIC: **3471** Electroplating of metals or formed products

**(P-8974)**
**INTERNTIONAL PHOTO PLATES CORP**
Also Called: Nanofilm
2641 Townsgate Rd Ste 100, Westlake Village (91361-2724)
PHONE..............................805 496-5031
Valdis Sneberg, *Pr*
Dorothy Cesari, *
Maria Flores, *
Dale Burow, *
▲ EMP: 25 EST: 1989
SQ FT: 8,000
SALES (est): 2.33MM **Privately Held**
SIC: **3471** 2796 Plating and polishing; Platemaking services

**(P-8975)**
**INVECO INC**
Also Called: Mighty Green
440 Fair Dr Ste 200, Costa Mesa (92626-6222)

PHONE..............................949 378-3850
Dennis D'alessio, *Pr*
EMP: 30 EST: 2013
SALES (est): 18MM **Privately Held**
SIC: **3471** Cleaning, polishing, and finishing

**(P-8976)**
**JCR AIRCRAFT DEBURRING LLC**
Also Called: Jcr Deburring
221 Foundation Ave, La Habra (90631-6812)
PHONE..............................714 870-4427
Juan Carlos Ruiz, *CEO*
Juan Carlos Ruiz, *Managing Member*
Omar Ruiz, *
EMP: 80 EST: 1986
SALES (est): 10.62MM **Privately Held**
Web: www.jcrindustries.com
SIC: **3471** 3541 3444 3542 Electroplating of metals or formed products; Deburring machines; Forming machine work, sheet metal; Machine tools, metal forming type

**(P-8977)**
**JD PROCESSING INC**
2220 Cape Cod Way, Santa Ana (92703-3563)
PHONE..............................714 972-8161
Thomas Scimeca, *CEO*
EMP: 50 EST: 2014
SALES (est): 4.77MM **Privately Held**
Web: www.jdprocessinginc.com
SIC: **3471** 3559 Anodizing (plating) of metals or formed products; Anodizing equipment

**(P-8978)**
**KRYLER CORP**
Also Called: Pecific Grinding
1217 E Ash Ave, Fullerton (92831-5019)
PHONE..............................714 871-9611
Chet Krygier Senior, *Pr*
Phyllis Krygier, *
EMP: 37 EST: 1977
SQ FT: 900
SALES (est): 2.42MM **Privately Held**
Web: www.krylercorporation.com
SIC: **3471** Electroplating of metals or formed products

**(P-8979)**
**LUCKINTA CORPORATION**
7307 Alexis Manor Pl, San Jose (95120-3407)
EMP: 33 EST: 1978
SALES (est): 7.76MM **Privately Held**
Web: www.intatech.com
SIC: **3471** 2891 Electroplating of metals or formed products; Sealants

**(P-8980)**
**M & R PLATING CORPORATION**
12375 Montague St, Pacoima (91331-2214)
PHONE..............................818 896-2700
Andres Rauda, *CEO*
EMP: 17 EST: 1976
SQ FT: 11,000
SALES (est): 1.88MM **Privately Held**
Web: www.m-rplatingcorp.com
SIC: **3471** Electroplating of metals or formed products

**(P-8981)**
**MAIN STEEL LLC**
3100 Jefferson St, Riverside (92504-4343)
PHONE..............................951 231-4949
Mike Folley, *Brnch Mgr*
EMP: 63
SALES (corp-wide): 1.54B **Privately Held**

Web: www.mainsteel.com
SIC: **3471** Polishing, metals or formed products
HQ: Main Steel, Llc
 2200 E Pratt Blvd
 Elk Grove Village IL 60007
 847 916-1220

**(P-8982)**
**MAKPLATE INC**
Also Called: Makplate
5780 Obata Way Ste F, Gilroy (95020-7092)
PHONE..............................408 842-7572
Zain Yahya, *Pr*
Naaim Ali Yahya, *
EMP: 43 EST: 1996
SQ FT: 5,000
SALES (est): 4.1MM **Privately Held**
Web: www.makplate.com
SIC: **3471** Gold plating

**(P-8983)**
**MECLEC METAL FINISHING INC**
5945 E Harvard Ave, Fresno (93727-8621)
PHONE..............................559 797-0101
Rod Bandy, *Owner*
EMP: 30 EST: 2005
SALES (est): 2.44MM **Privately Held**
Web: www.meclec.com
SIC: **3471** Electroplating of metals or formed products

**(P-8984)**
**METAL CHEM INC**
Also Called: Metal Chem
21514 Nordhoff St, Chatsworth (91311-5822)
PHONE..............................818 727-9951
Carlos Pongo, *Pr*
EMP: 30 EST: 1997
SALES (est): 6.15MM **Privately Held**
Web: www.metalcheminc.com
SIC: **3471** 3443 Plating of metals or formed products; Fabricated plate work (boiler shop)

**(P-8985)**
**METAL SURFACES INTL LLC**
6060 Shull St, Bell Gardens (90201-6297)
P.O. Box 5001 (90202-5001)
PHONE..............................562 927-1331
Olaf Schubert, *Pr*
Charles K Bell, *
Sam Bell, *
EMP: 150 EST: 1954
SQ FT: 85,000
SALES (est): 18.65MM **Privately Held**
Web: www.metalsurfaces.com
SIC: **3471** Electroplating of metals or formed products

**(P-8986)**
**MORRELLS ELECTRO PLATING INC**
Also Called: Morrell's Metal Finishing
436 E Euclid Ave, Compton (90222-2810)
P.O. Box 3085 (90223-3085)
PHONE..............................310 639-1024
Cyrus Gipoor, *Pr*
EMP: 30 EST: 1948
SQ FT: 20,000
SALES (est): 4.6MM **Privately Held**
Web: www.morrellsplating.com
SIC: **3471** Electroplating of metals or formed products

## 3471 - Plating And Polishing (P-8987)

**(P-8987)**
**MULTICHROME COMPANY INC (PA)**
Also Called: Microplate
1013 W Hillcrest Blvd, Inglewood (90301-2019)
PHONE................310 216-1086
Steven A Peterman, Pr
EMP: 26 EST: 1962
SQ FT: 5,000
SALES (est): 2.57MM
SALES (corp-wide): 2.57MM Privately Held
Web: www.multiplate.com
SIC: 3471 Electroplating of metals or formed products

**(P-8988)**
**NASMYTH TMF INC**
29102 Hancock Pkwy, Valencia (91355-1066)
PHONE................818 954-9504
Peter Smith, CEO
EMP: 54 EST: 2014
SQ FT: 10,000
SALES (est): 6.22MM
SALES (corp-wide): 253.95K Privately Held
Web: www.technicalmetalfinishing.com
SIC: 3471 3479 Anodizing (plating) of metals or formed products; Coating of metals and formed products
HQ: Ngl Realisations Limited
Nasmyth House
Coventry W MIDLANDS CV7 9

**(P-8989)**
**NXEDGE CSL LLC**
Also Called: C S L
529 Aldo Ave, Santa Clara (95054-2205)
PHONE................408 727-0893
Mahesh Naik, Pr
Tim Mickael, *
▲ EMP: 55 EST: 2011
SQ FT: 16,000
SALES (est): 4.39MM Privately Held
Web: www.nxedge.com
SIC: 3471 Anodizing (plating) of metals or formed products

**(P-8990)**
**OLD SPC INC**
202 W 140th St, Los Angeles (90061-1006)
PHONE................310 533-0748
Mary Mcmeans, CEO
Donna Martinez, VP
Jesus Diaz, Sec
EMP: 25 EST: 1999
SQ FT: 60,000
SALES (est): 3.3MM Privately Held
Web: www.spectrumplating.com
SIC: 3471 Electroplating of metals or formed products

**(P-8991)**
**OMNI METAL FINISHING INC (PA)**
11639 Coley River Cir, Fountain Valley (92708-4216)
PHONE................714 979-9414
Victor M Salazar, Pr
Ramiro Salazar, *
Filiberto Hernandez, *
EMP: 99 EST: 1980
SQ FT: 34,000
SALES (est): 15.79MM
SALES (corp-wide): 15.79MM Privately Held
Web: www.omnimetal.com

**SIC: 3471** Electroplating of metals or formed products

**(P-8992)**
**OPTI-FORMS INC**
42310 Winchester Rd, Temecula (92590-4810)
PHONE................951 296-1300
Kevin Thompson, Pr
Robert Brunson, *
Clint Tinker, *
EMP: 45 EST: 1984
SQ FT: 61,000
SALES (est): 9.96MM Privately Held
Web: www.optiforms.com
SIC: 3471 3827 Plating of metals or formed products; Optical instruments and lenses

**(P-8993)**
**P K SELECTIVE METAL PLTG INC**
415 Mathew St, Santa Clara (95050-3105)
PHONE................408 988-1910
Peter Kellett, Pr
EMP: 16 EST: 1975
SQ FT: 21,000
SALES (est): 828.65K Privately Held
Web: www.pkselective.com
SIC: 3471 Electroplating of metals or formed products

**(P-8994)**
**PENTRATE METAL PROCESSING**
3517 E Olympic Blvd, Los Angeles (90023-3976)
PHONE................323 269-2121
John J Grana, Pr
Vincent Grana, *
Nick Grana, *
Nick Gran, Genl Mgr
EMP: 30 EST: 1945
SQ FT: 18,000
SALES (est): 3.03MM Privately Held
Web: www.pentrate.com
SIC: 3471 Electroplating of metals or formed products

**(P-8995)**
**PLASMA RGGEDIZED SOLUTIONS INC**
5452 Business Dr, Huntington Beach (92649-1226)
PHONE................714 893-6063
Bob Marla, Brnch Mgr
EMP: 27
Web: www.plasmarugged.com
SIC: 3471 3479 Electroplating and plating; Coating of metals and formed products
PA: Plasma Ruggedized Solutions, Inc.
2284 Ringwood Ave Ste A

**(P-8996)**
**PLATERONICS PROCESSING INC**
Also Called: Plateronics Processing
9164 Independence Ave, Chatsworth (91311-5902)
PHONE................818 341-2191
Joseph Roter, Pr
Marvin Roter, *
Lee F Roter, *
EMP: 35 EST: 1959
SQ FT: 6,500
SALES (est): 3MM Privately Held
Web: www.plateronics.com
SIC: 3471 5051 Finishing, metals or formed products; Metals service centers and offices

**(P-8997)**
**PRECIOUS METALS PLATING CO INC**
2635 Orange Ave, Santa Ana (92707-3738)
PHONE................714 546-6271
Chad Wayne Bird, Pr
Betty Bird, Sec
EMP: 15 EST: 1957
SQ FT: 6,500
SALES (est): 2.16MM Privately Held
Web: www.pmplating.com
SIC: 3471 Electroplating of metals or formed products

**(P-8998)**
**PRECISION ANODIZING & PLTG INC**
Also Called: P A P
1601 N Miller St, Anaheim (92806-1469)
PHONE................714 996-1601
Jose A Salazar, CEO
EMP: 89 EST: 1971
SQ FT: 44,000
SALES (est): 9.94MM Privately Held
Web: www.precisionanodizingandplating.com
SIC: 3471 Electroplating of metals or formed products

**(P-8999)**
**PROCESS STAINLESS LAB INC (PA)**
Also Called: Advance Elctro Polishing
1280 Memorex Dr, Santa Clara (95050-2812)
PHONE................408 980-0535
Clay Hudson, Owner
David Hays, *
EMP: 27 EST: 1993
SQ FT: 8,000
SALES (est): 7.74MM Privately Held
Web: www.pslinc.com
SIC: 3471 Polishing, metals or formed products

**(P-9000)**
**PRODIGY SURFACE TECH INC**
Also Called: Arrhenius
807 Aldo Ave Ste 103, Santa Clara (95054-2254)
PHONE................408 492-9390
John Shaw, Pr
Mark Danitschek, *
EMP: 38 EST: 2002
SQ FT: 14,500
SALES (est): 1.9MM Privately Held
Web: www.prodigysurfacetech.com
SIC: 3471 Electroplating of metals or formed products

**(P-9001)**
**QUAKER CITY PLATING**
Also Called: Quaker City Plating & Silvrsm
11729 Washington Blvd, Whittier (90606-2498)
P.O. Box 2406 (90610-2406)
PHONE................562 945-3721
Michael Crain, Mng Pt
Angelo Dirado, Mng Pt
▲ EMP: 220 EST: 1937
SQ FT: 48,000
SALES (est): 23.36MM Privately Held
Web: www.qcpent.com
SIC: 3471 Plating of metals or formed products

**(P-9002)**
**QUALITY CONTROL PLATING INC**

4425 E Airport Dr Ste 113, Ontario (91761-7815)
PHONE................909 605-0206
Jay J Singh, VP
Mona Singh, Pr
EMP: 22 EST: 1991
SQ FT: 3,500
SALES (est): 1.51MM Privately Held
SIC: 3471 Plating of metals or formed products

**(P-9003)**
**RAVLICH ENTERPRISES LLC**
Also Called: Spectrum Plating Company
202 W 140th St, Los Angeles (90061-1006)
PHONE................310 533-0748
Anthony Ravlich, Brnch Mgr
EMP: 41
SALES (corp-wide): 10.45MM Privately Held
Web: www.neutronicstamping.com
SIC: 3471 Plating and polishing
PA: Ravlich Enterprises, Llc
100 Business Center Dr
714 964-8900

**(P-9004)**
**RAVLICH ENTERPRISES LLC (PA)**
Also Called: Neutronic Stamping & Plating
100 Business Center Dr, Corona (92878-3224)
PHONE................714 964-8900
Anthony Ravlich, CEO
Nicholas Ravlich, CFO
EMP: 27 EST: 2003
SQ FT: 27,000
SALES (est): 10.45MM
SALES (corp-wide): 10.45MM Privately Held
Web: www.neutronicstamping.com
SIC: 3471 3469 Electroplating of metals or formed products; Metal stampings, nec

**(P-9005)**
**REAL PLATING INC**
1245 W 2nd St, Pomona (91766-1310)
PHONE................909 623-2304
Juan Real, CEO
EMP: 25 EST: 2007
SQ FT: 5,264
SALES (est): 2.05MM Privately Held
Web: www.realplating.com
SIC: 3471 Electroplating of metals or formed products

**(P-9006)**
**ROSE MANUFACTURING GROUP INC**
Also Called: Elite Metal Finishing
2525 Jason Ct Ste 102, Oceanside (92056-3000)
PHONE................760 407-0232
Dan Rose, Pr
EMP: 21 EST: 2000
SQ FT: 3,300
SALES (est): 2.74MM Privately Held
Web: www.elite-metalfinishing.com
SIC: 3471 Plating of metals or formed products

**(P-9007)**
**SAFE PLATING INC**
18001 Railroad St, City Of Industry (91748-1215)
PHONE................626 810-1872
Magdy Seif, Pr
Mario Gomez, *
EMP: 58 EST: 1979
SQ FT: 35,000

# PRODUCTS & SERVICES SECTION
## 3471 - Plating And Polishing (P-9029)

SALES (est): 4.81MM **Privately Held**
Web: www.safeplatinginc.com
SIC: **3471** Electroplating of metals or formed products

### (P-9008)
### SANTA ANA PLATING (PA)
1726 E Rosslynn Ave, Fullerton (92831-5111)
PHONE.................310 923-8305
Tony Kakuk, *Pr*
EMP: 55 EST: 1954
SQ FT: 17,100
SALES (est): 952.53K
SALES (corp-wide): 952.53K **Privately Held**
SIC: **3471** Finishing, metals or formed products

### (P-9009)
### SANTA CLARA PLATING CO INC
1773 Grant St, Santa Clara (95050-3974)
PHONE.................408 727-9315
Thomas L Coss, *Pr*
Wendy Coss, *Stockholder\**
EMP: 85 EST: 1974
SQ FT: 13,000
SALES (est): 6.98MM **Privately Held**
Web: www.santaclaraplating.com
SIC: **3471** Electroplating of metals or formed products

### (P-9010)
### SANTOSHI CORPORATION
Also Called: Entrance Tech
2439 Seaman Ave, El Monte (91733-1936)
PHONE.................626 444-7118
Hershad Shah, *Pr*
Raksha Shah, *\**
EMP: 33 EST: 1971
SQ FT: 15,000
SALES (est): 6.36MM **Privately Held**
Web: www.alumacoat.com
SIC: **3471** Coloring and finishing of aluminum or formed products

### (P-9011)
### SCHMIDT INDUSTRIES INC
Also Called: Prime Plating
11321 Goss St, Sun Valley (91352-3206)
P.O. Box 1843 (91353-1843)
PHONE.................818 768-9100
Fred Schmidt, *Pr*
Jennifer Schmidt, *\**
EMP: 90 EST: 1986
SQ FT: 30,000
SALES (est): 1.24MM **Privately Held**
Web: www.prime-plating.com
SIC: **3471** Electroplating of metals or formed products

### (P-9012)
### SEMANO INC
31757 Knapp St, Hayward (94544-7827)
PHONE.................510 489-2360
Frank Largusa, *Pr*
Terry Dillon, *\**
▲ EMP: 35 EST: 1993
SQ FT: 13,000
SALES (est): 4.57MM **Privately Held**
Web: www.semanoinc.com
SIC: **3471** Electroplating of metals or formed products

### (P-9013)
### SHEFFIELD PLATERS INC
9850 Waples St, San Diego (92121-2921)
PHONE.................858 546-8484
Dale Watkins Junior, *Pr*
Mark Watkins, *\**
Shelley Watkins, *Stockholder\**
EMP: 85 EST: 1946
SQ FT: 20,000
SALES (est): 4.75MM **Privately Held**
Web: www.sheffieldplaters.com
SIC: **3471** Plating of metals or formed products

### (P-9014)
### SHEILA STREET PROPERTIES INC (PA)
5900 Sheila St, Commerce (90040-2403)
P.O. Box 911458 (90091-1238)
PHONE.................323 838-9208
EMP: 51 EST: 1931
SALES (est): 13MM
SALES (corp-wide): 13MM **Privately Held**
Web: www.valleyplating.com
SIC: **3471** Plating of metals or formed products

### (P-9015)
### SOUTHERN CALIFORNIA PLATING CO
3261 National Ave, San Diego (92113-2636)
PHONE.................619 231-1481
Paul Hummell Junior, *Pr*
EMP: 30 EST: 1946
SQ FT: 13,000
SALES (est): 1.5MM **Privately Held**
Web: www.socalplating.com
SIC: **3471** Electroplating of metals or formed products

### (P-9016)
### STABILE PLATING COMPANY INC
1150 E Edna Pl, Covina (91724-2592)
PHONE.................626 339-9091
David Crest, *Pr*
Eric Crest, *VP*
Steven Crest, *VP*
EMP: 22 EST: 1959
SQ FT: 6,000
SALES (est): 2.3MM **Privately Held**
Web: www.stabileplating.com
SIC: **3471** 3444 3353 Plating of metals or formed products; Sheet metalwork; Aluminum sheet, plate, and foil

### (P-9017)
### STUART-DEAN CO INC
14731 Franklin Ave Ste L, Tustin (92780-7221)
PHONE.................714 544-4460
Steven Materazzo, *Mgr*
EMP: 30
SALES (corp-wide): 65.45MM **Privately Held**
Web: www.stuartdean.com
SIC: **3471** Polishing, metals or formed products
PA: Stuart-Dean Co. Inc.
43-50 10th St
800 322-3180

### (P-9018)
### SUPERIOR CONNECTOR PLATING INC
Also Called: Superior Plating
1901 E Cerritos Ave, Anaheim (92805-6427)
PHONE.................714 774-1174
Juan Martin, *Pr*
EMP: 22 EST: 1994
SQ FT: 7,500
SALES (est): 2.46MM **Privately Held**
Web: www.superiorplatingca.com
SIC: **3471** Electroplating of metals or formed products

### (P-9019)
### SYMCOAT METAL PROCESSING INC
7887 Dunbrook Rd Ste C, San Diego (92126-4382)
PHONE.................858 451-3313
Sylvia Twiggs, *Pr*
Michelle Kanganis, *VP*
EMP: 24 EST: 1994
SQ FT: 12,000
SALES (est): 967.55K **Privately Held**
SIC: **3471** 3341 Finishing, metals or formed products; Secondary nonferrous metals

### (P-9020)
### TECHNIC INC
1170 N Hawk Cir, Anaheim (92807-1789)
PHONE.................714 632-0200
Mike Chicos, *Mgr*
EMP: 30
SALES (corp-wide): 159.53MM **Privately Held**
Web: www.technic.com
SIC: **3471** 2899 3678 3672 Plating of metals or formed products; Plating compounds; Electronic connectors; Printed circuit boards
PA: Technic, Inc.
47 Molter St
401 781-6100

### (P-9021)
### TEIKURO CORPORATION
Also Called: Hayward Plant
31499 Hayman St, Hayward (94544-7123)
PHONE.................510 487-4797
EMP: 41
Web: www.teikuro.com
SIC: **3471** Electroplating of metals or formed products
HQ: Teikuro Corporation
101a Clay St Ste 128
San Francisco CA 94111
415 273-2650

### (P-9022)
### TEMECULA QUALITY PLATING INC
42147 Roick Dr, Temecula (92590-3695)
PHONE.................951 296-9875
Duc Vo, *Pr*
Dat Vo, *\**
EMP: 32 EST: 2011
SALES (est): 1.82MM **Privately Held**
Web: www.temeculaplating.com
SIC: **3471** Electroplating of metals or formed products

### (P-9023)
### THERMIONICS LABORATORY INC
Thermionics Metal Proc Inc
3118 Depot Rd, Hayward (94545-2708)
PHONE.................510 786-0680
Al Nielsen, *Mgr*
EMP: 75
SQ FT: 1,300
SALES (corp-wide): 24.98MM **Privately Held**
Web: www.thermionics.com
SIC: **3471** 8711 7342 Cleaning and descaling metal products; Engineering services; Disinfecting and pest control services
HQ: Thermionics Laboratory, Inc.
3118 Depot Rd
Hayward CA 94545
510 538-3304

### (P-9024)
### TRIDENT PLATING INC
10046 Romandel Ave, Santa Fe Springs (90670-3424)
PHONE.................562 906-2556
Maty Rodriguez, *Pr*
Juan Carlos Rodriguez, *\**
Ian Holmber, *\**
EMP: 28 EST: 1981
SQ FT: 18,197
SALES (est): 2.46MM **Privately Held**
Web: www.tridentplating.com
SIC: **3471** Electroplating of metals or formed products

### (P-9025)
### TRIUMPH PROC - EMBEE DIV INC
2158 S Hathaway St, Santa Ana (92705-5249)
PHONE.................714 546-9842
EMP: 400
SALES (est): 10.75MM **Privately Held**
SIC: **3471** Electroplating and plating

### (P-9026)
### TRIUMPH PROCESSING INC
Also Called: Valence Lynwood
2605 Industry Way, Lynwood (90262-4007)
PHONE.................323 563-1338
Peter Labarbera, *CEO*
Richard C III, *\**
EMP: 103 EST: 1968
SQ FT: 140,000
SALES (est): 20.15MM
SALES (corp-wide): 138.9MM **Privately Held**
Web: www.valencesurfacetech.com
SIC: **3471** 3398 3356 Anodizing (plating) of metals or formed products; Metal heat treating; Nonferrous rolling and drawing, nec
PA: Valence Surface Technologies Llc
300 Cntnntal Blvd Ste 600
888 540-0878

### (P-9027)
### ULTRAMET
12173 Montague St, Pacoima (91331-2210)
PHONE.................818 899-0236
Andrew Duffy, *CEO*
Walter Abrams, *\**
Richard B Kaplan, *Stockholder\**
James Kaplan, *Stockholder\**
▲ EMP: 79 EST: 1970
SQ FT: 43,000
SALES (est): 16.07MM **Privately Held**
Web: www.ultramet.com
SIC: **3471** 8731 Electroplating and plating; Commercial physical research

### (P-9028)
### UNIVERSAL METAL PLATING
704 S Taylor Ave, Montebello (90640-5562)
PHONE.................626 969-7932
Guadalupe Martinez, *Pt*
EMP: 15
SALES (corp-wide): 338.17K **Privately Held**
Web: www.universalplating.com
SIC: **3471** Chromium plating of metals or formed products
PA: Universal Metal Plating
626 1/2 S Gerhart Ave
626 969-7931

### (P-9029)
### V & M COMPANY
14024 Avalon Blvd, Los Angeles (90061-2636)

# 3471 - Plating And Polishing (P-9030)

PHONE..................310 532-5633
Anthony Babiak, *Pr*
Timothy Babiak, *VP*
▲ **EMP:** 19 **EST:** 1948
**SQ FT:** 7,500
**SALES (est):** 762.33K **Privately Held**
**Web:** www.vmplating.com
**SIC: 3471** Electroplating of metals or formed products

### (P-9030)
### VALEX CORP (HQ)
6080 Leland St, Ventura (93003-7605)
PHONE..................805 658-0944
▲ **EMP:** 83 **EST:** 1976
**SALES (est):** 36.16MM
**SALES (corp-wide):** 14.81B **Publicly Held**
**Web:** www.valex.com
**SIC: 3471** 3317 3494 Polishing, metals or formed products; Steel pipe and tubes; Valves and pipe fittings, nec
**PA:** Reliance, Inc.
16100 N 71st St Ste 400
480 564-5700

### (P-9031)
### VALLEY CHROME PLATING INC (PA)
Also Called: Wing Master
1028 Hoblitt Ave, Clovis (93612-2805)
P.O. Box 189 (93613-0189)
PHONE..................559 298-8094
Thomas A Lucas, *CEO*
Ray Lucas, *Pr*
Greg Lucas, *VP*
Matthew Lucas, *VP*
Catherine L Booey, *Sec*
▲ **EMP:** 62 **EST:** 1961
**SQ FT:** 30,000
**SALES (est):** 24.66MM
**SALES (corp-wide):** 24.66MM **Privately Held**
**Web:** www.valleychrome.com
**SIC: 3471** 3714 Plating of metals or formed products; Bumpers and bumperettes, motor vehicle

### (P-9032)
### WEST COAST PVD INC
3280 Corporate Vw, Vista (92081-8528)
PHONE..................714 822-6362
Brian T Nevill, *CEO*
**EMP:** 21 **EST:** 2006
**SALES (est):** 418.84K **Privately Held**
**Web:** www.westcoastpvd.com
**SIC: 3471** Plating and polishing

### (P-9033)
### WEST VALLEY PLATING INC
21061 Superior St Ste A, Chatsworth (91311-4330)
PHONE..................818 709-1684
Josephina Campos, *Pr*
**EMP:** 15 **EST:** 2000
**SALES (est):** 915.97K **Privately Held**
**SIC: 3471** Plating of metals or formed products

---

## 3479 Metal Coating And Allied Services

### (P-9034)
### ABACUS POWDER COATING
1829 Tyler Ave, South El Monte (91733-3617)
PHONE..................626 443-7556
Esther Davidoff, *Pr*
**EMP:** 25 **EST:** 2006
**SALES (est):** 2.44MM **Privately Held**
**Web:** www.abacuspowder.com
**SIC: 3479** Coating of metals and formed products

### (P-9035)
### ACI ALLOYS INC
1458 Seareel Pl, San Jose (95131-1572)
PHONE..................408 259-7337
Paul Albert, *Pr*
Larry Albert, *VP*
Charles Albert, *VP*
**EMP:** 15 **EST:** 1982
**SQ FT:** 4,800
**SALES (est):** 2.42MM **Privately Held**
**Web:** www.acialloys.com
**SIC: 3479** Coating of metals and formed products

### (P-9036)
### ACTION POWDER COATING LLC
7949 Stromesa Ct Ste D, San Diego (92126-6338)
PHONE..................858 566-2288
Chuck Dewent, *Managing Member*
**EMP:** 18 **EST:** 1993
**SQ FT:** 20,000
**SALES (est):** 1.37MM **Privately Held**
**Web:** www.actionpowdercoating.com
**SIC: 3479** Coating of metals and formed products

### (P-9037)
### ADFA INCORPORATED
Also Called: A&A Jewelry Supply
319 W 6th St, Los Angeles (90014-1703)
PHONE..................213 627-8004
Robert Adem, *Pr*
Naim Farah, *
▲ **EMP:** 45 **EST:** 1986
**SALES (est):** 4.4MM **Privately Held**
**Web:** www.aajewelry.com
**SIC: 3479** 3548 3172 Engraving jewelry, silverware, or metal; Electric welding equipment; Cases, jewelry

### (P-9038)
### ADVANCED FABRICATION TECHNOLOGY LLC
31154 San Benito St, Hayward (94544-7912)
PHONE..................510 489-6218
**EMP:** 66 **EST:** 1984
**SALES (est):** 4.89MM **Privately Held**
**Web:** www.aftmetal.com
**SIC: 3479** 3444 Painting of metal products; Sheet metalwork

### (P-9039)
### ADVANCED GRINDING INCORPORATED
812 49th Ave, Oakland (94601-5136)
PHONE..................510 536-3465
Ronald L Wegstein, *Pr*
Karen Wegstein, *
Ronald Wegstein, *
**EMP:** 30 **EST:** 1980
**SQ FT:** 13,000
**SALES (est):** 4.19MM **Privately Held**
**Web:** www.advancedgrindinginc.com
**SIC: 3479** Coating of metals and formed products

### (P-9040)
### AHC ENTERPRISES INC
Also Called: Advanced Industrial Coatings
950 Industrial Dr, Stockton (95206-3927)
PHONE..................209 234-2700
**TOLL FREE:** 877
Ronald Cymanski, *Pr*
David Arney, *
Steve Hockett, *
Marianne Arney, *
**EMP:** 53 **EST:** 1984
**SQ FT:** 48,000
**SALES (est):** 7.6MM **Privately Held**
**Web:** www.aic-coatings.com
**SIC: 3479** Coating of metals and formed products

### (P-9041)
### AIRCOAT INC
13405 S Broadway, Los Angeles (90061-1127)
PHONE..................310 527-2258
Francisco Ramirez, *Pr*
**EMP:** 15 **EST:** 1995
**SQ FT:** 20,000
**SALES (est):** 478.87K **Privately Held**
**Web:** www.aircoatinc.com
**SIC: 3479** Painting of metal products

### (P-9042)
### ALL SOURCE COMPANY BLDG GROUP
10625 Scripps Ranch Blvd Ste D, San Diego (92131-1012)
PHONE..................858 586-0903
Jerry Zumbro, *Pr*
**EMP:** 21 **EST:** 2008
**SQ FT:** 2,000
**SALES (est):** 5.17MM **Privately Held**
**Web:** www.allsourceco.com
**SIC: 3479** 1721 Aluminum coating of metal products; Painting and paper hanging

### (P-9043)
### ALPHACOAT FINISHING LLC
9350 Cabot Dr, San Diego (92126-4311)
PHONE..................949 748-7796
Vaishali Joshi, *
**EMP:** 28 **EST:** 2017
**SALES (est):** 2.5MM **Privately Held**
**Web:** www.alphacoatfinishing.com
**SIC: 3479** Coating of metals and formed products

### (P-9044)
### AMADA AMERICA INC
100 S Puente St, Brea (92821-3813)
PHONE..................714 739-2111
**EMP:** 64
**Web:** www.amada.com
**SIC: 3479** Aluminum coating of metal products
**HQ:** Amada America, Inc.
7025 Firestone Blvd
Buena Park CA 90621
714 739-2111

### (P-9045)
### AMCS
125 N Aspan Ave, Azusa (91702-4231)
PHONE..................626 334-9160
An Tien Chung, *Admn*
**EMP:** 18 **EST:** 2010
**SALES (est):** 303.62K **Privately Held**
**Web:** www.amcsgroup.com
**SIC: 3479** Coating of metals and formed products

### (P-9046)
### AMERICAN ETCHING & MFG
13730 Desmond St, Pacoima (91331-2706)
PHONE..................323 875-3910
Gary Kipka, *Pr*
**EMP:** 45 **EST:** 1972
**SQ FT:** 20,000
**SALES (est):** 4.21MM **Privately Held**
**Web:** www.aemetch.com
**SIC: 3479** Etching on metals

### (P-9047)
### APPLIED COATINGS & LININGS
3224 Rosemead Blvd, El Monte (91731-2807)
PHONE..................626 280-6354
**EMP:** 24
**SQ FT:** 150,000
**SALES (est):** 2.7MM **Privately Held**
**Web:** www.appliedcoatings.com
**SIC: 3479** 3471 Coating of metals and formed products; Plating and polishing

### (P-9048)
### APPLIED POWDERCOAT INC
3101 Camino Del Sol, Oxnard (93030-8999)
PHONE..................805 981-1991
Victor Anselmo, *Pr*
J Michael Hagan, *
Deborah Anselmo, *
**EMP:** 45 **EST:** 1989
**SQ FT:** 30,000
**SALES (est):** 4.17MM **Privately Held**
**Web:** www.appliedpowder.com
**SIC: 3479** Coating of metals and formed products

### (P-9049)
### ARNACO INDUSTRIAL COATINGS
8445 Warvale St, Pico Rivera (90660-4316)
PHONE..................562 222-1022
Edawrd Gomez, *Pr*
Jose Vasquez, *Prin*
**EMP:** 20 **EST:** 2016
**SALES (est):** 2.26MM **Privately Held**
**Web:** www.aicindustrialcoatings.com
**SIC: 3479** Coating of metals and formed products

### (P-9050)
### ASTRO CHROME AND POLSG CORP
8136 Lankershim Blvd, North Hollywood (91605-1611)
PHONE..................818 781-1463
Jesse Gonzalez, *Pr*
**EMP:** 23 **EST:** 1981
**SQ FT:** 3,000
**SALES (est):** 410.01K **Privately Held**
**Web:** www.astroplating.com
**SIC: 3479** Coating of metals and formed products

### (P-9051)
### ATLAS GALVANIZING LLC
2639 Leonis Blvd, Vernon (90058-2203)
PHONE..................323 587-6247
Patricia New, *
**EMP:** 36 **EST:** 1936
**SQ FT:** 20,000
**SALES (est):** 2.79MM **Privately Held**
**Web:** www.atlasgalv.com
**SIC: 3479** Coating of metals and formed products

### (P-9052)
### B & C PAINTING SOLUTIONS INC
107 Val Dervin Pkwy, Stockton (95206-4001)
PHONE..................209 982-0422
Gary Maggard, *CEO*
**EMP:** 28 **EST:** 2002
**SQ FT:** 40,000
**SALES (est):** 2.35MM **Privately Held**
**Web:** www.bcpaintingsolutions.com

# PRODUCTS & SERVICES SECTION
## 3479 - Metal Coating And Allied Services (P-9074)

SIC: 3479 Coating of metals and formed products

**(P-9053)**
**B R & F SPRAY INC**
3380 De La Cruz Blvd, Santa Clara (95054-2608)
PHONE..............................408 988-7582
Ronald Grainger, *Pr*
Florence Grainger, *Sec*
EMP: 20 EST: 1972
SQ FT: 14,000
SALES (est): 1.66MM **Privately Held**
Web: www.brf-spray.com
SIC: 3479 3471 Painting of metal products; Plating and polishing

**(P-9054)**
**BELL POWDER COATING INC**
4747 Mcgrath St, Ventura (93003-6495)
P.O. Box 7117 (93006-7117)
PHONE..............................805 658-2233
Carl Bell, *Pr*
Judith Bell, *VP*
EMP: 15 EST: 1986
SQ FT: 16,500
SALES (est): 1.59MM **Privately Held**
SIC: 3479 Coating of metals and formed products

**(P-9055)**
**BJS&T ENTERPRISES INC**
Also Called: San Diego Powder Coating
1702 N Magnolia Ave, El Cajon (92020-1287)
PHONE..............................619 448-7795
Philip Johnson, *Pr*
Bob Johnson, *
Stephen Johnson, *
EMP: 50 EST: 2001
SQ FT: 7,000
SALES (est): 4.12MM **Privately Held**
Web: www.sandiegopowdercoating.com
SIC: 3479 Coating of metals and formed products

**(P-9056)**
**CALWEST GALVANIZING CORP**
Also Called: Calwest Galvanizing
2226 E Dominguez St, Carson (90810-1086)
PHONE..............................310 549-2200
TOLL FREE: 888
Isaac Malbonado, *Genl Mgr*
▲ EMP: 18 EST: 1984
SQ FT: 20,000
SALES (est): 4.3MM
SALES (corp-wide): 4.17B **Publicly Held**
Web: www.valmontcoatings.com
SIC: 3479 3317 Galvanizing of iron, steel, or end-formed products; Steel pipe and tubes
PA: Valmont Industries, Inc.
15000 Valmont Plz
402 963-1000

**(P-9057)**
**CERTIFIED ENAMELING INC (PA)**
Also Called: Certified Archtctral Fbrction
3342 Emery St, Los Angeles (90023-3810)
PHONE..............................323 264-4403
Vicki Ziegel, *CEO*
Glenn Ziegel, *
EMP: 91 EST: 1953
SQ FT: 50,000
SALES (est): 12MM
SALES (corp-wide): 12MM **Privately Held**
Web: www.certifiedenameling.com
SIC: 3479 Coating of metals and formed products

**(P-9058)**
**CLASS A POWDERCOAT INC**
7506 Henrietta Dr, Sacramento (95822-5145)
PHONE..............................916 681-7474
Klay Stubbs, *Pr*
Kirk Stubbs, *
EMP: 25 EST: 1991
SALES (est): 2.56MM **Privately Held**
Web: www.classapc.com
SIC: 3479 3471 Painting of metal products; Sand blasting of metal parts

**(P-9059)**
**COURT GALVANIZING INC**
4937 Allison Pkwy, Vacaville (95688-9346)
PHONE..............................707 448-4848
EMP: 15 EST: 1966
SALES (est): 3.42MM **Privately Held**
Web: www.courtgalvanizinginc.com
SIC: 3479 Galvanizing of iron, steel, or end-formed products

**(P-9060)**
**CREST COATING INC**
1361 S Allec St, Anaheim (92805-6304)
PHONE..............................714 635-7090
TOLL FREE: 800
Michael D Erickson, *CEO*
Bonnie George, *
▲ EMP: 60 EST: 1968
SQ FT: 55,000
SALES (est): 9.3MM **Privately Held**
Web: www.crestcoating.com
SIC: 3479 Coating of metals and formed products

**(P-9061)**
**DENMAC INDUSTRIES INC**
7616 Rosecrans Ave, Paramount (90723-2508)
P.O. Box 2144 (90723-8144)
PHONE..............................562 634-2714
Mark Plechot, *Pr*
Maurice Plechot, *
James Campagna, *
▲ EMP: 40 EST: 1974
SQ FT: 20,000
SALES (est): 4.9MM **Privately Held**
Web: www.denmac-ind.com
SIC: 3479 Coating of metals and formed products

**(P-9062)**
**DURA COAT PRODUCTS INC (PA)**
5361 Via Ricardo, Riverside (92509-2414)
PHONE..............................951 341-6500
Myung K Hong, *CEO*
Lorrie Y Hong, *
Suzanne Faust, *
◆ EMP: 64 EST: 1986
SQ FT: 29,000
SALES (est): 45.96MM
SALES (corp-wide): 45.96MM **Privately Held**
Web: www.axalta.com
SIC: 3479 2851 Aluminum coating of metal products; Paints and allied products

**(P-9063)**
**DURABLE COATING INC**
28716 Garnet Canyon Dr, Santa Clarita (91390-4296)
PHONE..............................805 299-8750
EMP: 15
SALES (corp-wide): 96.52K **Privately Held**
Web: www.durablecoatinginc.com
SIC: 3479 Coating of metals and formed products
PA: Durable Coating Inc.
21163 Centre Pointe Pkwy

**(P-9064)**
**E-FAB INC**
1075 Richard Ave, Santa Clara (95050-2815)
P.O. Box 239 (95052-0239)
PHONE..............................408 727-5218
James W Scales, *Pr*
Jerry Banks, *VP*
EMP: 22 EST: 1981
SQ FT: 4,000
SALES (est): 6.07MM **Privately Held**
Web: www.e-fab.com
SIC: 3479 Etching and engraving

**(P-9065)**
**ELECTRO STAR INDUS COATING INC**
Also Called: Electro Star Powder Coatings
1945 Airport Blvd, Red Bluff (96080-4518)
PHONE..............................530 527-5400
Baron A Pierce, *Pr*
Susan Pierce, *CFO*
EMP: 15 EST: 1979
SQ FT: 4,000
SALES (est): 825.66K **Privately Held**
Web: www.electrostar.net
SIC: 3479 Coating of metals and formed products

**(P-9066)**
**ELECTRO TECH COATINGS INC**
Also Called: Electro Tech Powder Coating
836 Rancheros Dr Ste A, San Marcos (92069-7035)
PHONE..............................760 746-0292
Adam P Mitchell, *Pr*
Allen L Mitchell, *VP*
Denise Mitchell, *Sec*
Linda Mitchell, *CFO*
EMP: 20 EST: 1994
SQ FT: 13,000
SALES (est): 3.36MM **Privately Held**
Web: www.electrotechcoatings.com
SIC: 3479 3471 Coating of metals and formed products; Sand blasting of metal parts

**(P-9067)**
**ELYTE INC**
Also Called: Quality Powder Coating
4516 District Blvd, Bakersfield (93313-2314)
PHONE..............................661 832-1000
Marco Amavizca, *Pr*
Marco Amavizca, *Prin*
EMP: 18 EST: 2006
SALES (est): 1.97MM **Privately Held**
SIC: 3479 Coating of metals and formed products

**(P-9068)**
**ETS EXPRESS LLC (DH)**
Also Called: Ets Express
420 Lombard St, Oxnard (93030-5100)
PHONE..............................805 278-7771
Sharon Eyal, *Pr*
Taly Eyal, *CFO*
▲ EMP: 28 EST: 1998
SQ FT: 40,000
SALES (est): 24.8MM **Privately Held**
Web: www.etsexpress.com
SIC: 3479 3231 Etching and engraving; Cut and engraved glassware: made from purchased glass
HQ: Leedsworld, Inc.
400 Hunt Valley Rd
New Kensington PA 15068
724 334-9000

**(P-9069)**
**FLAME-SPRAY INC**
4674 Alvarado Canyon Rd, San Diego (92120-4304)
PHONE..............................619 283-2007
Larry Suhl, *Pr*
Darrel Suhl, *VP*
Roxy Suhl, *Dir*
Pam Scalzo, *Stockholder*
▲ EMP: 20 EST: 1969
SQ FT: 20,000
SALES (est): 4.88MM **Privately Held**
Web: www.flamesprayinc.com
SIC: 3479 Coating of metals and formed products

**(P-9070)**
**FLETCHER COATING CO**
Also Called: Fletcher Coating
426 W Fletcher Ave, Orange (92865-2612)
PHONE..............................714 637-4763
Kurtis Breeding, *CEO*
▲ EMP: 50 EST: 1971
SQ FT: 37,500
SALES (est): 4.78MM **Privately Held**
Web: www.fletcherkote.com
SIC: 3479 Coating of metals and formed products

**(P-9071)**
**FUSION COATINGS INC**
6589 Las Positas Rd, Livermore (94551-5157)
PHONE..............................925 443-8083
Paul Fleury, *Pr*
EMP: 15 EST: 1984
SQ FT: 7,000
SALES (est): 1.73MM **Privately Held**
Web: www.fusioncoatingsonline.com
SIC: 3479 Coating of metals and formed products

**(P-9072)**
**FUSION FINISH LLC**
2527 Ximeno Ave, Long Beach (90815-1843)
PHONE..............................562 619-1189
Cord D Rodman, *Brnch Mgr*
EMP: 16
SALES (corp-wide): 494K **Privately Held**
Web: www.fusionfinishwheels.com
SIC: 3479 Coating of metals and formed products
PA: Fusion Finish Llc
800 Santiago Ave
562 773-5303

**(P-9073)**
**FVO SOLUTIONS INC**
Also Called: Foothill Vctonal Opportunities
789 N Fair Oaks Ave, Pasadena (91103-3045)
PHONE..............................626 449-0218
▲ EMP: 75
Web: www.fvosolutions.com
SIC: 3479 3999 Coating of metals and formed products; Gold stamping, except books

**(P-9074)**
**GEMTECH INDS GOOD EARTH MFG**
Also Called: Gemtech International
2737 S Garnsey St, Santa Ana (92707-3340)
P.O. Box 15506 (92735-0506)
PHONE..............................714 848-2517

## 3479 - Metal Coating And Allied Services (P-9075)

Shig Shiwota, *Pr*
Maya Shiwota, *
David Shiwota, *
▲ **EMP:** 24 **EST:** 1971
**SQ FT:** 10,500
**SALES (est):** 2.38MM **Privately Held**
**Web:** www.gemtechcoatings.com
**SIC: 3479** Coating of metals and formed products

### (P-9075)
### GILBERT SPRAY COAT INC
Also Called: Gilbert Spray Coat
300 Laurelwood Rd, Santa Clara (95054-2311)
**PHONE**.................................408 988-0747
Todd Mclean, *Pr*
Lisa Mclean, *VP*
**EMP:** 16 **EST:** 1939
**SQ FT:** 5,000
**SALES (est):** 1.91MM **Privately Held**
**Web:** www.gilbertspray.com
**SIC: 3479** Coating of metals and formed products

### (P-9076)
### HAI ADVNCED MTL SPCIALISTS INC
Also Called: H A I
1600 E Miraloma Ave, Placentia (92870-6622)
**PHONE**.................................714 414-0575
Daren J Gansert, *Pr*
Debra Gansert, *VP*
▲ **EMP:** 15 **EST:** 2003
**SALES (est):** 851.89K **Privately Held**
**Web:** www.haiinc.com
**SIC: 3479** Coating of metals and formed products

### (P-9077)
### HALEY INDUS CTINGS LININGS INC
2919 Tanager Ave, Commerce (90040-2723)
**PHONE**.................................323 588-8086
Yvonne P Haley, *Pr*
**EMP:** 21 **EST:** 1993
**SALES (est):** 3.33MM **Privately Held**
**Web:** www.haleyindustrial.com
**SIC: 3479** 1771 Coating of metals and formed products; Flooring contractor

### (P-9078)
### INLAND PACIFIC COATINGS INC
3556 Lytle Creek Rd, Lytle Creek (92358-9776)
**PHONE**.................................909 822-0594
Ciro Hernandez, *Prin*
**EMP:** 20 **EST:** 2012
**SALES (est):** 1.81MM **Privately Held**
**SIC: 3479** 1721 7389 Metal coating and allied services; Painting and paper hanging; Business Activities at Non-Commercial Site

### (P-9079)
### INLAND POWDER COATING CORP
Also Called: Prs Industries
1656 S Bon View Ave Ste F, Ontario (91761-4419)
P.O. Box 3427 (91761-0943)
**PHONE**.................................909 947-1122
David Paul Flatten, *Pr*
Debbie Flatten, *
**EMP:** 104 **EST:** 1983
**SQ FT:** 83,000
**SALES (est):** 16.91MM **Privately Held**
**Web:** www.inlandpowder.com

**SIC: 3479** 3471 Coating of metals and formed products; Sand blasting of metal parts

### (P-9080)
### INNOVATIVE COATINGS TECHNOLOGY CORPORATION
Also Called: Incotec
1347 Poole St 106, Mojave (93501-1658)
**PHONE**.................................661 824-8101
**EMP:** 127 **EST:** 1992
**SALES (est):** 22.04MM **Privately Held**
**Web:** www.incoteccorp.com
**SIC: 3479** 8732 Coating of metals with plastic or resins; Research services, except laboratory

### (P-9081)
### INOVATI
1522 Cook Pl, Goleta (93117-3124)
P.O. Box 60007 (93160-0007)
**PHONE**.................................805 571-8384
Sky Ternahan, *Engr*
**EMP:** 24 **EST:** 1989
**SALES (est):** 1.68MM **Privately Held**
**Web:** www.inovati.com
**SIC: 3479** Coating of metals and formed products

### (P-9082)
### ISLAND POWDER COATING
Also Called: Powder Coating
1830 Tyler Ave, South El Monte (91733-3618)
**PHONE**.................................626 279-2460
Joe Graham, *Owner*
**EMP:** 30 **EST:** 1994
**SALES (est):** 2.17MM **Privately Held**
**Web:** www.abacuspowder.com
**SIC: 3479** Coating of metals and formed products

### (P-9083)
### ITALIX COMPANY INC
120 Mast St Ste A, Morgan Hill (95037-5154)
**PHONE**.................................408 988-2487
Robert L Armanasco, *Pr*
Frank Fantino, *CEO*
**EMP:** 19 **EST:** 1977
**SQ FT:** 8,000
**SALES (est):** 2.35MM **Privately Held**
**Web:** www.italix.com
**SIC: 3479** 3471 Etching, photochemical; Finishing, metals or formed products

### (P-9084)
### JAN-KENS ENAMELING COMPANY INC
715 E Cypress Ave, Monrovia (91016-4254)
**PHONE**.................................626 358-1849
**EMP:** 24
**Web:** www.jankens.com
**SIC: 3479** Coating of metals and formed products

### (P-9085)
### KENNEDY NAME PLATE CO
4501 Pacific Blvd, Vernon (90058-2207)
**PHONE**.................................323 585-0121
William J Kennedy Junior, *Pr*
Mike Kennedy, *
**EMP:** 25 **EST:** 1921
**SQ FT:** 36,000
**SALES (est):** 2.53MM **Privately Held**
**Web:** www.knpco.com

**SIC: 3479** 7336 3993 3444 Name plates: engraved, etched, etc.; Silk screen design; Signs and advertising specialties; Sheet metalwork

### (P-9086)
### KENS SPRAY EQUIPMENT LLC
Also Called: Ken's Spray Equipment, Inc.
1900 W Walnut St, Compton (90220-5019)
**PHONE**.................................310 635-9995
Joseph I Snowden, *Pr*
**EMP:** 133 **EST:** 1979
**SALES (est):** 29.74MM
**SALES (corp-wide):** 364.48B **Publicly Held**
**Web:** www.pccaero.com
**SIC: 3479** Painting of metal products
**HQ:** Precision Castparts Corp.
5885 Meadows Rd Ste 620
Lake Oswego OR 97035
503 946-4800

### (P-9087)
### LOS ANGELES GALVANIZING CO
2518 E 53rd St, Huntington Park (90255-2505)
**PHONE**.................................323 583-2263
Lance Michael Rosenkranz, *CEO*
Jamie Rosenkranz, *
Tim Rosenkranz, *
Lance Rosenkranz, *
**EMP:** 58 **EST:** 1932
**SQ FT:** 26,000
**SALES (est):** 9.76MM **Privately Held**
**Web:** www.lagalvanizing.com
**SIC: 3479** Coating of metals and formed products

### (P-9088)
### MAAS BROTHERS INC
Also Called: Maas Brothers Powder Coating
285 S Vasco Rd, Livermore (94551-9203)
**PHONE**.................................925 294-8200
Kevin Maas, *Pr*
Kraig Maas, *
**EMP:** 75 **EST:** 1998
**SQ FT:** 80,000
**SALES (est):** 4.62MM **Privately Held**
**Web:** www.maasbrothersinc.com
**SIC: 3479** Coating of metals and formed products

### (P-9089)
### MABEL BAAS INC
Also Called: Royal Coatings
3960 Royal Ave, Simi Valley (93063-3380)
**PHONE**.................................805 520-8075
Marilyn Teperson, *Pr*
**EMP:** 50 **EST:** 1991
**SALES (est):** 4.16MM **Privately Held**
**Web:** www.royalcoatings.com
**SIC: 3479** Coating of metals and formed products

### (P-9090)
### MASTER POWDER COATING INC
13721 Bora Dr, Santa Fe Springs (90670-5007)
**PHONE**.................................562 863-4135
Judith Flores, *CEO*
Juan Renteria, *
**EMP:** 15 **EST:** 2006
**SALES (est):** 4.79MM **Privately Held**
**Web:** www.masterpowdercoating.com
**SIC: 3479** Coating of metals and formed products

### (P-9091)
### MELROSE NAMEPLATE LABEL CO INC (PA)
Also Called: Melrose
26575 Corporate Ave, Hayward (94545-3920)
**PHONE**.................................510 732-3100
Chris Somers, *Pr*
Kathy Brenner, *
▼ **EMP:** 28 **EST:** 1939
**SQ FT:** 33,000
**SALES (est):** 4.54MM
**SALES (corp-wide):** 4.54MM **Privately Held**
**Web:** www.melrose-nl.com
**SIC: 3479** 3993 3643 3355 Name plates: engraved, etched, etc.; Signs and advertising specialties; Current-carrying wiring services; Aluminum rolling and drawing, nec

### (P-9092)
### MERCURY METAL DIE & LTR CO INC (PA)
Also Called: Hts Division
600 3rd St Ste A, Lake Elsinore (92530-2748)
P.O. Box 86 (92531-0086)
**PHONE**.................................951 674-8717
Hugh Mosbacher, *Pr*
▲ **EMP:** 15 **EST:** 1946
**SQ FT:** 10,000
**SALES (est):** 2.47MM
**SALES (corp-wide):** 2.47MM **Privately Held**
**Web:** www.mercurymarking.com
**SIC: 3479** 3953 3544 Engraving jewelry, silverware, or metal; Marking devices; Diamond dies, metalworking

### (P-9093)
### METAL COATERS CALIFORNIA INC
Also Called: Metal Coaters System
9123 Center Ave, Rancho Cucamonga (91730-5312)
**PHONE**.................................909 987-4681
Norman C Chambers, *CEO*
Dick Klein, *
Tom Scarinza, *
**EMP:** 75 **EST:** 1998
**SALES (est):** 2.39MM
**SALES (corp-wide):** 5.58B **Privately Held**
**Web:** www.metalcoaters.com
**SIC: 3479** Painting of metal products
**HQ:** Cornerstone Building Brands, Inc.
5020 Weston Pkwy
Cary NC 27513
281 897-7788

### (P-9094)
### MOORE QUALITY GALVANIZING INC
3001 Falcon Dr, Madera (93637-8601)
P.O. Box 420 (93639-0420)
**PHONE**.................................559 673-2822
Thomas E Moore, *Pr*
Marie Moore, *
Kellie Moore, *
**EMP:** 26 **EST:** 1984
**SQ FT:** 11,000
**SALES (est):** 4.74MM **Privately Held**
**Web:** www.mooregalvanizing.com
**SIC: 3479** Coating of metals and formed products

### (P-9095)
### NELSON NAME PLATE COMPANY (PA)

## 3479 - Metal Coating And Allied Services (P-9116)

Also Called: Nelson-Miller
708 Nogales St, City Of Industry (91748-1306)
PHONE..................323 663-3971
Jim Kaldem, Pr
▲ **EMP:** 48 **EST:** 1946
**SALES (est):** 43.25MM
**SALES (corp-wide):** 43.25MM **Privately Held**
Web: www.nelson-miller.co
**SIC: 3479** 3993  Name plates: engraved, etched, etc.; Signs and advertising specialties

### (P-9096)
### NM HOLDCO INC
2800 Casitas Ave, Los Angeles (90039-2942)
PHONE..................323 663-3971
Mark Carroll, Dir
William Mckinley, Dir
**EMP:** 200 **EST:** 2011
**SALES (est):** 877.12K **Privately Held**
**SIC: 3479** 3993  Name plates: engraved, etched, etc.; Signs and advertising specialties
PA: Superior Capital Partners Llc
    418 N Main St

### (P-9097)
### OPTICAL COATING LABORATORY LLC (HQ)
Also Called: Ocli
2789 Northpoint Pkwy, Santa Rosa (95407-7397)
PHONE..................707 545-6440
Fred Van Milligen, Pr
**EMP:** 400 **EST:** 1963
**SQ FT:** 490,000
**SALES (est):** 18.35MM
**SALES (corp-wide):** 1B **Publicly Held**
**SIC: 3479** 3577 3827  Coating of metals and formed products; Computer peripheral equipment, nec; Optical instruments and lenses
PA: Viavi Solutions Inc.
    1445 S Spctrum Blvd Ste 1
    408 404-3600

### (P-9098)
### PACIFIC GALVANIZING INC
715 46th Ave, Oakland (94601-5096)
PHONE..................510 261-7331
William Branagh, Pr
**EMP:** 25 **EST:** 1969
**SQ FT:** 16,000
**SALES (est):** 5.15MM
**SALES (corp-wide):** 26.21MM **Privately Held**
Web: www.pacificgalvanizing.com
**SIC: 3479**  Coating of metals and formed products
PA: Branagh Inc.
    750 Kevin Ct
    510 638-6455

### (P-9099)
### PACIFIC POWDER COATING INC
8637 23rd Ave, Sacramento (95826-4903)
PHONE..................916 381-1154
Jeffrey M Rochester, Pr
▲ **EMP:** 30 **EST:** 1987
**SQ FT:** 40,000
**SALES (est):** 6.31MM **Privately Held**
Web: www.pacpowder.com
**SIC: 3479** 3449  Coating of metals and formed products; Miscellaneous metalwork

### (P-9100)
### PACIFIC SHORING PRODUCTS LLC (PA)
265 Roberts Ave, Santa Rosa (95407-6925)
PHONE..................707 575-9014
Bruce Russell, CEO
Robert Pitts, Managing Member
**EMP:** 19 **EST:** 2006
**SALES (est):** 10.46MM
**SALES (corp-wide):** 10.46MM **Privately Held**
Web: www.pacificshoring.com
**SIC: 3479** 3334  Aluminum coating of metal products; Primary aluminum

### (P-9101)
### PARYLENE COATING SERVICES INC
Also Called: Polymer Coating Services
35 Argonaut, Aliso Viejo (92656-4151)
PHONE..................281 391-7665
**EMP:** 25
**SIC: 3479**  Coating of metals and formed products

### (P-9102)
### PDU LAD CORPORATION (PA)
Also Called: Plastic Dress-Up
11165 Valley Spring Ln, North Hollywood (91602-2646)
P.O. Box 3897 (91733-0897)
PHONE..................626 442-7711
Loren Funk, CEO
Dennis Funk, *
Allen Greenblat, *
◆ **EMP:** 38 **EST:** 1990
**SALES (est):** 8.8MM **Privately Held**
Web: www.pdu.com
**SIC: 3479**  Name plates: engraved, etched, etc.

### (P-9103)
### PEARSON ENGINEERING CORP
Also Called: Vaga Industries
2505 Loma Ave, South El Monte (91733-1417)
PHONE..................626 442-7436
Jeff Trost, Pr
Jimmy Trost, Pr
**EMP:** 15 **EST:** 1965
**SQ FT:** 10,000
**SALES (est):** 1.96MM **Privately Held**
Web: www.vaga.com
**SIC: 3479**  Etching, photochemical

### (P-9104)
### PELTEK HOLDINGS INC
35 Argonaut Ste A1, Laguna Hills (92656-4151)
PHONE..................949 855-8010
Jeffrey Stewart, Pr
Paul Stewart, *
Joyce Stewart, *
▲ **EMP:** 30 **EST:** 1974
**SQ FT:** 10,560
**SALES (est):** 2.33MM **Privately Held**
Web: www.peltekfab.com
**SIC: 3479** 5169  Bonderizing of metal or metal products; Chemicals and allied products, nec

### (P-9105)
### PERFORMANCE POWDER INC
2940 E La Jolla St Ste A, Anaheim (92806-1349)
PHONE..................714 632-0600
Kevin Aaberg, Pr
Robert Goldberg, *
**EMP:** 29 **EST:** 1993
**SALES (est):** 4.71MM **Privately Held**
Web: www.performancepowder.com
**SIC: 3479**  Coating of metals and formed products

### (P-9106)
### PLASMA COATING CORPORATION
1900 W Walnut St, Compton (90220-5019)
PHONE..................310 532-1951
James M Emery, Pr
Willard A Emery, VP
**EMP:** 22 **EST:** 1972
**SALES (est):** 9.2MM
**SALES (corp-wide):** 364.48B **Publicly Held**
**SIC: 3479**  Coating of metals and formed products
HQ: Southwest United Industries, Inc.
    422 S Saint Louis Ave
    Tulsa OK 74120
    918 587-4161

### (P-9107)
### PLASMA RGGEDIZED SOLUTIONS INC (PA)
2284 Ringwood Ave Ste A, San Jose (95131-1722)
PHONE..................408 954-8405
Jim Stameson, CEO
Evan Persky, *
**EMP:** 68 **EST:** 2008
**SALES (est):** 24.88MM **Privately Held**
Web: www.plasmarugged.com
**SIC: 3479**  Coating of metals and formed products

### (P-9108)
### PLASMA TECHNOLOGY INCORPORATED (PA)
Also Called: P T I
1754 Crenshaw Blvd, Torrance (90501-3384)
PHONE..................310 320-3373
Robert Donald Dowell, CEO
Burnard Fosket, *
Malcom Jones, *
John Nikitich, *
▲ **EMP:** 73 **EST:** 1984
**SQ FT:** 40,000
**SALES (est):** 12.34MM
**SALES (corp-wide):** 12.34MM **Privately Held**
Web: www.ptise.com
**SIC: 3479**  Coating of metals and formed products

### (P-9109)
### POWDERCOAT SERVICES LLC
1747 W Lincoln Ave Ste K, Anaheim (92801-6770)
PHONE..................714 533-2251
Ravi Rao, Pr
▲ **EMP:** 38 **EST:** 1981
**SQ FT:** 75,000
**SALES (est):** 1.43MM **Privately Held**
Web: www.powdercoatservices.com
**SIC: 3479** 7211  Coating of metals and formed products; Power laundries, family and commercial

### (P-9110)
### PREMIER COATINGS INC
Also Called: Premier Finishing
7910 Longe St, Stockton (95206-3933)
PHONE..................209 982-5585
Craig M Walters, Pr
Thom Foulks, *
Wendy Foulks, *
**EMP:** 75 **EST:** 1996
**SQ FT:** 30,000
**SALES (est):** 10.21MM **Privately Held**
Web: www.premiercoatingsscorp.com
**SIC: 3479**  Coating of metals and formed products

### (P-9111)
### PROCESSES BY MARTIN INC
12150 Alameda St, Lynwood (90262-4005)
PHONE..................310 637-1855
Irene Romero, Pr
Cathleen Fuentes, *
**EMP:** 45 **EST:** 1993
**SQ FT:** 200,000
**SALES (est):** 4.76MM **Privately Held**
Web: www.processesbymartin.com
**SIC: 3479**  Coating of metals and formed products

### (P-9112)
### PROFESSIONAL FINISHING INC
770 Market Ave, Richmond (94801-1303)
PHONE..................510 233-7629
Ricardo E Gomez, Pr
**EMP:** 60 **EST:** 1979
**SQ FT:** 18,000
**SALES (est):** 5.45MM **Privately Held**
Web: www.professionalfinishing.com
**SIC: 3479**  Coating of metals and formed products

### (P-9113)
### PVD COATINGS LLC
5271 Argosy Ave, Huntington Beach (92649-1015)
PHONE..................714 899-4892
Red Silversterstein, Managing Member
**EMP:** 18 **EST:** 2001
**SALES (est):** 1.71MM **Privately Held**
Web: www.pvdcoatings.net
**SIC: 3479**  Coating of metals and formed products

### (P-9114)
### RGF ENTERPRISES INC
220 Citation Cir, Corona (92878-5022)
PHONE..................951 734-6922
Rodney G Fisher, Pr
**EMP:** 26 **EST:** 1976
**SQ FT:** 15,000
**SALES (est):** 2.15MM **Privately Held**
Web: www.rgfcoatings.com
**SIC: 3479**  Coating of metals and formed products

### (P-9115)
### RTS POWDER COATING INC (PA)
15121 Sierra Bonita Ln, Chino (91710-8904)
PHONE..................909 393-5404
Donald D Reed Senior, Pr
**EMP:** 20 **EST:** 1991
**SQ FT:** 8,100
**SALES (est):** 721.26K **Privately Held**
**SIC: 3479**  Coating of metals and formed products

### (P-9116)
### S C COATINGS CORPORATION
41775 Elm St Ste 302, Murrieta (92562-9267)
PHONE..................951 461-9777
Michael Podratz, Pr
Victor Lopez, *
**EMP:** 48 **EST:** 2000
**SALES (est):** 4.55MM **Privately Held**
Web: www.sccoatingscorp.com

## 3479 - Metal Coating And Allied Services (P-9117)

SIC: 3479 Coating of metals and formed products

### (P-9117)
**SCIENTIFIC METAL FINISHING INC**
3180 Molinaro St, Santa Clara (95054-2425)
PHONE..................................408 970-9011
Theodore G Otto Iii, *Pr*
Kathleen Otto, *
EMP: 20 EST: 1987
SQ FT: 18,000
SALES (est): 3.95MM **Privately Held**
Web: www.scientificmetal.com
SIC: 3479 2851 Coating of metals and formed products; Paints and allied products

### (P-9118)
**SDC TECHNOLOGIES INC (HQ)**
45 Parker Ste 100, Irvine (92618-1605)
PHONE..................................714 939-8300
Richard Chang, *Pr*
▲ EMP: 25 EST: 1986
SQ FT: 16,800
SALES (est): 52.08MM **Privately Held**
Web: www.sdctech.com
SIC: 3479 Coating of metals and formed products
PA: Mitsui Chemicals, Inc.
2-2-1, Yaesu

### (P-9119)
**SHMAZE INDUSTRIES INC**
Also Called: Shmaze Custom Coatings
20792 Canada Rd, Lake Forest (92630-6732)
PHONE..................................949 583-1448
Michael Shamassian, *Pr*
Joanne Shamassian, *
EMP: 50 EST: 1987
SQ FT: 21,500
SALES (est): 5.13MM **Privately Held**
Web: www.shmaze.com
SIC: 3479 Coating of metals with plastic or resins

### (P-9120)
**SILICOR MATERIALS INC**
Also Called: Silicor Materials
985 Almanor Ave, Sunnyvale (94085-2903)
P.O. Box 610220 (95161-0220)
PHONE..................................408 962-3100
▲ EMP: 75
Web: www.silicormaterials.com
SIC: 3479 Coating of metals with silicon

### (P-9121)
**SOCCO PLASTIC COATING COMPANY**
11251 Jersey Blvd, Rancho Cucamonga (91730-5147)
PHONE..................................909 987-4753
Peter M Smits, *Pr*
Peter M Smits Junior, *Pr*
Rose Smits, *
EMP: 25 EST: 1945
SQ FT: 60,000
SALES (est): 2.36MM **Privately Held**
Web: www.soccoplastics.com
SIC: 3479 3444 3088 2851 Coating of metals with plastic or resins; Sheet metalwork; Plastics plumbing fixtures; Paints and allied products

### (P-9122)
**SPECIALIZED COATING SVCS LLC (HQ)** ◊
Also Called: Specialized Coating Services
42680 Christy St, Fremont (94538-3135)
PHONE..................................510 226-8700
EMP: 43 EST: 2023
SALES (est): 12.22MM
SALES (corp-wide): 68.36MM **Privately Held**
SIC: 3479 Coating of metals and formed products
PA: Tide Rock Holdings, Llc
343 S Highway 101
858 204-7438

### (P-9123)
**SPECIALTY COATING SYSTEMS INC**
4435 E Airport Dr Ste 100, Ontario (91761-7816)
PHONE..................................909 390-8818
Steven Frease, *Brnch Mgr*
EMP: 99
Web: www.scscoatings.com
SIC: 3479 Coating of metals and formed products
HQ: Specialty Coating Systems, Inc.
7645 Woodland Dr
Indianapolis IN 46278

### (P-9124)
**STEELSCAPE LLC**
11200 Arrow Rte, Rancho Cucamonga (91730-4805)
PHONE..................................909 987-4711
Ron Hurst, *Brnch Mgr*
EMP: 19
SALES (corp-wide): 106.42MM **Privately Held**
Web: www.steelscape.com
SIC: 3479 Coating of metals and formed products
PA: Steelscape, Llc
222 W Kalama River Rd
360 673-8200

### (P-9125)
**STRIKER CO**
1230 N Jefferson St, Anaheim (92807)
PHONE..................................562 861-2216
Jack E Young, *Pr*
Grace Young, *Sec*
Don Schram, *VP*
EMP: 15 EST: 1966
SALES (est): 1.14MM **Privately Held**
Web: www.a-1engraving.com
SIC: 3479 Engraving jewelry, silverware, or metal

### (P-9126)
**SUNDIAL INDUSTRIES INC**
Also Called: Powder Painting By Sundial
8421 Telfair Ave, Sun Valley (91352-3926)
PHONE..................................818 767-4477
TOLL FREE: 866
Hasu Bhakta, *Pr*
Naseen Khan, *
Gurtreet Riaz, *
▲ EMP: 30 EST: 1980
SQ FT: 13,000
SALES (est): 2.43MM **Privately Held**
Web: www.sundialpowdercoating.com
SIC: 3479 Coating of metals and formed products

### (P-9127)
**SUNDIAL POWDER COATINGS INC**
Also Called: Bottle Coatings
8421 Telfair Ave, Sun Valley (91352-3926)
PHONE..................................818 767-4477
Hasu Bhakta, *CEO*
EMP: 25 EST: 1995
SALES (est): 2.61MM **Privately Held**
Web: www.sundialpowdercoating.com
SIC: 3479 Coating of metals and formed products

### (P-9128)
**TIODIZE CO INC (PA)**
Also Called: Tiodize
5858 Engineer Dr, Huntington Beach (92649-1166)
PHONE..................................714 898-4377
Thomas R Adams, *CEO*
EMP: 17 EST: 1966
SQ FT: 26,000
SALES (est): 9.73MM
SALES (corp-wide): 9.73MM **Privately Held**
Web: www.tiodize.com
SIC: 3479 Coating of metals and formed products

### (P-9129)
**TORTOISE INDUSTRIES INC**
Also Called: Tortoise Tube
3052 Treadwell St, Los Angeles (90065-1423)
PHONE..................................323 258-7776
EMP: 40 EST: 1981
SALES (est): 2.43MM **Privately Held**
Web: www.tortoiseindustries.com
SIC: 3479 3498 1799 Painting, coating, and hot dipping; Tube fabricating (contract bending and shaping); Exterior cleaning, including sandblasting

### (P-9130)
**ULTIMATE METAL FINISHING CORP**
6150 Sheila St, Commerce (90040-2407)
PHONE..................................323 890-9100
John Ondrasik, *Pr*
James M Sales, *Genl Mgr*
EMP: 44 EST: 1983
SQ FT: 4,800
SALES (est): 346K
SALES (corp-wide): 22.58MM **Privately Held**
SIC: 3479 Coating of metals and formed products
PA: Precision Wire Products, Inc.
6150 Sheila St
323 890-9100

### (P-9131)
**UNITED WESTERN ENTERPRISES INC**
Also Called: Uwe
850 Flynn Rd Ste 200, Camarillo (93012-8783)
PHONE..................................805 389-1077
Gerald Williams, *Pr*
Mike Lynch, *
EMP: 29 EST: 1969
SQ FT: 21,000
SALES (est): 4.99MM
SALES (corp-wide): 4.99MM **Privately Held**
Web: www.uweinc.com
SIC: 3479 Etching, photochemical
PA: Pma Industries
18008 N Black Canyon Hwy
602 607-4155

### (P-9132)
**VALMONT INDUSTRIES INC**
Also Called: Valmont Ctngs Clwest Glvnizing
2226 E Dominguez St, Long Beach (90810-1008)
PHONE..................................310 549-2200
EMP: 50
SALES (corp-wide): 4.17B **Publicly Held**
Web: www.valmontcoatings.com
SIC: 3479 Coating of metals and formed products
PA: Valmont Industries, Inc.
15000 Valmont Plz
402 963-1000

### (P-9133)
**VIVID INC**
180 E Sunnyoaks Ave Bldg 1, Campbell (95008-6631)
P.O. Box 320486 (95032-0108)
PHONE..................................408 982-9101
John Comeau, *Pr*
John Comeau, *Pr*
Stephanie Comeau, *
▲ EMP: 35 EST: 1989
SQ FT: 38,800
SALES (est): 4.52MM **Privately Held**
Web: www.vividinc.com
SIC: 3479 Coating of metals and formed products

## 3483 Ammunition, Except For Small Arms, Nec

### (P-9134)
**FIELD TIME TARGET TRAINING LLC**
Also Called: Ft3 Tactical
8230 Electric Ave, Stanton (90680-2640)
P.O. Box 1219 (90680-1219)
PHONE..................................714 677-2841
Michael R Kaplan, *Managing Member*
EMP: 24 EST: 2010
SALES (est): 3.6MM **Privately Held**
Web: www.fieldtimetargetandtraining.com
SIC: 3483 7999 Ammunition, except for small arms, nec; Shooting range operation

## 3484 Small Arms

### (P-9135)
**INTEGRIS COMPOSITES INC (DH)**
120 Cremona Dr Ste 130, Goleta (93117-3159)
PHONE..................................740 928-0326
Donald Andrew Bonham, *CEO*
Joseph Dobriski, *
Michael Gilbert, *
Peter J Schoomaker, *
James Allen, *
EMP: 22 EST: 2007
SALES (est): 33.15MM **Privately Held**
Web: www.integriscomposites.com
SIC: 3484 Small arms
HQ: Integris Composites Holding B.V.
De Entree 143
Amsterdam NH

### (P-9136)
**SAI INDUSTRIES**
Also Called: Standard Armament
631 Allen Ave, Glendale (91201-2013)
PHONE..................................818 842-6144
Curtis Correll, *CEO*
Gary Correll, *
Marcene Correll, *
Cathy Joens, *
Kriti Ahuja, *
◆ EMP: 40 EST: 1950
SQ FT: 24,000
SALES (est): 4.55MM **Privately Held**
Web: www.standardarmament.com

# PRODUCTS & SERVICES SECTION

## 3491 - Industrial Valves (P-9156)

SIC: **3484** Guns (firearms) or gun parts, 30 mm. and below

### 3489 Ordnance And Accessories, Nec

**(P-9137)**
**ARMTEC DEFENSE PRODUCTS CO (DH)**
Also Called: Armtec Defense Technologies
85901 Avenue 53, Coachella (92236-2607)
PHONE..................................760 398-0143
Robert W Cremin, *CEO*
◆ **EMP:** 330 **EST:** 1968
**SQ FT:** 108,000
**SALES (est):** 114.97MM
**SALES (corp-wide):** 7.94B **Publicly Held**
Web: www.armtecdefense.com
SIC: **3489** Artillery or artillery parts, over 30 mm.
HQ: Esterline Technologies Corp
1350 Euclid Ave Ste 1600
Cleveland OH 44114
216 706-2960

**(P-9138)**
**CONCEALED CARRIER LLC**
Also Called: Tacticon Armament
11315 Sunrise Gold Cir Ste F, Rancho Cordova (95742-6534)
PHONE..................................916 530-6205
Jacob Dines, *Managing Member*
**EMP:** 21 **EST:** 2015
**SALES (est):** 15.4MM **Privately Held**
Web: www.tacticon.com
SIC: **3489** Ordnance and accessories, nec

**(P-9139)**
**NETWORKS ELECTRONIC CO LLC**
9750 De Soto Ave, Chatsworth (91311-4409)
PHONE..................................818 341-0440
Tamara Marie Christen, *Managing Member*
Andrew Campany, *
▼ **EMP:** 26 **EST:** 2005
**SQ FT:** 25,000
**SALES (est):** 5.35MM **Privately Held**
Web: www.networkselectronic.com
SIC: **3489** Ordnance and accessories, nec

**(P-9140)**
**ROBERTS RESEARCH LABORATORY**
23150 Kashiwa Ct, Torrance (90505-4027)
PHONE..................................310 320-7310
David Roberts, *Pr*
A L Roberts, *Pr*
David E Roberts, *VP*
Kathryn Roberts, *Sec*
**EMP:** 15 **EST:** 1964
**SQ FT:** 10,000
**SALES (est):** 2.03MM **Privately Held**
SIC: **3489** 8731 Ordnance and accessories, nec; Commercial research laboratory

**(P-9141)**
**VECTOR LAUNCH LLC (PA)**
Also Called: Vector
15261 Connector Ln, Huntington Beach (92649-1117)
PHONE..................................202 888-3063
Jim Penrose, *CEO*
Robert Spalding, *Pr*
Robert Cleave, *CRO*
Stephanie Koster, *CFO*
Eric Besnard, *VP*
**EMP:** 50 **EST:** 2016
**SALES (est):** 9.59MM
**SALES (corp-wide):** 9.59MM **Privately Held**
Web: www.vector-launch.com
SIC: **3489** Rocket launchers

### 3491 Industrial Valves

**(P-9142)**
**ACRO ASSOCIATES INC**
Also Called: Acro Associates
1990 Olivera Rd Ste A, Concord (94520-5455)
PHONE..................................925 676-8828
**EMP:** 100 **EST:** 1960
**SALES (est):** 4.97MM
**SALES (corp-wide):** 2.74B **Privately Held**
Web: www.norgren.com
SIC: **3491** Automatic regulating and control valves
HQ: Bimba Llc
25150 S Governors Hwy
University Park IL 60484
708 534-8544

**(P-9143)**
**AQUASYN LLC**
9525 Owensmouth Ave Ste E, Chatsworth (91311-8006)
PHONE..................................818 350-0423
Dean Richards, *Brnch Mgr*
**EMP:** 19
**SALES (corp-wide):** 5.93MM **Privately Held**
Web: www.aquasyn.com
SIC: **3491** Industrial valves
PA: Aquasyn, Llc
1771 South Sutro Ter
818 350-0423

**(P-9144)**
**ASEPCO**
Also Called: Watson Marlow Fluid Tech Group
5002 Elester Dr, San Jose (95124)
▲ **EMP:** 19 **EST:** 1989
**SALES (est):** 3.39MM
**SALES (corp-wide):** 4.46MM **Privately Held**
Web: www.wmftg.com
SIC: **3491** Industrial valves
PA: Watson-Marlow America Manufacturing Inc
37 Upton Dr
800 282-8823

**(P-9145)**
**BAILEY VALVE INC**
264 W Fallbrook Ave Ste 105, Fresno (93711-5807)
PHONE..................................559 434-2838
Eric Brewer, *Pr*
John Edward, *
▲ **EMP:** 35 **EST:** 2004
**SQ FT:** 3,500
**SALES (est):** 3.69MM **Privately Held**
Web: www.baileyvalve.com
SIC: **3491** Industrial valves

**(P-9146)**
**BERMINGHAM CNTRLS INC A CAL CO (PA)**
Also Called: Capital Westward
11144 Business Cir, Cerritos (90703-5523)
PHONE..................................562 860-0463
Gregory Gass, *Pr*
Edwin Bonner, *
Kevin Mulholland, *
**EMP:** 37 **EST:** 1961
**SQ FT:** 20,000
**SALES (est):** 1.39MM
**SALES (corp-wide):** 1.39MM **Privately Held**
Web: www.bermingham.com
SIC: **3491** 3823 5084 Industrial valves; Process control instruments; Industrial machinery and equipment

**(P-9147)**
**BVI INTERNATIONAL INC**
4301 Yeager Way, Bakersfield (93313-2018)
PHONE..................................661 834-1775
◆ **EMP:** 20
SIC: **3491** Industrial valves

**(P-9148)**
**CIRCOR AEROSPACE INC (DH)**
2301 Wardlow Cir, Corona (92878-5101)
P.O. Box 2824 (29304-2824)
PHONE..................................951 270-6200
Carl Nasca, *Pr*
Christopher Celtruda, *
Kathy Fazio, *
Michael Dill, *
Renuka Ayer, *
◆ **EMP:** 245 **EST:** 1947
**SQ FT:** 100,000
**SALES (est):** 69.36MM **Publicly Held**
Web: www.circoraerospace.com
SIC: **3491** 3494 3769 5085 Pressure valves and regulators, industrial; Plumbing and heating valves; Space vehicle equipment, nec; Seals, industrial
HQ: Circor International, Inc.
30 Corporate Dr Ste 200
Burlington MA 01803
781 270-1200

**(P-9149)**
**CRANE INSTRMNTTION SMPLING INC**
2301 Wardlow Cir, Corona (92878-5101)
PHONE..................................951 270-6200
Andy Brandenburg, *Genl Mgr*
**EMP:** 80
**SALES (corp-wide):** 2.09B **Publicly Held**
Web: www.circor.com
SIC: **3491** Industrial valves
HQ: Crane Instrumentation & Sampling, Inc.
405 Centura Ct
Spartanburg SC 29303
864 574-7966

**(P-9150)**
**CURTISS-WRIGHT CORPORATION**
Also Called: Defense Solutions
28965 Avenue Penn, Santa Clarita (91355-4185)
PHONE..................................661 257-4430
**EMP:** 56
**SALES (corp-wide):** 2.85B **Publicly Held**
Web: www.curtisswright.com
SIC: **3491** Industrial valves
PA: Curtiss-Wright Corporation
130 Harbour Pl Dr Ste 300
704 869-4600

**(P-9151)**
**CURTISS-WRIGHT CORPORATION**
1675 Brandywine Ave Ste F, Chula Vista (91911-6064)
PHONE..................................619 482-3405
David Schurra, *Brnch Mgr*
**EMP:** 85
**SALES (corp-wide):** 2.85B **Publicly Held**
Web: www.curtisswright.com
SIC: **3491** Industrial valves
PA: Curtiss-Wright Corporation
130 Harbour Pl Dr Ste 300
704 869-4600

**(P-9152)**
**CURTISS-WRIGHT FLOW CONTROL**
Penny & Giles
28965 Avenue Penn, Valencia (91355-4185)
PHONE..................................626 851-3100
**EMP:** 160
**SALES (corp-wide):** 2.41B **Publicly Held**
SIC: **3491** Industrial valves
HQ: Curtiss-Wright Flow Control Corporation
1966 Broadhollow Rd Ste E
Farmingdale NY 11735
631 293-3800

**(P-9153)**
**CURTISS-WRIGHT FLOW CTRL CORP**
Also Called: Collins Technologies
2950 E Birch St, Brea (92821-6246)
PHONE..................................949 271-7500
Glenn Roberts, *Mgr*
**EMP:** 31
**SALES (corp-wide):** 2.85B **Publicly Held**
Web: www.curtisswright.com
SIC: **3491** Industrial valves
HQ: Curtiss-Wright Flow Control Corporation
1966 Broadhollow Rd Ste E
Farmingdale NY 11735
631 293-3800

**(P-9154)**
**CURTISS-WRIGHT FLOW CTRL CORP**
Also Called: Curtiss-Wrght Nclear Div Enrte
260 Ranger Ave, Brea (92821-6215)
PHONE..................................714 528-2301
**EMP:** 68
**SALES (corp-wide):** 2.85B **Publicly Held**
Web: www.cwnuclear.com
SIC: **3491** Industrial valves
HQ: Curtiss-Wright Flow Control Corporation
2950 E Birch St
Brea CA 92821
714 528-1365

**(P-9155)**
**DANCO VALVE COMPANY**
15230 Lakewood Blvd, Bellflower (90706-4240)
PHONE..................................562 925-2588
Mike Dante, *Pr*
**EMP:** 28 **EST:** 1985
**SQ FT:** 27,000
**SALES (est):** 1.11MM **Privately Held**
Web: www.dantevalve.com
SIC: **3491** 5085 Industrial valves; Industrial supplies

**(P-9156)**
**IMI CRITICAL ENGINEERING LLC (DH)**
Also Called: IMI CCI
22591 Avenida Empresa, Rcho Sta Marg (92688-2003)
PHONE..................................949 858-1877
Kevin Mckown, *Pr*
Abhijit Rao, *CFO*
◆ **EMP:** 365 **EST:** 1961
**SQ FT:** 75,000
**SALES (est):** 61.92MM

# 3491 - Industrial Valves

**(P-9157)**
SALES (corp-wide): 2.74B **Privately Held**
Web: www.retrofit3d.com
SIC: **3491** Process control regulator valves
HQ: Imi Americas Inc.
5400 S Delaware St
Littleton CO 80120
763 488-5400

**(P-9157)**
**JAMES JONES COMPANY**
1470 S Vintage Ave, Ontario (91761-3646)
PHONE..................................909 418-2558
Jerry Schnelzer, *Genl Mgr*
◆ EMP: 3988 EST: 1892
SQ FT: 68,000
SALES (est): 3.08MM
SALES (corp-wide): 1.28B **Publicly Held**
Web: www.joneswaterproducts.com
SIC: **3491 3494** Fire hydrant valves; Pipe fittings
HQ: Mueller Group, Llc
1200 Abrnthy Rd Ne Ste 12
Atlanta GA 30328
770 206-4200

**(P-9158)**
**LUBRICATION SCIENTIFICS INC**
Also Called: All Technology Machine
17651 Armstrong Ave, Irvine (92614-5727)
PHONE..................................714 557-0664
Richard T Hanley, *Pr*
EMP: 15 EST: 1993
SQ FT: 6,000
SALES (est): 3.93MM **Privately Held**
Web: www.lubricationscientifics.com
SIC: **3491** Industrial valves

**(P-9159)**
**MDC PRECISION LLC**
23874b Cabot Blvd, Hayward (94545-1661)
PHONE..................................510 265-3500
EMP: 49
SALES (corp-wide): 113.45MM **Privately Held**
Web: www.mdcprecision.com
SIC: **3491** Industrial valves
PA: Mdc Precision, Llc
30962 Santana St
510 265-3500

**(P-9160)**
**PACIFIC SEISMIC PRODUCTS INC**
233 E Avenue H8, Lancaster (93535-1821)
PHONE..................................661 942-4499
Etsuko Ikegaya, *Pr*
Shigeko I Aramaki, *
EMP: 24 EST: 1989
SQ FT: 10,000
SALES (est): 1.77MM **Privately Held**
Web: www.pspvalves.com
SIC: **3491** Industrial valves

**(P-9161)**
**RELIANCE WORLDWIDE CORPORATION**
2750 E Mission Blvd, Ontario (91761-2909)
PHONE..................................770 863-4005
EMP: 59
Web: www.rwc.com
SIC: **3491** Industrial valves
HQ: Reliance Worldwide Corporation
2300 Defoor Hills Rd Nw
Atlanta GA 30318
770 863-4005

**(P-9162)**
**STORM MANUFACTURING GROUP INC**
Also Called: Smg
23201 Normandie Ave, Torrance (90501-5050)
PHONE..................................310 326-8287
Dale Philippi, *CEO*
Russell Kneipp, *
Georgia S Claessens, *
Rick Ward, *
◆ EMP: 74 EST: 1908
SQ FT: 41,936
SALES (est): 6.04MM
SALES (corp-wide): 44.12MM **Privately Held**
Web: www.getsuperior.com
SIC: **3491 3494** Industrial valves; Sprinkler systems, field
PA: Storm Industries, Inc.
970 W 190th St
310 534-5232

**(P-9163)**
**WATTS REGULATOR CO**
Also Called: Watts Water Technology
1485 Tanforan Ave, Woodland (95776-6108)
PHONE..................................530 666-2493
EMP: 161
SALES (corp-wide): 2.06B **Publicly Held**
Web: www.watts.com
SIC: **3491** Pressure valves and regulators, industrial
HQ: Watts Regulator Co.
815 Chestnut St
North Andover MA 01845
978 689-6000

**(P-9164)**
**WESTERN VALVE INC**
Also Called: Western Valve
201 Industrial St, Bakersfield (93307-2703)
P.O. Box 10628 (93389-0628)
PHONE..................................661 327-7660
▲ EMP: 41 EST: 1991
SALES (est): 9.36MM **Privately Held**
Web: www.westernvalve.com
SIC: **3491** Industrial valves

## 3492 Fluid Power Valves And Hose Fittings

**(P-9165)**
**ACOUSTICFAB LLC (DH)**
28150 Industry Dr, Valencia (91355-4100)
PHONE..................................661 257-2242
EMP: 59 EST: 2008
SQ FT: 12,000
SALES (est): 5.64MM
SALES (corp-wide): 3.28B **Publicly Held**
SIC: **3492 3812 3728** Control valves, aircraft: hydraulic and pneumatic; Acceleration indicators and systems components, aerospace; Aircraft body and wing assemblies and parts
HQ: Itt Aerospace Controls Llc
28150 Industry Dr
Valencia CA 91355
315 568-7258

**(P-9166)**
**CRANE CO**
Also Called: CRANE CO.
3201 Walnut Ave, Long Beach (90755-5225)
PHONE..................................562 426-2531
Kevin Mckown, *Mgr*
EMP: 110
SALES (corp-wide): 3.37B **Privately Held**
Web: www.craneco.com
SIC: **3492** Fluid power valves and hose fittings
HQ: Redco Corporation
100 1st Stamford Pl
Stamford CT 06902
203 363-7300

**(P-9167)**
**ELECTROFILM MFG CO LLC**
Also Called: Hartzell Aerospace
28150 Industry Dr, Valencia (91355-4100)
PHONE..................................661 257-2242
David Schmidt, *
Joseph W Brown, *
Simon Shackelton, *
EMP: 80 EST: 2008
SQ FT: 43,000
SALES (est): 6.44MM
SALES (corp-wide): 3.28B **Publicly Held**
Web: www.ittaerospace.com
SIC: **3492 3728 3812** Control valves, aircraft: hydraulic and pneumatic; Aircraft body and wing assemblies and parts; Acceleration indicators and systems components, aerospace
HQ: Itt Aerospace Controls Llc
28150 Industry Dr
Valencia CA 91355
315 568-7258

**(P-9168)**
**FABER ENTERPRISES INC**
14800 S Figueroa St, Gardena (90248-1719)
PHONE..................................310 323-6200
Kevin M Stein, *CEO*
Esther Faber, *
Ronald E Spencer, *
Marilyn Spencer, *
Loretta Appel, *
EMP: 110 EST: 1947
SALES (est): 2.73MM **Privately Held**
Web: www.pccfluidfittings.com
SIC: **3492** Control valves, aircraft: hydraulic and pneumatic

**(P-9169)**
**INDUSTRIAL TUBE COMPANY LLC**
Also Called: Industrial Tube Company
28150 Industry Dr, Valencia (91355-4100)
PHONE..................................661 295-4000
Farrokh Batliwala, *CEO*
EMP: 99 EST: 2008
SQ FT: 28,000
SALES (est): 5.61MM
SALES (corp-wide): 3.28B **Publicly Held**
SIC: **3492 3728 3812** Control valves, aircraft: hydraulic and pneumatic; Aircraft body and wing assemblies and parts; Acceleration indicators and systems components, aerospace
HQ: Itt Aerospace Controls Llc
28150 Industry Dr
Valencia CA 91355
315 568-7258

**(P-9170)**
**S & H MACHINE INC**
9928 Hayward Way, South El Monte (91733-3114)
PHONE..................................626 448-5062
David Fisher, *Pr*
EMP: 23
SALES (corp-wide): 7.33MM **Privately Held**
Web: www.shmachine.com
SIC: **3492 3728** Fluid power valves and hose fittings; Aircraft parts and equipment, nec
PA: S & H Machine, Inc.
900 N Lake St
818 846-9847

**(P-9171)**
**SENIOR OPERATIONS LLC**
Senior Aerospace Spencer
28510 Industry Dr, Valencia (91355-5442)
PHONE..................................818 350-8499
Steven Spencer, *Pr*
EMP: 60
SALES (corp-wide): 1.2B **Privately Held**
Web: www.sajetproducts.com
SIC: **3492** Hose and tube fittings and assemblies, hydraulic/pneumatic
HQ: Senior Operations Llc
300 E Devon Ave
Bartlett IL 60103
630 372-3500

## 3493 Steel Springs, Except Wire

**(P-9172)**
**AMERICAN SPRING INC**
321 W 135th St, Los Angeles (90061-1001)
PHONE..................................310 324-2181
Ty Kehlenbec, *Pr*
▲ EMP: 16 EST: 2004
SQ FT: 25,000
SALES (est): 2.47MM **Privately Held**
Web: www.americanspring.com
SIC: **3493 3446** Coiled flat springs; Acoustical suspension systems, metal

**(P-9173)**
**ARGO SPRING MFG CO INC**
13930 Shoemaker Ave, Norwalk (90650-4534)
PHONE..................................800 252-2740
TOLL FREE: 800
Gene Fox, *Pr*
Michael Fox, *
Kay Greathouse, *
▲ EMP: 55 EST: 1966
SQ FT: 20,000
SALES (est): 4.04MM **Privately Held**
Web: www.argospringmfg.com
SIC: **3493 3495 3469 3599** Coiled flat springs; Wire springs; Stamping metal for the trade; Custom machinery

**(P-9174)**
**EIBACH INC**
Also Called: Eibach Springs, Inc.
264 Mariah Cir, Corona (92879-1706)
PHONE..................................951 256-8300
Greg Cooley, *Pr*
Gary Peek, *
Sieglinde Eibach, *
◆ EMP: 60 EST: 1987
SQ FT: 52,000
SALES (est): 15.49MM
SALES (corp-wide): 116.99MM **Privately Held**
Web: www.eibach.com
SIC: **3493** Steel springs, except wire
HQ: Heinrich Eibach Gmbh
Am Lennedamm 1
Finnentrop NW 57413
27215110

**(P-9175)**
**HERAEUS MEDICAL COMPONENTS LLC**
4090 Nelson Ave, Concord (94520-8513)
PHONE..................................925 798-4080
Mark Kempf, *Brnch Mgr*
EMP: 95
SALES (corp-wide): 2.67MM **Privately Held**

## PRODUCTS & SERVICES SECTION
### 3495 - Wire Springs (P-9195)

Web: www.heraeus-group.com
SIC: 3493 Steel springs, except wire
HQ: Heraeus Medical Components, Llc
  5030 Centerville Rd
  Saint Paul MN 55127

**(P-9176)**
**JUENGERMANN INC**
Also Called: Spring Industries
1899 Palma Dr Ste A, Ventura
(93003-5719)
PHONE.................805 644-7165
Peter Juengermann, Pr
EMP: 40 EST: 1974
SQ FT: 21,600
SALES (est): 4.53MM Privately Held
Web: www.springind.com
SIC: 3493 3495 Steel springs, except wire; Wire springs

**(P-9177)**
**MATTHEW WARREN INC**
Also Called: Helical Products
901 W Mccoy Ln, Santa Maria
(93455-1109)
P.O. Box 1069 (93456-1069)
PHONE.................805 928-3851
Leroy Mcchesney, Brnch Mgr
EMP: 30
SALES (corp-wide): 1.05B Privately Held
Web: www.mwcomponents.com
SIC: 3493 Helical springs, hot wound; railroad equip., etc.
HQ: Matthew Warren, Inc.
  3426 Tringdon Way Ste 400
  Charlotte NC 28277
  704 837-0331

**(P-9178)**
**OHARA METAL PRODUCTS**
4949 Fulton Dr Ste E, Fairfield
(94534-1648)
PHONE.................707 863-9090
Tim Ives, Pr
Irene O'hara, CEO
Kathleen O'hara, Bd of Dir
EMP: 30 EST: 1964
SQ FT: 20,000
SALES (est): 2.42MM Privately Held
Web: www.oharamfg.com
SIC: 3493 3721 5051 5085 Steel springs, except wire; Helicopters; Metals service centers and offices; Industrial supplies

**(P-9179)**
**SUPERSPRINGS INTERNATIONAL INC**
5251 6th St, Carpinteria (93013-2402)
PHONE.................805 745-5553
Gerry Lamberti, CEO
Ryan Dougan, *
EMP: 32 EST: 1998
SALES (est): 4.82MM Privately Held
Web: www.superspringsinternational.com
SIC: 3493 Automobile springs

---

### 3494 Valves And Pipe Fittings, Nec

**(P-9180)**
**ALLAN AIRCRAFT SUPPLY CO LLC**
11643 Vanowen St, North Hollywood
(91605-6128)
PHONE.................818 765-4992
Robert Kahmann, Managing Member
Mary Katz, Contrlr
EMP: 45 EST: 1952
SQ FT: 30,000
SALES (est): 9.01MM Privately Held
Web: www.allanaircraft.com
SIC: 3494 Pipe fittings

**(P-9181)**
**AMERON INTERNATIONAL CORP**
Ameron Concrete & Steel Pipe
10100 W Linne Rd, Tracy (95377-9128)
PHONE.................209 836-5050
Lynn Pindar, Brnch Mgr
EMP: 60
SALES (corp-wide): 8.58B Publicly Held
SIC: 3494 3317 3272 Pipe fittings; Steel pipe and tubes; Concrete products, nec
HQ: Ameron International Corporation
  7909 Parkwood Circle Dr
  Houston TX 77036
  713 375-3700

**(P-9182)**
**ANCO INTERNATIONAL INC**
Also Called: Anco
19851 Cajon Blvd, San Bernardino
(92407-1828)
PHONE.................909 887-2521
Marjorie A Nielsen, Pr
EMP: 36 EST: 1978
SQ FT: 13,500
SALES (est): 6.39MM Privately Held
Web: www.ancointernational.com
SIC: 3494 3599 3492 Valves and pipe fittings, nec; Machine shop, jobbing and repair; Fluid power valves and hose fittings

**(P-9183)**
**BERMAD INC (PA)**
Also Called: Bermad Control Valves
3816 S Willow Ave Ste 101, Fresno
(93725-9241)
PHONE.................877 577-4283
Nadav Yakir, Pr
▲ EMP: 34 EST: 1977
SQ FT: 10,000
SALES (est): 5.51MM
SALES (corp-wide): 5.51MM Privately Held
Web: www.bermad.com
SIC: 3494 Sprinkler systems, field

**(P-9184)**
**CURTISS-WRIGHT FLOW CTRL CORP (DH)**
Also Called: Paul-Munroe Entertech Division
2950 E Birch St, Brea (92821-6246)
PHONE.................714 528-1365
Frank U Erlach, Pr
Paul Mawn, VP
James Leachman, VP
Dan Miller, Genl Mgr
Jubel Easaw, Prin
▲ EMP: 80 EST: 1996
SQ FT: 30,550
SALES (est): 11.36MM
SALES (corp-wide): 2.85B Publicly Held
Web: www.curtisswright.com
SIC: 3494 3625 Valves and pipe fittings, nec; Actuators, industrial
HQ: Curtiss-Wright Flow Control Corporation
  1966 Broadhollow Rd Ste E
  Farmingdale NY 11735
  631 293-3800

**(P-9185)**
**FEDERAL INDUSTRIES INC**
Also Called: FI
645 Hawaii St, El Segundo (90245-4814)
PHONE.................310 297-4040
Avi Wacht, Pr
Asher Bartov, CEO
EMP: 23 EST: 1981
SALES (est): 3.34MM Privately Held
Web: www.fedindustries.com
SIC: 3494 3728 Valves and pipe fittings, nec; Aircraft parts and equipment, nec

**(P-9186)**
**G-G DISTRIBUTION & DEV CO INC**
Also Called: G/G Industries
28545 Livingston Ave, Valencia
(91355-4166)
PHONE.................661 257-5700
John Gedney, Pr
Mary Ellen, *
Richard Greenberg, *
◆ EMP: 120 EST: 1974
SALES (est): 3MM Privately Held
SIC: 3494 3088 Plumbing and heating valves; Plastics plumbing fixtures

**(P-9187)**
**GRISWOLD CONTROLS LLC (PA)**
Also Called: Griswold Controls
1700 Barranca Pkwy, Irvine (92606-4824)
P.O. Box 19612 (92623-9612)
PHONE.................949 559-6000
Brooks Sherman, CEO
◆ EMP: 100 EST: 1960
SALES (est): 21.09MM
SALES (corp-wide): 21.09MM Privately Held
Web: www.griswoldcontrols.com
SIC: 3494 3491 Valves and pipe fittings, nec; Industrial valves

**(P-9188)**
**MISSION RUBBER COMPANY LLC**
1660 Leeson Ln, Corona (92879-2061)
PHONE.................951 736-1313
EMP: 64
SALES (corp-wide): 66.6MM Privately Held
Web: www.missionrubber.com
SIC: 3494 Couplings, except pressure and soil pipe
HQ: Mission Rubber Company Llc
  1660 Leeson Ln
  Corona CA 92879
  951 736-1313

**(P-9189)**
**MORRILL INDUSTRIES INC**
24754 E River Rd, Escalon (95320-8601)
PHONE.................209 838-2550
Ken Morrill, Pr
Wayne Morrill, *
Diane Cordray, *
▲ EMP: 55 EST: 1954
SALES (est): 4.4MM Privately Held
Web: www.morrillinc.com
SIC: 3494 Sprinkler systems, field

**(P-9190)**
**NOR-CAL PRODUCTS INC (DH)**
Also Called: Pfeiffer Vacuum Valves & Engrg
1967 S Oregon St, Yreka (96097-3462)
P.O. Box 518 (96097-0518)
PHONE.................530 842-4457
Tom Deany, Pr
David Stone, *
▲ EMP: 140 EST: 1946
SQ FT: 57,000
SALES (est): 23.53MM
SALES (corp-wide): 1.72B Privately Held
Web: www.n-c.com
SIC: 3494 Valves and pipe fittings, nec
HQ: Pfeiffer Vacuum, Inc.
  24 Trafalgar Sq
  Nashua NH 03063

**(P-9191)**
**RAIN BIRD CORPORATION (PA)**
Also Called: Rain Bird
970 W Sierra Madre Ave, Azusa
(91702-1873)
PHONE.................626 812-3400
Michael L Donoghue, CEO
◆ EMP: 125 EST: 1933
SALES (est): 433.78MM
SALES (corp-wide): 433.78MM Privately Held
Web: www.rainbird.com
SIC: 3494 3432 3523 Sprinkler systems, field; Lawn hose nozzles and sprinklers; Farm machinery and equipment

**(P-9192)**
**VACCO INDUSTRIES (DH)**
10350 Vacco St, South El Monte
(91733-3316)
PHONE.................626 443-7121
Antonio E Gonzalez, CEO
Robert Mc Creadie, *
Paul Rowan, *
EMP: 248 EST: 1954
SALES (est): 97.3MM Publicly Held
Web: www.vacco.com
SIC: 3494 3492 3728 Valves and pipe fittings, nec; Fluid power valves and hose fittings; Aircraft parts and equipment, nec
HQ: Esco Technologies Holding Llc
  9900a Clayton Rd
  Saint Louis MO 63124
  314 213-7200

**(P-9193)**
**VALTERRA PRODUCTS LLC (HQ)**
15235 Brand Blvd Ste A101, Mission Hills
(91345-1445)
PHONE.................818 898-1671
Bryan Fletcher, Managing Member
▲ EMP: 20 EST: 1981
SQ FT: 50,000
SALES (est): 45.07MM
SALES (corp-wide): 2.84B Privately Held
Web: www.valterra.com
SIC: 3494 3088 3949 3432 Valves and pipe fittings, nec; Plastics plumbing fixtures; Skateboards; Plumbing fixture fittings and trim
PA: Dometic Group Ab (Publ)
  Hemvarnsgatan 15
  101729780

**(P-9194)**
**WATERMAN INDUSTRIES INC**
Also Called: Waterman Industries
25500 Road 204, Exeter (93221-9655)
P.O. Box 458 (93221-0458)
PHONE.................559 562-8661
▲ EMP: 70
SIC: 3494 3523 Valves and pipe fittings, nec; Farm machinery and equipment

---

### 3495 Wire Springs

**(P-9195)**
**AARD INDUSTRIES INC**
Also Called: Aard Spring & Stamping
42075 Avenida Alvarado, Temecula
(92590-3486)
PHONE.................951 296-0844
William Verstegen, Pr

# 3495 - Wire Springs (P-9196)

**EMP:** 22 **EST:** 1970
**SQ FT:** 5,000
**SALES (est):** 2.45MM **Privately Held**
**Web:** www.aard.com
**SIC:** 3495 3469  Wire springs; Metal stampings, nec

### (P-9196)
### AMERICAN PRECISION SPRING CORP
1513 Arbuckle Ct, Santa Clara (95054-3401)
**PHONE**.................................408 986-1020
Kathleen Chu, *Pr*
Mike Remily, *VP*
**EMP:** 23 **EST:** 1979
**SQ FT:** 1,500
**SALES (est):** 3.46MM **Privately Held**
**Web:** www.americanprecspring.com
**SIC:** 3495  Mechanical springs, precision

### (P-9197)
### BAL SEAL ENGINEERING LLC (DH)
19650 Pauling, Foothill Ranch (92610-2610)
**PHONE**.................................949 460-2100
Richard Dawson, *CEO*
Peter J Balsells, *Ch*
Jacques Naviaux, *Vice Chairman*
Andrew Wiggins, *Contrlr*
▲ **EMP:** 202 **EST:** 1959
**SQ FT:** 325,000
**SALES (est):** 92.5MM
**SALES (corp-wide):** 775.85MM **Privately Held**
**Web:** www.balseal.com
**SIC:** 3495 3053  Wire springs; Gaskets and sealing devices
**HQ:** Kaman Acquisition Usa, Inc.
   1332 Blue Hills Ave
   Bloomfield CT 06002
   860 243-7100

### (P-9198)
### BETTS COMPANY (PA)
Also Called: Betts Spring Manufacturing
2843 S Maple Ave, Fresno (93725-2217)
**PHONE**.................................559 498-3304
William Betts Iv, *Ch Bd*
William Betts V, *Pr*
Bill Betts, *
Donald Devany, *
▲ **EMP:** 75 **EST:** 1873
**SQ FT:** 7,500
**SALES (est):** 39.88MM
**SALES (corp-wide):** 39.88MM **Privately Held**
**Web:** www.betts1868.com
**SIC:** 3495 3493  Wire springs; Automobile springs

### (P-9199)
### BETTS COMPANY
Also Called: Betts Truck Parts
10007 Elm Ave, Fontana (92335-6318)
**PHONE**.................................909 427-9988
**TOLL FREE:** 800
Dan Paul, *Mgr*
**EMP:** 26
**SALES (corp-wide):** 39.88MM **Privately Held**
**Web:** www.betts1868.com
**SIC:** 3495 3493  Wire springs; Automobile springs
**PA:** Betts Company
   2843 S Maple Ave
   559 498-3304

### (P-9200)
### FOREMOST SPRING COMPANY INC
Also Called: Foremost Spring & Mfg
11876 Burke St, Santa Fe Springs (90670-2536)
**PHONE**.................................562 923-0791
Forrest Gardner, *Pr*
Forrest Gardner, *Pr*
Christine Brown, *VP*
Jesus Silva, *Sec*
**EMP:** 15 **EST:** 1968
**SQ FT:** 20,000
**SALES (est):** 2.33MM **Privately Held**
**Web:** www.foremostspring.com
**SIC:** 3495 3469 3493  Mechanical springs, precision; Stamping metal for the trade; Steel springs, except wire

### (P-9201)
### ICONN ENGINEERING LLC
6882 Preakness Dr, Huntington Beach (92648-1567)
**PHONE**.................................714 696-8826
Jay Huang, *Pr*
**EMP:** 25 **EST:** 2011
**SALES (est):** 387.1K **Privately Held**
**Web:** www.iconneng.com
**SIC:** 3495  Wire springs

### (P-9202)
### MATTHEW WARREN INC
Also Called: Century Spring
5959 Triumph St, Commerce (90040-1609)
**PHONE**.................................800 237-5225
Bill Cook, *Prin*
**EMP:** 75
**SALES (corp-wide):** 1.05B **Privately Held**
**Web:** www.centuryspring.com
**SIC:** 3495  Wire springs
**HQ:** Matthew Warren, Inc.
   3426 Toringdon Way # 100
   Charlotte NC 28277
   704 837-0331

### (P-9203)
### NEWCOMB SPRING CORP
Also Called: Newcomb Spring of California
8380 Cerritos Ave, Stanton (90680-2514)
**PHONE**.................................714 995-5341
Robert Guard, *Mgr*
**EMP:** 25
**SALES (corp-wide):** 42.63MM **Privately Held**
**Web:** www.newcombspring.com
**SIC:** 3495 3469 5085  Wire springs; Stamping metal for the trade; Springs
**PA:** Newcomb Spring Corp.
   3155 North Point Pkwy G220
   770 981-2803

### (P-9204)
### ORLANDO SPRING CORP
Also Called: Orlando Precision
5341 Argosy Ave, Huntington Beach (92649-1036)
**PHONE**.................................562 594-8411
Frank Mauro, *Pr*
Zachary Fischer, *
**EMP:** 40 **EST:** 1957
**SQ FT:** 20,000
**SALES (est):** 8.49MM **Privately Held**
**Web:** www.orlandospring.com
**SIC:** 3495  Wire springs

### (P-9205)
### PENINSULA SPRING CORPORATION
6750 Silacci Way, Gilroy (95020-7035)
P.O. Box 1782 (95021-1782)
**PHONE**.................................408 848-3361
Joe Kilmer, *Pr*
Muriel Kilmer, *VP*
Laura Hampel, *Off Mgr*
**EMP:** 18 **EST:** 1977
**SQ FT:** 10,000
**SALES (est):** 2.36MM **Privately Held**
**Web:** www.peninsulaspring.com
**SIC:** 3495 3444 3498 3496  Precision springs ; Forming machine work, sheet metal; Fabricated pipe and fittings; Miscellaneous fabricated wire products

### (P-9206)
### PRECISION COIL SPRING COMPANY
10107 Rose Ave, El Monte (91731-1801)
**PHONE**.................................626 444-0561
Albert H Goering, *CEO*
Bert Goering, *
Don Adkins, *
William Turek, *VP Mfg*
Gustavo Arenas, *VP Engg*
**EMP:** 111 **EST:** 1951
**SQ FT:** 45,000
**SALES (est):** 8.43MM **Privately Held**
**Web:** www.pcspring.com
**SIC:** 3495  Wire springs

### (P-9207)
### STECHER ENTERPRISES INC
Also Called: C&F Wire Products
8536 Central Ave, Stanton (90680-2718)
**PHONE**.................................714 484-6900
Fred Stecher, *Dir*
Tammy Stecher, *Pr*
Carol Stecher, *VP*
**EMP:** 15 **EST:** 1995
**SQ FT:** 10,000
**SALES (est):** 1.76MM **Privately Held**
**Web:** stecher.openfos.com
**SIC:** 3495  Instrument springs, precision

### (P-9208)
### SUPERIOR SPRING COMPANY
1260 S Talt Ave, Anaheim (92806-5533)
**PHONE**.................................714 490-0881
**TOLL FREE:** 800
Robert De Long Junior, *Pr*
**EMP:** 25 **EST:** 1958
**SQ FT:** 17,000
**SALES (est):** 4.62MM **Privately Held**
**Web:** www.superiorspring.com
**SIC:** 3495  Wire springs

## 3496 Miscellaneous Fabricated Wire Products

### (P-9209)
### AMERICAN WIRE INC
784 S Lugo Ave, San Bernardino (92408-2236)
**PHONE**.................................909 884-9990
Bambang Rahardjanoto, *CEO*
▲ **EMP:** 19 **EST:** 1991
**SQ FT:** 12,000
**SALES (est):** 1.96MM **Privately Held**
**Web:** www.americanwirecorp.com
**SIC:** 3496  Mesh, made from purchased wire

### (P-9210)
### ANAHEIM WIRE PRODUCTS INC
1009 E Vermont Ave, Anaheim (92805-5618)
**PHONE**.................................714 563-8300
**TOLL FREE:** 800
Michael Lewis, *Pr*
▲ **EMP:** 20 **EST:** 1985
**SQ FT:** 14,000
**SALES (est):** 2.47MM **Privately Held**
**Web:** www.anaheimwire.com
**SIC:** 3496  Miscellaneous fabricated wire products

### (P-9211)
### C M C STEEL FABRICATORS INC
Also Called: Fontana Steel
1455 Auto Center Dr Ste 200, Ontario (91761-2239)
P.O. Box 2219 (91729-2219)
**PHONE**.................................909 899-9993
Deborah Marshall, *Brnch Mgr*
**EMP:** 20
**SALES (corp-wide):** 7.93B **Publicly Held**
**Web:** www.cmc.com
**SIC:** 3496 3441 1791  Miscellaneous fabricated wire products; Fabricated structural metal; Concrete reinforcement, placing of
**HQ:** C M C Steel Fabricators, Inc.
   1 Steel Mill Dr
   Seguin TX 78155
   830 372-8200

### (P-9212)
### CABLE MOORE INC (PA)
4700 Coliseum Way, Oakland (94601-5008)
P.O. Box 4067 (94614-4067)
**PHONE**.................................510 436-8000
Sandra Moore, *CEO*
Gregory Moore, *
▲ **EMP:** 30 **EST:** 1986
**SQ FT:** 12,500
**SALES (est):** 9.72MM
**SALES (corp-wide):** 9.72MM **Privately Held**
**Web:** www.cablemoore.com
**SIC:** 3496  Wire chain

### (P-9213)
### CALIFORNIA WIRE PRODUCTS CORP
Also Called: Cal-Monarch
1316 Railroad St, Corona (92882-1840)
**PHONE**.................................951 371-7730
John G Frei, *CEO*
Samuel A Agajanian, *
Sam Agajanian, *
▲ **EMP:** 30 **EST:** 1948
**SQ FT:** 34,000
**SALES (est):** 4.4MM **Privately Held**
**Web:** www.cawire.com
**SIC:** 3496 2542  Screening, woven wire: made from purchased wire; Partitions for floor attachment, prefabricated: except wood

### (P-9214)
### CIRCLE W ENTERPRISES INC
Also Called: Wirenetics Co
27737 Avenue Hopkins, Valencia (91355-1223)
**PHONE**.................................661 257-2400
Howard Weiss, *CEO*
Michael Weiss, *
Phyllis G Weiss, *
Mark Lee, *
▲ **EMP:** 50 **EST:** 1969
**SQ FT:** 65,000
**SALES (est):** 8.86MM
**SALES (corp-wide):** 512.41MM **Privately Held**
**SIC:** 3496  Miscellaneous fabricated wire products
**HQ:** B.J.G. Electronics, Inc.
   141 Remington Blvd
   Ronkonkoma NY 11779
   631 737-1234

PRODUCTS & SERVICES SECTION  
3496 - Miscellaneous Fabricated Wire Products (P-9237)

**(P-9215)**
**DHA AMERICA INC**
5403 Harvest Run Dr, San Diego (92130-4879)
PHONE..................................858 925-3246
Heon Young Ha, *Pr*
Duck Peerl Ha, *Sec*
▲ EMP: 54 EST: 1996
SALES (est): 9.99MM **Privately Held**
Web: www.dha-america.com
SIC: **3496** Wire winding
PA: Dae Ha Cable Co.,Ltd.
   2022 Deogyeong-Daero, Giheung-Gu

**(P-9216)**
**EJAY FILTRATION INC**
3036 Durahart St, Riverside (92507-3446)
P.O. Box 5268 (92517-5268)
PHONE..................................951 683-0805
Jerry Green, *CEO*
Cheryl Young, *
Bob Rostig, *
EMP: 33 EST: 1988
SQ FT: 14,000
SALES (est): 4.46MM **Privately Held**
Web: www.ejayfiltration.com
SIC: **3496** Mesh, made from purchased wire

**(P-9217)**
**FEENEY INC**
Also Called: Feeney Wire Rope & Rigging
2603 Union St, Oakland (94607-2423)
PHONE..................................510 893-9473
TOLL FREE: 800
Grissell Ralston, *CEO*
Katrina Ralston, *
Richard Ralston, *
Steven Imbrenda, *
▼ EMP: 48 EST: 1948
SQ FT: 29,000
SALES (est): 8.96MM **Privately Held**
Web: www.feeneyinc.com
SIC: **3496** Miscellaneous fabricated wire products

**(P-9218)**
**FITTINGS THAT FIT INC**
4628 Mission Blvd, Montclair (91763-6135)
PHONE..................................909 248-2808
Eric C Wang, *Pr*
▲ EMP: 15 EST: 1947
SALES (est): 2.24MM **Privately Held**
Web: www.ftf99.com
SIC: **3496** Fencing, made from purchased wire

**(P-9219)**
**GROSSI FABRICATION INC**
3200 Tully Rd, Hughson (95326-9816)
P.O. Box 937 (95326-0937)
PHONE..................................209 883-2817
Larry Grossi, *Pr*
Shanon Grossi, *VP*
EMP: 15 EST: 1998
SALES (est): 2.46MM **Privately Held**
Web: www.grossifabrication.com
SIC: **3496** Netting, woven wire: made from purchased wire

**(P-9220)**
**INNOVIVE LLC (PA)**
10019 Waples Ct, San Diego (92121-2962)
PHONE..................................858 309-6620
Dee Conger, *CEO*
Joanna Xiong, *
◆ EMP: 40 EST: 2006
SQ FT: 50,000
SALES (est): 10.28MM **Privately Held**
Web: www.innovive.com
SIC: **3496** Cages, wire

**(P-9221)**
**KEVIN WHALEY**
Also Called: Whaley, Kevin Enterprises
9565 Pathway St, Santee (92071-4184)
PHONE..................................619 596-4000
Kevin M Whaley, *Owner*
▼ EMP: 30 EST: 1976
SQ FT: 24,000
SALES (est): 3.3MM **Privately Held**
Web: www.kwcages.com
SIC: **3496** Cages, wire

**(P-9222)**
**LEXCO IMPORTS INC**
1455 S Campus Ave, Ontario (91761-4369)
P.O. Box 271 (91763-0271)
PHONE..................................800 883-1454
▲ EMP: 26 EST: 2001
SALES (est): 921.68K **Privately Held**
SIC: **3496** Miscellaneous fabricated wire products

**(P-9223)**
**NASHVILLE WIRE PDTS MFG CO LLC**
10727 Commerce Way Ste C, Fontana (92337-8246)
PHONE..................................714 736-0081
George Alvarez, *Asstg*
▲ EMP: 19 EST: 2006
SALES (est): 180.29K **Privately Held**
Web: www.nashvillewire.com
SIC: **3496** Miscellaneous fabricated wire products

**(P-9224)**
**PACIFIC WIRE PRODUCTS INC**
10725 Vanowen St, North Hollywood (91605-6402)
PHONE..................................818 755-6400
Charles L Swick, *Pr*
EMP: 25 EST: 1984
SQ FT: 28,000
SALES (est): 3.44MM **Privately Held**
Web: www.prontoproducts.com
SIC: **3496** Miscellaneous fabricated wire products

**(P-9225)**
**PHIFER INCORPORATED**
Also Called: Phifer Western
14408 Nelson Ave, City Of Industry (91744-3513)
PHONE..................................626 968-0438
Joel Hartig, *Mgr*
EMP: 56
SQ FT: 23,182
SALES (corp-wide): 286.29MM **Privately Held**
Web: www.phifer.com
SIC: **3496** Miscellaneous fabricated wire products
PA: Phifer Incorporated
   4400 Reese Phifer Ave
   205 345-2120

**(P-9226)**
**PRECISION WIRE PRODUCTS INC (PA)**
6150 Sheila St, Commerce (90040-2407)
PHONE..................................323 890-9100
Vladimir John Ondrasik Junior, *Prin*
V John Ondrasik, *
◆ EMP: 200 EST: 1946
SQ FT: 200,000
SALES (est): 22.58MM
SALES (corp-wide): 22.58MM **Privately Held**
Web: www.precisionwireproducts.com

SIC: **3496** Grocery carts, made from purchased wire

**(P-9227)**
**R & B WIRE PRODUCTS INC**
2902 W Garry Ave, Santa Ana (92704-6510)
PHONE..................................714 549-3355
Richard G Rawlins, *CEO*
◆ EMP: 50 EST: 1948
SQ FT: 20,000
SALES (est): 1.08MM **Privately Held**
Web: www.rbwire.com
SIC: **3496** Miscellaneous fabricated wire products

**(P-9228)**
**RAMPONE INDUSTRIES LLC**
168 E Liberty Ave, Anaheim (92801-1011)
PHONE..................................714 265-0200
Horacio Rampone, *Managing Member*
▲ EMP: 30 EST: 2003
SALES (est): 4.37MM **Privately Held**
Web: www.ramponeindustries.com
SIC: **3496** Miscellaneous fabricated wire products

**(P-9229)**
**RAPID MFG A CAL LTD PARTNR (PA)**
Also Called: Rapid Manufacturing
8080 E Crystal Dr, Anaheim (92807-2524)
PHONE..................................714 974-2432
Patricia Engler Howard, *Genl Pt*
Ronald W Howard, *
EMP: 180 EST: 1986
SQ FT: 19,500
SALES (est): 48.52MM
SALES (corp-wide): 48.52MM **Privately Held**
Web: www.rapidmfg.com
SIC: **3496** Miscellaneous fabricated wire products

**(P-9230)**
**RDS WIRE & CABLE INCORPORATED**
225 E Gardena Blvd, Gardena (90248-2835)
PHONE..................................310 323-7131
R Douglas Stott, *CEO*
John Stott, *Pr*
Jesse Luna, *VP*
EMP: 15 EST: 1985
SQ FT: 13,000
SALES (est): 2.17MM **Privately Held**
Web: www.rdswire.com
SIC: **3496** Miscellaneous fabricated wire products

**(P-9231)**
**RFC WIRE FORMS INC**
Also Called: Rfc Wire Forms
525 Brooks St, Ontario (91762-3702)
PHONE..................................909 467-0559
Donald C Kemby, *CEO*
Christine Kemby, *
▲ EMP: 70 EST: 1946
SQ FT: 29,000
SALES (est): 8.73MM **Privately Held**
Web: www.rfcwireforms.com
SIC: **3496** Miscellaneous fabricated wire products

**(P-9232)**
**RPS INC**
20331 Corisco St, Chatsworth (91311-6120)
PHONE..................................818 350-8088

Travis Miller, *Pr*
EMP: 25 EST: 2017
SQ FT: 1,000
SALES (est): 429.95K **Privately Held**
SIC: **3496** 7389 Miscellaneous fabricated wire products; Design services

**(P-9233)**
**STANDARD CABLE USA INC**
Also Called: Conductive
23126 Arroyo Vis, Rcho Sta Marg (92688-2608)
PHONE..................................949 888-0842
Selvin Kao, *Head Officer*
Ann Tai, *Treas*
▲ EMP: 15 EST: 1999
SQ FT: 10,000
SALES (est): 4.53MM **Privately Held**
SIC: **3496** Miscellaneous fabricated wire products

**(P-9234)**
**SUMIDEN WIRE PRODUCTS CORP**
1412 El Pinal Dr, Stockton (95205-2642)
PHONE..................................615 446-3199
EMP: 24
Web: www.sumidenwire.com
SIC: **3496** Miscellaneous fabricated wire products
HQ: Sumiden Wire Products Corp
   710 Marshall Stuart Dr
   Dickson TN 37055
   615 446-3199

**(P-9235)**
**SYNERGISTIC RESEARCH INC**
11208 Young River Ave, Fountain Valley (92708-4109)
PHONE..................................949 476-0000
Theodore Denney Iii, *Pr*
▲ EMP: 15 EST: 1999
SALES (est): 2.14MM **Privately Held**
Web: www.synergisticresearch.com
SIC: **3496** Cable, uninsulated wire: made from purchased wire

**(P-9236)**
**TOP-SHELF FIXTURES LLC**
5263 Schaefer Ave, Chino (91710-5554)
P.O. Box 2470 (91708-2470)
PHONE..................................909 627-7423
Alonso Munoz, *Managing Member*
EMP: 95 EST: 2002
SQ FT: 90,000
SALES (est): 20.98MM **Privately Held**
Web: www.topshelffixtures.com
SIC: **3496** Miscellaneous fabricated wire products

**(P-9237)**
**TREE ISLAND WIRE (USA) INC**
Also Called: Tree Island Wire USA
5080 Hallmark Pkwy, San Bernardino (92407-1835)
P.O. Box 90100 (92427-1100)
PHONE..................................909 899-1673
Daryl Young Opts, *Mgr*
EMP: 115
SALES (corp-wide): 185.25MM **Privately Held**
Web: www.treeisland.com
SIC: **3496** Miscellaneous fabricated wire products
HQ: Tree Island Wire (Usa), Inc.
   3880 Valley Blvd
   Walnut CA 91789

## 3496 - Miscellaneous Fabricated Wire Products (P-9238)

**(P-9238)**
**UNI-FAB INDUSTRIES INC**
5020 Brandin Ct, Fremont (94538-3140)
PHONE...............................408 945-9733
EMP: 75 EST: 1985
SALES (est): 9.77MM Privately Held
Web: www.uni-fab.com
SIC: 3496 Miscellaneous fabricated wire products

**(P-9239)**
**UNITED SUNSHINE AMERICAN INDUSTRIES CORPORATION**
Also Called: USA Industries
2808 E Marywood Ln, Orange (92867-1912)
EMP: 25 EST: 1948
SALES (est): 698.27K Privately Held
Web: www.usa-industries.com
SIC: 3496 Fencing, made from purchased wire

**(P-9240)**
**US RIGGING SUPPLY CORP**
1600 E Mcfadden Ave, Santa Ana (92705-4310)
PHONE...............................714 545-7444
Richard T Walker, CEO
▲ EMP: 50 EST: 1974
SQ FT: 20,000
SALES (est): 5.68MM Privately Held
Web: www.usrigging.com
SIC: 3496 5051 Miscellaneous fabricated wire products; Rope, wire (not insulated)

**(P-9241)**
**VOLK ENTERPRISES INC**
618 S Kilroy Rd, Turlock (95380-9531)
PHONE...............................209 632-3826
Anthony Volks, Mgr
EMP: 60
Web: www.volkenterprises.com
SIC: 3496 3089 Miscellaneous fabricated wire products; Plastics processing
PA: Volk Enterprises, Inc.
1335 Ridgeland Pkwy # 120

**(P-9242)**
**WHITMOR PLSTIC WIRE CABLE CORP (PA)**
Also Called: Whitmor Wire and Cable
27737 Avenue Hopkins, Santa Clarita (91355-1223)
PHONE...............................661 257-2400
Michael Weiss, Pr
Jeff Siebert, *
Mark Lee, *
Dwight Van Lake, *
Stella Reaza, *
▼ EMP: 50 EST: 1959
SQ FT: 50,000
SALES (est): 9.22MM
SALES (corp-wide): 9.22MM Privately Held
Web: www.wireandcable.com
SIC: 3496 5063 3357 Cable, uninsulated wire: made from purchased wire; Electrical apparatus and equipment; Nonferrous wiredrawing and insulating

**(P-9243)**
**WHITMOR PLSTIC WIRE CABLE CORP**
Also Called: Whitmor Wirenetics
28420 Avenue Stanford, Valencia (91355-3982)
PHONE...............................661 257-2400
Jeff Siebert, VP Mfg
EMP: 42
SALES (corp-wide): 9.22MM Privately Held
Web: www.wireandcable.com
SIC: 3496 5063 Cable, uninsulated wire: made from purchased wire; Electrical apparatus and equipment
PA: Whitmor Plastic Wire And Cable Corp.
27737 Avenue Hopkins
661 257-2400

**(P-9244)**
**WYREFAB INC**
15711 S Broadway, Gardena (90248-2401)
P.O. Box 3767 (90247-7467)
PHONE...............................310 523-2147
Charles Nick, Pr
John P Massey, *
EMP: 42 EST: 1948
SQ FT: 55,000
SALES (est): 4.42MM Privately Held
Web: www.wyrefab.com
SIC: 3496 Miscellaneous fabricated wire products

## 3498 Fabricated Pipe And Fittings

**(P-9245)**
**ACCURATE TUBE BENDING INC**
Also Called: Accurate
37770 Timber St, Newark (94560-4443)
P.O. Box 990 (94537-0990)
PHONE...............................510 790-6500
Jon Morrow, Pr
EMP: 33 EST: 1994
SQ FT: 28,000
SALES (est): 7.43MM Privately Held
Web: www.atbending.com
SIC: 3498 Tube fabricating (contract bending and shaping)

**(P-9246)**
**AEROFIT LLC**
1425 S Acacia Ave, Fullerton (92831-5317)
PHONE...............................714 521-5060
Jordan A Law, Managing Member
David A Werner, *
▲ EMP: 150 EST: 1968
SQ FT: 67,000
SALES (est): 22.92MM
SALES (corp-wide): 15.78B Publicly Held
Web: www.aerofit.com
SIC: 3498 Pipe fittings, fabricated from purchased pipe
HQ: Consolidated Aerospace Manufacturing, Llc
1425 S Acacia Ave
Fullerton CA 92831
714 989-2797

**(P-9247)**
**AMERIFLEX INC**
Also Called: Mw Components - Corona
2390 Railroad St, Corona (92878-5410)
PHONE...............................951 737-5557
John Bagnuolo, CEO
Chester Kwasniak, CFO
▲ EMP: 76 EST: 1981
SQ FT: 32,000
SALES (est): 7.33MM
SALES (corp-wide): 1.05B Privately Held
Web: www.mwcomponents.com
SIC: 3498 3494 3674 Fabricated pipe and fittings; Valves and pipe fittings, nec; Semiconductors and related devices
HQ: Mw Industries, Inc.
2400 Farrell Rd
Houston TX 77073
800 875-3510

**(P-9248)**
**ASC ENGINEERED SOLUTIONS LLC**
551 N Loop Dr, Ontario (91761-8629)
PHONE...............................909 418-3233
Gwyn Lundy, Crdt Mgr
EMP: 51
SALES (corp-wide): 836.12MM Privately Held
Web: www.asc-es.com
SIC: 3498 3321 3317 Fabricated pipe and fittings; Gray and ductile iron foundries; Steel pipe and tubes
PA: Asc Engineered Solutions, Llc
2001 Spring Rd Ste 300
800 301-2701

**(P-9249)**
**ASC ENGINEERED SOLUTIONS LLC**
2867 Vail Ave, Commerce (90040-2613)
PHONE...............................800 766-0076
EMP: 65
SALES (corp-wide): 836.12MM Privately Held
Web: www.asc-es.com
SIC: 3498 Fabricated pipe and fittings
PA: Asc Engineered Solutions, Llc
2001 Spring Rd Ste 300
800 301-2701

**(P-9250)**
**BASSANI MANUFACTURING**
Also Called: Bassani Exhaust
2900 E La Jolla St, Anaheim (92806-1305)
PHONE...............................714 630-1821
Darryl Bassani, Pr
Becky Bassani, *
▲ EMP: 46 EST: 1969
SQ FT: 20,791
SALES (est): 9.45MM Privately Held
Web: www.bassani.com
SIC: 3498 3599 Fabricated pipe and fittings; Machine shop, jobbing and repair

**(P-9251)**
**BCC DISSOLUTION INC**
2929 S Santa Fe Ave, Los Angeles (90058)
P.O. Box 7249 (91327)
PHONE...............................323 583-3444
Ramendra Satyarthi, Pr
▲ EMP: 35 EST: 1982
SQ FT: 65,000
SALES (est): 3.73MM Privately Held
Web: www.bakercouplingcompany.com
SIC: 3498 Couplings, pipe: fabricated from purchased pipe

**(P-9252)**
**CAL PIPE MANUFACTURING INC (PA)**
Also Called: Calpipe Security Bollards
12160 Woodruff Ave, Downey (90241-5606)
PHONE...............................562 803-4388
Dan Markus, Pr
Sheri Caine-markus, VP
▲ EMP: 37 EST: 1986
SQ FT: 125,000
SALES (est): 3.08MM
SALES (corp-wide): 3.08MM Privately Held
Web: www.atkore.com
SIC: 3498 Tube fabricating (contract bending and shaping)

**(P-9253)**
**CRYOTECH INTERNATIONAL INC**
Also Called: Chart
161 Baypointe Pkwy, San Jose (95134-1622)
PHONE...............................408 371-3303
▲ EMP: 40
SIC: 3498 Fabricated pipe and fittings

**(P-9254)**
**CRYOWORKS INC**
3309 Grapevine St, Mira Loma (91752-3503)
PHONE...............................951 360-0920
Timothy L Mast, Pr
Donna J Mast, VP
Tamara Sipos, CFO
▲ EMP: 85 EST: 2009
SALES (est): 10.36MM Privately Held
Web: www.cryoworks.net
SIC: 3498 1711 Fabricated pipe and fittings; Plumbing contractors

**(P-9255)**
**CUNICO CORPORATION**
1910 W 16th St, Long Beach (90813-1137)
P.O. Box 9010 (90810-0010)
PHONE...............................562 733-4600
▲ EMP: 45 EST: 1951
SALES (est): 2.98MM
SALES (corp-wide): 9.45MM Privately Held
Web: www.bwxt.com
SIC: 3498 Pipe fittings, fabricated from purchased pipe
PA: Citadel Capital Corporation
1910 W 16th St
562 733-4600

**(P-9256)**
**CUSTOM PIPE & FABRICATION INC (HQ)**
10560 Fern Ave, Stanton (90680-2648)
P.O. Box 978 (90680-0978)
PHONE...............................800 553-3058
Danny Daniel, CEO
Leonard Shapiro, Treas
Jerry Witkow, Sec
▲ EMP: 60 EST: 1972
SQ FT: 8,000
SALES (est): 117.01MM
SALES (corp-wide): 134.62MM Privately Held
Web: www.custompipe.com
SIC: 3498 Tube fabricating (contract bending and shaping)
PA: Shapco Inc.
1666 20th St Ste 100
310 264-1666

**(P-9257)**
**EDMUND A GRAY CO (PA)**
2277 E 15th St, Los Angeles (90021-2852)
PHONE...............................213 625-0376
Lawrence Gray Junior, CEO
Lawrence Gray Iii, VP
Patricia Gray, *
▲ EMP: 75 EST: 1910
SQ FT: 50,000
SALES (est): 13.68MM
SALES (corp-wide): 13.68MM Privately Held
Web: www.eagray.com
SIC: 3498 Pipe fittings, fabricated from purchased pipe

**(P-9258)**
**EPS CORPORATE HOLDINGS INC (DH)**
3100 Donald Douglas Loop N Hngr 3, Santa Monica (90405-3085)
PHONE...............................310 204-7238
Greg Boiko, Pr

## 3499 - Fabricated Metal Products, Nec (P-9278)

Alan Shapiro, *
Trish Dougherty, *
**EMP:** 16 **EST:** 1993
**SQ FT:** 200,000
**SALES (est):** 48.42MM **Privately Held**
**SIC: 3498** 5074 Pipe fittings, fabricated from purchased pipe; Plumbing and hydronic heating supplies
**HQ:** Express Pipe & Supply Co., Llc
  1235 S Lewis St
  Santa Monica CA 90404
  310 204-7238

**(P-9259)**
### FLEXIBLE METAL INC
Also Called: FMI
1685 Brandywine Ave, Chula Vista (91911-6020)
**PHONE**....................734 516-3017
Michael Nocholson, *CEO*
▲ **EMP:** 180 **EST:** 1986
**SALES (est):** 40.23MM
**SALES (corp-wide):** 115.37MM **Privately Held**
**Web:** www.flexiblemetal.com
**SIC: 3498** Fabricated pipe and fittings
**PA:** Hyspan Precision Products, Inc.
  1685 Brandywine Ave
  619 421-1355

**(P-9260)**
### FLO-MAC INC
1846 E 60th St, Los Angeles (90001-1420)
P.O. Box 1078 (90255-1078)
**PHONE**....................323 583-8751
Larry Smith, *Pr*
Scott Crane, *VP*
Mark Smith, *Treas*
**EMP:** 16 **EST:** 1974
**SQ FT:** 14,000
**SALES (est):** 645.65K **Privately Held**
**Web:** www.flo-mac.net
**SIC: 3498** Pipe fittings, fabricated from purchased pipe

**(P-9261)**
### ILCO INDUSTRIES INC
Also Called: Ilco Industries
1308 W Mahalo Pl, Compton (90220-5418)
**PHONE**....................310 631-8655
Elias Awad, *Pr*
**EMP:** 35 **EST:** 1936
**SQ FT:** 23,000
**SALES (est):** 5.84MM **Privately Held**
**Web:** www.ilcoind.com
**SIC: 3498** 3492 Manifolds, pipe: fabricated from purchased pipe; Hose and tube fittings and assemblies, hydraulic/pneumatic

**(P-9262)**
### JIFCO INC (PA)
Also Called: Jifco Fabaricated Piping
571 Exchange Ct, Livermore (94550-2400)
P.O. Box 589 (94551-0589)
**PHONE**....................925 449-4665
Jay Forni Junior, *Pr*
Kevin N Krausgill, *
Monica Spina Forni, *
Jeffrey Hill, *
**EMP:** 47 **EST:** 1983
**SALES (est):** 5.62MM
**SALES (corp-wide):** 5.62MM **Privately Held**
**Web:** www.jifco.com
**SIC: 3498** Tube fabricating (contract bending and shaping)

**(P-9263)**
### KAISER ENTERPRISES INC
Also Called: Insight Manufacturing Services
11375 Sunrise Park Dr Ste 500, Rancho Cordova (95742-6592)
**PHONE**....................916 203-9797
**EMP:** 30
**Web:** www.insightmanufacturing.com
**SIC: 3498** Coils, pipe: fabricated from purchased pipe
**PA:** Kaiser Enterprises Inc.
  798 Murphys Creek Rd

**(P-9264)**
### KAISER ENTERPRISES INC (PA)
Also Called: Insight Mfg Services
798 Murphys Creek Rd, Murphys (95247-9562)
P.O. Box 2609 (95247-2609)
**PHONE**....................209 728-2091
Loretta Dietz Kaiser, *Pr*
Herman Kaiser, *
**EMP:** 45 **EST:** 2007
**SQ FT:** 6,900
**SALES (est):** 11.23MM **Privately Held**
**Web:** www.insightmanufacturing.com
**SIC: 3498** Coils, pipe: fabricated from purchased pipe

**(P-9265)**
### MARINE & INDUSTRIAL SVCS INC
2391 W 10th St, Antioch (94509-1366)
P.O. Box 2236 (94531-2236)
**PHONE**....................925 757-8791
Thomas M Hannaford, *Pr*
**EMP:** 16 **EST:** 1988
**SQ FT:** 21,000
**SALES (est):** 3.39MM **Privately Held**
**SIC: 3498** Pipe fittings, fabricated from purchased pipe

**(P-9266)**
### MD STAINLESS SERVICES
8241 Phlox St, Downey (90241-4841)
**PHONE**....................562 904-7022
Marvin Davis, *Pr*
Sunshine Olsen, *Treas*
**EMP:** 20 **EST:** 1988
**SQ FT:** 15,000
**SALES (est):** 5.06MM **Privately Held**
**Web:** www.mdstainless.com
**SIC: 3498** 1711 Fabricated pipe and fittings; Process piping contractor

**(P-9267)**
### ONE-WAY MANUFACTURING INC
1195 N Osprey Cir, Anaheim (92807-1709)
**PHONE**....................714 630-8833
Sue Huang, *CEO*
Ike Huang, *COO*
**EMP:** 23 **EST:** 2005
**SQ FT:** 19,400
**SALES (est):** 6.58MM **Privately Held**
**Web:** www.onewaymfg.com
**SIC: 3498** 3599 1541 7692 Tube fabricating (contract bending and shaping); Machine and other job shop work; Truck and automobile assembly plant construction; Welding repair

**(P-9268)**
### RIGHT MANUFACTURING LLC
7949 Stromesa Ct Ste G, San Diego (92126-6338)
**PHONE**....................858 566-7002
▲ **EMP:** 30 **EST:** 1971
**SQ FT:** 15,000
**SALES (est):** 5.89MM **Privately Held**
**Web:** www.rightmfg.com
**SIC: 3498** 3444 Tube fabricating (contract bending and shaping); Sheet metalwork

**(P-9269)**
### RUSSELL FABRICATION CORP
Also Called: American Fabrication
4940 Gilmore Ave, Bakersfield (93308-6150)
**PHONE**....................661 861-8495
Kevin Russell, *Pr*
**EMP:** 45 **EST:** 1985
**SALES (est):** 4.44MM **Privately Held**
**Web:** www.americanfabandpowdercoating.com
**SIC: 3498** 3444 Fabricated pipe and fittings; Sheet metalwork

**(P-9270)**
### SF TUBE INC
23099 Connecticut St, Hayward (94545-1605)
**PHONE**....................510 785-9148
Michelle Valdez, *Off Mgr*
**EMP:** 46
**SALES (corp-wide):** 505.7MM **Privately Held**
**Web:** www.sftubebending.com
**SIC: 3498** Tube fabricating (contract bending and shaping)
**HQ:** Sf Tube, Inc.
  640 N Lasalle Dr Ste 670
  Chicago IL 60654
  312 374-4829

**(P-9271)**
### SHAPCO INC
5220 S Peach Ave, Fresno (93725-9708)
**PHONE**....................559 834-1342
Garette Scott, *Brnch Mgr*
**EMP:** 98
**SALES (corp-wide):** 134.62MM **Privately Held**
**Web:** www.custompipe.com
**SIC: 3498** Fabricated pipe and fittings
**PA:** Shapco Inc.
  1666 20th St Ste 100
  310 264-1666

**(P-9272)**
### TRINITY PROCESS SOLUTIONS INC
4740 E Bryson St, Anaheim (92807-1901)
**PHONE**....................714 701-1112
Jack Brunner, *Pr*
Candace Brunner, *VP*
**EMP:** 20 **EST:** 2005
**SQ FT:** 13,000
**SALES (est):** 3.9MM
**SALES (corp-wide):** 700MM **Privately Held**
**Web:** www.trinityprocesssolutions.com
**SIC: 3498** 3317 8711 Fabricated pipe and fittings; Welded pipe and tubes; Engineering services
**PA:** Legence Holdings Llc
  1601 Las Plumas Ave
  408 347-3400

**(P-9273)**
### WESSEX INDUSTRIES INC
8619 Red Oak St, Rancho Cucamonga (91730-4820)
**PHONE**....................562 944-5760
Archie Castillo, *Pr*
Edward Mojica, *
Linne A Castillo, *
**EMP:** 25 **EST:** 1985
**SQ FT:** 30,000
**SALES (est):** 2.44MM **Privately Held**
**SIC: 3498** 8742 Pipe fittings, fabricated from purchased pipe; Management consulting services

## 3499 Fabricated Metal Products, Nec

**(P-9274)**
### AMERICAN SECURITY PRODUCTS CO
Also Called: Amsec
11925 Pacific Ave, Fontana (92337-8205)
P.O. Box 317001 (92331-7001)
**PHONE**....................951 685-9680
David Lazier, *CEO*
Thomas Cassutt, *CFO*
Robert Sallee, *VP*
◆ **EMP:** 237 **EST:** 1946
**SQ FT:** 150,000
**SALES (est):** 44.62MM **Privately Held**
**Web:** www.americansecuritysafes.com
**SIC: 3499** 1731 Safes and vaults, metal; Safety and security specialization

**(P-9275)**
### ARTISAN HOUSE INC
Also Called: ARTISAN HOUSE, INC
8238 Lankershim Blvd, North Hollywood (91605-1613)
**PHONE**....................818 767-7476
Dennis Damore, *Brnch Mgr*
**EMP:** 30
**SALES (corp-wide):** 1.45MM **Privately Held**
**Web:** www.artisanhouse.com
**SIC: 3499** Novelties and specialties, metal
**PA:** Artisan House, Inc.
  3750 Cohasset St
  818 565-5030

**(P-9276)**
### BEY-BERK INTERNATIONAL (PA)
9145 Deering Ave, Chatsworth (91311-5802)
**PHONE**....................818 773-7534
Kurken Y Berksanlar, *Pr*
Serop Beylerian, *
◆ **EMP:** 23 **EST:** 1980
**SQ FT:** 19,800
**SALES (est):** 2.88MM
**SALES (corp-wide):** 2.88MM **Privately Held**
**Web:** www.bey-berk.com
**SIC: 3499** 3873 Novelties and giftware, including trophies; Clocks, assembly of

**(P-9277)**
### BISHOP-WISECARVER CORPORATION (PA)
2104 Martin Way, Pittsburg (94565-5027)
**PHONE**....................925 439-8272
Pamela Kan, *CEO*
Suzanne Methe, *
Judith S Wiscarver, *
Shelley Galvin, *
Warren R Wisecarver, *
▲ **EMP:** 54 **EST:** 1950
**SQ FT:** 80,000
**SALES (est):** 9.84MM
**SALES (corp-wide):** 9.84MM **Privately Held**
**Web:** www.bwc.com
**SIC: 3499** 5085 3823 Machine bases, metal; Bearings; Process control instruments

**(P-9278)**
### CAL-WELD INC
4308 Solar Way, Fremont (94538-6335)
**PHONE**....................510 226-0100
Maurice Carson, *Pr*
**EMP:** 116 **EST:** 1978
**SALES (est):** 19.46MM

## 3499 - Fabricated Metal Products, Nec (P-9279)

SALES (corp-wide): 811.12MM **Publicly Held**
Web: www.cal-weld.com
SIC: **3499** Aerosol valves, metal
HQ: Ichor Holdings, Llc
9660 Sw Herman Rd
Tualatin OR 97062
503 625-2251

### (P-9279)
### CHATSWORTH PRODUCTS INC (PA)
Also Called: C P I
4175 Guardian St, Simi Valley (93063-3382)
PHONE...............................818 735-6100
Michael Custer, *CEO*
Larry Renaud, *
Larry Varblow, *
Tom Jorgenson, *
Ted Behrens, *
◆ EMP: 25 EST: 1990
SALES (est): 107.78MM **Privately Held**
Web: www.chatsworth.com
SIC: **3499** 2542 Machine bases, metal; Partitions and fixtures, except wood

### (P-9280)
### CRYSTAL BLUE INC
236 S Puente Dr, Tracy (95391-2044)
PHONE...............................510 783-5888
Feng Hsu Kuo, *Admn*
◆ EMP: 22 EST: 2014
SALES (est): 1.01MM **Privately Held**
Web: www.crystalblueusa.com
SIC: **3499** 5199 Novelties and giftware, including trophies; Gifts and novelties

### (P-9281)
### DO IT AMERICAN MFG COMPANY LLC
137 Vander St, Corona (92878-3252)
PHONE...............................951 254-9204
Moises Vasquez, *Managing Member*
EMP: 16 EST: 2008
SQ FT: 20,000
SALES (est): 4.01MM **Privately Held**
Web: www.doitamerican.net
SIC: **3499** 3545 8711 Machine bases, metal; Machine tool accessories; Engineering services

### (P-9282)
### DOT BLUE SAFES CORPORATION
2707 N Garey Ave, Pomona (91767-1809)
PHONE...............................909 445-8888
Berge Jalakian, *CEO*
◆ EMP: 42 EST: 2004
SQ FT: 90,000
SALES (est): 9.01MM **Privately Held**
Web: www.bluedotsafes.com
SIC: **3499** 8741 Safes and vaults, metal; Management services

### (P-9283)
### ECOOLTHING CORP
Also Called: Cool Things
1321 E Saint Gertrude Pl Ste A, Santa Ana (92705-5241)
P.O. Box 6022 (92616-6022)
PHONE...............................714 368-4791
Connie Wang, *Pr*
Linda Wang, *
▲ EMP: 50 EST: 2001
SQ FT: 10,000
SALES (est): 2.33MM **Privately Held**

SIC: **3499** 5199 Novelties and giftware, including trophies; Gifts and novelties

### (P-9284)
### ENERGY ABSORPTION SYSTEMS INC
Also Called: ENERGY ABSORPTION SYSTEMS, INC.
3617 Cincinnati Ave, Rocklin (95765-1202)
PHONE...............................916 645-8181
Barry Stephens, *Mgr*
EMP: 155
SQ FT: 22,968
SALES (corp-wide): 2.98B **Publicly Held**
Web: www.valtir.com
SIC: **3499** 3842 3669 3823 Barricades, metal; Surgical appliances and supplies; Transportation signaling devices; Absorption analyzers: infrared, x-ray, etc.: industrial
HQ: Energy Absorption Systems, Llc
70 W Madison St Ste 2350
Chicago IL 60602
312 467-6750

### (P-9285)
### EVANS INDUSTRIES INC
Darnell-Rose Div
17915 Railroad St, City Of Industry (91748-1113)
PHONE...............................626 912-1688
Bob Batistic, *Mgr*
EMP: 58
SALES (corp-wide): 16.83MM **Privately Held**
Web: www.mmgmfg.com
SIC: **3499** 5072 Wheels: wheelbarrow, stroller, etc.: disc, stamped metal; Casters and glides
HQ: Evans Industries, Inc.
3150 Livernois Rd Ste 170
Troy MI 48083
313 259-2266

### (P-9286)
### EXECUTIVE SAFE AND SEC CORP
Also Called: Amphion
10722 Edison Ct, Rancho Cucamonga (91730-4845)
PHONE...............................909 947-7020
Scott C Denton, *Pr*
Robyn Denton, *
◆ EMP: 30 EST: 1999
SQ FT: 11,000
SALES (est): 3.86MM **Privately Held**
Web: www.amphion.biz
SIC: **3499** 5072 7382 5099 Safes and vaults, metal; Security devices, locks; Confinement surveillance systems maintenance and monitoring; Locks and lock sets

### (P-9287)
### GIFTS INTERNATIONAL INC
5620 Villa Mar Pl, Malibu (90265-6320)
PHONE...............................909 854-3977
Mingsong Yao, *Pr*
▲ EMP: 18 EST: 2004
SQ FT: 130,000
SALES (est): 1.71MM **Privately Held**
Web: www.giftsintl-us.com
SIC: **3499** Novelties and giftware, including trophies

### (P-9288)
### INTEGRATED TECH GROUP INC (PA)
11250 Playa Ct, Culver City (90230-6127)
PHONE...............................310 391-7213

Anil Anji, *CEO*
EMP: 20 EST: 2006
SQ FT: 50,000
SALES (est): 46.01MM
SALES (corp-wide): 46.01MM **Privately Held**
Web: www.intetechgroup.com
SIC: **3499** Magnetic shields, metal

### (P-9289)
### INTRA STORAGE SYSTEMS INC
Also Called: Gibo/Kodama Chairs
7100 Honold Cir, Garden Grove (92841-1424)
PHONE...............................714 373-2346
▲ EMP: 30 EST: 1983
SALES (est): 4MM **Privately Held**
Web: www.intrastorage.com
SIC: **3499** 5084 3535 2599 Chair frames, metal; Materials handling machinery; Belt conveyor systems, general industrial use; Factory furniture and fixtures

### (P-9290)
### L A PROPOINT INC
10870 La Tuna Canyon Rd, Sun Valley (91352-2009)
PHONE...............................818 767-6800
Mark Riddlesperger, *Pr*
James Hartman, *
▼ EMP: 30 EST: 2002
SQ FT: 28,000
SALES (est): 4.57MM **Privately Held**
Web: www.lapropoint.com
SIC: **3499** 3449 Metal household articles; Miscellaneous metalwork

### (P-9291)
### LAMINATED SHIM COMPANY INC
1691 California Ave, Corona (92881-3375)
PHONE...............................951 273-3900
EMP: 25 EST: 1982
SALES (est): 3.45MM **Privately Held**
Web: www.laminatedshim.com
SIC: **3499** Shims, metal

### (P-9292)
### MAGNETIC COMPONENT ENGRG LLC (PA)
Also Called: M C E
2830 Lomita Blvd, Torrance (90505-5101)
PHONE...............................310 784-3100
Linda Montgomerie, *CEO*
▲ EMP: 93 EST: 1973
SQ FT: 50,000
SALES (est): 13.38MM
SALES (corp-wide): 13.38MM **Privately Held**
Web: www.mceproducts.com
SIC: **3499** 3677 Magnets, permanent: metallic; Electronic coils and transformers

### (P-9293)
### MATERIAL CONTROL INC
Also Called: Cotterman Company
6901 District Blvd Ste A, Bakersfield (93313-2071)
PHONE...............................661 617-6033
Tony Ortiz, *Brnch Mgr*
EMP: 74
SALES (corp-wide): 49.54MM **Privately Held**
Web: www.cotterman.com
SIC: **3499** Metal ladders
PA: Material Control, Inc.
130 Seltzer Rd
630 892-4274

### (P-9294)
### MOHIN INC
5040 Commercial Cir Ste A, Concord (94520-1250)
P.O. Box 1798 (94565-0179)
PHONE...............................925 798-5572
Kirana Banga, *Pr*
EMP: 24 EST: 2019
SALES (est): 1.14MM **Privately Held**
SIC: **3499** Machine bases, metal

### (P-9295)
### OLDCASTLE INFRASTRUCTURE INC
Also Called: Utility Vault
801 S Pine St, Madera (93637-5219)
PHONE...............................559 674-8093
William Wood, *Mgr*
EMP: 58
SQ FT: 8,000
SALES (corp-wide): 34.95B **Privately Held**
Web: www.oldcastleinfrastructure.com
SIC: **3499** 1799 3444 3443 Safes and vaults, metal; Welding on site; Sheet metalwork; Fabricated plate work (boiler shop)
HQ: Oldcastle Infrastructure, Inc.
7000 Central Pkwy Ste 800
Atlanta GA 30328
770 270-5000

### (P-9296)
### PHIL WOOD & COMPANY
1125 N 7th St # A, San Jose (95112-4428)
P.O. Box 90389 (95109-3389)
PHONE...............................408 298-1540
Peter Enright, *Pr*
EMP: 15 EST: 1971
SQ FT: 6,000
SALES (est): 782.33K **Privately Held**
Web: www.philwood.com
SIC: **3499** Wheels: wheelbarrow, stroller, etc.: disc, stamped metal

### (P-9297)
### PSM INDUSTRIES INC (PA)
14000 Avalon Blvd, Los Angeles (90061-2636)
PHONE...............................888 663-8256
Craig Paullin, *CEO*
Susan Paullin, *
Mary Sherrill, *
▲ EMP: 60 EST: 1956
SALES (est): 23.24MM
SALES (corp-wide): 23.24MM **Privately Held**
Web: www.psmindustries.com
SIC: **3499** Friction material, made from powdered metal

### (P-9298)
### R & K INDUSTRIAL PRODUCTS CO
Also Called: R&K Industrial Wheels
1945 7th St, Richmond (94801-1639)
PHONE...............................510 234-7212
Jorge Ramirez, *Pr*
EMP: 30 EST: 1945
SQ FT: 48,000
SALES (est): 4.95MM **Privately Held**
Web: www.rkwheels.com
SIC: **3499** Wheels: wheelbarrow, stroller, etc.: disc, stamped metal

### (P-9299)
### SPORTSMEN STEEL SAFE FABG CO (PA)
Also Called: Sportsman Steel Gun Safe
6311 N Paramount Blvd, Long Beach (90805-3301)

PHONE..................562 984-0244
Kevin Hand, *CEO*
Chris Cude, *CFO*
▲ **EMP**: 20 **EST**: 1988
**SQ FT**: 30,000
**SALES (est)**: 2.31MM
**SALES (corp-wide)**: 2.31MM **Privately Held**
Web: www.sportsmansteelsafes.com
**SIC**: **3499** 5999 Safes and vaults, metal; Safety supplies and equipment

**(P-9300)**
### STRYKER ENTERPRISES INC
Also Called: Recognition Products Mfg
1358 E San Fernando St, San Jose (95116-2329)
PHONE..................408 295-6300
William J Stryker Junior, *Pr*
▲ **EMP**: 19 **EST**: 1948
**SQ FT**: 12,000
**SALES (est)**: 2.41MM **Privately Held**
Web: www.plaque.com
**SIC**: **3499** Trophies, metal, except silver

**(P-9301)**
### VAULT PRO
13607 Pumice St, Santa Fe Springs (90670-5105)
PHONE..................800 299-6929
Tony Darling, *Prin*
Dick Slater, *CFO*
▲ **EMP**: 17 **EST**: 2013
**SALES (est)**: 2.96MM **Privately Held**
Web: www.vaultprousa.com
**SIC**: **3499** Fabricated metal products, nec

**(P-9302)**
### VIGILANT DRONE DEFENSE INC
1055 W 7th St 33rd Fl, Los Angeles (90017-2577)
PHONE..................424 275-8282
Paul Tremaine, *Pr*
**EMP**: 20 **EST**: 2017
**SALES (est)**: 1.39MM **Privately Held**
Web: www.vigilantdronedefense.com
**SIC**: **3499** 3728 Target drones, for use by ships: metal; Target drones

**(P-9303)**
### WERNER CO
1810 Grogan Ave, Merced (95341-6404)
PHONE..................209 383-3989
Saied Djavadi, *Brnch Mgr*
**EMP**: 24
Web: www.wernerco.com
**SIC**: **3499** Ladders, portable: metal
**HQ**: Werner Co.
555 Pierce Rd Ste 300
Itasca IL 60143

**(P-9304)**
### WESTERN FAB INC
Also Called: Western Fabricators
9823 E Ave, Hesperia (92345-6280)
PHONE..................760 949-1441
Bryon Porter, *Pr*
Mandi Porter, *Sec*
**EMP**: 15 **EST**: 1990
**SQ FT**: 4,800
**SALES (est)**: 2.81MM **Privately Held**
Web: www.westernfabricators.com
**SIC**: **3499** Welding tips, heat resistant: metal

**(P-9305)**
### WOODSIDE INVESTMENT INC
Also Called: Michael and Company
12405 E Brandt Rd, Lockeford (95237-9571)
P.O. Box 1100 (95237-1100)

PHONE..................209 787-8040
Dennis E Wood, *CEO*
Dennis Wood, *
Jung Kamburov, *Prin*
**EMP**: 70 **EST**: 1991
**SQ FT**: 50,000
**SALES (est)**: 9.08MM **Privately Held**
**SIC**: **3499** Aerosol valves, metal

---

## 3511 Turbines And Turbine Generator Sets

**(P-9306)**
### AERO TURBINE INC
6800 Lindbergh St, Stockton (95206-3934)
PHONE..................209 983-1112
Douglas R Clayton, *Pr*
David Mattson, *
C W Bill Dinsley, *Treas*
▲ **EMP**: 60 **EST**: 1978
**SQ FT**: 51,000
**SALES (est)**: 11.62MM **Privately Held**
Web: www.aeroturbine.aero
**SIC**: **3511** Turbines and turbine generator sets

**(P-9307)**
### ALTURDYNE POWER SYSTEMS INC
1405 N Johnson Ave, El Cajon (92020-1615)
PHONE..................619 343-3204
Frank Verbeke, *Pr*
**EMP**: 30 **EST**: 2013
**SQ FT**: 3,000
**SALES (est)**: 4.72MM **Privately Held**
Web: www.alturdyne.com
**SIC**: **3511** 1731 Gas turbine generator set units, complete; Electric power systems contractors

**(P-9308)**
### BABCOCK & WILCOX COMPANY
Also Called: Babcock and Wilcox
710 Airpark Rd, Napa (94558-7518)
PHONE..................707 259-1122
David Pavlik, *Genl Mgr*
**EMP**: 38
**SALES (corp-wide)**: 999.35MM **Publicly Held**
Web: www.babcock.com
**SIC**: **3511** Turbines and turbine generator sets
**HQ**: The Babcock & Wilcox Company
1200 E Market St Ste 650
Akron OH 44305
330 753-4511

**(P-9309)**
### CAPSTONE DSTR SPPORT SVCS CORP (PA)
Also Called: Capstone
16640 Stagg St, Van Nuys (91406-1630)
PHONE..................818 734-5300
Robert C Flexon, *Pr*
Robert C Flexon, *Pr*
Scott Robinson, *Interim Chief Financial Officer*
John J Juric, *CFO*
◆ **EMP**: 121 **EST**: 1988
**SQ FT**: 79,000
**SALES (est)**: 69.64MM **Privately Held**
Web: www.capstonegreenenergy.com
**SIC**: **3511** Turbines and turbine generator sets

**(P-9310)**
### CLIPPER WINDPOWER PLC
Also Called: Clipper Windpower
6305 Carpinteria Ave Ste 300, Carpinteria (93013-2968)
PHONE..................805 690-3275
Michael Keane, *
**EMP**: 740 **EST**: 2005
**SALES (est)**: 66.33MM **Privately Held**
**SIC**: **3511** Turbines and turbine generator sets

**(P-9311)**
### GE RENEWABLES NORTH AMER LLC
13681 Chantico Rd, Tehachapi (93561-8188)
PHONE..................661 823-6423
Gerlad Turk, *Mgr*
**EMP**: 212
**SALES (corp-wide)**: 67.95B **Publicly Held**
**SIC**: **3511** Turbines and turbine generator sets
**HQ**: Ge Renewables North Amer Llc
8301 Scenic Hwy
Pensacola FL 32514
850 474-4011

**(P-9312)**
### LA TURBINE (HQ)
28557 Industry Dr, Valencia (91355-5424)
PHONE..................661 294-8290
John Maskaluk, *CEO*
Danny Mascari, *
Christian Maskaluk, *
Idris Kebir, *
Richard Samson, *
▼ **EMP**: 69 **EST**: 2003
**SQ FT**: 90,000
**SALES (est)**: 19MM **Publicly Held**
Web: www.chartindustries.com
**SIC**: **3511** Turbines and turbine generator sets and parts
**PA**: Chart Industries, Inc.
2200 Arprt Indus Dr Ste 1

**(P-9313)**
### MODULAR WIND ENERGY INC
1709 Apollo Ct, Seal Beach (90740-5617)
PHONE..................562 304-6782
**EMP**: 53 **EST**: 2007
**SALES (est)**: 1.83MM **Privately Held**
Web: www.modwind.com
**SIC**: **3511** Turbines and turbine generator sets

**(P-9314)**
### PRECISION ENGINE CONTROLS CORP (DH)
Also Called: Pecc
11661 Sorrento Valley Rd, San Diego (92121-1083)
P.O. Box 7734 (44306-0734)
PHONE..................858 792-3217
**EMP**: 102 **EST**: 1992
**SALES (est)**: 12.25MM
**SALES (corp-wide)**: 19.93B **Publicly Held**
**SIC**: **3511** Gas turbine generator set units, complete
**HQ**: Meggitt Limited
Ansty Bus.
Coventry W MIDLANDS CV7 9
247 682-6900

**(P-9315)**
### SOLAR TURBINES INCORPORATED (HQ)
2200 Pacific Hwy, San Diego (92101-1773)
P.O. Box 85376 (92186)

PHONE..................619 544-5352
Derrick York, *Pr*
P Browning, *
Robert May, *
◆ **EMP**: 3890 **EST**: 1927
**SQ FT**: 1,080,000
**SALES (est)**: 1.88B
**SALES (corp-wide)**: 67.06B **Publicly Held**
Web: www.solarturbines.com
**SIC**: **3511** Gas turbine generator set units, complete
**PA**: Caterpillar Inc.
5205 N Ocnnor Blvd Ste 10
972 891-7700

**(P-9316)**
### SOLAR TURBINES INCORPORATED
2660 Sarnen St, San Diego (92154-6216)
PHONE..................619 544-5321
**EMP**: 25
**SALES (corp-wide)**: 67.06B **Publicly Held**
Web: www.solarturbines.com
**SIC**: **3511** Gas turbine generator set units, complete
**HQ**: Solar Turbines Incorporated
2200 Pacific Hwy
San Diego CA 92101
619 544-5352

**(P-9317)**
### SOLAR TURBINES INCORPORATED
9330 Sky Park Ct, San Diego (92123-4304)
PHONE..................858 694-6110
Stephen Kanyr, *Prin*
**EMP**: 200
**SALES (corp-wide)**: 67.06B **Publicly Held**
Web: www.solarturbines.com
**SIC**: **3511** Gas turbine generator set units, complete
**HQ**: Solar Turbines Incorporated
2200 Pacific Hwy
San Diego CA 92101
619 544-5352

**(P-9318)**
### SOLAR TURBINES INCORPORATED
9250 Sky Park Ct A, San Diego (92123-4302)
PHONE..................858 715-2060
**EMP**: 52
**SQ FT**: 60,155
**SALES (corp-wide)**: 67.06B **Publicly Held**
Web: www.solarturbines.com
**SIC**: **3511** Gas turbine generator set units, complete
**HQ**: Solar Turbines Incorporated
2200 Pacific Hwy
San Diego CA 92101
619 544-5352

**(P-9319)**
### SOLAR TURBINES INTL CO (DH)
2200 Pacific Hwy, San Diego (92101-1773)
P.O. Box 85376 (92186-5376)
PHONE..................619 544-5000
Thomas Pellette, *CEO*
Steve Gosslin, *Pr*
D M Lehmann, *VP*
D W Esbeck, *VP*
Greg Barr, *VP*
**EMP**: 20 **EST**: 1977
**SALES (est)**: 15.39MM
**SALES (corp-wide)**: 67.06B **Publicly Held**
Web: www.solarturbines.com
**SIC**: **3511** Gas turbine generator set units, complete
**HQ**: Solar Turbines Incorporated
2200 Pacific Hwy

# 3511 - Turbines And Turbine Generator Sets (P-9320)

San Diego CA 92101
619 544-5352

**(P-9320)**
**TURBINE REPAIR SERVICES LLC (PA)**
1838 E Cedar St, Ontario (91761-7763)
PHONE..................................909 947-2256
Victor M Sanchez, *Managing Member*
Dave Meyer, *
Michael Dorrel, *Managing Member**
Cesar Siordia, *
Danny Sanchez, *
**EMP:** 39 **EST:** 2000
**SQ FT:** 12,000
**SALES (est):** 16.3MM **Privately Held**
Web: www.turbinerepairservices.com
**SIC: 3511** Turbines and turbine generator sets

**(P-9321)**
**WEPOWER LLC**
32 Journey Ste 250, Aliso Viejo (92656-5329)
PHONE..................................866 385-9463
Marvin Winkler, *Managing Member*
Howard Makler, *Pr*
Kevin B Donovan, *Dir*
▲ **EMP:** 26 **EST:** 2008
**SALES (est):** 981.66K **Privately Held**
**SIC: 3511** Turbines and turbine generator set units, complete

## 3519 Internal Combustion Engines, Nec

**(P-9322)**
**CUMMINS PACIFIC LLC**
3061 S Riverside Ave, Bloomington (92316-3527)
PHONE..................................909 877-0433
Brandon Daste, *Prin*
**EMP:** 15
**SALES (corp-wide):** 34.06B **Publicly Held**
Web: www.cummins.com
**SIC: 3519** Internal combustion engines, nec
HQ: Cummins Pacific, Llc
1939 Deere Ave
Irvine CA 92606

**(P-9323)**
**CUMMINS PACIFIC LLC**
2755 S Cherry Ave, Fresno (93706-5423)
PHONE..................................559 277-6760
Joseph Ayerza Suzanne, *Prin*
**EMP:** 22
**SALES (corp-wide):** 34.06B **Publicly Held**
Web: www.cummins.com
**SIC: 3519** Internal combustion engines, nec
HQ: Cummins Pacific, Llc
1939 Deere Ave
Irvine CA 92606

**(P-9324)**
**CUMMINS PACIFIC LLC (HQ)**
Also Called: Cummins
1939 Deere Ave, Irvine (92606-4818)
PHONE..................................949 253-6000
**TOLL FREE:** 800
Mark Yragui, *Pr*
▲ **EMP:** 85 **EST:** 2002
**SALES (est):** 87.89MM
**SALES (corp-wide):** 34.06B **Publicly Held**
Web: www.cumminspacific.com
**SIC: 3519** 5063 7538 Internal combustion engines, nec; Generators; General automotive repair shops

PA: Cummins Inc.
500 Jackson St
812 377-5000

**(P-9325)**
**CUMMINS PACIFIC LLC**
Also Called: Cummins
310 N Johnson Ave, El Cajon (92020-3114)
PHONE..................................619 593-3093
Steve Gallant, *Brnch Mgr*
**EMP:** 16
**SALES (corp-wide):** 34.06B **Publicly Held**
Web: www.cummins.com
**SIC: 3519** Internal combustion engines, nec
HQ: Cummins Pacific, Llc
1939 Deere Ave
Irvine CA 92606

**(P-9326)**
**CUMMINS PACIFIC LLC**
Also Called: Cummins
3958 Transport St, Ventura (93003-5128)
PHONE..................................805 644-7281
Dan Elliott, *Mgr*
**EMP:** 16
**SALES (corp-wide):** 34.06B **Publicly Held**
Web: www.cummins.com
**SIC: 3519** 5063 Internal combustion engines, nec; Generators
HQ: Cummins Pacific, Llc
1939 Deere Ave
Irvine CA 92606

**(P-9327)**
**DETROIT DIESEL CORPORATION**
10645 Studebaker Rd 2nd Fl, Downey (90241-3173)
PHONE..................................562 929-7016
Glen Nutting, *VP*
**EMP:** 68
**SALES (corp-wide):** 60.75B **Privately Held**
Web: www.demanddetroit.com
**SIC: 3519** Engines, diesel and semi-diesel or dual-fuel
HQ: Detroit Diesel Corporation
13400 W Outer Dr
Detroit MI 48239
313 592-5000

**(P-9328)**
**GALE BANKS ENGINEERING**
Also Called: Banks Power Products
546 S Duggan Ave, Azusa (91702-5136)
PHONE..................................626 969-9600
Gale C Banks Iii, *Pr*
Vicki L Banks, *
▲ **EMP:** 195 **EST:** 1970
**SQ FT:** 121,000
**SALES (est):** 22.57MM **Privately Held**
Web: www.bankspower.com
**SIC: 3519** 3714 Parts and accessories, internal combustion engines; Motor vehicle parts and accessories

**(P-9329)**
**PACMET AEROSPACE LLC**
Also Called: Pacmet Aerospace
224 Glider Cir, Corona (92878-5033)
PHONE..................................909 218-8889
David Janes, *CEO*
David A Janes Junior, *Managing Member*
◆ **EMP:** 76 **EST:** 2005
**SQ FT:** 45,000
**SALES (est):** 9.77MM **Privately Held**
Web: www.pacmetaerospace.com
**SIC: 3519** Jet propulsion engines

**(P-9330)**
**SOUTHWEST PRODUCTS CORPORATION**
2875 Cherry Ave, Signal Hill (90755-1908)
PHONE..................................360 887-7400
Jason Hair, *Brnch Mgr*
**EMP:** 15
**SALES (corp-wide):** 18.16MM **Privately Held**
Web: www.assemblysystems.com
**SIC: 3519** Diesel engine rebuilding
HQ: Southwest Products Corporation
11690 N 132nd Ave
Surprise AZ 85379
602 269-3581

**(P-9331)**
**SOUTHWEST PRODUCTS CORPORATION**
85 Enterprise Ct Ste B, Galt (95632-8162)
PHONE..................................209 745-6000
Patrick Cofild, *Brnch Mgr*
**EMP:** 35
**SALES (corp-wide):** 18.16MM **Privately Held**
Web: www.assemblysystems.com
**SIC: 3519** Diesel engine rebuilding
HQ: Southwest Products Corporation
11690 N 132nd Ave
Surprise AZ 85379
602 269-3581

**(P-9332)**
**TRACY INDUSTRIES INC**
Also Called: Genuine Parts Distributors
3200 E Guasti Rd Ste 100, Ontario (91761-8661)
P.O. Box 1260 (91762-0260)
PHONE..................................562 692-9034
Timothy Engvall, *CEO*
David Rosenberger, *
Erma Jean Tracy, *
Timothy Engvall, *Treas*
▲ **EMP:** 216 **EST:** 1946
**SALES (est):** 18.84MM **Privately Held**
**SIC: 3519** 7538 Internal combustion engines, nec; Engine rebuilding: automotive

**(P-9333)**
**TRANSONIC COMBUSTION INC**
461 Calle San Pablo, Camarillo (93012-8506)
PHONE..................................805 465-5145
Wolfgang Bullmer, *Pr*
Timothy Noonan, *
Mike Cheiky, *
**EMP:** 40 **EST:** 2006
**SALES (est):** 7.15MM **Privately Held**
Web: www.tscombustion.com
**SIC: 3519** Internal combustion engines, nec

## 3523 Farm Machinery And Equipment

**(P-9334)**
**AG INDUSTRIAL MFG INC**
Also Called: Aim
110 S Beckman Rd, Lodi (95240-3102)
P.O. Box 53 (95241-0053)
PHONE..................................209 369-1994
**EMP:** 35 **EST:** 1979
**SALES (est):** 2.99MM **Privately Held**
Web: www.agindustrialmanufacturing.com
**SIC: 3523** Harvesters, fruit, vegetable, tobacco, etc.

**(P-9335)**
**AGRIFIM IRRIGATION PDTS INC**
Also Called: Nds
2855 S East Ave, Fresno (93725-1908)
PHONE..................................559 443-6680

Rael Sacks, *Pr*
▲ **EMP:** 15 **EST:** 1985
**SQ FT:** 15,200
**SALES (est):** 3.9MM **Privately Held**
**SIC: 3523** Farm machinery and equipment
HQ: National Diversified Sales, Inc.
21300 Vctory Blvd Ste 215
Woodland Hills CA 91367
559 562-9888

**(P-9336)**
**ALBERS MFG CO INC (PA)**
Also Called: Albers Dairy Equipment. Inc
14323 Albers Way, Chino (91710-1134)
PHONE..................................909 597-5537
Teo Albers Junior, *Pr*
◆ **EMP:** 21 **EST:** 1949
**SQ FT:** 10,000
**SALES (est):** 5.22MM
**SALES (corp-wide):** 5.22MM **Privately Held**
**SIC: 3523** Barn stanchions and standards

**(P-9337)**
**AMARILLO WIND MACHINE LLC**
20513 Avenue 256, Exeter (93221-9656)
P.O. Box 96809 (60693-6809)
PHONE..................................559 592-4256
Steven Chaloupka, *Pr*
**EMP:** 18 **EST:** 1989
**SQ FT:** 12,000
**SALES (est):** 2.79MM
**SALES (corp-wide):** 364.48B **Publicly Held**
Web: www.amarillowind.com
**SIC: 3523** 7699 Farm machinery and equipment; Agricultural equipment repair services
HQ: Amarillo Gear Company Llc
2401 W Sundown Ln
Amarillo TX 79118
806 622-1273

**(P-9338)**
**AMERICAN INTERNATIONAL MFG CO**
Also Called: Aim Mail Centers
1230 Fortna Ave, Woodland (95776-5905)
PHONE..................................530 666-2446
John Bridges, *CEO*
David Neilson, *
Chistophre Neilson, *
**EMP:** 29 **EST:** 1973
**SQ FT:** 23,000
**SALES (est):** 4.85MM **Privately Held**
Web: www.aimfab.com
**SIC: 3523** 3556 Farm machinery and equipment; Food products machinery

**(P-9339)**
**AWETA-AUTOLINE INC (DH)**
4516 E Citron, Fresno (93725-9861)
PHONE..................................559 244-8340
Otto Vink, *CEO*
Art Lopez, *
▲ **EMP:** 45 **EST:** 1995
**SQ FT:** 20,000
**SALES (est):** 5.13MM **Privately Held**
**SIC: 3523** Grading, cleaning, sorting machines, fruit, grain, vegetable
HQ: Aweta Holding B.V.
Kwakelweg 2
Pijnacker ZH 2641
886688000

**(P-9340)**
**B W IMPLEMENT CO**
288 W Front St, Buttonwillow (93206)
P.O. Box 758 (93206-0758)
PHONE..................................661 764-5254

## 3523 - Farm Machinery And Equipment (P-9362)

John C Blair, *Pr*
Alene Parsons, *Sec*
Julien Parsons, *Treas*
**EMP:** 22 **EST:** 1948
**SQ FT:** 85,000
**SALES (est):** 2.58MM **Privately Held**
**Web:** www.bwimp.com
**SIC: 3523** 5083 5999   Tractors, farm; Farm implements; Farm machinery, nec

### (P-9341)
### BIANCHI ORCHARD SYSTEMS INC
Also Called: Orchard Equipment Mfg
1221 Independence Pl, Gridley (95948-9341)
P.O. Box 743  (96073-0743)
**PHONE**.................................530 846-5625
◆ **EMP:** 130
**SIC: 3523**   Farm machinery and equipment

### (P-9342)
### BLUE RIVER TECHNOLOGY INC
3303 Scott Blvd, Santa Clara  (95054-3102)
**PHONE**.................................408 733-2583
Jorge Heraud, *CEO*
Lee Redden, *
Scott Kimmel, *
▲ **EMP:** 70 **EST:** 2011
**SALES (est):** 24.96MM
**SALES (corp-wide):** 61.25B **Publicly Held**
**Web:** www.bluerivertechnology.com
**SIC: 3523**   Farm machinery and equipment
**PA:** Deere & Company
   1 John Deere Pl
   309 765-8000

### (P-9343)
### BRITZ FERTILIZERS INC
12498 11th Ave, Hanford  (93230-9523)
**PHONE**.................................559 582-0942
Keith Roberts, *Mgr*
**EMP:** 49
**SALES (corp-wide):** 35.15MM **Privately Held**
**SIC: 3523** 2873   Spreaders, fertilizer; Nitrogenous fertilizers
**HQ:** Britz Fertilizers Inc.
   3265 W Figarden Dr
   Fresno CA 93711
   559 448-8000

### (P-9344)
### CAGECO INC
16225 Beaver Rd, Adelanto  (92301-3908)
**PHONE**.................................800 605-4859
Mike Alexander, *Pr*
**EMP:** 38 **EST:** 2012
**SALES (est):** 5.65MM **Privately Held**
**Web:** www.cagecoinc.com
**SIC: 3523**   Barn, silo, poultry, dairy, and livestock machinery

### (P-9345)
### COE ORCHARD EQUIPMENT INC
Also Called: Coe
3453 Riviera Rd, Live Oak  (95953-9713)
**PHONE**.................................530 695-5121
Lyman Coe, *CEO*
Lois A Coe, *
▲ **EMP:** 570 **EST:** 1970
**SQ FT:** 45,000
**SALES (est):** 21.16MM
**SALES (corp-wide):** 67.29MM **Privately Held**
**Web:** www.coeshakers.com
**SIC: 3523**   Harvesters, fruit, vegetable, tobacco, etc.
**PA:** Flory Industries
   4737 Toomes Rd
   209 545-1167

### (P-9346)
### D&M MANUFACTURING CO  LLC
5400 S Villa Ave, Fresno  (93725-9798)
P.O. Box 308  (93625-0308)
**PHONE**.................................559 834-4668
Judy Tolentino, *Owner*
**EMP:** 18 **EST:** 1987
**SQ FT:** 10,000
**SALES (est):** 4.06MM **Privately Held**
**Web:** www.dnmmfgco.com
**SIC: 3523**   Fertilizing, spraying, dusting, and irrigation machinery

### (P-9347)
### D-K-P  INC
275 N Marks Ave, Fresno  (93706-1102)
**PHONE**.................................559 266-2695
Douglas R King, *Pr*
**EMP:** 15 **EST:** 1969
**SQ FT:** 12,000
**SALES (est):** 1.84MM
**SALES (corp-wide):** 5.14MM **Privately Held**
**SIC: 3523**   Cotton pickers and strippers
**PA:** R. M. King Company Exports
   315 N Marks Ave
   559 266-0258

### (P-9348)
### DAVIS MACHINE SHOP  INC
Also Called: Meridian Supply
15805 Central St, Meridian  (95957-9517)
**PHONE**.................................530 696-2577
Clifton Davis, *CEO*
Thomas Davis, *
**EMP:** 34 **EST:** 1913
**SQ FT:** 5,000
**SALES (est):** 3.97MM **Privately Held**
**Web:** www.davismachineshop.net
**SIC: 3523** 3599 5251   Farm machinery and equipment; Machine shop, jobbing and repair; Hardware stores

### (P-9349)
### DIG CORPORATION
1210 Activity Dr, Vista  (92081-8510)
**PHONE**.................................760 727-0914
David Levy, *Pr*
Racquell Bibens, *
Greg Smith, *
Duy Johnson, *
◆ **EMP:** 43 **EST:** 1982
**SQ FT:** 45,000
**SALES (est):** 9.39MM **Privately Held**
**Web:** www.digcorp.com
**SIC: 3523**   Irrigation equipment, self-propelled

### (P-9350)
### DOMRIES ENTERPRISES  INC
12281 Road 29, Madera  (93638-8332)
**PHONE**.................................559 485-4306
Candyce L Domries, *CEO*
Lorraine Domries, *VP*
▲ **EMP:** 35 **EST:** 1924
**SQ FT:** 65,000
**SALES (est):** 8.88MM **Privately Held**
**Web:** www.domries.com
**SIC: 3523** 5084   Soil preparation machinery, except turf and grounds; Industrial machinery and equipment

### (P-9351)
### DOWDYS SALES AND SERVICES INC
15185 Avenue 224, Tulare  (93274-9305)
**PHONE**.................................559 688-6973
Brad Dowdy, *Pr*
Melinda Dowdy, *Sec*
**EMP:** 15 **EST:** 1987
**SALES (est):** 2.44MM **Privately Held**
**Web:** www.dowdys.com
**SIC: 3523**   Farm machinery and equipment

### (P-9352)
### DRTS ENTERPRISES LTD
Also Called: Drip Research Technology Svcs
7979 Stromesa Ct Ste A, San Diego (92126-4329)
**PHONE**.................................858 270-7244
▲ **EMP:** 20
**Web:** www.drts.com
**SIC: 3523**   Irrigation equipment, self-propelled

### (P-9353)
### EXETER MERCANTILE COMPANY
Also Called: Ace Hardware
258 E Pine St, Exeter  (93221-1750)
P.O. Box 67  (93221-0067)
**PHONE**.................................559 592-2121
Robert G Schelling, *Pr*
Brian Schelling, *VP*
Sidney Schelling Junior, *Sec*
▲ **EMP:** 19 **EST:** 1916
**SQ FT:** 22,000
**SALES (est):** 2.22MM **Privately Held**
**Web:** www.exetermercantile.com
**SIC: 3523** 3537 5072 5251   Tractors, farm; Industrial trucks and tractors; Hardware; Hardware stores

### (P-9354)
### FLORY INDUSTRIES (PA)
4737 Toomes Rd, Salida  (95368)
P.O. Box P O Box 908  (95368)
**PHONE**.................................209 545-1167
Jason Flory, *Ch*
Mike Eger, *
**EMP:** 80 **EST:** 1904
**SQ FT:** 12,000
**SALES (est):** 67.29MM
**SALES (corp-wide):** 67.29MM **Privately Held**
**Web:** www.goflory.com
**SIC: 3523** 5083 3441 0173   Harvesters, fruit, vegetable, tobacco, etc.; Farm equipment parts and supplies; Fabricated structural metal; Tree nuts

### (P-9355)
### GREENBROZ INC
955 Vernon Way, El Cajon  (92020-1832)
**PHONE**.................................844 379-8746
Cullen Raichart, *CEO*
**EMP:** 16 **EST:** 2012
**SQ FT:** 7,000
**SALES (est):** 2.25MM **Privately Held**
**Web:** www.greenbroz.com
**SIC: 3523**   Farm machinery and equipment

### (P-9356)
### GUSS AUTOMATION LLC
2545 Simpson St, Kingsburg  (93631-9501)
**PHONE**.................................559 897-0245
Dave Crinklaw, *Managing Member*
**EMP:** 15 **EST:** 2019
**SALES (est):** 2.66MM **Privately Held**
**Web:** www.gussag.com
**SIC: 3523**   Sprayers and spraying machines, agricultural

### (P-9357)
### HUNTER INDUSTRIES INCORPORATED
3950 N Chestnut Ave Ste 101, Fresno (93726-4728)
**PHONE**.................................559 347-0816
Ken Withwerow, *Genl Mgr*
**EMP:** 20
**Web:** www.hunterindustries.com
**SIC: 3523**   Irrigation equipment, self-propelled
**PA:** Hunter Industries Incorporated
   1940 Diamond St

### (P-9358)
### HYDROPOINT DATA SYSTEMS INC
Also Called: Hydropoint
1720 Corporate Cir, Petaluma (94954-6924)
**PHONE**.................................707 769-9696
Chris Spain, *CEO*
Paul Ciandrini, *Pr*
▲ **EMP:** 50 **EST:** 2002
**SQ FT:** 18,000
**SALES (est):** 15.5MM **Privately Held**
**Web:** www.hydropoint.com
**SIC: 3523**   Irrigation equipment, self-propelled

### (P-9359)
### INTERNATIONAL HORT TECH LLC
Also Called: Interntional Horticulture Tech
150 Acquistapace Rd, Hollister (95023-9350)
P.O. Box 1035  (95024-1035)
**PHONE**.................................831 637-1800
Gary R Hartman, *Managing Member*
▲ **EMP:** 25 **EST:** 1998
**SQ FT:** 60,000
**SALES (est):** 2.44MM **Privately Held**
**Web:** www.ihort.com
**SIC: 3523**   Farm machinery and equipment

### (P-9360)
### INVELOP INC
Also Called: Double K Industries
9711 Mason Ave, Chatsworth  (91311-5208)
**PHONE**.................................818 772-2887
Gregory S Crisp, *Pr*
◆ **EMP:** 30 **EST:** 1982
**SQ FT:** 20,700
**SALES (est):** 827.43K **Privately Held**
**Web:** www.bootguard.com
**SIC: 3523** 3999 3841   Clippers, for animal use: hand or electric; Pet supplies; Veterinarians' instruments and apparatus

### (P-9361)
### IRRITEC USA  INC
1420 N Irritec Way, Fresno  (93703-4432)
**PHONE**.................................559 275-8825
Mitchell Martin, *CEO*
◆ **EMP:** 56 **EST:** 2009
**SALES (est):** 13.93MM **Privately Held**
**Web:** www.irritec.com
**SIC: 3523**   Irrigation equipment, self-propelled

### (P-9362)
### JACKRABBIT
Also Called: Dakota AG Welding
1318 Dakota Ave, Modesto  (95358-9505)
**PHONE**.................................209 521-9325
Earl Anderson, *Brnch Mgr*
**EMP:** 15
**SALES (corp-wide):** 9.01MM **Privately Held**
**Web:** www.jackrabbitequipment.com
**SIC: 3523** 7692   Farm machinery and equipment; Welding repair
**PA:** Jackrabbit
   471 Industrial Ave
   209 599-6118

---

(PA)=Parent Co  (HQ)=Headquarters
✪ = New Business established in last 2 years

## 3523 - Farm Machinery And Equipment (P-9363)

**(P-9363)**
**JACKRABBIT (PA)**
Also Called: Dakota AG Welding
471 Industrial Ave, Ripon (95366-2768)
PHONE.....................209 599-6118
Bill Kirkendall, CEO
▲ EMP: 60 EST: 1983
SQ FT: 15,000
SALES (est): 9.01MM
SALES (corp-wide): 9.01MM Privately Held
Web: www.jackrabbitequipment.com
SIC: 3523 Harvesters, fruit, vegetable, tobacco, etc.

**(P-9364)**
**KAMPER FABRICATION INC**
20107 N Ripon Rd, Ripon (95366-9758)
P.O. Box 177 (95366-0177)
PHONE.....................209 599-7137
Richard Kamper, Pr
Brenda Kamper, Sec
EMP: 23 EST: 1983
SQ FT: 24,800
SALES (est): 7.07MM Privately Held
Web: www.kamperfab.com
SIC: 3523 Farm machinery and equipment

**(P-9365)**
**KINGSBURG CULTIVATOR INC**
40190 Road 36, Kingsburg (93631-9621)
PHONE.....................559 897-3662
Clint Erling, Pr
Allen Scheidt, VP
EMP: 23 EST: 1954
SQ FT: 1,400
SALES (est): 2.88MM Privately Held
Web: www.kcimfg.com
SIC: 3523 Harvesters, fruit, vegetable, tobacco, etc.

**(P-9366)**
**KIRBY MANUFACTURING INC (PA)**
484 S Hwy 59, Merced (95341-6541)
P.O. Box 989 (95341-0989)
PHONE.....................209 723-0778
Richard M Kirby, Pr
Madeleine Kirby Davenport, *
William T Kirby, *
Kelly Sellers, *
◆ EMP: 68 EST: 1970
SQ FT: 45,000
SALES (est): 12.87MM
SALES (corp-wide): 12.87MM Privately Held
Web: www.kirbymanufacturing.com
SIC: 3523 Cattle feeding, handling, and watering equipment

**(P-9367)**
**LAIRD MFG LLC (PA)**
Also Called: Laird Manufacturing
531 S State Highway 59, Merced (95341-6925)
P.O. Box 1053 (95341-1053)
PHONE.....................209 722-4145
Issac Isako, *
◆ EMP: 40 EST: 1937
SQ FT: 15,000
SALES (est): 11.61MM
SALES (corp-wide): 11.61MM Privately Held
Web: www.lairdmanufacturing.com
SIC: 3523 7692 Cattle feeding, handling, and watering equipment; Welding repair

**(P-9368)**
**LIMITED ACCESS UNLIMITED INC**
Also Called: Pacific Drilling Co.
5220 Anna Ave Ste A, San Diego (92110-4019)
PHONE.....................619 294-3682
Tod Clark, CEO
Craig Roberts, VP
EMP: 16 EST: 1986
SALES (est): 2MM Privately Held
Web: www.pacdrill.com
SIC: 3523 1781 Soil sampling machines; Water well drilling

**(P-9369)**
**MARIE EDWARD VINEYARDS INC**
6901 E Brundage Ln, Bakersfield (93307-3057)
PHONE.....................661 363-5038
Matthew E Brock, Pr
EMP: 35 EST: 1988
SALES (est): 3.35MM Privately Held
Web: www.brockstrailersinc.com
SIC: 3523 5013 7539 5511 Trailers and wagons, farm; Trailer parts and accessories; Trailer repair; Trucks, tractors, and trailers: new and used

**(P-9370)**
**MIDLAND TRACTOR COMPANY**
1901 W Cleveland Ave, Madera (93637-8705)
P.O. Box 1227 (93639-1227)
PHONE.....................559 674-8757
EMP: 52 EST: 1969
SALES (est): 35MM Privately Held
Web: www.midlandtractor.com
SIC: 3523 Farm machinery and equipment

**(P-9371)**
**MINERAL EARTH SCIENCES LLC**
100 Mayfield Ave, Mountain View (94043-4122)
PHONE.....................650 532-9590
Elliott Grant, CEO
EMP: 80
SALES (est): 867.7K Privately Held
SIC: 3523 7371 Farm machinery and equipment; Computer software development and applications

**(P-9372)**
**NIKKEL IRON WORKS CORPORATION**
17045 S Central Valley Hwy, Shafter (93263-2704)
P.O. Box 1597 (93263-1597)
PHONE.....................661 746-4904
Andrew Cummings, Pr
Shirley Cummings, Sec
EMP: 17 EST: 1924
SQ FT: 26,000
SALES (est): 3.65MM Privately Held
Web: www.nikkelironworks.com
SIC: 3523 Farm machinery and equipment

**(P-9373)**
**OLSON IRRIGATION SYSTEMS**
Also Called: Olson Industrial Systems
10910 Wheatlands Ave Ste A, Santee (92071-2867)
P.O. Box 711570 (92072-1570)
PHONE.....................619 562-3100
Donald Olson, Pr
Kathleen Baldwin, *
▲ EMP: 28 EST: 1976
SQ FT: 17,000
SALES (est): 2.24MM Publicly Held
SIC: 3523 Sprayers and spraying machines, agricultural
HQ: Evoqua Water Technologies Llc
210 6th Ave Ste 3300
Pittsburgh PA 15222
724 772-0044

**(P-9374)**
**ORCHARD MACHINERY CORP DISC (PA)**
Also Called: Orchard Harvest
2700 Colusa Hwy, Yuba City (95993-8927)
PHONE.....................530 673-2822
Don Mayo, CEO
Brian Anderson, *
Joe Martinez, *
Greg Kriss, *
Tom Thomas, *
▲ EMP: 60 EST: 1961
SQ FT: 70,000
SALES (est): 23.5MM
SALES (corp-wide): 23.5MM Privately Held
Web: www.shakermaker.com
SIC: 3523 Shakers, tree: nuts, fruits, etc.

**(P-9375)**
**PELLENC AMERICA INC (DH)**
3171 Guerneville Rd, Santa Rosa (95401-4028)
PHONE.....................707 568-7286
Marc Paisnel, Pr
Roger Pellenc, *
J P Pettavino, *
J L Guigues, *
▲ EMP: 24 EST: 1996
SQ FT: 50,000
SALES (est): 5.85MM
SALES (corp-wide): 2.67MM Privately Held
Web: www.pellencus.com
SIC: 3523 Farm machinery and equipment
HQ: Pellenc
Quartier Notre Dames Des Anges
Pertuis PAC 84120
490094700

**(P-9376)**
**PERRYS CUSTOM CHOPPING LLC**
21365 Williams Ave, Hilmar (95324-9602)
PHONE.....................209 667-8777
Jeff Perry, Prin
EMP: 15 EST: 2003
SALES (est): 2.62MM Privately Held
SIC: 3523 Harvesters, fruit, vegetable, tobacco, etc.

**(P-9377)**
**RAIN BIRD CORPORATION**
9491 Ridgehaven Ct, San Diego (92123-5601)
PHONE.....................619 674-4068
Eileen Collins, Mgr
EMP: 41
SALES (corp-wide): 433.78MM Privately Held
Web: www.rainbird.com
SIC: 3523 Farm machinery and equipment
PA: Rain Bird Corporation
970 W Sierra Madre Ave
626 812-3400

**(P-9378)**
**RAMSAY HIGHLANDER INC**
Also Called: Highlander Harvesting Aid
45 Gonzales River Rd, Gonzales (93926)
PHONE.....................831 675-3453
Frank Maconachy, Pr
David Offerdahl, VP
Chris Garnett, VP
Michele Maconachy, Sec
▲ EMP: 38 EST: 1964
SQ FT: 34,000
SALES (est): 4.65MM Privately Held
Web: www.ramsayhighlander.com
SIC: 3523 5999 7692 7699 Farm machinery and equipment; Farm machinery, nec; Welding repair; Hydraulic equipment repair

**(P-9379)**
**RANCH SYSTEMS INC**
Also Called: Manufacturer
865 Sweetser Ave Ste A, Novato (94945-2490)
PHONE.....................415 884-2770
Jacob Christfort, CEO
EMP: 16 EST: 2005
SALES (est): 1.67MM Privately Held
Web: www.ranchsystems.com
SIC: 3523 Irrigation equipment, self-propelled

**(P-9380)**
**RIVULIS IRRIGATION INC (HQ)**
Also Called: John Deere Water
7545 Carroll Rd, San Diego (92121-2401)
PHONE.....................858 578-1860
◆ EMP: 20 EST: 1977
SALES (est): 97.26MM Privately Held
Web: www.rivulis.com
SIC: 3523 Fertilizing, spraying, dusting, and irrigation machinery
PA: Rivulis Irrigation Ltd
98 Alon Yigal

**(P-9381)**
**SIGNATURE CONTROL SYSTEMS**
16485 Laguna Canyon Rd Ste 130, Irvine (92618-3848)
PHONE.....................949 580-3640
Brian Smith, Pr
◆ EMP: 100 EST: 2000
SQ FT: 7,000
SALES (est): 5.11MM Privately Held
Web: www.signaturecontrolsystems.com
SIC: 3523 Irrigation equipment, self-propelled

**(P-9382)**
**SPECIALIZED DAIRY SERVICE INC**
Also Called: S D S
1710 E Philadelphia St, Ontario (91761-7705)
PHONE.....................909 923-3420
Joe T Trujillo, CEO
Joe Trujillo, VP
EMP: 22 EST: 2004
SQ FT: 25,000
SALES (est): 4.75MM Privately Held
Web: www.sdsdairy.com
SIC: 3523 3556 5083 Dairy equipment (farm), nec; Dairy and milk machinery; Dairy machinery and equipment

**(P-9383)**
**SPRAYING DEVICES INC**
Also Called: S D I
447 E Caldwell Ave, Visalia (93277-7609)
P.O. Box 3107 (93278-3107)
PHONE.....................559 734-5555
William S Bennet Ii, Pr
Denise Bennett, VP
EMP: 17 EST: 1982
SQ FT: 16,000
SALES (est): 2.48MM Privately Held
Web: www.sprayingdevices.com
SIC: 3523 Farm machinery and equipment

## PRODUCTS & SERVICES SECTION
## 3531 - Construction Machinery (P-9406)

**(P-9384)**
**STORM INDUSTRIES INC (PA)**
Also Called: Storm
970 W 190th St, Torrance  (90502-1000)
PHONE.................................310 534-5232
Dale R Philippi, *CEO*
Guy E Marge, *
Georgia Claessens, *
Jonathan Corbin, *
▲ **EMP:** 100 **EST:** 1977
**SALES (est):** 44.12MM
**SALES (corp-wide):** 44.12MM **Privately Held**
Web: www.stormind.com
**SIC: 3523** 6552  Irrigation equipment, self-propelled; Subdividers and developers, nec

**(P-9385)**
**STOUT INDUSTRIAL TECH INC**
90 Monterey Salinas Hwy, Salinas (93908-8976)
PHONE.................................831 455-1004
Scott Grabau, *CEO*
**EMP:** 17 **EST:** 2019
**SALES (est):** 4.42MM **Privately Held**
Web: www.stout.ai
**SIC: 3523** 7371  Farm machinery and equipment; Computer software development and applications

**(P-9386)**
**TORO COMPANY**
1588 N Marshall Ave, El Cajon (92020-1523)
PHONE.................................619 562-2950
Timothy Young, *Mgr*
**EMP:** 132
**SQ FT:** 86,578
**SALES (corp-wide):** 4.55B **Publicly Held**
Web: www.thetorocompany.com
**SIC: 3523**  Irrigation equipment, self-propelled
**PA:** The Toro Company
   8111 Lyndale Ave S
   952 888-8201

**(P-9387)**
**TORO COMPANY**
5825 Jasmine St, Riverside  (92504-1183)
P.O. Box 489  (92502-0489)
PHONE.................................951 688-9221
Kendrick Melrose, *Mgr*
**EMP:** 197
**SALES (corp-wide):** 4.55B **Publicly Held**
Web: www.thetorocompany.com
**SIC: 3523**  Irrigation equipment, self-propelled
**PA:** The Toro Company
   8111 Lyndale Ave S
   952 888-8201

**(P-9388)**
**VAL PLASTIC USA L L C**
4570 Eucalyptus Ave Ste C, Chino (91710-9200)
PHONE.................................909 390-9600
Dablu Kundu, *Genl Mgr*
▲ **EMP:** 15 **EST:** 1992
**SQ FT:** 11,000
**SALES (est):** 2.22MM **Privately Held**
Web: www.valplasticusa.com
**SIC: 3523**  Fertilizing, spraying, dusting, and irrigation machinery

**(P-9389)**
**VALLEY FABRICATION INC**
1056 Pellet Ave, Salinas (93901-4359)
P.O. Box 3618 (93912-3618)
PHONE.................................831 757-5151
George Glen Heffington, *CEO*
Peter De Groot, *
▲ **EMP:** 60 **EST:** 1988

**SQ FT:** 86,000
**SALES (est):** 10.46MM **Privately Held**
Web: www.valleyfabrication.com
**SIC: 3523** 7699 5013  Farm machinery and equipment; Farm machinery repair; Truck parts and accessories

**(P-9390)**
**VALMETAL TULARE INC**
2955 S K St, Tulare  (93274-7164)
PHONE.................................559 685-0340
▲ **EMP:** 75 **EST:** 1979
**SALES (est):** 9.75MM
**SALES (corp-wide):** 22.2MM **Privately Held**
Web: www.usfarmsystems.com
**SIC: 3523** 7699  Dairy equipment (farm), nec; Agricultural equipment repair services
**PA:** Valmetal Inc
   230 Boul Industriel
   819 395-4282

**(P-9391)**
**VERDANT ROBOTICS INC**
3167 Corporate Pl, Hayward  (94545-3915)
PHONE.................................202 510-5040
Gerardo Adame, *CFO*
**EMP:** 25 **EST:** 2019
**SALES (est):** 5MM **Privately Held**
Web: www.verdantrobotics.com
**SIC: 3523**  Farm machinery and equipment

**(P-9392)**
**WARREN & BAERG MFG INC**
39950 Road 108, Dinuba  (93618-9518)
PHONE.................................559 591-6790
Robert Baerg, *CEO*
Robert L Baerg, *
Randy R Baerg, *
▲ **EMP:** 30 **EST:** 1968
**SQ FT:** 15,000
**SALES (est):** 5.24MM **Privately Held**
Web: www.warrenbaerg.com
**SIC: 3523**  Planting, haying, harvesting, and processing machinery

**(P-9393)**
**WASCO HARDFACING CO**
4585 E Citron Ave, Fresno  (93725)
P.O. Box 2395  (93745)
PHONE.................................559 485-5860
Robin R Messick, *CEO*
▲ **EMP:** 60 **EST:** 1952
**SQ FT:** 20,000
**SALES (est):** 9.68MM **Privately Held**
Web: www.wascohardfacing.com
**SIC: 3523**  Farm machinery and equipment

**(P-9394)**
**WEISS-MCNAIR LLC (DH)**
100 Loren Ave, Chico (95928-7450)
PHONE.................................530 891-6214
Larry Demmer, *Pr*
Glenn Stanley, *
Lawrence Demmer, *
▲ **EMP:** 80 **EST:** 1974
**SQ FT:** 32,000
**SALES (est):** 24.51MM **Privately Held**
Web: www.weissmcnair.com
**SIC: 3523**  Farm machinery and equipment
**HQ:** Gould Paper Corporation
   360 Madison Ave 9th Fl
   New York NY 10017
   212 301-0000

**(P-9395)**
**WELDCRAFT INDUSTRIES INC**
18794 Avenue 96, Terra Bella (93270-9630)
P.O. Box 11104 (93270-1104)

PHONE.................................559 784-4322
Gerald R Micke, *Pr*
Dixie L Micke, *VP*
▲ **EMP:** 18 **EST:** 1972
**SALES (est):** 2.32MM **Privately Held**
Web: www.weldcraftindustries.com
**SIC: 3523** 5191  Harvesters, fruit, vegetable, tobacco, etc.; Farm supplies

**(P-9396)**
**WILCOX BROTHERS INC**
Also Called: Wilcox AG Products
14180 State Highway 160, Walnut Grove (95690-9741)
P.O. Box 70  (95690-0070)
PHONE.................................916 776-1784
Alan Wilcox, *Pr*
Bruce Wilcox, *
▲ **EMP:** 57 **EST:** 1983
**SQ FT:** 10,800
**SALES (est):** 6.11MM **Privately Held**
**SIC: 3523**  Farm machinery and equipment

## 3524 Lawn And Garden Equipment

**(P-9397)**
**MCLANE MANUFACTURING INC**
6814 Foster Bridge Blvd, Bell Gardens (90201-2032)
PHONE.................................562 633-8158
Elmer E Malchow, *Ch Bd*
Ronald Mc Lane, *
Olivia Osorio, *
▲ **EMP:** 65 **EST:** 1942
**SALES (est):** 3.59MM **Privately Held**
Web: www.mclaneedgers.com
**SIC: 3524**  Lawnmowers, residential: hand or power

**(P-9398)**
**POWER - TRIM CO**
6060 Phyllis Dr, Cypress  (90630-5243)
P.O. Box 18380  (92623)
PHONE.................................714 523-8560
James O Dykes, *CEO*
James O Dykes, *Pr*
Philip Shearer, *VP*
Barbara Dykes, *Sec*
▼ **EMP:** 15 **EST:** 1953
**SALES (est):** 577.15K **Privately Held**
Web: www.powertrim.com
**SIC: 3524** 5083  Edgers, lawn; Lawn and garden machinery and equipment

**(P-9399)**
**R&M SUPPLY INC**
420 Harley Knox Blvd, Perris  (92571-7566)
PHONE.................................951 552-9860
◆ **EMP:** 100
Web: www.randmsupply.com
**SIC: 3524**  Lawn and garden equipment

**(P-9400)**
**SCOTTS TEMECULA OPERATIONS LLC (DH)**
42375 Remington Ave, Temecula (92590-2512)
PHONE.................................951 719-1700
Jim Hagedorn, *Ch*
Barry Sanders, *Pr*
▲ **EMP:** 41 **EST:** 2001
**SQ FT:** 400,000
**SALES (est):** 39.85MM
**SALES (corp-wide):** 3.55B **Publicly Held**
**SIC: 3524**  Lawn and garden equipment
**HQ:** The Scotts Company Llc
   14111 Scottslawn Rd
   Marysville OH 43040
   937 644-0011

**(P-9401)**
**TRU-CUT INC**
141 E 157th St, Gardena  (90248-2508)
P.O. Box 642475  (90064-8137)
PHONE.................................310 630-0422
Nabi Merchant, *CEO*
▲ **EMP:** 35 **EST:** 1953
**SQ FT:** 28,620
**SALES (est):** 2.1MM **Privately Held**
Web: www.trucutmower.com
**SIC: 3524** 5083  Lawn and garden mowers and accessories; Lawn and garden machinery and equipment

**(P-9402)**
**WESTERN CACTUS GROWERS INC**
1860 Monte Vista Dr, Vista  (92084-7124)
P.O. Box 2018  (92085-2018)
PHONE.................................760 726-1710
Thomas Hans Britsch, *CEO*
Margaret Britsch, *
▲ **EMP:** 25 **EST:** 1974
**SQ FT:** 6,000
**SALES (est):** 2.55MM **Privately Held**
**SIC: 3524** 0181  Lawn and garden equipment; Florists' greens and flowers

## 3531 Construction Machinery

**(P-9403)**
**ADEL PARK LLC**
350 Carlson Blvd, Richmond  (94804-3117)
PHONE.................................510 620-9670
Tommy Le, *Mgr*
**EMP:** 15 **EST:** 2017
**SALES (est):** 186.02K **Privately Held**
**SIC: 3531**  Concrete plants

**(P-9404)**
**ALTEC INC**
1127 Carrier Parkway Ave, Bakersfield (93308-9666)
PHONE.................................661 679-4177
**EMP:** 26
**SALES (corp-wide):** 1.21B **Privately Held**
Web: www.altec.com
**SIC: 3531**  Construction machinery
**PA:** Altec, Inc.
   210 Inverness Center Dr
   205 991-7733

**(P-9405)**
**ALTEC INDUSTRIES INC**
1450 N 1st St, Dixon  (95620-9798)
PHONE.................................707 678-0800
Adam Baxandall, *Brnch Mgr*
**EMP:** 16
**SALES (corp-wide):** 1.21B **Privately Held**
Web: www.altec.com
**SIC: 3531**  Construction machinery
**HQ:** Altec Industries, Inc.
   210 Inverness Center Drv
   Birmingham AL 35242
   205 991-7733

**(P-9406)**
**ALTEC INDUSTRIES INC**
325 Industrial Way, Dixon  (95620-9763)
PHONE.................................707 678-0800
James Pitts, *Mgr*
**EMP:** 30
**SQ FT:** 17,664
**SALES (corp-wide):** 1.21B **Privately Held**
Web: www.altec.com

## 3531 - Construction Machinery (P-9407)

**PRODUCTS & SERVICES SECTION**

SIC: **3531** 3536 3713 3537  Derricks, except oil and gas field; Cranes, overhead traveling ; Truck bodies (motor vehicles); Industrial trucks and tractors
HQ: Altec Industries, Inc.
   210 Inverness Center Drv
   Birmingham AL 35242
   205 991-7733

### (P-9407)
### AMERICAN COMPACTION EQP INC
Also Called: Compaction American
29380 Hunco Way, Lake Elsinore (92530-2757)
PHONE..............................949 661-2921
Richard S Anderson, *CEO*
Monty Ihde, *
Darryl Kanell, *
Kelly Ihde, *
Mike Shoemaker, *
▲ **EMP:** 24 **EST:** 1987
**SQ FT:** 8,500
**SALES (est):** 9.81MM **Privately Held**
Web: www.acewheels.com
SIC: **3531** 7353  Soil compactors: vibratory; Heavy construction equipment rental
HQ: Cascade Corporation
   2201 Ne 201st Ave
   Fairview OR 97024
   503 669-6300

### (P-9408)
### ARCBYT INC (PA)
Also Called: Petra
548 Market St Pmb 39975, San Francisco (94104-5401)
PHONE..............................415 449-4852
Kimberly Abrams, *CEO*
**EMP:** 16 **EST:** 2018
**SALES (est):** 2.71MM
**SALES (corp-wide):** 2.71MM **Privately Held**
Web: www.petra.cc
SIC: **3531**  Construction machinery

### (P-9409)
### BLACK DIAMOND BLADE COMPANY (PA)
Also Called: Cutting Edge Supply
234 E O St, Colton (92324-3466)
PHONE..............................800 949-9014
John Brenner, *CEO*
Franklin J Brenner Senior, *Pr*
Hoby Brenner, *Treas*
◆ **EMP:** 35 **EST:** 1950
**SQ FT:** 16,000
**SALES (est):** 24.83MM
**SALES (corp-wide):** 24.83MM **Privately Held**
Web: www.cuttingedgesupply.com
SIC: **3531**  Blades for graders, scrapers, dozers, and snow plows

### (P-9410)
### BRODERICK GENERAL ENGINEERING
21750 8th St E Ste B, Sonoma (95476-9803)
PHONE..............................707 996-7809
Jeffrey Carlson, *Prin*
Jesus Fernandez, *Prin*
Sean Martin, *Prin*
Ryan Poore, *Prin*
Nik Patridis, *Prin*
**EMP:** 68 **EST:** 1998
**SALES (est):** 5.47MM **Privately Held**
Web: www.broderickge.com
SIC: **3531**  Construction machinery

### (P-9411)
### BUGGY WHIP INC
3245 Production Ave, Oceanside (92058-1339)
P.O. Box 576 (92065-0576)
PHONE..............................760 789-3230
Russell Porter, *CEO*
Russell T Porter, *Pr*
**EMP:** 15 **EST:** 1967
**SALES (est):** 1.07MM **Privately Held**
Web: www.buggywhip.com
SIC: **3531** 3532  Construction machinery; Mining machinery

### (P-9412)
### CAL VSTA EROSION CTRL PDTS LLC
459 Country Rd 99w, Arbuckle (95912)
PHONE..............................530 476-0706
Renee Shadinger, *CEO*
Bryan Shadinger, *Pr*
John Shadinger, *CFO*
**EMP:** 35 **EST:** 2006
**SALES (est):** 3.54MM **Privately Held**
Web: www.calvistaerosion.com
SIC: **3531**  Construction machinery

### (P-9413)
### CALIFORNIA MFG & ENGRG CO LLC
1401 S Madera Ave, Kerman (93630-9139)
PHONE..............................559 842-1500
Karen Emery, *
Richard Spencer, *
▲ **EMP:** 130 **EST:** 2004
**SALES (est):** 7.69MM **Privately Held**
Web: www.mecawp.com
SIC: **3531**  Construction machinery

### (P-9414)
### CARON COMPACTOR CO
Also Called: Aron
1204 Ullrey Ave, Escalon (95320-8618)
PHONE..............................800 448-8236
James O Caron, *CEO*
Judith S Caron, *
▲ **EMP:** 25 **EST:** 1969
**SQ FT:** 18,000
**SALES (est):** 3.74MM **Privately Held**
Web: www.caroncompactor.com
SIC: **3531** 3441  Construction machinery attachments; Fabricated structural metal

### (P-9415)
### CAVOTEC INET US INC
5665 Corporate Ave, Cypress (90630-4727)
PHONE..............................714 947-0005
Mike Larkin, *Pr*
Dorothy Chen, *
▼ **EMP:** 70 **EST:** 2011
**SALES (est):** 7.3MM **Privately Held**
Web: www.cavotec.com
SIC: **3531**  Airport construction machinery
HQ: Cavotec Us Holdings, Inc.
   5665 Corporate Ave
   Cypress CA 90630
   714 545-7900

### (P-9416)
### CLEASBY MANUFACTURING CO INC (PA)
1414 Bancroft Ave, San Francisco (94124-3603)
P.O. Box 24132 (94124-0132)
PHONE..............................415 822-6565
Leslie John Cleasby, *Pr*
John Cleasby, *Pr*
**EMP:** 20 **EST:** 1949
**SQ FT:** 21,000
**SALES (est):** 4.36MM
**SALES (corp-wide):** 4.36MM **Privately Held**
Web: www.cleasby.com
SIC: **3531** 5033  Roofing equipment; Roofing and siding materials

### (P-9417)
### COUNTY OF LOS ANGELES
Also Called: Public Works, Dept of
3637 Winter Canyon Rd, Malibu (90265-4834)
PHONE..............................310 456-8014
Mark Sanchez, *Mgr*
**EMP:** 41
Web: www.lacounty.gov
SIC: **3531** 9621  Graders, road (construction machinery); Regulation, administration of transportation
PA: County Of Los Angeles
   500 W Temple St Ste 437
   213 974-1101

### (P-9418)
### COUNTY OF LOS ANGELES
Also Called: Public Works, Dept of
14959 Proctor Ave, La Puente (91746-3206)
PHONE..............................626 968-3312
Mike Lee, *Mgr*
**EMP:** 31
Web: www.lacounty.info
SIC: **3531** 9111  Road construction and maintenance machinery; Executive offices
PA: County Of Los Angeles
   500 W Temple St Ste 437
   213 974-1101

### (P-9419)
### CUSTOM BUILDING PRODUCTS INC
Also Called: Custom Building Products, Inc.
3525 Zephyr Ct, Stockton (95206-4210)
PHONE..............................209 983-8322
**EMP:** 40
Web: www.custombuildingproducts.com
SIC: **3531**  Concrete grouting equipment
HQ: Custom Building Products Llc
   7711 Center Ave Ste 500
   Huntington Beach CA 92647
   800 272-8786

### (P-9420)
### EAGLE ROCK INCORPORATED
40029 La Grange Rd, Junction City (96048)
P.O. Box 1498 (96093-1498)
PHONE..............................530 623-4444
Larry E Yingling, *Pr*
David W Yingling, *VP*
**EMP:** 15 **EST:** 1980
**SQ FT:** 720
**SALES (est):** 2.5MM **Privately Held**
Web: eagle-rock-incorporated.sbcontract.com
SIC: **3531** 2951 1423  Rock crushing machinery, portable; Asphalt and asphaltic paving mixtures (not from refineries); Crushed and broken granite

### (P-9421)
### EMPIRE SOUTHWEST LLC
Also Called: Caterpillar Authorized Dealer
3393 Us Highway 86, Imperial (92251-9527)
P.O. Box 936 (92251-0936)
PHONE..............................760 545-6200
Diane Madrigal, *Mgr*
**EMP:** 31
**SALES (corp-wide):** 616.2MM **Privately Held**
Web: www.empire-cat.com
SIC: **3531**  Construction machinery
PA: Empire Southwest, Llc
   1725 S Country Club Dr
   480 633-4000

### (P-9422)
### ENDEAVOR HOMES INC
655 Cal Oak Rd, Oroville (95965-9621)
P.O. Box 1947 (95965-1947)
PHONE..............................530 534-0300
Del Fleener, *Pr*
William Wicklas, *VP*
Shonie Schufeldt, *Treas*
**EMP:** 20 **EST:** 1996
**SALES (est):** 2.17MM **Privately Held**
Web: www.endeavorhomes.com
SIC: **3531** 2439  Construction machinery; Trusses, wooden roof

### (P-9423)
### GLOBAL RENTAL CO INC
Also Called: Global Equipment Rental Co
325 Industrial Way, Dixon (95620-9763)
PHONE..............................707 693-2520
Pete Garcia, *Mgr*
**EMP:** 120
**SQ FT:** 4,000
**SALES (corp-wide):** 1.21B **Privately Held**
Web: www.altec.com
SIC: **3531**  Construction machinery
HQ: Global Rental Co., Inc.
   33 Inverness Center Pkwy # 250
   Hoover AL 35242

### (P-9424)
### GROUND HOG INC
1470 Victoria Ct, San Bernardino (92408-2831)
P.O. Box 290 (92402-0290)
PHONE..............................909 478-5700
Edward Carlson, *Pr*
Jack Carlson, *
▼ **EMP:** 25 **EST:** 1948
**SQ FT:** 52,000
**SALES (est):** 5.69MM **Privately Held**
Web: www.groundhoginc.com
SIC: **3531**  Posthole diggers, powered

### (P-9425)
### H & L TOOTH COMPANY (PA)
Also Called: H & L Forge Company
1540 S Greenwood Ave, Montebello (90640-6536)
P.O. Box 48 (74055-0048)
PHONE..............................323 721-5146
Richard L Launder, *Ch Bd*
Brian L Launder, *
▲ **EMP:** 85 **EST:** 1931
**SQ FT:** 220,000
**SALES (est):** 1.26MM
**SALES (corp-wide):** 1.26MM **Privately Held**
Web: www.hltooth.com
SIC: **3531**  Bucket or scarifier teeth

### (P-9426)
### HARCON PRECISION METALS INC
1790 Dornoch Ct, Chula Vista (91910)
PHONE..............................619 423-5544
**EMP:** 50 **EST:** 1971
**SALES (est):** 4.55MM **Privately Held**
Web: www.harcon-precision.com
SIC: **3531** 3444  Construction machinery; Sheet metalwork

## 3532 - Mining Machinery (P-9448)

**(P-9427)**
**HIROK INC**
Also Called: Spitzlift
5644 Kearny Mesa Rd Ste H, San Diego (92111-1311)
P.O. Box 3423 (92065-0959)
PHONE..................................619 713-5066
Michael Spitsbergen, *CEO*
Mark Spitsbergen, *VP*
**EMP:** 20 **EST:** 2005
**SQ FT:** 2,500
**SALES (est):** 3.7MM **Privately Held**
Web: www.spitzlist.com
SIC: **3531** Construction machinery

**(P-9428)**
**JLG INDUSTRIES INC**
Also Called: Jlg Serviceplus
7820 Lincoln Ave, Riverside (92504-4443)
PHONE..................................951 358-1915
Eric Golden, *Mgr*
**EMP:** 23
**SALES (corp-wide):** 9.66B **Publicly Held**
Web: www.jlg.com
SIC: **3531** Cranes, nec
HQ: Jlg Industries, Inc.
1 Jlg Dr
Mc Connellsburg PA 17233
717 485-5161

**(P-9429)**
**KDF ENTERPRISES LLC**
3941 Park Dr, El Dorado Hills (95762-4549)
PHONE..................................803 928-7073
James Dearing, *Dir*
**EMP:** 250
**SALES (corp-wide):** 8.3MM **Privately Held**
Web: www.kdfglobal.co
SIC: **3531** Construction machinery
PA: Kdf Enterprises Llc
3512 Godwin Ct Ste A
205 687-1875

**(P-9430)**
**KENCO ENGINEERING INC**
Also Called: Kenco Wear Parts
2155 Pfe Rd, Roseville (95747-9765)
P.O. Box 1467 (95678-8467)
PHONE..................................916 782-8494
David Lutz, *Pr*
Donald Lutz, *
**EMP:** 30 **EST:** 1957
**SQ FT:** 25,000
**SALES (est):** 5.24MM **Privately Held**
Web: www.kencoengineering.com
SIC: **3531** 5082 Construction machinery attachments; General construction machinery and equipment

**(P-9431)**
**MARINE CORPS UNITED STATES**
Usmc, Barstow (92311)
PHONE..................................760 577-6716
**EMP:** 155
Web: www.marines.mil
SIC: **3531** Marine related equipment
HQ: United States Marine Corps
Branch Hlth Clnic Bldg #5
Beaufort SC 29904

**(P-9432)**
**MESA INDUSTRIES INC**
Gunite Supplies & Equipment
1419 Palomares St, La Verne (91750-5234)
PHONE..................................626 712-1708
Kent Sexton, *Mgr*
**EMP:** 20
**SQ FT:** 18,286
**SALES (corp-wide):** 9.91MM **Privately Held**
Web: www.mesa-intl.com
SIC: **3531** Concrete gunning equipment
PA: Mesa Industries, Inc.
4027 Eastern Ave
513 321-2950

**(P-9433)**
**MIXMOR INC**
3131 Casitas Ave, Los Angeles (90039-2499)
PHONE..................................323 664-1941
Michael K Mcnamara, *CEO*
Ann B Mc Namara, *Sec*
**EMP:** 19 **EST:** 1935
**SQ FT:** 17,000
**SALES (est):** 2.64MM **Privately Held**
Web: www.mixmor.com
SIC: **3531** Construction machinery

**(P-9434)**
**PB LOADER CORPORATION**
5778 W Barstow Ave, Fresno (93722-5024)
PHONE..................................800 350-8521
▼ **EMP:** 35 **EST:** 1960
**SALES (est):** 1.19MM **Privately Held**
Web: www.pbloader.com
SIC: **3531** 3714 Backfillers, self-propelled; Dump truck lifting mechanism

**(P-9435)**
**REED INTERNATIONAL**
Vss Macropaver
13024 Lake Rd, Hickman (95323-9667)
P.O. Box 178 (95323-0178)
PHONE..................................209 874-2719
**EMP:** 17
**SALES (corp-wide):** 163.99MM **Privately Held**
Web: www.macropaver.com
SIC: **3531** Drags, road (construction and road maintenance equipment)
HQ: Reed International
13024 Lake Rd
Hickman CA 95323
209 874-2357

**(P-9436)**
**SCHWING AMERICA INC**
3351 Grapevine St Bldg A, Jurupa Valley (91752-3510)
PHONE..................................909 681-6430
Albert Ornelas, *Mgr*
**EMP:** 244
**SALES (corp-wide):** 12.98B **Privately Held**
Web: www.schwing.com
SIC: **3531** Bituminous, cement and concrete related products and equip.
HQ: Schwing America, Inc.
5900 Centerville Rd
Saint Paul MN 55127
651 429-0999

**(P-9437)**
**SOLARJUICE AMERICAN INC (PA)**
Also Called: Solar 4 America
6764 Preston Ave Ste A, Livermore (94551-9431)
PHONE..................................925 474-8821
Denton Teng, *Pr*
**EMP:** 272 **EST:** 2019
**SALES (est):** 4.58MM
**SALES (corp-wide):** 4.58MM **Privately Held**
Web: www.solar4america.com
SIC: **3531** 5211 Roofing equipment; Solar heating equipment

**(P-9438)**
**STURGEON SERVICES INTL INC**
Ssi
3511 Gilmore Ave, Bakersfield (93308-6205)
P.O. Box 936 (93302-0936)
PHONE..................................661 322-4408
Ollie Sturgeon, *Brnch Mgr*
**EMP:** 400
Web: www.sturgeonservices.com
SIC: **3531** Construction machinery
PA: Sturgeon Services International, Inc.
3511 Gilmore Ave

**(P-9439)**
**SUPERWINCH HOLDING LLC**
3945 Freedom Cir Ste 560, Santa Clara (95054-1269)
PHONE..................................860 412-1476
**EMP:** 70 **EST:** 2009
**SALES (est):** 2.74MM **Privately Held**
Web: www.superwinch.com
SIC: **3531** Winches

**(P-9440)**
**TANFIELD ENGRG SYSTEMS US INC**
Also Called: Upright
2686 S Maple Ave, Fresno (93725-2108)
PHONE..................................559 443-6602
Roy Stanley, *Pr*
Charles Brooks, *CFO*
Darren Kell, *Bus Dev Di*
David Sternweis Ctrll, *Prin*
**EMP:** 15 **EST:** 2006
**SQ FT:** 67,727
**SALES (est):** 2.95MM
**SALES (corp-wide):** 3.72MM **Privately Held**
SIC: **3531** Aerial work platforms: hydraulic/elec. truck/carrier mounted
PA: Tanfield Group Plc
Weightmans Ltd
345 073-9900

**(P-9441)**
**TINK INC**
2361 Durham Dayton Hwy, Durham (95938-9604)
PHONE..................................530 895-0897
Robert J Du Bose, *CEO*
Dan M Du Bose, *
**EMP:** 40 **EST:** 1977
**SQ FT:** 53,000
**SALES (est):** 5.81MM **Privately Held**
Web: www.tinkinc.com
SIC: **3531** 3444 Construction machinery; Sheet metalwork

**(P-9442)**
**TNT INDUSTRIAL CONTRACTORS INC (PA)**
3800 Happy Ln, Sacramento (95827-9721)
PHONE..................................916 395-8400
Josh Twist, *CEO*
**EMP:** 35 **EST:** 1991
**SQ FT:** 4,000
**SALES (est):** 16.19MM **Privately Held**
Web: www.tntindustrial.com
SIC: **3531** Construction machinery

**(P-9443)**
**TRAVIS SNYDER**
Also Called: Advantage Backhoes
27248 Hwy 189 Ste Ab-06, Blue Jay (92317)
P.O. Box 647 (92325-0647)
PHONE..................................909 338-6302
Travis Snyder, *Prin*
**EMP:** 15 **EST:** 2006
**SALES (est):** 4.38MM **Privately Held**
Web: www.advantagebackhoes.com
SIC: **3531** Backhoes

**(P-9444)**
**TRIO ENGINEERED PRODUCTS INC (HQ)**
Also Called: Trio
505 W Foothill Blvd, Azusa (91702-2345)
PHONE..................................626 851-3966
Michael Francis Burke, *CEO*
Eugene Xue, *
◆ **EMP:** 25 **EST:** 2002
**SALES (est):** 5.27MM
**SALES (corp-wide):** 3.29B **Privately Held**
Web: www.global.weir
SIC: **3531** Construction machinery attachments
PA: Weir Group Plc(The)
1 West Regent Street
141 637-7111

**(P-9445)**
**US SAWS INC (PA)**
Also Called: U S Saw & Blades
3702 W Central Ave, Santa Ana (92704-5832)
PHONE..................................860 668-2402
Bruce Root, *CEO*
C W Duncan, *Pr*
Bill Glynn, *VP*
▲ **EMP:** 18 **EST:** 2004
**SQ FT:** 4,000
**SALES (est):** 8.27MM
**SALES (corp-wide):** 8.27MM **Privately Held**
Web: www.ussaws.com
SIC: **3531** 5082 Blades for graders, scrapers, dozers, and snow plows; Road construction and maintenance machinery

**(P-9446)**
**WEST POINT SPC CONTG INC**
2704 Transportation Ave Ste C, National City (91950-8783)
PHONE..................................619 784-2524
Scott Larzalere, *CEO*
Raymond S Jennings, *Sec*
**EMP:** 15 **EST:** 2020
**SALES (est):** 2.87MM **Privately Held**
SIC: **3531** Tractors, construction

**(P-9447)**
**WESTERN EQUIPMENT MFG INC**
Also Called: Western Equipment Mfg
1160 Olympic Dr, Corona (92881-3390)
PHONE..................................951 284-2000
Kenneth R Thompson, *CEO*
William Weihl, *Pr*
▲ **EMP:** 49 **EST:** 2010
**SALES (est):** 3.91MM **Privately Held**
Web: www.western-emi.com
SIC: **3531** Finishers and spreaders (construction equipment)

## 3532 Mining Machinery

**(P-9448)**
**CAVOTEC US HOLDINGS INC (HQ)**
Also Called: Cavotec Inet
5665 Corporate Ave, Cypress (90630-4727)
PHONE..................................714 545-7900
Michael Larkin, *Pr*
**EMP:** 17 **EST:** 2008
**SALES (est):** 35.16MM **Privately Held**
Web: www.cavotec.com

# 3532 - Mining Machinery

**(P-9449)**
SIC: 3532 3569 Drills, bits, and similar equipment; Filters
PA: Cavotec Sa
Corso Elvezia 16

**(P-9449)**
**POLYALLOYS INJECTED METALS INC**
14000 Avalon Blvd, Los Angeles (90061-2636)
PHONE..............................310 715-9800
Craig Paulin, *CEO*
EMP: 75 EST: 2001
SALES (est): 2.64MM
SALES (corp-wide): 23.24MM **Privately Held**
Web: www.psmindustries.com
SIC: 3532 Amalgamators (metallurgical or mining machinery)
PA: Psm Industries, Inc.
14000 Avalon Blvd
888 663-8256

**(P-9450)**
**REED INTERNATIONAL (HQ)**
Also Called: Sauneo Air Technologies
13024 Lake Rd, Hickman (95323-9667)
P.O. Box 178 (95323-0178)
PHONE..............................209 874-2357
Wendell Reed, *Pr*
▼ EMP: 28 EST: 1973
SALES (est): 6.3MM
SALES (corp-wide): 163.99MM **Privately Held**
Web: www.macropaver.com
SIC: 3532 5531 3564 3444 Mining machinery; Auto and home supply stores; Blowers and fans; Sheet metalwork
PA: Reed Family Companies
928 12th St Ste 700
209 521-9771

**(P-9451)**
**SOTEC USA LLC**
3076 S Edenglen Ave, Ontario (91761-2626)
PHONE..............................909 525-5861
Gang Ye, *Managing Member*
EMP: 18
Web: www.sotecusa.com
SIC: 3532 Crushing, pulverizing, and screening equipment
HQ: Sotec Usa Llc
17870 Castleton St # 338
City Of Industry CA 91748
909 930-2792

**(P-9452)**
**SPAULDING EQUIPMENT COMPANY (PA)**
Also Called: Spaulding Crusher Parts
75 Paseo Adelanto, Perris (92570-9343)
P.O. Box 1807 (92572-1807)
PHONE..............................951 943-4531
George E Spaulding, *Ch Bd*
James Michael Spaulding, *
Norman Vetter, *
Fred Stemrich, *
◆ EMP: 47 EST: 1966
SALES (est): 5.08MM
SALES (corp-wide): 5.08MM **Privately Held**
Web: www.spauldingequipment.com
SIC: 3532 5082 7699 Mineral beneficiation equipment; Mineral beneficiation machinery; Industrial machinery and equipment repair

---

## 3533 Oil And Gas Field Machinery

**(P-9453)**
**AERA ENERGY SERVICES COMPANY**
29010 Shell Rd, Coalinga (93210-9235)
PHONE..............................559 935-7418
Kevin Peck, *Brnch Mgr*
EMP: 170
SALES (corp-wide): 316.62B **Privately Held**
Web: www.aeraenergy.com
SIC: 3533 1311 Oil and gas drilling rigs and equipment; Crude petroleum and natural gas production
HQ: Aera Energy Services Company
10000 Ming Ave
Bakersfield CA 93311
661 665-5000

**(P-9454)**
**AQUEOS CORPORATION**
2550 Eastman Ave, Ventura (93003-7714)
PHONE..............................805 676-4330
Theodore Roche, *Brnch Mgr*
EMP: 121
SALES (corp-wide): 38.64MM **Privately Held**
Web: www.aqueossubsea.com
SIC: 3533 Oil and gas field machinery
PA: Aqueos Corporation
418 Chapala St Ste E
805 364-0570

**(P-9455)**
**AQUEOS CORPORATION (PA)**
418 Chapala St Ste E, Santa Barbara (93101-8056)
PHONE..............................805 364-0570
Theodore Roche Iv, *Pr*
Bradley Parro, *
Michael Pfau, *
Larry Barels, *
Eric Legendre, *
EMP: 50 EST: 2000
SQ FT: 23,000
SALES (est): 38.64MM
SALES (corp-wide): 38.64MM **Privately Held**
Web: www.aqueossubsea.com
SIC: 3533 Oil and gas field machinery

**(P-9456)**
**BARDEX CORPORATION (PA)**
6338 Lindmar Dr, Goleta (93117-3112)
PHONE..............................805 964-7747
Thomas Miller, *CEO*
◆ EMP: 71 EST: 1963
SQ FT: 80,000
SALES (est): 20.77MM
SALES (corp-wide): 20.77MM **Privately Held**
Web: www.bardex.com
SIC: 3533 Oil and gas field machinery

**(P-9457)**
**CAMERON INTERNATIONAL CORP**
535 Getty Ct Ste A, Benicia (94510-1179)
PHONE..............................707 752-8800
EMP: 30
Web: www.slb.com
SIC: 3533 Oil field machinery and equipment
HQ: Cameron International Corporation
1333 West Loop S Ste 1700
Houston TX 77027

**(P-9458)**
**CHANCELLOR OIL TOOLS INC**
3521 Gulf St, Bakersfield (93308-5210)
PHONE..............................661 324-2213
EMP: 40
SIC: 3533 Drilling tools for gas, oil, or water wells

**(P-9459)**
**CONTROL SYSTEMS INTL INC**
35 Parker, Irvine (92618-1605)
PHONE..............................949 238-4150
Rob Lewis, *Genl Mgr*
EMP: 85
SALES (corp-wide): 7.83B **Privately Held**
Web: www.technipfmc.com
SIC: 3533 Oil and gas field machinery
HQ: Control Systems International, Inc.
8040 Nieman Rd
Shawnee Mission KS 66214
913 599-5010

**(P-9460)**
**DAWSON ENTERPRISES (PA)**
Also Called: Cavins Oil Well Tools
2853 Cherry Ave, Signal Hill (90755-1908)
P.O. Box 6039 (90806-0039)
PHONE..............................562 424-8564
James M Dawson, *CEO*
Harry Dawson, *
◆ EMP: 36 EST: 1928
SQ FT: 19,000
SALES (est): 12.79MM
SALES (corp-wide): 12.79MM **Privately Held**
Web: www.cavins.com
SIC: 3533 7359 Bits, oil and gas field tools: rock; Garage facility and tool rental

**(P-9461)**
**DOWNHOLE STABILIZATION INC**
3515 Thomas Way, Bakersfield (93308-6215)
P.O. Box 2467 (93303-2467)
PHONE..............................661 631-1044
Jim Calanchini, *Pr*
Mike Jarboe, *
Jacob Banducci, *
Diane Calanchini, *
▲ EMP: 38 EST: 1989
SQ FT: 8,800
SALES (est): 4.83MM **Privately Held**
Web: www.downholestabilization.com
SIC: 3533 5082 3599 1389 Drilling tools for gas, oil, or water wells; Construction and mining machinery; Amusement park equipment; Construction, repair, and dismantling services

**(P-9462)**
**FMC TECHNOLOGIES INC**
260 Cousteau Pl, Davis (95618-5490)
PHONE..............................530 753-6718
John T Gremp, *Ch Bd*
EMP: 25
SALES (corp-wide): 7.83B **Privately Held**
Web: www.technipfmc.com
SIC: 3533 Oil and gas field machinery
HQ: Fmc Technologies, Inc.
13460 Lockwood Rd
Houston TX 77044
281 591-4000

**(P-9463)**
**GLOBAL ELASTOMERIC PDTS INC**
5551 District Blvd, Bakersfield (93313-2126)
PHONE..............................661 831-5380
Phil W Embury, *Pr*
Sandy Embury, *
▲ EMP: 55 EST: 1963
SQ FT: 20,000
SALES (est): 8.36MM **Privately Held**
Web: www.globaleee.com
SIC: 3533 5084 Oil and gas field machinery; Oil refining machinery, equipment, and supplies

**(P-9464)**
**KBA ENGINEERING LLC**
2157 Mohawk St, Bakersfield (93308-6020)
P.O. Box 1200 (93302-1200)
PHONE..............................661 323-0487
Richard C Jones, *Managing Member*
EMP: 95 EST: 1997
SQ FT: 45,000
SALES (est): 3.3MM **Privately Held**
Web: www.kbaeng.com
SIC: 3533 3462 Oil and gas field machinery; Gear and chain forgings

**(P-9465)**
**NOV INC**
759 N Eckhoff St, Orange (92868-1005)
P.O. Box 6626 (92863-6626)
PHONE..............................714 978-1900
Owen Unruh, *Prin*
EMP: 23
SALES (corp-wide): 8.58B **Publicly Held**
Web: www.nov.com
SIC: 3533 Oil field machinery and equipment
PA: Nov Inc.
10353 Richmond Ave
346 223-3000

**(P-9466)**
**SMITH INTERNATIONAL INC**
Also Called: Omni Seals
11031 Jersey Blvd Ste A, Rancho Cucamonga (91730-5150)
PHONE..............................909 906-7900
EMP: 130
Web: www.smithcodevelopment.com
SIC: 3533 Oil and gas field machinery
HQ: Smith International, Llc
5599 San Felipe St
Houston TX 77056
281 443-3370

**(P-9467)**
**SOUTH COAST SCREEN AND CASING**
19112 S Santa Fe Ave, Compton (90221-5910)
PHONE..............................310 632-3200
Tyson Scimo, *CEO*
EMP: 15 EST: 2011
SALES (est): 532.25K **Privately Held**
Web: www.southcoastsc.com
SIC: 3533 Oil and gas drilling rigs and equipment

**(P-9468)**
**TECHNIPFMC USA INC**
6400 Oak Cyn Ste 100, Irvine (92618-5204)
PHONE..............................949 238-4150
EMP: 17
SALES (corp-wide): 7.83B **Privately Held**
Web: www.technipfmc.com
SIC: 3533 Oil field machinery and equipment
HQ: Technipfmc Usa, Inc.
13460 Lockwood Rd
Houston TX 77044
281 591-4000

## 3534 Elevators And Moving Stairways

**(P-9469)**
**BLISSERA CORP**
101 Jefferson Dr, Menlo Park (94025-1114)
PHONE.....................844 960-4141
Alex Alexanian, *CEO*
Alex Alexahian, *Prin*
**EMP:** 15 **EST:** 2019
**SALES (est):** 1.46MM **Privately Held**
Web: www.blissera.com
**SIC: 3534** 8712 1796 Elevators and equipment; Architectural engineering; Elevator installation and conversion

**(P-9470)**
**ELEVATOR INDUSTRIES INC**
110 Main Ave, Sacramento (95838-2015)
PHONE.....................916 921-1495
Guy Buckman, *Pr*
Jason Buckman, *VP*
▲ **EMP:** 16 **EST:** 2013
**SALES (est):** 3.81MM **Privately Held**
Web: www.elevator-industries.com
**SIC: 3534** 7699 Elevators and equipment; Elevators: inspection, service, and repair

**(P-9471)**
**ELEVATOR RESEARCH & MFG CO**
1417 Elwood St, Los Angeles (90021-2812)
PHONE.....................213 746-1914
Frank Edward Ed, *Park President*
Lynn Park, *
**EMP:** 19 **EST:** 1964
**SQ FT:** 5,000
**SALES (est):** 4.23MM
**SALES (corp-wide):** 73.15MM **Privately Held**
Web: www.elevatorresearch.com
**SIC: 3534** Elevators and equipment
**PA:** Dewhurst Group Plc
Unit 9
208 744-8200

**(P-9472)**
**GMS ELEVATOR SERVICES INC**
Also Called: Gms Elevator Services
401 Borrego Ct, San Dimas (91773-2971)
PHONE.....................909 599-3904
G Matthew Simpkins, *Pr*
Pamela Simpkins, *
**EMP:** 35 **EST:** 1987
**SQ FT:** 4,000
**SALES (est):** 5.42MM **Privately Held**
Web: www.gmselevator.com
**SIC: 3534** 1796 Elevators and equipment; Elevator installation and conversion

**(P-9473)**
**MOTION CONTROL ENGINEERING INC**
11380 White Rock Rd, Rancho Cordova (95742-6522)
PHONE.....................916 638-4011
◆ **EMP:** 400
Web: acim.nidec.com
**SIC: 3534** 3613 Elevators and equipment; Switchgear and switchboard apparatus

**(P-9474)**
**NIDEC MOTOR CORPORATION**
Also Called: McE
11380 White Rock Rd, Rancho Cordova (95742-6522)
PHONE.....................916 463-9200
**EMP:** 400
Web: acim.nidec.com
**SIC: 3534** 3613 Elevators and equipment; Switchgear and switchboard apparatus
**HQ:** Nidec Motor Corporation
8050 W Florissant Ave
Saint Louis MO 63136

**(P-9475)**
**POWERLIFT DUMBWAITERS INC**
2444 Georgia Slide Rd, Georgetown (95634-2201)
PHONE.....................800 409-5438
John B Reite, *CEO*
▲ **EMP:** 16 **EST:** 2000
**SQ FT:** 7,500
**SALES (est):** 3.02MM **Privately Held**
Web: www.dumbwaiters.com
**SIC: 3534** Dumbwaiters

**(P-9476)**
**SCHINDLER ELEVATOR CORPORATION**
Also Called: Schindler
555 Mccormick St, San Leandro (94577-1107)
PHONE.....................510 382-2075
Dennis Devos, *Mgr*
**EMP:** 30
Web: www.schindler.com
**SIC: 3534** 1796 7699 Elevators and equipment; Elevator installation and conversion; Elevators: inspection, service, and repair
**HQ:** Schindler Elevator Corporation
20 Whippany Rd
Morristown NJ 07960
973 397-6500

**(P-9477)**
**TL SHIELD & ASSOCIATES INC**
Also Called: Inclinator of California
1030 Arroyo St, San Fernando (91340-1822)
P.O. Box 6845 (91359-6845)
PHONE.....................818 509-8228
Thomas Louis Shield, *Pr*
**EMP:** 35 **EST:** 1982
**SQ FT:** 2,000
**SALES (est):** 6.62MM **Privately Held**
Web: www.tlshield.com
**SIC: 3534** 1796 Elevators and equipment; Elevator installation and conversion

**(P-9478)**
**WINTER & BAIN MFG INC (PA)**
1417 Elwood St, Los Angeles (90021-2812)
PHONE.....................213 749-3568
Henry Spencer, *Owner*
Henry W Spencer, *Pr*
**EMP:** 16 **EST:** 1984
**SQ FT:** 8,000
**SALES (est):** 2.38MM
**SALES (corp-wide):** 2.38MM **Privately Held**
Web: www.elevatorresearch.com
**SIC: 3534** Elevators and moving stairways

## 3535 Conveyors And Conveying Equipment

**(P-9479)**
**AIR TUBE TRANSFER SYSTEMS INC**
Also Called: A T T
715 N Cypress St, Orange (92867-6605)
PHONE.....................714 363-0700
Rick Blodgett, *Pr*
**EMP:** 15 **EST:** 1996
**SQ FT:** 10,000
**SALES (est):** 5.15MM **Privately Held**
Web: www.attsystems.com
**SIC: 3535** 1796 7699 3494 Pneumatic tube conveyor systems; Machinery installation; Industrial equipment services; Valves and pipe fittings, nec

**(P-9480)**
**AMERICAN ULTRAVIOLET WEST INC**
Also Called: Lesco
23555 Telo Ave, Torrance (90505-4012)
PHONE.....................310 784-2930
Meredith C Stines, *Pr*
▲ **EMP:** 21 **EST:** 1978
**SQ FT:** 22,775
**SALES (est):** 2.73MM **Privately Held**
Web: www.americanultraviolet.com
**SIC: 3535** 5065 Conveyors and conveying equipment; Electronic parts

**(P-9481)**
**APEX CONVEYOR CORP**
40001 Via Caseta, Murrieta (92562)
P.O. Box 812 (92564)
PHONE.....................951 304-7808
**EMP:** 17 **EST:** 1995
**SALES (est):** 951.73K **Privately Held**
Web: www.nicolejanowicz.com
**SIC: 3535** Conveyors and conveying equipment

**(P-9482)**
**COMPASS EQUIPMENT INC (PA)**
4688 Pacific Heights Rd, Oroville (95965-9239)
P.O. Box 1048 (95965-1048)
PHONE.....................530 533-7284
Stephen Appleby, *Pr*
Stephen Appleby, *Prin*
Victor Abreo, *
Ron Moras, *
**EMP:** 22 **EST:** 1976
**SQ FT:** 22,400
**SALES (est):** 8.45MM
**SALES (corp-wide):** 8.45MM **Privately Held**
Web: www.compassequip.com
**SIC: 3535** Belt conveyor systems, general industrial use

**(P-9483)**
**CONVEYOR MFG & SVC INC**
771 Marylind Ave, Claremont (91711-3531)
PHONE.....................909 621-0406
Jesus Dehorta, *Pr*
Josefina Dehorta, *Sec*
**EMP:** 15 **EST:** 1989
**SQ FT:** 30,000
**SALES (est):** 2.7MM **Privately Held**
Web: www.conveyormfg.com
**SIC: 3535** Conveyors and conveying equipment

**(P-9484)**
**CONVEYOR SERVICE & ELECTRIC**
9550 Ann St, Santa Fe Springs (90670-2616)
PHONE.....................562 777-1221
Patricia Moseley, *Pt*
Richard Moseley, *Pt*
Efren Alcantar, *Pt*
**EMP:** 23 **EST:** 1995
**SQ FT:** 13,000
**SALES (est):** 2.6MM **Privately Held**
Web: www.conserel.com

**SIC: 3535** 1796 Conveyors and conveying equipment; Machinery installation

**(P-9485)**
**FLO STOR ENGINEERING INC (PA)**
Also Called: Flostor
21371 Cabot Blvd, Hayward (94545-1650)
PHONE.....................510 887-7179
Robert Weeks, *Owner*
▼ **EMP:** 22 **EST:** 1983
**SALES (est):** 5.49MM **Privately Held**
Web: www.flostor.com
**SIC: 3535** Conveyors and conveying equipment

**(P-9486)**
**HECO-PACIFIC MANUFACTURING INC**
1510 Pacific St, Union City (94587-2015)
PHONE.....................510 487-1155
Malik A Alarab, *Pr*
Allan M Alarab, *Sec*
▼ **EMP:** 25 **EST:** 1961
**SQ FT:** 34,000
**SALES (est):** 6.8MM **Privately Held**
Web: www.hecopacific.com
**SIC: 3535** 3536 3531 Conveyors and conveying equipment; Cranes, overhead traveling; Construction machinery

**(P-9487)**
**INGALLS CONVEYORS INC**
1005 W Olympic Blvd, Montebello (90640-5121)
PHONE.....................323 837-9900
**TOLL FREE:** 888
Maged Labib Nakla, *CEO*
Steve Ingalls, *Treas*
Colleen Ingalls, *Sec*
**EMP:** 21 **EST:** 1976
**SQ FT:** 174,000
**SALES (est):** 4.97MM **Privately Held**
Web: www.ingallsconveyors.com
**SIC: 3535** 8711 Conveyors and conveying equipment; Consulting engineer

**(P-9488)**
**JOSE PEREZ**
Also Called: J&E Conveyor Services
41403 Stork Ct, Lake Elsinore (92532-1665)
PHONE.....................920 318-6527
Jose Perez, *Owner*
**EMP:** 25 **EST:** 2022
**SALES (est):** 779.19K **Privately Held**
**SIC: 3535** 7389 Conveyors and conveying equipment; Business Activities at Non-Commercial Site

**(P-9489)**
**OMRON ROBOTICS SAFETY TECH INC (HQ)**
4225 Hacienda Dr, Pleasanton (94588-2720)
PHONE.....................925 245-3400
Rob Cain, *Pr*
Seth Halio, *
Deron Jackson, *
▲ **EMP:** 157 **EST:** 2005
**SQ FT:** 57,000
**SALES (est):** 50.54MM **Privately Held**
Web: robotics.omron.com
**SIC: 3535** 7372 Robotic conveyors; Prepackaged software
**PA:** Omron Corporation
801, Horikawahigashiiruminamifudodocho, Shiokojidoori, Shimogyo-

## 3535 - Conveyors And Conveying Equipment (P-9490)

**(P-9490)**
**PNEUMATIC CONVEYING INC (PA)**
960 E Grevillea Ct, Ontario  (91761-5612)
PHONE..................866 557-5214
**EMP:** 16 **EST:** 1978
**SALES (est):** 9.47MM
**SALES (corp-wide):** 9.47MM **Privately Held**
**Web:** www.pneumaticconveyingsolutions.com
**SIC: 3535** 3548  Pneumatic tube conveyor systems; Arc welding generators, a.c. and d.c.

**(P-9491)**
**PRIDE CONVEYANCE SYSTEMS INC (PA)**
Also Called: P C S
1700 Shelton Dr, Hollister  (95023-9404)
PHONE..................831 637-1787
Shannon Pride, *Pr*
Pat Jordon, *
Bill Stewart, *CUS SVR*
Mike Zgragen, *
Ruben Padilla, *
◆ **EMP:** 75 **EST:** 1990
**SQ FT:** 36,000
**SALES (est):** 16.33MM **Privately Held**
**Web:** www.roeslein.com
**SIC: 3535**  Conveyors and conveying equipment

**(P-9492)**
**RALPHS-PUGH CO INC**
Also Called: Ralphs-Pugh Co.
3931 Oregon St, Benicia  (94510-1101)
PHONE..................707 745-6222
William G Pugh, *CEO*
Tom Anderson, *VP*
Deborah Pugh, *Sec*
**EMP:** 65 **EST:** 1912
**SQ FT:** 36,000
**SALES (est):** 9.42MM **Privately Held**
**Web:** www.ralphs-pugh.com
**SIC: 3535**  Conveyors and conveying equipment

**(P-9493)**
**SCREW CONVEYOR PACIFIC CORP**
7807 W Doe Ave, Visalia  (93291-9275)
PHONE..................559 651-2131
Randy Smith, *Prin*
**EMP:** 112
**SALES (corp-wide):** 8.74MM **Privately Held**
**Web:** www.screwconveyor.com
**SIC: 3535**  Conveyors and conveying equipment
**PA:** Screw Conveyor Pacific Corp
  700 Hoffman St
  219 931-1450

**(P-9494)**
**SDI INDUSTRIES INC (DH)**
Also Called: Autostore Integrator
24307 Magic Mountain Pkwy # 443, Valencia  (91355-3402)
PHONE..................818 890-6002
Krish Nathan, *CEO*
Mark Conrad, *
▲ **EMP:** 150 **EST:** 1978
**SALES (est):** 48.64MM
**SALES (corp-wide):** 2.67MM **Privately Held**
**Web:** www.sdi.systems

**SIC: 3535** 3537 8748 8711  Conveyors and conveying equipment; Industrial trucks and tractors; Business consulting, nec; Engineering services
**HQ:** Element Logic As
  Dyrskuevegen 26
  Klofta 2040

**(P-9495)**
**SOFTBANK ROBOTICS AMERICA INC (DH)**
2 Embarcadero Ctr Fl 8, San Francisco  (94111-3833)
PHONE..................844 737-7371
Brady Watkins, *Pr*
Bee Bee Nie Vpf, *Prin*
**EMP:** 15 **EST:** 2010
**SALES (est):** 26.35MM
**SALES (corp-wide):** 2.62B **Privately Held**
**Web:** us.softbankrobotics.com
**SIC: 3535** 5099  Robotic conveyors; Robots, service or novelty
**HQ:** Aldebaran
  43 Rue Du Colonel Pierre Avia
  Paris 15 IDF 75015
  177371752

**(P-9496)**
**STOCKTON TRI-INDUSTRIES LLC**
2141 E Anderson St, Stockton  (95205-7010)
P.O. Box 6097  (95206-0097)
PHONE..................209 948-9701
Courtney Rogers, *Managing Member*
Ray Smith, *
Harrison Freddie Wells, *
**EMP:** 39 **EST:** 1976
**SQ FT:** 32,000
**SALES (est):** 5.45MM **Privately Held**
**Web:** www.stocktontri.com
**SIC: 3535** 3599  Conveyors and conveying equipment; Machine shop, jobbing and repair

**(P-9497)**
**TERRA NOVA TECHNOLOGIES INC**
10770 Rockville St Ste A, Santee  (92071-8505)
PHONE..................619 596-7400
Ronald Kelly, *Pr*
**EMP:** 80 **EST:** 2019
**SQ FT:** 8,366
**SALES (est):** 2.41MM **Privately Held**
**Web:** www.tntinc.com
**SIC: 3535** 8742  Bulk handling conveyor systems; Industrial consultant
**HQ:** Cementation Usa Inc.
  10150 S Cntnnial Pkwy Ste
  Sandy UT 84070

**(P-9498)**
**TIG/M LLC**
9160 Jordan Ave, Chatsworth  (91311-5707)
PHONE..................818 709-8500
Alvaro Villa, *CEO*
Brad Read, *
David Hall, *
Bradley Read, *
**EMP:** 30 **EST:** 2005
**SQ FT:** 2,000
**SALES (est):** 4.94MM **Privately Held**
**Web:** www.tig-m.com
**SIC: 3535**  Trolley conveyors

## 3536 Hoists, Cranes, And Monorails

**(P-9499)**
**CARPENTER GROUP (PA)**
Also Called: Cable-Cisco
28800 Hesperian Blvd, Hayward  (94545-5038)
PHONE..................415 285-1954
**TOLL FREE:** 800
Bernard L Martin, *CEO*
Bruce Yoder, *
Frank Joost, *
Patty Oliverio, *
▲ **EMP:** 33 **EST:** 1950
**SALES (est):** 24.59MM
**SALES (corp-wide):** 24.59MM **Privately Held**
**Web:** www.thecarpentergroup.com
**SIC: 3536** 2394 5085 3496  Hoists; Liners and covers, fabric: made from purchased materials; Industrial supplies; Cable, uninsulated wire: made from purchased wire

**(P-9500)**
**CRANEVEYOR CORP (PA)**
1524 Potrero Ave, El Monte  (91733-3017)
P.O. Box 3727  (91733)
PHONE..................626 442-1524
Frank Gaetano Trimboli, *CEO*
Hector Valiente, *
John Lehman, *
Greg Bischoff, *
Michael Williams, *
▲ **EMP:** 67 **EST:** 1946
**SQ FT:** 41,200
**SALES (est):** 28.25MM
**SALES (corp-wide):** 28.25MM **Privately Held**
**Web:** www.craneveyor.com
**SIC: 3536** 3446  Cranes, overhead traveling; Railings, banisters, guards, etc: made from metal pipe

**(P-9501)**
**KONECRANES INC**
1620 S Carlos Ave, Ontario  (91761-7601)
PHONE..................909 930-0108
Amy Gonzalez, *Brnch Mgr*
**EMP:** 24
**Web:** www.konecranes.com
**SIC: 3536**  Hoists, cranes, and monorails
**HQ:** Konecranes, Inc.
  4401 Gateway Blvd
  Springfield OH 45502

**(P-9502)**
**KONECRANES INC**
10310 Pioneer Blvd Ste 2, Santa Fe Springs  (90670-3732)
PHONE..................562 903-1371
Ari Ramo, *Brnch Mgr*
**EMP:** 45
**Web:** www.konecranes.com
**SIC: 3536**  Hoists, cranes, and monorails
**HQ:** Konecranes, Inc.
  4401 Gateway Blvd
  Springfield OH 45502

**(P-9503)**
**MOBILE EQUIPMENT COMPANY**
Also Called: Mobile Equipment Appraisers
3610 Gilmore Ave, Bakersfield  (93308-6208)
P.O. Box 80776  (93380-0776)
PHONE..................661 327-8476
Evelyn Stanfill, *Pr*
Paul J Faulconer, *VP*
Gary Stanfill, *Genl Mgr*

Felecia Stanfill, *Sec*
**EMP:** 20 **EST:** 1960
**SQ FT:** 18,580
**SALES (est):** 3.01MM **Privately Held**
**Web:** www.mobile-equipment.com
**SIC: 3536** 8748 3559  Cranes, overhead traveling; Safety training service; Automotive related machinery

**(P-9504)**
**WESTMONT INDUSTRIES LLC (PA)**
10805 Painter Ave Uppr, Santa Fe Springs  (90670-4526)
PHONE..................562 944-6137
Diane Henderson, *Pr*
David Chetwood, *
▼ **EMP:** 15 **EST:** 1951
**SALES (est):** 24.58MM
**SALES (corp-wide):** 24.58MM **Privately Held**
**Web:** www.westmont.com
**SIC: 3536** 3533  Cranes, industrial plant; Oil and gas field machinery

## 3537 Industrial Trucks And Tractors

**(P-9505)**
**ANCRA INTERNATIONAL LLC**
Aircraft Systems Division
601 S Vincent Ave, Azusa  (91702-5102)
PHONE..................626 765-4818
Ed Dugic, *Mgr*
**EMP:** 226
**Web:** www.ancraaircraft.com
**SIC: 3537** 2298  Industrial trucks and tractors ; Cargo nets
**HQ:** Ancra International Llc
  601 S Vincent Ave
  Azusa CA 91702

**(P-9506)**
**ANCRA INTERNATIONAL LLC (HQ)**
Also Called: Delaware Ancra Intl LLC
601 S Vincent Ave, Azusa  (91702-5102)
PHONE..................626 765-4800
Steve Frediani, *CEO*
Nelson Fong, *
▲ **EMP:** 130 **EST:** 1996
**SALES (est):** 76.8MM **Privately Held**
**Web:** www.ancraaircraft.com
**SIC: 3537**  Lift trucks, industrial: fork, platform, straddle, etc.
**PA:** The Heico Companies L L C
  70 W Madison Ste 5600

**(P-9507)**
**ANTHONY WELDED PRODUCTS INC (PA)**
1447 S Lexington St, Delano  (93215-9700)
P.O. Box 299  (93062-0299)
PHONE..................661 721-7211
Frank S Salvucci Senior, *Ch*
Elsie Salvucci, *Pr*
**EMP:** 20 **EST:** 1958
**SQ FT:** 25,000
**SALES (est):** 9.98MM
**SALES (corp-wide):** 9.98MM **Privately Held**
**Web:** www.anthonycarts.com
**SIC: 3537** 3444 3443  Dollies (hand or power trucks), industrial,except mining; Sheet metalwork; Fabricated plate work (boiler shop)

## 3537 - Industrial Trucks And Tractors (P-9529)

**(P-9508)**
**CALIFORNIA PCF TRDG CO II INC**
Also Called: Electrolift
1320 Riverview Dr, San Bernardino (92408-2944)
PHONE..................................951 218-8253
Humberto Michel, *Pr*
**EMP:** 15 **EST:** 2003
**SALES (est):** 5.6MM **Privately Held**
**Web:** www.electroliftrentals.com
**SIC: 3537** 7359 Forklift trucks; Equipment rental and leasing, nec

**(P-9509)**
**CONSOLIDATED FRT SYSTEMS LLC**
Also Called: CFS
24407 Shoshone Rd, Apple Valley (92307-6741)
PHONE..................................310 424-9924
Jose Luis Hernandez, *CEO*
**EMP:** 23 **EST:** 2020
**SALES (est):** 3.9MM **Privately Held**
**SIC: 3537** Trucks: freight, baggage, etc.: industrial, except mining

**(P-9510)**
**CRANEWORKS SOUTHWEST INC**
1312 E Barham Dr, San Marcos (92078-4503)
PHONE..................................760 735-9793
Marise Williams, *Off Mgr*
**EMP:** 18 **EST:** 2015
**SALES (est):** 5.7MM **Privately Held**
**Web:** www.crane-works.com
**SIC: 3537** 7353 Cranes, industrial truck; Cranes and aerial lift equipment, rental or leasing

**(P-9511)**
**CROWN EQUIPMENT CORPORATION**
Also Called: Crown Lift Trucks
1355 E Fontana Ave Ste 102, Fresno (93725)
P.O. Box 641173 (45264-1173)
PHONE..................................559 585-8000
Keith Heinke, *Genl Mgr*
**EMP:** 17
**SALES (corp-wide):** 7.12B **Privately Held**
**Web:** www.crown.com
**SIC: 3537** Forklift trucks
**PA:** Crown Equipment Corporation
44 S Washington St
419 629-2311

**(P-9512)**
**CROWN EQUIPMENT CORPORATION**
Also Called: Crown Lift Trucks
1300 Palomares St, La Verne (91750-5232)
PHONE..................................626 968-0556
Kevin Mccarthy, *Mgr*
**EMP:** 27
**SQ FT:** 28,000
**SALES (corp-wide):** 7.12B **Privately Held**
**Web:** www.crown.com
**SIC: 3537** Lift trucks, industrial: fork, platform, straddle, etc.
**PA:** Crown Equipment Corporation
44 S Washington St
419 629-2311

**(P-9513)**
**CROWN EQUIPMENT CORPORATION**
Also Called: Crown Lift Trucks
4250 Greystone Dr, Ontario (91761-3104)
PHONE..................................909 923-8357
Mike Lammers, *Mgr*
**EMP:** 51
**SALES (corp-wide):** 7.12B **Privately Held**
**Web:** www.crown.com
**SIC: 3537** Lift trucks, industrial: fork, platform, straddle, etc.
**PA:** Crown Equipment Corporation
44 S Washington St
419 629-2311

**(P-9514)**
**CROWN EQUIPMENT CORPORATION**
Also Called: Crown Lift Trucks
1400 Crocker Ave, Hayward (94544-7031)
PHONE..................................510 471-7272
Scott Walter, *Mgr*
**EMP:** 50
**SALES (corp-wide):** 7.12B **Privately Held**
**Web:** www.crown.com
**SIC: 3537** Lift trucks, industrial: fork, platform, straddle, etc.
**PA:** Crown Equipment Corporation
44 S Washington St
419 629-2311

**(P-9515)**
**CROWN EQUIPMENT CORPORATION**
Also Called: Crown Lift Trucks
1420 Enterprise Blvd, West Sacramento (95691-3485)
PHONE..................................916 373-8980
Ron Bensman, *Mgr*
**EMP:** 48
**SALES (corp-wide):** 7.12B **Privately Held**
**Web:** www.crown.com
**SIC: 3537** Lift trucks, industrial: fork, platform, straddle, etc.
**PA:** Crown Equipment Corporation
44 S Washington St
419 629-2311

**(P-9516)**
**CROWN EQUIPMENT CORPORATION**
Also Called: Crown Lift Trucks
4061 Via Oro Ave, Long Beach (90810-1458)
PHONE..................................310 952-6600
Tom Labrador, *Brnch Mgr*
**EMP:** 64
**SALES (corp-wide):** 7.12B **Privately Held**
**Web:** www.crown.com
**SIC: 3537** Lift trucks, industrial: fork, platform, straddle, etc.
**PA:** Crown Equipment Corporation
44 S Washington St
419 629-2311

**(P-9517)**
**DAYTON SUPERIOR CORPORATION**
Also Called: American Highway Technology
5300 Claus Rd Ste 7, Modesto (95357-1665)
PHONE..................................209 869-1201
Wesley Tilton, *Mgr*
**EMP:** 26
**SALES (corp-wide):** 7.35B **Privately Held**
**Web:** www.daytonsuperior.com
**SIC: 3537** Loading docks: portable, adjustable, and hydraulic
**HQ:** Dayton Superior Corporation
1125 Byers Rd
Miamisburg OH 45342
937 866-0711

**(P-9518)**
**FREMONT PACKAGE EXPRESS**
734 Still Breeze Way, Sacramento (95831-5544)
PHONE..................................916 541-1812
Terrence Wong, *Owner*
**EMP:** 15 **EST:** 2015
**SALES (est):** 1.14MM **Privately Held**
**SIC: 3537** Trucks: freight, baggage, etc.: industrial, except mining

**(P-9519)**
**GLEASON INDUSTRIAL PDTS INC**
Also Called: Milwaukee Hand Truck
10474 Santa Monica Blvd Ste 400, Los Angeles (90025-6929)
PHONE..................................574 533-1141
Morton Kay, *CEO*
Shirley Kotler, *
Howard Simon, *
▲ **EMP:** 200 **EST:** 1891
**SQ FT:** 200,000
**SALES (est):** 20.58MM **Privately Held**
**SIC: 3537** Industrial trucks and tractors

**(P-9520)**
**GOLDEN GATE FREIGHTLINER INC**
Also Called: Golden Gate Truck Center
2727 E Central Ave, Fresno (93725-2425)
P.O. Box 12346 (93777-2346)
PHONE..................................559 486-4310
**EMP:** 300
**SALES (corp-wide):** 47.73MM **Privately Held**
**Web:** www.freightliner.com
**SIC: 3537** 5511 Trucks: freight, baggage, etc.: industrial, except mining; New and used car dealers
**HQ:** Golden Gate Freightliner Inc.
8200 Baldwin St
Oakland CA 94621
559 486-4310

**(P-9521)**
**GOLDEN STATE TRCK TRLR REPR IN**
1354 Dayton St, Salinas (93901-4426)
PHONE..................................888 881-8825
Rene Manzur, *CEO*
**EMP:** 24
**SALES (est):** 3.4MM **Privately Held**
**Web:** www.goldenstatetruckrepair.com
**SIC: 3537** Trucks, tractors, loaders, carriers, and similar equipment

**(P-9522)**
**GOLDEN VALLEY & ASSOCIATES INC**
Also Called: Cal Central Catering Trailers
3511 Finch Rd # A, Modesto (95357-4143)
PHONE..................................209 549-1549
Estafani Ochoa, *CEO*
**EMP:** 22 **EST:** 2004
**SQ FT:** 30,000
**SALES (est):** 6.26MM **Privately Held**
**SIC: 3537** Aircraft engine cradles

**(P-9523)**
**HYDRAULIC SHOP INC**
2753 S Vista Ave, Bloomington (92316-3269)
PHONE..................................909 875-9336
Christopher O Kirk, *Pr*
**EMP:** 20 **EST:** 2006
**SQ FT:** 4,500
**SALES (est):** 5.94MM **Privately Held**
**Web:** www.hydraulicshopinc.com
**SIC: 3537** Industrial trucks and tractors

**(P-9524)**
**INDUSTRIAL DESIGN PRODUCTS INC**
2700 Pomona Blvd, Pomona (91768-3222)
P.O. Box 7846 (92860-8095)
PHONE..................................909 468-0693
Richard Fleischhacker Junior, *Pr*
Jose Pizarro, *Ex VP*
**EMP:** 21 **EST:** 1999
**SQ FT:** 14,000
**SALES (est):** 732.01K **Privately Held**
**Web:** www.toprevenuegate.com
**SIC: 3537** 5084 2542 Platforms, stands, tables, pallets, and similar equipment; Materials handling machinery; Pallet racks: except wood

**(P-9525)**
**J&S GOODWIN INC (HQ)**
5753 E Santa Ana Canyon Rd Ste G-355, Anaheim (92807-3230)
PHONE..................................714 956-4040
Arthur J Goodwin, *CEO*
Sharon Goodwin, *
Mark Mcgregor, *CFO*
Scott Currie, *
Dan Broschak, *
◆ **EMP:** 65 **EST:** 1989
**SQ FT:** 3,000
**SALES (est):** 35.64MM
**SALES (corp-wide):** 8.93B **Publicly Held**
**SIC: 3537** 5088 5084 Trucks, tractors, loaders, carriers, and similar equipment; Golf carts; Materials handling machinery
**PA:** Polaris Inc.
2100 Highway 55
763 542-0500

**(P-9526)**
**JE THOMSON & COMPANY LLC**
Also Called: Carousel USA
15206 Ceres Ave, Fontana (92335-4311)
PHONE..................................626 334-7190
▲ **EMP:** 15 **EST:** 2004
**SALES (est):** 4.86MM **Privately Held**
**Web:** www.carousel-usa.com
**SIC: 3537** 3535 Tables, lift: hydraulic; Trolley conveyors

**(P-9527)**
**JS TRUCKING INC**
Also Called: Js Trucking
2930 Geer Rd, Turlock (95382-1142)
PHONE..................................209 252-0007
Balbir Dhaliwal, *Pr*
**EMP:** 40 **EST:** 2010
**SALES (est):** 3.05MM **Privately Held**
**SIC: 3537** Trucks: freight, baggage, etc.: industrial, except mining

**(P-9528)**
**MEEM WORLDWIDE LOGISTICS LLC**
5756 Jean Dr, Union City (94587-5182)
PHONE..................................347 666-9680
**EMP:** 15
**SALES (est):** 1.12MM **Privately Held**
**SIC: 3537** 7389 Trucks, tractors, loaders, carriers, and similar equipment; Business services, nec

**(P-9529)**
**PAPE MATERIAL HANDLING INC**
2600 Peck Rd, City Of Industry (90601-1620)
P.O. Box 60007 (91716-0007)
PHONE..................................562 692-9311

## 3537 - Industrial Trucks And Tractors (P-9530)

Steve Smith, *Mgr*
**EMP:** 100
**Web:** www.papemh.com
**SIC: 3537** 5084 Forklift trucks; Industrial machinery and equipment
**HQ:** Pape' Material Handling, Inc.
355 Goodpasture Island Rd
Eugene OR 97401

### (P-9530)
### POWER PT INC
9292 Nancy St, Cypress (90630-3318)
**PHONE**....................714 826-7407
Tyson Paulis, *Brnch Mgr*
**EMP:** 36
**SALES (corp-wide):** 5.96MM **Privately Held**
**SIC: 3537** Platforms, stands, tables, pallets, and similar equipment
**PA:** Power Pt Inc
1500 Crafton Ave Bldg 100
951 490-4149

### (P-9531)
### POWER PT INC (PA)
Also Called: AAA Pallet
1500 Crafton Ave Bldg 100, Mentone (92359-1315)
**PHONE**....................951 490-4149
Tyson Paulis, *CEO*
**EMP:** 32 **EST:** 2018
**SALES (est):** 5.96MM
**SALES (corp-wide):** 5.96MM **Privately Held**
**SIC: 3537** Platforms, stands, tables, pallets, and similar equipment

### (P-9532)
### PRODUCTBOARD INC (PA)
333 Bush St, San Francisco (94104-2832)
**PHONE**....................844 472-6273
Hubert Palan, *CEO*
Noah Barr, *
**EMP:** 233 **EST:** 2014
**SALES (est):** 14.29MM
**SALES (corp-wide):** 14.29MM **Privately Held**
**Web:** www.productboard.com
**SIC: 3537** Platforms, cargo

### (P-9533)
### PROFESSIONAL LUMPER SVC INC
1943 Alex Way, Turlock (95382-9207)
P.O. Box 729 (95307-0729)
**PHONE**....................209 613-5397
Tony Kauffman, *Pr*
**EMP:** 35 **EST:** 2004
**SALES (est):** 1.37MM **Privately Held**
**Web:** www.prolumpers.com
**SIC: 3537** Trucks, tractors, loaders, carriers, and similar equipment

### (P-9534)
### SUPERIOR TRAILER WORKS
13700 Slover Ave, Fontana (92337-7067)
**PHONE**....................909 350-0185
Jack N Pocock, *CEO*
Jay Pocock, *
▲ **EMP:** 50 **EST:** 1935
**SQ FT:** 4,000
**SALES (est):** 4.35MM **Privately Held**
**Web:** www.superiortrailerworks.com
**SIC: 3537** 7539 Industrial trucks and tractors; Trailer repair

### (P-9535)
### TAYLOR-DUNN MANUFACTURING LLC (HQ)
2114 W Ball Rd, Anaheim (92804-5498)
**PHONE**....................714 956-4040
Keith Simon, *CEO*
◆ **EMP:** 100 **EST:** 1949
**SQ FT:** 145,000
**SALES (est):** 23.4MM
**SALES (corp-wide):** 50.09MM **Privately Held**
**Web:** www.taylor-dunn.com
**SIC: 3537** Trucks, tractors, loaders, carriers, and similar equipment
**PA:** Waev Inc.
2114 W Ball Rd
714 956-4040

### (P-9536)
### WAEV INC (PA)
2114 W Ball Rd, Anaheim (92804-5417)
**PHONE**....................714 956-4040
Keith Simon, *Pr*
Paul Vitrano, *Legal*
Cosmin Batrin, *Sr VP*
Jon Conlon, *Sr VP*
Luke Mulvaney, *Sr VP*
**EMP:** 48 **EST:** 2021
**SALES (est):** 50.09MM
**SALES (corp-wide):** 50.09MM **Privately Held**
**Web:** www.waevinc.com
**SIC: 3537** Trucks, tractors, loaders, carriers, and similar equipment

### (P-9537)
### WAKOOL TRANSPORT
19130 San Jose Ave, Rowland Heights (91748-1415)
**PHONE**....................626 723-3100
Willie Wu, *CEO*
Hong Zhu, *
**EMP:** 72 **EST:** 2022
**SALES (est):** 3.18MM **Privately Held**
**Web:** www.wakooltransport.com
**SIC: 3537** Trucks: freight, baggage, etc.: industrial, except mining

## 3541 Machine Tools, Metal Cutting Type

### (P-9538)
### ACCEL MANUFACTURING INC
Also Called: Accel Manufacturing
1709 Grant St, Santa Clara (95050-3939)
**PHONE**....................408 727-5883
Loc Pham, *Pr*
**EMP:** 15 **EST:** 2010
**SALES (est):** 4.66MM **Privately Held**
**Web:** www.accelmfg.com
**SIC: 3541** Machine tool replacement & repair parts, metal cutting types

### (P-9539)
### AM AND S MFG INC
Also Called: AM&s Mnufactruing Design Group
1394 Tully Rd Ste 203-207 Pmb 213-215, San Jose (95122-3057)
**PHONE**....................408 396-3027
Andrew Le, *CEO*
Vincent Rondas, *
**EMP:** 35 **EST:** 2012
**SALES (est):** 5.64MM **Privately Held**
**Web:** www.amnsmfg.com
**SIC: 3541** 3599 3728 3548 Lathes; Machine shop, jobbing and repair; Aircraft body and wing assemblies and parts; Welding wire, bare and coated

### (P-9540)
### APT MANUFACTURING LLC
Also Called: Stellar Engineering
2899 E Coronado St Ste E, Anaheim (92806-2535)
**PHONE**....................714 632-0040
**EMP:** 18 **EST:** 2012
**SALES (est):** 2.72MM **Privately Held**
**SIC: 3541** 3451 Plasma process metal cutting machines; Screw machine products

### (P-9541)
### BERNHARDT AND BERNHARDT INC
Also Called: Protool Co
14771 Myford Rd Ste D, Tustin (92780-7206)
**PHONE**....................714 544-0708
Anton Bernhardt, *Pr*
Norbert Bernhardt, *Pr*
**EMP:** 21 **EST:** 1972
**SQ FT:** 4,600
**SALES (est):** 2.63MM **Privately Held**
**Web:** www.protoolco.com
**SIC: 3541** Numerically controlled metal cutting machine tools

### (P-9542)
### BERTRAM CAPITAL MANAGEMENT LLC (PA)
Also Called: Bertram Capital
950 Tower Ln Ste 1000, Foster City (94404-4244)
**PHONE**....................650 358-5000
Ingrid Swenson, *
Kevin Yamashita, *
David Hellier, *
Jared Ruger, *
**EMP:** 136 **EST:** 2006
**SALES (est):** 668.04MM **Privately Held**
**Web:** www.bertramcapital.com
**SIC: 3541** 3556 Machine tools, metal cutting type; Cutting, chopping, grinding, mixing, and similar machinery

### (P-9543)
### CERATIZIT LOS ANGELES LLC
11312 Sunrise Gold Cir, Rancho Cordova (95742-6508)
**PHONE**....................310 464-8050
Mark Nunez, *Pr*
Salvador Nunez, *
Carmen Nunez, *
▲ **EMP:** 85 **EST:** 2016
**SALES (est):** 23.14MM
**SALES (corp-wide):** 242.12K **Privately Held**
**Web:** www.bestcarbide.com
**SIC: 3541** Machine tools, metal cutting type
**HQ:** Ceratizit S.A.
Route De Holzem 101
Mamer 8232
3120851

### (P-9544)
### CREMACH TECH INC (DH)
Also Called: Creative Machine Technology
369 Meyer Cir, Corona (92879-1078)
**PHONE**....................951 735-3194
Mike Mcneeley, *CEO*
Mike Mcneeley, *Prin*
Jae Wan Choi, *
**EMP:** 23 **EST:** 2000
**SQ FT:** 34,000
**SALES (est):** 23.18MM
**SALES (corp-wide):** 16.11B **Publicly Held**
**Web:** www.cmtus.com
**SIC: 3541** 8711 Machine tools, metal cutting type; Engineering services
**HQ:** Brooks Instrument Llc
407 W Vine St
Hatfield PA 19440

### (P-9545)
### CREMACH TECH INC
Also Called: Creative Machine Technology
400 E Parkridge Ave, Corona (92879-6618)
**PHONE**....................951 735-3194
Mike Mcneeley, *Brnch Mgr*
**EMP:** 117
**SALES (corp-wide):** 16.11B **Publicly Held**
**Web:** www.cmtus.com
**SIC: 3541** Machine tools, metal cutting type
**HQ:** Cremach Tech, Inc.
369 Meyer Cir
Corona CA 92879

### (P-9546)
### CTD MACHINES INC
7355 E Slauson Ave, Commerce (90040-3626)
**PHONE**....................213 689-4455
Kiwon Ban, *Genl Mgr*
Thomas Orlando, *Pr*
Seymour Lehrer, *VP*
Shirley Lehrer, *VP*
Ellen Orlando, *Sec*
**EMP:** 18 **EST:** 1967
**SALES (est):** 3.84MM **Privately Held**
**Web:** www.ctdsaw.com
**SIC: 3541** Cutoff machines (metalworking machinery)

### (P-9547)
### DAC INTERNATIONAL INC
Also Called: D A C
6390 Rose Ln, Carpinteria (93013-2922)
**PHONE**....................805 684-8307
Kenneth R Payne, *Pr*
Joyce Kawachi, *
▲ **EMP:** 34 **EST:** 1999
**SQ FT:** 17,500
**SALES (est):** 4.78MM **Privately Held**
**Web:** www.dac-intl.com
**SIC: 3541** Machine tools, metal cutting type

### (P-9548)
### DEVELOPMENT ASSOCIATES CONTRLS
Also Called: D A C
6390 Rose Ln, Carpinteria (93013-2922)
**PHONE**....................805 684-8307
Edward W Vernon, *Pr*
**EMP:** 32 **EST:** 1994
**SALES (est):** 2.99MM
**SALES (corp-wide):** 2.55MM **Privately Held**
**Web:** www.dac-intl.com
**SIC: 3541** Lathes, metal cutting and polishing
**HQ:** Dac Vision Incorporated
3630 W Miller Rd Ste 350
Garland TX 75041
972 677-2700

### (P-9549)
### DMG MORI MANUFACTURING USA INC (HQ)
Also Called: DTL Research & Technical Ctr
3601 Faraday Ave, Davis (95618-7776)
**PHONE**....................530 746-7400
Adam Hansel, *Pr*
Zach Piner, *
Natsuo Okada, *
Hiroshi Takami, *
▲ **EMP:** 63 **EST:** 2011
**SALES (est):** 10.33MM **Privately Held**
**Web:** us.dmgmori.com
**SIC: 3541** Machine tools, metal cutting type
**PA:** Dmg Mori Co., Ltd.
2-3-23, Shiomi

## 3541 - Machine Tools, Metal Cutting Type (P-9571)

**(P-9550)**
**DMG MORI MANUFACTURING USA INC**
3601 Faraday Ave, Davis (95618-7776)
PHONE....................530 746-3140
Dan Letamendi, *Prin*
EMP: 57
Web: us.dmgmori.com
SIC: 3541 Machine tools, metal cutting type
HQ: Dmg Mori Manufacturing Usa, Inc.
  3601 Faraday Ave
  Davis CA 95618
  530 746-7400

**(P-9551)**
**DOLLAR SHAVE CLUB INC (HQ)**
13335 Maxella Ave, Marina Del Rey (90292-5619)
PHONE....................310 975-8528
Jason Goldberger, *CEO*
Janet Song, *
Danny Miles, *
EMP: 110 EST: 2011
SALES (est): 94.1MM
SALES (corp-wide): 64.79B Privately Held
Web: us.dollarshaveclub.com
SIC: 3541 3991 2844 Shaving machines (metalworking); Shaving brushes; Shaving preparations
PA: Unilever Plc
  Unilever House
  207 572-1202

**(P-9552)**
**DORINGER MANUFACTURING CO INC**
13400 Estrella Ave, Gardena (90248-1513)
PHONE....................310 366-7766
William Bailey, *Pr*
Lisa Pomeroy, *Treas*
EMP: 15 EST: 1982
SQ FT: 50,000
SALES (est): 2.58MM
SALES (corp-wide): 5.78MM Privately Held
Web: www.doringer.com
SIC: 3541 Machine tools, metal cutting type
PA: Cold Saws Of America, Inc.
  13400 Estrella Ave
  310 366-7766

**(P-9553)**
**DOWNEY GRINDING CO**
12323 Bellflower Blvd, Downey (90242-2829)
P.O. Box 583 (90241-0583)
PHONE....................562 803-5556
Larry Sequeira, *Pr*
Darla Sequeira, *
▲ EMP: 26 EST: 1960
SQ FT: 27,000
SALES (est): 3.61MM Privately Held
Web: www.downeygrinding.com
SIC: 3541 3599 Machine tools, metal cutting type; Machine shop, jobbing and repair

**(P-9554)**
**ENSIGN US DRLG CAL INC (HQ)**
7001 Charity Ave, Bakersfield (93308-5824)
PHONE....................661 589-0111
Selby Porter, *Pr*
Loys Honeycutt, *Prin*
EMP: 21 EST: 1962
SALES (est): 24.45MM
SALES (corp-wide): 1.3B Privately Held
Web: www.ensignusd.com
SIC: 3541 Drilling and boring machines
PA: Ensign Energy Services Inc
  1000-400 5 Ave Sw
  403 262-1361

**(P-9555)**
**GNB CORPORATION**
Also Called: GNB Vacuum Excellence Defined
3200 Dwight Rd Ste 100, Elk Grove (95758-6461)
PHONE....................916 395-3003
Thomas Dobler, *CEO*
Chris Long, *
Klaus Rindt, *
Donald A Bendix, *
▲ EMP: 60 EST: 1968
SQ FT: 62,500
SALES (est): 23.88MM Privately Held
Web: www.vacuumchamber.com
SIC: 3541 3491 Machine tools, metal cutting type; Industrial valves
HQ: Ellison Technologies, Inc.
  9828 Arlee Ave
  Santa Fe Springs CA 90670
  562 949-8311

**(P-9556)**
**HAAS AUTOMATION INC (PA)**
2800 Sturgis Rd, Oxnard (93030-8901)
PHONE....................805 278-1800
◆ EMP: 1521 EST: 1983
SALES (est): 437.22MM
SALES (corp-wide): 437.22MM Privately Held
Web: www.haascnc.com
SIC: 3541 Machine tools, metal cutting type

**(P-9557)**
**J&N ENGINEERING INC**
1310 N 4th St, San Jose (95112-4713)
PHONE....................408 680-1810
John Pham, *CEO*
Tu Pham, *Dir*
EMP: 20 EST: 2017
SALES (est): 2.34MM Privately Held
Web: www.j-n-engineering.com
SIC: 3541 Machine tools, metal cutting type

**(P-9558)**
**K-V ENGINEERING INC**
2411 W 1st St, Santa Ana (92703-3509)
PHONE....................714 229-9977
Duong Vu, *Pr*
Christie Vu, *
EMP: 60 EST: 1984
SQ FT: 22,000
SALES (est): 9.15MM Privately Held
Web: www.kvengineering.com
SIC: 3541 3542 Milling machines; Machine tools, metal forming type

**(P-9559)**
**KYOCERA TYCOM CORPORATION**
Also Called: Kyoceara
3565 Cadillac Ave, Costa Mesa (92626-1401)
PHONE....................714 428-3600
▲ EMP: 500
SIC: 3541 3845 3843 3841 Machine tools, metal cutting type; Endoscopic equipment, electromedical, nec; Cutting instruments, dental; Surgical and medical instruments

**(P-9560)**
**MELFRED BORZALL INC**
2712 Airpark Dr, Santa Maria (93455-1418)
PHONE....................805 614-4344
Dick Melsheimer, *Prin*
Larry Coots, *Prin*
▲ EMP: 40 EST: 1946
SQ FT: 30,000
SALES (est): 5.31MM Privately Held
Web: www.melfredborzall.com
SIC: 3541 Machine tools, metal cutting type

**(P-9561)**
**METLSAW SYSTEMS INC**
2950 Bay Vista Ct, Benicia (94510-1123)
PHONE....................707 746-6200
Lisa Kvech, *CEO*
◆ EMP: 21 EST: 1984
SQ FT: 30,000
SALES (est): 7.36MM Privately Held
Web: www.metlsaw.com
SIC: 3541 Saws and sawing machines

**(P-9562)**
**PRECISION DEBURRING SERVICES**
4440 Manning Rd, Pico Rivera (90660-2164)
PHONE....................562 944-4497
Darren Smith, *Pr*
▲ EMP: 24 EST: 1984
SALES (est): 810.31K Privately Held
Web: www.pdsdeburring.com
SIC: 3541 Machine tools, metal cutting type

**(P-9563)**
**PROMAX TOOLS LP**
Also Called: Design Rite Xl
11312 Sunrise Gold Cir, Rancho Cordova (95742-6508)
PHONE....................916 638-0501
▲ EMP: 42 EST: 1967
SALES (est): 3.68MM Privately Held
Web: www.promaxtools.com
SIC: 3541 Machine tools, metal cutting type

**(P-9564)**
**R H STRASBAUGH (PA)**
Also Called: Strasbaugh
825 Buckley Rd, San Luis Obispo (93401-8192)
PHONE....................805 541-6424
Alan Strasbaugh, *CF*
Brad Diaz, *VP*
Eric Jacobson, *CUST SERV*
Michael Kirkpatrick, *S&M/Dir*
EMP: 50 EST: 1964
SQ FT: 135,000
SALES (est): 9.74MM
SALES (corp-wide): 9.74MM Privately Held
Web: www.gainliftoff.com
SIC: 3541 3559 5065 Grinding, polishing, buffing, lapping, and honing machines; Semiconductor manufacturing machinery; Electronic parts and equipment, nec

**(P-9565)**
**REPUBLIC MACHINERY CO INC (PA)**
Also Called: Lagun Engineering Solutions
800 Sprucelake Dr, Harbor City (90710-1607)
PHONE....................310 518-1100
Vivian Bezic, *CEO*
Joseph Bezic, *
Nicole Bezic, *
◆ EMP: 22 EST: 1969
SQ FT: 30,000
SALES (est): 4.73MM
SALES (corp-wide): 4.73MM Privately Held
Web: www.lagun.com
SIC: 3541 3542 3549 3545 Drilling and boring machines; Arbor presses; Metalworking machinery, nec; Machine knives, metalworking

**(P-9566)**
**ROBB-JACK CORPORATION (PA)**
3300 Nicolaus Rd Ste 1, Lincoln (95648-9574)
PHONE....................916 645-6045
David Baker, *Pr*
Steve Handrop, *
EMP: 74 EST: 1959
SQ FT: 42,000
SALES (est): 9.58MM
SALES (corp-wide): 9.58MM Privately Held
Web: www.robbjack.com
SIC: 3541 Machine tools, metal cutting type

**(P-9567)**
**RYTAN INC**
1648 W 134th St, Gardena (90249-2014)
PHONE....................310 328-6553
Carol J Silbaugh, *CEO*
▲ EMP: 18 EST: 1983
SQ FT: 20,400
SALES (est): 2.56MM Privately Held
Web: www.rytan.com
SIC: 3541 Keysetting machines

**(P-9568)**
**S L FUSCO INC (PA)**
1966 E Via Arado, Rancho Dominguez (90220)
P.O. Box 5924 (90224)
PHONE....................310 868-1010
Jerald C Rosin, *CEO*
Eric Rosin, *
Arlene Rosin, *
Barrie Williams, *
Tom Burke, *
◆ EMP: 45 EST: 1941
SQ FT: 40,000
SALES (est): 24.65MM
SALES (corp-wide): 24.65MM Privately Held
Web: www.slfusco.com
SIC: 3541 Machine tools, metal cutting type

**(P-9569)**
**S S SCHAFFER CO INC**
Also Called: Steel Services Co
5637 District Blvd, Vernon (90058-5518)
PHONE....................323 560-1430
Steven Schaffer Junior, *Pr*
Marcia Schaffer, *Treas*
William Salenbach, *Sec*
Caroline Sallenbach, *VP*
EMP: 15 EST: 1940
SQ FT: 30,000
SALES (est): 1.81MM Privately Held
SIC: 3541 Grinding machines, metalworking

**(P-9570)**
**SAFETY PRODUCTS HOLDINGS LLC**
170 Technology Dr, Irvine (92618-2401)
PHONE....................714 662-1033
Andreas Kieper, *of Glbl Sls*
EMP: 50 EST: 2016
SALES (est): 3.42MM Privately Held
Web: www.phcsafety.com
SIC: 3541 3556 Machine tools, metal cutting type; Cutting, chopping, grinding, mixing, and similar machinery
PA: Bertram Capital Management, Llc
  950 Tower Ln Ste 1000

**(P-9571)**
**SHERLINE PRODUCTS INCORPORATED**
Also Called: Sherline Products
3235 Executive Rdg, Vista (92081-8527)

# 3541 - Machine Tools, Metal Cutting Type (P-9572)

PHONE..................760 727-5181
Joe Martin, *Pr*
Karl W Rohlin Iii, *CEO*
Charla Papp, *
▲ EMP: 30 EST: 1973
SQ FT: 65,000
SALES (est): 6.04MM Privately Held
Web: www.sherlineipd.com
SIC: 3541 3545 Lathes, metal cutting and polishing; Machine tool accessories

### (P-9572)
### SOUTHWESTERN INDUSTRIES INC (PA)
Also Called: Trak Machine Tools
2615 Homestead Pl, Rancho Dominguez (90220-5610)
P.O. Box 9066 (90224-9066)
PHONE..................310 608-4422
Stephen F Pinto, *CFO*
Richard W Leonhard, *
John Arroues, *
John Baumhauer, *
Mark Eisen, *
▲ EMP: 70 EST: 1951
SALES (est): 34.9MM
SALES (corp-wide): 34.9MM Privately Held
Web: www.southwesternindustries.com
SIC: 3541 Machine tools, metal cutting type

### (P-9573)
### SUPERTEC MACHINERY INC
Also Called: St Supertec
6435 Alondra Blvd, Paramount (90723-3758)
PHONE..................562 220-1675
Johnny Kao, *CEO*
Randy Chu, *Pr*
Yanlin Qiao, *Acctnt*
▲ EMP: 15 EST: 1994
SQ FT: 8,420
SALES (est): 2.35MM Privately Held
Web: www.supertecusa.com
SIC: 3541 3542 7389 Grinding, polishing, buffing, lapping, and honing machines; Machine tools, metal forming type; Grinding, precision: commercial or industrial

### (P-9574)
### US UNION TOOL INC (HQ)
1260 N Fee Ana St, Anaheim (92807-1817)
PHONE..................714 521-6242
Hideo Hirano, *Pr*
Robert Smallwood, *
▲ EMP: 45 EST: 1981
SQ FT: 44,000
SALES (est): 5.75MM Privately Held
Web: www.uniontool.co.jp
SIC: 3541 Machine tools, metal cutting type
PA: Union Tool Co.
    6-17-1, Minamioi

---

## 3542 Machine Tools, Metal Forming Type

### (P-9575)
### ADDITION MANUFACTURING TECHNOLOGIES CA INC
1391 Specialty Dr Ste A, Vista (92081-8521)
PHONE..................760 597-5220
▲ EMP: 35
SIC: 3542 Bending machines

### (P-9576)
### AMBRIT INDUSTRIES INC
432 Magnolia Ave, Glendale (91204-2406)
PHONE..................818 243-1224
Paul Yaussi, *Pr*
Louis A Yaussi, *
Michelle Taylor, *
EMP: 38 EST: 1946
SQ FT: 9,184
SALES (est): 6.37MM Privately Held
Web: www.ambritindustries.com
SIC: 3542 3363 Die casting machines; Aluminum die-castings

### (P-9577)
### AMERICAN PNEUMATIC TOOLS INC
Also Called: APT
1000 S Grand Ave, Santa Ana (92705-4122)
PHONE..................562 204-1555
Kim Eads, *Pr*
Dan O Brien, *CFO*
▲ EMP: 16 EST: 1938
SQ FT: 15,000
SALES (est): 2.42MM Privately Held
Web: www.apt-tools.com
SIC: 3542 3541 3546 3532 Machine tools, metal forming type; Machine tools, metal cutting type; Power-driven handtools; Mining machinery

### (P-9578)
### AMERICAN PRECISION HYDRAULICS
5601 Research Dr, Huntington Beach (92649-1620)
PHONE..................714 903-8610
Susan Smith, *Pr*
Steve Smith, *
EMP: 23 EST: 1996
SQ FT: 6,500
SALES (est): 2.69MM Privately Held
Web: www.americanprecisionassembly.com
SIC: 3542 Presses: hydraulic and pneumatic, mechanical and manual

### (P-9579)
### ANGELUS MACHINE CORP INTL
4900 Pacific Blvd, Vernon (90058-2214)
PHONE..................323 583-2171
Maurice Koeberle, *Ch Bd*
Chuck Deane, *
EMP: 45 EST: 1910
SQ FT: 295,000
SALES (est): 4.42MM Privately Held
SIC: 3542 Metal container making machines: cans, etc.
HQ: Angelus Sanitary Can Machine Company
    4900 Pacific Blvd
    Vernon CA 90058
    314 862-8000

### (P-9580)
### BORDEN MANUFACTURING
3314 Pacific Trail, Cottonwood (96022)
PHONE..................530 347-6642
Ralph Borden, *Pt*
Karen Borden, *Pt*
EMP: 25 EST: 1996
SQ FT: 7,200
SALES (est): 1.15MM Privately Held
Web: www.stretcherbars.net
SIC: 3542 Stretching machines

### (P-9581)
### BROTHERS MACHINE & TOOL INC
11095 Inland Ave, Jurupa Valley (91752-1155)
PHONE..................951 361-9454
Jose E Razo, *Pr*
EMP: 20
SIC: 3542 Machine tools, metal forming type
PA: Brothers Machine & Tool, Inc.
    11098 Inland Ave

### (P-9582)
### CARANDO TECHNOLOGIES INC
345 N Harrison St, Stockton (95203-2801)
P.O. Box 1167 (95201-1167)
PHONE..................209 948-6500
Sidney A Scheutz, *Pr*
Laura Keir, *
▼ EMP: 25 EST: 2003
SQ FT: 35,000
SALES (est): 3.65MM Privately Held
Web: www.carando.net
SIC: 3542 3548 3599 Machine tools, metal forming type; Welding apparatus; Custom machinery

### (P-9583)
### HORN MACHINE TOOLS INC (PA)
Also Called: H M T
40455 Brickyard Dr Ste 101, Madera (93636-9516)
PHONE..................559 431-4131
Kent Horn, *Pr*
▲ EMP: 21 EST: 1996
SALES (est): 5.43MM
SALES (corp-wide): 5.43MM Privately Held
Web: www.hornmachinetools.com
SIC: 3542 5084 Bending machines; Industrial machinery and equipment

### (P-9584)
### MAGNETIC METALS CORPORATION
2475 W La Palma Ave, Anaheim (92801-2610)
PHONE..................714 828-4625
Linda Cannon, *Brnch Mgr*
EMP: 15
SQ FT: 50,400
SALES (corp-wide): 645.5MM Privately Held
Web: www.magneticmetals.com
SIC: 3542 Magnetic forming machines
HQ: Magnetic Metals Corporation
    1950 Marlton Pike E # 103
    Cherry Hill NJ 08003
    856 964-7842

### (P-9585)
### MEDLIN RAMPS
14903 Marquardt Ave, Santa Fe Springs (90670-5128)
PHONE..................877 463-3546
Mark Medlin, *Prin*
▲ EMP: 42 EST: 1990
SQ FT: 10,000
SALES (est): 4.98MM Privately Held
Web: www.medlinramps.com
SIC: 3542 5084 3441 Machine tools, metal forming type; Materials handling machinery; Fabricated structural metal

### (P-9586)
### MJC ENGINEERING AND TECH INC
15401 Assembly Ln, Huntington Beach (92649-1329)
PHONE..................714 890-0618
Carl Lorentzen, *Pr*
Per Carlson, *VP*
Gro Jensen, *Treas*
Kristi Jensen, *Sec*
Bernd Hermann, *CFO*
◆ EMP: 18 EST: 1993
SQ FT: 10,000
SALES (est): 4.98MM Privately Held
Web: www.mjcengineering.com
SIC: 3542 Spinning machines, metal

### (P-9587)
### PHI (PA)
Also Called: PHI Hydraulics
14955 Salt Lake Ave, City Of Industry (91746-3133)
PHONE..................626 968-9680
Anthony Morrow, *Pr*
▼ EMP: 18 EST: 2010
SQ FT: 25,930
SALES (est): 7.75MM
SALES (corp-wide): 7.75MM Privately Held
Web: www.phihydraulics.com
SIC: 3542 3549 Presses: hydraulic and pneumatic, mechanical and manual; Metalworking machinery, nec

### (P-9588)
### SAMTECH AUTOMOTIVE USA INC
Also Called: Samtech International
1130 E Dominguez St, Carson (90746-3518)
PHONE..................310 638-9955
Yoshiki Sakaguchi, *Pr*
Don Zimmerman, *
▲ EMP: 50 EST: 1996
SQ FT: 27,812
SALES (est): 11.04MM Privately Held
Web: www.samtechintl.com
SIC: 3542 Machine tools, metal forming type
PA: Samtech Corp.
    1000-18, Emmyocho

### (P-9589)
### SYNVENTIVE ENGINEERING INC
Also Called: Demand Cnc
3301 Michelson Dr Apt 1534, Irvine (92612-7684)
PHONE..................312 848-8717
Greg Field, *Pr*
James Bloomfield, *
EMP: 38 EST: 2017
SALES (est): 5MM Privately Held
SIC: 3542 Machine tools, metal forming type

### (P-9590)
### UNIVERSAL PUNCH CORP
4001 W Macarthur Blvd, Santa Ana (92704-6307)
P.O. Box 26879 (92799-6879)
PHONE..................714 556-4488
Kenneth L Williams, *Pr*
Kevin Williams, *
Joan Williams, *
▲ EMP: 55 EST: 1974
SQ FT: 52,000
SALES (est): 5.47MM Privately Held
Web: www.universalpunch.com
SIC: 3542 3545 3544 3452 Punching and shearing machines; Machine tool accessories; Special dies, tools, jigs, and fixtures; Bolts, nuts, rivets, and washers

### (P-9591)
### US INDUSTRIAL TOOL & SUP CO
Also Called: Usit Co
14083 S Normandie Ave, Gardena (90249-2614)
P.O. Box 2589 (90247-0589)
PHONE..................310 464-8400
Keith Rowland, *CEO*
▲ EMP: 47 EST: 1955

## PRODUCTS & SERVICES SECTION
### 3544 - Special Dies, Tools, Jigs, And Fixtures (P-9612)

SQ FT: 35,000
SALES (est): 4.89MM **Privately Held**
Web: www.ustool.com
SIC: **3542** 3546  Machine tools, metal forming type; Power-driven handtools

**(P-9592)**
**WEST COAST-ACCUDYNE INC**
Also Called: Accudyne Engineering & Eqp
7180 Scout Ave, Bell  (90201-3202)
P.O. Box 2159  (90202-2159)
PHONE.............................562 927-2546
George F Schofhauser, *Pr*
Kurt Anderegg, *VP*
Jill Wigney, *Sec*
▲ **EMP:** 20 **EST:** 1954
SALES (est): 3.35MM **Privately Held**
Web: www.accudyneeng.com
SIC: **3542** 5084  Presses: forming, stamping, punching, sizing (machine tools); Machine tools and accessories

**(P-9593)**
**XY CORP INC**
Also Called: E P S Products
1258 Montalvo Way Ste A, Palm Springs  (92262-5441)
PHONE.............................760 323-0333
Jerry Good, *Pr*
Greg Good, *VP*
**EMP:** 15 **EST:** 1991
SQ FT: 14,000
SALES (est): 2.39MM **Privately Held**
SIC: **3542** 3299  Presses: hydraulic and pneumatic, mechanical and manual; Ornamental and architectural plaster work

---

### 3544 Special Dies, Tools, Jigs, And Fixtures

**(P-9594)**
**ACE CLEARWATER ENTERPRISES INC**
1614 Kona Dr, Compton  (90220-5412)
PHONE.............................310 538-5380
James D Dodson, *Brnch Mgr*
**EMP:** 35
SALES (corp-wide): 19.32MM **Privately Held**
Web: www.aceclearwater.com
SIC: **3544** 3728 3769  Special dies, tools, jigs, and fixtures; Aircraft parts and equipment, nec; Space vehicle equipment, nec
PA:  Ace Clearwater Enterprises, Inc.
     19815 Magellan Dr
     310 323-2140

**(P-9595)**
**ADVANCED MACHINING TOOLING INC**
Also Called: C S C
13535 Danielson St, Poway  (92064-6868)
PHONE.............................858 486-9050
Terry A Deane, *CEO*
Tony Cerda, *
Jodi Deane, *
**EMP:** 46 **EST:** 1989
SQ FT: 31,000
SALES (est): 7.47MM **Privately Held**
Web: www.amtmfg.com
SIC: **3544** 3599  Special dies, tools, jigs, and fixtures; Machine shop, jobbing and repair

**(P-9596)**
**ADVANCED MOLD TECHNOLOGY INC**
16507 Celadon Ct, Chino Hills  (91709-4611)
◆ **EMP:** 19 **EST:** 1984
SALES (est): 848.92K **Privately Held**
Web: www.advancedmold.com
SIC: **3544**  Special dies and tools

**(P-9597)**
**ALCO MANUFACTURING INC**
207 E Alton Ave, Santa Ana  (92707-4416)
P.O. Box 672  (92629-0672)
PHONE.............................714 549-5007
Frank Reuland, *Pr*
Frank Reuland, *VP*
Ingrid Reuland, *Sec*
**EMP:** 15 **EST:** 1980
SQ FT: 11,000
SALES (est): 1.92MM **Privately Held**
Web: www.alcomanufacturing.com
SIC: **3544** 3469 3444  Special dies and tools; Stamping metal for the trade; Sheet metalwork

**(P-9598)**
**AMBRIT ENGINEERING CORPORATION**
2640 Halladay St, Santa Ana  (92705-5649)
PHONE.............................714 557-1074
Terrence Saul, *CEO*
John F Mattimoe, *
Thomas W Vickers, *
▲ **EMP:** 65 **EST:** 1972
SQ FT: 32,000
SALES (est): 17.92MM **Privately Held**
Web: www.ambritengineering.com
SIC: **3544**  Forms (molds), for foundry and plastics working machinery

**(P-9599)**
**AMERICAN PLASTIC PRODUCTS INC**
9243 Glenoaks Blvd, Sun Valley  (91352-2614)
PHONE.............................818 504-1073
Roupen Yegavian, *Pr*
Varosh Petrosian, *
▲ **EMP:** 75 **EST:** 1991
SQ FT: 35,000
SALES (est): 9.07MM **Privately Held**
Web: www.americanplasticproductsinc.com
SIC: **3544**  Special dies and tools

**(P-9600)**
**ART MOLD DIE CASTING INC**
11872 Sheldon St, Sun Valley  (91352-1507)
PHONE.............................818 767-6464
Leo Benavides, *Pr*
Arman Sarkissian, *
**EMP:** 57 **EST:** 1965
SQ FT: 14,000
SALES (est): 976.47K **Privately Held**
Web: www.artmoldinc.com
SIC: **3544** 3369 3363  Industrial molds; Nonferrous foundries, nec; Aluminum die-castings

**(P-9601)**
**ATS TOOL INC**
Also Called: Ats Workholding
30222 Esperanza, Rcho Sta Marg  (92688-2121)
PHONE.............................949 888-1744
William Murphy, *Pr*
Sean Murphy, *VP*
▲ **EMP:** 25 **EST:** 1991
SALES (est): 1.28MM **Privately Held**
Web: www.atssystems.us
SIC: **3544**  Jigs and fixtures

**(P-9602)**
**AVIS ROTO DIE CO**
1560 N San Fernando Rd, Los Angeles  (90065-1225)
P.O. Box 65617  (90065-0617)
PHONE.............................323 255-7070
Avetis Iskanian, *CEO*
**EMP:** 30 **EST:** 1982
SQ FT: 32,000
SALES (est): 4.62MM **Privately Held**
Web: www.avisrd.com
SIC: **3544**  Paper cutting dies

**(P-9603)**
**AW DIE ENGRAVING  INC**
8550 Roland St, Buena Park  (90621-3199)
PHONE.............................714 521-7910
Arnold Werdin, *Pr*
Art Chavez, *
**EMP:** 30 **EST:** 1972
SQ FT: 9,000
SALES (est): 1.05MM **Privately Held**
Web: www.awdie.com
SIC: **3544**  Dies and die holders for metal cutting, forming, die casting

**(P-9604)**
**B&R MOLD  INC**
4564 E Los Angeles Ave Ste C, Simi Valley  (93063-3428)
PHONE.............................805 526-8665
Brent Robinson, *Pr*
**EMP:** 15 **EST:** 1986
SALES (est): 926.85K **Privately Held**
Web: www.brmold.com
SIC: **3544**  Special dies and tools

**(P-9605)**
**BALDA C BREWER  INC (DH)**
Also Called: C Brewer Company
4501 E Wall St, Ontario  (91761-8143)
PHONE.............................909 212-0290
Fabio Vanin, *CEO*
Steve Holland, *Pr*
Harold Hee, *VP*
Francesco Cavalieri, *CFO*
Sergio Stevanato, *Dir*
▲ **EMP:** 66 **EST:** 1968
SQ FT: 60,000
SALES (est): 21.18MM
SALES (corp-wide): 2.67MM **Privately Held**
SIC: **3544** 3089  Special dies, tools, jigs, and fixtures; Molding primary plastics
HQ:  Clere Ag
     Schluterstr. 45
     Berlin BE 10707
     302 130-0430

**(P-9606)**
**BARROT CORPORATION**
1881 Kaiser Ave, Irvine  (92614-5707)
PHONE.............................949 852-1640
Jesus Barrot, *Pr*
Carlos Barrot, *VP*
Robert Barrot, *Treas*
James Barrot, *Sec*
**EMP:** 22 **EST:** 1983
SQ FT: 15,000
SALES (est): 2.72MM **Privately Held**
Web: www.barrotcorp.com
SIC: **3544** 3769  Special dies and tools; Space vehicle equipment, nec

**(P-9607)**
**BENDA TOOL & MODEL WORKS  INC**
Also Called: A & B Diecasting
900 Alfred Nobel Dr, Hercules  (94547-1814)
PHONE.............................510 741-3170
Robert Dathe, *Pr*
Stephen Dathe, *
▲ **EMP:** 35 **EST:** 1946
SQ FT: 60,000
SALES (est): 5.78MM **Privately Held**
Web: www.bendatool.com
SIC: **3544**  Dies, steel rule

**(P-9608)**
**CACO-PACIFIC CORPORATION (PA)**
813 N Cummings Rd, Covina  (91724-2597)
PHONE.............................626 331-3361
Robert G Hoffmann, *Pr*
Manfred Hoffman, *Ch Bd*
Thom Williams, *Sec*
◆ **EMP:** 142 **EST:** 1985
SQ FT: 45,000
SALES (est): 20.83MM
SALES (corp-wide): 20.83MM **Privately Held**
Web: www.cacopacific.com
SIC: **3544**  Industrial molds

**(P-9609)**
**CAST-RITE CORPORATION**
515 E Airline Way, Gardena  (90248-2593)
PHONE.............................310 532-2080
Donald De Haan, *Pr*
Wynn Chapman, *VP*
Howard Watkins, *CFO*
▲ **EMP:** 98 **EST:** 1941
SQ FT: 74,712
SALES (est): 6.24MM
SALES (corp-wide): 23.12MM **Privately Held**
Web: www.cast-rite.com
SIC: **3544** 3471 3363  Special dies and tools; Plating and polishing; Aluminum die-castings
PA:  Alloy Die Casting Co.
     6550 Caballero Blvd
     714 521-9800

**(P-9610)**
**CHARLES MEISNER  INC**
201 Sierra Pl Ste A, Upland  (91786-5627)
PHONE.............................909 946-8216
Charles Meisner, *Pr*
Carol Meisner, *
**EMP:** 25 **EST:** 1972
SQ FT: 19,000
SALES (est): 2.42MM **Privately Held**
Web: www.charlesmeisnerinc.com
SIC: **3544** 3599  Special dies and tools; Machine shop, jobbing and repair

**(P-9611)**
**CHIP-MAKERS TOOLING SUPPLY INC**
33867 Petunia St, Murrieta  (92563-3491)
PHONE.............................562 698-5840
Stephen Smith, *CEO*
Paul Hartman, *Pr*
Patty Rivera, *Treas*
**EMP:** 17 **EST:** 1990
SALES (est): 961.2K **Privately Held**
Web: www.chip-makers.com
SIC: **3544**  Special dies and tools

**(P-9612)**
**COAST AEROSPACE MFG INC**
Also Called: Coast Aerospace
950 Richfield Rd, Placentia  (92870-6732)
PHONE.............................714 893-8066
Louis Ponce, *Pr*
Frank Fleck, *
Steven Castillo, *
David Rodriguez, *Design Vice President*

## 3544 - Special Dies, Tools, Jigs, And Fixtures (P-9613)

**EMP:** 43 **EST:** 1999
**SALES (est):** 10.8MM **Privately Held**
**Web:** www.coastaero.com
**SIC: 3544** 3441 3728 3291 Special dies and tools; Fabricated structural metal; Aircraft parts and equipment, nec; Abrasive products

### (P-9613)
### COLBRIT MANUFACTURING CO INC
9666 Owensmouth Ave Ste G, Chatsworth (91311-8050)
**PHONE**..................818 709-3608
Gerardo Cruz, *Pr*
Marina Cruz, *
▲ **EMP:** 30 **EST:** 1979
**SQ FT:** 6,000
**SALES (est):** 5.03MM **Privately Held**
**Web:** www.colbrit.com
**SIC: 3544** Special dies and tools

### (P-9614)
### COMPUTER PLASTICS
1914 National Ave, Hayward (94545-1784)
**PHONE**..................510 785-3600
**TOLL FREE:** 800
Wayne L Harshbarger, *Pr*
**EMP:** 21 **EST:** 1969
**SQ FT:** 12,700
**SALES (est):** 4.67MM **Privately Held**
**Web:** www.computerplastics.com
**SIC: 3544** 3089 Special dies and tools; Molding primary plastics

### (P-9615)
### CRENSHAW DIE AND MFG CORP
7432 Prince Dr, Huntington Beach (92647-4553)
**PHONE**..................949 475-5505
**TOLL FREE:** 800
James V Ireland, *CEO*
Dale Congelliere, *
Sharon Piers, *
**EMP:** 55 **EST:** 1962
**SQ FT:** 38,000
**SALES (est):** 2.42MM **Privately Held**
**Web:** www.crenshawdiemfg.com
**SIC: 3544** Special dies and tools

### (P-9616)
### DAUNTLESS INDUSTRIES INC
Also Called: Dauntless Molds
806 N Grand Ave, Covina (91724-2418)
**PHONE**..................626 966-4494
George R Payton, *Pr*
Norm Holt, *
**EMP:** 25 **EST:** 1975
**SQ FT:** 15,000
**SALES (est):** 5.36MM **Privately Held**
**Web:** www.dauntlessmolds.com
**SIC: 3544** Special dies and tools

### (P-9617)
### DAVID ENGINEERING & MANUFACTURING INC
1230 Quarry St, Corona (92879-1708)
**PHONE**..................951 735-5200
▲ **EMP:** 30
**SIC: 3544** 3469 Special dies and tools; Metal stampings, nec

### (P-9618)
### DIE SHOP
7302 Adams St, Paramount (90723-4008)
**PHONE**..................562 630-4400
Hector Ramirez, *Owner*
▲ **EMP:** 15 **EST:** 1997
**SQ FT:** 4,000

**SALES (est):** 1.86MM **Privately Held**
**Web:** www.tdsfinishing.com
**SIC: 3544** Special dies and tools

### (P-9619)
### EDRO ENGINEERING LLC (DH)
Also Called: Voestalpine High Prfmce Mtls
20500 Carrey Rd, Walnut (91789-2417)
**PHONE**..................909 594-5751
Terry Henn, *CEO*
Eric Henn, *
Mike Guscott, *
Laurinda Diaz, *Stockholder*
Kevin Ewing, *
◆ **EMP:** 36 **EST:** 1976
**SQ FT:** 60,000
**SALES (est):** 20.09MM
**SALES (corp-wide):** 19.29B **Privately Held**
**Web:** www.edro.com
**SIC: 3544** 3599 Special dies and tools; Machine shop, jobbing and repair
**HQ:** Voestalpine High Performance Metals Llc
2505 Millennium Dr
Elgin IL 60123
877 992-8764

### (P-9620)
### ENSTROM MOLD & ENGINEERING INC
235 Trade St, San Marcos (92078-4373)
**PHONE**..................760 744-1880
Fred Enstrom, *Pr*
Janice Enstrom, *Sec*
Greg Metzger, *VP*
**EMP:** 17 **EST:** 1986
**SQ FT:** 12,500
**SALES (est):** 3.5MM **Privately Held**
**Web:** www.enstrommold.com
**SIC: 3544** 3089 Industrial molds; Plastics processing

### (P-9621)
### EXPRESS DIE SUPPLY INC
10020 Freeman Ave, Santa Fe Springs (90670-3406)
**PHONE**..................562 903-1700
Jeff Tsui, *Pr*
Jess Tsui, *
**EMP:** 20 **EST:** 2001
**SALES (est):** 1.62MM **Privately Held**
**Web:** www.expressdie.com
**SIC: 3544** Special dies and tools

### (P-9622)
### FAIRWAY INJECTION MOLDS INC
Also Called: Westfall Technik
20109 Paseo Del Prado, Walnut (91789-2665)
**PHONE**..................909 595-2201
Darrel Zamora, *CEO*
▲ **EMP:** 54 **EST:** 1977
**SQ FT:** 31,147
**SALES (est):** 9.82MM
**SALES (corp-wide):** 500.49MM **Privately Held**
**Web:** www.fairwaymolds.com
**SIC: 3544** Industrial molds
**PA:** Westfall Technik, Llc
9280 S Kyrene Rd
702 659-9898

### (P-9623)
### FLOTRON
2630 Progress St, Vista (92081-8412)
**PHONE**..................760 727-2700
Danny K Horrell, *Pr*
**EMP:** 24 **EST:** 1991
**SQ FT:** 25,000

**SALES (est):** 11.02MM **Privately Held**
**Web:** www.flotron.com
**SIC: 3544** Special dies and tools

### (P-9624)
### FUSION PRODUCT MFG INC
24024 Humphries Rd Bldg 1, Tecate (91980-4008)
**PHONE**..................619 819-5521
Adalberto L Ramirez, *Pr*
Jose Ramirez, *
Simon Ramirez, *
▼ **EMP:** 72 **EST:** 2004
**SQ FT:** 36,000
**SALES (est):** 4.4MM **Privately Held**
**Web:** www.fusionpm.com
**SIC: 3544** Forms (molds), for foundry and plastics working machinery

### (P-9625)
### GEMINI MFG & ENGRG INC
1020 E Vermont Ave, Anaheim (92805-5617)
**PHONE**..................714 999-0010
Sandra Lowry, *Pr*
David Lowry, *VP*
**EMP:** 20 **EST:** 1979
**SQ FT:** 40,000
**SALES (est):** 2.63MM **Privately Held**
**Web:** www.geminimfg.com
**SIC: 3544** 3599 Subpresses, metalworking; Machine shop, jobbing and repair

### (P-9626)
### GRUBER SYSTEMS INC
29071 The Old Rd, Valencia (91355-1083)
**PHONE**..................661 257-0464
John Hoskinson, *Ch Bd*
Jim Thiessen, *
Steve Miller, *
Diana Arima, *
Katherine Pavard, *
◆ **EMP:** 45 **EST:** 1968
**SALES (est):** 9.88MM **Privately Held**
**Web:** www.grubersystems.com
**SIC: 3544** 3842 3531 3537 Industrial molds; Whirlpool baths, hydrotherapy equipment; Construction machinery; Industrial trucks and tractors

### (P-9627)
### HIGHTOWER METAL PRODUCTS LLC
2090 N Glassell St, Orange (92865)
P.O. Box P.O. Box 5586 (92863)
**PHONE**..................714 637-7000
Kurt Koch, *Pr*
Mark Koch, *
**EMP:** 66 **EST:** 1945
**SQ FT:** 20,000
**SALES (est):** 6.13MM **Privately Held**
**SIC: 3544** Special dies and tools

### (P-9628)
### HUGHES BROS AIRCRAFTERS INC
11010 Garfield Pl, South Gate (90280-7512)
**PHONE**..................323 773-4541
Susan Hughes, *Pr*
James P Hughes, *
Michael Hall, *
**EMP:** 43 **EST:** 1947
**SQ FT:** 15,000
**SALES (est):** 4.51MM **Privately Held**
**Web:** www.hbai.com
**SIC: 3544** 3449 3444 Die sets for metal stamping (presses); Plastering accessories, metal; Sheet metalwork

### (P-9629)
### IDEA TOOLING AND ENGRG INC
13915 S Main St, Los Angeles (90061-2151)
**PHONE**..................310 608-7488
Peter Janner, *Pr*
Monica Janner, *
Moe Sumbulan, *
Inga Janner, *
▲ **EMP:** 56 **EST:** 1973
**SALES (est):** 3.78MM **Privately Held**
**Web:** www.ideatooling.com
**SIC: 3544** 3061 Special dies and tools; Mechanical rubber goods

### (P-9630)
### JW MOLDING INC
2523 Calcite Cir, Newbury Park (91320-1204)
**PHONE**..................805 499-2682
Ralf Wolters, *Pr*
Bridgette Wolters, *Sec*
**EMP:** 15 **EST:** 1980
**SQ FT:** 16,000
**SALES (est):** 2.3MM **Privately Held**
**Web:** www.jwmolding.com
**SIC: 3544** 3089 Forms (molds), for foundry and plastics working machinery; Injection molding of plastics

### (P-9631)
### KINGSON MOLD & MACHINE INC
1350 Titan Way, Brea (92821-3707)
**PHONE**..................714 871-0221
Gregory S Rex, *CEO*
**EMP:** 27 **EST:** 1977
**SQ FT:** 8,500
**SALES (est):** 5.01MM **Privately Held**
**Web:** www.kingsonmold.com
**SIC: 3544** 5031 Industrial molds; Molding, all materials

### (P-9632)
### KIPE MOLDS INC
340 E Crowther Ave, Placentia (92870-6419)
**PHONE**..................714 572-9576
George B Kipe Junior, *Pr*
George B Kipe Senior, *Sec*
Rebbeca L Kipe, *Treas*
**EMP:** 15 **EST:** 1970
**SQ FT:** 15,000
**SALES (est):** 2.44MM **Privately Held**
**Web:** www.kipemolds.com
**SIC: 3544** Industrial molds

### (P-9633)
### MACDONALD CARBIDE CO
525 S Prospero Dr, West Covina (91791-2931)
**PHONE**..................626 960-4034
Amy Mac Donald, *Pr*
◆ **EMP:** 20 **EST:** 1967
**SALES (est):** 2.02MM **Privately Held**
**Web:** www.macdonaldcarbide.com
**SIC: 3544** 3545 Special dies and tools; Machine tool accessories

### (P-9634)
### MAGOR MOLD LLC
420 S Lone Hill Ave, San Dimas (91773-4600)
**PHONE**..................909 592-3663
Wolfgang Buhler, *Pr*
Martin Schottli, *
▲ **EMP:** 68 **EST:** 1967
**SQ FT:** 15,000
**SALES (est):** 4.28MM **Privately Held**
**Web:** www.husky.co

## PRODUCTS & SERVICES SECTION
### 3544 - Special Dies, Tools, Jigs, And Fixtures (P-9656)

SIC: 3544 Industrial molds

**(P-9635)**
**MANTLE INC**
1950 Cesar Chavez, San Francisco (94124-1132)
PHONE..................415 655-3555
Theodore Sorom, CEO
James Groves, *
Mary Walls, *
**EMP:** 43 **EST:** 2015
**SALES (est):** 11.07MM Privately Held
**Web:** www.mantle3d.com
**SIC:** 3544 Industrial molds

**(P-9636)**
**MARMAN INDUSTRIES INC**
1701 Earhart, La Verne (91750-5827)
PHONE..................909 392-2136
**EMP:** 90 **EST:** 1985
**SALES (est):** 15.08MM Privately Held
**Web:** www.marman.com
**SIC:** 3544 3089 Industrial molds; Plastics containers, except foam

**(P-9637)**
**MR MOLD & ENGINEERING CORP**
1150 Beacon St, Brea (92821-2936)
PHONE..................714 996-5511
Richard Finnie Ii, Pr
Marilyn Finnie, *
**EMP:** 31 **EST:** 1985
**SALES (est):** 4.64MM Privately Held
**Web:** www.mrmold.com
**SIC:** 3544 Special dies and tools

**(P-9638)**
**NIRON INC**
20541 Earlgate St, Walnut (91789-2909)
PHONE..................909 598-1526
Glen Nieberle, Pr
Cheryl Nieberle, *
**EMP:** 17 **EST:** 1974
**SQ FT:** 17,000
**SALES (est):** 522.89K Privately Held
**Web:** www.niron.com
**SIC:** 3544 3089 Industrial molds; Injection molding of plastics

**(P-9639)**
**PACE PUNCHES INC**
297 Goddard, Irvine (92618-4604)
PHONE..................949 428-2750
Edward W Pepper, Pr
▲ **EMP:** 55 **EST:** 1978
**SQ FT:** 30,000
**SALES (est):** 4.57MM Privately Held
**Web:** www.pacepunches.com
**SIC:** 3544 Punches, forming and stamping

**(P-9640)**
**PRECISE DIE AND FINISHING**
9400 Oso Ave, Chatsworth (91311-6020)
PHONE..................818 773-9337
David Rewers, CEO
**EMP:** 27 **EST:** 2016
**SQ FT:** 15,000
**SALES (est):** 4.59MM Privately Held
**Web:** www.precisedf.com
**SIC:** 3544 Special dies and tools

**(P-9641)**
**PRECISION FORGING DIES INC**
Also Called: C&C Aerol Machining
10710 Sessler St, South Gate (90280-7221)
PHONE..................562 861-1878
Dan Kloss, CEO

Dan Kloss, Pr
**EMP:** 20 **EST:** 2001
**SALES (est):** 4.28MM Privately Held
**Web:** www.precisionforgingdies.com
**SIC:** 3544 Special dies and tools

**(P-9642)**
**PRESTIGE MOLD INCORPORATED**
11040 Tacoma Dr, Rancho Cucamonga (91730-4857)
PHONE..................909 980-6600
Donna C Pursell, CEO
Lance Spangler, *
▲ **EMP:** 98 **EST:** 1982
**SQ FT:** 28,500
**SALES (est):** 8.21MM
**SALES (corp-wide):** 9.02MM Privately Held
**Web:** www.prestigemold.com
**SIC:** 3544 Industrial molds
**PA:** Pres-Tek Plastics, Inc.
10700 7th St
909 360-1600

**(P-9643)**
**PRODUCT SLINGSHOT INC (DH)**
Also Called: Forecast 3d
2221 Rutherford Rd, Carlsbad (92008-8815)
PHONE..................760 929-9380
Corey Douglas Weber, Pr
Donovan Weber, *
**EMP:** 24 **EST:** 1994
**SQ FT:** 28,000
**SALES (est):** 44.44MM
**SALES (corp-wide):** 6.06B Privately Held
**Web:** www.forecast3d.com
**SIC:** 3544 3082 3089 3555 Industrial molds; Unsupported plastics profile shapes; Casting of plastics; Printing trades machinery
**HQ:** Gkn Powder Metallurgy Holdings Limited
Rhodium Building,Central Boulevard
Solihull W MIDLANDS B90 8

**(P-9644)**
**PUNCH PRESS PRODUCTS INC**
Also Called: Auto Trend Products
2035 E 51st St, Vernon (90058-2818)
PHONE..................323 581-7151
Delmo Molinari, Ch
Cj Matiszik, *
Helen Wesley, *
Joseph Mcclure, Genl Mgr
▲ **EMP:** 67 **EST:** 1953
**SQ FT:** 150,000
**SALES (est):** 9.45MM Privately Held
**Web:** www.punch-press.com
**SIC:** 3544 3469 3471 Special dies and tools; Metal stampings, nec; Plating and polishing

**(P-9645)**
**PYRAMID MOLD & TOOL**
10155 Sharon Cir, Rancho Cucamonga (91730-5300)
PHONE..................909 476-2555
Stephen Hoare, Pr
Brandan Heyes, *
**EMP:** 62 **EST:** 1995
**SQ FT:** 30,300
**SALES (est):** 8.13MM
**SALES (corp-wide):** 63.22MM Privately Held
**Web:** www.pyramidmold.net
**SIC:** 3544 Industrial molds
**PA:** Sybridge Technologies U.S. Inc.
265 Spring Lake Dr
814 474-9100

**(P-9646)**
**S & S CARBIDE TOOL INC**
2830 Via Orange Way Ste D, Spring Valley (91978-1743)
PHONE..................619 670-5214
Dennis Strong, Pr
Gary Stewart, *
**EMP:** 25 **EST:** 1986
**SQ FT:** 6,000
**SALES (est):** 5.76MM Privately Held
**Web:** www.sscarbide.com
**SIC:** 3544 Special dies and tools

**(P-9647)**
**SANTA FE ENTERPRISES INC**
Also Called: SFE
11654 Pike St, Santa Fe Springs (90670-2938)
PHONE..................562 692-7596
David Warner, Pr
Bob Becker, *
**EMP:** 27 **EST:** 1980
**SQ FT:** 20,000
**SALES (est):** 4.83MM Privately Held
**Web:** www.santafeenterprises.com
**SIC:** 3544 Special dies and tools

**(P-9648)**
**SCHREY & SONS MOLD CO INC**
24735 Avenue Rockefeller, Valencia (91355-3466)
PHONE..................661 294-2260
Walter Schrey, Pr
Thomas Schrey, *
William Schrey, *
Gertrude Schrey, *
**EMP:** 35 **EST:** 1969
**SQ FT:** 53,000
**SALES (est):** 6.38MM Privately Held
**Web:** www.schrey.com
**SIC:** 3544 Industrial molds

**(P-9649)**
**SUPERIOR JIG INC**
1540 N Orangethorpe Way, Anaheim (92801-1289)
PHONE..................714 525-4777
John Morrissey, Pr
Tracy Reed, Sec
**EMP:** 22 **EST:** 1960
**SQ FT:** 14,000
**SALES (est):** 12.18MM Privately Held
**Web:** www.superiorjiginc.com
**SIC:** 3544 3599 Special dies and tools; Machine shop, jobbing and repair

**(P-9650)**
**SUPERIOR MOLD CO**
3122 Maple St, Santa Ana (92707-4408)
PHONE..................714 751-7084
Codet Anthony, Prin
**EMP:** 27 **EST:** 2012
**SALES (est):** 3.62MM Privately Held
**SIC:** 3544 Industrial molds

**(P-9651)**
**SYBRIDGE TECHNOLOGIES ALA INC**
10155 Sharon Cir, Rancho Cucamonga (91730-5300)
PHONE..................909 476-2555
**EMP:** 17
**SALES (corp-wide):** 63.22MM Privately Held
**Web:** www.sybridge.com
**SIC:** 3544 Industrial molds
**HQ:** Sybridge Technologies Alabama, Inc.
651 24th St Sw
Cullman AL 35055
256 255-1100

**(P-9652)**
**TEAM TECHNOLOGIES INC**
Also Called: Precision Die Cutting, LLC
4675 Vinita Ct, Chino (91710-5731)
PHONE..................626 334-5000
Marshall White, Brnch Mgr
**EMP:** 60
**Web:** www.teamtechinc.net
**SIC:** 3544 Special dies and tools
**HQ:** Team Technologies, Inc.
5949 Commerce Blvd
Morristown TN 37814
423 587-2199

**(P-9653)**
**UNITED CALIFORNIA CORPORATION**
12200 Woodruff Ave, Downey (90241-5608)
P.O. Box 4250 (90241-1250)
PHONE..................562 803-1521
Dale L Bethke, Pr
Billie Huckins, *
**EMP:** 22 **EST:** 1974
**SQ FT:** 85,000
**SALES (est):** 494.3K Privately Held
**Web:** www.ucc-udb.com
**SIC:** 3544 Special dies and tools

**(P-9654)**
**UPM INC**
Also Called: Universal Plastic Mold
13245 Los Angeles St, Baldwin Park (91706-2295)
PHONE..................626 962-4001
Jason Dowling, Pr
Jason Dowling, CEO
Steve Dowling, *
Don Ashleigh, *
◆ **EMP:** 290 **EST:** 1962
**SQ FT:** 100,000
**SALES (est):** 29.13MM Privately Held
**Web:** www.upminc.com
**SIC:** 3544 3089 Forms (molds), for foundry and plastics working machinery; Injection molding of plastics

**(P-9655)**
**US DIES INC (PA)**
1992 Rockefeller Dr Ste 300, Ceres (95307-7274)
PHONE..................209 664-1402
Thomas Mason, Pr
Ken Thomas, *
Diana L Mason, *
**EMP:** 23 **EST:** 1971
**SQ FT:** 21,000
**SALES (est):** 1.29MM
**SALES (corp-wide):** 1.29MM Privately Held
**SIC:** 3544 Dies, steel rule

**(P-9656)**
**VALCO PLANER WORKS INC**
Also Called: Valco Precision Works
6131 Maywood Ave, Huntington Park (90255-3213)
PHONE..................323 582-6355
Leonel F Valerio, Pr
Leonel G Valerio Junior, VP
Carlos Valerio, *
▼ **EMP:** 25 **EST:** 1953
**SQ FT:** 10,000
**SALES (est):** 4.65MM Privately Held
**SIC:** 3544 3545 Special dies, tools, jigs, and fixtures; Machine tool accessories

## 3544 - Special Dies, Tools, Jigs, And Fixtures (P-9657)

**(P-9657)**
**WAGNER DIE SUPPLY INC (PA)**
2041 Elm Ct, Ontario (91761-7619)
PHONE..............................909 947-3044
Ellsworth Knutson, *Pr*
John Knutson, *
Tom Knutson, *
Mike Knutson, *
▲ **EMP:** 36 **EST:** 1947
**SALES (est):** 9.89MM
**SALES (corp-wide):** 9.89MM **Privately Held**
**Web:** www.wagnerdiesupply.com
**SIC: 3544** Dies, steel rule

**(P-9658)**
**WRIGHT ENGINEERED PLASTICS LLC**
Also Called: Wright Engineered Plastics Inc
3681 N Laughlin Rd, Santa Rosa (95403-1027)
PHONE..............................707 575-1218
Barbara F Roberts, *Pr*
Mike Nellis, *
▲ **EMP:** 47 **EST:** 1970
**SQ FT:** 25,000
**SALES (est):** 10.24MM
**SALES (corp-wide):** 1.21B **Privately Held**
**Web:** www.wepmolding.com
**SIC: 3544** 3089 Special dies, tools, jigs, and fixtures; Plastics hardware and building products
**HQ:** Seaway Plastics Engineering Llc
6006 Siesta Ln
Port Richey FL 34668

### 3545 Machine Tool Accessories

**(P-9659)**
**AMERICAN QUALITY TOOLS INC**
Also Called: American Quality Tools
12650 Magnolia Ave Ste B, Riverside (92503-4690)
PHONE..............................951 280-4700
Mukesh Aghi, *Pr*
Rakesh Aghi, *
▲ **EMP:** 45 **EST:** 1989
**SQ FT:** 22,000
**SALES (est):** 6.98MM **Privately Held**
**Web:** www.cobracarbide.com
**SIC: 3545** Cutting tools for machine tools

**(P-9660)**
**ATS WORKHOLDING LLC (PA)**
Also Called: Ats Systems
30222 Esperanza, Rancho Santa Margari (92688-2121)
PHONE..............................800 321-1833
Kenneth Erkenbrack, *Managing Member*
Charles A Goad, *
Wu Robert, *
Carlos Hernandez, *
▲ **EMP:** 43 **EST:** 1981
**SQ FT:** 22,840
**SALES (est):** 10.15MM
**SALES (corp-wide):** 10.15MM **Privately Held**
**Web:** www.atssystems.us
**SIC: 3545** Milling machine attachments (machine tool accessories)

**(P-9661)**
**BARRANCA HOLDINGS LTD**
Also Called: Barranca Diamond Products
22815 Frampton Ave, Torrance (90501-5034)
PHONE..............................310 523-5867
Brian Delahaut, *Pr*
▲ **EMP:** 104 **EST:** 1998
**SALES (est):** 876.4K
**SALES (corp-wide):** 27.31MM **Privately Held**
**Web:** www.barrancadiamond.com
**SIC: 3545** Diamond cutting tools for turning, boring, burnishing, etc.
**PA:** Diamond Mk Products Inc
1315 Storm Pkwy
310 539-5221

**(P-9662)**
**BMW OF PALM SPRINGS**
3737 E Palm Canyon Dr, Palm Springs (92264-5205)
PHONE..............................760 324-7071
Frank Hickinbotham, *Prin*
**EMP:** 52 **EST:** 2015
**SALES (est):** 5.67MM **Privately Held**
**Web:** www.bmwpalmsprings.com
**SIC: 3545** 5511 Thread cutting dies; Automobiles, new and used

**(P-9663)**
**BROACH MASTERS INC**
2160 Precision Pl, Auburn (95603-9096)
PHONE..............................530 885-1939
Mark Vian, *Pr*
Elizabeth Vian, *
**EMP:** 27 **EST:** 1978
**SALES (est):** 3.33MM **Privately Held**
**Web:** www.broachmasters.com
**SIC: 3545** 3599 Precision tools, machinists'; Machine shop, jobbing and repair

**(P-9664)**
**CAL-CRAFT DESIGN INTL INC**
1615 Riverview Dr Ste A, San Bernardino (92408-3010)
PHONE: **EMP:** 15 **EST:** 1990
**SQ FT:** 10,500
**SALES (est):** 2.5MM **Privately Held**
**Web:** www.cal-craft.net
**SIC: 3545** 3599 Tools and accessories for machine tools; Machine shop, jobbing and repair

**(P-9665)**
**CAMPBELL ENGINEERING INC**
Also Called: Campbell Engineering
20412 Barents Sea Cir, Lake Forest (92630-8807)
PHONE..............................949 859-3306
James J Campbell, *CEO*
Carolyn Campbell, *
**EMP:** 24 **EST:** 1994
**SQ FT:** 3,800
**SALES (est):** 2.9MM **Privately Held**
**Web:** www.campbellcnc.com
**SIC: 3545** 3541 Precision measuring tools; Lathes, metal cutting and polishing

**(P-9666)**
**CENTURY DESIGN INC**
Also Called: CDI
7485 Trade St Ste A, San Diego (92121-3436)
PHONE..............................858 292-1212
◆ **EMP:** 16 **EST:** 1964
**SALES (est):** 3.48MM **Privately Held**
**Web:** www.centurydesign.com
**SIC: 3545** Machine tool accessories

**(P-9667)**
**COASTAL CNTING INDUS SCALE INC**
Also Called: Actionpac Scales & Automation
270 Quail Ct Ste 100, Santa Paula (93060-9205)
PHONE..............................805 487-0403
John W Dishion, *CEO*
▲ **EMP:** 22 **EST:** 1982
**SALES (est):** 4.15MM **Privately Held**
**Web:** www.actionpacusa.com
**SIC: 3545** 3565 Machine tool accessories; Packaging machinery

**(P-9668)**
**CONCEPT PART SOLUTIONS INC**
2047 Zanker Rd, San Jose (95131-2107)
PHONE..............................408 748-1244
Richard L Diehl, *CEO*
**EMP:** 23 **EST:** 2007
**SALES (est):** 5.07MM **Privately Held**
**Web:** www.conceptpartsolutions.com
**SIC: 3545** Machine tool accessories

**(P-9669)**
**COPLAN & COPLAN INC**
Also Called: Speedpress Sign Supply
2270 Camino Vida Roble Ste H, Carlsbad (92011-1503)
PHONE..............................760 268-0583
Jacob Coplan, *CEO*
◆ **EMP:** 20 **EST:** 1989
**SQ FT:** 14,000
**SALES (est):** 2.57MM **Privately Held**
**Web:** www.speedpress.com
**SIC: 3545** Tools and accessories for machine tools

**(P-9670)**
**CRAIG TOOLS INC**
142 Lomita St, El Segundo (90245-4113)
PHONE..............................310 322-0614
William B Cleveland, *Pr*
Don Tripler, *
▼ **EMP:** 37 **EST:** 1958
**SQ FT:** 13,000
**SALES (est):** 6.78MM **Privately Held**
**Web:** www.craigtools.com
**SIC: 3545** Precision tools, machinists'

**(P-9671)**
**CRITERION MACHINE WORKS**
765 W 16th St, Costa Mesa (92627-4302)
**EMP:** 40 **EST:** 1935
**SALES (est):** 2.57MM **Privately Held**
**Web:** www.criterionmachineworks.com
**SIC: 3545** Machine tool attachments and accessories

**(P-9672)**
**CTE CALIFORNIA TL & ENGRG INC**
Also Called: California Tool & Engineering
7801 Bolero Dr, Jurupa Valley (92509-5219)
▲ **EMP:** 25 **EST:** 1987
**SQ FT:** 14,000
**SALES (est):** 1.77MM **Privately Held**
**SIC: 3545** 7389 2819 Cutting tools for machine tools; Grinding, precision: commercial or industrial; Carbides

**(P-9673)**
**CURRY COMPANY LLC**
Also Called: Carbro Company
15724 Condon Ave, Lawndale (90260-2531)
P.O. Box 278 (90260-0278)
PHONE..............................310 643-8400
Patrick Curry, *Managing Member*
**EMP:** 40 **EST:** 2019
**SALES (est):** 3.23MM
**SALES (corp-wide):** 21MM **Privately Held**
**Web:** www.carbrocorp.com

**SIC: 3545** End mills
**PA:** Fullerton Tool Company, Inc.
121 Perry St
989 799-4550

**(P-9674)**
**DEWEYL TOOL CO INC**
959 Transport Way, Petaluma (94954-1474)
PHONE..............................707 765-5779
William Cline, *Pr*
Linda Cline, *
Susan Blow, *
**EMP:** 35 **EST:** 1969
**SQ FT:** 20,000
**SALES (est):** 3.86MM **Privately Held**
**Web:** www.deweyl.com
**SIC: 3545** Machine tool attachments and accessories

**(P-9675)**
**DMG MORI DIGITAL TECH LAB CORP**
Also Called: DTL Mori Seiki
3601 Faraday Ave, Davis (95618-7776)
PHONE..............................530 746-7400
Zach Piner, *Pr*
Adam Hansel, *
Natsuo Okada, *
Hiroshi Takami, *
▲ **EMP:** 67 **EST:** 2002
**SALES (est):** 9.95MM **Privately Held**
**Web:** us.dmgmori.com
**SIC: 3545** Machine tool accessories
**HQ:** Dmg Mori Usa, Inc.
2400 Huntington Blvd
Hoffman Estates IL 60192
847 593-5400

**(P-9676)**
**DRILLING & TRENCHING SUP INC (PA)**
Also Called: Drilling World
1458 Mariani Ct, Tracy (95376-2825)
PHONE..............................510 895-1650
**TOLL FREE:** 800
David Wellington Moran, *CEO*
Erin B Moran, *Sec*
▲ **EMP:** 17 **EST:** 1987
**SQ FT:** 52,000
**SALES (est):** 9.31MM
**SALES (corp-wide):** 9.31MM **Privately Held**
**Web:** www.drillingworld.com
**SIC: 3545** Drilling machine attachments and accessories

**(P-9677)**
**ELCON PRECISION LLC**
1009 Timothy Dr, San Jose (95133-1043)
PHONE..............................408 292-7800
Dan Brumlik, *Ch*
Pater Smith, *Pr*
Jamie Howton, *Managing Member*
**EMP:** 64 **EST:** 2011
**SALES (est):** 5.99MM **Privately Held**
**Web:** www.elconprecision.com
**SIC: 3545** Precision tools, machinists'

**(P-9678)**
**GUHRING INC**
15581 Computer Ln, Huntington Beach (92649-1605)
PHONE..............................714 841-3582
**EMP:** 50
**SALES (corp-wide):** 1.03B **Privately Held**
**Web:** www.guhring.com
**SIC: 3545** Cutting tools for machine tools
**HQ:** Guhring, Inc.
1445 Commerce Ave

PRODUCTS & SERVICES SECTION  
3545 - Machine Tool Accessories (P-9699)

Brookfield WI 53045
262 784-6730

**(P-9679)**
**KARBIDE INC**
12650 Magnolia Ave Ste B, Riverside (92503-4690)
PHONE....................951 354-0900
Rakesh Aghi, *CEO*
▲ **EMP:** 23 **EST:** 2012
**SALES (est):** 2.31MM **Privately Held**
**SIC: 3545** Cutting tools for machine tools

**(P-9680)**
**KEMPTON MACHINE WORKS INC**
4070 E Leaverton Ct, Anaheim (92807-1610)
PHONE....................714 990-0596
Greg Kempton, *Pr*
**EMP:** 17 **EST:** 1983
**SQ FT:** 14,000
**SALES (est):** 1.95MM **Privately Held**
**Web:** www.kemptonmachineworksinc.com
**SIC: 3545** 3599 Tools and accessories for machine tools; Machine shop, jobbing and repair

**(P-9681)**
**KYOCERA SGS PRECISION TLS INC**
Also Called: Kyocera Precision Tools
1814 W Collins Ave, Orange (92867-5425)
PHONE....................888 848-9266
Csr Paul, *Brnch Mgr*
**EMP:** 85
**SALES (corp-wide):** 36.3MM **Privately Held**
**Web:** www.kyocera-sgstool.com
**SIC: 3545** 3541 3845 3843 Machine tool accessories; Machine tools, metal cutting type; Electromedical equipment; Dental equipment and supplies
**PA:** Kyocera Sgs Precision Tools, Inc.
150 Marc Dr
330 688-6667

**(P-9682)**
**MAKINO INC**
17800 Newhope St Ste H, Fountain Valley (92708-5443)
PHONE....................714 444-4334
Jonathan Haye, *Brnch Mgr*
**EMP:** 26
**Web:** www.makino.com
**SIC: 3545** Tools and accessories for machine tools
**HQ:** Makino Inc.
7680 Innovation Way
Mason OH 45040
513 573-7200

**(P-9683)**
**MEYCO MACHINE AND TOOL INC**
11579 Martens River Cir, Fountain Valley (92708-4201)
P.O. Box 9659 (92728-9659)
PHONE....................714 435-1546
Manuel Gomez, *CEO*
Victor Salazar, *
Max Gomez, *
Edith Martinez, *
Lorena Estrada, *
**EMP:** 38 **EST:** 1996
**SQ FT:** 12,500
**SALES (est):** 3.11MM **Privately Held**
**Web:** www.meycomachine.com

**SIC: 3545** Tools and accessories for machine tools

**(P-9684)**
**MICRO TOOL & MANUFACTURING INC**
6494 Federal Blvd, Lemon Grove (91945-1376)
PHONE....................619 582-2884
Fae Galea, *Pr*
Charles Galea, *VP*
Michael H Galea, *Sec*
Steve J Galea, *Asst VP*
John Galea, *Asst VP*
**EMP:** 22 **EST:** 1964
**SQ FT:** 10,000
**SALES (est):** 2.85MM **Privately Held**
**Web:** www.microtoolmfginc.com
**SIC: 3545** 3544 Precision tools, machinists'; Jigs: inspection, gauging, and checking

**(P-9685)**
**NORANCO MANUFACTURING (USA) ACQUISITION CORP**
Also Called: Noranco Corona Division
345 Cessna Cir Ste 102, Corona (92880-2519)
PHONE....................951 721-8400
▲ **EMP:** 125 **EST:** 2013
**SALES (est):** 37.41MM
**SALES (corp-wide):** 364.48B **Publicly Held**
**SIC: 3545** 3728 Machine tool attachments and accessories; Aircraft parts and equipment, nec
**HQ:** Noranco Inc
710 Rowntree Dairy Rd
Woodbridge ON L4L 5
905 264-2050

**(P-9686)**
**OMEGA DIAMOND INC**
10125 Ophir Rd, Newcastle (95658-9504)
PHONE....................530 889-8977
Samuel Devai, *Pr*
Roneily Devai, *Sec*
▲ **EMP:** 17 **EST:** 1987
**SQ FT:** 3,000
**SALES (est):** 2.56MM **Privately Held**
**Web:** www.omegadiamond.com
**SIC: 3545** Diamond cutting tools for turning, boring, burnishing, etc.

**(P-9687)**
**PELAGIC PRESSURE SYSTEMS CORP**
480 Mccormick St, San Leandro (94577-1106)
PHONE....................510 569-3100
Michael Hollis, *CEO*
Robert Hollis, *
Paul Elsinga, *
▲ **EMP:** 75 **EST:** 1979
**SALES (est):** 6.9MM
**SALES (corp-wide):** 1.74MM **Privately Held**
**Web:** www.pelagicnet.com
**SIC: 3545** Gauges (machine tool accessories)
**HQ:** Aqua-Lung America, Inc.
8880 Nw 20th St
Doral FL 33172
760 376-9813

**(P-9688)**
**PENNOYER-DODGE CO**
6650 San Fernando Rd, Glendale (91201-1745)
P.O. Box 5105 (91221-1017)

PHONE....................818 547-2100
Hazel Dodge, *Pr*
Karen Dodge, *
**EMP:** 40 **EST:** 1946
**SALES (est):** 4.96MM **Privately Held**
**Web:** www.pdgage.com
**SIC: 3545** 8734 5084 3643 Gauges (machine tool accessories); Calibration and certification; Instruments and control equipment; Current-carrying wiring services

**(P-9689)**
**PICOSYS INCORPORATED**
Also Called: Invenios
320 N Nopal St, Santa Barbara (93103-3225)
PHONE....................805 962-3333
**EMP:** 70
**SIC: 3545** 3821 Precision measuring tools; Micromanipulator

**(P-9690)**
**PIONEER BROACH COMPANY (PA)**
6434 Telegraph Rd, Commerce (90040-2593)
PHONE....................323 728-1263
Gary M Ezor, *CEO*
Robert Ezor, *
Karin Ezor, *
▲ **EMP:** 50 **EST:** 1939
**SQ FT:** 22,000
**SALES (est):** 4.83MM
**SALES (corp-wide):** 4.83MM **Privately Held**
**Web:** www.pioneerbroach.com
**SIC: 3545** 3599 3541 Broaches (machine tool accessories); Machine shop, jobbing and repair; Machine tools, metal cutting type

**(P-9691)**
**PRECISION CUTTING TOOLS INC**
5572 Fresca Dr, La Palma (90623-1007)
PHONE....................562 921-7898
Audrey Sheth, *CEO*
▲ **EMP:** 30 **EST:** 1979
**SALES (est):** 2.17MM **Privately Held**
**Web:** www.pct-imc.com
**SIC: 3545** 3541 Cutting tools for machine tools; Drilling machine tools (metal cutting)

**(P-9692)**
**PRECISION CUTTING TOOLS LLC**
5572 Fresca Dr, La Palma (90623-1007)
PHONE....................562 921-7898
Nikhil Sheth, *Prin*
Mehar Grewal, *Prin*
Audrey Sheth, *Prin*
Jacob Harpaz, *Prin*
**EMP:** 48 **EST:** 2018
**SALES (est):** 4.33MM **Privately Held**
**Web:** www.pct-imc.com
**SIC: 3545** Cutting tools for machine tools

**(P-9693)**
**PRO TOOL SERVICES INC**
1704 Sunnyside Ct, Bakersfield (93308-6859)
P.O. Box 80235 (93380-0235)
PHONE....................661 393-9222
Ron Jacobs, *Pr*
Mark Gardener, *
**EMP:** 19 **EST:** 2000
**SQ FT:** 4,000
**SALES (est):** 3.14MM **Privately Held**
**Web:** www.protoolservices.com

**SIC: 3545** Tools and accessories for machine tools

**(P-9694)**
**QUALITY GRINDING CO INC**
6800 Caballero Blvd, Buena Park (90620-1136)
P.O. Box 5968 (90622-5968)
PHONE....................714 228-2100
Cornel Feceu, *Pr*
**EMP:** 16 **EST:** 1946
**SQ FT:** 29,000
**SALES (est):** 1.62MM **Privately Held**
**Web:** www.qualitygrinding.net
**SIC: 3545** 3599 Precision tools, machinists'; Machine shop, jobbing and repair

**(P-9695)**
**RAFCO-BRICKFORM LLC (PA)**
Also Called: Rafco Products Brickform
11061 Jersey Blvd, Rancho Cucamonga (91730-5135)
PHONE....................909 484-3399
Robert Freis, *Managing Member*
Matt Bissantti, *Managing Member*
▲ **EMP:** 72 **EST:** 1973
**SQ FT:** 79,000
**SALES (est):** 1.73MM
**SALES (corp-wide):** 1.73MM **Privately Held**
**SIC: 3545** 5169 Machine tool accessories; Adhesives, chemical

**(P-9696)**
**RON WITHERSPOON INC (PA)**
Also Called: R W I
1551 Dell Ave, Campbell (95008-6903)
PHONE....................408 370-6620
▲ **EMP:** 49 **EST:** 1978
**SALES (est):** 8.26MM
**SALES (corp-wide):** 8.26MM **Privately Held**
**Web:** www.rwinc.com
**SIC: 3545** Precision tools, machinists'

**(P-9697)**
**SCIENTIFIC CUTTING TOOLS INC**
220 W Los Angeles Ave, Simi Valley (93065-1650)
PHONE....................805 584-9495
Dale Christopher, *Pr*
Jan Kaye, *
Gary Christopher, *
**EMP:** 37 **EST:** 1963
**SALES (est):** 5.26MM **Privately Held**
**Web:** www.sct-usa.com
**SIC: 3545** Machine tool accessories

**(P-9698)**
**SOUTHLAND TOOL MFG INC**
1430 N Hundley St, Anaheim (92806-1322)
PHONE....................714 632-8198
David Pryor, *Pr*
▲ **EMP:** 16 **EST:** 2010
**SALES (est):** 2.31MM **Privately Held**
**Web:** www.southlandtool.com
**SIC: 3545** Machine tool accessories

**(P-9699)**
**STADCO (HQ)**
Also Called: Standard Tool & Die Co
107 S Avenue 20, Los Angeles (90031-1709)
PHONE....................323 227-8888
Doug Paletz, *Pr*
Bob Parsi, *
Bret Matta, *
**EMP:** 86 **EST:** 1945
**SQ FT:** 15,000
**SALES (est):** 29.25MM **Publicly Held**

(PA)=Parent Co (HQ)=Headquarters
✪ = New Business established in last 2 years

## 3545 - Machine Tool Accessories (P-9700)

Web: www.stadco.com
SIC: **3545** 3599 Precision tools, machinists'; Machine shop, jobbing and repair
PA: Techprecision Corporation
  1 Bella Dr

### (P-9700)
### STARRETT KINEMETRIC ENGRG INC
26052 Merit Cir Ste 103, Laguna Hills (92653-7004)
PHONE..................................949 348-1213
Douglas Starrett, *Pr*
**EMP:** 26 **EST:** 2007
**SALES (est):** 5.03MM
**SALES (corp-wide):** 256.18MM **Privately Held**
Web: www.starrettmetrology.com
SIC: **3545** Machine tool accessories
PA: The L S Starrett Company
  121 Crescent St
  978 249-3551

### (P-9701)
### STEP TOOLS UNLIMITED INC
Also Called: Destiny Tool
18434 Technology Dr, Morgan Hill (95037-2844)
PHONE..................................408 988-8898
Guy Calamia, *Pr*
Nettie Calamia, *
**EMP:** 36 **EST:** 1980
**SALES (est):** 9.28MM **Privately Held**
Web: www.destinytool.com
SIC: **3545** Cutting tools for machine tools

### (P-9702)
### STEWART TOOL COMPANY
3647 Omec Cir, Rancho Cordova (95742-7302)
PHONE..................................916 635-8321
Mark Richard Stewart, *CEO*
Craig Harrington, *
Dave Hassemeyer, *
**EMP:** 55 **EST:** 1968
**SQ FT:** 22,000
**SALES (est):** 9.02MM **Privately Held**
Web: www.stewarttool.com
SIC: **3545** 3544 7692 Precision tools, machinists'; Jigs and fixtures; Welding repair

### (P-9703)
### TOOL ALLIANCE CORPORATION
Also Called: Roundtool Laboratories
5372 Mcfadden Ave, Huntington Beach (92649-1239)
PHONE..................................714 373-5864
Keith Dennis, *Mgr*
**EMP:** 45
**SALES (corp-wide):** 5.34MM **Privately Held**
Web: www.toolalliance.com
SIC: **3545** Cutting tools for machine tools
PA: Tool Alliance Corporation
  5451 Mcfadden Ave
  714 898-9224

### (P-9704)
### UNITED DRILL BUSHING CORP
Also Called: United California
12200 Woodruff Ave, Downey (90241-5608)
P.O. Box 4250 (90241-1250)
PHONE..................................562 803-1521
Dale L Bethke, *Pr*
Billie Huckins, *
**EMP:** 150 **EST:** 1964
**SQ FT:** 80,000
**SALES (est):** 7.04MM **Privately Held**
Web: www.ucc-udb.com

SIC: **3545** 3544 Drill bushings (drilling jig); Special dies, tools, jigs, and fixtures

### (P-9705)
### VERIDIAM INC (DH)
1717 N Cuyamaca St, El Cajon (92020-1110)
PHONE..................................619 448-1000
Brian Joyal, *CEO*
Jennifer Bowman, *
Robert Oevson, *
Scott Rogow, *
▲ **EMP:** 53 **EST:** 1996
**SQ FT:** 250,000
**SALES (est):** 64.67MM
**SALES (corp-wide):** 98MM **Privately Held**
Web: www.veridiam.com
SIC: **3545** 3317 3354 3312 Precision tools, machinists'; Tubes, seamless steel; Tube, extruded or drawn, aluminum; Tubes, steel and iron
HQ: Whi Capital Partners
  191 N Wacker Dr Ste 1500
  Chicago IL 60606

### (P-9706)
### VIKING PRODUCTS INC
20 Doppler, Irvine (92618-4306)
PHONE..................................949 379-5100
Marc Kaplan, *CEO*
**EMP:** 40 **EST:** 1981
**SQ FT:** 12,000
**SALES (est):** 5.02MM **Privately Held**
Web: www.vikingproducts.com
SIC: **3545** Precision measuring tools

### (P-9707)
### WESTERN GAGE CORPORATION
3316 Maya Linda Ste A, Camarillo (93012-8059)
PHONE..................................805 445-1410
Donald E Moors, *Pr*
Nanette Moors, *
**EMP:** 24 **EST:** 1968
**SQ FT:** 22,000
**SALES (est):** 3.65MM **Privately Held**
Web: www.westerngage.com
SIC: **3545** Gauges (machine tool accessories)

### (P-9708)
### WETMORE TOOL AND ENGRG CO
Also Called: Wetmore Cutting Tools
5091 G St, Chino (91710-5141)
PHONE..................................909 364-1000
Jerome David, *CEO*
Phil Kurtz, *Pr*
Mike Gallegos, *CFO*
Keith Rowland, *Ex VP*
▲ **EMP:** 75 **EST:** 1999
**SQ FT:** 32,000
**SALES (est):** 9.03MM
**SALES (corp-wide):** 12.03B **Privately Held**
Web: www.dormerpramet.com
SIC: **3545** 5084 3544 3541 Cutting tools for machine tools; Industrial machinery and equipment; Special dies, tools, jigs, and fixtures; Machine tools, metal cutting type
HQ: Dormer Pramet Ab
  Tre Hjartans Vag 2
  Halmstad 302 4
  35165200

## 3546 Power-driven Handtools

### (P-9709)
### BLACK & DECKER CORPORATION
Also Called: Black & Decker
19701 Da Vinci, El Toro (92610-2622)
PHONE..................................949 672-4000
Chris Metz, *Mgr*
**EMP:** 26
**SALES (corp-wide):** 15.78B **Publicly Held**
Web: www.blackanddecker.com
SIC: **3546** 3553 Power-driven handtools; Woodworking machinery
HQ: The Black & Decker Corporation
  701 E Joppa Rd
  Towson MD 21286
  410 716-3900

### (P-9710)
### CALIFORNIA AIR TOOLS INC
8560 Siempre Viva Rd, San Diego (92154-6270)
PHONE..................................619 407-7905
Manuel Gonicman, *CEO*
Larry Cerneka, *Pr*
◆ **EMP:** 30 **EST:** 2002
**SQ FT:** 10,000
**SALES (est):** 5.43MM **Privately Held**
Web: www.californiaairtools.com
SIC: **3546** 3563 5072 Cartridge-activated hand power tools; Air and gas compressors; Power tools and accessories

### (P-9711)
### GEORGE JUE MFG CO INC
Also Called: Paramount Metal & Supply Co
8140 Rosecrans Ave, Paramount (90723-2794)
PHONE..................................562 634-8181
Vincent Jue, *CEO*
George Jue, *
Elenor Sylva, *
◆ **EMP:** 60 **EST:** 1946
**SQ FT:** 80,000
**SALES (est):** 9.47MM **Privately Held**
SIC: **3546** Drills and drilling tools

### (P-9712)
### GRANBERG PUMP AND METER LTD
Also Called: Granberg International
1051 Los Medanos St, Pittsburg (94565-2561)
PHONE..................................707 562-2099
Erik Granberg, *Pr*
◆ **EMP:** 19 **EST:** 1956
**SQ FT:** 9,000
**SALES (est):** 4.71MM **Privately Held**
Web: www.granberg.com
SIC: **3546** Power-driven handtools

### (P-9713)
### MK DIAMOND PRODUCTS INC (PA)
1315 Storm Pkwy, Torrance (90501-5041)
P.O. Box 2803 (90509-2803)
PHONE..................................310 539-5221
Robert J Delahaut, *Pr*
Brian Delahaut, *CFO*
David W Riley, *Sec*
◆ **EMP:** 96 **EST:** 1945
**SQ FT:** 35,000
**SALES (est):** 27.31MM
**SALES (corp-wide):** 27.31MM **Privately Held**
Web: www.mkdiamond.com

SIC: **3546** 3425 Saws and sawing equipment; Saw blades and handsaws

### (P-9714)
### SEESCAN INC (PA)
Also Called: Seektech
3855 Ruffin Rd, San Diego (92123-1813)
PHONE..................................858 244-3300
Mark Olsson, *Pr*
John Chew, *
▲ **EMP:** 178 **EST:** 1983
**SQ FT:** 63,641
**SALES (est):** 47.11MM
**SALES (corp-wide):** 47.11MM **Privately Held**
Web: www.seescan.com
SIC: **3546** Power-driven handtools

### (P-9715)
### ZEPHYR MANUFACTURING CO INC
Also Called: Zephyr Tool Group
201 Hindry Ave, Inglewood (90301-1519)
PHONE..................................310 410-4907
Ray Chin, *VP Fin*
Earl Houston, *
Tom Houstan, *
Robert Szanter, *
▲ **EMP:** 100 **EST:** 1939
**SQ FT:** 60,000
**SALES (est):** 3.89MM **Privately Held**
Web: www.zephyrtoolgroup.com
SIC: **3546** 3545 3423 Power-driven handtools; Machine tool accessories; Hand and edge tools, nec
PA: Shg Holdings Corp
  201 Hindry Ave

### (P-9716)
### ZIRCON CORPORATION (HQ)
Also Called: Zircon
1580 Dell Ave, Campbell (95008-6992)
PHONE..................................408 866-8600
John Stauss, *Pr*
John R Stauss, *
Charles J Stauss, *
Robert Wyler, *
◆ **EMP:** 45 **EST:** 1977
**SQ FT:** 6,000
**SALES (est):** 23.54MM
**SALES (corp-wide):** 6.67K **Privately Held**
Web: www.zircon.com
SIC: **3546** Power-driven handtools
PA: Zrcn Inc.
  165 Broadway, Flr 23
  212 602-1188

## 3547 Rolling Mill Machinery

### (P-9717)
### ENGINEERED MACHINERY GROUP INC
Also Called: Macbee Engineering
1042 N Mountain Ave Ste B561, Upland (91786-3695)
PHONE..................................909 579-0088
**EMP:** 17
Web: www.emc-wire.com
SIC: **3547** Steel rolling machinery

### (P-9718)
### JOHN LIST CORPORATION
Also Called: Protocast
9732 Cozycroft Ave, Chatsworth (91311-4498)
PHONE..................................818 882-7848
John List, *Pr*
Susan List, *
**EMP:** 47 **EST:** 1966

SQ FT: 16,000
SALES (est): 8.39MM **Privately Held**
Web: www.protocastjlc.com
SIC: **3547** 3365 3369 3366 Ferrous and nonferrous mill equipment, auxiliary; Aluminum and aluminum-based alloy castings; Nonferrous foundries, nec; Copper foundries

**(P-9719)**
**OLD COUNTRY MILLWORK INC (PA)**
Also Called: O C M
5855 Hooper Ave, Los Angeles (90001-1280)
PHONE...............................323 234-2940
Gerard J Kilgallon, *CEO*
▲ EMP: 24 EST: 1984
SQ FT: 36,000
SALES (est): 9.11MM
SALES (corp-wide): 9.11MM **Privately Held**
Web: www.ocmcoil.com
SIC: **3547** 3479 Rolling mill machinery; Painting, coating, and hot dipping

**(P-9720)**
**VEST TUBE LLC**
6023 Alcoa Ave, Los Angeles (90058-3901)
P.O. Box 58827 (90058-0827)
PHONE...............................800 421-6370
Yoshiki Murakami, *Pr*
Sean Mccaughan, *Pr*
Iwaki Sugimoto, *
Tomoya Shiraishi, *
Hideki Matsumoto, *
▲ EMP: 77 EST: 1970
SQ FT: 312,000
SALES (est): 13.89MM **Privately Held**
Web: www.vesttubellc.com
SIC: **3547** 3317 Rolling mill machinery; Tubes, wrought: welded or lock joint
HQ: Shoji Jfe America Holdings Inc
301 E Ocean Blvd Ste 1750
Long Beach CA 90802
562 637-3500

### 3548 Welding Apparatus

**(P-9721)**
**AMADA WELD TECH INC (HQ)**
1820 S Myrtle Ave, Monrovia (91016-4833)
PHONE...............................626 303-5676
David Fawcett, *Pr*
Mark G Rodighiero, *
Kunio Minejima, *
James E Malloy, *
David Cielinski, *
◆ EMP: 33 EST: 1994
SQ FT: 70,000
SALES (est): 50.39MM **Privately Held**
Web: www.amadaweldtech.com
SIC: **3548** 3699 3829 Soldering equipment, except hand soldering irons; Laser welding, drilling, and cutting equipment; Measuring and controlling devices, nec
PA: Amada Co., Ltd.
200, Ishida

**(P-9722)**
**BELHOME INC**
Also Called: Technical Devices Company
560 Alaska Ave, Torrance (90503)
P.O. Box 329 (90507)
PHONE...............................310 618-8437
Douglas N Winther, *CEO*
Rey Malazo, *
EMP: 48 EST: 1977
SQ FT: 35,000
SALES (est): 2.49MM

SALES (corp-wide): 11.25MM **Privately Held**
Web: www.technicaldev.com
SIC: **3548** 3471 3544 3423 Soldering equipment, except hand soldering irons; Cleaning, polishing, and finishing; Special dies and tools; Hand and edge tools, nec
PA: Winther Technologies, Inc.
560 Alaska Ave
310 618-8437

**(P-9723)**
**BROCO INC**
Also Called: Broco
400 S Rockefeller Ave, Ontario (91761-8144)
PHONE...............................909 483-3222
◆ EMP: 25 EST: 1968
SALES (est): 3.66MM **Privately Held**
Web: www.broco-rankin.com
SIC: **3548** Welding and cutting apparatus and accessories, nec

**(P-9724)**
**CREATIVE PATHWAYS INC**
20815 Higgins Ct, Torrance (90501-1830)
PHONE...............................310 530-1965
Brent Daldo, *CEO*
Timothy Rohrberg, *
Patrica Rohrberg, *
EMP: 35 EST: 1969
SQ FT: 29,000
SALES (est): 8.22MM **Privately Held**
Web: www.creativepathways.com
SIC: **3548** Welding and cutting apparatus and accessories, nec

**(P-9725)**
**DIAMOND GROUND PRODUCTS INC**
2651 Lavery Ct, Newbury Park (91320-1502)
PHONE...............................805 498-3837
Robert Elizarraz, *CEO*
James C Elizarraz, *
▲ EMP: 30 EST: 1992
SQ FT: 40,000
SALES (est): 4.92MM **Privately Held**
Web: www.diamondground.com
SIC: **3548** Electrodes, electric welding

**(P-9726)**
**LODESTONE LLC**
Also Called: Weldstone Portable Welders
4769 E Wesley Dr, Anaheim (92807-1941)
PHONE...............................714 970-0900
EMP: 20 EST: 2007
SALES (est): 813.68K **Privately Held**
Web: www.lodestonepacific.com
SIC: **3548** 8742 Welding apparatus; Management consulting services

**(P-9727)**
**M K PRODUCTS INC**
Also Called: Mk Manufacturing
16882 Armstrong Ave, Irvine (92606-4975)
PHONE...............................949 798-1234
Chris Westlake, *Pr*
Dana E Paquin, *
▲ EMP: 80 EST: 1966
SQ FT: 80,000
SALES (est): 18.57MM **Privately Held**
Web: www.mkproducts.com
SIC: **3548** Electric welding equipment

**(P-9728)**
**OK INTERNATIONAL INC (DH)**
Also Called: Metcal
10800 Valley View St, Cypress (90630-5016)

PHONE...............................714 799-9910
◆ EMP: 224 EST: 1982
SALES (est): 45.72MM
SALES (corp-wide): 8.44B **Publicly Held**
Web: www.okinternational.com
SIC: **3548** Soldering equipment, except hand soldering irons
HQ: Dover Engineered Products Segment, Inc.
3005 Hghland Pkwy Ste 200
Downers Grove IL 60515
630 541-1540

**(P-9729)**
**ONEX RF INC**
1824 Flower Ave, Duarte (91010-2931)
PHONE...............................626 358-6639
Onik Bogosyan, *Pr*
EMP: 22 EST: 1991
SALES (est): 2.38MM **Privately Held**
Web: www.onexrf.com
SIC: **3548** Welding apparatus

**(P-9730)**
**SENSBEY INC (PA)**
833 Mahler Rd Ste 3, Burlingame (94010-1609)
PHONE...............................650 697-2032
Katsuhiro Enokawa, *Pr*
Hiro Ito, *VP*
▲ EMP: 15 EST: 1988
SQ FT: 22,000
SALES (est): 626.31K
SALES (corp-wide): 626.31K **Privately Held**
Web: www.sensbey.com
SIC: **3548** 3634 3822 Soldering equipment, except hand soldering irons; Heating units, for electric appliances; Built-in thermostats, filled system and bimetal types

**(P-9731)**
**SSCO MANUFACTURING INC**
Also Called: ARC Products
8155 Mercury Ct Ste 100, San Diego (92111-1227)
PHONE...............................619 628-1022
Victor B Miller, *Pr*
Susan D Miller, *
Lane A Litke, *
EMP: 35 EST: 1988
SALES (est): 9.59MM
SALES (corp-wide): 4.19B **Publicly Held**
Web: mechanized.lincolnelectric.com
SIC: **3548** 5085 7629 7699 Electric welding equipment; Welding supplies; Circuit board repair; Welding equipment repair
PA: Lincoln Electric Holdings, Inc.
22801 St Clair Ave
216 481-8100

**(P-9732)**
**WINTHER TECHNOLOGIES INC (PA)**
Also Called: Technical Devices
560 Alaska Ave, Torrance (90503-3904)
P.O. Box 329 (90507-0129)
PHONE...............................310 618-8437
Douglas N Winther, *Pr*
▲ EMP: 46 EST: 1986
SQ FT: 32,000
SALES (est): 11.25MM
SALES (corp-wide): 11.25MM **Privately Held**
SIC: **3548** 3544 3542 3471 Soldering equipment, except hand soldering irons; Special dies and tools; Machine tools, metal forming type; Cleaning and descaling metal products

### 3549 Metalworking Machinery, Nec

**(P-9733)**
**ADAPT AUTOMATION INC**
1661 Palm St Ste A, Santa Ana (92701-5190)
PHONE...............................714 662-4454
Case Van Mechelen, *Prin*
Case V Mechelen, *
Tim Van Mechelen, *Prin*
Tia V Mechelen, *
Peter Smit, *
EMP: 34 EST: 1988
SQ FT: 50,000
SALES (est): 6.78MM **Privately Held**
Web: www.adaptautomation.com
SIC: **3549** Assembly machines, including robotic

**(P-9734)**
**BMCI INC**
Also Called: Bergandi Machinery Company
1689 S Parco Ave, Ontario (91761-8308)
P.O. Box 3790 (91761-0977)
PHONE...............................951 361-8000
Scott Barsotti, *Pr*
Jose Garcia, *
Gary Costanzo, *
▼ EMP: 45 EST: 1994
SQ FT: 45,000
SALES (est): 4.49MM **Privately Held**
Web: www.bergandi.com
SIC: **3549** 3548 Wiredrawing and fabricating machinery and equipment, ex. die; Welding apparatus

**(P-9735)**
**BRIGHT MACHINES INC (PA)**
2445 16th St, San Francisco (94103-4210)
PHONE...............................415 867-4402
Lior Susan, *CEO*
Gillian Bregman, *
EMP: 392 EST: 2018
SALES (est): 42.77MM
SALES (corp-wide): 42.77MM **Privately Held**
Web: www.brightmachines.com
SIC: **3549** Assembly machines, including robotic

**(P-9736)**
**EUBANKS ENGINEERING CO (PA)**
1921 S Quaker Ridge Pl, Ontario (91761-8041)
PHONE...............................909 483-2456
David C Eubanks, *Prin*
EMP: 21 EST: 1951
SQ FT: 34,000
SALES (est): 6.51MM
SALES (corp-wide): 6.51MM **Privately Held**
Web: www.eubanks.com
SIC: **3549** 3825 Wiredrawing and fabricating machinery and equipment, ex. die; Test equipment for electronic and electrical circuits

**(P-9737)**
**FOOMA AMERICA INC**
12735 Stanhill Dr, La Mirada (90638-1937)
PHONE...............................310 921-0717
Soohyung Kim, *CEO*
EMP: 30 EST: 2019
SALES (est): 1.22MM **Privately Held**
SIC: **3549** Cutting and slitting machinery

## 3549 - Metalworking Machinery, Nec (P-9738)

**(P-9738)**
**GOLDEN STATE ENGINEERING INC**
15338 Garfield Ave, Paramount (90723-4092)
PHONE..................562 634-3125
Alexandra Rostovski, *CEO*
Mary Saguini, *
Eugenio Rostovski, *
Tom Scroggin, *
**EMP:** 120 **EST:** 1968
**SQ FT:** 65,000
**SALES (est):** 20.59MM **Privately Held**
**Web:** www.goldenstateeng.com
**SIC: 3549** 3541 3451 8711 Metalworking machinery, nec; Grinding, polishing, buffing, lapping, and honing machines; Screw machine products; Engineering services

**(P-9739)**
**LTI BOYD**
600 S Mcclure Rd, Modesto (95357-0520)
PHONE..................800 554-0200
Mitch Aiello, *Pr*
Kurt Wetzel, *
▲ **EMP:** 574 **EST:** 2011
**SALES (est):** 2.19MM **Privately Held**
**Web:** www.boydcorp.com
**SIC: 3549** 3053 8711 Metalworking machinery, nec; Gaskets; packing and sealing devices; Industrial engineers
**PA:** Sentinel Capital Partners Llc
51 E 42nd St Fl 53

**(P-9740)**
**MASTERBILT ATMTN SOLUTIONS INC**
12568 Kirkham Ct, Poway (92064-8899)
PHONE..................858 748-6700
Robert Michalak, *CEO*
Charles D Ross, *Pr*
**EMP:** 22 **EST:** 1992
**SQ FT:** 12,000
**SALES (est):** 3.78MM **Privately Held**
**Web:** www.masterbiltautomationsolutions.com
**SIC: 3549** Assembly machines, including robotic

**(P-9741)**
**MYTRA INC**
111 Pine Ave, South San Francisco (94080-2964)
PHONE..................650 539-8070
Chris Walti, *CEO*
**EMP:** 20 **EST:** 2022
**SALES (est):** 5.95MM **Privately Held**
**Web:** www.mytra.ai
**SIC: 3549** Assembly machines, including robotic

**(P-9742)**
**NEATO ROBOTICS INC (HQ)**
3590 N 1st St Ste 200, San Jose (95134-2137)
P.O. Box 612797 (95161-2797)
PHONE..................510 795-1351
Thomas Nedder, *CEO*
Bruce Mcallister, *CFO*
♦ **EMP:** 25 **EST:** 2005
**SALES (est):** 22.57MM
**SALES (corp-wide):** 3.29B **Privately Held**
**Web:** www.neatorobotics.it
**SIC: 3549** 3524 Assembly machines, including robotic; Blowers and vacuums, lawn
**PA:** Vorwerk Se & Co. Kg
Muhlenweg 17-37
2025640

**(P-9743)**
**OHMNILABS INCORPORATED**
591 Yosemite Dr, Milpitas (95035-5448)
PHONE..................408 675-9565
Thuc Vu, *CEO*
**EMP:** 92 **EST:** 2016
**SALES (est):** 5.72MM **Privately Held**
**Web:** www.ohmnilabs.com
**SIC: 3549** Assembly machines, including robotic

**(P-9744)**
**POSITRONICS INCORPORATED**
173 Spring St Ste 120, Pleasanton (94566-9401)
PHONE..................925 931-0211
Howard Miles, *Pr*
Vincent Leung, *VP*
**EMP:** 28 **EST:** 2001
**SQ FT:** 2,200
**SALES (est):** 2.21MM **Privately Held**
**Web:** www.posincorp.com
**SIC: 3549** Assembly machines, including robotic

**(P-9745)**
**SAILDRONE INC**
Also Called: Saildrone
1050 W Tower Ave, Alameda (94501-5003)
PHONE..................415 670-9700
Richard Jenkins, *CEO*
Michael Mullen, *
Barak Ben-gal, *CFO*
**EMP:** 250 **EST:** 2012
**SQ FT:** 32,500
**SALES (est):** 34.24MM **Privately Held**
**Web:** www.saildrone.com
**SIC: 3549** 3812 Assembly machines, including robotic; Nautical instruments

**(P-9746)**
**TELEDYNE SEABOTIX INC**
2877 Historic Decatur Rd Ste 100, San Diego (92106-6177)
PHONE..................619 239-5959
**EMP:** 68
**SIC: 3549** Propeller straightening presses

**(P-9747)**
**TRINITY ROBOTICS AUTOMTN LLC**
4582 Brickell Privado St, Ontario (91761-7827)
PHONE..................562 690-4525
**EMP:** 16 **EST:** 2014
**SALES (est):** 1.87MM **Privately Held**
**Web:** www.trinityautomation.com
**SIC: 3549** Assembly machines, including robotic

**(P-9748)**
**UBTECH ROBOTICS CORP**
767 S Alameda St Ste 250, Los Angeles (90021-1665)
PHONE..................213 261-7153
John Rhee, *CEO*
**EMP:** 30 **EST:** 2015
**SALES (est):** 4.4MM **Privately Held**
**Web:** www.ubtrobot.com
**SIC: 3549** Assembly machines, including robotic
**PA:** Ubtech Robotics Corp Ltd
Room 2201, Building C1, Nanshan Zhiyuan, No. 1001 Xueyuan Avenue

**(P-9749)**
**WALLNER EXPAC INC (PA)**
Also Called: W T E
1274 S Slater Cir, Ontario (91761-1522)

PHONE..................909 481-8800
Sophia Wallner, *Ch Bd*
Michael Wallner, *
Paul Wallner, *
♦ **EMP:** 55 **EST:** 1959
**SALES (est):** 29.77MM
**SALES (corp-wide):** 29.77MM **Privately Held**
**Web:** www.expac.com
**SIC: 3549** 3542 Metalworking machinery, nec; Machine tools, metal forming type

## 3552 Textile Machinery

**(P-9750)**
**DILCO INDUSTRIAL INC**
205 E Bristol Ln, Orange (92865-2715)
PHONE..................714 998-5266
Jay R Dille, *Pr*
Jay R Dille Junior, *VP*
Tina Dille, *Sec*
**EMP:** 15 **EST:** 1974
**SQ FT:** 6,000
**SALES (est):** 2.45MM **Privately Held**
**Web:** www.dilco.com
**SIC: 3552** 3993 Silk screens for textile industry; Signs and advertising specialties

**(P-9751)**
**LYTLE SCREEN PRINTING INC**
21572 Surveyor Cir, Huntington Beach (92646-7067)
PHONE..................714 969-2424
Tim Mcmillen, *Pr*
Mark Lytle, *Pr*
**EMP:** 18 **EST:** 1988
**SQ FT:** 6,000
**SALES (est):** 1.69MM **Privately Held**
**Web:** www.lysphb.com
**SIC: 3552** 7336 2759 Silk screens for textile industry; Silk screen design; Screen printing

**(P-9752)**
**SURFACE ENGINEERING SPC**
919 Hamlin Ct, Sunnyvale (94089-1402)
PHONE..................408 734-8810
Richard Peattie, *Pr*
Jane Peattie, *VP*
**EMP:** 20 **EST:** 1976
**SQ FT:** 18,000
**SALES (est):** 4.79MM **Privately Held**
**Web:** www.surfeng.com
**SIC: 3552** 7389 Spindles, textile; Grinding, precision: commercial or industrial

**(P-9753)**
**TAJIMA USA INC**
19925 S Susana Rd, Compton (90221-5726)
PHONE..................310 604-8200
Ron Krasnitz, *Pr*
▲ **EMP:** 35 **EST:** 1996
**SQ FT:** 25,000
**SALES (est):** 2.21MM **Privately Held**
**SIC: 3552** Embroidery machines
**PA:** Tajima Industries Ltd.
1800, Ushiyamacho

## 3553 Woodworking Machinery

**(P-9754)**
**KVAL INC**
Also Called: Kval Machinery Co
825 Petaluma Blvd S, Petaluma (94952-5134)
PHONE..................707 762-4363
Gerald Kvalheim, *CEO*
Gerald Kvalheim, *Pr*

Dave Kvalheim, *
Mark Kvalheim, *
Andrew M Kvalheim, *
▲ **EMP:** 125 **EST:** 1950
**SALES (est):** 19.92MM **Privately Held**
**Web:** www.kvalinc.com
**SIC: 3553** 5084 Woodworking machinery; Industrial machinery and equipment

**(P-9755)**
**MADE AND MODERN HARD GOODS INC**
2260 Cordelia Rd Ste 400, Fairfield (94534-1914)
PHONE..................707 366-9180
Amrit Rao, *CEO*
**EMP:** 90 **EST:** 2020
**SALES (est):** 9.18MM **Privately Held**
**Web:** www.madeandmodern.com
**SIC: 3553** Furniture makers machinery, woodworking

**(P-9756)**
**NORFIELD ACQUISITION LLC (HQ)**
422 Otterson Dr, Chico (95928-8206)
PHONE..................800 824-6242
**EMP:** 24 **EST:** 1959
**SALES (est):** 11.13MM
**SALES (corp-wide):** 51.06MM **Privately Held**
**Web:** www.norfield.com
**SIC: 3553** 5085 Woodworking machinery; Tools, nec
**PA:** Ged Integrated Solutions, Inc.
31100 Diamond Pkwy
330 963-5401

**(P-9757)**
**VOORWOOD COMPANY**
Also Called: Turbosand
2350 Barney Rd, Anderson (96007-4306)
PHONE..................530 365-3311
Adam Britton, *CEO*
Larry Ackernecht, *
Steve Shifflet, *
▼ **EMP:** 30 **EST:** 1961
**SQ FT:** 60,000
**SALES (est):** 7.21MM **Privately Held**
**Web:** www.voorwood.com
**SIC: 3553** Woodworking machinery

**(P-9758)**
**WANESHEAR TECHNOLOGIES LLC**
3471 N State St, Ukiah (95482-3080)
PHONE..................707 462-4761
Ron Mcgehee, *Mng Pt*
Ron Mc Gehee, *
Clark Mcgehee, *Mng Pt*
▼ **EMP:** 35 **EST:** 2011
**SALES (est):** 2.5MM **Privately Held**
**SIC: 3553** Sawmill machines

## 3554 Paper Industries Machinery

**(P-9759)**
**ELLISON EDUCATIONAL EQP INC (PA)**
Also Called: Sizzix
25671 Commercentre Dr, Lake Forest (92630-8801)
PHONE..................949 598-8822
Richard Birse, *CEO*
Kristin Highberg, *
▲ **EMP:** 38 **EST:** 1981
**SQ FT:** 132,000

**PRODUCTS & SERVICES SECTION**  **3556 - Food Products Machinery (P-9780)**

SALES (est): 12.04MM
SALES (corp-wide): 12.04MM **Privately Held**
Web: www.ellison.com
SIC: **3554** Cutting machines, paper

**(P-9760)**
**GEO M MARTIN COMPANY (PA)**
1250 67th St, Emeryville (94608-1121)
PHONE............................510 652-2200
Merrill D Martin, *Ch*
Robert A Morgan, *
George R Martin, *
Lillian Martin, *
Daniel J D'angelo, *VP*
▲ **EMP:** 99 **EST:** 1957
**SQ FT:** 50,000
**SALES (est):** 24.58MM
**SALES (corp-wide):** 24.58MM **Privately Held**
Web: www.geomartin.com
SIC: **3554** Corrugating machines, paper

## 3555 Printing Trades Machinery

**(P-9761)**
**4L TECHNOLOGIES INC**
Also Called: Catridge Return Center
325 Weakley St, Calexico (92231-9659)
PHONE............................817 538-0974
**EMP:** 1047
**SALES (corp-wide):** 26.47MM **Privately Held**
Web: www.clovertech.com
SIC: **3555** Printing trades machinery
HQ: 4l Technologies Inc.
122 W Madison St
Ottawa IL 61350
815 431-8100

**(P-9762)**
**ANAJET LLC**
1100 Valencia Ave, Tustin (92780-6428)
PHONE............................714 662-3200
▲ **EMP:** 20 **EST:** 2005
**SALES (est):** 5.78MM **Privately Held**
Web: www.ricohdtg.com
SIC: **3555** Printing trades machinery

**(P-9763)**
**CAL PLATE (PA)**
17110 Jersey Ave, Artesia (90701-2694)
PHONE............................562 403-3000
Richard Borelli, *Pr*
**EMP:** 63 **EST:** 1966
**SQ FT:** 33,000
**SALES (est):** 8.97MM
**SALES (corp-wide):** 8.97MM **Privately Held**
Web: www.calplate.com
SIC: **3555** 3423 3544 Printing plates; Cutting dies, except metal cutting; Special dies, tools, jigs, and fixtures

**(P-9764)**
**CONTAINER GRAPHICS CORP**
1137 Graphics Dr, Modesto (95351-1501)
PHONE............................209 577-0181
Brian Bennett, *Mgr*
**EMP:** 61
**SALES (corp-wide):** 3.99MM **Privately Held**
Web: www.containergraphics.com
SIC: **3555** Printing trades machinery
PA: Container Graphics Corp.
114 Ednbrgh S Drv Ste 104
919 481-4200

**(P-9765)**
**COUNT NUMBERING MACHINE INC**
Also Called: Count Machinery Co
2128 Auto Park Way, Escondido (92029-1344)
PHONE............................760 739-9357
◆ **EMP:** 20
Web: www.count-usa.com
SIC: **3555** 3554 Printing trades machinery; Folding machines, paper

**(P-9766)**
**FABRIC8LABS INC**
11075 Roselle St, San Diego (92121-1204)
PHONE............................858 215-1142
Jeff Herman, *CEO*
David Pain, *
**EMP:** 60 **EST:** 2016
**SALES (est):** 1.01MM **Privately Held**
Web: www.fabric8labs.com
SIC: **3555** Printing trades machinery

**(P-9767)**
**GRAPHICS MICROSYSTEMS LLC (DH)**
484 Oakmead Pkwy, Sunnyvale (94085-4708)
**EMP:** 70 **EST:** 1983
**SQ FT:** 20,000
**SALES (est):** 3MM
**SALES (corp-wide):** 23.89B **Publicly Held**
SIC: **3555** Printing trades machinery
HQ: Advanced Vision Technology (A.V.T.) Ltd.
4 Hayam Rd.
Kfar Saba

**(P-9768)**
**HARRIS & BRUNO MACHINE CO INC (PA)**
Also Called: Harris & Bruno International
8555 Washington Blvd, Roseville (95678-5901)
PHONE............................916 781-7676
Nick Bruno, *CEO*
▲ **EMP:** 64 **EST:** 1944
**SQ FT:** 45,000
**SALES (est):** 21.21MM
**SALES (corp-wide):** 21.21MM **Privately Held**
Web: www.harris-bruno.com
SIC: **3555** Printing trades machinery

**(P-9769)**
**IMPERIAL RUBBER PRODUCTS INC**
5691 Gates St, Chino (91710-7603)
PHONE............................909 393-0528
Ronald Hill, *CEO*
Bob Schwartz, *
Steve Huff, *
▲ **EMP:** 35 **EST:** 1989
**SQ FT:** 20,000
**SALES (est):** 4.69MM **Privately Held**
Web: www.imperialrubber.com
SIC: **3555** Printing trades machinery

**(P-9770)**
**LITH-O-ROLL CORPORATION**
9521 Telstar Ave, El Monte (91731-2994)
P.O. Box 5328 (91734-1328)
PHONE............................626 579-0340
Rita Sepe, *Pr*
**EMP:** 50 **EST:** 1957
**SQ FT:** 30,000
**SALES (est):** 9.49MM **Privately Held**
Web: www.lithoroll.com

SIC: **3555** Printing trades machinery

**(P-9771)**
**ONE TOUCH SOLUTIONS INC**
Also Called: One Touch Office Technology
370 Amapola Ave Ste 106, Torrance (90501-7241)
P.O. Box 2226 (90247-0226)
PHONE............................310 320-6868
William Rees, *CEO*
Mark Stratton, *CFO*
Jayson Beasley, *COO*
**EMP:** 15 **EST:** 2005
**SQ FT:** 5,182
**SALES (est):** 6.12MM **Privately Held**
Web: www.1touchoffice.com
SIC: **3555** Printing trades machinery

**(P-9772)**
**PACIFIC BARCODE INC**
27531 Enterprise Cir W Ste 201c, Temecula (92590-4864)
PHONE............................951 587-8717
Michael Meadors, *Pr*
Michael Meadors, *Pr*
Michelle Meadors, *
**EMP:** 37 **EST:** 1999
**SQ FT:** 8,600
**SALES (est):** 5.03MM **Privately Held**
Web: www.pacificbarcode.com
SIC: **3555** 2759 3565 3577 Printing trades machinery; Commercial printing, nec; Labeling machines, industrial; Bar code (magnetic ink) printers

**(P-9773)**
**PARA-PLATE & PLASTICS CO INC**
Also Called: Para Plate
15910 Shoemaker Ave, Cerritos (90703-2200)
PHONE............................562 404-3434
Shane Pearson, *Pr*
Robert J Clapp, *
John Greenamyer, *
Steve Binnard, *
**EMP:** 27 **EST:** 1945
**SQ FT:** 17,000
**SALES (est):** 2.49MM **Privately Held**
Web: www.paraplate.com
SIC: **3555** 7336 2796 Printing plates; Commercial art and graphic design; Platemaking services

**(P-9774)**
**RIMA ENTERPRISES INC**
Also Called: Rima-System
16417 Ladona Cir, Huntington Beach (92649-2133)
PHONE............................714 893-4534
Horst K Steinhart, *CEO*
▲ **EMP:** 62 **EST:** 1970
**SALES (est):** 7.41MM **Privately Held**
SIC: **3555** Bookbinding machinery

**(P-9775)**
**THISTLE ROLLER CO INC**
209 Van Norman Rd, Montebello (90640-5393)
PHONE............................323 685-5322
Lizbeth Karpynec, *CEO*
Eric Karpynetz, *
▲ **EMP:** 35 **EST:** 1957
**SQ FT:** 45,000
**SALES (est):** 3.74MM **Privately Held**
Web: www.thistleroller.com
SIC: **3555** 3312 2796 Printing trades machinery; Blast furnaces and steel mills; Platemaking services

**(P-9776)**
**VELO3D INC (PA)**
511 Division St, Campbell (95008-6905)
PHONE............................408 610-3915
Brad Kreger, *Interim Chief Executive Officer*
Carl Bass, *Ch Bd*
Hull Xu, *CFO*
Nancy Krystal, *VP*
**EMP:** 23 **EST:** 2014
**SALES (est):** 77.44MM
**SALES (corp-wide):** 77.44MM **Publicly Held**
Web: www.velo3d.com
SIC: **3555** 7372 Printing trades machinery; Prepackaged software

**(P-9777)**
**XEROX INTERNATIONAL PARTNERS (DH)**
Also Called: Fuji Xerox
2100 Geng Rd Ste 210, Palo Alto (94303-3307)
▲ **EMP:** 43 **EST:** 1991
**SALES (est):** 38.49MM
**SALES (corp-wide):** 6.89B **Publicly Held**
SIC: **3555** Leads, printers'
HQ: Xerox Corporation
201 Merritt 7
Norwalk CT 06851
203 849-5216

## 3556 Food Products Machinery

**(P-9778)**
**ATLAS PACIFIC ENGINEERING CO**
Also Called: Sinclair Systems
3115 S Willow Ave, Fresno (93725-9349)
PHONE............................559 233-4500
Don Freeman, *Prin*
**EMP:** 28
**SALES (corp-wide):** 103.68MM **Privately Held**
Web: www.atlaspacific.com
SIC: **3556** Food products machinery
HQ: Atlas Pacific Engineering Company
1 Atlas Ave
Pueblo CO 81002
719 948-3040

**(P-9779)**
**BILLINGTON WELDING & MFG INC**
Also Called: Bwm
1442 N Emerald Ave, Modesto (95351-1115)
P.O. Box 4460 (95352-4460)
PHONE............................209 526-0846
Timothy Ryan Billington, *CEO*
Francis Billington, *
**EMP:** 60 **EST:** 1969
**SQ FT:** 26,000
**SALES (est):** 2.42MM **Privately Held**
SIC: **3556** 3535 Food products machinery; Conveyors and conveying equipment

**(P-9780)**
**BLENTECH CORPORATION**
2899 Dowd Dr, Santa Rosa (95407-7897)
PHONE............................707 523-5949
Darrell Horn, *Pr*
Daniel Voit, *
▲ **EMP:** 60 **EST:** 1986
**SQ FT:** 27,000
**SALES (est):** 15.13MM **Privately Held**
Web: www.blentech.com

## 3556 - Food Products Machinery (P-9781)

SIC: 3556 Mixers, commercial, food

**(P-9781)**
**CALPACK FOODS LLC**
22625 S Western Ave, Torrance (90501-4950)
PHONE..................................310 320-0141
Susan Ricci, *Managing Member*
EMP: 24 EST: 2012
SALES (est): 1.3MM Privately Held
Web: www.calpackfoods.com
SIC: 3556 Food products machinery

**(P-9782)**
**CAPNA FABRICATION**
Also Called: Capna Systems
9801 Independence Ave, Chatsworth (91311-4320)
PHONE..................................888 416-6777
Vitaly Mekk, *CEO*
Gene Galyuk, *
EMP: 30 EST: 2017
SALES (est): 7.55MM Privately Held
SIC: 3556 Oilseed crushing and extracting machinery

**(P-9783)**
**CASA HERRERA INC (PA)**
2655 Pine St, Pomona (91767-2115)
PHONE..................................909 392-3930
Michael L Herrera, *CEO*
Ronald L Meade, *
Alfred J Herrera, *
Frank J Herrera, *
Susan A Herrera, *
◆ EMP: 100 EST: 1970
SQ FT: 100,000
SALES (est): 20.67MM
SALES (corp-wide): 20.67MM Privately Held
Web: www.casaherrera.com
SIC: 3556 Food products machinery

**(P-9784)**
**CHOOLJIAN & SONS INC**
Also Called: Del Ray Packaging
Del Rey Ave, Del Rey (93616)
P.O. Box 160 (93616-0160)
PHONE..................................559 888-2031
Gerald Chooljian, *Sec*
EMP: 20
SQ FT: 1,152
SALES (corp-wide): 9.53MM Privately Held
Web: www.delreypacking.com
SIC: 3556 Dehydrating equipment, food processing
PA: Chooljian & Sons, Inc.
5287 S Del Rey Ave
559 888-2031

**(P-9785)**
**COMMERCIAL MANUFACTURING**
2432 S East Ave, Fresno (93706-5119)
P.O. Box 947 (93714-0947)
PHONE..................................559 237-1855
Larry Hagopian, *Pr*
EMP: 45 EST: 1938
SQ FT: 45,000
SALES (est): 3.59MM Privately Held
Web: www.commercialmfg.com
SIC: 3556 Food products machinery

**(P-9786)**
**CRIVELLER CALIFORNIA CORP**
185 Grant Ave, Healdsburg (95448-9539)
PHONE..................................707 431-2211
Bruno Criveller, *Pr*
Mario Creveller, *VP*
▲ EMP: 15 EST: 2000
SALES (est): 3.19MM Privately Held
Web: www.criveller.com
SIC: 3556 Brewers' and maltsters' machinery

**(P-9787)**
**EBARA MIXERS INC**
Also Called: Scott Turbon Mixer Inc.
9351 Industrial Way, Adelanto (92301-3932)
P.O. Box 160 (92301-0160)
PHONE..................................760 246-3430
EMP: 30 EST: 1980
SALES (est): 6.58MM Privately Held
Web: www.haywardgordon.com
SIC: 3556 Cutting, chopping, grinding, mixing, and similar machinery
HQ: Hayward Gordon Us, Inc.
1541 S 92nd Pl
Seattle WA 98108
206 767-5660

**(P-9788)**
**FOOD & BEV INNOVATIONS LLC**
1801 Century Park E Ste 1420, Los Angeles (90067-2316)
PHONE..................................888 491-3772
Stan Levitsky, *PRODUCT Development*
EMP: 15 EST: 2012
SALES (est): 1.05MM Privately Held
SIC: 3556 Beverage machinery

**(P-9789)**
**FOODTOOLS CONSOLIDATED INC (PA)**
315 Laguna St, Santa Barbara (93101-1716)
PHONE..................................805 962-8383
Martin Grano, *Ch Bd*
Matt Browne, *
Doug Petrovich, *
◆ EMP: 20 EST: 1983
SQ FT: 8,500
SALES (est): 13.41MM
SALES (corp-wide): 13.41MM Privately Held
Web: www.foodtools.com
SIC: 3556 2679 Slicers, commercial, food; Paper products, converted, nec

**(P-9790)**
**FOTIS AND SON IMPORTS INC (PA)**
15451 Electronic Ln, Huntington Beach (92649-1333)
PHONE..................................714 894-9022
Peter Georgatsos, *Pr*
Russ Hillas, *
Laura Georgatsos, *
Eleni Hillas, *
▲ EMP: 38 EST: 1976
SQ FT: 34,000
SALES (est): 11.42MM
SALES (corp-wide): 11.42MM Privately Held
Web: www.fotisandsonimports.com
SIC: 3556 Food products machinery

**(P-9791)**
**FPEC CORPORATION A CAL CORP (PA)**
Also Called: Food Processing Equipment Co
13623 Pumice St, Santa Fe Springs (90670-5105)
PHONE..................................562 802-3727
Alan Davison, *CEO*
Ethel Davison, *Sec*
EMP: 18 EST: 1969
SQ FT: 18,000
SALES (est): 8.18MM
SALES (corp-wide): 8.18MM Privately Held
Web: www.fpec.com
SIC: 3556 Food products machinery

**(P-9792)**
**FRESH VENTURE FOODS LLC**
1205 Craig Dr, Santa Maria (93458)
P.O. Box 1023 (93458)
PHONE..................................805 928-3374
John Schaefer, *Managing Member*
Jeff Lundberg, *
EMP: 239 EST: 2012
SQ FT: 70
SALES (est): 22.38MM Privately Held
Web: www.freshventurefoods.com
SIC: 3556 Dehydrating equipment, food processing

**(P-9793)**
**G & I ISLAS INDUSTRIES INC (PA)**
Also Called: G & I Industries
12860 Schabarum Ave, Baldwin Park (91706-6801)
P.O. Box 1262 (91706-7262)
PHONE..................................626 960-5020
Gonzalo R Islas, *CEO*
Sara Islas, *
▲ EMP: 23 EST: 1988
SQ FT: 12,500
SALES (est): 2.73MM
SALES (corp-wide): 2.73MM Privately Held
Web: www.giislasindustries.com
SIC: 3556 5084 Bakery machinery; Food industry machinery

**(P-9794)**
**GOLDEN PACIFIC SEAFOODS INC**
700 S Raymond Ave, Fullerton (92831-5233)
PHONE..................................714 589-8888
Tony Zavala, *Pr*
EMP: 45 EST: 2016
SALES (est): 3.6MM Privately Held
SIC: 3556 Meat, poultry, and seafood processing machinery

**(P-9795)**
**HACKETT INDUSTRIES INC**
Also Called: West Star Industries
4445 E Fremont St, Stockton (95215-4007)
PHONE..................................209 955-8220
Michelle E Focke, *CEO*
Richard Hackett, *
Carolyn Hackett, *
Mark Lathrop, *
EMP: 43 EST: 1973
SQ FT: 90,000
SALES (est): 4.16MM Privately Held
Web: www.weststarindustries.com
SIC: 3556 3444 3431 Food products machinery; Sheet metalwork; Metal sanitary ware

**(P-9796)**
**HEINZEN MANUFACTURING INC**
Also Called: Heinzen Manufacturing Intl
405 Mayock Rd, Gilroy (95020-7040)
PHONE..................................408 842-7233
EMP: 97 EST: 1978
SALES (est): 17.39MM Privately Held
Web: www.heinzen.com
SIC: 3556 Food products machinery

**(P-9797)**
**HNY RAMEN INC**
Also Called: Hironori Ramen Factory
17109 Edwards Rd, Cerritos (90703-2423)
PHONE..................................626 586-7209
Yohei Uchida, *Sec*
EMP: 15 EST: 2018
SALES (est): 2.65MM Privately Held
SIC: 3556 Pasta machinery

**(P-9798)**
**INTERSTATE MEAT CO INC**
Also Called: Sterling Pacific Meat Co.
6114 Scott Way, Commerce (90040-3518)
PHONE..................................323 838-9400
James T Asher, *Pr*
EMP: 49 EST: 1996
SALES (est): 10.65MM Privately Held
Web: www.sterlingpacificmeat.com
SIC: 3556 Meat processing machinery

**(P-9799)**
**J C FORD COMPANY (HQ)**
Also Called: JC Ford
901 S Leslie St, La Habra (90631)
PHONE..................................714 871-7361
Scott D Ruhe, *CEO*
◆ EMP: 43 EST: 1945
SALES (est): 38.16MM Privately Held
Web: www.jcford.com
SIC: 3556 Food products machinery
PA: Ruhe Corporation
901 S Leslie St

**(P-9800)**
**JOHN BEAN TECHNOLOGIES CORP**
1660 Iowa Ave Ste 100, Riverside (92507-0501)
P.O. Box 5710 (92517-5710)
PHONE..................................951 222-2300
Thomas Brickweg, *Prin*
EMP: 88
Web: www.jbtc.com
SIC: 3556 3542 3523 Dairy and milk machinery; Nail heading machines; Dairy equipment (farm), nec
PA: John Bean Technologies Corporation
70 W Madison St Ste 4400

**(P-9801)**
**JOHN BEAN TECHNOLOGIES CORP**
Also Called: Jbt Food Tech Madera
2300 W Industrial Ave, Madera (93637-5210)
PHONE..................................559 661-3200
Eric Madsen, *Brnch Mgr*
EMP: 165
Web: www.jbtc.com
SIC: 3556 Food products machinery
PA: John Bean Technologies Corporation
70 W Madison St Ste 4400

**(P-9802)**
**JUICY WHIP INC**
1668 Curtiss Ct, La Verne (91750-5848)
PHONE..................................909 392-7500
TOLL FREE: 800
Gus Stratton, *Pr*
▲ EMP: 28 EST: 1981
SQ FT: 23,000
SALES (est): 6.37MM Privately Held
Web: www.juicywhip.com
SIC: 3556 2033 Beverage machinery; Fruit juices: fresh

▲ = Import ▼ = Export
◆ = Import/Export

## PRODUCTS & SERVICES SECTION
### 3559 - Special Industry Machinery, Nec (P-9824)

**(P-9803)**
**LAWRENCE EQUIPMENT LEASING INC (PA)**
Also Called: Lawrence Equipment
2034 Peck Rd, El Monte (91733-3727)
PHONE..............................626 442-2894
John Lawrence, *CEO*
Linda Lawrence, *
Glenn Shelton, *
Jack Kirkpatrick, *Stockholder*
▲ **EMP:** 190 **EST:** 1981
**SQ FT:** 50,000
**SALES (est):** 48.74MM
**SALES (corp-wide):** 48.74MM **Privately Held**
Web: www.lawrenceequipment.com
**SIC: 3556** Flour mill machinery

**(P-9804)**
**MACHINE BUILDING SPC INC**
Also Called: Conveyor Concepts
1977 Blake Ave, Los Angeles (90039-3832)
PHONE..............................323 666-8289
Charles Conaway, *Ch Bd*
Dennis James Conaway, *
Sandra Conaway, *
Sharon Conaway, *
**EMP:** 25 **EST:** 1960
**SQ FT:** 17,000
**SALES (est):** 3.09MM **Privately Held**
Web: www.machinebuildingspecialties.com
**SIC: 3556** 3535 Bakery machinery; Belt conveyor systems, general industrial use

**(P-9805)**
**MEAT PACKERS BUTCHERS SUP INC**
Also Called: Mpbs Industries
2820 E Washington Blvd, Los Angeles (90023-4274)
PHONE..............................323 268-8514
Jimmy Jin, *CEO*
Shaofa Jin, *Ch Bd*
▲ **EMP:** 17 **EST:** 1939
**SQ FT:** 16,000
**SALES (est):** 3.25MM **Privately Held**
Web: www.mpbs.com
**SIC: 3556** Food products machinery

**(P-9806)**
**MEMC LIQUIDATING CORPORATION**
Also Called: Mc Cann's Engineering & Mfg Co
4570 Colorado Blvd, La Mirada (90638)
P.O. Box 39100 (90039-0100)
PHONE..............................818 637-7200
▲ **EMP:** 250
**SIC: 3556** 3586 3585 3581 Beverage machinery; Measuring and dispensing pumps; Refrigeration and heating equipment; Automatic vending machines

**(P-9807)**
**NATIONAL BAND SAW COMPANY**
1055 W Avenue L12, Lancaster (93534-7045)
PHONE..............................661 294-9552
Harley Frank, *Pr*
Norman Frank, *Ch Bd*
▲ **EMP:** 17 **EST:** 1953
**SQ FT:** 12,000
**SALES (est):** 3.17MM **Privately Held**
Web: www.nbsparts.com
**SIC: 3556** Meat processing machinery

**(P-9808)**
**O H I COMPANY**
820 S Pershing Ave, Stockton (95206-1176)
P.O. Box 622 (95201-0622)
PHONE..............................209 466-8921
Thomas W Hubbard, *CEO*
Ben Wallace, *
▲ **EMP:** 26 **EST:** 1970
**SQ FT:** 40,000
**SALES (est):** 2.52MM **Privately Held**
Web: www.ohicompany.com
**SIC: 3556** 3443 Food products machinery; Fabricated plate work (boiler shop)

**(P-9809)**
**ODENBERG INC**
Also Called: Tomra
875 Embarcadero Dr, West Sacramento (95605-1503)
PHONE..............................916 371-0700
▲ **EMP:** 25
**SIC: 3556** 3523 3823 Food products machinery; Dairy equipment (farm), nec; Industrial process control instruments

**(P-9810)**
**PACIFIC PACKAGING MCHY LLC**
Also Called: Pack West Machinery
200 River Rd, Corona (92878-1435)
PHONE..............................951 393-2200
Gerald Carpino, *CEO*
Jerry Carpino, *
▲ **EMP:** 25 **EST:** 1962
**SQ FT:** 30,000
**SALES (est):** 7.55MM **Privately Held**
Web: www.pacificpak.com
**SIC: 3556** 3565 Food products machinery; Packaging machinery
HQ: Pro Mach, Inc.
50 E Rvrcnter Blvd Ste 18
Covington KY 41011
513 831-8778

**(P-9811)**
**RBM CONVEYOR SYSTEMS INC**
1570 W Mission Blvd, Pomona (91766-1247)
PHONE..............................909 620-1333
Roobik Kureghian, *Pr*
Armine Kureghian, *Treas*
▲ **EMP:** 20 **EST:** 1980
**SALES (est):** 3.1MM **Privately Held**
**SIC: 3556** 8711 3537 3535 Food products machinery; Engineering services; Industrial trucks and tractors; Conveyors and conveying equipment

**(P-9812)**
**RESERS FINE FOODS INC**
3261 Lionshead Ave Ste 100, Carlsbad (92010-4710)
PHONE..............................503 643-6431
**EMP:** 18
**SALES (corp-wide):** 347.92MM **Privately Held**
Web: www.resers.com
**SIC: 3556** Food products machinery
PA: Reser's Fine Foods, Inc.
15570 Sw Jenkins Rd
503 643-6431

**(P-9813)**
**RESERS FINE FOODS INC**
3285 Corporate Vw, Vista (92081-8528)
PHONE..............................503 643-6431
**EMP:** 37
**SALES (corp-wide):** 347.92MM **Privately Held**
Web: www.resers.com

**SIC: 3556** Food products machinery
PA: Reser's Fine Foods, Inc.
15570 Sw Jenkins Rd
503 643-6431

**(P-9814)**
**REXNORD INDUSTRIES LLC**
Also Called: Industrial Components Div
2175 Union Pl, Simi Valley (93065-1661)
PHONE..............................805 583-5514
Dave Kleinhaus, *Mgr*
**EMP:** 45
**SALES (corp-wide):** 6.25B **Publicly Held**
**SIC: 3556** 3568 Food products machinery; Couplings, shaft: rigid, flexible, universal joint, etc.
HQ: Rexnord Industries, Llc
111 W Michigan St
Milwaukee WI 53203
414 643-3000

**(P-9815)**
**RIPON MFG CO**
Also Called: RMC
652 S Stockton Ave, Ripon (95366-2798)
PHONE..............................209 599-2148
Glenn Navarro, *Pr*
Ursula Navarro, *Sec*
**EMP:** 20 **EST:** 1964
**SQ FT:** 45,000
**SALES (est):** 4.92MM **Privately Held**
Web: www.riponmfgco.com
**SIC: 3556** 3535 Food products machinery; Conveyors and conveying equipment

**(P-9816)**
**SHAVER SPECIALTY CO INC**
20608 Earl St, Torrance (90503-3009)
PHONE..............................310 370-6941
George Shaver, *Pr*
Ronald Shaver, *VP*
▲ **EMP:** 22 **EST:** 1937
**SQ FT:** 20,000
**SALES (est):** 2.99MM **Privately Held**
Web: www.shaverkeenkutter.com
**SIC: 3556** 3599 Choppers, commercial, food ; Machine shop, jobbing and repair

**(P-9817)**
**STALFAB INC**
131 Algen Ln, Watsonville (95076-8624)
P.O. Box 780 (95077-0780)
PHONE..............................831 786-1600
Eric Buksa, *Prin*
**EMP:** 21 **EST:** 1994
**SQ FT:** 5,000
**SALES (est):** 976.38K **Privately Held**
**SIC: 3556** Food products machinery

**(P-9818)**
**SUNKIST GROWERS INC**
Sunkist RES Technical Svcs Div
10730 Bell Ct, Rancho Cucamonga (91730-4834)
PHONE..............................844 694-5406
Alex Paradiang, *Genl Mgr*
**EMP:** 20
**SALES (corp-wide):** 81.32MM **Privately Held**
Web: www.sunkistequipment.com
**SIC: 3556** Food products machinery
PA: Sunkist Growers, Inc.
27770 Entertainment Dr
661 290-8900

**(P-9819)**
**SUPERIOR FOOD MACHINERY INC**
8311 Sorensen Ave, Santa Fe Springs (90670-2125)
PHONE..............................562 949-0396
Danny Reyes, *Pr*
Polo Reyes, *Pr*
Marc Reyes, *VP*
**EMP:** 23 **EST:** 1975
**SQ FT:** 14,000
**SALES (est):** 4.96MM **Privately Held**
Web: www.superiorinc.com
**SIC: 3556** Food products machinery

**(P-9820)**
**TBDX INC**
Also Called: Xbloom
1212 Broadway Plz Ste 2100, Walnut Creek (94596-5129)
PHONE..............................415 225-1391
Qiliang Xu, *CEO*
**EMP:** 30 **EST:** 2021
**SALES (est):** 985.61K **Privately Held**
**SIC: 3556** 5046 Roasting machinery: coffee, peanut, etc.; Coffee brewing equipment and supplies

**(P-9821)**
**TOUCHSTONE PISTACHIO CO LLC**
19570 Avenue 88, Terra Bella (93270-9705)
PHONE..............................559 535-0110
Farid Assemi, *Mgr*
**EMP:** 250
**SALES (corp-wide):** 29.94MM **Privately Held**
Web: www.touchstonepistachio.com
**SIC: 3556** Food products machinery
PA: Touchstone Pistachio Company, Llc
5260 N Palm Ave Ste 421
559 440-8350

**(P-9822)**
**VALLEY PACKLINE SOLUTIONS**
5259 Avenue 408, Reedley (93654-9131)
PHONE..............................559 638-7821
Jim Parra, *Pr*
**EMP:** 30 **EST:** 2008
**SALES (est):** 4.53MM **Privately Held**
Web: www.packlinesolutions.com
**SIC: 3556** Dehydrating equipment, food processing

### 3559 Special Industry Machinery, Nec

**(P-9823)**
**ACME CRYOGENICS INC**
Also Called: Cryogenic Experts
531 Sandy Cir, Oxnard (93036-0971)
PHONE..............................805 981-4500
Robert Worcester Junior, *Brnch Mgr*
**EMP:** 30
**SALES (corp-wide):** 8.44B **Publicly Held**
Web: www.opwces.com
**SIC: 3559** Cryogenic machinery, industrial
HQ: Acme Cryogenics, Inc.
2801 Mitchell Ave
Allentown PA 18103
610 966-4488

**(P-9824)**
**ADVANCED INDUS CERAMICS LLC**
2449 Zanker Rd, San Jose (95131-1116)
PHONE..............................408 955-9990
Chau Nguyen, *CEO*
Chau Nguyen, *Prin*
**EMP:** 49 **EST:** 2002
**SQ FT:** 7,500
**SALES (est):** 9.18MM **Privately Held**

# 3559 - Special Industry Machinery, Nec (P-9825)

**Web:** www.aiceramics.com
**SIC: 3559** 3674 Semiconductor manufacturing machinery; Stud bases or mounts for semiconductor devices

### (P-9825)
### ALTAIR TECHNOLOGIES INC
41970 Christy St, Fremont (94538-3160)
**PHONE**..................650 508-8700
▼ **EMP:** 30
**Web:** www.altairusa.com
**SIC: 3559** 7692 Electronic component making machinery; Brazing

### (P-9826)
### AMERGENCE TECHNOLOGY INC
295 Brea Canyon Rd, Walnut (91789-3049)
**PHONE**..................909 859-8400
Shavonne Tran, *Pr*
▲ **EMP:** 29 **EST:** 2006
**SQ FT:** 40,000
**SALES (est):** 2.59MM **Privately Held**
**Web:** www.amergenceinc.com
**SIC: 3559** Recycling machinery

### (P-9827)
### AMERICAN INDUSTRIAL PARTNERS LP
1 Maritime Plz Ste 1925, San Francisco (94111-3530)
**PHONE**..................415 788-7354
**EMP:** 1428
**SIC: 3559** 7371 Foundry machinery and equipment; Custom computer programming services

### (P-9828)
### AMREP MANUFACTURING CO LLC
1555 S Cucamonga Ave, Ontario (91761-4512)
**PHONE**..................877 468-9278
Martin Bryant, *CEO*
**EMP:** 500 **EST:** 2019
**SALES (est):** 10.12MM **Privately Held**
**Web:** www.amrepproducts.com
**SIC: 3559** Semiconductor manufacturing machinery

### (P-9829)
### APERIA TECHNOLOGIES INC (PA)
3160 Corporate Pl, Hayward (94545-3916)
**PHONE**..................650 741-3231
Joshua Carter, *CEO*
Bill Hoover, *CFO*
▲ **EMP:** 99 **EST:** 2010
**SALES (est):** 25.37MM **Privately Held**
**Web:** www.aperiatech.com
**SIC: 3559** Automotive maintenance equipment

### (P-9830)
### APPLIED MATERIALS INC (PA)
Also Called: APPLIED MATERIALS
3050 Bowers Ave, Santa Clara (95054-3298)
P.O. Box 58039 (95052)
**PHONE**..................408 727-5555
Gary E Dickerson, *Pr*
Thomas J Iannotti, *
Brice Hill, *Sr VP*
Teri Little, *CLO*
Omkaram Nalamasu, *Sr VP*
▲ **EMP:** 1489 **EST:** 1967
**SALES (est):** 26.52B
**SALES (corp-wide):** 26.52B **Publicly Held**
**Web:** www.appliedmaterials.com

**SIC: 3559** 3674 Semiconductor manufacturing machinery; Semiconductors and related devices

### (P-9831)
### AQUA PRO PROPERTIES VII LP
Also Called: Village Marine Technology
2000 W 135th St, Gardena (90249-2456)
**PHONE**..................310 516-9911
▲ **EMP:** 256
**Web:** www.villagemarine.com
**SIC: 3559** Desalination equipment

### (P-9832)
### ASC PROCESS SYSTEMS INC (PA)
Also Called: ASC
28402 Livingston Ave, Valencia (91355-4172)
**PHONE**..................818 833-0088
David C Mason, *Pr*
Dave Mason, *
Gudrun Mason, *
◆ **EMP:** 240 **EST:** 1988
**SQ FT:** 41,000
**SALES (est):** 39.43MM
**SALES (corp-wide):** 39.43MM **Privately Held**
**Web:** www.aschome.com
**SIC: 3559** 3443 3567 Sewing machines and hat and zipper making machinery; Fabricated plate work (boiler shop); Industrial furnaces and ovens

### (P-9833)
### ASML US INC
Also Called: ASML US, Inc.
1 Viper Way Ste A, Vista (92081-7809)
**PHONE**..................760 443-6244
Jenna Moggio, *Prin*
**EMP:** 308
**SALES (corp-wide):** 21.99B **Privately Held**
**Web:** www.asml.com
**SIC: 3559** Semiconductor manufacturing machinery
**HQ:** Asml Us, Llc
2625 W Geronimo Pl
Chandler AZ 85224
480 696-2888

### (P-9834)
### ASML US LLC
17075 Thornmint Ct, San Diego (92127-2413)
**PHONE**..................858 385-6500
**EMP:** 476
**SALES (corp-wide):** 21.99B **Privately Held**
**Web:** www.asml.com
**SIC: 3559** Semiconductor manufacturing machinery
**HQ:** Asml Us, Llc
2625 W Geronimo Pl
Chandler AZ 85224
480 696-2888

### (P-9835)
### ATI LIQUIDATING INC
Also Called: Spp Process Technology Systems
1150 Ringwood Ct, San Jose (95131-1726)
**PHONE**..................831 438-2100
Jerauld J Cutini, *Ch Bd*
Jerauld J Cutini, *Ch Bd*
Patrick C O'connor, *Ex VP*
John Macneil Ph.d., *Ex VP*
Subrata Chatterji, *VP*
**EMP:** 491 **EST:** 2003
**SQ FT:** 213,000
**SALES (est):** 3.63MM **Privately Held**

**SIC: 3559** Semiconductor manufacturing machinery

### (P-9836)
### AVANZATO TECHNOLOGY CORP
5335 Mcconnell Ave, Los Angeles (90066-7025)
**PHONE**..................312 509-0506
Carissa Davino, *CEO*
Jeremy Green, *Dir Opers*
**EMP:** 20 **EST:** 2016
**SALES (est):** 1.45MM **Privately Held**
**SIC: 3559** 5065 Electronic component making machinery; Electronic parts

### (P-9837)
### BARKENS HARDCHROME INC
Also Called: Bhc Industries
239 E Greenleaf Blvd, Compton (90220-4913)
**PHONE**..................310 632-2000
Gary Barken, *CEO*
Carol Barken, *VP*
**EMP:** 25 **EST:** 1942
**SQ FT:** 60,000
**SALES (est):** 4.84MM **Privately Held**
**Web:** www.barkenshardchrome.com
**SIC: 3559** 5082 Metal finishing equipment for plating, etc.; Oil field equipment

### (P-9838)
### BENDPAK INC (PA)
30440 Agoura Rd, Agoura Hills (91301-2145)
**PHONE**..................805 933-9970
Jeffrey Kritzer, *Pr*
Donald R Henthorn, *
◆ **EMP:** 138 **EST:** 1965
**SALES (est):** 26.45MM
**SALES (corp-wide):** 26.45MM **Privately Held**
**Web:** www.bendpak.com
**SIC: 3559** 3537 Automotive related machinery; Industrial trucks and tractors

### (P-9839)
### BOOM INDUSTRIAL INC
2010 Wright Ave, La Verne (91750-5821)
**PHONE**..................909 495-3555
Huiwen Chen, *CEO*
**EMP:** 60 **EST:** 2016
**SALES (est):** 2.04MM **Privately Held**
**Web:** www.boomindustrial.com
**SIC: 3559** 3069 Rubber working machinery, including tires; Rubber automotive products

### (P-9840)
### BROOKS AUTOMATION US LLC
46702 Bayside Pkwy, Fremont (94538-6582)
**PHONE**..................510 661-5132
Kevin Matsumoto, *Prin*
**EMP:** 21
**SALES (est):** 4.38MM **Privately Held**
**SIC: 3559** Semiconductor manufacturing machinery

### (P-9841)
### CHA INDUSTRIES INC
Also Called: Cha Vacuum Technology
250 S Vasco Rd, Livermore (94551-9060)
**PHONE**..................510 683-8554
Stephen Kaplan, *Pr*
Stephen Dipietro, *
Sharon Krawiecki, *
▼ **EMP:** 25 **EST:** 1953
**SALES (est):** 5.8MM **Privately Held**
**Web:** www.chaindustries.com
**SIC: 3559** Semiconductor manufacturing machinery

### (P-9842)
### COSMODYNE LLC
Also Called: Nikkiso Cosmodyne
3010 Old Ranch Pkwy Ste 300, Seal Beach (90740-2750)
**PHONE**..................562 795-5990
Peter Wagner, *Pr*
◆ **EMP:** 25 **EST:** 1997
**SQ FT:** 125,000
**SALES (est):** 16.94MM **Privately Held**
**Web:** www.nikkisoceig.com
**SIC: 3559** 3443 Smelting and refining machinery and equipment; Cryogenic tanks, for liquids and gases
**HQ:** Cryogenic Industries, Inc.
27710 Jffrson Ave Ste 301
Temecula CA 92590
951 677-2081

### (P-9843)
### CP MANUFACTURING INC (HQ)
Also Called: CP Manufacturing
6795 Calle De Linea, San Diego (92154-8017)
**PHONE**..................619 477-3175
Robert M Davis, *Pr*
Ruth Davis, *
Theodora Davis Inman, *
Michael W Howard, *
John O Willis, *General Vice President*
▲ **EMP:** 104 **EST:** 1977
**SQ FT:** 60,572
**SALES (est):** 25.22MM
**SALES (corp-wide):** 81.98MM **Privately Held**
**Web:** www.cpgrp.com
**SIC: 3559** Recycling machinery
**PA:** Ims Recycling Services, Inc.
2697 Main St
619 231-2521

### (P-9844)
### CRIST GROUP INC
Also Called: Manufacturing
1324 E Beamer St, Woodland (95776-6003)
**PHONE**..................530 661-0700
Paul Crist, *Pr*
Jennifer Pebley, *
**EMP:** 35 **EST:** 2000
**SALES (est):** 6.05MM
**SALES (corp-wide):** 450.67MM **Privately Held**
**Web:** www.cristgroup.com
**SIC: 3559** 3821 2821 Semiconductor manufacturing machinery; Laboratory apparatus and furniture; Polytetrafluoroethylene resins, teflon
**PA:** Harrington Industrial Plastics Llc
14480 Yorba Ave
909 597-8641

### (P-9845)
### CRYOGENIC EXPERTS INC
Also Called: Cexi
531 Sandy Cir, Oxnard (93036-0971)
**PHONE**..................805 981-4500
**EMP:** 30
**SIC: 3559** Cryogenic machinery, industrial

### (P-9846)
### CRYOGENIC INDUSTRIES INC
1326 N Santiago St, Santa Ana (92701-2515)
**PHONE**..................714 568-0201
**EMP:** 20
**Web:** www.nikkisoceig.com

# PRODUCTS & SERVICES SECTION
## 3559 - Special Industry Machinery, Nec (P-9867)

SIC: 3559 3443 6719 Cryogenic machinery, industrial; Cryogenic tanks, for liquids and gases; Investment holding companies, except banks
HQ: Cryogenic Industries, Inc.
27710 Jffrson Ave Ste 301
Temecula CA 92590
951 677-2081

**(P-9847)**
**CRYOPORT SYSTEMS LLC (HQ)**
19000 Macarthur Blvd Ste 800, Irvine (92612-1438)
PHONE..................................949 470-2300
Jerrell W Shelton, *Pr*
Dee Kelly, *VP*
Robert S Stefanovich, *CFO*
**EMP:** 17 **EST:** 1999
**SQ FT:** 28,000
**SALES (est):** 11.35MM **Publicly Held**
Web: www.cryoport.com
SIC: 3559 Cryogenic machinery, industrial
PA: Cryoport, Inc.
112 Westwood Pl Ste 350

**(P-9848)**
**CRYST MARK INC A SWAN TECHNO C**
Also Called: Crystal Mark
613 Justin Ave, Glendale (91201-2326)
PHONE..................................818 240-7520
John Swan, *Pr*
Marko S Swan, *
E Michael Swan, *
Pauline Swan, *
**EMP:** 40 **EST:** 1968
**SQ FT:** 18,000
**SALES (est):** 1.7MM **Privately Held**
Web: www.crystalmarkinc.com
SIC: 3559 3471 Semiconductor manufacturing machinery; Sand blasting of metal parts

**(P-9849)**
**DEK INDUSTRY INC**
Also Called: Trademark Plastics, Inc.
807 Palmyrita Ave, Riverside (92507-1805)
PHONE..................................909 941-8810
Alex Wang, *CEO*
Erin Carty, *
Kris Carty, *Sec*
David Carty, *COO*
◆ **EMP:** 150 **EST:** 1988
**SQ FT:** 100,000
**SALES (est):** 25.82MM **Privately Held**
Web: www.trademarkplastics.com
SIC: 3559 3089 Plastics working machinery; Injection molding of plastics
PA: Zhejiang Gongdong Medical Technology Co., Ltd.
No.10,Beiyuan Ave.,Huangyan Dist.

**(P-9850)**
**EKSO BIONICS INC (PA)**
Also Called: Ekso Bionics
101 Glacier Pt Ste A, San Rafael (94901-5547)
PHONE..................................510 984-1761
Scott Davis, *CEO*
Eythor Bender, *
Nathan Harding, *
**EMP:** 44 **EST:** 2005
**SALES (est):** 19.63MM
**SALES (corp-wide):** 19.63MM **Privately Held**
Web: www.eksobionics.com
SIC: 3559 Cryogenic machinery, industrial

**(P-9851)**
**ELITE SERVICE EXPERTS INC (PA)**
819 Striker Ave, Sacramento (95834-1129)
PHONE..................................916 568-1400
Roy Hill, *CEO*
**EMP:** 26 **EST:** 2017
**SALES (est):** 1.31MM
**SALES (corp-wide):** 1.31MM **Privately Held**
Web: www.elite.gs
SIC: 3559 1711 0782 1731 Parking facility equipment and supplies; Plumbing contractors; Landscape contractors; Electrical work

**(P-9852)**
**ENERGY RECOVERY INC (PA)**
Also Called: ENERGY RECOVERY
1717 Doolittle Dr, San Leandro (94577-2231)
PHONE..................................510 483-7370
David W Moon, *Pr*
Pamela Tondreau, *Ch Bd*
Michael Mancini, *CFO*
William W Yeung, *CLO*
▲ **EMP:** 263 **EST:** 1992
**SQ FT:** 171,000
**SALES (est):** 128.35MM **Publicly Held**
Web: www.energyrecovery.com
SIC: 3559 Desalination equipment

**(P-9853)**
**ENVIROKINETICS INC (PA)**
101 S Milliken Ave, Ontario (91761-7836)
PHONE..................................909 621-7599
Henry Seal, *Pr*
Long Le, *VP*
**EMP:** 15 **EST:** 2000
**SQ FT:** 6,000
**SALES (est):** 7.91MM **Privately Held**
Web: www.envirokinetics.com
SIC: 3559 Petroleum refinery equipment

**(P-9854)**
**EPOCH INTERNATIONAL ENTPS INC (PA)**
2383 Bering Dr, San Jose (95131-1125)
PHONE..................................510 556-1225
Foad Ghalili, *Pr*
Ladon Ghalili, *
▲ **EMP:** 35 **EST:** 1993
**SQ FT:** 5,550
**SALES (est):** 8.66MM **Privately Held**
Web: www.epoch-int.com
SIC: 3559 Electronic component making machinery

**(P-9855)**
**EXCELLON ACQUISITION LLC (HQ)**
Also Called: Excellon Automation Co
16130 Gundry Ave, Paramount (90723-4831)
PHONE..................................310 668-7700
**EMP:** 38 **EST:** 1962
**SALES (est):** 10.67MM
**SALES (corp-wide):** 10.67MM **Privately Held**
Web: www.excellon.com
SIC: 3559 Semiconductor manufacturing machinery
PA: Turning Point Capital, Llc
138 Del Prado St

**(P-9856)**
**FANUC AMERICA CORPORATION**
Also Called: Fanuc Robotics West
25951 Commercentre Dr, Lake Forest (92630-8805)
PHONE..................................949 595-2700
Mike Hollingsworth, *Mgr*
**EMP:** 57
Web: www.fanucamerica.com
SIC: 3559 3548 3569 Metal finishing equipment for plating, etc.; Electric welding equipment; Robots, assembly line: industrial and commercial
HQ: Fanuc America Corporation
3900 W Hamlin Rd
Rochester Hills MI 48309
248 377-7000

**(P-9857)**
**FLAT PLANET INC**
618 Hampton Dr, Venice (90291-8625)
PHONE..................................888 656-6872
Michael Lee Simpson, *CEO*
Erik Mickelson, *Contrlr*
**EMP:** 20 **EST:** 2006
**SALES (est):** 200K **Privately Held**
Web: www.flatplanetltd.com
SIC: 3559 Tobacco products machinery

**(P-9858)**
**FLIGHT MICROWAVE CORPORATION**
410 S Douglas St, El Segundo (90245-4628)
PHONE..................................310 607-9819
Rolf Kich, *Pr*
Mike Callas, *
**EMP:** 26 **EST:** 2004
**SQ FT:** 8,000
**SALES (est):** 6.56MM **Publicly Held**
Web: www.flightmicrowave.com
SIC: 3559 Electronic component making machinery
HQ: Lucix Corporation
800 Avenida Acaso Ste E
Camarillo CA 93012
805 987-6645

**(P-9859)**
**GARAGE EQUIPMENT SUPPLY INC**
16000 Ventura Blvd Ste 1000, Encino (91436-2762)
PHONE..................................805 530-0027
Danette Henthorn, *CEO*
Gary Henthorn, *Pr*
▲ **EMP:** 15 **EST:** 2003
**SALES (est):** 2.04MM **Privately Held**
Web: www.dannmar.com
SIC: 3559 Automotive maintenance equipment

**(P-9860)**
**GLASTAR CORPORATION**
Also Called: Glastar
8425 Canoga Ave, Canoga Park (91304-2607)
PHONE..................................818 341-0301
Lorie Mitchell, *Pr*
**EMP:** 20 **EST:** 1978
**SQ FT:** 14,000
**SALES (est):** 2.22MM **Privately Held**
Web: www.glastar.com
SIC: 3559 3563 3231 Glass making machinery: blowing, molding, forming, etc.; Spraying and dusting equipment; Products of purchased glass

**(P-9861)**
**GOLDEN BY-PRODUCTS INC**
Also Called: Scrap Tire Company
13000 Newport Rd, Ballico (95303-9704)
P.O. Box 1 (95303-0001)
PHONE..................................209 668-4855
**EMP:** 70
Web: www.goldenscraptire.com
SIC: 3559 0173 Tire grooving machines; Almond grove

**(P-9862)**
**HANTRONIX INC**
10080 Bubb Rd, Cupertino (95014-4132)
PHONE..................................408 252-1100
Richard E Choi, *CEO*
Wayne Choi, *Dir*
Jane Choi, *CFO*
▲ **EMP:** 22 **EST:** 1975
**SQ FT:** 10,000
**SALES (est):** 2.66MM **Privately Held**
Web: www.hantronix.com
SIC: 3559 5065 3577 Electronic component making machinery; Electronic parts and equipment, nec; Computer peripheral equipment, nec

**(P-9863)**
**HESSE MECHATRONICS INC**
3002 Dow Ave Ste 308, Tustin (92780-7234)
PHONE..................................657 720-1233
Frank Rondinelli, *Pr*
▲ **EMP:** 20 **EST:** 2002
**SQ FT:** 1,500
**SALES (est):** 3.54MM **Privately Held**
Web: www.wirebonddemo.com
SIC: 3559 Semiconductor manufacturing machinery

**(P-9864)**
**HEXCO INTERNATIONAL**
Also Called: Cryogenic Industries
25720 Jefferson Ave, Murrieta (92562-6929)
PHONE..................................951 677-2081
◆ **EMP:** 117
SIC: 3559 3561 3443 Cryogenic machinery, industrial; Pumps and pumping equipment; Fabricated plate work (boiler shop)

**(P-9865)**
**IMG ALTAIR LLC**
41970 Christy St, Fremont (94538-3160)
PHONE..................................650 508-8700
Chris Ferrari, *CEO*
**EMP:** 56 **EST:** 2019
**SALES (est):** 8.43MM
**SALES (corp-wide):** 811.12MM **Publicly Held**
Web: www.altairusa.com
SIC: 3559 7692 Electronic component making machinery; Brazing
HQ: Img Companies, Llc
225 Mountain Vista Pkwy
Livermore CA 94551

**(P-9866)**
**IMTEC ACCULINE LLC**
Also Called: Intelligent Quartz Solutions
48625 Warm Springs Blvd, Fremont (94539-7782)
PHONE..................................510 770-1800
Paul V Mendes, *Managing Member*
▲ **EMP:** 24 **EST:** 1977
**SALES (est):** 4.74MM **Privately Held**
Web: www.wkfluidhandling.com
SIC: 3559 Semiconductor manufacturing machinery

**(P-9867)**
**INDUSTRIAL DYNAMICS CO LTD (PA)**
Also Called: Filtec
3100 Fujita St, Torrance (90505-4007)

## 3559 - Special Industry Machinery, Nec (P-9868)

P.O. Box 2945 (90509-2945)
PHONE.................310 325-5633
James Kearbey, *CEO*
▲ **EMP:** 125 **EST:** 1960
**SQ FT:** 155,000
**SALES (est):** 27.94MM
**SALES (corp-wide):** 27.94MM **Privately Held**
Web: www.filtec.com
**SIC: 3559** 3829 Screening equipment, electric; Measuring and controlling devices, nec

### (P-9868)
### INDUSTRIAL TOOLS INC
1800 Avenue Of The Stars, Los Angeles (90067-4216)
PHONE.................805 483-1111
Donald O Murphy, *Pr*
John E Anderson, *
Kay Nolan, *
**EMP:** 50 **EST:** 1961
**SALES (est):** 4.97MM **Privately Held**
Web: www.iti-abrasives.com
**SIC: 3559** 3545 3544 3541 Semiconductor manufacturing machinery; Machine tool accessories; Special dies, tools, jigs, and fixtures; Machine tools, metal cutting type

### (P-9869)
### INNOVATED SOLUTIONS INC
Also Called: Integrated Solutions
7201 Garden Grove Blvd Ste C, Garden Grove (92841-4220)
PHONE.................949 222-1088
Joe Whann, *Pr*
◆ **EMP:** 15 **EST:** 2002
**SQ FT:** 1,600
**SALES (est):** 2.72MM **Privately Held**
Web: www.integratedsolutionsco.com
**SIC: 3559** Ammunition and explosives, loading machinery

### (P-9870)
### INTEGRTED CRYGNIC SLUTIONS LLC
Also Called: Nikkiso Cryoquip
2835 Progress Pl, Escondido (92029-1516)
PHONE.................951 234-0899
Peter Wagner, *Managing Member*
**EMP:** 35 **EST:** 2014
**SALES (est):** 1.99MM **Privately Held**
Web: www.nikkisoceig.com
**SIC: 3559** Cryogenic machinery, industrial

### (P-9871)
### INTEVAC INC
Intevac Fabrication Center
3560 Bassett St, Santa Clara (95054-2704)
PHONE.................408 986-9888
Don Cordoni, *Mgr*
**EMP:** 16
Web: www.intevac.com
**SIC: 3559** 3674 Semiconductor manufacturing machinery; Semiconductors and related devices
**PA:** Intevac, Inc.
3560 Bassett St

### (P-9872)
### JOHN CURRIE PERFORMANCE GROUP
Also Called: Rockjock
1592 Jenks Dr, Corona (92878-5008)
PHONE.................714 367-1580
Stephen E Blaine, *Ch Bd*
**EMP:** 22 **EST:** 2019
**SALES (est):** 4MM **Privately Held**
Web: www.rockjock4x4.com

**SIC: 3559** Automotive maintenance equipment

### (P-9873)
### KVR INVESTMENT GROUP INC
Also Called: Pacific Plating
12113 Branford St, Sun Valley (91352-5710)
PHONE.................818 896-1102
Rakesh Bajaria, *Pr*
Ken Pansuria, *
Harry Thummar, *
Benny Kadhrota, *
**EMP:** 60 **EST:** 1997
**SALES (est):** 4.67MM **Privately Held**
**SIC: 3559** 3471 Metal finishing equipment for plating, etc.; Plating and polishing

### (P-9874)
### MEEDER EQUIPMENT COMPANY (PA)
Also Called: Ransome Manufacturing
3495 S Maple Ave, Fresno (93725-2494)
P.O. Box 12446 (93777-2446)
PHONE.................559 485-0979
Jeffrey D Vertz, *Pr*
Jeffrey Vertz, *
Wane Morgan, *
James Moe, *
▲ **EMP:** 45 **EST:** 1954
**SQ FT:** 13,000
**SALES (est):** 26.58MM
**SALES (corp-wide):** 26.58MM **Privately Held**
Web: www.meeder.com
**SIC: 3559** 5084 3714 8711 Refinery, chemical processing, and similar machinery; Industrial machinery and equipment; Propane conversion equipment, motor vehicle; Building construction consultant

### (P-9875)
### MEI RIGGING & CRATING LLC
Also Called: Dunkel Bros. Machinery Moving
14555 Alondra Blvd, La Mirada (90638-5602)
P.O. Box 1630 (97321-0477)
PHONE.................714 712-5888
Dan Cappello, *Prin*
Sondra Ludwick, *
Seth Christensen, *
Patrick Moore, *
Terry Shain, *
**EMP:** 60 **EST:** 2018
**SALES (est):** 5.42MM **Privately Held**
Web: www.dunkelbros.com
**SIC: 3559** Special industry machinery, nec

### (P-9876)
### MERITEK ELECTRONICS CORP (PA)
Also Called: Ralec USA Electronic Corp
5160 Rivergrade Rd, Baldwin Park (91706-1406)
PHONE.................626 373-1728
Pa-shih Oliver Su, *CEO*
◆ **EMP:** 75 **EST:** 1993
**SQ FT:** 60,000
**SALES (est):** 20.99MM **Privately Held**
Web: www.meritekusa.com
**SIC: 3559** 5065 Electronic component making machinery; Electronic parts

### (P-9877)
### MMR TECHNOLOGIES INC
72 Bonaventura Dr, San Jose (95134-2123)
PHONE.................650 962-9620
**EMP:** 19
Web: www.lboerestaurant.com

**SIC: 3559** Cryogenic machinery, industrial

### (P-9878)
### MOREHOUSE-COWLES LLC
Also Called: Epworth Morehouse Cowles
13930 Magnolia Ave, Chino (91710-7029)
PHONE.................909 627-7222
**EMP:** 25 **EST:** 2004
**SALES (est):** 5.48MM
**SALES (corp-wide):** 6.97B **Publicly Held**
Web: www.morehousecowles.com
**SIC: 3559** Chemical machinery and equipment
**HQ:** Nusil Technology Llc
1050 Cindy Ln
Carpinteria CA 93013
805 684-8780

### (P-9879)
### MORGAN POLYMER SEALS LLC
3303 2475a Paseo De Las Americas, San Diego (92154)
PHONE.................619 498-9221
Kevin A Morgan, *CEO*
Todd Tesky, *VP Sls*
**EMP:** 400 **EST:** 1997
**SALES (est):** 3.75MM **Privately Held**
Web: www.morganpolymerseals.com
**SIC: 3559** 5211 3663 3365 Automotive related machinery; Energy conservation products; Space satellite communications equipment; Aerospace castings, aluminum

### (P-9880)
### MT SYSTEMS INC
Also Called: Micro Tech Systems
580 Cottonwood Dr, Milpitas (95035-7403)
PHONE.................510 651-5277
Thomas Mike Vukosav, *Pr*
▼ **EMP:** 17 **EST:** 2000
**SALES (est):** 4.69MM **Privately Held**
Web: www.microtechprocess.com
**SIC: 3559** Semiconductor manufacturing machinery

### (P-9881)
### MULTIBEAM CORPORATION
3951 Burton Dr, Santa Clara (95054-1583)
PHONE.................408 980-1800
Doctor David K Lam, *Ch Bd*
Lynn Barringer, *
Ted Prescop, *
Ben Quinones, *Sec*
Jasin D.o.s., *Sr VP*
**EMP:** 35 **EST:** 2011
**SALES (est):** 8.2MM **Privately Held**
Web: www.multibeamcorp.com
**SIC: 3559** Semiconductor manufacturing machinery

### (P-9882)
### NEWPORT ELECTRONICS INC
2229 S Yale St, Santa Ana (92704-4401)
PHONE.................714 540-4914
▲ **EMP:** 90
**SIC: 3559** 3829 3822 3825 Electronic component making machinery; Temperature sensors, except industrial process and aircraft; Temperature controls, automatic; Measuring instruments and meters, electric

### (P-9883)
### NORCHEM CORPORATION (PA)
5649 Alhambra Ave, Los Angeles (90032-3107)
PHONE.................323 221-0221
Gevork Minissian, *CEO*
▲ **EMP:** 50 **EST:** 1980
**SQ FT:** 50,000

**SALES (est):** 10.63MM
**SALES (corp-wide):** 10.63MM **Privately Held**
Web: www.norchemcorp.com
**SIC: 3559** 2842 2841 Chemical machinery and equipment; Laundry cleaning preparations; Soap and other detergents

### (P-9884)
### NOVELLUS SYSTEMS INC
4000 N 1st St, San Jose (95134-1568)
PHONE.................408 943-9700
**EMP:** 2855
Web: www.novellus.com
**SIC: 3559** Semiconductor manufacturing machinery

### (P-9885)
### NURO INC
1300 Terra Bella Ave Ste 200, Mountain View (94043-1850)
PHONE.................650 476-2687
Jiajun Zhu, *CEO*
David Ferguson, *
**EMP:** 671 **EST:** 2016
**SALES (est):** 47.32MM **Privately Held**
Web: www.nuro.ai
**SIC: 3559** Robots, molding and forming plastics

### (P-9886)
### P & L SPECIALTIES
1650 Almar Pkwy, Santa Rosa (95403-8253)
PHONE.................707 573-3141
Edwin Barr, *Pr*
Lisa Hyde, *VP*
◆ **EMP:** 15 **EST:** 1984
**SQ FT:** 15,000
**SALES (est):** 4.1MM **Privately Held**
Web: www.pnlspecialties.com
**SIC: 3559** 3556 Recycling machinery; Beverage machinery

### (P-9887)
### PACIFIC COAST OPTICS LLC
10604 Industrial Ave # 100, Roseville (95678-6227)
PHONE.................916 789-0111
**EMP:** 15 **EST:** 2016
**SALES (est):** 1.01MM **Privately Held**
Web: www.pcoptics.com
**SIC: 3559** Optical lens machinery

### (P-9888)
### PALOMAR TECHNOLOGIES INC (PA)
6305 El Camino Real, Carlsbad (92009-1606)
PHONE.................760 931-3600
Bruce Hueners, *CEO*
Carl Hempel, *CFO*
**EMP:** 50 **EST:** 1975
**SQ FT:** 40,000
**SALES (est):** 24.68MM **Privately Held**
Web: www.palomartechnologies.com
**SIC: 3559** Semiconductor manufacturing machinery

### (P-9889)
### PEABODY ENGINEERING & SUP INC
Also Called: Peabody Engineering
13435 Estelle St, Corona (92879-1877)
PHONE.................951 734-7711
Mark Peabody, *CEO*
Larry Peabody, *
◆ **EMP:** 25 **EST:** 1952
**SQ FT:** 32,400

## PRODUCTS & SERVICES SECTION
### 3559 - Special Industry Machinery, Nec (P-9911)

SALES (est): 5.71MM **Privately Held**
Web: www.4peabody.com
SIC: **3559** 5084 Chemical machinery and equipment; Industrial machinery and equipment

**(P-9890)**
**PERCEPTIMED INC**
365 San Antonio Rd, Mountain View (94040-1213)
P.O. Box 731338 (95173)
PHONE..............................650 941-7000
Frank Starn, CEO
Alan Jacobs, *
Hamutal Anavi Russo, *
Frank Maione, Chief Business Officer*
Terry Cater, Marketing*
**EMP:** 27 **EST:** 2011
SALES (est): 4.63MM **Privately Held**
Web: www.perceptimed.com
SIC: **3559** Pharmaceutical machinery

**(P-9891)**
**PHILLIPS 66 CO CARBON GROUP**
2555 Willow Rd, Arroyo Grande (93420-5731)
PHONE..............................805 489-4050
**EMP:** 26 **EST:** 2004
SALES (est): 4.08MM **Privately Held**
SIC: **3559** Petroleum refinery equipment

**(P-9892)**
**PROLINE CONCRETE TOOLS INC**
4645 North Ave Ste 102, Oceanside (92056-3593)
PHONE..............................760 758-7240
Jeff Irwin, CEO
Kellen Irwin, *
Tyler Irwin, *
▼ **EMP:** 27 **EST:** 1990
SALES (est): 5.2MM **Privately Held**
Web: www.prolinestamps.com
SIC: **3559** 1771 Concrete products machinery; Patio construction, concrete

**(P-9893)**
**PURFRESH INC**
Also Called: Pfi Acquisition
1350 Willow Rd Ste 102, Menlo Park (94025-1544)
PHONE..............................510 580-0700
**EMP:** 25 **EST:** 1996
SALES (est): 2.62MM **Privately Held**
Web: www.purfreshclean.com
SIC: **3559** 4731 Ozone machines; Freight forwarding

**(P-9894)**
**PUROTECS INC**
216 Lindbergh Ave, Livermore (94551-9512)
PHONE..............................925 215-0380
Ken Stevens, Prin
**EMP:** 17 **EST:** 2012
SALES (est): 3.15MM **Privately Held**
Web: www.purotecs.com
SIC: **3559** Chemical machinery and equipment

**(P-9895)**
**QUALITY MACHINING & DESIGN INC**
2857 Aiello Dr, San Jose (95111-2155)
PHONE..............................408 224-7976
Ryszard Ott, Pr
**EMP:** 30 **EST:** 1998
SQ FT: 23,000

SALES (est): 4.39MM **Privately Held**
Web: www.qualitymd.com
SIC: **3559** 3365 Semiconductor manufacturing machinery; Aerospace castings, aluminum

**(P-9896)**
**RUCKER & KOLLS INC (PA)**
1064 Yosemite Dr, Milpitas (95035-5410)
PHONE..............................408 934-9875
Arlen Chou, Pr
Hsun Chou, Dir
**EMP:** 17 **EST:** 1976
SQ FT: 6,000
SALES (est): 4.63MM **Privately Held**
Web: www.ruckerkolls.com
SIC: **3559** 3825 Semiconductor manufacturing machinery; Instruments to measure electricity

**(P-9897)**
**RXSAFE LLC**
Also Called: Rxsafe
2453 Cades Way Bldg A, Vista (92081-7831)
PHONE..............................760 593-7161
William Holmes, Managing Member
Shawn Orr, *
**EMP:** 68 **EST:** 2008
SALES (est): 23.02MM **Privately Held**
Web: www.rxsafe.com
SIC: **3559** Pharmaceutical machinery

**(P-9898)**
**SCREEN SPE USA LLC (DH)**
Also Called: Dns Electronics
3151 Jay St Ste 210, Santa Clara (95054-3335)
PHONE..............................408 523-9140
Laszlo Mikulas, Pr
Scott Prengle, OF INTERNAL STRATEGIC Operations*
▲ **EMP:** 30 **EST:** 1984
SQ FT: 28,400
SALES (est): 24.31MM **Privately Held**
Web: www.screen-spe.com
SIC: **3559** Semiconductor manufacturing machinery
HQ: Screen North America Holdings, Inc.
150 Innovation Dr Ste A
Elk Grove Village IL 60007
847 870-7400

**(P-9899)**
**SILITRONICS SOLUTIONS INC**
2388 Walsh Ave, Santa Clara (95051-1301)
PHONE..............................408 605-1148
Dhiraj Bora, Pr
**EMP:** 30 **EST:** 2017
SALES (est): 2.17MM **Privately Held**
SIC: **3559** Semiconductor manufacturing machinery

**(P-9900)**
**SPTS TECHNOLOGIES INC (HQ)**
Also Called: Spts
2381 Bering Dr, San Jose (95131-1125)
PHONE..............................408 571-1400
**EMP:** 108 **EST:** 1995
SALES (est): 42.56MM
SALES (corp-wide): 9.81B **Publicly Held**
Web: www.kla.com
SIC: **3559** Semiconductor manufacturing machinery
PA: Kla Corporation
1 Technology Dr
408 875-3000

**(P-9901)**
**STARCO ENTERPRISES INC (PA)**
Also Called: Four Star Chemical
3137 E 26th St, Los Angeles (90058-8006)
PHONE..............................323 266-7111
George D Stroesenreuther, CEO
Ross Sklar, *
▲ **EMP:** 74 **EST:** 1973
SQ FT: 25,000
SALES (est): 16.32MM
SALES (corp-wide): 16.32MM **Privately Held**
Web: www.thestarcogroup.com
SIC: **3559** 5169 5191 Degreasing machines, automotive and industrial; Specialty cleaning and sanitation preparations; Farm supplies

**(P-9902)**
**SUSS MICROTEC INC (HQ)**
2520 Palisades Dr, Corona (92882-0632)
PHONE..............................408 940-0300
Frank Averdung, Pr
Franz Richter, *
Peter Szafir, *
Stewart Mc C0naughy, *
Stefan Schneidewind, *
**EMP:** 130 **EST:** 1980
SALES (est): 23.07MM
SALES (corp-wide): 330.72MM **Privately Held**
Web: www.suss.com
SIC: **3559** 3825 3674 Semiconductor manufacturing machinery; Instruments to measure electricity; Semiconductors and related devices
PA: Suss Microtec Se
SchleiBheimer Str. 90
89320070

**(P-9903)**
**TIMEC COMPANIES INC**
Also Called: Timec Southern California
6861 Charity Ave, Bakersfield (93308-5918)
PHONE..............................661 322-8177
Will Nord, Site Superintendent
**EMP:** 50
Web: www.timec.com
SIC: **3559** Refinery, chemical processing, and similar machinery
HQ: Timec Companies Inc
473 E Channel Rd
Benicia CA 94510
707 642-2222

**(P-9904)**
**TITANS OF CNC INC**
4041 Alvis Ct, Rocklin (95677-4011)
PHONE..............................916 203-2430
Titan Gilroy, Prin
**EMP:** 43 **EST:** 2016
SALES (est): 1.51MM **Privately Held**
Web: www.titansofcnc.com
SIC: **3559** Special industry machinery, nec

**(P-9905)**
**TRI-C MANUFACTURING INC**
517 Houston St, West Sacramento (95691-2213)
P.O. Box 83478 (97283-0478)
PHONE..............................916 371-1700
Lilburn Clyde Lamar, Pr
**EMP:** 20 **EST:** 1969
SALES (est): 2.37MM
SALES (corp-wide): 5.64MM **Privately Held**
Web: www.tri-cshredders.com

SIC: **3559** Rubber working machinery, including tires
PA: Tri-C Machine Corporation
520 Harbor Blvd
916 371-8090

**(P-9906)**
**ULTRA TEC MANUFACTURING INC**
1025 E Chestnut Ave, Santa Ana (92701-6425)
PHONE..............................714 542-0608
Joseph I Rubin, Pr
Robert Rubin, VP
Maxine Rubin, Sec
**EMP:** 15 **EST:** 1966
SQ FT: 7,000
SALES (est): 2.22MM **Privately Held**
Web: www.ultratecusa.com
SIC: **3559** 3541 Synthetic filament extruding machines; Grinding, polishing, buffing, lapping, and honing machines

**(P-9907)**
**ULTRATECH INC**
Also Called: Ultratech
3050 Zanker Rd, San Jose (95134-2126)
PHONE..............................408 321-8835
**EMP:** 312
Web: www.ultratechinc.com
SIC: **3559** Semiconductor manufacturing machinery

**(P-9908)**
**UNITED SURFACE SOLUTIONS LLC**
11901 Burke St, Santa Fe Springs (90670-2507)
PHONE..............................562 693-0202
Ken Bagdasarian, CEO
**EMP:** 27 **EST:** 2010
SQ FT: 20,000
SALES (est): 4.71MM **Privately Held**
Web: www.deburring.com
SIC: **3559** 3541 Metal finishing equipment for plating, etc.; Deburring machines

**(P-9909)**
**VECTRON INC**
345 6th Ave, San Diego (92101-7005)
PHONE..............................858 621-2400
Joseph L Vilella, Pr
**EMP:** 18 **EST:** 1992
SQ FT: 20,000
SALES (est): 651.76K **Privately Held**
SIC: **3559** Refinery, chemical processing, and similar machinery

**(P-9910)**
**VIZUALOGIC LLC**
1493 E Bentley Dr, Corona (92879-5102)
PHONE..............................407 509-3421
Janis Patterson, *
**EMP:** 200 **EST:** 2015
SQ FT: 3,000
SALES (est): 6.38MM **Privately Held**
Web: www.vizualogicdirect.com
SIC: **3559** Automotive related machinery

**(P-9911)**
**WEST COAST CRYOGENICS INC**
Also Called: West Coast Cryogenics Services
503 W Larch Rd Ste K, Tracy (95304-1670)
PHONE..............................800 657-0545
Danny Silveira, Pr
Krystal Silveria, VP
**EMP:** 21 **EST:** 2013
SALES (est): 3.62MM **Privately Held**
Web: www.westcoastcryo.com

# 3559 - Special Industry Machinery, Nec (P-9912)

**SIC: 3559** Cryogenic machinery, industrial

### (P-9912)
### WESTCOAST PRECISION INC
2091 Fortune Dr, San Jose (95131-1824)
PHONE..................408 943-9998
Sang A Nhin, *CEO*
Sang A Nhin, *Pr*
Helen Nhin, *
**EMP:** 55 **EST:** 2004
**SALES (est):** 3.85MM **Privately Held**
**Web:** www.westcoastprecision.com
**SIC: 3559** Semiconductor manufacturing machinery

### (P-9913)
### ZAMBONI COMPANY USA INC
Also Called: Zamboni
15714 Colorado Ave, Paramount (90723-4211)
PHONE..................562 633-0751
▲ **EMP:** 35 **EST:** 1949
**SALES (est):** 10.67MM **Privately Held**
**Web:** www.zamboni.com
**SIC: 3559** Ice resurfacing machinery

## 3561 Pumps And Pumping Equipment

### (P-9914)
### AQUASTAR POOL PRODUCTS INC
Also Called: Aquastar Pool Productions
2340 Palma Dr Ste 104, Ventura (93003-8091)
PHONE..................877 768-2717
Olaf Mjelde, *CEO*
▲ **EMP:** 46 **EST:** 2003
**SALES (est):** 6.06MM **Privately Held**
**Web:** www.aquastarpoolproducts.com
**SIC: 3561** Pumps, domestic: water or sump

### (P-9915)
### AQUATEC INTERNATIONAL INC
Also Called: Aquatec Water Systems
17422 Pullman St, Irvine (92614-5527)
PHONE..................949 225-2200
Bryan Hausner, *CEO*
Sami Levi, *
Isak Levi, *
Ivar Schoenmeyr, *
▲ **EMP:** 95 **EST:** 1986
**SQ FT:** 30,000
**SALES (est):** 22.79MM **Privately Held**
**Web:** www.aquatec.com
**SIC: 3561** Pumps and pumping equipment

### (P-9916)
### BORIN MANUFACTURING INC
5741 Buckingham Pkwy Ste B, Culver City (90230-6520)
PHONE..................310 822-1000
Frank William Borin, *CEO*
Gregg Steele, *
**EMP:** 40 **EST:** 1976
**SALES (est):** 9.95MM **Privately Held**
**Web:** www.borin.com
**SIC: 3561** 3443 3317 3494 Pumps and pumping equipment; Fabricated plate work (boiler shop); Steel pipe and tubes; Valves and pipe fittings, nec

### (P-9917)
### CASCADE PUMP COMPANY
10107 Norwalk Blvd, Santa Fe Springs (90670-3354)
P.O. Box 2767 (90670-0767)
PHONE..................562 946-1414
T W Summerfield, *CEO*
John Summerfield, *
**EMP:** 60 **EST:** 1948
**SQ FT:** 120,000
**SALES (est):** 9.16MM **Privately Held**
**Web:** www.cascadepump.com
**SIC: 3561** 3594 Pumps, domestic: water or sump; Fluid power pumps and motors

### (P-9918)
### CRYOSTAR USA LLC
13117 Meyer Rd, Whittier (90605-3555)
PHONE..................562 903-1290
▲ **EMP:** 63 **EST:** 2014
**SALES (est):** 11.78MM **Privately Held**
**Web:** www.cryostar.com
**SIC: 3561** Pump jacks and other pumping equipment
**HQ:** Cryostar Sas
2 Rue De L Industrie
Hesingue 68220
389702727

### (P-9919)
### ELLIOTT COMPANY
51 Main Ave, Sacramento (95838-2014)
PHONE..................916 920-5451
Evertt Hylton, *Brnch Mgr*
**EMP:** 27
**Web:** www.elliott-turbo.com
**SIC: 3561** Pumps and pumping equipment
**HQ:** Elliott Company
901 N 4th St
Jeannette PA 15644
724 527-2811

### (P-9920)
### EMR FINAL CTRL US HOLDG CORP
Also Called: Pentair
7328 Trade St, San Diego (92121)
PHONE..................858 740-2471
Bill Brancaniello, *Pr*
**EMP:** 15
**SALES (corp-wide):** 17.49B **Publicly Held**
**SIC: 3561** 3589 3569 3469 Pumps and pumping equipment; Swimming pool filter and water conditioning systems; Filters; Electronic enclosures, stamped or pressed metal
**HQ:** Emr Final Control Us Holding Corporation
5500 Wayzata Blvd Ste 800
Minneapolis MN 55416
763 545-1730

### (P-9921)
### FLOWSERVE CORPORATION
Flowserve
2300 E Vernon Ave Stop 76, Vernon (90058-1609)
PHONE..................323 584-1890
Rick Soldo, *Brnch Mgr*
**EMP:** 342
**SALES (corp-wide):** 4.32B **Publicly Held**
**Web:** www.flowserve.com
**SIC: 3561** Pumps and pumping equipment
**PA:** Flowserve Corporation
5215 N Ocnnor Blvd Ste 70
972 443-6500

### (P-9922)
### FLOWSERVE CORPORATION
Flowserve
1909 E Cashdan St, Compton (90220-6422)
PHONE..................310 667-4220
Dan Lattimore, *Mgr*
**EMP:** 79
**SALES (corp-wide):** 4.32B **Publicly Held**
**Web:** www.flowserve.com
**SIC: 3561** Industrial pumps and parts
**PA:** Flowserve Corporation
5215 N Ocnnor Blvd Ste 70
972 443-6500

### (P-9923)
### FLOWSERVE CORPORATION
Flowserve
6077 Egret Ct, Benicia (94510-1205)
PHONE..................707 748-4900
Keith Slothers, *Mgr*
**EMP:** 17
**SALES (corp-wide):** 4.32B **Publicly Held**
**Web:** www.flowserve.com
**SIC: 3561** Industrial pumps and parts
**PA:** Flowserve Corporation
5215 N Ocnnor Blvd Ste 70
972 443-6500

### (P-9924)
### FLOWSERVE CORPORATION
Flowserve
27455 Tierra Alta Way Ste C, Temecula (92590-3498)
PHONE..................951 296-2464
Paul Cortenbach, *Brnch Mgr*
**EMP:** 87
**SALES (corp-wide):** 4.32B **Publicly Held**
**Web:** www.flowserve.com
**SIC: 3561** 3053 Industrial pumps and parts; Gaskets; packing and sealing devices
**PA:** Flowserve Corporation
5215 N Ocnnor Blvd Ste 70
972 443-6500

### (P-9925)
### GRISWOLD PUMP COMPANY
22069 Van Buren St, Grand Terrace (92313-5607)
PHONE..................909 422-1700
Dale Pavlovich, *Pr*
Edward Vaughn, *VP Engg*
Dave Spitzer, *VP*
Michael Boul, *VP*
◆ **EMP:** 25 **EST:** 1996
**SQ FT:** 25,000
**SALES (est):** 13.48MM
**SALES (corp-wide):** 8.44B **Publicly Held**
**Web:** www.griswoldpump.com
**SIC: 3561** 5084 Industrial pumps and parts; Industrial machinery and equipment
**HQ:** Psg California Llc
22069 Van Buren St
Grand Terrace CA 92313
909 422-1700

### (P-9926)
### GROVER SMITH MFG CORP
Also Called: Grover Manufacturing
9717 Factorial Way, South El Monte (91733-1724)
P.O. Box 986 (90640-0986)
PHONE..................323 724-3444
Marilyn Schirmer, *Corporate President*
Marilyn Schirmer, *Pr*
Lino Paras, *
W Michael Meeker, *
**EMP:** 30 **EST:** 1925
**SALES (est):** 5.88MM **Privately Held**
**Web:** www.grovermfg.com
**SIC: 3561** 3569 Pumps and pumping equipment; Lubrication equipment, industrial

### (P-9927)
### GRUNDFOS PUMPS MANUFACTURING CORPORATION (DH)
5900 E Shields Ave, Fresno (93727)
PHONE..................559 292-8000
◆ **EMP:** 250 **EST:** 1973
**SALES (est):** 41.23MM
**SALES (corp-wide):** 5.02B **Privately Held**
**Web:** www.grundfos.com
**SIC: 3561** Pumps and pumping equipment
**HQ:** Grundfos Holding Ag
C/O Bratschi Ag, Zweigniederlassung
Zug
Zug ZG 6300

### (P-9928)
### HASKEL INTERNATIONAL LLC (HQ)
100 E Graham Pl, Burbank (91502-2027)
PHONE..................818 843-4000
Chris Krieps, *CEO*
Dave Alan Barta, *
Elmer Lee Doty, *
Maria Blase, *
▲ **EMP:** 125 **EST:** 1986
**SQ FT:** 78,000
**SALES (est):** 51MM
**SALES (corp-wide):** 6.88B **Publicly Held**
**Web:** www.haskel.com
**SIC: 3561** 3594 5084 5085 Pumps and pumping equipment; Fluid power pumps; Hydraulic systems equipment and supplies; Hose, belting, and packing
**PA:** Ingersoll Rand Inc.
525 Harbor Pl Dr Ste 600
704 896-4000

### (P-9929)
### HP WATER SYSTEMS INC
9338 W Whites Bridge Ave, Fresno (93706-9515)
PHONE..................559 268-4751
Hollis Priest Junior, *Pr*
Joyce Priest, *
**EMP:** 30 **EST:** 1995
**SQ FT:** 3,000
**SALES (est):** 4.56MM **Privately Held**
**Web:** www.hepelectricinc.com
**SIC: 3561** 1781 Pumps and pumping equipment; Water well drilling

### (P-9930)
### LOS ANGLES PUMP VALVE PDTS INC
Also Called: Los Angeles Brass Products
2528 E 57th St, Huntington Park (90255-2521)
P.O. Box 2007 (90255-1307)
PHONE..................323 277-7788
Santos J Pinto, *Pr*
Phil Pinto, *VP*
**EMP:** 20 **EST:** 1975
**SQ FT:** 11,000
**SALES (est):** 2.56MM **Privately Held**
**Web:** www.lapumpandvalve.com
**SIC: 3561** Pump jacks and other pumping equipment

### (P-9931)
### MJW INC
Also Called: American Lab and Systems
1328 W Slauson Ave, Los Angeles (90044-2824)
PHONE..................323 778-8900
Mike Curry, *Pr*
Linda Curry, *
**EMP:** 65 **EST:** 1978
**SQ FT:** 30,000
**SALES (est):** 4.77MM **Privately Held**
**Web:** modern-jewelry-and-watches.business.site
**SIC: 3561** Industrial pumps and parts

## PRODUCTS & SERVICES SECTION
## 3562 - Ball And Roller Bearings (P-9952)

**(P-9932)**
**MOLEAER INC**
3232 W El Segundo Blvd, Hawthorne (90250-4823)
PHONE.............................424 558-3567
Nicholas Dyner, *CEO*
Warren Russell, *
Bruce Scholten, *
Bryan Brister, *
Hoshang Subawalla, *Chief Business Officer*
**EMP:** 85 **EST:** 2016
**SALES (est):** 13.51MM **Privately Held**
**Web:** www.moleaer.com
**SIC: 3561** Pumps and pumping equipment

**(P-9933)**
**PENGUIN PUMPS INCORPORATED**
Also Called: Filter Pump Industries
7932 Ajay Dr, Sun Valley (91352-5315)
PHONE.............................818 504-2391
Jerome S Hollander, *Pr*
▲ **EMP:** 50 **EST:** 1972
**SQ FT:** 20,000
**SALES (est):** 7.61MM
**SALES (corp-wide):** 24.11MM **Privately Held**
**Web:** www.filterpump.com
**SIC: 3561** 3569 Pumps and pumping equipment; Filters, general line: industrial
**PA:** Finish Thompson, Inc.
921 Greengarden Rd
814 455-4478

**(P-9934)**
**POLARIS E-COMMERCE INC**
1941 E Occidental St, Santa Ana (92705-5115)
PHONE.............................714 907-0582
Insoo Hwang, *CEO*
▲ **EMP:** 25 **EST:** 2010
**SALES (est):** 2.71MM **Privately Held**
**Web:** www.officesmartlabels.com
**SIC: 3561** Industrial pumps and parts

**(P-9935)**
**PROVAC SALES INC**
3131 Soquel Dr Ste A, Soquel (95073-2098)
PHONE.............................831 462-8900
Paul Flood, *CEO*
**EMP:** 23 **EST:** 1990
**SALES (est):** 3.11MM **Privately Held**
**Web:** www.provac.com
**SIC: 3561** 5084 Pumps and pumping equipment; Pumps and pumping equipment, nec

**(P-9936)**
**PSG CALIFORNIA LLC (HQ)**
Also Called: Wilden Pump
22069 Van Buren St, Grand Terrace (92313-5607)
PHONE.............................909 422-1700
Denny L Buskirk, *Managing Member*
Daniel Anderson, *
◆ **EMP:** 295 **EST:** 1998
**SQ FT:** 153,000
**SALES (est):** 49.05MM
**SALES (corp-wide):** 8.44B **Publicly Held**
**Web:** www.wildenpump.com
**SIC: 3561** Industrial pumps and parts
**PA:** Dover Corporation
3005 Highland Pkwy
630 541-1540

**(P-9937)**
**REED LLC**
Also Called: Reed Manufacturing
13822 Oaks Ave, Chino (91710-7008)
PHONE.............................909 287-2100
James W Shea, *Managing Member*
Cliff Kao, *VP*
◆ **EMP:** 40 **EST:** 1957
**SQ FT:** 69,000
**SALES (est):** 9.93MM **Privately Held**
**Web:** www.reedpumps.com
**SIC: 3561** 3531 Pumps and pumping equipment; Bituminous, cement and concrete related products and equip.

**(P-9938)**
**ROBOTIC SOFTWARE SOLUTIONS INC**
Also Called: Robot27
550 Wald, Irvine (92618-4637)
PHONE.............................855 762-6827
Douglas Robert Spinn, *CEO*
**EMP:** 28 **EST:** 2017
**SALES (est):** 1.2MM **Privately Held**
**SIC: 3561** Pumps and pumping equipment

**(P-9939)**
**SCHROFF INC**
Also Called: Pep West, Inc.
7328 Trade St, San Diego (92121-3435)
PHONE.............................800 525-4682
Beth Wozniak, *CEO*
Bill Biancaniello, *Pr*
Judy Carle, *VP Fin*
Michael Meyer, *Treas*
▲ **EMP:** 800 **EST:** 2005
**SALES (est):** 15.89MM **Privately Held**
**SIC: 3561** Pumps and pumping equipment
**HQ:** Schroff, Inc.
170 Commerce Dr
Warwick RI 02886
763 204-7700

**(P-9940)**
**SHURFLO LLC**
Also Called: Pentair Water Treatment
3545 Harbor Gtwy S Ste 103, Costa Mesa (92626-1457)
PHONE.............................714 371-1550
▲ **EMP:** 430
**Web:** www.shurflo.com
**SIC: 3561** Pumps and pumping equipment

**(P-9941)**
**SULZER PUMP SERVICES (US) INC**
Also Called: Sulzer Bingham Pumps
9856 Jordan Cir, Santa Fe Springs (90670-3303)
P.O. Box 3904 (90670-1904)
PHONE.............................562 903-1000
Tim Voyles, *Mgr*
**EMP:** 20
**SQ FT:** 18,968
**SIC: 3561** Pumps and pumping equipment
**HQ:** Sulzer Pump Services (Us) Inc.
900 Thrdneedle St Ste 700
Houston TX 77079
281 417-7110

**(P-9942)**
**SULZER PUMP SOLUTIONS US INC**
1650 Bell Ave Ste 140, Sacramento (95838-2869)
PHONE.............................916 925-8508
Dale Gretzinger, *Mgr*
**EMP:** 25
**SALES (corp-wide):** 8.81MM **Privately Held**
**SIC: 3561** Pumps and pumping equipment
**PA:** Sulzer Pump Solutions (Us) Inc.
108 Leigus Rd
203 238-2700

**(P-9943)**
**TOTAL PROCESS SOLUTIONS LLC**
1400 Norris Rd, Bakersfield (93308-2232)
PHONE.............................661 829-7910
Eddie L Rice, *Managing Member*
Stan Ellis, *Managing Member**
Travis Ellis, *Managing Member**
Joey L Taylor, *Managing Member**
**EMP:** 30 **EST:** 2012
**SALES (est):** 4.45MM **Privately Held**
**SIC: 3561** 3563 Cylinders, pump; Air and gas compressors including vacuum pumps

**(P-9944)**
**TRANE TECHNOLOGIES COMPANY LLC**
Also Called: Ingersoll-Rand
2845 Pellissier Pl, City Of Industry (90601-1512)
PHONE.............................323 583-4771
**EMP:** 17
**Web:** www.tranetechnologies.com
**SIC: 3561** Pumps and pumping equipment
**HQ:** Trane Technologies Company Llc
800-E Beaty St
Davidson NC 28036
704 655-4000

**(P-9945)**
**TRILLIUM PUMPS USA INC (HQ)**
Also Called: Trillium Pump USA
2495 S Golden State Blvd, Fresno (93706-4533)
P.O. Box 164 (93707-0164)
PHONE.............................559 442-4000
John Kavalam, *Pr*
◆ **EMP:** 130 **EST:** 1934
**SQ FT:** 128,000
**SALES (est):** 49.37MM
**SALES (corp-wide):** 144.07MM **Privately Held**
**Web:** www.trilliumflow.com
**SIC: 3561** Industrial pumps and parts
**PA:** First Reserve Corporation, L.L.C.
290 Harbor Dr
203 661-6601

**(P-9946)**
**XYLEM WATER SOLUTIONS USA INC**
17942 Cowan, Irvine (92614-6026)
PHONE.............................949 474-1679
**EMP:** 53
**Web:** www.xylem.com
**SIC: 3561** Pumps and pumping equipment
**HQ:** Xylem Water Solutions U.S.A., Inc.
4828 Parkway Plz Blvd 200
Charlotte NC 28217

**(P-9947)**
**XYLEM WATER SYSTEMS (CALIFORNIA) INC**
830 Bay Blvd Ste 101, Chula Vista (91911-1683)
PHONE.............................619 575-7466
▲ **EMP:** 26
**SIC: 3561** 3443 Pumps and pumping equipment; Fabricated plate work (boiler shop)

## 3562 Ball And Roller Bearings

**(P-9948)**
**AMERICAN METAL BEARING COMPANY**
7191 Acacia Ave, Garden Grove (92841-5297)
PHONE.............................714 892-5527
Alfred A Anawati, *CEO*
Michael Litton, *VP*
Jim Demaio, *Sec*
▲ **EMP:** 21 **EST:** 1921
**SQ FT:** 40,000
**SALES (est):** 9.49MM
**SALES (corp-wide):** 44.47MM **Privately Held**
**Web:** www.ambco.net
**SIC: 3562** 7699 3568 Ball bearings and parts; Rebabbitting; Power transmission equipment, nec
**PA:** Marisco, Ltd.
91-607 Malakole St
808 682-1333

**(P-9949)**
**CLEAN WAVE MANAGEMENT INC**
Also Called: Impact Bearing
1291 Puerta Del Sol, San Clemente (92673-6310)
PHONE.............................949 370-0740
Richard D Kay Junior, *CEO*
Michael Bartlett, *
◆ **EMP:** 30 **EST:** 1995
**SQ FT:** 20,000
**SALES (est):** 4.62MM **Privately Held**
**Web:** www.impactbearing.com
**SIC: 3562** Ball bearings and parts

**(P-9950)**
**INDUSTRIAL TCTNICS BRINGS CORP (DH)**
18301 S Santa Fe Ave, E Rncho Dmngz (90221-5519)
PHONE.............................310 537-3750
Michael J Hartnett, *CEO*
**EMP:** 111 **EST:** 1990
**SQ FT:** 70,000
**SALES (est):** 42.07MM
**SALES (corp-wide):** 1.56B **Publicly Held**
**Web:** www.rbcbearings.com
**SIC: 3562** 5085 Roller bearings and parts; Bearings
**HQ:** Roller Bearing Company Of America, Inc.
102 Willenbrock Rd
Oxford CT 06478
203 267-7001

**(P-9951)**
**INTEGRATED ENERGY TECHNOLOGIES INC**
Also Called: Doncasters Gce Integrated
1478 Santa Sierra Dr, Chula Vista (91913-2862)
PHONE.............................619 421-1151
**EMP:** 160
**SIC: 3562** Casters

**(P-9952)**
**NEXT POINT BEARING GROUP LLC**
28364 Avenue Crocker, Valencia (91355-1250)
PHONE.............................818 988-1880
Mark Mickelson, *Managing Member*
John Burroughs, *
▲ **EMP:** 28 **EST:** 2012

# 3562 - Ball And Roller Bearings (P-9953)

SQ FT: 27,000
**SALES (est):** 8.29MM **Privately Held**
**Web:** www.nextpointbearing.com
**SIC: 3562** 5085  Ball and roller bearings; Bearings

## (P-9953)
### NMB (USA) INC (HQ)
Also Called: NMB Tech
9730 Independence Ave, Chatsworth (91311-4323)
**PHONE**...............................818 709-1770
◆ **EMP:** 50 **EST:** 1983
**SALES (est):** 451.49MM **Privately Held**
**Web:** www.nmbtc.com
**SIC: 3562** 5063 5084 3728  Ball bearings and parts; Motors, electric; Fans, industrial; Aircraft propellers and associated equipment
**PA:** Minebea Mitsumi Inc.
  1-9-3, Higashishimbashi

## (P-9954)
### SCHAEFFLER GROUP USA INC
34700 Pacific Coast Hwy Ste 203, Capistrano Beach (92624-1349)
**PHONE**...............................949 234-9799
Rich Peterson, *Brnch Mgr*
**EMP:** 29
**SALES (corp-wide):** 66.25B **Privately Held**
**Web:** www.schaeffler.us
**SIC: 3562**  Ball and roller bearings
**HQ:** Schaeffler Group Usa Inc.
  308 Springhill Farm Rd
  Fort Mill SC 29715
  803 548-8500

## (P-9955)
### SPECIALTY MOTIONS INC
5480 Smokey Mountain Way, Yorba Linda (92887-4247)
**PHONE**...............................951 735-8722
Thomas Corey, *CEO*
Dorothy Corey, *Sec*
**EMP:** 20 **EST:** 1990
SQ FT: 13,000
**SALES (est):** 2.1MM **Privately Held**
**SIC: 3562** 5085  Ball and roller bearings; Bearings

## (P-9956)
### WEARTECH INTERNATIONAL INC
1177 N Grove St, Anaheim (92806-2110)
**PHONE**...............................714 683-2430
▲ **EMP:** 43
**Web:** www.weartech.net
**SIC: 3562** 3313 3548 3496  Ball bearings and parts; Alloys, additive, except copper: not made in blast furnaces; Welding apparatus; Miscellaneous fabricated wire products

---

# 3563 Air And Gas Compressors

## (P-9957)
### ATLAS COPCO COMPRESSORS LLC
Also Called: Accurate Air Engineering
16207 Carmenita Rd, Cerritos (90703-2212)
**PHONE**...............................562 484-6370
John T Lague, *Pr*
**EMP:** 35
**Web:** www.accurateair.com
**SIC: 3563**  Air and gas compressors
**HQ:** Atlas Copco Compressors Llc
  300 Tchnlogy Ctr Dr Ste 5
  Rock Hill SC 29730
  866 472-1015

## (P-9958)
### C M AUTOMOTIVE SYSTEMS INC (PA)
5646 W Mission Blvd, Ontario (91762-4652)
**PHONE**...............................909 869-7912
Chander Mittal, *Pr*
Sameer Mittal, *CFO*
▲ **EMP:** 23 **EST:** 1986
**SALES (est):** 4.47MM
**SALES (corp-wide):** 4.47MM **Privately Held**
**Web:** www.cmautomotive.com
**SIC: 3563**  Air and gas compressors

## (P-9959)
### COMPUVAC INDUSTRIES INC
18381 Mount Langley St, Fountain Valley (92708-6904)
**PHONE**...............................949 574-5085
David Donnelly, *Pr*
▲ **EMP:** 16 **EST:** 2001
SQ FT: 13,000
**SALES (est):** 2.44MM **Privately Held**
**Web:** www.compuvacind.com
**SIC: 3563**  Vacuum (air extraction) systems, industrial

## (P-9960)
### DRESSER-RAND COMPANY
18502 Dominguez Hill Dr, Rancho Dominguez (90220-6415)
**PHONE**...............................310 223-0600
**EMP:** 43
**SALES (corp-wide):** 73.09B **Privately Held**
**SIC: 3563**  Air and gas compressors
**HQ:** Dresser-Rand Company
  500 Paul Clark Dr
  Olean NY 14870
  716 375-3000

## (P-9961)
### EBARA TECHNOLOGIES INC (DH)
Also Called: Ebara
51 Main Ave, Sacramento (95838)
**PHONE**...............................916 920-5451
Nasao Asami, *Ch Bd*
Naoki Ando, *
Mitsuhiko Shirakashi, *
Tadashi Urata, *
Ray Campbell, *
▲ **EMP:** 100 **EST:** 1991
SQ FT: 160,000
**SALES (est):** 46.65MM **Privately Held**
**Web:** www.ebaratech.com
**SIC: 3563**  Vacuum pumps, except laboratory
**HQ:** Ebara America Corporation
  809 Walker Ave Apt 1
  Oakland CA 94610

## (P-9962)
### ELLIOTT COMPANY
6014 Bloomfield Rd, Petaluma (94952-9708)
**PHONE**...............................707 665-5307
**EMP:** 19
**Web:** www.elliott-turbo.com
**SIC: 3563**  Air and gas compressors
**HQ:** Elliott Company
  901 N 4th St
  Jeannette PA 15644
  724 527-2811

## (P-9963)
### HUNTINGTON MECHANICAL LABS INC
Also Called: Huntington Mechanical Labs
13355 Nevada City Ave, Grass Valley (95945-9091)
**PHONE**...............................530 273-9533
Ronald Scott Hooper, *CEO*
Ron Hooper, *
**EMP:** 36 **EST:** 1969
SQ FT: 45,000
**SALES (est):** 4.74MM **Privately Held**
**Web:** www.huntvac.com
**SIC: 3563**  Vacuum pumps, except laboratory

## (P-9964)
### KOBELCO COMPRESSORS AMER INC
301 N Smith Ave, Corona (92878-3242)
**PHONE**...............................951 739-3030
**EMP:** 75
**Web:** www.kobelco-machinery-energy.com
**SIC: 3563**  Air and gas compressors
**HQ:** Kobelco Compressors America, Inc.
  1450 W Rincon St
  Corona CA 92880

## (P-9965)
### KOBELCO COMPRESSORS AMER INC (DH)
1450 W Rincon St, Corona (92880)
**PHONE**...............................951 739-3030
Teruhiko Murata, *Pr*
◆ **EMP:** 260 **EST:** 1990
**SALES (est):** 55.25MM **Privately Held**
**Web:** www.kobelco-machinery-energy.com
**SIC: 3563**  Air and gas compressors including vacuum pumps
**HQ:** Kobe Steel Usa Holdings Inc.
  535 Madison Ave, 5th Fl
  New York NY 10022

## (P-9966)
### MDC PRECISION LLC (PA)
Also Called: Mdc Vacuum
30962 Santana St, Hayward (94544-7058)
P.O. Box 398436 (94139-8436)
**PHONE**...............................510 265-3500
David Dutton, *CEO*
Paul Downey, *
▲ **EMP:** 100 **EST:** 1975
SQ FT: 45,000
**SALES (est):** 113.45MM
**SALES (corp-wide):** 113.45MM **Privately Held**
**Web:** www.mdcprecision.com
**SIC: 3563**  Vacuum pumps, except laboratory

## (P-9967)
### NORDSON CORPORATION
2747 Loker Ave W, Carlsbad (92010-6601)
**PHONE**...............................760 419-6551
Dave Padgett, *Brnch Mgr*
**EMP:** 81
**SALES (corp-wide):** 2.63B **Publicly Held**
**Web:** www.nordson.com
**SIC: 3563**  Air and gas compressors
**PA:** Nordson Corporation
  28601 Clemens Rd
  440 892-1580

## (P-9968)
### NORDSON CORPORATION
Also Called: Nordson Asymtek
2747 Loker Ave W, Carlsbad (92010-6601)
**PHONE**...............................760 431-1919
**EMP:** 212
**SALES (corp-wide):** 2.63B **Publicly Held**
**Web:** www.nordson.com
**SIC: 3563**  Air and gas compressors
**PA:** Nordson Corporation
  28601 Clemens Rd
  440 892-1580

## (P-9969)
### NORDSON CORPORATION
Also Called: Nordon Yestech
2765 Loker Ave W, Carlsbad (92010-6601)
**PHONE**...............................760 431-1919
Carla Loeffler, *Brnch Mgr*
**EMP:** 34
**SALES (corp-wide):** 2.63B **Publicly Held**
**Web:** www.nordson.com
**SIC: 3563**  Spraying outfits: metals, paints, and chemicals (compressor)
**PA:** Nordson Corporation
  28601 Clemens Rd
  440 892-1580

## (P-9970)
### NORDSON MARCH INC (HQ)
Also Called: March Plasma Systems
2470 Bates Ave Ste A, Concord (94520-1294)
**PHONE**...............................925 827-1240
James Getty, *CEO*
Raymond L Cushing, *
Robert E Veillette, *Prin*
▲ **EMP:** 24 **EST:** 1984
SQ FT: 6,000
**SALES (est):** 7.91MM
**SALES (corp-wide):** 2.63B **Publicly Held**
**Web:** www.nordson.com
**SIC: 3563**  Air and gas compressors
**PA:** Nordson Corporation
  28601 Clemens Rd
  440 892-1580

## (P-9971)
### NORDSON MARCH INC
2762 Loker Ave W, Carlsbad (92010-6603)
**PHONE**...............................925 827-1240
Jerry Wilder, *Brnch Mgr*
**EMP:** 75
**SALES (corp-wide):** 2.63B **Publicly Held**
**Web:** www.nordson.com
**SIC: 3563**  Air and gas compressors
**HQ:** March Nordson Inc
  2470 Bates Ave Ste A
  Concord CA 94520
  925 827-1240

## (P-9972)
### NORDSON TEST INSPTN AMRCAS INC
2765 Loker Ave W, Carlsbad (92010-6601)
**PHONE**...............................760 918-8471
Don Miller, *Pr*
Christine Schwarzmann, *
Robert E Veillette, *
**EMP:** 32 **EST:** 2002
SQ FT: 10,000
**SALES (est):** 3.16MM
**SALES (corp-wide):** 2.63B **Publicly Held**
**Web:** www.nordson.com
**SIC: 3563**  Air and gas compressors
**PA:** Nordson Corporation
  28601 Clemens Rd
  440 892-1580

## (P-9973)
### NU VENTURE DIVING CO
Also Called: Nuvair
1600 Beacon Pl, Oxnard (93033-2433)
**PHONE**...............................805 815-4044
Glenn Huebner, *CEO*
Glenn A Huebner, *CEO*
Janet Huebner, *VP*

◆ EMP: 22 EST: 1988
SQ FT: 27,000
SALES (est): 4.53MM Privately Held
Web: www.nuvair.com
SIC: 3563 Air and gas compressors

**(P-9974)**
**RIX INDUSTRIES (PA)**
4900 Industrial Way, Benicia (94510-1006)
PHONE.................707 747-5900
◆ EMP: 90 EST: 1966
SALES (est): 23.71MM
SALES (corp-wide): 23.71MM Privately Held
Web: www.rixindustries.com
SIC: 3563 Air and gas compressors including vacuum pumps

**(P-9975)**
**SIEMENS ENERGY INC**
18502 S Dominguez Hills Dr, Rancho Dominguez (90220-6415)
PHONE.................310 223-0660
EMP: 36
SALES (corp-wide): 33.81B Privately Held
Web: www.siemens-energy.com
SIC: 3563 Air and gas compressors
HQ: Siemens Energy, Inc.
4400 N Alafaya Trl
Orlando FL 32826
407 736-2000

**(P-9976)**
**TAYLOR INVESTMENTS LLC**
Also Called: Global Precision Manufacturing
13355 Nevada City Ave, Grass Valley (95945-9091)
PHONE.................530 273-4135
Edwin Taylor, Pr
Ronald Hooper, VP
EMP: 34 EST: 2007
SALES (est): 6.17MM Privately Held
Web: www.huntvac.com
SIC: 3563 Air and gas compressors

## 3564 Blowers And Fans

**(P-9977)**
**ADWEST TECHNOLOGIES INC (HQ)**
Also Called: Adwest
4222 E La Palma Ave, Anaheim (92807-1816)
PHONE.................714 632-8595
Brian Cannon, VP
Craig Bayer, *
Richard Whitford, *
Maryann Erickson, *
EMP: 35 EST: 1988
SQ FT: 23,500
SALES (est): 4.72MM Publicly Held
SIC: 3564 3585 3826 Air purification equipment; Heating equipment, complete; Thermal analysis instruments, laboratory type
PA: Ceco Environmental Corp.
5080 Spectrum Dr Ste 800e

**(P-9978)**
**AIRGARD INC (PA)**
1755 Mccarthy Blvd, Milpitas (95035-7416)
PHONE.................408 573-0701
Dan White, Pr
Mark Johnsgard, VP
Dyana Chargin, VP
Joe Ploshay Ii, VP Opers
Kevin Mcginnis, VP
▲ EMP: 22 EST: 1988
SALES (est): 6.11MM Privately Held
Web: www.airgard.net
SIC: 3564 Air purification equipment

**(P-9979)**
**AMERICAN METAL FILTER COMPANY**
Also Called: Metal Air Filters
611 Marsat Ct, Chula Vista (91911-4648)
PHONE.................619 628-1917
Valentine C Deilgat, Pr
EMP: 17 EST: 1986
SALES (est): 5.2MM Privately Held
Web: www.amfco.com
SIC: 3564 Filters, air: furnaces, air conditioning equipment, etc.

**(P-9980)**
**ATLAS COPCO MAFI-TRENCH CO LLC (DH)**
Also Called: Atlas Copco
3037 Industrial Pkwy, Santa Maria (93455-1807)
PHONE.................805 928-5757
◆ EMP: 208 EST: 2007
SQ FT: 90,000
SALES (est): 97.4MM Privately Held
SIC: 3564 3533 8744 Turbo-blowers, industrial; Oil and gas field machinery; Facilities support services
HQ: Atlas Copco North America Llc
6 Century Dr Ste 310
Parsippany NJ 07054

**(P-9981)**
**CAMFIL FARR INC**
3625 Del Amo Blvd Ste 260, Torrance (90503-1688)
PHONE.................973 616-7300
Frank Shahin, Prin
EMP: 26 EST: 2010
SALES (est): 817.3K Privately Held
SIC: 3564 Blowers and fans

**(P-9982)**
**CAMFIL USA INC**
500 Industrial Ave, Corcoran (93212-9629)
PHONE.................559 992-5118
Fausto Chavez, Brnch Mgr
EMP: 46
SALES (corp-wide): 95.11K Privately Held
Web: www.camfil.com
SIC: 3564 Dust or fume collecting equipment, industrial
HQ: Camfil Usa, Inc.
1 N Corporate Dr
Riverdale NJ 07457
973 616-7300

**(P-9983)**
**CENTRAL BLOWER CO**
3427 Pomona Blvd, Pomona (91768-3260)
PHONE.................626 330-3182
TOLL FREE: 800
David Roger Petersen, Pr
Eleanor Petersen, VP
Mary Petersen, Stockholder
EMP: 20 EST: 1979
SALES (est): 2.75MM Privately Held
Web: www.centralblower.com
SIC: 3564 Exhaust fans: industrial or commercial

**(P-9984)**
**ENVION LLC**
14724 Ventura Blvd Fl 200, Sherman Oaks (91403-3514)
PHONE.................818 217-2500
▲ EMP: 85 EST: 2003
SQ FT: 36,000
SALES (est): 1.84MM
SALES (corp-wide): 3.71MM Privately Held
Web: www.envion.com
SIC: 3564 Air purification equipment
PA: Sylmark Inc.
7821 Orion Ave Ste 200
818 217-2000

**(P-9985)**
**ENVIROCARE INTERNATIONAL INC**
507 Green Island Rd, American Canyon (94503-9649)
PHONE.................707 638-6800
John Tate Iii, Pr
Lisa Helfond, VP
Russell Helfond, COO
EMP: 22 EST: 1991
SQ FT: 10,000
SALES (est): 4.5MM Privately Held
Web: www.envirocare.com
SIC: 3564 Air cleaning systems

**(P-9986)**
**FILTRATION GROUP LLC**
498 Aviation Blvd, Santa Rosa (95403-1069)
PHONE.................707 525-8633
Dean Kerstetter, Dir
EMP: 124
SALES (corp-wide): 1.05B Privately Held
Web: www.filtrationgroup.com
SIC: 3564 Filters, air: furnaces, air conditioning equipment, etc.
HQ: Filtration Group Llc
912 E Washington St Ste 1
Joliet IL 60433
803 628-2410

**(P-9987)**
**GREENHECK FAN CORPORATION**
3034 Peacekeeper Way, Mcclellan (95652-2536)
PHONE.................916 643-4616
EMP: 66
SALES (corp-wide): 1.29B Privately Held
Web: www.greenheck.com
SIC: 3564 Blowers and fans
PA: Greenheck Fan Corporation
1100 Greenheck Dr
715 359-6171

**(P-9988)**
**GREENHECK FAN CORPORATION**
170 Cyber Ct, Rocklin (95765-1205)
PHONE.................916 626-3400
Mike Venturi, Mgr
EMP: 63
SALES (corp-wide): 1.29B Privately Held
Web: www.greenheck.com
SIC: 3564 Blowers and fans
PA: Greenheck Fan Corporation
1100 Greenheck Dr
715 359-6171

**(P-9989)**
**HEPA CORPORATION**
3071 E Coronado St, Anaheim (92806-2698)
PHONE.................714 630-5700
EMP: 100 EST: 1968
SALES (est): 2.2MM Privately Held
Web: www.hepa.com
SIC: 3564 Air purification equipment

**(P-9990)**
**IQAIR NORTH AMERICA INC**
14351 Firestone Blvd, La Mirada (90638-5527)
PHONE.................877 715-4247
Glory Z Dolphin, CEO
Frank Hammes, *
▲ EMP: 48 EST: 1991
SQ FT: 40,000
SALES (est): 22.9MM Privately Held
Web: www.iqair.com
SIC: 3564 8742 5999 Air cleaning systems; Materials mgmt. (purchasing, handling, inventory) consultant; Air purification equipment
PA: Icleen Entwicklungs- Und Vertriebsanstalt Fur Umweltprodukte C/O Jgt Treuunternehmen Reg.

**(P-9991)**
**M D H BURNER & BOILER CO INC**
12106 Center St, South Gate (90280-8046)
PHONE.................562 630-2875
Mauro Donate, CEO
EMP: 18 EST: 1992
SQ FT: 5,000
SALES (est): 3.03MM Privately Held
SIC: 3564 7699 3443 3433 Air purification equipment; Boiler repair shop; Fabricated plate work (boiler shop); Heating equipment, except electric

**(P-9992)**
**MACROAIR TECHNOLOGIES INC (PA)**
Also Called: Macro Air Technologies
794 S Allen St, San Bernardino (92408-2210)
P.O. Box 1467 (92324-0805)
PHONE.................909 890-2270
TOLL FREE: 800
Edward Boyd, CEO
◆ EMP: 45 EST: 1979
SQ FT: 15,000
SALES (est): 19MM
SALES (corp-wide): 19MM Privately Held
Web: www.macroairfans.com
SIC: 3564 Ventilating fans: industrial or commercial

**(P-9993)**
**MARS AIR SYSTEMS LLC**
Also Called: Mars Air Curtains
14716 S Broadway, Gardena (90248-1814)
PHONE.................310 532-1555
▼ EMP: 75 EST: 1961
SALES (est): 9.34MM Privately Held
Web: www.marsair.com
SIC: 3564 Blowers and fans

**(P-9994)**
**PACWEST AIR FILTER LLC**
26550 Adams Ave, Murrieta (92562-7085)
PHONE.................951 698-2228
Buddy Olds, CEO
EMP: 44 EST: 2009
SQ FT: 5,000
SALES (est): 4.74MM Privately Held
Web: www.pacwestfilter.com
SIC: 3564 5085 Filters, air: furnaces, air conditioning equipment, etc.; Filters, industrial

**(P-9995)**
**QC MANUFACTURING INC**
26040 Ynez Rd, Temecula (92591-6033)
PHONE.................951 325-6340
Dane Stevenson, Pr

# 3564 - Blowers And Fans (P-9996)

▲ **EMP:** 65 **EST:** 2009
**SALES (est):** 20.16MM **Privately Held**
Web: www.quietcoolsystems.com
**SIC: 3564** Blowers and fans

### (P-9996)
### ROTRON INCORPORATED
Ametek Rotron
474 Raleigh Ave, El Cajon (92020-3138)
**PHONE**..................619 593-7400
Fred Taylor, *Mgr*
**EMP:** 120
**SALES (corp-wide):** 6.6B **Publicly Held**
Web: www.rotron.com
**SIC: 3564** Blowers and fans
**HQ:** Rotron Incorporated
  55 Hasbrouck Ln
  Woodstock NY 12498
  845 679-2401

### (P-9997)
### STANDARD FILTER CORPORATION (PA)
3801 Ocean Ranch Blvd Ste 107, Oceanside (92056-8603)
**PHONE**..................866 443-3615
Tobey Wiik, *Pr*
◆ **EMP:** 26 **EST:** 1973
**SALES (est):** 6.22MM
**SALES (corp-wide):** 6.22MM **Privately Held**
Web: www.standardfilter.com
**SIC: 3564** 5199 Filters, air; furnaces, air conditioning equipment, etc.; Felt

### (P-9998)
### SUN INDUSTRIES CORPORATION
Also Called: Sun Industries
370 Amapola Ave Ste 101, Torrance (90501-7239)
**PHONE**..................310 782-1188
▲ **EMP:** 21 **EST:** 1981
**SALES (est):** 925.2K **Privately Held**
Web: www.sunindustries.com
**SIC: 3564** 5065 5013 3569 Filters, air: furnaces, air conditioning equipment, etc.; Electronic parts; Filters, air and oil; Filters

### (P-9999)
### SUN INDUSTRIES FILTRATION CORP ✪
Also Called: Sun Industries Filtration
14322 Bonelli St, City Of Industry (91746)
**PHONE**..................310 782-1188
Seo Son, *Prin*
Joey Choo, *Prin*
Kim Park, *Prin*
Logan Jung, *Prin*
**EMP:** 21 **EST:** 2024
**SALES (est):** 1.24MM **Privately Held**
**SIC: 3564** 5013 Filters, air: furnaces, air conditioning equipment, etc.; Filters, air and oil

### (P-10000)
### SUNON INC (PA)
Also Called: Eme Fan & Motor
1760 Yeager Ave, La Verne (91750-5850)
**PHONE**..................714 255-0208
Yin Su Hong, *CEO*
▲ **EMP:** 30 **EST:** 1998
**SALES (est):** 3.34MM
**SALES (corp-wide):** 3.34MM **Privately Held**
Web: www.sunonusa.com
**SIC: 3564** Blowers and fans

### (P-10001)
### TEMPEST TECHNOLOGY CORPORATION
4708 N Blythe Ave, Fresno (93722-3930)
**PHONE**..................800 346-2143
Leroy B Coffman Ii, *CEO*
Leroy B Coffman Iii, *Pr*
▲ **EMP:** 25 **EST:** 1982
**SQ FT:** 22,000
**SALES (est):** 6.34MM **Privately Held**
Web: tempest.us.com
**SIC: 3564** Ventilating fans: industrial or commercial

### (P-10002)
### TERRA UNIVERSAL INC (PA)
800 S Raymond Ave, Fullerton (92831-5234)
**PHONE**..................714 526-0100
G H Sadaghiani, *CEO*
▲ **EMP:** 99 **EST:** 1975
**SQ FT:** 88,000
**SALES (est):** 41.62MM
**SALES (corp-wide):** 41.62MM **Privately Held**
Web: www.terrauniversal.com
**SIC: 3564** 3567 3569 3572 Purification and dust collection equipment; Heating units and devices, industrial: electric; Filters; Computer storage devices

### (P-10003)
### TRI-DIM FILTER CORPORATION
26550 Adams Ave, Murrieta (92562-7085)
**PHONE**..................626 826-5893
Scott Breckenridge, *Mgr*
**EMP:** 30
**SALES (corp-wide):** 1.42MM **Privately Held**
Web: airfiltration.mann-hummel.com
**SIC: 3564** Filters, air: furnaces, air conditioning equipment, etc.
**HQ:** Tri-Dim Filter Corporation
  93 Industrial Dr
  Louisa VA 23093
  540 967-2600

### (P-10004)
### VENTUREDYNE LTD
Climet Instruments Company
1320 W Colton Ave, Redlands (92374-2864)
P.O. Box 1760 (92373-0543)
**PHONE**..................909 793-2788
Ray Felbinger, *Mgr*
**EMP:** 65
**SALES (corp-wide):** 178 **Privately Held**
Web: www.venturedyne.com
**SIC: 3564** 3829 3825 3823 Blowing fans: industrial or commercial; Measuring and controlling devices, nec; Instruments to measure electricity; Process control instruments
**PA:** Venturedyne, Ltd.
  600 College Ave
  262 691-9900

### (P-10005)
### VORTECH ENGINEERING INC
Also Called: Vortech
1650 Pacific Ave, Oxnard (93033-2746)
**PHONE**..................805 247-0226
Jim Middlebrook, *CEO*
Randolf Riley, *
▲ **EMP:** 42 **EST:** 2001
**SALES (est):** 10.26MM **Privately Held**
Web: www.vortechsuperchargers.com
**SIC: 3564** Blowing fans: industrial or commercial

### (P-10006)
### VORTOX AIR TECHNOLOGY INC
121 S Indian Hill Blvd, Claremont (91711-4997)
**PHONE**..................909 621-3843
**EMP:** 23 **EST:** 1917
**SALES (est):** 2.36MM **Privately Held**
Web: www.vortox.com
**SIC: 3564** 3444 3829 Air cleaning systems; Sheet metalwork; Measuring and controlling devices, nec

### (P-10007)
### WEMS INC (PA)
Also Called: Wems Electronics
4650 W Rosecrans Ave, Hawthorne (90250-6841)
P.O. Box 528 (90251-0528)
**PHONE**..................310 644-0251
Ronald Hood, *CEO*
Nancy Howe, *Information Technology**
Carroll Whitney, *
Charles Wilson, *
**EMP:** 84 **EST:** 1960
**SQ FT:** 78,000
**SALES (est):** 20.45MM
**SALES (corp-wide):** 20.45MM **Privately Held**
Web: www.wems.com
**SIC: 3564** 3612 6513 Blowers and fans; Transformers, except electric; Apartment building operators

### (P-10008)
### WHIPPLE INDUSTRIES INC
Also Called: Whipple Superchargers
3292 N Weber Ave, Fresno (93722-4942)
**PHONE**..................559 442-1261
Arthur Whipple, *CEO*
Sherry Anderson, *Sec*
▲ **EMP:** 15 **EST:** 1989
**SQ FT:** 5,258
**SALES (est):** 6.6MM **Privately Held**
Web: www.whipplesuperchargers.com
**SIC: 3564** 3732 3724 3714 Turbo-blowers, industrial; Boatbuilding and repairing; Aircraft engines and engine parts; Motor vehicle parts and accessories

## 3565 Packaging Machinery

### (P-10009)
### ACCUTEK PACKAGING EQUIPMENT CO (PA)
Also Called: Kiss Packaging Systems
2980 Scott St, Vista (92081-8321)
**PHONE**..................760 734-4177
Edward Chocholek, *Prin*
Drew Chocholek, *
Darren Chocholek, *
Drake Chocholek, *
◆ **EMP:** 25 **EST:** 1987
**SALES (est):** 9.54MM **Privately Held**
Web: www.accutekpackaging.com
**SIC: 3565** Packaging machinery

### (P-10010)
### ADCO MANUFACTURING
2170 Academy Ave, Sanger (93657-3795)
**PHONE**..................559 875-5563
Kate King, *Pr*
Frank Hoffman, *
Glen Long, *
◆ **EMP:** 150 **EST:** 1957
**SQ FT:** 75,000
**SALES (est):** 24.83MM **Privately Held**
Web: www.adcomfg.com
**SIC: 3565** Carton packing machines

### (P-10011)
### ALINE SYSTEMS CORPORATION
Also Called: Aline Systems
13844 Struikman Rd, Cerritos (90703-1032)
**PHONE**..................562 229-9727
**EMP:** 20
**SIC: 3565** Packaging machinery

### (P-10012)
### AVP TECHNOLOGY LLC
4140 Business Center Dr, Fremont (94538-6354)
**PHONE**..................510 683-0157
Hugh Chau, *CEO*
Lynn Chau, *Managing Member**
▲ **EMP:** 45 **EST:** 2005
**SQ FT:** 4,000
**SALES (est):** 5.01MM **Privately Held**
Web: www.avptechnologyllc.com
**SIC: 3565** Vacuum packaging machinery

### (P-10013)
### B & H MANUFACTURING CO INC (PA)
Also Called: B & H Labeling Systems
3461 Roeding Rd, Ceres (95307-9442)
P.O. Box 247 (95307-0247)
**PHONE**..................209 537-5785
Roman M Eckols, *CEO*
Calvin E Bright, *
Lyn E Bright, *
Marjorie Bright, *
Bob Adamson, *
◆ **EMP:** 149 **EST:** 1969
**SQ FT:** 65,000
**SALES (est):** 19.96MM
**SALES (corp-wide):** 19.96MM **Privately Held**
Web: www.bhlabeling.com
**SIC: 3565** Labeling machines, industrial

### (P-10014)
### BELCO PACKAGING SYSTEMS INC
910 S Mountain Ave, Monrovia (91016-3641)
**PHONE**..................626 357-9566
**TOLL FREE:** 800
Helen V Misik, *CEO*
A Michael Misik, *
▲ **EMP:** 25 **EST:** 1959
**SQ FT:** 35,000
**SALES (est):** 8.36MM **Privately Held**
Web: www.belcopackaging.com
**SIC: 3565** Packing and wrapping machinery

### (P-10015)
### BLC WC INC
Also Called: Imperial System
2900 Faber St, Union City (94587-1228)
**PHONE**..................510 489-5400
John Kramer, *Brnch Mgr*
**EMP:** 35
**SALES (corp-wide):** 11.19MM **Privately Held**
Web: www.resourcelabel.com
**SIC: 3565** 2679 3953 2672 Labeling machines, industrial; Labels, paper: made from purchased material; Marking devices; Paper; coated and laminated, nec
**PA:** Blc Wc, Inc.
  13260 Moore St
  562 926-1452

### (P-10016)
### CAN LINES ENGINEERING INC (PA)
Also Called: C L E

**PRODUCTS & SERVICES SECTION**  
**3565 - Packaging Machinery (P-10037)**

9839 Downey Norwalk Rd, Downey (90241-5596)
PHONE..................562 861-2996
Donald Koplien, *CEO*
Keenan Koplien, *
Erik Koplien, *
EMP: 89 EST: 1960
SQ FT: 40,000
SALES (est): 23.71MM
SALES (corp-wide): 23.71MM Privately Held
Web: www.canlines.com
SIC: 3565 3556 Canning machinery, food; Food products machinery

**(P-10017)**
**CVC TECHNOLOGIES INC**
10861 Business Dr, Fontana (92337-8235)
PHONE..................909 355-0311
Sheng Hui Yang, *CEO*
K Joe Yang, *Pr*
▲ EMP: 21 EST: 1998
SQ FT: 29,000
SALES (est): 12.8MM Privately Held
Web: www.cvctechnologies.com
SIC: 3565 Labeling machines, industrial
PA: Cvc Technologies Inc.
   No. 190, Gongye 9th Rd.

**(P-10018)**
**FUTURE COMMODITIES INTL INC**
Also Called: Bestpack Packaging Systems
1425 S Campus Ave, Ontario (91761-4366)
PHONE..................888 588-2378
David L Lim, *Pr*
Chery Co Lim, *Ex VP*
▲ EMP: 27 EST: 1984
SQ FT: 27,500
SALES (est): 7.83MM Privately Held
Web: www.bestpack.com
SIC: 3565 Packaging machinery

**(P-10019)**
**HANNAN PRODUCTS CORP (PA)**
9106 Pulsar Ct Ste C, Corona (92883-4632)
P.O. Box 954 (92878-0954)
PHONE..................951 735-1587
TOLL FREE: 800
Henry H Jenkins, *Pr*
Lawrence Jenkins, *VP Sls*
Alfred Ramos, *VP*
Nancy P Jenkins, *Stockholder*
EMP: 16 EST: 1966
SALES (est): 2.42MM
SALES (corp-wide): 2.42MM Privately Held
Web: www.hannanpak.com
SIC: 3565 3053 3554 3549 Packaging machinery; Packing materials; Paper industries machinery; Cutting and slitting machinery

**(P-10020)**
**HIS INDUSTRIES INC**
Also Called: Phoenix Engineering
1202 W Shelley Ct, Orange (92868-1239)
PHONE..................949 383-4308
Lynn Worthington, *Pr*
▲ EMP: 20 EST: 1997
SQ FT: 6,000
SALES (est): 4.6MM Privately Held
Web: www.pouchmachines.com
SIC: 3565 Packaging machinery

**(P-10021)**
**JACKSAM CORPORATION**
Also Called: JACKSAM CORP BLACKOUT
4440 Von Karman Ave Ste 220, Newport Beach (92660-2011)
PHONE..................800 605-3580
Mark Adams, *Pr*
Michael Sakala, *
EMP: 25 EST: 1989
SALES (est): 1.46MM Privately Held
Web: www.convectium.com
SIC: 3565 Bottling machinery: filling, capping, labeling

**(P-10022)**
**KLIPPENSTEIN CORPORATION**
2246 E Date Ave, Fresno (93706-5425)
PHONE..................559 834-4258
Kenneth Klippenstein, *Pr*
Kenneth Ray Klippenstein, *
Richard Klippenstein, *
Wendy Klippenstein, *
▲ EMP: 25 EST: 1979
SALES (est): 7.25MM Privately Held
Web: www.klippenstein.com
SIC: 3565 Packaging machinery

**(P-10023)**
**KODIAK CARTONERS INC**
Also Called: Ywd Cartoners
2550 Se Ave, Ste 101, Fresno (93706-5121)
PHONE..................559 266-4844
Casandra Tanney, *Pr*
EMP: 18 EST: 1997
SALES (est): 952K Privately Held
Web: www.kodiakcartoners.com
SIC: 3565 Packing and wrapping machinery

**(P-10024)**
**LABEL-AIRE INC (PA)**
Also Called: Label-Aire
550 Burning Tree Rd, Fullerton (92833-1449)
PHONE..................714 449-5155
▲ EMP: 67 EST: 1968
SALES (est): 10.59MM
SALES (corp-wide): 10.59MM Privately Held
Web: www.label-aire.com
SIC: 3565 Labeling machines, industrial

**(P-10025)**
**M & O PERRY INDUSTRIES INC**
Also Called: Perry Industries
412 N Smith Ave, Corona (92878-4303)
PHONE..................951 734-9838
Phillip Osterhaus, *CEO*
▲ EMP: 40 EST: 1987
SQ FT: 20,000
SALES (est): 7.67MM Privately Held
Web: www.moperry.com
SIC: 3565 8711 7629 5084 Packaging machinery; Engineering services; Electrical repair shops; Conveyor systems

**(P-10026)**
**MAF INDUSTRIES INC (HQ)**
36470 Highway 99, Traver (93673-7120)
P.O. Box 218 (93673-0218)
PHONE..................559 897-2905
Thomas Blanc, *Pr*
Philippe Blanc, *
Raul Mejia, *
▲ EMP: 80 EST: 1989
SQ FT: 30,000
SALES (est): 24.64MM Privately Held
Web: www.maf-roda.com
SIC: 3565 5084 Packing and wrapping machinery; Food industry machinery
PA: Maf
    Cbi

**(P-10027)**
**P R P MULTISOURCE INC**
3836 Wacker Dr, Jurupa Valley (91752-1147)
PHONE..................951 681-6100
Phil Woss, *Pr*
Kurt Fisch, *Treas*
▲ EMP: 20 EST: 1994
SQ FT: 25,000
SALES (est): 3.5MM Privately Held
Web: www.multisource.us
SIC: 3565 5084 Vacuum packaging machinery; Packaging machinery and equipment

**(P-10028)**
**PACKLINE TECHNOLOGIES INC**
5929 Avenue 408, Dinuba (93618-9791)
P.O. Box 636 (93631-0636)
PHONE..................559 591-3150
Lorin R Reed, *Pr*
EMP: 30 EST: 2011
SALES (est): 1.39MM Privately Held
Web: www.packlinetech.com
SIC: 3565 5084 Packaging machinery; Packaging machinery and equipment

**(P-10029)**
**SARDEE INDUSTRIES INC**
Also Called: Sardee
2731 E Myrtle St, Stockton (95205-4718)
PHONE..................209 466-1526
Alan Basset, *Brnch Mgr*
EMP: 33
SALES (corp-wide): 9.43MM Privately Held
Web: www.sardee.com
SIC: 3565 3536 Packaging machinery; Hoists, cranes, and monorails
PA: Sardee Industries, Inc.
   5100 Academy Dr Ste 400
   630 824-4200

**(P-10030)**
**SERPA PACKAGING SOLUTIONS LLC**
Also Called: Serpa Packaging Solutions
7020 W Sunnyview Ave, Visalia (93291-9639)
PHONE..................559 651-2339
Fernando M Serpa, *Pr*
Joseph Scalia, *
Manuela Parreira, *
◆ EMP: 100 EST: 1985
SQ FT: 62,000
SALES (est): 23.37MM Privately Held
Web: www.serpapackaging.com
SIC: 3565 Carton packing machines
HQ: Pro Mach, Inc.
   50 E Rvrcnter Blvd Ste 18
   Covington KY 41011
   513 831-8778

**(P-10031)**
**SIMPLEX FILLER INC**
Also Called: Simplex Filler Co
640 Airpark Rd Ste A, Napa (94558-7569)
PHONE..................707 265-6801
Alexandra Kaether, *CEO*
EMP: 15 EST: 1966
SQ FT: 15,500
SALES (est): 3.13MM Privately Held
Web: www.simplexfiller.com
SIC: 3565 Packaging machinery

**(P-10032)**
**SYSTEMS TECHNOLOGY INC**
Also Called: Delaware Systems Technology
1350 Riverview Dr, San Bernardino (92408-2944)
PHONE..................909 799-9950
David R Landon, *CEO*
John G Stjohn, *
▲ EMP: 65 EST: 1998
SQ FT: 43,000
SALES (est): 2.43MM Privately Held
Web: www.systems-technology-inc.com
SIC: 3565 Packing and wrapping machinery

**(P-10033)**
**THIELE TECHNOLOGIES INC**
1949 E Manning Ave, Reedley (93654-9462)
PHONE..................559 638-8484
Ed Suarez, *Mgr*
EMP: 64
Web: www.bwflexiblesystems.com
SIC: 3565 Packaging machinery
HQ: Thiele Technologies, Inc.
   9360 W Broadway Ave
   Minneapolis MN 55445
   612 782-1200

**(P-10034)**
**UNITED BAKERY EQUIPMENT CO INC (PA)**
Also Called: Hartman Slicer Div
15315 Marquardt Ave, Santa Fe Springs (90670-5709)
PHONE..................310 635-8121
Dulce Sohm, *CFO*
◆ EMP: 99 EST: 1966
SALES (est): 19.16MM
SALES (corp-wide): 19.16MM Privately Held
Web: www.ubeusa.com
SIC: 3565 3556 Packaging machinery; Bakery machinery

**(P-10035)**
**VANOMATION INC**
9241 Research Dr, Irvine (92618-4286)
PHONE..................877 228-2992
Van Le, *CEO*
EMP: 15 EST: 2012
SQ FT: 1,200
SALES (est): 248.56K Privately Held
Web: www.vanomation.com
SIC: 3565 Packaging machinery

**(P-10036)**
**VERICOOL INC**
7066 Las Positas Rd Ste C, Livermore (94551-5134)
PHONE..................925 337-0808
Darrell Jobe, *CEO*
EMP: 24 EST: 2016
SALES (est): 9.45MM Privately Held
Web: www.vericoolpackaging.com
SIC: 3565 Packaging machinery

**(P-10037)**
**W E PLEMONS MCHY SVCS INC**
13479 E Industrial Dr, Parlier (93648-9678)
P.O. Box 787 (93648-0787)
PHONE..................559 646-6630
William Plemons, *Pr*
Edward Baskette, *
Jeff Winters, *
Olivia Kozera, *
John Robinson, *Stockholder*
▲ EMP: 25 EST: 1986
SQ FT: 30,000
SALES (est): 5.28MM Privately Held
Web: www.weplemons.com
SIC: 3565 7699 Packaging machinery; Industrial machinery and equipment repair

## 3566 Speed Changers, Drives, And Gears

**(P-10038)**
**AMERICAN PRECISION GEAR CO**
365 Foster City Blvd, Foster City (94404-1104)
PHONE..................650 627-8060
Steve W Lefczik, *Pr*
**EMP:** 20 **EST:** 1956
**SQ FT:** 22,000
**SALES (est):** 6.52MM **Privately Held**
Web: www.amgear.com
**SIC: 3566** Gears, power transmission, except auto

**(P-10039)**
**HARMONIC DRIVE LLC**
333 W San Carlos St Ste 1070, San Jose (95110-2726)
PHONE..................800 921-3332
**EMP:** 22
Web: www.harmonicdrive.net
**SIC: 3566** Speed changers, drives, and gears
HQ: Harmonic Drive L.L.C.
42 Dunham Ridge
Beverly MA 01915

**(P-10040)**
**HECO INC**
Also Called: Pascal Systems
2350 Del Monte St, West Sacramento (95691-3807)
P.O. Box 1388 (95691-1388)
PHONE..................916 372-5411
Michael H Jacobs, *Pr*
Allen Rasmussen, *VP*
◆ **EMP:** 18 **EST:** 1975
**SQ FT:** 10,000
**SALES (est):** 3.76MM **Privately Held**
Web: www.hecogear.com
**SIC: 3566** Speed changers (power transmission equipment), except auto

**(P-10041)**
**MARPLES GEARS INC**
1310 Mountain View Cir, Azusa (91702-1648)
PHONE..................626 570-1744
**TOLL FREE:** 800
James A Phillips Iv, *CEO*
**EMP:** 23 **EST:** 1937
**SALES (est):** 6.28MM **Privately Held**
Web: www.marplesgears.com
**SIC: 3566** Speed changers, drives, and gears

**(P-10042)**
**MARTIN SPROCKET & GEAR INC**
1199 Vine St, Sacramento (95811-0426)
PHONE..................916 441-7172
Steve Delay, *Brnch Mgr*
**EMP:** 97
**SQ FT:** 100,000
**SALES (corp-wide):** 292.47MM **Privately Held**
Web: www.martinsprocket.com
**SIC: 3566** 3535 3534 3462 Gears, power transmission, except auto; Conveyors and conveying equipment; Elevators and moving stairways; Iron and steel forgings
PA: Martin Sprocket & Gear, Inc.
3100 Sprocket Dr
817 258-3000

**(P-10043)**
**MARTIN SPROCKET & GEAR INC**
5920 Triangle Dr, Commerce (90040-3688)
PHONE..................323 728-8117
Gus Diaz, *Mgr*
**EMP:** 18
**SQ FT:** 8,500
**SALES (corp-wide):** 292.47MM **Privately Held**
Web: www.martinsprocket.com
**SIC: 3566** 5085 3568 Gears, power transmission, except auto; Sprockets; Power transmission equipment, nec
PA: Martin Sprocket & Gear, Inc.
3100 Sprocket Dr
817 258-3000

**(P-10044)**
**SEW-EURODRIVE INC**
30599 San Antonio St, Hayward (94544-7101)
PHONE..................510 487-3560
Marvin Leeper, *Brnch Mgr*
**EMP:** 44
**SALES (corp-wide):** 4.27B **Privately Held**
Web: www.seweurodrive.com
**SIC: 3566** Speed changers, drives, and gears
HQ: Sew-Eurodrive, Inc.
1295 Old Spartanburg Hwy
Lyman SC 29365
864 439-7537

**(P-10045)**
**UNIVERSAL MOTION COMPONENTS CO INC**
Also Called: U M C
2920 Airway Ave, Costa Mesa (92626-6008)
PHONE..................714 437-9600
▲ **EMP:** 50 **EST:** 1978
**SALES (est):** 9.32MM **Privately Held**
Web: www.umcproducts.com
**SIC: 3566** 5013 3523 3429 Gears, power transmission, except auto; Truck parts and accessories; Irrigation equipment, self-propelled; Marine hardware

## 3567 Industrial Furnaces And Ovens

**(P-10046)**
**BAKER FURNACE INC**
Also Called: Baker Furnace
2680 Orbiter St, Brea (92821-6265)
PHONE..................714 223-7262
Ernest E Bacon, *Pr*
Diane Bacon, *Sec*
▼ **EMP:** 19 **EST:** 1980
**SALES (est):** 3.14MM
**SALES (corp-wide):** 85.81MM **Privately Held**
Web: www.bakerfurnace.com
**SIC: 3567** Heating units and devices, industrial: electric
HQ: Tps, Llc
2821 Old Rte 15
New Columbia PA 17856
570 538-7200

**(P-10047)**
**CIRCLE INDUSTRIAL MFG CORP (PA)**
Also Called: Cim Services
1613 W El Segundo Blvd, Compton (90222-1024)
PHONE..................310 638-5101
Ronald M La Forest, *Pr*
John La Forest, *
Karen La Forest, *
**EMP:** 23 **EST:** 1953
**SQ FT:** 3,500
**SALES (est):** 6.07MM
**SALES (corp-wide):** 6.07MM **Privately Held**
Web: www.circleindustrial.com
**SIC: 3567** 3542 3535 3444 Industrial furnaces and ovens; Sheet metalworking machines; Conveyors and conveying equipment; Sheet metalwork

**(P-10048)**
**DICK FARRELL INDUSTRIES INC**
Also Called: D.F. Industries
5071 Lindsay Ct, Chino (91710-5757)
PHONE..................909 613-9424
Timothy Farrell, *Prin*
Richard Farrell, *VP*
Lisa Van Den Berg, *Sec*
▲ **EMP:** 17 **EST:** 1978
**SQ FT:** 25,000
**SALES (est):** 2.66MM **Privately Held**
Web: dickf.openfos.com
**SIC: 3567** 3312 7699 Industrial furnaces and ovens; Ferroalloys, produced in blast furnaces; Industrial machinery and equipment repair

**(P-10049)**
**DICKEN ENTERPRISES INC**
22060 Bear Valley Rd, Apple Valley (92308-7209)
PHONE..................760 246-7333
Micahei T Dicken, *Pr*
Michael T Dicken, *Pr*
Marilyn Dicken, *Sec*
**EMP:** 21 **EST:** 1979
**SQ FT:** 25,000
**SALES (est):** 5.61MM **Privately Held**
Web: www.inductiontech.com
**SIC: 3567** 7699 Induction heating equipment ; Industrial machinery and equipment repair

**(P-10050)**
**DS FIBERTECH CORP**
Also Called: Interntonal Thermoproducts Div
11015 Mission Park Ct, Santee (92071-5601)
PHONE..................619 562-7001
Duong Minh Nguyen, *CEO*
Son Dinh Nguyen, *
Eric Ulrich, *
▲ **EMP:** 45 **EST:** 1993
**SQ FT:** 14,000
**SALES (est):** 4.42MM **Privately Held**
Web: www.dsfibertech.com
**SIC: 3567** Heating units and devices, industrial: electric

**(P-10051)**
**FURNACE SUPER HEROS INC**
Also Called: Heatech
920 S Placentia Ave Ste A, Placentia (92870-8000)
PHONE..................714 238-9009
Kevin J Davis, *Pr*
**EMP:** 15 **EST:** 1989
**SQ FT:** 5,000
**SALES (est):** 2.83MM **Privately Held**
Web: www.bakerfurnace.com
**SIC: 3567** Heating units and devices, industrial: electric

**(P-10052)**
**HEATER DESIGNS INC**
2211 S Vista Ave, Bloomington (92316-2921)
PHONE..................909 421-0971
James Fan, *Ch*
Tom Odendahl, *
**EMP:** 30 **EST:** 1986
**SQ FT:** 14,500
**SALES (est):** 2.96MM **Privately Held**
Web: www.heaterdesigns.com
**SIC: 3567** Heating units and devices, industrial: electric

**(P-10053)**
**INDUCTION TECHNOLOGY CORP**
22060 Bear Valley Rd, Apple Valley (92308-7209)
PHONE..................760 246-7333
**EMP:** 30 **EST:** 2019
**SALES (est):** 3.67MM **Privately Held**
**SIC: 3567** Induction heating equipment

**(P-10054)**
**INDUSTRIAL PROCESS EQP INC**
Also Called: I P E
1700 Industrial Ave, Norco (92860-2949)
PHONE..................714 447-0171
Michael J Waggoner, *CEO*
James Waggoner, *Pr*
▼ **EMP:** 16 **EST:** 1984
**SQ FT:** 30,220
**SALES (est):** 6.22MM **Privately Held**
Web: www.ipeontime.com
**SIC: 3567** Industrial furnaces and ovens

**(P-10055)**
**JHAWAR INDUSTRIES LLC**
Also Called: G-M Enterprises
525 Klug Cir, Corona (92878-5452)
PHONE..................951 340-4646
Jean-francois Cloutier, *Managing Member*
▼ **EMP:** 41 **EST:** 1975
**SQ FT:** 50,000
**SALES (est):** 10.39MM **Privately Held**
**SIC: 3567** Vacuum furnaces and ovens

**(P-10056)**
**L C MILLER COMPANY**
717 Monterey Pass Rd, Monterey Park (91754-3606)
PHONE..................323 268-3611
Dolores Naimy, *Pr*
Victor De Lucia, *
Dave Vito, *
**EMP:** 27 **EST:** 1956
**SQ FT:** 14,000
**SALES (est):** 4.91MM **Privately Held**
Web: www.lcmiller.com
**SIC: 3567** 3546 3625 3398 Heating units and devices, industrial: electric; Saws and sawing equipment; Industrial electrical relays and switches; Metal heat treating

**(P-10057)**
**PRIME HEAT INCORPORATED**
1844 Friendship Dr Ste A, El Cajon (92020-1115)
PHONE..................619 449-6623
Herb Boekamp, *Pr*
▲ **EMP:** 18 **EST:** 1988
**SQ FT:** 20,500
**SALES (est):** 3.08MM **Privately Held**
Web: www.primeheatsystems.com
**SIC: 3567** Heating units and devices, industrial: electric

**(P-10058)**
**RAMA CORPORATION**
600 W Esplanade Ave, San Jacinto (92583-4999)
PHONE..................951 654-7351
Peggy Renshaw, *Pr*

**PRODUCTS & SERVICES SECTION**  3569 - General Industrial Machinery, (P-10077)

EMP: 45 EST: 1947
SQ FT: 25,000
SALES (est): 3.94MM
SALES (corp-wide): 8.78MM Privately Held
Web: www.ramacorporation.com
SIC: 3567 3634 Heating units and devices, industrial: electric; Electric housewares and fans
PA: Amark Industries, Inc.
600 W Esplanade Ave
951 654-7351

**(P-10059)**
**SIERRATHERMAL INC (DH)**
Also Called: Schmid
200 Westridge Dr, Watsonville (95076-4172)
PHONE................................831 763-0113
Thomas Stewart, CEO
William Daley, Sec
◆ EMP: 21 EST: 1993
SQ FT: 34,000
SALES (est): 43.48MM Privately Held
Web: www.sierratherm.com
SIC: 3567 3674 3559 Electrical furnaces, ovens, & heating devices, exc.induction; Semiconductors and related devices; Broom making machinery
HQ: Gebr. Schmid Gmbh
Robert-Bosch-Str. 32-36
Freudenstadt BW 72250
74415380

**(P-10060)**
**THERMTRONIX CORPORATION (PA)**
17129 Muskrat Ave, Adelanto (92301-2260)
P.O. Box 100 (92301-0100)
PHONE................................760 246-4500
Robert Nealon, Pr
Deborah Nealon, Sec
▲ EMP: 21 EST: 1984
SQ FT: 12,000
SALES (est): 2.74MM
SALES (corp-wide): 2.74MM Privately Held
Web: www.thermtronix.com
SIC: 3567 Metal melting furnaces, industrial: electric

**(P-10061)**
**TP SOLAR INC**
Also Called: Tpsi
16310 Downey Ave, Paramount (90723-5500)
PHONE................................562 808-2171
Alex Rey, Pr
Peter Ragay, VP
▼ EMP: 16 EST: 2005
SQ FT: 4,000
SALES (est): 479.85K Privately Held
Web: www.tpsolar.com
SIC: 3567 Industrial furnaces and ovens

**(P-10062)**
**W P KEITH CO INC**
Also Called: Keith Co
8323 Loch Lomond Dr, Pico Rivera (90660-2588)
PHONE................................562 948-3636
Reto Fehr, CEO
Carol N Keith, *
Wendell P Keith Junior, Pr
▲ EMP: 25 EST: 1954
SQ FT: 19,200
SALES (est): 4.54MM Privately Held
Web: www.keithcompany.com
SIC: 3567 Kilns, nsk

**(P-10063)**
**WARMBOARD INC**
100 Enterprise Way Ste G300, Scotts Valley (95066-3245)
PHONE................................831 685-9276
Terry Alberg, Pr
EMP: 20 EST: 2001
SQ FT: 1,250
SALES (est): 7.17MM Privately Held
Web: www.warmboard.com
SIC: 3567 Radiant heating systems, industrial process

## 3568 Power Transmission Equipment, Nec

**(P-10064)**
**ANACO INC**
311 Corporate Terrace Cir, Corona (92879-6028)
PHONE................................951 372-2732
Leon Nolen Iii, Pr
▲ EMP: 140 EST: 1986
SALES (est): 23.67MM
SALES (corp-wide): 970.37MM Privately Held
Web: www.anaco-husky.com
SIC: 3568 Couplings, shaft: rigid, flexible, universal joint, etc.
PA: Mcwane, Inc.
2900 Hwy 280 S Ste 300
205 414-3100

**(P-10065)**
**ATR SALES INC**
Also Called: Atra-Flex
110 E Garry Ave, Santa Ana (92707-4201)
PHONE................................714 432-8411
Jerry Hauck, CEO
Raymond Hoyt, *
EMP: 26 EST: 1980
SQ FT: 12,000
SALES (est): 4.38MM Privately Held
Web: www.atra-flex.com
SIC: 3568 Couplings, shaft: rigid, flexible, universal joint, etc.
HQ: U.S. Tsubaki Holdings, Inc.
301 E Marquardt Dr
Wheeling IL 60090
847 459-9500

**(P-10066)**
**BALL SCREWS & ACTUATORS CO INC (DH)**
Also Called: B S A
48767 Kato Rd, Fremont (94538-7313)
PHONE................................510 770-5932
Steve Randazzo, Pr
▲ EMP: 73 EST: 1971
SQ FT: 30,000
SALES (est): 8.59MM
SALES (corp-wide): 6.25B Publicly Held
Web: www.thomsonlinear.com
SIC: 3568 3625 3593 3562 Power transmission equipment, nec; Actuators, industrial; Fluid power cylinders and actuators; Ball and roller bearings
HQ: Altra Industrial Motion Corp.
300 Granite St Ste 201
Braintree MA 02184
781 917-0600

**(P-10067)**
**FERROTEC (USA) CORPORATION (HQ)**
566 Exchange Ct, Livermore (94550-2400)
PHONE................................408 964-7700
Eiji Miyamaga, CEO
Akira Yamamura, Ch
Nigel Hunton, Pr
Barry Moskoitz, Marketing
Bob Otey P Te Engg, Prin
◆ EMP: 90 EST: 1968
SQ FT: 55,000
SALES (est): 138.53MM Privately Held
Web: www.ferrotec.com
SIC: 3568 3053 Bearings, bushings, and blocks; Gaskets and sealing devices
PA: Ferrotec Holdings Corporation
2-3-4, Nihombashi

**(P-10068)**
**FORWARD**
13020 Pacific Promenade, Los Angeles (90094-4017)
PHONE................................310 962-2522
Johnny Ward, Prin
EMP: 38 EST: 2011
SALES (est): 1.61MM Privately Held
Web: www.foodforward.org
SIC: 3568 Railroad car journal bearings

**(P-10069)**
**HELICAL PRODUCTS COMPANY INC**
901 W Mccoy Ln, Santa Maria (93455-1196)
P.O. Box 1069 (93456-1069)
PHONE................................805 928-3851
EMP: 120
SIC: 3568 3495 3493 Couplings, shaft: rigid, flexible, universal joint, etc.; Instrument springs, precision; Steel springs, except wire

**(P-10070)**
**HYSPAN PRECISION PRODUCTS INC (PA)**
Also Called: Hyspan
1685 Brandywine Ave, Chula Vista (91911-6097)
PHONE................................619 421-1355
Eric Barnes, CEO
Donald R Heye, *
Phillip Ensz, *
Eric Barnes, CFO
◆ EMP: 100 EST: 1974
SQ FT: 54,000
SALES (est): 115.37MM
SALES (corp-wide): 115.37MM Privately Held
Web: www.hyspan.com
SIC: 3568 3496 3441 Ball joints, except aircraft and auto; Woven wire products, nec; Expansion joints (structural shapes), iron or steel

**(P-10071)**
**INDU-ELECTRIC NORTH AMER INC (PA)**
27756 Avenue Hopkins, Valencia (91355-1222)
PHONE................................310 578-2144
Martin Gerber, CEO
▲ EMP: 47 EST: 2002
SQ FT: 11,000
SALES (est): 9MM
SALES (corp-wide): 9MM Privately Held
Web: www.indu-electric.com
SIC: 3568 5063 Power transmission equipment, nec; Power transmission equipment, electric

**(P-10072)**
**INDUSTRIAL SPROCKETS GEARS INC**
13650 Rosecrans Ave, Santa Fe Springs (90670-5025)
PHONE................................323 233-7221
Max R Patridge, CEO
Monty Patridge, VP
Connie Patridge-eason, Sec
Mark Partridge, Treas
EMP: 21 EST: 1971
SQ FT: 18,000
SALES (est): 1.91MM Privately Held
Web: www.industrialsprocketsandgears.com
SIC: 3568 3566 3462 Drives, chains, and sprockets; Drives, high speed industrial, except hydrostatic; Iron and steel forgings

**(P-10073)**
**POWERSPHYR INC**
4115 Blackhawk Plaza Cir Ste 100, Danville (94506-4901)
PHONE................................925 736-8299
David F Meng, CEO
Bill Lombardi, CIO
Robert Klosterboer Indep, Dir
EMP: 28 EST: 2016
SALES (est): 1.46MM Privately Held
Web: www.powersphyr.com
SIC: 3568 Power transmission equipment, nec

**(P-10074)**
**WEST COAST YAMAHA INC**
Also Called: West Coast Motor Sports
1622 Illinois Ave, Perris (92571-9374)
PHONE................................951 943-2061
Gerald Morris Langston, CEO
Margret Mckinley, Sec
EMP: 25 EST: 1998
SALES (est): 3.2MM Privately Held
Web: www.yamaha-motor.com
SIC: 3568 5571 5561 Power transmission equipment, nec; Motorcycle dealers; Recreational vehicle dealers

## 3569 General Industrial Machinery,

**(P-10075)**
**AVX FILTERS CORPORATION**
11144 Penrose St, Sun Valley (91352-2756)
PHONE................................818 767-6770
John Gilbertson, Pr
▲ EMP: 90 EST: 1981
SQ FT: 25,000
SALES (est): 4.29MM Privately Held
Web: www.kyocera-avx.com
SIC: 3569 3675 Filters; Electronic capacitors
HQ: Kyocera Avx Components Corporation
1 Avx Blvd
Fountain Inn SC 29644
864 967-2150

**(P-10076)**
**BAY AREA INDUS FILTRATION INC**
6355 Coliseum Way, Oakland (94621-3793)
P.O. Box 2071 (94577-0207)
PHONE................................510 562-6373
Thomas S Schneider, Pr
Diana E Schneider, *
EMP: 24 EST: 1972
SALES (est): 4.12MM Privately Held
Web: www.bayareafiltration.com
SIC: 3569 5085 3564 2674 Filters, general line: industrial; Filters, industrial; Blowers and fans; Bags: uncoated paper and multiwall

**(P-10077)**
**BEAM ON TECHNOLOGY CORPORATION**

# 3569 - General Industrial Machinery, (P-10078)

317 Brokaw Rd, Santa Clara (95050-4335)
PHONE...................408 982-0161
Rajoo Venkat, Pr
Herbert Martinez, *
**EMP:** 27 **EST:** 1992
**SALES (est):** 4.63MM **Privately Held**
Web: www.beamon.com
**SIC: 3569** 3544 3543 Assembly machines, non-metalworking; Special dies, tools, jigs, and fixtures; Industrial patterns

### (P-10078)
### BLUELAB CORPORATION USA INC
437 S Cataract Ave, San Dimas (91773-2973)
PHONE...................909 599-1940
Rick Jaries, Pr
**EMP:** 50 **EST:** 2010
**SALES (est):** 2.37MM **Privately Held**
**SIC: 3569** Testing chambers for altitude, temperature, ordnance, power

### (P-10079)
### CAMPBELL MEMBRANE TECH INC
1168 N Johnson Ave, El Cajon (92020-1917)
PHONE...................619 938-2481
Jeffrey Campbell, CEO
◆ **EMP:** 50 **EST:** 2007
**SALES (est):** 4.71MM **Privately Held**
Web: www.campbellsengineering.com
**SIC: 3569** Filter elements, fluid, hydraulic line

### (P-10080)
### CAPSTONE FIRE MANAGEMENT INC (PA)
2240 Auto Park Way, Escondido (92029-1249)
PHONE...................760 839-2290
Jerry Dusa, Pr
Christopher Dusa, *
Matthew Dusa, *
**EMP:** 31 **EST:** 1989
**SALES (est):** 4.91MM
**SALES (corp-wide):** 4.91MM **Privately Held**
Web: www.capstonefire.com
**SIC: 3569** Firefighting and related equipment

### (P-10081)
### CENTRIFUGE-SYSTEMS LLC
Also Called: Centrisys/Cnp West
825 Performance Dr, Stockton (95206-4974)
PHONE...................209 583-3753
Mickey Balash, Brnch Mgr
**EMP:** 117
**SALES (corp-wide):** 25.96MM **Privately Held**
Web: www.centrisys-cnp.com
**SIC: 3569** Centrifuges, industrial
PA: Centrifuge-Systems, Llc
9586 58th Pl
262 654-6006

### (P-10082)
### CLAYTON MANUFACTURING COMPANY (PA)
Also Called: Clayton Industries
17477 Hurley St, City Of Industry (91744-5106)
PHONE...................626 443-9381
John Clayton, Pr
Boyd A Calvin, *
Phyllis Nielson, *
Alexander Smirnoff, *
Allen L Cluer, *

▲ **EMP:** 147 **EST:** 1930
**SQ FT:** 215,000
**SALES (est):** 48.23MM
**SALES (corp-wide):** 48.23MM **Privately Held**
Web: www.claytonindustries.com
**SIC: 3569** 3829 3511 Generators: steam, liquid oxygen, or nitrogen; Dynamometer instruments; Turbines and turbine generator sets

### (P-10083)
### CLAYTON MANUFACTURING INC (HQ)
17477 Hurley St, City Of Industry (91744-5106)
PHONE...................626 443-9381
William Clayton Junior, CEO
Boyd A Calvin, *
Allen L Cluer, *
John Clayton, *
▼ **EMP:** 80 **EST:** 1930
**SQ FT:** 215,000
**SALES (est):** 22.22MM
**SALES (corp-wide):** 48.23MM **Privately Held**
Web: www.claytonindustries.com
**SIC: 3569** 3829 Generators: steam, liquid oxygen, or nitrogen; Dynamometer instruments
PA: Clayton Manufacturing Company
17477 Hurley St
626 443-9381

### (P-10084)
### CODE-IN-MOTION LLC
1307 Calle Avanzado, San Clemente (92673-6351)
PHONE...................949 361-2633
**EMP:** 15 **EST:** 2004
**SALES (est):** 3.99MM **Privately Held**
Web: www.code-in-motion.com
**SIC: 3569** 3565 Robots, assembly line: industrial and commercial; Labeling machines, industrial

### (P-10085)
### DELTA DESIGN INC (HQ)
12367 Crosthwaite Cir, Poway (92064-6817)
PHONE...................858 848-8000
Samer Aabbani, Pr
Charles A Schwan, *
James A Donahue, *
James Mcfarlane, Sr VP
Jeff Jose, *
▲ **EMP:** 400 **EST:** 1957
**SQ FT:** 334,000
**SALES (est):** 37.41MM
**SALES (corp-wide):** 636.32MM **Publicly Held**
Web: www.cohu.com
**SIC: 3569** 3825 3674 Testing chambers for altitude, temperature, ordnance, power; Test equipment for electronic and electrical circuits; Semiconductors and related devices
PA: Cohu, Inc.
12367 Crosthwaite Cir
858 848-8100

### (P-10086)
### DELTA TAU DATA SYSTEMS INC CAL (HQ)
Also Called: Omron Delta Tau
21314 Lassen St, Chatsworth (91311-4254)
PHONE...................818 998-2095
Yasuto Ikuta, Pr
Tamara Dimitri, *
James Fornear, *

**EMP:** 129 **EST:** 1976
**SALES (est):** 21MM **Privately Held**
Web: automation.omron.com
**SIC: 3569** 7372 3625 3577 Robots, assembly line: industrial and commercial; Prepackaged software; Relays and industrial controls; Computer peripheral equipment, nec
PA: Omron Corporation
801,
Horikawahigashiiruminamifudodocho, Shiokojidoori, Shimogyo-

### (P-10087)
### ENTEGRIS GP INC
4175 Santa Fe Rd, San Luis Obispo (93401-8159)
PHONE...................805 541-9299
Bertrand Loy, Pr
◆ **EMP:** 130 **EST:** 1975
**SQ FT:** 50,000
**SALES (est):** 27.53MM
**SALES (corp-wide):** 3.52B **Publicly Held**
Web: www.entegris.com
**SIC: 3569** Gas producers, generators, and other gas related equipment
PA: Entegris, Inc.
129 Concord Rd
978 436-6500

### (P-10088)
### FIGURE AI INC
1247 Elko Dr, Sunnyvale (94089-2211)
PHONE...................716 830-0904
Brett Adcock, CEO
**EMP:** 50 **EST:** 2022
**SALES (est):** 1.81MM **Privately Held**
**SIC: 3569** Robots, assembly line: industrial and commercial

### (P-10089)
### FIREBLAST GLOBAL INC
Also Called: Fireblast
41633 Eastman Dr, Murrieta (92562-7054)
PHONE...................951 277-8319
Richard Egelin, CEO
**EMP:** 25 **EST:** 2000
**SALES (est):** 6.69MM **Privately Held**
Web: www.fireblast.com
**SIC: 3569** 8711 Firefighting apparatus; Engineering services

### (P-10090)
### FIREQUICK PRODUCTS INC
1137 Red Rock Inyokern Rd, Inyokern (93527)
P.O. Box 910 (93527-0910)
PHONE...................760 371-4279
Beth Sumners, Pr
Beth J Sumners, Pr
Bill Sumners, VP
**EMP:** 18 **EST:** 2004
**SALES (est):** 1.27MM **Privately Held**
Web: www.firequick.com
**SIC: 3569** Firefighting and related equipment

### (P-10091)
### GRINNELL LLC
3077 Wiljan Ct Ste B, Santa Rosa (95407-5764)
PHONE...................707 578-3212
Mark Watson, Dist Mgr
**EMP:** 214
**SQ FT:** 1,200
**SIC: 3569** 1711 3498 3669 Sprinkler systems, fire: automatic; Fire sprinkler system installation; Pipe fittings, fabricated from purchased pipe; Smoke detectors
HQ: Grinnell Llc
1501 Nw 51st St

Boca Raton FL 33431
561 988-3658

### (P-10092)
### GUSMER ENTERPRISES INC
Also Called: Cellulo Co Division
81 M St, Fresno (93721-3215)
PHONE...................908 301-1811
Fred Mazanec, Mgr
**EMP:** 34
**SQ FT:** 18,644
**SALES (corp-wide):** 48.93MM **Privately Held**
Web: www.gusmerdistilling.com
**SIC: 3569** Filters, general line: industrial
PA: Gusmer Enterprises, Inc.
1165 Globe Ave
908 301-1811

### (P-10093)
### HF GROUP INC
Also Called: Beale Air Force Base
5801 C St, Marysville (95903-1510)
P.O. Box 390 (95901-0009)
PHONE...................530 788-0288
Paul Lindke, Mgr
**EMP:** 15
**SALES (corp-wide):** 7.95MM **Privately Held**
Web: www.hf76.com
**SIC: 3569** Gas producers, generators, and other gas related equipment
PA: Hf Group, Inc.
203 W Artesia Blvd
310 605-0755

### (P-10094)
### HONEYBEE ROBOTICS LLC
2408 Lincoln Ave, Altadena (91001-5436)
PHONE...................303 774-7613
**EMP:** 67
Web: www.honeybeerobotics.com
**SIC: 3569** Filters
HQ: Honeybee Robotics, Llc
1830 Lefthand Cir
Longmont CO 80501
303 774-7613

### (P-10095)
### HONEYBEE ROBOTICS LLC
398 W Washington Blvd Ste 200, Pasadena (91103-2000)
PHONE...................510 207-4555
Stephen Gorvan, Brnch Mgr
**EMP:** 67
Web: www.honeybeerobotics.com
**SIC: 3569** Filters
HQ: Honeybee Robotics, Llc
1830 Lefthand Cir
Longmont CO 80501
303 774-7613

### (P-10096)
### INDUSTRIAL FIRE SPRNKLR CO INC
3845 Imperial Ave, San Diego (92113-1702)
PHONE...................619 266-6030
L David Sandage, Pr
**EMP:** 35 **EST:** 1986
**SALES (est):** 4.67MM **Privately Held**
Web: www.indfire.net
**SIC: 3569** 1731 Sprinkler systems, fire: automatic; Fire detection and burglar alarm systems specialization

### (P-10097)
### JOHNSTON INTERNATIONAL CORPORATION

## PRODUCTS & SERVICES SECTION
### 3569 - General Industrial Machinery, (P-10119)

Also Called: Kingman Industries
14272 Chambers Rd, Tustin (92780-6994)
PHONE..................................714 542-4487
▲ EMP: 25 EST: 1970
SALES (est): 5MM **Privately Held**
Web: www.plasties.com
SIC: 3569  Assembly machines, non-metalworking

### (P-10098)
### KNIGHT LLC (HQ)
15340 Barranca Pkwy, Irvine (92618-2215)
PHONE..................................949 595-4800
Don Julienne, *Dir*
Diane Peterson, *Dir*
◆ EMP: 100 EST: 1972
SQ FT: 46,000
SALES (est): 23.79MM
SALES (corp-wide): 3.27B **Publicly Held**
Web: www.knightequip.com
SIC: 3569 3582 3589  Liquid automation machinery and equipment; Commercial laundry equipment; Dishwashing machines, commercial
PA: Idex Corporation
    3100 Sanders Rd Ste 301
    847 498-7070

### (P-10099)
### LUBRICATION SCIENTIFICS LLC
17651 Armstrong Ave, Irvine (92614-5727)
PHONE..................................714 557-0664
Richard Hanley, *Managing Member*
EMP: 48 EST: 2014
SALES (est): 5.1MM **Privately Held**
Web: www.lubricationscientifics.com
SIC: 3569  Lubricating equipment

### (P-10100)
### MYERS MIXERS LLC
8376 Salt Lake Ave, Cudahy (90201-5817)
PHONE..................................323 560-4723
EMP: 41 EST: 2014
SALES (est): 5.22MM **Privately Held**
Web: www.myersmixers.com
SIC: 3569  Centrifuges, industrial

### (P-10101)
### NEWLIFE2 (PA)
4855 Morabito Pl, San Luis Obispo (93401-8748)
PHONE..................................805 549-8093
Kim Boege, *CEO*
EMP: 24 EST: 1954
SQ FT: 7,000
SALES (est): 2.97MM
SALES (corp-wide): 2.97MM **Privately Held**
Web: www.tankcleaningmachines.com
SIC: 3569  Liquid automation machinery and equipment

### (P-10102)
### NORCO INDUSTRIES INC (PA)
Also Called: Flo Dynamics
365 W Victoria St, Compton (90220-6029)
PHONE..................................310 639-4000
◆ EMP: 137 EST: 1964
SALES (est): 82.94MM
SALES (corp-wide): 82.94MM **Privately Held**
Web: www.norcoind.com
SIC: 3569 2531 5085 3537  Jacks, hydraulic; Seats, automobile; Industrial supplies; Industrial trucks and tractors

### (P-10103)
### PACIFIC CONSOLIDATED INDS LLC
Also Called: PCI
12201 Magnolia Ave, Riverside (92503-4820)
PHONE..................................951 479-0860
Bob Eng, *Managing Member*
Paul Stevens, *
Robert Eng, *
Alicia Fernandez, *
John Horton, *
◆ EMP: 77 EST: 2003
SQ FT: 85,000
SALES (est): 23.82MM
SALES (corp-wide): 27.01MM **Privately Held**
Web: www.pcigases.com
SIC: 3569 1382  Gas separators (machinery); Oil and gas exploration services
PA: Pci Holding Company, Inc.
    12201 Magnolia Ave
    951 479-0860

### (P-10104)
### PALL CORPORATION
4116 Sorrento Valley Blvd, San Diego (92121-1407)
PHONE..................................858 455-7264
Richard Mc Donald, *Genl Mgr*
EMP: 136
SALES (corp-wide): 23.89B **Publicly Held**
Web: www.pall.com
SIC: 3569  Filters
HQ: Pall Corporation
    25 Harbor Park Dr
    Port Washington NY 11050
    516 484-5400

### (P-10105)
### PHENIX TECHNOLOGY CORPORATION (PA)
Also Called: Phenix Technology
3453 Durahart St, Riverside (92507-3452)
PHONE..................................951 272-4938
Raymond M Russell, *Ch Bd*
Angel Sanchez, *CEO*
EMP: 17 EST: 1971
SALES (est): 2.91MM
SALES (corp-wide): 2.91MM **Privately Held**
Web: www.phenixfirehelmets.com
SIC: 3569  Firefighting and related equipment

### (P-10106)
### PIPELINE PRODUCTS INC
1650 Linda Vista Dr Ste 110, San Marcos (92078-3810)
PHONE..................................760 744-8907
Scott Higley, *Pr*
EMP: 17 EST: 1962
SQ FT: 20,000
SALES (est): 4.88MM **Privately Held**
Web: www.pipelineproducts.com
SIC: 3569  Filter elements, fluid, hydraulic line

### (P-10107)
### POLLEY INC (PA)
Also Called: Kelco Sales & Engineering
11936 Front St, Norwalk (90650-2911)
P.O. Box 305 (90651-0305)
PHONE..................................562 868-9861
Tracy Polley, *Pr*
▲ EMP: 15 EST: 1950
SQ FT: 24,000
SALES (est): 6.72MM
SALES (corp-wide): 6.72MM **Privately Held**
Web: www.kelcosales.com
SIC: 3569 5084  Assembly machines, non-metalworking; Industrial machinery and equipment

### (P-10108)
### PREMIER FILTERS INC
Also Called: OEM
952 N Elm St, Orange (92867-5441)
PHONE..................................657 226-0091
Bob Singh, *CEO*
Bob Singh, *Admn*
EMP: 40 EST: 2018
SALES (est): 2.51MM **Privately Held**
Web: www.premieremc.com
SIC: 3569  Filters, general line: industrial

### (P-10109)
### REC INC
Also Called: Ridgeline Engineering Company
2442 Cades Way, Vista (92081-7830)
PHONE..................................760 727-8006
Patrick Falley, *Pr*
EMP: 15 EST: 1998
SQ FT: 13,500
SALES (est): 5.88MM **Privately Held**
Web: www.rdgln.com
SIC: 3569  Liquid automation machinery and equipment

### (P-10110)
### RELAY ROBOTICS INC
271 E Hacienda Ave, Campbell (95008-6616)
PHONE..................................833 735-2976
Michael Odonnell, *CEO*
Izumi Yaskawa, *VP*
Steve Croft, *COO*
Bill Booth, *Sr VP*
EMP: 38 EST: 2021
SALES (est): 7MM **Privately Held**
Web: www.relayrobotics.com
SIC: 3569  Robots, assembly line: industrial and commercial

### (P-10111)
### RESCUE 42 INC
370 Ryan Ave Ste 120, Chico (95973-9530)
P.O. Box 1242 (95927-1242)
PHONE..................................530 891-3473
Tim Oconnell, *Pr*
EMP: 15 EST: 1995
SALES (est): 4.32MM **Privately Held**
Web: www.rescue42.com
SIC: 3569  Firefighting and related equipment

### (P-10112)
### SENJU FIRE PROTECTION CORP
Also Called: Senju Sprinkler
8850 Research Dr, Irvine (92618-4223)
PHONE..................................949 333-1281
Mitsuhiro Uchimura, *Pr*
▲ EMP: 16 EST: 2015
SALES (est): 6.53MM **Privately Held**
Web: www.senjusprinkler.com
SIC: 3569  Sprinkler systems, fire: automatic

### (P-10113)
### SEPARATION ENGINEERING INC
931 S Andreasen Dr Ste A, Escondido (92029-1959)
PHONE..................................760 489-0101
Charles E Hull, *Pr*
▲ EMP: 28 EST: 1980
SQ FT: 20,000
SALES (est): 5.78MM **Privately Held**
SIC: 3569  Filters, general line: industrial

### (P-10114)
### SERVE ROBOTICS INC
730 Broadway St, Redwood City (94063-3124)
PHONE..................................818 860-1352
Ali Kashani, *Ch Bd*
Touraj Parang, *
Brian Read, *CFO*
Euan Abraham, *Hardware Engineer*
EMP: 69 EST: 2021
SQ FT: 4,200
SALES (est): 207.54K **Privately Held**
Web: www.serverobotics.com
SIC: 3569  Robots, assembly line: industrial and commercial

### (P-10115)
### SOUTH SKYLINE FIREFIGHTERS
Also Called: South Skyline Vlntr Fire Rscue
12900 Skyline Blvd, Los Gatos (95033-9401)
PHONE..................................408 354-0025
Greg Redden, *Ex Dir*
Captain Arnie Wernick, *Prin*
EMP: 18 EST: 1983
SALES (est): 427.4K **Privately Held**
Web: www.southskyline.org
SIC: 3569  Firefighting and related equipment

### (P-10116)
### SPINTEK FILTRATION INC
10863 Portal Dr, Los Alamitos (90720-2508)
PHONE..................................714 236-9190
William A Greene, *CEO*
Patricia Kirk, *VP*
◆ EMP: 15 EST: 2001
SQ FT: 3,000
SALES (est): 2.61MM **Privately Held**
Web: www.spintek.com
SIC: 3569 3069 8711  Filters and strainers, pipeline; Roofing, membrane rubber; Engineering services

### (P-10117)
### STEARNS PRODUCT DEV CORP (PA)
Also Called: Doughpro
20281 Harvill Ave, Perris (92570-7235)
PHONE..................................951 657-0379
Steven Raio, *Pr*
▲ EMP: 91 EST: 1971
SQ FT: 50,000
SALES (est): 21.39MM
SALES (corp-wide): 21.39MM **Privately Held**
Web: www.proluxe.com
SIC: 3569 3444  Assembly machines, non-metalworking; Sheet metalwork

### (P-10118)
### TOMRA SORTING INC
Also Called: Tomra Food
728 N American St, Visalia (93291-4067)
PHONE..................................877 402-1755
EMP: 44
Web: www.tomra.com
SIC: 3569  Assembly machines, non-metalworking
HQ: Tomra Sorting, Inc.
    875 Embarcadero Dr
    West Sacramento CA 95605
    720 870-2240

### (P-10119)
### TRIFO INC
Also Called: Trifo
4633 Old Ironsides Dr Ste 300, Santa Clara (95054-1807)
PHONE..................................408 326-2242
Zhe Zhang, *CEO*
Shaoshan Liu, *Prin*
Jiao Zhang, *Prin*
EMP: 20 EST: 2016
SALES (est): 1.69MM **Privately Held**
Web: www.trifo.com

## 3569 - General Industrial Machinery, (P-10120)

SIC: **3569** 8742 Robots, assembly line: industrial and commercial; Automation and robotics consultant

### (P-10120)
**WALIN GROUP INC**
Also Called: Brilliant AV
1117 Baker St Ste A, Costa Mesa (92626-4159)
P.O. Box 2074 (92859-0074)
PHONE.....................................714 444-5980
Matthew James Walin, *CEO*
**EMP:** 42 **EST:** 2011
**SALES (est):** 5.48MM **Privately Held**
Web: www.brilliantav.com
SIC: **3569** 3699 3645 3651 Liquid automation machinery and equipment; Security devices; Residential lighting fixtures; Home entertainment equipment, electronic, nec

### (P-10121)
**WASSER FILTRATION INC (PA)**
Also Called: Pacific Press
1215 N Fee Ana St, Anaheim (92807-1804)
PHONE.....................................714 696-6450
Sean Duby, *Pr*
▲ **EMP:** 70 **EST:** 1987
**SQ FT:** 20,000
**SALES (est):** 4.78MM
**SALES (corp-wide):** 4.78MM **Privately Held**
Web: www.pacpress.com
SIC: **3569** 5084 Filters, general line: industrial; Industrial machinery and equipment

### (P-10122)
**WATER FILTER EXCHANGE INC**
Also Called: American Filter Company
875 N Todd Ave, Azusa (91702-2224)
PHONE.....................................818 808-2541
Alex Chividian, *CEO*
Mireille Chividian, *CEO*
**EMP:** 16 **EST:** 2010
**SQ FT:** 5,000
**SALES (est):** 768.25K **Privately Held**
SIC: **3569** 5999 Filters; Water purification equipment

### (P-10123)
**WESTERN FILTER A DIVISION OF DONALDSON COMPANY INC**
26235 Technology Dr, Valencia (91355-1147)
P.O. Box 1299 (55440-1299)
PHONE.....................................661 295-0800
▲ **EMP:** 100
Web: shop.donaldson.com
SIC: **3569** Filters

### (P-10124)
**WORKING ROBOT INC**
Also Called: Savioke
583c Division St, Campbell (95008-6905)
PHONE.....................................408 809-5600
Steve Cousins, *CEO*
**EMP:** 29 **EST:** 2022
**SALES (est):** 1.24MM **Privately Held**
SIC: **3569** Robots, assembly line: industrial and commercial

## 3571 Electronic Computers

### (P-10125)
**3PAR INC (HQ)**
4209 Technology Dr, Fremont (94538-6339)
PHONE.....................................510 445-1046
David C Scott, *Pr*
Adriel G Lares, *
Ashok Singhal Ph.d., *Chief Technology Officer System Architecture*
Alastair A Short, *General Vice President**
**EMP:** 188 **EST:** 1999
**SQ FT:** 263,000
**SALES (est):** 10.63MM
**SALES (corp-wide):** 29.14B **Publicly Held**
Web: www.hpe.com
SIC: **3571** 2542 Electronic computers; Partitions and fixtures, except wood
PA: Hewlett Packard Enterprise Company
1701 E Mossy Oaks Rd
678 259-9860

### (P-10126)
**ACCURATE ALWAYS INC**
127 Ocean Blvd, Half Moon Bay (94019-4042)
PHONE.....................................650 728-9428
Yousef Shemisa, *CEO*
Kate Haley, *CMO**
Kate Shemisa, *
**EMP:** 25 **EST:** 2004
**SQ FT:** 3,500
**SALES (est):** 2.42MM **Privately Held**
Web: www.accuratealways.com
SIC: **3571** Electronic computers

### (P-10127)
**ACME PORTABLE MACHINES INC**
1330 Mountain View Cir, Azusa (91702-1648)
PHONE.....................................626 610-1888
James Cheng, *Pr*
▲ **EMP:** 30 **EST:** 1994
**SQ FT:** 12,200
**SALES (est):** 4.59MM **Privately Held**
Web: www.acmeportable.com
SIC: **3571** Electronic computers

### (P-10128)
**AIVRES SYSTEMS INC (PA)**
615 N King Rd, San Jose (95133-1707)
PHONE.....................................866 687-1430
Ziliang Leon Zheng, *CEO*
Yichen Chen, *
Jungang Li, *CFO*
▲ **EMP:** 50 **EST:** 2015
**SALES (est):** 21.97MM
**SALES (corp-wide):** 21.97MM **Privately Held**
Web: www.aivres.com
SIC: **3571** Electronic computers

### (P-10129)
**AIVRES SYSTEMS INC**
Also Called: Inspur US R&D Technology Ctr
3347 Gateway Blvd, Fremont (94538-6526)
PHONE.....................................510 400-7599
**EMP:** 125
**SALES (corp-wide):** 21.97MM **Privately Held**
Web: www.aivres.com
SIC: **3571** Electronic computers
PA: Aivres Systems Inc.
615 N King Rd
866 687-1430

### (P-10130)
**AIVRES SYSTEMS INC**
1501 Mccarthy Blvd, Milpitas (95035)
PHONE.....................................866 687-1430
**EMP:** 125
**SALES (corp-wide):** 21.97MM **Privately Held**
Web: www.aivres.com
SIC: **3571** Electronic computers
PA: Aivres Systems Inc.
615 N King Rd
866 687-1430

### (P-10131)
**ALERATEC INC**
21722 Lassen St, Chatsworth (91311-3623)
▲ **EMP:** 24 **EST:** 2000
**SALES (est):** 2.6MM **Privately Held**
Web: www.aleratec.com
SIC: **3571** 5045 Electronic computers; Computer peripheral equipment

### (P-10132)
**ALLHEALTH**
515 S Figueroa St Ste 1300, Los Angeles (90071-3301)
PHONE.....................................213 538-0762
John R Cochran, *CEO*
**EMP:** 24 **EST:** 1998
**SALES (est):** 964.16K **Privately Held**
Web: www.allhealthinc.com
SIC: **3571** 7381 Electronic computers; Security guard service

### (P-10133)
**ALPHA RESEARCH & TECH INC**
Also Called: Art
5175 Hillsdale Cir Ste 100, El Dorado Hills (95762-5776)
PHONE.....................................916 431-9340
Deann Smith, *CEO*
Deann Kerr, *
**EMP:** 73 **EST:** 1993
**SQ FT:** 22,000
**SALES (est):** 10.7MM **Privately Held**
Web: www.artruggedsystems.com
SIC: **3571** Electronic computers

### (P-10134)
**AMERICAN RELIANCE INC**
Also Called: Amrel
789 N Fair Oaks Ave, Pasadena (91103-3045)
PHONE.....................................626 443-6818
Edward Chen, *CEO*
Shelly Chen, *
▲ **EMP:** 45 **EST:** 1985
**SALES (est):** 4.44MM **Privately Held**
Web: www.amrel.com
SIC: **3571** Electronic computers

### (P-10135)
**AMPERE COMPUTING LLC**
Also Called: Ampere
4655 Great America Pkwy Ste 601, Santa Clara (95054)
PHONE.....................................669 770-3700
Renee J James, *CEO*
Todd Underwood, *CFO*
**EMP:** 23 **EST:** 2017
**SALES (est):** 24.74MM **Privately Held**
Web: www.amperecomputing.com
SIC: **3571** Personal computers (microcomputers)

### (P-10136)
**AMPRO ADLINK TECHNOLOGY INC**
Also Called: Adlink Technology
6450 Via Del Oro, San Jose (95119-1208)
PHONE.....................................408 360-0200
Elizabeth Campbell, *CEO*
Mark Peterson, *
Joanne M Williams, *
Al Rosenbaum, *
Len Backus, *
▲ **EMP:** 65 **EST:** 1995
**SQ FT:** 25,000
**SALES (est):** 20.69MM **Privately Held**
Web: www.adlinktech.com
SIC: **3571** Electronic computers
PA: Adlink Technology Inc.
No. 66, Huaya 1st Rd.

### (P-10137)
**AYAR LABS INC (PA)**
695 River Oaks Pkwy, San Jose (95134-1907)
PHONE.....................................650 963-7200
Mark Wade, *CEO*
Lisa Cummins Dulchinos, *CFO*
Alex Wright-gladstein, *CSO*
Maria Del Rosario, *Acctg Mgr*
**EMP:** 82 **EST:** 2015
**SALES (est):** 17.22MM
**SALES (corp-wide):** 17.22MM **Privately Held**
Web: www.ayarlabs.com
SIC: **3571** Electronic computers

### (P-10138)
**B-REEL FILMS INC**
8383 Wilshire Blvd Ste 1000, Beverly Hills (90211-2439)
PHONE.....................................917 388-3836
Anders Wahlquist, *Pr*
**EMP:** 39 **EST:** 2007
**SALES (est):** 2MM **Privately Held**
Web: www.b-reel.com
SIC: **3571** Computers, digital, analog or hybrid

### (P-10139)
**BOLD DATA TECHNOLOGY INC**
Also Called: Crown Micro
47540 Seabridge Dr, Fremont (94538-6547)
PHONE.....................................510 490-8296
Eugene Kiang, *Pr*
Winston Xia, *
Marco Yee, *
▲ **EMP:** 45 **EST:** 1991
**SQ FT:** 50,000
**SALES (est):** 7.9MM **Privately Held**
Web: www.boldata.com
SIC: **3571** 3577 3674 Personal computers (microcomputers); Computer peripheral equipment, nec; Computer logic modules

### (P-10140)
**BRELYON INC**
930 Park Pl, San Mateo (94403-1907)
PHONE.....................................650 246-9426
Alok Mehta, *Managing Member*
Barmak Heshmat, *
Alok Mehta, *Prin*
Reza Khorasaninejad, *
Trevor Pan, *
**EMP:** 33 **EST:** 2019
**SALES (est):** 3.75MM **Privately Held**
Web: www.brelyon.com
SIC: **3571** Electronic computers

### (P-10141)
**CEMTROL INC**
3035 E La Jolla St, Anaheim (92806-1303)
PHONE.....................................714 666-6606
Sharon Paz, *Pr*
**EMP:** 15 **EST:** 2010
**SALES (est):** 3.95MM **Privately Held**
Web: www.cemtrol.com
SIC: **3571** Electronic computers

### (P-10142)
**COBALT ROBOTICS INC**
Also Called: Cobalt Ai
526 2nd St, San Francisco (94107)
PHONE.....................................650 781-3623
Travis Deyle, *CEO*
Ken Wolf, *

# PRODUCTS & SERVICES SECTION
## 3571 - Electronic Computers (P-10162)

Angela Kabana, *
Tyler Bayne, *
**EMP:** 60 **EST:** 2016
**SALES (est):** 9.39MM **Privately Held**
Web: www.cobaltai.com
**SIC: 3571** Electronic computers

### (P-10143)
### COLFAX INTERNATIONAL
2805 Bowers Ave Ste 230, Santa Clara (95051-0971)
**PHONE**..................................408 730-2275
Gautam Shah, *CEO*
Barbara Karvonen, *
▼ **EMP:** 31 **EST:** 1987
**SALES (est):** 12.36MM **Privately Held**
Web: www.colfax-intl.com
**SIC: 3571** Electronic computers

### (P-10144)
### CONTINUOUS COMPUTING CORP
Also Called: Ccpu
10431 Wateridge Cir Ste 110, San Diego (92121-5703)
**PHONE**..................................858 882-8800
Mike Dagenais, *CEO*
Ron Pyles, *
Erez Barnavon, *
Robert Telles, *
Michael Coward, *
**EMP:** 132 **EST:** 1998
**SQ FT:** 48,000
**SALES (est):** 4.85MM **Privately Held**
**SIC: 3571** 3661 4812 5045 Computers, digital, analog or hybrid; Telephone and telegraph apparatus; Radiotelephone communication; Computers, peripherals, and software
**HQ:** Radisys Corporation
8900 Ne Walker Rd Ste 130
Hillsboro OR 97006
503 615-1100

### (P-10145)
### CTS ELECTRONICS MANUFACTURING SOLUTIONS (SANTA CLARA) INC
5550 Hellyer Ave, San Jose (95138-1005)
**PHONE**..................................408 754-9800
▲ **EMP:** 290
**SIC: 3571** Electronic computers

### (P-10146)
### CYBERNET MANUFACTURING INC
5 Holland Ste 201, Irvine (92618-2574)
**PHONE**..................................949 600-8000
Pouran Shoaee, *CEO*
Joe Divino, *
Tina Jo Wentz, *
◆ **EMP:** 720 **EST:** 1996
**SALES (est):** 48MM **Privately Held**
Web: www.cybernetman.com
**SIC: 3571** 3577 Electronic computers; Computer peripheral equipment, nec

### (P-10147)
### DYNABOOK AMERICAS INC (HQ)
5241 California Ave Ste 100, Irvine (92617-3052)
**PHONE**..................................949 583-3000
Ikuaki Takayama, *Pr*
Takayuki Tono, *Sr VP*
James Robbins, *Genl Mgr*
**EMP:** 298 **EST:** 2018
**SALES (est):** 26.28MM **Privately Held**
Web: us.dynabook.com

**SIC: 3571** Electronic computers
**PA:** Sharp Corporation
1, Takumicho, Sakai-Ku

### (P-10148)
### ECHO LABS
235 Alma St, Palo Alto (94301-1017)
**PHONE**..................................650 561-3446
**EMP:** 21 **EST:** 2016
**SALES (est):** 866.7K **Privately Held**
Web: www.echolabs.net
**SIC: 3571** Computers, digital, analog or hybrid

### (P-10149)
### EDGE SOLUTIONS CONSULTING INC (PA)
5126 Clareton Dr Ste 160, Agoura Hills (91301-4529)
P.O. Box 661480 (91066-1480)
**PHONE**..................................818 591-3500
Marti Reeder, *Pr*
Marti R Hedge, *Pr*
**EMP:** 32 **EST:** 1999
**SQ FT:** 600
**SALES (est):** 8.62MM
**SALES (corp-wide):** 8.62MM **Privately Held**
Web: www.edgesolutionsandconsulting.com
**SIC: 3571** Mainframe computers

### (P-10150)
### ELMA ELECTRONIC INC (HQ)
44350 S Grimmer Blvd, Fremont (94538-6327)
**PHONE**..................................510 656-3400
Fred Ruegg, *CEO*
Shan Morgan, *
Peter Brunner, *
Ram Rajan, *
Badri Rajan, *
▲ **EMP:** 150 **EST:** 1985
**SQ FT:** 100,000
**SALES (est):** 68.28MM **Privately Held**
Web: www.elma.com
**SIC: 3571** 3575 3577 Electronic computers; Computer terminals; Computer peripheral equipment, nec
**PA:** Elma Electronic Ag
Hofstrasse 93

### (P-10151)
### ENTERPRISE SVCS ASIA PCF CORP
Also Called: HP
3000 Hanover St, Palo Alto (94304-1112)
**PHONE**..................................650 857-1501
**EMP:** 46
**SALES (corp-wide):** 13.67B **Publicly Held**
**SIC: 3571** Personal computers (microcomputers)
**HQ:** Enterprise Services Asia Pacific Corporation
5400 Legacy Dr
Plano TX 75024
703 245-9675

### (P-10152)
### EZCHIP SEMICONDUCTOR INC
Also Called: Tilera
2700 Zanker Rd, San Jose (95134-2139)
**PHONE**..................................408 520-3700
**EMP:** 20
**SIC: 3571** Electronic computers

### (P-10153)
### GARNER HOLT PRODUCTIONS INC

Also Called: Garner Holt Productions
1255 Research Dr, Redlands (92374-4541)
**PHONE**..................................909 799-3030
Garner L Holt, *Pr*
Michelle Berg, *
**EMP:** 50 **EST:** 1977
**SQ FT:** 50,000
**SALES (est):** 12.37MM **Privately Held**
Web: www.garnerholt.com
**SIC: 3571** Electronic computers

### (P-10154)
### GATEWAY INC
Also Called: Gateway
12750 Gateway Park Rd # 124, Poway (92064-2050)
**PHONE**..................................858 451-9933
**EMP:** 46
Web: www.acer.com
**SIC: 3571** Personal computers (microcomputers)
**HQ:** Gateway, Inc.
7565 Irvine Center Dr # 150
Irvine CA 92618
949 471-7000

### (P-10155)
### GATEWAY INC (DH)
Also Called: Gateway
7565 Irvine Center Dr Ste 150, Irvine (92618-4933)
**PHONE**..................................949 471-7000
Ed Coleman, *CEO*
Neal E West, *Contrlr*
John Goldsberry, *CFO*
Craig Calle, *Treas*
◆ **EMP:** 250 **EST:** 1985
**SQ FT:** 98,000
**SALES (est):** 223.23MM **Privately Held**
Web: www.acer.com
**SIC: 3571** 3577 Personal computers (microcomputers); Computer peripheral equipment, nec
**HQ:** Acer American Holdings Corp.
1730 N 1st St Ste 400
San Jose CA 95112

### (P-10156)
### GATEWAY US RETAIL INC
7565 Irvine Center Dr, Irvine (92618-4918)
**PHONE**..................................949 471-7000
Wayne R Inouye, *Pr*
Brian Firestone, *Executive Strategy Vice President*
▲ **EMP:** 29 **EST:** 1998
**SQ FT:** 147,000
**SALES (est):** 1.55MM **Privately Held**
**SIC: 3571** 3577 5045 Electronic computers; Computer peripheral equipment, nec; Computers, peripherals, and software
**HQ:** Gateway, Inc.
7565 Irvine Center Dr # 150
Irvine CA 92618
949 471-7000

### (P-10157)
### GENERAL DYNMICS MSSION SYSTEMS
General Dynmics Advnced Info S
100 Ferguson Dr, Mountain View (94043-5239)
P.O. Box 7188 (94039)
**PHONE**..................................650 966-2000
John Stewart, *Brnch Mgr*
**EMP:** 71
**SALES (corp-wide):** 42.27B **Publicly Held**
Web: www.gdmissionsystems.com
**SIC: 3571** 8731 Electronic computers; Commercial physical research

**HQ:** General Dynamics Mission Systems, Inc.
12450 Fair Lakes Cir
Fairfax VA 22033
877 449-0600

### (P-10158)
### HEWLETT-PACKARD ENTPS LLC (PA)
3000 Hanover St, Palo Alto (94304-1112)
**PHONE**..................................650 687-5817
Dion J Weisler, *CEO*
**EMP:** 15 **EST:** 2006
**SALES (est):** 55.3MM **Privately Held**
**SIC: 3571** Electronic computers

### (P-10159)
### HP INC
HP
303 2nd St Ste S500, San Francisco (94107-1373)
**PHONE**..................................415 979-3700
Ben Nelson, *Genl Mgr*
**EMP:** 70
**SALES (corp-wide):** 53.72B **Publicly Held**
Web: www.hp.com
**SIC: 3571** Personal computers (microcomputers)
**PA:** Hp Inc.
1501 Page Mill Rd
650 857-1501

### (P-10160)
### HP HEWLETT PACKARD GROUP LLC
1501 Page Mill Rd, Palo Alto (94304-1126)
**PHONE**..................................650 857-1501
Charles V Bergh, *Ch Bd*
**EMP:** 19 **EST:** 2015
**SALES (est):** 4.49MM
**SALES (corp-wide):** 53.72B **Publicly Held**
Web: www.hp.com
**SIC: 3571** Personal computers (microcomputers)
**PA:** Hp Inc.
1501 Page Mill Rd
650 857-1501

### (P-10161)
### HP INC (PA)
Also Called: HP
1501 Page Mill Rd, Palo Alto (94304-1126)
P.O. Box 10301 (94303)
**PHONE**..................................650 857-1501
Enrique Lores, *Pr*
Charles V Bergh, *
Stephanie Liebman, *FCO*
Karen Parkhill, *CFO*
Julie Jacobs, *CLO*
**EMP:** 1679 **EST:** 1939
**SALES (est):** 53.72B
**SALES (corp-wide):** 53.72B **Publicly Held**
Web: www.hp.com
**SIC: 3571** 7372 3861 3577 Personal computers (microcomputers); Prepackaged software; Cameras, still and motion picture (all types); Printers, computer

### (P-10162)
### HP INC
Also Called: HP
16399 W Bernardo Dr Bldg 61, San Diego (92127-1801)
**PHONE**..................................858 924-5117
Philip Liebscher, *Brnch Mgr*
**EMP:** 350
**SALES (corp-wide):** 53.72B **Publicly Held**
Web: www.hp.com
**SIC: 3571** Personal computers (microcomputers)

# 3571 - Electronic Computers (P-10163)

PA: Hp Inc.
1501 Page Mill Rd
650 857-1501

### (P-10163)
### HP INC
Also Called: HP
3495 Deer Creek Rd, Palo Alto
(94304-1316)
P.O. Box 10301 (94303-0890)
PHONE..................650 857-1501
Deidre Hoehn, *Brnch Mgr*
**EMP:** 17
**SALES (corp-wide):** 53.72B **Publicly Held**
Web: www.hp.com
**SIC: 3571** Personal computers (microcomputers)
PA: Hp Inc.
1501 Page Mill Rd
650 857-1501

### (P-10164)
### I/O MAGIC CORPORATION
4 Marconi, Irvine (92618-2525)
PHONE..................949 707-4800
Tony Shahbaz, *CEO*
Steve Gillings, *CFO*
**EMP:** 30 **EST:** 2000
**SALES (est):** 3.85MM **Privately Held**
Web: www.iomagic.com
**SIC: 3571** 3652 Computers, digital, analog or hybrid; Compact laser discs, prerecorded

### (P-10165)
### INDIGO AMERICA INC
1501 Page Mill Rd, Palo Alto (94304-1126)
PHONE..................650 857-1501
Catherine A Lesjak, *Brnch Mgr*
**EMP:** 86
**SALES (corp-wide):** 53.72B **Publicly Held**
**SIC: 3571** 7372 Personal computers (microcomputers); Prepackaged software
HQ: Indigo America Inc
165 Dascomb Rd Ste 1
Andover MA 01810

### (P-10166)
### INNERS TASKS LLC
Also Called: Remstek Corp
27708 Jefferson Ave Ste 201, Temecula (92590-2641)
PHONE..................951 225-9696
Jason Patrick, *Managing Member*
James Stewart, *Managing Member*
Ryan Wetmore, *Managing Member*
**EMP:** 38 **EST:** 2015
**SALES (est):** 2.48MM **Privately Held**
**SIC: 3571** Electronic computers

### (P-10167)
### INNOWI INC
Also Called: Deskless.ai
3240 Scott Blvd, Santa Clara (95054-3011)
PHONE..................408 609-9404
Zia Hasnain, *CEO*
Asis Reo, *Pr*
Saisel Seed, *CIO**
◆ **EMP:** 40 **EST:** 2014
**SALES (est):** 7.82MM **Privately Held**
Web: www.innowi.com
**SIC: 3571** Electronic computers

### (P-10168)
### INTERNATIONAL BUS MCHS CORP
IBM
600 Anton Blvd Ste 400, Costa Mesa (92626-7677)
PHONE..................714 472-2237
Jim Steele, *Genl Mgr*
**EMP:** 27
**SALES (corp-wide):** 61.86B **Publicly Held**
Web: www.ibm.com
**SIC: 3571** 5045 1731 Computers, digital, analog or hybrid; Computers, nec; Computer installation
PA: International Business Machines Corporation
1 New Orchard Rd
914 499-1900

### (P-10169)
### INTERNATIONAL BUS MCHS CORP
Also Called: IBM
400 N Brand Blvd Fl 7, Glendale (91203-2364)
PHONE..................818 553-8100
**EMP:** 700
**SALES (corp-wide):** 61.86B **Publicly Held**
Web: www.ibm.com
**SIC: 3571** Minicomputers
PA: International Business Machines Corporation
1 New Orchard Rd
914 499-1900

### (P-10170)
### ISTARUSA GROUP
727 Phillips, Rowland Heights (91748-1147)
PHONE..................888 989-1189
Kuo An Wang, *CEO*
**EMP:** 28 **EST:** 2020
**SALES (est):** 3.35MM **Privately Held**
Web: www.istarusa.com
**SIC: 3571** Electronic computers

### (P-10171)
### IXI TECHNOLOGY INC
Also Called: Ixi Technology
22705 Savi Ranch Pkwy Ste 200, Yorba Linda (92887-4604)
PHONE..................714 221-5000
Michael Carter, *CEO*
Thomas Bell, *
**EMP:** 40 **EST:** 1986
**SQ FT:** 40,000
**SALES (est):** 11.68MM **Privately Held**
**SIC: 3571** 3672 Electronic computers; Printed circuit boards

### (P-10172)
### KEY CODE MEDIA INC (PA)
270 S Flower St, Burbank (91502-2101)
PHONE..................818 303-3900
Michael Cavanagh, *CEO*
Ka Man Chan, *
**EMP:** 36 **EST:** 2001
**SQ FT:** 13,000
**SALES (est):** 48.61MM
**SALES (corp-wide):** 48.61MM **Privately Held**
Web: www.keycodemedia.com
**SIC: 3571** Computers, digital, analog or hybrid

### (P-10173)
### KONTRON AMERICA INCORPORATED (PA)
9477 Waples St Ste 150, San Diego (92121-2937)
PHONE..................800 822-7522
John Goode Junior, *Pr*
Ken Lowe, *CFO*
Thomas Sparrvik, *COO*
▲ **EMP:** 15 **EST:** 1999
**SQ FT:** 40,000
**SALES (est):** 8.94MM
**SALES (corp-wide):** 8.94MM **Privately Held**
Web: www.kontron.com
**SIC: 3571** 7373 Electronic computers; Computer integrated systems design

### (P-10174)
### LEADMAN ELECTRONICS USA INC (PA)
Also Called: APM Electronics USA
382 Laurelwood Rd, Santa Clara (95054-2311)
PHONE..................408 380-4567
Cherngi Dior Wu, *Pr*
◆ **EMP:** 49 **EST:** 1986
**SQ FT:** 12,000
**SALES (est):** 7.7MM
**SALES (corp-wide):** 7.7MM **Privately Held**
Web: www.leadman.com
**SIC: 3571** 5734 5045 Electronic computers; Computer and software stores; Computer peripheral equipment

### (P-10175)
### LENOVO (UNITED STATES) INC
602 Charcot Ave, San Jose (95131-2204)
PHONE..................510 813-3331
**EMP:** 93
Web: www.lenovo.com
**SIC: 3571** Electronic computers
HQ: Lenovo (United States) Inc.
8001 Development Dr
Morrisville NC 27560
855 253-6686

### (P-10176)
### MAGNELL ASSOCIATE INC
Also Called: Newegg.com
17708 Rowland St, City Of Industry (91748-1119)
PHONE..................626 271-1320
Fred Chang, *Pr*
**EMP:** 256
**SALES (corp-wide):** 2.38B **Publicly Held**
Web: www.absgamingpc.com
**SIC: 3571** 5961 5045 Personal computers (microcomputers); Computers and peripheral equipment, mail order; Computers, peripherals, and software
HQ: Magnell Associate, Inc.
21688 Gtwy Ctr Dr Ste 300
Diamond Bar CA 91765

### (P-10177)
### MATRI KART
448 W Market St, San Diego (92101-6703)
PHONE..................858 609-0933
**EMP:** 50 **EST:** 2020
**SALES (est):** 2.59MM **Privately Held**
**SIC: 3571** Electronic computers

### (P-10178)
### MEDIATEK USA INC (HQ)
Also Called: Mediatek
2840 Junction Ave, San Jose (95134-1922)
PHONE..................408 526-1899
Ming-kai Tsai, *Ch Bd*
Jyh-jer Cho, *Vice Chairman*
Ching-jiang Hsieh, *Pr*
Cheng-te Chuang, *Sr VP*
Jeffrey Ju, *Sr VP*
▲ **EMP:** 21 **EST:** 1997
**SALES (est):** 45.3MM **Privately Held**
**SIC: 3571** 3674 Electronic computers; Semiconductors and related devices
PA: Mediatek Inc.
No. 1, Dusing Rd. 1, Hsinchu Science Park,

### (P-10179)
### MEDIATEK USA INC
1 Ada Ste 200, Irvine (92618-5341)
PHONE..................408 526-1899
**EMP:** 154
Web: www.mediatek.com
**SIC: 3571** 3674 Electronic computers; Semiconductors and related devices
HQ: Mediatek Usa Inc.
2840 Junction Ave
San Jose CA 95134
408 526-1899

### (P-10180)
### MERCURY COMPUTER SYSTEM INC
1815 Aston Ave Ste 107, Carlsbad (92008-7340)
PHONE..................760 494-9600
Lance Turner, *CEO*
**EMP:** 35 **EST:** 2007
**SALES (est):** 2.85MM **Privately Held**
**SIC: 3571** Electronic computers

### (P-10181)
### MERCURY SYSTEMS INC
48025 Fremont Blvd, Fremont (94538-6541)
PHONE..................510 252-0870
**EMP:** 65
**SALES (corp-wide):** 835.27MM **Publicly Held**
Web: www.mrcy.com
**SIC: 3571** Electronic computers
PA: Mercury Systems, Inc.
50 Minuteman Rd
978 256-1300

### (P-10182)
### MERCURY SYSTEMS - TRUSTED MISSION SOLUTIONS INC
Also Called: Mercury Systems - Trsted Mssio
47200 Bayside Pkwy, Fremont (94538-6567)
PHONE..................510 252-0870
**EMP:** 65
Web: www.themis.com
**SIC: 3571** Electronic computers

### (P-10183)
### MICRO/SYS INC
158 W Pomona Ave, Monrovia (91016-4558)
PHONE..................818 244-4600
Susan Wooley, *Pr*
James K Finster, *
**EMP:** 30 **EST:** 1976
**SALES (est):** 4.33MM **Privately Held**
Web: www.embeddedsys.com
**SIC: 3571** 3674 Electronic computers; Semiconductors and related devices

### (P-10184)
### MITAC INFORMATION SYSTEMS CORP
Also Called: Blue Coat
44131 Nobel Dr, Fremont (94538-3173)
PHONE..................510 668-3507
Karen Soong, *CFO*
**EMP:** 24
Web: www.mitac.com
**SIC: 3571** Electronic computers
HQ: Mitac Information Systems Corp.
39889 Eureka Dr
Newark CA 94560

## 3571 - Electronic Computers (P-10206)

**(P-10185)**
**ORACLE AMERICA INC**
Also Called: Sun Microsystems
4220 Network Cir, Santa Clara
(95054-1780)
PHONE..................................408 276-4300
Mark Toliver, *Pr*
EMP: 25
SALES (corp-wide): 52.96B Publicly Held
Web: www.oracle.com
SIC: 3571 Minicomputers
HQ: Oracle America, Inc.
500 Oracle Pkwy
Redwood Shores CA 94065
650 506-7000

**(P-10186)**
**ORACLE AMERICA INC (HQ)**
Also Called: Sun Microsystems
500 Oracle Pkwy, Redwood Shores
(94065-1677)
PHONE..................................650 506-7000
Jeffrey O Henley, *Ch*
Safra A Catz, *
Dorian Daley, *
Cindy Reese, *
Steve Au Yeung, *
▲ EMP: 3500 EST: 1986
SALES (est): 2.72B
SALES (corp-wide): 52.96B Publicly Held
Web: www.oracle.com
SIC: 3571 7379 7373 7372 Minicomputers; Computer related consulting services; Systems integration services; Operating systems computer software
PA: Oracle Corporation
2300 Oracle Way
737 867-1000

**(P-10187)**
**ORACLE AMERICA INC**
Also Called: Sun Microsystems
1001 Sunset Blvd, Rocklin (95765-3702)
PHONE..................................303 272-6473
Mark Kulaga, *Brnch Mgr*
EMP: 15
SALES (corp-wide): 52.96B Publicly Held
Web: www.oracle.com
SIC: 3571 Minicomputers
HQ: Oracle America, Inc.
500 Oracle Pkwy
Redwood Shores CA 94065
650 506-7000

**(P-10188)**
**ORACLE AMERICA INC**
Also Called: Sun Microsystems
5815 Owens Dr, Pleasanton (94588-3939)
PHONE..................................925 694-3314
Terri Beck, *Mgr*
EMP: 19
SALES (corp-wide): 52.96B Publicly Held
Web: www.oracle.com
SIC: 3571 Minicomputers
HQ: Oracle America, Inc.
500 Oracle Pkwy
Redwood Shores CA 94065
650 506-7000

**(P-10189)**
**ORACLE AMERICA INC**
Also Called: Sun Microsystems
9540 Towne Centre Dr, San Diego
(92121-1988)
PHONE..................................858 625-5044
Steven Nathan, *Mgr*
EMP: 16
SALES (corp-wide): 52.96B Publicly Held
Web: www.oracle.com
SIC: 3571 Minicomputers

HQ: Oracle America, Inc.
500 Oracle Pkwy
Redwood Shores CA 94065
650 506-7000

**(P-10190)**
**ORACLE AMERICA INC**
Also Called: Sun Microsystems
4230 Leonard Stocking Dr, Santa Clara
(95054-1777)
PHONE..................................408 276-7534
Denise Shiffman, *VP Mktg*
EMP: 44
SALES (corp-wide): 52.96B Publicly Held
Web: www.oracle.com
SIC: 3571 Minicomputers
HQ: Oracle America, Inc.
500 Oracle Pkwy
Redwood Shores CA 94065
650 506-7000

**(P-10191)**
**OXIDE COMPUTER COMPANY**
1251 Park Ave, Emeryville (94608-3630)
PHONE..................................510 922-1392
Steven Tuck, *Pr*
EMP: 25 EST: 2019
SALES (est): 8.17MM Privately Held
Web: www.oxide.computer
SIC: 3571 5734 Electronic computers; Computer and software stores

**(P-10192)**
**PARALLAX INCORPORATED**
Also Called: Parallax Research
599 Menlo Dr Ste 100, Rocklin
(95765-3725)
PHONE..................................916 624-8333
Charles Gracey Iii, *Pr*
Charles Gracey Ii, *Treas*
▲ EMP: 33 EST: 1987
SQ FT: 11,000
SALES (est): 8.15MM Privately Held
Web: www.parallax.com
SIC: 3571 5045 3577 Minicomputers; Computers, peripherals, and software; Computer peripheral equipment, nec

**(P-10193)**
**PIRANHA EMS INC**
2681 Zanker Rd, San Jose (95134-2107)
PHONE..................................408 520-3963
Richard Walkup, *CEO*
Roger Malmrose, *
Richard Walkup, *Ex VP*
EMP: 45 EST: 2013
SALES (est): 7.73MM Privately Held
Web: www.piranhaems.com
SIC: 3571 Electronic computers

**(P-10194)**
**PLANTRONICS INC**
Ameriphone Products
12082 Western Ave, Garden Grove
(92841-2913)
PHONE..................................714 897-0808
George Cheung, *Brnch Mgr*
EMP: 56
SALES (corp-wide): 53.72B Publicly Held
Web: www.hp.com
SIC: 3571 Personal computers (microcomputers)
HQ: Plantronics, Inc.
100 Enterprise Way
Scotts Valley CA 95066
831 420-3002

**(P-10195)**
**POLYCOM INC**
4750 Willow Rd, Pleasanton (94588-2959)

PHONE..................................925 924-6151
Barbara Gstalder, *Brnch Mgr*
EMP: 39
SALES (corp-wide): 53.72B Publicly Held
Web: www.hp.com
SIC: 3571 Personal computers (microcomputers)
HQ: Polycom, Inc.
6001 America Center Dr
San Jose CA 95002

**(P-10196)**
**POLYCOM INC**
25212 S Schulte Rd, Tracy (95377-9703)
PHONE..................................209 830-5083
Wendy Wam, *Brnch Mgr*
EMP: 23
SALES (corp-wide): 53.72B Publicly Held
Web: www.hp.com
SIC: 3571 Personal computers (microcomputers)
HQ: Polycom, Inc.
6001 America Center Dr
San Jose CA 95002

**(P-10197)**
**PREMIO INC (PA)**
918 Radecki Ct, City Of Industry
(91748-1132)
PHONE..................................626 839-3100
Crystal Tsao, *CEO*
Tom Tsao, *
Ken Szeto, *
Eliza Leung, *
▲ EMP: 120 EST: 1989
SQ FT: 140,000
SALES (est): 41.5MM Privately Held
Web: www.premioinc.com
SIC: 3571 7373 7378 Personal computers (microcomputers); Computer integrated systems design; Computer maintenance and repair

**(P-10198)**
**PSIQUANTUM CORP (PA)**
700 Hansen Way, Palo Alto (94304-1016)
PHONE..................................650 427-0000
Jeremy O'brien, *CEO*
EMP: 19 EST: 2015
SALES (est): 25.08MM
SALES (corp-wide): 25.08MM Privately Held
Web: www.psiquantum.com
SIC: 3571 Electronic computers

**(P-10199)**
**QANTEL TECHNOLOGIES INC**
9812 Vasquez Cir, Loomis (95650-8535)
PHONE..................................510 731-2080
Michael Galvin, *Pr*
EMP: 21 EST: 1996
SALES (est): 2.43MM Privately Held
Web: www.qantel.com
SIC: 3571 7371 Electronic computers; Computer software development

**(P-10200)**
**RUGGED SYSTEMS INC**
Also Called: Core Systems
13000 Danielson St Ste Q, Poway
(92064-6827)
PHONE..................................858 391-1006
Chris O Brien, *CEO*
Chris Alan Schaffner, *
EMP: 156 EST: 2006
SQ FT: 63,000
SALES (est): 10.01MM Privately Held
Web: www.ruggedcomputersystems.com
SIC: 3571 7373 Electronic computers; Computer integrated systems design

**(P-10201)**
**SHASTA ELECTRONIC MFG SVCS INC**
Also Called: Shasta Ems
525 E Brokaw Rd, San Jose (95112-1004)
PHONE..................................408 436-1267
Vinh Nguyen, *Pr*
Rang Nguyen, *VP*
EMP: 17 EST: 2006
SQ FT: 11,000
SALES (est): 2.41MM Privately Held
Web: www.shastaems.com
SIC: 3571 Electronic computers

**(P-10202)**
**SIGMA MFG & LOGISTICS LLC**
851 Eagle Ridge Cir, Folsom (95630-6241)
PHONE..................................916 781-3052
EMP: 20 EST: 2002
SALES (est): 2.26MM Privately Held
Web: www.sigmamfg.com
SIC: 3571 Computers, digital, analog or hybrid

**(P-10203)**
**SILICON GRAPHICS INTL INC**
900 N Mccarthy Blvd, Milpitas
(95035-5128)
PHONE..................................669 900-8000
▲ EMP: 17
SALES (est): 2.38MM
SALES (corp-wide): 50.12B Publicly Held
SIC: 3571 3577 3674 Personal computers (microcomputers); Computer peripheral equipment, nec; Microprocessors
HQ: Silicon Graphics International Corp.
900 N Mccarthy Blvd
Milpitas CA 95035

**(P-10204)**
**SOLARFLARE COMMUNICATIONS INC (DH)**
7505 Irvine Center Dr Ste 100, Irvine
(92618-2991)
PHONE..................................949 581-6830
Russell Stern, *Pr*
Mary Jane Abalos, *
EMP: 97 EST: 2001
SQ FT: 22,097
SALES (est): 15.97MM
SALES (corp-wide): 22.68B Publicly Held
Web: www.xilinx.com
SIC: 3571 Electronic computers
HQ: Xilinx, Inc.
2100 Logic Dr
San Jose CA 95124
408 559-7778

**(P-10205)**
**SOURCE CODE LLC**
Also Called: Aberdeen
9808 Alburtis Ave, Santa Fe Springs
(90670-3208)
PHONE..................................562 903-1500
EMP: 48
Web: www.thinkmate.com
SIC: 3571 3572 Electronic computers; Computer storage devices
PA: Source Code, Llc
232 Vanderbilt Ave

**(P-10206)**
**SUPER MICRO COMPUTER INC (PA)**
Also Called: Supermicro
980 Rock Ave, San Jose (95131-1615)
PHONE..................................408 503-8000
Charles Liang, *Ch Bd*
David Weigand, *CCO*

## 3571 - Electronic Computers (P-10207)

Don Clegg, *Senior Vice President Worldwide Sales*
George Kao, *VP Opers*
Sara Liu, *
▲ **EMP:** 2291 **EST:** 1993
**SQ FT:** 2,273,000
**SALES (est):** 7.12B **Publicly Held**
**Web:** www.supermicro.com
**SIC:** 3571 3572 7372 Electronic computers; Computer storage devices; Prepackaged software

### (P-10207)
### SYNERGY MICROSYSTEMS INC
28965 Avenue Penn, Valencia (91355-4185)
**PHONE**.................................858 452-0020
Chris Wiltsey, *Dir*
**EMP:** 110 **EST:** 1985
**SALES (est):** 3.6MM
**SALES (corp-wide):** 2.85B **Publicly Held**
**Web:** www.curtisswright.com
**SIC:** 3571 Computers, digital, analog or hybrid
**HQ:** Curtiss-Wright Controls, Inc.
15801 Brixham Hill Ave # 200
Charlotte NC 28277
704 869-4600

### (P-10208)
### TALL TREE INSURANCE COMPANY
1501 Page Mill Rd, Palo Alto (94304-1126)
**PHONE**.................................650 857-1501
William Hewlet, *CEO*
**EMP:** 57 **EST:** 1939
**SALES (est):** 2.55MM
**SALES (corp-wide):** 53.72B **Publicly Held**
**SIC:** 3571 Electronic computers
**PA:** Hp Inc.
1501 Page Mill Rd
650 857-1501

### (P-10209)
### TARACOM CORPORATION
1735 N 1st St Ste 301a, San Jose (95112-4511)
**PHONE**.................................408 691-6655
Farhad Haghighi, *CEO*
**EMP:** 15 **EST:** 2006
**SALES (est):** 2.5MM **Privately Held**
**Web:** www.taracom.net
**SIC:** 3571 Electronic computers

### (P-10210)
### TD SYNNEX CORPORATION
6551 W Schulte Rd Ste 100, Tracy (95377-8130)
**PHONE**.................................510 656-3333
**EMP:** 17
**SALES (corp-wide):** 31.61B **Publicly Held**
**Web:** www.tdsynnex.com
**SIC:** 3571 Personal computers (microcomputers)
**PA:** Td Synnex Corporation
44201 Nobel Dr
510 656-3333

### (P-10211)
### TENSTORRENT USA INC
2600 Great America Way Ste 501, Santa Clara (95054)
**PHONE**.................................737 262-8464
**EMP:** 37 **EST:** 2017
**SALES (est):** 6.8MM **Privately Held**
**Web:** www.tenstorrent.com
**SIC:** 3571 Electronic computers

### (P-10212)
### TERADATA OPERATIONS INC (HQ)
17095 Via Del Campo, San Diego (92127-1711)
**PHONE**.................................937 242-4030
Steve Mcmillan, *Pr*
**EMP:** 100 **EST:** 2007
**SALES (est):** 363.12MM **Publicly Held**
**Web:** www.teradata.com
**SIC:** 3571 7379 Electronic computers; Computer related consulting services
**PA:** Teradata Corporation
17095 Via Del Campo

### (P-10213)
### TOSHIBA AMER INFO SYSTEMS INC
9740 Irvine Blvd Fl 1, Irvine (92618-1651)
**PHONE**.................................949 583-3000
Bill Goodwin, *Mgr*
**EMP:** 120
**Web:** www.toshiba.com
**SIC:** 3571 Electronic computers
**HQ:** Toshiba America Information Systems, Inc.
1251 Ave Of The Amrcas St
New York NY 10020
949 583-3000

### (P-10214)
### TRANSLATTICE INC (PA)
3398 Londonderry Dr, Santa Clara (95050-6619)
**PHONE**.................................408 749-8478
Frank Huerta, *CEO*
Michael Lyle, *Pr*
**EMP:** 15 **EST:** 2007
**SQ FT:** 4,197
**SALES (est):** 2.41MM
**SALES (corp-wide):** 2.41MM **Privately Held**
**Web:** www.translattice.com
**SIC:** 3571 Electronic computers

### (P-10215)
### UNITEK TECHNOLOGY INC
10211 Bellegrave Ave, Jurupa Valley (91752-1919)
**PHONE**.................................909 930-5700
Yubo Ho, *Pr*
**EMP:** 15 **EST:** 1990
**SQ FT:** 21,000
**SALES (est):** 2.32MM **Privately Held**
**Web:** www.unitektechnologyinc.com
**SIC:** 3571 5734 Electronic computers; Computer and software stores

### (P-10216)
### VECTOR DATA LLC
801 Addison St, Berkeley (94710-2053)
**PHONE**.................................408 933-3266
Timothy Naple, *Managing Member*
Bryan Foster, *Mgr*
**EMP:** 76 **EST:** 2006
**SALES (est):** 1.43MM **Privately Held**
**Web:** www.vectordata.com
**SIC:** 3571 Electronic computers

### (P-10217)
### VOICEBOARD CORPORATION
473 Post St, Camarillo (93010-8553)
**PHONE**.................................805 389-3100
Greg Peacock, *Pr*
**EMP:** 16 **EST:** 1989
**SQ FT:** 10,000
**SALES (est):** 954.13K **Privately Held**
**Web:** www.voiceboard.com

**SIC:** 3571 Electronic computers

### (P-10218)
### XMULTIPLE TECHNOLOGIES (PA)
Also Called: Xmultiple/Xrjax
1919 Williams St Ste 325, Simi Valley (93065-7848)
**PHONE**.................................805 579-1100
Alan Pocrass, *CEO*
Alan Pocrass, *Pr*
Drew Storberg, *VP*
▲ **EMP:** 22 **EST:** 1982
**SALES (est):** 7.37MM
**SALES (corp-wide):** 7.37MM **Privately Held**
**Web:** www.xmultiple.com
**SIC:** 3571 3663 3661 3577 Electronic computers; Multiplex equipment; Telephone and telegraph apparatus; Computer peripheral equipment, nec

---

## 3572 Computer Storage Devices

### (P-10219)
### ADD-ON CMPT PERIPHERALS LLC
Also Called: Addon Networks
15775 Gateway Cir, Tustin (92780-6470)
**PHONE**.................................949 546-8200
Matt Mccormick, *CEO*
Scott Krzywicki, *
Katie Patton Ctrl, *Prin*
▲ **EMP:** 73 **EST:** 1999
**SALES (est):** 19.59MM
**SALES (corp-wide):** 12.55B **Publicly Held**
**Web:** www.addonnetworks.com
**SIC:** 3572 3577 5045 Computer storage devices; Computer peripheral equipment, nec; Computers and accessories, personal and home entertainment
**PA:** Amphenol Corporation
358 Hall Ave
203 265-8900

### (P-10220)
### ADVANCED HPC INC
7879 Raytheon Rd, San Diego (92111-1604)
**PHONE**.................................858 716-8262
Toni Falcone, *CEO*
Toni Falcone, *Pr*
Jeff Tomlinson, *VP*
**EMP:** 18 **EST:** 2009
**SALES (est):** 4.68MM **Privately Held**
**Web:** www.advancedhpc.com
**SIC:** 3572 3571 Computer storage devices; Electronic computers

### (P-10221)
### AFERIN LLC
9808 Alburtis Ave, Santa Fe Springs (90670-3208)
**PHONE**.................................562 903-1500
▲ **EMP:** 48
**SIC:** 3572 3571 Computer storage devices; Electronic computers

### (P-10222)
### ALLSTAR MICROELECTRONICS INC
Also Called: Allstarshop.com
30191 Avenida De Las Bandera, Rancho Santa Margari (92688-2168)
**PHONE**.................................949 546-0888
Ming-chyi Chiang, *Pr*
**EMP:** 18 **EST:** 1995

**SQ FT:** 12,843
**SALES (est):** 3.63MM **Privately Held**
**Web:** www.allstarshop.com
**SIC:** 3572 Computer storage devices

### (P-10223)
### AMPEX DATA SYSTEMS CORPORATION (HQ)
26460 Corporate Ave, Hayward (94545-3914)
**PHONE**.................................650 367-2011
Gary Thom, *Pr*
▲ **EMP:** 58 **EST:** 1990
**SQ FT:** 15,661
**SALES (est):** 13.04MM
**SALES (corp-wide):** 41.45MM **Privately Held**
**Web:** www.ampex.com
**SIC:** 3572 Computer storage devices
**PA:** Delta Information Systems, Inc.
747 Dresher Rd Ste 125
215 657-5270

### (P-10224)
### APPLIED MICRO CIRCUITS CORP
Amcc
455 W Maude Ave, Sunnyvale (94085-3540)
**PHONE**.................................408 523-1000
Faye Pairman, *Brnch Mgr*
**EMP:** 20
**Web:** www.macom.com
**SIC:** 3572 8731 3613 3577 Computer auxiliary storage units; Computer (hardware) development; Switchgear and switchboard apparatus; Computer peripheral equipment, nec
**HQ:** Applied Micro Circuits Corp
4555 Great America Pkwy # 6
Santa Clara CA 95054
408 542-8600

### (P-10225)
### APPRO INTERNATIONAL INC (DH)
Also Called: Cray Cluster Solutions
220 Devcon Dr, San Jose (95112-4210)
**PHONE**.................................408 941-8100
Daniel Kim, *Pr*
James Yi, *
Giri Chukkapalli, *
▲ **EMP:** 75 **EST:** 1991
**SQ FT:** 40,000
**SALES (est):** 7.63MM
**SALES (corp-wide):** 29.14B **Publicly Held**
**Web:** www.hpe.com
**SIC:** 3572 3577 3571 Computer storage devices; Computer peripheral equipment, nec; Electronic computers
**HQ:** Cray Inc.
901 5th Ave Ste 1000
Seattle WA 98164
206 701-2000

### (P-10226)
### BLUEARC CORPORATION
50 Rio Robles, San Jose (95134-1806)
**PHONE**.................................408 576-6600
**EMP:** 271
**SIC:** 3572 Computer storage devices

### (P-10227)
### BNL TECHNOLOGIES INC
Also Called: Fantom Drives
22301 S Western Ave Ste 101, Torrance (90501-4155)
**PHONE**.................................310 320-7272
Hamid Khorsandi, *CEO*

## PRODUCTS & SERVICES SECTION
### 3572 - Computer Storage Devices (P-10248)

Farhad Fred Bokhoor, *
▲ **EMP:** 25 **EST:** 1998
**SALES (est):** 7.57MM **Privately Held**
Web: www.fantomdrives.com
**SIC: 3572** Computer storage devices

### (P-10228)
### CALDIGIT INC
1941 E Miraloma Ave Ste B, Placentia (92870-6770)
**PHONE**....................714 572-6668
Po Hung Chen, *CEO*
▲ **EMP:** 15 **EST:** 2006
**SALES (est):** 2.22MM **Privately Held**
Web: www.caldigit.com
**SIC: 3572** Disk drives, computer

### (P-10229)
### CAMEO TECHNOLOGIES INC
20511 Lake Forest Dr, Lake Forest (92630-7741)
**PHONE**....................949 672-7000
Matthew Massingel, *CEO*
**EMP:** 20 **EST:** 2012
**SALES (est):** 1.45MM
**SALES (corp-wide):** 13B **Publicly Held**
**SIC: 3572** Disk drives, computer
**HQ:** Western Digital Technologies, Inc.
5601 Great Oaks Pkwy
San Jose CA 95119

### (P-10230)
### CENTON ELECTRONICS INC (PA)
Also Called: Centon
27 Journey Ste 100, Aliso Viejo (92656-3320)
**PHONE**....................949 855-9111
Jennifer Miscione, *CEO*
Gene Miscione, *
Laura Miscione, *
Laura Wellman, *
Janet Miscione, *
◆ **EMP:** 60 **EST:** 1978
**SQ FT:** 20,000
**SALES (est):** 10.29MM
**SALES (corp-wide):** 10.29MM **Privately Held**
Web: www.centon.com
**SIC: 3572** 5734 7379 Computer storage devices; Computer software and accessories; Computer related consulting services

### (P-10231)
### CERTANCE LLC (HQ)
Also Called: Quantum Corporation
141 Innovation Dr, Irvine (92617-3211)
**PHONE**....................949 856-7800
Howard L Matthews, *Pr*
Donald L Waite, *
**EMP:** 300 **EST:** 2000
**SALES (est):** 8.54MM
**SALES (corp-wide):** 311.6MM **Publicly Held**
Web: www.quantum.com
**SIC: 3572** Computer tape drives and components
**PA:** Quantum Corporation
224 Airport Pkwy Ste 550
408 944-4000

### (P-10232)
### CHENBRO MICOM (USA) INC
2800 Jurupa St, Ontario (91761-2903)
**PHONE**....................909 937-0100
Mei Chi Chen, *Pr*
▲ **EMP:** 20 **EST:** 1983
**SALES (est):** 14.06MM **Privately Held**
Web: www.chenbro.com

**SIC: 3572** Computer storage devices
**PA:** Chenbro Micom Co., Ltd.
18f, No. 558, Zhongyuan Rd.

### (P-10233)
### COMPUCASE CORPORATION
Also Called: Orion Tech
16720 Chestnut St Ste C, City Of Industry (91748-1038)
**PHONE**....................626 336-6588
Doung Fu Hsu, *Pr*
Aaron Tao, *
Phillip Liu, *
▲ **EMP:** 1500 **EST:** 1995
**SQ FT:** 30,000
**SALES (est):** 7.83MM **Privately Held**
Web: www.hecgroupusa.com
**SIC: 3572** Computer storage devices
**PA:** Compucase Enterprise Co., Ltd.
No. 225, Lane 54, Sec. 2, An Ho Rd.

### (P-10234)
### EMC CORPORATION
No Physicla Address, Santa Clara (95054)
P.O. Box 45076 (94145-0076)
**PHONE**....................408 646-4406
**EMP:** 47
Web: www.emc.com
**SIC: 3572** Computer storage devices
**HQ:** Emc Corporation
176 S St
Hopkinton MA 01748
508 435-1000

### (P-10235)
### EMC CORPORATION
6801 Koll Center Pkwy, Pleasanton (94566-7076)
**PHONE**....................925 600-6800
Kelly Campos, *Brnch Mgr*
**EMP:** 119
Web: www.emc.com
**SIC: 3572** Computer storage devices
**HQ:** Emc Corporation
176 S St
Hopkinton MA 01748
508 435-1000

### (P-10236)
### EP HOLDINGS INC
Also Called: Ep Memory
30442 Esperanza, Rcho Sta Marg (92688-2144)
**PHONE**....................949 713-4600
Eric Krantz, *CEO*
**EMP:** 20 **EST:** 2005
**SALES (est):** 9.49MM **Privately Held**
Web: www.epholdingsinc.com
**SIC: 3572** Computer storage devices

### (P-10237)
### EYE-FI INC
967 N Shoreline Blvd, Mountain View (94043-1932)
**PHONE**....................650 969-3162
▲ **EMP:** 28
Web: www.eyefi.com
**SIC: 3572** 4813 Computer storage devices; Internet host services

### (P-10238)
### GIGAMEM LLC
9 Spectrum Pointe Dr, Lake Forest (92630-2242)
**PHONE**....................949 461-9999
Keller J Lee, *Managing Member*
▲ **EMP:** 15 **EST:** 1996
**SQ FT:** 9,500
**SALES (est):** 4.64MM
**SALES (corp-wide):** 4.64MM **Privately Held**

**SIC: 3572** Computer storage devices
**PA:** Memoryten, Inc.
2995 Mead Ave
408 516-4141

### (P-10239)
### GLOBAL SILICON ELECTRONICS INC
Also Called: Buslink Media
440 Cloverleaf Dr, Baldwin Park (91706-6500)
**PHONE**....................626 336-1888
James Djen, *CEO*
Jie Zhu, *
▲ **EMP:** 39 **EST:** 2004
**SQ FT:** 50,000
**SALES (est):** 2.19MM **Privately Held**
Web: www.buslink.com
**SIC: 3572** Computer storage devices

### (P-10240)
### H CO COMPUTER PRODUCTS (PA)
Also Called: Thinkcp Technologies
16812 Hale Ave, Irvine (92606-5021)
**PHONE**....................949 833-3222
Ali Hojreh, *CEO*
Mark Hojreh, *
Saed Hojreh, *
Mohammad Hojreh, *
◆ **EMP:** 25 **EST:** 1987
**SQ FT:** 15,600
**SALES (est):** 10MM **Privately Held**
Web: www.thinkcp.com
**SIC: 3572** 3577 Computer storage devices; Computer peripheral equipment, nec

### (P-10241)
### HEADWAY TECHNOLOGIES INC
682 S Hillview Dr, Milpitas (95035-5457)
**PHONE**....................408 934-5300
Mao-min Chen, *Pr*
Gary Pester, *
Thomas Surran, *
▲ **EMP:** 3139 **EST:** 1994
**SALES (est):** 487.39MM **Privately Held**
Web: www.headway.com
**SIC: 3572** Magnetic storage devices, computer
**PA:** Tdk Corporation
2-5-1, Nihombashi

### (P-10242)
### HGST INC (DH)
5601 Great Oaks Pkwy, San Jose (95119-1003)
**PHONE**....................408 717-6000
John Coyne, *CEO*
Stephen Milligan, *Pr*
Douglas A Gross, *COO*
Phillip Duncan, *CAO*
Craig Haught, *CIO*
▲ **EMP:** 195 **EST:** 2002
**SALES (est):** 193.15MM
**SALES (corp-wide):** 13B **Publicly Held**
Web: www.westerndigital.com
**SIC: 3572** Computer storage devices
**HQ:** Western Digital Technologies, Inc.
5601 Great Oaks Pkwy
San Jose CA 95119

### (P-10243)
### HIGHPOINT TECHNOLOGIES INC
41650 Christy St, Fremont (94538-3114)
**PHONE**....................408 942-5800
Michael Whang, *Pr*
Yuan-lang Chang, *CFO*
◆ **EMP:** 24 **EST:** 1995

**SQ FT:** 14,500
**SALES (est):** 5.58MM **Privately Held**
Web: www.highpoint-tech.com
**SIC: 3572** 8731 Computer disk and drum drives and components; Computer (hardware) development

### (P-10244)
### HITACHI VANTARA CORPORATION (DH)
2535 Augustine Dr, Santa Clara (95054-3003)
**PHONE**....................858 225-2095
Minoru Kosuge, *Ch Bd*
Jack Domme, *Pr*
Brian Householder, *Pr*
Randy Demont, *GLOBAL SLS*
Rex Carter, *CIO*
▲ **EMP:** 450 **EST:** 1979
**SQ FT:** 250,000
**SALES (est):** 1.77B **Privately Held**
Web: www.hitachivantara.com
**SIC: 3572** Computer storage devices
**HQ:** Hitachi Data Systems Holding Corporation
2535 Augustine Dr
Santa Clara CA 95054
408 970-1000

### (P-10245)
### I/OMAGIC CORPORATION (PA)
20512 Crescent Bay Dr, Lake Forest (92630-8847)
**PHONE**....................949 707-4800
Tony Shahbaz, *Ch Bd*
Tony Shahbaz, *Interim Chief Financial Officer*
Mary St George, *
▲ **EMP:** 30 **EST:** 1992
**SQ FT:** 52,000
**SALES (est):** 8.75MM **Privately Held**
Web: www.iomagic.com
**SIC: 3572** 3651 Computer storage devices; Home entertainment equipment, electronic, nec

### (P-10246)
### IN WIN DEVELOPMENT USA INC
188 Brea Canyon Rd, Walnut (91789-3086)
**PHONE**....................909 348-0588
Wen Hsien Lai, *
Wen Hsien Lai, *Pr*
Paul Hao, *Ex VP*
▲ **EMP:** 20 **EST:** 1989
**SQ FT:** 50,000
**SALES (est):** 4.59MM **Privately Held**
Web: www.in-win.com
**SIC: 3572** Computer tape drives and components
**PA:** In Win Development Inc.
57, Lane 350, Nan Shang Rd.,

### (P-10247)
### INTELLIGENT STORAGE SOLUTION
2073 Otoole Ave, San Jose (95131-1303)
**PHONE**....................408 428-0105
Dat D.o.s., *Pr*
Ian Wallace, *
▲ **EMP:** 18 **EST:** 2004
**SALES (est):** 800.63K **Privately Held**
Web: www.iss-phil.com
**SIC: 3572** Computer disk and drum drives and components

### (P-10248)
### IOSAFE INC
10600 Industrial Ave Ste 120, Roseville (95678-6209)
**PHONE**....................888 984-6723

## 3572 - Computer Storage Devices (P-10249)

Robb Moore, *CEO*
Andrea Moore, *Treas*
▲ **EMP:** 18 **EST:** 2005
**SQ FT:** 20,000
**SALES (est):** 1.83MM **Privately Held**
Web: www.iosafe.com
**SIC: 3572** Computer storage devices

### (P-10249)
### JTS CORPORATION
Also Called: Atari
166 Baypointe Pkwy, San Jose
(95134-1621)
**PHONE**..................................408 468-1800
David T Mitchell, *Pr*
Sirjang Lal Tandon, *
David T Mitchell, *Pr*
Steven L Kaczeus, *Chief Technical Officer*
**EMP:** 6000 **EST:** 1994
**SQ FT:** 52,000
**SALES (est):** 4.38MM **Privately Held**
**SIC: 3572** Disk drives, computer

### (P-10250)
### KINGSTON TECHNOLOGY COMPANY
17600 Newhope St, Fountain Valley
(92708-4298)
**PHONE**..................................310 729-3394
John Tu, *CEO*
**EMP:** 3000 **EST:** 1999
**SALES (est):** 3.31MM **Privately Held**
**SIC: 3572** Computer storage devices

### (P-10251)
### LGARDE INC
15181 Woodlawn Ave, Tustin (92780-6487)
**PHONE**..................................714 259-0771
Gayle D Bilyeu, *Ch Bd*
Constantine Cassapakis, *Pr*
Gordon Veal, *Sec*
Alan R Hirasuna, *Treas*
Mitch Thomas, *Bd of Dir*
**EMP:** 24 **EST:** 1971
**SQ FT:** 19,000
**SALES (est):** 6.49MM **Privately Held**
Web: www.lgarde.com
**SIC: 3572** 8731 2822 3769 Tape recorders for computers; Engineering laboratory, except testing; Acrylic rubbers, polyacrylate ; Space vehicle equipment, nec

### (P-10252)
### MAGIC TECHNOLOGIES INC
463 S Milpitas Blvd, Milpitas (95035-5438)
**PHONE**..................................408 263-1484
◆ **EMP:** 1917
**SIC: 3572** Computer storage devices

### (P-10253)
### MEMORY EXPERTS INTL USA INC (HQ)
2102 Business Center Dr, Irvine
(92612-1001)
**PHONE**..................................714 258-3000
Guadulupe Reusing, *Ch Bd*
Lawrence Reusing, *Pr*
Julian Reusing, *VP*
Gerard Reusing, *CEO*
Rino Lampasona, *VP*
▲ **EMP:** 22 **EST:** 1996
**SALES (est):** 21.65MM
**SALES (corp-wide):** 35.77MM **Privately Held**
Web: www.memoryexpertsinc.com
**SIC: 3572** 3577 Computer storage devices; Computer peripheral equipment, nec
**PA:** Les Experts En Memoire Internationale Inc
2321 Rue Cohen

514 333-5010

### (P-10254)
### MITAC INFORMATION SYSTEMS CORP (DH)
39889 Eureka Dr, Newark (94560-4811)
**PHONE**..................................510 284-3000
Charlotte Chou, *Pr*
Karen Soong, *
Matthew Miau, *
Billy Ho, *
◆ **EMP:** 103 **EST:** 2010
**SQ FT:** 240,000
**SALES (est):** 53.15MM **Privately Held**
Web: www.mitac.com
**SIC: 3572** Computer storage devices
**HQ:** Mitac International Corporation
No. 1, Yanfa 2nd Rd., Hsinchu Science Park,
Baoshan Township HSI 30800

### (P-10255)
### NETAPP INC (PA)
Also Called: Netapp
3060 Olsen Dr, San Jose (95128-2155)
**PHONE**..................................408 822-6000
George Kurian, *CEO*
T Michael Nevens, *
Cesar Cernuda, *Pr*
Michael J Berry, *Ex VP*
Harvinder S Bhela, *CPO*
▲ **EMP:** 1600 **EST:** 1992
**SQ FT:** 300,000
**SALES (est):** 6.36B **Publicly Held**
Web: www.netapp.com
**SIC: 3572** 7373 7372 Computer storage devices; Computer integrated systems design; Prepackaged software

### (P-10256)
### NEXSAN TECHNOLOGIES (US) LL
1287 Anvilwood Ave, Sunnyvale
(94089-2204)
P.O. Box 61687 (94088-1687)
**PHONE**..................................408 724-9809
Dan Shimmerman, *Managing Member*
**EMP:** 15
**SALES (est):** 1.28MM **Privately Held**
**SIC: 3572** Computer storage devices

### (P-10257)
### NEXSAN TECHNOLOGIES INC
Also Called: Nexsan
1289 Anvilwood Ave, Sunnyvale
(94089-2204)
▲ **EMP:** 149 **EST:** 2001
**SALES (est):** 13.15MM
**SALES (corp-wide):** 14.25MM **Privately Held**
Web: www.nexsan.com
**SIC: 3572** Computer storage devices
**PA:** Nexsan Corporation
1289 Anvilwood Ave
408 724-9809

### (P-10258)
### NGD SYSTEMS INC
3019 Wilshire Blvd, Santa Monica
(90403-2301)
**PHONE**..................................949 870-9148
Mohammad Nader Salessi, *CEO*
**EMP:** 30 **EST:** 2016
**SALES (est):** 5.75MM **Privately Held**
Web: www.ngdsystems.com
**SIC: 3572** Computer storage devices

### (P-10259)
### NIMBLE STORAGE INC
900 N Mccarthy Blvd, Milpitas
(95035-5132)
**PHONE**..................................408 432-9600
Suresh Vasudevan, *CEO*
Umesh Maheshwari, *
Varun Mehta, *CSO**
Anup Singh, *
Janet Matsuda, *CMO**
▲ **EMP:** 1300 **EST:** 2007
**SALES (est):** 30.13MM
**SALES (corp-wide):** 29.14B **Publicly Held**
Web: www.hpe.com
**SIC: 3572** Computer storage devices
**PA:** Hewlett Packard Enterprise Company
1701 E Mossy Oaks Rd
678 259-9860

### (P-10260)
### NWE TECHNOLOGY INC
1688 Richard Ave, Santa Clara
(95050-2844)
**PHONE**..................................408 919-6100
S C Huang, *Pr*
▲ **EMP:** 150 **EST:** 1998
**SQ FT:** 63,000
**SALES (est):** 5.09MM **Privately Held**
Web: www.nwetechnology.com
**SIC: 3572** Computer disk and drum drives and components

### (P-10261)
### ORYX ADVANCED MATERIALS INC (PA)
Also Called: Oryx
46458 Fremont Blvd, Fremont
(94538-6469)
**PHONE**..................................510 249-1157
Victor Tan, *CEO*
Kwei-san Teng, *VP*
Tan Geok San, *
Emily Tan, *
▲ **EMP:** 25 **EST:** 1976
**SQ FT:** 7,000
**SALES (est):** 7.33MM
**SALES (corp-wide):** 7.33MM **Privately Held**
Web: www.oryxadv.com
**SIC: 3572** Disk drives, computer

### (P-10262)
### OVERLAND STORAGE INC (HQ)
Also Called: Overland-Tandberg
2633 Camino Ramon Ste 325, San Ramon
(94583-9149)
**PHONE**..................................408 283-4700
Eric L Kelly, *Ch*
Peter Tassiopoulos, *Vice Chairman*
Kurt L Kalbfleisch, *CFO*
◆ **EMP:** 96 **EST:** 1980
**SALES (est):** 36.86MM
**SALES (corp-wide):** 36.86MM **Privately Held**
Web: www.overlandtandberg.com
**SIC: 3572** 7372 Computer storage devices; Prepackaged software
**PA:** Silicon Valley Technology Partners, Inc.
12645 Cambridge Dr
408 255-0580

### (P-10263)
### OVERLAND STORAGE INC
2633 Camino Ramon, San Ramon
(94583-9132)
**PHONE**..................................858 571-5555
**EMP:** 351
**SALES (corp-wide):** 36.86MM **Privately Held**
Web: www.overlandtandberg.com

**SIC: 3572** Computer storage devices
**HQ:** Overland Storage, Inc.
2633 Camino Ramon Ste 325
San Ramon CA 94583
408 283-4700

### (P-10264)
### PHILIPS LT-ON DGTAL SLTONS USA (DH)
Also Called: P L D S
720 S Hillview Dr, Milpitas (95035-5455)
**PHONE**..................................510 687-1800
Charlie Pseng, *Pr*
Armando Abella, *
Walker Su, *Corporate Secretary**
▼ **EMP:** 50 **EST:** 2006
**SQ FT:** 17,088
**SALES (est):** 16.38MM
**SALES (corp-wide):** 18.51B **Privately Held**
**SIC: 3572** Disk drives, computer
**HQ:** Philips & Lite-On Digital Solutions Corporation
16f, 392, Rueykuang Rd.,
Taipei City TAP 11406

### (P-10265)
### PILLAR DATA SYSTEMS INC
2840 Junction Ave, San Jose (95134-1922)
**PHONE**..................................408 503-4000
Michael L Workman, *CEO*
Adrian Jones, *Senior Vice President Worldwide Sales**
Warren Webster, *
Edward Hayes, *
Nancy Holleran, *
**EMP:** 409 **EST:** 1993
**SQ FT:** 80,000
**SALES (est):** 17.54MM
**SALES (corp-wide):** 52.96B **Publicly Held**
**SIC: 3572** Computer storage devices
**PA:** Oracle Corporation
2300 Oracle Way
737 867-1000

### (P-10266)
### POSTVISION INC
Also Called: Archion
2605 E Foothill Blvd Ste 103, Glendora
(91740-4003)
**PHONE**..................................818 840-0777
Reuben Lima, *CEO*
Mark Bianchi, *CEO*
Reuben Lima, *COO*
Daniel Stern, *Ex VP*
**EMP:** 17 **EST:** 1998
**SQ FT:** 6,000
**SALES (est):** 655.15K **Privately Held**
**SIC: 3572** Computer storage devices

### (P-10267)
### PSSC LABS
20432 N Sea Cir, Lake Forest
(92630-8806)
**PHONE**..................................949 380-7288
Janice Lesser, *Pr*
Larry Lesser, *VP*
▲ **EMP:** 15 **EST:** 1990
**SQ FT:** 2,500
**SALES (est):** 3.73MM **Privately Held**
Web: www.pssclabs.com
**SIC: 3572** 5734 Computer storage devices; Computer and software stores

### (P-10268)
### QUANTUM
220 S Glasgow Ave, Inglewood
(90301-2102)
**PHONE**..................................323 709-8880
**EMP:** 20 **EST:** 2018
**SALES (est):** 1.03MM **Privately Held**

# PRODUCTS & SERVICES SECTION
## 3572 - Computer Storage Devices (P-10288)

SIC: 3572 Computer storage devices

### (P-10269)
**QUANTUM CORPORATION (PA)**
Also Called: QUANTUM
224 Airport Pkwy Ste 550, San Jose (95110-1097)
PHONE..............................408 944-4000
James J Lerner, *Ch Bd*
Kenneth P Gianella, *CFO*
Brian E Cabrera, *Legal*
John Hurley, *CRO*
Lewis Moorehead, *CAO*
▲ **EMP:** 170 **EST:** 1980
**SALES (est):** 311.6MM
**SALES (corp-wide):** 311.6MM **Publicly Held**
Web: www.quantum.com
SIC: 3572 Computer storage devices

### (P-10270)
**QUANTUM CORPORATION**
141 Innovation Dr Ste 100, Irvine (92617-3212)
PHONE..............................949 856-7800
Lisa Ewbank, *Brnch Mgr*
**EMP:** 37
**SALES (corp-wide):** 311.6MM **Publicly Held**
Web: www.quantum.com
SIC: 3572 Computer storage devices
PA: Quantum Corporation
224 Airport Pkwy Ste 550
408 944-4000

### (P-10271)
**QUANTUMCAMP INC**
4010 Opal St, Oakland (94609-2616)
PHONE..............................650 933-5467
**EMP:** 16 **EST:** 2018
**SALES (est):** 483.4K **Privately Held**
Web: www.quantumcamp.com
SIC: 3572 Computer storage devices

### (P-10272)
**RADIAN MEMORY SYSTEMS INC**
5010 N Pkwy Ste 205, Calabasas (91302)
PHONE..............................818 222-4080
Michael Jadon, *CEO*
Brian Dexheimer, *Board Director**
Ted Samford, *Board Director**
**EMP:** 26 **EST:** 2011
**SALES (est):** 10MM **Privately Held**
Web: www.radianmemory.com
SIC: 3572 Computer storage devices

### (P-10273)
**SALE 121 CORP (PA)**
1467 68th Ave, Sacramento (95822-4728)
P.O. Box 190969 (11219-0969)
PHONE..............................888 233-7667
Mohammad Naz, *Prin*
**EMP:** 31 **EST:** 2014
**SQ FT:** 3,500
**SALES (est):** 2.39MM
**SALES (corp-wide):** 2.39MM **Privately Held**
SIC: 3572 8748 7373 Disk drives, computer; Systems engineering consultant, ex. computer or professional; Systems software development services

### (P-10274)
**SANDISK LLC (DH)**
Also Called: Western Digital
951 Sandisk Dr, Milpitas (95035-9801)
PHONE..............................408 801-1000
Sanjay Mehrotra, *Pr*
Michael Marks, *
Judy Bruner, *
Sumit Sadana, *Chief Strategy Officer**
Shuki Nir Senior, *Corporate Marketing Vice President*
▲ **EMP:** 141 **EST:** 1988
**SQ FT:** 589,000
**SALES (est):** 201.54MM
**SALES (corp-wide):** 13B **Publicly Held**
Web: www.westerndigital.com
SIC: 3572 Computer storage devices
HQ: Western Digital Technologies, Inc.
5601 Great Oaks Pkwy
San Jose CA 95119

### (P-10275)
**SCALE COMPUTING INC**
2121 S El Camino Real Ste 500, San Mateo (94403-1859)
PHONE..............................650 212-0132
Jeff Ready, *CEO*
**EMP:** 18
**SALES (corp-wide):** 22.8MM **Privately Held**
Web: www.scalecomputing.com
SIC: 3572 Computer storage devices
PA: Scale Computing, Inc.
525 S Meridian St Ste 3e
317 856-9959

### (P-10276)
**SCALITY INC**
149 New Montgomery St Fl 4, San Francisco (94105-3740)
PHONE..............................650 356-8500
Peter Brennan, *CEO*
Jerome Lecat, *
Giorgio Regni, *
Erwan Menard, *
Philippe Mechanick, *
**EMP:** 45 **EST:** 2010
**SALES (est):** 11.14MM
**SALES (corp-wide):** 27.89MM **Privately Held**
Web: www.scality.com
SIC: 3572 Computer storage devices
PA: Scality
11 Rue Tronchet
142948470

### (P-10277)
**SEAGATE SYSTEMS (US) INC (DH)**
Also Called: Xyratex
46831 Lakeview Blvd, Fremont (94538-6552)
PHONE..............................510 687-5200
Steve J Luczo, *Prin*
Ernest Sampias, *
Richard Pearce, *
Ahmed Shihab, *
Ed Prager, *
▲ **EMP:** 70 **EST:** 1986
**SALES (est):** 14.73MM **Privately Held**
Web: www.seagate.com
SIC: 3572 Disk drives, computer
HQ: Seagate Technology Llc
47488 Kato Rd
Fremont CA 94538
800 732-4283

### (P-10278)
**SEAGATE TECHNOLOGY LLC**
10200 S De Anza Blvd, Cupertino (95014-3029)
P.O. Box 30000 (94538-0017)
PHONE..............................405 324-4799
Alan Shugart, *Brnch Mgr*
**EMP:** 342
Web: www.seagate.com
SIC: 3572 Disk drives, computer
HQ: Seagate Technology Llc
47488 Kato Rd
Fremont CA 94538
800 732-4283

### (P-10279)
**SEAGATE TECHNOLOGY LLC (DH)**
Also Called: Seagate Technology
47488 Kato Rd, Fremont (94538-7319)
P.O. Box 4030 (95015-4030)
PHONE..............................800 732-4283
Dave Mosley, *CEO*
Gianluca Romano, *
B S Teh, *CCO**
Patricia Frost, *CRO**
▲ **EMP:** 3000 **EST:** 2000
**SQ FT:** 383,000
**SALES (est):** 1.45B **Privately Held**
Web: www.seagate.com
SIC: 3572 Computer storage devices
HQ: Seagate Technology (Us) Holdings, Inc.
10200 S De Anza Blvd
Cupertino CA 95014
831 438-6550

### (P-10280)
**SEAGATE TECHNOLOGY LLC**
Also Called: Seagate Systems
47488 Kato Rd, Fremont (94538-7319)
PHONE..............................510 624-3728
James Smith, *Mgr*
**EMP:** 333
Web: www.seagate.com
SIC: 3572 Computer storage devices
HQ: Seagate Technology Llc
47488 Kato Rd
Fremont CA 94538
800 732-4283

### (P-10281)
**SEAGATE US LLC**
10200 S De Anza Blvd, Cupertino (95014-3029)
PHONE..............................408 658-1000
Stephen J Luczo, *CEO*
**EMP:** 18 **EST:** 2000
**SALES (est):** 2.64MM **Privately Held**
Web: www.seagate.com
SIC: 3572 Magnetic storage devices, computer
HQ: Seagate Technology Unlimited Company
38/39 Fitzwilliam Square West
Dublin 2 D02NX

### (P-10282)
**SHAXON INDUSTRIES INC**
337 W Freedom Ave, Orange (92865)
PHONE..............................714 779-1140
Ahmet Erdogan, *CEO*
Yuksel Acik, *
Bahadir Tulunay, *
Bekir Aydinoglu, *
Christina Rodriguez, *
▲ **EMP:** 85 **EST:** 1978
**SALES (est):** 15.45MM **Privately Held**
Web: www.shaxon.com
SIC: 3572 5045 3678 3661 Computer storage devices; Computers and accessories, personal and home entertainment; Electronic connectors; Telephone and telegraph apparatus

### (P-10283)
**SHOP4TECHCOM**
Also Called: Leda Multimedia
13745 Seminole Dr, Chino (91710-5515)
PHONE..............................909 248-2725
Danny Wang, *Pr*
▲ **EMP:** 45 **EST:** 1999
**SQ FT:** 25,500
**SALES (est):** 1.28MM
**SALES (corp-wide):** 1.28MM **Privately Held**
Web: www.shop4tech.com
SIC: 3572 5731 Computer tape drives and components; Video recorders, players, disc players, and accessories
PA: Plc Multimedia, Inc.
398 Lemon Creek Dr Ste K
909 248-2680

### (P-10284)
**SILICON TECH INC**
Also Called: Silicontech
3009 Daimler St, Santa Ana (92705-5812)
PHONE..............................949 476-1130
Manouch Moshayedi, *CEO*
Mike Moshayedi, *
Mark Moshayedi, *
**EMP:** 555 **EST:** 1998
**SALES (est):** 1.89MM
**SALES (corp-wide):** 13B **Publicly Held**
SIC: 3572 Computer storage devices
HQ: Stec, Inc.
3355 Michelson Dr Ste 100
Irvine CA 92612

### (P-10285)
**SL3 TECHNOLOGIES LLC**
416 W San Ysidro Blvd Ste L-5, San Ysidro (92173-2443)
PHONE..............................619 365-4275
**EMP:** 15 **EST:** 2012
**SALES (est):** 1.08MM **Privately Held**
SIC: 3572 8711 1731 Computer tape drives and components; Engineering services; Computer installation

### (P-10286)
**SQUARE INTERNATIONAL SVCS INC**
1955 Broadway Ste 600, Oakland (94612-2205)
PHONE..............................415 375-3176
Chrysty Esperanza, *Pr*
**EMP:** 80
**SALES (est):** 3.79MM **Privately Held**
SIC: 3572 Computer storage devices

### (P-10287)
**STEC INC (HQ)**
3355 Michelson Dr Ste 100, Irvine (92612-5694)
PHONE..............................415 222-9996
Stephen D Milligan, *Pr*
▲ **EMP:** 340 **EST:** 1990
**SQ FT:** 73,100
**SALES (est):** 10.97MM
**SALES (corp-wide):** 13B **Publicly Held**
SIC: 3572 3674 3577 Computer storage devices; Semiconductors and related devices; Computer peripheral equipment, nec
PA: Western Digital Corporation
5601 Great Oaks Pkwy
408 717-6000

### (P-10288)
**SYPRIS DATA SYSTEMS INC (HQ)**
160 Via Verde, San Dimas (91773-3901)
PHONE..............................909 962-9400
Darrell Robertson, *Pr*
▲ **EMP:** 50 **EST:** 1957
**SQ FT:** 30,000
**SALES (est):** 263.39MM
**SALES (corp-wide):** 136.22MM **Publicly Held**

## 3572 - Computer Storage Devices (P-10289)

SIC: **3572** 3651 Computer tape drives and components; Tape recorders: cassette, cartridge or reel: household use
PA: Sypris Solutions, Inc.
   101 Bullitt Ln Ste 450
   502 329-2000

### (P-10289)
### TOSHIBA AMER ELCTRNIC CMPNNTS
2610 Orchard Pkwy, San Jose (95134-2020)
PHONE.................................408 526-2400
**EMP:** 323
Web: www.toshiba.com
SIC: **3572** Computer storage devices
HQ: Toshiba America Electronic Components Inc
   5231 California Ave
   Irvine CA 92617

### (P-10290)
### US CRITICAL LLC (PA)
Also Called: US Critical
6 Orchard Ste 150, Lake Forest (92630-8352)
PHONE.................................949 916-9326
Thomas Horton, *Dir*
John Lightman, *
Kurt Dunteman, *
Angela Lunt, *
**EMP:** 44 **EST:** 2013
**SQ FT:** 12,000
**SALES (est):** 7.87MM
**SALES (corp-wide):** 7.87MM **Privately Held**
Web: www.approvednetworks.com
SIC: **3572** Computer disk and drum drives and components

### (P-10291)
### US CRITICAL LLC
25422 Trabuco Rd # 320, Lake Forest (92630-2791)
PHONE.................................800 884-8945
Thomas Horton, *Dir*
**EMP:** 21
**SALES (corp-wide):** 7.87MM **Privately Held**
Web: www.approvednetworks.com
SIC: **3572** Computer disk and drum drives and components
PA: Us Critical Llc
   6 Orchard Ste 150
   949 916-9326

### (P-10292)
### VIGOBYTE TAPE CORPORATION
2498 Roll Dr Ste 916, San Diego (92154-7213)
PHONE.................................866 803-8446
▲ **EMP:** 700
SIC: **3572** Magnetic storage devices, computer

### (P-10293)
### VIOLIN MEMORY INC (PA)
4555 Great America Pkwy Ste 150, Santa Clara (95054-1243)
PHONE.................................650 396-1500
**EMP:** 129 **EST:** 2005
**SALES (est):** 10.99MM **Privately Held**
Web: www.violin-memory.com
SIC: **3572** 8731 Computer storage devices; Computer (hardware) development

### (P-10294)
### WD MEDIA LLC
1710 Automation Pkwy, San Jose (95131-1873)
PHONE.................................408 576-2000
Timothy D Harris, *CEO*
Kathleen A Bayless, *
Edward J Casey, *
Tsutomu T Yamashita, *
Peter S Norris, *Strategy Business Development*
▲ **EMP:** 426 **EST:** 1983
**SQ FT:** 188,000
**SALES (est):** 3.7MM
**SALES (corp-wide):** 13B **Publicly Held**
Web: www.westerndigital.com
SIC: **3572** Computer storage devices
PA: Western Digital Corporation
   5601 Great Oaks Pkwy
   408 717-6000

### (P-10295)
### WESTERN DIGITAL CORPORATION (PA)
Also Called: WESTERN DIGITAL
5601 Great Oaks Pkwy, San Jose (95119-1003)
PHONE.................................408 717-6000
David V Goeckeler, *CEO*
Matthew E Massengill, *Non-Executive Chairman of the Board*
Wissam G Jabre, *Ex VP*
Robert W Soderbery, *Ex VP*
▲ **EMP:** 1158 **EST:** 1970
**SQ FT:** 2,205,000
**SALES (est):** 13B
**SALES (corp-wide):** 13B **Publicly Held**
Web: www.westerndigital.com
SIC: **3572** Computer storage devices

### (P-10296)
### WESTERN DIGITAL CORPORATION
Also Called: Fremont Office
3337 Michelson Dr, Irvine (92612-1699)
PHONE.................................949 672-7000
**EMP:** 31
**SALES (corp-wide):** 13B **Publicly Held**
Web: www.westerndigital.com
SIC: **3572** Disk drives, computer
PA: Western Digital Corporation
   5601 Great Oaks Pkwy
   408 717-6000

### (P-10297)
### WESTERN DIGITAL TECH INC (HQ)
Also Called: WD
5601 Great Oaks Pkwy, San Jose (95119-1003)
PHONE.................................408 801-1000
David Goeckeler, *CEO*
John F Coyne, *
Steven Campbell, *
Jacqueline Demaria, *
Michael D Cordano, *
▲ **EMP:** 4300 **EST:** 1986
**SQ FT:** 257,000
**SALES (est):** 2.38B
**SALES (corp-wide):** 13B **Publicly Held**
Web: www.westerndigital.com
SIC: **3572** Disk drives, computer
PA: Western Digital Corporation
   5601 Great Oaks Pkwy
   408 717-6000

### (P-10298)
### WMN CORP
Also Called: Synapsense
340 Palladio Pkwy Ste 530, Folsom (95630-8833)
PHONE.................................916 294-0110
Bart Tichelman, *Pr*
**EMP:** 35 **EST:** 2006
**SALES (est):** 7.34MM
**SALES (corp-wide):** 13MM **Privately Held**
Web: www.vigilent.com
SIC: **3572** Computer storage devices
PA: Vigilent Corporation
   1111 Broadway Fl 3
   888 305-4451

### (P-10299)
### ZADARA STORAGE INC
6 Venture Ste 140, Irvine (92618-3742)
PHONE.................................949 251-0360
Nelson Nahum, *CEO*
Nir Ben Zvi, *
Yair Hershko, *
Vladimir Popovski, *
Doug Jury, *
▲ **EMP:** 82 **EST:** 2011
**SALES (est):** 8.77MM **Privately Held**
Web: www.zadara.com
SIC: **3572** Computer storage devices

### (P-10300)
### ZCO LIQUIDATING CORPORATION
Also Called: Ocz Enterprise
6373 San Ignacio Ave, San Jose (95119-1200)
PHONE.................................408 733-8400
◆ **EMP:** 597
SIC: **3572** Computer storage devices

---

## 3575 Computer Terminals

### (P-10301)
### ACCO BRANDS CORPORATION
Also Called: Kensington Computer Pdts Group
1350 Bayshore Hwy Ste 825, Burlingame (94010-1848)
PHONE.................................650 572-2700
**EMP:** 16
**SALES (corp-wide):** 1.83B **Publicly Held**
Web: www.accobrands.com
SIC: **3575** Keyboards, computer, office machine
PA: Acco Brands Corporation
   4 Corporate Dr
   847 541-9500

### (P-10302)
### ACCO BRANDS USA LLC
Kensington Computer Pdts Group
1350 Bayshore Hwy Ste 825, Burlingame (94010-1848)
PHONE.................................650 572-2700
Patty Coffee, *Brnch Mgr*
**EMP:** 100
**SALES (corp-wide):** 1.83B **Publicly Held**
Web: www.accobrands.com
SIC: **3575** Keyboards, computer, office machine
HQ: Acco Brands Usa Llc
   4 Corporate Dr
   Lake Zurich IL 60047
   800 222-6462

### (P-10303)
### AG NEOVO TECHNOLOGY CORP
48501 Warm Springs Blvd Ste 114, Fremont (94539-7750)
PHONE.................................408 321-8210
Phillip Chang, *Pr*
▲ **EMP:** 18 **EST:** 1999
**SALES (est):** 4.82MM **Privately Held**
Web: healthcare.agneovo.com
SIC: **3575** Computer terminals, monitors and components
PA: Associated Industries China, Inc.
   5f-1, No. 3-1, Park St.

### (P-10304)
### DIAMANTI INC (PA)
111 N Market St Ste 800, San Jose (95113-1102)
PHONE.................................408 645-5111
Tom Barton, *CEO*
Karthik Govindhasamy, *COO*
**EMP:** 38 **EST:** 2014
**SALES (est):** 5.39MM
**SALES (corp-wide):** 5.39MM **Privately Held**
Web: www.diamanti.com
SIC: **3575** Keyboards, computer, office machine

### (P-10305)
### GATEWAY MANUFACTURING LLC
7565 Irvine Center Dr, Irvine (92618-4918)
PHONE.................................949 471-7000
Gary Fan, *Prin*
**EMP:** 21 **EST:** 2002
**SALES (est):** 849.4K **Privately Held**
SIC: **3575** Computer terminals
HQ: Gateway, Inc.
   7565 Irvine Center Dr # 150
   Irvine CA 92618
   949 471-7000

### (P-10306)
### IMC NETWORKS CORP (PA)
25531 Commercentre Dr Ste 200, Lake Forest (92630-8873)
PHONE.................................949 465-3000
Jerry Roby, *Ch Bd*
Michael Dailey, *
▲ **EMP:** 40 **EST:** 1988
**SQ FT:** 35,000
**SALES (est):** 9.49MM
**SALES (corp-wide):** 9.49MM **Privately Held**
Web: www.opm25.com
SIC: **3575** 3577 Computer terminals, monitors and components; Computer peripheral equipment, nec

### (P-10307)
### JUPITER SYSTEMS INC
Also Called: Infocus Jupiter
31015 Huntwood Ave, Hayward (94544-7007)
PHONE.................................510 675-1000
Sidney Rittenberg Junior, *CEO*
Jack Klingelhofer, *
Robert Worthington, *
Bob Worthington, *
Daniel Lecour, *
◆ **EMP:** 42 **EST:** 1981
**SQ FT:** 33,000
**SALES (est):** 9.15MM **Privately Held**
Web: www.jupiter.com
SIC: **3575** Computer terminals
HQ: Infocus Corporation
   13190 Sw 68th Pkwy Ste 12
   Portland OR 97223
   503 207-4700

### (P-10308)
### MTA MOVING TECH IN AMER INC
Also Called: MTA
10065 Via De La Amistad Ste A1, San Diego (92154)
PHONE.................................619 651-7208
Edgar Vargas, *CEO*
Michelle Lynn Perez, *Pr*
James Stearrett, *CFO*
Alexandrina Perez, *Treas*
▼ **EMP:** 20 **EST:** 2004
**SQ FT:** 6,200
**SALES (est):** 124.11MM **Privately Held**

## PRODUCTS & SERVICES SECTION
### 3577 - Computer Peripheral Equipment, Nec (P-10327)

Web: www.mtaus.com
SIC: **3575** 5045 3571 7373  Computer terminals, monitors and components; Computer peripheral equipment; Electronic computers; Computer-aided engineering (CAE) systems service

**(P-10309)**
**OCP GROUP  INC**
7130 Engineer Rd, San Diego (92111-1422)
PHONE..................................858 279-7400
Neil Gleason, *Pr*
Tracy Sommer, *VP*
▲ **EMP:** 22 **EST:** 1989
**SALES (est):** 8.47MM **Privately Held**
Web: www.ocp.com
SIC: **3575** 5051 7549  Computer terminals, monitors and components; Cable, wire; Automotive maintenance services

**(P-10310)**
**SGB ENTERPRISES  INC**
24844 Anza Dr Ste A, Valencia (91355-1286)
PHONE..................................661 294-8306
Joseph Padula, *Pr*
Joseph Padula, *CEO*
Chuck Burkholder, *CFO*
**EMP:** 22 **EST:** 1991
**SQ FT:** 9,600
**SALES (est):** 9.02MM **Privately Held**
Web: www.sgbent.com
SIC: **3575** 5999 3728 3699  Cathode ray tube (CRT), computer terminal; Training materials, electronic; Aircraft training equipment; Flight simulators (training aids), electronic

**(P-10311)**
**SMK MANUFACTURING  INC**
Also Called: SMK
1055 Tierra Del Rey Ste F, Chula Vista (91910-7875)
PHONE..................................619 216-6400
Nobuyuki Suzuki, *CEO*
Naomasa Miyata, *VP*
Mathoru Hurukawa, *CFO*
▲ **EMP:** 50 **EST:** 1979
**SQ FT:** 14,688
**SALES (est):** 21.08MM **Privately Held**
Web: www.smkusa.com
SIC: **3575**  Keyboards, computer, office machine
HQ: Smk Electronics Corporation Usa
1055 Tierra Del Rey Ste H
Chula Vista CA 91910
619 216-6400

**(P-10312)**
**TRANSPARENT PRODUCTS  INC**
28064 Avenue Stanford Unit E, Valencia (91355-1160)
PHONE..................................661 294-9787
Fred Bonyadian, *Pr*
John Mcvay, *Pr*
▲ **EMP:** 50 **EST:** 1992
**SQ FT:** 18,000
**SALES (est):** 8.67MM **Privately Held**
Web: www.touchpage.com
SIC: **3575** 7371  Computer terminals, monitors and components; Computer software systems analysis and design, custom

---

### 3577 Computer Peripheral Equipment, Nec

**(P-10313)**
**3DCONNEXION INC**
6505 Kaiser Dr, Fremont (94555-3614)
PHONE..................................510 713-6000
Rory Dooley, *Pr*
James V Mccanna, *CFO*
Lew Epstein, *
Niraj Swarup, *
**EMP:** 75 **EST:** 2001
**SALES (est):** 2.19MM **Privately Held**
Web: www.3dconnexion.com
SIC: **3577** 5045  Computer peripheral equipment, nec; Computers and accessories, personal and home entertainment
HQ: Logitech Inc.
3930 N 1st St
San Jose CA 95134
510 795-8500

**(P-10314)**
**ACCES I/O PRODUCTS  INC**
10623 Roselle St, San Diego (92121-1506)
PHONE..................................858 550-9559
John Persidok, *Pr*
Marty Wingett, *Quality*
**EMP:** 17 **EST:** 1984
**SQ FT:** 9,447
**SALES (est):** 8.42MM **Privately Held**
Web: www.accesio.com
SIC: **3577**  Computer peripheral equipment, nec

**(P-10315)**
**ACER AMERICAN HOLDINGS CORP (DH)**
Also Called: Acer America
1730 N 1st St Ste 400, San Jose (95112-4642)
PHONE..................................408 533-7700
Emmanuel Fromont, *CEO*
J T Wang, *CEO*
**EMP:** 15 **EST:** 2007
**SALES (est):** 1.77B **Privately Held**
Web: www.acer.com
SIC: **3577** 3571  Computer peripheral equipment, nec; Electronic computers
HQ: Boardwalk Capital Holdings Limited
C/O: Harneys Corporate Services Limited
Road Town

**(P-10316)**
**ADD-ON CMPT PERIPHERALS INC**
15775 Gateway Cir, Tustin (92780-6470)
PHONE..................................949 546-8200
James Patton, *CEO*
Matthew Mccormick, *VP*
Brent Loomis, *
Thomas Virden, *
▲ **EMP:** 130 **EST:** 2000
**SQ FT:** 11,000
**SALES (est):** 12.17MM **Privately Held**
Web: www.addonnetworks.com
SIC: **3577** 5045  Computer peripheral equipment, nec; Computers, peripherals, and software

**(P-10317)**
**ALL AMERICAN PRINT SUPPLY CO**
17511 Valley View Ave, Cerritos (90703-7002)
PHONE..................................714 616-5834
**EMP:** 34 **EST:** 1986
**SALES (est):** 1.98MM **Privately Held**
Web: www.aaprintsupplyco.com
SIC: **3577** 5045  Printers, computer; Printers, computer

**(P-10318)**
**ALLIED TELESIS  INC**
468 S Abbott Ave, Milpitas (95035-5258)
PHONE..................................408 519-6700
Takayoshi Oshima, *Brnch Mgr*
**EMP:** 98
Web: www.alliedtelesis.com
SIC: **3577**  Computer peripheral equipment, nec
HQ: Allied Telesis, Inc.
10521 19th Ave Se Ste 200
Everett WA 98208
408 519-8700

**(P-10319)**
**ALLIED TELESIS  INC**
Also Called: Tokalabs
3041 Orchard Pkwy, San Jose (95134-2017)
PHONE..................................408 519-8700
Taki Oshima, *Mgr*
**EMP:** 20
Web: www.alliedtelesis.com
SIC: **3577**  Computer peripheral equipment, nec
HQ: Allied Telesis, Inc.
10521 19th Ave Se Ste 200
Everett WA 98208
408 519-8700

**(P-10320)**
**AMAG TECHNOLOGY  INC (DH)**
2205 W 126th St Ste B, Hawthorne (90250-3367)
PHONE..................................310 518-2380
Matt Barnette, *Ch Bd*
N Keith Whitelock, *
Robert A Sawyer Junior, *Pr*
Robert Causee, *
Gary Thorington-jones, *Treas*
▲ **EMP:** 48 **EST:** 1971
**SALES (est):** 24.89MM
**SALES (corp-wide):** 2.67MM **Privately Held**
Web: www.amag.com
SIC: **3577**  Decoders, computer peripheral equipment
HQ: G4s Technology Limited
New Challenge House
Tewkesbury GLOS GL20

**(P-10321)**
**APEM  INC (HQ)**
970 Park Center Dr, Vista (92081-8301)
PHONE..................................978 372-1602
Peter Brouilette, *CEO*
Laurel Pittera, *
Marc Enjalbert, *
◆ **EMP:** 30 **EST:** 2008
**SALES (est):** 38MM **Privately Held**
Web: www.apem.com
SIC: **3577** 3679  Computer peripheral equipment, nec; Electronic switches
PA: Idec Corporation
2-6-64, Nishimiyahara, Yodogawa-Ku

**(P-10322)**
**APPLIED SYSTEMS ENGRG INC**
2105 S Bascom Ave Ste 155, Campbell (95008-3276)
PHONE..................................408 364-0500
Prasanth Gopalakrishnan, *CEO*
**EMP:** 16 **EST:** 1982
**SALES (est):** 2.28MM **Privately Held**

Web: www.ase-systems.com
SIC: **3577** 7371 7379 3663  Computer peripheral equipment, nec; Computer software development; Computer related consulting services; Mobile communication equipment

**(P-10323)**
**APRICORN LLC**
12191 Kirkham Rd, Poway (92064-6870)
PHONE..................................858 513-2000
Paul Brown, *Pr*
Michael Gordon, *
▲ **EMP:** 29 **EST:** 1983
**SQ FT:** 21,000
**SALES (est):** 7.09MM **Privately Held**
Web: www.apricorn.com
SIC: **3577** 5734  Computer peripheral equipment, nec; Computer and software stores

**(P-10324)**
**ARIES RESEARCH  INC**
Also Called: Aries Solutions
46750 Fremont Blvd Ste 107, Fremont (94538-6573)
P.O. Box 1112 (94507-7112)
PHONE..................................925 818-1078
Lawrence T Kou, *CEO*
Ilain Kou, *Pr*
**EMP:** 32 **EST:** 1989
**SQ FT:** 8,600
**SALES (est):** 788.27K **Privately Held**
SIC: **3577** 3571  Computer peripheral equipment, nec; Electronic computers

**(P-10325)**
**ARISTA NETWORKS INC (PA)**
Also Called: ARISTA
5453 Great America Pkwy, Santa Clara (95054-3645)
PHONE..................................408 547-5500
**EMP:** 100 **EST:** 2011
**SALES (est):** 5.86B **Publicly Held**
Web: www.arista.com
SIC: **3577** 4813 7372  Computer peripheral equipment, nec; Online service providers; Prepackaged software

**(P-10326)**
**ARUBA NETWORKS  INC**
1322 Crossman Ave, Sunnyvale (94089-1113)
PHONE..................................408 227-4500
Amol Kelkar, *Brnch Mgr*
**EMP:** 622
**SALES (corp-wide):** 29.14B **Publicly Held**
Web: www.hpe.com
SIC: **3577**  Computer peripheral equipment, nec
HQ: Aruba Networks, Inc.
6280 America Center Dr
San Jose CA 95002
408 941-4300

**(P-10327)**
**ARUBA NETWORKS  INC (HQ)**
Also Called: Aruba Networks Cafe
6280 America Center Dr, San Jose (95002-2563)
P.O. Box 2000 (95002-2000)
PHONE..................................408 941-4300
Keerti Melkote, *Pr*
Jon Faust, *
Partha Narasimhan, *
Vishal Lall, *
**EMP:** 270 **EST:** 2002
**SALES (est):** 479.38MM
**SALES (corp-wide):** 29.14B **Publicly Held**
Web: www.hpe.com

# 3577 - Computer Peripheral Equipment, Nec (P-10328)

SIC: 3577 3663 7371 Computer peripheral equipment, nec; Mobile communication equipment; Computer software development
PA: Hewlett Packard Enterprise Company
1701 E Mossy Oaks Rd
678 259-9860

### (P-10328)
### ARUBA NETWORKS INC
634 E Caribbean Dr, Sunnyvale (94089-1108)
PHONE.................408 227-4500
EMP: 622
SALES (corp-wide): 29.14B **Publicly Held**
Web: www.hpe.com
SIC: 3577 Computer peripheral equipment, nec
HQ: Aruba Networks, Inc.
6280 America Center Dr
San Jose CA 95002
408 941-4300

### (P-10329)
### ASANTE TECHNOLOGIES INC (PA)
2223 Oakland Rd, San Jose (95131-1402)
PHONE.................408 435-8388
Jeff Yuan-kai Lin, *Pr*
Phil Berkowitz, *VP Sls*
David Kichar, *Ex VP*
EMP: 29 EST: 1988
SQ FT: 7,000
SALES (est): 2.35MM
SALES (corp-wide): 2.35MM **Privately Held**
Web: www.asante.com
SIC: 3577 Computer peripheral equipment, nec

### (P-10330)
### ATELIERE CRTIVE TECH HLDG CORP
315 S Beverly Dr Ste 315, Beverly Hills (90212-4309)
PHONE.................855 466-9696
Dan Goman, *CEO*
Rick Capstraw, *CRO*
EMP: 24 EST: 2017
SALES (est): 3.68MM **Privately Held**
SIC: 3577 Data conversion equipment, media-to-media: computer

### (P-10331)
### BAR CODE SPECIALTIES INC
Also Called: Quest Solution
12272 Monarch St, Garden Grove (92841-2907)
PHONE.................877 411-2633
EMP: 30
Web: www.barcodespecialties.com
SIC: 3577 5045 Bar code (magnetic ink) printers; Computer peripheral equipment

### (P-10332)
### BDR INDUSTRIES INC
Also Called: Rnd Enterprises
9700 Owensmouth Ave Lbby, Chatsworth (91311-8073)
PHONE.................818 341-2112
Scott Riddle, *Brnch Mgr*
EMP: 20
SALES (corp-wide): 24.38MM **Privately Held**
Web: www.rndcable.com
SIC: 3577 Computer peripheral equipment, nec
PA: B.D.R. Industries, Inc.
820 E Avenue L12
661 940-8554

### (P-10333)
### BELKIN INTERNATIONAL INC (DH)
Also Called: Belkin Components
555 S Aviation Blvd Ste 180, El Segundo (90245-4852)
PHONE.................310 751-5100
Steven Malony, *CEO*
Chester Pipkin, *
Jasjit Jay Singh, *
◆ EMP: 450 EST: 1983
SQ FT: 218,000
SALES (est): 473.4MM **Privately Held**
Web: www.belkin.com
SIC: 3577 5045 5065 Computer peripheral equipment, nec; Computers and accessories, personal and home entertainment; Intercommunication equipment, electronic
HQ: Foxconn Interconnect Technology Limited
C/O Conyers Trust Company (Cayman) Limited
George Town GR CAYMAN KY1-1

### (P-10334)
### BEST DATA PRODUCTS INC
Also Called: Diamond Multimedia
7801 Alabama Ave, Canoga Park (91304-4903)
PHONE.................818 534-1414
Behrouz Zamanzadeh, *CEO*
Bruce Zaman, *
Shirley Zaman, *
▲ EMP: 85 EST: 1983
SALES (est): 9.88MM **Privately Held**
Web: www.diamondmm.com
SIC: 3577 Computer peripheral equipment, nec

### (P-10335)
### BESTEK MANUFACTURING INC
675 Sycamore Dr # 170, Milpitas (95035-7469)
PHONE.................408 321-8834
Frank Dang, *Pr*
EMP: 40 EST: 1994
SQ FT: 8,000
SALES (est): 11.54MM **Privately Held**
Web: www.bestekmfg.com
SIC: 3577 3679 3672 Computer peripheral equipment, nec; Harness assemblies, for electronic use: wire or cable; Printed circuit boards

### (P-10336)
### BIXOLON AMERICA INC
2575 W 237th St, Torrance (90505-5216)
PHONE.................858 764-4580
Chan Young Hwang, *CEO*
Yon H Son, *Pr*
◆ EMP: 23 EST: 2005
SALES (est): 5.19MM **Privately Held**
Web: www.bixolonusa.com
SIC: 3577 Printers, computer
PA: Bixolon Co., Ltd
344 Pangyo-Ro, Bundang-Gu

### (P-10337)
### BLACK DIAMOND VIDEO INC
503 Canal Blvd, Richmond (94804-3517)
PHONE.................510 439-4500
Peter Metcalf, *CEO*
▲ EMP: 90 EST: 2004
SQ FT: 30,000
SALES (est): 8.98MM **Privately Held**
SIC: 3577 3679 Computer peripheral equipment, nec; Electronic switches
HQ: Steris Corporation
5960 Heisley Rd
Mentor OH 44060
440 354-2600

### (P-10338)
### BLUE CEDAR NETWORKS INC
325 Pacific Ave Fl 1, San Francisco (94111-1711)
PHONE.................415 329-0401
John Aisien, *CEO*
Chris Ford, *Chief Product Officer*
Jeanne Angelo-pardo, *CFO*
EMP: 36 EST: 2016
SQ FT: 8,000
SALES (est): 2.99MM **Privately Held**
Web: www.bluecedar.com
SIC: 3577 Computer peripheral equipment, nec

### (P-10339)
### BROCADE CMMNCTIONS SYSTEMS LLC (DH)
3421 Hillview Ave, Palo Alto (94304-1320)
PHONE.................408 333-8000
Hock E Tan, *Pr*
Thomas H Krause Junior, *CFO*
Jean Samuel Furter, *
EMP: 800 EST: 1995
SQ FT: 562,000
SALES (est): 221.03MM
SALES (corp-wide): 35.82B **Publicly Held**
Web: www.broadcom.com
SIC: 3577 4813 Computer peripheral equipment, nec; Proprietary online service networks
HQ: Lsi Corporation
1320 Ridder Park Dr
San Jose CA 95131
408 433-8000

### (P-10340)
### CALIFORNIA DIGITAL INC (PA)
6 Saddleback Rd, Rolling Hills (90274-5141)
P.O. Box 3399 (90510-3399)
PHONE.................310 217-0500
Terry Reiter, *Pr*
Wade Wood, *
Floyd Pothoven, *
EMP: 67 EST: 1973
SQ FT: 30,000
SALES (est): 2.54MM
SALES (corp-wide): 2.54MM **Privately Held**
Web: www.florod.com
SIC: 3577 3571 3699 Computer peripheral equipment, nec; Mainframe computers; Electrical equipment and supplies, nec

### (P-10341)
### CARBON INC (PA)
Also Called: Carbon3d
1089 Mills Way, Redwood City (94063-3119)
PHONE.................650 285-6307
Ellen J Kullman, *Pr*
Joseph M Desimone, *Ofcr*
Elisa De Martel, *CFO*
EMP: 102 EST: 2013
SQ FT: 87,000
SALES (est): 59.2MM
SALES (corp-wide): 59.2MM **Privately Held**
Web: www.carbon3d.com
SIC: 3577 3841 Computer peripheral equipment, nec; Surgical and medical instruments

### (P-10342)
### CIPHERTEX LLC
Also Called: Ciphertex Data Security
9301 Jordan Ave Ste 105a, Chatsworth (91311-5863)
PHONE.................818 773-8989
Jerry Kaner, *CEO*
▲ EMP: 18 EST: 2009
SALES (est): 2.08MM **Privately Held**
Web: www.ciphertex.com
SIC: 3577 3572 Computer peripheral equipment, nec; Computer storage devices

### (P-10343)
### CISCO SYSTEMS INC
Also Called: Cisco Systems
755 Sycamore Dr, Milpitas (95035-7411)
PHONE.................408 526-6200
John Chambers, *Mgr*
EMP: 53
SALES (corp-wide): 53.8B **Publicly Held**
Web: www.cisco.com
SIC: 3577 Computer peripheral equipment, nec
PA: Cisco Systems, Inc.
170 W Tasman Dr
408 526-4000

### (P-10344)
### CISCO SYSTEMS INC
3675 Cisco Way, San Jose (95134-2204)
PHONE.................408 216-3440
EMP: 29
SALES (corp-wide): 53.8B **Publicly Held**
Web: www.cisco.com
SIC: 3577 Data conversion equipment, media-to-media: computer
PA: Cisco Systems, Inc.
170 W Tasman Dr
408 526-4000

### (P-10345)
### CISCO SYSTEMS INC (PA)
Also Called: Cisco Systems
170 W Tasman Dr, San Jose (95134-1706)
PHONE.................408 526-4000
Charles H Robbins, *Ch Bd*
R Scott Herren, *Ex VP*
Deborah L Stahlkopf, *CLO*
Jeetu Patel, *CPO*
EMP: 3534 EST: 1984
SALES (est): 53.8B
SALES (corp-wide): 53.8B **Publicly Held**
Web: www.cisco.com
SIC: 3577 7379 Data conversion equipment, media-to-media: computer; Online services technology consultants

### (P-10346)
### CISCO SYSTEMS INC
Also Called: Cisco Systems
4464 Willow Rd Ste 102, Pleasanton (94588-8593)
PHONE.................925 225-2111
Rick Degabrielle, *Brnch Mgr*
EMP: 40
SALES (corp-wide): 53.8B **Publicly Held**
Web: www.cisco.com
SIC: 3577 Data conversion equipment, media-to-media: computer
PA: Cisco Systems, Inc.
170 W Tasman Dr
408 526-4000

### (P-10347)
### CISCO SYSTEMS INC
Also Called: Cisco Systems
85 2nd St Ste 710, San Francisco (94105-3465)
PHONE.................415 845-8008
David Mcmullin, *CFO*
EMP: 24
SALES (corp-wide): 53.8B **Publicly Held**

Web: www.cisco.com
SIC: 3577 Data conversion equipment, media-to-media: computer
PA: Cisco Systems, Inc.
170 W Tasman Dr
408 526-4000

**(P-10348)**
**CMS PRODUCTS LLC**
29620 Skyline Dr, Tehachapi (93561-8571)
PHONE.................................714 424-5520
Les Kristof, *Pr*
EMP: 40 EST: 2015
SALES (est): 3.58MM **Privately Held**
Web: www.cmsproducts.com
SIC: 3577 Decoders, computer peripheral equipment

**(P-10349)**
**COMEXPOSIUM US LLC**
5455 Wilshire Blvd Ste 1150, Los Angeles (90036-4201)
PHONE.................................310 598-1376
Stephen Corrick, *Prin*
EMP: 15 EST: 2017
SALES (est): 514.35K **Privately Held**
Web: www.comexposium.com
SIC: 3577 Computer peripheral equipment, nec

**(P-10350)**
**CONGATEC INC**
6262 Ferris Sq, San Diego (92121-3205)
PHONE.................................858 457-2600
Ronald F Mazza, *Pr*
EMP: 33 EST: 2008
SALES (est): 4.45MM
SALES (corp-wide): 355.83K **Privately Held**
Web: www.congatec.com
SIC: 3577 Computer peripheral equipment, nec
HQ: Congatec Gmbh
Auwiesenstr. 5
Deggendorf BY 94469
991 270-0100

**(P-10351)**
**CORSAIR COMPONENTS INC**
47100 Bayside Pkwy, Fremont (94538-6563)
PHONE.................................510 657-8747
EMP: 1000
Web: www.corsair.com
SIC: 3577 Computer peripheral equipment, nec

**(P-10352)**
**CORSAIR GAMING INC (HQ)**
Also Called: CORSAIR
115 N Mccarthy Blvd, Milpitas (95035-5102)
PHONE.................................510 657-8747
Andrew J Paul, *CEO*
Thi L La, *Pr*
Michael G Potter, *CFO*
EMP: 20 EST: 1994
SQ FT: 118,000
SALES (est): 1.46B **Publicly Held**
Web: www.corsair.com
SIC: 3577 5045 5734 Computer peripheral equipment, nec; Computer peripheral equipment; Computer peripheral equipment
PA: Corsair Group (Cayman) Lp
C/O Maples Corporate Services Limited

**(P-10353)**
**CPACKET NETWORKS INC**
Also Called: Cwr Labs
480 N Mccarthy Blvd Ste 100, Milpitas (95035-5129)
P.O. Box 430 (95002)
PHONE.................................650 969-9500
Brendan O'flaherty, *CEO*
EMP: 22 EST: 2002
SALES (est): 11.18MM **Privately Held**
Web: www.cpacket.com
SIC: 3577 Computer peripheral equipment, nec

**(P-10354)**
**CS SYSTEMS INC**
Also Called: Cs Electronics
16781 Noyes Ave, Irvine (92606-5123)
PHONE.................................949 475-9100
Christian Schwartz, *Pr*
Gayle Schwartz, *
▲ EMP: 25 EST: 1982
SQ FT: 33,200
SALES (est): 4.97MM **Privately Held**
Web: www.cs-electronics.com
SIC: 3577 3677 Computer peripheral equipment, nec; Coil windings, electronic

**(P-10355)**
**CYBERDATA CORPORATION**
3 Justin Ct, Monterey (93940-5733)
PHONE.................................831 373-2601
Phil Lembo, *Pr*
◆ EMP: 33 EST: 1974
SQ FT: 30,000
SALES (est): 5.4MM **Privately Held**
Web: www.cyberdata.net
SIC: 3577 7379 Computer peripheral equipment, nec; Computer related consulting services

**(P-10356)**
**DELKIN DEVICES INC (PA)**
Also Called: Delkin Devices
13350 Kirkham Way, Poway (92064-7117)
PHONE.................................858 391-1234
◆ EMP: 100 EST: 1986
SALES (est): 13.42MM
SALES (corp-wide): 13.42MM **Privately Held**
Web: www.delkin.com
SIC: 3577 5734 3861 Computer peripheral equipment, nec; Computer and software stores; Photographic equipment and supplies

**(P-10357)**
**DELPHI DISPLAY SYSTEMS INC**
3550 Hyland Ave, Costa Mesa (92626-1438)
PHONE.................................714 825-3400
Ken Neeld, *CEO*
David Skinner, *VP Sls*
Doug Gordon, *Contrlr*
Michael Deson, *CEO*
▲ EMP: 55 EST: 1997
SQ FT: 10,000
SALES (est): 8.27MM
SALES (corp-wide): 3.87B **Publicly Held**
Web: www.delphidisplay.com
SIC: 3577 Computer peripheral equipment, nec
PA: Toast, Inc.
333 Summer St
617 297-1005

**(P-10358)**
**DOCUMENT CAPTURE TECHNOLOGIES INC**
41332 Christy St, Fremont (94538-3115)
PHONE.................................408 436-9888
▲ EMP: 28
Web: www.docketport.com
SIC: 3577 Optical scanning devices

**(P-10359)**
**EFAXCOM (DH)**
Also Called: Jetfax
6922 Hollywood Blvd Fl 5, Los Angeles (90028-6125)
PHONE.................................323 817-3207
Ronald Brown, *Pr*
John H Harris, *INT'L Operations*
Gary P Kapner, *Vice President North America*
EMP: 80 EST: 1988
SALES (est): 21.9MM
SALES (corp-wide): 1.36B **Publicly Held**
Web: www.ziffdavis.com
SIC: 3577 Computer peripheral equipment, nec
HQ: J2 Cloud Services, Llc
700 S Flower St Fl 15
Los Angeles CA 90017

**(P-10360)**
**EFAXCOM**
Also Called: J2 Global Communications
5385 Hollister Ave Ste 208, Santa Barbara (93111-2389)
PHONE.................................805 692-0064
Stephen Zendjahas, *Mgr*
EMP: 41
SALES (corp-wide): 1.36B **Publicly Held**
Web: www.ziffdavis.com
SIC: 3577 Computer peripheral equipment, nec
HQ: Efax.Com
6922 Hollywood Blvd Fl 5
Los Angeles CA 90028
323 817-3207

**(P-10361)**
**ELISITY INC**
6203 San Ignacio Ave Ste 110, San Jose (95119-1371)
PHONE.................................408 839-3971
James Winebrenner, *CEO*
Matthew Krieg, *VP Sls*
EMP: 15 EST: 2018
SALES (est): 7.56MM **Privately Held**
Web: www.elisity.com
SIC: 3577 Computer output to microfilm units

**(P-10362)**
**ELITEGROUP CMPT SYSTEMS INC**
6851 Mowry Ave, Newark (94560-4925)
PHONE.................................510 226-7333
Ray Lin, *CEO*
See See Lo, *
Lena Ruan, *
◆ EMP: 200 EST: 1990
SQ FT: 60,000
SALES (est): 7.98MM **Privately Held**
Web: www.ecsusa.com
SIC: 3577 Computer peripheral equipment, nec
HQ: Ecs Holding (America) Co.
6600 Sands Point Dr # 288
Houston TX

**(P-10363)**
**EMULEX CORPORATION (DH)**
5300 California Ave, Irvine (92617-3038)
▲ EMP: 124 EST: 1979
SQ FT: 180,000
SALES (est): 31.01MM
SALES (corp-wide): 35.82B **Publicly Held**
Web: www.broadcom.com
SIC: 3577 3661 Input/output equipment, computer; Telephone and telegraph apparatus
HQ: Avago Technologies Wireless (U.S.A.) Manufacturing Llc
4380 Ziegler Rd
Fort Collins CO 80525

**(P-10364)**
**ENCRYPTED ACCESS CORPORATION**
1730 Redhill Ave, Irvine (92697-0001)
PHONE.................................714 371-4125
Hirihisa Matsunaga, *Brnch Mgr*
EMP: 110
SIC: 3577 Punch card equipment: readers, tabulators, sorters, etc.
PA: Encrypted Access Corporation
600 Anton Blvd Fl 11

**(P-10365)**
**EPSON AMERICA INC (DH)**
Also Called: Seiko Epson
3131 Katella Ave, Los Alamitos (90720-2335)
P.O. Box 93012 (90809-3012)
PHONE.................................800 463-7766
John Lang, *Pr*
John D Lang, *
Genevieve Walker, *
◆ EMP: 510 EST: 1975
SQ FT: 163,000
SALES (est): 359.49MM **Privately Held**
Web: www.epson.com
SIC: 3577 Computer peripheral equipment, nec
HQ: U.S. Epson, Inc.
3131 Katella Ave
Los Alamitos CA 90720

**(P-10366)**
**EXCE LP**
Also Called: C Enterprises, Inc.
16868 Via Del Campo Ct Ste 200, San Diego (92127-1771)
PHONE.................................858 549-6340
Brian Tauber, *Pr*
Steven Yamasaki, *COO*
EMP: 64 EST: 1984
SALES (est): 9.81MM
SALES (corp-wide): 72.17MM **Publicly Held**
Web: www.rfindustries.com
SIC: 3577 5045 3357 3229 Computer peripheral equipment, nec; Computers and accessories, personal and home entertainment; Nonferrous wiredrawing and insulating; Pressed and blown glass, nec
PA: Rf Industries, Ltd.
16868 Via Del Cmpo Ct Ste
858 549-6340

**(P-10367)**
**FINIS LLC**
3347 Michelson Dr Ste 100, Irvine (92612)
P.O. Box 17192 (92623)
PHONE.................................949 250-4929
EMP: 80 EST: 2015
SALES (est): 11.75MM
SALES (corp-wide): 32.46MM **Privately Held**
Web: www.incipio.com
SIC: 3577 Computer peripheral equipment, nec
PA: Incipio Technologies, Inc.
190 Nwport Ctr Dr Ste 150
888 893-1638

**(P-10368)**
**FIRETIDE INC (DH)**
Also Called: Firetide
2105 S Bascom Ave Ste 220, Campbell (95008-3292)

## 3577 - Computer Peripheral Equipment, Nec (P-10369)

PHONE.................................408 399-7771
Corry S Hong, Pr
▲ EMP: 34 EST: 2001
SQ FT: 30,000
SALES (est): 3.68MM
SALES (corp-wide): 579.13MM Privately Held
Web: www.firetide.com
SIC: 3577 3825 4899 Computer peripheral equipment, nec; Network analyzers; Communication signal enhancement network services
HQ: Unicom Systems Inc.
   15535 San Frnndo Mssion B
   Mission Hills CA 91345
   818 838-0606

### (P-10369)
### FORESEESON CUSTOM DISPLAYS INC (PA)
2210 E Winston Rd, Anaheim (92806-5536)
PHONE.................................714 300-0540
Insik Kang, Pr
▲ EMP: 20 EST: 2000
SQ FT: 8,000
SALES (est): 4.22MM
SALES (corp-wide): 4.22MM Privately Held
Web: www.foreseesonusa.com
SIC: 3577 Computer peripheral equipment, nec

### (P-10370)
### FOUNDRY NETWORKS INC
1745 Technology Dr, San Jose (95110-3728)
PHONE.................................408 207-1700
▲ EMP: 981
Web: www.healthcarefuture.com
SIC: 3577 Computer peripheral equipment, nec

### (P-10371)
### FUJIFILM DIMATIX INC (DH)
2250 Martin Ave, Santa Clara (95050-2704)
PHONE.................................408 565-9150
Steve Billow, Pr
Kenji Sukeno, *
◆ EMP: 84 EST: 1996
SQ FT: 125,000
SALES (est): 123.23MM Privately Held
Web: www.fujifilm.com
SIC: 3577 Printers, computer
HQ: Fujifilm Corporation
   9-7-3, Akasaka
   Minato-Ku TKY 107-0

### (P-10372)
### FUJITSU MANAGEMENT SERVICES OF AMERICA INC
Also Called: Fujitsu Software
1250 E Arques Ave, Sunnyvale (94085-5401)
PHONE.................................408 746-6000
◆ EMP: 115
SIC: 3577 8721 Computer peripheral equipment, nec; Accounting, auditing, and bookkeeping

### (P-10373)
### GDCA INC
1799 Portola Ave Ste 1, Livermore (94551-7947)
PHONE.................................925 456-9900
Ethan Plotkin, CEO
Corinne Weber, *
Arlin Niernberger, *
Kip Kingsland, *
Kaye Porter, *
EMP: 38 EST: 1993
SQ FT: 6,000
SALES (est): 7.48MM Privately Held
Web: www.gdca.com
SIC: 3577 3571 Computer peripheral equipment, nec; Electronic computers

### (P-10374)
### GIGAMON INC (HQ)
3300 Olcott St, Santa Clara (95054-3005)
PHONE.................................408 831-4000
Paul Hooper, CEO
Shane Buckley, Pr
Christel Ventura, CPO
▲ EMP: 88 EST: 2009
SQ FT: 105,600
SALES (est): 310.86MM Privately Held
Web: www.gigamon.com
SIC: 3577 7372 Computer peripheral equipment, nec; Prepackaged software
PA: Elliott Management Corporation
   40 W 57th St

### (P-10375)
### HANAPS ENTERPRISES
Also Called: Digital Storm
8100 Camino Arroyo, Gilroy (95020)
PHONE.................................669 235-3810
Paramjit Chana, CEO
Surnderjit Chana, *
Navjitpal Chana, *
Harjitpal Chana, *
▲ EMP: 70 EST: 2003
SALES (est): 9.28MM Privately Held
Web: www.digitalstorm.com
SIC: 3577 7379 Computer peripheral equipment, nec; Computer related maintenance services

### (P-10376)
### HP IT SERVICES INCORPORATED
1506 W Flower Ave, Fullerton (92833-3952)
PHONE.................................714 844-7737
Brian White, CEO
EMP: 25 EST: 2019
SALES (est): 250K Privately Held
Web: www.raditservices.com
SIC: 3577 7372 7382 Computer peripheral equipment, nec; Operating systems computer software; Confinement surveillance systems maintenance and monitoring

### (P-10377)
### IDENTIV INC (PA)
Also Called: IDENTIV
2201 Walnut Ave Ste 100, Fremont (94538-2334)
PHONE.................................949 250-8888
Steven Humphreys, CEO
James E Ousley, Ch Bd
Justin Scarpulla, CFO
EMP: 62 EST: 1990
SQ FT: 3,082
SALES (est): 116.38MM Publicly Held
Web: www.identiv.com
SIC: 3577 7372 Computer peripheral equipment, nec; Prepackaged software

### (P-10378)
### INCAL TECHNOLOGY INC
46420 Fremont Blvd, Fremont (94538-6469)
PHONE.................................510 657-8405
Cary Caywood, CEO
Bruce Simikowski, *
John Pioorda, *
EMP: 25 EST: 1988
SQ FT: 7,500
SALES (est): 8.57MM Privately Held
Web: www.incal.com
SIC: 3577 Computer peripheral equipment, nec

### (P-10379)
### INCIPIO TECHNOLOGIES INC (PA)
Also Called: Incipio Group
190 Newport Ctr Dr Ste 150, Irvine (92612)
P.O. Box 17192 (92623-7192)
PHONE.................................888 893-1638
Brian Stech, CEO
Stephen Finney, *
◆ EMP: 26 EST: 2000
SALES (est): 32.46MM
SALES (corp-wide): 32.46MM Privately Held
Web: www.incipio.com
SIC: 3577 Computer peripheral equipment, nec

### (P-10380)
### INDUSTRIAL ELCTRNIC ENGNERS IN
Also Called: Iee
13170 Telfair Ave, Sylmar (91342-3573)
PHONE.................................818 787-0311
Thomas Whinfrey, Pr
Thomas Whinfrey, Pr
Donald G Gumpertz, Ch
Alan R Wolen, Sec
▲ EMP: 100 EST: 1947
SALES (est): 22.12MM Privately Held
Web: www.ieeinc.com
SIC: 3577 3575 Graphic displays, except graphic terminals; Keyboards, computer, office machine

### (P-10381)
### INFINEON TECH AMERICAS CORP
Interntnal Rctfier/Hexget Amer
41915 Business Park Dr, Temecula (92590-3637)
PHONE.................................951 375-6008
Marc Rougee, Brnch Mgr
EMP: 710
SALES (corp-wide): 17.72B Privately Held
Web: www-blue.infineon.com
SIC: 3577 3674 Computer peripheral equipment, nec; Semiconductor circuit networks
HQ: Infineon Technologies Americas Corp.
   101 N Pacific Coast Hwy
   El Segundo CA 90245
   310 726-8200

### (P-10382)
### INFINETA SYSTEMS INC
1100 La Avenida St Ste A, Mountain View (94043-1453)
PHONE.................................408 514-6650
Raj Kinaya, Pr
Ainslie Mayberry, CFO
Larry Lang, Prin
EMP: 21 EST: 2008
SQ FT: 15,000
SALES (est): 413.24K Privately Held
Web: www.riverbed.com
SIC: 3577 Computer peripheral equipment, nec

### (P-10383)
### INNOVATIVE TECH & ENGRG INC
Also Called: Innov8v
2691 Richter Ave Ste 124, Irvine (92606-5124)
PHONE.................................949 955-2501
Hassan Siddiqi, Pr
EMP: 23 EST: 1997
SQ FT: 2,200
SALES (est): 728.92K Privately Held
Web: www.innov8v.com
SIC: 3577 5961 1731 5999 Computer peripheral equipment, nec; Computers and peripheral equipment, mail order; Safety and security specialization; Audio-visual equipment and supplies

### (P-10384)
### INPUT/OUTPUT TECHNOLOGY INC
28415 Industry Dr Ste 520, Valencia (91355-4161)
PHONE.................................661 257-1000
Ted Drapala, Pr
EMP: 20 EST: 1977
SALES (est): 2.32MM Privately Held
Web: www.iotechnology.com
SIC: 3577 3823 Input/output equipment, computer; Process control instruments

### (P-10385)
### INTEL CORP PRFIT SHRING RTRMEN
2200 Mission College Blvd, Santa Clara (95054-1549)
PHONE.................................408 765-8080
Andy D Bryant, Ch
EMP: 20 EST: 2014
SALES (est): 2.33MM
SALES (corp-wide): 54.23B Publicly Held
Web: www.intel.com
SIC: 3577 Computer peripheral equipment, nec
PA: Intel Corporation
   2200 Mission College Blvd
   408 765-8080

### (P-10386)
### INTEL CORPORATION
Also Called: Intel
2300 Mission College Blvd, Santa Clara (95054-1531)
PHONE.................................408 425-8398
Ziya Ma, Mgr
EMP: 200
SALES (corp-wide): 54.23B Publicly Held
Web: www.intel.com
SIC: 3577 Computer peripheral equipment, nec
PA: Intel Corporation
   2200 Mission College Blvd
   408 765-8080

### (P-10387)
### INTEL CORPORATION
Also Called: Intel
101 Innovation Dr Bldg 1, San Jose (95134-1941)
PHONE.................................408 544-7000
Dan Mcnamara, Brnch Mgr
EMP: 3000
SALES (corp-wide): 54.23B Publicly Held
Web: www.intel.com
SIC: 3577 Computer peripheral equipment, nec
PA: Intel Corporation
   2200 Mission College Blvd
   408 765-8080

### (P-10388)
### INTEL SERVICES LLC (HQ)
2200 Mission College Blvd Sc4-203, Santa Clara (95054-1549)
PHONE.................................408 765-8080
EMP: 19 EST: 1968
SALES (est): 1.28MM

## PRODUCTS & SERVICES SECTION
### 3577 - Computer Peripheral Equipment, Nec (P-10409)

SALES (corp-wide): 54.23B **Publicly Held**
Web: www.intel.com
SIC: **3577** Computer peripheral equipment, nec
PA: Intel Corporation
2200 Mission College Blvd
408 765-8080

**(P-10389)**
**INTEL TECHNOLOGIES INC (HQ)**
Also Called: Intel
2200 Mission College Blvd, Santa Clara (95054-1549)
PHONE.................................408 765-8080
Roger Whittier, *Prin*
**EMP: 17 EST:** 1991
**SALES (est):** 5.17MM
SALES (corp-wide): 54.23B **Publicly Held**
Web: www.intel.com
SIC: **3577** Computer peripheral equipment, nec
PA: Intel Corporation
2200 Mission College Blvd
408 765-8080

**(P-10390)**
**INTERNET MACHINES CORPORATION (PA)**
30501 Agoura Rd Ste 203, Agoura Hills (91301-4389)
PHONE.................................818 575-2100
Christopher Hoogenboom, *CEO*
Christopher Hoogenboom, *Pr*
Frank Knuettel Ii, *CFO*
Chris Haywood, *VP Engg*
Aloke Gupta, *VP Mktg*
**EMP: 70 EST:** 1999
**SQ FT:** 18,500
**SALES (est):** 1.17MM
SALES (corp-wide): 1.17MM **Privately Held**
Web: www.internetmachines.com
SIC: **3577** Computer peripheral equipment, nec

**(P-10391)**
**ITUNER NETWORKS CORPORATION**
44244 Fremont Blvd, Fremont (94538-6000)
PHONE.................................510 573-0783
Andrei Bulucea, *Pr*
Raluca Neacsu, *VP*
▲ **EMP: 15 EST:** 1999
**SALES (est):** 3.33MM **Privately Held**
Web: www.mini-box.com
SIC: **3577** 5961 5045 Computer peripheral equipment, nec; Computers and peripheral equipment, mail order; Computer peripheral equipment

**(P-10392)**
**JUNIPER NETWORKS INC (PA)**
Also Called: JUNIPER NETWORKS
1133 Innovation Way, Sunnyvale (94089-1228)
PHONE.................................408 745-2000
Rami Rahim, *CEO*
Scott Kriens, *
Manoj Leelanivas, *Ex VP*
Kenneth B Miller, *Ex VP*
Christopher Kaddaras, *Ex VP*
**EMP: 868 EST:** 1996
**SALES (est):** 5.56B **Publicly Held**
Web: www.juniper.net
SIC: **3577** 7372 Computer peripheral equipment, nec; Prepackaged software

**(P-10393)**
**KINGSTON DIGITAL INC (DH)**
17600 Newhope St, Fountain Valley (92708-4220)
PHONE.................................714 435-2600
John Tu, *Pr*
David Sun, *Prin*
▲ **EMP: 21 EST:** 2007
**SALES (est):** 4.18MM **Privately Held**
Web: www.kingston.com
SIC: **3577** Computer peripheral equipment, nec
HQ: Kingston Technology Company, Inc.
17600 Newhope St
Fountain Valley CA 92708
714 435-2600

**(P-10394)**
**KINGSTON TECHNOLOGY CORP (PA)**
17600 Newhope St, Fountain Valley (92708-4298)
PHONE.................................714 435-2600
John Tu, *CEO*
David Sun, *
▲ **EMP: 500 EST:** 1987
**SALES (est):** 1.08B **Privately Held**
Web: www.kingston.com
SIC: **3577** Computer peripheral equipment, nec

**(P-10395)**
**LASERGRAPHICS INC**
Also Called: Lasergraphics General Business
20 Ada, Irvine (92618-2303)
PHONE.................................949 753-8282
Mihai Demetrescu Ph.d., *Pr*
Stefan Demetrescu Ph.d., *Senior Vice President Research & Development*
Stefan Demetrescu, *Senior Vice President Research & Development*
David Boyd, *
▲ **EMP: 40 EST:** 1981
**SQ FT:** 20,000
**SALES (est):** 4.68MM **Privately Held**
Web: www.lasergraphics.com
SIC: **3577** 7371 3823 Graphic displays, except graphic terminals; Custom computer programming services; Process control instruments

**(P-10396)**
**LITE-ON TECHNOLOGY INTL INC (HQ)**
720 S Hillview Dr, Milpitas (95035-5455)
PHONE.................................408 945-0222
Kung Soong, *Prin*
Daisy Young, *
▲ **EMP: 38 EST:** 1994
**SALES (est):** 9.11MM **Privately Held**
Web: us.liteon.com
SIC: **3577** 3572 Computer peripheral equipment, nec; Computer storage devices
PA: Lite-On Technology Corporation
No. 392, Ruiguang Rd.,

**(P-10397)**
**LIVESCRIBE INC**
930 Roosevelt, Irvine (92620-3664)
▲ **EMP: 50**
Web: www.livescribe.com
SIC: **3577** 3951 Computer peripheral equipment, nec; Pens and mechanical pencils

**(P-10398)**
**LOGICUBE INC (PA)**
Also Called: Logicube
19755 Nordhoff Pl, Chatsworth (91311-6606)
PHONE.................................888 494-8832
Farid Emrani, *Pr*
Jack M Schuster, *Ch Bd*
Jeffrey Schuster, *CFO*
▲ **EMP: 20 EST:** 1993
**SALES (est):** 2.71MM **Privately Held**
Web: www.logicube.com
SIC: **3577** Computer peripheral equipment, nec

**(P-10399)**
**LOGITECH INC**
3 Jenner Ste 180, Irvine (92618-3835)
PHONE.................................510 795-8500
Darrell Bracken, *Brnch Mgr*
**EMP: 839**
Web: www.logitech.com
SIC: **3577** Computer peripheral equipment, nec
HQ: Logitech Inc.
3930 N 1st St
San Jose CA 95134
510 795-8500

**(P-10400)**
**LOGITECH INC**
2053 E Jay St, Ontario (91764-1847)
PHONE.................................972 947-7100
**EMP: 301**
Web: www.logitech.com
SIC: **3577** Computer peripheral equipment, nec
HQ: Logitech Inc.
3930 N 1st St
San Jose CA 95134
510 795-8500

**(P-10401)**
**LOGITECH INC (HQ)**
3930 N 1st St, San Jose (95134-1501)
PHONE.................................510 795-8500
Bracken P Darrell, *Pr*
Chuck Boynton, *
◆ **EMP: 276 EST:** 1982
**SALES (est):** 415.52MM **Privately Held**
Web: www.logitech.com
SIC: **3577** Input/output equipment, computer
PA: Logitech International S.A.
Route De Pampigny 20

**(P-10402)**
**LYNN PRODUCTS INC**
Also Called: Pureformance Cables
2645 W 237th St, Torrance (90505-5269)
PHONE.................................310 530-5966
Hsinyu Lin, *Pr*
Eric Tseng, *
Chen Huei Tseng, *
Chun Mei Shei, *Treas*
▲ **EMP: 1000 EST:** 1982
**SQ FT:** 35,000
**SALES (est):** 23.35MM **Privately Held**
Web: www.lynnprod.com
SIC: **3577** 3357 Computer peripheral equipment, nec; Fiber optic cable (insulated)

**(P-10403)**
**MAD CATZ INC**
Also Called: Mad Catz
10680 Treena St Ste 500, San Diego (92131-2447)
PHONE.................................858 790-5008
▲ **EMP: 250**
SIC: **3577** 5734 Computer peripheral equipment, nec; Software, computer games

**(P-10404)**
**MAGIC RAM INC**
3540 Wilshire Blvd Ste 716, Los Angeles (90010-3934)
PHONE.................................213 380-5555
Eddie Mirarooni, *Ch Bd*
Alan Nouray, *VP*
Meheran Michael Navidbakhsh, *CFO*
**EMP: 16 EST:** 1988
**SQ FT:** 65,000
**SALES (est):** 7MM **Privately Held**
Web: www.magicram.com
SIC: **3577** Computer peripheral equipment, nec

**(P-10405)**
**MAGMA INC**
9918 Via Pasar, San Diego (92126-4559)
PHONE.................................858 530-2511
▲ **EMP: 30**
Web: www.magma.com
SIC: **3577** Computer peripheral equipment, nec

**(P-10406)**
**MAGTEK INC (PA)**
1710 Apollo Ct, Seal Beach (90740-5617)
PHONE.................................562 546-6400
Ann Marle Hart, *Pr*
Louis E Struett, *
▲ **EMP: 200 EST:** 1972
**SQ FT:** 48,000
**SALES (est):** 50.18MM
SALES (corp-wide): 50.18MM **Privately Held**
Web: www.magtek.com
SIC: **3577** 3674 Readers, sorters, or inscribers, magnetic ink; Semiconductors and related devices

**(P-10407)**
**MARBURG TECHNOLOGY INC**
Also Called: Glide-Write
304 Turquoise St, Milpitas (95035-5431)
PHONE.................................408 262-8400
Francis Burga, *CEO*
Mohammad Ebrahimi, *
Francis Guevara, *
▲ **EMP: 18 EST:** 1988
**SALES (est):** 4.14MM **Privately Held**
Web: www.glidewrite.com
SIC: **3577** Disk and diskette equipment, except drives

**(P-10408)**
**MARWAY POWER SYSTEMS INC (PA)**
Also Called: Marway Power Solutions
1721 S Grand Ave, Santa Ana (92705)
P.O. Box 30118 (92735)
PHONE.................................714 917-6200
TOLL FREE: 800
Paul Patel, *Pr*
Kevin Jacobs, *
◆ **EMP: 39 EST:** 1979
**SQ FT:** 33,400
**SALES (est):** 9.7MM
SALES (corp-wide): 9.7MM **Privately Held**
Web: www.marway.com
SIC: **3577** 8711 Computer peripheral equipment, nec; Engineering services

**(P-10409)**
**MEGA FORCE CORPORATION**
Also Called: Megaforce
2035 Otoole Ave, San Jose (95131-1301)
PHONE.................................408 956-9989
Stanley Trenh, *Pr*
**EMP: 45 EST:** 1994
**SQ FT:** 15,000
**SALES (est):** 13.25MM **Privately Held**
Web: www.megaforcecorp.com
SIC: **3577** Computer peripheral equipment, nec

## 3577 - Computer Peripheral Equipment, Nec (P-10410)

**(P-10410)**
**METROMEDIA TECHNOLOGIES INC**
311 Parkside Dr, San Fernando (91340-3036)
PHONE...............................818 552-6500
Paul Havig, *Brnch Mgr*
**EMP:** 26
**SALES (corp-wide):** 20.45MM **Privately Held**
Web: www.mmt.com
**SIC: 3577** Graphic displays, except graphic terminals
**PA:** Metromedia Technologies, Inc.
810 7th Ave Fl 29
212 273-2100

**(P-10411)**
**MICRO CONNECTORS INC**
2700 Mccone Ave, Hayward (94545-1615)
PHONE...............................510 266-0299
Charlie Lin, *Pr*
▲ **EMP:** 29 **EST:** 1986
**SALES (est):** 2.44MM **Privately Held**
Web: www.microconnectors.com
**SIC: 3577** Computer peripheral equipment, nec

**(P-10412)**
**MOTION ENGINEERING INC (DH)**
Also Called: M E I
33 S La Patera Ln, Santa Barbara (93117-3214)
PHONE...............................805 696-1200
**EMP:** 60 **EST:** 1987
**SQ FT:** 21,000
**SALES (est):** 3.87MM
**SALES (corp-wide):** 6.25B **Publicly Held**
Web: www.motioneng.com
**SIC: 3577** 8711 3823 Computer peripheral equipment, nec; Engineering services; Process control instruments
**HQ:** Altra Industrial Motion Corp.
300 Granite St Ste 201
Braintree MA 02184
781 917-0600

**(P-10413)**
**MOXA AMERICAS INC**
601 Valencia Ave Ste 100, Brea (92823-6357)
PHONE...............................714 528-6777
Tein Shun, *CEO*
Ben Chen, *
Tein Shun Chen, *
▲ **EMP:** 50 **EST:** 2002
**SQ FT:** 8,000
**SALES (est):** 24.36MM **Privately Held**
Web: www.moxa.com
**SIC: 3577** Input/output equipment, computer
**PA:** Moxa Inc.
13f, No. 3, Xinbei Blvd., Sec. 4,

**(P-10414)**
**MPD HOLDINGS INC**
Also Called: Mousepad Designs
16200 Commerce Way, Cerritos (90703-2324)
PHONE...............................213 210-2591
Glenn M Boghosian, *Pr*
▲ **EMP:** 34 **EST:** 1993
**SALES (est):** 1.21MM **Privately Held**
Web: www.mpdholdings.company
**SIC: 3577** 2822 Computer peripheral equipment, nec; Ethylene-propylene rubbers, EPDM polymers

**(P-10415)**
**OLEA KIOSKS INC**
13845 Artesia Blvd, Cerritos (90703-9000)
PHONE...............................562 924-2644
Francisco Olea, *CEO*
Shauna Olea, *
▲ **EMP:** 54 **EST:** 1975
**SQ FT:** 50,000
**SALES (est):** 13.91MM **Privately Held**
Web: www.olea.com
**SIC: 3577** Computer peripheral equipment, nec

**(P-10416)**
**OMNIPRINT INC**
1923 E Deere Ave, Santa Ana (92705-5715)
PHONE...............................949 833-0080
Fardin Mostafavi, *Pr*
▲ **EMP:** 24 **EST:** 1984
**SQ FT:** 22,000
**SALES (est):** 2.63MM **Privately Held**
Web: www.omniprintinc.com
**SIC: 3577** 5045 Printers and plotters; Printers, computer

**(P-10417)**
**ONE STOP SYSTEMS INC (PA)**
Also Called: Oss
2235 Enterprise St Ste 110, Escondido (92029-2074)
PHONE...............................760 745-9883
David Raun, *Pr*
Kenneth Potashner, *Ch Bd*
Daniel Gabel, *CFO*
Jim Ison, *CPO*
**EMP:** 30 **EST:** 1998
**SQ FT:** 29,342
**SALES (corp-wide):** 60.9MM
**SALES (corp-wide):** 60.9MM **Publicly Held**
Web: www.onestopsystems.com
**SIC: 3577** 3571 Computer peripheral equipment, nec; Electronic computers

**(P-10418)**
**ONE STOP SYSTEMS INC**
Also Called: Magma
2235 Enterprise St Ste 110, Escondido (92029-2074)
PHONE...............................858 530-2511
Timothy Miller, *Prin*
**EMP:** 26
**SALES (corp-wide):** 60.9MM **Publicly Held**
Web: www.onestopsystems.com
**SIC: 3577** Computer peripheral equipment, nec
**PA:** One Stop Systems, Inc.
2235 Entp St Ste 110
760 745-9883

**(P-10419)**
**OPTIBASE INC (HQ)**
931 Benecia Ave, Sunnyvale (94085-2805)
P.O. Box 448 (94042)
PHONE...............................800 451-5101
Tom Wyler, *CEO*
Amir Philips, *
Alex Schwartz, *
**EMP:** 27 **EST:** 1991
**SQ FT:** 15,000
**SALES (est):** 9.81MM **Privately Held**
**SIC: 3577** Computer peripheral equipment, nec
**PA:** Optibase Ltd.
8 Hamanofim

**(P-10420)**
**PANO LOGIC INC**
1100 La Avenida Dr Ste A, Mountain View (94043-1453)
PHONE...............................650 743-1773
John Kish, *Pr*
Nils Bunger, *VP Engg*
▲ **EMP:** 43 **EST:** 2006
**SQ FT:** 11,800
**SALES (est):** 1.85MM **Privately Held**
**SIC: 3577** Computer peripheral equipment, nec

**(P-10421)**
**PRINCETON TECHNOLOGY INC**
1691 Browning, Irvine (92606-4808)
PHONE...............................949 851-7776
Nasir Javed, *CEO*
▲ **EMP:** 30 **EST:** 1990
**SQ FT:** 14,000
**SALES (est):** 4.71MM **Privately Held**
Web: www.princetonusa.com
**SIC: 3577** 5045 3674 Computer peripheral equipment, nec; Computers, peripherals, and software; Semiconductors and related devices

**(P-10422)**
**PRINTRONIX LLC (PA)**
7700 Irvine Center Dr Ste 700, Irvine (92618-3042)
PHONE...............................714 368-2300
Werner Heid, *CEO*
Sean Irby, *
Bill Matthewes, *
▲ **EMP:** 50 **EST:** 1974
**SALES (est):** 9.65MM
**SALES (corp-wide):** 9.65MM **Privately Held**
Web: www.printronix.com
**SIC: 3577** Printers, computer

**(P-10423)**
**PRINTWORX INC**
195 Aviation Way Ste 201, Watsonville (95076-2059)
PHONE...............................831 722-7147
James B Riches, *Ch Bd*
David Willmon, *Pr*
**EMP:** 17 **EST:** 1987
**SQ FT:** 15,000
**SALES (est):** 550.81K **Privately Held**
**SIC: 3577** 5112 7378 3861 Printers, computer; Computer and photocopying supplies; Computer and data processing equipment repair/maintenance; Photographic equipment and supplies

**(P-10424)**
**PROPHECY TECHNOLOGY LLC**
Also Called: Maxus Group
339 Cheryl Ln, Walnut (91789-3003)
PHONE...............................909 598-7998
▲ **EMP:** 15 **EST:** 1995
**SALES (est):** 1.05MM **Privately Held**
Web: www.maxususa.com
**SIC: 3577** Computer peripheral equipment, nec

**(P-10425)**
**QUALITYLOGIC INC**
2245 1st St Ste 103, Simi Valley (93065-0904)
PHONE...............................208 424-1905
Joe Walker, *Mgr*
**EMP:** 109
**SALES (corp-wide):** 8.71MM **Privately Held**
Web: www.qualitylogic.com

**SIC: 3577** 8748 Computer peripheral equipment, nec; Testing services
**PA:** Qualitylogic, Inc.
9576 W Emerald St
208 424-1905

**(P-10426)**
**RAISE 3D TECHNOLOGIES INC**
43 Tesla, Irvine (92618-4603)
PHONE...............................949 482-2040
Hua Feng, *CEO*
**EMP:** 23 **EST:** 2018
**SALES (est):** 9.33MM **Privately Held**
Web: www.raise3d.com
**SIC: 3577** 7372 7336 Printers, computer; Prepackaged software; Graphic arts and related design
**PA:** Shanghai Fusion Tech Co., Ltd.
Room 402,403,404, No.68, 1688 Lane, Guoquan N. Road, Yangpu Dist

**(P-10427)**
**REVERA INCORPORATED**
3090 Oakmead Village Dr, Santa Clara (95051-0862)
PHONE...............................408 510-7400
Glyn Davies, *Pr*
Timothy Welch, *
Dave Reed, *
▲ **EMP:** 40 **EST:** 2003
**SQ FT:** 20,000
**SALES (est):** 2.39MM **Privately Held**
Web: www.novami.com
**SIC: 3577** Optical scanning devices
**PA:** Nova Ltd
5 David Fikes

**(P-10428)**
**RGB SPECTRUM**
1101 Marina Village Pkwy Ste 101, Alameda (94501-1044)
PHONE...............................510 814-7000
Robert Marcus, *CEO*
Scott Norder, *
Jed Deame, *
Tony Spica, *
Jason Tirado, *
▲ **EMP:** 81 **EST:** 1987
**SALES (est):** 10MM **Privately Held**
Web: www.rgb.com
**SIC: 3577** 5731 3679 Graphic displays, except graphic terminals; Video cameras, recorders, and accessories; Recording and playback apparatus, including phonograph

**(P-10429)**
**RGB SYSTEMS INC (PA)**
Also Called: Extron Electronics
1025 E Ball Rd Ste 100, Anaheim (92805-5957)
PHONE...............................714 491-1500
Andrew C Edwards, *CEO*
◆ **EMP:** 185 **EST:** 1983
**SQ FT:** 160,000
**SALES (est):** 174.47MM
**SALES (corp-wide):** 174.47MM **Privately Held**
Web: www.extron.com
**SIC: 3577** Computer output to microfilm units

**(P-10430)**
**RICOH PRTG SYSTEMS AMER INC (HQ)**
2390 Ward Ave Ste A, Simi Valley (93065-1859)
PHONE...............................805 578-4000
Osamu Namikawa, *Pr*
Leonard Stone, *VP*
Hiroyuki Kajiyama, *Pr*
◆ **EMP:** 400 **EST:** 1962

**PRODUCTS & SERVICES SECTION**

**3577 - Computer Peripheral Equipment, Nec (P-10450)**

SQ FT: 97,400
SALES (est): 30.72MM **Privately Held**
Web: rpsa.ricoh.com
SIC: **3577** 3861 3955 Printers, computer; Toners, prepared photographic (not made in chemical plants); Ribbons, inked: typewriter, adding machine, register, etc.
PA: Ricoh Company, Ltd.
1-3-6, Nakamagome

*(P-10431)*
**RUGGED INFO TECH EQP CORP**
Also Called: Ritec
25 E Easy St, Simi Valley (93065-7707)
PHONE.................................805 577-9710
Carl C Stella, *Pr*
Harry P Alteri, *
Vincent Stella, *
Roger Lazer, *
◆ EMP: 86 EST: 1996
SQ FT: 25,000
SALES (est): 12MM **Privately Held**
Web: www.ritecrugged.com
SIC: **3577** Computer peripheral equipment, nec

*(P-10432)*
**SEAGRA TECHNOLOGY INC**
816 W Ahwanee Ave, Sunnyvale (94085-1409)
PHONE.................................408 230-8706
EMP: 23
Web: www.seagra.com
SIC: **3577** Computer peripheral equipment, nec
PA: Seagra Technology Inc.
14252 Culver Dr

*(P-10433)*
**SECUGEN CORPORATION**
2445 Augustine Dr Ste 150, Santa Clara (95054-3032)
PHONE.................................408 727-7787
Won Lee, *CEO*
Won Lee, *Pr*
◆ EMP: 30 EST: 2006
SALES (est): 3.34MM **Privately Held**
Web: www.secugen.com
SIC: **3577** Computer peripheral equipment, nec

*(P-10434)*
**SEGMENTIO INC**
101 Spear St Fl 1, San Francisco (94105-1580)
PHONE.................................844 611-0621
Peter Kristian Reinhardt, *Pr*
Sandra Smith, *
EMP: 313 EST: 2011
SALES (est): 33.73MM
SALES (corp-wide): 4.15B **Publicly Held**
Web: www.segment.com
SIC: **3577** Data conversion equipment, media-to-media: computer
PA: Twilio Inc.
101 Spear St Fl 5
415 390-2337

*(P-10435)*
**SEMTEK INNVTIVE SOLUTIONS CORP**
12777 High Bluff Dr Ste 225, San Diego (92130-2224)
PHONE.................................858 436-2270
John Sarkisian, *Ch Bd*
Patrick Hazel, *Pr*
▲ EMP: 18 EST: 1998
SQ FT: 10,000
SALES (est): 1.23MM **Privately Held**
Web: www.semtek.com

SIC: **3577** Readers, sorters, or inscribers, magnetic ink

*(P-10436)*
**SILICON GRAPHICS INTL CORP (HQ)**
940 N Mccarthy Blvd, Milpitas (95035-5128)
PHONE.................................669 900-8000
Jorge L Titinger, *CEO*
Mack Asrat, *
Cassio Conceicao, *
Eng Lim Goh, *
Peter E Hilliard, *CAO*
▲ EMP: 126 EST: 2002
SALES (est): 532.93MM
SALES (corp-wide): 29.14B **Publicly Held**
Web: www.hpe.com
SIC: **3577** 7371 Computer peripheral equipment, nec; Computer software development and applications
PA: Hewlett Packard Enterprise Company
1701 E Mossy Oaks Rd
678 259-9860

*(P-10437)*
**SONY ELECTRONICS INC**
Also Called: Sony Broadcast Products
1730 N 1st St, San Jose (95112-4642)
PHONE.................................408 352-4000
Elizabeth Boukis, *Mgr*
EMP: 41
Web: www.visual-imaging-solutions.com
SIC: **3577** 3571 8731 8711 Computer peripheral equipment, nec; Electronic computers; Commercial physical research; Engineering services
HQ: Sony Electronics Inc.
16535 Via Esprillo Bldg 1
San Diego CA 92127
858 942-2400

*(P-10438)*
**SP CONTROLS INC**
930 Linden Ave, South San Francisco (94080-1754)
PHONE.................................650 392-7880
Paul Anson Brown, *CEO*
Gary Arcudi, *Ex VP*
▲ EMP: 15 EST: 1997
SQ FT: 5,000
SALES (est): 2.75MM **Privately Held**
Web: www.spcontrols.com
SIC: **3577** Computer peripheral equipment, nec

*(P-10439)*
**SPYRUS INC (PA)**
103 Bonaventura Dr, San Jose (95134-2106)
PHONE.................................408 392-9131
Sue Pontius, *CEO*
Ed Almojuela, *Finance & Operations*
Tom Dickens, *COO*
EMP: 20 EST: 1992
SQ FT: 15,000
SALES (est): 5.58MM **Privately Held**
Web: www.spyrus.com
SIC: **3577** 7371 7372 Computer peripheral equipment, nec; Computer software development; Prepackaged software

*(P-10440)*
**SYNAPTICS INC**
1929 Main St Ste 105, Irvine (92614-6524)
PHONE.................................949 483-5594
EMP: 15 EST: 2018
SALES (est): 5.47MM **Privately Held**
Web: www.synaptics.com

SIC: **3577** Computer peripheral equipment, nec

*(P-10441)*
**SYNAPTICS INCORPORATED (PA)**
Also Called: SYNAPTICS
1109 Mckay Dr, San Jose (95131-1706)
PHONE.................................408 904-1100
Michael Hurlston, *Pr*
Nelson C Chan, *Ch Bd*
Vikram Gupta, *CPO*
Saleel Awsare, *Sr VP*
John Mcfarland, *Sr VP*
EMP: 266 EST: 1986
SQ FT: 111,000
SALES (est): 959.4MM
SALES (corp-wide): 959.4MM **Publicly Held**
Web: www.synaptics.com
SIC: **3577** 7372 Computer peripheral equipment, nec; Application computer software

*(P-10442)*
**SYNAPTICS LLC**
1109 Mckay Dr, San Jose (95131-1706)
PHONE.................................408 904-1100
EMP: 382 EST: 2014
SALES (est): 1.59MM
SALES (corp-wide): 959.4MM **Publicly Held**
Web: www.synaptics.com
SIC: **3577** Computer peripheral equipment, nec
PA: Synaptics Incorporated
1109 Mckay Dr
408 904-1100

*(P-10443)*
**SYNCHRONIZED TECHNOLOGIES INC**
Also Called: Synchrotech
7536 Tyrone Ave, Van Nuys (91405-1447)
PHONE.................................213 368-3760
Eric Hartouni, *Pr*
John Melikian, *Treas*
▲ EMP: 15 EST: 1991
SALES (est): 1.96MM **Privately Held**
Web: www.synchrotech.com
SIC: **3577** Computer peripheral equipment, nec

*(P-10444)*
**TERARECON INC**
93141 Civic Ct Dr, Fremont (94538)
PHONE.................................650 372-1100
Jeff Sorenson, *Brnch Mgr*
EMP: 35
SALES (corp-wide): 27.42MM **Privately Held**
Web: www.terarecon.com
SIC: **3577** 5734 Computer peripheral equipment, nec; Computer and software stores
PA: Terarecon Inc.
4309 Emperor Blvd Ste 310
650 372-1100

*(P-10445)*
**TOPAZ SYSTEMS INC (PA)**
Also Called: Esign Emcee
875 Patriot Dr Ste A, Moorpark (93021-3351)
PHONE.................................805 520-8282
Anthony Zank, *Pr*
▲ EMP: 25 EST: 1995
SQ FT: 16,000
SALES (est): 12.92MM **Privately Held**
Web: www.topazsystems.com

SIC: **3577** 7371 Graphic displays, except graphic terminals; Custom computer programming services

*(P-10446)*
**TRI-NET TECHNOLOGY INC**
21709 Ferrero, Walnut (91789-5209)
PHONE.................................909 598-8818
Tom Chung, *CEO*
Tom Chung, *Pr*
Lisa Chung, *
Akinori Ogawa, *
▲ EMP: 100 EST: 1992
SQ FT: 35,000
SALES (est): 3.19MM **Privately Held**
Web: www.trinetusa.com
SIC: **3577** 3571 Computer peripheral equipment, nec; Electronic computers

*(P-10447)*
**US COMPUTERS INC**
Also Called: U S Technical Institute
181 W Orangethorpe Ave Ste C, Placentia (92870-6931)
PHONE.................................714 528-0514
Uzma Sheikh, *Pr*
Saleem Sheikh, *VP*
EMP: 19 EST: 1997
SQ FT: 3,500
SALES (est): 2.48MM **Privately Held**
Web: www.uscomputersinc.com
SIC: **3577** 8249 Computer peripheral equipment, nec; Vocational schools, nec

*(P-10448)*
**VERIFONE INC**
440 Stevens Ave Ste 200, Solana Beach (92075-2059)
PHONE.................................858 436-2270
John Sarkisian, *Brnch Mgr*
EMP: 16
SALES (corp-wide): 695.17MM **Privately Held**
Web: www.verifone.com
SIC: **3577** Readers, sorters, or inscribers, magnetic ink
HQ: Verifone, Inc.
2744 N University Dr
Coral Springs FL 33065
800 837-4366

*(P-10449)*
**VIEWSONIC CORPORATION (PA)**
Also Called: Viewsonic
10 Pointe Dr Ste 200, Brea (92821-7620)
PHONE.................................909 444-8888
James Chu, *Ch Bd*
Jeff Volpe, *
Brian Igoe, *
Sung Yi, *
Bonny Cheng, *
◆ EMP: 140 EST: 1987
SQ FT: 298,050
SALES (est): 81.88MM
SALES (corp-wide): 81.88MM **Privately Held**
Web: www.viewsonic.com
SIC: **3577** 3575 5045 Computer peripheral equipment, nec; Computer terminals, monitors and components; Computer peripheral equipment

*(P-10450)*
**VIPTELA INC**
510 Mccarthy Blvd, Milpitas (95035-7908)
PHONE.................................408 663-6759
EMP: 44 EST: 2017
SALES (est): 790.61K
SALES (corp-wide): 53.8B **Publicly Held**

# 3577 - Computer Peripheral Equipment, Nec (P-10451)

SIC: **3577** Data conversion equipment, media-to-media: computer
PA: Cisco Systems, Inc.
170 W Tasman Dr
408 526-4000

**(P-10451)**
**VISIONEER INC (PA)**
5696 Stewart Ave, Fremont (94538-3174)
PHONE.....................925 251-6300
J Larry Smart, *Ch Bd*
Walt Thinsen, *
▲ **EMP:** 42 **EST:** 1994
**SALES (est):** 18.4MM
**SALES (corp-wide):** 18.4MM **Privately Held**
Web: www.visioneer.com
SIC: **3577** Computer peripheral equipment, nec

**(P-10452)**
**WESTERN TELEMATIC INC**
5 Sterling, Irvine (92618-2517)
PHONE.....................949 586-9950
Daniel Morrison, *CEO*
Herbert Hoover Iii, *Ch Bd*
▲ **EMP:** 50 **EST:** 1964
**SQ FT:** 24,000
**SALES (est):** 8.87MM **Privately Held**
Web: www.wti.com
SIC: **3577** 5065 Computer peripheral equipment, nec; Electronic parts and equipment, nec

**(P-10453)**
**WORTH DATA INC**
623 Swift St, Santa Cruz (95060-5825)
PHONE.....................831 458-9938
▲ **EMP:** 15 **EST:** 1984
**SALES (est):** 2.14MM **Privately Held**
Web: www.barcodehq.com
SIC: **3577** 5961 Readers, sorters, or inscribers, magnetic ink; Computers and peripheral equipment, mail order

**(P-10454)**
**ZEBRA TECHNOLOGIES CORPORATION**
Also Called: Eltron International
30601 Agoura Rd, Agoura Hills (91301-2147)
PHONE.....................805 579-1800
Don Skinner, *Brnch Mgr*
**EMP:** 54
**SALES (corp-wide):** 4.58B **Publicly Held**
Web: www.zebra.com
SIC: **3577** Bar code (magnetic ink) printers
PA: Zebra Technologies Corporation
3 Overlook Pt
847 634-6700

**(P-10455)**
**ZNYX NETWORKS INC**
Also Called: Znyx
48421 Milmont Dr, Fremont (94538-3274)
P.O. Box 14796 (94539-1796)
**EMP:** 95
Web: www.znyx.com
SIC: **3577** Computer peripheral equipment, nec

## 3578 Calculating And Accounting Equipment

**(P-10456)**
**ASTERES INC (PA)**
10650 Treena St Ste 105, San Diego (92131-2436)
PHONE.....................858 777-8600
Linda Pinney, *CEO*
Martin Bridges, *
▲ **EMP:** 27 **EST:** 2003
**SALES (est):** 7.73MM
**SALES (corp-wide):** 7.73MM **Privately Held**
Web: www.asteres.com
SIC: **3578** Cash registers

**(P-10457)**
**CAR ENTERPRISES INC**
Also Called: C.A.R ENTERPRISES, INC.
13100 Main St, Hesperia (92345-4625)
PHONE.....................760 947-6411
Sam Anabi, *Pr*
**EMP:** 20
**SALES (corp-wide):** 5.89MM **Privately Held**
Web: www.shell.com
SIC: **3578** Automatic teller machines (ATM)
PA: C.A.R. Enterprises, Inc.
1450 N Benson Ave Unit A
909 932-9242

**(P-10458)**
**CAR ENTERPRISES INC**
Also Called: C.A.R ENTERPRISES, INC.
12301 Heacock St, Moreno Valley (92557-7108)
PHONE.....................951 413-6262
Carl Cox, *Brnch Mgr*
**EMP:** 15
**SALES (corp-wide):** 95.36MM **Privately Held**
Web: www.shell.com
SIC: **3578** Automatic teller machines (ATM)
PA: C.A.R. Enterprises, Inc.
1450 N Benson Ave Unit A
909 932-9242

**(P-10459)**
**CLOVER NETWORK INC**
415 N Mathilda Ave, Sunnyvale (94085-4222)
PHONE.....................650 210-7888
Leonard Speiser, *CEO*
John Beatty, *
**EMP:** 65 **EST:** 2010
**SQ FT:** 8,200
**SALES (est):** 10.96MM
**SALES (corp-wide):** 19.09B **Publicly Held**
Web: www.clover.com
SIC: **3578** 4813 Calculating and accounting equipment; Internet connectivity services
HQ: First Data Corporation
600 N Vel R Phillips Ave
Milwaukee WI 53203

**(P-10460)**
**SUZHOU SOUTH**
18351 Colima Rd Ste 82, Rowland Heights (91748-2791)
PHONE.....................626 322-0101
Joel Wynne, *Dir*
**EMP:** 300 **EST:** 2017
**SALES (est):** 2.32MM **Privately Held**
SIC: **3578** Banking machines

**(P-10461)**
**VERIFONE INTRMDATE HLDINGS INC**
2099 Gateway Pl, San Jose (95110-1093)
PHONE.....................408 232-7800
**EMP:** 188 **EST:** 2002
**SALES (est):** 10.34MM
**SALES (corp-wide):** 695.17MM **Privately Held**
Web: www.verifone.com

SIC: **3578** Point-of-sale devices
HQ: Verifone, Inc.
2744 N University Dr
Coral Springs FL 33065
800 837-4366

## 3579 Office Machines, Nec

**(P-10462)**
**LYNDE-ORDWAY COMPANY INC**
5402 Commercial Dr, Huntington Beach (92649-1232)
P.O. Box 8709 (92708)
PHONE.....................714 957-1311
**TOLL FREE:** 800
Thomas Ordway, *Pr*
Penny Ordway, *Sec*
**EMP:** 18 **EST:** 1925
**SALES (est):** 1.74MM **Privately Held**
Web: www.lynde-ordway.com
SIC: **3579** 5999 5044 7359 Paper handling machines; Business machines and equipment; Office equipment; Equipment rental and leasing, nec

**(P-10463)**
**PARKER POWIS INC**
2929 5th St, Berkeley (94710-2736)
PHONE.....................510 848-2463
Kevin Parker, *Pr*
Tony Cheng, *
Charles Marino, *
▲ **EMP:** 75 **EST:** 1982
**SQ FT:** 54,000
**SALES (est):** 9.98MM **Privately Held**
Web: www.mypowis.com
SIC: **3579** Binding machines, plastic and adhesive

**(P-10464)**
**PROTEMPIS (USA) LLC**
2151 Otoole Ave Ste 60, San Jose (95131-1330)
PHONE.....................408 410-3222
Karen Guldan, *Managing Member*
**EMP:** 30 **EST:** 2022
**SALES (est):** 2.98MM **Privately Held**
Web: www.protempis.com
SIC: **3579** Time clocks and time recording devices

**(P-10465)**
**RICOH ELECTRONICS INC**
17482 Pullman St, Irvine (92614-5527)
PHONE.....................714 259-1220
Paul Bakonyi, *Mgr*
**EMP:** 88
**SQ FT:** 49,359
Web: rei.ricoh.com
SIC: **3579** 3571 Mailing, letter handling, and addressing machines; Electronic computers
HQ: Ricoh Electronics, Inc.
1125 Hurricane Shoals Rd
Lawrenceville GA 30043
714 566-2500

**(P-10466)**
**SOLARIS PAPER INC**
505 N Euclid St Ste 630, Anaheim (92801-5506)
PHONE.....................714 687-6657
▲ **EMP:** 197 **EST:** 2005
**SALES (est):** 748.42K **Privately Held**
Web: www.solarispaper.com
SIC: **3579** Paper handling machines
HQ: Solaris Paper, Inc.
770 The Cy Dr S Ste 3000
Orange CA 92868

**(P-10467)**
**WHITTIER MAILING PRODUCTS INC (PA)**
13019 Park St, Santa Fe Springs (90670-4005)
PHONE.....................562 464-3000
Richard A Casford, *Pr*
**EMP:** 17 **EST:** 1991
**SQ FT:** 5,000
**SALES (est):** 4.73MM
**SALES (corp-wide):** 4.73MM **Privately Held**
Web: www.wmpwebstore.com
SIC: **3579** Mailing, letter handling, and addressing machines

**(P-10468)**
**XEROX**
12833 Monarch St, Garden Grove (92841-3921)
PHONE.....................714 895-7500
Monica Navarro, *Prin*
**EMP:** 20 **EST:** 2016
**SALES (est):** 394.88K **Privately Held**
Web: www.xerox.com
SIC: **3579** Office machines, nec

## 3581 Automatic Vending Machines

**(P-10469)**
**AVT INC**
341 Bonnie Cir Ste 102, Corona (92880-2895)
PHONE.....................951 737-1057
▲ **EMP:** 38
Web: www.autoretail.com
SIC: **3581** Automatic vending machines

**(P-10470)**
**CARACAL ENTERPRISES LLC**
Also Called: Ventek International
1260 Holm Rd Ste A, Petaluma (94954-7152)
PHONE.....................707 773-3373
Bob Forsyth, *
▲ **EMP:** 30 **EST:** 2003
**SALES (est):** 6.66MM **Privately Held**
Web: www.ventek-intl.com
SIC: **3581** Automatic vending machines

**(P-10471)**
**IMPULSE INDUSTRIES INC**
Also Called: Impulse Amusement
9281 Borden Ave, Sun Valley (91352-2034)
PHONE.....................818 767-4258
◆ **EMP:** 24 **EST:** 1986
**SALES (est):** 6.31MM **Privately Held**
Web: www.impulseindustries.com
SIC: **3581** 3999 Automatic vending machines; Coin-operated amusement machines

**(P-10472)**
**VENTEK INTERNATIONAL INC**
1260 Holm Rd Ste A, Petaluma (94954-7152)
PHONE.....................707 773-3373
▲ **EMP:** 20 **EST:** 1976
**SALES (est):** 4.5MM **Privately Held**
Web: www.ventek-intl.com
SIC: **3581** Locks, coin-operated

PRODUCTS & SERVICES SECTION  
3585 - Refrigeration And Heating Equipment (P-10493)

## 3582 Commercial Laundry Equipment

**(P-10473)**  
**ALLIANCE LAUNDRY SYSTEMS LLC**  
162 Harbor Ct, Pittsburg (94565-5063)  
PHONE..................800 464-6866  
Michael D Schoeb, *Brnch Mgr*  
**EMP:** 24  
**SALES (corp-wide):** 631.85MM **Privately Held**  
Web: distribution.alliancelaundry.com  
SIC: **3582** Commercial laundry equipment  
HQ: Alliance Laundry Systems Llc  
221 Shepard St  
Ripon WI 54971  
920 748-3121  

**(P-10474)**  
**DENIM-TECH LLC**  
375 E 2nd St Apt 604, Los Angeles (90012-4154)  
PHONE..................323 277-8998  
▲ **EMP:** 100  
Web: www.denim-tech.com  
SIC: **3582** Commercial laundry equipment  

**(P-10475)**  
**WESTERN STATE DESIGN INC**  
2331 Tripaldi Way, Hayward (94545-5022)  
PHONE..................510 786-9271  
**EMP:** 80 **EST:** 2016  
**SALES (est):** 4.78MM **Publicly Held**  
Web: www.westernstatedesign.com  
SIC: **3582** Commercial laundry equipment  
PA: Evi Industries, Inc.  
4500 Bscayne Blvd Ste 340  

## 3585 Refrigeration And Heating Equipment

**(P-10476)**  
**ACCO ENGINEERED SYSTEMS INC**  
3559 Landco Dr Ste B, Bakersfield (93308-6169)  
PHONE..................661 631-1975  
**EMP:** 23  
**SALES (corp-wide):** 1.51B **Privately Held**  
Web: www.accoes.com  
SIC: **3585** Air conditioning equipment, complete  
PA: Acco Engineered Systems, Inc.  
888 East Walnut St  
818 244-6571  

**(P-10477)**  
**ACE HEATERS LLC**  
130 Klug Cir, Corona (92878-5424)  
PHONE..................951 738-2230  
Robin Cruse, *CEO*  
William Newbauer Iii, *Pr*  
**EMP:** 20 **EST:** 2016  
**SQ FT:** 40,000  
**SALES (est):** 3.43MM  
**SALES (corp-wide):** 104.4MM **Privately Held**  
Web: www.aceheaters.com  
SIC: **3585** 3443 Heating equipment, complete; Boiler and boiler shop work  
PA: The Nudyne Group Llc  
45 Seymour St  
203 378-2659  

**(P-10478)**  
**ALLIANCE AIR PRODUCTS LLC**  
9565 Heinrich Hertz Dr Ste 1, San Diego (92154-7920)  
PHONE..................619 664-0027  
**EMP:** 1053  
Web: www.allianceairproducts.com  
SIC: **3585** Refrigeration and heating equipment  
HQ: Alliance Air Products, Llc.  
2285 Mchael Frday Dr Ste  
San Diego CA 92154  
619 428-9688  

**(P-10479)**  
**ALLIANCE AIR PRODUCTS LLC (DH)**  
Also Called: Especializados Del Aire  
2285 Michael Faraday Dr Ste 15, San Diego (92154-7926)  
PHONE..................619 428-9688  
Luis Plascencia, *Pr*  
**EMP:** 47 **EST:** 2004  
**SQ FT:** 3,300  
**SALES (est):** 5.74MM **Privately Held**  
Web: www.allianceairproducts.com  
SIC: **3585** Air conditioning units, complete: domestic or industrial  
HQ: Daikin Applied Americas Inc.  
13600 Industrial Pk Blvd  
Minneapolis MN 55441  
763 553-5330  

**(P-10480)**  
**AMERICAN CONDENSER & COIL LLC**  
Also Called: American Condenser  
1628 W 139th St, Gardena (90249-3003)  
PHONE..................310 327-8600  
▲ **EMP:** 75  
Web: www.american-coil.com  
SIC: **3585** Air conditioning condensers and condensing units  

**(P-10481)**  
**ANTHONY INC (DH)**  
Also Called: Anthony International  
12391 Montero Ave, Sylmar (91342-5370)  
PHONE..................818 365-9451  
Jeffrey Clark, *CEO*  
Michael Murth, *  
David Lautenschaelger, *  
Craig Little, *  
◆ **EMP:** 850 **EST:** 1998  
**SQ FT:** 350,000  
**SALES (est):** 486.02MM  
**SALES (corp-wide):** 8.44B **Publicly Held**  
Web: www.anthonyintl.com  
SIC: **3585** Refrigeration and heating equipment  
HQ: Dover Refrigeration & Food Equipment, Inc.  
3005 Highland Pkwy # 200  
Downers Grove IL 60515  
513 878-4400  

**(P-10482)**  
**ARI INDUSTRIES INC**  
Also Called: Airdyne Refrigeration  
17018 Edwards Rd, Cerritos (90703-2422)  
PHONE..................714 993-3700  
R Tony Bedi, *Pr*  
Ruth Lee Bedi, *  
**EMP:** 80 **EST:** 1995  
**SQ FT:** 20,000  
**SALES (est):** 3.1MM **Privately Held**  
Web: www.airdyne.com  
SIC: **3585** Refrigeration equipment, complete  

**(P-10483)**  
**AUTOMATIC BAR CONTROLS INC (HQ)**  
Also Called: Wunder-Bar  
2060 Cessna Dr #100, Vacaville (95688-8712)  
PHONE..................707 448-5151  
▲ **EMP:** 47 **EST:** 1994  
**SALES (est):** 32.31MM  
**SALES (corp-wide):** 4.04B **Publicly Held**  
Web: www.wunderbar.com  
SIC: **3585** Cold drink dispensing equipment (not coin-operated)  
PA: The Middleby Corporation  
1400 Toastmaster Dr  
847 741-3300  

**(P-10484)**  
**AVIATE ENTERPRISES INC**  
5844 Price Ave, Mcclellan (95652-2407)  
PHONE..................916 993-4000  
Timothy Devine, *CEO*  
**EMP:** 27 **EST:** 2014  
**SQ FT:** 3,700  
**SALES (est):** 10.07MM **Privately Held**  
Web: www.aviateinc.com  
SIC: **3585** 3843 5599 3629 Refrigeration and heating equipment; Dental equipment and supplies; Golf cart, powered; Electronic generation equipment  

**(P-10485)**  
**BALTIMORE AIRCOIL COMPANY INC**  
B A C  
15341 Road 28 1/2, Madera (93638-2395)  
P.O. Box 960 (93639-0960)  
PHONE..................559 673-9231  
Han Yen, *Brnch Mgr*  
**EMP:** 150  
**SQ FT:** 45,000  
**SALES (corp-wide):** 3.96B **Privately Held**  
Web: www.baltimoreaircoil.com  
SIC: **3585** Condensers, refrigeration  
HQ: Baltimore Aircoil Company, Inc.  
7600 Dorsey Run Rd  
Jessup MD 20794  
410 799-6200  

**(P-10486)**  
**BIGFOGG INC (PA)**  
30818 Wealth St, Murrieta (92563-2534)  
PHONE..................951 587-2460  
Christopher Miehl, *Pr*  
Chris Miehl, *Pr*  
**EMP:** 17 **EST:** 2000  
**SALES (est):** 5.84MM  
**SALES (corp-wide):** 5.84MM **Privately Held**  
Web: www.bigfogg.com  
SIC: **3585** Air conditioning condensers and condensing units  

**(P-10487)**  
**CALIFRNIA INDUS RFRGN MCHS INC**  
Also Called: California Industrial  
3197 Cornerstone Dr, Eastvale (91752-1028)  
PHONE..................951 361-0040  
TOLL FREE: 800  
Shahnaz Ghelani, *Sec*  
Mansoor Ghelani, *VP*  
Rahim Ghelani, *Pr*  
**EMP:** 15 **EST:** 1984  
**SALES (est):** 2.45MM **Privately Held**  
Web: www.caindustrial.com  

SIC: **3585** 5075 1711 1731 Air conditioning equipment, complete; Compressors, air conditioning; Heating and air conditioning contractors; General electrical contractor  

**(P-10488)**  
**CLASSIC TENTS**  
Also Called: Classic Tents  
19119 S Reyes Ave, Compton (90221-5811)  
PHONE..................310 328-5060  
▲ **EMP:** 45  
Web: www.bright.com  
SIC: **3585** 7359 1731 Air conditioning equipment, complete; Business machine and electronic equipment rental services; General electrical contractor  

**(P-10489)**  
**COLD STORAGE MANUFACTURING INC**  
740 Bradford Way, Union City (94587)  
PHONE..................510 476-1700  
**EMP:** 22 **EST:** 1972  
**SALES (est):** 10.28MM **Privately Held**  
Web: www.coldstoragemfg.com  
SIC: **3585** Refrigeration equipment, complete  

**(P-10490)**  
**COMMERCIAL DISPLAY SYSTEMS LLC**  
Also Called: C D S  
17341 Sierra Hwy, Canyon Country (91351-1625)  
PHONE..................818 361-8160  
Fernando Calderon, *Managing Member*  
John T Karnes, *Managing Member*  
Duane Beswick, *  
**EMP:** 30 **EST:** 2002  
**SQ FT:** 17,000  
**SALES (est):** 4.96MM **Privately Held**  
Web: www.cdsdoors.net  
SIC: **3585** Refrigeration and heating equipment  

**(P-10491)**  
**COMPU AIRE INC**  
8167 Byron Rd, Whittier (90606-2615)  
PHONE..................562 945-8971  
Balbir Narang, *Pr*  
Robert Narang, *  
▲ **EMP:** 150 **EST:** 1980  
**SQ FT:** 75,000  
**SALES (est):** 6.44MM **Privately Held**  
Web: www.compu-aire.com  
SIC: **3585** Air conditioning units, complete: domestic or industrial  

**(P-10492)**  
**COOLTEC REFRIGERATION CORP**  
1250 E Franklin Ave Unit B, Pomona (91766-5449)  
P.O. Box 1150 (91769-1150)  
PHONE..................909 865-2229  
Paul Bedi, *CEO*  
George Share, *Sec*  
**EMP:** 22 **EST:** 2005  
**SQ FT:** 50,000  
**SALES (est):** 4.94MM **Privately Held**  
Web: www.cooltecrefrigeration.com  
SIC: **3585** Refrigeration equipment, complete  

**(P-10493)**  
**CROWNTONKA CALIFORNIA INC**  
Also Called: Thermal Rite  
6514 E 26th St, Commerce (90040-3240)  
PHONE..................909 230-6720  
Dave Jett, *Genl Mgr*

## 3585 - Refrigeration And Heating Equipment (P-10494)

EMP: 46
Web: www.everidge.com
SIC: 3585 Refrigeration and heating equipment
HQ: Crowntonka California, Inc.
15600 37th Ave N Ste 100
Minneapolis MN 55446
763 543-2386

**(P-10494)**
**DAIKIN COMFORT TECH MFG LP**
3018 Alvarado St Ste C, San Leandro (94577-5726)
PHONE.................................510 265-1212
Toni Boglin, *Brnch Mgr*
EMP: 292
Web: www.goodmanmfg.com
SIC: 3585 Refrigeration and heating equipment
HQ: Daikin Comfort Technologies Manufacturing, L.P.
19001 Kermier Rd
Waller TX 77484
877 254-4729

**(P-10495)**
**DAIKIN COMFORT TECH MFG LP**
15024 Anacapa Rd, Victorville (92392-2509)
PHONE.................................760 955-7770
Don Johnston, *Brnch Mgr*
EMP: 292
Web: www.goodmanmfg.com
SIC: 3585 Air conditioning equipment, complete
HQ: Daikin Comfort Technologies Manufacturing, L.P.
19001 Kermier Rd
Waller TX 77484
877 254-4729

**(P-10496)**
**DATA AIRE INC (HQ)**
230 W Blueridge Ave, Orange (92865-4225)
P.O. Box 7064 (92863)
PHONE.................................800 347-2473
Duncan Moffatt, *Pr*
Edward J Altieri, *
▲ EMP: 60 EST: 1979
SALES (est): 27.32MM
SALES (corp-wide): 496.1MM **Privately Held**
Web: www.dataaire.com
SIC: 3585 Air conditioning units, complete: domestic or industrial
PA: Construction Specialties, Inc.
3 Werner Way
908 236-0800

**(P-10497)**
**ELCO RFRGN SOLUTIONS LLC**
Also Called: Craft
2554 Commercial St, San Diego (92113-1132)
PHONE.................................858 888-9447
Dean Rafiee, *Ex Dir*
EMP: 5000 EST: 2014
SALES (est): 9.61MM **Privately Held**
Web: www.icraft.us
SIC: 3585 3499 3999 Refrigeration and heating equipment; Fire- or burglary-resistive products; Barber and beauty shop equipment

**(P-10498)**
**ENLINK GEOENERGY SERVICES INC**
2630 Homestead Pl, Rancho Dominguez (90220-5610)
PHONE.................................424 242-1200
Mark Mizrahi, *Pr*
Howard Johnson, *CIO*
▲ EMP: 35 EST: 2004
SQ FT: 12,000
SALES (est): 728.35K **Privately Held**
SIC: 3585 Heat pumps, electric

**(P-10499)**
**EVAPCO INC**
Also Called: Evapco West
1900 W Almond Ave, Madera (93637-5208)
PHONE.................................559 673-2207
Steve Levake, *Mgr*
EMP: 82
SQ FT: 88,250
SALES (corp-wide): 490.01MM **Privately Held**
Web: www.evapco.com
SIC: 3585 Air conditioning units, complete: domestic or industrial
PA: Evapco, Inc.
5151 Allendale Ln
410 756-2600

**(P-10500)**
**EVERIDGE INC**
Also Called: Thermalrite
8886 White Oak Ave, Rancho Cucamonga (91730-5106)
PHONE.................................909 605-6419
Chris Kahler, *Brnch Mgr*
EMP: 47
Web: www.everidge.com
SIC: 3585 Refrigeration and heating equipment
PA: Everidge, Inc.
15600 37th Ave N Ste 100

**(P-10501)**
**HARVEST THERMAL INC**
663 Coventry Rd, Kensington (94707-1329)
PHONE.................................408 597-7152
Jane Melia, *CEO*
Dan Johnson, *Sec*
Pierre Delforge, *Treas*
EMP: 17 EST: 2019
SALES (est): 2.9MM **Privately Held**
Web: www.harvest-thermal.com
SIC: 3585 7389 Refrigeration and heating equipment; Business services, nec

**(P-10502)**
**HUSSMANN CORPORATION**
13770 Ramona Ave, Chino (91710-5423)
P.O. Box 5133 (91708-5133)
PHONE.................................909 590-4910
Mike Gleason, *Genl Mgr*
EMP: 350
Web: www.hussmann.com
SIC: 3585 7623 Refrigeration and heating equipment; Refrigeration service and repair
HQ: Hussmann Corporation
12999 St Charles Rock Rd
Bridgeton MO 63044
314 291-2000

**(P-10503)**
**J P LAMBORN CO (PA)**
Also Called: J P L
3663 E Wawona Ave, Fresno (93725-9236)
PHONE.................................559 650-2120
John P Lamborn Junior, *CEO*
Pam Lamborn, *
▲ EMP: 25 EST: 1961
SQ FT: 125,000
SALES (est): 9.9MM
SALES (corp-wide): 9.9MM **Privately Held**
Web: www.jplflex.com

SIC: 3585 Heating and air conditioning combination units

**(P-10504)**
**KOOLFOG INC (PA)**
31290 Plantation Dr, Thousand Palms (92276-6604)
PHONE.................................760 321-9203
Bryan Roe, *Pr*
EMP: 15 EST: 1987
SQ FT: 4,000
SALES (est): 4.97MM **Privately Held**
Web: www.koolfog.com
SIC: 3585 7819 Humidifiers and dehumidifiers; Visual effects production

**(P-10505)**
**LENNOX INTERNATIONAL INC**
Also Called: Lennox
1155 E North Ave Ste 102, Fresno (93725-1947)
PHONE.................................559 490-0078
EMP: 213
SALES (corp-wide): 4.98B **Publicly Held**
Web: www.lennoxpros.com
SIC: 3585 Refrigeration and heating equipment
PA: Lennox International Inc.
2140 Lake Park Blvd
972 497-5000

**(P-10506)**
**LMW ENTERPRISES LLC**
Also Called: Lrc Coil Company
10558 Norwalk Blvd, Santa Fe Springs (90670-3836)
PHONE.................................562 944-1969
EMP: 22
SALES (corp-wide): 5.39MM **Privately Held**
Web: www.lrccoil.com
SIC: 3585 Refrigeration equipment, complete
PA: Lmw Enterprises Llc
3861 E 42nd Pl
562 944-1969

**(P-10507)**
**MACINTYRE CORP**
5285 Diamond Heights Blvd, San Francisco (94131-2147)
PHONE.................................800 229-3560
John-paul Farsight, *CEO*
EMP: 25 EST: 2020
SALES (est): 692.91K **Privately Held**
Web: www.mcintyrecorp.com
SIC: 3585 Refrigeration and heating equipment

**(P-10508)**
**MESTEK INC**
Also Called: Anemostat Products
1220 E Watson Center Rd, Carson (90745-4206)
PHONE.................................310 835-7500
Chang Hung, *Mgr*
EMP: 200
SALES (corp-wide): 689.94MM **Privately Held**
Web: www.mestek.com
SIC: 3585 3549 3542 3354 Heating equipment, complete; Metalworking machinery, nec; Punching, shearing, and bending machines; Shapes, extruded aluminum, nec
PA: Mestek, Inc.
260 N Elm St
413 568-9571

**(P-10509)**
**MYDAX INC**
12260 Shale Ridge Ln Ste 4, Auburn (95602-8400)
PHONE.................................530 888-6662
Thomas Spesick, *Pr*
Richard S Frankel, *CEO*
Thomas Spesick, *VP*
EMP: 19 EST: 1986
SQ FT: 15,000
SALES (est): 3.53MM **Privately Held**
Web: www.mydax.com
SIC: 3585 Refrigeration and heating equipment

**(P-10510)**
**PAC-REFCO INC**
Also Called: Pacific Refrigerator Company
2230 Ottawa Rd Ste A, Apple Valley (92307)
PHONE.................................760 956-8600
John Gomez, *Pr*
Kim Lipka, *
Paul Jett, *
EMP: 25 EST: 1944
SQ FT: 25,000
SALES (est): 2.49MM **Privately Held**
SIC: 3585 Refrigeration equipment, complete

**(P-10511)**
**R-COLD INC**
1221 S G St, Perris (92570-2477)
PHONE.................................951 436-5476
Michael Mulcahy, *Pr*
Ernest Gaston, *
EMP: 65 EST: 1982
SQ FT: 28,000
SALES (est): 10.84MM **Privately Held**
Web: www.r-cold.com
SIC: 3585 1541 Refrigeration and heating equipment; Industrial buildings and warehouses

**(P-10512)**
**RAHN INDUSTRIES INCORPORATED (PA)**
Also Called: Rahn Industries
2630 Pacific Park Dr, Whittier (90601-1611)
PHONE.................................562 908-0680
John Hancock, *Pr*
Jeff Meier, *
Claudia Maytum, *
▲ EMP: 46 EST: 1979
SQ FT: 25,000
SALES (est): 9.29MM
SALES (corp-wide): 9.29MM **Privately Held**
Web: www.rahnindustries.com
SIC: 3585 Refrigeration and heating equipment

**(P-10513)**
**REFRIGERATOR MANUFACTURERS LLC**
Also Called: Airdyne Refrigeration
17018 Edwards Rd, Cerritos (90703-2422)
PHONE.................................562 926-2006
Tony Bedi, *Pr*
EMP: 47 EST: 2015
SALES (est): 5.99MM **Privately Held**
Web: www.rmi-econocold.com
SIC: 3585 Condensers, refrigeration

**(P-10514)**
**SEAWARD PRODUCTS CORP**
3721 Capitol Ave, City Of Industry (90601-1732)
PHONE.................................562 699-7997
◆ EMP: 55 EST: 1975

## PRODUCTS & SERVICES SECTION
## 3589 - Service Industry Machinery, Nec (P-10536)

SALES (est): 4.49MM **Privately Held**
**SIC: 3585** 3634 Heating equipment, complete; Hot plates, electric

**(P-10515)**
**SMART FOG**
1017 L St Pmb 319, Sacramento (95814-3805)
PHONE.................................800 921-5230
Adaya Goldstein, *CEO*
**EMP:** 20 **EST:** 2017
SALES (est): 2.13MM **Privately Held**
Web: www.smartfog.com
**SIC: 3585** Humidifiers and dehumidifiers

**(P-10516)**
**SUMMIT ESP LLC**
27655 Avenue Hopkins Unit B, Santa Clarita (91355-3493)
PHONE.................................805 585-0595
**EMP:** 17 **EST:** 2016
SALES (est): 300.33K **Privately Held**
Web: www.halliburton.com
**SIC: 3585** Refrigeration and heating equipment

**(P-10517)**
**TEAM AIR INC (PA)**
Also Called: Team Air Conditioning Eqp
12771 Brown Ave, Riverside (92509-1831)
PHONE.................................909 823-1957
Thirusenthil Nathan, *Pr*
Oliver Corbala, *
**EMP:** 35 **EST:** 1999
SALES (est): 8.2MM **Privately Held**
Web: www.teamairinc.com
**SIC: 3585** Air conditioning equipment, complete

**(P-10518)**
**THERMOCRAFT**
2554 Commercial St, San Diego (92113-1132)
PHONE.................................619 813-2985
Dean Rafiee, *Pr*
Dean Ideen Rafiee, *
**EMP:** 100 **EST:** 2016
SALES (est): 1.87MM **Privately Held**
**SIC: 3585** 5078 5031 Refrigeration and heating equipment; Commercial refrigeration equipment; Doors, garage

**(P-10519)**
**TRANE US INC**
Also Called: Trane
20450 E Walnut Dr N, Walnut (91789-2921)
PHONE.................................626 913-7913
**EMP:** 26
Web: www.trane.com
**SIC: 3585** Refrigeration and heating equipment
HQ: Trane U.S. Inc.
800-E Beaty St
Davidson NC 28036
704 655-4000

**(P-10520)**
**TRANE US INC**
Also Called: Trane
3565 Corporate Ct Fl 1, San Diego (92123-2415)
PHONE.................................858 292-0833
Tyler Clemmer, *Brnch Mgr*
**EMP:** 132
Web: www.trane.com
**SIC: 3585** Refrigeration and heating equipment
HQ: Trane U.S. Inc.
800-E Beaty St
Davidson NC 28036
704 655-4000

**(P-10521)**
**TRANE US INC**
Also Called: Southern California Trane
3253 E Imperial Hwy, Brea (92821-6722)
PHONE.................................626 913-7123
John Clark, *Brnch Mgr*
**EMP:** 100
Web: www.trane.com
**SIC: 3585** Heating and air conditioning combination units
HQ: Trane U.S. Inc.
800-E Beaty St
Davidson NC 28036
704 655-4000

**(P-10522)**
**TREAU INC**
Also Called: Gradient
375 Alabama St Ste 220, San Francisco (94110-1361)
PHONE.................................866 945-3514
Vincent Romanin, *Pr*
**EMP:** 22 **EST:** 2017
SALES (est): 2.75MM **Privately Held**
Web: www.gradientcomfort.com
**SIC: 3585** 8731 Air conditioning condensers and condensing units; Energy research

**(P-10523)**
**TRUMED SYSTEMS INCORPORATED**
4370 La Jolla Village Dr Ste 200, San Diego (92122-1233)
PHONE.................................844 878-6331
Jesper Jensen, *CEO*
Jesper Jensen, *Pr*
Joe Milkovits, *
Jim Martindale, *Field Operations Vice President*
**EMP:** 29 **EST:** 2013
SALES (est): 9.62MM **Privately Held**
Web: www.trumedsystems.com
**SIC: 3585** 5078 Refrigeration and heating equipment; Commercial refrigeration equipment

**(P-10524)**
**UTILITY REFRIGERATOR**
12160 Sherman Way, North Hollywood (91605-5501)
P.O. Box 570782 (91357-0782)
PHONE.................................818 764-6200
Michael Michrowski, *Pr*
▲ **EMP:** 26 **EST:** 2007
SALES (est): 4.12MM **Privately Held**
Web: www.utilityrefrigerator.com
**SIC: 3585** Parts for heating, cooling, and refrigerating equipment

**(P-10525)**
**VEGE-MIST INC**
Also Called: Alco Designs
407 E Redondo Beach Blvd, Gardena (90248-2312)
PHONE.................................310 353-2300
Samuel Cohen, *CEO*
▲ **EMP:** 61 **EST:** 1988
**SQ FT:** 8,000
SALES (est): 1.24MM **Privately Held**
Web: www.alcodesigns.com
**SIC: 3585** 2541 5074 2542 Humidifying equipment, except portable; Store and office display cases and fixtures; Water purification equipment; Partitions and fixtures, except wood

**(P-10526)**
**VINOTHEQUE WINE CELLARS**
1738 E Alpine Ave, Stockton (95205-2505)
PHONE.................................209 466-9463

TOLL FREE: 800
Thomas R Schneider, *CEO*
▼ **EMP:** 16 **EST:** 1999
**SQ FT:** 30,000
SALES (est): 5.69MM **Privately Held**
Web: www.vinotheque.com
**SIC: 3585** Refrigeration equipment, complete

**(P-10527)**
**WELBILT FDSRVICE COMPANIES LLC**
Also Called: Chester Paul Company
1210 N Red Gum St, Anaheim (92806-1820)
PHONE.................................323 245-3761
**EMP:** 281
SALES (corp-wide): 4.8B **Privately Held**
Web: direct.welbilt.us
**SIC: 3585** Refrigeration and heating equipment
HQ: Welbilt Foodservice Companies, Llc
2227 Welbilt Blvd
Trinity FL 34655

**(P-10528)**
**WESTAIRE ENGINEERING INC**
5820 S Alameda St, Vernon (90058-3432)
PHONE.................................323 587-3347
Vazgen Galadjian, *Pr*
Shane Bekian, *VP*
Kevin Galadjian, *VP*
▲ **EMP:** 15 **EST:** 1993
**SQ FT:** 50,000
SALES (est): 2.37MM **Privately Held**
Web: www.westaireengineering.com
**SIC: 3585** 5075 Air conditioning units, complete: domestic or industrial; Ventilating equipment and supplies

**(P-10529)**
**WILLIAMS FURNACE CO (DH)**
Also Called: Williams Comfort Products
250 W Laurel St, Colton (92324-1435)
PHONE.................................562 450-3602
Michael Markowich, *Pr*
James Gidwitz, *
Joseph Sum, *
Mark Nichter, *
Ruth Ann Davis, *
▲ **EMP:** 173 **EST:** 1916
**SQ FT:** 400,000
SALES (est): 43.34MM
SALES (corp-wide): 113.28MM **Privately Held**
Web: www.williamscomfort.com
**SIC: 3585** 3433 Refrigeration and heating equipment; Heating equipment, except electric
HQ: Riverbend Industries Inc.
440 S La Salle St # 3100
Chicago IL 60605
312 541-7200

**(P-10530)**
**YORK INTERNATIONAL CORPORATION**
1307 Striker Ave Ste 100, Sacramento (95834-1181)
PHONE.................................916 283-7650
Lee Howard, *Pr*
**EMP:** 15
Web: www.mapleton.us
**SIC: 3585** Refrigeration and heating equipment
HQ: York International Corporation
5005 York Dr
Norman OK 73069
800 481-9738

---

### 3589 Service Industry Machinery, Nec

**(P-10531)**
**ACM RESEARCH INC (PA)**
Also Called: SAPS
42307 Osgood Rd Ste I, Fremont (94539-5062)
PHONE.................................510 445-3700
David H Wang, *Pr*
Mark A Mckechnie, *Ex VP*
Howard Chen, *Corporate Strategy Vice President*
**EMP:** 165 **EST:** 1998
SALES (est): 557.72MM **Publicly Held**
Web: www.acmr.com
**SIC: 3589** Commercial cleaning equipment

**(P-10532)**
**ADVANCED UV INC (PA)**
16350 Manning Way, Cerritos (90703-2224)
PHONE.................................562 407-0299
Kiyomitsu Kevin Toma, *CEO*
▲ **EMP:** 25 **EST:** 1996
**SQ FT:** 30,000
SALES (est): 9.36MM
SALES (corp-wide): 9.36MM **Privately Held**
Web: www.advanceduv.com
**SIC: 3589** Water purification equipment, household type

**(P-10533)**
**AMIAD USA INC**
Also Called: West Coast Sales Office & Whse
1251 Maulhardt Ave, Oxnard (93030-7990)
PHONE.................................805 988-3323
**EMP:** 23
Web: us.amiad.com
**SIC: 3589** Water treatment equipment, industrial
HQ: Amiad U.S.A., Inc.
120 Talbert Rd Ste J
Mooresville NC 28117
704 662-3133

**(P-10534)**
**AMIAD USA INC**
Also Called: Amiad Filtration Systems
1251 Maulhardt Ave, Oxnard (93030-7990)
P.O. Box 5547 (93031-5547)
PHONE.................................805 988-3323
Tom Akehurst, *Pr*
Issac Orlans, *Stockholder*
▲ **EMP:** 35 **EST:** 1981
**SQ FT:** 30,000
SALES (est): 3.56MM **Privately Held**
Web: www.amiad.com
**SIC: 3589** Water treatment equipment, industrial
PA: Amiad Water Systems Ltd
Kibbutz

**(P-10535)**
**AMPAC USA INC**
5255 State St 5275, Montclair (91763-6236)
PHONE.................................435 291-0961
Hunter Tyson, *Prin*
**EMP:** 50 **EST:** 2021
SALES (est): 4.62MM **Privately Held**
Web: www.ampac1.com
**SIC: 3589** Water purification equipment, household type

**(P-10536)**
**APPLIED MEMBRANES INC**
Also Called: Wateranywhere

## 3589 - Service Industry Machinery, Nec (P-10537)

2450 Business Park Dr, Vista (92081-8847)
PHONE..........................760 727-3711
Gulshan Dhawan, *CEO*
◆ **EMP:** 178 **EST:** 1983
**SQ FT:** 55,000
**SALES (est):** 25.41MM **Privately Held**
Web: www.appliedmembranes.com
**SIC: 3589** 5074 Water purification equipment, household type; Water heaters and purification equipment

### (P-10537)
### AQUA PRODUCTS INC (DH)
2882 Whiptail Loop Ste 100, Carlsbad (92010-6758)
PHONE..........................973 857-2700
Giora Erlich, *Pr*
Joseph Porat, *
Kathleen A Mcclarnon, *Sec*
◆ **EMP:** 24 **EST:** 1964
**SALES (est):** 6.81MM
**SALES (corp-wide):** 362.18K **Privately Held**
Web: www.aquaproducts.com
**SIC: 3589** Swimming pool filter and water conditioning systems
**HQ:** Foridra Srl
Strada Statale 16 Adriatica 16 17/A
Castelfidardo AN 60022

### (P-10538)
### AQUAFINE CORPORATION (HQ)
29010 Avenue Paine, Valencia (91355-4198)
PHONE..........................661 257-4770
Roberta Veloz, *Ch*
Michael Murphy, *
◆ **EMP:** 72 **EST:** 1949
**SQ FT:** 100,000
**SALES (est):** 24.33MM
**SALES (corp-wide):** 23.89B **Publicly Held**
Web: www.trojantechnologies.com
**SIC: 3589** Water treatment equipment, industrial
**PA:** Danaher Corporation
2200 Pa Ave Nw Ste 800w
202 828-0850

### (P-10539)
### AQUAMOR LLC (PA)
Also Called: Watersentinel
42188 Rio Nedo, Temecula (92590-3717)
PHONE..........................951 541-9517
▲ **EMP:** 100 **EST:** 2004
**SALES (est):** 14.91MM
**SALES (corp-wide):** 14.91MM **Privately Held**
Web: www.aquamor.com
**SIC: 3589** Water filters and softeners, household type

### (P-10540)
### AQUEOUS TECHNOLOGIES CORP
1678 N Maple St, Corona (92878-3206)
PHONE..........................909 944-7771
Michael Konrad, *CEO*
▲ **EMP:** 23 **EST:** 1992
**SQ FT:** 15,000
**SALES (est):** 4.2MM **Privately Held**
Web: www.aqueoustech.com
**SIC: 3589** 3829 5084 7699 High pressure cleaning equipment; Physical property testing equipment; Cleaning equipment, high pressure, sand or steam; Industrial machinery and equipment repair

### (P-10541)
### AXEON WATER TECHNOLOGIES
40980 County Center Dr Ste 100, Temecula (92591-6052)
PHONE..........................760 723-5417
Augustin R Pavel, *Pr*
Jeanette Pavel, *
◆ **EMP:** 85 **EST:** 1989
**SQ FT:** 47,000
**SALES (est):** 24.17MM **Privately Held**
Web: www.axeonwater.com
**SIC: 3589** 5999 Water filters and softeners, household type; Water purification equipment

### (P-10542)
### B AND F SOLUTIONS INC
Also Called: Water Treatment Services
2377 Ivy St, Chico (95928-7178)
PHONE..........................530 343-5100
William Bocast, *Pr*
**EMP:** 20 **EST:** 2021
**SALES (est):** 1.18MM **Privately Held**
**SIC: 3589** 7699 Water treatment equipment, industrial; Construction equipment repair

### (P-10543)
### B&W CUSTOM RESTAURANT EQP INC
541 E Jamie Ave, La Habra (90631-6642)
PHONE..........................714 578-0332
Nathan Bojorquez, *Pr*
**EMP:** 20 **EST:** 1990
**SALES (est):** 3.95MM **Privately Held**
Web: www.bwcustom.com
**SIC: 3589** 8711 2599 Cooking equipment, commercial; Industrial engineers; Carts, restaurant equipment

### (P-10544)
### BLUE DESERT INTERNATIONAL INC
Also Called: Hydro Quip
510 N Sheridan St Ste A, Corona (92878-4024)
PHONE..........................951 273-7575
Christopher W Kuttig, *Pr*
◆ **EMP:** 80 **EST:** 1994
**SQ FT:** 31,000
**SALES (est):** 8.14MM **Privately Held**
Web: www.hydroquip.com
**SIC: 3589** Swimming pool filter and water conditioning systems

### (P-10545)
### CHEMICAL METHODS ASSOC LLC (DH)
Also Called: CMA Dish Machines
17707 Valley View Ave, Cerritos (90703-7004)
PHONE..........................714 898-8781
Fred G Palmer, *Pr*
▲ **EMP:** 30 **EST:** 1970
**SALES (est):** 13.4MM
**SALES (corp-wide):** 4.8B **Privately Held**
Web: www.cmadishmachines.com
**SIC: 3589** Dishwashing machines, commercial
**HQ:** Ali Group North America Corporation
101 Corporate Woods Pkwy
Vernon Hills IL 60061
847 215-6565

### (P-10546)
### CHEMICAL TECHNOLOGIES INTL INC
Also Called: CTI
2747 Mercantile Dr Ste 200, Rancho Cordova (95742-6618)
P.O. Box 968 (95741-0968)
PHONE..........................916 638-1315
Clint Townsend, *CEO*
Risa Townsend, *Sec*
▲ **EMP:** 18 **EST:** 1998
**SQ FT:** 50,000
**SALES (est):** 3.29MM **Privately Held**
Web: www.proschoice.com
**SIC: 3589** 2842 Commercial cleaning equipment; Cleaning or polishing preparations, nec

### (P-10547)
### CITY OF DELANO
Also Called: Delano Waste Water Treatment
1107 Lytle Ave, Delano (93215-9389)
PHONE..........................661 721-3352
Bill Hylton, *Mgr*
**EMP:** 28
**SALES (corp-wide):** 39.7MM **Privately Held**
Web: www.cityofdelano.org
**SIC: 3589** Water treatment equipment, industrial
**PA:** City Of Delano
1015 11th Ave
661 721-3300

### (P-10548)
### CITY OF RIVERSIDE
Also Called: Water Treatment Plant
5950 Acorn St, Riverside (92504-1036)
PHONE..........................951 351-6140
Richard Pallante, *Genl Mgr*
**EMP:** 106
Web: www.riversideca.gov
**SIC: 3589** 9111 Water treatment equipment, industrial; Mayors' office
**PA:** City Of Riverside
3900 Main St 7 Fl
951 826-5311

### (P-10549)
### CITY OF SANTA MONICA
Also Called: City Snta Mnica Wtr Trtmnt Pla
1228 S Bundy Dr, Los Angeles (90025-1102)
PHONE..........................310 826-6712
Myriam Cardenas, *Brnch Mgr*
**EMP:** 247
**SQ FT:** 2,500
**SALES (corp-wide):** 546.23MM **Privately Held**
Web: www.santamonica.gov
**SIC: 3589** Sewage and water treatment equipment
**PA:** City Of Santa Monica
1685 Main St
310 458-8411

### (P-10550)
### CLEAN WATER TECHNOLOGY INC (HQ)
Also Called: CWT
13008 S Western Ave, Gardena (90249-1920)
PHONE..........................310 380-4648
Ariel Lechter, *CEO*
Gerald Friedman, *
▲ **EMP:** 50 **EST:** 1996
**SALES (est):** 13.83MM
**SALES (corp-wide):** 149.54MM **Privately Held**
Web: www.cwt-global.com
**SIC: 3589** Water treatment equipment, industrial
**PA:** Marvin Engineering Co., Inc.
261 W Beach Ave
310 674-5030

### (P-10551)
### CLEARLY FILTERED INC
23121 Antonio Pkwy, Rcho Sta Marg (92688-2658)
PHONE..........................877 876-2740
Asaiah Simeon Passwater, *CEO*
**EMP:** 21 **EST:** 2015
**SALES (est):** 2.13MM **Privately Held**
Web: www.clearlyfiltered.com
**SIC: 3589** Water filters and softeners, household type

### (P-10552)
### CM BREWING TECHNOLOGIES LLC
Also Called: Ss Brewtech
42245 Remington Ave, Temecula (92590-2566)
PHONE..........................888 391-9990
Mitchell Thomson, *CEO*
Michael Fabian, *COO*
**EMP:** 15 **EST:** 2013
**SALES (est):** 4.71MM
**SALES (corp-wide):** 4.04B **Publicly Held**
**SIC: 3589** 5046 Coffee brewing equipment; Coffee brewing equipment and supplies
**PA:** The Middleby Corporation
1400 Toastmaster Dr
847 741-3300

### (P-10553)
### COMCO INC
2151 N Lincoln St, Burbank (91504-3392)
PHONE..........................818 333-8500
Colin Weightman, *Pr*
**EMP:** 36 **EST:** 1965
**SQ FT:** 12,500
**SALES (est):** 8.03MM **Privately Held**
Web: www.comcoinc.com
**SIC: 3589** 3291 Sandblasting equipment; Abrasive products

### (P-10554)
### COMPASS WATER SOLUTIONS INC (HQ)
15542 Mosher Ave, Tustin (92780-6425)
PHONE..........................949 222-5777
Thomas Farshler, *CEO*
Bill Tidmore, *
▲ **EMP:** 50 **EST:** 1983
**SQ FT:** 3,000
**SALES (est):** 11.08MM **Publicly Held**
Web: www.compasswater.com
**SIC: 3589** Water treatment equipment, industrial
**PA:** Ceco Environmental Corp.
5080 Spectrum Dr Ste 800e

### (P-10555)
### DE NORA WATER TECHNOLOGIES LLC
1230 Rosecrans Ave Ste 300, Manhattan Beach (90266-2477)
PHONE..........................310 618-9700
Marwan Nesicolaci, *VP*
**EMP:** 19
**SALES (corp-wide):** 930.89MM **Privately Held**
**SIC: 3589** Water treatment equipment, industrial
**HQ:** De Nora Water Technologies Llc
3000 Advance Ln
Colmar PA 18915
215 997-4000

### (P-10556)
### DYNAMIC COOKING SYSTEMS INC
Also Called: Fisher & Paykel
695 Town Center Dr Ste 180, Costa Mesa (92626-1924)
PHONE..........................714 372-7000
Laurence Mawhinney, *CEO*

# PRODUCTS & SERVICES SECTION
## 3589 - Service Industry Machinery, Nec (P-10576)

Stuart Broadhurst, *
▲ **EMP:** 700 **EST:** 1987
**SQ FT:** 140,000
**SALES (est):** 29.65MM **Privately Held**
**SIC: 3589** Cooking equipment, commercial
**HQ:** Fisher & Paykel Appliances Usa
   Holdings Inc.
   695 Town Center Dr # 180
   Costa Mesa CA 92626

### (P-10557)
### ENAQUA (DH)
1350 Specialty Dr Ste D, Vista (92081-8565)
**PHONE**................................760 599-2644
Manoj Kumar Jhawar, *CEO*
Mark Maki, *
Rudra Mishra, *
▲ **EMP:** 18 **EST:** 1985
**SQ FT:** 26,000
**SALES (est):** 8.67MM
**SALES (corp-wide):** 5.02B **Privately Held**
**Web:** www.enaqua.com
**SIC: 3589** Water treatment equipment, industrial
**HQ:** Grundfos Ab
   Lunnagardsgatan 6
   Molndal 431 9
   771322300

### (P-10558)
### ENGINEERED FOOD SYSTEMS
2490 Anselmo Dr, Corona (92879-8089)
P.O. Box 28321 (92809-0144)
**PHONE**................................714 921-9913
Martin Olguin, *Pr*
Irma Olguin, *
▲ **EMP:** 25 **EST:** 2008
**SQ FT:** 18,000
**SALES (est):** 4.51MM **Privately Held**
**Web:** www.efs-eng.com
**SIC: 3589** 5084 Food warming equipment, commercial; Food product manufacturing machinery

### (P-10559)
### FLUIDRA NORTH AMERICA LLC (HQ)
Also Called: Zodiac Pool Solutions
2882 Whiptail Loop Ste 100, Carlsbad (92010-6758)
**PHONE**................................760 599-9600
Lennie Rhodes, *Pr*
**EMP:** 61 **EST:** 2016
**SALES (est):** 489.08MM **Privately Held**
**Web:** www.fluidrausa.com
**SIC: 3589** Swimming pool filter and water conditioning systems
**PA:** Fluidra, Sa
   Avenida Alcalde Barnils 69

### (P-10560)
### FLUIDRA USA LLC (PA)
2882 Whiptail Loop Ste 100, Carlsbad (92010-6758)
**PHONE**................................904 378-0999
Eloy P Corts, *Ch Bd*
Pere Ballart, *
Stephen B De Bever, *
Janice Hague, *
◆ **EMP:** 20 **EST:** 1993
**SQ FT:** 43,000
**SALES (est):** 11.72MM **Privately Held**
**Web:** www.fluidrausa.com
**SIC: 3589** 3561 5091 Swimming pool filter and water conditioning systems; Pumps and pumping equipment; Sporting and recreation goods

### (P-10561)
### G A SYSTEMS INC
226 W Carleton Ave, Orange (92867-3608)
**PHONE**................................714 848-7529
Steven Anderson, *Pr*
**EMP:** 15 **EST:** 1968
**SQ FT:** 19,400
**SALES (est):** 3.08MM **Privately Held**
**Web:** www.gasystemsmfg.com
**SIC: 3589** Commercial cooking and foodwarming equipment

### (P-10562)
### GORLITZ SEWER & DRAIN INC
10132 Norwalk Blvd, Santa Fe Springs (90670-3326)
**PHONE**................................562 944-3060
James Kruger, *CEO*
Gerd Kruger, *
Elba Kruger, *
▲ **EMP:** 30 **EST:** 1974
**SQ FT:** 33,300
**SALES (est):** 4.85MM **Privately Held**
**Web:** www.gorlitz.com
**SIC: 3589** Sewer cleaning equipment, power

### (P-10563)
### HANNAH INDUSTRIES INC
Also Called: South Coast Water
401 S Santa Fe St, Santa Ana (92705-4139)
P.O. Box 247 (92856-6247)
**PHONE**................................714 939-7873
Roy Hall, *Pr*
**EMP:** 15 **EST:** 1984
**SQ FT:** 15,000
**SALES (est):** 3.46MM **Privately Held**
**Web:** www.sch2o.com
**SIC: 3589** 5074 Water treatment equipment, industrial; Water purification equipment

### (P-10564)
### HYDROCOMPONENTS & TECH INC
Also Called: Hydro Components and Tech
1175 Park Center Dr Ste H, Vista (92081-8303)
**PHONE**................................760 598-0189
Robert Williamson, *Pr*
John Snyder, *VP*
Elizabeth Pierce, *Sec*
▲ **EMP:** 15 **EST:** 1991
**SQ FT:** 5,500
**SALES (est):** 2.38MM **Privately Held**
**Web:** www.hcti.com
**SIC: 3589** Water treatment equipment, industrial

### (P-10565)
### HYDRODEX LLC
31225 La Baya Dr, Westlake Village (91362-4019)
**PHONE**................................800 218-8813
**EMP:** 20 **EST:** 2019
**SALES (est):** 926.52K **Privately Held**
**Web:** www.hydrodex.com
**SIC: 3589** Water treatment equipment, industrial

### (P-10566)
### INTEGRITY MUNICPL SYSTEMS LLC
Also Called: Integrity Municipal Systems
13135 Danielson St Ste 204, Poway (92064-8874)
**PHONE**................................858 486-1620
Khaled Roueiheb, *Prin*
Georgios Ioannou, *Prin*
Rich Pasquesi, *Prin*
◆ **EMP:** 16 **EST:** 2006
**SALES (est):** 4.25MM **Privately Held**
**Web:** www.integritymunicipalsystems.com
**SIC: 3589** 1629 8711 Water treatment equipment, industrial; Waste water and sewage treatment plant construction; Engineering services

### (P-10567)
### J F DUNCAN INDUSTRIES INC (PA)
Also Called: Duray
4380 Ayers Ave, Vernon (90058-4306)
**PHONE**................................562 862-4269
Johnny F Wong, *CEO*
Don Durward, *
▲ **EMP:** 86 **EST:** 1988
**SALES (est):** 21.51MM **Privately Held**
**Web:** www.durayduncan.com
**SIC: 3589** Cooking equipment, commercial

### (P-10568)
### JACUZZI INC (DH)
Also Called: Jacuzzi Outdoor Products
17872 Gillette Ave Ste 300, Irvine (92614-6573)
**PHONE**................................909 606-7733
Roy A Jacuzzi, *Ch Bd*
Thomas Koos, *
Donald C Devine, *
◆ **EMP:** 110 **EST:** 1979
**SALES (est):** 457.27MM
**SALES (corp-wide):** 440.01K **Privately Held**
**Web:** www.jacuzzi.com
**SIC: 3589** 3088 Swimming pool filter and water conditioning systems; Hot tubs, plastics or fiberglass
**HQ:** Jacuzzi Brands Llc
   17872 Gllette Ave Ste 300
   Irvine CA 92614
   909 606-1416

### (P-10569)
### JWC ENVIRONMENTAL INC
Also Called: Disposable Waste System
2600 S Garnsey St, Santa Ana (92707-3339)
**PHONE**................................714 662-5829
Steve Glomb, *CFO*
**EMP:** 100
**SQ FT:** 45,637
**Web:** www.jwce.com
**SIC: 3589** Sewage treatment equipment
**HQ:** Jwc Environmental Inc.
   2850 Redhill Ave Ste 125
   Santa Ana CA 92705

### (P-10570)
### KELLERMYER BERGENSONS SVCS LLC (PA)
3605 Ocean Ranch Blvd Ste 200, Oceanside (92056-2696)
**PHONE**................................760 631-5111
Mark Minasian, *CEO*
Christian Cornelius-knudsen, *Pr*
Aj Long, *
Zulfiqar Rashid, *CIO*
Nathaniel Shaw, *Chief Commercial Officer*
◆ **EMP:** 28 **EST:** 2001
**SALES (est):** 620.83MM
**SALES (corp-wide):** 620.83MM **Privately Held**
**Web:** www.kbs-services.com
**SIC: 3589** Commercial cleaning equipment

### (P-10571)
### LAS COLINAS
600 S Jefferson St Ste M, Placentia (92870-6634)
**PHONE**................................714 528-8100
C Christine Licata, *Pr*
Catharine Christine Licata, *Pr*
Anthony Licata, *CFO*
**EMP:** 15 **EST:** 2000
**SALES (est):** 2.28MM **Privately Held**
**Web:** www.lascolinasco.com
**SIC: 3589** 1711 Asbestos removal equipment; Plumbing contractors

### (P-10572)
### LIFESOURCE WATER SYSTEMS INC (PA)
911 E Colorado Blvd Ste 100, Pasadena (91106-1700)
**PHONE**................................626 792-4214
B J Wright, *Pr*
**EMP:** 22 **EST:** 1984
**SQ FT:** 10,000
**SALES (est):** 7.72MM
**SALES (corp-wide):** 7.72MM **Privately Held**
**Web:** www.lifesourcewater.com
**SIC: 3589** 5074 Water purification equipment, household type; Plumbing and hydronic heating supplies

### (P-10573)
### M D MANUFACTURING INC
34970 Mcmurtrey Ave, Bakersfield (93308-9578)
P.O. Box 70277 (93387-0277)
**PHONE**................................661 283-7550
Raymond Stewart, *Pr*
◆ **EMP:** 19 **EST:** 1961
**SQ FT:** 34,000
**SALES (est):** 4.67MM **Privately Held**
**Web:** www.builtinvacuum.com
**SIC: 3589** Vacuum cleaners and sweepers, electric: industrial

### (P-10574)
### MANN+HMMEL WTR FLUID SLTONS IN (DH)
93 S La Patera Ln, Goleta (93117-3246)
**PHONE**................................805 964-8003
Peter Knappe, *Pr*
Kevin Edberg, *
◆ **EMP:** 90 **EST:** 1990
**SQ FT:** 40,000
**SALES (est):** 29.1MM
**SALES (corp-wide):** 5.01B **Privately Held**
**Web:** water-membrane-solutions.mann-hummel.com
**SIC: 3589** Water treatment equipment, industrial
**HQ:** Mann+Hummel Water & Fluid
   Solutions Gmbh
   Kasteler Str. 45
   Wiesbaden HE 65203
   61171187480

### (P-10575)
### MAR COR PURIFICATION INC
6351 Orangethorpe Ave, Buena Park (90620-1340)
**PHONE**................................800 633-3080
Sean West, *Brnch Mgr*
**EMP:** 27
**SIC: 3589** Water treatment equipment, industrial
**HQ:** Mar Cor Purification, Inc.
   4450 Township Line Rd
   Skippack PA 19474
   800 633-3080

### (P-10576)
### MAR COR PURIFICATION INC
2606 Barrington Ct, Hayward (94545-1100)

## 3589 - Service Industry Machinery, Nec (P-10577)

PHONE...............510 397-0025
**EMP:** 18
**SIC: 3589** Water treatment equipment, industrial
**HQ:** Mar Cor Purification, Inc.
4450 Township Line Rd
Skippack PA 19474
800 633-3080

### (P-10577)
### MAZZEI INJECTOR COMPANY LLC
500 Rooster Dr, Bakersfield (93307-9555)
PHONE...............661 363-6500
Angelo Mazzei, *CEO*
Geofffrey Whynot, *Pr*
Mary Mazzei, *Bd of Dir*
▲ **EMP:** 24 **EST:** 1978
**SALES (est):** 2.49MM
**SALES (corp-wide):** 4.19MM **Privately Held**
**Web:** www.mazzei.net
**SIC: 3589** Water treatment equipment, industrial
**PA:** Mazzei Injector Corporation
500 Rooster Dr
661 363-6500

### (P-10578)
### MCC CONTROL SYSTEMS LP
Also Called: McC Control Systems
859 Cotting Ct Ste G, Vacaville (95688-9354)
PHONE...............707 449-0341
**EMP:** 26
**SIC: 3589** Water treatment equipment, industrial

### (P-10579)
### MCC CONTROLS LLC
Also Called: Primex
859 Cotting Ct Ste G, Vacaville (95688-9354)
P.O. Box 1708 (56502-1708)
PHONE...............218 847-1317
David Thomas, *Pr*
Taunia Suckert, *
**EMP:** 27 **EST:** 2016
**SALES (est):** 3.76MM **Privately Held**
**Web:** www.primexcontrols.com
**SIC: 3589** Sewage and water treatment equipment

### (P-10580)
### MEDIA BLAST & ABRASIVE INC
591 Apollo St, Brea (92821-3127)
PHONE...............714 257-0484
Ronald Storer, *Pr*
**EMP:** 19 **EST:** 1997
**SALES (est):** 4.58MM **Privately Held**
**Web:** www.mediablast.com
**SIC: 3589** 3822 Sandblasting equipment; Environmental controls

### (P-10581)
### MEISSNER MFG CO INC (PA)
Also Called: Unicel
21701 Prairie St, Chatsworth (91311-5835)
PHONE...............818 678-0400
**EMP:** 53 **EST:** 1958
**SALES (est):** 7.84MM
**SALES (corp-wide):** 7.84MM **Privately Held**
**SIC: 3589** Swimming pool filter and water conditioning systems

### (P-10582)
### MONTAGUE COMPANY
1830 Stearman Ave, Hayward (94545-1018)
P.O. Box 4954 (94540-4954)
PHONE...............510 785-8822
Thomas M Whalen, *Pr*
Robert M Whalen, *
Joe Deckelman, *
George A Malloch, *
◆ **EMP:** 105 **EST:** 1857
**SQ FT:** 100,000
**SALES (est):** 22.44MM **Privately Held**
**Web:** www.montaguecompany.com
**SIC: 3589** Cooking equipment, commercial

### (P-10583)
### MYTEE PRODUCTS INC
13655 Stowe Dr, Poway (92064-6873)
PHONE...............858 679-1191
John La Barbera, *Pr*
Paul La Barbera, *
Gina La Barbera, *
◆ **EMP:** 43 **EST:** 1991
**SQ FT:** 45,000
**SALES (est):** 8.91MM **Privately Held**
**Web:** www.mytee.com
**SIC: 3589** Commercial cleaning equipment

### (P-10584)
### N/S CORPORATION (PA)
Also Called: NS Wash Systems
28309 Avenue Crocker, Valencia (91355-1251)
PHONE...............310 412-7074
G Thomas Ennis Senior, *CEO*
Francis Penggardjaja, *
Lumen Ong, *
◆ **EMP:** 84 **EST:** 1967
**SQ FT:** 80,000
**SALES (est):** 20.74MM
**SALES (corp-wide):** 20.74MM **Privately Held**
**Web:** www.nswash.com
**SIC: 3589** Car washing machinery

### (P-10585)
### NALCO WTR PRTRTMENT SLTONS LLC
Also Called: Nalco Water
1961 Petra Ln, Placentia (92870-6749)
PHONE...............714 792-0708
**EMP:** 28
**SALES (corp-wide):** 15.32B **Publicly Held**
**SIC: 3589** Water treatment equipment, industrial
**HQ:** Nalco Water Pretreatment Solutions, Llc
1601 W Diehl Rd
Naperville IL 60563
708 754-2550

### (P-10586)
### NEW WAVE INDUSTRIES LTD (DH)
Also Called: Pur-Clean Pressure Car Wash
3315 Orange Grove Ave, North Highlands (95660-5807)
PHONE...............800 882-8854
Michael Gillen, *CEO*
Matt Pronk, *CFO*
Jesse Wurth, *Sec*
**EMP:** 16 **EST:** 1985
**SQ FT:** 24,000
**SALES (est):** 11.41MM
**SALES (corp-wide):** 978.45MM **Privately Held**
**Web:** www.purclean.com
**SIC: 3589** Car washing machinery
**HQ:** Zep Inc.
600 Galleria Pkwy Se
Atlanta GA 30339
877 428-9937

### (P-10587)
### NIECO CORPORATION
7950 Cameron Dr, Windsor (95492-8594)
PHONE...............707 838-3226
Edward D Baker Senior, *Pr*
Edward Baker Junior, *VP*
Matthew Baker, *
Patrick Baker, *
Thomas Baker, *
◆ **EMP:** 70 **EST:** 1972
**SQ FT:** 80,000
**SALES (est):** 24.5MM
**SALES (corp-wide):** 4.04B **Publicly Held**
**Web:** www.nieco.com
**SIC: 3589** Commercial cooking and foodwarming equipment
**PA:** The Middleby Corporation
1400 Toastmaster Dr
847 741-3300

### (P-10588)
### NIMBUS WATER SYSTEMS
42445 Avenida Alvarado, Temecula (92590-3461)
P.O. Box 1478 (92593-1478)
**EMP:** 15 **EST:** 1968
**SQ FT:** 25,000
**SALES (est):** 6.17MM
**SALES (corp-wide):** 267.31MM **Privately Held**
**Web:** www.nimbuswater.com
**SIC: 3589** Water purification equipment, household type
**HQ:** Kinetico Incorporated
10845 Kinsman Rd
Newbury OH 44065
440 564-9111

### (P-10589)
### OSMOSIS TECHNOLOGY INC
Also Called: Osmotik
6900 Hermosa Cir, Buena Park (90620-1151)
PHONE...............714 670-9303
Mike Joulakian, *Pr*
Sonia Joulakian, *VP*
**EMP:** 21 **EST:** 1984
**SQ FT:** 13,000
**SALES (est):** 2.9MM **Privately Held**
**Web:** www.osmotik.com
**SIC: 3589** Water filters and softeners, household type

### (P-10590)
### OZOTECH INC (PA)
1015 S Main St, Yreka (96097-3324)
PHONE...............530 842-4189
Stephen Christiansen, *Pr*
▲ **EMP:** 18 **EST:** 1986
**SALES (est):** 3.58MM
**SALES (corp-wide):** 3.58MM **Privately Held**
**Web:** www.ozotech.com
**SIC: 3589** Water purification equipment, household type

### (P-10591)
### PRODUCT SOLUTIONS INC
1182 N Knollwood Cir, Anaheim (92801-1307)
P.O. Box 6601 (92607-6601)
PHONE...............714 545-9757
Robert Kreaton, *CEO*
Judith Keaton, *
▲ **EMP:** 50 **EST:** 1993
**SQ FT:** 25,000
**SALES (est):** 4.76MM **Privately Held**
**Web:** www.fastproductsolutions.com

**SIC: 3589** 3631 Commercial cooking and foodwarming equipment; Household cooking equipment

### (P-10592)
### PRONTO PRODUCTS CO (PA)
9850 Siempre Viva Rd, San Diego (92154-7247)
PHONE...............619 661-6995
Carlos Matos, *CEO*
William E Parrot, *
Martha J Wagner, *
Barbara Parrot, *
**EMP:** 39 **EST:** 1962
**SALES (est):** 4.42MM
**SALES (corp-wide):** 4.42MM **Privately Held**
**Web:** www.prontoproducts.com
**SIC: 3589** 3496 Commercial cooking and foodwarming equipment; Miscellaneous fabricated wire products

### (P-10593)
### PURI TECH INC
Also Called: Everfilt
3167 Progress Cir, Jurupa Valley (91752-1112)
PHONE...............951 360-8380
Barbara J Andrew, *Pr*
**EMP:** 22 **EST:** 1979
**SQ FT:** 10,600
**SALES (est):** 1.08MM **Privately Held**
**Web:** www.everfilt.com
**SIC: 3589** 5074 Water treatment equipment, industrial; Water purification equipment

### (P-10594)
### PURONICS INCORPORATED (HQ)
7503 Southfront Rd, Livermore (94551-8226)
PHONE...............925 456-7000
Gregg C Sengstack, *CEO*
**EMP:** 32 **EST:** 2005
**SALES (est):** 12.71MM
**SALES (corp-wide):** 2.07B **Publicly Held**
**Web:** www.puronics.com
**SIC: 3589** Swimming pool filter and water conditioning systems
**PA:** Franklin Electric Co., Inc.
9255 Coverdale Rd
260 824-2900

### (P-10595)
### QMP INC
25070 Avenue Tibbitts, Valencia (91355-3447)
PHONE...............661 294-6860
Freddy Vidal, *Pr*
Irma Vidal, *
▲ **EMP:** 45 **EST:** 1994
**SQ FT:** 40,000
**SALES (est):** 4.65MM **Privately Held**
**Web:** www.qmpusa.com
**SIC: 3589** Sewage and water treatment equipment

### (P-10596)
### RANKIN-DELUX INC (PA)
3245 Corridor Dr, Eastvale (91752-1030)
PHONE...............951 685-0081
L Vasan, *Pr*
William A Rankin, *Stockholder*
▲ **EMP:** 15 **EST:** 1965
**SQ FT:** 25,000
**SALES (est):** 2.44MM
**SALES (corp-wide):** 2.44MM **Privately Held**
**Web:** www.rankindelux.com

## PRODUCTS & SERVICES SECTION
## 3589 - Service Industry Machinery, Nec (P-10616)

SIC: 3589 Cooking equipment, commercial

**(P-10597)**
**SANSANI CLEANING SOLUTIONS LLC**
551 E 64th St Apt 3, Long Beach (90805-2395)
PHONE.............................310 630-9033
EMP: 15 EST: 2020
SALES (est): 615.09K Privately Held
SIC: 3589 Commercial cleaning equipment

**(P-10598)**
**SEACO TECHNOLOGIES INC**
280 El Cerrito Dr, Bakersfield (93305-1328)
PHONE.............................661 326-1522
Bob Beck, Brnch Mgr
EMP: 28
Web: www.seacotech.com
SIC: 3589 Water treatment equipment, industrial
PA: Seaco Technologies, Inc.
3220 Patton Way

**(P-10599)**
**SEWER RODDING EQUIPMENT CO (PA)**
Also Called: Flexible Video Systems
3217 Carter Ave, Marina Del Rey (90292-5554)
PHONE.............................310 301-9009
Patrick Crane, CEO
EMP: 25 EST: 1932
SQ FT: 24,000
SALES (est): 3.04MM
SALES (corp-wide): 3.04MM Privately Held
SIC: 3589 Sewer cleaning equipment, power

**(P-10600)**
**SHEPARD BROS INC (PA)**
503 S Cypress St, La Habra (90631-6126)
PHONE.............................562 697-1366
Ronald Shepard, CEO
Duane Shepard, *
Jon Wynkoop, *
◆ EMP: 119 EST: 1976
SQ FT: 57,830
SALES (est): 23.33MM
SALES (corp-wide): 23.33MM Privately Held
Web: www.shepardbros.com
SIC: 3589 5169 Sewage and water treatment equipment; Chemicals and allied products, nec

**(P-10601)**
**SNOWPURE LLC**
Also Called: Snowpure Water Technologies
130 Calle Iglesia Ste A, San Clemente (92672-7535)
P.O. Box 73368 (92673-0113)
PHONE.............................949 240-2188
Michael Snow, Managing Member
◆ EMP: 30 EST: 1979
SALES (est): 7.87MM Privately Held
Web: www.snowpure.com
SIC: 3589 5074 Water purification equipment, household type; Water purification equipment

**(P-10602)**
**SOUTH GATE BREWING COMPANY**
40233 Enterprise Dr, Oakhurst (93644-8839)
PHONE.............................559 692-2739
Steven Hawkins, CEO
EMP: 25 EST: 2013
SQ FT: 1,550
SALES (est): 3.84MM Privately Held
Web: www.southgatebrewco.com
SIC: 3589 5812 5813 Coffee brewing equipment; American restaurant; Bars and lounges

**(P-10603)**
**SPENUZZA INC (HQ)**
Also Called: Imperial Coml Cooking Eqp
1128 Sherborn St, Corona (92879-2089)
PHONE.............................951 281-1830
Peter Spenuzza, CEO
◆ EMP: 71 EST: 1957
SQ FT: 100,000
SALES (est): 24.97MM
SALES (corp-wide): 4.04B Publicly Held
Web: www.imperialrange.com
SIC: 3589 3556 Cooking equipment, commercial; Food products machinery
PA: The Middleby Corporation
1400 Toastmaster Dr
847 741-3300

**(P-10604)**
**STANTEC CONSULTING SVCS INC**
1245 Fiddyment Rd, Lincoln (95648-9504)
P.O. Box 1050 (95648-1050)
PHONE.............................916 434-5062
Sarah Mckelroy, Brnch Mgr
EMP: 24
SALES (corp-wide): 4.23B Privately Held
Web: www.stantec.com
SIC: 3589 Water treatment equipment, industrial
HQ: Stantec Consulting Services Inc.
475 5th Ave Fl 12
New York NY 10017
212 366-5600

**(P-10605)**
**THERMIONICS LABORATORY INC**
10230 Twin Pines Pl, Grass Valley (95949-9530)
PHONE.............................530 272-3436
Steve Rolland, Prin
EMP: 48
SALES (corp-wide): 36.36MM Privately Held
Web: www.thermionics.com
SIC: 3589 Asbestos removal equipment
HQ: Thermionics Laboratory, Inc.
3118 Depot Rd
Hayward CA 94545
510 538-3304

**(P-10606)**
**TIMBUCKTOO MANUFACTURING INC**
Also Called: T M I
1633 W 134th St, Gardena (90249-2013)
PHONE.............................310 323-1134
Juen Lee, CEO
Kyu Lee, *
▲ EMP: 43 EST: 1974
SQ FT: 50,000
SALES (est): 4.69MM Privately Held
Web: www.timbucktoomfg.com
SIC: 3589 Car washing machinery

**(P-10607)**
**TOPPER MANUFACTURING CORP**
23880 Madison St, Torrance (90505-6009)
PHONE.............................310 375-5000
Timothy A Beall, CEO
EMP: 15 EST: 2015
SQ FT: 11,000
SALES (est): 2.1MM Privately Held
Web: www.wowwater.com
SIC: 3589 Water filters and softeners, household type

**(P-10608)**
**VANDER LANS & SONS INC (PA)**
Also Called: Lansas Products
1320 S Sacramento St, Lodi (95240-5705)
P.O. Box 758 (95241-0758)
PHONE.............................209 334-4115
Gerald Vanderlans, Pr
Victor Schuh, *
Nick Bettencourt, *
▲ EMP: 41 EST: 1958
SQ FT: 30,000
SALES (est): 10.44MM
SALES (corp-wide): 10.44MM Privately Held
Web: www.lansas.com
SIC: 3589 5084 Commercial cleaning equipment; Industrial machinery and equipment

**(P-10609)**
**VEOLIA WTS SERVICES USA INC**
7777 Industry Ave, Pico Rivera (90660-4303)
PHONE.............................562 942-2200
Michael Dimick, Brnch Mgr
EMP: 60
SQ FT: 32,091
Web: www.suezwatertechnologies.com
SIC: 3589 Water treatment equipment, industrial
HQ: Veolia Wts Services Usa, Inc.
4545 Patent Rd
Norfolk VA 23502
757 855-9000

**(P-10610)**
**WATER ONE INDUSTRIES INC (PA)**
Also Called: Water One
5410 Gateway Plaza Dr, Benicia (94510-2122)
PHONE.............................707 747-4300
Hans-erik Fuchs, CEO
Tim Russell, *
Erin Steiger, *
EMP: 25 EST: 2006
SQ FT: 3,500
SALES (est): 4.01MM Privately Held
Web: www.wateroneonline.com
SIC: 3589 Water treatment equipment, industrial

**(P-10611)**
**WATER WORKS INC**
5490 Complex St Ste 601, San Diego (92123-1126)
PHONE.............................858 499-0119
John Warmes, Pr
EMP: 27 EST: 2006
SALES (est): 5.79MM Privately Held
Web: www.ultrapurewaterworks.com
SIC: 3589 Water treatment equipment, industrial

**(P-10612)**
**WATERMAN VALVE LLC (HQ)**
Also Called: Waterman Industries
25500 Road 204, Exeter (93221-9655)
P.O. Box 458 (93221-0458)
PHONE.............................559 562-4000
Marcus Shiveley, Pr
▲ EMP: 126 EST: 2005
SQ FT: 175,000
SALES (est): 24.92MM
SALES (corp-wide): 970.37MM Privately Held
Web: www.watermanusa.com
SIC: 3589 Water treatment equipment, industrial
PA: Mcwane, Inc.
2900 Hwy 280 S Ste 300
205 414-3100

**(P-10613)**
**WESFAC INC (HQ)**
Also Called: Wespac
9300 Hall Rd, Downey (90241-5309)
PHONE.............................562 861-2160
Don Hyatt, Pr
Julie Hyatt, *
EMP: 17 EST: 1982
SQ FT: 55,000
SALES (est): 985.15K
SALES (corp-wide): 4.19MM Privately Held
Web: www.omniteaminc.com
SIC: 3589 3431 Commercial cooking and foodwarming equipment; Metal sanitary ware
PA: Omniment Industries, Inc
4380 Ayers Ave
562 923-9660

**(P-10614)**
**WHITTIER FILTRATION INC (DH)**
120 S State College Blvd Ste 175, Brea (92821-5834)
PHONE.............................714 986-5300
Jim Brown, Pr
John M Santelli, Sec
◆ EMP: 21 EST: 1977
SQ FT: 80,000
SALES (est): 8.98MM Privately Held
Web: www.veoliawatertech.com
SIC: 3589 Water treatment equipment, industrial
HQ: Veolia Water Technologies, Inc.
4001 Weston Pkwy
Cary NC 27513

**(P-10615)**
**YANCHEWSKI & WARDELL ENTPS INC**
Also Called: Ecowater Systems
2241 La Mirada Dr, Vista (92081-8828)
PHONE.............................760 754-1960
Ryan Wardell, Pr
EMP: 95 EST: 2006
SALES (est): 8.15MM Privately Held
Web: www.ecowatersocal.com
SIC: 3589 3677 3639 Water purification equipment, household type; Filtration devices, electronic; Hot water heaters, household

**(P-10616)**
**YARDNEY WATER MGT SYSTEMS INC**
Also Called: Yardney Water MGT Systems
6666 Box Springs Blvd, Riverside (92507-0736)
PHONE.............................951 656-6716
Chris Phillips, Pr
◆ EMP: 40 EST: 1948
SQ FT: 55,000
SALES (est): 7.15MM Privately Held
Web: www.yardneyfilters.com
SIC: 3589 Water treatment equipment, industrial

# 3589 - Service Industry Machinery, Nec (P-10617)

**(P-10617)**
**YUBA CY WSTE WTR TRTMNT FCILTY**
302 Burns Dr, Yuba City (95991-7205)
PHONE..................................530 822-7698
John Buckland, *Mayor*
**EMP:** 24 **EST:** 2003
**SALES (est):** 2.97MM **Privately Held**
**Web:** www.yubacity.net
**SIC: 3589** Water treatment equipment, industrial

**(P-10618)**
**Z P M INC**
5770 Thornwood Dr Ste C, Goleta (93117-3812)
PHONE..................................805 681-3511
Dwayne Morse, *Pr*
Marlow Baar, *Treas*
**EMP:** 22 **EST:** 1994
**SQ FT:** 2,400
**SALES (est):** 1.01MM **Privately Held**
**SIC: 3589** 5999 Water treatment equipment, industrial; Water purification equipment

**(P-10619)**
**ZODIAC POOL SYSTEMS LLC (DH)**
Also Called: Jandy Pool Products
2882 Whiptail Loop Ste 100, Carlsbad (92010-6758)
PHONE..................................760 599-9600
Bruce Brooks, *CEO*
Anthony Prudhomme, *
Mike Allanc, *
◆ **EMP:** 250 **EST:** 1999
**SALES (est):** 489.08MM **Privately Held**
**Web:** www.fluidrausa.com
**SIC: 3589** 3999 Swimming pool filter and water conditioning systems; Hot tub and spa covers
**HQ:** Fluidra North America Llc
   2882 Whiptail Loop # 100
   Carlsbad CA 92010
   760 599-9600

## 3592 Carburetors, Pistons, Rings, Valves

**(P-10620)**
**CP-CARRILLO INC**
17401 Armstrong Ave, Irvine (92614-5723)
PHONE..................................949 567-9000
Barry Calvert, *Managing Member*
**EMP:** 30
**SALES (corp-wide):** 3.83B **Privately Held**
**Web:** www.cp-carrillo.com
**SIC: 3592** 3714 Pistons and piston rings; Connecting rods, motor vehicle engine
**HQ:** Cp-Carrillo, Inc.
   1902 Mcgaw Ave
   Irvine CA 92614

**(P-10621)**
**CP-CARRILLO INC (DH)**
1902 Mcgaw Ave, Irvine (92614-0910)
PHONE..................................949 567-9000
Barry Calvert, *CEO*
Peter Calvert, *
Wolfgang Plasser, *
Harry Glieder, *
▲ **EMP:** 160 **EST:** 2011
**SQ FT:** 31,840
**SALES (est):** 27.09MM
**SALES (corp-wide):** 3.39B **Privately Held**
**Web:** www.cp-carrillo.com

**SIC: 3592** 3714 Pistons and piston rings; Connecting rods, motor vehicle engine
**HQ:** Pankl Holdings, Inc.
   1902 Mcgaw Ave
   Irvine CA 92614

**(P-10622)**
**PACIFIC PISTON RING CO INC**
3620 Eastham Dr, Culver City (90232-2411)
P.O. Box 927 (90232-0927)
PHONE..................................310 836-3322
Forest Shannon, *Pr*
Michael Shannon, *
Christina Davis, *
**EMP:** 58 **EST:** 1921
**SQ FT:** 35,000
**SALES (est):** 8.06MM **Privately Held**
**Web:** www.pacificpistonring.com
**SIC: 3592** Pistons and piston rings

**(P-10623)**
**PERFORMANCE MOTORSPORTS INC**
5100 Campus Dr Ste 100, Newport Beach (92660-2191)
PHONE..................................714 898-9763
▲ **EMP:** 265
**SIC: 3592** Pistons and piston rings

**(P-10624)**
**ROSS RACING PISTONS**
625 S Douglas St, El Segundo (90245-4812)
PHONE..................................310 536-0100
Ken Roble, *Pr*
J B Moe Mills, *VP*
Joy Roble, *
**EMP:** 55 **EST:** 1979
**SQ FT:** 25,000
**SALES (est):** 4.89MM **Privately Held**
**Web:** www.rosspistons.com
**SIC: 3592** Pistons and piston rings

**(P-10625)**
**RTR INDUSTRIES LLC (PA)**
Also Called: Grant Piston Rings
4430 E Miraloma Ave Ste B, Anaheim (92807-1840)
PHONE..................................714 996-0050
▲ **EMP:** 27 **EST:** 2002
**SALES (est):** 4.94MM
**SALES (corp-wide):** 4.94MM **Privately Held**
**Web:** www.grantpistonrings.com
**SIC: 3592** Pistons and piston rings

**(P-10626)**
**SEABISCUIT MOTORSPORTS INC**
10800 Valley View St, Cypress (90630-5016)
PHONE..................................714 898-9763
**EMP:** 30
**SALES (corp-wide):** 8.44B **Publicly Held**
**Web:** www.wiseco.com
**SIC: 3592** 3714 Pistons and piston rings; Motor vehicle parts and accessories
**HQ:** Seabiscuit Motorsports, Inc.
   7201 Industrial Park Blvd
   Mentor OH 44060
   440 951-6600

## 3593 Fluid Power Cylinders And Actuators

**(P-10627)**
**GENERAL GRINDING & MFG CO LLC**
Also Called: General Grinding
15100 Valley View Ave, La Mirada (90638-5226)
PHONE..................................562 921-7033
**EMP:** 15 **EST:** 1947
**SQ FT:** 25,000
**SALES (est):** 2.77MM **Privately Held**
**Web:** www.generalgrinding.com
**SIC: 3593** 3599 3471 Fluid power cylinders, hydraulic or pneumatic; Grinding castings for the trade; Plating and polishing

**(P-10628)**
**HYDRAULIC PNEUMATIC INC**
Also Called: Hpi Cylinders
13766 Milroy Pl, Santa Fe Springs (90670-5131)
PHONE..................................562 926-1122
James Whitney, *Pr*
**EMP:** 17 **EST:** 1946
**SQ FT:** 18,000
**SALES (est):** 2.8MM **Privately Held**
**Web:** www.hpicylinders.com
**SIC: 3593** 3599 Fluid power cylinders, hydraulic or pneumatic; Machine shop, jobbing and repair

**(P-10629)**
**RTC ARSPACE - CHTSWRTH DIV INC (PA)**
20409 Prairie St, Chatsworth (91311-6029)
PHONE..................................818 341-3344
James B Hart, *CEO*
Bj Schramm, *Pr*
Bill Hart, *
Elizabeth Hart, *
◆ **EMP:** 84 **EST:** 1958
**SQ FT:** 42,000
**SALES (est):** 30.6MM
**SALES (corp-wide):** 30.6MM **Privately Held**
**Web:** www.rtcaerospace.com
**SIC: 3593** 3594 3599 Fluid power cylinders and actuators; Fluid power pumps and motors; Machine shop, jobbing and repair

## 3594 Fluid Power Pumps And Motors

**(P-10630)**
**BERNELL HYDRAULICS INC (PA)**
8821 Etiwanda Ave, Rancho Cucamonga (91739-9625)
P.O. Box 417 (91739-0417)
PHONE..................................909 899-1751
**TOLL FREE:** 800
Terrance B Jones Senior, *Ch Bd*
Rhonda A Garness, *
John S Clemons, *
**EMP:** 28 **EST:** 1977
**SALES (est):** 15.99MM
**SALES (corp-wide):** 15.99MM **Privately Held**
**Web:** www.bernellhydraulics.com
**SIC: 3594** 5084 3621 3593 Pumps, hydraulic power transfer; Hydraulic systems equipment and supplies; Motors and generators; Fluid power cylinders and actuators

**(P-10631)**
**CRISSAIR INC**
28909 Avenue Williams, Valencia (91355-4183)
PHONE..................................661 367-3300
Michael Alfred, *Pr*
Patrick Lacanfora, *Sr VP*
Eric Grupp, *VP*
Beverly Miller, *VP*
**EMP:** 185 **EST:** 1954
**SQ FT:** 40,000
**SALES (est):** 45.98MM **Publicly Held**
**Web:** www.crissair.com
**SIC: 3594** 3492 Motors, pneumatic; Fluid power valves and hose fittings
**PA:** Esco Technologies Inc.
   9900 A Clayton Rd

**(P-10632)**
**HYPERION MOTORS LLC**
1032 W Taft Ave, Orange (92865-4119)
PHONE..................................714 363-5858
Angelo Kafantaris, *Prin*
**EMP:** 50 **EST:** 2011
**SALES (est):** 5.28MM **Privately Held**
**Web:** www.hyperion.inc
**SIC: 3594** Fluid power pumps and motors

**(P-10633)**
**PARKER-HANNIFIN CORPORATION**
Composite Sealing Systems Div
7664 Panasonic Way, San Diego (92154-8206)
PHONE..................................619 661-7000
Jim Rando, *Mgr*
**EMP:** 130
**SALES (corp-wide):** 19.93B **Publicly Held**
**Web:** www.parker.com
**SIC: 3594** Fluid power pumps and motors
**PA:** Parker-Hannifin Corporation
   6035 Parkland Blvd
   216 896-3000

**(P-10634)**
**PARKER-HANNIFIN CORPORATION**
Also Called: Cylinder Division
221 Helicopter Cir, Corona (92878-5032)
PHONE..................................951 280-3800
Donald P Szmania, *Brnch Mgr*
**EMP:** 73
**SALES (corp-wide):** 19.93B **Publicly Held**
**Web:** www.parker.com
**SIC: 3594** 3728 3593 Fluid power pumps and motors; Aircraft parts and equipment, nec; Fluid power cylinders and actuators
**PA:** Parker-Hannifin Corporation
   6035 Parkland Blvd
   216 896-3000

**(P-10635)**
**PARKER-HANNIFIN CORPORATION**
5500 Business Park Dr, Rohnert Park (94928-7904)
PHONE..................................707 584-7558
**EMP:** 28
**SALES (corp-wide):** 19.93B **Publicly Held**
**Web:** www.parker.com
**SIC: 3594** Fluid power pumps and motors
**PA:** Parker-Hannifin Corporation
   6035 Parkland Blvd
   216 896-3000

**(P-10636)**
**WESTERN HYDROSTATICS INC (PA)**
1956 Keats Dr, Riverside (92501-1747)

# PRODUCTS & SERVICES SECTION
## 3599 - Industrial Machinery, Nec (P-10658)

PHONE..................951 784-2133
**TOLL FREE:** 800
John Starke Scott, *Pr*
Tandy W Scott, *
Barnett Totten, *
▲ **EMP:** 28 **EST:** 1985
**SALES (est):** 4.44MM
**SALES (corp-wide):** 4.44MM **Privately Held**
Web: www.weshyd.com
**SIC: 3594** 7699 5084  Hydrostatic drives (transmissions); Hydraulic equipment repair ; Hydraulic systems equipment and supplies

## 3596 Scales And Balances, Except Laboratory

**(P-10637)**
**BURAN AND REED  INC (PA)**
Also Called: Acme Scale
1801 Adams Ave, San Leandro (94577-1003)
P.O. Box 1922  (94577-0285)
PHONE..................888 638-5040
**TOLL FREE:** 800
Louis G Buran, *CEO*
**EMP:** 20 **EST:** 1984
**SQ FT:** 30,000
**SALES (est):** 4.93MM
**SALES (corp-wide):** 4.93MM **Privately Held**
Web: www.mt.com
**SIC: 3596**  Scales and balances, except laboratory

**(P-10638)**
**JONEL ENGINEERING**
500 E Walnut Ave, Fullerton  (92832-2540)
P.O. Box 798  (92836-0798)
PHONE..................714 879-2360
John Lawson, *Ch*
Mike Lawson, *Pr*
▼ **EMP:** 20 **EST:** 1963
**SQ FT:** 8,000
**SALES (est):** 7.58MM **Privately Held**
Web: www.jonel.com
**SIC: 3596** 5045  Weighing machines and apparatus; Computers, nec

## 3599 Industrial Machinery, Nec

**(P-10639)**
**3-D PRECISION MACHINE INC**
42132 Remington Ave, Temecula (92590-2547)
PHONE..................951 296-5449
Linda Luoma, *Pr*
Roy Luoma, *VP*
**EMP:** 30 **EST:** 2006
**SQ FT:** 14,000
**SALES (est):** 12.51MM **Privately Held**
Web: www.3dprecisionmachine.com
**SIC: 3599**  Machine shop, jobbing and repair

**(P-10640)**
**3D MACHINE CO  INC**
4790 E Wesley Dr, Anaheim  (92807-1941)
PHONE..................714 777-8985
Maria Falcusan, *Pr*
Constantine Falcusan, *
**EMP:** 30 **EST:** 1996
**SQ FT:** 3,300
**SALES (est):** 4.24MM **Privately Held**
Web: www.3dmachineco.com
**SIC: 3599**  Machine shop, jobbing and repair

**(P-10641)**
**3DCAM INTERNATIONAL CORP**
9801 Variel Ave, Chatsworth  (91311-4317)
PHONE..................818 773-8777
Gary Vassighi, *Pr*
**EMP:** 18 **EST:** 2004
**SALES (est):** 2.38MM **Privately Held**
Web: www.3d-cam.com
**SIC: 3599** 3089  Machine shop, jobbing and repair; Injection molding of plastics

**(P-10642)**
**478826 LIMITED**
Also Called: Zi Machine Manufacturing
5050 Hillsdale Cir, El Dorado Hills (95762-5706)
PHONE..................916 933-5280
Steve Zeldag, *CEO*
Terry Young, *Genl Mgr*
**EMP:** 21 **EST:** 1983
**SQ FT:** 26,000
**SALES (est):** 4.85MM **Privately Held**
Web: www.zimachine.com
**SIC: 3599**  Machine shop, jobbing and repair

**(P-10643)**
**5TH AXIS  INC (PA)**
7140 Engineer Rd, San Diego (92111-1422)
PHONE..................858 505-0432
▲ **EMP:** 200 **EST:** 2005
**SQ FT:** 21,000
**SALES (est):** 28MM
**SALES (corp-wide):** 28MM **Privately Held**
Web: www.5thaxis.com
**SIC: 3599**  Machine shop, jobbing and repair

**(P-10644)**
**A & A MACHINE & DEV CO INC**
16625 Gramercy Pl, Gardena  (90247-5201)
PHONE..................310 532-7706
Arlene Hymovitz, *Pr*
Eric Hymovitz, *VP*
**EMP:** 18 **EST:** 1972
**SQ FT:** 12,000
**SALES (est):** 3.24MM **Privately Held**
Web: www.aamach.com
**SIC: 3599**  Machine shop, jobbing and repair

**(P-10645)**
**A & B AEROSPACE  INC**
612 S Ayon Ave, Azusa  (91702-5122)
PHONE..................626 334-2976
Kenneth Smith, *Pr*
Malcolm Smith, *
**EMP:** 35 **EST:** 1950
**SQ FT:** 23,000
**SALES (est):** 8.46MM **Privately Held**
Web: www.abaerospace.com
**SIC: 3599**  Machine shop, jobbing and repair

**(P-10646)**
**A & D PRECISION MACHINING INC**
Also Called: A & D Precision
4155 Business Center Dr, Fremont (94538-6355)
PHONE..................510 657-6781
David A Dreifort, *CEO*
Diane Dreifort, *
**EMP:** 45 **EST:** 1977
**SQ FT:** 28,000
**SALES (est):** 9.43MM **Privately Held**
Web: www.adprecision.com
**SIC: 3599**  Machine shop, jobbing and repair

**(P-10647)**
**A & D PRECISION MFG INC**
4751 E Hunter Ave, Anaheim  (92807-1940)
PHONE..................714 779-2714
Phong Vo, *CEO*
Newton Pham, *CFO*
**EMP:** 21 **EST:** 1988
**SQ FT:** 9,000
**SALES (est):** 3.14MM **Privately Held**
Web: www.adprecisionmfg.com
**SIC: 3599** 3728  Machine shop, jobbing and repair; Aircraft parts and equipment, nec

**(P-10648)**
**A & M ENGINEERING  INC**
15854 Salvatierra St, Irwindale (91706-6603)
PHONE..................626 813-2020
Boris Beljak Senior, *Pr*
Boris Beljak Senior, *Pr*
Boris Beljak Junior, *VP*
Roy Beljak, *
Anita Beljak, *
**EMP:** 80 **EST:** 1973
**SQ FT:** 25,000
**SALES (est):** 9.79MM **Privately Held**
Web: www.amengineeringinc.com
**SIC: 3599** 3812 3537  Machine shop, jobbing and repair; Search and navigation equipment; Industrial trucks and tractors

**(P-10649)**
**A & R ENGINEERING CO  INC**
Also Called: A & R
1053 E Bedmar St, Carson  (90746-3601)
PHONE..................310 603-9060
Murat Sehidoglu, *Pr*
**EMP:** 72 **EST:** 1982
**SQ FT:** 23,334
**SALES (est):** 9.73MM **Privately Held**
Web: www.arengr.com
**SIC: 3599**  Machine shop, jobbing and repair

**(P-10650)**
**A&G MACHINE SHOP  INC**
1352 Burton Ave Ste B, Salinas (93901-4417)
P.O. Box 6190  (93912-6190)
PHONE..................831 759-2261
Anuar Molina, *Pr*
Edna Molina, *VP*
**EMP:** 29 **EST:** 1995
**SQ FT:** 5,500
**SALES (est):** 1.18MM **Privately Held**
**SIC: 3599**  Machine shop, jobbing and repair

**(P-10651)**
**A&T PRECISION MACHINING INC**
Also Called: A&T Precision
330 Piercy Rd, San Jose  (95138-1401)
PHONE..................408 363-1198
James Le, *Pt*
James Le, *Pr*
An Le, *Pt*
Hieu Le, *Pr*
**EMP:** 18 **EST:** 1993
**SALES (est):** 2.92MM **Privately Held**
**SIC: 3599**  Machine shop, jobbing and repair

**(P-10652)**
**A&W PRECISION MACHINING INC**
16320 S Main St, Gardena  (90248-2822)
PHONE..................310 527-7242
Walter Galich, *Pr*
Adelfo Varela, *VP*
**EMP:** 15 **EST:** 2006
**SALES (est):** 1.54MM **Privately Held**
**SIC: 3599**  Machine shop, jobbing and repair

**(P-10653)**
**A-1 JAYS MACHINING  INC (PA)**
2228 Oakland Rd, San Jose  (95131-1414)
PHONE..................408 262-1845
James K Machathil, *CEO*
**EMP:** 84 **EST:** 1990
**SQ FT:** 10,000
**SALES (est):** 22MM **Privately Held**
Web: www.a1jays.com
**SIC: 3599**  Machine shop and repair

**(P-10654)**
**A-1 MACHINE MANUFACTURING INC (PA)**
490 Gianni St, Santa Clara  (95054-2413)
PHONE..................408 727-0880
Yong Kil, *Pr*
Yong Su Pak, *
▲ **EMP:** 49 **EST:** 1986
**SQ FT:** 250,000
**SALES (est):** 11.79MM
**SALES (corp-wide):** 11.79MM **Privately Held**
**SIC: 3599**  Machine shop, jobbing and repair

**(P-10655)**
**A-Z MFG INC**
Also Called: AZ Manufacturing
3101 W Segerstrom Ave, Santa Ana (92704-5811)
PHONE..................714 444-4446
Ann Lukas, *Prin*
Gary Lukas, *
**EMP:** 40 **EST:** 1993
**SQ FT:** 16,096
**SALES (est):** 10.07MM **Privately Held**
Web: www.azmfginc.com
**SIC: 3599**  Machine shop, jobbing and repair

**(P-10656)**
**ABEN MACHINE PRODUCTS INC**
Also Called: Aben
9550 Owensmouth Ave, Chatsworth (91311-4801)
PHONE..................818 960-4502
Nabeel Saoud, *Pr*
Nabeel Saoud, *Pr*
Esdras Giron, *Product Vice President*
**EMP:** 17 **EST:** 1998
**SALES (est):** 2.46MM **Privately Held**
Web: www.abenusa.com
**SIC: 3599**  Machine shop, jobbing and repair

**(P-10657)**
**ABLE WIRE EDM  INC**
440 Atlas St Ste A, Brea  (92821-3136)
PHONE..................714 255-1967
John Marquardt, *Pr*
Barbara Marquardt, *Sec*
Chris Marks, *Mgr*
**EMP:** 15 **EST:** 1988
**SQ FT:** 5,500
**SALES (est):** 2.12MM **Privately Held**
Web: www.electricaldischargemachining.com
**SIC: 3599**  Machine shop, jobbing and repair

**(P-10658)**
**ABSOLUTE MACHINE INC**
5020 Mountain Lakes Blvd, Redding (96003-1457)
PHONE..................530 242-6840
Alfred Madena, *Pr*
**EMP:** 15 **EST:** 2004
**SALES (est):** 1.15MM **Privately Held**
Web: www.absolutem.com
**SIC: 3599**  Machine shop, jobbing and repair

# 3599 - Industrial Machinery, Nec (P-10659)

**(P-10659)**
**ACC PRECISION INC**
321 Hearst Dr, Oxnard (93030-5158)
PHONE..............................805 278-9801
Arturo Alfaro, *Pr*
**EMP:** 15 **EST:** 2003
**SQ FT:** 6,000
**SALES (est):** 2.33MM **Privately Held**
**Web:** www.accprecision.com
**SIC: 3599** Machine shop, jobbing and repair

**(P-10660)**
**ACCU MACHINE INC**
440 Aldo Ave, Santa Clara (95054-2301)
**EMP:** 23 **EST:** 2006
**SALES (est):** 1.75MM **Privately Held**
**Web:** accumachineinc.weebly.com
**SIC: 3599** Machine shop, jobbing and repair

**(P-10661)**
**ACCU-TECH LASER PROCESSING INC**
1175 Linda Vista Dr, San Marcos (92078-3811)
PHONE..............................760 744-6692
Michael C Gericke, *Pr*
Roger Underwood, *
**EMP:** 33 **EST:** 2006
**SQ FT:** 6,500
**SALES (est):** 2.67MM **Privately Held**
**Web:** www.accutechlaser.com
**SIC: 3599** Machine shop, jobbing and repair

**(P-10662)**
**ACCURATE PRFMCE MACHINING INC**
2255 S Grand Ave, Santa Ana (92705-5206)
PHONE..............................714 434-7811
Robert Keith Fischer, *CEO*
Larry Taylor, *VP*
Karen Fischer, *VP*
**EMP:** 21 **EST:** 1996
**SQ FT:** 3,200
**SALES (est):** 3.28MM **Privately Held**
**Web:** www.cncapm.com
**SIC: 3599** Machine shop, jobbing and repair

**(P-10663)**
**ACCURATE TECHNOLOGY MFG INC**
Also Called: Accurate Technology Mfg
930 Thompson Pl, Sunnyvale (94085-4517)
PHONE..............................408 733-4344
Ivo Dukanovic, *CEO*
John Dukanovic, *
**EMP:** 60 **EST:** 1994
**SQ FT:** 40,000
**SALES (est):** 4.71MM **Privately Held**
**Web:** www.accuratetm.com
**SIC: 3599** Machine shop, jobbing and repair

**(P-10664)**
**ACE AIR MANUFACTURING**
1430 W 135th St, Gardena (90249-2218)
PHONE..............................310 323-7246
Aldo Lemus, *CEO*
**EMP:** 17 **EST:** 1957
**SQ FT:** 12,000
**SALES (est):** 3.63MM **Privately Held**
**Web:** www.aceairmfg.com
**SIC: 3599** Machine shop, jobbing and repair

**(P-10665)**
**ACE INDUSTRIES INC**
195 Mace St, Chula Vista (91911-5820)
PHONE..............................619 482-2700
Bobby Yoo, *CEO*
Bobby Yoo, *Pr*
Joy Yoo, *Treas*
▲ **EMP:** 20 **EST:** 1998
**SQ FT:** 15,000
**SALES (est):** 1.32MM **Privately Held**
**Web:** www.aceindustriesinc.com
**SIC: 3599** Machine shop, jobbing and repair

**(P-10666)**
**ACE MACHINE SHOP INC**
11200 Wright Rd, Lynwood (90262-3124)
P.O. Box 97 (91709)
PHONE..............................310 608-2277
Pedro Gallinucci, *Pr*
Lucia Gallinucci, *
**EMP:** 70 **EST:** 1956
**SQ FT:** 35,000
**SALES (est):** 6.24MM **Privately Held**
**Web:** www.isconcepts.com
**SIC: 3599** Machine shop, jobbing and repair

**(P-10667)**
**ACE TUBE BENDING**
14 Journey, Aliso Viejo (92656-3317)
PHONE..............................949 362-2220
**EMP:** 22 **EST:** 1978
**SALES (est):** 2.64MM **Privately Held**
**Web:** www.acetubebending.com
**SIC: 3599** Machine shop, jobbing and repair

**(P-10668)**
**ACM MACHINING INC (PA)**
11390 Gold Dredge Way, Rancho Cordova (95742-6867)
PHONE..............................916 852-8600
Alfred Balbach, *Pr*
Carlos Balbachas, *
▲ **EMP:** 41 **EST:** 1974
**SQ FT:** 29,000
**SALES (est):** 8.63MM
**SALES (corp-wide):** 8.63MM **Privately Held**
**Web:** www.acmmachining.com
**SIC: 3599** Machine shop, jobbing and repair

**(P-10669)**
**ACM MACHINING INC**
Also Called: Alfred's Machining
240 State Highway 16 Unit 18, Plymouth (95669-9701)
PHONE..............................916 804-9489
Carlos Balbacas, *Owner*
**EMP:** 35
**SALES (corp-wide):** 8.63MM **Privately Held**
**Web:** www.acmmachining.com
**SIC: 3599** 3494 Machine shop, jobbing and repair; Valves and pipe fittings, nec
**PA:** Acm Machining, Inc.
11390 Gold Dredge Way
916 852-8600

**(P-10670)**
**ACUNA DIONISIO ABLE**
Also Called: A & L Engineering
12629 Prairie Ave, Hawthorne (90250-4611)
PHONE..............................310 978-4741
Dionasio Abel Acuna, *Owner*
**EMP:** 15 **EST:** 1993
**SQ FT:** 3,700
**SALES (est):** 1.25MM **Privately Held**
**SIC: 3599** 8711 5049 Machine shop, jobbing and repair; Industrial engineers; Engineers' equipment and supplies, nec

**(P-10671)**
**ADEM LLC**
Also Called: Advanced Design Engrg & Mfg
1040 Di Giulio Ave Ste 160, Santa Clara (95050-2847)
PHONE..............................408 727-8955
**EMP:** 30 **EST:** 1997
**SQ FT:** 11,000
**SALES (est):** 4.98MM **Privately Held**
**Web:** www.ademllc.com
**SIC: 3599** 8711 Machine shop, jobbing and repair; Engineering services

**(P-10672)**
**ADVANCED CERAMIC TECHNOLOGY**
803 W Angus Ave, Orange (92868-1307)
PHONE..............................714 538-2524
Eric Roberts, *Pr*
Eric Andrew Roberts, *Pr*
William Roberts, *VP*
**EMP:** 16 **EST:** 1983
**SQ FT:** 9,900
**SALES (est):** 1.8MM **Privately Held**
**Web:** www.advancedceramictech.com
**SIC: 3599** Machine shop, jobbing and repair

**(P-10673)**
**ADVANCED ENGINEERING & EDM INC**
13007 Kirkham Way Ste A, Poway (92064-7152)
PHONE..............................858 679-6800
Norm Turoff, *CEO*
Lindy Bauer, *Contrlr*
**EMP:** 17 **EST:** 2013
**SALES (est):** 913.04K **Privately Held**
**Web:** www.aeedm.com
**SIC: 3599** Machine shop, jobbing and repair

**(P-10674)**
**ADVANCED ENGINERING AND EDM**
13007 Kirkham Way Ste A, Poway (92064-7152)
PHONE..............................858 679-6800
William J Bauer, *Mng Pt*
Norm Turoff, *Mng Pt*
**EMP:** 20 **EST:** 2011
**SALES (est):** 4.91MM **Privately Held**
**Web:** www.aeedm.com
**SIC: 3599** Machine shop, jobbing and repair

**(P-10675)**
**ADVANCED JOINING TECHNOLOGIES INC**
3030 Red Hill Ave, Santa Ana (92705-5823)
PHONE..............................949 756-8091
**EMP:** 25
**Web:** www.ajt-inc.com
**SIC: 3599** Machine shop, jobbing and repair

**(P-10676)**
**ADVANCED MCHNING SOLUTIONS INC**
3523 Main St Ste 606, Chula Vista (91911-0803)
PHONE..............................619 671-3055
Pamela Yuhm, *Pr*
**EMP:** 35 **EST:** 2005
**SALES (est):** 2.58MM **Privately Held**
**Web:** www.amssd.com
**SIC: 3599** Machine shop, jobbing and repair

**(P-10677)**
**ADVANCED MCHNING TCHNIQUES INC**
16205 Vineyard Blvd, Morgan Hill (95037-7124)
PHONE..............................408 778-4500
Frank C Dutra, *Pr*
Susan Dutra, *

**EMP:** 49 **EST:** 1985
**SQ FT:** 24,000
**SALES (est):** 5.65MM **Privately Held**
**Web:** www.amtcal.com
**SIC: 3599** Machine shop, jobbing and repair

**(P-10678)**
**ADVANCED PRECISION INC**
13445 Yorba Ave, Chino (91710-5055)
PHONE..............................909 591-4244
Craig G Rohde, *CFO*
**EMP:** 16 **EST:** 2013
**SALES (est):** 2.96MM **Privately Held**
**Web:** www.advanced-precision.com
**SIC: 3599** Machine shop, jobbing and repair

**(P-10679)**
**ADVANCED TECH MACHINING INC**
28909 Avenue Williams, Valencia (91355)
PHONE..............................661 257-2313
Herbert Joe Howton, *CEO*
Vickie Howton, *Pr*
Joe Howton, *VP*
**EMP:** 15 **EST:** 1987
**SALES (est):** 2.12MM **Privately Held**
**Web:** www.crissair.com
**SIC: 3599** Machine shop, jobbing and repair

**(P-10680)**
**ADVOQUE GROUP LLC**
1030 Commercial St Ste 108, San Jose (95112-1436)
PHONE..............................408 560-2990
Jason Azevedo, *CEO*
**EMP:** 50 **EST:** 2021
**SALES (est):** 3.78MM **Privately Held**
**Web:** www.advoquesafeguard.com
**SIC: 3599** Custom machinery

**(P-10681)**
**AERO CHIP INC**
13563 Freeway Dr, Santa Fe Springs (90670-5633)
PHONE..............................562 404-6300
Solomon M Gavrila, *CEO*
Liviu Pribac, *
**EMP:** 50 **EST:** 1988
**SQ FT:** 17,000
**SALES (est):** 8.38MM **Privately Held**
**Web:** www.aerochip.com
**SIC: 3599** Machine shop, jobbing and repair

**(P-10682)**
**AERO DYNAMIC MACHINING INC**
7472 Chapman Ave, Garden Grove (92841-2106)
PHONE..............................714 379-1073
Wendy Nguyen, *Ch Bd*
David Nguyen, *
Wendy Nguyen, *VP*
Kevin Tran, *
▲ **EMP:** 65 **EST:** 1998
**SALES (est):** 10.52MM **Privately Held**
**Web:** www.aerodynamicinc.com
**SIC: 3599** 3499 Machine shop, jobbing and repair; Fire- or burglary-resistive products

**(P-10683)**
**AERO INDUSTRIES LLC**
139 Industrial Way, Buellton (93427-9592)
P.O. Box 198 (93427-0198)
PHONE..............................805 688-6734
Dave Watkins, *Mgr*
**EMP:** 340 **EST:** 2007
**SALES (est):** 2.97MM
**SALES (corp-wide):** 40.31MM **Privately Held**

## PRODUCTS & SERVICES SECTION
### 3599 - Industrial Machinery, Nec (P-10707)

Web: www.aero-cnc.com
SIC: 3599 Machine shop, jobbing and repair
PA: Gavial Holdings, Inc.
1435 W Mccoy Ln
805 614-0060

**(P-10684)**
**AERO MECHANISM PRECISION INC**
21700 Marilla St, Chatsworth (91311-4125)
PHONE..............................818 886-1855
Palminder Sehmbey, *Pr*
EMP: 34 EST: 1996
SQ FT: 8,000
SALES (est): 4.53MM **Privately Held**
Web: www.aeromechanism.com
SIC: 3599 Machine shop, jobbing and repair

**(P-10685)**
**AERO-K**
2040 E Dyer Rd, Santa Ana (92705-5710)
PHONE..............................626 350-5125
Robert Krusic, *Pr*
EMP: 45 EST: 1983
SALES (est): 4.23MM **Privately Held**
Web: www.aero-k.com
SIC: 3599 Machine shop, jobbing and repair

**(P-10686)**
**AERO-MECHANICAL ENGRG INC**
5945 Engineer Dr, Huntington Beach (92649-1129)
PHONE..............................323 682-0961
Anders Ahlstrom, *CEO*
John Ahlstrom, *Pr*
Anders Ahlstrom, *Ch Bd*
EMP: 16 EST: 1974
SQ FT: 4,150
SALES (est): 2.35MM **Privately Held**
Web: www.aero-mechanical.com
SIC: 3599 Machine shop, jobbing and repair

**(P-10687)**
**AERODYNAMIC ENGINEERING INC**
15495 Graham St, Huntington Beach (92649-1205)
PHONE..............................714 891-2651
Bob Waddell, *
Alfred Mayer, *
Ewald Eisel, *
Mark Schultz, *Manager*
▲ EMP: 40 EST: 1968
SQ FT: 12,000
SALES (est): 5.29MM **Privately Held**
Web: www.aerodynamic.net
SIC: 3599 3769 Machine shop, jobbing and repair; Space vehicle equipment, nec

**(P-10688)**
**AERODYNE PRCSION MACHINING INC**
5471 Argosy Ave, Huntington Beach (92649-1038)
PHONE..............................714 891-1311
Raymond Krispel, *Pr*
Otto Schulz, *
Veronica Schultz, *
▲ EMP: 25 EST: 1986
SQ FT: 20,000
SALES (est): 7.73MM **Privately Held**
Web: www.aerodyneprecision.com
SIC: 3599 Machine shop, jobbing and repair

**(P-10689)**
**AEROLIANT MANUFACTURING INC**
Also Called: Fordon Grind Industries
1613 Lockness Pl, Torrance (90501-5119)
PHONE..............................310 257-1903
Patricia A Wiacek, *Pr*
Greg Wiacek, *
EMP: 20 EST: 2009
SQ FT: 7,200
SALES (est): 990.42K **Privately Held**
Web: www.amratec.com
SIC: 3599 Machine shop, jobbing and repair

**(P-10690)**
**AEROSPACE AND COML TOOLING INC**
Also Called: A C T
1866 S Lake Pl, Ontario (91761-5788)
PHONE..............................909 930-5780
Oscar Borello, *Pr*
EMP: 16 EST: 1989
SQ FT: 20,000
SALES (est): 2.64MM **Privately Held**
Web: www.actooling.com
SIC: 3599 Machine shop, jobbing and repair

**(P-10691)**
**AEROTECH PRECISION MACHINING**
42541 6th St E Ste 17, Lancaster (93535-5201)
PHONE..............................661 802-7185
Jose Reyes, *CEO*
EMP: 15 EST: 2018
SALES (est): 3.42MM **Privately Held**
Web: www.aerotechpmi.com
SIC: 3599 Machine shop, jobbing and repair

**(P-10692)**
**AEROTEK INC**
2751 Park View Ct Ste 221, Oxnard (93036-5450)
PHONE..............................805 604-3000
EMP: 1439
SALES (corp-wide): 14.88B **Privately Held**
Web: www.aerotek.com
SIC: 3599 Machine and other job shop work
HQ: Aerotek, Inc.
7301 Pkwy Dr
Hanover MD 21076
410 694-5100

**(P-10693)**
**ALCO ENGRG & TOOLING CORP**
Also Called: Alco Metal Fab
3001 Oak St, Santa Ana (92707-4235)
PHONE..............................714 556-6060
Frank Vallefuoco, *Pr*
Frank Vallefuoco, *CEO*
Tom Hare, *
Angelo D'eramo, *Sec*
EMP: 40 EST: 1944
SQ FT: 32,000
SALES (est): 5.16MM **Privately Held**
Web: www.alcoge.com
SIC: 3599 Machine shop, jobbing and repair

**(P-10694)**
**ALL 4-PCB NORTH AMERICA INC**
345 Mira Loma Ave, Glendale (91204-2912)
PHONE..............................866 734-9403
Torsten Reckert, *Pr*
Roland Lacap, *VP*
▲ EMP: 17 EST: 2001
SQ FT: 4,000
SALES (est): 2.72MM **Privately Held**
Web: www.all4-pcb.us
SIC: 3599 3545 3541 3672 Chemical milling job shop; Milling machine attachments (machine tool accessories); Chemical milling machines; Printed circuit boards

**(P-10695)**
**ALL DIAMETER GRINDING INC**
725 N Main St, Orange (92868-1105)
PHONE..............................714 744-1200
Marvin W Goodwin, *Pr*
Jeff Goodwin, *VP*
Barbara Goodwin, *Sec*
EMP: 22 EST: 1960
SQ FT: 9,500
SALES (est): 2.22MM **Privately Held**
Web: www.alldiametergrinding.com
SIC: 3599 Machine shop, jobbing and repair

**(P-10696)**
**ALL STAR PRECISION**
8739 Lion St, Rancho Cucamonga (91730-4428)
PHONE..............................909 944-8373
Scott Jackson, *Owner*
Ron Jackson, *Pt*
EMP: 23 EST: 2004
SALES (est): 3.66MM **Privately Held**
Web: www.allstarprecision.com
SIC: 3599 Machine shop, jobbing and repair

**(P-10697)**
**ALL SWISS TURNING** ✪
7745 Alabama Ave Ste 13, Canoga Park (91304-6639)
PHONE..............................818 466-3076
Juan R Olivas, *Pr*
EMP: 25 EST: 2024
SALES (est): 1.27MM **Privately Held**
Web: www.allswissturning.com
SIC: 3599 Machine shop, jobbing and repair

**(P-10698)**
**ALL-IN MACHINING LLC**
157 Sloan Ct Ste B, Tracy (95304-1649)
PHONE..............................209 839-8672
EMP: 18 EST: 2017
SALES (est): 6.18MM **Privately Held**
Web: www.allinmach.com
SIC: 3599 Machine shop, jobbing and repair

**(P-10699)**
**ALL-TECH MACHINE & ENGRG INC**
2700 Prune Ave, Fremont (94539-6780)
PHONE..............................510 353-2000
Richard M Gale, *CEO*
Boydine Michaels, *
EMP: 49 EST: 1987
SALES (est): 2.52MM **Privately Held**
Web: www.alltechinc.com
SIC: 3599 Machine shop, jobbing and repair

**(P-10700)**
**ALLIED ENGINEERING AND PRODUCTION CORPORATION**
2421 Blanding Ave, Alameda (94501-1503)
PHONE..............................510 522-1500
◆ EMP: 36
SIC: 3599 Machine shop, jobbing and repair

**(P-10701)**
**ALLOY MACHINING AND HONING INC**
2808 Supply Ave, Commerce (90040-2706)
PHONE..............................323 726-8248
Paul Muscet, *Pr*
Nada Muscet, *Sec*
EMP: 15 EST: 1991
SQ FT: 12,000
SALES (est): 891.65K **Privately Held**
Web: www.alloymachiningservices.com
SIC: 3599 Machine shop, jobbing and repair

**(P-10702)**
**ALPHA AVIATION COMPONENTS INC (PA)**
16772 Schoenborn St, North Hills (91343-6108)
PHONE..............................818 894-8801
Lidia Gorko, *Pr*
William Tudor, *
EMP: 25 EST: 1954
SQ FT: 18,000
SALES (est): 8.18MM
SALES (corp-wide): 8.18MM **Privately Held**
Web: www.alphaaci.com
SIC: 3599 3451 3728 Machine shop, jobbing and repair; Screw machine products; Aircraft parts and equipment, nec

**(P-10703)**
**ALPHA MACHINE COMPANY INC**
Also Called: Alpha Machine Co
933 Chittenden Ln Ste A, Capitola (95010-3600)
PHONE..............................831 462-7400
Pemo Saraliev, *Pr*
EMP: 18 EST: 1978
SQ FT: 12,000
SALES (est): 2.5MM **Privately Held**
Web: www.alphamco.com
SIC: 3599 Machine shop, jobbing and repair

**(P-10704)**
**ALTAMONT MANUFACTURING INC**
241 Rickenbacker Cir, Livermore (94551-7216)
PHONE..............................925 371-5401
Robert Stivers, *Pr*
Richard Stivers, *VP*
EMP: 18 EST: 2003
SALES (est): 2.28MM **Privately Held**
Web: www.altamontmfg.com
SIC: 3599 Machine shop, jobbing and repair

**(P-10705)**
**ALTEST CORPORATION**
Also Called: Altest
898 Faulstich Ct, San Jose (95112-1361)
PHONE..............................408 436-9900
Savann Seng, *CEO*
Brian Sen, *
Amy Tung, *
EMP: 29 EST: 1998
SQ FT: 30,000
SALES (est): 10.49MM **Privately Held**
Web: www.altestcorp.com
SIC: 3599 3672 Machine shop, jobbing and repair; Printed circuit boards

**(P-10706)**
**ALTS TOOL & MACHINE INC**
10926 Woodside Ave N, Santee (92071-3272)
P.O. Box 712485 (92072-2485)
PHONE..............................619 562-6653
EMP: 55
Web: www.altstool.com
SIC: 3599 Machine shop, jobbing and repair

**(P-10707)**
**ALVELLAN INC**
Also Called: East Bay Machine and Shtmtl
1030 Shary Ct, Concord (94518-2409)
P.O. Box 1206 (94522-1206)
PHONE..............................925 689-2421
Sean M Mclellan, *CEO*
Tim Alvey, *
EMP: 28 EST: 2006
SQ FT: 30,000

# 3599 - Industrial Machinery, Nec (P-10708)

**SALES (est): 3.97MM Privately Held**
Web: www.eastbaymachine.com
SIC: **3599** 5083  Machine shop, jobbing and repair; Lawn and garden machinery and equipment

## (P-10708)
### AM-TEK ENGINEERING INC
1180 E Francis St Ste C, Ontario (91761-4802)
PHONE.............................909 673-1633
Boone Bounyaseng, *CEO*
**EMP:** 18 **EST:** 1998
**SQ FT:** 10,000
**SALES (est):** 3.06MM **Privately Held**
Web: www.amtekeng.com
SIC: **3599**  Machine shop, jobbing and repair

## (P-10709)
### AMERICAN DEBURRING INC
Also Called: A Fab
20742 Linear Ln, Lake Forest (92630-7804)
PHONE.............................949 457-9790
Robert L Campbell, *Pr*
Theresa Cook, *
**EMP:** 25 **EST:** 1973
**SQ FT:** 11,000
**SALES (est):** 3.2MM **Privately Held**
Web: www.afabcnc.com
SIC: **3599**  Machine shop, jobbing and repair

## (P-10710)
### ANGULAR MACHINING INC
2040 Hartog Dr, San Jose (95131-2214)
PHONE.............................408 954-8326
Kiet Nguyen, *Pr*
**EMP:** 21 **EST:** 2001
**SALES (est):** 3.92MM **Privately Held**
Web: www.angularmachining.com
SIC: **3599**  Machine shop, jobbing and repair

## (P-10711)
### ANTRIN MINIATURE SPC INC
342 Industrial Way Ste 201, Fallbrook (92028-2352)
PHONE.............................760 723-7605
Anne Odermatt, *CEO*
Oscar Lomeli, *Pr*
Anne Odermatt, *VP*
**EMP:** 15 **EST:** 1987
**SQ FT:** 5,000
**SALES (est):** 2.13MM **Privately Held**
Web: www.antrinminiature.com
SIC: **3599**  Machine shop, jobbing and repair

## (P-10712)
### APEX MACHINING INC
1997 Hartog Dr, San Jose (95131-2222)
PHONE.............................408 441-1335
Carl Kennedy, *Genl Mgr*
**EMP:** 23 **EST:** 1993
**SQ FT:** 1,200
**SALES (est):** 1.5MM **Privately Held**
Web: www.apexmachining.net
SIC: **3599**  Machine shop, jobbing and repair

## (P-10713)
### APOGEE MANUFACTURING
28231 Avenue Crocker Ste 90, Valencia (91355-1249)
PHONE.............................661 467-0440
Chad Jensen, *Pr*
Glen Jelletich, *VP*
◆ **EMP:** 15 **EST:** 2003
**SQ FT:** 800
**SALES (est):** 1.01MM **Privately Held**
SIC: **3599**  Machine shop, jobbing and repair

## (P-10714)
### ARANDA TOOLING LLC
13950 Yorba Ave, Chino (91710-5520)
PHONE.............................714 379-6565
Pedro Aranda, *Pr*
Martha Aranda, *
▲ **EMP:** 70 **EST:** 1976
**SQ FT:** 60,000
**SALES (est):** 18.58MM **Privately Held**
Web: www.arandatooling.com
SIC: **3599** 3469 3544 3465  Machine shop, jobbing and repair; Metal stampings, nec; Special dies, tools, jigs, and fixtures; Automotive stampings

## (P-10715)
### AREMAC ASSOCIATES INC
2004 S Myrtle Ave, Monrovia (91016-4837)
PHONE.............................626 303-8795
Scott Sher, *CEO*
Mariela Vinas, *
**EMP:** 35 **EST:** 1963
**SQ FT:** 12,500
**SALES (est):** 2.3MM **Privately Held**
SIC: **3599** 3444  Machine shop, jobbing and repair; Sheet metalwork

## (P-10716)
### ARMSTRONG TECHNOLOGY SV INC
Also Called: Armstrong Technology
1271 Anvilwood Ave, Sunnyvale (94089-2204)
PHONE.............................408 734-4434
**EMP:** 19
**SALES (corp-wide):** 13.84MM **Privately Held**
Web: www.armstrong-tech.com
SIC: **3599**  Machine shop, jobbing and repair
PA: Armstrong Technology S.V., Inc.
 1121 Elko Dr
 408 734-4434

## (P-10717)
### ARMSTRONG TECHNOLOGY SV INC
12780 Earhart Ave, Auburn (95602-9027)
PHONE.............................530 888-6262
Arthur Armstrong, *Brnch Mgr*
**EMP:** 19
**SALES (corp-wide):** 13.84MM **Privately Held**
Web: www.armstrong-tech.com
SIC: **3599**  Machine shop, jobbing and repair
PA: Armstrong Technology S.V., Inc.
 1121 Elko Dr
 408 734-4434

## (P-10718)
### ARMSTRONG TECHNOLOGY SV INC (PA)
1121 Elko Dr, Sunnyvale (94089-2208)
PHONE.............................408 734-4434
**EMP:** 53 **EST:** 1966
**SALES (est):** 9.27MM
**SALES (corp-wide):** 9.27MM **Privately Held**
Web: www.armstrong-tech.com
SIC: **3599**  Machine and other job shop work

## (P-10719)
### ARNOLD-GONSALVES ENGRG INC
5731 Chino Ave, Chino (91710-5226)
PHONE.............................909 465-1579
Manuel Gonsalves, *Pr*
Mike Arnold, *
**EMP:** 35 **EST:** 1969
**SQ FT:** 10,000
**SALES (est):** 3.21MM **Privately Held**
Web: www.arnoldgonsalveseng.com
SIC: **3599** 3444  Machine shop, jobbing and repair; Sheet metal specialties, not stamped

## (P-10720)
### ARROW ENGINEERING
4946 Azusa Canyon Rd, Irwindale (91706-1940)
PHONE.............................626 960-2806
John Beaman, *Pr*
Jim Ballantyne, *
**EMP:** 36 **EST:** 1974
**SQ FT:** 18,000
**SALES (est):** 5.66MM **Privately Held**
Web: www.arrow-engineering.com
SIC: **3599**  Machine shop, jobbing and repair

## (P-10721)
### ARROW SCREW PRODUCTS INC
941 W Mccoy Ln, Santa Maria (93455-1109)
PHONE.............................805 928-2269
Robert Vine, *CEO*
Tim Vine, *
Hoang Vine, *
**EMP:** 33 **EST:** 1956
**SQ FT:** 10,000
**SALES (est):** 5.35MM **Privately Held**
Web: www.aspsmca.com
SIC: **3599** 3541  Machine shop, jobbing and repair; Machine tools, metal cutting type

## (P-10722)
### ASIGMA CORPORATION
2930 San Luis Rey Rd, Oceanside (92058-1220)
PHONE.............................760 966-3103
C Dale Chudomelka, *Pr*
Doug Chudomelka, *VP*
Darryl Chudomelka, *VP*
▲ **EMP:** 16 **EST:** 1992
**SQ FT:** 6,500
**SALES (est):** 2.46MM **Privately Held**
SIC: **3599**  Custom machinery

## (P-10723)
### ASSEMBLY AUTOMATION INDUSTRIES
Also Called: Assembly Automation
1849 Business Center Dr, Duarte (91010-2902)
PHONE.............................626 303-2777
Francis E Frost, *CEO*
Elizabeth Frost, *
**EMP:** 21 **EST:** 1978
**SQ FT:** 10,000
**SALES (est):** 2.78MM **Privately Held**
Web: www.assemblyauto.com
SIC: **3599**  Machine shop, jobbing and repair

## (P-10724)
### AUGER INDUSTRIES INC
390 E Crowther Ave, Placentia (92870-6419)
PHONE.............................714 577-9350
John Auger, *Pr*
Francoise Auger, *Stockholder*
**EMP:** 17 **EST:** 1969
**SQ FT:** 12,000
**SALES (est):** 2.42MM **Privately Held**
Web: www.augerind.com
SIC: **3599**  Machine shop, jobbing and repair

## (P-10725)
### AUTO-CHLOR SYSTEM OF MID S LLC
450 Ferguson Dr, Mountain View (94043-5214)
PHONE.............................650 967-3085
**EMP:** 76
**SALES (corp-wide):** 285.79MM **Privately Held**
Web: www.autochlor.com
SIC: **3599**  Air intake filters, internal combustion engine, except auto
HQ: Auto-Chlor System Of The Mid South, Llc
 746 Poplar Ave
 Memphis TN 38105

## (P-10726)
### AUTOCAM ACQUISITION INC
Also Called: Autocam California
1209 San Luis Obispo St, Hayward (94544-7915)
**EMP:** 20 **EST:** 1992
**SALES (est):** 2.79MM
**SALES (corp-wide):** 489.27MM **Publicly Held**
SIC: **3599** 7692 3545  Machine shop, jobbing and repair; Welding repair; Machine tool accessories
HQ: Autocam Corporation
 4180 40th St Se
 Kentwood MI 49512
 616 698-0707

## (P-10727)
### AVATAR MACHINE LLC
18100 Mount Washington St, Fountain Valley (92708-6121)
PHONE.............................714 434-2737
**EMP:** 23 **EST:** 2008
**SALES (est):** 9.4MM **Privately Held**
Web: www.avatarmachine.com
SIC: **3599** 5049  Machine shop, jobbing and repair; Precision tools

## (P-10728)
### AXXIS CORPORATION
Also Called: Axxis Arms
1535 Nandina Ave, Perris (92571-7010)
PHONE.............................951 436-9921
Brandy Tidball, *Pr*
Brandy Tidball, *Pr*
Susan Tidball, *
Jo Olchawa, *
**EMP:** 35 **EST:** 2007
**SALES (est):** 4.82MM **Privately Held**
Web: www.axxiscorp.us
SIC: **3599**  Machine shop, jobbing and repair

## (P-10729)
### AZURE MICRODYNAMICS INC
19652 Descartes, Foothill Ranch (92610-2600)
PHONE.............................949 699-3344
Stanislaw Sulek, *Pr*
Zyta Sulek, *Stockholder**
Oliver Sulek, *
Christopher Hughes, *
**EMP:** 77 **EST:** 1997
**SALES (est):** 15.2MM **Privately Held**
Web: www.azuremd.com
SIC: **3599** 3544  Machine shop, jobbing and repair; Special dies, tools, jigs, and fixtures

## (P-10730)
### B & B PIPE AND TOOL CO
2301 Parker Ln, Bakersfield (93308-6006)
PHONE.............................661 323-8208
Joe Keller, *Genl Mgr*
**EMP:** 29
**SALES (corp-wide):** 7.08MM **Privately Held**
Web: www.bbpipe.com
SIC: **3599**  Machine shop, jobbing and repair
PA: B & B Pipe And Tool Co.
 3035 Walnut Ave

## PRODUCTS & SERVICES SECTION
### 3599 - Industrial Machinery, Nec (P-10753)

562 424-0704

**(P-10731)**
**B & G PRECISION INC**
45450 Industrial Pl Ste 9, Fremont (94538-6474)
**PHONE**.................................510 438-9785
Daniel Datta, *CEO*
**EMP:** 19 **EST:** 1986
**SQ FT:** 3,600
**SALES (est):** 2.04MM **Privately Held**
**Web:** www.bgprecisioninc.com
**SIC:** 3599 Machine shop, jobbing and repair

**(P-10732)**
**B P I CORP**
Also Called: Banbury Precision
1208 Norman Ave Ste B, Santa Clara (95054-2068)
**PHONE**.................................408 988-7888
Gordon Banbury Junior, *Pr*
**EMP:** 15 **EST:** 1978
**SQ FT:** 6,000
**SALES (est):** 450.7K **Privately Held**
**SIC:** 3599 Machine shop, jobbing and repair

**(P-10733)**
**B&B MANUFACTURING CO (PA)**
27940 Beale Ct, Santa Clarita (91355-1210)
**PHONE**.................................661 257-2161
Kenneth Gentry, *CEO*
Fred Duncan, *
▲ **EMP:** 192 **EST:** 1961
**SQ FT:** 180,000
**SALES (est):** 21.4MM
**SALES (corp-wide):** 21.4MM **Privately Held**
**Web:** www.bbmfg.com
**SIC:** 3599 Machine shop, jobbing and repair

**(P-10734)**
**B&Z MANUFACTURING COMPANY INC**
1478 Seareel Ln, San Jose (95131-1567)
**PHONE**.................................408 943-1117
Dennis Kimball, *Pr*
Thomas Simpson, *
**EMP:** 42 **EST:** 1960
**SQ FT:** 18,000
**SALES (est):** 4.39MM **Privately Held**
**Web:** www.bzmfg.com
**SIC:** 3599 Machine shop, jobbing and repair

**(P-10735)**
**BABBITT BEARING CO INC**
Also Called: B B C
1170 N 5th St, San Jose (95112-4483)
**PHONE**.................................408 298-1101
Stanley Sinn, *Pr*
Jerry Mann, *
**EMP:** 25 **EST:** 1946
**SQ FT:** 16,000
**SALES (est):** 5.18MM **Privately Held**
**Web:** www.bbcmachine.com
**SIC:** 3599 Machine shop, jobbing and repair

**(P-10736)**
**BAKERSFIELD MACHINE CO INC**
Also Called: BMC Industries
5605 North Chester Ave Ext, Bakersfield (93308)
P.O. Box 122 (93302-0122)
**PHONE**.................................661 709-1992
John L Meyer, *Pr*
Alfred T Meyer Junior, *VP*
▲ **EMP:** 55 **EST:** 1924
**SQ FT:** 8,276
**SALES (est):** 8.97MM **Privately Held**

**Web:** www.bakersfieldmachinerymovers.com
**SIC:** 3599 Machine shop, jobbing and repair

**(P-10737)**
**BARBER WELDING AND MFG CO**
7171 Scout Ave, Bell Gardens (90201-3201)
P.O. Box 635 (92885-0635)
**PHONE**.................................562 928-2570
C Douglas Barber, *CEO*
Yvonne M Barber, *
**EMP:** 25 **EST:** 1943
**SQ FT:** 15,000
**SALES (est):** 2.46MM **Privately Held**
**SIC:** 3599 3443 Machine shop, jobbing and repair; Tanks for tank trucks, metal plate

**(P-10738)**
**BAUMANN ENGINEERING**
212 S Cambridge Ave, Claremont (91711-4843)
**PHONE**.................................909 621-4181
Fred Baumann, *Pr*
Isolde Doll, *
**EMP:** 85 **EST:** 1961
**SQ FT:** 18,057
**SALES (est):** 5.03MM **Privately Held**
**Web:** www.becontrols.com
**SIC:** 3599 Machine shop, jobbing and repair

**(P-10739)**
**BAY PRECISION MACHINING INC**
Also Called: Emkay Mfg.
815 Sweeney Ave Ste D, Redwood City (94063-3029)
**PHONE**.................................650 365-3010
Anne Feher, *Pr*
George Koncz, *
**EMP:** 17 **EST:** 1978
**SQ FT:** 7,500
**SALES (est):** 3.06MM **Privately Held**
**SIC:** 3599 Machine shop, jobbing and repair

**(P-10740)**
**BAYLESS MANUFACTURING LLC**
Also Called: Fabcon
26140 Avenue Hall, Valencia (91355-4808)
**PHONE**.................................661 257-3373
Robert Lummus, *Pr*
**EMP:** 235 **EST:** 1978
**SALES (est):** 8.11MM **Privately Held**
**Web:** www.fabcon.com
**SIC:** 3599 3444 Machine shop, jobbing and repair; Sheet metalwork

**(P-10741)**
**BECHLER CAMS INC**
1313 S State College Pkwy, Anaheim (92806-5298)
**PHONE**.................................714 774-5150
Daniel Lennert, *Pr*
Laura Stearman, *Sec*
**EMP:** 16 **EST:** 1957
**SQ FT:** 11,500
**SALES (est):** 1.54MM **Privately Held**
**Web:** www.bechlercams.com
**SIC:** 3599 Machine shop, jobbing and repair

**(P-10742)**
**BEGOVIC INDUSTRIES INC**
Also Called: B & H Engineering Company
1725 Old County Rd, San Carlos (94070-5206)
**PHONE**.................................650 594-2861
Bakir Begovic, *CEO*

Kenan Begovic, *Pr*
Hamida Begovic, *VP*
**EMP:** 20 **EST:** 1972
**SALES (est):** 4.73MM **Privately Held**
**Web:** www.bhengineering.com
**SIC:** 3599 3444 Machine shop, jobbing and repair; Sheet metalwork

**(P-10743)**
**BEL-AIR MACHINING CO**
151 E Columbine Ave, Santa Ana (92707-4401)
**PHONE**.................................714 953-6616
Moon H Choi, *Owner*
**EMP:** 15 **EST:** 1984
**SQ FT:** 5,000
**SALES (est):** 3.4MM **Privately Held**
**Web:** www.belairmachine.com
**SIC:** 3599 Machine shop, jobbing and repair

**(P-10744)**
**BENDER CCP INC (PA)**
Also Called: Bender US
2150 E 37th St, Vernon (90058-1417)
P.O. Box 847 (94510)
**PHONE**.................................323 232-2371
Michael Potter, *Pr*
Randall Potter, *
▲ **EMP:** 105 **EST:** 2007
**SALES (est):** 50MM
**SALES (corp-wide):** 50MM **Privately Held**
**Web:** www.benderccp.com
**SIC:** 3599 3731 Custom machinery; Shipbuilding and repairing

**(P-10745)**
**BENDER CCP INC**
757 Main St Unit 102, Chula Vista (91911-6168)
**PHONE**.................................619 232-5719
Briana Velasco, *Mgr*
**EMP:** 42
**SALES (corp-wide):** 50MM **Privately Held**
**Web:** www.benderccp.com
**SIC:** 3599 Custom machinery
**PA:** Bender Ccp, Inc.
  2150 E 37th St
  323 232-2371

**(P-10746)**
**BENDICK PRECISION INC**
56 La Porte St, Arcadia (91006-2827)
**PHONE**.................................626 445-0217
Christie Joseph, *Pr*
Benny Joseph, *Sec*
**EMP:** 16 **EST:** 1975
**SQ FT:** 5,000
**SALES (est):** 3.08MM **Privately Held**
**Web:** www.bendick.com
**SIC:** 3599 3061 Machine shop, jobbing and repair; Medical and surgical rubber tubing (extruded and lathe-cut)

**(P-10747)**
**BEONCA MACHINE INC**
1680 Curtiss Ct, La Verne (91750-5848)
**PHONE**.................................909 392-9991
Johann Bock, *Pr*
Danny Bock, *Pr*
Dennis Bock, *VP*
Jame Bock, *Corporate Secretary*
**EMP:** 17 **EST:** 1973
**SQ FT:** 7,000
**SALES (est):** 3.2MM **Privately Held**
**Web:** www.beoncamachine.com
**SIC:** 3599 Machine shop, jobbing and repair

**(P-10748)**
**BERANEK LLC**
2340 W 205th St, Torrance (90501-1436)

**PHONE**.................................310 328-9094
Hector Beranek, *Pr*
Sean Holly, *
Christoper Lin, *
Tucker Cowden, *
Stephen Cook, *
**EMP:** 36 **EST:** 1978
**SQ FT:** 20,000
**SALES (est):** 8.38MM
**SALES (corp-wide):** 13.91MM **Privately Held**
**Web:** www.beranekinc.com
**SIC:** 3599 Machine shop, jobbing and repair
**PA:** J&E Precision Tool Holdings, Llc
  107 Valley Rd
  413 527-8778

**(P-10749)**
**BERNS BROS INC**
Also Called: De Berns Company
1250 W 17th St, Long Beach (90813-1310)
**PHONE**.................................562 437-0471
Steven Berns, *Pr*
Sue Porter, *VP*
▲ **EMP:** 17 **EST:** 1957
**SQ FT:** 20,000
**SALES (est):** 2.95MM **Privately Held**
**Web:** www.thebernscompany.com
**SIC:** 3599 Machine and other job shop work

**(P-10750)**
**BMW PRECISION MACHINING INC**
2379 Industry St, Oceanside (92054-4803)
**PHONE**.................................760 439-6813
Richard Blakely, *Pr*
**EMP:** 25 **EST:** 1981
**SQ FT:** 17,400
**SALES (est):** 2.57MM **Privately Held**
**Web:** www.bmwprecision.com
**SIC:** 3599 Machine shop, jobbing and repair

**(P-10751)**
**BNLE BERG HOLDINGS LLC**
Also Called: Bnle Berg Holdings
408 Aldo Ave, Santa Clara (95054-2301)
**PHONE**.................................408 727-2374
Travis Sessions, *CEO*
Jamie Berg, *
**EMP:** 63 **EST:** 2014
**SALES (est):** 6.62MM **Privately Held**
**Web:** www.bergmanufacturinginc.com
**SIC:** 3599 Crankshafts and camshafts, machining
**HQ:** Biomerics, Llc
  6030 W Harold Gatty Dr
  Salt Lake City UT 84116

**(P-10752)**
**BOUDRAUX PRCSION MCHINING CORP**
11762 Western Ave Ste G, Stanton (90680-3481)
**PHONE**.................................714 894-4523
Mike Boudreaux, *Pr*
Steve Boudreaux, *
**EMP:** 25 **EST:** 1990
**SQ FT:** 3,750
**SALES (est):** 1.72MM **Privately Held**
**Web:** boudreaux-precision-machining-ca.hub.biz
**SIC:** 3599 Machine shop, jobbing and repair

**(P-10753)**
**BREK MANUFACTURING CO**
1513 W 132nd St, Gardena (90249)
**PHONE**.................................310 329-7638
▲ **EMP:** 169 **EST:** 1968
**SALES (est):** 56.04MM
**SALES (corp-wide):** 56.04MM **Privately Held**

## 3599 - Industrial Machinery, Nec (P-10754)

Web: www.brek.aero
SIC: **3599** Machine shop, jobbing and repair
PA: Aernnova Engineering Us, Inc.
1513 W 132nd St
310 329-7638

**(P-10754)**
**BROTHERS MACHINE & TOOL INC (PA)**
Also Called: Brothers Machine & Toolinc.
11098 Inland Ave, Jurupa Valley (91752-1154)
PHONE.....................951 361-2909
Jose E Razzo, *Pr*
Jose F Razzo, *VP*
Jose L Razzo, *Treas*
**EMP:** 15 **EST:** 1990
**SALES (est):** 3.05MM **Privately Held**
**SIC: 3599** Machine shop, jobbing and repair

**(P-10755)**
**BTL MACHINE**
Also Called: Apex Design Tech.
1168 Sherborn St, Corona (92879-2089)
PHONE.....................951 808-9929
▲ **EMP:** 65
Web: www.btlmachine.com
**SIC: 3599** Machine shop, jobbing and repair

**(P-10756)**
**BUENA PARK TOOL & ENGRG INC**
Also Called: Buena Park Tool
7661 Windfield Dr, Huntington Beach (92647-7100)
PHONE.....................714 843-6215
Leo Gomez, *CEO*
Leo Gomez Junior, *VP*
Teresa Gomez, *Pr*
**EMP:** 16 **EST:** 1972
**SQ FT:** 11,000
**SALES (est):** 261.75K **Privately Held**
Web: www.buenaparktool.com
**SIC: 3599** 7692 3544 Machine shop, jobbing and repair; Welding repair; Special dies, tools, jigs, and fixtures

**(P-10757)**
**BULLSEYE LEAK DETECTION INC**
4015 Seaport Blvd, West Sacramento (95691-3416)
P.O. Box 73114 (95617-3114)
PHONE.....................916 760-8944
Daniel Spatz, *Pr*
**EMP:** 25 **EST:** 2009
**SALES (est):** 5.31MM **Privately Held**
Web: www.bullseyeleak.com
**SIC: 3599** 1623 Water leak detectors; Pipe laying construction

**(P-10758)**
**C & H MACHINE INC**
Also Called: Support Equipment
943 S Andreasen Dr, Escondido (92029-1934)
PHONE.....................760 746-6459
Lyle J Anderson, *Ex VP*
Charles Gohlich, *
**EMP:** 70 **EST:** 1964
**SQ FT:** 13,000
**SALES (est):** 7.38MM **Privately Held**
Web: www.c-hmachine.com
**SIC: 3599** Machine shop, jobbing and repair

**(P-10759)**
**C L HANN INDUSTRIES INC**
7200 Alexander St, Gilroy (95020-6907)
PHONE.....................408 293-4800
Pete Hann, *Pr*
Art Korp, *VP*
Georgette Hann, *Off Mgr*
Cheyne Hann, *CFO*
**EMP:** 16 **EST:** 1971
**SALES (est):** 2.19MM **Privately Held**
Web: www.clhann.com
**SIC: 3599** Machine shop, jobbing and repair

**(P-10760)**
**CALMAX TECHNOLOGY INC**
558 Laurelwood Rd, Santa Clara (95054-2418)
PHONE.....................408 506-2035
Boguslaw J Marcinkowski, *Brnch Mgr*
**EMP:** 15
Web: www.calmaxtechnology.com
**SIC: 3599** Machine shop, jobbing and repair
PA: Calmax Technology, Inc.
3491 Lafayette St

**(P-10761)**
**CALMAX TECHNOLOGY INC**
526 Laurelwood Rd, Santa Clara (95054-2418)
PHONE.....................408 513-2139
**EMP:** 20
Web: www.calmaxtechnology.com
**SIC: 3599** Machine shop, jobbing and repair
PA: Calmax Technology, Inc.
3491 Lafayette St

**(P-10762)**
**CALMAX TECHNOLOGY INC (PA)**
3491 Lafayette St, Santa Clara (95054-2707)
PHONE.....................408 748-8660
Boguslaw J Marcinkowski, *CEO*
**EMP:** 50 **EST:** 1987
**SALES (est):** 26.2MM **Privately Held**
Web: www.calmaxtechnology.com
**SIC: 3599** Machine shop, jobbing and repair

**(P-10763)**
**CAMPBELL GRINDING INC**
1003 E Vine St, Lodi (95240-3127)
PHONE.....................209 339-8838
Dan Fritz, *Pr*
**EMP:** 19 **EST:** 1980
**SQ FT:** 17,000
**SALES (est):** 491.43K **Privately Held**
**SIC: 3599** Machine shop, jobbing and repair

**(P-10764)**
**CARDIC MACHINE PRODUCTS INC**
17000 Keegan Ave, Carson (90746-1309)
PHONE.....................310 884-3400
Joseph Trumpio, *CEO*
Calvin Crockett, *VP*
**EMP:** 15 **EST:** 1951
**SQ FT:** 10,900
**SALES (est):** 2.92MM **Privately Held**
Web: www.cardicmachine.com
**SIC: 3599** Machine shop, jobbing and repair

**(P-10765)**
**CAVALLO & CAVALLO INC**
Also Called: Production Engineering & Mch
14955 Hilton Dr, Fontana (92336-2082)
P.O. Box 907 (91711-0907)
PHONE.....................909 428-6994
Thomas H Kearns, *Pr*
**EMP:** 16 **EST:** 1967
**SQ FT:** 16,400
**SALES (est):** 2.12MM **Privately Held**
Web: www.pemmachining.com

**SIC: 3599** Machine shop, jobbing and repair

**(P-10766)**
**CAVANAUGH MACHINE WORKS INC**
1540 Santa Fe Ave, Long Beach (90813-1239)
PHONE.....................562 437-1126
John Wells, *Pr*
Michael Wells, *
**EMP:** 40 **EST:** 1946
**SQ FT:** 19,000
**SALES (est):** 4.9MM **Privately Held**
Web: www.cavmachine.com
**SIC: 3599** 3731 3441 Machine shop, jobbing and repair; Shipbuilding and repairing; Fabricated structural metal

**(P-10767)**
**CDS ENGINEERING INC**
Also Called: Cds Leopold
40725 Encyclopedia Cir, Fremont (94538-2451)
PHONE.....................510 252-2100
▲ **EMP:** 110
**SIC: 3599** 3542 Machine shop, jobbing and repair; Plasma jet spray metal forming machines

**(P-10768)**
**CENCAL CNC INC**
2491 Simpson St, Kingsburg (93631-9501)
PHONE.....................559 897-8706
Abe Wiebe, *Pr*
Ann Wiebe, *
**EMP:** 25 **EST:** 2006
**SQ FT:** 5,000
**SALES (est):** 5.28MM **Privately Held**
Web: www.cencalcnc.com
**SIC: 3599** Electrical discharge machining (EDM)

**(P-10769)**
**CENTERPOINT MFG CO INC**
2625 N San Fernando Blvd, Burbank (91504-3220)
PHONE.....................818 842-2147
John C Rotunno, *Pr*
Carmen Rotunno, *
**EMP:** 40 **EST:** 1966
**SQ FT:** 12,000
**SALES (est):** 5.11MM **Privately Held**
Web: www.centerpointmfgco.com
**SIC: 3599** Machine shop, jobbing and repair

**(P-10770)**
**CENTURY PARTS INC**
913 W 223rd St, Torrance (90502-2246)
PHONE.....................310 328-0281
Lynn Hale, *CEO*
**EMP:** 16 **EST:** 1969
**SQ FT:** 12,500
**SALES (est):** 486.57K **Privately Held**
**SIC: 3599** Machine shop, jobbing and repair

**(P-10771)**
**CENTURY PRECISION ENGRG INC**
2141 W 139th St, Gardena (90249-2451)
PHONE.....................310 538-0015
Myron Yoo, *Pr*
Bruce Lee, *
**EMP:** 25 **EST:** 1980
**SQ FT:** 20,000
**SALES (est):** 3.84MM **Privately Held**
Web: www.centurype.com
**SIC: 3599** Machine shop, jobbing and repair

**(P-10772)**
**CERAMIC TECH INC**
Also Called: Fralock
46211 Research Ave, Fremont (94539-6113)
PHONE.....................510 252-8500
Kanu Gandhi, *Pr*
Vivek Gandhi, *
**EMP:** 30 **EST:** 1989
**SQ FT:** 30,000
**SALES (est):** 7.79MM
**SALES (corp-wide):** 153.54MM **Privately Held**
Web: www.fralock.com
**SIC: 3599** 3264 Machine and other job shop work; Porcelain electrical supplies
PA: Fralock Holdings Llc
28525 W Industry Dr
661 702-6999

**(P-10773)**
**CHE PRECISION INC**
2586 Calcite Cir, Newbury Park (91320-1203)
PHONE.....................805 499-8885
Charles Holguin, *Pr*
Claude Holguin, *Pr*
Charlie Holguin, *VP*
▲ **EMP:** 20 **EST:** 1989
**SALES (est):** 2.59MM **Privately Held**
Web: www.cheprecision.com
**SIC: 3599** Machine shop, jobbing and repair

**(P-10774)**
**CHEEK MACHINE CORP**
1312 S Allec St, Anaheim (92805-6303)
PHONE.....................714 279-9486
Tatiana Cheek, *Pr*
Christopher Cheek, *VP*
**EMP:** 21 **EST:** 1994
**SQ FT:** 5,000
**SALES (est):** 4.01MM **Privately Held**
Web: www.cheekmachine.com
**SIC: 3599** Machine shop, jobbing and repair

**(P-10775)**
**CHIPMASTERS MANUFACTURING INC (PA)**
Also Called: Chipmasters Manufacturing
798 N Coney Ave, Azusa (91702-2239)
P.O. Box 408 (92391-0408)
PHONE.....................626 804-8178
Richard Jacobsen, *Pr*
**EMP:** 16 **EST:** 1973
**SQ FT:** 15,400
**SALES (est):** 4.16MM **Privately Held**
Web: www.chipmastersmfg.com
**SIC: 3599** Machine shop, jobbing and repair

**(P-10776)**
**CITROGENE INC**
2528 Qume Dr Ste 6, San Jose (95131-1836)
PHONE.....................408 930-5070
Sam Kiamanesh, *Prin*
**EMP:** 18 **EST:** 2018
**SALES (est):** 2.94MM **Privately Held**
Web: www.citrogene.com
**SIC: 3599** Machine shop, jobbing and repair

**(P-10777)**
**CJ ADVISORS INC**
6900 8th St, Buena Park (90620-1036)
PHONE.....................714 956-3388
Jason Cho, *CEO*
**EMP:** 23 **EST:** 1993
**SALES (est):** 1.74MM **Privately Held**
Web: www.hqmachine.com

## PRODUCTS & SERVICES SECTION
## 3599 - Industrial Machinery, Nec (P-10800)

SIC: 3599 Machine and other job shop work

**(P-10778)**
**CLASSIC WIRE CUT COMPANY INC**
28210 Constellation Rd, Valencia (91355-5000)
PHONE..............................661 257-0558
Brett Bannerman, *Prin*
▲ **EMP:** 150 **EST:** 1984
**SQ FT:** 80,000
**SALES (est):** 19.19MM **Privately Held**
Web: www.classicwirecut.com
SIC: 3599 3841 Electrical discharge machining (EDM); Surgical instruments and apparatus

**(P-10779)**
**CM MACHINE INC**
560 S Grand Ave, San Jacinto (92582-3832)
PHONE..............................951 654-6019
Carmel Tomoni, *Pr*
Michael Tomoni, *Genl Mgr*
**EMP:** 15 **EST:** 1993
**SQ FT:** 6,000
**SALES (est):** 1.37MM **Privately Held**
Web: www.cmmachineinc.com
SIC: 3599 Machine shop, jobbing and repair

**(P-10780)**
**CNC MACHINING INC**
510 S Fairview Ave, Goleta (93117-3617)
PHONE..............................805 681-8855
Gary Brous, *Pr*
Greg Brous, *VP*
Shirley Brous, *Sec*
**EMP:** 15 **EST:** 1985
**SQ FT:** 2,000
**SALES (est):** 2.04MM **Privately Held**
Web: www.cncmachining.com
SIC: 3599 Machine shop, jobbing and repair

**(P-10781)**
**CNI MFG INC**
Also Called: Computer-Nozzles
15627 Arrow Hwy, Irwindale (91706-2004)
PHONE..............................626 962-6646
Toby Argandona, *Pr*
David Argandona, *VP*
Yolanda Pullen, *Sec*
**EMP:** 18 **EST:** 1969
**SQ FT:** 32,200
**SALES (est):** 2.47MM **Privately Held**
Web: www.cni-mfg.com
SIC: 3599 3443 Custom machinery; Fabricated plate work (boiler shop)

**(P-10782)**
**COAST COMPOSITES LLC**
7 Burroughs, Irvine (92618-2804)
PHONE..............................949 455-0665
Brendan Buckel, *Mgr*
**EMP:** 30
**SALES (corp-wide):** 7.68MM **Privately Held**
Web: www.ascentaerospace.com
SIC: 3599 Machine shop, jobbing and repair
PA: Coast Composites, Llc
5 Burroughs
949 455-0665

**(P-10783)**
**CODY CYLINDER SERVICE LLC**
1393 Dodson Way Ste A, Riverside (92507-2073)
P.O. Box 56099 (92517-0999)
PHONE..............................951 786-3650
Art Pastoor, *Pr*
Jolene Cody Patoor, *VP*
**EMP:** 21 **EST:** 2018
**SALES (est):** 3.5MM **Privately Held**
SIC: 3599 7379 Machine shop, jobbing and repair; Tape recertification service

**(P-10784)**
**COLLEEN & HERB ENTERPRISES INC**
Also Called: C & H Enterprises
46939 Bayside Pkwy, Fremont (94538-6527)
PHONE..............................510 226-6083
Herbert Schmidt, *CEO*
Colleen Schmidt, *
Jake Schmidt, *
**EMP:** 115 **EST:** 1984
**SQ FT:** 50,000
**SALES (est):** 16.74MM **Privately Held**
Web: www.candhenterprises.com
SIC: 3599 7692 Machine shop, jobbing and repair; Welding repair

**(P-10785)**
**COMPUTER ASSISTED MFG TECH LLC**
Also Called: Camtech
8710 Research Dr 8750, Irvine (92618-4222)
PHONE..............................949 263-8911
Mike Dennis, *CEO*
**EMP:** 40 **EST:** 1982
**SQ FT:** 50,000
**SALES (est):** 5.69MM
**SALES (corp-wide):** 5.69MM **Privately Held**
SIC: 3599 Machine shop, jobbing and repair
HQ: Cam Holdco, Llc
8710 Research Dr
Irvine CA

**(P-10786)**
**COMPUTER INTGRTED MCHINING INC**
10940 Wheatlands Ave, Santee (92071-2857)
PHONE..............................619 596-9246
Michael J Brown, *Pr*
**EMP:** 21 **EST:** 1995
**SQ FT:** 20,000
**SALES (est):** 4.49MM **Privately Held**
Web: www.cimsd.com
SIC: 3599 Machine shop, jobbing and repair

**(P-10787)**
**CONNELLY MACHINE WKS**
Also Called: Acme Tool Grinding Company
420 N Terminal St, Santa Ana (92701-4927)
PHONE..............................714 558-6855
Ray Connelly, *Pr*
Scott Connelly, *VP*
**EMP:** 22 **EST:** 1946
**SQ FT:** 17,000
**SALES (est):** 3.57MM **Privately Held**
Web: www.connellymachine.com
SIC: 3599 3492 Machine shop, jobbing and repair; Fluid power valves and hose fittings

**(P-10788)**
**CONQUIP INC**
11255 Pyrites Way Ste 100, Gold River (95670-6336)
PHONE..............................916 379-8200
✪ **EMP:** 54
Web: www.wxati.us
SIC: 3599 Custom machinery

**(P-10789)**
**CONSOLDTED HNGE MNFCTURED PDTS**
Also Called: Champ Co
1150b Dell Ave, Campbell (95008-6640)
PHONE..............................408 379-6550
Karl L Herbst, *Pr*
Alfred Riesenhuber, *VP*
Ursula Gueldner, *Treas*
**EMP:** 17 **EST:** 1969
**SQ FT:** 23,000
**SALES (est):** 2.67MM **Privately Held**
Web: consolidatedhinampman.mfgpages.com
SIC: 3599 Machine shop, jobbing and repair

**(P-10790)**
**COREDUX USA LLC**
6721 Cobra Way, San Diego (92121-4110)
PHONE..............................858 642-0713
Jan Hennipman, *CEO*
**EMP:** 100 **EST:** 1988
**SQ FT:** 23,800
**SALES (est):** 21.59MM **Privately Held**
Web: www.pyramidprecision.com
SIC: 3599 Machine shop, jobbing and repair

**(P-10791)**
**CPK MANUFACTURING INC**
2188 Del Franco St Ste 70, San Jose (95131-1583)
PHONE..............................408 971-4019
Khamsy Syluangkhot, *Pr*
Paul Wendall, *VP*
**EMP:** 16 **EST:** 1995
**SALES (est):** 2.37MM **Privately Held**
Web: www.cpkmfg.net
SIC: 3599 Machine shop, jobbing and repair

**(P-10792)**
**CRESCO MANUFACTURING INC**
Also Called: Crescomfg.com
1614 N Orangethorpe Way, Anaheim (92801-1227)
PHONE..............................714 525-2326
Jon Spielman, *Pr*
Alberta Spielman, *
**EMP:** 40 **EST:** 1981
**SQ FT:** 14,000
**SALES (est):** 3.67MM **Privately Held**
Web: petespielman.weebly.com
SIC: 3599 Machine shop, jobbing and repair

**(P-10793)**
**CRUSH MASTER GRINDING CORP**
Also Called: Evolution Industries
755 Penarth Ave, Walnut (91789-3028)
PHONE..............................909 595-2249
Sherman Durousseau, *Pr*
Jeanne Durousseau, *
**EMP:** 35 **EST:** 1976
**SQ FT:** 11,800
**SALES (est):** 5.29MM **Privately Held**
Web: www.crushmastergrinding.com
SIC: 3599 Machine shop, jobbing and repair

**(P-10794)**
**CUSTOM MICRO MACHINING INC**
365 Reed St, Santa Clara (95050-3107)
PHONE..............................510 651-9434
Tao Chou, *Pr*
Victor Nguyen, *
David Chow, *
**EMP:** 32 **EST:** 1990
**SQ FT:** 8,000
**SALES (est):** 2.49MM **Privately Held**
Web: www.cmmusa.com

SIC: 3599 Machine shop, jobbing and repair

**(P-10795)**
**CUTTING EDGE MACHINING INC (PA)**
1331 Old County Rd, Belmont (94002-3967)
PHONE..............................408 738-8677
Jack Corey, *CEO*
Gloria L Corey, *
**EMP:** 25 **EST:** 1973
**SALES (est):** 2.04MM
**SALES (corp-wide):** 2.04MM **Privately Held**
Web: www.cemachining.com
SIC: 3599 Machine shop, jobbing and repair

**(P-10796)**
**D & H MFG CO**
49235 Milmont Dr, Fremont (94538-7349)
PHONE..............................510 770-5100
**EMP:** 118
SIC: 3599 Machine shop, jobbing and repair

**(P-10797)**
**D G A MACHINE SHOP INC**
Also Called: D G A Mch Sp Blnchard Grinding
5825 Ordway St, Riverside (92504-1132)
PHONE..............................951 354-2113
Angelo Diguglielmo, *CEO*
**EMP:** 15 **EST:** 1980
**SALES (est):** 2.31MM **Privately Held**
Web: www.dgamachineshop.com
SIC: 3599 Machine shop, jobbing and repair

**(P-10798)**
**D MILLS GRNDING MACHINING INC**
1738 N Neville St, Orange (92865-4214)
PHONE..............................951 697-6847
Anthony Puccio, *Pr*
Gilles Madelmont, *
Joe Puccio, *
**EMP:** 150 **EST:** 1973
**SALES (est):** 2.65MM
**SALES (corp-wide):** 43.53MM **Privately Held**
Web: d-mills-grinding-machining-co-inc.hub.biz
SIC: 3599 Grinding castings for the trade
PA: Manufacturing Solutions, Inc.
1738 N Neville St
714 453-0100

**(P-10799)**
**DARCY AK CORPORATION**
Also Called: AK Darcy
1760 Monrovia Ave Ste A22, Costa Mesa (92627-4433)
PHONE..............................949 650-5566
Darrell Gilbert, *CEO*
**EMP:** 15 **EST:** 1988
**SQ FT:** 9,000
**SALES (est):** 1.6MM **Privately Held**
SIC: 3599 5085 Machine shop, jobbing and repair; Valves and fittings

**(P-10800)**
**DARKO PRECISION INC**
470 Gianni St, Santa Clara (95054-2413)
PHONE..............................408 988-6133
Dardo Simunic, *Pr*
Vesna Simunic, *
**EMP:** 78 **EST:** 1987
**SQ FT:** 35,000
**SALES (est):** 8.76MM **Privately Held**
Web: www.darkoprecision.com
SIC: 3599 Machine shop, jobbing and repair

## 3599 - Industrial Machinery, Nec (P-10801)

**(P-10801)**
**DARMARK CORPORATION**
13225 Gregg St, Poway (92064-7120)
PHONE..............................858 679-3970
Darwin Mark Zavadil, *Pr*
Martin T Drake, *
Lori Zavadil, *
Jackie Williams, *
**EMP:** 90 **EST:** 1979
**SQ FT:** 28,000
**SALES (est):** 17.49MM **Privately Held**
**Web:** www.darmark.com
**SIC: 3599** Machine shop, jobbing and repair

**(P-10802)**
**DCPM INC**
Also Called: DC Valve Mfg & Precision Mchs
885 Jarvis Dr, Morgan Hill (95037-2858)
PHONE..............................408 928-2510
Cuu Banh, *CEO*
**EMP:** 43 **EST:** 1998
**SQ FT:** 3,200
**SALES (est):** 5.51MM **Privately Held**
**SIC: 3599** Machine shop, jobbing and repair

**(P-10803)**
**DELAFIELD CORPORATION (PA)**
Also Called: Delafield Fluid Technology
1520 Flower Ave, Duarte (91010-2925)
PHONE..............................626 303-0740
Nik Ray, *Pr*
Jim Martin, *
Henry Custodia, *
◆ **EMP:** 120 **EST:** 1949
**SQ FT:** 90,000
**SALES (est):** 40.45MM
**SALES (corp-wide):** 40.45MM **Privately Held**
**Web:** www.dftcorp.com
**SIC: 3599** 5085 3498 3492 Hose, flexible metallic; Valves, pistons, and fittings; Tube fabricating (contract bending and shaping); Fluid power valves and hose fittings

**(P-10804)**
**DELONG MANUFACTURING CO INC**
967 Parker Ct, Santa Clara (95050-2808)
PHONE..............................408 727-3348
David De Long, *CEO*
William A De Long Junior, *Sec*
**EMP:** 16 **EST:** 1966
**SQ FT:** 8,400
**SALES (est):** 3.16MM **Privately Held**
**Web:** www.delongmfg.com
**SIC: 3599** Machine shop, jobbing and repair

**(P-10805)**
**DELTA FABRICATION INC**
9600 De Soto Ave, Chatsworth (91311-5012)
PHONE..............................818 407-4000
Chava Ostrowsky, *CEO*
Joe Ostrowsky, *
**EMP:** 90 **EST:** 1996
**SQ FT:** 20,000
**SALES (est):** 4.33MM **Privately Held**
**Web:** www.deltahi-tech.com
**SIC: 3599** Machine shop, jobbing and repair

**(P-10806)**
**DELTA HI-TECH**
9600 De Soto Ave, Chatsworth (91311-5012)
PHONE..............................818 407-4000
Joe Ostrowsky, *CEO*
Ilan Ostrowsky, *
Gregory Elkhunovich, *
Chava Ostrowsky, *
▲ **EMP:** 130 **EST:** 1985
**SQ FT:** 40,000
**SALES (est):** 19.97MM **Privately Held**
**Web:** www.deltahi-tech.com
**SIC: 3599** Machine shop, jobbing and repair

**(P-10807)**
**DELTA MATRIX INC**
Also Called: Delta Machine
2180 Oakland Rd, San Jose (95131-1571)
P.O. Box 320370 (95032-0106)
PHONE..............................408 955-9140
Tad Slowikowski, *Pr*
Yolanda Slowikowski, *
**EMP:** 38 **EST:** 2001
**SQ FT:** 9,000
**SALES (est):** 10.2MM **Privately Held**
**SIC: 3599** Machine shop, jobbing and repair

**(P-10808)**
**DESCO MANUFACTURING COMPANY (PA)**
23031 Arroyo Vis Ste A, Rcho Sta Marg (92688-2605)
PHONE..............................949 858-7400
Ralph L Fabian, *Pr*
William Cobble, *VP*
Ruth Sistrunk, *Executive Administrator*
▲ **EMP:** 16 **EST:** 1962
**SALES (est):** 4.71MM
**SALES (corp-wide):** 4.71MM **Privately Held**
**Web:** www.descomfg.com
**SIC: 3599** Custom machinery

**(P-10809)**
**DETENTION DEVICE SYSTEMS**
Also Called: DDS
25545 Seaboard Ln, Hayward (94545-3209)
PHONE..............................510 783-0771
Steven R Allington, *Pr*
Tom Heath, *
**EMP:** 45 **EST:** 1985
**SQ FT:** 20,000
**SALES (est):** 3.31MM **Privately Held**
**Web:** www.detentiondevicesystems.com
**SIC: 3599** 3429 Machine shop, jobbing and repair; Locks or lock sets

**(P-10810)**
**DIAL PRECISION INC**
17235 Darwin Ave, Hesperia (92345-5178)
P.O. Box 402259 (92340-2259)
PHONE..............................760 947-3557
Darryl L Tarullo, *Ch Bd*
Jeff Marousek, *Prin*
Linda James, *Prin*
**EMP:** 95 **EST:** 1958
**SQ FT:** 15,000
**SALES (est):** 4.86MM **Privately Held**
**Web:** www.dialprecision.com
**SIC: 3599** 3545 Machine shop, jobbing and repair; Machine tool accessories

**(P-10811)**
**DIAMOND TOOL AND DIE INC**
Also Called: Lab Clear
508 29th Ave, Oakland (94601-2198)
PHONE..............................510 534-7050
Darrell G Holt, *Pr*
Daniel Walter, *
▲ **EMP:** 32 **EST:** 1967
**SQ FT:** 22,000
**SALES (est):** 8MM **Privately Held**
**Web:** www.dtdjobshop.com
**SIC: 3599** Machine shop, jobbing and repair

**(P-10812)**
**DILIGENT SOLUTIONS INC**
Also Called: Absolute EDM
3240 Grey Hawk Ct, Carlsbad (92010-6651)
P.O. Box 985 (92564-0985)
PHONE..............................760 814-8960
Stephen A Bowles, *Pr*
**EMP:** 20 **EST:** 2001
**SALES (est):** 2.36MM **Privately Held**
**SIC: 3599** Machine shop, jobbing and repair

**(P-10813)**
**DKW PRECISION MACHINING INC**
17731 Ideal Pkwy, Manteca (95336-8991)
PHONE..............................209 824-7899
Kurt Franklin, *Pr*
**EMP:** 20 **EST:** 1984
**SQ FT:** 10,000
**SALES (est):** 3.88MM **Privately Held**
**Web:** www.dkwmachine.com
**SIC: 3599** Machine shop, jobbing and repair

**(P-10814)**
**DL HORTON ENTERPRISES INC**
Also Called: Warmelin Precision Products
12705 Daphne Ave, Hawthorne (90250-3311)
PHONE..............................323 777-1700
**EMP:** 55
**SIC: 3599** Machine shop, jobbing and repair

**(P-10815)**
**DONAL MACHINE INC**
591 N Mcdowell Blvd, Petaluma (94954-2340)
P.O. Box 750637 (94975-0637)
PHONE..............................707 763-6625
John Chris Bergstedt, *Pr*
Robert Bergstedt, *
Donna Bergstedt, *
**EMP:** 31 **EST:** 1969
**SQ FT:** 30,000
**SALES (est):** 4.11MM **Privately Held**
**Web:** www.donalmachine.com
**SIC: 3599** 3444 3548 Machine shop, jobbing and repair; Sheet metalwork; Welding and cutting apparatus and accessories, nec

**(P-10816)**
**DOW HYDRAULIC SYSTEMS INC**
2895 Metropolitan Pl, Pomona (91767-1853)
PHONE..............................909 596-6602
Richard P Dow, *Pr*
Ryan K Dow, *
Bryan Dow, *
Keith Dow, *
**EMP:** 60 **EST:** 1968
**SALES (est):** 9.33MM **Privately Held**
**Web:** www.dowhydraulics.com
**SIC: 3599** 3594 Machine shop, jobbing and repair; Fluid power pumps and motors

**(P-10817)**
**DYNAMIC ENTERPRISES INC**
Also Called: D E I
2081 Rancho Hills Dr, Chino Hills (91709-4763)
PHONE..............................562 944-0271
Mildred Sudduth, *Pr*
Alan Sudduth, *VP*
Deanna Mansfield, *Sec*
◆ **EMP:** 21 **EST:** 1959
**SALES (est):** 3.11MM **Privately Held**
**Web:** www.dynamic-ent.com
**SIC: 3599** Machine shop, jobbing and repair

**(P-10818)**
**E & S PRECISION MACHINE INC**
4631 Enterprise Way, Modesto (95356-8715)
PHONE..............................209 545-6161
Jim Elzner, *Pr*
Donita Elzner, *CFO*
**EMP:** 18 **EST:** 1989
**SQ FT:** 5,000
**SALES (est):** 2.66MM **Privately Held**
**Web:** esprecision.comcastbiz.net
**SIC: 3599** Machine shop, jobbing and repair

**(P-10819)**
**ED STIGLIC**
Also Called: Stigtec Mfg
1125 Linda Vista Dr Ste 110, San Marcos (92078-3819)
PHONE..............................760 744-7239
Ed Stiglic, *Owner*
Teresa Stiglic, *Prin*
**EMP:** 19 **EST:** 1988
**SQ FT:** 10,000
**SALES (est):** 2.16MM **Privately Held**
**Web:** www.stigtec.com
**SIC: 3599** Machine shop, jobbing and repair

**(P-10820)**
**EH SUDA INC (PA)**
Also Called: Fabtron
1811 Jefferson Ave, Redwood City (94062-2003)
PHONE..............................650 622-9700
Edwin H Suda, *CEO*
**EMP:** 15 **EST:** 1979
**SALES (est):** 2.11MM
**SALES (corp-wide):** 2.11MM **Privately Held**
**SIC: 3599** Machine shop, jobbing and repair

**(P-10821)**
**EH SUDA INC**
Also Called: Fabtron
210 Texas Ave, Lewiston (96052)
P.O. Box 171 (96052-0171)
PHONE..............................530 778-9830
Mark Suda, *Brnch Mgr*
**EMP:** 20
**SALES (corp-wide):** 2.29MM **Privately Held**
**SIC: 3599** Machine shop, jobbing and repair
**PA:** E.H. Suda, Inc.
1811 Jefferson Ave
650 622-9700

**(P-10822)**
**EJAYS MACHINE CO INC**
1108 E Valencia Dr, Fullerton (92831-4627)
PHONE..............................714 879-0558
Denise Eastin, *Pr*
Schuyler Eastin, *VP*
**EMP:** 20 **EST:** 1965
**SALES (est):** 2.71MM **Privately Held**
**Web:** www.ejaysmachine.com
**SIC: 3599** Machine shop, jobbing and repair

**(P-10823)**
**EL CAMINO MACHINE & WLDG LLC (PA)**
296 El Camino Real S, Salinas (93901-4511)
PHONE..............................831 758-8309
**EMP:** 26 **EST:** 1978
**SQ FT:** 4,800
**SALES (est):** 5.91MM
**SALES (corp-wide):** 5.91MM **Privately Held**
**Web:** www.elcaminomachine.com

SIC: 3599 7692 Machine shop, jobbing and repair; Welding repair

**(P-10824)**
**ELCON INC**
1009 Timothy Dr, San Jose (95133-1043)
PHONE.................................408 292-7800
Anthony J Barraco, *CEO*
Steve Loveless, *
EMP: 50 EST: 1967
SQ FT: 31,000
SALES (est): 3.77MM **Privately Held**
Web: www.elconprecision.com
SIC: 3599 Machine shop, jobbing and repair

**(P-10825)**
**ELY CO INC**
3046 Kashiwa St, Torrance (90505-4009)
PHONE.................................310 539-5831
Walter Senff, *CEO*
Kurt Senff, *
Judith Senff, *
Bill Senff, *
EMP: 36 EST: 1953
SQ FT: 11,500
SALES (est): 5.28MM **Privately Held**
Web: www.elyco.com
SIC: 3599 Machine shop, jobbing and repair

**(P-10826)**
**EME TECHNOLOGIES INC**
3485 Victor St, Santa Clara (95054-2319)
PHONE.................................408 720-8817
Walter Nguyen, *Pr*
▲ EMP: 21 EST: 1986
SQ FT: 20,000
SALES (est): 804.48K **Privately Held**
Web: www.emetec.com
SIC: 3599 Machine shop, jobbing and repair

**(P-10827)**
**ENERGY LINK INDUS SVCS INC**
11439 S Enos Ln, Bakersfield (93311-9452)
P.O. Box 10716 (93389-0716)
PHONE.................................661 765-4444
James R Miller Iii, *CEO*
Ray Miller, *
Matt Knight, *Stockholder**
West Moore, *Stockholder**
Joe Yrigoyen Stckhldrs, *Prin*
EMP: 34 EST: 2000
SALES (est): 11.9MM **Privately Held**
Web: www.energylink1.com
SIC: 3599 7699 Bellows, industrial: metal; Compressor repair

**(P-10828)**
**ERC CONCEPTS CO INC**
1255 Birchwood Dr, Sunnyvale (94089-2206)
P.O. Box 62019 (94088-2019)
PHONE.................................408 734-5345
Felix Oramas, *Pr*
Reina Oramas, *
EMP: 18 EST: 1993
SQ FT: 17,000
SALES (est): 3.52MM **Privately Held**
Web: www.erc-concepts.com
SIC: 3599 Machine shop, jobbing and repair

**(P-10829)**
**EXCEL CNC MACHINING INC**
Also Called: Excel Machining
3185 De La Cruz Blvd, Santa Clara (95054-2405)
PHONE.................................408 970-9460
Krzysztof Wisinski, *Pr*
EMP: 48 EST: 1996
SALES (est): 8.91MM **Privately Held**
Web: www.excel-cnc.com

SIC: 3599 Machine shop, jobbing and repair

**(P-10830)**
**EXCEL MANUFACTURING INC**
20409 Prairie St, Chatsworth (91311-6029)
PHONE.................................661 257-1900
Susan Halliday, *Pr*
EMP: 46 EST: 1992
SQ FT: 14,000
SALES (est): 3MM
SALES (corp-wide): 30.6MM **Privately Held**
Web: www.excelbalermfg.com
SIC: 3599 Machine shop, jobbing and repair
PA: Rtc Aerospace - Chatsworth Division, Inc.
20409 Prairie St
818 341-3344

**(P-10831)**
**EXPAND MACHINERY LLC**
Also Called: Expand Toolroom Solutions
20869 Plummer St, Chatsworth (91311-5005)
PHONE.................................818 349-9166
EMP: 18 EST: 2012
SALES (est): 4MM **Privately Held**
Web: www.expandmachinery.com
SIC: 3599 Machine shop, jobbing and repair

**(P-10832)**
**EXPEDITE PRECISION WORKS INC**
931 Berryessa Rd, San Jose (95133-1002)
PHONE.................................408 573-9600
Orlando Teixeira, *CEO*
EMP: 45 EST: 1994
SQ FT: 5,500
SALES (est): 5.03MM **Privately Held**
Web: www.expediteprecision.com
SIC: 3599 3089 Machine shop, jobbing and repair; Plastics hardware and building products

**(P-10833)**
**EXTREME PRECISION INC**
7855 Prestwick Cir, San Jose (95135-2143)
PHONE.................................408 275-8365
Matthew Ellis, *Pr*
EMP: 15 EST: 1993
SALES (est): 2.24MM **Privately Held**
SIC: 3599 Machine shop, jobbing and repair

**(P-10834)**
**F & L TOOLS CORPORATION**
Also Called: F & L Tls Precision Machining
245 Jason Ct, Corona (92879-6199)
PHONE.................................951 279-1555
Tracey Pratt, *Pr*
Tracey Pratt, *VP*
Larry Pratt, *Prin*
EMP: 18 EST: 1972
SQ FT: 8,100
SALES (est): 4.98MM **Privately Held**
Web: www.fltcorp.com
SIC: 3599 Machine shop, jobbing and repair

**(P-10835)**
**FARRELL BROTHERS HOLDING CORP**
Also Called: Swiss Machine Products
1137 N Armando St, Anaheim (92806-2609)
PHONE.................................714 630-3417
Doug Farrell, *Pr*
Ruby Farrell, *Sec*
Myra Farrell, *Treas*
EMP: 16 EST: 1966
SQ FT: 10,000

SALES (est): 4.03MM **Privately Held**
Web: www.swissmachine.com
SIC: 3599 Machine shop, jobbing and repair

**(P-10836)**
**FERAL PRODUCTIONS LLC**
1935 N Macarthur Dr, Tracy (95376-2833)
PHONE.................................510 791-5392
Lynn Potts, *
EMP: 28 EST: 1997
SQ FT: 10,400
SALES (est): 3MM **Privately Held**
Web: www.feralprodinc.com
SIC: 3599 Machine shop, jobbing and repair

**(P-10837)**
**FIBREFORM ELECTRONICS INC**
Also Called: Fibreform Precision Machining
5341 Argosy Ave, Huntington Beach (92649-1036)
PHONE.................................714 898-9641
Zachary Fischer, *Ch Bd*
Zachary Fischer, *Ch Bd*
Frank Mauro, *
Todd Crow, *
EMP: 30 EST: 1945
SQ FT: 30,000
SALES (est): 4.57MM **Privately Held**
Web: www.fibreformprecision.com
SIC: 3599 Machine shop, jobbing and repair

**(P-10838)**
**FM INDUSTRIES INC (DH)**
Also Called: FM Industries
221 E Warren Ave, Fremont (94539-7916)
PHONE.................................510 668-1900
Hidenori Nanto, *Ch*
David S Miller, *
EMP: 110 EST: 1989
SQ FT: 56,000
SALES (est): 49.81MM **Privately Held**
Web: www.fmindustries.com
SIC: 3599 3544 3999 Machine shop, jobbing and repair; Special dies, tools, jigs, and fixtures; Atomizers, toiletry
HQ: Ngk North America, Inc.
1105 N Market St Ste 1300
Wilmington DE 19801
302 654-1344

**(P-10839)**
**FORM GRIND CORPORATION**
Also Called: Form Products
30062 Aventura, Rcho Sta Marg (92688-2010)
PHONE.................................949 858-7000
Ernest Treichler, *CEO*
Gary Treichler, *
Joan Treichler, *
EMP: 27 EST: 1963
SQ FT: 30,000
SALES (est): 4.83MM **Privately Held**
Web: www.formgrind.com
SIC: 3599 5084 Machine shop, jobbing and repair; Industrial machinery and equipment

**(P-10840)**
**FORTNER ENG & MFG INC**
2927 N Ontario St, Burbank (91504-2017)
P.O. Box 30015 (84130-0015)
PHONE.................................818 240-7740
David W Fortner, *Pr*
EMP: 30 EST: 1952
SQ FT: 24,000
SALES (est): 14.54MM **Publicly Held**
Web: www.fortnereng.com
SIC: 3599 Machine shop, jobbing and repair
HQ: Wencor Group, Llc
416 Dividend Dr
Peachtree City GA 30269
678 490-0140

**(P-10841)**
**FORTUNE MANUFACTURING INC**
13849 Magnolia Ave, Chino (91710-7028)
PHONE.................................909 591-1547
EMP: 45
SIC: 3599 Machine shop, jobbing and repair

**(P-10842)**
**FRANK RUSSELL INC**
341 Pacific Ave, Shafter (93263-2046)
PHONE.................................661 324-5575
Andrew Russell, *Pr*
EMP: 17 EST: 1939
SQ FT: 13,000
SALES (est): 2.96MM **Privately Held**
Web: www.frankrussellinc.com
SIC: 3599 5251 Machine shop, jobbing and repair; Hardware stores

**(P-10843)**
**FRANKLINS INDS SAN DIEGO INC**
12135 Dearborn Pl, Poway (92064-7111)
PHONE.................................858 486-9399
Kelly Franklin, *Pr*
EMP: 44 EST: 1980
SQ FT: 20,000
SALES (est): 9.22MM **Privately Held**
Web: www.franklin-ind.com
SIC: 3599 Machine shop, jobbing and repair

**(P-10844)**
**FRED MATTER INC**
Also Called: Alloy Metal Products
7801 Las Positas Rd, Livermore (94551-8206)
PHONE.................................925 371-1234
Fred Matter, *Pr*
EMP: 21 EST: 1977
SQ FT: 30,000
SALES (est): 3.48MM **Privately Held**
Web: www.alloymp.com
SIC: 3599 Machine shop, jobbing and repair

**(P-10845)**
**FRONTIER ENGRG & MFG TECH INC (PA)**
Also Called: Frontier Technologies
800 W 16th St, Long Beach (90813-1413)
PHONE.................................310 767-1227
John Tsai, *CEO*
Steve Hoekstra, *Pr*
▲ EMP: 33 EST: 1994
SQ FT: 30,000
SALES (est): 10.4MM
SALES (corp-wide): 10.4MM **Privately Held**
Web: www.ftmfg.com
SIC: 3599 8711 Machine shop, jobbing and repair; Engineering services

**(P-10846)**
**FUTURE TECH METALS INC**
719 Palmyrita Ave, Riverside (92507-1811)
PHONE.................................951 781-4801
Tim Gearhardt, *Owner*
EMP: 20 EST: 1998
SALES (est): 4.82MM **Privately Held**
Web: www.futuretechmetals.com
SIC: 3599 Machine shop, jobbing and repair

**(P-10847)**
**FUTURISTICS MACHINE INC**
7014 Carroll Rd, San Diego (92121-2213)
PHONE.................................858 450-0644
Mark Mcginn, *CEO*
EMP: 35 EST: 2016
SALES (est): 2.54MM **Privately Held**
Web: www.futuristicsmachine.com

## 3599 - Industrial Machinery, Nec (P-10848)

SIC: 3599 Machine shop, jobbing and repair

### (P-10848)
**G P MANUFACTURING INC**
Also Called: Protype
541 W Briardale Ave, Orange (92865-4207)
PHONE...................714 974-0288
Greg Gilbert, *Pr*
Lewis Pearmain, *VP*
EMP: 16 EST: 1984
SQ FT: 13,500
SALES (est): 1.63MM **Privately Held**
SIC: 3599 3444 Machine shop, jobbing and repair; Sheet metalwork

### (P-10849)
**G V INDUSTRIES INC**
1346 Cleveland Ave, National City (91950-4207)
PHONE...................619 474-3013
Gregory J Verdon, *Pr*
Joseph Verdon, *
Linda Verdon, *Corporate Vice President**
EMP: 38 EST: 1978
SQ FT: 14,000
SALES (est): 5.21MM **Privately Held**
Web: www.gvindustries.biz
SIC: 3599 Machine shop, jobbing and repair

### (P-10850)
**GAMMA AEROSPACE LLC**
1461 S Balboa Ave, Ontario (91761-7609)
PHONE...................310 532-4480
Thomas C Hutton, *Managing Member*
EMP: 32
SALES (corp-wide): 24.83MM **Privately Held**
Web: www.gammaaero.com
SIC: 3599 Machine shop, jobbing and repair
PA: Gamma Aerospace Llc
601 Airport Dr Ste 2718
817 477-2193

### (P-10851)
**GARABEDIAN BROS INC (PA)**
Also Called: Valley Welding & Machine Works
2543 S Orange Ave, Fresno (93725-1329)
P.O. Box 2455 (93745-2455)
PHONE...................559 268-5014
Michael J Garabedian, *CEO*
Joanne Garabedian, *
▼ EMP: 30 EST: 1946
SQ FT: 45,000
SALES (est): 4.67MM
SALES (corp-wide): 4.67MM **Privately Held**
Web: www.vwmworks.com
SIC: 3599 3523 Machine shop, jobbing and repair; Driers (farm): grain, hay, and seed

### (P-10852)
**GARRETT PRECISION INC**
25082 La Suen Rd, Laguna Hills (92653-5102)
PHONE...................949 855-9710
Justin S Osborn, *CEO*
Dean Garrett, *Pr*
Lynn Sandra Garrett, *VP*
EMP: 19 EST: 1978
SQ FT: 6,500
SALES (est): 1.44MM **Privately Held**
SIC: 3599 Machine shop, jobbing and repair

### (P-10853)
**GATEWAY PRECISION INC**
480 Vista Way, Milpitas (95035-5406)
PHONE...................408 942-8849
Duy Kevin Nguyen, *CEO*
EMP: 40 EST: 2000
SALES (est): 4.68MM **Privately Held**
Web: www.gatewayprecision.com
SIC: 3599 3559 Machine shop, jobbing and repair; Semiconductor manufacturing machinery

### (P-10854)
**GBF ENTERPRISES INC**
2709 Halladay St, Santa Ana (92705-5618)
PHONE...................714 979-7131
Cheryl Nowak, *Pr*
EMP: 25 EST: 1976
SQ FT: 17,000
SALES (est): 5.31MM **Privately Held**
Web: www.gbfenterprises.com
SIC: 3599 Machine shop, jobbing and repair

### (P-10855)
**GEIGER MANUFACTURING INC**
1110 E Scotts Ave, Stockton (95205-6148)
P.O. Box 1449 (95201-1449)
PHONE...................209 464-7746
Roger Haack, *Pr*
Dennis D Geiger, *Treas*
EMP: 16 EST: 1904
SQ FT: 27,250
SALES (est): 3.35MM **Privately Held**
Web: www.geigermfg.com
SIC: 3599 Machine shop, jobbing and repair

### (P-10856)
**GENERAL GRINDING INC**
Also Called: Stailess Polishing Co.
801 51st Ave, Oakland (94601-5694)
PHONE...................510 261-5557
TOLL FREE: 800
Michael Bardon, *Pr*
Daniel Bardon, *
EMP: 34 EST: 1944
SQ FT: 22,500
SALES (est): 2.36MM **Privately Held**
Web: www.generalgrindinginc.com
SIC: 3599 Machine shop, jobbing and repair

### (P-10857)
**GENERAL INDUSTRIAL REPAIR**
6865 Washington Blvd, Montebello (90640-5434)
PHONE...................323 278-0873
Henry Biazus, *Pr*
Richard Biazus, *
EMP: 25 EST: 1995
SALES (est): 4.2MM **Privately Held**
Web: www.girepair.us
SIC: 3599 Machine shop, jobbing and repair

### (P-10858)
**GENTEC MANUFACTURING INC**
Also Called: Machined-Art
2241 Ringwood Ave, San Jose (95131)
PHONE...................408 432-6220
Mark Diaz, *Pr*
EMP: 15 EST: 1976
SQ FT: 5,700
SALES (est): 3.38MM **Privately Held**
Web: www.gentecmfg.com
SIC: 3599 Machine shop, jobbing and repair

### (P-10859)
**GEORGE FISCHER INC (HQ)**
5462 Irwindale Ave Ste A, Baldwin Park (91706-2074)
PHONE...................626 571-2770
Chris Blumer, *CEO*
Daniel Vaterlaus, *VP*
◆ EMP: 239 EST: 1954
SALES (est): 314.98MM **Privately Held**
Web: www.georgfischer.com
SIC: 3599 5074 3829 3559 Electrical discharge machining (EDM); Pipes and fittings, plastic; Testing equipment: abrasion, shearing strength, etc.; Foundry machinery and equipment
PA: Georg Fischer Ag
Amsler-Laffon-Strasse 9

### (P-10860)
**GERMAN MACHINED PRODUCTS INC**
Also Called: German Machine Products
1415 W 178th St, Gardena (90248-3201)
PHONE...................310 532-4480
EMP: 32
SIC: 3599 Machine shop, jobbing and repair

### (P-10861)
**GLENDEE CORP (PA)**
Also Called: Metalagraphics
5390 Gabbert Rd, Moorpark (93021-1772)
PHONE...................805 523-2422
EMP: 41 EST: 1975
SALES (est): 10.92MM
SALES (corp-wide): 10.92MM **Privately Held**
Web: www.mgius.com
SIC: 3599 3444 Machine and other job shop work; Sheet metalwork

### (P-10862)
**GLENDEE CORP**
Also Called: Metalagraphics
5151 N Commerce Ave, Moorpark (93021-1763)
PHONE...................805 523-2422
EMP: 20
SALES (corp-wide): 9.95MM **Privately Held**
Web: www.mgius.com
SIC: 3599 3444 Machine and other job shop work; Sheet metalwork
PA: Glendee Corp.
5390 Gabbert Rd
805 523-2422

### (P-10863)
**GOLDEN WEST MACHINE INC**
9930 Jordan Cir, Santa Fe Springs (90670-3305)
PHONE...................562 903-1111
Dan Goodman, *Prin*
Al Schlunegger, *
EMP: 35 EST: 1982
SQ FT: 25,000
SALES (est): 6.02MM **Privately Held**
Web: www.goldenwestmachine.com
SIC: 3599 7699 Machine shop, jobbing and repair; Industrial machinery and equipment repair

### (P-10864)
**HAIG PRECISION MFG CORP**
3616 Snell Ave, San Jose (95136-1305)
PHONE...................408 378-4920
Daniel S Sarkisian, *CEO*
Paul Sarkisian, *
▲ EMP: 60 EST: 1960
SQ FT: 26,000
SALES (est): 4.4MM **Privately Held**
Web: www.haigprecision.com
SIC: 3599 7692 Machine shop, jobbing and repair; Welding repair

### (P-10865)
**HALES ENGINEERING CO INC**
18 Wood Rd, Camarillo (93010-8327)
EMP: 49 EST: 1966
SALES (est): 3.65MM **Privately Held**

SIC: 3599 1791 3441 Machine shop, jobbing and repair; Structural steel erection; Fabricated structural metal

### (P-10866)
**HAMMOND ENTERPRISES INC**
1911 Tarob Ct, Milpitas (95035-7114)
PHONE...................925 432-3537
Melissa Kozar, *Pr*
▲ EMP: 20 EST: 1990
SALES (est): 4.44MM **Privately Held**
Web: www.hammondenterprises.com
SIC: 3599 Machine shop, jobbing and repair

### (P-10867)
**HANSEN ENGINEERING CO**
24020 Frampton Ave, Harbor City (90710-2102)
PHONE...................310 534-3870
EMP: 86 EST: 1962
SALES (est): 4.25MM **Privately Held**
Web: www.hansenengineering.com
SIC: 3599 Machine shop, jobbing and repair

### (P-10868)
**HEIGHTEN AMERICA INC**
Also Called: Heighten Manfacturing
1144 Post Rd, Oakdale (95361-9384)
PHONE...................209 845-0455
Linda Smeck, *Pr*
Jerrold W Smeck, *Treas*
EMP: 21 EST: 1984
SQ FT: 8,000
SALES (est): 5.08MM **Privately Held**
Web: www.hi10usa.com
SIC: 3599 Machine shop, jobbing and repair

### (P-10869)
**HENRY MACHINE INC**
2316 La Mirada Dr, Vista (92081-7862)
EMP: 15 EST: 1992
SALES (est): 2.62MM **Privately Held**
Web: www.henrymachine.com
SIC: 3599 Machine shop, jobbing and repair

### (P-10870)
**HERA TECHNOLOGIES LLC**
1055 E Francis St, Ontario (91761-5633)
PHONE...................951 751-6191
Didi Truong, *CEO*
Aaron Evans, *
Eugene Chuck, *
EMP: 50 EST: 2015
SALES (est): 5.48MM **Privately Held**
Web: www.heratechnologies.com
SIC: 3599 Machine shop, jobbing and repair

### (P-10871)
**HI-TECH LABELS INCORPORATED**
Also Called: Hi-Tech Products
8530 Roland St, Buena Park (90621-3124)
PHONE...................714 670-2150
Jeffrey T Ruch, *CEO*
▲ EMP: 34 EST: 1983
SQ FT: 24,000
SALES (est): 6.75MM **Privately Held**
Web: www.hi-tech-products.com
SIC: 3599 Machine shop, jobbing and repair

### (P-10872)
**HIGH PRCSION GRNDING MCHNING I**
1130 Pioneer Way, El Cajon (92020-1925)
PHONE...................619 440-0303
Keith Brawner, *Pr*
Ken Gerhart, *
Shanda Brawner, *
EMP: 18 EST: 1971

# PRODUCTS & SERVICES SECTION

## 3599 - Industrial Machinery, Nec (P-10896)

SQ FT: 20,000
SALES (est): 2.41MM **Privately Held**
Web: www.highprecisiongrinding.com
SIC: **3599** Machine shop, jobbing and repair

**(P-10873)**
**HMCOMPANY**
4464 Mcgrath St Ste 111, Ventura (93003-7764)
PHONE..................................805 650-2651
Mark Woellert, *Owner*
EMP: 18 EST: 1977
SQ FT: 3,500
SALES (est): 458.36K **Privately Held**
Web: www.hm-company.net
SIC: **3599** Machine shop, jobbing and repair

**(P-10874)**
**HOEFNER CORPORATION**
9722 Rush St, South El Monte (91733-1777)
PHONE..................................626 443-3258
Gerald Hoefner, *Pr*
Karen Hoefner, *Sec*
EMP: 20 EST: 1946
SQ FT: 14,800
SALES (est): 5.6MM **Privately Held**
Web: www.hoefnercorp.com
SIC: **3599** 3429 Machine shop, jobbing and repair; Hardware, nec

**(P-10875)**
**HOLLAND & HERRING MFG INC**
Also Called: H & H Manufacturing
661 E Monterey Ave, Pomona (91767-5607)
PHONE..................................909 469-4700
Jerry C Holland, *Pr*
Lawrence P Saylor, *Sec*
Debbie Krakowe, *CFO*
Mark B Herring, *Stockholder*
Bruce N Herring, *Stockholder*
EMP: 29 EST: 1991
SQ FT: 15,000
SALES (est): 1.02MM **Privately Held**
SIC: **3599** 3471 Machine shop, jobbing and repair; Cleaning, polishing, and finishing

**(P-10876)**
**HOUSTON ONTIC INC**
20400 Plummer St, Chatsworth (91311-5372)
PHONE..................................818 678-6555
EMP: 19 EST: 2016
SALES (est): 6.22MM **Privately Held**
Web: www.ontic.com
SIC: **3599** Machine shop, jobbing and repair

**(P-10877)**
**HTE ACQUISITION LLC**
Also Called: Hi-Tech Engineering
4610 Calle Quetzal, Camarillo (93012-8558)
PHONE..................................805 987-0520
Shaffiq Rahim, *Pr*
EMP: 20 EST: 2019
SQ FT: 15,000
SALES (est): 5.21MM **Privately Held**
Web: www.htemfg.com
SIC: **3599** Machine shop, jobbing and repair

**(P-10878)**
**HUGO VENTURE SOLUTIONS CORP**
6325 Carpinteria Ave, Carpinteria (93013)
P.O. Box 87 (93014)
PHONE..................................805 684-0593
Alberto Hugo, *CEO*
Roger Hugo, *
Richard Hugo, *

EMP: 43 EST: 1961
SQ FT: 12,000
SALES (est): 6.44MM **Privately Held**
Web: www.rinconengineering.com
SIC: **3599** 3444 3441 Machine shop, jobbing and repair; Sheet metalwork; Fabricated structural metal

**(P-10879)**
**HYTRON MFG CO INC**
15582 Chemical Ln, Huntington Beach (92649-1505)
PHONE..................................714 903-6701
James C Rehling, *Pr*
Robert Rehling, *
Cheryll Rehling, *
Deborah Strickland, *
EMP: 50 EST: 1963
SQ FT: 13,370
SALES (est): 3.75MM **Privately Held**
Web: www.hytronmanufacturing.com
SIC: **3599** Machine shop, jobbing and repair

**(P-10880)**
**I COPY INC**
Also Called: Ibe Digital
11266 Monarch St Ste B, Garden Grove (92841-1450)
PHONE..................................562 921-0202
Ronald Varing, *Pr*
EMP: 50 EST: 2001
SALES (est): 6.25MM **Privately Held**
Web: www.ibedigital.com
SIC: **3599** 5044 5999 Amusement park equipment; Duplicating machines; Business machines and equipment

**(P-10881)**
**I M T PRECISION INC**
31902 Hayman St, Hayward (94544-7925)
PHONE..................................510 324-8926
Timoteo Ilario, *Pr*
EMP: 50 EST: 1993
SQ FT: 50,000
SALES (est): 9.69MM **Privately Held**
Web: www.imtp.com
SIC: **3599** Machine shop, jobbing and repair

**(P-10882)**
**IMG COMPANIES LLC (HQ)**
Also Called: IMG
225 Mountain Vista Pkwy, Livermore (94551-8210)
PHONE..................................925 273-1100
Kam Pasha, *CEO*
Kiran Mukkamala, *
Mahesh Kumar, *
▲ EMP: 70 EST: 2004
SALES (est): 45.07MM
SALES (corp-wide): 811.12MM **Publicly Held**
Web: www.imgprecision.com
SIC: **3599** Machine shop, jobbing and repair
PA: Ichor Holdings, Ltd.
3185 Laurelview Ct
510 897-5200

**(P-10883)**
**IMMOTION VR LTD**
1067 Gayley Ave, Los Angeles (90024-3401)
PHONE..................................818 813-3923
Rodey Findley, *Managing Member*
EMP: 20
SALES (est): 1.4MM **Privately Held**
SIC: **3599** Amusement park equipment

**(P-10884)**
**INFINITY PRECISION INC**
Also Called: Design Engineering

730 E Easy St, Simi Valley (93065-1810)
PHONE..................................818 727-0504
Evelina Martirosova, *CEO*
EMP: 20 EST: 2007
SQ FT: 6,000
SALES (est): 2.88MM **Privately Held**
Web: www.ipinc-usa.com
SIC: **3599** 3441 Machine shop, jobbing and repair; Fabricated structural metal

**(P-10885)**
**INFOCUS CNC MACHINING INC**
11245 Young River Ave, Fountain Valley (92708-4108)
PHONE..................................714 979-1253
Vinny Tran, *Prin*
EMP: 20 EST: 2007
SQ FT: 7,972
SALES (est): 2.76MM **Privately Held**
Web: www.infocuscnc.com
SIC: **3599** Machine shop, jobbing and repair

**(P-10886)**
**INNO TECH MANUFACTURING INC**
10109 Carroll Canyon Rd, San Diego (92131-1109)
PHONE..................................858 565-4556
Marek Prochazka, *Pr*
Gail Prochazka, *CFO*
▲ EMP: 19 EST: 1996
SALES (est): 3.98MM **Privately Held**
Web: www.innotech-mfg.com
SIC: **3599** Machine shop, jobbing and repair

**(P-10887)**
**INNOVATIVE MACHINING INC**
845 Yosemite Way, Milpitas (95035-6329)
PHONE..................................408 262-2270
Thang Vo, *Pr*
Bich Nguyen, *
EMP: 26 EST: 1997
SQ FT: 3,000
SALES (est): 4.69MM **Privately Held**
Web: www.innomachcorp.com
SIC: **3599** Machine shop, jobbing and repair

**(P-10888)**
**INTER-CITY MANUFACTURING INC**
507 Redwood Ave, Seaside (93955-3029)
PHONE..................................831 899-3636
Douglas A Learned, *Pr*
Karen Learned, *Sec*
EMP: 21 EST: 1975
SQ FT: 12,000
SALES (est): 3.02MM **Privately Held**
Web: www.fastforwardracingcomponents.com
SIC: **3599** Machine shop, jobbing and repair

**(P-10889)**
**INTERNATIONAL PRECISION INC**
Also Called: I P
9526 Vassar Ave, Chatsworth (91311-4168)
P.O. Box 4839 (91313-4839)
PHONE..................................818 882-3933
Renee M Brendel-konrad, *Pr*
Kalei Kaumaka Konrad, *VP*
◆ EMP: 18 EST: 1968
SQ FT: 12,000
SALES (est): 5.15MM **Privately Held**
Web: www.intlprecision.com
SIC: **3599** 3728 Machine shop, jobbing and repair; Aircraft parts and equipment, nec

**(P-10890)**
**INTRA AEROSPACE LLC**
10671 Civic Center Dr, Rancho Cucamonga (91730-3804)
PHONE..................................909 476-0343
Robert Sayig, *Prin*
EMP: 35 EST: 2018
SALES (est): 1.3MM **Privately Held**
Web: www.intra-aerospace.com
SIC: **3599** Machine shop, jobbing and repair

**(P-10891)**
**INTRI-PLEX TECHNOLOGIES INC (HQ)**
751 S Kellogg Ave, Goleta (93117-3806)
PHONE..................................805 683-3414
David Dexter, *CEO*
▲ EMP: 126 EST: 1987
SQ FT: 46,000
SALES (est): 20.93MM
SALES (corp-wide): 21.69MM **Privately Held**
Web: www.intriplex.com
SIC: **3599** Machine shop, jobbing and repair
PA: Ipt Holding Inc
751 S Kellogg Ave
805 683-3414

**(P-10892)**
**INVERSE SOLUTIONS INC**
3922 Valley Ave Ste A, Pleasanton (94566-4864)
P.O. Box 1059 (94566-0906)
PHONE..................................925 931-9500
David Jordan, *Prin*
Ronda Jordan, *
EMP: 24 EST: 1999
SQ FT: 12,500
SALES (est): 4.78MM **Privately Held**
Web: www.inversesolutionsinc.com
SIC: **3599** Machine shop, jobbing and repair

**(P-10893)**
**ITSJ GROUP INC**
148 E Brokaw Rd, San Jose (95112-4203)
PHONE..................................408 609-6392
Chau Tran, *CEO*
EMP: 20 EST: 2020
SALES (est): 2.78MM **Privately Held**
Web: www.itsj-group.com
SIC: **3599** Machine and other job shop work

**(P-10894)**
**J & F MACHINE INC**
6401 Global Dr, Cypress (90630-5227)
PHONE..................................714 527-3499
Micheline Varnum, *Pr*
Richard Varnum, *VP*
EMP: 22 EST: 1977
SQ FT: 8,500
SALES (est): 3.25MM **Privately Held**
Web: www.jandfmachine.com
SIC: **3599** Machine shop, jobbing and repair

**(P-10895)**
**J & R MACHINE WORKS**
45420 60th St W, Lancaster (93536-8322)
PHONE..................................661 945-8826
Jesse Alvarado, *Pt*
Rudy Alvarado, *Pt*
EMP: 21 EST: 1989
SQ FT: 3,500
SALES (est): 794.51K **Privately Held**
Web: www.jrmachineworks.com
SIC: **3599** Machine shop, jobbing and repair

**(P-10896)**
**J & S INC**
229 E Gardena Blvd, Gardena (90248-2800)

## 3599 - Industrial Machinery, Nec (P-10897)

PHONE..................310 719-7144
Joseph Brown, *Pr*
Margaret Brown, *
Sheryl Zamora, *
**EMP:** 33 **EST:** 1981
**SQ FT:** 6,141
**SALES (est):** 3.11MM **Privately Held**
**SIC: 3599** Machine shop, jobbing and repair

### (P-10897)
### J A-CO MACHINE WORKS LLC
Also Called: Jaco Machine Works
4 Carbonero Way, Scotts Valley (95066-4200)
PHONE..................877 429-8175
Andy Smith, *Managing Member*
Jeffrey A Smith, *Mng Pt*
**EMP:** 20 **EST:** 1979
**SQ FT:** 9,000
**SALES (est):** 3.9MM **Privately Held**
Web: www.jacoworks.com
**SIC: 3599** Machine shop, jobbing and repair

### (P-10898)
### J AND K MANUFACTURING INC
14701 Garfield Ave, Paramount (90723-3412)
PHONE..................562 630-8417
▲ **EMP:** 28 **EST:** 1978
**SALES (est):** 6.65MM **Privately Held**
**SIC: 3599** Machine shop, jobbing and repair

### (P-10899)
### J B TOOL INC
350 E Orangethorpe Ave Ste 6, Placentia (92870-6504)
PHONE..................714 993-7173
Robert Barna, *Pr*
**EMP:** 17 **EST:** 1975
**SQ FT:** 12,000
**SALES (est):** 515.01K **Privately Held**
Web: www.jbtoolinc.com
**SIC: 3599** Machine shop, jobbing and repair

### (P-10900)
### J I MACHINE COMPANY INC
9720 Distribution Ave, San Diego (92121-2310)
PHONE..................858 695-1787
Ila Ree Piel, *Pr*
James Piel, *VP*
Mark Jay Piel, *VP*
Wendy Anne Piel, *VP*
▲ **EMP:** 24 **EST:** 1976
**SQ FT:** 15,400
**SALES (est):** 3.47MM **Privately Held**
Web: www.jimachine.com
**SIC: 3599** 3812 Machine shop, jobbing and repair; Search and navigation equipment

### (P-10901)
### JACO ENGINEERING
879 S East St, Anaheim (92805-5391)
PHONE..................714 991-1680
H J Meagher, *Pr*
Barbara Meagher, *
**EMP:** 35 **EST:** 1964
**SQ FT:** 10,000
**SALES (est):** 5.13MM **Privately Held**
Web: www.jacoengineering.com
**SIC: 3599** Machine shop, jobbing and repair

### (P-10902)
### JAFFA PRECISION ENGRG INC
12117 Madera Way, Riverside (92503-4849)
PHONE..................951 278-8797
Raida Sayegh, *Pr*
Mark Sayegh, *Mgr*
**EMP:** 15 **EST:** 1986
**SQ FT:** 12,500
**SALES (est):** 2.8MM **Privately Held**
Web: www.jaffaprecision.com
**SIC: 3599** Machine shop, jobbing and repair

### (P-10903)
### JAMES STOUT
Also Called: Stg Machine
481 Gianni St, Santa Clara (95054-2414)
PHONE..................408 988-8582
Jim Stout, *Owner*
**EMP:** 30 **EST:** 1987
**SQ FT:** 15,000
**SALES (est):** 6.13MM **Privately Held**
Web: www.stgmachine.com
**SIC: 3599** Machine shop, jobbing and repair

### (P-10904)
### JARVIS MANUFACTURING INC
210 Hillsdale Ave, San Jose (95136-1392)
PHONE..................408 226-2600
Tony Grewal, *CEO*
**EMP:** 17 **EST:** 1957
**SALES (est):** 3.02MM **Privately Held**
Web: www.jarvismfg.com
**SIC: 3599** Machine shop, jobbing and repair

### (P-10905)
### JCPM INC
Also Called: J C Precision
8576 Red Oak St, Rancho Cucamonga (91730-4822)
PHONE..................909 484-9040
Carlos Cajas, *Pr*
**EMP:** 23 **EST:** 1995
**SQ FT:** 5,200
**SALES (est):** 919.89K **Privately Held**
Web: www.jcpm-inc.com
**SIC: 3599** Machine shop, jobbing and repair

### (P-10906)
### JENSON MECHANICAL INC
Also Called: J M I
32420 Central Ave, Union City (94587-2007)
P.O. Box 1006 (95378-1006)
PHONE..................510 429-8078
Greg Jenson, *Pr*
**EMP:** 20 **EST:** 1976
**SQ FT:** 30,000
**SALES (est):** 2.48MM **Privately Held**
Web: www.jensonmechanical.com
**SIC: 3599** 7699 Custom machinery; Industrial machinery and equipment repair

### (P-10907)
### JESSEE BROTHERS MACHINE SP INC
Also Called: J B Precision
1640 Dell Ave, Campbell (95008-6901)
PHONE..................408 866-1755
Chett Jessee, *Pr*
**EMP:** 16 **EST:** 1975
**SQ FT:** 12,500
**SALES (est):** 2.78MM **Privately Held**
Web: www.jesseebrothersinc.com
**SIC: 3599** Machine shop, jobbing and repair

### (P-10908)
### JET CUTTING SOLUTIONS INC
10853 Bell Ct, Rancho Cucamonga (91730-4835)
PHONE..................909 948-2424
Louis Mammolito, *Pr*
Thomas Ribas, *
Louis Mammooito, *
**EMP:** 45 **EST:** 2005
**SALES (est):** 6.36MM **Privately Held**
Web: www.jetcuttingsolutions.com
**SIC: 3599** Machine shop, jobbing and repair

### (P-10909)
### JL HALEY ENTERPRISES INC
3510 Luyung Dr, Rancho Cordova (95742-6872)
PHONE..................916 631-6375
James L Haley, *CEO*
◆ **EMP:** 140 **EST:** 1971
**SQ FT:** 67,000
**SALES (est):** 24.9MM
**SALES (corp-wide):** 138.57MM **Privately Held**
Web: www.vantedgemedical.com
**SIC: 3599** 3312 7692 Machine shop, jobbing and repair; Blast furnaces and steel mills; Welding repair
PA: Vander-Bend Manufacturing, Inc.
2701 Orchard Pkwy
408 245-5150

### (P-10910)
### JMC CLOSING CO LLC
Also Called: Ever-Pac
1499 Palmyrita Ave, Riverside (92507)
PHONE..................951 278-9900
Ron Vangrouw, *Brnch Mgr*
**EMP:** 25
**SQ FT:** 12,400
**SALES (corp-wide):** 5.97MM **Privately Held**
Web: www.quinncompany.com
**SIC: 3599** 3444 3441 Machine shop, jobbing and repair; Sheet metalwork; Fabricated structural metal
PA: Jmc Closing Co. Llc
2900 Adams St U C230

### (P-10911)
### JMG MACHINE INC
17037 Industry Pl, La Mirada (90638-5819)
PHONE..................714 522-6221
Juan Manuel Guillen, *CEO*
**EMP:** 20 **EST:** 1994
**SQ FT:** 10,000
**SALES (est):** 2.77MM **Privately Held**
Web: www.jmgmachine.com
**SIC: 3599** Machine shop, jobbing and repair

### (P-10912)
### JNS INDUSTRIES INC
Also Called: Jns Industries
5120 Hamner Ave, Eastvale (91752-1051)
PHONE..................909 923-8334
Janet Sheikh, *Pr*
**EMP:** 15 **EST:** 2000
**SALES (est):** 1.71MM **Privately Held**
Web: www.jnsindustries.com
**SIC: 3599** Machine shop, jobbing and repair

### (P-10913)
### JOHNSON MANUFACTURING INC
15201 Connector Ln, Huntington Beach (92649-1117)
PHONE..................714 903-0393
Colleen Johnson, *CEO*
Allan Johnson, *
**EMP:** 35 **EST:** 1981
**SQ FT:** 13,000
**SALES (est):** 4.96MM **Privately Held**
Web: www.johnsonmfginc.com
**SIC: 3599** Machine shop, jobbing and repair

### (P-10914)
### JOHNSON PRECISION PRODUCTS LLC
1308 E Wakeham Ave, Santa Ana (92705-4145)
PHONE..................714 824-6971
Paul Cronin, *Pr*
**EMP:** 19 **EST:** 1961
**SQ FT:** 4,000
**SALES (est):** 5.44MM **Privately Held**
Web: www.johnsonprecisionmachining.com
**SIC: 3599** Machine shop, jobbing and repair

### (P-10915)
### JR MACHINE COMPANY INC
13245 Florence Ave, Santa Fe Springs (90670-4509)
PHONE..................562 903-9477
Gilbert Reyes, *Pr*
**EMP:** 29 **EST:** 1973
**SQ FT:** 12,000
**SALES (est):** 2.47MM **Privately Held**
**SIC: 3599** Machine shop, jobbing and repair

### (P-10916)
### JWP MANUFACTURING LLC
3500 De La Cruz Blvd, Santa Clara (95054-2111)
PHONE..................408 970-0641
Jerzy W Prokop, *Managing Member*
Suzanna Prokop, *
Zuzanna Prokop, *Managing Member*
**EMP:** 25 **EST:** 1986
**SQ FT:** 12,000
**SALES (est):** 7.11MM **Privately Held**
Web: www.jwpmfg.com
**SIC: 3599** Machine shop, jobbing and repair

### (P-10917)
### K-P ENGINEERING CORP
2614 Rousselle St, Santa Ana (92707-3729)
PHONE..................714 545-7045
Kemal Pepic, *CEO*
**EMP:** 21 **EST:** 1980
**SQ FT:** 7,000
**SALES (est):** 3.3MM **Privately Held**
Web: www.kpe.com
**SIC: 3599** 8711 Machine shop, jobbing and repair; Professional engineer

### (P-10918)
### K-TECH MACHINE INC
1377 Armorlite Dr, San Marcos (92069-1341)
PHONE..................800 274-9424
Kenneth Russell, *Pr*
Stuart John Russell, *
**EMP:** 134 **EST:** 1990
**SQ FT:** 16,000
**SALES (est):** 24.39MM **Privately Held**
Web: www.k-techmachine.com
**SIC: 3599** 3444 Machine shop, jobbing and repair; Sheet metalwork

### (P-10919)
### KADAN CONSULTANTS INCORPORATED
5662 Research Dr, Huntington Beach (92649-1615)
PHONE..................562 988-1165
Rhoda Sjoberg, *CEO*
**EMP:** 15 **EST:** 2001
**SQ FT:** 17,000
**SALES (est):** 2.71MM **Privately Held**
Web: www.kadaninc.net
**SIC: 3599** 3728 3544 8711 Machine shop, jobbing and repair; Aircraft parts and equipment, nec; Special dies, tools, jigs, and fixtures; Engineering services

# PRODUCTS & SERVICES SECTION
## 3599 - Industrial Machinery, Nec (P-10944)

**(P-10920)**
**KALMAN MANUFACTURING INC**
780 Jarvis Dr Ste 150, Morgan Hill (95037-2886)
PHONE..................................408 776-7664
Alan D Kalman, *Pr*
Freia Kalman, *
EMP: 43 EST: 1983
SQ FT: 35,000
SALES (est): 8.39MM **Privately Held**
Web: www.kalman.com
SIC: 3599 Machine shop, jobbing and repair

**(P-10921)**
**KAP MANUFACTURING INC**
327 W Allen Ave, San Dimas (91773-1441)
PHONE..................................909 599-2525
Michael D' Amato, *CFO*
Michael D Amato, *
Kathleen D Amato, *
Bryan D'amato, *VP*
EMP: 27 EST: 1999
SQ FT: 6,000
SALES (est): 4.07MM **Privately Held**
Web: www.kapmfg.com
SIC: 3599 Machine shop, jobbing and repair

**(P-10922)**
**KAY & JAMES INC**
Also Called: J&S Machine Works
14062 Balboa Blvd, Sylmar (91342-1005)
PHONE..................................818 998-0357
Kye Sook So, *CEO*
Jung M So, *
EMP: 75 EST: 1981
SQ FT: 25,000
SALES (est): 8.83MM **Privately Held**
SIC: 3599 Machine shop, jobbing and repair

**(P-10923)**
**KDF INC**
Also Called: Pro-Cision Machining
15875 Concord Cir, Morgan Hill (95037-5448)
PHONE..................................408 779-3731
Ken Fredenburg, *Pr*
EMP: 30 EST: 1984
SQ FT: 20,000
SALES (est): 3.92MM **Privately Held**
Web: www.procisionmachining.com
SIC: 3599 Machine shop, jobbing and repair

**(P-10924)**
**KEMAC TECHNOLOGY INC**
503 S Vincent Ave, Azusa (91702-5131)
PHONE..................................626 334-1519
EMP: 40
Web: www.tecometetch.com
SIC: 3599 3479 Chemical milling job shop; Etching and engraving

**(P-10925)**
**KERLEYLEGACY63 INC**
3000-3010 La Jolla St, Anaheim (92806)
PHONE..................................714 630-7286
EMP: 100
SIC: 3599 3469 3444 3061 Machine and other job shop work; Machine parts, stamped or pressed metal; Sheet metalwork ; Mechanical rubber goods

**(P-10926)**
**KHUUS INC**
Also Called: Kamet
1778 Mccarthy Blvd, Milpitas (95035-7421)
PHONE..................................408 522-8000
Peter Khuu, *Pr*
Donald Cheng, *Genl Mgr*
John Gitonga, *Mgr*
▲ EMP: 60 EST: 1986
SQ FT: 25,000
SALES (est): 9.36MM **Privately Held**
Web: www.kamet.com
SIC: 3599 Machine shop, jobbing and repair

**(P-10927)**
**KILGORE MACHINE COMPANY INC**
2312 S Susan St, Santa Ana (92704-4421)
PHONE..................................714 540-3659
Bryant Kilgore, *Pr*
Doree Kilgore, *VP*
Linda Mckenzie, *Prin*
Lisa Damico, *Prin*
EMP: 22 EST: 1968
SQ FT: 8,000
SALES (est): 2.78MM **Privately Held**
Web: www.kilgoremachinecompany.com
SIC: 3599 Machine shop, jobbing and repair

**(P-10928)**
**KIMBERLY MACHINE INC**
12822 Joy St, Garden Grove (92840-6350)
PHONE..................................714 539-0151
Khanh Cao, *CEO*
Tam Nguyen, *
EMP: 35 EST: 1975
SQ FT: 10,300
SALES (est): 4.3MM **Privately Held**
Web: www.kimberlymachine.com
SIC: 3599 Machine shop, jobbing and repair

**(P-10929)**
**KITCH ENGINEERING INC**
12320 Montague St, Pacoima (91331-2213)
PHONE..................................818 897-7133
Steven Kitching, *Pr*
Terry Kitching, *
Kerri Kitching, *
EMP: 30 EST: 1984
SQ FT: 6,000
SALES (est): 4.92MM **Privately Held**
Web: www.kitchengineering.com
SIC: 3599 3751 Machine shop, jobbing and repair; Motorcycles, bicycles and parts

**(P-10930)**
**KNT INC**
Also Called: Knt Manufacturing
39760 Eureka Dr, Newark (94560-4808)
PHONE..................................510 651-7163
Keith Ngo, *CEO*
EMP: 150 EST: 2001
SQ FT: 50,000
SALES (est): 23.39MM **Privately Held**
Web: www.kntmfg.com
SIC: 3599 Machine shop, jobbing and repair

**(P-10931)**
**KODIAK PRECISION INC (PA)**
444 S 1st St, Richmond (94804)
PHONE..................................510 234-4165
Paul Bacchi, *Pr*
Neil Divers, *VP*
Dave Harris, *VP*
EMP: 17 EST: 1976
SQ FT: 10,000
SALES (est): 3.72MM
SALES (corp-wide): 3.72MM **Privately Held**
Web: www.kodiakprecision.com
SIC: 3599 Machine shop, jobbing and repair

**(P-10932)**
**KQ INTEGRATED SOLUTIONS INC**
3380 Keller St, Santa Clara (95054-2612)
PHONE..................................408 654-0428
EMP: 125 EST: 1994
SALES (est): 8.5MM **Privately Held**
Web: www.kqisi.com
SIC: 3599 Machine shop, jobbing and repair

**(P-10933)**
**KT ENGINEERING CORPORATION**
2016 E Vista Bella Way, Rancho Dominguez (90220-6109)
PHONE..................................310 537-3818
John Tajirian, *CEO*
EMP: 16 EST: 1986
SQ FT: 3,500
SALES (est): 4.31MM **Privately Held**
Web: www.ktengineering.com
SIC: 3599 8711 Machine shop, jobbing and repair; Aviation and/or aeronautical engineering

**(P-10934)**
**L & T PRECISION ENGRG INC**
2395 Qume Dr, San Jose (95131-1813)
PHONE..................................408 441-1890
Luc Tran, *Pr*
EMP: 40 EST: 1988
SALES (est): 5.19MM **Privately Held**
Web: www.lt-engineering.com
SIC: 3599 8711 Machine shop, jobbing and repair; Consulting engineer

**(P-10935)**
**L A GAUGE COMPANY INC**
7440 San Fernando Rd, Sun Valley (91352-4398)
PHONE..................................818 767-7193
Harbans Bawa, *Pr*
EMP: 74 EST: 1954
SQ FT: 26,682
SALES (est): 16.89MM **Privately Held**
Web: www.lagauge.com
SIC: 3599 Machine shop, jobbing and repair

**(P-10936)**
**LANDMARK MFG INC**
Also Called: Landmark Motor Cycle ACC
4112 Avenida De La Plata, Oceanside (92056-6099)
PHONE..................................760 941-6626
Tom Allen, *Pr*
Lowell Allen, *VP*
Pat Allen, *Sec*
EMP: 23 EST: 1979
SQ FT: 17,000
SALES (est): 2.56MM **Privately Held**
Web: www.landmarkmfg.com
SIC: 3599 3751 Machine shop, jobbing and repair; Motorcycle accessories

**(P-10937)**
**LANGE PRECISION INC**
1106 E Elm Ave, Fullerton (92831-5024)
PHONE..................................714 870-5420
Gregory R Lange, *Pr*
Lisa Lange, *CFO*
EMP: 18 EST: 1967
SQ FT: 35,000
SALES (est): 2.9MM **Privately Held**
Web: www.langeprecision.biz
SIC: 3599 Machine shop, jobbing and repair

**(P-10938)**
**LANGILLS GENERAL MACHINE INC**
7850 14th Ave, Sacramento (95826-4302)
PHONE..................................916 452-0167
James Langill Senior, *Pr*
EMP: 35 EST: 1969
SQ FT: 10,000
SALES (est): 4.62MM **Privately Held**
Web: www.langills.com
SIC: 3599 Machine shop, jobbing and repair

**(P-10939)**
**LANSAIR CORPORATION**
25228 Anza Dr, Santa Clarita (91355-3496)
PHONE..................................661 294-9503
John Voshell, *Pr*
Eleanor Voshell, *VP*
EMP: 15 EST: 1966
SQ FT: 15,000
SALES (est): 1.45MM **Privately Held**
Web: www.lansaircorp.com
SIC: 3599 Machine shop, jobbing and repair

**(P-10940)**
**LARKIN PRECISION MACHINING INC**
Also Called: Precision Cnc Mil & Turning
175 El Pueblo Rd Ste 10, Scotts Valley (95066-4260)
PHONE..................................831 438-2700
EMP: 35
Web: www.lpmachining.com
SIC: 3599 Amusement park equipment

**(P-10941)**
**LASER INDUSTRIES INC**
1351 Manhattan Ave, Fullerton (92831-5216)
PHONE..................................714 532-3271
Robert Karim, *Pr*
John Krickl, *
Joseph Butterly, *
Gary Nadau, *
EMP: 65 EST: 1986
SQ FT: 17,500
SALES (est): 9.25MM **Privately Held**
Web: www.laserindustries.com
SIC: 3599 Machine shop, jobbing and repair

**(P-10942)**
**LASEROD TECHNOLOGIES LLC**
20312 Gramercy Pl, Torrance (90501-1511)
PHONE..................................310 328-5869
Charles T Moffitt, *Managing Member*
David V Adams Junior, *Managing Member*
▼ EMP: 20 EST: 2011
SQ FT: 8,000
SALES (est): 1.9MM **Privately Held**
Web: www.laserod.com
SIC: 3599 Machine shop, jobbing and repair

**(P-10943)**
**LENZ PRECISION TECHNOLOGY INC**
Also Called: Lenz Technology
355 Pioneer Way Ste A, Mountain View (94041-1542)
PHONE..................................650 966-1784
Eric Lenz, *Pr*
Valerie Lenz, *Sec*
EMP: 23 EST: 1972
SQ FT: 18,000
SALES (est): 3.02MM **Privately Held**
Web: www.lenztech.com
SIC: 3599 Machine shop, jobbing and repair

**(P-10944)**
**LIBERTY INDUSTRIES**
10754 Lower Azusa Rd, El Monte (91731-1391)
PHONE..................................626 575-3206
William Carter, *Pr*
EMP: 15 EST: 1966
SQ FT: 9,000
SALES (est): 1.89MM **Privately Held**

## 3599 - Industrial Machinery, Nec (P-10945)

Web: www.liberty-ind.com
SIC: 3599 Machine shop, jobbing and repair

**(P-10945)**
**LOCK-N-STITCH INC**
1015 S Soderquist Rd, Turlock (95380-5726)
PHONE.................................209 632-2345
Gary J Reed, CEO
Louise Reed, *
Brandi Rollins, *
▲ EMP: 42 EST: 1990
SQ FT: 33,000
SALES (est): 8.86MM
SALES (corp-wide): 6.54B Privately Held
Web: www.locknstitch.com
SIC: 3599 Machine shop, jobbing and repair
PA: Wartsila Oyj Abp
Hiililaiturinkuja 2
107090000

**(P-10946)**
**LONG MACHINE INC**
27450 Colt Ct, Temecula (92590-3673)
PHONE.................................951 296-0194
Larry Long, Pr
Vicki Long, VP
EMP: 21 EST: 1979
SQ FT: 15,000
SALES (est): 2.66MM Privately Held
Web: www.longmachine.com
SIC: 3599 Machine shop, jobbing and repair

**(P-10947)**
**LURAN INC**
24927 Avenue Tibbitts Ste K, Valencia (91355-1268)
PHONE.................................661 257-6303
Terry Decker Junior, Pr
Terry Decker, *
EMP: 18 EST: 1970
SQ FT: 20,000
SALES (est): 1.03MM Privately Held
Web: www.luraninc.com
SIC: 3599 Machine shop, jobbing and repair

**(P-10948)**
**LUSK QUALITY MACHINE PRODUCTS**
39457 15th St E, Palmdale (93550-3445)
P.O. Box 901030 (93590-1030)
PHONE.................................661 272-0630
Randall J Lusk, CEO
Lloyd Lusk, *
EMP: 27 EST: 1971
SQ FT: 25,000
SALES (est): 4.77MM Privately Held
Web: www.luskquality.com
SIC: 3599 3451 Machine shop, jobbing and repair; Screw machine products

**(P-10949)**
**M & L PRECISION MACHINING INC (PA)**
18665 Madrone Pkwy, Morgan Hill (95037-2868)
PHONE.................................408 436-3955
Mark Laisure, Pr
Karen Laisure, VP
Ross Laisure, VP
Harold Laisure, VP
▲ EMP: 20 EST: 1971
SQ FT: 10,000
SALES (est): 5.75MM
SALES (corp-wide): 5.75MM Privately Held
Web: www.mlprecision.com
SIC: 3599 3451 3444 Machine shop, jobbing and repair; Screw machine products; Sheet metalwork

**(P-10950)**
**M & W ENGINEERING INC**
3880 Dividend Dr Ste 100, Shingle Springs (95682-7229)
PHONE.................................530 676-7185
Frank E Marsh, Pr
Kim Waters, VP
EMP: 20 EST: 1979
SQ FT: 10,800
SALES (est): 4.88MM Privately Held
SIC: 3599 Machine shop, jobbing and repair

**(P-10951)**
**M-INDUSTRIAL ENTERPRISES LLC**
Also Called: Project Management
11 Via Onagro, Rcho Sta Marg (92688-4126)
PHONE.................................949 413-7513
Zahid Nazarzai, Owner
EMP: 25 EST: 2001
SALES (est): 1.17MM Privately Held
SIC: 3599 Industrial machinery, nec

**(P-10952)**
**MACHINE CRAFT OF SAN DIEGO**
7204 Babilonia St, Carlsbad (92009-6510)
PHONE.................................858 642-0509
Chinta M Sawh, Pr
Deo Sawh, *
Indra Starr, *
EMP: 19 EST: 1981
SALES (est): 440.46K Privately Held
SIC: 3599 3812 Machine shop, jobbing and repair; Search and navigation equipment

**(P-10953)**
**MACHINE PRECISION COMPONENTS**
14014 Dinard Ave, Santa Fe Springs (90670-4923)
PHONE.................................562 404-0500
Mauro Michel, CEO
EMP: 18 EST: 2004
SALES (est): 1.97MM Privately Held
Web: www.mpcmachining.com
SIC: 3599 Machine shop, jobbing and repair

**(P-10954)**
**MADSEN PRODUCTS INCORPORATED**
Also Called: Huntington Beach Machining
15321 Connector Ln, Huntington Beach (92649-1119)
PHONE.................................714 894-1816
Robert Madsen, Pr
Erik Madsen, VP
Linda Adkison, VP
EMP: 16 EST: 1975
SQ FT: 11,345
SALES (est): 3.83MM Privately Held
Web: www.madsenproductions.com
SIC: 3599 5961 Machine shop, jobbing and repair; Mail order house, nec

**(P-10955)**
**MAGNA TOOL INC**
5594 Market Pl, Cypress (90630-4710)
PHONE.................................714 826-2500
Bob Melton, Pr
Cindy Melton, CFO
EMP: 20 EST: 1977
SQ FT: 8,500
SALES (est): 4.47MM Privately Held
Web: www.magnatoolinc.com
SIC: 3599 Machine shop, jobbing and repair

**(P-10956)**
**MALMBERG ENGINEERING INC**
655 Deep Valley Dr Ste 125, Rllng Hls Est (90274-3688)
PHONE.................................925 606-6500
▼ EMP: 40
Web: www.malmbergeng.com
SIC: 3599 Custom machinery

**(P-10957)**
**MAR ENGINEERING COMPANY**
7350 Greenbush Ave, North Hollywood (91605-4003)
PHONE.................................818 765-4805
Monte Markowitz, CEO
Samuel Markowitz, *
Barbara Markowitz, *
EMP: 29 EST: 1957
SQ FT: 12,000
SALES (est): 3.04MM Privately Held
Web: www.marengineering.com
SIC: 3599 Machine shop, jobbing and repair

**(P-10958)**
**MARONEY COMPANY**
9016 Winnetka Ave, Northridge (91324-3235)
PHONE.................................818 882-2722
John C Maroney Senior, Pr
Francine L Maroney, Sr VP
EMP: 17 EST: 1955
SQ FT: 12,500
SALES (est): 2.37MM Privately Held
Web: www.maroneycompany.com
SIC: 3599 Machine shop, jobbing and repair

**(P-10959)**
**MARS ENGINEERING COMPANY INC (PA)**
Also Called: Vin-Max
699 Montague St, San Leandro (94577-4323)
PHONE.................................510 483-0541
Manny Ambrosio, Pr
Christy Ambrosio, Sec
EMP: 24 EST: 1964
SQ FT: 15,000
SALES (est): 9.14MM
SALES (corp-wide): 9.14MM Privately Held
Web: www.marseng.com
SIC: 3599 Machine shop, jobbing and repair

**(P-10960)**
**MARTINEZ AND TUREK INC**
Also Called: Martinez & Turek
300 S Cedar Ave, Rialto (92376-9100)
PHONE.................................909 820-6800
Larry Tribe, Pr
Donald A Turek, *
Thomas J Martinez, Testing Vice President*
Laurence Martinez, *
John Romero, *
EMP: 120 EST: 1980
SQ FT: 139,000
SALES (est): 19.67MM Privately Held
Web: www.mandtinc.com
SIC: 3599 Machine shop, jobbing and repair

**(P-10961)**
**MASTER PRECISION MACHINING**
2199 Ronald St, Santa Clara (95050-2883)
PHONE.................................408 727-0185
Richard Rossi, Pr
William Regnani, *
Robert Paolinetti, *
EMP: 30 EST: 1969
SQ FT: 10,000
SALES (est): 2.53MM Privately Held
Web: www.master-precision.com
SIC: 3599 Machine shop, jobbing and repair

**(P-10962)**
**MATHY MACHINE INC**
9315 Wheatlands Rd, Santee (92071-2860)
PHONE.................................619 448-0404
Jay Mathy, Pr
EMP: 30 EST: 1979
SQ FT: 14,000
SALES (est): 4.43MM Privately Held
Web: www.mathymachine.com
SIC: 3599 Machine shop, jobbing and repair

**(P-10963)**
**MAUL MFG INC (PA)**
3041 S Shannon St, Santa Ana (92704-6320)
PHONE.................................714 641-0727
Tony Johnson, Pr
Lori Deorio, *
EMP: 20 EST: 1975
SQ FT: 10,080
SALES (est): 3.76MM
SALES (corp-wide): 3.76MM Privately Held
Web: www.ysc-mmi.com
SIC: 3599 3491 3492 Machine shop, jobbing and repair; Solenoid valves; Control valves, aircraft: hydraulic and pneumatic

**(P-10964)**
**MAX PROCESS EQP GLOBL LLC** ✪
Also Called: Max Process Equipment
1420 Healdsburg Ave, Healdsburg (95448-3207)
PHONE.................................707 433-7281
Ilya Kravtchouk, Managing Member
EMP: 30 EST: 2024
SALES (est): 1.23MM Privately Held
SIC: 3599 Custom machinery

**(P-10965)**
**MCCAIN & MCCAIN INC**
Also Called: B&G Machine Shop
3801 Gilmore Ave, Bakersfield (93308-6211)
PHONE.................................661 322-7764
Jim Mccain, Pr
Gary Mccain, Sec
EMP: 15 EST: 1951
SQ FT: 10,000
SALES (est): 2.93MM Privately Held
Web: www.bgmach.com
SIC: 3599 Machine shop, jobbing and repair

**(P-10966)**
**MCCOPPIN ENTERPRISES**
Also Called: Accurate Manufacturing Company
6641 San Fernando Rd, Glendale (91201-1702)
PHONE.................................818 240-4840
Richard J Mc Coppin, Pr
Robert R Gagliardi, VP
John Gagliardi, VP
Carol Park, Stockholder
EMP: 22 EST: 1945
SQ FT: 25,000
SALES (est): 2.29MM Privately Held
Web: www.accuratemfgco.com
SIC: 3599 3544 3441 Machine shop, jobbing and repair; Dies and die holders for metal cutting, forming, die casting; Fabricated structural metal

# PRODUCTS & SERVICES SECTION
## 3599 - Industrial Machinery, Nec (P-10989)

**(P-10967)**
**MCGUIRE GRINDING INC**
2754 Concrete Ct, Paso Robles (93446-5936)
PHONE..................................805 238-9000
Scott Mcguire, *CEO*
Rachel Mcguire, *Prin*
**EMP:** 16 **EST:** 2006
**SALES (est):** 429.92K **Privately Held**
**SIC: 3599** Machine shop, jobbing and repair

**(P-10968)**
**MD ENGINEERING INC**
1550 Consumer Cir, Corona (92878-3225)
PHONE..................................951 736-5390
Mike Morgan, *Pr*
Ryan Cortes, *
Kurt Bryan Qco, *Prin*
**EMP:** 37 **EST:** 1999
**SQ FT:** 16,000
**SALES (est):** 5.61MM **Privately Held**
**Web:** www.mdengineeringonline.com
**SIC: 3599** Machine shop, jobbing and repair

**(P-10969)**
**MECPRO INC**
980 George St, Santa Clara (95054-2705)
PHONE..................................408 727-9757
Son Ho, *Pr*
Kelly Ho, *
Colin Wintrup, *
**EMP:** 23 **EST:** 1979
**SQ FT:** 15,000
**SALES (est):** 4.43MM **Privately Held**
**Web:** www.mecproinc.com
**SIC: 3599** Machine shop, jobbing and repair

**(P-10970)**
**MEDLIN AND SON ENGRG SVC INC**
Also Called: Medlin & Sons
12484 Whittier Blvd, Whittier (90602-1017)
PHONE..................................562 464-5889
George W Medlin Ii, *CEO*
Susan Medlin, *
**EMP:** 45 **EST:** 1959
**SQ FT:** 26,000
**SALES (est):** 4.76MM **Privately Held**
**Web:** www.medlinandson.com
**SIC: 3599** Machine shop, jobbing and repair

**(P-10971)**
**MENCHES TOOL & DIE INC**
30995 San Benito St, Hayward (94544-7936)
PHONE..................................510 476-1160
John Menches Junior, *CEO*
Rosa Menches, *Sec*
**EMP:** 20 **EST:** 1965
**SQ FT:** 22,400
**SALES (est):** 2.23MM **Privately Held**
**Web:** www.menches.com
**SIC: 3599** Machine shop, jobbing and repair

**(P-10972)**
**MERRY AN CEJKA**
Also Called: Scott Craft Co
4601 Cecilia St, Cudahy (90201-5813)
P.O. Box 430 (90201-0430)
PHONE..................................323 560-3949
Merry An Cejka, *Owner*
Amelia Leal-lee, *Prin*
Robert Cejka, *Prin*
Veronica Zazueta, *Prin*
**EMP:** 25 **EST:** 1966
**SQ FT:** 12,000
**SALES (est):** 3.54MM **Privately Held**
**Web:** www.scottcraftco.com

**SIC: 3599** 3544 Custom machinery; Special dies, tools, jigs, and fixtures

**(P-10973)**
**METAL CUTTING SERVICE**
16233 Gale Ave, City Of Industry (91745-1719)
PHONE..................................626 968-4764
David Viel, *Pr*
Milon Viel, *CEO*
Earl Viel, *Sec*
**EMP:** 18 **EST:** 1956
**SQ FT:** 32,000
**SALES (est):** 2.47MM **Privately Held**
**Web:** www.metalcut.com
**SIC: 3599** Machine shop, jobbing and repair

**(P-10974)**
**METALORE INC**
750 S Douglas St, El Segundo (90245-4901)
PHONE..................................310 643-0360
Kenneth Hill, *Pr*
▲ **EMP:** 30 **EST:** 1961
**SALES (est):** 2.39MM **Privately Held**
**Web:** www.metalore.com
**SIC: 3599** Machine shop, jobbing and repair

**(P-10975)**
**METRIC MACHINING (PA)**
Also Called: Master Machine Products
3263 Trade Center Dr, Riverside (92507-3432)
PHONE..................................909 947-9222
Drake Archer, *Pr*
Maggie Lopez, *
▲ **EMP:** 50 **EST:** 1973
**SQ FT:** 45,000
**SALES (est):** 41.2MM
**SALES (corp-wide):** 41.2MM **Privately Held**
**Web:** www.metricorp.com
**SIC: 3599** Machine shop, jobbing and repair

**(P-10976)**
**MEZIERE ENTERPRISES INC**
220 S Hale Ave Ste A, Escondido (92029-1719)
PHONE..................................800 208-1755
Michael Meziere, *Pr*
Don Meziere, *
Dave Meziere, *
▲ **EMP:** 30 **EST:** 1980
**SQ FT:** 15,000
**SALES (est):** 4.15MM **Privately Held**
**Web:** www.meziere.com
**SIC: 3599** Machine shop, jobbing and repair

**(P-10977)**
**MICRON MACHINE COMPANY**
3337 Highway 67, Ramona (92065-7119)
PHONE..................................858 486-5900
Mark Conley, *CEO*
Donna Conley, *VP*
**EMP:** 22 **EST:** 1977
**SALES (est):** 2.53MM **Privately Held**
**Web:** www.micronmachine.com
**SIC: 3599** 8731 3462 3369 Machine shop, jobbing and repair; Commercial physical research; Iron and steel forgings; Nonferrous foundries, nec

**(P-10978)**
**MIKE DYELL MACHINE SHOP INC (PA)**
160 S Linden Ave, Rialto (92376-6204)
P.O. Box 974 (92377-0974)
PHONE..................................909 350-4101
Edith Dyell, *CEO*
Tom Bradley, *Pr*

**EMP:** 17 **EST:** 1968
**SQ FT:** 20,000
**SALES (est):** 3.87MM
**SALES (corp-wide):** 3.87MM **Privately Held**
**Web:** www.dyellmachine.com
**SIC: 3599** 5084 7699 Machine shop, jobbing and repair; Hydraulic systems equipment and supplies; Hydraulic equipment repair

**(P-10979)**
**MIKE KENNEY TOOL INC**
Also Called: Mkt Innovations
588 Porter Way, Placentia (92870-6453)
PHONE..................................714 577-9262
Mike Kenney, *Pr*
Julie Kenney, *
▲ **EMP:** 37 **EST:** 1980
**SALES (est):** 2.2MM **Privately Held**
**Web:** www.mkti.com
**SIC: 3599** Machine shop, jobbing and repair

**(P-10980)**
**MIKELSON MACHINE SHOP INC**
2546 Merced Ave, South El Monte (91733-1924)
PHONE..................................626 448-3920
James Michaelson, *Pr*
James M Mikelson, *
▼ **EMP:** 23 **EST:** 1967
**SQ FT:** 14,000
**SALES (est):** 4.32MM **Privately Held**
**Web:** www.mikelson.net
**SIC: 3599** Machine shop, jobbing and repair

**(P-10981)**
**MILCO WIRE EDM INC**
Also Called: Milco Waterjet
15221 Connector Ln, Huntington Beach (92649-1117)
PHONE..................................714 373-0098
Steven R Miller, *Pr*
**EMP:** 17 **EST:** 1990
**SQ FT:** 14,000
**SALES (est):** 3.34MM **Privately Held**
**Web:** www.milcowireedm.com
**SIC: 3599** 3541 Electrical discharge machining (EDM); Machine tools, metal cutting type

**(P-10982)**
**MILLER CASTINGS INC**
12245 Coast Dr, Whittier (90601-1608)
PHONE..................................562 695-0461
**EMP:** 42
**SALES (corp-wide):** 49.35MM **Privately Held**
**Web:** www.millercastings.com
**SIC: 3599** Machine shop, jobbing and repair
**PA:** Miller Castings, Inc.
2503 Pacific Pk Dr
562 695-0461

**(P-10983)**
**MILLER MACHINE WORKS LLC**
Also Called: Miller Cnc
789 Anita St, Chula Vista (91911-3901)
PHONE..................................619 501-9866
Todd Cuffaro, *CEO*
**EMP:** 17 **EST:** 2007
**SQ FT:** 7,500
**SALES (est):** 3.75MM **Privately Held**
**Web:** www.millercnc.com
**SIC: 3599** Machine shop, jobbing and repair

**(P-10984)**
**MILLIPART INC (PA)**
412 W Carter Dr, Glendora (91740-5998)
PHONE..................................626 963-4101
Scot Jamison, *Pr*

**EMP:** 18 **EST:** 1954
**SQ FT:** 4,000
**SALES (est):** 6.38MM
**SALES (corp-wide):** 6.38MM **Privately Held**
**Web:** www.millipart.com
**SIC: 3599** Machine shop, jobbing and repair

**(P-10985)**
**MILLWORX PRCSION MACHINING INC**
Also Called: Millworx
506 Malloy Ct, Corona (92878-4045)
PHONE..................................951 371-2683
Stacy Wilson, *Pr*
Terry Windust, *VP*
Vince M, *Dir*
**EMP:** 22 **EST:** 2003
**SQ FT:** 3,500
**SALES (est):** 6.86MM **Privately Held**
**Web:** www.millworxprecision.com
**SIC: 3599** Machine shop, jobbing and repair

**(P-10986)**
**MISSION TOOL AND MFG CO INC**
3440 Arden Rd, Hayward (94545-3906)
PHONE..................................510 782-8383
Gary W Smith, *Pr*
Carol Smith, *
Robert Diaz, *Dir*
▲ **EMP:** 40 **EST:** 1968
**SQ FT:** 28,000
**SALES (est):** 8MM **Privately Held**
**Web:** www.missiontool.com
**SIC: 3599** 3465 3469 3544 Machine and other job shop work; Automotive stampings; Metal stampings, nec; Special dies, tools, jigs, and fixtures

**(P-10987)**
**MITCO INDUSTRIES INC (PA)**
2235 S Vista Ave, Bloomington (92316-2921)
PHONE..................................909 877-0800
Larry Mitchell, *Pr*
Sammy Mitchell, *
**EMP:** 26 **EST:** 1972
**SQ FT:** 11,000
**SALES (est):** 4.89MM
**SALES (corp-wide):** 4.89MM **Privately Held**
**Web:** vdi.mitcoind.servve.com
**SIC: 3599** 3533 Machine shop, jobbing and repair; Drilling tools for gas, oil, or water wells

**(P-10988)**
**MKT INNOVATIONS**
Also Called: Cooljet Systems
588 Porter Way, Placentia (92870-6453)
PHONE..................................714 524-7668
Mike Kenney, *CEO*
Kathy Jackson, *
▲ **EMP:** 68 **EST:** 2002
**SALES (est):** 4.95MM **Privately Held**
**Web:** www.mkti.com
**SIC: 3599** 3523 Machine shop, jobbing and repair; Farm machinery and equipment

**(P-10989)**
**MODERN ENGINE INC**
701 Sonora Ave, Glendale (91201-2431)
PHONE..................................818 409-9494
Vachagan Aslanian, *Pr*
Razmik Aslanian, *
Armond Aslanian, *
Nora Aslanian, *
▲ **EMP:** 43 **EST:** 1979
**SQ FT:** 26,000
**SALES (est):** 4.78MM **Privately Held**

# 3599 - Industrial Machinery, Nec (P-10990)

**PRODUCTS & SERVICES SECTION**

Web: www.meparts.com
SIC: **3599** 7539  Machine shop, jobbing and repair; Machine shop, automotive

### (P-10990)
### MOLNAR ENGINEERING INC
Also Called: Lee's Enterprise
20731 Marilla St, Chatsworth  (91311-4408)
PHONE.................................818 993-3495
Laszlo Molnar, *CEO*
Linda D Molnar, *
Tom Molnar, *
Michael Molnar, *
▲ **EMP:** 37 **EST:** 1975
**SQ FT:** 12,000
**SALES (est):** 6.2MM **Privately Held**
Web: www.leesenterprise.com
SIC: **3599**  Machine shop, jobbing and repair

### (P-10991)
### MOMENI ENGINEERING LLC
Also Called: Essex Industries
5451 Argosy Ave, Huntington Beach  (92649-1038)
PHONE.................................714 897-9301
Ahmad Momeni, *Managing Member*
**EMP:** 28 **EST:** 1982
**SALES (est):** 3.72MM **Privately Held**
Web: www.essexindustries.com
SIC: **3599** 3841  Machine shop, jobbing and repair; Surgical and medical instruments

### (P-10992)
### MONARCH PRCSION DEBURRING INC
1514 E Edinger Ave Ste C, Santa Ana  (92705-4918)
PHONE.................................714 258-0342
Russell F Little, *CEO*
Russ Little, *Pr*
**EMP:** 15 **EST:** 1968
**SQ FT:** 6,100
**SALES (est):** 652.04K **Privately Held**
Web: www.monarchprecisiondeburring.com
SIC: **3599**  Machine shop, jobbing and repair

### (P-10993)
### MONO ENGINEERING CORP
20977 Knapp St, Chatsworth  (91311-5926)
PHONE.................................818 772-4998
Siamak Morini, *CEO*
**EMP:** 50 **EST:** 1994
**SQ FT:** 40,000
**SALES (est):** 5.3MM **Privately Held**
Web: www.monoengineering.com
SIC: **3599** 3444 8711  Machine shop, jobbing and repair; Sheet metalwork; Industrial engineers

### (P-10994)
### MOONEY INDS PRCSION MCHNING IN
8744 Remmet Ave, Canoga Park  (91304-1588)
PHONE.................................818 998-0199
Alan Mooney, *CFO*
Joyce Mooney, *VP*
Brian Mooney, *Pr*
**EMP:** 15 **EST:** 1962
**SQ FT:** 9,000
**SALES (est):** 3.23MM **Privately Held**
SIC: **3599**  Machine shop, jobbing and repair

### (P-10995)
### MOSEYS PRODUCTION MACHINISTS INC (PA)
1550 Lakeview Loop, Anaheim  (92807-1819)
PHONE.................................714 693-4840
**EMP:** 42 **EST:** 1975
**SALES (est):** 5.92MM
**SALES (corp-wide):** 5.92MM **Privately Held**
Web: www.moseys.com
SIC: **3599**  Machine shop, jobbing and repair

### (P-10996)
### MOSS PRECISION INC
Also Called: Moss Prcsion McHning Shetmetal
3200 Arden Rd, Hayward  (94545-3902)
PHONE.................................510 785-2235
**EMP:** 85 **EST:** 1968
**SALES (est):** 21.28MM **Privately Held**
Web: www.mossprecision.com
SIC: **3599** 3444  Machine shop, jobbing and repair; Sheet metalwork

### (P-10997)
### MOTIV DESIGN GROUP INC
430 Perrymont Ave, San Jose  (95125-1444)
PHONE.................................408 441-0611
Lino R Covarrubias, *CEO*
Carlos Barrientos, *VP*
**EMP:** 16 **EST:** 2006
**SQ FT:** 2,400
**SALES (est):** 2.89MM **Privately Held**
Web: www.motiv-dgi.com
SIC: **3599**  Custom machinery

### (P-10998)
### MOTORVAC TECHNOLOGIES INC
1431 Village Way, Santa Ana  (92705-4714)
PHONE.................................714 558-4822
Mark J Hallsman, *Pr*
John A Rome, *VP*
Gerry Quinn Bdmem, *Prin*
Ron Monark, *Ch Bd*
Stephen Greaves Bdmem, *Prin*
**EMP:** 30 **EST:** 1992
**SQ FT:** 24,360
**SALES (est):** 3.09MM **Privately Held**
Web: www.cpsproducts.com
SIC: **3599** 2899 2842 5013  Gasoline filters, internal combustion engine, except auto; Fuel tank or engine cleaning chemicals; Polishes and sanitation goods; Automotive servicing equipment
PA: Erin Mills International Investment Corp.
C/O Dr. Trevor Carmichael

### (P-10999)
### MS-TECH CORPORATION
1911 Sampson Ave, Corona  (92879-6006)
PHONE.................................562 404-9727
Charlie Kong, *Pr*
Susan Han, *Treas*
**EMP:** 20 **EST:** 1990
**SALES (est):** 1.06MM **Privately Held**
Web: www.ms-tech.com
SIC: **3599**  Machine shop, jobbing and repair

### (P-11000)
### MUTH MACHINE WORKS (HQ)
8042 Katella Ave, Stanton  (90680-3207)
PHONE.................................714 527-2239
Richard Muth, *Pr*
Lynn Muth, *VP*
Dwayne Gleason, *VP Opers*
Peter G Muth, *Treas*
▲ **EMP:** 20 **EST:** 1993
**SQ FT:** 2,000
**SALES (est):** 6.21MM
**SALES (corp-wide):** 23.6MM **Privately Held**
SIC: **3599**  Machine shop, jobbing and repair
PA: Orco Block & Hardscape
11100 Beach Blvd
714 527-2239

### (P-11001)
### MY MACHINE INC
5140 Commerce Dr, Baldwin Park  (91706-1450)
PHONE.................................626 214-9223
Jamie Scott Young, *CEO*
Pedro Ignico Martinez, *VP*
**EMP:** 15 **EST:** 2008
**SALES (est):** 2.21MM **Privately Held**
Web: www.mymachineinc.com
SIC: **3599**  Machine shop, jobbing and repair

### (P-11002)
### NANEZ MFG INC (PA)
164 Commercial St, Sunnyvale  (94086-5201)
PHONE.................................408 830-9903
Francisco Nanez, *Pr*
**EMP:** 19 **EST:** 2012
**SQ FT:** 500
**SALES (est):** 4.82MM
**SALES (corp-wide):** 4.82MM **Privately Held**
Web: www.nanezmfg.com
SIC: **3599**  Machine shop, jobbing and repair

### (P-11003)
### NC DYNAMICS INCORPORATED
Also Called: Ncdi
6925 Downey Ave, Long Beach  (90805-1823)
PHONE.................................562 634-7392
Kevin Minter, *CEO*
Randall L Bazz, *
▲ **EMP:** 151 **EST:** 1979
**SALES (est):** 10.1MM
**SALES (corp-wide):** 92.77MM **Privately Held**
Web: www.ncdynamics.com
SIC: **3599**  Machine shop, jobbing and repair
PA: Harlow Aerostructures Llc
1501 S Mclean Blvd
316 265-5268

### (P-11004)
### NC DYNAMICS LLC
Also Called: NC Dynamics
3401 E 69th St, Long Beach  (90805-1872)
PHONE.................................562 634-7392
Phillip Friedman, *Managing Member*
**EMP:** 150 **EST:** 2017
**SALES (est):** 9.1MM
**SALES (corp-wide):** 92.77MM **Privately Held**
Web: www.ncdynamics.com
SIC: **3599**  Machine shop, jobbing and repair
PA: Harlow Aerostructures Llc
1501 S Mclean Blvd
316 265-5268

### (P-11005)
### NELGO INDUSTRIES INC
Also Called: Nelgo Manufacturing
598 Airport Rd, Oceanside  (92058-1207)
PHONE.................................760 433-6434
Peter Edward Goethel, *CEO*
**EMP:** 32 **EST:** 1966
**SALES (est):** 4.93MM **Privately Held**
Web: www.nelgo.com
SIC: **3599**  Machine shop, jobbing and repair

### (P-11006)
### NEXT INTENT INC
Also Called: Next Intent
865 Via Esteban, San Luis Obispo  (93401-7178)
PHONE.................................805 781-6755
Rodney Babcock, *CEO*
Catherine B Babcock, *
**EMP:** 30 **EST:** 1996
**SQ FT:** 8,500
**SALES (est):** 4.67MM **Privately Held**
Web: www.nextintent.com
SIC: **3599**  Machine shop, jobbing and repair

### (P-11007)
### NGK NORTH AMERICA INC
7100 National Dr, Livermore  (94550-8815)
PHONE.................................925 292-5372
**EMP:** 17
Web: www.fmindustries.com
SIC: **3599**  Machine shop, jobbing and repair
HQ: Ngk North America, Inc.
1105 N Market St Ste 1300
Wilmington DE 19801
302 654-1344

### (P-11008)
### NIEDWICK CORPORATION
Also Called: Niedwick Machine Co
967 N Eckhoff St, Orange  (92867-5432)
P.O. Box 63851 (92602-6132)
PHONE.................................714 771-9999
Theodore R Niedwick, *Pr*
**EMP:** 45 **EST:** 1992
**SQ FT:** 8,200
**SALES (est):** 5.2MM **Privately Held**
Web: www.niedwickmachine.com
SIC: **3599**  Machine shop, jobbing and repair

### (P-11009)
### NJ MC CUTCHEN INC
Also Called: N J M
123 W Sonora St, Stockton  (95203-3415)
PHONE.................................209 466-9704
**EMP:** 25 **EST:** 1976
**SALES (est):** 5.38MM **Privately Held**
Web: www.njminc.com
SIC: **3599**  Machine and other job shop work

### (P-11010)
### NM MACHINING INC
175 Lewis Rd Ste 25, San Jose  (95111-2175)
PHONE.................................408 972-8978
Mike Tran, *Pr*
**EMP:** 22 **EST:** 1995
**SQ FT:** 8,272
**SALES (est):** 1.53MM **Privately Held**
Web: www.nmmachining.com
SIC: **3599**  Machine shop, jobbing and repair

### (P-11011)
### NOROTOS INC
201 E Alton Ave, Santa Ana  (92707-4416)
PHONE.................................714 662-3113
Ronald Soto, *Pr*
John Soto, *
▲ **EMP:** 116 **EST:** 1985
**SQ FT:** 12,000
**SALES (est):** 9.98MM **Privately Held**
Web: www.norotos.com
SIC: **3599** 3842  Machine shop, jobbing and repair; Surgical appliances and supplies

### (P-11012)
### NTL PRECISION MACHINING INC
1355 Vander Way, San Jose  (95112-2809)
PHONE.................................408 298-6650
Henry Ngo, *CEO*
Hai Ngo, *VP*
Thao Ngo, *Sec*
**EMP:** 15 **EST:** 1996
**SQ FT:** 7,500
**SALES (est):** 2.32MM **Privately Held**

▲ = Import  ▼ = Export
◆ = Import/Export

# PRODUCTS & SERVICES SECTION

## 3599 - Industrial Machinery, Nec (P-11035)

Web: www.ntlprecision.com
SIC: 3599 Machine shop, jobbing and repair

**(P-11013)**
**NUSPACE INC (HQ)**
4401 E Donald Douglas Dr, Long Beach (90808-1732)
PHONE..................................562 497-3200
Ian Ballinger, CEO
Lili Zhou, *
◆ EMP: 25 EST: 1907
SQ FT: 60,000
SALES (est): 2.86MM
SALES (corp-wide): 2.86MM Privately Held
Web: www.keyengco.com
SIC: 3599 Air intake filters, internal combustion engine, except auto
PA: Ke Company Acquisition Corp.
4401 E Donald Douglas Dr
562 497-3200

**(P-11014)**
**O & S PRECISION INC**
20630 Nordhoff St, Chatsworth (91311-6114)
PHONE..................................818 718-8876
Scott Onasch, CEO
EMP: 20 EST: 1996
SQ FT: 5,000
SALES (est): 4.17MM Privately Held
Web: www.oands.com
SIC: 3599 Machine shop, jobbing and repair

**(P-11015)**
**OEM LLC**
311 S Highland Ave, Fullerton (92832-2398)
PHONE..................................714 449-7500
John B Copp, CEO
▲ EMP: 23 EST: 1985
SQ FT: 40,000
SALES (est): 2.08MM Privately Held
Web: www.oempresssystems.com
SIC: 3599 Machine shop, jobbing and repair

**(P-11016)**
**OMEGA PRECISION**
13040 Telegraph Rd, Santa Fe Springs (90670-4078)
PHONE..................................562 946-2491
Richard Venegas, CEO
Joseph M Venegas, *
Richard M Venegas, *
Steve Venegas, *
EMP: 25 EST: 1965
SQ FT: 16,332
SALES (est): 2.64MM Privately Held
Web: www.omegaprecision.us
SIC: 3599 Machine shop, jobbing and repair

**(P-11017)**
**ORANGE COUNTY SCREW PDTS INC**
2993 E La Palma Ave, Anaheim (92806-2620)
PHONE..................................714 630-7433
Robert Andri, Pr
EMP: 20 EST: 1967
SQ FT: 8,000
SALES (est): 682.51K Privately Held
SIC: 3599 3451 Machine shop, jobbing and repair; Screw machine products

**(P-11018)**
**OT PRECISION MACHINING INC**
1450 Seareel Ln, San Jose (95131-1580)
PHONE..................................408 435-8818
Tam Dang, Pr
EMP: 25 EST: 1995
SQ FT: 2,000
SALES (est): 2.86MM Privately Held
Web: www.otprecision.com
SIC: 3599 Machine shop, jobbing and repair

**(P-11019)**
**OWENS DESIGN INCORPORATED (PA)**
47427 Fremont Blvd, Fremont (94538-6504)
PHONE..................................510 659-1800
John Apgar, Pr
EMP: 35 EST: 1983
SQ FT: 30,000
SALES (est): 9.28MM
SALES (corp-wide): 9.28MM Privately Held
Web: www.owensdesign.com
SIC: 3599 Custom machinery

**(P-11020)**
**P M S D INC (PA)**
Also Called: Danco Machine
3411 Leonard Ct, Santa Clara (95054-2053)
PHONE..................................408 988-5235
Timothy Rohr, CEO
EMP: 92 EST: 1986
SALES (est): 16.94MM
SALES (corp-wide): 16.94MM Privately Held
Web: www.dancomachine.com
SIC: 3599 Machine shop, jobbing and repair

**(P-11021)**
**P M S D INC**
Also Called: K-Fab
3411 Leonard Ct, Santa Clara (95054-2053)
PHONE..................................408 727-5322
EMP: 40
SALES (corp-wide): 16.94MM Privately Held
Web: www.dancomachine.com
SIC: 3599 Machine shop, jobbing and repair
PA: P M S D Inc
3411 Leonard Ct
408 988-5235

**(P-11022)**
**PACIFIC BROACH & ENGRG ASSOC**
1513 N Kraemer Blvd, Anaheim (92806-1407)
PHONE..................................714 632-5678
Steven R Yetzke, Pr
Michael Yetzke, VP
Elaine Montgomery, Sec
▲ EMP: 19 EST: 1943
SQ FT: 18,000
SALES (est): 1.72MM Privately Held
Web: www.bdlind.com
SIC: 3599 Machine shop, jobbing and repair

**(P-11023)**
**PACIFIC MFG INC SAN DIEGO**
1520 Corporate Center Dr, San Diego (92154-6634)
PHONE..................................619 423-0316
Raymundo Montalvo, Pr
Maria A Montalvo, VP
EMP: 20 EST: 1977
SQ FT: 9,500
SALES (est): 936.88K Privately Held
Web: www.pacmfginc.com
SIC: 3599 Machine shop, jobbing and repair

**(P-11024)**
**PACIFIC ROLLER DIE CO INC**
Also Called: Prd Company
1321 W Winton Ave, Hayward (94545-1407)
PHONE..................................510 244-7286
Robert F Miller, CEO
◆ EMP: 16 EST: 1961
SQ FT: 25,000
SALES (est): 4.58MM Privately Held
Web: www.prdcompany.com
SIC: 3599 3547 3542 Machine shop, jobbing and repair; Rolling mill machinery; Machine tools, metal forming type

**(P-11025)**
**PACIFIC SCREW PRODUCTS INC**
Also Called: Rollin J. Lobaugh
1331 Old County Rd Ste C, Belmont (94002-3968)
P.O. Box 98 (94002)
PHONE..................................650 583-9682
Jack Corey, Pr
Gloria Corey, *
EMP: 52 EST: 1922
SQ FT: 24,000
SALES (est): 1.24MM Privately Held
SIC: 3599 Machine shop, jobbing and repair

**(P-11026)**
**PACON MFG INC**
Also Called: Pacon
4777 Bennett Dr Ste H, Livermore (94551-4860)
P.O. Box 400034 (89140-0034)
PHONE..................................925 961-0445
Steven Mcclure, CEO
EMP: 20 EST: 2013
SALES (est): 7.45MM Privately Held
Web: www.paconquality.com
SIC: 3599 Machine shop, jobbing and repair

**(P-11027)**
**PAMCO MACHINE WORKS INC**
9359 Feron Blvd, Rancho Cucamonga (91730-4516)
PHONE..................................909 941-7260
James Fredrick Wilkinson, CEO
Diane Wilkinson, Sec
EMP: 20 EST: 1956
SQ FT: 17,000
SALES (est): 4.45MM Privately Held
Web: www.pamcomachine.com
SIC: 3599 3462 Machine shop, jobbing and repair; Iron and steel forgings

**(P-11028)**
**PARAGON MACHINE WORKS INC**
253 S 25th St, Richmond (94804-2856)
PHONE..................................510 232-3223
Mark Norstad, Owner
EMP: 60 EST: 1983
SQ FT: 55,000
SALES (est): 3.73MM Privately Held
Web: www.paragonmachineworks.com
SIC: 3599 Machine shop, jobbing and repair

**(P-11029)**
**PARAGON SWISS**
545 Aldo Ave Ste 1, Santa Clara (95054-2206)
PHONE..................................408 748-1617
Kevin Beatty, Pr
David R Beatty, *
Joanne Beatty, *
EMP: 30 EST: 1984
SQ FT: 10,200
SALES (est): 3.69MM Privately Held
Web: www.paragonswiss.com
SIC: 3599 3451 Machine shop, jobbing and repair; Screw machine products

**(P-11030)**
**PARAMETRIC MANUFACTURING INC**
3465 Edward Ave, Santa Clara (95054-2131)
PHONE..................................408 654-9845
Jon Drury, Pr
EMP: 16 EST: 2005
SQ FT: 7,500
SALES (est): 3.81MM Privately Held
Web: www.parametric-usa.com
SIC: 3599 Machine shop, jobbing and repair

**(P-11031)**
**PARAMOUNT MACHINE CO INC**
10824 Edison Ct, Rancho Cucamonga (91730-3868)
P.O. Box 8068 (91701-0068)
PHONE..................................909 484-3600
Gregory A Harsen, Pr
Gail Harsen, *
EMP: 36 EST: 1964
SQ FT: 12,000
SALES (est): 5.7MM Privately Held
Web: www.paramountmachine.com
SIC: 3599 Machine shop, jobbing and repair

**(P-11032)**
**PARK ENGINEERING AND MFG CO**
Also Called: Pem
6430 Roland St, Buena Park (90621-3122)
P.O. Box 2275 (90621-0775)
PHONE..................................714 521-4660
Joanna Tenney, CEO
Jeff Tenney, *
EMP: 30 EST: 1959
SQ FT: 6,000
SALES (est): 942.66K Privately Held
Web: www.roguefishmedia.com
SIC: 3599 Machine shop, jobbing and repair

**(P-11033)**
**PAULCO PRECISION INC**
Also Called: Precision Resources
13916 Cordary Ave, Hawthorne (90250-7916)
PHONE..................................310 679-4900
Paul Ruby, Pr
EMP: 16 EST: 1989
SQ FT: 15,000
SALES (est): 2.48MM Privately Held
Web: www.precisionresources.com
SIC: 3599 Machine shop, jobbing and repair

**(P-11034)**
**PAULI SYSTEMS INC**
1820 Walters Ct, Fairfield (94533)
PHONE..................................707 429-2434
Robert Pauli, CEO
EMP: 22 EST: 1996
SQ FT: 13,500
SALES (est): 3.77MM Privately Held
Web: www.paulisystems.com
SIC: 3599 Custom machinery

**(P-11035)**
**PEDAVENA MOULD AND DIE CO INC**
12464 Mccann Dr, Santa Fe Springs (90670-3335)
PHONE..................................310 327-2814
Steve Scardenzan, Pr
Paul Weisbrich, *

## 3599 - Industrial Machinery, Nec (P-11036)

▲ EMP: 28 EST: 1964
SQ FT: 12,000
SALES (est): 4.83MM Privately Held
Web: www.pmdprecision.com
SIC: 3599 Machine and other job shop work

**(P-11036)**
**PEN MANUFACTURING LLC**
Also Called: Pen Manufacturing
1808 N American St, Anaheim (92801-1001)
PHONE.................714 992-0950
TOLL FREE: 800
Robert D Pendarvis, *CEO*
Brian Pendarvis, *
EMP: 25 EST: 1982
SQ FT: 8,000
SALES (est): 1.07MM Privately Held
Web: www.pendarvismanufacturing.com
SIC: 3599 Machine shop, jobbing and repair

**(P-11037)**
**PERFORMANCE MACHINE TECH INC**
25141 Avenue Stanford, Valencia (91355-1227)
PHONE.................661 294-8617
Dennis Moran, *Pr*
Carolyn Moran, *
EMP: 38 EST: 1995
SQ FT: 10,000
SALES (est): 4.98MM Privately Held
Web: www.pmtinc.org
SIC: 3599 Machine shop, jobbing and repair

**(P-11038)**
**PERFORMEX MACHINING INC**
963 Terminal Way, San Carlos (94070-3224)
PHONE.................650 595-2228
Joseph Iffla, *Owner*
EMP: 20 EST: 1977
SQ FT: 5,600
SALES (est): 4.15MM Privately Held
Web: www.performexmachining.com
SIC: 3599 Machine shop, jobbing and repair

**(P-11039)**
**PETERSEN PRECISION ENGRG LLC**
Also Called: Petersen Precision
611 Broadway St, Redwood City (94063-3102)
PHONE.................650 365-4373
Fred Petersen, *CEO*
Fred Petersen, *Managing Member*
Milton Philip Olson, *
EMP: 120 EST: 1999
SQ FT: 55,000
SALES (est): 16.52MM Privately Held
Web: www.petersenprecision.com
SIC: 3599 Machine shop, jobbing and repair

**(P-11040)**
**PIEDRAS MACHINE CORPORATION**
15154 Downey Ave Ste B, Paramount (90723-4595)
PHONE.................562 602-1500
Salvador Piedra, *Pr*
Ruben Piedra, *CFO*
Lucia Piedra, *Sec*
EMP: 19 EST: 2006
SALES (est): 980.16K Privately Held
Web: www.piedrasmachine.com
SIC: 3599 Machine shop, jobbing and repair

**(P-11041)**
**PL MACHINE CORPORATION**
10716 Reagan St, Los Alamitos (90720-2431)
PHONE.................714 892-1100
Andrew Dinh, *Ex Dir*
EMP: 25 EST: 2009
SALES (est): 5.34MM Privately Held
Web: www.plmachinecorp.com
SIC: 3599 Machine shop, jobbing and repair

**(P-11042)**
**PLEASANTON TOOL & MFG INC**
1181 Quarry Ln Ste 450, Pleasanton (94566-8460)
PHONE.................925 426-0500
Chester Thomas, *Pr*
Shirley Thomas, *
Rich Thomas, *
EMP: 25 EST: 1989
SQ FT: 18,000
SALES (est): 3.65MM Privately Held
Web: www.pleasantontool.com
SIC: 3599 Machine shop, jobbing and repair

**(P-11043)**
**PNM COMPANY**
2547 N Business Park Ave, Fresno (93727-8637)
PHONE.................559 291-1986
Dave Counts, *Pt*
Mark Winters, *Pt*
Mario Persicone, *Dir*
Bev Caldwell, *Off Mgr*
▲ EMP: 48 EST: 1987
SQ FT: 5,500
SALES (est): 8.4MM Privately Held
Web: www.pnmcnc.com
SIC: 3599 Machine shop, jobbing and repair

**(P-11044)**
**POLYTEC PRODUCTS CORPORATION**
3390 Valley Square Ln, San Jose (95117-3068)
PHONE.................650 322-7555
John Parissenti, *Pr*
Tony Hertado, *
EMP: 45 EST: 1968
SALES (est): 1.4MM Privately Held
Web: www.polytecproducts.com
SIC: 3599 Machine shop, jobbing and repair

**(P-11045)**
**PRECISION ARCFT MACHINING INC**
Also Called: Pamco
10640 Elkwood St, Sun Valley (91352-4631)
PHONE.................818 768-5900
Donald A Pisano, *Pr*
Joyce Pisano, *
Kimberly Pisano, *
▲ EMP: 50 EST: 1961
SQ FT: 6,500
SALES (est): 6.86MM Privately Held
Web: www.pamco-usa.com
SIC: 3599 3678 Machine shop, jobbing and repair; Electronic connectors

**(P-11046)**
**PRECISION MANUFACTURING**
301 Derek Pl, Roseville (95678-7026)
PHONE.................408 460-2435
Kelly Johnson, *Pr*
EMP: 16 EST: 2015
SALES (est): 1.76MM Privately Held
Web: www.pmccnc.com

SIC: 3599 Machine and other job shop work

**(P-11047)**
**PRECISION WATERJET INC**
Also Called: Precision Machining & Fab
4900 E Hunter Ave, Anaheim (92807-2057)
PHONE.................888 538-9287
Shane Strowski, *Pr*
EMP: 39 EST: 2011
SALES (est): 16.45MM Privately Held
Web: www.h2ojet.com
SIC: 3599 Machine shop, jobbing and repair

**(P-11048)**
**PREFERRED MFG SVCS INC (PA)**
Also Called: Snowline Engineering
4261 Business Dr, Cameron Park (95682-7217)
PHONE.................530 677-2675
Calvin Reynolds, *Pr*
Lee Block, *
EMP: 65 EST: 1998
SQ FT: 34,000
SALES (est): 3.46MM
SALES (corp-wide): 3.46MM Privately Held
Web: www.snowlineengineering.com
SIC: 3599 Machine shop, jobbing and repair

**(P-11049)**
**PRICE PRODUCTS INCORPORATED**
106 State Pl, Escondido (92029-1323)
PHONE.................760 745-5602
John Price, *Pr*
Robert Price, *
Shirley L Price, *
EMP: 34 EST: 1968
SQ FT: 15,000
SALES (est): 4.22MM Privately Held
Web: www.priceproducts.com
SIC: 3599 Machine shop, jobbing and repair

**(P-11050)**
**PROCESS FAB INC**
13153 Lakeland Rd, Santa Fe Springs (90670-4520)
P.O. Box 314 (90670)
PHONE.................562 921-1979
EMP: 180
SIC: 3599 8711 Machine shop, jobbing and repair; Industrial engineers

**(P-11051)**
**PRODUCTION LAPPING COMPANY**
120 E Chestnut Ave Pmb 124, Monrovia (91016-3432)
PHONE.................626 359-0611
Hans J Herzig, *Pr*
Gertrude Herzig, *Sec*
Seon Park, *Genl Mgr*
Evangeline Lozada, *Acctg Mgr*
Melissa Lozada, *Mgr*
EMP: 16 EST: 1968
SQ FT: 9,000
SALES (est): 1.53MM Privately Held
Web: www.productionlapping.com
SIC: 3599 Machine shop, jobbing and repair

**(P-11052)**
**PROMINEX INC**
6181 Cornerstone Ct E Ste 106, San Diego (92121-4727)
PHONE.................858 242-1541
EMP: 17 EST: 1995
SALES (est): 2.1MM Privately Held
Web: www.prominex.com

SIC: 3599 Industrial machinery, nec

**(P-11053)**
**PRONTO PRODUCTS CO**
1801 W Olympic Blvd, Pasadena (91199-0001)
PHONE.................800 377-6680
EMP: 21
SALES (corp-wide): 4.42MM Privately Held
Web: www.prontoproducts.com
SIC: 3599 Machine shop, jobbing and repair
PA: Pronto Products Co.
9850 Siempre Viva Rd
619 661-6995

**(P-11054)**
**PROTOTEK DGTAL MFG SCRMNTO LLC**
Also Called: Sacramento E.D.M., Inc.
11341 Sunrise Park Dr, Rancho Cordova (95742-6532)
PHONE.................916 851-9285
Daniel Folk, *CEO*
EMP: 27 EST: 1983
SQ FT: 20,000
SALES (est): 4.96MM
SALES (corp-wide): 10.02MM Privately Held
Web: www.sacedm.com
SIC: 3599 Machine shop, jobbing and repair
PA: Prototek Holdings Llc
215 Devcon Dr
800 403-9777

**(P-11055)**
**PSCMB REPAIRS INC**
Also Called: Quality Industry Repair
12145 Slauson Ave, Santa Fe Springs (90670-2619)
PHONE.................626 448-7778
Stephany Castellanos, *CEO*
EMP: 40 EST: 2012
SALES (est): 7.32MM Privately Held
Web: www.qir-usa.com
SIC: 3599 Machine shop, jobbing and repair

**(P-11056)**
**PTR MANUFACTURING INC**
Also Called: Ptr Sheet Metal & Fabrication
33390 Transit Ave, Union City (94587-2014)
PHONE.................510 477-9654
Sai La, *Pr*
EMP: 40 EST: 1994
SQ FT: 45,000
SALES (est): 4.88MM Privately Held
Web: www.ptrmanufacturing.com
SIC: 3599 3444 Machine shop, jobbing and repair; Sheet metalwork

**(P-11057)**
**PVA TEPLA AMERICA INC (HQ)**
Also Called: Plasma Division
251 Corporate Terrace St, Corona (92879-6000)
PHONE.................951 371-2500
Bill Marsh, *Pr*
EMP: 20 EST: 1971
SQ FT: 15,000
SALES (est): 8.51MM
SALES (corp-wide): 8.51MM Privately Held
Web: www.pvateplaamerica.com
SIC: 3599 Custom machinery
PA: Pva Holding, Llc
251 Corporate Terrace St
951 270-3949

## PRODUCTS & SERVICES SECTION
### 3599 - Industrial Machinery, Nec (P-11081)

**(P-11058)**
**QUALITASK INC**
2840 E Gretta Ln, Anaheim (92806-2512)
PHONE.............................714 237-0900
Som Suntharaphat, *Pr*
Eduvigis Suntharaphat, *
Deb Beds, *
EMP: 26 EST: 1992
SQ FT: 13,100
SALES (est): 2.44MM **Privately Held**
Web: www.qualitask.com
SIC: 3599 Machine shop, jobbing and repair

**(P-11059)**
**QUALITY CONTROLLED MFG INC**
9429 Abraham Way, Santee (92071-2854)
PHONE.............................619 443-3997
William Grande, *Pr*
James Hiebing, *
Jane Currie, *
EMP: 70 EST: 1978
SQ FT: 25,000
SALES (est): 8.73MM **Privately Held**
Web: www.qualitycontrolledmanufacturinginc.com
SIC: 3599 Machine shop, jobbing and repair

**(P-11060)**
**QUALITY INDUSTRY REPAIR INC**
1815 Potrero Ave, South El Monte (91733-3022)
PHONE.............................626 448-7778
Patricia Castellanos, *Pr*
EMP: 16 EST: 2007
SALES (est): 619.92K **Privately Held**
Web: www.qir-usa.com
SIC: 3599 Machine shop, jobbing and repair

**(P-11061)**
**QUALITY MACHINE ENGRG INC**
2559 Grosse Ave, Santa Rosa (95404-2608)
PHONE.............................707 528-1900
Rudy Hirschnitz, *Pr*
John F Wright, *
Shawn Barnett, *
John Wright, *
EMP: 29 EST: 1991
SQ FT: 13,500
SALES (est): 488.96K **Privately Held**
Web: www.qme1.com
SIC: 3599 Machine shop, jobbing and repair

**(P-11062)**
**R & G PRECISION MACHINING INC**
2585 Jason Ct, Oceanside (92056-3592)
PHONE.............................760 630-8602
Paul Ryan, *Pr*
Dax Harrison, *
EMP: 25 EST: 2004
SALES (est): 4.44MM **Privately Held**
Web: www.rgprecision.com
SIC: 3599 Machine and other job shop work

**(P-11063)**
**R & L ENTERPRISES INC**
Also Called: Rand Machine Works
1955 S Mary St, Fresno (93721-3309)
PHONE.............................559 233-1608
Robert Rand, *Pr*
Linda Rand, *
EMP: 26 EST: 1980
SQ FT: 27,000
SALES (est): 4.85MM **Privately Held**
Web: www.randmachineworks.com
SIC: 3599 7692 Machine shop, jobbing and repair; Welding repair

**(P-11064)**
**R C I P INC**
Also Called: R C Industries
1476 N Hundley St, Anaheim (92806-1322)
PHONE.............................714 630-1239
Robert Champlin, *CEO*
EMP: 16 EST: 1997
SQ FT: 4,400
SALES (est): 2.6MM **Privately Held**
Web: www.rcind.net
SIC: 3599 Machine shop, jobbing and repair

**(P-11065)**
**R M BAKER MACHINE AND TL INC**
815 W Front St, Covina (91722-3613)
PHONE.............................562 697-4007
Richard Baker, *Pr*
Faith Baker, *Sec*
EMP: 16 EST: 1980
SQ FT: 6,700
SALES (est): 2.48MM **Privately Held**
Web: www.rmbakermachine.com
SIC: 3599 Machine shop, jobbing and repair

**(P-11066)**
**RA INDUSTRIES LLC**
900 Glenneyre St, Laguna Beach (92651-2707)
PHONE.............................714 557-2322
Thomas Hyland, *
Carole A Follman, *
◆ EMP: 30 EST: 1969
SALES (est): 4.93MM **Privately Held**
Web: www.ra-industries.com
SIC: 3599 3593 Machine shop, jobbing and repair; Fluid power cylinders and actuators

**(P-11067)**
**RALPH E AMES MACHINE WORKS**
2301 Dominguez Way, Torrance (90501-6200)
PHONE.............................310 328-8523
Mike Ames, *Pr*
Ron Ames, *
EMP: 45 EST: 1942
SQ FT: 11,000
SALES (est): 8.48MM **Privately Held**
Web: www.amesmachine.com
SIC: 3599 Machine shop, jobbing and repair

**(P-11068)**
**RAMKO MFG INC**
3500 Tanya Ave, Hemet (92545-9410)
PHONE.............................951 652-3510
EMP: 100 EST: 1981
SALES (est): 1.41MM **Privately Held**
Web: www.ramko.com
SIC: 3599 Machine shop, jobbing and repair

**(P-11069)**
**RAMP ENGINEERING INC**
6850 Walthall Way, Paramount (90723-2028)
PHONE.............................562 531-8030
Mark Scott, *CEO*
Robert C Scott, *
Lisa Scott, *
EMP: 24 EST: 1998
SQ FT: 12,000
SALES (est): 2.22MM **Privately Held**
Web: www.rampengineering.com
SIC: 3599 Machine shop, jobbing and repair

**(P-11070)**
**RAPID PRECISION MFG INC**
1516 Montague Expy, San Jose (95131-1408)
PHONE.............................408 617-0771
Paul Yi, *CEO*
EMP: 35 EST: 2006
SQ FT: 11,000
SALES (est): 11.24MM **Privately Held**
Web: www.rapidprecision.net
SIC: 3599 Machine shop, jobbing and repair

**(P-11071)**
**RAPID PRODUCT SOLUTIONS INC**
2240 Celsius Ave Ste D, Oxnard (93030-8015)
PHONE.............................805 485-7234
Max Gerdts, *Pr*
Douglas Wallis, *
Richard Fitch, *
▲ EMP: 30 EST: 1998
SQ FT: 10,000
SALES (est): 5.05MM **Privately Held**
Web: www.rapid-products.com
SIC: 3599 Machine shop, jobbing and repair

**(P-11072)**
**RDC MACHINE INC**
2011 Stone Ave, San Jose (95125-1447)
PHONE.............................408 970-0721
Randolph D Cuilla, *Pr*
Mark Cuilla, *
Janene Cuilla, *
EMP: 26 EST: 1991
SALES (est): 4.93MM **Privately Held**
Web: www.rdcmachine.com
SIC: 3599 Machine shop, jobbing and repair

**(P-11073)**
**REDLINE PRCISION MACHINING INC**
907 E Francis St, Ontario (91761-5631)
PHONE.............................909 483-1273
Jon Bouch, *CEO*
Cheryl Bouch, *Sec*
EMP: 15 EST: 1997
SQ FT: 10,000
SALES (est): 1.6MM **Privately Held**
Web: www.redlineprecision.com
SIC: 3599 Machine shop, jobbing and repair

**(P-11074)**
**REID PRODUCTS INC**
Also Called: Reid Products
21430 Waalew Rd, Apple Valley (92307-1026)
P.O. Box 1507 (92307-0028)
PHONE.............................760 240-1355
Kevin Reid, *Pr*
Shelby Reid, *
Lisa Grinser, *
Cliff R Carter, *
EMP: 48 EST: 1980
SQ FT: 15,000
SALES (est): 9.69MM **Privately Held**
Web: www.reidproducts.com
SIC: 3599 Machine shop, jobbing and repair

**(P-11075)**
**RELIANCE MACHINE PRODUCTS INC**
4265 Solar Way, Fremont (94538-6389)
PHONE.............................510 438-6760
Kelly L Hill, *Pr*
EMP: 45 EST: 1981
SQ FT: 12,000
SALES (est): 4.22MM **Privately Held**
Web: www.rmp-inc.com
SIC: 3599 Machine shop, jobbing and repair

**(P-11076)**
**REMCO MCH & FABRICATION INC**
1966 S Date Ave, Bloomington (92316-2442)
PHONE.............................909 877-3530
Jacque Lewis Russell, *CEO*
Jerry Gilson, *VP*
▲ EMP: 19 EST: 1979
SALES (est): 4.96MM **Privately Held**
SIC: 3599 3441 Machine shop, jobbing and repair; Fabricated structural metal

**(P-11077)**
**RESEARCH METAL INDUSTRIES INC**
1970 W 139th St, Gardena (90249-2408)
PHONE.............................310 352-3200
Harish Brahmbhatt, *Pr*
◆ EMP: 35 EST: 1964
SQ FT: 24,000
SALES (est): 11.17MM **Privately Held**
Web: www.researchmetal.com
SIC: 3599 3469 Electrical discharge machining (EDM); Spinning metal for the trade

**(P-11078)**
**RICAURTE PRECISION INC**
1550 E Mcfadden Ave, Santa Ana (92705-4308)
PHONE.............................714 667-0632
Luis Ricaurte, *CEO*
Marina Ricaurte, *Pr*
EMP: 22 EST: 1985
SQ FT: 72,000
SALES (est): 841.48K **Privately Held**
Web: www.ricaurteprecision.com
SIC: 3599 Machine shop, jobbing and repair

**(P-11079)**
**RICHARDS MACHINING CO INC**
382 Martin Ave, Santa Clara (95050-3112)
PHONE.............................408 526-9219
Gustavo Chavez, *Pr*
Odin Chavez, *VP*
Yamir Chavez, *Sec*
EMP: 16 EST: 1988
SALES (est): 3.84MM **Privately Held**
Web: www.rmco-inc.com
SIC: 3599 Machine shop, jobbing and repair

**(P-11080)**
**RINCON ENGINEERING TECH**
6325 Carpinteria Ave, Carpinteria (93013-2901)
PHONE.............................805 684-4144
Edward Avetisian, *Prin*
EMP: 29
SALES (corp-wide): 3.64MM **Privately Held**
SIC: 3599 Machine shop, jobbing and repair
PA: Rincon Engineering Technologies
3 Caelum Court

**(P-11081)**
**RMC ENGINEERING CO INC (PA)**
255 Mayock Rd, Gilroy (95020-7032)
P.O. Box 575 (95021-0575)
PHONE.............................408 842-2525
Betty Mc Kenzie, *Pr*
Kevin Mc Kenzie, *
Scott Mc Kenzie, *
Shawna Mc Kenzie, *
▲ EMP: 30 EST: 1978
SQ FT: 14,000
SALES (est): 4.48MM
SALES (corp-wide): 4.48MM **Privately Held**

## 3599 - Industrial Machinery, Nec (P-11082)

Web: www.rmcengineering.com
SIC: 3599 7692 7538 3715 Machine shop, jobbing and repair; Automotive welding; General automotive repair shops; Truck trailers

### (P-11082)
### ROBERT H OLIVA INC
Also Called: Romakk Engineering
19863 Nordhoff St, Northridge (91324-3331)
PHONE.................818 700-1035
Robert Oliva, Pr
Kim Oliva, *
EMP: 25 EST: 1975
SQ FT: 4,000
SALES (est): 3.55MM Privately Held
Web: www.romakk.com
SIC: 3599 Machine shop, jobbing and repair

### (P-11083)
### ROBERTS PRECISION ENGRG INC
Also Called: Robert's Engineering
1345 S Allec St, Anaheim (92805-6304)
PHONE.................714 635-4485
Robert Flores Ii, Pr
EMP: 25 EST: 1979
SQ FT: 23,000
SALES (est): 4.2MM Privately Held
Web: www.roberts-eng.com
SIC: 3599 Machine shop, jobbing and repair

### (P-11084)
### ROBSON TECHNOLOGIES INC
Also Called: R T I
135 E Main Ave Ste 130, Morgan Hill (95037-7522)
PHONE.................408 779-8008
William W Robson, Pr
Lori Robson, *
Ryan Block, *
EMP: 27 EST: 1989
SQ FT: 3,000
SALES (est): 5.31MM Privately Held
Web: www.testfixtures.com
SIC: 3599 3823 Machine shop, jobbing and repair; Computer interface equipment, for industrial process control

### (P-11085)
### ROC-AIRE CORP
2198 Pomona Blvd, Pomona (91768-3332)
PHONE.................909 784-3385
Thomas L Collins, CEO
Jason Collins, Sec
EMP: 22 EST: 1958
SQ FT: 52,000
SALES (est): 2.54MM Privately Held
Web: www.rocaire.com
SIC: 3599 Machine shop, jobbing and repair

### (P-11086)
### ROCKET COMPOSITES INC
1790 Terminal St, West Sacramento (95691-3822)
PHONE.................916 873-8840
Paul A Hewitt, Prin
EMP: 22 EST: 2016
SALES (est): 5.33MM Privately Held
Web: www.rocketcomposites.com
SIC: 3599 Machine shop, jobbing and repair

### (P-11087)
### ROMEROS ENGINEERING INC
Also Called: American Turn-Key Fabricators
9175 Milliken Ave, Rancho Cucamonga (91730-5509)
PHONE.................909 481-1170
George Romero, Pr
EMP: 25 EST: 2005
SALES (est): 10.43MM Privately Held
Web: www.atf1.com
SIC: 3599 Machine and other job shop work

### (P-11088)
### RON WITHERSPOON INC
13525 Blackie Rd, Castroville (95012-3211)
PHONE.................831 633-3568
Les Oglesby, Mgr
EMP: 69
SALES (corp-wide): 8.26MM Privately Held
Web: www.rwinc.com
SIC: 3599 Machine shop, jobbing and repair
PA: Ron Witherspoon, Inc.
  1551 Dell Ave
  408 370-6620

### (P-11089)
### RONCELLI PLASTICS INC
330 W Duarte Rd, Monrovia (91016-4584)
PHONE.................800 250-6516
Gino Roncelli, CEO
Riley Cole, *
Bingo Roncelli, *
EMP: 151 EST: 1970
SQ FT: 11,000
SALES (est): 24.01MM Privately Held
Web: www.roncelli.com
SIC: 3599 Machine shop, jobbing and repair

### (P-11090)
### RONLO ENGINEERING LTD
955 Flynn Rd, Camarillo (93012-8704)
PHONE.................805 388-3227
Ronnie Lowe, CEO
Rick Slaney, *
Karen Mc Master, *
Tracy Slaney, *
Patricia Lowe Stkhlr, Prin
EMP: 30 EST: 1969
SQ FT: 23,650
SALES (est): 6.46MM Privately Held
Web: www.ronlo.com
SIC: 3599 Machine shop, jobbing and repair

### (P-11091)
### ROTHLISBERGER MFG A CAL CORP
Also Called: R M I
14718 Arminta St, Van Nuys (91402-5904)
PHONE.................818 786-9462
Jerry Rothlisberger, Pr
Korena Rothlisberger, Sec
EMP: 16 EST: 1967
SQ FT: 8,000
SALES (est): 2.27MM Privately Held
Web: www.rmi-mfg.com
SIC: 3599 Machine shop, jobbing and repair

### (P-11092)
### ROUTER WORKS INC
Also Called: Diversified Mfg Cal Inc
2555 Progress St, Vista (92081-8423)
PHONE.................760 599-9280
Thane D Rivers, Pr
Jerri Rivers, VP
▲ EMP: 15 EST: 2000
SQ FT: 10,000
SALES (est): 2.1MM
SALES (corp-wide): 2.1MM Privately Held
Web: www.dmoc.us
SIC: 3599 3083 Machine shop, jobbing and repair; Laminated plastics sheets
PA: North American Specialty Laminations Llc
  51149 Whitetail Rd
  715 597-6525

### (P-11093)
### S & S NUMERICAL CONTROL INC
Also Called: Satterfield Aerospace
19841 Nordhoff St, Northridge (91324-3331)
PHONE.................818 341-4141
John Satterfield, Pr
Roberta J Satterfield, Sec
EMP: 20 EST: 1982
SQ FT: 9,000
SALES (est): 2.45MM Privately Held
Web: www.ssnumerical.com
SIC: 3599 Machine shop, jobbing and repair

### (P-11094)
### S J AUTOMOTIVE LLC
Also Called: Lexus of Stevens Creek
3333 Stevens Creek Blvd, San Jose (95117-1038)
PHONE.................408 296-2223
EMP: 16 EST: 2013
SALES (est): 5.84MM Privately Held
SIC: 3599 Industrial machinery, nec

### (P-11095)
### S R MACHINING INC
640 Parkridge Ave, Norco (92860-3124)
PHONE.................951 520-9486
Lawrence T Kaford, Pr
EMP: 28 EST: 2003
SALES (est): 3.94MM Privately Held
Web: www.srmachining.com
SIC: 3599 Machine shop, jobbing and repair

### (P-11096)
### S R MACHINING-PROPERTIES LLC
Also Called: S R Machining
640 Parkridge Ave, Norco (92860-3124)
PHONE.................951 520-9486
Lawrence Kaford, Pr
▲ EMP: 134 EST: 1998
SQ FT: 28,000
SALES (est): 6.31MM Privately Held
Web: www.srmachining.com
SIC: 3599 3089 Machine shop, jobbing and repair; Injection molding of plastics

### (P-11097)
### S&S PRECISION MFG INC
2101 S Yale St, Santa Ana (92704-4424)
PHONE.................714 754-6664
David Mosier, Pr
EMP: 45 EST: 1987
SQ FT: 10,000
SALES (est): 4.16MM Privately Held
Web: www.ssprecisionmfg.com
SIC: 3599 Machine shop, jobbing and repair

### (P-11098)
### SAMAX PRECISION INC
926 W Evelyn Ave, Sunnyvale (94086-5957)
PHONE.................408 245-9555
Vicki Murray, Pr
Jodi Mccash, Sec
EMP: 36 EST: 1963
SQ FT: 10,000
SALES (est): 4.49MM Privately Held
Web: www.samaxinc.com
SIC: 3599 Custom machinery

### (P-11099)
### SANTA FE MACHINE WORKS INC
14578 Rancho Vista Dr, Fontana (92335-4277)
PHONE.................909 350-6877
Todd Kelly, Pr
Dennis Kelly, *
Gilbert Robinson, *
Patricia Kelly, *
Todd Kelly, Sec
EMP: 29 EST: 1923
SQ FT: 30,000
SALES (est): 4.45MM Privately Held
Web: www.santafemachine.com
SIC: 3599 Machine shop, jobbing and repair

### (P-11100)
### SAVAGE MACHINING INC
2235 1st St Ste 116, Simi Valley (93065-0903)
PHONE.................805 584-8047
Wade Savage, Pr
EMP: 23 EST: 2001
SALES (est): 4.31MM Privately Held
Web: www.savagemachininginc.com
SIC: 3599 Machine shop, jobbing and repair

### (P-11101)
### SCHNEIDERS MANUFACTURING INC
11122 Penrose St, Sun Valley (91352-2724)
PHONE.................818 771-0082
Nick Schneider, Pr
Tom Schneider, *
Trudy Schneider, *
EMP: 30 EST: 1967
SQ FT: 18,000
SALES (est): 4.06MM Privately Held
Web: www.schneidersmanufacturing.com
SIC: 3599 Machine shop, jobbing and repair

### (P-11102)
### SCREWMATIC INC
925 W 1st St, Azusa (91702-4222)
P.O. Box 518 (91702-0518)
PHONE.................626 334-7831
Louis E Zimmerli, CEO
Alice Zimmerli, *
Jeff Clow, *
EMP: 65 EST: 1953
SQ FT: 40,000
SALES (est): 4.92MM Privately Held
Web: www.screwmaticinc.com
SIC: 3599 Machine shop, jobbing and repair

### (P-11103)
### SDI LLC
21 Morgan Ste 150, Irvine (92618-2086)
PHONE.................949 351-1866
Jon Korbonski, Pr
EMP: 20 EST: 2017
SALES (est): 2.89MM Privately Held
Web: www.sdinetwork.com
SIC: 3599 Custom machinery

### (P-11104)
### SENGA ENGINEERING INC
1525 E Warner Ave, Santa Ana (92705-5419)
PHONE.................714 549-8011
Roy Jones, Pr
EMP: 48 EST: 1976
SQ FT: 25,000
SALES (est): 1.62MM Privately Held
Web: www.senga-eng.com
SIC: 3599 Machine shop, jobbing and repair

### (P-11105)
### SENIOR OPERATIONS LLC
Senior Aerospace
9150 Balboa Ave, San Diego (92123-1512)
PHONE.................858 278-8400
Willis Fletcher, Brnch Mgr

**PRODUCTS & SERVICES SECTION**  **3599 - Industrial Machinery, Nec (P-11127)**

**EMP:** 151
**SALES (corp-wide):** 1.2B **Privately Held**
**Web:** www.sajetproducts.com
**SIC: 3599** Machine shop, jobbing and repair
**HQ:** Senior Operations Llc
  300 E Devon Ave
  Bartlett IL 60103
  630 372-3500

*(P-11106)*
**SENIOR OPERATIONS LLC**
Also Called: Senior Flexonics
9106 Balboa Ave, San Diego (92123-1512)
**PHONE**....................858 278-8400
James Young, *VP*
**EMP:** 75
**SALES (corp-wide):** 1.2B **Privately Held**
**Web:** www.sajetproducts.com
**SIC: 3599** Bellows, industrial: metal
**HQ:** Senior Operations Llc
  300 E Devon Ave
  Bartlett IL 60103
  630 372-3500

*(P-11107)*
**SENIOR OPERATIONS LLC**
Also Called: Capo Industries Division
790 Greenfield Dr, El Cajon (92021-3101)
**PHONE**....................909 627-2723
**EMP:** 70
**SALES (corp-wide):** 1.43B **Privately Held**
**SIC: 3599** Hose, flexible metallic
**HQ:** Senior Operations Llc
  300 E Devon Ave
  Bartlett IL 60103
  630 372-3500

*(P-11108)*
**SENIOR OPERATIONS LLC**
Also Called: Jet Products
9106 Balboa Ave, San Diego (92123-1512)
**PHONE**....................858 278-8400
Damon Evans, *Brnch Mgr*
**EMP:** 236
**SALES (corp-wide):** 1.2B **Privately Held**
**Web:** www.sajetproducts.com
**SIC: 3599** Hose, flexible metallic
**HQ:** Senior Operations Llc
  300 E Devon Ave
  Bartlett IL 60103
  630 372-3500

*(P-11109)*
**SERAMPORE INDS PRIVATE LTD INC**
8333 Almeria Ave, Fontana (92335-3283)
**PHONE**....................877 921-6111
**EMP:** 17
**SALES (corp-wide):** 22.77MM **Privately Held**
**Web:** www.sipindustries.com
**SIC: 3599** Grinding castings for the trade
**PA:** Serampore Industries Private (Ltd.), Inc.
  8876 Gulf Fwy Ste 500
  713 923-6111

*(P-11110)*
**SERRANO INDUSTRIES INC**
9922 Tabor Pl, Santa Fe Springs (90670-3300)
**PHONE**....................562 777-8180
Hoberto Serrano, *Pr*
Maria Serrano, *
Bobby Serrano, *
**EMP:** 34 **EST:** 1990
**SQ FT:** 30,000
**SALES (est):** 4.13MM **Privately Held**
**Web:** www.serrano-ind.com

*(P-11111)*
**SERTEC PRECISION MACHINING**
16787 Beach Blvd, Huntington Beach (92647-4848)
**PHONE**....................714 842-2023
Brian Geisert, *CEO*
Kenneth Geisert, *Pr*
**EMP:** 16 **EST:** 2000
**SQ FT:** 3,600
**SALES (est):** 475.08K **Privately Held**
**Web:** www.sertecprecision.com
**SIC: 3599** Machine shop, jobbing and repair

*(P-11112)*
**SHARP DIMENSION INC**
4240 Business Center Dr, Fremont (94538-6356)
**PHONE**....................510 656-8938
Scott Vo, *Pr*
**EMP:** 21 **EST:** 1991
**SQ FT:** 12,000
**SALES (est):** 6.85MM **Privately Held**
**Web:** www.sharpdimension.com
**SIC: 3599** Machine shop, jobbing and repair

*(P-11113)*
**SHEFFIELD MANUFACTURING INC**
9131 Glenoaks Blvd, Sun Valley (91352-2692)
**PHONE**....................310 320-1473
**EMP:** 70
**SIC: 3599** 3444 3548 3812 Machine shop, jobbing and repair; Sheet metalwork; Electric welding equipment; Search and navigation equipment

*(P-11114)*
**SILICON VALLEY MFG INC**
6520 Central Ave, Newark (94560-3933)
**PHONE**....................510 791-9450
Mark Serpa, *Prin*
**EMP:** 26 **EST:** 2007
**SALES (est):** 3.99MM **Privately Held**
**Web:** www.svmfg.com
**SIC: 3599** Machine shop, jobbing and repair

*(P-11115)*
**SMI CA INC**
Also Called: Saeilo Manufacturing Inds
14340 Iseli Rd, Santa Fe Springs (90670-5204)
**PHONE**....................562 926-9407
Katsuhiko Tsukamoto, *CEO*
David Tsukamoto, *
Erik Kawakami, *
**EMP:** 26 **EST:** 1999
**SQ FT:** 10,000
**SALES (est):** 4.95MM
**SALES (corp-wide):** 19.09MM **Privately Held**
**Web:** www.smi-ca.com
**SIC: 3599** Machine shop, jobbing and repair
**PA:** Saeilo Enterprises Inc
  105 Kahr Ave
  845 735-6500

*(P-11116)*
**SMITH BROTHERS MFG CORP**
Also Called: Smith Brothers
5304 Banks St, San Diego (92110-4008)
**PHONE**....................619 296-3171
Larry D Smith, *Pr*
Billie L Mc Farland, *VP*
Karen Amberg, *Treas*
**EMP:** 18 **EST:** 1945
**SQ FT:** 5,700
**SALES (est):** 2.73MM **Privately Held**
**Web:** www.smithbrosmfg.com
**SIC: 3599** 3548 Machine shop, jobbing and repair; Electrodes, electric welding

*(P-11117)*
**SOLO ENTERPRISE CORP**
Also Called: Solo Golf
220 N California Ave, City Of Industry (91744-4323)
P.O. Box 607 (91747-0607)
**PHONE**....................626 961-3591
Richard F Mugica, *CEO*
Edward A Mugica, *
**EMP:** 50 **EST:** 1966
**SQ FT:** 20,000
**SALES (est):** 4.26MM **Privately Held**
**Web:** www.soloenterprisecorp.com
**SIC: 3599** 3812 Machine shop, jobbing and repair; Search and navigation equipment

*(P-11118)*
**SONSRAY INC**
23935 Madison St, Torrance (90505-6010)
**PHONE**....................323 585-1271
Matthew Hoelscher, *Prin*
**EMP:** 25 **EST:** 2014
**SALES (est):** 5.4MM **Privately Held**
**Web:** www.sonsray.com
**SIC: 3599** Industrial machinery, nec

*(P-11119)*
**SOUTH BAY SOLUTIONS INC (PA)**
Also Called: SBS
37399 Centralmont Pl, Fremont (94536-6549)
**PHONE**....................650 843-1800
Adam Drewniany, *CEO*
**EMP:** 30 **EST:** 1992
**SQ FT:** 20,000
**SALES (est):** 24.08MM **Privately Held**
**Web:** www.southbaysolutions.com
**SIC: 3599** Machine shop, jobbing and repair

*(P-11120)*
**SOUTHERN CAL TCHNICAL ARTS INC**
Also Called: Technical Arts
370 E Crowther Ave, Placentia (92870-6419)
**PHONE**....................714 524-2626
John H Robson Iv, *Pr*
John H Robson Iv, *Pr*
Christine Robson, *
Matt Robson, *
Kristi A Robson, *
**EMP:** 48 **EST:** 1970
**SQ FT:** 9,400
**SALES (est):** 9.94MM
**SALES (corp-wide):** 489.27MM **Publicly Held**
**Web:** www.technicalarts.net
**SIC: 3599** 3827 Machine shop, jobbing and repair; Optical instruments and lenses
**PA:** Nn, Inc.
  6210 Ardrey Kell Rd Ste 1
  980 264-4300

*(P-11121)*
**SPARTAN MANUFACTURING CO**
7081 Patterson Dr, Garden Grove (92841-1435)
**PHONE**....................714 894-1955
R J Horton, *Pr*
Terry Danielson, *
**EMP:** 26 **EST:** 1957
**SQ FT:** 16,000
**SALES (est):** 3.66MM **Privately Held**
**Web:** www.spartanmfg.com
**SIC: 3599** Machine shop, jobbing and repair

*(P-11122)*
**SPEC ENGINEERING COMPANY INC**
13754 Saticoy St, Panorama City (91402-6518)
**PHONE**....................818 780-3045
Gregory Viksman, *Pr*
Anna Viksman, *
**EMP:** 25 **EST:** 1987
**SQ FT:** 5,200
**SALES (est):** 2.74MM **Privately Held**
**Web:** www.specengco.com
**SIC: 3599** 3412 Machine shop, jobbing and repair; Metal barrels, drums, and pails

*(P-11123)*
**SPRAY SYSTEMS INC**
1363 E Grand Ave, Pomona (91766-3867)
**PHONE**....................909 397-7511
▲ **EMP:** 20 **EST:** 1978
**SALES (est):** 3.65MM **Privately Held**
**Web:** www.spraysystems.com
**SIC: 3599** 3444 Custom machinery; Sheet metalwork

*(P-11124)*
**SQUAGLIA MANUFACTURING COMPANY (PA)**
275 Polaris Ave, Mountain View (94043-4588)
**PHONE**....................650 965-9644
Pat Pellizzari, *Pr*
Ken Pellizzari, *VP*
**EMP:** 35 **EST:** 1962
**SQ FT:** 10,000
**SALES (est):** 2.5MM
**SALES (corp-wide):** 2.5MM **Privately Held**
**Web:** www.squaglia.com
**SIC: 3599** Machine shop, jobbing and repair

*(P-11125)*
**STINES MACHINE INC**
2481 Coral St, Vista (92081-8431)
**PHONE**....................760 599-9955
Edward L Huston, *Pr*
Tri Tran, *
**EMP:** 35 **EST:** 1969
**SQ FT:** 15,000
**SALES (est):** 2.11MM **Privately Held**
**Web:** www.stinesmachine.com
**SIC: 3599** Machine shop, jobbing and repair

*(P-11126)*
**SUN PRECISION MACHINING INC**
1651 Market St Ste A, Corona (92880-1710)
**PHONE**....................951 817-0056
**EMP:** 17
**SALES (est):** 2.68MM **Privately Held**
**SIC: 3599** Machine shop, jobbing and repair

*(P-11127)*
**SUPERIOR THREAD ROLLING CO**
12801 Wentworth St, Arleta (91331-4332)
**PHONE**....................818 504-3626
**EMP:** 82 **EST:** 1952
**SALES (est):** 18.28MM **Privately Held**
**Web:** www.superiorthread.com
**SIC: 3599** 3542 3429 Machine shop, jobbing and repair; Thread rolling machines; Aircraft hardware

## 3599 - Industrial Machinery, Nec (P-11128)

**(P-11128)**
**SUPREME MACHINE PRODUCTS INC**
302 Sequoia Ave, Ontario (91761-1543)
PHONE..............................909 974-0349
Harold Hal Peterson, *Pr*
Isac Gomez, *VP*
**EMP:** 18 **EST:** 1955
**SQ FT:** 7,800
**SALES (est):** 1.61MM **Privately Held**
**Web:** www.suprememachineproducts.com
**SIC: 3599** Machine shop, jobbing and repair

**(P-11129)**
**SVM MACHINING INC**
Also Called: Silicon Valley Mfg.
6520 Central Ave, Newark (94560-3933)
PHONE..............................510 791-9450
Mark Serpa, *Pr*
**EMP:** 18 **EST:** 1997
**SQ FT:** 21,000
**SALES (est):** 2.98MM **Privately Held**
**Web:** www.svmfg.com
**SIC: 3599** Machine shop, jobbing and repair

**(P-11130)**
**SWISS SCREW PRODUCTS INC**
339 Mathew St, Santa Clara (95050-3113)
PHONE..............................408 748-8400
Sung H Hwang, *Pr*
Young S Hwang, *
**EMP:** 25 **EST:** 1969
**SQ FT:** 12,750
**SALES (est):** 2.56MM **Privately Held**
**Web:** www.swissscrew.com
**SIC: 3599** 3541 3451 Machine shop, jobbing and repair; Machine tools, metal cutting type; Screw machine products

**(P-11131)**
**SWISS WIRE EDM**
3505 Cadillac Ave Ste J1, Costa Mesa (92626-1401)
PHONE..............................714 540-2903
Malcolm Schneer, *Pr*
Nola Schneer, *VP*
**EMP:** 15 **EST:** 1979
**SQ FT:** 10,000
**SALES (est):** 3.79MM **Privately Held**
**Web:** www.swedm.com
**SIC: 3599** Machine shop, jobbing and repair

**(P-11132)**
**T & M MACHINING**
331 Irving Dr, Oxnard (93030-5172)
PHONE..............................805 983-6716
Mario Mangone, *Pr*
Kay Mangone, *Contrlr*
**EMP:** 20 **EST:** 1979
**SALES (est):** 2.43MM **Privately Held**
**Web:** www.tmmachining.com
**SIC: 3599** 3544 Machine shop, jobbing and repair; Special dies, tools, jigs, and fixtures

**(P-11133)**
**T E B INC**
14288 Central Ave Ste B, Chino (91710-5779)
PHONE..............................909 941-8100
Ignacio Flores, *Pr*
**EMP:** 15 **EST:** 1961
**SQ FT:** 8,500
**SALES (est):** 2.7MM **Privately Held**
**Web:** www.tebincca.com
**SIC: 3599** Machine shop, jobbing and repair

**(P-11134)**
**T I B INC**
Also Called: B.T.i Tool Engineering
9525 Pathway St, Santee (92071-4170)
PHONE..............................619 562-3071
James W Jim Barnhill, *Pr*
James T Todd Barnhill, *VP*
Chris Barnhill, *VP*
**EMP:** 18 **EST:** 1967
**SQ FT:** 1,000
**SALES (est):** 3.12MM **Privately Held**
**Web:** www.bti-tool.com
**SIC: 3599** Machine shop, jobbing and repair

**(P-11135)**
**T/Q SYSTEMS INC**
25131 Arctic Ocean Dr, Lake Forest (92630-8852)
PHONE..............................949 455-0478
Victor Buytkus, *Pr*
Scott Moebius, *
**EMP:** 40 **EST:** 1988
**SALES (est):** 4.65MM **Privately Held**
**Web:** www.tqsystems.net
**SIC: 3599** Machine shop, jobbing and repair

**(P-11136)**
**TALOS CORPORATION**
Also Called: Paramount Tool & Machine Co
512 2nd Ave, Redwood City (94063-3848)
PHONE..............................713 328-3071
Gerald G Popplewell, *Pr*
Adelina Popplewell, *Sec*
**EMP:** 20 **EST:** 1962
**SQ FT:** 20,000
**SALES (est):** 695.26K **Privately Held**
**Web:** www.talos.com
**SIC: 3599** Machine shop, jobbing and repair

**(P-11137)**
**TAPEMATION MACHINING INC (PA)**
13 Janis Way, Scotts Valley (95066-3537)
PHONE..............................831 438-3069
Ericka Stevens, *Pr*
Josolyn Bradshaw, *VP*
**EMP:** 25 **EST:** 1961
**SALES (est):** 6.59MM
**SALES (corp-wide):** 6.59MM **Privately Held**
**Web:** www.tapemation.com
**SIC: 3599** Machine shop, jobbing and repair

**(P-11138)**
**TAURUS FABRICATION INC**
22838 Industrial Pl, Grass Valley (95949-6326)
PHONE..............................530 268-2650
Beau Huiskens, *Pr*
Beau Huisaens, *
**EMP:** 25 **EST:** 2015
**SQ FT:** 1,200
**SALES (est):** 4.84MM **Privately Held**
**Web:** www.taurusfab.com
**SIC: 3599** 3499 3999 3446 Machine shop, jobbing and repair; Fire- or burglary-resistive products; Barber and beauty shop equipment; Gratings, tread: fabricated metal

**(P-11139)**
**TECFAR MANUFACTURING INC**
8525 Telfair Ave, Sun Valley (91352-3928)
PHONE..............................818 767-0677
Charles Ahn, *CEO*
**EMP:** 17 **EST:** 1976
**SQ FT:** 8,500
**SALES (est):** 4.02MM **Privately Held**
**Web:** www.tecfar.com

**(P-11140)**
**TECHNIFORM INTERNATIONAL CORP**
375 S Cactus Ave, Rialto (92376-6320)
PHONE..............................909 877-6886
Richard S Jones, *Pr*
**EMP:** 176 **EST:** 1989
**SQ FT:** 60,000
**SALES (est):** 3.49MM **Privately Held**
**Web:** www.plantprefab.com
**SIC: 3599** 3469 3444 Machine shop, jobbing and repair; Metal stampings, nec; Sheet metalwork

**(P-11141)**
**TEDON SPECIALTIES A CAL CORP**
Also Called: Rock Systems
1255 Vista Way, Red Bluff (96080-4506)
P.O. Box 1236 (96080-1236)
PHONE..............................530 527-6600
Donald E Hake, *Pr*
**EMP:** 15 **EST:** 1980
**SQ FT:** 14,000
**SALES (est):** 2.33MM **Privately Held**
**Web:** tedon-specialties.hub.biz
**SIC: 3599** Machine shop, jobbing and repair

**(P-11142)**
**THIESSEN PRODUCTS INC**
Also Called: Jim's Machining
555 Dawson Dr Ste A, Camarillo (93012-5085)
PHONE..............................805 482-6913
Jim Thiessen, *Pr*
Debra Thiessen, *
Jay R Thiessen, *
**EMP:** 130 **EST:** 1971
**SQ FT:** 44,000
**SALES (est):** 16.05MM **Privately Held**
**Web:** www.jimsusa.com
**SIC: 3599** Machine shop, jobbing and repair

**(P-11143)**
**THOMSON INDUSTRIES INC**
Also Called: Thomson Lnear Motion Optimized
2695 Customhouse Ct, San Diego (92154-7645)
PHONE..............................619 661-6292
**EMP:** 30
**SALES (corp-wide):** 6.25B **Publicly Held**
**Web:** www.thomsonlinear.com
**SIC: 3599** Air intake filters, internal combustion engine, except auto
**HQ:** Thomson Industries, Inc.
 203a W Rock Rd
 Radford VA 24141
 540 633-3549

**(P-11144)**
**THUNDERBOLT MANUFACTURING INC**
641 S State College Blvd, Fullerton (92831-5115)
PHONE..............................714 632-0397
Minh Son To, *Pr*
**EMP:** 26 **EST:** 1990
**SQ FT:** 5,800
**SALES (est):** 6.94MM **Privately Held**
**Web:** www.thunderboltmfg.com
**SIC: 3599** Machine shop, jobbing and repair

**(P-11145)**
**TMX ENGINEERING AND MFG CORP**
2141 S Standard Ave, Santa Ana (92707-3034)
PHONE..............................714 641-5884
Souhil Toubia, *CEO*
Gus Toubia, *
Ali Ossaily, *
Steve Korn, *
Mauricio Escarcega, *
**EMP:** 75 **EST:** 1985
**SQ FT:** 23,000
**SALES (est):** 3.78MM **Privately Held**
**Web:** www.tmxengineering.com
**SIC: 3599** 3728 3544 Machine shop, jobbing and repair; Aircraft parts and equipment, nec; Special dies, tools, jigs, and fixtures

**(P-11146)**
**TOMI ENGINEERING INC**
414 E Alton Ave, Santa Ana (92707-4242)
PHONE..............................714 556-1474
Michael F Falbo, *CEO*
Anthony Falbo, *
**EMP:** 52 **EST:** 1975
**SQ FT:** 15,000
**SALES (est):** 8.37MM **Privately Held**
**Web:** www.tomiengineering.com
**SIC: 3599** Machine shop, jobbing and repair

**(P-11147)**
**TOSCO - TOOL SPECIALTY COMPANY**
Also Called: Tool Specialty Co
1011 E Slauson Ave, Los Angeles (90011-5296)
P.O. Box 512157 (90051-0157)
PHONE..............................323 232-3561
Jerry Tetzlaff, *Pr*
Ted Tetzlaff, *
▲ **EMP:** 25 **EST:** 1943
**SQ FT:** 19,500
**SALES (est):** 2.36MM **Privately Held**
**Web:** www.toolspecialty.com
**SIC: 3599** Machine shop, jobbing and repair

**(P-11148)**
**TOWER INDUSTRIES INC**
Also Called: Allied Mechanical Products
1720 S Bon View Ave, Ontario (91761-4411)
PHONE..............................909 947-2723
Mark Slater, *Mgr*
**EMP:** 110
**SQ FT:** 60,794
**SALES (corp-wide):** 28.17MM **Privately Held**
**Web:** metal-stamping-companies.cmac.ws
**SIC: 3599** Machine shop, jobbing and repair
**PA:** Tower Industries, Inc.
 1518 N Endeavor Ln Ste C

**(P-11149)**
**TREPANNING SPECIALITIES INC**
Also Called: Trepanning Specialities
16201 Illinois Ave, Paramount (90723-4996)
PHONE..............................562 633-8110
Donald B Laughlin, *Pr*
Patricia Laughlin, *VP*
▲ **EMP:** 23 **EST:** 1973
**SQ FT:** 7,000
**SALES (est):** 2.92MM **Privately Held**
**Web:** www.trepanningspec.com
**SIC: 3599** Machine shop, jobbing and repair

**(P-11150)**
**TRIANGLE TOOL & DIE CORP**
Also Called: Trianglehardalloys
13189 Flores St, Santa Fe Springs (90670-4041)
PHONE..............................562 944-2117
Michael J Beyer, *Prin*

## PRODUCTS & SERVICES SECTION
## 3599 - Industrial Machinery, Nec (P-11171)

Michael J Beyer, *Pr*
Barbara Beyer, *VP*
**EMP:** 15 **EST:** 1968
**SQ FT:** 14,000
**SALES (est):** 2.42MM **Privately Held**
**SIC: 3599** 3542  Electrical discharge machining (EDM); Die casting and extruding machines

### (P-11151)
### TRIDECS CORPORATION
3513 Arden Rd, Hayward  (94545-3907)
**PHONE**..............................510 785-2620
Frank Schenkhuizen Senior, *Ch Bd*
Frank Schenkhuizen Junior, *Pr*
Emma J Schenkhuizen, *
**EMP:** 25 **EST:** 1970
**SQ FT:** 15,000
**SALES (est):** 4.05MM **Privately Held**
**Web:** www.tridecs.com
**SIC: 3599**  Machine shop, jobbing and repair

### (P-11152)
### TRONSON MANUFACTURING INC
3421 Yale Way, Fremont  (94538-6171)
**PHONE**..............................408 533-0369
Michael Lieu, *Pr*
▲ **EMP:** 20 **EST:** 1998
**SQ FT:** 11,040
**SALES (est):** 4.86MM **Privately Held**
**Web:** www.tronsonmfg.com
**SIC: 3599**  Machine shop, jobbing and repair

### (P-11153)
### TRU MACHINING
45979 Warm Springs Blvd Ste 8, Fremont  (94539-6765)
**PHONE**..............................510 573-3408
Quocthuy Truong, *Pr*
Diep Nguyen, *Dir*
**EMP:** 15 **EST:** 2013
**SALES (est):** 1.61MM **Privately Held**
**Web:** www.trumachining.com
**SIC: 3599** 3569  Machine shop, jobbing and repair; Liquid automation machinery and equipment

### (P-11154)
### TRUE POSITION TECHNOLOGIES LLC
24900 Avenue Stanford, Valencia  (91355-1272)
**PHONE**..............................661 294-0030
Allen Sumian, *Pr*
**EMP:** 82 **EST:** 1990
**SQ FT:** 25,000
**SALES (est):** 12.9MM
**SALES (corp-wide):** 241.4MM **Privately Held**
**Web:** www.truepositiontech.com
**SIC: 3599**  Machine shop, jobbing and repair
**PA:** Hbd Industries, Inc.
 5200 Upper Metro Pl # 110
 614 526-7000

### (P-11155)
### TRUE PRECISION MACHINING INC
175 Industrial Way, Buellton  (93427-9592)
**PHONE**..............................805 964-4545
Todd Ackert, *Pr*
**EMP:** 22 **EST:** 1998
**SQ FT:** 17,000
**SALES (est):** 3.86MM **Privately Held**
**Web:** www.trueprecisionmachining.com
**SIC: 3599**  Machine shop, jobbing and repair

### (P-11156)
### TSC PRECISION MACHINING INC
1311 E Saint Gertrude Pl Ste A, Santa Ana  (92705-5216)
**PHONE**..............................714 542-3182
Steve Salazar, *Pr*
**EMP:** 15 **EST:** 1994
**SQ FT:** 6,298
**SALES (est):** 2.3MM **Privately Held**
**Web:** www.tscprecision.com
**SIC: 3599** 3452 8711  Machine shop, jobbing and repair; Bolts, nuts, rivets, and washers; Mechanical engineering

### (P-11157)
### TTN MACHINING  INC
9105 Olive Dr, Spring Valley  (91977-2304)
**PHONE**..............................619 303-4573
Hung Troung, *Pr*
**EMP:** 16 **EST:** 2004
**SALES (est):** 2.06MM **Privately Held**
**Web:** www.ttnmachining.com
**SIC: 3599**  Machine shop, jobbing and repair

### (P-11158)
### TURRET LATHE SPECIALISTS INC
875 S Rose Pl, Anaheim  (92805-5337)
**PHONE**..............................714 520-0058
Robert Mcbride, *Pr*
**EMP:** 18 **EST:** 1973
**SQ FT:** 6,000
**SALES (est):** 2.59MM **Privately Held**
**Web:** www.turretlathespecialists.com
**SIC: 3599**  Machine shop, jobbing and repair

### (P-11159)
### UNICO MECHANICAL CORP (PA)
Also Called: Unico Mechanical
1209 Polk St, Benicia  (94510-2906)
P.O. Box 847  (94510-0847)
**PHONE**..............................707 745-9970
Randall Potter, *CEO*
Michael Guthrie, *CFO*
▲ **EMP:** 41 **EST:** 2006
**SQ FT:** 80,000
**SALES (est):** 19.92MM **Privately Held**
**Web:** www.unicomechanical.com
**SIC: 3599**  Machine shop, jobbing and repair

### (P-11160)
### UNITED PRECISION CORP
20810 Plummer St, Chatsworth  (91311)
**PHONE**..............................818 576-9540
Robert Hawrylo, *CEO*
Robert Stanley Hawrylo, *
**EMP:** 40 **EST:** 2014
**SQ FT:** 7,500
**SALES (est):** 7.08MM **Privately Held**
**Web:** www.upc-usa.com
**SIC: 3599** 3812  Machine shop, jobbing and repair; Defense systems and equipment

### (P-11161)
### UNITED WESTERN INDUSTRIES INC
3515 N Hazel Ave, Fresno  (93722-4913)
P.O. Box 13099  (93794-3099)
**PHONE**..............................559 226-7236
Camilo Salas, *Pr*
Anthony Bandy, *
**EMP:** 49 **EST:** 1971
**SQ FT:** 15,000
**SALES (est):** 9.77MM **Privately Held**
**Web:** www.uwi.us
**SIC: 3599** 3469 3544  Custom machinery; Metal stampings, nec; Die sets for metal stamping (presses)

### (P-11162)
### UNIVERSAL PLANT SVCS CAL INC
20545 Belshaw Ave # A, Carson  (90746-3505)
**PHONE**..............................310 618-1600
Stewart Jones, *Brnch Mgr*
**EMP:** 92
**SALES (corp-wide):** 273.28MM **Privately Held**
**Web:** www.universalplant.com
**SIC: 3599**  Custom machinery
**HQ:** Universal Plant Services Of California, Inc.
 20545a Belshaw Ave
 Carson CA 90746
 310 618-1600

### (P-11163)
### UPLAND FAB  INC
1445 Brooks St Ste L, Ontario  (91762-3665)
**PHONE**..............................909 986-6565
Paul Sapra, *CEO*
Patsy Sapra, *
Steven Sapra, *
Jackson Sapra, *Stockholder*
**EMP:** 30 **EST:** 1970
**SQ FT:** 12,000
**SALES (est):** 4.63MM **Privately Held**
**Web:** www.uplandfab.com
**SIC: 3599** 2679 3083  Machine shop, jobbing and repair; Honeycomb core and board: made from purchased material; Plastics finished products, laminated

### (P-11164)
### V & S ENGINEERING COMPANY LTD
5766 Research Dr, Huntington Beach  (92649-1617)
**PHONE**..............................714 898-7869
Dino Dukovic, *Pr*
Dino Dokovic, *Pr*
**EMP:** 27 **EST:** 1979
**SQ FT:** 10,000
**SALES (est):** 581.03K **Privately Held**
**Web:** www.vseng.biz
**SIC: 3599**  Machine shop, jobbing and repair

### (P-11165)
### V-TECH MANUFACTURING  INC
Also Called: V Tech
505 Baldwin Rd, Patterson  (95363-8859)
P.O. Box 293  (94042-0293)
**PHONE**..............................408 730-9200
Robert Gluchowski, *Pr*
Jamie Sandidge, *
**EMP:** 25 **EST:** 1995
**SQ FT:** 2,000
**SALES (est):** 2.42MM **Privately Held**
**Web:** www.vtechmanufacturing.com
**SIC: 3599**  Machine shop, jobbing and repair

### (P-11166)
### VALLEY PERFORATING  LLC
3201 Gulf St, Bakersfield  (93308-4905)
**PHONE**..............................661 324-4964
Mike Dover, *Pr*
Dorothy Reynolds, *
Alice Lomas, *
**EMP:** 65 **EST:** 1970
**SQ FT:** 10,440
**SALES (est):** 5.18MM **Privately Held**
**Web:** www.valleyperf.com
**SIC: 3599**  Machine shop, jobbing and repair

### (P-11167)
### VALLEY TOOL & MFG CO INC
2507 Tully Rd, Hughson  (95326-9824)
P.O. Box 220  (95326-0220)
**PHONE**..............................209 883-4093
Fred G Brenda, *CEO*
Daniel C Finn, *
Carol Finn, *
▲ **EMP:** 40 **EST:** 1969
**SQ FT:** 50,000
**SALES (est):** 9.2MM **Privately Held**
**Web:** www.valleytoolmfg.com
**SIC: 3599**  Machine shop, jobbing and repair

### (P-11168)
### VALLEY TOOL AND MACHINE CO INC
111 Explorer St, Pomona  (91768-3278)
**PHONE**..............................909 595-2205
Chuck Rogers, *CEO*
Jim Rogers, *
Nancy Larson, *
**EMP:** 68 **EST:** 1982
**SQ FT:** 34,000
**SALES (est):** 2.33MM **Privately Held**
**Web:** www.valleytool-inc.com
**SIC: 3599** 7692 3544  Machine shop, jobbing and repair; Welding repair; Special dies, tools, jigs, and fixtures

### (P-11169)
### VANDER-BEND MANUFACTURING INC
Also Called: J.L. Haley
3510 Luyung Dr, Rancho Cordova  (95742-6872)
**PHONE**..............................916 631-6375
Steve Butts, *Brnch Mgr*
**EMP:** 140
**SALES (corp-wide):** 138.57MM **Privately Held**
**Web:** www.vantedgemedical.com
**SIC: 3599** 3312 7692  Machine shop, jobbing and repair; Blast furnaces and steel mills; Welding repair
**PA:** Vander-Bend Manufacturing, Inc.
 2701 Orchard Pkwy
 408 245-5150

### (P-11170)
### VANDERHORST BROTHERS INDUSTRIES INC
Also Called: V B I
1715 Surveyor Ave, Simi Valley  (93063-3374)
**PHONE**..............................805 583-3333
**EMP:** 60 **EST:** 2000
**SALES (est):** 11.51MM
**SALES (corp-wide):** 31.13MM **Privately Held**
**Web:** www.vbinc.com
**SIC: 3599** 3542 3728  Machine shop, jobbing and repair; Knurling machines; Aircraft parts and equipment, nec
**PA:** Rtc Aerospace Llc
 7215 45th St Ct E
 918 407-0291

### (P-11171)
### VANDERHULST ASSOCIATES INC
3300 Victor Ct, Santa Clara  (95054-2316)
**PHONE**..............................408 727-1313
Hank Vanderhulst Junior, *CEO*
Hank Vanderhulst, *CEO*
Sandy Thompson, *
Corrie Vanderhulst, *
**EMP:** 30 **EST:** 1975
**SQ FT:** 11,000

# 3599 - Industrial Machinery, Nec (P-11172)

SALES (est): 2.25MM **Privately Held**
Web: www.vanderhulst.com
SIC: **3599** Machine shop, jobbing and repair

*(P-11172)*
**VANS MANUFACTURING INC**
330 E Easy St Ste C, Simi Valley (93065-7526)
PHONE.................805 522-6267
Louis Tignac, *Pr*
EMP: 19 EST: 1976
SQ FT: 8,500
SALES (est): 3.27MM **Privately Held**
SIC: **3599** Machine shop, jobbing and repair

*(P-11173)*
**VEECO PROCESS EQUIPMENT INC**
Slider Process Division
112 Robin Hill Rd, Goleta (93117-3107)
PHONE.................805 967-2700
Ed Wagner, *Mgr*
EMP: 52
Web: www.veeco.com
SIC: **3599** 3545 3544 3291 Machine shop, jobbing and repair; Machine tool accessories; Special dies, tools, jigs, and fixtures; Abrasive products
HQ: Veeco Process Equipment Inc.
1 Terminal Dr
Plainview NY 11803

*(P-11174)*
**VENTURA HYDRULIC MCH WORKS INC**
1555 Callens Rd, Ventura (93003-5606)
PHONE.................805 656-1760
Fred H Malzacher, *Pr*
Elaine Z Malzacher, *VP*
EMP: 20 EST: 1965
SQ FT: 15,700
SALES (est): 2.96MM **Privately Held**
Web: www.venturahydraulics.com
SIC: **3599** Machine shop, jobbing and repair

*(P-11175)*
**VESCIO THREADING CO**
Also Called: Vescio Manufacturing Intl
14002 Anson Ave, Santa Fe Springs (90670-5202)
PHONE.................562 802-1868
Gregory Vescio, *CEO*
Greg Vescio, *
Robert Vescio, *
Verna Vescio, *
Bob Vescio, *
EMP: 73 EST: 1947
SQ FT: 13,000
SALES (est): 8.9MM **Privately Held**
Web: www.vesciomfg.com
SIC: **3599** Machine shop, jobbing and repair

*(P-11176)*
**VETPOWERED LLC**
Also Called: Vetpowered
2717 Boston Ave, San Diego (92113-3707)
PHONE.................619 269-7116
Hernan Luis Y Prado, *CEO*
Hernan B Luis Y Prado, *CEO*
EMP: 16 EST: 2009
SQ FT: 32,000
SALES (est): 2.19MM **Privately Held**
Web: www.vetpowered.com
SIC: **3599** 7359 7699 3589 Machine shop, jobbing and repair; Home cleaning and maintenance equipment rental services; Industrial machinery and equipment repair; Commercial cooking and foodwarming equipment

*(P-11177)*
**VIAN ENTERPRISES INC**
2120 Precision Pl, Auburn (95603-9096)
PHONE.................530 885-1997
Christopher Vian, *CEO*
Liz Popsicle, *Pr*
Carol Ann Vian, *VP*
William Kirby, *CFO*
EMP: 87 EST: 1968
SALES (est): 12.66MM
SALES (corp-wide): 2.09B **Publicly Held**
Web: www.vianenterprises.com
SIC: **3599** Machine shop, jobbing and repair
PA: Crane Company
100 1st Stmford Pl Ste 40
203 363-7300

*(P-11178)*
**VIANH COMPANY INC**
13841 A Better Way Ste 10c, Garden Grove (92843-3930)
PHONE.................714 590-9808
Tam Nguyen, *Pr*
EMP: 15 EST: 1989
SQ FT: 8,000
SALES (est): 2.26MM **Privately Held**
Web: www.vianhcompany.com
SIC: **3599** Machine shop, jobbing and repair

*(P-11179)*
**VISTA INDUSTRIAL PRODUCTS INC**
3210 Executive Rdg, Vista (92081-8527)
PHONE.................760 599-5050
EMP: 160 EST: 1968
SALES (est): 22.59MM **Privately Held**
Web: www.vista-industrial.com
SIC: **3599** Machine shop, jobbing and repair

*(P-11180)*
**W MACHINE WORKS INC**
13814 Del Sur St, San Fernando (91340-3440)
PHONE.................818 890-8049
Marzel Neckien, *Pr*
Randy Neckien, *
EMP: 45 EST: 1977
SQ FT: 25,000
SALES (est): 9.01MM **Privately Held**
Web: www.wmwcnc.com
SIC: **3599** Machine shop, jobbing and repair

*(P-11181)*
**WAHLCO INC**
Also Called: Wahlco
4774 Murrieta St Ste 3, Chino (91710-5155)
PHONE.................714 979-7300
Alonso Munoz, *CEO*
Robert R Wahler, *
Barry J Southam, *
Dennis Nickel, *
◆ EMP: 106 EST: 1972
SALES (est): 6.53MM **Privately Held**
Web: www.wahlco.com
SIC: **3599** Custom machinery

*(P-11182)*
**WALLACE E MILLER INC**
Also Called: Micro-TEC
9155 Alabama Ave Ste B, Chatsworth (91311-5867)
PHONE.................818 998-0444
Gary Case, *Pr*
Roxanne Case, *VP*
EMP: 16 EST: 1987
SQ FT: 8,000
SALES (est): 2.95MM **Privately Held**
SIC: **3599** Machine shop, jobbing and repair

*(P-11183)*
**WATTS MACHINING INC**
3370 Victor Ct, Santa Clara (95054-2316)
PHONE.................408 654-9300
Doug Watts, *Pr*
EMP: 30 EST: 1982
SALES (est): 2.37MM **Privately Held**
Web: www.wattsmachining.com
SIC: **3599** Machine shop, jobbing and repair

*(P-11184)*
**WB MACHINING & MECH DESIGN**
1670 Zanker Rd, San Jose (95112-1134)
PHONE.................408 453-5005
Max Ho, *CEO*
EMP: 22 EST: 1992
SQ FT: 20,000
SALES (est): 2.3MM **Privately Held**
Web: www.wb-precision.com
SIC: **3599** 3569 3699 Machine shop, jobbing and repair; Assembly machines, non-metalworking; Electrical equipment and supplies, nec

*(P-11185)*
**WEBER DRILLING CO INC**
4028 W 184th St, Torrance (90504-4712)
PHONE.................310 670-7708
Marlene Wood, *Pr*
Ronald Wood, *
EMP: 25 EST: 1947
SALES (est): 2.35MM **Privately Held**
SIC: **3599** Machine shop, jobbing and repair

*(P-11186)*
**WELDMAC MANUFACTURING COMPANY**
1451 N Johnson Ave, El Cajon (92020-1615)
PHONE.................619 440-2300
Marshall J Rugg, *Pr*
Barbara Bloomfield, *
Robert L Rugg, *
EMP: 122 EST: 1968
SQ FT: 100,000
SALES (est): 13.4MM **Privately Held**
Web: www.weldmac.com
SIC: **3599** 3444 7692 Machine shop, jobbing and repair; Sheet metalwork; Brazing

*(P-11187)*
**WELDMAC MANUFACTURING COMPANY**
1533 N Johnson Ave, El Cajon (92020-1683)
PHONE.................619 440-2300
Marshall J Rugg, *CEO*
EMP: 38 EST: 1969
SALES (est): 5.24MM **Privately Held**
Web: www.weldmac.com
SIC: **3599** Machine shop, jobbing and repair

*(P-11188)*
**WES MANUFACTURING INC**
431 Greenwood Dr, Santa Clara (95054-2134)
PHONE.................408 727-0750
Garn Nelson, *CEO*
Dennis Whightman, *VP*
Carl Michaels, *VP*
EMP: 20 EST: 1995
SALES (est): 3.2MM **Privately Held**
Web: www.wesmfg.com
SIC: **3599** 8711 Machine shop, jobbing and repair; Consulting engineer

*(P-11189)*
**WEST BOND INC (PA)**
1551 S Harris Ct, Anaheim (92806-5932)
PHONE.................714 978-1551
John C Price, *Pr*
Gary Phillips, *
Phyllis Eppig, *
▼ EMP: 47 EST: 1966
SQ FT: 38,000
SALES (est): 9.98MM
SALES (corp-wide): 9.98MM **Privately Held**
Web: www.westbond.com
SIC: **3599** Machine shop, jobbing and repair

*(P-11190)*
**WEST COAST MACHINING INC**
14560 Marquardt Ave, Santa Fe Springs (90670-5121)
PHONE.................562 229-1087
Sonia Duran, *CEO*
Carolina Beas, *CFO*
EMP: 15 EST: 1997
SQ FT: 18,000
SALES (est): 2.45MM **Privately Held**
Web: www.westcoastmachining.com
SIC: **3599** Machine shop, jobbing and repair

*(P-11191)*
**WESTERN CNC INC**
1001 Park Center Dr, Vista (92081-8340)
PHONE.................760 597-7000
Danny Ashcraft, *Pr*
Carolyn Ashcraft, *
April Ashcraft Ramirez, *
EMP: 100 EST: 1980
SQ FT: 57,000
SALES (est): 2.02MM **Privately Held**
Web: www.westerncnc.com
SIC: **3599** Machine shop, jobbing and repair

*(P-11192)*
**WESTERN GRINDING SERVICE INC**
2375 De La Cruz Blvd, Santa Clara (95050-2920)
PHONE.................650 591-2635
David P Wilson, *Ch Bd*
Ethan C Wilson, *
EMP: 30 EST: 1953
SQ FT: 28,000
SALES (est): 5.43MM **Privately Held**
Web: www.westerngrinding.com
SIC: **3599** Machine shop, jobbing and repair

*(P-11193)*
**WESTERN PRECISION AERO LLC**
11600 Monarch St, Garden Grove (92841-1817)
PHONE.................714 893-7999
Ed Mckenna, *Managing Member*
Norma Davis, *
EMP: 37 EST: 2009
SQ FT: 16,000
SALES (est): 10.47MM
SALES (corp-wide): 1.56B **Publicly Held**
Web: www.rbcbearings.com
SIC: **3599** Machine shop, jobbing and repair
PA: Rbc Bearings Incorporated
1 Tribiology Ctr
203 267-7001

*(P-11194)*
**WILCOX MACHINE CO**
7180 Scout Ave, Bell Gardens (90201-3202)
P.O. Box 2159 (90202-2159)
PHONE.................562 927-5353

**PRODUCTS & SERVICES SECTION**

**3612 - Transformers, Except Electric (P-11216)**

George Schofhauser, *Pr*
Kurt Anderegg, *
Jill Wigney, *
Tom Anderegg, *
◆ **EMP:** 60 **EST:** 1955
**SALES (est):** 7.53MM **Privately Held**
**Web:** www.wilcoxmachine.com
**SIC: 3599** Machine shop, jobbing and repair

**(P-11195)**
**WILLIS MACHINE INC**
11000 Alto Dr, Oak View (93022-9569)
**PHONE**.................805 604-4500
Harlan Willis, *Pr*
**EMP:** 23 **EST:** 1977
**SALES (est):** 2.52MM **Privately Held**
**Web:** www.willismachine.com
**SIC: 3599** Machine shop, jobbing and repair

**(P-11196)**
**WILSHIRE PRECISION PDTS INC**
7353 Hinds Ave, North Hollywood (91605-3704)
**PHONE**.................818 765-4571
Thomas G Lewis, *Pr*
Wendy Lewis, *
Dana Lewis, *
Shoshona Lewis, *
**EMP:** 31 **EST:** 1951
**SQ FT:** 10,000
**SALES (est):** 8.32MM **Privately Held**
**Web:** www.wilshireprecision.com
**SIC: 3599** 3621 Machine shop, jobbing and repair; Motors, electric

**(P-11197)**
**WIRE CUT COMPANY INC**
6750 Caballero Blvd, Buena Park (90620-1134)
**PHONE**.................714 994-1170
Sydney Omar, *Pr*
Sydney Omar, *CEO*
Milton M Thomas, *
Tina Thomas, *
**EMP:** 30 **EST:** 1978
**SQ FT:** 20,000
**SALES (est):** 4.48MM **Privately Held**
**Web:** www.wirecutcompany.com
**SIC: 3599** Machine shop, jobbing and repair

**(P-11198)**
**YOUNG MACHINE INC**
Also Called: California Machine Specialties
12282 Colony Ave, Chino (91710-2095)
**PHONE**.................909 464-0405
Anand Jagani, *Pr*
Gilbert Fresquez, *Cnslt*
**EMP:** 19 **EST:** 1970
**SQ FT:** 11,000
**SALES (est):** 3.37MM **Privately Held**
**Web:** www.calmachine.com
**SIC: 3599** Machine shop, jobbing and repair

**(P-11199)**
**YUHAS TOOLING & MACHINING INC**
Also Called: Slawomira Sobczyk
1031 Pecten Ct, Milpitas (95035-6804)
**PHONE**.................408 934-9196
Slava Sobczyk, *CEO*
**EMP:** 15 **EST:** 1993
**SQ FT:** 6,000
**SALES (est):** 462.31K **Privately Held**
**Web:** www.yuhasmachining.com
**SIC: 3599** Machine shop, jobbing and repair

**(P-11200)**
**ZET-TEK PRECISION MACHINING (PA)**
Also Called: Zet-Tek Machining
22951 La Palma Ave, Yorba Linda (92887-6701)
**PHONE**.................714 777-8770
Daniel Zettler, *CEO*
Sandra Rubino, *VP Opers*
**EMP:** 15 **EST:** 1988
**SQ FT:** 25,000
**SALES (est):** 2.39MM
**SALES (corp-wide):** 2.39MM **Privately Held**
**Web:** www.cristek.com
**SIC: 3599** 3444 Machine shop, jobbing and repair; Sheet metalwork

## 3612 Transformers, Except Electric

**(P-11201)**
**ABB INC**
1321 Harbor Bay Pkwy Ste 101, Alameda (94502-6582)
**PHONE**.................510 987-7111
Beth Reid, *Brnch Mgr*
**EMP:** 45
**Web:** www.abb.com
**SIC: 3612** Transformers, except electric
**HQ:** Abb Inc.
305 Gregson Dr
Cary NC 27511

**(P-11202)**
**ABBOTT TECHNOLOGIES INC**
8203 Vineland Ave, Sun Valley (91352-3956)
**PHONE**.................818 504-0644
Kerima Marie Batte, *CEO*
**EMP:** 40 **EST:** 1961
**SQ FT:** 12,000
**SALES (est):** 8.24MM **Privately Held**
**Web:** www.abbott-tech.com
**SIC: 3612** 3559 3677 Transformers, except electric; Electronic component making machinery; Transformers power supply, electronic type

**(P-11203)**
**ALECTRO INC**
Also Called: Protech Systems
6770 Central Ave Ste B, Riverside (92504-1443)
**PHONE**.................909 590-9521
Jorge Rios, *CEO*
Tim Stevens, *CEO*
Gail A Stephens, *Pr*
**EMP:** 15 **EST:** 1978
**SQ FT:** 18,000
**SALES (est):** 2.34MM **Privately Held**
**SIC: 3612** 1731 Transformers, except electric; Safety and security specialization

**(P-11204)**
**ALGONQUIN POWER SANGER LLC**
1125 Muscat Ave, Sanger (93657-4000)
P.O. Box 397 (93657-0397)
**PHONE**.................559 875-0800
Ian Robertson, *Managing Member*
**EMP:** 22 **EST:** 1988
**SQ FT:** 16,225
**SALES (est):** 5.97MM
**SALES (corp-wide):** 2.7B **Privately Held**
**Web:** www.sanger.org
**SIC: 3612** Power transformers, electric
**PA:** Algonquin Power & Utilities Corp
354 Davis Rd
905 465-4500

**(P-11205)**
**ARNOLD MAGNETICS CORPORATION**
Also Called: Arnold Magnetics
841 Avenida Acaso Ste A, Camarillo (93012-8798)
**PHONE**.................805 484-4221
**EMP:** 52 **EST:** 1956
**SALES (est):** 9.92MM **Privately Held**
**Web:** www.amcpower.com
**SIC: 3612** 3679 Transformers, except electric; Power supplies, all types: static

**(P-11206)**
**CALIFORNIA PAK INTL INC**
17706 S Main St, Gardena (90248-3517)
**PHONE**.................310 223-2500
Byung Yull Kwon, *CEO*
Jeong Yang Kwon, *CFO*
▲ **EMP:** 20 **EST:** 1989
**SQ FT:** 15,000
**SALES (est):** 8.33MM **Privately Held**
**Web:** www.calpaktravel.com
**SIC: 3612** Distribution transformers, electric

**(P-11207)**
**CORE BRANDS LLC**
Also Called: Furman
1800 S Mcdowell Boulevard Ext, Petaluma (94954-6962)
**PHONE**.................707 283-5900
◆ **EMP:** 70
**SIC: 3612** Transformers, except electric

**(P-11208)**
**CUSTOM MAGNETICS CAL INC**
15142 Vista Del Rio Ave, Chino (91710-9694)
**PHONE**.................909 620-3877
Christopher Cimino, *CEO*
▲ **EMP:** 27 **EST:** 2013
**SALES (est):** 4.37MM **Privately Held**
**Web:** www.cmi-power.com
**SIC: 3612** Transformers, except electric

**(P-11209)**
**DATATRONIC DISTRIBUTION INC**
28151 Us Highway 74, Romoland (92585-8915)
P.O. Box 1580 (92585-1580)
▲ **EMP:** 19 **EST:** 2000
**SQ FT:** 8,200
**SALES (est):** 4.87MM **Privately Held**
**Web:** www.datatronics.com
**SIC: 3612** Transformers, except electric
**HQ:** Datatronic Limited
19/F North Point Indl Bldg
North Point HK

**(P-11210)**
**DATATRONICS ROMOLAND INC**
Also Called: Datatronics
28151 Us Highway 74, Menifee (92585-8916)
P.O. Box 1579 (92585-1579)
**PHONE**.................951 928-7700
Paul Y Siu, *Pr*
Wai M Siu Shui, *
▲ **EMP:** 70 **EST:** 1989
**SQ FT:** 38,800
**SALES (est):** 16.36MM **Privately Held**
**Web:** www.datatronics.com
**SIC: 3612** 3677 Transformers, except electric; Inductors, electronic

**(P-11211)**
**DOW-ELCO INC**
1313 W Olympic Blvd, Montebello (90640-5010)
P.O. Box 669 (90640-0669)
**PHONE**.................323 723-1288
Linda Su, *Pr*
Cecile Se Kay, *VP*
Grace Park, *
Ronald Cheung, *
Annie Su, *
**EMP:** 25 **EST:** 1946
**SQ FT:** 8,100
**SALES (est):** 2.45MM **Privately Held**
**SIC: 3612** 3829 3061 Vibrators, interrupter; Measuring and controlling devices, nec; Mechanical rubber goods

**(P-11212)**
**ENERGY CNVRSION APPLCTIONS INC**
Also Called: Eca
582 Explorer St, Brea (92821-3108)
**PHONE**.................714 256-2166
Akbal Grewal, *CEO*
**EMP:** 17 **EST:** 1989
**SQ FT:** 10,000
**SALES (est):** 3.98MM **Privately Held**
**Web:** www.eca-mfg.com
**SIC: 3612** 8748 Transformers, except electric; Telecommunications consultant

**(P-11213)**
**FULHAM CO INC**
12705 S Van Ness Ave, Hawthorne (90250-3322)
**PHONE**.................323 779-2980
Antony Corrie, *CEO*
James Cooke, *CFO*
Harry Libby, *VP*
Mike Hu, *VP*
Deborah Knuckles, *CFO*
▲ **EMP:** 40 **EST:** 1994
**SQ FT:** 48,000
**SALES (est):** 8.52MM **Privately Held**
**Web:** www.fulham.com
**SIC: 3612** Ballasts for lighting fixtures
**HQ:** Fulham Company Gmbh
Torstr. 138
Berlin BE 10119

**(P-11214)**
**GRAND GENERAL ACCESSORIES LLC**
Also Called: Grand General
1965 E Vista Bella Way, Rancho Dominguez (90220-6106)
**PHONE**.................310 631-2589
Shu-hui Sophia Lin Huang, *CEO*
Nan-huang Huang, *Sec*
▲ **EMP:** 39 **EST:** 1984
**SALES (est):** 2.84MM **Privately Held**
**Web:** www.grandgeneral.com
**SIC: 3612** 5531 3713 Transformers, except electric; Truck equipment and parts; Truck and bus bodies

**(P-11215)**
**JACKSON ENGINEERING CO INC**
9411 Winnetka Ave # A, Chatsworth (91311-6035)
**PHONE**.................818 886-9567
Ron Jackson, *Pr*
Dennis Elliott, *
**EMP:** 40 **EST:** 1951
**SQ FT:** 10,000
**SALES (est):** 920.19K **Privately Held**
**Web:** www.jacksonengineering.com
**SIC: 3612** Electronic meter transformers

**(P-11216)**
**JUSTIN INC**
Also Called: Justin
2663 Lee Ave, El Monte (91733-1411)

## 3612 - Transformers, Except Electric (P-11217)

PHONE..................................626 444-4516
Frank Justin Junior, *Pr*
Jeff Justin, *
Jeffrey Ross Justin, *
**EMP:** 50 **EST:** 1956
**SQ FT:** 4,000
**SALES (est):** 4.16MM **Privately Held**
Web: www.justininc.com
**SIC: 3612** Specialty transformers

**(P-11217)**
**MGM TRANSFORMER CO**
5701 Smithway St, Commerce (90040-1583)
PHONE..................................323 726-0888
Patrick Gogerchin, *CEO*
Patrick Gogerchin, *Pr*
Luis Otero, *
Bianca Kaveh, *
Sherry Bouloury, *
◆ **EMP:** 70 **EST:** 1975
**SQ FT:** 40,000
**SALES (est):** 99.19MM **Privately Held**
Web: www.mgmtransformer.com
**SIC: 3612** Transformers, except electric

**(P-11218)**
**NUVVE HOLDING CORP (PA)**
2488 Historic Decatur Rd Ste 300, San Diego (92106-6134)
PHONE..................................619 456-5161
Gregory Poilasne, *CEO*
Jon M Montgomery, *Interim Chairman of the Board*
Ted Smith, *Pr*
David G Robson, *CFO*
**EMP:** 38 **EST:** 1996
**SALES (est):** 8.33MM
**SALES (corp-wide):** 8.33MM **Publicly Held**
Web: www.nuvve.com
**SIC: 3612** Power and distribution transformers

**(P-11219)**
**OHMEGA SOLENOID CO INC**
10912 Painter Ave, Santa Fe Springs (90670-4529)
P.O. Box 2747 (90670-0747)
PHONE..................................562 944-7948
**EMP:** 47 **EST:** 1967
**SALES (est):** 5.86MM **Privately Held**
Web: www.ohmegasolenoid.com
**SIC: 3612 3679 3677** Power and distribution transformers; Solenoids for electronic applications; Electronic coils and transformers

**(P-11220)**
**ON-LINE POWER INCORPORATED (PA)**
Also Called: Power Services
14000 S Broadway, Los Angeles (90061-1018)
PHONE..................................323 721-5017
Abbie Gougerchian, *CEO*
▲ **EMP:** 46 **EST:** 1980
**SQ FT:** 36,000
**SALES (est):** 9.49MM
**SALES (corp-wide):** 9.49MM **Privately Held**
Web: www.onlinepower.com
**SIC: 3612 3621 3613 3677** Transformers, except electric; Motors and generators; Regulators, power; Electronic coils and transformers

**(P-11221)**
**ONYX POWER INC**
4011 W Carriage Dr, Santa Ana (92704-6301)

PHONE..................................714 513-1500
**EMP:** 104
**SIC: 3612** Power and distribution transformers

**(P-11222)**
**PACIFIC TRANSFORMER CORP**
5399 E Hunter Ave, Anaheim (92807-2054)
PHONE..................................714 779-0450
Patrick A Thomas, *CEO*
Justin Richardson, *
▲ **EMP:** 85 **EST:** 1981
**SQ FT:** 37,000
**SALES (est):** 14.29MM **Privately Held**
Web: www.pactran.com
**SIC: 3612** Power transformers, electric

**(P-11223)**
**PIONEER CUSTOM ELEC PDTS CORP**
10640 Springdale Ave, Santa Fe Springs (90670-3843)
PHONE..................................562 944-0626
Geo Murickan, *Pr*
**EMP:** 68 **EST:** 2013
**SALES (est):** 12.84MM **Publicly Held**
Web: www.pioneercep.com
**SIC: 3612** Electronic meter transformers
**PA:** Pioneer Power Solutions, Inc.
    400 Kelby St Fl 12

**(P-11224)**
**POWERTRONIX INC**
1120 Chess Dr, Foster City (94404-1103)
PHONE..................................650 345-6800
**EMP:** 23 **EST:** 2021
**SALES (est):** 4.2MM **Privately Held**
Web: www.powertronix.com
**SIC: 3612** Transformers, except electric
**PA:** Astrodyne Corporation
    36 Newburgh Rd

**(P-11225)**
**PULSE ELECTRONICS INC (HQ)**
15255 Innovation Dr Ste 100, San Diego (92128-3400)
PHONE..................................858 674-8100
Mark Twaalfhoven, *CEO*
Renuka Ayer, *
John Houston, *
John R D Dickson, *
Mike Bond, *
▲ **EMP:** 270 **EST:** 1955
**SQ FT:** 49,750
**SALES (est):** 60MM **Privately Held**
Web: www.pulseelectronics.com
**SIC: 3612 3674 3677** Specialty transformers ; Modules, solid state; Filtration devices, electronic
**PA:** Yageo Corporation
    3f, No.233-1, Pao Chiao Rd.,

**(P-11226)**
**QUALITY TRANSFORMER & ELEC**
Also Called: Quality Transformer & Elec Co
963 Ames Ave, Milpitas (95035-6326)
PHONE..................................408 935-0231
Carl Clift, *CEO*
Frank W Hendershot, *
▲ **EMP:** 40 **EST:** 1964
**SQ FT:** 32,500
**SALES (est):** 12.69MM **Privately Held**
Web: www.qte.com
**SIC: 3612** Transformers, except electric

**(P-11227)**
**RING LLC (HQ)**
Also Called: Ring

12515 Cerise Ave, Hawthorne (90250-4801)
PHONE..................................310 929-7085
Jamie Siminoff, *Managing Member*
▲ **EMP:** 300 **EST:** 2013
**SQ FT:** 40,000
**SALES (est):** 67.88MM **Publicly Held**
Web: www.ring.com
**SIC: 3612 5065** Doorbell transformers, electric; Security control equipment and systems
**PA:** Amazon.Com, Inc.
    410 Terry Ave N

**(P-11228)**
**RWNM INC**
1240 Simpson Way, Escondido (92029-1406)
▲ **EMP:** 33 **EST:** 1995
**SQ FT:** 2,200
**SALES (est):** 2.05MM **Privately Held**
**SIC: 3612** Transformers, except electric

**(P-11229)**
**SEMPRA GLOBAL (HQ)**
488 8th Ave, San Diego (92101-7123)
PHONE..................................619 696-2000
Mark A Snell, *CEO*
**EMP:** 60 **EST:** 1997
**SALES (est):** 1.68MM
**SALES (corp-wide):** 16.72B **Publicly Held**
Web: www.sempra.com
**SIC: 3612** Transformers, except electric
**PA:** Sempra
    488 8th Ave
    619 696-2000

**(P-11230)**
**SIWIBI WHOLESALE**
625 Ellis St, Mountain View (94043-2226)
PHONE..................................650 448-1041
**EMP:** 30 **EST:** 2020
**SALES (est):** 1.32MM **Privately Held**
**SIC: 3612** Distribution transformers, electric

**(P-11231)**
**STREAMLINE AVIONICS INC**
17672 Armstrong Ave, Irvine (92614-5728)
PHONE..................................949 861-8151
Daniel Frahm, *Pr*
**EMP:** 22 **EST:** 2010
**SALES (est):** 2.49MM **Privately Held**
Web: www.streamlineavionics.com
**SIC: 3612** Transformers, except electric

**(P-11232)**
**ZETTLER MAGNETICS INC**
2410 Birch St, Vista (92081-8472)
PHONE..................................949 831-5000
Gunther Rueb, *CEO*
▲ **EMP:** 190 **EST:** 1997
**SQ FT:** 80,000
**SALES (est):** 2.28MM **Privately Held**
Web: www.zettlercontrols.com
**SIC: 3612** Transformers, except electric
**PA:** Zettler Components, Inc.
    75 Columbia

## 3613 Switchgear And Switchboard Apparatus

**(P-11233)**
**AEMI HOLDINGS LLC**
6610 Cobra Way, San Diego (92121-4107)
PHONE..................................858 481-0210
Daniel H Chang, *Pr*
Xiang Ming Li, *Sr VP*
Caili Chang, *

▲ **EMP:** 77 **EST:** 1986
**SQ FT:** 45,000
**SALES (est):** 9.21MM **Privately Held**
Web: www.aem-usa.com
**SIC: 3613 3677 7699** Fuses and fuse equipment; Inductors, electronic; Metal reshaping and replating services

**(P-11234)**
**AGE INCORPORATED**
14831 Spring Ave, Santa Fe Springs (90670-5109)
PHONE..................................562 483-7300
Vasken Imasdounian, *Pr*
Daniel Imasdounian, *
Annie Imasdounian, *
▲ **EMP:** 35 **EST:** 1975
**SALES (est):** 4.2MM **Privately Held**
Web: www.agenameplate.com
**SIC: 3613 3625** Control panels, electric; Electric controls and control accessories, industrial

**(P-11235)**
**AMTEC INDUSTRIES INC**
7079 Commerce Cir, Pleasanton (94588-8008)
PHONE..................................510 887-2289
▲ **EMP:** 32 **EST:** 1983
**SALES (est):** 5.14MM **Privately Held**
Web: www.amtec1.com
**SIC: 3613 8711** Control panels, electric; Electrical or electronic engineering

**(P-11236)**
**BRILLIANT HOME TECHNOLOGY INC**
28 E 3rd Ave, San Mateo (94401)
PHONE..................................855 650-0940
Aaron Emigh, *CEO*
Steven Stanek, *
Brian Cardanha, *
Laurie Chan, *
**EMP:** 69 **EST:** 2016
**SALES (est):** 8.53MM **Privately Held**
Web: www.brilliant.tech
**SIC: 3613** Switchgear and switchboard apparatus

**(P-11237)**
**COBEL TECHNOLOGIES INC**
822 N Grand Ave, Covina (91724-2418)
PHONE..................................626 332-2100
Mike Warner, *Pr*
**EMP:** 16 **EST:** 1985
**SQ FT:** 5,600
**SALES (est):** 2.94MM **Privately Held**
Web: www.cobeltech.com
**SIC: 3613 3625** Control panels, electric; Relays and industrial controls

**(P-11238)**
**CROWN TECHNICAL SYSTEMS (PA)**
13470 Philadelphia Ave, Fontana (92337-7700)
PHONE..................................951 332-4170
Naim Siddiqui, *Pr*
Howard Siddiqui, *
▲ **EMP:** 198 **EST:** 1996
**SQ FT:** 92,000
**SALES (est):** 61.35MM **Privately Held**
Web: www.crowntechnicalsystems.com
**SIC: 3613** Control panels, electric

**(P-11239)**
**CUSTOM CONTROL SENSORS LLC (PA)**
Also Called: Custom Aviation Supply

# PRODUCTS & SERVICES SECTION
## 3621 - Motors And Generators (P-11258)

21111 Plummer St, Chatsworth (91311-4905)
P.O. Box 3535 (91313-3535)
PHONE..................................818 341-4610
Henry P Acuff, *Pr*
Thomas Pilgrim, *
Joann D Acuff, *
**EMP:** 113 **EST:** 1957
**SALES (est):** 21.88MM
**SALES (corp-wide):** 21.88MM **Privately Held**
**Web:** www.ccsdualsnap.com
**SIC:** 3613 3643 3625  Switches, electric power except snap, push button, etc.; Current-carrying wiring services; Relays and industrial controls

### (P-11240)
### ELECTRO SWITCH CORP
Also Called: Digitran
10410 Trademark St, Rancho Cucamonga (91730-5826)
PHONE..................................909 581-0855
Robert M Pineau, *Pr*
**EMP:** 69
**SALES (corp-wide):** 39.86MM **Privately Held**
**Web:** www.digitran-switches.com
**SIC:** 3613 3625  Switches, electric power except snap, push button, etc.; Industrial controls: push button, selector switches, pilot
**HQ:** Electro Switch Corp.
775 Pleasant St Ste 1
Weymouth MA 02189
781 335-1195

### (P-11241)
### FACTORY TECHNOLOGIES INC
627 Bitritto Ct Ste A, Modesto (95356-9276)
PHONE..................................209 248-8420
Jared Dean Hoefle, *CEO*
Lula Kavanaugh, *
**EMP:** 30 **EST:** 2013
**SALES (est):** 6MM **Privately Held**
**Web:** www.factorytechnologies.com
**SIC:** 3613 7373  Control panels, electric; Systems integration services

### (P-11242)
### GENERAL SWITCHGEAR INC
14729 Spring Ave, Santa Fe Springs (90670-5107)
**EMP:** 30 **EST:** 1983
**SALES (est):** 2.27MM **Privately Held**
**SIC:** 3613 5063  Switchgear and switchgear accessories, nec; Electrical apparatus and equipment

### (P-11243)
### HYDRA-ELECTRIC COMPANY (PA)
3151 N Kenwood St, Burbank (91505)
PHONE..................................818 843-6211
Tc Queener, *Pr*
Len Torres, *
**EMP:** 178 **EST:** 1950
**SQ FT:** 90,000
**SALES (est):** 22.61MM
**SALES (corp-wide):** 22.61MM **Privately Held**
**Web:** www.hydraelectric.com
**SIC:** 3613  Switches, electric power except snap, push button, etc.

### (P-11244)
### ICONN INC
Also Called: Iconn Technologies
8909 Irvine Center Dr, Irvine (92618-4249)
PHONE..................................800 286-6742
Turker Hidirlar, *CEO*
Jon Harrison, *
Raif Tunc Elmas, *
▲ **EMP:** 56 **EST:** 2007
**SQ FT:** 9,920
**SALES (est):** 9.05MM **Privately Held**
**Web:** www.iconn-ems.com
**SIC:** 3613 3714 3678 3351  Power connectors, electric; Booster (jump-start) cables, automotive; Electronic connectors; Wire, copper and copper alloy
**PA:** Cape Ems Berhad
Plo 227a Jalan Cyber 1a

### (P-11245)
### INDUSTRIAL ELECTRIC MFG INC
48205 Warm Springs Blvd, Fremont (94539-7654)
PHONE..................................510 656-1600
**EMP:** 160
**SIC:** 3613  Switchboards and parts, power

### (P-11246)
### MARWELL CORPORATION
1094 Wabash Ave, Mentone (92359)
P.O. Box 139 (92359-0139)
PHONE..................................909 794-4192
Larry R Blackwell, *Pr*
Kelle A Blackwell, *Sec*
**EMP:** 18 **EST:** 1979
**SQ FT:** 3,500
**SALES (est):** 2.97MM **Privately Held**
**Web:** www.marwellcorp.com
**SIC:** 3613  Panel and distribution boards and other related apparatus

### (P-11247)
### NEW IEM LLC
Also Called: Industrial Electric Mfg
48205 Warm Springs Blvd, Fremont (94539-7654)
PHONE..................................510 656-1600
Clayton Such, *CEO*
Doug Kristensen, *
Zhana Goldblatt, *
Sean Goforth, *
▲ **EMP:** 384 **EST:** 2003
**SQ FT:** 131,000
**SALES (est):** 715MM
**SALES (corp-wide):** 955MM **Privately Held**
**Web:** www.iemfg.com
**SIC:** 3613  Switchboards and parts, power
**HQ:** Iem New Sub 2 Llc
48205 Warm Springs Blvd
Fremont CA
510 656-1600

### (P-11248)
### PHAOSTRON INSTR ELECTRONIC CO
Also Called: Phaostron Instr Electronic Co
717 N Coney Ave, Azusa (91702-2205)
PHONE..................................626 969-6801
Paul R Mc Guirk, *Pr*
Andrew Mcguirk, *VP*
Jacqueline Cangialosi, *
**EMP:** 80 **EST:** 1937
**SQ FT:** 50,000
**SALES (est):** 4.35MM **Privately Held**
**Web:** www.phaostron.com
**SIC:** 3613  Metering panels, electric
**PA:** Westbase, Inc.
717 N Coney Ave

### (P-11249)
### ROMAC SUPPLY CO INC
Also Called: Romac
17722 Neff Ranch Rd, Yorba Linda (92886-9013)
PHONE..................................323 721-5810
**TOLL FREE:** 800
David B Rosenfield, *Pr*
Lisa R Podolsky, *
Phillip Rosenfield, *
Edith Rosenfield, *
Victoria Rosenfield, *
**EMP:** 60 **EST:** 1955
**SALES (est):** 5.12MM **Privately Held**
**Web:** www.tauberaronsinc.com
**SIC:** 3613 3621 3612 5063  Switchgear and switchgear accessories, nec; Motors and generators; Transformers, except electric; Motors, electric

### (P-11250)
### STACO SYSTEMS INC (HQ)
Also Called: Staco Switch
7 Morgan, Irvine (92618-2005)
PHONE..................................949 297-8700
Patrick Hutchins, *Pr*
Jeffrey Nick, *VP*
Brett Meinsen, *VP Fin*
Tom Lanni, *VP*
Jeff Bowen, *VP Sls*
◆ **EMP:** 69 **EST:** 1957
**SQ FT:** 35,000
**SALES (est):** 9.91MM
**SALES (corp-wide):** 46.24MM **Privately Held**
**Web:** www.stacosystems.com
**SIC:** 3613  Switches, electric power except snap, push button, etc.
**PA:** Components Corporation Of America
5950 Berkshire Ln # 1500
214 969-0166

### (P-11251)
### TRAYER ENGINEERING CORPORATION
1569 Alvarado St, San Leandro (94577-2640)
PHONE..................................415 285-7770
John Trayer, *Pr*
Kirit Patel, *
▼ **EMP:** 84 **EST:** 1962
**SQ FT:** 21,000
**SALES (est):** 9.39MM **Privately Held**
**Web:** www.trayer.com
**SIC:** 3613  Switchgear and switchgear accessories, nec

### (P-11252)
### W A BENJAMIN ELECTRIC CO
1615 Staunton Ave, Los Angeles (90021-3118)
PHONE..................................213 749-7731
D E Benjamin, *Pr*
**EMP:** 50 **EST:** 1911
**SALES (est):** 10.27MM **Privately Held**
**Web:** www.benjaminelectric.com
**SIC:** 3613  Panelboards and distribution boards, electric

### (P-11253)
### WEST COAST SWITCHGEAR (DH)
13837 Bettencourt St, Cerritos (90703-1009)
PHONE..................................562 802-3441
Alfred P Cisternelli, *CEO*
▲ **EMP:** 93 **EST:** 2003
**SQ FT:** 20,000
**SALES (est):** 3.96MM **Privately Held**
**Web:** www.westcoastswitchgear.com
**SIC:** 3613 5063  Power circuit breakers; Switchgear
**HQ:** Resa Power, Llc
8723 Fallbrook Dr
Houston TX 77064
832 900-8340

## 3621 Motors And Generators

### (P-11254)
### AC PROPULSION INC
441 Borrego Ct, San Dimas (91773-2971)
PHONE..................................909 592-5399
▲ **EMP:** 20 **EST:** 1992
**SALES (est):** 2.44MM **Privately Held**
**Web:** www.acpropulsion.com
**SIC:** 3621  Electric motor and generator parts

### (P-11255)
### ASI HOLDCO INC
780 Montague Expy Ste 508, San Jose (95131-1319)
PHONE..................................408 913-1300
Howe Yuen Lim, *CEO*
**EMP:** 32 **EST:** 2012
**SALES (est):** 2.79MM **Privately Held**
**Web:** www.akribis-sys.com
**SIC:** 3621 5084  Servomotors, electric; Industrial machinery and equipment
**HQ:** Akribis Systems Pte. Ltd.
56 Serangoon North Avenue 4
Singapore 55585

### (P-11256)
### BARTA - SCHOENEWALD INC (PA)
Also Called: Advanced Motion Controls
3805 Calle Tecate, Camarillo (93012-5068)
PHONE..................................805 389-1935
Sandor Barta, *Pr*
Daniel Schoenewald, *
▲ **EMP:** 116 **EST:** 1986
**SQ FT:** 86,000
**SALES (est):** 34.72MM
**SALES (corp-wide):** 34.72MM **Privately Held**
**Web:** www.a-m-c.com
**SIC:** 3621 3699  Servomotors, electric; Electrical equipment and supplies, nec

### (P-11257)
### CAL LLC POWERFLEX SYSTEMS
15445 Innovation Dr, San Diego (92128)
P.O. Box 3155 (94024)
PHONE..................................650 469-3392
Raphael Declercq, *CEO*
Bryan Towe, *
**EMP:** 24 **EST:** 2016
**SALES (est):** 3.07MM **Privately Held**
**Web:** www.powerflex.com
**SIC:** 3621  Generators for gas-electric or oil-electric vehicles
**PA:** Edf Renewables, Inc.
15445 Innovation Dr

### (P-11258)
### CALNETIX TECHNOLOGIES LLC (HQ)
16323 Shoemaker Ave, Cerritos (90703-2244)
PHONE..................................562 293-1660
Vatche Artinian, *Ch*
Ian Hart, *
Andrea Matiauda, *
Herman Artinian, *UPLING LLC**
Pana Shenoy, *
**EMP:** 67 **EST:** 2011
**SALES (est):** 22MM
**SALES (corp-wide):** 100.4MM **Privately Held**
**Web:** www.calnetix.com
**SIC:** 3621  Motors and generators
**PA:** Calnetix, Inc.
16323 Shoemaker Ave
562 293-1660

## 3621 - Motors And Generators (P-11259)

**(P-11259)**
**CHARGIE LLC**
3947 Landmark St, Culver City (90232-2315)
PHONE..................310 621-0024
Zach Jennings, *Managing Member*
**EMP:** 49 **EST:** 2020
**SALES (est):** 4.37MM **Privately Held**
**Web:** www.chargie.com
**SIC: 3621** Electric motor and generator parts

**(P-11260)**
**CMI INTEGRATED TECH INC**
11250 Playa Ct, Culver City (90230-6127)
**EMP:** 35 **EST:** 1989
**SQ FT:** 6,600
**SALES (est):** 1.55MM **Privately Held**
**SIC: 3621** 3825 Electric motor and generator auxiliary parts; Instruments to measure electricity

**(P-11261)**
**COLE INSTRUMENT CORP**
2650 S Croddy Way, Santa Ana (92704-5238)
PHONE..................714 556-3100
Ric Garcia, *Pr*
Manuel Garcia, *
Muse Khawaja, *
**EMP:** 70 **EST:** 1965
**SQ FT:** 16,000
**SALES (est):** 8.37MM **Privately Held**
**Web:** www.cole-switches.com
**SIC: 3621** 3679 Motors and generators; Electronic switches

**(P-11262)**
**CONTROLOMATIC INC**
12146 Charles Dr Ste 7-8, Grass Valley (95945-9562)
PHONE..................530 205-4520
Melinda Kohnke, *CEO*
Scott Lenney, *Pr*
Terri Van Wagner, *Opers Mgr*
**EMP:** 20 **EST:** 2008
**SALES (est):** 2.96MM **Privately Held**
**Web:** www.controlomatic.com
**SIC: 3621** Motors and generators

**(P-11263)**
**DIRECT DRIVE SYSTEMS INC**
621 Burning Tree Rd, Fullerton (92833-1448)
PHONE..................714 872-5500
James Pribble, *CEO*
Michael Slater, *
Robert Clark, *
**EMP:** 57 **EST:** 2005
**SALES (est):** 3.69MM
**SALES (corp-wide):** 7.83B **Privately Held**
**SIC: 3621** Electric motor and generator parts
**HQ:** Fmc Technologies, Inc.
13460 Lockwood Rd
Houston TX 77044
281 591-4000

**(P-11264)**
**EROAD INC**
15110 Avenue Of Science Ste 100, San Diego (92128-3405)
P.O. Box 23846 (97281-3846)
PHONE..................503 305-2255
Brian Michie, *Pr*
**EMP:** 77 **EST:** 2012
**SALES (est):** 10.54MM **Privately Held**
**Web:** www.eroad.com
**SIC: 3621** Storage battery chargers, motor and engine generator type
**PA:** Eroad Limited
260 Oteha Valley Road

**(P-11265)**
**ES WEST COAST LLC**
Also Called: Energy Systems
7100 Longe St Ste 300, Stockton (95206-3962)
PHONE..................209 870-1900
Don Richter, *Pr*
**EMP:** 45 **EST:** 2012
**SALES (est):** 5.53MM
**SALES (corp-wide):** 113.94MM **Privately Held**
**SIC: 3621** Electric motor and generator auxiliary parts
**HQ:** The Shane Group Llc
215 W Mechanic St
Hillsdale MI 49242
517 439-4316

**(P-11266)**
**EURUS ENERGY AMERICA CORP (DH)**
9255 Towne Centre Dr Ste 840, San Diego (92121-3041)
PHONE..................858 638-7115
Mark E Anderson, *Pr*
Yoko Rover, *Asstg*
**EMP:** 16 **EST:** 1988
**SQ FT:** 3,000
**SALES (est):** 19.07MM **Privately Held**
**Web:** www.eurusenergy.com
**SIC: 3621** Windmills, electric generating
**HQ:** Eurus Energy Holdings Corporation
4-3-13, Toranomon
Minato-Ku TKY 105-0

**(P-11267)**
**FARASIS ENERGY USA INC**
21363 Cabot Blvd, Hayward (94545-1650)
PHONE..................510 732-6600
Yu Wang, *CEO*
**EMP:** 67 **EST:** 2019
**SALES (est):** 6.97MM **Privately Held**
**SIC: 3621** Generators for storage battery chargers

**(P-11268)**
**FREEWIRE TECHNOLOGIES INC (PA)**
7200 Gateway Blvd, Newark (94560-8001)
PHONE..................415 779-5515
Arcady Sosinov, *CEO*
Martin Lynch, *COO*
Michael Beer, *CFO*
**EMP:** 47 **EST:** 2014
**SALES (est):** 12.21MM
**SALES (corp-wide):** 12.21MM **Privately Held**
**Web:** www.freewiretech.com
**SIC: 3621** 3714 7389 Storage battery chargers, motor and engine generator type; Motor vehicle electrical equipment; Business Activities at Non-Commercial Site

**(P-11269)**
**G3 VIRTUS SOLUTIONS INC** ✪
12850 Florence Ave, Santa Fe Springs (90670-4540)
PHONE..................323 724-6771
Enrique C Gonzalez, *CEO*
Esmeralda Gonzalez, *Sec*
**EMP:** 20 **EST:** 2023
**SALES (est):** 804.98K **Privately Held**
**SIC: 3621** Coils, for electric motors or generators

**(P-11270)**
**GLENTEK INC**
208 Standard St, El Segundo (90245-3834)
PHONE..................310 322-3026
Richard Vasak, *CEO*
Helen Sysel, *
◆ **EMP:** 84 **EST:** 1964
**SQ FT:** 105,000
**SALES (est):** 11.21MM **Privately Held**
**Web:** www.glentek.com
**SIC: 3621** Motors and generators

**(P-11271)**
**GOHZ INC**
23555 Golden Springs Dr Ste K1, Diamond Bar (91765-2176)
PHONE..................800 603-1219
Zhuge Fusheng, *Pr*
**EMP:** 30 **EST:** 2015
**SQ FT:** 1,200
**SALES (est):** 558.71K **Privately Held**
**Web:** www.gohz.com
**SIC: 3621** Frequency converters (electric generators)

**(P-11272)**
**HITACHI AUTOMOTIVE SYSTEMS**
Also Called: Los Angeles Plant
6200 Gateway Dr, Cypress (90630-4842)
PHONE..................310 212-0200
**EMP:** 100
**SIC: 3621** 3714 Electric motor and generator parts; Motor vehicle parts and accessories
**HQ:** Hitachi Automotive Systems Americas, Inc.
955 Warwick Rd
Harrodsburg KY 40330
859 734-9451

**(P-11273)**
**INTEGRATED MAGNETICS INC**
11250 Playa Ct, Culver City (90230-6127)
PHONE..................310 391-7213
Anil Nanji, *Pr*
**EMP:** 40 **EST:** 2012
**SQ FT:** 120,000
**SALES (est):** 2.28MM
**SALES (corp-wide):** 46.01MM **Privately Held**
**Web:** www.intemag.com
**SIC: 3621** 3679 3764 Rotors, for motors; Cores, magnetic; Rocket motors, guided missiles
**PA:** Integrated Technologies Group, Inc.
11250 Playa Ct
310 391-7213

**(P-11274)**
**KOLLMORGEN CORPORATION**
33 S La Patera Ln, Santa Barbara (93117-3214)
PHONE..................805 696-1236
**EMP:** 79
**SALES (corp-wide):** 6.25B **Publicly Held**
**Web:** www.kollmorgen.com
**SIC: 3621** Servomotors, electric
**HQ:** Kollmorgen Corporation
203a W Rock Rd
Radford VA 24141
540 639-9045

**(P-11275)**
**LEOCH BATTERY CORPORATION (DH)**
20322 Valencia Cir, Lake Forest (92630-8158)
PHONE..................949 588-5853
Hui Peng, *Pr*
Lili Shi, *
◆ **EMP:** 100 **EST:** 2003
**SALES (est):** 47.56MM **Privately Held**
**Web:** www.leochamericas.com
**SIC: 3621** Storage battery chargers, motor and engine generator type
**HQ:** Leoch International Technology Limited
C/O Conyers Trust Company (Cayman) Limited
George Town GR CAYMAN KY1-1

**(P-11276)**
**LIN ENGINEERING INC**
16245 Vineyard Blvd, Morgan Hill (95037-7123)
PHONE..................408 919-0200
Ted T Lin, *Pr*
Cynthia Lin, *
Rouyu Loughry, *
▲ **EMP:** 125 **EST:** 1987
**SQ FT:** 16,000
**SALES (est):** 24.96MM
**SALES (corp-wide):** 293.57K **Privately Held**
**Web:** www.linengineering.com
**SIC: 3621** Motors, electric
**HQ:** Moons' International Trading (Shanghai) Co., Ltd.
Caohejing Hi-Tech Zone
Shanghai SH 20023

**(P-11277)**
**MAC M MC CULLY CORPORATION**
Also Called: Mac M McCully Co
5316 Kazuko Ct, Moorpark (93021-1790)
PHONE..................805 529-0661
Guy Mc Cully, *Pr*
**EMP:** 35 **EST:** 1979
**SALES (est):** 5.17MM
**SALES (corp-wide):** 23.52MM **Privately Held**
**Web:** www.windings.com
**SIC: 3621** Motors, electric
**PA:** Careen, Inc.
15 Somsen St
800 795-8533

**(P-11278)**
**MAGICALL INC**
4550 Calle Alto, Camarillo (93012-8509)
P.O. Box 3730 (93011-3730)
PHONE..................805 484-4300
Joel Wacknov, *CEO*
▲ **EMP:** 21 **EST:** 2004
**SALES (est):** 4.36MM **Privately Held**
**Web:** www.magicall.biz
**SIC: 3621** 3612 3677 3679 Motors and generators; Power transformers, electric; Electronic coils and transformers; Static power supply converters for electronic applications

**(P-11279)**
**NANTENERGY LLC**
2040 E Mariposa Ave, El Segundo (90245-5027)
PHONE..................310 905-4866
**EMP:** 75 **EST:** 2019
**SALES (est):** 2.12MM **Privately Held**
**SIC: 3621** 8731 Storage battery chargers, motor and engine generator type; Energy research

**(P-11280)**
**NATURENER USA LLC (HQ)**
435 Pacific Ave Fl 4, San Francisco (94133)
PHONE..................415 217-5500
**EMP:** 25 **EST:** 2007
**SALES (est):** 9.4MM **Privately Held**
**Web:** www.naturener.net
**SIC: 3621** Windmills, electric generating
**PA:** Grupo Naturener, Sa
Calle Nulez De Balboa 120

# PRODUCTS & SERVICES SECTION
## 3624 - Carbon And Graphite Products (P-11300)

**(P-11281)**
**OHMIO INC**
1900 Powell St Ste 700, Emeryville (94608-1811)
PHONE..................818 818-8268
Mohammed Hikmet, *CEO*
**EMP:** 15
**SALES (est):** 1.4MM **Privately Held**
**SIC:** 3621  Motors, electric

**(P-11282)**
**R K LARRABEE COMPANY INC**
Also Called: Construction Electrical Pdts
7800 Las Positas Rd, Livermore (94551-8240)
PHONE..................925 828-9420
Robert Larrabee, *Pr*
Nancy Larrabee, *VP*
◆ **EMP:** 65 **EST:** 1977
**SALES (est):** 18.66MM
**SALES (corp-wide):** 1.7B **Privately Held**
**Web:** www.cepnow.com
**SIC:** 3621 3699 3648 3646  Power generators; Electrical equipment and supplies, nec; Lighting equipment, nec; Commercial lighting fixtures
**PA:** Southwire Company, Llc
   One Southwire Dr
   770 832-4529

**(P-11283)**
**RESMED MOTOR TECHNOLOGIES INC**
Also Called: Resmed
9540 De Soto Ave, Chatsworth (91311-5010)
PHONE..................818 428-6400
David B Sears, *CEO*
▲ **EMP:** 170 **EST:** 2002
**SQ FT:** 35,000
**SALES (est):** 49.25MM **Publicly Held**
**SIC:** 3621 3714 3841  Coils, for electric motors or generators; Propane conversion equipment, motor vehicle; Surgical and medical instruments
**PA:** Resmed Inc.
   9001 Spectrum Center Blvd

**(P-11284)**
**REULAND ELECTRIC CO (PA)**
17969 Railroad St, City Of Industry (91748-1192)
P.O. Box 1464 (91749-1464)
PHONE..................626 964-6411
Noel C Reuland, *Pr*
William Kramer Iii, *VP*
▲ **EMP:** 130 **EST:** 1937
**SQ FT:** 100,000
**SALES (est):** 50.09MM
**SALES (corp-wide):** 50.09MM **Privately Held**
**Web:** www.reuland.com
**SIC:** 3621 3566 3363 3625  Motors, electric; Drives, high speed industrial, except hydrostatic; Aluminum die-castings; Electric controls and control accessories, industrial

**(P-11285)**
**SEA ELECTRIC LLC**
436 Alaska Ave, Torrance (90503-3902)
PHONE..................424 376-3660
**EMP:** 29
**SALES (est):** 10.75MM **Privately Held**
**Web:** www.sea-electric.com
**SIC:** 3621 3711  Motors and generators; Motor vehicles and car bodies

**(P-11286)**
**SIERRAMOTION INC**
3295 Swetzer Rd, Loomis (95650-9525)
PHONE..................916 259-1868
Robert Mastromattei, *CEO*
**EMP:** 15 **EST:** 2019
**SALES (est):** 2.57MM
**SALES (corp-wide):** 2.57MM **Privately Held**
**Web:** www.sierramotion.com
**SIC:** 3621  Electric motor and generator auxiliary parts
**PA:** Allient Inc.
   23 Inverness Way E # 150
   303 799-8520

**(P-11287)**
**SKURKA AEROSPACE INC (DH)**
4600 Calle Bolero, Camarillo (93012-8575)
P.O. Box 2869 (93011-2869)
PHONE..................805 484-8884
Michael Lisman, *CEO*
Lisa Sabol, *
Halle Terrion, *
**EMP:** 47 **EST:** 2004
**SQ FT:** 70,000
**SALES (est):** 40.15MM
**SALES (corp-wide):** 7.94B **Publicly Held**
**Web:** www.skurka-aero.com
**SIC:** 3621 3679  Motors, electric; Transducers, electrical
**HQ:** Transdigm, Inc.
   1350 Euclid Ave
   Cleveland OH 44115

**(P-11288)**
**SMI HOLDINGS INC**
Also Called: Specialty Motors
28420 Witherspoon Pkwy, Valencia (91355-4167)
PHONE..................800 232-2612
▲ **EMP:** 25
**SIC:** 3621  Motors, electric

**(P-11289)**
**STEM INC (PA)**
100 California St Ste 1400, San Francisco (94111-4519)
PHONE..................877 374-7836
David Buzby, *CEO*
Doran Hole, *Ex VP*
Mark Triplett, *COO*
Alan Russo, *CRO*
**EMP:** 33 **EST:** 2018
**SQ FT:** 23,500
**SALES (est):** 461.51MM
**SALES (corp-wide):** 461.51MM **Publicly Held**
**Web:** www.stem.com
**SIC:** 3621 7372  Storage battery chargers, motor and engine generator type; Prepackaged software

**(P-11290)**
**SURE POWER INC**
9255 Customhouse Plz, San Diego (92154-7636)
PHONE..................619 661-6292
**EMP:** 18
**Web:** www.eaton.com
**SIC:** 3621  Motors and generators
**HQ:** Sure Power, Inc.
   10955 Sw Avery St
   Tualatin OR 97062
   503 692-5360

**(P-11291)**
**THINGAP INC**
Also Called: Thingap
4035 Via Pescador, Camarillo (93012-5050)
PHONE..................805 477-9741
John Baumann, *CEO*
**EMP:** 33 **EST:** 2012
**SALES (est):** 4.51MM
**SALES (corp-wide):** 578.63MM **Publicly Held**
**Web:** www.thingap.com
**SIC:** 3621  Coils, for electric motors or generators
**PA:** Allient Inc.
   495 Commerce Dr Ste 3
   716 242-8634

**(P-11292)**
**TSDI AMERICA INC**
1065 E Hillsdale Blvd Ste 416, Foster City (94404-1613)
PHONE..................650 430-3776
Donglin Yang, *Pr*
**EMP:** 18 **EST:** 2010
**SALES (est):** 659.56K
**SALES (corp-wide):** 174.14B **Privately Held**
**SIC:** 3621  Railway motors and control equipment, electric
**HQ:** China Railway Design Corporation
   No.109, East 7 Road, (Airport Economic Zone), Tianjin Pilot Free
   Tianjin TJ 30030

**(P-11293)**
**TURNONGREEN INC**
1421 Mccarthy Blvd, Milpitas (95035-7433)
PHONE..................510 657-2635
Amos Kohn, *Ch Bd*
Marcus Charuvastra, *Pr*
David J Katzoff, *CFO*
**EMP:** 22 **EST:** 2005
**SQ FT:** 31,165
**SALES (est):** 4.2MM
**SALES (corp-wide):** 207.19MM **Publicly Held**
**Web:** www.turnongreen.com
**SIC:** 3621  Storage battery chargers, motor and engine generator type
**HQ:** Hyperscale Data, Inc.
   11411 Sthern Hghlnds Pkwy
   Las Vegas NV 89141
   949 444-5464

**(P-11294)**
**TURNTIDE TECHNOLOGIES INC (PA)**
1295 Forgewood Ave, Sunnyvale (94089-2216)
PHONE..................877 776-8470
Ryan Morris, *CEO*
Mark Johnston, *CEO*
Carl Burrow, *CRO*
**EMP:** 25 **EST:** 2013
**SALES (est):** 26.14MM
**SALES (corp-wide):** 26.14MM **Privately Held**
**Web:** www.turntide.com
**SIC:** 3621 7389  Motors, electric; Design services

**(P-11295)**
**VALLEY POWER SERVICES INC**
425 S Hacienda Blvd, City Of Industry (91745-1123)
PHONE..................909 969-9345
Clark Lee, *Pr*
▲ **EMP:** 64 **EST:** 1999
**SQ FT:** 17,802
**SALES (est):** 3.98MM **Privately Held**
**Web:** www.valleypowersystems.com
**SIC:** 3621  Motor housings

**(P-11296)**
**ZAPWORLDCOM**
300 Stony Point Rd Spc 249, Petaluma (94952-8113)
PHONE..................707 525-8658
▲ **EMP:** 435
**SIC:** 3621 3751  Motors, electric; Motorcycles, bicycles and parts

## 3624 Carbon And Graphite Products

**(P-11297)**
**ADVANCE CARBON PRODUCTS INC**
2036 National Ave, Hayward (94545-1712)
PHONE..................510 293-5930
Ronald D Crader, *Pr*
James Michael Crader, *
**EMP:** 40 **EST:** 1955
**SQ FT:** 20,000
**SALES (est):** 4.65MM **Privately Held**
**Web:** store.advancecarbon.com
**SIC:** 3624 3678 3643 3568  Brush blocks, carbon or molded graphite; Electronic connectors; Current-carrying wiring services; Power transmission equipment, nec

**(P-11298)**
**ALLIANCE SPACESYSTEMS LLC**
4398 Corporate Center Dr, Los Alamitos (90720-2537)
PHONE..................714 226-1400
Rick Byrens, *Pr*
**EMP:** 155 **EST:** 1997
**SQ FT:** 101,000
**SALES (est):** 21.5MM
**SALES (corp-wide):** 189.21MM **Privately Held**
**Web:** www.appliedcomposites.com
**SIC:** 3624  Carbon and graphite products
**PA:** Applied Composites Holdings, Llc
   25692 Atlantic Ocean Dr
   949 716-3511

**(P-11299)**
**KBR INC**
Also Called: Electro-Tech Machining Div
2000 W Gaylord St, Long Beach (90813-1032)
P.O. Box 92610 (14692-0610)
PHONE..................562 436-9281
Ryan Mcmahon, *Pr*
▲ **EMP:** 32 **EST:** 1977
**SQ FT:** 39,000
**SALES (est):** 4.87MM **Privately Held**
**Web:** www.etmgraphite.com
**SIC:** 3624  Carbon and graphite products

**(P-11300)**
**MITSUBSHI CHEM CRBN FIBR CMPST (DH)**
5900 88th St, Sacramento (95828-1109)
PHONE..................916 386-1733
Susumu Sasaki, *CEO*
Takeshi Sasaki, *
Masayoshi Ozeki, *General Vice President*
Donald Carter, *
▲ **EMP:** 125 **EST:** 1991
**SQ FT:** 60,000
**SALES (est):** 98.55MM **Privately Held**
**Web:** www.mccfc.com
**SIC:** 3624  Fibers, carbon and graphite
**HQ:** Mitsubishi Chemical Corporation
   1-1-1, Marunouchi
   Chiyoda-Ku TKY 100-8

## 3624 - Carbon And Graphite Products (P-11301)

**(P-11301)**
**SANGRAF INTERNATIONAL INC**
3171 Independence Dr, Livermore (94551-7595)
PHONE..................................216 800-9999
Jamie Hansen, *CEO*
Helen Hou, *CFO*
**EMP:** 23 **EST:** 2012
**SALES (est):** 2.8MM **Privately Held**
**Web:** www.sangrafintl.com
**SIC: 3624** Carbon and graphite products

**(P-11302)**
**TORAY PRFMCE MTLS CORP USA**
Also Called: Toray PMC
1150 Calle Suerte, Camarillo (93012-8051)
PHONE..................................805 402-6664
**EMP:** 18 **EST:** 2020
**SALES (est):** 5.97MM **Privately Held**
**Web:** www.toray.us
**SIC: 3624** Fibers, carbon and graphite

## 3625 Relays And Industrial Controls

**(P-11303)**
**A P SEEDORFF & COMPANY INC**
Also Called: Seedorff Acme
1338 N Knollwood Cir, Anaheim (92801-1311)
PHONE..................................714 252-5330
Kurt Simon, *Pr*
Helmut Simon, *Treas*
**EMP:** 15 **EST:** 1948
**SQ FT:** 10,000
**SALES (est):** 2.46MM **Privately Held**
**Web:** www.seedorffacme.com
**SIC: 3625** Resistance welder controls

**(P-11304)**
**ABSOLUTE GRAPHIC TECH USA INC**
Also Called: Agt
235 Jason Ct, Corona (92879-6199)
PHONE..................................909 597-1133
Steven J Barberi, *Pr*
**EMP:** 49 **EST:** 2006
**SQ FT:** 25,800
**SALES (est):** 9.17MM **Privately Held**
**Web:** www.agt-usa.com
**SIC: 3625** 3577 Industrial electrical relays and switches; Printers and plotters

**(P-11305)**
**AIRSPACE SYSTEMS INC**
1933 Davis St Ste 229, San Leandro (94577-1257)
P.O. Box 998 (94023-0998)
PHONE..................................415 226-7779
Jasminder Banga, *CEO*
Guy Bar-nahum, *VP*
Steve Schimmel, *
Rob Coneybeer, *
**EMP:** 30 **EST:** 2015
**SALES (est):** 3.29MM **Privately Held**
**Web:** www.airspace.co
**SIC: 3625** Control equipment, electric

**(P-11306)**
**AMES FIRE WATERWORKS**
Also Called: Ames
1485 Tanforan Ave, Woodland (95776-6108)
PHONE..................................530 666-2493
Nancy West, *CEO*
▲ **EMP:** 88 **EST:** 1910
**SQ FT:** 10,000
**SALES (est):** 10.54MM
**SALES (corp-wide):** 2.06B **Publicly Held**
**Web:** www.watts.com
**SIC: 3625** 3494 Relays and industrial controls; Valves and pipe fittings, nec
**PA:** Watts Water Technologies, Inc.
815 Chestnut St
978 688-1811

**(P-11307)**
**ANAHEIM AUTOMATION INC**
4985 E Landon Dr, Anaheim (92807-1972)
PHONE..................................714 992-6990
Joanne Dargan, *CEO*
Alan Harmon, *
Faithe Reimbold, *
Jhon Witt, *
◆ **EMP:** 42 **EST:** 1966
**SQ FT:** 9,000
**SALES (est):** 8.73MM **Privately Held**
**Web:** www.anaheimautomation.com
**SIC: 3625** 3545 3566 Control equipment, electric; Machine tool accessories; Speed changers, drives, and gears

**(P-11308)**
**ANIMATICS CORPORATION**
3200 Patrick Henry Dr Ste 110, Santa Clara (95054-1865)
PHONE..................................408 748-8721
▲ **EMP:** 36 **EST:** 1987
**SALES (est):** 2.63MM
**SALES (corp-wide):** 3.32B **Publicly Held**
**Web:** www.animatics.com
**SIC: 3625** Control equipment, electric
**PA:** Moog Inc.
400 Jamison Rd
716 652-2000

**(P-11309)**
**AP PARPRO INC**
2700 S Fairview St, Santa Ana (92704-5947)
PHONE..................................619 498-9004
Hsiu Pi Wu, *Pr*
Po Ju Shih, *Sec*
**EMP:** 47 **EST:** 2005
**SALES (est):** 5.64MM **Privately Held**
**Web:** www.parpro.com
**SIC: 3625** Relays and industrial controls

**(P-11310)**
**APPLIED CONTROL ELECTRONICS**
5480 Merchant Cir, Placerville (95667-8250)
PHONE..................................530 626-5181
Terry Burke, *Pr*
Natalie Burke, *CFO*
**EMP:** 22 **EST:** 1988
**SQ FT:** 10,000
**SALES (est):** 4.07MM **Privately Held**
**Web:** www.appconx.com
**SIC: 3625** 8711 Motor controls and accessories; Electrical or electronic engineering

**(P-11311)**
**BALBOA WATER GROUP LLC (HQ)**
Also Called: Controlmyspa
3030 Airway Ave Ste B, Costa Mesa (92626-6036)
PHONE..................................714 384-0384
Eric Kownacki, *CEO*
David J Cline, *
Jean-pierre Parent, *Sr VP*
◆ **EMP:** 66 **EST:** 2007
**SALES (est):** 100.57MM
**SALES (corp-wide):** 835.6MM **Publicly Held**
**Web:** www.balboawater.com
**SIC: 3625** 3599 Electric controls and control accessories, industrial; Machine shop, jobbing and repair
**PA:** Helios Technologies, Inc.
7456 16th St E
941 362-1200

**(P-11312)**
**CAL-COMP ELECTRONICS (USA) CO LTD**
Also Called: Ccsd
9877 Waples St, San Diego (92121-2922)
PHONE..................................858 587-6900
▲ **EMP:** 299
**SIC: 3625** Actuators, industrial

**(P-11313)**
**CONTROL SWITCHES INTL INC**
2425 Mira Mar Ave, Long Beach (90815-1757)
P.O. Box 92349 (90809-2349)
PHONE..................................562 498-7331
Margerate Turner, *Ex VP*
Peggy Turner, *
Judith Steward, *
Susan Moore, *
Jane Armstrong, *
**EMP:** 25 **EST:** 1977
**SQ FT:** 10,000
**SALES (est):** 3.49MM
**SALES (corp-wide):** 7.85MM **Privately Held**
**Web:** www.controlswitches.com
**SIC: 3625** Switches, electronic applications
**PA:** Control Switches, Inc.
2425 Mira Mar Ave
562 498-7331

**(P-11314)**
**CRYDOM INC (DH)**
2320 Paseo De Las Americas Ste 201, San Diego (92154-7273)
PHONE..................................619 210-1590
Bob Ciurczak, *Pr*
▲ **EMP:** 47 **EST:** 2005
**SQ FT:** 20,000
**SALES (est):** 41.7MM
**SALES (corp-wide):** 4.05B **Privately Held**
**Web:** www.sensata.com
**SIC: 3625** 5065 3674 3643 Control equipment, electric; Electronic parts and equipment, nec; Semiconductors and related devices; Current-carrying wiring services
**HQ:** Sensata Technologies, Inc.
529 Pleasant St
Attleboro MA 02703

**(P-11315)**
**CTI-CONTROLTECH INC**
Also Called: Cti-Controltech
22 Beta Ct, San Ramon (94583-1202)
PHONE..................................925 208-4250
George P Constas, *Pr*
**EMP:** 15 **EST:** 1976
**SQ FT:** 5,000
**SALES (est):** 2.93MM **Privately Held**
**Web:** www.cti-ct.com
**SIC: 3625** 5084 Relays and industrial controls; Controlling instruments and accessories

**(P-11316)**
**CURTISS-WRGHT CNTRLS ELCTRNIC (DH)**
Also Called: Curtiss-Wrght Cntrls Elctrnic
28965 Avenue Penn, Santa Clarita (91355-4185)
PHONE..................................661 257-4430
Thomas P Quinly, *CEO*
David Dietz, *
**EMP:** 172 **EST:** 1985
**SQ FT:** 18,700
**SALES (est):** 38.8MM
**SALES (corp-wide):** 2.85B **Publicly Held**
**Web:** www.curtisswright.com
**SIC: 3625** 8731 8711 3769 Relays and industrial controls; Commercial physical research; Consulting engineer; Space vehicle equipment, nec
**HQ:** Curtiss-Wright Controls, Inc.
15801 Brixham Hill Ave # 200
Charlotte NC 28277
704 869-4600

**(P-11317)**
**CUSTOM CONTROL SENSORS INC**
21111 Plummer St, Chatsworth (91311-4905)
P.O. Box 3535 (91313-3535)
PHONE..................................818 341-4610
**EMP:** 17 **EST:** 2015
**SALES (est):** 3.52MM **Privately Held**
**Web:** www.ccsdualsnap.com
**SIC: 3625** Relays and industrial controls

**(P-11318)**
**DOW-KEY MICROWAVE CORPORATION**
Also Called: Dow-Key Microwave
4822 Mcgrath St, Ventura (93003-7718)
PHONE..................................805 650-0260
David Wightman, *Pr*
**EMP:** 150 **EST:** 1970
**SQ FT:** 26,000
**SALES (est):** 20.31MM
**SALES (corp-wide):** 8.44B **Publicly Held**
**Web:** www.mpgdover.com
**SIC: 3625** 3678 3643 3613 Switches, electronic applications; Electronic connectors; Current-carrying wiring services; Switchgear and switchboard apparatus
**PA:** Dover Corporation
3005 Highland Pkwy
630 541-1540

**(P-11319)**
**EAGLE ACCESS CTRL SYSTEMS INC**
12953 Foothill Blvd, Sylmar (91342-4929)
PHONE..................................818 837-7900
Yossi Afriat, *CEO*
Avi Afriat, *VP Opers*
Oren Afriat, *CFO*
◆ **EMP:** 22 **EST:** 1996
**SQ FT:** 13,000
**SALES (est):** 5.03MM **Privately Held**
**Web:** www.eagleoperators.com
**SIC: 3625** Control equipment, electric

**(P-11320)**
**EATON ELECTRICAL INC**
13201 Dahlia St, Fontana (92337-6971)
PHONE..................................951 685-5788
**EMP:** 154
**SIC: 3625** Motor controls and accessories
**HQ:** Eaton Electrical Inc.
1000 Cherrington Pkwy
Moon Township PA 15108

**(P-11321)**
**ELEVATOR CONTROLS COMPANY LLC**
6150 Warehouse Way, Sacramento (95826-4908)
PHONE..................................916 428-1708
**EMP:** 72 **EST:** 1986

## PRODUCTS & SERVICES SECTION
## 3625 - Relays And Industrial Controls (P-11339)

**SALES (est):** 21.6MM
**SALES (corp-wide):** 1.42B **Privately Held**
Web: www.elevatorcontrols.com
**SIC: 3625** 3534 Relays and industrial controls; Elevators and moving stairways
HQ: G.A.L. Manufacturing Company, Llc
50 E 153rd St
Bronx NY 10451
718 292-9000

### (P-11322)
### EMBEDDED SYSTEMS INC
Also Called: Esi Motion
2250a Union Pl, Simi Valley (93065-1660)
**PHONE**.................................805 624-6030
Earnie Beem, *Pr*
Sheila D'angelo, *VP*
**EMP:** 40 **EST:** 2005
**SALES (est):** 8.24MM **Privately Held**
Web: www.esimotion.com
**SIC: 3625** Motor starters and controllers, electric

### (P-11323)
### GENERAL DYNAMICS MISSION
General Dynamics Global
7603 Saint Andrews Ave Ste H, San Diego (92154-8216)
**PHONE**.................................619 671-5400
Bud Jenkins, *Ofcr*
**EMP:** 107
**SALES (corp-wide):** 42.27B **Publicly Held**
Web: www.gdmissionsystems.com
**SIC: 3625** 3824 3825 3621 Relays and industrial controls; Fluid meters and counting devices; Instruments to measure electricity; Motors and generators
HQ: General Dynamics Mission Systems, Inc.
12450 Fair Lakes Cir
Fairfax VA 22033
877 449-0600

### (P-11324)
### H2W TECHNOLOGIES INC
26380 Ferry Ct, Santa Clarita (91350)
**PHONE**.................................661 291-1620
Mark Philip Wilson, *CEO*
Alexander Hinds, *Ex VP*
**EMP:** 16 **EST:** 2000
**SQ FT:** 12,000
**SALES (est):** 2.4MM **Privately Held**
Web: www.h2wtech.com
**SIC: 3625** Relays and industrial controls

### (P-11325)
### HONGFA AMERICA INC
Also Called: Xiamen Hongfa Electroacoustic
20381 Hermana Cir, Lake Forest (92630-8701)
**PHONE**.................................714 669-2888
Guo Manjin, *CEO*
▲ **EMP:** 22 **EST:** 2015
**SALES (est):** 8.69MM **Privately Held**
Web: www.hongfa.com
**SIC: 3625** 6719 Electric controls and control accessories, industrial; Investment holding companies, except banks
HQ: Xiamen Hongfa Electroacoustic Co., Ltd.
No.91-101, Sunban South Road, Beibu Industrial Zone, Jimei
Xiamen FJ 36102

### (P-11326)
### ITT CANNON LLC
Also Called: BIW Connector Systems
56 Technology Dr, Irvine (92618-2301)
**PHONE**.................................714 557-4700
Farrokh Batliwala, *Prin*

Farrokh Batliwala, *Pr*
Mary Beth Gustafsson, *
Philip Bordages, *
John Capela, *CAO**
**EMP:** 132 **EST:** 2011
**SALES (est):** 28.52MM
**SALES (corp-wide):** 3.28B **Publicly Held**
Web: www.ittcannon.com
**SIC: 3625** Control equipment, electric
HQ: Itt Industries Holdings, Inc
100 Wshington Blvd Fl 6 Flr 6
Stamford CT 06902
914 641-2000

### (P-11327)
### ITT LLC
ITT Goulds Pumps
3951 Capitol Ave, City Of Industry (90601-1734)
P.O. Box 1254 (91749-1254)
**PHONE**.................................562 908-4144
Shashank Patel, *Genl Mgr*
**EMP:** 75
**SQ FT:** 85,000
**SALES (corp-wide):** 3.28B **Publicly Held**
Web: www.itt.com
**SIC: 3625** Control equipment, electric
HQ: Itt Llc
1133 Westchester Ave
White Plains NY 10604
914 641-2000

### (P-11328)
### ITT LLC
ITT BIW Connector Systems
500 Tesconi Cir, Santa Rosa (95401-4665)
**PHONE**.................................707 523-2300
Robert Roeser, *Brnch Mgr*
**EMP:** 109
**SQ FT:** 35,000
**SALES (corp-wide):** 3.28B **Publicly Held**
Web: www.itt.com
**SIC: 3625** Control equipment, electric
HQ: Itt Llc
1133 Westchester Ave
White Plains NY 10604
914 641-2000

### (P-11329)
### KAPSCH TRAFFICCOM USA INC
4256 Hacienda Dr Ste 100, Pleasanton (94588-8595)
**PHONE**.................................925 225-1600
David Dimlich, *Pr*
**EMP:** 110
**SALES (corp-wide):** 593.49MM **Privately Held**
Web: www.kapsch.net
**SIC: 3625** Industrial electrical relays and switches
HQ: Kapsch Trafficcom Usa, Inc.
2855 Premiere Pkwy Ste F
Duluth GA 30097
678 473-6400

### (P-11330)
### KENSINGTON LABORATORIES LLC (PA)
6200 Village Pkwy, Dublin (94568-3004)
**PHONE**.................................510 324-0126
Raj Kaul, *Managing Member*
**EMP:** 17 **EST:** 1972
**SQ FT:** 72,000
**SALES (est):** 8.77MM
**SALES (corp-wide):** 8.77MM **Privately Held**
Web: www.kensingtonlabs.com

**SIC: 3625** 3825 3674 Positioning controls, electric; Measuring instruments and meters, electric; Semiconductors and related devices

### (P-11331)
### LUMENS
Also Called: LUMENS
1906 L St, Sacramento (95811-4002)
**PHONE**.................................916 231-1952
Ken Plumlee, *Brnch Mgr*
**EMP:** 26
**SALES (corp-wide):** 2.67MM **Privately Held**
Web: www.lumens.com
**SIC: 3625** Switches, electronic applications
HQ: Lumens Llc
2020 L St Ste Ll10
Sacramento CA 95811
916 444-5885

### (P-11332)
### M W SAUSSE & CO INC (PA)
Also Called: Vibrex
28744 Witherspoon Pkwy, Valencia (91355-5425)
**PHONE**.................................661 257-3311
Torbjorn Helland, *Pr*
Dan Robinson, *
Paul Azevedo, *
Gregory Hall, *
▲ **EMP:** 59 **EST:** 1961
**SQ FT:** 12,000
**SALES (est):** 9.82MM
**SALES (corp-wide):** 9.82MM **Privately Held**
Web: www.vibrex.net
**SIC: 3625** Control equipment, electric

### (P-11333)
### MICROSEMI CORP-POWER MGT GROUP
11861 Western Ave, Garden Grove (92841-2119)
**PHONE**.................................714 994-6500
James J Peterson, *Pr*
John W Hohener, *
David Goren, *
Rob Warren, *General Vice President**
**EMP:** 249 **EST:** 1977
**SQ FT:** 135,000
**SALES (est):** 3.89MM
**SALES (corp-wide):** 7.63B **Publicly Held**
Web: www.microsemi.com
**SIC: 3625** 3677 3679 3613 Relays, for electronic use; Electronic transformers; Liquid crystal displays (LCD); Switchgear and switchboard apparatus
HQ: Microsemi Corp.-Power Management Group Holding
11861 Western Ave
Garden Grove CA 92841
714 994-6500

### (P-11334)
### MICROSEMI FREQUENCY TIME CORP (DH)
3870 N 1st St, San Jose (95134-1702)
**PHONE**.................................480 792-7200
Ganesh Moorthy, *Pr*
Steve Sanghi, *
J Eric Bjornholt, *
▲ **EMP:** 170 **EST:** 2001
**SALES (est):** 101.08MM
**SALES (corp-wide):** 7.63B **Publicly Held**
Web: www.microsemi.com
**SIC: 3625** 7372 Timing devices, electronic; Business oriented computer software
HQ: Microsemi Corporation
11861 Western Ave

Garden Grove CA 92841
949 380-6100

### (P-11335)
### MOOG INC
Also Called: Moog Jon Street Warehouse
1218 W Jon St, Torrance (90502-1208)
**PHONE**.................................310 533-1178
Alberto Bilalon, *Mgr*
**EMP:** 500
**SALES (corp-wide):** 3.32B **Publicly Held**
Web: www.moog.com
**SIC: 3625** 8711 3812 Relays and industrial controls; Aviation and/or aeronautical engineering; Aircraft/aerospace flight instruments and guidance systems
PA: Moog Inc.
400 Jamison Rd
716 652-2000

### (P-11336)
### NEXTINPUT INC (HQ)
980 Linda Vista Ave, Mountain View (94043-1903)
**PHONE**.................................408 770-9293
Ali Foughi, *CEO*
Philip Thach, *VP*
**EMP:** 41 **EST:** 2012
**SALES (est):** 9.33MM
**SALES (corp-wide):** 3.77B **Publicly Held**
Web: www.nextinput.com
**SIC: 3625** Switches, electronic applications
PA: Qorvo, Inc.
7628 Thorndike Rd
336 664-1233

### (P-11337)
### NOVATE SOLUTIONS INC
4781 Pell Dr, Sacramento (95838-2047)
**PHONE**.................................916 641-2725
Carlos W Rogers, *Prin*
**EMP:** 19
**SALES (corp-wide):** 6.4MM **Privately Held**
Web: www.novate.com
**SIC: 3625** Control equipment, electric
PA: Novate Solutions, Inc.
2101 Stone Blvd Ste 210
866 668-2830

### (P-11338)
### PARKER-HANNIFIN CORPORATION
Compumotor
5500 Business Park Dr, Rohnert Park (94928-7904)
**PHONE**.................................707 584-7558
Kenneth Sweet, *Mgr*
**EMP:** 132
**SQ FT:** 32,000
**SALES (corp-wide):** 19.93B **Publicly Held**
Web: www.parker.com
**SIC: 3625** 3823 Motor controls, electric; Process control instruments
PA: Parker-Hannifin Corporation
6035 Parkland Blvd
216 896-3000

### (P-11339)
### PECO INSPX
1616 Culpepper Ave Ste A, Modesto (95351-1220)
**PHONE**.................................209 576-3345
Jeff Souza, *Mgr*
**EMP:** 17
**SALES (corp-wide):** 11.66MM **Privately Held**
Web: www.peco-inspx.com
**SIC: 3625** Relays and industrial controls
PA: Peco Inspx
1835 Rollins Rd

## 3625 - Relays And Industrial Controls (P-11340)

209 576-3345

**(P-11340)**
**PIVOTAL SYSTEMS CORPORATION**
Also Called: Pivotal Systems
48389 Fremont Blvd Ste 100, Fremont (94538)
PHONE...................510 770-9125
John Hoffman, *CEO*
**EMP:** 20 **EST:** 2003
**SQ FT:** 1,000
**SALES (est):** 6.73MM **Privately Held**
Web: www.pivotalsys.com
**SIC: 3625** Control equipment, electric

**(P-11341)**
**Q COM INC**
17782 Cowan, Irvine (92614-6030)
PHONE...................949 833-1000
Robert Elders, *CEO*
Frederick P Kaiser, *
**EMP:** 26 **EST:** 1980
**SALES (est):** 576.95K **Privately Held**
**SIC: 3625** 3822 3564 Control equipment, electric; Environmental controls; Blowers and fans

**(P-11342)**
**RACEAMERICA INC**
62 Bonaventura Dr, San Jose (95134-2123)
PHONE...................408 988-6188
Dennis Laczny, *Owner*
**EMP:** 16 **EST:** 2016
**SALES (est):** 2.78MM **Privately Held**
Web: www.raceamerica.com
**SIC: 3625** Relays and industrial controls

**(P-11343)**
**RCD ENGINEERING INC**
17100 Salmon Mine Rd, Nevada City (95959-9350)
P.O. Box 119 (95960-0119)
PHONE...................530 292-3133
Steve Leach, *CEO*
Pat Leach, *Sec*
**EMP:** 24 **EST:** 1967
**SQ FT:** 12,000
**SALES (est):** 2.43MM **Privately Held**
Web: www.rcdengineering.com
**SIC: 3625** 3714 Motor controls and accessories; Motor vehicle parts and accessories

**(P-11344)**
**RIGHT HAND MANUFACTURING INC**
180 Otay Lakes Rd Ste 205, Bonita (91902-2444)
PHONE...................619 819-5056
▲ **EMP:** 150 **EST:** 2003
**SALES (est):** 10.01MM **Privately Held**
Web: www.righthandmanufacturing.com
**SIC: 3625** Control circuit devices, magnet and solid state

**(P-11345)**
**ROSEMOUNT ANALYTICAL INC**
2400 Barranca Pkwy, Irvine (92606-5018)
Rural Route 22737 (60673-0001)
PHONE...................713 396-8880
◆ **EMP:** 1100
**SIC: 3625** 3825 3823 3564 Relays and industrial controls; Instruments to measure electricity; Process control instruments; Blowers and fans

**(P-11346)**
**S R C DEVICES INCCUSTOMER**
6295 Ferris Sq Ste D, San Diego (92121-3248)
PHONE...................866 772-8668
Richard W Carlyle, *Pr*
Mark Mccabe, *Sr VP*
**EMP:** 303 **EST:** 2001
**SQ FT:** 2,000
**SALES (est):** 2.76MM **Privately Held**
**SIC: 3625** 3643 5065 Switches, electronic applications; Current-carrying wiring services; Electronic parts and equipment, nec

**(P-11347)**
**SILICON MICROSTRUCTURES INC**
1701 Mccarthy Blvd, Milpitas (95035-7416)
PHONE...................408 473-9700
Frank D Guidone, *Pr*
▲ **EMP:** 76 **EST:** 1991
**SQ FT:** 34,000
**SALES (est):** 8.64MM
**SALES (corp-wide):** 400.61MM **Privately Held**
Web: www.te.com
**SIC: 3625** 3823 Relays and industrial controls; Process control instruments
**PA:** Measurement Specialties, Inc.
1000 Lucas Way
757 766-1500

**(P-11348)**
**SILVERON INDUSTRIES INC**
182 S Brent Cir, City Of Industry (91789-3050)
PHONE...................909 598-4533
Steve Lee, *Pr*
▲ **EMP:** 16 **EST:** 1977
**SQ FT:** 24,000
**SALES (est):** 5.9MM **Privately Held**
**SIC: 3625** 5065 Industrial controls: push button, selector switches, pilot; Electronic parts

**(P-11349)**
**SOUNDCOAT COMPANY INC**
16901 Armstrong Ave, Irvine (92606-4914)
PHONE...................631 242-2200
Clay Simpson, *Brnch Mgr*
**EMP:** 69
**SALES (corp-wide):** 130.22MM **Privately Held**
Web: www.soundcoat.com
**SIC: 3625** 3086 3296 Noise control equipment; Plastics foam products; Mineral wool
**HQ:** The Soundcoat Company, Inc.
1 Burt Dr
Deer Park NY 11729
631 242-2200

**(P-11350)**
**SURFACE TECHNOLOGIES CORP**
3170 Commercial St, San Diego (92113-1427)
PHONE...................619 564-8320
Bernard Meartz, *Mgr*
**EMP:** 31
**SQ FT:** 29,617
**SALES (corp-wide):** 24.92MM **Privately Held**
Web: www.surfacetechnologiescorp.com
**SIC: 3625** Marine and navy auxiliary controls
**PA:** Surface Technologies Corporation
2440 Mayport Rd Ste 7
904 241-1501

**(P-11351)**
**SYSTEMS MCHS ATMTN CMPNNTS COR (PA)**
Also Called: Smac
5807 Van Allen Way, Carlsbad (92008-7309)
PHONE...................760 929-7575
Ed Neff, *CEO*
Robert Berry, *
▲ **EMP:** 165 **EST:** 1990
**SALES (est):** 35.4MM **Privately Held**
Web: www.smac-mca.com
**SIC: 3625** 2822 3549 Actuators, industrial; Synthetic rubber; Assembly machines, including robotic

**(P-11352)**
**TE CONNECTIVITY CORPORATION**
Also Called: Kilovac
550 Linden Ave, Carpinteria (93013-2038)
PHONE...................805 684-4560
Mike Moschitto, *Brnch Mgr*
**EMP:** 30
**SALES (corp-wide):** 9.17B **Privately Held**
Web: www.te.com
**SIC: 3625** Relays, for electronic use
**HQ:** Te Connectivity Corporation
1050 Westlakes Dr
Berwyn PA 19312
610 893-9800

**(P-11353)**
**TEAL ELECTRONICS CORPORATION (PA)**
10350 Sorrento Valley Rd, San Diego (92121-1642)
PHONE...................858 558-9000
Glen Kassan, *Ch Bd*
Donald Klein, *CEO*
William Bickel, *VP Fin*
David Nuzzo, *Treas*
◆ **EMP:** 79 **EST:** 1983
**SQ FT:** 36,059
**SALES (est):** 6.42MM
**SALES (corp-wide):** 6.42MM **Privately Held**
**SIC: 3625** 2631 3612 Noise control equipment; Transformer board; Transformers, except electric

**(P-11354)**
**UNIVERSAL CTRL SOLUTIONS CORP**
Also Called: Dnf Controls
19770 Bahama St, Northridge (91324-3303)
PHONE...................818 898-3380
Daniel Fogel, *CEO*
▲ **EMP:** 15 **EST:** 1990
**SALES (est):** 2.97MM
**SALES (corp-wide):** 10.27MM **Privately Held**
Web: www.tslproducts.com
**SIC: 3625** Control equipment, electric
**HQ:** Tsl Professional Products Ltd.
Unit 1
Marlow BUCKS SL7 1
162 856-4610

**(P-11355)**
**WOODWARD HRT INC (HQ)**
25200 Rye Canyon Rd, Santa Clarita (91355-1204)
PHONE...................661 294-6000
Charles Blankenship, *CEO*
Tom Cromwell, *COO*
Bill Lacey, *CFO*
▲ **EMP:** 650 **EST:** 1954
**SQ FT:** 200,000
**SALES (est):** 80.49MM
**SALES (corp-wide):** 2.91B **Publicly Held**
**SIC: 3625** 3492 Actuators, industrial; Electrohydraulic servo valves, metal
**PA:** Woodward, Inc.
1081 Woodward Way
970 482-5811

**(P-11356)**
**ZBE INC**
1035 Cindy Ln, Carpinteria (93013-2905)
PHONE...................805 576-1600
Zac Bogart, *Pr*
▲ **EMP:** 45 **EST:** 1980
**SQ FT:** 7,500
**SALES (est):** 3.76MM **Privately Held**
Web: www.zbe.com
**SIC: 3625** 3861 3577 Electric controls and control accessories, industrial; Photographic equipment and supplies; Computer peripheral equipment, nec

**(P-11357)**
**ZMP AQUISITION CORPORATION**
Also Called: Adams Rite Aerospace
4141 N Palm St, Fullerton (92835-1025)
PHONE...................714 278-6500
Charles Collins, *Pr*
**EMP:** 16 **EST:** 1986
**SQ FT:** 100,000
**SALES (est):** 308.78K **Privately Held**
Web: www.adamsriteaerospace.org
**SIC: 3625** 3743 3728 3429 Electric controls and control accessories, industrial; Railroad locomotives and parts, electric or nonelectric; Aircraft parts and equipment, nec; Aircraft hardware

## 3629 Electrical Industrial Apparatus

**(P-11358)**
**ADVANCED CHARGING TECH LLC**
Also Called: A C T
17260 Newhope St, Fountain Valley (92708)
PHONE...................877 228-5922
Robert J Istwan, *Pr*
Chris Oltman, *Coordtr*
Anthony Capalino, *Sec*
▲ **EMP:** 21 **EST:** 2008
**SALES (est):** 7.54MM **Privately Held**
Web: www.act-chargers.com
**SIC: 3629** 3691 Battery chargers, rectifying or nonrotating; Alkaline cell storage batteries

**(P-11359)**
**APOLLO MANUFACTURING SERVICES**
10360 Sorrento Valley Rd Ste A, San Diego (92121-1600)
PHONE...................858 271-8009
Jenny Truong, *Pr*
**EMP:** 15 **EST:** 2007
**SQ FT:** 5,000
**SALES (est):** 2.72MM **Privately Held**
**SIC: 3629** 8742 Battery chargers, rectifying or nonrotating; Manufacturing management consultant

**(P-11360)**
**ARECONT VISION LLC**
425 E Colorado St Fl 7, Glendale (91205)
PHONE...................818 937-0700
◆ **EMP:** 103

## 3629 - Electrical Industrial Apparatus (P-11381)

SIC: 3629 Electronic generation equipment

**(P-11361)**
**AVEOX INC**
2265 Ward Ave Ste A, Simi Valley (93065-1864)
PHONE .................................. 805 915-0200
David Palombo, Pr
▲ EMP: 35 EST: 1992
SQ FT: 22,000
SALES (est): 9.27MM Privately Held
Web: www.aveox.com
SIC: 3629 Electronic generation equipment

**(P-11362)**
**CAPAX TECHNOLOGIES INC**
24842 Avenue Tibbitts, Valencia (91355-3404)
PHONE .................................. 661 257-7666
Jagdish Patel, Pr
Nina Patel, *
EMP: 28 EST: 1988
SQ FT: 17,000
SALES (est): 2.63MM Privately Held
Web: www.capaxtechnologies.com
SIC: 3629 3675 Capacitors, fixed or variable; Electronic capacitors

**(P-11363)**
**CHARGEPOINT INC (HQ)**
240 E Hacienda Ave, Campbell (95008-6617)
PHONE .................................. 408 841-4500
Colleen Jansen, CMO
Rex Jackson, *
Michael Hughes Ccro, Prin
◆ EMP: 120 EST: 2007
SQ FT: 120,000
SALES (est): 476.84MM
SALES (corp-wide): 506.64MM Publicly Held
Web: www.chargepoint.com
SIC: 3629 Battery chargers, rectifying or nonrotating
PA: Chargepoint Holdings, Inc.
240 E Hacienda Ave
408 841-4500

**(P-11364)**
**CLEAREDGE POWER INC**
920 Thompson Pl 100, Sunnyvale (94085-4628)
PHONE .................................. 877 257-3343
▲ EMP: 180
SIC: 3629 Electrochemical generators (fuel cells)

**(P-11365)**
**COMPOSITE TECHNOLOGY CORP**
2026 Mcgaw Ave, Irvine (92614-0911)
PHONE .................................. 949 428-8500
Benton H Wilcoxon, Ch Bd
◆ EMP: 104 EST: 2001
SALES (est): 3.24MM Privately Held
SIC: 3629 8711 Mercury arc rectifiers (electrical apparatus); Engineering services

**(P-11366)**
**CONCURRENT HOLDINGS LLC**
11150 Santa Monica Blvd Ste 825, Los Angeles (90025-3314)
PHONE .................................. 310 473-3065
Benjamin Teno, Managing Member
▲ EMP: 750 EST: 2012
SALES (est): 2.32MM
SALES (corp-wide): 406.38MM Privately Held

SIC: 3629 3679 Electronic generation equipment; Harness assemblies, for electronic use: wire or cable
PA: Balmoral Funds Llc
11150 Snta Mnica Blvd Ste
310 473-3065

**(P-11367)**
**COOPER BUSSMANN LLC**
Also Called: Cooper Bussmann-Automotive
5735 W Las Positas Blvd Ste 100, Pleasanton (94588-4002)
PHONE .................................. 925 924-8500
Hundi Kamath, Mgr
EMP: 161
SIC: 3629 5065 Capacitors and condensers; Capacitors, electronic
HQ: Cooper Bussmann, Llc
114 Old State Rd
Ellisville MO 63021
636 394-2877

**(P-11368)**
**CURRENT WAYS INC**
10221 Buena Vista Ave, Santee (92071-4484)
PHONE .................................. 619 596-3984
James Gevarges, Pr
Forest Tracko, CFO
Craig Miller, Sec
EMP: 15 EST: 2010
SQ FT: 26,000
SALES (est): 3.91MM Privately Held
Web: www.currentways.com
SIC: 3629 Battery chargers, rectifying or nonrotating

**(P-11369)**
**DESCO INDUSTRIES INC (PA)**
Also Called: Desco
3651 Walnut Ave, Chino (91710-2904)
PHONE .................................. 909 627-8178
◆ EMP: 75 EST: 1965
SALES (est): 48.53MM
SALES (corp-wide): 48.53MM Privately Held
Web: www.descoindustries.com
SIC: 3629 Static elimination equipment, industrial

**(P-11370)**
**ENGINEERED MAGNETICS INC**
Also Called: Aap Division
10524 S La Cienega Blvd, Inglewood (90304-1116)
PHONE .................................. 310 649-9000
Josh Shachar, Ch Bd
Kathy Tran, *
Maya Vu, *
Isabella Yi Sha Li, Dir
EMP: 26 EST: 2000
SQ FT: 57,000
SALES (est): 4.43MM Privately Held
Web: www.engineeredmagnetics.net
SIC: 3629 3812 3369 Power conversion units, a.c. to d.c.: static-electric; Missile guidance systems and equipment; Aerospace castings, nonferrous: except aluminum

**(P-11371)**
**EPC POWER CORP (PA)**
13250 Gregg St Ste A2, Poway (92064-7164)
PHONE .................................. 858 748-5590
Devin Dilley, CEO
Mary Loomas, CFO
Allan Abela, COO
▼ EMP: 113 EST: 2010
SQ FT: 10,000

SALES (est): 38.82MM Privately Held
Web: www.epcpower.com
SIC: 3629 Battery chargers, rectifying or nonrotating

**(P-11372)**
**EVOQUA WATER TECHNOLOGIES LLC**
Also Called: Pacific Ozone Technology, Inc.
6160 Egret Ct, Benicia (94510-1269)
PHONE .................................. 707 747-9600
EMP: 21 EST: 1996
SALES (est): 2.15MM Publicly Held
Web: www.evoqua.com
SIC: 3629 3559 Electronic generation equipment; Ozone machines
HQ: Benson Neptune Inc
334 Knight St Unit 3100
Warwick RI 02886
401 821-7140

**(P-11373)**
**IAMPLUS LLC**
809 N Cahuenga Blvd, Los Angeles (90038-3703)
PHONE .................................. 323 210-3852
Phil Molyneux, Pr
Chandrasekar Rathakrishnan, Dir
Rosemary Peschken, CFO
EMP: 56 EST: 2012
SQ FT: 3,900
SALES (est): 6.28MM
SALES (corp-wide): 9.1MM Privately Held
Web: www.iamplus.com
SIC: 3629 Electronic generation equipment
PA: I.Am.Plus Electronics, Inc.
809 N Cahuenga Blvd
323 210-3852

**(P-11374)**
**INTELLIGENT TECHNOLOGIES LLC**
Also Called: Itech
9454 Waples St, San Diego (92121-2919)
PHONE .................................. 858 458-1500
Rod Bolton, Pr
Frank Cooper, *
▲ EMP: 125 EST: 1997
SQ FT: 17,846
SALES (est): 23.49MM
SALES (corp-wide): 86.13MM Privately Held
Web: www.itecheng.com
SIC: 3629 3356 Battery chargers, rectifying or nonrotating; Battery metal
PA: Universal Power Group, Inc.
120 Dividend Dr Ste 100
469 892-1122

**(P-11375)**
**INTERCONNECT SOLUTIONS CO LLC (PA)**
17595 Mount Herrmann St, Fountain Valley (92708-4160)
PHONE .................................. 714 556-7007
Nick Kendall-jones, CEO
▲ EMP: 70 EST: 2018
SQ FT: 15,000
SALES (est): 49.73MM
SALES (corp-wide): 49.73MM Privately Held
Web: www.interconnectsolutions.com
SIC: 3629 Electronic generation equipment

**(P-11376)**
**MAXWELL TECHNOLOGIES INC**
3912 Calle Fortunata, San Diego (92123-1827)
PHONE .................................. 858 503-3493

EMP: 71
SALES (corp-wide): 96.77B Publicly Held
Web: www.maxwell.com
SIC: 3629 Capacitors and condensers
HQ: Maxwell Technologies, Inc.
3888 Calle Fortunada
San Diego CA 92123
858 503-3300

**(P-11377)**
**PHOENIX MOTOR INC**
140 Blue Ravine Rd, Folsom (95630-4703)
PHONE .................................. 909 987-0815
EMP: 29
Web: www.spigroups.com
SIC: 3629 Electrochemical generators (fuel cells)
HQ: Phoenix Motor Inc.
1500 Lakeview Loop
Anaheim CA 92807
909 987-0815

**(P-11378)**
**Q C M INC**
Also Called: Veris Manufacturing
285 Gemini Ave, Brea (92821-3704)
PHONE .................................. 714 414-1173
Jay Cadler, CEO
Larry Ching, *
▲ EMP: 45 EST: 2006
SALES (est): 27.29MM
SALES (corp-wide): 144.18MM Privately Held
Web: www.emeraldems.com
SIC: 3629 Electronic generation equipment
PA: Megatronics Us Ultimate Holdco Llc
2243 Lundy Ave
888 706-0230

**(P-11379)**
**SCHNEIDER ELECTRIC SOLAR INVERTERS USA INC**
Also Called: Schneder Elc Slar Invrters USA
250 S Vasco Rd, Livermore (94551-9060)
PHONE .................................. 925 245-1935
◆ EMP: 500 EST: 1985
SALES (est): 3.19MM
SALES (corp-wide): 82.05K Privately Held
Web: www.se-solar-docs.com
SIC: 3629 Inverters, nonrotating: electrical
PA: Schneider Electric Se
35 Rue Joseph Monier
146046982

**(P-11380)**
**SCIENTFIC APPLCTONS RES ASSOC (PA)**
Also Called: Sara
6300 Gateway Dr, Cypress (90630-4844)
PHONE .................................. 714 224-4410
Parviz Parhami, CEO
James Wes, *
Wes Addington, *
Amy Dockenhorf, *
EMP: 58 EST: 1989
SQ FT: 43,000
SALES (est): 41.76MM Privately Held
Web: www.sara.com
SIC: 3629 Electronic generation equipment

**(P-11381)**
**SCOTT MFG SOLUTIONS INC**
Also Called: Scott Manufacturing Solutions
5051 Edison Ave, Chino (91710-5716)
PHONE .................................. 909 594-9637
Luis Ernesto Lujan, CEO
Deborah N Davis, *
Jason J Huitrado, *
▲ EMP: 120 EST: 1967
SQ FT: 102,660

## 3629 - Electrical Industrial Apparatus (P-11382)

SALES (est): 21.34MM **Privately Held**
Web: www.scottmfgsolutions.com
SIC: **3629** 3613 Electronic generation equipment; Switchgear and switchboard apparatus

**(P-11382)**
### SEACOMP INC (PA)
1525 Faraday Ave, Carlsbad (92008-7319)
PHONE.....................760 918-6722
Michael Szymanski, *CEO*
Terry Arbaugh, *
Robert Marshal, *
▲ EMP: 148 EST: 1989
SALES (est): 13.93MM
SALES (corp-wide): 13.93MM **Privately Held**
Web: www.seacomp.com
SIC: **3629** Battery chargers, rectifying or nonrotating

**(P-11383)**
### SKYWORKS SOLUTIONS INC
1767 Carr Rd Ste 105, Calexico (92231-9506)
PHONE.....................301 874-6408
David J Aldrich, *Brnch Mgr*
▲ EMP: 18
SALES (corp-wide): 4.77B **Publicly Held**
Web: www.skyworksinc.com
SIC: **3629** Capacitors and condensers
PA: Skyworks Solutions, Inc.
5260 California Ave
949 231-3000

**(P-11384)**
### SOLAREDGE TECHNOLOGIES INC (PA)
Also Called: Solaredge
700 Tasman Dr, Milpitas (95035-7456)
PHONE.....................510 498-3200
Ronen Faier, *Interim Chief Executive Officer*
Nadav Zafrir, *Ch Bd*
Uri Bechor, *COO*
Yogev Barak, *CMO*
Meir Adest, *PRODUCT*
◆ EMP: 96 EST: 2006
SALES (est): 3.11B
SALES (corp-wide): 3.11B **Privately Held**
Web: www.solaredge.com
SIC: **3629** Power conversion units, a.c. to d.c.; static-electric

**(P-11385)**
### ZPOWER LLC
5171 Clareton Dr, Agoura Hills (91301-4523)
PHONE.....................805 445-7789
Herbert V Weigel Ii, *COO*
Dennis J Dugan, *
Barry A Freeman, *
Damon Mikoy, *
EMP: 210 EST: 1996
SALES (est): 14.99MM **Privately Held**
Web: www.riotenergy.com
SIC: **3629** Battery chargers, rectifying or nonrotating

## 3631 Household Cooking Equipment

**(P-11386)**
### CAPTIVATE BRANDS USA INC
19781 Pauling, Foothill Ranch (92610-2606)
PHONE.....................949 229-8927
Alan Taylor, *CEO*
Rick Jones, *Prin*
EMP: 15 EST: 2018

SALES (est): 1.02MM **Privately Held**
SIC: **3631** Barbecues, grills, and braziers (outdoor cooking)

**(P-11387)**
### DCEC HOLDINGS INC
Also Called: Twin Eagles, Inc.
13259 166th St, Cerritos (90703)
PHONE.....................562 802-3488
Dante L Cantal, *Pr*
Epifania Cantal, *
▲ EMP: 101 EST: 1999
SQ FT: 45,000
SALES (est): 18.18MM
SALES (corp-wide): 2.84B **Privately Held**
Web: www.twineaglesgrills.com
SIC: **3631** Barbecues, grills, and braziers (outdoor cooking)
HQ: Dometic Corporation
5600 N River Rd Ste 250
Rosemont IL 60018

**(P-11388)**
### DSP WINNER INC
1641 W Main St Ste 222, Alhambra (91801-1900)
PHONE.....................858 336-9471
Jinsong Zou, *Pr*
EMP: 15 EST: 2020
SALES (est): 1.11MM **Privately Held**
SIC: **3631** Household cooking equipment

**(P-11389)**
### DURO CORPORATION
Also Called: Nexrange Industries
918 Canada Ct, City Of Industry (91748-1136)
▲ EMP: 15 EST: 2003
SALES (est): 4.34MM **Privately Held**
Web: www.nxrproducts.com
SIC: **3631** Gas ranges, domestic

**(P-11390)**
### JADE RANGE LLC
Also Called: Jade Products
2650 Orbiter St, Brea (92821-6265)
PHONE.....................714 961-2400
Martin M Lindsay, *
▲ EMP: 120 EST: 1998
SALES (est): 25.51MM
SALES (corp-wide): 4.04B **Publicly Held**
Web: www.jaderange.com
SIC: **3631** 3589 Household cooking equipment; Commercial cooking and foodwarming equipment
PA: The Middleby Corporation
1400 Toastmaster Dr
847 741-3300

**(P-11391)**
### MAGMA PRODUCTS LLC
3940 Pixie Ave, Lakewood (90712-4136)
PHONE.....................562 627-0500
James Mashburn, *
◆ EMP: 70 EST: 1976
SQ FT: 22,000
SALES (est): 9.73MM **Privately Held**
Web: www.magmaproducts.com
SIC: **3631** 3634 Barbecues, grills, and braziers (outdoor cooking); Griddles or grills, electric: household

**(P-11392)**
### MIRAMA ENTERPRISES INC
Also Called: Aroma Housewares
6469 Flanders Dr, San Diego (92121-4104)
PHONE.....................858 587-8866
Chung Yuan Peter Chang, *CEO*
Shiu Run Shirley Chang, *
Tom Kho-hong Kao, *Sec*

◆ EMP: 68 EST: 1996
SQ FT: 60,000
SALES (est): 13.58MM **Privately Held**
Web: www.aroma-housewares.com
SIC: **3631** Household cooking equipment

**(P-11393)**
### PACIFIC COAST MFG INC
5270 Edison Ave, Chino (91710-5719)
PHONE.....................909 627-7040
Bruce Doran, *Pr*
James Poremba, *
▲ EMP: 72 EST: 2011
SQ FT: 40,000
SALES (est): 9.87MM **Privately Held**
Web: www.pcmbbq.com
SIC: **3631** Barbecues, grills, and braziers (outdoor cooking)

**(P-11394)**
### RH PETERSON CO (PA)
Also Called: Robert H Peterson Company
14724 Proctor Ave, City Of Industry (91746-3202)
PHONE.....................626 369-5085
◆ EMP: 170 EST: 1949
SALES (est): 22.45MM
SALES (corp-wide): 22.45MM **Privately Held**
Web: www.rhpeterson.com
SIC: **3631** 3433 Barbecues, grills, and braziers (outdoor cooking); Logs, gas fireplace

**(P-11395)**
### ROYAL RANGE CALIFORNIA INC
Also Called: Royal Industries
3245 Corridor Dr, Eastvale (91752-1030)
PHONE.....................951 360-1600
L Vasan, *CEO*
Patricia Woods, *
▼ EMP: 65 EST: 1995
SQ FT: 52,000
SALES (est): 9.46MM **Privately Held**
Web: www.royalranges.com
SIC: **3631** Household cooking equipment

**(P-11396)**
### SUNBEAM PRODUCTS INC
Also Called: Sunbeam
13052 Jurupa Ave, Fontana (92337-6912)
PHONE.....................951 727-3901
EMP: 17
SALES (corp-wide): 8.13B **Publicly Held**
Web: www.newellbrands.com
SIC: **3631** 3634 3089 Barbecues, grills, and braziers (outdoor cooking); Electric housewares and fans; Plastics containers, except foam
HQ: Sunbeam Products, Inc.
6655 Pachtree Dunwoody Rd
Atlanta GA 30328
770 418-7000

**(P-11397)**
### SUPERIOR EQUIPMENT SOLUTIONS
1085 Bixby Dr, City Of Industry (91745-1704)
PHONE.....................323 722-7900
Jeffrey Bernstein, *CEO*
Stephan Bernstein, *
▲ EMP: 60 EST: 2001
SQ FT: 45,000
SALES (est): 13.99MM **Privately Held**
Web: www.sesbrands.com
SIC: **3631** 5046 Household cooking equipment; Restaurant equipment and supplies, nec

## 3632 Household Refrigerators And Freezers

**(P-11398)**
### REFRIDERATOR MANUFACTERS LLC
17018 Edwards Rd, Cerritos (90703-2422)
PHONE.....................562 229-0500
EMP: 42 EST: 2014
SQ FT: 40,000
SALES (est): 1.36MM **Privately Held**
SIC: **3632** Freezers, home and farm

**(P-11399)**
### REFRIGERATOR MANUFACTERS INC (PA)
Also Called: Econocold Refrigerators
17018 Edwards Rd, Cerritos (90703-2422)
PHONE.....................562 926-2006
Lawrence E Jaffe, *Pr*
Leo R Lewis, *Ex VP*
Russell E Anthony, *Ex VP*
EMP: 20 EST: 1945
SQ FT: 40,000
SALES (est): 9.87MM
SALES (corp-wide): 9.87MM **Privately Held**
Web: www.rmi-econocold.com
SIC: **3632** 3585 Household refrigerators and freezers; Refrigeration and heating equipment

## 3634 Electric Housewares And Fans

**(P-11400)**
### BRANDS REPUBLIC INC
10333 Rush St, South El Monte (91733-3341)
PHONE.....................302 401-1195
Asif Kashif, *Prin*
EMP: 50
SALES (est): 1.6MM **Privately Held**
SIC: **3634** Electric housewares and fans

**(P-11401)**
### BRAVA HOME INC
Also Called: Brava Oven
2211 Warm Springs Ct, Fremont (94539-6773)
PHONE.....................855 276-6767
John Pleasants, *CEO*
Shih Yu Cheng, *
Dan Yue, *CPO*
Mark Janoff, *
EMP: 26 EST: 2015
SALES (est): 4.63MM
SALES (corp-wide): 4.04B **Publicly Held**
Web: www.brava.com
SIC: **3634** Ovens, portable: household
PA: The Middleby Corporation
1400 Toastmaster Dr
847 741-3300

**(P-11402)**
### CAPITAL BRANDS DISTRIBUTION L (PA)
11601 Wilshire Blvd Ste 2300, Los Angeles (90025-0509)
PHONE.....................800 523-5993
Lenny Sands, *
EMP: 62 EST: 2015
SALES (est): 47.46MM
SALES (corp-wide): 47.46MM **Privately Held**
Web: www.capitalbrands.com

SIC: 3634 Blenders, electric

**(P-11403)**
**CRYOGENIC INDUSTRIES INC**
25720 Jefferson Ave, Murrieta (92562-6929)
PHONE.................................951 677-2060
Peter Wagner, *CEO*
EMP: 200 EST: 2016
SALES (est): 9.81MM **Privately Held**
Web: www.nikkisoceig.com
SIC: 3634 Vaporizers, electric: household

**(P-11404)**
**FELLOW INDUSTRIES INC**
Also Called: Fellow
1342 1/2 Abbot Kinney Blvd, Venice (90291-3778)
PHONE.................................415 649-0361
Jacob Miller, *CEO*
EMP: 49
SALES (corp-wide): 8.2MM **Privately Held**
Web: www.fellowproducts.com
SIC: 3634 Electric housewares and fans
PA: Fellow Industries Inc.
320 Florida St
415 649-0361

**(P-11405)**
**FOLDIMATE INC**
879 White Pine Ct, Oak Park (91377-4769)
PHONE.................................805 876-4418
Gal Rozov, *CEO*
Ori Kaplan, *COO*
EMP: 22 EST: 2012
SALES (est): 1.83MM **Privately Held**
Web: www.foldimate.com
SIC: 3634 Personal electrical appliances

**(P-11406)**
**INSEAT SOLUTIONS LLC**
1871 Wright Ave, La Verne (91750-5817)
PHONE.................................562 447-1780
▲ EMP: 22 EST: 2000
SALES (est): 7.23MM **Privately Held**
Web: www.relaxor.com
SIC: 3634 Massage machines, electric, except for beauty/barber shops

**(P-11407)**
**KATADYN DESALINATION LLC**
Also Called: Spectra Watermakers
2220 S Mcdowell Boulevard Ext, Petaluma (94954)
PHONE.................................415 526-2780
Shawn Hostetter, *Managing Member*
EMP: 20 EST: 2014
SQ FT: 8,400
SALES (est): 5.07MM **Privately Held**
Web: www.spectrawatermakers.com
SIC: 3634 3732 Water pulsating devices, electric; Yachts, building and repairing

**(P-11408)**
**LUMA COMFORT LLC**
Also Called: Luma Comfort
6600 Katella Ave, Cypress (90630-5104)
PHONE.................................855 963-9247
Luke Peters, *Pr*
Luke Peters, *CEO*
Mariella Peters, *
▲ EMP: 50 EST: 2011
SQ FT: 30,000
SALES (est): 2.44MM **Privately Held**
Web: www.lumacomfort.com
SIC: 3634 Electric housewares and fans

**(P-11409)**
**MILA USA INC**
1 Belvedere Pl Ste 200, Mill Valley (94941-2493)
PHONE.................................540 206-4306
Grant Prigge, *CEO*
Riaz Khan, *CFO*
EMP: 20 EST: 2018
SALES (est): 1.04MM **Privately Held**
SIC: 3634 7389 Air purifiers, portable; Business Activities at Non-Commercial Site

**(P-11410)**
**MILL INDUSTRIES INC**
950 Elm Ave Ste 200, San Bruno (94066-3029)
PHONE.................................415 862-4394
Matthew Rogers, *CEO*
Harry Tannenbaum, *
EMP: 100 EST: 2020
SALES (est): 23.36MM **Privately Held**
Web: www.mill.com
SIC: 3634 Housewares, excluding cooking appliances and utensils

**(P-11411)**
**MJC AMERICA LTD (PA)**
Also Called: Soleus International
20035 E Walnut Dr N, Walnut (91789-2922)
P.O. Box 472 (91788-0472)
PHONE.................................888 876-5387
Simon Chu, *CEO*
◆ EMP: 35 EST: 1998
SQ FT: 100,000
SALES (est): 3.69MM
SALES (corp-wide): 3.69MM **Privately Held**
Web: www.soleusair.com
SIC: 3634 Electric housewares and fans

**(P-11412)**
**OLISO INC**
1200 Harbour Way S # 215, Richmond (94804-3636)
PHONE.................................415 864-7600
Ehsan Alipour, *CEO*
▲ EMP: 16 EST: 2004
SQ FT: 7,000
SALES (est): 2.33MM **Privately Held**
Web: www.oliso.com
SIC: 3634 Personal electrical appliances

**(P-11413)**
**SAMVCO**
Also Called: Sam Israel Viner
14016 Bora Bora Way, Marina Del Rey (90292-6889)
PHONE.................................310 980-5680
Sam Israel Viner, *Owner*
▲ EMP: 15 EST: 1982
SQ FT: 3,500
SALES (est): 969.92K **Privately Held**
Web: www.samvco.com
SIC: 3634 3714 Electric household cooking appliances; Motor vehicle parts and accessories

**(P-11414)**
**T3 MICRO INC (PA)**
301 Arizona Ave Ste 230, Santa Monica (90401-1457)
PHONE.................................310 452-2888
Kent Yu, *Pr*
Anish Agarwal, *Sec*
▲ EMP: 17 EST: 2005
SALES (est): 6.24MM
SALES (corp-wide): 6.24MM **Privately Held**
Web: www.t3micro.com

SIC: 3634 5199 Hair dryers, electric; Hairbrushes

## 3635 Household Vacuum Cleaners

**(P-11415)**
**BETTER CLEANING SYSTEMS INC**
Also Called: Kleenrite
1122 Maple St, Madera (93637-5368)
P.O. Box 359 (93639-0359)
PHONE.................................559 673-5700
William Hachtmann, *CEO*
Bill Hachtmann, *
◆ EMP: 37 EST: 1975
SQ FT: 27,620
SALES (est): 5.82MM **Privately Held**
Web: www.kleenritemfg.com
SIC: 3635 Carpet shampooer

## 3639 Household Appliances, Nec

**(P-11416)**
**BRENTWOOD APPLIANCES INC**
Also Called: Import
3088 E 46th St, Vernon (90058-2422)
PHONE.................................323 266-4600
Poorad Beni Panahi, *CEO*
Poorad Beni Panahi, *CEO*
Maurice Araghi, *
John Yadgari, *
◆ EMP: 36 EST: 2009
SQ FT: 65,000
SALES (est): 5.03MM **Privately Held**
Web: www.brentwoodus.com
SIC: 3639 Major kitchen appliances, except refrigerators and stoves

**(P-11417)**
**BREVILLE USA INC**
Also Called: Breville
19400 S Western Ave, Torrance (90501-1119)
PHONE.................................310 755-3000
Stephen Krauss, *CEO*
Michelle Waters, *
Barbara Dirsa, *
◆ EMP: 50 EST: 1989
SQ FT: 135,000
SALES (est): 24.19MM **Privately Held**
Web: www.breville.com
SIC: 3639 3634 5722 Major kitchen appliances, except refrigerators and stoves; Coffee makers, electric: household; Microwave ovens
HQ: Breville Holdings Pty Limited
G Se 2 170 Bourke Rd
Alexandria NSW 2015

**(P-11418)**
**FISHER & PAYKEL APPLIANCES INC (DH)**
695 Town Center Dr Ste 180, Costa Mesa (92626-1902)
PHONE.................................949 790-8900
Peter Lockwell, *Pr*
◆ EMP: 22 EST: 1996
SQ FT: 26,000
SALES (est): 42.56MM **Privately Held**
Web: www.fisherpaykel.com
SIC: 3639 3631 5064 5078 Dishwashing machines, household; Household cooking equipment; Electric household appliances, nec; Refrigeration equipment and supplies

HQ: Fisher & Paykel Appliances Usa Holdings Inc.
695 Town Center Dr # 180
Costa Mesa CA 92626

**(P-11419)**
**HESTAN COMMERCIAL CORPORATION**
3375 E La Palma Ave, Anaheim (92806-2815)
P.O. Box 887 (92811-0887)
PHONE.................................714 869-2380
Stanley Kin Sui Cheng, *CEO*
Eric Deng, *
Barry Needleman Ctrl, *Prin*
▲ EMP: 125 EST: 2013
SQ FT: 70,000
SALES (est): 24.42MM **Privately Held**
Web: commercial.hestan.com
SIC: 3639 Major kitchen appliances, except refrigerators and stoves
HQ: Meyer Corporation, U.S.
1 Meyer Plz
Vallejo CA 94590
707 551-2800

**(P-11420)**
**TLM INTERNATIONAL INC**
Also Called: Dr Heater USA
860 Mahler Rd, Burlingame (94010-1604)
PHONE.................................650 952-2257
James Tan, *Pr*
Vincent Ma, *VP*
EMP: 15 EST: 2008
SALES (est): 2.72MM **Privately Held**
Web: www.drheaterusa.com
SIC: 3639 2519 3634 Hot water heaters, household; Household furniture, except wood or metal: upholstered; Massage machines, electric, except for beauty/barber shops

## 3641 Electric Lamps

**(P-11421)**
**APPLIED PHOTON TECHNOLOGY INC**
3346 Arden Rd, Hayward (94545-3923)
PHONE.................................510 780-9500
Leonard Goldfine, *Pr*
Rodney Romero, *
Rafael Olano, *
▲ EMP: 29 EST: 2002
SQ FT: 12,850
SALES (est): 5MM **Privately Held**
Web: www.appliedphoton.com
SIC: 3641 Ultraviolet lamps

**(P-11422)**
**CANDLE LAMP HOLDINGS LLC**
949 S Coast Dr Ste 650, Costa Mesa (92626-7737)
PHONE.................................951 682-9600
Don Hinshaw, *CEO*
John Clark, *Managing Member*
EMP: 310 EST: 2006
SALES (est): 1.37MM **Privately Held**
SIC: 3641 3645 3589 3634 Electric lamps; Table lamps; Food warming equipment, commercial; Chafing dishes, electric

**(P-11423)**
**DASOL INC**
Also Called: Coronet Lighting
9004 Meredith Pl, Beverly Hills (90210-1841)
P.O. Box 2065 (90247-0010)
PHONE.................................310 327-6700
Sol Smith, *Ch Bd*

## 3641 - Electric Lamps (P-11424)

David Smith, *
Mark Smith, *
◆ **EMP:** 225 **EST:** 1944
**SALES (est):** 4.5MM **Privately Held**
**SIC: 3641** Electric lamps and parts for generalized applications

**(P-11424)**
**DELTA ULTRAVIOLET CORPORATION**
1535 W Rosecrans Ave, Gardena (90249-2635)
**PHONE**...................310 323-6400
◆ **EMP:** 15
**SIC: 3641** Health lamps, infrared or ultraviolet

**(P-11425)**
**IRTRONIX INC**
Also Called: Euri Lighting
20900 Normandie Ave Bldg B, Torrance (90502-1602)
**PHONE**...................310 787-1100
Danny Joon Oh, *CEO*
▲ **EMP:** 22 **EST:** 2000
**SQ FT:** 23,000
**SALES (est):** 15MM **Privately Held**
Web: www.irtronix.com
**SIC: 3641** 5065 Electric lamps and parts for generalized applications; Semiconductor devices

**(P-11426)**
**IWORKS US INC**
Also Called: Iworks
2501 S Malt Ave, Commerce (90040-3203)
**PHONE**...................323 278-8363
Eric Dortch, *CEO*
◆ **EMP:** 53 **EST:** 1988
**SQ FT:** 35,000
**SALES (est):** 9.44MM **Privately Held**
Web: www.iworksus.com
**SIC: 3641** Electric lamps and parts for generalized applications

**(P-11427)**
**LEDVANCE LLC**
1651 S Archibald Ave, Ontario (91761-7651)
**PHONE**...................909 923-3003
Jane Running, *Owner*
**EMP:** 26 **EST:** 2017
**SALES (est):** 6.51MM **Privately Held**
**SIC: 3641** Electric lamps

**(P-11428)**
**LITEGEAR INC**
Also Called: Litegear
4406 W Vanowen St, Burbank (91505-1134)
**PHONE**...................818 358-8542
Albert M Demayo, *Pr*
**EMP:** 45 **EST:** 2006
**SALES (est):** 7.59MM **Privately Held**
Web: www.litegear.com
**SIC: 3641** Electric lamps

**(P-11429)**
**LUXIM CORP**
3542 Bassett St, Santa Clara (95054-2704)
**PHONE**...................408 734-1096
**EMP:** 18 **EST:** 2019
**SALES (est):** 475.17K **Privately Held**
**SIC: 3641** Electric lamps

**(P-11430)**
**OSRAM SYLVANIA INC**
13350 Gregg St Ste 101, Poway (92064-7137)

**PHONE**...................858 748-5077
Dennis Cohen, *Brnch Mgr*
**EMP:** 76
**SALES (corp-wide):** 5B **Privately Held**
Web: www.sylvania-automotive.com
**SIC: 3641** Electric lamps
**HQ:** Osram Sylvania Inc.
200 Ballardvale St Bldg 2
Wilmington MA 01887
978 570-3000

**(P-11431)**
**SWITCH BULB COMPANY INC**
Also Called: Switch Lighting
225 Charcot Ave, San Jose (95131-1107)
**PHONE**...................408 457-3821
**EMP:** 85
Web: www.revolights.com
**SIC: 3641** Electric lamps

**(P-11432)**
**TANGO SYSTEMS LLC**
1980 Concourse Dr, San Jose (95131-1719)
**PHONE**...................408 526-2330
Jeff Turner, *CEO*
**EMP:** 70 **EST:** 2005
**SQ FT:** 15,000
**SALES (est):** 11.23MM
**SALES (corp-wide):** 26.52B **Publicly Held**
Web: www.tangosystems.com
**SIC: 3641** 3679 Lamps, vapor; Attenuators
**PA:** Applied Materials, Inc.
3050 Bowers Ave
408 727-5555

**(P-11433)**
**TIVOLI LLC**
17110 Armstrong Ave, Irvine (92614-5718)
**PHONE**...................714 957-6101
Jannhuan Jang, *CEO*
Targetti Poulsen, *Managing Member*
Eric Kramer, *Managing Member*
Susan Larson, *
▲ **EMP:** 50 **EST:** 2003
**SALES (est):** 9.22MM **Privately Held**
Web: www.tivolilighting.com
**SIC: 3641** 3646 Tubes, electric light; Ceiling systems, luminous

**(P-11434)**
**TOLEMAR LLC**
6412 Maple Ave, Westminster (92683-3609)
**PHONE**...................657 200-3840
Eric Ison, *Managing Member*
**EMP:** 45 **EST:** 2017
**SALES (est):** 1.46MM **Privately Held**
**SIC: 3641** Electric lamps

**(P-11435)**
**VISUALIZELED INC**
Also Called: Visualize Led
1531 Rigel St, San Diego (92113-3807)
**PHONE**...................703 919-5559
Jose Rubalcaba, *CEO*
**EMP:** 16 **EST:** 2014
**SALES (est):** 1.06MM **Privately Held**
Web: www.visualizeled.com
**SIC: 3641** Electric lamps

**(P-11436)**
**WESTERN QUARTZ PRODUCTS INC**
2432 Spring St, Paso Robles (93446-1296)
**PHONE**...................805 238-3524
**EMP:** 15
Web: www.westernquartz.com

**SIC: 3641** Health lamps, infrared or ultraviolet

## 3643 Current-carrying Wiring Devices

**(P-11437)**
**ABRAMS ELECTRONICS INC**
Also Called: Thor Electronics of California
420 W Market St, Salinas (93901-1422)
**PHONE**...................831 758-6400
Stephen Abrams, *Pr*
Jeff Abrams, *
**EMP:** 15 **EST:** 1966
**SQ FT:** 28,000
**SALES (est):** 4.26MM **Privately Held**
Web: www.thorconnect.com
**SIC: 3643** 3496 Connectors and terminals for electrical devices; Cable, uninsulated wire: made from purchased wire

**(P-11438)**
**AERO-ELECTRIC CONNECTOR INC (PA)**
2280 W 208th St, Torrance (90501-1452)
**PHONE**...................310 618-3737
Walter Neubauer, *Ch*
Walter Neubauer Junior, *CEO*
**EMP:** 344 **EST:** 1982
**SQ FT:** 65,000
**SALES (est):** 45.47MM
**SALES (corp-wide):** 45.47MM **Privately Held**
Web: www.aero-electric.com
**SIC: 3643** 3678 Connectors and terminals for electrical devices; Electronic connectors

**(P-11439)**
**ALLAN KIDD**
Also Called: AK Industries
3115 E Las Hermanas St, Compton (90221-5512)
**PHONE**...................310 762-1600
Allan Kidd, *Owner*
**EMP:** 20 **EST:** 1995
**SQ FT:** 17,000
**SALES (est):** 4MM **Privately Held**
Web: www.ak-ind.com
**SIC: 3643** Electric connectors

**(P-11440)**
**AMPHENOL DC ELECTRONICS INC**
Also Called: DC Electronics
1870 Little Orchard St, San Jose (95125-1041)
P.O. Box 28463 (95159-8463)
**PHONE**...................408 947-4500
Ruben Matias, *Genl Mgr*
David Cianciulli Junior, *Pr*
Eric Hynes, *
**EMP:** 300 **EST:** 1979
**SQ FT:** 33,000
**SALES (est):** 22.12MM
**SALES (corp-wide):** 12.55B **Publicly Held**
Web: www.dcelectronics.com
**SIC: 3643** Current-carrying wiring services
**PA:** Amphenol Corporation
358 Hall Ave
203 265-8900

**(P-11441)**
**AUTOSPLICE PARENT INC (PA)**
Also Called: Autosplice
10431 Wateridge Cir Ste 110, San Diego (92121-5797)
**PHONE**...................858 535-0077
Santosh Rao, *CEO*

Ken Krone, *
Jeffrey Cartwright, *
Kevin Barry, *
▲ **EMP:** 200 **EST:** 1954
**SQ FT:** 20,000
**SALES (est):** 23.46MM
**SALES (corp-wide):** 23.46MM **Privately Held**
Web: www.autosplice.com
**SIC: 3643** Electric connectors

**(P-11442)**
**BIZLINK TECHNOLOGY INC (HQ)**
47211 Bayside Pkwy, Fremont (94538-6517)
**PHONE**...................510 252-0786
Annie Kuo, *Pr*
Roger Liang, *VP*
◆ **EMP:** 80 **EST:** 1996
**SQ FT:** 62,000
**SALES (est):** 81.55MM **Privately Held**
Web: www.bizlinktech.com
**SIC: 3643** Current-carrying wiring services
**PA:** Bizlink Holding Inc
C/O: Corporate Filing Services Ltd

**(P-11443)**
**CABLE CONNECTION INC**
Also Called: Lorom West
1035 Mission Ct, Fremont (94539-8203)
**PHONE**...................510 249-9000
Greg Gaches, *Pr*
▲ **EMP:** 100 **EST:** 1992
**SQ FT:** 55,000
**SALES (est):** 17.62MM **Privately Held**
Web: www.cable-connection.com
**SIC: 3643** Current-carrying wiring services

**(P-11444)**
**CALPICO INC**
1387 San Mateo Ave, South San Francisco (94080-6511)
**PHONE**...................650 588-2241
Carey Wilson, *Pr*
Edna Wilson, *
▲ **EMP:** 23 **EST:** 1963
**SQ FT:** 20,000
**SALES (est):** 3.53MM **Privately Held**
Web: www.calpicoinc.com
**SIC: 3643** 3317 3089 3498 Current-carrying wiring services; Steel pipe and tubes; Plastics hardware and building products; Fabricated pipe and fittings

**(P-11445)**
**CELESTICA LLC**
280 Campillo St Ste G, Calexico (92231-3200)
**PHONE**...................760 357-4880
Michael Garmon, *Brnch Mgr*
**EMP:** 72
**SALES (corp-wide):** 7.96B **Privately Held**
Web: www.celestica.com
**SIC: 3643** Current-carrying wiring services
**HQ:** Celestica Llc
400 Glleria Pkwy Ste 1500
Atlanta GA 30339

**(P-11446)**
**CONNECTEC COMPANY INC (PA)**
Also Called: MANUFACTURE
1701 Reynolds Ave, Irvine (92614-5711)
**PHONE**...................949 252-1077
Rassool Kavezade, *CEO*
Lora Taleb, *
Mike Taleb, *
▲ **EMP:** 74 **EST:** 1988
**SQ FT:** 12,000
**SALES (est):** 20.09MM

# PRODUCTS & SERVICES SECTION
## 3643 - Current-carrying Wiring Devices (P-11467)

SALES (corp-wide): 20.09MM **Privately Held**
Web: www.connectecco.com
**SIC: 3643** 3678 Electric connectors; Electronic connectors

### (P-11447)
### CTC GLOBAL CORPORATION (PA)
Also Called: Ctc Global
2026 Mcgaw Ave, Irvine (92614-0911)
**PHONE**.................................949 428-8500
J D Sitton, *CEO*
Dean Hagen, *
Anne Mcdowell, *Commercial Vice President*
John Mansfield, *Strategy Vice President*
Eric Johnson, *OF FIELD Technology SRVS*
▲ **EMP:** 146 **EST:** 2011
**SALES (est):** 34.71MM
**SALES (corp-wide):** 34.71MM **Privately Held**
Web: www.ctcglobal.com
**SIC: 3643** Power line cable

### (P-11448)
### DC ELECTRONICS INC
1870 Little Orchard St, San Jose (95125-1041)
P.O. Box 67126 (95067-7126)
**PHONE**.................................408 947-4500
Dave Cianciulli, *Pr*
Ruben Macias Junior, *COO*
Steve Gulesserian, *VP*
Eric Hynes, *CFO*
Alice Cheung, *Dir*
**EMP:** 23 **EST:** 1983
**SALES (est):** 6.24MM **Privately Held**
Web: www.dcelectronics.com
**SIC: 3643** Current-carrying wiring services

### (P-11449)
### DDH ENTERPRISE INC (PA)
2220 Oak Ridge Way, Vista (92081-8341)
**PHONE**.................................760 599-0171
David Du, *CEO*
Danny Du, *
▲ **EMP:** 100 **EST:** 1988
**SQ FT:** 42,000
**SALES (est):** 30.55MM
**SALES (corp-wide):** 30.55MM **Privately Held**
Web: www.ddhent.com
**SIC: 3643** 3644 3699 Current-carrying wiring services; Noncurrent-carrying wiring devices; Electrical equipment and supplies, nec

### (P-11450)
### DMC POWER INC (PA)
623 E Artesia Blvd, Carson (90746)
**PHONE**.................................310 323-1616
Tony Ward, *CEO*
Michael Yazdanpanah, *
Eben Kane, *
Ed Cox, *
▲ **EMP:** 50 **EST:** 2009
**SQ FT:** 40,000
**SALES (est):** 27.99MM **Privately Held**
Web: www.dmcpower.com
**SIC: 3643** Current-carrying wiring services

### (P-11451)
### ELECTRO ADAPTER INC
Also Called: Plating
20640 Nordhoff St, Chatsworth (91311-6114)
P.O. Box 2560 (91313-2560)
**PHONE**.................................818 998-1198
Ray Fish, *Pr*
Terrill Fish, *
**EMP:** 100 **EST:** 1969
**SQ FT:** 54,000
**SALES (est):** 12.11MM **Privately Held**
Web: www.electro-adapter.com
**SIC: 3643** Electric connectors
**PA:** Intritec
20640 Nordhoff St

### (P-11452)
### EMP CONNECTORS INC
2280 W 208th St, Torrance (90501-1452)
**PHONE**.................................310 533-6799
Walter Neubauer, *Prin*
Walter Neubauer Junior, *Pr*
Erika Neubauer, *Prin*
**EMP:** 20 **EST:** 1987
**SQ FT:** 39,000
**SALES (est):** 2.42MM **Privately Held**
Web: www.conesys.com
**SIC: 3643** 3678 3612 Electric connectors; Electronic connectors; Transformers, except electric

### (P-11453)
### ESL POWER SYSTEMS INC
2800 Palisades Dr, Corona (92878-9427)
**PHONE**.................................800 922-4188
Michael Hellmers, *Pr*
David Hellmers, *
◆ **EMP:** 55 **EST:** 1995
**SQ FT:** 36,000
**SALES (est):** 15.95MM **Privately Held**
Web: www.eslpwr.com
**SIC: 3643** Outlets, electric: convenience

### (P-11454)
### FOXLINK INTERNATIONAL INC (HQ)
3010 Saturn St Ste 200, Brea (92821-6220)
**PHONE**.................................714 256-1777
Ching Fan Pu, *CEO*
James Lee, *
▲ **EMP:** 44 **EST:** 1994
**SALES (est):** 12.81MM **Privately Held**
**SIC: 3643** 3678 3679 3691 Current-carrying wiring services; Electronic connectors; Electronic circuits; Storage batteries
**PA:** Cheng Uei Precision Industry Co., Ltd.
No.18, Chung Shan Rd.,

### (P-11455)
### G D M ELECTRONIC ASSEMBLY INC
Also Called: Gdm Electronic & Medical
740 S Milpitas Blvd, Milpitas (95035-5449)
**PHONE**.................................408 945-4100
Michael Sobolewski, *CEO*
Grant Murphy, *Pt*
Susie Perches, *Pt*
**EMP:** 77 **EST:** 1983
**SALES (est):** 4.42MM **Privately Held**
Web: www.gdm1.com
**SIC: 3643** 3565 Current-carrying wiring services; Packaging machinery

### (P-11456)
### GLENAIR INC (PA)
Also Called: Papi
1211 Air Way, Glendale (91201-2497)
**PHONE**.................................818 247-6000
**EMP:** 371 **EST:** 1956
**SALES (est):** 782.53MM
**SALES (corp-wide):** 782.53MM **Privately Held**
Web: www.glenair.com
**SIC: 3643** 3825 3357 Connectors and terminals for electrical devices; Test equipment for electronic and electrical circuits; Nonferrous wiredrawing and insulating

### (P-11457)
### GOLD TECHNOLOGIES INC
Also Called: Goldtec USA
1648 Mabury Rd Ste A, San Jose (95133-1097)
**PHONE**.................................408 321-9568
Patricia Tran, *Pr*
**EMP:** 25 **EST:** 1998
**SQ FT:** 12,000
**SALES (est):** 2.45MM **Privately Held**
Web: www.goldtec.com
**SIC: 3643** Electric connectors

### (P-11458)
### HI REL CONNECTORS INC
Also Called: Hirel Connectors
760 Wharton Dr, Claremont (91711-4800)
**PHONE**.................................909 626-1820
Fred Baumann, *CEO*
Frederick Bb Baumann, *
**EMP:** 300 **EST:** 1967
**SQ FT:** 25,000
**SALES (est):** 23.04MM **Privately Held**
Web: www.hirelco.net
**SIC: 3643** 3678 Connectors and terminals for electrical devices; Electronic connectors

### (P-11459)
### IMPULSE ENTERPRISE
Also Called: Teledyne Impulse
9855 Carroll Canyon Rd, San Diego (92131-1103)
**PHONE**.................................858 565-7050
▲ **EMP:** 17 **EST:** 2015
**SALES (est):** 5.92MM **Privately Held**
Web: www.teledynemarine.com
**SIC: 3643** Connectors and terminals for electrical devices

### (P-11460)
### JOY SIGNAL TECHNOLOGY LLC
1020 Marauder St Ste A, Chico (95973-9028)
**PHONE**.................................530 891-3551
**EMP:** 50 **EST:** 1987
**SQ FT:** 21,000
**SALES (est):** 4.97MM
**SALES (corp-wide):** 34.19MM **Privately Held**
Web: www.joysignal.com
**SIC: 3643** Power line cable
**PA:** Ohio Associated Enterprises Llc
1382 W Jackson St
440 354-2106

### (P-11461)
### JUDCO MANUFACTURING INC (PA)
1429 240th St, Harbor City (90710-1306)
P.O. Box 487 (90710-0487)
**PHONE**.................................310 534-0959
▲ **EMP:** 200 **EST:** 1980
**SALES (est):** 21.81MM
**SALES (corp-wide):** 21.81MM **Privately Held**
Web: www.judco.net
**SIC: 3643** Electric switches

### (P-11462)
### LEVITON MANUFACTURING CO INC
6020 Progressive Ave Ste 500, San Diego (92154-6633)
**PHONE**.................................619 205-8600
John Nelson, *Prin*
**EMP:** 15
**SALES (corp-wide):** 1.46B **Privately Held**
Web: www.leviton.com

**SIC: 3643** Current-carrying wiring services
**PA:** Leviton Manufacturing Co., Inc.
201 N Service Rd
800 323-8920

### (P-11463)
### LYNCOLE GRUNDING SOLUTIONS LLC
Also Called: Lyncole Xit Grounding
369 Van Ness Way, Torrance (90501-1489)
**PHONE**.................................310 214-4000
**EMP:** 25 **EST:** 1985
**SALES (est):** 2.67MM **Privately Held**
Web: www.vfclp.com
**SIC: 3643** 8711 Current-carrying wiring services; Consulting engineer

### (P-11464)
### MERCOTAC INC
6195 Corte Del Cedro Ste 100, Carlsbad (92011-1549)
**PHONE**.................................760 431-7723
Timothy Leslie, *Pr*
Dave Brunet, *VP*
Chris Rechlin, *Sec*
▼ **EMP:** 17 **EST:** 1978
**SQ FT:** 12,000
**SALES (est):** 2.51MM **Privately Held**
Web: www.mercotac.com
**SIC: 3643** Connectors and terminals for electrical devices

### (P-11465)
### NEWVAC LLC (HQ)
9330 De Soto Ave, Chatsworth (91311-4926)
**PHONE**.................................310 525-1205
Ted Anderson, *CEO*
Mike Davidson, *CFO*
Garrett Hoffman, *General Vice President*
Heather Wynne, *Contrlr*
**EMP:** 16 **EST:** 2019
**SQ FT:** 44,000
**SALES (est):** 3.88MM
**SALES (corp-wide):** 96.54MM **Privately Held**
Web: www.newvac-llc.com
**SIC: 3643** Current-carrying wiring services
**PA:** Adi American Distributors, Llc
2 Emery Ave Ste 1
973 328-1181

### (P-11466)
### NIVEK INDUSTRIES INC
Also Called: International Component Tech
230 E Dyer Rd Ste K, Santa Ana (92707-3751)
**PHONE**.................................714 545-8855
Kevin Pezzolla, *Pr*
**EMP:** 48 **EST:** 1987
**SQ FT:** 8,000
**SALES (est):** 5.15MM **Privately Held**
Web: www.intcomptech.com
**SIC: 3643** Current-carrying wiring services

### (P-11467)
### PLT ENTERPRISES INC
Also Called: So-Cal Value Added
809 Calle Plano, Camarillo (93012-8516)
**PHONE**.................................805 389-5335
Pamela L Tunis, *Pr*
Peter L Tunis, *
Peter Tunis Junior, *Genl Mgr*
**EMP:** 75 **EST:** 1996
**SQ FT:** 41,000
**SALES (est):** 8.45MM **Privately Held**
**SIC: 3643** 3679 Current-carrying wiring services; Harness assemblies, for electronic use: wire or cable

## 3643 - Current-carrying Wiring Devices (P-11468)

**(P-11468)**
**PRECISION STAMPINGS INC (PA)**
Also Called: P S I
500 Egan Ave, Beaumont (92223-2132)
PHONE..................................951 845-1174
Herman Viets, *Ch Bd*
Steven Morgan, *
Frauke Roth, *Stockholder**
Peter Gailing, *Stockholder**
Herta Viets, *Stockholder**
**EMP:** 32 **EST:** 1966
**SQ FT:** 25,000
**SALES (est):** 8.95MM
**SALES (corp-wide):** 8.95MM **Privately Held**
Web: www.precisionstampingsinc.com
**SIC: 3643** 5084 7539  Contacts, electrical; Tool and die makers equipment; Machine shop, automotive

**(P-11469)**
**SAFRAN USA INC**
Also Called: Safran Aerospace
1500 Glenn Curtiss St, Carson (90746-4012)
PHONE..................................310 884-7198
**EMP:** 512
**SALES (corp-wide):** 940.23MM **Privately Held**
Web: www.safran-group.com
**SIC: 3643** 3621 7699 3724  Connectors and terminals for electrical devices; Motors and generators; Engine repair and replacement, non-automotive; Aircraft engines and engine parts
HQ: Safran Usa, Inc.
  700 S Washington St # 320
  Alexandria VA 22314
  703 351-9898

**(P-11470)**
**SOURIAU USA INC (DH)**
1740 Commerce Way, Paso Robles (93446-3620)
PHONE..................................805 238-2840
Rob Hanes, *Pr*
◆ **EMP:** 46 **EST:** 2003
**SQ FT:** 55,000
**SALES (est):** 23.19MM **Privately Held**
Web: usa.souriau.com
**SIC: 3643**  Bus bars (electrical conductors)
HQ: Eaton Corporation
  1000 Eaton Blvd
  Cleveland OH 44122
  440 523-5000

**(P-11471)**
**SPIRE MANUFACTURING INC**
2526 Qume Dr Ste 18, San Jose (95131-1870)
PHONE..................................510 226-1070
Christine Bui, *CEO*
Achilleas Vezirir, *Pr*
▲ **EMP:** 20 **EST:** 2008
**SALES (est):** 2.55MM **Privately Held**
Web: www.spiremfg.com
**SIC: 3643** 3674  Power outlets and sockets; Integrated circuits, semiconductor networks, etc.

**(P-11472)**
**SULLINS ELECTRONICS CORP**
Also Called: Sullins Connector Solutions
801 E Mission Rd # B, San Marcos (92069-3002)
PHONE..................................760 744-0125
Kayvan Sullins, *CEO*
▲ **EMP:** 75 **EST:** 1969
**SQ FT:** 33,000
**SALES (est):** 8.11MM **Privately Held**
Web: www.sullinscorp.com
**SIC: 3643** 3678  Connectors and terminals for electrical devices; Electronic connectors

**(P-11473)**
**TECHNICAL RESOURCE INDUSTRIES (PA)**
Also Called: T R I
12854 Daisy Ct, Yucaipa (92399-2026)
PHONE..................................909 446-1109
Reinhard Thalmayer, *Pr*
**EMP:** 25 **EST:** 1988
**SQ FT:** 5,000
**SALES (est):** 468.89K
**SALES (corp-wide):** 468.89K **Privately Held**
**SIC: 3643**  Electric connectors

**(P-11474)**
**TELEDYNE INSTRUMENTS INC**
Also Called: Teledyne Impulse
9855 Carroll Canyon Rd, San Diego (92131-1103)
PHONE..................................858 842-3100
Kenneth Mendoza, *Fin Mgr*
**EMP:** 79
**SALES (corp-wide):** 5.64B **Publicly Held**
Web: www.teledyne.com
**SIC: 3643**  Electric connectors
HQ: Teledyne Instruments, Inc.
  16830 Chestnut St
  City Of Industry CA 91748
  626 934-1500

**(P-11475)**
**TOBAR INDUSTRIES INC**
912 Olinder Ct, San Jose (95122-2619)
PHONE..................................408 494-3530
Elias Antoun, *CEO*
Farid Ghantous, *
William Delaney, *
**EMP:** 95 **EST:** 1976
**SQ FT:** 58,516
**SALES (est):** 8.87MM **Privately Held**
Web: www.tobar-ind.com
**SIC: 3643** 3444  Current-carrying wiring services; Sheet metalwork

**(P-11476)**
**UNIVERSAL SWITCHING CORP**
Also Called: U S C
7671 N San Fernando Rd, Burbank (91505-1073)
PHONE..................................818 785-0200
**EMP:** 28 **EST:** 1992
**SALES (est):** 4.68MM **Privately Held**
Web: www.uswi.com
**SIC: 3643**  Electric switches

**(P-11477)**
**WASCO SALES AND MARKETING INC**
Also Called: Wasco Switches & Sensors
2245 A St, Santa Maria (93455-1008)
PHONE..................................805 739-2747
Ronald Way, *Pr*
Dana Way, *Sec*
Dave Way, *Genl Mgr*
Carrie Way, *Mgr*
◆ **EMP:** 20 **EST:** 1987
**SQ FT:** 9,000
**SALES (est):** 5.7MM **Privately Held**
Web: www.wascoinc.com
**SIC: 3643**  Electric switches

**(P-11478)**
**YC CABLE USA INC (HQ)**
48010 Fremont Blvd, Fremont (94538-6500)
PHONE..................................510 824-2788
Gary Hsu, *CEO*
Kao Y Fang, *Stockholder*
▲ **EMP:** 70 **EST:** 1991
**SQ FT:** 45,000
**SALES (est):** 16.47MM **Privately Held**
Web: www.yccable.com
**SIC: 3643**  Power line cable
PA: Y.C. Cable Co., Ltd.
  5f, No. 12, Lane 270, Beishen Rd., Sec. 3

## 3644 Noncurrent-carrying Wiring Devices

**(P-11479)**
**FRASE ENTERPRISES**
Also Called: Kortick Manufacturer Co
2261 Carion Ct, Pittsburg (94565-4029)
PHONE..................................510 856-3600
Robert C Frase, *CEO*
Robert Spigel, *
▲ **EMP:** 26 **EST:** 1891
**SQ FT:** 90,000
**SALES (est):** 7.68MM **Privately Held**
Web: www.kortick.com
**SIC: 3644** 3462  Insulators and insulation materials, electrical; Pole line hardware forgings, ferrous

**(P-11480)**
**GUND COMPANY INC**
4701 E Airport Dr, Ontario (91761-7817)
PHONE..................................909 890-9300
Ricardo Beinar, *Mgr*
**EMP:** 15
**SALES (corp-wide):** 55.91MM **Privately Held**
Web: www.thegundcompany.com
**SIC: 3644**  Insulators and insulation materials, electrical
PA: The Gund Company Inc
  9333 Dielman Indus Dr
  314 423-5200

**(P-11481)**
**SAF-T-CO SUPPLY**
Also Called: All American Pipe Bending
1300 E Normandy Pl, Santa Ana (92705-4138)
PHONE..................................714 547-9975
Patricia Mcdonald, *Pr*
Robyn Dague, *
Paul Mcdonald, *Sec*
**EMP:** 50 **EST:** 1987
**SQ FT:** 24,000
**SALES (est):** 24.58MM **Privately Held**
Web: www.saftco.com
**SIC: 3644** 5063 5032 5074  Noncurrent-carrying wiring devices; Electrical apparatus and equipment; Brick, stone, and related material; Pipes and fittings, plastic

**(P-11482)**
**SPEED VENTURES**
901 N Fairfax Ave # 207, West Hollywood (90046-7271)
PHONE..................................323 461-4795
Aaron Bitterman, *Prin*
**EMP:** 20 **EST:** 2007
**SALES (est):** 949.34K **Privately Held**
Web: www.speedventures.com
**SIC: 3644**  Raceways

**(P-11483)**
**TODAY PVC BENDING INC**
995 E Discovery Ln, Anaheim (92801-1147)
PHONE..................................714 953-5707
Joe Castro, *CEO*
Joe Castro, *Pr*
Juan Martinez, *Prin*
Marcellino Rios, *Prin*
**EMP:** 20 **EST:** 2011
**SALES (est):** 2.32MM **Privately Held**
Web: www.todaypvcbending.com
**SIC: 3644**  Electric conduits and fittings

**(P-11484)**
**WESTERN TUBE & CONDUIT CORP (HQ)**
2001 E Dominguez St, Long Beach (90810-1088)
P.O. Box 608 (16161-0608)
PHONE..................................310 537-6300
Barry Zekelman, *CEO*
▲ **EMP:** 88 **EST:** 2004
**SQ FT:** 420,000
**SALES (est):** 45.35MM **Privately Held**
Web: www.westerntube.com
**SIC: 3644** 3446 3317  Electric conduits and fittings; Fences or posts, ornamental iron or steel; Tubing, mechanical or hypodermic sizes: cold drawn stainless
PA: Zekelman Industries, Inc.
  227 W Monroe St Ste 2600

## 3645 Residential Lighting Fixtures

**(P-11485)**
**ALEO LIGHTING INC**
Also Called: Aleo
10988 Bloomfield Ave, Santa Fe Springs (90670-3904)
PHONE..................................877 358-8825
Brandon Yuan, *Pr*
**EMP:** 16 **EST:** 2016
**SALES (est):** 3.96MM **Privately Held**
Web: www.aleolighting.com
**SIC: 3645** 3646  Residential lighting fixtures; Commercial lighting fixtures

**(P-11486)**
**ALGER-TRITON INC**
Also Called: Alger International
5600 W Jefferson Blvd, Los Angeles (90016-3131)
PHONE..................................310 229-9500
Mishel Michael, *Prin*
Clark Scott, *Prin*
Michelle Seminaris Bass, *Prin*
Rick Cooley, *Prin*
◆ **EMP:** 28 **EST:** 1993
**SALES (est):** 3.98MM **Privately Held**
Web: www.studio-at.com
**SIC: 3645**  Residential lighting fixtures

**(P-11487)**
**AMERICAN NAIL PLATE LTG INC**
Also Called: Anp Lighting
9044 Del Mar Ave, Montclair (91763-1627)
PHONE..................................909 982-1807
Harry Foster, *CEO*
Joan Foster, *
Ron Foster, *
Bob Foster, *
▲ **EMP:** 70 **EST:** 1976
**SQ FT:** 13,000
**SALES (est):** 8.33MM **Privately Held**
Web: www.anplighting.com
**SIC: 3645** 3646  Residential lighting fixtures; Commercial lighting fixtures

**(P-11488)**
**ANTHONY CALIFORNIA INC (PA)**
14485 Monte Vista Ave, Chino (91710-5728)
PHONE..................................909 627-0351

# PRODUCTS & SERVICES SECTION
## 3645 - Residential Lighting Fixtures (P-11508)

Kuei-Ian Yeh, *CEO*
Cindy Chang, *
◆ **EMP:** 23 **EST:** 1983
**SALES (est):** 4.79MM
**SALES (corp-wide):** 4.79MM **Privately Held**
Web: www.anthonyshowrooms.com
**SIC: 3645** 5063 5023 Residential lighting fixtures; Lighting fixtures; Lamps: floor, boudoir, desk

### (P-11489)
### ARTIVA USA INC
Also Called: Artiva
12866 Ann St Ste 1, Santa Fe Springs (90670-3064)
PHONE.....................562 298-8968
Jane Wang, *Mgr*
**EMP:** 42
Web: www.artivaus.com
**SIC: 3645** 5063 Residential lighting fixtures; Lighting fixtures
PA: Artiva Usa Inc.
   13901 Magnolia Ave

### (P-11490)
### ARTIVA USA INC (PA)
Also Called: Artiva
13901 Magnolia Ave, Chino (91710-7030)
PHONE.....................909 628-1388
Po Y Webb, *Pr*
Gina Yeh, *VP*
▲ **EMP:** 35 **EST:** 2008
**SQ FT:** 20,000
**SALES (est):** 2.63MM **Privately Held**
Web: www.artivaus.com
**SIC: 3645** 5063 Residential lighting fixtures; Lighting fixtures

### (P-11491)
### B-K LIGHTING INC
40429 Brickyard Dr, Madera (93636-9515)
PHONE.....................559 438-5800
Douglas W Hagen, *Pr*
Nathan Sloan, *
▲ **EMP:** 90 **EST:** 1985
**SQ FT:** 70,000
**SALES (est):** 19.96MM **Privately Held**
Web: www.bklighting.com
**SIC: 3645** 3646 5063 Residential lighting fixtures; Commercial lighting fixtures; Electrical apparatus and equipment

### (P-11492)
### BASE LITE CORPORATION
Also Called: Baselite
12260 Eastend Ave, Chino (91710-2008)
PHONE.....................909 444-2776
Moaaa A Teixeira, *CEO*
**EMP:** 38 **EST:** 1997
**SQ FT:** 10,000
**SALES (est):** 4.48MM **Privately Held**
Web: www.baselite.com
**SIC: 3645** 3646 Residential lighting fixtures; Commercial lighting fixtures

### (P-11493)
### DAB INC
Also Called: Spectrum Lighting
13415 Marquardt Ave, Santa Fe Springs (90670-5012)
PHONE.....................562 623-4773
David A Boose, *Pr*
▲ **EMP:** 52 **EST:** 1978
**SQ FT:** 31,000
**SALES (est):** 2.44MM **Privately Held**
Web: www.scll.com
**SIC: 3645** 3648 3646 Residential lighting fixtures; Decorative area lighting fixtures; Commercial lighting fixtures

### (P-11494)
### DMF INC
Also Called: Dmf Lighting
1118 E 223rd St Unit 1, Carson (90745-4210)
PHONE.....................323 934-7779
Morteza Danesh, *Pr*
Fariba Danesh, *
Michael Danesh, *
▲ **EMP:** 51 **EST:** 1989
**SQ FT:** 8,000
**SALES (est):** 15.07MM **Privately Held**
Web: www.dmflighting.com
**SIC: 3645** 5063 Residential lighting fixtures; Lighting fixtures, commercial and industrial

### (P-11495)
### FEIT ELECTRIC COMPANY INC (PA)
Also Called: Feit Electric
4901 Gregg Rd, Pico Rivera (90660-2108)
PHONE.....................562 463-2852
Aaron Feit, *CEO*
Alan Feit, *
Toby S Feit, *
John Mcmillin, *CFO*
◆ **EMP:** 141 **EST:** 1978
**SQ FT:** 300,000
**SALES (est):** 43.92MM
**SALES (corp-wide):** 43.92MM **Privately Held**
Web: www.feit.com
**SIC: 3645** 3641 5023 3646 Residential lighting fixtures; Electric light bulbs, complete; Homefurnishings; Commercial lighting fixtures

### (P-11496)
### GLOBALUX LIGHTING LLC
773 S Benson Ave, Ontario (91762-4750)
PHONE.....................909 591-7506
Zeeshan Parekh, *Managing Member*
▲ **EMP:** 16 **EST:** 2011
**SALES (est):** 3.87MM **Privately Held**
Web: www.globaluxlighting.com
**SIC: 3645** 3646 5063 Residential lighting fixtures; Commercial lighting fixtures; Lighting fittings and accessories

### (P-11497)
### LIGHTS OF AMERICA INC (PA)
13602 12th St Ste B, Chino (91710-5200)
PHONE.....................909 594-7883
Usman Vakil, *CEO*
Farooq Vakil, *
◆ **EMP:** 500 **EST:** 1977
**SQ FT:** 210,000
**SALES (est):** 14.27MM
**SALES (corp-wide):** 14.27MM **Privately Held**
Web: www.lightsofamerica.com
**SIC: 3645** 3646 3641 Fluorescent lighting fixtures, residential; Fluorescent lighting fixtures, commercial; Electric lamps

### (P-11498)
### MAXIM LIGHTING INTL INC
247 Vineland Ave, City Of Industry (91746-2319)
PHONE.....................626 956-4200
**EMP:** 51
**SALES (corp-wide):** 47.04MM **Privately Held**
Web: www.maximlighting.com
**SIC: 3645** Residential lighting fixtures
PA: Maxim Lighting International, Inc.
   253 N Vineland Ave
   626 956-4200

### (P-11499)
### NL&A COLLECTIONS INC
Also Called: Nova
6323 Maywood Ave, Huntington Park (90255-4531)
P.O. Box 661820 (90066-8820)
PHONE.....................323 277-6266
Daniel Edelist, *Pr*
◆ **EMP:** 40 **EST:** 1980
**SQ FT:** 48,675
**SALES (est):** 1.96MM **Privately Held**
Web: www.novaofcalifornia.com
**SIC: 3645** 5023 Boudoir lamps; Lamps: floor, boudoir, desk

### (P-11500)
### PHILIPS NORTH AMERICA LLC
11201 Iberia St Ste A, Jurupa Valley (91752-3280)
PHONE.....................909 574-1800
Kenneth Parivar, *Brnch Mgr*
**EMP:** 148
**SALES (corp-wide):** 18.51B **Privately Held**
Web: usa.philips.com
**SIC: 3645** 3648 3646 Residential lighting fixtures; Outdoor lighting equipment; Ceiling systems, luminous
HQ: Philips North America Llc
   222 Jacobs St Fl 3
   Cambridge MA 02141
   617 245-5900

### (P-11501)
### PHOENIX DAY INC
3431 Regatta Blvd, Richmond (94804-4594)
PHONE.....................415 822-4414
Tony Brenta, *Pr*
▲ **EMP:** 15 **EST:** 1850
**SQ FT:** 8,000
**SALES (est):** 3.32MM **Privately Held**
Web: www.phoenixday.com
**SIC: 3645** 3646 3446 Residential lighting fixtures; Commercial lighting fixtures; Ornamental metalwork

### (P-11502)
### SPECTRUM SYSTEMS SF
1331 Old County Rd, Belmont (94002-3968)
PHONE.....................415 361-2429
Timothy Brian Smith, *Prin*
**EMP:** 31 **EST:** 2016
**SALES (est):** 1.95MM **Privately Held**
Web: www.spectrumsystemssf.net
**SIC: 3645** Residential lighting fixtures

### (P-11503)
### TECHTRON PRODUCTS INC
2694 W Winton Ave, Hayward (94545-1108)
PHONE.....................510 293-3500
William Swen, *Pr*
Shiow Shya Swen, *
**EMP:** 43 **EST:** 1977
**SQ FT:** 50,500
**SALES (est):** 3.91MM **Privately Held**
Web: www.techtronproducts.com
**SIC: 3645** 5063 Residential lighting fixtures; Lighting fixtures, residential

### (P-11504)
### TROY-CSL LIGHTING INC
14508 Nelson Ave, City Of Industry (91744-3514)
P.O. Box 514310 (90051-4310)
PHONE.....................626 336-4511
David Littman, *CEO*
Steve Nadell, *
Anne Wilcox, *
Ian Wilcox, *
◆ **EMP:** 205 **EST:** 1970
**SALES (est):** 40.47MM **Privately Held**
Web: www.csllighting.com
**SIC: 3645** 3646 Wall lamps; Ornamental lighting fixtures, commercial

### (P-11505)
### VIDESSENCE LLC (PA)
10768 Lower Azusa Rd, El Monte (91731-1306)
PHONE.....................626 579-0943
Toni Swarens, *Pr*
▲ **EMP:** 25 **EST:** 1951
**SQ FT:** 35,000
**SALES (est):** 4.6MM
**SALES (corp-wide):** 4.6MM **Privately Held**
Web: www.videssence.tv
**SIC: 3645** 3648 Residential lighting fixtures; Stage lighting equipment

### (P-11506)
### VODE LIGHTING LLC
Also Called: Vode
21684 8th St E Ste 700, Sonoma (95476-2818)
PHONE.....................707 996-9898
Ann Schiffers, *CEO*
Scott Yu, *Chief Creative Officer*
George Mieling, *Business Development Advisor*
▲ **EMP:** 19 **EST:** 2005
**SALES (est):** 9.5MM
**SALES (corp-wide):** 70.73MM **Privately Held**
Web: www.vode.com
**SIC: 3645** 3646 Residential lighting fixtures; Commercial lighting fixtures
PA: Lmpg Inc
   1220 Boul Marie-Victorin
   514 937-3003

### (P-11507)
### WANGS ALLIANCE CORPORATION
Also Called: Wac Lighting
1750 S Archibald Ave, Ontario (91761-1239)
PHONE.....................909 230-9401
Nina Chou, *Prin*
**EMP:** 20
**SALES (corp-wide):** 48.43MM **Privately Held**
Web: www.waclighting.com
**SIC: 3645** Residential lighting fixtures
PA: Wangs Alliance Corporation
   44 Harbor Park Dr
   516 515-5000

### (P-11508)
### WASHOE EQUIPMENT INC
Also Called: Sunoptics Prismatic Skylights
6201 27th St, Sacramento (95822-3712)
PHONE.....................916 395-4700
**TOLL FREE:** 800
Jim Blomberg, *Pr*
Jerry Blomberg, *
Thomas Blomberg, *
Grant Grabble, *
▼ **EMP:** 19 **EST:** 1978
**SQ FT:** 16,000
**SALES (est):** 6.13MM
**SALES (corp-wide):** 3.84B **Publicly Held**
Web: www.aessunoptics.com
**SIC: 3645** 3646 5031 Residential lighting fixtures; Commercial lighting fixtures; Skylights, all materials
PA: Acuity Brands, Inc.
   1170 Pchtree St Ne Ste 23
   404 853-1400

# 3645 - Residential Lighting Fixtures

**(P-11509)**
**XICATO INC**
102 Cooper Ct, Los Gatos (95032-7604)
PHONE...........................866 223-8395
Amir Zoufonoun, *CEO*
Mark Pugh, *
Joanna Brace, *
Steve Workman, *
Menko Deroos, *
▲ **EMP:** 39 **EST:** 2007
**SALES (est):** 8.69MM **Privately Held**
Web: www.xicato.com
**SIC: 3645** Garden, patio, walkway and yard lighting fixtures: electric

**(P-11510)**
**YAWITZ INC**
Also Called: Evergreen Lighting
1379 Ridgeway St, Pomona (91768-2701)
PHONE...........................909 865-5599
John Klena, *CEO*
George Cole Iii, *Marketing*
Victor Rosen, *
▲ **EMP:** 42 **EST:** 1997
**SQ FT:** 23,000
**SALES (est):** 5.53MM **Privately Held**
Web: www.evergreenlighting.com
**SIC: 3645 3646** Fluorescent lighting fixtures, residential; Fluorescent lighting fixtures, commercial

**(P-11511)**
**ZUO MODERN CONTEMPORARY INC (PA)**
Also Called: Zuo
80 Swan Way Ste 150, Oakland (94621-1451)
PHONE...........................510 877-4087
Luis Ruesga, *CEO*
Steven Poon, *
Terrence Tam, *
◆ **EMP:** 26 **EST:** 2004
**SQ FT:** 64,000
**SALES (est):** 9.5MM
**SALES (corp-wide):** 9.5MM **Privately Held**
Web: www.zuomod.com
**SIC: 3645 5021** Residential lighting fixtures; Office furniture, nec

## 3646 Commercial Lighting Fixtures

**(P-11512)**
**1LE CALIFORNIA INC**
3224 Mchenry Ave Ste F, Modesto (95350-1442)
PHONE...........................209 846-7541
**EMP:** 40
**SIC: 3646 3645** Commercial lighting fixtures; Residential lighting fixtures

**(P-11513)**
**A V POLES AND LIGHTING INC**
43827 Division St, Lancaster (93535-4061)
P.O. Box 9054 (93539-9054)
PHONE...........................661 945-2731
Luis Romero, *CEO*
Roberta Wood, *Pr*
▼ **EMP:** 20 **EST:** 2013
**SQ FT:** 12,000
**SALES (est):** 2.35MM **Privately Held**
Web: www.avpolesandlighting.com
**SIC: 3646** Commercial lighting fixtures

**(P-11514)**
**ACCLAIM LIGHTING LLC**
6122 S Eastern Ave, Commerce (90040-3402)
PHONE...........................323 213-4626
Charles J Davies, *Prin*
▲ **EMP:** 25 **EST:** 2003
**SALES (est):** 3.74MM **Privately Held**
Web: www.acclaimlighting.com
**SIC: 3646 3679 5063** Commercial lighting fixtures; Electronic loads and power supplies; Wire and cable

**(P-11515)**
**ACUITY BRANDS LIGHTING INC**
Peerless Lighting
55 Harrison St Ste 200, Oakland (94607-3772)
P.O. Box 6143 (94524-1143)
PHONE...........................510 845-2760
Thor Scordelis, *Mgr*
**EMP:** 31
**SALES (corp-wide):** 3.84B **Publicly Held**
Web: lithonia.acuitybrands.com
**SIC: 3646** Fluorescent lighting fixtures, commercial
HQ: Acuity Brands Lighting, Inc.
1170 Pchtree St Ne Ste 23
Atlanta GA 30309

**(P-11516)**
**ACUITY BRANDS LIGHTING INC**
12281 Bradley Avenue, City Of Industry (91748)
P.O. Box 8550 (91748-0550)
PHONE...........................626 965-0711
**EMP:** 22
**SALES (corp-wide):** 3.84B **Publicly Held**
Web: lithonia.acuitybrands.com
**SIC: 3646 5063** Fluorescent lighting fixtures, commercial; Electrical apparatus and equipment
HQ: Acuity Brands Lighting, Inc.
1170 Pchtree St Ne Ste 23
Atlanta GA 30309

**(P-11517)**
**AGNETIX INC**
7965 Dunbrook Rd Ste I, San Diego (92126-6325)
P.O. Box 5414 (94805)
PHONE...........................833 246-3849
Jordan Miles, *CEO*
Elisa Danielson, *CFO*
Nicholas Maderas, *Sec*
**EMP:** 15 **EST:** 2017
**SALES (est):** 6.23MM **Privately Held**
Web: www.agnetix.com
**SIC: 3646** Commercial lighting fixtures

**(P-11518)**
**ALCON LIGHTING INC**
2845 S Robertson Blvd, Los Angeles (90034-2439)
PHONE...........................310 733-1248
**EMP:** 20 **EST:** 2016
**SALES (est):** 3.8MM **Privately Held**
Web: www.alconlighting.com
**SIC: 3646** Commercial lighting fixtures

**(P-11519)**
**ARTE DE MEXICO INC**
Also Called: Arte De Mexico
5506 Riverton Ave, North Hollywood (91601-2815)
PHONE...........................818 753-4510
David Staffers, *Mgr*
**EMP:** 71
**SALES (corp-wide):** 8.01MM **Privately Held**
Web: www.artedemexico.com
**SIC: 3646 3446** Commercial lighting fixtures; Architectural metalwork
PA: Arte De Mexico, Inc.
1000 Chestnut St
818 753-4559

**(P-11520)**
**BLUE PLANET ENERGY SOLUTIONS**
4370 La Jolla Village Dr Ste 660, San Diego (92122-6244)
P.O. Box 910757 (92191-0757)
PHONE...........................858 947-0100
Michael Lance Copelin, *CEO*
**EMP:** 15 **EST:** 2010
**SALES (est):** 3.03MM **Privately Held**
Web: www.blueplanetes.com
**SIC: 3646 5063** Commercial lighting fixtures; Electrical apparatus and equipment

**(P-11521)**
**BORDEN LIGHTING**
2355 Verna Ct, San Leandro (94577-4205)
P.O. Box 2817 (94501-0817)
PHONE...........................510 357-0171
Randy Borden, *Prin*
James Borden, *
Allen Reaves, *Prin*
Karla Paredes-perez, *Prin*
Isaiah Goff, *Prin*
**EMP:** 24 **EST:** 1962
**SALES (est):** 891K **Privately Held**
Web: www.bordenlighting.com
**SIC: 3646 3645** Fluorescent lighting fixtures, commercial; Fluorescent lighting fixtures, residential

**(P-11522)**
**BOYD LIGHTING FIXTURE COMPANY (PA)**
Also Called: Boyd Lighting
200a Harbor Dr, Sausalito (94965-1427)
PHONE...........................415 778-4300
John S Sweet Junior, *Pr*
Udell Blackham, *CFO*
◆ **EMP:** 20 **EST:** 1921
**SQ FT:** 13,000
**SALES (est):** 9.65MM
**SALES (corp-wide):** 9.65MM **Privately Held**
Web: www.boydlighting.com
**SIC: 3646 3645** Commercial lighting fixtures; Residential lighting fixtures

**(P-11523)**
**C W COLE & COMPANY INC**
Also Called: Cole Lighting
2560 Rosemead Blvd, South El Monte (91733-1593)
PHONE...........................626 443-2473
Russell W Cole, *Ch Bd*
Stephen W Cole, *
Donald Cole, *
**EMP:** 41 **EST:** 1911
**SQ FT:** 25,000
**SALES (est):** 3.22MM **Privately Held**
Web: www.colelighting.com
**SIC: 3646** Commercial lighting fixtures

**(P-11524)**
**DECO ENTERPRISES INC**
Also Called: Deco Lighting
2917 Vail Ave, Commerce (90040-2615)
PHONE...........................323 726-2575
Saman Sinai, *Prin*
Saman Sinai, *CEO*
Ben Peterson, *
Benjamin Pouladian, *
▲ **EMP:** 60 **EST:** 2005
**SQ FT:** 100,000
**SALES (est):** 19.81MM **Privately Held**
Web: www.getdeco.com
**SIC: 3646** Commercial lighting fixtures

**(P-11525)**
**DSA PHOTOTECH LLC**
Also Called: DSA Signage
2321 E Gladwick St, Rancho Dominguez (90220-6209)
PHONE...........................866 868-1602
▲ **EMP:** 50 **EST:** 1974
**SALES (est):** 14.07MM **Privately Held**
Web: www.dsasignage.com
**SIC: 3646 3648** Commercial lighting fixtures; Lighting equipment, nec

**(P-11526)**
**EDISON PRICE LIGHTING INC (PA)**
Also Called: Epl
5424 E Slauson Ave, Commerce (90040-2919)
PHONE...........................718 685-0700
Emma Price, *Pr*
Joel R Siegel, *VP*
James D Vizzini, *VP*
Gregory Mortman, *VP*
▲ **EMP:** 119 **EST:** 1952
**SALES (est):** 7.05MM
**SALES (corp-wide):** 7.05MM **Privately Held**
Web: www.epl.com
**SIC: 3646** Ceiling systems, luminous

**(P-11527)**
**ELEMENT CONTROLS CORP**
2917 Vail Ave, Commerce (90040-2615)
PHONE...........................323 727-2737
◆ **EMP:** 15
Web: www.elementcontrols.com
**SIC: 3646** Commercial lighting fixtures

**(P-11528)**
**ENERTRON TECHNOLOGIES INC**
3525 Del Mar Heights Rd, San Diego (92130-2199)
PHONE...........................800 537-7649
Ronald Curley, *Pr*
**EMP:** 50 **EST:** 1985
**SALES (est):** 2.34MM **Privately Held**
**SIC: 3646 3645** Fluorescent lighting fixtures, commercial; Fluorescent lighting fixtures, residential

**(P-11529)**
**ENLIGHTED INC**
46897 Bayside Pkwy, Fremont (94538)
PHONE...........................650 964-1094
Stefan Schwab, *CEO*
Jens Stottmann, *
Tanuj Mohan, *
▲ **EMP:** 91 **EST:** 2009
**SALES (est):** 24.26MM
**SALES (corp-wide):** 84.48B **Privately Held**
Web: www.enlightedinc.com
**SIC: 3646** Commercial lighting fixtures
HQ: Siemens Industry, Inc.
1000 Deerfield Pkwy
Buffalo Grove IL 60089
847 215-1000

**(P-11530)**
**EXIT LIGHT CO INC**
Also Called: Light Fixture Industries
3170 Scott St, Vista (92081-8318)
PHONE...........................877 352-3948
Jeannette Carrico, *Pr*
Paul Carrico, *CFO*
◆ **EMP:** 15 **EST:** 2000
**SQ FT:** 11,000
**SALES (est):** 3.42MM **Privately Held**
Web: www.exitlightco.com

## PRODUCTS & SERVICES SECTION
### 3646 - Commercial Lighting Fixtures (P-11552)

SIC: **3646** 5063 3993 Commercial lighting fixtures; Signaling equipment, electrical; Electric signs

**(P-11531)**
**FINELITE INC (PA)**
Also Called: Finelite
30500 Whipple Rd, Union City (94587-1530)
PHONE..................510 441-1100
Jerome Mix, *CEO*
Walter B Clark, *Ch*
Jane White, *Marketing*
Margaret Fenton, *CFO*
Mark Benguerel, *COO*
◆ **EMP:** 137 **EST:** 1991
**SQ FT:** 140,132
**SALES (est):** 58.1MM **Privately Held**
Web: www.finelite.com
SIC: **3646** Commercial lighting fixtures

**(P-11532)**
**FLEXFIRE LEDS INC**
Also Called: Evoralight
3554 Business Park Dr Ste F, Costa Mesa (92626-1423)
PHONE..................925 273-9080
Brenton Mauriello, *CEO*
**EMP:** 24 **EST:** 2011
**SQ FT:** 4,600
**SALES (est):** 2.22MM **Privately Held**
Web: www.flexfireleds.com
SIC: **3646** 5063 Commercial lighting fixtures; Lighting fixtures

**(P-11533)**
**FLO KINO INC**
2840 N Hollywood Way, Burbank (91505-1023)
PHONE..................818 767-6528
**EMP:** 103 **EST:** 1984
**SALES (est):** 4.81MM **Privately Held**
SIC: **3646** Commercial lighting fixtures

**(P-11534)**
**FLUORESCENT SUPPLY CO INC**
Also Called: Fsc
9120 Center Ave, Rancho Cucamonga (91730-5310)
PHONE..................909 948-8878
Vincent Alonzi, *Pr*
▲ **EMP:** 48 **EST:** 1969
**SQ FT:** 80,000
**SALES (est):** 22.04MM
**SALES (corp-wide):** 22.04MM **Privately Held**
Web: www.fsclighting.com
SIC: **3646** 3645 Commercial lighting fixtures; Residential lighting fixtures
PA: Onward Capital Llc
525 W Monroe St Ste 22109
847 983-0869

**(P-11535)**
**FOCUS INDUSTRIES INC**
Also Called: Focus Landscape
25301 Commercentre Dr, Lake Forest (92630-8808)
PHONE..................949 830-1350
Stan Shibata, *Pr*
June Shibata, *
▲ **EMP:** 100 **EST:** 1989
**SQ FT:** 40,000
**SALES (est):** 22.55MM **Privately Held**
Web: www.focusindustries.com
SIC: **3646** 5063 Commercial lighting fixtures; Electrical apparatus and equipment

**(P-11536)**
**HALLMARK LIGHTING LLC**
Also Called: Hallmark Lighting
1945 S Tubeway Ave, Commerce (90040-1611)
PHONE..................818 885-5010
Christopher Larocca, *CEO*
Robert Godlewski, *
Julie Winfield, *
◆ **EMP:** 80 **EST:** 1978
**SALES (est):** 5.35MM **Privately Held**
Web: www.hallmarklighting.com
SIC: **3646** 3645 3641 Commercial lighting fixtures; Wall lamps; Electric lamps

**(P-11537)**
**HI-LITE MANUFACTURING CO INC**
13450 Monte Vista Ave, Chino (91710-5149)
PHONE..................909 465-1999
Dorothy A Ohai, *Pr*
◆ **EMP:** 90 **EST:** 1959
**SQ FT:** 157,000
**SALES (est):** 3.61MM **Privately Held**
Web: www.hilitemfg.com
SIC: **3646** 3645 Commercial lighting fixtures; Residential lighting fixtures

**(P-11538)**
**HOLOPHANE CORPORATION**
2231 4th St, Berkeley (94710-2214)
PHONE..................510 540-0156
Denise Bernard, *Prin*
**EMP:** 1910
**SALES (corp-wide):** 3.84B **Publicly Held**
Web: holophane.acuitybrands.com
SIC: **3646** Commercial lighting fixtures
HQ: Holophane Corporation
3825 Columbus Rd Bldg A
Granville OH 43023

**(P-11539)**
**INTENSE LIGHTING LLC**
3340 E La Palma Ave, Anaheim (92806-2814)
PHONE..................714 630-9877
Roger Weisenaur, *
Kenneth Eidsvold, *
Tom Elam, *Prin*
Allan Gray, *Prin*
◆ **EMP:** 80 **EST:** 2001
**SQ FT:** 153,000
**SALES (est):** 22.26MM
**SALES (corp-wide):** 1.46B **Privately Held**
Web: www.intenselighting.com
SIC: **3646** 3645 Commercial lighting fixtures; Residential lighting fixtures
PA: Leviton Manufacturing Co., Inc.
201 N Service Rd
800 323-8920

**(P-11540)**
**LA SPEC INDUSTRIES INC**
Also Called: Laspec Lighting
2315 E 52nd St, Vernon (90058-3499)
PHONE..................323 588-8746
Jacob Melamed, *Prin*
J Melamed, *
▲ **EMP:** 15 **EST:** 1984
**SQ FT:** 30,000
**SALES (est):** 2.94MM **Privately Held**
Web: www.laspec.com
SIC: **3646** 3648 Commercial lighting fixtures; Decorative area lighting fixtures

**(P-11541)**
**LAMPS PLUS INC**
Also Called: Pacific Coast Lighting
4723 Telephone Rd, Ventura (93003-5242)
PHONE..................805 642-9007
David Hillard, *Mgr*
**EMP:** 23
**SALES (corp-wide):** 490.53MM **Privately Held**
Web: www.lampsplus.com
SIC: **3646** 5719 5064 Commercial lighting fixtures; Lamps and lamp shades; Fans, household: electric
PA: Lamps Plus, Inc.
20250 Plummer St
818 886-5267

**(P-11542)**
**LEXSTAR INC (PA)**
Also Called: Lites On West Soho
4959 Kalamis Way, Oceanside (92056-7411)
PHONE..................845 947-1415
Uri Redlich, *Pr*
▲ **EMP:** 15 **EST:** 1973
**SQ FT:** 15,000
**SALES (est):** 2.4MM
**SALES (corp-wide):** 2.4MM **Privately Held**
Web: www.lexstar.com
SIC: **3646** Commercial lighting fixtures

**(P-11543)**
**LF ILLUMINATION LLC**
Also Called: Formed Lighting
9200 Deering Ave, Chatsworth (91311-5803)
PHONE..................818 885-1335
Loren Kessel, *Pr*
Eileen S Cheng, *
▲ **EMP:** 51 **EST:** 2013
**SALES (est):** 9.68MM **Privately Held**
Web: www.lfillumination.com
SIC: **3646** 3645 5719 Commercial lighting fixtures; Residential lighting fixtures; Lighting fixtures

**(P-11544)**
**LIGHTWAY INDUSTRIES**
28435 Industry Dr, Valencia (91355-4107)
PHONE..................661 257-0286
Jeffrey Bargman, *Pr*
Gary N Patten, *
**EMP:** 15 **EST:** 1980
**SQ FT:** 22,300
**SALES (est):** 4.75MM **Privately Held**
Web: www.lightwayind.com
SIC: **3646** 3645 Commercial lighting fixtures; Residential lighting fixtures

**(P-11545)**
**LUMIGROW INC**
6550 Vallejo St Ste 200, Emeryville (94608-1112)
PHONE..................800 514-0487
Jay Albere Ii, *CEO*
Kevin Wells, *
**EMP:** 28 **EST:** 2008
**SALES (est):** 2.47MM **Privately Held**
Web: www.lumigrow.com
SIC: **3646** Ornamental lighting fixtures, commercial

**(P-11546)**
**MEDICAL ILLUMINATION INTERNATIONAL INC (PA)**
Also Called: Nuvo
19749 Dearborn St, Chatsworth (91311-6510)
PHONE..................818 838-3025
◆ **EMP:** 17 **EST:** 1978
**SALES (est):** 17.45MM
**SALES (corp-wide):** 17.45MM **Privately Held**
Web: www.medillum.com
SIC: **3646** 3841 Fluorescent lighting fixtures, commercial; Surgical and medical instruments

**(P-11547)**
**MODERN WOODWORKS INC**
Also Called: Modern Woodworks
7949 Deering Ave, Canoga Park (91304-5009)
PHONE..................800 575-3475
George Mekhtarian, *CEO*
Allen Mekhtarian, *
▲ **EMP:** 35 **EST:** 2000
**SQ FT:** 10,000
**SALES (est):** 4.04MM **Privately Held**
Web: www.californialightworks.com
SIC: **3646** Commercial lighting fixtures

**(P-11548)**
**NOMOFLO ENTERPRISES INC**
Also Called: Kino Flo Lighting Systems
2840 N Hollywood Way, Burbank (91505-1023)
PHONE..................818 767-6528
Frieder Hochheim, *Pr*
Gary Swink, *VP*
▲ **EMP:** 51 **EST:** 1987
**SALES (est):** 22.93MM **Privately Held**
Web: www.kinoflo.com
SIC: **3646** Commercial lighting fixtures

**(P-11549)**
**OPTIC ARTS HOLDINGS INC**
716 Monterey Pass Rd, Monterey Park (91754-3607)
PHONE..................213 250-6069
Jason Mullen, *CEO*
Dorian L Hicklin, *
Mason Barker, *
**EMP:** 47 **EST:** 2011
**SQ FT:** 15,750
**SALES (est):** 7.17MM
**SALES (corp-wide):** 21.63MM **Privately Held**
Web: www.luminii.com
SIC: **3646** 3645 3648 Commercial lighting fixtures; Residential lighting fixtures; Decorative area lighting fixtures
PA: Luminii Llc
7777 N Merrimac Ave
224 333-6033

**(P-11550)**
**ORION CHANDELIER INC**
2202 S Wright St, Santa Ana (92705-5316)
PHONE..................714 668-9668
Paul Depersis, *Pr*
Kirk Fisher, *Asst VP*
◆ **EMP:** 17 **EST:** 1998
**SQ FT:** 3,000
**SALES (est):** 2.79MM **Privately Held**
Web: www.orionchandelier.com
SIC: **3646** Commercial lighting fixtures

**(P-11551)**
**PACIFIC LTG & STANDARDS CO**
2815 Los Flores Blvd, Lynwood (90262-2416)
PHONE..................310 603-9344
Frank Munoz, *Pr*
Enrique Garcia, *
▲ **EMP:** 34 **EST:** 1982
**SQ FT:** 17,000
**SALES (est):** 3.31MM **Privately Held**
Web: www.pacificlighting.com
SIC: **3646** Commercial lighting fixtures

**(P-11552)**
**PACLIGHTS LLC (PA)**
Also Called: Paclights

# 3646 - Commercial Lighting Fixtures (P-11553)

15318 El Prado Rd, Chino (91708)
P.O. Box 928 (91709)
PHONE..................................800 980-6386
Tommy Zhen, CEO
Fiona Zhao, Pr
▲ EMP: 19 EST: 2013
SQ FT: 20,000
SALES (est): 5.29MM
SALES (corp-wide): 5.29MM Privately Held
Web: www.paclights.com
SIC: 3646 Commercial lighting fixtures

**(P-11553)**
**PRUDENTIAL LIGHTING CORP (PA)**
Also Called: P L M
1774 E 21st St, Los Angeles (90058-1007)
P.O. Box 58736 (90058-0736)
PHONE..................................213 477-1694
Stanely J Ellis, CEO
Jeffrey Ellis, *
Elliot Ellis, *
Jolie Ellis, *
▲ EMP: 120 EST: 1955
SQ FT: 112,000
SALES (est): 21.31MM
SALES (corp-wide): 21.31MM Privately Held
Web: www.prulite.com
SIC: 3646 Fluorescent lighting fixtures, commercial

**(P-11554)**
**R W SWARENS ASSOCIATES INC**
Also Called: Engineered Lighting Products
10768 Lower Azusa Rd, El Monte (91731-1306)
PHONE..................................626 579-0943
Toni Swarens, CEO
Lauri Maines, *
▲ EMP: 33 EST: 1984
SALES (est): 2.08MM Privately Held
Web: www.elplighting.com
SIC: 3646 Commercial lighting fixtures

**(P-11555)**
**SAPPHIRE CHANDELIER LLC**
505 Porter Way, Placentia (92870-6454)
PHONE..................................714 879-3660
Hector Garibay, Pt
Hector Garibay, Managing Member
▲ EMP: 61 EST: 2009
SQ FT: 10,000
SALES (est): 6.88MM Privately Held
Web: www.sapphirechandelier.com
SIC: 3646 Commercial lighting fixtures

**(P-11556)**
**SCOTT LAMP COMPANY INC**
Also Called: Scott Architectural
355 Watt Dr, Fairfield (94534-4207)
PHONE..................................707 864-2066
Dennis J Scott, CEO
Dennis Scott, *
Paul R Scott, *
Eileen K Scott-emerson, Sec
▲ EMP: 90 EST: 1957
SQ FT: 71,000
SALES (est): 19.89MM Privately Held
Web: www.scottlamp.com
SIC: 3646 3645 Ceiling systems, luminous; Residential lighting fixtures

**(P-11557)**
**SIGNIFY NORTH AMERICA CORP**
3350 Enterprise Dr, Bloomington (92316-3538)
PHONE..................................732 563-3000
EMP: 110

Web: www.signify.com
SIC: 3646 Commercial lighting fixtures
HQ: Signify North America Corporation
400 Crossing Blvd Ste 600
Bridgewater NJ 08807
732 563-3000

**(P-11558)**
**SPOTLITE POWER CORPORATION**
9937 Jefferson Blvd Ste 110, Culver City (90232-3528)
PHONE..................................310 838-2367
Halston Mikail, Pr
▲ EMP: 28 EST: 2016
SALES (est): 636.19K
SALES (corp-wide): 2.17MM Privately Held
SIC: 3646 Commercial lighting fixtures
PA: Spotlite America Corporation
9937 Jefferson Blvd # 110
310 829-0200

**(P-11559)**
**SUN VALLEY LTG STANDARDS INC**
Also Called: US Architectural Lighting
660 W Avenue O, Palmdale (93551-3610)
PHONE..................................661 233-2000
Joseph Straus, Pr
Judith Straus, VP
EMP: 52 EST: 1984
SQ FT: 30,000
SALES (est): 2.52MM
SALES (corp-wide): 24.01MM Privately Held
Web: www.usaltg.com
SIC: 3646 5063 3648 Ornamental lighting fixtures, commercial; Electrical apparatus and equipment; Lighting equipment, nec
PA: U.S. Pole Company, Inc.
660 W Avenue O
800 877-6537

**(P-11560)**
**T-1 LIGHTING INC**
9929 Pioneer Blvd, Santa Fe Springs (90670-3219)
PHONE..................................626 234-2328
Artur Saakyan, CEO
Pang Chun Zhang, CFO
An Bao Vu, COO
EMP: 16 EST: 2016
SQ FT: 19,660
SALES (est): 4.71MM Privately Held
Web: www.t1-lighting.com
SIC: 3646 Commercial lighting fixtures

**(P-11561)**
**TANKO STREETLIGHTING INC**
Also Called: Tanko Streetlighting Services
220 Bay Shore Blvd, San Francisco (94124-1323)
PHONE..................................415 254-7579
Jason Tanko, Pr
Clare Bressani, *
▲ EMP: 31 EST: 2004
SQ FT: 5,000
SALES (est): 4.96MM Privately Held
Web: www.tankolighting.com
SIC: 3646 Commercial lighting fixtures

**(P-11562)**
**TOPAZ LIGHTING COMPANY LLC**
225 Parkside Dr, San Fernando (91340-3033)
PHONE..................................818 838-3123
EMP: 25
SALES (corp-wide): 1.7B Privately Held
Web: www.southwire.com

SIC: 3646 Commercial lighting fixtures
HQ: Topaz Lighting Company Llc
3241 Route 112 Ste 7
Medford NY 11763
800 666-2852

**(P-11563)**
**TRITON CHANDELIER INC**
Also Called: Triton
1301 Dove St Ste 900, Newport Beach (92660-2473)
PHONE..................................714 957-9600
Richard Cooley, Pr
▲ EMP: 18 EST: 1995
SQ FT: 10,000
SALES (est): 851.62K Privately Held
SIC: 3646 Chandeliers, commercial

**(P-11564)**
**TUJAYAR ENTERPRISES INC**
Also Called: Tube Lighting Products
1346 Pioneer Way, El Cajon (92020-1626)
PHONE..................................619 442-0577
Rick Tempkin, Pr
▲ EMP: 21 EST: 1989
SQ FT: 9,000
SALES (est): 2.25MM Privately Held
Web: www.tubelightingproducts.com
SIC: 3646 3645 Commercial lighting fixtures; Residential lighting fixtures

**(P-11565)**
**US ENERGY TECHNOLOGIES INC**
Also Called: US Lighting Tech
14370 Myford Road Ste 100, Walnut (91789)
P.O. Box 365 (90621-0365)
PHONE..................................714 617-8800
◆ EMP: 50
Web: www.uslightingtech.com
SIC: 3646 Commercial lighting fixtures

**(P-11566)**
**US POLE COMPANY INC (PA)**
Also Called: U S Architectural Lighting
660 W Avenue O, Palmdale (93551-3610)
PHONE..................................800 877-6537
Joseph Straus, Pr
◆ EMP: 97 EST: 1984
SQ FT: 112,000
SALES (est): 24.01MM
SALES (corp-wide): 24.01MM Privately Held
Web: www.usaltg.com
SIC: 3646 Commercial lighting fixtures

**(P-11567)**
**VISION ENGRG MET STAMPING INC**
Also Called: Vision Engineering
114 Grand Cypress Ave, Palmdale (93551-3617)
P.O. Box 901780 (93590-1780)
PHONE..................................661 575-0933
Joseph Avila, CEO
EMP: 100 EST: 1997
SQ FT: 72,000
SALES (est): 2.4MM Privately Held
Web: www.visionengineering.com
SIC: 3646 Ceiling systems, luminous

**(P-11568)**
**VISIONAIRE LIGHTING LLC**
Also Called: Visionaire Lighting
3780 Kilroy Airport Way, Long Beach (90806)
PHONE..................................310 512-6480
Bryan Fried, CEO

Cheryl Moorman, *
◆ EMP: 89 EST: 2000
SALES (est): 24.64MM Privately Held
Web: www.visionairelighting.com
SIC: 3646 Commercial lighting fixtures

**(P-11569)**
**WPMG INC**
Also Called: Tempo Industries
1961 Mcgaw Ave, Irvine (92614-0909)
PHONE..................................949 442-1601
Dennis Pearson, CEO
▲ EMP: 31 EST: 1986
SQ FT: 27,000
SALES (est): 7.81MM Privately Held
Web: www.tempollc.com
SIC: 3646 Commercial lighting fixtures

**(P-11570)**
**YANKON INDUSTRIES INC (PA)**
Also Called: Energetic Lighting
13445 12th St, Chino (91710-5206)
PHONE..................................909 591-2345
Wei Chen, CEO
David Liu, CEO
Kristen Tai, CFO
▲ EMP: 23 EST: 2009
SQ FT: 100,627
SALES (est): 8.07MM
SALES (corp-wide): 8.07MM Privately Held
Web: www.energeticlighting.com
SIC: 3646 Commercial lighting fixtures

## 3647 Vehicular Lighting Equipment

**(P-11571)**
**AMP PLUS INC**
Also Called: Elco Lighting
2042 E Vernon Ave, Los Angeles (90058-1613)
PHONE..................................323 231-2600
Steve Cohen, Pr
◆ EMP: 55 EST: 1991
SQ FT: 100,000
SALES (est): 8.41MM Privately Held
Web: www.elcolighting.com
SIC: 3647 5063 3645 Vehicular lighting equipment; Electrical apparatus and equipment; Residential lighting fixtures

**(P-11572)**
**EXCELLENCE OPTO INC (PA)**
Also Called: E O I
21858 Garcia Ln, Walnut (91789-0941)
PHONE..................................909 468-0550
Cheryl Huang, Ch Bd
Fang-yue Huang, Pr
▲ EMP: 21 EST: 2001
SQ FT: 18,000
SALES (est): 6.93MM
SALES (corp-wide): 6.93MM Privately Held
Web: www.eoius.com
SIC: 3647 3669 3648 Automotive lighting fixtures, nec; Traffic signals, electric; Street lighting fixtures

**(P-11573)**
**JKL COMPONENTS CORPORATION**
13343 Paxton St, Pacoima (91331-2340)
PHONE..................................818 896-0019
Joseph Velas, Pr
Kent Koerting, *
EMP: 32 EST: 1974
SQ FT: 7,000
SALES (est): 4.46MM Privately Held

## PRODUCTS & SERVICES SECTION

**3648 - Lighting Equipment, Nec (P-11597)**

Web: www.jkllamps.com
SIC: 3647 3827 3699 Automotive lighting fixtures, nec; Optical instruments and lenses ; Electrical equipment and supplies, nec

**(P-11574)**
**KC HILITES INC**
13637 Cimarron Ave, Gardena (90249-2461)
PHONE.....................928 635-2607
Michael Dehaas, *Pr*
◆ EMP: 36 EST: 1970
SQ FT: 25,000
SALES (est): 2.98MM **Privately Held**
Web: www.kchilites.com
SIC: 3647 Vehicular lighting equipment

**(P-11575)**
**SIERRA DESIGN MFG INC (PA)**
Also Called: Dry Launch Light Co
2602 Superior Dr, Livermore (94550-6614)
PHONE.....................925 443-3140
Dennis Moore, *Pr*
Cindy Moore, *VP*
◆ EMP: 20 EST: 1969
SALES (est): 1.89MM
SALES (corp-wide): 1.89MM **Privately Held**
SIC: 3647 Taillights, motor vehicle

**(P-11576)**
**SODERBERG MANUFACTURING CO INC**
20821 Currier Rd, Walnut (91789-3018)
PHONE.....................909 595-1291
B W Soderberg, *CEO*
Kathy Kirkeby, *
Rick Soderberg, *
Kari Levario, *
EMP: 85 EST: 1946
SALES (est): 7.62MM **Privately Held**
Web: www.soderberg.aero
SIC: 3647 3812 Aircraft lighting fixtures; Search and navigation equipment

**(P-11577)**
**ZO MOTORS NORTH AMERICA LLC** ✪
Also Called: Zm Trucks
21250 Hawthorne Blvd Ste 500, Torrance (90503-5514)
PHONE.....................310 792-7077
Jeroen J De Bris, *Managing Member*
EMP: 50 EST: 2023
SALES (est): 2.71MM **Privately Held**
SIC: 3647 Vehicular lighting equipment

---

## 3648 Lighting Equipment, Nec

**(P-11578)**
**ALL ACCESS STGING PRDCTONS INC (PA)**
1320 Storm Pkwy, Torrance (90501-5041)
PHONE.....................310 784-2464
Clive Forrester, *CEO*
Erik Eastland, *
Robert Achlimbari, *
▲ EMP: 45 EST: 1997
SQ FT: 42,000
SALES (est): 13.74MM
SALES (corp-wide): 13.74MM **Privately Held**
Web: www.allaccessinc.com
SIC: 3648 Stage lighting equipment

**(P-11579)**
**AMERICAN GRIP INC**
8468 Kewen Ave, Sun Valley (91352-3118)
PHONE.....................818 768-8922
Lance Snoke, *Pr*
EMP: 25 EST: 1984
SQ FT: 15,000
SALES (est): 5.04MM **Privately Held**
Web: www.americangrip.com
SIC: 3648 3861 Stage lighting equipment; Stands, camera and projector

**(P-11580)**
**AMERICAN POWER SOLUTIONS INC**
14355 Industry Cir, La Mirada (90638-5810)
PHONE.....................714 626-0300
Bansik Yoon, *CEO*
▲ EMP: 20 EST: 2001
SALES (est): 6.06MM **Privately Held**
Web: www.americanpowersolutions.com
SIC: 3648 Lighting equipment, nec

**(P-11581)**
**AMERILLUM LLC**
Also Called: Alumen-8
3728 Maritime Way, Oceanside (92056-2702)
PHONE.....................760 727-7675
Ronald S Lancial, *Managing Member*
Serge Lambert, *
Guy St Pierre, *
▲ EMP: 54 EST: 2010
SQ FT: 27,000
SALES (est): 14.17MM
SALES (corp-wide): 3.84B **Publicly Held**
Web: www.alights.com
SIC: 3648 Lighting equipment, nec
PA: Acuity Brands, Inc.
1170 Pchtree St Ne Ste 23
404 853-1400

**(P-11582)**
**BEGA NORTH AMERICA INC**
Also Called: Bega
1000 Bega Way, Carpinteria (93013-2902)
PHONE.....................805 684-0533
Don Kinderdick, *CEO*
◆ EMP: 100 EST: 1985
SQ FT: 60,000
SALES (est): 22.22MM **Privately Held**
Web: www.bega-us.com
SIC: 3648 3646 Outdoor lighting equipment; Commercial lighting fixtures

**(P-11583)**
**BIRCHWOOD LIGHTING INC**
3340 E La Palma Ave, Anaheim (92806-2814)
PHONE.....................714 550-7118
EMP: 25 EST: 1993
SQ FT: 1,900
SALES (est): 9.06MM
SALES (corp-wide): 1.46B **Privately Held**
Web: www.birchwoodlighting.com
SIC: 3648 3646 3645 Decorative area lighting fixtures; Commercial lighting fixtures ; Residential lighting fixtures
PA: Leviton Manufacturing Co., Inc.
201 N Service Rd
800 323-8920

**(P-11584)**
**BIRNS OCEANOGRAPHICS INC**
Also Called: Birns
1720 Fiske Pl, Oxnard (93033-1863)
PHONE.....................805 487-5393
▼ EMP: 19 EST: 1978
SALES (est): 2.68MM **Privately Held**
Web: www.birns.com
SIC: 3648 3643 Underwater lighting fixtures; Electric connectors

**(P-11585)**
**BLISS HOLDINGS LLC**
745 S Vinewood St, Escondido (92029-1928)
PHONE.....................626 506-8696
▲ EMP: 50 EST: 2006
SALES (est): 2.11MM **Privately Held**
SIC: 3648 Lighting equipment, nec

**(P-11586)**
**BLISSLIGHTS LLC**
2449 Cades Way, Vista (92081-7873)
PHONE.....................888 868-4603
Ravi Bhagavatula, *Managing Member*
EMP: 15 EST: 2016
SALES (est): 3.69MM **Privately Held**
Web: www.blisslights.com
SIC: 3648 Lighting equipment, nec

**(P-11587)**
**CLEAR BLUE ENERGY CORP**
Also Called: Cbec
17150 Via Del Campo Ste 203, San Diego (92127-2139)
P.O. Box 532086 (92153)
PHONE.....................858 451-1549
Paul Santina, *CEO*
Jim Kelly, *
EMP: 80 EST: 2009
SALES (est): 9.98MM **Privately Held**
Web: www.cbesco.com
SIC: 3648 1731 Lighting equipment, nec; Lighting contractor

**(P-11588)**
**COOPER LIGHTING LLC**
Also Called: Cooper Lighting
3350 Enterprise Dr, Bloomington (92316-3538)
PHONE.....................909 605-6615
John Seiler, *Mgr*
EMP: 488
Web: www.cooperlighting.com
SIC: 3648 Lighting equipment, nec
HQ: Cooper Lighting, Llc
1121 Hwy 74 S
Peachtree City GA 30269
770 486-4800

**(P-11589)**
**DANA CREATH DESIGNS LTD**
3030 Kilson Dr, Santa Ana (92707-4203)
PHONE.....................714 662-0111
Dana E Creath, *Pt*
James K Creath, *
Raylene R Creath, *
EMP: 30 EST: 1968
SALES (est): 2.44MM **Privately Held**
Web: www.danacreath.com
SIC: 3648 3646 3645 Lighting equipment, nec; Commercial lighting fixtures; Residential lighting fixtures

**(P-11590)**
**DEEPSEA POWER & LIGHT INC**
4033 Ruffin Rd, San Diego (92123-1817)
PHONE.....................858 576-1261
EMP: 23
SIC: 3648 Underwater lighting fixtures

**(P-11591)**
**EEMA INDUSTRIES INC**
Also Called: Liton Lighting
5461 W Jefferson Blvd, Los Angeles (90016-3715)
PHONE.....................323 904-0200
Amir Esmail Zadeh, *Pr*
◆ EMP: 40 EST: 1998
SQ FT: 40,000
SALES (est): 4.32MM **Privately Held**
Web: www.liton.com
SIC: 3648 5063 Lighting equipment, nec; Electrical apparatus and equipment

**(P-11592)**
**ELATION LIGHTING INC**
Also Called: Elation Professional
6122 S Eastern Ave, Commerce (90040-3402)
PHONE.....................323 582-3322
Toby Velazquez, *Pr*
Charles J Davies, *
▲ EMP: 60 EST: 1992
SQ FT: 50,000
SALES (est): 4.91MM **Privately Held**
Web: www.elationlighting.com
SIC: 3648 Lighting equipment, nec

**(P-11593)**
**ELITE LIGHTING**
Also Called: Elite Lighting
5424 E Slauson Ave, Commerce (90040-2919)
PHONE.....................323 888-1973
Babak Rashididoust, *CEO*
◆ EMP: 200 EST: 1998
SQ FT: 25,000
SALES (est): 52.36MM **Privately Held**
Web: www.iuseelite.com
SIC: 3648 3646 3645 Lighting equipment, nec; Commercial lighting fixtures; Boudoir lamps

**(P-11594)**
**EMAZING LIGHTS LLC**
240 S Loara St, Anaheim (92802-1020)
PHONE.....................626 628-6482
Brian Lim, *Managing Member*
▲ EMP: 18 EST: 2010
SALES (est): 3.69MM **Privately Held**
Web: www.gloving.com
SIC: 3648 3229 Spotlights; Bulbs for electric lights

**(P-11595)**
**EXCELITAS TECHNOLOGIES CORP**
6701 Koll Center Pkwy Unit 400, Pleasanton (94566-8061)
PHONE.....................510 979-6500
John Lucero, *Brnch Mgr*
EMP: 208
SALES (corp-wide): 1.48B **Privately Held**
Web: www.excelitas.com
SIC: 3648 3845 Lighting equipment, nec; Electromedical apparatus
HQ: Excelitas Technologies Corp.
200 W St 4th Fl E
Waltham MA 02451

**(P-11596)**
**EXCELITAS TECHNOLOGIES CORP**
Also Called: Excelitas Tech Illumination
6701 Koll Center Pkwy # 400, Pleasanton (94566-8061)
PHONE.....................510 979-6500
EMP: 50
SALES (corp-wide): 1.48B **Privately Held**
Web: www.excelitas.com
SIC: 3648 Lighting equipment, nec
HQ: Excelitas Technologies Corp.
200 W St 4th Fl E
Waltham MA 02451

**(P-11597)**
**FOXFURY LLC**
Also Called: Foxfury Lighting Solution

## 3648 - Lighting Equipment, Nec (P-11598)

3544 Seagate Way, Oceanside (92056-6041)
PHONE..............................760 945-4231
▲ EMP: 24 EST: 2005
SALES (est): 4.81MM **Privately Held**
Web: www.foxfury.com
SIC: 3648 Lighting equipment, nec

### (P-11598)
### GALLAGHER RENTAL INC
15701 Heron Ave, La Mirada (90638-5206)
PHONE..............................714 690-1559
Joseph Gallagher, CEO
Megan Gallagher, *
EMP: 30 EST: 2012
SALES (est): 3.89MM **Privately Held**
Web: www.gallagherstaging.com
SIC: 3648 Stage lighting equipment

### (P-11599)
### GREENSHINE NEW ENERGY LLC
23661 Birtcher Dr, Lake Forest (92630-1770)
PHONE..............................949 609-9636
Alex Chen, Managing Member
Scott Douglas, Genl Mgr
◆ EMP: 100 EST: 2010
SQ FT: 200
SALES (est): 7.83MM **Privately Held**
Web: www.greenshine-solar.com
SIC: 3648 Lighting equipment, nec

### (P-11600)
### HYDROFARM LLC (HQ)
1304 Southpoint Blvd Ste 200, Petaluma (94954-7464)
PHONE..............................707 765-9990
William Toler, Managing Member
Peter Wardenburg, *
Jeffrey Peterson, *
◆ EMP: 28 EST: 1977
SALES (est): 23.24MM
SALES (corp-wide): 226.58MM **Publicly Held**
Web: www.hydrofarm.com
SIC: 3648 3999 Lighting equipment, nec; Hydroponic equipment
PA: Hydrofarm Holdings Group, Inc.
    1510 Main St
    707 765-9990

### (P-11601)
### HYDROFARM LLC
2225 Huntington Dr, Fairfield (94533-9732)
PHONE..............................707 765-9990
EMP: 51
SALES (corp-wide): 226.58MM **Publicly Held**
Web: www.hydrofarm.eu
SIC: 3648 Lighting equipment, nec
HQ: Hydrofarm, Llc
    1304 Sthpint Blvd Ste 200
    Petaluma CA 94954
    707 765-9990

### (P-11602)
### INNOVALIGHT INC
965 W Maude Ave, Sunnyvale (94085-2802)
PHONE..............................408 419-4400
Thomas Linn, CEO
Conrad Burke, *
Michael Johnson, *
▲ EMP: 40 EST: 2001
SALES (est): 2MM
SALES (corp-wide): 17.23B **Publicly Held**
Web: www.dupont.com
SIC: 3648 Lighting equipment, nec
HQ: Eidp, Inc.
    9330 Zionsville Rd
    Indianapolis IN 46268
    833 267-8382

### (P-11603)
### JIMWAY INC
Also Called: Altair Lighting
20101 S Santa Fe Ave, Compton (90221-5917)
PHONE..............................310 886-3718
Hsing-min Keng, CEO
Irene Wang, *
▲ EMP: 100 EST: 1982
SQ FT: 200,000
SALES (est): 19.89MM **Privately Held**
Web: www.jimway.com
SIC: 3648 3221 5063 Lighting equipment, nec; Glass containers; Electrical apparatus and equipment

### (P-11604)
### KIM LIGHTING INC
Also Called: Kim Lighting & Mfg
16555 Gale Ave, City Of Industry (91745-1713)
P.O. Box 1275 (91716)
PHONE..............................626 968-5666
▲ EMP: 550
SIC: 3648 3646 3317 Outdoor lighting equipment; Commercial lighting fixtures; Steel pipe and tubes

### (P-11605)
### LEDCONN CORP
Also Called: Ledconn
301 Thor Pl, Brea (92821-4133)
PHONE..............................714 256-2111
Tsanyu Wang, Pr
Wan Ting Huang, *
▲ EMP: 25 EST: 2008
SQ FT: 2,000
SALES (est): 4.82MM **Privately Held**
Web: www.ledconn.com
SIC: 3648 3993 7389 Lighting equipment, nec; Signs and advertising specialties; Interior decorating

### (P-11606)
### LG-LED SOLUTIONS LIMITED
15902 Halliburton Rd Ste A, Hacienda Heights (91745-3500)
PHONE..............................626 587-8506
Zegao Hu, CEO
EMP: 50 EST: 2015
SALES (est): 1.81MM **Privately Held**
SIC: 3648 Lighting equipment, nec

### (P-11607)
### LIGHT & MOTION INDUSTRIES
711 Neeson Rd, Marina (93933-5104)
PHONE..............................831 645-1525
Daniel T Emerson, Pr
▲ EMP: 55 EST: 1989
SALES (est): 9.8MM **Privately Held**
Web: www.lightandmotion.com
SIC: 3648 Underwater lighting fixtures

### (P-11608)
### LIGHT VAST INC
1202 Monte Vista Ave Ste 1, Upland (91786-8208)
PHONE..............................800 358-0499
Leo Mao, CEO
EMP: 24 EST: 2015
SALES (est): 811.93K **Privately Held**
Web: www.lightvast.com
SIC: 3648 Lighting equipment, nec

### (P-11609)
### LIGHTING CONTROL & DESIGN INC
Also Called: LCD&d
9144 Deering Ave, Chatsworth (91311-5801)
PHONE..............................323 226-0000
EMP: 46 EST: 1987
SALES (est): 6.1MM
SALES (corp-wide): 3.84B **Publicly Held**
Web: www.acuitybrands.com
SIC: 3648 3643 5719 Lighting equipment, nec; Current-carrying wiring services; Lighting fixtures
PA: Acuity Brands, Inc.
    1170 Pchtree St Ne Ste 23
    404 853-1400

### (P-11610)
### LUMINUS INC (HQ)
Also Called: Lightera
1145 Sonora Ct, Sunnyvale (94086-5384)
PHONE..............................408 708-7000
Decai Sun, CEO
EMP: 120 EST: 2012
SALES (est): 33.42MM **Privately Held**
Web: www.luminus.com
SIC: 3648 Lighting equipment, nec
PA: Sanan Optoelectronics Co.,Ltd.
    No.1721-1725, Lvling Road, Siming District

### (P-11611)
### LUMINUS DEVICES INC
Also Called: Luminus
1145 Sonora Ct, Sunnyvale (94086-5384)
PHONE..............................978 528-8000
Mark Pugh, CEO
James Loo, *
Shaohua Huang, *
▲ EMP: 156 EST: 2002
SALES (est): 5.67MM **Privately Held**
Web: www.luminus.com
SIC: 3648 Lighting equipment, nec
HQ: Luminus, Inc.
    1145 Sonora Ct
    Sunnyvale CA 94086
    408 708-7000

### (P-11612)
### MAG INSTRUMENT INC (PA)
2001 S Hellman Ave, Ontario (91761-8019)
P.O. Box 50600 (91761-1083)
PHONE..............................909 947-1006
Anthony Maglica, CEO
James Zecchini, *
Thomas K Richardson, *
Malissa Peace, *
Brent Flaharty, *
▲ EMP: 406 EST: 1955
SQ FT: 1,000,000
SALES (est): 83.32MM
SALES (corp-wide): 83.32MM **Privately Held**
Web: www.maglite.com
SIC: 3648 Flashlights

### (P-11613)
### MOLE-RICHARDSON CO LTD (PA)
Also Called: Studio Depot
12154 Montague St, Pacoima (91331-2209)
PHONE..............................323 851-0111
▲ EMP: 100 EST: 1927
SALES (est): 9.65MM
SALES (corp-wide): 9.65MM **Privately Held**
Web: www.mole.com

### (P-11614)
### MW MCWONG INTERNATIONAL INC (PA)
Also Called: Pacific Lighting & Electrical
1921 Arena Blvd, Sacramento (95834-3770)
PHONE..............................916 371-8080
Margaret Wong, Pr
Blane Goettle, *
Yan Zhou, *
Emily Mei, CFO
▲ EMP: 19 EST: 1984
SQ FT: 47,430
SALES (est): 8.5MM
SALES (corp-wide): 8.5MM **Privately Held**
Web: www.mcwonginc.info
SIC: 3648 Lighting fixtures, except electric: residential

### (P-11615)
### NEW BEDFORD PANORAMEX CORP
Also Called: Nbp
1480 N Claremont Blvd, Claremont (91711-3538)
PHONE..............................909 982-9806
Steven Robert Ozuna, Pr
James Casso, *
Bryce Nielsen, *
EMP: 35 EST: 1966
SQ FT: 65,000
SALES (est): 10.3MM **Privately Held**
Web: www.nbpcorp.com
SIC: 3648 Airport lighting fixtures: runway approach, taxi, or ramp

### (P-11616)
### NITERDER TCHNCAL LTG VDEO SYST
Also Called: Niterider
12255 Crosthwaite Cir Ste A, Poway (92064-8825)
PHONE..............................858 268-9316
Thomas Edward Carroll, CEO
Mark Schultz, *
▲ EMP: 35 EST: 1989
SALES (est): 5.59MM **Privately Held**
Web: www.niterider.com
SIC: 3648 3646 Lighting equipment, nec; Commercial lighting fixtures

### (P-11617)
### PACIFIC COAST LIGHTING INC (HQ)
Also Called: Pacific Coast Lighting Group
20238 Plummer St, Chatsworth (91311-5365)
PHONE..............................800 709-9004
Clark Linstone, CEO
Dennis K Swanson, Ch
Manja Swanson, Sec
◆ EMP: 19 EST: 1979
SQ FT: 100,000
SALES (est): 18.91MM
SALES (corp-wide): 490.53MM **Privately Held**
Web: www.pacificcoastlighting.com
SIC: 3648 3641 5719 Lighting fixtures, except electric: residential; Electric lamp (bulb) parts; Lighting fixtures
PA: Lamps Plus, Inc.
    20250 Plummer St
    818 886-5267

## PRODUCTS & SERVICES SECTION
### 3651 - Household Audio And Video Equipment (P-11638)

**(P-11618)**
**PELICAN PRODUCTS INC (PA)**
Also Called: Pelican
23215 Early Ave, Torrance (90505-4002)
PHONE.................................310 326-4700
James Curleigh, CEO
Scott Ermeti, INTL Business*
Dave Pres Biothermal Div Williams, Prin
Chris Favreau, *
George Platisa, *
◆ EMP: 245 EST: 2007
SQ FT: 150,000
SALES (est): 564.44MM
SALES (corp-wide): 564.44MM Privately Held
Web: www.pelican.com
SIC: 3648 3161 3089 Flashlights; Luggage; Plastics containers, except foam

**(P-11619)**
**PROJECT SUTTER HOLDINGS LLC (HQ)**
Also Called: Dynamic Digital Displays
11370 Sunrise Park Dr, Rancho Cordova (95742-6542)
PHONE.................................916 669-7408
◆ EMP: 20 EST: 2005
SQ FT: 60,000
SALES (est): 22.37MM
SALES (corp-wide): 198.04MM Privately Held
Web: www.rossvideo.com
SIC: 3648 3993 Lighting equipment, nec; Signs and advertising specialties
PA: Ross Video Limited
8 John St
613 652-4886

**(P-11620)**
**Q TECHNOLOGY INC**
336 Lindbergh Ave, Livermore (94551-9511)
PHONE.................................925 373-3456
Samuel S Lee, Pr
◆ EMP: 30 EST: 1992
SQ FT: 10,000
SALES (est): 2.58MM Privately Held
Web: www.q-techinc.com
SIC: 3648 Lighting equipment, nec

**(P-11621)**
**REMOTE OCEAN SYSTEMS INC (PA)**
Also Called: R O S
9581 Ridgehaven Ct, San Diego (92123-1624)
PHONE.................................858 565-8500
Robert Acks, CEO
Christine Acks, *
EMP: 34 EST: 1975
SALES (est): 9.47MM
SALES (corp-wide): 9.47MM Privately Held
Web: www.rosys.com
SIC: 3648 3861 3812 3643 Underwater lighting fixtures; Photographic equipment and supplies; Search and navigation equipment; Current-carrying wiring services

**(P-11622)**
**SHIMADA ENTERPRISES INC**
Also Called: Celestial Lighting
14009 Dinard Ave, Santa Fe Springs (90670-4922)
PHONE.................................562 802-8811
Tak Shimada, Pr
Mick Shimada, *
▲ EMP: 30 EST: 1975
SQ FT: 11,000
SALES (est): 5.29MM Privately Held

Web: www.celestiallighting.com
SIC: 3648 Decorative area lighting fixtures

**(P-11623)**
**STERIL-AIRE INC**
25060 Avenue Stanford Ste 160, Valencia (91355-3915)
PHONE.................................818 565-1128
Robert Scheir, Pr
◆ EMP: 23 EST: 1995
SALES (est): 7.34MM Privately Held
Web: www.steril-aire.com
SIC: 3648 Ultraviolet lamp fixtures

**(P-11624)**
**SUN POWER SOURCE (PA)**
1650 Palma Dr, Ventura (93003-5749)
PHONE.................................805 644-2520
Sean Frye, Pr
Tammy Frye, VP
EMP: 15 EST: 1989
SQ FT: 1,850
SALES (est): 1.39MM Privately Held
SIC: 3648 7299 Sun tanning equipment, incl. tanning beds; Tanning salon

**(P-11625)**
**SUREFIRE LLC (PA)**
18300 Mount Baldy Cir, Fountain Valley (92708-6122)
PHONE.................................714 545-9444
Sean Vo, *
Joel Smith, CAO*
◆ EMP: 175 EST: 2000
SQ FT: 45,000
SALES (est): 97.06MM
SALES (corp-wide): 97.06MM Privately Held
Web: www.surefire.com
SIC: 3648 3699 Flashlights; Laser systems and equipment

**(P-11626)**
**TEC LIGHTING INC**
115 Arovista Cir, Brea (92821-3830)
PHONE.................................714 529-5068
Kamal S Hodhodc, CEO
David Hodhod, Pr
▲ EMP: 15 EST: 2001
SALES (est): 5.02MM Privately Held
Web: www.teclighting.com
SIC: 3648 Lighting equipment, nec

**(P-11627)**
**THIN-LITE CORPORATION**
530 Constitution Ave, Camarillo (93012-8595)
PHONE.................................805 987-5021
Alan Griffin, Pr
Lilian Cross Szymanek, *
▲ EMP: 47 EST: 1970
SQ FT: 27,000
SALES (est): 7.75MM Privately Held
Web: www.thinlite.com
SIC: 3648 3612 3646 Lighting equipment, nec; Transformers, except electric; Fluorescent lighting fixtures, commercial

**(P-11628)**
**TOTAL STRUCTURES INC**
Also Called: Total Structures
1696 Walter St, Ventura (93003-5619)
PHONE.................................805 676-3322
William Scott Johnson, CEO
◆ EMP: 45 EST: 1995
SQ FT: 24,000
SALES (est): 5.22MM Privately Held
Web: www.totalstructures.com
SIC: 3648 3441 Lighting equipment, nec; Fabricated structural metal

HQ: Eurotruss B.V.
Castorweg 2
Leeuwarden FR 8938
582158888

**(P-11629)**
**TRULY GREEN SOLUTIONS LLC**
Also Called: Tgs
9601 Variel Ave, Chatsworth (91311-4914)
PHONE.................................818 206-4404
Rubina Jadwet, CEO
▲ EMP: 22 EST: 2010
SALES (est): 3.69MM Privately Held
Web: www.trulygreensolutions.com
SIC: 3648 3645 Lighting equipment, nec; Residential lighting fixtures

**(P-11630)**
**UNIQUE LIGHTING SYSTEMS INC**
5825 Jasmine St, Riverside (92504-1144)
PHONE.................................800 955-4831
Randy Weisser, Pr
EMP: 38 EST: 2014
SALES (est): 2.44MM Privately Held
Web: www.uniquelighting.com
SIC: 3648 Lighting equipment, nec

### 3651 Household Audio And Video Equipment

**(P-11631)**
**ABSOLUTE USA INC**
Also Called: Absolute Pro Music
1800 E Washington Blvd, Los Angeles (90021-3127)
PHONE.................................213 744-0044
Mohammad K Razipour, Pr
Sasha Razipour, *
◆ EMP: 47 EST: 2002
SQ FT: 35,000
SALES (est): 16MM Privately Held
Web: www.absolutepromusic.com
SIC: 3651 Audio electronic systems

**(P-11632)**
**ACTI CORPORATION INC**
Also Called: California Acti
18 Technology Dr Ste 139, Irvine (92618-2311)
PHONE.................................949 753-0352
Juber Chu, Pr
Jesse Kuo, COO
EMP: 20 EST: 2008
SALES (est): 5.6MM Privately Held
Web: www.acti.com
SIC: 3651 3663 3699 Household audio and video equipment; Cameras, television; Security devices
PA: Acti Corporation
7f, No. 1, Alley 20, Lane 407, Sec. 2, Tiding Blvd.

**(P-11633)**
**ACTIVEON INC (PA)**
10905 Technology Pl, San Diego (92127-1811)
PHONE.................................858 798-3300
John Lee, CEO
Jonathan Zupnik, VP
▲ EMP: 49 EST: 2006
SALES (est): 1.01MM Privately Held
Web: www.activeon.com
SIC: 3651 Household audio and video equipment

**(P-11634)**
**AL SHELLCO LLC (HQ)**
9330 Scranton Rd Ste 600, San Diego (92121-7706)
PHONE.................................570 296-6444
Mark Lucas, Managing Member
Edward Anchel, *
Richard P Horner, *
Ross Gatlin, *
▲ EMP: 160 EST: 1953
SQ FT: 120,000
SALES (est): 3.14MM
SALES (corp-wide): 691.84MM Privately Held
SIC: 3651 3577 Radio receiving sets; Computer peripheral equipment, nec
PA: Prophet Equity Lp
1460 Main St Ste 200
817 898-1500

**(P-11635)**
**ANACOM GENERAL CORPORATION**
Also Called: Anacom Medtek
1240 S Claudina St, Anaheim (92805-6232)
PHONE.................................714 774-8484
Daniel S Haines, Pr
William K Haines, *
▲ EMP: 48 EST: 1967
SQ FT: 20,000
SALES (est): 9.87MM Privately Held
Web: www.anacom-medtek.com
SIC: 3651 3577 Speaker monitors; Computer peripheral equipment, nec

**(P-11636)**
**ANCHOR AUDIO INC**
5931 Darwin Ct, Carlsbad (92008)
PHONE.................................760 827-7100
Janet Jacobs, CEO
David Jacobs, *
Dwight Garbe, *
▲ EMP: 58 EST: 1973
SQ FT: 31,200
SALES (est): 9.88MM Privately Held
Web: www.anchoraudio.com
SIC: 3651 Public address systems

**(P-11637)**
**APOGEE ELECTRONICS CORPORATION**
Also Called: Apogee Electronics
1715 Berkeley St, Santa Monica (90404-4104)
PHONE.................................310 584-9394
Betty A Bennett, CEO
▲ EMP: 35 EST: 1985
SQ FT: 5,000
SALES (est): 4.87MM Privately Held
Web: www.apogeedigital.com
SIC: 3651 3621 8748 Audio electronic systems; Motors and generators; Communications consulting

**(P-11638)**
**ARLO TECHNOLOGIES INC (PA)**
Also Called: ARLO
2200 Faraday Ave Ste 150, Carlsbad (92008-7224)
PHONE.................................408 890-3900
Matthew Mcrae, CEO
Ralph E Faison, Ch Bd
Kurtis Binder, CFO
Brian Busse, Corporate Secretary
EMP: 86 EST: 2014
SQ FT: 43,500
SALES (est): 491.18MM
SALES (corp-wide): 491.18MM Publicly Held
Web: www.arlo.com

## 3651 - Household Audio And Video Equipment (P-11639)

**PRODUCTS & SERVICES SECTION**

SIC: **3651** 7372 Household audio and video equipment; Application computer software

**(P-11639)**
**AUDIO VISUAL MGT SOLUTIONS LLC**
3425 Solano Ave, Napa (94558-2709)
PHONE.................................707 254-3395
Jason Woods, *Brnch Mgr*
**EMP:** 59
Web: www.pinnaclelive.com
SIC: **3651** Electronic kits for home assembly: radio, TV, phonograph
PA: Audio Visual Management Solutions, Llc
814 6th Ave S

**(P-11640)**
**AURASOUND INC**
1801 E Edinger Ave Ste 190, Santa Ana (92705-4754)
PHONE.................................949 829-4000
**EMP:** 72
Web: www.aurasound.com
SIC: **3651** Household audio equipment

**(P-11641)**
**AV NOW INC**
231 Technology Cir, Scotts Valley (95066-3525)
PHONE.................................831 425-2500
Robert Dehart, *Pr*
▲ **EMP:** 20 **EST:** 1987
**SQ FT:** 2,000
**SALES (est):** 4.82MM **Privately Held**
Web: www.avnow.com
SIC: **3651** 7929 Audio electronic systems; Disc jockey service

**(P-11642)**
**BALTIC LTVIAN UNVRSAL ELEC LLC**
Also Called: Blue Microphone
5706 Corsa Ave, Westlake Village (91362-4057)
PHONE.................................818 879-5200
John Maier, *CEO*
Bart E Thielen, *
Bernard Wise, *
Martin Saulespurens, *
▲ **EMP:** 35 **EST:** 1998
**SALES (est):** 2.77MM **Privately Held**
SIC: **3651** 5731 Microphones; Consumer electronic equipment, nec
PA: Logitech International S.A.
Route De Pampigny 20

**(P-11643)**
**BEATS ELECTRONICS LLC**
Also Called: Beats By Dre
8600 Hayden Pl, Culver City (90232-2902)
PHONE.................................424 326-4679
Timothy Cook, *CEO*
▲ **EMP:** 500 **EST:** 2006
**SALES (est):** 20.37MM
**SALES (corp-wide):** 391.04B **Publicly Held**
Web: www.beatsbydre.com
SIC: **3651** 3679 Speaker systems; Headphones, radio
PA: Apple Inc.
1 Apple Park Way
408 996-1010

**(P-11644)**
**BELKIN INC**
Also Called: Belkin
555 S Aviation Blvd, El Segundo (90245-4852)
PHONE.................................800 223-5546
Chester J Pipkin, *Pr*
George Platisa, *
◆ **EMP:** 775 **EST:** 2003
**SALES (est):** 18.66MM **Privately Held**
Web: www.belkin.com
SIC: **3651** Electronic kits for home assembly: radio, TV, phonograph
HQ: Belkin International, Inc.
555 S Avi Blvd Ste 180
El Segundo CA 90245
310 751-5100

**(P-11645)**
**BIG 5 ELECTRONICS INC**
Also Called: Big Five Electronics
13452 Alondra Blvd, Cerritos (90703-2315)
PHONE.................................562 941-4669
Amina Bawaney, *CEO*
Latif Bawaney, *Pr*
Rizwan Bawaney, *CFO*
▲ **EMP:** 22 **EST:** 2003
**SQ FT:** 4,500
**SALES (est):** 7.54MM **Privately Held**
Web: www.big5electronics.com
SIC: **3651** 5099 5065 Audio electronic systems; Video and audio equipment; Electronic parts and equipment, nec

**(P-11646)**
**COUNTRYMAN ASSOCIATES INC**
Also Called: Countryman Associates
195 Constitution Dr, Menlo Park (94025-1106)
PHONE.................................650 364-9988
Carl Countryman, *Pr*
Carolyn Countryman, *Sec*
▲ **EMP:** 17 **EST:** 1967
**SQ FT:** 4,000
**SALES (est):** 3.03MM **Privately Held**
Web: www.countryman.com
SIC: **3651** 5065 Audio electronic systems; Electronic parts and equipment, nec

**(P-11647)**
**DANA INNOVATIONS (PA)**
Also Called: Sonance
991 Calle Amanecer, San Clemente (92673-6212)
PHONE.................................949 492-7777
Ari Supran, *CEO*
Scott Struthers, *Pr*
Geoffrey L Spencer, *Sec*
Mike Simmons, *CFO*
◆ **EMP:** 156 **EST:** 1981
**SQ FT:** 42,320
**SALES (est):** 49.59MM
**SALES (corp-wide):** 49.59MM **Privately Held**
Web: www.sonance.com
SIC: **3651** 5731 7629 Speaker systems; Radio, television, and electronic stores; Electrical repair shops

**(P-11648)**
**DIGITAL PERIPH SOLUTIONS INC**
Also Called: Q-See
160 S Old Springs Rd Ste 220, Anaheim (92808-1260)
PHONE.................................714 998-3440
Priti Sharma, *Pr*
Rajeev Sharma, *
▲ **EMP:** 40 **EST:** 2002
**SQ FT:** 30,000
**SALES (est):** 4.27MM **Privately Held**
Web: www.q-see.com

SIC: **3651** 7382 Video camera-audio recorders, household use; Confinement surveillance systems maintenance and monitoring

**(P-11649)**
**DOLBY LABORATORIES INC**
999 Brannan St, San Francisco (94103-4999)
PHONE.................................415 645-5000
John Neary, *Dir*
**EMP:** 125
**SALES (corp-wide):** 1.3B **Publicly Held**
Web: www.dolby.com
SIC: **3651** Audio electronic systems
PA: Dolby Laboratories, Inc.
1275 Market St
415 558-0200

**(P-11650)**
**DOLBY LABORATORIES INC**
432 Lakeside Dr, Sunnyvale (94085-4703)
PHONE.................................408 730-5543
Carlo Basile, *Pr*
**EMP:** 40
**SALES (corp-wide):** 1.3B **Publicly Held**
Web: www.dolby.com
SIC: **3651** Audio electronic systems
PA: Dolby Laboratories, Inc.
1275 Market St
415 558-0200

**(P-11651)**
**DOLBY LABORATORIES INC**
Also Called: Doremi Labs
1020 Chestnut St, Burbank (91506-1623)
PHONE.................................818 562-1101
**EMP:** 25
**SALES (corp-wide):** 1.3B **Publicly Held**
Web: www.dolby.com
SIC: **3651** Audio electronic systems
PA: Dolby Laboratories, Inc.
1275 Market St
415 558-0200

**(P-11652)**
**DOLBY LABORATORIES INC (PA)**
Also Called: Dolby
1275 Market St Fl 15, San Francisco (94103-1426)
PHONE.................................415 558-0200
Kevin Yeaman, *Pr*
Peter Gotcher, *
Andy Sherman, *Corporate Secretary*
Robert Park, *Sr VP*
Todd Pendleton, *CMO*
▲ **EMP:** 429 **EST:** 1965
**SALES (est):** 1.3B
**SALES (corp-wide):** 1.3B **Publicly Held**
Web: www.dolby.com
SIC: **3651** 7819 6794 Audio electronic systems; Laboratory service, motion picture ; Music licensing and royalties

**(P-11653)**
**DOLBY LABS LICENSING CORP**
1275 Market St Fl 15, San Francisco (94103-1426)
PHONE.................................415 558-0200
Ray Dolby, *Ch*
N William Jasper Junior, *Pr*
▲ **EMP:** 125 **EST:** 1965
**SQ FT:** 50,000
**SALES (est):** 44.08MM
**SALES (corp-wide):** 1.3B **Publicly Held**
Web: www.dolby.com
SIC: **3651** Audio electronic systems
PA: Dolby Laboratories, Inc.
1275 Market St

415 558-0200

**(P-11654)**
**DOREMI LABS INC**
Also Called: Doremi
1020 Chestnut St, Burbank (91506-1623)
PHONE.................................818 562-1101
▲ **EMP:** 40
SIC: **3651** Audio electronic systems

**(P-11655)**
**DWI ENTERPRISES**
11081 Winners Cir Ste 100, Los Alamitos (90720-2894)
PHONE.................................714 842-2236
Fred Delgleize, *Pr*
Dan Delgleize, *
Dave Dain, *
Amanda Delgleize, *
◆ **EMP:** 25 **EST:** 1980
**SQ FT:** 9,500
**SALES (est):** 2.02MM **Privately Held**
Web: www.dwienterprises.com
SIC: **3651** 3669 Audio electronic systems; Visual communication systems

**(P-11656)**
**EARTHQUAKE SOUND CORPORATION**
Also Called: Earthquake Audio Products
2727 Mccone Ave, Hayward (94545-1614)
PHONE.................................510 732-1000
Sabina Hohmann, *Pr*
Joseph Sahyoun, *VP*
◆ **EMP:** 15 **EST:** 1988
**SQ FT:** 60,088
**SALES (est):** 2.42MM **Privately Held**
Web: www.earthquakesound.com
SIC: **3651** Household audio and video equipment

**(P-11657)**
**ECOLINK INTELLIGENT TECH INC**
2055 Corte Del Nogal, Carlsbad (92011-1412)
PHONE.................................855 432-6546
Michael Lamb, *CEO*
**EMP:** 18 **EST:** 2007
**SALES (est):** 2.34MM **Publicly Held**
Web: www.discoverecolink.com
SIC: **3651** Video triggers (remote control TV devices)
PA: Universal Electronics Inc.
15147 N Scttsdale Rd Ste

**(P-11658)**
**EI CORP**
13355 Grass Valley Ave Ste A, Grass Valley (95945-9521)
PHONE.................................530 274-1240
Michael Castorino, *Prin*
Ram Narayanan, *
Syed Zaidi, *
Michael Ahmadi, *
**EMP:** 22 **EST:** 1975
**SQ FT:** 27,000
**SALES (est):** 2.58MM **Privately Held**
Web: www.eigen.com
SIC: **3651** 3845 3841 Recording machines, except dictation and telephone answering; Electromedical equipment; Surgical and medical instruments

**(P-11659)**
**ETI SOUND SYSTEMS INC**
Also Called: Eti B Si Professional
5300 Harbor St, Commerce (90040-3927)
PHONE.................................323 835-6660

## PRODUCTS & SERVICES SECTION
### 3651 - Household Audio And Video Equipment (P-11680)

Eli El-kiss, *Pr*
Avi El-kiss, *VP*
◆ **EMP:** 45 **EST:** 1989
**SALES (est):** 6.84MM **Privately Held**
**Web:** www.b-52pro.com
**SIC: 3651** Speaker monitors

**(P-11660)**
### FRESNO DISTRIBUTING CO
Also Called: FRESNO "D"
2055 E Mckinley Ave, Fresno (93703-2997)
P.O. Box 6078 (93703-6078)
**PHONE**.................................559 442-8800
Stephen Ronald Cloud, *CEO*
Ryan Cloud, *
Steve Cloud Junior, *VP*
Mary Iness, *
**EMP:** 33 **EST:** 1946
**SALES (est):** 4.68MM **Privately Held**
**Web:** www.fresnod.com
**SIC: 3651** 3494  Home entertainment equipment, electronic, nec; Plumbing and heating valves

**(P-11661)**
### FUNAI CORPORATION INC (DH)
12489 Lakeland Rd, Santa Fe Springs (90670-3938)
**PHONE**.................................310 787-3000
Yoshihiro Sasaki, *CEO*
Hiroyuki Anabe, *
Ryo Fukuda, *
George Kanazawa, *
Yoichi Kanazawa, *
▲ **EMP:** 25 **EST:** 1991
**SALES (est):** 12.06MM **Privately Held**
**Web:** www.funai.us
**SIC: 3651** 3955  Television receiving sets; Print cartridges for laser and other computer printers
**HQ:** Funai Group Co., Ltd.
7-7-1, Nakagaito
Daito OSK 574-0

**(P-11662)**
### FUNAI CORPORATION INC
Also Called: Funai Electric Co.
19900 Van Ness Ave, Torrance (90501-1143)
**PHONE**.................................201 727-4560
◆ **EMP:** 77
**SIC: 3651** Household audio and video equipment

**(P-11663)**
### GALLIEN TECHNOLOGY INC (PA)
Also Called: Galliien Krueger
2234 Industrial Dr, Stockton (95206-4937)
**PHONE**.................................209 234-7300
Robert Gallien, *Pr*
◆ **EMP:** 59 **EST:** 1970
**SQ FT:** 21,000
**SALES (est):** 7.28MM **Privately Held**
**Web:** www.gallien-krueger.com
**SIC: 3651** Amplifiers: radio, public address, or musical instrument

**(P-11664)**
### GOTO CALIFORNIA INC (HQ)
Also Called: GCI
6120 Business Center Ct Ste F200, San Diego (92154-6652)
**PHONE**.................................619 691-8722
Saburo Goto, *CEO*
◆ **EMP:** 15 **EST:** 1996
**SALES (est):** 8.3MM **Privately Held**
**Web:** www.goto-california.com
**SIC: 3651** Speaker systems
**PA:** Goto Densan, Y.K.
1-2-44, Minamiharamachi

**(P-11665)**
### HARMAN PROFESSIONAL INC
24950 Grove View Rd, Moreno Valley (92551-9552)
**PHONE**.................................951 242-2927
**EMP:** 140
**Web:** www.jblpro.com
**SIC: 3651** Household audio equipment
**HQ:** Harman Professional, Inc.
8500 Balboa Blvd
Northridge CA 91329
818 893-8411

**(P-11666)**
### HARMAN PROFESSIONAL INC
14780 Bar Harbor Rd, Fontana (92336-4254)
**PHONE**.................................844 776-4899
**EMP:** 159
**Web:** www.jblpro.com
**SIC: 3651** Audio electronic systems
**HQ:** Harman Professional, Inc.
8500 Balboa Blvd
Northridge CA 91329
818 893-8411

**(P-11667)**
### HARMAN PROFESSIONAL INC (DH)
Also Called: Harman Professional
8500 Balboa Blvd, Northridge (91329-0003)
P.O. Box 2200 (91329)
**PHONE**.................................818 893-8411
Brian Divine, *CEO*
◆ **EMP:** 300 **EST:** 2006
**SALES (est):** 165.47MM **Privately Held**
**Web:** www.jblpro.com
**SIC: 3651** Audio electronic systems
**HQ:** Harman International Industries Incorporated
400 Atlantic St Fl 15
Stamford CT 06901
203 328-3500

**(P-11668)**
### HENRYS ADIO VSUAL SLUTIONS INC
Also Called: Audio Images
18002 Cowan, Irvine (92614-6812)
**PHONE**.................................714 258-7238
Mark Ontiveros, *CEO*
**EMP:** 30 **EST:** 1998
**SALES (est):** 5.71MM **Privately Held**
**Web:** www.audioimages.tv
**SIC: 3651** Household audio and video equipment

**(P-11669)**
### ISOLATION NETWORK INC (PA)
Also Called: Ingrooves
55 Francisco St Ste 350, San Francisco (94133-2112)
**PHONE**.................................818 212-2600
Robert D Roback, *CEO*
Adam Hiles, *Pr*
Clifton Wong, *CFO*
Vincent Freda, *COO*
**EMP:** 79 **EST:** 2003
**SQ FT:** 5,000
**SALES (est):** 12.38MM
**SALES (corp-wide):** 12.38MM **Privately Held**
**Web:** www.virginmusic.com
**SIC: 3651** 7929  Music distribution apparatus ; Musical entertainers

**(P-11670)**
### JEFF BURGESS & ASSOCIATES INC (DH)
Also Called: JB&a Distribution
1050 Northgate Dr Ste 200, San Rafael (94903-2562)
**PHONE**.................................415 256-2800
Jeff Burgess, *CEO*
Gregory Burgess, *
**EMP:** 25 **EST:** 1996
**SQ FT:** 10,000
**SALES (est):** 10.01MM **Privately Held**
**Web:** www.jbanda.com
**SIC: 3651** Household audio equipment
**HQ:** Exertis Supply Chain Services, Inc.
1550 The Alameda Ste 211
San Jose CA 95126

**(P-11671)**
### KSC INDUSTRIES INC
9771 Clairemont Mesa Blvd Ste E, San Diego (92124-1300)
**PHONE**.................................619 671-0110
Jeffrey W King Junior, *Pr*
Malcolm Hollombe, *VP*
William Mccarty, *VP*
Lisa Michaud, *VP*
Mary Beth King-fuller, *Dir*
◆ **EMP:** 26 **EST:** 1973
**SQ FT:** 10,000
**SALES (est):** 1.95MM **Privately Held**
**Web:** www.kscind.com
**SIC: 3651** Speaker systems

**(P-11672)**
### M KLEMME TECHNOLOGY CORP
Also Called: K-Tek
1384 Poinsettia Ave Ste F, Vista (92081-8505)
**PHONE**.................................760 727-0593
Brenda L Parker, *Pr*
▲ **EMP:** 26 **EST:** 1996
**SALES (est):** 3.17MM **Privately Held**
**Web:** www.ktekpro.com
**SIC: 3651** Audio electronic systems

**(P-11673)**
### MAGICO LLC
3170 Corporate Pl, Hayward (94545-3916)
**PHONE**.................................510 649-9700
Peter Maher, *
Tuan Trinh, *
▲ **EMP:** 26 **EST:** 1996
**SQ FT:** 12,000
**SALES (est):** 4.53MM **Privately Held**
**Web:** www.magicoaudio.com
**SIC: 3651** Speaker systems

**(P-11674)**
### MAGNASYNC/MOVIOLA CORPORATION
Also Called: Magnasync-Moviola
1400 W Burbank Blvd, Burbank (91506-1308)
**PHONE**.................................818 845-8066
**EMP:** 20
**SALES (corp-wide):** 22.49MM **Privately Held**
**Web:** www.filmtools.com
**SIC: 3651** Household audio and video equipment
**PA:** Magnasync/Moviola Corporation
1015 N Hollywood Way
818 845-8066

**(P-11675)**
### MARSHALL ELECTRONICS INC (PA)
Also Called: Mogami
20608 Madrona Ave, Torrance (90503-3715)
**PHONE**.................................310 333-0606
▲ **EMP:** 90 **EST:** 1979
**SALES (est):** 12.02MM
**SALES (corp-wide):** 12.02MM **Privately Held**
**Web:** www.marshall-usa.com
**SIC: 3651** 5961  Electronic kits for home assembly: radio, TV, phonograph; Electronic kits and parts, mail order

**(P-11676)**
### MESA/BOOGIE LIMITED (HQ)
1317 Ross St, Petaluma (94954-1124)
**PHONE**.................................707 765-1805
▲ **EMP:** 100 **EST:** 1975
**SQ FT:** 47,000
**SALES (est):** 24.42MM
**SALES (corp-wide):** 438.34MM **Privately Held**
**Web:** www.mesaboogie.com
**SIC: 3651** 5736  Amplifiers: radio, public address, or musical instrument; Musical instrument stores
**PA:** Gibson Brands, Inc.
209 10th Ave S Ste 460
615 871-4500

**(P-11677)**
### MEYER SOUND LABORATORIES INC (PA)
Also Called: Meyer Sound Labs
2832 San Pablo Ave, Berkeley (94702-2204)
**PHONE**.................................510 486-1166
John D Meyer, *Pr*
Brad Friedman, *
Helen Meyer, *
◆ **EMP:** 140 **EST:** 1979
**SQ FT:** 15,800
**SALES (est):** 43.73MM
**SALES (corp-wide):** 43.73MM **Privately Held**
**Web:** www.meyersound.com
**SIC: 3651** Loudspeakers, electrodynamic or magnetic

**(P-11678)**
### MJ BEST VIDEOGRAPHER LLC
14005 S Berendo Ave Apt 3, Gardena (90247-2248)
**PHONE**.................................209 208-8432
John S Morris, *CEO*
**EMP:** 209 **EST:** 2020
**SALES (est):** 300.82K **Privately Held**
**SIC: 3651** Video camera-audio recorders, household use

**(P-11679)**
### MR DJ INC
1800 E Washington Blvd, Los Angeles (90021-3127)
**PHONE**.................................213 744-0044
Mike Razipour, *CEO*
Shahzad Fatemi, *
▲ **EMP:** 50 **EST:** 2009
**SALES (est):** 1.33MM **Privately Held**
**Web:** www.mrdjusa.com
**SIC: 3651** Audio electronic systems

**(P-11680)**
### NADY SYSTEMS INC
3341 Vincent Rd, Pleasant Hill (94523-4354)
**PHONE**.................................510 652-2411
John Nady, *Pr*
▲ **EMP:** 24 **EST:** 1976
**SALES (est):** 1.77MM **Privately Held**
**Web:** www.nady.com

## 3651 - Household Audio And Video Equipment (P-11681)

**PRODUCTS & SERVICES SECTION**

SIC: **3651** 3669 Audio electronic systems; Intercommunication systems, electric

### (P-11681)
### NCA LABORATORIES INC
Also Called: The Clearwater Company
11305 Sunrise Gold Cir, Rancho Cordova (95742-7213)
P.O. Box 428 (95763-0428)
PHONE..............................916 852-7029
Glenn A Stasky, *Pr*
◆ **EMP:** 37 **EST:** 2001
**SALES (est):** 934.16K
**SALES (corp-wide):** 659.7MM **Publicly Held**
Web: www.ncalaboratories.com
SIC: **3651** Audio electronic systems
HQ: Simpson Performance Products, Inc.
328 Fm 306
New Braunfels TX 78130
830 625-1774

### (P-11682)
### NEW CENTURY AUDIO / VIDEO INC
Also Called: Century Stereo
450 El Paseo De Saratoga, San Jose (95130-1619)
PHONE..............................408 341-1950
**EMP:** 17
SIC: **3651** Household audio and video equipment

### (P-11683)
### NOOPL INC
Also Called: Noopl
1210 G St Ste B, Sacramento (95814-1516)
PHONE..............................916 400-3976
Tim Trine, *CEO*
Steven Verdooner, *Ch*
Jean Yoo, *CFO*
**EMP:** 20 **EST:** 2015
**SALES (est):** 325.57K **Privately Held**
Web: www.noopl.com
SIC: **3651** Audio electronic systems

### (P-11684)
### OLIVE MEDIA PRODUCTS INC
Also Called: Save The Sound
555 Howard St, San Francisco (94105-3014)
PHONE..............................415 908-3870
**EMP:** 17
Web: www.olive.us
SIC: **3651** Household audio and video equipment

### (P-11685)
### PASS LABORATORIES INC
13395 New Airport Rd Ste G, Auburn (95602-7419)
P.O. Box 219 (95631-0219)
PHONE..............................530 878-5350
Desmond Harrinton, *Pr*
Desmond Harrington, *Pr*
▲ **EMP:** 15 **EST:** 1991
**SQ FT:** 4,000
**SALES (est):** 2.48MM **Privately Held**
Web: www.passlabs.com
SIC: **3651** Amplifiers: radio, public address, or musical instrument

### (P-11686)
### PETCUBE INC (PA)
555 De Haro St Ste 280a, San Francisco (94107-2363)
PHONE..............................424 302-6107
Iaroslav Azhniuk, *CEO*
Alexander Neskin, *
Andrii Kulbaba, *
**EMP:** 27 **EST:** 2013
**SALES (est):** 10.48MM
**SALES (corp-wide):** 10.48MM **Privately Held**
Web: www.petcube.com
SIC: **3651** Video camera-audio recorders, household use

### (P-11687)
### PHILIPS
3721 Valley Centre Dr Ste 500, San Diego (92130-3328)
PHONE..............................916 337-8008
**EMP:** 86 **EST:** 2018
**SALES (est):** 4.41MM **Privately Held**
Web: usa.philips.com
SIC: **3651** Household audio and video equipment

### (P-11688)
### PIONEER SPEAKERS INC
2050 W 190th St Ste 100, Torrance (90504-6229)
PHONE..............................310 952-2000
◆ **EMP:** 1250
Web: www.pioneerdj.com
SIC: **3651** Speaker systems

### (P-11689)
### QSC LLC (PA)
Also Called: Qsc Audio
1675 Macarthur Blvd, Costa Mesa (92626-1468)
PHONE..............................800 854-4079
Joe Pham, *CEO*
Jatan Shah, *
Barry Ferrell, *
Ray Van Straten, *
Anna Csontos, *
◆ **EMP:** 175 **EST:** 1979
**SQ FT:** 180,000
**SALES (est):** 101.64MM
**SALES (corp-wide):** 101.64MM **Privately Held**
Web: www.qsc.com
SIC: **3651** Household audio equipment

### (P-11690)
### RENKUS-HEINZ INC (PA)
19201 Cook St, Foothill Ranch (92610-3501)
PHONE..............................949 588-9997
Harro Heinz, *Ch*
Roscoe L Anthony Iii, *CEO*
Erika Heinz, *
▲ **EMP:** 79 **EST:** 1979
**SQ FT:** 48,500
**SALES (est):** 9.86MM
**SALES (corp-wide):** 9.86MM **Privately Held**
Web: www.renkus-heinz.com
SIC: **3651** Audio electronic systems

### (P-11691)
### ROBOT-GXG INC
8960 Toronto Ave, Rancho Cucamonga (91730-5411)
PHONE..............................660 324-0030
Xiwen Xu, *Prin*
**EMP:** 20 **EST:** 2019
**SALES (est):** 194.36K **Privately Held**
SIC: **3651** Home entertainment equipment, electronic, nec

### (P-11692)
### ROCK-OLA MANUFACTURING CORP
Also Called: Antique Apparatus Company
1445 Sepulveda Blvd, Torrance (90501-5004)
PHONE..............................310 328-1306
Glenn S Streeter, *Pr*
◆ **EMP:** 80 **EST:** 1994
**SALES (est):** 9.98MM **Privately Held**
Web: www.rock-ola.com
SIC: **3651** Coin-operated phonographs, juke boxes

### (P-11693)
### RODE MICROPHONES LLC (DH)
2745 Raymond Ave, Signal Hill (90755-2129)
P.O. Box 91028 (90809-1028)
PHONE..............................310 328-7456
Mark Ludmer, *CEO*
Peter Freedmon, *
Brian Swbaringen, *
▲ **EMP:** 140 **EST:** 2001
**SALES (est):** 51.04MM **Privately Held**
Web: www.rode.com
SIC: **3651** Microphones
HQ: Freedman Electronics Pty Ltd
107 Carnarvon St
Silverwater NSW 2128

### (P-11694)
### S2E INC
Also Called: Mee Audio
817 Lawson St, City Of Industry (91748-1104)
PHONE..............................626 965-1008
Martie Shieh, *Pr*
Jerry Shieh, *VP*
▲ **EMP:** 15 **EST:** 2005
**SQ FT:** 7,000
**SALES (est):** 2.39MM **Privately Held**
Web: www.meeaudio.com
SIC: **3651** Household audio and video equipment

### (P-11695)
### SANYO MANUFACTURING CORPORATION
2055 Sanyo Ave, San Diego (92154-6234)
P.O. Box 2000 (72336-2000)
PHONE..............................619 661-1134
◆ **EMP:** 100
SIC: **3651** Television receiving sets

### (P-11696)
### SCOSCHE INDUSTRIES INC
1550 Pacific Ave, Oxnard (93033-2451)
P.O. Box 2901 (93034-2901)
PHONE..............................805 486-4450
Roger J Alves, *CEO*
Scotia Alves, *
Kasidy Alves, *
Vincent Alves, *
Steven Klinger, *
◆ **EMP:** 180 **EST:** 1980
**SQ FT:** 83,000
**SALES (est):** 24.51MM **Privately Held**
Web: www.scosche.com
SIC: **3651** Audio electronic systems

### (P-11697)
### SIGMATRONIX INC
2109 S Susan St, Santa Ana (92704-4416)
PHONE..............................714 436-1618
Michael Dang, *Pr*
**EMP:** 15 **EST:** 2005
**SQ FT:** 5,600
**SALES (est):** 4.66MM **Privately Held**
Web: www.sigmatronix.com
SIC: **3651** Electronic kits for home assembly: radio, TV, phonograph

### (P-11698)
### SONANCE
212 Avenida Fabricante, San Clemente (92672-7538)
PHONE..............................949 492-7777
**EMP:** 19 **EST:** 2022
**SALES (est):** 1.47MM **Privately Held**
Web: iport.squarespace.com
SIC: **3651** Household audio and video equipment

### (P-11699)
### SONOS INC (PA)
Also Called: Sonos
301 Coromar Dr, Goleta (93117-3286)
PHONE..............................805 965-3001
Patrick Spence, *Pr*
Julius Genachowski, *
Saori Casey, *CFO*
Edward Lazarus, *CSO CLO*
Nicholas Millington, *CIO*
◆ **EMP:** 91 **EST:** 2002
**SALES (est):** 1.66B
**SALES (corp-wide):** 1.66B **Publicly Held**
Web: www.sonos.com
SIC: **3651** Household audio and video equipment

### (P-11700)
### SONY ELECTRONICS INC (DH)
16535 Via Esprillo 1, San Diego (92127-1738)
PHONE..............................858 942-2400
Shigeki Ishizuka, *Pr*
Phil Molyneux, *
Hideki Komiyama, *
Rintaro Miyoshi, *
William A Glaser, *
◆ **EMP:** 1000 **EST:** 1988
**SALES (est):** 1.41B **Privately Held**
Web: www.sony.com
SIC: **3651** 5064 3695 3671 Household audio and video equipment; Electrical appliances, television and radio; Video recording tape, blank; Television tubes
HQ: Sony Corporation Of America
25 Madison Ave Fl 27
New York NY 10010

### (P-11701)
### SONY ELECTRONICS INC
Also Called: Sony Style
16530 Via Esprillo, San Diego (92127-1708)
PHONE..............................858 942-2400
Bill Lunger, *Prin*
**EMP:** 224
Web: www.sony.com
SIC: **3651** Household audio and video equipment
HQ: Sony Electronics Inc.
16535 Via Esprillo Bldg 1
San Diego CA 92127
858 942-2400

### (P-11702)
### SPEAKERCRAFT LLC
12471 Riverside Dr, Mira Loma (91752-1007)
P.O. Box 9003 (92008)
PHONE..............................951 685-1759
◆ **EMP:** 100
Web: www.speakercraft.com
SIC: **3651** 5731 Household audio equipment ; High fidelity stereo equipment

### (P-11703)
### SYNG INC (PA)
120 Mildred Ave, Venice (90291-4227)
PHONE..............................770 354-0915

# PRODUCTS & SERVICES SECTION
## 3652 - Prerecorded Records And Tapes (P-11725)

Christopher Stringer, *CEO*
Damon Way, *
**EMP:** 60 **EST:** 2018
**SALES (est):** 9.51MM
**SALES (corp-wide):** 9.51MM **Privately Held**
**Web:** www.syngspace.com
**SIC: 3651** Loudspeakers, electrodynamic or magnetic

### (P-11704)
### TECHNICOLOR USA INC
Also Called: Technicolor Connected USA
4049 Industrial Parkway Dr, Lebec (93243-9719)
**PHONE**..................661 496-1309
**EMP:** 599
**Web:** www.technicolor.com
**SIC: 3651** Household audio and video equipment
**HQ:** Technicolor Usa, Inc.
6040 W Sunset Blvd
Hollywood CA 90028
317 587-4287

### (P-11705)
### TECHNICOLOR USA INC (HQ)
Also Called: Technicolor
6040 W Sunset Blvd, Hollywood (90028-6402)
P.O. Box 1976 (46206-1976)
**PHONE**..................317 587-4287
◆ **EMP:** 800 **EST:** 1987
**SALES (est):** 576.79MM **Privately Held**
**Web:** www.technicolor.com
**SIC: 3651** 3861 3661 Household audio and video equipment; Cameras, microfilm; Telephone sets, all types except cellular radio
**PA:** Vantiva
10 Boulevard De Grenelle

### (P-11706)
### TOSHIBA AMER ELCTRNIC CMPNNTS (DH)
Also Called: Toshiba
5231 California Ave, Irvine (92617-3235)
**PHONE**..................949 462-7700
Hideya Yamaguchi, *CEO*
Hitoshi Otsuka, *
Ichiro Hirata, *
Richard Tobias, *
Farhad Mafie, *
◆ **EMP:** 300 **EST:** 1998
**SQ FT:** 100,000
**SALES (est):** 412.02MM **Privately Held**
**Web:** www.toshiba.com
**SIC: 3651** 3631 3674 3679 Television receiving sets; Microwave ovens, including portable; household; Semiconductors and related devices; Electronic circuits
**HQ:** Toshiba America Inc
1251 Ave Of Amrcas Ste 41
New York NY 10020
212 596-0600

### (P-11707)
### TOSHIBA AMERICA INC
5241 California Ave Ste 200, Irvine (92617-3052)
**PHONE**..................212 596-0600
**EMP:** 1074
**Web:** www.toshiba.com
**SIC: 3651** 3631 5075 3571 Television receiving sets; Microwave ovens, including portable; household; Compressors, air conditioning; Personal computers (microcomputers)
**HQ:** Toshiba America Inc
1251 Ave Of Amrcas Ste 41
New York NY 10020
212 596-0600

### (P-11708)
### ULTIMATE SOUND INC
1200 S Diamond Bar Blvd Ste 200, Diamond Bar (91765-2298)
**PHONE**..................909 861-6200
Robert Chiu, *Pr*
Cindy Chiu, *
◆ **EMP:** 300 **EST:** 1978
**SQ FT:** 20,000
**SALES (est):** 5.74MM **Privately Held**
**SIC: 3651** 5731 Loudspeakers, electrodynamic or magnetic; Radio, television, and electronic stores

### (P-11709)
### ULTIMATUM RECORDS LLC
4695 Chabot Dr Ste 200, Pleasanton (94588-2756)
**PHONE**..................925 353-5202
**EMP:** 16 **EST:** 2021
**SALES (est):** 944.48K **Privately Held**
**SIC: 3651** Music distribution apparatus

### (P-11710)
### VANDERSTEEN AUDIO
116 W 4th St, Hanford (93230-5021)
**PHONE**..................559 582-0324
Richard J Vandersteen, *Pr*
Eneke Vandersteen, *Prin*
▲ **EMP:** 21 **EST:** 1977
**SQ FT:** 20,000
**SALES (est):** 2.18MM **Privately Held**
**Web:** www.vandersteen.com
**SIC: 3651** 5731 Speaker systems; Radio, television, and electronic stores

### (P-11711)
### VANTAGE POINT PRODUCTS CORP (PA)
Also Called: Vpt Direct
9234 Hall Rd, Downey (90241-5308)
P.O. Box 2485 (90670-0485)
**PHONE**..................562 946-1718
Donald R Burns, *CEO*
Mick Mulcahey, *Pr*
▲ **EMP:** 33 **EST:** 1988
**SALES (est):** 4.72MM **Privately Held**
**Web:** www.thinkvp.com
**SIC: 3651** Audio electronic systems

### (P-11712)
### VELODYNE ACOUSTICS INC
850 Tanglewood Dr, Lafayette (94549-4929)
**PHONE**..................408 465-2800
David Hall, *CEO*
Bruce Hall, *
Michael Jellen, *
Vincent C Hall, *Stockholder**
Joseph B Culkin, *Stockholder**
▲ **EMP:** 70 **EST:** 1983
**SALES (est):** 4.41MM **Privately Held**
**Web:** www.velodynelidar.com
**SIC: 3651** 5731 Speaker systems; Radio, television, and electronic stores

### (P-11713)
### VIZIO INC
2601 S Bdwy Unit B, Los Angeles (90007-2731)
**PHONE**..................213 746-7730
**EMP:** 122
**SALES (corp-wide):** 1.68B **Publicly Held**
**Web:** www.vizio.com
**SIC: 3651** Television receiving sets
**HQ:** Vizio, Inc.
39 Tesla
Irvine CA 92618
855 833-3221

### (P-11714)
### VIZIO INC (HQ)
39 Tesla, Irvine (92618-4603)
**PHONE**..................855 833-3221
William Wang, *CEO*
Adam Townsend, *
Jerry Huang, *
◆ **EMP:** 154 **EST:** 2002
**SQ FT:** 27,300
**SALES (est):** 90.48MM
**SALES (corp-wide):** 1.68B **Publicly Held**
**Web:** www.vizio.com
**SIC: 3651** Television receiving sets
**PA:** Vizio Holding Corp.
39 Tesla
949 428-2525

### (P-11715)
### VIZIO HOLDING CORP (PA)
Also Called: VIZIO
39 Tesla, Irvine (92618-4603)
**PHONE**..................949 428-2525
William Wang, *Ch Bd*
Ben Wong, *Pr*
Adam Townsend, *CFO*
Michael O'donnell, *CRO*
**EMP:** 31 **EST:** 2003
**SALES (est):** 1.68B
**SALES (corp-wide):** 1.68B **Publicly Held**
**Web:** www.vizio.com
**SIC: 3651** Household audio and video equipment

### (P-11716)
### VTL AMPLIFIERS INC
4774 Murrietta St Ste 10, Chino (91710-5155)
**PHONE**..................909 627-5944
Luke Manley, *Pr*
▲ **EMP:** 24 **EST:** 2000
**SQ FT:** 6,000
**SALES (est):** 2.88MM **Privately Held**
**Web:** www.vtl.com
**SIC: 3651** Audio electronic systems

### (P-11717)
### WESTLAKE AUDIO INC (PA)
2696 Lavery Ct Ste 18, Newbury Park (91320-1591)
**PHONE**..................805 499-3686
Glenn Phoenix, *Pr*
**EMP:** 15 **EST:** 1970
**SQ FT:** 6,500
**SALES (est):** 4.42MM
**SALES (corp-wide):** 4.42MM **Privately Held**
**Web:** www.westlakeaudio.com
**SIC: 3651** Home entertainment equipment, electronic, nec

### (P-11718)
### WINNOV INC
3945 Freedom Cir Ste 560, Santa Clara (95054-1269)
**PHONE**..................888 315-9460
Olivier Garbe, *CEO*
**EMP:** 24 **EST:** 1992
**SALES (est):** 1.86MM **Privately Held**
**Web:** www.winnov.com
**SIC: 3651** Household audio and video equipment

### (P-11719)
### WIRELESS TECHNOLOGY INC
Also Called: Wti
2064 Eastman Ave Ste 113, Ventura (93003-7787)
**PHONE**..................805 339-9696
Phil Fancher, *CEO*
Arlene Fancher, *
**EMP:** 30 **EST:** 1987
**SQ FT:** 7,000
**SALES (est):** 4.73MM **Privately Held**
**Web:** www.gotowti.com
**SIC: 3651** Household audio and video equipment

### (P-11720)
### X HYPER
17600 Newhope St, Fountain Valley (92708-4220)
P.O. Box 237 (95982-0237)
**PHONE**..................530 673-7099
Dennis Eugene Matthews, *Prin*
**EMP:** 36 **EST:** 2010
**SALES (est):** 153.7K **Privately Held**
**SIC: 3651** Audio electronic systems

### (P-11721)
### X-1 AUDIO INC
Also Called: H2o Audio
5771 Copley Dr, San Diego (92111-7905)
P.O. Box 712332 (92171-2332)
**PHONE**..................858 623-0339
▲ **EMP:** 15
**Web:** www.h2oaudio.com
**SIC: 3651** Household audio and video equipment

### (P-11722)
### XANTECH LLC
1690 Corporate Cir, Petaluma (94954-6912)
P.O. Box 9003 (92008)
**PHONE**..................818 362-0353
▲ **EMP:** 39
**Web:** www.xantech.com
**SIC: 3651** Electronic kits for home assembly: radio, TV, phonograph

## 3652 Prerecorded Records And Tapes

### (P-11723)
### CAPITOL-EMI MUSIC INC
Also Called: E M D
1750b Vine St, Los Angeles (90028-5209)
**PHONE**..................323 462-6252
**EMP:** 1500
**SIC: 3652** Compact laser discs, prerecorded

### (P-11724)
### CLINCAPTURE
1428 Bush St, San Francisco (94109-5521)
P.O. Box 15069 (94115-0069)
**PHONE**..................408 412-7256
Amanda Mclean, *Prin*
**EMP:** 50 **EST:** 2017
**SALES (est):** 1.41MM **Privately Held**
**Web:** www.clincapture.com
**SIC: 3652** Prerecorded records and tapes

### (P-11725)
### CMH RECORDS INC
Also Called: Dwell Records
2898 Rowena Ave Ste 201, Los Angeles (90039-2096)
P.O. Box 39439 (90039-0439)
**PHONE**..................323 663-8098
David Haerle, *Pr*
**EMP:** 38 **EST:** 1975
**SQ FT:** 3,303
**SALES (est):** 1.52MM **Privately Held**
**Web:** www.cmhrecords.com

# 3652 - Prerecorded Records And Tapes (P-11726)

**SIC: 3652** 7929 Phonograph records, prerecorded; Entertainers and entertainment groups

### (P-11726)
**CPAPERLESS LLC**
605 1/2 Orchid Ave, Corona Del Mar (92625-2461)
P.O. Box 1113 (92625-6113)
PHONE..................949 510-3365
**EMP:** 41 **EST:** 2018
**SALES (est):** 380.87K **Privately Held**
Web: www.safesend.com
**SIC: 3652** Prerecorded records and tapes

### (P-11727)
**DIGITAL FLEX MEDIA INC**
Also Called: CD Digital
11150 White Birch Dr, Rancho Cucamonga (91730-3819)
PHONE..................909 484-8440
**EMP:** 90
Web: www.digitalflexmedia.com
**SIC: 3652** Compact laser discs, prerecorded

### (P-11728)
**DISC REPLICATOR INC**
21137 Commerce Point Dr, Walnut (91789-3054)
PHONE..................909 385-0118
Jingtao Xie, *CEO*
**EMP:** 15 **EST:** 2014
**SALES (est):** 2.01MM **Privately Held**
Web: www.discreplicator.com
**SIC: 3652** Compact laser discs, prerecorded

### (P-11729)
**DISCOPYLABS**
Also Called: Dcl
4455 E Philadelphia St, Ontario (91761-2329)
PHONE..................909 390-3800
Larry Shaker, *Dir*
**EMP:** 21
**SALES (corp-wide):** 81.65MM **Privately Held**
Web: www.dclcorp.com
**SIC: 3652** 4225 7379 7389 Prerecorded records and tapes; General warehousing and storage; Diskette duplicating service
PA: Discopylabs
48641 Milmont Dr
510 651-5100

### (P-11730)
**DYNAMIC VISION INC**
550 Seagaze Dr Apt 32, Oceanside (92054-3075)
PHONE..................858 877-6200
**EMP:** 20 **EST:** 2019
**SALES (est):** 175.08K **Privately Held**
Web: www.dynamicvision.ca
**SIC: 3652** Prerecorded records and tapes

### (P-11731)
**ERIKA RECORDS INC**
6300 Caballero Blvd, Buena Park (90620-1126)
PHONE..................714 228-5420
Liz Dunster, *Pr*
Erzsebet Dunster, *CEO*
▲ **EMP:** 20 **EST:** 1981
**SALES (est):** 2.87MM **Privately Held**
Web: www.erikarecords.com
**SIC: 3652** 5735 Phonograph records, prerecorded; Records

### (P-11732)
**EXTREME GROUP HOLDINGS LLC**
Also Called: Extreme Production Music
1531 14th St, Santa Monica (90404-3302)
PHONE..................310 899-3200
Emanuel Russell, *Brnch Mgr*
**EMP:** 19
Web: www.extrememusic.com
**SIC: 3652** Prerecorded records and tapes
HQ: Extreme Group Holdings Llc
25 Madison Ave
New York NY 10010

### (P-11733)
**FEATHERSOFT INC**
600 N Mountain Ave Ste C100, Upland (91786-4331)
PHONE..................925 230-0740
George Varghese, *CEO*
**EMP:** 29 **EST:** 2018
**SALES (est):** 286.74K **Privately Held**
Web: www.feathersoft.com
**SIC: 3652** Prerecorded records and tapes

### (P-11734)
**GC INTERNATIONAL INC**
Also Called: Al Johnson Company
4671 Calle Carga, Camarillo (93012-8560)
PHONE..................805 389-4631
Mark Griffith, *Prin*
**EMP:** 20
**SALES (corp-wide):** 10.1MM **Privately Held**
Web: www.aljcast.com
**SIC: 3652** 3369 Phonograph record blanks; Lead, zinc, and white metal
PA: Gc International, Inc.
4671 Calle Carga
805 389-4631

### (P-11735)
**HOLLYWOOD RECORDS INC**
Also Called: Andanov Music
500 S Buena Vista St, Burbank (91521-0002)
PHONE..................818 560-5670
Abbey Konowitch, *Genl Mgr*
**EMP:** 50 **EST:** 1990
**SALES:** 1.6MM
**SALES (corp-wide):** 88.9B **Publicly Held**
Web: www.hollywoodrecords.com
**SIC: 3652** Prerecorded records and tapes
HQ: Walt Disney Music Company
500 S Buena Vista St
Burbank CA 91521
818 560-1000

### (P-11736)
**ISOMEDIA LLC**
43297 Osgood Rd, Fremont (94539-5657)
PHONE..................510 668-1656
▲ **EMP:** 25 **EST:** 2004
**SALES (est):** 782.34K **Privately Held**
Web: www.isomediainc.com
**SIC: 3652** Compact laser discs, prerecorded

### (P-11737)
**MOTIVEMETRICS**
425 Sherman Ave Ste 300, Palo Alto (94306-1851)
PHONE..................800 216-5207
**EMP:** 43 **EST:** 2019
**SALES (est):** 801.03K **Privately Held**
Web: www.motivemetrics.com
**SIC: 3652** Prerecorded records and tapes

### (P-11738)
**NCC GROUP ESCROW ASSOC LLC**
123 Mission St Ste 900, San Francisco (94105-5124)
PHONE..................678 381-2768
**EMP:** 19 **EST:** 2014
**SALES (est):** 618.6K **Privately Held**
**SIC: 3652** Prerecorded records and tapes

### (P-11739)
**PANASONIC DISC MANUFACTURING CORPORATION OF AMERICA**
20000 Mariner Ave Ste 200, Torrance (90503-1670)
PHONE..................310 783-4800
▲ **EMP:** 200
Web: pdmc.panasonic.com
**SIC: 3652** Compact laser discs, prerecorded

### (P-11740)
**PARTNERS 1993 INC**
3501 Ocean View Blvd, Glendale (91208-1211)
PHONE..................818 352-7800
**EMP:** 18 **EST:** 2019
**SALES (est):** 176.16K **Privately Held**
**SIC: 3652** Prerecorded records and tapes

### (P-11741)
**PRECISE MEDIA SERVICES INC**
Also Called: Precise-Full Service Media
888 Vintage Ave, Ontario (91764-5392)
PHONE..................909 481-3305
Choy Tim Lee, *CEO*
Robert Miller, *
▲ **EMP:** 25 **EST:** 1991
**SQ FT:** 112,000
**SALES (est):** 2.15MM **Privately Held**
Web: www.precisemedia.com
**SIC: 3652** 7819 Prerecorded records and tapes; Video tape or disk reproduction

### (P-11742)
**RAINBO RECORD MFG CORP (PA)**
Also Called: Rainbo Records & Cassettes
8960 Eton Ave, Canoga Park (91304-1621)
P.O. Box 280700 (91328-0700)
PHONE..................818 280-1100
Jack Brown, *Prin*
Steve Sheldon, *Prin*
▲ **EMP:** 50 **EST:** 1939
**SQ FT:** 50,000
**SALES (est):** 3.85MM
**SALES (corp-wide):** 3.85MM **Privately Held**
Web: www.urpressing.com
**SIC: 3652** 5099 Compact laser discs, prerecorded; Compact discs

### (P-11743)
**RECORD TECHNOLOGY INC (PA)**
486 Dawson Dr Ste 4s, Camarillo (93012-8049)
PHONE..................805 484-2747
Don Mac Innis, *Pr*
Melodie Mac Innis, *
▲ **EMP:** 24 **EST:** 1972
**SQ FT:** 30,000
**SALES (est):** 2.47MM
**SALES (corp-wide):** 2.47MM **Privately Held**
Web: www.recordtech.com
**SIC: 3652** Master records or tapes, preparation of

### (P-11744)
**SITETRAKER**
420 Florence St, Palo Alto (94301-1741)
PHONE..................650 868-5164
Lauren Cheek, *Prin*
**EMP:** 37 **EST:** 2018
**SALES (est):** 252.68K **Privately Held**
Web: www.sitetracker.com
**SIC: 3652** Prerecorded records and tapes

### (P-11745)
**SUITECENTRIC LCC**
5857 Owens Ave Ste 300, Carlsbad (92008-5507)
PHONE..................760 520-1611
**EMP:** 36 **EST:** 2019
**SALES (est):** 2.87MM **Privately Held**
Web: www.suitecentric.com
**SIC: 3652** Prerecorded records and tapes

### (P-11746)
**THROUGHPUT INC**
2100 Geng Rd, Palo Alto (94303-3343)
PHONE..................215 606-8552
Ali Raza, *CEO*
Khizer Hayat, *Prin*
Seth Page, *COO*
**EMP:** 15 **EST:** 2016
**SALES (est):** 1.34MM **Privately Held**
Web: www.throughput.world
**SIC: 3652** Prerecorded records and tapes

## 3661 Telephone And Telegraph Apparatus

### (P-11747)
**ACCORDION NETWORKS INC**
990 Yakima Dr, Fremont (94539-7211)
PHONE..................510 623-2876
Gautam Chanda, *Pr*
Rajan Aiyer, *VP Mktg*
**EMP:** 20 **EST:** 1998
**SQ FT:** 12,000
**SALES (est):** 638.98K **Privately Held**
**SIC: 3661** Telephone and telegraph apparatus

### (P-11748)
**ACTELIS NETWORKS INC (PA)**
Also Called: Actelis Networks
4039 Clipper Ct, Fremont (94538-6540)
PHONE..................510 545-1045
Tuvia Barlev, *Ch Bd*
Yoav Efron, *CFO*
Yaron Altit, *International Sales Vice President*
**EMP:** 29 **EST:** 1998
**SQ FT:** 3,000
**SALES (est):** 5.61MM **Publicly Held**
Web: www.actelis.com
**SIC: 3661** Telephone and telegraph apparatus

### (P-11749)
**ALCATEL-LUCENT USA INC**
Also Called: ALCATEL-LUCENT USA INC.
777 E Middlefield Rd, Mountain View (94043-4023)
PHONE..................650 623-3300
Sudhanshu Jain, *Prin*
**EMP:** 58
**SALES (corp-wide):** 24.19B **Privately Held**
Web: www.nokia.com
**SIC: 3661** Telephone and telegraph apparatus
HQ: Nokia Of America Corporation
600 Mountain Ave Ste 700
Murray Hill NJ 07974

## 3661 - Telephone And Telegraph Apparatus (P-11769)

**(P-11750)**
**ALLEGIANCE SUPPLY INCORPORATED**
6354 Corte Del Abeto Ste D, Carlsbad (92011-1479)
PHONE...................760 230-8018
John Mckinley, Pr
EMP: 21 EST: 2008
SALES (est): 1.08MM Privately Held
Web: www.alleglancesupply.com
SIC: 3661 Fiber optics communications equipment

**(P-11751)**
**ALTIGEN COMMUNICATIONS INC**
670 N Mccarthy Blvd Ste 200, Milpitas (95035-5119)
PHONE...................408 597-9000
Jeremiah J Fleming, Pr
Mike Plumer, *
Simon Chouldjian, *
Shirley Sun, *
Philip M Mcdermott, CFO
▲ EMP: 115 EST: 1994
SQ FT: 27,576
SALES (est): 9.47MM Privately Held
Web: www.altigen.com
SIC: 3661 1731 Telephone and telegraph apparatus; Communications specialization

**(P-11752)**
**AYANTRA INC**
47873 Fremont Blvd, Fremont (94538-6506)
PHONE...................510 623-7526
Ashok Teckchandani, Pr
Harbans Rattia, VP
▲ EMP: 15 EST: 1995
SQ FT: 2,300
SALES (est): 2.53MM Privately Held
Web: www.ayantra.com
SIC: 3661 Telephone and telegraph apparatus

**(P-11753)**
**BALAJI TRADING INC**
Also Called: City of Industry
4850 Eucalyptus Ave, Chino (91710-9255)
PHONE...................909 444-7999
Mukesh Batta, CEO
▲ EMP: 91 EST: 2010
SALES (est): 2.47MM Privately Held
Web: www.balajiwireless.com
SIC: 3661 Headsets, telephone

**(P-11754)**
**BLACK POINT PRODUCTS INC**
650 Central Ave, Alameda (94501-7803)
P.O. Box 70074 (94807-0074)
PHONE...................510 232-7723
Thomas Tognetti, Pr
Karin M Ashford, *
▲ EMP: 30 EST: 1985
SALES (est): 2.43MM Privately Held
Web: www.blkpoint.com
SIC: 3661 3651 Telephones and telephone apparatus; Video cassette recorders/players and accessories

**(P-11755)**
**CALIENT TECHNOLOGIES INC (PA)**
Also Called: Calient Technologies
120 Cremona Dr Ste 160, Goleta (93117-3168)
PHONE...................805 695-4800
Arjun Gutpa, Ofcr
Kevin Welsh, *
Jitender Miglani, *
Daniel Tardent, *
Jag Setlur, *
▲ EMP: 30 EST: 1999
SQ FT: 150,000
SALES (est): 21.37MM
SALES (corp-wide): 21.37MM Privately Held
Web: www.calient.net
SIC: 3661 Fiber optics communications equipment

**(P-11756)**
**CALMAR OPTCOM INC**
Also Called: Calmar Laser, Inc.
951 Commercial St, Palo Alto (94303-4908)
PHONE...................408 733-7800
Anthony Lin, Pr
EMP: 20 EST: 1996
SQ FT: 7,000
SALES (est): 2.33MM Privately Held
Web: www.calmarlaser.com
SIC: 3661 3699 Fiber optics communications equipment; Pulse amplifiers

**(P-11757)**
**COADNA PHOTONICS INC (HQ)**
1012 Stewart Dr, Sunnyvale (94085-3914)
PHONE...................408 736-1100
Jim Yuan, CEO
Jack Kelly, VP
Irene Yum, CFO
Fang Wang, COO
▲ EMP: 60 EST: 2000
SQ FT: 12,000
SALES (est): 6.29MM
SALES (corp-wide): 4.71B Publicly Held
SIC: 3661 Fiber optics communications equipment
PA: Coherent Corp.
375 Saxonburg Blvd
724 352-4455

**(P-11758)**
**COASTAL CONNECTIONS**
2085 Sperry Ave Ste B, Ventura (93003-7452)
PHONE...................805 644-5051
Andrew Devine, Pr
Nancy Devine, *
◆ EMP: 37 EST: 2002
SQ FT: 9,000
SALES (est): 2.74MM Privately Held
Web: www.coastalcon.com
SIC: 3661 Fiber optics communications equipment

**(P-11759)**
**DANTEL INC**
Also Called: Whistlestop MTA
4210 N Brawley Ave # 108, Fresno (93722-3979)
PHONE...................559 292-1111
Alan J Brown, Ch
Alan G Hutcheson, *
EMP: 23 EST: 1971
SALES (est): 4.98MM Privately Held
Web: www.dantel.com
SIC: 3661 Telephones and telephone apparatus

**(P-11760)**
**DITECH NETWORKS INC (DH)**
3099 N 1st St, San Jose (95134)
PHONE...................408 883-3636
Thomas L Beaudoin, Pr
Paul A Ricci, CEO
William Tamblyn, VP
EMP: 24 EST: 1983
SQ FT: 20,100
SALES (est): 2.28MM
SALES (corp-wide): 245.12B Publicly Held
SIC: 3661 Telephones and telephone apparatus
HQ: Nuance Communications, Inc.
1 Wayside Rd
Burlington MA 01803

**(P-11761)**
**ENABLENCE USA COMPONENTS INC**
2933 Bayview Dr, Fremont (94538-6520)
PHONE...................510 226-8900
Evan Chen, CEO
Jacob Sun, *
Andy Spector Senior, Sls Dir
Peter Sung, *
Fang Wang, *
EMP: 98 EST: 2003
SQ FT: 26,000
SALES (est): 20.71MM
SALES (corp-wide): 1.96MM Privately Held
Web: www.enablence.com
SIC: 3661 Fiber optics communications equipment
PA: Enablence Technologies Inc
119-390 March Rd
613 656-2850

**(P-11762)**
**EPIC TECHNOLOGIES LLC**
Also Called: Natel Engineering
9340 Owensmouth Ave, Chatsworth (91311)
PHONE...................908 707-4085
Sudesh Arora, Ch
John J Sammut, *
Robert T Howard, *
Jochen Lipp, *
Marcus Wedner, *
▲ EMP: 1750 EST: 2004
SQ FT: 52,000
SALES (est): 361.03MM
SALES (corp-wide): 1.43B Privately Held
Web: www.neotech.com
SIC: 3661 3577 3679 Telephone and telegraph apparatus; Computer peripheral equipment, nec; Electronic circuits
PA: Natel Engineering Company, Llc
9340 Owensmouth Ave
818 495-8617

**(P-11763)**
**FINISAR CORPORATION (HQ)**
Also Called: Finisar
1830 Bering Dr, San Jose (95112-4212)
PHONE...................408 548-1000
Walter R Bashaw Ii, Pr
Mary Jane Raymond, CAO*
▲ EMP: 24 EST: 1987
SQ FT: 92,000
SALES (est): 1.92MM
SALES (corp-wide): 4.71B Publicly Held
Web: www.coherent.com
SIC: 3661 3663 Fiber optics communications equipment; Antennas, transmitting and communications
PA: Coherent Corp.
375 Saxonburg Blvd
724 352-4455

**(P-11764)**
**FONEGEAR LLC**
13953 Ramona Ave, Chino (91710-5428)
P.O. Box 2606 (91709-0087)
PHONE...................909 627-7999
▲ EMP: 15 EST: 2003
SALES (est): 2.38MM Privately Held
Web: www.fonegear.com
SIC: 3661 Carrier equipment, telephone or telegraph

**(P-11765)**
**FRANKLIN WIRELESS CORP**
Also Called: Franklin Wireless
3940 Ruffin Rd Ste C, San Diego (92123-1844)
PHONE...................858 623-0000
Ok Chae Kim, Pr
Gary Nelson, *
Yun J David Lee, VP Sls
Bill Bauer, Interim Chief Financial Officer
▲ EMP: 69 EST: 1981
SALES (est): 30.8MM Privately Held
Web: www.franklinwireless.com
SIC: 3661 Fiber optics communications equipment

**(P-11766)**
**GENERAL PHOTONICS CORP**
Also Called: General Photonics
14351 Pipeline Ave, Chino (91710-5642)
PHONE...................909 590-5473
Steve Yao, Pr
Bruce Pazouki, VP
Helen Ren, Contrlr
Shasha Luo, Acctnt
▲ EMP: 51 EST: 1995
SQ FT: 20,000
SALES (est): 8.25MM Publicly Held
Web: www.lunainc.com
SIC: 3661 Fiber optics communications equipment
HQ: Luna Technologies, Inc.
301 1st St Sw Ste 200
Roanoke VA 24011
540 769-8400

**(P-11767)**
**GRASS VALLEY USA LLC (PA)**
310 Providence Mine Rd Ste 200, Nevada City (95959-2959)
P.O. Box 599000 (95959-7900)
PHONE...................800 547-8949
Timothy Shoulders, Pr
Michael Prinn, CFO
▲ EMP: 300 EST: 2010
SALES (est): 85.55MM Privately Held
Web: www.grassvalley.com
SIC: 3661 3999 3663 3651 Telephone sets, all types except cellular radio; Radio and t.v. communications equipment; Television receiving sets

**(P-11768)**
**INFINERA CORPORATION (PA)**
Also Called: Infinera
6373 San Ignacio Ave, San Jose (95119-1200)
PHONE...................408 572-5200
David W Heard, CEO
George A Riedel, *
Nancy L Erba, CFO
Regan Macpherson, CLO
David F Welch, CIO*
▼ EMP: 450 EST: 2000
SQ FT: 82,000
SALES (est): 1.61B
SALES (corp-wide): 1.61B Publicly Held
Web: www.infinera.com
SIC: 3661 7372 Fiber optics communications equipment; Prepackaged software

**(P-11769)**
**INFINERA INTERNATIONAL CORP (HQ)**
6373 San Ignacio Ave, San Jose (95119-1200)

## 3661 - Telephone And Telegraph Apparatus (P-11770)

PHONE.................................408 572-5200
EMP: 19 EST: 2004
SALES (est): 4.08MM
SALES (corp-wide): 1.61B Publicly Held
Web: www.infinera.com
SIC: 3661 Fiber optics communications equipment
PA: Infinera Corporation
6373 San Ignacio Ave
408 572-5200

### (P-11770)
### INFINERA OPTICAL NETWORKS INC (HQ)
6373 San Ignacio Ave, San Jose (95119-1200)
PHONE.................................630 798-8800
David W Heard, Pr
Shaygan Kheradpir, CEO
Gary Spitz, CFO
Uwe Fischer, Ex VP
Homayoun Razavi, CCO
▲ EMP: 20 EST: 1991
SQ FT: 850,000
SALES (est): 23.11MM
SALES (corp-wide): 1.61B Publicly Held
SIC: 3661 Telephone and telegraph apparatus
PA: Infinera Corporation
6373 San Ignacio Ave
408 572-5200

### (P-11771)
### INTEMATIX CORPORATION
351 Rheem Blvd, Moraga (94556-1541)
PHONE.................................925 631-9005
Yi-qun Li, Pr
EMP: 16 EST: 2000
SQ FT: 10,000
SALES (est): 1.73MM Privately Held
Web: www.intematix.com
SIC: 3661 Telephone and telegraph apparatus

### (P-11772)
### INTERNTNAL CNNCTORS CABLE CORP
Also Called: I C C
1270 N Hancock St, Anaheim (92807-1922)
PHONE.................................888 275-4422
Mike Lin, Pr
Mike Lin, Pr
Eugene Chyun Tsai, Stockholder*
▲ EMP: 110 EST: 1984
SQ FT: 38,720
SALES (est): 9.22MM Privately Held
Web: www.icc.com
SIC: 3661 5065 Telephone and telegraph apparatus; Telephone and telegraphic equipment

### (P-11773)
### JETSTREAM COMMUNICATIONS INC
5400 Hellyer Ave, San Jose (95138-1019)
PHONE.................................408 361-7000
Sundi Sundaresh, Pr
David Frankel, *
John Niedermaier, *
Stephen Ashurkoff, Worldwide Sales Vice President*
EMP: 100 EST: 1994
SALES (est): 1.58MM Privately Held
SIC: 3661 7371 Telephone and telegraph apparatus; Custom computer programming services

### (P-11774)
### LG-ERICSSON USA INC
20 Mason, Irvine (92618-2706)
PHONE.................................877 828-2673
◆ EMP: 47
Web: www.lgericssonus.com
SIC: 3661 5065 Telephone sets, all types except cellular radio; Modems, computer

### (P-11775)
### NETGEAR INC (PA)
350 E Plumeria Dr, San Jose (95134-1911)
PHONE.................................408 907-8000
Charles Prober, CEO
Thomas H Waechter, *
Bryan D Murray, CFO
Michael F Falcon, COO
Andrew W Kim, CLO
◆ EMP: 130 EST: 1996
SQ FT: 142,700
SALES (est): 740.84MM Publicly Held
Web: www.netgear.com
SIC: 3661 4813 Fiber optics communications equipment; Telephone communication, except radio

### (P-11776)
### NOKIA OF AMERICA CORPORATION
Also Called: Alcatel-Lucent
2000 Corporate Center Dr, Newbury Park (91320-1400)
PHONE.................................818 880-3500
Menandro Canelo, Ofcr
EMP: 34
SALES (corp-wide): 24.19B Privately Held
Web: www.nokia.com
SIC: 3661 Telephone and telegraph apparatus
HQ: Nokia Of America Corporation
600 Mountain Ave Ste 700
Murray Hill NJ 07974

### (P-11777)
### OCLARO (NORTH AMERICA) INC (DH)
252 Charcot Ave, San Jose (95131)
PHONE.................................408 383-1400
Jerry Turin, CEO
Pete Mangan, *
Kate Rundle, *
EMP: 433 EST: 2000
SQ FT: 54,000
SALES (est): 3.88MM
SALES (corp-wide): 1.36B Publicly Held
SIC: 3661 Fiber optics communications equipment
HQ: Oclaro, Inc.
400 N Mccarthy Blvd
Milpitas CA 95035

### (P-11778)
### OCLARO SUBSYSTEMS INC
400 N Mccarthy Blvd, Milpitas (95035-9100)
PHONE.................................408 383-1400
Jerry Turin, CEO
Shri Dodani, *
John Ralston, *
Pat Rezza, *
Bryson Wallace, *
▲ EMP: 200 EST: 2008
SALES (est): 78.67MM
SALES (corp-wide): 1.36B Publicly Held
SIC: 3661 Fiber optics communications equipment
HQ: Oclaro Fiber Optics, Inc.
400 N Mccarthy Blvd
Milpitas CA 95035
408 383-1400

### (P-11779)
### OPTICAL ZONU CORPORATION
Also Called: Zonu
7510 Hazeltine Ave, Van Nuys (91405-1419)
PHONE.................................818 780-9701
Meir Bartur, Pr
Frazad Ghadooshay, VP
Meir Bartur, Prin
▲ EMP: 18 EST: 2003
SALES (est): 6.16MM Privately Held
Web: www.opticalzonu.com
SIC: 3661 Fiber optics communications equipment

### (P-11780)
### OPTOPLEX CORPORATION
48500 Kato Rd, Fremont (94538-7338)
PHONE.................................510 490-9930
James C Sha, Pr
Dar-yuan Song, Ex VP
EMP: 300 EST: 2000
SQ FT: 16,000
SALES (est): 17.18MM Privately Held
Web: www.optoplex.com
SIC: 3661 7361 3827 Fiber optics communications equipment; Employment agencies; Optical instruments and lenses

### (P-11781)
### POLYCOM INC (DH)
6001 America Center Dr, San Jose (95002-2562)
PHONE.................................831 426-5858
Robert C Hagerty, Ch
Chuck Boynton, *
Alex Bustamante, *
Anja Hamilton, Chief Human Resource Officer*
Mary Huser, Co-Vice President*
▲ EMP: 99 EST: 1990
SALES (est): 445.81MM
SALES (corp-wide): 53.72B Publicly Held
Web: www.hp.com
SIC: 3661 3679 Telephones and telephone apparatus; Headphones, radio
HQ: Plantronics, Inc.
100 Enterprise Way
Scotts Valley CA 95066
831 420-3002

### (P-11782)
### PREMISYS COMMUNICATIONS INC (HQ)
70011 Oakport St, Oakland (94621)
PHONE.................................510 777-7000
Mory Ejabat, CEO
Michael A Graves, CIO
EMP: 200 EST: 1994
SQ FT: 96,000
SALES (est): 2.79MM
SALES (corp-wide): 244.54MM Publicly Held
SIC: 3661 Switching equipment, telephone
PA: Dzs Inc.
5700 Tnnyson Pkwy Ste 400
469 327-1531

### (P-11783)
### RLH INDUSTRIES INC
936 N Main St, Orange (92867-5403)
PHONE.................................714 532-1672
James B Harris, CEO
Carol E Harris, *
Tristan Harris, *
▲ EMP: 40 EST: 1988
SQ FT: 16,000
SALES (est): 9.35MM Privately Held
Web: www.fiberopticlink.com

SIC: 3661 5065 5999 Telephone and telegraph apparatus; Communication equipment; Telephone equipment and systems

### (P-11784)
### SIEMENS MED SOLUTIONS USA INC
757 Arnold Dr, Martinez (94553-6598)
PHONE.................................925 293-5430
Ken Duplantis, Brnch Mgr
EMP: 375
SALES (corp-wide): 84.48B Privately Held
Web: www.siemens.com
SIC: 3661 Telephones and telephone apparatus
HQ: Siemens Medical Solutions Usa, Inc.
40 Liberty Blvd
Malvern PA 19355
888 826-9702

### (P-11785)
### SIEMENS MOBILITY INC
1026 E Lacy Ave, Anaheim (92805-5651)
PHONE.................................714 284-0206
David Hopping, Brnch Mgr
EMP: 23
SALES (corp-wide): 84.48B Privately Held
Web: www.siemens.com
SIC: 3661 Telephones and telephone apparatus
HQ: Siemens Mobility, Inc.
1 Penn Plz Ste 1100
New York NY 10119
212 672-4000

### (P-11786)
### SONIM TECHNOLOGIES INC (PA)
4445 Eastgate Mall Ste 200, San Diego (92121-1979)
PHONE.................................650 378-8100
Peter Hao Liu, CEO
Michael Mulica, Ch Bd
Clay Crolius, CFO
Charles Becher, CCO
▲ EMP: 36 EST: 1999
SALES (est): 93.63MM
SALES (corp-wide): 93.63MM Publicly Held
Web: www.sonimtech.com
SIC: 3661 4812 Telephones and telephone apparatus; Cellular telephone services

### (P-11787)
### SORRENTO NETWORKS CORPORATION (HQ)
7195 Oakport St, Oakland (94621-1947)
PHONE.................................510 577-1400
Phillip W Arneson, Pr
Richard L Jacobson, Senior Vice President Legal
Joe R Armstrong, CFO
EMP: 18 EST: 1981
SQ FT: 36,000
SALES (est): 3.1MM
SALES (corp-wide): 244.54MM Publicly Held
Web: www.sorrentonet.com
SIC: 3661 Telephones and telephone apparatus
PA: Dzs Inc.
5700 Tnnyson Pkwy Ste 400
469 327-1531

### (P-11788)
### SORRENTO NETWORKS I INC
55 Almaden Blvd, San Jose (95113-1608)
PHONE.................................303 803-9405

# PRODUCTS & SERVICES SECTION
## 3663 - Radio And T.v. Communications Equipment (P-11807)

**EMP:** 70
**SIC: 3661** Telephone and telegraph apparatus

### (P-11789)
### SYSTEM STUDIES INCORPORATED (PA)
21340 E Cliff Dr, Santa Cruz (95062-4862)
**PHONE**..........................831 475-5777
Robert A Simpkins, *Pr*
William D Simpkins, *
Diane Bordoni, *
**EMP:** 42 **EST:** 1980
**SQ FT:** 11,000
**SALES (est):** 9.08MM
**SALES (corp-wide):** 9.08MM **Privately Held**
**Web:** www.airtalk.com
**SIC: 3661** Telephone and telegraph apparatus

### (P-11790)
### SYSTEM STUDIES INCORPORATED
2900 Research Park Dr, Soquel (95073-2253)
**PHONE**..........................831 475-5777
Gary Cramer, *Brnch Mgr*
**EMP:** 38
**SALES (corp-wide):** 9.08MM **Privately Held**
**Web:** www.airtalk.com
**SIC: 3661** Telephone and telegraph apparatus
**PA:** System Studies Incorporated
21340 E Cliff Dr
831 475-5777

### (P-11791)
### U-BLOX SAN DIEGO INC
12626 High Bluff Dr Ste 200, San Diego (92130-2070)
**PHONE**..........................858 847-9611
David W Carey, *Pr*
**EMP:** 21 **EST:** 2009
**SALES (est):** 7.49MM **Privately Held**
**SIC: 3661** 3571 5045 Modems; Personal computers (microcomputers); Computers, peripherals, and software
**HQ:** U-Blox Ag
Zurcherstrasse 68
Thalwil ZH 8800

### (P-11792)
### VELLO SYSTEMS INC
1530 Obrien Dr, Menlo Park (94025-1454)
**PHONE**..........................650 324-7688
Karl May, *CEO*
Armineh Baghoomian, *CFO*
**EMP:** 15 **EST:** 2009
**SALES (est):** 1.86MM **Privately Held**
**Web:** www.vellosystems.com
**SIC: 3661** 5999 5065 7622 Telephone station equipment and parts, wire; Communication equipment; Communication equipment; Communication equipment repair

### (P-11793)
### VOX NETWORK SOLUTIONS INC
130 Produce Ave Ste C, South San Francisco (94080-6523)
**PHONE**..........................650 989-1000
Scott Landis, *Pr*
Craig Schneider, *
Aaron Wilson, *
**EMP:** 150 **EST:** 2006
**SALES (est):** 37.22MM
**SALES (corp-wide):** 90.06MM **Privately Held**
**Web:** www.voxns.com
**SIC: 3661** 8748 4813 Switching equipment, telephone; Telecommunications consultant; Internet host services
**PA:** Waterfield Technologies, Inc.
110 S Hartford Ave # 2502
918 858-6400

### (P-11794)
### WEST COAST VENTURE CAPITAL LLC (PA)
10050 Bandley Dr, Cupertino (95014-2102)
**PHONE**..........................408 725-0700
Carl Berg, *Pr*
**EMP:** 54 **EST:** 1981
**SALES (est):** 2.81MM
**SALES (corp-wide):** 2.81MM **Privately Held**
**SIC: 3661** Telephone and telegraph apparatus

### (P-11795)
### Y B S ENTERPRISES INC
Also Called: Electro-Comm
3114 W Vanowen St, Burbank (91505-1237)
**PHONE**..........................818 848-7790
Steven Song, *Managing Member*
Y B Song, *Pr*
Grace Song, *Sec*
**EMP:** 15 **EST:** 1986
**SQ FT:** 30,000
**SALES (est):** 7.38MM **Privately Held**
**SIC: 3661** Communication headgear, telephone

## 3663 Radio And T.v. Communications Equipment

### (P-11796)
### 24/7 STUDIO EQUIPMENT INC
Also Called: Hertz Entertainment Services
3111 N Kenwood St, Burbank (91505-1041)
**PHONE**..........................818 840-8247
Lance Sorenson, *Pr*
Gary Mielke, *
**EMP:** 19 **EST:** 2006
**SALES (est):** 6.59MM
**SALES (corp-wide):** 9.37B **Publicly Held**
**SIC: 3663** Studio equipment, radio and television broadcasting
**PA:** Hertz Global Holdings, Inc.
8501 Williams Rd Fl 3
239 301-7000

### (P-11797)
### ACROAMATICS INC
Also Called: Telemetry Systems
125 Cremona Dr Ste 130, Goleta (93117-3083)
**PHONE**..........................805 967-9909
Geoffrey Johnson, *Pr*
John Foondle, *VP*
Robert Danford, *VP*
Patricia Johnson, *CFO*
**EMP:** 15 **EST:** 1971
**SALES (est):** 2.5MM **Privately Held**
**Web:** www.gdpspace.com
**SIC: 3663** 7373 Telemetering equipment, electronic; Computer integrated systems design

### (P-11798)
### ADAPTIVE DIGITAL SYSTEMS INC
20322 Sw Acacia St Ste 200, Newport Beach (92660-1702)
**PHONE**..........................949 955-3116
Attila W Mathe, *Pr*
Ralph Boehringer, *
Susan Cameron, *
▲ **EMP:** 27 **EST:** 1979
**SQ FT:** 6,500
**SALES (est):** 4.02MM **Privately Held**
**Web:** www.adaptivedigitalsystems.com
**SIC: 3663** Marine radio communications equipment

### (P-11799)
### AETHERCOMM INC
3205 Lionshead Ave, Carlsbad (92010-4710)
**PHONE**..........................760 208-6002
William Todd Thornton, *CEO*
Todd Thornton, *
Terri Thornton, *
Richard Martinez, *
Mark Bahu, *
**EMP:** 125 **EST:** 1999
**SQ FT:** 46,000
**SALES (est):** 23.11MM **Privately Held**
**Web:** www.aethercomm.com
**SIC: 3663** Radio and t.v. communications equipment
**HQ:** Frontgrade Technologies Llc
4350 Centennial Blvd
Colorado Springs CO 80907

### (P-11800)
### AIRGAIN INC (PA)
Also Called: AIRGAIN
3611 Valley Centre Dr Ste 150, San Diego (92130-3331)
**PHONE**..........................760 579-0200
Jacob Suen, *Pr*
James K Sims, *Ch Bd*
Michael Elbaz, *CFO*
**EMP:** 21 **EST:** 1995
**SQ FT:** 10,300
**SALES (est):** 56.04MM
**SALES (corp-wide):** 56.04MM **Publicly Held**
**Web:** www.airgain.com
**SIC: 3663** Antennas, transmitting and communications

### (P-11801)
### ALDETEC INC
3560 Business Dr Ste 100, Sacramento (95820-2161)
**PHONE**..........................916 453-3382
Jon Alt, *Managing Member*
Jon Alt, *CEO*
**EMP:** 45 **EST:** 1999
**SQ FT:** 16,038
**SALES (est):** 11.63MM **Privately Held**
**Web:** www.aldetec.com
**SIC: 3663** Amplifiers, RF power and IF
**HQ:** Ust-Aldetec Holding Company, Llc
1700 Pollitt Dr
Fair Lawn NJ 07410
201 475-8700

### (P-11802)
### ALE USA INC
Also Called: Alcatel-Lucent Enterprise USA
2000 Corporate Center Dr, Thousand Oaks (91320-1400)
**PHONE**..........................818 880-3500
Stephan Robineau, *Pr*
Louise Kuphal, *
**EMP:** 550 **EST:** 2014
**SQ FT:** 50,000
**SALES (est):** 61.7MM **Privately Held**
**Web:** www.al-enterprise.com
**SIC: 3663** 3613 Mobile communication equipment; Switchgear and switchboard apparatus
**HQ:** China Huaxin Post And Telecommunications Technology Co.,Ltd.
Room 1219, Building 4, No. 389 Ningqiao Road, China (Shanghai) P
Shanghai SH 20120
105 852-9297

### (P-11803)
### ALIEN TECHNOLOGY LLC (PA)
300 Piercy Rd, San Jose (95138-1401)
**PHONE**..........................408 782-3900
Weijie Yun, *CEO*
Duane E Zitzner, *Ch Bd*
Robert K Eulau, *Ex VP*
Stavro Prodromou, *Executive Advisor*
David A Aaron, *VP*
▲ **EMP:** 50 **EST:** 1994
**SALES (est):** 24.41MM **Privately Held**
**Web:** www.alientechnology.com
**SIC: 3663** Radio broadcasting and communications equipment

### (P-11804)
### ALTINEX INC
Also Called: Air Gap International
500 S Jefferson St, Placentia (92870-6617)
**PHONE**..........................714 990-0877
Jack Gershfeld, *Pr*
▲ **EMP:** 50 **EST:** 1993
**SALES (est):** 10.55MM **Privately Held**
**Web:** www.altinex.com
**SIC: 3663** 3577 3651 5099 Radio and t.v. communications equipment; Computer peripheral equipment, nec; Household audio and video equipment; Video and audio equipment

### (P-11805)
### AMINO TECHNOLOGIES (US) LLC (HQ)
20863 Stevens Creek Blvd Ste 300, Cupertino (95014-2113)
**PHONE**..........................408 861-1400
Donald Mcgarva, *CEO*
◆ **EMP:** 30 **EST:** 2006
**SALES (est):** 2.67MM **Privately Held**
**Web:** www.amino.tv
**SIC: 3663** 5064 Television broadcasting and communications equipment; Electrical appliances, television and radio
**PA:** Aferian Plc
Prospect House

### (P-11806)
### AMPEX CORPORATION
500 Broadway St, Redwood City (94063-3199)
**PHONE**..........................650 367-2011
▲ **EMP:** 112
**Web:** www.ampex.com
**SIC: 3663** 3861 Radio and t.v. communications equipment; Cameras and related equipment

### (P-11807)
### AMPLIFIER TECHNOLOGIES INC (HQ)
901 S Greenwood Ave, Montebello (90640-5835)
**PHONE**..........................323 278-0001
Morris Kessler, *Pr*
▲ **EMP:** 25 **EST:** 1981
**SALES (est):** 6.18MM
**SALES (corp-wide):** 7.09MM **Privately Held**
**Web:** www.ati-amp.com
**SIC: 3663** Television broadcasting and communications equipment
**PA:** Macey Investment Corp.
1749 Chapin Rd

## 3663 - Radio And T.v. Communications Equipment (P-11808)

323 278-0001

**(P-11808)**
**ANACOM INC**
11682 Vineyard Spring Ct, Cupertino (95014-5135)
PHONE....................408 519-2062
James Tom, *CEO*
May Tom, *
▲ **EMP:** 40 **EST:** 1991
**SALES (est):** 3.77MM **Privately Held**
**Web:** www.anacominc.com
**SIC: 3663** Receiver-transmitter units (transceiver)

**(P-11809)**
**ANRITSU COMPANY (DH)**
490 Jarvis Dr, Morgan Hill (95037-2809)
P.O. Box 39000 (94139-0001)
PHONE....................800 267-4878
Hirokazu Hashimoto, *CEO*
Junkichi Shirono, *
Toshihiko Takahashi, *
Stephen Vonderach, *
Donn Mulder, *
▲ **EMP:** 485 **EST:** 1960
**SQ FT:** 242,000
**SALES (est):** 96.57MM **Privately Held**
**Web:** us.anritsu.com
**SIC: 3663** 3825 Radio and t.v. communications equipment; Instruments to measure electricity
**HQ:** Anritsu U.S. Holding, Inc.
490 Jarvis Dr
Morgan Hill CA 95037
408 778-2000

**(P-11810)**
**ANTCOM CORPORATION**
Also Called: Antcom
367 Van Ness Way Ste 602, Torrance (90501-6246)
PHONE....................310 782-1076
Michael Ritter, *CEO*
Sean Huynh, *VP*
Doug Reid, *Genl Mgr*
Linda Cupchak, *Contrlr*
**EMP:** 45 **EST:** 1997
**SQ FT:** 15,000
**SALES (est):** 9.68MM
**SALES (corp-wide):** 2.5MM **Privately Held**
**Web:** www.antcom.com
**SIC: 3663** Antennas, transmitting and communications
**HQ:** Novatel Inc
10921 14 St Ne
Calgary AB T3K 2
403 295-4500

**(P-11811)**
**ANYDATA CORPORATION**
5405 Alton Pkwy, Irvine (92604-3717)
PHONE....................949 900-6040
**EMP:** 100
**SIC: 3663** Mobile communication equipment

**(P-11812)**
**APPLE INC (PA)**
Also Called: Apple
1 Apple Park Way, Cupertino (95014-0642)
PHONE....................408 996-1010
Tim Cook, *CEO*
Arthur D Levinson, *
Luca Maestri, *Sr VP*
Kate Adams, *Sr VP*
Deirdre O'brien, *Sr VP*
◆ **EMP:** 1310 **EST:** 1977
**SALES (est):** 391.04B
**SALES (corp-wide):** 391.04B **Publicly Held**
**Web:** www.apple.com
**SIC: 3663** 3571 3575 3577 Mobile communication equipment; Personal computers (microcomputers); Computer terminals, monitors and components; Printers, computer

**(P-11813)**
**ARCTIC SEMICONDUCTOR**
2216 Ringwood Ave, San Jose (95131-1714)
PHONE....................408 712-3350
Vahid Toosi, *CEO*
Marzieh Veyseh, *
Sam Heidari, *
**EMP:** 35 **EST:** 2006
**SQ FT:** 3,200
**SALES (est):** 4.14MM **Privately Held**
**Web:** www.situne-ic.com
**SIC: 3663** Television closed circuit equipment

**(P-11814)**
**ARUBA NETWORKS INC**
390 W Caribbean Dr, Sunnyvale (94089-1010)
PHONE....................408 227-4500
**EMP:** 622
**SALES (corp-wide):** 29.14B **Publicly Held**
**Web:** www.hpe.com
**SIC: 3663** 3577 7371 Mobile communication equipment; Data conversion equipment, media-to-media: computer; Computer software development
**HQ:** Aruba Networks, Inc.
6280 America Center Dr
San Jose CA 95002
408 941-4300

**(P-11815)**
**ASTRANIS SPACE TECH CORP (PA)**
575 20th St, San Francisco (94107-4345)
PHONE....................408 829-1101
John Gedmark, *CEO*
Miki Heller, *Business Operations Vice President*
**EMP:** 67 **EST:** 2015
**SQ FT:** 13,000
**SALES (est):** 32.07MM
**SALES (corp-wide):** 32.07MM **Privately Held**
**Web:** www.astranis.com
**SIC: 3663** Satellites, communications

**(P-11816)**
**ATX NETWORKS (SAN DIEGO) CORP (DH)**
Also Called: Atx Networks San Diego
2800 Whiptail Loop Ste 6, Carlsbad (92010)
PHONE....................858 546-5050
Dan Whalen, *Pr*
Ian A Lerner, *Chief Product Officer*
Carlos Shteremberg, *
Anthony Tibbs, *
Andrew Isherwood, *
◆ **EMP:** 27 **EST:** 1983
**SALES (est):** 24.76MM
**SALES (corp-wide):** 66.29MM **Privately Held**
**Web:** www.atx.com
**SIC: 3663** 5065 3678 Radio and t.v. communications equipment; Electronic parts and equipment, nec; Electronic connectors
**HQ:** Atx Networks Corp
8-1602 Tricont Ave
Whitby ON L1N 7
905 428-6068

**(P-11817)**
**AVID SYSTEMS INC (DH)**
280 Bernardo Ave, Mountain View (94043-5238)
PHONE....................650 526-1600
Ken A Sexton, *CEO*
Patti S Hart, *
Ajay Chopra, *MEDIA DIV*
Arthur D Chadwick, *
Georg Blinn, *WEB VIDEO DIV*
▲ **EMP:** 225 **EST:** 1986
**SQ FT:** 106,000
**SALES (est):** 5.5MM
**SALES (corp-wide):** 566.89MM **Privately Held**
**SIC: 3663** 3577 Radio and t.v. communications equipment; Computer peripheral equipment, nec
**HQ:** Avid Technology, Inc.
75 Blue Sky Dr
Burlington MA 01803
978 640-3000

**(P-11818)**
**BIGBAND NETWORKS INC**
475 Broadway St, Redwood City (94063-3136)
PHONE....................650 995-5000
▲ **EMP:** 465
**Web:** www.bigbandnet.com
**SIC: 3663** Radio and t.v. communications equipment

**(P-11819)**
**BITTREE INCORPORATED**
600 W Elk Ave, Glendale (91204-1404)
P.O. Box 3764 (91221-0764)
PHONE....................818 500-8142
▲ **EMP:** 29 **EST:** 1977
**SALES (est):** 2.12MM **Privately Held**
**Web:** www.bittree.com
**SIC: 3663** Radio and t.v. communications equipment

**(P-11820)**
**BOEING SATELLITE SYSTEMS INC (HQ)**
Also Called: Boeing
900 N Pacific Coast Hwy, El Segundo (90245-2710)
P.O. Box 92919 (90009-2919)
PHONE....................310 791-7450
Craig R Cooning, *Pr*
Dave Ryan, *General Vice President*
Charles Toups, *Operations*
◆ **EMP:** 25 **EST:** 1995
**SALES (est):** 1.23B
**SALES (corp-wide):** 77.79B **Publicly Held**
**Web:** www.boeing.com
**SIC: 3663** Satellites, communications
**PA:** The Boeing Company
929 Long Bridge Dr
703 465-3500

**(P-11821)**
**BROADCAST MICROWAVE SVCS LLC (PA)**
Also Called: B M S
13475 Danielson St Ste 130, Poway (92064-8858)
PHONE....................858 391-3050
Harry Davoody, *CEO*
Mike Sieglen, *
Kristina Clark, *
**EMP:** 109 **EST:** 1982
**SQ FT:** 37,000
**SALES (est):** 23.63MM
**SALES (corp-wide):** 23.63MM **Privately Held**
**Web:** www.bms-inc.com
**SIC: 3663** Microwave communication equipment

**(P-11822)**
**CANARY COMMUNICATIONS INC**
6040 Hellyer Ave Ste 150, San Jose (95138-1041)
PHONE....................408 365-0609
Vinh Tran, *Pr*
Roland Yamaguchi, *VP Opers*
▲ **EMP:** 15 **EST:** 1987
**SALES (est):** 2.65MM **Privately Held**
**Web:** www.canarycom.com
**SIC: 3663** Receiver-transmitter units (transceiver)

**(P-11823)**
**CARLSON WIRELESS TECH INC**
Also Called: Carlson Wireless
3134 Jacobs Ave Ste C, Eureka (95501-0960)
PHONE....................707 443-0100
James R Carlson, *CEO*
Mindy Hiley, *Dir Opers*
**EMP:** 15 **EST:** 1998
**SQ FT:** 6,000
**SALES (est):** 1.79MM **Privately Held**
**Web:** www.carlsonwireless.com
**SIC: 3663** Airborne radio communications equipment

**(P-11824)**
**CELLPHONE-MATE INC**
Also Called: Surecall
48346 Milmont Dr, Fremont (94538-7324)
PHONE....................510 770-0469
Hongtao Zhan, *Pr*
▲ **EMP:** 52 **EST:** 2001
**SQ FT:** 22,800
**SALES (est):** 9.46MM **Privately Held**
**Web:** www.surecall.com
**SIC: 3663** Amplifiers, RF power and IF

**(P-11825)**
**CENTRON INDUSTRIES INC**
441 W Victoria St, Gardena (90248-3528)
PHONE....................310 324-6443
Yong W Kim, *CEO*
Hye S Kim, *Sec*
◆ **EMP:** 37 **EST:** 1984
**SQ FT:** 10,000
**SALES (est):** 9.93MM **Privately Held**
**Web:** www.centronind.com
**SIC: 3663** Radio and t.v. communications equipment

**(P-11826)**
**CLEAR-COM LLC (HQ)**
Also Called: Clear-Com Communications
1301 Marina Village Pkwy Ste 105, Alameda (94501-1028)
PHONE....................510 337-6600
Mitzi Dominguez, *CEO*
Bob Boster, *
Harry Miyahira, *
Helen Miyahira, *
▲ **EMP:** 768 **EST:** 1968
**SQ FT:** 23,700
**SALES (est):** 92.6MM
**SALES (corp-wide):** 452.77MM **Privately Held**
**Web:** www.clearcom.com
**SIC: 3663** Radio and t.v. communications equipment
**PA:** H.M. Electronics, Inc.
2848 Whiptail Loop
858 535-6000

▲ = Import ▼ = Export
◆ = Import/Export

## PRODUCTS & SERVICES SECTION
## 3663 - Radio And T.v. Communications Equipment (P-11848)

**(P-11827)**
**COASTLINE HIGH PRFMCE CTNGS LT**
7181 Orangewood Ave, Garden Grove (92841-1409)
PHONE..................714 372-3263
Phil Viljoen, *Pr*
**EMP:** 15 **EST:** 2003
**SALES (est):** 2.38MM **Privately Held**
Web: www.coastlinehpc.com
**SIC: 3663** Satellites, communications

**(P-11828)**
**COMMSCOPE**
3839 Spinnaker Ct, Fremont (94538-6537)
PHONE..................408 952-2454
Brett Roach, *Mgr*
**EMP:** 36 **EST:** 2016
**SALES (est):** 3.26MM **Privately Held**
Web: www.commscope.com
**SIC: 3663** Radio and t.v. communications equipment

**(P-11829)**
**COMMSCOPE**
350 W Java Dr, Sunnyvale (94089-1026)
PHONE..................650 265-4200
**EMP:** 16 **EST:** 2020
**SALES (est):** 5.54MM **Privately Held**
Web: www.commscope.com
**SIC: 3663** Radio and t.v. communications equipment

**(P-11830)**
**COMMUNICATIONS & PWR INDS LLC**
CPI
811 Hansen Way, Palo Alto (94304-1031)
PHONE..................650 846-3494
Michael Cheng, *Brnch Mgr*
**EMP:** 109
**SQ FT:** 25,000
Web: www.cpii.com
**SIC: 3663** Radio and t.v. communications equipment
**HQ:** Communications & Power Industries Llc
811 Hansen Way
Palo Alto CA 94304

**(P-11831)**
**COMMUNICATIONS & PWR INDS LLC**
Also Called: CPI
811 Hansen Way, Palo Alto (94304-1031)
PHONE..................650 846-3729
Robert Sickett, *Mgr*
**EMP:** 1500
**SQ FT:** 25,000
Web: www.cpii.com
**SIC: 3663** Radio and t.v. communications equipment
**HQ:** Communications & Power Industries Llc
811 Hansen Way
Palo Alto CA 94304

**(P-11832)**
**COMMUNICATIONS & PWR INDS LLC**
CPI
6385 San Ignacio Ave, San Jose (95119-1206)
P.O. Box 51110 (94303-0687)
PHONE..................650 846-2900
**EMP:** 19
Web: www.cpii.com
**SIC: 3663** Radio and t.v. communications equipment

**HQ:** Communications & Power Industries Llc
811 Hansen Way
Palo Alto CA 94304

**(P-11833)**
**COMMUNICATIONS & PWR INDS LLC**
Also Called: Microwave Power Products Div
811 Hansen Way, Palo Alto (94304-1031)
PHONE..................650 846-2900
**EMP:** 58
Web: www.cpii.com
**SIC: 3663** Radio and t.v. communications equipment
**HQ:** Communications & Power Industries Llc
811 Hansen Way
Palo Alto CA 94304

**(P-11834)**
**COMTECH STLLITE NTWRK TECH INC**
Also Called: Comtech Xicom Technology
3550 Bassett St, Santa Clara (95054-2704)
PHONE..................408 213-3000
Kevin Kirkpatrick, *Mgr*
**EMP:** 160
**SALES (corp-wide):** 540.4MM **Publicly Held**
Web: www.xicomtech.com
**SIC: 3663** 3679 Amplifiers, RF power and IF; Power supplies, all types: static
**HQ:** Comtech Satellite Network Technologies, Inc.
305 N 54th St
Chandler AZ 85226

**(P-11835)**
**CPI MALIBU DIVISION**
3623 Old Conejo Rd Ste 205, Newbury Park (91320-0803)
PHONE..................805 383-1829
Joel Littman, *CFO*
**EMP:** 80 **EST:** 1975
**SALES (est):** 3.94MM **Privately Held**
**SIC: 3663** Antennas, transmitting and communications
**HQ:** Communications & Power Industries Llc
811 Hansen Way
Palo Alto CA 94304

**(P-11836)**
**CPI SATCOM & ANTENNA TECH INC**
2205 Fortune Dr, San Jose (95131-1806)
PHONE..................408 955-1900
Steve Michaud, *Brnch Mgr*
**EMP:** 70
Web: www.cpii.com
**SIC: 3663** Radio and t.v. communications equipment
**HQ:** Cpi Satcom & Antenna Technologies Inc.
1700 Cable Dr Ne
Conover NC 28613
704 462-7330

**(P-11837)**
**CPI SATCOM & ANTENNA TECH INC**
3111 Fujita St, Torrance (90505-4006)
PHONE..................310 539-6704
Sandra Seto, *Brnch Mgr*
**EMP:** 221
Web: www.cpii.com
**SIC: 3663** Antennas, transmitting and communications

**HQ:** Cpi Satcom & Antenna Technologies Inc.
1700 Cable Dr Ne
Conover NC 28613
704 462-7330

**(P-11838)**
**CREDENCE ID LLC**
2335 Broadway Ste 100, Oakland (94612-2495)
PHONE..................888 243-5452
Bruce Hanson, *Pr*
Yash Shah, *
Chip Shimer, *
Kai Aiello, *
Aranesh Chandra, *
**EMP:** 32 **EST:** 2012
**SALES (est):** 2.84MM **Privately Held**
Web: www.credenceid.com
**SIC: 3663** Mobile communication equipment

**(P-11839)**
**D X COMMUNICATIONS INC**
Also Called: Tpl Communications
8160 Van Nuys Blvd, Panorama City (91402-4806)
PHONE..................323 256-3000
Richard H Myers, *CEO*
Richard Myers, *
John Ehret, *
**EMP:** 28 **EST:** 1971
**SALES (est):** 2.78MM **Privately Held**
Web: www.tplcom.com
**SIC: 3663** Satellites, communications

**(P-11840)**
**DENSO WIRELESS SYSTEMS AMERICA INC**
2251 Rutherford Rd # 100, Carlsbad (92008-8815)
PHONE..................760 734-4600
◆ **EMP:** 191
**SIC: 3663** 3714 Cellular radio telephone; Motor vehicle electrical equipment

**(P-11841)**
**DIGITAL PROTOTYPE SYSTEMS INC**
Also Called: Dps Telecom
4955 E Yale Ave, Fresno (93727-1523)
PHONE..................559 454-1600
Robert A Berry, *CEO*
Marshall Denhartog, *
Ron Stover, *
**EMP:** 46 **EST:** 1986
**SQ FT:** 50,000
**SALES (est):** 10.83MM **Privately Held**
Web: www.dpstele.com
**SIC: 3663** Telemetering equipment, electronic

**(P-11842)**
**DJH ENTERPRISES**
Also Called: Channel Vision Technology
23011 Moulton Pkwy Ste B6, Laguna Hills (92653-1222)
PHONE..................714 424-6500
Darrel Eugene Hauk, *Pr*
◆ **EMP:** 35 **EST:** 1993
**SALES (est):** 4.4MM **Privately Held**
**SIC: 3663** Radio and t.v. communications equipment

**(P-11843)**
**DOLBY LABORATORIES INC**
Also Called: Dolby Labs
175 S Hill Dr, Brisbane (94005-1203)
PHONE..................415 715-2500
Jeff Griffith, *OK Vice President*

**EMP:** 23
**SALES (corp-wide):** 1.3B **Publicly Held**
Web: www.dolby.com
**SIC: 3663** 3651 Radio broadcasting and communications equipment; Household audio and video equipment
**PA:** Dolby Laboratories, Inc.
1275 Market St
415 558-0200

**(P-11844)**
**DX RADIO SYSTEMS INC**
10941 Pendleton St, Sun Valley (91352-1522)
PHONE..................818 252-6700
◆ **EMP:** 15
Web: dxradiosystemsy.openfos.com
**SIC: 3663** Radio broadcasting and communications equipment

**(P-11845)**
**DYNAMIC SCIENCES INTL INC**
9400 Lurline Ave Unit B, Chatsworth (91311-6022)
PHONE..................818 226-6262
Eli Shiri, *Pr*
Robert Cook, *
Oren Shiri, *
**EMP:** 35 **EST:** 1972
**SQ FT:** 20,000
**SALES (est):** 1.32MM **Privately Held**
**SIC: 3663** Radio receiver networks

**(P-11846)**
**E-BAND COMMUNICATIONS LLC**
82 Coromar Dr, Goleta (93117-3024).
PHONE..................858 408-0660
Jamal Hamdani, *CEO*
Saul Umbrasas, *
Russ Kinsch, *
**EMP:** 30 **EST:** 2003
**SALES (est):** 2.32MM
**SALES (corp-wide):** 27.29MM **Privately Held**
Web: www.e-band.com
**SIC: 3663** Carrier equipment, radio communications
**PA:** Axxcss Wireless Solutions Inc
82 Coromar Dr
805 968-9621

**(P-11847)**
**ECTRON CORPORATION**
9340 Hazard Way Ste B2, San Diego (92123)
PHONE..................858 278-0600
E Earl Cunningham, *Pr*
Carol C Cunningham, *
Karl E Cunningham, *
**EMP:** 44 **EST:** 1964
**SALES (est):** 4.74MM **Privately Held**
Web: www.ectron.com
**SIC: 3663** 3829 3577 3823 Amplifiers, RF power and IF; Measuring and controlling devices, nec; Data conversion equipment, media-to-media: computer; Process control instruments

**(P-11848)**
**EEG 3 LLC (DH)**
Also Called: Maritime Telecom Netwrk Inc
6080 Center Dr Ste 1200, Los Angeles (90045-9209)
◆ **EMP:** 200 **EST:** 1990
**SALES (est):** 30.13MM
**SALES (corp-wide):** 656.88MM **Privately Held**
**SIC: 3663** Satellites, communications

## 3663 - Radio And T.v. Communications Equipment (P-11849)

**PRODUCTS & SERVICES SECTION**

HQ: Emerging Markets Communications, Llc
1821 E Dyer Rd Ste 125
Santa Ana CA 92705

### (P-11849)
### ELVE INC
1440 Drew Ave Ste 150, Davis (95618-6160)
PHONE.................................734 846-2705
Diana Gamzina, *CEO*
John Collman, *CEO*
EMP: 15 EST: 2021
SALES (est): 6.35MM **Privately Held**
Web: www.elvespeed.com
SIC: 3663 Radio and t.v. communications equipment

### (P-11850)
### EMPOWER RF SYSTEMS INC (PA)
Also Called: Empower Rf
316 W Florence Ave, Inglewood (90301)
PHONE.................................310 412-8100
Barry Phelps, *Ch Bd*
Jon Jacocks, *
Larisa Stanisic, *
EMP: 76 EST: 1999
SQ FT: 30,000
SALES (est): 16.8MM
SALES (corp-wide): 16.8MM **Privately Held**
Web: www.empowerrf.com
SIC: 3663 Amplifiers, RF power and IF

### (P-11851)
### ENERGOUS CORPORATION
Also Called: ENERGOUS
3590 N 1st St Ste 210, San Jose (95134-1812)
PHONE.................................408 963-0200
Mallorie Burak, *Interim Chief Executive Officer*
David Roberson, *
EMP: 37 EST: 2012
SALES (est): 474.18K **Privately Held**
Web: www.energous.com
SIC: 3663 3674 Radio broadcasting and communications equipment; Semiconductors and related devices

### (P-11852)
### ENSEMBLE COMMUNICATIONS INC
2223 Avenida De La Playa, La Jolla (92037-3200)
PHONE.................................858 458-1400
Rami Hadar, *Pr*
Sheldon Gilbert, *
EMP: 140 EST: 1997
SQ FT: 63,000
SALES (est): 1.72MM **Privately Held**
SIC: 3663 Radio and t.v. communications equipment

### (P-11853)
### ESCAPE COMMUNICATIONS INC
2790 Skypark Dr Ste 203, Torrance (90505-5345)
PHONE.................................310 997-1300
Micheal Stewart, *Pr*
Gregory Caso Ph.d., *Ex VP*
James Nadeau, *Sec*
EMP: 17 EST: 1998
SQ FT: 5,300
SALES (est): 2.93MM **Privately Held**
Web: www.escapecom.com
SIC: 3663 8711 8731 Microwave communication equipment; Engineering services; Commercial physical research

### (P-11854)
### EUPHONIX INC (DH)
280 Bernardo Ave, Mountain View (94043-5238)
PHONE.................................650 526-1600
Jeffrey A Chew, *CEO*
Paul L Hammel, *
▲ EMP: 95 EST: 1988
SQ FT: 40,000
SALES (est): 5.89MM
SALES (corp-wide): 566.89MM **Privately Held**
SIC: 3663 Studio equipment, radio and television broadcasting
HQ: Avid Technology, Inc.
75 Blue Sky Dr
Burlington MA 01803
978 640-3000

### (P-11855)
### EXALT COMMUNICATIONS INC
530 Division St, Campbell (95008-6906)
PHONE.................................408 688-0200
▲ EMP: 60
Web: www.starmicrowave.com
SIC: 3663 Cellular radio telephone

### (P-11856)
### FISICA APPLIED TECH INC
Also Called: Randtron Antenna Systems
150 Constitution Dr, Menlo Park (94025-1107)
PHONE.................................650 326-9500
EMP: 160
SALES (corp-wide): 175.58MM **Privately Held**
Web: www.l3harris.com
SIC: 3663 Telemetering equipment, electronic
HQ: Fisica Applied Technologies, Inc.
1025 W Nasa Blvd
Melbourne FL 32919
858 404-7824

### (P-11857)
### FLEET MANAGEMENT SOLUTIONS INC
310 Commerce Ste 100, Irvine (92602-1360)
PHONE.................................800 500-6009
Tony Eales, *CEO*
EMP: 26 EST: 2002
SALES (est): 904.87K
SALES (corp-wide): 3.1B **Publicly Held**
Web: www.fleetmanagementsolutions.com
SIC: 3663 4899 Radio and t.v. communications equipment; Satellite earth stations
HQ: Teletrac Navman (Uk) Ltd
First Floor
Milton Keynes BUCKS MK7 6

### (P-11858)
### GLOBAL MICROWAVE SYSTEMS INC
Also Called: G M S
1916 Palomar Oaks Way Ste 100, Carlsbad (92008-6510)
PHONE.................................760 496-0046
EMP: 47
SIC: 3663 7359 Microwave communication equipment; Business machine and electronic equipment rental services

### (P-11859)
### GRASS VALLEY INC (HQ)
310 Providence Mine Rd, Nevada City (95959-2959)
P.O. Box 1658 (95959-1658)
PHONE.................................530 265-1000
Strath Goodship, *CEO*
Sydney Lovely, *
EMP: 87 EST: 1999
SALES (est): 12.31MM
SALES (corp-wide): 13.38MM **Privately Held**
Web: www.grassvalley.com
SIC: 3663 Radio and t.v. communications equipment
PA: Black Dragon Capital, Llc
6400 W Boynton Beach Blvd
978 640-5010

### (P-11860)
### GROUND CONTROL INC
1485 Bay Shore Blvd Ste 451, San Francisco (94124-4010)
PHONE.................................415 508-8589
Jae Shin, *Pr*
EMP: 20 EST: 2018
SALES (est): 5.26MM **Privately Held**
Web: www.groundci.com
SIC: 3663 Satellites, communications

### (P-11861)
### HADRIAN AUTOMATION INC
Also Called: Hadrian
19501 S Western Ave, Torrance (90502)
PHONE.................................503 807-4490
Christopher Power, *CEO*
Lars Lider, *
Sarah Annin, *
Dave Malcher, *Head OF Finance*
EMP: 100 EST: 2018
SALES (est): 10.73MM **Privately Held**
Web: www.hadrian.co
SIC: 3663 Space satellite communications equipment

### (P-11862)
### HARMONIC INC (PA)
Also Called: HARMONIC
2590 Orchard Pkwy, San Jose (95131-1033)
PHONE.................................408 542-2500
Patrick J Harshman, *Pr*
Patrick Gallagher, *
Nimrod Ben-natan, *CABLE ACCESS Business*
Neven Haltmayer Senior, *Site Vice President*
Ian Graham, *Senior Vice President Global Sales*
◆ EMP: 57 EST: 1988
SALES (est): 607.91MM **Publicly Held**
Web: www.harmonicinc.com
SIC: 3663 3823 Television broadcasting and communications equipment; Process control instruments

### (P-11863)
### HEROTEK INC (PA)
155 Baytech Dr, San Jose (95134-2303)
PHONE.................................408 941-8399
Cheng W Lai, *Pr*
EMP: 41 EST: 1982
SQ FT: 9,600
SALES (est): 5.01MM
SALES (corp-wide): 5.01MM **Privately Held**
Web: www.herotek.com
SIC: 3663 3812 Microwave communication equipment; Search and navigation equipment

### (P-11864)
### HIGHER GROUND LLC (PA)
2595 E Bayshore Rd Ste 200, Palo Alto (94303-3240)
Rural Route 2625 Middlefield (94306)
PHONE.................................650 322-3958
Robert Reis, *Pr*
EMP: 19 EST: 2012
SALES (est): 2.51MM
SALES (corp-wide): 2.51MM **Privately Held**
Web: www.higherground.earth
SIC: 3663 Satellites, communications

### (P-11865)
### HILLSIDE CAPITAL INC
6222 Fallbrook Ave, Woodland Hills (91367-1601)
PHONE.................................650 367-2011
Becky Tran, *Pr*
EMP: 115 EST: 2008
SALES (est): 753.64K **Privately Held**
SIC: 3663 Radio and t.v. communications equipment

### (P-11866)
### HUAWEI DEVICE USA INC
345 E Middlefield Rd, Mountain View (94043-4003)
PHONE.................................408 306-7171
EMP: 144
SIC: 3663 Cellular radio telephone
HQ: Huawei Device Usa Inc.
5700 Tennyson Pkwy # 300
Plano TX 75024
214 919-6688

### (P-11867)
### INGENU INC (PA)
Also Called: Ingenu
10301 Meanley Dr, San Diego (92131-3011)
P.O. Box 22628 (92192)
PHONE.................................858 201-6000
John Horn, *Prin*
John Horn, *CEO*
Tom Gregor, *Pr*
James Seines, *VP*
Jason Wilson, *Sr VP*
EMP: 20 EST: 2008
SALES (est): 6.98MM **Privately Held**
Web: www.ingenu.com
SIC: 3663 Radio and t.v. communications equipment

### (P-11868)
### INTERDIGITAL INC
Also Called: INTERDIGITAL, INC.
9276 Scranton Rd Ste 300, San Diego (92121-7700)
PHONE.................................858 210-4800
Julie Mcdonough, *Brnch Mgr*
EMP: 64
SALES (corp-wide): 549.59MM **Publicly Held**
Web: www.interdigital.com
SIC: 3663 Mobile communication equipment
HQ: Interdigital Wireless, Inc.
200 Bellevue Pkwy Ste 300
Wilmington DE 19809

### (P-11869)
### JAMPRO ANTENNAS INC (PA)
6340 Sky Creek Dr, Sacramento (95828-1025)
PHONE.................................916 383-1177
Alex Perchevitch, *Pr*
Doug Mccabe, *COO*
Cyndi Sanderson, *
Ken Mueller, *
◆ EMP: 49 EST: 1986
SQ FT: 12,000
SALES (est): 8.39MM
SALES (corp-wide): 8.39MM **Privately Held**

▲ = Import ▼ = Export
◆ = Import/Export

# PRODUCTS & SERVICES SECTION
## 3663 - Radio And T.v. Communications Equipment (P-11889)

Web: www.jampro.com
SIC: 3663  Antennas, transmitting and communications

**(P-11870)**
**KATEEVA INC (PA)**
7015 Gateway Blvd, Newark  (94560-1011)
PHONE..............................800 385-7802
May Su, *CEO*
Conor Madigan, *
Eli Vronsky, *CPO*
▲ EMP: 179 EST: 2007
SQ FT: 11,000
SALES (est): 52.53MM
SALES (corp-wide): 52.53MM **Privately Held**
Web: www.kateeva.com
SIC: 3663  Cable television equipment

**(P-11871)**
**KATZ MILLENNIUM SLS & MKTG INC**
Also Called: Clear Channel Radio Sales
5700 Wilshire Blvd Ste 100, Los Angeles  (90036-3659)
PHONE..............................323 966-5066
Nathan Brown, *Mgr*
EMP: 227
Web: www.raisingthevolume.com
SIC: 3663  Radio receiver networks
HQ: Katz Millennium Sales & Marketing Inc.
    125 W 55th St Frnt 3
    New York NY 10019

**(P-11872)**
**KRATOS MICROWAVE INC**
Also Called: CTT Inc.
5870 Hellyer Ave Ste 70, San Jose  (95138)
PHONE..............................408 541-0596
David Tai, *CEO*
Thanh Thai, *
John Campbell, *
▼ EMP: 81 EST: 1981
SQ FT: 45,000
SALES (est): 7.31MM **Publicly Held**
Web: www.cttinc.com
SIC: 3663  Microwave communication equipment
PA: Kratos Defense & Security Solutions, Inc.
    10680 Treena St Ste 600

**(P-11873)**
**KYOCERA AVX CMPNNTS SAN DEGO I (DH)**
Also Called: AVX Antenna, Inc.
5501 Oberlin Dr Ste 100, San Diego  (92121-1718)
PHONE..............................858 550-3820
Laurent Desclos, *Pr*
Laurent Desclos, *CEO*
Vahid Manian, *COO*
Rick Johnson, *CFO*
Sebastian Rowson, *Chief Scientist*
▲ EMP: 21 EST: 2000
SALES (est): 9.43MM **Privately Held**
Web: www.kyocera-avx.com
SIC: 3663  Antennas, transmitting and communications
HQ: Kyocera Avx Components Corporation
    1 Avx Blvd
    Fountain Inn SC 29644
    864 967-2150

**(P-11874)**
**L3 TECHNOLOGIES INC**
15825 Roxford St, Sylmar  (91342-3537)
PHONE..............................818 367-0111
EMP: 91
SALES (corp-wide): 19.42B **Publicly Held**
Web: www.l3harris.com
SIC: 3663  Radio and t.v. communications equipment
HQ: L3 Technologies, Inc.
    600 3rd Ave Fl 34
    New York NY 10016
    321 727-9100

**(P-11875)**
**L3 TECHNOLOGIES INC**
Also Called: Communction Systms-Wst/Lnkabit
9020 Balboa Ave, San Diego  (92123-1510)
PHONE..............................858 552-9500
Andrew Ivers, *Brnch Mgr*
EMP: 325
SALES (corp-wide): 19.42B **Publicly Held**
Web: www.l3harris.com
SIC: 3663  Space satellite communications equipment
HQ: L3 Technologies, Inc.
    600 3rd Ave Fl 34
    New York NY 10016
    321 727-9100

**(P-11876)**
**L3 TECHNOLOGIES INC**
Also Called: L-3 Telemetry & Rf Products
9020 Balboa Ave, San Diego  (92123-1510)
PHONE..............................858 279-0411
Burt Smith, *Brnch Mgr*
EMP: 358
SALES (corp-wide): 19.42B **Publicly Held**
Web: www.l3harris.com
SIC: 3663 3669 3812 3679  Telemetering equipment, electronic; Signaling apparatus, electric; Search and navigation equipment; Microwave components
HQ: L3 Technologies, Inc.
    600 3rd Ave Fl 34
    New York NY 10016
    321 727-9100

**(P-11877)**
**L3 TECHNOLOGIES INC**
602 E Vermont Ave, Anaheim  (92805-5607)
PHONE..............................714 758-4222
Robert Vanwechel, *Brnch Mgr*
EMP: 220
SALES (corp-wide): 19.42B **Publicly Held**
Web: www.l3harris.com
SIC: 3663  Telemetering equipment, electronic
HQ: L3 Technologies, Inc.
    600 3rd Ave Fl 34
    New York NY 10016
    321 727-9100

**(P-11878)**
**L3 TECHNOLOGIES INC**
Also Called: Maripro
7414 Hollister Ave, Goleta  (93117-2583)
PHONE..............................805 683-3881
EMP: 90
SALES (corp-wide): 19.42B **Publicly Held**
Web: www.l3harris.com
SIC: 3663  Telemetering equipment, electronic
HQ: L3 Technologies, Inc.
    600 3rd Ave Fl 34
    New York NY 10016
    321 727-9100

**(P-11879)**
**L3 TECHNOLOGIES INC**
L3 Rccs
10180 Barnes Canyon Rd, San Diego  (92121-2724)
PHONE..............................858 552-9716
Jonathan Roy, *CFO*
EMP: 100
SALES (corp-wide): 19.42B **Publicly Held**
Web: www.l3harris.com
SIC: 3663  Telemetering equipment, electronic
HQ: L3 Technologies, Inc.
    600 3rd Ave Fl 34
    New York NY 10016
    321 727-9100

**(P-11880)**
**L3 TECHNOLOGIES INC**
Also Called: L-3 Communication
2700 Merced St, San Leandro  (94577-5602)
PHONE..............................858 499-0284
Jim Clemmons, *Brnch Mgr*
EMP: 112
SALES (corp-wide): 19.42B **Publicly Held**
Web: www.l3harris.com
SIC: 3663  Telemetering equipment, electronic
HQ: L3 Technologies, Inc.
    600 3rd Ave Fl 34
    New York NY 10016
    321 727-9100

**(P-11881)**
**L3HARRIS INTERSTATE ELEC CORP**
604 E Vermont Ave, Anaheim  (92805-5607)
PHONE..............................714 758-3395
Thomas Jackson, *Brnch Mgr*
EMP: 72
SALES (corp-wide): 19.42B **Publicly Held**
Web: www.l3harris.com
SIC: 3663 3621  Telemetering equipment, electronic; Motors and generators
HQ: L3harris Interstate Electronics Corporation
    602 E Vermont Ave
    Anaheim CA 92805
    714 758-0500

**(P-11882)**
**LENNTEK CORPORATION**
Also Called: Sonix
1610 Lockness Pl, Torrance  (90501-5119)
PHONE..............................310 534-2738
Danny Tsai, *Prin*
▲ EMP: 50 EST: 2007
SQ FT: 15,000
SALES (est): 3.11MM **Privately Held**
Web: www.shopsonix.com
SIC: 3663  Mobile communication equipment

**(P-11883)**
**LGC WIRELESS LLC**
541 E Trimble Rd, San Jose  (95131-1224)
PHONE..............................408 952-2400
Ian Sugarbroad, *Pr*
Dermot Conlon, *
Michael Frausing, *
John Niedermaier, *
▲ EMP: 227 EST: 1995
SQ FT: 30,000
SALES (est): 82.09M **Publicly Held**
SIC: 3663  Carrier equipment, radio communications
HQ: Commscope Technologies Llc
    4 Westbrook Corp Ctr Ste
    Westchester IL 60154
    800 366-3891

**(P-11884)**
**LOCKHEED MARTIN CORPORATION**
Also Called: Lockheed Martin
1111 Lockheed Martin Way, Sunnyvale  (94089-1212)
P.O. Box 3504  (94088-3504)
PHONE..............................408 742-4321
Christin Kulinski, *CEO*
EMP: 43
Web: www.lockheedmartin.com
SIC: 3663 3761  Radio and t.v. communications equipment; Ballistic missiles, complete
PA: Lockheed Martin Corporation
    6801 Rockledge Dr

**(P-11885)**
**LOCKHEED MARTIN CORPORATION**
Also Called: Lockheed Martin
3130 Zanker Rd, San Jose  (95134-1965)
P.O. Box 3504  (94088-3504)
PHONE..............................408 473-3000
Magda Clyne, *Mgr*
EMP: 82
Web: www.lockheedmartin.com
SIC: 3663 7373 8711  Satellites, communications; Computer integrated systems design; Engineering services
PA: Lockheed Martin Corporation
    6801 Rockledge Dr

**(P-11886)**
**MACOM TECHNOLOGY SOLUTIONS INC**
18275 Serene Dr, Morgan Hill  (95037-2860)
PHONE..............................408 542-8872
EMP: 70
Web: www.macom.com
SIC: 3663 3679 3674  Radio and t.v. communications equipment; Microwave components; Semiconductors and related devices
HQ: Macom Technology Solutions Inc.
    100 Chelmsford St
    Lowell MA 01851

**(P-11887)**
**MAINLINE EQUIPMENT INC**
Also Called: Mainline
20917 Higgins Ct, Torrance  (90501-1723)
PHONE..............................800 444-2288
EMP: 52 EST: 1986
SALES (est): 2.88MM **Privately Held**
Web: www.main-line-inc.com
SIC: 3663 7629  Satellites, communications; Electrical equipment repair services

**(P-11888)**
**MANLEY LABORATORIES INC**
Also Called: Manufacturing
13880 Magnolia Ave, Chino  (91710-7027)
PHONE..............................909 627-4256
Eveanna Manley, *Pr*
Eveanna Manley-collins, *Pr*
▲ EMP: 32 EST: 1992
SQ FT: 11,000
SALES (est): 3.97MM **Privately Held**
Web: www.manley.com
SIC: 3663 3651  Radio and t.v. communications equipment; Audio electronic systems

**(P-11889)**
**MAXAR SPACE LLC**
5130 Robert J Mathews Pkwy, El Dorado Hills  (95762-5703)
PHONE..............................916 605-5448
Bob White, *Brnch Mgr*
EMP: 580
SALES (corp-wide): 1.6B **Privately Held**
Web: www.maxar.com
SIC: 3663  Space satellite communications equipment

## 3663 - Radio And T.v. Communications Equipment (P-11890)

HQ: Maxar Space Llc
3875 Fabian Way
Palo Alto CA 94303
650 852-4000

**(P-11890)**
**MICRO-MODE PRODUCTS INC**
1870 John Towers Ave, El Cajon
(92020-1193)
PHONE..................................619 449-3844
Vincent De Marco, Pr
Michael Cuban, *
Ruby Marco, *
**EMP:** 170 **EST:** 1971
**SALES (est):** 22.77MM
**SALES (corp-wide):** 3.28B **Publicly Held**
Web: www.micromode.com
**SIC: 3663** 3678 7389 Microwave communication equipment; Electronic connectors; Business Activities at Non-Commercial Site
PA: Itt Inc.
100 Washington Blvd Fl 6
914 641-2000

**(P-11891)**
**MICROWAVE DYNAMICS LLC**
Also Called: Quantic Mwd
16541 Scientific, Irvine (92618-4356)
PHONE..................................949 679-7788
Joe Svoboda, Managing Member
**EMP:** 18 **EST:** 1992
**SQ FT:** 10,000
**SALES (est):** 3.25MM **Privately Held**
Web: www.quanticmwd.com
**SIC: 3663** 5065 Microwave communication equipment; Electronic parts and equipment, nec

**(P-11892)**
**MILLENNIUM SPACE SYSTEMS INC (HQ)**
2265 E El Segundo Blvd, El Segundo (90245-4608)
PHONE..................................310 683-5840
Stan Dubyn, CEO
Tiffany Guthrie, *
Laura White, *
**EMP:** 32 **EST:** 2001
**SQ FT:** 10,000
**SALES (est):** 99.74MM
**SALES (corp-wide):** 77.79B **Publicly Held**
Web: www.millennium-space.com
**SIC: 3663** Space satellite communications equipment
PA: The Boeing Company
929 Long Bridge Dr
703 465-3500

**(P-11893)**
**MIRAPOINT SOFTWARE INC**
1600 Seaport Blvd Ste 400, Redwood City (94063-5564)
PHONE..................................650 286-7200
**EMP:** 96
**SIC: 3663** Radio and t.v. communications equipment

**(P-11894)**
**MISSION MICROWAVE TECH LLC (PA)**
6060 Phyllis Dr, Cypress (90630-5243)
PHONE..................................951 893-4925
Francis Auricchio, CEO
Michael Delisio, *
John Ocampo, *
**EMP:** 70 **EST:** 2014
**SALES (est):** 10.1MM
**SALES (corp-wide):** 10.1MM **Privately Held**

Web: www.missionmicrowave.com
**SIC: 3663** Satellites, communications

**(P-11895)**
**MODULAR COMMUNICATIONS SYSTEMS**
Also Called: Moducom
2629 Foothill Blvd, La Crescenta (91214-3511)
PHONE..................................818 764-1333
Robert A Moesch, Pr
Bernard Brandt, VP
Peter Hong, VP Opers
**EMP:** 17 **EST:** 1978
**SALES (est):** 2.77MM **Privately Held**
Web: www.moducom.com
**SIC: 3663** Radio and t.v. communications equipment

**(P-11896)**
**MOPHIE INC (DH)**
15495 Sand Canyon Ave Ste 400, Irvine (92618-3153)
PHONE..................................888 866-7443
Daniel Huang, CEO
▲ **EMP:** 75 **EST:** 2005
**SALES (est):** 10.05MM
**SALES (corp-wide):** 198.79MM **Privately Held**
Web: www.zagg.com
**SIC: 3663** Mobile communication equipment
HQ: Zagg Inc
910 W Lgacy Ctr Way Ste 5
Midvale UT 84047

**(P-11897)**
**MOTOROLA MOBILITY LLC**
2121 Tasman Dr, Santa Clara (95054-1027)
PHONE..................................408 919-0600
**EMP:** 26
Web: www.motorola.com
**SIC: 3663** Radio and t.v. communications equipment
HQ: Motorola Mobility Llc
222 W Mdse Mart Plz Ste 1
Chicago IL 60654

**(P-11898)**
**MOTOROLA MOBILITY LLC**
Also Called: Motorola
809 Eleventh Ave Bldg 4, Sunnyvale (94089-4731)
PHONE..................................847 576-5000
**EMP:** 43
Web: www.motorola.com
**SIC: 3663** Radio and t.v. communications equipment
HQ: Motorola Mobility Llc
222 W Mdse Mart Plz Ste 1
Chicago IL 60654

**(P-11899)**
**MOTOROLA SLTONS CNNCTIVITY INC (HQ)**
42555 Rio Nedo, Temecula (92590-3726)
P.O. Box 9007 (92589)
PHONE..................................951 719-2100
Gino Bonanotte, CEO
John Jack Molloy, Pr
Andrew Sinclair, *
Uygar Gazioglu, *
Daniel Pekofske, Care Vice President*
▲ **EMP:** 99 **EST:** 1967
**SQ FT:** 100,000
**SALES (est):** 56.28MM
**SALES (corp-wide):** 9.98B **Publicly Held**
Web: www.motorolasolutions.com
**SIC: 3663** Radio and t.v. communications equipment
PA: Motorola Solutions, Inc.
500 W Monroe St Ste 4400

847 576-5000

**(P-11900)**
**MTI LABORATORY INC**
Also Called: Mtil
201 Continental Blvd Ste 300, El Segundo (90245-4500)
PHONE..................................310 955-3700
Davis Kent, Pr
Alister Hsu, CFO
▼ **EMP:** 26 **EST:** 2006
**SQ FT:** 12,000
**SALES (est):** 6.7MM **Privately Held**
Web: www.mtigroup.com
**SIC: 3663** Microwave communication equipment
PA: Microelectronics Technology, Inc.
No. 1, Chuangxin 2nd Rd., Science-Based Industrial Park,

**(P-11901)**
**NAVCOM TECHNOLOGY INC (HQ)**
20780 Madrona Ave, Torrance (90503-3777)
PHONE..................................310 381-2000
Tony Thelen, CEO
Craig Fawcept, *
Michael Linzy, *
**EMP:** 100 **EST:** 1997
**SQ FT:** 55,000
**SALES (est):** 10.87MM
**SALES (corp-wide):** 61.25B **Publicly Held**
Web: www.navcomtech.com
**SIC: 3663** 8748 Satellites, communications; Communications consulting
PA: Deere & Company
1 John Deere Pl
309 765-8000

**(P-11902)**
**NERDIST CHANNEL LLC**
Also Called: Nerdist Industries
2900 W Alameda Ave Unit 1500, Burbank (91505-4220)
PHONE..................................818 333-2705
**EMP:** 30 **EST:** 2011
**SALES (est):** 3.96MM **Privately Held**
Web: www.nerdist.com
**SIC: 3663** Digital encoders

**(P-11903)**
**NEXTIVITY INC (PA)**
16550 W Bernardo Dr Ste 550, San Diego (92127-1870)
PHONE..................................858 485-9442
Werner Sievers, CEO
Michiel Lotter, *
Carol Lee, *
George Lamb, *
Thomas Cooper, Business Development*
▲ **EMP:** 49 **EST:** 2006
**SALES (est):** 53.53MM **Privately Held**
Web: www.nextivityinc.com
**SIC: 3663** Airborne radio communications equipment

**(P-11904)**
**NOKIA INC**
200 S Mathilda Ave, Sunnyvale (94086-6135)
P.O. Box 22720 (71903-2720)
PHONE..................................408 530-7600
▲ **EMP:** 2500
**SIC: 3663** 5065 3661 3577 Cellular radio telephone; Mobile telephone equipment; Telephone and telegraph apparatus; Computer peripheral equipment, nec

**(P-11905)**
**NORDEN MILLIMETER INC**
5441 Merchant Cir Ste C, Placerville (95667-8643)
PHONE..................................530 642-9123
Jc Rosenberg, Ch
Pete Hamlin, Dir
Kary Robertson, Treas
Duncan Smith, Pr
**EMP:** 22 **EST:** 2001
**SQ FT:** 10,000
**SALES (est):** 7.82MM **Privately Held**
Web: www.nordengroup.com
**SIC: 3663** Amplifiers, RF power and IF

**(P-11906)**
**NORTHROP GRUMMAN SYSTEMS CORP**
Space Systems Division
1 Space Park Blvd, Redondo Beach (90278-1071)
PHONE..................................310 812-5149
**EMP:** 101
Web: www.northropgrumman.com
**SIC: 3663** 3674 3679 3761 Airborne radio communications equipment; Semiconductors and related devices; Antennas, satellite: household use; Guided missiles and space vehicles
HQ: Northrop Grumman Systems Corporation
2980 Fairview Park Dr
Falls Church VA 22042
703 280-2900

**(P-11907)**
**NVIDIA US INVESTMENT COMPANY**
2701 San Tomas Expy, Santa Clara (95050-2519)
PHONE..................................408 615-2500
Jen-hsun Huang, Pr
**EMP:** 45 **EST:** 2000
**SALES (est):** 2.92MM **Publicly Held**
Web: www.nvidia.com
**SIC: 3663** Radio and t.v. communications equipment
PA: Nvidia Corporation
2788 San Tomas Expy

**(P-11908)**
**OPHIR RF INC**
Also Called: Ophir Rf
5300 Beethoven St Fl 3, Los Angeles (90066-7015)
PHONE..................................310 306-5556
Ilan Israely, Pr
Albert Barrios, *
**EMP:** 42 **EST:** 1992
**SQ FT:** 11,800
**SALES (est):** 9.04MM **Privately Held**
Web: www.ophirrf.com
**SIC: 3663** Amplifiers, RF power and IF

**(P-11909)**
**ORCA TECHNOLOGIES LLC**
Also Called: Orca Technologies
934 Calle Negocio Ste B, San Clemente (92673-6210)
P.O. Box 73394 (92673)
PHONE..................................949 682-3289
Gary Geil, Managing Member
**EMP:** 15 **EST:** 2007
**SALES (est):** 2.85MM **Privately Held**
Web: www.orcatechnologies.com
**SIC: 3663** Radio and t.v. communications equipment

## PRODUCTS & SERVICES SECTION
## 3663 - Radio And T.v. Communications Equipment (P-11930)

**(P-11910)**
**OTI ENGINEERING CONS INC**
24926 State Highway 108, Mi Wuk Village (95346-9714)
PHONE..................209 586-1022
Thomas A Olson, CEO
Janice Sue Olson, *
EMP: 30 EST: 1985
SQ FT: 2,600
SALES (est): 2.5MM
SALES (corp-wide): 38.23MM Privately Held
Web: www.olsontech.com
SIC: 3663 Cable television equipment
HQ: Antronix Of California, Inc.
  24926 State Highway 108
  Mi Wuk Village CA 95346
  800 545-1022

**(P-11911)**
**OVATION R&G LLC (PA)**
2850 Ocean Park Blvd Ste 225, Santa Monica (90405-2955)
PHONE..................310 430-7575
Ken Solomon, *
Phil Gilligan, *
Liz Janneman, *
Brad Samuels, *
EMP: 19 EST: 2009
SALES (est): 3MM Privately Held
Web: www.ovationtv.com
SIC: 3663 Satellites, communications

**(P-11912)**
**PACIFIC CREST CORPORATION (HQ)**
510 De Guigne Dr, Sunnyvale (94085-3920)
PHONE..................408 481-8070
EMP: 51 EST: 1977
SALES (est): 1.09MM
SALES (corp-wide): 3.8B Publicly Held
Web: www.pacificcrest.com
SIC: 3663 Transmitting apparatus, radio or television
PA: Trimble Inc.
  10368 Westmoor Dr
  720 887-6100

**(P-11913)**
**PACIFIC WAVE SYSTEMS INC**
2525 W 190th St, Torrance (90504-6002)
PHONE..................714 893-0152
Carl Esposito, CEO
John J Tus, *
Victor Jay Miller, *
Robert B Topolski, *
EMP: 68 EST: 1992
SALES (est): 9.87MM Privately Held
Web: www.pacificwavesystems.com
SIC: 3663 Satellites, communications

**(P-11914)**
**PALM INC (HQ)**
950 W Maude Ave, Sunnyvale (94085-2801)
PHONE..................408 617-7000
Jonathan J Rubinstein, Pr
▲ EMP: 400 EST: 1999
SQ FT: 347,144
SALES (est): 42.32MM Privately Held
Web: www.palmsource.com
SIC: 3663 Mobile communication equipment
PA: Tcl Communications Technology Co., Ltd.

**(P-11915)**
**PHONESUIT INC**
1431 7th St Ste 201, Santa Monica (90401-2638)
PHONE..................310 774-0282
Sumeet Gupta, CEO
EMP: 25 EST: 2012
SQ FT: 4,000
SALES (est): 2.42MM Privately Held
Web: www.phonesuit.com
SIC: 3663 Mobile communication equipment

**(P-11916)**
**PLANET LABS PBC (PA)**
Also Called: Planet
645 Harrison St Fl 4, San Francisco (94107-3624)
PHONE..................415 829-3313
William Marshall, CEO
Robert Schingler Junior, CSO
Ashley Fieglein Johnson, CFO
EMP: 51 EST: 2010
SQ FT: 65,000
SALES (est): 220.7MM
SALES (corp-wide): 220.7MM Publicly Held
Web: www.dmytechnology.com
SIC: 3663 Satellites, communications

**(P-11917)**
**PRECISION CONTACTS INC**
990 Suncast Ln, El Dorado Hills (95762-9626)
PHONE..................916 939-4147
Mat Wroblewski, Pr
Mathew Wroblewski, *
Nancy Wroblewski, *
Steven Wroblewski, *
Dean Wroblewski, *
EMP: 37 EST: 1976
SQ FT: 24,000
SALES (est): 2.44MM Privately Held
Web: www.precisioncontacts.com
SIC: 3663 3829 Radio and t.v. communications equipment; Measuring and controlling devices, nec

**(P-11918)**
**PREMIER WIRELESS INC**
4010 Watson Plaza Dr Ste 245, Lakewood (90712-4044)
P.O. Box 1876 (91077-1876)
PHONE..................925 776-1070
Mike Long, Pr
Rowland Lee, *
EMP: 29 EST: 1994
SQ FT: 5,000
SALES (est): 2.53MM Privately Held
SIC: 3663 4812 Radio and t.v. communications equipment; Cellular telephone services

**(P-11919)**
**PROSHOT INVESTORS LLC**
Also Called: Proshot Golf
14 Corporate Plaza Dr Ste 120, Newport Beach (92660-7995)
P.O. Box 9939 (92658-1939)
PHONE..................949 586-9500
David Kuhn, Pr
▲ EMP: 17 EST: 2001
SALES (est): 1.33MM
SALES (corp-wide): 1.8MM Privately Held
Web: www.proshotgolf.com
SIC: 3663 Global positioning systems (GPS) equipment
PA: Prelude Financial, Inc.
  2600 N Central Ave # 1700
  480 626-2423

**(P-11920)**
**PUREWAVE NETWORKS INC**
3951 Burton Dr, Santa Clara (95054-1583)
P.O. Box 970 (94566-0970)
PHONE..................650 528-5200
▲ EMP: 35 EST: 2003
SALES (est): 1.6MM Privately Held
Web: www.pwnets.com
SIC: 3663 Light communications equipment

**(P-11921)**
**QUALCOMM INCORPORATED**
Also Called: Qualcomm
4243 Campus Point Ct, San Diego (92121-1513)
PHONE..................858 587-1121
EMP: 142
SALES (corp-wide): 38.96B Publicly Held
Web: www.qualcomm.com
SIC: 3663 Radio and t.v. communications equipment
PA: Qualcomm Incorporated
  5775 Morehouse Dr
  858 587-1121

**(P-11922)**
**QUALCOMM INCORPORATED**
Also Called: Qualcomm
5775 Morehouse Dr, San Diego (92121-1714)
P.O. Box 10300 (92121)
PHONE..................202 263-0008
EMP: 28
SALES (corp-wide): 38.96B Publicly Held
Web: www.qualcomm.com
SIC: 3663 Radio and t.v. communications equipment
PA: Qualcomm Incorporated
  5775 Morehouse Dr
  858 587-1121

**(P-11923)**
**QUALCOMM INCORPORATED**
Also Called: Qualcomm
3165 Kifer Rd, Santa Clara (95051-0804)
PHONE..................858 587-1121
Stephen Zee, Brnch Mgr
EMP: 287
SALES (corp-wide): 38.96B Publicly Held
Web: www.qualcomm.com
SIC: 3663 Radio and t.v. communications equipment
PA: Qualcomm Incorporated
  5775 Morehouse Dr
  858 587-1121

**(P-11924)**
**QUALCOMM INCORPORATED (PA)**
Also Called: Qualcomm
5775 Morehouse Dr, San Diego (92121-1714)
PHONE..................858 587-1121
Cristiano R Amon, Pr
Mark D Mclaughlin, Ch Bd
Akash Palkhiwala, CFO
James J Cathey, CCO
EMP: 1430 EST: 1985
SALES (est): 38.96B
SALES (corp-wide): 38.96B Publicly Held
Web: www.qualcomm.com
SIC: 3663 3674 7372 6794 Mobile communication equipment; Semiconductors and related devices; Business oriented computer software; Patent buying, licensing, leasing

**(P-11925)**
**RADIAN AUDIO ENGINEERING INC**
2720 Kimball Ave, Pomona (91767-2200)
PHONE..................714 288-8900
Richard Kontrimas, CEO
Raimonda Kontrimas, Sec
◆ EMP: 20 EST: 1988
SALES (est): 2.26MM Privately Held
Web: www.radianaudio.com
SIC: 3663 5731 3651 Radio broadcasting and communications equipment; Radio, television, and electronic stores; Household audio and video equipment

**(P-11926)**
**RADITEK INC (PA)**
1702I Meridian Ave Ste 127, San Jose (95125-5586)
PHONE..................408 266-7404
Peter Corbett, CEO
Malcolm R Lee, *
Peter Corbett, COO
▲ EMP: 69 EST: 1993
SALES (est): 2.69MM Privately Held
Web: www.raditek.com
SIC: 3663 Microwave communication equipment

**(P-11927)**
**RAMONA RESEARCH INC**
Also Called: Mastiff Design
13741 Danielson St Ste J, Poway (92064-6895)
PHONE..................858 679-0717
Todd Jones, Genl Mgr
Carlos Macau, Treas
Dean Lentz, General Vice President
EMP: 19 EST: 2002
SALES (est): 5.63MM Publicly Held
Web: www.ramonaresearch.com
SIC: 3663 Microwave communication equipment
PA: Heico Corporation
  3000 Taft St

**(P-11928)**
**RANTEC MICROWAVE SYSTEMS INC**
Microwave Specialty Company
2066 Wineridge Pl, Escondido (92029-1930)
PHONE..................760 744-1544
Ben Walpole, Pr
EMP: 27
SALES (corp-wide): 12.58MM Privately Held
Web: www.rantecantennas.com
SIC: 3663 Radio and t.v. communications equipment
PA: Rantec Microwave Systems, Inc.
  31186 La Baya Dr
  818 223-5000

**(P-11929)**
**RAVEON TECHNOLOGIES CORP**
2320 Cousteau Ct, Vista (92081-8363)
PHONE..................760 444-5995
John Richard Sonnenberg, Pr
EMP: 37 EST: 2003
SQ FT: 7,300
SALES (est): 5.14MM Privately Held
Web: www.raveon.com
SIC: 3663 Airborne radio communications equipment

**(P-11930)**
**RAYTHEON APPLIED SGNAL TECH IN**
2000 E El Segundo Blvd, El Segundo (90245-4501)
PHONE..................310 436-7000
John R Treichler, CEO
EMP: 109
SALES (corp-wide): 68.92B Publicly Held
Web: www.appsig.com

# 3663 - Radio And T.v. Communications Equipment (P-11931)

**SIC: 3663** 8711 Radio and t.v. communications equipment; Engineering services
**HQ:** Raytheon Applied Signal Technology, Inc.
100 Headquarters Dr
San Jose CA 95134
408 749-1888

## (P-11931)
### RAYTHEON APPLIED SGNAL TECH IN (DH)
100 Headquarters Dr, San Jose (95134-1370)
**PHONE**..................................408 749-1888
John R Treichler, *CEO*
William B Van Vleet Iii, *CEO*
James E Doyle, *VP Fin*
R Fred Roscher, *BROADBAND Communications SYSTEMS*
Joseph Leonelli, *Strategy Vice President*
**EMP:** 95 **EST:** 1984
**SALES (est):** 412.75K
**SALES (corp-wide):** 68.92B **Publicly Held**
**Web:** www.appsig.com
**SIC: 3663** Radio and t.v. communications equipment
**HQ:** Raytheon Company
870 Winter St
Waltham MA 02451
781 522-3000

## (P-11932)
### REMEC BRDBAND WRLESS NTWRKS LL
82 Coromar Dr, Goleta (93117-3024)
**PHONE**..................................858 312-6900
Jamal Hamdani, *CEO*
Bruce Tarr, *
**EMP:** 180 **EST:** 2015
**SALES (est):** 2.29MM
**SALES (corp-wide):** 27.29MM **Privately Held**
**Web:** www.sagesat.com
**SIC: 3663** Mobile communication equipment
**PA:** Axxcss Wireless Solutions Inc
82 Coromar Dr
805 968-9621

## (P-11933)
### REMEC BROADBAND WIRELESS LLC
82 Coromar Dr, Goleta (93117-3024)
**PHONE**..................................858 312-6900
David K Newman, *Managing Member*
**EMP:** 102 **EST:** 2005
**SALES (est):** 19.75MM **Privately Held**
**Web:** www.remecbroadband.com
**SIC: 3663** Radio and t.v. communications equipment

## (P-11934)
### REVIVERMX INC
Also Called: Reviver
4170 Douglas Blvd Ste 200, Granite Bay (95746-9704)
**PHONE**..................................916 580-3495
Robert Wood, *CEO*
Mark Luhdorff, *Prin*
Neville Boston, *Prin*
**EMP:** 21 **EST:** 2017
**SALES (est):** 8.59MM **Privately Held**
**Web:** www.reviver.com
**SIC: 3663** 3469 5531 Mobile communication equipment; Automobile license tags, stamped metal; Automotive parts

## (P-11935)
### ROSELM INDUSTRIES INC
2510 Seaman Ave, South El Monte (91733-1928)
**PHONE**..................................626 442-6840
Conrad Arguijo, *Pr*
**EMP:** 20 **EST:** 1965
**SQ FT:** 13,000
**SALES (est):** 3.2MM **Privately Held**
**Web:** www.roselmindustries.com
**SIC: 3663** Radio and t.v. communications equipment

## (P-11936)
### ROTATING PRCSION MCHANISMS INC
Also Called: RPM
8750 Shirley Ave, Northridge (91324)
**PHONE**..................................818 349-9774
Kathy Flynn-nikolai, *CEO*
Daniel P Flynn, *
Jerome Smith, *Stockholder**
**EMP:** 46 **EST:** 1986
**SQ FT:** 40,000
**SALES (est):** 11.33MM **Privately Held**
**Web:** www.rpm-psi.com
**SIC: 3663** Radio and t.v. communications equipment

## (P-11937)
### RUCKUS WIRELESS LLC (DH)
Also Called: Ruckus Networks
350 W Java Dr, Sunnyvale (94089-1026)
**PHONE**..................................650 265-4200
Ken Cheng, *CEO*
Ellen O Donnell, *
Jean Furter, *
Kyle D Lorentzen, *
▲ **EMP:** 36 **EST:** 2004
**SQ FT:** 95,000
**SALES (est):** 1.43B **Publicly Held**
**Web:** www.ruckusnetworks.com
**SIC: 3663** 4813 5045 Radio and t.v. communications equipment; Internet connectivity services; Computers, peripherals, and software
**HQ:** Arris International Limited
12 New Fetter Lane
London
127 453-2000

## (P-11938)
### SALEM MUSIC NETWORK INC
4880 Santa Rosa Rd Ste 300, Camarillo (93012-5190)
**PHONE**..................................805 987-0400
Stuart W Epperson, *Prin*
**EMP:** 17 **EST:** 2001
**SALES (est):** 237.53K **Privately Held**
**Web:** www.salemmusicnetwork.com
**SIC: 3663** Radio broadcasting and communications equipment

## (P-11939)
### SATELLITE SECURITY CORPORATION
6779 Mesa Ridge Rd Ste 100, San Diego (92121-2996)
**PHONE**..................................877 437-4199
John Phillips, *CEO*
**EMP:** 26 **EST:** 1998
**SALES (est):** 1.51MM **Privately Held**
**Web:** www.kratosdefense.com
**SIC: 3663** Space satellite communications equipment

## (P-11940)
### SEASPACE CORPORATION
9155 Brown Deer Rd, San Diego (92121-2260)
**PHONE**..................................858 746-1100
Eric Park, *CEO*
Erik Park, *
Daniel Lee, *
Jihong Park, *
**EMP:** 25 **EST:** 1982
**SALES (est):** 8.52MM **Privately Held**
**Web:** www.seaspace.com
**SIC: 3663** 3829 Satellites, communications; Measuring and controlling devices, nec

## (P-11941)
### SEATEL INC (DH)
Also Called: Cobham Satcom
4030 Nelson Ave, Concord (94520-1200)
**PHONE**..................................925 798-7979
◆ **EMP:** 150 **EST:** 1980
**SALES (est):** 29.72MM
**SALES (corp-wide):** 2.67MM **Privately Held**
**SIC: 3663** Marine radio communications equipment
**HQ:** Cobham Limited
Basepoint Business Centre
Christchurch
120 288-2020

## (P-11942)
### SECURE COMM SYSTEMS INC (HQ)
Also Called: Benchmark Secure Technology
1740 E Wilshire Ave, Santa Ana (92705-4615)
**PHONE**..................................714 547-1174
Edward Hanrahan, *Pr*
Michael Buseman, *
Roop Lakkaraju, *
Kenneth Dorfman, *
▲ **EMP:** 147 **EST:** 2014
**SQ FT:** 38,000
**SALES (est):** 104.75MM
**SALES (corp-wide):** 2.84B **Publicly Held**
**Web:** www.bench.com
**SIC: 3663** 3829 3577 3571 Encryption devices; Vibration meters, analyzers, and calibrators; Computer peripheral equipment, nec; Electronic computers
**PA:** Benchmark Electronics, Inc.
56 S Rockford Dr
623 300-7000

## (P-11943)
### SEKAI ELECTRONICS INC (PA)
38 Waterworks Way, Irvine (92618-3107)
**PHONE**..................................949 783-5740
Roland Soohoo, *CEO*
**EMP:** 25 **EST:** 1982
**SQ FT:** 7,000
**SALES (est):** 7.9MM
**SALES (corp-wide):** 7.9MM **Privately Held**
**Web:** www.sekai-electronics.com
**SIC: 3663** 5065 Radio and t.v. communications equipment; Video equipment, electronic

## (P-11944)
### SIDUS SOLUTIONS LLC
7352 Trade St, San Diego (92121-2422)
P.O. Box 420698 (92142-0698)
**PHONE**..................................619 275-5533
Leonard Pool, *Managing Member*
**EMP:** 19 **EST:** 2000
**SQ FT:** 1,000
**SALES (est):** 4.23MM **Privately Held**
**Web:** www.sidus-solutions.com
**SIC: 3663** Radio and t.v. communications equipment

## (P-11945)
### SIERRA AUTOMATED SYS/ENG CORP
Also Called: Sierra Automated Systems
2821 Burton Ave, Burbank (91504-3224)
**PHONE**..................................818 840-6749
Edward O Fritz, *Pr*
Al Salci, *VP*
**EMP:** 20 **EST:** 1987
**SALES (est):** 2.52MM **Privately Held**
**Web:** www.sasaudio.com
**SIC: 3663** Radio broadcasting and communications equipment

## (P-11946)
### SIERRA NEVADA CORPORATION
Also Called: SIERRA NEVADA CORPORATION
39465 Paseo Padre Pkwy Ste 2900, Fremont (94538-5350)
**PHONE**..................................510 446-8400
Fatih Ozmen, *Brnch Mgr*
**EMP:** 68
**SALES (corp-wide):** 2.38B **Privately Held**
**Web:** www.sncorp.com
**SIC: 3663** 4812 Radio and t.v. communications equipment; Radiotelephone communication
**PA:** Sierra Nevada Company, Llc
444 Salomon Cir
775 331-0222

## (P-11947)
### SILVUS TECHNOLOGIES INC (PA)
10990 Wilshire Blvd Ste 1500, Los Angeles (90024-3957)
**PHONE**..................................310 479-3333
Babak Daneshrad, *Ch*
Jimi Henderson, *
Weijun Zhu, *
Gorik Hossepian, *
Eduardo Iniguez, *
**EMP:** 44 **EST:** 2004
**SQ FT:** 7,200
**SALES (est):** 34.21MM
**SALES (corp-wide):** 34.21MM **Privately Held**
**Web:** www.silvustechnologies.com
**SIC: 3663** 8731 Radio and t.v. communications equipment; Commercial physical research

## (P-11948)
### SOLECTEK CORPORATION
8375 Camino Santa Fe Ste A, San Diego (92121-2634)
**PHONE**..................................858 450-1220
Seung Joon Lee, *CEO*
Eric Lee, *Pr*
◆ **EMP:** 20 **EST:** 1997
**SQ FT:** 10,000
**SALES (est):** 3.05MM **Privately Held**
**Web:** www.solectek.com
**SIC: 3663** Television broadcasting and communications equipment

## (P-11949)
### SPACE MICRO INC
15378 Avenue Of Science Ste 200, San Diego (92128-3451)
**PHONE**..................................858 332-0700
David Czajkowski, *CEO*
David J Strobel, *
David R Czajkowski, *
Patricia Ellison, *
Michael Jacox, *
**EMP:** 107 **EST:** 2002
**SALES (est):** 20.22MM **Privately Held**
**Web:** www.spacemicro.com

# PRODUCTS & SERVICES SECTION — 3663 - Radio And T.v. Communications Equipment (P-11970)

SIC: 3663 Space satellite communications equipment

**(P-11950)**
**SPIRENT COMMUNICATIONS INC**
2350 Mission College Blvd, Santa Clara (95054-1532)
PHONE..............................408 752-7100
Laura Chavez, *Mgr*
EMP: 111
SALES (corp-wide): 474.3MM **Privately Held**
Web: www.spirent.com
SIC: 3663 3825 3829 Radio and t.v. communications equipment; Instruments to measure electricity; Measuring and controlling devices, nec
HQ: Spirent Communications Inc.
27349 Agoura Rd
Calabasas CA 91301

**(P-11951)**
**SSL MDA HOLDINGS INC**
3825 Fabian Way, Palo Alto (94303-4604)
PHONE..............................650 852-4000
Michelle Kaey, *Prin*
EMP: 18 EST: 2016
SALES (est): 2.4MM **Privately Held**
Web: www.sslmda.com
SIC: 3663 Satellites, communications

**(P-11952)**
**STELLANT SYSTEMS INC**
Also Called: Narda Microwave West
107 Woodmere Rd, Folsom (95630-4706)
PHONE..............................916 351-4500
Adam Erskine, *Brnch Mgr*
EMP: 165
SALES (corp-wide): 296.08MM **Privately Held**
Web: www.stellantsystems.com
SIC: 3663 Telemetering equipment, electronic
HQ: Stellant Systems, Inc.
3100 W Lomita Blvd
Torrance CA 90505

**(P-11953)**
**STONECROP TECHNOLOGIES LLC**
103 H St Ste B, Petaluma (94952-5125)
P.O. Box 550 (94953-0550)
PHONE..............................781 659-0007
EMP: 30
Web: www.stonecroptech.com
SIC: 3663 Microwave communication equipment
PA: Stonecrop Technologies, Llc
80 Washington St Ste M50

**(P-11954)**
**SUNBRITETV LLC (DH)**
2630 Townsgate Rd Ste F, Westlake Village (91361-2780)
PHONE..............................805 214-7250
Cameron Hill, *Managing Member*
▲ EMP: 19 EST: 2010
SALES (est): 3.72MM
SALES (corp-wide): 6.24B **Publicly Held**
Web: www.sunbritetv.com
SIC: 3663 Transmitting apparatus, radio or television
HQ: Sunbrite Holding Corporation
2001 Anchor Ct
Thousand Oaks CA 91320
805 214-7250

**(P-11955)**
**SUNTECH INTERNATIONAL USA LLC**
6060 Corte Del Cedro, Carlsbad (92011)
PHONE..............................833 282-3731
Robert Martin, *CEO*
EMP: 15 EST: 2016
SALES (est): 5.01MM **Privately Held**
Web: www.suntechint.com
SIC: 3663 Global positioning systems (GPS) equipment

**(P-11956)**
**TARANA WIRELESS INC (PA)**
630 Alder Dr, Milpitas (95035-7435)
PHONE..............................408 351-4085
Basil Alwan, *CEO*
Sergiu Nedeski, *Pr*
Rabin K Patra, *VP*
EMP: 15 EST: 2009
SALES (est): 50.58MM **Privately Held**
Web: www.taranawireless.com
SIC: 3663 Radio and t.v. communications equipment

**(P-11957)**
**TATUNG COMPANY AMERICA INC (HQ)**
2157 Mount Shasta Dr, San Pedro (90732-1334)
PHONE..............................310 637-2105
Huei-jihn Jih, *Pr*
Danny Huang, *
Christina Sun, *
▲ EMP: 98 EST: 1972
SALES (est): 21.24MM **Privately Held**
Web: www.tatungusa.com
SIC: 3663 3575 3944 3651 Television closed circuit equipment; Computer terminals, monitors and components; Video game machines, except coin-operated; Television receiving sets
PA: Tatung Company
22 Chungshan North Road,3rd Sec.,

**(P-11958)**
**TCI INTERNATIONAL INC (DH)**
3541 Gateway Blvd, Fremont (94538-6585)
PHONE..............................510 687-6100
Slobodan Tkalcevic, *VP*
Stephen Stein, *
Roy Woolsey, *
▲ EMP: 103 EST: 1986
SQ FT: 60,000
SALES (est): 24.89MM
SALES (corp-wide): 1.83B **Privately Held**
Web: www.tcibr.com
SIC: 3663 3812 3661 Radio broadcasting and communications equipment; Antennas, radar or communications; Modems
HQ: Canvas Sx, Llc
6325 Ardrey Kell Rd Ste 4
Charlotte NC 28277
980 474-3700

**(P-11959)**
**TECHNICOLOR USA INC**
400 Providence Mine Rd, Nevada City (95959-2953)
PHONE..............................530 478-3000
Jeff Rosica, *Sr VP*
EMP: 247
Web: www.technicolor.com
SIC: 3663 Radio and t.v. communications equipment
HQ: Technicolor Usa, Inc.
6040 W Sunset Blvd
Hollywood CA 90028
317 587-4287

**(P-11960)**
**TECHNOCONCEPTS INC**
6060 Sepulveda Blvd Ste 202, Van Nuys (91411-2512)
PHONE..............................818 988-3364
Antonio Turgeon, *CEO*
Eric Pommer, *
Michael Handelman, *
Richard A Hahn, *
Kevin Worth, *
EMP: 33 EST: 2004
SALES (est): 924.76K **Privately Held**
SIC: 3663 Cellular radio telephone

**(P-11961)**
**TELECOMMUNICATIONS ENGRG ASSOC**
1160 Industrial Rd Ste 15, San Carlos (94070-4128)
PHONE..............................650 590-1801
Daryl Jones, *Pr*
EMP: 17 EST: 1974
SQ FT: 5,500
SALES (est): 442.56K **Privately Held**
Web: www.tcomeng.com
SIC: 3663 7622 Radio and t.v. communications equipment; Communication equipment repair

**(P-11962)**
**TELEDYNE ETM INC (HQ)**
Also Called: ETM Teledyne
35451 Dumbarton Ct, Newark (94560-1100)
PHONE..............................510 797-1100
Robert Mehrabian, *Pr*
◆ EMP: 97 EST: 1973
SQ FT: 56,000
SALES (est): 23.03MM
SALES (corp-wide): 5.64B **Publicly Held**
Web: www.teledyneetm.com
SIC: 3663 3825 Microwave communication equipment; Test equipment for electronic and electric measurement
PA: Teledyne Technologies Inc
1049 Camino Dos Rios
805 373-4545

**(P-11963)**
**TELEMTRY CMMNCTONS SYSTEMS INC**
Also Called: TCS
10020 Remmet Ave, Chatsworth (91311-3854)
PHONE..............................818 718-6248
Sarin Michel Roy, *Pr*
Mihail Mateescu, *
EMP: 24 EST: 1999
SQ FT: 14,500
SALES (est): 5.88MM
SALES (corp-wide): 41.45MM **Privately Held**
Web: www.delta-telemetry.com
SIC: 3663 Antennas, transmitting and communications
PA: Delta Information Systems, Inc.
747 Dresher Rd Ste 125
215 657-5270

**(P-11964)**
**TELEWAVE INC**
48421 Milmont Dr, Fremont (94538-7327)
PHONE..............................408 929-4400
Roberta Boward, *Pr*
Allen Collins, *
Scott Wiebe, *
◆ EMP: 46 EST: 1972
SALES (est): 9.38MM **Privately Held**
Web: www.telewave.com

SIC: 3663 Radio broadcasting and communications equipment

**(P-11965)**
**TERRASAT COMMUNICATIONS INC**
315 Digital Dr, Morgan Hill (95037-2878)
PHONE..............................408 782-5911
Jit Patel, *Pr*
Carl Hurst, *
Jose Hecht, *
Rod Benson, *
▲ EMP: 47 EST: 1994
SALES (est): 15.28MM **Privately Held**
Web: www.terrasatinc.com
SIC: 3663 Satellites, communications

**(P-11966)**
**THOMSON REUTERS CORPORATION**
Also Called: Reuters Television La
5161 Lankershim Blvd, North Hollywood (91601-4963)
PHONE..............................877 518-2761
Kevin Regan, *Brnch Mgr*
EMP: 31
SALES (corp-wide): 10.66B **Publicly Held**
Web: www.thomsonreuters.com
SIC: 3663 Satellites, communications
HQ: Thomson Reuters Corporation
333 Bay St
Toronto ON M5H 2
416 687-7500

**(P-11967)**
**TRANSCOM TELECOMMUNICATION INC**
1390 E Burnett St Ste C, Signal Hill (90755-3559)
PHONE..............................562 424-9616
EMP: 27 EST: 2019
SALES (est): 4.97MM **Privately Held**
Web: www.transcomla.com
SIC: 3663 Radio and t.v. communications equipment

**(P-11968)**
**TRICOM RESEARCH INC**
17791 Sky Park Cir Ste J, Irvine (92614-6150)
PHONE..............................949 250-6024
Paula Wright, *Pr*
John W Wright, *
EMP: 64 EST: 2012
SALES (est): 3.26MM **Privately Held**
Web: www.tricomresearch.com
SIC: 3663 Radio and t.v. communications equipment

**(P-11969)**
**TRICOM RESEARCH INC**
17791 Sky Park Cir Ste J, Irvine (92614-6118)
PHONE..............................949 250-6024
◆ EMP: 64
SQ FT: 25,000
SALES (est): 4.22MM **Privately Held**
SIC: 3663 Radio and t.v. communications equipment

**(P-11970)**
**TRIQUINT WJ INC**
3099 Orchard Dr, San Jose (95134-2005)
PHONE..............................408 577-6200
W Dexter Paine Iii, *Ch Bd*
Ralph G Quinsey, *CEO*
Bruce W Diamond, *Pr*
R Gregory Miller, *VP*
Mark S Knoch, *VP Opers*

# 3663 - Radio And T.v. Communications Equipment (P-11971)

**EMP:** 92 **EST:** 2000
**SQ FT:** 124,000
**SALES (est):** 6.13MM
**SALES (corp-wide):** 3.77B **Publicly Held**
**Web:** www.qorvo.com
**SIC: 3663** 3674 Radio broadcasting and communications equipment; Semiconductors and related devices
**HQ:** Qorvo Us, Inc.
2300 Ne Brookwood Pkwy
Hillsboro OR 97124
503 615-9000

### (P-11971)
### VIASAT INC (PA)
Also Called: VIASAT
6155 El Camino Real, Carlsbad (92009-1602)
**PHONE**.................................760 476-2200
Mark Dankberg, *Ch Bd*
K Guru Gowrappan, *Pr*
Robert Blair, *Sr VP*
Kevin Harkenrider, *CCO*
Shawn Duffy, *Chief Accounting Officer*
▲ **EMP:** 1169 **EST:** 1986
**SALES (est):** 4.28B
**SALES (corp-wide):** 4.28B **Publicly Held**
**Web:** www.viasat.com
**SIC: 3663** 4899 Space satellite communications equipment; Data communication services

### (P-11972)
### VIDOVATION CORPORATION
1035 N Armando St Ste V, Anaheim (92806-2607)
**PHONE**.................................949 777-5435
Shannon Jachetta, *CEO*
James Jachetta, *COO*
**EMP:** 16 **EST:** 2010
**SALES (est):** 3.09MM **Privately Held**
**Web:** www.vidovation.com
**SIC: 3663** Radio and t.v. communications equipment

### (P-11973)
### VIGOR SYSTEMS INC
4660 La Jolla Village Dr Ste 500, San Diego (92122-4601)
**PHONE**.................................866 748-4467
Magnus Sorlander, *CEO*
Shayna Smith, *
▲ **EMP:** 35 **EST:** 2002
**SALES (est):** 7.75MM **Privately Held**
**Web:** www.edisen.com
**SIC: 3663** Studio equipment, radio and television broadcasting

### (P-11974)
### VISTA POINT TECHNOLOGIES INC
847 Gibraltar Dr, Milpitas (95035-6332)
**PHONE**.................................408 576-7000
Walter Sheram, *Prin*
**EMP:** 27 **EST:** 2008
**SALES (est):** 2.34MM
**SALES (corp-wide):** 388.79MM **Publicly Held**
**SIC: 3663** Cellular radio telephone
**HQ:** Fotonation Corporation
3025 Orchard Packway
San Jose CA 95101

### (P-11975)
### W B WALTON ENTERPRISES INC
4185 Hallmark Pkwy, San Bernardino (92407-1832)
P.O. Box 9010 (92427-0010)
**PHONE**.................................951 683-0930
William B Walton Junior, *Pr*
Jane Walton, *
**EMP:** 26 **EST:** 1979
**SQ FT:** 30,000
**SALES (est):** 4.94MM **Privately Held**
**Web:** www.de-ice.com
**SIC: 3663** 1731 Satellites, communications; Electrical work

### (P-11976)
### WATER ASSOCIATES LLC
Also Called: Redtrac
5060 California Ave, Bakersfield (93309-0728)
**PHONE**.................................661 281-6077
Jeff Young, *Managing Member*
**EMP:** 20 **EST:** 2002
**SALES (est):** 4.29MM **Privately Held**
**Web:** www.red-trac.com
**SIC: 3663** 3523 Radio and t.v. communications equipment; Irrigation equipment, self-propelled

### (P-11977)
### WEST-COM NRSE CALL SYSTEMS INC (PA)
Also Called: Wc
2200 Cordelia Rd, Fairfield (94534-1912)
**PHONE**.................................707 428-5900
C Larry Peters, *CEO*
Denise Peters, *
Dania Atanassova-een, *CFO*
**EMP:** 24 **EST:** 1988
**SQ FT:** 15,000
**SALES (est):** 11.07MM **Privately Held**
**Web:** www.westcomncs.com
**SIC: 3663** Radio broadcasting and communications equipment

### (P-11978)
### WI2WI INC (PA)
Also Called: Wi2wi
1879 Lundy Ave Ste 218, San Jose (95131-1881)
**PHONE**.................................408 416-4200
Zachariah J Mathews, *Pr*
**EMP:** 26 **EST:** 2005
**SALES (est):** 8.35MM **Privately Held**
**Web:** www.wi2wi.com
**SIC: 3663** Radio and t.v. communications equipment

### (P-11979)
### WOHLER TECHNOLOGIES INC
1280 San Luis Obispo St, Hayward (94544-7916)
**PHONE**.................................510 870-0810
Michael Kelly, *Pr*
John Palmer, *Ch*
Aaron Aiken, *Sec*
▲ **EMP:** 25 **EST:** 1991
**SALES (est):** 4.75MM **Privately Held**
**Web:** www.wohler.com
**SIC: 3663** Radio and t.v. communications equipment

### (P-11980)
### WV COMMUNICATIONS INC
1125 Business Center Cir Ste A, Newbury Park (91320-1186)
**PHONE**.................................805 376-1820
Uri Yulzari, *CEO*
Jim Tranovich, *VP*
Gerri L Yulzari, *Sec*
▲ **EMP:** 40 **EST:** 1998
**SQ FT:** 18,000
**SALES (est):** 4.96MM **Privately Held**
**Web:** www.wv-comm.com
**SIC: 3663** Microwave communication equipment

### (P-11981)
### YAESU USA INC
6125 Phyllis Dr, Cypress (90630-5242)
**PHONE**.................................714 827-7600
Jun Hasegawa, *CEO*
▲ **EMP:** 40 **EST:** 2012
**SALES (est):** 5.39MM **Privately Held**
**Web:** www.yaesu.com
**SIC: 3663** Radio and t.v. communications equipment

## 3669 Communications Equipment, Nec

### (P-11982)
### 71YRS INC (PA)
Also Called: Contract Furn & Ancillary Pdts
6525 Flotilla St, Commerce (90040-1713)
P.O. Box 5769 (90224-5769)
**PHONE**.................................310 639-0390
◆ **EMP:** 65 **EST:** 1952
**SALES (est):** 10.18MM
**SALES (corp-wide):** 10.18MM **Privately Held**
**Web:** www.peterpepper.com
**SIC: 3669** Visual communication systems

### (P-11983)
### BDFCO INC
Also Called: Damac
1926 Kauai Dr, Costa Mesa (92626-3542)
**PHONE**.................................714 228-2900
Frank J Kubat Junior, *CEO*
Daniel L Davis, *
Robert Mc Clory, *Stockholder*
▲ **EMP:** 80 **EST:** 1984
**SQ FT:** 120,000
**SALES (est):** 4.41MM **Privately Held**
**SIC: 3669** Intercommunication systems, electric

### (P-11984)
### BITMAX LLC (PA)
6255 W Sunset Blvd Ste 1515, Los Angeles (90028-7416)
**PHONE**.................................323 978-7878
Nancy Bennett, *Managing Member*
**EMP:** 21 **EST:** 1998
**SQ FT:** 7,500
**SALES (est):** 5MM
**SALES (corp-wide):** 5MM **Privately Held**
**Web:** www.bitmax.net
**SIC: 3669** 7929 Visual communication systems; Entertainment service

### (P-11985)
### BLUE SQUIRREL INC
8295 Aero Pl, San Diego (92123-2031)
**PHONE**.................................858 268-0717
Steve Deal, *CEO*
Dan Patton, *
Larry Cleary, *
Jay Standiford, *
Bill Kepner, *
▲ **EMP:** 80 **EST:** 1989
**SQ FT:** 20,000
**SALES (est):** 9.66MM **Privately Held**
**Web:** www.indyme.com
**SIC: 3669** 3663 Burglar alarm apparatus, electric; Airborne radio communications equipment

### (P-11986)
### CANOGA PERKINS CORPORATION (HQ)
20600 Prairie St, Chatsworth (91311-6008)
**PHONE**.................................818 718-6300
Alfred Tim Champion, *Pr*
James Heney, *
◆ **EMP:** 100 **EST:** 1965
**SQ FT:** 64,000
**SALES (est):** 24.61MM
**SALES (corp-wide):** 645.5MM **Privately Held**
**Web:** www.canoga.com
**SIC: 3669** Intercommunication systems, electric
**PA:** Inductotherm Group, Llc
10 Indel Ave
609 267-9000

### (P-11987)
### CARLOS A GARCIA
Also Called: All States Elc & Fire Alarm
582 Market St Ste 204, San Francisco (94104-5303)
**PHONE**.................................888 410-1648
Carlos A Garcia, *Owner*
**EMP:** 57 **EST:** 2007
**SALES (est):** 2.78MM **Privately Held**
**Web:** www.asefas.com
**SIC: 3669** Fire alarm apparatus, electric

### (P-11988)
### COMPUTER SERVICE COMPANY
Also Called: Steiny & Company
210 N Delilah St, Corona (92879-1883)
**PHONE**.................................951 738-1444
Justin Cataldo, *Mgr*
**EMP:** 49
**SALES (corp-wide):** 4.98MM **Privately Held**
**SIC: 3669** 7629 Traffic signals, electric; Electrical repair shops
**PA:** Computer Service Company
5463 Diaz St
951 738-1444

### (P-11989)
### D-TECH OPTOELECTRONICS INC
18062 Rowland St, City Of Industry (91748-1205)
**PHONE**.................................626 956-1100
An Baoxin, *Pr*
**EMP:** 20 **EST:** 2007
**SALES (est):** 2.59MM **Privately Held**
**Web:** www.dtechopto.com
**SIC: 3669** Intercommunication systems, electric
**PA:** Gcs Holdings, Inc.
115 S 4th St W

### (P-11990)
### DEI HEADQUARTERS INC
Also Called: Sound United
3002 Wintergreen Dr, Carlsbad (92008-6883)
**PHONE**.................................760 598-6200
James E Minarik, *Pr*
Kevin P Duffy, *
Veysel P Goker, *
Crystal L Biggs, *
Josh Talge, *CMO*
▲ **EMP:** 385 **EST:** 2002
**SALES (est):** 6.15MM **Privately Held**
**SIC: 3669** Burglar alarm apparatus, electric
**HQ:** Dei Holdings, Inc.
5541 Fermi Ct
Carlsbad CA 92008
760 598-6200

### (P-11991)
### DEI HOLDINGS INC (HQ)
Also Called: Masimo Consumer
5541 Fermi Ct, Carlsbad (92008-7348)
**PHONE**.................................760 598-6200
Paul Hataishi, *Pr*

## PRODUCTS & SERVICES SECTION
## 3669 - Communications Equipment, Nec (P-12011)

Anthony Blair Tripodi, *COO*
Tom Mcclenahan, *Sec*
◆ **EMP:** 30 **EST:** 1999
**SQ FT:** 198,000
**SALES (est):** 112.67MM **Privately Held**
**Web:** www.masimo.com
**SIC: 3669** 3651 Burglar alarm apparatus, electric; Amplifiers: radio, public address, or musical instrument
**PA:** Viper Holdings Corporation
200 Clarendon St Fl 54

**(P-11992)**
### ECONOLITE CONTROL PRODUCTS INC (PA)
1250 N Tustin Ave, Anaheim (92807-1617)
P.O. Box 6150 (92816-0150)
**PHONE**....................714 630-3700
Michael C Doyle, *Ch*
Christian Haas, *
John Tracey, *
▼ **EMP:** 160 **EST:** 1933
**SQ FT:** 95,000
**SALES (est):** 90.02MM
**SALES (corp-wide):** 90.02MM **Privately Held**
**Web:** www.econolite.com
**SIC: 3669** Traffic signals, electric

**(P-11993)**
### ESCO TECHNOLOGIES INC
501 Del Norte Blvd, Oxnard (93030-7983)
**PHONE**....................805 604-3875
**EMP:** 48
**Web:** www.escotechnologies.com
**SIC: 3669** Intercommunication systems, electric
**PA:** Esco Technologies Inc.
9900 A Clayton Rd

**(P-11994)**
### EXIGENT SENSORS LLC
11441 Markon Dr, Garden Grove (92841-1404)
**PHONE**....................949 439-1321
Jeff Buss, *Managing Member*
▲ **EMP:** 27 **EST:** 2007
**SALES (est):** 4.98MM **Privately Held**
**SIC: 3669** Fire alarm apparatus, electric

**(P-11995)**
### GENERAL DYNAMICS MISSION
2688 Orchard Pkwy, San Jose (95134-2020)
**PHONE**....................408 908-7300
Christopher Brady, *Pr*
**EMP:** 449
**SALES (corp-wide):** 42.27B **Publicly Held**
**Web:** www.gdmissionsystems.com
**SIC: 3669** 3812 Transportation signaling devices; Search and navigation equipment
**HQ:** General Dynamics Mission Systems, Inc.
12450 Fair Lakes Cir
Fairfax VA 22033
877 449-0600

**(P-11996)**
### GENERAL MONITORS INC (DH)
16782 Von Karman Ave Ste 14, Irvine (92606-2417)
**PHONE**....................949 581-4464
Richard Lamishaw, *CFO*
◆ **EMP:** 110 **EST:** 1961
**SALES (est):** 47.52MM
**SALES (corp-wide):** 1.79B **Publicly Held**
**Web:** www.generalmonitors.com
**SIC: 3669** 1799 3812 Fire detection systems, electric; Gas leakage detection; Infrared object detection equipment

**HQ:** Msa Safety Sales, Llc
1000 Cranberry Woods Dr
Cranberry Township PA 16066
800 672-2222

**(P-11997)**
### H M ELECTRONICS INC
Also Called: H. M. ELECTRONICS, INC.
2848 Whiptail Loop, Carlsbad (92010-6708)
**PHONE**....................858 535-6139
Mike Grell, *Brnch Mgr*
**EMP:** 21
**SALES (corp-wide):** 452.77MM **Privately Held**
**Web:** www.hme.com
**SIC: 3669** Intercommunication systems, electric
**PA:** H.M. Electronics, Inc.
2848 Whiptail Loop
858 535-6000

**(P-11998)**
### HIGHBALL SIGNAL INC
Also Called: Railroad Signals
6767 Di Carlo Pl, Rancho Cucamonga (91739-9155)
**PHONE**....................310 961-1122
Lupita Mejia, *Managing Member*
Lupita Mejia, *Pr*
Miguel Mejia Junior, *VP*
**EMP:** 20 **EST:** 2012
**SALES (est):** 2.98MM **Privately Held**
**Web:** www.highballsignal.com
**SIC: 3669** Railroad signaling devices, electric

**(P-11999)**
### HONEYWELL SEC AMERICAS LLC
Also Called: Utc, Mas
2955 Red Hill Ave Ste 100, Costa Mesa (92626-1207)
**PHONE**....................949 737-7800
Shin Voeks, *Genl Mgr*
**EMP:** 86
**SALES (corp-wide):** 36.66B **Publicly Held**
**Web:** corporate.carrier.com
**SIC: 3669** 5063 Burglar alarm apparatus, electric; Alarm systems, nec
**HQ:** Honeywell Security Americas, Llc
855 S Mint St
Charlotte NC 28202

**(P-12000)**
### INDYME SOLUTIONS LLC
8295 Aero Pl Ste 260, San Diego (92123-2029)
**PHONE**....................858 268-0717
Joe Joseph Eudano, *CEO*
Bill Kepner, *
James Doss, *
Philip Joostens, *
**EMP:** 50 **EST:** 1980
**SQ FT:** 18,000
**SALES (est):** 5.95MM **Privately Held**
**Web:** www.indyme.com
**SIC: 3669** Burglar alarm apparatus, electric

**(P-12001)**
### ITERIS INC
2150 Shattuck Ave Ste 175, Berkeley (94704-1356)
**PHONE**....................510 540-7647
Karl Petty, *Brnch Mgr*
**EMP:** 15
**SALES (corp-wide):** 156.05MM **Privately Held**
**Web:** www.iteris.com
**SIC: 3669** Emergency alarms
**PA:** Iteris, Inc.
1250 S Cpitl Of Txas Hwy

512 716-0808

**(P-12002)**
### JOHNSON CNTRLS FIRE PRTCTION L
Also Called: Simplexgrinnell
3568 Ruffin Rd, San Diego (92123-2597)
P.O. Box 23080 (92193-3080)
**PHONE**....................858 633-9100
Bob Jamieson, *Brnch Mgr*
**EMP:** 150
**SIC: 3669** 1731 1711 3873 Emergency alarms; Fire detection and burglar alarm systems specialization; Fire sprinkler system installation; Watches, clocks, watchcases, and parts
**HQ:** Johnson Controls Fire Protection Lp
6600 Congress Ave
Boca Raton FL 33487
561 988-7200

**(P-12003)**
### LUMENTUM HOLDINGS INC (PA)
Also Called: LUMENTUM
1001 Ridder Park Dr, San Jose (95131-2314)
**PHONE**....................408 546-5483
Alan S Lowe, *Pr*
Wajid Ali, *Ex VP*
Vincent Retort, *Ex VP*
Jason Reinhardt, *Ex VP*
Judy Hamel, *Sr VP*
**EMP:** 249 **EST:** 1979
**SQ FT:** 238,000
**SALES (est):** 1.36B
**SALES (corp-wide):** 1.36B **Publicly Held**
**Web:** www.lumentum.com
**SIC: 3669** 3674 Intercommunication systems, electric; Semiconductors and related devices

**(P-12004)**
### MERU NETWORKS INC (HQ)
Also Called: Meru Networks
894 Ross Dr, Sunnyvale (94089-1403)
**PHONE**....................408 215-5300
Ken Xie, *CEO*
Michael Xie, *
Andrew Del Matto, *
▲ **EMP:** 16 **EST:** 2002
**SQ FT:** 44,000
**SALES (est):** 26.11MM
**SALES (corp-wide):** 5.3B **Publicly Held**
**Web:** www.merunetworks.com
**SIC: 3669** Intercommunication systems, electric
**PA:** Fortinet, Inc.
909 Kifer Rd
408 235-7700

**(P-12005)**
### MK DAVIDSON INC
3333 W Coast Hwy Ste 200, Newport Beach (92663-4040)
**PHONE**....................949 698-2963
Darren Davidson, *CEO*
**EMP:** 32 **EST:** 2022
**SALES (est):** 916.65K **Privately Held**
**Web:** www.mkdavidson.com
**SIC: 3669** Communications equipment, nec

**(P-12006)**
### OPTEX INCORPORATED
10741 Walker St, Cypress (90630-4720)
**PHONE**....................800 966-7839
Makoto Kokobo, *CEO*
Tohru Kobayashi, *Ch Bd*
James Quick, *Pr*
Michael La Chere, *VP*
▲ **EMP:** 40 **EST:** 1992

**SALES (est):** 10.24MM **Privately Held**
**Web:** www.optexamerica.com
**SIC: 3669** Emergency alarms
**PA:** Optex Group Company, Limited
4-7-5, Nionohama

**(P-12007)**
### PALOMAR PRODUCTS INC
23042 Arroyo Vis, Rcho Sta Marg (92688-2617)
**PHONE**....................949 766-5300
Kevin Moschetti, *CEO*
Val Policky, *
Fred Ekstein, *
**EMP:** 79 **EST:** 1995
**SQ FT:** 35,000
**SALES (est):** 25.04MM
**SALES (corp-wide):** 7.94B **Publicly Held**
**Web:** www.palomar.com
**SIC: 3669** Intercommunication systems, electric
**PA:** Transdigm Group Incorporated
1350 Euclid Ave Ste 1600
216 706-2960

**(P-12008)**
### PI VARIABLES INC
Also Called: PI Variables
3002 Dow Ave Ste 138, Tustin (92780-7248)
**PHONE**....................949 415-9411
James Selevan, *CEO*
Kathleen Selevan, *Pr*
**EMP:** 20 **EST:** 2013
**SALES (est):** 2.39MM **Privately Held**
**Web:** www.pi-lit.com
**SIC: 3669** Traffic signals, electric

**(P-12009)**
### PRESENTERTEK INC
3710 N Lakeshore Blvd, Loomis (95650-9789)
**PHONE**....................916 251-7190
Thomas J Tanner, *CEO*
Steven Mcnerney, *Pr*
**EMP:** 22 **EST:** 2017
**SQ FT:** 2,500
**SALES (est):** 1.82MM **Privately Held**
**Web:** www.presentertek.com
**SIC: 3669** Visual communication systems

**(P-12010)**
### PROTO SERVICES INC
Also Called: PSI
1991 Concourse Dr, San Jose (95131-1708)
**PHONE**....................408 719-9088
Nicky Wu, *CEO*
**EMP:** 40 **EST:** 1998
**SQ FT:** 25,000
**SALES (est):** 6.93MM **Privately Held**
**Web:** www.protoservices.com
**SIC: 3669** Visual communication systems

**(P-12011)**
### PROXIM WIRELESS CORPORATION (PA)
2114 Ringwood Ave, San Jose (95131-1715)
**PHONE**....................408 383-7600
Greg Marzullo, *Pr*
David L Renauld, *
Steve Button, *
David Porte, *
David Sumi, *
▲ **EMP:** 55 **EST:** 2003
**SQ FT:** 42,500
**SALES (est):** 47.07MM
**SALES (corp-wide):** 47.07MM **Privately Held**

## 3669 - Communications Equipment, Nec (P-12012)

Web: www.proxim.com
SIC: 3669 Signaling apparatus, electric

**(P-12012)**
**QUALCOMM MEMS TECHNOLOGIES INC**
5775 Morehouse Dr, San Diego (92121-1714)
PHONE.................................858 587-1121
Greg Heinzinger, *Sr VP*
Derek Aberle, *
EMP: 25 EST: 1998
SQ FT: 9,000
SALES (est): 6.33MM
SALES (corp-wide): 38.96B **Publicly Held**
SIC: 3669 Visual communication systems
PA: Qualcomm Incorporated
    5775 Morehouse Dr
    858 587-1121

**(P-12013)**
**RAYTHEON APPLIED SGNAL TECH IN**
160 N Riverview Dr Ste 300, Anaheim (92808-2295)
PHONE.................................714 917-0255
John Mcgrory, *Brnch Mgr*
EMP: 94
SALES (corp-wide): 68.92B **Publicly Held**
Web: www.appsig.com
SIC: 3669 Signaling apparatus, electric
HQ: Raytheon Applied Signal Technology, Inc.
    100 Headquarters Dr
    San Jose CA 95134
    408 749-1888

**(P-12014)**
**SAFETY NTWRK TRAFFIC SIGNS INC**
Also Called: Safety Network
1345 N Rabe Ave, Fresno (93727-2249)
PHONE.................................559 291-8000
Russ Johnson, *Pr*
EMP: 20 EST: 2014
SALES (est): 2.26MM **Privately Held**
Web: www.safetynetworkinc.com
SIC: 3669 Traffic signals, electric

**(P-12015)**
**SENSYS NETWORKS INC**
Also Called: Senetrics International
1608 4th St Ste 110, Berkeley (94710-1749)
PHONE.................................510 548-4620
Amine Haoui, *Pr*
Robert Kavaler, *
Hamed Benouar, *
Brian Fuller, *
Carolyn Owens, *
▲ EMP: 80 EST: 2003
SALES (est): 21.59MM
SALES (corp-wide): 10.97MM **Privately Held**
Web: www.sensysnetworks.com
SIC: 3669 Transportation signaling devices
PA: Tagmaster Ab
    Kronborgs Grand 11
    86321950

**(P-12016)**
**SIEMENS RAIL AUTOMATION CORP**
9568 Archibald Ave, Rancho Cucamonga (91730-5744)
PHONE.................................909 532-5405
Jay Aslam, *Mgr*
EMP: 84
SALES (corp-wide): 84.48B **Privately Held**
Web: www.siemens.com
SIC: 3669 Railroad signaling devices, electric
HQ: Siemens Rail Automation Corporation
    2400 Nelson Miller Pkwy
    Louisville KY 40223
    800 626-2710

**(P-12017)**
**SIGTRONICS CORPORATION**
178 E Arrow Hwy, San Dimas (91773-3336)
PHONE.................................909 305-9399
Mark Kelley, *Pr*
Frank M Sigona, *Prin*
Jane Sigona, *Prin*
EMP: 20 EST: 1974
SQ FT: 12,000
SALES (est): 3.67MM **Privately Held**
Web: www.sigtronics.com
SIC: 3669 Intercommunication systems, electric

**(P-12018)**
**STATEWIDE TRFFIC SFETY SGNS IN (HQ)**
2722 S Fairview St Fl 2, Santa Ana (92704-5947)
PHONE.................................949 553-8272
Rob Sehnert, *CEO*
EMP: 39 EST: 1987
SALES (est): 24.12MM
SALES (corp-wide): 539.72MM **Privately Held**
Web: www.statewidess.com
SIC: 3669 Pedestrian traffic control equipment
PA: Awp, Inc.
    4244 Mount Pleasant St Nw
    330 677-7401

**(P-12019)**
**SYSTECH CORPORATION**
Also Called: Systech
118 State Pl Ste 101, Escondido (92029-1324)
PHONE.................................858 674-6500
D Mark Fowler, *Pr*
Don Armerding, *
Jon Goby, *
Cheri Houchin, *
Zenon Barelka, *
▲ EMP: 35 EST: 1980
SALES (est): 8.21MM **Privately Held**
Web: www.systech.com
SIC: 3669 7371 3661 3577 Intercommunication systems, electric; Custom computer programming services; Telephone and telegraph apparatus; Computer peripheral equipment, nec

**(P-12020)**
**TACTICAL COMMAND INDS INC (DH)**
4700 E Airport Dr, Ontario (91761-7875)
PHONE.................................925 219-1097
Scott O'brien, *CEO*
EMP: 23 EST: 1996
SALES (est): 4.43MM
SALES (corp-wide): 482.53MM **Publicly Held**
Web: www.safariland.com
SIC: 3669 Intercommunication systems, electric
HQ: Safariland, Llc
    13386 International Pkwy
    Jacksonville FL 32218
    904 741-5400

**(P-12021)**
**TACTICAL COMMUNICATIONS CORP**
473 Post St, Camarillo (93010-8553)
PHONE.................................805 987-4100
Gregory Peacock, *CHBGREGORY PEACOCK CEO CHBGREGORY PEACOCK*
EMP: 25 EST: 2009
SQ FT: 11,000
SALES (est): 5.2MM **Privately Held**
Web: www.tacticalcommunications.com
SIC: 3669 8999 Intercommunication systems, electric; Communication services

**(P-12022)**
**TELLABS ACCESS LLC (HQ)**
338 Pier Ave, Hermosa Beach (90254-3617)
PHONE.................................630 798-8671
Mike Dagenais, *Pr*
Robb Warwick, *VP*
Doug Bayerd, *VP*
Jeff Carnes, *VP*
EMP: 44 EST: 2014
SALES (est): 16.5MM **Privately Held**
Web: www.tellabs.com
SIC: 3669 Intercommunication systems, electric
PA: Marlin Equity Partners, Llc
    1301 Manhattan Ave

**(P-12023)**
**TRAFFIX DEVICES INC (PA)**
Also Called: Vizcon
160 Avenida La Pata, San Clemente (92673-6304)
PHONE.................................949 361-5663
Jack H Kulp, *Pr*
Brent M Kulp, *VP*
Suzanne Kulp, *Sec*
◆ EMP: 15 EST: 1986
SQ FT: 10,000
SALES (est): 20.25MM
SALES (corp-wide): 20.25MM **Privately Held**
Web: www.traffixdevices.com
SIC: 3669 Traffic signals, electric

**(P-12024)**
**VOCERA COMMUNICATIONS INC (HQ)**
Also Called: Vocera
3030 Orchard Pkwy, San Jose (95134-2028)
PHONE.................................408 882-5100
J Andrew Pierce, *Pr*
Steven J Anheier, *CFO*
William E Berry Junior, *VP*
Jeanne M Blondia, *VP*
Sean C Etheridge, *VP*
▲ EMP: 162 EST: 2000
SQ FT: 70,000
SALES (est): 234.19MM
SALES (corp-wide): 20.5B **Publicly Held**
Web: www.stryker.com
SIC: 3669 Intercommunication systems, electric
PA: Stryker Corporation
    1941 Stryker Way
    269 385-2600

**(P-12025)**
**WALTON ELECTRIC CORPORATION**
755 N Central Ave Ste A, Upland (91786-9475)
P.O. Box 1599 (91711-8599)
PHONE.................................909 981-5051
Tanyon D Dunkley, *CEO*
Don R Davis, *
Ron C Stickel, *
EMP: 150 EST: 1985
SQ FT: 10,150
SALES (est): 35.19MM **Privately Held**
Web: www.waltonelectriccorp.com
SIC: 3669 1731 Fire alarm apparatus, electric ; Electrical work

**(P-12026)**
**WESTERN PACIFIC SIGNAL LLC**
15890 Foothill Blvd, San Leandro (94577)
PHONE.................................510 276-6400
Heidi Shupp, *Pr*
EMP: 15 EST: 1997
SQ FT: 6,500
SALES (est): 3.39MM
SALES (corp-wide): 90.02MM **Privately Held**
Web: www.wpsignal.com
SIC: 3669 Traffic signals, electric
HQ: Econolite Group Inc.
    1250 N Tustin Ave
    Anaheim CA 92807
    714 630-3700

**(P-12027)**
**ZETTLER COMPONENTS INC (PA)**
75 Columbia, Orange (92868)
PHONE.................................949 831-5000
Kurt Rexius, *Genl Mgr*
▲ EMP: 250 EST: 1996
SQ FT: 27,000
SALES (est): 43.13MM **Privately Held**
Web: www.zettlercomponents.com
SIC: 3669 5065 5087 Intercommunication systems, electric; Intercommunication equipment, electronic; Firefighting equipment

### 3671 Electron Tubes

**(P-12028)**
**COMMUNICATIONS & PWR INDS LLC**
CPI International
1318 Commerce Ave, Woodland (95776-5908)
PHONE.................................530 662-7553
EMP: 73
Web: www.cpii.com
SIC: 3671 3679 3699 3663 Vacuum tubes; Microwave components; Electrical equipment and supplies, nec; Radio and t.v. communications equipment
HQ: Communications & Power Industries Llc
    811 Hansen Way
    Palo Alto CA 94304

**(P-12029)**
**COMMUNICATIONS & PWR INDS LLC (HQ)**
Also Called: CPI
811 Hansen Way, Palo Alto (94304-1021)
PHONE.................................650 846-2900
Robert A Fickett, *Pr*
Joel A Littman, *
Don C Coleman, *
John Beighley, *
Laura Kowalchik, *
◆ EMP: 720 EST: 1950
SQ FT: 429,000
SALES (est): 687.25MM **Privately Held**
Web: www.cpii.com

**PRODUCTS & SERVICES SECTION**  **3672 - Printed Circuit Boards (P-12051)**

SIC: **3671** 3679 3699 3663  Vacuum tubes; Microwave components; Electrical equipment and supplies, nec; Radio and t.v. communications equipment
PA: Cpi Satcom & Antenna Technologies Inc.
811 Hansen Way

*(P-12030)*
### DCX-CHOL ENTERPRISES INC
Also Called: Masterite Division
12831 S Figueroa St, Los Angeles (90061-1157)
PHONE.................................310 516-1692
Brian Gamberg, *Brnch Mgr*
EMP: 16
SALES (corp-wide): 112.69MM **Privately Held**
Web: www.dcxchol.com
SIC: **3671** 3365  Electron tubes; Aerospace castings, aluminum
PA: Dcx-Chol Enterprises, Inc.
12831 S Figueroa St
310 516-1692

*(P-12031)*
### ECOATM LLC
900 Dana Dr, Redding  (96003-4053)
PHONE.................................858 255-4111
EMP: 27
SALES (corp-wide): 32.64B **Publicly Held**
Web: www.ecoatm.com
SIC: **3671**  Electron tubes
HQ: Ecoatm, Llc
10121 Barnes Canyon Rd
San Diego CA 92121

*(P-12032)*
### ECOATM  LLC (DH)
10121 Barnes Canyon Rd, San Diego (92121-2725)
PHONE.................................858 999-3200
David Mersten, *
EMP: 250 EST: 2008
SALES (est): 105.7MM
SALES (corp-wide): 32.64B **Publicly Held**
Web: www.ecoatm.com
SIC: **3671**  Electron tubes
HQ: Apollo Asset Management, Inc.
9 W 57th St Fl 42
New York NY 10019

*(P-12033)*
### HEATWAVE LABS  INC
195 Aviation Way Ste 100, Watsonville (95076-2059)
PHONE.................................831 722-9081
Kim Gunther, *Pr*
EMP: 18 EST: 1994
SQ FT: 10,000
SALES (est): 2.28MM **Privately Held**
Web: www.cathode.com
SIC: **3671**  Electron tubes

*(P-12034)*
### LEEMAH CORPORATION (PA)
155 S Hill Dr, Brisbane  (94005-1203)
PHONE.................................415 394-1288
Efrem Mah, *CEO*
Bing Hong Mah, *
Dick Wong, *
Warren Gee, *
▲ EMP: 150 EST: 1971
SQ FT: 60,000
SALES (est): 127.87MM
SALES (corp-wide): 127.87MM **Privately Held**
Web: www.leemah.com

SIC: **3671** 3672 3669 3663  Electron tubes; Printed circuit boards; Intercommunication systems, electric; Radio and t.v. communications equipment

*(P-12035)*
### MICROWAVE POWER PRODUCTS INC ✪
811 Hansen Way, Palo Alto  (94304-1031)
PHONE.................................650 846-2900
Amanda Garcia, *Pr*
EMP: 458 EST: 2024
SALES (est): 3.23MM **Privately Held**
SIC: **3671**  Electron tubes

*(P-12036)*
### NEWVAC  LLC
Also Called: Newvac Division
9330 De Soto Ave, Chatsworth (91311-4926)
PHONE.................................310 990-0401
Garrett Hoffman, *Brnch Mgr*
EMP: 114
SALES (corp-wide): 96.54MM **Privately Held**
Web: www.newvac-llc.com
SIC: **3671** 3678 3679  Electron tubes; Electronic connectors; Harness assemblies, for electronic use: wire or cable
HQ: Newvac, Llc
9330 De Soto Ave
Chatsworth CA 91311
310 525-1205

*(P-12037)*
### PENTA FINANCIAL  INC
Also Called: Penta Laboratories
14399 Princeton Ave, Moorpark  (93021)
PHONE.................................818 882-3872
Steve Sanett, *Pr*
Steve Sanett, *CEO*
▲ EMP: 15 EST: 1993
SQ FT: 28,000
SALES (est): 2.25MM **Privately Held**
Web: pentafinancial.openfos.com
SIC: **3671** 3589  Electron tubes; Microwave ovens (cooking equipment), commercial

*(P-12038)*
### PENTA LABORATORIES  LLC
14399 Princeton Ave, Moorpark (93021-1481)
PHONE.................................818 882-3872
▲ EMP: 15 EST: 1951
SALES (est): 2.93MM **Privately Held**
Web: www.pentalabs.com
SIC: **3671** 5065  Electron tubes; Electronic tubes: receiving and transmitting, or industrial

## 3672 Printed Circuit Boards

*(P-12039)*
### A & M ELECTRONICS  INC
25018 Avenue Kearny, Valencia (91355-1253)
PHONE.................................661 257-3680
Ron Simpson, *Pr*
Tiffiny Simpson, *
EMP: 30 EST: 1977
SQ FT: 12,000
SALES (est): 7.32MM **Privately Held**
Web: www.aandmelectronics.com
SIC: **3672**  Circuit boards, television and radio printed

*(P-12040)*
### ACCU-SEMBLY  INC
1835 Huntington Dr, Duarte  (91010-2635)
PHONE.................................626 357-3447
John Hykes, *CEO*
Marilyn Hykes, *
Jan Shimmin, *Stockholder*
John Shimmin, *Stockholder*
▲ EMP: 95 EST: 1983
SQ FT: 15,000
SALES (est): 22.18MM **Privately Held**
Web: www.accu-sembly.com
SIC: **3672**  Printed circuit boards

*(P-12041)*
### ACCURATE CIRCUIT ENGRG INC
Also Called: Ace
3019 Kilson Dr, Santa Ana  (92707-4202)
PHONE.................................714 546-2162
Charles Lowe, *CEO*
▲ EMP: 70 EST: 1984
SQ FT: 15,000
SALES (est): 9.13MM **Privately Held**
Web: www.ace-pcb.com
SIC: **3672**  Printed circuit boards

*(P-12042)*
### ACCURATE ENGINEERING  INC
8710 Telfair Ave, Sun Valley  (91352-2530)
PHONE.................................818 768-3919
Shitalkumar Desai, *Pr*
Rush Patel, *
Hiten Golakiea, *
Suresh Jasani, *
Gautam Jasani, *
EMP: 25 EST: 1996
SQ FT: 15,000
SALES (est): 2.44MM **Privately Held**
Web: www.accueng.com
SIC: **3672**  Printed circuit boards

*(P-12043)*
### ADDISON TECHNOLOGY  INC
Also Called: Addison Engineering
3350 Scott Blvd, Santa Clara  (95054-3121)
PHONE.................................408 749-1000
Gibson Cobb, *Pr*
Jim Landis, *
▲ EMP: 45 EST: 1983
SALES (est): 5.29MM **Privately Held**
Web: www.addisonengineering.com
SIC: **3672** 5065  Printed circuit boards; Semiconductor devices

*(P-12044)*
### ADVANCED CIRCUITS  INC
17067 Cantara St, Van Nuys  (91406-1112)
PHONE.................................818 345-1993
Ralph Richart, *Brnch Mgr*
EMP: 33
Web: www.4pcb.com
SIC: **3672**  Printed circuit boards
PA: Advanced Circuits, Inc.
21101 E 32nd Pkwy

*(P-12045)*
### ADVANCED CIRCUITS  INC
Also Called: Coastal Circuit
1602 Tacoma Way, Redwood City (94063-1109)
PHONE.................................415 602-6834
Ralph Richart Junior, *Pr*
EMP: 113
Web: www.4pcb.com
SIC: **3672**  Circuit boards, television and radio printed
PA: Advanced Circuits, Inc.
21101 E 32nd Pkwy

*(P-12046)*
### AIR ADHART  INC
41549 Cherry St, Murrieta  (92562)
P.O. Box 1031 (92564)
PHONE.................................951 698-4452
Clark M Steddom, *Pr*
Mark Chiang, *Prin*
EMP: 20 EST: 2005
SALES (est): 2.56MM **Privately Held**
Web: www.cmscircuits.com
SIC: **3672**  Circuit boards, television and radio printed

*(P-12047)*
### ALL QUALITY & SERVICES  INC (PA)
Also Called: Aqs
47817 Fremont Blvd, Fremont (94538-6506)
PHONE.................................510 249-5800
So Jin Lee, *Pr*
▲ EMP: 84 EST: 1991
SALES (est): 27.02MM **Privately Held**
Web: www.aqs-inc.com
SIC: **3672** 3651  Printed circuit boards; Electronic kits for home assembly: radio, TV, phonograph

*(P-12048)*
### ALPHA EMS CORPORATION
44193 S Grimmer Blvd, Fremont (94538-6350)
PHONE.................................510 498-8788
Eric Chang, *Pr*
Chingping Chang, *
Eric Liaw, *
Bill Yee, *
EMP: 138 EST: 2002
SQ FT: 50,000
SALES (est): 43.09MM **Privately Held**
Web: www.alphaemscorp.com
SIC: **3672**  Printed circuit boards

*(P-12049)*
### ALTA MANUFACTURING  INC
47650 Westinghouse Dr, Fremont (94539-7473)
PHONE.................................510 668-1870
Anne Lee, *CEO*
EMP: 30 EST: 1998
SQ FT: 24,000
SALES (est): 5.37MM **Privately Held**
Web: www.altamfg.com
SIC: **3672**  Printed circuit boards

*(P-12050)*
### ALTAFLEX
336 Martin Ave, Santa Clara  (95050-3112)
PHONE.................................408 727-6614
Paul Morben, *Pr*
Robert Jung, *
EMP: 70 EST: 2000
SQ FT: 20,200
SALES (est): 9.64MM
SALES (corp-wide): 1.54B **Publicly Held**
Web: www.altaflex.com
SIC: **3672**  Printed circuit boards
HQ: Osi Electronics, Inc.
12533 Chadron Ave
Hawthorne CA 90250
310 978-0516

*(P-12051)*
### AMERICAN CIRCUIT TECH INC (PA)
5330 E Hunter Ave, Anaheim  (92807-2053)
PHONE.................................714 777-2480
Ravi Kheni, *Pr*
Giradhar Butani, *

## 3672 - Printed Circuit Boards (P-12052)

**PRODUCTS & SERVICES SECTION**

Labheu Zalavadia, *
Kanu Patel, *
**EMP:** 36 **EST:** 1975
**SQ FT:** 22,000
**SALES (est):** 4.33MM
**SALES (corp-wide):** 4.33MM **Privately Held**
**Web:** www.excello.com
**SIC: 3672** Circuit boards, television and radio printed

**(P-12052)**
**AMPRO SYSTEMS INC**
2950 Merced St Ste 114, San Leandro (94577-5636)
**PHONE**.................510 624-9000
Elliot Wang, Pr
▲ **EMP:** 42 **EST:** 1997
**SALES (est):** 1.75MM **Privately Held**
**Web:** www.amprosystems.com
**SIC: 3672** Printed circuit boards

**(P-12053)**
**AMTECH MICROELECTRONICS INC**
485 Cochrane Cir, Morgan Hill (95037-2831)
**PHONE**.................408 612-8888
Walter Chavez, Pr
**EMP:** 42 **EST:** 1993
**SQ FT:** 14,500
**SALES (est):** 9.59MM **Privately Held**
**Web:** www.amtechmicro.com
**SIC: 3672** Printed circuit boards

**(P-12054)**
**ANC TECHNOLOGY INC**
Also Called: Shanghai Anc Electronic Tech
10195 Stockton Rd, Moorpark (93021-9755)
**PHONE**.................805 530-3958
Dennis Noble, CEO
▲ **EMP:** 100 **EST:** 1994
**SQ FT:** 60,000
**SALES (est):** 6.91MM **Privately Held**
**Web:** www.anctech.com
**SIC: 3672** 5083 Printed circuit boards; Irrigation equipment

**(P-12055)**
**APCT INC (HQ)**
Also Called: (Former: Advanced Printed Circuit Technology)
3495 De La Cruz Blvd, Santa Clara (95054-2110)
**PHONE**.................408 727-6442
Steve Robinson, CEO
Bill Boyle, *
Greg Elder, *
▲ **EMP:** 110 **EST:** 1977
**SQ FT:** 30,000
**SALES (est):** 39.34MM
**SALES (corp-wide):** 87.73MM **Privately Held**
**Web:** www.apct.com
**SIC: 3672** Circuit boards, television and radio printed
**PA:** Apct Holdings, Llc
3495 De La Cruz Blvd
408 727-6442

**(P-12056)**
**APCT HOLDINGS LLC (PA)**
Also Called: Apct
3495 De La Cruz Blvd, Santa Clara (95054-2110)
**PHONE**.................408 727-6442
Steve Robinson, CEO
Greg Elder, CFO
**EMP:** 185 **EST:** 2013
**SQ FT:** 30,000
**SALES (est):** 87.73MM
**SALES (corp-wide):** 87.73MM **Privately Held**
**Web:** www.apct.com
**SIC: 3672** Printed circuit boards

**(P-12057)**
**APCT-WALLINGFORD INC**
Also Called: Tech Circuits
3495 De La Cruz Blvd, Santa Clara (95054-2110)
P.O. Box 309 (06492-0309)
**PHONE**.................203 269-3311
Steve Robinson, Pr
Greg Elder, *
**EMP:** 45 **EST:** 1979
**SALES (est):** 4.89MM
**SALES (corp-wide):** 87.73MM **Privately Held**
**Web:** www.apct.com
**SIC: 3672** Circuit boards, television and radio printed
**HQ:** Apct, Inc.
3495 De La Cruz Blvd
Santa Clara CA 95054
408 727-6442

**(P-12058)**
**APT ELECTRONICS INC**
Also Called: APT Electronics
241 N Crescent Way, Anaheim (92801-6704)
**PHONE**.................714 687-6760
Tae Myoung Kim, CEO
**EMP:** 112 **EST:** 1999
**SQ FT:** 20,000
**SALES (est):** 24.76MM **Privately Held**
**Web:** www.aptelectronics.com
**SIC: 3672** Printed circuit boards

**(P-12059)**
**ARDENT SYSTEMS INC**
2040 Ringwood Ave, San Jose (95131-1728)
**PHONE**.................408 526-0100
Thomas Han, Pr
Young C Kang, *
**EMP:** 20 **EST:** 1989
**SQ FT:** 8,000
**SALES (est):** 2.47MM **Privately Held**
**Web:** www.ardentsi.com
**SIC: 3672** Printed circuit boards

**(P-12060)**
**ASTEELFLASH CALIFORNIA INC**
Also Called: Asteelflash Group
4211 Starboard Dr, Fremont (94538-6427)
**PHONE**.................510 440-2840
▲ **EMP:** 611
**SIC: 3672** Printed circuit boards

**(P-12061)**
**ASTEELFLASH USA CORP (DH)**
Also Called: Asteelflash Fremont
1940 Milmont Dr, Milpitas (95035-2578)
**PHONE**.................510 440-2840
Gilles Benhamou, CEO
Claude Savard, *
Vince Pradia, *
Pierre Laboisse, *
Albert Yanez, *
▲ **EMP:** 28 **EST:** 2011
**SALES (est):** 116.59MM
**SALES (corp-wide):** 12.35MM **Privately Held**
**Web:** www.asteelflash.com
**SIC: 3672** 3679 Printed circuit boards; Electronic circuits
**HQ:** Asteelflash France
1 Rue Royale
Saint-Cloud IDF 92210

**(P-12062)**
**ASTRONIC**
2 Orion, Aliso Viejo (92656-4200)
**PHONE**.................949 454-1180
Sang H Choi, CEO
Ok Kay Choi, Sec
▲ **EMP:** 143 **EST:** 1976
**SQ FT:** 41,000
**SALES (est):** 7.68MM **Privately Held**
**Web:** www.astronic-ems.com
**SIC: 3672** 1742 Printed circuit boards; Acoustical and insulation work

**(P-12063)**
**AVANTEC MANUFACTURING INC**
1811 N Case St, Orange (92865-4234)
**PHONE**.................714 532-6197
Alan E Mcneeney, CEO
▲ **EMP:** 20 **EST:** 2003
**SALES (est):** 5.1MM **Privately Held**
**Web:** www.avantecusa.com
**SIC: 3672** Printed circuit boards

**(P-12064)**
**BAY AREA CIRCUITS INC**
44358 Old Warm Springs Blvd, Fremont (94538-6148)
**PHONE**.................510 933-9000
Barbara Nobriga, Pr
▲ **EMP:** 48 **EST:** 1975
**SQ FT:** 7,500
**SALES (est):** 9.06MM **Privately Held**
**Web:** www.bayareacircuits.com
**SIC: 3672** Circuit boards, television and radio printed

**(P-12065)**
**BAY ELCTRNIC SPPORT TRNICS INC**
Also Called: Bestronics
2090 Fortune Dr, San Jose (95131-1823)
**PHONE**.................408 432-3222
Nat Mani, CEO
Ron Menigoz, *
▲ **EMP:** 155 **EST:** 1990
**SQ FT:** 150,000
**SALES (est):** 49.03MM
**SALES (corp-wide):** 49.03MM **Privately Held**
**Web:** www.emeraldems.com
**SIC: 3672** Circuit boards, television and radio printed
**PA:** Bestronics Holdings, Inc.
2090 Fortune Dr
408 385-7777

**(P-12066)**
**BEMA ELECTRONIC MFG INC**
4545 Cushing Pkwy, Fremont (94538-6466)
**PHONE**.................510 490-7770
Helen Kwong, Pr
Suju Kwong, *
▲ **EMP:** 100 **EST:** 1999
**SQ FT:** 26,205
**SALES (est):** 23.8MM **Privately Held**
**Web:** www.bemaelectronics.com
**SIC: 3672** Printed circuit boards

**(P-12067)**
**BENCHMARK ELEC MFG SLTIONS INC (HQ)**
5550 Hellyer Ave, San Jose (95138-1005)
**PHONE**.................805 222-1303
Jayne Desorcie, Admn
▲ **EMP:** 100 **EST:** 1986
**SQ FT:** 80,000
**SALES (est):** 38.36MM
**SALES (corp-wide):** 2.84B **Publicly Held**
**Web:** www.bench.com
**SIC: 3672** Printed circuit boards
**PA:** Benchmark Electronics, Inc.
56 S Rockford Dr
623 300-7000

**(P-12068)**
**BENCHMARK ELEC MFG SLTONS MRPA**
Also Called: Benchmark
200 Science Dr, Moorpark (93021-2003)
**PHONE**.................805 532-2800
Jayne Desorcie, Pr
**EMP:** 523 **EST:** 1986
**SALES (est):** 18.58MM
**SALES (corp-wide):** 2.84B **Publicly Held**
**Web:** www.bench.com
**SIC: 3672** Printed circuit boards
**HQ:** Benchmark Electronics Manufacturing Solutions Inc.
5550 Hellyer Ave
San Jose CA 95138
805 222-1303

**(P-12069)**
**BENCHMARK ELEC PHOENIX INC**
1659 Gailes Blvd, San Diego (92154-8230)
**PHONE**.................619 397-2402
Roberto Perez, Brnch Mgr
**EMP:** 300
**SALES (corp-wide):** 2.84B **Publicly Held**
**Web:** www.bench.com
**SIC: 3672** 3577 Printed circuit boards; Computer peripheral equipment, nec
**HQ:** Benchmark Electronics Phoenix, Inc.
56 S Rockford Dr
Tempe AZ 85288
623 300-7000

**(P-12070)**
**BENCHMARK ELECTRONICS INC**
42701 Christy St, Fremont (94538-3146)
**PHONE**.................510 360-2800
Robert Pruett, VP
**EMP:** 21
**SALES (corp-wide):** 2.84B **Publicly Held**
**Web:** www.bench.com
**SIC: 3672** Printed circuit boards
**PA:** Benchmark Electronics, Inc.
56 S Rockford Dr
623 300-7000

**(P-12071)**
**BENCHMARK ELECTRONICS INC**
2301 Arnold Industrial Way Ste G, Concord (94520-5379)
**PHONE**.................925 363-1151
Steve Tate, Brnch Mgr
**EMP:** 39
**SALES (corp-wide):** 2.84B **Publicly Held**
**Web:** www.bench.com
**SIC: 3672** Printed circuit boards
**PA:** Benchmark Electronics, Inc.
56 S Rockford Dr
623 300-7000

**(P-12072)**
**CAL-COMP USA (SAN DIEGO) INC**
1940 Camino Vida Roble, Carlsbad (92008-6516)
**PHONE**.................858 587-6900
Wei-chang Chen, CEO
**EMP:** 215 **EST:** 1995

## PRODUCTS & SERVICES SECTION
### 3672 - Printed Circuit Boards (P-12094)

SQ FT: 65,000
SALES (est): 19.58MM **Privately Held**
Web: www.calcompusa.com
SIC: 3672 Circuit boards, television and radio printed
HQ: Cal-Comp Electronics (Usa) Co., Ltd.
1940 Camino Vida Roble
Carlsbad CA
858 587-6900

### (P-12073)
### CALPAK USA INC
13748 Prairie Ave, Hawthorne (90250-7359)
PHONE.................................310 937-7335
Danish Qureshi, *Pr*
▲ EMP: 20 EST: 1978
SALES (est): 3.72MM **Privately Held**
Web: www.calpak-usa.com
SIC: 3672 3679 8742 4813 Printed circuit boards; Commutators, electronic; Management consulting services; Telephone communication, except radio

### (P-12074)
### CARTEL ELECTRONICS LLC
Also Called: Apct Orange County
1900 Petra Ln Ste C, Placentia (92870-6758)
PHONE.................................714 993-0270
▲ EMP: 85 EST: 1994
SALES (est): 20.69MM
SALES (corp-wide): 87.73MM **Privately Held**
Web: www.apct.com
SIC: 3672 Printed circuit boards
PA: Apct Holdings, Llc
3495 De La Cruz Blvd
408 727-6442

### (P-12075)
### CELESTICA AEROSPACE TECH CORP
Also Called: Celestica-Aerospace
895 S Rockefeller Ave Ste 102, Ontario (91761-8145)
PHONE.................................512 310-7540
Jeffrey Bain, *Pr*
Thomas Lovelock, *
Leslie K Sladek, *
▲ EMP: 200 EST: 2002
SQ FT: 55,000
SALES (est): 95.39MM
SALES (corp-wide): 7.96B **Privately Held**
Web: www.elitehealthchoices.com
SIC: 3672 Printed circuit boards
PA: Celestica Inc
1900-5140 Yonge St
416 448-5800

### (P-12076)
### CHAD INDUSTRIES INCORPORATED
Also Called: Chad
1565 S Sinclair St, Anaheim (92806-5934)
PHONE.................................714 938-0080
Scott W Klimczak, *Pr*
Wayne Rapp, *
▲ EMP: 40 EST: 1973
SQ FT: 31,000
SALES (est): 4.77MM **Privately Held**
SIC: 3672 Printed circuit boards

### (P-12077)
### CHOOSE MANUFACTURING CO LLC
24 Passion Flower, Irvine (92618-2252)
PHONE.................................714 327-1698
Herbert Chiu, *Managing Member*
▲ EMP: 20 EST: 2000
SALES (est): 2.26MM **Privately Held**
Web: www.choosemfg.com
SIC: 3672 Printed circuit boards

### (P-12078)
### CIRCUIT SERVICES LLC
Also Called: Career Tech Circuit Services
9134 Independence Ave, Chatsworth (91311-5902)
PHONE.................................818 701-5391
Marc Haugen, *CEO*
EMP: 43 EST: 1998
SALES (est): 32.62MM
SALES (corp-wide): 153.54MM **Privately Held**
Web: www.careertech-usa.com
SIC: 3672 Printed circuit boards
PA: Fralock Holdings Llc
28525 W Industry Dr
661 702-6999

### (P-12079)
### CIREXX INTERNATIONAL INC (PA)
791 Nuttman St, Santa Clara (95054-2623)
PHONE.................................408 988-3980
Philip Menges, *Pr*
Kurt H Menges, *
EMP: 115 EST: 2005
SALES (est): 21.46MM **Privately Held**
Web: www.cirexx.com
SIC: 3672 Circuit boards, television and radio printed

### (P-12080)
### COAST TO COAST CIRCUITS INC (PA)
Also Called: Speedy Circuits
5331 Mcfadden Ave, Huntington Beach (92649-1204)
PHONE.................................714 891-9441
Edward Porter, *CEO*
Ronald Scott Lawhead, *
◆ EMP: 41 EST: 1985
SQ FT: 40,000
SALES (est): 13.55MM **Privately Held**
Web: www.excello.com
SIC: 3672 Circuit boards, television and radio printed

### (P-12081)
### CONCEPT DEVELOPMENT LLC
Also Called: CDI
1881 Langley Ave, Irvine (92614-5623)
PHONE.................................949 623-8000
James M Reardon, *Pr*
EMP: 20 EST: 1972
SQ FT: 12,880
SALES (est): 2.45MM
SALES (corp-wide): 60.9MM **Publicly Held**
Web: www.onestopsystems.com
SIC: 3672 Printed circuit boards
PA: One Stop Systems, Inc.
2235 Entp St Ste 110
760 745-9883

### (P-12082)
### COPPER CLAD MLTILAYER PDTS INC
Also Called: C C M P
1150 N Hawk Cir, Anaheim (92807-1708)
PHONE.................................714 237-1388
Fred Ohanian, *Pr*
William Schwerter, *
▲ EMP: 25 EST: 1994
SQ FT: 13,200
SALES (est): 3.74MM **Privately Held**

### (P-12083)
### CREATION TECH CALEXICO INC (HQ)
Also Called: Aisling Industries
1778 Zinetta Rd Ste F, Calexico (92231-9510)
P.O. Box 1833 (92244)
▲ EMP: 25 EST: 1995
SQ FT: 10,000
SALES (est): 85.94MM
SALES (corp-wide): 656.54MM **Privately Held**
SIC: 3672 3679 Printed circuit boards; Electronic circuits
PA: Creation Technologies International Inc.
1 Beacon St
877 734-7456

### (P-12084)
### CTS CORPORATION
Also Called: CTS
2271 Ringwood Ave, San Jose (95131-1717)
PHONE.................................408 955-9001
Richard Dinh, *Mgr*
EMP: 17
SALES (corp-wide): 550.42MM **Publicly Held**
Web: www.ctscorp.com
SIC: 3672 Printed circuit boards
PA: Cts Corporation
4925 Indiana Ave
630 577-8800

### (P-12085)
### DALLAS ELECTRONICS INC
2151 Delaware Ave Ste A, Santa Cruz (95060-5788)
P.O. Box 2489 (95063-2489)
PHONE.................................831 457-3610
▲ EMP: 50
Web: www.dallaselectronics.com
SIC: 3672 3674 Printed circuit boards; Semiconductors and related devices

### (P-12086)
### DE LEON ENTPS ELEC SPCLIST INC
Also Called: De Leon Enterprises
11934 Allegheny St, Sun Valley (91352-1833)
PHONE.................................818 252-6690
Miguel De Leon, *Pr*
▲ EMP: 24 EST: 1994
SQ FT: 11,000
SALES (est): 2.6MM **Privately Held**
Web: www.deleonenterprises.com
SIC: 3672 Printed circuit boards

### (P-12087)
### DIGICOM ELECTRONICS INC
Also Called: Digicom Electronics
7799 Pardee Ln, Oakland (94621-1425)
PHONE.................................510 639-7003
Mohammed Ohady, *CEO*
Mohammed R Ohady, *
EMP: 32 EST: 1982
SALES (est): 6.63MM **Privately Held**
Web: www.digicom.org
SIC: 3672 Printed circuit boards

### (P-12088)
### DYNASTY ELECTRONIC COMPANY LLC
Also Called: Dec
1790 E Mcfadden Ave Ste 105, Santa Ana (92705-4638)
PHONE.................................714 550-1197
Fredrick Rodenhuis, *Managing Member*
Mark Clark, *
EMP: 65 EST: 2008
SQ FT: 10,000
SALES (est): 8.57MM **Privately Held**
Web: www.dec-assembly.com
SIC: 3672 Printed circuit boards

### (P-12089)
### ELECTRO SURFACE TECH INC
Also Called: E S T
2281 Las Palmas Dr # 101, Carlsbad (92011-1527)
PHONE.................................760 431-8306
Hiroo Kirpalani, *Pr*
EMP: 42 EST: 1989
SQ FT: 31,500
SALES (est): 2.41MM **Privately Held**
Web: www.est.com
SIC: 3672 Circuit boards, television and radio printed

### (P-12090)
### ELECTROMAX INC
1960 Concourse Dr, San Jose (95131-1719)
PHONE.................................408 428-9474
Aaron Wong, *Pr*
Ken Wong, *
▲ EMP: 50 EST: 1991
SQ FT: 30,000
SALES (est): 9.48MM **Privately Held**
Web: www.electromaxinc.com
SIC: 3672 Printed circuit boards

### (P-12091)
### ELECTRONIC SURFC MOUNTED INDS
Also Called: Esmi
6731 Cobra Way, San Diego (92121-4110)
PHONE.................................858 455-1710
Henry Kim, *Pr*
Lynn Kim, *
▼ EMP: 40 EST: 1986
SQ FT: 25,000
SALES (est): 5.59MM **Privately Held**
Web: www.esmiinc.com
SIC: 3672 Printed circuit boards

### (P-12092)
### ELECTROTEK CORPORATION
1108 W Evelyn Ave, Sunnyvale (94086-5742)
PHONE.................................414 762-1390
John Johnson, *Pr*
Michael Swerdlow, *
▲ EMP: 140 EST: 1968
SALES (est): 7.57MM **Privately Held**
Web: www.boards4u.com
SIC: 3672 Printed circuit boards

### (P-12093)
### ELMA BUSTRONIC CORP
44350 S Grimmer Blvd, Fremont (94538-6385)
PHONE.................................510 490-7388
EMP: 28
Web: www.elmabustronic.com
SIC: 3672 Printed circuit boards

### (P-12094)
### EMSOLUTIONS INC
2152 Zanker Rd, San Jose (95131-2113)
PHONE.................................510 668-1118
Jun Huo, *CEO*
EMP: 21 EST: 2008
SQ FT: 5,000
SALES (est): 2.6MM **Privately Held**
Web: www.emsolutionstech.com

# 3672 - Printed Circuit Boards (P-12095)

SIC: 3672 Printed circuit boards

**(P-12095)**
**ETI PARTNERS IV LLC**
901 Washington Blvd Ste 208, Marina Del Rey (90292)
PHONE..................949 273-4990
EMP: 20 EST: 2015
SALES (est) 526.92K Privately Held
SIC: 3672 Printed circuit boards

**(P-12096)**
**EXCELLO CIRCUITS INC**
Also Called: Speedy Circuits
5330 E Hunter Ave, Anaheim (92807-2053)
PHONE..................714 993-0560
Rax Ribadia, Pr
Sam Bhayani, *
Rax Ribadia, VP
Tushar Patel, *
EMP: 72 EST: 1992
SQ FT: 11,000
SALES (est): 9.11MM Privately Held
Web: www.excello.com
SIC: 3672 Printed circuit boards

**(P-12097)**
**EXPERT ASSEMBLY SERVICES INC**
Also Called: Expert Ems
14312 Chambers Rd Ste B, Tustin (92780-6912)
PHONE..................714 258-8880
Jack Quinn, CEO
EMP: 50 EST: 1997
SALES (est): 12.13MM Privately Held
Web: www.expertassembly.com
SIC: 3672 Printed circuit boards

**(P-12098)**
**FABRICATED COMPONENTS CORP**
Also Called: Summit Interconnect Orange
130 W Bristol Ln, Orange (92865-2640)
PHONE..................714 974-8590
Shane Whiteside, Pr
▼ EMP: 140 EST: 1979
SQ FT: 40,000
SALES (est): 9.93MM Privately Held
Web: www.fabricatedcomponents.com
SIC: 3672 Printed circuit boards

**(P-12099)**
**FABRINET WEST INC**
Also Called: Fabrinet West
4900 Patrick Henry Dr, Santa Clara (95054-1822)
PHONE..................408 748-0900
Tom Mitchell, CEO
▲ EMP: 89 EST: 2015
SALES (est): 25.05MM Privately Held
Web: www.fabrinet.com
SIC: 3672 3999 Printed circuit boards; Atomizers, toiletry
PA: Fabrinet
C/O Intertrust Corporate Services (Cayman) Limited

**(P-12100)**
**FINE LINE CIRCUITS & TECH INC**
594 Apollo St Ste A, Brea (92821-3134)
PHONE..................714 529-2942
Rick Bajaria, Pr
Ken Pansuria, *
Vinny Kathrotia, *
EMP: 30 EST: 1995
SQ FT: 20,000
SALES (est): 4.47MM Privately Held
Web: www.finelinecircuits.com

SIC: 3672 Circuit boards, television and radio printed

**(P-12101)**
**FINE PTCH ELCTRNIC ASSMBLY LLC**
Also Called: Fine Pitch
5106 Azusa Canyon Rd, Irwindale (91706-1846)
PHONE..................626 337-2800
Ashish Sheladiya, Managing Member
EMP: 20 EST: 2004
SQ FT: 15,000
SALES (est): 4.12MM Privately Held
Web: www.finepitchassembly.com
SIC: 3672 Printed circuit boards

**(P-12102)**
**FLEX INTERCONNECT TECH INC**
Also Called: Flex Interconnect Technologies
1603 Watson Ct, Milpitas (95035-6806)
PHONE..................408 956-8204
Chetan Shah, CEO
Dean Matsuo, *
EMP: 41 EST: 1998
SQ FT: 15,000
SALES (est): 5.49MM Privately Held
Web: www.fit4flex.com
SIC: 3672 Printed circuit boards

**(P-12103)**
**FLEXTRONICS AMERICA LLC**
6201 America Center Dr, Alviso (95002-2563)
PHONE..................512 425-4129
EMP: 121
Web: www.flex.com
SIC: 3672 Printed circuit boards
HQ: Flextronics America, Llc
12455 Research Blvd
Austin TX 78759
408 576-7000

**(P-12104)**
**FLEXTRONICS AMERICA LLC**
777 Gibraltar Dr, Milpitas (95035-6328)
PHONE..................408 576-7156
EMP: 142
Web: www.flex.com
SIC: 3672 Printed circuit boards
HQ: Flextronics America, Llc
12455 Research Blvd
Austin TX 78759
408 576-7000

**(P-12105)**
**FLEXTRONICS INTL PA INC**
677 Gibraltar Dr, Milpitas (95035-6335)
PHONE..................408 577-2489
EMP: 15
Web: www.flex.com
SIC: 3672 Printed circuit boards
HQ: Flextronics International Pa, Inc.
6201 America Ctr Dr
San Jose CA 95002
408 576-7000

**(P-12106)**
**FLEXTRONICS INTL USA INC**
727 Gibraltar Dr, Milpitas (95035-6328)
PHONE..................408 576-7492
EMP: 69
Web: www.flex.com
SIC: 3672 Printed circuit boards
HQ: Flextronics International Usa, Inc.
6201 America Ctr Dr
San Jose CA 95002

**(P-12107)**
**FLEXTRONICS INTL USA INC**
260 S Milpitas Blvd Bldg 15, Milpitas (95035-5420)
PHONE..................408 576-7000
Matt Bryan, Brnch Mgr
EMP: 309
Web: www.flex.com
SIC: 3672 3679 Printed circuit boards; Power supplies, all types: static
HQ: Flextronics International Usa, Inc.
6201 America Ctr Dr
San Jose CA 95002

**(P-12108)**
**FLEXTRONICS INTL USA INC**
927 Gibraltar Dr, Milpitas (95035-6336)
PHONE..................510 814-7000
EMP: 135
Web: www.flex.com
SIC: 3672 Printed circuit boards
HQ: Flextronics International Usa, Inc.
6201 America Ctr Dr
San Jose CA 95002

**(P-12109)**
**FLEXTRONICS INTL USA INC**
1177 Gibraltar Dr Bldg 9, Milpitas (95035-6337)
PHONE..................408 678-3268
EMP: 48
Web: www.flex.com
SIC: 3672 Printed circuit boards
HQ: Flextronics International Usa, Inc.
6201 America Ctr Dr
San Jose CA 95002

**(P-12110)**
**FLEXTRONICS INTL USA INC**
777 Gibraltar Dr, Milpitas (95035-6328)
PHONE..................408 577-4874
EMP: 131
Web: www.flex.com
SIC: 3672 Printed circuit boards
HQ: Flextronics International Usa, Inc.
6201 America Ctr Dr
San Jose CA 95002

**(P-12111)**
**FLEXTRONICS INTL USA INC**
1077 Gibraltar Dr, Milpitas (95035-6324)
PHONE..................408 577-7044
Kevin Daugherty, Brnch Mgr
EMP: 150
Web: www.flex.com
SIC: 3672 Printed circuit boards
HQ: Flextronics International Usa, Inc.
6201 America Ctr Dr
San Jose CA 95002

**(P-12112)**
**FLEXTRONICS INTL USA INC**
847 Gibraltar Dr, Milpitas (95035-6332)
PHONE..................408 576-7076
EMP: 113
Web: www.flex.com
SIC: 3672 Printed circuit boards
HQ: Flextronics International Usa, Inc.
6201 America Ctr Dr
San Jose CA 95002

**(P-12113)**
**FLEXTRONICS INTL USA INC**
925 Lightpost Way, Morgan Hill (95037-2869)
PHONE..................408 577-2262
EMP: 263
Web: www.flex.com

SIC: 3672 Printed circuit boards
HQ: Flextronics International Usa, Inc.
6201 America Ctr Dr
San Jose CA 95002

**(P-12114)**
**FLEXTRONICS INTL USA INC**
6201 America Center Dr, San Jose (95002-2563)
PHONE..................408 576-7000
EMP: 2000
Web: www.flex.com
SIC: 3672 Printed circuit boards
HQ: Flextronics International Usa, Inc.
6201 America Center Dr
San Jose CA 95002

**(P-12115)**
**FLEXTRONICS INTL USA INC (HQ)**
Also Called: Flex
6201 America Center Dr, San Jose (95002-2563)
PHONE..................408 576-7000
Revathi Advaithi, CEO
Jason Spicer, *
David Bennett, *
▲ EMP: 892 EST: 1987
SQ FT: 100,000
SALES (est): 2.17B Privately Held
Web: www.flex.com
SIC: 3672 Printed circuit boards
PA: Flex Ltd.
2 Changi South Lane

**(P-12116)**
**FLEXTRONICS INTL USA INC**
Also Called: Flextronics Global Services
890 Yosemite Dr, Milpitas (95035-5437)
PHONE..................408 576-6769
Mike Mcnamara, Prin
EMP: 152
Web: www.flex.com
SIC: 3672 Printed circuit boards
HQ: Flextronics International Usa, Inc.
6201 America Center Dr
San Jose CA 95002

**(P-12117)**
**FLEXTRONICS LOGISTICS USA INC (DH)**
Also Called: Flex
6201 America Center Dr Fl 6, San Jose (95101)
PHONE..................408 576-7000
Jason D Spicer, CEO
Timothy Stewart, Sec
Daniel Wendler, CFO
▲ EMP: 65 EST: 2001
SALES (est): 24.68MM Privately Held
SIC: 3672 Printed circuit boards
HQ: Flextronics International Usa, Inc.
6201 America Ctr Dr
San Jose CA 95002

**(P-12118)**
**FTG CIRCUITS INC (DH)**
20750 Marilla St, Chatsworth (91311-4407)
PHONE..................818 407-4024
Brad Bourne, CEO
Michael Labrador, *
Joe Ricci, *
Ed Hanna, *
▼ EMP: 91 EST: 1956
SQ FT: 38,000
SALES (est): 15.39MM
SALES (corp-wide): 98.06MM Privately Held
Web: www.ftgcorp.com

## PRODUCTS & SERVICES SECTION
### 3672 - Printed Circuit Boards (P-12141)

SIC: 3672 3644 Printed circuit boards;
Terminal boards
HQ: Firan Technology Group (Usa)
Corporation
20750 Marilla St
Chatsworth CA 91311
818 407-4024

**(P-12119)**
**G2 MICROSYSTEMS INC**
1999 S Baston Ave, Campbell (95008)
PHONE.................................408 879-2614
Geoff Smith, *Pr*
EMP: 50 EST: 2004
SALES (est): 2.28MM **Privately Held**
SIC: 3672 Printed circuit boards

**(P-12120)**
**GAVIAL ENGINEERING & MFG INC**
1435 W Mccoy Ln, Santa Maria (93455-1002)
PHONE.................................805 614-0060
Don Connors, *Pr*
Ken Hicks, *
Stanley D Connors, *
EMP: 50 EST: 2012
SQ FT: 25,000
SALES (est): 3.56MM
SALES (corp-wide): 40.31MM **Privately Held**
Web: www.gavial.com
SIC: 3672 3679 Printed circuit boards;
Electronic circuits
PA: Gavial Holdings, Inc.
1435 W Mccoy Ln
805 614-0060

**(P-12121)**
**GEERIRAJ INC**
Also Called: Mer-Mar Electronics
7042 Santa Fe Ave E Ste A1, Hesperia (92345-5711)
PHONE.................................760 244-6149
Kanjibhai Ghadia, *Pr*
Suresh Patel, *
EMP: 28 EST: 1974
SQ FT: 22,000
SALES (est): 4.95MM **Privately Held**
SIC: 3672 Printed circuit boards

**(P-12122)**
**GENERAL ELEC ASSEMBLY INC**
1525 Atteberry Ln, San Jose (95131-1412)
PHONE.................................408 980-8819
Eric Chang, *Pr*
EMP: 45 EST: 1992
SQ FT: 16,000
SALES (est): 5.27MM **Privately Held**
Web: www.geamfg.com
SIC: 3672 Wiring boards

**(P-12123)**
**GOLDEN WEST TECHNOLOGY**
1180 E Valencia Dr, Fullerton (92831-4627)
PHONE.................................714 738-3775
Dan P Rieth, *Pr*
EMP: 60 EST: 1974
SQ FT: 30,000
SALES (est): 9.21MM **Privately Held**
Web: www.goldenwesttech.com
SIC: 3672 Printed circuit boards

**(P-12124)**
**GORILLA CIRCUITS (PA)**
1445 Oakland Rd, San Jose (95112-1203)
PHONE.................................408 294-9897
Hershel Petty, *CEO*
Jaime Gutierrez, *
▲ EMP: 166 EST: 1967
SQ FT: 60,000
SALES (est): 45.11MM
SALES (corp-wide): 45.11MM **Privately Held**
Web: www.gorillacircuits.com
SIC: 3672 Circuit boards, television and radio printed

**(P-12125)**
**GRAPHIC RESEARCH INC**
3339 Durham Ct, Burbank (91504-1600)
PHONE.................................818 886-7340
Govind R Vaghashia, *Pr*
Pete Vaghashia, *
▲ EMP: 50 EST: 1966
SALES (est): 3.88MM **Privately Held**
Web: www.graphicresearch.com
SIC: 3672 Printed circuit boards

**(P-12126)**
**GREEN CIRCUITS INC**
1130 Ringwood Ct, San Jose (95131-1726)
PHONE.................................408 526-1700
Michael Hinshaw, *CEO*
Mark Evans, *
Richard Dutton, *
Jennie Tran Senior, *Prs Dir*
Adam Szychonski, *Marketing*
▲ EMP: 187 EST: 2006
SQ FT: 15,000
SALES (est): 55.31MM **Privately Held**
Web: www.greencircuits.com
SIC: 3672 Printed circuit boards

**(P-12127)**
**HAMBY CORPORATION**
27704 Avenue Scott, Valencia (91355-1218)
PHONE.................................661 257-1924
EMP: 23 EST: 1956
SALES (est): 828.51K **Privately Held**
Web: www.hambycorp.com
SIC: 3672 Printed circuit boards

**(P-12128)**
**HARBOR ELECTRONICS INC (PA)**
3021 Kenneth St, Santa Clara (95054-3416)
PHONE.................................408 988-6544
Christopher Cuda, *Pr*
Thomas Bleakley, *
Qing Lin, *
EMP: 190 EST: 2016
SQ FT: 50,000
SALES (est): 56.75MM
SALES (corp-wide): 56.75MM **Privately Held**
Web: www.harbor-electronics.com
SIC: 3672 Printed circuit boards

**(P-12129)**
**HI TECH ELECTRONIC MFG CORP**
Also Called: Hitem
1938 Avenida Del Oro, Oceanside (92056-5803)
PHONE.................................858 657-0908
Thai Nguyen, *CEO*
Vinh Lam, *
Tran Vu, *
▲ EMP: 82 EST: 1997
SALES (est): 11MM **Privately Held**
Web: www.hitem.com
SIC: 3672 Circuit boards, television and radio printed

**(P-12130)**
**HUGHES CIRCUITS INC (PA)**
Also Called: Hci
546 S Pacific St, San Marcos (92078)
PHONE.................................760 744-0300
Barbara Hughes, *CEO*
Jerry Hughes, *
Michelle Glatts, *
Joe Hughes, *
Steve Hughes, *
EMP: 99 EST: 1999
SQ FT: 50,000
SALES (est): 36.08MM
SALES (corp-wide): 36.08MM **Privately Held**
Web: www.hughescircuits.com
SIC: 3672 3679 8711 3444 Printed circuit boards; Electronic circuits; Engineering services; Sheet metalwork

**(P-12131)**
**HUGHES CIRCUITS INC**
Also Called: Pcb Fabrication Facility
540 S Pacific St, San Marcos (92078-4050)
PHONE.................................760 744-0300
Barbara Hughes, *Brnch Mgr*
EMP: 126
SALES (corp-wide): 36.08MM **Privately Held**
Web: www.hughescircuits.com
SIC: 3672 Circuit boards, television and radio printed
PA: Hughes Circuits, Inc.
546 S Pacific St
760 744-0300

**(P-12132)**
**HYBOND INC**
330 State Pl, Escondido (92029-1364)
PHONE.................................760 746-7105
Hanns Lindberg, *CEO*
EMP: 15 EST: 1980
SQ FT: 7,500
SALES (est): 2.56MM **Privately Held**
Web: www.hybond.com
SIC: 3672 Printed circuit boards

**(P-12133)**
**HYTEK R&D INC (PA)**
Also Called: R & D Tech
2044 Corporate Ct, Milpitas (95035)
PHONE.................................408 761-5266
Dave Linedaugh, *Pr*
EMP: 22 EST: 2008
SALES (est): 1.76MM **Privately Held**
SIC: 3672 5063 Printed circuit boards; Electrical supplies, nec

**(P-12134)**
**IMPACT PROJECT MANAGEMENT INC**
2872 S Santa Fe Ave, San Marcos (92069-6046)
PHONE.................................760 747-6616
Randy Scott Walker, *Pr*
Debbie Walker, *
▲ EMP: 19 EST: 2001
SALES (est): 3.23MM **Privately Held**
Web: www.impactprojects.com
SIC: 3672 Printed circuit boards

**(P-12135)**
**INDTEC CORPORATION**
3348 Paul Davis Dr Ste 109, Marina (93933-2258)
P.O. Box 1998 (93955-1998)
PHONE.................................831 582-9388
Dung Van Trinh, *Pr*
Lily Pham, *Sec*
EMP: 34 EST: 1991
SQ FT: 5,000
SALES (est): 6.81MM **Privately Held**
Web: www.indtec.net
SIC: 3672 Circuit boards, television and radio printed

**(P-12136)**
**INNERSTEP BSE**
4742 Scotts Valley Dr, Scotts Valley (95066-4231)
PHONE.................................831 461-5600
▲ EMP: 63
SIC: 3672 3679 Printed circuit boards; Power supplies, all types: static

**(P-12137)**
**IPC CAL FLEX INC**
13337 South St # 307, Cerritos (90703-7308)
PHONE.................................714 952-0373
Scott Kohno, *Pr*
EMP: 25 EST: 1980
SQ FT: 25,000
SALES (est): 1.62MM **Privately Held**
SIC: 3672 Printed circuit boards

**(P-12138)**
**IRVINE ELECTRONICS LLC**
Also Called: Irvine Electronics Inc
1601 Alton Pkwy Ste A, Irvine (92606-4801)
PHONE.................................949 250-0315
Jane Zerounian, *Pr*
Onnig Zerounian, *
EMP: 100 EST: 1969
SQ FT: 48,000
SALES (est): 24.05MM
SALES (corp-wide): 912.8MM **Privately Held**
Web: www.volex.com
SIC: 3672 Circuit boards, television and radio printed
PA: Volex Plc
Unit C
203 370-8830

**(P-12139)**
**ISU PETASYS CORP**
12930 Bradley Ave, Sylmar (91342-3829)
PHONE.................................818 833-5800
Yong Kyoun Kim, *Pr*
▲ EMP: 95 EST: 1997
SQ FT: 50,000
SALES (est): 21.11MM **Privately Held**
Web: www.isupetasys.com
SIC: 3672 Printed circuit boards
PA: Isu Chemical Co., Ltd.
84 Sapyeong-Daero, Seocho-Gu

**(P-12140)**
**JABIL INC**
4050 Technology Pl, Fremont (94538-6362)
PHONE.................................510 353-1000
EMP: 112
SALES (corp-wide): 28.88B **Publicly Held**
Web: www.jabil.com
SIC: 3672 Printed circuit boards
PA: Jabil Inc.
10800 Roosevelt Blvd N
727 577-9749

**(P-12141)**
**JABIL INC**
Also Called: Jabil
1925 Lundy Ave, San Jose (95131-1847)
PHONE.................................408 361-3200
Thomas Costkel, *Mgr*
EMP: 74
SALES (corp-wide): 28.88B **Publicly Held**
Web: www.jabil.com

## 3672 - Printed Circuit Boards (P-12142)

SIC: 3672 Printed circuit boards
PA: Jabil Inc.
    10800 Roosevelt Blvd N
    727 577-9749

**(P-12142)**
**JABIL INC**
Stackvelocity
6375 San Ignacio Ave, San Jose (95119-1200)
PHONE..................408 360-3475
EMP: 218
SALES (corp-wide): 28.88B Publicly Held
Web: www.jabil.com
SIC: 3672 Printed circuit boards
PA: Jabil Inc.
    10800 Roosevelt Blvd N
    727 577-9749

**(P-12143)**
**JABIL INC**
Also Called: Jabil Chad Automation
1565 S Sinclair St, Anaheim (92806-5934)
PHONE..................714 938-0080
Babak Naderi, *Dir Opers*
EMP: 50
SALES (corp-wide): 28.88B Publicly Held
Web: www.jabil.com
SIC: 3672 Printed circuit boards
PA: Jabil Inc.
    10800 Roosevelt Blvd N
    727 577-9749

**(P-12144)**
**JABIL INC**
122 Lindbergh Ave, Livermore (94551-9569)
PHONE..................925 447-2000
EMP: 32 EST: 2017
SALES (est): 7.43MM Privately Held
Web: www.jabil.com
SIC: 3672 Printed circuit boards

**(P-12145)**
**JABIL INC**
Also Called: Jabil Circuit
30 Great Oaks Blvd, San Jose (95119-1309)
PHONE..................408 361-3200
EMP: 500
SALES (corp-wide): 28.88B Publicly Held
Web: www.jabil.com
SIC: 3672 Printed circuit boards
PA: Jabil Inc.
    10800 Roosevelt Blvd N
    727 577-9749

**(P-12146)**
**JATON CORPORATION**
Also Called: Holy High Wines
47677 Lakeview Blvd, Fremont (94538-6544)
PHONE..................510 933-8888
Vicky Hong, *Pr*
J S Chiang, *
▲ EMP: 24 EST: 1982
SQ FT: 85,000
SALES (est): 962.59K Privately Held
Web: www.jaton.com
SIC: 3672 3674 3661 3577 Printed circuit boards; Modules, solid state; Modems; Computer peripheral equipment, nec

**(P-12147)**
**K L ELECTRONIC INC**
3083 S Harbor Blvd, Santa Ana (92704-6448)
PHONE..................714 751-5611
Khanh Ton, *Pr*
Luon Ton, *Sec*
Michael Ton, *CEO*
EMP: 46 EST: 1981
SQ FT: 4,000
SALES (est): 3.13MM Privately Held
Web: www.klelectronics.com
SIC: 3672 Printed circuit boards

**(P-12148)**
**KCA ELECTRONICS INC**
Also Called: Summit Interconnect - Anaheim
223 N Crescent Way, Anaheim (92801-6704)
PHONE..................714 239-2433
Shane Whiteside, *Pr*
▲ EMP: 180 EST: 1992
SQ FT: 60,000
SALES (est): 14.03MM
SALES (corp-wide): 1.78B Privately Held
Web: www.kcamerica.com
SIC: 3672 Circuit boards, television and radio printed
HQ: Equity Hci Management L P
    1730 Pennsylvania Ave Nw # 525
    Washington DC

**(P-12149)**
**KIMBALL ELECTRONICS IND INC**
Also Called: Global Equipment Services
5215 Hellyer Ave Ste 130, San Jose (95138-1090)
PHONE..................669 234-1110
Christopher Thyen, *VP*
Christopher Thyen, *OF NEW PLATFORMS*
EMP: 40 EST: 2018
SQ FT: 154
SALES (est): 1.2B
SALES (corp-wide): 1.71B Publicly Held
Web: www.kimballelectronics.com
SIC: 3672 8711 7371 Printed circuit boards; Engineering services; Computer software development
PA: Kimball Electronics, Inc.
    1205 Kimball Blvd
    812 634-4000

**(P-12150)**
**LAMINATING COMPANY OF AMERICA**
Also Called: Lcoa
20322 Windrow Dr Ste 100, Lake Forest (92630-8150)
PHONE..................949 587-3300
Tim Redfern, *Pr*
Brad Biddol, *
▲ EMP: 30 EST: 1971
SALES (est): 2.25MM Privately Held
Web: www.lcoa.com
SIC: 3672 Printed circuit boards

**(P-12151)**
**LARITECH INC**
5898 Condor Dr, Moorpark (93021-2603)
PHONE..................805 529-5000
William Larrick, *CEO*
Terry Gonzales, *
Joel Butler, *
EMP: 111 EST: 2001
SQ FT: 13,000
SALES (est): 32.82MM Privately Held
Web: www.laritech.com
SIC: 3672 Printed circuit boards

**(P-12152)**
**LEEMAH ELECTRONICS INC (HQ)**
155 S Hill Dr, Brisbane (94005-1203)
PHONE..................415 394-1288
▲ EMP: 40 EST: 1984
SALES (est): 56.83MM
SALES (corp-wide): 127.87MM Privately Held
Web: www.leemah.com
SIC: 3672 Printed circuit boards
PA: Leemah Corporation
    155 S Hill Dr
    415 394-1288

**(P-12153)**
**LENTHOR ENGINEERING INC**
Also Called: Fralock
311 Turquoise St, Milpitas (95035-5432)
PHONE..................408 945-8787
EMP: 190 EST: 1977
SALES (est): 35MM
SALES (corp-wide): 153.54MM Privately Held
Web: www.lenthor.com
SIC: 3672 Printed circuit boards
PA: Fralock Holdings Llc
    28525 W Industry Dr
    661 702-6999

**(P-12154)**
**LIFETIME MEMORY PRODUCTS INC**
2505 Da Vinci Ste A, Irvine (92614-0170)
P.O. Box 1207 (92652-1207)
PHONE..................949 794-9000
Paul Columbus, *CEO*
Cameron Hum, *
◆ EMP: 40 EST: 1981
SQ FT: 16,000
SALES (est): 852.13K Privately Held
Web: www.lifetimememory.com
SIC: 3672 5045 3674 Printed circuit boards; Computers, peripherals, and software; Semiconductors and related devices

**(P-12155)**
**MARCEL ELECTRONICS INC**
130 W Bristol Ln, Orange (92865-2637)
PHONE..................714 974-8590
EMP: 34 EST: 2014
SALES (est): 5.18MM Privately Held
SIC: 3672 Printed circuit boards

**(P-12156)**
**MATRIX USA INC**
2730 S Main St, Santa Ana (92707-3435)
PHONE..................714 825-0404
Kieran Healy, *Pr*
George Potocska, *
Sharon Nioson, *Branch Administrator**
▲ EMP: 25 EST: 2005
SALES (est): 11.37MM
SALES (corp-wide): 9.15MM Privately Held
Web: www.matrixelectronics.com
SIC: 3672 Printed circuit boards
HQ: Matrix Electronics Limited
    1124 Mid-Way Blvd
    Mississauga ON L5T 2
    905 670-8400

**(P-12157)**
**MAXTROL CORPORATION**
1701 E Edinger Ave Ste B6, Santa Ana (92705-5010)
PHONE..................714 245-0506
Uri Ranon, *Pr*
Leo Pardo, *
EMP: 40 EST: 1990
SQ FT: 5,000
SALES (est): 2.44MM Privately Held
Web: www.maxtrol.com
SIC: 3672 Printed circuit boards

**(P-12158)**
**MC ELECTRONICS LLC**
1891 Airway Dr, Hollister (95023-9099)
PHONE..................831 637-1651
EMP: 399 EST: 1981
SQ FT: 6,000
SALES (est): 25.26MM
SALES (corp-wide): 912.8MM Privately Held
Web: www.volex.com
SIC: 3672 Printed circuit boards
PA: Volex Plc
    Unit C
    203 370-8830

**(P-12159)**
**MER-MAR ELECTRONICS INC**
7042 Santa Fe Ave E Ste A1, Hesperia (92345-5711)
PHONE..................760 244-6149
EMP: 15 EST: 2021
SALES (est): 5.63MM Privately Held
Web: www.mermarinc.com
SIC: 3672 Printed circuit boards

**(P-12160)**
**MERCURY SYSTEMS INC**
400 Del Norte Blvd, Oxnard (93030-7997)
PHONE..................805 388-1345
Deepak Alagh, *Brnch Mgr*
EMP: 110
SALES (corp-wide): 835.27MM Publicly Held
Web: www.mrcy.com
SIC: 3672 Printed circuit boards
PA: Mercury Systems, Inc.
    50 Minuteman Rd
    978 256-1300

**(P-12161)**
**MERCURY SYSTEMS INC**
300 Del Norte Blvd, Oxnard (93030-7217)
PHONE..................805 751-1100
Deepak Alagh, *Brnch Mgr*
EMP: 153
SALES (corp-wide): 835.27MM Publicly Held
Web: www.mrcy.com
SIC: 3672 Printed circuit boards
PA: Mercury Systems, Inc.
    50 Minuteman Rd
    978 256-1300

**(P-12162)**
**MERITRONICS INC (PA)**
500 Yosemite Dr Ste 108, Milpitas (95035-5467)
PHONE..................408 969-0888
Cherng Dior Wu, *Pr*
▲ EMP: 29 EST: 1995
SQ FT: 34,000
SALES (est): 13.36MM Privately Held
Web: www.meritronics.com
SIC: 3672 Printed circuit boards

**(P-12163)**
**MERITRONICS MATERIALS INC**
Also Called: Merit Assembly
42660 Christy St, Fremont (94538-3135)
PHONE..................408 390-5642
Richard Maldonado, *Pr*
EMP: 18 EST: 2017
SALES (est): 4.34MM Privately Held
SIC: 3672 3679 Printed circuit boards; Electronic circuits

**(P-12164)**
**MFLEX DELAWARE INC**
101 Academy Ste 250, Irvine (92617-3035)
PHONE..................949 453-6800
Reza A Meshgin, *CEO*
EMP: 4933 EST: 2019
SALES (est): 1.1MM Privately Held

## 3672 - Printed Circuit Boards (P-12186)

SIC: 3672 Printed circuit boards
HQ: Multi-Fineline Electronix, Inc.
   101 Academy Ste 250
   Irvine CA 92617
   949 453-6800

**(P-12165)**
**MODALAI INC**
10855 Sorrento Valley Rd Ste 2, San Diego (92121-1616)
PHONE..............................858 247-7053
Charles Sweet Iii, CEO
Charles Wheeler Sweet Iii, CEO
EMP: 38 EST: 2018
SALES (est): 5.37MM Privately Held
Web: www.modalai.com
SIC: 3672 Printed circuit boards

**(P-12166)**
**MORGAN-ROYCE INDUSTRIES INC**
Also Called: Morgan-Royce Industries
47730 Westinghouse Dr, Fremont (94539-7475)
PHONE..............................510 440-8500
EMP: 23 EST: 1991
SALES (est): 4.75MM Privately Held
Web: www.morganroyce.com
SIC: 3672 3679 3613 Printed circuit boards; Electronic circuits; Control panels, electric
PA: Golden State Assembly, Inc.
   47823 Westinghouse Dr

**(P-12167)**
**MULTI-FINELINE ELECTRONIX INC (HQ)**
Also Called: Mflex
101 Academy Ste 250, Irvine (92617-3035)
PHONE..............................949 453-6800
Reza Meshgin, Pr
Christine Besnard, *
Tom Kampfer, *
Neil Liu, CIO*
Thomas Lee, *
EMP: 583 EST: 1984
SQ FT: 20,171
SALES (est): 33.12MM Privately Held
Web: www.mflex.com
SIC: 3672 Printed circuit boards
PA: Suzhou Dongshan Precision Manufacturing Co., Ltd.
   8 Fenghuangshan Road Dongshan Town, Wuzhong District

**(P-12168)**
**MULTILAYER PROTOTYPES INC**
Also Called: Mpi
2320 Terra Bella Ln, Camarillo (93012-9080)
PHONE..............................805 498-9390
Steve Ferris, Pr
Dara Garza, Sec
EMP: 19 EST: 1981
SALES (est): 2.5MM Privately Held
Web: www.mpi-pcb.com
SIC: 3672 Circuit boards, television and radio printed

**(P-12169)**
**MULTIMEK INC**
357 Reed St, Santa Clara (95050-3107)
PHONE..............................408 653-1300
Doug Mccown, Pr
EMP: 20 EST: 1980
SQ FT: 8,000
SALES (est): 2.56MM Privately Held
Web: www.multimek.com
SIC: 3672 Printed circuit boards

**(P-12170)**
**MURRIETTA CIRCUITS**
5000 E Landon Dr, Anaheim (92807-1978)
PHONE..............................714 970-2430
Andrew Murrietta, CEO
Albert G Murrietta, *
Albert A Murrietta, *
Josh Murrietta, OK Vice President*
Helen Murrietta, *
EMP: 105 EST: 1992
SQ FT: 48,500
SALES (est): 21.95MM Privately Held
Web: www.murrietta.com
SIC: 3672 8711 Printed circuit boards; Engineering services

**(P-12171)**
**NAPROTEK LLC (PA)**
90 Rose Orchard Way, San Jose (95134-1356)
PHONE..............................408 830-5000
Teh-kuang Lung, Pr
EMP: 43 EST: 1995
SQ FT: 24,000
SALES (est): 31.45MM Privately Held
Web: www.naprotek.com
SIC: 3672 Circuit boards, television and radio printed

**(P-12172)**
**NASO INDUSTRIES CORPORATION**
Also Called: Naso Technologies
3007 Bunsen Ave Ste Q, Ventura (93003-7634)
PHONE..............................805 650-1231
Jahansooz Saleh, CEO
Namdar Saleh, *
Bryan Howe, *
Mike White, *
Soraya Saleh, *
EMP: 40 EST: 1990
SQ FT: 20,000
SALES (est): 15.68MM Privately Held
Web: www.naso.com
SIC: 3672 3599 Printed circuit boards; Machine shop, jobbing and repair

**(P-12173)**
**NATEL ENGINEERING HOLDINGS INC**
9340 Owensmouth Ave, Chatsworth (91311-6915)
PHONE..............................818 734-6500
EMP: 65 EST: 2015
SALES (est): 5.68MM Privately Held
Web: www.neotech.com
SIC: 3672 Printed circuit boards

**(P-12174)**
**NBS DESIGN INC**
1940 Milmont Dr, Milpitas (95035-2578)
PHONE..............................805 966-9383
▲ EMP: 265
SIC: 3672 Printed circuit boards

**(P-12175)**
**NEO TECH INC**
48119 Warm Springs Blvd, Fremont (94539-7498)
PHONE..............................510 360-2222
EMP: 16 EST: 2017
SALES (est): 4.81MM Privately Held
Web: www.neotech.com
SIC: 3672 Printed circuit boards

**(P-12176)**
**NEW BRUNSWICK INDUSTRIES INC**
5656 La Jolla Blvd, La Jolla (92037-7523)
PHONE..............................619 448-4900
Jim Krehbiel, Pr
Sue Harnack, *
Sue Krehbiel, *
EMP: 30 EST: 1982
SALES (est): 4.29MM Privately Held
Web: www.nbiinc.com
SIC: 3672 Circuit boards, television and radio printed

**(P-12177)**
**NEXLOGIC TECHNOLOGIES LLC**
2085 Zanker Rd, San Jose (95131)
PHONE..............................408 436-8150
Zulki Khan, Pr
▲ EMP: 76 EST: 1995
SALES (est): 8.19MM Privately Held
Web: www.naprotek.com
SIC: 3672 Printed circuit boards
PA: Naprotek, Llc
   90 Rose Orchard Way

**(P-12178)**
**NORTHWEST CIRCUITS CORP**
8660 Avenida Costa Blanca, San Diego (92154-6232)
PHONE..............................619 661-1701
Toribio Lobato, Pr
▲ EMP: 65 EST: 1991
SQ FT: 12,000
SALES (est): 10.65MM Privately Held
Web: www.nwcircuits.com
SIC: 3672 Printed circuit boards

**(P-12179)**
**NPI SERVICES INC**
1580 Corporate Dr Ste 124, Costa Mesa (92626-1460)
PHONE..............................714 850-0550
Judith Greenspon, CEO
Judith Greenspon, Pr
Juliann Ranieri, Contrlr
EMP: 15 EST: 1998
SQ FT: 5,880
SALES (est): 6.09MM Privately Held
Web: www.npiservices.com
SIC: 3672 3825 7389 8742 Printed circuit boards; Test equipment for electronic and electric measurement; Printed circuitry graphic layout; Management engineering

**(P-12180)**
**ONCORE MANUFACTURING LLC**
6600 Stevenson Blvd, Fremont (94538-2471)
PHONE..............................510 516-5488
James Liow, Brnch Mgr
EMP: 99
SALES (corp-wide): 1.43B Privately Held
Web: www.neotech.com
SIC: 3672 8711 Printed circuit boards; Electrical or electronic engineering
HQ: Oncore Manufacturing Llc
   9340 Owensmouth Ave
   Chatsworth CA 91311

**(P-12181)**
**ONCORE MANUFACTURING LLC**
Also Called: Oncore Velocity
237 Via Vera Cruz, San Marcos (92078-2617)
PHONE..............................760 737-6777
Arnulfo Villa, Prin
EMP: 110
SALES (corp-wide): 1.43B Privately Held
Web: www.neotech.com
SIC: 3672 Printed circuit boards
HQ: Oncore Manufacturing Llc
   9340 Owensmouth Ave
   Chatsworth CA 91311

**(P-12182)**
**ONCORE MANUFACTURING SVCS INC**
Also Called: Neo Tech Natel Epic Oncore
9340 Owensmouth Ave, Chatsworth (91311-6915)
PHONE..............................510 360-2222
Sudesh Arora, CEO
David Brakenwagen, Sr VP
Sajjad Malik, Ex VP
Magdy Henry, VP
Zareen Mohta, VP
▲ EMP: 230 EST: 2007
SALES (est): 88.4MM
SALES (corp-wide): 1.43B Privately Held
Web: www.neotech.com
SIC: 3672 Printed circuit boards
PA: Natel Engineering Company, Llc
   9340 Owensmouth Ave
   818 495-8617

**(P-12183)**
**OSI ELECTRONICS INC (HQ)**
12533 Chadron Ave, Hawthorne (90250-4807)
PHONE..............................310 978-0516
Paul Morben, Pr
Bruce Macdonald, *
Lou Campana, *
Alex Colquhoun, *
▲ EMP: 52 EST: 1995
SQ FT: 60,000
SALES (est): 90.28MM
SALES (corp-wide): 1.54B Publicly Held
Web: www.osielectronics.com
SIC: 3672 Printed circuit boards
PA: Osi Systems, Inc.
   12525 Chadron Ave
   310 978-0516

**(P-12184)**
**PACTRON**
Also Called: Pactron
3000 Patrick Henry Dr, Santa Clara (95054-1814)
PHONE..............................408 329-5500
Sriram S Iyer, CEO
K Prakash, *
EMP: 99 EST: 1995
SQ FT: 35,000
SALES (est): 33.08MM Privately Held
Web: www.pactroninc.com
SIC: 3672 Printed circuit boards

**(P-12185)**
**PALPILOT INTERNATIONAL CORP (PA)**
500 Yosemite Dr, Milpitas (95035)
PHONE..............................408 855-8866
Eddy Niu, Pr
Yi-chien Hwang, Sec
May Huang, CFO
▲ EMP: 40 EST: 1992
SQ FT: 7,000
SALES (est): 9.82MM Privately Held
Web: www.palpilot.com
SIC: 3672 Wiring boards

**(P-12186)**
**PARAMIT CORPORATION (PA)**
Also Called: Lathrop Engineering
18735 Madrone Pkwy, Morgan Hill (95037-2876)
PHONE..............................408 782-5600
Faiyaz Syed, *
Tania Micki, CFO
Mary Flores, Sec
▲ EMP: 63 EST: 1990

# 3672 - Printed Circuit Boards (P-12187)

SQ FT: 150,000
SALES (est): 102.42MM
SALES (corp-wide): 102.42MM **Privately Held**
Web: www.paramit.com
SIC: 3672  Printed circuit boards

### (P-12187)
### PARPRO TECHNOLOGIES INC
Also Called: P T I
2700 S Fairview St, Santa Ana (92704-5947)
PHONE..................714 545-8886
Thomas Sparrvik, *CEO*
Keith Knight, *Pr*
Ngathuong Le, *COO*
Eduardo Serrano, *CFO*
EMP: 210 EST: 1998
SALES (est): 77.67MM **Privately Held**
Web: www.parpro.com
SIC: 3672  Printed circuit boards
PA: Parpro Corporation
 No. 67-1, Dongyuan Rd.

### (P-12188)
### PDM SOLUTIONS  INC
Also Called: Protech Design & Manufacturing
8451 Miralani Dr Ste J, San Diego (92126-4388)
PHONE..................858 348-1000
James O'shea, *Pr*
Michelle Kim, *VP*
EMP: 20 EST: 1998
SQ FT: 5,700
SALES (est): 4.67MM **Privately Held**
Web: www.pdmsolutions.net
SIC: 3672  Printed circuit boards

### (P-12189)
### PHOTO FABRICATORS  INC
7648 Burnet Ave, Van Nuys (91405-1043)
PHONE..................818 781-1010
Steve L Brooks, *Pr*
John R Brooks, *
Susan Brooks, *
▲ EMP: 75 EST: 1973
SQ FT: 14,000
SALES (est): 8.32MM **Privately Held**
Web: www.photofabricators.com
SIC: 3672  Circuit boards, television and radio printed

### (P-12190)
### PIONEER CIRCUITS  INC
3021 S Shannon St, Santa Ana (92704-6320)
PHONE..................714 641-3132
Robert Lee, *CEO*
James Y Lee, *
EMP: 290 EST: 1981
SQ FT: 50,000
SALES (est): 58.9MM **Privately Held**
Web: www.pioneercircuits.com
SIC: 3672 3812  Printed circuit boards; Defense systems and equipment

### (P-12191)
### POWER DESIGN MANUFACTURING LLC
Also Called: Power Design Services
1130 Ringwood Ct, San Jose (95131-1726)
PHONE..................408 437-1931
EMP: 23
SIC: 3672  Circuit boards, television and radio printed

### (P-12192)
### PREFERRED TESTING LABS INC
Also Called: Element Materials Tech Anaheim
1435 S Allec St, Anaheim (92805-6306)
PHONE..................714 999-1616
Mack Dixon, *Pr*
Mclellan Dixon, *Pr*
Major Mirza, *Prin*
◆ EMP: 19 EST: 1990
SALES (est): 5MM **Privately Held**
Web: www.element.com
SIC: 3672  Printed circuit boards

### (P-12193)
### PRIME TECHNOLOGIES
19850 Pacific Coast Hwy, Malibu (90265-5424)
PHONE..................818 568-0482
Aaron Landau, *Prin*
EMP: 17 EST: 2010
SALES (est): 2.13MM **Privately Held**
Web: www.primetechpa.com
SIC: 3672  Printed circuit boards

### (P-12194)
### QOSTRONICS INC
2044 Corporate Ct, San Jose (95131-1753)
PHONE..................408 719-1286
Shawn D.o.s., *Prin*
Mai Tran, *Sec*
EMP: 33 EST: 2002
SQ FT: 5,500
SALES (est): 8.64MM **Privately Held**
Web: www.qostronics.com
SIC: 3672 3845  Circuit boards, television and radio printed; Electromedical equipment

### (P-12195)
### QUAL-PRO CORPORATION (HQ)
18510 S Figueroa St, Gardena (90248-4519)
PHONE..................310 329-7535
Brian Jeffrey Shane, *CEO*
Richard Fitzgerald, *
EMP: 200 EST: 1971
SQ FT: 55,000
SALES (est): 61.65MM **Privately Held**
Web: www.qual-pro.com
SIC: 3672  Circuit boards, television and radio printed
PA: Sfo Technologies Private Limited
 Plot No. 02, Cochin Special Economic Zone

### (P-12196)
### QUALITEK  INC (HQ)
Also Called: Westak
1116 Elko Dr, Sunnyvale (94089-2207)
PHONE..................408 734-8686
Louise Crisham, *CEO*
▲ EMP: 75 EST: 1972
SQ FT: 20,000
SALES (est): 6.34MM
SALES (corp-wide): 36.57MM **Privately Held**
Web: www.westak.com
SIC: 3672  Printed circuit boards
PA: Westak, Inc.
 1116 Elko Dr
 408 734-8686

### (P-12197)
### QUALITEK  INC
Also Called: Westak
1272 Forgewood Ave, Sunnyvale (94089-2215)
PHONE..................408 752-8422
Ray Giancola, *Mgr*
EMP: 75
SALES (corp-wide): 36.57MM **Privately Held**
Web: www.westak.com
SIC: 3672  Printed circuit boards
HQ: Qualitek, Inc.
 1116 Elko Dr
 Sunnyvale CA 94089

### (P-12198)
### QUALITY CIRCUIT ASSEMBLY INC
Also Called: Q C A
161 Baypointe Pkwy, San Jose (95134-1622)
PHONE..................408 441-1001
Jeff Moss, *CEO*
Dwight Hargrave, *
EMP: 65 EST: 1988
SQ FT: 30,000
SALES (est): 9.75MM **Privately Held**
Web: www.qcamfg.com
SIC: 3672  Circuit boards, television and radio printed

### (P-12199)
### QUALITY SYSTEMS INTGRATED CORP
7098 Miratech Dr Ste 170, San Diego (92121-3111)
PHONE..................858 536-3128
EMP: 120
Web: www.qsic.com
SIC: 3672  Printed circuit boards
PA: Quality Systems Integrated Corporation
 6740 Top Gun St

### (P-12200)
### QUALITY SYSTEMS INTGRATED CORP (PA)
Also Called: Quality Systems
6740 Top Gun St, San Diego (92121-4114)
PHONE..................858 587-9797
Kiem T Le, *CEO*
Minh Nguyen, *Dir*
Hai Bach, *Prin*
Thui Trong, *Prin*
Cecile Le, *CFO*
▲ EMP: 155 EST: 1994
SQ FT: 50,000
SALES (est): 47.28MM **Privately Held**
Web: www.qsic.com
SIC: 3672  Printed circuit boards

### (P-12201)
### ROCKET EMS  INC
2950 Patrick Henry Dr, Santa Clara (95054-1813)
PHONE..................408 727-3700
Michael D Kottke, *CEO*
EMP: 266 EST: 2010
SQ FT: 40,000
SALES (est): 120.04MM **Privately Held**
Web: www.rocketems.com
SIC: 3672  Printed circuit boards

### (P-12202)
### ROGER INDUSTRY
11552 Knott St Ste 5, Garden Grove (92841-1833)
PHONE..................714 896-0765
Shann-mou Lee, *Pr*
Jiin-sheue Lee, *VP*
▲ EMP: 16 EST: 1985
SQ FT: 10,000
SALES (est): 2.28MM **Privately Held**
SIC: 3672 3479  Printed circuit boards; Coating of metals with plastic or resins

### (P-12203)
### ROYAL CIRCUIT SOLUTIONS LLC (DH)
Also Called: Summit Interconnect Hollister
21 Hamilton Ct, Hollister (95023-2535)
PHONE..................831 636-7789
Milan Shah, *Pr*
▲ EMP: 100 EST: 2008
SQ FT: 15,000
SALES (est): 11.48MM
SALES (corp-wide): 1.78B **Privately Held**
Web: www.royalcircuits.com
SIC: 3672  Circuit boards, television and radio printed
HQ: Summit Interconnect, Inc.
 223 N Crescent Way
 Anaheim CA 92801
 714 239-2433

### (P-12204)
### SAEHAN ELECTRONICS AMERICA INC (PA)
7880 Airway Rd Ste B5g, San Diego (92154-8308)
PHONE..................858 496-1500
Bongsu Jeong, *CEO*
John Kim, *Pr*
Bok Geun Song, *CFO*
▲ EMP: 53 EST: 1994
SALES (est): 8.06MM **Privately Held**
Web: www.saehanusa.com
SIC: 3672  Printed circuit boards

### (P-12205)
### SAN DIEGO PCB DESIGN  LLC
461 Whitby Gln, Escondido (92027-2912)
PHONE..................858 271-5722
P Michael Stoehr, *Managing Member*
EMP: 18 EST: 2016
SALES (est): 1.25MM **Privately Held**
Web: www.sdpcb.com
SIC: 3672  Circuit boards, television and radio printed

### (P-12206)
### SANMINA CORPORATION
San Jose Plant 1337
2700 N 1st St, San Jose (95134-2015)
PHONE..................408 964-3500
EMP: 20
Web: www.sanmina.com
SIC: 3672  Printed circuit boards
PA: Sanmina Corporation
 2700 N 1st St

### (P-12207)
### SANMINA CORPORATION
2701 Zanker Rd, San Jose (95134-2112)
PHONE..................408 964-3500
Paul Hopwood, *Brnch Mgr*
EMP: 21
SQ FT: 77,712
Web: www.sanmina.com
SIC: 3672  Printed circuit boards
PA: Sanmina Corporation
 2700 N 1st St

### (P-12208)
### SANMINA CORPORATION
2050 Bering Dr, San Jose (95131-2009)
PHONE..................408 964-6400
Eileen Card, *Brnch Mgr*
EMP: 375
Web: www.sanmina.com
SIC: 3672  Printed circuit boards
PA: Sanmina Corporation
 2700 N 1st St

### (P-12209)
### SANMINA CORPORATION
Also Called: Sanmina-Sci
2036 Bering Dr, San Jose (95131-2009)
PHONE..................408 964-3500
Norman Evans, *Brnch Mgr*
EMP: 45
Web: www.sanmina.com

▲ = Import ▼ = Export
◆ = Import/Export

## PRODUCTS & SERVICES SECTION

### 3672 - Printed Circuit Boards (P-12230)

SIC: 3672 Printed circuit boards
PA: Sanmina Corporation
2700 N 1st St

**(P-12210)**
### SANMINA CORPORATION
60 E Plumeria Dr Bldg 2, San Jose (95134-2102)
PHONE....................408 557-7210
Randy Furr, *Pr*
EMP: 116
Web: www.sanmina.com
SIC: 3672 3643 Printed circuit boards; Current-carrying wiring services
PA: Sanmina Corporation
2700 N 1st St

**(P-12211)**
### SANMINA CORPORATION
2945 Airway Ave, Costa Mesa (92626-6007)
PHONE....................714 371-2800
Dox Scream, *Mgr*
EMP: 51
SQ FT: 60,580
Web: www.sanmina.com
SIC: 3672 Printed circuit boards
PA: Sanmina Corporation
2700 N 1st St

**(P-12212)**
### SANMINA CORPORATION (PA)
Also Called: Sanmina
2700 N 1st St, San Jose (95134-2015)
P.O. Box 7 (35804-0007)
PHONE....................408 964-3500
Jure Sola, *Ch Bd*
Jonathan Faust, *Ex VP*
Alan Reid, *Executive Global Human Resources Vice-President*
Charles C Mason, *Executive Worldwide Sales Vice-President*
Brent Billinger Senior, *Corporate Vice President*
▲ EMP: 2139 EST: 1980
SALES (est) 8.94B **Publicly Held**
Web: www.sanmina.com
SIC: 3672 3674 Printed circuit boards; Semiconductors and related devices

**(P-12213)**
### SANMINA CORPORATION
8455 Cabot Ct, Newark (94560-3336)
PHONE....................510 494-2421
Lyn Morris, *Brnch Mgr*
EMP: 200
Web: www.sanmina.com
SIC: 3672 Printed circuit boards
PA: Sanmina Corporation
2700 N 1st St

**(P-12214)**
### SANMINA CORPORATION
Viking Modular Solutions
2950 Red Hill Ave, Costa Mesa (92626-5935)
PHONE....................714 913-2200
Hamid Shokrgovar, *Pr*
EMP: 110
Web: www.sanmina.com
SIC: 3672 Printed circuit boards
PA: Sanmina Corporation
2700 N 1st St

**(P-12215)**
### SEMI-KINETICS INC
20191 Windrow Dr Ste A, Lake Forest (92630-8161)
PHONE....................949 830-7364
Gary H Gonzalez, *CEO*
▲ EMP: 95 EST: 1981
SALES (est): 20.71MM
SALES (corp-wide): 75MM **Privately Held**
Web: www.semi-kinetics.com
SIC: 3672 Circuit boards, television and radio printed
PA: Gonzalez Production Systems, Inc.
1670 Highwood E
248 745-1200

**(P-12216)**
### SIERRA ASSEMBLY TECHNOLOGY LLC
14764 Yorba Ct Unit T1, Chino (91710-9210)
PHONE....................909 606-7700
EMP: 16 EST: 2019
SALES (est): 6.36MM **Privately Held**
Web: www.sierraassembly.com
SIC: 3672 Printed circuit boards

**(P-12217)**
### SIERRA CIRCUITS INC (PA)
Also Called: Sierra Proto Express
1108 W Evelyn Ave, Sunnyvale (94086-5745)
PHONE....................408 735-7137
Kenneth Bahl, *CEO*
S Bala Bahl, *
▲ EMP: 79 EST: 1978
SQ FT: 22,000
SALES (est): 46.33MM
SALES (corp-wide): 46.33MM **Privately Held**
Web: www.protoexpress.com
SIC: 3672 Printed circuit boards

**(P-12218)**
### SIERRA ELECTROTEK LLC
1108 W Evelyn Ave, Sunnyvale (94086-5742)
PHONE....................414 762-1390
Steve Dutton, *Pr*
EMP: 60 EST: 2022
SALES (est): 1.99MM **Privately Held**
Web: www.sierraelectrotek.com
SIC: 3672 Printed circuit boards

**(P-12219)**
### SMART ELEC & ASSEMBLY INC
Also Called: Smart Electronics
2000 W Corporate Way, Anaheim (92801-5373)
PHONE....................714 772-2651
Robert Swelgin, *Pr*
Shou-lee Wang, *CEO*
James Wang, *
Dave Wopschall, *
Getaneh Bekele, *
▲ EMP: 120 EST: 1994
SQ FT: 34,500
SALES (est): 100.25MM
SALES (corp-wide): 2.84B **Publicly Held**
SIC: 3672 Printed circuit boards
HQ: Secure Communication Systems, Inc.
1740 E Wilshire Ave
Santa Ana CA 92705
714 547-1174

**(P-12220)**
### SMTC MANUFACTURING CORP CAL
431 Kato Ter, Fremont (94539-8333)
PHONE....................510 737-0700
Larry Silber, *CEO*
Alex Walker, *
Paul Blom, *
John Caldwell, *
David Sandberg, *
▲ EMP: 1875 EST: 1994
SALES (est): 21.89MM **Privately Held**
Web: www.smtc.com
SIC: 3672 Printed circuit boards
HQ: Smtc Manufacturing Corporation Of Canada
7050 Woodbine Ave Suite 215
Markham ON L3R 5
905 479-1810

**(P-12221)**
### SNA ELECTRONICS INC
3249 Laurelview Ct, Fremont (94538-6535)
PHONE....................510 656-3903
Sung W Shin, *CEO*
Chi Shin, *CFO*
EMP: 44 EST: 2002
SQ FT: 40,800
SALES (est): 10.86MM **Privately Held**
Web: www.sna-electronic.com
SIC: 3672 Printed circuit boards

**(P-12222)**
### SOLDERMASK INC
17905 Metzler Ln, Huntington Beach (92647-6258)
PHONE....................714 842-1987
Frank S Kurisu, *Pr*
▲ EMP: 15 EST: 1985
SQ FT: 10,000
SALES (est): 2.39MM **Privately Held**
Web: www.soldermask.com
SIC: 3672 3577 Printed circuit boards; Printers and plotters

**(P-12223)**
### SOMACIS INC
13500 Danielson St, Poway (92064-6874)
PHONE....................858 513-2200
Giovanni Tridenti, *CEO*
▲ EMP: 120 EST: 1970
SQ FT: 76,000
SALES (est): 17.52MM
SALES (corp-wide): 2.67MM **Privately Held**
Web: www.hallmarkcircuits.com
SIC: 3672 Circuit boards, television and radio printed
HQ: So.Ma.Ci.S. Spa
Via Jesina 17
Castelfidardo AN 60022
071721531

**(P-12224)**
### SONIC MANUFACTURING TECH INC
47931 Westinghouse Dr, Fremont (94539-7483)
PHONE....................510 580-8551
EMP: 71
Web: www.sonicmfg.com
SIC: 3672 Printed circuit boards
PA: Sonic Manufacturing Technologies, Inc.
47951 Westinghouse Dr

**(P-12225)**
### SONIC MANUFACTURING TECH INC
44051 Nobel Dr, Fremont (94538-3162)
PHONE....................510 573-3065
EMP: 71
Web: www.sonicmfg.com
SIC: 3672 Printed circuit boards
PA: Sonic Manufacturing Technologies, Inc.
47951 Westinghouse Dr

**(P-12226)**
### SONIC MANUFACTURING TECH INC (PA)
47951 Westinghouse Dr, Fremont (94539-7483)
PHONE....................510 580-8500
Kenneth Raab, *Pr*
Kenneth Raab, *CEO*
Robert Pereyda, *VP*
Henry Woo, *VP*
▲ EMP: 158 EST: 1996
SQ FT: 80,000
SALES (est): 59.61MM **Privately Held**
Web: www.sonicmfg.com
SIC: 3672 Printed circuit boards

**(P-12227)**
### SOUTH COAST CIRCUITS LLC
Also Called: Summit Interconnect
3506 W Lake Center Dr Ste A, Santa Ana (92704-6985)
PHONE....................714 966-2108
Milan Shah, *CEO*
▲ EMP: 87 EST: 1983
SQ FT: 30,000
SALES (est): 9.5MM
SALES (corp-wide): 1.78B **Privately Held**
Web: www.sccircuits.com
SIC: 3672 Circuit boards, television and radio printed
HQ: Royal Circuit Solutions, Llc
21 Hamilton Ct
Hollister CA 95023
831 636-7789

**(P-12228)**
### SPARQTRON CORPORATION
5079 Brandin Ct, Fremont (94538-3140)
PHONE....................510 657-7198
Shu Hung Kung, *CEO*
Mitchell Kung, *
Lee Ai, *
▲ EMP: 100 EST: 1998
SQ FT: 70,000
SALES (est): 20.55MM **Privately Held**
Web: www.sparqtron.com
SIC: 3672 Printed circuit boards

**(P-12229)**
### SPECTRUM ASSEMBLY INC
Also Called: Spectrum Electronics
6300 Yarrow Dr Ste 100, Carlsbad (92011-1542)
PHONE....................760 930-4000
Ronald Topp, *Pr*
Ronald Tupp, *
Michael Baldwin, *
EMP: 147 EST: 1993
SQ FT: 20,000
SALES (est): 24.05MM **Privately Held**
Web: www.saicorp.com
SIC: 3672 3569 3315 3999 Printed circuit boards; Assembly machines, non-metalworking; Wire and fabricated wire products; Barber and beauty shop equipment

**(P-12230)**
### STREAMLINE CIRCUITS LLC
Also Called: Summit Intrconnect Santa Clara
1410 Martin Ave, Santa Clara (95050-2621)
PHONE....................408 727-1418
Shane Whiteside, *CEO*
Thomas P Caldwell, *
◆ EMP: 300 EST: 2003
SALES (est): 28.6MM
SALES (corp-wide): 1.78B **Privately Held**
Web: www.summitinterconnect.com
SIC: 3672 Printed circuit boards
HQ: Summit Interconnect, Inc.
223 N Crescent Way
Anaheim CA 92801
714 239-2433

## 3672 - Printed Circuit Boards (P-12231)

**(P-12231)**
**STREAMLINE ELECTRONICS MFG INC**
Also Called: S E M
4285 Technology Dr, Fremont (94538-6339)
PHONE.................408 263-3600
Shahab Jafri, *Pr*
**EMP:** 50 **EST:** 1975
**SQ FT:** 26,000
**SALES (est):** 6.13MM **Privately Held**
**Web:** www.sem-inc.com
**SIC:** 3672 8711 2542 Printed circuit boards; Engineering services; Partitions and fixtures, except wood

**(P-12232)**
**SUBA TECHNOLOGY INC**
Also Called: Suba Tech
46501 Landing Pkwy, Fremont (94538-6421)
PHONE.................408 434-6500
Rolando M Suba, *CEO*
Alex Obice, *COO*
**EMP:** 53 **EST:** 2001
**SQ FT:** 35,000
**SALES (est):** 6.12MM **Privately Held**
**Web:** www.subatech.com
**SIC:** 3672 Printed circuit boards

**(P-12233)**
**SUMITRONICS USA INC**
9335 Airway Rd Ste 212, San Diego (92154-7930)
PHONE.................619 661-0450
Jiro Hashiguchi, *CEO*
Ryuji Sumi, *CFO*
◆ **EMP:** 30 **EST:** 2007
**SQ FT:** 800
**SALES (est):** 30.6MM **Privately Held**
**Web:** www.sumitronics.com
**SIC:** 3672 Printed circuit boards
**HQ:** Sumitronics Corporation
   1-2-2, Hitotsubashi
   Chiyoda-Ku TKY 100-0

**(P-12234)**
**SUMMIT INTERCONNECT INC (HQ)**
223 N Crescent Way, Anaheim (92801-6704)
PHONE.................714 239-2433
Shane Whiteside, *Pr*
**EMP:** 150 **EST:** 2016
**SALES (est):** 154.36MM
**SALES (corp-wide):** 1.78B **Privately Held**
**Web:** www.summitinterconnect.com
**SIC:** 3672 Printed circuit boards
**PA:** Goldberg Lindsay & Co. Llc
   630 Fifth Ave 30th Fl
   212 651-1100

**(P-12235)**
**SUMMIT INTERCONNECT INC**
Also Called: Santa Clara Facility
1401 Martin Ave, Santa Clara (95050-2614)
PHONE.................408 727-1418
Shane Whiteside, *Brnch Mgr*
**EMP:** 240
**SALES (corp-wide):** 1.78B **Privately Held**
**Web:** www.summitinterconnect.com
**SIC:** 3672 Printed circuit boards
**HQ:** Summit Interconnect, Inc.
   223 N Crescent Way
   Anaheim CA 92801
   714 239-2433

**(P-12236)**
**SUNNYTECH BIZ INC**
150 River Oaks Pkwy Ste 100, San Jose (95134-2525)
PHONE.................408 943-8100
Siu Fong Chow, *CEO*
Virgil Chen, *CFO*
▲ **EMP:** 18 **EST:** 1986
**SQ FT:** 5,500
**SALES (est):** 2.5MM **Privately Held**
**Web:** www.sunnytechbiz.com
**SIC:** 3672 Printed circuit boards

**(P-12237)**
**SYMPROTEK CO**
950 Yosemite Dr, Milpitas (95035-5452)
PHONE.................408 956-0700
Eric Chon, *Pr*
▲ **EMP:** 35 **EST:** 1994
**SQ FT:** 36,000
**SALES (est):** 4.65MM **Privately Held**
**Web:** www.symprotek.com
**SIC:** 3672 Printed circuit boards

**(P-12238)**
**TECHNOTRONIX INC**
1381 N Hundley St, Anaheim (92806-1301)
PHONE.................714 630-9200
Jayshree Kapuria, *CEO*
**EMP:** 20 **EST:** 2012
**SALES (est):** 6.25MM **Privately Held**
**Web:** www.technotronix.us
**SIC:** 3672 Printed circuit boards

**(P-12239)**
**TELIRITE TECHNICAL SVCS INC**
2857 Lakeview Ct, Fremont (94538-6534)
PHONE.................510 440-3888
Patrick Chan, *CEO*
Kue Chau Loh, *VP*
▲ **EMP:** 22 **EST:** 1995
**SQ FT:** 12,000
**SALES (est):** 4.47MM **Privately Held**
**Web:** www.telirite.com
**SIC:** 3672 Printed circuit boards

**(P-12240)**
**TIGER BUSINESS HOLDINGS INC**
32052 Sea Island Dr, Dana Point (92629-3629)
PHONE.................714 763-4180
Thomas Meeker, *Pr*
Masayuki Kojima, *VP*
Sherlene Meeker, *CFO*
◆ **EMP:** 18 **EST:** 1980
**SALES (est):** 3.31MM **Privately Held**
**Web:** www.taiyocircuitautomation.com
**SIC:** 3672 Printed circuit boards

**(P-12241)**
**TRANSLINE TECHNOLOGY INC**
1106 S Technology Cir, Anaheim (92805-6329)
PHONE.................714 533-8300
Kishor Patel, *Pr*
Larry Padmani, *
▲ **EMP:** 33 **EST:** 1996
**SQ FT:** 20,000
**SALES (est):** 4.83MM **Privately Held**
**Web:** www.translinetech.com
**SIC:** 3672 Printed circuit boards

**(P-12242)**
**TRANTRONICS INC**
1822 Langley Ave, Irvine (92614-5624)
PHONE.................949 553-1234
Tom Tran, *Pr*
**EMP:** 32 **EST:** 1997
**SALES (est):** 9.92MM **Privately Held**
**Web:** www.trantronics.com
**SIC:** 3672 3599 Printed circuit boards; Machine and other job shop work

**(P-12243)**
**TRI-STAR LAMINATES INC**
Also Called: Laminating Company of America
20322 Windrow Dr Ste 100, Lake Forest (92630-8150)
PHONE.................949 587-3200
Patrick Redfern, *Pr*
**EMP:** 33 **EST:** 2000
**SQ FT:** 50,000
**SALES (est):** 2.72MM **Privately Held**
**SIC:** 3672 Printed circuit boards

**(P-12244)**
**TTM PRINTED CIRCUIT GROUP INC**
407 Mathew St, Santa Clara (95050-3105)
PHONE.................408 486-3100
Jeff Gonsman, *Mgr*
**EMP:** 149
**SALES (corp-wide):** 2.23B **Publicly Held**
**Web:** www.ttm.com
**SIC:** 3672 Printed circuit boards
**HQ:** Ttm Printed Circuit Group, Inc.
   2630 S Harbor Blvd
   Santa Ana CA 92704

**(P-12245)**
**TTM PRINTED CIRCUIT GROUP INC (HQ)**
2630 S Harbor Blvd, Santa Ana (92704-5829)
PHONE.................714 327-3000
Thomas T Edman, *Pr*
Steve Richards, *CFO*
▲ **EMP:** 156 **EST:** 2006
**SALES (est):** 26.58MM
**SALES (corp-wide):** 2.23B **Publicly Held**
**Web:** www.ttm.com
**SIC:** 3672 Printed circuit boards
**PA:** Ttm Technologies, Inc.
   200 Sndpointe Ave Ste 400
   714 327-3000

**(P-12246)**
**TTM TECHNOLOGIES INC**
407 Mathew St, Santa Clara (95050-3105)
PHONE.................408 486-3100
**EMP:** 260
**SALES (corp-wide):** 2.23B **Publicly Held**
**Web:** www.ttm.com
**SIC:** 3672 Printed circuit boards
**PA:** Ttm Technologies, Inc.
   200 Sndpointe Ave Ste 400
   714 327-3000

**(P-12247)**
**TTM TECHNOLOGIES INC**
2630 S Harbor Blvd, Santa Ana (92704-5829)
PHONE.................714 241-0303
Dale Anderson, *Prin*
**EMP:** 300
**SALES (corp-wide):** 2.23B **Publicly Held**
**Web:** www.ttm.com
**SIC:** 3672 Printed circuit boards
**PA:** Ttm Technologies, Inc.
   200 Sndpointe Ave Ste 400
   714 327-3000

**(P-12248)**
**TTM TECHNOLOGIES INC (PA)**
Also Called: TTM
200 Sandpointe Ave Ste 400, Santa Ana (92707-5747)
PHONE.................714 327-3000
Thomas T Edman, *Pr*
Rex D Geveden, *Non-Executive Chairman of the Board*
Daniel L Boehle, *Ex VP*
Philip Titterton, *Ex VP*
Douglas L Soder, *Ex VP*
**EMP:** 500 **EST:** 1978
**SQ FT:** 14,472
**SALES (est):** 2.23B
**SALES (corp-wide):** 2.23B **Publicly Held**
**Web:** www.ttm.com
**SIC:** 3672 Printed circuit boards

**(P-12249)**
**TTM TECHNOLOGIES INC**
3140 E Coronado St, Anaheim (92806-1914)
PHONE.................714 688-7200
**EMP:** 290
**SALES (corp-wide):** 2.23B **Publicly Held**
**Web:** www.ttm.com
**SIC:** 3672 Printed circuit boards
**PA:** Ttm Technologies, Inc.
   200 Sndpointe Ave Ste 400
   714 327-3000

**(P-12250)**
**TTM TECHNOLOGIES INC**
5037 Ruffner St, San Diego (92111-1107)
PHONE.................858 874-2701
Mark Micale, *Mgr*
**EMP:** 149
**SALES (corp-wide):** 2.23B **Publicly Held**
**Web:** www.ttm.com
**SIC:** 3672 Printed circuit boards
**PA:** Ttm Technologies, Inc.
   200 Sndpointe Ave Ste 400
   714 327-3000

**(P-12251)**
**TTM TECHNOLOGIES INC**
355 Turtle Creek Ct, San Jose (95125-1316)
PHONE.................408 280-0422
Arnold Amaral, *Brnch Mgr*
**EMP:** 118
**SALES (corp-wide):** 2.23B **Publicly Held**
**Web:** www.ttm.com
**SIC:** 3672 Printed circuit boards
**PA:** Ttm Technologies, Inc.
   200 Sndpointe Ave Ste 400
   714 327-3000

**(P-12252)**
**UNITED INTERNATIONAL TECH INC**
9207 Deering Ave Ste B, Chatsworth (91311-6960)
PHONE.................818 772-9400
Edmundo Espindola, *CEO*
Edmundo Espindolo, *
**EMP:** 36 **EST:** 2008
**SALES (est):** 5.21MM **Privately Held**
**Web:** www.uitpcb.com
**SIC:** 3672 7629 Circuit boards, television and radio printed; Circuit board repair

**(P-12253)**
**VALLEY SERVICES ELECTRONICS**
6190 San Ignacio Ave, San Jose (95119-1378)
PHONE.................408 284-7700
Andy Pecota, *CEO*
Beth Kendrick, *
**EMP:** 160 **EST:** 1978
**SQ FT:** 52,000
**SALES (est):** 24.23MM **Privately Held**
**Web:** www.vse.com
**SIC:** 3672 Printed circuit boards

# PRODUCTS & SERVICES SECTION

## 3674 - Semiconductors And Related Devices (P-12274)

**(P-12254)**
**VECTOR ELECTRONICS & TECH INC**
11115 Vanowen St, North Hollywood (91605-6371)
PHONE.............................818 985-8208
Rakesh Bajaria, *CEO*
Ken Pansuriah, *
Viny Kathrotia, *
▲ **EMP:** 25 **EST:** 2001
**SALES (est):** 4.06MM **Privately Held**
**Web:** www.vectorelect.com
**SIC: 3672** Printed circuit boards

**(P-12255)**
**VEECO ELECTRO FAB INC**
1176 N Osprey Cir, Anaheim (92807-1709)
PHONE.............................714 630-8020
**EMP:** 21
**SQ FT:** 10,000
**SALES (est):** 2.57MM **Privately Held**
**SIC: 3672** 7629 Printed circuit boards; Circuit board repair

**(P-12256)**
**VINATRONIC INC**
15571 Industry Ln, Huntington Beach (92649-1534)
PHONE.............................714 845-3480
Lan Nguyen, *CEO*
Kem Strano, *
**EMP:** 18 **EST:** 1988
**SQ FT:** 13,000
**SALES (est):** 3.72MM **Privately Held**
**Web:** www.vinatronic.com
**SIC: 3672** Printed circuit boards

**(P-12257)**
**VITRON ELECTRONIC SERVICES INC**
Also Called: Vitron Electronics Mfg & Svcs
5400 Hellyer Ave, San Jose (95138-1019)
PHONE.............................408 251-1600
Huan Cong Tran, *CEO*
▲ **EMP:** 60 **EST:** 1988
**SQ FT:** 3,500
**SALES (est):** 9.07MM **Privately Held**
**Web:** www.vitronmfg.com
**SIC: 3672** Printed circuit boards

**(P-12258)**
**WE IMAGINE INC**
9371 Canoga Ave, Chatsworth (91311-5879)
P.O. Box 5696 (91313-5696)
PHONE.............................818 709-0064
**EMP:** 53 **EST:** 1974
**SALES (est):** 2.94MM **Privately Held**
**SIC: 3672** Printed circuit boards

**(P-12259)**
**WESTAK INC (PA)**
Also Called: A2
1116 Elko Dr, Sunnyvale (94089-2207)
PHONE.............................408 734-8686
Louise Crisham, *CEO*
Dicie Hinaga, *
**EMP:** 100 **EST:** 1972
**SQ FT:** 20,000
**SALES (est):** 36.57MM
**SALES (corp-wide):** 36.57MM **Privately Held**
**Web:** www.westak.com
**SIC: 3672** Circuit boards, television and radio printed

**(P-12260)**
**WESTAK INTERNATIONAL SALES INC (HQ)**
1116 Elko Dr, Sunnyvale (94089-2207)
PHONE.............................408 734-8686
Louise Crisham, *Pr*
▲ **EMP:** 130 **EST:** 1982
**SQ FT:** 20,000
**SALES (est):** 5.15MM
**SALES (corp-wide):** 36.57MM **Privately Held**
**Web:** www.westak.com
**SIC: 3672** Printed circuit boards
**PA:** Westak, Inc.
1116 Elko Dr
408 734-8686

**(P-12261)**
**WFB ARCHIVES INC**
13500 Danielson St, Poway (92064-6874)
**EMP:** 80
**SIC: 3672** Printed circuit boards

**(P-12262)**
**WHIZZ SYSTEMS INC (PA)**
Also Called: Whizz Systems
3240 Scott Blvd, Santa Clara (95054-3011)
PHONE.............................408 207-0400
Munawar Karimjee, *CEO*
Muhammad Irfan, *
Yome Salinas, *
▲ **EMP:** 33 **EST:** 1999
**SQ FT:** 35,000
**SALES (est):** 23.46MM
**SALES (corp-wide):** 23.46MM **Privately Held**
**Web:** www.whizzsystems.com
**SIC: 3672** Printed circuit boards

**(P-12263)**
**WINONICS INC**
Also Called: Bench 2 Bench Technologies
1257 S State College Blvd, Fullerton (92831-5336)
PHONE.............................714 626-3755
Tom Sciulli, *Genl Mgr*
**EMP:** 120
**SALES (corp-wide):** 35.2MM **Privately Held**
**Web:** www.winonics.com
**SIC: 3672** Printed circuit boards
**HQ:** Winonics Llc
660 N Puente St
Brea CA
714 256-8700

**(P-12264)**
**YUN INDUSTRIAL CO LTD**
Also Called: Y I C
161 Selandia Ln, Carson (90746-1412)
PHONE.............................310 715-1898
Ilun Yun, *Pr*
William Yun, *
Stephen Yun, *
◆ **EMP:** 40 **EST:** 1990
**SQ FT:** 16,000
**SALES (est):** 10.68MM **Privately Held**
**Web:** www.yic-assm.com
**SIC: 3672** Printed circuit boards

**(P-12265)**
**ZF ARRAY TECHNOLOGY INC**
2302 Trade Zone Blvd, San Jose (95131-1819)
PHONE.............................408 433-9920
Robert Zinn, *CEO*
Jim Viviani, *
Richard Freiberger, *
▲ **EMP:** 26 **EST:** 2003
**SQ FT:** 33,000
**SALES (est):** 1.59MM **Privately Held**
**SIC: 3672** Printed circuit boards

**HQ:** Smtc Manufacturing Corporation Of Canada
7050 Woodbine Ave Suite 215
Markham ON L3R 5
905 479-1810

**(P-12266)**
**ZOLLNER ELECTRONICS INC**
575 Cottonwood Dr, Milpitas (95035-7402)
PHONE.............................408 434-5400
Markus Aschenbrenner, *Bd of Dir*
Stephan Weiss, *
Nessa Hunt, *
▲ **EMP:** 29 **EST:** 1965
**SALES (est):** 16.9MM
**SALES (corp-wide):** 3.67B **Privately Held**
**Web:** www.zollner-electronics.com
**SIC: 3672** Printed circuit boards
**PA:** Zollner Elektronik Ag
Manfred-Zollner-Str. 1
99442010

**(P-12267)**
**ZYTEK CORP (PA)**
Also Called: Zytek Ems
1755 Mccarthy Blvd, Milpitas (95035-7416)
PHONE.............................408 520-4287
Rabia Khan, *Pr*
**EMP:** 39 **EST:** 2011
**SQ FT:** 21,000
**SALES (est):** 1.91MM
**SALES (corp-wide):** 1.91MM **Privately Held**
**SIC: 3672** Printed circuit boards

## 3674 Semiconductors And Related Devices

**(P-12268)**
**ABB ENTERPRISE SOFTWARE INC**
Also Called: ABB ENTERPRISE SOFTWARE INC.
4600 Colorado Blvd, Los Angeles (90039-1106)
PHONE.............................213 743-4819
Carol Clemons, *Brnch Mgr*
▲ **EMP:** 60
**Web:** new.abb.com
**SIC: 3674** Microcircuits, integrated (semiconductor)
**HQ:** Abb Inc.
305 Gregson Dr
Cary NC 27511

**(P-12269)**
**ACACIA COMMUNICATIONS INC**
2700 Zanker Rd Ste 160, San Jose (95134-2139)
PHONE.............................212 331-8417
**EMP:** 86
**SALES (corp-wide):** 53.8B **Publicly Held**
**Web:** www.acacia-inc.com
**SIC: 3674** Semiconductors and related devices
**HQ:** Acacia Communications, Inc.
3 Mill & Main Pl Ste 400
Maynard MA 01754
978 938-4896

**(P-12270)**
**ACCELERATED MEMORY PROD INC**
Also Called: AMP
1317 E Edinger Ave, Santa Ana (92705-4416)
PHONE.............................714 460-9800
Richard Mccauley, *Pr*

Cathleen Mccauley, *VP*
◆ **EMP:** 49 **EST:** 2007
**SQ FT:** 10,000
**SALES (est):** 3.69MM **Privately Held**
**Web:** www.ampinc.com
**SIC: 3674** Semiconductors and related devices

**(P-12271)**
**ACHRONIX SEMICONDUCTOR CORP (PA)**
2903 Bunker Hill Ln Ste 200, Santa Clara (95054-1141)
PHONE.............................408 889-4100
Robert Blake, *Pr*
John Holt, *
Mark Voll, *
Virantha Ekanayake, *
Kamal Chaudhary, *OK Vice President*
**EMP:** 40 **EST:** 2006
**SQ FT:** 25,000
**SALES (est):** 21.27MM
**SALES (corp-wide):** 21.27MM **Privately Held**
**Web:** www.achronix.com
**SIC: 3674** Integrated circuits, semiconductor networks, etc.

**(P-12272)**
**ACTSOLAR INC**
2900 Semiconductor Dr, Santa Clara (95051-0606)
PHONE.............................408 721-5000
Andrew Foss, *Pr*
Brian Dupin, *VP*
**EMP:** 57 **EST:** 2006
**SQ FT:** 3,000
**SALES (est):** 3.92MM
**SALES (corp-wide):** 17.52B **Publicly Held**
**SIC: 3674** Semiconductors and related devices
**HQ:** National Semiconductor Corporation
2900 Semiconductor Dr
Santa Clara CA 95051
408 721-5000

**(P-12273)**
**ADESTO TECHNOLOGIES CORP (DH)**
Also Called: Adesto
6024 Silver Creek Valley Rd, San Jose (95138-1011)
PHONE.............................408 400-0578
Narbeh Derhacobian, *Pr*
Nelson Chan, *Ch Bd*
Ron Shelton, *CFO*
Sohrab Modi, *CSO*
◆ **EMP:** 25 **EST:** 2006
**SALES (est):** 118.17MM **Privately Held**
**Web:** www.adestotech.com
**SIC: 3674** Semiconductors and related devices
**HQ:** Dialog Semiconductor Limited
Dukes Meadow Millboard Road
Bourne End BUCKS SL8 5
179 375-7700

**(P-12274)**
**ADEX ELECTRONICS INC**
3 Watson, Irvine (92618-2716)
PHONE.............................949 597-1772
Casey Huang, *Pr*
Cheryl Roberts, *Treas*
▲ **EMP:** 15 **EST:** 1985
**SQ FT:** 10,330
**SALES (est):** 2.18MM **Privately Held**
**Web:** www.adexelec.com
**SIC: 3674** 8711 Semiconductors and related devices; Engineering services

## 3674 - Semiconductors And Related Devices (P-12275)

**(P-12275)**
**ADTECH PHOTONICS INC**
Also Called: Adtech Optics
18007 Cortney Ct, City Of Industry
(91748-1203)
PHONE..................................626 956-1000
Mary Fong, *CEO*
EMP: 25 EST: 2012
SALES (est): 2.3MM **Privately Held**
Web: www.atoptics.com
SIC: **3674** Semiconductors and related devices

**(P-12276)**
**ADVANCED ANALOGIC TECH INC**
2740 Zanker Rd, San Jose (95134)
PHONE..................................408 330-1400
Richard K Williams, *Pr*
Ashok Chandran, *Interim Chief Financial Officer\**
Parviz Ghaffaripour, *\**
Bijan Mohandes, *\**
Yee W Seto, *\**
EMP: 45 EST: 1962
SQ FT: 42,174
SALES (est): 5.94MM
SALES (corp-wide): 4.77B **Publicly Held**
Web: www.skyworksinc.com
SIC: **3674** Integrated circuits, semiconductor networks, etc.
PA: Skyworks Solutions, Inc.
5260 California Ave
949 231-3000

**(P-12277)**
**ADVANCED COMPONENT LABS INC**
Also Called: A C L
990 Richard Ave Ste 118, Santa Clara (95050-2828)
PHONE..................................408 327-0200
Michael J Oswald, *CEO*
EMP: 20 EST: 1994
SQ FT: 20,000
SALES (est): 2.28MM **Privately Held**
Web: www.aclusa.com
SIC: **3674** Semiconductor circuit networks

**(P-12278)**
**ADVANCED SEMICONDUCTOR INC**
Also Called: A S I
24955 Avenue Kearny, Valencia (91355-1252)
PHONE..................................818 982-1400
Fred Golob, *CEO*
▲ EMP: 58 EST: 1979
SQ FT: 9,000
SALES (est): 3.64MM **Privately Held**
Web: www.advancedsemiconductor.com
SIC: **3674** Integrated circuits, semiconductor networks, etc.

**(P-12279)**
**ADVANTEST AMERICA INC (HQ)**
3061 Zanker Rd, San Jose (95134-2127)
PHONE..................................408 456-3600
Douglas Lefever, *CEO*
Keith Hardwick, *\**
▲ EMP: 90 EST: 1982
SALES (est): 278.64MM **Privately Held**
Web: www.advantest.com
SIC: **3674** Semiconductors and related devices
PA: Advantest Corporation
1-6-2, Marunouchi

**(P-12280)**
**ADVANTEST TEST SOLUTIONS INC**
26211 Enterprise Way, Lake Forest (92630-8402)
PHONE..................................949 523-6900
Jonathan Sinskie, *CEO*
Keith Sinskie, *CFO*
EMP: 66 EST: 2018
SALES (est): 22.4MM **Privately Held**
Web: www.advantest.com
SIC: **3674** Semiconductors and related devices
HQ: Advantest America, Inc.
3061 Zanker Rd
San Jose CA 95134

**(P-12281)**
**AEROFLEX INCORPORATED**
15375 Barranca Pkwy Ste F106, Irvine (92618-2217)
PHONE..................................800 843-1553
Len Burrows, *Brnch Mgr*
EMP: 45
SALES (corp-wide): 2.67MM **Privately Held**
Web: www.caes.com
SIC: **3674** Semiconductors and related devices
HQ: Aeroflex Incorporated
2121 Crystal Dr Ste 800
Arlington VA 22202
516 694-6700

**(P-12282)**
**AIXTRON INC**
1700 Wyatt Dr Ste 15, Santa Clara (95054-1541)
PHONE..................................669 228-3759
Martin Goetzeler, *CEO*
Randy Singh, *\**
▲ EMP: 156 EST: 1981
SQ FT: 100,500
SALES (est): 196.48K
SALES (corp-wide): 684.66MM **Privately Held**
Web: www.aixtron.com
SIC: **3674** Semiconductors and related devices
PA: Aixtron Se
Dornkaulstr. 2
240790300

**(P-12283)**
**AKEANA USA INC**
3131 Jay St Ste 210, Santa Clara (95054-3340)
PHONE..................................408 332-3005
Rabin Sugumar, *CEO*
EMP: 40 EST: 2021
SALES (est): 263.6K **Privately Held**
SIC: **3674** Semiconductors and related devices

**(P-12284)**
**AKM SEMICONDUCTOR INC**
Also Called: A K M
1731 Technology Dr Ste 500, San Jose (95110-1327)
PHONE..................................408 436-8580
S Kido, *Pr*
Makoto Konosu, *CEO*
Lyle Knudsen, *VP*
▲ EMP: 23 EST: 1995
SQ FT: 5,402
SALES (est): 4.48MM **Privately Held**
Web: www.akm.com
SIC: **3674** Semiconductors and related devices
HQ: Asahi Kasei Microdevices Corporation
1-1-2, Yurakucho
Chiyoda-Ku TKY 100-0

**(P-12285)**
**AKT AMERICA INC (HQ)**
3101 Scott Blvd Bldg 91, Santa Clara (95054-3318)
PHONE..................................408 563-5455
In Doo Kang, *VP*
▲ EMP: 400 EST: 1994
SQ FT: 200,000
SALES (est): 11.5MM
SALES (corp-wide): 26.52B **Publicly Held**
SIC: **3674** Semiconductors and related devices
PA: Applied Materials, Inc.
3050 Bowers Ave
408 727-5555

**(P-12286)**
**AKT AMERICA INC**
1245 Walsh Ave, Santa Clara (95050-2662)
PHONE..................................408 563-5455
EMP: 400
SALES (corp-wide): 26.52B **Publicly Held**
SIC: **3674** Semiconductors and related devices
HQ: Akt America, Inc.
3101 Scott Blvd Bldg 91
Santa Clara CA 95054
408 563-5455

**(P-12287)**
**ALACRITECH INC**
Also Called: Alacritech
1995 N 1st St Ste 200, San Jose (95112-4220)
PHONE..................................408 867-3809
Larry Boucher, *Pr*
Esther Lee, *\**
Richard Blackborow, *\**
Russ Lait, *\**
Doug Rainbolt, *\**
EMP: 39 EST: 1997
SQ FT: 10,600
SALES (est): 4.91MM **Privately Held**
Web: www.alacritech.com
SIC: **3674** Semiconductors and related devices

**(P-12288)**
**ALION ENERGY INC**
Also Called: Alion Energy
2200 Central St # D, Richmond (94801-1213)
PHONE..................................510 965-0868
Mark Kingsley, *Pr*
Jesse Atkinson, *\**
▲ EMP: 51 EST: 2008
SALES (est): 7.74MM **Privately Held**
Web: www.alionenergy.com
SIC: **3674** Solar cells

**(P-12289)**
**ALL SENSORS CORPORATION**
16035 Vineyard Blvd, Morgan Hill (95037-5480)
PHONE..................................408 776-9434
Dennis Dauenhauer, *Pr*
◆ EMP: 38 EST: 1999
SQ FT: 20,000
SALES (est): 9.95MM
SALES (corp-wide): 12.55B **Publicly Held**
Web: www.allsensors.com
SIC: **3674** Infrared sensors, solid state
PA: Amphenol Corporation
358 Hall Ave
203 265-8900

**(P-12290)**
**ALLVIA INC**
Also Called: Allvia
445 Fairway Dr, Half Moon Bay (94019-2200)
PHONE..................................408 234-8778
Sergey Savastiouk, *CEO*
EMP: 20 EST: 1996
SALES (est): 2.13MM **Privately Held**
Web: www.allvia.com
SIC: **3674** Integrated circuits, semiconductor networks, etc.

**(P-12291)**
**ALPHA AND OMEGA SEMICDTR INC (HQ)**
475 Oakmead Pkwy, Sunnyvale (94085-4709)
PHONE..................................408 789-0008
Mike F Chang, *CEO*
Hamza Yilmaz, *\**
Mary Dotz, *\**
Michael L Pfeiffer, *\**
▲ EMP: 28 EST: 2000
SQ FT: 50,000
SALES (est): 54.44MM **Privately Held**
Web: www.aosmd.com
SIC: **3674** Semiconductors and related devices
PA: Alpha And Omega Semiconductor Limited
C/O Conyers Corporate Services (Bermuda) Limited

**(P-12292)**
**ALPHAWAVE SEMI INC (HQ)**
Also Called: Openfive
1730 N 1st St, San Jose (95112-4642)
PHONE..................................408 240-5700
Tony Pialis, *CEO*
Sameer Ladiwala, *CAO\**
EMP: 33 EST: 2003
SALES (est): 21.93MM
SALES (corp-wide): 321.72MM **Privately Held**
Web: www.awavesemi.com
SIC: **3674** Integrated circuits, semiconductor networks, etc.
PA: Alphawave Ip Group Plc
85 Gresham Street
203 901-7895

**(P-12293)**
**ALTA DEVICES INC**
545 Oakmead Pkwy, Sunnyvale (94085-4023)
PHONE..................................408 988-8600
Doctor Jian Ding, *CEO*
Jose Corbacho, *\**
Rich Kapusta, *CMO*
Mallorie Burak, *\**
Harry Atwater, *\**
EMP: 250 EST: 2013
SQ FT: 115,000
SALES (est): 28.12MM **Privately Held**
Web: www.altadevices.com
SIC: **3674** Semiconductors and related devices
PA: Jinjiang Hydropower Group Co., Ltd.
Room 105, No. 680, Tanghekou Street, Tanghekou Town, Huairou Dis

**(P-12294)**
**ALTERA CORPORATION (HQ)**
Also Called: Altera
101 Innovation Dr, San Jose (95134-1941)
PHONE..................................408 544-7000
John P Daane, *Pr*
Danny Biran, *Senior Vice President Corporate Strategy\**

## PRODUCTS & SERVICES SECTION
## 3674 - Semiconductors And Related Devices (P-12316)

William Y Hata, *Senior Vice President Worldwide Operation\**
Bradley Howe, *Senior Vice President Research & Development\**
Kevin H Lyman, *Senior Vice President Human Resources\**
▲ **EMP:** 224 **EST:** 1983
**SQ FT:** 505,000
**SALES (est):** 73.62MM
**SALES (corp-wide):** 54.23B **Publicly Held**
**Web:** www.intel.com
**SIC: 3674** 7371 Semiconductors and related devices; Computer software development and applications
**PA:** Intel Corporation
  2200 Mission College Blvd
  408 765-8080

### (P-12295)
### ALTIERRE CORPORATION
1980 Concourse Dr, San Jose (95131-1719)
P.O. Box 640527 (95164-0527)
**PHONE**..............................408 435-7343
Tony Alvarez, *CEO*
Anurag Goel, *VP*
Dave Wetle, *VP*
Shan Kumar, *CFO*
▲ **EMP:** 50 **EST:** 2003
**SQ FT:** 85,367
**SALES (est):** 6.38MM **Privately Held**
**Web:** www.altierre.com
**SIC: 3674** Integrated circuits, semiconductor networks, etc.

### (P-12296)
### AMAT
3101 Scott Blvd, Santa Clara (95054-3318)
**PHONE**..............................408 563-5385
**EMP:** 37 **EST:** 2018
**SALES (est):** 3.19MM **Privately Held**
**Web:** www.appliedmaterials.com
**SIC: 3674** Semiconductors and related devices

### (P-12297)
### AMBARELLA INC (PA)
Also Called: Ambarella
3101 Jay St, Santa Clara (95054-3329)
**PHONE**..............................408 734-8888
Feng-ming Wang, *Ch Bd*
Brian C White, *CFO*
Chan W Lee, *COO*
**EMP:** 667 **EST:** 2004
**SQ FT:** 58,700
**SALES (est):** 226.47MM
**SALES (corp-wide):** 226.47MM **Publicly Held**
**Web:** www.ambarella.com
**SIC: 3674** Semiconductors and related devices

### (P-12298)
### AMBER SEMICONDUCTOR INC
Also Called: Amber
6400 Sierra Ct Ste F, Danville (94506)
**PHONE**..............................510 364-4680
Thar Casey, *CEO*
**EMP:** 36 **EST:** 2016
**SALES (est):** 619.68K **Privately Held**
**Web:** www.ambersi.com
**SIC: 3674** Semiconductors and related devices

### (P-12299)
### AMD FAR EAST LTD (HQ)
1 Amd Pl, Sunnyvale (94085-3905)
**PHONE**..............................408 749-4000
**EMP:** 15 **EST:** 1987
**SALES (est):** 843.61K

**SALES (corp-wide):** 22.68B **Publicly Held**
**SIC: 3674** Integrated circuits, semiconductor networks, etc.
**PA:** Advanced Micro Devices, Inc.
  2485 Augustine Dr
  408 749-4000

### (P-12300)
### AMERICAN ARIUM
Also Called: Arium
17791 Fitch, Irvine (92614-6019)
**PHONE**..............................949 623-7090
Larry Traylor, *Pr*
Diane Dirks, *\**
**EMP:** 40 **EST:** 1977
**SQ FT:** 32,330
**SALES (est):** 2.6MM **Privately Held**
**Web:** www.asset-intertech.com
**SIC: 3674** 3577 Microprocessors; Computer peripheral equipment, nec

### (P-12301)
### AMERICAN SOLAR ADVANTAGE INC
Also Called: Asa Power BDH Engrg & Cnstr
13348 Monte Vista Ave, Chino (91710-5147)
**PHONE**..............................877 765-2388
Bobby D Harris, *Pr*
**EMP:** 20 **EST:** 2016
**SALES (est):** 3.5MM **Privately Held**
**Web:** www.asa.solar
**SIC: 3674** 1731 Solar cells; Electrical work

### (P-12302)
### AMLOGIC INC
Also Called: Amlogic
2518 Mission College Blvd Ste 120, Santa Clara (95054-1239)
**PHONE**..............................408 850-9688
John Zhong, *Pr*
**EMP:** 20 **EST:** 1995
**SALES (est):** 4.29MM **Privately Held**
**Web:** www.amlogiccorp.com
**SIC: 3674** Integrated circuits, semiconductor networks, etc.

### (P-12303)
### AMONIX INC
1709 Apollo Ct, Seal Beach (90740-5617)
**PHONE**..............................562 344-4750
▲ **EMP:** 120
**SIC: 3674** Solar cells

### (P-12304)
### ANALOG BITS INC (HQ)
945 Stewart Dr, Sunnyvale (94085-3861)
**PHONE**..............................650 279-9323
Alan Rogers, *CEO*
**EMP:** 16 **EST:** 1996
**SALES (est):** 10.37MM **Privately Held**
**Web:** www.analogbits.com
**SIC: 3674** Semiconductors and related devices
**PA:** Semifive Inc.
  Rm 603, 605 6/F Korea Design Center

### (P-12305)
### ANALOG DEVICES INC
160 Rio Robles, San Jose (95134-1813)
**PHONE**..............................408 428-2050
**EMP:** 58
**SALES (corp-wide):** 12.31B **Publicly Held**
**Web:** www.analog.com
**SIC: 3674** Integrated circuits, semiconductor networks, etc.
**PA:** Analog Devices, Inc.
  1 Analog Way
  781 935-5565

### (P-12306)
### ANALOG DEVICES INC
160 Rio Robles, San Jose (95134-1813)
**PHONE**..............................408 432-1900
Lothar Maier, *Pr*
**EMP:** 101
**SALES (corp-wide):** 12.31B **Publicly Held**
**Web:** www.analog.com
**SIC: 3674** Integrated circuits, semiconductor networks, etc.
**PA:** Analog Devices, Inc.
  1 Analog Way
  781 935-5565

### (P-12307)
### ANALOG DEVICES INC
160 Rio Robles, San Jose (95134-1813)
**PHONE**..............................408 727-9222
Jerry Fishman, *Mgr*
**EMP:** 85
**SALES (corp-wide):** 12.31B **Publicly Held**
**Web:** www.analog.com
**SIC: 3674** Integrated circuits, semiconductor networks, etc.
**PA:** Analog Devices, Inc.
  1 Analog Way
  781 935-5565

### (P-12308)
### ANALOG INFERENCE INC
2350 Mission College Blvd Ste 300, Santa Clara (95054-1532)
**PHONE**..............................408 771-6413
**EMP:** 44 **EST:** 2018
**SALES (est):** 5.67MM **Privately Held**
**Web:** www.analog-inference.com
**SIC: 3674** Semiconductors and related devices

### (P-12309)
### ANALOGIX SEMICONDUCTOR INC (PA)
Also Called: Pacific Analogix Semiconductor
2350 Mission College Blvd Ste 1100, Santa Clara (95054-1566)
**PHONE**..............................408 988-8848
Kewei Yang, *CEO*
Shuran Wei, *VP*
Ted Rado, *\**
Bill Eichen, *\**
Ning Zhu, *\**
▲ **EMP:** 24 **EST:** 2002
**SALES (est):** 131.4MM
**SALES (corp-wide):** 131.4MM **Privately Held**
**Web:** www.analogix.com
**SIC: 3674** Integrated circuits, semiconductor networks, etc.

### (P-12310)
### ANCHOR BAY TECHNOLOGIES INC
Also Called: Dvdo
564 Crawford Dr, Sunnyvale (94087-7307)
**PHONE**..............................888 651-1765
▲ **EMP:** 34 **EST:** 2001
**SALES (est):** 3.9MM **Privately Held**
**SIC: 3674** 5731 Semiconductors and related devices; Consumer electronic equipment, nec

### (P-12311)
### APIC CORPORATION
5800 Uplander Way, Culver City (90230-6608)
**PHONE**..............................310 642-7975
James Chan, *VP*
Birendra Dutt, *\**
Koichi Sayano, *\**

Anguel Nikolov, *\**
**EMP:** 58 **EST:** 2001
**SQ FT:** 14,416
**SALES (est):** 6.2MM **Privately Held**
**Web:** www.apichip.com
**SIC: 3674** Semiconductors and related devices

### (P-12312)
### APPLIED CERAMICS INC (PA)
Also Called: Applied Ceramics
48630 Milmont Dr, Fremont (94538-7353)
**PHONE**..............................510 249-9700
Matt Darko Sertic, *CEO*
▲ **EMP:** 123 **EST:** 1994
**SQ FT:** 57,000
**SALES (est):** 20.34MM **Privately Held**
**Web:** www.appliedceramics.net
**SIC: 3674** 3264 Semiconductors and related devices; Porcelain electrical supplies

### (P-12313)
### APPLIED MANUFACTURING GROUP
Also Called: Manufacturing/Machining
941 George St, Santa Clara (95054-2706)
**PHONE**..............................408 855-8857
Ewa Gregorczuk, *Pr*
Eddie Ng, *CEO*
Ewa Gregorczuk, *Ch Bd*
Jackie Ng, *COO*
**EMP:** 20 **EST:** 2003
**SALES (est):** 5.04MM **Privately Held**
**Web:** www.appliedmfrgroup.com
**SIC: 3674** 3999 Semiconductors and related devices; Barber and beauty shop equipment

### (P-12314)
### APPLIED MATERIALS INC
Also Called: Applied Materials
3320 Scott Blvd, Santa Clara (95054-3101)
**PHONE**..............................408 727-5555
Mary Ryan, *Brnch Mgr*
**EMP:** 27
**SALES (corp-wide):** 26.52B **Publicly Held**
**Web:** www.appliedmaterials.com
**SIC: 3674** Semiconductors and related devices
**PA:** Applied Materials, Inc.
  3050 Bowers Ave
  408 727-5555

### (P-12315)
### APPLIED MATERIALS INC
Also Called: Applied Materials
1285 Walsh Ave, Santa Clara (95050-2662)
**PHONE**..............................406 752-2107
**EMP:** 21
**SALES (corp-wide):** 26.52B **Publicly Held**
**Web:** www.appliedmaterials.com
**SIC: 3674** Semiconductors and related devices
**PA:** Applied Materials, Inc.
  3050 Bowers Ave
  408 727-5555

### (P-12316)
### APPLIED MATERIALS INC
Also Called: Applied Materials
3340 Scott Blvd, Santa Clara (95054-3101)
**PHONE**..............................408 727-5555
**EMP:** 56
**SALES (corp-wide):** 26.52B **Publicly Held**
**Web:** www.appliedmaterials.com
**SIC: 3674** Semiconductors and related devices
**PA:** Applied Materials, Inc.
  3050 Bowers Ave
  408 727-5555

## 3674 - Semiconductors And Related Devices (P-12317)

**(P-12317)**
**APPLIED MATERIALS INC**
Also Called: Applied Materials
3101 Scott Blvd, Santa Clara (95054-3318)
PHONE.................512 272-3692
**EMP:** 26
**SALES (corp-wide):** 26.52B **Publicly Held**
Web: www.appliedmaterials.com
**SIC: 3674** Semiconductors and related devices
PA: Applied Materials, Inc.
3050 Bowers Ave
408 727-5555

**(P-12318)**
**APPLIED MATERIALS INC**
Also Called: Applied Materials
974 E Arques Ave Bldg 81, Sunnyvale (94085-4520)
PHONE.................408 727-5555
James Morgan, *Brnch Mgr*
**EMP:** 48
**SALES (corp-wide):** 26.52B **Publicly Held**
Web: www.appliedmaterials.com
**SIC: 3674** Semiconductors and related devices
PA: Applied Materials, Inc.
3050 Bowers Ave
408 727-5555

**(P-12319)**
**APPLIED MATERIALS INC**
Also Called: Applied Materials
2821 Scott Blvd Bldg 17, Santa Clara (95050-2549)
P.O. Box 58039 (95052-8039)
PHONE.................408 727-5555
Johnny Singh, *Prin*
**EMP:** 24
**SALES (corp-wide):** 26.52B **Publicly Held**
Web: www.appliedmaterials.com
**SIC: 3674** Semiconductors and related devices
PA: Applied Materials, Inc.
3050 Bowers Ave
408 727-5555

**(P-12320)**
**APPLIED MATERIALS (HOLDINGS) (HQ)**
Also Called: Applied Materials
3050 Bowers Ave, Santa Clara (95054-3298)
P.O. Box 58039 (95052-8039)
PHONE.................408 727-5555
Michael R Splinter, *CEO*
Gary E Dickerson, *
George S Davise, *
Randhir Thakur, *
Joseph Flanagan, *
**EMP:** 34 **EST:** 1982
**SALES (est):** 6.65MM
**SALES (corp-wide):** 26.52B **Publicly Held**
Web: www.appliedmaterials.com
**SIC: 3674** Semiconductors and related devices
PA: Applied Materials, Inc.
3050 Bowers Ave
408 727-5555

**(P-12321)**
**APPLIED MICRO CIRCUITS CORP (HQ)**
4555 Great America Pkwy # 6, Santa Clara (95054-1243)
PHONE.................408 542-8600
Paramesh Gopi, *Pr*
Martin S Mcdermut, *CFO*
L William Caraccio, *CLO*
▲ **EMP:** 138 **EST:** 1979

**SQ FT:** 55,000
**SALES (est):** 34.2MM **Publicly Held**
Web: www.macom.com
**SIC: 3674** Microcircuits, integrated (semiconductor)
PA: Macom Technology Solutions Holdings, Inc.
100 Chelmsford St

**(P-12322)**
**APPLIED MICRO CIRCUITS CORP**
Also Called: Amcc Sales
4555 Great America Pkwy Ste 601, Santa Clara (95054-1243)
PHONE.................408 542-8600
Kambiz Hooshmand, *Mgr*
**EMP:** 25
Web: www.macom.com
**SIC: 3674** Microcircuits, integrated (semiconductor)
HQ: Applied Micro Circuits Corp
4555 Great America Pkwy # 6
Santa Clara CA 95054
408 542-8600

**(P-12323)**
**APPLIED MTLS ASIA-PACIFIC LLC (HQ)**
Also Called: Applied Materials
3050 Bowers Ave, Santa Clara (95054-3201)
P.O. Box 58039 (95052-8039)
PHONE.................408 727-5555
Franz Janker, *Pr*
**EMP:** 103 **EST:** 1989
**SQ FT:** 3,000
**SALES (est):** 20.71MM
**SALES (corp-wide):** 26.52B **Publicly Held**
Web: www.appliedmaterials.com
**SIC: 3674** Semiconductors and related devices
PA: Applied Materials, Inc.
3050 Bowers Ave
408 727-5555

**(P-12324)**
**APPLIED THIN-FILM PRODUCTS (PA)**
Also Called: Atp
3620 Yale Way, Fremont (94538-6182)
PHONE.................510 661-4287
David J Adams, *CEO*
Franco Pietroforte, *
**EMP:** 112 **EST:** 1995
**SQ FT:** 18,000
**SALES (est):** 24.68MM **Privately Held**
Web: www.thinfilm.com
**SIC: 3674** Semiconductors and related devices

**(P-12325)**
**APTA GROUP INC**
Also Called: Advanced Packaging Tech Amer
7580 Britannia Ct, San Diego (92154-7424)
PHONE.................619 710-8170
Per Tonnesen, *Pr*
**EMP:** 21 **EST:** 1993
**SQ FT:** 25,000
**SALES (est):** 2.95MM **Privately Held**
Web: www.perfectdomain.com
**SIC: 3674** Hybrid integrated circuits

**(P-12326)**
**APTINA LLC**
Also Called: Aptina Imaging
2660 Zanker Rd, San Jose (95134-2700)
PHONE.................408 660-2699
Joseph Passarello, *Managing Member*

**EMP:** 650 **EST:** 2006
**SALES (est):** 94.46MM
**SALES (corp-wide):** 8.25B **Publicly Held**
Web: www.aptina.com
**SIC: 3674** 7336 Semiconductors and related devices; Graphic arts and related design
PA: On Semiconductor Corporation
5701 N Pima Rd
602 244-6600

**(P-12327)**
**AQT SOLAR INC**
1145 Sonora Ct, Sunnyvale (94086-5384)
P.O. Box 2699 (95055-2699)
▲ **EMP:** 40
Web: www.aqtsolar.com
**SIC: 3674** Semiconductors and related devices

**(P-12328)**
**AQUANTIA CORP (DH)**
Also Called: Aquantia
5488 Marvell Ln, Santa Clara (95054-3606)
PHONE.................408 228-8300
Matt Murphy, *Pr*
**EMP:** 22 **EST:** 2004
**SALES (est):** 19.56MM
**SALES (corp-wide):** 5.51B **Publicly Held**
Web: www.marvell.com
**SIC: 3674** Semiconductors and related devices
HQ: Marvell Technology Group Ltd.
C/O Appleby
Hamilton

**(P-12329)**
**ARM INC**
5375 Mira Sorrento Pl Ste 540, San Diego (92121-3804)
PHONE.................858 453-1900
Todd Vierra, *Brnch Mgr*
**EMP:** 1151
**SALES (corp-wide):** 8.87B **Privately Held**
Web: www.arm.com
**SIC: 3674** Integrated circuits, semiconductor networks, etc.
HQ: Arm, Inc.
120 Rose Orchard Way
San Jose CA 95134

**(P-12330)**
**ARM INC (DH)**
120 Rose Orchard Way, San Jose (95134)
PHONE.................408 576-1500
Simon Segars, *CEO*
Graham Budd, *
**EMP:** 270 **EST:** 1991
**SALES (est):** 1.04B
**SALES (corp-wide):** 8.87B **Privately Held**
Web: www.arm.com
**SIC: 3674** Integrated circuits, semiconductor networks, etc.
HQ: Svf Holdco (Uk) Limited
69 Grosvenor Street
London W1K 3

**(P-12331)**
**ARRIVE TECHNOLOGIES INC**
3693 Westchester Dr, Roseville (95747-6353)
PHONE.................916 715-9775
Peter W Keeler, *Ch Bd*
Murat Uraz, *Pr*
**EMP:** 15 **EST:** 2001
**SALES (est):** 740.37K **Privately Held**
Web: www.arrivetechnologies.com
**SIC: 3674** Integrated circuits, semiconductor networks, etc.

**(P-12332)**
**ARTERIS INC (PA)**
900 E Hamilton Ave Ste 300, Campbell (95008-0672)
PHONE.................408 470-7300
K Charles Janac, *Ch Bd*
Laurent R Moll, *COO*
Nicholas B Hawkins, *VP*
Paul L Alpern, *VP*
**EMP:** 189 **EST:** 2004
**SALES (est):** 53.67MM **Publicly Held**
Web: www.arteris.com
**SIC: 3674** Semiconductors and related devices

**(P-12333)**
**ARTERIS HOLDINGS INC**
Also Called: Arteris
591 W Hamilton Ave Ste 250, Campbell (95008-0559)
PHONE.................408 470-7300
Charles K Janac, *Pr*
Stephane Mehat, *
Ty Garibay, *
**EMP:** 45 **EST:** 2007
**SQ FT:** 4,500
**SALES (est):** 5.18MM **Privately Held**
Web: www.arteris.com
**SIC: 3674** Semiconductors and related devices

**(P-12334)**
**ASC GROUP INC**
12243 Branford St, Sun Valley (91352-1010)
PHONE.................818 896-1101
Chuck Rogers, *Pr*
**EMP:** 344 **EST:** 1988
**SQ FT:** 80,000
**SALES (est):** 9.66MM
**SALES (corp-wide):** 1.71B **Privately Held**
Web: www.pmcglobalinc.com
**SIC: 3674** Semiconductors and related devices
HQ: Pmc, Inc.
12243 Branford St
Sun Valley CA 91352
818 896-1101

**(P-12335)**
**ASI SEMICONDUCTOR INC**
Also Called: A S I
24955 Avenue Kearny, Valencia (91355-1252)
PHONE.................818 982-1200
Steve Golob, *Prin*
Mike Lincoln, *
Fred Golob, *
**EMP:** 25 **EST:** 2011
**SALES (est):** 3.78MM **Privately Held**
Web: www.advancedsemiconductor.com
**SIC: 3674** Semiconductors and related devices

**(P-12336)**
**ASTERA LABS INC (PA)**
Also Called: ASTERA LABS
2901 Tasman Dr Ste 205, Santa Clara (95054-1138)
PHONE.................408 337-9056
Jitendra Mohan, *CEO*
Manuel Alba, *Non-Executive Chairman of the Board*
Sanjay Gajendra, *Pr*
Michael Tate, *CFO*
**EMP:** 256 **EST:** 2017
**SQ FT:** 51,320
**SALES (est):** 115.79MM
**SALES (corp-wide):** 115.79MM **Publicly Held**

# PRODUCTS & SERVICES SECTION
## 3674 - Semiconductors And Related Devices (P-12359)

Web: www.asteralabs.com
SIC: 3674 Integrated circuits, semiconductor networks, etc.

**(P-12337)**
**ASYST TECHNOLOGIES INC**
46897 Bayside Pkwy, Fremont (94538-6572)
P.O. Box 4118 (95056-4118)
PHONE.............................408 329-6661
▲ EMP: 1002
SIC: 3674 Semiconductors and related devices

**(P-12338)**
**ATMEL CORPORATION**
1600 Technology Dr, San Jose (95110-1382)
PHONE.............................408 735-9110
EMP: 5200
Web: www.microchip.com
SIC: 3674 3714 3545 Microcircuits, integrated (semiconductor); Motor vehicle electrical equipment; Wheel turning equipment, diamond point or other

**(P-12339)**
**ATOMICA CORP**
Also Called: IMT Analytical
75 Robin Hill Rd, Goleta (93117-3108)
PHONE.............................805 681-2807
Eric Sigler, CEO
Jim Mcgibbon, CFO
Chris Gudeman, *
Dave Chrishna, *
EMP: 115 EST: 1987
SQ FT: 130,000
SALES (est): 42.81MM Privately Held
Web: www.atomica.com
SIC: 3674 Semiconductors and related devices

**(P-12340)**
**ATP ELECTRONICS INC**
Also Called: Atp Electronics
2590 N 1st St Ste 150, San Jose (95131-1049)
PHONE.............................408 732-5000
Jeffray Hsieh, CEO
Dean Chang, Ch Bd
Danny Lin, Genl Mgr
▲ EMP: 23 EST: 1991
SQ FT: 10,000
SALES (est): 5.41MM Privately Held
Web: www.atpinc.com
SIC: 3674 Semiconductors and related devices
PA: Atp Electronics Taiwan Inc.
10f, No. 185, Tiding Blvd., Sec. 2,

**(P-12341)**
**ATTOLLO ENGINEERING LLC**
Also Called: Attollo Engineering
160 Camino Ruiz, Camarillo (93012-6700)
PHONE.............................805 384-8046
Michael Macdougal, Pr
Michael Macdougal, Owner
EMP: 52 EST: 2012
SALES (est): 5.29MM Privately Held
Web: www.attolloengineering.com
SIC: 3674 Semiconductors and related devices

**(P-12342)**
**AUDIENCE INC**
331 Fairchild Dr, Mountain View (94043-2200)
PHONE.............................650 254-2800
EMP: 349
Web: www.audience.com

SIC: 3674 Microprocessors

**(P-12343)**
**AUXIN SOLAR INC**
6835 Via Del Oro, San Jose (95119-1315)
PHONE.............................408 225-4380
Sherry Tai, CEO
Mamum Rashid, *
▲ EMP: 45 EST: 2008
SQ FT: 100,000
SALES (est): 8.74MM Privately Held
Web: www.auxinsolar.com
SIC: 3674 Solar cells

**(P-12344)**
**AVAGO TECHNOLOGIES US INC**
1730 Fox Dr, San Jose (95131-2311)
PHONE.............................408 433-4068
EMP: 812
SALES (corp-wide): 35.82B Publicly Held
Web: www.broadcom.com
SIC: 3674 Semiconductors and related devices
HQ: Avago Technologies U.S. Inc.
1320 Ridder Park Dr
San Jose CA 95131

**(P-12345)**
**AVAGO TECHNOLOGIES US INC**
408 E Plumeria Dr, San Jose (95134-1912)
PHONE.............................408 433-8000
Hock Tan, Brnch Mgr
EMP: 812
SALES (corp-wide): 35.82B Publicly Held
Web: www.broadcom.com
SIC: 3674 Semiconductors and related devices
HQ: Avago Technologies U.S. Inc.
1320 Ridder Park Dr
San Jose CA 95131

**(P-12346)**
**AVALANCHE TECHNOLOGY INC**
3450 W Warren Ave, Fremont (94538-6425)
PHONE.............................510 438-0148
Petro Estakhri, Pr
Bob Netter, *
Michael Ofstedahl, *
Yiming Huai, *
Ebrahim Abedifard, *
EMP: 25 EST: 2006
SALES (est): 7.06MM Privately Held
Web: www.avalanche-technology.com
SIC: 3674 Magnetic bubble memory device

**(P-12347)**
**AVID IDNTIFICATION SYSTEMS INC (PA)**
Also Called: Avid
3185 Hamner Ave, Norco (92860-1937)
PHONE.............................951 371-7505
Hannis L Stoddard, CEO
Hannis L Stoddard, Pr
Peter Troesch, *
▲ EMP: 100 EST: 1986
SQ FT: 30,000
SALES (est): 9.83MM Privately Held
Web: www.avidid.com
SIC: 3674 5999 Semiconductors and related devices; Pets and pet supplies

**(P-12348)**
**AVOGY INC**
677 River Oaks Pkwy, San Jose (95134-1907)
PHONE.............................408 684-5200
EMP: 20
Web: www.avogy.com

SIC: 3674 Semiconductor diodes and rectifiers

**(P-12349)**
**AWBSCQEMGK INC**
545 Oakmead Pkwy, Sunnyvale (94085-4023)
PHONE.............................408 988-8600
EMP: 50
SIC: 3674 Solar cells

**(P-12350)**
**AXT INC (PA)**
Also Called: AXT
4281 Technology Dr, Fremont (94538-6339)
PHONE.............................510 438-4700
Morris S Young, Ch Bd
Gary L Fischer, Corporate Secretary
▲ EMP: 24 EST: 1986
SQ FT: 19,467
SALES (est): 75.8MM
SALES (corp-wide): 75.8MM Publicly Held
Web: www.axt.com
SIC: 3674 Semiconductors and related devices

**(P-12351)**
**AXT INC**
Also Called: American Etal Technology
4311 Solar Way, Fremont (94538-6389)
PHONE.............................510 683-5900
Maureen Wang, Mgr
EMP: 412
SALES (corp-wide): 75.8MM Publicly Held
Web: www.axt.com
SIC: 3674 Integrated circuits, semiconductor networks, etc.
PA: Axt, Inc.
4281 Technology Dr
510 438-4700

**(P-12352)**
**AXT-TONGMEI INC**
4281 Technology Dr, Fremont (94538-6339)
PHONE.............................510 438-4700
Doctor Morris Young, CEO
Alan Chan, Contrlr
EMP: 26 EST: 2020
SALES (est): 6.62MM
SALES (corp-wide): 75.8MM Publicly Held
SIC: 3674 Semiconductor diodes and rectifiers
PA: Axt, Inc.
4281 Technology Dr
510 438-4700

**(P-12353)**
**AZIMUTH INDUSTRIAL CO INC**
Also Called: Azimuth Semiconductor Assembly
30593 Union City Blvd Ste 110, Union City (94587-1515)
PHONE.............................510 441-6000
David Lee, Pr
Sandra Lee, Ofcr
▲ EMP: 20 EST: 1988
SQ FT: 16,000
SALES (est): 3.11MM Privately Held
Web: www.azimuthsemi.com
SIC: 3674 Semiconductors and related devices

**(P-12354)**
**BAE SYSTEMS IMGING SLTIONS INC**
1841 Zanker Rd Ste 50, San Jose (95112-4223)

PHONE.............................408 433-2500
Kwang Bo Cho, Pr
EMP: 99 EST: 2001
SQ FT: 60,000
SALES (est): 20.28MM
SALES (corp-wide): 28.77B Privately Held
SIC: 3674 3577 Semiconductors and related devices; Computer peripheral equipment, nec
HQ: Bae Systems Information And Electronic Systems Integration Inc.
65 Spit Brook Rd
Nashua NH 03060
603 885-4321

**(P-12355)**
**BAR MANUFACTURING INC**
3921 Sandstone Dr Ste 1, El Dorado Hills (95762-9343)
P.O. Box 4664 (95762-0022)
PHONE.............................916 939-0551
S S Wong, Ch Bd
◆ EMP: 62 EST: 2003
SALES (est): 2.9MM Privately Held
SIC: 3674 Semiconductor circuit networks
HQ: Compart Engineering, Inc.
1730 E Philadelphia St
Ontario CA 91761
909 947-6688

**(P-12356)**
**BAYWA RE EPC LLC**
17901 Von Karman Ave Ste 1050, Irvine (92614-5254)
PHONE.............................949 398-3915
Baywa R E Solar, Project LLC
EMP: 32 EST: 2015
SALES (est): 1.05MM Privately Held
Web: us.baywa-re.com
SIC: 3674 Solar cells

**(P-12357)**
**BAYWA RE SOLAR PROJECTS LLC (DH)**
Also Called: Baywa R.E.renewable Energy
18575 Jamboree Rd Ste 850, Irvine (92612-2558)
PHONE.............................949 398-3915
▲ EMP: 15 EST: 2014
SALES (est): 318.57MM
SALES (corp-wide): 26.03B Privately Held
Web: www.baywa-re.com
SIC: 3674 Solar cells
HQ: Baywa R.E. Ag
Arabellastr. 4
Munchen BY 81925

**(P-12358)**
**BEAM GLOBAL (PA)**
5660 Eastgate Dr, San Diego (92121-2816)
PHONE.............................858 799-4583
Desmond Wheatley, Ch Bd
Katherine Mcdermott, CFO
Mark Myers, COO
EMP: 103 EST: 2006
SQ FT: 53,000
SALES (est): 67.35MM Publicly Held
Web: www.beamforall.com
SIC: 3674 Solar cells

**(P-12359)**
**BEAMREACH SOLAR INC**
Also Called: Beamreach Solar
1530 Mccarthy Blvd, Milpitas (95035-7405)
PHONE.............................408 240-3800
EMP: 30
Web: www.beamreachsolar.com
SIC: 3674 Solar cells

# 3674 - Semiconductors And Related Devices (P-12360)

**(P-12360)**
**BLAIZE INC**
4659 Golden Foothill Pkwy, El Dorado Hills (95762-9742)
PHONE.................916 347-0050
Dinakar C Munagala, *CEO*
Leo Merle, *
**EMP:** 300 **EST:** 2011
**SALES (est):** 23.8MM **Privately Held**
Web: www.blaize.com
SIC: **3674** Semiconductors and related devices

**(P-12361)**
**BLOOM ENERGY CORPORATION (PA)**
Also Called: BLOOM ENERGY
4353 N 1st St, San Jose (95134-1259)
PHONE.................408 543-1500
K R Sridhar, *Ch Bd*
Gregory Cameron, *Pr*
Aman Joshi, *CCO*
Satish Chitoori, *COO*
Shawn M Soderberg, *CLO*
▲ **EMP:** 300 **EST:** 2001
**SQ FT:** 183,000
**SALES (est):** 1.33B
**SALES (corp-wide):** 1.33B **Publicly Held**
Web: www.bloomenergy.com
SIC: **3674** Fuel cells, solid state

**(P-12362)**
**BROADCOM CORPORATION**
1465 N Mcdowell Blvd Ste 140, Petaluma (94954-6571)
PHONE.................707 792-9000
Joy Hinke, *Mgr*
**EMP:** 27
**SALES (corp-wide):** 35.82B **Publicly Held**
Web: www.broadcom.com
SIC: **3674** Semiconductors and related devices
HQ: Broadcom Corporation
1320 Ridder Park Dr
San Jose CA 95131

**(P-12363)**
**BROADCOM CORPORATION**
15101 Alton Pkwy, Irvine (92618-2372)
PHONE.................949 926-5000
**EMP:** 224
**SALES (corp-wide):** 35.82B **Publicly Held**
Web: www.broadcom.com
SIC: **3674** Semiconductors and related devices
HQ: Broadcom Corporation
1320 Ridder Park Dr
San Jose CA 95131

**(P-12364)**
**BROADCOM CORPORATION**
Also Called: Broadcom Limited Bldg 2
15191 Alton Pkwy, Irvine (92618-2300)
PHONE.................714 376-5029
**EMP:** 35
**SALES (corp-wide):** 35.82B **Publicly Held**
Web: www.broadcom.com
SIC: **3674** Semiconductors and related devices
HQ: Broadcom Corporation
1320 Ridder Park Dr
San Jose CA 95131

**(P-12365)**
**BROADCOM CORPORATION**
250 Innovation Dr, San Jose (95134-3390)
PHONE.................408 922-7000
Carol Barrett, *Brnch Mgr*
**EMP:** 39
**SALES (corp-wide):** 35.82B **Publicly Held**
Web: www.broadcom.com
SIC: **3674** Integrated circuits, semiconductor networks, etc.
HQ: Broadcom Corporation
1320 Ridder Park Dr
San Jose CA 95131

**(P-12366)**
**BROADCOM CORPORATION (HQ)**
1320 Ridder Park Dr, San Jose (95131-2313)
P.O. Box 57013 (92619-7013)
PHONE.................408 433-8000
Hock Tan, *CEO*
Kristen Spears, *
Charlie Kawwas, *CSO*
Henry Samueli, *
▲ **EMP:** 456 **EST:** 1991
**SALES (est):** 2.45B
**SALES (corp-wide):** 35.82B **Publicly Held**
Web: www.broadcom.com
SIC: **3674** Integrated circuits, semiconductor networks, etc.
PA: Broadcom Inc.
3421 Hillview Ave
650 427-6000

**(P-12367)**
**BROADCOM CORPORATION**
16340 W Bernardo Dr Bldg A, San Diego (92127-1802)
PHONE.................858 385-8800
Bell Philip Andrew, *Brnch Mgr*
**EMP:** 142
**SALES (corp-wide):** 35.82B **Publicly Held**
Web: www.broadcom.com
SIC: **3674** Integrated circuits, semiconductor networks, etc.
HQ: Broadcom Corporation
1320 Ridder Park Dr
San Jose CA 95131

**(P-12368)**
**BROADCOM INC (PA)**
Also Called: Broadcom
3421 Hillview Ave, Palo Alto (94304-1320)
PHONE.................650 427-6000
Hock E Tan, *Pr*
Henry Samueli, *Ch Bd*
Kirsten M Spears, *CAO*
Mark D Brazeal, *Legal CORP AFFAIRS*
**EMP:** 1712 **EST:** 1960
**SALES (est):** 35.82B
**SALES (corp-wide):** 35.82B **Publicly Held**
Web: www.broadcom.com
SIC: **3674** Semiconductor diodes and rectifiers

**(P-12369)**
**BROADCOM INC**
1730 Fox Dr, San Jose (95131-2311)
PHONE.................650 427-6000
**EMP:** 16
**SALES (corp-wide):** 35.82B **Publicly Held**
Web: www.broadcom.com
SIC: **3674** Semiconductor diodes and rectifiers
PA: Broadcom Inc.
3421 Hillview Ave
650 427-6000

**(P-12370)**
**BROADCOM TECHNOLOGIES INC (HQ)**
1320 Ridder Park Dr, San Jose (95131-2313)
PHONE.................408 433-8000
**EMP:** 63 **EST:** 2018
**SALES (est):** 3.03MM
**SALES (corp-wide):** 35.82B **Publicly Held**
Web: www.broadcom.com
SIC: **3674** Semiconductors and related devices
PA: Broadcom Inc.
3421 Hillview Ave
650 427-6000

**(P-12371)**
**BROADLIGHT INC**
2901 Tasman Dr Ste 218, Santa Clara (95054-1138)
PHONE.................408 982-4210
Raanan Gewirtzman, *CEO*
Didi Ivancovsky, *VP*
Dror Heldenberg, *CFO*
Raanan Gewirtzman, *COO*
**EMP:** 29 **EST:** 2003
**SALES (est):** 1.31MM
**SALES (corp-wide):** 35.82B **Publicly Held**
Web: www.broadcom.com
SIC: **3674** Semiconductors and related devices
HQ: Broadcom Corporation
1320 Ridder Park Dr
San Jose CA 95131

**(P-12372)**
**C & D SEMICONDUCTOR SVCS INC (PA)**
Also Called: C&D Precision Machining
1110 Ringwood Ct, San Jose (95131-1726)
PHONE.................408 383-1888
Dong Van Nguyen, *CEO*
Tien Nguyen, *
◆ **EMP:** 60 **EST:** 1990
**SQ FT:** 47,000
**SALES (est):** 9.38MM **Privately Held**
Web: www.cdsemi.com
SIC: **3674** Semiconductors and related devices

**(P-12373)**
**CA INC**
Also Called: CA
6000 Shoreline Ct Ste 300, South San Francisco (94080-7606)
PHONE.................650 534-9000
Lillie Moreci, *Brnch Mgr*
**EMP:** 22
**SALES (corp-wide):** 35.82B **Publicly Held**
Web: www.broadcom.com
SIC: **3674** Semiconductors and related devices
HQ: Ca, Inc.
3421 Hillview Ave
Palo Alto CA 94304
800 225-5224

**(P-12374)**
**CA INC**
Also Called: CA
3013 Douglas Blvd Ste 120, Roseville (95661-3842)
PHONE.................800 405-5540
Larry Lynch, *Mgr*
**EMP:** 37
**SALES (corp-wide):** 35.82B **Publicly Held**
Web: www.broadcom.com
SIC: **3674** Semiconductors and related devices
HQ: Ca, Inc.
3421 Hillview Ave
Palo Alto CA 94304
800 225-5224

**(P-12375)**
**CAELUX CORPORATION**
404 N Halstead St, Pasadena (91107-3124)
PHONE.................626 502-7033
Scott Graybeal, *CEO*
John Iannellli, *Pr*
Jeremy Ferrell, *CFO*
**EMP:** 27 **EST:** 2014
**SALES (est):** 7.6MM **Privately Held**
SIC: **3674** Semiconductors and related devices

**(P-12376)**
**CAVIUM LLC (DH)**
5488 Marvell Ln, Santa Clara (95054-3606)
PHONE.................408 222-2500
Jean Hu, *Pr*
**EMP:** 30 **EST:** 2000
**SALES (est):** 230.23MM
**SALES (corp-wide):** 5.51B **Publicly Held**
Web: www.marvell.com
SIC: **3674** Semiconductors and related devices
HQ: Marvell Technology Group Ltd.
C/O Appleby
Hamilton

**(P-12377)**
**CAVIUM NETWORKS INTL INC**
2315 N 1st St, San Jose (95131-1010)
PHONE.................650 625-7000
Syed Ali, *CEO*
**EMP:** 85 **EST:** 2005
**SALES (est):** 21.6MM
**SALES (corp-wide):** 5.51B **Publicly Held**
Web: www.marvell.com
SIC: **3674** Semiconductor diodes and rectifiers
HQ: Cavium, Llc
5488 Marvell Ln
Santa Clara CA 95054

**(P-12378)**
**CAVLI INC**
99 Almaden Blvd Ste 600, San Jose (95113-1605)
PHONE.................650 605-8166
John Mathew, *CEO*
Tarun Thomas George, *COO*
**EMP:** 20 **EST:** 2022
**SALES (est):** 4.3MM **Privately Held**
SIC: **3674** Semiconductors and related devices

**(P-12379)**
**CELESTICA LLC**
5325 Hellyer Ave, San Jose (95138-1013)
PHONE.................408 574-6000
Joel Bustos, *Genl Mgr*
**EMP:** 133
**SALES (corp-wide):** 7.96B **Privately Held**
Web: www.celestica.com
SIC: **3674** Semiconductors and related devices
HQ: Celestica Llc
400 Glleria Pkwy Ste 1500
Atlanta GA 30339

**(P-12380)**
**CEVA DEVELOPMENT INC (HQ)** ✪
1174 Castro St Ste 275, Mountain View (94040-2571)
PHONE.................650 417-7900
**EMP:** 18 **EST:** 2024
**SALES (est):** 8.88MM
**SALES (corp-wide):** 97.42MM **Publicly Held**
Web: www.ceva-dsp.com
SIC: **3674** Semiconductors and related devices
PA: Ceva, Inc.
15245 Shady Grove Rd Ste
240 308-8328

## 3674 - Semiconductors And Related Devices (P-12401)

**(P-12381)**
**CHRONTEL INC (PA)**
2210 Otoole Ave Ste 100, San Jose (95131-1300)
PHONE..............................408 383-9328
Bruce Wooley, *Ch Bd*
David C Soo, *Pr*
James Lin, *
EMP: 70 EST: 1986
SQ FT: 40,000
SALES (est): 9.17MM **Privately Held**
Web: www.chrontel.com
SIC: 3674 8711 Integrated circuits, semiconductor networks, etc.; Engineering services

**(P-12382)**
**CLARIPHY COMMUNICATIONS INC (DH)**
15485 Sand Canyon Ave, Irvine (92618-3154)
PHONE..............................949 861-3074
Nariman Yousefi, *Pr*
William J Ruehle, *
Norman L Swenson, *
EMP: 78 EST: 2004
SALES (est): 11.02MM
SALES (corp-wide): 5.51B **Publicly Held**
Web: www.marvell.com
SIC: 3674 Integrated circuits, semiconductor networks, etc.
HQ: Inphi Corporation
110 Rio Robles
San Jose CA 95134

**(P-12383)**
**CLEARWELL SYSTEMS INC**
350 Ellis St, Mountain View (94043-2202)
PHONE..............................877 253-2793
Aaref Hilaly, *CEO*
Venkat Rangan, *
Anup Singh, *
▼ EMP: 110 EST: 2004
SQ FT: 17,000
SALES (est): 9.13MM
SALES (corp-wide): 3.81B **Publicly Held**
Web: www.broadcom.com
SIC: 3674 Semiconductors and related devices
PA: Gen Digital Inc.
60 E Rio Slado Pkwy Ste 1
650 527-8000

**(P-12384)**
**CM MANUFACTURING INC**
6321 San Ignacio Ave, San Jose (95119-1202)
PHONE..............................408 284-7200
▲ EMP: 228
SIC: 3674 Semiconductors and related devices

**(P-12385)**
**CNEX LABS INC (PA)**
2390 Bering Dr, San Jose (95131-1121)
PHONE..............................408 695-1045
Alan Armstrong, *CEO*
Joe Defranco, *
Ronnie Huang, *
EMP: 30 EST: 2013
SALES (est): 5.33MM
SALES (corp-wide): 5.33MM **Privately Held**
Web: www.cnexlabs.com
SIC: 3674 Semiconductors and related devices

**(P-12386)**
**CONCEPT SYSTEMS MFG INC**
2047 Zanker Rd, San Jose (95131-2107)
PHONE..............................408 855-8595
Richard Diehl, *Pr*
▲ EMP: 21 EST: 2006
SALES (est): 568.66K **Privately Held**
Web: www.csmanufacturing.net
SIC: 3674 Semiconductors and related devices

**(P-12387)**
**CONDOR RELIABILITY SVCS INC**
3400 De La Cruz Blvd, Santa Clara (95054-2609)
PHONE..............................408 486-9600
Punam Patel, *Pr*
EMP: 26 EST: 1980
SALES (est): 1.76MM **Privately Held**
Web: www.crsigroup.com
SIC: 3674 8999 8734 8731 Semiconductors and related devices; Weather related services; Testing laboratories; Commercial physical research

**(P-12388)**
**CONEXANT HOLDINGS INC**
4000 Macarthur Blvd, Newport Beach (92660-2558)
PHONE..............................415 983-2706
EMP: 600
SIC: 3674 5065 Semiconductors and related devices; Semiconductor devices

**(P-12389)**
**CONEXANT SYSTEMS LLC (HQ)**
1901 Main St Ste 300, Irvine (92614-0512)
PHONE..............................949 483-4600
Jan Johannessen, *CEO*
EMP: 23 EST: 2013
SQ FT: 140,000
SALES (est): 3.13MM
SALES (corp-wide): 959.4MM **Publicly Held**
SIC: 3674 5065 Semiconductors and related devices; Semiconductor devices
PA: Synaptics Incorporated
1109 Mckay Dr
408 904-1100

**(P-12390)**
**CONTECH SOLUTIONS INCORPORATED**
631 Montague St, San Leandro (94577-4323)
PHONE..............................510 357-7900
Afshin Nouri, *Pr*
Jafarzaden Mehran, *Mng Dir*
Mehran Jafarcadeh, *VP*
EMP: 21 EST: 1995
SQ FT: 4,000
SALES (est): 2.29MM **Privately Held**
Web: www.contechsolutions.com
SIC: 3674 Semiconductors and related devices

**(P-12391)**
**COOPER MICROELECTRONICS INC**
Also Called: CMI
1671 Reynolds Ave, Irvine (92614-5709)
PHONE..............................949 553-8352
Kenneth B Cooper Iii, *Pr*
Lily Cooper, *
▲ EMP: 37 EST: 1985
SQ FT: 10,000
SALES (est): 5.69MM **Privately Held**
Web: www.coopermicro.com

**(P-12392)**
**CORE SYSTEMS LLC**
2121 Zanker Rd, San Jose (95131-2109)
PHONE..............................510 933-2300
Donald W Lindsey, *CEO*
Steve Lindsey, *
Walter J Wriggins, *
▲ EMP: 25 EST: 1990
SALES (est): 9.22MM **Privately Held**
Web: www.coresystems.com
SIC: 3674 Semiconductors and related devices

**(P-12393)**
**CORSAIR MEMORY INC (DH)**
Also Called: Corsair
115 N Mccarthy Blvd, Milpitas (95035-5102)
PHONE..............................510 657-8747
Andrew Paul, *CEO*
Ronald Van Veen, *VP Fin*
Michael G Potter, *CFO*
Thi La, *Pr*
◆ EMP: 128 EST: 1994
SALES (est): 35.31MM **Publicly Held**
Web: www.corsair.com
SIC: 3674 7373 8731 Memories, solid state; Computer integrated systems design; Computer (hardware) development
HQ: Corsair Gaming, Inc.
115 N Mccarthy Blvd
Milpitas CA 95035
510 657-8747

**(P-12394)**
**CORTINA SYSTEMS INC (DH)**
2953 Bunker Hill Ln Ste 300, Santa Clara (95054-1131)
PHONE..............................408 481-2300
Amir Nayyerhabibi, *Pr*
Bruce Margtson, *
EMP: 120 EST: 2001
SQ FT: 41,645
SALES (est): 17.44MM
SALES (corp-wide): 5.51B **Publicly Held**
Web: www.marvell.com
SIC: 3674 Integrated circuits, semiconductor networks, etc.
HQ: Inphi Corporation
110 Rio Robles
San Jose CA 95134

**(P-12395)**
**CREDO SEMICONDUCTOR INC**
Also Called: Credo
110 Rio Robles Fl 1, San Jose (95134-1813)
PHONE..............................408 906-8557
William Brennan, *CEO*
Dan Fleming, *
Lawrence Cheng, *
Job Lam, *
EMP: 92 EST: 2015
SALES (est): 12.96MM **Privately Held**
Web: www.credosemi.com
SIC: 3674 Integrated circuits, semiconductor networks, etc.
PA: Credo Technology Group Holding Ltd
C/O: Maples Corporate Services Limited

**(P-12396)**
**CROSSBAR INC**
2055 Laurelwood Rd, Santa Clara (95054-2729)
PHONE..............................408 884-0281
George Minassian, *CEO*
EMP: 20 EST: 2008
SALES (est): 4.61MM **Privately Held**
Web: www.crossbar-inc.com
SIC: 3674 Semiconductors and related devices

**(P-12397)**
**CYPRESS SEMICONDUCTOR CORP (HQ)**
Also Called: Cypress
198 Champion Ct, San Jose (95134-1709)
PHONE..............................408 943-2600
Robert Lefort, *Pr*
Jack Artman, *
◆ EMP: 650 EST: 1982
SQ FT: 171,370
SALES (est): 1.78B
SALES (corp-wide): 17.72B **Privately Held**
Web: www.cypress.com
SIC: 3674 Semiconductors and related devices
PA: Infineon Technologies Ag
Am Campeon 1-15
892340

**(P-12398)**
**CYPRESS SEMICONDUCTOR INTL INC (DH)**
4001 N 1st St, San Jose (95134-1503)
PHONE..............................408 943-2600
EMP: 21 EST: 1982
SALES (est): 4.22MM
SALES (corp-wide): 17.72B **Privately Held**
SIC: 3674 Semiconductors and related devices
HQ: Cypress Semiconductor Corporation
198 Champion Ct
San Jose CA 95134
408 943-2600

**(P-12399)**
**D-TEK MANUFACTURING**
3245 Woodward Ave, Santa Clara (95054-2626)
PHONE..............................408 588-1574
Dung Nguyen, *Pr*
Thanh L Dang, *VP*
EMP: 20 EST: 2010
SQ FT: 5,000
SALES (est): 1.26MM **Privately Held**
Web: www.d-tekmfg.com
SIC: 3674 Semiconductors and related devices

**(P-12400)**
**DATA DEVICE CORPORATION**
13000 Gregg St Ste C, Poway (92064-7151)
PHONE..............................858 503-3300
Dan Veenstra, *Brnch Mgr*
EMP: 35
SALES (corp-wide): 7.94B **Publicly Held**
Web: www.ddc-web.com
SIC: 3674 Semiconductors and related devices
HQ: Data Device Corporation
105 Wilbur Pl
Bohemia NY 11716
631 567-5600

**(P-12401)**
**DAYLIGHT SOLUTIONS INC (DH)**
Also Called: Drs Daylight Solutions
16465 Via Esprillo Ste 100, San Diego (92127-1701)
PHONE..............................858 432-7500
Timothy Day, *CEO*
Paul Larson, *Pr*
EMP: 101 EST: 2004
SALES (est): 40.72MM

## 3674 - Semiconductors And Related Devices (P-12402)

SALES (corp-wide): 16.62B **Publicly Held**
Web: www.daylightsolutions.com
SIC: **3674** 5084 3826 Molecular devices, solid state; Instruments and control equipment; Analytical instruments
HQ: Leonardo Drs, Inc.
2345 Crystal Dr Ste 1000
Arlington VA 22202
703 416-8000

### (P-12402)
### DAYSTAR TECHNOLOGIES INC
1010 S Milpitas Blvd, Milpitas (95035-6307)
PHONE.................................408 582-7100
Tina Carrillo, *Brnch Mgr*
EMP: 60
SALES (corp-wide): 3MM **Privately Held**
Web: www.daystartech.com
SIC: **3674** Solar cells
PA: Daystar Technologies Inc.
3556 Alvarado Niles Rd S
408 582-7100

### (P-12403)
### DISCERA INC
950 Tower Ln Ste 700, Foster City (94404-4254)
P.O. Box 725 (95015-0725)
EMP: 15 EST: 2004
SALES (est): 2.43MM **Privately Held**
SIC: **3674** Semiconductors and related devices

### (P-12404)
### DISPLAY PRODUCTS INC
Also Called: Data Display Products
445 S Douglas St, El Segundo (90245-4630)
PHONE.................................310 640-0442
EMP: 48 EST: 1970
SALES (est): 5MM **Privately Held**
Web: www.vcclite.com
SIC: **3674** 3679 Semiconductors and related devices; Electronic circuits

### (P-12405)
### DOLPHIN TECHNOLOGY INC
333 W Santa Clara St Ste 920, San Jose (95113-1713)
PHONE.................................408 392-0012
Mohammad Tamjidi, *Pr*
EMP: 24 EST: 1996
SALES (est): 2.15MM **Privately Held**
Web: www.dolphin-ic.com
SIC: **3674** Semiconductors and related devices

### (P-12406)
### DPA LABS INC
Also Called: Dpa Components International
2251 Ward Ave, Simi Valley (93065-7556)
PHONE.................................805 581-9200
Douglas Young, *Pr*
Philip Young, *VP*
EMP: 50 EST: 1979
SQ FT: 38,000
SALES (est): 12.15MM **Privately Held**
Web: www.dpaci.com
SIC: **3674** 8734 Semiconductors and related devices; Testing laboratories

### (P-12407)
### DREAMBIG SEMICONDUCTOR INC
2860 Zanker Rd Ste 210, San Jose (95134-2120)
PHONE.................................408 839-1232
Sohail A Syed, *CEO*
EMP: 75 EST: 2019
SALES (est): 5.25MM **Privately Held**
Web: www.dreambigsemi.com
SIC: **3674** Semiconductor circuit networks

### (P-12408)
### DRS NTWORK IMAGING SYSTEMS LLC
Also Called: Drs Network & Imaging Systems
10600 Valley View St, Cypress (90630-4833)
PHONE.................................714 220-3800
EMP: 100 EST: 2009
SALES (est): 23.98MM
SALES (corp-wide): 16.62B **Publicly Held**
Web: www.leonardodrs.com
SIC: **3674** 8731 Infrared sensors, solid state; Commercial physical research
HQ: Leonardo Drs, Inc.
2345 Crystal Dr Ste 1000
Arlington VA 22202
703 416-8000

### (P-12409)
### DSP GROUP INC (HQ)
Also Called: Dsp Group
2055 Gateway Pl Ste 480, San Jose (95110-1019)
PHONE.................................408 986-4300
Michael Hurlston, *Pr*
Dean Butler, *
Venkat Kodavati, *
Divyesh Shah, *
EMP: 67 EST: 1987
SQ FT: 1,723
SALES (est): 114.48MM
SALES (corp-wide): 959.4MM **Publicly Held**
Web: www.dspg.com
SIC: **3674** 7371 Integrated circuits, semiconductor networks, etc.; Computer software development
PA: Synaptics Incorporated
1109 Mckay Dr
408 904-1100

### (P-12410)
### DUST NETWORKS INC
32990 Alvarado Niles Rd Ste 910, Union City (94587-8106)
PHONE.................................510 400-2900
Joy Weiss, *Pr*
Dave Lynch, *
Brenda Glaze, *
Eva Chen, *
EMP: 25 EST: 2002
SQ FT: 15,000
SALES (est): 2.31MM
SALES (corp-wide): 12.31B **Publicly Held**
SIC: **3674** Semiconductors and related devices
HQ: Linear Technology Llc
1630 Mccarthy Blvd
Milpitas CA 95035
408 432-1900

### (P-12411)
### DYNAMIC INTGRTED SOLUTIONS LLC
1710 Fortune Dr, San Jose (95131-1744)
PHONE.................................408 727-3400
EMP: 30
Web: www.dynamicsolutionsusa.com
SIC: **3674** Semiconductors and related devices
PA: Dynamic Integrated Solutions Llc
3964 Rvermark Plz Ste 104

### (P-12412)
### DYNAMIC INTGRTED SOLUTIONS LLC (PA)
3964 Rivermark Plz Ste 104, Santa Clara (95054)
PHONE.................................408 727-3400
EMP: 16 EST: 2006
SALES (est): 7.58MM **Privately Held**
Web: www.dynamicsolutionsusa.com
SIC: **3674** Semiconductors and related devices

### (P-12413)
### ECOMICRON INC
2161 Otoole Ave Ste 30, San Jose (95131)
PHONE.................................408 526-1020
Jae Hwan Hong, *CEO*
EMP: 16 EST: 2008
SALES (est): 32MM **Privately Held**
Web: www.ecomicron.com
SIC: **3674** Semiconductor diodes and rectifiers

### (P-12414)
### EDGEQ INC
Also Called: Edgeq
2550 Great America Way Ste 125, Santa Clara (95054-1159)
PHONE.................................408 209-0368
Vinay Ravuri, *CEO*
EMP: 25 EST: 2018
SALES (est): 5.84MM **Privately Held**
Web: www.edgeq.io
SIC: **3674** Semiconductors and related devices

### (P-12415)
### EDISON OPTO USA CORPORATION
1809 Excise Ave Ste 201, Ontario (91761-8558)
PHONE.................................909 284-9710
Wen-jui Cheng, *CEO*
Adrian Cheng, *Prin*
▲ EMP: 30 EST: 2010
SALES (est): 1.8MM **Privately Held**
Web: www.edison-opto.com
SIC: **3674** Light emitting diodes

### (P-12416)
### EMAGIN CORPORATION
3140 De La Cruz Blvd, Santa Clara (95054-2406)
PHONE.................................408 327-8500
EMP: 40
Web: www.emagin.com
SIC: **3674** Semiconductors and related devices
HQ: Emagin Corporation
700 South Dr Ste 201
Hopewell Junction NY 12533

### (P-12417)
### EMAGIN CORPORATION
3080 Olcott St Ste C100, Santa Clara (95054-3263)
PHONE.................................845 838-7989
EMP: 40
Web: www.emagin.com
SIC: **3674** Light emitting diodes
HQ: Emagin Corporation
700 South Dr Ste 201
Hopewell Junction NY 12533

### (P-12418)
### EMCORE CORPORATION
2700 Systron Dr, Concord (94518-1355)
PHONE.................................925 979-4500
EMP: 105
SALES (corp-wide): 97.72MM **Publicly Held**
Web: www.emcore.com
SIC: **3674** Integrated circuits, semiconductor networks, etc.
PA: Emcore Corporation
2015 Chestnut St
626 293-3400

### (P-12419)
### EMCORE CORPORATION (PA)
Also Called: Emcore
2015 Chestnut St, Alhambra (91803-1542)
PHONE.................................626 293-3400
Jeffrey Rittichier, *CEO*
Stephen L Domenik, *
Tom Minichiello, *CFO*
Iain Black, *Sr VP*
▲ EMP: 188 EST: 1984
SQ FT: 50,000
SALES (est): 97.72MM
SALES (corp-wide): 97.72MM **Publicly Held**
Web: www.emcore.com
SIC: **3674** 3559 Integrated circuits, semiconductor networks, etc.; Semiconductor manufacturing machinery

### (P-12420)
### ENERVENUE INC
3500 Gateway Blvd, Fremont (94538-6584)
PHONE.................................408 664-0355
Jorg Heinemann, *CEO*
Yi Cui, *Technology Advisor*
Frank Blohm, *COO*
EMP: 146 EST: 2020
SALES (est): 18.43MM **Privately Held**
Web: www.enervenue.com
SIC: **3674** Semiconductors and related devices

### (P-12421)
### ENFABRICA CORPORATION
295 Bernardo Ave Ste 200, Mountain View (94043-5205)
PHONE.................................650 206-8533
Rochan Sankar, *Pr*
EMP: 30 EST: 2021
SALES (est): 4.95MM **Privately Held**
SIC: **3674** Semiconductors and related devices

### (P-12422)
### ENPHASE ENERGY INC (PA)
Also Called: Enphase Energy
47281 Bayside Pkwy, Fremont (94538-6517)
PHONE.................................707 774-7000
Badrinarayanan Kothandaraman, *
Badrinarayanan Kothandaraman, *
Steven J Gomo, *
Mandy Yang, *Ex VP*
Mary Erginsoy, *CAO*
▲ EMP: 1460 EST: 2006
SQ FT: 40,446
SALES (est): 2.29B **Publicly Held**
Web: www.enphase.com
SIC: **3674** Semiconductors and related devices

### (P-12423)
### EPSON ELECTRONICS AMERICA INC (DH)
3131 Katella Ave, Los Alamitos (90720-2335)
PHONE.................................408 922-0200
Koji Abe, *Pr*
Craig Hodowski, *Sec*
▲ EMP: 32 EST: 1997
SALES (est): 7.67MM **Privately Held**
Web: www.epson.com

## PRODUCTS & SERVICES SECTION
### 3674 - Semiconductors And Related Devices (P-12442)

SIC: **3674** 5065 8731 Semiconductors and related devices; Electronic parts and equipment, nec; Commercial physical research
HQ: U.S. Epson, Inc.
3131 Katella Ave
Los Alamitos CA 90720

**(P-12424)**
### ESILICON CORPORATION (DH)
2130 Gold St Ste 100, San Jose (95002-3700)
**EMP:** 187 **EST:** 1999
**SALES (est):** 29.52MM
**SALES (corp-wide):** 5.51B **Publicly Held**
Web: www.marvell.com
SIC: **3674** Integrated circuits, semiconductor networks, etc.
HQ: Inphi Corporation
110 Rio Robles
San Jose CA 95134

**(P-12425)**
### ESPERANTO TECHNOLOGIES INC (PA)
Also Called: Esperanto.ai
800 W El Camino Real Ste 410, Mountain View (94040-2577)
**PHONE**.............................650 319-7357
Arthur L Swift, *CEO*
Ralph J Harms, *
Mark A Leahy, *
**EMP:** 91 **EST:** 2014
**SALES (est):** 12.01MM
**SALES (corp-wide):** 12.01MM **Privately Held**
Web: www.esperanto.ai
SIC: **3674** 7371 Integrated circuits, semiconductor networks, etc.; Computer software development

**(P-12426)**
### ESS TECHNOLOGY HOLDINGS INC (HQ)
Also Called: Ess Technology
109 Bonaventura Dr, San Jose (95134-2106)
**PHONE**.............................408 643-8818
Robert L Blair, *Pr*
John A Marsh, *VP*
Gilbert Amelio, *
Dan Christman, *CMO*
▲ **EMP:** 45 **EST:** 1984
**SALES (est):** 23.79MM **Privately Held**
Web: www.esstech.com
SIC: **3674** Microcircuits, integrated (semiconductor)
PA: Imperium Partners Group, Llc
509 Madison Ave

**(P-12427)**
### ESSEX ELECTRONICS INC
1130 Mark Ave, Carpinteria (93013-2918)
**PHONE**.............................805 684-7601
Stewart Frisch, *Ch Bd*
Jesse Moore, *CEO*
Fred Zimmermann, *Pr*
Garrett Kaufman, *Pr*
Dean Benjamin, *Prin*
▲ **EMP:** 23 **EST:** 1991
**SQ FT:** 7,000
**SALES (est):** 4.8MM **Privately Held**
Web: www.keyless.com
SIC: **3674** Semiconductors and related devices

**(P-12428)**
### EXAR CORPORATION (HQ)
Also Called: Exar
1060 Rincon Cir, San Jose (95131)
**PHONE**.............................669 265-6100
Ryan A Benton, *
Ryan A Benton, *
Keith Tainsky, *
Sherry Lin, *CAO*
Jessica Wu, *Corporate Secretary*
**EMP:** 50 **EST:** 1971
**SQ FT:** 151,000
**SALES (est):** 7.95MM
**SALES (corp-wide):** 693.26MM **Publicly Held**
Web: www.maxlinear.com
SIC: **3674** Integrated circuits, semiconductor networks, etc.
PA: Maxlinear, Inc.
5966 La Place Ct Ste 100
760 692-0711

**(P-12429)**
### EXPERT SEMICONDUCTOR TECH INC
Also Called: Expertech
10 Victor Sq Ste 100, Scotts Valley (95066-3562)
P.O. Box 66508 (95067-6508)
**PHONE**.............................831 439-9300
Jonathan George, *CEO*
Jonathan George, *Pr*
Mark Cooper, *
**EMP:** 25 **EST:** 1992
**SQ FT:** 40,000
**SALES (est):** 4.47MM **Privately Held**
Web: www.exper-tech.com
SIC: **3674** Semiconductors and related devices

**(P-12430)**
### FAIRCHILD SEMICDTR INTL INC (HQ)
Also Called: On Semiconductor
1272 Borregas Ave, Sunnyvale (94089-1310)
**PHONE**.............................408 822-2000
Keith D Jackson, *Pr*
Bernard Gutmann, *Ex VP*
William A Schromm, *Ex VP*
George H Cave, *Compliance ETHICS*
Paul Rolls, *Executive Sales & Marketing Vice President*
**EMP:** 286 **EST:** 1959
**SALES (est):** 310.06MM
**SALES (corp-wide):** 8.25B **Publicly Held**
SIC: **3674** Semiconductors and related devices
PA: On Semiconductor Corporation
5701 N Pima Rd
602 244-6600

**(P-12431)**
### FERROTEC (USA) CORPORATION
Also Called: Meivac
5830 Hellyer Ave, San Jose (95138-1004)
**PHONE**.............................408 362-1000
Eiji Miyamaga, *CEO*
**EMP:** 30
Web: www.ferrotec.com
SIC: **3674** Semiconductors and related devices
HQ: Ferrotec (Usa) Corporation
566 Exchange Ct
Livermore CA 94550
408 964-7700

**(P-12432)**
### FINISAR CORPORATION
41762 Christy St, Fremont (94538-5106)
**PHONE**.............................408 548-1000
Fariba Daneh, *Mgr*
**EMP:** 15
**SALES (corp-wide):** 4.71B **Publicly Held**
Web: www.coherent.com
SIC: **3674** Semiconductors and related devices
HQ: Finisar Corporation
1830 Bering Dr
San Jose CA 95112
408 548-1000

**(P-12433)**
### FLEX LOGIX TECHNOLOGIES INC
Also Called: Flex Logix Technologies
2465 Latham St Ste 100, Mountain View (94040-4792)
P.O. Box 458 (94035-0458)
**PHONE**.............................650 867-2904
Geoffrey Tate, *CEO*
Cheng Wang, *
**EMP:** 80 **EST:** 2014
**SALES (est):** 8.03MM **Privately Held**
Web: www.flex-logix.com
SIC: **3674** Integrated circuits, semiconductor networks, etc.

**(P-12434)**
### FLEXTRONICS SEMICONDUCTOR (DH)
2241 Lundy Ave Bldg 2, San Jose (95131-1822)
**PHONE**.............................408 576-7000
Ash Bhardwaj, *Pr*
Duncan Robertson, *
**EMP:** 40 **EST:** 1976
**SQ FT:** 54,000
**SALES (est):** 25.13K **Privately Held**
SIC: **3674** 8711 Semiconductors and related devices; Engineering services
HQ: Flextronics Holding Usa, Inc.
2090 Fortune Dr
San Jose CA 95131

**(P-12435)**
### FORMER LUNA SUBSIDIARY INC (HQ)
**PHONE**.............................805 987-0146
**EMP:** 55 **EST:** 1998
**SALES (est):** 23.61MM **Publicly Held**
SIC: **3674** Semiconductors and related devices
PA: Luna Innovations Incorporated
301 1st St Sw Ste 200

**(P-12436)**
### FORMFACTOR INC (PA)
Also Called: FORMFACTOR
7005 Southfront Rd, Livermore (94551-8201)
**PHONE**.............................925 290-4000
Michael D Slessor, *Pr*
Thomas St Dennis, *
Shai Shahar, *CAO*
▲ **EMP:** 188 **EST:** 1993
**SQ FT:** 259,000
**SALES (est):** 663.1MM **Publicly Held**
Web: www.formfactor.com
SIC: **3674** 3825 Semiconductors and related devices; Instruments to measure electricity

**(P-12437)**
### FORTEMEDIA INC (PA)
2150 Gold St Ste 250, San Jose (95002-3702)
P.O. Box 280 (95002-0280)
**PHONE**.............................408 716-8028
Paul Huang, *CEO*
▼ **EMP:** 25 **EST:** 1996
**SQ FT:** 9,000
**SALES:** 9.73MM
**SALES (corp-wide):** 9.73MM **Privately Held**
Web: www.fortemedia.com
SIC: **3674** Semiconductors and related devices

**(P-12438)**
### FOVEON INC
2249 Zanker Rd, San Jose (95131-1120)
P.O. Box 791 (95009-0791)
**PHONE**.............................408 855-6800
Carver A Mead, *Ch Bd*
Jim Lau, *
**EMP:** 50 **EST:** 1997
**SALES (est):** 6.75MM **Privately Held**
Web: www.sigma-global.com
SIC: **3674** 7221 Light sensitive devices, solid state; Photographic studios, portrait

**(P-12439)**
### FRONTIER SEMICONDUCTOR (PA)
Also Called: Fsm
165 Topaz St, Milpitas (95035-5430)
**PHONE**.............................408 432-8338
Yuen F Lim, *CEO*
**EMP:** 31 **EST:** 1988
**SQ FT:** 40,000
**SALES (est):** 5.23MM
**SALES (corp-wide):** 5.23MM **Privately Held**
Web: www.frontiersemi.com
SIC: **3674** Integrated circuits, semiconductor networks, etc.

**(P-12440)**
### FULCRUM MICROSYSTEMS INC
26630 Agoura Rd, Calabasas (91302-1954)
**PHONE**.............................818 871-8100
Robert R Nunn, *CEO*
Dale Bartos, *
Mike Zeile, *
Uri Cummings, *
**EMP:** 58 **EST:** 1999
**SQ FT:** 17,077
**SALES (est):** 5.6MM
**SALES (corp-wide):** 54.23B **Publicly Held**
Web: www.fulcrummicro.com
SIC: **3674** Semiconductors and related devices
PA: Intel Corporation
2200 Mission College Blvd
408 765-8080

**(P-12441)**
### GAINSPAN CORP
125 S Market St Ste 400, San Jose (95113-2241)
**PHONE**.............................408 627-6500
**EMP:** 20 **EST:** 2019
**SALES (est):** 4.36MM **Privately Held**
Web: www.telit.com
SIC: **3674** Semiconductors and related devices

**(P-12442)**
### GEN DIGITAL INC
Also Called: Symantec
380 Ellis St, Mountain View (94043-2202)
**PHONE**.............................781 530-2200
Greg Gotta, *Mgr*
**EMP:** 28
**SALES (corp-wide):** 3.81B **Publicly Held**
Web: www.nortonlifelock.com
SIC: **3674** Semiconductors and related devices
PA: Gen Digital Inc.
60 E Rio Slado Pkwy Ste 1
650 527-8000

## 3674 - Semiconductors And Related Devices (P-12443)

**(P-12443)**
**GEO SEMICONDUCTOR INC (PA)**
Also Called: Geo
181 Metro Dr, San Jose (95110-1317)
PHONE..................................408 638-0400
Paul Russo, *Ch*
Simon Westbrook, *
Michael Hopton, *
Madhu Rayabhari, *Business Development*
Chris Candler, *
**EMP:** 18 **EST:** 2009
**SALES (est):** 5.05MM **Privately Held**
Web: www.geosemi.com
**SIC: 3674** Semiconductors and related devices

**(P-12444)**
**GIGAMAT TECHNOLOGIES INC**
47358 Fremont Blvd, Fremont (94538-6501)
PHONE..................................510 770-8008
Edmond Abrahamians, *CEO*
**EMP:** 17 **EST:** 2002
**SQ FT:** 7,000
**SALES (est):** 7.41MM **Privately Held**
Web: www.gigamat.com
**SIC: 3674** Semiconductors and related devices

**(P-12445)**
**GIGPEAK INC (DH)**
6024 Silver Creek Valley Rd, San Jose (95138-1011)
PHONE..................................408 546-3316
Gregory L Waters, *Pr*
Brian C White, *
Matthew D Brandalise, *
**EMP:** 132 **EST:** 2008
**SQ FT:** 32,805
**SALES (est):** 17.02MM **Privately Held**
Web: www.gigpeak.com
**SIC: 3674** Integrated circuits, semiconductor networks, etc.
HQ: Renesas Electronics America Inc.
6024 Silver Creek Vly Rd
San Jose CA 95138
408 284-8200

**(P-12446)**
**GLF INTEGRATED POWER INC**
Also Called: Semiconductor
4500 Great America Pkwy Rm 1045, Santa Clara (95054-1283)
PHONE..................................408 239-4326
Ni Sun, *CEO*
**EMP:** 15 **EST:** 2013
**SALES (est):** 1.88MM **Privately Held**
Web: www.glfipower.com
**SIC: 3674** Integrated circuits, semiconductor networks, etc.

**(P-12447)**
**GLOBAL COMM SEMICONDUCTORS LLC**
Also Called: G C S
23155 Kashiwa Ct, Torrance (90505-4026)
PHONE..................................310 530-7274
Bau-hsing Brian Ann, *Pr*
Mark L Raggio, *Sec*
Ta-lun Darren Huang, *Ch*
**EMP:** 20 **EST:** 1997
**SQ FT:** 38,000
**SALES (est):** 18.09MM **Privately Held**
Web: www.gcsincorp.com
**SIC: 3674** Semiconductors and related devices
PA: Gcs Holdings, Inc.
115 S 4th St W

**(P-12448)**
**GLOBAL TESTING CORPORATION**
225 Pamela Dr Apt 205, Mountain View (94040-3236)
PHONE..................................408 745-0718
Jon Hwu, *CEO*
**EMP:** 76 **EST:** 1998
**SQ FT:** 12,000
**SALES (est):** 1.22MM **Privately Held**
**SIC: 3674** Semiconductors and related devices
HQ: Global Testing Corporation
75 & 77, Guangfu Rd.,
Hukou Township HSI 30303

**(P-12449)**
**GLOBALFOUNDRIES DRESDEN**
1050 E Arques Ave, Sunnyvale (94085-4601)
PHONE..................................408 462-3900
Hans Deppe, *
James E Doran, *
**EMP:** 1206 **EST:** 2004
**SALES (est):** 2.54MM **Privately Held**
Web: www.gf.com
**SIC: 3674** 3369 Integrated circuits, semiconductor networks, etc.; Nonferrous foundries, nec
PA: Globalfoundries U.S. Inc.
400 Stonebreak Ext

**(P-12450)**
**GLOBALFOUNDRIES US 2 LLC**
2600 Great America Way, Santa Clara (95054-1169)
PHONE..................................408 462-3900
**EMP:** 35
Web: www.gf.com
**SIC: 3674** Semiconductors and related devices
HQ: Globalfoundries U.S. 2 Llc
2070 Rte 52
Hopewell Junction NY 12533
512 457-3900

**(P-12451)**
**GLOBALFOUNDRIES US INC**
2600 Great America Way, Santa Clara (95054-1169)
PHONE..................................971 285-7461
**EMP:** 568
Web: www.gf.com
**SIC: 3674** Semiconductors and related devices
PA: Globalfoundries U.S. Inc.
400 Stonebreak Ext

**(P-12452)**
**GLOBALFOUNDRIES US INC**
1278 Reamwood Ave, Sunnyvale (94089-2233)
PHONE..................................408 462-3900
**EMP:** 426
Web: www.gf.com
**SIC: 3674** Semiconductors and related devices
PA: Globalfoundries U.S. Inc.
400 Stonebreak Ext

**(P-12453)**
**GLP GERMAN LIGHT PRODUCTS INC**
16170 Stagg St, Van Nuys (91406-1713)
PHONE..................................818 767-8899
Mark Ravenhill, *Pr*
Udo Kunzler, *Treas*
Kasper Gissel, *Sec*
▲ **EMP:** 15 **EST:** 2009
**SALES (est):** 4.1MM **Privately Held**
Web: www.germanlightproducts.com
**SIC: 3674** Light emitting diodes

**(P-12454)**
**GREENLIANT SYSTEMS INC**
3970 Freedom Cir Ste 100, Santa Clara (95054-1204)
PHONE..................................408 217-7400
**EMP:** 105 **EST:** 2010
**SALES (est):** 14.45MM **Privately Held**
Web: www.greenliant.com
**SIC: 3674** 5065 Semiconductors and related devices; Electronic parts and equipment, nec

**(P-12455)**
**GRINDING & DICING SERVICES INC**
Also Called: Gdsi
925 Berryessa Rd, San Jose (95133-1002)
PHONE..................................408 451-2000
Joe D Collins, *CEO*
Saira Haq, *
Laila H Collins, *
▲ **EMP:** 38 **EST:** 1992
**SQ FT:** 14,500
**SALES (est):** 5.88MM
**SALES (corp-wide):** 27.12MM **Publicly Held**
Web: www.stealthdicing.com
**SIC: 3674** 2672 Semiconductors and related devices; Adhesive papers, labels, or tapes: from purchased material
HQ: Akoustis, Inc.
9805 Northcross Center Ct
Huntersville NC 28078
704 997-5735

**(P-12456)**
**GSI TECHNOLOGY INC (PA)**
1213 Elko Dr, Sunnyvale (94089-2211)
PHONE..................................408 331-8800
Lee-lean Shu, *Ch Bd*
Robert Yau, *
Didier Lasserre, *VP Sls*
Bor-tay Wu V, *Tribal President*
Ping Wu V, *US Operations President*
**EMP:** 51 **EST:** 1995
**SQ FT:** 44,277
**SALES (est):** 21.77MM **Publicly Held**
Web: www.gsitechnology.com
**SIC: 3674** 3572 Integrated circuits, semiconductor networks, etc.; Computer storage devices

**(P-12457)**
**GYRFALCON TECHNOLOGY INC (PA)**
1900 Mccarthy Blvd Ste 412, Milpitas (95035-7436)
PHONE..................................408 944-9219
Jianguo Lin, *CEO*
**EMP:** 25 **EST:** 2016
**SALES (est):** 3.22MM
**SALES (corp-wide):** 3.22MM **Privately Held**
Web: www.gyrfalcontech.ai
**SIC: 3674** Semiconductors and related devices

**(P-12458)**
**H-SQUARE CORPORATION**
Also Called: H2 Co
3100 Patrick Henry Dr, Santa Clara (95054-1850)
PHONE..................................408 982-9108
Bud Barclay, *Pr*
Larry Dean, *Stockholder*
▲ **EMP:** 42 **EST:** 1975
**SQ FT:** 20,000
**SALES (est):** 6MM **Privately Held**
Web: www.h-square.com
**SIC: 3674** Semiconductor circuit networks

**(P-12459)**
**HANERGY HOLDING (AMERICA) LLC (HQ)**
1350 Bayshore Hwy Ste 825, Burlingame (94010-1823)
PHONE..................................650 288-3722
Yi Wu, *CEO*
**EMP:** 100 **EST:** 2010
**SALES (est):** 94.3MM **Privately Held**
**SIC: 3674** 6719 Solar cells; Investment holding companies, except banks
PA: Jinjiang Hydropower Group Co., Ltd.
Room 105, No. 680, Tangkekou Street, Tangkekou Town, Huairou Dis

**(P-12460)**
**HANWHA ENRGY USA HOLDINGS CORP (HQ)**
Also Called: 174 Power Global
400 Spectrum Center Dr Ste 1400, Irvine (92618-5021)
PHONE..................................949 748-5996
Henry Yun, *Pr*
David Kim, *CFO*
**EMP:** 28 **EST:** 2013
**SALES (est):** 45.71MM **Privately Held**
Web: www.174powerglobal.com
**SIC: 3674** 1711 Solar cells; Solar energy contractor
PA: Hanwha Corporation
86 Cheonggyecheon-Ro, Jung-Gu

**(P-12461)**
**HANWHA Q CELLS USA INC**
300 Spectrum Center Dr Ste 500, Irvine (92618-4989)
PHONE..................................706 671-3077
Byeong Young Choi, *CEO*
Hyunkwang Cho, *
**EMP:** 34 **EST:** 2018
**SALES (est):** 2.87MM **Privately Held**
Web: www.q-cells.de
**SIC: 3674** Solar cells

**(P-12462)**
**HAYWARD QUARTZ TECHNOLOGY INC**
1700 Corporate Way, Fremont (94539-6107)
PHONE..................................510 657-9605
Nhe Thi Le, *CEO*
Ha Vinh Ly, *
Chris Quang D Le, *
▲ **EMP:** 250 **EST:** 1989
**SQ FT:** 250,000
**SALES (est):** 22.82MM **Privately Held**
Web: www.haywardquartz.com
**SIC: 3674** Semiconductor circuit networks

**(P-12463)**
**HELITEK COMPANY LTD**
4033 Clipper Ct, Fremont (94538-6540)
PHONE..................................510 933-7688
Ping-hai Chiao, *Pr*
▲ **EMP:** 46 **EST:** 1994
**SQ FT:** 30,000
**SALES (est):** 3.45MM **Privately Held**
**SIC: 3674** Semiconductors and related devices
PA: Wafer Works Corporation
No.100, Longyuan 1 St Rd., Longtan Science Park,

# PRODUCTS & SERVICES SECTION
## 3674 - Semiconductors And Related Devices (P-12482)

**(P-12464)**
**HI RELBLITY MCRELECTRONICS INC**
1804 Mccarthy Blvd, Milpitas (95035-7410)
PHONE.................408 764-5500
Zafar Malik, *Pr*
Alex Barrios, *
Larry Jorstad, *
Catherine Tijo, *Finance**
**EMP:** 52 **EST:** 2008
**SALES (est):** 4.66MM
**SALES (corp-wide):** 340.38MM **Privately Held**
**Web:** www.micross.com
**SIC: 3674** 7389 Semiconductors and related devices; Inspection and testing services
**HQ:** Silicon Turnkey Solutions, Inc.
1804 Mccarthy Blvd
Milpitas CA 95035
408 904-0200

**(P-12465)**
**I2A TECHNOLOGIES INC**
3399 W Warren Ave, Fremont (94538-6424)
PHONE.................510 770-0322
▲ **EMP:** 40
**Web:** www.ipac.com
**SIC: 3674** 8711 Semiconductors and related devices; Engineering services

**(P-12466)**
**IC SENSORS INC**
45738 Northport Loop W, Fremont (94538-6476)
PHONE.................510 498-1570
Frank Guibone, *Pr*
Victor Chatigny, *
**EMP:** 248 **EST:** 1982
**SQ FT:** 34,000
**SALES (est):** 2.33MM
**SALES (corp-wide):** 400.61MM **Privately Held**
**SIC: 3674** 8711 3625 Semiconductors and related devices; Engineering services; Switches, electronic applications
**PA:** Measurement Specialties, Inc.
1000 Lucas Way
757 766-1500

**(P-12467)**
**ICHIA USA INC**
509 Telegraph Canyon Rd, Chula Vista (91910-6436)
PHONE.................619 482-2222
Simon Goh, *Genl Mgr*
◆ **EMP:** 57 **EST:** 1993
**SQ FT:** 3,000
**SALES (est):** 5.2MM **Privately Held**
**SIC: 3674** Semiconductors and related devices
**PA:** Ichia Technologies, Inc.
No. 268, Huaya 2nd Rd.

**(P-12468)**
**ICHOR HOLDINGS LTD (PA)**
Also Called: Ichor
3185 Laurelview Ct, Fremont (94538-6535)
PHONE.................510 897-5200
Jeffrey S Andreson, *CEO*
Thomas M Rohrs, *Ch Bd*
Greg Swyt, *CFO*
Bruce Ragsdale, *COO*
**EMP:** 57 **EST:** 1999
**SQ FT:** 865,700
**SALES (est):** 811.12MM
**SALES (corp-wide):** 811.12MM **Publicly Held**
**Web:** www.ichorsystems.com

**SIC: 3674** 8711 3559 Wafers (semiconductor devices); Engineering services; Semiconductor manufacturing machinery

**(P-12469)**
**ICHOR SYSTEMS INC**
Also Called: US Weldments
4308 Solar Way, Fremont (94538-6335)
PHONE.................510 226-0100
**EMP:** 86
**SALES (corp-wide):** 811.12MM **Publicly Held**
**Web:** www.ichorsystems.com
**SIC: 3674** Semiconductors and related devices
**HQ:** Ichor Systems, Inc.
3185 Laurelview Ct
Fremont CA 94538

**(P-12470)**
**ICHOR SYSTEMS INC**
4302 Solar Way, Fremont (94538-6335)
PHONE.................510 226-0100
**EMP:** 50
**SALES (corp-wide):** 811.12MM **Publicly Held**
**Web:** www.ichorsystems.com
**SIC: 3674** Semiconductors and related devices
**HQ:** Ichor Systems, Inc.
3185 Laurelview Ct
Fremont CA 94538

**(P-12471)**
**ICHOR SYSTEMS INC (HQ)**
Also Called: Talon Innovations
3185 Laurelview Ct, Fremont (94538)
PHONE.................510 897-5200
Jeffrey Anderson, *CEO*
Greg Swyt, *Prin*
▲ **EMP:** 20 **EST:** 2009
**SALES (est):** 253.95MM
**SALES (corp-wide):** 811.12MM **Publicly Held**
**Web:** www.ichorsystems.com
**SIC: 3674** Semiconductors and related devices
**PA:** Ichor Holdings, Ltd.
3185 Laurelview Ct
510 897-5200

**(P-12472)**
**IKANOS COMMUNICATIONS INC (DH)**
5775 Morehouse Dr, San Diego (92121-1714)
PHONE.................858 587-1121
Rahul Patel, *Pr*
Sanjay Mehta, *
▲ **EMP:** 18 **EST:** 1999
**SQ FT:** 73,500
**SALES (est):** 5.68MM
**SALES (corp-wide):** 38.96B **Publicly Held**
**SIC: 3674** Integrated circuits, semiconductor networks, etc.
**HQ:** Qualcomm Atheros, Inc.
1700 Technology Dr
San Jose CA 95110
408 773-5200

**(P-12473)**
**ILLINOIS TOOL WORKS INC**
ITW Rippey
5000 Hillsdale Cir, El Dorado Hills (95762-5706)
PHONE.................916 939-4332
Brent Best, *Mgr*
**EMP:** 69
**SALES (corp-wide):** 16.11B **Publicly Held**
**Web:** www.itw.com

**SIC: 3674** Semiconductors and related devices
**PA:** Illinois Tool Works Inc.
155 Harlem Ave
847 724-7500

**(P-12474)**
**INAPAC TECHNOLOGY INC**
46848 Lakeview Blvd, Fremont (94538-6543)
PHONE.................408 746-0614
Richard Egan, *Pr*
Jean Pierre Braun, *
Adrian Ong, *
Fan Ho, *
**EMP:** 34 **EST:** 2000
**SQ FT:** 10,000
**SALES (est):** 850.42K **Privately Held**
**SIC: 3674** Integrated circuits, semiconductor networks, etc.

**(P-12475)**
**INDIE SEMICONDUCTOR INC (PA)**
Also Called: INDIE
32 Journey Ste 100, Aliso Viejo (92656-5329)
PHONE.................949 608-0854
Donald Mcclymont, *CEO*
David Aldrich, *Ch Bd*
Ichiro Aoki, *Pr*
Steven Machuga, *COO*
**EMP:** 26 **EST:** 2019
**SQ FT:** 18,000
**SALES (est):** 223.17MM
**SALES (corp-wide):** 223.17MM **Publicly Held**
**Web:** www.indiesemi.com
**SIC: 3674** Semiconductors and related devices

**(P-12476)**
**INFINEON TECH AMERICAS CORP**
Crydom Controls
233 Kansas St, El Segundo (90245-4316)
PHONE.................310 726-8000
Derek Lidow, *Mgr*
**EMP:** 47
**SALES (corp-wide):** 17.72B **Privately Held**
**Web:** www-blue.infineon.com
**SIC: 3674** Semiconductors and related devices
**HQ:** Infineon Technologies Americas Corp.
101 N Pacific Coast Hwy
El Segundo CA 90245
310 726-8200

**(P-12477)**
**INFINEON TECH AMERICAS CORP**
198 Champion Ct, San Jose (95134-1709)
PHONE.................866 951-9519
Robert Lefort, *Pr*
**EMP:** 1200
**SALES (corp-wide):** 17.72B **Privately Held**
**Web:** www-blue.infineon.com
**SIC: 3674** Semiconductors and related devices
**HQ:** Infineon Technologies Americas Corp.
101 N Pacific Coast Hwy
El Segundo CA 90245
310 726-8200

**(P-12478)**
**INFINEON TECH AMERICAS CORP**
1521 E Grand Ave, El Segundo (90245-4339)

P.O. Box 2788 (91729-2788)
PHONE.................310 252-7116
**EMP:** 123
**SALES (corp-wide):** 17.72B **Privately Held**
**Web:** www-blue.infineon.com
**SIC: 3674** Semiconductors and related devices
**HQ:** Infineon Technologies Americas Corp.
101 N Pacific Coast Hwy
El Segundo CA 90245
310 726-8200

**(P-12479)**
**INFINEON TECH AMERICAS CORP (HQ)**
101 N Pacific Coast Hwy, El Segundo (90245-4318)
PHONE.................310 726-8200
Oleg Khaykin, *CEO*
Ilan Daskal, *
▲ **EMP:** 900 **EST:** 1979
**SALES (est):** 303.11MM
**SALES (corp-wide):** 17.72B **Privately Held**
**Web:** www-blue.infineon.com
**SIC: 3674** Integrated circuits, semiconductor networks, etc.
**PA:** Infineon Technologies Ag
Am Campeon 1-15
892340

**(P-12480)**
**INFINEON TECH N AMER CORP (DH)**
198 Champion Ct, San Jose (95134-1709)
PHONE.................866 951-9519
Robert Lefort, *Pr*
Andrew Prillwitz, *
▲ **EMP:** 500 **EST:** 1982
**SALES (est):** 11.21MM
**SALES (corp-wide):** 17.72B **Privately Held**
**SIC: 3674** Semiconductors and related devices
**HQ:** Infineon Technologies Us Holdco Inc.
198 Champion Ct
San Jose CA 95134
866 951-9519

**(P-12481)**
**INFINEON TECH N AMER CORP**
30805 Santana St, Hayward (94544-7030)
P.O. Box 60000 File 0670 (94102)
PHONE.................919 768-0315
Robert Lefort, *Pr*
**EMP:** 233
**SALES (corp-wide):** 17.72B **Privately Held**
**SIC: 3674** Semiconductors and related devices
**HQ:** Infineon Technologies North America Corporation
198 Champion Ct
San Jose CA 95134
866 951-9519

**(P-12482)**
**INFINEON TECH US HOLDCO INC (HQ)**
Also Called: Infineon Technologies AG
198 Champion Ct, San Jose (95134-1709)
PHONE.................866 951-9519
David Lewis, *CEO*
Andrew Prillwitz, *
Oleg Frimershtein, *
**EMP:** 100 **EST:** 2014
**SALES (est):** 21.34MM
**SALES (corp-wide):** 17.72B **Privately Held**
**SIC: 3674** Integrated circuits, semiconductor networks, etc.
**PA:** Infineon Technologies Ag
Am Campeon 1-15
892340

## 3674 - Semiconductors And Related Devices (P-12483)

**(P-12483)**
**INFINEON TECHNOLOGIES**
18225 Serene Dr, Morgan Hill (95037-2860)
PHONE...............................408 779-2367
**EMP:** 15 **EST:** 2019
**SALES (est):** 2.15MM **Privately Held**
**Web:** www-blue.infineon.com
**SIC: 3674** Semiconductors and related devices

**(P-12484)**
**INNODISK USA CORPORATION**
42996 Osgood Rd, Fremont (94539-5627)
PHONE...............................510 770-9421
Victor Le, *Pr*
▲ **EMP:** 30 **EST:** 2011
**SALES (est):** 9.54MM **Privately Held**
**Web:** www.innodisk.com
**SIC: 3674** Random access memory (RAM)
**PA:** Innodisk Corporation
5f, No. 237, Datong Rd., Sec. 1,

**(P-12485)**
**INNOGRIT CORPORATION**
1735 Technology Dr Ste 600, San Jose (95110-1332)
PHONE...............................408 785-3678
Zining Wu, *CEO*
**EMP:** 34 **EST:** 2016
**SALES (est):** 3.14MM **Privately Held**
**Web:** www.innogritcorp.com
**SIC: 3674** Semiconductors and related devices

**(P-12486)**
**INNOPHASE INC**
Also Called: Innophase
5880 Oberlin Dr Ste 600, San Diego (92121-4762)
PHONE...............................619 541-8280
Yang Xu, *CEO*
Thomas Lee, *
**EMP:** 100 **EST:** 2011
**SALES (est):** 9.66MM **Privately Held**
**Web:** www.innophaseinc.com
**SIC: 3674** Semiconductors and related devices

**(P-12487)**
**INNOVION LLC (HQ)**
Also Called: Core System
2121 Zanker Rd, San Jose (95131-2109)
PHONE...............................408 501-9140
**EMP:** 57 **EST:** 1981
**SALES (est):** 24.72MM
**SALES (corp-wide):** 4.71B **Publicly Held**
**Web:** www.ii-vi.com
**SIC: 3674** Silicon wafers, chemically doped
**PA:** Coherent Corp.
375 Saxonburg Blvd
724 352-4455

**(P-12488)**
**INPHENIX INC**
250 N Mines Rd, Livermore (94551-2238)
PHONE...............................925 606-8809
David Eu, *Pr*
**EMP:** 25 **EST:** 2003
**SALES (est):** 9.06MM **Privately Held**
**Web:** www.inphenix.com
**SIC: 3674** Semiconductors and related devices

**(P-12489)**
**INPHI CORPORATION (HQ)**
Also Called: Inphi
110 Rio Robles, San Jose (95134-1813)
**EMP:** 229 **EST:** 2000
**SQ FT:** 110,611
**SALES (est):** 682.95MM
**SALES (corp-wide):** 5.51B **Publicly Held**
**Web:** www.marvell.com
**SIC: 3674** Integrated circuits, semiconductor networks, etc.
**PA:** Marvell Technology, Inc.
1000 N West St Ste 1200
302 295-4840

**(P-12490)**
**INPHI INTERNATIONAL PTE LTD**
112 S Lakeview Canyon Rd Ste 100, Westlake Village (91362-3925)
PHONE...............................805 719-2300
Ford Tamer, *Pr*
John Edmunds, *CFO*
**EMP:** 21 **EST:** 2017
**SALES (est):** 1.29MM **Privately Held**
**Web:** www.marvell.com
**SIC: 3674** Semiconductors and related devices

**(P-12491)**
**INTEGRA TECH SILICON VLY LLC (DH)**
1635 Mccarthy Blvd, Milpitas (95035-7415)
PHONE...............................408 618-8700
Matt Bergeron, *CEO*
Joe Foerstel, *
**EMP:** 109 **EST:** 1990
**SQ FT:** 48,000
**SALES (est):** 24.39MM **Privately Held**
**Web:** www.corwil.com
**SIC: 3674** 3825 Semiconductors and related devices; Semiconductor test equipment
**HQ:** Integra Technologies Inc.
3450 N Rock Rd Ste 100
Wichita KS 67226
316 630-6800

**(P-12492)**
**INTEGRA TECHNOLOGIES INC**
321 Coral Cir, El Segundo (90245-4620)
PHONE...............................310 606-0855
Paul Aken, *Pr*
Jeff Burger, *
**EMP:** 50 **EST:** 1997
**SQ FT:** 15,000
**SALES (est):** 9.43MM **Privately Held**
**Web:** www.integratech.com
**SIC: 3674** Modules, solid state

**(P-12493)**
**INTEGRTED SILICON SOLUTION INC (PA)**
1623 Buckeye Dr, Milpitas (95035-7423)
PHONE...............................408 969-6600
Jimmy Lee, *CEO*
Scott Howarth, *
Kong Yeu Han, *
▲ **EMP:** 440 **EST:** 1988
**SQ FT:** 55,612
**SALES (est):** 23.27MM **Privately Held**
**Web:** www.issi.com
**SIC: 3674** Semiconductors and related devices

**(P-12494)**
**INTEL CORPORATION (PA)**
2200 Mission College Blvd, Santa Clara (95054-1549)
P.O. Box 58119 (95052-8119)
PHONE...............................408 765-8080
Patrick P Gelsinger, *CEO*
Frank D Yeary, *Non-Executive Chairman of the Board*
David Zinsner, *Ex VP*
April Miller Boise, *CLO*
Michelle Johnston Holthaus, *Ex VP*
◆ **EMP:** 2463 **EST:** 1968
**SALES (est):** 54.23B
**SALES (corp-wide):** 54.23B **Publicly Held**
**Web:** www.intel.com
**SIC: 3674** 3577 7372 Microprocessors; Computer peripheral equipment, nec; Prepackaged software

**(P-12495)**
**INTEL SEMICONDUCTOR (US) LLC (HQ)**
2200 Mission College Blvd, Santa Clara (95054-1549)
PHONE...............................408 765-8080
Robert H Swan, *CEO*
▲ **EMP:** 25 **EST:** 1996
**SALES (est):** 5.63MM
**SALES (corp-wide):** 54.23B **Publicly Held**
**Web:** www.intel.com
**SIC: 3674** 7372 Semiconductors and related devices; Prepackaged software
**PA:** Intel Corporation
2200 Mission College Blvd
408 765-8080

**(P-12496)**
**INTERCONNECT SYSTEMS INTL LLC (DH)**
Also Called: Interconnect Systems, Inc.
741 Flynn Rd, Camarillo (93012-8056)
PHONE...............................805 482-2870
Mark Gilliam, *Pr*
William P Miller, *
Glen Griswold, *
Louis Buldain, *
Thomas Casey, *
▲ **EMP:** 90 **EST:** 1987
**SQ FT:** 48,000
**SALES (est):** 30.05MM
**SALES (corp-wide):** 64.37B **Privately Held**
**Web:** www.isipkg.com
**SIC: 3674** Computer logic modules
**HQ:** Molex, Llc
2222 Wellington Ct
Lisle IL 60532
630 969-4550

**(P-12497)**
**INTERMOLECULAR INC (HQ)**
Also Called: Intermolecular
3011 N 1st St, San Jose (95134-2004)
PHONE...............................408 582-5700
Chris Kramer, *Pr*
Bruce M Mcwilliams, *Ex Ch Bd*
C Richard Neely, *CAO*
Scot A Griffin, *Corporate Secretary*
**EMP:** 16 **EST:** 2004
**SQ FT:** 146,000
**SALES (est):** 33.66MM
**SALES (corp-wide):** 22.82B **Privately Held**
**Web:** www.intermolecular.com
**SIC: 3674** Integrated circuits, semiconductor networks, etc.
**PA:** Merck Kg Auf Aktien
Frankfurter Str. 250
6151720

**(P-12498)**
**INTERSIL COMMUNICATIONS LLC**
1001 Murphy Ranch Rd, Milpitas (95035-7912)
PHONE...............................408 432-8888
◆ **EMP:** 1017
**SIC: 3674** Semiconductors and related devices

**(P-12499)**
**INVECAS INC (HQ)**
Also Called: Invecas
2655 Seely Ave, San Jose (95134-1931)
PHONE...............................408 758-5636
Dasaradha Gude, *CEO*
**EMP:** 23 **EST:** 2014
**SALES (est):** 5.8MM
**SALES (corp-wide):** 4.09B **Publicly Held**
**Web:** www.invecas.com
**SIC: 3674** Semiconductors and related devices
**PA:** Cadence Design Systems, Inc.
2655 Seely Ave Bldg 5
408 943-1234

**(P-12500)**
**INVENLUX CORPORATION**
168 Mason Way Ste B5, City Of Industry (91746-2339)
PHONE...............................626 277-4163
Chunhui Yan, *Pr*
**EMP:** 23 **EST:** 2008
**SQ FT:** 18,000
**SALES (est):** 519.39K **Privately Held**
**SIC: 3674** Light emitting diodes

**(P-12501)**
**INVENSAS CORPORATION**
3025 Orchard Pkwy, San Jose (95134-2017)
PHONE...............................408 324-5100
Craig Mitchell, *Pr*
**EMP:** 16 **EST:** 2008
**SALES (est):** 1.9MM
**SALES (corp-wide):** 388.79MM **Publicly Held**
**Web:** www.adeia.com
**SIC: 3674** Integrated circuits, semiconductor networks, etc.
**HQ:** Tessera Technologies, Inc.
3025 Orchard Pkwy
San Jose CA 95134
408 321-6000

**(P-12502)**
**IO SEMICONDUCTOR INCORPORATED**
Also Called: Iosemi
4795 Eastgate Mall, San Diego (92121-1971)
P.O. Box 910674 (92191-0674)
PHONE...............................858 362-4074
◆ **EMP:** 22
**SIC: 3674** Semiconductors and related devices

**(P-12503)**
**IOG PRODUCTS LLC**
Also Called: Impact-O-Graph Devices
9737 Lurline Ave, Chatsworth (91311-4404)
PHONE...............................818 350-5070
**EMP:** 15 **EST:** 2010
**SALES (est):** 2.13MM **Privately Held**
**Web:** www.impactograph.com
**SIC: 3674** 3669 Radiation sensors; Visual communication systems

**(P-12504)**
**IQ-ANALOG CORPORATION**
12348 High Bluff Dr Ste 110, San Diego (92130-3545)
PHONE...............................858 200-0388
Michael S Kappes, *Pr*
Randy Wayland, *
**EMP:** 25 **EST:** 2005
**SALES (est):** 5.39MM **Privately Held**
**Web:** www.iqanalog.com

# PRODUCTS & SERVICES SECTION
## 3674 - Semiconductors And Related Devices (P-12525)

SIC: 3674 Semiconductors and related devices

**(P-12505)**
**IRVINE SENSORS CORPORATION**
3000 Airway Ave Ste A1, Costa Mesa (92626-6033)
PHONE.................................714 444-8700
John C Carson, Pr
James Justice, *
Anthony Mastrangelo, *
EMP: 43 EST: 2013
SALES (est): 5.38MM Privately Held
Web: www.irvine-sensors.com
SIC: 3674 8731 Semiconductors and related devices; Electronic research

**(P-12506)**
**IWATT INC (DH)**
Also Called: Dialog Semiconductor
6024 Silver Creek Valley Rd, San Jose (95138-1011)
PHONE.................................408 374-4200
Ronald P Edgerton, CEO
James V Mccanna, VP
Alex Sinar, *
Kaj Den Daas, *
Brian Mcdonald, Prin
▲ EMP: 45 EST: 1999
SALES (est): 32.63MM Privately Held
SIC: 3674 Semiconductors and related devices
HQ: Renesas Design Germany Gmbh
Neue Str. 95
Kirchheim Unter Teck BW 73230
70218050

**(P-12507)**
**IXYS LLC (HQ)**
1590 Buckeye Dr, Milpitas (95035-7418)
PHONE.................................408 457-9000
Nathan Zommer, *
EMP: 66 EST: 1983
SQ FT: 51,000
SALES (est): 85.7MM
SALES (corp-wide): 2.36B Publicly Held
Web: www.ixys.com
SIC: 3674 Integrated circuits, semiconductor networks, etc.
PA: Littelfuse, Inc.
8755 W Higgins Rd Ste 500
773 628-1000

**(P-12508)**
**IXYS INTGRTED CRCITS DIV AV IN**
145 Columbia, Aliso Viejo (92656-1413)
PHONE.................................949 831-4622
Nathan Zommer, Ch Bd
Uzi Sasson, *
EMP: 621 EST: 1983
SQ FT: 28,000
SALES (est): 4.35MM
SALES (corp-wide): 2.36B Publicly Held
SIC: 3674 7389 Microcircuits, integrated (semiconductor); Design services
HQ: Ixys, Llc
1590 Buckeye Dr
Milpitas CA 95035
408 457-9000

**(P-12509)**
**IXYS LONG BEACH INC (DH)**
2500 Mira Mar Ave, Long Beach (90815-1758)
PHONE.................................562 296-6584
Nathan Zommer, CEO
Arnold Agbayani, *
▲ EMP: 25 EST: 1980

SQ FT: 20,000
SALES (est): 11.49MM
SALES (corp-wide): 2.36B Publicly Held
Web: www.littelfuse.com
SIC: 3674 5065 Semiconductors and related devices; Electronic parts and equipment, nec
HQ: Ixys, Llc
1590 Buckeye Dr
Milpitas CA 95035
408 457-9000

**(P-12510)**
**JINKOSOLAR (US) INC**
1901 S Bascom Ave, Campbell (95008-2215)
PHONE.................................415 402-0502
Xiande Li, CEO
Miao Gen, *
▲ EMP: 23 EST: 2010
SALES (est): 25.29MM Privately Held
Web: www.jinkosolar.us
SIC: 3674 Semiconductors and related devices
HQ: Jinkosolar (U.S.) Holding Inc.
1901 S Bascom Ave
Campbell CA 95008
415 402-0502

**(P-12511)**
**JIREH SEMICONDUCTOR INC**
475 Oakmead Pkwy, Sunnyvale (94085-4709)
EMP: 30 EST: 2011
SALES (est): 7.9MM Privately Held
Web: www.aosmd.com
SIC: 3674 Wafers (semiconductor devices)

**(P-12512)**
**KEYSSA INC (PA)**
3945 Freedom Cir Ste 560, Santa Clara (95054-1269)
PHONE.................................408 637-2300
Tony Fadell, CEO
Gordon Almquist, *
Srikanth Gondi, *
Roger Isaac, *
Nick Antonopoulos, *
EMP: 37 EST: 2009
SALES (est): 9.58MM Privately Held
Web: experience.molex.com
SIC: 3674 3577 Semiconductors and related devices; Computer peripheral equipment, nec

**(P-12513)**
**KIOXIA AMERICA INC (PA)**
2610 Orchard Pkwy, San Jose (95134-2020)
PHONE.................................408 526-2400
Toshiaki Fujikawa, CEO
Takanori Nakazawa, *
EMP: 200 EST: 2017
SQ FT: 60,000
SALES (est): 38.94MM
SALES (corp-wide): 38.94MM Privately Held
Web: www.kioxia.com
SIC: 3674 Semiconductors and related devices

**(P-12514)**
**KLA CORPORATION**
Also Called: Promesys Division
5451 Patrick Henry Dr, Santa Clara (95054-1167)
PHONE.................................408 986-5600
EMP: 16
SALES (corp-wide): 9.81B Publicly Held
Web: www.kla.com

SIC: 3674 Semiconductors and related devices
PA: Kla Corporation
1 Technology Dr
408 875-3000

**(P-12515)**
**KOVIO INC**
2865 Zanker Rd, San Jose (95134-2101)
PHONE.................................408 503-7300
EMP: 55
Web: www.kovio.com
SIC: 3674 Semiconductors and related devices

**(P-12516)**
**KSM CORP**
102 Persian Dr Ste 203, Sunnyvale (94089-1561)
PHONE.................................408 514-2400
Jooswan Kim, CEO
Harvinder P Singh, Pr
EMP: 48 EST: 2003
SQ FT: 18,000
SALES (est): 4.63MM Privately Held
Web: www.ksmusa.com
SIC: 3674 Semiconductors and related devices
PA: Ksm Component Co., Ltd.
90 Wolha-Ro 589beon-Gil, Haseong-Myeon

**(P-12517)**
**KTC-TU CORPORATION**
17600 Newhope St, Fountain Valley (92708-4220)
PHONE.................................714 435-2600
John Tu, Pr
EMP: 20 EST: 2001
SALES (est): 497.77K Privately Held
Web: www.kingston.com
SIC: 3674 Magnetic bubble memory device

**(P-12518)**
**KULR TECHNOLOGY CORPORATION**
4863 Shawline St Ste B, San Diego (92111-1435)
PHONE.................................408 663-5247
Michael Mo, CEO
EMP: 64 EST: 2013
SALES (est): 10MM
SALES (corp-wide): 9.83MM Publicly Held
Web: www.kulrtechnology.com
SIC: 3674 3624 Semiconductors and related devices; Carbon and graphite products
PA: Kulr Technology Group, Inc.
4863 Shawline St Ste B
408 663-5247

**(P-12519)**
**KUPRION INC**
4425 Fortran Dr, San Jose (95134-2300)
PHONE.................................408 206-0122
Nicholas Antonopoulos, CEO
Alfred Zinn, *
EMP: 32 EST: 2016
SALES (est): 5.03MM Privately Held
Web: www.kuprioninc.com
SIC: 3674 Semiconductors and related devices

**(P-12520)**
**KYOCERA AMERICA INC**
8611 Balboa Ave, San Diego (92123-1580)
PHONE.................................858 576-2600
▲ EMP: 50

SIC: 3674 Integrated circuits, semiconductor networks, etc.

**(P-12521)**
**KYOCERA INTERNATIONAL INC (HQ)**
8611 Balboa Ave, San Diego (92123-1501)
PHONE.................................858 492-1456
Robert Whisler, Vice Chairman
Nick Huntalas, Pr
William Edwards, VP
George Woodworth, VP
Franklin Kim, Div VP
◆ EMP: 100 EST: 1969
SQ FT: 16,000
SALES (est): 113.45MM Publicly Held
Web: global.kyocera.com
SIC: 3674 5023 5731 Semiconductors and related devices; Kitchen tools and utensils, nec; Radio, television, and electronic stores
PA: Kyocera Corporation
6, Takedatobadonocho, Fushimi-Ku

**(P-12522)**
**LABARGE/STC INC**
600 Anton Blvd, Costa Mesa (92626)
PHONE.................................281 207-1400
Anthony J Reardon, Pr
Samuel D Williams, VP
Weems Turner, *
James S Heiser, Sec
EMP: 42 EST: 1985
SALES (est): 1.27MM
SALES (corp-wide): 756.99MM Publicly Held
SIC: 3674 Hybrid integrated circuits
HQ: Ducommun Labarge Technologies, Inc.
689 Craig Rd Ste 200
Saint Louis MO 63141
314 997-0800

**(P-12523)**
**LAM RESEARCH CORPORATION**
3590 N 1st St Ste 200, San Jose (95134-2137)
PHONE.................................408 434-6109
John Newman, Prin
EMP: 29
SALES (corp-wide): 14.91B Publicly Held
Web: www.lamresearch.com
SIC: 3674 Semiconductors and related devices
PA: Lam Research Corporation
4650 Cushing Pkwy
510 572-0200

**(P-12524)**
**LAM RESEARCH CORPORATION**
1 Portola Ave, Livermore (94551-7647)
PHONE.................................510 572-8400
EMP: 25
SALES (corp-wide): 14.91B Publicly Held
Web: www.lamresearch.com
SIC: 3674 Semiconductors and related devices
PA: Lam Research Corporation
4650 Cushing Pkwy
510 572-0200

**(P-12525)**
**LAM RESEARCH CORPORATION**
1201 Voyager St, Livermore (94550-2568)
PHONE.................................209 597-2194
EMP: 15 EST: 2011
SALES (est): 364.56K Privately Held
Web: www.lamresearch.com
SIC: 3674 Semiconductors and related devices

## 3674 - Semiconductors And Related Devices (P-12526)

**(P-12526)**
**LAM RESEARCH CORPORATION (PA)**
Also Called: LAM RESEARCH
4650 Cushing Pkwy, Fremont (94538-6401)
PHONE.................510 572-0200
Timothy M Archer, *Pr*
Abhijit Y Talwalkar, *
Douglas R Bettinger, *Ex VP*
Patrick J Lord, *Ex VP*
Vahid Vahedi, *Sr VP*
**EMP:** 1413 **EST:** 1980
**SALES (est):** 14.91B
**SALES (corp-wide):** 14.91B **Publicly Held**
Web: www.lamresearch.com
SIC: **3674** Wafers (semiconductor devices)

**(P-12527)**
**LASER OPERATIONS LLC**
Also Called: Qpc Laser
15632 Roxford St, Rancho Cascades (91342-1265)
PHONE.................818 986-0000
Morris Lichtenstein, *Managing Member*
Mikhail Leibov, *
Jeffrey Ungar, *
Elyahu Pendler, *Managing Member*
**EMP:** 27 **EST:** 2009
**SQ FT:** 40,320
**SALES (est):** 4.53MM **Privately Held**
Web: www.qpclasers.com
SIC: **3674** Semiconductors and related devices

**(P-12528)**
**LATTICE SEMICONDUCTOR CORP**
2115 Onel Dr, San Jose (95131-2032)
PHONE.................408 826-6000
Al Chan, *Mgr*
**EMP:** 300
**SALES (corp-wide):** 737.15MM **Publicly Held**
Web: www.latticesemi.com
SIC: **3674** Integrated circuits, semiconductor networks, etc.
PA: Lattice Semiconductor Corp
   5555 Ne Moore Ct
   503 268-8000

**(P-12529)**
**LEDENGIN INC**
651 River Oaks Pkwy, San Jose (95134-1907)
PHONE.................408 922-7200
▲ **EMP:** 35
SIC: **3674** Light emitting diodes

**(P-12530)**
**LEDTRONICS INC (PA)**
23105 Kashiwa Ct, Torrance (90505-4026)
PHONE.................310 534-1505
Pervaiz Lodhie, *Pr*
Almas Lodhie, *
▲ **EMP:** 40 **EST:** 1983
**SQ FT:** 60,000
**SALES (est):** 20.66MM
**SALES (corp-wide):** 20.66MM **Privately Held**
Web: web.ledtronics.com
SIC: **3674** 3825 3641 Light emitting diodes; Instruments to measure electricity; Electric lamps

**(P-12531)**
**LINEAR INTEGRATED SYSTEMS INC**
4042 Clipper Ct, Fremont (94538-6540)
PHONE.................510 490-9160
Cindy Cook Johnson, *CEO*
Tim Mccune, *Pr*
Timothy Mccune, *Pr*
**EMP:** 15 **EST:** 1987
**SQ FT:** 5,000
**SALES (est):** 2.92MM **Privately Held**
Web: www.linearsystems.com
SIC: **3674** Integrated circuits, semiconductor networks, etc.

**(P-12532)**
**LINEAR TECHNOLOGY LLC (HQ)**
1630 Mccarthy Blvd, Milpitas (95035-7487)
PHONE.................408 432-1900
Lothar Maier, *CEO*
Donald P Zerio, *VP Fin*
Robert C Dobkin, *VP Engg*
Alexander R Mccann, *VP*
▲ **EMP:** 900 **EST:** 1981
**SQ FT:** 430,000
**SALES (est):** 499.99MM
**SALES (corp-wide):** 12.31B **Publicly Held**
Web: www.analog.com
SIC: **3674** Integrated circuits, semiconductor networks, etc.
PA: Analog Devices, Inc.
   1 Analog Way
   781 935-5565

**(P-12533)**
**LOCKWOOD INDUSTRIES LLC (HQ)**
Also Called: Fralock
28525 Industry Dr, Valencia (91355-5424)
PHONE.................661 702-6999
Marc Haugen, *CEO*
Bobbi Booher, *
**EMP:** 105 **EST:** 1966
**SQ FT:** 62,500
**SALES (est):** 49.22MM
**SALES (corp-wide):** 153.54MM **Privately Held**
Web: www.fralock.com
SIC: **3674** 3842 3089 2891 Semiconductors and related devices; Prosthetic appliances; Plastics containers, except foam; Sealants
PA: Fralock Holdings Llc
   28525 W Industry Dr
   661 702-6999

**(P-12534)**
**LRE SILICON SERVICES**
Also Called: L R Enterprises
1235 Torres Ave, Milpitas (95035-4015)
P.O. Box 360869 (95036-0869)
PHONE.................408 262-8725
Linda Robinson, *Owner*
**EMP:** 18 **EST:** 1999
**SALES (est):** 774.42K **Privately Held**
SIC: **3674** Silicon wafers, chemically doped

**(P-12535)**
**LSI CORPORATION (DH)**
Also Called: LSI Logic
1320 Ridder Park Dr, San Jose (95131-2313)
PHONE.................408 433-8000
Hock E Tan, *CEO*
Jean F Rankin, *
▲ **EMP:** 2400 **EST:** 1980
**SQ FT:** 240,000
**SALES (est):** 1.71B
**SALES (corp-wide):** 35.82B **Publicly Held**
Web: www.landscapeservicesinc.com
SIC: **3674** Microcircuits, integrated (semiconductor)
HQ: Avago Technologies Wireless (U.S.A.) Manufacturing Llc
   4380 Ziegler Rd
   Fort Collins CO 80525

**(P-12536)**
**LUXTERA LLC**
2320 Camino Vida Roble Ste 100, Carlsbad (92011-1562)
PHONE.................760 448-3520
**EMP:** 162 **EST:** 2001
**SALES (est):** 71.65MM
**SALES (corp-wide):** 53.8B **Publicly Held**
Web: www.cisco.com
SIC: **3674** Semiconductors and related devices
PA: Cisco Systems, Inc.
   170 W Tasman Dr
   408 526-4000

**(P-12537)**
**M-PULSE MICROWAVE INC**
576 Charcot Ave, San Jose (95131-2201)
PHONE.................408 432-1480
Billy Long, *Pr*
Hector Flores, *
Wendell Sanders, *Stockholder*
**EMP:** 25 **EST:** 1987
**SQ FT:** 24,000
**SALES (est):** 2.52MM **Privately Held**
Web: www.mpulsemw.com
SIC: **3674** Integrated circuits, semiconductor networks, etc.

**(P-12538)**
**MACKENZIE LABORATORIES INC**
1163 Nicole Ct, Glendora (91740)
P.O. Box 1416 (91740)
PHONE.................909 394-9007
Nagy Khattar, *Pr*
▲ **EMP:** 15 **EST:** 1952
**SQ FT:** 20,000
**SALES (est):** 4.34MM **Privately Held**
Web: www.macklabs.com
SIC: **3674** 3663 Semiconductors and related devices; Radio and t.v. communications equipment

**(P-12539)**
**MACOM TECHNOLOGY SOLUTIONS INC**
471 El Camino Real Ste 210, Santa Clara (95050-4482)
PHONE.................408 387-7741
Dean Drako, *Pr*
**EMP:** 34
Web: www.macom.com
SIC: **3674** Semiconductors and related devices
HQ: Macom Technology Solutions Inc.
   100 Chelmsford St
   Lowell MA 01851

**(P-12540)**
**MAGNACHIP SEMICONDUCTOR CORP**
60 S Market St Ste 750, San Jose (95113-2362)
PHONE.................408 625-5999
Young-joon Kim, *CEO*
Young Soo Woo, *CFO*
**EMP:** 17 **EST:** 2010
**SALES (est):** 1.94MM **Privately Held**
Web: www.magnachip.com
SIC: **3674** Semiconductors and related devices

**(P-12541)**
**MAGNUM SEMICONDUCTOR INC**
6024 Silver Creek Valley Rd, San Jose (95138-1011)
PHONE.................408 934-3700
Gopal Solanki, *Pr*
Terry Griffin, *
▲ **EMP:** 233 **EST:** 2005
**SALES (est):** 16.83MM **Privately Held**
Web: www.renesas.com
SIC: **3674** Integrated circuits, semiconductor networks, etc.
HQ: Gigpeak, Inc.
   6024 Silver Creek Vly Rd
   San Jose CA 95138
   408 546-3316

**(P-12542)**
**MARSEILLE NETWORKS INC**
3211 Scott Blvd Ste 205, Santa Clara (95054-3009)
PHONE.................408 689-0303
Amine Chabane, *Pr*
▼ **EMP:** 17 **EST:** 2005
**SQ FT:** 2,500
**SALES (est):** 3.25MM **Privately Held**
Web: www.marseilleinc.com
SIC: **3674** Semiconductors and related devices

**(P-12543)**
**MARVELL SEMICONDUCTOR INC**
890 Glenn Dr, Folsom (95630-3185)
PHONE.................916 605-3700
**EMP:** 49
**SALES (corp-wide):** 5.51B **Publicly Held**
Web: www.marvell.com
SIC: **3674** Semiconductors and related devices
HQ: Marvell Semiconductor, Inc.
   5488 Marvell Ln
   Santa Clara CA 95054

**(P-12544)**
**MARVELL SEMICONDUCTOR INC**
15485 Sand Canyon Ave, Irvine (92618-3154)
PHONE.................949 614-7700
Robert E Romney, *Prin*
**EMP:** 882
**SALES (corp-wide):** 5.51B **Publicly Held**
Web: www.marvell.com
SIC: **3674** Semiconductors and related devices
HQ: Marvell Semiconductor, Inc.
   5488 Marvell Ln
   Santa Clara CA 95054

**(P-12545)**
**MARVELL SEMICONDUCTOR INC (HQ)**
Also Called: Marvell
5488 Marvell Ln, Santa Clara (95054-3606)
PHONE.................408 222-2500
Matthew Murphy, *CEO*
Jean Hu, *
Neil Kim, *
◆ **EMP:** 900 **EST:** 1995
**SALES (est):** 678.65MM
**SALES (corp-wide):** 5.51B **Publicly Held**
Web: www.marvell.com
SIC: **3674** Semiconductors and related devices
PA: Marvell Technology, Inc.
   1000 N West St Ste 1200
   302 295-4840

**(P-12546)**
**MARVELL TECHNOLOGY GROUP LTD**
5488 Marvell Ln, Santa Clara (95054-3606)
PHONE.................408 222-2500

## PRODUCTS & SERVICES SECTION
### 3674 - Semiconductors And Related Devices (P-12566)

EMP: 193 EST: 1991
SALES (est): 4.5MM **Privately Held**
Web: www.marvell.com
SIC: 3674 Semiconductors and related devices

**(P-12547)**
**MASIMO SEMICONDUCTOR INC**
52 Discovery, Irvine (92618-3105)
PHONE..................603 595-8900
Mark P De Raad, *Pr*
Gerry Hammarth, *VP*
EMP: 16 EST: 2012
SALES (est): 4.54MM **Publicly Held**
Web: professional.masimo.com
SIC: 3674 Light emitting diodes
PA: Masimo Corporation
52 Discovery

**(P-12548)**
**MATTSON TECHNOLOGY INC (HQ)**
47131 Bayside Pkwy, Fremont (94538-6517)
PHONE..................510 657-5900
Allen Lu, *Pr*
Michael Yang, *
Subhash Deshmukh, *Chief Business Officer*
Frank Moreman, *
Curtis Liang, *
▲ EMP: 45 EST: 1988
SQ FT: 101,000
SALES (est): 77.43MM
SALES (corp-wide): 706.59MM **Privately Held**
Web: www.mattson.com
SIC: 3674 Semiconductors and related devices
PA: Beijing E-Town International Investment & Development Co.,Ltd.
2501, 25/F, Building 1, No.22 Courtyard, Ronghua Middle Road, Be
108 105-7856

**(P-12549)**
**MAXIM INTEGRATED PRODUCTS LLC (HQ)**
Also Called: Maxim Integrated
160 Rio Robles, San Jose (95134-1813)
PHONE..................408 601-1000
Tunc Doluca, *Pr*
William P Sullivan, *Ch Bd*
Brian C White, *Sr VP*
Edwin B Medlin, *CLO CCO*
Vivek Jain, *Sr VP*
EMP: 956 EST: 1983
SQ FT: 435,000
SALES (est): 2.63B
SALES (corp-wide): 12.31B **Publicly Held**
Web: www.analog.com
SIC: 3674 Semiconductors and related devices
PA: Analog Devices, Inc.
1 Analog Way
781 935-5565

**(P-12550)**
**MAXIM INTERNATIONAL HOLDG INC (DH)**
160 Rio Robles, San Jose (95134-1813)
PHONE..................408 737-7600
EMP: 20 EST: 1999
SALES (est): 3.31MM
SALES (corp-wide): 12.31B **Publicly Held**
SIC: 3674 Semiconductors and related devices
HQ: Maxim Integrated Products, Llc
160 Rio Robles
San Jose CA 95134
408 601-1000

**(P-12551)**
**MAXLINEAR INC (PA)**
5966 La Place Ct Ste 100, Carlsbad (92008-8830)
PHONE..................760 692-0711
Kishore Seendripu, *Ch Bd*
Steven G Litchfield, *CORP*
Connie Kwong, *CAO*
Michael J Lachance, *VP Opers*
▲ EMP: 45 EST: 2003
SQ FT: 68,000
SALES (est): 693.26MM
SALES (corp-wide): 693.26MM **Publicly Held**
Web: www.maxlinear.com
SIC: 3674 Semiconductors and related devices

**(P-12552)**
**MAXLINEAR COMMUNICATIONS LLC (HQ)**
5966 La Place Ct Ste 100, Carlsbad (92008-8895)
▲ EMP: 16 EST: 2001
SQ FT: 90,000
SALES (est): 5.78MM
SALES (corp-wide): 693.26MM **Publicly Held**
Web: www.maxlinear.com
SIC: 3674 7372 Semiconductor circuit networks; Prepackaged software
PA: Maxlinear, Inc.
5966 La Place Ct Ste 100
760 692-0711

**(P-12553)**
**MEGA FLUID SYSTEMS INC**
6161 Industrial Way Ste A, Livermore (94551-9712)
PHONE..................971 277-9000
Kevin Bradey, *CEO*
EMP: 33
SALES (corp-wide): 242.12K **Privately Held**
Web: www.kinetics.net
SIC: 3674 Wafers (semiconductor devices)
HQ: Mega Fluid Systems, Inc.
9398 Sw Tltin Sherwood Rd
Tualatin OR 97062

**(P-12554)**
**MEGACHIPS LSI USA CORPORATION**
910 E Hamilton Ave Ste 120, Campbell (95008-0612)
PHONE..................408 570-0555
Ikuo Iwama, *CEO*
Akihide Maeda, *
EMP: 75 EST: 2018
SALES (est): 4.96MM **Privately Held**
Web: www.megachips.co.jp
SIC: 3674 5065 Semiconductors and related devices; Semiconductor devices
PA: Megachips Corporation
1-1-1, Miyahara, Yodogawa-Ku

**(P-12555)**
**MEGACHIPS TECHNOLOGY AMERICA CORPORATION**
Also Called: Kawasaki Micro Elec Amer
2755 Orchard Pkwy, San Jose (95134-2008)
PHONE..................408 570-0555
▲ EMP: 75
Web: www.megachips.co.jp
SIC: 3674 Integrated circuits, semiconductor networks, etc.

**(P-12556)**
**MELLANOX TECHNOLOGIES INC**
Also Called: Accounts Payable
2530 Zanker Rd, San Jose (95131-1127)
P.O. Box 67143 (95067-7143)
PHONE..................408 970-3400
Eyal Waldman, *CEO*
EMP: 154
Web: www.nvidia.com
SIC: 3674 Semiconductors and related devices
HQ: Mellanox Technologies, Inc.
2530 Zanker Rd
San Jose CA 95131
408 970-3400

**(P-12557)**
**MELLANOX TECHNOLOGIES INC (DH)**
2530 Zanker Rd, San Jose (95131-1127)
PHONE..................408 970-3400
Eyal Waldman, *West Chief Executive Officer*
Eyal Waldman, *Ch Bd*
Roni Ashuri, *VP*
Michael Kagan, *VP*
Marc Sultzbaugh, *VP*
EMP: 34 EST: 1999
SALES (est): 1.33B **Publicly Held**
Web: www.nvidia.com
SIC: 3674 Integrated circuits, semiconductor networks, etc.
HQ: Mellanox Technologies, Ltd.
26 Hakidma
Yokneam Illit 20667

**(P-12558)**
**MERLIN SOLAR TECHNOLOGIES INC (HQ)**
5225 Hellyer Ave Ste 200, San Jose (95138-1021)
PHONE..................844 637-5461
Arthur Tan, *
Olaf Gresens, *
Chi Miller, *CFO*
EMP: 25 EST: 2016
SALES (est): 1.4MM
SALES (corp-wide): 1.4MM **Privately Held**
Web: www.merlinsolar.com
SIC: 3674 Solar cells
PA: Aci Solar Holdings Na, Inc.
3220 Nw 101st Ave
650 227-3271

**(P-12559)**
**MIASOLE**
2590 Walsh Ave, Santa Clara (95051-1315)
PHONE..................408 919-5700
Jeff Zhou, *CEO*
Merle Mcclendon, *CFO*
Atiye Bayman, *
▲ EMP: 315 EST: 2001
SALES (est): 2.81MM **Privately Held**
Web: www.miasole.com
SIC: 3674 Solar cells

**(P-12560)**
**MIASOLE HI-TECH CORP (DH)**
Also Called: Miasole
3211 Scott Blvd Ste 201, Santa Clara (95054-3010)
PHONE..................408 919-5700
Jie Zhang, *CEO*
Lyndsey Zhang, *
Atiye Bayman, *
EMP: 250 EST: 2012
SALES (est): 20.78MM **Privately Held**
Web: www.miasole.com

SIC: 3674 5074 Solar cells; Heating equipment and panels, solar
HQ: Hanergy Holding (America) Llc
1350 Bayshore Hwy
Burlingame CA 94010
650 288-3722

**(P-12561)**
**MICREL INCORPORATED**
Also Called: Micrel Semiconductor
2180 Fortune Dr, San Jose (95131-1815)
PHONE..................408 944-0800
EMP: 728
SIC: 3674 Integrated circuits, semiconductor networks, etc.

**(P-12562)**
**MICREL LLC**
Also Called: Micrel Semiconductor
1849 Fortune Dr, San Jose (95131-1724)
PHONE..................408 944-0800
Mark Lunsford, *Brnch Mgr*
EMP: 899
SALES (corp-wide): 7.63B **Publicly Held**
SIC: 3674 Semiconductors and related devices
HQ: Micrel Llc
2355 W Chandler Blvd
Chandler AZ 85224
480 792-7200

**(P-12563)**
**MICREL LLC**
1931 Fortune Dr, San Jose (95131-1724)
PHONE..................408 944-0800
Jung-chen Lin, *Brnch Mgr*
EMP: 353
SALES (corp-wide): 7.63B **Publicly Held**
SIC: 3674 Semiconductors and related devices
HQ: Micrel Llc
2355 W Chandler Blvd
Chandler AZ 85224
480 792-7200

**(P-12564)**
**MICREL LLC**
2180 Fortune Dr, San Jose (95131-1815)
PHONE..................408 944-0800
Raymond Zinn, *CEO*
EMP: 728
SALES (corp-wide): 7.63B **Publicly Held**
SIC: 3674 Integrated circuits, semiconductor networks, etc.
HQ: Micrel Llc
2355 W Chandler Blvd
Chandler AZ 85224
480 792-7200

**(P-12565)**
**MICRO ANALOG INC**
Also Called: Analog
1861 Puddingstone Dr, La Verne (91750-5825)
PHONE..................909 392-8277
Hung T Nguyen, *CEO*
Khanh Van Nguyen, *
▲ EMP: 160 EST: 1991
SQ FT: 27,000
SALES (est): 24.75MM **Privately Held**
Web: www.micro-analog.com
SIC: 3674 Semiconductors and related devices

**(P-12566)**
**MICROCHIP TECHNOLOGY**
1931 Fortune Dr, San Jose (95131-1724)
PHONE..................408 474-3640
Thomas Mendoza, *Mgr*
EMP: 37 EST: 2015

## 3674 - Semiconductors And Related Devices (P-12567)

SALES (est): 5.95MM **Privately Held**
Web: www.microsemi.com
SIC: **3674** Semiconductors and related devices

### (P-12567)
### MICROCHIP TECHNOLOGY INC
450 Holger Way, San Jose (95134-1368)
PHONE.................................408 735-9110
Greg Winner, *CEO*
EMP: 48
SALES (corp-wide): 7.63B **Publicly Held**
Web: www.microchip.com
SIC: **3674** Integrated circuits, semiconductor networks, etc.
PA: Microchip Technology Inc
2355 W Chandler Blvd
480 792-7200

### (P-12568)
### MICRON TECHNOLOGY INC
2235 Iron Point Rd, Folsom (95630-8765)
PHONE.................................916 458-3003
Glen Hawk, *Brnch Mgr*
EMP: 181
SALES (corp-wide): 15.54B **Publicly Held**
Web: www.micron.com
SIC: **3674** Integrated circuits, semiconductor networks, etc.
PA: Micron Technology, Inc.
8000 S Federal Way
208 368-4000

### (P-12569)
### MICROSEMI COMMUNICATIONS INC (DH)
Also Called: Catawba County Schools
4721 Calle Carga, Camarillo (93012)
PHONE.................................805 388-3700
Christopher R Gardner, *Pr*
Martin S Mcdermut, *CFO*
Jacob Nielsen, *CIO**
EMP: 53 EST: 1987
SQ FT: 111,000
SALES (est): 33.76MM
SALES (corp-wide): 7.63B **Publicly Held**
Web: www.microsemi.com
SIC: **3674** Semiconductors and related devices
HQ: Microsemi Corporation
11861 Western Ave
Garden Grove CA 92841
949 380-6100

### (P-12570)
### MICROSEMI CORP - ANLOG MXED SG
3850 N 1st St, San Jose (95134-1702)
PHONE.................................408 643-6000
Shafy Eltoukhy, *Genl Mgr*
EMP: 1222
SALES (corp-wide): 7.63B **Publicly Held**
Web: www.microsemi.com
SIC: **3674** Semiconductors and related devices
HQ: Microsemi Corp. - Analog Mixed Signal Group
11861 Western Ave
Garden Grove CA 92841

### (P-12571)
### MICROSEMI CORP - ANLOG MXED SG (DH)
Also Called: Linfinity Microelectronics
11861 Western Ave, Garden Grove (92841-2119)
PHONE.................................714 898-8121
James Peterson, *CEO*
John Hohener, *CFO*

Paul Pickle, *COO*
Steve Litchfield, *CSO*
EMP: 78 EST: 1968
SALES (est): 16.54MM
SALES (corp-wide): 7.63B **Publicly Held**
Web: www.microsemi.com
SIC: **3674** Semiconductors and related devices
HQ: Microsemi Corporation
11861 Western Ave
Garden Grove CA 92841
949 380-6100

### (P-12572)
### MICROSEMI CORP- RF INTEGRATED
3870 N 1st St, San Jose (95134-1702)
PHONE.................................408 954-8314
FAX: 408 451-9243
EMP: 15
SALES (corp-wide): 1.66B **Publicly Held**
SIC: **3674** Semiconductors and related devices
HQ: Microsemi Corp- Rf Integrated Solutions
105 Lake Forest Way
Folsom CA 95630

### (P-12573)
### MICROSEMI CORPORATION
Also Called: Microsemi Corp - Santa Ana
11861 Western Ave, Garden Grove (92841-2119)
PHONE.................................714 898-7112
Lane Jorgensen, *Mgr*
EMP: 244
SQ FT: 93,000
SALES (corp-wide): 7.63B **Publicly Held**
Web: www.microsemi.com
SIC: **3674** Semiconductors and related devices
HQ: Microsemi Corporation
11861 Western Ave
Garden Grove CA 92841
949 380-6100

### (P-12574)
### MICROSEMI CORPORATION
3850 N 1st St, San Jose (95134-1702)
PHONE.................................408 643-6000
Jim Peterson, *CEO*
EMP: 21
SALES (corp-wide): 7.63B **Publicly Held**
Web: www.microsemi.com
SIC: **3674** Semiconductors and related devices
HQ: Microsemi Corporation
11861 Western Ave
Garden Grove CA 92841
949 380-6100

### (P-12575)
### MICROSEMI CORPORATION
3870 N 1st St, San Jose (95134-1702)
PHONE.................................650 318-4200
Pierre Irisso, *Brnch Mgr*
EMP: 123
SALES (corp-wide): 7.63B **Publicly Held**
Web: www.microsemi.com
SIC: **3674** Semiconductors and related devices
HQ: Microsemi Corporation
11861 Western Ave
Garden Grove CA 92841
949 380-6100

### (P-12576)
### MICROSEMI CORPORATION (HQ)
Also Called: Microsemi
11861 Western Ave, Garden Grove (92841-2119)

PHONE.................................949 380-6100
Steve Sanghi, *Ch*
Eric Bjornholt, *
Ganesh Moorthy, *
EMP: 50 EST: 1960
SALES (est): 1.45B
SALES (corp-wide): 7.63B **Publicly Held**
Web: www.microsemi.com
SIC: **3674** Integrated circuits, semiconductor networks, etc.
PA: Microchip Technology Inc
2355 W Chandler Blvd
480 792-7200

### (P-12577)
### MICROSEMI CRP- RF INTGRTED SLT (DH)
Also Called: Microsemi Rfis
105 Lake Forest Way, Folsom (95630-4708)
PHONE.................................916 850-8640
James J Peterson, *Pr*
Ralph Brandi, *
John W Hohener, *
David H Hall, *MICROSEMI RFIS**
▲ EMP: 115 EST: 2009
SALES (est): 74.71MM
SALES (corp-wide): 7.63B **Publicly Held**
SIC: **3674** Semiconductors and related devices
HQ: Microsemi Corporation
11861 Western Ave
Garden Grove CA 92841
949 380-6100

### (P-12578)
### MICROSEMI FREQUENCY TIME CORP
2300 Orchard Pkwy, San Jose (95131-1017)
P.O. Box 39000 (94139-0001)
PHONE.................................408 433-0910
EMP: 64
SALES (corp-wide): 7.63B **Publicly Held**
Web: www.microsemi.com
SIC: **3674** Semiconductors and related devices
HQ: Microsemi Frequency And Time Corporation
3870 N 1st St
San Jose CA 95134
480 792-7200

### (P-12579)
### MICROSEMI SOC CORP (DH)
3850 N 1st St, San Jose (95134-1702)
PHONE.................................408 643-6000
James J Peterson, *CEO*
John W Hohener, *
Esmat Z Hamdy, *Senior Vice President Technology**
Fares N Mubarak, *Marketing**
David L Van De Hey, *
▲ EMP: 78 EST: 1985
SQ FT: 158,000
SALES (est): 34.99MM
SALES (corp-wide): 7.63B **Publicly Held**
Web: www.microsemi.com
SIC: **3674** 7371 Microcircuits, integrated (semiconductor); Computer software development
HQ: Microsemi Corporation
11861 Western Ave
Garden Grove CA 92841
949 380-6100

### (P-12580)
### MICROSEMI SOC CORP
2051 Stierlin Ct, Mountain View (94043-4655)

PHONE.................................650 318-4200
Mary Segura, *Crdt Mgr*
EMP: 161
SALES (corp-wide): 7.63B **Publicly Held**
Web: www.microsemi.com
SIC: **3674** Microcircuits, integrated (semiconductor)
HQ: Microsemi Soc Corp.
3850 N 1st St
San Jose CA 95134
408 643-6000

### (P-12581)
### MICROSEMI STOR SOLUTIONS INC (DH)
1380 Bordeaux Dr, Sunnyvale (94089-1005)
PHONE.................................408 239-8000
Paul Pickle, *Pr*
John W Hohener, *
EMP: 85 EST: 1983
SQ FT: 85,000
SALES (est): 49.39MM
SALES (corp-wide): 7.63B **Publicly Held**
Web: www.microsemi.com
SIC: **3674** Modules, solid state
HQ: Microsemi Corporation
11861 Western Ave
Garden Grove CA 92841
949 380-6100

### (P-12582)
### MICROSEMI STOR SOLUTIONS INC
101 Creekside Ridge Ct Ste 100, Roseville (95678-3595)
PHONE.................................916 788-3300
Jim Dabney, *CEO*
EMP: 30
SALES (corp-wide): 7.63B **Publicly Held**
Web: www.microsemi.com
SIC: **3674** Semiconductors and related devices
HQ: Microsemi Storage Solutions, Inc.
1380 Bordeaux Dr
Sunnyvale CA 94089
408 239-8000

### (P-12583)
### MICROSS HI REL PWR SLTIONS INC
2520 Junction Ave, San Jose (95134-1902)
PHONE.................................408 434-5000
Vincent Buffa, *CEO*
EMP: 179
SALES (corp-wide): 8.56MM **Privately Held**
SIC: **3674** 3663 Microcircuits, integrated (semiconductor); Receiver-transmitter units (transceiver)
PA: Micross Hi Rel Power Solutions, Inc.
2520 Junction Ave Bldg D
408 944-0308

### (P-12584)
### MICROSS HOLDINGS INC
11150 Santa Monica Blvd Ste 750, Los Angeles (90025-3380)
PHONE.................................215 997-3200
F Michael Pisch, *CFO*
EMP: 99 EST: 2010
SALES (est): 4.4MM **Privately Held**
SIC: **3674** Semiconductors and related devices

### (P-12585)
### MINDSPEED TECHNOLOGIES LLC (HQ)
Also Called: Macom

## PRODUCTS & SERVICES SECTION
## 3674 - Semiconductors And Related Devices (P-12606)

4000 Macarthur Blvd, Newport Beach (92660-2558)
PHONE.............................949 579-3000
Raouf Y Halim, *CEO*
Stephen N Ananias, *
Gerald J Hamilton, *Senior Vice President Worldwide Sales**
Allison K Musetich, *Senior Vice President Human Resources**
Najabat H Bajwa, *
**EMP:** 54 **EST:** 2002
**SQ FT:** 97,000
**SALES (est):** 22.17MM **Publicly Held**
Web: www.macom.com
**SIC: 3674** Semiconductors and related devices
**PA:** Macom Technology Solutions Holdings, Inc.
100 Chelmsford St

**(P-12586)**
### MIXEL INC
Also Called: Semiconductors
97 E Brokaw Rd Ste 250, San Jose (95112-1032)
PHONE.............................408 436-8500
Ashraf Takla, *Pr*
**EMP:** 85 **EST:** 1999
**SQ FT:** 2,500
**SALES (est):** 10.95MM **Privately Held**
Web: www.mixel.com
**SIC: 3674** Semiconductors and related devices

**(P-12587)**
### MOBIVEIL INC
2535 Augustine Dr, Santa Clara (95054)
PHONE.............................408 791-2977
Ravikumar R Thummarukudy, *CEO*
Gopa Periyadan, *Cncil Mbr*
Amit Saxena, *VP*
Dale Olstinske, *VP*
D Srinivasan, *Prin*
**EMP:** 24 **EST:** 2011
**SALES (est):** 1.88MM **Privately Held**
Web: www.mobiveil.com
**SIC: 3674** Semiconductors and related devices

**(P-12588)**
### MONTAGE TECHNOLOGY INC
101 Metro Dr Ste 500, San Jose (95110-1342)
PHONE.............................408 982-2788
Howard Yang, *Prin*
**EMP:** 46 **EST:** 2005
**SALES (est):** 2.38MM **Privately Held**
Web: www.montage-tech.com
**SIC: 3674** Semiconductors and related devices

**(P-12589)**
### MORSE MICRO INC
40 Waterworks Way, Irvine (92618-3107)
PHONE.............................949 501-7080
Michael De Nil, *CEO*
**EMP:** 85 **EST:** 2019
**SALES (est):** 5.21MM **Privately Held**
Web: www.morsemicro.com
**SIC: 3674** Integrated circuits, semiconductor networks, etc.

**(P-12590)**
### MPI AMERICA INC
2360 Qume Dr Ste C, San Jose (95131-1812)
PHONE.............................408 770-3650
Richard William Dock, *Pr*
**EMP:** 17 **EST:** 2017
**SALES (est):** 16.82MM **Privately Held**
Web: www.mpi-corporation.com
**SIC: 3674** Semiconductors and related devices

**(P-12591)**
### MPS INTERNATIONAL LTD
79 Great Oaks Blvd, San Jose (95119-1311)
PHONE.............................408 826-0600
Michael R Hsing, *CEO*
▼ **EMP:** 27 **EST:** 1997
**SQ FT:** 100,000
**SALES (est):** 3.34MM **Publicly Held**
**SIC: 3674** Semiconductors and related devices
**PA:** Monolithic Power Systems, Inc.
5808 Lake Wash Blvd Ne

**(P-12592)**
### MRV COMMUNICATIONS INC
Also Called: Mrv
20520 Nordhoff St, Chatsworth (91311-6113)
PHONE.............................818 773-0900
▲ **EMP:** 268
**SIC: 3674** Integrated circuits, semiconductor networks, etc.

**(P-12593)**
### MULTICHIP ASSEMBLY INC
270 E Brokaw Rd, San Jose (95112-4205)
PHONE.............................408 451-2345
Donald Macintyre, *Pr*
**EMP:** 30 **EST:** 1991
**SQ FT:** 12,500
**SALES (est):** 2.36MM **Privately Held**
**SIC: 3674** Semiconductors and related devices

**(P-12594)**
### NANOSILICON INC
2461 Autumnvale Dr, San Jose (95131-1802)
PHONE.............................408 263-7341
Lincoln Bejan, *Pr*
Jackie Bejan, *CFO*
John Ayala, *VP Opers*
**EMP:** 22 **EST:** 2009
**SQ FT:** 30,000
**SALES (est):** 2.53MM **Privately Held**
Web: www.nanosiliconinc.com
**SIC: 3674** Semiconductors and related devices

**(P-12595)**
### NANOSYS INC (HQ)
Also Called: Nanosys
233 S Hillview Dr, Milpitas (95035-5417)
PHONE.............................408 240-6700
Jason Hartlove, *CEO*
John Hanlow, *
Peter S Garcia, *
**EMP:** 48 **EST:** 2001
**SQ FT:** 32,000
**SALES (est):** 35.53MM
**SALES (corp-wide):** 35.53MM **Privately Held**
Web: www.nanosys.com
**SIC: 3674** Semiconductors and related devices
**PA:** Shoei Electronic Materials, Inc.
1100 Ne Circle Blvd # 110

**(P-12596)**
### NATIONAL SEMICONDUCTOR CORP (HQ)
2900 Semiconductor Dr, Santa Clara (95051-0606)
PHONE.............................408 721-5000
Ellen L Barker, *CEO*
Lewis Chew, *
Todd M Duchene, *
Edward J Sweeney, *Senior Vice President Human Resources**
Jamie E Samath, *Corporate Controller**
▲ **EMP:** 1700 **EST:** 1959
**SALES (est):** 106.92MM
**SALES (corp-wide):** 17.52B **Publicly Held**
Web: www.ti.com
**SIC: 3674** Microprocessors
**PA:** Texas Instruments Incorporated
12500 Ti Blvd
214 479-3773

**(P-12597)**
### NDSP DELAWARE INC
Also Called: Ndsp Crp
224 Airport Pkwy Ste 400, San Jose (95110-1095)
PHONE.............................408 626-1640
Ven L Lee, *Pr*
Ven L Lee, *Pr*
Leonard Liu, *Ch*
**EMP:** 30 **EST:** 1997
**SQ FT:** 9,285
**SALES (est):** 631.15K
**SALES (corp-wide):** 59.68MM **Publicly Held**
**SIC: 3674** Integrated circuits, semiconductor networks, etc.
**PA:** Pixelworks, Inc.
226 Airport Pkwy Ste 595
408 200-9200

**(P-12598)**
### NEOCONIX INC
4020 Moorpark Ave Ste 108, San Jose (95117-1845)
PHONE.............................408 530-9393
Asuri Raghavan, *Pr*
Dirk Brown, *
Jim Witham, *
Dinesh Kalakkad, *
Phil Damberg, *
**EMP:** 40 **EST:** 2002
**SQ FT:** 5,000
**SALES (est):** 1.88MM **Privately Held**
Web: www.neoconix.com
**SIC: 3674** Semiconductors and related devices

**(P-12599)**
### NETHRA IMAGING INC (PA)
2855 Bowers Ave, Santa Clara (95051-0917)
PHONE.............................408 257-5880
Ramesh Singh, *Pr*
**EMP:** 30 **EST:** 2003
**SALES (est):** 1.57MM
**SALES (corp-wide):** 1.57MM **Privately Held**
Web: www.nethra-imaging.com
**SIC: 3674** Semiconductors and related devices

**(P-12600)**
### NETLIST INC (PA)
Also Called: NETLIST
111 Academy Ste 100, Irvine (92617-3046)
PHONE.............................949 435-0025
Chun K Hong, *CEO*
Gail Sasaki, *VP*
**EMP:** 50 **EST:** 2000
**SQ FT:** 14,809
**SALES (est):** 69.2MM
**SALES (corp-wide):** 69.2MM **Publicly Held**
Web: www.netlist.com
**SIC: 3674** Semiconductors and related devices

**(P-12601)**
### NETLOGIC MICROSYSTEMS LLC
Also Called: Broadcom
3975 Freedom Cir, Santa Clara (95054-1255)
P.O. Box 57013 (95054)
PHONE.............................408 454-3000
**EMP:** 645
Web: www.netlogicmicro.com
**SIC: 3674** Integrated circuits, semiconductor networks, etc.

**(P-12602)**
### NEWPORT FAB LLC
Also Called: Jazz Semiconductor
4321 Jamboree Rd, Newport Beach (92660-3007)
PHONE.............................949 435-8000
**EMP:** 99 **EST:** 2002
**SALES (est):** 3.84MM **Privately Held**
Web: www.towersemi.com
**SIC: 3674** Wafers (semiconductor devices)
**HQ:** Tower Semiconductor Newport Beach, Inc.
4321 Jamboree Rd
Newport Beach CA 92660
949 435-8000

**(P-12603)**
### NEXGEN POWER SYSTEMS INC
3151 Jay St Ste 201, Santa Clara (95054-3308)
PHONE.............................408 230-7698
Dinesh Ramanathan, *Pr*
Narayanan Karu, *
**EMP:** 30 **EST:** 2017
**SALES (est):** 5.16MM **Privately Held**
Web: www.nexgenpowersystems.com
**SIC: 3674** Semiconductor circuit networks

**(P-12604)**
### NEXT SEMICONDUCTOR TECH INC
4115 Sorrento Valley Blvd, San Diego (92121-1406)
PHONE.............................858 707-7060
Mickey Rushing, *CEO*
Robert Kummer, *CFO*
**EMP:** 20 **EST:** 2020
**SALES (est):** 1.3MM **Privately Held**
**SIC: 3674** Semiconductors and related devices

**(P-12605)**
### NGCODEC INC
440 N Wolfe Rd Ste 2187, Sunnyvale (94085-3869)
PHONE.............................408 766-4382
Oliver Gunasekara, *CEO*
Alberto Duenas, *Ch*
Adam Malamy, *VP*
**EMP:** 20 **EST:** 2012
**SALES (est):** 2.29MM
**SALES (corp-wide):** 22.68B **Publicly Held**
Web: www.xilinx.com
**SIC: 3674** Semiconductors and related devices
**HQ:** Xilinx, Inc.
2100 Logic Dr
San Jose CA 95124
408 559-7778

**(P-12606)**
### NIMSOFT INC (HQ)
3965 Freedom Cir Fl 6, Santa Clara (95054-1286)
PHONE.............................408 796-3400
Chris O'malley, *CEO*
Lokesh Jindal, *
Mark Harris, *

## 3674 - Semiconductors And Related Devices (P-12607)

EMP: 30 EST: 2004
SQ FT: 6,000
SALES (est): 5.83MM
SALES (corp-wide): 35.82B **Publicly Held**
SIC: **3674** Semiconductors and related devices
PA: Broadcom Inc.
   3421 Hillview Ave
   650 427-6000

**(P-12607)**
**NOKIA OF AMERICA CORPORATION**
520 Almanor Ave, Sunnyvale (94085-3533)
PHONE.................................408 878-6500
Oscar Rodriguez, *Mgr*
EMP: 15
SALES (corp-wide): 24.19B **Privately Held**
Web: www.nokia.com
SIC: **3674** Integrated circuits, semiconductor networks, etc.
HQ: Nokia Of America Corporation
   600 Mountain Ave Ste 700
   Murray Hill NJ 07974

**(P-12608)**
**NURLINK TECHNOLOGY CORP**
5910 Pacific Center Blvd Ste 310, San Diego (92121-6303)
PHONE.................................408 205-5363
EMP: 18 EST: 2018
SALES (est): 1.97MM **Privately Held**
SIC: **3674** Semiconductors and related devices

**(P-12609)**
**NUVIA INC**
2811 Mission College Blvd Fl 7, Santa Clara (95054-1884)
PHONE.................................408 654-9696
Gerard Williams, *CEO*
EMP: 20 EST: 2019
SALES (est): 4.4MM
SALES (corp-wide): 38.96B **Publicly Held**
SIC: **3674** 8731 Metal oxide silicon (MOS) devices; Computer (hardware) development
HQ: Qualcomm Technologies, Inc.
   5775 Morehouse Dr
   San Diego CA 92121
   858 587-1121

**(P-12610)**
**NUVOSUN INC**
1565 Barber Ln, Milpitas (95035-7409)
PHONE.................................510 304-2351
EMP: 25 EST: 2019
SALES (est): 2.19MM
SALES (corp-wide): 44.62B **Publicly Held**
Web: www.nuvosun.com
SIC: **3674** Semiconductors and related devices
PA: Dow Inc.
   2211 H H Dow Way
   989 636-1000

**(P-12611)**
**NVIDIA CORPORATION**
2530 Zanker Rd, San Jose (95131-1127)
PHONE.................................408 486-2715
EMP: 20
Web: www.nvidia.com
SIC: **3674** Semiconductors and related devices
PA: Nvidia Corporation
   2788 San Tomas Expy

**(P-12612)**
**NVIDIA CORPORATION (PA)**
Also Called: Nvidia
2788 San Tomas Expy, Santa Clara (95051-0952)
PHONE.................................408 486-2000
Jen-hsun Huang, *Pr*
Colette M Kress, *Ex VP*
Timothy S Teter, *Ex VP*
Debora Shoquist, *Operations*
Ajay K Puri, *Executive Worldwide Field Operations Vice President*
◆ EMP: 911 EST: 1993
SALES (est): 60.92B **Publicly Held**
Web: www.nvidia.com
SIC: **3674** Semiconductors and related devices

**(P-12613)**
**NXP SEMICONDUCTORS USA INC**
Also Called: Nxp
411 E Plumeria Dr, San Jose (95134-1924)
PHONE.................................408 518-5500
▲ EMP: 5000
SIC: **3674** Integrated circuits, semiconductor networks, etc.

**(P-12614)**
**NXP USA INC**
Also Called: Philips Semiconductors
411 E Plumeria Dr, San Jose (95134-1924)
PHONE.................................408 518-5500
EMP: 500
SALES (corp-wide): 13.28B **Privately Held**
Web: www.nxp.com
SIC: **3674** Integrated circuits, semiconductor networks, etc.
HQ: Nxp Usa, Inc.
   6501 W William Cannon Dr
   Austin TX 78735
   512 933-8214

**(P-12615)**
**OCLARO FIBER OPTICS INC (DH)**
Also Called: Oclaro
400 N Mccarthy Blvd, Milpitas (95035-9100)
PHONE.................................408 383-1400
Harry L Bosco, *Pr*
Robert J Nobile, *
Atsushi Horiuchi, *Senior Vice President Global Sales*
Justin J O'neill, *Corporate Secretary*
EMP: 223 EST: 2000
SALES (est): 6.7MM
SALES (corp-wide): 1.36B **Publicly Held**
SIC: **3674** Photoconductive cells
HQ: Oclaro, Inc.
   400 N Mccarthy Blvd
   Milpitas CA 95035

**(P-12616)**
**OEPIC SEMICONDUCTORS INC**
1231 Bordeaux Dr, Sunnyvale (94089-1203)
PHONE.................................408 747-0388
Yi-ching Pao, *Pr*
EMP: 35 EST: 2000
SQ FT: 18,000
SALES (est): 5.42MM **Privately Held**
Web: www.oepic.com
SIC: **3674** Semiconductors and related devices

**(P-12617)**
**OMNISIL**
5401 Everglades St, Ventura (93003-6523)
PHONE.................................805 644-2514
David Clark, *Pr*
Dennis Strang, *VP*
Karin Clark, *Sec*
▲ EMP: 21 EST: 1986
SQ FT: 9,800
SALES (est): 1.9MM **Privately Held**
Web: www.omnisil.com
SIC: **3674** Silicon wafers, chemically doped

**(P-12618)**
**OMNIVISION TECHNOLOGIES INC (PA)**
4275 Burton Dr, Santa Clara (95054-1512)
PHONE.................................408 567-3000
Henry Yang, *Pr*
Shaw Hong, *
Raymond Wu, *
Henry Yang, *COO*
Anson Chan, *
▲ EMP: 1545 EST: 1995
SQ FT: 207,000
SALES (est): 97.97MM **Privately Held**
Web: www.ovt.com
SIC: **3674** Semiconductors and related devices

**(P-12619)**
**ON SEMCNDCTOR CNNCTVITY SLTONS**
1704 Automation Pkwy, San Jose (95131-1873)
PHONE.................................669 209-5500
Keith D Jackson, *Pr*
Lionel Bonnot, *Business Development*
David Carroll, *Senior Vice President Worldwide Sales*
EMP: 325 EST: 2005
SQ FT: 84,000
SALES (est): 27.42MM
SALES (corp-wide): 8.25B **Publicly Held**
SIC: **3674** Semiconductors and related devices
PA: On Semiconductor Corporation
   5701 N Pima Rd
   602 244-6600

**(P-12620)**
**OORJA CORPORATION**
45473 Warm Springs Blvd, Fremont (94539-6104)
PHONE.................................510 659-1899
EMP: 50 EST: 2018
SALES (est): 4.59MM **Privately Held**
SIC: **3674** Semiconductors and related devices

**(P-12621)**
**OPTO DIODE CORPORATION**
1260 Calle Suerte, Camarillo (93012-8053)
PHONE.................................805 499-0335
EMP: 40
Web: www.optodiode.com
SIC: **3674** Diodes, solid state (germanium, silicon, etc.)

**(P-12622)**
**ORBOTECH LT SOLAR LLC**
Also Called: Olt Solar
5970 Optical Ct, San Jose (95138-1400)
PHONE.................................408 414-3777
Georg Bremer, *Managing Member*
EMP: 20 EST: 2009
SALES (est): 3.15MM
SALES (corp-wide): 9.81B **Publicly Held**
Web: www.kla.com
SIC: **3674** Integrated circuits, semiconductor networks, etc.
PA: Kla Corporation
   1 Technology Dr
   408 875-3000

**(P-12623)**
**ORCA SYSTEMS INC**
3990 Old Town Ave Ste C307, San Diego (92110-2930)
PHONE.................................858 679-9175
John G Mcdonough, *CEO*
Sagar Pushpala, *Bd of Dir*
Raghuveer Mendu, *Bd of Dir*
EMP: 18 EST: 2004
SALES (est): 2.64MM **Privately Held**
Web: www.orcasystems.com
SIC: **3674** Semiconductors and related devices

**(P-12624)**
**OSI OPTOELECTRONICS INC**
Also Called: Advanced Photonix
1240 Avenida Acaso, Camarillo (93012-8727)
PHONE.................................805 987-0146
Jean-pierre Maufras, *Genl Mgr*
EMP: 50
SALES (corp-wide): 1.54B **Publicly Held**
Web: www.osioptoelectronics.com
SIC: **3674** Semiconductors and related devices
HQ: Osi Optoelectronics, Inc.
   12525 Chadron Ave
   Hawthorne CA 90250

**(P-12625)**
**OSI OPTOELECTRONICS INC (HQ)**
Also Called: United Detector Technology
12525 Chadron Ave, Hawthorne (90250-4807)
PHONE.................................310 978-0516
▲ EMP: 113 EST: 1967
SALES (est): 103.75MM
SALES (corp-wide): 1.54B **Publicly Held**
Web: www.osioptoelectronics.com
SIC: **3674** 3827 3812 3672 Photoconductive cells; Optical instruments and lenses; Search and navigation equipment; Printed circuit boards
PA: Osi Systems, Inc.
   12525 Chadron Ave
   310 978-0516

**(P-12626)**
**OSI SYSTEMS INC (PA)**
12525 Chadron Ave, Hawthorne (90250-4807)
PHONE.................................310 978-0516
Deepak Chopra, *Ch Bd*
Alan Edrick, *Ex VP*
Ajay Mehra, *OF OSI SOLUTIONS Business*
Victor Sze, *Ex VP*
Glenn Grindstaff, *Chief Human Resources Officer*
EMP: 624 EST: 1987
SQ FT: 88,000
SALES (est): 1.54B
SALES (corp-wide): 1.54B **Publicly Held**
Web: www.osi-systems.com
SIC: **3674** 3845 Integrated circuits, semiconductor networks, etc.; Electromedical equipment

**(P-12627)**
**OUTSOURCE MANUFACTURING INC**
2460 Ash St, Vista (92081-8424)
PHONE.................................760 795-1295
▲ EMP: 60
Web: www.outsourcemanufacturing.com
SIC: **3674** Solid state electronic devices, nec

**(P-12628)**
**PATRIOT MEMORY INC (PA)**
Also Called: Patriot Memory
2925 Bayview Dr, Fremont (94538-6520)
PHONE.................................510 979-1021
Paul Jones, *Managing Member*

## PRODUCTS & SERVICES SECTION
### 3674 - Semiconductors And Related Devices (P-12650)

Doug Diggs, *
▲ **EMP:** 125 **EST:** 1985
**SALES (est):** 9.23MM
**SALES (corp-wide):** 9.23MM **Privately Held**
**Web:** www.patriotmemory.com
**SIC: 3674** 5045 Semiconductors and related devices; Computers, nec

**(P-12629)**
**PEAK TECHNOLOGY INC**
1835 S Centre City Pkwy, Escondido (92025-6581)
**PHONE**..................760 745-8297
Michael Douglas Lawrence, *Pr*
**EMP:** 15 **EST:** 1991
**SALES (est):** 367.57K **Privately Held**
**Web:** www.peaktechnologyinc.com
**SIC: 3674** Semiconductors and related devices

**(P-12630)**
**PENGUIN SOLUTIONS INC (PA)**
Also Called: Penguin Solutions
1390 Mccarthy Blvd, Milpitas (95035-7434)
**PHONE**..................510 623-1231
Mark Adams, *Pr*
Penelope Herscher, *Ch Bd*
Jack Pacheco, *MEMORY SOLUTIONS*
Nate Olmstead, *Sr VP*
Anne Kuykendall, *CLO*
**EMP:** 164 **EST:** 1988
**SQ FT:** 21,000
**SALES (est):** 1.17B
**SALES (corp-wide):** 1.17B **Publicly Held**
**Web:** www.penguinsolutions.com
**SIC: 3674** Semiconductors and related devices

**(P-12631)**
**PERMLIGHT PRODUCTS INC**
Also Called: Perm Light
420 W 6th St, Tustin (92780-4334)
**PHONE**..................714 508-0729
▲ **EMP:** 20
**Web:** www.permlight.com
**SIC: 3674** Light emitting diodes

**(P-12632)**
**PIEZO-METRICS INC (PA)**
Also Called: Micron Instruments
4584 Runway St, Simi Valley (93063-3449)
**PHONE**..................805 522-4676
Herbert Chelner, *Pr*
Sharon Chelner, *
**EMP:** 25 **EST:** 1967
**SQ FT:** 9,000
**SALES (est):** 3.88MM
**SALES (corp-wide):** 3.88MM **Privately Held**
**Web:** www.microninstruments.com
**SIC: 3674** 3829 Strain gages, solid state; Pressure transducers

**(P-12633)**
**PLANSEE USA LLC**
Also Called: E/G Electro-Graph
1491 Poinsettia Ave Ste 138, Vista (92081-8541)
**PHONE**..................760 438-9090
**EMP:** 60
**SALES (corp-wide):** 242.12K **Privately Held**
**Web:** www.plansee.com
**SIC: 3674** Semiconductor diodes and rectifiers
**HQ:** Plansee Usa Llc
115 Constitution Blvd
Franklin MA 02038
508 553-3800

**(P-12634)**
**POLISHING CORPORATION AMERICA**
Also Called: PCA
442 Martin Ave, Santa Clara (95050-2911)
**PHONE**..................888 892-3377
Stuart Becker, *CEO*
▲ **EMP:** 16 **EST:** 1970
**SQ FT:** 10,000
**SALES (est):** 4.6MM **Privately Held**
**Web:** www.pcasilicon.com
**SIC: 3674** Silicon wafers, chemically doped

**(P-12635)**
**POLYFET RF DEVICES INC**
1110 Avenida Acaso, Camarillo (93012-8725)
**PHONE**..................805 484-9582
S K Leong, *Pr*
**EMP:** 25 **EST:** 1984
**SQ FT:** 7,500
**SALES (est):** 5.61MM **Privately Held**
**Web:** www.polyfet.com
**SIC: 3674** Transistors

**(P-12636)**
**POWER INTEGRATIONS INC (PA)**
Also Called: POWER INTEGRATIONS
5245 Hellyer Ave, San Jose (95138-1002)
**PHONE**..................408 414-9200
Balu Balakrishnan, *Ch*
Sandeep Nayyar, *VP Fin*
Mike Matthews, *VP Fin*
Sunil Gupta, *VP Opers*
**EMP:** 395 **EST:** 1997
**SALES (est):** 444.54MM
**SALES (corp-wide):** 444.54MM **Publicly Held**
**Web:** www.power.com
**SIC: 3674** Integrated circuits, semiconductor networks, etc.

**(P-12637)**
**PREMIER SOLAR ENERGY INC**
1359 E Lassen Ave, Chico (95973-7824)
**PHONE**..................530 450-9450
Andres Murillo, *CEO*
Hugo Guardado, *CFO*
Tracie Kandler, *Sec*
**EMP:** 24 **EST:** 2019
**SALES (est):** 3.17MM **Privately Held**
**Web:** www.premiersolarservices.com
**SIC: 3674** Solar cells

**(P-12638)**
**PRIMENANO INC**
4701 Patrick Henry Dr Bldg 8, Santa Clara (95054-1863)
**PHONE**..................650 300-5115
Eduard Weichselbaumer, *CEO*
**EMP:** 15 **EST:** 2010
**SALES (est):** 1.2MM **Privately Held**
**Web:** www.primenanoinc.com
**SIC: 3674** Semiconductors and related devices

**(P-12639)**
**PRINTEC HT ELECTRONICS LLC**
501 Sally Pl, Fullerton (92831-5014)
**PHONE**..................714 484-7597
▲ **EMP:** 50 **EST:** 2011
**SQ FT:** 12,000
**SALES (est):** 7.58MM **Privately Held**
**Web:** www.printec-ht.com
**SIC: 3674** 3629 Modules, solid state; Electronic generation equipment
**PA:** Printec H. T. Electronics Corp.
No. 38, Liyan St.

**(P-12640)**
**PROCESS SPECIALTIES INC**
1660 W Linne Rd Ste A, Tracy (95377-8025)
**PHONE**..................209 832-1344
Edward Morris, *Pr*
Mark Hinkle, *VP*
Manny D Arroz, *Sec*
**EMP:** 22 **EST:** 1988
**SQ FT:** 35,910
**SALES (est):** 4.74MM **Privately Held**
**Web:** www.processspecialties.com
**SIC: 3674** Wafers (semiconductor devices)

**(P-12641)**
**PROMEX INDUSTRIES INCORPORATED (PA)**
Also Called: Promex
3075 Oakmead Village Dr, Santa Clara (95051-0811)
**PHONE**..................408 496-0222
Richard F Otte, *CEO*
Chris Pugh, *VP*
Doctor Edward Binkley, *Prin*
▲ **EMP:** 65 **EST:** 1999
**SQ FT:** 30,000
**SALES (est):** 22.62MM
**SALES (corp-wide):** 22.62MM **Privately Held**
**Web:** www.promex-ind.com
**SIC: 3674** Modules, solid state

**(P-12642)**
**PROTONEX LLC**
Also Called: Pni Sensor
2331 Circadian Way, Santa Rosa (95407-5437)
**PHONE**..................707 566-2260
**EMP:** 18 **EST:** 2017
**SALES (est):** 6.87MM **Privately Held**
**Web:** www.pnicorp.com
**SIC: 3674** Radiation sensors

**(P-12643)**
**PSEMI CORPORATION (DH)**
9369 Carroll Park Dr, San Diego (92121-2257)
**PHONE**..................858 731-9400
Tatsuo Bizen, *CEO*
James S Cable, *
Takaki Muratajay C Biskupski, *
Takaki Murata, *HIGH PERFORMANCE ANALOG HP S UNIT*
▲ **EMP:** 70 **EST:** 1990
**SQ FT:** 96,384
**SALES (est):** 117.71MM **Privately Held**
**Web:** www.psemi.com
**SIC: 3674** Silicon wafers, chemically doped
**HQ:** Murata Electronics North America, Inc.
3330 Cumberland Blvd Se
Atlanta GA 30339
770 436-1300

**(P-12644)**
**PURE WAFER INC**
Also Called: Wrs Materials
2240 Ringwood Ave, San Jose (95131-1716)
**PHONE**..................408 945-8112
Jerry Winters, *CEO*
**EMP:** 235
**SALES (corp-wide):** 50.03MM **Privately Held**
**Web:** www.purewafer.com
**SIC: 3674** 8742 Integrated circuits, semiconductor networks, etc.; Financial consultant
**HQ:** Pure Wafer, Inc.
2575 Melville Rd
Prescott AZ 86301

**(P-12645)**
**PVD MODULAR LLC**
1684 Decoto Rd Ste 215, Union City (94587-3544)
**PHONE**..................510 962-5100
Nick Glinkowski, *Managing Member*
**EMP:** 25 **EST:** 2017
**SALES (est):** 1.27MM **Privately Held**
**Web:** www.pvdmodular.com
**SIC: 3674** Semiconductors and related devices

**(P-12646)**
**QLOGIC LLC (DH)**
15485 Sand Canyon Ave, Irvine (92618-3154)
**PHONE**..................949 389-6000
Arthur Chadwick, *
M Hussain, *
▲ **EMP:** 138 **EST:** 1992
**SQ FT:** 161,000
**SALES (est):** 52.07MM
**SALES (corp-wide):** 5.51B **Publicly Held**
**Web:** www.marvell.com
**SIC: 3674** Integrated circuits, semiconductor networks, etc.
**HQ:** Cavium, Llc
5488 Marvell Ln
Santa Clara CA 95054

**(P-12647)**
**QORVO US INC**
3099 Orchard Dr, San Jose (95134-2005)
**PHONE**..................408 493-4304
Timothy R Richardson, *Mgr*
**EMP:** 90
**SALES (corp-wide):** 3.77B **Publicly Held**
**Web:** www.qorvo.com
**SIC: 3674** Integrated circuits, semiconductor networks, etc.
**HQ:** Qorvo Us, Inc.
2300 Ne Brookwood Pkwy
Hillsboro OR 97124
503 615-9000

**(P-12648)**
**QUADRICIO INC**
330 Primrose Rd Ste 306, Burlingame (94010-4028)
**PHONE**..................408 337-2429
Veerbhan Kheterpal, *CEO*
**EMP:** 25 **EST:** 2016
**SALES (est):** 5.34MM **Privately Held**
**Web:** www.quadric.io
**SIC: 3674** Semiconductors and related devices

**(P-12649)**
**QUALCOMM ATHEROS INC (HQ)**
1700 Technology Dr, San Jose (95110-1383)
**PHONE**..................408 773-5200
Cristiano Amon, *Pr*
▲ **EMP:** 600 **EST:** 1998
**SALES (est):** 129.04MM
**SALES (corp-wide):** 38.96B **Publicly Held**
**SIC: 3674** 4899 Integrated circuits, semiconductor networks, etc.; Communication signal enhancement network services
**PA:** Qualcomm Incorporated
5775 Morehouse Dr
858 587-1121

**(P-12650)**
**QUALCOMM DATACENTER TECH INC (HQ)**
5775 Morehouse Dr, San Diego (92121-1714)
**PHONE**..................858 567-1121

## 3674 - Semiconductors And Related Devices (P-12651)

Dileep Bhandarkar, *Pr*
Anand Chandrasekher, *VP*
**EMP:** 41 **EST:** 2016
**SALES (est):** 6.7MM
**SALES (corp-wide):** 38.96B **Publicly Held**
**SIC: 3674** Integrated circuits, semiconductor networks, etc.
**PA:** Qualcomm Incorporated
5775 Morehouse Dr
858 587-1121

*(P-12651)*
### QUALCOMM INCORPORATED
Also Called: Qualcomm
2016 Palomar Airport Rd Ste 100, Carlsbad (92011-4400)
**PHONE**..................................858 651-8481
David Lieber, *Prin*
**EMP:** 27
**SALES (corp-wide):** 38.96B **Publicly Held**
**Web:** www.qualcomm.com
**SIC: 3674** Integrated circuits, semiconductor networks, etc.
**PA:** Qualcomm Incorporated
5775 Morehouse Dr
858 587-1121

*(P-12652)*
### QUALCOMM INCORPORATED
Also Called: Qualcomm
3135 Kifer Rd, Santa Clara (95051-0804)
**PHONE**..................................408 216-6797
Vincent Jones, *Brnch Mgr*
**EMP:** 21
**SALES (corp-wide):** 38.96B **Publicly Held**
**Web:** www.qualcomm.com
**SIC: 3674** Integrated circuits, semiconductor networks, etc.
**PA:** Qualcomm Incorporated
5775 Morehouse Dr
858 587-1121

*(P-12653)*
### QUALCOMM INCORPORATED
Also Called: Qualcomm
1700 Technology Dr, San Jose (95110-1383)
**PHONE**..................................408 546-2000
**EMP:** 52
**SALES (corp-wide):** 38.96B **Publicly Held**
**Web:** www.qualcomm.com
**SIC: 3674** Integrated circuits, semiconductor networks, etc.
**PA:** Qualcomm Incorporated
5775 Morehouse Dr
858 587-1121

*(P-12654)*
### QUALCOMM INCORPORATED
Also Called: Qualcomm
5828 Pacific Center Blvd Ste 100, San Diego (92121-4253)
**PHONE**..................................619 341-2920
**EMP:** 22
**SALES (corp-wide):** 38.96B **Publicly Held**
**Web:** www.qualcomm.com
**SIC: 3674** Integrated circuits, semiconductor networks, etc.
**PA:** Qualcomm Incorporated
5775 Morehouse Dr
858 587-1121

*(P-12655)*
### QUALCOMM INCORPORATED
Also Called: Qualcomm
5751 Pacific Center Blvd, San Diego (92121-4252)
**PHONE**..................................858 909-0316
Margaret L Johnson, *Brnch Mgr*
**EMP:** 42

**SALES (corp-wide):** 38.96B **Publicly Held**
**Web:** www.qualcomm.com
**SIC: 3674** Integrated circuits, semiconductor networks, etc.
**PA:** Qualcomm Incorporated
5775 Morehouse Dr
858 587-1121

*(P-12656)*
### QUALCOMM INCORPORATED
Also Called: Qualcomm
9393 Waples St Ste 150, San Diego (92121-3931)
**PHONE**..................................858 587-1121
**EMP:** 106
**SALES (corp-wide):** 38.96B **Publicly Held**
**Web:** www.qualcomm.com
**SIC: 3674** 7372 Integrated circuits, semiconductor networks, etc.; Prepackaged software
**PA:** Qualcomm Incorporated
5775 Morehouse Dr
858 587-1121

*(P-12657)*
### QUALCOMM INCORPORATED
Also Called: Qualcomm
10555 Sorrento Valley Rd, San Diego (92121-1608)
**PHONE**..................................858 587-1121
Jim Callaghen, *Brnch Mgr*
**EMP:** 100
**SALES (corp-wide):** 38.96B **Publicly Held**
**Web:** www.qualcomm.com
**SIC: 3674** Integrated circuits, semiconductor networks, etc.
**PA:** Qualcomm Incorporated
5775 Morehouse Dr
858 587-1121

*(P-12658)*
### QUALCOMM INCORPORATED
Also Called: Qualcomm
5525 Morehouse Dr, San Diego (92121-1710)
**PHONE**..................................858 587-1121
Derek May, *Sr VP*
**EMP:** 55
**SALES (corp-wide):** 38.96B **Publicly Held**
**Web:** www.qualcomm.com
**SIC: 3674** Integrated circuits, semiconductor networks, etc.
**PA:** Qualcomm Incorporated
5775 Morehouse Dr
858 587-1121

*(P-12659)*
### QUALCOMM TECHNOLOGIES INC (HQ)
5775 Morehouse Dr, San Diego (92121-1714)
P.O. Box 919042 (92191-9042)
**PHONE**..................................858 587-1121
Cristiano Amon, *CEO*
James Thompson, *
Kevin Frizzell, *
Jim Cathey, *CCO**
▲ **EMP:** 299 **EST:** 2011
**SALES (est):** 1.88B
**SALES (corp-wide):** 38.96B **Publicly Held**
**Web:** www.qualcomm.com
**SIC: 3674** 7372 6794 Integrated circuits, semiconductor networks, etc.; Business oriented computer software; Patent buying, licensing, leasing
**PA:** Qualcomm Incorporated
5775 Morehouse Dr
858 587-1121

*(P-12660)*
### QUALCOMM TECHNOLOGIES INC
5745 Pacific Center Blvd, San Diego (92121-4203)
**PHONE**..................................858 587-1121
**EMP:** 25
**SALES (corp-wide):** 38.96B **Publicly Held**
**Web:** www.qualcomm.com
**SIC: 3674** Integrated circuits, semiconductor networks, etc.
**HQ:** Qualcomm Technologies, Inc.
5775 Morehouse Dr
San Diego CA 92121
858 587-1121

*(P-12661)*
### QUALCOMM TECHNOLOGIES INC
Also Called: BP
10350 Sorrento Valley Rd, San Diego (92121-1642)
**PHONE**..................................858 658-3040
**EMP:** 28
**SALES (corp-wide):** 38.96B **Publicly Held**
**Web:** www.qualcomm.com
**SIC: 3674** Integrated circuits, semiconductor networks, etc.
**HQ:** Qualcomm Technologies, Inc.
5775 Morehouse Dr
San Diego CA 92121
858 587-1121

*(P-12662)*
### QUANTUMSCAPE BATTERY INC
1730 Technology Dr, San Jose (95110-1331)
**PHONE**..................................408 452-2000
**EMP:** 121 **EST:** 2010
**SALES (est):** 26.91MM **Publicly Held**
**Web:** www.quantumscape.com
**SIC: 3674** Semiconductors and related devices
**PA:** Quantumscape Corporation
1730 Technology Dr
408 452-2000

*(P-12663)*
### QUANTUMSCAPE CORPORATION (PA)
1730 Technology Dr, San Jose (95110-1331)
**PHONE**..................................408 452-2000
Siva Sivaram, *CEO*
Jagdeep Singh, *Ch*
Kevin Hettrich, *CFO*
**EMP:** 729 **EST:** 2020
**Web:** www.quantumscape.com
**SIC: 3674** Semiconductors and related devices

*(P-12664)*
### QUARTICS INC
15241 Laguna Canyon Rd Ste 200, Irvine (92618-3146)
P.O. Box 54648 (92619-4648)
**PHONE**..................................949 679-2672
Sherjil Ahmed, *Pr*
Adeel Ahmed, *
▲ **EMP:** 31 **EST:** 2005
**SALES (est):** 1.92MM **Privately Held**
**Web:** www.quartics.com
**SIC: 3674** Semiconductors and related devices

*(P-12665)*
### QUICKLOGIC CORPORATION (PA)
Also Called: QUICKLOGIC
2220 Lundy Ave, San Jose (95131-1816)
**PHONE**..................................408 990-4000
Brian C Faith, *Pr*
Michael R Farese, *Ch Bd*
Elias Nader, *VP Fin*
Rajiv Jain, *Worldwide Operations Vice President*
**EMP:** 44 **EST:** 1988
**SQ FT:** 24,164
**SALES (est):** 21.2MM **Publicly Held**
**Web:** www.quicklogic.com
**SIC: 3674** 3823 Integrated circuits, semiconductor networks, etc.; Programmers, process type

*(P-12666)*
### R2 SEMICONDUCTOR INC
3600 W Bayshore Rd Ste 205, Palo Alto (94303-4237)
**PHONE**..................................408 745-7400
David Fisher, *Pr*
Frank Sasselli, *VP*
Andrew Hartland, *Prin*
Ravi Ramachandran, *Prin*
Larry Burns, *Prin*
**EMP:** 18 **EST:** 2008
**SALES (est):** 2.26MM **Privately Held**
**Web:** www.r2semi.com
**SIC: 3674** Integrated circuits, semiconductor networks, etc.

*(P-12667)*
### RAMBUS INC
Lighting Technology Division
4353 N 1st St # 100, San Jose (95134-1259)
**PHONE**..................................408 462-8000
Jeff Parker, *Sr VP*
**EMP:** 31
**Web:** www.rambus.com
**SIC: 3674** Semiconductors and related devices
**PA:** Rambus Inc.
4453 N 1st St Ste 100

*(P-12668)*
### RAMBUS INC
4453 N 1st St, San Jose (95134-1260)
**PHONE**..................................919 960-6600
Fred Heaton, *Mgr*
**EMP:** 21
**Web:** www.rambus.com
**SIC: 3674** Semiconductors and related devices
**PA:** Rambus Inc.
4453 N 1st St Ste 100

*(P-12669)*
### RAMBUS INC (PA)
Also Called: RAMBUS
4453 N 1st St Ste 100, San Jose (95134)
**PHONE**..................................408 462-8000
Luc Seraphin, *Pr*
Charles Kissner, *Non-Executive Chairman of the Board*
Desmond Lynch, *VP Fin*
Sean Fan, *Sr VP*
John Shinn, *CCO*
◆ **EMP:** 200 **EST:** 1990
**SALES (est):** 461.12MM **Publicly Held**
**Web:** www.rambus.com
**SIC: 3674** 6794 Integrated circuits, semiconductor networks, etc.; Patent owners and lessors

*(P-12670)*
### REACTION TECHNOLOGY INC (HQ)
1590 Buckeye Dr, Milpitas (95035-7418)
**PHONE**..................................408 970-9601

# PRODUCTS & SERVICES SECTION
## 3674 - Semiconductors And Related Devices (P-12689)

Uzi Sasson, *CEO*
James Jacobson, *Pr*
David Sallous, *VP*
Janice Baker, *Off Mgr*
**EMP:** 21 **EST:** 1991
**SALES (est):** 11.89MM
**SALES (corp-wide):** 2.36B **Publicly Held**
**Web:** www.reactiontechnology.com
**SIC: 3674** Integrated circuits, semiconductor networks, etc.
**PA:** Littelfuse, Inc.
8755 W Higgins Rd Ste 500
773 628-1000

### (P-12671)
### RENESAS DESIGN NORTH AMER INC (DH)
6024 Silver Creek Valley Rd, San Jose (95138-1011)
P.O. Box 2369 (07015-2369)
**PHONE**.................................408 845-8500
Jalal Bagherli, *CEO*
Karim Arabi, *VP*
Andrew Austin, *VP*
Christophe Chene, *VP*
Mohamed Djadoudi, *VP*
**EMP:** 35 **EST:** 1998
**SALES (est):** 32.34MM **Privately Held**
**Web:** www.renesas.com
**SIC: 3674** Semiconductors and related devices
**HQ:** Renesas Design Germany Gmbh
Neue Str. 95
Kirchheim Unter Teck BW 73230
70218050

### (P-12672)
### RENESAS DESIGN NORTH AMER INC
1515 Wyatt Dr, Santa Clara (95054-1586)
**PHONE**.................................408 327-8800
**EMP:** 235
**Web:** www.renesas.com
**SIC: 3674** Semiconductors and related devices
**HQ:** Renesas Design North America Inc.
6024 Silver Creek Vly Rd
San Jose CA 95138
408 845-8500

### (P-12673)
### RENESAS ELECTRONICS AMER INC
915 Murphy Ranch Rd, Milpitas (95035-7912)
**PHONE**.................................408 432-8888
**EMP:** 363
**Web:** www.renesas.com
**SIC: 3674** Semiconductors and related devices
**HQ:** Renesas Electronics America Inc.
6024 Silver Creek Vly Rd
San Jose CA 95138
408 284-8200

### (P-12674)
### RENESAS ELECTRONICS AMER INC
Also Called: Intersil Techwell
240a Lawrence Ave, South San Francisco (94080-6817)
**PHONE**.................................408 588-6750
**EMP:** 600
**Web:** www.renesas.com
**SIC: 3674** Semiconductors and related devices
**HQ:** Renesas Electronics America Inc.
6024 Silver Creek Vly Rd
San Jose CA 95138
408 284-8200

### (P-12675)
### RENESAS ELECTRONICS AMER INC
1001 Murphy Ranch Rd, Milpitas (95035-7912)
**PHONE**.................................408 432-8888
**EMP:** 93
**Web:** www.renesas.com
**SIC: 3674** Integrated circuits, semiconductor networks, etc.
**HQ:** Renesas Electronics America Inc.
6024 Silver Creek Vly Rd
San Jose CA 95138
408 284-8200

### (P-12676)
### RESONANT INC
Also Called: Resonant
1875 S Grant St Ste 750, San Mateo (94402-2670)
**PHONE**.................................805 308-9803
George B Holmes, *Ch Bd*
Martin S Mcdermut, *CFO*
Dylan J Kelly, *COO*
**EMP:** 77 **EST:** 2007
**SALES (est):** 2.18MM **Privately Held**
**Web:** www.resonant.com
**SIC: 3674** Semiconductors and related devices
**HQ:** Murata Electronics North America, Inc.
3330 Cumberland Blvd Se
Atlanta GA 30339
770 436-1300

### (P-12677)
### REVASUM INC
825 Buckley Rd, San Luis Obispo (93401-8192)
**PHONE**.................................805 541-6424
Bill Kalenian, *Interim Chief Executive Officer*
Eric Jacobson, *OK Vice President*
Sarah Okada, *
Belinda Reyna, *
Dennis Riccio, *
**EMP:** 106 **EST:** 2016
**SALES (est):** 18.19MM **Privately Held**
**Web:** www.revasum.com
**SIC: 3674** Semiconductors and related devices

### (P-12678)
### RF DIGITAL CORPORATION
1601 Pacific Coast Hwy Ste 290, Hermosa Beach (90254-3283)
**PHONE**.................................949 610-0008
Armen Kazanchian, *Pr*
Rod Landers, *
**EMP:** 103 **EST:** 1999
**SQ FT:** 5,000
**SALES (est):** 2.24MM
**SALES (corp-wide):** 5B **Privately Held**
**SIC: 3674** Modules, solid state
**HQ:** Heptagon Usa, Inc.
465 N Whisman Rd Ste 200
Mountain View CA 94043
650 336-7990

### (P-12679)
### RFAXIS INC
7595 Irvine Center Dr Ste 200, Irvine (92618-2963)
**PHONE**.................................949 825-6300
**EMP:** 15
**SIC: 3674** Semiconductors and related devices

### (P-12680)
### ROCKLEY PHOTONICS INC (HQ)
17252 Armstrong Ave Ste E, Irvine (92614-5737)
**PHONE**.................................626 304-9960
Andrew George Rickman, *CEO*
**EMP:** 192 **EST:** 2013
**SALES (est):** 68.55MM
**SALES (corp-wide):** 30K **Privately Held**
**Web:** www.rockleyphotonics.com
**SIC: 3674** Semiconductors and related devices
**PA:** Rockley Photonics Limited
57 Woodstock Road Clarendon
Business Centre Belsyre Court
186 529-2017

### (P-12681)
### ROCKLEY PHOTONICS INC
333 W San Carlos St Ste 850, San Jose (95110-2711)
**PHONE**.................................408 579-9210
Andrew George Rickman, *Brnch Mgr*
**EMP:** 15
**SALES (corp-wide):** 30K **Privately Held**
**Web:** www.rockleyphotonics.com
**SIC: 3674** Semiconductors and related devices
**HQ:** Rockley Photonics, Inc.
17252 Armstrong Ave
Irvine CA 92614
626 304-9960

### (P-12682)
### S3 GRAPHICS INC
940 Mission Ct, Fremont (94539-8202)
**PHONE**.................................510 687-4900
Wenchih Chen, *Pr*
**EMP:** 22 **EST:** 2000
**SALES (est):** 5.32MM **Privately Held**
**SIC: 3674** Semiconductors and related devices
**PA:** S3 Graphics Co., Ltd
C/O: Card Corporate Services Ltd

### (P-12683)
### SAC-TEC LABS INC (PA)
24311 Wilmington Ave, Carson (90745-6139)
**PHONE**.................................310 375-5295
Robert Kunesh, *Pr*
Bruce Kaufman, *Bd of Dir*
Marylin Hafermalz, *Stockholder*
**EMP:** 20 **EST:** 1991
**SALES (est):** 2.74MM **Privately Held**
**Web:** www.sactec.com
**SIC: 3674** Semiconductors and related devices

### (P-12684)
### SANTIER INC
10103 Carroll Canyon Rd, San Diego (92131-1109)
**PHONE**.................................858 271-1993
Kevin Cotner, *CEO*
Warren Bartholomew, *
▼ **EMP:** 64 **EST:** 1991
**SQ FT:** 23,000
**SALES (est):** 10.72MM
**SALES (corp-wide):** 19.17MM **Privately Held**
**Web:** www.santier.com
**SIC: 3674** Semiconductors and related devices
**HQ:** Egide (Usa), Llc
4 Washington St
Cambridge MD 21613
410 901-6100

### (P-12685)
### SCINTERA NETWORKS INC
160 Rio Robles, San Jose (95134-1813)
**PHONE**.................................408 636-2600
Davin Lee, *CEO*
Scott M Gibson, *
Rajeev Krishnamoorthy, *
Kris Rausch, *
Steffen Hahn, *
**EMP:** 32 **EST:** 2001
**SQ FT:** 20,000
**SALES (est):** 2.93MM **Privately Held**
**SIC: 3674** Semiconductors and related devices

### (P-12686)
### SEMI AUTOMATION & TECH INC
Also Called: Noel Technologies
1510 Dell Ave Ste C, Campbell (95008-6917)
**PHONE**.................................408 374-9549
Kristin Boyce, *Pr*
Brenda Hill, *
▲ **EMP:** 42 **EST:** 1996
**SQ FT:** 7,500
**SALES (est):** 4.71MM **Privately Held**
**Web:** www.noeltech.com
**SIC: 3674** Semiconductors and related devices

### (P-12687)
### SEMICNDCTOR CMPONENTS INDS LLC
Also Called: On Semiconductor
3001 Stender Way, Santa Clara (95054-3216)
**PHONE**.................................408 660-2699
**EMP:** 30
**SALES (corp-wide):** 8.25B **Publicly Held**
**Web:** www.onsemi.com
**SIC: 3674** 3825 3651 Semiconductors and related devices; Diode and transistor testers; Amplifiers: radio, public address, or musical instrument
**HQ:** Semiconductor Components Industries, Llc
5701 N Pima Rd
Scottsdale AZ 85250
602 244-6600

### (P-12688)
### SEMICNDCTOR CMPONENTS INDS LLC
Also Called: On Semiconductor
2975 Stender Way, Santa Clara (95054-3214)
**PHONE**.................................408 542-1000
Gelu Voicu, *Mgr*
**EMP:** 19
**SALES (corp-wide):** 8.25B **Publicly Held**
**Web:** www.onsemi.com
**SIC: 3674** Semiconductors and related devices
**HQ:** Semiconductor Components Industries, Llc
5701 N Pima Rd
Scottsdale AZ 85250
602 244-6600

### (P-12689)
### SEMICOA CORPORATION
333 Mccormick Ave, Costa Mesa (92626-3479)
**PHONE**.................................714 979-1900
Thomas E Epley, *CEO*
Ramesh Ramchandani, *
Gary B Joyce, *Interim Chief Financial Officer*
Perry Denning, *
▲ **EMP:** 60 **EST:** 2009
**SALES (est):** 8.69MM **Privately Held**
**Web:** www.semicoa.com
**SIC: 3674** Semiconductors and related devices

# 3674 - Semiconductors And Related Devices (P-12690)

**(P-12690)**
**SEMICONDUCTOR EQUIPMENT CORP**
Also Called: SEC
5154 Goldman Ave, Moorpark (93021-1760)
PHONE..................805 529-2293
Donald I Moore, *CEO*
Richard Folsom, *Treas*
▲ **EMP:** 16 **EST:** 1974
**SQ FT:** 12,500
**SALES (est):** 3.06MM **Privately Held**
Web: www.semicorp.com
SIC: 3674 Semiconductors and related devices

**(P-12691)**
**SEMICONDUCTOR PROCESS EQP LLC**
Also Called: Spec
27963 Franklin Pkwy, Valencia (91355-4110)
PHONE..................661 257-0934
Arnold Gustin, *CEO*
Robin Douglas, *
Kevin Mcgillivray, *VP*
◆ **EMP:** 29 **EST:** 1986
**SQ FT:** 139,000
**SALES (est):** 9.64MM
**SALES (corp-wide):** 45.63MM **Privately Held**
Web: www.team-spec.com
SIC: 3674 Semiconductors and related devices
PA: Yield Engineering Systems, Inc.
3178 Laurelview Ct
510 954-6889

**(P-12692)**
**SEMIQ INCORPORATED**
20692 Prism Pl, Lake Forest (92630-7803)
PHONE..................949 273-4373
Sung Joon Kim, *Pr*
**EMP:** 16 **EST:** 2010
**SALES (est):** 4.08MM **Privately Held**
Web: www.semiq.com
SIC: 3674 Semiconductors and related devices

**(P-12693)**
**SEMTECH CORPORATION (PA)**
Also Called: Semtech
200 Flynn Rd, Camarillo (93012-8790)
PHONE..................805 498-2111
Hong Q Hou, *Pr*
Rockell N Hankin, *
Mark Lin, *Ex VP*
Asaf Silberstein, *Ex VP*
J Michael Wilson, *Co-Vice President*
▲ **EMP:** 180 **EST:** 1960
**SQ FT:** 88,000
**SALES (est):** 868.76MM
**SALES (corp-wide):** 868.76MM **Publicly Held**
Web: www.semtech.com
SIC: 3674 Semiconductors and related devices

**(P-12694)**
**SENSEMETRICS INC**
750 B St Ste 1630, San Diego (92101-8131)
P.O. Box 16727 (80216-0727)
PHONE..................619 738-8300
Cory Stewart Baldwin, *CEO*
**EMP:** 29 **EST:** 2014
**SALES (est):** 3.2MM
**SALES (corp-wide):** 965.05MM **Publicly Held**
Web: www.infrastructureiot.com

SIC: 3674 Infrared sensors, solid state
PA: Bentley Systems, Incorporated
685 Stockton Dr
610 458-5000

**(P-12695)**
**SI-WARE SYSTEMS INC**
101 Jefferson Dr Fl 1, Menlo Park (94025-1114)
PHONE..................650 257-9680
Youssri Helmy, *CEO*
Nevine Mounib, *
**EMP:** 100 **EST:** 2011
**SALES (est):** 21.98MM **Privately Held**
Web: www.si-ware.com
SIC: 3674 Semiconductors and related devices
PA: Si-Ware Systems
3, Khaled Ibn Al Waleed Street,
Sheraton Building, Heliopolis

**(P-12696)**
**SIFIVE INC (PA)**
2625 Augustine Dr Ste 201, Santa Clara (95054)
PHONE..................415 673-2836
Patrick Little, *Pr*
Naveed Sherwani, *
Shiva Natarajan, *
Keith Witek, *
Stuart Ching, *
**EMP:** 83 **EST:** 2016
**SALES (est):** 90.62MM
**SALES (corp-wide):** 90.62MM **Privately Held**
Web: www.sifive.com
SIC: 3674 Integrated circuits, semiconductor networks, etc.

**(P-12697)**
**SIGMA DESIGNS INC**
Also Called: Sigma
47467 Fremont Blvd, Fremont (94538-6504)
PHONE..................510 897-0200
▲ **EMP:** 718
SIC: 3674 Semiconductors and related devices

**(P-12698)**
**SILC TECHNOLOGIES INC**
181 W Huntington Dr Ste 200, Monrovia (91016-3456)
PHONE..................626 375-1231
Bradley Luff, *Prin*
**EMP:** 96 **EST:** 2018
**SALES (est):** 6.67MM **Privately Held**
Web: www.silc.com
SIC: 3674 Semiconductors and related devices

**(P-12699)**
**SILICON GENESIS CORPORATION**
46816 Lakeview Blvd, Fremont (94538-6543)
PHONE..................408 228-5885
Theodore E Fong, *Brnch Mgr*
**EMP:** 42
Web: www.sigen.net
SIC: 3674 Semiconductors and related devices
PA: Silicon Genesis Corporation
145 Baytech Dr

**(P-12700)**
**SILICON GENESIS CORPORATION (PA)**
Also Called: Sigen

145 Baytech Dr, San Jose (95134-2303)
PHONE..................408 228-5858
Theodore E Fong, *CEO*
Theodore Fong, *CEO*
Francois J Henley, *Pr*
▲ **EMP:** 28 **EST:** 1997
**SALES (est):** 4.62MM **Privately Held**
Web: www.sigen.net
SIC: 3674 8731 Semiconductors and related devices; Commercial physical research

**(P-12701)**
**SILICON IMAGE INC (HQ)**
2115 Onel Dr, San Jose (95131-2032)
PHONE..................408 616-4000
Joe Bedewi, *Corporate Vice President*
Byron Milstead, *Corporate Vice President**
David L Rutledge, *
Khurram Sheikh Csto, *Prin*
Kurt Thielen, *
▲ **EMP:** 28 **EST:** 1995
**SQ FT:** 128,154
**SALES (est):** 9.59MM
**SALES (corp-wide):** 737.15MM **Publicly Held**
SIC: 3674 7371 Semiconductors and related devices; Computer software development and applications
PA: Lattice Semiconductor Corp
5555 Ne Moore Ct
503 268-8000

**(P-12702)**
**SILICON LIGHT MACHINES CORP (DH)**
6660 Via Del Oro, San Jose (95119-1392)
PHONE..................408 240-4700
Lars Eng, *CEO*
Ken Fukui, *Sr VP*
**EMP:** 19 **EST:** 1994
**SALES (est):** 4MM **Privately Held**
Web: www.siliconlight.com
SIC: 3674 Semiconductors and related devices
HQ: Screen North America Holdings, Inc.
150 Innovation Dr Ste A
Elk Grove Village IL 60007
847 870-7400

**(P-12703)**
**SILICON MOTION INC**
690 N Mccarthy Blvd Ste 200, Milpitas (95035-5113)
PHONE..................408 501-5300
Wallace Kou, *Pr*
Richard Chang, *
**EMP:** 60 **EST:** 1995
**SQ FT:** 12,000
**SALES (est):** 6.02MM **Privately Held**
Web: www.siliconmotion.com
SIC: 3674 Integrated circuits, semiconductor networks, etc.
PA: Silicon Motion Technology Corporation
C/O: Conyers Trust Company (Cayman) Limited

**(P-12704)**
**SILICON QUEST INTERNATIONAL INC**
Also Called: S Q I
4425 Fortran Dr, San Jose (95134-2300)
PHONE..................408 496-1000
▲ **EMP:** 70
Web: www.siliconquest.com
SIC: 3674 Semiconductors and related devices

**(P-12705)**
**SILICON TURNKEY SOLUTIONS INC (HQ)**
Also Called: SILICON TURNKEY SOLUTIONS INC. DBA HI RELIABILITY MICROELECTRONICS
1804 Mccarthy Blvd, Milpitas (95035-7410)
PHONE..................408 904-0200
Richard Kingdon, *Pr*
Michael Rooney, *CFO*
**EMP:** 17 **EST:** 2000
**SQ FT:** 35,000
**SALES (est):** 21.76MM
**SALES (corp-wide):** 340.38MM **Privately Held**
Web: www.micross.com
SIC: 3674 5065 Microcircuits, integrated (semiconductor); Semiconductor devices
PA: Micross Inc.
225 Bradhollow Rd Ste 305
407 298-7100

**(P-12706)**
**SILICON VLY MCRELECTRONICS INC**
2985 Kifer Rd, Santa Clara (95051-0802)
PHONE..................408 844-7100
Patrick Callinan, *Pr*
Shirley Sun, *
◆ **EMP:** 30 **EST:** 1993
**SQ FT:** 30,000
**SALES (est):** 9.78MM **Privately Held**
Web: www.svmi.com
SIC: 3674 Silicon wafers, chemically doped

**(P-12707)**
**SILICONCORE TECHNOLOGY INC (PA)**
Also Called: Siliconcore
890 Hillview Ct Ste 120, Milpitas (95035)
PHONE..................408 946-8185
Eric Li, *Pr*
▲ **EMP:** 15 **EST:** 1997
**SQ FT:** 6,000
**SALES (est):** 2.06MM
**SALES (corp-wide):** 2.06MM **Privately Held**
Web: www.silicon-core.com
SIC: 3674 Integrated circuits, semiconductor networks, etc.

**(P-12708)**
**SILICONIX INCORPORATED (HQ)**
2585 Junction Ave, San Jose (95134-1923)
PHONE..................408 988-8000
Serge Jaunay, *CEO*
King Owyang, *
Nick Bacile, *
▲ **EMP:** 610 **EST:** 1962
**SQ FT:** 220,100
**SALES (est):** 24.59MM
**SALES (corp-wide):** 3.4B **Publicly Held**
SIC: 3674 Transistors
PA: Vishay Intertechnology, Inc.
63 Lancaster Ave
610 644-1300

**(P-12709)**
**SILVER PEAK SYSTEMS LLC (HQ)**
2860 De La Cruz Blvd Ste 100, Santa Clara (95050-2635)
PHONE..................408 935-1800
David Hughes, *Managing Member*
**EMP:** 101 **EST:** 2004
**SQ FT:** 29,000
**SALES (est):** 49.4MM
**SALES (corp-wide):** 29.14B **Publicly Held**
Web: www.hpe.com

**PRODUCTS & SERVICES SECTION**        **3674 - Semiconductors And Related Devices (P-12730)**

SIC: **3674** Integrated circuits, semiconductor networks, etc.
PA: Hewlett Packard Enterprise Company
1701 E Mossy Oaks Rd
678 259-9860

**(P-12710)**
**SIMPLE SOLAR INDUSTRIES LLC**
661 Brea Canyon Rd Ste 1, Walnut (91789-3044)
PHONE.................................844 907-0705
Moe Falah, *Managing Member*
EMP: 50 EST: 2022
SALES (est): 1.27MM **Privately Held**
SIC: **3674** Semiconductors and related devices

**(P-12711)**
**SIRF TECHNOLOGY HOLDINGS INC**
1060 Rincon Cir, San Jose (95131-1325)
PHONE.................................408 523-6500
Diosdado B Banatao, *Ch Bd*
Diosdado P Banatao, *
Geoffrey Ribar, *Sr VP*
Kanwar Chadha, *VP Mktg*
Atul P Shingal, *Prin*
EMP: 753 EST: 2001
SQ FT: 48,000
SALES (est): 13.49MM
SALES (corp-wide): 38.96B **Publicly Held**
SIC: **3674** 3663 Semiconductors and related devices; Global positioning systems (GPS) equipment
HQ: Csr Limited
Churchill House
Cambridge CAMBS CB4 0
122 369-2000

**(P-12712)**
**SITEK PROCESS SOLUTIONS**
233 Technology Way Ste 3, Rocklin (95765-1208)
PHONE.................................916 797-9000
James Mullany, *CEO*
James Mullany, *Pr*
Terri Mullany, *VP*
▲ EMP: 21 EST: 1998
SQ FT: 8,000
SALES (est): 4.84MM **Privately Held**
Web: www.sitekprocess.com
SIC: **3674** Semiconductors and related devices

**(P-12713)**
**SITIME CORPORATION (PA)**
Also Called: SITIME
5451 Patrick Henry Dr, Santa Clara (95054-1167)
PHONE.................................408 328-4400
Rajesh Vashist, *Ch Bd*
Samsheer Ahmad, *CAO*
Elizabeth A Howe, *Ex VP*
Vincent P Pangrazio, *Corporate Secretary*
Fariborz Assaderaghi, *TECH AND ENGINEERING*
EMP: 295 EST: 2003
SQ FT: 50,400
SALES (est): 143.99MM
SALES (corp-wide): 143.99MM **Publicly Held**
Web: www.sitime.com
SIC: **3674** Semiconductors and related devices

**(P-12714)**
**SK HYNIX MMORY SLTONS AMER INC**
3103 N 1st St, San Jose (95134-1934)
PHONE.................................408 514-3500
Tony Yoon, *CEO*
Sang Soo Son, *CFO*
EMP: 270 EST: 2004
SALES (est): 22.73MM **Privately Held**
Web: www.skhms.com
SIC: **3674** Semiconductors and related devices
PA: Sk Hynix Inc.
2091 Gyeongchung-Daero, Bubal-Eup

**(P-12715)**
**SK HYNIX NAND PDT SLTIONS CORP (HQ)**
Also Called: Solidigm
10951 White Rock Rd, Rancho Cordova (95670)
PHONE.................................858 863-3069
Jongwon Noh, *Pr*
EMP: 115 EST: 2021
SALES (est): 44.9MM **Privately Held**
Web: www.solidigmtechnology.com
SIC: **3674** Semiconductor circuit networks
PA: Sk Hynix Inc.
2091 Gyeongchung-Daero, Bubal-Eup

**(P-12716)**
**SKYWORKS SOLUTIONS INC**
1778 Zinetta Rd Ste A, Calexico (92231-9511)
PHONE.................................949 231-3550
EMP: 15
SALES (corp-wide): 4.77B **Publicly Held**
Web: www.skyworksinc.com
SIC: **3674** Semiconductors and related devices
PA: Skyworks Solutions, Inc.
5260 California Ave
949 231-3000

**(P-12717)**
**SKYWORKS SOLUTIONS INC**
2427 W Hillcrest Dr, Newbury Park (91320-2202)
PHONE.................................805 480-4400
Michael Gooch, *Mgr*
EMP: 43
SALES (corp-wide): 4.77B **Publicly Held**
Web: www.skyworksinc.com
SIC: **3674** Semiconductors and related devices
PA: Skyworks Solutions, Inc.
5260 California Ave
949 231-3000

**(P-12718)**
**SKYWORKS SOLUTIONS INC**
730 Lawrence Dr, Newbury Park (91320-2207)
PHONE.................................805 480-4227
EMP: 42
SALES (corp-wide): 4.77B **Publicly Held**
Web: www.skyworksinc.com
SIC: **3674** Semiconductors and related devices
PA: Skyworks Solutions, Inc.
5260 California Ave
949 231-3000

**(P-12719)**
**SKYWORKS SOLUTIONS INC (PA)**
Also Called: Skyworks
5260 California Ave, Irvine (92617-3228)
PHONE.................................949 231-3000
Liam K Griffin, *Pr*
Robert J Terry, *Sr VP*
Kris Sennesael, *Chief Financial Officer USA*
Reza Kasnavi, *Sr VP*
Carlos S Bori, *Sr VP*
▲ EMP: 535 EST: 1962
SQ FT: 218,000
SALES (est): 4.77B
SALES (corp-wide): 4.77B **Publicly Held**
Web: www.skyworksinc.com
SIC: **3674** Integrated circuits, semiconductor networks, etc.

**(P-12720)**
**SMALL PRECISION TOOLS INC**
Also Called: Wire Bonding Tools
1330 Clegg St, Petaluma (94954-1127)
PHONE.................................707 762-5880
Peter Glutz, *Pr*
Joe Gracia, *
▲ EMP: 94 EST: 1969
SQ FT: 25,000
SALES (est): 16.59MM **Privately Held**
Web: www.smallprecisiontools.com
SIC: **3674** Semiconductors and related devices
PA: Spt Roth Ag
Werkstrasse 28

**(P-12721)**
**SMART MODULAR TECH DE INC (HQ)**
45800 Northport Loop W, Fremont (94538-6413)
PHONE.................................510 623-1231
Jack Pacheco, *CEO*
EMP: 110 EST: 2004
SALES (est): 67.37MM
SALES (corp-wide): 1.17B **Publicly Held**
Web: www.smartm.com
SIC: **3674** Semiconductors and related devices
PA: Penguin Solutions, Inc.
1390 Mccarthy Blvd
510 623-1231

**(P-12722)**
**SMART MODULAR TECHNOLOGIES (WWH) INC**
39870 Eureka Dr, Newark (94560-4809)
PHONE.................................510 623-1231
▲ EMP: 1100
SIC: **3674** 3577 3679 Integrated circuits, semiconductor networks, etc.; Computer peripheral equipment, nec; Liquid crystal displays (LCD)

**(P-12723)**
**SMART MODULAR TECHNOLOGIES INC (HQ)**
39870 Eureka Dr, Newark (94560-4809)
PHONE.................................510 623-1231
Jack Pacheco, *CEO*
Mike Rubino, *
Kiwan Kim, *
▲ EMP: 232 EST: 1988
SALES (est): 374.79MM
SALES (corp-wide): 1.17B **Publicly Held**
Web: www.smartm.com
SIC: **3674** Semiconductors and related devices
PA: Penguin Solutions, Inc.
1390 Mccarthy Blvd
510 623-1231

**(P-12724)**
**SOLID STATE DEVICES INC**
Also Called: Ssdi
14701 Firestone Blvd, La Mirada (90638-5918)
PHONE.................................562 404-4474
Arnold N Applebaum, *Pr*
David Franz, *
▲ EMP: 110 EST: 1967
SQ FT: 32,000
SALES (est): 20.29MM **Privately Held**
Web: www.ssdi-power.com
SIC: **3674** Diodes, solid state (germanium, silicon, etc.)

**(P-12725)**
**SORAA INC (PA)**
6500 Kaiser Dr Ste 110, Fremont (94555-3662)
PHONE.................................510 456-2200
Jeffery Parker, *Ch Bd*
▲ EMP: 90 EST: 2007
SQ FT: 50,000
SALES (est): 17.85MM **Privately Held**
Web: www.soraa.com
SIC: **3674** 3641 Semiconductors and related devices; Electric lamps

**(P-12726)**
**SOURCE PHOTONICS USA INC (PA)**
8521 Fallbrook Ave Ste 200, West Hills (91304-3239)
PHONE.................................818 773-9044
Doug Wright, *CEO*
EMP: 249 EST: 1999
SALES (est): 3.67MM **Privately Held**
Web: www.sourcephotonics.com
SIC: **3674** Semiconductors and related devices

**(P-12727)**
**SOURCE PHOTONICS USA INC**
8917 Fullbright Ave, Chatsworth (91311-6124)
PHONE.................................818 407-5007
EMP: 19
Web: www.sourcephotonics.com
SIC: **3674** Semiconductors and related devices
PA: Source Photonics Usa, Inc.
8521 Fllbrook Ave Ste 200

**(P-12728)**
**SPANSION LLC (DH)**
198 Champion Ct, San Jose (95134)
P.O. Box 3453 (94088)
PHONE.................................512 691-8500
Thad Trent, *Pr*
Tom Moon, *
▲ EMP: 160 EST: 2003
SALES (est): 107.13MM
SALES (corp-wide): 17.72B **Privately Held**
Web: www.infineon.com
SIC: **3674** Semiconductors and related devices
HQ: Cypress Semiconductor Corporation
198 Champion Ct
San Jose CA 95134
408 943-2600

**(P-12729)**
**SPI ENERGY CO LTD**
4803 Urbani Ave, Mcclellan (95652-2000)
PHONE.................................408 919-8000
Xiaofeng Peng, *Brnch Mgr*
EMP: 316
SIC: **3674** Semiconductors and related devices
PA: Spi Energy Co, Ltd
C/O Harneys Fiduciary (Cayman) Limited

**(P-12730)**
**SPT MICROTECHNOLOGIES**
1755 Junction Ave, San Jose (95112-1029)
PHONE.................................408 571-1400
EMP: 22 EST: 2016

# 3674 - Semiconductors And Related Devices (P-12731)

SALES (est): 2.65MM **Privately Held**
Web: www.sptmicro.com
SIC: **3674** Semiconductors and related devices

**(P-12731)**
## SST RG LLC
1171 Sonora Ct, Sunnyvale (94086-5384)
PHONE..................408 735-9110
**EMP:** 500 **EST:** 1998
**SQ FT:** 19,440
**SALES (est):** 102.23MM
**SALES (corp-wide):** 6.82B **Publicly Held**
SIC: **3674** Memories, solid state
HQ: Silicon Storage Technology, Inc.
1020 Kifer Rd
Sunnyvale CA 94086

**(P-12732)**
## SST TECHNOLOGIES
Also Called: Sst Vacuum Reflow Systems
6305 El Camino Real, Carlsbad (92009-1606)
PHONE..................562 803-3361
Anthony Wilson, *Pr*
Ralph Burroughs, *
◆ **EMP:** 30 **EST:** 1969
**SALES (est):** 4.63MM **Privately Held**
Web: www.palomartechnologies.com
SIC: **3674** Semiconductors and related devices
PA: Palomar Technologies, Inc.
6305 El Camino Real

**(P-12733)**
## STARTECH SEMICONDUCTOR INC
48720 Kato Rd, Fremont (94538-7312)
PHONE..................510 668-7000
**EMP:** 63 **EST:** 2002
**SALES (est):** 2.32MM
**SALES (corp-wide):** 693.26MM **Publicly Held**
SIC: **3674** Semiconductors and related devices
HQ: Exar Corporation
1060 Rincon Cir
San Jose CA 95131
669 265-6100

**(P-12734)**
## STATS CHIPPAC INC (DH)
880 N Mccarthy Blvd Ste 250, Milpitas (95035-5121)
PHONE..................510 979-8000
Tan Lay Koon, *Pr*
Tan Lay Koon, *CEO*
Janet Taylor, *
John Lau Tai Chong, *
Wan Choong Hoe, *
▲ **EMP:** 50 **EST:** 2000
**SALES (est):** 6.71MM
**SALES (corp-wide):** 2.1MM **Privately Held**
Web: www.jcetglobal.com
SIC: **3674** Integrated circuits, semiconductor networks, etc.
HQ: Stats Chippac Pte. Ltd.
5 Yishun Street 23
Singapore 76844

**(P-12735)**
## STATS CHIPPAC TEST SVCS INC (DH)
Also Called: Fastramp
46429 Landing Pkwy, Fremont (94538-6496)
PHONE..................510 979-8000
Tan Lay Koon, *Pr*
David Goldberg, *Corporate Secretary*
**EMP:** 15 **EST:** 2001

SALES (est): 4.94MM
**SALES (corp-wide):** 2.1MM **Privately Held**
SIC: **3674** Semiconductors and related devices
HQ: Stats Chippac Pte. Ltd.
5 Yishun Street 23
Singapore 76844

**(P-12736)**
## STELLAR MICROELECTRONICS INC
9340 Owensmouth Ave, Chatsworth (91311-6915)
PHONE..................661 775-3500
Sudesh Arora, *Pr*
**EMP:** 239 **EST:** 1974
**SQ FT:** 140,000
**SALES (est):** 17.96MM
**SALES (corp-wide):** 1.43B **Privately Held**
Web: www.neotech.com
SIC: **3674** Semiconductors and related devices
PA: Natel Engineering Company, Llc
9340 Owensmouth Ave
818 495-8617

**(P-12737)**
## STMICROELECTRONICS INC
2755 Great America Way, Santa Clara (95054-1166)
PHONE..................408 919-8400
Ted Daniels, *Mgr*
**EMP:** 15
**SALES (corp-wide):** 17.29B **Privately Held**
SIC: **3674** Semiconductors and related devices
HQ: Stmicroelectronics, Inc.
750 Canyon Dr Ste 300
Coppell TX 75019
972 466-6000

**(P-12738)**
## STRATEDGE CORPORATION
Also Called: Strat Edge
9424 Abraham Way, Santee (92071-5640)
PHONE..................866 424-4962
Tim Going, *Pr*
Josie Santos, *
**EMP:** 40 **EST:** 1985
**SALES (est):** 4.65MM **Privately Held**
Web: www.stratedge.com
SIC: **3674** Semiconductors and related devices

**(P-12739)**
## SUBSTANCE ABUSE PROGRAM
1370 S State St Ste A, Hemet (92543)
PHONE..................951 791-3350
Mark Thuve, *Mgr*
**EMP:** 30 **EST:** 2010
**SALES (est):** 1.33MM **Privately Held**
SIC: **3674** Semiconductors and related devices

**(P-12740)**
## SUMCO USA SALES CORPORATION
Also Called: Cincinnati Div
2099 Gateway Pl Ste 400, San Jose (95110-1017)
PHONE..................408 352-3880
▲ **EMP:** 1300
SIC: **3674** Silicon wafers, chemically doped

**(P-12741)**
## SUMMIT MICROELECTRONICS INC
757 N Mary Ave, Sunnyvale (94085-2909)
PHONE..................408 523-1000

**EMP:** 45
Web: www.qualcomm.com
SIC: **3674** Integrated circuits, semiconductor networks, etc.

**(P-12742)**
## SUNCORE INC
15 Hubble Ste 200, Irvine (92618-4268)
PHONE..................949 450-0054
Steven Brimmer, *Pr*
Donald A Nevins, *
Richard Sanett, *
Arthur Kozak, *
▲ **EMP:** 31 **EST:** 2004
**SQ FT:** 5,000
**SALES (est):** 1.05MM **Privately Held**
Web: www.suncoresolar.com
SIC: **3674** 5063 5065 Solar cells; Batteries; Electronic parts and equipment, nec

**(P-12743)**
## SUNLINK CORPORATION
2131 Williams St, San Leandro (94577-3224)
PHONE..................415 925-9650
**EMP:** 15
Web: www.nov.com
SIC: **3674** Stud bases or mounts for semiconductor devices

**(P-12744)**
## SUNPOWER CORPORATION (HQ)
Also Called: Sunpower
880 Harbour Way S Ste 600, Richmond (94804-3650)
PHONE..................408 240-5500
Elizabeth Eby, *CAO*
Tony Garzolini, *CRO*
Eileen Evans, *CLO*
▲ **EMP:** 234 **EST:** 1985
**SQ FT:** 163,000
**SALES (est):** 1.13B
**SALES (corp-wide):** 1.13B **Privately Held**
Web: us.sunpower.com
SIC: **3674** 3679 Solar cells; Power supplies, all types: static
PA: Sol Holding, Llc
1201 La St Ste 1800

**(P-12745)**
## SUNPREME INC
4701 Patrick Henry Dr Bldg 25, Santa Clara (95054-1863)
PHONE..................408 419-9281
Ashok K Sinha, *CEO*
Surinder S Bedi, *
Hema Sundarraj, *
Ratson Morad, *
Homi Fateni Senior, *Development*
▲ **EMP:** 30 **EST:** 2009
**SALES (est):** 2.18MM **Privately Held**
Web: www.sunpreme.com
SIC: **3674** Solar cells

**(P-12746)**
## SUNSYSTEM TECHNOLOGY LLC
Also Called: Next Phase Solar
2802 10th St, Berkeley (94710-2711)
PHONE..................510 984-2027
Adam Burstein, *Brnch Mgr*
**EMP:** 160
**SALES (corp-wide):** 49.25MM **Privately Held**
Web: www.sstsolar.com
SIC: **3674** Photovoltaic devices, solid state
PA: Sunsystem Technology, Llc
2731 Citrus Rd Ste D
916 671-3351

**(P-12747)**
## SUPERTEX INC (HQ)
1235 Bordeaux Dr, Sunnyvale (94089-1203)
PHONE..................408 222-8888
Henry C Pao Ph.d., *Finance Officer*
▲ **EMP:** 77 **EST:** 1975
**SQ FT:** 42,000
**SALES (est):** 9.6MM
**SALES (corp-wide):** 7.63B **Publicly Held**
SIC: **3674** Integrated circuits, semiconductor networks, etc.
PA: Microchip Technology Inc
2355 W Chandler Blvd
480 792-7200

**(P-12748)**
## SURFACE ART ENGINEERING INC
Also Called: Surface Art Ems
81 Bonaventura Dr, San Jose (95134-2105)
PHONE..................408 433-4700
Jennifer Lee, *CEO*
Richard Kundert, *
▲ **EMP:** 50 **EST:** 1993
**SQ FT:** 24,000
**SALES (est):** 9.8MM **Privately Held**
Web: www.surfaceart.com
SIC: **3674** Computer logic modules

**(P-12749)**
## SWAVE PHOTONICS INC
1610 Canary Dr, Sunnyvale (94087-4632)
PHONE..................408 963-9958
Michael Noonen, *CEO*
Dmitri Choutov, *COO*
Theo Marescaux, *CPO*
**EMP:** 25 **EST:** 2022
**SALES (est):** 1.02MM **Privately Held**
SIC: **3674** Semiconductors and related devices

**(P-12750)**
## SWIFT SOLAR INC
981 Bing St, San Carlos (94070-5321)
PHONE..................650 297-7943
Joel Jean, *CEO*
**EMP:** 20 **EST:** 2017
**SALES (est):** 1.38MM **Privately Held**
Web: www.swiftsolar.com
SIC: **3674** Solar cells

**(P-12751)**
## SYMANTEC SEC HOLDINGS I INC
350 Ellis St, Mountain View (94043-2202)
PHONE..................650 527-8000
**EMP:** 28 **EST:** 2019
**SALES (est):** 7.27MM
**SALES (corp-wide):** 3.81B **Publicly Held**
SIC: **3674** Semiconductors and related devices
PA: Gen Digital Inc.
60 E Rio Slado Pkwy Ste 1
650 527-8000

**(P-12752)**
## SYNAPSE SEMICONDUCTOR CORP
Also Called: Solid State Optronics
15 Great Oaks Blvd, San Jose (95119-1242)
PHONE..................408 293-4600
Juan Kadah, *Ex Dir*
**EMP:** 55 **EST:** 2004
**SALES (est):** 1.23MM **Privately Held**
Web: synapsesemiconductor.mfgpages.com

# PRODUCTS & SERVICES SECTION
## 3674 - Semiconductors And Related Devices (P-12771)

SIC: **3674** 3625  Semiconductors and related devices; Relays, for electronic use

### (P-12753)
### SYNTIANT CORP (PA)
7555 Irvine Center Dr Ste 200, Irvine (92618-2912)
PHONE.....................949 774-4887
Kurt Busch, *CEO*
Paul Henderson, *
Pieter Vorenkamp, *
**EMP:** 50 **EST:** 2017
**SALES (est):** 10.22MM
**SALES (corp-wide):** 10.22MM **Privately Held**
Web: www.syntiant.com
SIC: **3674**  Semiconductors and related devices

### (P-12754)
### TALMO & CHINN INC
9537 Telstar Ave Ste 131, El Monte (91731-2912)
PHONE.....................626 443-1741
Bruce Talmo, *Pr*
Martin Chinn, *
**EMP:** 35 **EST:** 1972
**SQ FT:** 9,000
**SALES (est):** 3.06MM **Privately Held**
SIC: **3674**  Semiconductors and related devices

### (P-12755)
### TECHNOPROBE AMERICA INC
2526 Qume Dr Ste 27, San Jose (95131-1870)
PHONE.....................408 573-9911
Stefano Felici, *Pr*
**EMP:** 25 **EST:** 2007
**SQ FT:** 800
**SALES (est):** 4.12MM **Privately Held**
Web: www.technoprobe.com
SIC: **3674**  Semiconductors and related devices

### (P-12756)
### TELEDYNE DEFENSE ELEC LLC
Also Called: Teledyne E2v Hirel Electronics
765 Sycamore Dr, Milpitas (95035-7465)
PHONE.....................408 737-0992
**EMP:** 105
**SALES (corp-wide):** 5.64B **Publicly Held**
Web: www.teledynelecroy.com
SIC: **3674**  Semiconductors and related devices
HQ: Teledyne Defense Electronics, Llc
    1274 Terra Bella Ave
    Mountain View CA 94043
    650 691-9800

### (P-12757)
### TELEDYNE E2V INC
Also Called: Teledyne Hirel Electronics
765 Sycamore Dr, Milpitas (95035-7465)
PHONE.....................408 737-0992
**EMP:** 105
Web: www.teledyne-e2v.com
SIC: **3674**  Semiconductors and related devices

### (P-12758)
### TELEDYNE INSTRUMENTS INC
Also Called: Teledyne
9855 Carroll Canyon Rd, San Diego (92131-1103)
PHONE.....................858 842-3127
Mark Page, *Mgr*
**EMP:** 20
**SALES (corp-wide):** 5.64B **Publicly Held**
Web: www.teledyne.com

SIC: **3674** 3678 3613 3423  Semiconductors and related devices; Electronic connectors; Switchgear and switchboard apparatus; Hand and edge tools, nec
HQ: Teledyne Instruments, Inc.
    16830 Chestnut St
    City Of Industry CA 91748
    626 934-1500

### (P-12759)
### TENSORCOM INC
3530 John Hopkins Ct, San Diego (92121-1121)
PHONE.....................760 496-3264
Patrick Soon-shiong, *CEO*
◆ **EMP:** 22 **EST:** 2007
**SQ FT:** 5,000
**SALES (est):** 4.46MM **Privately Held**
Web: www.tensorcom.com
SIC: **3674**  Microcircuits, integrated (semiconductor)

### (P-12760)
### TERIDIAN SEMICONDUCTOR CORP (DH)
6440 Oak Cyn Ste 100, Irvine (92618-5208)
PHONE.....................714 508-8800
Mark Casper, *CEO*
Pete Todd, *Worldwide Sales Vice President*
John Silk, *
David Gruetter, *
**EMP:** 90 **EST:** 1996
**SALES (est):** 2.08MM
**SALES (corp-wide):** 12.31B **Publicly Held**
Web: www.teridian.com
SIC: **3674**  Semiconductors and related devices
HQ: Teridian Semiconductor Holdings Corp.
    6440 Oak Cyn Ste 100
    Irvine CA 92618

### (P-12761)
### TERIDIAN SMICDTR HOLDINGS CORP (DH)
6440 Oak Cyn Ste 100, Irvine (92618-5208)
PHONE.....................714 508-8800
Gerald Fitch, *Pr*
John Silk, *VP Opers*
**EMP:** 15 **EST:** 2005
**SALES (est):** 2.2MM
**SALES (corp-wide):** 12.31B **Publicly Held**
SIC: **3674**  Semiconductors and related devices
HQ: Maxim Integrated Products, Llc
    160 Rio Robles
    San Jose CA 95134
    408 601-1000

### (P-12762)
### TESSERA INC (DH)
Also Called: Tessera
3025 Orchard Pkwy, San Jose (95134-2017)
PHONE.....................408 321-6000
Richard Chernicoff, *Pr*
Simon Mcelrea, *Pr*
Christopher Pickett, *Prin*
Bernard Cassidy, *Prin*
Robert A Young, *Prin*
**EMP:** 37 **EST:** 1992
**SQ FT:** 51,000
**SALES (est):** 26.23MM
**SALES (corp-wide):** 388.79MM **Publicly Held**
Web: www.adeia.com
SIC: **3674** 8999  Integrated circuits, semiconductor networks, etc.; Inventor
HQ: Tessera Technologies, Inc.
    3025 Orchard Pkwy
    San Jose CA 95134
    408 321-6000

### (P-12763)
### TESSERA GLOBAL SERVICES INC
140 Scott Dr, Menlo Park (94025-1008)
PHONE.....................408 321-6000
**EMP:** 16 **EST:** 2012
**SALES (est):** 2.02MM
**SALES (corp-wide):** 388.79MM **Publicly Held**
SIC: **3674**  Semiconductors and related devices
HQ: Tessera Technologies, Inc.
    3025 Orchard Pkwy
    San Jose CA 95134
    408 321-6000

### (P-12764)
### TESSERA INTELLECTUAL PRPTS INC
3025 Orchard Pkwy, San Jose (95134-2017)
PHONE.....................408 321-6000
Tom Lacey, *Prin*
**EMP:** 43 **EST:** 2012
**SALES (est):** 1.88MM
**SALES (corp-wide):** 388.79MM **Publicly Held**
SIC: **3674**  Integrated circuits, semiconductor networks, etc.
HQ: Tessera, Inc.
    3025 Orchard Pkwy
    San Jose CA 95134

### (P-12765)
### TESSERA INTLLCTUAL PRPRTY CORP
3025 Orchard Pkwy, San Jose (95134-2017)
PHONE.....................408 321-6000
Tom Lacey, *CEO*
Murali Dharan, *
Robert Andersen, *
Robert A Young Ph.d., *Pr*
**EMP:** 16 **EST:** 2011
**SALES (est):** 1.65MM
**SALES (corp-wide):** 388.79MM **Publicly Held**
Web: www.adeia.com
SIC: **3674**  Microcircuits, integrated (semiconductor)
HQ: Tessera Technologies, Inc.
    3025 Orchard Pkwy
    San Jose CA 95134
    408 321-6000

### (P-12766)
### TESSERA TECHNOLOGIES INC (DH)
3025 Orchard Pkwy, San Jose (95134-2017)
PHONE.....................408 321-6000
Tom Lacey, *CEO*
Jon E Kirchner, *Pr*
Robert Andersen, *CFO*
Kris M Graves, *Chief Human Resources Officer*
▲ **EMP:** 104 **EST:** 1990
**SALES (est):** 29.21MM
**SALES (corp-wide):** 388.79MM **Publicly Held**
Web: www.adeia.com
SIC: **3674** 6794  Integrated circuits, semiconductor networks, etc.; Patent buying, licensing, leasing
HQ: Adeia Holdings Inc.
    3025 Orchard Pkwy
    San Jose CA 95134
    408 473-2500

### (P-12767)
### TEXAS INSTRUMENTS INCORPORATED
Also Called: Texas Instruments
2900 Semiconductor Dr, Santa Clara (95051-0606)
PHONE.....................669 721-5000
**EMP:** 50
**SALES (corp-wide):** 17.52B **Publicly Held**
Web: www.ti.com
SIC: **3674** 3613 3822 3578  Microprocessors; Power circuit breakers; Thermostats and other environmental sensors; Calculators and adding machines
PA: Texas Instruments Incorporated
    12500 Ti Blvd
    214 479-3773

### (P-12768)
### THERMAL CONDUCTIVE BONDING INC (PA)
Also Called: T C B
6210 88th St, Sacramento (95828-1140)
PHONE.....................408 920-0255
Wayne Simpson, *Pr*
Ryan Scatena, *
**EMP:** 22 **EST:** 2012
**SALES (est):** 9.29MM
**SALES (corp-wide):** 9.29MM **Privately Held**
Web: www.tcbonding.com
SIC: **3674**  Semiconductors and related devices

### (P-12769)
### TOWER SEMICDTR NEWPORT BCH INC (DH)
Also Called: Towerjazz
4321 Jamboree Rd, Newport Beach (92660-3007)
PHONE.....................949 435-8000
Russell Ellwanger, *CEO*
Itzhak Edrei, *
Rafi Mor, *
Oren Shirazi, *
▲ **EMP:** 700 **EST:** 2002
**SQ FT:** 300,000
**SALES (est):** 77.27MM **Privately Held**
Web: www.towersemi.com
SIC: **3674**  Wafers (semiconductor devices)
HQ: Tower Us Holdings Inc.
    4321 Jamboree Rd
    Newport Beach CA 92660

### (P-12770)
### TOWER SEMICONDUCTOR USA INC
2570 N 1st St Ste 480, San Jose (95131-1018)
PHONE.....................408 770-1320
Doron Simon, *Pr*
Oren Shirazi, *Dir*
Russell Ellwanger, *Dir*
**EMP:** 15 **EST:** 1996
**SQ FT:** 4,100
**SALES (est):** 5.02MM **Privately Held**
Web: www.towersemi.com
SIC: **3674**  Semiconductors and related devices
PA: Tower Semiconductor Ltd
    20 Shaul Amor Blvd

### (P-12771)
### TRANSPHORM INC (DH)
75 Castilian Dr Ste 200, Goleta (93117-5580)
PHONE.....................805 456-1300
Primit Parikh, *Pr*
**EMP:** 102 **EST:** 2017

# 3674 - Semiconductors And Related Devices (P-12772)

SQ FT: 27,800
SALES (est): 16.51MM **Privately Held**
Web: www.transphormusa.com
SIC: **3674** Microcircuits, integrated (semiconductor)
HQ: Renesas Electronics America Inc.
6024 Silver Creek Vly Rd
San Jose CA 95138
408 284-8200

**(P-12772)**
**TRIDENT MICROSYSTEMS INC**
1170 Kifer Rd, Sunnyvale (94086-5303)
PHONE..................................408 962-5000
▲ EMP: 1522
SIC: **3674** Semiconductors and related devices

**(P-12773)**
**TRIDENT SPACE & DEFENSE LLC**
Also Called: TCS Space & Component Tech
19951 Mariner Ave, Torrance (90503-1738)
PHONE..................................310 214-5500
EMP: 47
Web: www.tridentsd.com
SIC: **3674** 3812 8711 Semiconductors and related devices; Search and navigation equipment; Electrical or electronic engineering

**(P-12774)**
**TRIQUINT SEMICONDUCTOR INC**
3099 Orchard Dr, San Jose (95134-2005)
PHONE..................................408 577-6344
EMP: 18 EST: 2016
SALES (est): 4.26MM **Privately Held**
Web: www.qorvo.com
SIC: **3674** Semiconductors and related devices

**(P-12775)**
**TSMC TECHNOLOGY INC**
2851 Junction Ave, San Jose (95134-1910)
PHONE..................................408 382-8052
Lora Ho, *Pr*
Wendell Huang, *
Richard L Thurston, *
EMP: 16 EST: 1996
SALES (est): 9.67MM **Privately Held**
SIC: **3674** Semiconductor circuit networks
HQ: Tsmc Partners Ltd.
  C/O: Portcullis Trusnet (Bvi) Limited
  Road Town

**(P-12776)**
**ULTRA CLEAN TECH SYSTEMS SVC I (HQ)**
Also Called: Uct
26462 Corporate Ave, Hayward (94545-3914)
PHONE..................................510 576-4400
James P Scholhamer, *CEO*
Leonard Mezhvinsky, *
Bruce Wier, *
Lavi Lev, *
Deborah Hayward, *
▲ EMP: 120 EST: 1991
SQ FT: 12,000
SALES (est): 576.12MM
SALES (corp-wide): 1.73B **Publicly Held**
Web: www.uct.com
SIC: **3674** Semiconductors and related devices
PA: Ultra Clean Holdings, Inc.
  26462 Corporate Ave
  510 576-4400

**(P-12777)**
**ULTRASIL LLC**
3527 Breakwater Ave, Hayward (94545-3610)
PHONE..................................510 266-3700
Nghia Nguyen, *CEO*
Len Anderson, *VP*
EMP: 20 EST: 2019
SALES (est): 3.2MM **Privately Held**
Web: www.ultrasil.com
SIC: **3674** Silicon wafers, chemically doped

**(P-12778)**
**ULTRON SYSTEMS INC**
5105 Maureen Ln, Moorpark (93021-1783)
PHONE..................................805 529-1485
Aki Egerer, *Pr*
Aaron Chan, *VP*
▲ EMP: 17 EST: 1982
SQ FT: 8,000
SALES (est): 3.62MM **Privately Held**
Web: www.ultronsystems.com
SIC: **3674** Semiconductors and related devices

**(P-12779)**
**UMC GROUP (USA)**
Also Called: Umc
488 De Guigne Dr, Sunnyvale (94085-3903)
PHONE..................................408 523-7800
Robert Tsao, *Ch*
Jason S Wang, *
Ing-dar Liu, *Vice Chairman*
Peter Chang, *
Fu Tai Liou, *
▲ EMP: 75 EST: 1997
SQ FT: 40,000
SALES (est): 24.87MM **Privately Held**
Web: www.umc.com
SIC: **3674** 5065 Wafers (semiconductor devices); Electronic parts and equipment, nec
PA: United Microelectronics Corporation
  3, Li-Shin 2nd Rd., Hsinchu Science Park,

**(P-12780)**
**UNIGEN CORPORATION (PA)**
39730 Eureka Dr, Newark (94560-4808)
PHONE..................................510 896-1818
▲ EMP: 120 EST: 1991
SALES (est): 238.53MM **Privately Held**
Web: www.unigen.com
SIC: **3674** 3999 3572 Random access memory (RAM); Atomizers, toiletry; Computer storage devices

**(P-12781)**
**UNIREX CORP**
Also Called: Unirex Technologies
2288 E 27th St, Vernon (90058-1131)
PHONE..................................323 589-4000
Bijan Neman, *Pr*
Behzad Neman, *
▲ EMP: 25 EST: 1985
SQ FT: 33,000
SALES (est): 3.46MM **Privately Held**
Web: www.unirex.com
SIC: **3674** 3572 Magnetic bubble memory device; Computer storage devices

**(P-12782)**
**US SENSOR CORP**
1832 W Collins Ave, Orange (92867-5425)
PHONE..................................714 639-1000
Roger W Dankert, *CEO*
EMP: 100 EST: 1989
SQ FT: 30,000
SALES (est): 26.8MM

SALES (corp-wide): 2.36B **Publicly Held**
Web: www.littelfuse.com
SIC: **3674** 3676 Semiconductors and related devices; Thermistors, except temperature sensors
PA: Littelfuse, Inc.
  8755 W Higgins Rd Ste 500
  773 628-1000

**(P-12783)**
**VENTANA MICRO SYSTEMS INC**
20813 Stevens Creek Blvd Ste 250, Cupertino (95014-2185)
P.O. Box 10505 (95157-1505)
PHONE..................................408 816-8852
Balaji Baktha, *CEO*
EMP: 16 EST: 2019
SALES (est): 3.14MM **Privately Held**
Web: www.ventanamicro.com
SIC: **3674** Semiconductors and related devices

**(P-12784)**
**VENTURA TECHNOLOGY GROUP**
855 E Easy St Ste 104, Simi Valley (93065-1825)
PHONE..................................805 581-0800
Douglas E Lafountaine, *Pr*
EMP: 16 EST: 1994
SQ FT: 7,400
SALES (est): 1.06MM **Privately Held**
Web: www.venturatech.com
SIC: **3674** Random access memory (RAM)

**(P-12785)**
**VERISILICON INC (HQ)**
2150 Gold St Ste 200, San Jose (95002-3702)
P.O. Box 1090 (95108-1090)
PHONE..................................408 844-8560
Wayne Wei Ming Dai, *Pr*
Robert Brown, *CFO*
▲ EMP: 17 EST: 2003
SQ FT: 55,000
SALES (est): 8.77MM **Privately Held**
Web: www.verisilicon.com
SIC: **3674** Semiconductors and related devices
PA: Verisilicon Holdings Co., Ltd
  C/O: Maples Corporate Services Limited

**(P-12786)**
**VERTICAL CIRCUITS INC**
10 Victor Sq Ste 100, Scotts Valley (95066-3558)
PHONE..................................831 438-3887
EMP: 50
Web: www.verticalcircuits.com
SIC: **3674** 3675 3676 3572 Memories, solid state; Electronic capacitors; Electronic resistors; Computer storage devices

**(P-12787)**
**VIA TECHNOLOGIES INC**
Also Called: Via Embedded Store
940 Mission Ct, Fremont (94539-8202)
PHONE..................................510 683-3300
Wenchi Chen, *Pr*
Cher Wang, *
▲ EMP: 130 EST: 1993
SQ FT: 55,000
SALES (est): 12.56MM
SALES (corp-wide): 12.56MM **Privately Held**
Web: www.viatech.com
SIC: **3674** Semiconductors and related devices
PA: Via Usa Inc
  940 Mission Ct

510 683-3300

**(P-12788)**
**VIAVI SOLUTIONS INC**
Also Called: Jdsu
1750 Automation Pkwy, San Jose (95131-1873)
PHONE..................................408 546-5000
Garry Ronco, *Mgr*
EMP: 17
SALES (corp-wide): 1B **Publicly Held**
Web: www.viavisolutions.com
SIC: **3674** Semiconductors and related devices
PA: Viavi Solutions Inc.
  1445 S Spctrum Blvd Ste 1
  408 404-3600

**(P-12789)**
**VIAVI SOLUTIONS INC**
80 Rose Orchard Way, San Jose (95134-1356)
PHONE..................................408 577-1478
Sergei Pacht, *Brnch Mgr*
EMP: 52
SALES (corp-wide): 1B **Publicly Held**
Web: www.viavisolutions.com
SIC: **3674** Optical isolators
PA: Viavi Solutions Inc.
  1445 S Spctrum Blvd Ste 1
  408 404-3600

**(P-12790)**
**VIRAGE LOGIC CORPORATION (HQ)**
700 E Middlefield Rd Bldg C, Mountain View (94043-4024)
PHONE..................................650 584-5000
Alexander Shubat, *Pr*
Brian Sereda, *
EMP: 354 EST: 1995
SQ FT: 61,500
SALES (est): 5.92MM
SALES (corp-wide): 5.84B **Publicly Held**
Web: www.synopsys.com
SIC: **3674** Integrated circuits, semiconductor networks, etc.
PA: Synopsys, Inc.
  675 Almanor Ave
  650 584-5000

**(P-12791)**
**VIRTIUM TECHNOLOGY INC**
Also Called: Virtium
30052 Tomas, Rcho Sta Marg (92688-2127)
PHONE..................................949 888-2444
▲ EMP: 35
SIC: **3674** Semiconductors and related devices

**(P-12792)**
**VISHAY SILICONIX LLC**
2585 Junction Ave, San Jose (95134-1923)
PHONE..................................408 988-8000
Felix Zandman, *Ch Bd*
Peter G Henrici, *Sr VP*
▲ EMP: 700 EST: 1999
SALES (est): 23.62MM
SALES (corp-wide): 3.4B **Publicly Held**
Web: www.vishay.com
SIC: **3674** Semiconductors and related devices
HQ: Siliconix Incorporated
  2585 Junction Ave
  San Jose CA 95134
  408 988-8000

# PRODUCTS & SERVICES SECTION

## 3674 - Semiconductors And Related Devices (P-12813)

**(P-12793)**
**VISHAY THIN FILM LLC**
Also Called: Vishay Spectoral Electronics
4051 Greystone Dr, Ontario (91761-3100)
PHONE..................................909 923-3313
EMP: 23 EST: 2006
SALES (est): 461.2K **Privately Held**
SIC: 3674 Thin film circuits

**(P-12794)**
**VISIONARY ELECTRONICS INC**
141 Parker Ave, San Francisco (94118-2607)
PHONE..................................415 751-8811
Brad Mc Millan, *Pr*
Brad Mc Millan, *Ch Bd*
Jeff Fearn, *
Roger Peterson, *Stockholder*
EMP: 16 EST: 1974
SALES (est): 936.82K **Privately Held**
Web: www.viselect.com
SIC: 3674 3679 Microprocessors; Recording and playback heads, magnetic

**(P-12795)**
**VITESSE MANUFACTURING & DEV**
Also Called: Vitesse Semiconductor
11861 Western Ave, Garden Grove (92841-2119)
PHONE..................................805 388-3700
Chris Gardner, *Pr*
EMP: 200 EST: 1984
SALES (est): 15.87MM
SALES (corp-wide): 7.63B **Publicly Held**
Web: www.microsemi.com
SIC: 3674 Microcircuits, integrated (semiconductor)
HQ: Microsemi Communications, Inc.
4721 Calle Carga
Camarillo CA 93012
805 388-3700

**(P-12796)**
**VOLTAGE MULTIPLIERS INC (PA)**
Also Called: V M I
8711 W Roosevelt Ave, Visalia (93291-9458)
PHONE..................................559 651-1402
Dennis J Kemp, *Pr*
Kenneth Hage, *
John Yakura, *
EMP: 176 EST: 1980
SQ FT: 24,000
SALES (est): 23.64MM
SALES (corp-wide): 23.64MM **Privately Held**
Web: www.voltagemultipliers.com
SIC: 3674 Diodes, solid state (germanium, silicon, etc.)

**(P-12797)**
**VOLTERRA SEMICONDUCTOR LLC (DH)**
160 Rio Robles, San Jose (95134-1813)
PHONE..................................408 601-1000
Mark Casper, *Pr*
Craig Teuscher, *Sr VP*
William Numann, *Sr VP*
Mike Burns, *VP Fin*
Christopher Paisley, *Ch Bd*
EMP: 27 EST: 1996
SQ FT: 73,000
SALES (est): 13.28MM
SALES (corp-wide): 12.31B **Publicly Held**
SIC: 3674 3612 Semiconductors and related devices; Voltage regulators, transmission and distribution
HQ: Maxim Integrated Products, Llc
160 Rio Robles
San Jose CA 95134
408 601-1000

**(P-12798)**
**VOLTERRA SEMICONDUCTOR LLC**
3839 Spinnaker Ct, Fremont (94538-6537)
PHONE..................................510 743-1200
Jeff Staszak, *CEO*
EMP: 237
SALES (corp-wide): 12.31B **Publicly Held**
SIC: 3674 3612 Semiconductors and related devices; Voltage regulators, transmission and distribution
HQ: Volterra Semiconductor Llc
160 Rio Robles
San Jose CA 95134
408 601-1000

**(P-12799)**
**W G HOLT INC**
Also Called: Holt Integrated Circuits
101 Columbia, Aliso Viejo (92656-1458)
PHONE..................................949 859-8800
David Mead, *CEO*
EMP: 65 EST: 1976
SALES (est): 8.85MM **Privately Held**
Web: www.holtic.com
SIC: 3674 Integrated circuits, semiconductor networks, etc.

**(P-12800)**
**WAFER PROCESS SYSTEMS INC**
3641 Charter Park Dr, San Jose (95136-1312)
PHONE..................................408 445-3010
Douglas H Caldwell, *CEO*
Christopher J Schmitz, *VP*
EMP: 15 EST: 1983
SALES (est): 2.11MM **Privately Held**
Web: www.waferprocess.com
SIC: 3674 Semiconductors and related devices

**(P-12801)**
**WAFER RECLAIM SERVICES LLC**
Also Called: Wrs Materials
2240 Ringwood Ave, San Jose (95131-1716)
PHONE..................................408 945-8112
▲ EMP: 182
Web: www.purewafer.com
SIC: 3674 8742 Integrated circuits, semiconductor networks, etc.; Financial consultant

**(P-12802)**
**WAFERNET INC**
2142 Paragon Dr, San Jose (95131-1305)
PHONE..................................408 437-9747
Lori L Vann, *Pr*
Jon Mewes, *VP*
Dave Mewes, *VP*
▲ EMP: 17 EST: 1988
SALES (est): 3.98MM **Privately Held**
Web: www.wafernet.com
SIC: 3674 Semiconductors and related devices

**(P-12803)**
**WELDEX CORPORATION**
6751 Katella Ave, Cypress (90630-5105)
PHONE..................................714 761-2100
William Jung, *CEO*
▲ EMP: 300 EST: 1992
SQ FT: 15,000
SALES (est): 8.4MM **Privately Held**
Web: cms.weldex.com
SIC: 3674 3663 Light emitting diodes; Television closed circuit equipment

**(P-12804)**
**WINSLOW AUTOMATION INC**
Also Called: Six Sigma
905 Montague Expy, Milpitas (95035-6817)
PHONE..................................408 262-9004
Russell Winslow, *CEO*
Daryl Sawtelle, *
EMP: 58 EST: 1986
SQ FT: 24,784
SALES (est): 12.4MM **Privately Held**
Web: www.winslowautomation.com
SIC: 3674 Semiconductors and related devices

**(P-12805)**
**WINTEC INDUSTRIES INC (HQ)**
Also Called: Wintec
8674 Thornton Ave, Newark (94560-3330)
PHONE..................................510 953-7421
David Jeng, *CEO*
Sue Jeng, *
Jennifer Chen, *
Shu Hui C Jheng, *
Bhaskar Bhatt, *CIO*
▲ EMP: 22 EST: 1988
SQ FT: 85,000
SALES (est): 42.6MM
SALES (corp-wide): 45.76MM **Privately Held**
Web: www.wintecind.com
SIC: 3674 3571 8742 7389 Semiconductors and related devices; Electronic computers; Materials mgmt. (purchasing, handling, inventory) consultant; Inventory computing service
PA: Wintec Industries Holding Corp.
8674 Thornton Avenue
510 953-7421

**(P-12806)**
**WORLDWIDE ENERGY AND MFG USA (PA)**
Also Called: Worldwide
1800 S Myrtle Ave, Monrovia (91016-4833)
PHONE..................................650 692-7788
John Ballard, *Ch Bd*
Tiffany Margaret Shum, *Dir*
▲ EMP: 55 EST: 2000
SALES (est): 4.93MM
SALES (corp-wide): 4.93MM **Privately Held**
Web: www.wwmusa.com
SIC: 3674 Semiconductors and related devices

**(P-12807)**
**XEL USA INC**
Also Called: XEL Group
25231 Paseo De Alicia, Laguna Hills (92653)
PHONE..................................949 425-8686
Paul Kuszka, *CEO*
EMP: 25 EST: 2008
SALES (est): 836.87K **Privately Held**
Web: www.xelgroup.com
SIC: 3674 Magnetic bubble memory device

**(P-12808)**
**XILINX DEVELOPMENT CORPORATION (DH)**
2100 All Programable, San Jose (95124-4355)
P.O. Box 240010 (95154-2410)
PHONE..................................408 559-7778
Jon A Olson, *CEO*
EMP: 18 EST: 1993
SALES (est): 7.63MM
SALES (corp-wide): 22.68B **Publicly Held**
SIC: 3674 Semiconductors and related devices
HQ: Xilinx, Inc.
2100 Logic Dr
San Jose CA 95124
408 559-7778

**(P-12809)**
**YIELD ENGINEERING SYSTEMS INC (PA)**
3178 Laurelview Ct, Fremont (94538-6535)
PHONE..................................510 954-6889
Ramakanth Alapati, *CEO*
William A Moffat, *
Ken Macwilliams, *
Rezwan Lateef, *
Fred Garcy, *
EMP: 135 EST: 1980
SQ FT: 20,000
SALES (est): 52.68MM
SALES (corp-wide): 52.68MM **Privately Held**
Web: www.yieldengineering.com
SIC: 3674 Semiconductors and related devices

**(P-12810)**
**ZENVERGE INC**
2680 Zanker Rd Ste 200, San Jose (95134-2144)
PHONE..................................408 350-5052
Amir Mobini, *CEO*
Tony Masterson, *
Vincent A Mccord, *CFO*
Raghu Rao, *VP*
EMP: 70 EST: 2005
SALES (est): 1.91MM **Privately Held**
SIC: 3674 Semiconductors and related devices

**(P-12811)**
**ZEP SOLAR LLC (DH)**
161 Mitchell Blvd Ste 104, San Rafael (94903-2085)
PHONE..................................415 479-6900
Michael John Miskovsky, *CEO*
Christina Manansala, *
Jack West, *
Peter David, *
▲ EMP: 28 EST: 2009
SQ FT: 8,200
SALES (est): 6.09MM
SALES (corp-wide): 96.77B **Publicly Held**
SIC: 3674 Photovoltaic devices, solid state
HQ: Tesla Energy Operations, Inc.
3055 Clearview Way
San Mateo CA 94402

**(P-12812)**
**ZILOG INC**
6800 Santa Teresa Blvd, San Jose (95119-1238)
PHONE..................................408 513-1500
EMP: 36
SALES (corp-wide): 2.36B **Publicly Held**
Web: www.zilog.com
SIC: 3674 Microcircuits, integrated (semiconductor)
HQ: Zilog, Inc.
1590 Buckeye Dr
Milpitas CA 95035
408 513-1500

**(P-12813)**
**ZILOG INC (DH)**
1590 Buckeye Dr, Milpitas (95035-7418)
PHONE..................................408 513-1500
Darin G Billerbeck, *Pr*
Perry J Grace, *Ex VP*

## 3674 - Semiconductors And Related Devices (P-12814)

Mike Speckman, *Pr*
Dan Eaton, *VP*
**EMP:** 27 **EST:** 1997
**SQ FT:** 42,000
**SALES (est):** 9.09MM
**SALES (corp-wide):** 2.36B **Publicly Held**
**Web:** www.zilog.com
**SIC: 3674** Microcircuits, integrated (semiconductor)
**HQ:** Ixys, Llc
1590 Buckeye Dr
Milpitas CA 95035
408 457-9000

**(P-12814)**
**ZOLA ELECTRIC LABS INC**
3130 20th St Ste 225, San Francisco (94110-2700)
**PHONE**..................650 542-6939
Bill Lenihan, *CEO*
Guido Frantzen, *
**EMP:** 34 **EST:** 2015
**SQ FT:** 2,500
**SALES (est):** 17.86MM **Privately Held**
**SIC: 3674** Solar cells
**PA:** Off Grid Electric Ltd
C/O: Estera Trust (Cayman) Limited

## 3675 Electronic Capacitors

**(P-12815)**
**BESTRONICS HOLDINGS INC (PA)**
2090 Fortune Dr, San Jose (95131-1823)
**PHONE**..................408 385-7777
Nat Mani, *CEO*
Ron Menigoz, *
Steve Yetso, *
**EMP:** 30 **EST:** 2011
**SQ FT:** 73,000
**SALES (est):** 49.03MM
**SALES (corp-wide):** 49.03MM **Privately Held**
**Web:** www.emeraldems.com
**SIC: 3675** Electronic capacitors

**(P-12816)**
**CSI TECHNOLOGIES INC**
2540 Fortune Way, Vista (92081-8441)
**PHONE**..................760 682-2222
Gary W Greiser, *Pr*
Perry Sheth, *Stockholder*
Narendra C Soni, *Stockholder*
▲ **EMP:** 18 **EST:** 1969
**SQ FT:** 18,000
**SALES (est):** 4.77MM **Privately Held**
**Web:** www.csicapacitors.com
**SIC: 3675** Electronic capacitors

**(P-12817)**
**GENERAL ATOMICS ELECTRONIC SYSTEMS INC**
4949 Greencraig Ln, San Diego (92123-1675)
P.O. Box 85608 (92186-5608)
**PHONE**..................858 522-8495
◆ **EMP:** 300
**SIC: 3675** Electronic capacitors

**(P-12818)**
**INCA ONE CORPORATION**
1632 1/2 W 134th St, Gardena (90249-2014)
**PHONE**..................310 808-0001
Adriana Roberts, *Pr*
Tupac Roberts, *
▲ **EMP:** 35 **EST:** 1971
**SALES (est):** 4.87MM **Privately Held**
**Web:** www.inca-tvlifts.com

**SIC: 3675** Electronic capacitors

**(P-12819)**
**JENNINGS TECHNOLOGY CO LLC (DH)**
Also Called: Jennings
970 Mclaughlin Ave, San Jose (95122-2611)
**PHONE**..................408 292-4025
Kurt Gallo, *
Jamie Horton, *
Roderick Mosely, *
▲ **EMP:** 70 **EST:** 1942
**SALES (est):** 4.09MM **Privately Held**
**Web:** www.jenningsandcompany.com
**SIC: 3675** 3679 3625 Electronic capacitors; Electronic circuits; Relays, for electronic use
**HQ:** Abb Installation Products Inc.
860 Rdg Lake Blvd
Memphis TN 38120
901 252-5000

**(P-12820)**
**JOHANSON TECHNOLOGY INC**
4001 Calle Tecate, Camarillo (93012-5087)
**PHONE**..................805 575-0124
John Petrinec, *CEO*
▲ **EMP:** 130 **EST:** 1991
**SQ FT:** 30,000
**SALES (est):** 23.75MM **Privately Held**
**Web:** www.johansontechnology.com
**SIC: 3675** 5065 3674 Electronic capacitors; Electronic parts and equipment, nec; Semiconductors and related devices
**PA:** Johanson Ventures, Inc.
4001 Calle Tecate

**(P-12821)**
**NEWMAR POWER LLC**
1580 Sunflower Ave, Costa Mesa (92626-1511)
**PHONE**..................800 854-3906
Wolfgang Hombrecher, *Managing Member*
**EMP:** 250 **EST:** 1979
**SALES (est):** 26.52MM
**SALES (corp-wide):** 68.25MM **Privately Held**
**Web:** www.poweringthenetwork.com
**SIC: 3675** 3678 3679 Electronic capacitors; Electronic connectors; Electronic switches
**PA:** Mission Critical Electronics Llc
1580 Sunflower Ave
714 751-0488

## 3676 Electronic Resistors

**(P-12822)**
**DALE VISHAY ELECTRONICS LLC**
Also Called: Applied Thin-Film Products
3620 Yale Way, Fremont (94538-6182)
**PHONE**..................510 661-4287
**EMP:** 25
**SALES (corp-wide):** 3.4B **Publicly Held**
**Web:** www.vishay.com
**SIC: 3676** 3677 3678 Electronic resistors; Electronic coils and transformers; Electronic connectors
**HQ:** Vishay Dale Electronics, Llc
1122 23rd St
Columbus NE 68601
402 564-3131

**(P-12823)**
**RIEDON INC (PA)**
300 Cypress Ave, Alhambra (91801-3001)
▲ **EMP:** 150 **EST:** 1960
**SQ FT:** 12,000
**SALES (est):** 18.61MM **Privately Held**

**Web:** www.riedon.com
**SIC: 3676** Electronic resistors

**(P-12824)**
**YAGEO AMERICA CORPORATION**
Also Called: Yageo America
2550 N 1st St Ste 480, San Jose (95131-1038)
**PHONE**..................408 240-6200
Chi Wen Chang, *Pr*
▲ **EMP:** 20 **EST:** 2006
**SALES (est):** 4.99MM **Privately Held**
**Web:** www.yageo.com
**SIC: 3676** Electronic resistors
**PA:** Yageo Corporation
3f, No.233-1, Pao Chiao Rd.,

## 3677 Electronic Coils And Transformers

**(P-12825)**
**A M I/COAST MAGNETICS INC**
Also Called: Coast Magnetics
5333 W Washington Blvd, Los Angeles (90016-1191)
**PHONE**..................323 936-6188
Satya Dosaj, *CEO*
Dev Dosaj, *
Phillis Dosaj, *Stockholder*
**EMP:** 49 **EST:** 1965
**SQ FT:** 25,000
**SALES (est):** 4.97MM **Privately Held**
**Web:** www.coastmagnetics.com
**SIC: 3677** 3549 Electronic transformers; Coil winding machines for springs

**(P-12826)**
**AEM ELECTRONICS (USA) INC (PA)**
Also Called: Aem Components USA
6610 Cobra Way, San Diego (92121-4107)
**PHONE**..................858 481-0210
Rick Busch, *CEO*
Daniel H Chang, *Ch*
**EMP:** 17 **EST:** 2010
**SALES (est):** 22.93MM **Privately Held**
**Web:** www.aemcomponents.com
**SIC: 3677** 3613 8742 3559 Inductors, electronic; Fuses, electric; Planning consultant; Electronic component making machinery

**(P-12827)**
**ALLIED COMPONENTS INTL**
19671 Descartes, Foothill Ranch (92610-2609)
**PHONE**..................949 356-1780
Anuj Jain, *CEO*
Rakesh Gupta, *
▲ **EMP:** 25 **EST:** 1992
**SQ FT:** 9,000
**SALES (est):** 4.52MM **Privately Held**
**Web:** www.alliedcomponents.com
**SIC: 3677** Electronic coils and transformers

**(P-12828)**
**ARAS POWER TECHNOLOGIES (PA)**
371 Fairview Way, Milpitas (95035-3024)
**PHONE**..................408 935-8877
Fariborz Rad, *Pr*
▲ **EMP:** 18 **EST:** 2002
**SQ FT:** 5,000
**SALES (est):** 2.66MM
**SALES (corp-wide):** 2.66MM **Privately Held**
**Web:** www.araspower.com

**SIC: 3677** 3679 Transformers power supply, electronic type; Static power supply converters for electronic applications

**(P-12829)**
**ASTRON CORPORATION**
9 Autry, Irvine (92682-2768)
**PHONE**..................949 458-7277
Loren Pochirowski, *Pr*
William Pochirowski, *
▲ **EMP:** 40 **EST:** 1976
**SQ FT:** 18,000
**SALES (est):** 2.19MM **Privately Held**
**Web:** www.astroncorp.com
**SIC: 3677** 3679 Transformers power supply, electronic type; Electronic circuits

**(P-12830)**
**BECKER SPECIALTY CORPORATION**
15310 Arrow Blvd, Fontana (92335-3249)
**PHONE**..................909 356-1095
Jack Mcgrew, *Brnch Mgr*
**EMP:** 99
**SALES (corp-wide):** 856.87MM **Privately Held**
**SIC: 3677** Electronic coils and transformers
**HQ:** Becker Specialty Corporation
755 Il Route 83 Ste 223
Bensenville IL 60106

**(P-12831)**
**BEL POWER SOLUTIONS INC (HQ)**
Also Called: Power One
2390 Walsh Ave, Santa Clara (95051-1301)
**PHONE**..................866 513-2839
Steve Dawson, *Pr*
Colin Dunn, *VP Fin*
Steve Dawson, *Dir*
▲ **EMP:** 73 **EST:** 1949
**SALES (est):** 22.72MM
**SALES (corp-wide):** 639.81MM **Publicly Held**
**Web:** www.belfuse.com
**SIC: 3677** Electronic coils and transformers
**PA:** Bel Fuse Inc.
300 Executive Dr Ste 300
201 432-0463

**(P-12832)**
**BOURNS INC (PA)**
Also Called: Bourns
1200 Columbia Ave, Riverside (92507-2129)
**PHONE**..................951 781-5500
Gordon Bourns, *CEO*
Al Yost, *
James Heiken, *
Gregg Gibbons, *
◆ **EMP:** 171 **EST:** 1952
**SQ FT:** 205,000
**SALES (est):** 459.73MM
**SALES (corp-wide):** 459.73MM **Privately Held**
**Web:** www.bourns.com
**SIC: 3677** 3676 3661 3639 Electronic transformers; Electronic resistors; Telephone and telegraph apparatus; Major kitchen appliances, except refrigerators and stoves

**(P-12833)**
**COAST/DVNCED CHIP MGNETICS INC**
Also Called: Coast/A C M
4225 Spencer St, Torrance (90503-2421)
**PHONE**..................310 370-8188
Benjamin Nguyen, *CEO*

## PRODUCTS & SERVICES SECTION
## 3677 - Electronic Coils And Transformers (P-12856)

Ben Nguyen, *CEO*
Allen Adams, *Pr*
**EMP:** 19 **EST:** 1952
**SQ FT:** 3,000
**SALES (est):** 4.79MM **Privately Held**
**Web:** www.coastacm.com
**SIC:** 3677 Electronic coils and transformers

### (P-12834)
### COIL WINDING SPECIALIST INC
Also Called: Cws
353 W Grove Ave, Orange (92865-3205)
**PHONE**..................714 279-9010
James Lau, *Pr*
◆ **EMP:** 15 **EST:** 2006
**SQ FT:** 1,000
**SALES (est):** 4.9MM **Privately Held**
**Web:** www.coilws.com
**SIC:** 3677 Inductors, electronic

### (P-12835)
### CORONA MAGNETICS INC
Also Called: C M I
201 Corporate Terrace St, Corona (92879-6000)
P.O. Box 1355 (92878-1355)
**PHONE**..................951 735-7558
Jay Paasch, *CEO*
Heike Paasch, *
Cory Vila Managing, *Prin*
**EMP:** 120 **EST:** 1968
**SQ FT:** 17,000
**SALES (est):** 4.63MM **Privately Held**
**Web:** www.corona-magnetics.com
**SIC:** 3677 3679 Transformers power supply, electronic type; Electronic circuits

### (P-12836)
### CUSTOM COILS INC
4000 Industrial Way, Benicia (94510-1242)
**PHONE**..................707 752-8633
Tom Quinn, *Pr*
John Quinn, *CFO*
**EMP:** 15 **EST:** 1978
**SQ FT:** 7,200
**SALES (est):** 2.68MM **Privately Held**
**Web:** www.ccoils.com
**SIC:** 3677 Electronic coils and transformers

### (P-12837)
### CUSTOM SUPPRESSION INC
Also Called: Csi
26470 Ruether Ave Ste 106, Santa Clarita (91350-2972)
**PHONE**..................818 718-1040
Edward C Mcsweeney Junior, *Pr*
Genevieve Mc Sweeney, *Sec*
**EMP:** 17 **EST:** 1986
**SQ FT:** 7,000
**SALES (est):** 600.44K **Privately Held**
**SIC:** 3677 3678 Filtration devices, electronic; Electronic connectors

### (P-12838)
### DSPM INC
Also Called: Digital Signal Power Mfg
439 S Stoddard Ave, San Bernardino (92401-2025)
**PHONE**..................714 970-2304
Milton Hanson, *Pr*
▲ **EMP:** 30 **EST:** 2003
**SQ FT:** 30,000
**SALES (est):** 7.21MM **Privately Held**
**Web:** www.dspmanufacturing.com
**SIC:** 3677 Transformers power supply, electronic type

### (P-12839)
### FILTER CONCEPTS INCORPORATED
22895 Eastpark Dr, Yorba Linda (92887-4653)
**PHONE**..................714 545-7003
**EMP:** 38 **EST:** 1980
**SALES (est):** 1.98MM **Privately Held**
**Web:** www.filterconcepts.com
**SIC:** 3677 Filtration devices, electronic
**PA:** Astrodyne Corporation
36 Newburgh Rd

### (P-12840)
### FRONTIER ELECTRONICS CORP
667 Cochran St, Simi Valley (93065-1939)
**PHONE**..................805 522-9998
Jeannie Gu, *CEO*
Winston Gu, *VP*
Jay Valguna, *Contrlr*
Jean Pope, *Contrlr*
▲ **EMP:** 18 **EST:** 1985
**SQ FT:** 15,246
**SALES (est):** 2.47MM **Privately Held**
**Web:** www.frontierusa.com
**SIC:** 3677 3674 Inductors, electronic; Semiconductors and related devices

### (P-12841)
### GENERAL LINEAR SYSTEMS INC
4332 Artesia Ave, Fullerton (92833-2523)
**PHONE**..................714 994-4822
Jeffrey Steele, *Pr*
Garrett Hartney, *Pr*
Annette Hartney, *Sec*
James Mynatt, *VP*
**EMP:** 19 **EST:** 1972
**SQ FT:** 4,000
**SALES (est):** 2.48MM **Privately Held**
**Web:** www.coilwinder.com
**SIC:** 3677 Electronic coils and transformers

### (P-12842)
### GOODFOR LLC
Also Called: The Godfor Plbg Wtr Filtration
5927 Balfour Ct Ste 206, Carlsbad (92008-7377)
**PHONE**..................833 488-3489
Yevgenia Emma, *Managing Member*
**EMP:** 15 **EST:** 2018
**SALES (est):** 3.77MM **Privately Held**
**Web:** www.goodfortexas.com
**SIC:** 3677 1711 Filtration devices, electronic; Plumbing contractors

### (P-12843)
### JAMES L HALL CO INCORPORATED
Also Called: Jetronics Company
218 Roberts Ave, Santa Rosa (95401-6146)
P.O. Box U (95402-0280)
**PHONE**..................707 544-2436
Stephen Vallarino, *CEO*
**EMP:** 55 **EST:** 1961
**SALES (est):** 9.66MM
**SALES (corp-wide):** 9.66MM **Privately Held**
**Web:** www.jetronics.com
**SIC:** 3677 3679 Electronic coils and transformers; Electronic circuits
**PA:** James L. Hall Co., Incorporated
360 Tesconi Cir Ste B
707 547-0775

### (P-12844)
### MAGNETIC COILS INC
150 San Hedrin Cir, Willits (95490-8753)
**PHONE**..................707 459-5994
Don Setzco, *Mgr*
**EMP:** 61
**SALES (corp-wide):** 6.27MM **Privately Held**
**Web:** www.mcitransformer.com
**SIC:** 3677 Electronic coils and transformers
**PA:** Magnetic Coils Inc.
411 Manhattan Ave
631 587-0510

### (P-12845)
### MAGTECH & POWER CONVERSION INC
Also Called: Speciality Labs
1146 E Ash Ave, Fullerton (92831-5018)
**PHONE**..................714 451-0106
Viet Pho, *Pr*
Linh Pho, *
**EMP:** 40 **EST:** 1981
**SQ FT:** 9,000
**SALES (est):** 4.99MM **Privately Held**
**Web:** www.magtechpower.com
**SIC:** 3677 Electronic transformers

### (P-12846)
### MEISSNER CORPORATION
1001 Flynn Rd, Camarillo (93012-8706)
**PHONE**..................805 388-9911
Christopher A Meissner, *CEO*
**EMP:** 30 **EST:** 2018
**SALES (est):** 3.14MM **Privately Held**
**SIC:** 3677 Filtration devices, electronic

### (P-12847)
### MEISSNER FILTRATION PDTS INC (PA)
1001 Flynn Rd, Camarillo (93012)
**PHONE**..................805 388-9911
Christopher Meissner, *Pr*
Laura Meissner, *VP*
▲ **EMP:** 20 **EST:** 1989
**SQ FT:** 45,000
**SALES (est):** 13.6MM **Privately Held**
**Web:** www.meissner.com
**SIC:** 3677 5047 8071 Filtration devices, electronic; Medical laboratory equipment; Testing laboratories

### (P-12848)
### MERCURY MAGNETICS INC
Also Called: Gulf Enterprises
21520 Blythe St, Canoga Park (91304-4993)
**PHONE**..................818 998-7791
Sergio Hamernik, *Pr*
Susan Hamernik, *VP*
▲ **EMP:** 20 **EST:** 1968
**SALES (est):** 3.55MM **Privately Held**
**Web:** www.mercurymagnetics.com
**SIC:** 3677 Electronic transformers

### (P-12849)
### MIL-SPEC MAGNETICS INC
169 Pacific St, Pomona (91768-3215)
**PHONE**..................909 598-8116
Rohan Gunewardena, *Pr*
Shelton Gunewardena, *
Tony Gunewardena, *
Andrew Gunewardena, *
Athula Meepe, *
**EMP:** 78 **EST:** 1990
**SQ FT:** 6,000
**SALES (est):** 12.36MM **Privately Held**
**Web:** www.milspecmag.com
**SIC:** 3677 3675 Electronic transformers; Electronic capacitors

### (P-12850)
### PARKER-HANNIFIN CORPORATION
Also Called: Water Purification
19610 S Rancho Way, Rancho Dominguez (90220-6039)
**PHONE**..................310 608-5600
Jaime Garcia, *Prin*
**EMP:** 150
**SALES (corp-wide):** 19.93B **Publicly Held**
**Web:** www.parker.com
**SIC:** 3677 Filtration devices, electronic
**PA:** Parker-Hannifin Corporation
6035 Parkland Blvd
216 896-3000

### (P-12851)
### PAYNE MAGNETICS CORPORATION
854 W Front St, Covina (91722-3614)
**PHONE**..................626 332-6207
George Payne, *Ch*
Jon S Payne, *
▲ **EMP:** 100 **EST:** 1982
**SQ FT:** 6,600
**SALES (est):** 2.12MM **Privately Held**
**Web:** www.payne-magnetics.com
**SIC:** 3677 3699 Electronic transformers; Electrical equipment and supplies, nec

### (P-12852)
### PREMIER MAGNETICS INC
20381 Barents Sea Cir, Lake Forest (92630-8807)
**PHONE**..................949 452-0511
James Earley, *Pr*
▲ **EMP:** 30 **EST:** 1991
**SALES (est):** 4.99MM **Privately Held**
**Web:** www.premiermag.com
**SIC:** 3677 3612 Electronic coils and transformers; Specialty transformers

### (P-12853)
### PUROFLUX CORPORATION
2121 Union Pl, Simi Valley (93065-1661)
**PHONE**..................805 579-0216
Henry Nmi Greenberg, *Pr*
▼ **EMP:** 17 **EST:** 1994
**SQ FT:** 25,000
**SALES (est):** 4.47MM **Privately Held**
**Web:** www.puroflux.com
**SIC:** 3677 3613 Filtration devices, electronic; Control panels, electric

### (P-12854)
### R H BARDEN INC
Also Called: Lodestone Pacific
4769 E Wesley Dr, Anaheim (92807-1941)
**PHONE**..................714 970-0900
Richard H Barden Iii, *Pr*
◆ **EMP:** 15 **EST:** 1988
**SQ FT:** 12,000
**SALES (est):** 4.39MM **Privately Held**
**Web:** www.lodestonepacific.com
**SIC:** 3677 Electronic coils and transformers

### (P-12855)
### RAYCO ELECTRONIC MFG INC
1220 W 130th St, Gardena (90247-1502)
**PHONE**..................310 329-2660
Mahendra P Patel, *CEO*
Steve Mardani, *
Mayan Patel, *
**EMP:** 50 **EST:** 1941
**SQ FT:** 20,000
**SALES (est):** 4.81MM **Privately Held**
**Web:** www.raycoelectronics.com
**SIC:** 3677 3612 3621 Electronic transformers; Transformers, except electric; Motors and generators

### (P-12856)
### ROBERT M HADLEY COMPANY INC
4054 Transport St Ste B, Ventura (93003-5680)

## 3677 - Electronic Coils And Transformers (P-12857)

PHONE..................805 658-7286
E Christopher Waian, *CEO*
Jim Hadley, *
Mary Hadley Waian, *
**EMP:** 80 **EST:** 1929
**SQ FT:** 28,000
**SALES (est):** 4.14MM **Privately Held**
**Web:** www.rmhco.com
**SIC: 3677** Transformers power supply, electronic type

### (P-12857)
### SCOTTS VALLEY MAGNETICS INC
300 El Pueblo Rd Ste 107, Scotts Valley (95066-4238)
P.O. Box 66575 (95067-6575)
PHONE..................831 438-3600
Norma Humphries, *Pr*
John F Humphries, *
Karina Humphries, *
Jerry Humphries, *
▲ **EMP:** 24 **EST:** 1976
**SQ FT:** 15,000
**SALES (est):** 4.33MM **Privately Held**
**Web:** www.svmagnetics.com
**SIC: 3677** 3679 3829 Filtration devices, electronic; Power supplies, all types: static; Measuring and controlling devices, nec

### (P-12858)
### SI MANUFACTURING INC
Also Called: Standard Industries
1440 S Allec St, Anaheim (92805-6305)
PHONE..................714 956-7110
James R Reed, *Pr*
Ata Shafizadeh, *
▲ **EMP:** 50 **EST:** 2000
**SALES (est):** 9.2MM **Privately Held**
**Web:** www.simfg.com
**SIC: 3677** 3679 8711 3613 Electronic coils and transformers; Electronic loads and power supplies; Engineering services; Switchgear and switchboard apparatus

### (P-12859)
### SONOMA PHOTONICS INC
1750 Northpoint Pkwy Ste C, Santa Rosa (95407-7597)
PHONE..................707 568-1202
Mark A Caylor, *Pr*
Wesley G Bush, *
**EMP:** 50 **EST:** 2000
**SQ FT:** 30,000
**SALES (est):** 23.5MM **Publicly Held**
**Web:** www.sonomaphotonics.com
**SIC: 3677** 3827 Filtration devices, electronic; Optical instruments and lenses
**HQ:** Northrop Grumman Systems Corporation
2980 Fairview Park Dr
Falls Church VA 22042
703 280-2900

### (P-12860)
### STANGENES INDUSTRIES INC (PA)
1052 E Meadow Cir, Palo Alto (94303-4230)
PHONE..................650 855-9926
Magne Stangenes, *CEO*
Kari Stangenes, *
▲ **EMP:** 75 **EST:** 1974
**SQ FT:** 15,500
**SALES (est):** 23.07MM
**SALES (corp-wide):** 23.07MM **Privately Held**
**Web:** www.stangenes.com
**SIC: 3677** Electronic transformers

### (P-12861)
### SYNDER INC (PA)
Also Called: Synder Filtration
4941 Allison Pkwy, Vacaville (95688-8794)
PHONE..................707 451-6060
Edward Yeh, *CEO*
Joseph Y Wang, *
Y C Jao, *
▲ **EMP:** 29 **EST:** 1989
**SQ FT:** 26,000
**SALES (est):** 10.16MM **Privately Held**
**Web:** www.synderfiltration.com
**SIC: 3677** 8748 8742 Filtration devices, electronic; Systems analysis or design; Industry specialist consultants

### (P-12862)
### TUR-BO JET PRODUCTS CO INC
5025 Earle Ave, Rosemead (91770-1169)
PHONE..................626 285-1294
Richard Bloom, *Pr*
Richard L Bloom, *
▲ **EMP:** 95 **EST:** 1945
**SQ FT:** 27,000
**SALES (est):** 12.97MM **Privately Held**
**Web:** www.tbj.aero
**SIC: 3677** Coil windings, electronic

### (P-12863)
### VANGUARD ELECTRONICS COMPANY (PA)
18292 Enterprise Ln, Huntington Beach (92648-1217)
PHONE..................714 842-3330
**EMP:** 48 **EST:** 1952
**SALES (est):** 22.7MM
**SALES (corp-wide):** 22.7MM **Privately Held**
**Web:** www.ve1.com
**SIC: 3677** Electronic transformers

### (P-12864)
### WJLP COMPANY INC
Also Called: West Coast Magnetics
4848 Frontier Way Ste 100, Stockton (95215-9649)
P.O. Box 31330 (95213-1330)
PHONE..................800 628-1123
Weyman Lundquist, *Pr*
▲ **EMP:** 100 **EST:** 1974
**SQ FT:** 8,000
**SALES (est):** 30MM **Privately Held**
**Web:** www.wcmagnetics.com
**SIC: 3677** 3357 Electronic transformers; Coaxial cable, nonferrous

## 3678 Electronic Connectors

### (P-12865)
### AEROFLITE ENTERPRISES INC
261 Gemini Ave, Brea (92821-3704)
PHONE..................714 773-4251
◆ **EMP:** 52 **EST:** 1977
**SALES (est):** 4.45MM **Privately Held**
**Web:** www.aeroflite.com
**SIC: 3678** Electronic connectors

### (P-12866)
### BRANTNER AND ASSOCIATES INC (DH)
Also Called: Te Connectivity MOG
1700 Gillespie Way, El Cajon (92020-1874)
PHONE..................619 456-6827
Harold G Barksdale, *CEO*
Jean-jacques Fotzeu, *CFO*
▲ **EMP:** 142 **EST:** 1957
**SQ FT:** 35,000
**SALES (est):** 18.17MM
**SALES (corp-wide):** 74.18MM **Privately Held**
**Web:** www.te.com
**SIC: 3678** 3643 Electronic connectors; Current-carrying wiring services
**HQ:** Brantner Holding Llc
501 Oakside Ave
Redwood City CA 94063
650 361-5292

### (P-12867)
### BRANTNER HOLDING LLC (HQ)
501 Oakside Ave, Redwood City (94063-3800)
PHONE..................650 361-5292
Harold Barksdale, *Pr*
**EMP:** 17 **EST:** 2014
**SALES (est):** 18.17MM
**SALES (corp-wide):** 74.18MM **Privately Held**
**SIC: 3678** Electronic connectors
**PA:** Te Connectivity Mog Inc.
501 Oakside Ave
650 361-5292

### (P-12868)
### CALCULEX
131 Stony Cir Ste 500a, Santa Rosa (95401-9520)
PHONE..................707 578-2307
**EMP:** 50 **EST:** 1985
**SALES (est):** 6.17MM **Privately Held**
**SIC: 3678** Electronic connectors

### (P-12869)
### CIRCUIT ASSEMBLY CORP (PA)
6 Autry Ste 150, Irvine (92618-2735)
PHONE..................949 855-7887
Andrew Lang, *Pr*
Terri Lang, *
▲ **EMP:** 18 **EST:** 1969
**SALES (est):** 8.45MM
**SALES (corp-wide):** 8.45MM **Privately Held**
**Web:** www.circuitassembly.com
**SIC: 3678** Electronic connectors

### (P-12870)
### CLEARPATHGPS LLC
Also Called: Clearpathgps
3463 State St # 494, Santa Barbara (93105-2662)
PHONE..................805 979-3442
Christopher Fowler, *Managing Member*
Steve Wells, *Mng Pt*
**EMP:** 20 **EST:** 2013
**SALES (est):** 2.74MM **Privately Held**
**Web:** www.clearpathgps.com
**SIC: 3678** Electronic connectors

### (P-12871)
### COMPONENT EQUIPMENT COINC
Also Called: Ceco
3050 Camino Del Sol, Oxnard (93030-7275)
P.O. Box 600 (93066-0600)
PHONE..................805 988-8004
Bill Rigby, *Pr*
Thomas Conway, *
**EMP:** 25 **EST:** 1979
**SQ FT:** 32,000
**SALES (est):** 2.47MM **Privately Held**
**SIC: 3678** Electronic connectors

### (P-12872)
### CONESYS INC
548 Amapola Ave, Torrance (90501-1472)
PHONE..................310 212-0065
Teresa Lynn De Forest, *Admn*
**EMP:** 88
**SALES (corp-wide):** 33.1MM **Privately Held**
**Web:** www.conesys.com
**SIC: 3678** Electronic connectors
**PA:** Conesys, Inc.
2280 W 208th St
310 618-3737

### (P-12873)
### COOPER INTERCONNECT INC (DH)
750 W Ventura Blvd, Camarillo (93010-8382)
PHONE..................805 484-0543
Revathi Advaithi, *Pr*
**EMP:** 17 **EST:** 1945
**SQ FT:** 113,000
**SALES (est):** 21.34MM **Privately Held**
**SIC: 3678** 3643 Electronic connectors; Electric connectors
**HQ:** Eaton Corporation
1000 Eaton Blvd
Cleveland OH 44122
440 523-5000

### (P-12874)
### CORSAIR ELEC CONNECTORS INC
17100 Murphy Ave, Irvine (92614-5916)
PHONE..................949 833-0273
Amir Saket, *Pr*
Steve Simmons, *Finance*
**EMP:** 140 **EST:** 2009
**SQ FT:** 34,554
**SALES (est):** 19.57MM **Privately Held**
**Web:** www.corsairelectricalconnectors.com
**SIC: 3678** Electronic connectors

### (P-12875)
### CRISTEK INTERCONNECTS LLC (DH)
Also Called: Cristek
5395 E Hunter Ave, Anaheim (92807-2054)
PHONE..................714 696-5200
Keith Barclay, *Pr*
**EMP:** 135 **EST:** 1985
**SALES (est):** 46.53MM
**SALES (corp-wide):** 168.44MM **Privately Held**
**Web:** www.cristek.com
**SIC: 3678** Electronic connectors
**HQ:** Hermetic Solutions Group Inc.
16 Plains Rd
Essex CT 06426
215 645-9420

### (P-12876)
### DETORONICS CORP
13071 Rosecrans Ave, Santa Fe Springs (90670-4930)
PHONE..................626 579-7130
Kenneth S Clark, *CEO*
Marcia Baroda, *
**EMP:** 37 **EST:** 1959
**SQ FT:** 20,000
**SALES (est):** 4.66MM **Privately Held**
**Web:** www.detoronics.com
**SIC: 3678** Electronic connectors

### (P-12877)
### DUEL SYSTEMS INC
2025 Gateway Pl Ste 235, San Jose (95110-1000)
PHONE..................408 453-9500
Don Duda, *Pr*
▲ **EMP:** 18 **EST:** 1988
**SQ FT:** 34,000
**SALES (est):** 2.42MM

**PRODUCTS & SERVICES SECTION**      **3678 - Electronic Connectors (P-12898)**

SALES (corp-wide): 1.11B **Publicly Held**
**SIC: 3678** Electronic connectors
**PA:** Methode Electronics, Inc
   8750 W Bryn Mawr Ave Ste
   708 867-6777

### (P-12878)
### E & E TOA CORPORATION
11450 Sheldon St, Sun Valley (91352-1121)
▲ **EMP:** 15
**SIC: 3678** 5065 Electronic connectors;
   Electronic parts

### (P-12879)
### FLEXIBLE MANUFACTURING LLC
Also Called: F M I
1719 S Grand Ave, Santa Ana
(92705-4808)
**PHONE**...............................714 259-7996
Carlos Cortes, *
Bart Pacetti, *
Tom Rendina, *
▲ **EMP:** 100 **EST:** 2001
**SQ FT:** 15,000
**SALES (est):** 9.95MM **Privately Held**
**Web:** www.4fmi.com
**SIC: 3678** Electronic connectors

### (P-12880)
### GLEN - MAC SWISS CO
12848 Weber Way, Hawthorne
(90250-5537)
**PHONE**...............................310 978-4555
Torkom Postajian, *Pr*
Armen Postajian, *Sec*
▲ **EMP:** 27 **EST:** 1963
**SQ FT:** 12,676
**SALES (est):** 1.53MM **Privately Held**
**Web:** www.screwmachineshop.net
**SIC: 3678** 3429 3451 3599 Electronic
   connectors; Hardware, nec; Screw machine
   products; Machine shop, jobbing and repair

### (P-12881)
### HIGH CONNECTION DENSITY INC
542 Gibraltar Dr, Milpitas (95035-6315)
**PHONE**...............................408 743-9700
Tsuyoshi Taira, *Pr*
Charlie Stevenson, *
**EMP:** 25 **EST:** 2000
**SALES (est):** 3MM **Privately Held**
**Web:** www.hcdcorp.com
**SIC: 3678** 8734 Electronic connectors;
   Testing laboratories

### (P-12882)
### HOLLAND ELECTRONICS LLC
Also Called: Holland Electronics
2935 Golf Course Dr, Ventura (93003-7604)
**PHONE**...............................888 628-5411
◆ **EMP:** 48 **EST:** 1998
**SALES (est):** 10.06MM
**SALES (corp-wide):** 12.55B **Publicly Held**
**Web:** www.hollandelectronics.com
**SIC: 3678** 5063 Electronic connectors;
   Electrical apparatus and equipment
**PA:** Amphenol Corporation
   358 Hall Ave
   203 265-8900

### (P-12883)
### INFINITE ELECTRONICS INTL INC (DH)
17792 Fitch, Irvine (92614-6020)
**PHONE**...............................949 261-1920
Penny Cotner, *Pr*
Scott Rosner, *

Jim Dauw, *
Terry G Jarniga, *
▲ **EMP:** 51 **EST:** 1972
**SQ FT:** 40,000
**SALES (est):** 231.46MM
**SALES (corp-wide):** 1.84B **Privately Held**
**Web:** www.infiniteelectronics.com
**SIC: 3678** 3357 3651 3643 Electronic
   connectors; Coaxial cable, nonferrous;
   Household audio and video equipment;
   Current-carrying wiring services
**HQ:** Infinite Electronics, Inc.
   17792 Fitch Ave
   Irvine CA 92614
   949 261-1920

### (P-12884)
### INFINITE ELECTRONICS INTL INC
Pasternack Enterprises
17802 Fitch, Irvine (92614-6002)
**PHONE**...............................949 261-1920
**EMP:** 15
**SALES (corp-wide):** 1.84B **Privately Held**
**Web:** www.infiniteelectronics.com
**SIC: 3678** 3651 3357 3643 Electronic
   connectors; Household audio and video
   equipment; Coaxial cable, nonferrous;
   Current-carrying wiring services
**HQ:** Infinite Electronics International, Inc.
   17792 Fitch
   Irvine CA 92614
   949 261-1920

### (P-12885)
### J - T E C H
548 Amapola Ave, Torrance (90501-1472)
**PHONE**...............................310 533-6700
Walter Naubauer Junior, *CEO*
**EMP:** 136 **EST:** 1987
**SALES (est):** 4.44MM **Privately Held**
**SIC: 3678** Electronic connectors

### (P-12886)
### JOSLYN SUNBANK COMPANY LLC
1740 Commerce Way, Paso Robles
(93446-3620)
**PHONE**...............................805 238-2840
Mark Thek, *Genl Mgr*
Mike Ritter, *Dir Opers*
Kirsten Park, *VP*
**EMP:** 500 **EST:** 1997
**SQ FT:** 80,000
**SALES (est):** 21.45MM **Privately Held**
**Web:**
joslyn-sunbank-company-llc-in-paso-robles-ca.cityfos.com
**SIC: 3678** 3643 5065 Electronic connectors;
   Connectors and terminals for electrical
   devices; Connectors, electronic
**HQ:** Eaton Corporation
   1000 Eaton Blvd
   Cleveland OH 44122
   440 523-5000

### (P-12887)
### L & M MACHINING CORPORATION
550 S Melrose St, Placentia (92870-6327)
**PHONE**...............................714 414-0923
Mike Mai, *Pr*
**EMP:** 70 **EST:** 1985
**SQ FT:** 31,000
**SALES (est):** 8.47MM **Privately Held**
**Web:** www.lmcnc.com
**SIC: 3678** Electronic connectors

### (P-12888)
### LACO INC
6767 Preston Ave, Livermore (94551-8529)
P.O. Box 3069 (94526-8069)
**PHONE**...............................775 461-2960
**EMP:** 116
**Web:** www.lacoinc.com
**SIC: 3678** Electronic connectors
**PA:** Laco, Inc.
   1150 Trademark Dr Ste 111

### (P-12889)
### LIGHTBIT CORPORATION
411 Clyde Ave, Mountain View
(94043-2209)
**PHONE**...............................650 988-9500
Larry Marshall, *CEO*
Indra Singhal, *VP*
**EMP:** 18 **EST:** 2000
**SQ FT:** 10,560
**SALES (est):** 845.84K **Privately Held**
**SIC: 3678** Electronic connectors

### (P-12890)
### MIN-E-CON LLC
17312 Eastman, Irvine (92614-5522)
**PHONE**...............................949 250-0087
Wendell Jacob, *Managing Member*
John M Brown, *
Wendell P Jacob, *
▼ **EMP:** 60 **EST:** 1974
**SALES (est):** 9.99MM **Privately Held**
**Web:** www.min-e-con.com
**SIC: 3678** Electronic connectors

### (P-12891)
### NEA ELECTRONICS INC
14370 White Sage Rd, Moorpark
(93021-8720)
**PHONE**...............................805 292-4010
Steven Perkins, *Pr*
**EMP:** 24 **EST:** 1995
**SQ FT:** 20,000
**SALES (est):** 5.76MM
**SALES (corp-wide):** 696.33MM **Privately Held**
**Web:** www.ebad.com
**SIC: 3678** 3629 3592 Electronic connectors;
   Battery chargers, rectifying or nonrotating;
   Valves
**HQ:** Ensign-Bickford Aerospace & Defense Co
   640 Hopmeadow St
   Simsbury CT 06070
   860 843-2289

### (P-12892)
### NETWORK VIDEO TECHNOLOGIES INC (PA)
Also Called: Network Video Technologies
551 Brown Rd, Fremont (94539-7003)
**PHONE**...............................650 462-8100
▲ **EMP:** 25 **EST:** 1994
**SALES (est):** 2.7MM **Privately Held**
**SIC: 3678** Electronic connectors

### (P-12893)
### ONANON INC
720 S Milpitas Blvd, Milpitas (95035-5449)
**PHONE**...............................408 262-8990
Dennis Joel Johnson, *CEO*
Thomas R Sahakian, *
**EMP:** 49 **EST:** 1979
**SQ FT:** 25,000
**SALES (est):** 12.02MM
**SALES (corp-wide):** 12.55B **Publicly Held**
**Web:** www.onanon.com
**SIC: 3678** 3089 Electronic connectors;
   Laminating of plastics
**PA:** Amphenol Corporation
   358 Hall Ave

203 265-8900

### (P-12894)
### R KERN ENGINEERING & MFG CORP
Also Called: Kern Engineering
13912 Mountain Ave, Chino (91710-9018)
**PHONE**...............................909 664-2440
Richard Kern, *CEO*
Roland A Kern, *
Helga Kern, *
Jose Nunez, *
▲ **EMP:** 54 **EST:** 1966
**SQ FT:** 34,000
**SALES (est):** 9.06MM **Privately Held**
**Web:** www.kerneng.com
**SIC: 3678** 3599 Electronic connectors;
   Machine shop, jobbing and repair

### (P-12895)
### RF INDUSTRIES LTD (PA)
Also Called: Comppro
16868 Via Del Campo Ct Ste 200, San Diego (92127-1772)
**PHONE**...............................858 549-6340
Robert Dawson, *CEO*
Mark K Holdsworth, *
Peter Yin, *CFO*
Ray Bibisi, *Pr*
**EMP:** 89 **EST:** 1979
**SALES (est):** 72.17MM
**SALES (corp-wide):** 72.17MM **Publicly Held**
**Web:** www.rfindustries.com
**SIC: 3678** 3643 3663 Electronic connectors;
   Electric connectors; Transmitter-receivers, radio

### (P-12896)
### SABRITEC
1550 Scenic Ave Ste 150, Costa Mesa
(92626-1465)
**PHONE**...............................714 371-1100
**EMP:** 300
**SIC: 3678** Electronic connectors

### (P-12897)
### STAUBLI ELECTRICAL CONNECTORS INC (DH)
Also Called: Mc
100 Market St, Windsor (95492-7228)
**PHONE**...............................707 838-0530
**EMP:** 18 **EST:** 1982
**SALES (est):** 43.36MM **Privately Held**
**Web:** www.staubli.com
**SIC: 3678** 5063 3841 Electronic connectors;
   Lugs and connectors, electrical; Medical
   instruments and equipment, blood and
   bone work
**HQ:** Staubli Electrical Connectors Ag
   Stockbrunnenrain 8
   Allschwil BL 4123

### (P-12898)
### TE CONNECTIVITY CORPORATION
300 Constitution Dr, Menlo Park
(94025-1140)
**PHONE**...............................650 361-3333
Jeff Harrison, *Brnch Mgr*
**EMP:** 188
**SALES (corp-wide):** 9.17B **Privately Held**
**Web:** www.te.com
**SIC: 3678** Electronic connectors
**HQ:** Te Connectivity Corporation
   1050 Westlakes Dr
   Berwyn PA 19312
   610 893-9800

## 3678 - Electronic Connectors (P-12899)

**(P-12899)**
**TE CONNECTIVITY CORPORATION**
Deutsch Engnred Intrcnnect Slt
3390 Alex Rd, Oceanside (92058-1319)
PHONE..................760 757-7500
Ken Watkins, *Brnch Mgr*
EMP: 81
SALES (corp-wide): 9.17B **Privately Held**
Web: www.te.com
SIC: 3678 Electronic connectors
HQ: Te Connectivity Corporation
  1050 Westlakes Dr
  Berwyn PA 19312
  610 893-9800

**(P-12900)**
**TE CONNECTIVITY CORPORATION**
Also Called: Raychem Product Division
501 Oakside Ave Side, Redwood City (94063-3800)
PHONE..................650 361-2495
EMP: 53
SALES (corp-wide): 9.17B **Privately Held**
Web: www.te.com
SIC: 3678 Electronic connectors
HQ: Te Connectivity Corporation
  1050 Westlakes Dr
  Berwyn PA 19312
  610 893-9800

**(P-12901)**
**TEKTEST INC**
Also Called: E-Z-Hook Test Products Div
5108 Azusa Canyon Rd, Baldwin Park (91706-1846)
P.O. Box 660729 (91066-0729)
PHONE..................626 446-6175
Phelps M Wood, *Pr*
Beverly Wood, *VP*
EMP: 20 EST: 1970
SALES (est): 2.5MM **Privately Held**
Web: www.e-z-hook.com
SIC: 3678 Electronic connectors

**(P-12902)**
**TIMCO/CAL RF INC**
3910 Royal Ave Ste A, Simi Valley (93063-3270)
PHONE..................805 582-1777
EMP: 20 EST: 1960
SALES (est): 1.72MM **Privately Held**
SIC: 3678 Electronic connectors

**(P-12903)**
**WINCHSTER INTRCNNECT MICRO LLC**
1872 N Case St, Orange (92865-4233)
PHONE..................714 637-7099
Ross Sealfon, *Pr*
Bruce I Billington, *
Thierry Pombart, *
Frank Malczyk Global, *Sls Mgr*
▲ EMP: 113 EST: 1977
SQ FT: 11,000
SALES (est): 23.35MM **Privately Held**
Web: www.winconn.com
SIC: 3678 Electronic connectors
HQ: Winchester Interconnect Corporation
  185 Plains Rd
  Milford CT 06461

## 3679 Electronic Components, Nec

**(P-12904)**
**3Y POWER TECHNOLOGY INC**
80 Bunsen, Irvine (92618-4210)
PHONE..................949 450-0152
Yuan Yu, *Pr*
▲ EMP: 17 EST: 1985
SQ FT: 13,800
SALES (est): 2.64MM **Privately Held**
Web: www.3ypower.com
SIC: 3679 Power supplies, all types: static

**(P-12905)**
**AAVID THERMALLOY LLC**
Also Called: Aavid California Design Center
150 S 1st St Ste 200, San Jose (95113-2611)
PHONE..................408 522-8730
Avijit Goswami, *Pr*
EMP: 31
Web: www.boydcorp.com
SIC: 3679 Electronic circuits
HQ: Boyd Laconia, Llc
  1 Aavid Cir
  Laconia NH 03246
  603 528-3400

**(P-12906)**
**ABRACON**
30332 Esperanza, Rcho Sta Marg (92688-2118)
PHONE..................949 546-8000
EMP: 15 EST: 2019
SALES (est): 2.11MM **Privately Held**
Web: www.abracon.com
SIC: 3679 Electronic components, nec

**(P-12907)**
**ACCRATRONICS SEALS LLC**
Also Called: A T S
2211 Kenmere Ave, Burbank (91504-3493)
PHONE..................818 843-1500
William Fisch, *CEO*
Corby Jones, *
Delbert Jones, *
Deken Jones, *
EMP: 72 EST: 1960
SQ FT: 10,000
SALES (est): 7.99MM **Privately Held**
Web: www.accratronics.com
SIC: 3679 Hermetic seals, for electronic equipment

**(P-12908)**
**ADVANCED WAVEGUIDE TECH**
29 Musick, Irvine (92618-1638)
PHONE..................949 297-3564
Garrett Biele, *Owner*
Garrett Biele, *CEO*
EMP: 30 EST: 2013
SALES (est): 4.05MM **Privately Held**
SIC: 3679 Waveguides and fittings

**(P-12909)**
**AGILE RF INC**
93 Castilian Dr, Santa Barbara (93117-3026)
PHONE..................805 968-5159
Charles A Bischof, *Pr*
Tom Goodwin, *Pr*
EMP: 20 EST: 1999
SQ FT: 6,000
SALES (est): 907.89K **Privately Held**
Web: www.agilerf.com
SIC: 3679 Microwave components

**(P-12910)**
**AHEAD MAGNETICS INC**
Also Called: Aheadtek
6410 Via Del Oro, San Jose (95119-1208)
PHONE..................408 226-9800
Tim Higgins, *Prin*
Ed Soldani, *
▲ EMP: 78 EST: 1987
SQ FT: 32,000
SALES (est): 8.79MM **Privately Held**
Web: www.aheadtek.com
SIC: 3679 Recording and playback heads, magnetic
PA: Huritga International Holding (S) Pte. Ltd.
  10 Anson Road

**(P-12911)**
**ALYN INDUSTRIES INC**
Also Called: Electronic Source Company
16028 Arminta St, Van Nuys (91406)
PHONE..................818 988-7696
Scott J Alyn, *CEO*
▼ EMP: 100 EST: 1994
SALES (est): 22.66MM **Privately Held**
Web: www.electronic-source.com
SIC: 3679 Electronic circuits

**(P-12912)**
**AMERICAN AUDIO COMPONENT INC**
Also Called: AAC
20 Fairbanks Ste 198, Irvine (92618-1673)
PHONE..................909 596-3788
David Plekenpol, *CEO*
Richard Monk, *
Willie Maglonso, *
▲ EMP: 26 EST: 1996
SALES (est): 4.6MM **Privately Held**
SIC: 3679 Transducers, electrical
HQ: Aac Acoustic Technologies (Shenzhen) Co., Ltd.
  Block A, Nanjing University Research Center Shenzhen Branch, No.
  Shenzhen GD 51805

**(P-12913)**
**AMSCO US INC**
15341 Texaco Ave, Paramount (90723-3946)
PHONE..................562 630-0333
Mike Yazdi, *Pr*
EMP: 110 EST: 1998
SALES (est): 4.23MM **Privately Held**
Web: www.amscous.com
SIC: 3679 Harness assemblies, for electronic use: wire or cable

**(P-12914)**
**APEM INC**
Also Called: Ch Products
970 Park Center Dr, Vista (92081-8301)
PHONE..................760 598-2518
Peter Brouilette, *Pr*
EMP: 81
Web: www.chproducts.com
SIC: 3679 3577 Electronic switches; Computer peripheral equipment, nec
HQ: Apem, Inc.
  970 Park Center Dr
  Vista CA 92081

**(P-12915)**
**APPLIED THIN-FILM PRODUCTS**
3439 Edison Way, Fremont (94538-6179)
PHONE..................510 661-4287
David Adams, *Brnch Mgr*
EMP: 16
Web: www.thinfilm.com
SIC: 3679 Microwave components
PA: Applied Thin-Film Products
  3620 Yale Way

**(P-12916)**
**ARCH MEDICAL SOLUTIONS - SONORA LLC**
Also Called: Mmi Sonora
20555 N Sunshine Rd, Sonora (95370-8905)
PHONE..................209 533-1033
EMP: 51 EST: 1980
SALES (est): 5.37MM **Privately Held**
Web: www.archglobalprecision.com
SIC: 3679 3728 3845 Electronic circuits; Aircraft parts and equipment, nec; Electromedical apparatus

**(P-12917)**
**ASTRO SEAL INC**
827 Palmyrita Ave Ste B, Riverside (92507-1820)
PHONE..................951 787-6670
Michael Hammer, *Pr*
Roger Hammer, *
Karen Upfold, *
▲ EMP: 34 EST: 1964
SQ FT: 42,000
SALES (est): 4.75MM **Privately Held**
Web: www.astroseal.com
SIC: 3679 3678 Hermetic seals, for electronic equipment; Electronic connectors

**(P-12918)**
**AVR GLOBAL TECHNOLOGIES INC (PA)**
Also Called: Avr Global Tech
500 La Terraza Blvd Ste 150, Escondido (92025-3876)
P.O. Box 3814 (92629-8814)
PHONE..................949 391-1180
Andy Bowman, *CEO*
Andy Bowman, *Pr*
Val Pontes, *Treas*
EMP: 197 EST: 2016
SALES (est): 4.79MM
SALES (corp-wide): 4.79MM **Privately Held**
Web: www.avrglobaltech.com
SIC: 3679 3714 5065 5063 Harness assemblies, for electronic use: wire or cable ; Automotive wiring harness sets; Electronic parts and equipment, nec; Wire and cable

**(P-12919)**
**AZ DISPLAYS INC**
2410 Birch St, Vista (92081-8472)
PHONE..................949 831-5000
Reiner Moegling, *Pr*
▲ EMP: 50 EST: 1996
SALES (est): 21.22MM **Privately Held**
Web: www.azdisplays.com
SIC: 3679 Liquid crystal displays (LCD)
HQ: American Zettler Inc.
  2410 Birch St
  Vista CA 92081
  949 831-5000

**(P-12920)**
**B & G ELECTRONIC ASSEMBLY INC**
10350 Regis Ct, Rancho Cucamonga (91730-3055)
PHONE..................909 608-2077
Robert M Odell, *CEO*
Lillian Odell, *VP*
EMP: 18 EST: 1998
SQ FT: 8,900
SALES (est): 4.55MM **Privately Held**

## PRODUCTS & SERVICES SECTION
### 3679 - Electronic Components, Nec (P-12942)

Web: www.bgelectronic.com
SIC: 3679 Harness assemblies, for electronic use: wire or cable

**(P-12921)**
**BASIC ELECTRONICS INC**
11371 Monarch St, Garden Grove (92841-1406)
PHONE..............................714 530-2400
Nancy Balzano, Pr
Al Balzano, *
EMP: 27 EST: 1967
SQ FT: 20,000
SALES (est): 4.3MM Privately Held
Web: www.basicelectronicsinc.com
SIC: 3679 3672 3613 Electronic circuits; Printed circuit boards; Switchgear and switchboard apparatus

**(P-12922)**
**BENTEK CORPORATION**
Also Called: Bentek Solar
1991 Senter Rd, San Jose (95112-2631)
PHONE..............................408 954-9600
Mitchell Schoch, Pr
▲ EMP: 100 EST: 2005
SALES (est): 37.79MM Privately Held
Web: www.bentek.com
SIC: 3679 Electronic circuits

**(P-12923)**
**BI TECHNOLOGIES CORPORATION (HQ)**
Also Called: TT Electronics
120 S State College Blvd Ste 175, Brea (92821-5834)
PHONE..............................714 447-2300
▲ EMP: 260 EST: 1984
SALES (est): 64MM
SALES (corp-wide): 765.19MM Privately Held
Web: www.bitechnologies.com
SIC: 3679 5065 8711 Electronic circuits; Electronic parts and equipment, nec; Engineering services
PA: Tt Electronics Plc
   4th Floor St. Andrews House
   193 282-5300

**(P-12924)**
**BI-SEARCH INTERNATIONAL INC**
17550 Gillette Ave, Irvine (92614-5610)
PHONE..............................714 258-4500
Kevin Kim, Pr
◆ EMP: 40 EST: 1996
SQ FT: 45,000
SALES (est): 68.34MM Privately Held
Web: www.bisearch.com
SIC: 3679 Liquid crystal displays (LCD)

**(P-12925)**
**BIVAR INC**
Also Called: Bivar
4 Thomas, Irvine (92618-2593)
PHONE..............................949 951-8808
Thomas Silber, CEO
▲ EMP: 40 EST: 1965
SQ FT: 26,040
SALES (est): 6.78MM Privately Held
Web: www.bivar.com
SIC: 3679 Electronic circuits

**(P-12926)**
**BRANDT ELECTRONICS INC**
1971 Tarob Ct, Milpitas (95035-6825)
P.O. Box 3255 (95055-3255)
PHONE..............................408 240-0004
Phillip D Duvall, CEO

Steve Hall, *
EMP: 40 EST: 1979
SQ FT: 12,000
SALES (est): 5.3MM Privately Held
Web: www.brandtelectronics.com
SIC: 3679 Power supplies, all types: static

**(P-12927)**
**BREE ENGINEERING CORP**
1750 Marilyn Ln, San Marcos (92069-9780)
PHONE..............................760 510-4950
Dan Bree, Pr
EMP: 30 EST: 1999
SALES (est): 2.51MM Privately Held
Web: www.breeeng.com
SIC: 3679 Electronic circuits

**(P-12928)**
**C & S ASSEMBLY INC**
1150 N Armando St, Anaheim (92806-2609)
PHONE..............................866 779-8939
Sandra A Foley, Pr
Sandra A Foley, Pr
Christopher Foley, VP
EMP: 17 EST: 1997
SQ FT: 12,000
SALES (est): 4.65MM Privately Held
Web: www.cnsassembly.com
SIC: 3679 5063 Harness assemblies, for electronic use: wire or cable; Electronic wire and cable

**(P-12929)**
**CAES MISSION SYSTEMS LLC**
4820 Eastgate Mall Ste 200, San Diego (92121-1993)
PHONE..............................858 812-7300
EMP: 32
SALES (corp-wide): 4.59B Privately Held
Web: www.caes.com
SIC: 3679 Microwave components
HQ: Caes Mission Systems Llc
   3061 Industry Dr
   Lancaster PA 17603
   717 397-2777

**(P-12930)**
**CAL SOUTHERN BRAIDING INC**
Also Called: Scb Division
7450 Scout Ave, Bell Gardens (90201-4932)
PHONE..............................562 927-5531
Neal Castleman, Pr
EMP: 60 EST: 1976
SQ FT: 38,000
SALES (est): 5.41MM
SALES (corp-wide): 112.69MM Privately Held
SIC: 3679 Harness assemblies, for electronic use: wire or cable
PA: Dcx-Chol Enterprises, Inc.
   12831 S Figueroa St
   310 516-1692

**(P-12931)**
**CALI RESOURCES INC**
Also Called: Brimes International
2310 Michael Faraday Dr, San Diego (92154)
PHONE..............................619 661-5741
Carlos Kelvin, CEO
◆ EMP: 45 EST: 1995
SQ FT: 30,000
SALES (est): 7.29MM Privately Held
Web: www.caliresources.com
SIC: 3679 Electronic circuits

**(P-12932)**
**CARROS SENSORS AMERICAS LLC**
Also Called: Carros Americas, Inc.
2945 Townsgate Rd Ste 200, Westlake Village (91361-5866)
PHONE..............................805 267-7176
Eric Pilaud, Pr
Ben Watt, *
EMP: 150 EST: 2015
SALES (est): 6.96MM
SALES (corp-wide): 675.45K Privately Held
Web: www.crouzet.com
SIC: 3679 3577 Electronic circuits; Encoders, computer peripheral equipment
HQ: Lbo France Gestion
   148 Rue De L Universite
   Paris IDF 75007

**(P-12933)**
**CCM ASSEMBLY & MFG INC (PA)**
2275 Michael Faraday Dr Ste 6, San Diego (92154-7927)
PHONE..............................760 560-1310
Erika Marcela Murillo, CEO
Sergio Murillo, Pr
John Savage, *
▲ EMP: 28 EST: 1997
SQ FT: 10,000
SALES (est): 9.39MM
SALES (corp-wide): 9.39MM Privately Held
Web: www.ccmassembly.com
SIC: 3679 3441 Harness assemblies, for electronic use: wire or cable; Fabricated structural metal

**(P-12934)**
**CELESTICA LLC**
Also Called: D&H Manufacturing
49235 Milmont Dr, Fremont (94538-7349)
PHONE..............................510 770-5100
Mark Morris, Brnch Mgr
EMP: 200
SALES (corp-wide): 7.96B Privately Held
Web: www.celestica.com
SIC: 3679 Electronic circuits
HQ: Celestica Llc
   400 Glleria Pkwy Ste 1500
   Atlanta GA 30339

**(P-12935)**
**CELLINK CORPORATION (PA)**
610 Quarry Rd, San Carlos (94070-6224)
PHONE..............................650 799-3018
Kevin Coakley, CEO
EMP: 54 EST: 2012
SALES (est): 29.91MM
SALES (corp-wide): 29.91MM Privately Held
Web: www.cellinkcorp.com
SIC: 3679 Electronic circuits

**(P-12936)**
**CERNEX INC**
1710 Zanker Rd Ste 103, San Jose (95112-4219)
PHONE..............................408 541-9226
Chanh Huynh, Pr
▲ EMP: 18 EST: 1988
SQ FT: 5,200
SALES (est): 3.02MM Privately Held
Web: www.cernex.com
SIC: 3679 Microwave components

**(P-12937)**
**CIAO WIRELESS INC**
Also Called: Ciao
4000 Via Pescador, Camarillo (93012-5044)

PHONE..............................805 389-3224
Glen Wasylewski, Pr
▼ EMP: 70 EST: 2003
SQ FT: 42,000
SALES (est): 9.85MM Privately Held
Web: www.ciaowireless.com
SIC: 3679 3699 Microwave components; Pulse amplifiers

**(P-12938)**
**CICON ENGINEERING INC (PA)**
6633 Odessa Ave, Van Nuys (91406-5746)
PHONE..............................818 909-6060
Ali Kolahi, Pr
Laurie Kertenian, *
Hamid Kolahi, Stockholder*
Farah Kolahi, Stockholder*
Abdi Kolahi, *
EMP: 169 EST: 1990
SQ FT: 50,000
SALES (est): 20.17MM
SALES (corp-wide): 20.17MM Privately Held
Web: www.cicon.com
SIC: 3679 Harness assemblies, for electronic use: wire or cable

**(P-12939)**
**CITALA US INC**
1277 Reamwood Ave, Sunnyvale (94089-2234)
PHONE..............................408 745-8500
▲ EMP: 27
SIC: 3679 Electronic switches

**(P-12940)**
**CKS SOLUTION INCORPORATED**
556 Vanguard Way Ste C, Brea (92821-3929)
PHONE..............................714 292-6307
Patrick Park, Mgr
EMP: 34
SALES (corp-wide): 5.49MM Privately Held
Web: www.ckssolution.com
SIC: 3679 Liquid crystal displays (LCD)
PA: Cks Solution Incorporated
   4293 Muhlhauser Rd
   513 947-1277

**(P-12941)**
**CLARY CORPORATION**
150 E Huntington Dr, Monrovia (91016-3415)
PHONE..............................626 359-4486
John G Clary, Ch Bd
Donald G Ash, *
EMP: 40 EST: 1939
SQ FT: 26,000
SALES (est): 9.96MM Privately Held
Web: www.clary.com
SIC: 3679 3612 Electronic loads and power supplies; Transformers, except electric

**(P-12942)**
**COASTAL COMPONENT INDS INC**
Also Called: C C I
133 E Bristol Ln, Orange (92865-2749)
PHONE..............................714 685-6677
Mark Coe, Pr
Ronna Coe, Ch
Donald B Coe, CEO
Diana Romero, VP
EMP: 20 EST: 1990
SQ FT: 6,027
SALES (est): 4.97MM Privately Held
Web: www.ccicoastal.com

## 3679 - Electronic Components, Nec (P-12943)

SIC: **3679** 5065 3643 3678 Electronic circuits; Electronic parts and equipment, nec; Electric connectors; Electronic connectors

**(P-12943)**
### COHERENT ASIA INC (HQ)
5100 Patrick Henry Dr, Santa Clara (95054-1112)
PHONE.................................408 764-4000
Helene Simonet, *Ex VP*
**EMP:** 105 **EST:** 2006
**SALES (est):** 34.95MM
**SALES (corp-wide):** 4.71B **Publicly Held**
Web: www.coherent.com
SIC: **3679** 3827 Electronic crystals; Optical instruments and lenses
PA: Coherent Corp.
375 Saxonburg Blvd
724 352-4455

**(P-12944)**
### COMPASS COMPONENTS INC (PA)
Also Called: Compass Manufacturing Service
48133 Warm Springs Blvd, Fremont (94539-7498)
PHONE.................................510 656-4700
Jack Maxwell, *CEO*
Bob Duplantier, *
**EMP:** 110 **EST:** 1979
**SQ FT:** 36,000
**SALES (est):** 41.35MM
**SALES (corp-wide):** 41.35MM **Privately Held**
Web: www.compassmade.com
SIC: **3679** 5065 Harness assemblies, for electronic use: wire or cable; Electronic parts

**(P-12945)**
### COOPER INTERCONNECT INC
13039 Crossroads Pkwy S, City Of Industry (91746-3406)
PHONE.................................617 389-7080
Preston Shultz, *CEO*
**EMP:** 80
SIC: **3679** 3643 3812 3672 Harness assemblies, for electronic use: wire or cable; Current-carrying wiring services; Search and navigation equipment; Printed circuit boards
HQ: Cooper Interconnect, Inc.
750 W Ventura Blvd
Camarillo CA 93010
805 484-0543

**(P-12946)**
### CORELIS INC
13100 Alondra Blvd Ste 102, Cerritos (90703-2262)
PHONE.................................562 926-6727
George Lafever, *CEO*
**EMP:** 25 **EST:** 1991
**SQ FT:** 15,000
**SALES (est):** 6.72MM **Privately Held**
Web: www.corelis.com
SIC: **3679** Electronic circuits
HQ: Electronic Warfare Associates, Inc.
13873 Pk Ctr Rd Ste 500s
Herndon VA 20171
703 904-5700

**(P-12947)**
### CPI INTERNATIONAL HOLDING CORP
811 Hansen Way, Palo Alto (94304-1031)
PHONE.................................650 846-2900
O Joe Caldarelli, *CEO*
John Overstreet, *VP*
Robert A Fickett, *Pr*
John R Beighley, *VP*
Andrew E Tafler, *VP*
**EMP:** 16 **EST:** 2011
**SALES (est):** 1.65MM **Privately Held**
Web: www.cpii.com
SIC: **3679** Electronic circuits

**(P-12948)**
### CRANE CO
Also Called: Crane Valves Services Division
3948 Teal Ct, Benicia (94510-1202)
PHONE.................................707 748-7166
Evan Russell, *Mgr*
**EMP:** 32
**SALES (corp-wide):** 3.37B **Privately Held**
Web: www.craneco.com
SIC: **3679** Oscillators
HQ: Redco Corporation
100 1st Stamford Pl
Stamford CT 06902
203 363-7300

**(P-12949)**
### CRUCIAL POWER PRODUCTS
14000 S Broadway, Los Angeles (90061-1018)
PHONE.................................323 721-5017
Abbie Gougerchian, *Prin*
**EMP:** 17 **EST:** 1992
**SALES (est):** 567.58K **Privately Held**
Web: www.crucialpower.com
SIC: **3679** Electronic circuits

**(P-12950)**
### CSR TECHNOLOGY INC (DH)
1060 Rincon Cir, San Jose (95131-1325)
PHONE.................................408 523-6500
Brett Gladden, *CEO*
Ron Mackintosh, *Ch*
Chris Ladas, *Ex VP*
▲ **EMP:** 20 **EST:** 1995
**SALES (est):** 19.82MM
**SALES (corp-wide):** 38.96B **Publicly Held**
SIC: **3679** 3812 3674 Electronic circuits; Search and navigation equipment; Semiconductors and related devices
HQ: Qualcomm Technologies International, Ltd.
Churchill House
Cambridge CAMBS CB4 0
289 046-3140

**(P-12951)**
### CUSTOM SENSORS & TECH INC
2475 Paseo De Las Americas, San Diego (92154-7255)
PHONE.................................805 716-0322
Carlos Borboa, *Supervisor*
**EMP:** 293
**SALES (corp-wide):** 4.05B **Privately Held**
Web: www.cstsensors.com
SIC: **3679** Electronic circuits
HQ: Custom Sensors & Technologies, Inc.
1461 Lawrence Dr
Thousand Oaks CA 91320
805 716-0322

**(P-12952)**
### CUSTOM SENSORS & TECH INC (HQ)
Also Called: C S T
1461 Lawrence Dr, Thousand Oaks (91320-1303)
PHONE.................................805 716-0322
Martha Sullivan, *CEO*
▲ **EMP:** 801 **EST:** 1997
**SALES (est):** 470.66MM
**SALES (corp-wide):** 4.05B **Privately Held**
Web: www.cstsensors.com
SIC: **3679** Electronic circuits
PA: Sensata Technologies Holding Plc
Interface House
179 325-0031

**(P-12953)**
### DAICO INDUSTRIES INC
1070 E 233rd St, Carson (90745-6205)
PHONE.................................310 507-3242
**EMP:** 90 **EST:** 1965
**SALES (est):** 15.1MM **Privately Held**
Web: www.daico.com
SIC: **3679** 3674 Microwave components; Semiconductors and related devices

**(P-12954)**
### DAVBERTA INC
181 E Tasman Dr Ste 20, San Jose (95134-3389)
PHONE.................................408 453-3272
**EMP:** 65
SIC: **3679** 3643 3824 Harness assemblies, for electronic use: wire or cable; Current-carrying wiring services; Mechanical and electromechanical counters and devices

**(P-12955)**
### DCX-CHOL ENTERPRISES INC (PA)
12831 S Figueroa St, Los Angeles (90061-1157)
PHONE.................................310 516-1692
Neal Castleman, *Pr*
Brian Gamberg, *
Garret Hoffman, *
▲ **EMP:** 80 **EST:** 1997
**SQ FT:** 50,000
**SALES (est):** 112.69MM
**SALES (corp-wide):** 112.69MM **Privately Held**
Web: www.dcxchol.com
SIC: **3679** Electronic circuits

**(P-12956)**
### DE ANZA MANUFACTURING SVCS INC
1271 Reamwood Ave, Sunnyvale (94089-2275)
PHONE.................................408 734-2020
Art Takahara, *Pr*
Michael Takahara, *
▼ **EMP:** 60 **EST:** 1978
**SQ FT:** 24,000
**SALES (est):** 4.8MM **Privately Held**
Web: www.deanzamfg.com
SIC: **3679** 3643 Harness assemblies, for electronic use: wire or cable; Current-carrying wiring services

**(P-12957)**
### DELTA GROUP ELECTRONICS INC
Also Called: Delta Group Electronics
10180 Scripps Ranch Blvd, San Diego (92131-1234)
PHONE.................................858 569-1681
Bill West, *Genl Mgr*
**EMP:** 55
**SALES (corp-wide):** 81.36MM **Privately Held**
Web: www.deltagroupinc.com
SIC: **3679** 3577 3672 Electronic circuits; Computer peripheral equipment, nec; Printed circuit boards
PA: Delta Group Electronics, Inc.
4521a Osuna Rd Ne
505 883-7674

**(P-12958)**
### DELTA MICROWAVE LLC
300 Del Norte Blvd, Oxnard (93030-7217)
PHONE.................................805 751-1100
▼ **EMP:** 66
Web: www.mrcy.com
SIC: **3679** Microwave components

**(P-12959)**
### DENRON INC
2135 Ringwood Ave, San Jose (95131-1725)
P.O. Box 612797 (95161-2797)
PHONE.................................408 435-8588
Don Mills, *VP Opers*
**EMP:** 400 **EST:** 1980
**SQ FT:** 40,000
**SALES (est):** 1.81MM **Privately Held**
SIC: **3679** Harness assemblies, for electronic use: wire or cable

**(P-12960)**
### DICON FIBEROPTICS INC
Also Called: Kessil
1689 Regatta Blvd, Richmond (94804-7438)
PHONE.................................510 620-5000
Ho-shang Lee, *Pr*
Doctor Gilles Corcos, *Ch Bd*
Robert Schleicher, *
Gilles Corcos, *Ch Bd*
Dunson Cheng, *
▲ **EMP:** 400 **EST:** 1986
**SQ FT:** 202,000
**SALES (est):** 31.3MM **Privately Held**
Web: www.diconfiberoptics.com
SIC: **3679** 3827 Electronic switches; Optical instruments and lenses

**(P-12961)**
### DIGITAL POWER CORPORATION (HQ)
Also Called: Digital Power
1635 S Main St, Milpitas (95035)
PHONE.................................510 657-2635
Amos Kohn, *Interim Chief Financial Officer*
Milton C Ault Iii, *Ex Ch Bd*
Amos Kohn, *Pr*
William B Horne, *CFO*
▲ **EMP:** 22 **EST:** 1969
**SALES (est):** 26.51MM
**SALES (corp-wide):** 156.44MM **Publicly Held**
Web: www.digipwr.com
SIC: **3679** Electronic switches
PA: Ault Alliance, Inc.
11411 Sthern Hghlnds Pkwy
949 444-5464

**(P-12962)**
### DJ GREY COMPANY INC
455 Allan Ct, Healdsburg (95448-4802)
PHONE.................................707 431-2779
Marla J Grey, *Pr*
Michele Perry, *VP*
**EMP:** 15 **EST:** 1978
**SQ FT:** 4,500
**SALES (est):** 2.18MM **Privately Held**
Web: www.djgreycable.com
SIC: **3679** Electronic circuits

**(P-12963)**
### DREAMCTCHERS EMPWERMENT NETWRK
2201 Tuolumne St, Vallejo (94589-2524)
PHONE.................................707 558-1775
George Lytal, *BD*
George Lytal, *Ch Bd*
**EMP:** 25 **EST:** 2012

PRODUCTS & SERVICES SECTION  
3679 - Electronic Components, Nec (P-12984)

SALES (est): 1.12MM **Privately Held**
Web: www.dreamcatchersnetwork.org
SIC: **3679** Voice controls

**(P-12964)**
### DYNALLOY INC
2801 Mcgaw Ave, Irvine (92614-5835)
PHONE..................................714 436-1206
Wayne Brown, *CEO*
Jess Brown, *VP*
◆ **EMP:** 20 **EST:** 1989
SALES (est): 7.6MM **Privately Held**
Web: www.dynalloy.com
SIC: **3679** 3357 5065 Electronic circuits; Nonferrous wiredrawing and insulating; Electronic parts

**(P-12965)**
### DYTRAN INSTRUMENTS INC
21592 Marilla St, Chatsworth (91311-4137)
PHONE..................................818 700-7818
Benjamin Bryson, *CEO*
Anne Hackney, *
David Cianciosi, *
**EMP:** 194 **EST:** 1980
SQ FT: 8,000
SALES (est): 38.19MM
SALES (corp-wide): 1.81B **Privately Held**
Web: www.dytran.com
SIC: **3679** 3829 Transducers, electrical; Measuring and controlling devices, nec
HQ: Spectris Inc.
117 Flanders Rd
Westborough MA 01581
508 768-6400

**(P-12966)**
### ECLIPTEK INC
24422 Avenida De La Carlota Ste 290, Laguna Hills (92653-3648)
PHONE..................................714 433-1200
Cary Rosen, *CEO*
**EMP:** 18 **EST:** 1987
SALES (est): 2.72MM **Privately Held**
Web: www.abracon.com
SIC: **3679** 5065 3825 3677 Electronic crystals; Electronic parts and equipment, nec; Instruments to measure electricity; Electronic coils and transformers

**(P-12967)**
### ELECTRO SWITCH CORP
Also Called: Arga Cntrls A Unit Eltro Swtc
10410 Trademark St, Rancho Cucamonga (91730-5826)
PHONE..................................909 581-0855
Kathy Brown, *Brnch Mgr*
**EMP:** 20
SALES (corp-wide): 39.86MM **Privately Held**
Web: www.digitran-switches.com
SIC: **3679** Transducers, electrical
HQ: Electro Switch Corp.
775 Pleasant St Ste 1
Weymouth MA 02189
781 335-1195

**(P-12968)**
### ELECTRO-TECH PRODUCTS INC
Also Called: Electro-Tech Products
2001 E Gladstone St Ste A, Glendora (91740-5381)
PHONE..................................909 592-1434
Ramzi Bader, *Pr*
▲ **EMP:** 30 **EST:** 1984
SQ FT: 11,000
SALES (est): 2.79MM **Privately Held**
Web: www.etp-inc.com

SIC: **3679** Electronic circuits

**(P-12969)**
### ELECTROCUBE INC (PA)
Also Called: Southern Electronics
3366 Pomona Blvd, Pomona (91768-3234)
PHONE..................................909 595-1821
Langdon Clay Parrill, *Pr*
Donald Duquette, *
Scott Wieland, *
◆ **EMP:** 47 **EST:** 1961
SQ FT: 27,000
SALES (est): 9.95MM
SALES (corp-wide): 9.95MM **Privately Held**
Web: www.electrocube.com
SIC: **3679** 3675 Electronic circuits; Electronic capacitors

**(P-12970)**
### EMCO HIGH VOLTAGE CORPORATION
1 Emco Ct, Sutter Creek (95685-9590)
PHONE..................................209 267-1630
**EMP:** 60
SIC: **3679** Static power supply converters for electronic applications

**(P-12971)**
### EMERGING DISPLAY TECHNOLOGIES CORPORATION (HQ)
Also Called: Edt
390 Goddard, Irvine (92618-4601)
PHONE..................................949 296-8300
▲ **EMP:** 15 **EST:** 1994
SALES (est): 41.21MM **Privately Held**
Web: www.edtc.com
SIC: **3679** Liquid crystal displays (LCD)
PA: Emerging Display Technologies Corp.
5, Central 1st Rd., K.E.P.Z.

**(P-12972)**
### EMI SOLUTIONS LLC ✪
13805 Alton Pkwy Ste B, Irvine (92618-1690)
PHONE..................................949 206-9960
Julie Ydens, *Admn*
Julie Ydens, *Ch Bd*
Bob Ydens, *Pr*
▼ **EMP:** 20 **EST:** 2023
SQ FT: 6,500
SALES (est): 2.76MM **Privately Held**
Web: www.4emi.com
SIC: **3679** Electronic circuits

**(P-12973)**
### ENSURGE MICROPOWER INC
Also Called: NFC Innovation Center
2581 Junction Ave, San Jose (95134-1923)
PHONE..................................408 503-7300
Kevin Dale Barber, *CEO*
**EMP:** 70 **EST:** 2011
SQ FT: 61,000
SALES (est): 18.6MM **Privately Held**
Web: www.ensurge.com
SIC: **3679** Electronic circuits
PA: Ensurge Micropower Asa
House Of Business Fridtjof Nansens Plass 4

**(P-12974)**
### EXPRESS MANUFACTURING INC (PA)
3519 W Warner Ave, Santa Ana (92704-5214)
PHONE..................................714 979-2228
Chauk Pan Chin, *Pr*
Tony Chin, *

Catherine Lee Chin, *
C M Chin, *
▲ **EMP:** 320 **EST:** 1982
SQ FT: 96,000
SALES (est): 96.84MM
SALES (corp-wide): 96.84MM **Privately Held**
Web: www.eminc.com
SIC: **3679** 3672 Electronic circuits; Printed circuit boards

**(P-12975)**
### FABRI-TECH COMPONENTS INC
576 Sycamore Dr, Milpitas (95035-7412)
PHONE..................................510 249-2000
Terry Anest, *Pr*
Teo Seow Phong, *CEO*
**EMP:** 15 **EST:** 1998
SALES (est): 5.7MM **Privately Held**
Web: www.fabritech.net
SIC: **3679** Electronic circuits
PA: Fabri-Tech Components (S) Pte Ltd
3 Tuas Basin Link

**(P-12976)**
### FABRICAST INC (PA)
2517 Seaman Ave, South El Monte (91733-1927)
P.O. Box 3176 (91733-0176)
PHONE..................................626 443-3247
H Phelps Wood Iii, *Pr*
**EMP:** 21 **EST:** 1960
SQ FT: 6,250
SALES (est): 3.18MM
SALES (corp-wide): 3.18MM **Privately Held**
Web: www.fabricast.com
SIC: **3679** 3621 Electronic circuits; Motors and generators

**(P-12977)**
### FASTRAK MANUFACTURING SVCS INC
Also Called: Fastrak Manufacturing
1275 Alma Ct, San Jose (95112-5943)
PHONE..................................408 298-6414
Phillip Guzman, *CEO*
Michelle Hilty, *Pr*
**EMP:** 20 **EST:** 1985
SALES (est): 2.69MM **Privately Held**
Web: www.fastrakmfg.com
SIC: **3679** 8711 Harness assemblies, for electronic use: wire or cable; Electrical or electronic engineering

**(P-12978)**
### FEMA ELECTRONICS CORPORATION
22 Corporate Park, Irvine (92606-3112)
PHONE..................................714 825-0140
Bob Cheng, *CEO*
Chinyun Cheng, *
▲ **EMP:** 30 **EST:** 2010
SQ FT: 3,000
SALES (est): 4MM **Privately Held**
Web: www.femacorp.com
SIC: **3679** Electronic crystals

**(P-12979)**
### FLEXTRONICS AP LLC (DH)
6201 America Center Dr, Alviso (95002-2563)
PHONE..................................408 576-7000
Marc A Onetto, *Pr*
▲ **EMP:** 235 **EST:** 1998
SQ FT: 350,000
SALES (est): 58.64K **Privately Held**
Web: www.flex.com

SIC: **3679** 3577 3571 Electronic circuits; Computer peripheral equipment, nec; Electronic computers
HQ: Flextronics Holding Usa, Inc.
2090 Fortune Dr
San Jose CA 95131

**(P-12980)**
### FONG ENGINEERING ENTERPRISE
Also Called: Pierce Magnetics
166 University Pkwy, Pomona (91768-4300)
PHONE..................................909 598-8835
James Fong, *Pr*
Lily Fong, *Sec*
▲ **EMP:** 20 **EST:** 1973
SQ FT: 20,000
SALES (est): 580.61K **Privately Held**
SIC: **3679** Recording and playback heads, magnetic

**(P-12981)**
### FOX ENTERPRISES LLC (HQ)
Also Called: Fox Electronics
24422 Avenida De La Carlota Ste 290, Laguna Hills (92653-3648)
PHONE..................................239 693-0099
Eugene Trefethen, *Pr*
**EMP:** 24 **EST:** 1979
SALES (est): 3.72MM **Privately Held**
SIC: **3679** 5065 Quartz crystals, for electronic application; Electronic parts
PA: Abracon, Llc
5101 Hidden Creek Ln

**(P-12982)**
### GAR ENTERPRISES
Also Called: K.G.S.electronics
1396 W 9th St, Upland (91786-5724)
PHONE..................................909 985-4575
Alex Morales, *Mgr*
**EMP:** 28
SALES (corp-wide): 23.35MM **Privately Held**
Web: www.kgselectronics.com
SIC: **3679** 3621 3577 Electronic loads and power supplies; Motors and generators; Computer peripheral equipment, nec
PA: Gar Enterprises
418 E Live Oak Ave
626 574-1175

**(P-12983)**
### GAVIAL HOLDINGS INC (PA)
Also Called: Gavial Engineering & Mfg
1435 W Mc Coy Lane, Santa Maria (93455-1002)
PHONE..................................805 614-0060
Morgan Maxwell Connor, *CEO*
**EMP:** 15 **EST:** 1981
SQ FT: 24,500
SALES (est): 53.82MM
SALES (corp-wide): 53.82MM **Privately Held**
Web: www.gavial.com
SIC: **3679** 4911 6799 Electronic circuits; Electric services; Investors, nec

**(P-12984)**
### GENERAL POWER SYSTEMS INC
Also Called: General Power Systems
955 E Ball Rd, Anaheim (92805-5916)
PHONE..................................714 956-9321
David Noyes, *Pr*
Frank Castle, *
David Noyes, *Ex VP*
**EMP:** 30 **EST:** 1984
SQ FT: 30,000

---

(PA)=Parent Co (HQ)=Headquarters
✪ = New Business established in last 2 years

# 3679 - Electronic Components, Nec (P-12985)

SALES (est): 1.23MM
SALES (corp-wide): 46.24MM **Privately Held**
SIC: 3679 Power supplies, all types: static
PA: Components Corporation Of America
5950 Berkshire Ln # 1500
214 969-0166

**(P-12985)**
**GIGATERA COMMUNICATIONS**
Also Called: KMW Communications
1413 Vista Del Mar Dr, Fullerton (92831-1124)
PHONE.................714 515-1100
Duk Y Kim, *Ch Bd*
Duk Y Kim, *Pr*
Yeong Kim, *Pr*
Burton Calloway, *
▲ EMP: 65 EST: 1995
SALES (est): 9.16MM **Privately Held**
Web: www.gteracom.com
SIC: 3679 5063 Electronic circuits; Electrical apparatus and equipment
PA: Kmw Inc.
21 Dongtan-Daero 25-Gil

**(P-12986)**
**GLIMMERGLASS NETWORKS INC**
Also Called: Glimmerglass
3945 Freedom Cir Ste 560, Santa Clara (95054-1269)
PHONE.................510 780-1800
EMP: 40
Web: www.glimmerglass.com
SIC: 3679 Electronic loads and power supplies

**(P-12987)**
**GM ASSOCIATES INC**
Also Called: G M Quartz
9824 Kitty Ln, Oakland (94603-1070)
PHONE.................510 430-0806
Melvyn Nutter, *Pr*
Deborah Camp, *
▲ EMP: 58 EST: 1973
SQ FT: 8,000
SALES (est): 8.81MM **Privately Held**
Web: www.gm-quartz.com
SIC: 3679 3229 Quartz crystals, for electronic application; Scientific glassware

**(P-12988)**
**GOOCH & HOUSEGO PALO ALTO LLC (HQ)**
Also Called: Crystal Technology
44247 Nobel Dr, Fremont (94538-3178)
PHONE.................650 856-7911
Mark Batzdorf, *
▲ EMP: 50 EST: 1967
SQ FT: 25,000
SALES (est): 7.82MM
SALES (corp-wide): 187.38MM **Privately Held**
Web: www.gandh.com
SIC: 3679 Electronic crystals
PA: Gooch & Housego Plc
Dowlish Ford
146 025-6440

**(P-12989)**
**GOURMET ELECTRONICS LTD**
1805 Junction Ave, San Jose (95131-2101)
PHONE.................408 467-1100
EMP: 20 EST: 1983
SALES (est): 940.49K **Privately Held**
Web: www.gourmetelectronics.com
SIC: 3679 5065 Harness assemblies, for electronic use: wire or cable; Electronic parts

**(P-12990)**
**GTRAN INC (PA)**
829 Flynn Rd, Camarillo (93012-8702)
PHONE.................805 445-4500
Ray Yu, *Pr*
Deepak Mehrotra, *
Douglas Holmes, *
▲ EMP: 46 EST: 1999
SQ FT: 226,000
SALES (est): 2.62MM
SALES (corp-wide): 2.62MM **Privately Held**
Web: www.gtran.net
SIC: 3679 Electronic circuits

**(P-12991)**
**GUNJOY INC**
22895 Eastpark Dr, Yorba Linda (92887-4653)
PHONE.................714 289-0055
▲ EMP: 26
SIC: 3679 Power supplies, all types: static

**(P-12992)**
**HANNSPREE NORTH AMERICA INC**
13223 Black Mountain Rd, San Diego (92129-2698)
PHONE.................909 992-5025
▲ EMP: 60
SIC: 3679 Liquid crystal displays (LCD)

**(P-12993)**
**HARPER & TWO INC (PA)**
2937 Cherry Ave, Signal Hill (90755-1910)
PHONE.................562 424-3030
Dan Kilstofte, *Pr*
Jim Quilty, *Sec*
EMP: 18 EST: 1987
SALES (est): 2.36MM
SALES (corp-wide): 2.36MM **Privately Held**
Web: www.harperandtwo.com
SIC: 3679 Electronic circuits

**(P-12994)**
**HARWIL PRECISION PRODUCTS**
Also Called: Harwil
541 Kinetic Dr, Oxnard (93030-7923)
PHONE.................805 988-6800
Geoffrey Strand, *Pr*
Cynthia Strand, *
Teresa Bowmar, *
EMP: 35 EST: 1957
SQ FT: 33,000
SALES (est): 4.46MM **Privately Held**
Web: www.harwil.com
SIC: 3679 3625 3823 Electronic circuits; Flow actuated electrical switches; Process control instruments

**(P-12995)**
**HERMETIC SEAL CORPORATION (DH)**
Also Called: Ametek HCC
4232 Temple City Blvd, Rosemead (91770-1592)
PHONE.................626 443-8971
Andrew Goldfarb, *Pr*
EMP: 200 EST: 1945
SQ FT: 36,000
SALES (est): 28.03MM
SALES (corp-wide): 6.6B **Publicly Held**
Web: www.ametekinterconnect.com
SIC: 3679 3469 Hermetic seals, for electronic equipment; Metal stampings, nec
HQ: Hcc Industries Leasing, Inc.
4232 Temple City Blvd
Rosemead CA 91770
626 443-8933

**(P-12996)**
**HTI TURNKEY MANUFACTURING SVCS**
2200 Zanker Rd Ste A, San Jose (95131-1112)
PHONE.................408 955-0807
Mai Linh Tran, *CEO*
Thanah Mai Tran, *Sec*
EMP: 25 EST: 1998
SQ FT: 10,000
SALES (est): 2.48MM **Privately Held**
Web: www.hti9001.com
SIC: 3679 Harness assemblies, for electronic use: wire or cable

**(P-12997)**
**IJ RESEARCH INC**
Also Called: Hermetics Material Solutions
2919 S Tech Center Dr, Santa Ana (92705-5657)
PHONE.................714 546-8522
Rick Yoon, *Pr*
◆ EMP: 35 EST: 1988
SQ FT: 12,500
SALES (est): 3.53MM
SALES (corp-wide): 3.27B **Publicly Held**
Web: www.ijresearch.org
SIC: 3679 Hermetic seals, for electronic equipment
HQ: Superior Technical Ceramics Corporation
600 Industrial Park Rd
Saint Albans VT 05478
802 527-7726

**(P-12998)**
**IMPACT LLC**
7121 Magnolia Ave, Riverside (92504-3805)
PHONE.................714 546-6000
EMP: 28 EST: 1998
SALES (est): 2.66MM **Privately Held**
Web: www.capitolimpact.com
SIC: 3679 3829 Electronic circuits; Measuring and controlling devices, nec

**(P-12999)**
**INFINITE ELECTRONICS INC (HQ)**
Also Called: L-Com
17792 Fitch, Irvine (92614-6020)
PHONE.................949 261-1920
Penny Cotner, *Pr*
David Quinn, *CRO*
Emily Campbell, *CMO*
David Collier, *COO*
Alexander Arrieta, *Chief Human Resource Officer*
EMP: 47 EST: 2007
SQ FT: 40,000
SALES (est): 369.37MM
SALES (corp-wide): 1.84B **Privately Held**
Web: www.infiniteelectronics.com
SIC: 3679 Electronic circuits
PA: Warburg Pincus Llc
450 Lexington Ave
212 878-0600

**(P-13000)**
**INSULATION SOURCES INC (PA)**
Also Called: ICO Rally
2575 E Bayshore Rd, Palo Alto (94303-3210)
PHONE.................650 856-8378
Edwina Cioffi, *CEO*
▲ EMP: 45 EST: 1997
SQ FT: 15,000
SALES (est): 18.46MM
SALES (corp-wide): 18.46MM **Privately Held**
Web: www.icorally.com
SIC: 3679 Electronic circuits

**(P-13001)**
**INTEGRATED MICROWAVE CORP**
Also Called: Imcsd
11353 Sorrento Valley Rd, San Diego (92121-1303)
PHONE.................858 259-2600
John F Anderson, *Pr*
Steven Porter, *CFO*
Robert J Perna, *Sec*
◆ EMP: 85 EST: 1982
SQ FT: 24,142
SALES (est): 20.77MM
SALES (corp-wide): 707.6MM **Publicly Held**
Web: www.knowlescapacitors.com
SIC: 3679 Microwave components
HQ: Knowles Electronics, Llc
1151 Maplewood Dr
Itasca IL 60143
630 250-5100

**(P-13002)**
**INTERCONNECT SOLUTIONS CO LLC**
Also Called: Tri-Tek Electronics
25358 Avenue Stanford, Valencia (91355-1214)
PHONE.................661 295-0020
Tony Lopez, *Brnch Mgr*
EMP: 66
SALES (corp-wide): 49.73MM **Privately Held**
Web: www.interconnectsolutions.com
SIC: 3679 Harness assemblies, for electronic use: wire or cable
PA: Interconnect Solutions Company, Llc
17595 Mt Herrmann St
714 556-7007

**(P-13003)**
**INTERCTIVE DSPLAY SLUTIONS INC**
Also Called: Interactive Display Solutions
490 Wald, Irvine (92618-4638)
PHONE.................949 727-1959
Brian Chung, *Pr*
Paul Kitzerow Senior V Press, *Prin*
Son Park V Press, *Prin*
Danny Lee, *
▲ EMP: 26 EST: 2004
SALES (est): 5.4MM **Privately Held**
Web: www.idsdisplay.com
SIC: 3679 Liquid crystal displays (LCD)

**(P-13004)**
**INTERFACE MASTERS TECH INC**
48430 Lakeview Blvd, Fremont (94538-6532)
PHONE.................408 676-1086
Benjamin Askarinam, *CEO*
Sima Askarinam, *
EMP: 50 EST: 1997
SQ FT: 3,000
SALES (est): 13.42MM **Privately Held**
Web: www.interfacemasters.com
SIC: 3679 3571 Electronic switches; Electronic computers

**(P-13005)**
**INTERLOG CORPORATION**
Also Called: Interlog Construction
1295 N Knollwood Cir, Anaheim (92801-1310)
PHONE.................714 529-7808
Justin H Kwon, *CEO*

## PRODUCTS & SERVICES SECTION
### 3679 - Electronic Components, Nec (P-13027)

▲ EMP: 20 EST: 1989
SALES (est): 4.73MM **Privately Held**
Web: www.interlogcorp.com
SIC: 3679 Electronic circuits

*(P-13006)*
**IQD FREQUENCY PRODUCTS INC**
592 N Tercero Cir, Palm Springs (92262-6243)
PHONE..................................408 250-1435
Neil Floodgate, *Pr*
EMP: 43 EST: 2010
SALES (est): 1.03MM
SALES (corp-wide): 22.17B **Privately Held**
Web: www.iqdfrequencyproducts.com
SIC: 3679 Microwave components
HQ: Iqd Frequency Products Limited
Station Road
Crewkerne TA18
146 027-0200

*(P-13007)*
**ISOLINK INC**
880 Yosemite Way, Milpitas (95035-6360)
PHONE..................................408 946-1968
David Aldrich, *CEO*
Jorge Rosario, *
▲ EMP: 32 EST: 1987
SQ FT: 16,600
SALES (est): 10MM
SALES (corp-wide): 4.77B **Publicly Held**
SIC: 3679 3827 Electronic circuits; Optical instruments and lenses
PA: Skyworks Solutions, Inc.
5260 California Ave
949 231-3000

*(P-13008)*
**J L COOPER ELECTRONICS INC**
Also Called: Jlcooper
142 Arena St, El Segundo (90245-3901)
PHONE..................................310 322-9990
James Loren Cooper, *Pr*
▲ EMP: 44 EST: 1981
SALES (est): 10.5MM **Privately Held**
SIC: 3679 Recording and playback apparatus, including phonograph

*(P-13009)*
**J&M MANUFACTURING INC**
430 Aaron St, Cotati (94931-3016)
P.O. Box 2435 (94927-2435)
PHONE..................................707 795-8223
James O Judd Junior, *Pr*
Paul L Matthias, *
▲ EMP: 34 EST: 1984
SQ FT: 25,000
SALES (est): 2.96MM **Privately Held**
Web: www.jmmfg.com
SIC: 3679 3444 Electronic circuits; Metal housings, enclosures, casings, and other containers

*(P-13010)*
**JANCO CORPORATION**
Also Called: Esterline Mason
13955 Balboa Blvd, Rancho Cascades (91342-1084)
P.O. Box 3038 (91508-3038)
PHONE..................................818 361-3366
▼ EMP: 120 EST: 1947
SALES (est): 24.75MM
SALES (corp-wide): 7.94B **Publicly Held**
Web: www.esterline.com
SIC: 3679 3825 3643 5088 Electronic switches; Shunts, electrical; Bus bars (electrical conductors); Aircraft and parts, nec
HQ: Esterline Technologies Corp
1350 Euclid Ave Ste 1600
Cleveland OH 44114
216 706-2960

*(P-13011)*
**JASPER ELECTRONICS**
1580 N Kellogg Dr, Anaheim (92807-1902)
PHONE..................................714 917-0749
Robert Nishimoto, *CEO*
Hiroshi Tango, *
◆ EMP: 30 EST: 1995
SQ FT: 17,000
SALES (est): 4.62MM **Privately Held**
Web: www.jasperelectronics.com
SIC: 3679 Electronic loads and power supplies

*(P-13012)*
**JAVAD EMS INC**
900 Rock Ave, San Jose (95131-1615)
PHONE..................................408 770-1700
Javad Ashjaee, *Pr*
Gary Walker, *
Pam Walke, *
Linda Bezoni, *
Leigh Miller, *Prin*
▲ EMP: 95 EST: 2009
SALES (est): 16.47MM **Privately Held**
Web: www.javad.com
SIC: 3679 Electronic circuits

*(P-13013)*
**JAXX MANUFACTURING INC**
Also Called: Craig Kackert Design Tech
1912 Angus Ave, Simi Valley (93063-3494)
PHONE..................................805 526-4979
Greg Liu, *Pr*
Veronica Liu, *
EMP: 45 EST: 2001
SALES (est): 3.39MM **Privately Held**
Web: www.jaxxmfg.com
SIC: 3679 Electronic circuits

*(P-13014)*
**JAYCO/MMI INC**
1351 Pico St, Corona (92881-3373)
PHONE..................................951 738-2000
Shaila Mistry, *Pr*
Hemant Mistry, *
EMP: 42 EST: 1992
SQ FT: 24,000
SALES (est): 1.14MM **Privately Held**
Web: www.jaycopanels.com
SIC: 3679 5065 3577 2759 Electronic circuits; Electronic parts and equipment, nec; Computer peripheral equipment, nec; Commercial printing, nec

*(P-13015)*
**JIC INDUSTRIAL CO INC**
978 Hanson Ct, Milpitas (95035-3165)
PHONE..................................408 935-9880
Frank Yen, *Pr*
▲ EMP: 22 EST: 1988
SALES (est): 499.97K **Privately Held**
Web: www.jicusa.com
SIC: 3679 3678 3357 Electronic circuits; Electronic connectors; Nonferrous wiredrawing and insulating

*(P-13016)*
**KAVLICO CORPORATION (DH)**
1461 Lawrence Dr, Thousand Oaks (91320-1311)
PHONE..................................805 523-2000
Jeffrey J Cote, *CEO*
Martha Sullivan, *Pr*
▼ EMP: 1390 EST: 1962
SALES (est): 71.54MM
SALES (corp-wide): 4.05B **Privately Held**
Web: www.sensata.com
SIC: 3679 Transducers, electrical
HQ: Custom Sensors & Technologies, Inc.
1461 Lawrence Dr
Thousand Oaks CA 91320
805 716-0322

*(P-13017)*
**KELYTECH CORPORATION**
1482 Gladding Ct, Milpitas (95035-6831)
PHONE..................................408 935-0888
K C Wong, *Pr*
Irene Wong, *
Stanley Chiu, *
Kevin Wong, *
EMP: 40 EST: 1990
SQ FT: 8,500
SALES (est): 4.48MM **Privately Held**
Web: www.kelytech.com
SIC: 3679 Electronic circuits

*(P-13018)*
**KENJITSU USA CORP**
9830 Siempre Viva Rd Ste 14, San Diego (92154-7236)
PHONE..................................619 734-5862
Tien-chen Tsou, *Pr*
▲ EMP: 15 EST: 2008
SQ FT: 2,000
SALES (est): 217.13K **Privately Held**
Web: www.kenjitsuusa.com
SIC: 3679 2899 3674 Electronic loads and power supplies; Battery acid; Light emitting diodes

*(P-13019)*
**KG TECHNOLOGIES INC (PA)**
6028 State Farm Dr, Rohnert Park (94928-2133)
PHONE..................................888 513-1874
Erik Zhang, *Pr*
▲ EMP: 18 EST: 2009
SQ FT: 5,600
SALES (est): 2.73MM
SALES (corp-wide): 2.73MM **Privately Held**
Web: www.kgtechnologies.net
SIC: 3679 Electronic circuits

*(P-13020)*
**KRYTAR INC**
1288 Anvilwood Ave, Sunnyvale (94089-2203)
PHONE..................................408 734-5999
Nancy Russell, *CEO*
Douglas Hagan, *Pr*
EMP: 20 EST: 1975
SALES (est): 2.51MM **Privately Held**
Web: www.krytar.com
SIC: 3679 Microwave components

*(P-13021)*
**LANDMARK ELECTRONICS INC**
990 N Amelia Ave, San Dimas (91773-1401)
PHONE..................................626 967-2857
▲ EMP: 23
Web: www.landmarkelectronics.com
SIC: 3679 7699 5088 Static power supply converters for electronic applications; Aircraft flight instrument repair; Aircraft and space vehicle supplies and parts

*(P-13022)*
**LEYDEN ENERGY INC**
1100 La Avenida St Ste A, Mountain View (94043-1453)
PHONE..................................408 776-2779
▲ EMP: 49
SIC: 3679 Electronic loads and power supplies

*(P-13023)*
**LHV POWER CORPORATION (PA)**
10221 Buena Vista Ave Ste A, Santee (92071-4484)
PHONE..................................619 258-7700
James Gevarges, *Pr*
▲ EMP: 25 EST: 1991
SQ FT: 20,000
SALES (est): 4.8MM **Privately Held**
Web: www.lhvpower.com
SIC: 3679 Power supplies, all types: static

*(P-13024)*
**LIMINAL INSIGHTS INC**
1175 Park Ave, Emeryville (94608-3631)
PHONE..................................310 702-5803
Andrew Hsieh, *CEO*
Andrew Hsieh, *Pt*
James Carrington, *
Daniel Steingart, *
Barry Van Tassell, *
EMP: 45 EST: 2015
SALES (est): 10.22MM **Privately Held**
Web: www.liminalinsights.com
SIC: 3679 3823 3826 3829 Electronic circuits; Industrial process measurement equipment; Analytical instruments; Stress, strain, and flaw detecting/measuring equipment

*(P-13025)*
**LUCERO CABLES INC**
193 Stauffer Blvd, San Jose (95125-1042)
PHONE..................................408 498-6001
Madeline Eliasnia, *CEO*
Art Eliasnia, *Ch*
Surendra Gupta, *Pr*
Serjik Avanes, *VP*
Iraj Pessian, *Treas*
▲ EMP: 110 EST: 1978
SQ FT: 50,000
SALES (est): 5.15MM **Privately Held**
Web: www.luceromfg.com
SIC: 3679 3571 Harness assemblies, for electronic use: wire or cable; Electronic computers

*(P-13026)*
**LUCIX CORPORATION (HQ)**
Also Called: Lucix
800 Avenida Acaso Ste E, Camarillo (93012-8758)
PHONE..................................805 987-6645
Mark Shahriary, *Pr*
Cheryl Johnson, *
D Ick Fanucchi, *
▲ EMP: 83 EST: 1999
SQ FT: 48,000
SALES (est): 48.27MM **Publicly Held**
Web: www.lucix.com
SIC: 3679 8731 Microwave components; Commercial physical research
PA: Heico Corporation
3000 Taft St

*(P-13027)*
**M2 ANTENNA SYSTEMS INC**
Also Called: Msquared
4402 N Selland Ave, Fresno (93722-4191)
PHONE..................................559 221-2271
Myrna Staal, *Pr*
Mike Staal, *VP*
EMP: 15 EST: 1985
SQ FT: 10,000
SALES (est): 2.52MM **Privately Held**
Web: www.m2inc.com
SIC: 3679 5999 3625 Antennas, receiving; Mobile telephones and equipment; Positioning controls, electric

# 3679 - Electronic Components, Nec (P-13028)

**(P-13028)**
**MAGNETIC CIRCUIT ELEMENTS INC**
Also Called: M C E
1540 Moffett St, Salinas (93905-3351)
PHONE.................................831 757-8752
John S Conklin, *CEO*
Lisa Battaglia, *
**EMP:** 16 **EST:** 1957
**SQ FT:** 11,000
**SALES (est):** 4.29MM **Privately Held**
Web: www.mcemagnetics.com
**SIC: 3679** 3677 Electronic circuits; Electronic coils and transformers

**(P-13029)**
**MAGNETIC DESIGN LABS INC**
1636 E Edinger Ave Ste I, Santa Ana (92705-5020)
PHONE.................................714 558-3355
Abi Kazem, *Prin*
Judith Kazem, *Pr*
Kamran Kazem, *VP*
Judith A Kazem, *CEO*
**EMP:** 15 **EST:** 1985
**SQ FT:** 6,000
**SALES (est):** 2.72MM **Privately Held**
Web: www.magneticdesign.com
**SIC: 3679** 5065 Power supplies, all types: static; Electronic parts and equipment, nec

**(P-13030)**
**MAGNETIC SENSORS CORPORATION**
1365 N Mccan St, Anaheim (92806-1316)
PHONE.................................714 630-8380
Charles Boudakian, *Pr*
Don Payne, *
**EMP:** 43 **EST:** 1983
**SQ FT:** 15,000
**SALES (est):** 8.88MM **Privately Held**
Web: www.magsensors.com
**SIC: 3679** 3677 Transducers, electrical; Coil windings, electronic

**(P-13031)**
**MANUTRONICS INC**
736 S Hillview Dr, Milpitas (95035-5455)
PHONE.................................408 262-6579
Cuong Tran, *CEO*
**EMP:** 16 **EST:** 2013
**SALES (est):** 2.35MM **Privately Held**
Web: www.manutronics.net
**SIC: 3679** Electronic circuits

**(P-13032)**
**MAPLE IMAGING LLC (HQ)**
1049 Camino Dos Rios, Thousand Oaks (91360-2362)
PHONE.................................805 373-4545
Aldo Pichelli, *Pr*
**EMP:** 28 **EST:** 2019
**SALES (est):** 1.55MM
**SALES (corp-wide):** 5.64B **Publicly Held**
**SIC: 3679** Electronic circuits
**PA:** Teledyne Technologies Inc
1049 Camino Dos Rios
805 373-4545

**(P-13033)**
**MAXAR SPACE LLC**
3825 Fabian Way, Palo Alto (94303-4604)
PHONE.................................650 852-4000
**EMP:** 234 **EST:** 1961
**SALES (est):** 42.37MM
**SALES (corp-wide):** 1.77B **Publicly Held**
Web: www.maxar.com
**SIC: 3679** Antennas, satellite: household use
**PA:** Maxar Technologies Inc.
1300 W 120th Ave
303 684-2207

**(P-13034)**
**MERCURY LLC - RF INTEGRATED SOLUTIONS**
1000 Avenida Acaso, Camarillo (93012-8712)
PHONE.................................805 388-1345
▲ **EMP:** 110
**SIC: 3679** 3663 Microwave components; Amplifiers, RF power and IF

**(P-13035)**
**MICRO LAMBDA WIRELESS INC**
46515 Landing Pkwy, Fremont (94538-6421)
PHONE.................................510 770-9221
John Nguyen, *Pr*
Myra Verret, *
David Suddarth, *
**EMP:** 39 **EST:** 1990
**SQ FT:** 19,000
**SALES (est):** 4.87MM **Privately Held**
Web: www.microlambdawireless.com
**SIC: 3679** 5065 3663 Microwave components; Electronic parts and equipment, nec; Radio and t.v. communications equipment

**(P-13036)**
**MICROFABRICA INC**
7911 Haskell Ave, Van Nuys (91406-1909)
PHONE.................................888 964-2763
Eric Miller, *Prin*
Michael Lockard, *Prin*
Uri Frodis, *
Richard Chen, *
Greg Schmitz, *
**EMP:** 50 **EST:** 1999
**SQ FT:** 39,000
**SALES (est):** 23.8MM **Privately Held**
Web: www.microfabrica.com
**SIC: 3679** Electronic circuits

**(P-13037)**
**MICROMETALS INC (PA)**
5615 E La Palma Ave, Anaheim (92807-2109)
PHONE.................................714 970-9400
Richard H Barden, *CEO*
◆ **EMP:** 159 **EST:** 1951
**SQ FT:** 50,000
**SALES (est):** 27MM
**SALES (corp-wide):** 27MM **Privately Held**
Web: www.micrometals.com
**SIC: 3679** Cores, magnetic

**(P-13038)**
**MICROWAVE TECHNOLOGY INC (HQ)**
4268 Solar Way, Fremont (94538-6335)
PHONE.................................510 651-6700
Nathan Zommer, *CEO*
**EMP:** 46 **EST:** 1982
**SQ FT:** 30,800
**SALES (est):** 17.49MM
**SALES (corp-wide):** 29.05MM **Privately Held**
Web: www.mwtinc.com
**SIC: 3679** 3663 Commutators, electronic; Amplifiers, RF power and IF
**PA:** Cml Microsystems Plc
Oval Park
162 187-5500

**(P-13039)**
**MITSUBSHI ELC VSUAL SLTONS AME**
Also Called: Mevsa
10833 Valley View St Ste 300, Cypress (90630-5046)
PHONE.................................800 553-7278
Kenichiro Yamanishi, *Ch*
Tadashi Hiraoka, *
Perry Pappous, *
◆ **EMP:** 150 **EST:** 2011
**SALES (est):** 24.07MM **Privately Held**
Web: www.me-vis.com
**SIC: 3679** Liquid crystal displays (LCD)
**PA:** Mitsubishi Electric Corporation
2-7-3, Marunouchi

**(P-13040)**
**MTI CORPORATION**
Also Called: Material Technology Intl
860 S 19th St, Richmond (94804-3809)
PHONE.................................510 525-3070
Xiao Ping Jiang, *CEO*
Zhao Liu, *Sec*
◆ **EMP:** 43 **EST:** 1995
**SQ FT:** 5,000
**SALES (est):** 4.74MM **Privately Held**
Web: www.mtixtl.com
**SIC: 3679** Electronic crystals

**(P-13041)**
**MUNEKATA AMERICA INC**
2320 Paseo De Las Americas Ste 112, San Diego (92154-7281)
P.O. Box 15929 (92175-5929)
PHONE.................................619 661-8080
Nobumitsu Endo, *CEO*
Masayuki Sato, *
Naoharu Munekata, *
Koji Yanagida, *
▲ **EMP:** 500 **EST:** 1987
**SQ FT:** 700
**SALES (est):** 4.18MM **Privately Held**
Web: www.munekata.co.jp
**SIC: 3679** Electronic circuits
**PA:** Munekata Co.,Ltd.
1-11-1, Horaicho

**(P-13042)**
**MURDOC TECHNOLOGY LLC**
5683 E Fountain Way, Fresno (93727-7813)
PHONE.................................559 497-1580
▲ **EMP:** 40 **EST:** 1999
**SQ FT:** 12,000
**SALES (est):** 4.72MM **Privately Held**
Web: www.murdoc.com
**SIC: 3679** Electronic circuits

**(P-13043)**
**MYNTAHL CORPORATION**
Also Called: East Electronics
48273 Lakeview Blvd, Fremont (94538-6519)
PHONE.................................510 413-0002
Tingyi Xu, *CEO*
▲ **EMP:** 30 **EST:** 1996
**SQ FT:** 7,000
**SALES (est):** 3.39MM **Privately Held**
Web: www.east-elec.com
**SIC: 3679** Electronic circuits

**(P-13044)**
**N D E INC**
Also Called: New Dimension Electronics
3301 Keller St, Santa Clara (95054-2601)
PHONE.................................408 727-3955
Richard Le, *Owner*
Richard Le, *CEO*
**EMP:** 23 **EST:** 1991
**SQ FT:** 6,000
**SALES (est):** 1.95MM **Privately Held**
Web: www.nde-usa.com

**SIC: 3679** Harness assemblies, for electronic use: wire or cable

**(P-13045)**
**NATEL ENGINEERING COMPANY LLC (PA)**
Also Called: Neo Tech
9340 Owensmouth Ave, Chatsworth (91311-6915)
PHONE.................................818 495-8617
Kunal Sharma, *
Laura Siegal, *
Victor Yamauchi, *
John Lowrey, *
▲ **EMP:** 210 **EST:** 1975
**SQ FT:** 200,000
**SALES (est):** 1.43B
**SALES (corp-wide):** 1.43B **Privately Held**
Web: www.neotech.com
**SIC: 3679** 3674 Antennas, receiving; Semiconductors and related devices

**(P-13046)**
**NEONODE INC (PA)**
Also Called: Neonode
2880 Zanker Rd, San Jose (95134-2117)
PHONE.................................408 496-6722
Urban Forssell, *Pr*
Ulf Rosberg, *Ch Bd*
Maria Ek, *VP*
Fredrik Nihlen, *CFO*
**EMP:** 44 **EST:** 1997
**SALES (est):** 5.67MM **Privately Held**
Web: www.webzin.us
**SIC: 3679** 3826 Cryogenic cooling devices for infrared detectors, masers; Infrared analytical instruments

**(P-13047)**
**NEW VISION DISPLAY INC (DH)**
1430 Blue Oaks Blvd Ste 100, Roseville (95747-5156)
PHONE.................................916 786-8111
Jeffrey W Olyniec, *CEO*
Owen Chen, *
Alan M Lefko, *
◆ **EMP:** 28 **EST:** 2012
**SQ FT:** 2,000
**SALES (est):** 20.33MM **Privately Held**
Web: www.newvisiondisplay.com
**SIC: 3679** Liquid crystal displays (LCD)
**HQ:** New Vision Display (Shenzhen) Co., Ltd.
Building 6, No.102/108, Lijia Road, Henggang Sub-District, Longg Shenzhen GD 51811

**(P-13048)**
**NEWVAC LLC**
American Def Interconnect Div
9330 De Soto Ave, Chatsworth (91311-4926)
PHONE.................................747 202-7333
Garrett Hoffman, *General Vice President*
**EMP:** 26
**SALES (corp-wide):** 96.54MM **Privately Held**
Web: www.newvac-llc.com
**SIC: 3679** Harness assemblies, for electronic use: wire or cable
**HQ:** Newvac, Llc
9330 De Soto Ave
Chatsworth CA 91311
310 525-1205

**(P-13049)**
**NORTRA CABLES INC**
570 Gibraltar Dr, Milpitas (95035-6315)
PHONE.................................408 942-1106
Jim Love, *Pr*

## PRODUCTS & SERVICES SECTION
### 3679 - Electronic Components, Nec (P-13069)

Lyn Hickey, *Stockholder**
**EMP:** 60 **EST:** 1985
**SQ FT:** 14,000
**SALES (est):** 10.09MM **Privately Held**
**Web:** www.nortra-cables.com
**SIC: 3679** Harness assemblies, for electronic use: wire or cable

**(P-13050)**
### NRC MANUFACTURING INC
Also Called: NRC
500 Yosemite Dr Ste 108, Milpitas (95035-5467)
**PHONE**.................510 438-9400
Rata Chea, *Pr*
David Hang, *CFO*
**EMP:** 18 **EST:** 2008
**SALES (est):** 2.67MM **Privately Held**
**Web:** www.nrcmfg.com
**SIC: 3679** Electronic circuits

**(P-13051)**
### OASIS MATERIALS COMPANY LLC (DH)
Also Called: Oasis Materials
12131 Community Rd, Poway (92064-8893)
**PHONE**.................858 486-8846
Frank Polese, *Pr*
Stephen Nootens, *
Christopher Bateman, *
Boksun Kang, *
**EMP:** 22 **EST:** 2012
**SQ FT:** 22,000
**SALES (est):** 19.81MM
**SALES (corp-wide):** 153.54MM **Privately Held**
**Web:** www.fralock.com
**SIC: 3679** Electronic circuits
**HQ:** Fralock Llc
  28525 Industry Dr
  Valencia CA 91355
  800 372-5625

**(P-13052)**
### OCM PE HOLDINGS LP
333 S Grand Ave Fl 28, Los Angeles (90071-1530)
**PHONE**.................213 830-6213
Mark C J Twaalfhoven, *CEO*
**EMP:** 10000 **EST:** 2012
**SALES (est):** 5.53MM **Privately Held**
**SIC: 3679** 3612 3663 Electronic circuits; Transformers, except electric; Antennas, transmitting and communications

**(P-13053)**
### OMEGA LEADS INC
Also Called: Wire Harness & Cable Assembly
1509 Colorado Ave, Santa Monica (90404-3316)
**PHONE**.................310 394-6786
**TOLL FREE:** 800
Jeff Sweet Senior, *Pr*
**EMP:** 20 **EST:** 1960
**SQ FT:** 7,200
**SALES (est):** 4.03MM **Privately Held**
**Web:** www.omegaleads.com
**SIC: 3679** Harness assemblies, for electronic use: wire or cable

**(P-13054)**
### OMNI CONNECTION INTL INC
126 Via Trevizio, Corona (92879-1772)
**PHONE**.................951 898-6232
Henry Cheng, *Pr*
Phyllis Ting, *VP*
▲ **EMP:** 410 **EST:** 1992
**SQ FT:** 65,000
**SALES (est):** 17.1MM

**SALES (corp-wide):** 6.55B **Privately Held**
**Web:** www.omni-conn.com
**SIC: 3679** Harness assemblies, for electronic use: wire or cable
**HQ:** Electrical Components International, Inc.
  1 City Pl Dr Ste 450
  Saint Louis MO 63141

**(P-13055)**
### OMNIYIG INC
630 Chelsea Xing, San Jose (95138-3173)
**PHONE**.................408 988-0843
William Capogeannis, *Pr*
Cathleen Capogeannis, *
**EMP:** 26 **EST:** 1973
**SALES (est):** 2.6MM **Privately Held**
**Web:** www.omniyig.com
**SIC: 3679** Microwave components

**(P-13056)**
### ONSHORE TECHNOLOGIES INC
2771 Plaza Del Amo Ste 802-803, Torrance (90503-9308)
**PHONE**.................310 533-4888
Max Van Orden, *Pr*
Mark Wilkinson, *Prin*
**EMP:** 25 **EST:** 1992
**SALES (est):** 8.34MM **Privately Held**
**Web:** www.onshoretechnologies.com
**SIC: 3679** Harness assemblies, for electronic use: wire or cable

**(P-13057)**
### OPTO 22
43044 Business Park Dr, Temecula (92590-3614)
**PHONE**.................951 695-3000
Mark Engman, *Pr*
Benson Hougland, *
Bob Sheffres, *
Kathleen Roe, *
◆ **EMP:** 200 **EST:** 1974
**SQ FT:** 135,000
**SALES (est):** 29.45MM **Privately Held**
**Web:** www.opto22.com
**SIC: 3679** 3823 3625 Electronic switches; Process control instruments; Relays and industrial controls

**(P-13058)**
### ORMET CIRCUITS INC
6555 Nancy Ridge Dr Ste 200, San Diego (92121-3221)
**PHONE**.................858 831-0010
Till Langner, *CEO*
◆ **EMP:** 22 **EST:** 2001
**SQ FT:** 18,000
**SALES (est):** 2.44MM
**SALES (corp-wide):** 22.82B **Privately Held**
**Web:** www.ormetcircuits.com
**SIC: 3679** Electronic circuits
**HQ:** Emd Performance Materials Corp.
  1200 Intrepid Ave
  Philadelphia PA 19112
  888 367-3275

**(P-13059)**
### OXFORD INSTRS X-RAY TECH INC
Also Called: X-Ray Technology Group
360 El Pueblo Rd, Scotts Valley (95066-4228)
**PHONE**.................831 439-9729
Bernard Scanlan, *CEO*
▲ **EMP:** 69 **EST:** 1979
**SQ FT:** 6,600
**SALES (est):** 7.28MM
**SALES (corp-wide):** 596.99MM **Privately Held**

**Web:** www.oxinst.com
**SIC: 3679** 3844 Power supplies, all types: static; X-ray apparatus and tubes
**HQ:** Oxford Instruments Holdings, Inc.
  600 Milik St
  Carteret NJ 07008
  732 541-1300

**(P-13060)**
### PACMAG INC
Also Called: Pacific Magnetics
87 Georgina St, Chula Vista (91910-6121)
**PHONE**.................619 872-0343
Mary Hill, *Pr*
▲ **EMP:** 29 **EST:** 1978
**SALES (est):** 1.42MM
**SALES (corp-wide):** 23.52MM **Privately Held**
**SIC: 3679** Electronic circuits
**PA:** Careen, Inc.
  15 Somsen St
  800 795-8533

**(P-13061)**
### PIONEER MAGNETICS INC
1745 Berkeley St, Santa Monica (90404-4104)
**PHONE**.................310 829-6751
**EMP:** 110
**Web:** www.pioneermagnetics.com
**SIC: 3679** Power supplies, all types: static

**(P-13062)**
### PLANAR MONOLITHICS INDS INC
4921 Robert J Mathews Pkwy Ste 1, El Dorado Hills (95762-5772)
**PHONE**.................916 542-1401
Ashok Gorwara, *Pr*
**EMP:** 27
**SQ FT:** 40,000
**SALES (corp-wide):** 17.99MM **Privately Held**
**Web:** www.planarmonolithics.com
**SIC: 3679** 3677 Attenuators; Filtration devices, electronic
**HQ:** Planar Monolithics Industries, Inc.
  7309 Grove Rd
  Frederick MD 21704

**(P-13063)**
### PLANTRONICS INC (HQ)
Also Called: Plantronics
100 Enterprise Way Ste A300, Scotts Valley (95066-3272)
**PHONE**.................831 420-3002
David M Shull, *Pr*
Charles D Boynton, *CAO**
Warren Schlichting, *
Lisa Bodensteiner, *Legal Compliance**
Carl J Wiese, *CRO**
▲ **EMP:** 534 **EST:** 1988
**SALES (est):** 1.68B
**SALES (corp-wide):** 53.72B **Publicly Held**
**Web:** www.hp.com
**SIC: 3679** 3661 Headphones, radio; Telephones and telephone apparatus
**PA:** Hp Inc.
  1501 Page Mill Rd
  650 857-1501

**(P-13064)**
### POWERS HOLDINGS INC
Also Called: Curtis Industries
1601 Clancy Ct, Visalia (93291-9253)
**PHONE**.................559 651-2222
Edward Powers, *CEO*
**EMP:** 18
**SALES (corp-wide):** 35.15MM **Privately Held**

**Web:** www.curtisind.com
**SIC: 3679** 3677 Electronic switches; Filtration devices, electronic
**PA:** Powers Holdings, Inc.
  2400 S 43rd St
  414 649-4200

**(P-13065)**
### PPST INC (PA)
17692 Fitch, Irvine (92614-6022)
**PHONE**.................800 421-1921
Kevin J Voelcker, *Pr*
▲ **EMP:** 35 **EST:** 2003
**SALES (est):** 25.52MM
**SALES (corp-wide):** 25.52MM **Privately Held**
**Web:** www.pacificpower.com
**SIC: 3679** Power supplies, all types: static

**(P-13066)**
### PRECISION HERMETIC TECH INC
Also Called: Precision Hermetic
1940 W Park Ave, Redlands (92373-8042)
**PHONE**.................909 381-6011
Daniel B Schachtel, *Pr*
Sari Schachtel, *
**EMP:** 85 **EST:** 1989
**SQ FT:** 50,000
**SALES (est):** 13.87MM **Privately Held**
**Web:** www.precisionhermetic.com
**SIC: 3679** Hermetic seals, for electronic equipment

**(P-13067)**
### PRED TECHNOLOGIES USA INC
Also Called: Pred
4901 Morena Blvd, San Diego (92117-7319)
**PHONE**.................858 999-2114
Charles Speidel, *CEO*
**EMP:** 70 **EST:** 2016
**SALES (est):** 2.92MM **Privately Held**
**Web:** www.tokktech.com
**SIC: 3679** Headphones, radio

**(P-13068)**
### PTB SALES INC (PA)
Also Called: Ptb
1361 Mountain View Cir, Azusa (91702-1649)
**PHONE**.................626 334-0500
Patrick T Blackwell, *CEO*
Brendan Riley, *
Dean Scarborough, *
Carmen Williams, *
▲ **EMP:** 28 **EST:** 1995
**SQ FT:** 16,000
**SALES (est):** 12.41MM
**SALES (corp-wide):** 12.41MM **Privately Held**
**Web:** www.ptbsales.com
**SIC: 3679** 3563 Power supplies, all types: static; Air and gas compressors including vacuum pumps

**(P-13069)**
### PULSE ELECTRONICS CORPORATION (HQ)
Also Called: Pulse A Yageo Company
15255 Innovation Dr Ste 100, San Diego (92128-3410)
**PHONE**.................858 674-8100
Mark C J Twaalfhoven, *CEO*
▲ **EMP:** 45 **EST:** 1947
**SQ FT:** 50,000
**SALES (est):** 37.31MM **Privately Held**
**Web:** www.pulseelectronics.com

## 3679 - Electronic Components, Nec (P-13070)

SIC: **3679** 3612 3663  Electronic circuits; Transformers, except electric; Antennas, transmitting and communications
PA: Yageo Corporation
   3f, No.233-1, Pao Chiao Rd.,

### (P-13070)
**Q MICROWAVE INC**
1591 Pioneer Way, El Cajon  (92020-1637)
PHONE..................................619 258-7322
Eric Maat, *CEO*
Craig Higginson, *
Craig Shauan, *
EMP: 84 EST: 1998
SQ FT: 18,000
SALES (est): 14.9MM
SALES (corp-wide): 12.55B **Publicly Held**
Web: www.qmicrowave.com
SIC: **3679** 5065  Microwave components; Electronic parts and equipment, nec
PA: Amphenol Corporation
   358 Hall Ave
   203 265-8900

### (P-13071)
**Q-VIO LLC**
10211 Pacific Mesa Blvd Ste 401, San Diego  (92121-4327)
PHONE..................................858 777-8299
EMP: 15
Web: www.q-vio.com
SIC: **3679**  Liquid crystal displays (LCD)

### (P-13072)
**QORVO CALIFORNIA INC**
Also Called: Qorvo US
950 Lawrence Dr, Newbury Park  (91320-1522)
PHONE..................................805 480-5050
Charles J Abronson, *Ch Bd*
Ralph G Quinsey, *
Paul O Daughenbaugh, *
Mark Lampenfeld, *
Susan Liles, *
EMP: 49 EST: 1996
SQ FT: 11,000
SALES (est): 8.15MM
SALES (corp-wide): 3.77B **Publicly Held**
Web: www.qorvo.com
SIC: **3679**  Electronic circuits
HQ: Qorvo Us, Inc.
   2300 Ne Brookwood Pkwy
   Hillsboro OR 97124
   503 615-9000

### (P-13073)
**REACH TECHNOLOGY INC**
4575 Cushing Pkwy, Fremont  (94538-6466)
PHONE..................................510 770-1417
EMP: 20
Web: www.reachtech.com
SIC: **3679** 3825 8711  Liquid crystal displays (LCD); Digital test equipment, electronic and electrical circuits; Engineering services

### (P-13074)
**REEDEX INC**
15526 Commerce Ln, Huntington Beach  (92649-1602)
PHONE..................................714 894-0311
Dan Reed, *Pr*
Ted Reed, *
▲ EMP: 49 EST: 1972
SALES (est): 4.41MM **Privately Held**
Web: www.reedex.com
SIC: **3679**  Harness assemblies, for electronic use: wire or cable

### (P-13075)
**REGAL ELECTRONICS INC (PA)**
820 Charcot Ave, San Jose  (95131-2226)
P.O. Box 60008  (94088-0008)
PHONE..................................408 988-2288
Tony Lee, *Pr*
Madeleine Lee, *
▲ EMP: 20 EST: 1976
SALES (est): 3.53MM
SALES (corp-wide): 3.53MM **Privately Held**
Web: www.regalusa.com
SIC: **3679** 3678 3612  Electronic circuits; Electronic connectors; Transformers, except electric

### (P-13076)
**RENESAS ELECTRONICS AMERICA INC**
1001 Murphy Ranch Rd, Milpitas  (95035-7912)
PHONE..................................408 432-8888
▲ EMP: 1027
Web: www.renesas.com
SIC: **3679** 3674  Electronic circuits; Integrated circuits, semiconductor networks, etc.

### (P-13077)
**ROCKER SOLENOID COMPANY**
Also Called: Rocker Industries
5492 Bolsa Ave, Huntington Beach  (92649-1021)
PHONE..................................310 534-5660
John W Perry, *Pr*
Francis E Goodyear, *
Raymond Hatashita, *
Milton A Mather, *
▼ EMP: 88 EST: 1954
SQ FT: 23,000
SALES (est): 18.01MM **Privately Held**
Web: www.rockerindustries.com
SIC: **3679** 3672  Solenoids for electronic applications; Printed circuit boards

### (P-13078)
**ROGAR MANUFACTURING INC**
Also Called: Ro Gar Mfg
866 E Ross Ave, El Centro  (92243-9652)
PHONE..................................760 335-3700
Pat Lewis, *Prin*
EMP: 126
SALES (corp-wide): 20.67MM **Privately Held**
Web: www.rogarmfg.com
SIC: **3679**  Electronic circuits
PA: Rogar Manufacturing Incorporated
   866 E Ross Ave
   760 335-3700

### (P-13079)
**ROTECH ENGINEERING INC**
Also Called: Rotech Engineering
1020 S Melrose St Ste A, Placentia  (92870-7169)
PHONE..................................714 632-0532
Ralph Ono, *Pr*
EMP: 20 EST: 1994
SQ FT: 10,000
SALES (est): 3.35MM **Privately Held**
Web: www.rotech-busbar.com
SIC: **3679**  Electronic circuits

### (P-13080)
**RTIE HOLDINGS LLC**
1800 E Via Burton, Anaheim  (92806-1213)
PHONE..................................714 765-8200
EMP: 19 EST: 2010
SALES (est): 472.92K **Privately Held**

SIC: **3679**  Electronic circuits

### (P-13081)
**SANDBERG INDUSTRIES INC (PA)**
Also Called: E M S
2921 Daimler St, Santa Ana  (92705-5810)
PHONE..................................949 660-9473
J Sandberg, *CEO*
Steve Walker, *
Leo Boarts, *
John T Sandberg, *
Becky Tamblyn, *
EMP: 52 EST: 1978
SQ FT: 30,000
SALES (est): 3.14MM
SALES (corp-wide): 3.14MM **Privately Held**
Web: www.unitindustriesgroup.com
SIC: **3679** 3825 3672 3643  Electronic circuits ; Test equipment for electronic and electrical circuits; Printed circuit boards; Current-carrying wiring services

### (P-13082)
**SAS MANUFACTURING INC**
405 N Smith Ave, Corona  (92878-4305)
PHONE..................................951 734-1808
Theo F Smit Junior, *CEO*
Sharon Smit, *
EMP: 45 EST: 1990
SQ FT: 24,000
SALES (est): 9.86MM **Privately Held**
Web: www.sasmanufacturing.com
SIC: **3679**  Harness assemblies, for electronic use: wire or cable

### (P-13083)
**SCEPTRE INC**
Also Called: E-Scepter
16800 Gale Ave, City Of Industry  (91745-1804)
PHONE..................................626 369-3698
Stephen Liu, *CEO*
Cathy Liu, *
▲ EMP: 50 EST: 1984
SALES (est): 9.83MM **Privately Held**
Web: www.sceptre.com
SIC: **3679**  Liquid crystal displays (LCD)

### (P-13084)
**SIGNATURE TECH GROUP INC**
Also Called: A & A Electronic Assembly
11960 Borden Ave, San Fernando  (91340-1808)
PHONE..................................818 890-7611
Victor Castro, *Owner*
EMP: 15 EST: 1984
SQ FT: 10,000
SALES (est): 1.36MM **Privately Held**
Web: www.aapcbassembly.com
SIC: **3679** 3672  Electronic circuits; Printed circuit boards

### (P-13085)
**SILITRONICS INC**
Also Called: Silitronics
2388 Walsh Ave, Santa Clara  (95051-1301)
PHONE..................................408 605-1148
EMP: 30 EST: 2011
SALES (est): 6MM **Privately Held**
Web: www.silitronics.com
SIC: **3679** 3672  Electronic circuits; Printed circuit boards

### (P-13086)
**SMITHS INTERCONNECT INC**
375 Conejo Ridge Ave, Thousand Oaks  (91361-4928)
PHONE..................................805 267-0100

Dave Moorehouse, *Pr*
EMP: 68
SALES (corp-wide): 3.97B **Privately Held**
Web: www.smithsinterconnect.com
SIC: **3679**  Microwave components
HQ: Smiths Interconnect, Inc.
   4726 Eisenhower Blvd
   Tampa FL 33634
   813 901-7200

### (P-13087)
**SMITHS INTRCNNECT AMERICAS INC**
1231 E Dyer Rd Ste 235, Santa Ana  (92705-5665)
PHONE..................................714 371-1100
Dom Matos, *Pr*
EMP: 300
SALES (corp-wide): 3.97B **Privately Held**
Web: www.smithsinterconnect.com
SIC: **3679**  Microwave components
HQ: Smiths Interconnect Americas, Inc.
   2001 Ne 46th St Ste 188
   Kansas City MO 64116
   913 342-5544

### (P-13088)
**SOURCE ONE CABLE TECHNOLOGY INC**
Also Called: Source One Technologies
6680 Via Del Oro, San Jose  (95119-1392)
PHONE..................................408 376-3400
▲ EMP: 100
Web: www.source1cable.com
SIC: **3679**  Harness assemblies, for electronic use: wire or cable

### (P-13089)
**SPECTROLAB INC**
12500 Gladstone Ave, Sylmar  (91342-5373)
P.O. Box 9209  (91392-9209)
PHONE..................................818 365-4611
David Lillington, *Pr*
Edward Ringo, *
Jeff Peacock, *
Nasser Karam, *
Paul Ballew, *
EMP: 400 EST: 1956
SQ FT: 50,000
SALES (est): 36.72MM
SALES (corp-wide): 77.79B **Publicly Held**
Web: www.spectrolab.com
SIC: **3679** 3674  Power supplies, all types: static; Solar cells
HQ: Boeing Satellite Systems, Inc.
   900 N Pacific Coast Hwy
   El Segundo CA 90245

### (P-13090)
**STATEK CORPORATION (HQ)**
Also Called: Statek
512 N Main St, Orange  (92868-1102)
PHONE..................................714 639-7810
Michael Dastmalchian, *
Margaritha W Werren, *
▲ EMP: 129 EST: 1970
SQ FT: 71,000
SALES (est): 16.06MM
SALES (corp-wide): 54.21MM **Privately Held**
Web: www.statek.com
SIC: **3679**  Electronic circuits
PA: Technicorp International Ii, Inc.
   512 N Main St
   714 639-7810

## PRODUCTS & SERVICES SECTION
### 3679 - Electronic Components, Nec (P-13111)

**(P-13091)**
**STATEK CORPORATION**
1449 W Orange Grove Ave, Orange (92868-1120)
PHONE.............................714 639-7810
**EMP:** 121
**SALES (corp-wide):** 54.21MM **Privately Held**
**Web:** www.statek.com
**SIC: 3679** Electronic circuits
**HQ:** Statek Corporation
   512 N Main St
   Orange CA 92868
   714 639-7810

**(P-13092)**
**STORE INTELLIGENCE INC**
6700 Koll Center Pkwy Ste 109, Pleasanton (94566-7060)
PHONE.............................925 433-9520
Zachary Abrams, *Ofcr*
Simon Jones, *COO*
**EMP:** 30 **EST:** 2020
**SALES (est):** 6.7MM **Privately Held**
**SIC: 3679** Electronic circuits

**(P-13093)**
**STRIKE TECHNOLOGY INC**
Also Called: Wilorco
24311 Wilmington Ave, Carson (90745-6139)
PHONE.............................562 437-3428
Robert Kunesh, *Ch Bd*
**EMP:** 25 **EST:** 2001
**SQ FT:** 9,800
**SALES (est):** 4.52MM **Privately Held**
**Web:** www.wilorco.com
**SIC: 3679** Electronic circuits

**(P-13094)**
**SUNTSU ELECTRONICS INC (PA)**
Also Called: Suntsu
142 Technology Dr Ste 150, Irvine (92618-2429)
PHONE.............................949 783-7300
Casey Conlan, *Pr*
Jason Gann, *Sec*
▲ **EMP:** 17 **EST:** 2002
**SQ FT:** 14,000
**SALES (est):** 8.82MM
**SALES (corp-wide):** 8.82MM **Privately Held**
**Web:** www.suntsu.com
**SIC: 3679** 5065 Electronic circuits; Electronic parts and equipment, nec

**(P-13095)**
**SUPPORT SYSTEMS INTL CORP**
Also Called: Fiber Optic Cable Shop
136 S 2nd St Dept B, Richmond (94804-2110)
PHONE.............................510 234-9090
Ben G Parsons, *Pr*
Richard St John, *
▼ **EMP:** 65 **EST:** 1976
**SQ FT:** 15,000
**SALES (est):** 4.54MM **Privately Held**
**Web:** www.fiberopticcableshop.com
**SIC: 3679** Harness assemblies, for electronic use: wire or cable

**(P-13096)**
**SURE POWER INC**
Also Called: Martek Power
1111 Knox St, Torrance (90502-1034)
PHONE.............................310 542-8561
Maricela Sanchez, *Brnch Mgr*
**EMP:** 18
**Web:** www.eaton.com
**SIC: 3679** Power supplies, all types: static
**HQ:** Sure Power, Inc.
   10955 Sw Avery St
   Tualatin OR 97062
   503 692-5360

**(P-13097)**
**SYSTRON DONNER INERTIAL INC**
Also Called: Systron Donner Inertial
2700 Systron Dr, Concord (94518-1399)
PHONE.............................925 979-4400
Dave Peace, *CEO*
**EMP:** 117 **EST:** 2015
**SALES (est):** 7.02MM
**SALES (corp-wide):** 97.72MM **Publicly Held**
**Web:** www.emcore.com
**SIC: 3679** 3829 Electronic circuits; Accelerometers
**PA:** Emcore Corporation
   2015 Chestnut St
   626 293-3400

**(P-13098)**
**TDK ELECTRONICS INC**
8787 Complex Dr Ste 200, San Diego (92123-1451)
PHONE.............................858 715-4200
Wolfgang Till, *Prin*
**EMP:** 105
**Web:** tdk-electronics.tdk.com
**SIC: 3679** 5065 3546 Electronic crystals; Diskettes, computer; Power-driven handtools
**HQ:** Tdk Electronics Inc.
   10 Wodbrdge Ctr Dr Ste 13
   Woodbridge NJ 07095
   732 906-4300

**(P-13099)**
**TE CONNECTIVITY LTD**
Also Called: Te Circuit Protection
6900 Paseo Padre Pkwy, Fremont (94555-3641)
PHONE.............................650 361-4923
Thomas J Lynch, *CEO*
Terrence Curtin, *
Mario Calastri, *
John Jenkins, *
Rob Shaddock, *
**EMP:** 38 **EST:** 2014
**SALES (est):** 8.24MM
**SALES (corp-wide):** 2.36B **Publicly Held**
**SIC: 3679** Electronic circuits
**PA:** Littelfuse, Inc.
   8755 W Higgins Rd Ste 500
   773 628-1000

**(P-13100)**
**TECHNICAL CABLE CONCEPTS INC**
350 Lear Ave, Costa Mesa (92626-6015)
PHONE.............................714 835-1081
▲ **EMP:** 50 **EST:** 1989
**SALES (est):** 7.8MM **Privately Held**
**Web:** www.techcable.com
**SIC: 3679** 3229 Harness assemblies, for electronic use: wire or cable; Fiber optics strands

**(P-13101)**
**TELEDYNE COUGAR INC**
1274 Terra Bella Ave, Mountain View (94043-1820)
PHONE.............................408 522-3838
**EMP:** 120
**SIC: 3679** Microwave components

**(P-13102)**
**TELEDYNE DEFENSE ELEC LLC**
Also Called: Teledyne Microwave Solutions
11361 Sunrise Park Dr, Rancho Cordova (95742-6587)
PHONE.............................916 638-3344
Bob Dipple, *Brnch Mgr*
**EMP:** 200
**SALES (corp-wide):** 5.64B **Publicly Held**
**Web:** www.teledynedefenseelectronics.com
**SIC: 3679** 3672 3663 3651 Microwave components; Printed circuit boards; Radio and t.v. communications equipment; Household audio and video equipment
**HQ:** Teledyne Defense Electronics, Llc
   1274 Terra Bella Ave
   Mountain View CA 94043
   650 691-9800

**(P-13103)**
**TELEDYNE DEFENSE ELEC LLC (HQ)**
Also Called: Teledyne Microwave Solutions
1274 Terra Bella Ave, Mountain View (94043-1820)
PHONE.............................650 691-9800
Richard Palilonis, *CEO*
Robert Mehrabian, *
David Zavadil, *
Susan L Main, *
▲ **EMP:** 25 **EST:** 2003
**SALES (est):** 339.74MM
**SALES (corp-wide):** 5.64B **Publicly Held**
**Web:** www.teledynedefenseelectronics.com
**SIC: 3679** Microwave components
**PA:** Teledyne Technologies Inc
   1049 Camino Dos Rios
   805 373-4545

**(P-13104)**
**TELEDYNE TECHNOLOGIES INC**
Also Called: Teledyne Controls
501 Continental Blvd, El Segundo (90245-5036)
P.O. Box 1026 (90245-1026)
PHONE.............................310 765-3600
Masood Hassan, *Brnch Mgr*
**EMP:** 300
**SALES (corp-wide):** 5.64B **Publicly Held**
**Web:** www.teledyne.com
**SIC: 3679** 8731 3812 3519 Electronic circuits; Commercial physical research; Search and navigation equipment; Internal combustion engines, nec
**PA:** Teledyne Technologies Inc
   1049 Camino Dos Rios
   805 373-4545

**(P-13105)**
**TELEDYNE TECHNOLOGIES INC (PA)**
Also Called: TELEDYNE TECHNOLOGIES
1049 Camino Dos Rios, Thousand Oaks (91360-2362)
PHONE.............................805 373-4545
Edwin Roks, *CEO*
Robert Mehrabian, *
Jason Vanwees, *Vice Chairman*
George C Bobb Iii, *Pr*
Melanie S Cibik, *CCO*
**EMP:** 250 **EST:** 1960
**SALES (est):** 5.64B
**SALES (corp-wide):** 5.64B **Publicly Held**
**Web:** www.teledyne.com
**SIC: 3679** 3761 3519 3724 Electronic circuits; Guided missiles and space vehicles; Internal combustion engines, nec; Aircraft engines and engine parts

**(P-13106)**
**TELEDYNE TECHNOLOGIES INC**
Also Called: Teledyne
12964 Panama St, Los Angeles (90066-6534)
PHONE.............................310 822-8229
Bruce Gecks, *Mgr*
**EMP:** 360
**SALES (corp-wide):** 5.64B **Publicly Held**
**Web:** www.teledyne.com
**SIC: 3679** Electronic circuits
**PA:** Teledyne Technologies Inc
   1049 Camino Dos Rios
   805 373-4545

**(P-13107)**
**TERADYNE INC**
30701 Agoura Rd, Agoura Hills (91301-5928)
PHONE.............................818 991-2900
Greg Beecher, *Mgr*
**EMP:** 92
**SALES (corp-wide):** 2.68B **Publicly Held**
**Web:** www.teradyne.com
**SIC: 3679** Electronic circuits
**PA:** Teradyne, Inc.
   600 Riverpark Dr
   978 370-2700

**(P-13108)**
**THERMAL ELECTRONICS INC**
403 W Minthorn St, Lake Elsinore (92530-2801)
**EMP:** 15 **EST:** 1977
**SQ FT:** 10,000
**SALES (est):** 4MM **Privately Held**
**Web:** www.thermalelectronics.com
**SIC: 3679** Electronic circuits

**(P-13109)**
**THOMPSON MAGNETICS INC**
Also Called: Auto Doctor
42255 Baldaray Cir Ste C, Temecula (92590-3632)
P.O. Box 2019 (92593-2019)
PHONE.............................951 676-0243
Howard M Thompson Senior, *Ch Bd*
Howard M Thompson Junior, *VP*
Betty J Thompson, *Sec*
David Thompson, *VP*
**EMP:** 21 **EST:** 1969
**SQ FT:** 16,000
**SALES (est):** 654.95K **Privately Held**
**SIC: 3679** 7538 Cores, magnetic; General automotive repair shops

**(P-13110)**
**TR MANUFACTURING LLC (HQ)**
840 N Mccarthy Blvd, Milpitas (95035-5114)
PHONE.............................408 235-2900
Dom Tran, *CEO*
Jack Cho, *
▲ **EMP:** 250 **EST:** 2015
**SQ FT:** 52,000
**SALES (est):** 34.31MM
**SALES (corp-wide):** 12.59B **Publicly Held**
**SIC: 3679** Electronic circuits
**PA:** Corning Incorporated
   1 Riverfront Plz
   607 974-9000

**(P-13111)**
**TRANSICO INC**
Also Called: Eeco Switch
1240 Pioneer St Ste A, Brea (92821-3740)
PHONE.............................714 835-6000
▲ **EMP:** 24 **EST:** 1992
**SALES (est):** 970.57K **Privately Held**
**Web:** www.eecoswitch.com

## 3679 - Electronic Components, Nec (P-13112)

SIC: **3679** 3672 3643 3577 Electronic switches; Printed circuit boards; Current-carrying wiring services; Computer peripheral equipment, nec

**(P-13112)**
### TT ELCTRNICS PWR SLTNS US INC
1330 E Cypress St, Covina (91724-2103)
PHONE..................626 967-6021
Michael Joseph Leahan, *CEO*
Matthew Alexander Sweaney, *Sec*
Kumen Rey Call, *CFO*
**EMP:** 120 **EST:** 2019
**SALES (est):** 24.32MM
**SALES (corp-wide):** 765.19MM **Privately Held**
Web: www.ttelectronics.com
SIC: **3679** Electronic circuits
PA: Tt Electronics Plc
　4th Floor St. Andrews House
　193 282-5300

**(P-13113)**
### U S CIRCUIT INC
2071 Wineridge Pl, Escondido (92029-1931)
PHONE..................760 489-1413
Michael Fariba, *Pr*
T J Sojitra, *Sr VP*
Mukesh Patel, *VP*
**EMP:** 80 **EST:** 1985
**SQ FT:** 40,000
**SALES (est):** 10.22MM
**SALES (corp-wide):** 13.47MM **Privately Held**
Web: www.uscircuit.com
SIC: **3679** 3672 Electronic circuits; Printed circuit boards
PA: Ampel Incorporated
　925 Estes Ave
　847 952-1900

**(P-13114)**
### UNIQUIFY INC (PA)
2323 Owen St # 101, Santa Clara (95054-3211)
PHONE..................408 235-8810
Josh Lee, *CEO*
Jung Ho Lee, *
Robert Sheffield, *
Sam Kim, *
Robert Smith, *
**EMP:** 25 **EST:** 2005
**SALES (est):** 9.7MM **Privately Held**
Web: www.uniquify.com
SIC: **3679** Electronic circuits

**(P-13115)**
### VANDER-BEND MANUFACTURING INC (PA)
2701 Orchard Pkwy, San Jose (95131)
PHONE..................408 245-5150
Greg Biggs, *Pr*
Brian King, *
▲ **EMP:** 137 **EST:** 1999
**SQ FT:** 207,000
**SALES (est):** 138.57MM
**SALES (corp-wide):** 138.57MM **Privately Held**
Web: www.vantedgemedical.com
SIC: **3679** 3444 3549 3599 Harness assemblies, for electronic use: wire or cable; Sheet metalwork; Metalworking machinery, nec; Machine and other job shop work

**(P-13116)**
### VAS ENGINEERING INC
4750 Viewridge Ave, San Diego (92123-1640)
PHONE..................858 569-1601
Rohak Vora, *CEO*
Greg Atzmiller, *
T J Sojitra, *Stockholder*
▲ **EMP:** 50 **EST:** 1979
**SQ FT:** 19,200
**SALES (est):** 9.24MM **Privately Held**
Web: www.vasengineering.com
SIC: **3679** 3823 Electronic circuits; Temperature measurement instruments, industrial

**(P-13117)**
### VERTEX LCD INC
600 S Jefferson St Ste K, Placentia (92870-6634)
P.O. Box 206 (92871-0206)
PHONE..................714 223-7111
**EMP:** 35 **EST:** 1999
**SALES (est):** 1.13MM **Privately Held**
Web: www.vertexlcd.com
SIC: **3679** Liquid crystal displays (LCD)

**(P-13118)**
### VISUAL COMMUNICATIONS COMPANY LLC
Also Called: Vcc
2173 Salk Ave Ste 175, Carlsbad (92008-7836)
PHONE..................800 522-5546
**EMP:** 205 **EST:** 1976
**SALES (est):** 13.53MM **Privately Held**
Web: www.vcclite.com
SIC: **3679** Electronic circuits

**(P-13119)**
### VOICE ASSIST INC
Also Called: (A Development Stage Company)
100 Spectrum Center Dr Ste 900, Irvine (92618-4962)
PHONE..................949 655-6400
Michael Metcalf, *Interim Chief Financial Officer*
**EMP:** 16 **EST:** 2008
**SALES (est):** 2.28MM **Privately Held**
Web: www.voiceassist.com
SIC: **3679** Voice controls

**(P-13120)**
### WAVESTREAM CORPORATION (HQ)
545 W Terrace Dr, San Dimas (91773-2915)
PHONE..................909 599-9080
Robert Huffman, *CEO*
Nimrod Itach, *
Lanis Bell, *
James Rosenberg, *
**EMP:** 103 **EST:** 2006
**SQ FT:** 33,000
**SALES (est):** 22.05MM **Privately Held**
Web: www.wavestream.com
SIC: **3679** 8731 Microwave components; Commercial physical research
PA: Gilat Satellite Networks Ltd.
　21 Yegia Kapaim

**(P-13121)**
### WELLEX CORPORATION (PA)
551 Brown Rd, Fremont (94539-7003)
PHONE..................510 743-1818
Chiennan Huang, *CEO*
Richard Fitzgerald, *
Jackson Wang, *
▲ **EMP:** 147 **EST:** 1983
**SQ FT:** 88,516
**SALES (est):** 24.43MM
**SALES (corp-wide):** 24.43MM **Privately Held**
Web: www.wellex.com
SIC: **3679** 3672 Harness assemblies, for electronic use: wire or cable; Printed circuit boards

**(P-13122)**
### WESTERN DIGITAL
19600 S Western Ave, Torrance (90501-1117)
P.O. Box 5084 (92609-8584)
PHONE..................510 557-7553
**EMP:** 81 **EST:** 2019
**SALES (est):** 5.55MM **Privately Held**
Web: www.westerndigital.com
SIC: **3679** Electronic components, nec

**(P-13123)**
### WESTERN DIGITAL CORPORATION
Also Called: Western Digital
3355 Michelson Dr Ste 100, Irvine (92612-5694)
PHONE..................949 672-7000
**EMP:** 21
**SALES (corp-wide):** 13B **Publicly Held**
Web: www.westerndigital.com
SIC: **3679** Electronic circuits
PA: Western Digital Corporation
　5601 Great Oaks Pkwy
　408 717-6000

**(P-13124)**
### WINCHESTER SRC CABLES CORP
Also Called: SRC Haverhill
5590 Skylane Blvd, Santa Rosa (95403-1030)
PHONE..................707 573-1900
**EMP:** 19
Web: www.winconn.com
SIC: **3679** 3357 Harness assemblies, for electronic use: wire or cable; Coaxial cable, nonferrous

**(P-13125)**
### WINCHSTER INTERCONNECT RF CORP
Winchester Interconnect
5590 Skylane Blvd, Santa Rosa (95403-1030)
PHONE..................707 573-1900
Robert Wallick, *Engr*
**EMP:** 1115
Web: www.winconn.com
SIC: **3679** 3357 Harness assemblies, for electronic use: wire or cable; Coaxial cable, nonferrous
HQ: Winchester Interconnect Rf Corporation
　185 Plains Rd
　Milford CT 06461
　978 532-0775

**(P-13126)**
### WYVERN TECHNOLOGIES
1205 E Warner Ave, Santa Ana (92705-5431)
PHONE..................714 966-0710
James J Weber, *Pr*
**EMP:** 30 **EST:** 1984
**SQ FT:** 10,000
**SALES (est):** 1.74MM **Privately Held**
Web: www.wyverncorp.com
SIC: **3679** Microwave components

**(P-13127)**
### XIDAS INC
Also Called: Integra Devices
46 Waterworks Way, Irvine (92618-3107)
PHONE..................949 930-0147
Paul Dhillon, *CEO*
James Spoto, *COO*
**EMP:** 16 **EST:** 2015
**SALES (est):** 1.58MM **Privately Held**
Web: www.xidas.com
SIC: **3679** Microwave components

**(P-13128)**
### XP POWER INC
Also Called: Switching Systems
1590 S Sinclair St, Anaheim (92806-5933)
PHONE..................714 712-2642
Fred Mckirigan, *VP*
**EMP:** 64
Web: www.xppower.com
SIC: **3679** Power supplies, all types: static
HQ: Xp Power Inc.
　305 Foster St Ste 4
　Littleton MA 01460
　800 253-0490

**(P-13129)**
### Z-TRONIX INC
Also Called: Manufacturer
6327 Alondra Blvd, Paramount (90723-3750)
PHONE..................562 808-0800
Kamran Jahangard-mahboob, *CEO*
Roy R Jahangard, *Pr*
◆ **EMP:** 20 **EST:** 1997
**SQ FT:** 18,000
**SALES (est):** 3.92MM **Privately Held**
Web: www.z-tronix.com
SIC: **3679** 5063 5065 Harness assemblies, for electronic use: wire or cable; Wire and cable; Connectors, electronic

---

## 3691 Storage Batteries

**(P-13130)**
### AA PORTABLE POWER CORPORATION
Also Called: BATTERYSPACE.COM
825 S 19th St, Richmond (94804-3808)
PHONE..................510 525-2328
Xiao Ping Jiang, *Pr*
Reiko Aso, *
▲ **EMP:** 35 **EST:** 1995
**SQ FT:** 15,000
**SALES (est):** 50.08K **Privately Held**
Web: www.batteryspace.com
SIC: **3691** Storage batteries

**(P-13131)**
### BATTERY TECHNOLOGY INC (PA)
Also Called: B T I
16651 E Johnson Dr, City Of Industry (91745-2413)
PHONE..................626 336-6878
Christopher Chu, *Pr*
Andy Tong, *VP*
▲ **EMP:** 53 **EST:** 1992
**SQ FT:** 20,000
**SALES (est):** 3.88MM **Privately Held**
Web: www.batterytech.com
SIC: **3691** Storage batteries

**(P-13132)**
### CABAN SYSTEMS INC
858 Stanton Rd, Burlingame (94010)
P.O. Box 65 (94560)
PHONE..................831 245-1608

## PRODUCTS & SERVICES SECTION
## 3691 - Storage Batteries (P-13154)

Alexandra Rasch, *CEO*
**EMP:** 25 **EST:** 2018
**SALES (est):** 8.78MM **Privately Held**
**Web:** www.cabanenergy.com
**SIC: 3691** Storage batteries

### (P-13133)
### CLARIOS LLC
Also Called: Johnson Controls
2200 Mis, Santa Clara (95054)
**PHONE**..................408 346-9984
Ned Caufin, *Brnch Mgr*
**EMP:** 22
**SALES (corp-wide):** 69.83B **Privately Held**
**Web:** www.clarios.com
**SIC: 3691** Storage batteries
**HQ:** Clarios, Llc
5757 N Green Bay Ave Flor
Glendale WI 53209

### (P-13134)
### EAST PENN MANUFACTURING
2709 Via Orange Way Ste B, Spring Valley (91978-1708)
**PHONE**..................619 660-0016
Kathy Broding, *Pr*
**EMP:** 16 **EST:** 1962
**SQ FT:** 1,600
**SALES (est):** 693.17K **Privately Held**
**Web:** www.eastpennmanufacturing.com
**SIC: 3691** Storage batteries

### (P-13135)
### ENERGY VAULT INC (HQ)
4360 Park Terrace Dr Ste 100, Westlake Village (91361-4627)
**PHONE**..................805 852-0000
Robert Piconi, *CEO*
Andrea Wuttke, *
**EMP:** 38 **EST:** 2017
**SQ FT:** 15,767
**SALES (est):** 24.95MM
**SALES (corp-wide):** 341.54MM **Publicly Held**
**Web:** www.energyvault.com
**SIC: 3691** Storage batteries
**PA:** Energy Vault Holdings, Inc.
4360 Park Ter Dr Ste 100
805 852-0000

### (P-13136)
### ENERSYS
30069 Ahern Ave, Union City (94587-1234)
**PHONE**..................510 887-8080
Tom Larkin, *Brnch Mgr*
**EMP:** 23
**SALES (corp-wide):** 3.58B **Publicly Held**
**Web:** www.enersys.com
**SIC: 3691** Lead acid batteries (storage batteries)
**PA:** Enersys
2366 Bernville Rd
610 208-1991

### (P-13137)
### ENERSYS
5580 Edison Ave, Chino (91710-6936)
**PHONE**..................909 464-8251
Ken Hill, *Brnch Mgr*
**EMP:** 25
**SALES (corp-wide):** 3.58B **Publicly Held**
**Web:** www.enersys.com
**SIC: 3691** Lead acid batteries (storage batteries)
**PA:** Enersys
2366 Bernville Rd
610 208-1991

### (P-13138)
### ENEVATE CORPORATION
Also Called: Enevate
101 Theory Ste 200, Irvine (92617-3089)
**PHONE**..................949 243-0399
Bob Kruse, *Pr*
Kirk Shockley, *
Doctor Benjamin Park, *Prin*
Jarvis Tou, *
Doug A Morris, *Quality Vice President*
▲ **EMP:** 62 **EST:** 2005
**SQ FT:** 17,000
**SALES (est):** 9.44MM **Privately Held**
**Web:** www.enevate.com
**SIC: 3691** Storage batteries

### (P-13139)
### ENPOWER GREENTECH INC
333 W San Carlos St, San Jose (95110-2726)
**PHONE**..................916 220-6060
**EMP:** 20 **EST:** 2018
**SALES (est):** 243.02K **Privately Held**
**Web:** www.enpowerus.com
**SIC: 3691** Storage batteries

### (P-13140)
### EREPLACEMENTS LLC
16885 W Bernardo Dr Ste 370, San Diego (92127-1618)
**PHONE**..................714 361-2652
Thomas M Peck, *Brnch Mgr*
**EMP:** 30
**Web:** www.ereplacements.com
**SIC: 3691** Storage batteries
**PA:** Ereplacements, Llc
1300 Mnters Chpel Rd Ste

### (P-13141)
### FLUX POWER HOLDINGS INC (PA)
2685 S Melrose Dr, Vista (92081-8783)
**PHONE**..................877 505-3589
Ronald F Dutt, *Ch Bd*
Charles A Scheiwe, *Sec*
Jeffrey Mason, *VP Opers*
Kevin Royal, *CFO*
▲ **EMP:** 123 **EST:** 1998
**SQ FT:** 63,200
**SALES (est):** 66.34MM **Publicly Held**
**Web:** www.fluxpower.com
**SIC: 3691** 5063 Storage batteries; Storage batteries, industrial

### (P-13142)
### FRANKLINWH ENERGY STORAGE INC
1731 Technology Dr Ste 530, San Jose (95110-1329)
**PHONE**..................888 837-2655
**EMP:** 19 **EST:** 2021
**SALES (est):** 5.62MM **Privately Held**
**Web:** www.franklinwh.com
**SIC: 3691** 7371 Storage batteries; Computer software development and applications

### (P-13143)
### GOLD PEAK INDUSTRIES (NORTH AMERICA) INC
Also Called: GP Batteries
11245 W Bernardo Ct Ste 104, San Diego (92127-1676)
**PHONE**..................858 674-6099
▲ **EMP:** 40
**Web:** www.gpina.com
**SIC: 3691** Batteries, rechargeable

### (P-13144)
### INEVIT INC
541 Jefferson Ave Ste 100, Redwood City (94063-1700)
**PHONE**..................650 298-6001
Michael Miskovsky, *CEO*
Mark White, *Sec*
**EMP:** 108 **EST:** 2016
**SALES (est):** 903.41K **Privately Held**
**SIC: 3691** Storage batteries
**HQ:** Sf Motors, Inc.
1504 Mccarthy Blvd
Milpitas CA 95035
408 617-7878

### (P-13145)
### LITHOS ENERGY INC
28345 Industrial Blvd, Hayward (94545-4428)
**PHONE**..................415 944-5482
James Meredith, *CEO*
**EMP:** 25 **EST:** 2015
**SALES (est):** 9.87MM **Privately Held**
**Web:** www.lithosenergy.com
**SIC: 3691** Batteries, rechargeable

### (P-13146)
### NATRON ENERGY INC (PA)
3542 Bassett St, Santa Clara (95054-2704)
**PHONE**..................408 498-5828
Colin Wessells, *CEO*
**EMP:** 60 **EST:** 2012
**SQ FT:** 2,500
**SALES (est):** 12.68MM
**SALES (corp-wide):** 12.68MM **Privately Held**
**Web:** www.natron.energy
**SIC: 3691** 7389 Batteries, rechargeable; Business services, nec

### (P-13147)
### PALOS VERDES BUILDING CORP (PA)
Also Called: U.S. Battery Mfg Co
1675 Sampson Ave, Corona (92879-1889)
**PHONE**..................951 371-8090
◆ **EMP:** 115 **EST:** 1949
**SALES (est):** 47.38MM
**SALES (corp-wide):** 47.38MM **Privately Held**
**Web:** www.usbattery.com
**SIC: 3691** Storage batteries

### (P-13148)
### SILA NANOTECHNOLOGIES INC (PA)
2470 Mariner Square Loop, Alameda (94501-1010)
**PHONE**..................408 475-7452
Gene Berdichevsky, *CEO*
Bill Mulligan, *
Warren Desouza, *CFO*
**EMP:** 155 **EST:** 2011
**SQ FT:** 87,531
**SALES (est):** 65.15MM
**SALES (corp-wide):** 65.15MM **Privately Held**
**Web:** www.silanano.com
**SIC: 3691** Storage batteries

### (P-13149)
### SIMPLIPHI POWER INC
3100 Camino Del Sol, Oxnard (93030-7257)
**PHONE**..................805 640-6700
Stephen P Andrews, *CEO*
Mark A Schwertfeger, *
▲ **EMP:** 34 **EST:** 2001
**SQ FT:** 5,300

**SALES (est):** 15.72MM
**SALES (corp-wide):** 2.04B **Privately Held**
**Web:** energy.briggsandstratton.com
**SIC: 3691** Storage batteries
**HQ:** Briggs & Stratton, Llc
12301 W Wirth St
Wauwatosa WI 53222
414 259-5333

### (P-13150)
### STACKED ENERGY INC ✪
2380 Bering Dr, San Jose (95131-1121)
**PHONE**..................618 420-9244
Dylan Erb, *CEO*
**EMP:** 20 **EST:** 2024
**SALES (est):** 1.22MM **Privately Held**
**SIC: 3691** Storage batteries

### (P-13151)
### SUNFUSION ENERGY SYSTEMS INC
9020 Kenamar Dr Ste 204, San Diego (92121-2431)
**PHONE**..................800 544-0282
Walter Ellard, *Pr*
**EMP:** 24 **EST:** 2019
**SQ FT:** 6,000
**SALES (est):** 1.33MM **Privately Held**
**Web:** www.sunfusioness.com
**SIC: 3691** Storage batteries

### (P-13152)
### TELEDYNE TECHNOLOGIES INC
Also Called: Teledyne Battery Products
840 W Brockton Ave, Redlands (92374-2902)
P.O. Box 7950 (92375-1150)
**PHONE**..................909 793-3131
Greg Donahey, *Brnch Mgr*
**EMP:** 58
**SALES (corp-wide):** 5.64B **Publicly Held**
**Web:** www.teledyne.com
**SIC: 3691** 3692 Storage batteries; Primary batteries, dry and wet
**PA:** Teledyne Technologies Inc
1049 Camino Dos Rios
805 373-4545

### (P-13153)
### TENERGY CORPORATION
Also Called: All-Battery.com
436 Kato Ter, Fremont (94539)
**PHONE**..................510 687-0388
Xiangbing Li, *CEO*
Ling Ch Liang, *
▲ **EMP:** 90 **EST:** 2004
**SALES (est):** 10.43MM **Privately Held**
**Web:** www.tenergybattery.com
**SIC: 3691** 5063 Alkaline cell storage batteries; Batteries

### (P-13154)
### TROJAN BATTERY HOLDINGS LLC
12380 Clark St, Santa Fe Springs (90670-3804)
**PHONE**..................800 423-6569
**EMP:** 27 **EST:** 2013
**SALES (est):** 4.65MM
**SALES (corp-wide):** 3.44B **Privately Held**
**Web:** www.trojanbattery.com
**SIC: 3691** 3692 Lead acid batteries (storage batteries); Primary batteries, dry and wet
**HQ:** Trojan Battery Company, Llc
12380 Clark St
Santa Fe Springs CA 90670
562 236-3000

# 3691 - Storage Batteries (P-13155)

**(P-13155)**
**ZEROBASE ENERGY LLC**
Also Called: Zero Base
46609 Fremont Blvd, Fremont
(94538-6410)
PHONE..................888 530-9376
Steve Hogge, *Pr*
Wayne Labrie Prod, *Unit Director*
Mark Lucas, *Sls Dir*
EMP: 22 EST: 2009
SALES (est): 5.5MM **Privately Held**
Web: www.zerobaseenergy.com
SIC: 3691 3699 4911 Storage batteries; Generators, ultrasonic; Generation, electric power

## 3692 Primary Batteries, Dry And Wet

**(P-13156)**
**ASSA ABLOY AB**
Also Called: Hhi
19701 Da Vinci, Lake Forest (92610-2622)
PHONE..................949 672-4003
Lucas Boselli, *Division Head*
EMP: 700
SQ FT: 150,000
Web: www.assaabloy.com
SIC: 3692 Primary batteries, dry and wet
PA: Assa Abloy Ab
Klarabergsviadukten 90
850648500

**(P-13157)**
**B & B BATTERY (USA) INC (PA)**
6415 Randolph St, Commerce
(90040-3511)
PHONE..................323 278-1900
Jack Liu, *Pr*
George Liu, *VP*
▲ EMP: 18 EST: 1995
SQ FT: 20,000
SALES (est): 2.38MM **Privately Held**
SIC: 3692 Primary batteries, dry and wet

**(P-13158)**
**CORESHELL TECHNOLOGIES INC**
2625 Alcatraz Ave # 314, Berkeley (94705)
PHONE..................415 265-4887
Jonathan Shaopeng Tan, *CEO*
Roger Basu, *
John Nadaskay, *CFO*
EMP: 30 EST: 2017
SALES (est): 400K **Privately Held**
Web: www.coreshell.com
SIC: 3692 Primary batteries, dry and wet

**(P-13159)**
**ENOVIX CORPORATION (PA)**
Also Called: ENOVIX
3501 W Warren Ave, Fremont
(94538-6400)
PHONE..................510 695-2350
Raj Talluri, *Pr*
Thurman John Rodgers, *Ch Bd*
Farhan Ahmad, *CFO*
Ajay Marathe, *COO*
Arthi Chakravarthy, *CLO*
EMP: 89 EST: 2007
SQ FT: 68,500
SALES (est): 7.64MM
SALES (corp-wide): 7.64MM **Publicly Held**
Web: www.enovix.com
SIC: 3692 Primary batteries, dry and wet

**(P-13160)**
**ENOVIX OPERATIONS INC**
3501 W Warren Ave, Fremont
(94538-6400)
PHONE..................510 695-2399
Harrold Rust, *CEO*
Steffen Pietzke, *
EMP: 115 EST: 2006
SALES (est): 1.57MM
SALES (corp-wide): 7.64MM **Publicly Held**
Web: www.enovix.com
SIC: 3692 Primary batteries, dry and wet
PA: Enovix Corporation
3501 W Warren Ave
510 695-2350

**(P-13161)**
**IMPRINT ENERGY INC**
1320 Harbor Bay Pkwy Ste 110, Alameda
(94502-2208)
PHONE..................510 847-7027
Christine Ho, *CEO*
Eliodoro Batingana Junior, *CFO*
EMP: 20 EST: 2010
SALES (est): 2.28MM **Privately Held**
Web: www.imprintenergy.com
SIC: 3692 Primary batteries, dry and wet

**(P-13162)**
**PRIMUS POWER CORPORATION**
3967 Trust Way, Hayward (94545-3723)
P.O. Box 4557 (94540-4557)
PHONE..................510 342-7600
Thomas Stepien, *CEO*
Richard Winter, *
Jorg Heinemann, *Chief Commercial Officer**
EMP: 50 EST: 2009
SALES (est): 8.34MM **Privately Held**
Web: www.primuspower.com
SIC: 3692 Primary batteries, dry and wet

**(P-13163)**
**QUALLION LLC**
12744 San Fernando Rd Ste 100, Sylmar
(91342-3854)
PHONE..................818 833-2000
Jackie York, *
▲ EMP: 155 EST: 1998
SALES (est): 20.01MM
SALES (corp-wide): 3.58B **Publicly Held**
Web: www.enersys.com
SIC: 3692 Primary batteries, dry and wet
PA: Enersys
2366 Bernville Rd
610 208-1991

**(P-13164)**
**TROJAN BATTERY COMPANY LLC (DH)**
12380 Clark St, Santa Fe Springs
(90670-3804)
PHONE..................562 236-3000
TOLL FREE: 800
Richard A Heller, *CEO*
Alex Dimitrijevic, *CFO*
◆ EMP: 182 EST: 2013
SALES (est): 658.32MM
SALES (corp-wide): 3.44B **Privately Held**
Web: www.trojanbattery.com
SIC: 3692 3691 Primary batteries, dry and wet; Lead acid batteries (storage batteries)
HQ: C&D Technologies, Inc.
200 Precision Rd
Horsham PA 19044
215 619-2700

## 3694 Engine Electrical Equipment

**(P-13165)**
**AMERICAN INDUSTRIAL MANUFACTURING SERVICES INC**
41673 Corning Pl, Murrieta (92562-7023)
PHONE..................951 698-3379
▼ EMP: 107
SIC: 3694 Engine electrical equipment

**(P-13166)**
**ARRIVER HOLDCO INC**
5775 Morehouse Dr, San Diego
(92121-1714)
PHONE..................858 587-1121
Jacob Svanberg, *CEO*
EMP: 7543 EST: 2017
SALES (est): 1.66B
SALES (corp-wide): 38.96B **Publicly Held**
Web: www.veoneer.com
SIC: 3694 3714 Automotive electrical equipment, nec; Motor vehicle parts and accessories
PA: Qualcomm Incorporated
5775 Morehouse Dr
858 587-1121

**(P-13167)**
**BATTERY-BIZ INC**
Also Called: Ebatts.com
1380 Flynn Rd, Camarillo (93012-8016)
PHONE..................800 848-6782
Ophir Marish, *CEO*
Yossi Jakubovits, *
▲ EMP: 63 EST: 1988
SALES (est): 9.47MM **Privately Held**
Web: www.battery-biz.com
SIC: 3694 Battery charging generators, automobile and aircraft

**(P-13168)**
**DSM&T CO INC**
10609 Business Dr, Fontana (92337-8212)
PHONE..................909 357-7960
Sergio Corona, *CEO*
▲ EMP: 170 EST: 1982
SQ FT: 41,000
SALES (est): 24.97MM **Privately Held**
Web: www.dsmt.com
SIC: 3694 3357 3634 3643 Harness wiring sets, internal combustion engines; Nonferrous wiredrawing and insulating; Heating pads, electric; Cord connectors, electric

**(P-13169)**
**ELECTRICAL REBUILDERS SLS INC**
Also Called: Vapex-Genex-Precision
7603 Willow Glen Rd, Los Angeles
(90046-1608)
PHONE..................323 249-7545
Mike Klapper, *Pr*
David Klapper, *
Mary Ann Klapper, *
▲ EMP: 100 EST: 1966
SALES (est): 3.25MM **Privately Held**
SIC: 3694 3592 3714 Distributors, motor vehicle engine; Carburetors; Motor vehicle brake systems and parts

**(P-13170)**
**EV CHARGING SOLUTIONS INC**
11800 Clark St, Arcadia (91006-6000)
PHONE..................866 300-3827
Gustavo Fabian Occhiuzzo, *CEO*
EMP: 56 EST: 2018
SALES (est): 5.55MM **Privately Held**
Web: www.evconnect.com
SIC: 3694 Battery charging alternators and generators

**(P-13171)**
**GREENLANE INFRASTRUCTURE LLC**
Also Called: Drive Greenlane
3101 Ocean Park Blvd Ste 100, Santa Monica (90405-3029)
PHONE..................503 839-8116
EMP: 20 EST: 2022
SALES (est): 1.34MM **Privately Held**
SIC: 3694 Battery charging generators, automobile and aircraft

**(P-13172)**
**HL URIMAN INC (HQ)**
Also Called: Ashera Motorsports
650 N Puente St, Brea (92821)
PHONE..................714 257-2080
Ki Taek Song, *CEO*
Susie Chiang, *
Minjun Kim, *
Joon Bom Kim, *
◆ EMP: 18 EST: 1983
SQ FT: 42,144
SALES (est): 16.45MM **Privately Held**
Web: www.hlmandoparts.com
SIC: 3694 3625 3714 Alternators, automotive; Starter, electric motor; Power steering equipment, motor vehicle
PA: Hl D&I Halla Corporation
289 Olympic-Ro, Songpa-Gu

**(P-13173)**
**INTERNATIONAL RES DEV CORP NEV (PA)**
Also Called: IRD
5212 Chelsea St, La Jolla (92037-7910)
PHONE..................858 488-9900
Robert E Kane, *Pr*
Anthony Renda, *VP*
▲ EMP: 15 EST: 1979
SALES (est): 1.66MM
SALES (corp-wide): 1.66MM **Privately Held**
SIC: 3694 Automotive electrical equipment, nec

**(P-13174)**
**LILYPAD EV LLC**
4591 Pacheco Blvd, Martinez (94553-2233)
PHONE..................866 525-9723
Niazi Alzhouhbi, *CEO*
EMP: 20 EST: 2021
SALES (est): 4.62MM
SALES (corp-wide): 38.91MM **Privately Held**
Web: www.lilypadev.com
SIC: 3694 Automotive electrical equipment, nec
PA: Shields, Harper & Co.
4591 Pacheco Blvd
510 653-9119

**(P-13175)**
**LOOP INC**
115 Eucalyptus Dr, El Segundo
(90245-3839)
PHONE..................888 385-6674
Dustin Cavanaugh, *CEO*
EMP: 30 EST: 2019
SALES (est): 6.08MM **Privately Held**
Web: www.evloop.io
SIC: 3694 Battery charging generators, automobile and aircraft

## PRODUCTS & SERVICES SECTION

### 3695 - Magnetic And Optical Recording Media (P-13196)

**(P-13176)**
**LOW COST INTERLOCK INC**
2038 W Park Ave, Redlands (92373-6260)
P.O. Box 365 (92373-0121)
PHONE.................844 387-0326
Michael E Lyon, *CEO*
**EMP:** 78 **EST:** 2010
**SALES (est):** 2.96MM **Privately Held**
**Web:** www.lowcostinterlock.com
**SIC: 3694** Ignition apparatus and distributors

**(P-13177)**
**M & H ELECTRIC FABRICATORS INC**
13537 Alondra Blvd, Santa Fe Springs (90670-5602)
PHONE.................562 926-9552
▲ **EMP:** 30 **EST:** 1985
**SALES (est):** 4.69MM **Privately Held**
**Web:** www.wiringharness.com
**SIC: 3694** Automotive electrical equipment, nec

**(P-13178)**
**MAXWELL TECHNOLOGIES INC (HQ)**
Also Called: Maxwell
3888 Calle Fortunada, San Diego (92123-1825)
PHONE.................858 503-3300
Franz Fink, *Pr*
David Lyle, *
Emily Lough, *
▲ **EMP:** 94 **EST:** 1965
**SQ FT:** 30,500
**SALES (est):** 33.92MM
**SALES (corp-wide):** 96.77B **Publicly Held**
**Web:** www.maxwell.com
**SIC: 3694** 3629 Engine electrical equipment; Capacitors and condensers
**PA:** Tesla, Inc.
1 Tesla Rd
512 516-8177

**(P-13179)**
**MYOTEK INDUSTRIES INCORPORATED (DH)**
1278 Glenneyre St Ste 431, Laguna Beach (92651-3103)
PHONE.................949 502-3776
Robert Harrington, *Pr*
▲ **EMP:** 90 **EST:** 1998
**SQ FT:** 1,800
**SALES (est):** 28.81MM
**SALES (corp-wide):** 110.61MM **Privately Held**
**Web:** www.fordledfog.com
**SIC: 3694** 5013 Automotive electrical equipment, nec; Automotive servicing equipment
**HQ:** Myotek Holdings, Inc.
1176 Main St Ste B
Irvine CA 92614
949 502-3776

**(P-13180)**
**PERTRONIX INC**
Also Called: Patriot Products
15601 Cypress Ave Unit B, Irwindale (91706-2120)
PHONE.................909 599-5955
Jack Porter, *Mgr*
**EMP:** 26
**SALES (corp-wide):** 13.89MM **Privately Held**
**Web:** www.pertronixbrands.com
**SIC: 3694** 5013 Ignition apparatus, internal combustion engines; Automotive supplies and parts

**PA:** Pertronix, Llc
10955 Mill Creek Rd
909 599-5955

**(P-13181)**
**POLAR POWER INC**
Also Called: Polar Power
249 E Gardena Blvd, Gardena (90248-2813)
PHONE.................310 830-9153
**EMP:** 87 **EST:** 1979
**SALES (est):** 15.29MM **Privately Held**
**Web:** www.polarpower.com
**SIC: 3694** Engine electrical equipment

**(P-13182)**
**PRECO AIRCRAFT MOTORS INC**
1133 Mission St, South Pasadena (91030-3211)
P.O. Box 189 (91031-0189)
PHONE.................626 799-3549
Peter Kingston Junior, *Pr*
Peter Kingston Senior, *Ch*
Linda D Kingston, *VP*
**EMP:** 20 **EST:** 1945
**SQ FT:** 10,000
**SALES (est):** 394.12K **Privately Held**
**Web:** www.day-ray.com
**SIC: 3694** Motors, starting: automotive and aircraft

**(P-13183)**
**PROTERRA INC (PA)**
1815 Rollins Rd, Burlingame (94010-2204)
PHONE.................864 438-0000
Gareth T Joyce, *Pr*
Roger M Nielsen, *Ch Bd*
Justin Pugh, *CFO*
**EMP:** 607 **EST:** 2004
**SQ FT:** 34,400
**SALES (est):** 309.36MM
**SALES (corp-wide):** 309.36MM **Publicly Held**
**Web:** www.proterra.com
**SIC: 3694** 3625 Automotive electrical equipment, nec; Truck controls, industrial battery

**(P-13184)**
**PROTERRA POWERED LLC (DH)** ✪
1815 Rollins Rd, Burlingame (94010-2204)
PHONE.................864 516-0068
Chris Bailey, *CEO*
John Dostert, *Prin*
Gregory Higgins, *Prin*
Douglas Knebel, *
**EMP:** 450 **EST:** 2023
**SALES (est):** 16.03MM
**SALES (corp-wide):** 119.84MM **Privately Held**
**SIC: 3694** 3625 Automotive electrical equipment, nec; Truck controls, industrial battery
**HQ:** Mack Trucks, Inc.
7900 National Service Rd
Greensboro NC 27409
336 291-9001

**(P-13185)**
**SERES INC**
1504 Mccarthy Blvd, Milpitas (95035-7405)
PHONE.................214 585-3356
Mingxu Yao, *CEO*
**EMP:** 200 **EST:** 2019
**SALES (est):** 4.54MM **Privately Held**
**Web:** www.driveseres.com
**SIC: 3694** Motors, starting: automotive and aircraft

**(P-13186)**
**STABLE AUTO CORPORATION**
124 Jupiter St, Encinitas (92024-1449)
PHONE.................415 967-2719
Rohan Puri, *CEO*
**EMP:** 30 **EST:** 2019
**SALES (est):** 3.09MM **Privately Held**
**Web:** www.stable.auto
**SIC: 3694** Battery charging generators, automobile and aircraft

**(P-13187)**
**TAU MOTORS INC**
Also Called: Tau Motors
1104 Main St, Redwood City (94063-1913)
PHONE.................650 486-1033
Walter Pennington Iii, *CEO*
Matthew Rubin, *Engr*
Alexander Hitzinger, *Dir*
Jason Schroeder, *Dir*
**EMP:** 15 **EST:** 2017
**SALES (est):** 5.16MM **Privately Held**
**Web:** www.taumotors.com
**SIC: 3694** 3621 8711 Motor generator sets, automotive; Motors and generators; Electrical or electronic engineering

**(P-13188)**
**TERAWATT INFRASTRUCTURE INC**
85 2nd St, San Francisco (94105-3459)
PHONE.................785 251-0751
Neha Palmer, *CEO*
**EMP:** 18 **EST:** 2021
**SALES (est):** 5.17MM **Privately Held**
**Web:** www.terawattinfrastructure.com
**SIC: 3694** Battery charging alternators and generators

**(P-13189)**
**TERAWATT INFRASTRUCTURE INC**
49 Stevenson St Ste 600, San Francisco (94105-2953)
PHONE.................415 837-1946
**EMP:** 30
**SALES (est):** 1.21MM **Privately Held**
**SIC: 3694** Battery charging generators, automobile and aircraft

**(P-13190)**
**TRADEMARK CONSTRUCTION CO INC (PA)**
Also Called: Jmw Truss and Components
15916 Bernardo Center Dr, San Diego (92127-1828)
PHONE.................760 489-5647
Richard D Wilson, *Pr*
John Cao, *
Nancy Wilson, *
**EMP:** 60 **EST:** 1978
**SQ FT:** 12,000
**SALES (est):** 21.52MM
**SALES (corp-wide):** 21.52MM **Privately Held**
**Web:** www.jmwtruss.com
**SIC: 3694** Engine electrical equipment

**(P-13191)**
**VANTAGE VEHICLE INTL INC**
Also Called: Vantage Vehicle Group
1740 N Delilah St, Corona (92879-1893)
PHONE.................951 735-1200
Michael Pak, *Pr*
◆ **EMP:** 30 **EST:** 2002
**SQ FT:** 50,000
**SALES (est):** 4.83MM **Privately Held**
**Web:** www.vantagevehicle.com

**SIC: 3694** Distributors, motor vehicle engine

### 3695 Magnetic And Optical Recording Media

**(P-13192)**
**CAPELLA PHOTONICS INC**
1100 La Avenida St Ste A, Mountain View (94043-1453)
PHONE.................408 360-4240
Larry Schwerin, *Pr*
William O'hollaren, *VP*
Rafael Torres, *
Long Yang, *
Byron Trop, *
**EMP:** 50 **EST:** 2000
**SQ FT:** 6,600
**SALES (est):** 3.34MM
**SALES (corp-wide):** 24.19B **Privately Held**
**Web:** www.capellainc.com
**SIC: 3695** Optical disks and tape, blank
**HQ:** Nokia Of America Corporation
600 Mountain Ave Ste 700
Murray Hill NJ 07974

**(P-13193)**
**CD VIDEO MANUFACTURING INC**
Also Called: C D Video
12650 Westminster Ave, Santa Ana (92706)
PHONE.................714 265-0770
Minh T Nguyen, *Pr*
▲ **EMP:** 60 **EST:** 1995
**SQ FT:** 11,000
**SALES (est):** 11.02MM **Privately Held**
**Web:** www.cdvideomfg.com
**SIC: 3695** 3652 7819 Video recording tape, blank; Compact laser discs, prerecorded; Services allied to motion pictures

**(P-13194)**
**ELECTRONIC ARTS REDWOOD LLC**
Also Called: Ea Sports
209 Redwood Shores Pkwy, Redwood City (94065-1175)
PHONE.................650 628-1500
Larry Probst, *CEO*
**EMP:** 1000 **EST:** 1994
**SALES (est):** 2.18MM
**SALES (corp-wide):** 7.43B **Publicly Held**
**Web:** www.ea.com
**SIC: 3695** Video recording tape, blank
**PA:** Electronic Arts Inc.
209 Redwood Shores Pkwy
650 628-1500

**(P-13195)**
**ELM SYSTEM INC**
11622 El Camino Real Ste 100, San Diego (92130-2051)
PHONE.................408 694-2750
Ingyeom Kim, *CEO*
**EMP:** 18 **EST:** 2012
**SALES (est):** 256.65K **Privately Held**
**SIC: 3695** Computer software tape and disks: blank, rigid, and floppy

**(P-13196)**
**FARSTONE TECHNOLOGY INC**
184 Technology Dr Ste 205, Irvine (92618-2435)
PHONE.................949 336-4321
**EMP:** 110
**SALES (est):** 3.1MM **Privately Held**
**Web:** www.farstone.com

## 3695 - Magnetic And Optical Recording Media (P-13197)

SIC: **3695** Computer software tape and disks: blank, rigid, and floppy

**(P-13197)**
**LASERCARD CORPORATION**
1875 N Shoreline Blvd, Mountain View (94043-1319)
PHONE..................650 969-4428
▲ EMP: 82
SIC: **3695** Magnetic and optical recording media

**(P-13198)**
**MICROTECH SYSTEMS INC**
1336 Brommer St, Santa Cruz (95062-2947)
PHONE..................650 596-1900
Corwin Nichols, *CEO*
Michael Fallavollita, *VP*
Victoria Nichols, *Sec*
EMP: 15 EST: 1977
SALES (est): 4.25MM **Privately Held**
Web: www.microtech.com
SIC: **3695** Optical disks and tape, blank

**(P-13199)**
**MOTA GROUP INC (PA)**
Also Called: Unorth
60 S Market St Ste 1100, San Jose (95113-2366)
PHONE..................408 370-1248
Michael Faro, *CEO*
Jeffrey L Garon, *CFO*
Lily Q Ju, *Sec*
◆ EMP: 24 EST: 2003
SALES (est): 861.39K **Privately Held**
Web: www.mota.com
SIC: **3695** Computer software tape and disks: blank, rigid, and floppy

**(P-13200)**
**NORDSON CALIFORNIA INC**
Also Called: Nordson Asymtek
2747 Loker Ave W, Carlsbad (92010-6601)
PHONE..................760 918-8490
◆ EMP: 94
SIC: **3695** 3561 Computer software tape and disks: blank, rigid, and floppy; Pump jacks and other pumping equipment

**(P-13201)**
**RECOMMIND INC (HQ)**
550 Kearny St Ste 700, San Francisco (94108-2503)
PHONE..................415 394-7899
Steve King, *CEO*
Robert Pennant, *Executive Chief Executive Officer*
Bernard Huger, *CFO*
EMP: 100 EST: 2000
SQ FT: 15,000
SALES (est): 13.19MM
SALES (corp-wide): 5.77B **Privately Held**
Web: www.opentext.com
SIC: **3695** Computer software tape and disks: blank, rigid, and floppy
PA: Open Text Corporation
275 Frank Tompa Dr
519 888-7111

**(P-13202)**
**REEL PICTURE PRODUCTIONS LLC**
5330 Eastgate Mall, San Diego (92121-2804)
PHONE..................858 587-0301
Michael Ishayik, *Managing Member*
▲ EMP: 43 EST: 1997
SQ FT: 45,000
SALES (est): 1.98MM **Privately Held**
Web: www.reelpicture.com
SIC: **3695** Optical disks and tape, blank

**(P-13203)**
**TARGET TECHNOLOGY COMPANY LLC**
3420 Bristol St, Costa Mesa (92626-7133)
PHONE..................949 788-0909
EMP: 50 EST: 1998
SALES (est): 1.6MM **Privately Held**
Web: www.targettechnology.com
SIC: **3695** Magnetic and optical recording media

**(P-13204)**
**TECHNICOLOR DISC SERVICES CORP (HQ)**
3601 Calle Tecate Ste 120, Camarillo (93012-5097)
PHONE..................805 445-1122
Mary Fialkowski, *Pr*
O F Raimondo, *
▲ EMP: 200 EST: 1996
SALES (est): 49.93MM **Privately Held**
SIC: **3695** 7361 Computer software tape and disks: blank, rigid, and floppy; Employment agencies
PA: Vantiva
10 Boulevard De Grenelle

**(P-13205)**
**U-TECH MEDIA USA LLC**
1105 Montague Expy, Milpitas (95035-6845)
PHONE..................408 597-1600
▲ EMP: 220
SIC: **3695** 7389 Computer software tape and disks: blank, rigid, and floppy; Packaging and labeling services

## 3699 Electrical Equipment And Supplies, Nec

**(P-13206)**
**3D ROBOTICS INC (PA)**
Also Called: Diy Drones
1165 Miller Ave, Berkeley (94708-1754)
PHONE..................415 599-1404
Chris Anderson, *CEO*
Jordi Munoz, *
Andy Jensen, *
John Cherbini, *
▲ EMP: 70 EST: 2009
SALES (est): 11.51MM
SALES (corp-wide): 11.51MM **Privately Held**
Web: www.3dr.com
SIC: **3699** Electrical equipment and supplies, nec

**(P-13207)**
**A T PARKER INC (PA)**
Also Called: Solar Electronics Company
10866 Chandler Blvd, North Hollywood (91601-2945)
PHONE..................818 755-1700
Tom A Parker, *Pr*
Jo Ann Dennis, *VP*
Sue Parker, *Sec*
▼ EMP: 22 EST: 1960
SQ FT: 7,500
SALES (est): 4.54MM
SALES (corp-wide): 4.54MM **Privately Held**
Web: www.solar-emc.com
SIC: **3699** Electrical equipment and supplies, nec

**(P-13208)**
**ACCSYS TECHNOLOGY INC**
Also Called: Accsys
1177 Quarry Ln, Pleasanton (94566-4787)
PHONE..................925 462-6949
▲ EMP: 26
Web: www.accsys.com
SIC: **3699** 8731 3663 Linear accelerators; Commercial physical research; Amplifiers, RF power and IF

**(P-13209)**
**AGENTS WEST INC**
Also Called: Electrical Products Rep
6 Hughes Ste 210, Irvine (92618-2063)
PHONE..................949 614-0293
Aldo Pellicciotti, *Pr*
Stephen Benshoof, *VP*
Clyde Collins, *Treas*
Robert Rathburn, *Sec*
EMP: 38 EST: 1978
SQ FT: 30,000
SALES (est): 4.52MM **Privately Held**
Web: www.agentswest.com
SIC: **3699** 5063 Electrical equipment and supplies, nec; Electrical apparatus and equipment

**(P-13210)**
**AITECH DEFENSE SYSTEMS INC**
19756 Prairie St, Chatsworth (91311-6531)
PHONE..................818 700-2000
Moshe Tal, *CEO*
Erez Konfino, *CFO*
◆ EMP: 55 EST: 1990
SQ FT: 22,000
SALES (est): 22.56MM **Privately Held**
Web: www.aitechsystems.com
SIC: **3699** Electrical equipment and supplies, nec
PA: Aitech Rugged Group, Inc.
19756 Prairie St

**(P-13211)**
**AITECH RUGGED GROUP INC (PA)**
19756 Prairie St, Chatsworth (91311-6531)
PHONE..................818 700-2000
Moshe Tal, *CEO*
Erez Konfino, *
EMP: 50 EST: 2008
SALES (est): 29.92MM **Privately Held**
Web: www.aitechsystems.com
SIC: **3699** Electrical equipment and supplies, nec

**(P-13212)**
**APTIBLE INC**
548 Market St, San Francisco (94104-5401)
PHONE..................866 296-5003
Charles C Ballew Ii, *CEO*
EMP: 58 EST: 2017
SALES (est): 3.84MM **Privately Held**
Web: www.aptible.com
SIC: **3699** Security devices

**(P-13213)**
**ASCO POWER SERVICES INC**
120 S Chaparral Ct Ste 200, Anaheim (92808-2237)
PHONE..................714 283-4000
Les Baird, *Mgr*
EMP: 18
SALES (corp-wide): 82.05K **Privately Held**
Web: www.ascopower.com
SIC: **3699** Electrical equipment and supplies, nec
HQ: Asco Power Services, Inc.
160 Park Ave
Florham Park NJ 07932

**(P-13214)**
**ASCO POWER TECHNOLOGIES LP**
Also Called: Asco Power Tech
3400 E Eight Mile Rd Ste B, Stockton (95212-9507)
PHONE..................209 931-7700
EMP: 107
SALES (corp-wide): 82.05K **Privately Held**
Web: www.ascopower.com
SIC: **3699** Electrical equipment and supplies, nec
HQ: Asco Power Technologies, L.P.
160 Park Ave
Florham Park NJ 07932

**(P-13215)**
**BLISSLIGHTS INC**
2449 Cades Way, Vista (92081-7873)
PHONE..................888 868-4603
Alan Lee, *Pr*
▲ EMP: 26 EST: 2007
SALES (est): 4.78MM **Privately Held**
Web: www.blisslights.com
SIC: **3699** Laser systems and equipment

**(P-13216)**
**BRIX GROUP INC**
Also Called: Panapacific Shipping
80 Van Ness Ave, Fresno (93721-3223)
PHONE..................559 457-4750
Harrison Brix, *CEO*
EMP: 35
SALES (corp-wide): 40.19MM **Privately Held**
Web: www.panapacific.com
SIC: **3699** Electrical equipment and supplies, nec
PA: The Brix Group Inc
838 N Laverne Ave
559 457-4700

**(P-13217)**
**CALSTAR SYSTEMS GROUP INC**
Also Called: Quikstor
6345 Balboa Blvd Ste 105, Encino (91316-1517)
PHONE..................818 922-2000
Dennis Levitt, *Pr*
▲ EMP: 22 EST: 1982
SALES (est): 2.51MM **Privately Held**
Web: www.quikstor.com
SIC: **3699** 7371 Security devices; Computer software development

**(P-13218)**
**CARTTRONICS LLC (HQ)**
90 Icon, Foothill Ranch (92610-3000)
PHONE..................888 696-2278
◆ EMP: 27 EST: 1997
SALES (est): 4.87MM
SALES (corp-wide): 40.85MM **Privately Held**
Web: www.gatekeepersystems.com
SIC: **3699** 7382 5065 Security devices; Security systems services; Security control equipment and systems
PA: Gatekeeper Systems, Inc.
90 Icon
888 808-9433

**(P-13219)**
**CELESTICA INC**
Also Called: Celestica
5325 Hellyer Ave, San Jose (95138-1013)
PHONE..................416 448-5800
FAX: 408 229-6075
▲ EMP: 39

## 3699 - Electrical Equipment And Supplies, Nec (P-13238)

SALES (est): 6.5MM **Privately Held**
SIC: 3699 5731 Electrical equipment and supplies, nec; Consumer electronic equipment, nec

**(P-13220)**
### CENTRAL TECH INC
2271 Ringwood Ave, San Jose (95131-1717)
PHONE.................................408 955-0919
EMP: 26 EST: 2016
SALES (est): 5.58MM **Privately Held**
Web: www.centraltechinc.com
SIC: 3699 Electronic training devices

**(P-13221)**
### CLEAN AMERICA INC
Also Called: EDM Performance Accessories
1400 Pioneer St, Brea (92821-3720)
PHONE.................................800 336-2946
Jim E Swartzbaugh, Pr
Tom Adams, VP
▲ EMP: 15 EST: 1989
SQ FT: 14,000
SALES (est): 5.12MM **Privately Held**
Web: www.edmperformance.com
SIC: 3699 Electrical equipment and supplies, nec

**(P-13222)**
### COAST WIRE & PLASTIC TECH LLC
1048 E Burgrove St, Carson (90746-3514)
PHONE.................................310 639-9473
George Lopez, Co-Managing Member
George Lopez, Managing Member
Mark Vanderwoude, *
David Ibanez, *
EMP: 750 EST: 1993
SQ FT: 60,000
SALES (est): 4.65MM
SALES (corp-wide): 2.51B **Publicly Held**
SIC: 3699 3357 Electrical equipment and supplies, nec; Communication wire
PA: Belden Inc.
1 N Brentwood Blvd Fl 15
314 854-8000

**(P-13223)**
### CODA ENERGY HOLDINGS LLC
Also Called: Coda Energy
111 N Artsakh Ave Ste 300, Glendale (91206-4097)
PHONE.................................626 775-3900
Paul Detering, CEO
Peter Nortman, *
John Bryan, *
Davnette Librando, *
Edward Solar, *
▲ EMP: 16 EST: 2013
SALES (est): 1.76MM **Privately Held**
Web: www.codaenergy.com
SIC: 3699 Household electrical equipment

**(P-13224)**
### COHERENT CORP
Also Called: Coherent Auburn Group, The
5100 Patrick Henry Dr, Santa Clara (95054-1112)
PHONE.................................408 764-4000
Robin Henderson, Mgr
EMP: 38
SALES (corp-wide): 4.71B **Publicly Held**
Web: www.coherent.com
SIC: 3699 3827 3674 Laser systems and equipment; Optical instruments and lenses; Semiconductors and related devices
PA: Coherent Corp.
375 Saxonburg Blvd
724 352-4455

**(P-13225)**
### CONSTRUCTION INNOVATIONS LLC
Also Called: Ci
10630 Mather Blvd Ste 200, Mather (95655-4125)
PHONE.................................855 725-9555
James B Littlejohn, *
EMP: 150 EST: 2012
SQ FT: 17,000
SALES (est): 39.61MM
SALES (corp-wide): 95.93MM **Privately Held**
Web: www.constructioninnovations.com
SIC: 3699 8711 Electrical equipment and supplies, nec; Consulting engineer
PA: Bdg Innovations, Llc
6001 Outfall Cir
855 725-9555

**(P-13226)**
### COOPER CROUSE-HINDS LLC
Also Called: Cooper Interconnect
3350 Enterprise Dr, Bloomington (92316-3538)
PHONE.................................951 241-8766
Morris Townsend, Brnch Mgr
EMP: 35
Web: www.coopercrouse-hinds.com
SIC: 3699 Fire control or bombing equipment, electronic
HQ: Cooper Crouse-Hinds, Llc
1201 Wolf St
Syracuse NY 13208
315 477-7000

**(P-13227)**
### COZZIA USA LLC (HQ)
861 S Oak Park Rd, Covina (91724-3624)
PHONE.................................626 667-2272
Jimmy Lo, *
▲ EMP: 19 EST: 2009
SQ FT: 5,500
SALES (est): 38.43MM **Privately Held**
Web: www.cozziausa.com
SIC: 3699 Electrical equipment and supplies, nec
PA: Xiamen Comfort Science&Technology Group Co., Ltd.
Floor 8, No.31-37, Anling 2nd Road, Huli District

**(P-13228)**
### CUBIC DEFENSE APPLICATIONS INC
4285 Ponderosa Ave, San Diego (92123-1525)
PHONE.................................858 277-6780
EMP: 1039
SALES (corp-wide): 1.48B **Privately Held**
Web: www.cubic.com
SIC: 3699 Flight simulators (training aids), electronic
HQ: Cubic Defense Applications, Inc.
9233 Balboa Ave
San Diego CA 92123
858 776-5664

**(P-13229)**
### CUBIC DEFENSE APPLICATIONS INC (DH)
Also Called: Cubic Ground Training
9233 Balboa Ave, San Diego (92123-1513)
P.O. Box 85587 (92186)
PHONE.................................858 776-5664
Steven Slijepcevic, CEO
John D Thomas, *
James R Edwards, *
Mark A Harrison, *

Norman R Bishop, *
▼ EMP: 589 EST: 1987
SQ FT: 130,000
SALES (est): 497.76MM
SALES (corp-wide): 1.48B **Privately Held**
Web: www.cubic.com
SIC: 3699 3663 3812 Flight simulators (training aids), electronic; Radio and t.v. communications equipment; Aircraft/aerospace flight instruments and guidance systems
HQ: Cubic Corporation
9233 Balboa Ave
San Diego CA 92123
858 277-6780

**(P-13230)**
### CUBIC DEFENSE APPLICATIONS INC
CMS Secure Comms
9233 Balboa Ave, San Diego (92123-1513)
PHONE.................................858 505-2870
Jerry Madigan, VP
EMP: 200
SALES (corp-wide): 1.48B **Privately Held**
Web: www.cubic.com
SIC: 3699 7382 Security devices; Security systems services
HQ: Cubic Defense Applications, Inc.
9233 Balboa Ave
San Diego CA 92123
858 776-5664

**(P-13231)**
### CYMER LLC (HQ)
17075 Thornmint Ct, San Diego (92127-2413)
PHONE.................................858 385-7300
▲ EMP: 555 EST: 1996
SQ FT: 135,000
SALES (est): 659.74MM
SALES (corp-wide): 21.99B **Privately Held**
Web: www.cymer.com
SIC: 3699 3827 Laser systems and equipment; Lens mounts
PA: Asml Holding N.V.
De Run 6501
402683000

**(P-13232)**
### DISTRIBUTION ELECTRNICS VLUED
Also Called: Deva
2651 Dow Ave, Tustin (92780-7207)
PHONE.................................714 368-1717
Rodger Dale Baker, CEO
Ken Plock, *
◆ EMP: 23 EST: 1974
SQ FT: 13,800
SALES (est): 8.14MM **Privately Held**
Web: www.devainc.com
SIC: 3699 5065 Electrical equipment and supplies, nec; Electronic parts and equipment, nec
HQ: Deva, Inc.
555 Madison Ave Ste 1100
New York NY 10022
212 223-2466

**(P-13233)**
### DIY CO
3360 20th St, San Francisco (94110-2655)
PHONE.................................844 564-6349
Zach Klein, CEO
EMP: 16 EST: 2011
SALES (est): 5.54MM **Privately Held**
Web: www.diy.org
SIC: 3699 Teaching machines and aids, electronic
HQ: Littlebits Electronics Inc.
601 W 26th St Rm M274

New York NY 10001

**(P-13234)**
### DOORKING INC (PA)
Also Called: Doorking
120 S Glasgow Ave, Inglewood (90301-1502)
PHONE.................................310 645-0023
Thomas Richmond, Pr
Pat Kochie, *
Susan Richmond, *
◆ EMP: 185 EST: 1948
SQ FT: 16,000
SALES (est): 32.06MM
SALES (corp-wide): 32.06MM **Privately Held**
Web: www.doorking.com
SIC: 3699 5065 3829 Security control equipment and systems; Security control equipment and systems; Measuring and controlling devices, nec

**(P-13235)**
### DPSS LASERS INC
2525 Walsh Ave, Santa Clara (95051-1316)
PHONE.................................408 988-4300
Thomas Hogan, CEO
Alex Laymon, *
EMP: 30 EST: 1998
SQ FT: 25,000
SALES (est): 3.14MM
SALES (corp-wide): 827.24MM **Privately Held**
Web: www.dpss-lasers.com
SIC: 3699 Laser systems and equipment
HQ: Arch Cutting Tools - Flushing, Llc
7162 Sheridan Rd
Flushing MI 48433
810 638-5045

**(P-13236)**
### DUTEK INCORPORATED
2228 Oak Ridge Way, Vista (92081)
PHONE.................................760 566-8888
David Du, CEO
Bill Marsh, *
EMP: 50 EST: 2000
SQ FT: 4,500
SALES (est): 20.57MM
SALES (corp-wide): 30.55MM **Privately Held**
Web: www.dutek.com
SIC: 3699 3629 3643 Electrical equipment and supplies, nec; Electronic generation equipment; Current-carrying wiring services
PA: Ddh Enterprise, Inc.
2220 Oak Ridge Way
760 599-0171

**(P-13237)**
### ECOTALITY INC
1 Montgomery St Ste 2525, San Francisco (94104-5525)
P.O. Box 20336 (85036-0336)
PHONE.................................415 992-3000
EMP: 164
Web: www.ecotality.com
SIC: 3699 3621 Electrical equipment and supplies, nec; Storage battery chargers, motor and engine generator type

**(P-13238)**
### ELECTRIC GATE STORE INC
15342 Chatsworth St, Mission Hills (91345-2041)
PHONE.................................818 504-2300
Jorge Nunez, Pr
Karla Nunez, *
▲ EMP: 150 EST: 2001
SALES (est): 1.46MM **Privately Held**

## 3699 - Electrical Equipment And Supplies, Nec (P-13239)

Web: www.gatestore.com
SIC: 3699 Security devices

**(P-13239)**
**ENVIA SYSTEMS INC**
7979 Gateway Blvd Ste 101, Newark (94560-1157)
P.O. Box 14142 (94539-1342)
PHONE..................510 509-1367
Sujeet Kumar, Pr
▲ EMP: 50 EST: 2007
SALES (est): 5.06MM Privately Held
Web: www.ionblox.com
SIC: 3699 Electrical equipment and supplies, nec

**(P-13240)**
**ETON CORPORATION**
1015 Corporation Way, Palo Alto (94303-4305)
PHONE..................650 903-3866
Esmail Amid-hozour, CEO
John Smith, Sr VP
Hamid Shomali, Dir
◆ EMP: 21 EST: 1986
SQ FT: 10,400
SALES (est): 8.08MM Privately Held
Web: www.etoncorp.com
SIC: 3699 5731 Electrical equipment and supplies, nec; Radio, television, and electronic stores

**(P-13241)**
**FREEDOM PHOTONICS LLC**
41 Aero Camino, Santa Barbara (93117-3104)
PHONE..................805 967-4900
Leif Johansson, *
EMP: 50 EST: 2005
SQ FT: 14,500
SALES (est): 11.28MM
SALES (corp-wide): 69.78MM Publicly Held
Web: www.freedomphotonics.com
SIC: 3699 3827 3674 Laser systems and equipment; Optical test and inspection equipment; Light sensitive devices
PA: Luminar Technologies, Inc.
2603 Discovery Dr Ste 100
407 900-5259

**(P-13242)**
**GATEKEEPER SYSTEMS INC (PA)**
90 Icon, Foothill Ranch (92610-3000)
PHONE..................888 808-9433
Robert Harling, CEO
Jason Crowl, *
Keith Kato, *
Greg Meisenzahl, *
Robert Newbold, *
▲ EMP: 63 EST: 1998
SQ FT: 15,000
SALES (est): 40.85MM
SALES (corp-wide): 40.85MM Privately Held
Web: www.gatekeepersystems.com
SIC: 3699 Security devices

**(P-13243)**
**GEFEN LLC**
1800 S Mcdowell Boulevard Ext, Petaluma (94954-6962)
PHONE..................818 772-9100
Hagai Gefen, CEO
Tony Dowzall, *
Jill Gefen, *
Uri Ram, Sr VP
Aaron Hernandez, *
▲ EMP: 42 EST: 1987

SQ FT: 8,000
SALES (est): 3.61MM
SALES (corp-wide): 865.12MM Privately Held
Web: www.gefen.com
SIC: 3699 High-energy particle physics equipment
HQ: Nice North America Llc
5919 Sea Otter Pl Ste 100
Carlsbad CA 92010
760 438-7000

**(P-13244)**
**GHANGOR CLOUD INC**
2001 Gateway Pl Ste 710, San Jose (95110-1077)
PHONE..................408 713-3303
Tarique Mustafa, CEO
Bhanu Panda, *
John Racioppi, *
EMP: 65 EST: 2014
SALES (est): 1.45MM Privately Held
Web: www.ghangorcloud.com
SIC: 3699 7371 Security devices; Software programming applications

**(P-13245)**
**GORES RADIO HOLDINGS LLC**
10877 Wilshire Blvd Ste 1805, Los Angeles (90024-4373)
PHONE..................310 209-3010
Alex Gores, Pr
EMP: 56 EST: 2007
SALES (est): 4.71MM
SALES (corp-wide): 1.81B Privately Held
Web: www.gores.com
SIC: 3699 7382 Security devices; Security systems services
PA: The Gores Group Llc
9800 Wilshire Blvd
310 209-3010

**(P-13246)**
**GUZIK TECHNICAL ENTERPRISES (PA)**
2443 Wyandotte St, Mountain View (94043)
PHONE..................650 625-8000
Nahum Guzik, Pr
Anatoli Stein, *
▲ EMP: 46 EST: 1982
SQ FT: 60,000
SALES (est): 8.58MM
SALES (corp-wide): 8.58MM Privately Held
Web: www.guzik.com
SIC: 3699 3669 Sound signaling devices, electrical; Signaling apparatus, electric

**(P-13247)**
**HC WEST LLC**
7130 Convoy Ct, San Diego (92111-1019)
PHONE..................858 277-3473
Robert Hunter, Managing Member
EMP: 300 EST: 2020
SALES (est): 20.19MM Privately Held
SIC: 3699 Security control equipment and systems

**(P-13248)**
**HUNT ELECTRONIC USA INC**
Also Called: Hunt Electronic
11790 Jersey Blvd, Rancho Cucamonga (91730-4935)
PHONE..................909 987-6999
Po Wen Lu, CEO
Ivan Lu, VP
Karen Wang, CFO
◆ EMP: 19 EST: 1999
SQ FT: 23,000
SALES (est): 5.09MM Privately Held

Web: www.huntcctv.com
SIC: 3699 Security control equipment and systems

**(P-13249)**
**IJK & CO INC**
Also Called: Bayshore Lights
225 Industrial St, San Francisco (94124-1928)
PHONE..................415 826-8899
Michael Tseng, CEO
EMP: 50 EST: 1991
SALES (est): 9.45MM Privately Held
Web: www.bayshoresupply.com
SIC: 3699 5063 1711 7349 Electrical equipment and supplies, nec; Electrical supplies, nec; Plumbing, heating, air-conditioning; Lighting maintenance service

**(P-13250)**
**INNOVATIVETEK INC**
1271 W 9th St, Upland (91786-5706)
PHONE..................909 981-3401
Sandy Samudrala, Pr
Paul Trinh, VP
EMP: 16 EST: 2004
SALES (est): 2.45MM Privately Held
Web: www.innovativetek.com
SIC: 3699 Electronic training devices

**(P-13251)**
**INO-TECH LASER PROCESSING INC**
1060 Commercial St Ste 101, San Jose (95112-1437)
PHONE..................408 262-1845
EMP: 26
SALES (corp-wide): 4.05MM Privately Held
Web: www.inotechlaser.com
SIC: 3699 Laser systems and equipment
PA: Ino-Tech Laser Processing, Inc.
2228 Oakland Rd
408 262-1845

**(P-13252)**
**INSTRUMENTS INCORPORATED**
7263 Engineer Rd Ste G, San Diego (92111-1493)
PHONE..................858 571-1111
EMP: 28 EST: 1941
SALES (est): 5.32MM Privately Held
Web: www.instrumentsinc.com
SIC: 3699 Electrical equipment and supplies, nec

**(P-13253)**
**INTERGEN INC**
1145 Tasman Dr, Sunnyvale (94089-2228)
PHONE..................408 245-2737
Kris Madeyski, Pr
John Horn, Sec
EMP: 19 EST: 1992
SQ FT: 7,000
SALES (est): 688.42K Privately Held
Web: www.intergengroup.com
SIC: 3699 7371 Laser systems and equipment; Computer software development and applications

**(P-13254)**
**INTERMOLECULAR INC**
2865 Zanker Rd, San Jose (95134-2101)
PHONE..................408 416-2300
EMP: 80
SALES (corp-wide): 22.82B Privately Held
Web: www.intermolecular.com
SIC: 3699 Electrical equipment and supplies, nec
HQ: Intermolecular, Inc.
3011 N 1st St

San Jose CA 95134
408 582-5700

**(P-13255)**
**IRONWOOD ELECTRIC INC**
13 Ashton, Mission Viejo (92692-4731)
PHONE..................714 630-2350
Raymond Chafe, Prin
EMP: 28 EST: 2011
SALES (est): 5.25MM Privately Held
Web: www.albdinc.com
SIC: 3699 1731 Electrical equipment and supplies, nec; Electrical work

**(P-13256)**
**ISC8 INC**
Also Called: Irvine Sensors
151 Kalmus Dr Ste A203, Costa Mesa (92626-5999)
PHONE..................714 549-8211
EMP: 38
Web: www.isc8.com
SIC: 3699 3674 8731 Security control equipment and systems; Semiconductors and related devices; Electronic research

**(P-13257)**
**IWERKS ENTERTAINMENT INC**
Also Called: Simex-Iwerks
25040 Avenue Tibbitts Ste F, Valencia (91355-3946)
PHONE..................661 678-1800
Gary Matus, CEO
Jeff Dahl, *
Mark Cornell, *
Donald Stults, *
EMP: 75 EST: 1986
SALES (est): 6.79MM Privately Held
Web: www.simex-iwerks.com
SIC: 3699 7819 Electrical equipment and supplies, nec; Developing and printing of commercial motion picture film

**(P-13258)**
**JBB INC**
Also Called: Precision Waterjet
492 W Meats Ave, Orange (92865-2625)
PHONE..................888 538-9287
Jack Budd, Pr
EMP: 22 EST: 1995
SALES (est): 2.13MM Privately Held
Web: www.h2ojet.com
SIC: 3699 Laser welding, drilling, and cutting equipment

**(P-13259)**
**KANEX**
9377 Haven Ave, Rancho Cucamonga (91730-5340)
PHONE..................714 332-1681
Kelvin Yan, CEO
▲ EMP: 25 EST: 1987
SALES (est): 1.9MM Privately Held
Web: www.kanex.com
SIC: 3699 5065 Electrical equipment and supplies, nec; Electronic parts and equipment, nec

**(P-13260)**
**KELLY PNEUMATICS INC**
1611 Babcock St, Newport Beach (92663-2805)
PHONE..................800 704-7552
Ed Kelly, Pr
▲ EMP: 16 EST: 2003
SALES (est): 3.15MM Privately Held
Web: www.kellypneumatics.com
SIC: 3699 Electrical equipment and supplies, nec

## PRODUCTS & SERVICES SECTION
### 3699 - Electrical Equipment And Supplies, Nec (P-13281)

**(P-13261)**
**KERI SYSTEMS INC (PA)**
302 Enzo Dr Ste 190, San Jose (95138-1801)
PHONE..................408 435-8400
Ted Geiszler, *Pr*
Ken Geiszler, *
◆ EMP: 53 EST: 1990
SQ FT: 20,000
SALES (est): 9.58MM **Privately Held**
Web: www.kerisys.com
SIC: **3699** 3829 Security control equipment and systems; Measuring and controlling devices, nec

**(P-13262)**
**KNIGHTSCOPE INC**
Also Called: Knightscope
1070 Terra Bella Ave, Mountain View (94043-1830)
PHONE..................650 924-1025
William Santana Li, *Ch Bd*
Apoorv S Dwivedi, *Ex VP*
Stacy Dean Stephens, *CCO*
Mercedes Soria, *CIO*
Aaron J Lehnhardt, *CDO*
EMP: 95 EST: 2015
SALES (est): 12.8MM **Privately Held**
Web: www.knightscope.com
SIC: **3699** Security devices

**(P-13263)**
**KULICKE SFFA WEDGE BONDING INC**
Also Called: Kulicke & Soffa Industries
1821 E Dyer Rd Ste 200, Santa Ana (92705-5700)
PHONE..................949 660-0440
Scott Kulicke, *Pr*
▲ EMP: 200 EST: 2008
SALES (est): 43.75MM
SALES (corp-wide): 742.49MM **Publicly Held**
Web: www.kns.com
SIC: **3699** Electrical equipment and supplies, nec
PA: Kulicke And Soffa Industries, Inc.
1005 Virginia Dr
215 784-6000

**(P-13264)**
**KYOCERA SLD LASER INC (HQ)**
Also Called: Sld Laser
485 Pine Ave, Goleta (93117-3709)
PHONE..................805 696-6999
Steven Denbaars, *CEO*
Eric B Kim, *
Thomas Caulfield, *
George Stringer, *
Neal Woods, *
EMP: 39 EST: 2013
SQ FT: 3,000
SALES (est): 24.9MM **Privately Held**
Web: www.kyocera-sldlaser.com
SIC: **3699** Laser systems and equipment
PA: Kyocera Corporation
6, Takedatobadonocho, Fushimi-Ku

**(P-13265)**
**KYOCERA SLD LASER INC**
6500 Kaiser Dr, Fremont (94555-3661)
PHONE..................805 696-6999
Steven Denbaars, *CEO*
EMP: 21
Web: www.kyocera-sldlaser.com
SIC: **3699** Laser systems and equipment
HQ: Kyocera Sld Laser, Inc.
485 Pine Ave
Goleta CA 93117
805 696-6999

**(P-13266)**
**KYOCERA SLD LASER INC**
111 Castilian Dr, Goleta (93117-3025)
PHONE..................310 808-4542
EMP: 21
Web: www.kyocera-sldlaser.com
SIC: **3699** Laser systems and equipment
HQ: Kyocera Sld Laser, Inc.
485 Pine Ave
Goleta CA 93117
805 696-6999

**(P-13267)**
**L T SEROGE INC**
Also Called: Laser Tech
7400 Jurupa Ave, Riverside (92504-1030)
PHONE..................951 354-7141
Anthony Di Guglielmo, *CEO*
Chuck Markley, *Mgr*
EMP: 15 EST: 1989
SQ FT: 50,000
SALES (est): 4.3MM **Privately Held**
Web: www.lasertech911.com
SIC: **3699** Laser welding, drilling, and cutting equipment

**(P-13268)**
**LORENZ INC**
Also Called: Karel Manufacturing
1749 Stergios Rd, Calexico (92231-9657)
PHONE..................760 427-1815
Zaven Arakelian, *Pr*
▲ EMP: 47 EST: 1993
SQ FT: 73,000
SALES (est): 3.55MM **Privately Held**
SIC: **3699** Electrical equipment and supplies, nec

**(P-13269)**
**LUNAR ENERGY INC (PA)**
755 Ravendale Dr, Mountain View (94043-5219)
PHONE..................408 475-4137
Jeff Barnes, *CFO*
Grace Hsu, *Sec*
EMP: 17 EST: 2020
SALES (est): 25.49MM
SALES (corp-wide): 25.49MM **Privately Held**
Web: www.lunarenergy.com
SIC: **3699** Electrical equipment and supplies, nec

**(P-13270)**
**MARIAN INC**
19550 Vallco Pkwy Unit 214, Cupertino (95014-7157)
PHONE..................408 645-5355
EMP: 27
SALES (corp-wide): 281.83MM **Privately Held**
Web: www.marianinc.com
SIC: **3699** Electrical welding equipment
HQ: Marian, Inc.
1011 E St Clair St
Indianapolis IN 46202
317 638-6525

**(P-13271)**
**MEGGITT SAFETY SYSTEMS INC (DH)**
Also Called: Parker Meggitt
1785 Voyager Ave, Simi Valley (93063-3363)
PHONE..................805 584-4100
Michael Macgillis, *CEO*
Patrick Scott, *
Guy C Fabe, *
Daniel J Whitman, *
▲ EMP: 210 EST: 1999
SQ FT: 180,000
SALES (est): 118.2MM
SALES (corp-wide): 19.93B **Publicly Held**
Web: www.meggitt.com
SIC: **3699** 3724 3728 7389 Betatrons; Exhaust systems, aircraft; Aircraft parts and equipment, nec; Fire protection service other than forestry or public
HQ: Meggitt Limited
Ansty Bus.
Coventry W MIDLANDS CV7 9
247 682-6900

**(P-13272)**
**MEGGITT SAFETY SYSTEMS INC**
11661 Sorrento Valley Rd, San Diego (92121-1010)
PHONE..................442 792-3217
EMP: 97
SALES (corp-wide): 19.93B **Publicly Held**
Web: www.meggitt.com
SIC: **3699** Betatrons
HQ: Meggitt Safety Systems, Inc.
1785 Voyager Ave
Simi Valley CA 93063
805 584-4100

**(P-13273)**
**MERCURY SECURITY PRODUCTS LLC**
4811 Airport Plaza Dr Ste 300, Long Beach (90815-1372)
PHONE..................562 986-9105
Joseph Grillo, *CEO*
Hing Hung, *Ex VP*
▲ EMP: 19 EST: 2012
SALES (est): 4.92MM **Privately Held**
Web: www.mercury-security.com
SIC: **3699** 8742 Security control equipment and systems; Industry specialist consultants
HQ: Hid Global Corporation
611 Center Ridge Dr
Austin TX 78753

**(P-13274)**
**MYE TECHNOLOGIES INC**
25060 Avenue Stanford, Valencia (91355-3411)
PHONE..................661 964-0217
Anthony Garcia, *Pr*
▲ EMP: 45 EST: 2006
SALES (est): 4.83MM **Privately Held**
Web: www.myeinc.com
SIC: **3699** Electric sound equipment

**(P-13275)**
**NANOTRONICS IMAGING INC**
Also Called: Nanotronics Automation
777 Flynn Rd, Hollister (95023-9558)
PHONE..................831 630-0700
Randy Griffith, *Brnch Mgr*
EMP: 36
SALES (corp-wide): 24.23MM **Privately Held**
Web: www.nanotronics.co
SIC: **3699** Electronic training devices
PA: Nanotronics Imaging, Inc.
2251 Front St Ste 110
330 926-9809

**(P-13276)**
**NETWORKED ENERGY SERVICES CORP (PA)**
Also Called: Nes Holding GMBH
780 Montague Expy Ste 401, San Jose (95131-1318)
PHONE..................408 622-9900
Ghaith Madi, *CEO*

Will Mathieson, *CFO*
Larry Colton, *Dir*
Mike Weiss, *COO*
▲ EMP: 47 EST: 2014
SALES (est): 7.89MM
SALES (corp-wide): 7.89MM **Privately Held**
Web: www.networkedenergy.com
SIC: **3699** Grids, electric

**(P-13277)**
**NEWPORT CORPORATION**
Also Called: Spectra-Physics Laser Div
3635 Peterson Way, Santa Clara (95054-2809)
P.O. Box 7013 (94039)
PHONE..................408 980-4300
EMP: 66
SALES (corp-wide): 3.62B **Publicly Held**
Web: www.newport.com
SIC: **3699** 5049 Laser systems and equipment; Scientific instruments
HQ: Newport Corporation
1791 Deere Ave
Irvine CA 92606
949 863-3144

**(P-13278)**
**NUPHOTON TECHNOLOGIES INC**
41610 Corning Pl, Murrieta (92562-7023)
PHONE..................951 696-8366
Ramadas Pillai, *CEO*
Sindu Pillai, *VP*
Vish Govindan, *CFO*
Dan Vera, *COO*
EMP: 25 EST: 1996
SQ FT: 12,000
SALES (est): 13.25MM **Privately Held**
Web: www.nuphoton.com
SIC: **3699** Laser systems and equipment

**(P-13279)**
**O & S CALIFORNIA INC**
Also Called: Osca-Arcosa
9731 Siempre Viva Rd Ste E, San Diego (92154-7217)
PHONE..................619 661-1800
Kazuo Murata, *Pr*
Jos Luis Furlong, *
▲ EMP: 400 EST: 1986
SQ FT: 4,676
SALES (est): 48.08MM **Privately Held**
Web: www.osca-arcosa.com
SIC: **3699** Electrical equipment and supplies, nec
PA: Onamba Co.,Ltd.
4-1-2, Minamikyuhojimachi, Chuo-Ku

**(P-13280)**
**OBRYANT ELECTRIC INC**
3 Banting, Irvine (92618-3601)
PHONE..................949 341-0025
EMP: 40
SALES (corp-wide): 21.3MM **Privately Held**
Web: www.obryantelectric.com
SIC: **3699** 1731 Electrical equipment and supplies, nec; Electrical work
PA: O'bryant Electric, Inc.
9314 Eton Ave
818 407-1986

**(P-13281)**
**ONESOURCE DISTRIBUTORS LLC (DH)**
3951 Oceanic Dr, Oceanside (92056-5846)
PHONE..................760 966-4500
◆ EMP: 45 EST: 1983
SQ FT: 50,000

## 3699 - Electrical Equipment And Supplies, Nec (P-13282)

SALES (est): 492.79MM
SALES (corp-wide): 16.09MM **Privately Held**
Web: www.1sourcedist.com
SIC: **3699** 5063 5085 5084 Electrical equipment and supplies, nec; Electrical supplies, nec; Industrial supplies; Industrial machinery and equipment
HQ: Sonepar Management Us, Inc.
4400 Leeds Ave Ste 500
Charleston SC 29405
843 872-3500

**(P-13282)**
**ORTHODYNE ELECTRONICS CORPORATION (HQ)**
16700 Red Hill Ave, Irvine (92606-4802)
PHONE..................949 660-0440
▲ EMP: 249 EST: 1960
SALES (est): 10.44MM
SALES (corp-wide): 742.49MM **Publicly Held**
Web: www.orthodyneelectronics.com
SIC: **3699** Electrical equipment and supplies, nec
PA: Kulicke And Soffa Industries, Inc.
1005 Virginia Dr
215 784-6000

**(P-13283)**
**OSI SUBSIDIARY INC**
12525 Chadron Ave, Hawthorne (90250-4807)
PHONE..................310 978-0516
Deepak Chopra, *CEO*
Ajay Mehra, *Pr*
Alan Edrick, *CFO*
EMP: 18 EST: 1995
SALES (est): 6.39MM
SALES (corp-wide): 1.54B **Publicly Held**
Web: www.osi-systems.com
SIC: **3699** Laser systems and equipment
PA: Osi Systems, Inc.
12525 Chadron Ave
310 978-0516

**(P-13284)**
**PACIFIC UTILITY PRODUCTS INC**
2430 Railroad St, Corona (92880-5418)
PHONE..................951 493-8394
EMP: 20
SIC: **3699** Electrical equipment and supplies, nec

**(P-13285)**
**PALOMAR TECH COMPANIES (PA)**
6305 El Camino Real, Carlsbad (92009-1606)
PHONE..................760 931-3600
Gary E Gist, *CEO*
Bruce W Hurners, *Pr*
Dan Evans, *Corporate Secretary*
EMP: 59 EST: 1995
SALES (est): 2.57MM **Privately Held**
Web: www.palomartechnologies.com
SIC: **3699** 6512 Electrical equipment and supplies, nec; Nonresidential building operators

**(P-13286)**
**PENDULUM INSTRUMENTS INC**
Also Called: Pendulum Instruments
1123 Madison Ave, Redwood City (94061-1544)
PHONE..................866 644-1230
Harald Kruger, *Pr*
Eva Chapa Sales America, *Prin*
Marcin Sawicki, *Genl Mgr*
EMP: 22 EST: 2018
SALES (est): 250K **Privately Held**
Web: www.pendulum-instruments.com
SIC: **3699** 3825 Electrical equipment and supplies, nec; Instruments to measure electricity

**(P-13287)**
**PHANTOM ACCESS SYSTEMS LLC**
631 Wald, Irvine (92618-4628)
PHONE..................949 753-1280
Ali Tehranchi, *Managing Member*
▲ EMP: 15 EST: 2003
SALES (est): 4.31MM
SALES (corp-wide): 366.96K **Privately Held**
Web: www.vikingaccess.com
SIC: **3699** 3625 Security control equipment and systems; Relays and industrial controls
HQ: Faac International, Inc.
3160 Murrell Rd
Rockledge FL 32955
904 448-8952

**(P-13288)**
**PHILATRON INTERNATIONAL (PA)**
Also Called: Santa Fe Supply Company
15315 Cornet St, Santa Fe Springs (90670-5531)
PHONE..................562 802-0452
Phillip M Ramos Junior, *CEO*
Phillip M Ramos Senior, *Ex VP*
EMP: 99 EST: 1978
SQ FT: 100,000
SALES (est): 24.17MM
SALES (corp-wide): 24.17MM **Privately Held**
Web: www.philatron.com
SIC: **3699** 3694 3357 Electrical equipment and supplies, nec; Engine electrical equipment; Communication wire

**(P-13289)**
**PINE GROVE GROUP INC**
25500 State Highway 88, Pioneer (95666-9647)
PHONE..................209 295-7733
Dan Nolting, *CEO*
EMP: 30 EST: 1997
SQ FT: 8,000
SALES (est): 2.68MM **Privately Held**
Web: www.pinegrovegroup.com
SIC: **3699** Electrical equipment and supplies, nec

**(P-13290)**
**PIPELINE TRADING SYSTEMS LLC**
1 Market St, San Francisco (94105-1420)
PHONE..................415 293-8159
EMP: 35
SALES (corp-wide): 9.93MM **Privately Held**
Web: www.algotradingsystems.net
SIC: **3699** Electronic training devices
HQ: Pipeline Trading Systems Llc
60 E 42nd St Ste 624
New York NY 10165

**(P-13291)**
**PRO SPOT INTERNATIONAL INC**
5932 Sea Otter Pl, Carlsbad (92010-6630)
PHONE..................760 407-1414
Joran Olsson, *Pr*
Wendy Olsson, *Sec*
▲ EMP: 17 EST: 1986
SALES (est): 6.2MM **Privately Held**
Web: www.prospot.com
SIC: **3699** Electrical welding equipment

**(P-13292)**
**PROTOTYPE EXPRESS LLC**
3506 W Lake Center Dr Ste D, Santa Ana (92704-6985)
PHONE..................714 751-3533
Bob Tavi, *Managing Member*
EMP: 25 EST: 1995
SQ FT: 7,000
SALES (est): 3.75MM **Privately Held**
Web: www.prototypexpress.com
SIC: **3699** Electrical equipment and supplies, nec

**(P-13293)**
**PXISE ENERGY SOLUTIONS LLC**
1455 Frazee Rd Ste 150, San Diego (92108-4436)
PHONE..................619 696-2944
Patrick Lee, *CEO*
EMP: 36 EST: 2017
SALES (est): 4.2MM **Privately Held**
Web: www.pxise.com
SIC: **3699** Grids, electric
PA: Yokogawa Electric Corporation
2-9-32, Nakacho

**(P-13294)**
**RACO MANUFACTURING & ENGRG CO**
Also Called: Raco
727 Allston Way Ste B, Berkeley (94710-2284)
PHONE..................510 658-6713
Constance Brown, *Pr*
James Brown, *MTG*
EMP: 28 EST: 1947
SALES (est): 4.34MM **Privately Held**
Web: www.racoman.com
SIC: **3699** 3823 Electrical equipment and supplies, nec; Temperature instruments: industrial process type

**(P-13295)**
**RAYTHEON COMPANY**
Raytheon
6380 Hollister Ave, Goleta (93117-3114)
PHONE..................805 967-5511
Jack Gressingh, *Genl Mgr*
EMP: 200
SQ FT: 102,570
SALES (corp-wide): 68.92B **Publicly Held**
Web: www.rtx.com
SIC: **3699** 3812 Countermeasure simulators, electric; Search and navigation equipment
HQ: Raytheon Company
870 Winter St
Waltham MA 02451
781 522-3000

**(P-13296)**
**RELDOM CORPORATION**
3241 Industry Dr, Signal Hill (90755-4013)
PHONE..................562 498-3346
Peter Modler, *CEO*
EMP: 20 EST: 1979
SALES (est): 4.94MM **Privately Held**
Web: www.reldom.com
SIC: **3699** Security devices

**(P-13297)**
**RELIABLE FIRE SEC SLUTIONS INC**
6339 Highway 145, Madera (93637-9406)
PHONE..................559 277-3754
Obed Guerrero, *Pr*
EMP: 28 EST: 2017
SALES (est): 5.05MM **Privately Held**
SIC: **3699** Security control equipment and systems

**(P-13298)**
**RESONETICS LLC**
Also Called: Resonetics, LLC
4602 2nd St Ste 5, Davis (95618-9402)
PHONE..................603 886-6772
EMP: 15
Web: www.resonetics.com
SIC: **3699** Laser systems and equipment
PA: Resonetics Llc
26 Whipple St

**(P-13299)**
**RIOT GLASS INC**
17941 Brookshire Ln, Huntington Beach (92647-7132)
PHONE..................800 580-2303
Brad Campbell, *CEO*
Pat Glass, *
EMP: 30 EST: 2017
SALES (est): 4.64MM **Privately Held**
Web: www.riotglass.com
SIC: **3699** Security devices

**(P-13300)**
**RKS INC (HQ)**
1955 Cordell Ct Ste 104, El Cajon (92020-0901)
PHONE..................858 571-4444
Russell Leonard Scheppmann, *CEO*
Allen Thomas, *COO*
Scott Skillman, *CFO*
Brian Shultz, *VP*
Mike Mcminn, *VP*
EMP: 18 EST: 2002
SQ FT: 7,747
SALES (est): 3.09MM **Privately Held**
SIC: **3699** Door opening and closing devices, electrical
PA: Abb Ltd
Affolternstrasse 44

**(P-13301)**
**ROSEMEAD ELECTRICAL SUPPLY**
9150 Dice Rd, Santa Fe Springs (90670-2522)
PHONE..................562 298-4190
Rony Perez, *CEO*
EMP: 50 EST: 2019
SALES (est): 2.8MM **Privately Held**
Web: www.rosemeadelectricalsupply.com
SIC: **3699** High-energy particle physics equipment

**(P-13302)**
**SCHNEDER ELC BLDNGS AMRCAS INC**
Also Called: TAC Yamas
5735 W Las Positas Blvd Ste 400, Pleasanton (94588-4002)
PHONE..................925 463-7100
Daroowe Torkelson, *Mgr*
EMP: 45
SALES (corp-wide): 82.05K **Privately Held**
SIC: **3699** Electrical equipment and supplies, nec
HQ: Schneider Electric Buildings Americas, Inc.
1650 W Crosby Rd
Carrollton TX 75006
972 323-1111

## 3699 - Electrical Equipment And Supplies, Nec (P-13324)

**(P-13303)**
**SCHNEIDER ELC BUILDINGS LLC**
Also Called: Invensys Climate Controls
100 W Victoria St, Long Beach (90805-2147)
PHONE..................................310 900-2385
Michael Utzman, *Prin*
EMP: 108
SALES (corp-wide): 82.05K **Privately Held**
SIC: 3699 Electrical equipment and supplies, nec
HQ: Schneider Electric Buildings, Llc
839 N Perryville Rd
Rockford IL 61107
815 381-5000

**(P-13304)**
**SCHNEIDER ELECTRIC**
1660 Scenic Ave, Costa Mesa (92626-1410)
PHONE..................................949 713-9200
EMP: 27
SALES (est): 5.06MM **Privately Held**
Web: www.se.com
SIC: 3699 Electrical equipment and supplies, nec

**(P-13305)**
**SENFENG LASER USA INC**
5989 Rickenbacker Rd, Commerce (90040-3029)
PHONE..................................562 319-8053
Bin Han, *CEO*
EMP: 15 EST: 2021
SALES (est): 1.02MM **Privately Held**
Web: www.senfenglaserusa.com
SIC: 3699 Laser systems and equipment

**(P-13306)**
**SERRA LASER AND WATERJET INC**
1740 N Orangethorpe Park, Anaheim (92801-1138)
PHONE..................................714 680-6211
Glenn Kline, *CEO*
EMP: 30 EST: 2012
SALES (est): 6.3MM **Privately Held**
Web: www.serralaser.com
SIC: 3699 Laser welding, drilling, and cutting equipment

**(P-13307)**
**SERVEXO**
Also Called: Servexo Protective Service
1411 W 190th St Ste 475, Gardena (90248-4323)
P.O. Box 9017 (90734)
PHONE..................................323 527-9994
John Palmer, *Pr*
John Palmer, *CEO*
EMP: 200 EST: 2012
SALES (est): 8.68MM **Privately Held**
Web: www.servexousa.com
SIC: 3699 8744 7382 4813 Security control equipment and systems; Facilities support services; Security systems services; Telephone communication, except radio

**(P-13308)**
**SONNET TECHNOLOGIES INC**
Also Called: Manufacturer
25 Empire Dr Ste 200, Lake Forest (92630-8539)
PHONE..................................949 587-3500
Robert Farnsworth, *CEO*
Robert Farnsworth, *Pr*
Robert Rich, *
Angelia Farnsworth Magill, *
▲ EMP: 30 EST: 1986
SQ FT: 17,000
SALES (est): 7.87MM **Privately Held**
Web: www.sonnettech.com
SIC: 3699 Electrical equipment and supplies, nec

**(P-13309)**
**SOUNDCRAFT INC**
Also Called: Secura Key
20301 Nordhoff St, Chatsworth (91311-6128)
PHONE..................................818 882-0020
Joel Smulson, *Pr*
Martin Casden, *
▲ EMP: 35 EST: 1971
SQ FT: 12,000
SALES (est): 4.75MM **Privately Held**
Web: www.securakey.com
SIC: 3699 1731 3829 Security control equipment and systems; Safety and security specialization; Measuring and controlling devices, nec

**(P-13310)**
**SPECTRA-PHYSICS INC (DH)**
Also Called: Laser Division
1565 Barber Ln, Milpitas (95035-7409)
P.O. Box 19607 (92623)
PHONE..................................877 835-9620
Robert J Phillippy, *CEO*
▼ EMP: 90 EST: 1961
SQ FT: 129,500
SALES (est): 20.04MM
SALES (corp-wide): 3.62B **Publicly Held**
Web: www.spectra-physics.com
SIC: 3699 8731 Laser systems and equipment; Commercial physical research
HQ: Newport Corporation
1791 Deere Ave
Irvine CA 92606
949 863-3144

**(P-13311)**
**STEINER EOPTICS INC**
Also Called: LDI
70 Garden Ct Ste 200, Monterey (93940-5342)
PHONE..................................831 373-0701
EMP: 60
Web: www.steiner-optics.com
SIC: 3699 Laser systems and equipment

**(P-13312)**
**STRACON INC**
1672 Kaiser Ave Ste 1, Irvine (92614-5700)
PHONE..................................949 851-2288
Son Pham, *Pr*
EMP: 17 EST: 1986
SQ FT: 10,000
SALES (est): 4.36MM **Privately Held**
Web: www.straconinc.com
SIC: 3699 Electrical equipment and supplies, nec

**(P-13313)**
**SUMMIT ELECTRIC & DATA INC**
27913 Smyth Dr, Valencia (91355-4034)
PHONE..................................661 775-9901
Ray Vasquez, *Pr*
EMP: 18 EST: 2010
SALES (est): 2.24MM **Privately Held**
Web: www.summitelectservices.com
SIC: 3699 1731 Electrical equipment and supplies, nec; Electrical work

**(P-13314)**
**SURF LOCH LLC**
9747 Olson Dr, San Diego (92121-2802)
PHONE..................................858 454-1777
Thomas J Lochtefeld, *Managing Member*
EMP: 18 EST: 2016
SALES (est): 6.62MM **Privately Held**
Web: www.surfloch.com
SIC: 3699 Waveguide pressurization equipment

**(P-13315)**
**SUSS MCRTEC PHTNIC SYSTEMS INC**
2520 Palisades Dr, Corona (92882-0632)
PHONE..................................951 817-3700
Courtney T Sheets, *CEO*
Debora Blanchard, *
Debbie Brown, *
EMP: 90 EST: 1966
SALES (est): 5.64MM
SALES (corp-wide): 330.72MM **Privately Held**
Web: www.suss.com
SIC: 3699 7389 Electrical equipment and supplies, nec; Business services, nec
PA: Suss Microtec Se
SchleiBheimer Str. 90
89320070

**(P-13316)**
**SYSTON CABLE TECHNOLOGY CORP**
15278 El Prado Rd, Chino (91710-7623)
PHONE..................................888 679-7866
Yulin Wang, *CEO*
Daniel Wong, *Admn*
▲ EMP: 20 EST: 2014
SALES (est): 2.05MM **Privately Held**
Web: www.systoncable.com
SIC: 3699 4841 3351 3651 Electrical equipment and supplies, nec; Cable television services; Wire, copper and copper alloy; Household audio and video equipment

**(P-13317)**
**TACTICAL MICRO INC (DH)**
1740 E Wilshire Ave, Santa Ana (92705-4615)
PHONE..................................714 547-1174
Ed Hanrahan, *Pr*
Allen Romk, *
John Moulton, *
Michael Hayden, *
▲ EMP: 18 EST: 2005
SQ FT: 14,000
SALES (est): 4.5MM
SALES (corp-wide): 2.84B **Publicly Held**
Web: www.bench.com
SIC: 3699 Electrical equipment and supplies, nec
HQ: Secure Communication Systems, Inc.
1740 E Wilshire Ave
Santa Ana CA 92705
714 547-1174

**(P-13318)**
**TASCENT INC**
475 Alberto Way Ste 200, Los Gatos (95032-5480)
P.O. Box 9 (49468-0009)
PHONE..................................650 799-4611
Dean Senner, *CEO*
Joey Pritikin, *VP*
Alastair Partington, *VP*
Scott Clark, *VP*
EMP: 16 EST: 2015
SALES (est): 5.65MM **Privately Held**
Web: www.tascent.com
SIC: 3699 Security control equipment and systems

**(P-13319)**
**TURNER DSGNS HYDRCRBON INSTRS**
2023 N Gateway Blvd Ste 101, Fresno (93727-1623)
PHONE..................................559 253-1414
Gary Bartman, *Pr*
Mark Fletcher, *
EMP: 43 EST: 2002
SALES (est): 3.49MM **Privately Held**
Web: www.oilinwatermonitors.com
SIC: 3699 Electrical equipment and supplies, nec

**(P-13320)**
**ULTRA-STEREO LABS INC**
Also Called: U S L
181 Bonetti Dr, San Luis Obispo (93401-7310)
PHONE..................................805 549-0161
James A Cashin, *Pr*
Jack Cashin, *Pr*
▲ EMP: 25 EST: 2016
SQ FT: 15,000
SALES (est): 6.45MM
SALES (corp-wide): 101.64MM **Privately Held**
SIC: 3699 Electric sound equipment
PA: Qsc, Llc
1675 Mcarthur Blvd
800 854-4079

**(P-13321)**
**UNDERSEA SYSTEMS INTL INC**
Also Called: Ocean Technology Systems
3133 W Harvard St, Santa Ana (92704-3912)
PHONE..................................714 754-7848
Michael R Pelissier, *Pr*
Jerry Peck, *
▲ EMP: 62 EST: 1987
SQ FT: 18,000
SALES (est): 9.58MM **Privately Held**
Web: www.oceantechnologysystems.com
SIC: 3699 8711 Underwater sound equipment; Acoustical engineering

**(P-13322)**
**UNITED SECURITY PRODUCTS INC**
Also Called: Amtek
12675 Danielson Ct Ste 405, Poway (92064-6835)
P.O. Box 785 (92074-0785)
PHONE..................................800 227-1592
Ted R Greene, *Pr*
▲ EMP: 32 EST: 1972
SALES (est): 4.58MM **Privately Held**
Web: www.unitedsecurity.com
SIC: 3699 5999 Security devices; Alarm signal systems

**(P-13323)**
**UNIVERSAL SURVEILLANCE SYSTEMS LLC**
Also Called: Universal Surveillance Systems
11172 Elm Ave, Rancho Cucamonga (91730-7670)
PHONE..................................909 484-7870
▲ EMP: 80
SIC: 3699 Security control equipment and systems

**(P-13324)**
**USA VISION SYSTEMS INC (HQ)**
9301 Irvine Blvd, Irvine (92618-1669)
PHONE..................................949 583-1519
Kuang Cheng Tai, *Pr*

# 3699 - Electrical Equipment And Supplies, Nec (P-13325)

▲ **EMP:** 40 **EST:** 2003
**SALES (est):** 5.54MM **Privately Held**
**Web:** www.geovision.com.tw
**SIC: 3699** Security control equipment and systems
**PA:** Geovision, Inc.
9f, No. 246, Sec. 1, Neihu Rd.

### (P-13325)
### VEECO PROCESS EQUIPMENT INC
355 E Trimble Rd, San Jose (95131-1218)
**PHONE**.................................408 321-8835
John R Peeler, *CEO*
**EMP:** 58
**Web:** www.veeco.com
**SIC: 3699** High-energy particle physics equipment
**HQ:** Veeco Process Equipment Inc.
1 Terminal Dr
Plainview NY 11803

### (P-13326)
### VIAVI SOLUTIONS INC
Also Called: Jsdu
2789 Northpoint Pkwy, Santa Rosa (95407-7350)
**PHONE**.................................707 545-6440
Toni Mcwilliamns, *Principal B*
**EMP:** 200
**SALES (corp-wide):** 1B **Publicly Held**
**Web:** www.viavisolutions.com
**SIC: 3699** Laser systems and equipment
**PA:** Viavi Solutions Inc.
1445 S Spctrum Blvd Ste 1
408 404-3600

### (P-13327)
### VOLTPOST INC
1345 Howard St, San Francisco (94103)
**PHONE**.................................908 868-1527
Jeffrey Prosserman, *CEO*
Luke Mairo, *COO*
**EMP:** 20 **EST:** 2021
**SALES (est):** 1.01MM **Privately Held**
**Web:** www.voltpost.com
**SIC: 3699** Household electrical equipment

### (P-13328)
### VTI INSTRUMENTS CORPORATION (HQ)
2031 Main St, Irvine (92614-6509)
**PHONE**.................................949 955-1894
Paul Dhillon, *CEO*
Jasdeep Dhillon, *
▲ **EMP:** 30 **EST:** 1990
**SQ FT:** 11,500
**SALES (est):** 8.09MM
**SALES (corp-wide):** 6.6B **Publicly Held**
**Web:** www.vtiinstruments.com
**SIC: 3699** Electrical equipment and supplies, nec
**PA:** Ametek, Inc.
1100 Cassatt Rd
610 647-2121

### (P-13329)
### WEST COAST CHAIN MFG CO
Also Called: Key-Bak
4245 Pacific Privado, Ontario (91761-1588)
P.O. Box 9088 (91762-9088)
**PHONE**.................................909 923-7800
Boake Paugh, *Pr*
Mike Winegar, *
▲ **EMP:** 50 **EST:** 1948
**SQ FT:** 31,000
**SALES (est):** 9.51MM **Privately Held**
**Web:** www.keybak.com
**SIC: 3699** Security devices

### (P-13330)
### WEST COAST CORPORATION
4245 Pacific Privado, Ontario (91761-1588)
**PHONE**.................................909 923-7800
Boake Paugh, *Pr*
▲ **EMP:** 40 **EST:** 1986
**SALES (est):** 3.64MM **Privately Held**
**Web:** www.wcc-mfg.com
**SIC: 3699** Security devices

### (P-13331)
### WESTERN DNING - SCHNEIDER CAFE
3500 Never Forget Ln, Clovis (93612-5628)
**PHONE**.................................559 292-1981
▲ **EMP:** 15 **EST:** 2013
**SALES (est):** 2.96MM **Privately Held**
**SIC: 3699** Electrical equipment and supplies, nec

### (P-13332)
### WESTGATE MFG INC
Also Called: Westgate Manufacturing
2462 E 28th St, Vernon (90058-1402)
**PHONE**.................................323 826-9490
Isaac Hadjyan, *CEO*
Eryeh Hadjyan, *
Ebrahim Hadjyan, *
▲ **EMP:** 74 **EST:** 2008
**SALES (est):** 9.94MM **Privately Held**
**Web:** www.westgatemfg.com
**SIC: 3699** 5063 Electrical equipment and supplies, nec; Lighting fixtures

### (P-13333)
### WG SECURITY PRODUCTS INC (PA)
Also Called: Wg
591 W Hamilton Ave Ste 260, Campbell (95008-0500)
**PHONE**.................................408 241-8000
Xiao Hui Yang, *CEO*
Graham Handyside, *
▲ **EMP:** 30 **EST:** 1998
**SALES (est):** 4.99MM
**SALES (corp-wide):** 4.99MM **Privately Held**
**Web:** www.wgspi.com
**SIC: 3699** 5065 Security devices; Security control equipment and systems

### (P-13334)
### XIRGO TECHNOLOGIES LLC
188 Camino Ruiz Fl 2, Camarillo (93012)
**PHONE**.................................805 319-4079
Roberto Piolanti, *CEO*
Mark Grout, *
Shawn Aleman, *CMO**
Rich Farruggia, *Chief Human Resources Officer**
**EMP:** 62 **EST:** 2006
**SALES (est):** 14.96MM
**SALES (corp-wide):** 4.05B **Privately Held**
**Web:** www.sensatainsights.com
**SIC: 3699** Electronic training devices
**HQ:** Sensata Technologies Holding Company U.K.
Cannon Place
London EC4N

## 3711 Motor Vehicles And Car Bodies

### (P-13335)
### ALAN JOHNSON PRFMCE ENGRG INC
Also Called: Johnson Racing
1097 Foxen Canyon Rd, Santa Maria (93454-9146)
**PHONE**.................................805 922-1202
Alan P Johnson, *Pr*
▲ **EMP:** 24 **EST:** 1985
**SQ FT:** 25,000
**SALES (est):** 2.56MM **Privately Held**
**Web:** www.alanjohnsonperformance.com
**SIC: 3711** Motor vehicles and car bodies

### (P-13336)
### ALLIANZ SWEEPER COMPANY
5405 Industrial Pkwy, San Bernardino (92407-1803)
▼ **EMP:** 180
**SIC: 3711** Street sprinklers and sweepers (motor vehicles), assembly of

### (P-13337)
### AMERICAN CARRIER SYSTEMS
2285 E Date Ave, Fresno (93706-5426)
**PHONE**.................................559 442-1500
Philip Sweet, *Pr*
David Sweet, *Sec*
▲ **EMP:** 17 **EST:** 1974
**SQ FT:** 36,552
**SALES (est):** 490.59K **Privately Held**
**Web:** www.americancarrierequipment.com
**SIC: 3711** Motor vehicles and car bodies

### (P-13338)
### AMERICAN HX AUTO TRADE INC
Also Called: U.S. Specialty Vehicles
4845 Via Del Cerro, Yorba Linda (92887-2641)
**PHONE**.................................909 484-1010
▲ **EMP:** 72 **EST:** 2010
**SALES (est):** 4.63MM **Privately Held**
**SIC: 3711** Automobile bodies, passenger car, not including engine, etc.

### (P-13339)
### ARTISAN VEHICLE SYSTEMS INC
742 Pancho Rd, Camarillo (93012-8576)
**PHONE**.................................805 402-6856
Michael Kasaba, *Pr*
**EMP:** 60 **EST:** 2010
**SALES (est):** 18.94MM
**SALES (corp-wide):** 12.03B **Privately Held**
**Web:** www.rocktechnology.sandvik
**SIC: 3711** Personnel carriers (motor vehicles), assembly of
**PA:** Sandvik Ab
Spangvagen 10
26260000

### (P-13340)
### ATIEVA INC (HQ)
Also Called: Lucid
7373 Gateway Blvd, Newark (94560-1149)
**PHONE**.................................510 648-3553
Peter Rawlinson, *CEO*
**EMP:** 19 **EST:** 2021
**SALES (est):** 1.28MM
**SALES (corp-wide):** 595.27MM **Publicly Held**
**SIC: 3711** Motor vehicles and car bodies
**PA:** Lucid Group, Inc.
7373 Gateway Blvd
510 648-3553

### (P-13341)
### AZAA INVESTMENTS INC (PA)
6602 Convoy Ct Ste 200, San Diego (92111-1000)
P.O. Box 2198 (38101-2198)
**PHONE**.................................858 569-8111
William C Rhodes Iii, *Pr*
David Klein, *COO*
Jamere Jackson, *Sec*
Brian L Campbell, *Treas*
▼ **EMP:** 36 **EST:** 2012
**SALES (est):** 30.16MM
**SALES (corp-wide):** 30.16MM **Privately Held**
**Web:** www.americantrucks.com
**SIC: 3711** Motor vehicles and car bodies

### (P-13342)
### BAATZ ENTERPRISES INC
Also Called: Tow Industries
2223 W San Bernardino Rd, West Covina (91790-1008)
**PHONE**.................................323 660-4866
Mark Ormonde Baatz, *CEO*
John O Baatz, *
Helen Baatz, *
▼ **EMP:** 38 **EST:** 1988
**SALES (est):** 4.59MM **Privately Held**
**Web:** www.towindustries.com
**SIC: 3711** 5013 7538 Motor vehicles and car bodies; Truck parts and accessories; Truck engine repair, except industrial

### (P-13343)
### BECKER AUTOMOTIVE DESIGNS INC
Also Called: Becker Automotive Design USA
1711 Ives Ave, Oxnard (93033-1866)
**PHONE**.................................805 487-5227
Howard Bernard Becker, *CEO*
Debra Becker, *
▲ **EMP:** 33 **EST:** 1996
**SQ FT:** 35,000
**SALES (est):** 4.84MM **Privately Held**
**Web:** www.beckerautodesign.com
**SIC: 3711** Cars, armored, assembly of

### (P-13344)
### BYTON NORTH AMERICA CORP
4201 Burton Dr, Santa Clara (95054-1512)
**PHONE**.................................408 966-5078
Carsten Breitfield, *CEO*
Albert Li, *CFO*
**EMP:** 225 **EST:** 2016
**SALES (est):** 23.79MM **Privately Held**
**SIC: 3711** Cars, electric, assembly of

### (P-13345)
### COACHWORKS HOLDINGS INC
1863 Service Ct, Riverside (92507-2341)
**PHONE**.................................951 684-9585
Dale Carson, *Pr*
Terri L Carson, *Sec*
**EMP:** 18 **EST:** 2007
**SALES (est):** 4.65MM
**SALES (corp-wide):** 54.62MM **Privately Held**
**SIC: 3711** Motor buses, except trackless trollies, assembly of
**PA:** D/T Carson Enterprises, Inc.
42882 Ivy St
951 684-9585

### (P-13346)
### CYNGN INC (PA)
Also Called: CYNGN
1015 Obrien Dr, Menlo Park (94025-1408)
**PHONE**.................................650 924-5905
Lior Tal, *Ch Bd*
Donald Alvarez, *CFO*
**EMP:** 69 **EST:** 2013
**SQ FT:** 16,400
**SALES (est):** 1.49MM
**SALES (corp-wide):** 1.49MM **Publicly Held**
**Web:** www.cyngn.com
**SIC: 3711** Motor vehicles and car bodies

# PRODUCTS & SERVICES SECTION
## 3711 - Motor Vehicles And Car Bodies (P-13367)

### (P-13347)
**CZV INC**
Also Called: Czinger Vehicles
19601 Hamilton Ave, Torrance
(90502-1309)
PHONE....................424 603-1450
Kevin Czinger, *CEO*
Jens Sverdrup, *
EMP: 77 EST: 2010
SALES (est): 1.64MM **Privately Held**
Web: www.czvinc.com
SIC: 3711 Automobile assembly, including specialty automobiles

### (P-13348)
**EDISONFUTURE INC (HQ)**
4677 Old Ironsides Dr Ste 190, Santa Clara (95054-1809)
PHONE....................408 919-8000
Denton Peng, *CEO*
EMP: 16 EST: 2003
SALES (est): 26.24MM **Publicly Held**
Web: www.edisonfuture.com
SIC: 3711 Cars, electric, assembly of
PA: Spi Solar, Inc.
   4803 Urbani Ave

### (P-13349)
**ELECTRIC VEHICLES INTERNATIONAL LLC**
1627 Army Ct Ste 1, Stockton (95206-4100)
PHONE....................209 939-0405
▲ EMP: 47
SIC: 3711 Buses, all types, assembly of

### (P-13350)
**FISKER AUTOMOTIVE INC**
3080 Airway Ave, Costa Mesa (92626-6012)
▲ EMP: 53
SIC: 3711 7539 Motor vehicles and car bodies; Automotive repair shops, nec

### (P-13351)
**FISKER GROUP INC (HQ)**
Also Called: Fisker
14 Centerpointe Dr, La Palma (90623-1028)
PHONE....................833 434-7537
Henrik Fisker, *CEO*
John Finnucan, *Chief Accounting Officer**
EMP: 740 EST: 2016
SALES (corp-wide): 272.88MM **Publicly Held**
Web: www.fiskerinc.com
SIC: 3711 Cars, electric, assembly of
PA: Fisker Inc.
   14 Centerpointe Dr
   833 434-7537

### (P-13352)
**FISKER INC (PA)**
Also Called: Fisker
14 Centerpointe Dr, La Palma (90623-1028)
PHONE....................833 434-7537
Henrik Fisker, *Ch Bd*
Geeta Gupta Fisker, *CFO*
Angel Salinas, *CAO*
EMP: 27 EST: 2016
SALES (est): 272.88MM
SALES (corp-wide): 272.88MM **Publicly Held**
Web: www.fiskerinc.com
SIC: 3711 Motor vehicles and car bodies

### (P-13353)
**FLYER DEFENSE LLC**
151 W 135th St, Los Angeles (90061-1645)
PHONE....................310 324-5650
Oded Nechushtan, *CEO*
Steven Markowitz, *
▲ EMP: 75 EST: 2000
SALES (est): 12.4MM **Privately Held**
Web: www.flyerdefense.com
SIC: 3711 3714 Military motor vehicle assembly; Motor vehicle parts and accessories

### (P-13354)
**GLOBAL ENVIRONMENTAL PDTS INC**
Also Called: Global Sweeping Solutions
5405 Industrial Pkwy, San Bernardino (92407-1803)
PHONE....................909 713-1600
Walter Pusic, *Prin*
Walter Pusic, *Pr*
Jason Condon, *Prin*
Sebastian Mentelski, *
▲ EMP: 67 EST: 2011
SQ FT: 104,000
SALES (est): 8.7MM **Privately Held**
Web: www.globalsweeper.com
SIC: 3711 Street sprinklers and sweepers (motor vehicles), assembly of

### (P-13355)
**GOLDEN STATE FIRE APPRATUS INC**
7400 Reese Rd, Sacramento (95828-3706)
PHONE....................916 330-1638
Ryan Wright, *Pr*
Marie Wright, *Sec*
EMP: 16 EST: 1989
SQ FT: 5,000
SALES (est): 3.02MM **Privately Held**
Web: www.goldenstatefire.com
SIC: 3711 3713 Truck and tractor truck assembly; Truck and bus bodies

### (P-13356)
**GREENKRAFT INC**
2530 S Birch St, Santa Ana (92707-3444)
PHONE....................714 545-7777
George Gemayel, *Ch Bd*
Sosi Bardakjian, *CFO*
EMP: 18 EST: 2008
SQ FT: 51,942
SALES (est): 2.46MM **Privately Held**
Web: www.greenkraftinc.com
SIC: 3711 3519 Motor vehicles and car bodies; Internal combustion engines, nec

### (P-13357)
**GREENPOWER MOTOR COMPANY INC**
8885 Haven Ave Ste 200, Rancho Cucamonga (91730-5199)
PHONE....................909 308-0960
Fraser Atkinson, *CEO*
EMP: 52 EST: 2013
SALES (est): 12.09MM
SALES (corp-wide): 39.27MM **Privately Held**
Web: www.greenpowermotor.com
SIC: 3711 Motor vehicles and car bodies
PA: Greenpower Motor Company Inc
   240-209 Carrall St
   604 563-4144

### (P-13358)
**HALCORE GROUP INC**
Leader Industries
10941 Weaver Ave, South El Monte (91733-2752)
PHONE....................626 575-0880
Gary Hunter, *Mgr*
EMP: 36
SIC: 3711 Motor vehicles and car bodies
HQ: Halcore Group, Inc.
   3800 Mcdowell Rd
   Grove City OH 43123
   614 539-8181

### (P-13359)
**HARBINGER MOTORS INC**
12821 Knott St Ste A, Garden Grove (92841-3941)
PHONE....................714 684-1067
John Harris, *CEO*
Phillip Weicker, *
Will Eberts, *
Gilbert Passin, *CPO**
Benjamin Dusastre, *
EMP: 150 EST: 2021
SALES (est): 28.17MM **Privately Held**
Web: www.harbingermotors.com
SIC: 3711 Chassis, motor vehicle

### (P-13360)
**HI-TECH EMERGENCY VEHICLE SERVICE INC**
Also Called: HI Tech Fire Apparatus
444 Greger St, Oakdale (95361-8000)
P.O. Box 1616 (95361-1616)
PHONE....................209 847-3042
EMP: 39 EST: 1987
SALES (est): 4.14MM **Privately Held**
Web: www.hitechevs.com
SIC: 3711 Fire department vehicles (motor vehicles), assembly of

### (P-13361)
**KARMA AUTOMOTIVE LLC**
9950 Jeronimo Rd, Irvine (92618-2014)
PHONE....................855 565-2762
Marques Mccammon, *Pr*
Liang Zhou, *
John Maloney, *CRO**
Ashoka Achuthan, *
EMP: 896 EST: 2014
SQ FT: 262,463
SALES (est): 101.46MM **Privately Held**
Web: www.karmaautomotive.com
SIC: 3711 Automobile bodies, passenger car, not including engine, etc.
HQ: Wanxiang America Corporation
   88 Airport Rd
   Elgin IL 60123

### (P-13362)
**KOVATCH MOBILE EQUIPMENT CORP**
Also Called: Kme Fire
14562 Manzanita Dr, Fontana (92335-5377)
PHONE....................951 685-1224
Ken Creese, *Brnch Mgr*
EMP: 33
SIC: 3711 Motor vehicles and car bodies
HQ: Kovatch Mobile Equipment Corp.
   1 Industrial Complex
   Nesquehoning PA 18240
   570 669-9461

### (P-13363)
**LIPPERT COMPONENTS INC**
1270 Puerta Del Sol, San Clemente (92673-6310)
PHONE....................949 259-4000
EMP: 16
SALES (corp-wide): 3.78B **Publicly Held**
Web: corporate.lippert.com
SIC: 3711 3469 3714 3444 Chassis, motor vehicle; Stamping metal for the trade; Motor vehicle parts and accessories; Metal roofing and roof drainage equipment
HQ: Lippert Components, Inc.
   3501 County Rd 6 E
   Elkhart IN 46514
   574 535-1125

### (P-13364)
**LIPPERT COMPONENTS INC**
1361 Calle Avanzado, San Clemente (92673-6351)
PHONE....................574 312-6277
Randy Jacobucci, *Mgr*
EMP: 16
SALES (corp-wide): 3.78B **Publicly Held**
Web: corporate.lippert.com
SIC: 3711 3469 3444 3714 Chassis, motor vehicle; Stamping metal for the trade; Metal roofing and roof drainage equipment; Motor vehicle parts and accessories
HQ: Lippert Components, Inc.
   3501 County Rd 6 E
   Elkhart IN 46514
   574 535-1125

### (P-13365)
**LIPPERT COMPONENTS INC**
168 S Spruce Ave, Rialto (92376-9005)
PHONE....................909 873-0061
Andrew Zanschoick, *Mgr*
EMP: 21
SALES (corp-wide): 3.78B **Publicly Held**
Web: www.lci1.com
SIC: 3711 3469 3444 3714 Chassis, motor vehicle; Stamping metal for the trade; Metal roofing and roof drainage equipment; Motor vehicle parts and accessories
HQ: Lippert Components, Inc.
   3501 County Rd 6 E
   Elkhart IN 46514
   574 535-1125

### (P-13366)
**LUCID GROUP INC (PA)**
7373 Gateway Blvd, Newark (94560-1149)
PHONE....................510 648-3553
Turqi Alnowaiser, *
Marc Winterhoff, *COO*
Eric Bach, *Sr VP*
Gagan Dhingra, *Interim Vice President*
EMP: 1539 EST: 2007
SALES (est): 595.27MM
SALES (corp-wide): 595.27MM **Publicly Held**
Web: www.lucidmotors.com
SIC: 3711 Motor vehicles and car bodies

### (P-13367)
**LUCID USA INC (HQ)**
Also Called: Lucid Motors
7373 Gateway Blvd, Newark (94560-1149)
PHONE....................510 648-3553
Peter Rawlinson, *CEO*
Gagan Dhingra, *
Marc Winterhoff, *
Matthew Everitt, *
Steven David, *
▲ EMP: 163 EST: 2007
SQ FT: 65,000
SALES (est): 446.49MM
SALES (corp-wide): 595.27MM **Publicly Held**
Web: www.lucidmotors.com
SIC: 3711 8711 Motor vehicles and car bodies; Engineering services
PA: Lucid Group, Inc.
   7373 Gateway Blvd
   510 648-3553

## 3711 - Motor Vehicles And Car Bodies (P-13368)

**(P-13368)**
**MARTINS QUALITY TRUCK BODY INC**
1831 W El Segundo Blvd, Compton (90222-1026)
PHONE.................310 632-5978
Oscar Parra, *Owner*
Edith A Torres, *Prin*
**EMP:** 17 **EST:** 2012
**SALES (est):** 1.3MM **Privately Held**
**Web:** www.martinsqualitytruckbody.com
**SIC:** 3711 Motor vehicles and car bodies

**(P-13369)**
**MARVIN LAND SYSTEMS INC**
Also Called: Marvin Group The
261 W Beach Ave, Inglewood (90302-2904)
PHONE.................310 674-5030
Gerald M Friedman, *Pr*
Leon Tsimmerman, *
▲ **EMP:** 44 **EST:** 1995
**SQ FT:** 200,000
**SALES (est):** 23.87MM
**SALES (corp-wide):** 149.54MM **Privately Held**
**Web:** www.marvingroup.com
**SIC:** 3711 Military motor vehicle assembly
**PA:** Marvin Engineering Co., Inc.
261 W Beach Ave
310 674-5030

**(P-13370)**
**MAZDA MOTOR OF AMERICA INC (HQ)**
Also Called: Mazda North Amercn Operations
200 Spectrum Center Dr Ste 100, Irvine (92618-5004)
P.O. Box 19734 (92623)
PHONE.................949 727-1990
◆ **EMP:** 400 **EST:** 1970
**SALES (est):** 406.92MM **Privately Held**
**Web:** www.mazdausa.com
**SIC:** 3711 Motor vehicles and car bodies
**PA:** Mazda Motor Corporation
3-1, Shinchi, Fuchucho

**(P-13371)**
**MILLENWORKS**
1361 Valencia Ave, Tustin (92780-6459)
PHONE.................714 426-5500
▲ **EMP:** 75
**SIC:** 3711 5012 7549 8731 Military motor vehicle assembly; Commercial vehicles; Automotive customizing services, nonfactory basis; Electronic research

**(P-13372)**
**MULLEN TECHNOLOGIES INC (PA)**
Also Called: Mullen Auto Sales
1405 Pioneer St, Brea (92821-3721)
PHONE.................714 613-1900
David Michery, *CEO*
Jerry Alban, *
William Johnston, *
**EMP:** 40 **EST:** 2014
**SQ FT:** 24,730
**SALES (est):** 10.3MM
**SALES (corp-wide):** 10.3MM **Privately Held**
**Web:** www.mullenusa.com
**SIC:** 3711 5013 Motor vehicles and car bodies; Motor vehicle supplies and new parts

**(P-13373)**
**NEW FLYER OF AMERICA INC**
2880 Jurupa St, Ontario (91761-2903)
P.O. Box 1464 (91743-1464)
PHONE.................909 456-3566
**EMP:** 109
**SALES (corp-wide):** 2.05B **Privately Held**
**Web:** www.newflyer.com
**SIC:** 3711 Motor vehicles and car bodies
**HQ:** New Flyer Of America Inc.
6200 Glenn Carlson Dr
Saint Cloud MN 56301

**(P-13374)**
**NIO USA INC**
Also Called: Nextev
3151 Zanker Rd, San Jose (95134-1933)
PHONE.................408 518-7000
Padmasree Warrior, *CEO*
**EMP:** 167 **EST:** 2015
**SALES (est):** 9.41MM **Privately Held**
**Web:** www.nio.com
**SIC:** 3711 Motor vehicles and car bodies
**HQ:** Nio Co., Ltd.
Room 521, Floor 5, No. 388, Lane 1555, Jiangxi Road, Jinsha, Jia
Shanghai SH 20180

**(P-13375)**
**PHOENIX CARS LLC**
Also Called: Phoenix Motorcars
1500 Lakeview Loop, Anaheim (92807-1819)
PHONE.................909 987-0815
Joseph Mitchell, *CEO*
Yasmin Fallah, *
▲ **EMP:** 39 **EST:** 2009
**SQ FT:** 40,000
**SALES (est):** 10.36MM **Publicly Held**
**Web:** www.spigroups.com
**SIC:** 3711 Cars, electric, assembly of
**HQ:** Edisonfuture Inc.
4677 Old Ironsides Dr # 1
Santa Clara CA 95054
408 919-8000

**(P-13376)**
**PREVOST CAR (US) INC**
28702 Hall Rd, Hayward (94545-5012)
PHONE.................951 202-2064
**EMP:** 19
**SALES (corp-wide):** 119.84MM **Privately Held**
**Web:** www.prevostcar.com
**SIC:** 3711 Motor vehicles and car bodies
**HQ:** Prevost Car (Us) Inc.
7817 National Service Rd
Greensboro NC 27409
908 222-7211

**(P-13377)**
**PROTERRA OPERATING COMPANY INC**
393 Cheryl Ln, City Of Industry (91789-3003)
PHONE.................864 438-0000
**EMP:** 274
**SALES (corp-wide):** 309.36MM **Publicly Held**
**Web:** www.proterra.com
**SIC:** 3711 Automobile assembly, including specialty automobiles
**HQ:** Proterra Operating Company, Inc.
1815 Rollins Rd
Burlingame CA 94010

**(P-13378)**
**PROTERRA OPERATING COMPANY INC (HQ)**
1815 Rollins Rd, Burlingame (94010-2204)
▲ **EMP:** 92 **EST:** 2004
**SQ FT:** 14,000
**SALES (est):** 181.28MM
**SALES (corp-wide):** 309.36MM **Publicly Held**
**Web:** www.proterra.com
**SIC:** 3711 Bus and other large specialty vehicle assembly
**PA:** Proterra Inc
1815 Rollins Rd
864 438-0000

**(P-13379)**
**RIVIAN AUTOMOTIVE INC (PA)**
Also Called: Rivian
14600 Myford Rd, Irvine (92606-1005)
PHONE.................888 748-4261
Robert J Scaringe, *Ch Bd*
Claire Mcdonough, *Interim CAO*
Dagan Mishoulam, *Chief Commercial Officer*
**EMP:** 496 **EST:** 2009
**SALES (est):** 4.43B
**SALES (corp-wide):** 4.43B **Publicly Held**
**Web:** www.rivian.com
**SIC:** 3711 Motor vehicles and car bodies

**(P-13380)**
**RIVIAN AUTOMOTIVE LLC**
1648 Ashley Way, Colton (92324-4000)
PHONE.................309 249-8777
**EMP:** 97
**SALES (corp-wide):** 4.43B **Publicly Held**
**Web:** www.rivian.com
**SIC:** 3711 3714 Motor vehicles and car bodies; Motor vehicle parts and accessories
**HQ:** Rivian Automotive, Llc
13250 Haggerty Rd
Plymouth MI 48170
888 748-4261

**(P-13381)**
**RIVIAN AUTOMOTIVE LLC**
14451 Myford Rd, Tustin (92780-7023)
PHONE.................888 748-4261
**EMP:** 97
**SALES (corp-wide):** 4.43B **Publicly Held**
**Web:** www.rivian.com
**SIC:** 3711 Motor vehicles and car bodies
**HQ:** Rivian Automotive, Llc
13250 Haggerty Rd
Plymouth MI 48170
888 748-4261

**(P-13382)**
**SALEEN INCORPORATED (PA)**
2735 Wardlow Rd, Corona (92882-2869)
PHONE.................714 400-2121
Paul Wilbur, *Pr*
Stephen Saleen, *
Brian Walsh, *
Michael Simmons, *Chief Marketing**
◆ **EMP:** 200 **EST:** 1984
**SALES (est):** 6.36MM **Privately Held**
**Web:** www.saleen.com
**SIC:** 3711 Automobile assembly, including specialty automobiles

**(P-13383)**
**SF MOTORS INC (DH)**
Also Called: Seres
1504 Mccarthy Blvd, Milpitas (95035-7405)
PHONE.................408 617-7878
Michael Deng, *CEO*
Martin Eberhard, *Chief Innovation Officer**
Mike Miskovsky, *Chief Development Officer**
**EMP:** 250 **EST:** 2016
**SALES (est):** 27.79MM **Privately Held**
**Web:** www.driveseres.com
**SIC:** 3711 Cars, electric, assembly of
**HQ:** Seres Auto Co., Ltd.
No. 229, Fusheng Avenue, Jiangbei District
Chongqing CQ 40113

**(P-13384)**
**SHELBY CARROLL INTL INC (PA)**
7927 Garden Grove Blvd, Garden Grove (92841-4225)
PHONE.................310 327-5072
Carroll Shelby, *Prin*
**EMP:** 22 **EST:** 2009
**SALES (est):** 9.35MM **Privately Held**
**Web:** www.carrollshelby.com
**SIC:** 3711 Motor vehicles and car bodies

**(P-13385)**
**SHYFT GROUP INC**
1130 S Vail Ave, Montebello (90640-6021)
PHONE.................323 276-1933
**EMP:** 74
**SALES (corp-wide):** 872.2MM **Publicly Held**
**Web:** www.utilimaster.com
**SIC:** 3711 Motor vehicles and car bodies
**PA:** The Shyft Group Inc
41280 Bridge St
517 543-6400

**(P-13386)**
**SHYFT GROUP INC**
4242 Forcum Ave Bldg B-640, Mcclellan (95652-2110)
PHONE.................916 921-2639
**EMP:** 59
**SALES (corp-wide):** 872.2MM **Publicly Held**
**Web:** www.theshyftgroup.com
**SIC:** 3711 3714 7519 Chassis, motor vehicle; Motor vehicle parts and accessories; Utility trailer rental
**PA:** The Shyft Group Inc
41280 Bridge St
517 543-6400

**(P-13387)**
**SIEMENS MOBILITY INC**
7464 French Rd, Sacramento (95828-4600)
PHONE.................916 681-3000
**EMP:** 2228
**SALES (corp-wide):** 84.48B **Privately Held**
**Web:** www.siemens.com
**SIC:** 3711 3743 Motor vehicles and car bodies; Railway motor cars
**HQ:** Siemens Mobility, Inc.
1 Penn Plz Ste 1100
New York NY 10119
212 672-4000

**(P-13388)**
**TCI ENGINEERING INC**
Also Called: Total Cost Involved
1416 Brooks St, Ontario (91762-3613)
PHONE.................909 984-1773
Edward Moss, *Pr*
Edward Moss, *Pr*
Sherlly Prakarsa, *
**EMP:** 54 **EST:** 1974
**SQ FT:** 25,000
**SALES (est):** 8.82MM **Privately Held**
**Web:** www.totalcostinvolved.com
**SIC:** 3711 5531 3714 Chassis, motor vehicle; Auto and home supply stores; Motor vehicle parts and accessories

**(P-13389)**
**TEAM USA (PA)**
2154 E 51st St, Vernon (90058-2817)
PHONE.................323 826-9888
Tony Hur, *Pr*
◆ **EMP:** 15 **EST:** 1999
**SQ FT:** 9,000
**SALES (est):** 313.96K
**SALES (corp-wide):** 313.96K **Privately Held**

## PRODUCTS & SERVICES SECTION
## 3713 - Truck And Bus Bodies (P-13411)

Web: www.theteamusa.com
SIC: **3711** 5511 Automobile assembly, including specialty automobiles; New and used car dealers

### (P-13390)
### TESLA INC
18260 S Harlan Rd, Lathrop (95330-8757)
PHONE.................................209 647-7037
Robyn Denholm, *Ch Bd*
**EMP:** 335
**SALES (corp-wide):** 96.77B **Publicly Held**
Web: www.tesla.com
SIC: **3711** Motor vehicles and car bodies
PA: Tesla, Inc.
   1 Tesla Rd
   512 516-8177

### (P-13391)
### TESLA INC
Also Called: Tesla Factory
45500 Fremont Blvd, Fremont (94538-6326)
PHONE.................................510 249-3500
Ali Syed, *Brnch Mgr*
**EMP:** 242
**SALES (corp-wide):** 96.77B **Publicly Held**
Web: www.tesla.com
SIC: **3711** Motor vehicles and car bodies
PA: Tesla, Inc.
   1 Tesla Rd
   512 516-8177

### (P-13392)
### TESLA INC
Also Called: Tesla Motors
47700 Kato Rd, Fremont (94538-7307)
P.O. Box 416 (94070-0416)
PHONE.................................650 681-5000
**EMP:** 329
**SALES (corp-wide):** 96.77B **Publicly Held**
Web: www.tesla.com
SIC: **3711** Motor vehicles and car bodies
PA: Tesla, Inc.
   1 Tesla Rd
   512 516-8177

### (P-13393)
### TESLA INC
Also Called: Tesla Store Menlo Park
4180 El Camino Real, Palo Alto (94306-4008)
PHONE.................................650 681-5800
Dan Myggen, *Brnch Mgr*
**EMP:** 351
**SALES (corp-wide):** 96.77B **Publicly Held**
Web: www.tesla.com
SIC: **3711** Motor vehicles and car bodies
PA: Tesla, Inc.
   1 Tesla Rd
   512 516-8177

### (P-13394)
### TESLA INC
39800 Fremont Blvd, Fremont (94538-2678)
PHONE.................................510 690-5451
**EMP:** 18
**SALES (corp-wide):** 96.77B **Publicly Held**
Web: www.tesla.com
SIC: **3711** Automobile assembly, including specialty automobiles
PA: Tesla, Inc.
   1 Tesla Rd
   512 516-8177

### (P-13395)
### TESLA INC
Also Called: Tesla Factory
45500 Fremont Blvd, Fremont (94538-6326)
PHONE.................................510 249-3650
**EMP:** 3500
**SALES (corp-wide):** 7B **Publicly Held**
SIC: **3711** Cars, electric, assembly of
PA: Tesla, Inc.
   3500 Deer Creek Rd
   650 681-5000

### (P-13396)
### TESLA INC
901 Page Ave, Fremont (94538-7341)
PHONE.................................510 766-6688
**EMP:** 90
**SALES (corp-wide):** 96.77B **Publicly Held**
Web: www.tesla.com
SIC: **3711** Cars, electric, assembly of
PA: Tesla, Inc.
   1 Tesla Rd
   512 516-8177

### (P-13397)
### WARLOCK INDUSTRIES
Also Called: Tiffany Coach Builders
23129 Cajalco Rd Ste A, Perris (92570-7298)
PHONE.................................951 657-2680
▼ **EMP:** 46 **EST:** 2009
**SALES (est):** 898.28K **Privately Held**
SIC: **3711** Motor vehicles and car bodies

### (P-13398)
### XOS FLEET INC (HQ)
Also Called: Xos Trucks
3550 Tyburn St Ste 100, Los Angeles (90065-1427)
PHONE.................................818 316-1890
Dakota Semler, *CEO*
Giordano Sordoni, *
Liana Pogosyan, *
**EMP:** 50 **EST:** 2015
**SALES (est):** 34.17MM
**SALES (corp-wide):** 44.52MM **Publicly Held**
Web: www.xostrucks.com
SIC: **3711** 3713 Truck and tractor truck assembly; Truck bodies and parts
PA: Xos, Inc.
   3550 Tyburn St Ste 100
   818 316-1890

### (P-13399)
### ZOOX INC (HQ)
Also Called: Zoox Labs
1149 Chess Dr, Foster City (94404-1102)
PHONE.................................650 539-9669
Carl Bass, *Ch*
Aicha Evans, *
Ilan Hart, *
Jesse Levinson, *
**EMP:** 50 **EST:** 2014
**SALES (est):** 251MM **Publicly Held**
Web: www.zoox.com
SIC: **3711** Automobile assembly, including specialty automobiles
PA: Amazon.Com, Inc.
   410 Terry Ave N

## 3713 Truck And Bus Bodies

### (P-13400)
### AMERICAN TRCK TRLR BDY CO INC (PA)
100 W Valpico Rd Ste D, Tracy (95376-8198)
P.O. Box 820 (95336)
PHONE.................................209 836-8985
Clint Garner, *Pr*
Michael A Garner, *
Dallas Dodson, *
Scott Page, *
Guy Garner, *
**EMP:** 42 **EST:** 1992
**SQ FT:** 40,000
**SALES (est):** 9.95MM **Privately Held**
Web: www.attbcinc.com
SIC: **3713** Truck bodies (motor vehicles)

### (P-13401)
### ARROW TRUCK BODIES & EQP INC
1639 S Campus Ave, Ontario (91761-4364)
PHONE.................................909 947-3991
Raymond A Glaze, *Pr*
Keith Wysocki, *Pr*
Richard Rubio, *Sec*
**EMP:** 20 **EST:** 1963
**SQ FT:** 33,980
**SALES (est):** 698.51K **Privately Held**
SIC: **3713** Truck bodies (motor vehicles)

### (P-13402)
### CALIFORNIA SUPERTRUCKS INC
14385 Veterans Way, Moreno Valley (92553-9059)
PHONE.................................951 656-2903
Chris Robinson, *Pr*
Bradley Myers, *
Tim Clark, *
**EMP:** 15 **EST:** 1996
**SQ FT:** 20,000
**SALES (est):** 3.55MM **Privately Held**
Web: www.californiasupertrucks.com
SIC: **3713** 3011 5014 5013 Truck bodies and parts; Inner tubes, all types; Truck tires and tubes; Truck parts and accessories

### (P-13403)
### COMMERCIAL TRUCK EQP CO LLC
Also Called: Commercial Truck Equipment Co
12351 Bellflower Blvd, Downey (90242-2829)
PHONE.................................562 803-4466
James E Anderson, *Pr*
Lorena Anderson, *
**EMP:** 56 **EST:** 2008
**SALES (est):** 3.92MM **Privately Held**
Web: www.ctec-truckbody.com
SIC: **3713** Truck bodies (motor vehicles)

### (P-13404)
### COMPLETE TRUCK BODY REPAIR INC
1217 N Alameda St, Compton (90222-4102)
P.O. Box 1792 (90723-1792)
PHONE.................................323 445-2675
Rodrigo Robles, *CEO*
**EMP:** 23 **EST:** 2012
**SQ FT:** 10,225
**SALES (est):** 2.45MM **Privately Held**
Web: www.completetruckbody.com
SIC: **3713** Truck bodies and parts

### (P-13405)
### CTBLA INC
1740 Albion St, Los Angeles (90031-2520)
PHONE.................................323 276-1933
Kam C Law, *Pr*
Peter Lee, *
◆ **EMP:** 99 **EST:** 1995
**SALES (est):** 7.99MM **Privately Held**
SIC: **3713** Truck bodies (motor vehicles)

### (P-13406)
### CUSTOM TRUCK ONE SOURCE LP
4500 State Rd, Bakersfield (93308-4544)
PHONE.................................316 627-2608
**EMP:** 39
**SALES (corp-wide):** 1.57B **Publicly Held**
Web: www.customtruck.com
SIC: **3713** Truck and bus bodies
HQ: Custom Truck One Source, L.P.
   7701 E 24 Hwy
   Kansas City MO 64125
   855 931-1852

### (P-13407)
### DENBESTE MANUFACTURING INC
820 Den Beste Ct, Windsor (95492-6896)
PHONE.................................707 838-1407
Lori Denbeste, *Pr*
**EMP:** 25 **EST:** 2006
**SALES (est):** 1.84MM **Privately Held**
Web: www.denbeste.com
SIC: **3713** Tank truck bodies

### (P-13408)
### DOUGLASS TRUCK BODIES INC
231 21st St, Bakersfield (93301-4138)
PHONE.................................661 327-0258
**TOLL FREE:** 800
Rick Douglass, *Pr*
Deborah Douglass, *
Jean Raley, *
**EMP:** 24 **EST:** 1959
**SQ FT:** 5,000
**SALES (est):** 5.57MM **Privately Held**
Web: www.douglasstruckbodies.com
SIC: **3713** Truck bodies (motor vehicles)

### (P-13409)
### DYNAFLEX PRODUCTS (PA)
Also Called: Exhaust Tech
6466 Gayhart St, Commerce (90040-2506)
PHONE.................................323 724-1555
Robert L Mcgovern, *Pr*
Denise Pehrsson, *CEO*
Robert L Mcgovern, *Prin*
Gil Contreras, *
**EMP:** 75 **EST:** 1971
**SQ FT:** 64,000
**SALES (est):** 16.78MM
**SALES (corp-wide):** 16.78MM **Privately Held**
Web: www.dynaflexproducts.com
SIC: **3713** 3498 3714 Truck and bus bodies; Fabricated pipe and fittings; Exhaust systems and parts, motor vehicle

### (P-13410)
### EBUS INC
9250 Washburn Rd, Downey (90242-2909)
PHONE.................................562 904-3474
Anders B Eklov, *Ch Bd*
**EMP:** 16 **EST:** 1983
**SALES (est):** 2.56MM **Privately Held**
Web: fcebus.wixsite.com
SIC: **3713** Bus bodies (motor vehicles)

### (P-13411)
### ERF ENTERPRISES INC
Also Called: Colton Truck Terminal Garage
863 E Valley Blvd, Colton (92324-3125)
PHONE.................................909 825-4080
Ed Doltar, *Pr*
Rich Doltar, *Prin*
Fran Fields, *Prin*
**EMP:** 18 **EST:** 2019
**SALES (est):** 1.25MM **Privately Held**

# 3713 - Truck And Bus Bodies (P-13412)

SIC: 3713 Truck bodies (motor vehicles)

## (P-13412)
### FLEMING METAL FABRICATORS
874 Camino De Los Mares, San Clemente (92673-3122)
PHONE..................................323 723-8203
Wade M Fleming, Pr
Marc Fleming, *
EMP: 30 EST: 1918
SALES (est): 3.98MM **Privately Held**
Web: www.flemingmetal.com
SIC: 3713 3441 3714 3577 Truck bodies and parts; Fabricated structural metal; Motor vehicle parts and accessories; Computer peripheral equipment, nec

## (P-13413)
### GILLIG LLC (HQ)
451 Discovery Dr, Livermore (94551-9534)
PHONE..................................510 264-5000
Derek Maunus, Pr
▲ EMP: 191 EST: 1896
SQ FT: 150,000
SALES (est): 467.3MM
SALES (corp-wide): 2.12B **Publicly Held**
Web: www.gillig.com
SIC: 3713 Truck and bus bodies
PA: Henry Crown And Company
222 N La Slle St Ste 2000
312 236-6300

## (P-13414)
### HARBOR TRUCK BODIES INC
Also Called: Harbor Truck Body
255 Voyager Ave, Brea (92821)
PHONE..................................714 996-0411
Ken Lindt, Pr
EMP: 79 EST: 1973
SQ FT: 50,000
SALES (est): 8.69MM **Privately Held**
Web: www.harbortruckandvan.com
SIC: 3713 7532 Truck bodies (motor vehicles); Body shop, automotive

## (P-13415)
### KRYSTAL INFINITY LLC
Also Called: Krystal Enterprises
6915 Arlington Ave, Riverside (92504-1905)
EMP: 500
SIC: 3713 3711 Truck and bus bodies; Automobile assembly, including specialty automobiles

## (P-13416)
### LIMOS BY TIFFANY INC
Also Called: Tiffany Coachworks
23129 Cajalco Rd, Perris (92570-7298)
P.O. Box 46 (92572-0046)
PHONE..................................951 657-2680
EMP: 35 EST: 2001
SALES (est): 1.29MM **Privately Held**
SIC: 3713 Specialty motor vehicle bodies

## (P-13417)
### MCLELLAN EQUIPMENT INC
13221 Crown Ave, Hanford (93230-9508)
PHONE..................................559 582-8100
Scott Mclellan, VP
EMP: 35
SALES (corp-wide): 8.84MM **Privately Held**
Web: www.mclellanindustries.com
SIC: 3713 3532 7532 3312 Truck bodies (motor vehicles); Mining machinery; Tops (canvas or plastic), installation or repair: automotive; Blast furnaces and steel mills
PA: Mclellan Equipment, Inc.
251 Shaw Rd
650 873-8100

## (P-13418)
### MCLELLAN INDUSTRIES INC
13221 Crown Ave, Hanford (93230-9508)
PHONE..................................650 873-8100
Victor Resendez, Mgr
EMP: 80
SALES (corp-wide): 21.27MM **Privately Held**
Web: www.mclellanindustries.com
SIC: 3713 Truck bodies (motor vehicles)
PA: Mclellan Industries, Inc.
251 Shaw Rd
650 873-8100

## (P-13419)
### MCNEILUS TRUCK AND MFG INC
401 N Pepper Ave, Colton (92324-1817)
P.O. Box 1588 (92324-0849)
PHONE..................................909 370-2100
Liza Langley, Brnch Mgr
EMP: 33
SALES (corp-wide): 9.66B **Publicly Held**
Web: www.mcneilusgarbagetrucks.com
SIC: 3713 5511 3711 3531 Cement mixer bodies; Pickups, new and used; Truck and tractor truck assembly; Construction machinery
HQ: Mcneilus Truck And Manufacturing, Inc.
524 E Highway St
Dodge Center MN 55927
507 374-6321

## (P-13420)
### MOTIV POWER SYSTEMS INC
2745 Boeing Way, Stockton (95206-3983)
PHONE..................................650 458-4804
Matt Oleary, Pr
EMP: 128 EST: 2014
SALES (est): 2.63MM
SALES (corp-wide): 20.32MM **Privately Held**
SIC: 3713 Truck and bus bodies
PA: Motiv Power Systems, Inc.
330 Hatch Dr
650 458-4804

## (P-13421)
### NOR-CAL VANS INC
1100 Marauder St, Chico (95973-9038)
PHONE..................................530 892-0150
Todd Lapant, CEO
Laura Lapant, CFO
EMP: 15 EST: 1980
SALES (est): 2.44MM **Privately Held**
Web: www.driverge.com
SIC: 3713 Van bodies

## (P-13422)
### PACIFIC TRUCK TANK INC
7029 Florin Perkins Rd Ste A, Sacramento (95828-2656)
PHONE..................................916 379-9280
Kirby Fleming, Pr
Jerry Jones, VP
EMP: 20 EST: 1997
SQ FT: 22,000
SALES (est): 4.4MM **Privately Held**
Web: www.pacifictrucktank.com
SIC: 3713 Truck beds

## (P-13423)
### PHENIX ENTERPRISES INC (PA)
Also Called: Phenix Truck Bodies and Eqp
1785 Mount Vernon Ave, Pomona (91768-3330)
PHONE..................................909 469-0411
Rick Albertini, CEO
Benjamin Albertini, *
Norma E Albertini, *
Paul Albertini, *
EMP: 39 EST: 1978
SQ FT: 100,000
SALES (est): 13.85MM
SALES (corp-wide): 13.85MM **Privately Held**
Web: www.phenixent.com
SIC: 3713 3711 Truck bodies (motor vehicles); Motor vehicles and car bodies

## (P-13424)
### REALTRUCK ENTERPRISE INC
Also Called: Realtruck
1747 W Lincoln Ave Ste K, Anaheim (92801-6770)
PHONE..................................956 324-5337
Carl-martin Lindahl, Pr
EMP: 40
SALES (corp-wide): 829.18MM **Privately Held**
Web: www.realtruck.com
SIC: 3713 Truck bodies and parts
HQ: Realtruck Enterprise, Inc.
5400 Data Ct
Ann Arbor MI 48108
734 205-9093

## (P-13425)
### RENZENBERGER INC
2096 E Main St, Quincy (95971-9658)
PHONE..................................530 283-3314
EMP: 481
SALES (corp-wide): 440.84MM **Privately Held**
Web: www.renzenberger.com
SIC: 3713 Truck and bus bodies
HQ: Renzenberger, Inc.
14325 W 95th St
Lenexa KS 66215
913 631-0450

## (P-13426)
### SAF-T-CAB INC (PA)
3241 S Parkway Dr, Fresno (93725-2319)
P.O. Box 2587 (93745-2587)
PHONE..................................559 268-5541
Fred Mattern, Pr
Dan Lockie, *
▲ EMP: 41 EST: 1968
SQ FT: 12,000
SALES (est): 18.54MM
SALES (corp-wide): 18.54MM **Privately Held**
Web: www.saftcab.com
SIC: 3713 3532 Truck cabs, for motor vehicles; Mining machinery

## (P-13427)
### SCELZI ENTERPRISES INC (PA)
2286 E Date Ave, Fresno (93706-5425)
P.O. Box 12066 (93776-2066)
PHONE..................................559 237-5541
EMP: 44 EST: 1988
SALES (est): 26.84MM
SALES (corp-wide): 26.84MM **Privately Held**
Web: www.seinc.com
SIC: 3713 Truck bodies (motor vehicles)

## (P-13428)
### SKAUG TRUCK BODY WORKS
1404 1st St, San Fernando (91340-2795)
PHONE..................................818 365-9123
George L Skaug, Pr
William Bill Reeves, VP
EMP: 18 EST: 1946
SQ FT: 3,200
SALES (est): 2.15MM **Privately Held**
Web: www.skaugtruckbody.com

SIC: 3713 Truck bodies (motor vehicles)

## (P-13429)
### SOUTHERN CAL TRCK BDIES SLS IN
1131 E 2nd St, Pomona (91766-2115)
PHONE..................................909 469-1132
Miguel Sanchez, Pr
Silvia Sanchez, Sec
EMP: 15 EST: 2000
SQ FT: 6,035
SALES (est): 3.33MM **Privately Held**
Web: www.socaltrkbodies.com
SIC: 3713 5531 Truck bodies (motor vehicles); Automotive parts

## (P-13430)
### SPARTAN TRUCK COMPANY INC
12266 Branford St, Sun Valley (91352-1009)
PHONE..................................818 899-1111
Myan Spaccarelli, Pr
EMP: 35 EST: 1972
SQ FT: 25,000
SALES (est): 9.62MM **Privately Held**
Web: www.spartantruck.com
SIC: 3713 7532 3537 Garbage, refuse truck bodies; Top and body repair and paint shops; Industrial trucks and tractors

## (P-13431)
### SUPREME TRUCK BODIES CAL INC
Also Called: Wabash
22135 Alessandro Blvd, Moreno Valley (92553-8215)
PHONE..................................800 827-0753
Mark D Weber, Pr
EMP: 39 EST: 2013
SALES (est): 3.73MM
SALES (corp-wide): 2.54B **Publicly Held**
SIC: 3713 Truck bodies (motor vehicles)
HQ: Supreme Industries, Inc.
2581 Kercher Rd
Goshen IN 46528
574 642-3070

## (P-13432)
### TABC INC (DH)
6375 N Paramount Blvd, Long Beach (90805-3301)
PHONE..................................562 984-3305
Michael Bafan, CEO
Yoshiaki Nishino, *
◆ EMP: 215 EST: 1974
SQ FT: 8,820
SALES (est): 113.12MM **Privately Held**
SIC: 3713 3469 3714 Truck beds; Metal stampings, nec; Motor vehicle parts and accessories
HQ: Toyota Motor Engineering & Manufacturing North America, Inc.
6565 Hdqtr Dr W1-3c
Plano TX 75024

## (P-13433)
### TRI COUNTIES TRUCKING
1263 Reed Rd, Yuba City (95991-9111)
PHONE..................................530 692-5388
Charina Kelly, CEO
Kailani Nicole Kelly, CEO
Charina Layug Kelly, Prin
EMP: 20 EST: 2021
SALES (est): 1.33MM **Privately Held**
Web: www.tricountiestrucking.com
SIC: 3713 Dump truck bodies

# PRODUCTS & SERVICES SECTION
## 3714 - Motor Vehicle Parts And Accessories (P-13455)

**(P-13434)**
**VAHE ENTERPRISES INC**
Also Called: Aa Leasing
750 E Slauson Ave, Los Angeles (90011-5236)
PHONE..................................323 235-6657
Vahe Karapetian, *CEO*
▲ **EMP:** 90 **EST:** 1976
**SQ FT:** 60,000
**SALES (est):** 9.89MM **Privately Held**
Web: www.aacatertruck.com
**SIC: 3713** 7513  Truck bodies (motor vehicles); Truck leasing, without drivers

**(P-13435)**
**WESTERN TRUCK FABRICATION INC**
Also Called: W T F
1923 W Winton Ave, Hayward (94545-1205)
PHONE..................................510 785-9994
**EMP:** 35 **EST:** 1984
**SALES (est):** 7.34MM **Privately Held**
Web: www.westerntruckfab.com
**SIC: 3713**  Truck beds

## 3714 Motor Vehicle Parts And Accessories

**(P-13436)**
**89908 INC**
Also Called: AMP Research
15651 Mosher Ave, Tustin (92780-6426)
PHONE..................................949 221-0023
**EMP:** 35
Web: www.realtruck.com
**SIC: 3714**  Motor vehicle parts and accessories

**(P-13437)**
**ACHATES POWER INC**
4060 Sorrento Valley Blvd Ste A, San Diego (92121-1428)
PHONE..................................858 535-9920
David Crompton, *Pr*
David Johnson, *CEO*
John Koszewnik, *Prin*
Jerome Paye, *Dir Opers*
Carol Mottershead, *Finance*
**EMP:** 95 **EST:** 2003
**SALES (est):** 24.96MM **Privately Held**
Web: www.achatespower.com
**SIC: 3714** 8711  Motor vehicle engines and parts; Mechanical engineering

**(P-13438)**
**ACME HEADLINING CO**
Also Called: Acme Auto Headlining
550 W 16th St, Long Beach (90813-1510)
P.O. Box 847 (90801-0847)
PHONE..................................562 432-0281
Bob Westmoreland, *VP*
Don Young, *
▲ **EMP:** 75 **EST:** 1948
**SQ FT:** 18,000
**SALES (est):** 5.1MM **Privately Held**
Web: www.acmeautoheadlining.com
**SIC: 3714**  Tops, motor vehicle

**(P-13439)**
**ACSCO PRODUCTS INC**
313 N Lake St, Burbank (91502-1816)
PHONE..................................818 953-2240
Thomas W Mc Intyre, *Pr*
**EMP:** 20 **EST:** 1963
**SQ FT:** 4,000
**SALES (est):** 5.31MM **Privately Held**
Web: www.acsco.net

**SIC: 3714**  Motor vehicle parts and accessories

**(P-13440)**
**ADIENT US LLC**
Also Called: Adient Newark
6601 Overlake Pl, Newark (94560-1009)
PHONE..................................510 771-2300
**EMP:** 45
Web: www.adient.com
**SIC: 3714**  Motor vehicle parts and accessories
HQ: Adient Us Llc
   49200 Halyard Dr
   Plymouth MI 48170
   734 254-5000

**(P-13441)**
**ADVANCE ADAPTERS INC**
4320 Aerotech Center Way, Paso Robles (93446-8529)
P.O. Box 247 (93447-0247)
PHONE..................................805 238-7000
Mike Partridge, *Pr*
John Partridge, *
Angela Partridge, *Ofcr*
Randy Cronkright, *Pur Mgr*
▲ **EMP:** 44 **EST:** 1971
**SQ FT:** 44,000
**SALES (est):** 5.02MM **Privately Held**
Web: www.advanceadapters.com
**SIC: 3714**  Transmission housings or parts, motor vehicle

**(P-13442)**
**ADVANCE ADAPTERS LLC**
4320 Aerotech Center Way, Paso Robles (93446-8529)
PHONE..................................805 238-7000
John Upshur, *Prin*
**EMP:** 45 **EST:** 2017
**SALES (est):** 3.86MM **Privately Held**
Web: www.advanceadapters.com
**SIC: 3714**  Motor vehicle parts and accessories

**(P-13443)**
**ADVANCED CLUTCH TECHNOLOGY INC**
206 E Avenue K4, Lancaster (93535-4685)
PHONE..................................661 940-7555
Tracy Nunez, *CEO*
Dirk Starksen, *
Danette Starksen, *
▲ **EMP:** 30 **EST:** 1994
**SQ FT:** 18,000
**SALES (est):** 5.08MM **Privately Held**
Web: www.advancedclutch.com
**SIC: 3714**  Clutches, motor vehicle

**(P-13444)**
**ADVANCED FLOW ENGINEERING INC (PA)**
Also Called: Afe Power
252 Granite St, Corona (92879-1283)
PHONE..................................951 493-7155
Shahriar Nick Niakan, *Pr*
Stuart Miyagishima, *
David Howey, *
Eric Griffith, *
Chris Barron, *
▲ **EMP:** 44 **EST:** 1999
**SQ FT:** 60,000
**SALES (est):** 21.62MM
**SALES (corp-wide):** 21.62MM **Privately Held**
Web: www.afepower.com
**SIC: 3714**  Motor vehicle engines and parts

**(P-13445)**
**ADVANCED FLOW ENGINEERING INC**
Also Called: Afe Power
1375 Sampson Ave, Corona (92879-1748)
PHONE..................................951 493-7100
**EMP:** 21
**SALES (corp-wide):** 21.62MM **Privately Held**
Web: www.afepower.com
**SIC: 3714**  Motor vehicle engines and parts
PA: Advanced Flow Engineering, Inc.
   252 Granite St
   951 493-7155

**(P-13446)**
**ADVANCED TRANSIT DYNAMICS INC**
Also Called: Atdynamics
3150 Corporate Pl, Hayward (94545-3916)
P.O. Box 1989 (75606-1989)
PHONE..................................510 619-8245
**EMP:** 57
**SIC: 3714**  Motor vehicle parts and accessories

**(P-13447)**
**AEC GROUP INC**
Also Called: Advantage Engrg & Chemistry
3600 W Carriage Dr, Santa Ana (92704-6416)
PHONE..................................714 444-1395
Mike Lau, *Pr*
Erik Waelput, *VP*
**EMP:** 15 **EST:** 2000
**SQ FT:** 12,000
**SALES (est):** 2.09MM **Privately Held**
Web: www.aecgroup.net
**SIC: 3714**  Lubrication systems and parts, motor vehicle

**(P-13448)**
**AEVA TECHNOLOGIES INC (PA)**
Also Called: AEVA
555 Ellis St, Mountain View (94043-2214)
PHONE..................................650 481-7070
Soroush Salehian Dardashti, *CEO*
Mina Rezk, *Ch Bd*
Saurabh Sinha, *CFO*
**EMP:** 296 **EST:** 2017
**SALES (est):** 4.31MM
**SALES (corp-wide):** 4.31MM **Publicly Held**
Web: www.aeva.com
**SIC: 3714** 7372  Motor vehicle parts and accessories; Prepackaged software

**(P-13449)**
**AEYE INC (PA)**
4670 Willow Rd Ste 125, Pleasanton (94588-8590)
PHONE..................................925 400-4366
Matthew Fisch, *Ch Bd*
Conor B Tierney, *CAO*
**EMP:** 15 **EST:** 2013
**SQ FT:** 6,522
**SALES (est):** 1.46MM
**SALES (corp-wide):** 1.46MM **Publicly Held**
Web: www.aeye.ai
**SIC: 3714**  Motor vehicle parts and accessories

**(P-13450)**
**AGILITY FUEL SYSTEMS LLC (DH)**
1815 Carnegie Ave, Santa Ana (92705-5527)
PHONE..................................949 236-5520

Kathleen Ligocki, *CEO*
Ron Eickeleman, *Pr*
Tom Russell, *CFO*
Joe Pike, *VP*
Jeff Scott, *VP*
▲ **EMP:** 19 **EST:** 2010
**SALES (est):** 109.78MM **Privately Held**
Web: www.hexagonagility.com
**SIC: 3714**  Fuel systems and parts, motor vehicle
HQ: Agility Fuel Solutions Llc
   3335 Susan St Ste 100
   Costa Mesa CA 92626
   949 236-5520

**(P-13451)**
**AIR FLOW RESEARCH HEADS INC**
Also Called: Air Flow Research
28611 Industry Dr, Valencia (91355-5413)
PHONE..................................661 257-8124
Rick Sperling, *Pr*
▲ **EMP:** 40 **EST:** 1970
**SQ FT:** 14,000
**SALES (est):** 6.37MM **Privately Held**
Web: www.airflowresearch.com
**SIC: 3714**  Cylinder heads, motor vehicle

**(P-13452)**
**AISIN ELECTRONICS INC**
Also Called: Aisin
199 Frank West Cir, Stockton (95206-4002)
P.O. Box 30070 (95213)
PHONE..................................209 983-4988
Yasuhito Mori, *Pr*
Yuji Tomisawa, *
**EMP:** 230 **EST:** 1996
**SQ FT:** 22,000
**SALES (est):** 18.94MM **Privately Held**
Web: www.aisin-electronics.com
**SIC: 3714** 3625  Motor vehicle parts and accessories; Control circuit relays, industrial
HQ: Aisin Holdings Of America, Inc.
   1665 E 4th St
   Seymour IN 47274
   812 524-8144

**(P-13453)**
**AITA CLUTCH INC**
960 S Santa Fe Ave, Compton (90221-4333)
PHONE..................................323 585-4140
Guillermo Rios, *Pr*
Fred Rios, *
Albert Rios, *
**EMP:** 23 **EST:** 1982
**SALES (est):** 2.02MM **Privately Held**
**SIC: 3714** 5013  Clutches, motor vehicle; Automotive supplies and parts

**(P-13454)**
**ALLIED WHEEL COMPONENTS INC**
Also Called: Raceline Wheels
12300 Edison Way, Garden Grove (92841-2810)
P.O. Box 5667 (92846-0667)
PHONE..................................800 529-4335
Bruce Higginson, *CEO*
◆ **EMP:** 38 **EST:** 1996
**SQ FT:** 91,000
**SALES (est):** 15.44MM **Privately Held**
Web: www.alliedwheel.com
**SIC: 3714** 5531  Wheels, motor vehicle; Automotive tires

**(P-13455)**
**AMCOR INDUSTRIES INC**
Also Called: Gorilla Automotive Products
6131 Knott Ave, Buena Park (90620-1031)

## 3714 - Motor Vehicle Parts And Accessories (P-13456)

PHONE..................323 585-2852
Peter J Schermer, *Pr*
▲ **EMP:** 25 **EST:** 1983
**SQ FT:** 30,000
**SALES (est):** 5.31MM
**SALES (corp-wide):** 731.01MM **Privately Held**
Web: www.gorilla-auto.com
**SIC: 3714** 3429 Motor vehicle wheels and parts; Hardware, nec
HQ: Wheel Pros, Llc
5347 S Vlntia Way Ste 200
Greenwood Village CO 80111

**(P-13456)**
**AMERICAN FABRICATION CORP (PA)**
Also Called: American Best Car Parts
2891 E Via Martens, Anaheim (92806-1751)
PHONE..................714 632-1709
Greg Knox, *Pr*
Jodee Jensen Smith, *
▲ **EMP:** 70 **EST:** 1974
**SALES (est):** 2.34MM
**SALES (corp-wide):** 2.34MM **Privately Held**
Web: www.teamxenon.com
**SIC: 3714** Motor vehicle parts and accessories

**(P-13457)**
**AMERICAN RIM SUPPLY INC**
1955 Kellogg Ave, Carlsbad (92008-6582)
PHONE..................760 431-3666
Robert D Ward, *Pr*
▼ **EMP:** 40 **EST:** 1991
**SQ FT:** 20,000
**SALES (est):** 5.52MM **Privately Held**
Web: www.americanrim.com
**SIC: 3714** Wheel rims, motor vehicle

**(P-13458)**
**APEX PRECISION TECHNOLOGIES INC**
23622 Calabasas Rd Ste 323, Calabasas (91302-1549)
PHONE..................317 821-1000
**EMP:** 45 **EST:** 1951
**SALES (est):** 1.5MM **Privately Held**
**SIC: 3714** 3586 3498 3462 Motor vehicle parts and accessories; Measuring and dispensing pumps; Fabricated pipe and fittings; Iron and steel forgings

**(P-13459)**
**APTIV SERVICES US LLC**
5137 Clareton Dr Ste 220, Agoura Hills (91301-6311)
PHONE..................818 661-6667
**EMP:** 286
Web: www.aptiv.com
**SIC: 3714** Motor vehicle engines and parts
HQ: Aptiv Services Us, Llc
5725 Innovation Dr
Troy MI 48098

**(P-13460)**
**AUTO MOTIVE POWER INC**
11643 Telegraph Rd, Santa Fe Springs (90670-3656)
PHONE..................800 894-7104
Anil Paryani, *Pr*
Lionel Selwood, *
Michael Rice, *CSO**
**EMP:** 120 **EST:** 2020
**SALES (est):** 16.43MM
**SALES (corp-wide):** 176.19B **Publicly Held**
Web: www.amp.tech

**SIC: 3714** Motor vehicle electrical equipment
PA: Ford Motor Company
1 American Rd
313 322-3000

**(P-13461)**
**AUTOLIV INC**
9355 Airway Rd, San Diego (92154-7931)
PHONE..................619 661-0438
**EMP:** 21
**SALES (corp-wide):** 10.47B **Publicly Held**
Web: www.autoliv.com
**SIC: 3714** Motor vehicle parts and accessories
PA: Autoliv, Inc.
3350 Airport Rd
801 629-9800

**(P-13462)**
**AUTOMAX STYLING INC**
16833 Krameria Ave, Riverside (92504-6118)
PHONE..................951 530-1876
Guoxiang Zhou, *CEO*
**EMP:** 40 **EST:** 2005
**SQ FT:** 100,000
**SALES (est):** 944.86K **Privately Held**
Web: www.automaxstyling.com
**SIC: 3714** Motor vehicle parts and accessories

**(P-13463)**
**AZUSA ENGINEERING INC**
1542 W Industrial Park St, Covina (91722-3487)
P.O. Box 2909 (91722-8909)
PHONE..................626 966-4071
James M Patronite, *CEO*
Tom Patronite, *Pr*
Janice M Patronite Esq, *Sec*
▲ **EMP:** 17 **EST:** 1960
**SQ FT:** 17,000
**SALES (est):** 2.38MM **Privately Held**
Web: www.azusaeng.com
**SIC: 3714** Transmission housings or parts, motor vehicle

**(P-13464)**
**BAB STEERING HYDRAULICS (PA)**
Also Called: Bab Hydraulics
14554 Whittram Ave, Fontana (92335-3108)
PHONE..................208 573-4502
William Carlson, *Pr*
▲ **EMP:** 20 **EST:** 1989
**SQ FT:** 15,000
**SALES (est):** 4.49MM **Privately Held**
Web: www.babsteering.com
**SIC: 3714** 3713 5084 Hydraulic fluid power pumps, for auto steering mechanism; Truck and bus bodies; Hydraulic systems equipment and supplies

**(P-13465)**
**BORLA PERFORMANCE INDS INC (PA)**
Also Called: Borla Performance
701 Arcturus Ave, Oxnard (93033-9018)
PHONE..................805 986-8600
Alyse Borla, *CEO*
Allen N Stoner, *
▲ **EMP:** 130 **EST:** 1982
**SQ FT:** 325,000
**SALES (est):** 21.69MM
**SALES (corp-wide):** 21.69MM **Privately Held**
Web: www.borla.com
**SIC: 3714** 5531 Exhaust systems and parts, motor vehicle; Automotive parts

**(P-13466)**
**BUNKER CORP (PA)**
Also Called: Energy Suspension
1131 Via Callejon, San Clemente (92673-6230)
PHONE..................949 361-3935
Donald Bunker, *CEO*
Boni Cambel, *
▼ **EMP:** 100 **EST:** 1985
**SQ FT:** 78,000
**SALES (est):** 22.12MM
**SALES (corp-wide):** 22.12MM **Privately Held**
Web: www.teamenergysuspension.com
**SIC: 3714** Motor vehicle body components and frame

**(P-13467)**
**BYD MOTORS LLC (DH)**
888 E Walnut St Fl 2, Pasadena (91101-1897)
PHONE..................213 748-3980
Stella Li, *CEO*
Ke Li, *Pr*
▲ **EMP:** 39 **EST:** 2010
**SALES (est):** 29.53MM **Privately Held**
Web: en.byd.com
**SIC: 3714** Motor vehicle electrical equipment
HQ: Byd Us Holding Inc.
1800 S Figueroa St
Los Angeles CA 90015
213 748-3980

**(P-13468)**
**C R LAURENCE CO INC (HQ)**
Also Called: Crl
2503 E Vernon Ave, Los Angeles (90058-1826)
PHONE..................323 588-1281
Michael Marcely, *CEO*
Barbara Haaksma, *
Shirin Khosravi, *
Jacque Maples, *
Steve Whitcomb, *
◆ **EMP:** 380 **EST:** 1963
**SQ FT:** 170,000
**SALES (est):** 483.56MM
**SALES (corp-wide):** 34.95B **Privately Held**
Web: azure.crlaurence.com
**SIC: 3714** 5072 5039 Sun roofs, motor vehicle; Hand tools; Glass construction materials
PA: Crh Public Limited Company
Stonemason S Way
14041000

**(P-13469)**
**CANOO INC (PA)**
Also Called: Canoo
19951 Mariner Ave, Torrance (90503-1672)
PHONE..................424 271-2144
Tony Aquila, *Ex Ch Bd*
Josette Sheeran, *Pr*
Greg Ethridge, *CFO*
Ramesh Murthy, *CAO*
Hector Ruiz, *Corporate Secretary*
**EMP:** 45 **EST:** 2017
**SALES (est):** 886K
**SALES (corp-wide):** 886K **Publicly Held**
Web: www.canoo.com
**SIC: 3714** Motor vehicle parts and accessories

**(P-13470)**
**CAR SOUND EXHAUST SYSTEM INC (PA)**
Also Called: Magnaflow Performance
1901 Corporate Ctr, Oceanside (92056-5831)
PHONE..................949 858-5900

Jerry Paolone, *CEO*
Scott Krog, *Prin*
◆ **EMP:** 20 **EST:** 1981
**SQ FT:** 45,000
**SALES (est):** 89.19MM
**SALES (corp-wide):** 89.19MM **Privately Held**
Web: www.magnaflow.com
**SIC: 3714** Exhaust systems and parts, motor vehicle

**(P-13471)**
**CAR SOUND EXHAUST SYSTEM INC**
Also Called: Magnaslow
30142 Avenida De Las Bandera, Rcho Sta Marg (92688-2116)
PHONE..................949 858-5900
Don Billings, *Mgr*
**EMP:** 50
**SALES (corp-wide):** 89.19MM **Privately Held**
Web: www.magnaflow.com
**SIC: 3714** Exhaust systems and parts, motor vehicle
PA: Car Sound Exhaust System, Inc.
1901 Corporate Centre
949 858-5900

**(P-13472)**
**CAR SOUND EXHAUST SYSTEM INC**
23201 Antonio Pkwy, Rcho Sta Marg (92688-2653)
PHONE..................949 858-5900
Jerry Paolone, *Brnch Mgr*
**EMP:** 38
**SALES (corp-wide):** 89.19MM **Privately Held**
Web: www.magnaflow.com
**SIC: 3714** Exhaust systems and parts, motor vehicle
PA: Car Sound Exhaust System, Inc.
1901 Corporate Centre
949 858-5900

**(P-13473)**
**CARLSTAR GROUP LLC**
10730 Production Ave, Fontana (92337-8008)
PHONE..................909 829-1703
**EMP:** 118
**SALES (corp-wide):** 1.82B **Publicly Held**
Web: www.carlstargroup.com
**SIC: 3714** Motor vehicle parts and accessories
HQ: The Carlstar Group Llc
725 Cool Sprng Blvd Ste 5
Franklin TN 37067

**(P-13474)**
**CENTER LINE WHEEL CORPORATION**
Also Called: Center Line Performance Wheels
23 Corporate Plaza Dr Ste 150, Newport Beach (92660-7908)
PHONE..................562 921-9637
Ray Lipper, *Pr*
▲ **EMP:** 16 **EST:** 1963
**SALES (est):** 3.27MM **Privately Held**
Web: www.centerlinewheels.com
**SIC: 3714** Wheels, motor vehicle

**(P-13475)**
**CEPTON INC (PA)**
399 W Trimble Rd, San Jose (95131-1028)
PHONE..................408 459-7579
Jun Pei, *Ch Bd*
Dong Chang, *Interim Chief Financial Officer*

## PRODUCTS & SERVICES SECTION
### 3714 - Motor Vehicle Parts And Accessories (P-13496)

Liqun Han, *COO*
Mitchell Hourtienne, *CCO*
**EMP:** 18 **EST:** 2016
**SQ FT:** 25,000
**SALES (est):** 13.06MM
**SALES (corp-wide):** 13.06MM **Publicly Held**
**Web:** www.gcacorp.com
**SIC:** 3714 Motor vehicle parts and accessories

#### (P-13476)
**CEPTON TECHNOLOGIES INC**
399 W Trimble Rd, San Jose (95131-1028)
**PHONE**.............................408 493-6246
Jun Pei, *Pr*
Winston Fu, *
**EMP:** 139 **EST:** 2016
**SQ FT:** 25,000
**SALES (est):** 2.01MM
**SALES (corp-wide):** 13.06MM **Publicly Held**
**Web:** www.cepton.com
**SIC:** 3714 Motor vehicle parts and accessories
**PA:** Cepton, Inc.
399 W Trimble Rd
408 459-7579

#### (P-13477)
**COAST AUTONOMOUS INC (PA)**
23 E Colorado Blvd Ste 203, Pasadena (91105-3747)
**PHONE**.............................626 838-2469
David M Hickey, *CEO*
Adrian Sussman, *
**EMP:** 23 **EST:** 2017
**SALES (est):** 8.19MM
**SALES (corp-wide):** 8.19MM **Privately Held**
**Web:** www.coastautonomous.com
**SIC:** 3714 Motor vehicle electrical equipment

#### (P-13478)
**CRAIG MANUFACTURING COMPANY (PA)**
8129 Slauson Ave, Montebello (90640-6621)
**PHONE**.............................323 726-7355
Craig Taslitt, *Pr*
Julie Taslitt Gross, *
**EMP:** 60 **EST:** 1976
**SQ FT:** 16,000
**SALES (est):** 4.73MM
**SALES (corp-wide):** 4.73MM **Privately Held**
**Web:** www.craigattachments.com
**SIC:** 3714 Radiators and radiator shells and cores, motor vehicle

#### (P-13479)
**CROWER ENGRG & SLS CO INC**
Also Called: Crower Cams
6180 Business Center Ct, San Diego (92154-5604)
**PHONE**.............................619 661-6477
Barbara Crower, *Pr*
Loren Harris, *
Peter Harris, *
Donald Cave, *
Brett Cave, *
▲ **EMP:** 88 **EST:** 1955
**SQ FT:** 40,000
**SALES (est):** 7.13MM **Privately Held**
**Web:** www.crower.com
**SIC:** 3714 Camshafts, motor vehicle

#### (P-13480)
**CUMMINS PACIFIC LLC**
Also Called: Cummins
5150 Boyd Rd, Arcata (95521-4449)
**PHONE**.............................707 822-7392
**EMP:** 24
**SALES (corp-wide):** 34.06B **Publicly Held**
**Web:** www.cummins.com
**SIC:** 3714 Motor vehicle parts and accessories
**HQ:** Cummins Pacific, Llc
1939 Deere Ave
Irvine CA 92606

#### (P-13481)
**CURRIE ENTERPRISES**
382 N Smith Ave, Corona (92878-4371)
**PHONE**.............................714 528-6957
Raymond Currie, *Pr*
Raymond Currie, *Pr*
Charles Currie, *
John Currie, *
◆ **EMP:** 60 **EST:** 1960
**SQ FT:** 13,000
**SALES (est):** 11.01MM **Privately Held**
**Web:** www.currieenterprises.com
**SIC:** 3714 3599 Differentials and parts, motor vehicle; Machine shop, jobbing and repair

#### (P-13482)
**DANCHUK MANUFACTURING INC**
3211 Halladay St, Santa Ana (92705-5628)
**PHONE**.............................714 540-4363
Arthur Danchuk, *Pr*
Daniel Danchuk, *
▲ **EMP:** 71 **EST:** 1967
**SALES (est):** 2.91MM **Privately Held**
**Web:** www.danchuk.com
**SIC:** 3714 3465 Motor vehicle parts and accessories; Automotive stampings

#### (P-13483)
**DEE ENGINEERING INC**
6918 Ed Perkic St, Riverside (92504-1001)
**PHONE**.............................909 947-5616
Gary Fulton, *VP*
**EMP:** 25
**SALES (corp-wide):** 4.52MM **Privately Held**
**Web:** www.prothane.com
**SIC:** 3714 Mufflers (exhaust), motor vehicle
**PA:** Dee Engineering, Inc.
1284 E 10 S
714 979-4990

#### (P-13484)
**DEL WEST ENGINEERING INC (PA)**
Also Called: Del West USA
28128 Livingston Ave, Valencia (91355-4115)
**PHONE**.............................661 295-5700
Al Sommer, *Ch*
Mark Sommer, *
Rosemarie Chegwin, *
Guido Keijzers, *
**EMP:** 120 **EST:** 1973
**SQ FT:** 50,000
**SALES (est):** 20.98MM
**SALES (corp-wide):** 20.98MM **Privately Held**
**Web:** www.delwestengineering.com
**SIC:** 3714 Motor vehicle parts and accessories

#### (P-13485)
**DENSO PDTS & SVCS AMERICAS INC**
41673 Corning Pl, Murrieta (92562-7023)
**PHONE**.............................951 698-3379
Yoshihiko Yamada, *Pr*
**EMP:** 150
**Web:** www.densorobotics.com
**SIC:** 3714 Motor vehicle parts and accessories
**HQ:** Denso Products And Services Americas, Inc.
3900 Via Oro Ave
Long Beach CA 90810
310 834-6352

#### (P-13486)
**DINAN ENGINEERING INC**
865 Jarvis Dr, Morgan Hill (95037-2858)
**PHONE**.............................408 779-8584
▲ **EMP:** 48
**Web:** www.dinancars.com
**SIC:** 3714 7538 Motor vehicle parts and accessories; General automotive repair shops

#### (P-13487)
**DONALDSON COMPANY INC**
26235 Technology Dr, Valencia (91355-1147)
**PHONE**.............................661 295-0800
Paul Akian, *Pr*
**EMP:** 35
**SALES (corp-wide):** 3.59B **Publicly Held**
**Web:** www.donaldson.com
**SIC:** 3714 Mufflers (exhaust), motor vehicle
**PA:** Donaldson Company, Inc.
1400 W 94th St
952 887-3131

#### (P-13488)
**DOUGLAS TECHNOLOGIES GROUP INC**
Also Called: Douglas Wheel
42092 Winchester Rd Ste B, Temecula (92590-4805)
**PHONE**.............................760 758-5560
Johnny Leach, *Pr*
◆ **EMP:** 40 **EST:** 1982
**SQ FT:** 60,000
**SALES (est):** 4.29MM **Privately Held**
**Web:** www.dwtracing.com
**SIC:** 3714 Wheel rims, motor vehicle

#### (P-13489)
**DRIVESHAFTPRO**
7532 Anthony Ave, Garden Grove (92841-4006)
**PHONE**.............................714 893-4585
Ronald Hart, *Pr*
**EMP:** 32 **EST:** 2016
**SALES (est):** 838.82K **Privately Held**
**Web:** www.driveshaftpro.com
**SIC:** 3714 Motor vehicle parts and accessories

#### (P-13490)
**DYNATRAC PRODUCTS LLC**
7392 Count Cir, Huntington Beach (92647-4551)
**PHONE**.............................714 596-4461
Jim Mcgean, *Pr*
**EMP:** 27 **EST:** 2021
**SALES (est):** 2.55MM **Privately Held**
**Web:** www.dynatrac.com
**SIC:** 3714 5013 5531 Motor vehicle transmissions, drive assemblies, and parts; Motor vehicle supplies and new parts; Truck equipment and parts

#### (P-13491)
**DYNATRAC PRODUCTS CO INC**
7392 Count Cir, Huntington Beach (92647-4551)
**PHONE**.............................714 596-4461

Jim Mcgean, *Pr*
**EMP:** 15 **EST:** 1988
**SQ FT:** 1,600
**SALES (est):** 3.85MM **Privately Held**
**Web:** www.dynatrac.com
**SIC:** 3714 5013 5531 Motor vehicle transmissions, drive assemblies, and parts; Motor vehicle supplies and new parts; Truck equipment and parts

#### (P-13492)
**EDELBROCK LLC**
501 Amapola Ave, Torrance (90501-1466)
**PHONE**.............................310 781-2290
**EMP:** 20
**Web:** www.edelbrock.com
**SIC:** 3714 Motor vehicle parts and accessories
**HQ:** Edelbrock, Llc
8649 Hacks Cross Rd
Olive Branch MS 38654
310 781-2222

#### (P-13493)
**EGR INCORPORATED (DH)**
4000 Greystone Dr, Ontario (91761-3101)
**PHONE**.............................800 757-7075
Rod Horwill, *CEO*
Simon Mclellan, *CFO*
John Whitten, *
▲ **EMP:** 26 **EST:** 1993
**SQ FT:** 70,000
**SALES (est):** 24.8MM **Privately Held**
**Web:** www.egrusa.com
**SIC:** 3714 Motor vehicle parts and accessories
**HQ:** Oakmoore Pty. Ltd.
84 Evans Rd
Salisbury QLD 4107

#### (P-13494)
**ENDERLE FUEL INJECTION**
1830 Voyager Ave, Simi Valley (93063-3348)
**PHONE**.............................805 526-3838
Kent H Enderle, *Pr*
Joan C Enderle, *Sec*
Jim Rehfeld, *VP*
**EMP:** 20 **EST:** 1966
**SQ FT:** 18,000
**SALES (est):** 2.36MM **Privately Held**
**Web:** www.goodvibesracing.com
**SIC:** 3714 Fuel systems and parts, motor vehicle

#### (P-13495)
**ENGINE WORLD LLC**
1487 67th St, Emeryville (94608-1015)
**PHONE**.............................510 653-4444
Said Saffari, *
◆ **EMP:** 25 **EST:** 2003
**SQ FT:** 60,000
**SALES (est):** 3.79MM **Privately Held**
**Web:** www.engineworld.com
**SIC:** 3714 Rebuilding engines and transmissions, factory basis

#### (P-13496)
**ESSLINGER ENGINEERING INC**
5946 Freedom Dr, Chino (91710-7014)
**PHONE**.............................909 539-0544
Dwaine E Esslinger, *Pr*
Elizabeth Esslinger, *Sec*
Dan Esslinger, *VP*
▲ **EMP:** 20 **EST:** 1969
**SQ FT:** 4,000
**SALES (est):** 2.37MM **Privately Held**
**Web:** www.esslingeracing.com
**SIC:** 3714 Motor vehicle engines and parts

## 3714 - Motor Vehicle Parts And Accessories (P-13497)

**(P-13497)**
**EVANS WALKER INC**
Also Called: Evans, Walker Racing
2304 Fleetwood Dr, Riverside (92509)
P.O. Box 2469 (92516)
PHONE..................................951 784-7223
Walker Evans, *Pr*
Randall Anderson, *VP*
Phyllis Evans, *Sec*
▲ **EMP:** 20 **EST:** 1978
**SQ FT:** 20,000
**SALES (est):** 9.47MM **Privately Held**
Web: www.walkerevansracing.com
**SIC: 3714** Motor vehicle parts and accessories

**(P-13498)**
**FABCO HOLDINGS INC**
151 Lawrence Dr, Livermore (94551-5126)
PHONE..................................925 454-9500
Gerard Giucidi, *CEO*
Allen Sunderland, *
David Doden, *
Michael Chapman, *
▲ **EMP:** 2635 **EST:** 2011
**SALES (est):** 96.63MM **Privately Held**
**SIC: 3714** Axles, motor vehicle

**(P-13499)**
**FASTER FASTER INC**
Also Called: Alta Motors
185 Valley Dr, Brisbane (94005-1340)
PHONE..................................323 839-0654
Marc Daniel Fenigstein, *CEO*
Derek Dorresteyn, *
Jeff Sand, *CDO*
Victor Pritzker, *
Grant Ray, *
▲ **EMP:** 42 **EST:** 2010
**SQ FT:** 24,000
**SALES (est):** 6.45MM **Privately Held**
Web: www.altamotors.co
**SIC: 3714** Power transmission equipment, motor vehicle

**(P-13500)**
**FLOWMASTER INC**
100 Stony Point Rd Ste 125, Santa Rosa (95401-4131)
PHONE..................................707 544-4761
**EMP:** 95
**SALES (corp-wide):** 12.76MM **Privately Held**
Web: www.holley.com
**SIC: 3714** Motor vehicle parts and accessories
HQ: Flowmaster, Inc.
1801 Russellville Rd
Bowling Green KY 42101
707 544-4761

**(P-13501)**
**FOOTE AXLE & FORGE LLC**
250 W Duarte Rd Ste A, Monrovia (91016-7460)
PHONE..................................323 268-4151
Michael F Denton Senior, *Managing Member*
Merrie N Denton, *
▲ **EMP:** 32 **EST:** 1937
**SALES (est):** 924.09K **Privately Held**
Web: www.footeaxle.com
**SIC: 3714** Differentials and parts, motor vehicle

**(P-13502)**
**FORGIATO INC**
Also Called: Forgiato
11915 Wicks St, Sun Valley (91352)
PHONE..................................818 771-9779
Norman Celik, *CEO*
Nisan G Celik, *
▲ **EMP:** 62 **EST:** 2006
**SQ FT:** 60,000
**SALES (est):** 5.19MM **Privately Held**
Web: www.forgiato.com
**SIC: 3714** Motor vehicle wheels and parts

**(P-13503)**
**FOX FACTORY INC**
200 El Pueblo Rd, Scotts Valley (95066-4265)
PHONE..................................831 274-6545
**EMP:** 26 **EST:** 2011
**SALES (est):** 8.01MM
**SALES (corp-wide):** 1.46B **Publicly Held**
Web: www.ridefox.com
**SIC: 3714** Motor vehicle parts and accessories
PA: Fox Factory Holding Corp.
2055 Sgarloaf Cir Ste 300
831 274-6500

**(P-13504)**
**GARRISON MANUFACTURING INC**
3320 S Yale St, Santa Ana (92704-6447)
PHONE..................................714 549-4880
Venu Shan, *Pr*
Jake Ralli, *
**EMP:** 30 **EST:** 1939
**SQ FT:** 26,000
**SALES (est):** 2.73MM **Privately Held**
Web: www.garrisonmfg.com
**SIC: 3714** 7699 5084 3593 Steering mechanisms, motor vehicle; Industrial machinery and equipment repair; Hydraulic systems equipment and supplies; Fluid power cylinders and actuators

**(P-13505)**
**GEAR VENDORS INC**
Also Called: Gear Vendors
1717 N Magnolia Ave, El Cajon (92020-1243)
PHONE..................................619 562-0060
Ken R Johnson, *CEO*
Rick Johnson, *
▲ **EMP:** 35 **EST:** 1981
**SQ FT:** 35,000
**SALES (est):** 3.09MM **Privately Held**
Web: www.gearvendors.com
**SIC: 3714** Transmissions, motor vehicle

**(P-13506)**
**GERHARDT GEAR CO INC**
133 E Santa Anita Ave, Burbank (91502-1926)
PHONE..................................818 842-6700
Ronald J Gerhardt, *CEO*
Mitch Gerhardt, *
John Kim, *
Kurht Gerhardt, *
**EMP:** 46 **EST:** 1937
**SQ FT:** 30,000
**SALES (est):** 8.14MM **Privately Held**
Web: www.gerhardtgear.com
**SIC: 3714** 3728 3769 3462 Gears, motor vehicle; Gears, aircraft power transmission; Space vehicle equipment, nec; Iron and steel forgings

**(P-13507)**
**GIBSON PERFORMANCE CORPORATION**
Also Called: Gibson Exhaust Systems
1270 Webb Cir, Corona (92879-5760)
PHONE..................................951 372-1220
Ronald Gibson, *Pr*
Julie Gibson, *
▲ **EMP:** 75 **EST:** 1990
**SQ FT:** 50,000
**SALES (est):** 4.81MM **Privately Held**
Web: www.gibsonperformance.com
**SIC: 3714** 5013 Exhaust systems and parts, motor vehicle; Motor vehicle supplies and new parts

**(P-13508)**
**GRANATELLI MOTOR SPORTS INC**
1000 Yarnell Pl, Oxnard (93033-2454)
PHONE..................................805 486-6644
Joseph R Granatelli, *CEO*
▲ **EMP:** 31 **EST:** 1998
**SQ FT:** 49,000
**SALES (est):** 2.14MM **Privately Held**
Web: www.granatellimotorsports.com
**SIC: 3714** Fuel systems and parts, motor vehicle

**(P-13509)**
**GREDES CORPORATION**
15615 Alton Pkwy Ste 450, Irvine (92618-3308)
PHONE..................................714 262-9150
**EMP:** 20 **EST:** 2018
**SALES (est):** 638.23K **Privately Held**
**SIC: 3714** Motor vehicle parts and accessories

**(P-13510)**
**GROVER PRODUCTS CO**
3424 E Olympic Blvd, Los Angeles (90023-3000)
P.O. Box 23966 (90023-0966)
PHONE..................................323 263-9981
John A Roesch, *CEO*
▲ **EMP:** 100 **EST:** 1932
**SQ FT:** 60,000
**SALES (est):** 4.7MM **Privately Held**
Web: www.airhorns.com
**SIC: 3714** 3494 5999 Motor vehicle brake systems and parts; Valves and pipe fittings, nec; Plumbing and heating supplies

**(P-13511)**
**HEATSHIELD PRODUCTS INC**
1040 S Andreasen Dr Ste 110, Escondido (92029-1951)
P.O. Box 462500 (92046-2500)
PHONE..................................760 751-0441
Stephen Heye, *CEO*
Bruce Heye, *Pt*
Stephen J Heye, *Pt*
**EMP:** 20 **EST:** 1999
**SQ FT:** 500
**SALES (est):** 2.49MM **Privately Held**
Web: www.heatshieldproducts.com
**SIC: 3714** Motor vehicle parts and accessories

**(P-13512)**
**HEDMAN MANUFACTURING (PA)**
Also Called: Hedman Hedders
12438 Putnam St, Whittier (90602-1002)
PHONE..................................562 204-1031
Robert Bandergriff, *Pr*
Ron Funfar, *
▲ **EMP:** 45 **EST:** 1978
**SALES (est):** 6.06MM
**SALES (corp-wide):** 6.06MM **Privately Held**
Web: www.hedman.com
**SIC: 3714** Exhaust systems and parts, motor vehicle

**(P-13513)**
**HELLWIG PRODUCTS COMPANY INC**
16237 Avenue 296, Visalia (93292-9675)
PHONE..................................559 734-7451
Melanie White, *CEO*
Mark Hellwig, *
▲ **EMP:** 61 **EST:** 1946
**SQ FT:** 37,000
**SALES (est):** 11.07MM **Privately Held**
Web: www.hellwigproducts.com
**SIC: 3714** 3493 3499 Motor vehicle parts and accessories; Automobile springs; Stabilizing bars (cargo), metal

**(P-13514)**
**HITACHI ASTEMO AMERICAS INC**
1235 Graphite Dr, Corona (92881-7252)
PHONE..................................951 340-0702
Satoru Panno, *Brnch Mgr*
**EMP:** 279
Web: www.amshowa.com
**SIC: 3714** Motor vehicle parts and accessories
HQ: Hitachi Astemo Americas, Inc.
955 Warwick Rd
Harrodsburg KY 40330
859 734-9451

**(P-13515)**
**HT MULTINATIONAL INC**
Also Called: Unisun Multinational
501 W Foothill Blvd, Azusa (91702-2345)
PHONE..................................909 325-8582
Chunli Zhao, *CEO*
▲ **EMP:** 21 **EST:** 2011
**SALES (est):** 2.58MM **Privately Held**
**SIC: 3714** 3429 5072 Motor vehicle brake systems and parts; Hardware, nec; Hardware
HQ: Sinatex, S.A. De C.V.
Industriales No. 1188 Pte.
Cajeme SON 85210

**(P-13516)**
**ICARCOVER INC**
Also Called: Autopartsmarket
15529 Blackburn Ave, Norwalk (90650-6846)
PHONE..................................714 469-7759
Calvin Kim, *CEO*
**EMP:** 20 **EST:** 2019
**SALES (est):** 2.9MM **Privately Held**
Web: www.coverland.com
**SIC: 3714** Motor vehicle parts and accessories

**(P-13517)**
**IMPCO TECHNOLOGIES INC (HQ)**
Also Called: Impco
3030 S Susan St, Santa Ana (92704-6435)
PHONE..................................714 656-1200
Massimo Fracchia, *Genl Mgr*
Peter Chase, *
◆ **EMP:** 160 **EST:** 1958
**SQ FT:** 108,000
**SALES (est):** 29.5MM
**SALES (corp-wide):** 331.8MM **Privately Held**
Web: www.impcotechnologies.com
**SIC: 3714** 3592 7363 Fuel systems and parts, motor vehicle; Carburetors; Engineering help service
PA: Westport Fuel Systems Inc
1691 75th Ave W
604 718-2000

## PRODUCTS & SERVICES SECTION
### 3714 - Motor Vehicle Parts And Accessories (P-13538)

**(P-13518)**
**INLAND EMPIRE DRV LINE SVC INC (PA)**
4035 E Guasti Rd Ste 301, Ontario (91761-1532)
PHONE.................909 390-3030
Gregory Frick, *Pr*
Jeff Gilroy, *VP*
Carolyn Frick, *Sec*
**EMP:** 16 **EST:** 1981
**SQ FT:** 7,500
**SALES (est):** 2.35MM
**SALES (corp-wide):** 2.35MM **Privately Held**
Web: www.iedls.com
**SIC: 3714** 7539 Drive shafts, motor vehicle; Automotive repair shops, nec

**(P-13519)**
**INNOVA ELECTRONICS CORPORATION**
Also Called: Equipment & Tool Institute
17352 Von Karman Ave, Irvine (92614-6204)
PHONE.................714 241-6800
Ieon C Chenn, *Pr*
**EMP:** 29 **EST:** 1990
**SQ FT:** 12,000
**SALES (est):** 9.16MM **Privately Held**
Web: www.innova.com
**SIC: 3714** Motor vehicle electrical equipment

**(P-13520)**
**INOVIT INC**
5120 Commerce Dr, Baldwin Park (91706-1450)
PHONE.................626 444-4775
Lauren Bronson, *CEO*
Yingshen Mao, *CEO*
▲ **EMP:** 16 **EST:** 2008
**SALES (est):** 2.59MM **Privately Held**
Web: www.inovit.com
**SIC: 3714** Wheels, motor vehicle

**(P-13521)**
**IVU TRAFFIC TECHNOLOGIES INC**
2612 8th St Ste A, Berkeley (94710-2575)
PHONE.................415 655-2200
**EMP:** 15 **EST:** 2016
**SALES (est):** 187.93K **Privately Held**
Web: www.ivu.de
**SIC: 3714** Motor vehicle parts and accessories

**(P-13522)**
**JOHN BOYD ENTERPRISES INC (PA)**
Also Called: J B Enterprises
8401 Specialty Cir, Sacramento (95828-2523)
P.O. Box 292460 (95829-2460)
PHONE.................916 381-4790
Darin M Boyd, *CEO*
▲ **EMP:** 234 **EST:** 1974
**SQ FT:** 14,000
**SALES (est):** 22.83MM
**SALES (corp-wide):** 22.83MM **Privately Held**
Web: www.jbrspecialties.com
**SIC: 3714** 3433 Radiators and radiator shells and cores, motor vehicle; Heating equipment, except electric

**(P-13523)**
**K & G LATIROVIAN INC**
Also Called: Kahgo Truck Parts
11182 Penrose St, Sun Valley (91352-2724)
PHONE.................818 319-2862
Kabrail Latirovian, *CEO*
**EMP:** 54
Web: www.kahgotruckparts.com
**SIC: 3714** Motor vehicle parts and accessories
**PA:** K & G Latirovian, Inc.
8277 Lankershim Blvd

**(P-13524)**
**KF FIBERGLASS INC (PA)**
8247 Phlox St, Downey (90241-4841)
PHONE.................562 869-1536
Ron Belk, *Pr*
David Ruiz, *VP*
**EMP:** 16 **EST:** 1965
**SQ FT:** 35,000
**SALES (est):** 1.47MM
**SALES (corp-wide):** 1.47MM **Privately Held**
Web: www.kffiberglass.com
**SIC: 3714** Motor vehicle parts and accessories

**(P-13525)**
**KING SHOCK TECHNOLOGY INC**
12472 Edison Way, Garden Grove (92841-2821)
PHONE.................719 394-3754
Brett King, *CEO*
Brett King, *Pr*
Ross King, *
Lance King, *
Sharon King, *
✧ **EMP:** 99 **EST:** 2001
**SQ FT:** 18,000
**SALES (est):** 17.87MM **Privately Held**
Web: www.kingshocks.com
**SIC: 3714** Motor vehicle body components and frame

**(P-13526)**
**KROEGER EQP SUP CO A CAL CORP**
Also Called: Kroeger Equipment
2645 South Chestnut At Jensen, Fresno (93725-2113)
P.O. Box 2427 (93745-2427)
PHONE.................559 485-9900
Casey O Tharp, *CEO*
**EMP:** 27 **EST:** 1981
**SQ FT:** 53,000
**SALES (est):** 4.6MM **Privately Held**
Web: www.emtharp.com
**SIC: 3714** 5531 5013 Motor vehicle parts and accessories; Automotive parts; Truck parts and accessories
**PA:** E. M. Tharp, Inc.
15243 Rd 192

**(P-13527)**
**KW AUTOMOTIVE NORTH AMER INC**
300 W Pontiac Way, Clovis (93612-5606)
PHONE.................800 445-3767
Klaus M Wohlfarth, *Pr*
Darrell Edwards, *
▲ **EMP:** 40 **EST:** 2005
**SQ FT:** 115,000
**SALES (est):** 15.8MM
**SALES (corp-wide):** 121.77MM **Privately Held**
Web: www.kwsuspensions.com
**SIC: 3714** Motor vehicle parts and accessories
**PA:** Kw Automotive Gmbh
Aspachweg 14
797196300

**(P-13528)**
**LAPCO WEST LLC**
Also Called: Lapco West
13140 Midway Pl, Cerritos (90703-2233)
PHONE.................562 348-4850
Graem Elliot, *CEO*
**EMP:** 20 **EST:** 2004
**SALES (est):** 1.06MM **Privately Held**
Web: www.lapcowest.com
**SIC: 3714** Motor vehicle brake systems and parts

**(P-13529)**
**LEET TECHNOLOGY INC**
1427 S Robertson Blvd, Los Angeles (90035-3401)
PHONE.................877 238-4492
Ding Jung Long, *CEO*
Kamal Hamidon, *Principal Accounting Officer*
**EMP:** 17 **EST:** 2013
**SALES (est):** 151.98K **Privately Held**
**SIC: 3714** Motor vehicle parts and accessories

**(P-13530)**
**LLOYD DESIGN CORPORATION**
Also Called: Lloyd Mats
19731 Nordhoff St, Northridge (91324-3330)
PHONE.................818 768-6001
Lloyd S Levine, *CEO*
Brendan Dooley, *
▲ **EMP:** 55 **EST:** 1974
**SALES (est):** 4.9MM **Privately Held**
Web: www.lloydmats.com
**SIC: 3714** Motor vehicle parts and accessories

**(P-13531)**
**LOS ANGELES SLEEVE CO INC**
Also Called: L.A. Sleeve
12051 Rivera Rd, Santa Fe Springs (90670-2211)
PHONE.................562 945-7578
Nick G Metchkoff, *Pr*
David Metchkoff, *
James G Metchkoff, *
Sarah Metchkoff, *
▲ **EMP:** 29 **EST:** 1975
**SQ FT:** 33,000
**SALES (est):** 4.5MM **Privately Held**
Web: www.lasleeve.com
**SIC: 3714** Exhaust systems and parts, motor vehicle

**(P-13532)**
**LUND MOTION PRODUCTS INC**
Also Called: AMP Research
3172 Nasa St, Brea (92821-6234)
PHONE.................888 983-2204
Mitch Fogle, *Pr*
**EMP:** 35
**SALES (corp-wide):** 829.18MM **Privately Held**
Web: www.realtruck.com
**SIC: 3714** Motor vehicle parts and accessories
**HQ:** Lund Motion Products, Inc.
4325 Hamilton Mill Rd # 4
Buford GA 30518
678 804-3767

**(P-13533)**
**M E D INC**
14001 Marquardt Ave, Santa Fe Springs (90670-5088)
PHONE.................562 921-0464
Steven Moore, *CEO*
Susan Lowe, *CFO*
**EMP:** 70 **EST:** 1974
**SQ FT:** 40,000
**SALES (est):** 9.37MM **Privately Held**
Web: www.dme-mfg.com
**SIC: 3714** 3429 Exhaust systems and parts, motor vehicle; Clamps, couplings, nozzles, and other metal hose fittings

**(P-13534)**
**M P N INC**
Also Called: Active Radiator Supply
14600 Marquardt Ave, Santa Fe Springs (90670-5123)
PHONE.................562 921-0748
**EMP:** 15
Web: www.activeradiator.com
**SIC: 3714** Motor vehicle parts and accessories
**PA:** M. P. N., Inc.
3675 Amber St

**(P-13535)**
**MAGNUSON PRODUCTS LLC**
Also Called: Magnuson Superchargers
1990 Knoll Dr Ste A, Ventura (93003-7309)
PHONE.................805 642-8833
Kim Pendergast, *CEO*
Tim Krauskopf, *
**EMP:** 49 **EST:** 1970
**SQ FT:** 45,600
**SALES (est):** 12.41MM **Privately Held**
Web: www.magnusonsuperchargers.com
**SIC: 3714** Motor vehicle parts and accessories

**(P-13536)**
**MAXON INDUSTRIES INC**
11921 Slauson Ave, Santa Fe Springs (90670-2221)
P.O. Box 3434 (90051)
PHONE.................562 464-0099
Murray Lugash, *Pr*
Larry Lugash, *
Brenda Leung, *
**EMP:** 75 **EST:** 1957
**SQ FT:** 250,000
**SALES (est):** 10.67MM **Privately Held**
Web: www.maxonlift.com
**SIC: 3714** Motor vehicle parts and accessories

**(P-13537)**
**MCLEOD RACING LLC**
Also Called: McLeod Racing
1570 Lakeview Loop, Anaheim (92807-1819)
PHONE.................714 630-2764
Paul Lee, *Pr*
Lana Chrisman, *VP*
**EMP:** 22 **EST:** 2009
**SQ FT:** 17,500
**SALES (est):** 3.73MM **Privately Held**
Web: www.mcleodracing.com
**SIC: 3714** Clutches, motor vehicle

**(P-13538)**
**MGM BRAKES**
1184 S Cloverdale Blvd, Cloverdale (95425-4412)
P.O. Box 249 (95425-0249)
PHONE.................707 894-3333
Ron Parker, *Owner*
✧ **EMP:** 65 **EST:** 2015
**SALES (est):** 5.31MM **Privately Held**
Web: www.mgmbrakes.com
**SIC: 3714** 3625 Air brakes, motor vehicle; Brakes, electromagnetic

## 3714 - Motor Vehicle Parts And Accessories (P-13539)

**(P-13539)**
**MID-WEST FABRICATING CO**
Also Called: West Bent Bolt Division
8623 Dice Rd, Santa Fe Springs (90670-2511)
PHONE.................562 698-9615
Steve Petersen, Mgr
EMP: 46
SQ FT: 40,000
SALES (corp-wide): 28.07MM Privately Held
Web: www.midwestfab.com
SIC: 3714 3452 3316 3312 Tie rods, motor vehicle; Bolts, nuts, rivets, and washers; Cold finishing of steel shapes; Wire products, steel or iron
PA: Mid-West Fabricating Co.
   313 N Johns St
   740 969-4411

**(P-13540)**
**MILODON INCORPORATED**
2250 Agate Ct, Simi Valley (93065-1842)
PHONE.................805 577-5950
Steve Morrison, Pr
▲ EMP: 40 EST: 1957
SQ FT: 32,000
SALES (est): 4.99MM Privately Held
Web: www.milodon.com
SIC: 3714 Motor vehicle engines and parts

**(P-13541)**
**MOBIS PARTS AMERICA LLC**
Also Called: Mobis
10550 Talbert Ave # 4, Fountain Valley (92708-6031)
PHONE.................949 450-0014
EMP: 29
Web: www.mobisusa.com
SIC: 3714 Motor vehicle body components and frame
HQ: Mobis Parts America, Llc
   10550 Talbert Ave Fl 4
   Fountain Valley CA 92708
   786 515-1101

**(P-13542)**
**MOGUL**
10106 Sunbrook Dr, Beverly Hills (90210-2032)
PHONE.................424 245-4331
Deborah Harpur, Prin
EMP: 40 EST: 2011
SALES (est): 175.39K Privately Held
Web: www.mogul-inc.com
SIC: 3714 Motor vehicle parts and accessories

**(P-13543)**
**MOTORCAR PARTS OF AMERICA INC (PA)**
Also Called: MPA
2929 California St, Torrance (90503-3914)
PHONE.................310 212-7910
Selwyn Joffe, Ch Bd
David Lee, CFO
Kamlesh Shah, CAO
Douglas Schooner, CMO
Richard Mochulsky, S&M/VP
◆ EMP: 768 EST: 1968
SQ FT: 231,000
SALES (est): 717.68MM
SALES (corp-wide): 717.68MM Publicly Held
Web: www.motorcarparts.com
SIC: 3714 3694 3625 Motor vehicle parts and accessories; Alternators, automotive; Starter, electric motor

**(P-13544)**
**MYGRANT GLASS COMPANY INC**
10220 Camino Santa Fe, San Diego (92121-3105)
PHONE.................858 455-8022
Tom Andia, Pr
EMP: 25
SQ FT: 32,185
SALES (corp-wide): 168.98MM Privately Held
Web: www.mygrantglass.com
SIC: 3714 5013 Motor vehicle parts and accessories; Motor vehicle supplies and new parts
PA: Mygrant Glass Company, Inc.
   3271 Arden Rd
   510 785-4360

**(P-13545)**
**NEW CENTURY INDUSTRIES INC**
7231 Rosecrans Ave, Paramount (90723-2501)
P.O. Box 1845 (90723-1845)
PHONE.................562 634-9551
Michael Mason, CEO
EMP: 50 EST: 1991
SQ FT: 32,000
SALES (est): 9.57MM Privately Held
SIC: 3714 3465 3469 Wheels, motor vehicle; Automotive stampings; Stamping metal for the trade

**(P-13546)**
**NEW UNITED MOTOR MANUFACTURING INC**
Also Called: Nummi
45500 Fremont Blvd, Fremont (94538-6326)
P.O. Box 14440 (94539-1140)
PHONE.................510 498-5500
◆ EMP: 5000
SIC: 3714 3711 Motor vehicle parts and accessories; Automobile assembly, including specialty automobiles

**(P-13547)**
**NMSP INC (DH)**
Also Called: A E M
2205 W 126th St Ste A, Hawthorne (90250-3367)
PHONE.................310 484-2322
Gregory Neuwirth, Pr
Peter Neuwirth, *
◆ EMP: 53 EST: 1997
SQ FT: 78,000
SALES (est): 25.47MM
SALES (corp-wide): 659.7MM Publicly Held
SIC: 3714 Motor vehicle engines and parts
HQ: Holley Performance Products Inc.
   1801 Russellville Rd
   Bowling Green KY 42101
   270 782-2900

**(P-13548)**
**NMSP INC**
1451 E 6th St, Corona (92879-1715)
PHONE.................951 734-2453
Darrell Contreras, Mgr
EMP: 46
SALES (corp-wide): 659.7MM Publicly Held
SIC: 3714 Motor vehicle engines and parts
HQ: Nmsp, Inc.
   2205 126th St Unit A
   Hawthorne CA 90250
   310 484-2322

**(P-13549)**
**NOLOGY ENGINEERING INC**
1333 Keystone Way, Vista (92081-8311)
PHONE.................760 591-0888
Werner Funk, Pr
Jan Quigley, CFO
EMP: 16 EST: 1993
SQ FT: 11,000
SALES (est): 807.27K Privately Held
Web: www.nology.com
SIC: 3714 Motor vehicle parts and accessories

**(P-13550)**
**NORTHROP GRMMN SPCE & MSSN SYS**
2501 Santa Fe Ave, Redondo Beach (90278-1117)
PHONE.................310 812-4321
EMP: 334
SIC: 3714 7373 3663 3661 Motor vehicle parts and accessories; Computer integrated systems design; Radio and t.v. communications equipment; Telephone and telegraph apparatus
HQ: Northrop Grumman Space & Mission Systems Corp.
   6379 San Ignacio Ave
   San Jose CA 95119
   703 280-2900

**(P-13551)**
**NRG MOTORSPORTS INC**
Also Called: Boyd Coddington Wheels
861 E Lambert Rd, La Habra (90631-6143)
PHONE.................714 541-1173
Boyd Coddington, Pr
▲ EMP: 55 EST: 1998
SALES (est): 872.19K Privately Held
Web: www.nrgmotorsports.net
SIC: 3714 Wheels, motor vehicle

**(P-13552)**
**PANA-PACIFIC CORPORATION (HQ)**
838 N Laverne Ave, Fresno (93727-6868)
PHONE.................559 457-4700
Joseph Saoud, CEO
Jason Welsh, Prin
Harrison Brix, *
EMP: 20 EST: 2004
SALES (est): 24.79MM
SALES (corp-wide): 40.19MM Privately Held
Web: www.panapacific.com
SIC: 3714 Motor vehicle parts and accessories
PA: The Brix Group Inc
   838 N Laverne Ave
   559 457-4700

**(P-13553)**
**PANA-PACIFIC CORPORATION**
541 Division St, Campbell (95008-6905)
PHONE.................559 499-1891
EMP: 130
SALES (corp-wide): 40.19MM Privately Held
Web: www.panapacific.com
SIC: 3714 Motor vehicle parts and accessories
HQ: Pana-Pacific Corporation
   838 N Laverne Ave
   Fresno CA 93727
   559 457-4700

**(P-13554)**
**PANKL ENGINE SYSTEMS INC**
Also Called: Sp Crankshaft
1902 Mcgaw Ave, Irvine (92614-0910)
PHONE.................949 428-8788
▲ EMP: 31
Web: www.pankl.com
SIC: 3714 Crankshaft assemblies, motor vehicle

**(P-13555)**
**PEBBLE MOBILITY INC**
2800 Bayview Dr, Fremont (94538-6518)
PHONE.................650 209-0799
Bingrui Yang, CEO
Chi Miller, CFO
EMP: 50 EST: 2022
SALES (est): 6.25MM Privately Held
SIC: 3714 Motor vehicle electrical equipment

**(P-13556)**
**PHOENIX MOTOR INC (DH)**
Also Called: Phoenix Motorcars
1500 Lakeview Loop, Anaheim (92807-1819)
PHONE.................909 987-0815
Xiaofeng Denton Peng, Ch Bd
Wenbing Chris Wang, CFO
Tarek Helou, COO
Michael Yung, CFO
EMP: 29 EST: 2020
SALES (est): 3.12MM Publicly Held
Web: www.spigroups.com
SIC: 3714 Motor vehicle electrical equipment
HQ: Edisonfuture Inc.
   4677 Old Ironsides Dr # 1
   Santa Clara CA 95054
   408 919-8000

**(P-13557)**
**POWER-RIGHT INDUSTRIES LLC**
4722 W Mission Blvd, Ontario (91762-4413)
PHONE.................909 628-4397
EMP: 18 EST: 2003
SALES (est): 1.29MM
SALES (corp-wide): 1.96MM Privately Held
SIC: 3714 Oil pump, motor vehicle
PA: Lloyd's Equipment, Inc.
   4722 W Mission Blvd
   909 628-5586

**(P-13558)**
**PRIME WHEEL CORPORATION**
23920 Vermont Ave, Harbor City (90710-1602)
PHONE.................310 326-5080
Eddie Chen, Mgr
EMP: 453
SQ FT: 200,000
SALES (corp-wide): 315.67MM Privately Held
Web: www.primewheel.com
SIC: 3714 3471 5013 Motor vehicle wheels and parts; Plating and polishing; Automotive supplies and parts
PA: Prime Wheel Corporation
   17705 S Main St
   310 516-9126

**(P-13559)**
**PRIME WHEEL CORPORATION**
Also Called: Prime Wheel of Figueroa
17680 S Figueroa St, Gardena (90248-3419)
PHONE.................310 819-4123
Peter Liang, Brnch Mgr
EMP: 25
SALES (corp-wide): 315.67MM Privately Held
Web: www.primewheel.com

**PRODUCTS & SERVICES SECTION**

**3714 - Motor Vehicle Parts And Accessories (P-13581)**

SIC: 3714 Wheels, motor vehicle
PA: Prime Wheel Corporation
17705 S Main St
310 516-9126

**(P-13560)**
**PRIME WHEEL CORPORATION (PA)**
17705 S Main St, Gardena (90248-3516)
PHONE..................310 516-9126
Philip Chen, CEO
Henry Chen, *
Mitchell M Tung, *
Albert Huang, *
Webb Carter, Vice Chairman*
◆ EMP: 600 EST: 1989
SQ FT: 320,000
SALES (est): 315.67MM
SALES (corp-wide): 315.67MM Privately Held
Web: www.primewheel.com
SIC: 3714 Wheels, motor vehicle

**(P-13561)**
**QF LIQUIDATION INC (PA)**
Also Called: Quantum Technologies
25242 Arctic Ocean Dr, Lake Forest (92630-8821)
PHONE..................949 930-3400
W Brian Olson, Pr
Bradley J Timon, CFO
Kenneth R Lombardo, Corporate Secretary
Mark Arold, VP Opers
David M Mazaika, Development
◆ EMP: 140 EST: 2000
SQ FT: 156,000
SALES (est): 24.78MM Privately Held
Web: www.qtww.com
SIC: 3714 3764 8711 Motor vehicle parts and accessories; Space propulsion units and parts; Engineering services

**(P-13562)**
**R A PHILLIPS INDUSTRIES INC (PA)**
Also Called: Phillips Industries
12012 Burke St, Santa Fe Springs (90670)
PHONE..................562 781-2121
◆ EMP: 35 EST: 1969
SALES (est): 71.29MM
SALES (corp-wide): 71.29MM Privately Held
Web: www.phillipsind.com
SIC: 3714 5531 Motor vehicle body components and frame; Truck equipment and parts

**(P-13563)**
**R3 PERFORMANCE PRODUCTS INC**
531 Old Woman Springs Rd, Yucca Valley (92284-1613)
PHONE..................760 909-0846
Roger Ketelslger, CEO
Robert Istwan, CFO
EMP: 15 EST: 2017
SALES (est): 1MM Privately Held
Web: www.r3pp.com
SIC: 3714 Shock absorbers, motor vehicle

**(P-13564)**
**RACEPAK LLC**
30402 Esperanza, Rcho Sta Marg (92688-2144)
PHONE..................949 709-5555
Tom Tomlinson, Pr
EMP: 28 EST: 2014
SALES (est): 2.84MM
SALES (corp-wide): 659.7MM Publicly Held

Web: www.holley.com
SIC: 3714 Motor vehicle parts and accessories
HQ: Holley Performance Products Inc.
1801 Russellville Rd
Bowling Green KY 42101
270 782-2900

**(P-13565)**
**RACING POWER COMPANY**
815 Tucker Ln, Walnut (91789-2914)
PHONE..................909 468-3690
Te Ming Chung, CEO
▲ EMP: 20 EST: 1955
SQ FT: 2,000
SALES (est): 4.37MM Privately Held
Web: www.usrpc.com
SIC: 3714 Motor vehicle parts and accessories

**(P-13566)**
**RICARDO DEFENSE INC (DH)**
3757 State St, Santa Barbara (93105-3133)
PHONE..................805 882-1884
Chester Gryzcan, Pr
Brian Smith, *
EMP: 22 EST: 1995
SALES (est): 39.18MM
SALES (corp-wide): 603.67MM Privately Held
Web: www.ricardo.com
SIC: 3714 8711 Motor vehicle brake systems and parts; Consulting engineer
HQ: Ricardo Defense Systems, Llc
300 E Big Beaver Rd # 180
Troy MI 48083

**(P-13567)**
**ROLL ALONG VANS INC**
1350 E Yorba Linda Blvd, Placentia (92870-3833)
PHONE..................714 528-9600
Dan Williams, Mgr
EMP: 34 EST: 1976
SQ FT: 40,400
SALES (est): 1.22MM Privately Held
Web: www.rollalongvans.com
SIC: 3714 Motor vehicle parts and accessories

**(P-13568)**
**RUFFSTUFF INC**
3237 Rippey Rd Ste 200, Loomis (95650-7661)
PHONE..................916 600-1945
Daniel Fredrickson, CEO
EMP: 42 EST: 2015
SALES (est): 4.79MM Privately Held
Web: www.ruffstuffspecialties.com
SIC: 3714 Motor vehicle parts and accessories

**(P-13569)**
**RYVID INC (PA)**
12090 Carson St Ste H504, Hawaiian Gardens (90716-1142)
PHONE..................949 691-3495
EMP: 18 EST: 2021
SALES (est): 6.31MM
SALES (corp-wide): 6.31MM Privately Held
Web: www.ryvid.com
SIC: 3714 Motor vehicle parts and accessories

**(P-13570)**
**S C I INDUSTRIES INC**
Also Called: SCI
1433 Adelia Ave, El Monte (91733-3002)
EMP: 25 EST: 1950

SALES (est): 630.34K Privately Held
SIC: 3714 3599 Motor vehicle brake systems and parts; Machine shop, jobbing and repair

**(P-13571)**
**S&B FILTERS INC (PA)**
15461 Slover Ave Ste A, Fontana (92337-1306)
PHONE..................909 947-0015
Berry Carter, Pr
▲ EMP: 49 EST: 1981
SALES (est): 11.01MM
SALES (corp-wide): 11.01MM Privately Held
Web: www.sandbfilters.com
SIC: 3714 3564 Filters: oil, fuel, and air, motor vehicle; Filters, air: furnaces, air conditioning equipment, etc.

**(P-13572)**
**SANDRA GRUCA**
Also Called: Ding Sticks
16993 Bluewater Ln, Huntington Beach (92649-2928)
PHONE..................714 661-6464
Sandra Gruca, Owner
Jim Gruca, Pr
EMP: 41 EST: 2014
SALES (est): 800K Privately Held
SIC: 3714 Shock absorbers, motor vehicle

**(P-13573)**
**SANKO ELECTRONICS AMERICA INC (HQ)**
2587 Otay Center Dr, San Diego (92154-7612)
PHONE..................310 618-1677
Hironori Saigusa, CEO
Akio Saigusa, Pr
Toshiaki Yamashita, Pr
▲ EMP: 19 EST: 1988
SALES (est): 8.99MM Privately Held
Web: www.sanko-grp.co.jp
SIC: 3714 Motor vehicle parts and accessories
PA: Sanko Electric Co.,Ltd.
7-23, Tamanoicho, Atsuta-Ku

**(P-13574)**
**SHEPARD-THOMASON COMPANY**
901 S Leslie St, La Habra (90631-6841)
PHONE..................714 773-5539
Thomas A Ruhe, Pr
Connie Ruhe, *
EMP: 74 EST: 1913
SQ FT: 25,000
SALES (est): 1.36MM Privately Held
SIC: 3714 Clutches, motor vehicle
PA: Ruhe Corporation
901 S Leslie St

**(P-13575)**
**SINISTER MFG COMPANY INC**
Also Called: Mkm Customs
2025 Opportunity Dr Ste 7, Roseville (95678-3010)
PHONE..................916 772-9253
Brian P George, Pr
Mike Mitchell, *
▲ EMP: 45 EST: 2010
SQ FT: 11,000
SALES (est): 20MM Privately Held
Web: www.sinisterdiesel.com
SIC: 3714 Motor vehicle parts and accessories

**(P-13576)**
**SLAM SPECIALTIES LLC**
5837 E Brown Ave, Fresno (93727-1364)
PHONE..................559 348-9038
Harry Solakian, Managing Member
▼ EMP: 16 EST: 2001
SALES (est): 2.34MM Privately Held
Web: www.slamspecialties.com
SIC: 3714 Motor vehicle engines and parts

**(P-13577)**
**SPECIAL DEVICES INCORPORATED**
Also Called: Sdi
2655 1st St Ste 125, Simi Valley (93065-1548)
PHONE..................805 387-1000
Yasuhiro Sakaki, CEO
Kenichi Tanaka, *
Kenichi Yamada, *
Harry Rector, *
Nicholas J Bruge, CCO*
▲ EMP: 600 EST: 1959
SALES (est): 46.65MM Privately Held
Web: www.daicelssa.com
SIC: 3714 Motor vehicle parts and accessories
PA: Daicel Corporation
3-1, Ofukacho, Kita-Ku

**(P-13578)**
**SPIRATEC SOLUTIONS INC**
190 S Orchard Ave Ste B220, Vacaville (95688-3647)
PHONE..................925 357-1103
Andreas Schadt, CEO
EMP: 18 EST: 2018
SALES (est): 440.77K Privately Held
Web: www.spiratec.com
SIC: 3714 Motor vehicle parts and accessories

**(P-13579)**
**STOPTECH**
21046 Figueroa St, Carson (90745-1906)
PHONE..................310 933-1100
EMP: 15 EST: 2013
SALES (est): 2.16MM Privately Held
Web: www.centricparts.com
SIC: 3714 Motor vehicle parts and accessories

**(P-13580)**
**SWAY-A-WAY INC**
8031 Remmet Ave, Canoga Park (91304-4128)
PHONE..................818 700-9712
▲ EMP: 31 EST: 1988
SALES (est): 2.57MM Privately Held
Web: www.swayaway.com
SIC: 3714 Motor vehicle parts and accessories

**(P-13581)**
**TASKER METAL PRODUCTS**
1823 S Hope St, Los Angeles (90015-4197)
P.O. Box 15368 (90015-0368)
PHONE..................213 765-5400
Eugene L Golling, Pr
Rudy Verstegen, VP
▲ EMP: 15 EST: 1941
SQ FT: 12,000
SALES (est): 2.3MM Privately Held
Web: www.taskermetalproducts.com
SIC: 3714 Motor vehicle body components and frame

## 3714 - Motor Vehicle Parts And Accessories (P-13582)

**(P-13582)**
**TEECO PRODUCTS INC**
Paca
7471 Reese Rd, Sacramento (95828-3721)
PHONE..................................916 688-3535
Tom Valvered, *Mgr*
**EMP:** 44
**SALES (corp-wide):** 17.85MM **Privately Held**
Web: www.teecoproducts.com
**SIC: 3714** 5084 3443 Propane conversion equipment, motor vehicle; Propane conversion equipment; Fabricated plate work (boiler shop)
**PA:** Teeco Products, Inc.
  16881 Armstrong Ave
  949 261-6295

**(P-13583)**
**THERMAL SOLUTIONS MFG INC**
1390 S Tippecanoe Ave Ste B, San Bernardino (92408-2998)
PHONE..................................909 796-0754
Maureen Baker, *Brnch Mgr*
**EMP:** 33
**SALES (corp-wide):** 47.17MM **Privately Held**
Web: www.thermalsolutionsmfg.com
**SIC: 3714** Radiators and radiator shells and cores, motor vehicle
**PA:** Thermal Solutions Manufacturing, Inc.
  25 Century Blvd Ste 210
  800 359-9186

**(P-13584)**
**THMX HOLDINGS LLC**
Also Called: Thermal Dynamics
4850 E Airport Dr, Ontario (91761-7818)
PHONE..................................909 390-3944
▲ **EMP:** 187
**SIC: 3714** Motor vehicle parts and accessories

**(P-13585)**
**THYSSENKRUPP BILSTEIN AMER INC**
13225 Danielson St # 100, Poway (92064-6843)
PHONE..................................858 386-5900
Doug Robertson, *VP*
**EMP:** 42
**SALES (corp-wide):** 40.78B **Privately Held**
Web: www.bilstein.com
**SIC: 3714** 5013 Motor vehicle parts and accessories; Motor vehicle supplies and new parts
**HQ:** Thyssenkrupp Bilstein Of America, Inc.
  8685 Bilstein Blvd
  Hamilton OH 45015
  513 881-7600

**(P-13586)**
**TILTON ENGINEERING INC**
25 Easy St, Buellton (93427-9566)
P.O. Box 1787 (93427-1787)
PHONE..................................805 688-2353
Jason Wahl, *Pr*
Todd Cooper, *
▲ **EMP:** 50 **EST:** 1972
**SQ FT:** 15,000
**SALES (est):** 6.35MM **Privately Held**
Web: www.tiltonracing.com
**SIC: 3714** Motor vehicle parts and accessories

**(P-13587)**
**TMI PRODUCTS INC**
Also Called: TMI Visualogic
1493 E Bentley Dr Ste 102, Corona (92879-5102)
PHONE..................................951 272-1996
▲ **EMP:** 150 **EST:** 1982
**SALES (est):** 28.31MM **Privately Held**
Web: www.tmiproducts.com
**SIC: 3714** 2399 Motor vehicle parts and accessories; Seat covers, automobile

**(P-13588)**
**TOGETHERBUYCOM**
Also Called: Vorsteiner
11621 Markon Dr, Garden Grove (92841-1810)
PHONE..................................714 379-4600
Seung B Nam, *Pr*
▲ **EMP:** 15 **EST:** 2007
**SALES (est):** 2.73MM **Privately Held**
Web: www.vorsteiner.com
**SIC: 3714** Motor vehicle parts and accessories

**(P-13589)**
**TRANS-DAPT CALIFORNIA INC**
12438 Putnam St, Whittier (90602-1002)
PHONE..................................562 921-0404
Robert Vandergriff, *Pr*
Ron Funfar, *General Vice President**
Jan Garner, *
**EMP:** 40 **EST:** 1959
**SQ FT:** 37,000
**SALES (est):** 1.45MM **Privately Held**
Web: www.hedman.com
**SIC: 3714** Motor vehicle parts and accessories

**(P-13590)**
**TRANSFER FLOW INC**
1444 Fortress St, Chico (95973)
PHONE..................................530 893-5209
▲ **EMP:** 100 **EST:** 1983
**SALES (est):** 15.94MM **Privately Held**
Web: www.transferflow.com
**SIC: 3714** Fuel systems and parts, motor vehicle

**(P-13591)**
**TRANSGO LLC**
Also Called: Transco
2621 Merced Ave, El Monte (91733-1905)
PHONE..................................626 443-7456
Gilbert W Younger, *Prin*
**EMP:** 19 **EST:** 1976
**SQ FT:** 4,560
**SALES (est):** 4.87MM **Privately Held**
Web: www.transgo.com
**SIC: 3714** Motor vehicle parts and accessories

**(P-13592)**
**TRANSPORTATION POWER LLC**
Also Called: Transpower
2057 Aldergrove Ave, Escondido (92029-1902)
PHONE..................................858 248-4255
Michael C Simon, *Pr*
Paul Scott, *
James Burns, *
**EMP:** 45 **EST:** 2010
**SALES (est):** 12.77MM
**SALES (corp-wide):** 34.06B **Publicly Held**
Web: www.transpowerusa.com
**SIC: 3714** Motor vehicle parts and accessories
**HQ:** Meritor, Inc.
  2135 W Maple Rd
  Troy MI 48084

**(P-13593)**
**TROPOS TECHNOLOGIES INC**
16890 Church St Bldg 1a, Morgan Hill (95037-5114)
P.O. Box 51 (95046)
PHONE..................................408 571-6104
John Foster, *Sec*
John Bautista, *CFO*
**EMP:** 18 **EST:** 2016
**SALES (est):** 3.74MM **Privately Held**
Web: www.troposmotors.com
**SIC: 3714** Motor vehicle electrical equipment

**(P-13594)**
**TUBE TECHNOLOGIES INC**
Also Called: TTI Performance Exhaust
1555 Consumer Cir, Corona (92878-3226)
PHONE..................................951 371-4878
Sam Davis, *Pr*
Raul Rodriguez, *
Tom Nakawatase, *
Trini Respico, *
▲ **EMP:** 30 **EST:** 1988
**SQ FT:** 18,400
**SALES (est):** 2.69MM **Privately Held**
Web: www.ttiexhaust.com
**SIC: 3714** 3498 Exhaust systems and parts, motor vehicle; Tube fabricating (contract bending and shaping)
**PA:** Jindal Saw Limited
  Jindal Centre, 12 Bhikaiji

**(P-13595)**
**U S WHEEL CORPORATION**
Also Called: US Wheel
15702 Producer Ln, Huntington Beach (92649-1303)
PHONE..................................714 892-0021
Eliot Mason, *Pr*
◆ **EMP:** 20 **EST:** 1986
**SQ FT:** 135,000
**SALES (est):** 6.7MM **Privately Held**
Web: www.uswheel.com
**SIC: 3714** 5013 Wheels, motor vehicle; Wheels, motor vehicle

**(P-13596)**
**UFO DESIGNS**
Also Called: S F Technology
16730 Gridley Rd, Cerritos (90703-1730)
PHONE..................................562 924-5763
Jitu Patel, *Pr*
**EMP:** 22
**SALES (corp-wide):** 1.45MM **Privately Held**
Web: www.ufodesign.com
**SIC: 3714** 3089 Motor vehicle parts and accessories; Plastics processing
**PA:** U.F.O. Designs
  5812 Machine Dr
  714 892-4420

**(P-13597)**
**ULTRA WHEEL COMPANY**
Also Called: Platinum
586 N Gilbert St, Fullerton (92833-2549)
PHONE..................................714 449-7100
Sharon A Wood, *Pr*
Fred Dobler, *
James Smith, *Stockholder**
Jim Smith, *
▼ **EMP:** 25 **EST:** 1984
**SQ FT:** 65,000
**SALES (est):** 4.65MM **Privately Held**
Web: www.ultrawheel.com
**SIC: 3714** Motor vehicle parts and accessories

**(P-13598)**
**UNI FILTER INC**
1468 Manhattan Ave, Fullerton (92831-5222)
PHONE..................................714 535-6933
Lanny R Mitchell, *Pr*
Kathi Perry, *
Tom Gross, *
Robert A Nichols, *Stockholder**
Kenneth E Mitchell, *Stockholder**
**EMP:** 19 **EST:** 1971
**SQ FT:** 26,000
**SALES (est):** 2.42MM **Privately Held**
Web: www.unifilter.com
**SIC: 3714** Filters: oil, fuel, and air, motor vehicle

**(P-13599)**
**US HYBRID CORPORATION (HQ)**
2660 Columbia St, Torrance (90503-3802)
PHONE..................................310 212-1200
Gordon Abas Goodarzi, *CEO*
▲ **EMP:** 39 **EST:** 1999
**SALES (est):** 1.37MM **Publicly Held**
Web: www.ushybrid.com
**SIC: 3714** Motor vehicle engines and parts
**PA:** Ideanomics, Inc.
  1441 Broadway Ste 5116

**(P-13600)**
**US MOTOR WORKS LLC (PA)**
14722 Anson Ave, Santa Fe Springs (90670)
PHONE..................................562 404-0488
Gil Benjamin, *Pr*
Doron Goren, *
◆ **EMP:** 43 **EST:** 1995
**SQ FT:** 37,000
**SALES (est):** 25.02MM **Privately Held**
Web: www.usmotorworks.com
**SIC: 3714** Water pump, motor vehicle

**(P-13601)**
**US RADIATOR CORPORATION (PA)**
4423 District Blvd, Vernon (90058-3111)
P.O. Box 5486 (90255-9486)
PHONE..................................323 826-0965
Donald Armstrong, *Pr*
Tim Armstrong, *
William Zimmerman, *
▲ **EMP:** 29 **EST:** 1956
**SQ FT:** 35,000
**SALES (est):** 1.35MM
**SALES (corp-wide):** 1.35MM **Privately Held**
Web: www.usradiator.com
**SIC: 3714** Radiators and radiator shells and cores, motor vehicle

**(P-13602)**
**VELODYNE LIDAR USA INC (DH)**
5521 Hellyer Ave, San Jose (95138-1017)
PHONE..................................669 275-2251
Ted Tewksbury, *CEO*
David Hall, *Ch Bd*
Marta Hall, *VP*
Mark Weinswig, *CFO*
Rick Tewell, *COO*
**EMP:** 44 **EST:** 1983
**SALES (est):** 33.4MM
**SALES (corp-wide):** 113.39MM **Privately Held**
Web: www.velodynelidar.com
**SIC: 3714** Motor vehicle parts and accessories
**HQ:** Velodyne, Llc
  5521 Hellyer Ave
  San Jose CA 95138
  669 275-2251

**(P-13603)**
**VETRONIX CORPORATION**
2030 Alameda Padre Serra, Santa Barbara (93103-1716)
PHONE..................................805 966-2000

## PRODUCTS & SERVICES SECTION

**3715 - Truck Trailers (P-13624)**

EMP: 152
SIC: 3714 3829 Motor vehicle parts and accessories; Aircraft and motor vehicle measurement equipment

**(P-13604)**
**WALKER PRODUCTS**
Also Called: WALKER PRODUCTS
14291 Commerce Dr, Garden Grove (92843-4944)
PHONE..........................714 554-5151
Chris Weaver, Genl Mgr
EMP: 50
SALES (corp-wide): 49.38MM **Privately Held**
Web: www.walkerproducts.com
SIC: 3714 Motor vehicle parts and accessories
PA: Walker Products, Inc.
525 W Congress St
636 257-2400

**(P-13605)**
**WILWOOD ENGINEERING (PA)**
4700 Calle Bolero, Camarillo (93012-8561)
PHONE..........................805 388-1188
William H Wood, Pr
▲ EMP: 108 EST: 1977
SALES (est): 15.01MM
SALES (corp-wide): 15.01MM **Privately Held**
Web: www.wilwood.com
SIC: 3714 Motor vehicle parts and accessories

**(P-13606)**
**WRIGHTSPEED INC**
Also Called: Revo Powetrains
150 Almaden Blvd, San Jose (95113-2000)
PHONE..........................866 960-9482
Ian Wright, CEO
Mark Schmitz, *
▲ EMP: 39 EST: 2005
SALES (est): 5.44MM **Privately Held**
Web: www.wrightspeed.com
SIC: 3714 Differentials and parts, motor vehicle

**(P-13607)**
**WSW CORP (PA)**
Also Called: Waag
16000 Strathern St, Van Nuys (91406-1316)
PHONE..........................818 989-5008
Gary Waagenaar, CEO
Mike Calka, *
Jennifer Waagenaar, *
▲ EMP: 45 EST: 1978
SQ FT: 55,000
SALES (est): 5.23MM
SALES (corp-wide): 5.23MM **Privately Held**
Web: www.waag.com
SIC: 3714 5712 Motor vehicle parts and accessories; Beds and accessories

**(P-13608)**
**XOS INC (PA)**
Also Called: XOS
3550 Tyburn St Ste 100, Los Angeles (90065-1427)
PHONE..........................818 316-1890
Dakota Semler, Ch Bd
Giordano Sordoni, COO
Liana Pogosyan, VP Fin
EMP: 25 EST: 2020
SQ FT: 85,142
SALES (est): 44.52MM
SALES (corp-wide): 44.52MM **Publicly Held**
Web: www.xostrucks.com
SIC: 3714 3694 Motor vehicle engines and parts; Automotive electrical equipment, nec

**(P-13609)**
**YANFENG INTL AUTO TECH US I LL**
Also Called: Yanfeng
30559 San Antonio St, Hayward (94544-7101)
PHONE..........................616 886-3622
Phillip George, Brnch Mgr
EMP: 20
Web: www.yanfeng.com
SIC: 3714 Motor vehicle parts and accessories
HQ: Yanfeng International Automotive Technology Us I Llc
41935 W 12 Mile Rd
Novi MI 48377
248 319-7333

**(P-13610)**
**YINLUN TDI LLC (HQ)**
10668 N Trademark Pkwy, Rancho Cucamonga (91730-5934)
PHONE..........................909 390-3944
Zack Yang, Pr
EMP: 24 EST: 2012
SQ FT: 85,000
SALES (est): 29.58MM
SALES (corp-wide): 1.54B **Privately Held**
Web: www.yinluntdi.com
SIC: 3714 Motor vehicle engines and parts
PA: Zhejiang Yinlun Machinery Co.,Ltd.
No.8, Shifeng East Rd., Fuxi Street, Tiantai County
57683938250

## 3715 Truck Trailers

**(P-13611)**
**ANDERSEN INDUSTRIES INC**
17079 Muskrat Ave, Adelanto (92301-2259)
PHONE..........................760 246-8766
Steven Andersen, CEO
Wayne Andersen, *
Neil Andersen, *
EMP: 25 EST: 1980
SQ FT: 110,000
SALES (est): 4.88MM **Privately Held**
Web: www.andersenmp.com
SIC: 3715 3441 3444 Truck trailers; Fabricated structural metal; Hoppers, sheet metal

**(P-13612)**
**BEALL TRAILERS OF CALIFORNIA INC**
1301 South Ave, Turlock (95380-5108)
P.O. Box 310 (95381-0310)
PHONE..........................209 669-7151
EMP: 42
Web: www.bealcorp.com
SIC: 3715 7539 3714 Truck trailers; Trailer repair; Motor vehicle parts and accessories

**(P-13613)**
**BLACKSERIES CAMPERS INC**
Also Called: Black Series Campers
19501 E Walnut Dr S, City Of Industry (91748-2318)
PHONE..........................833 822-6737
Hongwei Qiu, CEO
Yichun Chen, Sec
EMP: 20 EST: 2017
SALES (est): 5.05MM **Privately Held**
Web: www.blackseries.net
SIC: 3715 Truck trailers

**(P-13614)**
**CIMC INTERMODAL EQUIPMENT LLC (HQ)**
Also Called: Cimc Intermodal Equipment
10530 Sessler St, South Gate (90280-7252)
PHONE..........................562 904-8600
Frank Sonzala, CEO
Trevor Ash, *
▲ EMP: 70 EST: 2007
SALES (est): 24.91MM **Privately Held**
Web: www.ciemanufacturing.com
SIC: 3715 7539 Truck trailer chassis; Trailer repair
PA: China International Marine Containers (Group) Co.,Ltd.
Floor 8, Zhongji Group Yanfa Center, No.2, Shekou Gangwan Avenue

**(P-13615)**
**COZAD TRAILER SALES LLC**
4907 E Waterloo Rd, Stockton (95215-2096)
PHONE..........................209 931-3000
Delores Pistacchio, *
Kara Kardashian, *
▲ EMP: 92 EST: 1953
SQ FT: 78,000
SALES (est): 17.32MM **Privately Held**
Web: www.cozadtrailers.com
SIC: 3715 7539 Trailer bodies; Trailer repair

**(P-13616)**
**DEXTER AXLE COMPANY**
Also Called: Unique Functional Products
135 Sunshine Ln, San Marcos (92069-1733)
PHONE..........................760 744-1610
Steve Moore, Dir
EMP: 51
SALES (corp-wide): 1.41B **Privately Held**
Web: www.dexteraxle.com
SIC: 3715 3714 Trailer bodies; Motor vehicle parts and accessories
HQ: Dexter Axle Company Llc
2900 Industrial Pkwy E
Elkhart IN 46516

**(P-13617)**
**OWEN TRAILERS INC**
9020 Jurupa Rd, Riverside (92509-3106)
P.O. Box 36 (90633-0036)
PHONE..........................951 361-4557
Loren Owen Junior, Pr
Angela P Owen, *
EMP: 25 EST: 1946
SQ FT: 34,000
SALES (est): 2.43MM **Privately Held**
Web: www.owentrailers.com
SIC: 3715 Truck trailers

**(P-13618)**
**PACIFICO INC**
Also Called: Murray Trailers
1754 E Mariposa Rd, Stockton (95205)
PHONE..........................209 466-0266
Douglas G Murray, Pr
EMP: 21 EST: 1946
SQ FT: 41,000
SALES (est): 4.36MM **Privately Held**
Web: www.murraytrailer.com
SIC: 3715 7539 Semitrailers for truck tractors; Trailer repair

**(P-13619)**
**REFRIGRATED TRCK SOLUTIONS LLC**
1115 E Dominguez St, Carson (90746-3517)
PHONE..........................323 594-4500
Frederick Lukken, Pr
EMP: 26 EST: 2015
SALES (est): 1.89MM **Privately Held**
Web: www.truckreefer.com
SIC: 3715 Truck trailers

**(P-13620)**
**UNIQUE FUNCTIONAL PRODUCTS**
Also Called: U F P
135 Sunshine Ln, San Marcos (92069-1733)
PHONE..........................760 744-1610
▲ EMP: 125
Web: www.dexteraxle.com
SIC: 3715 3714 Trailer bodies; Motor vehicle parts and accessories

**(P-13621)**
**UNITED STATES LOGISTICS GROUP**
Also Called: US Logistics
2700 Rose Ave Ste A, Signal Hill (90755-1929)
P.O. Box 10129 (91209-3129)
PHONE..........................562 989-9555
Khachatur Khudikyan, CEO
EMP: 32 EST: 2009
SALES (est): 2.65MM **Privately Held**
Web: www.uslginc.com
SIC: 3715 Truck trailers

**(P-13622)**
**UTILITY TRAILER MANUFACTURING (PA)**
17295 Railroad St Ste A, City Of Industry (91748-1043)
PHONE..........................626 965-1514
Paul F Bennett, CEO
Harold C Bennett, *
Craig M Bennett, *
Jeffrey J Bennett, *
Stephen F Bennett, *
◆ EMP: 300 EST: 1914
SQ FT: 50,000
SALES (est): 897.7MM
SALES (corp-wide): 897.7MM **Privately Held**
Web: www.utilitytrailer.com
SIC: 3715 Truck trailers

**(P-13623)**
**UTILITY TRAILER MFG CO**
Tautliner Division
17295 Railroad St Ste A, City Of Industry (91748-1043)
PHONE..........................909 594-6026
Linda Baker, Mgr
EMP: 152
SALES (corp-wide): 897.7MM **Privately Held**
Web: www.utilitytrailer.com
SIC: 3715 5199 Truck trailers; Tarpaulins
PA: Utility Trailer Manufacturing Company, Llc
17295 E Railroad St
626 965-1514

**(P-13624)**
**UTILITY TRAILER MFG CO**
Also Called: Utility Trlr Sls Southern Cal
15567 Valley Blvd, Fontana (92335-6351)
PHONE..........................909 428-8300
TOLL FREE: 800
Thayne Stanger, Brnch Mgr
EMP: 176
SALES (corp-wide): 897.7MM **Privately Held**

**3716 - Motor Homes (P-13625)**     **PRODUCTS & SERVICES SECTION**

Web: www.utilitytrailer.com
SIC: 3715  Semitrailers for truck tractors
PA: Utility Trailer Manufacturing Company, Llc
   17295 E Railroad St
   626 965-1514

## 3716 Motor Homes

**(P-13625)**
**REXHALL INDUSTRIES INC**
26857 Tannahill Ave, Canyon Country (91387-3969)
PHONE....................661 726-5470
William Jonathan Rex, *Ch Bd*
Cheryl Rex, *Corporate Secretary\**
James C Rex, *General Vice President\**
▲ EMP: 46 EST: 1986
SQ FT: 120,000
SALES (est): 4.99MM **Privately Held**
Web: www.rexhall.com
SIC: 3716  Motor homes

## 3721 Aircraft

**(P-13626)**
**AEROVIRONMENT INC**
1610 S Magnolia Ave, Monrovia (91016-4547)
PHONE....................626 357-9983
EMP: 37
SALES (corp-wide): 716.72MM **Publicly Held**
Web: www.avinc.com
SIC: 3721  Aircraft
PA: Aerovironment, Inc.
   241 18th St S Ste 415
   805 520-8350

**(P-13627)**
**AEROVIRONMENT INC**
222 E Huntington Dr Ste 118, Monrovia (91016-8014)
P.O. Box 5130 (93062-5130)
PHONE....................626 357-9983
EMP: 37
SALES (corp-wide): 716.72MM **Publicly Held**
Web: www.avinc.com
SIC: 3721  Aircraft
PA: Aerovironment, Inc.
   241 18th St S Ste 415
   805 520-8350

**(P-13628)**
**AEROVIRONMENT INC**
1035 N Mcdowell Blvd, Petaluma (94954-1173)
PHONE....................707 206-9372
EMP: 29
SALES (corp-wide): 716.72MM **Publicly Held**
Web: www.avinc.com
SIC: 3721  Aircraft
PA: Aerovironment, Inc.
   241 18th St S Ste 415
   805 520-8350

**(P-13629)**
**AEROVIRONMENT INC**
825 S Myrtle Ave, Monrovia (91016-8600)
PHONE....................626 357-9983
Stewart Hindle, *Mgr*
EMP: 42
SALES (corp-wide): 716.72MM **Publicly Held**
Web: www.avinc.com
SIC: 3721  Aircraft
PA: Aerovironment, Inc.
   241 18th St S Ste 415
   805 520-8350

**(P-13630)**
**AEROVIRONMENT INC**
900 Innovators Way, Simi Valley (93065-2072)
PHONE....................805 520-8350
Wahid Nawabi, *Pr*
EMP: 30
SALES (corp-wide): 716.72MM **Publicly Held**
Web: www.avinc.com
SIC: 3721  Gliders (aircraft)
PA: Aerovironment, Inc.
   241 18th St S Ste 415
   805 520-8350

**(P-13631)**
**AIBOT US OPERATION INC**
2883 E Spring St Ste 200, Long Beach (90806-2467)
PHONE....................562 283-3286
Jack Shen, *Off Mgr*
EMP: 21
SALES (est): 1.11MM **Privately Held**
SIC: 3721  Aircraft

**(P-13632)**
**ALLCLEAR INC**
200 N Pacific Coast Hwy Ste 1350, El Segundo (90245-5680)
PHONE....................424 316-1596
Darryl Mayhorn, *CEO*
EMP: 32 EST: 2020
SALES (est): 2.39MM **Privately Held**
Web: www.goallclear.com
SIC: 3721  Aircraft

**(P-13633)**
**AMERICAN SCENCE TECH AS T CORP (PA)**
Also Called: AS&t
50 California St Fl 21, San Francisco (94111-4624)
P.O. Box 9148 (92652-7142)
PHONE....................415 251-2800
James Johnson, *Pr*
Jake Soujah, *
EMP: 135 EST: 2006
SALES (est): 4.06MM
SALES (corp-wide): 4.06MM **Privately Held**
Web: www.ast-d.com
SIC: 3721  3724 3761 3764  Aircraft; Aircraft engines and engine parts; Guided missiles and space vehicles; Space propulsion units and parts

**(P-13634)**
**AMERICAN SCENCE TECH AS T CORP**
2372 Morse Ave Ste 571, Irvine (92614-6234)
PHONE....................310 773-1978
Kinda Assouad, *Brnch Mgr*
EMP: 85
SALES (corp-wide): 4.06MM **Privately Held**
Web: www.ast-d.com
SIC: 3721  3724 3761 3764  Aircraft; Aircraft engines and engine parts; Guided missiles and space vehicles; Space propulsion units and parts
PA: American Science & Technology (As&T) Corporation
   50 California St Fl 21
   415 251-2800

**(P-13635)**
**APM MANUFACTURING**
341 W Blueridge Ave, Orange (92865-4201)
PHONE....................714 453-0100
Gilles Madelmont, *Contrlr*
EMP: 128
SALES (corp-wide): 43.53MM **Privately Held**
Web: www.anaheimprecision.com
SIC: 3721  Aircraft
HQ: Apm Manufacturing
   1738 N Neville St
   Orange CA 92865
   714 453-0100

**(P-13636)**
**ARCHER AVIATION INC (PA)**
Also Called: ARCHER
190 W Tasman Dr, San Jose (95134-1700)
PHONE....................650 272-3233
Adam Goldstein, *CEO*
Mark Mesler, *CFO*
Andy Missan, *CLO*
Tosha Perkins, *CPO*
EMP: 152 EST: 2018
Web: www.archer.com
SIC: 3721  Aircraft

**(P-13637)**
**ARCHER AVIATION INC**
77 Rio Robles, San Jose (95134)
PHONE....................650 272-3233
Adam Goldstein, *Brnch Mgr*
EMP: 286
SIC: 3721  Aircraft
PA: Archer Aviation Inc.
   190 W Tasman Dr
   650 272-3233

**(P-13638)**
**ARCHER AVIATION OPERATING CORP**
190 W Tasman Dr, San Jose (95134-1700)
PHONE....................650 272-3233
Tom Muniz, *COO*
Ben Lu, *CFO*
Andy Missan, *CLO*
EMP: 188 EST: 2018
Web: www.archer.com
SIC: 3721  Aircraft
PA: Archer Aviation Inc.
   190 W Tasman Dr
   650 272-3233

**(P-13639)**
**BOEING**
15320 Barranca Pkwy, Irvine (92618-2215)
PHONE....................949 623-2222
EMP: 42 EST: 2019
SALES (est): 578.95K **Privately Held**
Web: jobs.boeing.com
SIC: 3721  Airplanes, fixed or rotary wing

**(P-13640)**
**BOEING AROSPC OPERATIONS INC**
Also Called: Boeing
640 E St, Fairfield (94535-5006)
PHONE....................707 437-3175
John Sidorck, *Mgr*
EMP: 30
SALES (corp-wide): 77.79B **Publicly Held**
SIC: 3721  Aircraft
HQ: Boeing Aerospace Operations, Inc.
   6001 S A Depo Blvd Ste E
   Oklahoma City OK 73150
   405 622-6000

**(P-13641)**
**BOEING COMPANY**
Also Called: Boeing
2220 E Carson St, Carson (90810-1226)
PHONE....................310 522-2809
Jim Brown, *Mgr*
EMP: 125
SQ FT: 71,912
SALES (corp-wide): 77.79B **Publicly Held**
Web: www.boeing.com
SIC: 3721  Aircraft
PA: The Boeing Company
   929 Long Bridge Dr
   703 465-3500

**(P-13642)**
**BOEING COMPANY**
Also Called: Boeing
Bldg-1454 Receiving, San Diego (92135)
PHONE....................619 545-8382
EMP: 996
SALES (corp-wide): 77.79B **Publicly Held**
Web: www.boeing.com
SIC: 3721  Airplanes, fixed or rotary wing
PA: The Boeing Company
   929 Long Bridge Dr
   703 465-3500

**(P-13643)**
**BOEING COMPANY**
Also Called: Boeing
4000 N Lakewood Blvd, Long Beach (90808-1700)
PHONE....................562 496-1000
Nan Bouchard, *VP*
EMP: 2000
SALES (corp-wide): 77.79B **Publicly Held**
Web: www.boeing.com
SIC: 3721  Airplanes, fixed or rotary wing
PA: The Boeing Company
   929 Long Bridge Dr
   703 465-3500

**(P-13644)**
**BOEING COMPANY**
Also Called: Boeing
4060 N Lakewood Blvd, Long Beach (90808-1700)
P.O. Box 200 (90801-0200)
PHONE....................562 593-5511
Linda Van Reeden, *Mgr*
EMP: 1400
SALES (corp-wide): 77.79B **Publicly Held**
Web: www.boeing.com
SIC: 3721  Airplanes, fixed or rotary wing
PA: The Boeing Company
   929 Long Bridge Dr
   703 465-3500

**(P-13645)**
**BOEING INTLLCTUAL PRPRTY LCNSI**
14441 Astronautics Ln, Huntington Beach (92647-2080)
PHONE....................562 797-2020
EMP: 245 EST: 2011
SALES (est): 12.76MM
SALES (corp-wide): 77.79B **Publicly Held**
Web: www.boeing.com
SIC: 3721  Airplanes, fixed or rotary wing
PA: The Boeing Company
   929 Long Bridge Dr
   703 465-3500

**(P-13646)**
**BOEING SATELLITE SYSTEMS INC**
Also Called: Boeing
2300 E Imperial Hwy, El Segundo (90245-2813)

# PRODUCTS & SERVICES SECTION
## 3721 - Aircraft (P-13667)

P.O. Box 92919 (90009-2919)
PHONE.................................310 568-2735
Steve Tsukamoto, *Mgr*
**EMP:** 4915
**SALES (corp-wide):** 77.79B **Publicly Held**
**Web:** www.boeing.com
**SIC:** 3721 Aircraft
**HQ:** Boeing Satellite Systems, Inc.
900 N Pacific Coast Hwy
El Segundo CA 90245

*(P-13647)*
### CHIPTON-ROSS INC
420 Culver Blvd, Playa Del Rey (90293-7706)
PHONE.................................310 414-7800
Judith Hinkley, *Pr*
**EMP:** 100 **EST:** 1983
**SQ FT:** 6,000
**SALES (est):** 9.01MM **Privately Held**
**Web:** www.chiptonross.com
**SIC:** 3721 3731 8731 7363 Motorized aircraft; Military ships, building and repairing; Commercial physical research; Temporary help service

*(P-13648)*
### COMAC AMERICA CORPORATION
4350 Von Karman Ave Ste 400, Newport Beach (92660-2007)
PHONE.................................760 616-9614
Wei Ye, *CEO*
**EMP:** 31 **EST:** 2013
**SALES (est):** 4.31MM **Privately Held**
**Web:** www.comacamerica.com
**SIC:** 3721 Aircraft
**PA:** Commercial Aircraft Corporation Of China,Ltd.
No.1919, Shibo Avenue, Pudong New District

*(P-13649)*
### DFC INC (PA)
Also Called: Advanced Helicopter Svs
17986 County Road 94b, Woodland (95695-9238)
PHONE.................................530 669-7115
Sparrow Tang, *Pr*
Carol Aronson, *VP*
Patricia Laustalot, *Treas*
**EMP:** 51 **EST:** 2001
**SQ FT:** 55,000
**SALES (est):** 1.63MM
**SALES (corp-wide):** 1.63MM **Privately Held**
**Web:** www.advancedhelicopterservices.com
**SIC:** 3721 Aircraft

*(P-13650)*
### EMPIRICAL SYSTEMS AROSPC INC (PA)
Also Called: Esaero
3580 Sueldo St, San Luis Obispo (93401-7338)
P.O. Box 595 (93448-0595)
PHONE.................................805 474-5900
Andrew Gibson, *Pr*
Benjamin Schiltgen, *
**EMP:** 124 **EST:** 2003
**SQ FT:** 1,000
**SALES (est):** 22.49MM
**SALES (corp-wide):** 22.49MM **Privately Held**
**Web:** www.esaero.com
**SIC:** 3721 Aircraft

*(P-13651)*
### FASTENER DIST HOLDINGS LLC
Also Called: Fdh Aero
5200 Sheila St, Commerce (90040-3906)
PHONE.................................213 620-9950
**EMP:** 21
**SALES (corp-wide):** 512.41MM **Privately Held**
**Web:** www.aircraftfast.com
**SIC:** 3721 Aircraft
**HQ:** Fastener Distribution Holdings, Llc
5200 Sheila St
Commerce CA 90040
213 620-9950

*(P-13652)*
### GENERAL ATMICS ARNTCAL SYSTEMS
11906 Tech Center Ct, Poway (92064-7139)
PHONE.................................858 455-3358
**EMP:** 150
**Web:** www.ga-asi.com
**SIC:** 3721 Aircraft
**HQ:** General Atomics Aeronautical Systems, Inc.
14200 Kirkham Way
Poway CA 92064

*(P-13653)*
### GENERAL ATMICS ARNTCAL SYSTEMS
13330 Evening Creek Dr N, San Diego (92128-4110)
PHONE.................................858 964-6700
Neal Blue, *Pr*
**EMP:** 313
**Web:** www.ga-asi.com
**SIC:** 3721 Aircraft
**HQ:** General Atomics Aeronautical Systems, Inc.
14200 Kirkham Way
Poway CA 92064

*(P-13654)*
### GENERAL ATMICS ARNTCAL SYSTEMS
13550 Stowe Dr, Poway (92064-6858)
PHONE.................................858 312-4247
**EMP:** 326
**Web:** www.ga-asi.com
**SIC:** 3721 Aircraft
**HQ:** General Atomics Aeronautical Systems, Inc.
14200 Kirkham Way
Poway CA 92064

*(P-13655)*
### GENERAL ATMICS ARNTCAL SYSTEMS
12220 Parkway Centre Dr, Poway (92064-6867)
PHONE.................................858 455-3000
Eric Jones, *Brnch Mgr*
**EMP:** 216
**Web:** www.ga-asi.com
**SIC:** 3721 Aircraft
**HQ:** General Atomics Aeronautical Systems, Inc.
14200 Kirkham Way
Poway CA 92064

*(P-13656)*
### GENERAL ATMICS ARNTCAL SYSTEMS
16761 Via Del Campo Ct, San Diego (92127-1713)
PHONE.................................858 762-6700
**EMP:** 541
**Web:** www.ga-asi.com
**SIC:** 3721 Aircraft
**HQ:** General Atomics Aeronautical Systems, Inc.
14200 Kirkham Way
Poway CA 92064

*(P-13657)*
### GENERAL ATMICS ARNTCAL SYSTEMS
14102 Stowe Dr Ste A47, Poway (92064-7147)
PHONE.................................858 312-2810
**EMP:** 182
**Web:** www.ga-asi.com
**SIC:** 3721 Aircraft
**HQ:** General Atomics Aeronautical Systems, Inc.
14200 Kirkham Way
Poway CA 92064

*(P-13658)*
### GENERAL ATMICS ARNTCAL SYSTEMS
Also Called: General Atomics
3550 General Atomics Ct, San Diego (92121-1122)
PHONE.................................858 455-2810
**EMP:** 500
**Web:** www.ga-asi.com
**SIC:** 3721 Aircraft
**HQ:** General Atomics Aeronautical Systems, Inc.
14200 Kirkham Way
Poway CA 92064

*(P-13659)*
### GENERAL ATMICS ARNTCAL SYSTEMS
12365 Crosthwaite Cir, Poway (92064-6817)
PHONE.................................858 762-6700
Cyndra Flanagen, *Dir*
**EMP:** 500
**Web:** www.ga-asi.com
**SIC:** 3721 Aircraft
**HQ:** General Atomics Aeronautical Systems, Inc.
14200 Kirkham Way
Poway CA 92064

*(P-13660)*
### GENERAL ATMICS ARNTCAL SYSTEMS (DH)
Also Called: Ga-Asi
14200 Kirkham Way, Poway (92064-7103)
PHONE.................................858 312-2810
Neal Blue, *Pr*
Brad Clark, *
Stacy Jakuttis, *
Tony Navarra, *
◆ **EMP:** 500 **EST:** 1992
**SQ FT:** 900,000
**SALES (est):** 1.59B **Privately Held**
**Web:** www.ga-asi.com
**SIC:** 3721 Aircraft
**HQ:** Aeronautical Systems Inc
16761 Via Del Campo Ct
San Diego CA 92127

*(P-13661)*
### GENERAL ATOMIC AERON
14040 Danielson St, Poway (92064-6857)
PHONE.................................858 455-4560
**EMP:** 164
**Web:** www.ga-asi.com
**SIC:** 3721 Aircraft

*(P-13662)*
### GENERAL ATOMIC AERON
13950 Stowe Dr, Poway (92064-8803)
PHONE.................................858 312-3428
James N Blue, *Brnch Mgr*
**EMP:** 213
**Web:** www.ga-asi.com
**SIC:** 3721 Aircraft
**HQ:** General Atomics Aeronautical Systems, Inc.
14200 Kirkham Way
Poway CA 92064

*(P-13663)*
### GENERAL ATOMIC AERON
Also Called: General Atomics
73 El Mirage Airport Rd Ste B, Adelanto (92301-9540)
PHONE.................................760 388-8208
Gary Bener, *Brnch Mgr*
**EMP:** 200
**SQ FT:** 34,425
**Web:** www.ga-asi.com
**SIC:** 3721 Aircraft
**HQ:** General Atomics Aeronautical Systems, Inc.
14200 Kirkham Way
Poway CA 92064

*(P-13664)*
### GENERAL ATOMIC AERON
14115 Stowe Dr, Poway (92064-7145)
PHONE.................................858 312-2543
**EMP:** 500
**Web:** www.ga-asi.com
**SIC:** 3721 Aircraft
**HQ:** General Atomics Aeronautical Systems, Inc.
14200 Kirkham Way
Poway CA 92064

*(P-13665)*
### GENERAL ELECTRIC COMPANY
Also Called: G E Aviation
18000 Phantom St, Victorville (92394-7913)
PHONE.................................760 530-5200
John Hardell, *Prin*
**EMP:** 50
**SALES (corp-wide):** 67.95B **Publicly Held**
**Web:** www.ge.com
**SIC:** 3721 Aircraft
**PA:** General Electric Company
1 Neumann Way
617 443-3000

*(P-13666)*
### GKN AEROSPACE
12122 Western Ave, Garden Grove (92841-2915)
PHONE.................................714 653-7531
Peter Dilnot, *CEO*
Matthew Gregory, *CFO*
Warren Fernandez, *Sec*
**EMP:** 91 **EST:** 2016
**SALES (est):** 10.29MM **Privately Held**
**Web:** www.gknaerospace.com
**SIC:** 3721 Aircraft

*(P-13667)*
### GULFSTREAM AEROSPACE CORP GA
Also Called: Gulfstream
16644 Roscoe Blvd, Van Nuys (91406-1103)
PHONE.................................805 236-5755

# 3721 - Aircraft (P-13668)

## PRODUCTS & SERVICES SECTION

**EMP:** 413
**SALES (corp-wide):** 42.27B **Publicly Held**
**SIC:** 3721 Aircraft
**HQ:** Gulfstream Aerospace Corporation
(Georgia)
500 Gulfstream Rd
Savannah GA 31408
912 965-3000

### (P-13668)
### GULFSTREAM AEROSPACE CORP GA
4150 E Donald Douglas Dr, Long Beach (90808-1725)
**PHONE**.................562 420-1818
Barry Russell, *Brnch Mgr*
**EMP:** 1033
**SALES (corp-wide):** 42.27B **Publicly Held**
**SIC:** 3721 Aircraft
**HQ:** Gulfstream Aerospace Corporation
(Georgia)
500 Gulfstream Rd
Savannah GA 31408
912 965-3000

### (P-13669)
### GULFSTREAM AEROSPACE CORP GA
9818 Mina Ave, Whittier (90605-3035)
**PHONE**.................562 907-9300
**EMP:** 207
**SALES (corp-wide):** 42.27B **Publicly Held**
**SIC:** 3721 Airplanes, fixed or rotary wing
**HQ:** Gulfstream Aerospace Corporation
(Georgia)
500 Gulfstream Rd
Savannah GA 31408
912 965-3000

### (P-13670)
### IMPOSSIBLE AEROSPACE CORP
1709 Junction Ct, San Jose (95112-1044)
P.O. Box 7468 (94026-7468)
**PHONE**.................707 293-9367
Albert Spencer Gore, *CEO*
**EMP:** 15 **EST:** 2017
**SALES (est):** 2.21MM **Privately Held**
**Web:** www.vayuaerospace.com
**SIC:** 3721 Aircraft

### (P-13671)
### JETZERO INC (PA)
4150 E Donald Douglas Dr, Long Beach (90808-1725)
**PHONE**.................949 474-8222
Thomas O'leary, *CEO*
**EMP:** 36 **EST:** 2021
**SALES (est):** 1.67MM
**SALES (corp-wide):** 1.67MM **Privately Held**
**Web:** www.jetzero.aero
**SIC:** 3721 Aircraft

### (P-13672)
### JOBY AERO INC (HQ)
333 Encinal St, Santa Cruz (95060-2132)
**PHONE**.................831 426-3733
Joeben Bevirt, *CEO*
**EMP:** 663 **EST:** 2010
**SALES (est):** 643.62K
**SALES (corp-wide):** 1.03MM **Publicly Held**
**Web:** www.jobyaviation.com
**SIC:** 3721 Aircraft
**PA:** Joby Aviation, Inc.
333 Encinal St
831 201-6006

### (P-13673)
### JOBY AVIATION INC (PA)
333 Encinal St, Santa Cruz (95060-2132)
**PHONE**.................831 201-6006
Joeben Bevirt, *Chief Architect*
Joeben Bevirt, *Chief Architect*
Paul Sciarra, *Ex Ch Bd*
Matthew Field, *CFO*
Kate Dehoff, *Corporate Secretary*
**EMP:** 354 **EST:** 2009
**SQ FT:** 23,000
**SALES (est):** 1.03MM
**SALES (corp-wide):** 1.03MM **Publicly Held**
**Web:** www.jobyaviation.com
**SIC:** 3721 Aircraft

### (P-13674)
### JVR SHEETMETAL FABRICATION INC
Also Called: Talsco
7101 Patterson Dr, Garden Grove (92841-1415)
**PHONE**.................714 841-2464
Jose Castaneda, *CEO*
**EMP:** 33 **EST:** 2003
**SQ FT:** 1,000
**SALES (est):** 4.58MM **Privately Held**
**Web:** www.talsco.com
**SIC:** 3721 Aircraft

### (P-13675)
### LEARJET INC
16750 Schoenborn St, North Hills (91343-6108)
**PHONE**.................818 894-8241
Tonya Sudduth, *Brnch Mgr*
**EMP:** 28
**SALES (corp-wide):** 8.05B **Privately Held**
**Web:** www.bombardier.com
**SIC:** 3721 Aircraft
**HQ:** Learjet Inc.
1 Learjet Way
Wichita KS 67209
316 946-2000

### (P-13676)
### LIGHT COMPOSITES INC
12170 Paine Pl, Poway (92064-7153)
**PHONE**.................619 339-0638
Ryan Hosmer, *CEO*
**EMP:** 35 **EST:** 2016
**SALES (est):** 5.5MM **Privately Held**
**Web:** www.lightcomposites.net
**SIC:** 3721 3841 3624 Aircraft; Surgical and medical instruments; Carbon and graphite products

### (P-13677)
### LOCKHEED MARTIN CORPORATION
Also Called: Lockheed Martin
669 Mary Evelyn Dr, San Jose (95123-5520)
**PHONE**.................408 761-1276
**EMP:** 430
**Web:** www.lockheedmartin.com
**SIC:** 3721 Aircraft
**PA:** Lockheed Martin Corporation
6801 Rockledge Dr

### (P-13678)
### LOCKHEED MARTIN CORPORATION
Also Called: Lockheed Martin
2655 S Macarthur Dr, Tracy (95376-8188)
**PHONE**.................408 756-3008
**EMP:** 430
**Web:** www.lockheedmartin.com
**SIC:** 3721 Aircraft
**PA:** Lockheed Martin Corporation
6801 Rockledge Dr

### (P-13679)
### MADN AIRCRAFT HINGE
26911 Ruether Ave Ste Q, Santa Clarita (91351-6513)
**PHONE**.................661 257-3430
Aroosh Shahbazian, *CEO*
**EMP:** 45 **EST:** 2020
**SALES (est):** 554.47K **Privately Held**
**Web:** www.madnaircrafthinge.com
**SIC:** 3721 3728 Aircraft; Aircraft parts and equipment, nec

### (P-13680)
### NORTHROP GRUMMAN SYSTEMS CORP
Also Called: Air Combat Systems
3520 E Avenue M, Palmdale (93550-7401)
**PHONE**.................661 272-7000
David G Hogarth, *Mgr*
**EMP:** 300
**Web:** www.northropgrumman.com
**SIC:** 3721 3812 3761 Aircraft; Search and navigation equipment; Guided missiles and space vehicles
**HQ:** Northrop Grumman Systems Corporation
2980 Fairview Park Dr
Falls Church VA 22042
703 280-2900

### (P-13681)
### NORTHROP GRUMMAN SYSTEMS CORP
Also Called: Northrop Grumman Mar Systems
401 E Hendy Ave Ms 33-3, Sunnyvale (94086-5100)
P.O. Box 3499 (94088-3499)
**PHONE**.................408 735-3011
J Hupton, *Brnch Mgr*
**EMP:** 554
**Web:** www.northropgrumman.com
**SIC:** 3721 3519 3511 Aircraft; Internal combustion engines, nec; Turbines and turbine generator sets
**HQ:** Northrop Grumman Systems Corporation
2980 Fairview Park Dr
Falls Church VA 22042
703 280-2900

### (P-13682)
### NORTHROP GRUMMAN SYSTEMS CORP
Also Called: Aerospace Systems
1 Space Park Blvd, Redondo Beach (90278-1071)
**PHONE**.................310 812-1089
Gary Ervin, *Brnch Mgr*
**EMP:** 305
**Web:** www.northropgrumman.com
**SIC:** 3721 3761 3728 3812 Airplanes, fixed or rotary wing; Guided missiles, complete; Fuselage assembly, aircraft; Inertial guidance systems
**HQ:** Northrop Grumman Systems Corporation
2980 Fairview Park Dr
Falls Church VA 22042
703 280-2900

### (P-13683)
### NORTHROP GRUMMAN SYSTEMS CORP
Northrop Grumman
1 Space Park Blvd # D1 1024, Redondo Beach (90278-1071)
**PHONE**.................310 812-4321
Bruce Gaines, *Prin*
**EMP:** 305
**Web:** www.northropgrumman.com
**SIC:** 3721 3761 3728 Airplanes, fixed or rotary wing; Guided missiles, complete; Fuselage assembly, aircraft
**HQ:** Northrop Grumman Systems Corporation
2980 Fairview Park Dr
Falls Church VA 22042
703 280-2900

### (P-13684)
### OVERAIR INC
3001 S Susan St, Santa Ana (92704-6434)
**PHONE**.................949 503-7503
Benjamin Tigner, *CEO*
Valerie Manning, *CCO**
**EMP:** 30 **EST:** 2019
**SALES (est):** 11.28MM **Privately Held**
**Web:** www.overair.com
**SIC:** 3721 Research and development on aircraft by the manufacturer

### (P-13685)
### PIVOTAL AERO LLC
1029 Corporation Way, Palo Alto (94303-4305)
**PHONE**.................404 641-9131
Kenneth Karklin, *CEO*
Marcus Leng, *Managing Member**
**EMP:** 100 **EST:** 2016
**SALES (est):** 5.14MM **Privately Held**
**Web:** www.pivotal.aero
**SIC:** 3721 Aircraft

### (P-13686)
### PTERODYNAMICS INC
Also Called: Pterodynamics
14165 Huron Ct, Moorpark (93021-3562)
**PHONE**.................719 257-3103
Matthew Graczyk, *CEO*
Matthew R Graczyk, *CEO*
**EMP:** 16 **EST:** 2017
**SALES (est):** 4.68MM **Privately Held**
**Web:** www.pterodynamics.com
**SIC:** 3721 Aircraft

### (P-13687)
### QUALITY TECH MFG INC
170 W Mindanao St, Bloomington (92316-2946)
**PHONE**.................909 465-9565
Rudolph A Gutierrez, *Pr*
Camilio Gutierrez, **
**EMP:** 37 **EST:** 1996
**SQ FT:** 18,000
**SALES (est):** 4.63MM **Privately Held**
**Web:** www.qualitytechmfg.com
**SIC:** 3721 Aircraft

### (P-13688)
### SCALED COMPOSITES LLC
1624 Flight Line, Mojave (93501-1663)
**PHONE**.................661 824-4541
Greg Morris, *Pr*
Mark Taylor, *VP*
Jennifer Santiago, *Ex VP*
Ben Diachun, *VP*
Jason Kelley, *VP*
**EMP:** 500 **EST:** 2000
**SQ FT:** 160,000
**SALES (est):** 98.52MM **Publicly Held**
**Web:** www.scaled.com
**SIC:** 3721 3999 8711 Aircraft; Models, except toy; Aviation and/or aeronautical engineering

HQ: Northrop Grumman Systems
Corporation
2980 Fairview Park Dr
Falls Church VA 22042
703 280-2900

**(P-13689)**
**SHIELD AI INC (PA)**
600 W Broadway Ste 250, San Diego
(92101-3357)
PHONE.............................619 719-5740
Brandon Tseng, *Ch Bd*
Ryan Tseng, *CEO*
Jim Carlson, *Sec*
Kingsley Afemikhe, *CFO*
Thomas Tull, *Dir*
**EMP:** 601 **EST:** 2015
**SQ FT:** 20,000
**SALES (est):** 90.64MM
**SALES (corp-wide):** 90.64MM **Privately Held**
Web: www.shield.ai
**SIC: 3721** Aircraft

**(P-13690)**
**SKYDIO INC (PA)**
3000 Clearview Way Bldg E, San Mateo
(94402-3710)
PHONE.............................855 463-5902
Adam P Bry, *CEO*
Matthew Donahoe, *
Abraham Bachrach, *
Benjamin Perry, *
**EMP:** 75 **EST:** 2014
**SALES (est):** 103.56MM
**SALES (corp-wide):** 103.56MM **Privately Held**
Web: www.skydio.com
**SIC: 3721** Nonmotorized and lighter-than-air aircraft

**(P-13691)**
**SOARING AMERICA CORPORATION**
Also Called: Mooney International
8354 Kimball Ave # F360, Chino
(91708-9267)
PHONE.............................909 270-2628
Cheng-yuan Jerry Chen, *CEO*
Albert Li, *CFO*
**EMP:** 45 **EST:** 2012
**SALES (est):** 3.02MM **Privately Held**
**SIC: 3721 3728** Research and development on aircraft by the manufacturer; R and D by manuf., aircraft parts and auxiliary equipment

**(P-13692)**
**SPACE EXPLORATION TECH CORP**
731 Kelp Rd Slc-4, Vandenberg Afb
(93437)
PHONE.............................310 848-4410
**EMP:** 157
**SALES (corp-wide):** 2.07B **Privately Held**
Web: www.spacex.com
**SIC: 3721** Aircraft
PA: Space Exploration Technologies Corp.
1 Rocket Rd
310 363-6000

**(P-13693)**
**SPORT KITES INC**
Also Called: Wills Wing
500 W Blueridge Ave, Orange
(92865-4206)
PHONE.............................714 998-6359
▲ **EMP:** 18 **EST:** 1973
**SQ FT:** 16,000
**SALES (est):** 2.52MM **Privately Held**

**SIC: 3721** Hang gliders

**(P-13694)**
**SWIFT AUTONOMY INC**
1141 A Via Callejon, San Clemente
(92673-6230)
PHONE.............................800 547-9438
Richard Heise, *CEO*
**EMP:** 25 **EST:** 2019
**SALES (est):** 2.13MM **Privately Held**
Web: www.swiftautonomy.com
**SIC: 3721** Aircraft

**(P-13695)**
**TEXTRON AVIATION INC**
Also Called: Cessna Scrmnto Ctation Svc Ctr
5850 Citation Way, Sacramento
(95837-1105)
PHONE.............................916 929-5656
Thomas Defoe, *Mgr*
**EMP:** 231
**SALES (corp-wide):** 12.87B **Publicly Held**
Web: www.txtav.com
**SIC: 3721** Aircraft
HQ: Textron Aviation Inc.
1 Cessna Blvd
Wichita KS 67215
316 517-6000

**(P-13696)**
**TRI MODELS INC**
5191 Oceanus Dr, Huntington Beach
(92649-1026)
PHONE.............................714 896-0823
Prince A Herzog Senior, *CEO*
Jeff Herzog, *
▲ **EMP:** 82 **EST:** 1972
**SALES (est):** 14.85MM **Privately Held**
Web: www.trimodels.com
**SIC: 3721** Airplanes, fixed or rotary wing

**(P-13697)**
**WISK AERO LLC (PA)**
2700 Broderick Way, Mountain View
(94043-1108)
PHONE.............................650 641-0920
Gary Gysin, *CEO*
Ricky Robinson, *
Yuichi Sakashita, *
Tyler Painter, *
**EMP:** 269 **EST:** 2019
**SALES (est):** 54.37MM
**SALES (corp-wide):** 54.37MM **Privately Held**
Web: www.wisk.aero
**SIC: 3721** Aircraft

**(P-13698)**
**WORLDWIDE AEROS CORP**
3971 Fredonia Dr, Los Angeles
(90068-1213)
PHONE.............................818 344-3999
Igor Pasternak, *CEO*
▲ **EMP:** 82 **EST:** 1987
**SALES (est):** 5.27MM **Privately Held**
Web: www.aeroscraft.com
**SIC: 3721 8711** Airships; Aviation and/or aeronautical engineering

## 3724 Aircraft Engines And Engine Parts

**(P-13699)**
**AC&A ENTERPRISES LLC (HQ)**
25671 Commercentre Dr, Lake Forest
(92630-8801)
PHONE.............................949 716-3511
Justin Uchida, *CEO*

Justin Schultz, *
▲ **EMP:** 34 **EST:** 2004
**SALES (est):** 25.48MM
**SALES (corp-wide):** 189.21MM **Privately Held**
Web: www.acamfg.com
**SIC: 3724 3511** Aircraft engines and engine parts; Turbines and turbine generator sets
PA: Applied Composites Holdings, Llc
25692 Atlantic Ocean Dr
949 716-3511

**(P-13700)**
**ACCURATE GRINDING AND MFG CORP**
807 E Parkridge Ave, Corona (92879-6609)
PHONE.............................951 479-0909
Douglas Nilsen, *CEO*
Hans J Nilsen, *
David Nilsen, *
▲ **EMP:** 35 **EST:** 1950
**SQ FT:** 15,000
**SALES (est):** 4.76MM **Privately Held**
Web: www.accuratefishing.com
**SIC: 3724 3812** Aircraft engines and engine parts; Search and navigation equipment

**(P-13701)**
**ADVANCED GRUND SYSTEMS ENGRG L (HQ)**
Also Called: Agse
10805 Painter Ave, Santa Fe Springs
(90670-4526)
PHONE.............................562 906-9300
Diane Henderson, *CEO*
David Chetwood, *
▲ **EMP:** 40 **EST:** 1973
**SALES (est):** 23.69MM
**SALES (corp-wide):** 24.58MM **Privately Held**
Web: www.agsecorp.com
**SIC: 3724** Aircraft engines and engine parts
PA: Westmont Industries Llc
10805 Painter Ave Uppr
562 944-6137

**(P-13702)**
**AEROJET ROCKETDYNE DE INC**
6633 Canoga Ave, Canoga Park
(91303-2703)
P.O. Box 7922 (91309-7922)
PHONE.............................818 586-1000
Jerry Jackson, *Brnch Mgr*
**EMP:** 359
**SALES (corp-wide):** 19.42B **Publicly Held**
Web: www.l3harris.com
**SIC: 3724** Aircraft engines and engine parts
HQ: Inc Aerojet Rocketdyne Of De
8900 De Soto Ave
Canoga Park CA 91304
818 586-1000

**(P-13703)**
**AMERICAN MTAL MFG RESOURCE INC**
Also Called: American Metal
1989 W Holt Ave, Pomona (91768-3352)
PHONE.............................909 620-4500
Vikas Sharma, *Pr*
**EMP:** 25 **EST:** 2007
**SQ FT:** 6,000
**SALES (est):** 2.38MM **Privately Held**
Web: www.ammrinc.com
**SIC: 3724 3999** Aircraft engines and engine parts; Barber and beauty shop equipment

**(P-13704)**
**CHROMALLOY COMPONENT SVCS INC**

Precision Component Tech
7007 Consolidated Way, San Diego
(92121-2604)
PHONE.............................858 877-2800
Nat Love, *Genl Mgr*
**EMP:** 45
**SALES (corp-wide):** 517.74MM **Privately Held**
Web: www.chromalloy.com
**SIC: 3724** Aircraft engines and engine parts
HQ: Chromalloy Component Services, Inc.
303 Industrial Park Rd
San Antonio TX 78226
210 331-2300

**(P-13705)**
**CHROMALLOY GAS TURBINE LLC**
Also Called: Chromalloy Southwest
1749 Stergios Rd Ste 2, Calexico
(92231-9657)
PHONE.............................760 768-3723
**EMP:** 88
**SALES (corp-wide):** 517.74MM **Privately Held**
Web: www.chromalloy.com
**SIC: 3724** Aircraft engines and engine parts
HQ: Chromalloy Gas Turbine Llc
4100 Rca Blvd
Palm Beach Gardens FL 33410
561 935-3571

**(P-13706)**
**DUCOMMUN AEROSTRUCTURES INC (HQ)**
600 Anton Blvd Ste 1100, Costa Mesa
(92626-7100)
PHONE.............................310 380-5390
Anthony Reardon, *CEO*
◆ **EMP:** 450 **EST:** 1949
**SQ FT:** 300,000
**SALES (est):** 434.48MM
**SALES (corp-wide):** 756.99MM **Publicly Held**
Web: www.ducommun.com
**SIC: 3724 3812 3728** Aircraft engines and engine parts; Search and navigation equipment; Aircraft parts and equipment, nec
PA: Ducommun Incorporated
600 Anton Blvd Ste 1100
657 335-3665

**(P-13707)**
**DUCOMMUN AEROSTRUCTURES INC**
1885 N Batavia St, Orange (92865-4105)
PHONE.............................714 637-4401
Kent T Christensen, *Brnch Mgr*
**EMP:** 108
**SALES (corp-wide):** 756.99MM **Publicly Held**
Web: www.ducommun.com
**SIC: 3724 3812 3728** Aircraft engines and engine parts; Search and navigation equipment; Aircraft parts and equipment, nec
HQ: Ducommun Aerostructures, Inc.
600 Anton Blvd Ste 1100
Costa Mesa CA 92626
310 380-5390

**(P-13708)**
**GARRETT TRANSPORTATION I INC (HQ)**
2525 W 190th St, Torrance (90504-6002)
PHONE.............................973 455-2000
Darius Adamczyk, *CEO*
**EMP:** 26 **EST:** 2018
**SALES (est):** 11.76MM

# 3724 - Aircraft Engines And Engine Parts (P-13709)

**SALES (corp-wide):** 3.89B **Privately Held**
**Web:** www.garrettmotion.com
**SIC:** 3724 Aircraft engines and engine parts
**PA:** Garrett Motion Inc.
  47548 Halyard Dr
  734 392-5500

## (P-13709)
### GKN AEROSPACE CHEM-TRONICS INC (DH)
Also Called: Chem-Tronics
1150 W Bradley Ave, El Cajon (92020-1504)
P.O. Box 1604 (92020)
**PHONE**.................................619 258-5000
James Wilson, *CEO*
Mark Fowler, *CFO*
Warren Fernandez, *Sec*
▲ **EMP:** 648 **EST:** 1953
**SQ FT:** 400,000
**SALES (est):** 194.63MM
**SALES (corp-wide):** 4.18B **Privately Held**
**Web:** www.gknaerospace.com
**SIC:** 3724 7699 Aircraft engines and engine parts; Aircraft and heavy equipment repair services
**HQ:** Gkn Limited
  11th Floor, The Colmore Building
  Birmingham W MIDLANDS B4 6A
  121 210-9800

## (P-13710)
### HONEYWELL INTERNATIONAL INC
Also Called: Honeywell
2525 W 190th St, Torrance (90504-6002)
**PHONE**.................................310 323-9500
Ken Defusco, *Brnch Mgr*
**EMP:** 1000
**SALES (corp-wide):** 36.66B **Publicly Held**
**Web:** www.honeywell.com
**SIC:** 3724 Aircraft engines and engine parts
**PA:** Honeywell International Inc.
  855 S Mint St
  704 627-6200

## (P-13711)
### HONEYWELL INTERNATIONAL INC
Also Called: Honeywell
233 Paulin Ave Box 8500, Calexico (92231-2615)
**PHONE**.................................760 312-5300
William Bouscher, *Prin*
**EMP:** 17
**SALES (corp-wide):** 36.66B **Publicly Held**
**Web:** www.honeywell.com
**SIC:** 3724 Aircraft engines and engine parts
**PA:** Honeywell International Inc.
  855 S Mint St
  704 627-6200

## (P-13712)
### HONEYWELL SAFETY PDTS USA INC
7828 Waterville Rd, San Diego (92154-8205)
**PHONE**.................................619 661-8383
Dave M Cote, *CEO*
**EMP:** 110
**SALES (corp-wide):** 36.66B **Publicly Held**
**Web:** www.honeywell.com
**SIC:** 3724 Aircraft engines and engine parts
**HQ:** Honeywell Safety Products Usa, Inc.
  855 S Mint St
  Charlotte NC 28202
  800 430-5490

## (P-13713)
### INTERNATIONAL WIND INC (PA)
137 N Joy St, Corona (92879-1321)
**PHONE**.................................562 240-3963
Cory Arendt, *Pr*
**EMP:** 49 **EST:** 2013
**SALES (est):** 7.67MM
**SALES (corp-wide):** 7.67MM **Privately Held**
**Web:** www.international-wind.com
**SIC:** 3724 8711 8742 Turbines, aircraft type; Engineering services; Management consulting services

## (P-13714)
### IRISH INTERNATIONAL
5511 Skylab Rd, Huntington Beach (92647)
**PHONE**.................................949 559-0930
Tom Mcfarland, *CEO*
Antonio Perez, *Corporate Secretary**
Jude Dozor, **
Mike Melancon, **
▲ **EMP:** 250 **EST:** 2015
**SQ FT:** 80,000
**SALES (est):** 9.35MM **Privately Held**
**Web:** www.encoregroup.aero
**SIC:** 3724 Aircraft engines and engine parts

## (P-13715)
### LOGISTICAL SUPPORT LLC
Also Called: RTC Aerospace
20409 Prairie St, Chatsworth (91311-6029)
**PHONE**.................................818 341-3344
**EMP:** 125 **EST:** 1997
**SQ FT:** 14,600
**SALES (est):** 1.83MM **Privately Held**
**Web:** www.rtcaerospace.com
**SIC:** 3724 Aircraft engines and engine parts

## (P-13716)
### MARTON PRECISION MFG LLC
1365 S Acacia Ave, Fullerton (92831-5315)
**PHONE**.................................714 808-6523
Daniel J Marton, *Pr*
Mary Marton, **
**EMP:** 47 **EST:** 1986
**SQ FT:** 20,000
**SALES (est):** 13.8MM **Privately Held**
**Web:** www.martoninc.com
**SIC:** 3724 3599 3827 Aircraft engines and engine parts; Machine and other job shop work; Optical instruments and apparatus

## (P-13717)
### PARKER-HANNIFIN CORPORATION
Fluid Systems Division
16666 Von Karman Ave, Irvine (92606-4997)
**PHONE**.................................949 833-3000
Matthew Stafford, *Mgr*
**EMP:** 246
**SALES (corp-wide):** 19.93B **Publicly Held**
**Web:** www.parker.com
**SIC:** 3724 3728 Aircraft engines and engine parts; Aircraft parts and equipment, nec
**PA:** Parker-Hannifin Corporation
  6035 Parkland Blvd
  216 896-3000

## (P-13718)
### PRATT & WHITNEY ENG SVCS INC
Also Called: Pratt Whitney Engine Services
11190 Valley View St, Cypress (90630-5231)
**PHONE**.................................714 373-0110
Oliver Ho, *Mgr*
**EMP:** 2381
**SALES (corp-wide):** 68.92B **Publicly Held**
**Web:** www.prattwhitney.com
**SIC:** 3724 Aircraft engines and engine parts
**HQ:** Pratt & Whitney Engine Services, Inc.
  1525 Midway Park Rd
  Bridgeport WV 26330
  304 842-5421

## (P-13719)
### PRINCETON TOOL INC
Also Called: Paragon Precision
25620 Rye Canyon Rd Ste A, Valencia (91355-1139)
**PHONE**.................................661 257-1380
Kenneth Bevington Iii, *CEO*
**EMP:** 18
**SALES (corp-wide):** 20.3MM **Privately Held**
**Web:** www.princetontool.com
**SIC:** 3724 Aircraft engines and engine parts
**PA:** Princeton Tool, Inc.
  7830 Division Dr
  440 290-8666

## (P-13720)
### ROLLS-ROYCE ENGINE SERVICES-OAKLAND INC
Also Called: Rolls Royce
7200 Earhart Rd, Oakland (94621-4511)
P.O. Box 6069 (94603-0069)
**PHONE**.................................510 635-1500
◆ **EMP:** 500
**SIC:** 3724 3519 Aircraft engines and engine parts; Jet propulsion engines

## (P-13721)
### RTX CORPORATION
Also Called: Chemical Systems Div
600 Metcalf Rd, San Jose (95138-9601)
**PHONE**.................................408 779-9121
Greg Fatobic, *Brnch Mgr*
**EMP:** 36
**SALES (corp-wide):** 68.92B **Publicly Held**
**Web:** www.rtx.com
**SIC:** 3724 3769 3489 Rocket motors, aircraft; Space vehicle equipment, nec; Ordnance and accessories, nec
**PA:** Rtx Corporation
  1000 Wilson Blvd
  781 522-3000

## (P-13722)
### SAFRAN PWR UNITS SAN DIEGO LLC
Also Called: Safran Power Units
4255 Ruffin Rd Ste 100, San Diego (92123-1247)
**PHONE**.................................858 223-2228
**EMP:** 70 **EST:** 2015
**SQ FT:** 22,000
**SALES (est):** 9.29MM
**SALES (corp-wide):** 940.23MM **Privately Held**
**Web:** www.melomano.us
**SIC:** 3724 Research and development on aircraft engines and parts
**HQ:** Safran Power Units
  8 Che Du Pont De Rupe
  Toulouse 31200
  561375500

## (P-13723)
### THERMAL STRUCTURES INC (DH)
2362 Railroad St, Corona (92878)
**PHONE**.................................951 736-9911
Vaughn Barnes, *Pr*
▲ **EMP:** 270 **EST:** 1952
**SQ FT:** 175,000
**SALES (est):** 31.98MM **Publicly Held**
**Web:** www.thermalstructures.com
**SIC:** 3724 Aircraft engines and engine parts
**HQ:** Heico Aerospace Holdings Corp.
  3000 Taft St
  Hollywood FL 33021
  954 987-4000

## (P-13724)
### THERMAL STRUCTURES INC
2380 Railroad St, Corona (92878-5471)
**PHONE**.................................951 256-8051
**EMP:** 20
**Web:** www.thermalstructures.com
**SIC:** 3724 Aircraft engines and engine parts
**HQ:** Thermal Structures, Inc.
  2362 Railroad St
  Corona CA 92878
  951 736-9911

## (P-13725)
### TURBINE ENG CMPNENTS TECH CORP
Also Called: Tect Aerospace
1211 Old Albany Road, San Francisco (94103)
**PHONE**.................................415 626-2000
**EMP:** 135
**SALES (corp-wide):** 48.64MM **Privately Held**
**SIC:** 3724 Turbines, aircraft type
**PA:** Turbine Engine Components Technologies Corporation
  1211 Old Albany Rd
  229 228-2600

## (P-13726)
### VERTECHS ENTERPRISES INC
San Diego Welding and Forming
400 Raleigh Ave, El Cajon (92020)
**PHONE**.................................858 578-3900
Geosef Straza, *Pr*
**EMP:** 17
**Web:** www.vertechsusa.com
**SIC:** 3724 3728 Airfoils, aircraft engine; Bodies, aircraft
**PA:** Vertechs Enterprises, Inc.
  1071 Industrial Pl

## (P-13727)
### VIP MANUFACTURING & ENGRG CORP
Also Called: VIP Mfg & Engr
1084 Martin Ave, Santa Clara (95050-2609)
P.O. Box 2314 (95031-2314)
**PHONE**.................................408 727-6545
L A Vargo Junior, *Pr*
Emma Vargo, *Sec*
**EMP:** 76 **EST:** 1963
**SQ FT:** 10,500
**SALES (est):** 809.13K **Privately Held**
**SIC:** 3724 3451 3599 Aircraft engines and engine parts; Screw machine products; Machine shop, jobbing and repair

## (P-13728)
### WKF (FRIEDMAN ENTERPRISES INC (PA)
Also Called: Eff Aero
2334 Stagecoach Rd Ste B, Stockton (95215-7939)
**PHONE**.................................925 673-9100
Wayne Friedman, *Pr*
**EMP:** 19 **EST:** 2011
**SALES (est):** 1.51MM
**SALES (corp-wide):** 1.51MM **Privately Held**
**SIC:** 3724 Aircraft engines and engine parts

## 3728 Aircraft Parts And Equipment, Nec

**(P-13729)**
**A & A AEROSPACE INC**
1987 W 16th St, Long Beach (90813-1136)
PHONE.............................562 901-6803
Arnie Puentes, Pr
EMP: 15
Web: www.aaaerospace.net
SIC: 3728 Aircraft parts and equipment, nec
PA: A & A Aerospace, Inc.
   13649 Pumice St

**(P-13730)**
**A-INFO INC**
60 Tesla, Irvine (92618-4603)
PHONE.............................949 346-7326
Linda Williams, Asst Mgr
EMP: 35 EST: 2017
SALES (est): 2.5MM Privately Held
Web: www.ainfoinc.com
SIC: 3728 3812 5049 Aircraft parts and equipment, nec; Antennas, radar or communications; Analytical instruments

**(P-13731)**
**ACE CLEARWATER ENTERPRISES INC (PA)**
19815 Magellan Dr, Torrance (90502-1107)
PHONE.............................310 323-2140
James D Dodson, Pr
Kellie Johnson, *
EMP: 100 EST: 1961
SALES (est): 19.32MM
SALES (corp-wide): 19.32MM Privately Held
Web: www.aceclearwater.com
SIC: 3728 3544 7692 3812 Aircraft parts and equipment, nec; Special dies, tools, jigs, and fixtures; Welding repair; Search and navigation equipment

**(P-13732)**
**ACROMIL LLC (HQ)**
18421 Railroad St, City Of Industry (91748-1233)
PHONE.............................626 964-2522
Gerald A Niznick, *
Jon Konheim, *
EMP: 144 EST: 2015
SQ FT: 96,000
SALES (est): 44.93MM
SALES (corp-wide): 44.93MM Privately Held
Web: www.acromil.com
SIC: 3728 Aircraft body and wing assemblies and parts
PA: Acromil Corporation
   18421 Railroad St
   626 964-2522

**(P-13733)**
**ACROMIL LLC**
1168 Sherborn St, Corona (92879-2089)
PHONE.............................951 808-9929
David Nguyen, Pr
EMP: 60
SALES (corp-wide): 44.93MM Privately Held
Web: www.acromil.com
SIC: 3728 Aircraft body and wing assemblies and parts
HQ: Acromil, Llc
   18421 Railroad St
   City Of Industry CA 91748
   626 964-2522

**(P-13734)**
**ACROMIL CORPORATION (PA)**
18421 Railroad St, City Of Industry (91748-1281)
PHONE.............................626 964-2522
Gerald A Niznick, Pr
Jeanne Aguilera, CFO
Jon Konheim, COO
◆ EMP: 104 EST: 1961
SQ FT: 100,000
SALES (est): 44.93MM
SALES (corp-wide): 44.93MM Privately Held
Web: www.acromil.com
SIC: 3728 Aircraft body and wing assemblies and parts

**(P-13735)**
**ACUFAST AIRCRAFT PRODUCTS INC**
12445 Gladstone Ave, Sylmar (91342-5321)
PHONE.............................818 365-7077
Art Dovlatian, Pr
Jaime Salazar, *
EMP: 40 EST: 2006
SALES (est): 9.4MM Privately Held
Web: www.acufastap.com
SIC: 3728 Aircraft parts and equipment, nec

**(P-13736)**
**ADAMS RITE AEROSPACE INC (DH)**
4141 N Palm St, Fullerton (92835-1025)
PHONE.............................714 278-6500
John Schaefer, Pr
EMP: 71 EST: 1973
SQ FT: 100,000
SALES (est): 41.7MM
SALES (corp-wide): 7.94B Publicly Held
Web: www.araero.com
SIC: 3728 Aircraft parts and equipment, nec
HQ: Transdigm, Inc.
   1350 Euclid Ave
   Cleveland OH 44115

**(P-13737)**
**ADAPTIVE AEROSPACE CORPORATION**
501 Bailey Ave, Tehachapi (93561-9012)
PHONE.............................661 300-0616
Bill Mccune, CEO
EMP: 25 EST: 2001
SALES (est): 3.45MM Privately Held
Web: www.adapt.aero
SIC: 3728 Aircraft parts and equipment, nec

**(P-13738)**
**ADEPT FASTENERS INC (PA)**
27949 Hancock Pkwy, Valencia (91355-4116)
P.O. Box 579 (91310)
PHONE.............................661 257-6600
Gary Young, Pr
Don List, *
EMP: 106 EST: 2001
SQ FT: 40,000
SALES (est): 35.47MM
SALES (corp-wide): 35.47MM Privately Held
Web: www.adeptfasteners.com
SIC: 3728 Aircraft parts and equipment, nec

**(P-13739)**
**ADVANCED DIGITAL MFG LLC**
Also Called: ADM Works
1343 E Wilshire Ave, Santa Ana (92705-4420)
PHONE.............................714 245-0536
Javier Valdiveso, Pr
Javier J Valdiveso, *
Jimmy Garcia, *
EMP: 27 EST: 2003
SALES (est): 2.56MM Privately Held
Web: www.adm-works.com
SIC: 3728 R and D by manuf., aircraft parts and auxiliary equipment

**(P-13740)**
**ADVANCED MTLS JOINING CORP (PA)**
Also Called: Advanced Technology Co
2858 E Walnut St, Pasadena (91107-3755)
PHONE.............................626 449-2696
Jean L De Silvestri, Pr
Mohammed Islam, *
EMP: 41 EST: 1971
SQ FT: 23,000
SALES (est): 9.37MM
SALES (corp-wide): 9.37MM Privately Held
Web: www.at-co.com
SIC: 3728 3724 Aircraft parts and equipment, nec; Aircraft engines and engine parts

**(P-13741)**
**AEG INDUSTRIES INC**
1219 Briggs Ave, Santa Rosa (95401-4761)
PHONE.............................707 575-0697
Peggy Mcilnay Moe, Pr
Peg Mcilnay-moe, Pr
Dennis Mcilnay Moe, VP
EMP: 22 EST: 1991
SQ FT: 6,500
SALES (est): 2.18MM Privately Held
Web: www.aegindustries.com
SIC: 3728 Aircraft parts and equipment, nec

**(P-13742)**
**AERO ENGINEERING & MFG CO LLC**
Also Called: Aero Engineering
28217 Avenue Crocker, Valencia (91355-1249)
PHONE.............................661 295-0875
Dennis L Junker, CEO
Lance R Junker, *
Richard Jucksch, *
▼ EMP: 55 EST: 1948
SQ FT: 21,000
SALES (est): 9.59MM Privately Held
Web: www.aeroeng.com
SIC: 3728 5088 Aircraft assemblies, subassemblies, and parts, nec; Aircraft and parts, nec

**(P-13743)**
**AERO PACIFIC CORPORATION**
Also Called: Merco Manufacturing Co
20445 E Walnut Dr N, Walnut (91789-2918)
PHONE.............................714 961-9200
Mark Heasley, Pr
EMP: 130 EST: 1961
SALES (est): 21.68MM Privately Held
Web: www.alignprecision.com
SIC: 3728 Aircraft parts and equipment, nec

**(P-13744)**
**AERO SENSE INC**
26074 Avenue Hall Ste 18, Valencia (91355-3445)
PHONE.............................661 257-1608
Sohail Tabrizi, Pr
Ro Missaghian, VP Fin
▲ EMP: 15 EST: 2007
SALES (est): 2.62MM Privately Held
Web: www.aerosenseinc.com

SIC: 3728 Aircraft parts and equipment, nec

**(P-13745)**
**AERO-CRAFT HYDRAULICS INC**
392 N Smith Ave, Corona (92878-4371)
PHONE.............................951 736-4690
Rod Guzman Senior, Pr
Brad Davidson, *
Cathy Norris, *
Suzane Treneer, *
EMP: 43 EST: 1963
SQ FT: 16,500
SALES (est): 6.83MM Privately Held
Web: www.aero-craft.com
SIC: 3728 5084 7699 Aircraft body and wing assemblies and parts; Hydraulic systems equipment and supplies; Aircraft and heavy equipment repair services

**(P-13746)**
**AERO-NASCH AVIATION INC**
6849 Hayvenhurst Ave, Van Nuys (91406-4718)
PHONE.............................818 786-5480
William Onasch, CEO
EMP: 16 EST: 2000
SALES (est): 2.33MM Privately Held
Web: www.aeronasch.com
SIC: 3728 Aircraft parts and equipment, nec

**(P-13747)**
**AEROJET ROCKETDYNE INC**
Also Called: Rocket Shop
1180 Iron Point Rd Ste 350, Folsom (95630-8321)
PHONE.............................916 355-4000
Craig Halterman, Prin
EMP: 150
SALES (corp-wide): 19.42B Publicly Held
Web: www.l3harris.com
SIC: 3728 Aircraft body and wing assemblies and parts
HQ: Aerojet Rocketdyne, Inc.
   2001 Aerojet Rd
   Rancho Cordova CA 95742
   916 355-4000

**(P-13748)**
**AEROMETALS INC**
3920 Sandstone Dr, El Dorado Hills (95762-9652)
PHONE.............................916 939-6888
Lorie Symon, CEO
Lorie Symon, Pr
◆ EMP: 175 EST: 1982
SQ FT: 150,000
SALES (est): 34.57MM Privately Held
Web: www.aerometals.aero
SIC: 3728 Aircraft parts and equipment, nec

**(P-13749)**
**AEROSHEAR AVIATION SVCS INC (PA)**
7701 Woodley Ave 200, Van Nuys (91406-1732)
PHONE.............................818 779-1650
Lonnie Paschal, CEO
Christine Paschal, *
Ryan Hogan, *
EMP: 32 EST: 1996
SQ FT: 42,000
SALES (est): 4.92MM
SALES (corp-wide): 4.92MM Privately Held
Web: www.aeroshearaviation.com
SIC: 3728 3599 1799 Aircraft parts and equipment, nec; Machine shop, jobbing and repair; Welding on site

## 3728 - Aircraft Parts And Equipment, Nec (P-13750)

**(P-13750)**
**AEROSPACE COMPOSITE PRODUCTS (PA)**
Also Called: Acp Composites
78 Lindbergh Ave, Livermore (94551-9503)
PHONE.................925 443-5900
George William Sparr, *Pr*
Barbara Sparr, *Sec*
**EMP:** 19 **EST:** 2003
**SALES (est):** 8.99MM
**SALES (corp-wide):** 8.99MM **Privately Held**
Web: www.acpcomposites.com
**SIC: 3728** 5961 3624  Aircraft assemblies, subassemblies, and parts; Mail order house, nec; Carbon and graphite products

**(P-13751)**
**AEROSPACE DRIVEN TECH INC**
Also Called: Driven Technologies
2807 Catherine Way, Santa Ana (92705-5708)
PHONE.................949 553-1606
Kathleen F Freeman, *CEO*
Roger H Gottfried, *Pr*
**EMP:** 18 **EST:** 2002
**SQ FT:** 10,000
**SALES (est):** 5.77MM **Privately Held**
Web: www.driven-technologies.com
**SIC: 3728**  Aircraft parts and equipment, nec

**(P-13752)**
**AEROSPACE DYNAMICS INTL INC**
25575 Rye Canyon Rd, Santa Clarita (91355-1108)
PHONE.................661 310-6986
**EMP:** 279
**SALES (corp-wide):** 364.48B **Publicly Held**
Web: www.pccaero.com
**SIC: 3728**  Aircraft parts and equipment, nec
HQ: Aerospace Dynamics International, Inc.
25540 Rye Canyon Rd
Valencia CA 91355

**(P-13753)**
**AEROSPACE DYNAMICS INTL INC (DH)**
Also Called: ADI
25540 Rye Canyon Rd, Valencia (91355-1169)
PHONE.................661 257-3535
Joseph I Snowden, *CEO*
◆ **EMP:** 171 **EST:** 1989
**SQ FT:** 250,000
**SALES (est):** 97.53MM
**SALES (corp-wide):** 364.48B **Publicly Held**
Web: www.pccaero.com
**SIC: 3728**  Aircraft parts and equipment, nec
HQ: Precision Castparts Corp.
5885 Meadows Rd Ste 620
Lake Oswego OR 97035
503 946-4800

**(P-13754)**
**AEROSPACE ENGINEERING LLC**
2141 S Standard Ave, Santa Ana (92707-3034)
PHONE.................714 641-5884
**EMP:** 31
Web: www.karman-sd.com
**SIC: 3728**  Aircraft parts and equipment, nec
PA: Aerospace Engineering, Llc
2632 Saturn St

**(P-13755)**
**AEROSPACE ENGINEERING LLC (PA)**
Also Called: AEC
2632 Saturn St, Brea (92821-6701)
PHONE.................714 996-8178
Mohammad Mahboubi, *Pr*
**EMP:** 89 **EST:** 2008
**SALES (est):** 27.29MM **Privately Held**
Web: www.karman-sd.com
**SIC: 3728** 3541 3599  Aircraft parts and equipment, nec; Numerically controlled metal cutting machine tools; Machine and other job shop work

**(P-13756)**
**AEROSPACE ENGRG SUPPORT CORP**
Also Called: J and L Industries
645 Hawaii St, El Segundo (90245-4814)
P.O. Box 999 (90245-0999)
PHONE.................310 297-4050
Asher Bartov, *CEO*
Abraham Wacht, *
**EMP:** 27 **EST:** 1987
**SQ FT:** 30,000
**SALES (est):** 3.83MM
**SALES (corp-wide):** 1.3B **Privately Held**
Web: www.aerospace.org
**SIC: 3728**  Aircraft parts and equipment, nec
PA: The Aerospace Corporation
14745 Lee Rd
310 336-5000

**(P-13757)**
**AEROSPACE PARTS HOLDINGS INC**
Also Called: Cadence Aerospace
3150 E Miraloma Ave, Anaheim (92806-1906)
PHONE.................949 877-3630
Olivier Jarrault, *CEO*
Ron Case, *
Don Devore, *
Mike Coburn, *
**EMP:** 1175 **EST:** 2012
**SALES (est):** 5.23MM **Privately Held**
Web: www.verusaerospace.com
**SIC: 3728**  Aircraft parts and equipment, nec

**(P-13758)**
**AEROSPACE SERVICE & CONTROLS**
28402 Livingston Ave, Valencia (91355-4172)
PHONE.................818 833-0088
Dave Mason, *Pr*
**EMP:** 15 **EST:** 2010
**SALES (est):** 757.61K **Privately Held**
Web: www.aschome.com
**SIC: 3728**  Aircraft parts and equipment, nec

**(P-13759)**
**AERWINS INC**
101 Jefferson Dr Fl 1, Menlo Park (94025-1114)
PHONE.................808 892-6611
Shuhei Komatsu, *CEO*
Kensuke Okabe, *
Kazuo Miura, *CPO**
**EMP:** 80 **EST:** 2022
**SALES (est):** 2.82MM **Privately Held**
**SIC: 3728**  Target drones
PA: Aerwins Technologies Inc.
3-1-8, Shibakoen

**(P-13760)**
**AHF-DUCOMMUN INCORPORATED (HQ)**
Also Called: Ducommun Arostructures-Gardena
268 E Gardena Blvd, Gardena (90248-2814)
PHONE.................310 380-5390
Joseph C Berenato, *Prin*
Eugene P Conese, *Prin*
Ralph D Crosby, *Prin*
Jay L Haberland, *Prin*
Robert D Paulson, *Prin*
◆ **EMP:** 250 **EST:** 1950
**SQ FT:** 105,000
**SALES (est):** 434.48MM
**SALES (corp-wide):** 756.99MM **Publicly Held**
Web: www.ducommun.com
**SIC: 3728** 3812 3769 3469  Aircraft body and wing assemblies and parts; Search and navigation equipment; Space vehicle equipment, nec; Metal stampings, nec
PA: Ducommun Incorporated
600 Anton Blvd Ste 1100
657 335-3665

**(P-13761)**
**AIR CABIN ENGINEERING INC**
231 W Blueridge Ave, Orange (92865-4226)
PHONE.................714 637-4111
**EMP:** 25 **EST:** 1981
**SALES (est):** 4.32MM **Privately Held**
Web: www.aircabin.com
**SIC: 3728**  Aircraft parts and equipment, nec

**(P-13762)**
**AIR COMPONENTS INC**
10235 Indiana Ct, Rancho Cucamonga (91730-5332)
PHONE.................909 980-8224
David Blocker, *Pr*
Robert Ames, *VP*
**EMP:** 20 **EST:** 1987
**SQ FT:** 7,800
**SALES (est):** 5.22MM **Privately Held**
Web: www.aircomponentsinc.com
**SIC: 3728**  Aircraft parts and equipment, nec

**(P-13763)**
**AIRBORNE TECHNOLOGIES INC**
Also Called: Airborne Technologies
999 Avenida Acaso, Camarillo (93012-8700)
P.O. Box 2210 (93011-2210)
PHONE.................805 389-3700
Greg Beason, *CEO*
Christopher Celtruda, *
Richard Drinkward, *
**EMP:** 232 **EST:** 1980
**SQ FT:** 40,000
**SALES (est):** 25.5MM
**SALES (corp-wide):** 75.91MM **Privately Held**
Web: www.goallclear.com
**SIC: 3728** 5088 7699 3812  Aircraft parts and equipment, nec; Aircraft equipment and supplies, nec; Aircraft and heavy equipment repair services; Search and navigation equipment
PA: Kellstrom Holding Corporation
100 N Pcf Cast Hwy Ste 19
561 222-7455

**(P-13764)**
**AIRCRAFT HINGE INC**
26074 Avenue Hall Ste 16, Valencia (91355-3445)
PHONE.................661 257-3434
Doug Silva, *Pr*
Terrina Arroyo, *Dir Fin*
Brianne Dautel, *Off Mgr*
▲ **EMP:** 20 **EST:** 1986
**SQ FT:** 11,000
**SALES (est):** 2.2MM **Privately Held**
Web: www.aircrafthinge.com
**SIC: 3728**  Aircraft parts and equipment, nec

**(P-13765)**
**AIRTECH INTERNATIONAL INC (PA)**
Also Called: Airtech Advanced Mtls Group
5700 Skylab Rd, Huntington Beach (92647-2055)
PHONE.................714 899-8100
William Dahlgren, *CEO*
Jeffrey Dahlgren, *CFO*
Audrey Dahlgren, *Sec*
Darren Carson, *Dir*
August Fester, *Dir*
◆ **EMP:** 130 **EST:** 1973
**SQ FT:** 150,000
**SALES (est):** 48.77MM
**SALES (corp-wide):** 48.77MM **Privately Held**
Web: www.airtechintl.com
**SIC: 3728** 3081 5088 2673  Aircraft parts and equipment, nec; Unsupported plastics film and sheet; Aeronautical equipment and supplies; Bags: plastic, laminated, and coated

**(P-13766)**
**ALATUS AEROSYSTEMS (PA)**
9301 Mason Ave, Chatsworth (91311-5202)
PHONE.................610 965-1630
Scott Holland, *CEO*
Joe Zarrilli, *
◆ **EMP:** 20 **EST:** 1953
**SALES (est):** 11.4MM
**SALES (corp-wide):** 11.4MM **Privately Held**
Web: www.alatusaero.com
**SIC: 3728** 3489  Aircraft parts and equipment, nec; Artillery or artillery parts, over 30 mm.

**(P-13767)**
**ALATUS AEROSYSTEMS**
Also Called: Triumph Structures - Brea
9301 Mason Ave, Chatsworth (91311-5202)
PHONE.................714 732-0559
Manny Chacon, *Mgr*
**EMP:** 87
**SALES (corp-wide):** 11.4MM **Privately Held**
Web: www.alatusaero.com
**SIC: 3728** 3489  Aircraft parts and equipment, nec; Artillery or artillery parts, over 30 mm.
PA: Alatus Aerosystems
9301 Mason Ave
610 965-1630

**(P-13768)**
**ALATUS AEROSYSTEMS**
9301 Mason Ave, Chatsworth (91311-5202)
PHONE.................626 498-7376
Richard Oak, *Mgr*
**EMP:** 80
**SALES (corp-wide):** 11.4MM **Privately Held**
Web: www.alatusaero.com
**SIC: 3728** 3489  Aircraft parts and equipment, nec; Artillery or artillery parts, over 30 mm.
PA: Alatus Aerosystems
9301 Mason Ave
610 965-1630

## 3728 - Aircraft Parts And Equipment, Nec (P-13788)

**(P-13769)**
**ALIGN AEROSPACE LLC (PA)**
9401 De Soto Ave, Chatsworth (91311-4920)
PHONE....................818 727-7800
EMP: 287 EST: 2011
SQ FT: 73,000
SALES (est): 98.89MM Privately Held
Web: www.alignaero.com
SIC: 3728 Aircraft parts and equipment, nec

**(P-13770)**
**ALIGN PRECISION - ANAHEIM INC (DH)**
7100 Belgrave Ave, Garden Grove (92841-2809)
PHONE....................714 961-9200
Mark Cherry, CEO
EMP: 80 EST: 2010
SALES (est): 27.6MM
SALES (corp-wide): 1.89B Privately Held
Web: www.alignprecision.com
SIC: 3728 Aircraft parts and equipment, nec
HQ: Align Precision Corp.
730 W 22nd St
Tempe AZ 85282
480 968-1778

**(P-13771)**
**ALL POWER MANUFACTURING CO**
13141 Molette St, Santa Fe Springs (90670-5500)
PHONE....................562 802-2640
Michael J Hartnett, CEO
▲ EMP: 130 EST: 1948
SALES (est): 14.71MM
SALES (corp-wide): 1.56B Publicly Held
Web: www.rbcbearings.com
SIC: 3728 2899 Aircraft assemblies, subassemblies, and parts, nec; Chemical preparations, nec
PA: Rbc Bearings Incorporated
1 Tribiology Ctr
203 267-7001

**(P-13772)**
**ALLCLEAR AEROSPACE & DEF INC**
1283 Flynn Rd, Camarillo (93012-8013)
PHONE....................805 446-2700
EMP: 54
SALES (corp-wide): 156.2MM Privately Held
Web: www.kellstromdefense.com
SIC: 3728 Aircraft parts and equipment, nec
HQ: Allclear Aerospace & Defense, Inc.
15501 Sw 29th St Ste 101
Miramar FL 33027
954 239-7844

**(P-13773)**
**ALLCLEAR AEROSPACE & DEF INC**
Also Called: Williams Aerospace and Mfg
757 Main St # 102, Chula Vista (91911-6168)
PHONE....................619 660-6220
EMP: 45
SALES (corp-wide): 156.2MM Privately Held
Web: www.kellstromdefense.com
SIC: 3728 Aircraft parts and equipment, nec
HQ: Allclear Aerospace & Defense, Inc.
15501 Sw 29th St Ste 101
Miramar FL 33027
954 239-7844

**(P-13774)**
**ALLCLEAR AEROSPACE & DEF INC**
2525 Collier Canyon Rd, Livermore (94551-7545)
PHONE....................954 239-7844
EMP: 24
SALES (corp-wide): 156.2MM Privately Held
Web: www.goallclear.com
SIC: 3728 Aircraft parts and equipment, nec
HQ: Allclear Aerospace & Defense, Inc.
15501 Sw 29th St Ste 101
Miramar FL 33027
954 239-7844

**(P-13775)**
**ALVA MANUFACTURING INC**
236 E Orangethorpe Ave, Placentia (92870-6442)
PHONE....................714 237-0925
Tam V Nguyen, CEO
Tam V Nguyen, Pr
EMP: 44 EST: 2011
SQ FT: 15,000
SALES (est): 4.48MM Privately Held
Web: www.alvamanufacturing.com
SIC: 3728 3599 Aircraft parts and equipment, nec; Machine and other job shop work

**(P-13776)**
**AMERICAN AIRFRAME INC**
Also Called: Pacific Airframe & Engineering
1201 Vanguard Dr, Oxnard (93033-2409)
PHONE....................805 240-1608
EMP: 21
Web: www.pacificairframe.com
SIC: 3728 Airframe assemblies, except for guided missiles

**(P-13777)**
**AMG TORRANCE LLC (DH)**
Also Called: Metric Precision
5401 Business Dr, Huntington Beach (92649-1225)
PHONE....................310 515-2584
Omar Khan, CEO
Angelique Flores, *
EMP: 15 EST: 2009
SQ FT: 37,800
SALES (est): 22.44MM Privately Held
SIC: 3728 Ailerons, aircraft
HQ: Aerospace Manufacturing Group Inc
5401 Business Dr
Huntington Beach CA 92649
714 894-9802

**(P-13778)**
**AMRO FABRICATING CORPORATION (PA)**
Also Called: Karman Missile & Space Systems
1430 Amro Way, South El Monte (91733-3046)
PHONE....................626 579-2200
John Hammond, Pr
Michael Riley, *
EMP: 238 EST: 1977
SQ FT: 150,000
SALES (est): 45.24MM
SALES (corp-wide): 45.24MM Privately Held
Web: www.karman-sd.com
SIC: 3728 3769 3544 5088 Aircraft parts and equipment, nec; Space vehicle equipment, nec; Special dies, tools, jigs, and fixtures; Aircraft and space vehicle supplies and parts

**(P-13779)**
**APM MANUFACTURING (HQ)**
Also Called: Anaheim Precision Mfg
1738 N Neville St, Orange (92865-4214)
PHONE....................714 453-0100
Anthony Puccio, CEO
Gilles Madelmont, *
Joe Puccio, *
EMP: 22 EST: 1986
SQ FT: 57,000
SALES (est): 20.07MM
SALES (corp-wide): 43.53MM Privately Held
Web: www.anaheimprecision.com
SIC: 3728 3429 3599 3444 Aircraft parts and equipment, nec; Aircraft hardware; Machine shop, jobbing and repair; Sheet metalwork
PA: Manufacturing Solutions, Inc.
1738 N Neville St
714 453-0100

**(P-13780)**
**APPLIED AROSPC STRUCTURES CORP (PA)**
Also Called: Aasc
3437 S Airport Way, Stockton (95206)
P.O. Box 6189 (95206)
PHONE....................209 982-0160
John E Rule, Pr
Burton Weil, *
Rhonda Ward, *
▲ EMP: 229 EST: 1995
SQ FT: 100,000
SALES (est): 107.48MM Privately Held
Web: www.aascworld.com
SIC: 3728 Aircraft parts and equipment, nec

**(P-13781)**
**APPLIED CMPSITE STRUCTURES INC (HQ)**
1195 Columbia St, Brea (92821-2922)
PHONE....................714 990-6300
David Horner, CEO
Jorge Garcia, *
Justin Uchida, *
EMP: 87 EST: 1975
SQ FT: 100,000
SALES (est): 50.87MM
SALES (corp-wide): 189.21MM Privately Held
Web: www.appliedcomposites.com
SIC: 3728 Aircraft parts and equipment, nec
PA: Applied Composites Holdings, Llc
25692 Atlantic Ocean Dr
949 716-3511

**(P-13782)**
**APPROVED AERONAUTICS LLC**
Also Called: Manufacturer and Distributor
9130 Pulsar Ct, Corona (92883-4630)
PHONE....................951 200-3730
Anthony Janes, CEO
EMP: 42 EST: 1999
SALES (est): 5.04MM Privately Held
Web: www.approvedaeronautics.com
SIC: 3728 Aircraft parts and equipment, nec

**(P-13783)**
**ARDEN ENGINEERING INC (DH)**
3130 E Miraloma Ave, Anaheim (92806-1906)
PHONE....................949 877-3642
Thomas Hutton, CEO
John R Meisenbach Senior, CEO
Michael J Stow, Pr
▲ EMP: 21 EST: 1971
SQ FT: 25,000
SALES (est): 47.79MM
SALES (corp-wide): 666.39MM Privately Held

Web: www.arden-engr.com
SIC: 3728 Aircraft body assemblies and parts
HQ: Arden Engineering Holdings, Inc.
1878 N Main St
Orange CA 92865
714 998-6410

**(P-13784)**
**ARDEN ENGINEERING INC**
1878 N Main St, Orange (92865-4117)
Rural Route 3130 (92806)
PHONE....................714 998-6410
Thorin Southworth, of Corp
EMP: 197
SALES (corp-wide): 666.39MM Privately Held
Web: www.arden-engr.com
SIC: 3728 Aircraft body assemblies and parts
HQ: Arden Engineering, Inc.
3130 E Miraloma Ave
Anaheim CA 92806
949 877-3642

**(P-13785)**
**ARDEN ENGINEERING HOLDINGS INC (DH)**
1878 N Main St, Orange (92865-4117)
PHONE....................714 998-6410
EMP: 21 EST: 2010
SALES (est): 47.79MM
SALES (corp-wide): 666.39MM Privately Held
SIC: 3728 Aircraft body assemblies and parts
HQ: Cadence Aerospace, Llc
3150 E Miraloma Ave
Anaheim CA 92806
949 877-3630

**(P-13786)**
**ARMORSTRUXX LLC**
850 Thurman St, Lodi (95240-8228)
PHONE....................209 365-9400
EMP: 24
Web: www.armorstruxx.com
SIC: 3728 3795 3711 Military aircraft equipment and armament; Tanks and tank components; Motor vehicles and car bodies

**(P-13787)**
**ARROWHEAD PRODUCTS CORPORATION**
Also Called: Arrowhead Products
4411 Katella Ave, Los Alamitos (90720-3599)
PHONE....................714 822-2513
Andrew Whelan, Pr
Bill Gardner, *
Erick Reinhold, *
Pete Kraft, *
▲ EMP: 640 EST: 1968
SQ FT: 250,000
SALES (est): 67.49MM
SALES (corp-wide): 459.42MM Privately Held
Web: www.arrowheadproducts.net
SIC: 3728 Accumulators, aircraft propeller
HQ: Industrial Manufacturing Company Llc
8223 Brcksvlle Rd Ste 100
Brecksville OH 44141
440 838-4700

**(P-13788)**
**ASTOR MANUFACTURING**
779 Anita St Ste B, Chula Vista (91911-3937)
PHONE....................661 645-5585
Erick Muschenheim, Pr
EMP: 25 EST: 2016
SQ FT: 3,500
SALES (est): 4.42MM Privately Held

## 3728 - Aircraft Parts And Equipment, Nec (P-13789)

Web: www.astormanufacturing.com
SIC: 3728 Aircraft body assemblies and parts

**(P-13789)**
**ASTRO SPAR INC**
3130 E Miraloma Ave, Anaheim (92806-1906)
PHONE................................626 839-7858
▲ EMP: 42
Web: www.astrospar.com
SIC: 3728 Aircraft assemblies, subassemblies, and parts, nec

**(P-13790)**
**ASTURIES MANUFACTURING CO INC**
310 Cessna Cir, Corona (92878-5009)
PHONE................................951 270-1766
Manuel Perez, Pr
Luis Perez, *
EMP: 25 EST: 1979
SQ FT: 50,850
SALES (est): 4.64MM Privately Held
SIC: 3728 3559 Aircraft parts and equipment, nec; Semiconductor manufacturing machinery

**(P-13791)**
**AVANTUS AEROSPACE INC (DH)**
29101 The Old Rd, Valencia (91355-1014)
PHONE................................661 295-8620
Brian Williams, CEO
Dennis Suedkamp, *
Scott Wilkinson, *
EMP: 125 EST: 2015
SQ FT: 75,000
SALES (est): 60.56MM
SALES (corp-wide): 123.82MM Privately Held
Web: www.avantusaerospace.com
SIC: 3728 Aircraft parts and equipment, nec
HQ: Avantus Aerospace Limited
Unit 7 Millington Road
Hayes MIDDX UB3 4

**(P-13792)**
**AVIATION DESIGN GROUP INC**
Also Called: Gst Industries, Inc.
9060 Winnetka Ave, Northridge (91324-3235)
PHONE................................818 350-1900
Michael Saville, Pr
EMP: 24 EST: 2005
SQ FT: 9,700
SALES (est): 974.46K
SALES (corp-wide): 9.05MM Privately Held
SIC: 3728 Aircraft assemblies, subassemblies, and parts, nec
PA: Infinity Aerospace, Inc.
9060 Winnetka Ave
818 998-9811

**(P-13793)**
**AVIBANK MFG INC (DH)**
Also Called: Avibank
11500 Sherman Way, North Hollywood (91605-5827)
P.O. Box 9909 (91609-1909)
PHONE................................818 392-2100
Dan Welter, Pr
John Duran, *
▲ EMP: 115 EST: 1945
SALES (est): 90.28MM
SALES (corp-wide): 364.48B Publicly Held
Web: www.avibank.com
SIC: 3728 Aircraft parts and equipment, nec
HQ: Sps Technologies, Llc
301 Highland Ave

Jenkintown PA 19046
215 572-3000

**(P-13794)**
**B & E MANUFACTURING CO INC**
12151 Monarch St, Garden Grove (92841-2927)
PHONE................................714 898-2269
Emmanuel Neildez, Pr
Jerome Guilloteau, Sec
EMP: 45 EST: 1981
SQ FT: 26,000
SALES (est): 10.02MM
SALES (corp-wide): 2.67MM Privately Held
Web: www.bandemfg.com
SIC: 3728 Aircraft parts and equipment, nec
HQ: Lisi
6 Rue Juvenal Viellard
Grandvillars 90600
384573000

**(P-13795)**
**B/E AEROSPACE INC**
7155 Fenwick Ln, Westminster (92683-5218)
PHONE................................714 896-9001
Jim Melrose, Mgr
EMP: 136
SALES (corp-wide): 68.92B Publicly Held
Web: www.collinsaerospace.com
SIC: 3728 3647 Aircraft parts and equipment, nec; Aircraft lighting fixtures
HQ: B/E Aerospace, Inc.
2730 West Tyvola Rd
Charlotte NC 28217
704 423-7000

**(P-13796)**
**B/E AEROSPACE MACROLINK**
1500 N Kellogg Dr, Anaheim (92807-1902)
PHONE................................714 777-8800
Mark Cordivari, Pr
EMP: 32 EST: 2015
SALES (est): 3.06MM Privately Held
SIC: 3728 Aircraft parts and equipment, nec

**(P-13797)**
**BANDY MANUFACTURING LLC**
3420 N San Fernando Blvd, Burbank (91504-2532)
P.O. Box 7716 (91510-7716)
PHONE................................818 846-9020
Tom Fulton, Pr
Kevin L Cummings, *
EMP: 93 EST: 1952
SQ FT: 60,000
SALES (est): 10.85MM Privately Held
Web: www.bandymanufacturing.com
SIC: 3728 Aircraft parts and equipment, nec

**(P-13798)**
**BISH INC**
2820 Via Orange Way Ste G, Spring Valley (91978-1742)
PHONE................................619 660-6220
William L Cary, Pr
Shane Nonthavet, VP
EMP: 23 EST: 1997
SQ FT: 16,000
SALES (est): 1.05MM Privately Held
SIC: 3728 Aircraft parts and equipment, nec

**(P-13799)**
**C&D ZODIAC AEROSPACE**
7330 Lincoln Way, Garden Grove (92841-1427)
PHONE................................714 891-0683
▲ EMP: 26 EST: 2015
SALES (est): 944.67K Privately Held

Web: www.zodiacaerospace.com
SIC: 3728 Aircraft parts and equipment, nec

**(P-13800)**
**CADENCE AEROSPACE LLC (HQ)**
Also Called: Arden Engineering
3150 E Miraloma Ave, Anaheim (92806)
PHONE................................949 877-3630
Olivier Jarrault, CEO
EMP: 94 EST: 2010
SQ FT: 5,000
SALES (est): 256.2MM
SALES (corp-wide): 666.39MM Privately Held
Web: www.verusaerospace.com
SIC: 3728 Aircraft body assemblies and parts
PA: Arlington Capital Partners Iv, L.P.
5425 Wsconsin Ave Ste 200
202 337-7500

**(P-13801)**
**CADENCE AEROSPACE LLC**
3130 E Miraloma Ave, Anaheim (92806-1906)
PHONE................................425 353-0405
EMP: 18
SALES (est): 1.15MM Privately Held
Web: www.cadenceaerospace.com
SIC: 3728 Aircraft parts and equipment, nec

**(P-13802)**
**CAL TECH PRECISION INC**
1830 N Lemon St, Anaheim (92801-1000)
PHONE................................714 992-4130
Guy Haarlammert, Pr
▲ EMP: 99 EST: 1989
SALES (est): 10.99MM Privately Held
Web: www.caltechprecision.com
SIC: 3728 Aircraft parts and equipment, nec

**(P-13803)**
**CAMAR AIRCRAFT PARTS CO**
Also Called: Camar Aircraft Parts Company
743 Flynn Rd, Camarillo (93012-8056)
P.O. Box 190 (93011-0190)
PHONE................................805 389-8944
EMP: 22 EST: 2007
SALES (est): 4.5MM Privately Held
Web: www.camarac.com
SIC: 3728 Aircraft parts and equipment, nec

**(P-13804)**
**CANYON COMPOSITES INCORPORATED**
1548 N Gemini Pl, Anaheim (92801-1152)
PHONE................................714 991-8181
Bj Rutkoski, Pr
Robert Gray, *
Eric Collins, *
EMP: 40 EST: 1996
SQ FT: 31,500
SALES (est): 8.17MM Privately Held
Web: www.canyoncomposites.com
SIC: 3728 8711 Aircraft parts and equipment, nec; Engineering services

**(P-13805)**
**CANYON ENGINEERING PDTS INC**
28909 Avenue Williams, Valencia (91355-4183)
PHONE................................661 294-0084
Todd Strickland, Pr
Paul Knerr, *
EMP: 88 EST: 1979
SQ FT: 70,000
SALES (est): 6.86MM Publicly Held
Web: www.crissair.com

SIC: 3728 Aircraft assemblies, subassemblies, and parts, nec
PA: Esco Technologies Inc.
9900 A Clayton Rd

**(P-13806)**
**CARBON BY DESIGN LLC**
1491 Poinsettia Ave Ste 136, Vista (92081-8541)
PHONE................................760 643-1300
EMP: 75 EST: 2003
SQ FT: 65,000
SALES (est): 8.83MM Publicly Held
Web: www.carbonbydesign.com
SIC: 3728 3761 Airframe assemblies, except for guided missiles; Guided missiles and space vehicles
HQ: Heico Flight Support Corp.
3000 Taft St
Hollywood FL 33021
954 987-4000

**(P-13807)**
**CARDONA MANUFACTURING CORP**
1869 N Victory Pl, Burbank (91504-3476)
PHONE................................818 841-8358
Louis Cardona, Pr
Jo Ann Cardona, *
EMP: 26 EST: 1971
SQ FT: 10,000
SALES (est): 2.48MM Privately Held
Web: www.cardonamfg.com
SIC: 3728 3812 Aircraft parts and equipment, nec; Search and navigation equipment

**(P-13808)**
**CAVOTEC DABICO US INC**
5665 Corporate Ave, Cypress (90630-4727)
PHONE................................714 947-0005
Gary Matthews, Pr
Christian Bernadotte, *
Dorothy Chen, *
▲ EMP: 36 EST: 2008
SALES (est): 5.21MM Privately Held
Web: www.cavotec.com
SIC: 3728 Aircraft parts and equipment, nec

**(P-13809)**
**COAST COMPOSITES LLC (PA)**
5 Burroughs, Irvine (92618-2804)
PHONE................................949 455-0665
Daniel Nowicki, CFO
◆ EMP: 80 EST: 1988
SQ FT: 60,000
SALES (est): 7.68MM
SALES (corp-wide): 7.68MM Privately Held
Web: www.ascentaerospace.com
SIC: 3728 3544 3599 Aircraft parts and equipment, nec; Special dies, tools, jigs, and fixtures; Machine shop, jobbing and repair

**(P-13810)**
**COATING SPECIALTIES INC**
Also Called: Aero Products Co.
815 E Rosecrans Ave, Los Angeles (90059-3510)
PHONE................................310 639-6900
Mitchell Grant, Pr
Mitchell Grant, CEO
William Johnson, CEO
EMP: 18 EST: 1973
SQ FT: 31,000
SALES (est): 2.52MM Privately Held
Web: www.coatingspecialties.com

# PRODUCTS & SERVICES SECTION
## 3728 - Aircraft Parts And Equipment, Nec (P-13831)

SIC: 3728 3812 Aircraft assemblies, subassemblies, and parts, nec; Search and navigation equipment

### (P-13811)
### COI CERAMICS INC
Also Called: Coic
7130 Miramar Rd Ste 100b, San Diego (92121-2340)
PHONE...................................858 621-5700
David A Shanahan, CEO
Steve Atmur, *
Andy Szweda, *
EMP: 41 EST: 1999
SQ FT: 3,000
SALES (est): 1.12MM Publicly Held
Web: www.coiceramics.com
SIC: 3728 Aircraft parts and equipment, nec
HQ: Northrop Grumman Innovation Systems, Inc.
2980 Fairview Park Dr
Falls Church VA 22042

### (P-13812)
### COLLINS AEROSPACE ✪
8200 Arlington Ave, Riverside (92503-0428)
PHONE...................................951 351-5659
EMP: 26 EST: 2023
SALES (est): 894.26K Privately Held
SIC: 3728 Aircraft body assemblies and parts

### (P-13813)
### COMPOSITES HORIZONS LLC
1471 W Industrial Park St, Covina (91722-3499)
PHONE...................................626 331-0861
EMP: 20
SALES (corp-wide): 364.48B Publicly Held
Web: www.pccstructurals.com
SIC: 3728 3844 Aircraft parts and equipment, nec; X-ray apparatus and tubes
HQ: Composites Horizons, Llc
1629 W Industrial Park St
Covina CA 91722
626 331-0861

### (P-13814)
### COMPUCRAFT INDUSTRIES INC
Also Called: Cii
8787 Olive Ln, Santee (92071-4137)
P.O. Box 712529 (92072-2529)
PHONE...................................619 448-0787
Maurice Brear, Pr
Margarita Brear, *
EMP: 50 EST: 1972
SQ FT: 85,000
SALES (est): 4.88MM Privately Held
Web: www.ccind.com
SIC: 3728 Aircraft assemblies, subassemblies, and parts, nec

### (P-13815)
### COPP INDUSTRIAL MFG INC
5510 Brooks St, Montclair (91763-4522)
PHONE...................................909 593-7448
Sanjaya Amarasinghe, CEO
Sanjaya Amarasinghe, Pr
EMP: 20 EST: 1964
SALES (est): 3.57MM Privately Held
Web: www.coppmfg.com
SIC: 3728 5088 3599 3444 Aircraft body and wing assemblies and parts; Aeronautical equipment and supplies; Machine shop, jobbing and repair; Culverts, flumes, and pipes

### (P-13816)
### CORONADO MANUFACTURING LLC
8991 Glenoaks Blvd, Sun Valley (91352-2038)
PHONE...................................818 768-5010
Allen F Gowing, Pr
Phillip Belmonte, *
▼ EMP: 50 EST: 1959
SQ FT: 19,000
SALES (est): 10.22MM Privately Held
Web: www.coronadomfg.com
SIC: 3728 5084 Military aircraft equipment and armament; Industrial machine parts

### (P-13817)
### CRANE AEROSPACE INC
Crane Aerospace & Electronics
3000 Winona Ave, Burbank (91504-2540)
PHONE...................................818 526-2600
Brendan Curran, AERO GROUP
EMP: 51
SALES (corp-wide): 2.09B Publicly Held
Web: www.craneae.com
SIC: 3728 Aircraft parts and equipment, nec
HQ: Crane Aerospace, Inc.
100 Stamford Pl
Stamford CT 06902

### (P-13818)
### CURTISS-WRIGHT CONTROLS INC
6940 Farmdale Ave, North Hollywood (91605-6210)
PHONE...................................818 503-0998
EMP: 28
SALES (corp-wide): 2.85B Publicly Held
Web: www.curtisswright.com
SIC: 3728 Aircraft assemblies, subassemblies, and parts, nec
HQ: Curtiss-Wright Controls, Inc.
15801 Brixham Hill Ave # 200
Charlotte NC 28277
704 869-4600

### (P-13819)
### D & D GEAR INCORPORATED
Also Called: Absolute Technologies
4890 E La Palma Ave, Anaheim (92807)
PHONE...................................714 692-6570
Bill Beverage, Pr
▲ EMP: 210 EST: 1969
SQ FT: 82,500
SALES (est): 19.04MM Privately Held
Web: www.absolutetechnologies.com
SIC: 3728 Aircraft parts and equipment, nec

### (P-13820)
### DASCO ENGINEERING CORP
24747 Crenshaw Blvd, Torrance (90505-5308)
PHONE...................................310 326-2277
Ward Olson, Pr
Glen Olson, *
John Karle, *
◆ EMP: 110 EST: 1964
SQ FT: 50,000
SALES (est): 19.53MM Privately Held
Web: www.dascoeng.com
SIC: 3728 Aircraft body and wing assemblies and parts

### (P-13821)
### DATRON ADVANCED TECH INC
200 W Los Angeles Ave, Simi Valley (93065)
PHONE...................................805 579-2966
Mellon C Baird, CEO
EMP: 120 EST: 1990
SALES (est): 3.19MM Privately Held
SIC: 3728 3663 1799 R and D by manuf., aircraft parts and auxiliary equipment; Satellites, communications; Antenna installation

### (P-13822)
### DESIGNED METAL CONNECTIONS INC (DH)
Also Called: Permaswage USA
14800 S Figueroa St, Gardena (90248-1719)
PHONE...................................310 323-6200
Thomas Mcdonnell, VP
▲ EMP: 500 EST: 2004
SQ FT: 175,000
SALES (est): 84.78MM
SALES (corp-wide): 364.48B Publicly Held
Web: www.pccfluidfittings.com
SIC: 3728 Aircraft parts and equipment, nec
HQ: Precision Castparts Corp.
5885 Meadows Rd Ste 620
Lake Oswego OR 97035
503 946-4800

### (P-13823)
### DIAGNOSTIC SOLUTIONS INTL LLC
2580 E Philadelphia St Ste C, Ontario (91761-8093)
PHONE...................................909 930-3600
Brian Hatcher, Managing Member
EMP: 16 EST: 2007
SQ FT: 5,000
SALES (est): 4.53MM Privately Held
Web: www.dsi-hums.com
SIC: 3728 Aircraft parts and equipment, nec

### (P-13824)
### DJI SERVICE LLC
17301 Edwards Rd, Cerritos (90703-2427)
PHONE...................................818 235-0788
EMP: 15 EST: 2016
SALES (est): 5.2MM Privately Held
SIC: 3728 Aircraft parts and equipment, nec

### (P-13825)
### DPI LABS INC
1350 Arrow Hwy, La Verne (91750-5218)
PHONE...................................909 392-5777
Vicki Brown, CEO
Al Snow, *
Greg Desmet, *
Pam Archibald, *
EMP: 35 EST: 1984
SALES (est): 5.04MM Privately Held
Web: www.dpilabs.com
SIC: 3728 Aircraft parts and equipment, nec

### (P-13826)
### DRETLOH AIRCRAFT SUPPLY INC
Also Called: A & D Foam Products
2830 E La Cresta Ave, Anaheim (92806-1816)
PHONE...................................714 632-6982
Eugene Holte, Pr
Randy Holte, VP Opers
Freda Holte, Sec
▲ EMP: 15 EST: 1975
SQ FT: 10,000
SALES (est): 2.58MM Privately Held
Web: www.dretloh.com
SIC: 3728 5199 Aircraft parts and equipment, nec; Foam rubber

### (P-13827)
### DUCOMMUN AEROSTRUCTURES INC
801 Royal Oaks Dr, Monrovia (91016-3630)
PHONE...................................626 358-3211
Maurice Harris, Genl Mgr
EMP: 30
SALES (corp-wide): 756.99MM Publicly Held
Web: www.ducommun.com
SIC: 3728 Aircraft parts and equipment, nec
HQ: Ducommun Aerostructures, Inc.
600 Anton Blvd Ste 1100
Costa Mesa CA 92626
310 380-5390

### (P-13828)
### DUCOMMUN AEROSTRUCTURES INC
4001 El Mirage Rd, Adelanto (92301-9489)
PHONE...................................760 246-4191
Art Mcfarlan, Mgr
EMP: 47
SQ FT: 1,152
SALES (corp-wide): 756.99MM Publicly Held
Web: www.ducommun.com
SIC: 3728 Aircraft parts and equipment, nec
HQ: Ducommun Aerostructures, Inc.
600 Anton Blvd Ste 1100
Costa Mesa CA 92626
310 380-5390

### (P-13829)
### DUCOMMUN AEROSTRUCTURES INC
23301 Wilmington Ave, Carson (90745-6209)
PHONE...................................310 513-7200
Eugene Conese Junior, Dir
EMP: 117
SALES (corp-wide): 756.99MM Publicly Held
Web: www.ducommun.com
SIC: 3728 Aircraft parts and equipment, nec
HQ: Ducommun Aerostructures, Inc.
600 Anton Blvd Ste 1100
Costa Mesa CA 92626
310 380-5390

### (P-13830)
### DUCOMMUN INCORPORATED
801 Royal Oaks Dr, Monrovia (91016-3630)
PHONE...................................626 358-3211
Bradley W Spahr, CEO
EMP: 27
SALES (corp-wide): 712.54MM Publicly Held
Web: www.ducommun.com
SIC: 3728 Aircraft parts and equipment, nec
PA: Ducommun Incorporated
600 Anton Blvd Ste 1100
657 335-3665

### (P-13831)
### DUCOMMUN INCORPORATED (PA)
Also Called: DUCOMMUN
600 Anton Blvd Ste 1100, Costa Mesa (92626-7100)
PHONE...................................657 335-3665
Stephen G Oswald, Ch Bd
Suman Mookerjim, CFO
Christopher D Wampler, CFO
Laureen S Gonzalez, Chief Human Resource Officer
▲ EMP: 216 EST: 1849
SALES (est): 756.99MM
SALES (corp-wide): 756.99MM Publicly Held

---

(PA)=Parent Co (HQ)=Headquarters
✪ = New Business established in last 2 years

## 3728 - Aircraft Parts And Equipment, Nec (P-13832)

Web: www.ducommun.com
SIC: **3728** 3679 Aircraft body and wing assemblies and parts; Microwave components

**(P-13832)**
**DUCOMMUN LABARGE TECH INC (HQ)**
Also Called: American Electronics
23301 Wilmington Ave, Carson (90745-6209)
PHONE.................................310 513-7200
Stephen G Oswald, *Pr*
Christopher Wampler, *VP*
Jerry Redondo, *VP*
Michelle Stein, *VP*
Rajiv Tata, *Sec*
▲ **EMP:** 180 **EST:** 1958
**SQ FT:** 117,000
**SALES (est):** 85.22MM
**SALES (corp-wide):** 756.99MM **Publicly Held**
Web: www.ducommun.com
SIC: **3728** 3769 5065 3812 Aircraft parts and equipment, nec; Space vehicle equipment, nec; Electronic parts and equipment, nec; Search and navigation equipment
PA: Ducommun Incorporated
  600 Anton Blvd Ste 1100
  657 335-3665

**(P-13833)**
**DYNAMATION RESEARCH INC**
2301 Pontius Ave, Los Angeles (90064-1809)
PHONE.................................909 864-2310
Gal Lipkin, *Pr*
**EMP:** 15 **EST:** 2006
**SQ FT:** 5,500
**SALES (est):** 2.36MM **Privately Held**
Web: www.dynamationresearch.com
SIC: **3728** 3812 Aircraft parts and equipment, nec; Search and navigation equipment

**(P-13834)**
**DYNAMIC FABRICATION INC**
890 Mariner St, Brea (92821-3831)
PHONE.................................714 662-2440
Andrew Crook, *Pr*
Olga Garcia Crook, *
**EMP:** 25 **EST:** 1991
**SQ FT:** 22,000
**SALES (est):** 1.17MM **Privately Held**
Web: www.dynamicfab.com
SIC: **3728** 3764 3761 3812 Aircraft parts and equipment, nec; Engines and engine parts, guided missile; Guided missiles and space vehicles; Defense systems and equipment

**(P-13835)**
**EATON CORPORATION**
Also Called: Ground Fueling
9650 Jeronimo Rd, Irvine (92618-2024)
PHONE.................................714 272-4700
Keith Mayer, *Brnch Mgr*
**EMP:** 18
Web: www.dix-eaton.com
SIC: **3728** 3594 3561 3492 Aircraft parts and equipment, nec; Fluid power pumps and motors; Pumps and pumping equipment; Fluid power valves and hose fittings
HQ: Eaton Corporation
  1000 Eaton Blvd
  Cleveland OH 44122
  440 523-5000

**(P-13836)**
**ENCORE SEATS INC**
Also Called: Lift By Encore

5511 Skylab Rd, Huntington Beach (92647-2068)
PHONE.................................949 559-0930
Thomas Mcfarland, *CEO*
Mike Melancon, *
Aram Krikorian, *
**EMP:** 46 **EST:** 2015
**SQ FT:** 80,000
**SALES (est):** 824.44K **Privately Held**
Web: www.encoregroup.aero
SIC: **3728** Aircraft assemblies, subassemblies, and parts, nec

**(P-13837)**
**ENGINEERING JK AEROSPACE & DEF**
23231 La Palma Ave, Yorba Linda (92887-4768)
PHONE.................................714 499-9092
Jonathan Crisan, *Pr*
**EMP:** 25 **EST:** 2012
**SALES (est):** 6.82MM **Privately Held**
Web: mfg.nytron.aero
SIC: **3728** 3724 Aircraft parts and equipment, nec; Aircraft engines and engine parts

**(P-13838)**
**ESTERLINE TECHNOLOGIES CORP**
1740 Commerce Way, Paso Robles (93446-3620)
PHONE.................................805 238-2840
Preston Cole, *Brnch Mgr*
**EMP:** 17
**SALES (corp-wide):** 7.94B **Publicly Held**
Web: www.transdigm.com
SIC: **3728** Aircraft parts and equipment, nec
HQ: Esterline Technologies Corp
  1350 Euclid Ave Ste 1600
  Cleveland OH 44114
  216 706-2960

**(P-13839)**
**FERRA AEROSPACE INC**
940 E Orangethorpe Ave Ste A, Anaheim (92801-1129)
PHONE.................................918 787-2220
**EMP:** 46
**SALES (corp-wide):** 23.49MM **Privately Held**
Web: www.ferra-group.com
SIC: **3728** Aircraft parts and equipment, nec
PA: Ferra Aerospace, Inc.
  64353 E 290 Rd
  918 787-2220

**(P-13840)**
**FLARE GROUP**
Also Called: Aviation Equipment Processing
1571 Macarthur Blvd, Costa Mesa (92626-1407)
PHONE.................................714 850-2080
Dennis Heider, *Pr*
Steve Osorio, *
Daryl Silva, *
Jim Vinyard, *
Eric Trainor, *
**EMP:** 25 **EST:** 2010
**SALES (est):** 5.78MM **Privately Held**
Web: www.aveprocessing.com
SIC: **3728** Aircraft parts and equipment, nec

**(P-13841)**
**FLEXCO INC**
6855 Suva St, Bell Gardens (90201-1999)
PHONE.................................562 927-2525
Erik Moller, *Pr*
**EMP:** 36 **EST:** 1966
**SQ FT:** 14,000

**SALES (est):** 4.15MM **Privately Held**
Web: www.flexcoinc.com
SIC: **3728** 3496 Aircraft parts and equipment, nec; Miscellaneous fabricated wire products

**(P-13842)**
**FLIGHT ENVIRONMENTS INC**
570 Linne Rd Ste 100, Paso Robles (93446-9460)
P.O. Box 3169 (93447-3169)
**EMP:** 25 **EST:** 1998
**SALES (est):** 2.25MM **Privately Held**
Web: www.luminary.aero
SIC: **3728** Aircraft parts and equipment, nec

**(P-13843)**
**FLIGHT LINE PRODUCTS INC**
Also Called: Flightways Manufacturing
28732 Witherspoon Pkwy, Valencia (91355-5425)
PHONE.................................661 775-8366
▲ **EMP:** 40
SIC: **3728** 5599 Aircraft parts and equipment, nec; Aircraft, self-propelled

**(P-13844)**
**FMH AEROSPACE CORP**
Also Called: F M H
17072 Daimler St, Irvine (92614-5548)
PHONE.................................714 751-1000
Rick Busch, *CEO*
David Difranco, *
Valerie Gorman, *
▲ **EMP:** 100 **EST:** 1991
**SQ FT:** 15,000
**SALES (est):** 41.21MM
**SALES (corp-wide):** 6.6B **Publicly Held**
Web: www.fmhaerospace.com
SIC: **3728** Aircraft parts and equipment, nec
PA: Ametek, Inc.
  1100 Cassatt Rd
  610 647-2121

**(P-13845)**
**FORREST MACHINING LLC**
Also Called: Forrestmachining.com
27756 Avenue Mentry, Valencia (91355-3453)
PHONE.................................661 257-0231
Tim Mickael, *CEO*
▲ **EMP:** 240 **EST:** 1979
**SALES (est):** 47.57MM
**SALES (corp-wide):** 47.57MM **Privately Held**
Web: www.fmiaerostructures.com
SIC: **3728** Aircraft parts and equipment, nec
PA: Dvsm, L.L.C.
  760 Sw 9th Ave Ste 2300
  503 223-2721

**(P-13846)**
**FRAZIER AVIATION INC**
445 N Fox St, San Fernando (91340-2501)
PHONE.................................818 898-1998
Robert L Frazier, *CEO*
Robert Frazier Iii, *Pr*
Charles E Ricard, *
Robert Frazier Iv, *Ex VP*
**EMP:** 44 **EST:** 1956
**SQ FT:** 44,000
**SALES (est):** 5.37MM **Privately Held**
Web: www.frazieraviation.com
SIC: **3728** 5088 Aircraft body assemblies and parts; Transportation equipment and supplies

**(P-13847)**
**GEAR MANUFACTURING INC**
Also Called: G M I

3701 E Miraloma Ave, Anaheim (92806-2123)
PHONE.................................714 792-2895
Gary M Smith, *CEO*
**EMP:** 50 **EST:** 1989
**SQ FT:** 26,500
**SALES (est):** 9.63MM **Privately Held**
Web: www.gearmfg.com
SIC: **3728** 3714 3566 3568 Gears, aircraft power transmission; Bearings, motor vehicle; Speed changers, drives, and gears; Power transmission equipment, nec

**(P-13848)**
**GENERAL DYNAMICS OTS CAL INC**
Also Called: GENERAL DYNAMICS OTS (CALIFORNIA), INC.
7603 Saint Andrews Ave Ste H, San Diego (92154-8216)
PHONE.................................619 671-5411
**EMP:** 121
**SALES (corp-wide):** 42.27B **Publicly Held**
Web: www.gd-ots.com
SIC: **3728** Military aircraft equipment and armament
HQ: General Dynamics-Ots, Inc.
  100 Carillon Pkwy Ste 100
  Saint Petersburg FL 33716
  727 578-8100

**(P-13849)**
**GENERAL DYNMICS OTS NCVLLE INC (DH)**
511 Grove St, Healdsburg (95448-4747)
PHONE.................................707 473-9200
Phebe N Novakovic, *CEO*
Richard Schroeder, *
**EMP:** 65 **EST:** 1999
**SQ FT:** 28,000
**SALES (est):** 8.5MM
**SALES (corp-wide):** 42.27B **Publicly Held**
Web: www.gd-ots.com
SIC: **3728** Aircraft parts and equipment, nec
HQ: General Dynamics Ordnance And Tactical Systems, Inc.
  100 Carillon Pkwy
  Saint Petersburg FL 33716
  727 578-8100

**(P-13850)**
**GIDDENS INDUSTRIES INC (DH)**
3130 E Miraloma Ave, Anaheim (92806-1906)
**EMP:** 150 **EST:** 1974
**SALES (est):** 8.75MM
**SALES (corp-wide):** 666.39MM **Privately Held**
Web: www.giddens.com
SIC: **3728** Aircraft parts and equipment, nec
HQ: Giddens Holdings, Inc.
  2600 94th St Sw Ste 150
  Everett WA 98204
  425 353-0405

**(P-13851)**
**GLEDHILL/LYONS INC**
Also Called: Accurate Technology
1521 N Placentia Ave, Anaheim (92806-1236)
PHONE.................................714 502-0274
David M Lyons, *Pr*
**EMP:** 43 **EST:** 2000
**SQ FT:** 31,200
**SALES (est):** 1.29MM **Privately Held**
Web: www.accuratetechnology.net
SIC: **3728** Aircraft parts and equipment, nec

## 3728 - Aircraft Parts And Equipment, Nec (P-13873)

**(P-13852)**
**GLOBAL AEROSPACE TECH CORP**
29077 Avenue Penn, Valencia (91355-5426)
PHONE.............................818 407-5600
Steve Cormier, *CEO*
**EMP:** 22 **EST:** 2006
**SALES (est):** 5.18MM **Privately Held**
Web: www.globalatcorp.com
**SIC: 3728** Aircraft parts and equipment, nec

**(P-13853)**
**GLOBAL AEROSTRUCTURES**
10291 Trademark St Ste C, Rancho Cucamonga (91730-5847)
PHONE.............................909 987-4888
Becky Landa, *CEO*
Michael Cabral, *Genl Mgr*
**EMP:** 15 **EST:** 2011
**SQ FT:** 10,000
**SALES (est):** 5.04MM **Privately Held**
Web: www.gacone.com
**SIC: 3728** Aircraft assemblies, subassemblies, and parts, nec

**(P-13854)**
**GOODRICH CORPORATION**
3355 E La Palma Ave, Anaheim (92806-2815)
PHONE.............................714 984-1461
Rob Gibbs, *Genl Mgr*
**EMP:** 140
**SALES (corp-wide):** 68.92B **Publicly Held**
Web: www.collinsaerospace.com
**SIC: 3728** Aircraft parts and equipment, nec
**HQ:** Goodrich Corporation
2730 W Tyvola Rd
Charlotte NC 28217
704 423-7000

**(P-13855)**
**GOODRICH CORPORATION**
Goodrich Wheel and Brake Svcs
9920 Freeman Ave, Santa Fe Springs (90670-3421)
PHONE.............................562 944-4441
Hosrow Bordbar, *Mgr*
**EMP:** 87
**SALES (corp-wide):** 68.92B **Publicly Held**
Web: www.collinsaerospace.com
**SIC: 3728** Aircraft parts and equipment, nec
**HQ:** Goodrich Corporation
2730 W Tyvola Rd
Charlotte NC 28217
704 423-7000

**(P-13856)**
**GOODRICH CORPORATION**
Also Called: Goodrich Rconnaissance Systems
5801 C St # 200, Beale Afb (95903-1510)
PHONE.............................530 788-9214
Manuel Nino, *Dir*
**EMP:** 15
**SALES (corp-wide):** 68.92B **Publicly Held**
Web: www.collinsaerospace.com
**SIC: 3728** Aircraft parts and equipment, nec
**HQ:** Goodrich Corporation
2730 W Tyvola Rd
Charlotte NC 28217
704 423-7000

**(P-13857)**
**HANSEN ENGINEERING CO**
Also Called: Plant 2
24050 Frampton Ave, Harbor City (90710-2197)
PHONE.............................310 534-3870
**EMP:** 28 **EST:** 2019

**SALES (est):** 4.96MM **Privately Held**
Web: www.hansenengineering.com
**SIC: 3728** Aircraft parts and equipment, nec

**(P-13858)**
**HELICOPTER TECH CO LTD PARTNR**
Also Called: Helicopter Technology Company
12902 S Broadway, Los Angeles (90061-1118)
PHONE.............................310 523-2750
Frank Palminteri, *Pr*
Gary Burdorf, *
◆ **EMP:** 24 **EST:** 1995
**SQ FT:** 197,000
**SALES (est):** 4.26MM **Privately Held**
Web: www.helicoptertech.com
**SIC: 3728** 3721 Aircraft parts and equipment, nec; Helicopters

**(P-13859)**
**HUTCHINSON AROSPC & INDUST INC**
Also Called: ARS
4510 W Vanowen St, Burbank (91505-1135)
PHONE.............................818 843-1000
Shano Cristilli, *Brnch Mgr*
**EMP:** 165
**SALES (corp-wide):** 5.46B **Privately Held**
Web: www.hutchinsonai.com
**SIC: 3728** Aircraft parts and equipment, nec
**HQ:** Hutchinson Aerospace & Industry, Inc.
82 South St
Hopkinton MA 01748
508 417-7000

**(P-13860)**
**HYDRAFLOW**
Also Called: Hydraflow
1881 W Malvern Ave, Fullerton (92833-2403)
PHONE.............................714 773-2600
**EMP:** 255 **EST:** 1961
**SALES (est):** 29.15MM **Privately Held**
Web: www.hydraflow.com
**SIC: 3728** 3492 Aircraft parts and equipment, nec; Fluid power valves for aircraft

**(P-13861)**
**HYDRAULICS INTERNATIONAL INC (PA)**
20961 Knapp St, Chatsworth (91311-5926)
PHONE.............................818 998-1231
Nicky Ghaemmaghami, *CEO*
Shah Banifazl, *
◆ **EMP:** 285 **EST:** 1976
**SQ FT:** 78,000
**SALES (est):** 107.64MM
**SALES (corp-wide):** 107.64MM **Privately Held**
Web: www.hiigroup.com
**SIC: 3728** Aircraft parts and equipment, nec

**(P-13862)**
**HYDRAULICS INTERNATIONAL INC**
9000 Mason Ave, Chatsworth (91311-6178)
PHONE.............................818 998-1236
Chuck Sherman, *Brnch Mgr*
**EMP:** 25
**SALES (corp-wide):** 107.64MM **Privately Held**
Web: www.hiinet.com
**SIC: 3728** Aircraft parts and equipment, nec
**PA:** Hydraulics International, Inc.
20961 Knapp St
818 998-1231

**(P-13863)**
**HYDRAULICS INTERNATIONAL INC**
9261 Independence Ave, Chatsworth (91311-5905)
PHONE.............................818 998-1231
**EMP:** 25
**SALES (corp-wide):** 107.64MM **Privately Held**
Web: www.hiigroup.com
**SIC: 3728** Aircraft parts and equipment, nec
**PA:** Hydraulics International, Inc.
20961 Knapp St
818 998-1231

**(P-13864)**
**HYDRO-AIRE INC (HQ)**
3000 Winona Ave, Burbank (91504-2540)
PHONE.............................818 526-2600
Brendan J Curran, *CEO*
Tazewell Rowe, *
▲ **EMP:** 101 **EST:** 1996
**SQ FT:** 173,000
**SALES (est):** 184.7MM
**SALES (corp-wide):** 2.09B **Publicly Held**
Web: www.craneae.com
**SIC: 3728** Aircraft parts and equipment, nec
**PA:** Crane Company
100 1st Stmford Pl Ste 40
203 363-7300

**(P-13865)**
**HYDRO-AIRE AEROSPACE CORP**
3000 Winona Ave, Burbank (91504-2540)
PHONE.............................818 526-2600
Jay Higgs, *Pr*
**EMP:** 200
**SALES (corp-wide):** 2.09B **Publicly Held**
**SIC: 3728** Aircraft parts and equipment, nec
**HQ:** Hydro-Aire Aerospace Corp.
249 Abbe Rd S
Elyria OH 44035
440 323-3211

**(P-13866)**
**HYDROFORM USA INCORPORATED**
2848 E 208th St, Carson (90810-1101)
PHONE.............................310 632-6353
Chester K Jablonski, *CEO*
Mauricio Salazar, *
Jeffrey Lake, *Corporate Counsel*
▼ **EMP:** 154 **EST:** 1982
**SQ FT:** 95,000
**SALES (est):** 23.87MM **Privately Held**
Web: www.hydroformusa.com
**SIC: 3728** Aircraft parts and equipment, nec

**(P-13867)**
**ICE MANAGEMENT SYSTEMS INC**
Also Called: IMS-Ess
27449 Colt Ct, Temecula (92590-3674)
PHONE.............................951 676-2751
**EMP:** 28
**SIC: 3728** 3694 3357 Deicing equipment, aircraft; Harness wiring sets, internal combustion engines; Aircraft wire and cable, nonferrous

**(P-13868)**
**ICON AIRCRAFT INC (PA)**
2141 Icon Way, Vacaville (95688-8766)
PHONE.............................707 564-4000
Thomas M Mccabe, *CRO*
Kirk Hawkins, *CEO*
Thomas Wieners, *COO*
Rich Bridge, *VP*

**EMP:** 94 **EST:** 2006
**SALES (est):** 41.4MM **Privately Held**
Web: www.iconaircraft.com
**SIC: 3728** Aircraft parts and equipment, nec

**(P-13869)**
**IKHANA GROUP LLC**
Also Called: Ikhana Aircraft Services
37260 Sky Canyon Dr Hngr 20, Murrieta (92563-2680)
PHONE.............................951 600-0009
Brian Raduenz, *CEO*
▲ **EMP:** 120 **EST:** 2007
**SALES (est):** 24.83MM **Privately Held**
Web: www.ikhanagroup.com
**SIC: 3728** Flaps, aircraft wing
**PA:** Aevex Aerospace, Llc
440 Stevens Ave Ste 150

**(P-13870)**
**IMPRESA AEROSPACE LLC**
344 W 157th St, Gardena (90248-2135)
PHONE.............................310 354-1200
Steve Loye, *
Dennis Fitzgerald, *
Marco Barrantes, *
**EMP:** 169 **EST:** 1987
**SQ FT:** 26,000
**SALES (est):** 42MM
**SALES (corp-wide):** 42.24MM **Privately Held**
Web: www.impresaaerospace.com
**SIC: 3728** 3444 Aircraft parts and equipment, nec; Sheet metalwork
**HQ:** Impresa Acquisition Corporation
344 W 157th St
Gardena CA

**(P-13871)**
**INET AIRPORT SYSTEMS INC**
Also Called: Inet
5665 Corporate Ave, Cypress (90630-4727)
PHONE.............................714 888-2700
**EMP:** 50
**SIC: 3728** 4581 5088 Aircraft parts and equipment, nec; Aircraft servicing and repairing; Aircraft and parts, nec

**(P-13872)**
**INFINITY AEROSPACE INC (PA)**
9060 Winnetka Ave, Northridge (91324-3235)
PHONE.............................818 998-9811
Chet Huffman, *CEO*
R Lloyd Huffman, *
Steve Lonngren, *
**EMP:** 50 **EST:** 1958
**SQ FT:** 30,000
**SALES (est):** 9.05MM
**SALES (corp-wide):** 9.05MM **Privately Held**
**SIC: 3728** Aircraft parts and equipment, nec

**(P-13873)**
**INFLIGHT WARNING SYSTEMS INC**
Also Called: Iws Predictive Technologies
3940 Prospect Ave Ste P, Yorba Linda (92886-1752)
PHONE.............................714 993-9394
Joseph Barclay, *Pr*
George Orff, *Sec*
Jeff Bulkin, *CFO*
**EMP:** 19 **EST:** 2002
**SQ FT:** 6,000
**SALES (est):** 1.84MM **Privately Held**
Web: www.inflightwarningsystems.com
**SIC: 3728** Aircraft assemblies, subassemblies, and parts, nec

## 3728 - Aircraft Parts And Equipment, Nec (P-13874)

**(P-13874)**
**INTEGRAL AEROSPACE LLC**
Also Called: Pcx Aerosystems - Santa Ana
2040 E Dyer Rd, Santa Ana (92705-5710)
PHONE.................949 250-3123
Thomas Holzthum, CEO
John Kutler, *
Bryan Mclean, VP
Alan Guzik, *
EMP: 190 EST: 2016
SQ FT: 270,000
SALES (est): 50MM
SALES (corp-wide): 151.59MM Privately Held
Web: www.integralaerospace.com
SIC: 3728  Aircraft parts and equipment, nec
PA: Pcx Aerostructures, Llc
   300 Fenn Rd
   860 666-2471

**(P-13875)**
**IRISH INTERIORS INC (HQ)**
Also Called: Lift By Encore
5511 Skylab Rd Ste 101, Huntington Beach (92647-2071)
PHONE.................949 559-0930
Thomas Mcfarland, Pr
Micheal Melancon, *
Karl Jonson, *
▲ EMP: 130 EST: 1972
SQ FT: 42,000
SALES (est): 81.25MM
SALES (corp-wide): 77.79B Publicly Held
Web: www.encoreaerospace.com
SIC: 3728 1799  Aircraft parts and equipment, nec; Renovation of aircraft interiors
PA: The Boeing Company
   929 Long Bridge Dr
   703 465-3500

**(P-13876)**
**IRISH INTERIORS INC**
5511 Skylab Rd Ste 101, Huntington Beach (92647-2071)
PHONE.................562 344-1700
Karl Jonson, VP
EMP: 200
SALES (corp-wide): 77.79B Publicly Held
Web: www.encoreaerospace.com
SIC: 3728  Aircraft parts and equipment, nec
HQ: Irish Interiors, Inc.
   5511 Skylab Rd Ste 101
   Huntington Beach CA 92647
   949 559-0930

**(P-13877)**
**IRISH INTERIORS HOLDINGS INC**
Also Called: IRISH INTERIORS HOLDINGS, INC.
1729 Apollo Ct, Seal Beach (90740-5617)
PHONE.................949 559-0930
EMP: 20
SALES (corp-wide): 77.79B Publicly Held
Web: www.encoreaerospace.com
SIC: 3728  Aircraft parts and equipment, nec
HQ: Irish Interiors, Inc.
   5511 Skylab Rd Ste 101
   Huntington Beach CA 92647
   949 559-0930

**(P-13878)**
**IRWIN AVIATION INC**
Also Called: Aero Performance
225 Airport Cir, Corona (92878-5027)
PHONE.................951 372-9555
James Irwin, CEO
Nanci Irwin, *
EMP: 30 EST: 2014
SALES (est): 4.75MM Privately Held
Web: www.aeroperformance.com
SIC: 3728  Aircraft parts and equipment, nec

**(P-13879)**
**ITT AEROSPACE CONTROLS LLC (HQ)**
28150 Industry Dr, Valencia (91355-4101)
PHONE.................315 568-7258
Steven Giuliano, *
▲ EMP: 78 EST: 2011
SALES (est): 19.26MM
SALES (corp-wide): 3.28B Publicly Held
Web: www.ittaerospace.com
SIC: 3728  Aircraft parts and equipment, nec
PA: Itt Inc.
   100 Washington Blvd Fl 6
   914 641-2000

**(P-13880)**
**ITT AEROSPACE CONTROLS LLC**
ITT Aerospace Controls Unit S
28150 Industry Dr, Valencia (91355-4101)
PHONE.................661 295-4000
Robert Briggs, Mgr
EMP: 300
SALES (corp-wide): 3.28B Publicly Held
Web: www.ittaerospace.com
SIC: 3728  Aircraft parts and equipment, nec
HQ: Itt Aerospace Controls Llc
   28150 Industry Dr
   Valencia CA 91355
   315 568-7258

**(P-13881)**
**JET AIR FBO LLC**
681 Kenney St, El Cajon (92020-1278)
PHONE.................619 448-5991
EMP: 30 EST: 2005
SQ FT: 250,000
SALES (est): 1.46MM Privately Held
Web: www.circleag.com
SIC: 3728  Refueling equipment for use in flight, airplane

**(P-13882)**
**JOHNSON CALDRAUL INC**
Also Called: Cal-Draulics
220 N Delilah St Ste 101, Corona (92879-1883)
PHONE.................951 340-1067
Douglas Johnson, Pr
Kenneth W Johnson, *
EMP: 30 EST: 1992
SQ FT: 12,000
SALES (est): 5.33MM Privately Held
Web: www.caldraulics.com
SIC: 3728 3593  Aircraft parts and equipment, nec; Fluid power cylinders and actuators

**(P-13883)**
**K & E INC**
Also Called: Micro Space Products
3906 W 139th St, Hawthorne (90250-7497)
PHONE.................310 675-3309
Alex Berger, CEO
Cathy Riegler, CEO
Rudi Riegler, Pr
◆ EMP: 19 EST: 1957
SQ FT: 10,000
SALES (est): 3.34MM Privately Held
Web: www.microspaceproducts.com
SIC: 3728  Aircraft parts and equipment, nec

**(P-13884)**
**KAISER AEROSPACE & ELECTRONICS CORPORATION**
2701 Orchard Pkwy Ste 100, San Jose (95134-2008)
PHONE.................949 250-1015
EMP: 3580
SIC: 3728  Aircraft parts and equipment, nec

**(P-13885)**
**KAREM AIRCRAFT INC**
1 Capital Dr, Lake Forest (92630-2203)
PHONE.................949 859-4444
EMP: 48 EST: 2004
SALES (est): 8.58MM Privately Held
Web: www.karemaircraft.com
SIC: 3728  Aircraft parts and equipment, nec

**(P-13886)**
**KIRKHILL INC (HQ)**
Also Called: Sfs
300 E Cypress St, Brea (92821-4007)
PHONE.................714 529-4901
Kevin Stein, Pr
EMP: 107 EST: 2018
SALES (est): 49.71MM
SALES (corp-wide): 7.94B Publicly Held
Web: www.kirkhill.com
SIC: 3728  Aircraft parts and equipment, nec
PA: Transdigm Group Incorporated
   1350 Euclid Ave Ste 1600
   216 706-2960

**(P-13887)**
**KLUNE INDUSTRIES INC (DH)**
Also Called: PCC Aerostructures
7323 Coldwater Canyon Ave, North Hollywood (91605-4206)
PHONE.................818 503-8100
Joseph I Snowden, CEO
Kenneth Ward, *
▲ EMP: 358 EST: 1972
SQ FT: 125,000
SALES (est): 131.11MM
SALES (corp-wide): 364.48B Publicly Held
Web: www.pccaero.com
SIC: 3728  Aircraft parts and equipment, nec
HQ: Klune Holdings, Inc.
   7323 Coldwater Canyon Ave
   North Hollywood CA 91605

**(P-13888)**
**KS ENGINEERING INC**
14948 Shoemaker Ave, Santa Fe Springs (90670-5552)
PHONE.................562 483-7788
Clifford Yu, Pr
Kap Yu, Mgr
EMP: 15 EST: 1984
SQ FT: 14,000
SALES (est): 1.78MM Privately Held
SIC: 3728  Aircraft body and wing assemblies and parts

**(P-13889)**
**LANIC ENGINEERING INC (PA)**
Also Called: Lanic Aerospace
12144 6th St, Rancho Cucamonga (91730-6111)
PHONE.................877 763-0411
S Robert Leaming, CEO
Shaun Arnold, *
Jason Arnold, Prin
EMP: 35 EST: 1984
SQ FT: 30,000
SALES (est): 17.35MM
SALES (corp-wide): 17.35MM Privately Held
Web: www.lanicaerospace.com
SIC: 3728 3721  Aircraft parts and equipment, nec; Aircraft

**(P-13890)**
**LAUNCHPINT ELC PRPLSION SLTONS**
Also Called: Launchpoint Eps
320 Storke Rd Ste 100, Goleta (93117-2992)
PHONE.................805 683-9659
Robert Reali, CEO
Robert Reali, Prin
Brian Clark, Prin
Christopher Grieco, Prin
Vicki Young, Prin
EMP: 20 EST: 2018
SALES (est): 4.6MM Privately Held
Web: www.launchpointeps.com
SIC: 3728  Aircraft parts and equipment, nec

**(P-13891)**
**LEACH INTERNATIONAL CORP (DH)**
6900 Orangethorpe Ave, Buena Park (90620-1390)
P.O. Box 5032 (90622-5032)
PHONE.................714 736-7537
Richard Brad Lawrence, CEO
Mark Thek, *
Alain Durand, *
Carsten Muller, *
EMP: 500 EST: 1919
SALES (est): 94.17MM
SALES (corp-wide): 7.94B Publicly Held
Web: www.leachcorp.com
SIC: 3728  Aircraft parts and equipment, nec
HQ: Esterline Technologies Corp
   1350 Euclid Ave Ste 1600
   Cleveland OH 44114
   216 706-2960

**(P-13892)**
**LEFIELL MANUFACTURING COMPANY**
Also Called: Lefiell
13700 Firestone Blvd, Santa Fe Springs (90670-5652)
PHONE.................562 921-3411
▲ EMP: 150 EST: 1930
SALES (est): 26.8MM Privately Held
Web: www.lefiell.com
SIC: 3728 3599 3724  Aircraft assemblies, subassemblies, and parts, nec; Machine shop, jobbing and repair; Aircraft engines and engine parts

**(P-13893)**
**LLAMAS PLASTICS INC**
12970 Bradley Ave, Sylmar (91342-3851)
PHONE.................818 362-0371
James Lee, Pr
Ricardo M Llamas, *
Jeff Mabry, *
Robert Young, *
Oswald Llamas, *
EMP: 105 EST: 1977
SQ FT: 37,000
SALES (est): 19.45MM Privately Held
Web: www.llamasplastics.com
SIC: 3728 3089 3083  Aircraft parts and equipment, nec; Plastics containers, except foam; Laminated plastics plate and sheet

**(P-13894)**
**LONG-LOK LLC**
20531 Belshaw Ave, Carson (90746-3505)
PHONE.................424 209-8726
EMP: 21
SALES (corp-wide): 9.6MM Privately Held
Web: www.longlok.com
SIC: 3728  R and D by manuf., aircraft parts and auxiliary equipment

# PRODUCTS & SERVICES SECTION
## 3728 - Aircraft Parts And Equipment, Nec (P-13914)

PA: Long-Lok, Llc
10630 Chester Rd
336 343-7319

### (P-13895)
### LUXFER INC (DH)
Also Called: Luxfer Gas Cylinder
3016 Kansas Ave Bldg 1, Riverside (92507-3445)
PHONE..................................951 684-5110
John Rhodes, Pr
◆ EMP: 70 EST: 1973
SQ FT: 120,000
SALES (est): 115.7MM
SALES (corp-wide): 405MM Privately Held
Web: www.luxfercylinders.com
SIC: 3728 3354 Aircraft parts and equipment, nec; Shapes, extruded aluminum, nec
HQ: Ba Holdings, Inc.
3016 Kansas Ave Bldg 1
Riverside CA 92507

### (P-13896)
### MACHINETEK LLC
1985 Palomar Oaks Way, Carlsbad (92011-1307)
PHONE..................................760 438-6644
EMP: 18 EST: 1992
SQ FT: 21,000
SALES (est): 2.82MM Privately Held
Web: www.machinetek.com
SIC: 3728 Aircraft assemblies, subassemblies, and parts, nec

### (P-13897)
### MANEY AIRCRAFT INC
Also Called: Maney Aircraft
1305 S Wanamaker Ave, Ontario (91761-2237)
PHONE..................................909 390-2500
Martin T Bright, CEO
David A Ederer, *
Michael Neely, *
EMP: 30 EST: 1955
SQ FT: 14,700
SALES (est): 4.02MM Privately Held
Web: www.maneyaircraft.com
SIC: 3728 5088 3829 3812 Aircraft assemblies, subassemblies, and parts, nec; Aircraft and parts, nec; Aircraft and motor vehicle measurement equipment; Search and navigation equipment

### (P-13898)
### MARINO ENTERPRISES INC
Also Called: Gear Technology
10671 Civic Center Dr, Rancho Cucamonga (91730-3804)
PHONE..................................909 476-0343
Thomas Marino, Pr
EMP: 35 EST: 1986
SQ FT: 16,320
SALES (est): 4.11MM Privately Held
Web: www.intra-aerospace.com
SIC: 3728 3769 Gears, aircraft power transmission; Space vehicle equipment, nec

### (P-13899)
### MASON ELECTRIC CO
13955 Balboa Blvd, Rancho Cascades (91342-1084)
PHONE..................................818 361-3366
Steven Brune, Pr
EMP: 350 EST: 1968
SQ FT: 105,000
SALES (est): 35.46MM
SALES (corp-wide): 7.94B Publicly Held
Web: www.masoncontrols.com
SIC: 3728 Aircraft parts and equipment, nec
HQ: Esterline Technologies Corp
1350 Euclid Ave Ste 1600
Cleveland OH 44114
216 706-2960

### (P-13900)
### MASTER RESEARCH & MFG INC
13528 Pumice St, Norwalk (90650-5249)
PHONE..................................562 483-8789
Enrique Viano, VP
EMP: 52 EST: 1977
SQ FT: 31,200
SALES (est): 9.2MM Privately Held
Web: www.master-research.com
SIC: 3728 Aircraft body assemblies and parts

### (P-13901)
### MATTERNET INC (PA)
355 Ravendale Dr, Mountain View (94043-5217)
PHONE..................................650 260-2727
Andreas Ratopoulos, CEO
Michael Whitaker Faa, Prin
Laurence Marton Ucsf, Prin
EMP: 23 EST: 2014
SALES (est): 9.92MM
SALES (corp-wide): 9.92MM Privately Held
Web: www.mttr.net
SIC: 3728 Target drones

### (P-13902)
### MAVERICK AEROSPACE INC
3718 Capitol Ave, City Of Industry (90601-1731)
PHONE..................................714 578-1700
David Feltch, CEO
George Ono, Pr
Nigel Young, VP
EMP: 16 EST: 2002
SQ FT: 12,000
SALES (est): 5.04MM Privately Held
Web: www.mavaero.com
SIC: 3728 Aircraft assemblies, subassemblies, and parts, nec

### (P-13903)
### MAVERICK AEROSPACE LLC
3718 Capitol Ave, City Of Industry (90601-1731)
PHONE..................................714 578-1700
Steve Crisanti, CEO
Steve Crisanti, Managing Member
George Ono, *
Val Darie, *
Scott Curry, *
EMP: 100 EST: 2017
SQ FT: 40,000
SALES (est): 10.93MM Privately Held
Web: www.mavaero.com
SIC: 3728 3544 3761 3441 Aircraft parts and equipment, nec; Special dies, tools, jigs, and fixtures; Guided missiles and space vehicles; Fabricated structural metal

### (P-13904)
### MEGGITT (SAN DIEGO) INC (HQ)
Also Called: Meggitt Polymers & Composites
6650 Top Gun St, San Diego (92121-4112)
PHONE..................................858 824-8976
Pablo Florin, Genl Mgr
EMP: 120 EST: 2008
SQ FT: 120,000
SALES (est): 39.97MM
SALES (corp-wide): 19.93B Publicly Held
Web: www.meggitt.com
SIC: 3728 Roto-blades for helicopters
PA: Parker-Hannifin Corporation
6035 Parkland Blvd
216 896-3000

### (P-13905)
### MEGGITT DEFENSE SYSTEMS INC
9801 Muirlands Blvd, Irvine (92618-2521)
PHONE..................................949 465-7700
Roger Brum, Pr
Greg Brostek, *
Bob Bettwy, *
EMP: 353 EST: 1998
SQ FT: 153,000
SALES (est): 64.83MM
SALES (corp-wide): 19.93B Publicly Held
Web: www.meggittdefense.com
SIC: 3728 Military aircraft equipment and armament
HQ: Meggitt Limited
Ansty Bus.
Coventry W MIDLANDS CV7 9
247 682-6900

### (P-13906)
### MEGGITT NORTH HOLLYWOOD INC
10092 Foxrun Rd, Santa Ana (92705-1407)
PHONE..................................818 691-6258
Jen Larsen, Brnch Mgr
EMP: 23
SALES (corp-wide): 19.93B Publicly Held
Web: www.meggitt.com
SIC: 3728 Aircraft parts and equipment, nec
HQ: Meggitt (North Hollywood), Inc.
12838 Saticoy St
North Hollywood CA 91605

### (P-13907)
### MEGGITT NORTH HOLLYWOOD INC (DH)
Also Called: Meggitt Control Systems
12838 Saticoy St, North Hollywood (91605-3505)
PHONE..................................818 765-8160
Dennis Hutton, CEO
▲ EMP: 230 EST: 1969
SQ FT: 10,000
SALES (est): 46.77MM
SALES (corp-wide): 19.93B Publicly Held
Web: www.meggitt.com
SIC: 3728 Aircraft parts and equipment, nec
HQ: Meggitt Limited
Ansty Bus.
Coventry W MIDLANDS CV7 9
247 682-6900

### (P-13908)
### MEGGITT SAFETY SYSTEMS INC
Also Called: Htl Manufacturing Div
1785 Voyager Ave, Simi Valley (93063-3363)
PHONE..................................805 584-4100
Dennis Hutton, Pr
EMP: 97
SALES (corp-wide): 19.93B Publicly Held
Web: www.meggitt.com
SIC: 3728 Aircraft parts and equipment, nec
HQ: Meggitt Safety Systems, Inc.
1785 Voyager Ave
Simi Valley CA 93063
805 584-4100

### (P-13909)
### MEGGITT-USA INC (DH)
Also Called: Meggitt Polymers & Composites
1955 Surveyor Ave, Simi Valley (93063-3369)
PHONE..................................805 526-5700
Eric Lardiere, Sr VP
Robert W Soukup, *
Greg Brostek, *
▲ EMP: 310 EST: 1980
SQ FT: 3,000
SALES (est): 317.2MM
SALES (corp-wide): 19.93B Publicly Held
Web: www.meggitt.com
SIC: 3728 3829 3679 Aircraft parts and equipment, nec; Vibration meters, analyzers, and calibrators; Electronic switches
HQ: Meggitt Limited
Ansty Bus.
Coventry W MIDLANDS CV7 9
247 682-6900

### (P-13910)
### MILITARY AIRCRAFT PARTS (PA)
116 Oxburough Dr, Folsom (95630-3293)
PHONE..................................916 635-8010
Robert E Marin, Pr
EMP: 43 EST: 2000
SALES (est): 4.45MM
SALES (corp-wide): 4.45MM Privately Held
Web: www.asapaog.com
SIC: 3728 Aircraft parts and equipment, nec

### (P-13911)
### MISSION CRTICAL COMPOSITES LLC
15400 Graham St Ste 102, Huntington Beach (92649-1257)
PHONE..................................714 831-2100
Robert Hartman, Managing Member
EMP: 22 EST: 2012
SALES (est): 16.17MM Privately Held
Web: www.missioncriticalcomposites.com
SIC: 3728 3721 3724 3761 Aircraft assemblies, subassemblies, and parts, nec; Aircraft; Aircraft engines and engine parts; Guided missiles and space vehicles

### (P-13912)
### MULGREW ARCFT COMPONENTS INC
1810 S Shamrock Ave, Monrovia (91016-4251)
PHONE..................................626 256-1375
Mike Houshiar, CEO
EMP: 58 EST: 1979
SQ FT: 45,000
SALES (est): 8.89MM Privately Held
Web: www.mulgrewaircraft.com
SIC: 3728 Aircraft assemblies, subassemblies, and parts, nec

### (P-13913)
### N2 DEVELOPMENT INC
Also Called: N2 Aero
6849 Hayvenhurst Ave, Van Nuys (91406-4718)
PHONE..................................323 210-3251
Gregory Nelson, Pr
Olen Nelson, VP
EMP: 15 EST: 2010
SALES (est): 1.59MM Privately Held
SIC: 3728 Aircraft parts and equipment, nec

### (P-13914)
### NASCO AIRCRAFT BRAKE INC
Also Called: Meggitt Arcft Braking Systems
13300 Estrella Ave, Gardena (90248-1519)
PHONE..................................310 532-4430
Daniel Aron, CEO
Phil Friedman, *
EMP: 100 EST: 1981
SQ FT: 25,000
SALES (est): 8.02MM

## 3728 - Aircraft Parts And Equipment, Nec (P-13915)

SALES (corp-wide): 19.93B **Publicly Held**
Web: www.nascoaircraft.com
SIC: **3728** Brakes, aircraft
HQ: Meggitt Aircraft Braking Systems Corporation
1204 Massillon Rd
Akron OH 44306
330 796-4400

### (P-13915)
### NEILL AIRCRAFT CO
1260 W 15th St, Long Beach (90813-1302)
PHONE.................................562 432-7981
Judith L Carpenter, *Pr*
**EMP:** 275 **EST:** 1956
**SQ FT:** 150,000
**SALES (est):** 26.73MM **Privately Held**
Web: www.neillaircraft.com
SIC: **3728** Aircraft body and wing assemblies and parts

### (P-13916)
### NOTTHOFF ENGINEERING L A INC
5416 Argosy Ave, Huntington Beach (92649-1039)
PHONE................................714 894-9802
Kelly Kaller, *CEO*
Karen Ewing, *
▲ **EMP:** 20 **EST:** 1941
**SALES (est):** 4.38MM **Privately Held**
Web: www.notthoff.com
SIC: **3728** 3599 Aircraft parts and equipment, nec; Machine shop, jobbing and repair

### (P-13917)
### ORCON AEROSPACE
2600 Central Ave Ste E, Union City (94587-3187)
P.O. Box 487 (94914-0487)
PHONE................................510 489-8100
Hollis Bascom, *Pr*
Dennis Murray, *VP*
**EMP:** 18 **EST:** 2006
**SQ FT:** 200,000
**SALES (est):** 840.76K **Privately Held**
Web: www.lamartcorp.com
SIC: **3728** Aircraft parts and equipment, nec

### (P-13918)
### OTTO INSTRUMENT SERVICE INC (PA)
1441 Valencia Pl, Ontario (91761-7639)
PHONE................................909 930-5800
William R Otto Junior, *Pr*
Lynne Amber Otto-miller, *BORN 1979 1999*
**EMP:** 45 **EST:** 1946
**SQ FT:** 36,800
**SALES (est):** 29.55MM
**SALES (corp-wide):** 29.55MM **Privately Held**
Web: www.ottoinstrument.com
SIC: **3728** 5088 7699 Aircraft parts and equipment, nec; Aircraft equipment and supplies, nec; Aircraft flight instrument repair

### (P-13919)
### PACIFIC CONTOURS CORPORATION
5340 E Hunter Ave, Anaheim (92807-2053)
PHONE................................714 693-1260
Tom Rapacz, *Pr*
Tim Anderson, *
Jon Stannard, *
**EMP:** 60 **EST:** 1997
**SQ FT:** 36,000
**SALES (est):** 11.75MM **Privately Held**
Web: www.pacificcontours.com
SIC: **3728** 5088 Aircraft assemblies, subassemblies, and parts, nec; Aircraft and parts, nec

### (P-13920)
### PACIFIC PRECISION PRODUCTS MFG INC
Also Called: Pacific Precision Products
9671 Irvine Ctr Dr Koll Ctr Ii Bldg 6, Irvine (92618)
PHONE................................949 727-3844
**EMP:** 40 **EST:** 1973
**SALES (est):** 3.43MM **Privately Held**
SIC: **3728** 3812 Oxygen systems, aircraft; Search and navigation equipment

### (P-13921)
### PACIFIC SKY SUPPLY INC
8230 San Fernando Rd, Sun Valley (91352-3218)
PHONE................................818 768-3700
Emilio B Perez, *CEO*
Emilio Perez, *
Kelly Anderson, *
**EMP:** 59 **EST:** 1954
**SQ FT:** 27,000
**SALES (est):** 9.14MM **Privately Held**
Web: www.pacsky.com
SIC: **3728** 3724 5088 Aircraft parts and equipment, nec; Aircraft engines and engine parts; Transportation equipment and supplies

### (P-13922)
### PARKER-HANNIFIN CORPORATION
Also Called: Stratoflex Product Division
3800 Calle Tecate, Camarillo (93012-5070)
PHONE................................805 484-8533
William Cartmill, *Brnch Mgr*
**EMP:** 46
**SALES (corp-wide):** 19.93B **Publicly Held**
Web: www.parker.com
SIC: **3728** 3769 3568 Aircraft parts and equipment, nec; Space vehicle equipment, nec; Power transmission equipment, nec
PA: Parker-Hannifin Corporation
6035 Parkland Blvd
216 896-3000

### (P-13923)
### PARKER-HANNIFIN CORPORATION
Also Called: Parker Aerospace
14300 Alton Pkwy, Irvine (92618-1898)
PHONE................................949 833-3000
Robert Bond, *Brnch Mgr*
**EMP:** 169
**SQ FT:** 180,000
**SALES (corp-wide):** 19.93B **Publicly Held**
Web: www.parker.com
SIC: **3728** Aircraft assemblies, subassemblies, and parts, nec
PA: Parker-Hannifin Corporation
6035 Parkland Blvd
216 896-3000

### (P-13924)
### PCA AEROSPACE INC (PA)
17800 Gothard St, Huntington Beach (92647-6217)
PHONE................................714 841-1750
Brian Murray, *CEO*
Gregory Ruffalo, *
▲ **EMP:** 71 **EST:** 1963
**SQ FT:** 58,000
**SALES (est):** 6.54MM
**SALES (corp-wide):** 6.54MM **Privately Held**
Web: www.lanicaerospace.com
SIC: **3728** 3599 Aircraft parts and equipment, nec; Machine shop, jobbing and repair

### (P-13925)
### PCA AEROSPACE INC
15282 Newsboy Cir, Huntington Beach (92649-1202)
PHONE................................714 901-5209
Ron Brandenburg, *Pr*
**EMP:** 26
**SALES (corp-wide):** 6.54MM **Privately Held**
Web: www.lanicaerospace.com
SIC: **3728** Aircraft parts and equipment, nec
PA: Pca Aerospace, Inc.
17800 Gothard St
714 841-1750

### (P-13926)
### PERFORMANCE PLASTICS INC
7919 Saint Andrews Ave, San Diego (92154-8224)
PHONE................................714 343-3928
Jim Renaud, *Pr*
**EMP:** 99 **EST:** 1977
**SQ FT:** 50,000
**SALES (est):** 22.56MM **Privately Held**
Web: www.perf-plastics.com
SIC: **3728** Aircraft parts and equipment, nec
PA: Rock West Composites, Inc.
7625 Panasonic Way

### (P-13927)
### PMC INC (HQ)
12243 Branford St, Sun Valley (91352-1010)
PHONE................................818 896-1101
Christopher Lette, *Pr*
**EMP:** 88 **EST:** 1962
**SALES (est):** 541.32MM
**SALES (corp-wide):** 1.71B **Privately Held**
Web: www.pmcglobalinc.com
SIC: **3728** 3724 Bodies, aircraft; Engine mount parts, aircraft
PA: Pmc Global, Inc.
12243 Branford St
818 896-1101

### (P-13928)
### PRECISION AEROSPACE CORP
11155 Jersey Blvd Ste A, Rancho Cucamonga (91730-5148)
PHONE................................909 945-9604
Jim Hudson, *Pr*
**EMP:** 70 **EST:** 1989
**SQ FT:** 50,000
**SALES (est):** 9.42MM **Privately Held**
Web: www.pac.cc
SIC: **3728** Aircraft assemblies, subassemblies, and parts, nec

### (P-13929)
### PRECISION FLUID CONTROLS INC
1751 Aviation Blvd Ste 200, Lincoln (95648-9687)
PHONE................................916 626-3029
Peggy Stevens, *Pr*
**EMP:** 125 **EST:** 2004
**SALES (est):** 16.89MM **Privately Held**
Web: www.precisionfluidcontrols.com
SIC: **3728** 5085 3491 Accumulators, aircraft propeller; Valves and fittings; Industrial valves

### (P-13930)
### PRECISION TUBE BENDING
13626 Talc St, Santa Fe Springs (90670-5114)
PHONE................................562 921-6723
Diane M Williams, *CEO*
**EMP:** 98 **EST:** 1957
**SQ FT:** 60,000
**SALES (est):** 18.84MM **Privately Held**
Web: www.precision-tube-bending.com
SIC: **3728** 3498 Aircraft parts and equipment, nec; Tube fabricating (contract bending and shaping)

### (P-13931)
### PTI TECHNOLOGIES INC (DH)
501 Del Norte Blvd, Oxnard (93030-7983)
PHONE................................805 604-3700
Rowland Ellis, *Pr*
Beth Kozlowski, *
▲ **EMP:** 212 **EST:** 1979
**SQ FT:** 225,000
**SALES (est):** 38.12MM **Publicly Held**
Web: www.ptitechnologies.com
SIC: **3728** Aircraft parts and equipment, nec
HQ: Esco Technologies Holding Llc
9900a Clayton Rd
Saint Louis MO 63124
314 213-7200

### (P-13932)
### Q1 TEST INC
1100 S Grove Ave Ste B2, Ontario (91761-4574)
PHONE................................909 390-9718
Allen Riley, *CEO*
Jason Riley, *Pr*
**EMP:** 21 **EST:** 2005
**SQ FT:** 10,500
**SALES (est):** 4.14MM **Privately Held**
Web: www.q1testinc.com
SIC: **3728** Turret test fixtures, aircraft

### (P-13933)
### QUALITY FORMING LLC
Also Called: Qfi Prv Aerospace
22906 Frampton Ave, Torrance (90501-5035)
PHONE................................310 539-2855
Mark Severns, *Pr*
▲ **EMP:** 100 **EST:** 1972
**SALES (est):** 9.86MM
**SALES (corp-wide):** 666.39MM **Privately Held**
Web: www.verusaerospace.com
SIC: **3728** Aircraft assemblies, subassemblies, and parts, nec
HQ: Qpi Holdings, Inc.
22906 Frampton Ave
Torrance CA 90501
310 539-2855

### (P-13934)
### QUATRO COMPOSITES LLC
Also Called: Quatro Composites
13250 Gregg St Ste A1, Poway (92064-7164)
PHONE................................712 707-9200
Karash Quepin, *Mgr*
**EMP:** 160
Web: www.sekisuiaerospace.com
SIC: **3728** Aircraft parts and equipment, nec
HQ: Quatro Composites, L.L.C.
403 14th St Se
Orange City IA 51041
712 707-9200

### (P-13935)
### ROBINSON HELICOPTER CO INC (PA)

# PRODUCTS & SERVICES SECTION
## 3728 - Aircraft Parts And Equipment, Nec (P-13953)

2901 Airport Dr, Torrance (90505-6115)
PHONE..................310 539-0508
David Smith, Pr
Frank Robinson, Pr
Tim Goetz, CFO
P Wayne Walden, VP Mfg
◆ EMP: 970 EST: 1973
SQ FT: 260,000
SALES (est): 171.82MM
SALES (corp-wide): 171.82MM Privately Held
Web: shop.robinsonheli.com
SIC: 3728  Aircraft parts and equipment, nec

### (P-13936)
### ROCKWELL COLLINS INC
Also Called: Collins Aerospace
3530 Branscombe Rd, Fairfield (94533)
P.O. Box Kk (94533-0659)
PHONE..................707 422-1880
Lance Schaeffer, Brnch Mgr
EMP: 437
SALES (corp-wide): 68.92B Publicly Held
Web: www.rockwellcollins.com
SIC: 3728  Aircraft parts and equipment, nec
HQ: Rockwell Collins, Inc.
    400 Collins Rd Ne
    Cedar Rapids IA 52498

### (P-13937)
### ROCKWELL COLLINS INC
1757 Carr Rd Ste 100, Calexico (92231-9781)
PHONE..................760 768-4732
Nicolas Pineda, Mgr
EMP: 25
SALES (corp-wide): 68.92B Publicly Held
Web: www.rockwellcollins.com
SIC: 3728  Aircraft parts and equipment, nec
HQ: Rockwell Collins, Inc.
    400 Collins Rd Ne
    Cedar Rapids IA 52498

### (P-13938)
### ROGERS HOLDING COMPANY INC
Also Called: V & M Precision Grinding Co.
1130 Columbia St, Brea (92821-2921)
PHONE..................714 257-4850
Aldo Devile, Prin
Tom Rogers, *
EMP: 20 EST: 1946
SQ FT: 65,000
SALES (est): 2.18MM Privately Held
Web: www.vmprecision.com
SIC: 3728  Alighting (landing gear) assemblies, aircraft

### (P-13939)
### ROHR INC (HQ)
Also Called: Collins Aerospace
850 Lagoon Dr, Chula Vista (91910-2001)
PHONE..................619 691-4111
Greg Peters, Pr
Curtis Reusser, *
Kenneth Wood, *
Robert A Gustafson, General Vice President *
Brian Broderick, *
▲ EMP: 2100 EST: 1969
SQ FT: 2,770,000
SALES (est): 1.06B
SALES (corp-wide): 68.92B Publicly Held
Web: www.roehrs-timm.de
SIC: 3728  Nacelles, aircraft
PA: Rtx Corporation
    1000 Wilson Blvd
    781 522-3000

### (P-13940)
### RSA ENGINEERED PRODUCTS LLC
Also Called: Trimas Aerospace
110 W Cochran St Ste A, Simi Valley (93065-6228)
PHONE..................805 584-4150
Ray Scarcello, CEO
◆ EMP: 90 EST: 2012
SQ FT: 43,000
SALES (est): 27.89MM
SALES (corp-wide): 893.55MM Publicly Held
Web: www.rsaeng.com
SIC: 3728  Aircraft parts and equipment, nec
PA: Trimas Corporation
    38505 Wodward Ave Ste 200
    248 631-5450

### (P-13941)
### SABRIN CORPORATION
Also Called: Astronics Company
2836 E Walnut St, Pasadena (91107-3755)
PHONE..................626 792-3813
Julian Doherty, CEO
▲ EMP: 19 EST: 1961
SQ FT: 8,000
SALES (est): 3.13MM Privately Held
Web: www.astroniccompany.com
SIC: 3728 3444 3544 3499  Aircraft parts and equipment, nec; Sheet metalwork; Special dies, tools, jigs, and fixtures; Shims, metal

### (P-13942)
### SAFRAN CABIN GALLEYS US INC (HQ)
17311 Nichols Ln, Huntington Beach (92647-5721)
PHONE..................714 861-7300
Matthew Stafford, CEO
Vincent Kozar, CFO
◆ EMP: 717 EST: 1986
SQ FT: 90,000
SALES (est): 57.57MM
SALES (corp-wide): 940.23MM Privately Held
SIC: 3728  Aircraft parts and equipment, nec
PA: Safran
    2 Boulevard Du General Martial Valin

### (P-13943)
### SAFRAN CABIN INC
Also Called: 4 Flight
8595 Milliken Ave Ste 101, Rancho Cucamonga (91730-4942)
PHONE..................909 652-9700
Tom Mcfarland, CEO
EMP: 158
SALES (corp-wide): 940.23MM Privately Held
Web: www.zodiacaerospace.com
SIC: 3728  Aircraft parts and equipment, nec
HQ: Safran Cabin Inc.
    5701 Bolsa Ave
    Huntington Beach CA 92647
    714 934-0000

### (P-13944)
### SAFRAN CABIN INC
12472 Industry St, Garden Grove (92841-2819)
PHONE..................714 901-2672
Mike Boyd, Brnch Mgr
EMP: 137
SALES (corp-wide): 940.23MM Privately Held
Web: www.safran-group.com
SIC: 3728  Aircraft parts and equipment, nec
HQ: Safran Cabin Inc.
    5701 Bolsa Ave
    Huntington Beach CA 92647
    714 934-0000

### (P-13945)
### SAFRAN CABIN INC
2850 Skyway Dr, Santa Maria (93455-1410)
PHONE..................805 922-3013
Jude F Dozor, Brnch Mgr
EMP: 140
SALES (corp-wide): 940.23MM Privately Held
Web: www.safran-group.com
SIC: 3728  Aircraft parts and equipment, nec
HQ: Safran Cabin Inc.
    5701 Bolsa Ave
    Huntington Beach CA 92647
    714 934-0000

### (P-13946)
### SAFRAN CABIN INC
Also Called: C&D Aerodesign
6754 Calle De Linea Ste 111, San Diego (92154-8021)
PHONE..................619 671-0430
Jose Martinez, Mgr
EMP: 223
SALES (corp-wide): 940.23MM Privately Held
Web: www.safran-group.com
SIC: 3728  Aircraft parts and equipment, nec
HQ: Safran Cabin Inc.
    5701 Bolsa Ave
    Huntington Beach CA 92647
    714 934-0000

### (P-13947)
### SAFRAN CABIN INC (HQ)
5701 Bolsa Ave, Huntington Beach (92647)
PHONE..................714 934-0000
Jorge Ortega, CEO
Norman Jordan, *
Scott Savian, *
Daniel Edmundson, *
Arnault Dumont Lauret, *
▲ EMP: 500 EST: 1972
SQ FT: 150,000
SALES (est): 493.55MM
SALES (corp-wide): 940.23MM Privately Held
Web: www.safran-group.com
SIC: 3728  Aircraft assemblies, subassemblies, and parts, nec
PA: Safran
    2 Boulevard Du General Martial Valin

### (P-13948)
### SAFRAN CABIN INC
Also Called: Safran Cabin - Cypress
12240 Warland Dr, Cypress (90630)
PHONE..................562 344-4780
Gary Reese, Brnch Mgr
EMP: 248
SALES (corp-wide): 940.23MM Privately Held
Web: www.safran-group.com
SIC: 3728  Aircraft assemblies, subassemblies, and parts, nec
HQ: Safran Cabin Inc.
    5701 Bolsa Ave
    Huntington Beach CA 92647
    714 934-0000

### (P-13949)
### SAFRAN CABIN INC
Also Called: Safran Cabin Tijuana S.a De Cv
2695 Customhouse Ct Ste 111, San Diego (92154-7645)
PHONE..................619 661-6292
EMP: 173
SALES (corp-wide): 940.23MM Privately Held
Web: www.safran-group.com
SIC: 3728  Aircraft assemblies, subassemblies, and parts, nec
HQ: Safran Cabin Inc.
    5701 Bolsa Ave
    Huntington Beach CA 92647
    714 934-0000

### (P-13950)
### SAFRAN CABIN INC
1500 Glenn Curtiss St, Carson (90746-4012)
PHONE..................714 934-0000
EMP: 96
SALES (corp-wide): 940.23MM Privately Held
Web: www.safran-group.com
SIC: 3728  Aircraft assemblies, subassemblies, and parts, nec
HQ: Safran Cabin Inc.
    5701 Bolsa Ave
    Huntington Beach CA 92647
    714 934-0000

### (P-13951)
### SAFRAN CABIN INC
Also Called: C & D Aerospace
7330 Lincoln Way, Garden Grove (92841-1427)
PHONE..................714 891-1906
Alec Azarian, Brnch Mgr
EMP: 140
SALES (corp-wide): 940.23MM Privately Held
Web: www.zodiacaerospace.com
SIC: 3728 3443  Aircraft assemblies, subassemblies, and parts, nec; Fabricated plate work (boiler shop)
HQ: Safran Cabin Inc.
    5701 Bolsa Ave
    Huntington Beach CA 92647
    714 934-0000

### (P-13952)
### SAFRAN SEATS SANTA MARIA LLC
2641 Airpark Dr, Santa Maria (93455-1415)
PHONE..................805 922-5995
▲ EMP: 638 EST: 2012
SALES (est): 48.96MM
SALES (corp-wide): 940.23MM Privately Held
Web: weber.zodiac.com
SIC: 3728  Aircraft parts and equipment, nec
HQ: Safran Seats Usa Llc
    2000 Weber Dr
    Gainesville TX 76240
    940 668-4825

### (P-13953)
### SANDERS COMPOSITES INC (HQ)
Also Called: Sanders Composites Industries
3701 E Conant St, Long Beach (90808-1783)
PHONE..................562 354-2800
Larry O'toole, CEO
EMP: 49 EST: 1988
SQ FT: 44,400
SALES (est): 4.54MM
SALES (corp-wide): 150.17MM Privately Held
Web: www.sanderscomposites.com
SIC: 3728  Aircraft assemblies, subassemblies, and parts, nec
PA: Sanders Industries Holdings, Inc.
    3701 E Conant St
    562 354-2920

(PA)=Parent Co  (HQ)=Headquarters
✪ = New Business established in last 2 years

## 3728 - Aircraft Parts And Equipment, Nec (P-13954)

**(P-13954)**
**SANTA MONICA PROPELLER SVC INC**
Also Called: Santa Monica Propeller
3135 Donald Douglas Loop S, Santa Monica (90405-3210)
PHONE..................310 390-6233
Leonid Polyakov, CEO
▲ EMP: 15 EST: 1963
SQ FT: 11,000
SALES (est): 1.87MM Privately Held
Web: www.santamonicapropeller.com
SIC: 3728 5088 Aircraft propellers and associated equipment; Aircraft and parts, nec

**(P-13955)**
**SENIOR OPERATIONS LLC**
Senior Aerospace SSP
2980 N San Fernando Blvd, Burbank (91504-2522)
PHONE..................818 260-2900
Launie Flemning, Mgr
EMP: 380
SALES (corp-wide): 1.2B Privately Held
Web: www.seniorssp.com
SIC: 3728 3599 Aircraft parts and equipment, nec; Bellows, industrial: metal
HQ: Senior Operations Llc
300 E Devon Ave
Bartlett IL 60103
630 372-3500

**(P-13956)**
**SHIM-IT CORPORATION**
1691 California Ave, Corona (92881-3375)
PHONE..................951 734-8300
Jennifer Steigner, CEO
Jeff Johnson, Pr
Diane Hesson, VP
EMP: 15 EST: 1961
SQ FT: 8,500
SALES (est): 1.5MM Privately Held
Web: www.shim-it.com
SIC: 3728 3542 Aircraft parts and equipment, nec; Machine tools, metal forming type

**(P-13957)**
**SKYLOCK INDUSTRIES LLC**
1290 W Optical Dr, Azusa (91702-3249)
PHONE..................626 334-2391
Jeff Creoiserat, Ch Bd
Jim Pease, *
EMP: 70 EST: 1973
SQ FT: 14,000
SALES (est): 19.69MM Privately Held
Web: www.skylock.com
SIC: 3728 Aircraft parts and equipment, nec

**(P-13958)**
**SOUTHWEST MACHINE & PLASTIC CO**
Also Called: Southwest Plastics Co
620 W Foothill Blvd, Glendora (91741-2403)
PHONE..................626 963-6919
W Thomas Jorgensen, Pr
Alfred D Jorgensen, *
▲ EMP: 30 EST: 1937
SALES (est): 5.53MM Privately Held
Web: www.southwestplastics.com
SIC: 3728 3089 3544 Aircraft parts and equipment, nec; Injection molding of plastics; Special dies, tools, jigs, and fixtures

**(P-13959)**
**SPACE-LOK INC**
13306 Halldale Ave, Gardena (90249-2204)
P.O. Box 2919 (90247-1119)
PHONE..................310 527-6150
Scott F Wade, Pr
Jeffrey Wade, *
EMP: 138 EST: 1962
SALES (est): 23.96MM
SALES (corp-wide): 218.18MM Privately Held
Web: space-lok.herokuapp.com
SIC: 3728 3542 3812 3452 Aircraft assemblies, subassemblies, and parts, nec; Machine tools, metal forming type; Search and navigation equipment; Bolts, nuts, rivets, and washers
HQ: Novaria Fastening Systems, Llc
6300 Ridglea Pl Ste 800
Fort Worth TX 76116
817 381-3810

**(P-13960)**
**SPEC TOOL COMPANY**
Also Called: Alice G Fink-Painter
11805 Wakeman St, Santa Fe Springs (90670-2130)
P.O. Box 1056 (90660-1056)
PHONE..................323 723-9533
Alice G Fink-painter, Pr
D B Fink, *
Albert G Fink Junior, VP
EMP: 50 EST: 1954
SALES (est): 5.78MM Privately Held
Web: www.spectoolgse.com
SIC: 3728 Aircraft parts and equipment, nec

**(P-13961)**
**SPS TECHNOLOGIES LLC**
Air Industries
12570 Knott St, Garden Grove (92841-3932)
PHONE..................714 892-5571
Michael Wu, Contrlr
EMP: 50
SALES (corp-wide): 364.48B Publicly Held
Web: www.pccfasteners.com
SIC: 3728 Aircraft parts and equipment, nec
HQ: Sps Technologies, Llc
301 Highland Ave
Jenkintown PA 19046
215 572-3000

**(P-13962)**
**SUMMIT MACHINE LLC**
2880 E Philadelphia St, Ontario (91761-8523)
PHONE..................909 923-2744
▼ EMP: 120 EST: 2003
SQ FT: 103,000
SALES (est): 22.83MM
SALES (corp-wide): 364.48B Publicly Held
Web: www.summitmachining.com
SIC: 3728 3599 Aircraft parts and equipment, nec; Machine shop, jobbing and repair
HQ: Precision Castparts Corp.
5885 Meadows Rd Ste 620
Lake Oswego OR 97035
503 946-4800

**(P-13963)**
**SUNGEAR INC**
8535 Arjons Dr Ste G, San Diego (92126-4360)
PHONE..................858 549-3166
Lee Miramontes, Managing Member
Glenn Wilcox, Mfg Mgr
Paul Scott, QA
EMP: 42 EST: 1982
SQ FT: 16,000
SALES (est): 9.19MM
SALES (corp-wide): 93.1MM Privately Held
Web: www.sungearinc.com
SIC: 3728 Gears, aircraft power transmission
PA: H-D Advanced Manufacturing Company
2418 Greens Rd
346 219-0320

**(P-13964)**
**SUNVAIR INC (HQ)**
Also Called: Sunvair
29145 The Old Rd, Valencia (91355-1015)
PHONE..................661 294-3777
Robert Dann, Pr
Edward Waschak, *
Melba Waschak, *
EMP: 32 EST: 1956
SQ FT: 26,000
SALES (est): 17.73MM
SALES (corp-wide): 30.17MM Privately Held
Web: www.sunvair.com
SIC: 3728 7699 Aircraft landing assemblies and brakes; Aircraft and heavy equipment repair services
PA: Sunvair Aerospace Group, Inc.
29145 The Old Rd
661 294-3777

**(P-13965)**
**SWIFT ENGINEERING INC**
Also Called: Swift Engineering
1141a Via Callejon, San Clemente (92673-6230)
PHONE..................949 492-6608
▲ EMP: 83 EST: 1982
SALES (est): 10.86MM Privately Held
Web: www.swiftengineering.com
SIC: 3728 3714 3624 Aircraft body and wing assemblies and parts; Motor vehicle parts and accessories; Fibers, carbon and graphite
PA: Matsushita International Corp
1141 Via Callejon

**(P-13966)**
**SYMBOLIC DISPLAYS INC**
1917 E Saint Andrew Pl, Santa Ana (92705-5143)
PHONE..................714 258-2811
Candy Suits, CEO
▼ EMP: 76 EST: 1964
SQ FT: 15,860
SALES (est): 9.75MM Privately Held
Web: www.symbolicdisplays.com
SIC: 3728 3812 3577 Aircraft parts and equipment, nec; Search and navigation equipment; Computer peripheral equipment, nec

**(P-13967)**
**SYNERGETIC TECH GROUP INC**
1712 Earhart, La Verne (91750-5826)
PHONE..................909 305-4711
Tony Espinoza, CEO
EMP: 27 EST: 1997
SQ FT: 2,400
SALES (est): 6.8MM Privately Held
Web: www.synergetic-us.com
SIC: 3728 Aircraft parts and equipment, nec

**(P-13968)**
**TALSCO INC**
7101 Patterson Dr, Garden Grove (92841-1415)
PHONE..................714 841-2464
EMP: 36
SIC: 3728 Aircraft assemblies, subassemblies, and parts, nec

**(P-13969)**
**TDG AEROSPACE INC**
2180 Chablis Ct Ste 106, Escondido (92029-2076)
PHONE..................760 466-1040
Virginia Richard, Ch Bd
Virginia Richard, Ch
Gerry Bench, Pr
Fred Bond, CFO
EMP: 18 EST: 1991
SALES (est): 2.64MM Privately Held
Web: www.tdgaerospace.com
SIC: 3728 Aircraft parts and equipment, nec

**(P-13970)**
**THALES AVIONICS INC**
48 Discovery, Irvine (92618-3170)
PHONE..................949 381-3033
Dominique Giannoni, Owner
EMP: 34
SALES (corp-wide): 269.57MM Privately Held
Web: www.thalesgroup.com
SIC: 3728 Aircraft parts and equipment, nec
HQ: Thales Avionics, Inc.
7415 Emrald Dnes Dr Ste 2
Orlando FL 32822
407 812-2600

**(P-13971)**
**THALES AVIONICS INC**
Also Called: Inflight Entrmt & Connectivity
51 Discovery Ste 100, Irvine (92618-3120)
PHONE..................949 790-2500
Brad Foreman, Mgr
EMP: 34
SALES (corp-wide): 269.57MM Privately Held
Web: www.thalesgroup.com
SIC: 3728 3663 Aircraft parts and equipment, nec; Radio and t.v. communications equipment
HQ: Thales Avionics, Inc.
7415 Emrald Dnes Dr Ste 2
Orlando FL 32822
407 812-2600

**(P-13972)**
**THALES AVIONICS INC**
9975 Toledo Way, Irvine (92618-1826)
PHONE..................949 829-5808
EMP: 34
SALES (corp-wide): 269.57MM Privately Held
Web: www.thalesgroup.com
SIC: 3728 Aircraft parts and equipment, nec
HQ: Thales Avionics, Inc.
7415 Emrald Dnes Dr Ste 2
Orlando FL 32822
407 812-2600

**(P-13973)**
**THOMPSON INDUSTRIES LTD**
Also Called: Thompson ADB Industries
7155 Fenwick Ln, Westminster (92683-5218)
PHONE..................310 679-9193
EMP: 109
SALES (est): 8.33MM Privately Held
SIC: 3728 Aircraft parts and equipment, nec

**(P-13974)**
**TJ AEROSPACE INC**
Also Called: Tj Aerospace
12601 Monarch St, Garden Grove (92841-3918)
PHONE..................714 891-3564
Tien Dang, CEO
Tien N Dang, CEO
EMP: 23 EST: 2007

## PRODUCTS & SERVICES SECTION
### 3728 - Aircraft Parts And Equipment, Nec (P-13995)

SQ FT: 6,000
SALES (est): 4.65MM **Privately Held**
Web: www.tjaerospace.com
SIC: **3728** 3541 Aircraft parts and equipment, nec; Machine tools, metal cutting type

**(P-13975)**
**TMW CORPORATION (PA)**
Also Called: Crown Discount Tools
15148 Bledsoe St, Sylmar (91342-3807)
PHONE......................................818 362-5665
William Windette, *Pr*
Gary Berger, *
EMP: 110 EST: 1973
SQ FT: 115,000
SALES (est): 4.96MM
SALES (corp-wide): 4.96MM **Privately Held**
SIC: **3728** Aircraft landing assemblies and brakes

**(P-13976)**
**TRANSDIGM INC**
Adel Wggins Grp-Commercial Div
5000 Triggs St, Commerce (90022-4833)
P.O. Box 22228 (90022-0228)
PHONE......................................323 269-9181
Cindy Terakawa, *Brnch Mgr*
EMP: 75
SALES (corp-wide): 7.94B **Publicly Held**
Web: www.transdigm.com
SIC: **3728** 3365 Aircraft parts and equipment, nec; Aerospace castings, aluminum
HQ: Transdigm, Inc.
   1350 Euclid Ave
   Cleveland OH 44115

**(P-13977)**
**TRI-FITTING MFG COMPANY**
Also Called: Tri-Fitting Mfg
10414 Rush St, South El Monte (91733-3344)
PHONE......................................626 442-2000
Ralph Bernal, *Pr*
EMP: 15 EST: 1977
SQ FT: 13,000
SALES (est): 3.31MM **Privately Held**
Web: www.trifittingmfg.com
SIC: **3728** 3494 3492 Aircraft assemblies, subassemblies, and parts, nec; Valves and pipe fittings, nec; Fluid power valves and hose fittings

**(P-13978)**
**TRI-TECH PRECISION INC**
1863 N Case St, Orange (92865-4234)
PHONE......................................714 970-1363
Ernie Husted, *Pr*
EMP: 17 EST: 1989
SALES (est): 2MM **Privately Held**
Web: www.tri-techprecision.com
SIC: **3728** 3544 Aircraft parts and equipment, nec; Special dies, tools, jigs, and fixtures

**(P-13979)**
**TRIO MANUFACTURING INC**
Also Called: Trio Manufacturing
601 Lairport St, El Segundo (90245-5005)
PHONE......................................310 640-6123
Michael Hunkins, *Pr*
Michael Hunkins, *Pr*
Brian Hunkins, *
▲ EMP: 125 EST: 1943
SALES (est): 24.47MM **Privately Held**
Web: www.triomfg.com

SIC: **3728** 3829 3812 3663 Aircraft parts and equipment, nec; Measuring and controlling devices, nec; Search and navigation equipment; Radio and t.v. communications equipment

**(P-13980)**
**TRIUMPH ACTTION SYSTEMS - VLNC**
Also Called: Triumph Group
28150 Harrison Pkwy, Valencia (91355-4109)
PHONE......................................661 702-7537
Daniel J Crowley, *Pr*
Jim Mccabe, *Sr VP*
Dan Ostrosky, *VP*
Gary Tenison, *
John B Wright Ii, *Sr VP*
EMP: 250 EST: 2001
SALES (est): 37.55MM **Publicly Held**
SIC: **3728** Aircraft parts and equipment, nec
PA: Triumph Group, Inc.
   555 E Lncster Ave Ste 400

**(P-13981)**
**TRIUMPH EQUIPMENT INC**
13434 S Ontario Ave, Ontario (91761-7956)
PHONE......................................909 947-5983
Brigitte A De Laura, *Pr*
EMP: 16 EST: 2000
SQ FT: 2,700
SALES (est): 256.23K **Privately Held**
SIC: **3728** Aircraft parts and equipment, nec

**(P-13982)**
**TRIUMPH INSULATION SYSTEMS LLC**
Also Called: Triumph Group
1754 Carr Rd Ste 103, Calexico (92231-9509)
PHONE......................................760 618-7543
▲ EMP: 900 EST: 1976
SALES (est): 35.91MM **Publicly Held**
SIC: **3728** Aircraft parts and equipment, nec
HQ: Triumph Aerospace Systems Group, Llc
   899 Cassatt Rd Ste 210
   Berwyn PA 19312

**(P-13983)**
**TRIUMPH STRUCTURES - EVERETT INC**
Also Called: Triumph Structures
17055 Gale Ave, City Of Industry (91745-1808)
PHONE......................................425 348-4100
▲ EMP: 202
SIC: **3728** Aircraft parts and equipment, nec

**(P-13984)**
**UNIVERSAL PROPULSION CO INC**
Also Called: Goodrich
3530 Branscombe Rd, Fairfield (94533)
P.O. Box P.O. Box Kk (94533-0659)
PHONE......................................707 399-1867
Jasper J Philip, *CEO*
Russell Murdergh, *VP Fin*
Bhatti Naadia, *Sec*
Sadler A Duane, *CFO*
EMP: 270 EST: 1959
SALES (est): 10.19MM
SALES (corp-wide): 68.92B **Publicly Held**
SIC: **3728** Seat ejector devices, aircraft
HQ: Goodrich Corporation
   2730 W Tyvola Rd
   Charlotte NC 28217
   704 423-7000

**(P-13985)**
**VANGUARD SPACE TECH INC**
Also Called: Alliance Spacesystems
4398 Corporate Center Dr, Los Alamitos (90720-2537)
PHONE......................................858 587-4210
Frank Belknap, *CEO*
Ronald Miller, *
John Richer, *
EMP: 101 EST: 1994
SQ FT: 50,000
SALES (est): 18.85MM
SALES (corp-wide): 244.59MM **Publicly Held**
Web: www.appliedcomposites.com
SIC: **3728** Aircraft parts and equipment, nec
HQ: Solaero Technologies Corp.
   10420 Res Rd Se Bldg 1
   Albuquerque NM 87123
   505 332-5000

**(P-13986)**
**VANTAGE ASSOCIATES INC**
Also Called: Vantage Master Machine Company
1565 Macarthur Blvd, Costa Mesa (92626-1407)
PHONE......................................562 968-1400
Paul Roy, *Brnch Mgr*
EMP: 40
SALES (est): 24.86MM **Privately Held**
Web: www.vantageassoc.com
SIC: **3728** Aircraft assemblies, subassemblies, and parts, nec
PA: Vantage Associates Inc.
   1565 Macarthur Blvd
   619 477-6940

**(P-13987)**
**VENTURA AEROSPACE INC**
31355 Agoura Rd, Westlake Village (91361-4610)
PHONE......................................818 540-3130
Mark L Snow, *CEO*
Mark L Snow, *VP*
Michael Snow, *Sec*
EMP: 16 EST: 1996
SQ FT: 2,000
SALES (est): 6.28MM **Privately Held**
Web: www.venturaaerospace.com
SIC: **3728** Aircraft parts and equipment, nec

**(P-13988)**
**VISION AEROSPACE LLC**
Also Called: Romakk Engineering
19863 Nordhoff St, Northridge (91324-3331)
PHONE......................................818 700-1035
EMP: 24 EST: 2018
SALES (est): 3.13MM **Privately Held**
SIC: **3728** Aircraft parts and equipment, nec

**(P-13989)**
**WESANCO INC**
14870 Desman Rd, La Mirada (90638-5746)
PHONE......................................714 739-4989
Brain Szymanski, *CFO*
▲ EMP: 30 EST: 1973
SQ FT: 30,000
SALES (est): 9.98MM
SALES (corp-wide): 242.37MM **Privately Held**
Web: www.wesanco.com
SIC: **3728** Oleo struts, aircraft
HQ: Zsi-Foster, Inc.
   1751 Summit Dr
   Auburn Hills MI 48326

**(P-13990)**
**WEST VALLEY AVIATION INC**
1011 12th St, Firebaugh (93622-2600)
PHONE......................................559 659-7378
Charlie Witrado, *Pr*
EMP: 15 EST: 2005
SALES (est): 2.03MM **Privately Held**
SIC: **3728** Dusting and spraying equipment, aircraft

**(P-13991)**
**WESTERN METHODS MACHINERY CORPORATION**
Also Called: Western Methods
2344 Pullman St, Santa Ana (92705-5507)
PHONE......................................949 252-6600
EMP: 120 EST: 1977
SALES (est): 1.57MM **Privately Held**
SIC: **3728** 3769 Aircraft parts and equipment, nec; Space vehicle equipment, nec

**(P-13992)**
**WHITTAKER CORPORATION**
1955 Surveyor Ave Fl 2, Simi Valley (93063-3369)
PHONE......................................805 526-5700
Erick Lardiere, *Pr*
▲ EMP: 40 EST: 1942
SQ FT: 276,000
SALES (est): 8.25MM
SALES (corp-wide): 19.93B **Publicly Held**
Web: www.whittakercorp.com
SIC: **3728** 3669 7373 Aircraft parts and equipment, nec; Fire detection systems, electric; Systems integration services
HQ: Meggitt Limited
   Ansty Bus.
   Coventry W MIDLANDS CV7 9
   247 682-6900

**(P-13993)**
**WOODWARD HRT INC**
Also Called: Woodward Duarte
1700 Business Center Dr, Duarte (91010-2859)
PHONE......................................626 359-9211
Don Grimes, *Mgr*
EMP: 250
SALES (corp-wide): 2.91B **Publicly Held**
SIC: **3728** 5084 Aircraft parts and equipment, nec; Hydraulic systems equipment and supplies
HQ: Woodward Hrt, Inc.
   25200 Rye Canyon Rd
   Santa Clarita CA 91355
   661 294-6000

**(P-13994)**
**ZENITH MANUFACTURING INC**
Also Called: Zipco
3087 12th St, Riverside (92507-4904)
PHONE......................................818 767-2106
James Phoung, *Pr*
EMP: 25 EST: 2006
SQ FT: 47,000
SALES (est): 2.53MM **Privately Held**
SIC: **3728** Aircraft parts and equipment, nec

**(P-13995)**
**ZODIAC AEROSPACE**
11340 Jersey Blvd, Rancho Cucamonga (91730-4919)
PHONE......................................909 652-9700
EMP: 20 EST: 2018
SALES (est): 3.22MM **Privately Held**
SIC: **3728** Aircraft parts and equipment, nec

## 3728 - Aircraft Parts And Equipment, Nec (P-13996)

**(P-13996)**
**ZODIAC INTERCONNECT US**
3780 Flightline Dr, Santa Rosa
(95403-1054)
PHONE....................707 535-2700
**EMP:** 18 **EST:** 2016
**SALES (est):** 1.27MM Privately Held
**SIC: 3728** Aircraft parts and equipment, nec

**(P-13997)**
**ZODIAC WTR WASTE AERO SYSTEMS**
Also Called: Monogram Systems
1500 Glenn Curtiss St, Carson
(90746-4012)
PHONE....................310 884-7000
**EMP:** 83 **EST:** 1958
**SALES (est):** 15.32MM
**SALES (corp-wide):** 650.78MM Privately Held
**SIC: 3728** Aircraft parts and equipment, nec
**PA:** Safran
2 Bd Du General Martial Valin

## 3731 Shipbuilding And Repairing

**(P-13998)**
**APR ENGINEERING INC**
Also Called: Oceanwide Repairs
1812 W 9th St, Long Beach (90813-2614)
P.O. Box 9100 (90810-0100)
PHONE....................562 983-3800
Roy Herington, Pr
Trina Young, *
▲ **EMP:** 33 **EST:** 1997
**SALES (est):** 2.02MM Privately Held
Web: www.oceanwiderepair.com
**SIC: 3731** Shipbuilding and repairing

**(P-13999)**
**BAE SYSTEMS SAN DEGO SHIP REPR**
2205 Belt St, San Diego (92113-3634)
P.O. Box 13308 (92170)
PHONE....................619 238-1000
Eric Icke, Pr
James M Blue, *
Alice M Eldridge, *
◆ **EMP:** 732 **EST:** 1976
**SALES (est):** 19.82MM
**SALES (corp-wide):** 28.77B Privately Held
**SIC: 3731** Shipbuilding and repairing
**HQ:** Bae Systems Ship Repair Inc.
750 W Berkley Ave
Norfolk VA 23523
757 494-4000

**(P-14000)**
**BAY SHIP & YACHT CO (PA)**
Also Called: Bay Ship & Yacht Co.
2900 Main St Ste 2100, Alameda
(94501-7739)
PHONE....................510 337-9122
William Elliott, CEO
Alan Cameron, *
Vicki Elliott, *
Leslie R Cameron, *
Bill Elliott, *
▲ **EMP:** 175 **EST:** 1990
**SQ FT:** 20,000
**SALES (est):** 39.69MM
**SALES (corp-wide):** 39.69MM Privately Held
Web: www.bay-ship.com
**SIC: 3731** 3732 Commercial cargo ships, building and repairing; Yachts, building and repairing

**(P-14001)**
**COLONNAS SHIPYARD WEST LLC**
2890 Faivre St Ste 150, Chula Vista
(91911-4983)
PHONE....................757 545-2414
Robert Boyd, Prin
Ana Nowland, Ofcr
**EMP:** 30 **EST:** 2017
**SALES (est):** 2.39MM Privately Held
Web: www.colonnaship.com
**SIC: 3731** Shipbuilding and repairing

**(P-14002)**
**CONTINENTAL MARITIME INDS INC**
1995 Bay Front St, San Diego
(92113-2122)
PHONE....................619 234-8851
David H Mc Queary, Pr
Lee E Wilson, *
**EMP:** 429 **EST:** 1990
**SQ FT:** 90,000
**SALES (est):** 45.21MM Publicly Held
Web: www.cmsd-msr.com
**SIC: 3731** Shipbuilding and repairing
**PA:** Huntington Ingalls Industries, Inc.
4101 Washington Ave

**(P-14003)**
**CRAFT LABOR & SUPPORT SVCS LLC**
1545 Tidelands Ave Ste C, National City
(91950-4240)
PHONE....................619 336-9977
Michael Greene, Brnch Mgr
**EMP:** 169
**SALES (corp-wide):** 8.27MM Privately Held
Web: www.craftlabor.com
**SIC: 3731** Shipbuilding and repairing
**PA:** Craft Labor And Support Services, Llc
7636 230th St Sw Apt B
206 304-4543

**(P-14004)**
**HII SAN DIEGO SHIPYARD INC**
1995 Bay Front St, San Diego
(92101-1951)
PHONE....................619 234-8851
Christopher Joseph Miner, CEO
Ronald Sugar, *
**EMP:** 325 **EST:** 1981
**SQ FT:** 90,000
**SALES (est):** 16.28MM Publicly Held
Web: www.cmsd-msr.com
**SIC: 3731** Military ships, building and repairing
**PA:** Huntington Ingalls Industries, Inc.
4101 Washington Ave

**(P-14005)**
**INTEGRATED MARINE SERVICES INC**
Also Called: IMS
2320 Main St, Chula Vista (91911-4610)
PHONE....................619 429-0300
Larry Samano, Pr
**EMP:** 55 **EST:** 2003
**SALES (est):** 9.4MM Privately Held
Web: www.imships.com
**SIC: 3731** Shipbuilding and repairing

**(P-14006)**
**KARGO TECHNOLOGIES CORP**
424 9th St, San Francisco (94103-4411)
PHONE....................312 925-1565
Samuel Lurye, CEO
**EMP:** 32 **EST:** 2019
**SALES (est):** 7.14MM Privately Held
Web: www.mykargo.com
**SIC: 3731** Commercial cargo ships, building and repairing

**(P-14007)**
**LARSON AL BOAT SHOP**
1046 S Seaside Ave, San Pedro
(90731-7334)
PHONE....................310 514-4100
Jack Wall, CEO
Gloria Wall, *
George Wall, *
▲ **EMP:** 70 **EST:** 1903
**SQ FT:** 65,000
**SALES (est):** 7.2MM Privately Held
Web: www.larsonboat.com
**SIC: 3731** 4493 Military ships, building and repairing; Marinas

**(P-14008)**
**MARE ISLAND DRY DOCK LLC**
1180 Nimitz Ave, Vallejo (94592-1053)
PHONE....................707 652-7356
Stephen Dileo, Managing Member
**EMP:** 60 **EST:** 2012
**SALES (est):** 19.14MM Privately Held
Web: www.middllc.com
**SIC: 3731** Shipbuilding and repairing

**(P-14009)**
**MARE ISLAND SHIP YARD LLC**
Also Called: Mare Island Ship Yard
1180 Nimitz Ave, Vallejo (94592-1053)
PHONE....................760 877-0291
**EMP:** 52
**SIC: 3731** Shipbuilding and repairing

**(P-14010)**
**MILLER MARINE**
2275 Manya St, San Diego (92154-4713)
PHONE....................619 791-1500
Pauline Senter, CEO
Edward Senter, *
Miller Marine, *
**EMP:** 45 **EST:** 1989
**SQ FT:** 13,500
**SALES (est):** 9.51MM Privately Held
Web: www.millermarine.us
**SIC: 3731** 7389 Shipbuilding and repairing; Grinding, precision: commercial or industrial

**(P-14011)**
**NASSCO**
7470 Mission Valley Rd, San Diego
(92108-4406)
PHONE....................619 929-3019
**EMP:** 36 **EST:** 2018
**SALES (est):** 846.26K Privately Held
Web: www.nassco.com
**SIC: 3731** Shipbuilding and repairing

**(P-14012)**
**NATIONAL STL & SHIPBUILDING CO (HQ)**
2798 Harbor Dr, San Diego (92113-3650)
P.O. Box 85278 (92186-5278)
PHONE....................619 544-3400
Michael Toner, Ch Bd
David Carver, *
Phebe Novakoviz, *
Blaise Brennan, *
Andrew Chen, *
◆ **EMP:** 477 **EST:** 1892
**SQ FT:** 100,000
**SALES (est):** 153.93MM
**SALES (corp-wide):** 42.27B Publicly Held
Web: www.nassco.com
**SIC: 3731** Military ships, building and repairing
**PA:** General Dynamics Corporation
11011 Sunset Hills Rd
703 876-3000

**(P-14013)**
**PACIFIC SHIP REPR FBRCTION INC (PA)**
1625 Rigel St, San Diego (92113-3887)
P.O. Box 13428 (92170-3428)
PHONE....................619 232-3200
David J Moore, CEO
Gary N Thomas, Contracts Director*
**EMP:** 287 **EST:** 1969
**SQ FT:** 136,000
**SALES (est):** 46.49MM
**SALES (corp-wide):** 46.49MM Privately Held
Web: www.pacship.com
**SIC: 3731** 3444 Combat vessels, building and repairing; Sheet metalwork

**(P-14014)**
**PAIGE SITTA & ASSOCIATES INC (PA)**
Also Called: Paige Floor Cvg Specialists
2050 Wilson Ave Ste B, National City
(91950)
PHONE....................619 233-5912
Scott Nicholson, Pr
Peter Sitta, *
Debbie Kelley, *
**EMP:** 22 **EST:** 1989
**SQ FT:** 9,000
**SALES (est):** 4.21MM
**SALES (corp-wide):** 4.21MM Privately Held
Web: www.paigefc.com
**SIC: 3731** 1752 Shipbuilding and repairing; Floor laying and floor work, nec

**(P-14015)**
**PUGLIA ENGINEERING INC**
Foot Of 20th St Pier 70, San Francisco
(94107)
PHONE....................415 861-7447
**EMP:** 150
**SALES (corp-wide):** 34.23MM Privately Held
**SIC: 3731** Commercial cargo ships, building and repairing
**PA:** Puglia Engineering, Inc.
201 Harris Ave
360 647-0080

**(P-14016)**
**PYR PRESERVATION SERVICES**
Also Called: Pyr
2393 Newton Ave Ste B, San Diego
(92113-3648)
PHONE....................619 338-8395
Daniel R Cummins, CEO
▲ **EMP:** 30 **EST:** 1997
**SQ FT:** 12,500
**SALES (est):** 2.5MM Privately Held
Web: www.pyrsd.com
**SIC: 3731** 3589 3479 2851 Commercial cargo ships, building and repairing; Sandblasting equipment; Etching and engraving; Epoxy coatings

**(P-14017)**
**SAN FRANCISCO SHIP REPAIR INC**
Foot Of 20th St Pier 70, San Francisco
(94107)
P.O. Box 7644 (94120-7644)
PHONE....................415 861-7447

## PRODUCTS & SERVICES SECTION
## 3732 - Boatbuilding And Repairing (P-14038)

▲ **EMP:** 150
**Web:** sub-zero-repair-san-francisco.site123.me
**SIC: 3731** Commercial cargo ships, building and repairing

**(P-14018)**
### TECNICO CORPORATION
3636 Gateway Center Ave, San Diego (92102-4508)
**PHONE**..................................619 426-7385
Jerald Steen, *Mgr*
**EMP:** 16
**Web:** www.tecnicocorp.com
**SIC: 3731** Shipbuilding and repairing
**PA:** Tecnico Corporation
831 Industrial Ave

**(P-14019)**
### TRIDENT MARITIME SYSTEMS INC
651 Drucker Ln, San Diego (92154)
**PHONE**..................................619 346-3800
**EMP:** 54
**SALES (corp-wide):** 449.31MM **Privately Held**
**Web:** www.tridentllc.com
**SIC: 3731** Shipbuilding and repairing
**HQ:** Trident Maritime Systems, Inc.
2011 Crystal Dr Ste 1102
Arlington VA 22202
703 236-1590

**(P-14020)**
### UNITED STATES DEPT OF NAVY
Also Called: Supervision of Shipbuilding
32nd St Naval Sta, San Diego (92136-0001)
P.O. Box 368119 (92136-0001)
**PHONE**..................................619 556-6033
Ron Craig, *Brnch Mgr*
**EMP:** 712
**Web:** www.navy.mil
**SIC: 3731** 9711 Shipbuilding and repairing; Navy
**HQ:** United States Department Of The Navy
1200 Navy Pentagon
Washington DC 20350

**(P-14021)**
### VALIANT TECHNICAL SERVICES INC
1785 Utah Ave, Lompoc (93437-6020)
**PHONE**..................................757 628-9500
Danny Schanick, *Mgr*
**EMP:** 57
**SQ FT:** 5,734
**SALES (corp-wide):** 562.85MM **Privately Held**
**Web:** www.onevaliant.com
**SIC: 3731** Shipbuilding and repairing
**HQ:** Valiant Technical Services Inc.
4465 Guthrie Hwy
Clarksville TN 37040

**(P-14022)**
### VIGOR MARINE LLC
1636 Wilson Ave, National City (91950-4449)
**PHONE**..................................619 474-4352
Shelton Smith, *Brnch Mgr*
**EMP:** 72
**SALES (corp-wide):** 1.05B **Privately Held**
**Web:** www.vigor.net
**SIC: 3731** Shipbuilding and repairing
**HQ:** Vigor Marine Llc
5555 N Channel Ave
Portland OR 97217

**(P-14023)**
### WALASHEK INDUSTRIAL & MAR INC
3890 Industrial Way, Benicia (94510-1200)
**PHONE**..................................206 624-2880
Frank Walashek, *Mgr*
**EMP:** 51
**SALES (corp-wide):** 30.82MM **Privately Held**
**Web:** www.walashek.com
**SIC: 3731** Shipbuilding and repairing
**HQ:** Walashek Industrial & Marine, Inc.
3411 Amherst St
Norfolk VA 23513

**(P-14024)**
### WALASHEK INDUSTRIAL & MAR INC
1428 Mckinley Ave, National City (91950-4217)
**PHONE**..................................619 498-1711
Frank Walashek, *Mgr*
**EMP:** 42
**SALES (corp-wide):** 30.82MM **Privately Held**
**Web:** www.walashek.com
**SIC: 3731** Shipbuilding and repairing
**HQ:** Walashek Industrial & Marine, Inc.
3411 Amherst St
Norfolk VA 23513

**(P-14025)**
### WALKER DESIGN INC
Also Called: Walker Engineering Enterprises
9255 San Fernando Rd, Sun Valley (91352-1416)
**PHONE**..................................818 252-7788
Robert A Walker Junior, *CEO*
Shari Goodgame, *
Michael Delillo, *
▲ **EMP:** 33 **EST:** 1976
**SQ FT:** 29,800
**SALES (est):** 5.83MM **Privately Held**
**Web:** www.walkerengineering.co
**SIC: 3731** Lighters, marine: building and repairing

---

## 3732 Boatbuilding And Repairing

**(P-14026)**
### ADEPT PROCESS SERVICES INC
Also Called: APS Marine
609 Anita St, Chula Vista (91911-4619)
P.O. Box 2130 (91933-2130)
**PHONE**..................................619 434-3194
Gary Southerland, *Pr*
**EMP:** 34 **EST:** 2005
**SALES (est):** 2.33MM **Privately Held**
**Web:** www.adeptworks.net
**SIC: 3732** 4493 7699 Boatbuilding and repairing; Boat yards, storage and incidental repair; Boat repair

**(P-14027)**
### AIR & GAS TECH INC
Also Called: Cem
11433 Woodside Ave, Santee (92071-4725)
**PHONE**..................................619 955-5980
Anthony Greenwell, *Pr*
Berenice Cossio, *
Jacob Meek, *
**EMP:** 25 **EST:** 1979
**SQ FT:** 18,000
**SALES (est):** 5.21MM **Privately Held**
**Web:** www.cemcorp.net
**SIC: 3732** Boatbuilding and repairing

**(P-14028)**
### ARC BOAT COMPANY
2261 Market St, San Francisco (94114-1612)
**PHONE**..................................877 272-2443
Mitchell Lee, *CEO*
Mitchell Lee, *Prin*
**EMP:** 100 **EST:** 2021
**SALES (est):** 1.95MM **Privately Held**
**Web:** www.arcboats.com
**SIC: 3732** Boatbuilding and repairing

**(P-14029)**
### BASIN MARINE INC
Also Called: Basin Marine Shipyard
829 Harbor Island Dr Ste A, Newport Beach (92660-7235)
**PHONE**..................................949 673-0360
Paul Smith, *Pr*
▲ **EMP:** 28 **EST:** 1956
**SQ FT:** 44,000
**SALES (est):** 2.77MM **Privately Held**
**Web:** www.basinmarine.com
**SIC: 3732** 5551 Boatbuilding and repairing; Marine supplies, nec

**(P-14030)**
### CATALINA YACHTS INC (PA)
Also Called: Morgan Marine
2259 Ward Ave, Simi Valley (93065-1863)
**PHONE**..................................818 884-7700
Frank W Butler, *Pr*
Sharon Day, *
◆ **EMP:** 50 **EST:** 1968
**SALES (est):** 16.95MM
**SALES (corp-wide):** 16.95MM **Privately Held**
**Web:** www.catalinayachts.com
**SIC: 3732** 5551 Sailboats, building and repairing; Boat dealers

**(P-14031)**
### DEEP OCEAN ENGINEERING INC
2261 Fortune Dr, San Jose (95131-1861)
**PHONE**..................................408 436-1102
Fang Li, *CEO*
**EMP:** 15 **EST:** 2010
**SALES (est):** 2.37MM **Privately Held**
**Web:** www.deepocean.com
**SIC: 3732** Boatbuilding and repairing

**(P-14032)**
### DRISCOLL INC
Also Called: Driscoll Boat Works
2500 Shelter Island Dr, San Diego (92106-3114)
**PHONE**..................................619 226-2500
Thomas Driscoll, *Pr*
John Gerald Driscoll, *
Joseph E Driscoll, *
Mary-carol Driscoll, *Sec*
▲ **EMP:** 50 **EST:** 1947
**SQ FT:** 2,400
**SALES (est):** 3.79MM **Privately Held**
**Web:** www.driscollinc.com
**SIC: 3732** Boatbuilding and repairing

**(P-14033)**
### FINELINE INDUSTRIES INC (PA)
Also Called: Centurion
2047 Grogan Ave, Merced (95341-6440)
**PHONE**..................................209 384-0255
Richard D Lee, *Pr*
Jeffrey Polan, *
Clark Bird, *
Pamela Lee, *
▼ **EMP:** 75 **EST:** 1983
**SQ FT:** 38,000
**SALES (est):** 26.65MM
**SALES (corp-wide):** 26.65MM **Privately Held**
**Web:** www.centurionboats.com
**SIC: 3732** Boats, fiberglass: building and repairing

**(P-14034)**
### GAMBOL INDUSTRIES INC
1880 Century Park E Ste 950, Los Angeles (90067-1612)
**PHONE**..................................562 901-2470
Robert A Stein, *Pr*
John Bridwell, *
▲ **EMP:** 45 **EST:** 1992
**SALES (est):** 8.37MM **Privately Held**
**Web:** www.gambolindustries.com
**SIC: 3732** 7699 4493 Yachts, building and repairing; Boat repair; Boat yards, storage and incidental repair

**(P-14035)**
### HOBIE CAT COMPANY (PA)
4925 Oceanside Blvd, Oceanside (92056-3044)
**PHONE**..................................760 758-9100
Richard Rogers, *CEO*
Doug Skidmore, *
Bill Baldwin, *
◆ **EMP:** 140 **EST:** 1995
**SQ FT:** 60,000
**SALES (est):** 35.3MM
**SALES (corp-wide):** 35.3MM **Privately Held**
**Web:** www.hobie.com
**SIC: 3732** Sailboats, building and repairing

**(P-14036)**
### INDEL ENGINEERING INC
Also Called: Marina Shipyard
6400 E Marina Dr, Long Beach (90803-4618)
**PHONE**..................................562 594-0995
D E Bud Tretter, *Pr*
Jerry Tretter, *
Kurt Tretter, *
**EMP:** 35 **EST:** 1964
**SQ FT:** 3,000
**SALES (est):** 2.61MM **Privately Held**
**Web:** www.marinashipyard.com
**SIC: 3732** Houseboats, building and repairing

**(P-14037)**
### INFINITY YACHTS INC
Also Called: Infinity Yacht Sales
1450 Harbor Island Dr Ste 208, San Diego (92101-1056)
**PHONE**..................................619 431-1194
Brian Donnelly, *CEO*
**EMP:** 15 **EST:** 2017
**SALES (est):** 494.13K **Privately Held**
**Web:** www.infinityyachtsales.com
**SIC: 3732** Boatbuilding and repairing

**(P-14038)**
### KAYE SANDY ENTERPRISES INC
Also Called: Porta-Bote International
344 Alameda De Las Pulgas, Redwood City (94062-2804)
**PHONE**..................................650 961-5334
Alex R Kaye, *Pr*
Frances Kaye, *
▼ **EMP:** 35 **EST:** 1973
**SALES (est):** 2.33MM **Privately Held**
**Web:** www.portabote.com
**SIC: 3732** 5551 Boatbuilding and repairing; Boat dealers

# 3732 - Boatbuilding And Repairing (P-14039)

## (P-14039)
**MARITIME SOLUTIONS LLC**
1616 Newton Ave, San Diego (92113-1013)
PHONE.................................619 234-2676
**EMP:** 30 **EST:** 1999
**SQ FT:** 4,000
**SALES (est):** 916.74K **Privately Held**
Web: www.maritimesolutions.com
**SIC: 3732** 3731 8711 Boatbuilding and repairing; Shipbuilding and repairing; Engineering services

## (P-14040)
**MATTHEW SMITH CRAMPTON**
Also Called: Marine Outfitters
300 Carlsbad Village Dr Ste 108a, Carlsbad (92008-2900)
PHONE.................................760 840-8404
Matthew C Smith, *Owner*
Matthew Smith, *Owner*
**EMP:** 22 **EST:** 1996
**SQ FT:** 15,000
**SALES (est):** 461.13K **Privately Held**
**SIC: 3732** 7699 Boatbuilding and repairing; Boat repair

## (P-14041)
**MAURER MARINE INC**
873 W 17th St, Costa Mesa (92627-4308)
PHONE.................................949 645-7673
Craig Maurer, *Pr*
Jay S Maurer, *VP*
**EMP:** 18 **EST:** 1979
**SALES (est):** 2.06MM **Privately Held**
Web: www.maurermarine.com
**SIC: 3732** 7389 Yachts, building and repairing; Yacht brokers

## (P-14042)
**MB SPORTS INC**
280 Airpark Rd, Atwater (95301-9535)
PHONE.................................209 357-4153
Myung Bo Hong, *CEO*
▲ **EMP:** 40 **EST:** 1993
**SQ FT:** 16,000
**SALES (est):** 5.1MM **Privately Held**
Web: www.mbsportsusa.com
**SIC: 3732** 5551 5091 Motorboats, inboard or outboard: building and repairing; Boat dealers; Boats, canoes, watercrafts, and equipment

## (P-14043)
**MOOSE BOATS LLC**
1175 Nimitz Ave Ste 150, Vallejo (94592-1003)
PHONE.................................707 778-9828
Christian Lind, *CEO*
Christian Lind, *Pr*
Roger N Fleck, *Ex VP*
Aaron Lind, *Treas*
**EMP:** 16 **EST:** 2016
**SQ FT:** 20,000
**SALES (est):** 3.34MM **Privately Held**
Web: www.mooseboats.com
**SIC: 3732** Boatbuilding and repairing

## (P-14044)
**OCEAN PROTECTA INCORPORATED**
14708 Biola Ave, La Mirada (90638-4450)
PHONE.................................714 891-2628
Edgar Chong Tan, *CEO*
Myron Reyes, *
**EMP:** 50 **EST:** 2014
**SALES (est):** 455.98K **Privately Held**
Web: www.oceanprotecta.com
**SIC: 3732** Boatbuilding and repairing

## (P-14045)
**TBYCI LLC**
Also Called: Boatyard-Channel Islands, The
3615 Victoria Ave, Oxnard (93035-4360)
PHONE.................................805 985-6800
Gregory Schem, *Managing Member*
Craig Campbell, *Genl Mgr*
**EMP:** 16 **EST:** 2013
**SQ FT:** 7,500
**SALES (est):** 1.62MM **Privately Held**
Web: www.seasideboatyard.com
**SIC: 3732** 3731 Motorized boat, building and repairing; Patrol boats, building and repairing

## (P-14046)
**VENTURA HARBOR BOATYARD INC**
1415 Spinnaker Dr, Ventura (93001-4339)
PHONE.................................805 654-1433
Robert Bartosh, *Pr*
Stephen James, *
Kim Morris, *
Dale Morris, *
**EMP:** 35 **EST:** 1986
**SQ FT:** 2,000
**SALES (est):** 4.57MM **Privately Held**
Web: www.vhby.com
**SIC: 3732** 4493 Boatbuilding and repairing; Boat yards, storage and incidental repair

## (P-14047)
**W D SCHOCK CORP**
1232 E Pomona St, Santa Ana (92707-2404)
P.O. Box 79184 (92877-0172)
PHONE.................................951 277-3377
Alexander Vucelic, *Pr*
▼ **EMP:** 30 **EST:** 1946
**SQ FT:** 30,000
**SALES (est):** 446.01K **Privately Held**
Web: www.wdschockcorp.com
**SIC: 3732** Sailboats, building and repairing

## (P-14048)
**WILLARD MARINE INC**
4602 North Ave, Oceanside (92056-3509)
PHONE.................................714 666-2150
Jordan Angle, *CEO*
Joseph Nangle, *
Justin Law, *
▲ **EMP:** 55 **EST:** 1957
**SALES (est):** 9.32MM **Privately Held**
Web: www.willardmarine.com
**SIC: 3732** Boats, fiberglass: building and repairing

## 3743 Railroad Equipment

## (P-14049)
**HYUNDAI ROTEM USA CORPORATION**
12750 Center Court Dr S, Cerritos (90703-8581)
PHONE.................................215 227-6836
O Hyun Kim, *CEO*
▲ **EMP:** 15 **EST:** 2004
**SALES (est):** 3.97MM **Privately Held**
**SIC: 3743** Railroad equipment
**PA:** Hyundai Rotem Company
488 Changwon-Daero, Seongsan-Gu

## (P-14050)
**KINKISHARYO (USA) INC**
300 Continental Blvd Ste 300, El Segundo (90245-5043)
PHONE.................................424 276-1803
▲ **EMP:** 146
Web: www.kinkisharyo.com
**SIC: 3743** Train cars and equipment, freight or passenger

## (P-14051)
**KINKISHARYO INT LLC (HQ)**
1960 E Grand Ave Ste 1210, El Segundo (90245-5061)
PHONE.................................424 276-1803
Hideki Hatai, *Managing Member*
▲ **EMP:** 19 **EST:** 1999
**SQ FT:** 6,000
**SALES (est):** 72MM **Privately Held**
Web: www.kinkisharyo.com
**SIC: 3743** 3321 Train cars and equipment, freight or passenger; Railroad car wheels and brake shoes, cast iron
**PA:** Kinki Sharyo Co., Ltd., The
2-2-46, Inadauemachi

## 3751 Motorcycles, Bicycles, And Parts

## (P-14052)
**ALL AMERICAN RACERS INC**
Also Called: Dan Gurneys All Amercn Racers
2334 S Broadway, Santa Ana (92707-3250)
P.O. Box 2186 (92707-0186)
PHONE.................................714 540-1771
Daniel S Gurney, *CEO*
Justin B Gurney, *
Kathy Weida, *
**EMP:** 162 **EST:** 1962
**SQ FT:** 25,000
**SALES (est):** 24.03MM **Privately Held**
Web: www.allamericanracers.com
**SIC: 3751** Motorcycles and related parts

## (P-14053)
**BARNETT TOOL & ENGINEERING**
Also Called: Barnett Performance Products
2238 Palma Dr, Ventura (93003-8068)
PHONE.................................805 642-9435
Michael Taylor, *Pr*
Colleen Taylor, *
**EMP:** 60 **EST:** 1948
**SQ FT:** 43,000
**SALES (est):** 4.58MM **Privately Held**
Web: www.barnettclutches.com
**SIC: 3751** Motorcycle accessories

## (P-14054)
**BELT DRIVES LTD**
Also Called: B D L
1959 N Main St, Orange (92865-4101)
PHONE.................................714 693-1313
Steve R Yetzke, *CEO*
Kathy Yetzke, *Stockholder*
**EMP:** 21 **EST:** 1990
**SALES (est):** 2.63MM **Privately Held**
Web: www.beltdrives.com
**SIC: 3751** Motorcycles and related parts

## (P-14055)
**CULT/CVLT LLC**
1555 E Saint Gertrude Pl, Santa Ana (92705-5309)
PHONE.................................714 435-2858
Robert Morales, *Prin*
▲ **EMP:** 20 **EST:** 2009
**SALES (est):** 1.26MM **Privately Held**
Web: www.cultcrew.com
**SIC: 3751** Motorcycles, bicycles and parts

## (P-14056)
**CURRIE ACQUISITIONS LLC**
Also Called: Currie Technologies
3850 Royal Ave Ste A, Simi Valley (93063-3267)
PHONE.................................805 915-4900
Larry Pizzi, *Managing Member*
**EMP:** 28 **EST:** 2008
**SALES (est):** 2.11MM
**SALES (corp-wide):** 2.67MM **Privately Held**
**SIC: 3751** 5012 8742 Motor scooters and parts; Motor scooters; Marketing consulting services
**HQ:** Accell Group B.V.
Industrieweg 4
Heerenveen FR
513638703

## (P-14057)
**FACTORY PIPE LLC**
Also Called: Factory Pipe Products
1307 Masonite Rd, Ukiah (95482-3400)
PHONE.................................707 463-1322
**EMP:** 30 **EST:** 1978
**SALES (est):** 4.85MM **Privately Held**
Web: www.factorypipe.com
**SIC: 3751** 5571 3732 Motorcycles and related parts; Motorcycle parts and accessories; Boatbuilding and repairing

## (P-14058)
**FMF RACING**
Also Called: Flying Machine Factory
18033 S Santa Fe Ave, Compton (90221-5514)
PHONE.................................310 631-4363
Don Emler, *CEO*
▲ **EMP:** 150 **EST:** 1985
**SALES (est):** 24.53MM **Privately Held**
Web: www.fmfracing.com
**SIC: 3751** 5571 Motorcycle accessories; Motorcycle parts and accessories

## (P-14059)
**GLOBAL MOTORSPORT PARTS INC**
15750 Vineyard Blvd Ste 100, Morgan Hill (95037-7119)
PHONE.................................408 778-0500
Joseph F Keenan, *Ch Bd*
Seth Murdock, *CFO*
◆ **EMP:** 97 **EST:** 1998
**SALES (est):** 826.24K **Privately Held**
Web: www.customchrome.com
**SIC: 3751** 5013 Motorcycle accessories; Motorcycle parts
**HQ:** Dae-Il Usa, Inc.
112 Robert Young Blvd
Murray KY 42071

## (P-14060)
**IMS PRODUCTS INC**
700 S Hathaway St, Banning (92220-5904)
P.O. Box 1088 (92220-0008)
PHONE.................................951 653-7720
C H Wheat, *Pr*
**EMP:** 16 **EST:** 1976
**SQ FT:** 10,000
**SALES (est):** 2.34MM **Privately Held**
Web: www.imsproducts.com
**SIC: 3751** 5571 Motorcycles and related parts; Motorcycle dealers

## (P-14061)
**K & N ENGINEERING INC (PA)**
Also Called: K&N
1455 Citrus St, Riverside (92507-1603)
P.O. Box 1329 (92502-1329)
PHONE.................................951 826-4000
Craige Scanlon, *CEO*
Chance Miller, *
Steve Williams, *

◆ EMP: 565 EST: 1964
SQ FT: 270,000
SALES (est): 140.52MM
SALES (corp-wide): 140.52MM **Privately Held**
Web: www.knfilters.com
SIC: **3751** 3599 3714 Handle bars, motorcycle and bicycle; Air intake filters, internal combustion engine, except auto; Filters: oil, fuel, and air, motor vehicle

**(P-14062)**
**KIBBLWHITE PRCSION MCHNING INC**
Also Called: Precision Machining
580 Crespi Dr Ste H, Pacifica (94044-3426)
PHONE.................650 359-4704
Will Kibblewhite, *Pr*
▲ EMP: 23 EST: 1961
SQ FT: 3,000
SALES (est): 2.37MM **Privately Held**
Web: www.kpmi.us
SIC: **3751** 3599 Motorcycles and related parts; Machine shop, jobbing and repair

**(P-14063)**
**LOADED BOARDS INC**
10575 Virginia Ave, Culver City (90232-3520)
PHONE.................310 839-1800
Don Tashman, *CEO*
◆ EMP: 17 EST: 2002
SQ FT: 5,500
SALES (est): 1.82MM **Privately Held**
Web: www.loadedboards.com
SIC: **3751** Bicycles and related parts

**(P-14064)**
**MAIER MANUFACTURING INC**
416 Crown Point Cir Ste 1, Grass Valley (95945-9558)
PHONE.................530 272-9036
Charles A Maier, *Pr*
George Maier, *
Mark Maier, *
▲ EMP: 45 EST: 1971
SQ FT: 79,000
SALES (est): 2.41MM **Privately Held**
Web: www.maierusa.com
SIC: **3751** 3082 Motorcycle accessories; Unsupported plastics profile shapes

**(P-14065)**
**MARKLAND INDUSTRIES INC (PA)**
21 Merano, Laguna Niguel (92677-8606)
PHONE.................714 245-2850
Donald R Markland, *Pr*
▲ EMP: 44 EST: 1978
SALES (est): 4.28MM
SALES (corp-wide): 4.28MM **Privately Held**
Web: www.marklandindustries.com
SIC: **3751** Motorcycle accessories

**(P-14066)**
**PERFORMANCE MACHINE INC**
Also Called: Performance Machine
6892 Marlin Cir, La Palma (90623-1017)
PHONE.................714 523-3000
▲ EMP: 200
SIC: **3751** 3714 Motorcycle accessories; Brake drums, motor vehicle

**(P-14067)**
**RAZOR USA LLC (PA)**
Also Called: Razor
12723 166th St, Cerritos (90703-2102)
P.O. Box 3610 (90703-3610)
PHONE.................562 345-6000
Carlton Calvin, *Managing Member*
Robert Chen, *Managing Member*
◆ EMP: 60 EST: 2000
SQ FT: 50,000
SALES (est): 24.75MM **Privately Held**
Web: www.razor.com
SIC: **3751** Motor scooters and parts

**(P-14068)**
**SANTA CRUZ BICYCLES LLC**
Also Called: Santa Cruz Bikes
2841 Mission St, Santa Cruz (95060-5705)
PHONE.................831 459-7560
◆ EMP: 70 EST: 2015
SQ FT: 70,000
SALES (est): 22MM
SALES (corp-wide): 11.09B **Privately Held**
Web: www.santacruzbicycles.com
SIC: **3751** 5941 Motorcycles, bicycles and parts; Bicycle and bicycle parts
HQ: Pon Holdings B.V.
Stadionplein 28
Amsterdam NH
202460900

**(P-14069)**
**SEGWAY INC**
405 E Santa Clara St Ste 100, Arcadia (91006-7219)
PHONE.................603 222-6000
Luke Gao, *CEO*
Chen Huang, *
Ye Wang, *
◆ EMP: 120 EST: 2000
SALES (est): 3.03MM
SALES (corp-wide): 5.08MM **Privately Held**
Web: www.segway.com
SIC: **3751** Motor scooters and parts
HQ: Nunn Bo (Tianjin) Technology Co., Ltd.
No.3, Tianrui Road, Qiche Industries Park, Wu Qing District
Tianjin TJ 30170

**(P-14070)**
**SONDORS INC**
2710 Yates Ave, Commerce (90040-2624)
PHONE.................323 372-3000
Storm Sondors, *CEO*
EMP: 20 EST: 2017
SALES (est): 3.24MM **Privately Held**
Web: www.sondors.com
SIC: **3751** Gears, motorcycle and bicycle

**(P-14071)**
**SPINERGY INC**
1709 La Costa Meadows Dr, San Marcos (92078-5105)
PHONE.................760 496-2121
Martin Connolly, *Pr*
▲ EMP: 80 EST: 1977
SQ FT: 63,000
SALES (est): 7.82MM **Privately Held**
Web: www.spinergy.com
SIC: **3751** 3949 7389 Bicycles and related parts; Exercise equipment; Design services

**(P-14072)**
**SUPER73 INC (PA)**
2722 Michelson Dr Ste 125, Irvine (92612-8907)
PHONE.................949 258-9245
Legrand Crewse, *CEO*
▼ EMP: 23 EST: 2018
SALES (est): 5.03MM
SALES (corp-wide): 5.03MM **Privately Held**
Web: www.super73.com

SIC: **3751** 5012 Motorcycles and related parts; Motorcycles

**(P-14073)**
**TWO BROTHERS RACING INC**
3474 Niki Way, Riverside (92507-6811)
PHONE.................714 550-6070
Craig A Erion, *Pr*
◆ EMP: 18 EST: 1985
SALES (est): 4.98MM **Privately Held**
Web: www.twobros.com
SIC: **3751** 5013 Motorcycles and related parts; Motorcycle parts

**(P-14074)**
**V&H PERFORMANCE LLC**
Also Called: Vance & Hines
13861 Rosecrans Ave, Santa Fe Springs (90670-5207)
PHONE.................562 921-7461
Andrew Graves, *CEO*
Mike Kennedy, *
Terry Vance, *
Byron Hines, *Stockholder*
▼ EMP: 65 EST: 2010
SQ FT: 12,000
SALES (est): 23.75MM
SALES (corp-wide): 251.1MM **Privately Held**
Web: www.vanceandhines.com
SIC: **3751** 5013 Motorcycles, bicycles and parts; Motorcycle parts
PA: Motorsport Aftermarket Group, Inc.
13861 Rosecrans Ave
917 838-4002

**(P-14075)**
**WESTERN MFG & DISTRG LLC**
Also Called: I.V. League Medical
835 Flynn Rd, Camarillo (93012-8702)
P.O. Box 7192 (92067-7192)
PHONE.................805 988-1010
EMP: 40 EST: 1970
SQ FT: 25,000
SALES (est): 2.55MM **Privately Held**
Web: www.westernmanufacturinganddistributing.com
SIC: **3751** 3841 3599 Motorcycles and related parts; Surgical and medical instruments; Machine shop, jobbing and repair

---

## 3761 Guided Missiles And Space Vehicles

**(P-14076)**
**ABL SPACE SYSTEMS COMPANY**
224 Oregon St, El Segundo (90245-4214)
P.O. Box 1608 (90245-6608)
PHONE.................424 321-6060
Harrison Fagan O'hanley, *CEO*
Daniel George Piemont, *
EMP: 60 EST: 2017
SALES (est): 22.47MM **Privately Held**
Web: www.ablspacesystems.com
SIC: **3761** Guided missiles and space vehicles

**(P-14077)**
**ASTRA SPACE INC (PA)**
Also Called: Astra
1900 Skyhawk St, Alameda (94501-6612)
PHONE.................866 278-7217
Chris Kemp, *Ch*
Axel Martinez, *CFO*
Martin Attiq, *Chief Business Officer*
EMP: 43 EST: 2016

SQ FT: 179,070
SALES (est): 3.87MM
SALES (corp-wide): 3.87MM **Privately Held**
Web: www.astra.com
SIC: **3761** Guided missiles and space vehicles

**(P-14078)**
**ASTROBOTIC TECHNOLOGY INC**
1570 Sabovich St, Mojave (93501-1681)
PHONE.................888 488-8455
David Masten, *Engr*
EMP: 92
SALES (corp-wide): 44.28MM **Privately Held**
Web: www.astrobotic.com
SIC: **3761** Guided missiles and space vehicles
PA: Astrobotic Technology, Inc.
1016 N Lincoln Ave
412 682-3282

**(P-14079)**
**BOEING COMPANY**
Also Called: Boeing
14441 Astronautics Ln, Huntington Beach (92647-2080)
PHONE.................714 896-3311
James Mcnerney, *Brnch Mgr*
EMP: 368
SQ FT: 2,200,000
SALES (corp-wide): 77.79B **Publicly Held**
Web: www.boeing.com
SIC: **3761** 3769 Guided missiles and space vehicles; Space vehicle equipment, nec
PA: The Boeing Company
929 Long Bridge Dr
703 465-3500

**(P-14080)**
**GALACTIC CO LLC (DH)**
Also Called: Spaceship Company, The
1700 Flight Way Ste 400, Tustin (92782)
PHONE.................661 824-6600
Michael Colglazier, *CEO*
Enrico Palermo, *
EMP: 21 EST: 2006
SQ FT: 200,000
SALES (est): 28.15MM
SALES (corp-wide): 6.8MM **Publicly Held**
Web: www.virgingalactic.com
SIC: **3761** Rockets, space and military, complete
HQ: Galactic Enterprises, Llc
166 N Roadrunner Pkwy
Las Cruces NM 88011

**(P-14081)**
**IMPULSE SPACE INC**
2651 Manhattan Beach Blvd, Redondo Beach (90278-1604)
PHONE.................949 315-5540
Thomas Mueller, *CEO*
EMP: 25 EST: 2021
SALES (est): 16.72MM **Privately Held**
Web: www.impulsespace.com
SIC: **3761** Guided missiles and space vehicles

**(P-14082)**
**KRATOS DEF & SEC SOLUTIONS INC (PA)**
Also Called: KRATOS
10680 Treena St Ste 600, San Diego (92131-2440)
PHONE.................858 812-7300
Eric Demarco, *Pr*
William Hoglund, *

## 3761 - Guided Missiles And Space Vehicles (P-14083)

Deanna Lund, *
Marie Mendoza, *Sr VP*
Benjamin Goodwin, *Senior Vice President Corporate Development*
**EMP:** 166 **EST:** 1995
**SALES (est):** 1.04B **Publicly Held**
**Web:** www.kratosdefense.com
**SIC: 3761** 3663 7382 8711  Guided missiles and space vehicles; Microwave communication equipment; Security systems services; Engineering services

### (P-14083)
### MASTEN SPACE SYSTEMS INC
Also Called: Masten Space
1570 Sabovich St 25, Mojave (93501-1681)
**PHONE**..................888 488-8455
**EMP:** 38 **EST:** 2004
**SQ FT:** 6,000
**SALES (est):** 5.11MM **Privately Held**
**Web:** www.masten.aero
**SIC: 3761**  Guided missiles and space vehicles

### (P-14084)
### ROCKET LAB USA INC (PA)
3881 Mcgowen St, Long Beach (90808-1702)
**PHONE**..................714 465-5737
Peter Beck, *Ch Bd*
Adam Spice, *CFO*
Shaun O'donnell, *Executive Global Operations Vice President*
Arjun Kampani, *Corporate Secretary*
Frank Klein, *COO*
**EMP:** 50 **EST:** 2006
**SALES (est):** 244.59MM
**SALES (corp-wide):** 244.59MM **Publicly Held**
**Web:** www.rocketlabusa.com
**SIC: 3761**  Guided missiles and space vehicles

### (P-14085)
### ROCKET LAB USA INC
4022 E Conant St, Long Beach (90808-1777)
**PHONE**..................714 465-5737
**EMP:** 32
**SALES (corp-wide):** 244.59MM **Publicly Held**
**Web:** www.rocketlabusa.com
**SIC: 3761**  Guided missiles and space vehicles, research and development
**PA:** Rocket Lab Usa, Inc.
3881 Mcgowen St
714 465-5737

### (P-14086)
### SPACE EXPLORATION TECH CORP
Also Called: Spacex
2980 Nimitz Rd, Long Beach (90802-1048)
**PHONE**..................310 363-6289
**EMP:** 157
**SALES (corp-wide):** 2.07B **Privately Held**
**Web:** www.spacex.com
**SIC: 3761**  Guided missiles and space vehicles
**PA:** Space Exploration Technologies Corp.
1 Rocket Rd
310 363-6000

### (P-14087)
### SPACE EXPLORATION TECH CORP
Also Called: Spacex
2700 Miner St, San Pedro (90731)
**PHONE**..................714 330-8668
**EMP:** 157

**SALES (corp-wide):** 2.07B **Privately Held**
**Web:** www.spacex.com
**SIC: 3761**  Rockets, space and military, complete
**PA:** Space Exploration Technologies Corp.
1 Rocket Rd
310 363-6000

### (P-14088)
### SPACE EXPLORATION TECH CORP
Also Called: Spacex Wilkie
12520 Wilkie Ave, Gardena (90249)
**PHONE**..................323 754-1285
**EMP:** 157
**SALES (corp-wide):** 2.07B **Privately Held**
**Web:** www.spacex.com
**SIC: 3761**  Rockets, space and military, complete
**PA:** Space Exploration Technologies Corp.
1 Rocket Rd
310 363-6000

### (P-14089)
### SPACE EXPLORATION TECH CORP
Also Called: Spacex
3976 Jack Northrop Ave, Hawthorne (90250-4441)
**PHONE**..................310 889-4968
**EMP:** 236
**SALES (corp-wide):** 2.07B **Privately Held**
**Web:** www.spacex.com
**SIC: 3761**  Rockets, space and military, complete
**PA:** Space Exploration Technologies Corp.
1 Rocket Rd
310 363-6000

### (P-14090)
### SPACE EXPLORATION TECH CORP (PA)
Also Called: Spacex
1 Rocket Rd, Hawthorne (90250-6844)
**PHONE**..................310 363-6000
Elon Musk, *CEO*
Gwynne Shotwell, *
Bret Johnsen, *
◆ **EMP:** 340 **EST:** 2002
**SQ FT:** 964,000
**SALES (est):** 2.07B
**SALES (corp-wide):** 2.07B **Privately Held**
**Web:** www.spacex.com
**SIC: 3761**  Rockets, space and military, complete

### (P-14091)
### SPACEX LLC
12533 Crenshaw Blvd, Hawthorne (90250-3302)
**PHONE**..................310 970-5845
**EMP:** 1496 **EST:** 2004
**SALES (est):** 8.48MM
**SALES (corp-wide):** 2.07B **Privately Held**
**Web:** www.spacex.com
**SIC: 3761**  Guided missiles and space vehicles
**PA:** Space Exploration Technologies Corp.
1 Rocket Rd
310 363-6000

### (P-14092)
### STELLAR EXPLORATION INC
835 Airport Dr, San Luis Obispo (93401-8370)
**PHONE**..................805 459-1425
Tomas Svitek, *Pr*
Tomas Svitek, *Pr*
Iva Svitek, *

**EMP:** 24 **EST:** 2001
**SQ FT:** 3,000
**SALES (est):** 3.17MM **Privately Held**
**Web:** www.stellar-exploration.com
**SIC: 3761**  Space vehicles, complete

### (P-14093)
### TAYCO ENGINEERING INC
10874 Hope St, Cypress (90630-5214)
P.O. Box 6034 (90630-0034)
**PHONE**..................714 952-2240
Jay Chung, *Pr*
Ann Taylor, *
Sheri T Nikolakopulos, *
**EMP:** 130 **EST:** 1971
**SQ FT:** 55,600
**SALES (est):** 15.87MM **Privately Held**
**Web:** www.taycoeng.com
**SIC: 3761**  Guided missiles and space vehicles

### (P-14094)
### TYVAK NN-SATELLITE SYSTEMS INC
1288 W Mccoy Ln, Santa Maria (93455-1048)
**PHONE**..................805 264-4319
**EMP:** 20
**SALES (corp-wide):** 135.91MM **Privately Held**
**Web:** www.tyvak.eu
**SIC: 3761**  Guided missiles and space vehicles
**HQ:** Tyvak Nano-Satellite Systems Inc.
15330 Barranca Pkwy
Irvine CA 92618

### (P-14095)
### TYVAK NN-SATELLITE SYSTEMS INC
400 Spectrum Center Dr, Irvine (92618-4934)
**PHONE**..................949 753-1020
Marc Bell, *Mgr*
**EMP:** 20
**SALES (corp-wide):** 135.91MM **Privately Held**
**Web:** www.tyvak.eu
**SIC: 3761**  Space vehicles, complete
**HQ:** Tyvak Nano-Satellite Systems Inc.
15330 Barranca Pkwy
Irvine CA 92618

### (P-14096)
### TYVAK NN-SATELLITE SYSTEMS INC (DH)
15330 Barranca Pkwy, Irvine (92618-2215)
**PHONE**..................949 753-1020
Marc Bell, *Pr*
Roger Teague, *
James Black, *
Gary Hobart, *
**EMP:** 35 **EST:** 2011
**SALES (est):** 22.29MM
**SALES (corp-wide):** 135.91MM **Privately Held**
**Web:** www.terranorbital.com
**SIC: 3761** 3764  Space vehicles, complete; Space propulsion units and parts
**HQ:** Terran Orbital Operating Corporation
6800 Brken Sund Pkwy Nw S
Boca Raton FL 33487
561 988-1704

### (P-14097)
### UNITED LAUNCH ALLIANCE LLC
1579 Utah Ave, Bldg. 7525, Vandenberg Afb (93437)

**PHONE**..................303 269-5876
Deborah Settit, *Prin*
**EMP:** 362
**Web:** www.ulalaunch.com
**SIC: 3761**  Guided missiles and space vehicles
**PA:** United Launch Alliance, L.L.C.
9501 E Panorama Cir

### (P-14098)
### VARDA SPACE INDUSTRIES INC
225 S Aviation Blvd, El Segundo (90245-4604)
**PHONE**..................833 707-0020
Delian Asparouhov, *Pr*
**EMP:** 70 **EST:** 2020
**SALES (est):** 10.15MM **Privately Held**
**Web:** www.varda.com
**SIC: 3761**  Space vehicles, complete

### (P-14099)
### VIRGIN GALACTIC HOLDINGS INC (PA)
Also Called: VIRGIN GALACTIC
1700 Flight Way Ste 400, Tustin (92782-1854)
**PHONE**..................949 774-7640
Michael Colglazier, *Pr*
Raymond Mabus Junior, *Ch Bd*
Doug Ahrens, *CFO*
Aparna Chitale, *CPO*
Sarah Kim, *CLO*
**EMP:** 35 **EST:** 2017
**SALES (est):** 6.8MM
**SALES (corp-wide):** 6.8MM **Publicly Held**
**Web:** www.virgingalactic.com
**SIC: 3761** 3812  Space vehicles, complete; Space vehicle guidance systems and equipment

### (P-14100)
### XCOR AEROSPACE INC
Also Called: Xcor
1314 Flight Line, Mojave (93501-1665)
P.O. Box 61310 (93501)
**PHONE**..................661 824-4714
▲ **EMP:** 87
**Web:** www.xcor.com
**SIC: 3761**  Guided missiles and space vehicles, research and development

## 3764 Space Propulsion Units And Parts

### (P-14101)
### AEROJET ROCKETDYNE INC (DH)
Also Called: Aerojet Rocketdyne
2001 Aerojet Rd, Rancho Cordova (95742-6418)
P.O. Box 13222 (95813-3222)
**PHONE**..................916 355-4000
Eileen Drake, *CEO*
John Joy, *
Kathleen Redd, *
Chris Conley, *
Christopher Cambria, *
▲ **EMP:** 1400 **EST:** 1944
**SALES (est):** 333.34MM
**SALES (corp-wide):** 19.42B **Publicly Held**
**Web:** www.l3harris.com
**SIC: 3764** 3728 3769 3761  Propulsion units for guided missiles and space vehicles; Aircraft body and wing assemblies and parts ; Space vehicle equipment, nec; Guided missiles and space vehicles
**HQ:** Aerojet Rocketdyne Holdings, Inc.
222 N Pcf Cast Hwy Ste 50
El Segundo CA 90245
310 252-8100

▲ = Import ▼ = Export
◆ = Import/Export

# PRODUCTS & SERVICES SECTION
## 3792 - Travel Trailers And Campers (P-14123)

**(P-14102)**
**MICROCOSM INC**
3111 Lomita Blvd, Torrance (90505-5108)
PHONE..................................310 539-2306
James Wertz, *Pr*
Alice Wertz, *
Robert E Conger, *
**EMP:** 40 **EST:** 1984
**SQ FT:** 50,000
**SALES (est):** 3.5MM **Privately Held**
Web: www.smad.com
**SIC:** 3764 2731 3769 Space propulsion units and parts; Book publishing; Space vehicle equipment, nec

**(P-14103)**
**MORPHEUS SPACE INC (PA)**
2101 E El Segundo Blvd, El Segundo (90245-4518)
PHONE..................................562 766-8470
Daniel Bock, *CEO*
Istvan Lorincz, *
Istan Lorincz, *
**EMP:** 17 **EST:** 2019
**SALES (est):** 3.77MM
**SALES (corp-wide):** 3.77MM **Privately Held**
Web: www.morpheus.space
**SIC:** 3764 Space propulsion units and parts

**(P-14104)**
**PHASE FOUR INC**
12605 S Van Ness Ave, Hawthorne (90250-3321)
PHONE..................................310 648-8454
Jonathan Jarvis, *CEO*
**EMP:** 17 **EST:** 2015
**SALES (est):** 7.14MM **Privately Held**
Web: www.phasefour.io
**SIC:** 3764 Space propulsion units and parts

**(P-14105)**
**RELATIVITY SPACE INC (PA)**
3500 E Burnett St, Long Beach (90815-1730)
PHONE..................................424 393-4309
Timothy Ellis, *CEO*
Jordan Noone, *
Alexander Kwan, *
Muhammad Shahzad, *
Roxanne Fung, *Corporate Controller*
**EMP:** 337 **EST:** 2015
**SQ FT:** 10,000
**SALES (est):** 135.25MM
**SALES (corp-wide):** 135.25MM **Privately Held**
Web: www.relativityspace.com
**SIC:** 3764 Space propulsion units and parts

**(P-14106)**
**SPINLAUNCH INC**
3816 Stineman Ct, Long Beach (90808-2572)
PHONE..................................650 516-7746
Jonathan Yaney, *Pr*
Domhnal Slattery, *
**EMP:** 166 **EST:** 2015
**SALES (est):** 7.8MM **Privately Held**
Web: www.spinlaunch.com
**SIC:** 3764 Propulsion units for guided missiles and space vehicles

## 3769 Space Vehicle Equipment, Nec

**(P-14107)**
**AEROWIND CORPORATION**
1959 John Towers Ave, El Cajon (92020-1117)
PHONE..................................619 569-1960
William L Kousens, *CEO*
**EMP:** 15 **EST:** 1946
**SQ FT:** 20,000
**SALES (est):** 843.13K **Privately Held**
Web: www.aerowind.com
**SIC:** 3769 3469 Guided missile and space vehicle parts and aux. equip., R&D; Machine parts, stamped or pressed metal

**(P-14108)**
**AMERICAN AUTOMATED ENGRG INC**
Also Called: A A E Aerospace & Coml Tech
5382 Argosy Ave, Huntington Beach (92649-1037)
PHONE..................................714 898-9951
Kenneth Christensen, *Pr*
**EMP:** 215 **EST:** 1967
**SQ FT:** 48,000
**SALES (est):** 8.78MM **Privately Held**
**SIC:** 3769 Space vehicle equipment, nec

**(P-14109)**
**CLIFFDALE MANUFACTURING LLC**
Also Called: RTC Aerospace
20409 Prairie St, Chatsworth (91311-6029)
PHONE..................................818 341-3344
Brad Hart, *CEO*
**EMP:** 200 **EST:** 1943
**SQ FT:** 42,000
**SALES (est):** 9.9MM **Privately Held**
Web: www.rtcaerospace.com
**SIC:** 3769 3599 Space vehicle equipment, nec; Machine shop, jobbing and repair

**(P-14110)**
**COMPOSITE OPTICS INCORPORATED**
Also Called: Atk
7130 Miramar Rd Ste 100b, San Diego (92121-2340)
PHONE..................................937 490-4145
**EMP:** 800
**SIC:** 3769 Space vehicle equipment, nec

**(P-14111)**
**DW AND BB CONSULTING INC**
11381 Bradley Ave, Pacoima (91331-2358)
PHONE..................................818 896-9899
David Wyckoff, *Pr*
Lee Brown, *
Ben Bensal, *
**EMP:** 70 **EST:** 1989
**SQ FT:** 10,000
**SALES (est):** 8.85MM **Privately Held**
Web: www.kdlprecision.com
**SIC:** 3769 2822 3061 Space vehicle equipment, nec; Silicone rubbers; Oil and gas field machinery rubber goods (mechanical)

**(P-14112)**
**HELIOSPACE CORPORATION**
2448 6th St, Berkeley (94710-2414)
PHONE..................................415 385-6803
Gregory Delory, *CEO*
Gregory Delroy, *
**EMP:** 45 **EST:** 2018
**SALES (est):** 2.49MM **Privately Held**
Web: www.helio.space
**SIC:** 3769 Space vehicle equipment, nec

**(P-14113)**
**HYDROMACH INC**
20400 Prairie St, Chatsworth (91311-8129)
PHONE..................................818 341-0915
Norberto A Cusinato, *CEO*
Jose Nicosia, *
Anna M Cusinato, *
**EMP:** 40 **EST:** 1976
**SQ FT:** 23,000
**SALES (est):** 5.61MM **Privately Held**
Web: www.hydromach.com
**SIC:** 3769 3599 Space vehicle equipment, nec; Machine shop, jobbing and repair

**(P-14114)**
**LEDA CORPORATION**
7080 Kearny Dr, Huntington Beach (92648-6254)
PHONE..................................714 841-7821
Joseph K Tung, *Pr*
Dorothy Tung, *
David Tung, *
**EMP:** 30 **EST:** 1985
**SQ FT:** 15,000
**SALES (est):** 5.58MM **Privately Held**
Web: www.ledacorp.net
**SIC:** 3769 Guided missile and space vehicle parts and aux. equip., R&D

**(P-14115)**
**MICRO STEEL INC**
7850 Alabama Ave, Canoga Park (91304-4905)
PHONE..................................818 348-8701
Lazar Hersko, *Pr*
Claudia Sceelo, *
Tova Hersko, *
**EMP:** 25 **EST:** 1986
**SQ FT:** 14,500
**SALES (est):** 3.5MM **Privately Held**
Web: www.microsteel.net
**SIC:** 3769 Space vehicle equipment, nec

**(P-14116)**
**STANFORD MU CORPORATION**
Also Called: Airborne Components
20725 Annalee Ave, Carson (90746-3503)
PHONE..................................310 605-2888
Stanford Mu, *Pr*
Lynn Price, *
Robert Friend, *
**EMP:** 40 **EST:** 1992
**SALES (est):** 7.57MM **Privately Held**
Web: www.stanfordmu.com
**SIC:** 3769 3764 7699 Space vehicle equipment, nec; Space propulsion units and parts; Aircraft and heavy equipment repair services

**(P-14117)**
**VANTAGE ASSOCIATES INC (PA)**
1565 Macarthur Blvd, Costa Mesa (92626-1407)
PHONE..................................619 477-6940
Mary Normand, *CEO*
Eric Clack, *
Andrea Alpinieri Glover, *
**EMP:** 35 **EST:** 1980
**SALES (est):** 24.86MM
**SALES (corp-wide):** 24.86MM **Privately Held**
Web: www.vantageassoc.com
**SIC:** 3769 2821 3728 3083 Space vehicle equipment, nec; Plastics materials and resins; Aircraft parts and equipment, nec; Laminated plastics plate and sheet

## 3792 Travel Trailers And Campers

**(P-14118)**
**BLUE SEA RESOURCES INC**
1400 Churchill Downs Ave Ste A, Woodland (95776-6146)
PHONE..................................530 666-1442
Tom Hanagan, *Pr*
▲ **EMP:** 25 **EST:** 1973
**SALES (est):** 9.25MM **Privately Held**
Web: www.fourwheelcampers.com
**SIC:** 3792 5561 Travel trailers and campers; Recreational vehicle dealers

**(P-14119)**
**CUSTOM FIBREGLASS MFG CO**
Also Called: Custom Hardtops
1711 Harbor Ave, Long Beach (90813-1300)
PHONE..................................562 432-5454
Hartmut W Schroeder, *Pr*
Joel Thiefburg, *
Robert L Edwards, *
◆ **EMP:** 165 **EST:** 1966
**SQ FT:** 135,000
**SALES (est):** 10.43MM
**SALES (corp-wide):** 1.62B **Privately Held**
Web: www.snugtop.com
**SIC:** 3792 Pickup covers, canopies or caps
**HQ:** Truck Accessories Group, Llc
28858 Ventura Dr
Elkhart IN 46517
574 522-5337

**(P-14120)**
**FLEETWOOD TRAVEL TRLRS IND INC (DH)**
3125 Myers St, Riverside (92503-5527)
P.O. Box 7638 (92513-7638)
PHONE..................................951 354-3000
Edward B Caudill, *Pr*
Edward B Caudill, *Pr*
Boyd R Plowman, *Ex VP*
Forrest D Theobald, *Sr VP*
Lyle N Larkin, *VP*
**EMP:** 143 **EST:** 1971
**SQ FT:** 262,900
**SALES (est):** 8.5MM **Privately Held**
**SIC:** 3792 Travel trailers and campers
**HQ:** Fleetwood Enterprises, Inc.
1351 Pomona Rd Ste 230
Corona CA 92882
951 354-3000

**(P-14121)**
**KENDON INDUSTRIES INC**
3711 E La Palma Ave, Anaheim (92806-2121)
PHONE..................................714 630-7144
▲ **EMP:** 15
**SIC:** 3792 Travel trailers and campers

**(P-14122)**
**PACIFIC COACHWORKS INC**
3411 N Perris Blvd Bldg 1, Perris (92571-3100)
PHONE..................................951 686-7294
Brett Bashaw, *CEO*
Michael Rhodes, *
**EMP:** 155 **EST:** 2006
**SALES (est):** 15.62MM **Privately Held**
Web: www.pacificcoachworks.com
**SIC:** 3792 Travel trailers and campers

**(P-14123)**
**PROTO HOMES LLC**
11301 W Olympic Blvd, Los Angeles (90064-1615)
PHONE..................................310 271-7544
**EMP:** 40 **EST:** 2009
**SALES (est):** 5.15MM **Privately Held**
Web: www.protohomes.com
**SIC:** 3792 House trailers, except as permanent dwellings

## 3795 Tanks And Tank Components

**(P-14124)**
**BRADLEY TANKS INC**
301 Durham Ct, Danville (94526-2911)
PHONE..................925 831-3562
Sharon Bonner, *CEO*
**EMP:** 45
**SALES (corp-wide):** 11.33MM **Privately Held**
**Web:** www.btienvironmental.com
**SIC: 3795** Tanks and tank components
**PA:** Bradley Tanks, Inc.
402 Hartz Ave
925 229-2900

**(P-14125)**
**DN TANKS INC**
Also Called: Dyk
351 Cypress Ln, El Cajon (92020-1603)
P.O. Box 696 (92022-0696)
PHONE..................619 440-8181
**EMP:** 149
**Web:** www.dntanks.com
**SIC: 3795** Tanks and tank components
**PA:** Dn Tanks, Inc.
11 Teal Rd

**(P-14126)**
**DYK INCORPORATED (HQ)**
Also Called: Dyk Prestressed Tanks
351 Cypress Ln, El Cajon (92020-1603)
P.O. Box 696 (92022-0696)
PHONE..................619 440-8181
Charles Crowley, *CEO*
Max R Dykmans, *
Bill Hendrickson, *
Bill Crowley, *
David Gourley, *
◆ **EMP:** 24 **EST:** 1989
**SALES (est):** 3.99MM **Privately Held**
**Web:** www.dntanks.com
**SIC: 3795** 8711 1542 Tanks and tank components; Engineering services; Nonresidential construction, nec
**PA:** Dn Tanks, Inc.
11 Teal Rd

**(P-14127)**
**SANTA ROSA STAIN**
1400 Airport Blvd, Santa Rosa (95403-1023)
P.O. Box 518 (95402-0518)
PHONE..................707 544-7777
Mark Ferronato, *Pr*
Rod Ferronato, *
Michele Cotta, *
**EMP:** 45 **EST:** 1969
**SQ FT:** 12,000
**SALES (est):** 5.19MM **Privately Held**
**Web:** www.srss.com
**SIC: 3795** Tanks and tank components

**(P-14128)**
**TIGER TANKS INC**
3397 Edison Hwy, Bakersfield (93307-2234)
P.O. Box 21041 (93390-1041)
PHONE..................661 363-8335
**TOLL FREE:** 888
Robert E Bimat, *Ch Bd*
Darryck Selk, *
Bryan Lewis, *
Carol Bimat, *
Roger Burns, *
**EMP:** 30 **EST:** 1997
**SQ FT:** 55,000
**SALES (est):** 4.78MM **Privately Held**
**Web:** www.tigertanksinc.com
**SIC: 3795** 3443 Tanks and tank components; Fabricated plate work (boiler shop)

## 3799 Transportation Equipment, Nec

**(P-14129)**
**DG PERFORMANCE SPC INC**
4100 E La Palma Ave, Anaheim (92807-1818)
PHONE..................714 961-8850
Mark W Dooley, *Pr*
William J Dooley, *
Joan K Dooley, *
**EMP:** 100 **EST:** 1972
**SQ FT:** 25,000
**SALES (est):** 1.83MM **Privately Held**
**Web:** www.dgperformance.com
**SIC: 3799** 3751 5012 5961 Recreational vehicles; Motorcycles and related parts; Recreation vehicles, all-terrain; Fitness and sporting goods, mail order

**(P-14130)**
**HALL ASSOCIATES RACG PDTS INC**
2711 Plaza Del Amo Ste 503, Torrance (90503-7344)
PHONE..................310 326-4111
Ammie Armstrong, *CEO*
Kennith C Hall, *Pr*
**EMP:** 17 **EST:** 1995
**SALES (est):** 813.45K **Privately Held**
**Web:** www.hallass.com
**SIC: 3799** 8733 3699 Recreational vehicles; Research institute; Security devices

**(P-14131)**
**NATIONAL SIGNAL LLC**
14489 Industry Cir, La Mirada (90638-5812)
PHONE..................714 441-7707
Alex Henderson, *
James M Welch, *
**EMP:** 99 **EST:** 2022
**SALES (est):** 10.41MM
**SALES (corp-wide):** 1.03B **Privately Held**
**SIC: 3799** 3669 Trailers and trailer equipment; Highway signals, electric
**PA:** Hill & Smith Plc
Westhaven House
121 704-7430

**(P-14132)**
**PREMIER TRAILER MFG INC**
30517 Ivy Rd, Visalia (93291-9553)
P.O. Box 191 (93279-0191)
PHONE..................559 651-2212
Gene A Cuelho Junior, *Pr*
Sally Cuelho, *
**EMP:** 29 **EST:** 1996
**SALES (est):** 5.93MM **Privately Held**
**SIC: 3799** Trailers and trailer equipment

**(P-14133)**
**SPORT BOAT TRAILERS**
430 C St, Patterson (95363-2724)
P.O. Box 1686 (95363-1686)
PHONE..................209 892-5388
Robert J Kehl, *Pr*
**EMP:** 17 **EST:** 1974
**SQ FT:** 3,700
**SALES (est):** 945.33K **Privately Held**
**Web:** www.sbtrailers.com
**SIC: 3799** 7539 Boat trailers; Trailer repair

## 3812 Search And Navigation Equipment

**(P-14134)**
**ACCUTURN CORPORATION**
7189 Old 215 Frontage Rd Ste 101, Moreno Valley (92553-7903)
PHONE..................951 656-6621
Ignatius C Araujo, *CEO*
Iggy Araujo, *
Mark Sayegh, *Stockholder*
Henri Rahmon, *Stockholder*
**EMP:** 26 **EST:** 1974
**SQ FT:** 15,000
**SALES (est):** 4.82MM **Privately Held**
**Web:** www.accuturninc.com
**SIC: 3812** 3089 3599 Acceleration indicators and systems components, aerospace; Automotive parts, plastic; Machine shop, jobbing and repair

**(P-14135)**
**AEROANTENNA TECHNOLOGY INC**
20732 Lassen St, Chatsworth (91311-4507)
PHONE..................818 993-3842
Yosef Klein, *Pr*
Joe Klein, *
Carmela Klein, *
▲ **EMP:** 140 **EST:** 1991
**SALES (est):** 26.05MM **Publicly Held**
**Web:** www.aeroantenna.com
**SIC: 3812** 3663 Antennas, radar or communications; Antennas, transmitting and communications
**HQ:** Heico Electronic Technologies Corp.
3000 Taft St
Hollywood FL 33021
954 987-6101

**(P-14136)**
**AEROJET RCKETDYNE HOLDINGS INC (HQ)**
222 N Pacific Coast Hwy Ste 500, El Segundo (90245-5603)
P.O. Box 537012 (95853-7012)
PHONE..................310 252-8100
Ross Niebergall, *Pr*
Joseph Chontos, *VP*
**EMP:** 75 **EST:** 1915
**SALES (est):** 2.24B
**SALES (corp-wide):** 19.42B **Publicly Held**
**Web:** www.l3harris.com
**SIC: 3812** 3764 3769 6552 Defense systems and equipment; Propulsion units for guided missiles and space vehicles; Space vehicle equipment, nec; Subdividers and developers, nec
**PA:** L3harris Technologies, Inc.
1025 W Nasa Blvd
321 727-9100

**(P-14137)**
**AEROJET ROCKETDYNE DE INC**
222 N Pacific Coast Hwy Ste 50, El Segundo (90245-5648)
PHONE..................310 414-0110
**EMP:** 655
**SALES (corp-wide):** 19.42B **Publicly Held**
**Web:** www.l3harris.com
**SIC: 3812** Defense systems and equipment
**HQ:** Inc Aerojet Rocketdyne Of De
8900 De Soto Ave
Canoga Park CA 91304
818 586-1000

**(P-14138)**
**ALLIANT TCHSYSTEMS OPRTONS LLC**
21250 Califa St, Woodland Hills (91367-5001)
PHONE..................818 887-8185
**EMP:** 19
**Web:** www.northropgrumman.com
**SIC: 3812** Search and navigation equipment
**HQ:** Alliant Techsystems Operations Llc
2980 Fairview Park Dr
Falls Church VA 22042

**(P-14139)**
**ALLIANT TCHSYSTEMS OPRTONS LLC**
9401 Corbin Ave, Northridge (91324-2400)
PHONE..................818 887-8195
Ronald Hill, *Prin*
**EMP:** 400 **EST:** 2002
**SALES (est):** 15.53MM **Publicly Held**
**SIC: 3812** Search and navigation equipment
**HQ:** Northrop Grumman Innovation Systems, Inc.
2980 Fairview Park Dr
Falls Church VA 22042

**(P-14140)**
**ALLIANT TCHSYSTEMS OPRTONS LLC**
151 Martinvale Ln Ste 150, San Jose (95119-1455)
PHONE..................408 513-3271
**EMP:** 19
**Web:** www.northropgrumman.com
**SIC: 3812** Search and navigation equipment
**HQ:** Alliant Techsystems Operations Llc
2980 Fairview Park Dr
Falls Church VA 22042

**(P-14141)**
**ALLIANT TCHSYSTEMS OPRTONS LLC**
9401 Corbin Ave, Northridge (91324-2400)
PHONE..................818 887-8195
Albert Calabrese, *Pr*
**EMP:** 27
**Web:** www.northropgrumman.com
**SIC: 3812** Search and navigation equipment
**HQ:** Alliant Techsystems Operations Llc
2980 Fairview Park Dr
Falls Church VA 22042

**(P-14142)**
**ANDURIL INDUSTRIES INC (PA)**
1400 Anduril, Costa Mesa (92626-1548)
PHONE..................949 891-1607
Brian Schimpf, *CEO*
Matthew Grimm, *
**EMP:** 596 **EST:** 2017
**SQ FT:** 155,000
**SALES (est):** 457.43MM
**SALES (corp-wide):** 457.43MM **Privately Held**
**Web:** www.anduril.com
**SIC: 3812** Search and navigation equipment

**(P-14143)**
**ANDURIL INDUSTRIES INC**
2910 S Tech Center Dr, Santa Ana (92705-5657)
PHONE..................949 891-1607
**EMP:** 43
**SALES (corp-wide):** 457.43MM **Privately Held**
**Web:** www.anduril.com
**SIC: 3812** Search and navigation equipment
**PA:** Anduril Industries, Inc.
1400 Anduril

## 3812 - Search And Navigation Equipment (P-14164)

949 891-1607

**(P-14144)**
**AO SKY CORPORATION**
20185 Skywest Dr, Hayward (94541-4606)
PHONE..............................510 264-0402
Craig Miller, *Pr*
**EMP:** 22
**SALES (corp-wide):** 997.56K **Privately Held**
Web: www.ao-sky.com
**SIC: 3812** Aircraft/aerospace flight instruments and guidance systems
**PA:** Sky Ao Corporation
  4989 Pedro Hill Rd
  415 717-9901

**(P-14145)**
**APEX TECHNOLOGY HOLDINGS INC**
Also Called: Apex Design Technology
2850 E Coronado St, Anaheim (92806-2503)
PHONE..............................321 270-3630
Lance Schroeder, *Pr*
**EMP:** 513 **EST:** 2005
**SQ FT:** 80,000
**SALES (corp-wide):** 3.75MM **Privately Held**
Web: www.apexdt.com
**SIC: 3812** Acceleration indicators and systems components, aerospace

**(P-14146)**
**ARETE ASSOCIATES (PA)**
Also Called: Arete Associates
9301 Corbin Ave Ste 2000, Northridge (91324-2508)
PHONE..............................818 885-2200
David Campion, *Pr*
Doug Deprospo, *CSO\**
Christopher Choi, *\**
Sallie Di Vincenzo, *CAO\**
**EMP:** 125 **EST:** 1975
**SQ FT:** 170,000
**SALES (est):** 100MM
**SALES (corp-wide):** 100MM **Privately Held**
Web: www.arete.com
**SIC: 3812** 3827 Aircraft/aerospace flight instruments and guidance systems; Sighting and fire control equipment, optical

**(P-14147)**
**ARGON ST INC**
329 Bernardo Ave, Mountain View (94043-5225)
PHONE..............................650 988-4700
Matthew Hoff, *Brnch Mgr*
**EMP:** 50
**SALES (corp-wide):** 77.79B **Publicly Held**
Web: www.argonst.com
**SIC: 3812** Search and navigation equipment
**HQ:** Argon St, Inc.
  12701 Fair Lkes Cir Ste 8
  Fairfax VA 22033
  703 322-0881

**(P-14148)**
**ARGON ST INC**
6696 Mesa Ridge Rd Ste A, San Diego (92121-2950)
PHONE..............................703 270-6927
Matthew Hoff, *Brnch Mgr*
**EMP:** 66
**SALES (corp-wide):** 77.79B **Publicly Held**
Web: www.argonst.com
**SIC: 3812** Search and navigation equipment
**HQ:** Argon St, Inc.
  12701 Fair Lkes Cir Ste 8
  Fairfax VA 22033
  703 322-0881

**(P-14149)**
**ARMTEC COUNTERMEASURES CO (DH)**
85901 Avenue 53, Coachella (92236-2607)
PHONE..............................760 398-0143
Paul Heidenreich, *VP*
◆ **EMP:** 17 **EST:** 2002
**SQ FT:** 100,000
**SALES (est):** 38.31MM
**SALES (corp-wide):** 7.94B **Publicly Held**
Web: www.armtecdefense.com
**SIC: 3812** Defense systems and equipment
**HQ:** Armtec Defense Products Co.
  85901 Avenue 53
  Coachella CA 92236

**(P-14150)**
**ASCENT AEROSPACE**
1395 S Lyon St, Santa Ana (92705-4608)
PHONE..............................586 726-0500
**EMP:** 58 **EST:** 2020
**SALES (est):** 8.66MM **Privately Held**
Web: www.ascentaerospace.com
**SIC: 3812** Search and navigation equipment

**(P-14151)**
**ASRC AEROSPACE CORP**
Also Called: ASRC AEROSPACE CORP Nasa Ames Research Center, Mountain View (94035)
PHONE..............................650 604-5946
Ted Price, *Mgr*
**EMP:** 348
**SALES (corp-wide):** 2.72B **Privately Held**
Web: www.asrcfederal.com
**SIC: 3812** 7371 7373 5088 Search and navigation equipment; Custom computer programming services; Computer integrated systems design; Transportation equipment and supplies
**HQ:** Asrc Aerospace Corp.
  7000 Muirkirk Meadows Dr # 100
  Beltsville MD 20705
  301 837-5500

**(P-14152)**
**ASTRO DIGITAL US INC**
3047 Orchard Pkwy Ste 20, San Jose (95134-2129)
PHONE..............................650 804-3210
Chris Biddy, *CEO*
**EMP:** 65 **EST:** 2015
**SALES (est):** 8.94MM **Privately Held**
Web: www.astrodigital.com
**SIC: 3812** Aircraft/aerospace flight instruments and guidance systems

**(P-14153)**
**ATK LAUNCH SYSTEMS LLC**
16707 Via Del Campo Ct, San Diego (92127-1713)
PHONE..............................858 592-2509
Audrey Clarck, *Brnch Mgr*
**EMP:** 464
Web: www.northropgrumman.com
**SIC: 3812** Search and navigation equipment
**HQ:** Atk Launch Systems Llc
  9160 N Highway 83
  Corinne UT 84307
  801 251-2512

**(P-14154)**
**ATK SPACE SYSTEMS LLC**
Space Components Business Unit
7130 Miramar Rd Ste 100b, San Diego (92121-2340)
PHONE..............................858 530-3047
**EMP:** 109
Web: www.psi-pci.com
**SIC: 3812** Search and navigation equipment
**HQ:** Atk Space Systems Llc
  6033 Bandini Blvd
  Commerce CA 90040
  323 722-0222

**(P-14155)**
**ATK SPACE SYSTEMS LLC (DH)**
Also Called: Space Components
6033 Bandini Blvd, Commerce (90040-2968)
PHONE..............................323 722-0222
Blake Larson, *Pr*
Daniel J Murphy, *\**
Ronald D Dittemore, *\**
James Armor, *\**
Thomas R Wilson, *\**
◆ **EMP:** 50 **EST:** 1963
**SQ FT:** 104,000
**SALES (est):** 76.83MM **Publicly Held**
Web: www.psi-pci.com
**SIC: 3812** Search and navigation equipment
**HQ:** Northrop Grumman Innovation Systems, Inc.
  2980 Fairview Park Dr
  Falls Church VA 22042

**(P-14156)**
**ATK SPACE SYSTEMS LLC**
Also Called: Space Components Division
7130 Miramar Rd Ste 100b, San Diego (92121-2340)
PHONE..............................858 621-5700
**EMP:** 94
Web: www.psi-pci.com
**SIC: 3812** Search and navigation equipment
**HQ:** Atk Space Systems Llc
  6033 Bandini Blvd
  Commerce CA 90040
  323 722-0222

**(P-14157)**
**ATK SPACE SYSTEMS LLC**
600 Pine Ave, Goleta (93117-3803)
PHONE..............................805 685-2262
Blake Larson, *CEO*
**EMP:** 94
Web: www.psi-pci.com
**SIC: 3812** Search and navigation equipment
**HQ:** Atk Space Systems Llc
  6033 Bandini Blvd
  Commerce CA 90040
  323 722-0222

**(P-14158)**
**ATK SPACE SYSTEMS LLC**
1960 E Grand Ave Ste 1150, El Segundo (90245-5166)
PHONE..............................310 343-3799
Dale Woolheater, *Brnch Mgr*
**EMP:** 62
Web: www.psi-pci.com
**SIC: 3812** Search and navigation equipment
**HQ:** Atk Space Systems Llc
  6033 Bandini Blvd
  Commerce CA 90040
  323 722-0222

**(P-14159)**
**ATK SPACE SYSTEMS LLC**
370 N Halstead St, Pasadena (91107-3122)
PHONE..............................626 351-0205
Joe Tellegrino, *Mgr*
**EMP:** 94
Web: www.psi-pci.com
**SIC: 3812** 3826 8711 Search and navigation equipment; Instruments measuring thermal properties; Engineering services
**HQ:** Atk Space Systems Llc
  6033 Bandini Blvd
  Commerce CA 90040
  323 722-0222

**(P-14160)**
**ATK SPACE SYSTEMS LLC**
Also Called: Atk Arspace Strctres Test Fclt
16707 Via Del Campo Ct, San Diego (92127-1713)
PHONE..............................858 487-0970
Brian Welge, *Mgr*
**EMP:** 109
Web: www.psi-pci.com
**SIC: 3812** Search and navigation equipment
**HQ:** Atk Space Systems Llc
  6033 Bandini Blvd
  Commerce CA 90040
  323 722-0222

**(P-14161)**
**BAE SYSTEMS LAND ARMAMENTS LP**
1650 Industrial Blvd, Chula Vista (91911-3922)
PHONE..............................619 455-0213
Todd Eden, *Brnch Mgr*
**EMP:** 37
**SALES (corp-wide):** 28.77B **Privately Held**
Web: www.baesystems.com
**SIC: 3812** Search and navigation equipment
**HQ:** Bae Systems Land & Armaments L.P.
  2941 Frview Pk Dr Ste 100
  Falls Church VA 22042
  571 461-6000

**(P-14162)**
**BAE SYSTEMS LAND ARMAMENTS LP**
900 John Smith Rd, Hollister (95023)
PHONE..............................831 637-0356
Steven Ayupan, *Brnch Mgr*
**EMP:** 79
**SALES (corp-wide):** 28.77B **Privately Held**
Web: www.baesystems.com
**SIC: 3812** Search and navigation equipment
**HQ:** Bae Systems Land & Armaments L.P.
  2941 Frview Pk Dr Ste 100
  Falls Church VA 22042
  571 461-6000

**(P-14163)**
**BAE SYSTEMS LAND ARMAMENTS LP**
6331 San Ignacio Ave, San Jose (95119-1202)
P.O. Box 53107 (95153-0107)
PHONE..............................408 289-0111
**EMP:** 287
**SALES (corp-wide):** 28.77B **Privately Held**
Web: www.baesystems.com
**SIC: 3812** Search and navigation equipment
**HQ:** Bae Systems Land & Armaments L.P.
  2941 Frview Pk Dr Ste 100
  Falls Church VA 22042
  571 461-6000

**(P-14164)**
**BAE SYSTEMS TECH SLTONS SVCS I**
9650 Chesapeake Dr, San Diego (92123-1307)
PHONE..............................858 278-3042
David Davis, *Brnch Mgr*
**EMP:** 53
**SALES (corp-wide):** 28.77B **Privately Held**
**SIC: 3812** Navigational systems and instruments
**HQ:** Bae Systems Technology Solutions & Services Inc.
  520 Gaither Rd

## 3812 - Search And Navigation Equipment (P-14165)

Rockville MD 20850
703 847-5820

**(P-14165)**
**CACI PHOTONICS LLC**
Also Called: SA Photonics, LLC
120 Knowles Dr, Los Gatos (95032-1828)
**PHONE**....................408 560-3500
John Mengucci, *CEO*
James Coward, *
Cynthia Gamble, *
Dave Pechner, *
Mustafa Veziroglu, *
**EMP:** 110 **EST:** 2002
**SQ FT:** 30,000
**SALES (est):** 24.36MM
**SALES (corp-wide):** 7.66B **Publicly Held**
**Web:** www.caci.com
**SIC: 3812** Defense systems and equipment
**PA:** Caci International Inc.
12021 Sunset Hills Rd
703 841-7800

**(P-14166)**
**CAES SYSTEMS LLC**
5300 Hellyer Ave, San Jose (95138-1003)
**PHONE**....................408 624-3000
Dave Young, *Brnch Mgr*
**EMP:** 316
**SALES (corp-wide):** 4.59B **Privately Held**
**Web:** www.caes.com
**SIC: 3812** 3679 Search and navigation equipment; Microwave components
**HQ:** Caes Systems Llc
305 Richardson Rd
Lansdale PA 19446

**(P-14167)**
**CAES SYSTEMS LLC**
9404 Chesapeake Dr, San Diego (92123-1303)
**PHONE**....................858 560-1301
Dave Young, *Brnch Mgr*
**EMP:** 208
**SALES (corp-wide):** 4.59B **Privately Held**
**Web:** www.caes.com
**SIC: 3812** Search and navigation equipment
**HQ:** Caes Systems Llc
305 Richardson Rd
Lansdale PA 19446

**(P-14168)**
**CAPELLA SPACE CORP**
438 Shotwell St, San Francisco (94110-1914)
**PHONE**....................650 334-7734
Frank Backes, *CEO*
**EMP:** 75 **EST:** 2016
**SALES (est):** 12.26MM **Privately Held**
**Web:** www.capellaspace.com
**SIC: 3812** Antennas, radar or communications

**(P-14169)**
**CHANNEL TECHNOLOGIES GROUP LLC**
Also Called: Ctg
879 Ward Dr, Santa Barbara (93111-2920)
**EMP:** 1356 **EST:** 2012
**SALES (est):** 2.6MM **Privately Held**
**SIC: 3812** Search and navigation equipment

**(P-14170)**
**COHERENT AEROSPACE & DEFENSE INC (HQ)**
Also Called: Ii-VI Aerospace & Defense Inc
36570 Briggs Rd, Murrieta (92563-2387)
**PHONE**....................951 926-2994
**EMP:** 121 **EST:** 1961

**SALES (est):** 60.26MM
**SALES (corp-wide):** 4.71B **Publicly Held**
**Web:** www.iiviad.com
**SIC: 3812** 3827 Infrared object detection equipment; Optical instruments and apparatus
**PA:** Coherent Corp.
375 Saxonburg Blvd
724 352-4455

**(P-14171)**
**CONDOR PACIFIC INDUSTRIES INC (PA)**
905 Rancho Conejo Blvd, Newbury Park (91320-1716)
**PHONE**....................818 889-2150
Sidney Meltzner, *Pr*
**EMP:** 21 **EST:** 2006
**SALES (est):** 4.92MM **Privately Held**
**Web:** www.condorpacific.com
**SIC: 3812** 3728 Gyroscopes; Aircraft parts and equipment, nec

**(P-14172)**
**CONSOLIDATED AEROSPACE MFG LLC (HQ)**
Also Called: CAM
1425 S Acacia Ave, Fullerton (92831-5317)
**PHONE**....................714 989-2797
Dave Werner, *Managing Member*
**EMP:** 46 **EST:** 2012
**SALES (est):** 434.9MM
**SALES (corp-wide):** 15.78B **Publicly Held**
**Web:** www.stanleyblackanddecker.com
**SIC: 3812** Search and navigation equipment
**PA:** Stanley Black & Decker, Inc.
1000 Stanley Dr
860 225-5111

**(P-14173)**
**CORETEX USA INC**
15110 Avenue Of Science Ste 100, San Diego (92128-3405)
**PHONE**....................877 247-8725
Selwyn Pellett, *CEO*
**EMP:** 16 **EST:** 2015
**SALES (est):** 15.98MM **Privately Held**
**Web:** www.coretex.com
**SIC: 3812** Acceleration indicators and systems components, aerospace
**HQ:** Coretex Limited
73 Remuera Road
Auckland AUK 1050

**(P-14174)**
**CUBIC CORPORATION (HQ)**
Also Called: Cubic
9233 Balboa Ave, San Diego (92123-1513)
**PHONE**....................858 277-6780
Stevan Slijepcevic, *Pr*
Anshooman Aga, *Ex VP*
Mark A Harrison, *CAO*
Grace G Lee, *Chief Human Resources Officer*
Hilary L Hageman, *Corporate Secretary*
**EMP:** 1243 **EST:** 1951
**SQ FT:** 265,000
**SALES (est):** 1.48B
**SALES (corp-wide):** 1.48B **Privately Held**
**Web:** www.cubic.com
**SIC: 3812** 3699 7372 3724 Defense systems and equipment; Flight simulators (training aids), electronic; Application computer software; Aircraft engines and engine parts
**PA:** Atlas Cc Acquisition Corp.
850 New Burton Rd Ste 201
858 277-6780

**(P-14175)**
**CUMMINS AEROSPACE LLC (PA)**
Also Called: Cummins Aerospace
2320 E Orangethorpe Ave, Anaheim (92806-1223)
**PHONE**....................714 879-2800
Sean Beriah Cummins, *CEO*
William Beriah Cummins, *
Tina Marie Cummins, *
Mary Ellen Cummins, *
Sean Beriah Cummins, *Dir*
**EMP:** 30 **EST:** 1978
**SQ FT:** 35,000
**SALES (est):** 11.98MM
**SALES (corp-wide):** 11.98MM **Privately Held**
**Web:** www.cumminsaerospace.com
**SIC: 3812** 3519 3728 Search and navigation equipment; Internal combustion engines, nec; Aircraft parts and equipment, nec

**(P-14176)**
**DAVIS INSTRUMENTS CORPORATION**
3465 Diablo Ave, Hayward (94545-2778)
**PHONE**....................510 732-9229
James S Acquistapace, *Ch Bd*
Robert W Selig Junior, *Pr*
Susan Tatum, *CFO*
Kevin Mccarthy, *COO*
◆ **EMP:** 100 **EST:** 1964
**SQ FT:** 77,000
**SALES (est):** 19.94MM **Privately Held**
**Web:** www.davisinstruments.com
**SIC: 3812** 3429 3829 3823 Navigational systems and instruments; Marine hardware; Measuring and controlling devices, nec; Process control instruments

**(P-14177)**
**DECA INTERNATIONAL CORP**
Also Called: Golf Buddy
10700 Norwalk Blvd, Santa Fe Springs (90670-3824)
**PHONE**....................714 367-5900
Seung Wook Jung, *CEO*
▲ **EMP:** 28 **EST:** 2005
**SQ FT:** 3,000
**SALES (est):** 4.96MM **Privately Held**
**SIC: 3812** Navigational systems and instruments

**(P-14178)**
**DECATUR ELECTRONICS INC (DH)**
15890 Bernardo Center Dr, San Diego (92127-2320)
**PHONE**....................888 428-4315
Brian Brown, *CEO*
Luisa Nechodom, *
◆ **EMP:** 70 **EST:** 1955
**SQ FT:** 10,000
**SALES (est):** 30.04MM
**SALES (corp-wide):** 179.22MM **Privately Held**
**Web:** www.decaturelectronics.com
**SIC: 3812** Radar systems and equipment
**HQ:** D & K Engineering
16990 Goldentop Rd
San Diego CA 92127

**(P-14179)**
**DECATUR ELECTRONICS INC**
Also Called: Thunderworks Division
10729 Wheatlands Ave Ste C, Santee (92071-2887)
**PHONE**....................619 596-1925
Kevin Mitchell, *Mgr*
**EMP:** 15
**SALES (corp-wide):** 179.22MM **Privately Held**

**Web:** www.decaturelectronics.com
**SIC: 3812** Radar systems and equipment
**HQ:** Decatur Electronics Inc.
15890 Bernardo Center Dr
San Diego CA 92127
888 428-4315

**(P-14180)**
**DG ENGINEERING CORP (PA)**
Also Called: Schulz Engineering
13326 Ralston Ave, Sylmar (91342-7608)
**PHONE**....................818 364-9024
Gary Gilmore, *Ch Bd*
Aret Demiral, *
▲ **EMP:** 20 **EST:** 1973
**SQ FT:** 7,000
**SALES (est):** 3.89MM
**SALES (corp-wide):** 3.89MM **Privately Held**
**Web:** www.dge-corp.com
**SIC: 3812** 3845 Aircraft control systems, electronic; Electromedical equipment

**(P-14181)**
**EATON AEROSPACE LLC**
Also Called: Eaton
9650 Jeronimo Rd, Irvine (92618-2024)
**PHONE**....................949 452-9500
Lily Bridenbaker, *Mgr*
**EMP:** 25
**SIC: 3812** 3365 Acceleration indicators and systems components, aerospace; Aerospace castings, aluminum
**HQ:** Eaton Aerospace Llc
1000 Eaton Blvd
Cleveland OH 44114
818 409-0200

**(P-14182)**
**EDGE AUTONOMY SLO LLC**
831 Buckley Rd, San Luis Obispo (93401-8130)
**PHONE**....................805 544-0932
John Purvis, *CEO*
Gordon Jennings, *
**EMP:** 41 **EST:** 1989
**SQ FT:** 19,000
**SALES (est):** 10.38MM
**SALES (corp-wide):** 1.05B **Privately Held**
**Web:** www.edgeautonomy.io
**SIC: 3812** 7371 3721 Electronic detection systems (aeronautical); Computer software development and applications; Aircraft
**HQ:** Edge Autonomy Bend, Llc
2789 Nw Lolo Dr
Bend OR 97703
541 678-0515

**(P-14183)**
**EDO COMMUNICATIONS AND COUNTERMEASURES SYSTEMS INC**
Also Called: Force Protection Systems
7821 Orion Ave, Van Nuys (91406-2029)
**PHONE**....................818 464-2475
**EMP:** 60
**SIC: 3812** 3663 3612 7371 Search and navigation equipment; Radio and t.v. communications equipment; Signaling transformers, electric; Custom computer programming services

**(P-14184)**
**EMPLOYER DEFENSE GROUP**
2390 E Orangewood Ave Ste 520, Anaheim (92806-6188)
**PHONE**....................949 200-0137
Michelle Oelhafen, *Prin*
**EMP:** 22 **EST:** 2017
**SALES (est):** 1.88MM **Privately Held**

## PRODUCTS & SERVICES SECTION
## 3812 - Search And Navigation Equipment (P-14204)

Web: www.edglaw.com
SIC: 3812 Defense systems and equipment

**(P-14185)**
**ENSIGN-BICKFORD AROSPC DEF CO**
14370 White Sage Rd, Moorpark (93021-8720)
P.O. Box 429 (93020-0429)
PHONE...................805 292-4000
Brendan Walsh, *General Vice President*
EMP: 153
SALES (corp-wide): 696.33MM Privately Held
Web: www.ensign-bickfordind.com
SIC: 3812 Search and navigation equipment
HQ: Ensign-Bickford Aerospace & Defense Co
640 Hopmeadow St
Simsbury CT 06070
860 843-2289

**(P-14186)**
**FIRAN TECH GROUP USA CORP (HQ)**
20750 Marilla St, Chatsworth (91311-4407)
PHONE...................818 407-4024
Brad Bourne, *Pr*
EMP: 65 EST: 2004
SALES (est): 98.57MM
SALES (corp-wide): 98.06MM Privately Held
Web: www.ftgcorp.com
SIC: 3812 Aircraft control systems, electronic
PA: Firan Technology Group Corporation
250 Finchdene Sq
416 299-4000

**(P-14187)**
**FORT ORD WORKS INC**
791 Neeson Rd, Marina (93933-5106)
P.O. Box 1169 (93933-1169)
PHONE...................831 275-1294
Joe Johnson, *CEO*
EMP: 20 EST: 2018
SALES (est): 1.18MM Privately Held
Web: www.fortordworks.com
SIC: 3812 Aircraft/aerospace flight instruments and guidance systems

**(P-14188)**
**FRONTGRADE TECHNOLOGIES LLC**
577 Burning Tree Rd, Fullerton (92833-1445)
PHONE...................714 870-2420
EMP: 66
Web: www.frontgrade.com
SIC: 3812 Search and navigation equipment
HQ: Frontgrade Technologies Llc
4350 Centennial Blvd
Colorado Springs CO 80907

**(P-14189)**
**GARMIN INTERNATIONAL INC**
135 S State College Blvd Ste 110, Brea (92821-5823)
PHONE...................909 444-5000
EMP: 296
Web: www.garmin.com
SIC: 3812 Navigational systems and instruments
HQ: Garmin International, Inc.
1200 E 151st St
Olathe KS 66062

**(P-14190)**
**GARNER PRODUCTS INC**
10620 Industrial Ave Ste 100, Roseville (95678-5902)
PHONE...................916 784-0200
Ronald Stofan, *CEO*
Michelle M Stofan, *Sec*
EMP: 15 EST: 1959
SQ FT: 24,000
SALES (est): 2.41MM Privately Held
Web: www.garnerproducts.com
SIC: 3812 3663 7389 Degaussing equipment; Radio broadcasting and communications equipment; Document and office record destruction

**(P-14191)**
**GENERAL DYNMICS OTS NCVLLE INC**
105 Lake Forest Way, Folsom (95630-4708)
PHONE...................916 355-7700
Marshall Cousineau, *Dir*
EMP: 60
SALES (corp-wide): 42.27B Publicly Held
Web: www.gd-ots.com
SIC: 3812 3769 Search and navigation equipment; Space vehicle equipment, nec
HQ: General Dynamics Ots (Niceville), Inc.
511 Grove St
Healdsburg CA 95448
707 473-9200

**(P-14192)**
**GENERAL FORMING CORPORATION**
640 Alaska Ave, Torrance (90503-5100)
PHONE...................310 326-0624
Ward Olson, *CEO*
EMP: 43 EST: 1956
SALES (est): 3.66MM Privately Held
Web: www.generalformingcorporation.com
SIC: 3812 3769 3444 3728 Search and navigation equipment; Space vehicle equipment, nec; Sheet metal specialties, not stamped; Aircraft parts and equipment, nec

**(P-14193)**
**GENERAL RADAR CORP (PA)**
616 Mountain View Ave, Belmont (94002-2533)
PHONE...................650 304-9033
Dmitry Turbiner, *CEO*
Sergio Rodriguera Junior, *CFO*
Tricia Nelson, *Sec*
EMP: 18 EST: 2015
SALES (est): 1.32MM
SALES (corp-wide): 1.32MM Privately Held
Web: www.genrad.com
SIC: 3812 Antennas, radar or communications

**(P-14194)**
**GLOBAL A LGISTICS TRAINING INC**
Also Called: Galt
3860 Calle Fortunada Ste 100, San Diego (92123-4802)
PHONE...................760 688-0365
John Kohut, *CEO*
Lili Topchev, *CFO*
David Heist, *CSO*
Mark Kempf, *COO*
EMP: 47 EST: 2015
SQ FT: 18,000
SALES (est): 22.43MM Privately Held
Web: www.galt.aero

SIC: 3812 3721 3728 8711 Aircraft/aerospace flight instruments and guidance systems; Research and development on aircraft by the manufacturer; Military aircraft equipment and armament; Engineering services

**(P-14195)**
**GOLDAK INC**
15835 Monte St Ste 104, Sylmar (91342-7674)
P.O. Box 1988 (91209-1988)
PHONE...................818 240-2666
Dan Mulcahey, *Pr*
Dan Mulcahey, *Pr*
Butch Mulcahey, *
Thomas Mulcahey, *
Jeanie Mulcahey, *
EMP: 25 EST: 1970
SQ FT: 3,000
SALES (est): 2.29MM Privately Held
Web: www.goldak.com
SIC: 3812 Detection apparatus: electronic/magnetic field, light/heat

**(P-14196)**
**INTELLISENSE SYSTEMS INC**
21041 S Western Ave, Torrance (90501-1727)
PHONE...................310 320-1827
Robert Waldo, *CEO*
Robert Waldo, *Pr*
Selvy Utama, *VP*
EMP: 146 EST: 2017
SQ FT: 43,000
SALES (est): 62.11MM Privately Held
Web: www.intellisenseinc.com
SIC: 3812 Search and navigation equipment

**(P-14197)**
**INTEROCEAN INDUSTRIES INC**
Also Called: Interocean Systems
9201 Isaac St Ste C, Santee (92071-5627)
PHONE...................858 292-0808
Michael Pearlman, *CEO*
Stephen Pearlman, *
▼ EMP: 31 EST: 1945
SALES (est): 4.48MM Privately Held
Web: www.interoceansystems.com
SIC: 3812 3699 3826 3531 Search and navigation equipment; Underwater sound equipment; Environmental testing equipment; Marine related equipment

**(P-14198)**
**INTEROCEAN SYSTEMS LLC**
9201 Isaac St Ste C, Santee (92071-5627)
PHONE...................858 565-8400
Michael D Pearlman, *Pr*
EMP: 35 EST: 2005
SALES (est): 3.94MM
SALES (corp-wide): 19.66MM Privately Held
Web: www.interoceansystems.com
SIC: 3812 3699 Search and navigation equipment; Underwater sound equipment
PA: Delmar Systems, Inc.
8114 Highway 90 E
337 365-0180

**(P-14199)**
**INVENSENSE INC (HQ)**
Also Called: Invensense
1745 Technology Dr Ste 200, San Jose (95110-3729)
PHONE...................408 501-2200
Amit Shah, *Ch Bd*
Behrooz Abdi, *
Mark Dentinger, *
Daniel Goehl, *Worldwide Sales Vice President**

Mo Maghsoudnia, *Technology Vice President*
EMP: 174 EST: 2004
SQ FT: 159,000
SALES (est): 50.55MM Privately Held
Web: invensense.tdk.com
SIC: 3812 Gyroscopes
PA: Tdk Corporation
2-5-1, Nihombashi

**(P-14200)**
**JARIET TECHNOLOGIES INC**
103 W Torrance Blvd, Redondo Beach (90277)
PHONE...................310 698-1000
Charles Harper, *CEO*
David Clark, *
Monica Gilbert, *
Matthew Hoppe, *
Craig Hornbuckle, *
EMP: 35 EST: 2015
SQ FT: 20,000
SALES (est): 12.51MM Privately Held
Web: www.jariettech.com
SIC: 3812 Search and navigation equipment

**(P-14201)**
**L3 TECHNOLOGIES INC**
901 E Ball Rd, Anaheim (92805-5916)
PHONE...................714 956-9200
EMP: 30
SALES (corp-wide): 19.42B Publicly Held
Web: www.l3harris.com
SIC: 3812 Search and navigation equipment
HQ: L3 Technologies, Inc.
600 3rd Ave Fl 34
New York NY 10016
321 727-9100

**(P-14202)**
**L3 TECHNOLOGIES INC**
Also Called: Photonics Division
5957 Landau Ct, Carlsbad (92008-8803)
PHONE...................760 431-6800
Tim Call, *VP*
EMP: 131
SALES (corp-wide): 19.42B Publicly Held
Web: www.l3harris.com
SIC: 3812 Search and navigation equipment
HQ: L3 Technologies, Inc.
600 3rd Ave Fl 34
New York NY 10016
321 727-9100

**(P-14203)**
**L3 TECHNOLOGIES INC**
Datron Advanced Tech Div
200 W Los Angeles Ave, Simi Valley (93065)
PHONE...................805 584-1717
John Digioia, *Brnch Mgr*
EMP: 100
SALES (corp-wide): 19.42B Publicly Held
Web: www.l3harris.com
SIC: 3812 Search and navigation equipment
HQ: L3 Technologies, Inc.
600 3rd Ave Fl 34
New York NY 10016
321 727-9100

**(P-14204)**
**L3 TECHNOLOGIES INC**
Ocean Systems Division
28022 Industry Dr, Valencia (91355-4191)
PHONE...................818 367-0111
David Defranco, *Brnch Mgr*
EMP: 200
SALES (corp-wide): 19.42B Publicly Held
Web: www.l3harris.com

## 3812 - Search And Navigation Equipment (P-14205)

**SIC: 3812** Search and navigation equipment
**HQ:** L3 Technologies, Inc.
600 3rd Ave Fl 34
New York NY 10016
321 727-9100

### (P-14205)
### L3HARRIS TECHNOLOGIES INC
Also Called: Harris
7821 Orion Ave, Van Nuys (91406-2029)
P.O. Box 7713 (91409-7713)
PHONE..................................818 901-2523
**EMP:** 350
**SALES (corp-wide):** 19.42B **Publicly Held**
**Web:** www.l3harris.com
**SIC: 3812** Search and navigation equipment
**PA:** L3harris Technologies, Inc.
1025 W Nasa Blvd
321 727-9100

### (P-14206)
### L3HARRIS TECHNOLOGIES INC
Also Called: Harris
12121 Wilshire Blvd Ste 910, Los Angeles (90025-1123)
PHONE..................................310 481-6000
**EMP:** 42
**SALES (corp-wide):** 19.42B **Publicly Held**
**Web:** www.l3harris.com
**SIC: 3812** 7371 Search and navigation equipment; Computer software development
**PA:** L3harris Technologies, Inc.
1025 W Nasa Blvd
321 727-9100

### (P-14207)
### L3HARRIS TECHNOLOGIES INC
1400 S Shamrock Ave, Monrovia (91016-4267)
PHONE..................................626 305-6230
Pat Carr, *Brnch Mgr*
**EMP:** 134
**SALES (corp-wide):** 19.42B **Publicly Held**
**Web:** www.l3harris.com
**SIC: 3812** Search and navigation equipment
**PA:** L3harris Technologies, Inc.
1025 W Nasa Blvd
321 727-9100

### (P-14208)
### LAIRD R & F PRODUCTS INC (DH)
2091 Rutherford Rd, Carlsbad (92008-7316)
PHONE..................................760 916-9410
Scott Griffiths, *Pr*
▲ **EMP:** 49 **EST:** 1996
**SQ FT:** 62,000
**SALES (est):** 21.48MM
**SALES (corp-wide):** 2.93B **Publicly Held**
**SIC: 3812** Radar systems and equipment
**HQ:** Laird Technologies, Inc.
16401 Swingley Ridge Rd
Chesterfield MO 63017
636 898-6000

### (P-14209)
### LG INNOTEK USA INC
Also Called: San Jose Office
2540 N 1st St Ste 400, San Jose (95131-1015)
PHONE..................................408 234-6356
**EMP:** 93
**Web:** www.lg.com
**SIC: 3812** Defense systems and equipment
**HQ:** Lg Innotek Usa, Inc.
2540 N 1st St Ste 400
San Jose CA 95131
408 955-0364

### (P-14210)
### LOCKHEED MARTIN CORPORATION
Lockheed Martin Metrology Svcs
1111 Lockheed Martin Way Bldg 195a, Sunnyvale (94089-1212)
PHONE..................................408 756-5751
**EMP:** 94
**Web:** www.lockheedmartin.com
**SIC: 3812** Search and navigation equipment
**PA:** Lockheed Martin Corporation
6801 Rockledge Dr

### (P-14211)
### LOCKHEED MARTIN CORPORATION
Also Called: Lockheed Martin
3251 Hanover St, Palo Alto (94304-1121)
PHONE..................................650 424-2000
Aram Mica, *VP*
**EMP:** 24
**SQ FT:** 350,000
**Web:** www.lockheedmartin.com
**SIC: 3812** Search and navigation equipment
**PA:** Lockheed Martin Corporation
6801 Rockledge Dr

### (P-14212)
### LOCKHEED MARTIN CORPORATION
Also Called: Lockheed Martin Aeronautics Co
1011 Lockheed Way, Palmdale (93599-0001)
PHONE..................................661 572-7428
Rick Baker, *VP*
**EMP:** 4000
**Web:** www.lockheedmartin.com
**SIC: 3812** Search and navigation equipment
**PA:** Lockheed Martin Corporation
6801 Rockledge Dr

### (P-14213)
### LOCKHEED MARTIN CORPORATION
Santa Barbara Focal Plane
346 Bollay Dr, Goleta (93117-5550)
PHONE..................................805 571-2346
Bryan Butler, *Mgr*
**EMP:** 25
**SQ FT:** 8,500
**Web:** www.lockheedmartin.com
**SIC: 3812** Search and navigation equipment
**PA:** Lockheed Martin Corporation
6801 Rockledge Dr

### (P-14214)
### LOCKHEED MARTIN CORPORATION
Also Called: Lockheed Martin
Nas North Island, Coronado (92118)
PHONE..................................619 437-7230
**EMP:** 232
**Web:** www.lockheedmartin.com
**SIC: 3812** Search and navigation equipment
**PA:** Lockheed Martin Corporation
6801 Rockledge Dr

### (P-14215)
### LOCKHEED MARTIN CORPORATION
Also Called: Helendale Lckheed Plant Prtcti
17452 Wheeler Rd, Helendale (92342-9677)
PHONE..................................760 952-4200
**EMP:** 51
**Web:** www.lockheedmartin.com
**SIC: 3812** Search and navigation equipment
**PA:** Lockheed Martin Corporation
6801 Rockledge Dr

### (P-14216)
### LOCKHEED MARTIN ORINCON CORP (HQ)
10325 Meanley Dr, San Diego (92131-3011)
PHONE..................................858 455-5530
Daniel Alspach, *Ch Bd*
**EMP:** 200 **EST:** 1973
**SQ FT:** 41,000
**SALES (est):** 12.35MM **Publicly Held**
**SIC: 3812** Search and navigation equipment
**PA:** Lockheed Martin Corporation
6801 Rockledge Dr

### (P-14217)
### LOCKHEED MRTIN UNMNNED INTGRTE
125 Venture Dr Ste 110, San Luis Obispo (93401-9103)
PHONE..................................805 503-4340
Jesse May, *CEO*
**EMP:** 40
**Web:** www.lockheedmartin.com
**SIC: 3812** Search and navigation equipment
**HQ:** Lockheed Martin Unmanned Integrated Systems, Inc.
133 W Park Loop Nw
Huntsville AL 35806

### (P-14218)
### LYTX INC (PA)
9785 Towne Centre Dr, San Diego (92121-1968)
PHONE..................................858 430-4000
Brandon Nixon, *CEO*
Paul J Pucino, *CFO*
Tom Fisher, *VP*
Drew Martin, *Ex VP*
David Riordan, *Ex VP*
**EMP:** 300 **EST:** 1998
**SQ FT:** 100,000
**SALES (est):** 123.43MM
**SALES (corp-wide):** 123.43MM **Privately Held**
**Web:** www.lytx.com
**SIC: 3812** Search and detection systems and instruments

### (P-14219)
### MAPQUEST HOLDINGS LLC
4235 Redwood Ave, Los Angeles (90066-5605)
PHONE..................................310 256-4882
Michael Blend, *CEO*
**EMP:** 400 **EST:** 2019
**SALES (est):** 1.32MM
**SALES (corp-wide):** 401.97MM **Publicly Held**
**Web:** www.mapquest.com
**SIC: 3812** Navigational systems and instruments
**PA:** System1, Inc.
4235 Redwood Ave
310 924-6037

### (P-14220)
### MEGGITT (ORANGE COUNTY) INC
Also Called: Meggitt Aerospace
355 N Pastoria Ave, Sunnyvale (94085-4110)
PHONE..................................408 739-3533
Joseph Fragala, *Prin*
**EMP:** 85
**SALES (corp-wide):** 19.93B **Publicly Held**
**Web:** www.reflection-dental.com
**SIC: 3812** 8731 3829 Search and navigation equipment; Commercial physical research; Measuring and controlling devices, nec
**HQ:** Meggitt (Orange County), Inc.
4 Marconi
Irvine CA 92618

### (P-14221)
### METROTECH CORPORATION (PA)
Also Called: Vivax-Metrotech
3251 Olcott St, Santa Clara (95054-3006)
PHONE..................................408 734-3880
Christian Stolz, *CEO*
Andrew Hoare, *
Mark Drew, *
Mark Royle, *
▲ **EMP:** 78 **EST:** 1976
**SQ FT:** 65,000
**SALES (est):** 19.94MM
**SALES (corp-wide):** 19.94MM **Privately Held**
**Web:** www.vivax-metrotech.de
**SIC: 3812** 3599 3829 Detection apparatus: electronic/magnetic field, light/heat; Water leak detectors; Measuring and controlling devices, nec

### (P-14222)
### MOOG INC
Also Called: Moog Aircraft Group
20263 S Western Ave, Torrance (90501-1310)
PHONE..................................310 533-1178
Alberto Bilalon, *Mgr*
**EMP:** 450
**SALES (corp-wide):** 3.32B **Publicly Held**
**Web:** www.moog.com
**SIC: 3812** Search and navigation equipment
**PA:** Moog Inc.
400 Jamison Rd
716 652-2000

### (P-14223)
### MOOG INC
21339 Nordhoff St, Chatsworth (91311-5819)
PHONE..................................818 341-5156
Ruben Nalbandian, *Sls Mgr*
**EMP:** 150
**SALES (corp-wide):** 3.32B **Publicly Held**
**Web:** www.moog.com
**SIC: 3812** Aircraft control systems, electronic
**PA:** Moog Inc.
400 Jamison Rd
716 652-2000

### (P-14224)
### MOOG INC
7406 Hollister Ave, Goleta (93117-2583)
PHONE..................................805 618-3900
Robert W Urban, *Genl Mgr*
**EMP:** 300
**SALES (corp-wide):** 3.32B **Publicly Held**
**Web:** www.moog.com
**SIC: 3812** 3492 3625 3769 Aircraft control systems, electronic; Electrohydraulic servo valves, metal; Relays and industrial controls; Space vehicle equipment, nec
**PA:** Moog Inc.
400 Jamison Rd
716 652-2000

### (P-14225)
### MP SOLUTIONS INC
21818 S Wilmington Ave Ste 411, Carson (90810-1642)
**EMP:** 20 **EST:** 1999
**SALES (est):** 1.45MM **Privately Held**
**Web:** www.simulatorps.com

## PRODUCTS & SERVICES SECTION
### 3812 - Search And Navigation Equipment (P-14247)

SIC: 3812 Aircraft control instruments

**(P-14226)**
**MTI DE BAJA INC**
915 Industrial Way, San Jacinto (92582-3890)
PHONE.................................951 654-2333
Monty Merkin, CEO
EMP: 24 EST: 2009
SALES (est): 999.25K Privately Held
Web: www.mtibaja.com
SIC: 3812 Acceleration indicators and systems components, aerospace

**(P-14227)**
**NEVWEST INC**
1225 Exposition Way Ste 140, San Diego (92154-6663)
PHONE.................................619 420-8100
Alfredo Liburd, Pr
Virginia Burd, *
EMP: 15 EST: 2004
SALES (est): 3.45MM Privately Held
Web: www.nevwestinc.com
SIC: 3812 Warfare counter-measure equipment

**(P-14228)**
**NIGHTHAWK FLIGHT SYSTEMS INC**
1370 Decision St Ste D, Vista (92081-8551)
PHONE.................................760 727-4900
Paul Martin, CEO
Richard Lanning, *
EMP: 25 EST: 2022
SALES (est): 3.94MM Privately Held
Web: www.nighthawkfs.com
SIC: 3812 Navigational systems and instruments

**(P-14229)**
**NORTHROP GRMMAN INNVTION SYSTE**
9401 Corbin Ave, Northridge (91324-2400)
PHONE.................................818 887-8100
EMP: 100
Web: www.northropgrumman.com
SIC: 3812 Search and navigation equipment
HQ: Northrop Grumman Innovation Systems, Inc.
2980 Fairview Park Dr
Falls Church VA 22042

**(P-14230)**
**NORTHROP GRMMAN INNVTION SYSTE**
Also Called: Ca75 Atk
9617 Distribution Ave, San Diego (92121-2307)
PHONE.................................858 621-5700
David W Thompson, Pr
EMP: 300
Web: www.northropgrumman.com
SIC: 3812 Search and navigation equipment
HQ: Northrop Grumman Innovation Systems, Inc.
2980 Fairview Park Dr
Falls Church VA 22042

**(P-14231)**
**NORTHROP GRUMMAN CORPORATION**
Northrop Grumman Aviation
1 Hornet Way, El Segundo (90245-2804)
PHONE.................................310 332-1000
Ray Pollok, Mgr
EMP: 200
Web: www.northropgrumman.com
SIC: 3812 Search and navigation equipment
PA: Northrop Grumman Corporation
2980 Fairview Park Dr

**(P-14232)**
**NORTHROP GRUMMAN CORPORATION**
Also Called: Northrop Grmman Arospc Systems
3520 E Avenue M, Palmdale (93550-7401)
PHONE.................................661 272-7334
EMP: 44
Web: www.northropgrumman.com
SIC: 3812 Search and navigation equipment
PA: Northrop Grumman Corporation
2980 Fairview Park Dr

**(P-14233)**
**NORTHROP GRUMMAN CORPORATION**
500 N Douglas St, El Segundo (90245)
PHONE.................................310 332-0461
EMP: 46 EST: 2011
SALES (est): 6.38MM Privately Held
Web: www.northropgrumman.com
SIC: 3812 Search and navigation equipment

**(P-14234)**
**NORTHROP GRUMMAN CORPORATION**
19782 Macarthur Blvd, Irvine (92612-2452)
PHONE.................................949 260-9800
Jeffrey Smith, Mgr
EMP: 46
Web: www.northropgrumman.com
SIC: 3812 Search and navigation equipment
PA: Northrop Grumman Corporation
2980 Fairview Park Dr

**(P-14235)**
**NORTHROP GRUMMAN CORPORATION**
198 Willow Grove Pl, Escondido (92027-5348)
PHONE.................................310 864-7342
EMP: 37
Web: www.northropgrumman.com
SIC: 3812 Search and navigation equipment
PA: Northrop Grumman Corporation
2980 Fairview Park Dr

**(P-14236)**
**NORTHROP GRUMMAN CORPORATION**
18701 Caminito Pasadero, San Diego (92128-6162)
PHONE.................................858 967-1221
Dagnall Barry, Brnch Mgr
EMP: 735
Web: www.northropgrumman.com
SIC: 3812 Search and detection systems and instruments
PA: Northrop Grumman Corporation
2980 Fairview Park Dr

**(P-14237)**
**NORTHROP GRUMMAN SYSTEMS CORP**
9326 Spectrum Center Blvd, San Diego (92123-1443)
PHONE.................................858 514-9020
EMP: 107
Web: www.northropgrumman.com
SIC: 3812 Search and navigation equipment
HQ: Northrop Grumman Systems Corporation
2980 Fairview Park Dr
Falls Church VA 22042
703 280-2900

**(P-14238)**
**NORTHROP GRUMMAN SYSTEMS CORP**
Also Called: Northrop Grmman Def Mssion Sys
9326 Spectrum Center Blvd, San Diego (92123-1443)
PHONE.................................410 765-5589
Steve Appel, Brnch Mgr
EMP: 2969
Web: www.northropgrumman.com
SIC: 3812 7379 Search and navigation equipment; Computer related consulting services
HQ: Northrop Grumman Systems Corporation
2980 Fairview Park Dr
Falls Church VA 22042
703 280-2900

**(P-14239)**
**NORTHROP GRUMMAN SYSTEMS CORP**
California Microwave Systems
21200 Burbank Blvd, Woodland Hills (91367-6675)
PHONE.................................818 715-2597
Roy Medlin, Brnch Mgr
EMP: 250
Web: www.northropgrumman.com
SIC: 3812 Search and navigation equipment
HQ: Northrop Grumman Systems Corporation
2980 Fairview Park Dr
Falls Church VA 22042
703 280-2900

**(P-14240)**
**NORTHROP GRUMMAN SYSTEMS CORP**
5627 Stoneridge Dr Ste 310, Pleasanton (94588-8503)
PHONE.................................925 416-1080
Mike Mcelroy, Brnch Mgr
EMP: 20
Web: www.northropgrumman.com
SIC: 3812 Search and navigation equipment
HQ: Northrop Grumman Systems Corporation
2980 Fairview Park Dr
Falls Church VA 22042
703 280-2900

**(P-14241)**
**NORTHROP GRUMMAN SYSTEMS CORP**
Building 806, Fort Irwin (92310)
PHONE.................................760 380-4268
EMP: 72
Web: www.northropgrumman.com
SIC: 3812 Search and navigation equipment
HQ: Northrop Grumman Systems Corporation
2980 Fairview Park Dr
Falls Church VA 22042
703 280-2900

**(P-14242)**
**NORTHROP GRUMMAN SYSTEMS CORP**
Also Called: Weapons System Division
9401 Corbin Ave, Northridge (91324-2400)
PHONE.................................818 887-8110
Richard Nolan, Brnch Mgr
EMP: 519
Web: www.northropgrumman.com
SIC: 3812 Search and navigation equipment
HQ: Northrop Grumman Systems Corporation
2980 Fairview Park Dr
Falls Church VA 22042
703 280-2900

**(P-14243)**
**NORTHROP GRUMMAN SYSTEMS CORP**
Also Called: Aeronitcs Systems Arspc Strctr
16707 Via Del Campo Ct, San Diego (92127-1713)
PHONE.................................858 592-2535
Audrey Clark, Brnch Mgr
EMP: 18
Web: www.northropgrumman.com
SIC: 3812 Search and navigation equipment
HQ: Northrop Grumman Systems Corporation
2980 Fairview Park Dr
Falls Church VA 22042
703 280-2900

**(P-14244)**
**NORTHROP GRUMMAN SYSTEMS CORP**
6379 San Ignacio Ave, San Jose (95119-1200)
PHONE.................................703 968-1239
Stacy Moffett, Brnch Mgr
EMP: 107
Web: www.northropgrumman.com
SIC: 3812 Search and navigation equipment
HQ: Northrop Grumman Systems Corporation
2980 Fairview Park Dr
Falls Church VA 22042
703 280-2900

**(P-14245)**
**NORTHROP GRUMMAN SYSTEMS CORP**
Strategic Deterrent Systems
1467 Fairway Dr, Santa Maria (93455-1404)
PHONE.................................805 315-5728
EMP: 72
Web: www.northropgrumman.com
SIC: 3812 Search and navigation equipment
HQ: Northrop Grumman Systems Corporation
2980 Fairview Park Dr
Falls Church VA 22042
703 280-2900

**(P-14246)**
**NORTHROP GRUMMAN SYSTEMS CORP**
15120 Innovation Dr, San Diego (92128-3402)
PHONE.................................858 592-4518
Chris Willenborg, Brnch Mgr
EMP: 483
SQ FT: 211,000
Web: www.northropgrumman.com
SIC: 3812 8711 7373 Search and navigation equipment; Engineering services; Computer integrated systems design
HQ: Northrop Grumman Systems Corporation
2980 Fairview Park Dr
Falls Church VA 22042
703 280-2900

**(P-14247)**
**NORTHROP GRUMMAN SYSTEMS CORP**
Also Called: Technical Services
P.O. Box 81 (94035-0081)

## 3812 - Search And Navigation Equipment (P-14248)

PHONE..................650 604-6056
James R Blount, *Mgr*
**EMP:** 72
**Web:** www.northropgrumman.com
**SIC: 3812** 7374 Search and navigation equipment; Computer processing services
**HQ:** Northrop Grumman Systems Corporation
2980 Fairview Park Dr
Falls Church VA 22042
703 280-2900

*(P-14248)*
**NORTHROP GRUMMAN SYSTEMS CORP**
760 Paseo Camarillo Ste 200, Camarillo (93010-6000)
PHONE..................805 987-8831
Steve Crans, *Mgr*
**EMP:** 170
**Web:** www.northropgrumman.com
**SIC: 3812** Search and navigation equipment
**HQ:** Northrop Grumman Systems Corporation
2980 Fairview Park Dr
Falls Church VA 22042
703 280-2900

*(P-14249)*
**NORTHROP GRUMMAN SYSTEMS CORP**
5161 Verdugo Way, Camarillo (93012-8603)
PHONE..................805 987-9739
Jim Lueck, *Brnch Mgr*
**EMP:** 54
**Web:** www.northropgrumman.com
**SIC: 3812** 8731 8711 7371 Search and navigation equipment; Commercial physical research; Engineering services; Custom computer programming services
**HQ:** Northrop Grumman Systems Corporation
2980 Fairview Park Dr
Falls Church VA 22042
703 280-2900

*(P-14250)*
**NORTHROP GRUMMAN SYSTEMS CORP**
2550 Honolulu Ave, Montrose (91020-1858)
PHONE..................818 249-5252
Arthur F Brown, *Mgr*
**EMP:** 89
**Web:** www.northropgrumman.com
**SIC: 3812** Search and navigation equipment
**HQ:** Northrop Grumman Systems Corporation
2980 Fairview Park Dr
Falls Church VA 22042
703 280-2900

*(P-14251)*
**NORTHROP GRUMMAN SYSTEMS CORP**
Also Called: Northrop Grmman Elctrnic Syste
1100 W Hollyvale St, Azusa (91702-3365)
P.O. Box 296 (91702-0296)
PHONE..................626 812-1000
Carl Fischer, *Mgr*
**EMP:** 4077
**Web:** www.northropgrumman.com
**SIC: 3812** Search and navigation equipment
**HQ:** Northrop Grumman Systems Corporation
2980 Fairview Park Dr
Falls Church VA 22042
703 280-2900

*(P-14252)*
**NORTHROP GRUMMAN SYSTEMS CORP**
Western Region
3520 E Avenue M, Palmdale (93550-7401)
PHONE..................661 540-0446
Jim Pace, *Brnch Mgr*
**EMP:** 72
**Web:** www.northropgrumman.com
**SIC: 3812** Search and navigation equipment
**HQ:** Northrop Grumman Systems Corporation
2980 Fairview Park Dr
Falls Church VA 22042
703 280-2900

*(P-14253)*
**NORTHROP GRUMMAN SYSTEMS CORP**
Northrop Grumman Info Systems
5441 Luce Ave, Mcclellan (95652-2417)
PHONE..................916 570-4454
John Dydiw, *Mgr*
**EMP:** 393
**Web:** www.northropgrumman.com
**SIC: 3812** Search and navigation equipment
**HQ:** Northrop Grumman Systems Corporation
2980 Fairview Park Dr
Falls Church VA 22042
703 280-2900

*(P-14254)*
**NORTHROP GRUMMAN SYSTEMS CORP**
Defense Systems Sector
1 Space Park Blvd, Redondo Beach (90278-1071)
PHONE..................855 737-8364
Jack Distaso, *Brnch Mgr*
**EMP:** 140
**SQ FT:** 500,000
**Web:** www.northropgrumman.com
**SIC: 3812** Search and navigation equipment
**HQ:** Northrop Grumman Systems Corporation
2980 Fairview Park Dr
Falls Church VA 22042
703 280-2900

*(P-14255)*
**NORTHROP GRUMMAN SYSTEMS CORP**
2477 Manhattan Beach Blvd, Redondo Beach (90278-1544)
PHONE..................310 812-4321
Bruce R Gerding, *VP*
**EMP:** 72
**Web:** www.northropgrumman.com
**SIC: 3812** Search and navigation equipment
**HQ:** Northrop Grumman Systems Corporation
2980 Fairview Park Dr
Falls Church VA 22042
703 280-2900

*(P-14256)*
**NORTHROP GRUMMAN SYSTEMS CORP**
1111 W 3rd St, Azusa (91702-3328)
PHONE..................626 812-1464
Michael Clayton, *Mgr*
**EMP:** 769
**Web:** www.northropgrumman.com
**SIC: 3812** Search and navigation equipment
**HQ:** Northrop Grumman Systems Corporation
2980 Fairview Park Dr
Falls Church VA 22042
703 280-2900

*(P-14257)*
**NORTHROP GRUMMAN SYSTEMS CORP**
Also Called: Northrop Grumman Space
9326 Spectrum Center Blvd, San Diego (92123-1443)
PHONE..................858 514-9000
Mike Twyman, *Brnch Mgr*
**EMP:** 89
**Web:** www.northropgrumman.com
**SIC: 3812** Search and navigation equipment
**HQ:** Northrop Grumman Systems Corporation
2980 Fairview Park Dr
Falls Church VA 22042
703 280-2900

*(P-14258)*
**NORTHROP GRUMMAN SYSTEMS CORP**
1 Hornet Way, El Segundo (90245-2804)
PHONE..................310 332-1000
Kevin Witherell, *Prin*
**EMP:** 411
**Web:** www.northropgrumman.com
**SIC: 3812** Search and navigation equipment
**HQ:** Northrop Grumman Systems Corporation
2980 Fairview Park Dr
Falls Church VA 22042
703 280-2900

*(P-14259)*
**NORTHROP GRUMMAN SYSTEMS CORP**
Also Called: Technical Services
862 E Hospitality Ln, San Bernardino (92408-3530)
PHONE..................703 713-4096
Ben Overall, *Mgr*
**EMP:** 54
**Web:** www.northropgrumman.com
**SIC: 3812** Search and navigation equipment
**HQ:** Northrop Grumman Systems Corporation
2980 Fairview Park Dr
Falls Church VA 22042
703 280-2900

*(P-14260)*
**NORTHROP GRUMMAN SYSTEMS CORP**
2700 Camino Del Sol, Oxnard (93030-7967)
PHONE..................805 278-2074
Pierre Courduroux, *Brnch Mgr*
**EMP:** 72
**Web:** www.northropgrumman.com
**SIC: 3812** Aircraft/aerospace flight instruments and guidance systems
**HQ:** Northrop Grumman Systems Corporation
2980 Fairview Park Dr
Falls Church VA 22042
703 280-2900

*(P-14261)*
**NORTHROP GRUMMAN SYSTEMS CORP**
7130 Miramar Rd Ste 100b, San Diego (92121-2340)
PHONE..................858 621-7395
**EMP:** 89
**Web:** www.northropgrumman.com
**SIC: 3812** Aircraft/aerospace flight instruments and guidance systems
**HQ:** Northrop Grumman Systems Corporation
2980 Fairview Park Dr
Falls Church VA 22042
703 280-2900

*(P-14262)*
**NORTHROP GRUMMAN SYSTEMS CORP**
6033 Bandini Blvd, Commerce (90040-2968)
PHONE..................714 240-6521
**EMP:** 197
**Web:** www.northropgrumman.com
**SIC: 3812** Aircraft/aerospace flight instruments and guidance systems
**HQ:** Northrop Grumman Systems Corporation
2980 Fairview Park Dr
Falls Church VA 22042
703 280-2900

*(P-14263)*
**NORTHROP GRUMMAN SYSTEMS CORP**
600 Pine Ave, Goleta (93117-3803)
PHONE..................714 240-6521
**EMP:** 89
**Web:** www.northropgrumman.com
**SIC: 3812** Aircraft/aerospace flight instruments and guidance systems
**HQ:** Northrop Grumman Systems Corporation
2980 Fairview Park Dr
Falls Church VA 22042
703 280-2900

*(P-14264)*
**NORTHROP GRUMMAN SYSTEMS CORP**
400 Continental Blvd, El Segundo (90245-5076)
PHONE..................480 355-7716
**EMP:** 72
**Web:** www.northropgrumman.com
**SIC: 3812** Aircraft/aerospace flight instruments and guidance systems
**HQ:** Northrop Grumman Systems Corporation
2980 Fairview Park Dr
Falls Church VA 22042
703 280-2900

*(P-14265)*
**NORTHROP GRUMMAN SYSTEMS CORP**
20 Ryan Ranch Rd Ste 214, Monterey (93940-6439)
PHONE..................703 406-5474
**EMP:** 72
**Web:** www.northropgrumman.com
**SIC: 3812** Aircraft/aerospace flight instruments and guidance systems
**HQ:** Northrop Grumman Systems Corporation
2980 Fairview Park Dr
Falls Church VA 22042
703 280-2900

*(P-14266)*
**NORTHROP GRUMMAN SYSTEMS CORP**
17066 Goldentop Rd, San Diego (92127-2412)
PHONE..................858 618-4349
Gerald Dufresne, *Mgr*
**EMP:** 304
**Web:** www.northropgrumman.com

## PRODUCTS & SERVICES SECTION
### 3812 - Search And Navigation Equipment (P-14285)

**SIC: 3812** 3761 7373 3721 Search and detection systems and instruments; Guided missiles, complete; Computer integrated systems design; Airplanes, fixed or rotary wing
**HQ:** Northrop Grumman Systems Corporation
2980 Fairview Park Dr
Falls Church VA 22042
703 280-2900

### (P-14267)
### NORTHROP GRUMMAN SYSTEMS CORP
Also Called: Electronic Systems Co Esco
401 E Hendy Ave, Sunnyvale (94086-5100)
P.O. Box 3499 (94088-3499)
**PHONE**.................................408 735-2241
William Pitts, *Brnch Mgr*
**EMP:** 305
**Web:** www.northropgrumman.com
**SIC: 3812** Search and navigation equipment
**HQ:** Northrop Grumman Systems Corporation
2980 Fairview Park Dr
Falls Church VA 22042
703 280-2900

### (P-14268)
### NORTHROP GRUMMAN SYSTEMS CORP
6411 W Imperial Hwy, Los Angeles (90045-6307)
**PHONE**.................................310 556-4911
Shea Mark, *Prin*
**EMP:** 303
**Web:** www.northropgrumman.com
**SIC: 3812** Search and navigation equipment
**HQ:** Northrop Grumman Systems Corporation
2980 Fairview Park Dr
Falls Church VA 22042
703 280-2900

### (P-14269)
### NORTHROP GRUMMAN SYSTEMS CORP
Litton Navigation Systems Div
21240 Burbank Blvd Ms 29, Woodland Hills (91367-6680)
**PHONE**.................................818 715-4040
Bill Allison, *Div Pres*
**EMP:** 1000
**Web:** www.northropgrumman.com
**SIC: 3812** Search and navigation equipment
**HQ:** Northrop Grumman Systems Corporation
2980 Fairview Park Dr
Falls Church VA 22042
703 280-2900

### (P-14270)
### NORTHROP GRUMMAN SYSTEMS CORP
2601 Camino Del Sol, Oxnard (93030-7996)
**PHONE**.................................805 684-6641
Kathy Warden, *CEO*
Richard Nelson, *
Alice Reed, *
**EMP:** 110 **EST:** 1999
**SQ FT:** 70,000
**SALES (est):** 35.8MM **Publicly Held**
**Web:** www.northropgrumman.com
**SIC: 3812** Search and navigation equipment
**HQ:** Northrop Grumman Systems Corporation
2980 Fairview Park Dr
Falls Church VA 22042
703 280-2900

### (P-14271)
### NORTHROP GRUMMAN SYSTEMS CORP
Also Called: Northrop Grumman CMS
21240 Burbank Blvd, Woodland Hills (91367-6680)
**PHONE**.................................818 715-4854
Roy Medland, *Brnch Mgr*
**EMP:** 393
**Web:** www.northropgrumman.com
**SIC: 3812** Search and navigation equipment
**HQ:** Northrop Grumman Systems Corporation
2980 Fairview Park Dr
Falls Church VA 22042
703 280-2900

### (P-14272)
### ONE STEP GPS LLC
675 Glenoaks Blvd Unit C, San Fernando (91340-4803)
**PHONE**.................................818 659-2031
Kevin Kenneth Dale, *
**EMP:** 52 **EST:** 2017
**SALES (est):** 5.44MM **Privately Held**
**Web:** www.onestepgps.com
**SIC: 3812** Search and navigation equipment

### (P-14273)
### ORBITAL SCIENCES LLC
Also Called: Space Systems Division
2401 E El Segundo Blvd Ste 200, El Segundo (90245-4631)
**PHONE**.................................703 406-5000
Antonio Elias, *Ex VP*
**EMP:** 238
**Web:** www.orbitalsciencesllc.com
**SIC: 3812** Search and navigation equipment
**HQ:** Orbital Sciences Llc
2980 Fairview Park Dr
Falls Church VA 22042
703 552-8203

### (P-14274)
### ORBITAL SCIENCES LLC
1151 W Reeves Ave, Ridgecrest (93555-2313)
**PHONE**.................................818 887-8345
David Rocca, *Brnch Mgr*
**EMP:** 238
**Web:** www.orbitalsciencesllc.com
**SIC: 3812** Search and navigation equipment
**HQ:** Orbital Sciences Llc
2980 Fairview Park Dr
Falls Church VA 22042
703 552-8203

### (P-14275)
### ORBITAL SCIENCES LLC
Talo Rd Bldg 1555, Lompoc (93437)
P.O. Box 5159 (93437-0159)
**PHONE**.................................805 734-5400
Eric Denbrook, *Mgr*
**EMP:** 318
**Web:** www.orbitalsciencesllc.com
**SIC: 3812** Search and navigation equipment
**HQ:** Orbital Sciences Llc
2980 Fairview Park Dr
Falls Church VA 22042
703 552-8203

### (P-14276)
### ORBITAL SCIENCES LLC
16707 Via Del Campo Ct, San Diego (92127-1713)
**PHONE**.................................858 618-1847
Brian Welge, *Brnch Mgr*
**EMP:** 238
**Web:** www.orbitalsciencesllc.com
**SIC: 3812** Search and navigation equipment
**HQ:** Orbital Sciences Llc
2980 Fairview Park Dr
Falls Church VA 22042
703 552-8203

### (P-14277)
### PACIFIC DEFENSE STRATEGIES INC (PA)
Also Called: Pacific Defense
400 Continental Blvd Ste 100, El Segundo (90245-5062)
**PHONE**.................................310 722-6050
Travis Slocumb, *CEO*
Scott Hoffman, *CFO*
Kent Mader, *COO*
**EMP:** 33 **EST:** 2020
**SALES (est):** 61MM
**SALES (corp-wide):** 61MM **Privately Held**
**Web:** www.pacific-defense.com
**SIC: 3812** 3731 Defense systems and equipment; Military ships, building and repairing

### (P-14278)
### PACIFIC SCIENTIFIC COMPANY (DH)
Also Called: Electro Kinetics Division
1785 Voyager Ave, Simi Valley (93063-3363)
**PHONE**.................................805 526-5700
James Simpkins, *Prin*
David Penner, *
James Healey, *
◆ **EMP:** 23 **EST:** 1998
**SALES (est):** 68.11MM
**SALES (corp-wide):** 19.93B **Publicly Held**
**Web:** www.hachultra.com
**SIC: 3812** 3669 3621 3694 Aircraft control systems, electronic; Fire detection systems, electric; Generators and sets, electric; Alternators, automotive
**HQ:** Meggitt-Usa, Inc.
1955 Surveyor Ave
Simi Valley CA 93063
805 526-5700

### (P-14279)
### PNEUDRAULICS INC
8575 Helms Ave, Rancho Cucamonga (91730-4591)
**PHONE**.................................909 980-5366
Michael Saville, *CEO*
Dain Miller, *
▼ **EMP:** 275 **EST:** 1956
**SQ FT:** 48,000
**SALES (est):** 24.91MM
**SALES (corp-wide):** 7.94B **Publicly Held**
**Web:** www.pneudraulics.com
**SIC: 3812** Acceleration indicators and systems components, aerospace
**PA:** Transdigm Group Incorporated
1350 Euclid Ave Ste 1600
216 706-2960

### (P-14280)
### QUANERGY PERCEPTION TECH INC (HQ)
433 Lakeside Dr, Sunnyvale (94085-4704)
**PHONE**.................................408 245-9500
Kevin J Kennedy, *CEO*
Louay Eldada, *Pr*
Tianyue Yu, *Sec*
Tamer Hassanein, *Prin*
James Disanto, *Prin*
**EMP:** 49 **EST:** 2012
**SALES (est):** 49.8MM **Privately Held**
**Web:** www.quanergy.com
**SIC: 3812** Infrared object detection equipment
**PA:** Quanergy Systems, Inc.
128 Baytech Dr

### (P-14281)
### QUANTUM3D INC (PA)
920 Hillview Ct Ste 145, Milpitas (95035-4558)
**PHONE**.................................408 600-2500
Clayton Conrad, *Pr*
Murat Kose, *CFO*
◆ **EMP:** 19 **EST:** 1994
**SQ FT:** 20,000
**SALES (est):** 4.75MM **Privately Held**
**Web:** www.quantum3d.com
**SIC: 3812** Aircraft control instruments

### (P-14282)
### RANTEC MICROWAVE SYSTEMS INC (PA)
31186 La Baya Dr, Westlake Village (91362-4003)
**PHONE**.................................818 223-5000
Carl Grindle, *CEO*
Carl E Grindle, *
Graham R Wilson, *
Steven B Chegwin, *
Steven Chegwin, *
**EMP:** 55 **EST:** 2000
**SQ FT:** 35,000
**SALES (est):** 12.58MM
**SALES (corp-wide):** 12.58MM **Privately Held**
**Web:** www.rantecantennas.com
**SIC: 3812** Antennas, radar or communications

### (P-14283)
### RAYTHEON COMPANY
Also Called: Raytheon
2000 E El Segundo Blvd, El Segundo (90245-4501)
P.O. Box 925 (90245-0925)
**PHONE**.................................310 647-9438
**EMP:** 50
**SALES (corp-wide):** 68.92B **Publicly Held**
**Web:** www.rtx.com
**SIC: 3812** Aircraft/aerospace flight instruments and guidance systems
**HQ:** Raytheon Company
870 Winter St
Waltham MA 02451
781 522-3000

### (P-14284)
### RAYTHEON COMPANY
Also Called: Raytheon
1921 E Mariposa Ave, El Segundo (90245-3445)
**PHONE**.................................310 647-1000
David Wajsgras, *Brnch Mgr*
**EMP:** 100
**SALES (corp-wide):** 68.92B **Publicly Held**
**Web:** www.rtx.com
**SIC: 3812** 4899 Sonar systems and equipment; Satellite earth stations
**HQ:** Raytheon Company
870 Winter St
Waltham MA 02451
781 522-3000

### (P-14285)
### RAYTHEON COMPANY
Also Called: Raytheon
1801 Hughes Dr, Fullerton (92833-2200)
P.O. Box 902 (90245-0902)
**PHONE**.................................714 446-2584
John Coarse, *Brnch Mgr*
**EMP:** 15
**SALES (corp-wide):** 68.92B **Publicly Held**
**Web:** www.rtx.com

## 3812 - Search And Navigation Equipment (P-14286)

SIC: **3812** Sonar systems and equipment
HQ: Raytheon Company
870 Winter St
Waltham MA 02451
781 522-3000

### (P-14286)
### RAYTHEON COMPANY
Raytheon
1801 Hughes Dr, Fullerton (92833-2200)
P.O. Box 3310 (92834-3310)
PHONE..................................714 732-0119
EMP: 115
SALES (corp-wide): 68.92B **Publicly Held**
Web: www.rtx.com
SIC: **3812** 7371 Sonar systems and equipment; Computer software development and applications
HQ: Raytheon Company
870 Winter St
Waltham MA 02451
781 522-3000

### (P-14287)
### RAYTHEON COMPANY
Also Called: Raytheon
75 Coromar Dr, Goleta (93117-3023)
PHONE..................................805 562-4611
Mike E Allgeier, *Brnch Mgr*
EMP: 171
SALES (corp-wide): 68.92B **Publicly Held**
Web: www.rtx.com
SIC: **3812** 8731 3845 3825 Sonar systems and equipment; Commercial research laboratory; Electromedical equipment; Instruments to measure electricity
HQ: Raytheon Company
870 Winter St
Waltham MA 02451
781 522-3000

### (P-14288)
### RAYTHEON COMPANY
Also Called: Raytheon
8650 Balboa Ave, San Diego (92123-1502)
PHONE..................................858 571-6598
EMP: 54
SALES (corp-wide): 68.92B **Publicly Held**
Web: www.rtx.com
SIC: **3812** Sonar systems and equipment
HQ: Raytheon Company
870 Winter St
Waltham MA 02451
781 522-3000

### (P-14289)
### RAYTHEON COMPANY
Also Called: Raytheon
2000 E El Segundo Blvd, El Segundo (90245-4501)
PHONE..................................310 647-1000
John Jones, *Mgr*
EMP: 500
SALES (corp-wide): 68.92B **Publicly Held**
Web: www.rtx.com
SIC: **3812** Defense systems and equipment
HQ: Raytheon Company
870 Winter St
Waltham MA 02451
781 522-3000

### (P-14290)
### RAYTHEON COMPANY
Also Called: Raytheon
2000 E El Segundo Blvd, El Segundo (90245-4501)
P.O. Box 902 (90245-0902)
PHONE..................................310 647-9438
Rick Yuse, *Brnch Mgr*
EMP: 10000

SALES (corp-wide): 68.92B **Publicly Held**
Web: www.rtx.com
SIC: **3812** Defense systems and equipment
HQ: Raytheon Company
870 Winter St
Waltham MA 02451
781 522-3000

### (P-14291)
### RAYTHEON DGITAL FORCE TECH LLC (DH)
Also Called: Digital Force Technologies
6779 Mesa Ridge Rd Ste 150, San Diego (92121-2909)
PHONE..................................858 546-1244
EMP: 38 **EST:** 2000
SQ FT: 14,500
SALES (est): 11.85MM
SALES (corp-wide): 68.92B **Publicly Held**
Web: www.digitalforcetech.com
SIC: **3812** 8711 Defense systems and equipment; Engineering services
HQ: Raytheon Bbn Technologies Corp.
10 Moulton St
Cambridge MA 02138
617 873-8000

### (P-14292)
### REMEC DEFENSE & SPACE INC
Also Called: Cobham
9404 Chesapeake Dr, San Diego (92123-1388)
PHONE..................................858 560-1301
EMP: 1000
Web: www.caes.com
SIC: **3812** Search and navigation equipment

### (P-14293)
### RKO GENERAL INC
Highway 50 & Aerojet Road, Rancho Cordova (95670)
PHONE..................................916 351-8515
EMP: 57 **EST:** 2009
SALES (est): 608.08K
SALES (corp-wide): 19.42B **Publicly Held**
SIC: **3812** Defense systems and equipment
HQ: Aerojet Rocketdyne Holdings, Inc.
222 N Pcf Cast Hwy Ste 50
El Segundo CA 90245
310 252-8100

### (P-14294)
### ROCKWELL COLLINS INC
1733 Alton Pkwy, Irvine (92606-4901)
PHONE..................................714 929-3000
EMP: 26
SALES (corp-wide): 68.92B **Publicly Held**
Web: www.rockwellcollins.com
SIC: **3812** Search and navigation equipment
HQ: Rockwell Collins, Inc.
400 Collins Rd Ne
Cedar Rapids IA 52498

### (P-14295)
### ROCKWELL COLLINS INC
1733 Alton Pkwy, Irvine (92606-4901)
PHONE..................................714 929-3000
EMP: 51
SALES (corp-wide): 68.92B **Publicly Held**
Web: www.rtx.com
SIC: **3812** Search and navigation equipment
HQ: Rockwell Collins, Inc.
400 Collins Rd Ne
Cedar Rapids IA 52498

### (P-14296)
### ROGERSON AIRCRAFT CORPORATION (PA)
16940 Von Karman Ave, Irvine (92606-4923)

PHONE..................................949 660-0666
Michael J Rogerson, *Pr*
Milton R Pizinger, *
Jonathan C Smith, *
EMP: 80 **EST:** 1975
SALES (est): 24.72MM
SALES (corp-wide): 24.72MM **Privately Held**
Web: www.rogerson.com
SIC: **3812** 3545 3492 3728 Aircraft flight instruments; Machine tool accessories; Fluid power valves and hose fittings; Fuel tanks, aircraft

### (P-14297)
### ROGERSON KRATOS
403 S Raymond Ave, Pasadena (91105-2609)
PHONE..................................626 449-3090
Lawrence Smith, *CEO*
Michael Rogerson, *
Milton R Pizinger, *
Cannon Mathews, *
Alice Williams Cstr Srv, *Prin*
EMP: 160 **EST:** 1981
SQ FT: 28,000
SALES (est): 9.99MM
SALES (corp-wide): 24.72MM **Privately Held**
Web: www.rogersonkratos.com
SIC: **3812** 3825 3699 Aircraft flight instruments; Instruments to measure electricity; Electrical equipment and supplies, nec
PA: Rogerson Aircraft Corporation
16940 Von Karman Ave
949 660-0666

### (P-14298)
### SANDEL AVIONICS INC
Also Called: Sandel Avionics
2405 Dogwood Way, Vista (92081-8409)
PHONE..................................760 727-4900
Gerald Block, *Brnch Mgr*
EMP: 169
SALES (corp-wide): 22.51MM **Privately Held**
Web: www.sandel.com
SIC: **3812** Aircraft control instruments
PA: Sandel Avionics, Inc.
1370 Decision St Ste D
760 727-4900

### (P-14299)
### SANDEL AVIONICS INC (PA)
Also Called: Sandel
1370 Decision St Ste D, Vista (92081-8551)
PHONE..................................760 727-4900
Steven Jeppson, *Pr*
Grant Miller, *
EMP: 31 **EST:** 1997
SALES (est): 22.51MM
SALES (corp-wide): 22.51MM **Privately Held**
Web: www.sandel.com
SIC: **3812** Aircraft control instruments

### (P-14300)
### SANTA BARBARA INFRARED INC (DH)
Also Called: Sbir
30 S Calle Cesar Chavez Ste D, Santa Barbara (93103-5652)
PHONE..................................805 965-3669
EMP: 90 **EST:** 1986
SALES (est): 15.79MM **Publicly Held**
Web: www.sbir.com
SIC: **3812** Infrared object detection equipment
HQ: Heico Electronic Technologies Corp.
3000 Taft St

Hollywood FL 33021
954 987-6101

### (P-14301)
### SCIENTIFIC-ATLANTA LLC
Scientific Atlanta
13112 Evening Creek Dr S, San Diego (92128-4108)
PHONE..................................619 679-6000
Richard Lapointe, *Contrlr*
EMP: 25
SALES (corp-wide): 53.8B **Publicly Held**
SIC: **3812** Navigational systems and instruments
HQ: Scientific-Atlanta, Llc
5030 Sugarloaf Pkwy # 1
Lawrenceville GA 30044
678 277-1000

### (P-14302)
### SENSOR CONCEPTS LLC
7950 National Dr, Livermore (94550-8811)
P.O. Box 2657 (94551-2657)
PHONE..................................925 443-9001
John Ashton, *Ex Dir*
John Ashton, *Mgr*
Hunter Isakson, *
EMP: 55 **EST:** 1995
SALES (est): 10.28MM **Privately Held**
Web: www.sensorconcepts.com
SIC: **3812** 3825 Radar systems and equipment; Instruments for measuring electrical quantities

### (P-14303)
### SENSOR SYSTEMS INC
8929 Fullbright Ave, Chatsworth (91311-6179)
PHONE..................................818 341-5366
Mary E Bazar, *CEO*
Si Robin, *
Dennis E Bazar, *
EMP: 258 **EST:** 1961
SQ FT: 60,000
SALES (est): 22.44MM **Publicly Held**
Web: www.sensorantennas.com
SIC: **3812** Aircraft flight instruments
HQ: Heico Electronic Technologies Corp.
3000 Taft St
Hollywood FL 33021
954 987-6101

### (P-14304)
### SIERRA NEVADA CORPORATION
Also Called: SIERRA NEVADA CORPORATION
985 University Ave Ste 4, Los Gatos (95032-7639)
PHONE..................................408 395-2004
Michael Weiland, *Brnch Mgr*
EMP: 122
SALES (corp-wide): 2.38B **Privately Held**
Web: www.sncorp.com
SIC: **3812** Search and navigation equipment
PA: Sierra Nevada Company, Llc
444 Salomon Cir
775 331-0222

### (P-14305)
### SIERRA NEVADA CORPORATION
Also Called: SIERRA NEVADA CORPORATION
145 Parkshore Dr, Folsom (95630-4734)
PHONE..................................916 985-8799
Carolyn Cain, *Brnch Mgr*
EMP: 68
SALES (corp-wide): 2.38B **Privately Held**
Web: www.sncorp.com
SIC: **3812** Search and navigation equipment
PA: Sierra Nevada Company, Llc
444 Salomon Cir

# PRODUCTS & SERVICES SECTION
## 3812 - Search And Navigation Equipment (P-14325)

775 331-0222

**(P-14306)**
**SIMULATOR PDT SOLUTIONS LLC**
Also Called: Panel Products
21818 S Wilmington Ave Ste 411, Long Beach (90810-1642)
**PHONE**...................310 830-3331
Nabil Abdou, *Pr*
**EMP:** 26 **EST:** 2021
**SQ FT:** 5,200
**SALES (est):** 10.54MM
**SALES (corp-wide):** 35.49MM **Publicly Held**
**SIC: 3812** Aircraft control instruments
**PA:** Orbit International Corp.
80 Cabot Ct
631 435-8300

**(P-14307)**
**SMITHS DETECTION INC**
39714 Eureka Dr, Newark (94560-4808)
**PHONE**...................410 612-2625
**EMP:** 124
**SALES (corp-wide):** 3.97B **Privately Held**
**Web:** www.smithsdetection.com
**SIC: 3812** Detection apparatus: electronic/magnetic field, light/heat
**HQ:** Smiths Detection Inc.
2202 Lakeside Blvd
Edgewood MD 21040
410 612-4000

**(P-14308)**
**SMITHS DETECTION LLC**
7151 Gateway Blvd, Newark (94560-1012)
P.O. Box 7247-7251 (19170-0001)
**PHONE**...................510 739-2400
▲ **EMP:** 1009
**Web:** www.smithsdetection.com
**SIC: 3812** Detection apparatus: electronic/magnetic field, light/heat

**(P-14309)**
**SPACE VECTOR CORPORATION**
20520 Nordhoff St, Chatsworth (91311)
**PHONE**...................818 734-2600
**EMP:** 37 **EST:** 1969
**SALES (est):** 7.45MM **Privately Held**
**SIC: 3812** 3691 3663 3761 Defense systems and equipment; Batteries, rechargeable; Global positioning systems (GPS) equipment; Guided missiles and space vehicles

**(P-14310)**
**STELLANT SYSTEMS INC (DH)**
Also Called: Electron Devices
3100 Lomita Blvd, Torrance (90505-5104)
P.O. Box 2999 (90509)
**PHONE**...................310 517-6000
Keith Barclay, *CEO*
Steve Shpock, *
Todd Hansen, *WILLIAMSPORT*
▲ **EMP:** 508 **EST:** 2000
**SALES (est):** 181.58MM
**SALES (corp-wide):** 296.08MM **Privately Held**
**Web:** www.stellantsystems.com
**SIC: 3812** 3764 3671 Navigational systems and instruments; Space propulsion units and parts; Traveling wave tubes
**HQ:** Stellant Midco, Llc
Torrance CA

**(P-14311)**
**TECHNOVATIVE APPLICATIONS**
3160 Enterprise St Ste A, Brea (92821-6288)
**PHONE**...................714 996-0104
**EMP:** 61 **EST:** 1987
**SALES (est):** 10.92MM **Privately Held**
**Web:** www.tnov.com
**SIC: 3812** Radar systems and equipment

**(P-14312)**
**TECNOVA ADVANCED SYSTEMS INC**
Also Called: Tecnadyne
9770 Carroll Centre Rd Ste A, San Diego (92126-6504)
P.O. Box 676086 (92067-6086)
**PHONE**...................858 586-9660
Andrew Bazeley, *Pr*
Ute Pelzer, *CFO*
**EMP:** 20 **EST:** 1984
**SQ FT:** 17,150
**SALES (est):** 5.89MM **Privately Held**
**Web:** www.tecnadyne.com
**SIC: 3812** Search and navigation equipment

**(P-14313)**
**TELEDYNE CONTROLS LLC**
501 Continental Blvd, El Segundo (90245)
P.O. Box 1026 (90245)
**PHONE**...................310 765-3600
George C Bobb Iii, *CEO*
Robert Mehrabian, *
Masood Hassan, *
Susan L Main, *
Melanie S Cibik, *
**EMP:** 616 **EST:** 2015
**SALES (est):** 123.25MM
**SALES (corp-wide):** 5.64B **Publicly Held**
**Web:** www.teledynecontrols.com
**SIC: 3812** Search and navigation equipment
**PA:** Teledyne Technologies Inc
1049 Camino Dos Rios
805 373-4545

**(P-14314)**
**TELEDYNE FLIR LLC**
6769 Hollister Ave, Goleta (93117-3001)
**PHONE**...................805 964-9797
James Woolaway, *CEO*
**EMP:** 110
**SALES (corp-wide):** 5.64B **Publicly Held**
**Web:** www.flir.com
**SIC: 3812** Aircraft/aerospace flight instruments and guidance systems
**HQ:** Teledyne Flir, Llc
27700 Sw Parkway Ave
Wilsonville OR 97070
503 498-3547

**(P-14315)**
**TELEDYNE INSTRUMENTS INC**
Also Called: Teledyne Rd Instruments
14020 Stowe Dr, Poway (92064-6846)
**PHONE**...................858 842-2600
Dennis Klahn, *Brnch Mgr*
**EMP:** 140
**SALES (corp-wide):** 5.64B **Publicly Held**
**Web:** www.teledynemarine.com
**SIC: 3812** 3829 Search and navigation equipment; Measuring and controlling devices, nec
**HQ:** Teledyne Instruments, Inc.
16830 Chestnut St
City Of Industry CA 91748
626 934-1500

**(P-14316)**
**TELEDYNE RD INSTRUMENTS INC**
14020 Stowe Dr, Poway (92064-6846)
**PHONE**...................858 842-2600
**EMP:** 200
**SIC: 3812** 3829 Search and navigation equipment; Measuring and controlling devices, nec

**(P-14317)**
**TELENAV INC (PA)**
Also Called: Telenav
2540 Mission College Blvd Ste 100, Santa Clara (95054-1215)
**PHONE**...................408 245-3800
Hp Jin, *Ch Bd*
Adeel Manzoor, *CFO*
Steve Debenham, *VP*
**EMP:** 641 **EST:** 1999
**SQ FT:** 55,000
**SALES (est):** 240.35MM **Privately Held**
**Web:** www.telenav.com
**SIC: 3812** Navigational systems and instruments

**(P-14318)**
**TELETRONICS TECHNOLOGY CORP**
Also Called: I A D S
190 Sierra Ct Ste A3, Palmdale (93550-7608)
**PHONE**...................661 273-7033
**EMP:** 22
**SALES (corp-wide):** 2.85B **Publicly Held**
**Web:** www.curtisswright.com
**SIC: 3812** Aircraft/aerospace flight instruments and guidance systems
**HQ:** Teletronics Technology Corp
15 Terry Dr
Newtown PA 18940

**(P-14319)**
**TINI AEROSPACE INC**
2505 Kerner Blvd, San Rafael (94901-5571)
**PHONE**...................415 524-2124
Michael Bokaie, *Pr*
Trudy Sachs, *
David Bokaie, *
Vicki Lasky, *
▼ **EMP:** 30 **EST:** 1996
**SQ FT:** 5,400
**SALES (est):** 4.4MM **Privately Held**
**Web:** www.ebad.com
**SIC: 3812** Search and navigation equipment

**(P-14320)**
**TINKER & RASOR**
791 S Waterman Ave, San Bernardino (92408-2331)
P.O. Box 1667 (92402-1667)
**PHONE**...................909 890-0700
Theodore Byerley, *Pr*
Denise Byerley, *
Mary Butcher, *
▲ **EMP:** 23 **EST:** 1948
**SQ FT:** 15,000
**SALES (est):** 2.41MM **Privately Held**
**Web:** www.tinker-rasor.com
**SIC: 3812** 3829 Detection apparatus: electronic/magnetic field, light/heat; Measuring and controlling devices, nec

**(P-14321)**
**TMC ICE PROTECTION SYSTEMS LLC**
Also Called: TMC Aero
25775 Jefferson Ave, Murrieta (92562-6903)
**PHONE**...................951 677-6934
Edward Rigney, *COO*
**EMP:** 20
**SALES (corp-wide):** 4.52MM **Privately Held**
**SIC: 3812** 8711 Aircraft/aerospace flight instruments and guidance systems; Aviation and/or aeronautical engineering
**PA:** Tmc Ice Protection Systems Llc
10850 Wilshire Blvd # 12
951 677-6934

**(P-14322)**
**TMC ICE PROTECTION SYSTEMS LLC (PA)**
Also Called: TMC Aero
10850 Wilshire Blvd Ste 1250, Los Angeles (90024-4305)
**PHONE**...................951 677-6934
Bob Yari, *CEO*
Edward Rigney, *COO*
Michael Heaton, *Ofcr*
**EMP:** 20 **EST:** 2014
**SQ FT:** 10,000
**SALES (est):** 4.52MM
**SALES (corp-wide):** 4.52MM **Privately Held**
**SIC: 3812** 8711 Acceleration indicators and systems components, aerospace; Aviation and/or aeronautical engineering

**(P-14323)**
**TOWER MECHANICAL PRODUCTS INC**
Also Called: Allied Mechanical Products
1720 S Bon View Ave, Ontario (91761-4411)
**PHONE**...................714 947-2723
Richard B Slater, *Pr*
James W Longcrier, *
Susan J Hardy, *
**EMP:** 126 **EST:** 1953
**SQ FT:** 148,000
**SALES (est):** 20.52MM
**SALES (corp-wide):** 28.17MM **Privately Held**
**Web:** www.alliedmech.com
**SIC: 3812** Acceleration indicators and systems components, aerospace
**PA:** Tower Industries, Inc.
1518 N Endeavor Ln Ste C

**(P-14324)**
**TRIMBLE INC**
1720 Prairie City Rd Ste 100, Folsom (95630-4044)
**PHONE**...................916 294-2000
**EMP:** 40
**SALES (corp-wide):** 3.8B **Publicly Held**
**Web:** www.trimble.com
**SIC: 3812** Navigational systems and instruments
**PA:** Trimble Inc.
10368 Westmoor Dr
720 887-6100

**(P-14325)**
**TRIMBLE MILITARY & ADVNCED SYS**
510 De Guigne Dr, Sunnyvale (94085-3920)
P.O. Box 3642 (94088-3642)
**PHONE**...................408 481-8000
Ron Smith, *Pr*
▼ **EMP:** 55 **EST:** 2007
**SQ FT:** 22,000
**SALES (est):** 22.5MM
**SALES (corp-wide):** 3.8B **Publicly Held**
**SIC: 3812** 3829 Search and navigation equipment; Measuring and controlling devices, nec
**PA:** Trimble Inc.
10368 Westmoor Dr
720 887-6100

# 3812 - Search And Navigation Equipment (P-14326)

## (P-14326)
**TUFFER MANUFACTURING CO INC**
163 E Liberty Ave, Anaheim (92801-1012)
PHONE...................................714 526-3077
Cathy Kim, *Pr*
Ken Kim, *
**EMP:** 39 **EST:** 1977
**SQ FT:** 12,000
**SALES (est):** 4.93MM **Privately Held**
Web: www.tuffermfg.com
**SIC: 3812** 3599  Search and navigation equipment; Machine shop, jobbing and repair

## (P-14327)
**VIRGIN ORBIT HOLDINGS INC (HQ)**
4022 E Conant St, Long Beach (90808-1777)
PHONE...................................562 388-4400
Daniel M Hart, *CEO*
Evan Lovell, *Ch Bd*
Brita O'rear, *CFO*
Jim Simpson, *CSO*
Derrick Boston, *CLO*
**EMP:** 19 **EST:** 2017
**SQ FT:** 151,000
**SALES (est):** 33.11MM **Publicly Held**
Web: www.virginorbit.com
**SIC: 3812** 3761  Space vehicle guidance systems and equipment; Space vehicles, complete
**PA:** Virgin Investments Limited
C/O Harney Corporate Services Limited

## (P-14328)
**VOTAW PRECISION TECHNOLOGIES**
Also Called: Votaw
13153 Lakeland Rd, Santa Fe Springs (90670-4542)
P.O. Box 314 (90740-0314)
PHONE...................................562 944-0661
Steve Lamb, *CEO*
David Takes, *Pr*
Jonathan Miller, *CFO*
▲ **EMP:** 140 **EST:** 1964
**SQ FT:** 240,000
**SALES (est):** 23.48MM **Privately Held**
Web: www.votaw.com
**SIC: 3812**  Acceleration indicators and systems components, aerospace

---

## 3821 Laboratory Apparatus And Furniture

## (P-14329)
**APPLIED CELLS INC**
3350 Scott Blvd Bldg 6, Santa Clara (95054-3108)
PHONE...................................800 960-3004
Yuchen Zhou, *CEO*
Yu Liping, *Pr*
**EMP:** 20 **EST:** 2017
**SALES (est):** 1.78MM **Privately Held**
Web: www.appliedcells.com
**SIC: 3821**  Sample preparation apparatus

## (P-14330)
**BERLIN FOOD & LAB EQUIPMENT CO**
43 S Linden Ave, South San Francisco (94080-6407)
PHONE...................................650 589-4231
Mark Cottonaro, *Pr*
Michael F Ulrich, *
**EMP:** 24 **EST:** 1941
**SQ FT:** 50,000
**SALES (est):** 4.28MM **Privately Held**
Web: www.berlinusa.com
**SIC: 3821** 1799  Laboratory apparatus and furniture; Home/office interiors finishing, furnishing and remodeling

## (P-14331)
**CERA INC**
14180 Live Oak Ave Ste I, Baldwin Park (91706-1350)
P.O. Box 1608 (91706-7608)
PHONE...................................626 814-2688
Philip Dimson, *Pr*
◆ **EMP:** 21 **EST:** 1987
**SQ FT:** 2,000
**SALES (est):** 2.45MM **Privately Held**
Web: www.cerasalonoc.com
**SIC: 3821**  Chemical laboratory apparatus, nec

## (P-14332)
**CHEMAT TECHNOLOGY INC**
Also Called: Chemat Vision
9036 Winnetka Ave, Northridge (91324-3235)
PHONE...................................818 727-9786
Haixing Zheng, *CEO*
▲ **EMP:** 32 **EST:** 1990
**SQ FT:** 30,000
**SALES (est):** 5MM **Privately Held**
Web: www.chemat.com
**SIC: 3821** 3827  Chemical laboratory apparatus, nec; Optical test and inspection equipment

## (P-14333)
**CLEATECH LLC**
Also Called: GLOBAL LAB SUPPLY
2106 N Glassell St, Orange (92865-3308)
PHONE...................................714 754-6668
Sam Kashanchi, *CEO*
**EMP:** 45 **EST:** 2010
**SALES (est):** 8.22MM **Privately Held**
Web: www.cleatech.com
**SIC: 3821**  Laboratory apparatus and furniture

## (P-14334)
**CV INGENUITY CORP**
6531 Dumbarton Cir, Fremont (94555-3619)
PHONE...................................508 261-8000
**EMP:** 30
Web: www.cvingenuity.com
**SIC: 3821**  Laboratory apparatus and furniture

## (P-14335)
**ENDRUN TECHNOLOGIES LLC**
2270 Northpoint Pkwy, Santa Rosa (95407-7398)
PHONE...................................707 573-8633
Bruce Penrod, *Prin*
**EMP:** 15 **EST:** 1998
**SQ FT:** 7,400
**SALES (est):** 2.54MM **Privately Held**
Web: www.endruntechnologies.com
**SIC: 3821** 3825  Time interval measuring equipment, electric (lab type); Frequency meters: electrical, mechanical, and electronic

## (P-14336)
**EVERGREEN INDUSTRIES INC (DH)**
Also Called: Evergreen Scientific
2254 E 49th St, Vernon (90058-2823)
PHONE...................................323 583-1331
◆ **EMP:** 73 **EST:** 1969
**SALES (est):** 2.82MM
**SALES (corp-wide):** 2.26B **Privately Held**
Web: www.evergreensci.com
**SIC: 3821**  Laboratory equipment: fume hoods, distillation racks, etc.
**HQ:** Caplugs, Inc.
2150 Elmwood Ave
Buffalo NY 14207
716 876-9855

## (P-14337)
**GARDNER SYSTEMS INC**
17891 Georgetown Ln, Huntington Beach (92647-7162)
PHONE...................................714 668-9018
Joe Gardner, *Pr*
Claudia Gardner, *Sec*
▲ **EMP:** 15 **EST:** 1983
**SALES (est):** 2.05MM **Privately Held**
Web: www.gardner-systems.com
**SIC: 3821**  Laboratory apparatus and furniture

## (P-14338)
**GENETRONICS INC**
11494 Sorrento Valley Rd Ste A, San Diego (92121-1318)
PHONE...................................858 597-6006
James Heppell, *Ch*
Avtar Dhillon, *
Peter Kies, *
Douglas Murdock, *
**EMP:** 26 **EST:** 1983
**SQ FT:** 25,000
**SALES (est):** 67.18K **Publicly Held**
**SIC: 3821** 8731 3826  Laboratory apparatus, except heating and measuring; Biotechnical research, commercial; Analytical instruments
**PA:** Inovio Pharmaceuticals, Inc.
660 W Grmntown Pike Ste 1

## (P-14339)
**HANSON LAB SOLUTIONS LLC**
747 Calle Plano, Camarillo (93012-8556)
PHONE...................................805 498-3121
Mike Hanson, *Pr*
Joe Matta, *
Joseph F Matta, *
▲ **EMP:** 30 **EST:** 1971
**SQ FT:** 40,000
**SALES (est):** 7.02MM **Privately Held**
Web: www.hansonlab.com
**SIC: 3821**  Laboratory furniture

## (P-14340)
**IDEX HEALTH & SCIENCE LLC (HQ)**
600 Park Ct, Rohnert Park (94928-7906)
PHONE...................................707 588-2000
Jeff Cannon, *Managing Member*
Mark F Gorman, *
Gerald F Carter, *
Frank Notaro, *
▲ **EMP:** 87 **EST:** 2002
**SQ FT:** 70,000
**SALES (est):** 195.45MM
**SALES (corp-wide):** 3.27B **Publicly Held**
Web: www.idex-hs.com
**SIC: 3821** 3829 3826 3823  Laboratory apparatus and furniture; Measuring and controlling devices, nec; Analytical instruments; Process control instruments
**PA:** Idex Corporation
3100 Sanders Rd Ste 301
847 498-7070

## (P-14341)
**ISEC INCORPORATED**
5735 Kearny Villa Rd Ste 105, San Diego (92123-1138)
PHONE...................................858 279-9085
Don Shaw, *Pr*
**EMP:** 102
**SALES (corp-wide):** 317.22MM **Privately Held**
Web: www.isecinc.com
**SIC: 3821**  Laboratory apparatus and furniture
**PA:** Isec, Incorporated
6000 Grnwood Plz Blvd Ste
303 790-1444

## (P-14342)
**LASER REFERENCE INC**
786 E Mcglincy Ln, Campbell (95008-5019)
PHONE...................................408 361-0220
Lee Robson, *Pr*
Mike Middleton, *
Christopher Middleton, *
▲ **EMP:** 15 **EST:** 1991
**SQ FT:** 9,500
**SALES (est):** 1.06MM **Privately Held**
Web: www.proshotlaser.com
**SIC: 3821** 3829 3699  Laser beam alignment devices; Measuring and controlling devices, nec; Electrical equipment and supplies, nec

## (P-14343)
**MARVAC SCIENTIFIC MFG CO**
3231 Monument Way Ste I, Concord (94518-2444)
PHONE...................................925 825-4636
George Marin, *Pr*
Douglas Marin, *VP*
Steve Marin, *Sec*
**EMP:** 18 **EST:** 1959
**SQ FT:** 20,000
**SALES (est):** 2.33MM **Privately Held**
Web: www.marvacscientific.com
**SIC: 3821**  Vacuum pumps, laboratory

## (P-14344)
**NEWPORT CORPORATION (HQ)**
Also Called: Newport
1791 Deere Ave, Irvine (92606-4814)
P.O. Box 19607 (92623-9607)
PHONE...................................949 863-3144
Seth Bagshaw, *Pr*
Kathleen Burke, *
Derek D'antilio, *Treas*
◆ **EMP:** 467 **EST:** 1938
**SALES (est):** 355.83MM
**SALES (corp-wide):** 3.62B **Publicly Held**
Web: www.newport.com
**SIC: 3821** 3699 3827 3826  Worktables, laboratory; Laser systems and equipment; Optical instruments and lenses; Analytical optical instruments
**PA:** Mks Instruments, Inc.
2 Tech Dr Ste 201
978 645-5500

## (P-14345)
**NORTHRDGE TR-MDLITY IMGING INC**
Also Called: Trifoil Imaging
2140 Eastman Ave, Ventura (93003-7786)
PHONE...................................818 709-2468
Kevin Parnham, *Pr*
Ryan Weirich, *CFO*
**EMP:** 15 **EST:** 2013
**SALES (est):** 2.78MM **Privately Held**
Web: www.trifoilimaging.com
**SIC: 3821** 7699  Clinical laboratory instruments, except medical and dental; Medical equipment repair, non-electric

## (P-14346)
**PROCISEDX INC**
9449 Carroll Park Dr, San Diego (92121-5202)
PHONE...................................858 382-4598

# PRODUCTS & SERVICES SECTION
## 3822 - Environmental Controls (P-14367)

Peter Westlake, *Pr*
Larry Mimms, *
**EMP:** 30 **EST:** 2019
**SALES (est):** 4.62MM **Privately Held**
**Web:** www.procisedx.com
**SIC: 3821** Balances, laboratory

### (P-14347)
### QUALIGEN INC (HQ)
2042 Corte Del Nogal Ste B, Carlsbad (92011-1438)
**PHONE**.................................760 918-9165
Paul A Rosinack, *CEO*
Michael S Poirier, *Sr VP*
Christopher L Lotz, *CFO*
Shishir K Sinha, *VP*
**EMP:** 21 **EST:** 1996
**SQ FT:** 23,000
**SALES (est):** 15.18MM
**SALES (corp-wide):** 49.52MM **Privately Held**
**Web:** www.qualigendiagnostics.com
**SIC: 3821 3841** Laboratory apparatus and furniture; Surgical and medical instruments
**PA:** Chembio Diagnostics, Inc.
 555 Wireless Blvd
 631 924-1135

### (P-14348)
### ROMAR INNOVATIONS INC
Also Called: Romar Innovations
38429 Innovation Ct, Murrieta (92563-2570)
**PHONE**.................................951 296-3480
**EMP:** 100 **EST:** 1998
**SALES (est):** 9.27MM **Privately Held**
**Web:** www.aquaultraviolet.com
**SIC: 3821** Sterilizers

### (P-14349)
### SURPLUS SOLUTIONS LLC
30220 Commerce Ct, Murrieta (92563-4880)
**PHONE**.................................760 696-8788
**EMP:** 15
**SALES (corp-wide):** 5.29MM **Privately Held**
**Web:** www.ssllc.com
**SIC: 3821 5047 5122** Laboratory equipment: fume hoods, distillation racks, etc.; Medical and hospital equipment; Pharmaceuticals
**PA:** Surplus Solutions Llc
 2010 Diamond Hill Rd
 401 526-0055

### (P-14350)
### TECAN SYSTEMS INC
Also Called: Tecan
18635 Sutter Blvd, Morgan Hill (95037)
**PHONE**.................................408 953-3100
David Martyr, *CEO*
Rudolf Eugster, *
Martin Brusdeilins, *
▲ **EMP:** 100 **EST:** 1972
**SALES (est):** 40.02MM **Privately Held**
**Web:** www.tecan.com
**SIC: 3821 3829 3561 3494** Laboratory apparatus, except heating and measuring; Measuring and controlling devices, nec; Pumps and pumping equipment; Valves and pipe fittings, nec
**HQ:** Tecan U.S. Group, Inc.
 9401 Globe Center Dr # 140
 Morrisville NC 27560
 919 361-5200

### (P-14351)
### THERMAL EQUIPMENT CORPORATION
Also Called: TEC
2146 E Gladwick St, Rancho Dominguez (90220-6203)
**PHONE**.................................310 328-6600
Nancy Huffman, *CEO*
Nancy Huffman, *Pr*
▼ **EMP:** 45 **EST:** 1969
**SALES (est):** 4.8MM **Privately Held**
**Web:** www.thermalequipment.com
**SIC: 3821 2842 3443** Laboratory apparatus and furniture; Polishes and sanitation goods ; Autoclaves, industrial
**PA:** Km3 Holdings, Inc.
 2030 E University Dr

### (P-14352)
### THERMIONICS LABORATORY INC (HQ)
Also Called: Tli-Grass Valley
3118 Depot Rd, Hayward (94545-2708)
P.O. Box 3711 (94540-3711)
**PHONE**.................................510 538-3304
**EMP:** 35 **EST:** 1955
**SALES (est):** 19.81MM
**SALES (corp-wide):** 24.98MM **Privately Held**
**Web:** www.thermionics.com
**SIC: 3821 3829 3491** Vacuum pumps, laboratory; Ion chambers; Industrial valves
**PA:** Tli Enterprises, Inc.
 3118 Depot Rd
 510 538-3304

### (P-14353)
### TLI ENTERPRISES INC (PA)
3118 Depot Rd, Hayward (94545-2708)
P.O. Box 3711 (94540-3711)
**PHONE**.................................510 538-3304
John Trujillo, *CEO*
Shawn Trujillo, *
**EMP:** 30 **EST:** 1937
**SQ FT:** 18,000
**SALES (est):** 36.36MM
**SALES (corp-wide):** 36.36MM **Privately Held**
**Web:** www.thermionics.com
**SIC: 3821 3471** Vacuum pumps, laboratory; Cleaning, polishing, and finishing

---

## 3822 Environmental Controls

### (P-14354)
### AUTOMATED SOLUTIONS GROUP INC
Also Called: ASG
2150 Bering Dr, San Jose (95131-2013)
**PHONE**.................................408 432-0300
Tony Skibinski, *Pr*
**EMP:** 43 **EST:** 2012
**SQ FT:** 2,500
**SALES (est):** 4.53MM **Privately Held**
**Web:** www.asgbms.com
**SIC: 3822** Building services monitoring controls, automatic

### (P-14355)
### BEAR STATE WATER HEATING LLC
43234 Business Park Dr Ste 105, Temecula (92590-3604)
**PHONE**.................................951 269-3753
**EMP:** 15 **EST:** 2020
**SALES (est):** 3.23MM **Privately Held**
**Web:** www.bearstatewaterheating.com
**SIC: 3822** Water heater controls

### (P-14356)
### CATALYTIC SOLUTIONS INC (HQ)
1700 Fiske Pl, Oxnard (93033-1863)
**PHONE**.................................805 486-4649
David Gann, *CEO*
Charlie Karl, *CEO*
Kevin Mcdonnell, *CFO*
Dan Mcguire, *VP*
▲ **EMP:** 24 **EST:** 1996
**SQ FT:** 75,000
**SALES (est):** 6.28MM **Privately Held**
**Web:** www.cdti.com
**SIC: 3822** Environmental controls
**PA:** Cdti Advanced Materials, Inc.
 1641 Fiske Pl

### (P-14357)
### CHEVRON ENERGY SOLUTIONS LP
Also Called: Chevron Energy Solutions Co
345 California St Fl 18, San Francisco (94104-2650)
**PHONE**.................................415 894-4188
**EMP:** 300
**SIC: 3822 6531 3823 3691** Energy cutoff controls, residential or commercial types; Buying agent, real estate; Process control instruments; Storage batteries

### (P-14358)
### CHRONOMITE LABORATORIES INC
17451 Hurley St, City Of Industry (91744-5106)
P.O. Box 3527 (91744-0527)
**PHONE**.................................310 534-2300
Donald E Morris, *CEO*
▲ **EMP:** 34 **EST:** 1967
**SALES (est):** 6.52MM
**SALES (corp-wide):** 99.75MM **Privately Held**
**Web:** www.chronomite.com
**SIC: 3822 8731 3432** Water heater controls; Commercial physical research; Plumbing fixture fittings and trim
**PA:** Acorn Engineering Company
 15125 E Proctor Ave
 800 488-8999

### (P-14359)
### CYPRESS ENVIROSYSTEMS INC
5883 Rue Ferrari Ste 100, San Jose (95119-1391)
**PHONE**.................................800 544-5411
Harry Sim, *CEO*
**EMP:** 25 **EST:** 2007
**SALES (est):** 5.12MM **Privately Held**
**Web:** www.cypressenvirosystems.com
**SIC: 3822 3823** Environmental controls; Industrial process control instruments

### (P-14360)
### ELECTRASEM CORP
372 Elizabeth Ln, Corona (92878-5028)
**PHONE**.................................951 371-6140
Don S Edwards, *Pr*
▲ **EMP:** 84 **EST:** 1980
**SALES (est):** 3.73MM
**SALES (corp-wide):** 1.79B **Publicly Held**
**SIC: 3822** Electric heat proportioning controls, modulating controls
**HQ:** General Monitors, Inc.
 16782 Von Krman Ave Ste 1
 Irvine CA 92606
 949 581-4464

### (P-14361)
### HONEYWELL INTERNATIONAL INC
Also Called: Honeywell
2055 Dublin Dr, San Diego (92154-8203)
**PHONE**.................................619 671-5612
Virgel Mccormick, *Mgr*
**EMP:** 110
**SALES (corp-wide):** 36.66B **Publicly Held**
**Web:** www.honeywell.com
**SIC: 3822 3494** Environmental controls; Valves and pipe fittings, nec
**PA:** Honeywell International Inc.
 855 S Mint St
 704 627-6200

### (P-14362)
### INTEMATIX CORPORATION (PA)
46410 Fremont Blvd, Fremont (94538-6469)
**PHONE**.................................510 933-3300
◆ **EMP:** 51 **EST:** 2000
**SALES (est):** 8.99MM **Privately Held**
**Web:** www.intematix.com
**SIC: 3822** Environmental controls

### (P-14363)
### KURZ INSTRUMENTS INC
2411 Garden Rd, Monterey (93940-5318)
**PHONE**.................................831 646-5911
**EMP:** 53 **EST:** 1977
**SALES (est):** 9.77MM **Privately Held**
**Web:** www.kurzinstruments.com
**SIC: 3822 5084 3824 3823** Environmental controls; Industrial machinery and equipment; Fluid meters and counting devices; Process control instruments

### (P-14364)
### MEGGITT WESTERN DESIGN INC
Also Called: Western Design
9801 Muirlands Blvd, Irvine (92618-2521)
**PHONE**.................................949 465-7700
▲ **EMP:** 104
**SIC: 3822 3483** Environmental controls; Ammunition components

### (P-14365)
### NVENT THERMAL LLC
899 Broadway St, Redwood City (94063)
**PHONE**.................................650 474-7414
**EMP:** 388
**Web:** www.nvent.com
**SIC: 3822 1711** Environmental controls; Heating and air conditioning contractors
**HQ:** Nvent Thermal Llc
 1665 Utica Ave S Ste 700
 St Louis Park MN 55416
 763 204-7700

### (P-14366)
### PARAGON CONTROLS INCORPORATED
Also Called: PCI
2371 Circadian Way, Santa Rosa (95407-5439)
P.O. Box 99 (95436-0099)
**PHONE**.................................707 579-1424
Richard Thomas Reis, *Pr*
Larry E Winterbourne, *VP*
Dennis Reis, *Sec*
Cheryl Reis, *Treas*
▲ **EMP:** 15 **EST:** 1984
**SQ FT:** 8,200
**SALES (est):** 2.63MM **Privately Held**
**Web:** www.paragoncontrols.com
**SIC: 3822 3823** Air flow controllers, air conditioning and refrigeration; Primary elements for process flow measurement

### (P-14367)
### ROBERTSHAW CONTROLS COMPANY
1751 3rd St Ste 102, Norco (92860-2670)

## 3822 - Environmental Controls (P-14368)

PHONE................................951 893-6233
Jeff From, *Brnch Mgr*
**EMP:** 55
**Web:** www.robertshaw.com
**SIC: 3822** Environmental controls
**HQ:** Robertshaw Controls Company
1222 Hamilton Pkwy
Itasca IL 60143

### (P-14368)
### SIEMENS INDUSTRY INC
7464 French Rd, Sacramento (95828)
PHONE................................916 681-3000
Oliver Hauck, *Brnch Mgr*
**EMP:** 200
**SALES (corp-wide):** 84.48B **Privately Held**
**Web:** www.siemens.com
**SIC: 3822** 5063 3669 1731 Air conditioning and refrigeration controls; Electric alarms and signaling equipment; Emergency alarms; Safety and security specialization
**HQ:** Siemens Industry, Inc.
1000 Deerfield Pkwy
Buffalo Grove IL 60089
847 215-1000

### (P-14369)
### SIEMENS INDUSTRY INC
3650 Industrial Blvd Ste 100, West Sacramento (95691)
PHONE................................916 553-4444
Rick Glaser, *Prin*
**EMP:** 21
**SALES (corp-wide):** 84.48B **Privately Held**
**Web:** www.siemens.com
**SIC: 3822** Thermostats and other environmental sensors
**HQ:** Siemens Industry, Inc.
1000 Deerfield Pkwy
Buffalo Grove IL 60089
847 215-1000

### (P-14370)
### SUPERIOR SENSOR TECHNOLOGY INC
103 Cooper Ct, Los Gatos (95032-7604)
PHONE................................408 703-2950
James Finch, *CEO*
**EMP:** 25 **EST:** 2016
**SALES (est):** 5.14MM **Privately Held**
**Web:** www.superiorsensors.com
**SIC: 3822** Pressure controllers, air-conditioning system type

### (P-14371)
### TELLKAMP SYSTEMS INC (PA)
15523 Carmenita Rd, Santa Fe Springs (90670-5609)
PHONE................................562 802-1621
◆ **EMP:** 49 **EST:** 1971
**SALES (est):** 4.39MM
**SALES (corp-wide):** 4.39MM **Privately Held**
**Web:** www.tellkamp.com
**SIC: 3822** 3564 Environmental controls; Air purification equipment

### (P-14372)
### TRANSFIRST CORPORATION
900 E Blanco Rd, Salinas (93901-4419)
P.O. Box 1788 (93902-1788)
PHONE................................831 424-2911
James Lugg, *Pr*
Richard Macleod, *
Teresa Scattini, *
▲ **EMP:** 24 **EST:** 1966
**SALES (est):** 5.14MM **Privately Held**
**Web:** www.transfresh.com
**SIC: 3822** Air conditioning and refrigeration controls

### (P-14373)
### TRUE FRESH HPP LLC
6535 Caballero Blvd Unit B, Buena Park (90620-8106)
PHONE................................949 922-8801
**EMP:** 35 **EST:** 2015
**SALES (est):** 5.92MM **Privately Held**
**Web:** www.truefreshhpp.com
**SIC: 3822** Refrigeration controls (pressure)

### (P-14374)
### VIGILENT CORPORATION (PA)
1111 Broadway Fl 3, Oakland (94607-4139)
PHONE................................888 305-4451
David Hudson, *CEO*
**EMP:** 35 **EST:** 2008
**SALES (est):** 13MM
**SALES (corp-wide):** 13MM **Privately Held**
**Web:** www.vigilent.com
**SIC: 3822** Environmental controls

### (P-14375)
### VIVINT INC
651 N Armstrong Ave Ste 101, Fresno (93727-2935)
PHONE................................805 790-7209
**EMP:** 405
**Web:** www.vivint.com
**SIC: 3822** Building services monitoring controls, automatic
**HQ:** Vivint, Inc.
4931 N 300 W
Provo UT 84604
801 377-9111

### (P-14376)
### VOLTUS INC
2443 Fillmore St Pmb 380-3427, San Francisco (94115-1814)
PHONE................................646 248-4342
Dana Guernsey, *CEO*
Matthew Plante, *Pr*
**EMP:** 38 **EST:** 2016
**SALES (est):** 12.17MM **Privately Held**
**Web:** www.voltus.co
**SIC: 3822** 3829 Environmental controls; Measuring and controlling devices, nec

### (P-14377)
### WESTERN ENVIRONMENTAL INC
62150 Gene Welmas Dr, Mecca (92254-6550)
PHONE................................760 396-0222
Ed Kennon, *Pt*
**EMP:** 30 **EST:** 2002
**SALES (est):** 3.6MM **Privately Held**
**Web:** www.wei-mecca.com
**SIC: 3822** Environmental controls

### (P-14378)
### X THERM
3325 Investment Blvd, Hayward (94545-3808)
PHONE................................510 441-7566
H Johnson, *Prin*
**EMP:** 22 **EST:** 2018
**SALES (est):** 5.02MM **Privately Held**
**Web:** www.therm-x.com
**SIC: 3822** Environmental controls

### (P-14379)
### XPOWER MANUFACTURE INC
668 S 6th Ave, City Of Industry (91746-3025)
PHONE................................626 285-3301
Keidy Gu, *CEO*
Guogen Cui, *
▲ **EMP:** 40 **EST:** 2011
**SALES (est):** 3.43MM **Privately Held**
**Web:** www.xpower.com
**SIC: 3822** 3999 3564 Air flow controllers, air conditioning and refrigeration; Pet supplies; Blowing fans: industrial or commercial
**PA:** Xinshengyuan Electrical Appliances Co., Ltd.
No.3, East Area No.3 Road, Xiantang Industrial Zone, Longjiang T

## 3823 Process Control Instruments

### (P-14380)
### 3D INSTRUMENTS LLC
Also Called: Sierra Precision
4990 E Hunter Ave, Anaheim (92807-2057)
PHONE................................714 399-9200
**EMP:** 100
**Web:** www.wika.com
**SIC: 3823** Pressure gauges, dial and digital

### (P-14381)
### ACS INSTRUMENTATION VALVES INC
3065 Richmond Pkwy Ste 106, Richmond (94806-5718)
P.O. Box 21645 (94820-1645)
PHONE................................510 262-1880
Elizabeth Niemczyk, *CEO*
**EMP:** 99 **EST:** 2017
**SALES (est):** 1.54MM **Privately Held**
**Web:** www.acs-sf.com
**SIC: 3823** Process control instruments

### (P-14382)
### ADVANCED ELECTROMAGNETICS INC
Also Called: Aemi
1320 Air Wing Rd Ste 101, San Diego (92154-7707)
PHONE................................619 449-9492
Per Iversen, *Pr*
Andrew Mcfadden, *Prin*
◆ **EMP:** 37 **EST:** 1980
**SQ FT:** 16,000
**SALES (est):** 13.47MM
**SALES (corp-wide):** 14.04MM **Privately Held**
**Web:** www.mvg-world.com
**SIC: 3823** 3825 Absorption analyzers: infrared, x-ray, etc.: industrial; Instruments to measure electricity
**HQ:** Orbit/Fr, Inc.
650 Louis Dr Ste 100
Warminster PA 18974

### (P-14383)
### ADVANCED PRESSURE TECHNOLOGY
Also Called: AP Tech
687 Technology Way, Napa (94558-7512)
PHONE................................707 259-0102
Rene Zakhour, *Pr*
▲ **EMP:** 95 **EST:** 1987
**SALES (est):** 20.18MM **Privately Held**
**Web:** www.aptech-online.com
**SIC: 3823** Pressure gauges, dial and digital

### (P-14384)
### AIR MONITOR CORPORATION (PA)
1050 Hopper Ave, Santa Rosa (95403-1613)
P.O. Box 6358 (95406-0358)
PHONE................................707 544-2706
Dean De Baun, *CEO*
Sharon Hughes, *
Chris De Baun, *
**EMP:** 70 **EST:** 1967
**SQ FT:** 50,000
**SALES (est):** 10.63MM
**SALES (corp-wide):** 10.63MM **Privately Held**
**Web:** www.airmonitor.com
**SIC: 3823** Process control instruments

### (P-14385)
### ALPHA TECHNICS INC
24024 Humphries Rd, Tecate (91980-4008)
PHONE................................949 250-6578
Lisa Marie Ryan, *Pr*
Dan Obrien, *
**EMP:** 200 **EST:** 2011
**SALES (est):** 6.36MM
**SALES (corp-wide):** 9.17B **Privately Held**
**SIC: 3823** Process control instruments
**PA:** Te Connectivity Inc.
601 13th St Nw Ste 850s
800 522-6752

### (P-14386)
### AMETEK AMERON LLC (HQ)
Also Called: Mass Systems
4750 Littlejohn St, Baldwin Park (91706-2274)
PHONE................................626 856-0101
Keith Marsicola, *Managing Member*
Steve Tanner, *Managing Member*
**EMP:** 55 **EST:** 1988
**SQ FT:** 2,600
**SALES (est):** 25.88MM
**SALES (corp-wide):** 6.6B **Publicly Held**
**Web:** www.ameronglobal.com
**SIC: 3823** 3999 3728 8711 Pressure gauges, dial and digital; Fire extinguishers, portable; Aircraft parts and equipment, nec; Industrial engineers
**PA:** Ametek, Inc.
1100 Cassatt Rd
610 647-2121

### (P-14387)
### ANALYTICAL INDUSTRIES INC
Also Called: Advanced Instruments
2855 Metropolitan Pl, Pomona (91767-1853)
PHONE................................909 392-6900
Frank S Gregus, *Pr*
Patrick J Prindible, *
Mohammad Razaq, *
**EMP:** 45 **EST:** 1994
**SQ FT:** 15,000
**SALES (est):** 9.3MM **Privately Held**
**Web:** www.aii1.com
**SIC: 3823** Process control instruments

### (P-14388)
### BAMBECK SYSTEMS INC (PA)
1921 Carnegie Ave Ste 3a, Santa Ana (92705-5510)
PHONE................................949 250-3100
Robert J Bambeck, *Pr*
Robert Deweerd, *VP*
**EMP:** 19 **EST:** 1980
**SQ FT:** 6,100
**SALES (est):** 2.51MM
**SALES (corp-wide):** 2.51MM **Privately Held**
**Web:** www.bambecksystems.com
**SIC: 3823** Boiler controls: industrial, power, and marine type

### (P-14389)
### BIODOT INC (HQ)
2852 Alton Pkwy, Irvine (92606-5104)
PHONE................................949 440-3685
Anthony Lemmo, *CEO*
**EMP:** 93 **EST:** 1994

▲ = Import ▼ = Export
◆ = Import/Export

**PRODUCTS & SERVICES SECTION**  **3823 - Process Control Instruments (P-14409)**

SQ FT: 24,000
SALES (est): 21.44MM
SALES (corp-wide): 2.24B **Privately Held**
Web: www.biodot.com
SIC: **3823** 3826  Process control instruments; Analytical instruments
PA: Ats Corporation
730 Fountain St N Bldg 3
604 332-2666

**(P-14390)**
**BRUKER-MICHROM INC**
61 Daggett Dr, San Jose (95134-2109)
PHONE.................................530 888-6498
EMP: 21
Web: www.michrom.com
SIC: **3823**  Process control instruments

**(P-14391)**
**CALIFORNIA DEPT WTR RESOURCES**
901 P St Lbby, Sacramento  (95814-6424)
PHONE.................................916 651-9203
Mark Cowin, *Brnch Mgr*
EMP: 27
SALES (corp-wide): 534.4MM **Privately Held**
Web: water.ca.gov
SIC: **3823**  Water quality monitoring and control systems
HQ: California Department Of Water Resources
715 P St,
Sacramento CA 95814
916 653-9394

**(P-14392)**
**CALIFRNIA ANLYTICAL INSTRS INC**
Also Called: Cai
1312 W Grove Ave, Orange (92865-4136)
PHONE.................................714 974-5560
R Pete Furton, *Ch*
Harold J Peper, *
Loren T Mathews, *
EMP: 61 EST: 1992
SQ FT: 26,400
SALES (est): 11.34MM **Privately Held**
Web: www.gasanalyzers.com
SIC: **3823**  Process control instruments

**(P-14393)**
**CAMERON TECHNOLOGIES US LLC**
Also Called: Cameron's Measurement Systems
4040 Capitol Ave, Whittier  (90601-1751)
PHONE.................................562 222-8440
Victor Hart, *Manager*
EMP: 26
SIC: **3823**  Industrial flow and liquid measuring instruments
HQ: Cameron Technologies Us, Llc
1000 Mcclaren Woods Dr
Coraopolis PA 15108

**(P-14394)**
**CK TECHNOLOGIES  INC (PA)**
Also Called: Ckt
3629 Vista Mercado, Camarillo (93012-8055)
PHONE.................................805 987-4801
Karl F Zimmermann, *Pr*
Karl F Zimmermann, *Pr*
Heidi Zimmerman, *
EMP: 19 EST: 1987
SQ FT: 34,000
SALES (est): 4.33MM
SALES (corp-wide): 4.33MM **Privately Held**

Web: www.ckt.com
SIC: **3823**  3825 5065  Water quality monitoring and control systems; Instruments to measure electricity; Electronic parts and equipment, nec

**(P-14395)**
**COLTER & PETERSON MICROSYSTEMS**
Also Called: C & P Microsystems
1260 Holm Rd Ste C, Petaluma (94954-7152)
PHONE.................................707 776-4500
Bruce Peterson, *Pr*
▲ EMP: 20 EST: 1979
SQ FT: 7,500
SALES (est): 4.02MM
SALES (corp-wide): 23.64MM **Privately Held**
Web: www.papercutters.com
SIC: **3823** 5084 3554  Computer interface equipment, for industrial process control; Printing trades machinery, equipment, and supplies; Paper mill machinery: plating, slitting, waxing, etc.
PA: Colter & Peterson, Inc.
19 Fairfield Pl
973 684-0901

**(P-14396)**
**COMPUTATIONAL SYSTEMS INC**
4301 Resnik Ct, Bakersfield (93313-4851)
PHONE.................................661 832-5306
Shannon Romine, *Brnch Mgr*
EMP: 91
SALES (corp-wide): 17.49B **Publicly Held**
Web: www.emerson.com
SIC: **3823**  Process control instruments
HQ: Computational Systems, Incorporated
8000 West Florissant Ave
Saint Louis MO 63136
314 553-2000

**(P-14397)**
**CONTINENTAL CONTROLS CORP**
Also Called: Manufacturing
7710 Kenamar Ct, San Diego (92121-2425)
PHONE.................................858 453-9880
David Fisher, *Pr*
David Fisher, *Pr*
Richard Fisher, *
Judith Fisher, *
Ross Fisher, *
▲ EMP: 28 EST: 1989
SQ FT: 17,000
SALES (est): 4.38MM **Privately Held**
Web: www.continentalcontrols.com
SIC: **3823** 3533  Process control instruments; Oil and gas field machinery

**(P-14398)**
**COSASCO  INC**
11841 Smith Ave, Santa Fe Springs (90670-3226)
PHONE.................................562 949-0123
EMP: 97 EST: 2015
SALES (est): 6.38MM **Privately Held**
Web: www.cosasco.com
SIC: **3823**  Process control instruments

**(P-14399)**
**COUNTY OF NAPA**
Also Called: Flood Ctrl Wtr Cnservation Dst
804 1st St, Napa  (94559-2623)
PHONE.................................707 259-8620
Robert Peterson, *Dir*
EMP: 22
Web: www.countyofnapa.org

SIC: **3823**  Water quality monitoring and control systems
PA: County Of Napa
1195 3rd St Ste 310
707 253-4421

**(P-14400)**
**CRYSTAL ENGINEERING CORP**
708 Fiero Ln Ste 9, San Luis Obispo (93401-7945)
P.O. Box 3033 (93403-3033)
PHONE.................................805 595-5477
David Porter, *Pr*
▲ EMP: 38 EST: 1981
SALES (est): 12.29MM
SALES (corp-wide): 6.6B **Publicly Held**
Web: www.crystalengineering.net
SIC: **3823**  Pressure gauges, dial and digital
PA: Ametek, Inc.
1100 Cassatt Rd
610 647-2121

**(P-14401)**
**DELPHI CONTROL SYSTEMS INC**
2806 Metropolitan Pl, Pomona (91767-1854)
PHONE.................................909 593-8099
Beth Barbone, *CEO*
Beth A Barbonc, *Pr*
Scott Crail, *VP*
EMP: 15 EST: 1976
SQ FT: 11,000
SALES (est): 3.2MM **Privately Held**
Web: www.delphicontrolsystems.com
SIC: **3823** 3613  Industrial process control instruments; Control panels, electric

**(P-14402)**
**DIGITAL DYNAMICS  INC**
5 Victor Sq, Scotts Valley  (95066-3531)
PHONE.................................831 438-4444
Mister Jerde, *Pr*
Carolyn Jerde, *
William P Ledeen, *
EMP: 45 EST: 1974
SQ FT: 18,000
SALES (est): 9.71MM **Privately Held**
Web: www.digitaldynamics.com
SIC: **3823**  Process control instruments

**(P-14403)**
**DIGIVISION  INC**
9830 Summers Ridge Rd, San Diego (92121-3083)
PHONE.................................858 530-0100
Randy Millar, *Ex VP*
Randy Millar, *VP*
Richard Hier, *VP*
EMP: 24 EST: 1982
SQ FT: 10,000
SALES (est): 720.08K **Privately Held**
SIC: **3823** 8731  Digital displays of process variables; Commercial physical research

**(P-14404)**
**DURO-SENSE CORPORATION**
869 Sandhill Ave, Carson (90746-1210)
PHONE.................................310 533-6877
Jay Waterman, *Pr*
Roger S Waterman, *Ch Bd*
EMP: 15 EST: 1979
SQ FT: 8,000
SALES (est): 2.09MM **Privately Held**
Web: www.duro-sense.com
SIC: **3823**  Temperature instruments: industrial process type

**(P-14405)**
**DUSOUTH INDUSTRIES**
Also Called: Dst Controls
651 Stone Rd, Benicia (94510-1141)
PHONE.................................707 745-5117
William Southard, *Pr*
Read Hayward, *
EMP: 30 EST: 1975
SQ FT: 14,000
SALES (est): 8.88MM
SALES (corp-wide): 68.93MM **Privately Held**
Web: www.dstcontrols.com
SIC: **3823**  Process control instruments
HQ: Ckc Automation, Llc
6617 San Leandro St
Oakland CA 94621
415 494-8225

**(P-14406)**
**E D Q INC**
2920 Halladay St, Santa Ana  (92705-5623)
PHONE.................................714 546-6010
Erik K Moller, *CEO*
Randy Heartfield, *
Mary C Heartfield, *
▲ EMP: 39 EST: 1960
SQ FT: 14,000
SALES (est): 5.3MM **Privately Held**
Web: www.qedaero.com
SIC: **3823** 3829 3812  Pressure gauges, dial and digital; Accelerometers; Aircraft/aerospace flight instruments and guidance systems

**(P-14407)**
**EAGLE TECH MANUFACTURING  INC**
841 Walker St, Watsonville  (95076-4116)
PHONE.................................831 768-7467
Alfredo Madrigal, *Pr*
Hector Madrigal, *VP*
▲ EMP: 26 EST: 1996
SQ FT: 5,000
SALES (est): 4.64MM **Privately Held**
Web: www.eagletechman.com
SIC: **3823**  Electrolytic conductivity instruments, industrial process

**(P-14408)**
**ELDRIDGE PRODUCTS  INC**
465 Reservation Rd, Marina  (93933-3430)
PHONE.................................831 648-7777
Mark F Eldridge, *Pr*
▼ EMP: 20 EST: 1988
SQ FT: 8,500
SALES (est): 4.83MM **Privately Held**
Web: www.epiflow.com
SIC: **3823** 3824  Flow instruments, industrial process type; Fluid meters and counting devices

**(P-14409)**
**EMBEDDED DESIGNS INC**
Also Called: K I C
16120 W Bernardo Dr Ste A, San Diego (92127-1875)
PHONE.................................858 673-6050
Casey Kazmierowicz, *Ch*
Bjorn Dahle, *
Henryk J Kazmier, *
Miles Moreau, *
Phil Kazmierowicz, *
EMP: 32 EST: 1984
SQ FT: 9,500
SALES (est): 6.05MM **Privately Held**
Web: www.kicthermal.com
SIC: **3823**  Temperature measurement instruments, industrial

## 3823 - Process Control Instruments (P-14410)

**(P-14410)**
**ETI SYSTEMS**
Also Called: Polaris Music
1800 Century Park E Ste 600, Los Angeles (90067-1501)
PHONE.................................310 684-3664
Bill Tice, *Pr*
Gayle Tice, *
**EMP:** 60 **EST:** 1962
**SQ FT:** 8,200
**SALES (est):** 1.8MM **Privately Held**
Web: www.etisystems.com
**SIC: 3823** Potentiometric self-balancing inst., except X-Y plotters

**(P-14411)**
**FLOWMETRICS INC**
9201 Independence Ave, Chatsworth (91311-5905)
PHONE.................................818 407-3420
Hormoz Ghaemmaghami, *Pr*
**EMP:** 15 **EST:** 1989
**SQ FT:** 4,000
**SALES (est):** 793.56K **Privately Held**
Web: www.flowmetrics.com
**SIC: 3823** Industrial flow and liquid measuring instruments

**(P-14412)**
**FLUID COMPONENTS INTL LLC (DH)**
Also Called: F C I
1755 La Costa Meadows Dr, San Marcos (92078-5115)
PHONE.................................760 744-6950
Dan Mcqueen, *CEO*
Daniel M Mcqueen, *Pr*
Ronald E Ogle, *Dir*
Barbara Succetti, *CFO*
▲ **EMP:** 17 **EST:** 1992
**SQ FT:** 49,000
**SALES (est):** 41.43MM
**SALES (corp-wide):** 231.49MM **Privately Held**
Web: www.fluidcomponents.com
**SIC: 3823** Process control instruments
HQ: Process Sensing Technologies Corp.
  135 Engineers Rd Ste 150
  Hauppauge NY 11788
  631 427-3898

**(P-14413)**
**FORTREND ENGINEERING CORP (PA)**
2220 Otoole Ave, San Jose (95131-1326)
PHONE.................................408 734-9311
Chris Wu Ph.d., *CEO*
Joseph Ma Ph.d., *Ch*
▲ **EMP:** 41 **EST:** 1979
**SQ FT:** 20,000
**SALES (est):** 6.46MM
**SALES (corp-wide):** 6.46MM **Privately Held**
Web: www.fortrend.com
**SIC: 3823** Process control instruments

**(P-14414)**
**FOX THERMAL INSTRUMENTS INC**
399 Reservation Rd, Marina (93933-3229)
PHONE.................................831 384-4300
William Roller, *CEO*
Bradley Philip Lesko, *Pr*
▲ **EMP:** 20 **EST:** 1993
**SQ FT:** 8,000
**SALES (est):** 8.56MM
**SALES (corp-wide):** 287.28MM **Privately Held**
Web: www.foxthermal.com

**SIC: 3823** Process control instruments
HQ: Onicon Incorporated
  11451 Belcher Rd S
  Largo FL 33773
  727 447-6140

**(P-14415)**
**FUNDAMENTAL TECH INTL INC**
Also Called: F T I
2900 E 29th St, Long Beach (90806-2315)
PHONE.................................562 595-0661
Maarten Propper, *CEO*
John Jacobson, *
▼ **EMP:** 24 **EST:** 1996
**SQ FT:** 20,000
**SALES (est):** 1.14MM **Privately Held**
**SIC: 3823** Liquid analysis instruments, industrial process type

**(P-14416)**
**FUTEK ADVANCED SENSOR TECH INC**
Also Called: Futek Advanced Sensor Tech
10 Thomas, Irvine (92618-2702)
PHONE.................................949 465-0900
Javad Mokhberi, *CEO*
Javad Mokhbery, *
▼ **EMP:** 140 **EST:** 1988
**SQ FT:** 23,000
**SALES (est):** 17.89MM **Privately Held**
Web: www.futek.com
**SIC: 3823** 8711 Process control instruments; Engineering services

**(P-14417)**
**GALIL MOTION CONTROL INC**
Also Called: Galil
270 Technology Way, Rocklin (95765-1228)
PHONE.................................800 377-6329
Jacob Tal, *Prin*
Wayne Baron, *
Lisa Wade, *
John Thompson, *
Brian Kambe, *
**EMP:** 36 **EST:** 1983
**SQ FT:** 30,000
**SALES (est):** 9.24MM **Privately Held**
Web: www.galil.com
**SIC: 3823** Process control instruments

**(P-14418)**
**GEORG FISCHER SIGNET LLC**
5462 Irwindale Ave Ste A, Baldwin Park (91706)
PHONE.................................626 571-2770
Charlotte Hill, *Managing Member*
James Jackson, *Prin*
John Pregenzer, *Prin*
▲ **EMP:** 90 **EST:** 1953
**SALES (est):** 20.69MM **Privately Held**
Web: www.gfsignet.com
**SIC: 3823** Process control instruments
HQ: Georg Fischer Spa
  Via Eugenio Villoresi 2/4
  Agrate Brianza MB 20864

**(P-14419)**
**GET ENGINEERING CORP**
Also Called: Get Engineering
9350 Bond Ave, El Cajon (92021-2850)
PHONE.................................619 443-8295
Roger Kuroda, *CEO*
Leslie Adams, *CEO*
Rodney Tuttle, *Prin*
**EMP:** 18 **EST:** 1982
**SQ FT:** 14,500
**SALES (est):** 3.83MM **Privately Held**
Web: www.gethdio.com

**SIC: 3823** 7373 3812 3679 Computer interface equipment, for industrial process control; Computer integrated systems design; Search and navigation equipment; Electronic circuits

**(P-14420)**
**GRAPHTEC AMERICA INC (DH)**
Also Called: Graphtec
17462 Armstrong Ave, Irvine (92614-5724)
PHONE.................................949 770-6010
Yasutaka Arakawa, *CEO*
◆ **EMP:** 49 **EST:** 1949
**SQ FT:** 35,000
**SALES (est):** 16.5MM **Privately Held**
Web: www.graphtecamerica.com
**SIC: 3823** 5064 Process control instruments; Video cassette recorders and accessories
HQ: Graphtec Corp.
  503-10, Shinanocho, Totsuka-Ku
  Yokohama KNG 244-0

**(P-14421)**
**HARDY PROCESS SOLUTIONS**
Also Called: Hardy Process Solutions
10075 Mesa Rim Rd, San Diego (92121-2913)
PHONE.................................858 278-2900
Eric Schellenberger, *Pr*
Steve Hanes, *
◆ **EMP:** 50 **EST:** 1980
**SALES (est):** 19.57MM
**SALES (corp-wide):** 6.18B **Publicly Held**
Web: www.hardysolutions.com
**SIC: 3823** 3829 3596 Process control instruments; Measuring and controlling devices, nec; Scales and balances, except laboratory
HQ: Dynamic Instruments, Inc.
  10737 Lexington Dr
  Knoxville TN 37932
  858 278-4900

**(P-14422)**
**HCC INDUSTRIES LEASING INC (HQ)**
4232 Temple City Blvd, Rosemead (91770-1552)
PHONE.................................626 443-8933
Richard Ferraid, *Pr*
**EMP:** 15 **EST:** 1945
**SQ FT:** 36,000
**SALES (est):** 58.04MM
**SALES (corp-wide):** 6.6B **Publicly Held**
**SIC: 3823** Process control instruments
PA: Ametek, Inc.
  1100 Cassatt Rd
  610 647-2121

**(P-14423)**
**INNOVATIVE INTEGRATION INC**
741 Flynn Rd, Camarillo (93012-8056)
PHONE.................................805 520-3300
Jim Henderson, *Pr*
Dan Mclane, *VP*
▲ **EMP:** 30 **EST:** 1988
**SQ FT:** 11,000
**SALES (est):** 2.05MM **Privately Held**
Web: www.isipkg.com
**SIC: 3823** 3571 Process control instruments; Electronic computers

**(P-14424)**
**INTEGRATED FLOW SYSTEMS LLC (HQ)**
Also Called: Advanced Integration Tech
26462 Corporate Ave, Hayward (94545-3914)
PHONE.................................510 659-4900
Michael Mallinen, *Managing Member*

Carrie Buchanan, *Contrlr*
◆ **EMP:** 80 **EST:** 1983
**SQ FT:** 3,000
**SALES (est):** 11.67MM
**SALES (corp-wide):** 1.73B **Publicly Held**
**SIC: 3823** Process control instruments
PA: Ultra Clean Holdings, Inc.
  26462 Corporate Ave
  510 576-4400

**(P-14425)**
**ITI ELECTRO-OPTIC CORPORATION (PA)**
Also Called: Ccd
11500 W Olympic Blvd Ste 400, Los Angeles (90064-1524)
PHONE.................................310 445-8900
Mei Shi, *Ch Bd*
Robert Nevins, *Pr*
John Sun, *Ex VP*
James Wang, *VP Fin*
Richard Caserio, *VP Mktg*
▲ **EMP:** 20 **EST:** 1985
**SQ FT:** 5,000
**SALES (est):** 1.06MM
**SALES (corp-wide):** 1.06MM **Privately Held**
Web: www.itieo.com
**SIC: 3823** Infrared instruments, industrial process type

**(P-14426)**
**ITI ELECTRO-OPTIC CORPORATION**
1500 Olympia Blvd Ste 400, Los Angeles (90021-1900)
PHONE.................................310 312-4526
John Sun, *Mgr*
**EMP:** 20
**SALES (corp-wide):** 4.65MM **Privately Held**
Web: www.itieo.com
**SIC: 3823** Infrared instruments, industrial process type
PA: Iti Electro-Optic Corporation
  11500 W Olympic Blvd
  310 445-8900

**(P-14427)**
**KEYSIGHT TECHNOLOGIES INC (PA)**
1400 Fountaingrove Pkwy, Santa Rosa (95403-1738)
P.O. Box 4026 (95403)
PHONE.................................800 829-4444
Satish C Dhanasekaran, *Pr*
Ronald S Nersesian, *
Neil Dougherty, *Sr VP*
Ingrid Estrada, *PEOPLE*
Jeffrey Li, *Sr VP*
**EMP:** 1370 **EST:** 1939
**SALES (est):** 5.46B
**SALES (corp-wide):** 5.46B **Publicly Held**
Web: www.keysight.com
**SIC: 3823** 3829 7629 Process control instruments; Measuring and controlling devices, nec; Electronic equipment repair

**(P-14428)**
**KING INSTRUMENT COMPANY INC**
12700 Pala Dr, Garden Grove (92841-3924)
PHONE.................................714 891-0008
Clyde F King, *Pr*
**EMP:** 50 **EST:** 1983
**SQ FT:** 46,000
**SALES (est):** 10.2MM **Privately Held**
Web: www.kinginstrumentco.com

# PRODUCTS & SERVICES SECTION
## 3823 - Process Control Instruments (P-14449)

SIC: **3823** Flow instruments, industrial process type

### (P-14429)
### KING NUTRONICS LLC
Also Called: King Nutronics Corporation
6421 Independence Ave, Woodland Hills (91367-2608)
PHONE.............................818 887-5460
Robert Welther, *Pr*
**EMP:** 34 **EST:** 1960
**SQ FT:** 21,000
**SALES (est):** 6.62MM
**SALES (corp-wide):** 17.9MM **Privately Held**
Web: www.raptor-scientific.com
SIC: **3823** 3825 Pressure measurement instruments, industrial; Instruments to measure electricity
PA: Raptor Scientific
  81 Fuller Way
  860 829-0001

### (P-14430)
### LAIRD TECHNOLOGIES INC
2040 Fortune Dr Ste 102, San Jose (95131-1823)
PHONE.............................408 544-9500
Troy Hodges, *Owner*
**EMP:** 27
**SALES (corp-wide):** 2.93B **Publicly Held**
Web: www.lairdtech.com
SIC: **3823** Absorption analyzers: infrared, x-ray, etc.: industrial
HQ: Laird Technologies, Inc.
  16401 Swingley Ridge Rd
  Chesterfield MO 63017
  636 898-6000

### (P-14431)
### MAX MACHINERY INC
33 Healdsburg Ave Ste A, Healdsburg (95448-4043)
PHONE.............................707 433-2662
Oliver Max, *Pr*
Sonia Max, *VP*
**EMP:** 21 **EST:** 1967
**SQ FT:** 10,000
**SALES (est):** 5.6MM **Privately Held**
Web: www.maxmachinery.com
SIC: **3823** Process control instruments

### (P-14432)
### MCCROMETER INC (HQ)
3255 W Stetson Ave, Hemet (92545-7763)
PHONE.............................951 652-6811
David Oveson, *CEO*
Sameer Ralhan, *
Jonathan Hinkemeyer, *
Michael Vagnini, *
◆ **EMP:** 214 **EST:** 1996
**SQ FT:** 9,090
**SALES (est):** 39.7MM
**SALES (corp-wide):** 1.73B **Publicly Held**
Web: www.mccrometer.com
SIC: **3823** Process control instruments
PA: Veralto Corporation
  225 Wyman St Ste 250
  781 755-3655

### (P-14433)
### MICRO LITHOGRAPHY INC
1247 Elko Dr, Sunnyvale (94089-2211)
PHONE.............................408 747-1769
Yung-tsai Yen, *CEO*
Chris Yen, *
Sandy Yen, *
▲ **EMP:** 225 **EST:** 1981
**SQ FT:** 100,000
**SALES (est):** 23.2MM **Privately Held**

Web: www.mliusa.com
SIC: **3823** 3674 Process control instruments; Semiconductors and related devices

### (P-14434)
### MICROCOOL
72216 Northshore St Ste 103, Thousand Palms (92276-2325)
PHONE.............................760 322-1111
Mike Lemche, *Pr*
Christopher Stanley, *VP*
James Murphy, *Sec*
▲ **EMP:** 15 **EST:** 2007
**SQ FT:** 5,800
**SALES (est):** 2.43MM **Privately Held**
Web: www.microcool.com
SIC: **3823** Humidity instruments, industrial process type

### (P-14435)
### MODUTEK CORP
6387 San Ignacio Ave, San Jose (95119-1206)
PHONE.............................408 362-2000
Douglas G Wagner, *Pr*
Robert Brody, *VP*
**EMP:** 21 **EST:** 1980
**SQ FT:** 21,000
**SALES (est):** 5.7MM **Privately Held**
Web: www.modutek.com
SIC: **3823** 7373 Temperature instruments: industrial process type; Systems integration services

### (P-14436)
### MOORE INDUSTRIES-INTERNATIONAL INC (PA)
Also Called: Moore Industries
16650 Schoenborn St, North Hills (91343-6106)
PHONE.............................818 894-7111
▲ **EMP:** 200 **EST:** 1965
**SALES (est):** 39.36MM
**SALES (corp-wide):** 39.36MM **Privately Held**
Web: www.miinet.com
SIC: **3823** 5084 Process control instruments; Industrial machinery and equipment

### (P-14437)
### MOUNTZ INC (HQ)
Also Called: Dg Mountz Associates
1080 N 11th St, San Jose (95112-2927)
PHONE.............................408 292-2214
Brad Mountz, *Pr*
David Aviles, *CFO*
▲ **EMP:** 43 **EST:** 1964
**SQ FT:** 30,000
**SALES (est):** 13.25MM
**SALES (corp-wide):** 4.73B **Publicly Held**
Web: www.mountztorque.com
SIC: **3823** 5085 Process control instruments; Fasteners and fastening equipment
PA: Snap-On Incorporated
  2801 80th St
  262 656-5200

### (P-14438)
### MYRON L COMPANY
2450 Impala Dr, Carlsbad (92010-7226)
PHONE.............................760 438-2021
Gary O Robinson, *Pr*
Jerry Adams, *
◆ **EMP:** 80 **EST:** 1957
**SQ FT:** 43,000
**SALES (est):** 23.98MM **Privately Held**
Web: www.myronl.com

SIC: **3823** 3825 3613 Electrodes used in industrial process measurement; Instruments to measure electricity; Switchgear and switchboard apparatus

### (P-14439)
### NORDSON ASYMTEK INC
Also Called: Nordson Asymtek
2747 Loker Ave W, Carlsbad (92010-6601)
PHONE.............................760 431-1919
▲ **EMP:** 250
Web: www.nordson.com
SIC: **3823** Industrial flow and liquid measuring instruments

### (P-14440)
### NUMATIC ENGINEERING INC
7915 Ajay Dr, Sun Valley (91352-5315)
P.O. Box 1477 (35201-1477)
PHONE.............................818 768-1200
▲ **EMP:** 38
SIC: **3823** Process control instruments

### (P-14441)
### OLEUMTECH CORPORATION
19762 Pauling, Foothill Ranch (92610-2611)
PHONE.............................949 305-9009
Paul Gregory, *CEO*
Vrej Isa, *COO*
**EMP:** 57 **EST:** 2002
**SQ FT:** 55,000
**SALES (est):** 9.59MM **Privately Held**
Web: www.oleumtech.com
SIC: **3823** Process control instruments

### (P-14442)
### ORBIS INTELLIGENT SYSTEMS INC
5675 Ruffin Rd Ste 110, San Diego (92123-1362)
PHONE.............................858 737-4469
Dan Squiller, *CEO*
**EMP:** 22 **EST:** 2017
**SALES (est):** 5.53MM **Privately Held**
Web: www.orbis-smart-networks.com
SIC: **3823** Process control instruments

### (P-14443)
### PARKER-HANNIFIN CORPORATION
Veriflo Division
250 Canal Blvd, Richmond (94804-2002)
PHONE.............................510 235-9590
Pera Horne, *Genl Mgr*
**EMP:** 135
**SALES (corp-wide):** 19.93B **Publicly Held**
Web: www.parker.com
SIC: **3823** 3842 3841 3625 Industrial process control instruments; Respirators; Surgical and medical instruments; Relays and industrial controls
PA: Parker-Hannifin Corporation
  6035 Parkland Blvd
  216 896-3000

### (P-14444)
### PRESSURE PROFILE SYSTEMS INC
5757 W Century Blvd Ste 600, Los Angeles (90045-6429)
PHONE.............................310 641-8100
Denis A O'connor, *CEO*
Jae S Son, *CEO*
Steven Sanchez, *Treas*
David Ables, *Sec*
**EMP:** 17 **EST:** 1996
**SALES (est):** 2.11MM **Privately Held**
Web: www.pressureprofile.com

SIC: **3823** Process control instruments

### (P-14445)
### PRIMORDIAL DIAGNOSTICS INC
Also Called: Pulse Instruments
3233 Mission Oaks Blvd Ste P, Camarillo (93012-5134)
PHONE.............................800 462-1926
Karan Khurana, *Pr*
Mridula Khurana, *
**EMP:** 25 **EST:** 1985
**SALES (est):** 2.69MM **Privately Held**
SIC: **3823** 5063 5074 Water quality monitoring and control systems; Electrical apparatus and equipment; Water purification equipment

### (P-14446)
### PROCESS INSGHTS - GDED WAVE IN
2121 Aviation Dr, Upland (91786)
PHONE.............................919 264-9651
Mark Morano, *Mgr*
**EMP:** 25
**SALES (corp-wide):** 45.56MM **Privately Held**
Web: www.process-insights.com
SIC: **3823** Process control instruments
HQ: Process Insights - Guided Wave, Inc.
  3033 Gold Canal Dr
  Rancho Cordova CA 95670
  916 638-4944

### (P-14447)
### PROTEUS INDUSTRIES INC
340 Pioneer Way, Mountain View (94041-1506)
PHONE.............................650 964-4163
Jon Heiner, *CEO*
Mark Nicewonger, *
▲ **EMP:** 50 **EST:** 1978
**SQ FT:** 40,000
**SALES (est):** 10.07MM **Privately Held**
Web: www.proteusind.com
SIC: **3823** 3829 3826 3824 Process control instruments; Measuring and controlling devices, nec; Analytical instruments; Fluid meters and counting devices

### (P-14448)
### PSI WATER TECHNOLOGIES INC
Also Called: PSI
550 Sycamore Dr, Milpitas (95035-7412)
PHONE.............................408 819-3043
Brent Simmons, *CEO*
Gunnar Thortarson, *
▲ **EMP:** 32 **EST:** 2003
**SALES (est):** 4.3MM **Privately Held**
Web: www.cleanwater1.com
SIC: **3823** Water quality monitoring and control systems

### (P-14449)
### RENAU CORPORATION
Also Called: Renau Electronic Laboratories
9309 Deering Ave, Chatsworth (91311-5858)
PHONE.............................818 341-1994
Karol Renau, *CEO*
Christine Renau, *Sec*
▲ **EMP:** 20 **EST:** 1981
**SQ FT:** 10,000
**SALES (est):** 6.69MM **Privately Held**
Web: www.renau.com
SIC: **3823** Controllers, for process variables, all types

## 3823 - Process Control Instruments (P-14450)

**(P-14450)**
**REOTEMP INSTRUMENT CORPORATION (PA)**
10656 Roselle St, San Diego (92121-1524)
PHONE..................858 784-0710
▲ EMP: 55 EST: 1965
SALES (est): 14.45MM
SALES (corp-wide): 14.45MM Privately Held
Web: www.reotemp.com
SIC: 3823 3829 3585 Thermometers, filled system: industrial process type; Thermometers and temperature sensors; Heating equipment, complete

**(P-14451)**
**ROHRBACK COSASCO SYSTEMS INC (DH)**
11841 Smith Ave, Santa Fe Springs (90670-3226)
PHONE..................562 949-0123
Bryan Sanderlin, CEO
▼ EMP: 71 EST: 1977
SQ FT: 37,000
SALES (est): 17.49MM
SALES (corp-wide): 2.58B Privately Held
Web: www.rohrbackcosasco.com
SIC: 3823 8742 Process control instruments; Industry specialist consultants
HQ: Halma Investment Holdings Limited
Misbourne Court Rectory Way
Amersham BUCKS HP7 0

**(P-14452)**
**RONAN ENGINEERING COMPANY (PA)**
Also Called: Ronan Engnrng/Rnan Msrment Div
28209 Avenue Stanford, Valencia (91355-3984)
P.O. Box 129 (91310-0129)
PHONE..................661 702-1344
John A Hewitson, CEO
▼ EMP: 56 EST: 1962
SQ FT: 50,000
SALES (est): 9.69MM
SALES (corp-wide): 9.69MM Privately Held
Web: www.ronan.com
SIC: 3823 3825 Process control instruments; Measuring instruments and meters, electric

**(P-14453)**
**SABIA INCORPORATED (PA)**
Also Called: Sabia
10919 Technology Pl Ste A, San Diego (92127-1882)
PHONE..................858 217-2200
Steve Foster, CEO
Clinton L Lingren, *
James Miller, *
Craig Belnap, *
Edward Nunn, *
EMP: 24 EST: 2000
SALES (est): 7.64MM
SALES (corp-wide): 7.64MM Privately Held
Web: www.sabiainc.com
SIC: 3823 Process control instruments

**(P-14454)**
**SANTA BARBARA CONTROL SYSTEMS**
Also Called: Chemtrol
5375 Overpass Rd, Santa Barbara (93111-3015)
PHONE..................805 683-8833
Pablo Navarro, Pr
Jacques Steininger, CEO
Joe Osuna, Acctnt
EMP: 19 EST: 1976
SQ FT: 8,000
SALES (est): 3.34MM Privately Held
Web: www.sbcontrol.com
SIC: 3823 3589 7699 Water quality monitoring and control systems; Swimming pool filter and water conditioning systems; Cash register repair

**(P-14455)**
**SEMIFAB INC**
2027 Otoole Ave, San Jose (95131-1301)
PHONE..................408 414-5928
Hauynium Kabir, Pr
Greg Krikorian, *
◆ EMP: 60 EST: 1978
SALES (est): 2.16MM Privately Held
Web: www.semifab.com
SIC: 3823 3822 Process control instruments; Temperature controls, automatic

**(P-14456)**
**SENSARRAY CORPORATION**
7 Technology Dr, Milpitas (95035-7916)
PHONE..................408 875-3000
EMP: 100 EST: 1987
SALES (est): 27.47MM
SALES (corp-wide): 9.81B Publicly Held
Web: www.kla.com
SIC: 3823 Temperature measurement instruments, industrial
PA: Kla Corporation
1 Technology Dr
408 875-3000

**(P-14457)**
**SENSOREX CORPORATION**
11751 Markon Dr, Garden Grove (92841)
PHONE..................714 895-4344
▲ EMP: 62 EST: 1972
SALES (est): 14.59MM
SALES (corp-wide): 2.58B Privately Held
Web: www.sensorex.com
SIC: 3823 3826 Process control instruments; PH meters, except industrial process type
HQ: Halma Holdings Inc.
535 Sprngfeld Ave Ste 110
Summit NJ 07901
513 772-5501

**(P-14458)**
**SENSOSCIENTIFIC LLC**
685 Cochran St Ste 200, Simi Valley (93065-1921)
PHONE..................800 279-3101
Masoud Zarei, Pr
Ramin Rostami, *
Mike Zarei, *
▲ EMP: 43 EST: 2005
SQ FT: 4,000
SALES (est): 9.57MM
SALES (corp-wide): 231.49MM Privately Held
Web: www.sensoscientific.com
SIC: 3823 Process control instruments
HQ: Process Sensing Technologies Corp.
135 Engineers Rd Ste 150
Hauppauge NY 11788
631 427-3898

**(P-14459)**
**SIERRA INSTRUMENTS INC (HQ)**
Also Called: Sierra CP Engineering
5 Harris Ct Bldg L, Monterey (93940-5752)
PHONE..................831 373-0200
EMP: 85 EST: 1987
SALES (est): 28.94MM
SALES (corp-wide): 287.28MM Privately Held
Web: www.sierrainstruments.com
SIC: 3823 Controllers, for process variables, all types
PA: Tasi Holdings, Inc.
40 Locke Dr Ste B
513 202-5182

**(P-14460)**
**SOFFA ELECTRIC INC**
5901 Corvette St, Commerce (90040-1601)
PHONE..................323 728-0230
EMP: 48 EST: 1971
SALES (est): 24.57MM Privately Held
Web: www.soffaelectric.com
SIC: 3823 1731 8711 8742 Process control instruments; General electrical contractor; Engineering services; Automation and robotics consultant

**(P-14461)**
**STAR-LUCK ENTERPRISE INC**
11807 Harrington St, Bakersfield (93311-9278)
PHONE..................661 665-9999
Xiaodong Zhou, Pr
Stephen Thompson, Sr VP
David Johnson, VP
◆ EMP: 16 EST: 2000
SQ FT: 11,800
SALES (est): 813.28K Privately Held
SIC: 3823 Pressure measurement instruments, industrial

**(P-14462)**
**TERN DESIGN LTD**
Also Called: Oceanscience
14020 Stowe Dr, Poway (92064-6846)
PHONE..................760 754-2400
Ronald George, Pr
EMP: 25 EST: 1995
SQ FT: 4,800
SALES (est): 1.98MM Privately Held
Web: www.teledynemarine.com
SIC: 3823 Buoyancy instruments, industrial process type

**(P-14463)**
**TEST ENTERPRISES INC (PA)**
Also Called: Thermonics
1288 Reamwood Ave, Sunnyvale (94089-2233)
PHONE..................408 542-5900
James C Kufis, CEO
▲ EMP: 20 EST: 1976
SQ FT: 22,000
SALES (est): 1.15MM
SALES (corp-wide): 1.15MM Privately Held
Web: www.testenterprises.com
SIC: 3823 3825 Temperature measurement instruments, industrial; Semiconductor test equipment

**(P-14464)**
**THERMOMETRICS CORPORATION (PA)**
18714 Parthenia St, Northridge (91324-3813)
PHONE..................818 886-3755
Jorge Hernandez, Pr
Robert Hernandez, *
EMP: 19 EST: 1965
SQ FT: 16,897
SALES (est): 5.49MM
SALES (corp-wide): 5.49MM Privately Held
Web: www.thermometricscorp.com
SIC: 3823 Process control instruments

**(P-14465)**
**TRANSLOGIC INCORPORATED**
5641 Engineer Dr, Huntington Beach (92649-1123)
PHONE..................714 890-0058
Donald Ross, CEO
Gregory Ross, *
EMP: 41 EST: 1979
SALES (est): 4.23MM Privately Held
Web: www.translogicinc.com
SIC: 3823 3829 Temperature instruments: industrial process type; Measuring and controlling devices, nec

**(P-14466)**
**UNITED STTES THRMLCTRIC CNSRTI**
Also Called: Ustc
13267 Contractors Dr Ste D, Chico (95973-8851)
PHONE..................530 345-8000
James M Kerner, CEO
▲ EMP: 20 EST: 1995
SALES (est): 6.63MM Privately Held
Web: www.ustechcon.com
SIC: 3823 3999 Process control instruments; Barber and beauty shop equipment

**(P-14467)**
**VEEX INC**
Also Called: Veex
2827 Lakeview Ct, Fremont (94538-6534)
PHONE..................510 651-0500
Cyrille Morelle, Pr
EMP: 19 EST: 2006
SQ FT: 8,000
SALES (est): 4.45MM Privately Held
Web: www.veexinc.com
SIC: 3823 Programmers, process type

**(P-14468)**
**VERTIV CORPORATION**
Also Called: Vertiv
35 Parker, Irvine (92618-1605)
PHONE..................949 457-3600
Anita Golden, Brnch Mgr
EMP: 52
SALES (corp-wide): 6.86B Publicly Held
Web: www.vertiv.com
SIC: 3823 Process control instruments
HQ: Vertiv Corporation
505 N Cleveland Ave
Westerville OH 43082
614 888-0246

**(P-14469)**
**WORLD WATER INC**
9848 Everest St, Downey (90242-3114)
P.O. Box 2331 (90662-2331)
PHONE..................562 940-1964
Fernando Guerrero, CEO
EMP: 40 EST: 2006
SQ FT: 1,000
SALES (est): 5.62MM Privately Held
Web: www.worldwaterinc.com
SIC: 3823 Water quality monitoring and control systems

**(P-14470)**
**WORLDWIDE ENVMTL PDTS INC (PA)**
Also Called: Imperials Sand Dunes
1100 Beacon St, Brea (92821-2936)
PHONE..................714 990-2700
William Oscar Delaney, CEO
EMP: 90 EST: 1991
SQ FT: 23,000
SALES (est): 20.12MM Privately Held
Web: www.wep-inc.com

# PRODUCTS & SERVICES SECTION
## 3825 - Instruments To Measure Electricity (P-14488)

SIC: 3823 3694 Process control instruments; Automotive electrical equipment, nec

### (P-14471)
**XIRRUS INC**
2545 W Hillcrest Dr Ste 220, Newbury Park (91320-2217)
PHONE..................805 262-1600
Shane Buckley, CEO
Dirk Gates, Ofcr
Patrick Parker, CDO
Sam Bass, VP
◆ EMP: 24 EST: 2004
SALES (est): 5.09MM Privately Held
Web: www.xirrus.com
SIC: 3823 Computer interface equipment, for industrial process control

### (P-14472)
**YOUNG ENGINEERING & MFG INC (PA)**
560 W Terrace Dr, San Dimas (91773-2914)
P.O. Box 3984 (91773-7984)
PHONE..................909 394-3225
Winston Young, Pr
Joanne Young, *
◆ EMP: 21 EST: 1980
SQ FT: 55,000
SALES (est): 7.68MM
SALES (corp-wide): 7.68MM Privately Held
Web: www.youngeng.com
SIC: 3823 5084 8711 5074 Process control instruments; Industrial machinery and equipment; Consulting engineer; Water purification equipment

## 3824 Fluid Meters And Counting Devices

### (P-14473)
**BLUE-WHITE INDUSTRIES LTD (PA)**
5300 Business Dr, Huntington Beach (92649-1224)
PHONE..................714 893-8529
Robert E Gledhill, Pr
Robert E Gledhill Iii, VP
Jeanne Hendrickson, *
Cindy Henderson, *
▲ EMP: 69 EST: 1957
SQ FT: 48,000
SALES (est): 19.72MM
SALES (corp-wide): 19.72MM Privately Held
Web: www.blue-white.com
SIC: 3824 3561 3589 Water meters; Industrial pumps and parts; Sewage and water treatment equipment

### (P-14474)
**BRITELAB INC**
Also Called: Britex
6341 San Ignacio Ave, San Jose (95119-1202)
PHONE..................650 961-0691
Robert De Neve, CEO
Paul Rogan, *
Saeed Seyed, *
Jae Jung, CSO*
▲ EMP: 65 EST: 2007
SQ FT: 52,000
SALES (est): 14.42MM Privately Held
Web: www.britelab.com
SIC: 3824 8741 8742 Mechanical and electromechanical counters and devices; Management services; Management consulting services

### (P-14475)
**COUNTY OF ALAMEDA**
Also Called: Registrar of Voters Office
1225 Fallon St Ste G1, Oakland (94612-4229)
PHONE..................510 272-6964
Bradley Clark, Prin
EMP: 25
Web: www.acvote.org
SIC: 3824 9199 Registers, linear tallying; General government administration
PA: County Of Alameda
1221 Oak St Rm 555
510 272-6691

### (P-14476)
**D & K ENGINEERING (HQ)**
16990 Goldentop Rd, San Diego (92127-2415)
PHONE..................760 840-2214
Jeffrey Moss, CEO
Alex Kunczynski, *
Diane Law, *
Bill Suttner, *
Peter Ma, VP
▲ EMP: 105 EST: 2000
SQ FT: 60,000
SALES (est): 97.11MM
SALES (corp-wide): 179.22MM Privately Held
Web: www.ascentialtech.com
SIC: 3824 8711 Mechanical and electromechanical counters and devices; Acoustical engineering
PA: Burke E. Porter Machinery Company
730 Plymouth Ave Ne
616 234-1200

### (P-14477)
**DEXERIALS AMERICA CORPORATION (HQ)**
215 Satellite Blvd Ne Ste 400, Santa Clara (95054)
PHONE..................770 945-3845
Noriyuki Nemoto, Pr
Hiraku Kominami, *
Tetsuji Ishikawa, *
▲ EMP: 24 EST: 1989
SALES (est): 15.83MM Privately Held
Web: www.dexerials.jp
SIC: 3824 3953 5169 Magnetic counters; Marking devices; Adhesives, chemical
PA: Dexerials Corporation
1724, Shimotsuboyama

### (P-14478)
**EMCOR FACILITIES SERVICES INC**
2 Cromwell, Irvine (92618-1816)
PHONE..................949 475-6020
EMP: 200
SALES (corp-wide): 12.58B Publicly Held
Web: www.emcorfacilities.com
SIC: 3824 Fluid meters and counting devices
HQ: Emcor Facilities Services, Inc.
9655 Reading Rd
Cincinnati OH 45215
888 846-9462

### (P-14479)
**EXELIXIS INC**
Division 1
1851 Harbor Bay Pkwy, Alameda (94502-3010)
PHONE..................650 837-7000
Michael M Morrissey, Pr
EMP: 371
Web: www.exelixis.com

SIC: 3824 8731 Fluid meters and counting devices; Commercial physical research
PA: Exelixis, Inc.
1851 Harbor Bay Pkwy

### (P-14480)
**INTERSCAN CORPORATION**
4590 Ish Dr Ste 110, Simi Valley (93063-7666)
PHONE..................805 823-8301
Richard Shaw, Pr
Michael Shaw, VP
Lorienne Shaw, VP
EMP: 23 EST: 1975
SQ FT: 10,000
SALES (est): 2.56MM Privately Held
Web: www.gasdetection.com
SIC: 3824 3829 Gasmeters, domestic and large capacity: industrial; Measuring and controlling devices, nec
PA: Chen Instrument Design Inc.
1554 Ne 3rd Ave

### (P-14481)
**IPS GROUP INC (PA)**
7737 Kenamar Ct, San Diego (92121-2425)
PHONE..................858 404-0607
David W King, CEO
Amir Sedadi, VP
Dario Paduano, CFO
Chad Randall, COO
▲ EMP: 36 EST: 2000
SALES (est): 58.9MM
SALES (corp-wide): 58.9MM Privately Held
Web: www.ipsgroupinc.com
SIC: 3824 4899 Parking meters; Communication signal enhancement network services

### (P-14482)
**MINDRUM PRECISION INC**
Also Called: Mindrum Precision Products
10000 4th St, Rancho Cucamonga (91730-5723)
PHONE..................909 989-1728
Diane Mindrum, CEO
Daniel Mindrum, *
Matt Wade, *
EMP: 49 EST: 1956
SQ FT: 30,000
SALES (est): 9.77MM Privately Held
Web: www.mindrum.com
SIC: 3824 3827 3823 3264 Fluid meters and counting devices; Optical instruments and lenses; Process control instruments; Porcelain electrical supplies

### (P-14483)
**SPARLING INSTRUMENTS LLC**
4097 Temple City Blvd, El Monte (91731-1046)
PHONE..................626 444-0571
Yosufi Tyebkhan, Managing Member
▲ EMP: 25 EST: 1996
SQ FT: 56,000
SALES (est): 4.8MM Privately Held
Web: www.sparlinginstruments.com
SIC: 3824 3823 5084 Fluid meters and counting devices; Process control instruments; Industrial machinery and equipment

### (P-14484)
**TRI-CONTINENT SCIENTIFIC INC**
12740 Earhart Ave, Auburn (95602-9027)
PHONE..................530 273-8888
Lee Carter, CEO
Brenton Hanlon, *
Sandra Zoch, *

▲ EMP: 85 EST: 1975
SQ FT: 34,000
SALES (est): 5.49MM
SALES (corp-wide): 6.88B Publicly Held
Web: www.tricontinent.com
SIC: 3824 3829 3821 3561 Integrating and totalizing meters for gas and liquids; Measuring and controlling devices, nec; Laboratory apparatus and furniture; Pumps and pumping equipment
HQ: G. Denver And Co., Llc
800-A Beaty St
Davidson NC 28036

## 3825 Instruments To Measure Electricity

### (P-14485)
**ADAPTECH CORPORATION**
Also Called: Adaptive Technology
301 Mission Ave Unit 505, Oceanside (92054-2594)
PHONE..................571 261-9823
Arthur Luna, Mgr
EMP: 15
Web: www.adapteq.com
SIC: 3825 Test equipment for electronic and electric measurement
PA: Adaptech Corporation
861 Harold Pl Ste 306

### (P-14486)
**AEHR TEST SYSTEMS (PA)**
Also Called: Aehr Test
400 Kato Ter, Fremont (94539-8332)
PHONE..................510 623-9400
Gayn Erickson, Pr
Rhea J Posedel, Ch Bd
Adil Engineer, COO
Chris P Siu, VP Fin
Vernon Rogers, Executive Sales & Marketing Vice President
▲ EMP: 90 EST: 1977
SQ FT: 51,289
SALES (est): 66.22MM
SALES (corp-wide): 66.22MM Publicly Held
Web: www.aehr.com
SIC: 3825 Test equipment for electronic and electrical circuits

### (P-14487)
**AEROFLEX HIGH SPEED TEST SOLUTIONS INC**
Also Called: Aeroflex Cupertino
256 Gibraltar Dr Ste 110, Sunnyvale (94089-1337)
P.O. Box 6022 (11803-0622)
PHONE..................516 694-6700
EMP: 46
SIC: 3825 3577 3823 3621 Lab standards, electric: resistance, inductance, capacitance; Computer peripheral equipment, nec; Process control instruments; Motors and generators

### (P-14488)
**AGILENT TECH WORLD TRADE INC (HQ)**
5301 Stevens Creek Blvd, Santa Clara (95051-7201)
PHONE..................408 345-8886
Adrian Dillon, CEO
D Craig Norlund, Sec
EMP: 64 EST: 1999
SALES (est): 3.12MM
SALES (corp-wide): 6.83B Publicly Held
Web: www.agilent.com

## 3825 - Instruments To Measure Electricity (P-14489)

**SIC: 3825** Instruments to measure electricity
**PA:** Agilent Technologies, Inc.
5301 Stevens Creek Blvd
800 227-9770

**(P-14489)**
**AGILENT TECHNOLOGIES INC**
91 Blue Ravine Rd, Folsom (95630-4720)
**PHONE** ................................ 916 985-7888
James T Olsen, *Brnch Mgr*
**EMP:** 98
**SALES (corp-wide):** 6.83B **Publicly Held**
**Web:** www.agilent.com
**SIC: 3825** Instruments to measure electricity
**PA:** Agilent Technologies, Inc.
5301 Stevens Creek Blvd
800 227-9770

**(P-14490)**
**AGILENT TECHNOLOGIES INC**
1170 Mark Ave, Carpinteria (93013-2918)
**PHONE** ................................ 805 566-6655
Britt Meelby Jensen, *Genl Mgr*
**EMP:** 46
**SALES (corp-wide):** 6.83B **Publicly Held**
**Web:** www.agilent.com
**SIC: 3825** Instruments to measure electricity
**PA:** Agilent Technologies, Inc.
5301 Stevens Creek Blvd
800 227-9770

**(P-14491)**
**AGILENT TECHNOLOGIES INC**
Agilent Santa Clara Site
5301 Stevens Creek Blvd, Santa Clara (95051-7201)
P.O. Box 58059 (95052-8059)
**PHONE** ................................ 408 345-8886
Bill Sullivan, *CEO*
**EMP:** 56
**SALES (corp-wide):** 6.83B **Publicly Held**
**Web:** www.agilent.com
**SIC: 3825** Instruments to measure electricity
**PA:** Agilent Technologies, Inc.
5301 Stevens Creek Blvd
800 227-9770

**(P-14492)**
**AGILENT TECHNOLOGIES INC**
11011 N Torrey Pines Rd, La Jolla (92037-1007)
**PHONE** ................................ 858 373-6300
Janet King, *Prin*
**EMP:** 53
**SALES (corp-wide):** 6.83B **Publicly Held**
**Web:** www.agilent.com
**SIC: 3825** Instruments to measure electricity
**PA:** Agilent Technologies, Inc.
5301 Stevens Creek Blvd
800 227-9770

**(P-14493)**
**AGILENT TECHNOLOGIES INC**
Also Called: Agilent Technologies
6392 Via Real, Carpinteria (93013-2921)
**PHONE** ................................ 805 566-1405
**EMP:** 44
**SALES (corp-wide):** 6.83B **Publicly Held**
**Web:** www.agilent.com
**SIC: 3825** Instruments to measure electricity
**PA:** Agilent Technologies, Inc.
5301 Stevens Creek Blvd
800 227-9770

**(P-14494)**
**AGILENT TECHNOLOGIES INC**
3175 Bowers Ave, Santa Clara (95054-3225)
P.O. Box 58059 (95052-8059)
**PHONE** ................................ 408 553-7777
Paul Sedlewicz, *Brnch Mgr*
**EMP:** 17
**SALES (corp-wide):** 6.83B **Publicly Held**
**Web:** www.agilent.com
**SIC: 3825** Instruments to measure electricity
**PA:** Agilent Technologies, Inc.
5301 Stevens Creek Blvd
800 227-9770

**(P-14495)**
**AMETEK PROGRAMMABLE POWER INC (HQ)**
Also Called: Ametek Programmable Power
9250 Brown Deer Rd, San Diego (92121-2267)
**PHONE** ................................ 858 450-0085
Matthew Mannell, *CEO*
Dalip Puri, *CFO*
▲ **EMP:** 350 **EST:** 2006
**SQ FT:** 110,000
**SALES (est):** 114.65MM
**SALES (corp-wide):** 6.6B **Publicly Held**
**Web:** www.programmablepower.com
**SIC: 3825** Instruments to measure electricity
**PA:** Ametek, Inc.
1100 Cassatt Rd
610 647-2121

**(P-14496)**
**ANRITSU US HOLDING INC (HQ)**
Also Called: Anritsu Company
490 Jarvis Dr, Morgan Hill (95037-2834)
**PHONE** ................................ 408 778-2000
Wade Hulon, *Pr*
▲ **EMP:** 500 **EST:** 1990
**SQ FT:** 244,000
**SALES (est):** 105.62MM **Privately Held**
**SIC: 3825** 3663 5065 Test equipment for electronic and electric measurement; Radio and t.v. communications equipment; Electronic parts and equipment, nec
**PA:** Anritsu Corporation
5-1-1, Onna

**(P-14497)**
**ARBITER SYSTEMS INCORPORATED (PA)**
1324 Vendels Cir Ste 121, Paso Robles (93446-3806)
**PHONE** ................................ 805 237-3831
Craig Armstrong, *Pr*
Bruce Roeder, *
**EMP:** 30 **EST:** 1973
**SQ FT:** 15,000
**SALES (est):** 6.05MM
**SALES (corp-wide):** 6.05MM **Privately Held**
**Web:** www.arbiter.com
**SIC: 3825** 3829 3663 Test equipment for electronic and electric measurement; Measuring and controlling devices, nec; Radio and t.v. communications equipment

**(P-14498)**
**ASHLAND GROUP LLC**
Also Called: Intercom
11693 San Vicente Blvd Pmb 213, Los Angeles (90049)
**PHONE** ................................ 213 749-3709
Behzad Soroudi, *Pr*
Perry Bakhtiari, *VP*
Victoria Goosey, *Sec*
**EMP:** 15 **EST:** 1983
**SQ FT:** 6,000
**SALES (est):** 1.05MM **Privately Held**
**SIC: 3825** 5063 Test equipment for electronic and electrical circuits; Electrical supplies, nec

**(P-14499)**
**ASTRONICS TEST SYSTEMS INC (HQ)**
2652 Mcgaw Ave, Irvine (92614-5840)
**PHONE** ................................ 800 722-2528
James Mulato, *Pr*
David Burney, *
Brian Price, *
◆ **EMP:** 130 **EST:** 2014
**SQ FT:** 98,600
**SALES (est):** 73.5MM
**SALES (corp-wide):** 689.21MM **Publicly Held**
**Web:** www.astronics.com
**SIC: 3825** Test equipment for electronic and electric measurement
**PA:** Astronics Corporation
130 Commerce Way
716 805-1599

**(P-14500)**
**BAE SYSTEMS INFO ELCTRNIC SYST**
Also Called: Bae Systems
10920 Technology Pl, San Diego (92127-1874)
**PHONE** ................................ 858 592-5000
Mark Gist, *Brnch Mgr*
**EMP:** 719
**SALES (corp-wide):** 28.77B **Privately Held**
**Web:** www.baesystems.com
**SIC: 3825** 7373 3812 Test equipment for electronic and electric measurement; Computer integrated systems design; Search and navigation equipment
**HQ:** Bae Systems Information And Electronic Systems Integration Inc.
65 Spit Brook Rd
Nashua NH 03060
603 885-4321

**(P-14501)**
**BAE SYSTEMS NATIONAL SECURITY SOLUTIONS INC**
10920 Technology Pl, San Diego (92127-1874)
P.O. Box 509008 (92150-9008)
**PHONE** ................................ 858 592-5000
▲ **EMP:** 2200
**SIC: 3825** 7373 3812 Test equipment for electronic and electric measurement; Computer integrated systems design; Search and navigation equipment

**(P-14502)**
**BOURNS INC**
Bourns Sensor Controls
1200 Columbia Ave, Riverside (92507-2129)
**PHONE** ................................ 951 781-5690
James Davis, *Pr*
**EMP:** 29
**SALES (corp-wide):** 459.73MM **Privately Held**
**Web:** www.bourns.com
**SIC: 3825** Instruments to measure electricity
**PA:** Bourns, Inc.
1200 Columbia Ave
951 781-5500

**(P-14503)**
**CALOGIC (PA)**
237 Whitney Pl, Fremont (94539-7664)
**PHONE** ................................ 510 656-2900
Jonathan Kaye, *Pr*
**EMP:** 21 **EST:** 2001
**SQ FT:** 10,314
**SALES (est):** 2.48MM
**SALES (corp-wide):** 2.48MM **Privately Held**
**Web:** www.calogic.net
**SIC: 3825** Instruments to measure electricity

**(P-14504)**
**CHILICON POWER LLC (PA)**
15415 W Sunset Blvd Ste 102, Pacific Palisades (90272-3546)
**PHONE** ................................ 310 800-1396
▲ **EMP:** 24 **EST:** 2011
**SALES (est):** 2.59MM
**SALES (corp-wide):** 2.59MM **Privately Held**
**Web:** www.chiliconpower.com
**SIC: 3825** Power measuring equipment, electrical

**(P-14505)**
**CHROMA SYSTEMS SOLUTIONS INC (HQ)**
19772 Pauling, Foothill Ranch (92610-2611)
**PHONE** ................................ 949 297-4848
Fred Sabatine, *Pr*
▲ **EMP:** 21 **EST:** 2001
**SQ FT:** 25,000
**SALES (est):** 25.09MM **Privately Held**
**Web:** www.chromausa.com
**SIC: 3825** Measuring instruments and meters, electric
**PA:** Chroma Ate Inc.
No. 88, Wenmao Rd.,

**(P-14506)**
**CHROMA SYSTEMS SOLUTIONS INC**
25612 Commercentre Dr, Lake Forest (92630-8813)
**PHONE** ................................ 949 600-6400
**EMP:** 27
**Web:** www.chromausa.com
**SIC: 3825** Measuring instruments and meters, electric
**HQ:** Chroma Systems Solutions, Inc.
19772 Pauling
Foothill Ranch CA 92610
949 297-4848

**(P-14507)**
**COHU INC (PA)**
Also Called: COHU
12367 Crosthwaite Cir, Poway (92064-6817)
**PHONE** ................................ 858 848-8100
Luis A Muller, *Pr*
James A Donahue, *Non-Executive Chairman of the Board*
Christopher G Bohrson, *CCO*
Ian P Lawee, *Sr VP*
Jeffrey D Jones, *VP Fin*
▲ **EMP:** 220 **EST:** 1947
**SQ FT:** 147,000
**SALES (est):** 636.32MM
**SALES (corp-wide):** 636.32MM **Publicly Held**
**Web:** www.cohu.com
**SIC: 3825** Semiconductor test equipment

**(P-14508)**
**COHU INTERFACE SOLUTIONS LLC (HQ)**
Also Called: Factron Test Fixtures
12367 Crosthwaite Cir, Poway (92064-6817)
**PHONE** ................................ 858 848-8000
Luis Muller, *CEO*
▲ **EMP:** 75 **EST:** 1965
**SALES (est):** 25.01MM
**SALES (corp-wide):** 636.32MM **Publicly Held**

## PRODUCTS & SERVICES SECTION
### 3825 - Instruments To Measure Electricity (P-14528)

Web: www.cohu.com
SIC: 3825 3678 Test equipment for electronic and electrical circuits; Electronic connectors
PA: Cohu, Inc.
12367 Crosthwaite Cir
858 848-8100

### (P-14509)
### CONCISYS
5452 Oberlin Dr, San Diego (92121)
PHONE..................858 292-5888
Giao Huu Nguyen, *Managing Member*
Vu Wing, *
▲ EMP: 40 EST: 2000
SALES (est): 17.55MM **Privately Held**
Web: www.concisys.com
SIC: 3825 Digital test equipment, electronic and electrical circuits

### (P-14510)
### DB CONTROL CORP (HQ)
1120 Auburn St, Fremont (94538-7328)
PHONE..................510 656-2325
EMP: 94 EST: 1990
SALES (est): 26.55MM **Publicly Held**
Web: www.dbcontrol.com
SIC: 3825 Radar testing instruments, electric
PA: Heico Corporation
3000 Taft St

### (P-14511)
### DELTA DESIGN (LITTLETON) INC
12367 Crosthwaite Cir, Poway (92064-6817)
PHONE..................858 848-8100
Charles A Schwan, *Ch Bd*
Nicholas J Cedrone, *
▲ EMP: 570 EST: 1994
SQ FT: 102,000
SALES (est): 3.6MM
SALES (corp-wide): 636.32MM **Publicly Held**
SIC: 3825 Test equipment for electronic and electrical circuits
PA: Cohu, Inc.
12367 Crosthwaite Cir
858 848-8100

### (P-14512)
### DIVERSFIED TCHNCAL SYSTEMS INC (HQ)
1720 Apollo Ct, Seal Beach (90740-5617)
PHONE..................562 493-0158
Stephen D Pruitt, *CEO*
Steve Pruitt, *
George M Beckage, *
Tim Kippen, *
Kirsten Larsen, *
▲ EMP: 29 EST: 1990
SQ FT: 55,000
SALES (est): 11.58MM
SALES (corp-wide): 355.05MM **Publicly Held**
Web: www.dtsweb.com
SIC: 3825 3679 3495 8731 Instruments to measure electricity; Electronic circuits; Clock springs, precision; Commercial physical research
PA: Vishay Precision Group, Inc.
3 Great Vly Pkwy Ste 150
484 321-5300

### (P-14513)
### ECHELON CORPORATION (DH)
6024 Silver Creek Valley Rd, San Jose (95138-1011)
PHONE..................408 938-5200
Ronald Sege, *Pr*
▲ EMP: 55 EST: 1988

SALES (est): 14.99MM **Privately Held**
Web: www.adestotech.com
SIC: 3825 7371 Network analyzers; Computer software systems analysis and design, custom
HQ: Adesto Technologies Corporation
6024 Silver Creek Vly Rd
San Jose CA 95138

### (P-14514)
### ECLYPSE INTERNATIONAL CORP (PA)
341 S Maple St, Corona (92878-4307)
PHONE..................951 371-8008
Tom Day, *Ch Bd*
C Alan Ferguson, *CEO*
Glen Coulter, *Stockholder*
Cris Teal, *Dir*
EMP: 15 EST: 1988
SQ FT: 2,000
SALES (est): 6.91MM **Privately Held**
Web: www.eclypse.org
SIC: 3825 8711 Test equipment for electronic and electrical circuits; Consulting engineer

### (P-14515)
### ELECRAFT INCORPORATED
125 Westridge Dr, Watsonville (95076-4167)
P.O. Box 69 (95001-0069)
PHONE..................831 763-4211
Eric Swartz, *Pr*
Wayne Burdick, *
Lisa Jones, *
EMP: 35 EST: 1997
SALES (est): 12.24MM **Privately Held**
Web: www.elecraft.com
SIC: 3825 Oscillators, audio and radio frequency (instrument types)

### (P-14516)
### ENERSPONSE INC
1148 Manhattan Ave, Manhattan Beach (90266-5323)
PHONE..................949 829-3901
EMP: 27 EST: 2016
SALES (est): 849.88K **Privately Held**
Web: www.enersponse.com
SIC: 3825 8748 1731 Electrical energy measuring equipment; Energy conservation consultant; Energy management controls

### (P-14517)
### EQUUS PRODUCTS INC
17352 Von Karman Ave, Irvine (92614-6204)
PHONE..................714 424-6779
Ieon C Chen, *CEO*
Cynthia H Tsai, *
Duke Chen Skthldr, *Prin*
Michael Chen Skthldr, *Prin*
◆ EMP: 31 EST: 1982
SQ FT: 36,000
SALES (est): 4.7MM **Privately Held**
Web: www.equusus.com
SIC: 3825 3545 3714 Electrical power measuring equipment; Machine tool accessories; Motor vehicle parts and accessories

### (P-14518)
### ERIDAN COMMUNICATIONS INC (PA)
400 W California Ave, Sunnyvale (94086-5155)
PHONE..................650 492-0657
Douglas Kirkpatrick, *CEO*
Earl Mccune, *Engr*
Eve Cohen, *

EMP: 25 EST: 2013
SALES (est): 6.97MM
SALES (corp-wide): 6.97MM **Privately Held**
Web: www.eridan.io
SIC: 3825 8731 Instruments to measure electricity; Electronic research

### (P-14519)
### ERP POWER LLC (PA)
2625 Townsgate Rd, Westlake Village (91361-5758)
PHONE..................805 517-1300
Jeffrey Frank, *CEO*
Abdul Sher-jan, *COO*
Andy Williams, *Ex VP*
EMP: 17 EST: 2005
SALES (est): 19.4MM **Privately Held**
Web: www.erp-power.com
SIC: 3825 Energy measuring equipment, electrical

### (P-14520)
### ESSAI INC (DH)
48580 Kato Rd, Fremont (94538-7338)
PHONE..................510 580-1700
Nasser Barabi, *CEO*
Keith Hardwick, *
EMP: 27 EST: 2003
SALES (est): 40.89MM **Privately Held**
Web: www.advantest.com
SIC: 3825 Semiconductor test equipment
HQ: Advantest America, Inc.
3061 Zanker Rd
San Jose CA 95134

### (P-14521)
### ETA COMPUTE INC
182 S Murphy Ave, Sunnyvale (94086-6112)
PHONE..................650 255-1293
EMP: 32 EST: 2015
SALES (est): 5.1MM **Privately Held**
Web: www.etacompute.com
SIC: 3825 3559 Semiconductor test equipment; Semiconductor manufacturing machinery

### (P-14522)
### EUGENUS INC (HQ)
677 River Oaks Pkwy, San Jose (95134-1907)
PHONE..................669 235-8244
Peter Um, *Ch*
Jin Woong Kim, *
EMP: 73 EST: 2009
SQ FT: 2,700
SALES (est): 61.95MM **Privately Held**
Web: www.eugenustech.com
SIC: 3825 3559 Semiconductor test equipment; Semiconductor manufacturing machinery
PA: Eugene Technology Co., Ltd.
42 Chugye-Ro, Yangji-Myeon, Cheoin-Gu

### (P-14523)
### EVERACTIVE INC
2150 Paragon Dr, San Jose (95131-1305)
PHONE..................517 256-0679
Bob Nunn, *CEO*
Benton Calhoun Md, *Co-Chief Technology Officer*
David Wentzloff Md, *Co-Chief Technology Officer*
EMP: 86 EST: 2012
SALES (est): 15.76MM **Privately Held**
Web: www.everactive.com

SIC: 3825 3674 Analog-digital converters, electronic instrumentation type; Semiconductors and related devices

### (P-14524)
### EXATRON INC
2842 Aiello Dr, San Jose (95111-2154)
PHONE..................408 629-7600
Robert Howell, *CEO*
Eric Hagquist, *
EMP: 25 EST: 1974
SQ FT: 15,500
SALES (est): 5.68MM **Privately Held**
Web: www.exatron.com
SIC: 3825 Integrated circuit testers

### (P-14525)
### EXCEL PRECISION CORP USA
Also Called: Excel Precision
3350 Scott Blvd Bldg 62, Santa Clara (95054-3125)
PHONE..................408 727-4260
John Tsai, *CEO*
Lon Allen, *
EMP: 25 EST: 1984
SQ FT: 5,500
SALES (est): 2.33MM **Privately Held**
Web: www.excelprecision.com
SIC: 3825 3829 3827 3826 Measuring instruments and meters, electric; Measuring and controlling devices, nec; Optical instruments and lenses; Analytical instruments

### (P-14526)
### FIELDPIECE INSTRUMENTS INC (PA)
Also Called: Fieldpiece
1636 W Collins Ave, Orange (92867-5421)
PHONE..................714 634-1844
Cameron Rouns, *CEO*
Tim J Way, *
▲ EMP: 38 EST: 1990
SQ FT: 4,000
SALES (est): 9.21MM **Privately Held**
Web: www.fieldpiece.com
SIC: 3825 3829 3826 3823 Instruments for measuring electrical quantities; Measuring and controlling devices, nec; Analytical instruments; Process control instruments

### (P-14527)
### FIRST LEGAL NETWORK
1517 Beverly Blvd, Los Angeles (90026-5704)
PHONE..................213 250-1111
Alex Martinez, *CEO*
EMP: 153 EST: 2015
SALES (est): 5.39MM **Privately Held**
Web: www.firstlegalnetwork.com
SIC: 3825 4899 Network analyzers; Communication signal enhancement network services

### (P-14528)
### FISCHER CSTM CMMUNICATIONS INC (PA)
19220 Normandie Ave Unit B, Torrance (90502-1011)
PHONE..................310 303-3300
David Fischer, *Pr*
Allen Fischer, *
EMP: 21 EST: 1971
SALES (est): 9.01MM
SALES (corp-wide): 9.01MM **Privately Held**
Web: www.fischercc.com
SIC: 3825 Digital test equipment, electronic and electrical circuits

---

(PA)=Parent Co (HQ)=Headquarters
✪ = New Business established in last 2 years

## 3825 - Instruments To Measure Electricity (P-14529)

**(P-14529)**
**GOLDEN ALTOS CORPORATION**
44061 Old Warm Springs Blvd, Fremont (94538-6158)
PHONE..................408 956-1010
Arlen Chou, *CEO*
Alexander H C Chang, *
Hsun K Chou, *
▲ **EMP:** 50 **EST:** 1991
**SQ FT:** 10,000
**SALES (est)** 9.8MM **Privately Held**
**Web:** www.goldenaltos.com
**SIC:** 3825 3674 3672 Integrated circuit testers; Semiconductors and related devices ; Printed circuit boards

**(P-14530)**
**GOULD & BASS COMPANY INC**
1431 W 2nd St, Pomona (91766-1299)
PHONE..................909 623-6793
John S Bass, *CEO*
**EMP:** 32 **EST:** 1971
**SQ FT:** 66,000
**SALES (est):** 6.3MM **Privately Held**
**Web:** www.gould-bass.net
**SIC:** 3825 3535 3556 Test equipment for electronic and electric measurement; Belt conveyor systems, general industrial use; Packing house machinery

**(P-14531)**
**GUIDETECH INC**
774 Charcot Ave, San Jose (95131-2224)
PHONE..................408 733-6555
Frank Mckiney, *Pr*
Hans Betz, *
▲ **EMP:** 25 **EST:** 1988
**SALES (est):** 1.62MM **Privately Held**
**Web:** www.guidetech.com
**SIC:** 3825 Test equipment for electronic and electric measurement

**(P-14532)**
**HEXAGON MFG INTELLIGENCE INC**
Romer Cimcore
3536 Seagate Way Ste 100, Oceanside (92056-2672)
PHONE..................760 994-1401
Steve Ilmrud, *Genl Mgr*
**EMP:** 60
**SALES (corp-wide):** 2.5MM **Privately Held**
**Web:** www.hexagon.com
**SIC:** 3825 Instruments to measure electricity
**HQ:** Hexagon Manufacturing Intelligence, Inc.
250 Circuit Dr
North Kingstown RI 02852
401 886-2000

**(P-14533)**
**HID GLOBAL CORPORATION**
15370 Barranca Pkwy, Irvine (92618-2215)
PHONE..................949 732-2000
**EMP:** 56
**Web:** www.hidglobal.com
**SIC:** 3825 Instruments to measure electricity
**HQ:** Hid Global Corporation
611 Center Ridge Dr
Austin TX 78753

**(P-14534)**
**HID GLOBAL CORPORATION**
53 Discovery, Irvine (92618-3106)
PHONE..................949 466-9508
Mark Rivoli, *Mgr*
**EMP:** 15
**Web:** www.hidglobal.com

**SIC:** 3825 1731 8741 Radio frequency measuring equipment; Access control systems specialization; Management services
**HQ:** Hid Global Corporation
611 Center Ridge Dr
Austin TX 78753

**(P-14535)**
**INEOQUEST TECHNOLOGIES INC (HQ)**
Also Called: Ineoquest
848 Gold Flat Rd, Nevada City (95959-3208)
PHONE..................508 339-2497
Calvin Harrison, *Pr*
Peter Dawson, *Ch Bd*
Steve Sanford, *CFO*
**EMP:** 18 **EST:** 2001
**SALES (est):** 27.94MM
**SALES (corp-wide):** 122.84MM **Privately Held**
**SIC:** 3825 Instruments to measure electricity
**PA:** Telestream, Llc
848 Gold Flat Rd
530 470-1300

**(P-14536)**
**INGRASYS TECHNOLOGY USA INC**
1768 Automation Pkwy, San Jose (95131-1873)
PHONE..................970 301-5069
**EMP:** 51
**Web:** www.ingrasys.com
**SIC:** 3825 4899 Network analyzers; Communication signal enhancement network services
**HQ:** Ingrasys Technology Usa Inc.
2025 Gateway Pl Ste 190
San Jose CA

**(P-14537)**
**INTELLIGENT CMPT SOLUTIONS INC (PA)**
8968 Fullbright Ave, Chatsworth (91311-6123)
PHONE..................818 998-5805
Uzi Kohavi, *Pr*
Gonen Ravid, *
▲ **EMP:** 25 **EST:** 1989
**SQ FT:** 21,000
**SALES (est):** 3.32MM **Privately Held**
**Web:** www.icsiq.com
**SIC:** 3825 3577 3572 Test equipment for electronic and electrical circuits; Computer peripheral equipment, nec; Computer storage devices

**(P-14538)**
**INTERNATIONAL TRANDUCER CORP**
Also Called: Channel Technologies Group
869 Ward Dr, Santa Barbara (93111-2920)
PHONE..................805 683-2575
Robert F Carlson, *
Kevin Ruelas, *
Brian Dolan, *
**EMP:** 160 **EST:** 1966
**SALES (est):** 7.53MM
**SALES (corp-wide):** 40.31MM **Privately Held**
**SIC:** 3825 3812 Transducers for volts, amperes, watts, vars, frequency, etc.; Search and navigation equipment
**PA:** Gavial Holdings, Inc.
1435 W Mccoy Ln
805 614-0060

**(P-14539)**
**IXIA (HQ)**
26601 Agoura Rd, Calabasas (91302-1959)
PHONE..................818 871-1800
Neil Dougherty, *Pr*
Jeffrey Li, *VP*
Jason Kary, *
Matthew S Alexander, *Corporate Secretary**
Stephen Williams, *
**EMP:** 231 **EST:** 1997
**SQ FT:** 116,000
**SALES (est):** 51.28MM
**SALES (corp-wide):** 5.46B **Publicly Held**
**Web:** support.ixiacom.com
**SIC:** 3825 7371 Network analyzers; Custom computer programming services
**PA:** Keysight Technologies, Inc.
1400 Fountaingrove Pkwy
800 829-4444

**(P-14540)**
**IXIA**
Also Called: Ixia Communications
26701 Agoura Rd, Calabasas (91302-1960)
PHONE..................818 871-1800
**EMP:** 37
**SALES (corp-wide):** 5.46B **Publicly Held**
**Web:** www.keysight.com
**SIC:** 3825 Network analyzers
**HQ:** Ixia
26601 Agoura Rd
Calabasas CA 91302
818 871-1800

**(P-14541)**
**J2M TEST SOLUTIONS INC**
13225 Gregg St, Poway (92064-7120)
PHONE..................571 333-0291
John Ronk, *Pr*
**EMP:** 80 **EST:** 2005
**SALES (est):** 1.48MM **Privately Held**
**SIC:** 3825 Instruments to measure electricity

**(P-14542)**
**KEYSIGHT TECHNOLOGIES INC**
5301 Stevens Creek Blvd, Santa Clara (95051-7201)
PHONE..................408 553-3290
**EMP:** 93
**SALES (corp-wide):** 5.46B **Publicly Held**
**Web:** www.keysight.com
**SIC:** 3825 Instruments to measure electricity
**PA:** Keysight Technologies, Inc.
1400 Fountaingrove Pkwy
800 829-4444

**(P-14543)**
**KEYSIGHT TECHNOLOGIES INC**
10090 Foothills Blvd, Roseville (95747-7102)
PHONE..................916 788-5571
**EMP:** 15
**SALES (corp-wide):** 5.46B **Publicly Held**
**Web:** www.keysight.com
**SIC:** 3825 Instruments to measure electricity
**PA:** Keysight Technologies, Inc.
1400 Fountaingrove Pkwy
800 829-4444

**(P-14544)**
**L3HARRIS INTERSTATE ELEC CORP**
Also Called: Integrated Technical Services
600 E Vermont Ave, Anaheim (92805-5607)
PHONE..................714 758-0500
Robert Schembre, *Brnch Mgr*
**EMP:** 48
**SALES (corp-wide):** 19.42B **Publicly Held**
**Web:** www.l3harris.com

**SIC:** 3825 Instruments to measure electricity
**HQ:** L3harris Interstate Electronics Corporation
602 E Vermont Ave
Anaheim CA 92805
714 758-0500

**(P-14545)**
**L3HARRIS INTERSTATE ELEC CORP (DH)**
Also Called: L-3 Interstate Electronics
602 E Vermont Ave, Anaheim (92805-5607)
P.O. Box 3117 (92803-3117)
PHONE..................714 758-0500
Christopher E Kubasik, *CEO*
Arthur H Lim, *Treas*
Scott T Mikuen, *Dir*
Kristene E Schumacher, *Dir*
**EMP:** 275 **EST:** 1955
**SQ FT:** 235,700
**SALES (est):** 65.62MM
**SALES (corp-wide):** 19.42B **Publicly Held**
**Web:** www.l3harris.com
**SIC:** 3825 3812 3679 Test equipment for electronic and electric measurement; Navigational systems and instruments; Liquid crystal displays (LCD)
**HQ:** L3 Technologies, Inc.
600 3rd Ave Fl 34
New York NY 10016
321 727-9100

**(P-14546)**
**L3HARRIS INTERSTATE ELEC CORP**
Also Called: Human Resources
708 E Vermont Ave, Anaheim (92805-5611)
PHONE..................714 758-0500
**EMP:** 72
**SALES (corp-wide):** 19.42B **Publicly Held**
**Web:** www.l3harris.com
**SIC:** 3825 Test equipment for electronic and electric measurement
**HQ:** L3harris Interstate Electronics Corporation
602 E Vermont Ave
Anaheim CA 92805
714 758-0500

**(P-14547)**
**L3HARRIS INTERSTATE ELEC CORP**
3033 Science Park Rd, San Diego (92121-1167)
PHONE..................858 552-9500
Andrew Leuthe, *Prin*
**EMP:** 72
**SALES (corp-wide):** 19.42B **Publicly Held**
**Web:** www.l3harris.com
**SIC:** 3825 7379 5045 Test equipment for electronic and electric measurement; Computer related consulting services; Computer software
**HQ:** L3harris Interstate Electronics Corporation
602 E Vermont Ave
Anaheim CA 92805
714 758-0500

**(P-14548)**
**LDDF INC**
9781 Point Lakeview Rd Ste 3, Kelseyville (95451-8517)
PHONE..................707 995-7145
David Collmann, *Pr*
**EMP:** 15
**SALES (corp-wide):** 7.58MM **Privately Held**
**Web:** www.appliedinstruments.com

# PRODUCTS & SERVICES SECTION
## 3825 - Instruments To Measure Electricity (P-14567)

SIC: **3825** 7629 Instruments to measure electricity; Electrical repair shops
PA: Lddf, Inc.
3317 El Salido Pkwy
737 800-1982

### (P-14549)
### LIQUID INSTRUMENTS INC (PA)
12526 High Bluff Dr Ste 150, San Diego (92130-3044)
PHONE..............................619 332-6230
Danielle Wuchenich, *Prin*
**EMP:** 18 **EST:** 2018
**SALES (est):** 5.21MM
**SALES (corp-wide):** 5.21MM **Privately Held**
Web: www.liquidinstruments.com
SIC: **3825** Instruments to measure electricity

### (P-14550)
### LUCAS/SIGNATONE CORPORATION (PA)
Also Called: Lucas Labs
393 Tomkins Ct Ste J, Gilroy (95020-3632)
PHONE..............................408 848-2851
Richard Dickson, *Pr*
Dennis Dickson, *
**EMP:** 21 **EST:** 1990
**SALES (est):** 5.2MM
**SALES (corp-wide):** 5.2MM **Privately Held**
Web: www.signatone.com
SIC: **3825** 3559 Semiconductor test equipment; Semiconductor manufacturing machinery

### (P-14551)
### LUMILEDS LLC (DH)
370 W Trimble Rd, San Jose (95131-1008)
PHONE..............................408 964-2900
Matt Roney, *CEO*
Jan Paul Teuwen, *
Oleg Shchekin, *
Cheree Mcalpine, *Sr VP*
◆ **EMP:** 40 **EST:** 1999
**SALES (est):** 174.77MM **Privately Held**
Web: www.lumileds.com
SIC: **3825** 3674 Instruments to measure electricity; Light emitting diodes
HQ: Bright Bidco B.V.
Evert Van De Beekstraat 1 The Base
Luchthaven Schiphol NH

### (P-14552)
### MAGNEBIT HOLDING CORP
9474 La Cuesta Dr, La Mesa (91941-5634)
PHONE..............................858 573-0727
Catherine Jacobson, *Pr*
Peter Jacobson, *
**EMP:** 25 **EST:** 1981
**SALES (est):** 2.07MM **Privately Held**
Web: www.magnebit.com
SIC: **3825** 3471 Instruments to measure electricity; Plating and polishing

### (P-14553)
### MARVIN TEST SOLUTIONS INC
1770 Kettering, Irvine (92614-5616)
PHONE..............................949 263-2222
Loofie Gutterman, *Pr*
Leon Tsimmerman, *
Gerald Friedman, *
**EMP:** 96 **EST:** 1987
**SQ FT:** 31,000
**SALES (est):** 17.55MM
**SALES (corp-wide):** 149.54MM **Privately Held**
Web: www.marvintest.com
SIC: **3825** Instruments to measure electricity
PA: Marvin Engineering Co., Inc.
261 W Beach Ave
310 674-5030

### (P-14554)
### MEASUREMENT SPECIALTIES INC
Also Called: Te Connectivity
424 Crown Point Cir, Grass Valley (95945-9089)
PHONE..............................530 273-4608
Frank Guidone, *CEO*
**EMP:** 60
**SALES (corp-wide):** 400.61MM **Privately Held**
Web: www.te.com
SIC: **3825** 3676 Instruments to measure electricity; Electronic resistors
PA: Measurement Specialties, Inc.
1000 Lucas Way
757 766-1500

### (P-14555)
### MRV SYSTEMS LLC
6370 Lusk Blvd Ste F100, San Diego (92121-2754)
PHONE..............................800 645-7114
Adam Razavian, *Pr*
Fredric Maas, *Managing Member*
**EMP:** 20 **EST:** 2010
**SALES (est):** 3.51MM **Privately Held**
Web: www.mrvsys.com
SIC: **3825** 3823 Instruments to measure electricity; Temperature measurement instruments, industrial

### (P-14556)
### MULTITEST ELCTRNIC SYSTEMS INC (DH)
3021 Kenneth St, Santa Clara (95054-3416)
PHONE..............................408 988-6544
Dave Tacelli, *Pr*
▲ **EMP:** 280 **EST:** 1986
**SQ FT:** 40,000
**SALES (est):** 4.74MM
**SALES (corp-wide):** 636.32MM **Publicly Held**
SIC: **3825** 3674 3624 Semiconductor test equipment; Semiconductors and related devices; Brushes and brush stock contacts, electric
HQ: Xcerra Corporation
825 University Ave
Norwood MA 02062
781 461-1000

### (P-14557)
### N H RESEARCH LLC (DH)
Also Called: Nhr
16601 Hale Ave, Irvine (92606-5049)
PHONE..............................949 474-3900
Eric H Starkloff, *Pr*
▲ **EMP:** 65 **EST:** 1965
**SALES (est):** 24.81MM
**SALES (corp-wide):** 17.49B **Publicly Held**
Web: www.nhresearch.com
SIC: **3825** 3829 Test equipment for electronic and electrical circuits; Measuring and controlling devices, nec
HQ: National Instruments Corporation
11500 N Mopac Expy
Austin TX 78759
512 683-0100

### (P-14558)
### NANOFOCUS INC
Also Called: Solarius Development, Inc.
2360 Qume Dr Ste B, San Jose (95131-1838)
PHONE..............................408 435-2777
Peter Joshua, *Pr*
**EMP:** 21 **EST:** 1998
**SALES (est):** 2.42MM **Privately Held**
Web: www.solarius-inc.com
SIC: **3825** Electrical energy measuring equipment

### (P-14559)
### NATIONAL INSTRUMENTS CORP
Also Called: Ni Microwave Components
4600 Patrick Henry Dr, Santa Clara (95054-1817)
PHONE..............................408 610-6800
Dirk De Mol, *Brnch Mgr*
**EMP:** 28
**SALES (corp-wide):** 17.49B **Publicly Held**
Web: www.ni.com
SIC: **3825** Instruments to measure electricity
HQ: National Instruments Corporation
11500 N Mopac Expy
Austin TX 78759
512 683-0100

### (P-14560)
### NEARFIELD SYSTEMS INC
19730 Magellan Dr, Torrance (90502-1104)
PHONE..............................310 525-7000
Greg Hindman, *Pr*
Dan Slater, *
Rod Douglass, *
▼ **EMP:** 62 **EST:** 1988
**SALES (est):** 4.95MM
**SALES (corp-wide):** 6.6B **Publicly Held**
Web: www.nearfield.com
SIC: **3825** 3829 Test equipment for electronic and electric measurement; Measuring and controlling devices, nec
HQ: Nsi-Mi Technologies Inc.
1125 Stllite Blvd Nw Ste
Suwanee GA 30024
678 475-8300

### (P-14561)
### NEILSEN-KULJIAN INC
Also Called: Nk Technologies
3511 Charter Park Dr, San Jose (95136-1346)
PHONE..............................800 959-4014
**EMP:** 20 **EST:** 1982
**SALES (est):** 4.89MM **Privately Held**
Web: www.nktechnologies.com
SIC: **3825** Current measuring equipment, nec

### (P-14562)
### NEOLOGY INC (PA)
Also Called: Neology
1917 Palomar Oaks Way Ste 110, Carlsbad (92008-5513)
PHONE..............................858 391-0260
Bradley Feldmann, *CEO*
Neil Jadhav, *CDO*
Steve Haddix, *Sr VP*
Aaron Moser, *CFO*
Jeffrey Lowinger, *COO*
◆ **EMP:** 85 **EST:** 1986
**SALES (est):** 28.19MM
**SALES (corp-wide):** 28.19MM **Privately Held**
Web: www.neology.net
SIC: **3825** Integrated circuit testers

### (P-14563)
### NEOSEM TECHNOLOGY INC (HQ)
4659 Las Positas Rd Ste C, Livermore (94551-9631)
PHONE..............................925 303-4613
Dh Yeom, *Pr*
Stephanie Xu, *Corporate Controller*
Mike Rogowski, *COO*
Jin Choi, *Global Vice President*
Daejin Kim, *CFO*
▲ **EMP:** 20 **EST:** 2006
**SQ FT:** 18,000
**SALES (est):** 9.52MM **Privately Held**
Web: www.neosem.com
SIC: **3825** Test equipment for electronic and electrical circuits
PA: Neosem Inc.
12-26 Simin-Daero 327beon-Gil, Dongan-Gu

### (P-14564)
### NEXTEST SYSTEMS CORPORATION
Also Called: Nextest Systems Teradyne Co
875 Embedded Way, San Jose (95138-1030)
PHONE..............................408 960-2331
Mark Jadiela, *CEO*
Tim F Moriarty, *
Howard D Marshall, *
Paul Barics, *
James P Moniz, *
▲ **EMP:** 125 **EST:** 1997
**SQ FT:** 33,200
**SALES (est):** 24.19MM
**SALES (corp-wide):** 2.68B **Publicly Held**
SIC: **3825** Instruments to measure electricity
PA: Teradyne, Inc.
600 Riverpark Dr
978 370-2700

### (P-14565)
### NIKON RESEARCH CORP AMERICA
Also Called: Nikon
1399 Shoreway Rd, Belmont (94002-4105)
PHONE..............................800 446-4566
W Thomas Novak, *CEO*
Donis Flagello, *Pr*
Hamid Zarringhalam, *Ex VP*
Mohamad Zarringhalam, *Sr VP*
Mitsuaki Yonekawa, *Sr VP*
**EMP:** 40 **EST:** 1996
**SQ FT:** 15,000
**SALES (est):** 11.05MM **Privately Held**
Web: www.nikonprecision.com
SIC: **3825** Semiconductor test equipment
HQ: Nikon Americas Inc.
1300 Walt Whitman Rd Fl 2
Melville NY 11747

### (P-14566)
### NOVA MEASURING INSTRUMENTS INC
3342 Gateway Blvd, Fremont (94538-6525)
PHONE..............................408 510-7400
May Su, *Pr*
Dror David, *
**EMP:** 45 **EST:** 1996
**SALES (est):** 24.47MM **Privately Held**
Web: www.novami.com
SIC: **3825** Semiconductor test equipment
PA: Nova Ltd
5 David Fikes

### (P-14567)
### ONTO INNOVATION INC
1550 Buckeye Dr, Milpitas (95035-7418)
PHONE..............................408 545-6000
Kirsten Marshall, *Mgr*
**EMP:** 142
**SALES (corp-wide):** 815.87MM **Publicly Held**
Web: www.ontoinnovation.com
SIC: **3825** Instruments to measure electricity
PA: Onto Innovation Inc.
16 Jonspin Rd
978 253-6200

# 3825 - Instruments To Measure Electricity (P-14568)

**(P-14568)**
**ONTO INNOVATION INC**
1550 Buckeye Dr, Milpitas (95035-7418)
PHONE..............................408 545-6000
EMP: 16
SALES (corp-wide): 788.9MM **Publicly Held**
Web: investors.ontoinnovation.com
SIC: 3825 Instruments to measure electricity
PA: Onto Innovation Inc.
   16 Jonspin Rd
   978 253-6200

**(P-14569)**
**PACIFIC WESTERN SYSTEMS INC (PA)**
505 E Evelyn Ave, Mountain View (94041-1613)
PHONE..............................650 961-8855
Daniel A Worsham, *Ch Bd*
Becky Worsham, *Sec*
EMP: 20 EST: 1967
SQ FT: 40,000
SALES (est): 1.72MM
SALES (corp-wide): 1.72MM **Privately Held**
SIC: 3825 3567 Semiconductor test equipment; Industrial furnaces and ovens

**(P-14570)**
**PERICOM SEMICONDUCTOR CORP (HQ)**
1545 Barber Ln, Milpitas (95035-7409)
PHONE..............................408 232-9100
Alex Chiming Hui, *Pr*
Kevin S Bauer, *CFO*
Chi-hung Hui, *Technology*
Angela Chen, *Financial Aid*
◆ EMP: 53 EST: 1990
SQ FT: 85,040
SALES (est): 17.62MM
SALES (corp-wide): 1.66B **Publicly Held**
Web: www.diodes.com
SIC: 3825 3674 Instruments to measure electricity; Integrated circuits, semiconductor networks, etc.
PA: Diodes Incorporated
   4949 Hedgcoxe Rd Ste 200
   972 987-3900

**(P-14571)**
**PHOTON DYNAMICS INC**
Flat Panel Display Division
5970 Optical Ct, San Jose (95138-1400)
PHONE..............................408 723-7118
Jeffrey Hawthorne, *Pr*
EMP: 156
SALES (corp-wide): 9.81B **Publicly Held**
Web: www.kla.com
SIC: 3825 Test equipment for electronic and electric measurement
HQ: Photon Dynamics, Inc.
   5970 Optical Ct
   San Jose CA 95138
   408 226-9900

**(P-14572)**
**PHOTON DYNAMICS INC**
17 Great Oaks Blvd, San Jose (95119-1359)
PHONE..............................408 226-9900
Malcolm J Thompson, *Mgr*
EMP: 156
SALES (corp-wide): 9.81B **Publicly Held**
Web: www.kla.com
SIC: 3825 Test equipment for electronic and electric measurement
HQ: Photon Dynamics, Inc.
   5970 Optical Ct
   San Jose CA 95138
   408 226-9900

**(P-14573)**
**PHOTON DYNAMICS INC (HQ)**
5970 Optical Ct, San Jose (95138-1400)
PHONE..............................408 226-9900
Malcolm J Thompson Ph.d., *Ch Bd*
Errol Moore, *
Amichai Steimberg, *
Steve Song, *Worldwide Sales Vice President**
Mark Merrill, *
▲ EMP: 112 EST: 1986
SQ FT: 128,520
SALES (est): 40.04MM
SALES (corp-wide): 9.81B **Publicly Held**
Web: www.kla.com
SIC: 3825 3829 Test equipment for electronic and electrical circuits; Measuring and controlling devices, nec
PA: Kla Corporation
   1 Technology Dr
   408 875-3000

**(P-14574)**
**POWER STANDARDS LAB INC**
Also Called: Powerside
980 Atlantic Ave Ste 100, Alameda (94501-1098)
PHONE..............................510 522-4400
Alex Mceachern, *Pr*
Barry Tangney, *COO*
EMP: 32 EST: 2000
SQ FT: 12,000
SALES (est): 13.11MM
SALES (corp-wide): 15.24MM **Privately Held**
Web: www.powerstandards.com
SIC: 3825 8734 Power measuring equipment, electrical; Testing laboratories
PA: Power Survey And Equipment Ltd
   7850 Rte Transcanadienne
   514 333-8392

**(P-14575)**
**PULSE INSTRUMENTS**
22301 S Western Ave Ste 107, Torrance (90501-4155)
PHONE..............................310 515-5330
Sylvia Kan, *Pr*
David Kan, *
EMP: 23 EST: 1975
SALES (est): 4.75MM **Privately Held**
Web: www.pulseinstruments.com
SIC: 3825 3823 Pulse (signal) generators; Process control instruments

**(P-14576)**
**QUALITAU INCORPORATED (PA)**
2270 Martin Ave, Santa Clara (95050-2704)
PHONE..............................408 675-3034
Gadi Krieger, *CEO*
Jacob Herschmann, *
Nava Ben-yehuda, *VP*
Peter Y Cuevas, *
Tony Chavez, *
EMP: 59 EST: 1990
SALES (est): 24.03MM **Privately Held**
Web: www.qualitau.com
SIC: 3825 Semiconductor test equipment

**(P-14577)**
**QXQ INC**
44113 S Grimmer Blvd, Fremont (94538-6350)
PHONE..............................510 252-1522
Roger Quan, *Pr*
Jack Jenkins, *
▲ EMP: 26 EST: 1992
SQ FT: 2,600
SALES (est): 4.68MM **Privately Held**
Web: www.qxq.com

**(P-14578)**
**RICHARDSON RFPD INC**
1732 N 1st St Ste 300, San Jose (95110)
PHONE..............................669 342-3985
EMP: 38
SALES (corp-wide): 33.11MM **Publicly Held**
Web: www.richardsonrfpd.com
SIC: 3825 Radio frequency measuring equipment
HQ: Richardson Rfpd, Inc.
   2001 Bttrfeld Rd Ste 1800
   Downers Grove IL 60515

**(P-14579)**
**ROHDE & SCHWARZ USA INC**
2255 N Ontario St Ste 150, Burbank (91504-3186)
PHONE..............................818 846-3600
EMP: 22
SALES (corp-wide): 2.98B **Privately Held**
Web: www.rohde-schwarz.com
SIC: 3825 Instruments to measure electricity
HQ: Rohde & Schwarz Usa, Inc.
   6821 Benjamin Franklin Dr
   Columbia MD 21046
   410 910-7800

**(P-14580)**
**ROHDE & SCHWARZ USA INC**
409 Dixon Landing Rd, Milpitas (95035-2579)
PHONE..............................818 846-3600
EMP: 26
SALES (corp-wide): 2.98B **Privately Held**
Web: www.rohde-schwarz.com
SIC: 3825 Instruments to measure electricity
HQ: Rohde & Schwarz Usa, Inc.
   6821 Benjamin Franklin Dr
   Columbia MD 21046
   410 910-7800

**(P-14581)**
**ROOS INSTRUMENTS INC**
Also Called: RI
2285 Martin Ave, Santa Clara (95050-2715)
PHONE..............................408 748-8589
Mark Roos, *CEO*
Mark D Roos, *Pr*
Catherine Roos, *CFO*
EMP: 21 EST: 1989
SQ FT: 22,000
SALES (est): 6.08MM **Privately Held**
Web: www.roos.com
SIC: 3825 Semiconductor test equipment

**(P-14582)**
**ROSS ENGINEERING CORPORATION**
540 Westchester Dr, Campbell (95008-5000)
PHONE..............................408 377-4621
EMP: 32 EST: 1964
SALES (est): 5.89MM **Privately Held**
Web: www.rossengineeringcorp.com
SIC: 3825 3625 3613 Electrical energy measuring equipment; Relays and industrial controls; Switchgear and switchboard apparatus

**(P-14583)**
**SAGE INSTRUMENTS INC**
135 Aviation Way Ste 19, Watsonville (95076-2071)
PHONE..............................831 761-1000
Dave Mcintosh, *CEO*
Brett M Mackinnon, *
EMP: 90 EST: 1984
SALES (est): 3.35MM **Privately Held**
Web: www.sageinst.com
SIC: 3825 Test equipment for electronic and electric measurement

**(P-14584)**
**SATELLITE TELEWORK CENTERS INC**
5900 Butler Ln Ste 103, Scotts Valley (95066-3566)
PHONE..............................831 222-2100
Barbara Sprenger, *Owner*
EMP: 15
SALES (corp-wide): 1.85MM **Privately Held**
Web: www.thesatelliteinc.com
SIC: 3825 7389 Network analyzers; Office facilities and secretarial service rental
PA: Satellite Telework Centers, Inc.
   6265 Highway 9
   831 222-2100

**(P-14585)**
**SENARIOTEK LLC**
1201 Corporate Cntr Pkwy, Santa Rosa (95407-5412)
PHONE..............................707 237-6822
EMP: 20
Web: www.senariotek.com
SIC: 3825 7389 Digital test equipment, electronic and electrical circuits; Design services

**(P-14586)**
**STEM US HOLDINGS INC (HQ)**
100 Rollins Rd, Millbrae (94030-3115)
◆ EMP: 80 EST: 2009
SQ FT: 20,000
SALES (est): 24.5MM
SALES (corp-wide): 461.51MM **Publicly Held**
Web: www.stem.com
SIC: 3825 Electrical power measuring equipment
PA: Stem, Inc.
   100 California St Fl 14
   877 374-7836

**(P-14587)**
**SURFACE OPTICS CORPORATION**
11555 Rancho Bernardo Rd, San Diego (92127-1441)
PHONE..............................858 675-7404
Jonathan Dummer, *CEO*
James C Jafolla, *
Mark Dombrowski, *
Marian Geremia, *
James Jafolla, *
EMP: 50 EST: 1977
SQ FT: 18,000
SALES (est): 12.16MM **Privately Held**
Web: www.surfaceoptics.com
SIC: 3825 8748 3829 8731 Instruments to measure electricity; Business consulting, nec; Measuring and controlling devices, nec; Commercial physical research

**(P-14588)**
**SV PROBE INC**
Also Called: SV PROBE, INC.
6680 Via Del Oro, San Jose (95119-1392)
PHONE..............................480 635-4700
Kevin Kurtz, *Prin*
EMP: 434
Web: www.svprobe.com
SIC: 3825 Test equipment for electronic and electrical circuits
HQ: Nidec Sv Probe, Inc.
   7810 S Hardy Dr Ste 113

▲ = Import ▼ = Export
◆ = Import/Export

## PRODUCTS & SERVICES SECTION
### 3826 - Analytical Instruments (P-14610)

Tempe AZ 85284

**(P-14589)**
**TASEON INC**
515 S Flower St Fl 25, Los Angeles (90071-2228)
PHONE..........................408 240-7800
Albert Wong, *CEO*
▲ **EMP:** 18 **EST:** 2007
**SQ FT:** 21,000
**SALES (est):** 766.56K **Privately Held**
**SIC: 3825** Network analyzers

**(P-14590)**
**TELEDYNE LECROY INC**
Also Called: Lecroy Prtocol Solutions Group
765 Sycamore Dr, Milpitas (95035-7465)
PHONE..........................408 727-6600
Jason Lebeck, *Brnch Mgr*
**EMP:** 136
**SALES (corp-wide):** 5.64B **Publicly Held**
Web: www.teledynelecroy.com
**SIC: 3825** 3829 Test equipment for electronic and electrical circuits; Measuring and controlling devices, nec
**HQ:** Teledyne Lecroy, Inc.
700 Chestnut Ridge Rd
Chestnut Ridge NY 10977
845 425-2000

**(P-14591)**
**TELEDYNE LECROY INC**
1049 Camino Dos Rios, Thousand Oaks (91360-2362)
PHONE..........................434 984-4500
**EMP:** 29
**SALES (corp-wide):** 5.64B **Publicly Held**
Web: www.teledynelecroy.com
**SIC: 3825** Oscillographs and oscilloscopes
**HQ:** Teledyne Lecroy, Inc.
700 Chestnut Ridge Rd
Chestnut Ridge NY 10977
845 425-2000

**(P-14592)**
**TERADYNE INC**
875 Embedded Way, San Jose (95138-1030)
PHONE..........................408 960-2400
Ron Butler, *Genl Mgr*
**EMP:** 16
**SALES (corp-wide):** 2.68B **Publicly Held**
Web: www.teradyne.com
**SIC: 3825** Test equipment for electronic and electric measurement
**PA:** Teradyne, Inc.
600 Riverpark Dr
978 370-2700

**(P-14593)**
**TESCO CONTROLS INC**
Also Called: TESCO CONTROLS, INC.
42015 Remington Ave Ste 102, Temecula (92590-2563)
PHONE..........................916 395-8800
Tracy Adams, *Pr*
**EMP:** 91
**SALES (corp-wide):** 100MM **Privately Held**
Web: www.tescocontrols.com
**SIC: 3825** 3571 3625 Meters: electric, pocket, portable, panelboard, etc.; Minicomputers; Relays and industrial controls
**PA:** Tesco Controls, Llc
8440 Florin Rd
916 395-8800

**(P-14594)**
**TRANSLARITY INC (PA)**
46575 Fremont Blvd, Fremont (94538-6409)
PHONE..........................510 371-7900
Dominik Schmidt, *Pr*
**EMP:** 19 **EST:** 2002
**SQ FT:** 20,000
**SALES (est):** 4.34MM
**SALES (corp-wide):** 4.34MM **Privately Held**
Web: www.translarity.com
**SIC: 3825** Semiconductor test equipment

**(P-14595)**
**TRI-NET INC**
14721 Hilton Dr, Fontana (92336-4013)
PHONE..........................909 483-3555
Rosemarie V Hall, *Pr*
**EMP:** 50 **EST:** 1991
**SQ FT:** 7,500
**SALES (est):** 1.89MM **Privately Held**
Web: www.trinet.com
**SIC: 3825** Test equipment for electronic and electric measurement

**(P-14596)**
**TTT-CUBED INC**
1120 Auburn St, Fremont (94538-7328)
PHONE..........................510 656-2325
Jeff Tindall, *Pr*
**EMP:** 90 **EST:** 2011
**SALES (est):** 942.17K **Publicly Held**
Web: www.dbcontrol.com
**SIC: 3825** Test equipment for electronic and electric measurement
**HQ:** Db Control Corp.
1120 Auburn St
Fremont CA 94538

**(P-14597)**
**VALDOR FIBER OPTICS INC (PA)**
1838 D St, Hayward (94541-4435)
PHONE..........................510 293-1212
Las Yabut, *Pr*
**EMP:** 15 **EST:** 1993
**SQ FT:** 12,000
**SALES (est):** 2.49MM **Privately Held**
**SIC: 3825** Measuring instruments and meters, electric

**(P-14598)**
**VELHER LLC**
350 10th Ave Ste 1000, San Diego (92101-8705)
PHONE..........................619 494-6310
Luis Velazquez, *Managing Member*
**EMP:** 50 **EST:** 2019
**SALES (est):** 2.34MM **Privately Held**
Web: www.velher.net
**SIC: 3825** Energy measuring equipment, electrical

**(P-14599)**
**VITREK LLC (PA)**
Also Called: Xitron Technologies
12169 Kirkham Rd Ste C, Poway (92064-8835)
PHONE..........................858 689-2755
Kevin Clark, *CEO*
Don Millstein, *
▲ **EMP:** 27 **EST:** 1990
**SQ FT:** 4,000
**SALES (est):** 22.23MM **Privately Held**
Web: www.vitrek.com
**SIC: 3825** Test equipment for electronic and electric measurement

**(P-14600)**
**WILMINGTON INSTRUMENT CO INC (PA)**
332 N Fries Ave, Wilmington (90744-5691)
PHONE..........................310 834-1133
▲ **EMP:** 15 **EST:** 1944
**SALES (est):** 2.39MM
**SALES (corp-wide):** 2.39MM **Privately Held**
Web: www.calcert.com
**SIC: 3825** Instruments to measure electricity

**(P-14601)**
**XANDEX INC**
1360 Redwood Way Ste A, Petaluma (94954-1104)
PHONE..........................707 763-7799
Kamran Shamsavari, *Pr*
Kamran Shamsavari, *Pr*
Nariman Manoochehri, *
▲ **EMP:** 42 **EST:** 1980
**SQ FT:** 20,000
**SALES (est):** 8.99MM **Privately Held**
Web: www.xandex.com
**SIC: 3825** 3674 Instruments to measure electricity; Wafers (semiconductor devices)

### 3826 Analytical Instruments

**(P-14602)**
**ACCESS SYSTEMS INC**
4947 Hillsdale, Cir, El Dorado Hills (95762-5707)
PHONE..........................916 941-8099
Michael Herd, *Pr*
**EMP:** 59 **EST:** 2002
**SQ FT:** 3,000
**SALES (est):** 4.4MM **Privately Held**
Web: www.accesssystems.us
**SIC: 3826** 3699 Integrators (mathematical instruments); Security control equipment and systems

**(P-14603)**
**AFFYMETRIX INC**
5893 Oberlin Dr, San Diego (92121)
PHONE..........................858 642-2058
**EMP:** 54
**SALES (corp-wide):** 42.86B **Publicly Held**
Web: www.affymetrix.com
**SIC: 3826** Analytical instruments
**HQ:** Affymetrix, Inc.
428 Oakmead Pkwy
Sunnyvale CA 94085

**(P-14604)**
**AFFYMETRIX INC**
3450 Central Expy, Santa Clara (95051)
PHONE..........................408 731-5000
Mirasol Abriam, *Brnch Mgr*
**EMP:** 42
**SALES (corp-wide):** 42.86B **Publicly Held**
Web: www.affymetrix.com
**SIC: 3826** 2835 Analytical instruments; Diagnostic substances
**HQ:** Affymetrix, Inc.
428 Oakmead Pkwy
Sunnyvale CA 94085

**(P-14605)**
**AFFYMETRIX INC (HQ)**
428 Oakmead Pkwy, Sunnyvale (94085)
PHONE..........................408 731-5000
Seth H Hoogasian, *Pr*
**EMP:** 235 **EST:** 1998
**SALES (est):** 56.87MM
**SALES (corp-wide):** 42.86B **Publicly Held**
Web: www.affymetrix.com
**SIC: 3826** Analytical instruments
**PA:** Thermo Fisher Scientific Inc.
168 3rd Ave
781 622-1000

**(P-14606)**
**AGILENT TECHNOLOGIES INC (PA)**
Also Called: Agilent
5301 Stevens Creek Blvd, Santa Clara (95051-7201)
P.O. Box 58059 (95052-8059)
PHONE..........................800 227-9770
Padraig Mcdonnell, *CEO*
Koh Boon Hwee, *Non-Executive Chairman of the Board**
Rodney Gonsalves, *Corporate Vice President*
Robert W Mcmahon, *Sr VP*
Michael Tang, *Sr VP*
▲ **EMP:** 2256 **EST:** 1999
**SALES (est):** 6.83B
**SALES (corp-wide):** 6.83B **Publicly Held**
Web: www.agilent.com
**SIC: 3826** 7372 1389 Analytical instruments; Prepackaged software; Testing, measuring, surveying, and analysis services

**(P-14607)**
**ALZA CORPORATION**
1010 Joaquin Rd, Mountain View (94043-1242)
PHONE..........................650 564-5000
Duane Frise, *Brnch Mgr*
**EMP:** 725
**SALES (corp-wide):** 85.16B **Publicly Held**
Web: www.alza.com
**SIC: 3826** Analytical instruments
**HQ:** Alza Corporation
700 Eubanks Dr
Vacaville CA 95688
707 453-6400

**(P-14608)**
**ALZA CORPORATION**
700 Eubanks Dr, Vacaville (95688-9470)
PHONE..........................707 453-6400
David Danks, *VP*
**EMP:** 650
**SQ FT:** 23,040
**SALES (corp-wide):** 85.16B **Publicly Held**
Web: www.alza.com
**SIC: 3826** Analytical instruments
**HQ:** Alza Corporation
700 Eubanks Dr
Vacaville CA 95688
707 453-6400

**(P-14609)**
**AMPLITUDE LASER INC (PA)**
Also Called: Amplitude
532 Gibraltar Dr, Milpitas (95035-6315)
PHONE..........................408 727-3240
Damien Buet, *Pr*
◆ **EMP:** 40 **EST:** 2002
**SQ FT:** 44,000
**SALES (est):** 22.19MM
**SALES (corp-wide):** 22.19MM **Privately Held**
Web: www.amplitude-laser.com
**SIC: 3826** Laser scientific and engineering instruments

**(P-14610)**
**ANALYTCAL SCENTIFIC INSTRS INC**
Also Called: A S I
3023 Research Dr, San Pablo (94806-5206)
PHONE..........................510 669-2250

## 3826 - Analytical Instruments (P-14611)

Stephen H Graham, *Pr*
Yasu Graham, *
**EMP:** 30 **EST:** 1989
**SQ FT:** 12,000
**SALES (est):** 4.81MM **Privately Held**
**Web:** www.hplc-asi.com
**SIC: 3826** 3494 Analytical instruments;
  Valves and pipe fittings, nec

### (P-14611)
### ANALYTIK JENA US LLC
2066 W 11th St, Upland (91786-3509)
**PHONE**.................................781 376-9899
Chris Griffith, *Mgr*
**EMP:** 18
**Web:** www.analytik-jena.us
**SIC: 3826** Analytical instruments
**HQ:** Analytik Jena Us Llc
  3 Highwood Dr Ste 103e
  Tewksbury MA 01876

### (P-14612)
### ANASYS INSTRUMENTS CORP
325 Chapala St, Santa Barbara
(93101-3407)
**PHONE**.................................805 730-3310
Roshan Shetty, *Pr*
Kevin Kjloer, *Ex VP*
**EMP:** 15 **EST:** 2005
**SQ FT:** 3,000
**SALES (est):** 2.41MM **Privately Held**
**Web:** www.bruker.com
**SIC: 3826** Analytical instruments

### (P-14613)
### APPLIED BIOSYSTEMS INC
850 Lincoln Centre Dr, Foster City
(94404-1128)
**PHONE**.................................800 327-3002
**EMP:** 77 **EST:** 2014
**SALES (est):** 5.03MM **Privately Held**
**Web:** www.thermofisher.com
**SIC: 3826** Analytical instruments

### (P-14614)
### APPLIED INSTRUMENT TECH INC
2121 Aviation Dr, Upland (91786-2195)
**PHONE**.................................909 204-3700
Joseph Laconte, *Pr*
**EMP:** 40 **EST:** 2010
**SALES (est):** 3.57MM
**SALES (corp-wide):** 82.05K **Privately Held**
**SIC: 3826** Analytical instruments
**HQ:** Schneider Electric Usa, Inc.
  One Boston Pl Ste 2700
  Boston MA 02108
  978 975-9600

### (P-14615)
### ART ROBBINS INSTRUMENTS LLC
1293 Mountain View Alviso Rd Ste D,
Sunnyvale (94089-2241)
**PHONE**.................................408 734-8400
Matt Robbins, *Pr*
Ian Shuttler, *Ofcr*
**EMP:** 21 **EST:** 2003
**SQ FT:** 6,000
**SALES (est):** 3.7MM **Privately Held**
**Web:** www.artrobbins.com
**SIC: 3826** Analytical instruments

### (P-14616)
### ASA CORPORATION
3111 Sunset Blvd Ste V, Rocklin
(95677-3090)
**PHONE**.................................530 305-3720
**EMP:** 15

**SALES (est):** 5MM **Privately Held**
**SIC: 3826** Surface area analyzers

### (P-14617)
### ATONARP US INC
Also Called: Smart Spectrometer
5960 Inglewood Dr Ste 100, Pleasanton
(94588-8611)
**PHONE**.................................650 714-6290
David King, *CEO*
Kirk Johnson, *CFO*
Prakash Murthy, *Prin*
**EMP:** 25 **EST:** 2015
**SALES (est):** 5.95MM **Privately Held**
**Web:** www.atonarp.com
**SIC: 3826** Spectrometers

### (P-14618)
### AUTONOMOUS MEDICAL DEVICES INC (PA)
3511 W Sunflower Ave, Santa Ana
(92704-6944)
P.O. Box 28404 (92799-8404)
**PHONE**.................................657 660-6800
David Okrongly, *CEO*
Christopher Bissell, *
**EMP:** 28 **EST:** 2013
**SQ FT:** 3,750
**SALES (est):** 11.04MM
**SALES (corp-wide):** 11.04MM **Privately Held**
**Web:** www.amdilabs.com
**SIC: 3826** Analytical instruments

### (P-14619)
### AUTONOMOUS MEDICAL DEVICES INC
10524 S La Cienega Blvd, Inglewood
(90304-1116)
**PHONE**.................................310 641-2700
**EMP:** 43
**SALES (corp-wide):** 11.04MM **Privately Held**
**Web:** www.amdilabs.com
**SIC: 3826** Analytical instruments
**PA:** Autonomous Medical Devices
  Incorporated
  3511 W Sunflower Ave
  657 660-6800

### (P-14620)
### AXYGEN INC (HQ)
Also Called: Axygen Scientific
33210 Central Ave, Union City
(94587-2010)
**PHONE**.................................510 494-8900
Hemant Gupta, *Pr*
Amit Bansal, *
◆ **EMP:** 67 **EST:** 1993
**SQ FT:** 33,000
**SALES (est):** 11.65MM
**SALES (corp-wide):** 12.59B **Publicly Held**
**Web:** www.corning.com
**SIC: 3826** Analytical instruments
**PA:** Corning Incorporated
  1 Riverfront Plz
  607 974-9000

### (P-14621)
### BAYSPEC INC
Also Called: Bayspec
1101 Mckay Dr, San Jose (95131-1706)
**PHONE**.................................408 512-5928
William Yang, *Pr*
Eric Bergles, *
**EMP:** 35 **EST:** 1999
**SQ FT:** 48,000
**SALES (est):** 6.63MM **Privately Held**
**Web:** www.bayspec.com

**SIC: 3826** Analytical instruments

### (P-14622)
### BECKMAN COULTER INC
2470 Faraday Ave, Carlsbad (92010-7224)
**PHONE**.................................760 438-9151
Claire O'donadan, *Mgr*
**EMP:** 125
**SALES (corp-wide):** 23.89B **Publicly Held**
**Web:** www.beckmancoulter.com
**SIC: 3826** Analytical instruments
**HQ:** Beckman Coulter, Inc.
  250 S Kraemer Blvd
  Brea CA 92821
  714 993-5321

### (P-14623)
### BECKMAN COULTER INC (HQ)
250 S Kraemer Blvd, Brea (92821-6232)
P.O. Box 2268 (92822-2268)
**PHONE**.................................714 993-5321
◆ **EMP:** 1200 **EST:** 1935
**SALES (est):** 274.59K
**SALES (corp-wide):** 23.89B **Publicly Held**
**Web:** www.beckmancoulter.com
**SIC: 3826** 3841 3821 Analytical instruments;
  Diagnostic apparatus, medical; Chemical
  laboratory apparatus, nec
**PA:** Danaher Corporation
  2200 Pa Ave Nw Ste 800w
  202 828-0850

### (P-14624)
### BECKMAN INSTRUMENTS INC
8733 Scott St, Rosemead (91770-1363)
**PHONE**.................................626 309-0110
J Cendejas, *Pr*
**EMP:** 86 **EST:** 2003
**SALES (est):** 2.73MM **Privately Held**
**Web:** www.beckman.com
**SIC: 3826** Analytical instruments

### (P-14625)
### BECTON DICKINSON AND COMPANY
Also Called: Bdc Distribution Center
2200 W San Bernardino Ave, Redlands
(92374-5008)
**PHONE**.................................909 748-7300
Ricardo Frias, *Brnch Mgr*
**EMP:** 51
**SALES (corp-wide):** 19.37B **Publicly Held**
**Web:** www.bd.com
**SIC: 3826** Elemental analyzers
**PA:** Becton, Dickinson And Company
  1 Becton Dr
  201 847-6800

### (P-14626)
### BEMCO INC (PA)
2255 Union Pl, Simi Valley (93065-1661)
**PHONE**.................................805 583-4970
Randy Jean Bruskrud, *Pr*
Brian Bruskrud, *
**EMP:** 24 **EST:** 1951
**SQ FT:** 50,000
**SALES (est):** 6.35MM
**SALES (corp-wide):** 6.35MM **Privately Held**
**Web:** www.bemcoinc.com
**SIC: 3826** Environmental testing equipment

### (P-14627)
### BIO-RAD LABORATORIES INC
Also Called: Bio-RAD Labs
3110 Regatta Ave, Richmond (94804-6427)
**PHONE**.................................510 232-7000
Michele Kabacinski, *Pr*
**EMP:** 22
**SALES (corp-wide):** 2.8B **Publicly Held**

**Web:** www.bio-rad.com
**SIC: 3826** Analytical instruments
**PA:** Bio-Rad Laboratories, Inc.
  1000 Alfred Nobel Dr
  510 724-7000

### (P-14628)
### BIO-RAD LABORATORIES INC
Bio-RAD U S S D
2000 Alfred Nobel Dr, Hercules
(94547-1804)
**PHONE**.................................510 741-1000
**EMP:** 106
**SQ FT:** 95,850
**SALES (corp-wide):** 2.8B **Publicly Held**
**Web:** www.bio-rad.com
**SIC: 3826** Analytical instruments
**PA:** Bio-Rad Laboratories, Inc.
  1000 Alfred Nobel Dr
  510 724-7000

### (P-14629)
### BIO-RAD LABORATORIES INC
2000 Alfred Nobel Dr, Hercules
(94547-1804)
**PHONE**.................................510 232-7000
**EMP:** 104
**SALES (corp-wide):** 2.8B **Publicly Held**
**Web:** www.bio-rad.com
**SIC: 3826** Analytical instruments
**PA:** Bio-Rad Laboratories, Inc.
  1000 Alfred Nobel Dr
  510 724-7000

### (P-14630)
### BIO-RAD LABORATORIES INC
Also Called: Lifescience
2000 Alfred Nobel Dr, Hercules
(94547-1804)
**PHONE**.................................510 741-6999
Burt Zabin, *Mgr*
**EMP:** 16
**SALES (corp-wide):** 2.8B **Publicly Held**
**Web:** www.bio-rad.com
**SIC: 3826** 3841 3829 Analytical instruments;
  Surgical and medical instruments;
  Measuring and controlling devices, nec
**PA:** Bio-Rad Laboratories, Inc.
  1000 Alfred Nobel Dr
  510 724-7000

### (P-14631)
### BIO-RAD LABORATORIES INC
Bio-RAD Clinical Systems Div
4000 Alfred Nobel Dr, Hercules
(94547-1810)
**PHONE**.................................510 741-6709
**EMP:** 35
**SALES (corp-wide):** 2.8B **Publicly Held**
**Web:** www.bio-rad.com
**SIC: 3826** Analytical instruments
**PA:** Bio-Rad Laboratories, Inc.
  1000 Alfred Nobel Dr
  510 724-7000

### (P-14632)
### BIO-RAD LABORATORIES INC (PA)
Also Called: Bio-RAD
1000 Alfred Nobel Dr, Hercules
(94547-1811)
**PHONE**.................................510 724-7000
Norman Schwartz, *Ch Bd*
Jon Divincenzo, *Pr*
Ilan Daskal, *Ex VP*
Timothy S Ernst, *Ex VP*
Michael Crowley, *Executive Global
Commercial Operation Vice-President*
◆ **EMP:** 1018 **EST:** 1952
**SALES (est):** 2.8B

# PRODUCTS & SERVICES SECTION
## 3826 - Analytical Instruments (P-14651)

SALES (corp-wide): 2.8B **Publicly Held**
Web: www.bio-rad.com
SIC: **3826** 3845 2835 Electrophoresis equipment; Electromedical equipment; Diagnostic substances

### (P-14633)
### BIO-RAD LABORATORIES INC
Also Called: Finance Department
225 Linus Pauling Dr Stop 225-101, Hercules (94547-1816)
PHONE..................510 741-6916
Lanette Ewing, *Brnch Mgr*
EMP: 1500
SALES (corp-wide): 2.8B **Publicly Held**
Web: www.bio-rad.com
SIC: **3826** Electrophoresis equipment
PA: Bio-Rad Laboratories, Inc.
1000 Alfred Nobel Dr
510 724-7000

### (P-14634)
### BIOLOG INC (PA)
21124 Cabot Blvd, Hayward (94545-1130)
PHONE..................800 284-4949
Robert Wicke, *CEO*
Edwin Fineman, *VP Fin*
Doug Rife, *VP Opers*
EMP: 40 EST: 1981
SQ FT: 25,000
SALES (est): 14.69MM
SALES (corp-wide): 14.69MM **Privately Held**
Web: www.biolog.com
SIC: **3826** Analytical instruments

### (P-14635)
### BIONANO GENOMICS INC (PA)
Also Called: Bionano Genomics
9540 Towne Centre Dr Ste 100, San Diego (92121-1989)
PHONE..................858 888-7600
R Erik Holmlin, *Pr*
David L Barker, *Ch Bd*
Mark Oldakowski, *COO*
Gulsen Kama, *CFO*
Alka Chaubey, *CMO*
EMP: 58 EST: 2003
SQ FT: 35,823
SALES (est): 36.12MM
SALES (corp-wide): 36.12MM **Publicly Held**
Web: www.bionano.com
SIC: **3826** Analytical instruments

### (P-14636)
### BIOPAC SYSTEMS INC
42 Aero Camino, Goleta (93117-3105)
PHONE..................805 685-0066
Alan Macy, *CEO*
William Mcmullen, *VP*
Marc Wester, *
EMP: 40 EST: 1986
SQ FT: 16,000
SALES (est): 9.16MM **Privately Held**
Web: www.biopac.com
SIC: **3826** Analytical instruments

### (P-14637)
### BROADLEY-JAMES CORPORATION (PA)
19 Thomas, Irvine (92618-2704)
PHONE..................949 829-5555
Scott Broadley, *Pr*
Leighton S Broadley, *
Scott T Broadley, *Prin*
Catherine A Broadley, *
EMP: 79 EST: 1967
SQ FT: 24,000
SALES (est): 16.17MM
SALES (corp-wide): 16.17MM **Privately Held**
Web: www.broadleyjames.com
SIC: **3826** 3823 Analytical instruments; Industrial process measurement equipment

### (P-14638)
### BRUKER CELLULAR ANALYSIS INC (HQ)
5858 Horton St Ste 320, Emeryville (94608-2183)
PHONE..................510 858-2855
Mark Munch, *Dir*
Gerald Herman, *Dir*
Brent Alldredge, *Dir*
EMP: 232 EST: 2011
SALES (est): 78.59MM
SALES (corp-wide): 2.96B **Publicly Held**
Web: www.berkeleylights.com
SIC: **3826** 8733 Analytical instruments; Research institute
PA: Bruker Corporation
40 Manning Rd
978 663-3660

### (P-14639)
### BRUKER CORPORATION
61 Daggett Dr, San Jose (95134-2109)
PHONE..................510 683-4300
EMP: 16
SALES (corp-wide): 2.96B **Publicly Held**
Web: www.bruker.com
SIC: **3826** Analytical instruments
PA: Bruker Corporation
40 Manning Rd
978 663-3660

### (P-14640)
### BRUKER CORPORATION
3601 Calle Tecate Ste C, Camarillo (93012-5069)
PHONE..................805 388-3326
Steve Minne, *Brnch Mgr*
EMP: 18
SALES (corp-wide): 2.96B **Publicly Held**
Web: www.bruker.com
SIC: **3826** Analytical instruments
PA: Bruker Corporation
40 Manning Rd
978 663-3660

### (P-14641)
### BRUKER NANO INC
Also Called: Silicon Valley X-Ray
70 Bonaventura Dr, San Jose (95134-2123)
PHONE..................408 230-7164
Mark Munch, *Brnch Mgr*
EMP: 42
SALES (corp-wide): 2.96B **Publicly Held**
Web: www.bruker.com
SIC: **3826** Analytical instruments
HQ: Bruker Nano, Inc.
5255 E Williams Cir # 2080
Tucson AZ 85711
520 741-1044

### (P-14642)
### CAPILLARY BIOMEDICAL INC
2 Wrigley Ste 101, Irvine (92618-2759)
PHONE..................949 317-1701
Paul Strasma, *Pr*
EMP: 28 EST: 2014
SALES (est): 2.41MM **Publicly Held**
Web: www.capillarybio.com
SIC: **3826** 3841 Analytical instruments; Surgical and medical instruments
PA: Tandem Diabetes Care, Inc.
12400 High Bluff Dr

### (P-14643)
### CEPHEID (HQ)
904 E Caribbean Dr, Sunnyvale (94089-1189)
PHONE..................408 541-4191
Vitor Rocha, *CEO*
Christopher Bouda, *
Brett Cornell, *
Frank Mcfaden, *VP*
James O'reilly, *VP*
◆ EMP: 514 EST: 1996
SALES (est): 538.58MM
SALES (corp-wide): 23.89B **Publicly Held**
Web: www.cepheid.com
SIC: **3826** 3841 Analytical instruments; Surgical and medical instruments
PA: Danaher Corporation
2200 Pa Ave Nw Ste 800w
202 828-0850

### (P-14644)
### CITY OF SAN DIEGO
Also Called: Public Utilites Emts
2392 Kincaid Rd, San Diego (92101-0811)
PHONE..................619 758-2310
Steve Meyer, *Mgr*
EMP: 176
SQ FT: 92,782
SALES (corp-wide): 2.9B **Privately Held**
Web: www.sandiego.gov
SIC: **3826** Sewage testing apparatus
PA: City Of San Diego
202 C St
619 236-6330

### (P-14645)
### COHERENT INC (HQ)
Also Called: Coherent
5100 Patrick Henry Dr, Santa Clara (95054-1112)
PHONE..................408 764-4000
Garry W Rogerson, *Ch Bd*
Mark Sobey, *
Bret Dimarco, *CLO**
Richard J Martucci, *
Bob Bashaw, *
▲ EMP: 1082 EST: 1966
SQ FT: 200,000
SALES (est): 1.23B
SALES (corp-wide): 4.71B **Publicly Held**
Web: www.coherent.com
SIC: **3826** 3845 3699 Laser scientific and engineering instruments; Laser systems and equipment, medical; Laser systems and equipment
PA: Coherent Corp.
375 Saxonburg Blvd
724 352-4455

### (P-14646)
### COHERENT TIOS INC
4040 Lakeside Dr, Richmond (94806-1936)
PHONE..................510 964-5600
EMP: 50 EST: 2015
SALES (est): 2.6MM
SALES (corp-wide): 4.71B **Publicly Held**
SIC: **3826** Laser scientific and engineering instruments
PA: Coherent Corp.
375 Saxonburg Blvd
724 352-4455

### (P-14647)
### COMBIMATRIX CORPORATION (HQ)
310 Goddard Ste 150, Irvine (92618-4617)
PHONE..................949 753-0624
Mark Mcdonough, *Pr*
R Judd Jessup, *Ch Bd*
Scott R Burell, *CFO*
EMP: 20 EST: 1995
SQ FT: 12,200
SALES (est): 9.34MM **Publicly Held**
Web: www.combimatrix.com
SIC: **3826** 8731 8071 Analytical instruments; Biotechnical research, commercial; Medical laboratories
PA: Invitae Corporation
1400 16th St

### (P-14648)
### CONDITION MONITORING SVCS LLC
Also Called: Condition Monitoring Services
855 San Ysidro Ln, Nipomo (93444-8500)
P.O. Box 278 (93444-0278)
PHONE..................888 359-3277
Kirk F Cormany, *Pr*
EMP: 21 EST: 2006
SALES (est): 2.68MM **Privately Held**
Web: www.conditionmonitoringservices.com
SIC: **3826** Infrared analytical instruments

### (P-14649)
### CYTEK BIOSCIENCES INC (PA)
47215 Lakeview Blvd, Fremont (94538-6530)
PHONE..................510 657-0102
Wenbin Jiang, *Pr*
Patrik Jeanmonod, *CFO*
Valerie Barnett, *Corporate Secretary*
Allen Poirson, *Sr VP*
EMP: 279 EST: 2014
SQ FT: 12,000
SALES (est): 193.01MM
SALES (corp-wide): 193.01MM **Publicly Held**
Web: www.cytekbio.com
SIC: **3826** Analytical instruments

### (P-14650)
### DIONEX CORPORATION
Also Called: Thermo Fisher
501 Mercury Dr, Sunnyvale (94085-4019)
P.O. Box 3603 (94088-3603)
PHONE..................408 737-0700
Lucis Brancil, *Mgr*
EMP: 16
SALES (corp-wide): 42.86B **Publicly Held**
Web: www.thermofisher.com
SIC: **3826** Analytical instruments
HQ: Dionex Corporation
1228 Titan Way Ste 1002
Sunnyvale CA 94085
408 737-0700

### (P-14651)
### DIONEX CORPORATION (HQ)
1228 Titan Way Ste 1002, Sunnyvale (94085-4074)
P.O. Box 3603 (94088-3603)
PHONE..................408 737-0700
Mark Casper, *Pr*
Craig A Mccollam, *Ex VP*
Bruce Barton, *Chief Commercial Officer**
EMP: 400 EST: 1986
SQ FT: 252,000
SALES (est): 64.56MM
SALES (corp-wide): 42.86B **Publicly Held**
Web: www.thermofisher.com
SIC: **3826** 2819 3087 3841 Chromatographic equipment, laboratory type; Chemicals, reagent grade: refined from technical grade; Custom compound purchased resins; Surgical and medical instruments
PA: Thermo Fisher Scientific Inc.
168 3rd Ave
781 622-1000

# 3826 - Analytical Instruments (P-14652)

**(P-14652)**
**DNA SCRIPT INC**
2001 Junipero Serra Blvd Ste 400, Daly City (94014-3891)
PHONE..................650 457-0844
Thomas Ybert, *CEO*
Sylvain Gariel, *CFO*
**EMP:** 47 **EST:** 2019
**SALES (est):** 13.84MM **Privately Held**
Web: www.dnascript.com
**SIC: 3826** Analytical instruments

**(P-14653)**
**DOE & INGALLS CAL OPER LLC**
1060 Citrus St, Riverside (92507-1730)
PHONE..................951 801-7175
John Hollenbach, *Managing Member*
**EMP:** 36 **EST:** 2008
**SQ FT:** 43,000
**SALES (est):** 3.63MM
**SALES (corp-wide):** 42.86B **Publicly Held**
**SIC: 3826** Analytical instruments
HQ: Doe & Ingalls Management, Llc
  4813 Emperor Blvd Ste 300
  Durham NC 27703

**(P-14654)**
**DOW PHARMACEUTICAL SCIENCES INC**
Also Called: Solano Clinical Research
1330 Redwood Way Ste C, Petaluma (94954-7122)
PHONE..................707 793-2600
**EMP:** 140
**SIC: 3826** Analytical instruments

**(P-14655)**
**DRSD INC**
90 Bonaventura Dr, San Jose (95134-2124)
PHONE..................408 230-7164
Scott Jewler, *Pr*
**EMP:** 42 **EST:** 2013
**SALES (est):** 1.71MM **Privately Held**
Web: www.svxr.com
**SIC: 3826** Analytical instruments

**(P-14656)**
**DRY VAC ENVIRONMENTAL INC (PA)**
864 Saint Francis Way, Rio Vista (94571-1250)
PHONE..................707 374-7500
Dan Simpson, *Pr*
Greg Crocco, *Stockholder\**
**EMP:** 25 **EST:** 1996
**SQ FT:** 50,000
**SALES (est):** 5.11MM **Privately Held**
Web: www.dryvac1.com
**SIC: 3826** 3531 Liquid testing apparatus; Construction machinery

**(P-14657)**
**DUKE SCIENTIFIC CORPORATION**
46360 Fremont Blvd, Fremont (94538-6406)
P.O. Box 50005 (94303-0005)
PHONE..................650 424-1177
Stanley D Duke, *CEO*
Heather Vail, *Sec*
Ellen Layendecker, *Treas*
Philip Warren, *Pr*
**EMP:** 62 **EST:** 1970
**SQ FT:** 14,000
**SALES (est):** 6.38MM
**SALES (corp-wide):** 42.86B **Publicly Held**
**SIC: 3826** Analytical instruments
PA: Thermo Fisher Scientific Inc.
  168 3rd Ave
  781 622-1000

**(P-14658)**
**EMD MILLIPORE CORPORATION**
25801 Industrial Blvd Ste B, Hayward (94545-2223)
PHONE..................510 576-1367
Lawrence F Bruder, *CEO*
**EMP:** 46
**SALES (corp-wide):** 22.82B **Privately Held**
Web: www.emdmillipore.com
**SIC: 3826** Analytical instruments
HQ: Emd Millipore Corporation
  400 Summit Dr
  Burlington MA 01803
  800 645-5476

**(P-14659)**
**EMD MILLIPORE CORPORATION**
26578 Old Julian Hwy, Ramona (92065-6733)
PHONE..................760 788-9692
Haizhen Liu, *Mgr*
**EMP:** 36
**SQ FT:** 9,694
**SALES (corp-wide):** 22.82B **Privately Held**
Web: www.emdmillipore.com
**SIC: 3826** Analytical instruments
HQ: Emd Millipore Corporation
  400 Summit Dr
  Burlington MA 01803
  800 645-5476

**(P-14660)**
**EMD MILLIPORE CORPORATION**
28835 Single Oak Dr, Temecula (92590-5501)
PHONE..................951 676-8080
Patrick Schneider, *Mgr*
**EMP:** 56
**SALES (corp-wide):** 22.82B **Privately Held**
Web: www.emdmillipore.com
**SIC: 3826** Analytical instruments
HQ: Emd Millipore Corporation
  400 Summit Dr
  Burlington MA 01803
  800 645-5476

**(P-14661)**
**ENDRESS & HAUSER CONDUCTA INC**
Also Called: Endresshauser Conducta
4123 E La Palma Ave St200, Anaheim (92807-1813)
PHONE..................800 835-5474
Manfred A Jagiella, *CEO*
Claude Genswein, *
**EMP:** 50 **EST:** 1976
**SQ FT:** 31,000
**SALES (est):** 12.5MM **Privately Held**
Web: www.analysis-oem.com
**SIC: 3826** 3823 Water testing apparatus; Process control instruments
HQ: Endress+Hauser Conducta Gmbh+Co. Kg
  Dieselstr. 24
  Gerlingen BW 70839
  71562090

**(P-14662)**
**ENDRESS+HSER OPTCAL ANALIS INC**
11027 Arrow Rte, Rancho Cucamonga (91730-4866)
PHONE..................909 477-2329
**EMP:** 32 **EST:** 2001
**SALES (est):** 1.81MM **Privately Held**
**SIC: 3826** Analytical instruments
PA: Endress+Hauser Ag
  Kagenstrasse 2

**(P-14663)**
**ENTECH INSTRUMENTS INC**
2207 Agate Ct, Simi Valley (93065-1839)
PHONE..................805 527-5939
Daniel B Cardin, *CEO*
▲ **EMP:** 55 **EST:** 1989
**SQ FT:** 25,000
**SALES (est):** 9.34MM **Privately Held**
Web: www.entechinst.com
**SIC: 3826** Environmental testing equipment

**(P-14664)**
**EUV TECH INC**
Also Called: Euv Tech
2830 Howe Rd Ste A, Martinez (94553-4000)
PHONE..................925 229-4388
Rupert Perera, *Pr*
Scott Bradley, *
**EMP:** 61 **EST:** 1996
**SALES (est):** 22.86MM **Privately Held**
Web: www.euvtech.com
**SIC: 3826** Laser scientific and engineering instruments

**(P-14665)**
**FEI EFA INC (DH)**
Also Called: Dcg Systems
3400 W Warren Ave, Fremont (94538-6425)
PHONE..................510 897-6800
Israel Niv, *CEO*
Ronen Benzion, *
Tameyasu Anayama, *
Bob Conners, *
**EMP:** 95 **EST:** 2008
**SQ FT:** 45,000
**SALES (est):** 229.01MM
**SALES (corp-wide):** 42.86B **Publicly Held**
**SIC: 3826** Analytical instruments
HQ: Fei Company
  5350 Ne Dawson Creek Dr
  Hillsboro OR 97124
  503 726-7500

**(P-14666)**
**FIBERLITE CENTRIFUGE LLC**
Also Called: Thermo Fisher Scientific
422 Aldo Ave, Santa Clara (95054-2301)
PHONE..................408 492-1109
Al Piramoon, *Managing Member*
▲ **EMP:** 70 **EST:** 1994
**SQ FT:** 18,000
**SALES (est):** 6.84MM
**SALES (corp-wide):** 42.86B **Publicly Held**
Web: www.thermofisher.com
**SIC: 3826** Analytical instruments
PA: Thermo Fisher Scientific Inc.
  168 3rd Ave
  781 622-1000

**(P-14667)**
**FILMETRICS INC (HQ)**
10655 Roselle St Ste 200, San Diego (92121-1557)
PHONE..................858 573-9300
Scott Chalmers, *Pr*
**EMP:** 20 **EST:** 1993
**SQ FT:** 2,691
**SALES (est):** 9.07MM
**SALES (corp-wide):** 9.81B **Publicly Held**
Web: www.filmetrics.com
**SIC: 3826** Analytical optical instruments
PA: Kla Corporation
  1 Technology Dr
  408 875-3000

**(P-14668)**
**GATAN INC (HQ)**
5794 W Las Positas Blvd, Pleasanton (94588-4083)
PHONE..................925 463-0200
Benjamin Wood, *Pr*
Jack Buhsmer, *
David Liner, *
Ed Morrissey, *
**EMP:** 50 **EST:** 1964
**SQ FT:** 30,000
**SALES (est):** 42.05MM
**SALES (corp-wide):** 6.6B **Publicly Held**
Web: www.gatan.com
**SIC: 3826** 8711 Analytical optical instruments; Designing: ship, boat, machine, and product
PA: Ametek, Inc.
  1100 Cassatt Rd
  610 647-2121

**(P-14669)**
**GATAN INTERNATIONAL INC**
5794a W Las Positas Blvd, Pleasanton (94588-4083)
PHONE..................925 463-0200
William E Offenberg, *Pr*
**EMP:** 50 **EST:** 1992
**SALES (est):** 10.83MM
**SALES (corp-wide):** 6.18B **Publicly Held**
Web: www.gatan.com
**SIC: 3826** Analytical optical instruments
PA: Roper Technologies, Inc.
  6496 University Pkwy
  941 556-2601

**(P-14670)**
**HAMILTON SUNDSTRAND CORP**
Collins Aerospace
960 Overland Ct, San Dimas (91773-1742)
P.O. Box 2801 (91769-2801)
PHONE..................909 593-5300
Bob Hertel, *Brnch Mgr*
**EMP:** 240
**SALES (corp-wide):** 68.92B **Publicly Held**
Web: www.collinsaerospace.com
**SIC: 3826** 3861 3812 Spectrometers; Cameras, still and motion picture (all types); Search and navigation equipment
HQ: Hamilton Sundstrand Corporation
  1 Hamilton Rd
  Windsor Locks CT 06096
  619 714-9442

**(P-14671)**
**HORIBA AMERICAS HOLDING INC (HQ)**
9755 Research Dr, Irvine (92618-4626)
PHONE..................949 250-4811
Juichi Saito, *CEO*
**EMP:** 1055 **EST:** 2017
**SALES (est):** 438.93MM **Privately Held**
Web: www.horiba.com
**SIC: 3826** Analytical instruments
PA: Horiba, Ltd.
  2, Kisshoimmiyanohigashicho, Minami-Ku

**(P-14672)**
**HORIBA INSTRUMENTS INC (DH)**
Also Called: Horiba Automotive Test Systems
9755 Research Dr, Irvine (92618-4626)
PHONE..................949 250-4811
Jai Hakhu, *Ch Bd*
▲ **EMP:** 195 **EST:** 1998
**SQ FT:** 80,000
**SALES (est):** 194.11MM **Privately Held**
Web: www.horiba.com
**SIC: 3826** 3829 3511 3825 Analytical instruments; Measuring and controlling devices, nec; Turbines and turbine generator set units, complete; Instruments to measure electricity
HQ: Horiba Americas Holding Incorporated
  9755 Research Dr

## PRODUCTS & SERVICES SECTION
### 3826 - Analytical Instruments (P-14693)

Irvine CA 92618
949 250-4811

**(P-14673)**
**ILLUMINA INC**
9885 Towne Centre Dr, San Diego (92121-1975)
PHONE....................800 809-4566
William Rastetter, *Ch*
**EMP:** 16
**SALES (corp-wide):** 4.5B **Publicly Held**
Web: www.illumina.com
**SIC: 3826** Analytical instruments
**PA:** Illumina, Inc.
  5200 Illumina Way
  858 202-4500

**(P-14674)**
**ILLUMINA INC (PA)**
Also Called: ILLUMINA
5200 Illumina Way, San Diego (92122-4616)
PHONE....................858 202-4500
Jacob Thaysen, *CEO*
Stephen P Macmillan, *
Kevin Pegels, *OF GLOBAL Operations*
Charles Dadswell, *Ch Bd*
▲ **EMP:** 483 **EST:** 1998
**SQ FT:** 859,000
**SALES (est):** 4.5B
**SALES (corp-wide):** 4.5B **Publicly Held**
Web: www.illumina.com
**SIC: 3826** 3821 Analytical instruments; Clinical laboratory instruments, except medical and dental

**(P-14675)**
**ILLUMINA INC**
25861 Industrial Blvd, Hayward (94545-2991)
PHONE....................510 670-9300
**EMP:** 42 **EST:** 2000
**SALES (est):** 3.16MM **Privately Held**
Web: www.illumina.com
**SIC: 3826** Analytical instruments

**(P-14676)**
**INFRASTRUCTUREWORLD LLC**
377 Margarita Dr, San Rafael (94901-2376)
PHONE....................415 699-1543
Barbara L Treat, *Managing Member*
**EMP:** 20 **EST:** 2010
**SALES (est):** 689.64K **Privately Held**
Web: www.infrastructureworld.com
**SIC: 3826** Infrared analytical instruments

**(P-14677)**
**INTEGENX INC (HQ)**
Also Called: Integenx
5720 Stoneridge Dr Ste 300, Pleasanton (94588)
PHONE....................925 701-3400
Robert A Schueren, *CEO*
David V Smith, *
David King, *Executive Product Development Vice President*
▲ **EMP:** 69 **EST:** 2003
**SQ FT:** 10,000
**SALES (est):** 5.46MM
**SALES (corp-wide):** 42.86B **Publicly Held**
Web: www.thermofisher.com
**SIC: 3826** Analytical instruments
**PA:** Thermo Fisher Scientific Inc.
  168 3rd Ave
  781 622-1000

**(P-14678)**
**INTERGLOBAL WASTE MGT INC**
820 Calle Plano, Camarillo (93012-8557)
PHONE....................805 388-1588
Harold Katersky, *Ch Bd*
Thomas Williams, *Stockholder**
**EMP:** 80 **EST:** 2000
**SALES (est):** 1.28MM **Privately Held**
**SIC: 3826** Analytical instruments

**(P-14679)**
**INVITROGEN CORP**
1600 Faraday Ave, Carlsbad (92008-7313)
PHONE....................760 476-7055
**EMP:** 15 **EST:** 2017
**SALES (est):** 976.25K **Privately Held**
Web: www.thermofisher.com
**SIC: 3826** Analytical instruments

**(P-14680)**
**INVITROGEN IP HOLDINGS INC**
5791 Van Allen Way, Carlsbad (92008-7321)
PHONE....................760 603-7200
Stuart Hepburn, *Pr*
**EMP:** 97 **EST:** 2003
**SALES (est):** 15.46MM
**SALES (corp-wide):** 42.86B **Publicly Held**
**SIC: 3826** Analytical instruments
**HQ:** Life Technologies Corporation
  5781 Van Allen Way
  Carlsbad CA 92008
  760 603-7200

**(P-14681)**
**KASHIYAMA-USA INC**
3765 Yale Way, Fremont (94538-6188)
PHONE....................510 979-0070
Shinichi Takeshige, *Pr*
Take Hiraboyashi, *Pr*
Takashi Higo, *Sec*
Kazuyuki Tanaka, *CFO*
▲ **EMP:** 17 **EST:** 1995
**SALES (est):** 5.45MM **Privately Held**
**SIC: 3826** 3563 3821 Electrolytic conductivity instruments; Air and gas compressors including vacuum pumps; Vacuum pumps, laboratory
**PA:** Kashiyama Industries, Ltd.
  1-1, Nenei

**(P-14682)**
**LAMBDA RESEARCH OPTICS INC**
1695 Macarthur Blvd, Costa Mesa (92626-1440)
PHONE....................714 327-0600
Mark Youn, *Pr*
▲ **EMP:** 65 **EST:** 1991
**SQ FT:** 3,500
**SALES (est):** 8.77MM **Privately Held**
Web: www.lambda.cc
**SIC: 3826** 3827 3229 Laser scientific and engineering instruments; Optical instruments and lenses; Pressed and blown glass, nec

**(P-14683)**
**LEICA BIOSYSTEMS IMAGING INC (HQ)**
Also Called: Aperio
1360 Park Center Dr, Vista (92081-8300)
PHONE....................760 539-1100
James F O'reilly, *VP*
Dirk G Soenksen, *Pr*
Greg Crandall, *VP Engg*
Jared N Schwartz, *Chief Medical Officer*
Keith B Hagen, *COO*
**EMP:** 127 **EST:** 2011
**SQ FT:** 37,000
**SALES (est):** 51.62MM
**SALES (corp-wide):** 23.89B **Publicly Held**
Web: www.leicabiosystems.com

**SIC: 3826** Analytical instruments
**PA:** Danaher Corporation
  2200 Pa Ave Nw Ste 800w
  202 828-0850

**(P-14684)**
**LIFE TECHNOLOGIES CORPORATION**
Also Called: Life Technologies
5791 Van Allen Way, Carlsbad (92008-7321)
PHONE....................760 918-0135
**EMP:** 369
**SALES (corp-wide):** 42.86B **Publicly Held**
Web: www.thermofisher.com
**SIC: 3826** Analytical instruments
**HQ:** Life Technologies Corporation
  5781 Van Allen Way
  Carlsbad CA 92008
  760 603-7200

**(P-14685)**
**LIFE TECHNOLOGIES CORPORATION**
Also Called: Supplier Diversity Program
5791 Van Allen Way, Carlsbad (92008-7321)
PHONE....................760 918-4259
**EMP:** 28
**SALES (corp-wide):** 42.86B **Publicly Held**
Web: www.thermofisher.com
**SIC: 3826** Analytical instruments
**HQ:** Life Technologies Corporation
  5781 Van Allen Way
  Carlsbad CA 92008
  760 603-7200

**(P-14686)**
**MARINE SPILL RESPONSE CORP**
990 W Waterfront Dr, Eureka (95501-0173)
PHONE....................707 442-6087
**EMP:** 20
Web: www.msrc.org
**SIC: 3826** Environmental testing equipment
**PA:** Marine Spill Response Corporation
  220 Spring St Ste 500

**(P-14687)**
**MEANS ENGINEERING INC**
5927 Geiger Ct, Carlsbad (92008-7305)
PHONE....................760 931-9452
David William Means, *CEO*
Lisa Means, *
**EMP:** 70 **EST:** 1996
**SQ FT:** 34,000
**SALES (est):** 16.4MM **Privately Held**
Web: www.meanseng.com
**SIC: 3826** 3699 3559 Analytical instruments; Electrical equipment and supplies, nec; Semiconductor manufacturing machinery

**(P-14688)**
**MEDICAL ANALYSIS SYSTEMS INC (DH)**
46360 Fremont Blvd, Fremont (94538-6406)
PHONE....................510 979-5000
Steve Kondor, *Pr*
Eric Scheinerman, *
**EMP:** 150 **EST:** 1974
**SQ FT:** 180,000
**SALES (est):** 27.59MM
**SALES (corp-wide):** 42.86B **Publicly Held**
**SIC: 3826** Analytical instruments
**HQ:** Fisher Scientific International Llc
  81 Wyman St
  Waltham MA 02451

**(P-14689)**
**MESOTECH INTERNATIONAL INC**
2731 Citrus Rd Ste D, Rancho Cordova (95742-6303)
PHONE....................916 368-2020
Michael Robie, *CEO*
Michael Lydon, *Pr*
Don Hillis, *Off Mgr*
**EMP:** 22 **EST:** 1992
**SALES (est):** 3.85MM **Privately Held**
Web: www.mesotech.com
**SIC: 3826** Analytical instruments

**(P-14690)**
**MICROGENICS CORPORATION (HQ)**
46500 Kato Rd, Fremont (94538)
PHONE....................510 979-9147
Seth H Hoogasian, *CEO*
David Rubinfien, *
▲ **EMP:** 230 **EST:** 1998
**SQ FT:** 108,000
**SALES (est):** 23.74MM
**SALES (corp-wide):** 42.86B **Publicly Held**
**SIC: 3826** Analytical instruments
**PA:** Thermo Fisher Scientific Inc.
  168 3rd Ave
  781 622-1000

**(P-14691)**
**MICROGENICS CORPORATION**
44660 Osgood Rd, Fremont (94539-6410)
PHONE....................510 979-5000
**EMP:** 5846
**SALES (corp-wide):** 42.86B **Publicly Held**
**SIC: 3826** Analytical instruments
**HQ:** Microgenics Corporation
  46500 Kato Rd
  Fremont CA 94538
  510 979-9147

**(P-14692)**
**MOLECULAR BIOPRODUCTS INC (DH)**
9389 Waples St, San Diego (92121-3903)
PHONE....................858 453-7551
Seth H Hoogasian, *CEO*
Gary J Marmontello, *
R Jeffrey Harris, *
Michael K Bresson, *
John Buono, *
◆ **EMP:** 110 **EST:** 1978
**SQ FT:** 45,000
**SALES (est):** 89.79MM
**SALES (corp-wide):** 42.86B **Publicly Held**
Web: www.thermofisher.com
**SIC: 3826** Analytical instruments
**HQ:** Fisher Scientific International Llc
  81 Wyman St
  Waltham MA 02451

**(P-14693)**
**MOLECULAR DEVICES LLC (HQ)**
3860 N 1st St, San Jose (95134-1702)
PHONE....................408 747-1700
Kevin Chance, *Managing Member*
Mary Duseau, *
Albert Acevedo, *
George Parker, *
▲ **EMP:** 125 **EST:** 2011
**SALES (est):** 89.65MM
**SALES (corp-wide):** 23.89B **Publicly Held**
Web: www.moleculardevices.com
**SIC: 3826** 3841 Analytical instruments; Surgical and medical instruments
**PA:** Danaher Corporation
  2200 Pa Ave Nw Ste 800w

# 3826 - Analytical Instruments (P-14694)

## PRODUCTS & SERVICES SECTION

202 828-0850

**(P-14694)**
**MOTIONLOFT INC**
13681 Newport Ave Ste 8, Tustin
(92780-7815)
PHONE.................................415 580-7671
Joyce Reitman, CEO
Chris Garrison, *
EMP: 39 EST: 2010
SALES (est): 2.62MM **Privately Held**
Web: www.motionloft.com
SIC: 3826 7372 Analytical instruments;
Application computer software

**(P-14695)**
**MP BIOMEDICALS LLC (HQ)**
Also Called: Mp Biomedicals
6 Thomas, Irvine (92618-2500)
PHONE.................................949 833-2500
Huanjie Wang, CEO
Tom Stankovich, CFO
▲ EMP: 20 EST: 2003
SALES (est): 71.71MM
SALES (corp-wide): 601.99MM **Privately Held**
Web: www.mpbio.com
SIC: 3826 Analytical instruments
PA: Valiant Co.,Ltd
No.11, Wuzhishan Road, Economic Technology Development Zone, Fus
535 637-8873

**(P-14696)**
**NANOVEA INC (PA)**
6 Morgan Ste 156, Irvine (92618-1922)
PHONE.................................949 461-9292
Pierre Leroux, CEO
Pierre Leroux, Pr
EMP: 22 EST: 2008
SALES (est): 8.5MM **Privately Held**
Web: www.nanovea.com
SIC: 3826 Analytical instruments

**(P-14697)**
**NOOMA BIO INC**
250 Natural Bridges Dr, Santa Cruz
(95060-5710)
PHONE.................................408 309-9375
Kevin Corcorcan, CEO
EMP: 17 EST: 2020
SALES (est): 2.38MM **Privately Held**
Web: www.nooma.bio
SIC: 3826 Analytical instruments

**(P-14698)**
**ONI INC**
101 Jefferson Dr, Menlo Park (94025-1114)
PHONE.................................415 301-8526
EMP: 30 EST: 1999
SALES (est): 571.96K **Privately Held**
Web: www.oni.bio
SIC: 3826 Analytical instruments

**(P-14699)**
**OSPREYDATA INC**
32242 Paseo Adelanto C, San Juan Capistrano (92675-3610)
PHONE.................................619 971-4662
EMP: 15 EST: 2018
SALES (est): 938.04K **Privately Held**
Web: www.ospreydata.com
SIC: 3826 Petroleum product analyzing apparatus

**(P-14700)**
**OXFORD INSTRS ASYLUM RES INC (HQ)**
Also Called: Asylum Research
7416 Hollister Ave, Santa Barbara
(93117-2583)
PHONE.................................805 696-6466
Jason Cleveland, CEO
Roger Proksch, *
John Green, *
Richard Clark, *
Dick Clark, *
EMP: 55 EST: 2012
SALES (est): 11.73MM
SALES (corp-wide): 596.99MM **Privately Held**
Web: www.oxinst.com
SIC: 3826 Analytical instruments
PA: Oxford Instruments Plc
Magnetic Resonance
186 539-3200

**(P-14701)**
**OXFORD NANOIMAGING INC**
11045 Roselle St Ste 3, San Diego
(92121-1218)
PHONE.................................858 999-8860
Paul Scagnetti, CEO
Feyo Sickinghe, *
James Smobry, *
Nick Dobbs, *
EMP: 95 EST: 2019
SALES (est): 4.06MM **Privately Held**
Web: www.oni.bio
SIC: 3826 Microscopes, electron and proton

**(P-14702)**
**PACIFIC BIOSCIENCES CAL INC (PA)**
Also Called: PACBIO
1305 Obrien Dr, Menlo Park (94025-1445)
PHONE.................................650 521-8000
Christian O Henry, Pr
John F Milligan, *
Mark Van Oene, COO
Susan G Kim, CFO
Jeff Eidelm, Chief Commercial Officer
EMP: 173 EST: 2000
SQ FT: 180,000
SALES (est): 200.52MM
SALES (corp-wide): 200.52MM **Publicly Held**
Web: www.pacb.com
SIC: 3826 Analytical instruments

**(P-14703)**
**PASCO SCIENTIFIC (PA)**
Also Called: Pasco Scientific
10101 Foothills Blvd, Roseville
(95747-7100)
PHONE.................................916 786-3800
◆ EMP: 155 EST: 1964
SALES (est): 23.65MM
SALES (corp-wide): 23.65MM **Privately Held**
Web: www.pasco.com
SIC: 3826 5049 3829 Analytical instruments;
Scientific and engineering equipment and supplies; Measuring and controlling devices, nec

**(P-14704)**
**PHENOMENEX INC (HQ)**
411 Madrid Ave, Torrance (90501-1430)
PHONE.................................310 212-0555
Farshad Mahjoor, Pr
James F O Reilly, *
Frank T Mcfaden, CFO
Kaveh Kahen, *
▲ EMP: 250 EST: 1982
SQ FT: 100,000
SALES (est): 132.13MM
SALES (corp-wide): 23.89B **Publicly Held**
Web: www.phenomenex.com

SIC: 3826 Analytical instruments
PA: Danaher Corporation
2200 Pa Ave Nw Ste 800w
202 828-0850

**(P-14705)**
**PICARRO INC (PA)**
3105 Patrick Henry Dr, Santa Clara
(95054-1815)
PHONE.................................408 962-3900
Alex Balkanski, CEO
Betsy Kais, *
Chandra Prakash, *
EMP: 146 EST: 2001
SQ FT: 15,250
SALES (est): 28.51MM
SALES (corp-wide): 28.51MM **Privately Held**
Web: www.picarro.com
SIC: 3826 Analytical instruments

**(P-14706)**
**PROCESS INSGHTS - GDED WAVE IN (HQ)**
Also Called: Guided Wave Inc.
3033 Gold Canal Dr, Rancho Cordova
(95670)
PHONE.................................916 638-4944
Susan Foulk, CEO
Don Goldman, *
William Grooms, *
Neil Hekking, *
EMP: 29 EST: 2001
SQ FT: 15,000
SALES (est): 10.13MM
SALES (corp-wide): 45.56MM **Privately Held**
Web: www.process-insights.com
SIC: 3826 Analytical instruments
PA: Process Insights, Inc.
14400 Hllster St Ste 800b
713 947-9591

**(P-14707)**
**PROGNOMIQ INC**
1900 Alameda De Las Pulgas, San Mateo
(94403-1222)
PHONE.................................774 254-1569
Philip Ma, CEO
David Siewers, *
EMP: 45 EST: 2020
SALES (est): 11.33MM **Privately Held**
Web: www.prognomiq.com
SIC: 3826 Protein analyzers, laboratory type

**(P-14708)**
**QUANTUM DESIGN INC (PA)**
Also Called: Quantum Design International
10307 Pacific Center Ct, San Diego
(92121-4340)
PHONE.................................858 481-4400
Greg Degeller, Pr
Michael B Simmonds, *
David Schultz, *
Martin Kugler, *
▲ EMP: 217 EST: 1982
SQ FT: 118,000
SALES (est): 35.39MM
SALES (corp-wide): 35.39MM **Privately Held**
Web: www.qdusa.com
SIC: 3826 Laser scientific and engineering instruments

**(P-14709)**
**QUANTUM MAGNETICS LLC**
1251 E Dyer Rd Ste 140, Santa Ana
(92705-5677)
PHONE.................................714 258-4400
EMP: 609

SIC: 3826 3812 Magnetic resonance imaging apparatus; Search and navigation equipment

**(P-14710)**
**RAINDANCE TECHNOLOGIES INC**
Also Called: Raindance
5731 W Las Positas Blvd, Pleasanton
(94588-4084)
PHONE.................................978 495-3300
Kathy Ordonez, CEO
Roch Kelly, *
Alan Sherr, *
Jonathan Rothberg, *
Andy Watson, CMO*
EMP: 45 EST: 2004
SALES (est): 2.66MM
SALES (corp-wide): 2.8B **Publicly Held**
Web: www.bio-rad.com
SIC: 3826 Analytical instruments
PA: Bio-Rad Laboratories, Inc.
1000 Alfred Nobel Dr
510 724-7000

**(P-14711)**
**REMEL INC**
46500 Kato Rd, Fremont (94538-7310)
PHONE.................................916 425-2651
EMP: 1091
SALES (corp-wide): 42.86B **Publicly Held**
Web: www.thermofisher.com
SIC: 3826 Analytical instruments
HQ: Remel Inc.
12076 Santa Fe Trail Dr
Lenexa KS 66215
800 255-6730

**(P-14712)**
**RTEC-INSTRUMENTS INC**
1810 Oakland Rd Ste B, San Jose
(95131-2316)
PHONE.................................408 456-0801
Vishal Khosla, CEO
Jun Xiao, *
EMP: 25 EST: 2012
SQ FT: 3,000
SALES (est): 4.31MM **Privately Held**
Web: www.rtec-instruments.com
SIC: 3826 Analytical instruments

**(P-14713)**
**SAFEGUARD ENVIROGROUP INC**
153 Lowell Ave, Glendora (91741-2449)
PHONE.................................626 512-7585
EMP: 24
SALES (est): 2.77MM **Privately Held**
Web: www.safeguardenviro.com
SIC: 3826 Moisture analyzers

**(P-14714)**
**SCREENING SYSTEMS INC (PA)**
36 Blackbird Ln, Aliso Viejo (92656)
P.O. Box 3931 (92654)
PHONE.................................949 855-1751
Susan L Baker, Pr
Susan Baker, *
EMP: 25 EST: 1979
SQ FT: 34,000
SALES (est): 823.63K
SALES (corp-wide): 823.63K **Privately Held**
Web: www.scrsys.com
SIC: 3826 3829 Environmental testing equipment; Measuring and controlling devices, nec

▲ = Import ▼ = Export
◆ = Import/Export

## PRODUCTS & SERVICES SECTION
### 3826 - Analytical Instruments (P-14735)

**(P-14715)**
**SEER INC (PA)**
Also Called: SEER
3800 Bridge Pkwy Ste 102, Redwood City (94065-1171)
PHONE..................................650 453-0000
Omid Farokhzad, Ch Bd
David R Horn, Pr
EMP: 132 EST: 2017
SQ FT: 51,000
SALES (est): 16.66MM
SALES (corp-wide): 16.66MM **Publicly Held**
Web: www.seer.bio
SIC: **3826** 8733 Analytical instruments; Medical research

**(P-14716)**
**SEPRAGEN CORPORATION**
33470 Western Ave, Union City (94587-3202)
PHONE..................................510 475-0650
Vinit Saxena, Pr
Henry N Edmunds, CFO
EMP: 32 EST: 1985
SQ FT: 23,000
SALES (est): 7.23MM **Privately Held**
Web: www.sepragen.com
SIC: **3826** Liquid chromatographic instruments

**(P-14717)**
**SHORE WESTERN MANUFACTURING**
19888 Quiroz Ct, Walnut (91789-2828)
PHONE..................................626 357-3251
Donald Schroeder, Pr
Alice Schroeder, *
▲ EMP: 34 EST: 1967
SALES (est): 4.23MM **Privately Held**
SIC: **3826** Environmental testing equipment

**(P-14718)**
**SINGULAR GENOMICS SYSTEMS INC (PA)**
Also Called: SINGULAR GENOMICS
3010 Science Park Rd, San Diego (92121-1102)
PHONE..................................858 333-7830
Andrew Spaventa, Ch Bd
Jyotsna Ghai, COO
Dalen Meeter, CFO
Eli Glezer, CSO
Jorge Velarde, Chief Business Officer
EMP: 166 EST: 2016
SQ FT: 135,000
SALES (est): 2.91MM
SALES (corp-wide): 2.91MM **Publicly Held**
Web: www.singulargenomics.com
SIC: **3826** Analytical instruments

**(P-14719)**
**SINGULAR GENOMICS SYSTEMS INC**
10010 Mesa Rim Rd, San Diego (92121-2912)
PHONE..................................619 703-8135
EMP: 99
SALES (corp-wide): 2.91MM **Publicly Held**
Web: www.singulargenomics.com
SIC: **3826** Analytical instruments
PA: Singular Genomics Systems, Inc.
3010 Science Park Rd
858 333-7830

**(P-14720)**
**SLOUBER ENTERPRISES INC (PA)**
Also Called: High Sierra Electronics
11885 Sunrise Ln, Grass Valley (95945-8898)
PHONE..................................530 273-2080
Katherine L Slouber, CEO
James E Slouber, VP
EMP: 22 EST: 1992
SQ FT: 13,500
SALES (est): 8.09MM **Privately Held**
Web: www.hsierra.com
SIC: **3826** 8748 8731 Environmental testing equipment; Communications consulting; Electronic research

**(P-14721)**
**SPECTRON LLC (PA)**
2291 Portola Rd Ste A, Ventura (93003-7853)
PHONE..................................805 642-0400
Genette Alcaraz, CEO
Gail Faulkner, VP
EMP: 22 EST: 1987
SALES (est): 6.52MM **Privately Held**
Web: www.spectronus.com
SIC: **3826** Analytical instruments

**(P-14722)**
**SPRITE INDUSTRIES INCORPORATED**
Also Called: Sprite Showers
1791 Railroad St, Corona (92880)
PHONE..................................951 735-1015
David K Farley, Pr
Sherry Farley, VP Sls
Kathleen Farley, Admn Execs
Doris Farley, Sec
▲ EMP: 20 EST: 1974
SQ FT: 25,000
SALES (est): 2.24MM **Privately Held**
Web: www.spriteshowers.com
SIC: **3826** 3589 Water testing apparatus; Water filters and softeners, household type

**(P-14723)**
**STANDARD BIOTOOLS INC (PA)**
Also Called: STANDARD BIOTOOLS
2 Tower Pl Ste 2000, South San Francisco (94080-1844)
PHONE..................................650 266-6000
Michael Egholm, Pr
Thomas Carey, Ch Bd
Hanjoon Alex Kim, Interim Chief Financial Officer
Jeremy Davis, CCO
EMP: 227 EST: 1999
SQ FT: 78,000
SALES (est): 106.34MM
SALES (corp-wide): 106.34MM **Publicly Held**
Web: www.standardbio.com
SIC: **3826** 8731 Analytical instruments; Biotechnical research, commercial

**(P-14724)**
**STANFORD RESEARCH SYSTEMS INC**
Also Called: SRS
1290 Reamwood Ave Ste D, Sunnyvale (94089-2233)
PHONE..................................408 744-9040
William R Green, Pr
John Willison, *
EMP: 51 EST: 1980
SQ FT: 20,000
SALES (est): 7.77MM **Privately Held**
Web: www.thinksrs.com

SIC: **3826** Analytical instruments

**(P-14725)**
**SUTTER INSTRUMENT CORP**
1 Digital Dr, Novato (94949)
PHONE..................................415 883-0128
EMP: 76 EST: 1977
SALES (est): 15.59MM **Privately Held**
Web: www.sutter.com
SIC: **3826** Analytical instruments

**(P-14726)**
**TED PELLA INC (PA)**
4595 Mountain Lakes Blvd, Redding (96003)
P.O. Box 492477 (96049)
PHONE..................................530 243-2200
▲ EMP: 49 EST: 1976
SALES (est): 12.76MM
SALES (corp-wide): 12.76MM **Privately Held**
Web: www.tedpella.com
SIC: **3826** 3845 3674 Microscopes, electron and proton; Electromedical equipment; Semiconductors and related devices

**(P-14727)**
**TELEDYNE FLIR COML SYSTEMS INC (DH)**
6769 Hollister Ave, Goleta (93117-3001)
PHONE..................................805 964-9797
Robert Mehrabian, CEO
Todd Booth, *
Melanie S Cibik, *
▲ EMP: 350 EST: 1996
SALES (est): 99.7MM
SALES (corp-wide): 5.64B **Publicly Held**
Web: www.flir.com
SIC: **3826** Analytical instruments
HQ: Teledyne Flir, Llc
27700 Sw Parkway Ave
Wilsonville OR 97070
503 498-3547

**(P-14728)**
**TELEDYNE HANSON RESEARCH INC**
9810 Variel Ave, Chatsworth (91311-4316)
PHONE..................................818 882-7266
▲ EMP: 31
SIC: **3826** Analytical instruments

**(P-14729)**
**TELEDYNE INSTRUMENTS INC**
Teledyne Hanson Research
9810 Variel Ave, Chatsworth (91311-4316)
PHONE..................................818 882-7266
Thomas Reslewic, Mgr
EMP: 31
SALES (corp-wide): 5.64B **Publicly Held**
Web: www.teledynelabs.com
SIC: **3826** Analytical instruments
HQ: Teledyne Instruments, Inc.
16830 Chestnut St
City Of Industry CA 91748
626 934-1500

**(P-14730)**
**TELEDYNE REDLAKE MASD LLC (DH)**
1049 Camino Dos Rios, Thousand Oaks (91360-2362)
PHONE..................................805 373-4545
Edwin Roks, Pr
EMP: 21 EST: 1999
SQ FT: 50,000
SALES (est): 3.33MM
SALES (corp-wide): 5.64B **Publicly Held**

SIC: **3826** 3861 3822 3812 Analytical instruments; Photographic equipment and supplies; Environmental controls; Search and navigation equipment
HQ: Teledyne Digital Imaging Us, Inc.
700 Tchnlogy Pk Dr Ste 11
Billerica MA 01821
978 670-2000

**(P-14731)**
**TELESIS BIO INC (PA)**
Also Called: TELESIS BIO
10431 Wateridge Cir Ste 150, San Diego (92121-5796)
PHONE..................................858 228-4115
Eric Esser, Pr
Franklin R Witney, Non-Executive Chairman of the Board
William Kullback, CFO
Robert H Cutler, CLO
EMP: 37 EST: 2011
SALES (est): 27.51MM
SALES (corp-wide): 27.51MM **Publicly Held**
Web: www.codexdna.com
SIC: **3826** Analytical instruments

**(P-14732)**
**TERUMO AMERICAS HOLDING INC**
Also Called: Cardiovascular Systems
1311 Valencia Ave, Tustin (92780-6447)
PHONE..................................714 258-8001
Kevin Hoffman, Brnch Mgr
EMP: 28
Web: www.terumo.com
SIC: **3826** Hemoglobinometers
HQ: Terumo Americas Holding, Inc.
265 Davidson Ave Ste 320
Somerset NJ 08873
732 302-4900

**(P-14733)**
**TETRA TECH EC INC**
17885 Von Karman Ave Ste 500, Irvine (92614-5227)
PHONE..................................949 809-5000
Andrew Brack, Brnch Mgr
EMP: 40
SALES (corp-wide): 4.52B **Publicly Held**
SIC: **3826** Environmental testing equipment
HQ: Tetra Tech Ec, Inc.
6 Century Dr Ste 3
Parsippany NJ 07054
973 630-8000

**(P-14734)**
**THERMAL IDNTIFICATION TECH INC (PA)**
2707 Saturn St, Brea (92821-6705)
PHONE..................................408 656-6809
Phuong Vu Pham, CEO
EMP: 15 EST: 2018
SALES (est): 5.8MM
SALES (corp-wide): 5.8MM **Privately Held**
Web: www.thermalidtech.com
SIC: **3826** Thermal analysis instruments, laboratory type

**(P-14735)**
**THERMO FINNIGAN LLC (HQ)**
355 River Oaks Pkwy, San Jose (95134)
PHONE..................................408 965-6000
Anthony H Smith, Managing Member
Jonathan C Wilk, *
▲ EMP: 500 EST: 2001
SALES (est): 53.92MM
SALES (corp-wide): 42.86B **Publicly Held**
SIC: **3826** Analytical instruments
PA: Thermo Fisher Scientific Inc.
168 3rd Ave

## 3826 - Analytical Instruments (P-14736)

781 622-1000

**(P-14736)**
**THERMO FISHER SCIENTIFIC**
750 Laurelwood Rd, Santa Clara (95054-2422)
PHONE..................................603 430-2203
EMP: 22
SALES (corp-wide): 42.86B **Publicly Held**
Web: www.marysittonteam.com
SIC: **3826** Analytical instruments
HQ: Thermo Fisher Scientific (Asheville) Llc
  275 Aiken Rd
  Asheville NC 28804
  828 658-2711

**(P-14737)**
**THERMO FISHER SCIENTIFIC**
Also Called: Thermofinnegan
355 River Oaks Pkwy, San Jose (95134-1908)
P.O. Box 49031 (95161-9031)
PHONE..................................408 894-9835
Ian Jardin, *Brnch Mgr*
EMP: 400
SALES (corp-wide): 42.86B **Publicly Held**
Web: www.marysittonteam.com
SIC: **3826** Analytical instruments
HQ: Thermo Fisher Scientific (Asheville) Llc
  275 Aiken Rd
  Asheville NC 28804
  828 658-2711

**(P-14738)**
**THERMO FISHER SCIENTIFIC INC**
5823 Newton Dr, Carlsbad (92008-7361)
PHONE..................................781 622-1000
EMP: 32
SALES (corp-wide): 42.86B **Publicly Held**
Web: www.thermofisher.com
SIC: **3826** Analytical instruments
PA: Thermo Fisher Scientific Inc.
  168 3rd Ave
  781 622-1000

**(P-14739)**
**THERMO FISHER SCIENTIFIC INC**
Also Called: Molecular Bio Products
9389 Waples St, San Diego (92121-3903)
PHONE..................................858 453-7551
Cesar Ramirez, *Brnch Mgr*
EMP: 70
SALES (corp-wide): 42.86B **Publicly Held**
Web: www.thermofisher.com
SIC: **3826** Analytical instruments
PA: Thermo Fisher Scientific Inc.
  168 3rd Ave
  781 622-1000

**(P-14740)**
**THERMO FISHER SCIENTIFIC INC**
3380 Central Expy, Santa Clara (95051-0704)
PHONE..................................408 731-5056
Gene Tanimoto, *Brnch Mgr*
EMP: 29
SALES (corp-wide): 42.86B **Publicly Held**
Web: www.thermofisher.com
SIC: **3826** Analytical instruments
PA: Thermo Fisher Scientific Inc.
  168 3rd Ave
  781 622-1000

**(P-14741)**
**THERMO FISHER SCIENTIFIC INC**
5791 Van Allen Way, Carlsbad (92008-7321)
PHONE..................................760 603-7200
EMP: 51
SALES (corp-wide): 42.86B **Publicly Held**
Web: www.thermofisher.com
SIC: **3826** Analytical instruments
PA: Thermo Fisher Scientific Inc.
  168 3rd Ave
  781 622-1000

**(P-14742)**
**THERMO FISHER SCIENTIFIC INC**
Also Called: Thermo Fisher Scientific
5781 Van Allen Way, Carlsbad (92008-7321)
PHONE..................................760 268-8641
Heather Schultheisz, *Brnch Mgr*
EMP: 17
SALES (corp-wide): 42.86B **Publicly Held**
Web: www.thermofisher.com
SIC: **3826** Analytical instruments
PA: Thermo Fisher Scientific Inc.
  168 3rd Ave
  781 622-1000

**(P-14743)**
**THERMO FISHER SCIENTIFIC INC**
Also Called: Applied Biosystems
6055 Sunol Blvd Bldg D, Pleasanton (94566-7853)
PHONE..................................925 600-2522
EMP: 20
SALES (corp-wide): 42.86B **Publicly Held**
Web: thermofisher.dejobs.org
SIC: **3826** Analytical instruments
PA: Thermo Fisher Scientific Inc.
  168 3rd Ave
  781 622-1000

**(P-14744)**
**THERMO FISHER SCIENTIFIC INC**
355 River Oaks Pkwy, San Jose (95134-1908)
PHONE..................................408 965-6200
EMP: 28
SALES (corp-wide): 42.86B **Publicly Held**
Web: www.thermofisher.com
SIC: **3826** Analytical instruments
PA: Thermo Fisher Scientific Inc.
  168 3rd Ave
  781 622-1000

**(P-14745)**
**THERMO FISHER SCIENTIFIC INC**
180 Oyster Point Blvd, South San Francisco (94080-1909)
PHONE..................................650 246-5265
EMP: 49
SALES (corp-wide): 42.86B **Publicly Held**
Web: www.thermofisher.com
SIC: **3826** Environmental testing equipment
PA: Thermo Fisher Scientific Inc.
  168 3rd Ave
  781 622-1000

**(P-14746)**
**THERMO FSHER SCNTIFIC PSG CORP (HQ)**
5791 Van Allen Way, Carlsbad (92008-7321)
PHONE..................................760 603-7200
Marc N Casper, *Pr*
EMP: 214 EST: 2020
SALES (est): 22.3MM
SALES (corp-wide): 42.86B **Publicly Held**
SIC: **3826** Analytical instruments
PA: Thermo Fisher Scientific Inc.
  168 3rd Ave
  781 622-1000

**(P-14747)**
**THERMO FSHER SCNTIFIC PSG CORP**
777 Mariposa St, San Francisco (94107-2516)
PHONE..................................609 865-5869
Dan Herring, *Genl Mgr*
EMP: 34
SALES (corp-wide): 42.86B **Publicly Held**
SIC: **3826** Analytical instruments
HQ: Thermo Fisher Scientific Psg Corporation
  5791 Van Allen Way
  Carlsbad CA 92008
  760 603-7200

**(P-14748)**
**TURNER DESIGNS INC**
1995 N 1st St, San Jose (95112-4218)
PHONE..................................408 749-0994
Jim Crawford, *Pr*
EMP: 45 EST: 1972
SQ FT: 20,000
SALES (est): 9.98MM **Privately Held**
Web: www.turnerdesigns.com
SIC: **3826** Analytical instruments

**(P-14749)**
**V & P SCIENTIFIC INC**
9823 Pacific Heights Blvd Ste T, San Diego (92121-4706)
PHONE..................................858 455-0643
Patrick H Cleveland, *Pr*
Victoria L Cleveland, *Sec*
▲ EMP: 19 EST: 1982
SQ FT: 7,000
SALES (est): 3.77MM **Privately Held**
Web: www.vp-sci.com
SIC: **3826** Analytical instruments

**(P-14750)**
**VARIAN INC**
3100 Hansen Way, Palo Alto (94304-1030)
P.O. Box 58059 (95052-8059)
PHONE..................................650 213-8000
◆ EMP: 3500
SIC: **3826** 3845 3829 3827 Analytical instruments; Electromedical equipment; Measuring and controlling devices, nec; Optical instruments and lenses

**(P-14751)**
**VEECO PROCESS EQUIPMENT INC**
Digital Instruments Div
112 Robin Hill Rd, Goleta (93117-3107)
PHONE..................................805 967-1400
Don Kenia, *CEO*
EMP: 101
Web: www.veeco.com
SIC: **3826** 3827 Microscopes, electron and proton; Optical instruments and lenses
HQ: Veeco Process Equipment Inc.
  1 Terminal Dr
  Plainview NY 11803

**(P-14752)**
**VIAVI SOLUTIONS INC**
430 N Mccarthy Blvd, Milpitas (95035-5112)
PHONE..................................408 546-5000
EMP: 191
SALES (corp-wide): 1B **Publicly Held**
Web: www.viavisolutions.com
SIC: **3826** 3674 Analytical instruments; Optical isolators
PA: Viavi Solutions Inc.
  1445 S Spctrum Blvd Ste 1
  408 404-3600

**(P-14753)**
**VIBRANT SCIENCES LLC**
3521 Leonard Ct, Santa Clara (95054-2043)
PHONE..................................408 203-9383
John Rajasekaran, *Managing Member*
EMP: 111 EST: 2011
SALES (est): 6.61MM **Privately Held**
SIC: **3826** Electrolytic conductivity instruments

**(P-14754)**
**W R GRACE & CO-CONN**
Also Called: Grace Dvson Discovery Sciences
17434 Mojave St, Hesperia (92345-7611)
PHONE..................................760 244-6107
EMP: 18
SALES (corp-wide): 6.35B **Privately Held**
Web: www.grace.com
SIC: **3826** Chromatographic equipment, laboratory type
HQ: W. R. Grace & Co.-Conn.
  7500 Grace Dr
  Columbia MD 21044

**(P-14755)**
**WAFERGEN BIO-SYSTEMS INC**
Also Called: Wafergen Biosystems
34700 Campus Dr, Fremont (94555-3612)
PHONE..................................877 923-3746
EMP: 54
Web: www.takarabio.com
SIC: **3826** 5999 Analytical instruments; Medical apparatus and supplies

**(P-14756)**
**WYATT TECHNOLOGY LLC (HQ)**
Also Called: Wyatt Technology
6330 Hollister Ave, Goleta (93117-3115)
PHONE..................................805 681-9009
Philip J Wyatt, *CEO*
Geoffrey K Wyatt, *
Clifford D Wyatt, *
Carolyn Walton, *
EMP: 118 EST: 1982
SQ FT: 30,000
SALES (est): 20.69MM **Publicly Held**
Web: www.wyatt.com
SIC: **3826** Laser scientific and engineering instruments
PA: Waters Corporation
  34 Maple St

**(P-14757)**
**ZYGO CORPORATION**
3350 Scott Blvd Ste 4901, Santa Clara (95054-3134)
PHONE..................................408 434-1000
Robert Plozl, *Mgr*
EMP: 26
SALES (corp-wide): 6.6B **Publicly Held**
Web: www.zygo.com
SIC: **3826** 3829 3827 Microscopes, electron and proton; Measuring and controlling devices, nec; Optical instruments and lenses
HQ: Zygo Corporation
  21 Laurel Brook Rd
  Middlefield CT 06455
  860 347-8506

## 3827 Optical Instruments And Lenses

**(P-14758)**
**AAREN SCIENTIFIC INC (DH)**
Also Called: Carl Zeiss Meditec,
9010 Hellman Ave, Rancho Cucamonga (91730-4425)
PHONE..................909 937-1033
Hans-joachim Miesner, *Pr*
Stevens Chevillotte, *
James Thornton, *
Victor Garcia, *
Jan Willem De Cler, *
▲ EMP: 21 EST: 2008
SALES (est): 9.28MM Privately Held
Web: www.aareninc.com
SIC: 3827 3851 Optical instruments and lenses; Ophthalmic goods
HQ: Carl Zeiss Meditec, Inc.
5300 Central Pkwy
Dublin CA 94568
925 557-4100

**(P-14759)**
**ABRISA INDUSTRIAL GLASS INC (HQ)**
200 Hallock Dr, Santa Paula (93060-9646)
P.O. Box 85055 (60680-0851)
PHONE..................805 525-4902
Rajiv Ahuja, *CEO*
▲ EMP: 90 EST: 1980
SQ FT: 93,000
SALES (est): 18.09MM Privately Held
Web: www.abrisatechnologies.com
SIC: 3827 Optical instruments and lenses
PA: Graham Partners, Inc.
3811 W Chster Pike Bldg 2

**(P-14760)**
**ABRISA TECHNOLOGIES**
200 Hallock Dr, Santa Paula (93060-9646)
P.O. Box 489 (93061-0489)
PHONE..................805 525-4902
Blake Fennell, *CEO*
Maartin Ostendorp, *CFO*
EMP: 97 EST: 2013
SALES (est): 9.75MM Privately Held
Web: www.abrisatechnologies.com
SIC: 3827 Optical instruments and lenses

**(P-14761)**
**ADVANCED SPECTRAL TECH INC**
74 W Cochran St Ste A, Simi Valley (93065-6214)
PHONE..................805 527-7657
Thomas Persico, *Pr*
Roy Brochtrup, *CEO*
EMP: 16 EST: 2013
SALES (est): 5.1MM Privately Held
Web: www.advancedspectral.com
SIC: 3827 Optical test and inspection equipment

**(P-14762)**
**AVANTIER INC**
681 Garland Ave Apt 74, Sunnyvale (94086-7924)
PHONE..................732 570-8800
Joanna Lee, *Mgr*
EMP: 88
Web: www.avantierinc.com
SIC: 3827 Optical instruments and lenses
PA: Avantier Inc
1100 Us Highway 22

**(P-14763)**
**BLUE SKY RESEARCH INCORPORATED (PA)**
510 Alder Dr, Milpitas (95035-7443)
PHONE..................408 941-6068
Christopher Gladding, *Pr*
Sandip Basu, *
Joe Kulakofsky, *
EMP: 48 EST: 1986
SQ FT: 21,000
SALES (est): 3.73MM Privately Held
Web: www.blueskyresearch.com
SIC: 3827 3674 Lenses, optical: all types except ophthalmic; Semiconductors and related devices

**(P-14764)**
**BUK OPTICS INC**
Also Called: Precision Glass & Optics
3600 W Moore Ave, Santa Ana (92704-6835)
PHONE..................714 384-9620
Daniel S Bukaty, *CEO*
Daniel Bukaty Junior, *Pr*
▲ EMP: 42 EST: 1985
SQ FT: 25,000
SALES (est): 5.1MM Privately Held
Web: www.pgo.com
SIC: 3827 Optical instruments and apparatus

**(P-14765)**
**CARL ZEISS MEDITEC INC**
607 N Mccarthy Blvd, Milpitas (95035-5108)
PHONE..................650 871-4747
EMP: 471
Web: www.zeiss.com
SIC: 3827 Optical instruments and lenses
HQ: Carl Zeiss Meditec, Inc.
5300 Central Pkwy
Dublin CA 94568
925 557-4100

**(P-14766)**
**CARL ZEISS MEDITEC INC (DH)**
5300 Central Pkwy, Dublin (94568-4999)
P.O. Box 100372 (91189-0003)
PHONE..................925 557-4100
James V Mazzo, *Pr*
Roberto Deger, *
Min Qu, *Asst Tr*
Steven C Schallhorn Md, *Chief Medical Officer*
Andrew Chang, *Head OF GLOBAL SALES OPTHALMIC DIAGNOSTICS*
▲ EMP: 30 EST: 2000
SALES (est): 177.51MM Privately Held
Web: www.zeiss.com
SIC: 3827 Optical instruments and apparatus
HQ: Carl Zeiss Meditec Ag
Goschwitzer Str. 51-52
Jena TH 07745
36412200

**(P-14767)**
**CARL ZEISS MEDITEC PROD LLC**
1040 S Vintage Ave Ste A, Ontario (91761-3631)
PHONE..................877 644-4657
Hans-joachim Miesner, *Pr*
James Thornton, *
Paul Yun, *
Min Qu, *
EMP: 99 EST: 2017
SQ FT: 67,000
SALES (est): 9.82MM Privately Held
Web: www.zeiss.com
SIC: 3827 Optical instruments and lenses
HQ: Carl Zeiss Meditec, Inc.
5300 Central Pkwy
Dublin CA 94568
925 557-4100

**(P-14768)**
**CARL ZEISS OPHTHALMIC SYSTEMS**
5300 Central Pkwy, Dublin (94568-4999)
PHONE..................925 557-4100
Lothar Coob, *Pr*
EMP: 16 EST: 2000
SALES (est): 2.11MM Privately Held
Web: www.zeiss.com
SIC: 3827 Optical instruments and lenses

**(P-14769)**
**COHERENT AEROSPACE & DEF INC**
14192 Chambers Rd, Tustin (92780-6908)
PHONE..................714 247-7100
Mark Maiberger, *Genl Mgr*
EMP: 60
SALES (corp-wide): 4.71B Publicly Held
Web: www.iiviad.com
SIC: 3827 7389 8748 Optical instruments and apparatus; Design services; Business consulting, nec
HQ: Coherent Aerospace & Defense, Inc.
36570 Briggs Rd
Murrieta CA 92563
951 926-2994

**(P-14770)**
**DELTRONIC CORPORATION**
Also Called: Hi-Precision Grinding
3900 W Segerstrom Ave, Santa Ana (92704-6312)
PHONE..................714 545-5800
Robert C Larzelere, *Pr*
Diane Larzelere, *
Sterling Sander, *
▼ EMP: 73 EST: 1955
SQ FT: 40,000
SALES (est): 9.15MM Privately Held
Web: www.deltronic.com
SIC: 3827 3545 Optical comparators; Gauges (machine tool accessories)

**(P-14771)**
**DIGILENS INC**
Also Called: Digilens
1276 Hammerwood Ave, Sunnyvale (94089-2232)
PHONE..................408 734-0219
Christopher Pickett, *CEO*
Jonathan David Waldern, *
Michael Angel, *
Ratson Morad, *
Remi Lacombe, *Technology*
EMP: 40 EST: 2003
SQ FT: 15,000
SALES (est): 10.63MM Privately Held
Web: www.digilens.com
SIC: 3827 Optical instruments and lenses

**(P-14772)**
**DIMAXX TECHNOLOGIES LLC**
11842 Kemper Rd, Auburn (95603-9531)
P.O. Box 21810 (97402-0412)
PHONE..................530 888-1942
EMP: 16 EST: 2000
SALES (est): 3.33MM Privately Held
Web: www.dimaxxtech.com
SIC: 3827 Optical instruments and lenses

**(P-14773)**
**ELECTRO-OPTICAL INDUSTRIES LLC**
859 Ward Dr, Santa Barbara (93111-2960)
PHONE..................805 964-6701
EMP: 20
Web: www.electro-optical.com
SIC: 3827 Optical instruments and apparatus

**(P-14774)**
**ENHANCED VISION SYSTEMS INC (HQ)**
15301 Springdale St, Huntington Beach (92649-1140)
PHONE..................800 440-9476
Tom Tiernan, *CEO*
Rose Mayer, *
◆ EMP: 65 EST: 1996
SALES (est): 21.72MM
SALES (corp-wide): 36.64MM Privately Held
Web: www.enhancedvision.com
SIC: 3827 Optical instruments and lenses
PA: Freedom Scientific Blv Group, Llc
17757 Us Highway 19 N # 200
727 803-8000

**(P-14775)**
**FLEX PRODUCTS INC**
1402 Mariner Way, Santa Rosa (95407-7370)
PHONE..................707 525-9200
Michael B Sullivan, *Pr*
Joseph Zils, *
EMP: 225 EST: 1988
SQ FT: 70,000
SALES (est): 4.96MM
SALES (corp-wide): 1B Publicly Held
SIC: 3827 3081 Lens coating equipment; Unsupported plastics film and sheet
HQ: Optical Coating Laboratory, Llc
2789 Northpoint Pkwy
Santa Rosa CA 95407
707 545-6440

**(P-14776)**
**FOREAL SPECTRUM INC**
2370 Qume Dr Ste A, San Jose (95131-1842)
PHONE..................408 923-1675
Anmin Zheng, *CEO*
Anmin Zheng, *Pr*
▲ EMP: 25 EST: 2003
SALES (est): 4.65MM Privately Held
Web: www.forealspectrum.com
SIC: 3827 Optical instruments and lenses

**(P-14777)**
**GAMDAN OPTICS INC**
1751 Fortune Dr Ste J, San Jose (95131-1705)
PHONE..................669 214-2100
Hanna Cai, *CEO*
EMP: 15 EST: 2006
SALES (est): 1.61MM Privately Held
Web: www.gamdan.com
SIC: 3827 Optical instruments and lenses

**(P-14778)**
**GMTO CORPORATION**
Also Called: Giant Mgllan Tlscope Orgnztion
300 N Lake Ave Fl 14, Pasadena (91101-4164)
PHONE..................626 204-0500
Robert Shelton, *Pr*
Alan Gordon, *
Amy Honbo, *
Doctor Robert N Shelton, *Pr*
Sara Lee Keller, *
▲ EMP: 70 EST: 2007
SALES (est): 8.77MM Privately Held
Web: www.giantmagellan.org
SIC: 3827 8733 Telescopes: elbow, panoramic, sighting, fire control, etc.; Noncommercial research organizations

## 3827 - Optical Instruments And Lenses (P-14779)

**(P-14779)**
**GOOCH AND HOUSEGO CAL LLC**
5390 Kazuko Ct, Moorpark (93021-1790)
PHONE.................................805 529-3324
Kenneth Neczypor, *Managing Member*
**EMP:** 80 **EST:** 2008
**SALES (est):** 9.47MM
**SALES (corp-wide):** 187.38MM **Privately Held**
Web: www.gandh.com
**SIC: 3827** 3823 Optical instruments and lenses; Process control instruments
PA: Gooch & Housego Plc
   Dowlish Ford
   146 025-6440

**(P-14780)**
**HOYA CORPORATION**
Also Called: Hoya San Diego
4255 Ruffin Rd, San Diego (92123-1232)
PHONE.................................858 309-6050
Charlie Pendrell, *Prin*
**EMP:** 30
Web: www.hoya.com
**SIC: 3827** Optical instruments and lenses
HQ: Hoya Corporation
   651 E Corporate Dr
   Lewisville TX 75057
   972 221-4141

**(P-14781)**
**HOYA HOLDINGS INC**
Hoya Corporation USA
425 E Huntington Dr, Monrovia (91016-3632)
PHONE.................................626 739-5200
Al Benzoni, *VP*
**EMP:** 151
Web: www.hoyaoptics.com
**SIC: 3827** Optical instruments and lenses
HQ: Hoya Holdings, Inc.
   820 N Mccarthy Blvd
   Milpitas CA 95035

**(P-14782)**
**I-COAT COMPANY LLC**
12020 Mora Dr Ste 2, Santa Fe Springs (90670-6082)
PHONE.................................562 941-9989
Arman Bernardi, *CEO*
▲ **EMP:** 50 **EST:** 2003
**SQ FT:** 6,000
**SALES (est):** 6.27MM
**SALES (corp-wide):** 2.55MM **Privately Held**
Web: www.icoatcompany.com
**SIC: 3827** Optical instruments and lenses
HQ: Essilor Of America, Inc.
   13555 N Stemmons Fwy
   Dallas TX 75234

**(P-14783)**
**IDEX HEALTH & SCIENCE LLC**
2051 Palomar Airport Rd Ste 200, Carlsbad (92011-1461)
PHONE.................................760 438-2131
Blake Fennell, *Brnch Mgr*
**EMP:** 103
**SALES (corp-wide):** 3.27B **Publicly Held**
Web: www.idex-hs.com
**SIC: 3827** 3699 Optical instruments and lenses; Laser systems and equipment
HQ: Idex Health & Science Llc
   600 Park Ct
   Rohnert Park CA 94928
   707 588-2000

**(P-14784)**
**INFINITE OPTICS INC**
1712 Newport Cir Ste F, Santa Ana (92705-5118)
PHONE.................................714 557-2299
Geza Keller, *Pr*
Daniel Houston, *
Joseph Goodhand, *
Steven Crawford, *
Denise Banionis, *
**EMP:** 24 **EST:** 2003
**SQ FT:** 12,860
**SALES (est):** 4.21MM **Privately Held**
Web: www.infiniteoptics.com
**SIC: 3827** Lens coating and grinding equipment

**(P-14785)**
**INNEOS LLC**
4255 Hopyard Rd, Pleasanton (94588-2770)
PHONE.................................925 226-0138
Brian C Peters, *Managing Member*
**EMP:** 27 **EST:** 2005
**SALES (est):** 6.2MM **Privately Held**
Web: www.inneos.com
**SIC: 3827** Optical elements and assemblies, except ophthalmic

**(P-14786)**
**INSCOPIX INC**
1212 Terra Bella Ave Ste 200, Mountain View (94043-1824)
PHONE.................................650 600-3886
Kunal Ghosh, *Pr*
Martin Verhoef, *CCO*
David Gray, *CSO*
**EMP:** 103 **EST:** 2010
**SQ FT:** 6,041
**SALES (est):** 25.76MM
**SALES (corp-wide):** 2.96B **Publicly Held**
Web: www.inscopix.com
**SIC: 3827** Microscopes, except electron, proton, and corneal
PA: Bruker Corporation
   40 Manning Rd
   978 663-3660

**(P-14787)**
**INTEVAC PHOTONICS INC (PA)**
3560 Bassett St, Santa Clara (95054-2704)
PHONE.................................408 986-9888
Joseph Pietras Iii, *Pr*
Timothy Justyn, *Ex VP*
**EMP:** 78 **EST:** 2008
**SALES (est):** 12MM **Privately Held**
Web: www.intevac.com
**SIC: 3827** Optical instruments and lenses

**(P-14788)**
**INTEVAC PHOTONICS INC**
Also Called: Intevac Vision Systems
5909 Sea Lion Pl Ste A, Carlsbad (92010-6634)
PHONE.................................760 476-0339
**EMP:** 22
**SALES (corp-wide):** 95.11MM **Publicly Held**
**SIC: 3827** Optical instruments and lenses
HQ: Intevac Photonics, Inc.
   3560 Bassett St
   Santa Clara CA 95054

**(P-14789)**
**IRCAMERA LLC**
30 S Calle Cesar Chavez, Santa Barbara (93103-5652)
PHONE.................................805 965-9650
Steve Mchugh, *Managing Member*
**EMP:** 20 **EST:** 2011
**SALES (est):** 4.7MM **Publicly Held**
Web: www.ircameras.com
**SIC: 3827** 3812 Optical test and inspection equipment; Infrared object detection equipment
HQ: Santa Barbara Infrared, Inc.
   30 S Clle Csar Chvez Ste
   Santa Barbara CA 93103
   805 965-3669

**(P-14790)**
**IT CONCEPTS LLC**
1244 Quarry Ln Ste B, Pleasanton (94566-4767)
PHONE.................................925 401-0010
▼ **EMP:** 17 **EST:** 2000
**SQ FT:** 9,000
**SALES (est):** 8.63MM **Privately Held**
Web: www.itconceptsworld.com
**SIC: 3827** Optical instruments and apparatus
PA: International Technology Concepts, Inc.
   1244 Quarry Ln Ste B

**(P-14791)**
**JENOPTIK OPTICAL SYSTEMS LLC**
39300 Civic Center Dr Ste 240, Fremont (94538-2338)
PHONE.................................510 676-0019
**EMP:** 47
**SALES (corp-wide):** 1.16B **Privately Held**
Web: www.jenoptik.us
**SIC: 3827** Optical instruments and lenses
HQ: Jenoptik Optical Systems Llc
   16490 Innovation Dr Ste A
   Jupiter FL 33478

**(P-14792)**
**KAMA-TECH CORPORATION**
3451 Main St Ste 109, Chula Vista (91911-5894)
PHONE.................................619 421-7858
Ichiro Kamakura, *Pr*
▲ **EMP:** 15 **EST:** 1987
**SALES (est):** 2.52MM **Privately Held**
**SIC: 3827** Binoculars

**(P-14793)**
**KLA CORPORATION (PA)**
Also Called: KLA-Tencor
1 Technology Dr, Milpitas (95035-7916)
PHONE.................................408 875-3000
Richard P Wallace, *Pr*
Bren D Higgins, *Ex VP*
Mary Beth Wilkinson, *CLO*
Brian Lorig, *Ex VP*
Oreste Donzella, *CSO*
◆ **EMP:** 300 **EST:** 1975
**SALES (est):** 9.81B
**SALES (corp-wide):** 9.81B **Publicly Held**
Web: www.kla.com
**SIC: 3827** 3825 7699 7629 Optical instruments and lenses; Semiconductor test equipment; Optical instrument repair; Electronic equipment repair

**(P-14794)**
**LIGHT LABS INC**
Also Called: Light
725 Shasta St, Redwood City (94063-2124)
PHONE.................................650 257-8100
Dave Grannan, *CEO*
Rajiv Laroia, *
Bradley Lautenbach, *
Prashant Velagaleti, *
**EMP:** 78 **EST:** 2013
**SALES (est):** 8.56MM **Privately Held**
**SIC: 3827** Optical instruments and lenses

**(P-14795)**
**LIGHTWORKS OPTICS INC**
14192 Chambers Rd, Tustin (92780-6908)
PHONE.................................714 247-7100
**EMP:** 60
Web: www.iiviad.com
**SIC: 3827** 7389 8748 Optical instruments and apparatus; Design services; Business consulting, nec

**(P-14796)**
**LUMINIT LLC**
1850 W 205th St, Torrance (90501-1526)
PHONE.................................310 320-1066
Engin Arik, *Managing Member*
Linh Whitaker, *
Jonathan Waldern, *
▲ **EMP:** 42 **EST:** 2005
**SALES (est):** 10.11MM **Privately Held**
Web: www.luminitco.com
**SIC: 3827** Optical instruments and lenses

**(P-14797)**
**MACHINE VISION PRODUCTS INC (PA)**
3270 Corporate Vw Ste D, Vista (92081-8570)
PHONE.................................760 438-1138
George T Ayoub, *CEO*
▲ **EMP:** 36 **EST:** 1993
**SQ FT:** 60,000
**SALES (est):** 10.51MM **Privately Held**
Web: www.visionpro.com
**SIC: 3827** 7371 3229 Optical instruments and lenses; Custom computer programming services; Pressed and blown glass, nec

**(P-14798)**
**MARK OPTICS INC**
1424 E Saint Gertrude Pl, Santa Ana (92705-5271)
PHONE.................................714 545-6684
Julie A Houser, *Pr*
Judy A Chapman, *CFO*
▲ **EMP:** 20 **EST:** 1994
**SALES (est):** 3.26MM **Privately Held**
Web: www.markoptics.com
**SIC: 3827** Optical elements and assemblies, except ophthalmic

**(P-14799)**
**MELLES GRIOT INC**
2051 Palomar Airport Rd, Carlsbad (92011-1462)
PHONE.................................760 438-2254
**EMP:** 85
Web: www.idex-hs.com
**SIC: 3827** 3699 Optical instruments and lenses; Laser systems and equipment

**(P-14800)**
**MICRO-VU CORP CALIFORNIA (PA)**
Also Called: Micro-Vu
7909 Conde Ln, Windsor (95492-9779)
PHONE.................................707 838-6272
Edward P Amormino, *Pr*
Virginia Amormino, *Sec*
◆ **EMP:** 79 **EST:** 1958
**SQ FT:** 60,000
**SALES (est):** 10.07MM
**SALES (corp-wide):** 10.07MM **Privately Held**
Web: www.microvu.com
**SIC: 3827** Optical comparators

## PRODUCTS & SERVICES SECTION
### 3827 - Optical Instruments And Lenses (P-14822)

**(P-14801)**
**NCSTAR INC**
18031 Cortney Ct, City Of Industry (91748-1203)
PHONE..................866 627-8278
EMP: 30 EST: 2014
SALES (est): 4.78MM Privately Held
Web: www.ncstar.com
SIC: 3827 Optical instruments and lenses

**(P-14802)**
**NEWPORT OPTCAL INDS HLDNGS LTD (PA)**
Also Called: Newport Glassworks
10564 Fern Ave, Stanton (90680-2648)
P.O. Box 127 (90680-0127)
PHONE..................714 484-8100
Ray Larsen, Pr
▲ EMP: 20 EST: 1979
SQ FT: 12,000
SALES (est): 2.31MM
SALES (corp-wide): 2.31MM Privately Held
SIC: 3827 5049 Lenses, optical: all types except ophthalmic; Optical goods

**(P-14803)**
**NIPRO OPTICS INC**
7 Marconi, Irvine (92618-2701)
PHONE..................949 215-1151
Tom Gross, Pr
EMP: 30 EST: 2005
SQ FT: 3,500
SALES (est): 2.73MM Privately Held
Web: www.niprooptics.com
SIC: 3827 Reflectors, optical

**(P-14804)**
**OCLARO TECHNOLOGY INC**
400 N Mccarthy Blvd, Milpitas (95035-5112)
PHONE..................408 383-1400
Greg Dougherty, CEO
Jim Haynes, *
Pete Mangan, *
Terry Unter, *
EMP: 800 EST: 1997
SALES (est): 14.57MM
SALES (corp-wide): 1.36B Publicly Held
SIC: 3827 Optical instruments and lenses
HQ: Oclaro, Inc.
    400 N Mccarthy Blvd
    Milpitas CA 95035

**(P-14805)**
**ONDAX INC**
850 E Duarte Rd, Monrovia (91016-4275)
PHONE..................626 357-9600
Randy Heyler, CEO
Christophe Moser, Pr
EMP: 15 EST: 2000
SQ FT: 60,000
SALES (est): 2.28MM
SALES (corp-wide): 4.71B Publicly Held
Web: www.coherent.com
SIC: 3827 Optical instruments and apparatus
PA: Coherent Corp.
    375 Saxonburg Blvd
    724 352-4455

**(P-14806)**
**ONYX OPTICS INC**
6551 Sierra Ln, Dublin (94568-2798)
PHONE..................925 833-1969
Helmuthe Meissner, Ch Bd
Stephanie Meissner, CEO
David Meissner, Pr
EMP: 15 EST: 1992
SQ FT: 8,500
SALES (est): 2.48MM Privately Held
Web: www.onyxoptics.com
SIC: 3827 Optical instruments and lenses

**(P-14807)**
**OPTICAL ASSOCIATES INC**
Also Called: Oai
464 S Hillview Dr, Milpitas (95035-5464)
PHONE..................408 232-0600
EMP: 30 EST: 1973
SALES (est): 4.48MM Privately Held
Web: www.oainet.com
SIC: 3827 Optical test and inspection equipment

**(P-14808)**
**OPTICAL CORPORATION (DH)**
9731 Topanga Canyon Pl, Chatsworth (91311-4135)
PHONE..................818 725-9750
Francis Dominic, Pr
EMP: 23 EST: 1932
SQ FT: 14,000
SALES (est): 2.74MM Publicly Held
Web: www.theopticalco.com
SIC: 3827 Optical instruments and lenses
HQ: Excel Technology, Inc.
    125 Middlesex Tpke
    Bedford MA 01730
    781 266-5700

**(P-14809)**
**OPTICAL PHYSICS COMPANY**
4133 Guardian St # G, Simi Valley (93063-3382)
PHONE..................818 880-2907
Richard A Hutchin, CEO
Marc Jacoby, Pr
A Thomas Stanley, VP
EMP: 18 EST: 2013
SQ FT: 12,000
SALES (est): 3.93MM Privately Held
Web: www.opci.com
SIC: 3827 Optical instruments and apparatus

**(P-14810)**
**OPTOSIGMA CORPORATION**
1540 Scenic Ave, Costa Mesa (92626-1408)
PHONE..................949 851-5881
Scott Rudder, Pr
Guy Ear, *
Roger Matsunaga, *
Steve Mcnamee, VP
EMP: 25 EST: 1995
SQ FT: 13,000
SALES (est): 10.33MM Privately Held
Web: www.optosigma.com
SIC: 3827 Optical instruments and lenses
PA: Sigma Koki Co.,Ltd.
    1-19-9, Midori

**(P-14811)**
**ORAYA THERAPEUTICS INC**
3 Twin Dolphin Dr Ste 175, Redwood City (94065-5160)
P.O. Box 5122 (94002-5122)
PHONE..................510 456-3700
Jim Taylor, Pr
Michael Gertner, Stockholder
▲ EMP: 22 EST: 2007
SALES (est): 2.54MM Privately Held
Web: www.orayainc.com
SIC: 3827 Optical instruments and lenses

**(P-14812)**
**PERISCOPE LLC**
3247 Bennett Dr, Los Angeles (90068-1701)
PHONE..................323 327-5115
James Walters, Prin
EMP: 21 EST: 2019
SALES (est): 1.16MM Privately Held
Web: www.periscopemedia.net
SIC: 3827 Periscopes

**(P-14813)**
**PHOTO RESEARCH INC**
Also Called: Photo Research
9731 Topanga Canyon Pl, Chatsworth (91311-4135)
PHONE..................818 341-5151
EMP: 24
SIC: 3827 Optical instruments and lenses

**(P-14814)**
**PVP ADVANCED EO SYSTEMS INC (DH)**
14312 Franklin Ave Ste 100, Tustin (92780-7011)
PHONE..................714 508-2740
Bruce E Ferguson, CEO
John Le Blanc, *
▲ EMP: 48 EST: 1997
SQ FT: 21,000
SALES (est): 14.7MM Privately Held
Web: www.advancedeo.systems
SIC: 3827 Optical instruments and apparatus
HQ: Rafael U.S.A., Inc.
    6903 Rockledge Dr Ste 850
    Bethesda MD 20817

**(P-14815)**
**REDFERN INTEGRATED OPTICS INC**
3350 Scott Blvd Bldg 1, Santa Clara (95054-3107)
PHONE..................408 970-3500
Larry Marshall, CEO
EMP: 20 EST: 2001
SALES (est): 4.33MM Publicly Held
Web: www.rio-lasers.com
SIC: 3827 Optical elements and assemblies, except ophthalmic
HQ: Optasense Holdings Limited
    Building 3
    Camberley
    125 239-2000

**(P-14816)**
**REYNARD CORPORATION**
1020 Calle Sombra, San Clemente (92673-6227)
PHONE..................949 366-8866
Forrest Reynard, Pr
Jean Reynard, *
Randy Reynard, *
EMP: 32 EST: 1984
SQ FT: 28,000
SALES (est): 4.72MM Privately Held
Web: www.reynardcorp.com
SIC: 3827 Mirrors, optical

**(P-14817)**
**RRDS INC (PA)**
12 Goodyear Ste 100, Irvine (92618-3743)
PHONE..................949 482-6200
Troy Barnes, CEO
▲ EMP: 15 EST: 2014
SALES (est): 5.96MM
SALES (corp-wide): 5.96MM Privately Held
Web: www.rrds.com
SIC: 3827 5012 3949 5045 Optical instruments and lenses; Automobiles and other motor vehicles; Sporting and athletic goods, nec; Computers, peripherals, and software

**(P-14818)**
**RVISION INC**
2992 Scott Blvd, Santa Clara (95054)
PHONE..................408 437-5777
Brian M Kelly, Pr
Brian M Kelly, Pr
Ryan Wald, Pr
Daniel Spradling, Sec
Lance Rosenzweig, Dir
EMP: 20 EST: 1997
SQ FT: 11,000
SALES (est): 884K
SALES (corp-wide): 4MM Privately Held
Web: www.rvisionusa.com
SIC: 3827 3861 1731 5063 Optical instruments and lenses; Cameras and related equipment; Electrical work; Electrical apparatus and equipment
PA: Industrial Security Alliance Partners, Inc.
    10350 Scnce Ctr Dr Ste 10
    619 232-7041

**(P-14819)**
**SAFRAN DEFENSE & SPACE INC**
2665 Park Center Dr Ste A, Simi Valley (93065-6200)
PHONE..................805 373-9340
Garrick Matheson, COO
EMP: 80
SALES (corp-wide): 940.23MM Privately Held
Web: www.optics1.com
SIC: 3827 Optical instruments and lenses
HQ: Safran Defense & Space, Inc.
    2 Cooper Ln
    Bedford NH 03110
    603 296-0469

**(P-14820)**
**SAFRAN DEFENSE & SPACE INC**
2960 Airway Ave Ste A103, Costa Mesa (92626-6001)
PHONE..................603 296-0469
EMP: 74
SALES (corp-wide): 940.23MM Privately Held
Web: www.optics1.com
SIC: 3827 Optical instruments and lenses
HQ: Safran Defense & Space, Inc.
    2 Cooper Ln
    Bedford NH 03110
    603 296-0469

**(P-14821)**
**SANTEC CALIFORNIA CORPORATION**
Also Called: Optotest Corp.
4750 Calle Quetzal, Camarillo (93012-8534)
PHONE..................805 987-1700
Taihei Miyakoshi, CEO
Richard Buerli, Pr
Ursula Buerli, Sec
EMP: 20 EST: 2002
SQ FT: 3,000
SALES (est): 7.67MM Privately Held
Web: inst.santec.com
SIC: 3827 Optical test and inspection equipment
PA: Santec Holdings Corporation
    5823, Toshiuesaka, Okusa

**(P-14822)**
**SCOPE CITY (PA)**
2978 Topaz Ave, Simi Valley (93063-2168)
P.O. Box 1630 (93062-1630)

## 3827 - Optical Instruments And Lenses (P-14823)

PHONE..................805 522-6646
Maurice Sweiss, CEO
▲ EMP: 35 EST: 1980
SQ FT: 35,000
SALES (est): 1.11MM
SALES (corp-wide): 1.11MM Privately Held
Web: www.scope.city
SIC: 3827 Optical instruments and lenses

### (P-14823)
### SELLERS OPTICAL INC
Also Called: Precision Optical
320 Kalmus Dr, Costa Mesa (92626-6013)
PHONE..................949 631-6800
Alan Mixon Lambert, Ch Bd
Paul Dimeck, *
Rod Randolph, *
Janice Lambert, *
Alan Lambert Junior, VP
EMP: 57 EST: 1981
SQ FT: 17,000
SALES (est): 10.12MM Privately Held
Web: www.precisionoptical.com
SIC: 3827 Optical instruments and apparatus

### (P-14824)
### SIERRA PRECISION OPTICS INC
12830 Earhart Ave, Auburn (95602-9027)
PHONE..................530 885-6979
Michael Dorich, CEO
Eloise Dorich, *
EMP: 25 EST: 2001
SQ FT: 15,000
SALES (est): 4MM Privately Held
Web: www.sierraoptics.com
SIC: 3827 Optical instruments and apparatus

### (P-14825)
### SPECTRUM SCIENTIFIC INC
16692 Hale Ave Ste A, Irvine (92606-5052)
PHONE..................949 260-9900
Daphnie Chakran, Pr
EMP: 27 EST: 2004
SALES (est): 2.4MM Privately Held
Web: www.ssioptics.com
SIC: 3827 Optical instruments and lenses

### (P-14826)
### SYNERGEYES INC (HQ)
Also Called: Synergeyes
2236 Rutherford Rd Ste 115, Carlsbad (92008-8836)
PHONE..................760 476-9410
James K Kirchner, Pr
Thomas M Crews, *
David Voris, *
James Gorechner, *
David Fancher, *
▲ EMP: 98 EST: 2005
SALES (est): 24.15MM
SALES (corp-wide): 3.59B Publicly Held
Web: www.synergeyes.com
SIC: 3827 Optical instruments and lenses
PA: The Cooper Companies Inc
  6101 Bllnger Cyn Rd Ste 5
  925 460-3600

### (P-14827)
### TELEDYNE SCENTIFIC IMAGING LLC
Also Called: Teledyne Optmum Optcal Systems
4153 Calle Tesoro, Camarillo (93012-8760)
EMP: 51
SALES (corp-wide): 5.64B Publicly Held
Web: www.teledyne-si.com
SIC: 3827 Optical instruments and lenses
HQ: Teledyne Scientific & Imaging, Llc
  1049 Camino Dos Rios
  Thousand Oaks CA 91360

### (P-14828)
### TFD INCORPORATED
Also Called: Thin Film Devices
39 Heritage, Irvine (92604-1957)
PHONE..................714 630-7127
Saleem Shaikh, CEO
Joy Shaikh, *
▲ EMP: 25 EST: 1984
SALES (est): 4.95MM Privately Held
Web: www.tfdinc.com
SIC: 3827 Optical instruments and lenses

### (P-14829)
### TOUCH INTERNATIONAL DISPLAY ENHANCEMENTS CORP
11231 Jola Ln, Garden Grove (92843-3515)
PHONE..................512 646-0310
EMP: 28
SIC: 3827 Optical instruments and lenses

### (P-14830)
### TWIN COAST METROLOGY INC (PA)
333 Washington Blvd Ste 362, Marina Del Rey (90292-5152)
PHONE..................310 709-2308
Eric Stone, Pr
Jason Remillard, Treas
Amy Remillard, Sec
EMP: 15 EST: 2008
SQ FT: 1,200
SALES (est): 966.52K
SALES (corp-wide): 966.52K Privately Held
Web: www.twincoastmetrology.com
SIC: 3827 Optical instruments and lenses

### (P-14831)
### UNITED SCOPE LLC (HQ)
Also Called: Amscope
3210 El Camino Real, Irvine (92602-1365)
PHONE..................714 942-3202
Frank Dai, CEO
Andrew Wu, VP
Mandy J Liu, CFO
Nathaniel Fasnacht, CFO
▲ EMP: 24 EST: 2013
SALES (est): 11.57MM
SALES (corp-wide): 333.76MM Privately Held
Web: www.unitedscope.com
SIC: 3827 5049 Optical instruments and lenses; Optical goods
PA: L Squared Capital Partners Llc
  3434 Via Lido Ste 300
  949 398-0168

### (P-14832)
### WINTRISS ENGINEERING CORP
9010 Kenamar Dr Ste 101, San Diego (92121-3437)
PHONE..................858 550-7300
Andrew W Ash, CEO
Vic Wintriss, *
Pete Burggren, Sls Dir
▲ EMP: 23 EST: 1986
SQ FT: 11,576
SALES (est): 11.41MM Privately Held
Web: www.weco.com
SIC: 3827 Optical test and inspection equipment

### (P-14833)
### WSGLASS HOLDINGS INC
Also Called: Western States Glass
180 Main Ave, Sacramento (95838-2015)
PHONE..................916 388-5885
Curt Colgan, Brnch Mgr
EMP: 19
Web: www.wsglass.com
SIC: 3827 Glasses, field or opera
HQ: Wsglass Holdings, Inc.
  3241 Darby Cmn
  Fremont CA 94539

### (P-14834)
### Z C & R COATING FOR OPTICS INC
1401 Abalone Ave, Torrance (90501-2889)
PHONE..................310 381-3060
Rajiv Ahuja, CEO
EMP: 43 EST: 1979
SQ FT: 21,781
SALES (est): 3.93MM Privately Held
Web: www.abrisatechnologies.com
SIC: 3827 Lens coating equipment
HQ: Abrisa Industrial Glass, Inc.
  200 Hallock Dr
  Santa Paula CA 93060
  805 525-4902

### (P-14835)
### ZYGO CORPORATION
Also Called: Zygo Optical Systems
2031 Main St, Irvine (92614-6509)
PHONE..................714 918-7433
Eric D'Ippolito, Mgr
EMP: 22
SALES (corp-wide): 6.6B Publicly Held
Web: www.zygo.com
SIC: 3827 Optical instruments and lenses
HQ: Zygo Corporation
  21 Laurel Brook Rd
  Middlefield CT 06455
  860 347-8506

### (P-14836)
### ZYGO EPO
3900 Lakeside Dr, Richmond (94806-1963)
PHONE..................510 243-7592
EMP: 19 EST: 2011
SALES (est): 5.09MM Privately Held
Web: www.zygo.com
SIC: 3827 Optical instruments and lenses

## 3829 Measuring And Controlling Devices, Nec

### (P-14837)
### A D A C LABORATORIES (INC)
Also Called: Adac Medical Systems
3860 N 1st St, San Jose (95134-1702)
PHONE..................408 321-9100
▼ EMP: 732
SIC: 3829 3844 7373 3571 Medical diagnostic systems, nuclear; Radiographic X-ray apparatus and tubes; Turnkey vendors, computer systems; Computers, digital, analog or hybrid

### (P-14838)
### ABAXIS INC (HQ)
3240 Whipple Rd, Union City (94587-1217)
PHONE..................510 675-6500
Clinton H Severson, CEO
Donald P Wood, Pr
Ross Taylor, CFO
◆ EMP: 180 EST: 1989
SQ FT: 158,378
SALES (est): 82.57MM
SALES (corp-wide): 8.54B Publicly Held
Web: www.abaxis.com
SIC: 3829 2835 Medical diagnostic systems, nuclear; Diagnostic substances
PA: Zoetis Inc.
  10 Sylvan Way
  973 822-7000

### (P-14839)
### ACTION FIRE FAB & SUPPLY INC
1600 W Linne Rd, Tracy (95377-8023)
PHONE..................209 834-3460
▲ EMP: 31
Web: www.ferguson.com
SIC: 3829 Fire detector systems, non-electric

### (P-14840)
### ADVANCED MICRO INSTRUMENTS INC
Also Called: AMI
225 Paularino Ave, Costa Mesa (92626-3313)
PHONE..................714 848-5533
Kenneth Biele, CEO
EMP: 23 EST: 1999
SQ FT: 2,500
SALES (est): 12.38MM
SALES (corp-wide): 1.06B Publicly Held
Web: www.amio2.com
SIC: 3829 Measuring and controlling devices, nec
PA: Enpro Inc.
  5605 Crnegie Blvd Ste 500
  704 731-1500

### (P-14841)
### ALL WEATHER INC
Also Called: AWI
1065 National Dr Ste 1, Sacramento (95834-1927)
PHONE..................916 928-1000
Jason Hall, Pr
Bob Perrin, *
Adam Thomas, *
◆ EMP: 65 EST: 2000
SQ FT: 50,000
SALES (est): 7.35MM Privately Held
Web: www.allweatherinc.com
SIC: 3829 8999 3674 Weather tracking equipment; Weather related services; Radiation sensors

### (P-14842)
### ALVARADO MANUFACTURING CO INC
12660 Colony Ct, Chino (91710-2975)
PHONE..................909 591-8431
Bret Armatas, CEO
◆ EMP: 108 EST: 1955
SQ FT: 69,000
SALES (est): 23.33MM Privately Held
Web: www.alvaradomfg.com
SIC: 3829 Turnstiles, equipped with counting mechanisms

### (P-14843)
### APPLIED PHYSICS SYSTEMS INC (PA)
425 Clyde Ave, Mountain View (94043-2209)
PHONE..................650 965-0500
William Goodman, Pr
Robert Goodman, *
Christine Goodman, *
EMP: 102 EST: 1978
SALES (est): 20.7MM
SALES (corp-wide): 20.7MM Privately Held
Web: www.appliedphysics.com
SIC: 3829 8711 Magnetometers; Consulting engineer

### (P-14844)
### APPLIED TECHNOLOGIES ASSOC INC (HQ)

## PRODUCTS & SERVICES SECTION
### 3829 - Measuring And Controlling Devices, Nec (P-14862)

Also Called: A T A
3025 Buena Vista Dr, Paso Robles (93446-8555)
PHONE.....................805 239-9100
William B Wade, *Pr*
William B Wade, *Pr*
George Walker, *
▲ EMP: 127 EST: 1981
SALES (est): 32.25MM
SALES (corp-wide): 400.64MM **Privately Held**
Web: www.ata-sd.com
SIC: **3829** 1381 Surveying instruments and accessories; Drilling oil and gas wells
PA: Scientific Drilling International, Inc.
1450 Lk Rbbins Dr Ste 200
281 443-3300

**(P-14845)**
**AQUA MEASURE INSTRUMENT CO**
Also Called: Moisture Register Products
9567 Arrow Rte Ste E, Rancho Cucamonga (91730-4550)
PHONE.....................909 941-7776
John W Lundstrom, *Prin*
Dean Curd, *Prin*
Arthur B Schultz, *Prin*
▲ EMP: 15 EST: 1978
SQ FT: 13,500
SALES (est): 1.06MM **Privately Held**
Web: www.finnasensors.com
SIC: **3829** 3826 Moisture density meters; Analytical instruments

**(P-14846)**
**AQUA SIERRA CONTROLS INC**
1650 Industrial Dr, Auburn (95603-9018)
PHONE.....................530 823-3241
EMP: 16 EST: 1979
SALES (est): 5.01MM **Privately Held**
Web: www.aquasierra.com
SIC: **3829** Accelerometers

**(P-14847)**
**AUTOMATIC CONTROL ENGRG CORP**
Also Called: Johnson Contrls Authorized Dlr
5735 W Las Positas Blvd Ste 400, Pleasanton (94588-4002)
P.O. Box 20788 (94546-8788)
PHONE.....................510 293-6040
Robert Crowder, *CEO*
Stephen Crowder, *
EMP: 46 EST: 1975
SALES (est): 4.72MM **Privately Held**
Web: www.johnsoncontrols.com
SIC: **3829** 5084 5075 Measuring and controlling devices, nec; Instruments and control equipment; Warm air heating and air conditioning

**(P-14848)**
**BARKSDALE INC (DH)**
3211 Fruitland Ave, Los Angeles (90058-3757)
P.O. Box 58843 (90058-0843)
PHONE.....................323 583-6243
Subramanya Prasad, *Pr*
▲ EMP: 100 EST: 1946
SQ FT: 115,000
SALES (est): 65.75MM
SALES (corp-wide): 2.09B **Publicly Held**
Web: www.barksdale.com
SIC: **3829** 3491 3823 3643 Measuring and controlling devices, nec; Industrial valves; Process control instruments; Current-carrying wiring services
HQ: Crane Controls, Inc.
100 Stamford Pl
Stamford CT 06902

**(P-14849)**
**BEI NORTH AMERICA LLC (DH)**
1461 Lawrence Dr, Thousand Oaks (91320-1303)
PHONE.....................805 716-0642
Martha Sullivan, *Pr*
Jeffrey Cote, *VP*
Alison Roelke, *VP*
EMP: 103 EST: 2015
SALES (est): 19.1MM
SALES (corp-wide): 4.05B **Privately Held**
SIC: **3829** Measuring and controlling devices, nec
HQ: Custom Sensors & Technologies, Inc.
1461 Lawrence Dr
Thousand Oaks CA 91320
805 716-0322

**(P-14850)**
**BRENNER-FIEDLER & ASSOC INC (PA)**
Also Called: B F
4059 Flat Rock Dr, Riverside (92505-5859)
P.O. Box 7938 (92513-7938)
PHONE.....................562 404-2721
James Kloman, *CEO*
EMP: 39 EST: 1957
SQ FT: 28,669
SALES (est): 12.74MM
SALES (corp-wide): 12.74MM **Privately Held**
Web: www.brenner-fiedler.com
SIC: **3829** 5085 Accelerometers; Hydraulic and pneumatic pistons and valves

**(P-14851)**
**C J INSTRUMENTS INCORPORATED**
Also Called: Pace Transducer Co
P.O. Box 570430 (91357-0430)
PHONE.....................818 996-4131
Charles Tucker, *Pr*
Marshal Canter, *Genl Mgr*
Joe Bisera, *Prin*
EMP: 20 EST: 1968
SQ FT: 1,500
SALES (est): 2MM **Privately Held**
SIC: **3829** 3641 3679 2819 Pressure transducers; Lead-in wires, electric lamp made from purchased wire; Transducers, electrical; Aluminum oxide

**(P-14852)**
**C&C BUILDING AUTOMATION CO INC**
23520 Foley St, Hayward (94545-2757)
PHONE.....................650 292-7450
Charles Chavez, *CEO*
EMP: 25 EST: 1988
SALES (est): 3.53MM **Privately Held**
Web: www.ccbac.com
SIC: **3829** Measuring and controlling devices, nec

**(P-14853)**
**CALIFORNIA DYNAMICS CORP (PA)**
Also Called: Caldyn
20500 Prairie St, Chatsworth (91311-6006)
PHONE.....................323 223-3882
Donald Benkert, *Pr*
Adell Benkert, *VP*
▲ EMP: 24 EST: 1966
SALES (est): 10.63MM
SALES (corp-wide): 10.63MM **Privately Held**
Web: www.caldyn.com
SIC: **3829** Vibration meters, analyzers, and calibrators

**(P-14854)**
**CALIFORNIA SENSOR CORPORATION**
Also Called: Calsense
2075 Corte Del Nogal Ste P, Carlsbad (92011-1415)
PHONE.....................760 438-0525
Adrianus Van De Ven, *CEO*
Ralph Miller, *
David L Byma, *
Robert Destremps, *
Richard Wilkinson, *
EMP: 38 EST: 1986
SQ FT: 6,000
SALES (est): 4.96MM **Privately Held**
Web: www.calsense.com
SIC: **3829** 5083 Measuring and controlling devices, nec; Irrigation equipment

**(P-14855)**
**CARROS SENSORS SYSTEMS CO LLC**
Also Called: Systron Donner Inertial
355 Lennon Ln, Walnut Creek (94598-2475)
PHONE.....................925 979-4400
EMP: 438
SALES (corp-wide): 4.05B **Privately Held**
Web: www.sensata.com
SIC: **3829** Measuring and controlling devices, nec
HQ: Carros Sensors & Systems Company, Llc
1461 Lawrence Dr
Thousand Oaks CA 91320

**(P-14856)**
**CARROS SENSORS SYSTEMS CO LLC (DH)**
Also Called: BEI Industrial Encoders
1461 Lawrence Dr, Thousand Oaks (91320-1303)
PHONE.....................805 968-0782
Eric Pilaud, *CEO*
Jean-yves Mouttet, *Treas*
Victor Copeland, *
▲ EMP: 125 EST: 1990
SALES (est): 15.94MM
SALES (corp-wide): 4.05B **Privately Held**
Web: www.sensata.com
SIC: **3829** Measuring and controlling devices, nec
HQ: Sensata Technologies, Inc.
529 Pleasant St
Attleboro MA 02703

**(P-14857)**
**COMET TECHNOLOGIES USA INC**
541 E Trimble Rd, San Jose (95131-1224)
PHONE.....................408 325-8770
Paul Smith, *Mgr*
EMP: 205
Web: pct.comet.tech
SIC: **3829** Measuring and controlling devices, nec
HQ: Comet Technologies Usa Inc.
100 Trap Falls Road Ext # 100
Shelton CT 06484
203 447-3200

**(P-14858)**
**CUBIC TRNSP SYSTEMS INC**
Also Called: Cubic Transportation System
1800 Sutter St Ste 900, Concord (94520-2536)
PHONE.....................925 348-9163
Derrick Benoit, *Mgr*
EMP: 24
SALES (corp-wide): 1.48B **Privately Held**
Web: www.cubic.com
SIC: **3829** Fare registers, for street cars, buses, etc.
HQ: Cubic Transportation Systems, Inc.
9233 Balboa Ave
San Diego CA 92123
858 268-3100

**(P-14859)**
**DAVIDSON OPTRONICS INC**
Also Called: Doi Venture
9087 Arrow Rte Ste 180, Rancho Cucamonga (91730-4451)
PHONE.....................626 962-5181
Eugene Dumitrascu, *Ch Bd*
Debra Richards, *Sec*
EMP: 22 EST: 1932
SQ FT: 40,000
SALES (est): 1.88MM
SALES (corp-wide): 1.16B **Privately Held**
Web: www.trioptics.com
SIC: **3829** 3827 Measuring and controlling devices, nec; Optical instruments and apparatus
HQ: Trioptics Llc
9087 Arrow Rte Ste 180
Rancho Cucamonga CA 91730
626 962-5181

**(P-14860)**
**DELTATRAK INC**
1236 Doker Dr, Modesto (95351-1587)
PHONE.....................209 579-5343
Allen Hui, *Mgr*
EMP: 50
SQ FT: 25,468
Web: www.deltatrak.com
SIC: **3829** Temperature sensors, except industrial process and aircraft
PA: Deltatrak, Inc.
6801 Koll Center Pkwy # 120

**(P-14861)**
**DELTATRAK INC (PA)**
Also Called: Deltatrak
6801 Koll Center Pkwy # 120, Pleasanton (94566-7076)
P.O. Box 398 (94566-0039)
PHONE.....................925 249-2250
Frederick L Wu, *CEO*
▲ EMP: 25 EST: 1989
SALES (est): 21.56MM **Privately Held**
Web: www.deltatrak.com
SIC: **3829** 3823 3822 Temperature sensors, except industrial process and aircraft; Process control instruments; Environmental controls

**(P-14862)**
**ECKERT ZEGLER ISOTOPE PDTS INC**
1800 N Keystone St, Burbank (91504-3417)
PHONE.....................661 309-1010
Karl Amlauer, *Brnch Mgr*
EMP: 33
SALES (corp-wide): 267.49MM **Privately Held**
Web: sales.isotopeproducts.com
SIC: **3829** Nuclear radiation and testing apparatus
HQ: Eckert & Ziegler Isotope Products, Inc.
24937 Avenue Tibbitts
Valencia CA 91355
661 309-1010

## 3829 - Measuring And Controlling Devices, Nec (P-14863)

**(P-14863)**
**ECKERT ZEGLER ISOTOPE PDTS INC (HQ)**
Also Called: Isotope Products Lab
24937 Avenue Tibbitts, Valencia (91355-3427)
PHONE..............................661 309-1010
Frank Yeager, *CEO*
Joe Hathcock, *
Karen Haskins, *
**EMP:** 45 **EST:** 1967
**SQ FT:** 40,000
**SALES (est):** 67.75MM
**SALES (corp-wide):** 267.49MM **Privately Held**
Web: www.isotopeproducts.com
**SIC: 3829** Nuclear radiation and testing apparatus
**PA:** Eckert & Ziegler Se
Robert-Rossle-Str. 10
309410840

**(P-14864)**
**ET WATER SYSTEMS LLC**
384 Bel Marin Keys Blvd Ste 145, Novato (94949-5361)
PHONE..............................415 945-9383
▲ **EMP:** 21 **EST:** 2002
**SALES (est):** 912.22K **Privately Held**
Web: www.jainsusa.com
**SIC: 3829** Measuring and controlling devices, nec

**(P-14865)**
**FAR WEST TECHNOLOGY INC**
330 S Kellogg Ave Ste B, Goleta (93117-3814)
PHONE..............................805 964-3615
John D Rickey, *CEO*
John Handloser Junior, *Ex VP*
▼ **EMP:** 17 **EST:** 1971
**SQ FT:** 6,100
**SALES (est):** 2.51MM **Privately Held**
Web: www.fwt.com
**SIC: 3829** Nuclear radiation and testing apparatus

**(P-14866)**
**FIRE & GAS DETECTION TECH INC**
2570 E Cerritos Ave, Anaheim (92806-5636)
PHONE..............................714 671-8500
Olden Carr, *Pr*
**EMP:** 15 **EST:** 2017
**SALES (est):** 4.64MM **Privately Held**
Web: www.fg-detection.com
**SIC: 3829** Measuring and controlling devices, nec

**(P-14867)**
**FITBIT LLC**
15255 Innovation Dr Ste 200, San Diego (92128-3410)
PHONE..............................415 513-1000
**EMP:** 209
**SALES (corp-wide):** 307.39B **Publicly Held**
Web: www.fitbit.com
**SIC: 3829** Measuring and controlling devices, nec
**HQ:** Fitbit Llc
199 Fremont St Fl 14
San Francisco CA 94105

**(P-14868)**
**FITBIT LLC (DH)**
Also Called: Fitbit
199 Fremont St Fl 14, San Francisco (94105-2253)
PHONE..............................415 513-1000
James Park, *Pr*
Andy Missan, *
Jeff Devine, *
Ronald W Kisling, *
Eric N Friedman, *
**EMP:** 218 **EST:** 2007
**SQ FT:** 260,000
**SALES (est):** 1.43B
**SALES (corp-wide):** 307.39B **Publicly Held**
Web: www.fitbit.com
**SIC: 3829** Measuring and controlling devices, nec
**HQ:** Google Llc
1600 Amphitheatre Pkwy
Mountain View CA 94043
650 253-0000

**(P-14869)**
**FLOWLINE INC**
Also Called: Flowline Liquid Intelligence
10500 Humbolt St, Los Alamitos (90720-2439)
PHONE..............................562 598-3015
Stephen E Olson, *Ch Bd*
Scott Olson, *
**EMP:** 25 **EST:** 1990
**SQ FT:** 8,000
**SALES (est):** 3.25MM **Privately Held**
Web: www.flowline.com
**SIC: 3829** 5084 Measuring and controlling devices, nec; Industrial machinery and equipment

**(P-14870)**
**GAMMA SCIENTIFIC INC**
Also Called: Road Vista
9925 Carroll Canyon Rd, San Diego (92131-1105)
PHONE..............................858 635-9008
Kong G Loh, *CEO*
▲ **EMP:** 48 **EST:** 1961
**SQ FT:** 20,000
**SALES (est):** 8.45MM **Privately Held**
Web: www.gamma-sci.com
**SIC: 3829** 3648 3821 Measuring and controlling devices, nec; Reflectors, for lighting equipment: metal; Calibration tapes, for physical testing machines

**(P-14871)**
**GANTNER INSTRUMENTS INC**
402 W Broadway Ste 400, San Diego (92101-3554)
PHONE..............................888 512-5788
Ravi Shukla, *CEO*
**EMP:** 50 **EST:** 2010
**SALES (est):** 2.11MM
**SALES (corp-wide):** 22.73MM **Privately Held**
Web: www.gantner-instruments.com
**SIC: 3829** Measuring and controlling devices, nec
**PA:** Gantner Instruments Gmbh
Montafoner StraBe 4
555 677-4630

**(P-14872)**
**GEOMETRICS INC**
2190 Fortune Dr, San Jose (95131-1815)
PHONE..............................408 428-4244
Mark Prouty, *Pr*
Mark Prouty, *Pr*
Ron Royal, *
Rod Bravo, *
Robert Huggins, *Marketing*
**EMP:** 80 **EST:** 1969
**SALES (est):** 24.74MM **Privately Held**
Web: www.geometrics.com
**SIC: 3829** Geophysical or meteorological electronic equipment
**HQ:** Oyo Corporation U.S.A.
245 N Carmelo Ave Ste 101
Pasadena CA 91107

**(P-14873)**
**GMW ASSOCIATES**
955 Industrial Rd, San Carlos (94070-4117)
PHONE..............................650 802-8292
Ian Walker, *VP*
**EMP:** 50 **EST:** 2018
**SALES (est):** 5.62MM **Privately Held**
Web: www.gmw.com
**SIC: 3829** Measuring and controlling devices, nec

**(P-14874)**
**H2SCAN CORPORATION (PA)**
27215 Turnberry Ln Unit A, Valencia (91355-1068)
PHONE..............................661 775-9575
Michael Allman, *CEO*
Dennis W Reid, *
**EMP:** 22 **EST:** 2002
**SQ FT:** 10,000
**SALES (est):** 8.74MM
**SALES (corp-wide):** 8.74MM **Privately Held**
Web: www.h2scan.com
**SIC: 3829** Hydrometers, except industrial process type

**(P-14875)**
**HAMILTON SUNDSTRAND SPC SYSTMS**
Also Called: Hsssi
960 Overland Ct, San Dimas (91773-1742)
PHONE..............................909 288-5300
Edward Francis, *Ex Dir*
Lawrence R Mcnamara, *Pr*
Daniel C Lee, *
Clinton Gardiner, *
Eugene Dougherty, *
**EMP:** 76 **EST:** 2002
**SQ FT:** 134,000
**SALES (est):** 20.27MM
**SALES (corp-wide):** 68.92B **Publicly Held**
Web: www.collinsaerospace.com
**SIC: 3829** Measuring and controlling devices, nec
**HQ:** Goodrich Corporation
2730 W Tyvola Rd
Charlotte NC 28217
704 423-7000

**(P-14876)**
**HIGHLAND TECHNOLOGY**
650 Potrero Ave, San Francisco (94110-2117)
PHONE..............................415 551-1700
John Larkin, *Pr*
Hugh Callahan, *VP*
Rebecca Mckee, *Sec*
Denise Thiry, *Stockholder*
**EMP:** 20 **EST:** 1984
**SQ FT:** 6,000
**SALES (est):** 6.23MM **Privately Held**
Web: www.highlandtechnology.com
**SIC: 3829** Measuring and controlling devices, nec

**(P-14877)**
**HILZ CABLE ASSEMBLIES INC**
31889 Corydon St Ste 110, Lake Elsinore (92530-8509)
PHONE..............................951 245-0499
Darlene Hilz, *Pr*
▲ **EMP:** 15 **EST:** 1997
**SALES (est):** 5.02MM **Privately Held**
**SIC: 3829** Cable testing machines

**(P-14878)**
**HITACHI PRTICLE ENGRG SVCS INC (DH)**
1177 Quarry Ln Ste A, Pleasanton (94566-4787)
PHONE..............................215 619-4920
Perry Walraven, *CEO*
Eric Schmidt, *CFO*
▲ **EMP:** 24 **EST:** 1970
**SQ FT:** 100,000
**SALES (est):** 1.86MM **Privately Held**
Web: www.pcipa.com
**SIC: 3829** Measuring and controlling devices, nec
**HQ:** Fujifilm Healthcare Manufacturing Corporation
2-1, Shintoyofuta
Kashiwa CHI 277-0

**(P-14879)**
**HORIBA INSTRUMENTS INC**
430 Indio Way, Sunnyvale (94085-4202)
PHONE..............................408 730-4772
Margarita Trujillo, *Opers Mgr*
**EMP:** 57
Web: www.horiba.com
**SIC: 3829** Measuring and controlling devices, nec
**HQ:** Horiba Instruments Incorporated
9755 Research Dr
Irvine CA 92618
949 250-4811

**(P-14880)**
**HORIBA INTERNATIONAL CORP**
9755 Research Dr, Irvine (92618-4626)
PHONE..............................949 250-4811
▲ **EMP:** 930
**SIC: 3829** Measuring and controlling devices, nec

**(P-14881)**
**HORIBA/STEC INCORPORATED**
Also Called: Horiba Semiconductor
430 Indio Way, Sunnyvale (94085-4202)
PHONE..............................408 730-4772
▲ **EMP:** 100
**SIC: 3829** Measuring and controlling devices, nec

**(P-14882)**
**IMAGEGRID INC**
5010 Campus Dr, Newport Beach (92660-2120)
PHONE..............................949 852-1000
**EMP:** 20 **EST:** 2006
**SALES (est):** 2.07MM **Privately Held**
Web: www.candelis.com
**SIC: 3829** Thermometers, including digital: clinical

**(P-14883)**
**IMDEX TECHNOLOGY USA LLC**
179 Cross St, San Luis Obispo (93401-7597)
PHONE..............................805 540-2017
**EMP:** 20 **EST:** 2011
**SALES (est):** 5.35MM **Privately Held**
**SIC: 3829** 8711 Surveying instruments and accessories; Engineering services
**PA:** Imdex Ltd
216 Balcatta Rd

**(P-14884)**
**INTELLIGUARD GROUP LLC**
Also Called: Intellgard Inventory Solutions
12220 World Trade Dr Ste 210, San Diego (92128-3900)

# PRODUCTS & SERVICES SECTION
## 3829 - Measuring And Controlling Devices, Nec (P-14903)

P.O. Box 10481 (83001)
PHONE.................................760 448-9500
Bob Howard, *CEO*
Jennifer Bees Ctrl, *Prin*
Rob Sobie, *Chief Product Officer**
EMP: 50 EST: 2000
SALES (est): 8.02MM **Privately Held**
Web: www.ig.solutions
SIC: **3829** Accelerometers

*(P-14885)*
### INTERNATIONAL SENSOR TECH
3 Whatney Ste 100, Irvine (92618-2836)
PHONE.................................949 452-9000
Thomas Jack Chou, *Pr*
Doris Chou, *
Daniel R Chuo, *
Tai Cam Luu, *Sec*
▲ EMP: 20 EST: 1972
SQ FT: 20,000
SALES (est): 1.71MM **Privately Held**
Web: www.intlsensor.com
SIC: **3829** Gas detectors

*(P-14886)*
### IRROMETER COMPANY INC
Also Called: Watermark
1425 Palmyrita Ave, Riverside (92507-1600)
PHONE.................................951 682-9505
Jeremy Sullivan, *Pr*
Thomas C Penning, *Pr*
Samuel Legget, *Treas*
Jeremy Sullivan, *VP*
EMP: 19 EST: 1951
SQ FT: 9,000
SALES (est): 2.8MM **Privately Held**
Web: www.irrometer.com
SIC: **3829** Measuring and controlling devices, nec

*(P-14887)*
### J L SHEPHERD AND ASSOC INC
1010 Arroyo St, San Fernando (91340-1822)
PHONE.................................818 898-2361
Dorothy Shepherd, *Pr*
Joseph L Shepherd, *
Diana Shepherd, *
Mary Shepherd, *
Dorothy Shepherd, *Sec*
▲ EMP: 27 EST: 1967
SQ FT: 15,000
SALES (est): 2.71MM **Privately Held**
Web: www.jlshepherd.com
SIC: **3829** 3844 Nuclear radiation and testing apparatus; Irradiation equipment, nec

*(P-14888)*
### KALILA MEDICAL INC
1400 Dell Ave Ste C, Campbell (95008-6620)
PHONE.................................408 819-5175
EMP: 25 EST: 2011
SQ FT: 12,536
SALES (est): 3.01MM **Privately Held**
SIC: **3829** Thermometers, including digital; clinical
HQ: Terumo Americas Holding, Inc.
    265 Davidson Ave Ste 320
    Somerset NJ 08873
    732 302-4900

*(P-14889)*
### KAP MEDICAL
1395 Pico St, Corona (92881-3373)
PHONE.................................951 340-4360
Raj K Gowda, *Pr*
Dave Lewis, *

Dan Rosenmayer, *
◆ EMP: 35 EST: 1999
SQ FT: 20,000
SALES (est): 7.42MM **Privately Held**
Web: www.kapmedical.com
SIC: **3829** 8711 Medical diagnostic systems, nuclear; Consulting engineer

*(P-14890)*
### KARL STORZ IMAGING INC (HQ)
Also Called: Optronics
1 S Los Carneros Rd, Goleta (93117-5506)
PHONE.................................805 968-5563
Miles Hartfield, *Genl Mgr*
EMP: 344 EST: 1984
SQ FT: 105,000
SALES (est): 102.5MM
SALES (corp-wide): 2.14B **Privately Held**
Web: www.karlstorz.com
SIC: **3829** 3841 Measuring and controlling devices, nec; Surgical and medical instruments
PA: Karl Storz Se & Co. Kg
    Dr.-Karl-Storz-Str. 34
    74617080

*(P-14891)*
### KWJ ENGINEERING INC (PA)
Also Called: Eco Sensors
8430 Central Ave Ste C, Newark (94560-3457)
PHONE.................................510 794-4296
Joseph R Stetter, *Pr*
Edward F Stetter, *CFO*
EMP: 20 EST: 1993
SQ FT: 10,000
SALES (est): 4.76MM **Privately Held**
Web: www.kwjengineering.com
SIC: **3829** 5084 Gas detectors; Instruments and control equipment

*(P-14892)*
### LEICA GEOSYSTEMS HDS LLC
5000 Executive Pkwy Ste 500, San Ramon (94583-4210)
PHONE.................................925 790-2300
EMP: 97 EST: 2000
SQ FT: 25,000
SALES (est): 12.63MM
SALES (corp-wide): 2.5MM **Privately Held**
Web: www.leica-geosystems.com
SIC: **3829** Measuring and controlling devices, nec
PA: Hexagon Ab
    Lilla Bantorget 15
    86012620

*(P-14893)*
### LOBBY TRAFFIC SYSTEMS INC (PA)
8583 Irvine Center Dr # 10, Irvine (92618-4298)
PHONE.................................800 486-8606
Jeffrey Haden, *Pr*
EMP: 16 EST: 1982
SQ FT: 1,500
SALES (est): 1.57MM
SALES (corp-wide): 1.57MM **Privately Held**
Web: www.crowdcontrol.net
SIC: **3829** 1731 Turnstiles, equipped with counting mechanisms; Safety and security specialization

*(P-14894)*
### MARATHON PRODUCTS INCORPORATED
14500 Doolittle Dr, San Leandro (94577-6615)
P.O. Box 21579 (94620-1579)

PHONE.................................510 562-6450
Jon Nakagawa, *Pr*
Kevin Flynn, *VP*
▲ EMP: 25 EST: 1991
SALES (est): 10.04MM
SALES (corp-wide): 119.3MM **Publicly Held**
Web: www.marathonproducts.com
SIC: **3829** Temperature sensors, except industrial process and aircraft
HQ: Shockwatch, Inc.
    5000 Quorum Dr Ste 550
    Dallas TX 75254

*(P-14895)*
### MEASURE UAS INC
Also Called: Pilatus Unmanned
5862 Bolsa Ave Ste 104, Huntington Beach (92649-1169)
PHONE.................................714 916-6166
Josh Kornoff, *Mgr*
EMP: 25
SALES (corp-wide): 5.56MM **Privately Held**
Web: www.ageagle.com
SIC: **3829** Surveying instruments and accessories
PA: Measure Uas, Inc.
    1701 Rhode Island Ave Nw
    202 793-3052

*(P-14896)*
### MEASUREMENT SPECIALTIES INC
9131 Oakdale Ave Ste 170, Chatsworth (91311-6502)
PHONE.................................818 701-2750
Robert Simon, *Brnch Mgr*
EMP: 187
SALES (corp-wide): 400.61MM **Privately Held**
Web: www.te.com
SIC: **3829** Measuring and controlling devices, nec
PA: Measurement Specialties, Inc.
    1000 Lucas Way
    757 766-1500

*(P-14897)*
### MECHANIZED SCIENCE SEALS INC
Also Called: Ms Bellows
5322 Mcfadden Ave, Huntington Beach (92649-1239)
PHONE.................................714 898-5602
Jon Hamren, *Pr*
Robin Hamren, *Sec*
Victoria Hamren, *Treas*
EMP: 22 EST: 1964
SQ FT: 10,000
SALES (est): 2.59MM **Privately Held**
Web: www.msbellows.com
SIC: **3829** Measuring and controlling devices, nec

*(P-14898)*
### MEGGITT (ORANGE COUNTY) INC (DH)
Also Called: Meggitt Sensing Systems
4 Marconi, Irvine (92618-2525)
PHONE.................................949 493-8181
▲ EMP: 230 EST: 1947
SALES (est): 35.88MM
SALES (corp-wide): 19.93B **Publicly Held**
Web: www.reflection-dental.com
SIC: **3829** Vibration meters, analyzers, and calibrators
HQ: Meggitt Limited
    Ansty Bus.
    Coventry W MIDLANDS CV7 9
    247 682-6900

*(P-14899)*
### METTLER-TOLEDO RAININ LLC (HQ)
7500 Edgewater Dr, Oakland (94621-3027)
PHONE.................................510 564-1600
Gerhard Keller, *Managing Member*
Edward P Weinsoff, *
James Petrek, *
Olivier Filliol, *
Shawn Vadala, *
▲ EMP: 120 EST: 1963
SQ FT: 55,000
SALES (est): 81.1MM
SALES (corp-wide): 3.79B **Publicly Held**
Web: www.mt.com
SIC: **3829** 3821 Measuring and controlling devices, nec; Pipettes, hemocytometer
PA: Mettler-Toledo International Inc.
    1900 Polaris Pkwy
    614 438-4511

*(P-14900)*
### MINUS K TECHNOLOGY INC
460 Hindry Ave Ste C, Inglewood (90301-2044)
PHONE.................................310 348-9656
David L Platus, *Pr*
Nancee Schwartz, *
EMP: 110 EST: 1991
SQ FT: 2,500
SALES (est): 5.25MM **Privately Held**
Web: www.minusk.com
SIC: **3829** Measuring and controlling devices, nec

*(P-14901)*
### MIRION TECHNOLOGIES (US) INC (HQ)
3000 Executive Pkwy Ste 518, San Ramon (94583-4355)
PHONE.................................925 543-0800
John Viscovic, *CEO*
Mike Brumbaugh, *
Seth Rosen, *
Michael Flynn, *
David Najjar, *
EMP: 158 EST: 2005
SQ FT: 10,300
SALES (est): 401.26MM
SALES (corp-wide): 800.9MM **Publicly Held**
Web: www.mirion.com
SIC: **3829** Measuring and controlling devices, nec
PA: Mirion Technologies, Inc.
    1218 Menlo Dr
    770 432-2744

*(P-14902)*
### MITCHELL INSTRUMENTS CO INC
Also Called: Mitchell Instruments
2875 Scott St Ste 101, Vista (92081-8559)
PHONE.................................760 744-2690
James Desportes, *CEO*
◆ EMP: 15 EST: 1970
SALES (est): 3.23MM **Privately Held**
Web: www.mitchellinstrument.com
SIC: **3829** Measuring and controlling devices, nec

*(P-14903)*
### NDC TECHNOLOGIES INC
5314 Irwindale Ave, Irwindale (91706-2070)
PHONE.................................626 960-3300
▲ EMP: 53
SALES (corp-wide): 2.63B **Publicly Held**
Web: www.ndc.com

## 3829 - Measuring And Controlling Devices, Nec (P-14904)

SIC: 3829 Measuring and controlling devices, nec
HQ: Ndc Technologies, Inc.
8001 Technology Blvd
Dayton OH 45424
937 233-9935

**(P-14904)**
**NOAH MEDICAL CORPORATION**
2075 Zanker Rd, San Jose (95131-2107)
PHONE..........................718 564-3717
Jian Zhang, *CEO*
Emma Yang, *
EMP: 75 EST: 2018
SALES (est): 10.94MM **Privately Held**
Web: www.noahmed.com
SIC: 3829 Medical diagnostic systems, nuclear

**(P-14905)**
**OMNI OPTICAL PRODUCTS INC (PA)**
17282 Eastman, Irvine (92614-5522)
PHONE..........................714 634-5700
Ken Panique, *Pr*
▲ EMP: 25 EST: 1986
SALES (est): 1.9MM
SALES (corp-wide): 1.9MM **Privately Held**
SIC: 3829 Surveying instruments and accessories

**(P-14906)**
**OPTIVUS PROTON THERAPY INC**
1475 Victoria Ct, San Bernardino (92408-2831)
P.O. Box 608 (92354-0608)
PHONE..........................909 799-8300
Jon W Slater, *CEO*
Daryl L Anderson, *
EMP: 75 EST: 1992
SQ FT: 35,000
SALES (est): 15.85MM **Privately Held**
Web: www.optivus.com
SIC: 3829 7371 8742 3699 Nuclear radiation and testing apparatus; Custom computer programming services; Maintenance management consultant; Electrical equipment and supplies, nec

**(P-14907)**
**OUSTER INC (PA)**
350 Treat Ave Ste 1, San Francisco (94110-1948)
PHONE..........................415 987-6972
Angus Pacala, *CEO*
Susan Heystee, *Ch Bd*
Mark Frichtl, *COO*
Oliver Hutaff, *CFO*
EMP: 37 EST: 2015
SALES (est): 113.39MM
SALES (corp-wide): 113.39MM **Privately Held**
Web: www.ouster.com
SIC: 3829 Surveying instruments and accessories

**(P-14908)**
**PACIFIC DIVERSIFIED CAPITAL CO**
101 Ash St, San Diego (92101-3017)
PHONE..........................619 696-2000
Steve Baum, *Ch Bd*
Thomas Page, *
Henry Huta, *
Michael Lowell, *
EMP: 39 EST: 1983
SALES (est): 4.94MM
SALES (corp-wide): 16.72B **Publicly Held**

SIC: 3829 Measuring and controlling devices, nec
HQ: San Diego Gas & Electric Company
8330 Century Park Ct
San Diego CA 92123
619 696-2000

**(P-14909)**
**PACIFIC INSTRUMENTS INC**
4080 Pike Ln, Concord (94520-1227)
PHONE..........................925 827-9010
John Hueckel, *Pr*
Norm Hueckel, *VP*
▲ EMP: 21 EST: 1966
SQ FT: 18,000
SALES (est): 4.93MM
SALES (corp-wide): 355.05MM **Publicly Held**
Web: www.pacificinstruments.com
SIC: 3829 Measuring and controlling devices, nec
HQ: Vishay Precision Israel Ltd
18 Tzela Hahar, Entrance
Modiin-Maccabim-Reut 71795

**(P-14910)**
**PROPRIETARY CONTROLS SYSTEMS**
Also Called: P C S C
3830 Del Amo Blvd # 102, Torrance (90503-2119)
PHONE..........................310 303-3600
Masami Kosaka, *Pr*
Robert K Takahashi, *
▲ EMP: 45 EST: 1983
SALES (est): 5.9MM
SALES (corp-wide): 9.94MM **Privately Held**
Web: www.pcscsecurity.com
SIC: 3829 3669 Measuring and controlling devices, nec; Burglar alarm apparatus, electric
PA: Ttik, Inc.
3541 Challenger St
310 303-3600

**(P-14911)**
**QUALITY CONTROL SOLUTIONS INC**
43339 Business Park Dr Ste 101, Temecula (92590-3636)
PHONE..........................951 676-1616
Louis Todd, *Pr*
Denise Todd, *Sec*
EMP: 16 EST: 1979
SQ FT: 7,500
SALES (est): 2.59MM **Privately Held**
Web: www.qc-solutions.com
SIC: 3829 5084 Measuring and controlling devices, nec; Instruments and control equipment

**(P-14912)**
**RADCAL CORPORATION**
Also Called: Mdh
426 W Duarte Rd, Monrovia (91016-4591)
PHONE..........................626 357-7921
Margarita Blinchik, *CEO*
Curt Harkless, *
▲ EMP: 35 EST: 1973
SQ FT: 10,000
SALES (est): 8.19MM
SALES (corp-wide): 339.04MM **Privately Held**
Web: www.radcal.com
SIC: 3829 Nuclear radiation and testing apparatus
PA: Ion Beam Applications
Chemin Du Cyclotron 3
10475811

**(P-14913)**
**RAE SYSTEMS INC (DH)**
1349 Moffett Park Dr, Sunnyvale (94089-1134)
PHONE..........................408 952-8200
Robert Chen, *Pr*
Michael Hansen, *CFO*
Peter C Hsi Ph.d., *VP*
Ming Ting Tang Ph.d., *Ofcr*
Mark Heap, *Corporate Controller*
▲ EMP: 27 EST: 2002
SQ FT: 67,000
SALES (est): 496.48MM
SALES (corp-wide): 36.66B **Publicly Held**
Web: www.honeywell.com
SIC: 3829 3812 3699 Gas detectors; Search and detection systems and instruments; Security control equipment and systems
HQ: Honeywell Analytics Inc.
405 Barclay Blvd
Lincolnshire IL 60069
847 955-4175

**(P-14914)**
**REDLINE DETECTION LLC (PA)**
828 W Taft Ave, Orange (92865-4232)
PHONE..........................714 579-6961
Zachary Parker, *CEO*
▲ EMP: 23 EST: 2004
SQ FT: 21,000
SALES (est): 14.62MM
SALES (corp-wide): 14.62MM **Privately Held**
Web: www.redlinedetection.com
SIC: 3829 Liquid leak detection equipment

**(P-14915)**
**SACRAMENTO COOLING SYSTEMS INC**
5466 E Lamona Ave Ste 1022, Fresno (93727-2359)
PHONE..........................559 253-9660
Kevin Castle, *Pr*
EMP: 15
SALES (corp-wide): 11.92MM **Privately Held**
Web: www.lhairco.com
SIC: 3829 Measuring and controlling devices, nec
PA: Sacramento Cooling Systems, Inc.
2530 Warren Dr
916 677-1000

**(P-14916)**
**SECO MANUFACTURING COMPANY INC**
4155 Oasis Rd, Redding (96003-0859)
PHONE..........................530 225-8155
Steven W Berglund, *CEO*
Mike Dahl, *
▲ EMP: 120 EST: 1978
SQ FT: 73,400
SALES (est): 24.79MM
SALES (corp-wide): 3.8B **Publicly Held**
Web: www.surveying.com
SIC: 3829 Surveying instruments and accessories
PA: Trimble Inc.
10368 Westmoor Dr
720 887-6100

**(P-14917)**
**SEMCO**
1495 S Gage St, San Bernardino (92408-2835)
PHONE..........................909 799-9666
Shawn Martin, *Owner*
▲ EMP: 25 EST: 1994
SQ FT: 5,400
SALES (est): 2.35MM **Privately Held**

Web: www.semco.com
SIC: 3829 3599 Physical property testing equipment; Machine shop, jobbing and repair

**(P-14918)**
**SENTRAN LLC (PA)**
4355 E Lowell St Ste F, Ontario (91761-2225)
PHONE..........................888 545-8988
▲ EMP: 15 EST: 1998
SQ FT: 5,000
SALES (est): 3.24MM
SALES (corp-wide): 3.24MM **Privately Held**
Web: www.sentranllc.com
SIC: 3829 Measuring and controlling devices, nec

**(P-14919)**
**SIERRA MONITOR CORPORATION (HQ)**
Also Called: Sierra Monitor
1991 Tarob Ct, Milpitas (95035-6840)
PHONE..........................408 262-6611
▲ EMP: 56 EST: 1967
SQ FT: 28,000
SALES (est): 7.24MM
SALES (corp-wide): 1.79B **Publicly Held**
Web: www.sierramonitor.com
SIC: 3829 3822 Measuring and controlling devices, nec; Environmental controls
PA: Msa Safety Incorporated
1000 Cranberry Woods Dr
724 776-8600

**(P-14920)**
**SKF CONDITION MONITORING INC (DH)**
Also Called: SKF Aptitude Exchange
9444 Balboa Ave Ste 150, San Diego (92123-4377)
PHONE..........................858 496-3400
Mark Mcginn, *CEO*
EMP: 120 EST: 1983
SQ FT: 31,000
SALES (est): 4.98MM
SALES (corp-wide): 740.17MM **Privately Held**
SIC: 3829 Vibration meters, analyzers, and calibrators
HQ: Skf Usa Inc.
801 Lakeview Dr Ste 120
Blue Bell PA 19422
267 436-6000

**(P-14921)**
**SOILMOISTURE EQUIPMENT CORP**
601 Pine Ave Ste A, Goleta (93117-3886)
P.O. Box 30025 (93130-0025)
PHONE..........................805 964-3525
Whitney Skaling, *CEO*
Percy E Skaling, *
Jan Skaling, *
Kenneth Macaulay, *
▲ EMP: 23 EST: 1950
SQ FT: 14,000
SALES (est): 4.86MM **Privately Held**
Web: www.soilmoisture.com
SIC: 3829 Measuring and controlling devices, nec
PA: Stevens Water Monitoring Systems, Inc.
12067 Ne Glenn Wding Dr S

**(P-14922)**
**SOLANO DIAGNOSTICS IMAGING**

## 3841 - Surgical And Medical Instruments (P-14941)

1101 B Gale Wilson Blvd Ste 100, Fairfield (94533-3771)
PHONE...............................707 646-4646
Adrian Ritts, *Mgr*
Laverna Hubbard, *Admn*
**EMP:** 17 **EST:** 1990
**SQ FT:** 4,000
**SALES (est):** 2.23MM **Privately Held**
**Web:** www.northbay.org
**SIC: 3829** 8071 8011  Medical diagnostic systems, nuclear; Medical laboratories; Radiologist

**(P-14923)**
**SOLMETRIC CORPORATION**
Also Called: Suneye
117 Morris St Ste 100, Sebastopol (95472-3846)
PHONE...............................707 823-4600
Macdonald Willand, *Pr*
Robert Macdonald, *VP Fin*
▲ **EMP:** 25 **EST:** 2006
**SALES (est):** 4.29MM
**SALES (corp-wide):** 6.07B **Publicly Held**
**Web:** www.solmetric.com
**SIC: 3829**  Solarimeters
**HQ:** Fluke Corporation
6920 Seaway Blvd
Everett WA 98203
425 347-6100

**(P-14924)**
**SPECTRAL DYNAMICS INC (PA)**
Also Called: Spectral Dynamics
2199 Zanker Rd, San Jose (95131-2109)
PHONE...............................760 761-0440
Stewart J Slykhous, *CEO*
James D Tucker, *CFO*
▲ **EMP:** 20 **EST:** 1988
**SQ FT:** 12,000
**SALES (est):** 7.93MM
**SALES (corp-wide):** 7.93MM **Privately Held**
**Web:** www.spectraldynamics.com
**SIC: 3829**  Measuring and controlling devices, nec

**(P-14925)**
**SPECTRAL LABS INCORPORATED**
Also Called: Spectral Labs
15920 Bernardo Center Dr, San Diego (92127-1828)
PHONE...............................858 451-0540
James H Winso, *Pr*
Eric Ackermann, *VP*
John Rolando, *Stockholder*
James Adams, *Proj Mgr*
**EMP:** 20 **EST:** 2008
**SQ FT:** 2,000
**SALES (est):** 3.32MM **Privately Held**
**Web:** www.spectrallabs.com
**SIC: 3829**  Measuring and controlling devices, nec

**(P-14926)**
**STRUCTURAL DIAGNOSTICS INC**
Also Called: S D I
650 Via Alondra, Camarillo (93012-3873)
PHONE...............................805 987-7755
Paul R Teagle, *Pr*
**EMP:** 33 **EST:** 1994
**SQ FT:** 30,000
**SALES (est):** 4MM **Privately Held**
**Web:** www.sdindt.com
**SIC: 3829**  Measuring and controlling devices, nec

**(P-14927)**
**TELATEMP CORP**
2910 E La Palma Ave Ste C, Anaheim (92806-2618)
PHONE...............................714 414-0343
Daniel Stack, *Pr*
Evelyn Darringer, *VP*
**EMP:** 15 **EST:** 1972
**SQ FT:** 3,200
**SALES (est):** 2.49MM **Privately Held**
**Web:** www.telatemp.com
**SIC: 3829**  Thermometers and temperature sensors

**(P-14928)**
**TELEDYNE DGITAL IMAGING US INC**
Also Called: Teledyne RAD-Icon Imaging
765 Sycamore Dr, Milpitas (95035-7465)
PHONE...............................408 736-6000
**EMP:** 15
**SALES (corp-wide):** 5.64B **Publicly Held**
**Web:** www.photometrics.com
**SIC: 3829** 3674  Measuring and controlling devices, nec; Semiconductors and related devices
**HQ:** Teledyne Digital Imaging Us, Inc.
700 Tchnlogy Pk Dr Ste 11
Billerica MA 01821
978 670-2000

**(P-14929)**
**TELEDYNE INSTRUMENTS INC**
Also Called: Teledyne API
9970 Carroll Canyon Rd Ste A, San Diego (92131-1106)
PHONE...............................619 239-5959
Jeff Franks, *Brnch Mgr*
**EMP:** 100
**SALES (corp-wide):** 5.64B **Publicly Held**
**Web:** www.teledyne-api.com
**SIC: 3829** 3823  Measuring and controlling devices, nec; Process control instruments
**HQ:** Teledyne Instruments, Inc.
16830 Chestnut St
City Of Industry CA 91748
626 934-1500

**(P-14930)**
**TELEDYNE INSTRUMENTS INC**
Also Called: Teledyne Analytical Instrs
16830 Chestnut St, City Of Industry (91748-1017)
PHONE...............................626 934-1500
Tom Compas, *Brnch Mgr*
**EMP:** 170
**SQ FT:** 70,000
**SALES (corp-wide):** 5.64B **Publicly Held**
**Web:** www.teledyne-ai.com
**SIC: 3829**  Measuring and controlling devices, nec
**HQ:** Teledyne Instruments, Inc.
16830 Chestnut St
City Of Industry CA 91748
626 934-1500

**(P-14931)**
**TELEDYNE INSTRUMENTS INC**
Teledyne Advnced Plltion Instr
9970 Carroll Canyon Rd, San Diego (92131-1106)
PHONE...............................858 657-9800
Robert Mehrabian, *CEO*
**EMP:** 49
**SALES (corp-wide):** 5.64B **Publicly Held**
**Web:** www.teledyne-api.com
**SIC: 3829**  Measuring and controlling devices, nec
**HQ:** Teledyne Instruments, Inc.
16830 Chestnut St
City Of Industry CA 91748
626 934-1500

**(P-14932)**
**TELEDYNE RAD-ICON IMAGING CORP**
765 Sycamore Dr, Milpitas (95035-7465)
PHONE...............................408 736-6000
▼ **EMP:** 15
**Web:** www.teledynedalsa.com
**SIC: 3829** 3674  Measuring and controlling devices, nec; Semiconductors and related devices

**(P-14933)**
**TEMPTRON ENGINEERING INC**
7823 Deering Ave, Canoga Park (91304-5006)
PHONE...............................818 346-4900
Edward Skei, *Pr*
Beverly Skei, *
**EMP:** 35 **EST:** 1971
**SQ FT:** 13,000
**SALES (est):** 6.85MM **Privately Held**
**Web:** www.temptronengineeringinc.com
**SIC: 3829** 3769 3823  Measuring and controlling devices, nec; Space vehicle equipment, nec; Temperature instruments: industrial process type

**(P-14934)**
**THERM-X OF CALIFORNIA INC (HQ)**
Also Called: E&S Precision Machine
3200 Investment Blvd, Hayward (94545-3807)
P.O. Box 768 (94507)
PHONE...............................510 441-7566
Dan Trujillo, *CEO*
Skip Johnson, *
Linda Trujillo, *
**EMP:** 74 **EST:** 1976
**SQ FT:** 74,300
**SALES (est):** 32.36MM
**SALES (corp-wide):** 4.57MM **Privately Held**
**Web:** www.therm-x.com
**SIC: 3829**  Measuring and controlling devices, nec
**PA:** Nibe Industrier Ab
Jarnvagsgatan 40
43373000

**(P-14935)**
**TOPCON POSITIONING SYSTEMS INC (DH)**
Also Called: Topcon
7400 National Dr, Livermore (94550-7340)
PHONE...............................925 245-8300
Ivan Di Federico, *Pr*
Raymond O'connor, *Ch Bd*
David Mudrick, *
M Yamazaki, *
James Orsino, *
◆ **EMP:** 122 **EST:** 1993
**SQ FT:** 80,000
**SALES (est):** 93.77MM **Privately Held**
**Web:** www.topconpositioning.com
**SIC: 3829** 3625 3823 3699  Surveying instruments and accessories; Relays and industrial controls; Process control instruments; Electrical equipment and supplies, nec
**HQ:** Topcon America Corporation
111 Bauer Dr
Oakland NJ 07436
201 599-5100

**(P-14936)**
**TRANSDUCER TECHNIQUES LLC**
42480 Rio Nedo, Temecula (92590-3734)
PHONE...............................951 719-3965
Randy A Baker, *Managing Member*
**EMP:** 37 **EST:** 1978
**SQ FT:** 27,000
**SALES (est):** 8.4MM **Privately Held**
**Web:** www.transducertechniques.com
**SIC: 3829**  Measuring and controlling devices, nec

**(P-14937)**
**VALIDYNE ENGINEERING CORP**
8626 Wilbur Ave, Northridge (91324-4438)
P.O. Box 8626 (91327-8626)
PHONE...............................818 886-8488
▲ **EMP:** 21 **EST:** 1968
**SALES (est):** 5.42MM **Privately Held**
**Web:** www.validyne.com
**SIC: 3829** 3669 3823  Pressure transducers; Signaling apparatus, electric; Process control instruments

**(P-14938)**
**VISBY MEDICAL INC**
3010 N 1st St, San Jose (95134-2023)
PHONE...............................408 650-8878
Thomas Prescott, *
Gary Schoolnik, *CMO**
**EMP:** 250 **EST:** 2012
**SALES (est):** 38.08MM **Privately Held**
**Web:** www.visbymedical.com
**SIC: 3829**  Medical diagnostic systems, nuclear

## 3841 Surgical And Medical Instruments

**(P-14939)**
**AALTO SCIENTIFIC LTD**
1959 Kellogg Ave, Carlsbad (92008-6582)
PHONE...............................800 748-6674
R Reynolds, *Director of Information*
**EMP:** 25 **EST:** 2018
**SALES (est):** 1.19MM **Privately Held**
**Web:** www.aaltoscientific.com
**SIC: 3841**  Surgical and medical instruments

**(P-14940)**
**ABBOTT LABORATORIES**
Also Called: Abbott Vascular
3200 Lakeside Dr, Santa Clara (95054-2807)
P.O. Box 58167 (95052-8167)
PHONE...............................408 845-3000
Jean Reyda, *Brnch Mgr*
**EMP:** 750
**SALES (corp-wide):** 40.11B **Publicly Held**
**Web:** www.abbott.com
**SIC: 3841** 8731  Surgical and medical instruments; Commercial physical research
**PA:** Abbott Laboratories
100 Abbott Park Rd
224 667-6100

**(P-14941)**
**ABBOTT LABORATORIES**
Also Called: Abbott Diagnostics Division
4551 Great America Pkwy, Santa Clara (95054-1208)
PHONE...............................408 330-0057
Jim Janik, *Brnch Mgr*
**EMP:** 450
**SQ FT:** 117,500
**SALES (corp-wide):** 40.11B **Publicly Held**
**Web:** www.abbott**

# 3841 - Surgical And Medical Instruments (P-14942)

**SIC: 3841** Medical instruments and equipment, blood and bone work
**PA:** Abbott Laboratories
100 Abbott Park Rd
224 667-6100

### (P-14942)
### ABBOTT VASCULAR INC
Also Called: Abbott Vascular
30590 Cochise Cir, Murrieta (92563-2501)
P.O. Box 3020 (60064-9320)
**PHONE**..................................408 845-3186
**EMP:** 568
**SALES (corp-wide):** 40.11B **Publicly Held**
**Web:** www.abbott.com
**SIC: 3841** Surgical instruments and apparatus
**HQ:** Abbott Vascular Inc.
3200 Lakeside Dr
Santa Clara CA 95054
408 845-3000

### (P-14943)
### ABBOTT VASCULAR INC
42301 Zevo Dr Ste D, Temecula (92590-3731)
**PHONE**..................................951 914-2400
Rhonda Reddick, *Mgr*
**EMP:** 665
**SALES (corp-wide):** 40.11B **Publicly Held**
**Web:** www.cardiovascular.abbott
**SIC: 3841** Catheters
**HQ:** Abbott Vascular Inc.
3200 Lakeside Dr
Santa Clara CA 95054
408 845-3000

### (P-14944)
### ABBOTT VASCULAR INC (HQ)
3200 Lakeside Dr, Santa Clara (95054-2807)
**PHONE**..................................408 845-3000
John M Capek, *Pr*
Charles D Foltz, *
Mark Murray, *
▲ **EMP:** 230 **EST:** 1995
**SQ FT:** 370,000
**SALES (est):** 686.57MM
**SALES (corp-wide):** 40.11B **Publicly Held**
**Web:** www.cardiovascular.abbott
**SIC: 3841** Surgical and medical instruments
**PA:** Abbott Laboratories
100 Abbott Park Rd
224 667-6100

### (P-14945)
### ABLACON INC
3350 Scott Blvd, Santa Clara (95054-3104)
**PHONE**..................................303 955-5620
Marty Grasse, *CEO*
**EMP:** 16 **EST:** 2015
**SALES (est):** 1.59MM **Privately Held**
**Web:** www.ablacon.com
**SIC: 3841** Surgical and medical instruments

### (P-14946)
### ACCESS CLOSURE INC
Also Called: Cardinal Health 245 Henrico Co
5452 Betsy Ross Dr, Santa Clara (95054-1101)
**PHONE**..................................408 610-6500
Gregory D Casciaro, *Pr*
John J Buckley, *
Susan Aloyan, *
Stephen Mackinnon, *
Ariel Sutton, *
**EMP:** 344 **EST:** 2002
**SQ FT:** 40,000
**SALES (est):** 15.91MM
**SALES (corp-wide):** 226.83B **Publicly Held**

**SIC: 3841** Surgical and medical instruments
**PA:** Cardinal Health, Inc.
7000 Cardinal Pl
614 757-5000

### (P-14947)
### ACCLARENT INC
31 Technology Dr Ste 200, Irvine (92618-2302)
**PHONE**..................................650 687-5888
David Shepherd, *Pr*
Cristina Todasco, *
**EMP:** 400 **EST:** 2004
**SALES (est):** 28.1MM **Publicly Held**
**Web:** www.acclarent.com
**SIC: 3841** Surgical and medical instruments
**PA:** Integra Lifesciences Holdings Corporation
1100 Campus Rd

### (P-14948)
### ACCRIVA DGNOSTICS HOLDINGS INC (DH)
Also Called: Itc Nexus Holding Company
6260 Sequence Dr, San Diego (92121-4358)
**PHONE**..................................858 404-8203
Scott Cramer, *CEO*
Greg Tibbitts, *CFO*
Tom Whalen, *CSO*
**EMP:** 350 **EST:** 2010
**SALES (est):** 55.46MM **Privately Held**
**Web:** www.werfen.com
**SIC: 3841** 2835 6719 Diagnostic apparatus, medical; Blood derivative diagnostic agents ; Investment holding companies, except banks
**HQ:** Instrumentation Laboratory Company
180 Hartwell Rd
Bedford MA 01730

### (P-14949)
### ACI MEDICAL LLC
1857 Diamond St Ste A, San Marcos (92078-5129)
**PHONE**..................................760 744-4400
**EMP:** 47 **EST:** 1984
**SALES (est):** 5.69MM **Privately Held**
**Web:** www.acimedical.com
**SIC: 3841** Diagnostic apparatus, medical

### (P-14950)
### ACUTUS MEDICAL INC
Also Called: Acutus Medical
2210 Faraday Ave Ste 100, Carlsbad (92008-7225)
**PHONE**..................................442 232-6080
David Roman, *Pr*
R Scott Huennekens, *
Takeo Mukai, *Sr VP*
Steven Mcquillan, *Sr VP*
**EMP:** 160 **EST:** 2011
**SQ FT:** 50,800
**SALES (est):** 7.16MM **Privately Held**
**Web:** www.acutusmedical.com
**SIC: 3841** Surgical and medical instruments

### (P-14951)
### ADVANCED STERLIZATION (HQ)
Also Called: A S P
33 Technology Dr, Irvine (92618-2346)
**PHONE**..................................800 595-0200
Bernard Zovighian, *CEO*
**EMP:** 104 **EST:** 1991
**SALES (est):** 21.23MM
**SALES (corp-wide):** 6.07B **Publicly Held**
**Web:** www.asp.com
**SIC: 3841** Surgical and medical instruments
**PA:** Fortive Corporation
6920 Seaway Blvd

425 446-5000

### (P-14952)
### AJINOMOTO ALTHEA INC (HQ)
Also Called: Ajinomoto Bio-Pharma Services
11040 Roselle St, San Diego (92121-1205)
**PHONE**..................................858 882-0123
David Enloe Junior, *Pr*
Martha J Demski, *
Chris Duffy, *
Ej Brandreth, *Regional*
Jack Wright, *
**EMP:** 25 **EST:** 1998
**SALES (est):** 81.4MM **Privately Held**
**Web:** www.ajibio-pharma.com
**SIC: 3841** 2836 Hypodermic needles and syringes; Coagulation products
**PA:** Ajinomoto Co., Inc.
1-15-1, Kyobashi

### (P-14953)
### AKURA MEDICAL INC
170 Knowles Dr, Los Gatos (95032-1833)
**PHONE**..................................408 560-2500
**EMP:** 38 **EST:** 2019
**SALES (est):** 4.79MM **Privately Held**
**Web:** www.akuramed.com
**SIC: 3841** Surgical and medical instruments

### (P-14954)
### ALCON LENSX INC (DH)
Also Called: Alcon
15800 Alton Pkwy, Irvine (92618-3818)
**PHONE**..................................949 753-1393
Kevin J Buehler, *CEO*
Elaine Whitbeck, *CLO*
**EMP:** 99 **EST:** 2006
**SQ FT:** 20,000
**SALES (est):** 15.8MM **Privately Held**
**Web:** www.myalcon.com
**SIC: 3841** Surgical lasers
**HQ:** Alcon, Inc.
1132 Ferris Rd
Amelia OH 45102
513 722-1037

### (P-14955)
### ALCON RESEARCH LTD
Also Called: ALCON RESEARCH, LTD.
15800 Alton Pkwy, Irvine (92618-3818)
**PHONE**..................................949 387-2142
Ed Richards, *Owner*
**EMP:** 51
**Web:** www.alcon.com
**SIC: 3841** Surgical instruments and apparatus
**HQ:** Alcon Research, Llc
6201 S Fwy
Fort Worth TX 76134
817 551-4555

### (P-14956)
### ALCON VISION LLC
24514 Sunshine Dr, Laguna Niguel (92677-7826)
**PHONE**..................................949 753-6218
**EMP:** 343
**Web:** www.alcon.com
**SIC: 3841** Surgical and medical instruments
**HQ:** Alcon Vision, Llc
6201 South Fwy
Fort Worth TX 76134
817 293-0450

### (P-14957)
### ALCON VISION LLC
Also Called: Alcon Surgical
15800 Alton Pkwy, Irvine (92618-3818)
P.O. Box 19587 (92623-9587)
**PHONE**..................................949 753-6488

Kenneth Lickel, *Mgr*
**EMP:** 600
**SQ FT:** 32,000
**Web:** www.alcon.com
**SIC: 3841** 3851 5049 Surgical and medical instruments; Ophthalmic goods; Optical goods
**HQ:** Alcon Vision, Llc
6201 South Fwy
Fort Worth TX 76134
817 293-0450

### (P-14958)
### ALL MANUFACTURERS INC
Also Called: Allied Harbor Aerospace Fas
1831 Commerce St Ste 101, Corona (92878-5026)
**PHONE**..................................951 280-4200
Jon R Gerwin, *CEO*
Ron Gerwin, *
**EMP:** 197 **EST:** 1993
**SALES (est):** 8.04MM **Privately Held**
**Web:** www.allied1.com
**SIC: 3841** 3694 Surgical and medical instruments; Motors, starting: automotive and aircraft

### (P-14959)
### ALLIANCE MEDICAL PRODUCTS INC (DH)
Also Called: Siegfried Irvine
9342 Jeronimo Rd, Irvine (92618-1903)
**PHONE**..................................949 768-4690
Robert Hughes, *CEO*
Brian Jones, *
Frank Pham, *
▲ **EMP:** 41 **EST:** 2001
**SQ FT:** 55,000
**SALES (est):** 49.25MM **Privately Held**
**Web:** www.siegfried.ch
**SIC: 3841** 7819 Medical instruments and equipment, blood and bone work; Laboratory service, motion picture
**HQ:** Siegfried Usa Holding , Inc.
33 Industrial Park Rd
Pennsville NJ 08070
856 678-3601

### (P-14960)
### ALLIANCE MEDICAL PRODUCTS INC
Also Called: Siegfried Irvine
9292 Jeronimo Rd, Irvine (92618-1905)
**PHONE**..................................949 664-9616
**EMP:** 45
**Web:** www.siegfried.ch
**SIC: 3841** Medical instruments and equipment, blood and bone work
**HQ:** Alliance Medical Products, Inc.
9342 Jeronimo Rd
Irvine CA 92618
949 768-4690

### (P-14961)
### ALPHATEC HOLDINGS INC (PA)
Also Called: ALPHATEC
1950 Camino Vida Roble, Carlsbad (92008-6505)
**PHONE**..................................760 431-9286
Patrick S Miles, *Pr*
Scott Lish, *COO*
J Todd Koning, *Ex VP*
Tyson Marshall, *Corporate Secretary*
**EMP:** 428 **EST:** 1990
**SQ FT:** 121,541
**SALES (est):** 482.26MM **Publicly Held**
**Web:** www.atecspine.com
**SIC: 3841** Surgical and medical instruments

## PRODUCTS & SERVICES SECTION
### 3841 - Surgical And Medical Instruments (P-14982)

**(P-14962)**
**ALPINE BIOMED CORP**
1501 Industrial Rd, San Carlos (94070-4111)
PHONE.................650 802-0400
**EMP:** 52 **EST:** 1994
**SQ FT:** 1,460
**SALES (est):** 9MM
**SALES (corp-wide):** 28.49MM Privately Held
**SIC: 3841** Catheters
**HQ:** Natus Medical Incorporated
6701 Koll Center Pkwy # 12
Pleasanton CA 94566
925 223-6700

**(P-14963)**
**AMADA WELD TECH INC**
245 E El Norte St, Monrovia (91016-4828)
PHONE.................626 303-5676
Susan Gu, *Mgr*
**EMP:** 30
**Web:** www.amadaweldtech.com
**SIC: 3841** Surgical and medical instruments
**HQ:** Amada Weld Tech Inc.
1820 S Myrtle Ave
Monrovia CA 91016

**(P-14964)**
**AMEDITECH INC**
9940 Mesa Rim Rd, San Diego (92121-2910)
PHONE.................858 535-1968
Robert Joel, *Prin*
▲ **EMP:** 118 **EST:** 1999
**SQ FT:** 47,000
**SALES (est):** 11.92MM
**SALES (corp-wide):** 40.11B Publicly Held
**SIC: 3841** Medical instruments and equipment, blood and bone work
**HQ:** Alere Inc.
51 Sawyer Rd Ste 200
Waltham MA 02453
781 647-3900

**(P-14965)**
**AMERICAN MSTR TECH SCNTFIC INC**
Also Called: American Histology Reagent Co
1330 Thurman St, Lodi (95240-3145)
P.O. Box 2539 (95241-2539)
PHONE.................209 368-4031
Dan Eckert, *CEO*
Brandon B Jones, *
Jeff Kupp, *
Kameron Teyes, *
▲ **EMP:** 126 **EST:** 1979
**SQ FT:** 25,000
**SALES (est):** 5.06MM
**SALES (corp-wide):** 50.28MM Privately Held
**Web:** www.statlab.com
**SIC: 3841** 2835 Medical instruments and equipment, blood and bone work; Cytology and histology diagnostic agents
**PA:** Slmp, Llc
2090 Commerce Dr
972 436-1010

**(P-14966)**
**AMO USA INC**
1700 E Saint Andrew Pl, Santa Ana (92705-4933)
PHONE.................714 247-8200
Tom Frinzi, *Pr*
**EMP:** 200 **EST:** 2002
**SQ FT:** 100,000
**SALES (est):** 4.01MM
**SALES (corp-wide):** 85.16B Publicly Held
**SIC: 3841** 3845 Surgical and medical instruments; Laser systems and equipment, medical
**HQ:** Johnson & Johnson Surgical Vision, Inc.
31 Technology Dr Bldg 29a
Irvine CA 92618
949 581-5799

**(P-14967)**
**ANCORA HEART INC**
4001 Burton Dr, Santa Clara (95054-1585)
PHONE.................408 727-1105
Jeffrey M Closs, *Pr*
Mark Miles, *CCO**
**EMP:** 50 **EST:** 2002
**SALES (est):** 7.51MM Privately Held
**Web:** www.ancoraheart.com
**SIC: 3841** Diagnostic apparatus, medical

**(P-14968)**
**ANGIOSCORE INC**
5055 Brandin Ct, Fremont (94538-3140)
PHONE.................510 933-7900
**EMP:** 140
**SIC: 3841** Surgical and medical instruments

**(P-14969)**
**APEX MEDICAL TECHNOLOGIES INC**
10064 Mesa Ridge Ct Ste 202, San Diego (92121-2948)
PHONE.................858 535-0012
▲ **EMP:** 20 **EST:** 1985
**SALES (est):** 3.55MM Privately Held
**Web:** www.apexmedtech.com
**SIC: 3841** 8731 Surgical and medical instruments; Medical research, commercial

**(P-14970)**
**APPLIED CARDIAC SYSTEMS INC**
1 Hughes Ste A, Irvine (92618-2021)
PHONE.................949 855-9366
Loren A Manera, *CEO*
Tricia Meads, *
Susan Marcus, *
Robert Wilks, *
▲ **EMP:** 64 **EST:** 1981
**SQ FT:** 18,000
**SALES (est):** 8.82MM Privately Held
**Web:** www.cardiacmonitoring.com
**SIC: 3841** Diagnostic apparatus, medical

**(P-14971)**
**APPLIED MANUFACTURING LLC**
22872 Avenida Empresa, Rancho Santa Margari (92688-2650)
PHONE.................949 713-8000
Tom Wachli, *Pr*
**EMP:** 1200 **EST:** 2017
**SALES (est):** 21.23MM
**SALES (corp-wide):** 699.84MM Privately Held
**Web:** www.appliedmed.com
**SIC: 3841** Surgical and medical instruments
**HQ:** Applied Medical Resources Corporation
22872 Avenida Empresa
Rancho Santa Margari CA 92688
949 713-8000

**(P-14972)**
**APPLIED MEDICAL CORPORATION (PA)**
Also Called: Applied Medical Resources
22872 Avenida Empresa, Rancho Santa Margari (92688-2650)
PHONE.................949 713-8000
Said Hilal, *CEO*
**EMP:** 225 **EST:** 1987
**SALES (est):** 699.84MM
**SALES (corp-wide):** 699.84MM Privately Held
**Web:** www.appliedmedical.com
**SIC: 3841** Surgical and medical instruments

**(P-14973)**
**APPLIED MEDICAL DIST CORP**
22872 Avenida Empresa, Rcho Sta Marg (92688-2650)
PHONE.................949 713-8000
Said Hilal, *CEO*
Stephen Stanley, *
**EMP:** 700 **EST:** 1998
**SALES (est):** 108.5MM
**SALES (corp-wide):** 699.84MM Privately Held
**Web:** www.appliedmedical.com
**SIC: 3841** Surgical and medical instruments
**HQ:** Applied Medical Resources Corporation
22872 Avenida Empresa
Rancho Santa Margari CA 92688
949 713-8000

**(P-14974)**
**APPLIED MEDICAL RESOURCES**
30152 Esperanza, Rcho Sta Marg (92688-2120)
PHONE.................949 459-1042
**EMP:** 54 **EST:** 2013
**SALES (est):** 3MM Privately Held
**Web:** www.appliedmedical.com
**SIC: 3841** Surgical and medical instruments

**(P-14975)**
**APPLIED MEDICAL RESOURCES CORP (HQ)**
Also Called: Applied Medical Distribution
22872 Avenida Empresa, Rancho Santa Margari (92688-2650)
PHONE.................949 713-8000
Said S Hilal, *Pr*
Stephen E Stanley, *Group President**
Nabil Hilal, *Group President**
Samir Tall, *
Gary Johnson, *Group President**
▲ **EMP:** 50 **EST:** 1987
**SQ FT:** 800,000
**SALES (est):** 649.89MM
**SALES (corp-wide):** 699.84MM Privately Held
**Web:** www.appliedmedical.com
**SIC: 3841** Surgical and medical instruments
**PA:** Applied Medical Corporation
22872 Avenida Empresa
949 713-8000

**(P-14976)**
**ARCH MED SLTONS - ESCNDIDO LLC**
950 Borra Pl, Escondido (92029-2011)
PHONE.................760 432-9785
Eli Crotzer, *CEO*
**EMP:** 212 **EST:** 2020
**SALES (est):** 6.35MM
**SALES (corp-wide):** 22.33MM Privately Held
**SIC: 3841** Surgical and medical instruments
**PA:** Arch Cutting Tools, Llc
2600 S Telegraph Rd
734 266-6900

**(P-14977)**
**ARTHREX INC**
Also Called: Arthrex California Technology
460 Ward Dr Ste C, Santa Barbara (93111-2351)
PHONE.................805 964-8104
Bob Weber, *Brnch Mgr*
**EMP:** 17
**SALES (corp-wide):** 501.69MM Privately Held
**Web:** www.arthrex.com
**SIC: 3841** Diagnostic apparatus, medical
**PA:** Arthrex, Inc.
1370 Creekside Blvd
239 643-5553

**(P-14978)**
**ARTHROCARE CORPORATION**
680 Vaqueros Ave, Sunnyvale (94085-3523)
PHONE.................408 736-0224
David Pelcic, *Brnch Mgr*
**EMP:** 29
**SALES (corp-wide):** 5.55B Privately Held
**Web:** www.smith-nephew.com
**SIC: 3841** Surgical and medical instruments
**HQ:** Arthrocare Corporation
7000 W Wlliam Cnon Bldg 1
Austin TX 78735

**(P-14979)**
**ASPEN MEDICAL PRODUCTS LLC**
6481 Oak Cyn, Irvine (92618-5202)
P.O. Box 22116 (91185-0001)
PHONE.................949 681-0200
Jim Cloar, *Pr*
▲ **EMP:** 70 **EST:** 1993
**SQ FT:** 52,000
**SALES (est):** 14.85MM
**SALES (corp-wide):** 104.87MM Privately Held
**Web:** www.aspenmp.com
**SIC: 3841** Surgical and medical instruments
**PA:** Cogr, Inc.
140 E 45th St 43rd Fl
212 370-5600

**(P-14980)**
**ATHELAS INC**
1300 Terra Bella Ave, Mountain View (94043-1850)
PHONE.................833 524-1318
Tanay Tandon, *CEO*
**EMP:** 37 **EST:** 2016
**SALES (est):** 10.61MM
**SALES (corp-wide):** 56.76MM Privately Held
**Web:** www.athelas.com
**SIC: 3841** Diagnostic apparatus, medical
**PA:** Commure, Inc.
1300 Trra Bella Ave # 200
415 991-3675

**(P-14981)**
**ATIA VISION INC**
550 Division St, Campbell (95008-6906)
PHONE.................408 805-0520
William Richter, *Admn*
**EMP:** 38 **EST:** 2012
**SALES (est):** 5.02MM Privately Held
**Web:** www.atiavision.com
**SIC: 3841** Ophthalmic instruments and apparatus

**(P-14982)**
**AURIS HEALTH INC (DH)**
150 Shoreline Dr, Redwood City (94065-1400)
PHONE.................650 610-0750
Frederic Moll, *CEO*
Josh Defonzo, *Chief Strategy Officer**
David M Styka, *
**EMP:** 126 **EST:** 2007
**SALES (est):** 39.18MM

# 3841 - Surgical And Medical Instruments (P-14983)

## PRODUCTS & SERVICES SECTION

SALES (corp-wide): 85.16B **Publicly Held**
Web: www.jnjmedtech.com
SIC: **3841** Surgical and medical instruments
HQ: Ethicon Inc.
1000 Route 202
Raritan NJ 08869
800 384-4266

### (P-14983)
### AVAIL MEDSYSTEMS INC
2953 Bunker Hill Ln Ste 101, Santa Clara (95054-1131)
P.O. Box 5835 (95056)
PHONE.................650 772-1529
Daniel Hawkins, *CEO*
**EMP:** 20 **EST:** 2012
SALES (est): 6.32MM **Privately Held**
Web: www.avail.io
SIC: **3841** Surgical and medical instruments

### (P-14984)
### AVAILS MEDICAL INC
1455 Adams Dr # 1288, Menlo Park (94025-1438)
PHONE.................650 427-0460
Oren Knopfmacher, *CEO*
Michael Vosgueritchian, *CFO*
**EMP:** 17 **EST:** 2013
SALES (est): 3.35MM **Privately Held**
Web: www.availsmedical.com
SIC: **3841** Diagnostic apparatus, medical

### (P-14985)
### AVANTEC VASCULAR CORPORATION
870 Hermosa Ave, Sunnyvale (94085)
PHONE.................408 329-5400
Kiminori Toda, *CEO*
Motasim Sirhan, *
Nat Bowditch, *
▲ **EMP:** 35 **EST:** 1999
SALES (est): 5.03MM **Privately Held**
Web: www.avantecvascular.com
SIC: **3841** Medical instruments and equipment, blood and bone work

### (P-14986)
### AVINGER INC
400 Chesapeake Dr, Redwood City (94063-4739)
PHONE.................650 241-7900
Jeffrey M Soinski, *Pr*
James G Cullen, *Non-Executive Chairman of the Board**
Nabeel Subainati, *VP Fin*
**EMP:** 72 **EST:** 2007
**SQ FT:** 44,200
SALES (est): 7.65MM **Privately Held**
Web: www.avinger.com
SIC: **3841** Catheters

### (P-14987)
### AXIOM MEDICAL INCORPORATED
19320 Van Ness Ave, Torrance (90501-1103)
PHONE.................310 533-9020
**EMP:** 40 **EST:** 1976
SALES (est): 4.37MM **Privately Held**
Web: www.axiommed.com
SIC: **3841** 3842 Surgical and medical instruments; Surgical appliances and supplies

### (P-14988)
### B BRAUN MEDICAL INC
1151 Mildred St Ste B, Ontario (91761-3504)
PHONE.................909 906-7575
**EMP:** 148
SALES (corp-wide): 960.97MM **Privately Held**
Web: www.bbraunusa.com
SIC: **3841** Surgical and medical instruments
HQ: B. Braun Medical Inc.
824 12th Ave
Bethlehem PA 18018
610 691-5400

### (P-14989)
### B BRAUN MEDICAL INC
Also Called: B Braun Medical
2206 Alton Pkwy, Irvine (92606-5000)
PHONE.................949 660-3151
**EMP:** 24
SALES (corp-wide): 960.97MM **Privately Held**
Web: www.bbraun.com
SIC: **3841** Surgical and medical instruments
HQ: B. Braun Medical Inc.
824 12th Ave
Bethlehem PA 18018
610 691-5400

### (P-14990)
### B BRAUN MEDICAL INC
2488 Alton Pkwy, Irvine (92606-5037)
PHONE.................949 660-2581
**EMP:** 19
SALES (corp-wide): 960.97MM **Privately Held**
Web: www.bbraunusa.com
SIC: **3841** Surgical and medical instruments
HQ: B. Braun Medical Inc.
824 12th Ave
Bethlehem PA 18018
610 691-5400

### (P-14991)
### B BRAUN MEDICAL INC
2525 Mcgaw Ave, Irvine (92614-5841)
P.O. Box 19791 (92623-9791)
PHONE.................610 691-5400
Keith Klaes, *Mgr*
**EMP:** 1300
SALES (corp-wide): 960.97MM **Privately Held**
Web: www.bbraunusa.com
SIC: **3841** Catheters
HQ: B. Braun Medical Inc.
824 12th Ave
Bethlehem PA 18018
610 691-5400

### (P-14992)
### BAXALTA US INC
1700 Rancho Conejo Blvd, Thousand Oaks (91320-1424)
PHONE.................805 498-8664
Paul Marshall, *Brnch Mgr*
**EMP:** 527
SIC: **3841** 2835 2389 3842 Surgical and medical instruments; Blood derivative diagnostic agents; Hospital gowns; Surgical appliances and supplies
HQ: Baxalta Us Inc.
1200 Lakeside Dr
Bannockburn IL

### (P-14993)
### BAXANO INC
655 River Oaks Pkwy, San Jose (95134-1907)
PHONE.................408 514-2200
**EMP:** 40
Web: www.baxano.com
SIC: **3841** Surgical and medical instruments

### (P-14994)
### BAXTER HEALTHCARE CORPORATION
Baxter Bentley
1402 Alton Pkwy, Irvine (92606-4838)
P.O. Box 11150 (92711-1150)
PHONE.................949 250-2500
Mike Musalem, *Pr*
**EMP:** 16
**SQ FT:** 72,000
SALES (corp-wide): 14.81B **Publicly Held**
Web: www.baxter.com
SIC: **3841** Surgical and medical instruments
HQ: Baxter Healthcare Corporation
1 Baxter Pkwy
Deerfield IL 60015
224 948-2000

### (P-14995)
### BAXTER HEALTHCARE CORPORATION
Also Called: Baxter Medication Delivery
17511 Armstrong Ave, Irvine (92614-5725)
PHONE.................949 474-6301
Michael Mussallem, *Mgr*
**EMP:** 250
SALES (corp-wide): 14.81B **Publicly Held**
Web: www.baxter.com
SIC: **3841** Surgical and medical instruments
HQ: Baxter Healthcare Corporation
1 Baxter Pkwy
Deerfield IL 60015
224 948-2000

### (P-14996)
### BAYER CORPORATION
Pharmaceutical Division
820 Parker, Berkeley (94710-2440)
P.O. Box 1986 (94701-1986)
PHONE.................510 705-5000
Wolfgang Plischke, *Pr*
**EMP:** 74
SALES (corp-wide): 51.78B **Privately Held**
Web: cropscience.bayer.com
SIC: **3841** 2834 Surgical and medical instruments; Pharmaceutical preparations
HQ: Bayer Corporation
100 Bayer Blvd
Whippany NJ 07981
412 777-2000

### (P-14997)
### BEAUTY HEALTH COMPANY (PA)
2165 E Spring St, Long Beach (90806-2114)
PHONE.................800 603-4996
Marla Beck, *Pr*
Brenton L Saunders, *
Michael Monahan, *CFO*
Daniel Watson, *CRO*
**EMP:** 350 **EST:** 1997
**SQ FT:** 23,000
SALES (est): 397.99MM
SALES (corp-wide): 397.99MM **Publicly Held**
SIC: **3841** Surgical and medical instruments

### (P-14998)
### BECKMAN COULTER INC
Beckman Coulter Diagnostics
250 S Kraemer Blvd, Brea (92821-6232)
P.O. Box 8000 (92822-8000)
PHONE.................818 970-2161
Albert Ziegler, *Mgr*
**EMP:** 200
SALES (corp-wide): 23.89B **Publicly Held**
Web: www.beckmancoulter.com
SIC: **3841** 3821 Surgical and medical instruments; Clinical laboratory instruments, except medical and dental
HQ: Beckman Coulter, Inc.
250 S Kraemer Blvd
Brea CA 92821
714 993-5321

### (P-14999)
### BECTON DICKINSON AND COMPANY
86 Montecito Vista Dr, San Jose (95111-3108)
PHONE.................734 812-5271
Adam Chiasson, *Brnch Mgr*
**EMP:** 60
SALES (corp-wide): 19.37B **Publicly Held**
Web: www.bd.com
SIC: **3841** Surgical and medical instruments
PA: Becton, Dickinson And Company
1 Becton Dr
201 847-6800

### (P-15000)
### BECTON DICKINSON AND COMPANY
155 N Mccarthy Blvd, Milpitas (95035-5102)
PHONE.................734 812-5271
Adam Chiasson, *Brnch Mgr*
**EMP:** 850
SALES (corp-wide): 19.37B **Publicly Held**
Web: www.bd.com
SIC: **3841** Surgical and medical instruments
PA: Becton, Dickinson And Company
1 Becton Dr
201 847-6800

### (P-15001)
### BECTON DICKINSON AND COMPANY
Also Called: Care Fusion Products
3750 Torrey View Ct, San Diego (92130-2622)
PHONE.................888 876-4287
**EMP:** 56
SALES (corp-wide): 19.37B **Publicly Held**
Web: www.bd.com
SIC: **3841** Medical instruments and equipment, blood and bone work
PA: Becton, Dickinson And Company
1 Becton Dr
201 847-6800

### (P-15002)
### BECTON DICKINSON AND COMPANY
Bd Biosciences
2350 Qume Dr, San Jose (95131-1812)
PHONE.................408 432-9475
William Rhodes, *Prin*
**EMP:** 332
SALES (corp-wide): 19.37B **Publicly Held**
Web: www.bd.com
SIC: **3841** 3826 2899 2835 Surgical and medical instruments; Analytical instruments; Chemical preparations, nec; Diagnostic substances
PA: Becton, Dickinson And Company
1 Becton Dr
201 847-6800

### (P-15003)
### BECTON DICKINSON AND COMPANY
3750 Torrey View Ct, San Diego (92130-2622)
PHONE.................858 617-2000
**EMP:** 26
SALES (corp-wide): 19.37B **Publicly Held**
Web: www.bd.com

# PRODUCTS & SERVICES SECTION
## 3841 - Surgical And Medical Instruments (P-15026)

SIC: 3841 Surgical and medical instruments
PA: Becton, Dickinson And Company
1 Becton Dr
201 847-6800

**(P-15004)**
**BENTEC MEDICAL**
1380 E Beamer St, Woodland (95776-6003)
PHONE..................530 406-3333
EMP: 60
Web: www.bentecmed.com
SIC: 3841 Surgical and medical instruments

**(P-15005)**
**BENTEC MEDICAL OPCO LLC**
1380 E Beamer St, Woodland (95776-6003)
PHONE..................530 406-3333
Jg Singh, CEO
EMP: 50 EST: 2016
SALES (est): 7.16MM Privately Held
Web: www.bentecmed.com
SIC: 3841 Surgical and medical instruments

**(P-15006)**
**BIO-MEDICAL DEVICES INC**
Also Called: Maxair Systems
17171 Daimler St, Irvine (92614-5508)
PHONE..................949 752-9642
Nick Herbert, Pr
Alan Davidner, Stockholder*
Harry N Herbert, *
▲ EMP: 37 EST: 1988
SQ FT: 40,000
SALES (est): 9.49MM Privately Held
Web: www.maxair-systems.com
SIC: 3841 2353 Surgical and medical instruments; Hats, caps, and millinery

**(P-15007)**
**BIO-MEDICAL DEVICES INTL INC**
17171 Daimler St, Irvine (92614-5508)
PHONE..................949 752-9642
Nicholas Herbert, Pr
Allan Schultz, *
EMP: 25 EST: 1998
SALES (est): 5.35MM Privately Held
Web: www.maxair-systems.com
SIC: 3841 2353 Surgical and medical instruments; Hats, caps, and millinery

**(P-15008)**
**BIOCHECK INC (HQ)**
425 Eccles Ave, South San Francisco (94080-1902)
PHONE..................650 573-1968
Roy Paxton Yih, CEO
EMP: 16 EST: 1996
SQ FT: 7,000
SALES (est): 15.56MM Privately Held
Web: www.biocheckinc.com
SIC: 3841 5047 Diagnostic apparatus, medical; Diagnostic equipment, medical
PA: Origene Technologies, Inc.
9620 Med Ctr Dr Ste 200

**(P-15009)**
**BIOFILM INC**
3225 Executive Rdg, Vista (92081-8527)
PHONE..................760 727-9030
Lisa A O'carroll, CEO
Daniel Wray, *
Mike Adams, *
Lois Wray, *
Natalie Garcia, *
EMP: 54 EST: 1991
SQ FT: 61,000
SALES (est): 13.28MM Privately Held
Web: www.biofilm.com

SIC: 3841 Surgical and medical instruments

**(P-15010)**
**BIOGENERAL INC**
9925 Mesa Rim Rd, San Diego (92121-2911)
PHONE..................858 453-4451
Victor Wild, Pr
▲ EMP: 30 EST: 1986
SALES (est): 5.6MM Privately Held
Web: www.biogeneral.com
SIC: 3841 Surgical and medical instruments

**(P-15011)**
**BIOGENEX LABORATORIES (PA)**
Also Called: Biogenex
48810 Kato Rd Ste 200, Fremont (94538-7311)
PHONE..................510 824-1400
Krishan Lal Kalra, CEO
Satya Kalra, *
Ajay Kumar Valluri, Finance*
◆ EMP: 24 EST: 1981
SALES (est): 8.54MM
SALES (corp-wide): 8.54MM Privately Held
Web: www.biogenex.com
SIC: 3841 2835 8731 2819 Diagnostic apparatus, medical; Cytology and histology diagnostic agents; Commercial physical research; Chemicals, reagent grade: refined from technical grade

**(P-15012)**
**BIOJECT INC**
6769 Mesa Ridge Rd Ste 99, San Diego (92121-2995)
PHONE..................503 692-8001
EMP: 20
SIC: 3841 Surgical instruments and apparatus

**(P-15013)**
**BIOPLATE INC**
570 S Melrose St, Placentia (92870-6327)
PHONE..................310 815-2100
Thomas Hopson, Pr
Tadeusz Wellisz, Ch Bd
EMP: 21 EST: 1994
SALES (est): 4.9MM Privately Held
Web: www.bioplate.com
SIC: 3841 Surgical and medical instruments

**(P-15014)**
**BIOSEAL**
167 W Orangethorpe Ave, Placentia (92870-6922)
PHONE..................714 528-4695
Bill Runion, Pr
Robert C Kopple, *
Jeff Myers, *
▲ EMP: 40 EST: 1988
SQ FT: 8,500
SALES (est): 13.71MM Privately Held
Web: www.biosealnet.com
SIC: 3841 5047 Surgical and medical instruments; Hospital equipment and furniture

**(P-15015)**
**BIOTRICITY INC**
275 Shoreline Dr Ste 150, Redwood City (94065-1494)
PHONE..................650 832-1626
Waqaas Al-siddiq, CEO
EMP: 25 EST: 2016
SALES (est): 12.06MM Privately Held
Web: www.biotricity.com
SIC: 3841 Surgical and medical instruments

**(P-15016)**
**BLOOMLIFE INC**
181 2nd St, San Francisco (94105-3808)
PHONE..................415 215-4251
Eric Dy, CEO
Julian Penders, COO
EMP: 20 EST: 2014
SALES (est): 3.71MM Privately Held
Web: www.bloom-life.com
SIC: 3841 7389 Surgical and medical instruments; Business services, nec

**(P-15017)**
**BOLT MEDICAL INC**
2131 Faraday Ave, Carlsbad (92008-7252)
PHONE..................949 287-3207
Keegan Harper, CEO
Scott Murano, *
EMP: 58 EST: 2019
SALES (est): 10.29MM Privately Held
SIC: 3841 8731 Surgical and medical instruments; Biological research

**(P-15018)**
**BOSTON SCIENTIFIC CORPORATION**
Also Called: Boston Scientific - Valencia
25155 Rye Canyon Loop, Valencia (91355-5004)
PHONE..................800 678-2575
Phill Tarves, Mgr
EMP: 45
SALES (corp-wide): 12.68B Publicly Held
Web: www.bostonscientific.com
SIC: 3841 Surgical and medical instruments
PA: Boston Scientific Corporation
300 Boston Scientific Way
508 683-4000

**(P-15019)**
**BRANAN MEDICAL CORPORATION (PA)**
9940 Mesa Rim Rd, San Diego (92121-2910)
PHONE..................949 598-7166
Cindy Horton, CEO
Raphael Wong, *
Beckie Chien, *
▲ EMP: 32 EST: 1998
SQ FT: 8,400
SALES (est): 4.07MM
SALES (corp-wide): 4.07MM Privately Held
SIC: 3841 Diagnostic apparatus, medical

**(P-15020)**
**BREG INC (HQ)**
2382 Faraday Ave Ste 300, Carlsbad (92008-7220)
PHONE..................760 599-3000
Dave Mowry, CEO
Brad Lee, *
Stuart M Essig, *
Aaron Heisler, *
Tom Sohn, *
◆ EMP: 171 EST: 1989
SALES (est): 24K Privately Held
Web: www.breg.com
SIC: 3841 Surgical and medical instruments
PA: Water Street Healthcare Partners Llc
444 W Lake St Ste 1800

**(P-15021)**
**BRIGHTWATER MEDICAL INC**
42580 Rio Nedo, Temecula (92590-3727)
P.O. Box 1286 (92564-1286)
PHONE..................951 290-3410
Harry Robert Smouse, CEO
EMP: 15 EST: 2014

SQ FT: 5,000
SALES (est): 3.68MM
SALES (corp-wide): 1.26B Publicly Held
SIC: 3841 Surgical and medical instruments
PA: Merit Medical Systems, Inc.
1600 W Merit Pkwy
801 253-1600

**(P-15022)**
**BRUIN BIOMETRICS LLC**
10877 Wilshire Blvd Ste 1600, Los Angeles (90024-4371)
PHONE..................310 268-9494
Scott Hayashi, CFO
EMP: 17 EST: 2009
SQ FT: 3,000
SALES (est): 4.52MM Privately Held
Web: www.bruinbiometrics.com
SIC: 3841 Diagnostic apparatus, medical
HQ: Arjo Ab (Publ)
Malmo
103354500

**(P-15023)**
**CALBIOTECH EXPORT INC**
1935 Cordell Ct, El Cajon (92020-0911)
PHONE..................619 660-6162
Noori Barka, Pr
▼ EMP: 38 EST: 1998
SQ FT: 22,500
SALES (est): 9.43MM Privately Held
Web: www.calbiotech.com
SIC: 3841 8731 8071 Diagnostic apparatus, medical; Medical research, commercial; Medical laboratories
HQ: Erba Diagnostics Mannheim Gmbh
Mallaustr. 69-73
Mannheim BW 68219

**(P-15024)**
**CALDERA MEDICAL INC (PA)**
4360 Park Terrace Dr Ste 140, Westlake Village (91361)
PHONE..................818 879-6555
Bryon L Merade, Pr
Jeff Hubauer, COO
John Pitstick, CFO
EMP: 70 EST: 2002
SQ FT: 25,000
SALES (est): 20.41MM
SALES (corp-wide): 20.41MM Privately Held
Web: www.calderamedical.com
SIC: 3841 Surgical and medical instruments

**(P-15025)**
**CANARY MEDICAL USA LLC**
2710 Loker Ave W Ste 350, Carlsbad (92010-6645)
PHONE..................760 448-5066
William Hunter, CEO
Jeffrey M Gross, *
EMP: 100 EST: 2018
SALES (est): 9.17MM Privately Held
Web: www.canarymedical.com
SIC: 3841 Surgical and medical instruments

**(P-15026)**
**CARDEON CORPORATION**
10161 Bubb Rd, Cupertino (95014-4133)
PHONE..................408 253-3319
Wilfred Samson, Pr
Michael Regan, *
Daryl Banks, *
EMP: 26 EST: 1996
SQ FT: 10,000
SALES (est): 2.4MM Privately Held
SIC: 3841 8011 Surgical instruments and apparatus; Offices and clinics of medical doctors

## 3841 - Surgical And Medical Instruments (P-15027)

**(P-15027)**
**CARDIVA MEDICAL INC**
1615 Wyatt Dr, Santa Clara (95054-1587)
PHONE..................................408 470-7100
John Russell, *Pr*
Rick Anderson, *
Glenn Foy, *
Malcolm Farnsworth, *
Randy Hubbell, *Chief Commercial Officer*
**EMP:** 135 **EST:** 2002
**SALES (est):** 22.42MM
**SALES (corp-wide):** 1.17B **Publicly Held**
**Web:** hospital.haemonetics.com
**SIC: 3841** Surgical and medical instruments
**PA:** Haemonetics Corporation
 125 Summer St
 781 848-7100

**(P-15028)**
**CAREFUSION 207 INC**
1100 Bird Center Dr, Palm Springs (92262-8000)
PHONE..................................760 778-7200
Edward Borkowski, *CFO*
Carol Zilm, *INFUS & RESP*
Cathy Cooney, *
Neil Ryding, *GLOBAL MFG SUPPLY*
Joan Stafslien, *
▲ **EMP:** 327 **EST:** 2005
**SALES (est):** 4.81MM
**SALES (corp-wide):** 1.8B **Privately Held**
**SIC: 3841** 8741 Surgical and medical instruments; Nursing and personal care facility management
**PA:** Vyaire Holding Company
 26125 N Riverwoods Blvd
 872 757-0114

**(P-15029)**
**CAREFUSION 213 LLC (DH)**
3750 Torrey View Ct, San Diego (92130-2622)
PHONE..................................800 523-0502
David L Schlotterbeck, *CEO*
Edward Borkowski, *
Dwight Windstead, *
◆ **EMP:** 450 **EST:** 2008
**SALES (est):** 133.71MM
**SALES (corp-wide):** 19.37B **Publicly Held**
**Web:** www.bd.com
**SIC: 3841** Surgical and medical instruments
**HQ:** Carefusion Corporation
 3750 Torrey View Ct
 San Diego CA 92130

**(P-15030)**
**CAREFUSION CORPORATION**
10020 Pacific Mesa Blvd Bldg A, San Diego (92121-4386)
PHONE..................................858 617-4271
**EMP:** 52
**SALES (corp-wide):** 19.37B **Publicly Held**
**Web:** www.bd.com
**SIC: 3841** Surgical and medical instruments
**HQ:** Carefusion Corporation
 3750 Torrey View Ct
 San Diego CA 92130

**(P-15031)**
**CAREFUSION CORPORATION**
1100 Bird Center Dr, Palm Springs (92262-8000)
PHONE..................................760 778-7200
Carol Zilm, *Pr*
**EMP:** 59
**SALES (corp-wide):** 19.37B **Publicly Held**
**Web:** www.bd.com
**SIC: 3841** Surgical and medical instruments
**HQ:** Carefusion Corporation
 3750 Torrey View Ct
 San Diego CA 92130

**(P-15032)**
**CAREFUSION CORPORATION**
22745 Savi Ranch Pkwy, Yorba Linda (92887-4668)
PHONE..................................800 231-2466
Bill Ross, *Brnch Mgr*
**EMP:** 73
**SALES (corp-wide):** 19.37B **Publicly Held**
**Web:** www.bd.com
**SIC: 3841** Surgical and medical instruments
**HQ:** Carefusion Corporation
 3750 Torrey View Ct
 San Diego CA 92130

**(P-15033)**
**CAREFUSION SOLUTIONS LLC (DH)**
3750 Torrey View Ct, San Diego (92130-2622)
PHONE..................................858 617-2100
Keiran Gallahue, *CEO*
Tom Leonard, *Pr*
James Hinrichs, *CFO*
Don Abbey, *Ex VP*
Scott Bostick, *Sr VP*
**EMP:** 600 **EST:** 2007
**SALES (est):** 487.4MM
**SALES (corp-wide):** 19.37B **Publicly Held**
**Web:** www.bd.com
**SIC: 3841** Surgical and medical instruments
**HQ:** Carefusion Corporation
 3750 Torrey View Ct
 San Diego CA 92130

**(P-15034)**
**CARLSMED INC**
1800 Aston Ave Ste 100, Carlsbad (92008-7399)
PHONE..................................760 766-1923
Sharon Schulzki, *COO*
Alexander Arrow, *CFO*
**EMP:** 15 **EST:** 2021
**SALES (est):** 6.59MM **Privately Held**
**Web:** www.carlsmed.com
**SIC: 3841** Surgical and medical instruments

**(P-15035)**
**CAROL COLE COMPANY**
Also Called: Nuface
1325 Sycamore Ave Ste A, Vista (92081-7810)
PHONE..................................888 360-9171
Carol Cole, *CEO*
Ted Schwarz, *
**EMP:** 123 **EST:** 1989
**SQ FT:** 3,000
**SALES (est):** 23.37MM **Privately Held**
**Web:** www.mynuface.com
**SIC: 3841** Skin grafting equipment

**(P-15036)**
**CAROLINA LQUID CHMISTRIES CORP**
510 W Central Ave Ste C, Brea (92821-3032)
P.O. Box 92249 (92822)
PHONE..................................336 722-8910
Phil Shugart, *Brnch Mgr*
**EMP:** 25
**Web:** www.carolinachemistries.com
**SIC: 3841** Surgical and medical instruments
**PA:** Carolina Liquid Chemistries Corporation
 313 Gallimore Dairy Rd

**(P-15037)**
**CAS MEDICAL SYSTEMS INC (HQ)**
1 Edwards Way, Irvine (92614-5688)
PHONE..................................203 488-6056
Thomas Patton, *Pr*
Jeffery Baird, *
Paul Benni, *CSO*
**EMP:** 53 **EST:** 2018
**SALES (est):** 21.92MM
**SALES (corp-wide):** 6B **Publicly Held**
**Web:** www.edwards.com
**SIC: 3841** Diagnostic apparatus, medical
**PA:** Edwards Lifesciences Corp
 1 Edwards Way
 949 250-2500

**(P-15038)**
**CETERIX ORTHOPAEDICS INC**
Also Called: Ceterix Orthopaedics
6500 Kaiser Dr Ste 120, Fremont (94555-3662)
PHONE..................................650 241-1748
John Mccutcheon, *Pr*
Michael Hendricksen, *
Justin Saliman, *CMO*
**EMP:** 28 **EST:** 2010
**SALES (est):** 7.72MM
**SALES (corp-wide):** 5.55B **Privately Held**
**Web:** www.ceterix.com
**SIC: 3841** Surgical instruments and apparatus
**PA:** Smith & Nephew Plc
 Building 5
 192 347-7100

**(P-15039)**
**CHANNEL MEDSYSTEMS INC**
2919 7th St, Berkeley (94710-2704)
PHONE..................................603 318-5084
Ric Cote, *CEO*
Ric Cote, *Pr*
Ian Vawter, *
Rebecca Furlong, *US Sales*
**EMP:** 35 **EST:** 2009
**SALES (est):** 6.52MM **Privately Held**
**Web:** www.cerene.com
**SIC: 3841** Surgical and medical instruments

**(P-15040)**
**CHART SEQUAL TECHNOLOGIES INC**
12230 World Trade Dr Ste 100, San Diego (92128-3796)
PHONE..................................858 202-3100
▲ **EMP:** 90
**Web:** www.caireinc.com
**SIC: 3841** Diagnostic apparatus, medical

**(P-15041)**
**CHEN-TECH INDUSTRIES INC (DH)**
Also Called: ATI Forged Products
9 Wrigley, Irvine (92618-2711)
PHONE..................................949 855-6716
Richard Harshman, *CEO*
Shannon Ko, *
**EMP:** 38 **EST:** 1979
**SQ FT:** 18,000
**SALES (est):** 12.39MM **Publicly Held**
**Web:** www.atimaterials.com
**SIC: 3841** 3769 3724 3463 Surgical and medical instruments; Space vehicle equipment, nec; Aircraft engines and engine parts; Aluminum forgings
**HQ:** Ati Ladish Llc
 5481 S Packard Ave
 Cudahy WI 53110
 414 747-2611

**(P-15042)**
**CHROMOLOGIC LLC**
Also Called: Chromologic
1225 S Shamrock Ave, Monrovia (91016-4244)
PHONE..................................626 381-9974
Naresh Menon, *Managing Member*
**EMP:** 28 **EST:** 2008
**SALES (est):** 5.12MM **Privately Held**
**Web:** www.chromologic.com
**SIC: 3841** Diagnostic apparatus, medical

**(P-15043)**
**CIRTEC MEDICAL CORP**
101b Cooper Ct, Los Gatos (95032-7604)
PHONE..................................408 395-0443
Michael Forman, *Brnch Mgr*
**EMP:** 60
**SALES (corp-wide):** 200MM **Privately Held**
**Web:** www.cirtecmed.com
**SIC: 3841** Surgical and medical instruments
**PA:** Cirtec Medical Corp.
 9200 Xylon Ave N
 763 493-8556

**(P-15044)**
**CLEARFLOW INC (PA)**
Also Called: Clearflow
16 Technology Dr Ste 150, Irvine (92618-2327)
PHONE..................................714 916-5010
Paul Molloy, *Pr*
Edward Boyle Junior, *Prin*
Al Diaz, *Ex VP*
**EMP:** 20 **EST:** 2008
**SALES (est):** 3.28MM **Privately Held**
**Web:** www.clearflow.com
**SIC: 3841** 3829 Surgical and medical instruments; Thermometers, including digital: clinical

**(P-15045)**
**CLEARPOINT NEURO INC (PA)**
120 S Sierra Ave Ste 100, Solana Beach (92075-1874)
PHONE..................................949 900-6833
Joseph M Burnett, *Pr*
R John Fletcher, *Ch Bd*
Danilo D' Alessandro, *CFO*
Mazin Sabra, *COO*
Jeremy L Stigall, *Ex VP*
**EMP:** 91 **EST:** 1998
**SQ FT:** 7,500
**SALES (est):** 23.95MM **Publicly Held**
**Web:** www.clearpointneuro.com
**SIC: 3841** Surgical and medical instruments

**(P-15046)**
**COMPANION MEDICAL INC**
11011 Via Frontera Ste D, San Diego (92127-1752)
PHONE..................................858 522-0252
Sean Saint, *CEO*
Michael Mensinger, *
**EMP:** 58 **EST:** 2015
**SALES (est):** 7.1MM **Privately Held**
**Web:** www.medtronicdiabetes.com
**SIC: 3841** Surgical and medical instruments
**PA:** Medtronic Public Limited Company
 20 Hatch Street Lower

**(P-15047)**
**COMPOSITE MANUFACTURING INC**
Also Called: CMI
970 Calle Amanecer Ste D, San Clemente (92673-6250)
PHONE..................................949 361-7580
Roger Malcolm, *Pr*

## PRODUCTS & SERVICES SECTION
### 3841 - Surgical And Medical Instruments (P-15070)

Tim Salter, *
**EMP:** 36 **EST:** 1995
**SQ FT:** 16,000
**SALES (est):** 5.36MM **Privately Held**
**Web:** www.carbonfiber.com
**SIC: 3841** 3624  Operating tables; Carbon and graphite products

**(P-15048)**
**CONFLUENT MEDICAL TECH INC**
Also Called: N D C
47600 Westinghouse Dr, Fremont (94539-7473)
**PHONE**..............................510 683-2000
Tom Duerig, *Brnch Mgr*
**EMP:** 20
**Web:** www.confluentmedical.com
**SIC: 3841** 5047  Surgical and medical instruments; Medical and hospital equipment
**PA:** Confluent Medical Technologies, Inc.
6263 N Scttsdale Rd Ste 2

**(P-15049)**
**CONFLUENT MEDICAL TECH INC**
Also Called: Interface Associates
27752 El Lazo, Laguna Niguel (92677-3914)
**PHONE**..............................949 448-7056
Gary D Curtis, *Brnch Mgr*
**EMP:** 103
**Web:** www.confluentmedical.com
**SIC: 3841**  Catheters
**PA:** Confluent Medical Technologies, Inc.
6263 N Scttsdale Rd Ste 2

**(P-15050)**
**CONFLUENT MEDICAL TECH INC**
27721 La Paz Rd, Laguna Niguel (92677-3948)
**PHONE**..............................949 448-7056
**EMP:** 54
**Web:** www.confluentmedical.com
**SIC: 3841** 5047  Surgical and medical instruments; Medical and hospital equipment
**PA:** Confluent Medical Technologies, Inc.
6263 N Scttsdale Rd Ste 2

**(P-15051)**
**COOPER MEDICAL  INC (HQ)**
6140 Stoneridge Mall Rd Ste 590, Pleasanton  (94588-3772)
**PHONE**..............................925 460-3600
Robert S Weiss, *CEO*
**EMP:** 32 **EST:** 2012
**SALES (est):** 184.17MM
**SALES (corp-wide):** 3.59B **Publicly Held**
**Web:** www.coopercos.com
**SIC: 3841**  Medical instruments and equipment, blood and bone work
**PA:** The Cooper Companies Inc
6101 Bllnger Cyn Rd Ste 5
925 460-3600

**(P-15052)**
**CORDIS CORPORATION**
5452 Betsy Ross Dr, Santa Clara (95054-1101)
**PHONE**..............................408 273-3700
**EMP:** 208
**SALES (corp-wide):** 226.83B **Publicly Held**
**Web:** www.cordis.us
**SIC: 3841** 3842  Surgical and medical instruments; Surgical appliances and supplies
**HQ:** Cordis Corporation
14201 Nw 60th Ave
Miami Lakes FL 33014
786 313-2000

**(P-15053)**
**CORNEAGEN LLC**
2019 Artisan Way Apt 312, Chula Vista (91915-2352)
**PHONE**..............................786 992-2688
**EMP:** 18
**SALES (corp-wide):** 40.4MM **Privately Held**
**Web:** www.corneagen.com
**SIC: 3841**  Surgical and medical instruments
**PA:** Corneagen Llc
1200 6th Ave Ste 300
206 701-5840

**(P-15054)**
**CORTEX  INC** ✪
3350 Scott Blvd Ste 37b, Santa Clara (95054-3120)
**PHONE**..............................916 501-7214
**EMP:** 30 **EST:** 2023
**SALES (est):** 2.74MM **Privately Held**
**SIC: 3841**  Surgical and medical instruments

**(P-15055)**
**CORZA MEDICAL INC**
Also Called: Surgical Specialties
2001 Sanyo Ave, San Diego  (92154-6212)
**PHONE**..............................619 671-0276
**EMP:** 17
**SALES (corp-wide):** 679.11MM **Privately Held**
**Web:** www.corza.com
**SIC: 3841** 3842  Needles, suture; Sutures, absorbable and non-absorbable
**HQ:** Surgical Specialties Corporation
247 Station Dr Ste Ne1
Westwood MA 02090
781 751-1000

**(P-15056)**
**COVIDIEN**
4651 E Francis St, Ontario  (91761-2205)
**PHONE**..............................909 605-6572
**EMP:** 15 **EST:** 2019
**SALES (est):** 1.29MM **Privately Held**
**Web:** www.covidien.com
**SIC: 3841**  Surgical and medical instruments

**(P-15057)**
**COVIDIEN HOLDING INC**
3062 Bunker Hill Ln, Santa Clara (95054-1105)
**PHONE**..............................408 585-7700
Jose E Almeida, *Ch*
**EMP:** 151
**Web:** www.covidien.com
**SIC: 3841**  Surgical and medical instruments
**HQ:** Covidien Holding Inc.
710 Medtronic Pkwy
Minneapolis MN 55432

**(P-15058)**
**COVIDIEN HOLDING INC**
2101 Faraday Ave, Carlsbad  (92008-7205)
**PHONE**..............................760 603-5020
**EMP:** 151
**Web:** www.medtronic.com
**SIC: 3841**  Surgical and medical instruments
**HQ:** Covidien Holding Inc.
710 Medtronic Pkwy
Minneapolis MN 55432

**(P-15059)**
**COVIDIEN HOLDING INC**
Also Called: Covidien
6531 Dumbarton Cir, Fremont (94555-3619)
**PHONE**..............................510 456-1500
Duke Rohlen, *Brnch Mgr*
**EMP:** 151
**Web:** www.medtronic.com
**SIC: 3841**  Surgical and medical instruments
**HQ:** Covidien Holding Inc.
710 Medtronic Pkwy
Minneapolis MN 55432

**(P-15060)**
**COVIDIEN HOLDING INC**
Also Called: Covidien Kenmex
2475 Paseo De Las Americas Ste A, San Diego  (92154-7255)
**PHONE**..............................619 690-8500
Javira Gonzales, *Mgr*
**EMP:** 151
**Web:** www.medtronic.com
**SIC: 3841**  Surgical and medical instruments
**HQ:** Covidien Holding Inc.
710 Medtronic Pkwy
Minneapolis MN 55432

**(P-15061)**
**COVIDIEN LP**
Also Called: Vascular Therapies
9775 Toledo Way, Irvine  (92618-1811)
**PHONE**..............................949 837-3700
Hal Hurwitz, *CFO*
**EMP:** 174
**Web:** global.medtronic.com
**SIC: 3841**  Surgical and medical instruments
**HQ:** Covidien Lp
15 Hampshire St
Mansfield MA 02048
763 514-4000

**(P-15062)**
**CREDENCE MEDSYSTEMS  INC**
1430 Obrien Dr Ste D, Menlo Park (94025-1446)
**PHONE**..............................844 263-3797
Doctor Frank Litvack, *Ch Bd*
Jeff F Shanley, *Pr*
Jeff Tillack, *COO*
Doctor Robert W Beart, *Prin*
Norman S Gordon, *Dir*
**EMP:** 22 **EST:** 2013
**SALES (est):** 5.76MM **Privately Held**
**Web:** www.credencemed.com
**SIC: 3841**  Surgical and medical instruments

**(P-15063)**
**DAVID KOPF INSTRUMENTS**
7324 Elmo St, Tujunga  (91042-2205)
P.O. Box 636  (91043-0636)
**PHONE**..............................818 352-3274
Carl Koph, *CEO*
J David Kopf, *
Carol Kopf, *
**EMP:** 28 **EST:** 1959
**SQ FT:** 13,836
**SALES (est):** 5.27MM **Privately Held**
**Web:** www.kopfinstruments.com
**SIC: 3841**  Veterinarians' instruments and apparatus

**(P-15064)**
**DEVAX  INC**
13900 Alton Pkwy Ste 125, Irvine (92618-1621)
**PHONE**..............................949 461-0450
Jeff Theil, *CEO*
**EMP:** 32 **EST:** 1999
**SQ FT:** 5,000
**SALES (est):** 2.43MM **Privately Held**
**SIC: 3841**  Surgical and medical instruments

**(P-15065)**
**DEX LIQUIDATING CO**
900 Saginaw Dr, Redwood City (94063-4753)
**PHONE**..............................650 364-9975
**EMP:** 50
**Web:** www.dexterasurgical.com
**SIC: 3841**  Surgical instruments and apparatus

**(P-15066)**
**DEXCOM  INC (PA)**
Also Called: Dexcom
6340 Sequence Dr, San Diego (92121-4356)
**PHONE**..............................858 200-0200
Kevin R Sayer, *Ch Bd*
Jereme M Sylvain, *CAO*
Jacob S Leach, *Ex VP*
Michael Brown, *CLO*
Girish Naganathan, *Ex VP*
**EMP:** 568 **EST:** 1999
**SALES (est):** 3.62B
**SALES (corp-wide):** 3.62B **Publicly Held**
**Web:** www.dexcom.com
**SIC: 3841**  Surgical and medical instruments

**(P-15067)**
**DFINE  INC (HQ)**
3047 Orchard Pkwy, San Jose (95134-2129)
**PHONE**..............................408 321-9999
Greg Barrett, *Pr*
Rick Short, *CFO*
Dan Balbierz, *CDO*
▲ **EMP:** 30 **EST:** 2004
**SQ FT:** 18,000
**SALES (est):** 6MM
**SALES (corp-wide):** 1.26B **Publicly Held**
**SIC: 3841**  Surgical and medical instruments
**PA:** Merit Medical Systems, Inc.
1600 W Merit Pkwy
801 253-1600

**(P-15068)**
**DIAGNOSTIXX OF CALIFORNIA CORP**
Also Called: Immunalysis
829 Towne Center Dr, Pomona (91767-5901)
**PHONE**..............................909 482-0840
▲ **EMP:** 22
**Web:** www.immunalysis.com
**SIC: 3841** 2835  Diagnostic apparatus, medical; Diagnostic substances

**(P-15069)**
**DIALITY INC**
181 Technology Dr Ste 150, Irvine  (92618)
**PHONE**..............................949 916-5851
Osman Khawar, *CEO*
Aaron Mishkin, *Sec*
Ather Khan, *CFO*
**EMP:** 79 **EST:** 2015
**SALES (est):** 9.85MM **Privately Held**
**Web:** www.diality.com
**SIC: 3841**  Hemodialysis apparatus

**(P-15070)**
**DIGITAL SURGERY SYSTEMS INC**
Also Called: True Digital Surgery
125 Cremona Dr Pmb 110, Goleta (93117-3083)
**PHONE**..............................805 978-5400
Aidan Foley, *Pr*
Arthur Rice, *
Simon Raab, *
Kevin Foley, *
J Flagg Flanagan, *
**EMP:** 34 **EST:** 2018
**SALES (est):** 9.45MM **Privately Held**
**Web:** www.truedigitalsurgery.com

## 3841 - Surgical And Medical Instruments (P-15071)

SIC: 3841 Surgical and medical instruments

**(P-15071)**
**DOSE MEDICAL CORPORATION**
229 Avenida Fabricante, San Clemente (92672-7531)
PHONE..............................949 367-9600
Thomas W Burns, CEO
EMP: 15 EST: 2009
SALES (est): 1.32MM
SALES (corp-wide): 314.71MM Publicly Held
Web: www.glaukos.com
SIC: 3841 Eye examining instruments and apparatus
PA: Glaukos Corporation
   1 Glaukos Way
   949 367-9600

**(P-15072)**
**DUKE EMPIRICAL INC**
Also Called: Duke Empirical
18705 Madrone Pkwy, Morgan Hill (95037-2830)
PHONE..............................831 420-1104
Robert C Laduca, CEO
Jennifer Ramirez, Prin
EMP: 60 EST: 2000
SALES (est): 9.43MM Privately Held
Web: www.dukeempirical.com
SIC: 3841 Diagnostic apparatus, medical

**(P-15073)**
**DUPACO INC**
4144 Avenida De La Plata Ste B, Oceanside (92056-6038)
PHONE..............................760 758-4550
Gregory Jordan, Pr
EMP: 43 EST: 1962
SQ FT: 30,000
SALES (est): 4.35MM Privately Held
Web: www.dupacoinc.com
SIC: 3841 3845 Medical instruments and equipment, blood and bone work; Electromedical equipment

**(P-15074)**
**EAGLE LABS LLC**
Also Called: Eagle Labs
10201a Trademark St Ste A, Rancho Cucamonga (91730-5849)
PHONE..............................909 481-0011
Richard J De Camp, Pr
EMP: 65 EST: 1988
SQ FT: 30,000
SALES (est): 7.53MM
SALES (corp-wide): 17.47MM Privately Held
Web: www.eaglelabs.com
SIC: 3841 Surgical and medical instruments
HQ: Summit Medical, Llc
   815 Northwest Pkwy # 100
   Saint Paul MN 55121
   651 789-3939

**(P-15075)**
**ECA MEDICAL INSTRUMENTS (DH)**
1107 Tourmaline Dr, Newbury Park (91320-1208)
PHONE..............................805 376-2509
John J Nino, Pr
EMP: 21 EST: 1979
SQ FT: 14,982
SALES (est): 10.87MM Publicly Held
Web: www.ecamedical.com
SIC: 3841 Surgical and medical instruments
HQ: Acas, Llc
   2 Bethsda Metro Ctr Fl 14
   Bethesda MD 20814
   301 951-6122

**(P-15076)**
**ELECTRONIC WAVEFORM LAB INC**
5702 Bolsa Ave, Huntington Beach (92649-1128)
PHONE..............................714 843-0463
Ryan Haney, Pr
William Jim Heaney, Pr
Patricia Heaney, *
Ryan Haney, Pr
EMP: 25 EST: 1981
SALES (est): 4.91MM Privately Held
Web: www.h-wave.com
SIC: 3841 Anesthesia apparatus

**(P-15077)**
**ELIXIR MEDICAL CORPORATION**
920 N Mccarthy Blvd, Milpitas (95035-5128)
PHONE..............................408 636-2000
Motasim Sirhan, CEO
Vinayak Bhat, Pr
Rupa Patel, CFO
EMP: 15 EST: 2005
SQ FT: 15,000
SALES (est): 5.78MM Privately Held
Web: www.elixirmedical.com
SIC: 3841 Surgical and medical instruments

**(P-15078)**
**EMED TECHNOLOGIES CORPORATION (PA)**
Also Called: Evans Medical
1262 Hawks Flight Ct Ste 200, El Dorado Hills (95762-9802)
PHONE..............................916 932-0071
Paul Lambert, CEO
Joe Barberie, Prin
▲ EMP: 15 EST: 1991
SQ FT: 17,000
SALES (est): 10.5MM Privately Held
Web: www.emedtc.com
SIC: 3841 Surgical and medical instruments

**(P-15079)**
**ENCHANNEL MEDICAL LTD**
555 Corporate Dr Ste 165, Ladera Ranch (92694-2170)
PHONE..............................949 694-6802
Jun Feng, CEO
EMP: 25 EST: 2021
SALES (est): 5.47MM Privately Held
SIC: 3841 Diagnostic apparatus, medical

**(P-15080)**
**ENDOLOGIX INC (PA)**
Also Called: Endologix
2 Musick, Irvine (92618-1631)
PHONE..............................949 595-7200
John Onopchenko, CEO
Daniel Lemaitre, *
Matthew Thompson, CMO
Jeff Fecho Cqo, Prin
Cindy Pinto, Interim Vice President
▲ EMP: 108 EST: 1992
SQ FT: 129,000
SALES (est): 143.37MM Privately Held
Web: www.endologix.com
SIC: 3841 Surgical and medical instruments

**(P-15081)**
**ENDOLOGIX CANADA LLC**
2 Musick, Irvine (92618-1631)
PHONE..............................949 595-7200
EMP: 79 EST: 2014
SALES (est): 4.23MM Privately Held
Web: www.endologix.com
SIC: 3841 Catheters
HQ: Trivascular, Inc.
   2 Musick

Irvine CA 92618

**(P-15082)**
**ENVVENO MEDICAL CORPORATION**
70 Doppler, Irvine (92618-4306)
PHONE..............................949 261-2900
Robert A Berman, CEO
Craig Glynn, CFO
Hamed Alavi, Sr VP
Marc H Glickman, CMO
EMP: 31 EST: 1999
SQ FT: 14,507
Web: www.envveno.com
SIC: 3841 Surgical and medical instruments

**(P-15083)**
**EPICA MEDICAL INNOVATIONS LLC**
901 Calle Amanecer Ste 150, San Clemente (92673-4219)
PHONE..............................949 238-6323
▲ EMP: 24 EST: 2012
SQ FT: 4,441
SALES (est): 2.69MM
SALES (corp-wide): 9.24MM Privately Held
Web: www.epicaanimalhealth.com
SIC: 3841 5047 Surgical and medical instruments; Medical equipment and supplies
PA: Epica International, Inc.
   901 Calle Amanecer # 150
   949 238-6323

**(P-15084)**
**EVOLVE MANUFACTURING TECH INC**
47300 Bayside Pkwy, Fremont (94538-6516)
PHONE..............................510 690-8959
Noreen King, Pr
Dave Devine, *
Douglas Fujii, *
Pete Pangelinan, *
James Han, *
▲ EMP: 65 EST: 1999
SQ FT: 45,000
SALES (est): 14.12MM Privately Held
Web: www.evolvemfg.com
SIC: 3841 3674 8731 Ultrasonic medical cleaning equipment; Semiconductors and related devices; Biotechnical research, commercial

**(P-15085)**
**EVOME MEDICAL TECHNOLOGIES INC (PA)**
3330 Caminito Daniella, Del Mar (92014-4154)
PHONE..............................800 760-6826
Michael Seckler, CEO
Mike Seckler, CEO
Les Cross, Non-Executive Chairman of the Board
Lana Newishy, Executive Vice Chairman of the Board
Natalia Vakhitova, CFO
EMP: 17 EST: 2020
SALES (est): 79.75MM
SALES (corp-wide): 79.75MM Privately Held
Web: www.evomemedical.com
SIC: 3841 Medical instruments and equipment, blood and bone work

**(P-15086)**
**FLUID LINE TECHNOLOGY CORP**
4590 Ish Dr, Simi Valley (93063-7682)

P.O. Box 3116 (91313-3116)
PHONE..............................818 998-8848
Joseph Marcilese, Pr
Phillip Jaramilla, *
▼ EMP: 25 EST: 1989
SALES (est): 5.59MM Privately Held
Web: www.fluidlinetech.com
SIC: 3841 2833 Surgical and medical instruments; Medicinals and botanicals

**(P-15087)**
**FLUXERGY INC**
15 Musick, Irvine (92618-1638)
PHONE..............................949 305-4201
Tej Patel, Brnch Mgr
EMP: 18
SALES (corp-wide): 10.44MM Privately Held
Web: www.fluxergy.com
SIC: 3841 Surgical and medical instruments
PA: Fluxergy, Inc.
   30 Fairbanks
   949 305-4201

**(P-15088)**
**FLUXERGY INC**
13766 Alton Pkwy, Irvine (92618-1639)
PHONE..............................949 305-4201
Tej Patel, Brnch Mgr
EMP: 18
SALES (corp-wide): 10.44MM Privately Held
Web: www.fluxergy.com
SIC: 3841 Surgical and medical instruments
PA: Fluxergy, Inc.
   30 Fairbanks
   949 305-4201

**(P-15089)**
**FLUXION BIOSCIENCES INC**
Also Called: Fluxion
1407 E 20th St, Oakland (94607)
PHONE..............................650 241-4577
Jeff Jenson, CEO
Cristian Ionescu Zanetti, *
Jody Beecher, *
Niall Murphy, *
▲ EMP: 30 EST: 2005
SQ FT: 10,000
SALES (est): 8.57MM Privately Held
Web: www.cellmicrosystems.com
SIC: 3841 Diagnostic apparatus, medical

**(P-15090)**
**FOUNDRY MED INNOVATIONS INC**
Also Called: Toolbox Medical Innovations
1965 Kellogg Ave, Carlsbad (92008-6582)
PHONE..............................888 445-2333
John K Zeis, Pr
EMP: 17 EST: 2014
SALES (est): 5.65MM Privately Held
SIC: 3841 Diagnostic apparatus, medical

**(P-15091)**
**FRESENIUS MED CARE HLDINGS INC**
4040 Nelson Ave, Concord (94520-1200)
PHONE..............................888 373-1470
EMP: 19
SALES (corp-wide): 21.15B Privately Held
Web: www.fmcna.com
SIC: 3841 Surgical and medical instruments
HQ: Fresenius Medical Care Holdings, Inc.
   920 Winter St
   Waltham MA 02451

# PRODUCTS & SERVICES SECTION
## 3841 - Surgical And Medical Instruments (P-15111)

**(P-15092)**
**FREUDENBERG MEDICAL LLC**
5050 Rivergrade Rd, Baldwin Park (91706-1405)
PHONE...............626 814-9684
Coburn Pharr, *Brnch Mgr*
**EMP:** 149
**SALES (corp-wide):** 12.96B **Privately Held**
Web: www.inhealth.com
**SIC: 3841** Surgical and medical instruments
**HQ:** Freudenberg Medical, Llc
1110 Mark Ave
Carpinteria CA 93013
805 684-3304

**(P-15093)**
**FUSION BIOTEC LLC**
160 S Cypress St Ste 400, Orange (92866-1314)
PHONE...............949 264-3437
Bruce Alan Sargeant, *CEO*
**EMP:** 50 **EST:** 2016
**SQ FT:** 3,000
**SALES (est):** 4.26MM **Privately Held**
Web: www.fusion-biotec.com
**SIC: 3841** Surgical and medical instruments

**(P-15094)**
**FZIOMED INC (PA)**
231 Bonetti Dr, San Luis Obispo (93401-7376)
PHONE...............805 546-0610
Paul Mraz, *Pr*
Ronald F Haynes, *
**EMP:** 39 **EST:** 1996
**SQ FT:** 36,000
**SALES (est):** 4.83MM **Privately Held**
Web: www.fziomed.com
**SIC: 3841** Surgical and medical instruments

**(P-15095)**
**GALAXY MEDICAL INC**
3200 Bridge Pkwy Ste 100, Redwood City (94065-1197)
PHONE...............510 847-5189
Jonathan Waldstreicher, *CEO*
**EMP:** 49 **EST:** 2020
**SALES (est):** 4.5MM **Privately Held**
**SIC: 3841** Stethoscopes and stethographs

**(P-15096)**
**GALVANIZE THERAPEUTICS INC (PA)**
3200 Bridge Pkwy Ste 100, Redwood City (94065-1197)
PHONE...............628 800-1154
Jonathan Waldstreicher, *CEO*
Doug Godshall, *Ofcr*
**EMP:** 16 **EST:** 2016
**SALES (est):** 6.36MM
**SALES (corp-wide):** 6.36MM **Privately Held**
Web: www.galvanizetx.com
**SIC: 3841** Surgical and medical instruments

**(P-15097)**
**GENALYTE INC (PA)**
6620 Mesa Ridge Rd Ste 100, San Diego (92121-3917)
PHONE...............858 956-1200
Cary Gunn, *CEO*
Kevin Lo, *Pr*
Martin Gleeson, *VP*
William A Hagstrom, *Prin*
**EMP:** 17 **EST:** 2007
**SALES (est):** 5.26MM **Privately Held**
Web: www.genalyte.com
**SIC: 3841** Diagnostic apparatus, medical

**(P-15098)**
**GENBODY AMERICA LLC**
3420 De Forest Cir, Jurupa Valley (91752-1165)
PHONE...............949 561-0664
David Yoo, *CEO*
**EMP:** 34 **EST:** 2020
**SALES (est):** 2.32MM **Privately Held**
Web: www.genbodyamerica.com
**SIC: 3841** 5047 2835 Diagnostic apparatus, medical; Medical equipment and supplies; Microbiology and virology diagnostic products

**(P-15099)**
**GENERAL SURGICAL INNOVATIONS**
10460 Bubb Rd, Cupertino (95014-4150)
PHONE...............408 863-2500
Gregory D Casciaro, *Pr*
Roderick A Young, *Ch*
James E Jervis, *VP*
Stephen J Bonelli, *VP*
**EMP:** 18 **EST:** 1992
**SQ FT:** 30,000
**SALES (est):** 458.65K **Privately Held**
**SIC: 3841** Surgical instruments and apparatus

**(P-15100)**
**GENMARK DIAGNOSTICS INC (DH)**
Also Called: Genmark
5964 La Place Ct Ste 100, Carlsbad (92008)
PHONE...............760 448-4300
Scott Mendel, *Pr*
Johnny Ek, *CFO*
Brian Mitchell, *VP Opers*
Eric Stier, *Sr VP*
Hollis Winkler, *Pers/VP*
**EMP:** 583 **EST:** 2020
**SALES (est):** 171.55MM **Privately Held**
Web: diagnostics.roche.com
**SIC: 3841** Surgical and medical instruments
**HQ:** Roche Holdings, Inc.
1 Dna Way
South San Francisco CA 94080
650 225-1000

**(P-15101)**
**GLAUKOS CORPORATION (PA)**
1 Glaukos Way, Aliso Viejo (92656-2704)
PHONE...............949 367-9600
Thomas W Burns, *Ch Bd*
Joseph E Gilliam, *Pr*
Tomas Navratil, *CDO*
Alex R Thurman, *Sr VP*
**EMP:** 208 **EST:** 1998
**SQ FT:** 160,000
**SALES (est):** 314.71MM
**SALES (corp-wide):** 314.71MM **Publicly Held**
Web: www.glaukos.com
**SIC: 3841** Eye examining instruments and apparatus

**(P-15102)**
**GLYSENS INCORPORATED**
3931 Sorrento Valley Blvd Ste 110, San Diego (92121-1402)
PHONE...............858 638-7708
Bill Markle, *CEO*
Timothy Routh, *
**EMP:** 30 **EST:** 1997
**SALES (est):** 5.27MM **Privately Held**
Web: www.glysens.com
**SIC: 3841** Surgical and medical instruments

**(P-15103)**
**GUIDANT SALES LLC**
825 E Middlefield Rd, Mountain View (94043-4025)
PHONE...............650 965-2634
**EMP:** 1008
**SALES (corp-wide):** 12.68B **Publicly Held**
Web: www.bostonscientific.com
**SIC: 3841** Surgical and medical instruments
**HQ:** Guidant Sales Llc
4100 Hamline Ave N
Saint Paul MN 55112

**(P-15104)**
**HANSEN MEDICAL INC**
Also Called: Braid Logistics
800 E Middlefield Rd, Mountain View (94043-4030)
PHONE...............650 404-5800
Cary Vance, *Pr*
Michael L Eagle, *
Cary G Vance, *
Christopher P Lowe, *Interim Chief Financial Officer*
Robert Cathcart, *Senior Vice President Global Sales*
**EMP:** 130 **EST:** 2002
**SQ FT:** 63,000
**SALES (est):** 21.72MM
**SALES (corp-wide):** 85.16B **Publicly Held**
Web: www.joyofsocks.com
**SIC: 3841** Catheters
**HQ:** Auris Health, Inc.
150 Shoreline Dr
Redwood City CA 94065
650 610-0750

**(P-15105)**
**HOLLISTER INCORPORATED**
5276 Hollister Ave Ste 45, Santa Barbara (93111-2073)
PHONE...............805 845-4785
**EMP:** 16
**SALES (corp-wide):** 709.48MM **Privately Held**
Web: www.hollister.com
**SIC: 3841** Surgical and medical instruments
**PA:** Hollister Incorporated
2000 Hollister Dr
847 680-1000

**(P-15106)**
**HOYA SURGICAL OPTICS INC**
110 Progress, Irvine (92618-0390)
PHONE...............909 680-3900
Yasuro Mori, *CFO*
Bruno Chermette, *Pr*
**EMP:** 17 **EST:** 2007
**SALES (est):** 4.68MM **Privately Held**
Web: www.hoyasurgicaloptics.com
**SIC: 3841** Surgical and medical instruments

**(P-15107)**
**HYCOR BIOMEDICAL LLC**
Also Called: Hycor
7272 Chapman Ave Ste A, Garden Grove (92841-2103)
PHONE...............714 933-3000
Dick Aderman, *Pr*
Richard Hockins, *
Phil Crusco, *
Mark Van Cleve, *
Eric Whitters, *
▲ **EMP:** 120 **EST:** 1985
**SQ FT:** 76,000
**SALES (est):** 24.7MM
**SALES (corp-wide):** 91.99MM **Privately Held**
Web: www.hycorbiomedical.com

**SIC: 3841** 2835 Surgical and medical instruments; Diagnostic substances
**PA:** Linden, Llc
111 S Wacker Dr Ste 3350
312 506-5657

**(P-15108)**
**HYDRAFACIAL LLC**
Also Called: Edge Systems
3600 E Burnett St, Long Beach (90815-1749)
PHONE...............562 391-2052
Evan Hoover, *Brnch Mgr*
**EMP:** 30
**SALES (corp-wide):** 397.99MM **Publicly Held**
Web: www.hydrafacial.com
**SIC: 3841** Surgical and medical instruments
**HQ:** Hydrafacial Llc
3600 E Burnett St
Long Beach CA 90815
800 603-4996

**(P-15109)**
**HYDRAFACIAL LLC (HQ)**
Also Called: Hydrafacial Company, The
3600 E Burnett St, Long Beach (90815-1749)
PHONE...............800 603-4996
Clint Carnell, *CEO*
Jeff Nardoci, *
Randy Sieve, *
Paul Bokota, *
Michael Monahan, *
▲ **EMP:** 102 **EST:** 2012
**SQ FT:** 22,515
**SALES (est):** 20.9MM
**SALES (corp-wide):** 397.99MM **Publicly Held**
Web: www.hydrafacial.com
**SIC: 3841** Surgical and medical instruments
**PA:** The Beauty Health Company
2165 Spring St
800 603-4996

**(P-15110)**
**I-FLOW LLC**
43 Discovery Ste 100, Irvine (92618-3773)
PHONE...............800 448-3569
Donald Earhart, *Pr*
James J Dal Porto, *
James R Talevich, *
**EMP:** 1100 **EST:** 1985
**SQ FT:** 66,675
**SALES (est):** 17.42MM
**SALES (corp-wide):** 20.43B **Publicly Held**
Web: www.iflo.com
**SIC: 3841** Surgical instruments and apparatus
**PA:** Kimberly-Clark Corporation
351 Phelps Dr
972 281-1200

**(P-15111)**
**ICU MEDICAL INC (PA)**
Also Called: CLAVE
951 Calle Amanecer, San Clemente (92673-6212)
PHONE...............949 366-2183
Vivek Jain, *Ch Bd*
Brian Bonnell, *CFO*
Christian B Voigtlander, *COO*
Daniel Woolson, *Corporate Vice President*
Virginia Sanzone, *Corporate Vice President*
▲ **EMP:** 503 **EST:** 1984
**SQ FT:** 19,958
**SALES (est):** 2.26B
**SALES (corp-wide):** 2.26B **Publicly Held**
Web: www.icumed.com
**SIC: 3841** 3845 IV transfusion apparatus; Pacemaker, cardiac

## 3841 - Surgical And Medical Instruments (P-15112)

**(P-15112)**
**ICU MEDICAL INC**
5729 Fontanoso Way, San Jose (95138-1015)
PHONE.....................408 284-7064
Joe Belloah, *Mgr*
**EMP:** 100
**SALES (corp-wide):** 2.26B **Publicly Held**
Web: www.icumed.com
SIC: **3841** Surgical and medical instruments
PA: Icu Medical, Inc.
   951 Calle Amanecer
   949 366-2183

**(P-15113)**
**IGENOMIX USA INC**
Also Called: Ivigen
383 Van Ness Ave Ste 1605, Torrance (90501-7225)
PHONE.....................818 919-1657
Refik Kayali, *Mgr*
**EMP:** 37
**SALES (corp-wide):** 4.47MM **Privately Held**
Web: www.igenomix.com
SIC: **3841** 8071 Biopsy instruments and equipment; Medical laboratories
HQ: Igenomix Usa, Inc.
   5201 Waterford Dst Dr
   Miami FL 33126
   305 501-4948

**(P-15114)**
**IMPEDIMED INC (HQ)**
5900 Pasteur Ct Ste 125, Carlsbad (92008-7334)
PHONE.....................760 585-2100
Richard Carreon, *CEO*
Don Myll, *CFO*
**EMP:** 20 **EST:** 2002
**SQ FT:** 15,000
**SALES (est):** 11.08MM **Privately Held**
Web: www.impedimed.com
SIC: **3841** Surgical and medical instruments
PA: Impedimed Limited
   U 1 50 Parker Ct

**(P-15115)**
**IMTEC BIOMEDICAL INC**
13193 Polvera Ave, San Diego (92128-1147)
P.O. Box 27225 (92198-1225)
PHONE.....................619 316-1207
Daniel A Cota, *Brnch Mgr*
**EMP:** 15
**SALES (corp-wide):** 71.78K **Privately Held**
Web: www.imtecbiomedical.com
SIC: **3841** Surgical and medical instruments
PA: Imtec Biomedical Inc.
   718 El Carmel Pl

**(P-15116)**
**INARI MEDICAL INC (PA)**
Also Called: Inari
6001 Oak Cyn Ste 100, Irvine (92618-5200)
PHONE.....................877 927-4747
Andrew Hykes, *Pr*
Donald Milder, *Ch Bd*
Kevin Strange, *CFO*
Thomas Tu, *CMO*
**EMP:** 1003 **EST:** 2011
**SQ FT:** 38,200
**SALES (est):** 493.63MM
**SALES (corp-wide):** 493.63MM **Publicly Held**
Web: www.inarimedical.com
SIC: **3841** Surgical and medical instruments

**(P-15117)**
**INOGEN INC (PA)**
Also Called: INOGEN
859 Ward Dr Ste 200, Goleta (93111-2920)
PHONE.....................805 562-0500
Kevin Rm Smith, *Pr*
Elizabeth Mora, *
Michael K Sergesketter, *Corporate Treasurer*
Gregoire Ramade, *CCO*
Kevin P Smith, *Corporate Secretary*
◆ **EMP:** 208 **EST:** 2001
**SQ FT:** 46,000
**SALES (est):** 315.66MM
**SALES (corp-wide):** 315.66MM **Publicly Held**
Web: www.inogen.com
SIC: **3841** 3842 7352 Surgical and medical instruments; Surgical appliances and supplies; Medical equipment rental

**(P-15118)**
**INOVA LABS INC**
9001 Spectrum Center Blvd Ste 200, San Diego (92123-1438)
P.O. Box 18536 (78760-8536)
PHONE.....................866 647-0691
Brooke Harding, *CEO*
John B Rush, *
Phil Martin, *
Randy Williams, *
Dragan Nebrigic, *
▲ **EMP:** 55 **EST:** 2008
**SALES (est):** 4.23MM **Publicly Held**
Web: www.ariahealth.com
SIC: **3841** Surgical and medical instruments
PA: Resmed Inc.
   9001 Spectrum Center Blvd

**(P-15119)**
**INSOUND MEDICAL INC**
47257 Fremont Blvd, Fremont (94538-6502)
PHONE.....................510 792-4000
David Thrower, *CEO*
Susan Whichard, *
Igal Ladabaum, *
**EMP:** 31 **EST:** 2001
**SQ FT:** 14,000
**SALES (est):** 2.47MM **Privately Held**
SIC: **3841** Surgical and medical instruments
PA: Sonova Holding Ag
   Laubisrutistrasse 28

**(P-15120)**
**INTEGER HOLDINGS CORPORATION**
Also Called: Greatbatch Medical
8830 Siempre Viva Rd Ste 100, San Diego (92101)
PHONE.....................619 498-9448
Raul Mata, *Brnch Mgr*
**EMP:** 26
**SALES (corp-wide):** 1.6B **Publicly Held**
Web: www.integer.net
SIC: **3841** Surgical and medical instruments
PA: Integer Holdings Corporation
   2595 Dallas Pkwy Ste 310
   214 618-5243

**(P-15121)**
**INTEGRA LFSCNCES HOLDINGS CORP**
5955 Pacific Center Blvd, San Diego (92121-4309)
PHONE.....................609 529-9748
Peter Arduini, *CEO*
**EMP:** 25
Web: marketing.integralife.com
SIC: **3841** 3845 Surgical and medical instruments; Electromedical equipment
PA: Integra Lifesciences Holdings Corporation
   1100 Campus Rd

**(P-15122)**
**INTERFACE ASSOCIATES INC**
Also Called: Interface Catheter Solutions
27741 La Paz Rd, Laguna Niguel (92677-3948)
PHONE.....................949 448-7056
**EMP:** 175
Web: www.interfaceusa.com
SIC: **3841** 5047 Surgical and medical instruments; Hospital equipment and furniture

**(P-15123)**
**INTERNATIONAL TECHNIDYNE CORP (DH)**
Also Called: Itc
6260 Sequence Dr, San Diego (92121-4358)
PHONE.....................858 263-2300
Scott Cramer, *Pr*
Greg Tibbitts, *
Tom Whalen, *
Matt Bastardi, *
Kimberly Ballard, *
**EMP:** 250 **EST:** 1969
**SQ FT:** 130,000
**SALES (est):** 32.68MM **Privately Held**
Web: www.werfen.com
SIC: **3841** 3829 Diagnostic apparatus, medical; Medical diagnostic systems, nuclear
HQ: Accriva Diagnostics Holdings, Inc.
   6260 Sequence Dr
   San Diego CA 92121
   858 404-8203

**(P-15124)**
**INTERSECT ENT INC**
1555 Adams Dr, Menlo Park (94025-1439)
PHONE.....................650 641-2100
Thomas A West, *Pr*
Kieran T Gallahue, *Ch Bd*
Richard A Meier, *Ex VP*
Patrick A Broderick, *Ex VP*
▲ **EMP:** 402 **EST:** 2003
**SQ FT:** 10,200
**SALES (est):** 106.75MM **Privately Held**
Web: www.intersectent.com
SIC: **3841** Surgical and medical instruments
HQ: Medtronic, Inc.
   710 Medtronic Pkwy
   Minneapolis MN 55432
   763 514-4000

**(P-15125)**
**INTERVENTIONAL SPINE INC**
30 Fairbanks Ste 100, Irvine (92618-1688)
PHONE.....................949 472-0006
Walter Ceuvas, *CEO*
Michael Henson, *Ch Bd*
Joseph Darling, *VP*
**EMP:** 15 **EST:** 2000
**SALES (est):** 3.1MM **Privately Held**
Web: www.i-spineinc.com
SIC: **3841** Surgical and medical instruments

**(P-15126)**
**INTUITIVE SRGCAL OPRATIONS INC (HQ)**
1020 Kifer Rd, Sunnyvale (94086-5301)
PHONE.....................408 523-2100
Gary S Guthart, *CEO*
**EMP:** 27 **EST:** 2009
**SALES (est):** 10.08MM **Publicly Held**
Web: www.intuitive.com
SIC: **3841** Surgical and medical instruments
PA: Intuitive Surgical, Inc.
   1020 Kifer Rd

**(P-15127)**
**INTUITIVE SURGICAL INC**
1266 Kifer Rd Bldg 101, Sunnyvale (94086-5304)
PHONE.....................408 523-4000
Lonnie Smith, *CEO*
**EMP:** 25
Web: www.intuitivesurgical.com
SIC: **3841** Surgical and medical instruments
PA: Intuitive Surgical, Inc.
   1020 Kifer Rd

**(P-15128)**
**INTUITIVE SURGICAL INC**
1250 Kifer Rd, Sunnyvale (94086-5304)
PHONE.....................408 523-7314
**EMP:** 21
Web: www.intuitivesurgical.com
SIC: **3841** Surgical and medical instruments
PA: Intuitive Surgical, Inc.
   1020 Kifer Rd

**(P-15129)**
**INTUITIVE SURGICAL INC**
Also Called: Diagnstic Intrvntonal Crdiolgy
3410 Central Expy, Santa Clara (95051-0703)
PHONE.....................408 523-7579
Edward Fox, *Mgr*
**EMP:** 15
Web: www.intuitivesurgical.com
SIC: **3841** Surgical and medical instruments
PA: Intuitive Surgical, Inc.
   1020 Kifer Rd

**(P-15130)**
**INTUITY MEDICAL INC**
Also Called: Rosedale Medical
3500 W Warren Ave, Fremont (94538-6499)
PHONE.....................408 530-1700
George Zamanakos, *CEO*
Robb Hesley, *
Kelley Lipman, *
Tammy Cameron, *
**EMP:** 97 **EST:** 2002
**SQ FT:** 18,000
**SALES (est):** 29.15MM **Privately Held**
Web: www.presspogo.com
SIC: **3841** Surgical and medical instruments

**(P-15131)**
**INVUITY INC**
Also Called: Intelligent Photonics
444 De Haro St Ste 110, San Francisco (94107-2350)
PHONE.....................415 665-2100
Kevin A Lobo, *Ch Bd*
James H Mackaness, *
▲ **EMP:** 172 **EST:** 2004
**SQ FT:** 38,135
**SALES (est):** 14.17MM
**SALES (corp-wide):** 20.5B **Publicly Held**
SIC: **3841** 5047 Surgical instruments and apparatus; Surgical equipment and supplies
PA: Stryker Corporation
   1941 Stryker Way
   269 385-2600

**(P-15132)**
**IRHYTHM TECHNOLOGIES INC (PA)**
699 8th St Ste 600, San Francisco (94103-4901)
PHONE.....................415 632-5700

▲ = Import ▼ = Export
◆ = Import/Export

## PRODUCTS & SERVICES SECTION
### 3841 - Surgical And Medical Instruments (P-15154)

Quentin Blackford, *Pr*
Abhijit Y Talwalkar, *
Daniel G Wilson, *Executive Strategy Vice President*
Chad Patterson, *CCO*
Mark J Day, *Executive Research & Development Vice President*
**EMP:** 30 **EST:** 2006
**SQ FT:** 117,560
**SALES (est):** 492.68MM **Publicly Held**
**Web:** www.irhythmtech.com
**SIC: 3841** 3845 Surgical and medical instruments; Electrocardiographs

**(P-15133)**
**IRVINE BIOMEDICAL INC**
2375 Morse Ave, Irvine (92614-6233)
**PHONE**.................................949 851-3053
**EMP:** 200
**SIC: 3841** Catheters

**(P-15134)**
**ISSAC MEDICAL INC**
2761 Walnut Ave, Tustin (92780-7051)
**PHONE**.................................805 239-4284
**EMP:** 320
**SIC: 3841** 2822 2821 Surgical and medical instruments; Synthetic rubber; Plastics materials and resins

**(P-15135)**
**IVANTIS INC (PA)**
201 Technology Dr, Irvine (92618-2400)
**PHONE**.................................949 600-9650
David Van Meter, *Pr*
**EMP:** 16 **EST:** 2008
**SALES (est):** 6.82MM
**SALES (corp-wide):** 6.82MM **Privately Held**
**Web:** www.myalcon.com
**SIC: 3841** Ophthalmic instruments and apparatus

**(P-15136)**
**JIT MANUFACTURING INC**
1610 Commerce Way, Paso Robles (93446-3699)
**PHONE**.................................805 238-5000
Sharon Smith, *CEO*
**EMP:** 50
**SALES (est):** 4.69MM **Privately Held**
**Web:** www.jitmfginc.com
**SIC: 3841** Medical instruments and equipment, blood and bone work

**(P-15137)**
**JOHNSON JHNSON SRGCAL VSION IN**
Also Called: Johnson & Johnson Vision
510 Cottonwood Dr, Milpitas (95035-7403)
**PHONE**.................................408 273-4100
Murthy Simhambhatla, *Brnch Mgr*
**EMP:** 490
**SALES (corp-wide):** 85.16B **Publicly Held**
**Web:** www.jnjvisionpro.com
**SIC: 3841** Ophthalmic instruments and apparatus
**HQ:** Johnson & Johnson Surgical Vision, Inc.
31 Technology Dr Bldg 29a
Irvine CA 92618
949 581-5799

**(P-15138)**
**JOHNSON MATTHEY INC**
Also Called: Shape Memory Applications
1070 Commercial St Ste 110, San Jose (95112-1420)
**PHONE**.................................408 727-2221
Brian Woodward, *Brnch Mgr*
**EMP:** 86
**SALES (corp-wide):** 16.3B **Privately Held**
**Web:** www.matthey.com
**SIC: 3841** 3496 3356 3357 Surgical and medical instruments; Miscellaneous fabricated wire products; Nonferrous rolling and drawing, nec; Nonferrous wiredrawing and insulating
**HQ:** Johnson Matthey Inc.
435 Devon Park Dr Ste 600
Wayne PA 19087
610 971-3000

**(P-15139)**
**JOIMAX INC**
140 Technology Dr Ste 150, Irvine (92618-2453)
**PHONE**.................................949 859-3472
Maximilian Ries, *Genl Mgr*
**EMP:** 38 **EST:** 2005
**SALES (est):** 4.64MM **Privately Held**
**Web:** www.joimax.com
**SIC: 3841** Surgical and medical instruments

**(P-15140)**
**KAINOS DENTAL TECHNOLOGIES LLC (PA)**
2975 Treat Blvd Bldg D, Concord (94518-3690)
**PHONE**.................................800 331-4834
William Gianni, *CEO*
Andrew Nam, *
Michael Finke, *
**EMP:** 24 **EST:** 2011
**SQ FT:** 3,000
**SALES (est):** 3.64MM
**SALES (corp-wide):** 3.64MM **Privately Held**
**Web:** www.kainosdental.com
**SIC: 3841** 3843 8072 Surgical and medical instruments; Dental equipment and supplies; Artificial teeth production

**(P-15141)**
**KARL STORZ ENDSCPY-AMERICA INC (HQ)**
Also Called: Karl Storz Intgrated Solutions
2151 E Grand Ave, El Segundo (90245-5017)
**PHONE**.................................424 218-8100
Charles Wilhelm, *CEO*
Mark Green, *
Sken Huang, *
Sonal Matai, *
▲ **EMP:** 220 **EST:** 1971
**SQ FT:** 90,000
**SALES (est):** 280.88MM
**SALES (corp-wide):** 2.14B **Privately Held**
**Web:** www.karlstorz.com
**SIC: 3841** 5047 Surgical and medical instruments; Medical equipment and supplies
**PA:** Karl Storz Se & Co. Kg
Dr.-Karl-Storz-Str. 34
74617080

**(P-15142)**
**KARL STORZ ENDSCPY-AMERICA INC**
1 N Los Carneros Dr, Goleta (93117)
**PHONE**.................................800 964-5563
**EMP:** 60
**SALES (corp-wide):** 2.14B **Privately Held**
**Web:** www.karlstorz.com
**SIC: 3841** 3845 Suction therapy apparatus; Endoscopic equipment, electromedical, nec
**HQ:** Karl Storz Endoscopy-America, Inc.
2151 Grand Ave
El Segundo CA 90245
424 218-8100

**(P-15143)**
**KARL STORZ IMAGING INC**
32 Aero Camino, Goleta (93117-3105)
**PHONE**.................................805 968-5563
**EMP:** 28
**SALES (corp-wide):** 2.14B **Privately Held**
**Web:** www.karlstorz.com
**SIC: 3841** Surgical and medical instruments
**HQ:** Karl Storz Imaging, Inc.
1 S Los Carneros Rd
Goleta CA 93117

**(P-15144)**
**KINEMATIC AUTOMATION INC**
Also Called: Kinematic
21085 Longeway Rd, Sonora (95370-8968)
P.O. Box 69 (95383-0069)
**PHONE**.................................209 532-3200
David Carlberg, *Pr*
Ted Meigs, *
**EMP:** 55 **EST:** 1980
**SQ FT:** 19,000
**SALES (est):** 9.74MM **Privately Held**
**Web:** www.kinematic.com
**SIC: 3841** 7389 Diagnostic apparatus, medical; Design, commercial and industrial

**(P-15145)**
**KONIGSBERG INSTRUMENTS INC**
1017 S Mountain Ave, Monrovia (91016-3642)
**PHONE**.................................626 775-6500
▼ **EMP:** 35
**SIC: 3841** Surgical and medical instruments

**(P-15146)**
**KOROS USA INC**
610 Flinn Ave, Moorpark (93021-2008)
**PHONE**.................................805 529-0825
Tibor Koros, *Pr*
▲ **EMP:** 25 **EST:** 1974
**SQ FT:** 12,000
**SALES (est):** 5.21MM **Privately Held**
**Web:** www.korosusa.com
**SIC: 3841** Diagnostic apparatus, medical

**(P-15147)**
**LEVITA MAGNETICS INTL CORP**
453 Ravendale Dr Ste G, Mountain View (94043-5221)
**PHONE**.................................530 456-6627
Alberto Rodriguez, *Admn*
**EMP:** 32 **EST:** 2014
**SALES (est):** 5.79MM **Privately Held**
**Web:** www.levita.com
**SIC: 3841** Surgical and medical instruments

**(P-15148)**
**LIFE SCIENCE OUTSOURCING INC**
Also Called: Medical Device Manufacturing
830 Challenger St, Brea (92821-2946)
**PHONE**.................................714 672-1090
Barry Kazemi, *Pr*
Charlie Ricci, *
Neil A Goldman, *
◆ **EMP:** 80 **EST:** 1997
**SQ FT:** 56,000
**SALES (est):** 21.53MM **Privately Held**
**Web:** www.lso-inc.com
**SIC: 3841** Surgical instruments and apparatus

**(P-15149)**
**LINKS MEDICAL PRODUCTS INC (PA)**
9249 Research Dr, Irvine (92618-4286)
**PHONE**.................................949 753-0001
Thomas L Buckley, *CEO*
Patrick Buckley, *
▲ **EMP:** 22 **EST:** 1996
**SALES (est):** 2.81MM **Privately Held**
**Web:** www.linksmed.com
**SIC: 3841** Medical instruments and equipment, blood and bone work

**(P-15150)**
**LISI AEROSPACE**
2600 Skypark Dr, Torrance (90505-5314)
**PHONE**.................................310 326-8110
**EMP:** 30 **EST:** 2019
**SALES (est):** 13.84MM **Privately Held**
**Web:** www.lisi-medical.com
**SIC: 3841** Surgical and medical instruments

**(P-15151)**
**LOMA VISTA MEDICAL INC**
863 Mitten Rd Ste A100a, Burlingame (94010-1303)
**PHONE**.................................650 490-4747
Alex Tilson, *CEO*
Mark Scheeff, *VP*
**EMP:** 19 **EST:** 2007
**SQ FT:** 4,500
**SALES (est):** 2.14MM
**SALES (corp-wide):** 19.37B **Publicly Held**
**SIC: 3841** Surgical and medical instruments
**PA:** Becton, Dickinson And Company
1 Becton Dr
201 847-6800

**(P-15152)**
**LOMBARD MEDICAL TECH INC (PA)**
6440 Oak Cyn Ste 200, Irvine (92618-5209)
**PHONE**.................................949 379-3750
Kurt Lemvigh, *CEO*
Simon Hubbert, *CEO*
Micheal Gioffredi, *VP*
William Kullback, *CFO*
Peter W Phillips, *Dir*
**EMP:** 20 **EST:** 2006
**SQ FT:** 17,000
**SALES (est):** 3.8MM **Privately Held**
**Web:** www.lombardmedical.com
**SIC: 3841** Surgical and medical instruments

**(P-15153)**
**LOVEIS CORP**
Also Called: Ladybug Medical Supply
9588 Topanga Canyon Blvd, Chatsworth (91311)
**PHONE**.................................818 408-9504
Barry Wright Junior, *CEO*
**EMP:** 15 **EST:** 2020
**SALES (est):** 42MM **Privately Held**
**SIC: 3841** 5047 Surgical and medical instruments; Medical equipment and supplies

**(P-15154)**
**LUMENIS BE INC**
2077 Gateway Pl Ste 300, San Jose (95110-1149)
**PHONE**.................................877 586-3647
Zipora Ozer-armon, *CEO*
Shy Basson, *CFO*
Nazeeh Saab, *Corporate Controller*
Eran Kuppermaan, *Treas*
Brad Oliver, *Pr*
**EMP:** 280 **EST:** 2021
**SQ FT:** 13,500
**SALES (est):** 49.93MM **Privately Held**
**Web:** www.lumenis.com
**SIC: 3841** Surgical and medical instruments
**HQ:** Lumenis Ltd.
6 Hakidma

## 3841 - Surgical And Medical Instruments (P-15155)

Yokneam Illit 20692

**(P-15155)**
**LUMENIS INC (HQ)**
2077 Gateway Pl Ste 300, San Jose (95110-1149)
PHONE..................................408 764-3000
Tzipi Ozer Armon, *CEO*
Shlomi Cohen, *CFO*
Brad Oliver, *Pr*
Ido Warshavski, *Sec*
Jason Stinger, *VP Fin*
▲ **EMP:** 150 **EST:** 1992
**SQ FT:** 13,500
**SALES (est):** 42.48MM
**SALES (corp-wide):** 12.68B **Publicly Held**
Web: www.lumenis.com
**SIC: 3841** Surgical and medical instruments
PA: Boston Scientific Corporation
  300 Boston Scientific Way
  508 683-4000

**(P-15156)**
**LUMINOSTICS INC**
Also Called: Clip Health
48389 Fremont Blvd, Fremont (94538-6558)
PHONE..................................408 858-7103
Balakrishnan Raja, *Dir*
Balakrishnan Raja Venkatasubramaniam, *Dir*
Andrew Paterson, *Dir*
Gavin Garvey, *Dir*
James Hodges, *Dir*
**EMP:** 20 **EST:** 2014
**SALES (est):** 6.39MM **Privately Held**
Web: www.luminostics.com
**SIC: 3841** Surgical and medical instruments

**(P-15157)**
**MAGNUS MEDICAL INC**
1350 Bayshore Hwy Ste 600, Burlingame (94010-1887)
PHONE..................................415 231-7407
Brett Wingeir, *CEO*
**EMP:** 54 **EST:** 2020
**SALES (est):** 5.4MM **Privately Held**
Web: www.magnusmed.com
**SIC: 3841** Surgical and medical instruments

**(P-15158)**
**MAHANA THERAPEUTICS INC (PA)**
201 Mission St Ste 1200, San Francisco (94105-1805)
PHONE..................................650 483-4720
Simon Levy, *CEO*
Myla Puyat, *
**EMP:** 68 **EST:** 2018
**SALES (est):** 8.08MM
**SALES (corp-wide):** 8.08MM **Privately Held**
Web: www.mahana.com
**SIC: 3841** 8082 7372 Surgical and medical instruments; Home health care services; Application computer software

**(P-15159)**
**MARLEE MANUFACTURING INC**
4711 E Guasti Rd, Ontario (91761-8106)
PHONE..................................909 390-3222
Russell Wells, *Pr*
Patricia Wells, *
Shawn Cory, *
**EMP:** 39 **EST:** 1984
**SQ FT:** 41,000
**SALES (est):** 3.3MM **Privately Held**
Web: www.marleemanufacturing.com

**SIC: 3841** 3599 Surgical and medical instruments; Machine shop, jobbing and repair

**(P-15160)**
**MASIMO AMERICAS INC**
52 Discovery, Irvine (92618-3105)
PHONE..................................949 297-7000
Rick Fishel, *CEO*
**EMP:** 27 **EST:** 2004
**SALES (est):** 6.81MM **Publicly Held**
Web: www.masimo.com
**SIC: 3841** Surgical and medical instruments
PA: Masimo Corporation
  52 Discovery

**(P-15161)**
**MAST BIOSURGERY USA INC**
Also Called: Mast Biosurgery
6749 Top Gun St Ste 108, San Diego (92121-4151)
PHONE..................................858 550-8050
Thomas Brooas, *Pr*
Thoms Brooas, *
**EMP:** 30 **EST:** 2004
**SQ FT:** 10,000
**SALES (est):** 5.29MM **Privately Held**
Web: www.mastbio.com
**SIC: 3841** Surgical and medical instruments

**(P-15162)**
**MEDEDGE INC**
319 Windward Ave, Venice (90291-3766)
P.O. Box 3028 (90294-3028)
PHONE..................................310 392-9843
William J Schubert Junior, *Pr*
Donna L Schubert, *Sec*
**EMP:** 16 **EST:** 1996
**SQ FT:** 2,000
**SALES (est):** 837.35K **Privately Held**
Web: www.mededge-inc.com
**SIC: 3841** Surgical and medical instruments

**(P-15163)**
**MEDEOLOGIX INC**
Also Called: Mediballoon, Inc.
32940 Alvarado Niles Rd Ste 400, Union City (94587)
PHONE..................................510 431-3221
Anant Hegde, *CEO*
**EMP:** 25 **EST:** 2018
**SALES (est):** 4.85MM **Privately Held**
Web: www.mediballoon.com
**SIC: 3841** Surgical and medical instruments
HQ: Medeologix Corporation
  2f, No. 30, Baogao Rd.
  New Taipei City TAP 23102

**(P-15164)**
**MEDEOLOGIX LLC**
Also Called: Second Source Medical LLC
2200 Zanker Rd Ste F, San Jose (95131-1111)
PHONE..................................408 432-6388
Shawn Davis, *COO*
Shawn W Davis, *
Elisa Huang, *
**EMP:** 40 **EST:** 2004
**SALES (est):** 10.84MM **Privately Held**
Web: www.secondsourcemed.com
**SIC: 3841** Diagnostic apparatus, medical
HQ: Medeologix Corporation
  2f, No. 30, Baogao Rd.
  New Taipei City TAP 23102

**(P-15165)**
**MEDEONBIO INC**
452 Oakmead Pkwy, Sunnyvale (94085-4708)
PHONE..................................650 397-5100

Yue-teh Jang, *CEO*
**EMP:** 19 **EST:** 2012
**SALES (est):** 4.07MM **Privately Held**
Web: www.medeonbiodesign.com
**SIC: 3841** Surgical and medical instruments
HQ: Medeologix Corporation
  2f, No. 30, Baogao Rd.
  New Taipei City TAP 23102

**(P-15166)**
**MEDICAL DEPOT INC**
Also Called: Drive Devilbiss Healthcare
548 W Merrill Ave, Rialto (92376-9101)
PHONE..................................877 224-0946
**EMP:** 70
**SALES (corp-wide):** 409.99MM **Privately Held**
Web: www.drivemedical.com
**SIC: 3841** Surgical and medical instruments
HQ: Medical Depot, Inc.
  99 Seaview Blvd
  Port Washington NY 11050

**(P-15167)**
**MEDICAL INSTR DEV LABS INC**
Also Called: Mid Labs
557 Mccormick St, San Leandro (94577-1107)
PHONE..................................510 357-3952
Doctor Rob Peabody Senior, *CEO*
Carl Wang, *
**EMP:** 35 **EST:** 1991
**SQ FT:** 17,000
**SALES (est):** 6.82MM **Privately Held**
Web: www.midlabs.com
**SIC: 3841** Ophthalmic instruments and apparatus

**(P-15168)**
**MEDICAL TACTILE INC**
5500 W Rosecrans Ave Ste A, Hawthorne (90250-6642)
PHONE..................................310 641-8228
Jae Son, *Ch*
Steven Sanchez, *Sec*
Denis O'connor, *CEO*
▼ **EMP:** 20 **EST:** 2004
**SALES (est):** 1.88MM **Privately Held**
Web: www.mybexa.com
**SIC: 3841** Diagnostic apparatus, medical

**(P-15169)**
**MEDICOOL INC**
Also Called: TEC-Pro
20460 Gramercy Pl, Torrance (90501-1513)
PHONE..................................310 782-2200
Steve Yeager, *Prin*
◆ **EMP:** 17 **EST:** 1986
**SQ FT:** 15,000
**SALES (est):** 2.61MM **Privately Held**
Web: www.medicool.com
**SIC: 3841** Inhalators, surgical and medical

**(P-15170)**
**MEDTRONIC INC**
Also Called: Medtronic
2101 Faraday Ave, Carlsbad (92008-7205)
PHONE..................................760 214-3009
**EMP:** 26
Web: medtronic.dejobs.org
**SIC: 3841** Surgical and medical instruments
HQ: Medtronic, Inc.
  710 Medtronic Pkwy
  Minneapolis MN 55432
  763 514-4000

**(P-15171)**
**MEDTRONIC INC**
Medtronic
1851 E Deere Ave, Santa Ana (92705)

PHONE..................................949 474-3943
Walter Cuevas, *Mgr*
**EMP:** 518
**SQ FT:** 47,000
Web: www.medtronic.com
**SIC: 3841** Surgical and medical instruments
HQ: Medtronic, Inc.
  710 Medtronic Pkwy
  Minneapolis MN 55432
  763 514-4000

**(P-15172)**
**MEDTRONIC INC**
Also Called: Medtronic
3062 Bunker Hill Ln, Santa Clara (95054-1105)
PHONE..................................408 548-6618
Richard Mott, *CEO*
**EMP:** 53
Web: www.medtronic.com
**SIC: 3841** Surgical and medical instruments
HQ: Medtronic, Inc.
  710 Medtronic Pkwy
  Minneapolis MN 55432
  763 514-4000

**(P-15173)**
**MEDTRONIC INC**
Also Called: Medtronic
1659 Gailes Blvd, San Diego (92154-8230)
PHONE..................................949 798-3934
Araceli Rodriguez, *Brnch Mgr*
**EMP:** 27
Web: www.medtronic.com
**SIC: 3841** Surgical and medical instruments
HQ: Medtronic, Inc.
  710 Medtronic Pkwy
  Minneapolis MN 55432
  763 514-4000

**(P-15174)**
**MEDTRONIC INC**
Also Called: Medtronic
9775 Toledo Way, Irvine (92618-1811)
PHONE..................................949 837-3700
Geoff Martha, *Ch Bd*
**EMP:** 200
Web: www.medtronic.com
**SIC: 3841** Surgical and medical instruments
HQ: Medtronic, Inc.
  710 Medtronic Pkwy
  Minneapolis MN 55432
  763 514-4000

**(P-15175)**
**MEDTRONIC INC**
5345 Skylane Blvd, Santa Rosa (95403-1044)
PHONE..................................707 541-3144
Eric Kunz, *Brnch Mgr*
**EMP:** 30
Web: www.medtronic.com
**SIC: 3841** 5047 5999 Surgical and medical instruments; Medical equipment and supplies; Medical apparatus and supplies
HQ: Medtronic, Inc.
  710 Medtronic Pkwy
  Minneapolis MN 55432
  763 514-4000

**(P-15176)**
**MEDTRONIC ATS MEDICAL INC**
1851 E Deere Ave, Santa Ana (92705-5720)
PHONE..................................949 380-9333
Walter Cuevas, *Brnch Mgr*
**EMP:** 133
Web: www.medtronic.com
**SIC: 3841** Surgical instruments and apparatus

## 3841 - Surgical And Medical Instruments (P-15196)

HQ: Medtronic Ats Medical, Inc.
710 Medtronic Pkwy
Minneapolis MN 55432
763 553-7736

**(P-15177)**
**MEDTRONIC CARDIOVASCULAR**
Also Called: Medtronic
3576 Unocal Pl, Santa Rosa (95403-1774)
P.O. Box 778 (55440-0778)
PHONE.....................707 545-1156
▲ EMP: 5038
Web: www.medtronic.com
SIC: 3841 Surgical instruments and apparatus

**(P-15178)**
**MEDTRONIC MINIMED INC (DH)**
Also Called: Medtronic
18000 Devonshire St, Northridge (91325)
PHONE.....................800 646-4633
Sean Salmon, *Pr*
Austin Domenici, *
Eric P Geismar, *
George J Montague, *
▲ EMP: 1200 EST: 1993
SQ FT: 250,000
SALES (est): 443.05MM Privately Held
Web: www.medtronicdiabetes.com
SIC: 3841 Surgical and medical instruments
HQ: Medtronic, Inc.
710 Medtronic Pkwy
Minneapolis MN 55432
763 514-4000

**(P-15179)**
**MEDTRONIC PS MEDICAL INC (DH)**
Also Called: Medtronic
5290 California Ave # 100, Irvine (92617-3229)
PHONE.....................805 571-3769
◆ EMP: 200 EST: 1978
SALES (est): 102.71MM Privately Held
Web: www.medtronic.com
SIC: 3841 Surgical and medical instruments
HQ: Medtronic, Inc.
710 Medtronic Pkwy
Minneapolis MN 55432
763 514-4000

**(P-15180)**
**MEDTRONIC SPINE LLC**
1221 Crossman Ave, Sunnyvale (94089-1103)
PHONE.....................408 548-6500
Bill Hawkins, *Pr*
Karen D Talmadge, *VP*
EMP: 1090 EST: 2008
SQ FT: 151,000
SALES (est): 7.46MM Privately Held
Web: www.medtronic.com
SIC: 3841 Surgical and medical instruments
HQ: Medtronic, Inc.
710 Medtronic Pkwy
Minneapolis MN 55432
763 514-4000

**(P-15181)**
**MEDWAND SOLUTIONS INC**
23162 Arroyo Vis, Rancho Santa Margari (92688-2608)
PHONE.....................770 363-7053
Todd Cornell, *CEO*
Samir Qamar, *Prin*
EMP: 20 EST: 2014
SQ FT: 1,000
SALES (est): 6.02MM Privately Held
Web: www.medwand.com
SIC: 3841 Surgical and medical instruments

**(P-15182)**
**MEDZON HEALTH**
2099 S State College Blvd Ste 360, Anaheim (92806-6142)
PHONE.....................844 860-8584
EMP: 24 EST: 2020
SALES (est): 4.5MM Privately Held
Web: www.medzonhealth.com
SIC: 3841 Surgical and medical instruments

**(P-15183)**
**MEMRY CORPORATION**
4065 Campbell Ave, Menlo Park (94025-1006)
PHONE.....................650 463-3400
Robert Richardson, *Prin*
EMP: 115
Web: www.memry.com
SIC: 3841 Surgical and medical instruments
HQ: Memry Corporation
3 Berkshire Boulevard
Bethel CT 06801
203 739-1100

**(P-15184)**
**MERAQI MEDICAL INC**
47225 Fremont Blvd, Fremont (94538-6502)
PHONE.....................669 222-7710
Alan Hershey, *CEO*
EMP: 40 EST: 2017
SALES (est): 5.06MM
SALES (corp-wide): 466.54MM Privately Held
Web: www.viantmedical.com
SIC: 3841 Surgical and medical instruments
HQ: Viant Medical, Llc
2 Hampshire St
Foxborough MA 02035

**(P-15185)**
**MERIT CABLES INCORPORATED**
830 N Poinsettia St, Santa Ana (92701-3853)
PHONE.....................714 918-1932
Ted Hendrickson, *CEO*
David Greenwald, *
Ruben Mauricio, *
Rich Mchugh, *Dir*
▼ EMP: 25 EST: 1986
SQ FT: 8,000
SALES (est): 2.59MM
SALES (corp-wide): 130.59MM Privately Held
Web: www.meritcables.com
SIC: 3841 Surgical and medical instruments
PA: Addvise Group Ab (Publ)
Grev Turegatan 30, 2 Tr
856485180

**(P-15186)**
**MERIT MEDICAL SYSTEMS INC**
6 Journey Ste 125, Aliso Viejo (92656-5319)
PHONE.....................801 208-4793
Judy Wagner, *Brnch Mgr*
EMP: 20
SALES (corp-wide): 1.26B Publicly Held
Web: www.merit.com
SIC: 3841 Surgical and medical instruments
PA: Merit Medical Systems, Inc.
1600 W Merit Pkwy
801 253-1600

**(P-15187)**
**METTLER ELECTRONICS CORP**
1333 S Claudina St, Anaheim (92805-6266)
PHONE.....................714 533-2221
Stephen C Mettler, *CEO*
Mark Mettler, *
Donna Mettler, *
Matthew Ferrari, *
▲ EMP: 42 EST: 1957
SQ FT: 22,500
SALES (est): 6.35MM Privately Held
Web: www.mettlerelectronics.com
SIC: 3841 Surgical and medical instruments

**(P-15188)**
**MICRO THERAPEUTICS INC (HQ)**
Also Called: Ev3 Neurovascular
9775 Toledo Way, Irvine (92618)
PHONE.....................949 837-3700
Thomas C Wilder Iii, *Pr*
Thomas Berryman, *CFO*
EMP: 29 EST: 1993
SQ FT: 43,000
SALES (est): 4.46MM Privately Held
Web: www.medtronic.com
SIC: 3841 Surgical and medical instruments
PA: Medtronic Public Limited Company
20 Hatch Street Lower

**(P-15189)**
**MICROVENTION INC (DH)**
Also Called: Microvention Terumo
35 Enterprise, Aliso Viejo (92656-2601)
PHONE.....................714 258-8000
Carsten Schroeder, *Pr*
Kazuaki Kitabatake, *
Bruce Canter, *
Thierry De Bosson, *
Jacques Dion, *
▲ EMP: 190 EST: 1997
SQ FT: 35,000
SALES (est): 222.49MM Privately Held
Web: www.microvention.com
SIC: 3841 Surgical and medical instruments
HQ: Terumo Americas Holding, Inc.
265 Davidson Ave Ste 320
Somerset NJ 08873
732 302-4900

**(P-15190)**
**MICRUS ENDOVASCULAR LLC (HQ)**
821 Fox Ln, San Jose (95131-1601)
PHONE.....................408 433-1400
P Laxminarain, *Pr*
John T Kilcoyne, *CEO*
Robert A Stern, *Pr*
Gordon T Sangster, *CFO*
Carolyn M Bruguera, *VP*
EMP: 139 EST: 1997
SQ FT: 42,000
SALES (est): 10.59MM
SALES (corp-wide): 85.16B Publicly Held
SIC: 3841 Surgical instruments and apparatus
PA: Johnson & Johnson
1 Johnson & Johnson Plz
732 524-0400

**(P-15191)**
**MINERVA SURGICAL INC**
Also Called: Minerva
4255 Burton Dr, Santa Clara (95054-1512)
PHONE.....................855 646-7874
Darin Hammers, *Pr*
Ross A Jaffe, *
Dominique J Filloux, *COO*
Joel R Jung, *CFO*
Evgueni V Skalnyi, *VP*
▲ EMP: 139 EST: 2008
SQ FT: 32,719
SALES (est): 50.29MM Privately Held
Web: www.minervasurgical.com

SIC: 3841 Surgical and medical instruments

**(P-15192)**
**MIZUHO ORTHOPEDIC SYSTEMS INC (HQ)**
Also Called: Mizuho OSI
30031 Ahern Ave, Union City (94587-1234)
P.O. Box 1468 (94587-6468)
PHONE.....................510 429-1500
Takashi Nemoto, *CEO*
Steve Lamb, *
Yosup Kim, *
Patrick Rimroth, *
◆ EMP: 50 EST: 1977
SQ FT: 111,100
SALES (est): 98.31MM Privately Held
Web: www.mizuhosi.com
SIC: 3841 Operating tables
PA: Mizuho Corporation
3-30-13, Hongo

**(P-15193)**
**MIZUHO ORTHOPEDIC SYSTEMS INC**
30063 Ahern Ave, Union City (94587-1234)
PHONE.....................510 429-1500
EMP: 249
Web: www.mizuhosi.com
SIC: 3841 Operating tables
HQ: Mizuho Orthopedic Systems, Inc.
30031 Ahern Ave
Union City CA 94587
510 429-1500

**(P-15194)**
**MODULAR MEDICAL INC (PA)**
Also Called: Modular Medical
10740 Thornmint Rd, San Diego (92127-2700)
PHONE.....................858 800-3500
James Besser, *CEO*
Paul Diperna, *Ch Bd*
Kevin Schmid, *COO*
EMP: 21 EST: 2015
SQ FT: 24,000
Web: www.modular-medical.com
SIC: 3841 Surgical and medical instruments

**(P-15195)**
**MONOBIND SALES INC (PA)**
100 N Pointe Dr, Lake Forest (92630-2270)
PHONE.....................949 951-2665
Frederick Jerome, *Pr*
Doctor Jay Singh, *VP*
▲ EMP: 25 EST: 1977
SQ FT: 18,000
SALES (est): 8.27MM
SALES (corp-wide): 8.27MM Privately Held
Web: www.monobind.com
SIC: 3841 Diagnostic apparatus, medical

**(P-15196)**
**MOXIMED INC (PA)**
46602 Landing Pkwy, Fremont (94538-6420)
PHONE.....................510 887-3300
Christopher Gleason, *Pr*
Kevin Sidow, *Pr*
Anton Clifford, *VP*
Karen Nguyen, *CFO*
EMP: 16 EST: 2006
SQ FT: 4,100
SALES (est): 5.25MM Privately Held
Web: www.moximed.com
SIC: 3841 Surgical and medical instruments

## 3841 - Surgical And Medical Instruments (P-15197)

**(P-15197)**
**MPS MEDICAL INC**
785 Challenger St, Brea (92821-2948)
PHONE..........................714 672-1090
Barry A Kazemi, *CEO*
**EMP:** 37 **EST:** 2014
**SALES (est):** 4.35MM
**SALES (corp-wide):** 46.95MM **Privately Held**
Web: www.mpsmedical-inc.com
**SIC: 3841** Surgical and medical instruments
PA: Innova Medical Group, Inc.
  800 E Colo Blvd Ste 288
  760 330-6123

**(P-15198)**
**NELLIX INC**
2 Musick, Irvine (92618-1631)
PHONE..........................650 213-8700
Robert D Mitchell, *Pr*
Doug Hughes, *
**EMP:** 29 **EST:** 2001
**SQ FT:** 7,500
**SALES (est):** 9.84MM **Privately Held**
**SIC: 3841** Surgical and medical instruments
PA: Endologix, Inc.
  2 Musick

**(P-15199)**
**NEOMEND INC**
60 Technology Dr, Irvine (92618-2301)
PHONE..........................949 783-3300
David Renzi, *Pr*
Kevin Cousins, *
David Hanson, *
Pete Davis, *
▼ **EMP:** 90 **EST:** 1999
**SQ FT:** 21,000
**SALES (est):** 23.51MM
**SALES (corp-wide):** 19.37B **Publicly Held**
**SIC: 3841** Surgical and medical instruments
HQ: C. R. Bard, Inc.
  1 Becton Dr
  Franklin Lakes NJ 07417
  201 847-6800

**(P-15200)**
**NEUROPACE INC**
Also Called: NEUROPACE
455 Bernardo Ave, Mountain View (94043-5237)
PHONE..........................650 237-2700
Joel Becker, *Pr*
Frank Fischer, *
Rebecca Kuhn, *Corporate Secretary*
Martha Morrell, *CMO*
**EMP:** 179 **EST:** 1997
**SQ FT:** 53,000
**SALES (est):** 65.42MM **Privately Held**
Web: www.neuropace.com
**SIC: 3841** Surgical and medical instruments

**(P-15201)**
**NEUROPTICS INC**
9223 Research Dr, Irvine (92618-4286)
PHONE..........................949 250-9792
William Worthen, *CEO*
Kamran Siminou, *
William Worthen, *Pr*
Deborah Fineberg, *Global Vice President*
▲ **EMP:** 45 **EST:** 1995
**SALES (est):** 7.57MM **Privately Held**
Web: www.neuroptics.com
**SIC: 3841** Surgical and medical instruments

**(P-15202)**
**NEUROVASC TECHNOLOGIES INC**
3 Jenner Ste 100, Irvine (92618-3827)
PHONE..........................949 258-9946
**EMP:** 26 **EST:** 2016
**SALES (est):** 5.1MM **Privately Held**
Web: www.neurovasctechnologies.com
**SIC: 3841** Surgical and medical instruments

**(P-15203)**
**NEVRO CORP (PA)**
1800 Bridge Pkwy, Redwood City (94065-1164)
PHONE..........................650 251-0005
Kevin Thornal, *Pr*
D Keith Grossman, *
Roderick H Macleod, *CFO*
Kashif Rashid, *Corporate Secretary*
Richard B Carter, *CAO*
**EMP:** 981 **EST:** 2006
**SQ FT:** 50,740
**SALES (est):** 425.17MM **Publicly Held**
Web: www.nevro.com
**SIC: 3841** Surgical and medical instruments

**(P-15204)**
**NEW WORLD MEDICAL INCORPORATED**
10763 Edison Ct, Rancho Cucamonga (91730-4844)
PHONE..........................909 466-4304
A Mateen Ahmed, *Pr*
Omar Ahmed, *VP*
**EMP:** 17 **EST:** 1990
**SQ FT:** 10,000
**SALES (est):** 4.64MM **Privately Held**
Web: www.newworldmedical.com
**SIC: 3841** Ophthalmic instruments and apparatus

**(P-15205)**
**NEWPORT MEDICAL INSTRS INC**
Also Called: Covidien
1620 Sunflower Ave, Costa Mesa (92626-1513)
PHONE..........................949 642-3910
Philippe Negre, *Pr*
◆ **EMP:** 89 **EST:** 1981
**SQ FT:** 33,328
**SALES (est):** 9.74MM **Privately Held**
Web: www.allenstethoscopes.com
**SIC: 3841** 3842 3845 Surgical and medical instruments; Respirators; Electromedical equipment
HQ: Covidien Limited
  20 Lower Hatch Street
  Dublin D02 H

**(P-15206)**
**NEXUS DX INC**
6759 Mesa Ridge Rd, San Diego (92121-4902)
PHONE..........................858 410-4600
Nam Shin, *CEO*
▼ **EMP:** 34 **EST:** 2009
**SQ FT:** 39,000
**SALES (est):** 8.02MM
**SALES (corp-wide):** 310.54K **Privately Held**
Web: www.nexus-dx.com
**SIC: 3841** Diagnostic apparatus, medical
HQ: Polaris Medinet, Llc
  13571 Zinnia Hills Pl
  San Diego CA 92130
  858 410-4600

**(P-15207)**
**NOBLES MEDICAL TECH INC**
17080 Newhope St, Fountain Valley (92708-4206)
PHONE..........................714 427-0398
Anthony A Nobles, *Prin*
**EMP:** 42 **EST:** 2009
**SALES (est):** 1.86MM **Privately Held**
**SIC: 3841** Medical instruments and equipment, blood and bone work

**(P-15208)**
**NORDSON MEDICAL (CA) LLC**
7612 Woodwind Dr, Huntington Beach (92647-7164)
PHONE..........................657 215-4200
David Zgonc, *Managing Member*
**EMP:** 51 **EST:** 1991
**SQ FT:** 40,000
**SALES (est):** 9.67MM
**SALES (corp-wide):** 2.63B **Publicly Held**
Web: www.nordson.com
**SIC: 3841** Surgical and medical instruments
PA: Nordson Corporation
  28601 Clemens Rd
  440 892-1580

**(P-15209)**
**NOVA EYE INC**
Also Called: Nova Eye
41316 Christy St, Fremont (94538-3115)
PHONE..........................510 291-1300
Victor Previn, *CEO*
Jennifer Hagan, *Sec*
**EMP:** 25 **EST:** 2013
**SALES (est):** 6.11MM **Privately Held**
Web: www.nova-eye.com
**SIC: 3841** Surgical and medical instruments

**(P-15210)**
**NU-HOPE LABORATORIES INC**
12640 Branford St, Pacoima (91331-3451)
P.O. Box 331150 (91333-1150)
PHONE..........................818 899-7711
Bradley Johnson Galindo, *CEO*
Estelle Galindo, *
▲ **EMP:** 38 **EST:** 1959
**SQ FT:** 25,000
**SALES (est):** 4.78MM **Privately Held**
Web: www.nu-hope.com
**SIC: 3841** Surgical and medical instruments

**(P-15211)**
**NUVASIVE INC**
4223 Ponderosa Ave Ste C, San Diego (92123-1529)
PHONE..........................858 909-1800
**EMP:** 18
**SALES (corp-wide):** 1.57B **Publicly Held**
Web: www.nuvasive.com
**SIC: 3841** Surgical and medical instruments
HQ: Nuvasive, Inc.
  7475 Lusk Blvd
  San Diego CA 92121
  858 909-1800

**(P-15212)**
**NUVASIVE INC (HQ)**
7475 Lusk Blvd, San Diego (92121-5707)
PHONE..........................858 909-1800
J Christopher Barry, *CEO*
Daniel J Wolterman, *
Rajesh J Asarpota, *CAO*
Carol A Cox, *External Affairs Vice President*
Joan B Stafslien, *Corporate Secretary*
▲ **EMP:** 75 **EST:** 1997
**SQ FT:** 152,000
**SALES (est):** 406.33MM
**SALES (corp-wide):** 1.57B **Publicly Held**
Web: www.nuvasive.com
**SIC: 3841** Surgical and medical instruments
PA: Globus Medical, Inc.
  2560 Gen Armistead Ave
  610 930-1800

**(P-15213)**
**OPTIMEDICA CORPORATION**
510 Cottonwood Dr, Milpitas (95035-7403)
PHONE..........................408 850-8600
Miles White, *CEO*
Mark J Forchette, *
Mark A Murray, *
**EMP:** 37 **EST:** 2004
**SALES (est):** 3.66MM
**SALES (corp-wide):** 85.16B **Publicly Held**
**SIC: 3841** Eye examining instruments and apparatus
PA: Johnson & Johnson
  1 Johnson & Johnson Plz
  732 524-0400

**(P-15214)**
**OPTISCAN BIOMEDICAL CORP**
Also Called: Optiscan
35452 Galen Pl, Fremont (94536-3321)
PHONE..........................510 342-5800
**EMP:** 50
Web: www.blackdogsecondchance.org
**SIC: 3841** Diagnostic apparatus, medical

**(P-15215)**
**ORCHID MPS**
3233 W Harvard St, Santa Ana (92704-3917)
PHONE..........................714 549-9203
Mark Deischter, *VP*
**EMP:** 100 **EST:** 2005
**SALES (est):** 4.82MM **Privately Held**
Web: www.orchid-ortho.com
**SIC: 3841** Surgical and medical instruments

**(P-15216)**
**ORTHOFIX MEDICAL INC**
501 Mercury Dr, Sunnyvale (94085-4019)
PHONE..........................214 937-2000
**EMP:** 24
**SALES (corp-wide):** 746.64MM **Privately Held**
Web: www.orthofix.com
**SIC: 3841** Surgical and medical instruments
PA: Orthofix Medical Inc.
  3451 Plano Pkwy
  214 937-2000

**(P-15217)**
**ORTHOGROUP INC**
11280 Sanders Dr Ste A, Rancho Cordova (95742-6888)
PHONE..........................916 859-0881
Henry Fletcher, *CEO*
**EMP:** 15 **EST:** 2005
**SALES (est):** 3.05MM **Privately Held**
Web: www.orthogroup.com
**SIC: 3841** Medical instruments and equipment, blood and bone work

**(P-15218)**
**OSSEON LLC**
2301 Circadian Way Ste 300, Santa Rosa (95407-5444)
PHONE..........................707 636-5940
**EMP:** 15 **EST:** 2014
**SQ FT:** 10,000
**SALES (est):** 976.74K **Privately Held**
Web: www.osseon.com
**SIC: 3841** Surgical and medical instruments

**(P-15219)**
**OSSEON THERAPEUTICS INC**
2305 Circadian Way, Santa Rosa (95407-5416)
PHONE..........................707 636-5940
**EMP:** 40
**SIC: 3841** Diagnostic apparatus, medical

▲ = Import  ▼ = Export
◆ = Import/Export

## PRODUCTS & SERVICES SECTION
### 3841 - Surgical And Medical Instruments (P-15242)

**(P-15220)**
**PACIFIC INTEGRATED MFG INC**
4364 Bonita Rd Ste 454, Bonita (91902-1421)
PHONE..................................619 921-3464
Stephen F Keane, *CEO*
Charles Peinado, *
**EMP:** 200 **EST:** 2000
**SALES (est):** 10.9MM **Privately Held**
**Web:** www.pacific-im.com
**SIC: 3841** Diagnostic apparatus, medical

**(P-15221)**
**PENUMBRA INC (PA)**
Also Called: PENUMBRA
1 Penumbra, Alameda (94502-7676)
PHONE..................................510 748-3200
Adam Elsesser, *Ch Bd*
Maggie Yuen, *CFO*
Lambert Shiu, *CAO*
Johanna Roberts, *Ex VP*
**EMP:** 485 **EST:** 2004
**SQ FT:** 600,000
**SALES (est):** 1.06B
**SALES (corp-wide):** 1.06B **Publicly Held**
**Web:** www.penumbrainc.com
**SIC: 3841** Surgical and medical instruments

**(P-15222)**
**PETER BRASSELER HOLDINGS LLC**
4837 Mcgrath St, Ventura (93003-6442)
PHONE..................................805 658-2643
Laura Kriese, *Brnch Mgr*
**EMP:** 74
**SALES (corp-wide):** 22.1MM **Privately Held**
**Web:** www.brasselerusa.com
**SIC: 3841** Surgical and medical instruments
**PA:** Peter Brasseler Holdings, Llc
  1 Brasseler Blvd
  912 925-8525

**(P-15223)**
**PHARMACO-KINESIS CORPORATION**
10604 S La Cienega Blvd, Inglewood (90304-1115)
PHONE..................................310 641-2700
Frank Adell, *Prin*
Thomas Chen, *
Peter Hirshfield, *
John Muthew, *
**EMP:** 26 **EST:** 2006
**SALES (est):** 4.94MM **Privately Held**
**Web:** www.pharmaco-kinesis.com
**SIC: 3841** Surgical and medical instruments

**(P-15224)**
**PHILLPS-MDISIZE COSTA MESA LLC**
3545 Harbor Blvd, Costa Mesa (92626-1406)
PHONE..................................949 477-9495
Bob Frank, *Genl Mgr*
**EMP:** 240 **EST:** 1997
**SQ FT:** 45,000
**SALES (est):** 31.09MM
**SALES (corp-wide):** 64.37B **Privately Held**
**Web:** www.phillipsmedisize.com
**SIC: 3841** Surgical and medical instruments
**HQ:** Molex, Llc
  2222 Wellington Ct
  Lisle IL 60532
  630 969-4550

**(P-15225)**
**PHOENIX DEVENTURES INC**
18655 Madrone Pkwy Ste 180, Morgan Hill (95037-8101)
PHONE..................................408 782-6240
Jeffrey Christian, *Pr*
**EMP:** 47 **EST:** 2000
**SQ FT:** 30,000
**SALES (est):** 9.24MM **Privately Held**
**Web:** www.phoenixdeventures.com
**SIC: 3841** Surgical and medical instruments

**(P-15226)**
**PLANET INNOVATION INC**
2720 Loker Ave W Ste P, Carlsbad (92010-6606)
PHONE..................................847 943-7270
Anthony White, *Pr*
**EMP:** 30 **EST:** 2013
**SALES (est):** 22.93MM **Privately Held**
**Web:** www.planetinnovation.com
**SIC: 3841** Surgical and medical instruments
**PA:** Planet Innovation Holdings Ltd
  436 Elgar Rd

**(P-15227)**
**PLASVACC USA INC**
1535 Templeton Rd, Templeton (93465-9694)
PHONE..................................805 434-0321
Andrew Mcarthur, *Pr*
**EMP:** 15 **EST:** 2005
**SALES (est):** 2.47MM **Privately Held**
**Web:** www.plasvacc.com
**SIC: 3841** Surgical and medical instruments

**(P-15228)**
**POTRERO MEDICAL INC**
Also Called: Accuryn Monitoring System
26142 Eden Landing Rd, Hayward (94545-3710)
PHONE..................................888 635-7280
Joe Urban, *CEO*
Myria Crawford, *VP*
Rich Keenan, *VP*
Kelly Stanton, *VP*
Sanjay Banerjee, *COO*
**EMP:** 52 **EST:** 2014
**SQ FT:** 15,000
**SALES (est):** 10.43MM **Privately Held**
**Web:** www.accuryn.com
**SIC: 3841** Diagnostic apparatus, medical

**(P-15229)**
**PRANALYTICA INC**
1101 Colorado Ave, Santa Monica (90401-3009)
PHONE..................................310 458-3345
C Kumar N Patel, *Pr*
Francis Mcguire, *VP Fin*
**EMP:** 15 **EST:** 1999
**SQ FT:** 7,350
**SALES (est):** 2.28MM **Privately Held**
**Web:** www.pranalytica.com
**SIC: 3841 3826** Surgical and medical instruments; Laser scientific and engineering instruments

**(P-15230)**
**PRO-DEX INC (PA)**
Also Called: PRO-DEX
2361 Mcgaw Ave, Irvine (92614-5831)
PHONE..................................949 769-3200
Richard L Van Kirk, *Pr*
Nicholas J Swenson, *
Alisha K Charlton, *CFO*
**EMP:** 120 **EST:** 1978
**SQ FT:** 28,000
**SALES (est):** 53.84MM **Publicly Held**
**Web:** www.pro-dex.com
**SIC: 3841 3843 7372 3594** Surgical and medical instruments; Dental equipment; Business oriented computer software; Motors, pneumatic

**(P-15231)**
**PROCEPT BIOROBOTICS CORP (PA)**
Also Called: PROCEPT BIOROBOTICS
150 Baytech Dr, San Jose (95134-2302)
PHONE..................................650 232-7200
Reza Zadno, *Pr*
Frederic Moll, *
Kevin Waters, *Ex VP*
Alaleh Nouri, *CLO*
Hisham Shiblaq, *Chief Commercial Officer*
**EMP:** 419 **EST:** 2007
**SALES (est):** 136.19MM
**SALES (corp-wide):** 136.19MM **Publicly Held**
**Web:** www.procept-biorobotics.com
**SIC: 3841** Surgical and medical instruments

**(P-15232)**
**PROSURG INC**
Also Called: Ximed Medical Systems
2195 Trade Zone Blvd, San Jose (95131-1743)
PHONE..................................408 945-4040
Ashvin H Desai, *Pr*
**EMP:** 40 **EST:** 1987
**SQ FT:** 14,800
**SALES (est):** 2.06MM **Privately Held**
**Web:** www.prosurg.com
**SIC: 3841 3823** Surgical and medical instruments; Process control instruments

**(P-15233)**
**PROVIDIEN LLC (HQ)**
6740 Nancy Ridge Dr, San Diego (92121-2230)
PHONE..................................480 344-5000
Jeffrey S Goble, *CEO*
Paul Jazwin, *CFO*
Charles Stroupe, *Ch Bd*
**EMP:** 114 **EST:** 2011
**SALES (est):** 46.89MM
**SALES (corp-wide):** 4.59B **Publicly Held**
**Web:** www.providienmedical.com
**SIC: 3841** Surgical and medical instruments
**PA:** Carlisle Companies Incorporated
  16430 N Scttsdale Rd Ste
  480 781-5000

**(P-15234)**
**PROVIDIEN MACHINING & METALS LLC**
Also Called: Providien Machining Mtls Corp
12840 Bradley Ave, Sylmar (91342)
PHONE..................................818 367-3161
◆ **EMP:** 70 **EST:** 1987
**SALES (est):** 8.39MM
**SALES (corp-wide):** 4.59B **Publicly Held**
**Web:** resource.dynaroll.com
**SIC: 3841** Surgical and medical instruments
**HQ:** Providien, Llc
  6740 Nancy Ridge Dr
  San Diego CA 92121

**(P-15235)**
**PRYOR PRODUCTS**
1819 Peacock Blvd, Oceanside (92056-3578)
PHONE..................................760 724-8244
Jeffrey Pryor, *CEO*
Paul Pryor, *
▲ **EMP:** 50 **EST:** 1971
**SQ FT:** 29,000
**SALES (est):** 8.96MM **Privately Held**
**Web:** www.pryorproducts.com
**SIC: 3841** IV transfusion apparatus

**(P-15236)**
**QAPEL MEDICAL INC**
4245 Technology Dr, Fremont (94538-6339)
PHONE..................................510 738-6255
Jodie Fam, *CEO*
**EMP:** 79 **EST:** 2015
**SALES (est):** 7.86MM **Privately Held**
**Web:** www.qapelmedical.com
**SIC: 3841** Surgical and medical instruments

**(P-15237)**
**R2 TECHNOLOGIES INC**
6517 Sierra Ln, Dublin (94568-2798)
PHONE..................................925 378-4400
Tim Holt, *CEO*
Rox Anderson, *
**EMP:** 45 **EST:** 2015
**SALES (est):** 5.3MM **Privately Held**
**Web:** www.r2derm.com
**SIC: 3841** Surgical and medical instruments

**(P-15238)**
**RADIOLOGY SUPPORT DEVICES INC**
1501 W 178th St, Gardena (90248-3203)
P.O. Box 7490 (90504-8890)
PHONE..................................310 518-0527
Matthew Alderson, *CEO*
**EMP:** 29 **EST:** 1989
**SQ FT:** 16,000
**SALES (est):** 2.49MM **Privately Held**
**Web:** www.rsdphantoms.com
**SIC: 3841 3844** Diagnostic apparatus, medical; X-ray apparatus and tubes

**(P-15239)**
**REBOUND THERAPEUTICS CORP**
13900 Alton Pkwy Ste 120, Irvine (92618-1621)
PHONE..................................949 305-8111
Jeffrey Valko, *CEO*
**EMP:** 26 **EST:** 2015
**SALES (est):** 2.38MM **Publicly Held**
**SIC: 3841** Surgical and medical instruments
**PA:** Integra Lifesciences Holdings Corporation
  1100 Campus Rd

**(P-15240)**
**RESMED CORP**
14040 Danielson St, Poway (92064-6857)
PHONE..................................858 746-2400
**EMP:** 22 **EST:** 2019
**SALES (est):** 5.75MM **Privately Held**
**Web:** www.resmed.co.in
**SIC: 3841** Surgical and medical instruments

**(P-15241)**
**RESMED INC (PA)**
Also Called: Resmed
9001 Spectrum Center Blvd, San Diego (92123-1438)
PHONE..................................858 836-5000
Michael Farrell, *Ch Bd*
Rob Douglas, *Pr*
Brett Sandercock, *CFO*
**EMP:** 702 **EST:** 1989
**SQ FT:** 230,000
**SALES (est):** 4.69B **Publicly Held**
**Web:** www.resmed.com
**SIC: 3841 7372** Diagnostic apparatus, medical; Application computer software

**(P-15242)**
**REVERSE MEDICAL CORPORATION**
Also Called: Reverse Medical

## 3841 - Surgical And Medical Instruments (P-15243)

13700 Alton Pkwy Ste 167, Irvine
(92618-1618)
PHONE..................................949 215-0660
Jeffrey Valko, *Pr*
**EMP:** 47 **EST:** 2007
**SALES (est):** 5.43MM **Privately Held**
Web: www.reversemed.com
**SIC: 3841** Surgical and medical instruments
HQ: Covidien Limited
  20 Lower Hatch Street
  Dublin D02 H

### (P-15243)
### RF SURGICAL SYSTEMS LLC
5927 Landau Ct, Carlsbad (92008-8803)
PHONE..................................855 522-7027
John Buhler, *Pr*
Ron Wangerin, *CFO*
▲ **EMP:** 55 **EST:** 2008
**SQ FT:** 24,000
**SALES (est):** 2.3MM **Privately Held**
**SIC: 3841** Surgical and medical instruments
HQ: Medtronic, Inc.
  710 Medtronic Pkwy
  Minneapolis MN 55432
  763 514-4000

### (P-15244)
### RH USA INC
Also Called: Lumenis
455 N Canyons Pkwy Ste B, Livermore
(94551-7682)
PHONE..................................925 245-7900
Jeannette Trujillo, *VP*
Bob Schultz, *
Gladys Copeland, *
Miranda Yee, *
▲ **EMP:** 42 **EST:** 2004
**SQ FT:** 40,000
**SALES (est):** 12.29MM **Privately Held**
Web: www.rh-global.com
**SIC: 3841** Surgical and medical instruments
PA: R.H. Technologies Ltd
  5 Hatzoref

### (P-15245)
### ROCHE SEQUENCING SOLUTIONS INC
2841 Scott Blvd, Santa Clara (95050-2549)
PHONE..................................925 854-6246
**EMP:** 15
**SIC: 3841** Surgical and medical instruments
HQ: Roche Sequencing Solutions, Inc.
  4300 Hacienda Dr
  Pleasanton CA 94588
  925 854-6246

### (P-15246)
### ROX MEDICAL INC (PA)
150 Calle Iglesia Ste A, San Clemente
(92672-7550)
P.O. Box 4078 (92629-9078)
PHONE..................................949 276-8968
Mike Mackinnon, *CEO*
Keegan Harper, *Ch Bd*
Jonathan Sackner-bernstein, *CMO*
**EMP:** 19 **EST:** 2003
**SQ FT:** 3,500
**SALES (est):** 2.48MM
**SALES (corp-wide):** 2.48MM **Privately Held**
Web: www.roxmedical.com
**SIC: 3841** Surgical and medical instruments

### (P-15247)
### SANOVAS INC
2597 Kerner Blvd, San Rafael
(94901-5571)
P.O. Box 2129 (94912-2129)
PHONE..................................415 729-9391
Lawrence Gerrans, *Pr*
William St John, *
Roy Morgan, *
Mike Humason, *
**EMP:** 36 **EST:** 2010
**SALES (est):** 4.1MM **Privately Held**
Web: www.sanovas.com
**SIC: 3841** Surgical and medical instruments

### (P-15248)
### SCHOLTEN SURGICAL INSTRS INC
170 Commerce St Ste 101, Lodi
(95240-0871)
PHONE..................................209 365-1393
Arie Scholten, *Pr*
Jim Van Andel, *COO*
**EMP:** 16 **EST:** 1978
**SALES (est):** 3.33MM **Privately Held**
Web: www.novatome.com
**SIC: 3841** Surgical and medical instruments

### (P-15249)
### SCITON INC (PA)
925 Commercial St, Palo Alto (94303-4908)
PHONE..................................650 493-9155
James Hobart, *CEO*
Daniel Negus, *
▼ **EMP:** 226 **EST:** 1997
**SQ FT:** 15,000
**SALES (est):** 43.96MM
**SALES (corp-wide):** 43.96MM **Privately Held**
Web: www.sciton.com
**SIC: 3841** Surgical lasers

### (P-15250)
### SECHRIST INDUSTRIES INC
4225 E La Palma Ave, Anaheim
(92807-1815)
PHONE..................................714 579-8400
Edward Pulwer, *CEO*
John Razzano, *
◆ **EMP:** 1225 **EST:** 1973
**SQ FT:** 74,000
**SALES (est):** 9.72MM
**SALES (corp-wide):** 85.84MM **Privately Held**
Web: www.sechristusa.com
**SIC: 3841** Surgical and medical instruments
HQ: Wound Care Holdings, Llc
  5220 Belfort Rd Ste 130
  Jacksonville FL 32256
  800 379-9774

### (P-15251)
### SEMLER SCIENTIFIC INC
Also Called: SEMLER SCIENTIFIC
2340-2348 Walsh Ave Ste 2344, Santa
Clara (95051)
PHONE..................................877 774-4211
Douglas Murphy-chutorian, *CEO*
Eric Semler, *
Renae Cormier, *CFO*
**EMP:** 92 **EST:** 2007
**SALES (est):** 68.18MM **Privately Held**
Web: www.semlerscientific.com
**SIC: 3841** 3845 Surgical and medical
  instruments; Electromedical equipment

### (P-15252)
### SENDX MEDICAL INC (DH)
1945 Palomar Oaks Way Ste 100, Carlsbad
(92011-1300)
PHONE..................................760 930-6300
Henrik Schimmell, *Pr*
▲ **EMP:** 22 **EST:** 1998
**SQ FT:** 35,000
**SALES (est):** 33.84MM
**SALES (corp-wide):** 23.89B **Publicly Held**
**SIC: 3841** Surgical and medical instruments
HQ: Radiometer America Inc.
  250 S Krmer Blvd Ms B1 Sw
  Brea CA 92821
  800 736-0600

### (P-15253)
### SEQUENT MEDICAL INC
35 Enterprise, Aliso Viejo (92656)
PHONE..................................949 830-9600
Thomas C Wilder, *Pr*
Kevin J Cousins, *
**EMP:** 65 **EST:** 2006
**SALES (est):** 5.9MM **Privately Held**
Web: www.microvention.com
**SIC: 3841** Surgical and medical instruments
HQ: Microvention, Inc.
  35 Enterprise
  Aliso Viejo CA 92656
  714 258-8000

### (P-15254)
### SHEATHING TECHNOLOGIES INC
675 Jarvis Dr Ste A, Morgan Hill
(95037-2815)
PHONE..................................408 782-2720
Larry Polayes, *Pr*
▲ **EMP:** 46 **EST:** 1992
**SQ FT:** 10,000
**SALES (est):** 5.12MM **Privately Held**
Web: www.sheathes.com
**SIC: 3841** Diagnostic apparatus, medical

### (P-15255)
### SHOCKWAVE MEDICAL INC (HQ)
5403 Betsy Ross Dr, Santa Clara
(95054-1162)
PHONE..................................510 279-4262
Isaac Zacharias, *Pr*
**EMP:** 284 **EST:** 2009
**SQ FT:** 35,000
**SALES (est):** 730.23MM
**SALES (corp-wide):** 85.16B **Publicly Held**
Web: www.shockwavemedical.com
**SIC: 3841** Diagnostic apparatus, medical
PA: Johnson & Johnson
  1 Johnson & Johnson Plz
  732 524-0400

### (P-15256)
### SIEMENS HLTHCARE DGNOSTICS INC
Also Called: Siemens Medical Solutions
5210 Pacific Concourse Dr, Los Angeles
(90045-6900)
PHONE..................................310 645-8200
Anthony Bihl, *Brnch Mgr*
**EMP:** 55
**SALES (corp-wide):** 84.48B **Privately Held**
Web: new.siemens.com
**SIC: 3841** 5047 8011 8734 Diagnostic
  apparatus, medical; Diagnostic equipment,
  medical; Hematologist; X-ray inspection
  service, industrial
HQ: Siemens Healthcare Diagnostics Inc.
  511 Benedict Ave
  Tarrytown NY 10591
  914 631-8000

### (P-15257)
### SIEMENS MED SOLUTIONS USA INC
Ultra Sound Division
3120 Hansen Way, Palo Alto (94304-1030)
P.O. Box 7393 (94039-7393)
PHONE..................................650 694-5747
Franz Wiehler, *CFO*
**EMP:** 300
**SALES (corp-wide):** 84.48B **Privately Held**
Web: new.siemens.com
**SIC: 3841** 3845 Surgical and medical
  instruments; Electromedical equipment
HQ: Siemens Medical Solutions Usa, Inc.
  40 Liberty Blvd
  Malvern PA 19355
  888 826-9702

### (P-15258)
### SIGHT SCIENCES INC (PA)
Also Called: SIGHT SCIENCES
4040 Campbell Ave Ste 100, Menlo Park
(94025-1053)
PHONE..................................877 266-1144
Paul Badawi, *Pr*
Staffan Encrantz, *Ch Bd*
Sam Park, *COO*
Alison Bauerlein, *CFO*
**EMP:** 191 **EST:** 2010
**SQ FT:** 11,000
**SALES (est):** 81.06MM **Publicly Held**
Web: www.sightsciences.com
**SIC: 3841** Surgical and medical instruments

### (P-15259)
### SILK ROAD MEDICAL INC
Also Called: Silk Road Medical
1213 Innsbruck Dr, Sunnyvale
(94089-1317)
PHONE..................................408 720-9002
Chas Mckhann, *CEO*
Lucas W Buchanan, *COO*
Andrew Davis, *CCO*
**EMP:** 474 **EST:** 2007
**SQ FT:** 31,000
**SALES (est):** 177.13MM **Privately Held**
Web: www.silkroadmed.com
**SIC: 3841** Surgical and medical instruments

### (P-15260)
### SOURCE SCIENTIFIC LLC
2144 Michelson Dr, Irvine (92612-1304)
PHONE..................................949 231-5096
▲ **EMP:** 39
Web: www.bit-group.com
**SIC: 3841** 8711 Surgical and medical
  instruments; Engineering services

### (P-15261)
### SPECIFIC DIAGNOSTICS INC
130 Baytech Dr, San Jose (95134-2302)
PHONE..................................650 938-6800
Paul Rhodes, *CEO*
Anthony Bazarko, *CCO**
**EMP:** 75 **EST:** 2011
**SALES (est):** 22.61MM
**SALES (corp-wide):** 7.5MM **Privately Held**
Web: www.specifictechnologies.net
**SIC: 3841** Surgical and medical instruments
HQ: Biomerieux Sa
  376 Chemin De L'orme
  Marcy-L'etoile 69280
  478872000

### (P-15262)
### SPECTRUM INC
Also Called: Spectrum Laboratories
18617 S Broadwick St, Rancho Dominguez
(90220-6435)
P.O. Box 512939 (90051-0939)
PHONE..................................310 885-4600
▲ **EMP:** 200
**SIC: 3841** 3821 3842 Surgical and medical
  instruments; Laboratory apparatus and
  furniture; Surgical appliances and supplies

# PRODUCTS & SERVICES SECTION
## 3841 - Surgical And Medical Instruments (P-15285)

**(P-15263)**
**SPINAL ELEMENTS HOLDINGS INC**
Also Called: Spinal Elements
3115 Melrose Dr Ste 200, Carlsbad (92010-6690)
PHONE.................................877 774-6255
Ronald Lloyd, *Pr*
Steven J Healy, *
Steve Mcgowan, *CFO*
Ricardo J Simmons, *CMO*
Paul Graveline, *Ex VP*
EMP: 120 EST: 2016
SQ FT: 42,000
SALES (est): 95.92MM **Privately Held**
Web: www.spinalelements.com
SIC: **3841** Surgical and medical instruments

**(P-15264)**
**SPINE VIEW INC**
110 Pioneer Way Ste A, Mountain View (94041-1519)
PHONE.................................510 490-1753
Roy Chin, *CEO*
Sam Park, *
EMP: 56 EST: 2004
SALES (est): 2.63MM **Privately Held**
Web: www.spineview.com
SIC: **3841** Surgical and medical instruments

**(P-15265)**
**SPIRACUR INC**
Also Called: Snap
1180 Bordeaux Dr, Sunnyvale (94089-1209)
PHONE.................................650 364-1544
EMP: 65
Web: www.spiracur.com
SIC: **3841** Surgical and medical instruments

**(P-15266)**
**SSCOR INC**
11064 Randall St, Sun Valley (91352-2621)
PHONE.................................818 504-4054
Samuel Say, *CEO*
Samuel D Say, *Pr*
Jonathan Kim, *VP*
Betty Say, *Sec*
▲ EMP: 16 EST: 1980
SQ FT: 12,000
SALES (est): 3.34MM **Privately Held**
Web: www.sscor.com
SIC: **3841** Suction therapy apparatus

**(P-15267)**
**ST JUDE MEDICAL LLC**
Also Called: Abbott
645 Almanor Ave, Sunnyvale (94085-2901)
PHONE.................................408 738-4883
Ron Matricaria, *Principal B*
EMP: 76
SALES (corp-wide): 40.11B **Publicly Held**
Web: www.cardiovascular.abbott
SIC: **3841** Medical instruments and equipment, blood and bone work
HQ: St. Jude Medical, Llc
1 Saint Jude Medical Dr
Saint Paul MN 55117
651 756-2000

**(P-15268)**
**STRYKER CORPORATION**
Also Called: Stryker Dre Ai
4085 Campbell Ave Ste 200, Menlo Park (94025-1940)
PHONE.................................650 667-4460
Steve Scherf, *VP Engg*
EMP: 20
SALES (corp-wide): 20.5B **Publicly Held**
Web: www.stryker.com
SIC: **3841** Ophthalmic instruments and apparatus
PA: Stryker Corporation
1941 Stryker Way
269 385-2600

**(P-15269)**
**STRYKER SALES LLC**
Also Called: Stryker Neurovascular
47900 Bayside Pkwy, Fremont (94538-6515)
PHONE.................................510 413-2500
EMP: 38
SALES (corp-wide): 20.5B **Publicly Held**
Web: www.stryker.com
SIC: **3841** Surgical and medical instruments
HQ: Stryker Sales, Llc
2825 Airview Blvd
Kalamazoo MI 49002

**(P-15270)**
**SUPIRA MEDICAL INC**
590 Division St, Campbell (95008-6906)
PHONE.................................408 560-2500
Amr Salahieh, *CEO*
EMP: 36 EST: 2019
SALES (est): 5.02MM **Privately Held**
Web: www.shifamed.com
SIC: **3841** Surgical and medical instruments

**(P-15271)**
**SURGISTAR INC (PA)**
Also Called: Sabel
2310 La Mirada Dr, Vista (92081-7862)
PHONE.................................760 598-2480
Jonathan Woodward, *Pr*
Hema Chaudhary, *
◆ EMP: 35 EST: 1992
SQ FT: 12,000
SALES (est): 4.99MM **Privately Held**
Web: www.surgistar.com
SIC: **3841** Surgical and medical instruments

**(P-15272)**
**SURGISTAR INC**
Also Called: Sable Industries
4751 Oceanside Blvd Ste G, Oceanside (92056-3060)
PHONE.................................760 431-7400
Alexandria Mondiadis, *Owner*
EMP: 18 EST: 1983
SQ FT: 5,000
SALES (est): 432.84K **Privately Held**
Web: www.surgistar.com
SIC: **3841** Surgical knife blades and handles

**(P-15273)**
**SWEDEN & MARTINA INC**
600 Anton Blvd Ste 1134, Costa Mesa (92626-7221)
PHONE.................................844 862-7846
Elisabetta Martina, *Pr*
EMP: 33 EST: 2014
SALES (est): 735.91K **Privately Held**
SIC: **3841** Medical instruments and equipment, blood and bone work

**(P-15274)**
**SYNERGY HEALTH AST LLC (DH)**
Also Called: Americas Regional Division
9020 Activity Rd Ste D, San Diego (92126-4454)
PHONE.................................858 586-1166
▲ EMP: 44 EST: 2004
SALES (est): 8.68MM **Privately Held**
SIC: **3841** Surgical and medical instruments
HQ: Steris Corporation
5960 Heisley Rd
Mentor OH 44060
440 354-2600

**(P-15275)**
**SYNVASIVE TECHNOLOGY INC**
4925 Robert J Mathews Pkwy Ste 130, El Dorado Hills (95762-5700)
PHONE.................................916 939-3913
Kelly Fisher, *Prin*
EMP: 17
SALES (corp-wide): 7.39B **Publicly Held**
Web: www.synvasive.com
SIC: **3841** Surgical knife blades and handles
HQ: Synvasive Technology, Inc.
8690 Technology Way
Reno NV 89521

**(P-15276)**
**TANDEM DIABETES CARE INC (PA)**
Also Called: TANDEM DIABETES CARE
12400 High Bluff Dr, San Diego (92130-3077)
PHONE.................................858 366-6900
John Sheridan, *Pr*
Jean-claude Kyrillos, *Ex VP*
Leigh Vosseller, *Ex VP*
Mark Novara, *CCO*
Elizabeth Gasser, *CSO CPO*
EMP: 2343 EST: 2006
SQ FT: 181,949
SALES (est): 747.72MM **Publicly Held**
Web: www.tandemdiabetes.com
SIC: **3841** 2833 Surgical and medical instruments; Insulin: bulk, uncompounded

**(P-15277)**
**TEARLAB CORPORATION**
42309 Winchester Rd Ste I, Temecula (92590-4859)
PHONE.................................858 455-6006
Kelley Hall, *Brnch Mgr*
EMP: 25
SALES (corp-wide): 8.76B **Privately Held**
Web: www.trukera.com
SIC: **3841** 3851 Eye examining instruments and apparatus; Ophthalmic goods
HQ: Tearlab Corporation
940 S Kimball Ave
Southlake TX 76092
855 832-7522

**(P-15278)**
**TECOMET INC**
Also Called: Tecomet
503 S Vincent Ave, Azusa (91702-5131)
PHONE.................................626 334-1519
EMP: 582
SALES (corp-wide): 832.81MM **Privately Held**
Web: www.tecometech.com
SIC: **3841** 3444 Diagnostic apparatus, medical; Sheet metalwork
HQ: Tecomet Inc.
18 Commerce Way Ste 4800
Woburn MA 01801
978 642-2400

**(P-15279)**
**TENEX HEALTH INC**
26902 Vista Ter, Lake Forest (92630-8123)
PHONE.................................949 454-7500
William Maya, *Pr*
Bernard Morrey, *Chief Medical Officer**
Ivan Mijatovic, *
Jagi Gill, *
▲ EMP: 70 EST: 2011
SQ FT: 15,000
SALES (est): 9.22MM **Privately Held**
Web: www.tenexhealth.com
SIC: **3841** Surgical and medical instruments

**(P-15280)**
**TENON MEDICAL INC**
Also Called: Tenon Medical
104 Cooper Ct, Los Gatos (95032-7604)
PHONE.................................408 649-5760
Steven M Foster, *Pr*
Richard Ferrari, *Ex Ch Bd*
EMP: 23 EST: 2012
SALES (est): 2.93MM **Privately Held**
Web: www.tenonmed.com
SIC: **3841** Surgical and medical instruments

**(P-15281)**
**THERAPEUTIC INDUSTRIES INC**
72096 Dunham Way Ste E, Thousand Palms (92276-3320)
P.O. Box 92 (92276-0092)
PHONE.................................760 343-2502
Chris Lehude, *Pr*
Merideth Laureno, *Bd of Dir*
EMP: 15 EST: 2014
SALES (est): 903.44K **Privately Held**
Web: www.therapeuticindustries.com
SIC: **3841** Surgical and medical instruments

**(P-15282)**
**THERASENSE INC**
1360 S Loop Rd, Alameda (94502-7000)
PHONE.................................510 749-5400
W Mark Lortz, *CEO*
EMP: 27 EST: 2007
SALES (est): 5.25MM
SALES (corp-wide): 40.11B **Publicly Held**
Web: www.abbott.com
SIC: **3841** Surgical and medical instruments
PA: Abbott Laboratories
100 Abbott Park Rd
224 667-6100

**(P-15283)**
**THERMOGENESIS HOLDINGS INC (PA)**
Also Called: CESCA THERAPEUTICS
2711 Citrus Rd, Rancho Cordova (95742-6228)
PHONE.................................916 858-5100
Xiaochun Xu, *Ch Bd*
Jeff Cauble, *CFO*
▲ EMP: 20 EST: 1986
SQ FT: 28,000
SALES (est): 9.45MM
SALES (corp-wide): 9.45MM **Publicly Held**
Web: www.thermogenesis.com
SIC: **3841** Surgical and medical instruments

**(P-15284)**
**THI INC**
1525 E Edinger Ave, Santa Ana (92705-4907)
PHONE.................................714 444-4643
Jim Willett, *CEO*
▲ EMP: 100 EST: 2000
SQ FT: 35,000
SALES (est): 7.71MM **Privately Held**
Web: www.tenacore.com
SIC: **3841** 7699 Surgical instruments and apparatus; Surgical instrument repair

**(P-15285)**
**TMJ SOLUTIONS LLC**
Also Called: TMJ Concepts
6059 King Dr, Ventura (93003-7607)
PHONE.................................805 650-3391
Heather Wise, *Pr*
EMP: 54 EST: 1989
SQ FT: 7,280
SALES (est): 3.98MM
SALES (corp-wide): 20.5B **Publicly Held**

## 3841 - Surgical And Medical Instruments (P-15286)

SIC: 3841 Surgical and medical instruments
PA: Stryker Corporation
   1941 Stryker Way
   269 385-2600

**(P-15286)**
**TOP SHELF MANUFACTURING LLC**
Also Called: Top Shelf Orthopedics
1851 Paradise Rd Ste A, Tracy (95304-8524)
PHONE..................209 834-8185
John Petlansky, *CEO*
▲ EMP: 15 EST: 2002
SALES (est): 5.86MM **Privately Held**
Web: www.topshelfortho.com
SIC: 3841 Diagnostic apparatus, medical
PA: Pacific Medical, Inc.
   1700 N Chrisman Rd

**(P-15287)**
**TRELLBORG SLING SLTIONS US INC (DH)**
Also Called: Issac
2761 Walnut Ave, Tustin (92780-7051)
PHONE..................714 415-0280
William Reising, *CEO*
Tom Mazelin, *
Ron Fraleigh, *
Kevin Beatty, *
Fiona Guo, *
EMP: 150 EST: 1993
SQ FT: 1,600
SALES (est): 43.74MM
SALES (corp-wide): 45.02B **Privately Held**
SIC: 3841 Surgical and medical instruments
HQ: Trelleborg Corporation
   200 Veterans Blvd Ste 3
   South Haven MI 49090
   269 639-9891

**(P-15288)**
**TRELLEBORG SEALING SOLUTIONS**
Also Called: TRELLEBORG SEALING SOLUTIONS TUSTIN, INC.
3034 Propeller Dr, Paso Robles (93446-9519)
PHONE..................805 239-4284
William E Reising, *Brnch Mgr*
EMP: 85
SALES (corp-wide): 45.02B **Privately Held**
SIC: 3841 Surgical and medical instruments
HQ: Trelleborg Sealing Solutions Us, Inc.
   2761 Walnut Ave
   Tustin CA 92780

**(P-15289)**
**TRIREME MEDICAL LLC**
7060 Koll Center Pkwy Ste 300, Pleasanton (94566-3171)
PHONE..................925 931-1300
Eitan Konstantino, *Pr*
EMP: 22 EST: 2005
SQ FT: 15,000
SALES (est): 4.67MM **Privately Held**
Web: www.triremedical.com
SIC: 3841 Suction therapy apparatus

**(P-15290)**
**TRIVASCULAR INC (DH)**
2 Musick, Irvine (92618-1631)
PHONE..................707 543-8800
John Onopchenko, *CEO*
EMP: 36 EST: 1998
SALES (est): 10.47MM **Privately Held**
Web: www.endologix.com
SIC: 3841 Surgical and medical instruments
HQ: Trivascular Technologies, Inc.
   2 Musik

Irvine CA 92618
707 543-8800

**(P-15291)**
**TRIVASCULAR TECHNOLOGIES INC (HQ)**
2 Musick, Irvine (92618)
PHONE..................707 543-8800
John Onopchenko, *CEO*
Christopher G Chavez, *Pr*
Michael R Kramer, *CFO*
EMP: 188 EST: 2008
SQ FT: 110,000
SALES (est): 19.97MM **Privately Held**
Web: www.endologix.com
SIC: 3841 Surgical and medical instruments
PA: Endologix, Inc.
   2 Musick

**(P-15292)**
**TRUEVISION SYSTEMS INC**
Also Called: Truevision 3d Surgical
315 Bollay Dr Ste 101, Goleta (93117-2948)
PHONE..................805 963-9700
A Burton Tripathi, *CEO*
Robert Reali, *
▲ EMP: 43 EST: 2003
SQ FT: 10,549
SALES (est): 6.12MM **Privately Held**
Web: www.myalcon.com
SIC: 3841 Surgical and medical instruments
HQ: Alcon, Inc.
   1132 Ferris Rd
   Amelia OH 45102
   513 722-1037

**(P-15293)**
**TULAVI THERAPEUTICS INC**
160 Knowles Dr, Los Gatos (95032-1828)
PHONE..................877 885-2841
Joshua Vose, *CEO*
EMP: 26 EST: 2018
SALES (est): 1.01MM **Privately Held**
Web: www.tulavi.com
SIC: 3841 Surgical and medical instruments

**(P-15294)**
**U S MEDICAL INSTRUMENTS INC (PA)**
888 Prospect St Ste 100, La Jolla (92037-8200)
P.O. Box 928439 (92192-8439)
PHONE..................619 661-5500
Matthew Mazur, *Ch*
George A Schapiro, *Sec*
Carlos H Manjarrez, *VP Opers*
Eldridge Fridge, *Dir*
A R Moosa, *Dir*
EMP: 33 EST: 1991
SQ FT: 60,000
SALES (est): 1.63MM **Privately Held**
SIC: 3841 Surgical and medical instruments

**(P-15295)**
**UNITED MEDICAL DEVICES LLC**
16250 Ventura Blvd, Encino (91436-2220)
PHONE..................310 551-4100
EMP: 20 EST: 2010
SALES (est): 1.87MM **Privately Held**
Web: www.playboycondoms.com
SIC: 3841 Surgical and medical instruments

**(P-15296)**
**UOC USA INC**
Also Called: United Orthopedic Corp USA
15251 Alton Pkwy Ste 100, Irvine (92618-2307)
PHONE..................949 328-3366

Calvin Lin, *Pr*
▲ EMP: 17 EST: 2012
SALES (est): 4.79MM **Privately Held**
Web: us.unitedorthopedic.com
SIC: 3841 Surgical and medical instruments
PA: United Orthopedic Corporation
   No. 57, Park Ave. 2

**(P-15297)**
**V-WAVE INC**
29219 Canwood St Ste 100, Agoura Hills (91301-1582)
PHONE..................818 629-2164
Neal L Eigler, *Admn*
EMP: 23 EST: 2015
SALES (est): 2.07MM **Privately Held**
Web: www.vwavemedical.com
SIC: 3841 Surgical and medical instruments

**(P-15298)**
**VARIAN MEDICAL SYSTEMS INC**
3120 Hansen Way, Palo Alto (94304-1030)
PHONE..................650 213-8000
George Zdasiuk, *VP*
EMP: 45
SALES (corp-wide): 84.48B **Privately Held**
Web: www.varian.com
SIC: 3841 Surgical and medical instruments
HQ: Varian Medical Systems, Inc.
   3100 Hansen Way
   Palo Alto CA 94304
   650 493-4000

**(P-15299)**
**VARIAN MEDICAL SYSTEMS INC**
3045 Hanover St, Palo Alto (94304-1129)
P.O. Box 10022 (94303-0922)
PHONE..................650 493-4000
Sharon Rylander, *Brnch Mgr*
EMP: 86
SALES (corp-wide): 84.48B **Privately Held**
Web: www.varian.com
SIC: 3841 Surgical and medical instruments
HQ: Varian Medical Systems, Inc.
   3100 Hansen Way
   Palo Alto CA 94304
   650 493-4000

**(P-15300)**
**VENTUS MEDICAL INC**
1100 La Avenida St Ste A, Mountain View (94043-1453)
PHONE..................408 200-5299
EMP: 25
Web: www.spiravent.com
SIC: 3841 Surgical and medical instruments

**(P-15301)**
**VENUS CONCEPT INC**
1800 Bering Dr, San Jose (95112-4212)
PHONE..................408 489-4925
Ryan Rhodes, *Pr*
EMP: 87
Web: www.venustreatments.com
SIC: 3841 5047 Surgical and medical instruments; Electro-medical equipment
HQ: Venus Concept Canada Corp
   900-235 Yorkland Blvd
   Toronto ON M2J 4
   888 907-0115

**(P-15302)**
**VERB SURGICAL INC**
5490 Great America Pkwy, Santa Clara (95054-3644)
PHONE..................408 438-3363
Kurt Azarbarzin, *Pr*
Pablo E Garcia Kilroy, *
Dave Scott, *
Dave Herrmann, *

Mary Lynn Gaddis, *
EMP: 60 EST: 2015
SALES (est): 9.83MM
SALES (corp-wide): 85.16B **Publicly Held**
SIC: 3841 Surgical and medical instruments
PA: Johnson & Johnson
   1 Johnson & Johnson Plz
   732 524-0400

**(P-15303)**
**VERSATILE POWER INC**
743 Camden Ave Ste B, Campbell (95008-4101)
PHONE..................408 341-4600
Jerry Price, *CEO*
Dave Hoffman, *Pr*
▲ EMP: 24 EST: 2002
SALES (est): 4.89MM
SALES (corp-wide): 1.66B **Publicly Held**
Web: www.advancedenergy.com
SIC: 3841 3825 Medical instruments and equipment, blood and bone work; Semiconductor test equipment
PA: Advanced Energy Industries, Inc.
   1595 Wynkoop St Ste 800
   970 407-6626

**(P-15304)**
**VERTIFLEX INC**
25155 Rye Canyon Loop, Valencia (91355-5004)
PHONE..................442 325-5900
Earl Fender, *CEO*
EMP: 40 EST: 2004
SALES (est): 4.56MM
SALES (corp-wide): 12.68B **Publicly Held**
Web: www.bostonscientific.com
SIC: 3841 Surgical and medical instruments
PA: Boston Scientific Corporation
   300 Boston Scientific Way
   508 683-4000

**(P-15305)**
**VERTOS MEDICAL INC LLC**
95 Enterprise Ste 325, Aliso Viejo (92656-2612)
PHONE..................949 349-0008
James M Corbett, *CEO*
Rebecca Colbert, *CFO*
Stephen E Paul, *Chief Commercial Officer*
EMP: 62 EST: 2005
SQ FT: 25,000
SALES (est): 9.06MM **Privately Held**
Web: www.vertosmed.com
SIC: 3841 3842 Medical instruments and equipment, blood and bone work; Surgical appliances and supplies

**(P-15306)**
**VIVANI MEDICAL INC (PA)**
Also Called: VIVANI
1350 S Loop Rd Ste 100, Alameda (94502-7081)
PHONE..................415 506-8462
Adam Mendelsohn, *CEO*
Gregg Williams, *Non-Executive Chairman of the Board*
Brigid A Makes, *CFO*
Truc Le, *COO*
Lisa Porter, *CMO*
EMP: 15 EST: 1998
Web: www.secondsight.com
SIC: 3841 Ophthalmic instruments and apparatus

**(P-15307)**
**VNUS MEDICAL TECHNOLOGIES INC**
5799 Fontanoso Way, San Jose (95138-1015)

# 3842 - Surgical Appliances And Supplies (P-15326)

PHONE..............................408 360-7200
Brian E Farley, *Pr*
Peter Osborne, *CFO*
Mohan F Sancheti, *VP Mfg*
Kirti Kamdar, *Senior Vice President Research & Development*
Mark S Saxton, *US Sales Vice President*
**EMP:** 39 **EST:** 1995
**SQ FT:** 93,650
**SALES (est):** 4.07MM **Privately Held**
**Web:** www.vnus.fr
**SIC:** 3841 Catheters
**HQ:** Covidien Lp
15 Hampshire St
Mansfield MA 02048
763 514-4000

*(P-15308)*
### W L GORE & ASSOCIATES INC
2890 De La Cruz Blvd, Santa Clara (95050-2619)
PHONE..............................928 864-2705
Mohan Sancheti, *Brnch Mgr*
**EMP:** 184
**SALES (corp-wide):** 4.98B **Privately Held**
**Web:** www.gore.com
**SIC:** 3841 Surgical and medical instruments
**PA:** W. L. Gore & Associates, Inc.
555 Paper Mill Rd
302 738-4880

*(P-15309)*
### XINTEC CORPORATION (PA)
Also Called: Convergent Laser Technologies
1660 S Loop Rd, Alameda (94502-7091)
PHONE..............................510 832-2130
Mark H K Chim, *Pr*
Marilyn M Chou, *
▲ **EMP:** 20 **EST:** 1984
**SQ FT:** 20,000
**SALES (est):** 6.62MM
**SALES (corp-wide):** 6.62MM **Privately Held**
**Web:** www.convergentlaser.com
**SIC:** 3841 Surgical and medical instruments

*(P-15310)*
### XOFT INC
101 Nicholson Ln, San Jose (95134-1359)
PHONE..............................408 493-1500
Ken Ferry, *CEO*
Kevin Burns, *
John A Delucia, *
Dan Arnoff, *
Robert Kirby, *
**EMP:** 26 **EST:** 2010
**SALES (est):** 5.97MM
**SALES (corp-wide):** 1.62B **Privately Held**
**Web:** www.elekta.com
**SIC:** 3841 Surgical and medical instruments
**PA:** Elekta Ab (Publ)
Kungstensgatan 18
858725400

*(P-15311)*
### ZEDA INC
47929 Fremont Blvd, Fremont (94538-6508)
PHONE..............................510 225-8412
Shrinivas Shetty, *CEO*
Shri Shetty, *CEO*
**EMP:** 18 **EST:** 2018
**SALES (est):** 8.12MM **Privately Held**
**Web:** www.z8a.com
**SIC:** 3841 Surgical and medical instruments

*(P-15312)*
### ZELTIQ AESTHETICS INC
Also Called: Coolssculpting
6723 Sierra Ct, Dublin (94568-2699)
PHONE..............................925 474-2519
Patrick Williams, *Prin*
**EMP:** 147
**SALES (corp-wide):** 54.32B **Publicly Held**
**Web:** www.coolsculpting.com
**SIC:** 3841 Surgical and medical instruments
**HQ:** Zeltiq Aesthetics, Inc.
4410 Rosewood Dr
Pleasanton CA 94588

*(P-15313)*
### ZELTIQ AESTHETICS INC
7085 Las Positas Rd Ste G, Livermore (94551-5142)
PHONE..............................925 474-2519
Glenn Genovea, *Prin*
**EMP:** 147
**SALES (corp-wide):** 54.32B **Publicly Held**
**Web:** www.coolsculpting.com
**SIC:** 3841 Surgical and medical instruments
**HQ:** Zeltiq Aesthetics, Inc.
4410 Rosewood Dr
Pleasanton CA 94588

*(P-15314)*
### ZELTIQ AESTHETICS INC
Also Called: Coolsculpting By Allergan
7041 Las Positas Rd, Livermore (94551-5125)
PHONE..............................925 474-2500
**EMP:** 147
**SALES (corp-wide):** 54.32B **Publicly Held**
**Web:** www.coolsculpting.com
**SIC:** 3841 Surgical and medical instruments
**HQ:** Zeltiq Aesthetics, Inc.
4410 Rosewood Dr
Pleasanton CA 94588

*(P-15315)*
### ZELTIQ AESTHETICS INC (DH)
Also Called: Coolsculpting
4410 Rosewood Dr, Pleasanton (94588-3050)
PHONE..............................925 474-2500
Mark J Foley, *Pr*
Taylor Harris, *
Sergio Garcia, *Corporate Secretary*
▲ **EMP:** 100 **EST:** 2005
**SQ FT:** 71,670
**SALES (est):** 66.26MM
**SALES (corp-wide):** 54.32B **Publicly Held**
**Web:** www.coolsculpting.com
**SIC:** 3841 Surgical and medical instruments
**HQ:** Allergan Holdco Us, Inc.
400 Intrspace Pkwy Bldg D
Parsippany NJ 07054
862 261-7000

## 3842 Surgical Appliances And Supplies

*(P-15316)*
### ADVANCED ARM DYNAMICS (PA)
123 W Torrance Blvd Ste 203, Redondo Beach (90277-3614)
PHONE..............................310 372-3050
John Miguelez, *Pr*
Creighton Uyechi, *
Dan Conyers, *
Tiffany Ryan, *
Misty Carver, *
**EMP:** 21 **EST:** 1998
**SALES (est):** 8.56MM
**SALES (corp-wide):** 8.56MM **Privately Held**
**Web:** www.armdynamics.com
**SIC:** 3842 Prosthetic appliances

*(P-15317)*
### ADVANCED BIONICS LLC (HQ)
Also Called: A B
12740 San Fernando Rd, Sylmar (91342-3700)
PHONE..............................661 362-1400
Rainer Platz, *CEO*
**EMP:** 450 **EST:** 1997
**SALES (est):** 23.32MM **Privately Held**
**Web:** www.advancedbionics.com
**SIC:** 3842 Hearing aids
**PA:** Sonova Holding Ag
Laubisrutistrasse 28

*(P-15318)*
### ADVANCED BIONICS CORPORATION (HQ)
28515 Westinghouse Pl, Valencia (91355-4833)
PHONE..............................661 362-1400
Rainer Platz, *CEO*
Alfred Mann, *
Jeffrey Goldberg, *
▲ **EMP:** 158 **EST:** 2007
**SALES (est):** 108.47MM **Privately Held**
**Web:** www.advancedbionics.com
**SIC:** 3842 Hearing aids
**PA:** Sonova Holding Ag
Laubisrutistrasse 28

*(P-15319)*
### ALPHATEC SPINE INC (HQ)
Also Called: Atec Spine
1950 Camino Vida Roble, Carlsbad (92008-6505)
PHONE..............................760 431-9286
James M Corbett, *CEO*
Patrick Ryan, *
Thomas Mcleer, *Sr VP*
Ebun S Garner, *
Michael O'neill, *CFO*
▲ **EMP:** 250 **EST:** 1990
**SALES (est):** 93.43MM **Publicly Held**
**Web:** www.atecspine.com
**SIC:** 3842 8711 5047 Surgical appliances and supplies; Engineering services; Medical equipment and supplies
**PA:** Alphatec Holdings, Inc.
1950 Camino Vida Roble

*(P-15320)*
### AMERICAN MED O & P CLINIC INC
4955 Van Nuys Blvd, Sherman Oaks (91403-1801)
PHONE..............................818 281-5747
Konstandin Kumuryan, *CEO*
**EMP:** 20 **EST:** 2020
**SALES (est):** 1.33MM **Privately Held**
**SIC:** 3842 Prosthetic appliances

*(P-15321)*
### AMERICH CORPORATION (PA)
13222 Saticoy St, North Hollywood (91605-3404)
PHONE..............................818 982-1711
Edward Richmond, *Pr*
Dino Pacifici, *
Greg Richmond, *
▲ **EMP:** 120 **EST:** 1982
**SALES (est):** 23.68MM
**SALES (corp-wide):** 23.68MM **Privately Held**
**Web:** www.americh.com
**SIC:** 3842 3432 3431 3261 Whirlpool baths, hydrotherapy equipment; Plumbing fixture fittings and trim; Metal sanitary ware; Vitreous plumbing fixtures

*(P-15322)*
### ANSELL SNDEL MED SOLUTIONS LLC
9301 Oakdale Ave Ste 300, Chatsworth (91311-6539)
PHONE..............................818 534-2500
Anthony B Lopez, *Pr*
Wendell Franke, *Associate Director Global Training*
Stephanie Barth, *
◆ **EMP:** 32 **EST:** 2002
**SQ FT:** 14,600
**SALES (est):** 6.94MM **Privately Held**
**Web:** www.ansell.com
**SIC:** 3842 Surgical appliances and supplies
**PA:** Ansell Limited
678 Victoria St

*(P-15323)*
### APPLIED ORTHOPEDIC DESIGN
Also Called: Nanoknee
860 Oak Park Blvd Ste 101, Arroyo Grande (93420-1800)
PHONE..............................805 481-3685
Thomas D Ferro, *Pr*
**EMP:** 26 **EST:** 2009
**SALES (est):** 841.6K **Privately Held**
**Web:** www.aodesign.net
**SIC:** 3842 Orthopedic appliances

*(P-15324)*
### AXIOM INDUSTRIES INC
Also Called: Prime Engineering
4202 W Sierra Madre Ave, Fresno (93722-3932)
PHONE..............................559 276-1310
Mary Wilson Boegel, *Pr*
Mark Allen, *
Bruce Boegel, *
◆ **EMP:** 26 **EST:** 1987
**SALES (est):** 3.37MM **Privately Held**
**Web:** www.primeengineering.com
**SIC:** 3842 Technical aids for the handicapped

*(P-15325)*
### BIOMET INC
181 Technology Dr, Irvine (92618-2484)
PHONE..............................949 453-3200
**EMP:** 29
**SALES (corp-wide):** 7.39B **Publicly Held**
**Web:** www.zimmerbiomet.com
**SIC:** 3842 Orthopedic appliances
**HQ:** Biomet, Inc.
345 East Main Str
Warsaw IN 46580
574 267-6639

*(P-15326)*
### BOSTON SCNTFIC NRMDLATION CORP (HQ)
25155 Rye Canyon Loop, Valencia (91355-5004)
PHONE..............................661 949-4310
Michael F Mahoney, *CEO*
Kevin Ballinger, *
Wendy Carruthers, *
Supratim Bose, *
Jeffrey D Capello, *
▲ **EMP:** 450 **EST:** 1993
**SQ FT:** 26,000
**SALES (est):** 32.14MM
**SALES (corp-wide):** 12.68B **Publicly Held**
**Web:** www.bostonscientific.com
**SIC:** 3842 3841 5047 Hearing aids; Surgical and medical instruments; Medical and hospital equipment
**PA:** Boston Scientific Corporation
300 Boston Scientific Way
508 683-4000

# 3842 - Surgical Appliances And Supplies (P-15327)

**(P-15327)**
**BOYD CHATSWORTH INC**
9959 Canoga Ave, Chatsworth (91311-3002)
PHONE..................818 998-1477
Douglas Britt, *CEO*
Jeremiah Shives, *
Kelly Weber, *
▲ EMP: 59 EST: 1972
SQ FT: 14,000
SALES (est): 24.27MM **Privately Held**
Web: www.boydcorp.com
SIC: **3842** Adhesive tape and plasters, medicated or non-medicated
HQ: Boyd Corporation
 5960 Inglewood Dr Ste 125
 Pleasanton CA 94588
 209 236-1111

**(P-15328)**
**BREATHE TECHNOLOGIES INC**
15091 Bake Pkwy, Irvine (92618-2501)
PHONE..................949 988-7700
Lawrence A Mastrovich, *Pr*
Paul J Lytle, *
John L Miclot, *
Rebecca Mabry, *
Gary Berman, *Chief Business Officer*
EMP: 39 EST: 2005
SALES (est): 9.84MM
SALES (corp-wide): 14.81B **Publicly Held**
Web: www.hillrom.com
SIC: **3842** Respirators
HQ: Hill-Rom, Inc.
 1069 State Rte 46 E
 Batesville IN 47006
 812 934-7777

**(P-15329)**
**CANYON PRODUCTS CORPORATION**
10173 Croydon Way Ste 1, Sacramento (95827-2108)
PHONE..................916 361-1687
Jeff Klemz, *Pr*
EMP: 40 EST: 1980
SQ FT: 29,600
SALES (est): 1.27MM
SALES (corp-wide): 741.73MM **Privately Held**
SIC: **3842** Wheelchairs
PA: Invacare Corporation
 1 Invacare Way
 440 329-6000

**(P-15330)**
**CURTISS-WRGHT CNTRLS INTGRTED**
Also Called: Penny & Giles Drive Technology
210 Ranger Ave, Brea (92821-6215)
PHONE..................714 982-1860
John Camp, *Pr*
EMP: 61
SALES (corp-wide): 2.85B **Publicly Held**
Web: www.curtisswright.com
SIC: **3842** Braces, elastic
HQ: Curtiss-Wright Controls Integrated Sensing, Inc.
 28965 Avenue Penn
 Valencia CA 91355
 661 257-4430

**(P-15331)**
**CUSTOM CARBON COMPOSITE CREATIONS INC**
Also Called: Foresee Orthopedic Product
693 Hi Tech Pkwy, Oakdale (95361-9372)
PHONE..................209 845-2930
EMP: 29
SIC: **3842** Surgical appliances and supplies

**(P-15332)**
**DIAMOND GLOVES**
1100 S Linwood Ave Ste A, Santa Ana (92705-4345)
PHONE..................714 667-0506
John Te, *CEO*
▲ EMP: 20 EST: 2009
SALES (est): 4.26MM **Privately Held**
Web: www.diamondglove.com
SIC: **3842** Gloves, safety

**(P-15333)**
**DJO LLC (HQ)**
5919 Sea Otter Pl Ste 200, Carlsbad (92010-6750)
PHONE..................800 321-9549
Brady Shirley, *CEO*
Gordon Briscoe, *
Bradley Tandy, *
Susan Crawford, *Managing Member*
Thomas A Capizzi, *
◆ EMP: 80 EST: 1999
SALES (est): 98.62MM
SALES (corp-wide): 1.71B **Publicly Held**
Web: www.djoglobal.com
SIC: **3842** Surgical appliances and supplies
PA: Enovis Corporation
 2711 Cntrville Rd Ste 400
 301 252-9160

**(P-15334)**
**DJO HOLDINGS LLC (DH)**
1430 Decision St, Vista (92081-8553)
PHONE..................760 727-1280
Brady R Shirley, *Pr*
▼ EMP: 22 EST: 2006
SALES (est): 16.31MM
SALES (corp-wide): 1.71B **Publicly Held**
Web: www.djoglobal.com
SIC: **3842** Surgical appliances and supplies
HQ: Djo Global, Inc.
 2900 Lk Vista Dr Ste 200
 Lewisville TX 75067

**(P-15335)**
**DRS OWN INC (PA)**
Also Called: Good Feet
5923 Farnsworth Ct, Carlsbad (92008-7303)
PHONE..................760 804-0751
David E Workman, *Pr*
◆ EMP: 20 EST: 1995
SQ FT: 18,400
SALES (est): 5.9MM
SALES (corp-wide): 5.9MM **Privately Held**
Web: www.goodfeet.com
SIC: **3842** Abdominal supporters, braces, and trusses

**(P-15336)**
**DYNAMICS ORTHTICS PRSTHTICS IN**
Also Called: Dynamics O&P
1830 W Olympic Blvd Ste 123, Los Angeles (90006-3734)
PHONE..................213 383-9212
Peter J Sean, *CEO*
EMP: 27 EST: 1988
SQ FT: 20,662
SALES (est): 4.39MM **Privately Held**
Web: www.walkagain.com
SIC: **3842** Orthopedic appliances

**(P-15337)**
**EARGO INC (PA)**
2665 N 1st St Ste 300, San Jose (95134-2035)
PHONE..................650 351-7700
William Brownie, *Interim Chief Executive Officer*
Donald Spence, *Non-Executive Chairman of the Board*
Mark Thorpe, *CAO*
EMP: 80 EST: 2010
SQ FT: 30,000
SALES (est): 37.25MM
SALES (corp-wide): 37.25MM **Privately Held**
Web: www.eargo.com
SIC: **3842** Hearing aids

**(P-15338)**
**EDWARDS LIFESCIENCES CORP**
Also Called: Edwards Life Sciences Cardio V
17221 Red Hill Ave, Irvine (92614-5688)
PHONE..................949 250-2500
EMP: 108
SALES (corp-wide): 6B **Publicly Held**
Web: www.edwards.com
SIC: **3842** Surgical appliances and supplies
PA: Edwards Lifesciences Corp
 1 Edwards Way
 949 250-2500

**(P-15339)**
**EDWARDS LIFESCIENCES CORP**
1402 Alton Pkwy, Irvine (92606-4838)
PHONE..................949 250-3522
Diane Nguyen, *Brnch Mgr*
EMP: 17
SALES (corp-wide): 6B **Publicly Held**
Web: www.edwards.com
SIC: **3842** Surgical appliances and supplies
PA: Edwards Lifesciences Corp
 1 Edwards Way
 949 250-2500

**(P-15340)**
**EDWARDS LIFESCIENCES CORP (PA)**
Also Called: EDWARDS
1 Edwards Way, Irvine (92614-5688)
PHONE..................949 250-2500
Bernard J Zovighian, *CEO*
Nicholas J Valeriani, *
Andrew M Dahl, *CAO*
Scott B Ullem, *Corporate Vice President*
Donald E Bobo Junior, *Corporate Vice President*
EMP: 1379 EST: 1958
SALES (est): 6B
SALES (corp-wide): 6B **Publicly Held**
Web: www.edwards.com
SIC: **3842** Surgical appliances and supplies

**(P-15341)**
**EDWARDS LIFESCIENCES CORP**
1212 Alton Pkwy, Irvine (92606-4837)
PHONE..................949 553-0611
Rita Hernandez, *Brnch Mgr*
EMP: 30
SALES (corp-wide): 6B **Publicly Held**
Web: www.edwards.com
SIC: **3842** Surgical appliances and supplies
PA: Edwards Lifesciences Corp
 1 Edwards Way
 949 250-2500

**(P-15342)**
**EKSO BIONICS HOLDINGS INC**
101 Glacier Pt Ste A, San Rafael (94901-5547)
PHONE..................510 984-1761
Scott G Davis, *CEO*
Jason C Jones, *COO*
Jerome Wong, *Corporate Secretary*
EMP: 72 EST: 2012
SQ FT: 45,000
SALES (est): 18.28MM **Privately Held**
Web: ir.eksobionics.com
SIC: **3842** 5999 Crutches and walkers; Medical apparatus and supplies

**(P-15343)**
**EMERGENT GROUP INC (DH)**
10939 Pendleton St, Sun Valley (91352-1522)
PHONE..................818 394-2800
Bruce J Haber, *CEO*
Louis Buther, *Pr*
William M Mckay, *CFO*
EMP: 55 EST: 1996
SQ FT: 13,000
SALES (est): 1.01MM
SALES (corp-wide): 1.23B **Privately Held**
Web: sun-valley-e-wire.sitey.me
SIC: **3842** 7352 Surgical appliances and supplies; Medical equipment rental
HQ: Agiliti Health, Inc.
 6625 W 78th St Ste 300
 Minneapolis MN 55439
 952 893-3200

**(P-15344)**
**ETHICON INC**
Also Called: Ethicon Endo - Surgery
700 Bay Rd, Redwood City (94063-2477)
P.O. Box 151 (08876-0151)
PHONE..................650 306-7900
Christopher Hubbard, *Prin*
EMP: 250
SALES (corp-wide): 85.16B **Publicly Held**
SIC: **3842** Ligatures, medical
HQ: Ethicon Inc.
 1000 Route 202
 Raritan NJ 08869
 800 384-4266

**(P-15345)**
**ETHICON INC**
33 Technology Dr, Irvine (92618-2346)
PHONE..................949 581-5799
Charles Austin, *Brnch Mgr*
EMP: 300
SALES (corp-wide): 85.16B **Publicly Held**
Web: www.jnj.com
SIC: **3842** Sutures, absorbable and non-absorbable
HQ: Ethicon Inc.
 1000 Route 202
 Raritan NJ 08869
 800 384-4266

**(P-15346)**
**FERRACO INC (HQ)**
Also Called: Human Dsgns Prsthtic Orthtic L
2933 Long Beach Blvd, Long Beach (90806-1517)
PHONE..................562 988-2414
Natalie Rose Cronin, *CEO*
Eric Ferraco, *
Brian Cronin, *
EMP: 23 EST: 1991
SALES (est): 9.13MM
SALES (corp-wide): 10.71MM **Privately Held**
Web: www.humandesigns.com
SIC: **3842** Surgical appliances and supplies
PA: Arc-V, Inc.
 1639 N Hollywood Way
 626 445-7797

**(P-15347)**
**FINEST HOUR HOLDINGS INC**
Also Called: Aos
3203 Kashiwa St, Torrance (90505-4020)
PHONE..................310 533-9966
Gary Sohngen, *CEO*

## PRODUCTS & SERVICES SECTION
## 3842 - Surgical Appliances And Supplies (P-15368)

Paul Doner, *
Barry Hubbard, *
Michael Payne, *
**EMP:** 34 **EST:** 2001
**SALES (est):** 4.4MM **Privately Held**
**Web:** www.aosortho.com
**SIC: 3842** Implants, surgical

*(P-15348)*
### FOOT IN MOTION INC
Also Called: Kevin Orthopedic
2239 Business Way, Riverside (92501-2231)
**PHONE**.............................312 752-0990
Kevin Rosenbloom, *Pr*
◆ **EMP:** 15 **EST:** 2008
**SALES (est):** 1.81MM **Privately Held**
**Web:** www.footinmotion.com
**SIC: 3842** Foot appliances, orthopedic

*(P-15349)*
### FREEDOM DESIGNS INC
2241 N Madera Rd, Simi Valley (93065-1762)
**PHONE**.............................805 582-0077
Kathleen Leneghan, *Pr*
▲ **EMP:** 120 **EST:** 1981
**SQ FT:** 40,000
**SALES (est):** 20.93MM
**SALES (corp-wide):** 741.73MM **Privately Held**
**Web:** www.freedomdesigns.com
**SIC: 3842** Wheelchairs
**PA:** Invacare Corporation
1 Invacare Way
440 329-6000

*(P-15350)*
### FREUDENBERG MEDICAL LLC
6385 Rose Ln Ste A, Carpinteria (93013-2941)
**PHONE**.............................805 576-5308
Belinda Jackson, *Mgr*
**EMP:** 66
**SALES (corp-wide):** 12.96B **Privately Held**
**Web:** www.freudenbergmedical.com
**SIC: 3842** Prosthetic appliances
**HQ:** Freudenberg Medical, Llc
1110 Mark Ave
Carpinteria CA 93013
805 684-3304

*(P-15351)*
### FREUDENBERG MEDICAL LLC
1009 Cindy Ln, Carpinteria (93013-2905)
**PHONE**.............................805 684-3304
Lorena Lundeen, *Mgr*
**EMP:** 49
**SALES (corp-wide):** 12.96B **Privately Held**
**Web:** www.freudenbergmedical.com
**SIC: 3842** Prosthetic appliances
**HQ:** Freudenberg Medical, Llc
1110 Mark Ave
Carpinteria CA 93013
805 684-3304

*(P-15352)*
### FREUDENBERG MEDICAL LLC (DH)
Also Called: Helix Medical
1110 Mark Ave, Carpinteria (93013-2918)
**PHONE**.............................805 684-3304
Jorg Schneewind, *CEO*
Thomas Vassalo, *
▲ **EMP:** 177 **EST:** 1984
**SQ FT:** 66,000
**SALES (est):** 89.6MM
**SALES (corp-wide):** 12.96B **Privately Held**
**Web:** www.freudenbergmedical.com
**SIC: 3842** Prosthetic appliances
**HQ:** Freudenberg North America Limited Partnership
47774 W Anchor Ct
Plymouth MI 48170

*(P-15353)*
### GARY BERKE MSCP PROSTHETICS
2001 Winward Way, San Mateo (94404-2469)
**PHONE**.............................650 570-5861
Gary Berke, *Owner*
**EMP:** 17 **EST:** 2017
**SALES (est):** 3.67MM **Privately Held**
**Web:** www.berke-prosthetics.com
**SIC: 3842** Orthopedic appliances

*(P-15354)*
### GAUSS SURGICAL INC
4085 Campbell Ave Ste 200, Menlo Park (94025-1940)
**PHONE**.............................650 919-4683
Siddarth Satish, *CEO*
Steve Scherf, *
Griffeth Tully, *Chief Medical Officer*
Mac Farnsworth, *
Douglas R Carroll, *Chief Commercial Officer*
**EMP:** 42 **EST:** 2011
**SALES (est):** 4.88MM
**SALES (corp-wide):** 20.5B **Publicly Held**
**Web:** www.gausssurgical.com
**SIC: 3842** Surgical appliances and supplies
**PA:** Stryker Corporation
1941 Stryker Way
269 385-2600

*(P-15355)*
### HAND BIOMECHANICS LAB INC
77 Scripps Dr Ste 104, Sacramento (95825-6209)
**PHONE**.............................916 923-5073
John Agee Md, *Pr*
**EMP:** 16 **EST:** 1982
**SQ FT:** 2,600
**SALES (est):** 2.91MM **Privately Held**
**Web:** www.handbiolab.com
**SIC: 3842** Orthopedic appliances

*(P-15356)*
### HANGER PRSTHTICS ORTHTICS W IN (HQ)
4155 E La Palma Ave Ste 400, Anaheim (92807-1857)
**PHONE**.............................714 961-2112
Vinit K Asar, *CEO*
**EMP:** 21 **EST:** 1970
**SALES (est):** 7.06MM
**SALES (corp-wide):** 1.12B **Privately Held**
**SIC: 3842** Orthopedic appliances
**PA:** Hanger, Inc.
10910 Domain Dr Ste 300
512 777-3800

*(P-15357)*
### HANGER PRSTHTICS ORTHTICS W IN
1127 Wilshire Blvd Ste 310, Los Angeles (90017-3901)
**PHONE**.............................213 250-7850
Rafael Bibbens, *Mgr*
**EMP:** 65
**SALES (corp-wide):** 1.12B **Privately Held**
**SIC: 3842** 5999 Orthopedic appliances; Orthopedic and prosthesis applications
**HQ:** Hanger Prosthetics & Orthotics West, Inc.
4155 E La Palma Ave B4
Anaheim CA 92807
714 961-2112

*(P-15358)*
### HORIZON SURGICAL SYSTEMS INC
Also Called: Horizon Surgical Systems
22619 Pacific Coast Hwy Ste C280, Malibu (90265-5054)
**PHONE**.............................310 876-2460
Jean-pierre Hubschman, *CEO*
Julie Sunderland, *CFO*
**EMP:** 15 **EST:** 2021
**SALES (est):** 1.09MM **Privately Held**
**Web:** www.horizonsurgicalsystems.com
**SIC: 3842** Surgical appliances and supplies

*(P-15359)*
### HOWMEDICA OSTEONICS CORP
6885 Flanders Dr Ste G, San Diego (92121-2933)
**PHONE**.............................800 621-6104
**EMP:** 108
**SALES (corp-wide):** 20.5B **Publicly Held**
**Web:** www.patientwebsitecontent.com
**SIC: 3842** Surgical appliances and supplies
**HQ:** Howmedica Osteonics Corp.
325 Corporate Dr
Mahwah NJ 07430
201 831-5000

*(P-15360)*
### IMPERATIVE CARE INC (PA)
1359 Dell Ave, Campbell (95008-6609)
**PHONE**.............................669 228-3814
Matthew Garrett, *CEO*
Shacey Petrovic, *V Ch Bd*
**EMP:** 443 **EST:** 2016
**SQ FT:** 20,000
**SALES (est):** 100MM
**SALES (corp-wide):** 100MM **Privately Held**
**Web:** www.imperativecare.com
**SIC: 3842** Surgical appliances and supplies

*(P-15361)*
### IMPLANTECH ASSOCIATES INC
Also Called: Allied Bio Medical
6025 Nicolle St Ste B, Ventura (93003-7602)
P.O. Box 392 (93002-0392)
**PHONE**.............................805 289-1665
William Binder, *Pr*
**EMP:** 30 **EST:** 1989
**SQ FT:** 11,000
**SALES (est):** 7.19MM **Privately Held**
**Web:** www.implantech.com
**SIC: 3842** Implants, surgical

*(P-15362)*
### INFAB LLC
1040 Avenida Acaso, Camarillo (93012-8712)
**PHONE**.............................805 987-5255
Brittany Lepley, *CEO*
Donald J Cusick, *
Justine Peterson, *
Daren Dickerson, *
◆ **EMP:** 57 **EST:** 1980
**SQ FT:** 40,000
**SALES (est):** 19.05MM **Privately Held**
**Web:** www.infabcorp.com
**SIC: 3842** Radiation shielding aprons, gloves, sheeting, etc.

*(P-15363)*
### INHEALTH TECHNOLOGIES
1110 Mark Ave, Carpinteria (93013-2918)
**PHONE**.............................800 477-5969
Ed Munoz, *Prin*
**EMP:** 44 **EST:** 2005
**SALES (est):** 1.29MM **Privately Held**
**Web:** www.inhealth.com
**SIC: 3842** Surgical appliances and supplies

*(P-15364)*
### INTERPORE CROSS INTL INC (DH)
181 Technology Dr, Irvine (92618-2484)
**PHONE**.............................949 453-3200
Dan Hann, *Pr*
Greg Hartman, *CFO*
▲ **EMP:** 58 **EST:** 1975
**SALES (est):** 8.42MM
**SALES (corp-wide):** 7.39B **Publicly Held**
**Web:** www.interpore.org
**SIC: 3842** 3843 Orthopedic appliances; Dental equipment and supplies
**HQ:** Biomet, Inc.
345 East Main Str
Warsaw IN 46580
574 267-6639

*(P-15365)*
### INTUITIVE SURGICAL INC (PA)
Also Called: INTUITIVE SURGICAL
1020 Kifer Rd, Sunnyvale (94086-5301)
**PHONE**.............................408 523-2100
Gary S Guthart, *CEO*
Craig H Barratt, *
Dave Rosa, *Pr*
Myriam J Curet, *CMO*
Jamie E Samath, *Sr VP*
▲ **EMP:** 183 **EST:** 1995
**SQ FT:** 1,800,000
**SALES (est):** 7.12B **Publicly Held**
**Web:** www.intuitivesurgical.com
**SIC: 3842** 3841 Surgical appliances and supplies; Surgical and medical instruments

*(P-15366)*
### ISOMEDIX OPERATIONS INC
Also Called: A Steris Company
1000 Sarah Pl, Ontario (91761-8621)
**PHONE**.............................909 390-9942
Michael Au, *Brnch Mgr*
**EMP:** 40
**Web:** www.steris.com
**SIC: 3842** Surgical appliances and supplies
**HQ:** Isomedix Operations Inc.
5960 Heisley Rd
Mentor OH 44060

*(P-15367)*
### ISOMEDIX OPERATIONS INC
Also Called: Steris Isomedix
43425 Business Park Dr, Temecula (92590-3647)
**PHONE**.............................951 694-9340
Chris Bares, *Mgr*
**EMP:** 57
**Web:** www.steris.com
**SIC: 3842** Surgical appliances and supplies
**HQ:** Isomedix Operations Inc.
5960 Heisley Rd
Mentor OH 44060

*(P-15368)*
### JOHNSON & JOHNSON
Also Called: Johnson & Johnson
365 Ravendale Dr, Mountain View (94043-5217)
**PHONE**.............................650 903-4800
**EMP:** 28
**SALES (corp-wide):** 71.89B **Publicly Held**
**SIC: 3842** Implants, surgical
**PA:** Johnson & Johnson
1 Johnson And Johnson Plz
732 524-0400

## 3842 - Surgical Appliances And Supplies (P-15369)

**(P-15369)**
**JOHNSON & JOHNSON**
15715 Arrow Hwy, Irwindale (91706-2006)
PHONE...............................909 839-8650
Cathy Somalis, *Mgr*
EMP: 300
SALES (corp-wide): 85.16B **Publicly Held**
Web: www.jnj.com
SIC: **3842** Dressings, surgical
PA: Johnson & Johnson
  1 Johnson & Johnson Plz
  732 524-0400

**(P-15370)**
**JOHNSON WILSHIRE INC**
17343 Freedom Way, City Of Industry (91748-1001)
PHONE...............................562 777-0088
David W Pang, *Pr*
EMP: 25 EST: 2007
SQ FT: 120,000
SALES (est): 1.23MM **Privately Held**
Web: www.johnsonwilshire.com
SIC: **3842** Personal safety equipment

**(P-15371)**
**KAISE PERMA SAN FRANC MEDIC CE**
2425 Geary Blvd, San Francisco (94115-3358)
PHONE...............................415 833-2000
Michael Alexander, *Sr VP*
EMP: 50 EST: 2013
SALES (est): 7.78MM **Privately Held**
Web: www.kp.org
SIC: **3842** Autoclaves, hospital and surgical

**(P-15372)**
**KINAMED INC**
820 Flynn Rd, Camarillo (93012-8701)
PHONE...............................805 384-2748
Clyde R Pratt, *Pr*
Vineet Sarin, *
Bob Bruce, *
EMP: 26 EST: 1987
SQ FT: 28,828
SALES (est): 8.41MM **Privately Held**
Web: www.kinamed.com
SIC: **3842** Implants, surgical
PA: Vme Acquisition Corp.
  820 Flynn Rd

**(P-15373)**
**KYOCERA MEDICAL TECH INC**
1289 Bryn Mawr Ave Ste A, Redlands (92374-0106)
PHONE...............................909 557-2360
Ken Kaneko, *Pr*
Takahiro Kobayashi, *
EMP: 50 EST: 2019
SALES (est): 5.68MM **Privately Held**
Web: www.kyocera-medical.com
SIC: **3842** Prosthetic appliances

**(P-15374)**
**MEDICAL DEVICE BUS SVCS INC**
Also Called: Depuy
5644 Kearny Mesa Rd Ste I, San Diego (92111-1311)
PHONE...............................858 560-4165
Jim Lent, *Pr*
EMP: 31
SALES (corp-wide): 85.16B **Publicly Held**
SIC: **3842** Surgical appliances and supplies
HQ: Medical Device Business Services, Inc.
  700 Orthopaedic Dr
  Warsaw IN 46582

**(P-15375)**
**MEDICAL DEVICE BUS SVCS INC**
1174 National Dr Ste 100, Sacramento (95834-2955)
PHONE...............................916 285-9125
EMP: 31
SALES (corp-wide): 85.16B **Publicly Held**
SIC: **3842** Surgical appliances and supplies
HQ: Medical Device Business Services, Inc.
  700 Orthopaedic Dr
  Warsaw IN 46582

**(P-15376)**
**MEDICAL PACKAGING CORPORATION**
Also Called: Hygenia
941 Avenida Acaso, Camarillo (93012-8700)
PHONE...............................805 388-2383
Frederic L Nason, *Pr*
Susan J Nason, *
EMP: 100 EST: 1974
SQ FT: 45,000
SALES (est): 4.91MM **Privately Held**
Web: www.medicalpackaging.com
SIC: **3842** 2835 Surgical appliances and supplies; Diagnostic substances

**(P-15377)**
**MEDLINE INDUSTRIES LP**
5701 Promontory Pkwy Ste 100, Tracy (95377-9201)
PHONE...............................209 585-3260
EMP: 77
SALES (corp-wide): 7.75B **Privately Held**
Web: www.medline.com
SIC: **3842** Surgical appliances and supplies
PA: Medline Industries, Lp
  3 Lakes Dr
  800 633-5463

**(P-15378)**
**MEDLINE INDUSTRIES LP**
42500 Winchester Rd, Temecula (92590-2570)
PHONE...............................951 296-2600
EMP: 25
SALES (corp-wide): 7.75B **Privately Held**
Web: www.medline.com
SIC: **3842** Surgical appliances and supplies
PA: Medline Industries, Lp
  3 Lakes Dr
  800 633-5463

**(P-15379)**
**MEDTRONIC INC**
Also Called: Medtronic
3576 Unocal Pl Bldg B, Santa Rosa (95403-1774)
PHONE...............................707 541-3281
Omar Ishrak, *Ch*
EMP: 166
Web: www.medtronic.com
SIC: **3842** 3841 3845 Surgical appliances and supplies; Surgical and medical instruments; Pacemaker, cardiac
HQ: Medtronic, Inc.
  710 Medtronic Pkwy
  Minneapolis MN 55432
  763 514-4000

**(P-15380)**
**MEDTRONIC VASCULAR INC**
3576 Unocal Pl, Santa Rosa (95403-1774)
PHONE...............................707 522-2250
Sean Salmon, *Pr*
Scott Ward, *
Michael J Coyle, *
EMP: 28 EST: 1991
SALES (est): 9.89MM **Privately Held**
Web: www.medtronic.com
SIC: **3842** 3841 3845 Surgical appliances and supplies; Surgical and medical instruments; Pacemaker, cardiac
HQ: Medtronic, Inc.
  710 Medtronic Pkwy
  Minneapolis MN 55432
  763 514-4000

**(P-15381)**
**MEGIDDO GLOBAL LLC**
17101 Central Ave Ste 1c, Carson (90746-1360)
PHONE...............................844 477-7007
EMP: 25 EST: 2017
SALES (est): 3.38MM **Privately Held**
Web: www.megiddo-global.com
SIC: **3842** 2393 2329 3728 Bulletproof vests; Textile bags; Field jackets, military; Military aircraft equipment and armament

**(P-15382)**
**MENTOR WORLDWIDE LLC (DH)**
31 Technology Dr Ste 200, Irvine (92618-2302)
PHONE...............................800 636-8678
David Shepherd, *Pr*
Joshua H Levine, *Managing Member*
Flavia Pease, *
▲ EMP: 250 EST: 1969
SALES (est): 455.62MM
SALES (corp-wide): 85.16B **Publicly Held**
Web: www.mentordirect.com
SIC: **3842** 3845 3841 Surgical appliances and supplies; Ultrasonic medical equipment, except cleaning; Medical instruments and equipment, blood and bone work
HQ: Ethicon Inc.
  1000 Route 202
  Raritan NJ 08869
  800 384-4266

**(P-15383)**
**MIST INC**
Also Called: Miradry
3333 Michelson Dr Ste 650, Irvine (92612-0681)
PHONE...............................408 940-8700
Ronald Menezes, *Pr*
Ron Menezes, *
Brigid A Makes, *
Steven W Kim, *
EMP: 102 EST: 2006
SALES (est): 22.19MM
SALES (corp-wide): 38.75MM **Privately Held**
Web: www.miradryhcp.com
SIC: **3842** Surgical appliances and supplies
PA: 1315 Capital Llc
  2929 Walnut St Ste 1240
  215 662-1315

**(P-15384)**
**MOLDEX-METRIC INC**
Also Called: Moldex
10111 Jefferson Blvd, Culver City (90232-3509)
PHONE...............................310 837-6500
Mark Magidson, *CEO*
Debra Magidson, *
◆ EMP: 500 EST: 1960
SQ FT: 80,000
SALES (est): 24.17MM **Privately Held**
Web: www.moldex.com
SIC: **3842** Personal safety equipment

**(P-15385)**
**MPS ANZON LLC**
Also Called: Orchid Orthopedis
11911 Clark St, Arcadia (91006-6026)
PHONE...............................626 471-3553
EMP: 112
SALES (est): 613.6K
SALES (corp-wide): 496.98MM **Privately Held**
SIC: **3842** Orthopedic appliances
PA: Tulip Us Holdings, Inc.
  1365 N Cedar Rd
  517 694-2300

**(P-15386)**
**NUPRODX INC**
161 S Vasco Rd Ste G, Livermore (94551-5131)
PHONE...............................415 472-1699
David Gaskell, *Pr*
EMP: 16 EST: 1998
SQ FT: 650
SALES (est): 3.86MM **Privately Held**
Web: www.nuprodx.com
SIC: **3842** Wheelchairs

**(P-15387)**
**ORTHO ENGINEERING INC (PA)**
17402 Chatsworth St Ste 200, Granada Hills (91344-7620)
PHONE...............................310 559-5996
Avo Ashkharikian, *Pr*
EMP: 22 EST: 1991
SQ FT: 4,000
SALES (est): 2.4MM **Privately Held**
Web: www.orthoengineering.com
SIC: **3842** Braces, orthopedic

**(P-15388)**
**OSSUR AMERICAS INC**
19762 Pauling, Foothill Ranch (92610-2611)
PHONE...............................949 382-3883
Edward Castillo, *Brnch Mgr*
EMP: 110
SALES (corp-wide): 787.61MM **Privately Held**
SIC: **3842** Prosthetic appliances
HQ: Ossur Americas, Inc.
  200 Spctrum Ctr Dr Ste 70
  Irvine CA 92618
  800 233-6263

**(P-15389)**
**OSSUR AMERICAS INC (HQ)**
200 Spectrum Center Dr Ste 700, Irvine (92618-5005)
PHONE...............................800 233-6263
Sveinn Solvason, *CEO*
◆ EMP: 55 EST: 1984
SALES (est): 98.04MM
SALES (corp-wide): 787.61MM **Privately Held**
SIC: **3842** Braces, orthopedic
PA: Embla Medical Hf.
  Grjothalsi 5
  4253400

**(P-15390)**
**OSTIAL CORPORATION**
747 Camden Ave, Campbell (95008-4147)
PHONE...............................408 541-1007
Samrand Hesami, *Mgr*
Farhad Khosravi, *CEO*
EMP: 24 EST: 2010
SALES (est): 2.26MM **Privately Held**
Web: www.ostialflash.com
SIC: **3842** Surgical appliances and supplies

**(P-15391)**
**PASSY-MUIR INC (PA)**
17992 Mitchell S Ste 200, Irvine (92614-6813)

## PRODUCTS & SERVICES SECTION
### 3842 - Surgical Appliances And Supplies (P-15412)

PHONE..................................949 833-8255
Cameron Jolly, *Pr*
**EMP:** 30 **EST:** 1985
**SQ FT:** 1,200
**SALES (est):** 6.69MM
**SALES (corp-wide):** 6.69MM **Privately Held**
**Web:** www.passy-muir.com
**SIC: 3842** Orthopedic appliances

### (P-15392)
### PATIENT SAFETY TECHNOLOGIES INC
15440 Laguna Canyon Rd Ste 150, Irvine (92618-2143)
PHONE..................................949 387-2277
**EMP:** 25
**Web:** www.safeor.com
**SIC: 3842** Surgical appliances and supplies

### (P-15393)
### PAULSON MANUFACTURING CORP (PA)
46752 Rainbow Canyon Rd, Temecula (92592-5984)
PHONE..................................951 676-2451
Roy Paulson, *Pr*
Thomas V Paulson, *
Joyce Paulson, *
▲ **EMP:** 95 **EST:** 1947
**SQ FT:** 42,000
**SALES (est):** 24.76MM
**SALES (corp-wide):** 24.76MM **Privately Held**
**Web:** www.paulsonmfg.com
**SIC: 3842** Personal safety equipment

### (P-15394)
### PRECISION SWISS PRODUCTS INC
1911 Tarob Ct, Milpitas (95035-6825)
**EMP:** 80 **EST:** 1974
**SALES (est):** 10.5MM **Privately Held**
**Web:** www.precisionswiss.com
**SIC: 3842** 3841 3451 Braces, orthopedic; Surgical and medical instruments; Screw machine products

### (P-15395)
### PROSTHTIC ORTHTIC GROUP ORNGE
26300 La Alameda Ste 120, Mission Viejo (92691-6380)
PHONE..................................949 242-2237
Chad Marquis, *Prin*
**EMP:** 16 **EST:** 2017
**SALES (est):** 2.5MM **Privately Held**
**Web:** www.p-o-group.com
**SIC: 3842** Prosthetic appliances

### (P-15396)
### PSYONIC INC
9999 Businesspark Ave Ste B, San Diego (92131-1174)
PHONE..................................888 779-6642
Aadeel Akhtar, *CEO*
**EMP:** 20 **EST:** 2015
**SQ FT:** 400
**SALES (est):** 1.6MM **Privately Held**
**Web:** www.psyonic.io
**SIC: 3842** 3821 Limbs, artificial; Incubators, laboratory

### (P-15397)
### RAYES INC (PA)
Also Called: W O K
252 Mariah Cir, Corona (92879-1751)
P.O. Box 320 (67637-0320)
PHONE..................................785 726-4885

Willard L Frickey, *Pr*
Jackie Frickey, *Sec*
Tracy Frickey, *CFO*
Tracy Hudson, *CFO*
▲ **EMP:** 15 **EST:** 1975
**SQ FT:** 37,000
**SALES (est):** 4.03MM **Privately Held**
**Web:** www.wheelchairsofkansas.com
**SIC: 3842** Wheelchairs

### (P-15398)
### REVA MEDICAL INC (PA)
5751 Copley Dr Ste B, San Diego (92111-7912)
PHONE..................................858 966-3000
Jeffrey Anderson, *CEO*
Jeff Anderson, *Pr*
C Raymond Larkin Junior, *Ch Bd*
Leigh F Elkolli, *Corporate Secretary*
**EMP:** 41 **EST:** 1998
**SQ FT:** 37,000
**SALES (est):** 7.88MM
**SALES (corp-wide):** 7.88MM **Privately Held**
**Web:** www.revamedical.com
**SIC: 3842** Surgical appliances and supplies

### (P-15399)
### RIZZO INC
Also Called: Om Tactical
7720 Airport Business Pkwy, Van Nuys (91406-1720)
PHONE..................................818 781-6891
▲ **EMP:** 23
**Web:** www.omtactical.com
**SIC: 3842** Personal safety equipment

### (P-15400)
### SAFARILAND LLC
4700 E Airport Dr, Ontario (91761-7875)
PHONE..................................909 923-7300
Warren B Kanders, *Brnch Mgr*
**EMP:** 354
**SALES (corp-wide):** 482.53MM **Publicly Held**
**Web:** www.safariland.com
**SIC: 3842** Bulletproof vests
**HQ:** Safariland, Llc
13386 International Pkwy
Jacksonville FL 32218
904 741-5400

### (P-15401)
### SAS SAFETY CORPORATION
Also Called: Sas Safety
17785 Center Court Dr N, Cerritos (90703-8573)
PHONE..................................562 427-2775
James Anthony Mccool, *Pr*
Daniel M Deambrosio, *
Daniel J Lett, *
Anh Phuong Katy Vu, *Treas*
◆ **EMP:** 60 **EST:** 1983
**SALES (est):** 8.37MM **Privately Held**
**Web:** www.sassafety.com
**SIC: 3842** Personal safety equipment

### (P-15402)
### SEASPINE INC
Also Called: Integra Lifesciences
5770 Armada Dr, Carlsbad (92048-4608)
PHONE..................................760 727-8399
Keith Valentine, *CEO*
**EMP:** 80 **EST:** 2002
**SQ FT:** 22,000
**SALES (est):** 16.03MM
**SALES (corp-wide):** 746.64MM **Privately Held**
**Web:** www.seaspine.com

**SIC: 3842** 5999 Orthopedic appliances; Orthopedic and prosthesis applications
**HQ:** Seaspine Orthopedics Corporation
5770 Armada Dr
Carlsbad CA 92008
866 942-8698

### (P-15403)
### SEASPINE ORTHOPEDICS CORP (DH)
5770 Armada Dr, Carlsbad (92008-4608)
PHONE..................................866 942-8698
Keith Valentine, *CEO*
**EMP:** 20 **EST:** 2015
**SALES (est):** 23.9MM
**SALES (corp-wide):** 746.64MM **Privately Held**
**Web:** www.seaspine.com
**SIC: 3842** 5999 Orthopedic appliances; Orthopedic and prosthesis applications
**HQ:** Seaspine Holdings Corporation
5770 Armada Dr
Carlsbad CA 92008
760 727-8399

### (P-15404)
### SI-BONE INC (PA)
Also Called: Si-Bone
471 El Camino Real Ste 101, Santa Clara (95050-4482)
PHONE..................................408 207-0700
Laura A Francis, *CEO*
Jeffrey W Dunn, *Ex Ch Bd*
Anshul Maheshwari, *CFO*
**EMP:** 321 **EST:** 2008
**SQ FT:** 21,848
**SALES (est):** 138.89MM **Publicly Held**
**Web:** www.si-bone.com
**SIC: 3842** Implants, surgical

### (P-15405)
### SIENTRA INC (HQ)
Also Called: Sientra
3333 Michelson Dr Ste 650, Irvine (92612-0681)
PHONE..................................805 562-3500
Ronald Menezes, *Pr*
Caroline Van Hove, *
Andy Schmidt, *Sr VP*
Oliver Bennett, *Legal CCDO*
**EMP:** 29 **EST:** 2003
**SQ FT:** 14,000
**SALES (est):** 47.49MM
**SALES (corp-wide):** 89.45MM **Publicly Held**
**Web:** www.sientra.com
**SIC: 3842** Surgical appliances and supplies
**PA:** Tiger Aesthetics Medical Llc
9630 S 54th St
888 694-6694

### (P-15406)
### SONOVA USA INC
47257 Fremont Blvd, Fremont (94538-6502)
PHONE..................................510 743-3900
**EMP:** 79
**Web:** www.phonak.com
**SIC: 3842** Hearing aids
**HQ:** Sonova Usa Inc.
444 Commerce St Ste 112
Aurora IL 60504
763 744-3300

### (P-15407)
### SPECTRUM PRSTHTCS/ RTHTICS RDDI
1844 South St, Redding (96001-1809)
PHONE..................................530 243-4500
Forest Sexton, *Pr*

Jeff Zeller, *Sec*
**EMP:** 24 **EST:** 2005
**SALES (est):** 3.52MM **Privately Held**
**Web:** www.spectrumoandp.com
**SIC: 3842** Limbs, artificial

### (P-15408)
### STERIS CORPORATION
Also Called: Steris
9020 Activity Rd Ste D, San Diego (92126-4454)
PHONE..................................858 586-1166
Walt Rosebrough, *Mgr*
**EMP:** 58
**Web:** www.steris.com
**SIC: 3842** Surgical appliances and supplies
**HQ:** Steris Corporation
5960 Heisley Rd
Mentor OH 44060
440 354-2600

### (P-15409)
### STERIS CORPORATION
Also Called: Vts Medical Systems
503 Canal Blvd, Richmond (94804-3517)
PHONE..................................510 439-4500
**EMP:** 143
**Web:** www.steris.com
**SIC: 3842** Surgical appliances and supplies
**HQ:** Steris Corporation
5960 Heisley Rd
Mentor OH 44060
440 354-2600

### (P-15410)
### STRYKER SALES LLC
Also Called: Stryker Endoscopy
5900 Optical Ct, San Jose (95138-1400)
PHONE..................................800 624-4422
Kim Gonia, *Dir*
**EMP:** 38
**SQ FT:** 20,000
**SALES (corp-wide):** 20.5B **Publicly Held**
**Web:** www.stryker.com
**SIC: 3842** Personal safety equipment
**HQ:** Stryker Sales, Llc
2825 Airview Blvd
Kalamazoo MI 49002

### (P-15411)
### SUREFIRE LLC
18300 Mount Baldy Cir, Fountain Valley (92708-6122)
PHONE..................................714 545-9444
Joel Smith, *Brnch Mgr*
**EMP:** 45
**SALES (corp-wide):** 97.06MM **Privately Held**
**Web:** www.surefire.com
**SIC: 3842** Surgical appliances and supplies
**PA:** Surefire, Llc
18300 Mount Baldy Cir
714 545-9444

### (P-15412)
### SUREFIRE LLC
17680 Newhope St Ste B, Fountain Valley (92708-4220)
PHONE..................................714 545-9444
Daniel Fischer, *Pdt Mgr*
**EMP:** 45
**SALES (corp-wide):** 97.06MM **Privately Held**
**Web:** www.surefire.com
**SIC: 3842** 3484 3648 Ear plugs; Guns (firearms) or gun parts, 30 mm. and below; Flashlights
**PA:** Surefire, Llc
18300 Mount Baldy Cir
714 545-9444

---
(PA)=Parent Co (HQ)=Headquarters
✪ = New Business established in last 2 years

## 3842 - Surgical Appliances And Supplies (P-15413)

**(P-15413)**
**SUREFIRE LLC**
17760 Newhope St Ste A, Fountain Valley (92708-5401)
PHONE..................714 545-9444
Daniel Fischer, *Pdt Mgr*
**EMP:** 45
**SALES (corp-wide):** 97.06MM **Privately Held**
Web: www.surefire.com
SIC: **3842** 3484 3648 Ear plugs; Guns (firearms) or gun parts, 30 mm. and below; Flashlights
PA: Surefire, Llc
  18300 Mount Baldy Cir
  714 545-9444

**(P-15414)**
**SUREFIRE LLC**
2110 S Anne St, Santa Ana (92704-4409)
PHONE..................714 641-0483
Gustav Bonse, *Mfg Mgr*
**EMP:** 45
**SALES (corp-wide):** 97.06MM **Privately Held**
Web: www.surefire.com
SIC: **3842** 3484 3648 Ear plugs; Guns (firearms) or gun parts, 30 mm. and below; Flashlights
PA: Surefire, Llc
  18300 Mount Baldy Cir
  714 545-9444

**(P-15415)**
**SUREFIRE LLC**
2121 S Yale St, Santa Ana (92704-4437)
PHONE..................714 545-9444
John D Matthews, *Brnch Mgr*
**EMP:** 45
**SALES (corp-wide):** 97.06MM **Privately Held**
Web: www.surefire.com
SIC: **3842** Ear plugs
PA: Surefire, Llc
  18300 Mount Baldy Cir
  714 545-9444

**(P-15416)**
**SUREFIRE LLC**
2300 S Yale St, Santa Ana (92704-5330)
PHONE..................714 641-0483
Gustav Bonse, *Mgr*
**EMP:** 45
**SALES (corp-wide):** 158.99MM **Privately Held**
Web: www.surefire.com
SIC: **3842** 3484 3648 Ear plugs; Guns (firearms) or gun parts, 30 mm. and below; Flashlights
PA: Surefire, Llc
  18300 Mount Baldy Cir
  714 545-9444

**(P-15417)**
**THINK SURGICAL INC**
Also Called: Think Surgical
47201 Lakeview Blvd, Fremont (94538-6530)
PHONE..................510 249-2300
Stuart F Simpson, *CEO*
David C Dvorak, *
Paul S Weiner, *
Patricia Davis, *
Chris Fronk, *CCO*
**EMP:** 160 **EST:** 2007
**SQ FT:** 70,000
**SALES (est):** 21.55MM **Privately Held**
Web: www.thinksurgical.com
SIC: **3842** Surgical appliances and supplies

**(P-15418)**
**TOTAL RESOURCES INTL INC (PA)**
420 S Lemon Ave, Walnut (91789-2956)
PHONE..................909 594-1220
George Rivera, *CEO*
Gregg Rivera, *
Merlyn Rivera, *
▲ **EMP:** 49 **EST:** 1993
**SQ FT:** 115,000
**SALES (est):** 9.69MM **Privately Held**
Web: www.trikits.com
SIC: **3842** First aid, snake bite, and burn kits

**(P-15419)**
**TOWNSEND INDUSTRIES INC**
4401 Stine Rd, Bakersfield (93313-2306)
PHONE..................661 837-1795
**EMP:** 65
**SALES (corp-wide):** 1.25MM **Privately Held**
Web: www.townsenddesign.com
SIC: **3842** Braces, orthopedic
HQ: Townsend Industries, Inc.
  4615 Shepard St
  Bakersfield CA 93313
  661 837-1795

**(P-15420)**
**TOWNSEND INDUSTRIES INC**
4833 N Hills Dr, Bakersfield (93308-1186)
PHONE..................661 837-1795
Rick Riley, *Brnch Mgr*
**EMP:** 65
**SALES (corp-wide):** 1.25MM **Privately Held**
Web: www.thuasneusa.com
SIC: **3842** Braces, orthopedic
HQ: Townsend Industries, Inc.
  4615 Shepard St
  Bakersfield CA 93313
  661 837-1795

**(P-15421)**
**TOWNSEND INDUSTRIES INC (DH)**
Also Called: Townsend Design
4615 Shepard St, Bakersfield (93313-2339)
PHONE..................661 837-1795
**EMP:** 130 **EST:** 1984
**SALES (est):** 31.67MM
**SALES (corp-wide):** 1.25MM **Privately Held**
Web: www.townsenddesign.com
SIC: **3842** Braces, orthopedic
HQ: Thuasne North America Inc.
  4615 Shepard St
  Bakersfield CA 93313
  800 432-3466

**(P-15422)**
**ULTIMATE EARS CONSUMER LLC**
3 Jenner Ste 180, Irvine (92618-3835)
PHONE..................949 502-8340
Mindy Harvey, *Owner*
▲ **EMP:** 285 **EST:** 2004
**SALES (est):** 2.02MM **Privately Held**
Web: www.ultimateears.com
SIC: **3842** Hearing aids
HQ: Logitech Inc.
  3930 N 1st St
  San Jose CA 95134
  510 795-8500

**(P-15423)**
**UNITED BIOLOGICS INC**
1642 Kaiser Ave, Irvine (92614-5700)
PHONE..................949 345-7490
Craig Johnson, *CEO*
John Barnhill, *
**EMP:** 37 **EST:** 2002
**SALES (est):** 4.88MM **Privately Held**
Web: www.unitedbiologics.com
SIC: **3842** Models, anatomical

**(P-15424)**
**US ARMOR CORPORATION**
10715 Bloomfield Ave, Santa Fe Springs (90670-3913)
PHONE..................562 207-4240
Stephen Armellino, *Pr*
Susan L Armellino, *
Jana Armellino, *CFO*
▲ **EMP:** 45 **EST:** 1986
**SQ FT:** 14,000
**SALES (est):** 8.14MM **Privately Held**
Web: www.usarmor.com
SIC: **3842** 2326 5999 Bulletproof vests; Men's and boy's work clothing; Safety supplies and equipment

**(P-15425)**
**VALEDA COMPANY LLC**
Also Called: Safe Haven
13571 Vaughn St Unit E, San Fernando (91340-3006)
PHONE..................800 421-8700
**EMP:** 47
**SALES (corp-wide):** 13.9MM **Privately Held**
Web: www.qstraint.com
SIC: **3842** Wheelchairs
PA: Valeda Company, Llc
  4031 Ne 12th Ter
  954 986-6665

**(P-15426)**
**VCP MOBILITY HOLDINGS INC**
Also Called: Sunrise Med HM Hlth Care Group
745 Design Ct Ste 602, Chula Vista (91911-6165)
PHONE..................619 213-6500
Steve Winston, *Mgr*
**EMP:** 25
**SALES (corp-wide):** 463.03MM **Privately Held**
SIC: **3842** Wheelchairs
HQ: Vcp Mobility Holdings, Inc.
  7477 Dry Creek Pkwy
  Niwot CO 80503
  303 218-4600

**(P-15427)**
**VISION QUEST INDUSTRIES INC**
Also Called: V Q Orthocare
1390 Decision St Ste A, Vista (92081-8578)
PHONE..................949 261-6382
James W Knape, *CEO*
Kevin Lunau, *
Bob Blachford, *
▲ **EMP:** 175 **EST:** 1989
**SALES (est):** 26.04MM **Privately Held**
Web: www.vqorthocare.com
SIC: **3842** 5999 Braces, orthopedic; Medical apparatus and supplies

**(P-15428)**
**VME ACQUISITION CORP (PA)**
Also Called: Kinamed
820 Flynn Rd, Camarillo (93012-8701)
PHONE..................805 384-2748
Clyde R Pratt, *Pr*
Lorraine Willis, *CFO*
**EMP:** 15 **EST:** 1993
**SQ FT:** 14,000
**SALES (est):** 8.41MM **Privately Held**
Web: www.kinamed.com
SIC: **3842** 7342 Surgical appliances and supplies; Disinfecting and pest control services

**(P-15429)**
**WEBER ORTHOPEDIC LP (PA)**
Also Called: Hely & Weber Orthopedic
1185 E Main St, Santa Paula (93060-2954)
P.O. Box 832 (93061-0832)
PHONE..................800 221-5465
Jim Weber, *Pt*
Jim Weber, *Pr*
John P Hely, *
▲ **EMP:** 62 **EST:** 1982
**SQ FT:** 28,000
**SALES (est):** 9.25MM
**SALES (corp-wide):** 9.25MM **Privately Held**
Web: www.hely-weber.com
SIC: **3842** 5047 Braces, orthopedic; Orthopedic equipment and supplies

**(P-15430)**
**XR LLC**
15251 Pipeline Ln, Huntington Beach (92649-1135)
PHONE..................714 847-9292
Ari Suss, *Managing Member*
Kelly Eberhard Allen, *
▲ **EMP:** 27 **EST:** 2002
**SQ FT:** 68,000
**SALES (est):** 5.04MM **Privately Held**
Web: www.xrllc.com
SIC: **3842** Personal safety equipment

**(P-15431)**
**ZIMMER BIOMET FEGAN INC**
1640 Jeni Ln, Fairfield (94534-1541)
PHONE..................707 863-0291
Harry Fegan, *CEO*
**EMP:** 15 **EST:** 2015
**SALES (est):** 101.4K **Privately Held**
Web: www.zimmerbiomet.com
SIC: **3842** Orthopedic appliances

**(P-15432)**
**ZIMMER DENTAL INC**
1900 Aston Ave, Carlsbad (92008-7308)
PHONE..................800 854-7019
**EMP:** 440 **EST:** 1981
**SALES (est):** 8.87MM
**SALES (corp-wide):** 7.39B **Publicly Held**
Web: www.zimvie.com
SIC: **3842** 8021 3843 Implants, surgical; Offices and clinics of dentists; Dental equipment and supplies
HQ: Zimmer, Inc.
  1800 W Center St
  Warsaw IN 46580
  800 348-9500

**(P-15433)**
**ZIMMER MELIA & ASSOCIATES INC (PA)**
6832 Presidio Dr, Huntington Beach (92648)
PHONE..................615 377-0118
K Michael Melia, *Pr*
**EMP:** 25 **EST:** 2005
**SALES (est):** 1.48MM **Privately Held**
Web: www.zimmerbiomet.com
SIC: **3842** Orthopedic appliances

## 3843 Dental Equipment And Supplies

**(P-15434)**
**3M COMPANY**

## 3843 - Dental Equipment And Supplies (P-15457)

**3M**
2111 Mcgaw Ave, Irvine (92614-0908)
PHONE..................................949 863-1360
David Goldinger, *Brnch Mgr*
EMP: 274
SQ FT: 77,656
SALES (corp-wide): 32.68B **Publicly Held**
Web: www.3m.com
SIC: 3843 5047 Dental equipment and supplies; Dental equipment and supplies
PA: 3m Company
3m Center
651 733-1110

**(P-15435)**
**3M UNITEK CORPORATION**
Also Called: 3M Unitek
2724 Peck Rd, Monrovia (91016-5005)
PHONE..................................626 445-7960
Mary Jo Abler, *CEO*
Fred Palensky, *
▲ EMP: 480 EST: 1948
SQ FT: 249,000
SALES (est): 32.23MM
SALES (corp-wide): 32.68B **Publicly Held**
SIC: 3843 Orthodontic appliances
PA: 3m Company
3m Center
651 733-1110

**(P-15436)**
**AALBA DENT INC**
5045 Fulton Dr Ste B, Fairfield (94534-1690)
PHONE..................................707 864-3334
EMP: 16 EST: 1968
SALES (est): 3.01MM **Privately Held**
Web: www.aalbadent.com
SIC: 3843 Dental alloys for amalgams

**(P-15437)**
**ALPHA DENTAL OF UTAH INC**
12898 Towne Center Dr, Cerritos (90703-8546)
PHONE..................................562 467-7759
Anthony S Barth, *Prin*
EMP: 27 EST: 2010
SALES (est): 3.55MM **Privately Held**
Web: www.delta.org
SIC: 3843 Dental equipment and supplies

**(P-15438)**
**AURIDENT INCORPORATED**
610 S State College Blvd, Fullerton (92831-5138)
P.O. Box 7200 (92834-7200)
PHONE..................................714 870-1851
Howard M Hoffman, *Pr*
David H Fell, *
Fredelle G Hoffman, *
EMP: 30 EST: 1974
SQ FT: 2,700
SALES (est): 2.55MM **Privately Held**
Web: www.aurident.com
SIC: 3843 Dental alloys for amalgams

**(P-15439)**
**BELPORT COMPANY INC (PA)**
Also Called: Gingi Pak
4825 Calle Alto, Camarillo (93012-8530)
P.O. Box 240 (93011-0240)
PHONE..................................805 484-1051
Jo Pennington, *Pr*
EMP: 19 EST: 1954
SQ FT: 22,000
SALES (est): 5MM
SALES (corp-wide): 5MM **Privately Held**
Web: www.gingi-pak.com
SIC: 3843 Dental hand instruments, nec

**(P-15440)**
**BIEN AIR USA INC**
Also Called: Bien Air
8861 Research Dr Ste 100, Irvine (92618-4255)
PHONE..................................949 477-6050
Arhur Mateen, *Pr*
Jean Claude Maeier, *
Arthur Mateen, *
EMP: 65 EST: 1959
SALES (est): 39.95MM **Privately Held**
Web: dental.bienair.com
SIC: 3843 7699 5047 Dental equipment; Dental instrument repair; Hospital equipment and furniture
HQ: Bien-Air Dental Sa
Langgasse 60
Biel-Bienne BE 2504

**(P-15441)**
**BIOLASE INC**
4225 Prado Rd Ste 102, Corona (92880)
PHONE..................................949 361-1200
Richard Whitt, *Brnch Mgr*
EMP: 75
SALES (corp-wide): 49.16MM **Publicly Held**
Web: www.biolase.com
SIC: 3843 Dental equipment and supplies
PA: Biolase, Inc.
27042 Twne Cntre Dr Ste 2

**(P-15442)**
**BIOLASE INC (PA)**
Also Called: BIOLASE
27042 Towne Centre Dr Ste 270, Lake Forest (92610-2811)
PHONE..................................
EMP: 52 EST: 1984
SQ FT: 20,000
SALES (est): 49.16MM
SALES (corp-wide): 49.16MM **Publicly Held**
Web: www.biolase.com
SIC: 3843 3841 Dental equipment and supplies; Surgical lasers

**(P-15443)**
**CONAMCO SA DE CV**
3008 Palm Hill Dr, Vista (92084-6555)
PHONE..................................760 586-4356
Jane Mitchell, *VP*
Herman Mitchell, *VP*
Alfredo Mobarak, *Ch Bd*
EMP: 75 EST: 2017
SQ FT: 20,000
SALES (est): 887.76K **Privately Held**
SIC: 3843 Cement, dental

**(P-15444)**
**CYBER MEDICAL IMAGING INC**
Also Called: Xdr Radiology
11300 W Olympic Blvd Ste 710, Los Angeles (90064-1637)
PHONE..................................888 937-9729
Douglas Yoon, *CEO*
Adam Chen, *
Joel Karafin, *
EMP: 25 EST: 2003
SQ FT: 2,800
SALES (est): 2.34MM **Privately Held**
Web: www.xdrradiology.com
SIC: 3843 Dental equipment and supplies

**(P-15445)**
**DANSEREAU HEALTH PRODUCTS**
1581 Commerce St, Corona (92878-3230)
PHONE..................................951 549-1400
▲ EMP: 36 EST: 1957
SALES (est): 3.5MM **Privately Held**
Web: www.dhpdental.com
SIC: 3843 Dental equipment and supplies

**(P-15446)**
**DANVILLE MATERIALS LLC (HQ)**
Also Called: Danville
2875 Loker Ave E, Carlsbad (92010-6626)
PHONE..................................760 743-7744
Steve Schiess, *Pr*
▲ EMP: 16 EST: 1997
SALES (est): 11.3MM
SALES (corp-wide): 21.51MM **Privately Held**
Web: www.zestdent.com
SIC: 3843 Dental equipment and supplies
PA: Zest Anchors, Inc.
2875 Loker Ave E
760 743-7744

**(P-15447)**
**DANVILLE MATERIALS LLC**
4020 E Leaverton Ct, Anaheim (92807-1610)
PHONE..................................714 399-0334
Greg Dorsman, *Mgr*
EMP: 20
SALES (corp-wide): 21.51MM **Privately Held**
Web: www.zestdent.com
SIC: 3843 Dental materials
HQ: Danville Materials, Llc
2875 Loker Ave E
Carlsbad CA 92010

**(P-15448)**
**DCII NORTH AMERICA LLC (HQ)**
200 S Kraemer Blvd Bldg E, Brea (92821-6208)
PHONE..................................714 817-7000
John Bedford, *VP*
EMP: 41 EST: 2018
SALES (est): 1.27MM
SALES (corp-wide): 2.57B **Publicly Held**
SIC: 3843 Dental equipment and supplies
PA: Envista Holdings Corporation
200 S Kraemer Blvd Bldg E
714 817-7000

**(P-15449)**
**DENOVO DENTAL INC**
Also Called: Denovo
5130 Commerce Dr, Baldwin Park (91706-1450)
P.O. Box 548 (91706-0548)
PHONE..................................626 480-0182
Richard R Parker, *Pr*
Joseph Parker, *VP*
Jeanette Parker, *Sec*
▼ EMP: 20 EST: 1981
SQ FT: 10,000
SALES (est): 5.27MM **Privately Held**
Web: www.denovodental.com
SIC: 3843 5047 Dental equipment and supplies; Dental equipment and supplies

**(P-15450)**
**DENTIS USA CORPORATION**
Also Called: Dentis
11095 Knott Ave Ste B, Cypress (90630-5136)
PHONE..................................323 677-4363
Sim Gibong, *CEO*
Kichul Sim, *CFO*
▲ EMP: 42 EST: 2010
SALES (est): 4.51MM **Privately Held**
Web: www.dentisusa.com
SIC: 3843 Dental materials

**(P-15451)**
**DENTISTS SUPPLY COMPANY**
1201 K St Ste 740, Sacramento (95814-4039)
PHONE..................................888 253-1223
James Wiggett, *CEO*
EMP: 19 EST: 2014
SALES (est): 899.81K **Privately Held**
Web: www.cda.org
SIC: 3843 Dental equipment and supplies

**(P-15452)**
**DENTTIO INC**
116 N Maryland Ave Ste 125, Glendale (91206-4235)
PHONE..................................323 254-1000
Young Han, *CEO*
EMP: 16 EST: 2011
SALES (est): 1.8MM **Privately Held**
Web: www.denttio.com
SIC: 3843 Dental equipment and supplies

**(P-15453)**
**DEXTA CORPORATION**
957 Enterprise Way, Napa (94558-6209)
PHONE..................................707 255-2454
Mark M Rusin, *Pr*
Paul Rusin, *
EMP: 52 EST: 1966
SQ FT: 19,000
SALES (est): 4.71MM **Privately Held**
Web: www.dexta.com
SIC: 3843 Dental chairs

**(P-15454)**
**DUX INDUSTRIES INC**
Also Called: Dux Dental Products
1717 W Collins Ave, Orange (92867-5422)
P.O. Box 14247 (92863-1447)
PHONE..................................805 488-1122
▲ EMP: 65
Web: www.duxdental.com
SIC: 3843 Dental equipment and supplies

**(P-15455)**
**ENVISTA HOLDINGS CORPORATION (PA)**
Also Called: ENVISTA
200 S Kraemer Blvd Bldg E, Brea (92821-6208)
PHONE..................................714 817-7000
Paul Keel, *Pr*
Scott Huennekens, *Ch Bd*
Mark E Nance, *Sr VP*
Mischa M Reis Senior, *Strategy Vice President*
Eric Hammes, *CFO*
EMP: 51 EST: 2018
SALES (est): 2.57B
SALES (corp-wide): 2.57B **Publicly Held**
Web: www.envistaco.com
SIC: 3843 Dental equipment and supplies

**(P-15456)**
**EVOLVE DENTAL TECHNOLOGIES INC**
5 Vanderbilt, Irvine (92618-2011)
PHONE..................................949 713-0909
Rodger Kurthy, *CEO*
Sharon Kurthy, *Pr*
EMP: 18 EST: 2007
SALES (est): 4.54MM **Privately Held**
Web: www.korwhitening.com
SIC: 3843 Dental equipment and supplies

**(P-15457)**
**HANDPIECE PARTS & PRODUCTS INC**

# 3843 - Dental Equipment And Supplies (P-15458)

707 W Angus Ave, Orange (92868-1305)
PHONE.....................714 997-4331
Steve Bowen, *Pr*
Lyla Bowen, *
EMP: 30 EST: 1992
SQ FT: 18,000
SALES (est): 2.22MM **Privately Held**
Web: www.handpieceparts.com
SIC: 3843  Dental materials

### (P-15458)
### IMPLANT DIRECT SYBRON INTL LLC (HQ)
3050 E Hillcrest Dr Ste 100, Westlake Village (91362-3195)
PHONE.....................818 444-3000
EMP: 52 EST: 2010
SALES (est): 5.38MM
SALES (corp-wide): 23.89B **Publicly Held**
Web: www.implantdirect.com
SIC: 3843  Dental equipment and supplies
PA:  Danaher Corporation
     2200 Pa Ave Nw Ste 800w
     202 828-0850

### (P-15459)
### IMPLANT DIRECT SYBRON MFG LLC
Also Called: Implant Direct
3050 E Hillcrest Dr, Thousand Oaks (91362)
PHONE.....................818 444-3300
Gerald A Niznick, *Managing Member*
Philip Davis, *
EMP: 200 EST: 2010
SQ FT: 45,622
SALES (est): 41.85MM
SALES (corp-wide): 23.89B **Publicly Held**
Web: www.implantdirect.com
SIC: 3843  Dental equipment and supplies
PA:  Danaher Corporation
     2200 Pa Ave Nw Ste 800w
     202 828-0850

### (P-15460)
### JENERIC/PENTRON INCORPORATED (HQ)
1717 W Collins Ave, Orange (92867-5422)
PHONE.....................203 265-7397
Gordon Cohen, *Pr*
Martin Schulman, *
EMP: 200 EST: 1977
SQ FT: 46,000
SALES (est): 3.35MM
SALES (corp-wide): 7.1MM **Privately Held**
SIC: 3843  Dental equipment
PA:  Pentron Corporation
     53 N Plains Industrial Rd
     203 265-7397

### (P-15461)
### KERR CORPORATION (HQ)
1717 W Collins Ave, Orange (92867-5422)
P.O. Box 14247 (92863-1447)
PHONE.....................714 516-7400
Damien Mcdonald, *CEO*
Steve Semmelmayer, *
Steve Dunkerken, *
Leo Pranitis, *
◆ EMP: 218 EST: 1891
SQ FT: 105,000
SALES (est): 44.87MM **Privately Held**
Web: www.kerrdental.com
SIC: 3843  Dental materials
PA:  Sybron Dental Specialties, Inc.
     1717 W Collins Ave

### (P-15462)
### KETTENBACH LP
16052 Beach Blvd Ste 221, Huntington Beach (92647-3855)
PHONE.....................877 532-2123
Daniel Parrilli, *Dir*
EMP: 44 EST: 2007
SALES (est): 2.52MM **Privately Held**
Web: www.kettenbach-dental.us
SIC: 3843 5047  Dental equipment and supplies; Dental equipment and supplies

### (P-15463)
### KEYSTONE DENTAL INC
5 Holland Ste 209, Irvine (92618-2576)
PHONE.....................781 328-3324
Michael Nealon, *Owner*
EMP: 37
Web: www.keystonedental.com
SIC: 3843  Dental equipment and supplies
PA:  Keystone Dental, Inc.
     154 Middlesex Tpke Ste 2

### (P-15464)
### KEYSTONE DENTAL INC
13645 Alton Pkwy Ste A, Irvine (92618-1693)
PHONE.....................781 328-3382
Michael Nealon, *Brnch Mgr*
EMP: 37
Web: www.keystonedental.com
SIC: 3843  Enamels, dentists'
PA:  Keystone Dental, Inc.
     154 Middlesex Tpke Ste 2

### (P-15465)
### LACLEDE INC
Also Called: Laclede Research Center
2103 E University Dr, Rancho Dominguez (90220-6413)
PHONE.....................310 605-4280
Michael Pellico, *Pr*
Stephen Pellico, *
◆ EMP: 35 EST: 1978
SQ FT: 25,000
SALES (est): 9.1MM **Privately Held**
Web: www.laclede.com
SIC: 3843  Dental equipment

### (P-15466)
### LANCER ORTHODONTICS INC (PA)
2726 Loker Ave W, Carlsbad (92010-6603)
PHONE.....................760 744-5585
Giorgio Beretta, *CEO*
Janet Moore, *Sec*
Lisa Li, *CFO*
▲ EMP: 20 EST: 1967
SALES (est): 3.58MM
SALES (corp-wide): 3.58MM **Privately Held**
Web: www.lancerortho.com
SIC: 3843 5047  Orthodontic appliances; Dental equipment and supplies

### (P-15467)
### LARES RESEARCH
295 Lockheed Ave, Chico (95973-9026)
PHONE.....................530 345-1767
Craig Lares, *Pr*
Michelle Jackson, *
EMP: 39 EST: 1956
SQ FT: 30,000
SALES (est): 7.02MM **Privately Held**
Web: www.laresdental.com
SIC: 3843 5047  Dental equipment and supplies; Dental equipment and supplies

### (P-15468)
### MICRODENTAL LABORATORIES INC
Also Called: Microdental Laboratories
7475 Southfront Rd, Livermore (94551-8224)
PHONE.....................800 229-0936
Dazia Bosworth, *Brnch Mgr*
EMP: 45
SALES (corp-wide): 10.8MM **Privately Held**
Web: www.microdentalca.com
SIC: 3843  Dental equipment and supplies
PA:  Microdental Laboratories, Inc.
     500 Stephenson Hwy
     877 711-8778

### (P-15469)
### ORMCO CORPORATION
200 S Kraemer Blvd, Brea (92821-6208)
PHONE.....................909 962-5705
EMP: 25
SALES (corp-wide): 2.57B **Publicly Held**
Web: www.ormco.com
SIC: 3843  Orthodontic appliances
HQ:  Ormco Corporation
     1717 W Collins Ave
     Orange CA 92867
     714 516-7400

### (P-15470)
### ORMCO CORPORATION (HQ)
Also Called: Sybron Endo
1717 W Collins Ave, Orange (92867-5422)
PHONE.....................714 516-7400
Patrik Eriksson, *CEO*
Jason R Davis, *VP*
◆ EMP: 100 EST: 1975
SQ FT: 104,000
SALES (est): 85.59MM
SALES (corp-wide): 2.57B **Publicly Held**
Web: www.ormco.com
SIC: 3843  Orthodontic appliances
PA:  Envista Holdings Corporation
     200 S Kraemer Blvd Bldg E
     714 817-7000

### (P-15471)
### ORTHO ORGANIZERS INC
Also Called: Henry Schein Orthodontics
1822 Aston Ave, Carlsbad (92008-7306)
PHONE.....................760 448-8600
David Parker, *Ch*
Russell J Bonafede, *
Robert Riley, *
Ted Dreifuss, *
Alison Weber, *
▲ EMP: 226 EST: 1975
SQ FT: 65,000
SALES (est): 22.93MM
SALES (corp-wide): 12.34B **Publicly Held**
Web: www.henryscheinortho.com
SIC: 3843 5047  Orthodontic appliances; Dental equipment and supplies
PA:  Henry Schein, Inc.
     135 Duryea Rd
     631 843-5500

### (P-15472)
### ORTHODENTAL INTERNATIONAL INC
280 Campillo St Ste J, Calexico (92231)
PHONE.....................760 357-8070
Armando Lozano, *Pr*
▲ EMP: 57 EST: 1994
SALES (est): 2.19MM
SALES (corp-wide): 3.96B **Publicly Held**
SIC: 3843  Orthodontic appliances
PA:  Dentsply Sirona Inc.
     13320 Ballantyne Corp Pl
     844 848-0137

### (P-15473)
### PAC-DENT INC
670 Endeavor Cir, Brea (92821-2949)
PHONE.....................909 839-0888
Daniel Wang, *CEO*
EMP: 49 EST: 2003
SALES (est): 2.67MM **Privately Held**
Web: www.pac-dent.com
SIC: 3843  Dental equipment and supplies

### (P-15474)
### PANADENT CORPORATION
580 S Rancho Ave, Colton (92324-3252)
PHONE.....................909 783-1841
Arlene Lee, *Ch Bd*
Thomas E Lee, *Pr*
EMP: 20 EST: 1966
SQ FT: 1,200
SALES (est): 2.42MM **Privately Held**
Web: www.panadent.com
SIC: 3843  Dental hand instruments, nec

### (P-15475)
### PATTERSON DENTAL SUPPLY INC
5087 Commercial Cir, Concord (94520-1268)
PHONE.....................925 603-6350
Mark Webb, *Brnch Mgr*
EMP: 43
SALES (corp-wide): 6.57B **Publicly Held**
Web: www.pattersondental.com
SIC: 3843  Dental equipment and supplies
HQ:  Patterson Dental Supply, Inc.
     1031 Mendota Heights Rd
     Saint Paul MN 55120
     651 686-1600

### (P-15476)
### PDMA VENTURES INC
Also Called: Zet-Tek Precision Machining
22951 La Palma Ave, Yorba Linda (92887-6701)
PHONE.....................714 777-8770
Charles Platt, *Pr*
Mark Deischter, *
EMP: 35 EST: 2016
SALES (est): 2.35MM **Privately Held**
SIC: 3843 3842 3841  Dental equipment and supplies; Surgical appliances and supplies; Surgical and medical instruments

### (P-15477)
### PRECISION ONE MEDICAL INC
3923 Oceanic Dr Ste 200, Oceanside (92056-5866)
PHONE.....................760 945-7966
J Todd Strong, *CEO*
David P Dutil, *
Mike Mills, *
EMP: 80 EST: 2009
SQ FT: 10,000
SALES (est): 8.66MM **Privately Held**
Web: www.precisiononemedical.com
SIC: 3843  Dental equipment and supplies

### (P-15478)
### PROMA INC
730 Kingshill Pl, Carson (90746-1219)
PHONE.....................310 327-0035
Raymond Tai, *CEO*
Harold Tai, *
▲ EMP: 40 EST: 1967
SQ FT: 37,000
SALES (est): 4.55MM **Privately Held**
Web: www.proma.us

# PRODUCTS & SERVICES SECTION
## 3844 - X-ray Apparatus And Tubes (P-15500)

SIC: 3843 Dental equipment and supplies

**(P-15479)**
**REPLACEMENT PARTS INDS INC**
Also Called: RPI
625 Cochran St, Simi Valley (93065-1939)
P.O. Box 940250 (93094-0250)
PHONE.............................818 882-8611
Ira Lapides, Pr
Albert M Lapides, *
Sherry Lapides, *
◆ EMP: 25 EST: 1972
SQ FT: 15,000
SALES (est): 6.32MM Privately Held
Web: www.rpiparts.com
SIC: 3843 3841 3821 Dental equipment; Surgical and medical instruments; Laboratory apparatus, except heating and measuring

**(P-15480)**
**RF AMERICA-IDS INC**
17609 Ventura Blvd Ste 115, Encino (91316-5131)
PHONE.............................866 578-5533
Jesse Pulido, Pr
Ofir Zaidenberg, VP
EMP: 15 EST: 2006
SQ FT: 2,100
SALES (est): 1.5MM Privately Held
Web: www.myrfamerica.com
SIC: 3843 5734 Dental equipment and supplies; Computer software and accessories

**(P-15481)**
**SCIENTIFIC PHARMACEUTICALS INC**
Also Called: SCI-Pharm
3221 Producer Way, Pomona (91768-3916)
PHONE.............................909 595-9922
▲ EMP: 40 EST: 1979
SALES (est): 5.54MM Privately Held
Web: www.scipharm.com
SIC: 3843 2891 Dental materials; Adhesives and sealants

**(P-15482)**
**SELANE PRODUCTS INC (PA)**
Also Called: Sml Space Maintainers Labs
9129 Lurline Ave, Chatsworth (91311-5922)
P.O. Box 2101 (91313-2101)
PHONE.............................818 998-7460
Rob Veis, CEO
▲ EMP: 60 EST: 1957
SQ FT: 12,000
SALES (est): 9.83MM
SALES (corp-wide): 9.83MM Privately Held
Web: www.smlglobal.com
SIC: 3843 8072 Orthodontic appliances; Dental laboratories

**(P-15483)**
**SONENDO INC (PA)**
Also Called: SONENDO
26061 Merit Cir Ste 102, Laguna Hills (92653-7010)
PHONE.............................949 766-3636
Bjarne Bergheim, Pr
Anthony P Bihl Iii, Ch Bd
John P Mcgaugh, VP Opers
Chris Guo, CORP CTRL
John Bostjancic, CFO
EMP: 214 EST: 2006
SQ FT: 55,000
SALES (est): 43.87MM Publicly Held
Web: www.sonendo.com
SIC: 3843 Dental equipment and supplies

**(P-15484)**
**SPRINTRAY INC (PA)**
2710 Media Center Dr, Los Angeles (90065-1746)
PHONE.............................800 914-8004
Amir Mansouri, CEO
Jing Zhang, *
Erich Kreidler, *
Arun Subramony, *
Jessie Zhang, *
EMP: 51 EST: 2017
SALES (est): 31.98MM
SALES (corp-wide): 31.98MM Privately Held
Web: www.sprintray.com
SIC: 3843 Dental equipment and supplies

**(P-15485)**
**STRAIGHT SMILE LLC (HQ)**
Also Called: Byte
3435 Ocean Park Blvd Ste 107-252, Santa Monica (90405-3301)
PHONE.............................424 389-4551
Neeraj Gunsagar, CEO
EMP: 17 EST: 2017
SQ FT: 1,900
SALES (est): 1.2MM
SALES (corp-wide): 3.96B Publicly Held
Web: www.byte.com
SIC: 3843 Dental equipment and supplies
PA: Dentsply Sirona Inc.
13320 Ballantyne Corp Pl
844 848-0137

**(P-15486)**
**SYBRON DENTAL SPECIALTIES INC**
1332 S Lone Hill Ave, Glendora (91740-5339)
PHONE.............................909 596-0276
Andy Astadurian, Brnch Mgr
EMP: 47
Web: www.peakdentalspecialists.com
SIC: 3843 Dental equipment and supplies
PA: Sybron Dental Specialties, Inc.
1717 W Collins Ave

**(P-15487)**
**SYBRON DENTAL SPECIALTIES INC (PA)**
Also Called: Analytic Endodontics
1717 W Collins Ave, Orange (92867-5422)
PHONE.............................714 516-7400
Damien Mcdonald, CEO
◆ EMP: 250 EST: 1993
SQ FT: 16,000
SALES (est): 375.07MM Privately Held
Web: www.kavokerr.com
SIC: 3843 2834 Dental laboratory equipment; Pharmaceutical preparations

**(P-15488)**
**TALLADIUM INC (PA)**
27360 Muirfield Ln, Valencia (91355-1010)
PHONE.............................661 295-0900
Eddie Harms, CEO
Geoff Harms, *
◆ EMP: 26 EST: 1980
SQ FT: 9,000
SALES (est): 7.46MM
SALES (corp-wide): 7.46MM Privately Held
Web: www.talladium.com
SIC: 3843 3541 5047 Investment material, dental; Milling machines; Dental equipment and supplies

**(P-15489)**
**TECH WEST VACUUM INC**
Also Called: Tech West
2625 N Argyle Ave, Fresno (93727-1304)
PHONE.............................559 291-1650
John Napier, Pr
▲ EMP: 22 EST: 1983
SQ FT: 30,000
SALES (est): 5.78MM Privately Held
Web: www.tech-west.com
SIC: 3843 Dental equipment

**(P-15490)**
**TRUABUTMENT INC (PA)**
17666 Fitch, Irvine (92614-6022)
PHONE.............................714 956-1488
Hyungick Kim, CEO
Sangho Yoo, *
EMP: 17 EST: 2013
SQ FT: 1,800
SALES (est): 7.53MM
SALES (corp-wide): 7.53MM Privately Held
Web: www.truabutment.com
SIC: 3843 Dental equipment and supplies

**(P-15491)**
**UNIVERSAL ORTHODONTIC LAB INC**
11917 Front St, Norwalk (90650-2900)
PHONE.............................562 484-0500
Young Paul Kim, Owner
EMP: 18 EST: 1995
SALES (est): 1.11MM Privately Held
Web: www.uniortholab.com
SIC: 3843 Dental equipment

**(P-15492)**
**US DENTAL INC**
Also Called: Young Dental
13043 166th St, Cerritos (90703-2201)
PHONE.............................562 404-3500
Young Hoon Park, CEO
EMP: 20 EST: 2015
SALES (est): 1.23MM Privately Held
Web: www.usdentalinc.com
SIC: 3843 Dental equipment and supplies

**(P-15493)**
**VMC INTERNATIONAL LLC**
Also Called: Vaniman Manufacturing
25799 Jefferson Ave, Murrieta (92562-6903)
P.O. Box 74 (92088-0074)
PHONE.............................760 723-1498
EMP: 16 EST: 1984
SQ FT: 7,000
SALES (est): 3.63MM Privately Held
Web: www.vaniman.com
SIC: 3843 Dental equipment

**(P-15494)**
**WELLS DENTAL INC**
Also Called: Wells Precision Machining
5860 Flynn Creek Rd, Comptche (95427-9500)
P.O. Box 106 (95427-0106)
PHONE.............................707 937-0521
Richard B Wells, Pr
Ginger Wells, VP
Marvin Wells, Sec
EMP: 15 EST: 1929
SQ FT: 15,000
SALES (est): 2.39MM Privately Held
Web: www.wellsdental.com
SIC: 3843 Dental laboratory equipment

**(P-15495)**
**WESTSIDE RESOURCES INC**
Also Called: Crystal Tip
8850 Research Dr, Irvine (92618-4223)
PHONE.............................800 944-3939
Donovan Berkely, CEO
Derek Jenkins, *
▲ EMP: 40 EST: 2000
SQ FT: 18,000
SALES (est): 3.66MM Privately Held
Web: www.naturestip.com
SIC: 3843 5047 Dental equipment and supplies; Medical and hospital equipment

**(P-15496)**
**ZYRIS INC**
6868 Cortona Dr Ste A, Santa Barbara (93117-1362)
PHONE.............................805 560-9888
Sandra Hirsch, CEO
Sandra Y Hirsch, *
James Hirsch, *
Rolando Mia, *
Catherine Gloster Vv, Pr
▲ EMP: 50 EST: 2001
SQ FT: 10,200
SALES (est): 8.97MM Privately Held
Web: www.zyris.com
SIC: 3843 5047 Dental equipment; Dental equipment and supplies

## 3844 X-ray Apparatus And Tubes

**(P-15497)**
**ALARA INC**
47505 Seabridge Dr, Fremont (94538-6546)
PHONE.............................510 315-5200
EMP: 40
SIC: 3844 X-ray apparatus and tubes

**(P-15498)**
**ASHTEL STUDIOS INC**
Also Called: Ashtel Dental
1610 E Philadelphia St, Ontario (91761-5759)
PHONE.............................909 434-0911
Anish Patel, Pr
Anish Patel, CEO
◆ EMP: 50 EST: 2006
SQ FT: 40,000
SALES (est): 132.27MM Privately Held
Web: www.ashtelstudios.com
SIC: 3844 3991 5122 X-ray apparatus and tubes; Toothbrushes, except electric; Toothbrushes, except electric

**(P-15499)**
**ASTROPHYSICS INC (PA)**
21481 Ferrero, City Of Industry (91789-5233)
PHONE.............................909 598-5488
Francois Zayek, CEO
Francois Zayek, Pr
John Pan, *
▼ EMP: 129 EST: 2002
SQ FT: 65,376
SALES (est): 59.64MM
SALES (corp-wide): 59.64MM Privately Held
Web: www.astrophysicsinc.com
SIC: 3844 X-ray apparatus and tubes

**(P-15500)**
**CARL ZISS X-RAY MICROSCOPY INC**
5300 Central Pkwy, Dublin (94568-4999)

(PA)=Parent Co (HQ)=Headquarters
✪ = New Business established in last 2 years

# 3844 - X-ray Apparatus And Tubes (P-15501)

PHONE.............................925 701-3600
Bobby Blair, CEO
Peter Jackson, *
Timothy Hart, *
Jin Yoon, *
**EMP:** 66 **EST:** 2000
**SALES (est):** 23.26MM **Privately Held**
Web: www.team-dignitas.net
**SIC: 3844** 5047 X-ray apparatus and tubes; X-ray machines and tubes
HQ: Carl Zeiss Microscopy Gmbh
Carl-Zeiss-Promenade 10
Jena TH 07745

## (P-15501)
### CARR CORPORATION (PA)
1547 11th St, Santa Monica (90401-2999)
PHONE.............................310 587-1113
John Carr, Pr
Paul Carr, *
Reese Carr, *
**EMP:** 25 **EST:** 1946
**SQ FT:** 25,000
**SALES (est):** 2.48MM
**SALES (corp-wide):** 2.48MM **Privately Held**
Web: www.carrcorporation.com
**SIC: 3844** 3861 3842 X-ray apparatus and tubes; Processing equipment, photographic; Surgical appliances and supplies

## (P-15502)
### HOLOGIC INC
1240 Elko Dr, Sunnyvale (94089-2212)
PHONE.............................408 745-0975
**EMP:** 22
**SALES (corp-wide):** 4.03B **Publicly Held**
Web: www.hologic.com
**SIC: 3844** X-ray apparatus and tubes
PA: Hologic, Inc.
250 Campus Dr
508 263-2900

## (P-15503)
### IMMPORT THERAPEUTICS INC
Also Called: Antigen Discovery
1 Technology Dr Ste E309, Irvine (92618-2343)
PHONE.............................949 679-4068
Philip Felgner, Pr
**EMP:** 15 **EST:** 2002
**SALES (est):** 2.97MM **Privately Held**
Web: www.antigendiscovery.com
**SIC: 3844** Therapeutic X-ray apparatus and tubes

## (P-15504)
### LYNCEAN TECHNOLOGIES INC
47633 Westinghouse Dr, Fremont (94539-7474)
PHONE.............................650 320-8300
Ronald Ruth, CEO
Jeff Rifkin, VP
Rod Loewen, Stockholder
▲ **EMP:** 17 **EST:** 2001
**SALES (est):** 4.73MM **Privately Held**
Web: www.lynceantech.com
**SIC: 3844** X-ray generators

## (P-15505)
### NORDSON DAGE INC
Also Called: Nordson
2747 Loker Ave W, Carlsbad (92010-6601)
PHONE.............................440 985-4496
John J Keane, CEO
Robert E Veillette, *
Phil Vere, *
▲ **EMP:** 30 **EST:** 1977
**SQ FT:** 6,000
**SALES (est):** 9.76MM
**SALES (corp-wide):** 2.63B **Publicly Held**
Web: www.nordson.com
**SIC: 3844** 3544 5065 3823 X-ray apparatus and tubes; Special dies, tools, jigs, and fixtures; Electronic parts; Process control instruments
PA: Nordson Corporation
28601 Clemens Rd
440 892-1580

## (P-15506)
### RAPISCAN LABORATORIES INC (HQ)
46718 Fremont Blvd, Fremont (94538-6538)
PHONE.............................408 961-9700
Shiva Kumar, CEO
▲ **EMP:** 60 **EST:** 1997
**SALES (est):** 8.35MM
**SALES (corp-wide):** 1.54B **Publicly Held**
Web: www.rapiscansystems.com
**SIC: 3844** X-ray apparatus and tubes
PA: Osi Systems, Inc.
12525 Chadron Ave
310 978-0516

## (P-15507)
### RAPISCAN LABORATORIES INC
3793 Spinnaker Ct, Fremont (94538-6537)
PHONE.............................510 399-7101
Liz Boyle, Prin
**EMP:** 30
**SALES (corp-wide):** 1.54B **Publicly Held**
Web: www.osi-systems.com
**SIC: 3844** X-ray apparatus and tubes
HQ: Rapiscan Laboratories, Inc.
46718 Fremont Blvd
Fremont CA 94538
408 961-9700

## (P-15508)
### RAPISCAN SYSTEMS INC (HQ)
2805 Columbia St, Torrance (90503-3804)
PHONE.............................310 978-1457
Deepak Chopra, CEO
Ajay Mehra, *
Eric Luiz, *
Andy Kotowski, *
◆ **EMP:** 114 **EST:** 1993
**SQ FT:** 93,000
**SALES (est):** 45.51MM
**SALES (corp-wide):** 1.54B **Publicly Held**
Web: www.rapiscansystems.com
**SIC: 3844** X-ray apparatus and tubes
PA: Osi Systems, Inc.
12525 Chadron Ave
310 978-0516

## (P-15509)
### STRATEGIC MEDICAL VENTURES LLC
280 Newport Center Dr, Newport Beach (92660-7526)
PHONE.............................949 355-5212
Antony Clarke, Managing Member
**EMP:** 20 **EST:** 2010
**SALES (est):** 2.1MM **Privately Held**
**SIC: 3844** X-ray apparatus and tubes

## (P-15510)
### TRUFOCUS CORPORATION
Also Called: Trufocus
468 Westridge Dr, Watsonville (95076-4159)
PHONE.............................831 761-9981
George G Howard, Pr
Kevin Bedolla, Sec
Dianne Moody, Ex Sec
**EMP:** 16 **EST:** 1987
**SQ FT:** 12,500
**SALES (est):** 2.14MM **Privately Held**
Web: www.trufocus.com
**SIC: 3844** X-ray apparatus and tubes

## (P-15511)
### VAREX IMAGING WEST LLC (HQ)
2175 Mission College Blvd, Santa Clara (95054-1520)
PHONE.............................408 565-0850
Brian Giambattista, Managing Member
◆ **EMP:** 23 **EST:** 2015
**SQ FT:** 74,000
**SALES (est):** 9.23MM
**SALES (corp-wide):** 893.4MM **Publicly Held**
Web: www.vareximaging.com
**SIC: 3844** X-ray apparatus and tubes
PA: Varex Imaging Corporation
1678 S Pioneer Rd
801 972-5000

# 3845 Electromedical Equipment

## (P-15512)
### AEREOTECH LLC
4572 Fellows St, Union City (94587-5451)
PHONE.............................626 319-5394
**EMP:** 15
**SALES (corp-wide):** 84.25K **Privately Held**
**SIC: 3845** Electromedical equipment
PA: Aereotech Llc
409 N Oak Ave
626 209-9196

## (P-15513)
### AMPRONIX LLC
15 Whatney, Irvine (92618-2808)
PHONE.............................949 273-8000
Burton Tripathi, Managing Member
◆ **EMP:** 62 **EST:** 1982
**SQ FT:** 58,000
**SALES (est):** 8.86MM **Privately Held**
Web: www.ampronix.com
**SIC: 3845** 5047 Electrotherapeutic apparatus; Diagnostic equipment, medical

## (P-15514)
### AVANTIS MEDICAL SYSTEMS INC
2367 Bering Dr, San Jose (95131-1125)
P.O. Box 70845 (94086-0845)
PHONE.............................408 733-1901
Matt Frushell, Pr
Anthony Ditonno, Ch Bd
Scott Dodson, Pr
Larry Tannenbaum, Sr VP
**EMP:** 38 **EST:** 2004
**SQ FT:** 4,700
**SALES (est):** 4.77MM **Privately Held**
Web: avantis.thirdeyecolonoscopy.com
**SIC: 3845** Endoscopic equipment, electromedical, nec

## (P-15515)
### AXELGAARD MANUFACTURING CO
Also Called: Axelgaard Manufacturing
329 W Aviation Rd, Fallbrook (92028-3201)
PHONE.............................760 723-7554
Yen Axelgaard, Mgr
**EMP:** 23
**SALES (corp-wide):** 24.9MM **Privately Held**
Web: www.axelgaard.com
**SIC: 3845** Electromedical equipment
PA: Axelgaard Manufacturing Co., Ltd
520 Industrial Way
760 723-7554

## (P-15516)
### AXELGAARD MANUFACTURING CO (PA)
Also Called: Axelgaard
520 Industrial Way, Fallbrook (92028-2244)
PHONE.............................760 723-7554
Jens Axelgaard, CSO
Dan Jeffery, *
▲ **EMP:** 92 **EST:** 1985
**SQ FT:** 33,000
**SALES (est):** 24.9MM
**SALES (corp-wide):** 24.9MM **Privately Held**
Web: www.axelgaard.com
**SIC: 3845** Electromedical equipment

## (P-15517)
### BETA BIONICS INC
11 Hughes, Irvine (92618-1902)
PHONE.............................949 297-6635
Edward Damiano, Brnch Mgr
**EMP:** 24
**SALES (corp-wide):** 17.41MM **Privately Held**
Web: www.betabionics.com
**SIC: 3845** Patient monitoring apparatus, nec
PA: Beta Bionics, Inc.
300 Baker Ave Ste 301
855 745-3800

## (P-15518)
### BIO-RAD EXPORT LLC (HQ)
1000 Alfred Nobel Dr, Hercules (94547-1811)
PHONE.............................510 724-7000
**EMP:** 17 **EST:** 1982
**SALES (corp-wide):** 2.8B **Publicly Held**
Web: www.bio-rad.com
**SIC: 3845** 2835 3826 Electromedical equipment; Diagnostic substances; Electrophoresis equipment
PA: Bio-Rad Laboratories, Inc.
1000 Alfred Nobel Dr
510 724-7000

## (P-15519)
### BIOINTELLISENSE INC
570 El Camino Real Ste 200, Redwood City (94063-1248)
PHONE.............................650 481-8140
James Mault, CEO
**EMP:** 39 **EST:** 2018
**SALES (est):** 6.3MM **Privately Held**
Web: www.biointellisense.com
**SIC: 3845** Electromedical apparatus

## (P-15520)
### BIONESS INC
25103 Rye Canyon Loop, Valencia (91355-5004)
PHONE.............................661 362-4850
Todd Cushman, Pr
Alfred E Mann, Ch
Jim Mchargue, COO
Dan Lutz, Sr VP
Perry Payne, VP Opers
▲ **EMP:** 190 **EST:** 2004
**SQ FT:** 29,000
**SALES (est):** 47.63MM
**SALES (corp-wide):** 512.35MM **Publicly Held**
Web: www.bionessrehab.com
**SIC: 3845** 5047 Transcutaneous electrical nerve stimulators (TENS); Medical and hospital equipment
PA: Bioventus Inc.
4721 Emperor Blvd Ste 100

# PRODUCTS & SERVICES SECTION
## 3845 - Electromedical Equipment (P-15540)

919 474-6700

**(P-15521)**
**BIOSENSE WEBSTER INC (HQ)**
31 Technology Dr Ste 200, Irvine (92618-2302)
PHONE.....................909 839-8500
Uri Yaron, CEO
Jasmina Brooks, *
Kevin Robert Costello, *
Gerianne T Sarte, *
▲ EMP: 150 EST: 1980
SALES (est): 146.03MM
SALES (corp-wide): 85.16B Publicly Held
Web: www.jnj.com
SIC: 3845 3841 Electromedical apparatus; Surgical and medical instruments
PA: Johnson & Johnson
 1 Johnson & Johnson Plz
 732 524-0400

**(P-15522)**
**CALA HEALTH INC**
1800 Gateway Dr Ste 120, San Mateo (94404-4072)
PHONE.....................415 890-3961
Deanna Harshbarger, CEO
Renee Ryan, *
Kathryn Rosenbluth, CSO*
EMP: 90 EST: 2013
SALES (est): 11.17MM Privately Held
Web: www.calahealth.com
SIC: 3845 7389 Transcutaneous electrical nerve stimulators (TENS); Business services, nec

**(P-15523)**
**CARE INNOVATIONS LLC**
950 Iron Point Rd Ste 160, Folsom (95630-9304)
PHONE.....................800 450-0970
Randy Swanson, CEO
Marcus Grindstaff, COO
Bruce Pruden, CFO
EMP: 50 EST: 2011
SALES (est): 8.13MM Privately Held
SIC: 3845 3641 Electromedical apparatus; Electrotherapeutic lamp units

**(P-15524)**
**CAREFUSION CORPORATION (HQ)**
Also Called: Bd Carefusion
3750 Torrey View Ct, San Diego (92130-2622)
PHONE.....................858 617-2000
Thomas E Polen Junior, Pr
Christopher R Reidy, *
▲ EMP: 474 EST: 2009
SALES (est): 2.32B
SALES (corp-wide): 19.37B Publicly Held
Web: www.bd.com
SIC: 3845 8742 3841 Electromedical equipment; Hospital and health services consultant; Surgical instruments and apparatus
PA: Becton, Dickinson And Company
 1 Becton Dr
 201 847-6800

**(P-15525)**
**CHRISTIE MEDICAL HOLDINGS INC**
Also Called: Veinviewer
10550 Camden Dr, Cypress (90630-4600)
PHONE.....................714 236-8610
George Pinho, Pr
Chris Schnee, S&M/VP
EMP: 20 EST: 2009
SALES (est): 1.95MM Privately Held

SIC: 3845 Electromedical equipment
HQ: Christie Digital Systems Usa, Inc.
 10550 Camden Dr
 Cypress CA 90630
 714 236-8610

**(P-15526)**
**COASTLINE INTERNATIONAL**
1207 Bangor St, San Diego (92106-2407)
PHONE.....................888 748-7177
Larry Angione, CEO
▲ EMP: 250 EST: 1982
SQ FT: 32,000
SALES (est): 1.61MM Privately Held
Web: www.coastlineintl.com
SIC: 3845 3841 Electromedical equipment; Surgical and medical instruments

**(P-15527)**
**CONOR MEDSYSTEMS LLC**
1003 Hamilton Ct, Menlo Park (94025-1422)
EMP: 22 EST: 1999
SQ FT: 55,000
SALES (est): 2.27MM
SALES (corp-wide): 226.83B Publicly Held
SIC: 3845 3841 Dialyzers, electromedical; Surgical and medical instruments
HQ: Cordis Corporation
 14201 Nw 60th Ave
 Miami Lakes FL 33014
 786 313-2000

**(P-15528)**
**CUTERA INC (PA)**
Also Called: CUTERA
3240 Bayshore Blvd, Brisbane (94005-1021)
PHONE.....................415 657-5500
Sheila Hopkins, Interim Chief Executive Officer
Janet Widmann, Ch Bd
Stuart Drummond, Interim Chief Financial Officer
Jeff Jones, COO
EMP: 227 EST: 1998
SQ FT: 66,000
SALES (est): 212.37MM
SALES (corp-wide): 212.37MM Publicly Held
Web: www.cutera.com
SIC: 3845 Electromedical equipment

**(P-15529)**
**DAYLIGHT DEFENSE LLC**
Also Called: Drs Daylight Defense
16465 Via Esprillo Ste 100, San Diego (92127-1701)
PHONE.....................858 432-7500
EMP: 175 EST: 2009
SALES (est): 26.73MM
SALES (corp-wide): 16.62B Publicly Held
Web: www.daylightsolutions.com
SIC: 3845 Laser systems and equipment, medical
HQ: Daylight Solutions, Inc.
 16465 Via Esprillo # 100
 San Diego CA 92127
 858 432-7500

**(P-15530)**
**DECISION SCIENCES MED CO LLC**
Also Called: Decision Medical
12345 First American Way Ste 100, Poway (92064-6828)
PHONE.....................858 602-1600
Stuart J Rabin, Managing Member
Jed A Palmacci, CEO

EMP: 20 EST: 2012
SALES (est): 3.26MM Privately Held
Web: www.dsmedco.com
SIC: 3845 3841 Electromedical equipment; Surgical and medical instruments

**(P-15531)**
**DOLPHIN MEDICAL INC (HQ)**
12525 Chadron Ave, Hawthorne (90250-4807)
PHONE.....................800 448-6506
Deepak Chopra, Pr
Thomas Scharf, *
▲ EMP: 100 EST: 2001
SALES (est): 6.62MM
SALES (corp-wide): 1.54B Publicly Held
SIC: 3845 Ultrasonic medical equipment, except cleaning
PA: Osi Systems, Inc.
 12525 Chadron Ave
 310 978-0516

**(P-15532)**
**EBR SYSTEMS INC (PA)**
480 Oakmead Pkwy, Sunnyvale (94085-4708)
PHONE.....................408 720-1906
John Mccutcheon, Pr
Allan Will, Ch Bd
Rick Riley, COO
Debra Echt, CMO
EMP: 18 EST: 2003
SQ FT: 8,500
SALES (est): 8.61MM
SALES (corp-wide): 8.61MM Privately Held
Web: www.ebrsystemsinc.com
SIC: 3845 Cardiographs

**(P-15533)**
**EDWARDS LIFESCIENCES US INC (HQ)**
Also Called: Edwards
1 Edwards Way, Irvine (92614-5688)
PHONE.....................949 250-2500
Michael A Mussallem, Ch
Dirksen J Lehman, VP
Christine Z Mccauley, VP
Stanton J Rowe, VP
Scott B Ullem, VP
EMP: 80 EST: 2011
SALES (est): 6.89MM
SALES (corp-wide): 6B Publicly Held
Web: www.edwards.com
SIC: 3845 Patient monitoring apparatus, nec
PA: Edwards Lifesciences Corp
 1 Edwards Way
 949 250-2500

**(P-15534)**
**EKO HEALTH INC**
Also Called: Eko Devices
2100 Powell St 3rd Fl, Emeryville (94608-1892)
PHONE.....................844 356-3384
Connor Landgraf, CEO
Adam Saltman, CMO*
Tyler Crouch, *
EMP: 100 EST: 2013
SALES (est): 10.3MM Privately Held
Web: www.ekohealth.com
SIC: 3845 5047 3841 Electromedical equipment; Medical and hospital equipment; Diagnostic apparatus, medical

**(P-15535)**
**EXAM ROOM SUPPLY LLC**
2419 Harbor Blvd Unit 126, Ventura (93001-3904)
PHONE.....................805 298-3631

Doctor Charles Solomon, Managing Member
Charles Solomon, Managing Member
M Wash, Managing Member
EMP: 15 EST: 2016
SALES (est): 877.6K Privately Held
SIC: 3845 3841 5047 5999 Electromedical apparatus; Diagnostic apparatus, medical; Medical and hospital equipment; Medical apparatus and supplies

**(P-15536)**
**EXO IMAGING INC**
4201 Burton Dr, Santa Clara (95054-1512)
PHONE.....................833 633-8396
Sandeep Akkaraju, CEO
Yusuf Haque, *
Lori Munoz, *
EMP: 175 EST: 2016
SALES (est): 33.28MM Privately Held
Web: www.exo-imaging.com
SIC: 3845 Ultrasonic medical equipment, except cleaning

**(P-15537)**
**EXPLORAMED NC7 LLC**
Also Called: Willow
1975 W El Camino Real Ste 306, Mountain View (94040-2218)
PHONE.....................650 559-5805
Naomi Kelman, Pr
EMP: 175 EST: 2014
SQ FT: 5,175
SALES (est): 6.44MM Privately Held
Web: www.exploramed.com
SIC: 3845 Electromedical apparatus

**(P-15538)**
**FLEXICARE INCORPORATED**
15281 Barranca Pkwy Ste D, Irvine (92618-2202)
PHONE.....................949 450-9999
Ghassem Poormand, Pr
▲ EMP: 43 EST: 2006
SALES (est): 10.95MM Privately Held
Web: www.flexicare.com
SIC: 3845 Electromedical equipment

**(P-15539)**
**GEN-PROBE SALES & SERVICE INC**
10210 Genetic Center Dr, San Diego (92121-4394)
PHONE.....................858 410-8000
Carl Hull, Pr
EMP: 48 EST: 2010
SALES (est): 5.59MM
SALES (corp-wide): 4.03B Publicly Held
Web: www.hologic.com
SIC: 3845 Electromedical equipment
PA: Hologic, Inc.
 250 Campus Dr
 508 263-2900

**(P-15540)**
**GIVEN IMAGING LOS ANGELES LLC**
5860 Uplander Way, Culver City (90230-6608)
PHONE.....................310 641-8492
Ron Mcintyre, Business Operations Vice President
Eric Finkelman, ENGG*
Jeffrey Sawyer, Global Marketing Director*
◆ EMP: 175 EST: 2003
SALES (est): 46.08MM Privately Held
SIC: 3845 Electromedical equipment
HQ: Given Imaging Ltd.
 2 Hacarmel
 Yokneam Illit

## 3845 - Electromedical Equipment (P-15541)

**(P-15541)**
**HALO NEURO INC**
Also Called: Halo Neuroscience
735 Market St Fl 4, San Francisco (94103-2034)
PHONE.................................415 851-3338
Daniel Chao, *CEO*
Mark Mastlier, *CMO*
EMP: 17 EST: 2013
SQ FT: 8,000
SALES (est): 1.88MM **Privately Held**
Web: www.amolsarva.com
SIC: 3845 Electrotherapeutic apparatus

**(P-15542)**
**HOLOGIC INC**
10210 Genetic Center Dr, San Diego (92121-4362)
PHONE.................................858 410-8000
Gonzalo Martinez, *Brnch Mgr*
EMP: 157
SALES (corp-wide): 4.03B **Publicly Held**
Web: www.hologic.com
SIC: 3845 Ultrasonic medical equipment, except cleaning
PA: Hologic, Inc.
   250 Campus Dr
   508 263-2900

**(P-15543)**
**HOLOGIC INC**
9393 Waples St, San Diego (92121-3907)
PHONE.................................858 410-8792
EMP: 23 EST: 1995
SALES (est): 2.38MM **Privately Held**
Web: www.hologic.com
SIC: 3845 Electromedical equipment

**(P-15544)**
**HOSPITAL SYSTEMS INC**
750 Garcia Ave, Pittsburg (94565-5012)
PHONE.................................925 427-7800
Jennifer M Miller, *Ch Bd*
Rebecca Miller, *
David H Miller, *
EMP: 72 EST: 1970
SQ FT: 20,000
SALES (est): 9.23MM **Privately Held**
Web: www.hsiheadwalls.com
SIC: 3845 Electromedical equipment

**(P-15545)**
**HYGEIA II MEDICAL GROUP INC**
Also Called: A Breast Pump and More
6241 Yarrow Dr Ste A, Carlsbad (92011-1541)
PHONE.................................714 515-7571
Brett Nakfoor, *CEO*
Mark Engler, *
Brett Nakfoor, *Pr*
▲ EMP: 40 EST: 2007
SALES (est): 4.94MM **Privately Held**
Web: www.hygeiahealth.com
SIC: 3845 Electromedical equipment

**(P-15546)**
**HYPERBARIC TECHNOLOGIES INC**
3224 Hoover Ave, National City (91950-7224)
PHONE.................................619 336-2022
W T Gurnee, *Pr*
EMP: 80 EST: 1992
SQ FT: 15,000
SALES (est): 7.61MM **Privately Held**

SIC: 3845 3841 7352 3443 Electromedical equipment; Medical instruments and equipment, blood and bone work; Medical equipment rental; Fabricated plate work (boiler shop)

**(P-15547)**
**INKSPACE IMAGING INC**
5635 W Las Positas Blvd Ste 403-404, Pleasanton (94588-8538)
PHONE.................................925 425-7410
Peter Fischer, *CEO*
Pierre Balthazar Lechene, *Sec*
EMP: 16 EST: 2016
SALES (est): 2.28MM **Privately Held**
Web: www.inkspaceimaging.com
SIC: 3845 Magnetic resonance imaging device, nuclear

**(P-15548)**
**IRIDEX CORPORATION (PA)**
Also Called: IRIDEX
1212 Terra Bella Ave, Mountain View (94043-1824)
PHONE.................................650 940-4700
David I Bruce, *Pr*
Scott Shuda, *Ch Bd*
Patrick Mercer, *COO*
Fuad Ahmad, *Interim Chief Financial Officer*
EMP: 103 EST: 1989
SQ FT: 37,166
SALES (est): 51.87MM **Publicly Held**
Web: www.iridex.com
SIC: 3845 Electromedical equipment

**(P-15549)**
**JOHNSON JHNSON SRGCAL VSION IN (HQ)**
Also Called: Johnson & Johnson Vision
31 Technology Dr Bldg 29a, Irvine (92618-2302)
P.O. Box 25929 (92799)
PHONE.................................949 581-5799
Warren C Foust, *CEO*
Craig S Virgil, *
Christian A Cuzick, *
▲ EMP: 300 EST: 2001
SALES (est): 371.04MM
SALES (corp-wide): 85.16B **Publicly Held**
Web: www.jnjvisionpro.com
SIC: 3845 3841 Laser systems and equipment, medical; Ophthalmic instruments and apparatus
PA: Johnson & Johnson
   1 Johnson & Johnson Plz
   732 524-0400

**(P-15550)**
**KYMA MEDICAL TECHNOLOGIES INC**
2000 Ringwood Ave, San Jose (95131-1728)
PHONE.................................650 386-5089
Assaf Bernstein, *CEO*
EMP: 16 EST: 2014
SALES (est): 384.67K **Privately Held**
SIC: 3845 Automated blood and body fluid analyzers, except lab
PA: Zoll Medical Israel Ltd
   14 Atirei Yeda

**(P-15551)**
**LOBUE LASER & EYE MEDICAL CTRS**
40740 California Oaks Rd, Murrieta (92562-5727)
PHONE.................................951 696-1135
EMP: 19
SALES (corp-wide): 11.48MM **Privately Held**

Web: www.lobue2020eyes.com
SIC: 3845 Laser systems and equipment, medical
PA: Lobue Laser & Eye Medical Ctrs Inc
   40700 California Oaks Rd
   951 696-1135

**(P-15552)**
**LUMASENSE TECHNOLOGIES INC (HQ)**
888 Tasman Dr # 100, Milpitas (95035-7439)
PHONE.................................408 727-1600
Steve Abely, *CEO*
Vivek Joshi, *
Subra Sankar, *
Ronald Sutton, *
Patricia Winter, *
▲ EMP: 80 EST: 2005
SALES (est): 20.73MM
SALES (corp-wide): 1.66B **Publicly Held**
Web: www.advancedenergy.com
SIC: 3845 3829 3825 3823 Electromedical equipment; Measuring and controlling devices, nec; Instruments to measure electricity; Temperature instruments: industrial process type
PA: Advanced Energy Industries, Inc.
   1595 Wynkoop St Ste 800
   970 407-6626

**(P-15553)**
**MASIMO CORPORATION**
40 Parker, Irvine (92618)
PHONE.................................949 297-7000
EMP: 50
Web: www.masimo.com
SIC: 3845 Electromedical equipment
PA: Masimo Corporation
   52 Discovery

**(P-15554)**
**MASIMO CORPORATION**
9600 Jeronimo Rd, Irvine (92618)
PHONE.................................949 297-7000
EMP: 50
Web: www.masimo.com
SIC: 3845 Electromedical equipment
PA: Masimo Corporation
   52 Discovery

**(P-15555)**
**MASIMO CORPORATION (PA)**
Also Called: MASIMO
52 Discovery, Irvine (92618-3105)
PHONE.................................949 297-7000
Michelle Brennan, *Interim Chief Executive Officer*
Micah Young, *Ex VP*
Tao Levy, *Ex VP*
Tom Mcclenahan, *Corporate Secretary*
▲ EMP: 350 EST: 1989
SQ FT: 314,400
SALES (est): 2.05B **Publicly Held**
Web: www.masimo.com
SIC: 3845 Electromedical equipment

**(P-15556)**
**MASIMO CORPORATION**
15776 Laguna Canyon Rd, Irvine (92618-3111)
PHONE.................................949 297-7000
EMP: 18
Web: www.masimo.com
SIC: 3845 Patient monitoring apparatus, nec
PA: Masimo Corporation
   52 Discovery

**(P-15557)**
**MAY HOLDINGS INC**
Also Called: Medivision Optics
4883 E La Palma Ave Ste 503, Anaheim (92807-1957)
PHONE.................................714 563-2772
Kevin May, *Pr*
EMP: 15 EST: 1994
SQ FT: 6,000
SALES (est): 5.07MM **Publicly Held**
Web: www.medivisionusa.com
SIC: 3845 7699 5047 Endoscopic equipment, electromedical, nec; Scientific equipment repair service; Physician equipment and supplies
PA: Hca Healthcare, Inc.
   1 Park Plz

**(P-15558)**
**MEDTRONIC 3F THERAPEUTICS INC**
1851 E Deere Ave, Santa Ana (92705-5720)
PHONE.................................949 399-1675
Donna Saito, *Brnch Mgr*
EMP: 15
Web: www.medtronic.com
SIC: 3845 3842 3841 Electromedical equipment; Surgical appliances and supplies; Surgical and medical instruments
HQ: Medtronic 3f Therapeutics, Inc.
   710 Medtronic Pkwy
   Minneapolis MN 55432
   763 514-4000

**(P-15559)**
**MIRADRY INC**
2790 Walsh Ave, Santa Clara (95051-0963)
PHONE.................................408 579-8700
Arash Khavei, *CEO*
EMP: 70 EST: 2021
SALES (est): 5.58MM **Privately Held**
Web: www.miradry.com
SIC: 3845 Laser systems and equipment, medical

**(P-15560)**
**MOVANO INC**
Also Called: Movano
6800 Koll Center Pkwy Ste 160, Pleasanton (94566-7044)
PHONE.................................408 393-1209
Michael Leabman, *Pr*
Emily Wang Fairbairn, *
Phil Kelly, *VP*
Jeremy J Cogan, *CFO*
EMP: 30 EST: 2018
Web: www.movanohealth.com
SIC: 3845 Electromedical equipment

**(P-15561)**
**NATUS MEDICAL INCORPORATED**
Also Called: Natus Newborn Care
6701 Koll Center Pkwy # 120, Pleasanton (94566-8061)
PHONE.................................650 802-0400
EMP: 100
SALES (corp-wide): 28.49MM **Privately Held**
Web: www.natus.com
SIC: 3845 Electromedical equipment
HQ: Natus Medical Incorporated
   6701 Koll Center Pkwy # 12
   Pleasanton CA 94566
   925 223-6700

## PRODUCTS & SERVICES SECTION
## 3845 - Electromedical Equipment (P-15581)

**(P-15562)**
**NATUS MEDICAL INCORPORATED**
5955 Pacific Center Blvd, San Diego (92121-4309)
PHONE..............................858 260-2590
Stephen Dirocco, *Dir Opers*
EMP: 71
SALES (corp-wide): 28.49MM **Privately Held**
Web: www.natus.com
SIC: **3845** 3841 Electromedical equipment; Surgical instruments and apparatus
HQ: Natus Medical Incorporated
6701 Koll Center Pkwy # 12
Pleasanton CA 94566
925 223-6700

**(P-15563)**
**NATUS MEDICAL INCORPORATED (HQ)**
Also Called: Natus
6701 Koll Center Pkwy Ste 120, Pleasanton (94566-8061)
PHONE..............................925 223-6700
Jonathan Kennedy, *Pr*
Robert A Gunst, *Ch Bd*
Drew Davies, *Ex VP*
Austin F Noll Iii, *CCO*
D Christopher Chung, *VP*
▲ EMP: 39 EST: 1987
SQ FT: 8,200
SALES (est): 473.44MM
SALES (corp-wide): 28.49MM **Privately Held**
Web: www.natus.com
SIC: **3845** Electromedical equipment
PA: Archimed Sas
9 Rue Des Cuirassiers
481113533

**(P-15564)**
**NEURASIGNAL INC**
Also Called: Novasignal
1109 Westwood Blvd, Los Angeles (90024-3411)
PHONE..............................877 638-7251
Robert Hamilton, *CEO*
EMP: 35
SALES (est): 7.28MM **Privately Held**
Web: www.novasignal.com
SIC: **3845** Electromedical equipment

**(P-15565)**
**NEW SOURCE TECHNOLOGY LLC**
6678 Owens Dr Ste 105, Pleasanton (94588-3324)
PHONE..............................925 462-6888
EMP: 15 EST: 1996
SALES (est): 1.6MM **Privately Held**
Web: www.newsourcetechnology.com
SIC: **3845** Laser systems and equipment, medical

**(P-15566)**
**OUTSET MEDICAL INC**
Also Called: OUTSET
3052 Orchard Dr, San Jose (95134-2011)
PHONE..............................669 231-8200
Leslie Trigg, *Ch Bd*
Marc Nash, *Sr VP*
Nabeel Ahmed, *CFO*
EMP: 480 EST: 2003
SQ FT: 40,413
SALES (est): 130.38MM **Privately Held**
Web: www.outsetmedical.com
SIC: **3845** 3841 Electromedical equipment; Surgical and medical instruments

**(P-15567)**
**PACESETTER INC**
4946 Florence Ave, Bell (90201-4319)
PHONE..............................323 773-0591
Rosa Martinez, *Brnch Mgr*
EMP: 268
SALES (corp-wide): 40.11B **Publicly Held**
SIC: **3845** Electromedical equipment
HQ: Pacesetter, Inc.
15900 Valley View Ct
Sylmar CA 91342

**(P-15568)**
**PACESETTER INC**
13150 Telfair Ave, Sylmar (91342-3573)
PHONE..............................818 493-2715
Ignacio Machuca, *Brnch Mgr*
▲ EMP: 270
SALES (corp-wide): 40.11B **Publicly Held**
SIC: **3845** Defibrillator
HQ: Pacesetter, Inc.
15900 Valley View Ct
Sylmar CA 91342

**(P-15569)**
**PACESETTER INC**
6035 Stoneridge Dr, Pleasanton (94588-3270)
PHONE..............................925 730-4171
David Villarreal, *Brnch Mgr*
EMP: 242
SALES (corp-wide): 40.11B **Publicly Held**
SIC: **3845** Defibrillator
HQ: Pacesetter, Inc.
15900 Valley View Ct
Sylmar CA 91342

**(P-15570)**
**PACESETTER INC (DH)**
Also Called: Ventritex
15900 Valley View Ct, Sylmar (91342)
P.O. Box 9221 (91392)
PHONE..............................818 362-6822
Eric S Fain, *CEO*
Ronald A Matricaria, *
▲ EMP: 725 EST: 1994
SALES (est): 113.43MM
SALES (corp-wide): 40.11B **Publicly Held**
SIC: **3845** Defibrillator
HQ: St. Jude Medical, Llc
1 Saint Jude Medical Dr
Saint Paul MN 55117
651 756-2000

**(P-15571)**
**PALYON MEDICAL CORPORATION**
28432 Constellation Rd, Valencia (91355-5081)
P.O. Box 2091 (85646-2091)
EMP: 25 EST: 2009
SALES (est): 3.95MM **Privately Held**
Web: www.palyonmedical.com
SIC: **3845** Ultrasonic scanning devices, medical

**(P-15572)**
**PHILIPS IMAGE GDED THRAPY CORP (DH)**
Also Called: Volcano
3721 Valley Centre Dr Ste 500, San Diego (92130-3328)
PHONE..............................800 228-4728
Ronald A Matricaria, *Ch Bd*
R Scott Huennekens, *
John T Dahldorf, *
Darin M Lippoldt, *Chief Compliance Officer*
John Onopchenko, *Executive Strategy Vice President*
▲ EMP: 300 EST: 2000
SQ FT: 92,602
SALES (est): 47.32MM
SALES (corp-wide): 18.51B **Privately Held**
SIC: **3845** Ultrasonic medical equipment, except cleaning
HQ: Philips Holding U.S.A., Inc.
222 Jacobs St
Cambridge MA 02141

**(P-15573)**
**PHILIPS IMAGE GDED THRAPY CORP**
Also Called: Volcano Therapeutics
2451 Mercantile Dr Ste 200, Rancho Cordova (95742-6326)
PHONE..............................916 281-2932
Saul Salayandia, *Mgr*
EMP: 317
SALES (corp-wide): 18.51B **Privately Held**
SIC: **3845** Electromedical equipment
HQ: Philips Image Guided Therapy Corporation
3721 Vly Cntre Dr Ste 500
San Diego CA 92130
800 228-4728

**(P-15574)**
**R & D NOVA INC**
2934 E Garvey Ave S Ste 104, West Covina (91791-2118)
PHONE..............................951 781-7332
Scott Snyder, *Pr*
EMP: 15 EST: 1984
SQ FT: 4,000
SALES (est): 1.3MM
SALES (corp-wide): 24.51MM **Privately Held**
Web: www.kromek.com
SIC: **3845** 3812 Magnetic resonance imaging device, nuclear; Search and detection systems and instruments
PA: Kromek Group Plc
Thomas Wright Way
174 062-6050

**(P-15575)**
**REFLEXION MEDICAL INC**
25841 Industrial Blvd Ste 275, Hayward (94545)
PHONE..............................650 239-9070
Samuel R Mazin, *Pr*
Akshay Nanduri, *
Todd Powell, *
Martyn Webster, *
EMP: 120 EST: 2009
SALES (est): 20.16MM **Privately Held**
Web: www.reflexion.com
SIC: **3845** Electromedical equipment

**(P-15576)**
**RESMED CORP (HQ)**
9001 Spectrum Center Blvd, San Diego (92123-1438)
PHONE..............................858 836-5000
Michael Farrell, *CEO*
Robert Douglas, *COO*
Brett Sandercock, *CFO*
David Pendarvis, *CAO*
Hemanth Reddy, *CSO*
EMP: 58 EST: 2016
SALES (est): 34.42MM **Publicly Held**
Web: www.resmedfoundation.org
SIC: **3845** Ultrasonic scanning devices, medical
PA: Resmed Inc.
9001 Spectrum Center Blvd

**(P-15577)**
**SALUTRON INCORPORATED (PA)**
8371 Central Ave Ste A, Newark (94560-3473)
PHONE..............................510 795-2876
Mike Tsai, *CEO*
◆ EMP: 20 EST: 1995
SQ FT: 11,000
SALES (est): 5MM **Privately Held**
Web: www.salutron.com
SIC: **3845** Patient monitoring apparatus, nec

**(P-15578)**
**SIEMENS MED SOLUTIONS USA INC**
Also Called: Oncology Care Systems Group
4040 Nelson Ave, Concord (94520-1200)
PHONE..............................925 246-8200
Ajit Singh, *Pr*
EMP: 1375
SALES (corp-wide): 84.48B **Privately Held**
Web: new.siemens.com
SIC: **3845** 3842 5047 Electromedical equipment; Surgical appliances and supplies; Hospital equipment and furniture
HQ: Siemens Medical Solutions Usa, Inc.
40 Liberty Blvd
Malvern PA 19355
888 826-9702

**(P-15579)**
**SOLTA MEDICAL DISTRIBUTION LLC**
25901 Industrial Blvd, Hayward (94545-2995)
PHONE..............................510 782-2286
Doug Heigo, *Brnch Mgr*
EMP: 150
SALES (corp-wide): 8.76B **Privately Held**
Web: www.solta.com
SIC: **3845** Electromedical equipment
HQ: Solta Medical Distribution Llc
400 Somerset Corp Blvd
Bridgewater NJ 08807
877 782-2286

**(P-15580)**
**SOTERA WIRELESS INC**
5841 Edison Pl Ste 140, Carlsbad (92008-6500)
PHONE..............................858 427-4620
Tom Watlington, *CEO*
Benjamin Kanter, *CMO*
Mark Spring, *CFO*
Jim Welch, *Ex VP*
EMP: 104 EST: 2002
SALES (est): 19.07MM **Privately Held**
Web: www.soteradigitalhealth.com
SIC: **3845** Electromedical equipment

**(P-15581)**
**STRAND PRODUCTS INC (PA)**
2233 Knoll Dr, Ventura (93003-7398)
P.O. Box 4610 (93140-4610)
PHONE..............................800 343-7985
Wesley Prunckle, *CEO*
James Wilson, *
Susana Loewe, *
John Hottinger, *
▲ EMP: 20 EST: 1972
SQ FT: 6,000
SALES (est): 5.1MM **Privately Held**
Web: www.strandproducts.com
SIC: **3845** 5063 Ultrasonic scanning devices, medical; Wire and cable

## 3845 - Electromedical Equipment (P-15582)

**(P-15582)**
**SYNERON INC (DH)**
Also Called: Syneron Candela
3 Goodyear Ste A, Irvine (92618-2050)
PHONE......................866 259-6661
Doctor Shimon Eckhouse, Ch Bd
Shimon Eckhouse, *
Doctor Opher Shapira, VP
Doron Gerstel, *
Leslie Rigali, *
**EMP:** 87 **EST:** 2000
**SALES (est):** 102.55MM **Privately Held**
Web: www.candelamedical.com
SIC: 3845 Laser systems and equipment, medical
HQ: Syneron Medical Ltd
26 Hakidma
Yokneam Illit 20667

**(P-15583)**
**TENSYS MEDICAL INC**
12625 High Bluff Dr Ste 213, San Diego (92130-2054)
PHONE......................858 552-1941
Stuart Gallant, CEO
**EMP:** 32 **EST:** 1995
**SQ FT:** 25,370
**SALES (est):** 1.9MM **Privately Held**
Web: www.tensysmedical.com
SIC: 3845 3841 Ultrasonic scanning devices, medical; Surgical and medical instruments

**(P-15584)**
**THORATEC LLC (HQ)**
6035 Stoneridge Dr, Pleasanton (94588-3270)
PHONE......................925 847-8600
Jason Zellers, *
▲ **EMP:** 193 **EST:** 1976
**SQ FT:** 66,000
**SALES (est):** 49.15MM
**SALES (corp-wide):** 40.11B **Publicly Held**
SIC: 3845 3841 Electromedical equipment; Surgical and medical instruments
PA: Abbott Laboratories
100 Abbott Park Rd
224 667-6100

**(P-15585)**
**TOSHIBA AMERICA INC**
280 Utah Ave, South San Francisco (94080-6812)
PHONE......................212 596-0600
**EMP:** 176
Web: www.toshiba.com
SIC: 3845 Electromedical equipment
HQ: Toshiba America Inc
1251 Ave Of Amrcas Ste 41
New York NY 10020
212 596-0600

**(P-15586)**
**TOSHIBA AMERICA MRI INC**
Also Called: Toshiba
280 Utah Ave Ste 200, South San Francisco (94080-6883)
PHONE......................650 737-6686
▲ **EMP:** 190
SIC: 3845 8731 Magnetic resonance imaging device, nuclear; Commercial physical research

**(P-15587)**
**TUSKER MEDICAL INC**
155 Jefferson Dr, Menlo Park (94025-1114)
PHONE......................650 223-6900
Amir Abolfathi, Pr
**EMP:** 23 **EST:** 2016
**SALES (est):** 4.12MM
**SALES (corp-wide):** 5.55B **Privately Held**

Web: www.smith-nephew.com
SIC: 3845 Audiological equipment, electromedical
PA: Smith & Nephew Plc
Building 5
192 347-7100

**(P-15588)**
**VARIAN MEDICAL SYSTEMS INC (DH)**
Also Called: Varian
3100 Hansen Way, Palo Alto (94304-1030)
PHONE......................650 493-4000
Arthur Kaindle, CEO
Christopher Toth, CEO
**EMP:** 1710 **EST:** 1948
**SQ FT:** 481,000
**SALES (est):** 3.42B
**SALES (corp-wide):** 84.48B **Privately Held**
Web: www.varian.com
SIC: 3845 7372 Electromedical equipment; Prepackaged software
HQ: Siemens Healthineers Ag
Siemensstr. 3
Forchheim BY 91301
800 188-1885

**(P-15589)**
**VAVE HEALTH INC**
3031 Tisch Way, San Jose (95128-2584)
PHONE......................650 387-7059
Amin Nikoozadeh, CEO
**EMP:** 15 **EST:** 2014
**SALES (est):** 2.78MM **Privately Held**
Web: www.vavehealth.com
SIC: 3845 Ultrasonic medical equipment, except cleaning

**(P-15590)**
**VITAL CONNECT INC**
2870 Zanker Rd Ste 100, San Jose (95134-2133)
PHONE......................408 963-4600
Nersi Nazari, Ch Bd
Nersi Nazari, Pr
Martin Webster, *
**EMP:** 146 **EST:** 2012
**SALES (est):** 24.86MM **Privately Held**
Web: www.vitalconnect.com
SIC: 3845 Ultrasonic scanning devices, medical

**(P-15591)**
**VIVOMETRICS INC**
16030 Ventura Blvd Ste 470, Encino (91436-2731)
PHONE......................805 667-2225
Howard R Baker, Pr
**EMP:** 24 **EST:** 1999
**SQ FT:** 8,220
**SALES (est):** 562.08K **Privately Held**
SIC: 3845 3842 Patient monitoring apparatus, nec; Surgical appliances and supplies

**(P-15592)**
**ZOLL CIRCULATION INC**
2000 Ringwood Ave, San Jose (95131-1728)
PHONE......................408 541-2140
Richard A Packer, CEO
James Palabzolo, *
Mark Weeks, *
Jonathan A Rennert, *
Kenneth E Ludlum, *
▲ **EMP:** 130 **EST:** 1997
**SALES (est):** 46.73MM **Privately Held**
Web: www.zoll.com
SIC: 3845 3841 Electromedical equipment; Surgical and medical instruments

HQ: Zoll Medical Corporation
269 Mill Rd
Chelmsford MA 01824
978 421-9655

## 3851 Ophthalmic Goods

**(P-15593)**
**ADVANCED VISION SCIENCE INC**
5743 Thornwood Dr, Goleta (93117-3801)
PHONE......................805 683-3851
Cynthia Bentley, Pr
**EMP:** 40 **EST:** 1976
**SQ FT:** 30,000
**SALES (est):** 8.67MM **Privately Held**
Web: www.santen.com
SIC: 3851 3841 8011 Intraocular lenses; Surgical and medical instruments; Offices and clinics of medical doctors
PA: Santen Pharmaceutical Co., Ltd.
4-20, Ofukacho, Kita-Ku

**(P-15594)**
**BARTON PERREIRA LLC**
459 Wald, Irvine (92618-4639)
PHONE......................949 305-5360
Patty Jo L Perreira, *
▲ **EMP:** 25 **EST:** 2006
**SALES (est):** 4.24MM **Privately Held**
Web: www.bartonperreira.com
SIC: 3851 Protective eyeware

**(P-15595)**
**BLENDERS EYEWEAR LLC**
Also Called: Blenders Eyewear
4683 Cass St, San Diego (92109-2808)
PHONE......................858 490-2178
Chase Fisher, CEO
**EMP:** 75 **EST:** 2012
**SALES (est):** 8.99MM **Privately Held**
Web: www.blenderseyewear.com
SIC: 3851 Glasses, sun or glare
HQ: Safilo America, Inc.
300 Lighting Way Ste 400
Secaucus NJ 07094

**(P-15596)**
**COOPER COMPANIES INC (PA)**
Also Called: COOPER
6101 Bollinger Canyon Rd Ste 500, San Ramon (94583-5177)
PHONE......................925 460-3600
Albert G White Iii, Pr
Robert S Weiss, Ch Bd
William A Kozy, V Ch Bd
Daniel G Mcbride, Ex VP
Brian G Andrews, Ex VP
**EMP:** 167 **EST:** 1980
**SQ FT:** 201,143
**SALES (est):** 3.59B
**SALES (corp-wide):** 3.59B **Publicly Held**
Web: www.coopercos.com
SIC: 3851 3842 Contact lenses; Surgical appliances and supplies

**(P-15597)**
**COOPERVISION INC**
6101 Bollinger Canyon Rd # 500, San Ramon (94583-5108)
PHONE......................925 251-6600
Stephen Fanning, CEO
**EMP:** 144
**SALES (corp-wide):** 3.59B **Publicly Held**
Web: www.coopervision.com
SIC: 3851 Contact lenses
HQ: Coopervision, Inc.
209 High Point Dr Ste 100
Victor NY 14564

**(P-15598)**
**COOPERVISION INC**
5870 Stoneridge Dr Ste 1, Pleasanton (94588-2733)
PHONE......................925 251-2032
**EMP:** 58
**SALES (est):** 3.96MM **Privately Held**
Web: www.coopervision.com
SIC: 3851 Contact lenses

**(P-15599)**
**DRAGON ALLIANCE INC**
Also Called: Dragon Alliance
971 Calle Amanecer, San Clemente (92673-4228)
PHONE......................760 931-4900
William H Howard, Pr
Ryan Vance, Sec
▲ **EMP:** 44 **EST:** 1993
**SQ FT:** 3,500
**SALES (est):** 8.45MM
**SALES (corp-wide):** 1.89B **Privately Held**
Web: www.dragonalliance.com
SIC: 3851 Glasses, sun or glare
HQ: Marchon Eyewear, Inc.
35 Hub Dr
Melville NY 11747
631 755-2020

**(P-15600)**
**ELECTRIC VISUAL EVOLUTION LLC (PA)**
Also Called: Electric
950 Calle Amanecer Ste 101, San Clemente (92673-4203)
PHONE......................949 940-9125
◆ **EMP:** 28 **EST:** 1999
**SQ FT:** 2,000
**SALES (est):** 8.57MM
**SALES (corp-wide):** 8.57MM **Privately Held**
Web: www.electriccalifornia.com
SIC: 3851 5094 5136 Glasses, sun or glare; Watchcases; Apparel belts, men's and boys'

**(P-15601)**
**EYEONICS INC**
Also Called: Bausch & Lomb Surgical Div
32 Discovery, Irvine (92618)
PHONE......................949 788-6000
Joseph F Gordon, CEO
**EMP:** 50 **EST:** 1998
**SALES (est):** 3.74MM
**SALES (corp-wide):** 8.76B **Privately Held**
SIC: 3851 Ophthalmic goods
HQ: Bausch & Lomb Incorporated
400 Somerset Corp Blvd
Bridgewater NJ 08807
866 246-8245

**(P-15602)**
**HOYA CORPORATION**
1400 Carpenter Ln, Modesto (95351-1102)
PHONE......................209 579-7739
**EMP:** 30
Web: www.hoyavision.com
SIC: 3851 Ophthalmic goods
HQ: Hoya Corporation
651 E Corporate Dr
Lewisville TX 75057
972 221-4141

**(P-15603)**
**HOYA OPTICAL INC (PA)**
1400 Carpenter Ln, Modesto (95351-1102)
P.O. Box 580870 (95358-0016)
PHONE......................209 579-7739
Fred Fink, CEO
**EMP:** 90 **EST:** 1954
**SQ FT:** 17,700

▲ = Import ▼ = Export
◆ = Import/Export

## PRODUCTS & SERVICES SECTION
### 3851 - Ophthalmic Goods (P-15624)

SALES (est): 2MM
SALES (corp-wide): 2MM **Privately Held**
Web: www.hoyavision.com
SIC: **3851** 8011 5995 5048  Ophthalmic goods; Offices and clinics of medical doctors; Optical goods stores; Ophthalmic goods

**(P-15604)**
**IRD ACQUISITIONS LLC**
Also Called: Trijicon Electro Optics
12810 Earhart Ave, Auburn  (95602-9027)
PHONE..................530 210-2966
Stephen Bindon, *CEO*
EMP: 18 EST: 2013
SQ FT: 7,500
SALES (est): 1.02MM
SALES (corp-wide): 54.78MM **Privately Held**
SIC: **3851** 3949 3827  Goggles: sun, safety, industrial, underwater, etc.; Target shooting equipment; Telescopes: elbow, panoramic, sighting, fire control, etc.
PA: Trijicon, Inc.
49385 Shafer Ct
248 960-7700

**(P-15605)**
**KAZAK-MARS INC**
Also Called: K Mars
16430 Vanowen St, Van Nuys  (91406-4729)
PHONE..................818 375-1033
Dan Sadovsky, *Pr*
▲ EMP: 22 EST: 1995
SQ FT: 7,000
SALES (est): 1.98MM **Privately Held**
Web: www.kmarsoptical.com
SIC: **3851**  Ophthalmic goods

**(P-15606)**
**LENS C-C INC (PA)**
Also Called: Con-Cise Contact Lens Co
1750 N Loop Rd Ste 150, Alameda  (94502-8013)
PHONE..................800 772-3911
Carl Moore, *Pr*
Lynda Baker, *
Dan Davis, *
EMP: 100 EST: 1949
SQ FT: 34,000
SALES (est): 22.75MM
SALES (corp-wide): 22.75MM **Privately Held**
SIC: **3851**  Contact lenses

**(P-15607)**
**LENSVECTOR INC**
6203 San Ignacio Ave Ste 110, San Jose  (95119-1358)
PHONE..................669 247-5095
Howard Earhart, *CEO*
Mark Gemello, *
EMP: 70 EST: 2006
SALES (est): 4.71MM **Privately Held**
Web: www.lensvector.com
SIC: **3851**  Ophthalmic goods

**(P-15608)**
**MARCH VISION CARE INC**
6701 Center Dr W Ste 790, Los Angeles  (90045-1563)
PHONE..................310 665-0975
EMP: 42 EST: 2005
SALES (est): 3.58MM
SALES (corp-wide): 371.62B **Publicly Held**
Web: www.marchvisioncare.com
SIC: **3851**  Frames, lenses, and parts, eyeglass and spectacle

HQ: March Holdings, Inc.
6701 Center Dr W Ste 790
Los Angeles CA 90045

**(P-15609)**
**MEDENNIUM INC (PA)**
9 Parker Ste 150, Irvine  (92618-1691)
PHONE..................949 789-9000
Jacob Feldman, *Pr*
James R Zullo, *
EMP: 40 EST: 1998
SQ FT: 20,000
SALES (est): 4.77MM
SALES (corp-wide): 4.77MM **Privately Held**
Web: www.medennium.com
SIC: **3851**  Intraocular lenses

**(P-15610)**
**NITINOL DEVELOPMENT CORP**
Also Called: Nitinol Devices & Components
47533 Westinghouse Dr, Fremont  (94539-7463)
PHONE..................510 683-2000
Tom Duerig, *Pr*
John Dicello, *
Chuck Faris, *OF QA*
Steve Kleshinski, *OF DEVICE CONCEPTS*
Jeff Lenigan, *VP Opers*
EMP: 600 EST: 1991
SQ FT: 30,000
SALES (est): 32.94MM **Privately Held**
Web: www.confluentmedical.com
SIC: **3851** 3496  Frames and parts, eyeglass and spectacle; Miscellaneous fabricated wire products

**(P-15611)**
**OAKLEY INC (DH)**
1 Icon, Foothill Ranch  (92610-3000)
PHONE..................949 951-0991
Colin Baden, *Pr*
D Scott Olivet, *
Jim Jannard, *
Gianluca Tagliabue, *
Jon Krause, *
◆ EMP: 900 EST: 1994
SQ FT: 550,000
SALES (est): 984.07MM
SALES (corp-wide): 2.55MM **Privately Held**
Web: www.oakley.com
SIC: **3851** 2339 3873 3143  Ophthalmic goods; Women's and misses' outerwear, nec; Watches, clocks, watchcases, and parts; Men's footwear, except athletic
HQ: Luxottica Of America Inc.
4000 Luxottica Pl
Mason OH 45040

**(P-15612)**
**OASIS MEDICAL INC (PA)**
510-528 S Vermont Ave, Glendora  (91741)
P.O. Box 1137  (91740-1137)
PHONE..................909 305-5400
Norman Delgado, *Ch Bd*
Craig Delgado, *
Arlene Delgado, *
◆ EMP: 55 EST: 1987
SQ FT: 14,000
SALES (est): 18.37MM
SALES (corp-wide): 18.37MM **Privately Held**
Web: www.oasismedical.com
SIC: **3851** 5048  Ophthalmic goods; Ophthalmic goods

**(P-15613)**
**OPHTHONIX INC**
900 Glenneyre St, Laguna Beach  (92651-2707)

PHONE..................760 842-5600
▲ EMP: 25 EST: 2000
SQ FT: 50,000
SALES (est): 2.21MM **Privately Held**
Web: www.ophthonix.com
SIC: **3851**  Eyes, glass and plastic

**(P-15614)**
**PRESBIBIO LLC**
Also Called: Presbia
36 Plateau, Aliso Viejo  (92656-8026)
PHONE..................949 502-7010
Vladimir Feingold, *
EMP: 45 EST: 2008
SALES (est): 4.68MM **Privately Held**
SIC: **3851**  Frames, lenses, and parts, eyeglass and spectacle

**(P-15615)**
**RXSIGHT INC (PA)**
Also Called: RXSIGHT
100 Columbia Ste 120, Aliso Viejo  (92656-4114)
PHONE..................949 521-7830
Ron Kurtz, *Pr*
J Andy Corley, *Ch Bd*
Shelley Thunen, *CFO*
Ilya Goldshleger, *COO*
Eric Weinberg, *CCO*
▼ EMP: 100 EST: 1997
SQ FT: 109,822
SALES (est): 89.08MM
SALES (corp-wide): 89.08MM **Publicly Held**
Web: www.rxsight.com
SIC: **3851**  Ophthalmic goods

**(P-15616)**
**SIGNET ARMORLITE INC (DH)**
5803 Newton Dr Ste A, Carlsbad  (92008-7312)
P.O. Box 3309  (60132-3309)
PHONE..................760 744-4000
Brad Staley, *Pr*
Bruno Salvadori, *
Andrea Moscatelli, *
M Kathryn Bernard, *
John Hingey, *
▲ EMP: 400 EST: 1969
SQ FT: 138,000
SALES (est): 19.2MM
SALES (corp-wide): 2.55MM **Privately Held**
Web: www.signetarmorlite.com
SIC: **3851**  Ophthalmic goods
HQ: Essilor Of America, Inc.
13555 N Stemmons Fwy
Dallas TX 75234

**(P-15617)**
**SOLO CLIP INC**
Also Called: Cliphouse
1988 W Holt Ave, Pomona  (91768-3305)
PHONE..................626 448-8118
Richard Chung, *Pr*
▲ EMP: 20 EST: 1997
SALES (est): 502.05K **Privately Held**
SIC: **3851**  Frames and parts, eyeglass and spectacle

**(P-15618)**
**SPORTIFEYE OPTICS INC**
1854 Business Center Dr, Duarte  (91010-2901)
PHONE..................877 742-5000
Tom Pfeiffer, *CEO*
EMP: 20 EST: 2017
SALES (est): 3.96MM **Privately Held**
Web: www.sportifeye.com

SIC: **3851**  Frames, lenses, and parts, eyeglass and spectacle

**(P-15619)**
**SPY INC (PA)**
1896 Rutherford Rd, Carlsbad  (92008-7326)
PHONE..................760 804-8420
Seth Hamot, *Interim Chief Executive Officer*
James Mcginty, *CFO*
Jim Sepanek, *Ex VP*
▲ EMP: 69 EST: 1994
SQ FT: 32,551
SALES (est): 1.93MM **Privately Held**
Web: www.spyoptic.com
SIC: **3851** 5099  Glasses, sun or glare; Sunglasses

**(P-15620)**
**STAAR SURGICAL COMPANY (PA)**
Also Called: STAAR
25510 Commercentre Dr, Lake Forest  (92630-8855)
PHONE..................626 303-7902
Thomas G Frinzi, *Ch Bd*
Scott Barnes, *CMO*
Warren Foust, *COO*
Patrick F Williams, *CFO*
▲ EMP: 880 EST: 1982
SALES (est): 322.42MM
SALES (corp-wide): 322.42MM **Publicly Held**
Web: www.staar.com
SIC: **3851**  Ophthalmic goods

**(P-15621)**
**STAAR SURGICAL COMPANY**
15102 Red Hill Ave, Tustin  (92780-6532)
PHONE..................626 303-7902
Keith Holiday, *Brnch Mgr*
EMP: 16
SALES (corp-wide): 322.42MM **Publicly Held**
Web: www.staar.com
SIC: **3851**  Ophthalmic goods
PA: Staar Surgical Company
25510 Commercentre Dr
626 303-7902

**(P-15622)**
**TANGIBLE SCIENCE LLC**
750 Broadway St, Redwood City  (94063-3124)
PHONE..................650 241-1045
Vic Mccray Md, *CEO*
Brandon Felkins, *COO*
EMP: 22 EST: 2012
SALES (est): 1.05MM **Privately Held**
Web: www.tangiblescience.com
SIC: **3851**  Contact lenses

**(P-15623)**
**TEKIA INC**
17 Hammond Ste 414, Irvine  (92618-1635)
PHONE..................949 699-1300
Gene Currie, *Pr*
Larry Blake, *VP Engg*
EMP: 20 EST: 1995
SQ FT: 5,000
SALES (est): 2.76MM **Privately Held**
Web: www.tekia.com
SIC: **3851** 8742  Intraocular lenses; Hospital and health services consultant

**(P-15624)**
**VISIONARY CONTACT LENS INC**
2940 E Miraloma Ave, Anaheim  (92806-1811)
PHONE..................714 237-1900

# 3851 - Ophthalmic Goods (P-15625)

Richard Belliveau, *Pr*
Cindy Belliveau, *Treas*
**EMP:** 24 **EST:** 1992
**SQ FT:** 16,000
**SALES (est):** 3.75MM **Privately Held**
**Web:** www.visionarylens.com
**SIC: 3851** 5048  Contact lenses; Contact lenses

## (P-15625)
### YOUNGER MFG CO (PA)
Also Called: Younger Optics
2925 California St, Torrance  (90503-3914)
**PHONE**.................................310 783-1533
Joseph David Rips, *CEO*
Tom Balch, *
Roshan Seresinhe, *
◆ **EMP:** 280 **EST:** 1955
**SQ FT:** 130,000
**SALES (est):** 44.68MM
**SALES (corp-wide):** 44.68MM **Privately Held**
**Web:** www.youngeroptics.com
**SIC: 3851**  Lens coating, ophthalmic

## (P-15626)
### ZENNI OPTICAL INC (PA)
448 Ignacio Blvd Ste 332, Novato  (94949-6085)
**PHONE**.................................800 211-2105
Julia Zhen, *CEO*
Levente Tibor Laczay, *Prin*
▲ **EMP:** 100 **EST:** 2007
**SALES (est):** 84.43MM
**SALES (corp-wide):** 84.43MM **Privately Held**
**Web:** www.zennioptical.com
**SIC: 3851** 5995  Eyeglasses, lenses and frames; Optical goods stores

---

## 3861 Photographic Equipment And Supplies

## (P-15627)
### ADVEXURE LLC
9281 Irvine Blvd, Irvine  (92618)
**PHONE**.................................920 917-9566
**EMP:** 22 **EST:** 2015
**SALES (est):** 3.55MM **Privately Held**
**Web:** www.advexure.com
**SIC: 3861**  Aerial cameras

## (P-15628)
### ANSCHUTZ FILM GROUP LLC (HQ)
10201 W Pico Blvd # 52, Los Angeles  (90064-2606)
**PHONE**.................................310 887-1000
Michael Bostick, *CEO*
▲ **EMP:** 30 **EST:** 2004
**SALES (est):** 939.77K **Privately Held**
**Web:** www.walden.com
**SIC: 3861**  Motion picture film
**PA:** The Anschutz Corporation
   555 17th St Ste 2400

## (P-15629)
### AVID TECHNOLOGY INC
2600 10th St, Berkeley  (94710-2595)
**PHONE**.................................510 486-8302
**EMP:** 30
**SALES (corp-wide):** 447.28MM **Privately Held**
**Web:** www.avid.com
**SIC: 3861**  Photographic equipment and supplies
**HQ:** Avid Technology, Inc.
   75 Blue Sky Dr
   Burlington MA 01803
   978 640-3000

## (P-15630)
### AVID TECHNOLOGY INC
Also Called: Avid
101 S 1st St Ste 200, Burbank  (91502-1938)
**PHONE**.................................818 557-2520
Kristin Bedient, *Mgr*
**EMP:** 60
**SALES (corp-wide):** 447.28MM **Privately Held**
**Web:** www.avid.com
**SIC: 3861**  Editing equipment, motion picture: viewers, splicers, etc.
**HQ:** Avid Technology, Inc.
   75 Blue Sky Dr
   Burlington MA 01803
   978 640-3000

## (P-15631)
### C CERONIX INCORPORATED
13350 New Airport Rd, Auburn  (95602-7419)
**PHONE**.................................530 886-6400
◆ **EMP:** 28 **EST:** 1984
**SALES (est):** 9.87MM **Privately Held**
**Web:** www.ceronix.com
**SIC: 3861** 3575  Screens, projection; Cathode ray tube (CRT), computer terminal

## (P-15632)
### CAROLENSE ENTRMT GROUP LLC
506 S Spring St, Los Angeles  (90013-3200)
**PHONE**.................................405 493-1120
Danesha Barber, *Managing Member*
**EMP:** 60 **EST:** 2022
**SALES (est):** 2.94MM **Privately Held**
**SIC: 3861** 7389  Film, sensitized motion picture, X-ray, still camera, etc.; Business services, nec

## (P-15633)
### CDS CALIFORNIA LLC
3330 Cahuenga Blvd W Ste 200, Los Angeles  (90068-1354)
**PHONE**.................................818 766-5000
**EMP:** 15 **EST:** 2012
**SALES (est):** 4.76MM **Privately Held**
**SIC: 3861**  Photographic equipment and supplies

## (P-15634)
### CHRISTIE DIGITAL SYSTEMS INC (HQ)
10550 Camden Dr, Cypress  (90630-4600)
**PHONE**.................................714 236-8610
Hideaki Onishi, *CEO*
Michael Phipps, *
**EMP:** 83 **EST:** 1999
**SALES (est):** 99.79MM **Privately Held**
**Web:** www.christiedigital.com
**SIC: 3861** 6719  Projectors, still or motion picture, silent or sound; Investment holding companies, except banks
**PA:** Ushio Inc.
   1-6-5, Marunouchi

## (P-15635)
### CLOVER ENVMTL SOLUTIONS LLC
Also Called: Clover Imaging
315 Weakley St Bldg 3, Calexico  (92231-9659)
**PHONE**.................................760 357-9277
Jim Cerkleski, *Ofcr*
**EMP:** 50
**SALES (corp-wide):** 173.68MM **Privately Held**
**Web:** www.cloverimaging.com
**SIC: 3861**  Printing equipment, photographic
**PA:** Clover Environmental Solutions Llc
   4200 Columbus St
   866 734-6548

## (P-15636)
### DJI TECHNOLOGY INC
17301 Edwards Rd, Cerritos  (90703-2427)
**PHONE**.................................818 235-0789
Jie Shen, *CEO*
**EMP:** 99 **EST:** 2015
**SALES (est):** 5.18MM **Privately Held**
**SIC: 3861**  Aerial cameras

## (P-15637)
### ELITE SCREENS INC
12282 Knott St, Garden Grove  (92841-2825)
**PHONE**.................................877 511-1211
Jeff Chen, *Pr*
Henry Yoh, *
◆ **EMP:** 30 **EST:** 2004
**SALES (est):** 6.64MM **Privately Held**
**Web:** www.elitescreens.com
**SIC: 3861**  Photographic equipment and supplies

## (P-15638)
### FASTEC IMAGING CORPORATION
17150 Via Del Campo Ste 301, San Diego  (92127-2111)
**PHONE**.................................858 592-2342
Stephen W Ferrell, *Pr*
Charles Mrdjenovich, *
**EMP:** 25 **EST:** 2003
**SALES (est):** 3.79MM **Privately Held**
**Web:** www.fastecimaging.com
**SIC: 3861**  Cameras and related equipment

## (P-15639)
### FPC INC
1017 N Las Palmas Ave, Los Angeles  (90038-2408)
**PHONE**.................................323 468-5778
◆ **EMP:** 40
**SIC: 3861** 7829  Photographic equipment and supplies; Motion picture distribution services

## (P-15640)
### FREESTYLE FILMWORKS LLC
Also Called: Freestyle Cinemas Rentals
1518 Talmadge St, Los Angeles  (90027-1535)
**PHONE**.................................818 660-2888
Michael Barnett, *Managing Member*
Gregory Barnett, *Prin*
**EMP:** 15 **EST:** 2010
**SALES (est):** 1.22MM **Privately Held**
**SIC: 3861**  Photographic equipment and supplies

## (P-15641)
### FUJIFILM RCRDING MEDIA USA INC
6200 Phyllis Dr, Cypress  (90630-5239)
**PHONE**.................................310 536-0800
**EMP:** 88
**Web:** www.fujifilm-ffem.com
**SIC: 3861**  Photographic equipment and supplies
**HQ:** Fujifilm Recording Media U.S.A., Inc.
   45 Crosby Dr
   Bedford MA 01730

## (P-15642)
### GOPRO INC (PA)
Also Called: Gopro
3025 Clearview Way, San Mateo  (94402-3709)
**PHONE**.................................650 332-7600
Nicholas Woodman, *Ch Bd*
Brian Mcgee, *Ex VP*
Eve Saltman, *CCO CLO*
Dean Jahnke, *Senior Vice President Global Sales*
Charles Lafrade, *CAO*
◆ **EMP:** 495 **EST:** 2004
**SQ FT:** 201,000
**SALES (est):** 1.01B
**SALES (corp-wide):** 1.01B **Publicly Held**
**Web:** www.gopro.com
**SIC: 3861** 7372  Cameras and related equipment; Prepackaged software

## (P-15643)
### HF GROUP INC (PA)
Also Called: Houston Fearless 76
203 W Artesia Blvd, Compton  (90220-5517)
**PHONE**.................................310 605-0755
Myung S Lee, *Ch Bd*
James H Lee, *
Scott Mccormack, *VP Fin*
Virginia C Clark, *
**EMP:** 28 **EST:** 1929
**SQ FT:** 45,000
**SALES (est):** 7.95MM
**SALES (corp-wide):** 7.95MM **Privately Held**
**Web:** www.hf76.com
**SIC: 3861**  Processing equipment, photographic

## (P-15644)
### HOYA HOLDINGS INC (HQ)
820 N Mccarthy Blvd Ste 220, Milpitas  (95035-5115)
**PHONE**.................................408 654-2300
Hiroshi Suzuki, *CEO*
Ryo Hirooka, *
Eiichiro Ikeda, *
▲ **EMP:** 180 **EST:** 1973
**SALES (est):** 32.38MM **Privately Held**
**Web:** www.hoya.com
**SIC: 3861** 3825 3827  Photographic sensitized goods, nec; Test equipment for electronic and electric measurement; Optical instruments and lenses
**PA:** Hoya Corporation
   6-10-1, Nishishinjuku

## (P-15645)
### JONDO LTD (HQ)
22700 Savi Ranch Pkwy, Yorba Linda  (92887-4608)
**PHONE**.................................714 279-2300
John Stuart Doe, *CEO*
**EMP:** 60 **EST:** 1989
**SQ FT:** 50,000
**SALES (est):** 8MM
**SALES (corp-wide):** 496.73MM **Privately Held**
**Web:** www.jondo.com
**SIC: 3861**  Photographic equipment and supplies
**PA:** Circle Graphics, Inc.
   120 9th Ave
   303 532-2370

## (P-15646)
### KALAP INC
401 N Brand Blvd Ste 814, Glendale  (91203-4434)
**PHONE**.................................818 332-6916
Karen Petrosyan, *CEO*
**EMP:** 18 **EST:** 2021
**SALES (est):** 1.2MM **Privately Held**

▲ = Import  ▼ = Export
◆ = Import/Export

# PRODUCTS & SERVICES SECTION
## 3861 - Photographic Equipment And Supplies (P-15666)

SIC: **3861** Sound recording and reproducing equipment, motion picture

**(P-15647)**
### L-3 CMMNICATIONS SONOMA EO INC
Also Called: Wescam Sonoma Operations
428 Aviation Blvd, Santa Rosa (95403-1069)
**PHONE**..................707 568-3000
Andy Fordham, *Pr*
**EMP:** 200 **EST:** 1997
**SQ FT:** 20,000
**SALES (est):** 24.09MM
**SALES (corp-wide):** 19.42B **Publicly Held**
SIC: **3861** 3812 Photographic equipment and supplies; Heads-up display systems (HUD), aeronautical
HQ: L3 Technologies, Inc.
600 3rd Ave Fl 34
New York NY 10016
321 727-9100

**(P-15648)**
### LASER TECHNOLOGIES & SERVICES LLC
Also Called: Laser Technologies
1175 Aviation Pl, San Fernando (91340-1460)
▲ **EMP:** 100
SIC: **3861** 5999 Reproduction machines and equipment; Telephone and communication equipment

**(P-15649)**
### LUCARE CORPORATION
Also Called: Outex
1292 Journeys End Dr, La Canada Flintridge (91011-1709)
**PHONE**..................818 583-7731
Jr Desouza, *Pr*
**EMP:** 15 **EST:** 2010
**SALES (est):** 512.52K **Privately Held**
Web: www.outex.com
SIC: **3861** Cameras and related equipment

**(P-15650)**
### LUMENS INTEGRATION INC
4116 Clipper Ct, Fremont (94538-6514)
**PHONE**..................510 657-8367
Andy Chang, *Pr*
◆ **EMP:** 26 **EST:** 2001
**SQ FT:** 5,200
**SALES (est):** 2.64MM **Privately Held**
Web: www.mylumens.com
SIC: **3861** 5043 Projectors, still or motion picture, silent or sound; Projection apparatus, motion picture and slide
PA: Lumens Digital Optics Inc.
5f-1, No. 20, Taiyuan St.,

**(P-15651)**
### MATTHEWS STUDIO EQUIPMENT INC
Also Called: M S E
4520 W Valerio St, Burbank (91505-1046)
**PHONE**..................818 843-6715
Edward Phillips Iii, *Pr*
▲ **EMP:** 29 **EST:** 1970
**SALES (est):** 3.49MM **Privately Held**
Web: www.msegrip.com
SIC: **3861** Motion picture apparatus and equipment

**(P-15652)**
### MODERN STUDIO EQUIPMENT INC
16200 Stagg St, Van Nuys (91406-1715)
**PHONE**..................818 764-8574

Seno Mousally, *Pr*
Rina Mousally, *VP*
**EMP:** 19 **EST:** 1980
**SALES (est):** 2.47MM **Privately Held**
Web: www.modernstudio.com
SIC: **3861** Motion picture apparatus and equipment

**(P-15653)**
### MOVING IMAGE TECHNOLOGIES LLC
17760 Newhope St Ste B, Fountain Valley (92708-5442)
**PHONE**..................714 751-7998
Glenn Sherman, *Managing Member*
Bevan Wright, *
Joe Delgado, *
Phil Rassnon, *
David Richards, *
▲ **EMP:** 32 **EST:** 2003
**SQ FT:** 18,000
**SALES (est):** 5.71MM
**SALES (corp-wide):** 20.14MM **Publicly Held**
Web: www.movingimagetech.com
SIC: **3861** Motion picture apparatus and equipment
PA: Moving Image Technologies, Inc.
17760 Newhope St
714 751-7998

**(P-15654)**
### MPO VIDEOTRONICS INC (PA)
5069 Maureen Ln, Moorpark (93021-7148)
**PHONE**..................805 499-8513
Larry Kaiser, *Pr*
Julius Barron, *
Don Gaston, *
**EMP:** 75 **EST:** 1947
**SALES (est):** 1.66MM
**SALES (corp-wide):** 1.66MM **Privately Held**
Web: www.mpo-video.com
SIC: **3861** 5065 7819 3823 Motion picture apparatus and equipment; Video equipment, electronic; Equipment rental, motion picture; Process control instruments

**(P-15655)**
### NEUVECTOR INC
2880 Zanker Rd Ste 100, San Jose (95134-2121)
**PHONE**..................408 455-4034
Fei Huang, *Pr*
**EMP:** 37 **EST:** 2016
**SALES (est):** 3.47MM
**SALES (corp-wide):** 355.83K **Privately Held**
Web: www.suse.com
SIC: **3861** Photographic equipment and supplies
HQ: Suse Software Solutions Germany Gmbh
Frankenstr. 146
Nurnberg BY 90461
911740530

**(P-15656)**
### OPTOMA TECHNOLOGY INC
Also Called: Optoma Technology
47697 Westinghouse Dr, Fremont (94539-7401)
**PHONE**..................510 897-8600
Robert Tick, *CEO*
Hans Wang, *
Sindy Yip Ctrl, *Prin*
Jon Grodem, *
Shih-yuan Chen, *Dir*
▲ **EMP:** 120 **EST:** 1995
**SQ FT:** 34,000

**SALES (est):** 24.71MM **Privately Held**
Web: www.optomausa.com
SIC: **3861** Projectors, still or motion picture, silent or sound

**(P-15657)**
### OVERVIEW CORPORATION
736 Clementina St, San Francisco (94103-3813)
**PHONE**..................415 795-9020
Christopher Van Dyke, *CEO*
**EMP:** 18 **EST:** 2018
**SALES (est):** 2.72MM **Privately Held**
Web: www.overview.ai
SIC: **3861** Photographic instruments, electronic

**(P-15658)**
### PANAVISION INC
Also Called: Panavision Hollywood
6735 Selma Ave, Los Angeles (90028-6134)
**PHONE**..................323 464-3800
Lisa Harp, *VP*
**EMP:** 29
Web: www.panavision.com
SIC: **3861** Photographic equipment and supplies
PA: Panavision Inc.
6101 Variel Ave

**(P-15659)**
### PANAVISION INTERNATIONAL LP (HQ)
6101 Variel Ave, Woodland Hills (91367-3722)
P.O. Box 4360 (91365-4360)
**PHONE**..................818 316-1080
Robert Beitcher, *Pr*
Ross Landfbuam, *
▲ **EMP:** 380 **EST:** 1991
**SQ FT:** 150,000
**SALES (est):** 99.32MM **Privately Held**
Web: www.panavision.com
SIC: **3861** Cameras and related equipment
PA: Panavision Inc.
6101 Variel Ave

**(P-15660)**
### PHOTO-SONICS INC (PA)
9131 Independence Ave, Chatsworth (91311-5903)
**PHONE**..................818 842-2141
**EMP:** 33 **EST:** 1928
**SALES (est):** 14.13MM
**SALES (corp-wide):** 14.13MM **Privately Held**
Web: www.photosonics.com
SIC: **3861**-3827 3663 7819 Photographic equipment and supplies; Lenses, optical: all types except ophthalmic; Phototransmission equipment; Equipment rental, motion picture

**(P-15661)**
### PHOTRONICS INC (DH)
Also Called: Photronics California
2428 N Ontario St, Burbank (91504-3119)
**PHONE**..................203 740-5653
James Mac Donald Junior, *Ch Bd*
Constantine Maristos, *
**EMP:** 280 **EST:** 1970
**SQ FT:** 30,000
**SALES (est):** 70.42MM
**SALES (corp-wide):** 892.08MM **Publicly Held**
Web: photronicsinc.gcs-web.com
SIC: **3861** Photographic equipment and supplies
HQ: Align-Rite International Limited
1 Technology Dr
Bridgend M GLAM

**(P-15662)**
### PHOTRONICS INC
1760 Arroyo Gln, Escondido (92026-1859)
**PHONE**..................760 294-1896
Bob Rhodes, *Mgr*
**EMP:** 160
**SALES (corp-wide):** 892.08MM **Publicly Held**
Web: www.photronics.com
SIC: **3861** Photographic equipment and supplies
HQ: Photronics Inc
2428 N Ontario St
Burbank CA 91504
203 740-5653

**(P-15663)**
### REDCOM LLC
Also Called: Red Digital Cinema Camera Co
94 Icon, Foothill Ranch (92610-3000)
**PHONE**..................949 404-4084
James H Jannard, *CEO*
Mike D Executive, *
Vince Hassel, *
Greg Weeks, *
Scott Olivet, *
▲ **EMP:** 498 **EST:** 1999
**SALES (est):** 17.97MM
**SALES (corp-wide):** 10.25MM **Privately Held**
Web: www.red.com
SIC: **3861** Motion picture apparatus and equipment
HQ: Red Europe Limited
Pinewood Road
Iver BUCKS SL0 0
175 378-5454

**(P-15664)**
### RICOH ELECTRONICS INC
2310 Redhill Ave, Santa Ana (92705-5538)
**PHONE**..................714 566-6079
**EMP:** 250
Web: rei.ricoh.com
SIC: **3861** 3695 Photocopy machines; Magnetic and optical recording media
HQ: Ricoh Electronics, Inc.
1125 Hurricane Shoals Rd
Lawrenceville GA 30043
714 566-2500

**(P-15665)**
### SANTA BARBARA INSTRUMENT GP INC
Also Called: Sbig Astronomical Instruments
150 Castilian Dr, Goleta (93117-3028)
**PHONE**..................925 463-3410
**EMP:** 23 **EST:** 1991
**SALES (est):** 2.11MM **Privately Held**
Web: www.diffractionlimited.com
SIC: **3861** Cameras and related equipment

**(P-15666)**
### SONY PICTURES ENTRMT INC
Also Called: Sony Pictures Mpic Group
10202 Washington Blvd, Culver City (90232-3119)
**PHONE**..................310 244-4000
Tom Rothman, *Ch*
**EMP:** 20
Web: www.sonypictures.com
SIC: **3861** Motion picture film
HQ: Sony Pictures Entertainment, Inc.
10202 W Washington Blvd
Culver City CA 90232
310 244-4000

# 3861 - Photographic Equipment And Supplies (P-15667)

## (P-15667)
### STEWART FILMSCREEN CORP (PA)
1161 Sepulveda Blvd, Torrance (90502-2797)
PHONE.................310 784-5300
Donald R Stewart, *Ex VP*
Thomas E Stewart, *
Adrian Silva, *
◆ **EMP:** 160 **EST:** 1947
**SQ FT:** 43,000
**SALES (est):** 24.61MM
**SALES (corp-wide):** 24.61MM **Privately Held**
Web: www.stewartfilmscreen.com
**SIC: 3861** Screens, projection

## (P-15668)
### SUSS MCRTEC PRCSION PHTMASK IN
Also Called: Image Technology
821 San Antonio Rd, Palo Alto (94303-4618)
PHONE.................415 494-3113
Frank Averdung, *CEO*
Alex Naderi, *Pr*
Patricia Christiansen, *CFO*
**EMP:** 18 **EST:** 1963
**SQ FT:** 10,000
**SALES (est):** 3.92MM
**SALES (corp-wide):** 330.72MM **Privately Held**
**SIC: 3861** Photographic equipment and supplies
HQ: Suss Microtec Inc.
2520 Palisades Dr
Corona CA 92882
408 940-0300

## (P-15669)
### THERMAPRINT CORPORATION
11 Autry Ste B, Irvine (92618-2766)
PHONE.................949 583-0800
Natalie J Hochner, *Pr*
Gary Larsen, *
▲ **EMP:** 25 **EST:** 1985
**SQ FT:** 14,500
**SALES (est):** 2.38MM **Privately Held**
Web: www.thermaprint.com
**SIC: 3861** 3443 3585 2759 Graphic arts plates, sensitized; Fabricated plate work (boiler shop); Parts for heating, cooling, and refrigerating equipment; Screen printing

## (P-15670)
### TRAVELLING PIC SHOW COMPANY
1000 Kenfield Ave, Los Angeles (90049-1406)
PHONE.................323 769-1115
John Noble, *Prin*
**EMP:** 16 **EST:** 2011
**SALES (est):** 1.35MM **Privately Held**
Web: www.thetpsc.com
**SIC: 3861** Motion picture film

## (P-15671)
### VITEK INDUS VIDEO PDTS INC
28492 Constellation Rd, Valencia (91355)
PHONE.................661 294-8043
Greg Alan Bier, *CEO*
◆ **EMP:** 20 **EST:** 1998
**SQ FT:** 9,200
**SALES (est):** 3.31MM **Privately Held**
Web: www.vitekcctv.com
**SIC: 3861** 5099 Cameras and related equipment; Video and audio equipment

## (P-15672)
### WBI INC
8201 Woodley Ave, Van Nuys (91406-1231)
PHONE.................800 673-4968
◆ **EMP:** 600
**SIC: 3861** Toners, prepared photographic (not made in chemical plants)

## 3873 Watches, Clocks, Watchcases, And Parts

## (P-15673)
### ACCUSPLIT (PA)
1262 Quarry Ln Ste B, Pleasanton (94566-4733)
PHONE.................925 290-1900
W Ron Sutton, *Pr*
▲ **EMP:** 17 **EST:** 1980
**SALES (est):** 2.45MM
**SALES (corp-wide):** 2.45MM **Privately Held**
Web: www.accusplit.com
**SIC: 3873** 3824 Watches and parts, except crystals and jewels; Controls, revolution and timing instruments

## (P-15674)
### AMG EMPLOYEE MANAGEMENT INC
Also Called: Time Masters
1220 S Central Ave Ste 203, Glendale (91204-2547)
PHONE.................323 254-7448
**TOLL FREE:** 800
Tigran Galstyan, *Pr*
▲ **EMP:** 17 **EST:** 1998
**SALES (est):** 2.92MM **Privately Held**
Web: www.amgtime.com
**SIC: 3873** 7371 7372 3579 Timers for industrial use, clockwork mechanism only; Computer software development; Business oriented computer software; Time clocks and time recording devices

## (P-15675)
### BETENSH LLC
1230 Santa Anita Ave Ste D, South El Monte (91733-3861)
PHONE.................626 841-8543
Carrie Huang, *Managing Member*
**EMP:** 15
**SALES (est):** 1.01MM **Privately Held**
**SIC: 3873** Watches, clocks, watchcases, and parts

## (P-15676)
### CHASE-DURER LTD (PA)
8455 Fountain Ave Unit 515, West Hollywood (90069-2543)
PHONE.................310 550-7280
Brandon Chase, *Pr*
▲ **EMP:** 19 **EST:** 1997
**SALES (est):** 574K
**SALES (corp-wide):** 574K **Privately Held**
Web: www.chase-durer.com
**SIC: 3873** Watches, clocks, watchcases, and parts

## (P-15677)
### MOD-ELECTRONICS INC
Also Called: Ese
142 Sierra St, El Segundo (90245-4117)
PHONE.................310 322-2136
William Kaiser, *Pr*
Brian Way, *
▲ **EMP:** 26 **EST:** 1971
**SQ FT:** 7,500
**SALES (est):** 2.19MM **Privately Held**
Web: www.ese-web.com
**SIC: 3873** 3663 3651 3625 Clocks, assembly of; Radio and t.v. communications equipment; Household audio and video equipment; Relays and industrial controls

## 3911 Jewelry, Precious Metal

## (P-15678)
### ALEX AND ANI LLC
Also Called: Alex and Ani
21540 Hawthorne Blvd, Torrance (90503-5707)
PHONE.................310 214-3587
**EMP:** 15
**SALES (corp-wide):** 17.51MM **Privately Held**
Web: www.alexandani.com
**SIC: 3911** Jewelry, precious metal
HQ: Alex And Ani, Llc
10 Briggs Dr
East Greenwich RI 02818

## (P-15679)
### ALLISON-KAUFMAN CO
7640 Haskell Ave, Van Nuys (91406-2005)
PHONE.................818 373-5100
Bart Kaufman, *CEO*
Jay A Kaufman, *
▲ **EMP:** 75 **EST:** 1946
**SQ FT:** 21,000
**SALES (est):** 3.97MM **Privately Held**
Web: www.allisonkaufman.com
**SIC: 3911** Jewel settings and mountings, precious metal

## (P-15680)
### ALOR INTERNATIONAL LTD
Also Called: Philippe Charriol USA
11722 Sorrento Valley Rd, San Diego (92121-1021)
PHONE.................858 454-0011
Jack Zemer, *CEO*
Sandy Zemer, *
Ori Zemer, *
Tal Zemer, *
▲ **EMP:** 45 **EST:** 1975
**SALES (est):** 3.72MM **Privately Held**
Web: www.alor.com
**SIC: 3911** 3172 3915 Vanity cases, precious metal; Personal leather goods, nec; Jewel preparing: instruments, tools, watches, and jewelry

## (P-15681)
### ALUMA USA INC
435 Tesconi Cir, Santa Rosa (95401-4619)
PHONE.................707 545-9344
▲ **EMP:** 22
**SQ FT:** 8,867
**SALES (est):** 15MM **Privately Held**
Web: www.alumausa.net
**SIC: 3911** Jewelry, precious metal

## (P-15682)
### AMERICAS GOLD INC
Also Called: Americas Gold - Amrcas Damonds
650 S Hill St Ste 224, Los Angeles (90014-1769)
PHONE.................213 688-4904
Rafi M Siddiqui, *Pr*
Samina Siddiqui, *
**EMP:** 30 **EST:** 1999
**SQ FT:** 4,500
**SALES (est):** 1.45MM **Privately Held**
Web: www.americasgold.com

**SIC: 3911** Jewelry, precious metal

## (P-15683)
### AMINCO INTERNATIONAL USA INC
Also Called: California Premium Incentives
20571 Crescent Bay Dr, Lake Forest (92630-8825)
PHONE.................949 457-3261
Ann Wu, *Ex Dir*
William Wu, *
Ann Wu, *Treas*
▲ **EMP:** 62 **EST:** 1978
**SQ FT:** 35,000
**SALES (est):** 9.62MM **Privately Held**
Web: www.amincousa.com
**SIC: 3911** 5099 Jewelry, precious metal; Brass goods

## (P-15684)
### ANATOMETAL LLC
165 Dubois St, Santa Cruz (95060)
PHONE.................831 454-9880
Barry Blanchard, *Pr*
**EMP:** 40 **EST:** 1990
**SALES (est):** 4.04MM **Privately Held**
Web: www.anatometal.com
**SIC: 3911** Jewelry, precious metal

## (P-15685)
### ARTS ELEGANCE INC
154 W Bellevue Dr, Pasadena (91105-2504)
PHONE.................626 793-4794
Arutiun Mikaelian, *Pr*
**EMP:** 45
**SALES (corp-wide):** 4.63MM **Privately Held**
**SIC: 3911** Jewelry, precious metal
PA: Art's Elegance, Inc.
739 E Walnut St Ste 200
626 405-1522

## (P-15686)
### BESTSIO LLC
1230 Santa Anita Ave Ste D, South El Monte (91733-3861)
PHONE.................626 841-8543
Maggie Qin, *Managing Member*
**EMP:** 18
**SALES (est):** 358.37K **Privately Held**
**SIC: 3911** Jewelry apparel

## (P-15687)
### BRILLIANT EARTH GROUP INC (PA)
300 Grant Ave Fl 3, San Francisco (94108-3629)
PHONE.................800 691-0952
Beth Gerstein, *CEO*
Eric Grossberg, *Ex Ch Bd*
Jeffrey Kuo, *CFO*
Pamela Catlett, *Chief Brand Officer*
Sharon Dziesietnik, *COO*
**EMP:** 579 **EST:** 2005
**SALES (est):** 446.38MM
**SALES (corp-wide):** 446.38MM **Publicly Held**
**SIC: 3911** Jewelry, precious metal

## (P-15688)
### CONNERS ORO-CAL MFG CO
1720 Bird St, Oroville (95965-4806)
PHONE.................530 533-5065
David J Conner, *Pr*
Susan Y Conner, *Sec*
**EMP:** 18 **EST:** 1941
**SQ FT:** 2,850
**SALES (est):** 1.55MM **Privately Held**

## PRODUCTS & SERVICES SECTION

### 3931 - Musical Instruments (P-15712)

Web: www.orocal.com
SIC: 3911 3873 5094 Jewelry, precious metal; Watches, clocks, watchcases, and parts; Jewelry and precious stones

**(P-15689)**
**CRISLU CORP**
20916 Higgins Ct, Torrance (90501-1722)
PHONE..............................310 322-3444
◆ EMP: 30 EST: 1961
SALES (est): 3MM Privately Held
Web: www.crislu.com
SIC: 3911 Jewel settings and mountings, precious metal

**(P-15690)**
**ELBA JEWELRY INC**
Also Called: Elba Company
910 N Amelia Ave, San Dimas (91773-1401)
PHONE..............................909 394-5803
Edouard Bachoura, Pr
▼ EMP: 19 EST: 1994
SQ FT: 10,000
SALES (est): 948.16K Privately Held
Web: www.trustmyjeweler.com
SIC: 3911 Jewelry, precious metal

**(P-15691)**
**GEM TECH JEWELRY CORPORATION**
3250 W Olympic Blvd Ste 207, Los Angeles (90006-2372)
PHONE..............................213 623-2222
Heung Joo Lee, Pr
EMP: 20 EST: 1989
SQ FT: 12,500
SALES (est): 330.47K Privately Held
Web: gem-tech-jewelry-corporation-los-angeles.jewelleryandgemstones.com
SIC: 3911 5094 3961 Jewelry apparel; Jewelry and precious stones; Costume jewelry

**(P-15692)**
**GIVING KEYS INC**
836 Traction Ave, Los Angeles (90013-1816)
PHONE..............................213 935-8791
Caitlin Crosby, CEO
Brit Gilmore, *
▲ EMP: 25 EST: 2012
SQ FT: 8,000
SALES (est): 759.78K Privately Held
Web: www.thegivingkeys.com
SIC: 3911 Jewelry, precious metal

**(P-15693)**
**GREENE & COMPANY**
9465 Wilshire Blvd Ste 820, Beverly Hills (90212-2612)
PHONE..............................212 203-1107
Michael Greene, Prin
EMP: 24 EST: 2012
SALES (est): 182.32K Privately Held
Web: www.greeneandco.com
SIC: 3911 Jewelry apparel

**(P-15694)**
**HOLLY YASHI INC**
1300 9th St, Arcata (95521-5703)
PHONE..............................707 822-0389
Paul S Lubitz, Pr
Holly A Hosterman, *
▲ EMP: 54 EST: 1981
SQ FT: 4,800
SALES (est): 2.9MM Privately Held
Web: www.hollyyashi.com

SIC: 3911 Earrings, precious metal

**(P-15695)**
**KESMOR ASSOCIATES**
Also Called: American Designs
610 S Broadway Ste 717, Los Angeles (90014-1814)
PHONE..............................213 629-2300
Joseph Keshoyan, Pr
Hasmik Keshoyan, VP
EMP: 20 EST: 1985
SQ FT: 6,000
SALES (est): 1.45MM Privately Held
SIC: 3911 Jewelry, precious metal

**(P-15696)**
**KRYSTAL VENTURES LLC**
Also Called: Gracek Jewelry
17 Shell Bch, Newport Coast (92657-2151)
PHONE..............................213 507-2215
Daniel Kang, Managing Member
Krystal Kang, *
EMP: 30 EST: 2016
SALES (est): 2.12MM Privately Held
SIC: 3911 4813 5734 Jewelry, precious metal; Online service providers; Software, business and non-game

**(P-15697)**
**L SPARK**
1140 Kendall Rd Ste A, San Luis Obispo (93401-8047)
PHONE..............................805 626-0511
Courtney Bonzi, CEO
EMP: 40 EST: 2016
SALES (est): 2.3MM Privately Held
Web: www.sparklbands.com
SIC: 3911 Jewelry apparel

**(P-15698)**
**LA GEM AND JEWELRY DESIGN**
3232 E Washington Blvd, Los Angeles (90058-8022)
PHONE..............................213 488-1290
Joseph W Behney, CEO
EMP: 63
SALES (corp-wide): 9.6MM Privately Held
Web: www.la-rocks.com
SIC: 3911 Jewelry, precious metal
PA: L.A. Gem And Jewelry Design, Inc
659 S Broadway Fl 7
213 488-1290

**(P-15699)**
**LA GEM AND JEWELRY DESIGN (PA)**
Also Called: La Rocks
659 S Broadway Fl 7, Los Angeles (90014-2291)
PHONE..............................213 488-1290
Ashish Arora, CEO
Elsa Behney, Sec
▲ EMP: 37 EST: 2002
SALES (est): 9.6MM
SALES (corp-wide): 9.6MM Privately Held
Web: www.la-rocks.com
SIC: 3911 5094 Jewelry, precious metal; Jewelry

**(P-15700)**
**LEONARD CRAFT CO LLC**
1815 Ritchey St Ste B, Santa Ana (92705-5124)
PHONE..............................714 549-0678
Stephen D Leonard, CEO
Stephen D Leonard, Managing Member
EMP: 95 EST: 2017
SALES (est): 4.64MM Privately Held

SIC: 3911 5947 Jewelry, precious metal; Gift shop

**(P-15701)**
**MALCOLM DEMILLE INC**
650 S Frontage Rd, Nipomo (93444-9148)
PHONE..............................805 929-4353
Malcolm Demille, Pr
Janet Demille, VP
EMP: 15 EST: 1989
SALES (est): 2.1MM Privately Held
Web: www.mdemille.com
SIC: 3911 Jewelry mountings and trimmings

**(P-15702)**
**MASHKA JEWELRY LLC**
1400 Grant Ave, San Francisco (94133-3304)
PHONE..............................415 273-9330
EMP: 20 EST: 2011
SALES (est): 1.29MM Privately Held
Web: www.mashka.com
SIC: 3911 Jewelry apparel

**(P-15703)**
**RASTACLAT LLC**
100 W Broadway Ste 3000, Long Beach (90802-4467)
PHONE..............................424 287-0902
EMP: 36 EST: 2010
SALES (est): 4.18MM Privately Held
Web: www.rastaclat.com
SIC: 3911 Bracelets, precious metal

**(P-15704)**
**ROBERTO MARTINEZ INC**
1050 Calle Cordillera Ste 103, San Clemente (92673-6240)
PHONE..............................800 257-6462
Roberto Martinez, CEO
Elsa Martinez-phillips, Pr
▲ EMP: 15 EST: 1976
SQ FT: 6,000
SALES (est): 742.44K Privately Held
Web: www.robertomartinez.com
SIC: 3911 5094 Jewelry apparel; Jewelry

**(P-15705)**
**SAGE GODDESS INC**
21010 Figueroa St, Carson (90745-1937)
PHONE..............................650 733-6639
Athena I Perrakis, CEO
David Maeizlik, *
EMP: 42 EST: 2013
SALES (est): 2.51MM Privately Held
Web: www.sagegoddess.com
SIC: 3911 5944 5999 Jewelry apparel; Jewelry, precious stones and precious metals; Perfumes and colognes

**(P-15706)**
**TEMPLE CUSTOM JEWELERS LLC**
1640 Camino Del Rio N Ste 220, San Diego (92108-1506)
PHONE..............................800 988-3844
Anthony Temple, CEO
EMP: 50 EST: 2016
SALES (est): 2.5MM Privately Held
SIC: 3911 5094 Jewelry mountings and trimmings; Jewelry and precious stones

### 3914 Silverware And Plated Ware

**(P-15707)**
**CAL SIMBA INC (PA)**
1283 Flynn Rd, Camarillo (93012-8013)

PHONE..............................805 240-1177
Jay Schechter, CEO
Stuart Seeler, *
John Stout, *
▲ EMP: 38 EST: 1974
SALES (est): 9.17MM
SALES (corp-wide): 9.17MM Privately Held
Web: www.simbaline.com
SIC: 3914 2672 3452 2821 Trophies, plated (all metals); Labels (unprinted), gummed: made from purchased materials; Pins; Polyurethane resins

**(P-15708)**
**STREIVOR INC**
Also Called: Streivor Air Systems
2150 Kitty Hawk Rd, Livermore (94551-9522)
PHONE..............................925 960-9090
Jeffrey S Lambertson, CEO
EMP: 18 EST: 1989
SQ FT: 35,250
SALES (est): 4.58MM Privately Held
Web: www.streivor.com
SIC: 3914 Stainless steel ware

### 3915 Jewelers' Materials And Lapidary Work

**(P-15709)**
**CGM INC**
Also Called: Cgm Findings
19611 Ventura Blvd Ste 211, Tarzana (91356-2907)
PHONE..............................818 609-7088
TOLL FREE: 800
Devinder Bindra, CEO
▲ EMP: 25 EST: 1984
SQ FT: 12,000
SALES (est): 1.22MM Privately Held
Web: www.cgmfindings.com
SIC: 3915 5094 Jewelers' materials and lapidary work; Precious metals

**(P-15710)**
**LUCENT DIAMONDS INC**
6303 Owensmouth Ave Fl 10, Woodland Hills (91367-2262)
PHONE..............................424 781-7127
Alex Grizenko, *
EMP: 31 EST: 2000
SALES (est): 850.83K Privately Held
Web: www.lucentdiamonds.com
SIC: 3915 5094 5999 Diamond cutting and polishing; Diamonds (gems); Gems and precious stones

### 3931 Musical Instruments

**(P-15711)**
**ALEMBIC INC**
240 Classic Ct, Rohnert Park (94928-1619)
PHONE..............................707 523-2611
Susan L Wickersham, Pr
Ron Wickersham, Treas
EMP: 18 EST: 1969
SALES (est): 436.47K Privately Held
Web: www.alembic.com
SIC: 3931 5736 Guitars and parts, electric and nonelectric; Musical instrument stores

**(P-15712)**
**BBE SOUND INC (PA)**
Also Called: G & L Musical Instruments
2548 Fender Ave, Fullerton (92831-4439)
PHONE..............................714 897-6766
David Mclaren, CEO

## 3931 - Musical Instruments (P-15713)

Shailesh Karia, *CFO*
Robert Ruzzito, *VP Sls*
John Mclaren, *Prin*
John T Davey, *Prin*
▲ **EMP:** 22 **EST:** 1984
**SQ FT:** 10,000
**SALES (est):** 6MM
**SALES (corp-wide):** 6MM **Privately Held**
**Web:** www.bbesound.com
**SIC: 3931** 3651 Guitars and parts, electric and nonelectric; Amplifiers: radio, public address, or musical instrument

### (P-15713)
### DUNCAN CARTER CORPORATION (PA)
Also Called: Seymour Duncan
5427 Hollister Ave, Santa Barbara (93111-2307)
**PHONE**...............805 964-9749
Seymour Duncan, *Ch*
Cathy Carter Duncan, *
▲ **EMP:** 99 **EST:** 1976
**SQ FT:** 20,000
**SALES (est):** 21.03MM
**SALES (corp-wide):** 21.03MM **Privately Held**
**Web:** www.seymourduncan.com
**SIC: 3931** 5736 3674 3651 Guitars and parts, electric and nonelectric; Musical instrument stores; Semiconductors and related devices; Household audio and video equipment

### (P-15714)
### DUNLOP MANUFACTURING INC (PA)
Also Called: Dunlop
150 Industrial Way, Benicia (94510-1112)
P.O. Box 846 (94510-0846)
**PHONE**...............707 745-2722
James Andrew Dunlop, *CEO*
Jasmin Powell, *
◆ **EMP:** 87 **EST:** 1977
**SQ FT:** 40,000
**SALES (est):** 22.83MM
**SALES (corp-wide):** 22.83MM **Privately Held**
**Web:** www.jimdunlop.com
**SIC: 3931** Guitars and parts, electric and nonelectric

### (P-15715)
### EMG INC
675 Aviation Blvd Ste B, Santa Rosa (95403-1025)
P.O. Box 4394 (95402-4394)
**PHONE**...............707 525-9941
Robert A Turner, *Pr*
Gary Rush, *
Andy Gravelle, *
**EMP:** 81 **EST:** 1977
**SQ FT:** 10,000
**SALES (est):** 7.87MM **Privately Held**
**Web:** www.emgpickups.com
**SIC: 3931** 5736 Guitars and parts, electric and nonelectric; Musical instrument stores

### (P-15716)
### ERNIE BALL INC (PA)
Also Called: Ernie Ball
4117 Earthwood Ln, San Luis Obispo (93401-7541)
**PHONE**...............805 544-7726
Brian Ball, *CEO*
Sterling C Ball, *VP*
▲ **EMP:** 29 **EST:** 1965
**SQ FT:** 50,000
**SALES (est):** 23.36MM
**SALES (corp-wide):** 23.36MM **Privately Held**
**Web:** www.ernieball.com
**SIC: 3931** Guitars and parts, electric and nonelectric

### (P-15717)
### FENDER MUSICAL INSTRS CORP
311 Cessna Cir, Corona (92878-5021)
**PHONE**...............480 596-9690
**EMP:** 800
**SALES (corp-wide):** 1.87B **Privately Held**
**Web:** www.fender.com
**SIC: 3931** 3651 Musical instruments; Amplifiers: radio, public address, or musical instrument
**HQ:** Fender Musical Instruments Corporation
17600 N Perimeter Dr # 100
Scottsdale AZ 85255
480 596-9690

### (P-15718)
### HARRIS ORGANS INC
Also Called: Harris' Precision Products
7047 Comstock Ave, Whittier (90602-1399)
**PHONE**...............562 693-3442
David C Harris, *Pr*
**EMP:** 21 **EST:** 1971
**SQ FT:** 12,000
**SALES (est):** 1.72MM **Privately Held**
**Web:** www.harrisorgans.com
**SIC: 3931** 3599 Pipes, organ; Machine shop, jobbing and repair

### (P-15719)
### KANSTUL MUSICAL INSTRS INC
Also Called: K M I
23772 Perth Bay, Dana Point (92629-4203)
**PHONE**...............714 563-1000
Zigmant J Kanstul, *Pr*
**EMP:** 42 **EST:** 1982
**SALES (est):** 676.06K **Privately Held**
**Web:** www.kanstul.com
**SIC: 3931** Brass instruments and parts

### (P-15720)
### PALADAR MFG INC
53973 Polk St, Coachella (92236-3816)
P.O. Box 4117 (93403-4117)
**PHONE**...............760 775-4222
Sterling C Ball, *Pr*
Roland S Ball, *
▲ **EMP:** 52 **EST:** 1979
**SQ FT:** 6,000
**SALES (est):** 6.65MM **Privately Held**
**Web:** www.bigpoppasmokers.com
**SIC: 3931** Strings, musical instrument

### (P-15721)
### REMO INC (PA)
28101 Industry Dr, Valencia (91355-4102)
**PHONE**...............661 294-5600
Remo D Belli, *Pr*
Fredy Shen, *
Douglas Sink, *
◆ **EMP:** 300 **EST:** 1957
**SQ FT:** 216,000
**SALES (est):** 44.59MM
**SALES (corp-wide):** 44.59MM **Privately Held**
**Web:** www.remo.com
**SIC: 3931** Heads, drum

### (P-15722)
### RICKENBACKER INTERNATIONAL CORPORATION
Also Called: Ric
3895 S Main St, Santa Ana (92707-5710)
**PHONE**...............714 545-5574
**EMP:** 75 **EST:** 1931
**SALES (est):** 4.55MM **Privately Held**
**Web:** www.rickenbacker.com
**SIC: 3931** Guitars and parts, electric and nonelectric

### (P-15723)
### SANTA CRUZ GUITAR CORPORATION
151 Harvey West Blvd Ste C, Santa Cruz (95060-2167)
**PHONE**...............831 425-0999
Richard Hoover, *Pr*
▲ **EMP:** 22 **EST:** 1976
**SQ FT:** 6,800
**SALES (est):** 2.4MM **Privately Held**
**Web:** www.santacruzguitar.com
**SIC: 3931** 5736 Guitars and parts, electric and nonelectric; Musical instrument stores

### (P-15724)
### SCHECTER GUITAR RESEARCH INC
10953 Pendleton St, Sun Valley (91352-1522)
**PHONE**...............818 767-1029
Michael Ciravolo, *Pr*
◆ **EMP:** 43 **EST:** 1987
**SQ FT:** 11,000
**SALES (est):** 6.37MM **Privately Held**
**Web:** www.schecterguitars.com
**SIC: 3931** Musical instruments

### (P-15725)
### TOM ANDERSON GUITARWORKS
845 Rancho Conejo Blvd, Newbury Park (91320-1794)
**PHONE**...............805 498-1747
Tom Anderson, *Owner*
Rachel Williams, *Off Mgr*
**EMP:** 17 **EST:** 2012
**SALES (est):** 981.21K **Privately Held**
**Web:** www.andersonguitarworks.com
**SIC: 3931** Guitars and parts, electric and nonelectric

### (P-15726)
### YAMAHA GUITAR GROUP INC (HQ)
26580 Agoura Rd, Calabasas (91302-1921)
**PHONE**...............818 575-3600
Joe Bentivegna, *Pr*
Christine Hagemann, *
◆ **EMP:** 120 **EST:** 1988
**SQ FT:** 20,000
**SALES (est):** 45.84MM **Privately Held**
**Web:** www.yamahaguitargroup.com
**SIC: 3931** Musical instruments
**PA:** Yamaha Corporation
10-1, Nakazawacho, Chuo-Ku

### (P-15727)
### YAMAHA GUITAR GROUP INC
26664 Agoura Rd, Calabasas (91302-1954)
**PHONE**...............818 575-3900
Paul Foeckler, *Pr*
**EMP:** 38
**Web:** www.line6.com
**SIC: 3931** Musical instruments
**HQ:** Yamaha Guitar Group, Inc.
26580 Agoura Rd
Calabasas CA 91302
818 575-3600

## 3942 Dolls And Stuffed Toys

### (P-15728)
### CLOUD B INC
150 W Walnut St Ste 100, Gardena (90248-3145)
**PHONE**...............310 781-3833
Linda Suh, *CEO*
◆ **EMP:** 22 **EST:** 2002
**SQ FT:** 4,100
**SALES (est):** 4.68MM
**SALES (corp-wide):** 9.79MM **Publicly Held**
**Web:** www.cloudb.com
**SIC: 3942** 5099 Stuffed toys, including animals; Baby carriages, strollers and related products
**PA:** Vinco Ventures, Inc.
6 N Main St
866 900-0992

### (P-15729)
### FAR OUT TOYS INC
300 N Pacific Coast Hwy Ste 1050, El Segundo (90245-4472)
**PHONE**...............310 480-7554
Keith Meggs, *CEO*
**EMP:** 20 **EST:** 2017
**SQ FT:** 3,700
**SALES (est):** 2.22MM **Privately Held**
**Web:** www.farouttoysinc.com
**SIC: 3942** 5092 Dolls and stuffed toys; Toys and games
**HQ:** Far Out Toys (Hk) Co., Limited
Rm 805 8/F Inter-Continental Plz
Tsim Sha Tsui East KLN

### (P-15730)
### HASBRO INC
Also Called: Hasbro
3333 W Empire Ave, Burbank (91504-3160)
**PHONE**...............818 478-4320
**EMP:** 15
**SALES (corp-wide):** 5B **Publicly Held**
**Web:** hasbro.gcs-web.com
**SIC: 3942** 3069 3944 Stuffed toys, including animals; Teething rings, rubber; Board games, children's and adults'
**PA:** Hasbro, Inc.
1027 Newport Ave
401 431-8697

### (P-15731)
### MAHAR MANUFACTURING CORP (PA)
Also Called: Fiesta Concession
2834 E 46th St, Vernon (90058-2404)
**PHONE**...............323 581-9988
Donald Mcintyre, *CEO*
Carol Reynolds, *
David Foster, *
◆ **EMP:** 39 **EST:** 1971
**SQ FT:** 100,000
**SALES (est):** 4.82MM
**SALES (corp-wide):** 4.82MM **Privately Held**
**Web:** www.fiestatoy.com
**SIC: 3942** Stuffed toys, including animals

### (P-15732)
### MATTEL INC (PA)
Also Called: Mattel
333 Continental Blvd, El Segundo (90245-5012)
**PHONE**...............310 252-2000
Ynon Kreiz, *Ch Bd*
Steve Totzke, *CCO*
Anthony Disilvestro, *CFO*

## PRODUCTS & SERVICES SECTION
### 3944 - Games, Toys, And Children's Vehicles (P-15752)

Jonathan Anschell, *CLO*
Yoon Hugh, *CAO*
◆ **EMP:** 1700 **EST:** 1945
**SQ FT:** 360,000
**SALES (est):** 5.44B
**SALES (corp-wide):** 5.44B **Publicly Held**
**Web:** about.mattel.com
**SIC: 3942** 3944 Dolls and stuffed toys; Games, toys, and children's vehicles

### (P-15733)
### MOOSE TOYS LLC
Also Called: Moose
737 Campus Sq W, El Segundo (90245-2567)
**PHONE**.................................310 341-4642
Manny Stul, *Ch*
**EMP:** 95 **EST:** 2018
**SALES (est):** 2.01MM **Privately Held**
**Web:** www.moosetoys.com
**SIC: 3942** 3944 5092 7389 Dolls and stuffed toys; Electronic games and toys; Toys and hobby goods and supplies; Business services, nec
**HQ:** Moose Toys Pty Ltd
29 Grange Road
Cheltenham VIC 3192

### (P-15734)
### RAYKORVAY INC
Also Called: Giant Teddy
1070 N Kraemer Pl, Anaheim (92806-2610)
**PHONE**.................................714 632-8680
Reza Khosravi, *CEO*
▲ **EMP:** 16 **EST:** 2007
**SQ FT:** 10,000
**SALES (est):** 1.21MM **Privately Held**
**Web:** www.giantteddy.com
**SIC: 3942** 5961 Stuffed toys, including animals; Toys and games (including dolls and models), mail order

### (P-15735)
### STROTTMAN INTERNATIONAL INC (PA)
Also Called: Strottman
28 Executive Park Ste 200, Irvine (92614-4741)
**PHONE**.................................949 623-7900
◆ **EMP:** 25 **EST:** 1983
**SALES (est):** 12.5MM
**SALES (corp-wide):** 12.5MM **Privately Held**
**Web:** www.strottman.com
**SIC: 3942** 5092 5145 Dolls and stuffed toys; Toy novelties and amusements; Confectionery

### (P-15736)
### UPD INC
Also Called: United Pacific Designs
4507 S Maywood Ave, Vernon (90058-2610)
**PHONE**.................................323 588-8811
Shahin Dardashty, *Pr*
Fred Dardashty, *
Ben Hooshim, *
◆ **EMP:** 60 **EST:** 1990
**SQ FT:** 140,000
**SALES (est):** 11.88MM **Privately Held**
**Web:** www.updinc.net
**SIC: 3942** 5112 3944 Dolls and stuffed toys; Pens and/or pencils; Puzzles

## 3944 Games, Toys, And Children's Vehicles

### (P-15737)
### ALIQUANTUM INTERNATIONAL INC
Also Called: Aqi
2009 S Parco Ave, Ontario (91761-5700)
**PHONE**.................................909 773-0880
David Ringer, *CEO*
Wayne Lin, *
▲ **EMP:** 40 **EST:** 2010
**SQ FT:** 15,000
**SALES (est):** 5.17MM **Privately Held**
**Web:** www.aqi-intl.com
**SIC: 3944** Games, toys, and children's vehicles

### (P-15738)
### AMBR INC (PA)
Also Called: American Medical Bill Review
1160 Industrial St, Redding (96002-0734)
P.O. Box 492710 (96049-2710)
**PHONE**.................................530 221-4759
William Hullinger, *CEO*
Kevin Bird, *
**EMP:** 44 **EST:** 1996
**SQ FT:** 9,800
**SALES (est):** 664.1K **Privately Held**
**SIC: 3944** Games, toys, and children's vehicles

### (P-15739)
### ASSOCIATED ELECTRICS INC (HQ)
21062 Bake Pkwy Ste 100, Lake Forest (92630-2182)
**PHONE**.................................949 544-7500
Sheng-chieh Su, *CEO*
Chung L Lai, *Pr*
Clifton Lett, *VP*
▲ **EMP:** 17 **EST:** 1965
**SALES (est):** 4.75MM **Privately Held**
**Web:** www.associatedelectrics.com
**SIC: 3944** Automobile and truck models, toy and hobby
**PA:** Thunder Tiger Corporation
No. 7, 6th Rd., Industry Park

### (P-15740)
### BANDAI NMCO TOYS CLLCTBLES AME (DH)
23 Odyssey, Irvine (92618-3144)
**PHONE**.................................949 271-6000
Shusuke Takahara, *CEO*
Atsushi Takeuchi, *
Katsushi Murakami, *
Takeshi Nojima, *
Brian Goldner, *
▲ **EMP:** 53 **EST:** 1978
**SQ FT:** 75,000
**SALES (est):** 16.9MM **Privately Held**
**Web:** www.bandai.com
**SIC: 3944** Games, toys, and children's vehicles
**HQ:** Bandai Namco Holdings Usa Inc.
2120 Park Pl Ste 120
El Segundo CA 90245

### (P-15741)
### BLACK BOX PROJECT LLC
Also Called: Infinite Rabbit Holes
87 E Green St Ste 210, Pasadena (91105-2072)
**PHONE**.................................626 356-1302
Susan Bonds, *Managing Member*
**EMP:** 20 **EST:** 2019
**SALES (est):** 350K **Privately Held**

**SIC: 3944** Board games, puzzles, and models, except electronic

### (P-15742)
### BRAINSTORMPRODUCTS LLC
1011 S Andreasen Dr Ste 100, Escondido (92029-1962)
**PHONE**.................................760 871-1135
Randal W Joe, *Pr*
Ryan Marsh, *Dir Opers*
◆ **EMP:** 22 **EST:** 2006
**SQ FT:** 4,000
**SALES (est):** 20.77MM **Privately Held**
**Web:** www.xkites.com
**SIC: 3944** Kites

### (P-15743)
### CAPERON DESIGNS INC
Also Called: Beco Baby Carrier
1733 Monrovia Ave Ste N, Costa Mesa (92627-4421)
**PHONE**.................................714 552-3201
Gabriela Caperon, *Pr*
Andrew Caperon, *VP*
▲ **EMP:** 15 **EST:** 2007
**SQ FT:** 3,000
**SALES (est):** 206.13K **Privately Held**
**SIC: 3944** Baby carriages and restraint seats

### (P-15744)
### CRYPTIC STUDIOS INC
980 University Ave, Los Gatos (95032-7620)
**PHONE**.................................408 399-1969
Jack Emmert, *CEO*
Michael C Lewis, *
**EMP:** 100 **EST:** 2000
**SALES (est):** 19.54MM **Privately Held**
**Web:** www.crypticstudios.com
**SIC: 3944** Games, toys, and children's vehicles
**HQ:** Perfect World Co., Ltd.
701-20, Floor 7, Building 5, No.1 Courtyard, Shangdi E. Road, Ha Beijing BJ 10008

### (P-15745)
### DREAMGEAR LLC
Also Called: Isound
20001 S Western Ave, Torrance (90501-1306)
P.O. Box 478 (90508-0478)
**PHONE**.................................310 222-5522
Yahya Ahdout, *CEO*
Richard Weston, *
◆ **EMP:** 49 **EST:** 2002
**SQ FT:** 60,000
**SALES (est):** 17.32MM **Privately Held**
**Web:** www.dreamgear.net
**SIC: 3944** Electronic games and toys

### (P-15746)
### DT MATTSON ENTERPRISES INC
Also Called: Protoform
201 W Lincoln St, Banning (92220-4933)
P.O. Box 456 (92223-0456)
**PHONE**.................................951 849-9781
Todd Mattson, *CEO*
▲ **EMP:** 40 **EST:** 1983
**SQ FT:** 20,000
**SALES (est):** 5.05MM **Privately Held**
**Web:** www.prolineracing.com
**SIC: 3944** 5521 Games, toys, and children's vehicles; Trucks, tractors, and trailers; used

### (P-15747)
### EXPLODING KITTENS LLC
101 S La Brea Ave Ste A, Los Angeles (90036-2998)

**PHONE**.................................310 788-8699
Matthew Inman, *
◆ **EMP:** 29 **EST:** 2015
**SALES (est):** 5.26MM **Privately Held**
**Web:** www.explodingkittens.com
**SIC: 3944** 7371 Board games, children's and adults'; Computer software development and applications
**PA:** Asmodee Group
Quartier Villaroy

### (P-15748)
### FARALLON BRANDS INC (PA)
Also Called: Peanut Shell
33300 Central Ave, Union City (94587-2044)
**PHONE**.................................510 550-4299
Michael R Roach, *CEO*
William T Tauscher, *Ch Bd*
Laura Tauscher, *CFO*
Kyleigh Michelle Greely, *Sec*
◆ **EMP:** 17 **EST:** 2007
**SQ FT:** 27,000
**SALES (est):** 2.82MM **Privately Held**
**Web:** www.farallonbrands.com
**SIC: 3944** 2392 5137 Baby carriages and restraint seats; Blankets, comforters and beddings; Baby goods

### (P-15749)
### FUN-GI GAMES LLC
Also Called: Fun-GI
880 Apollo St Ste 229, El Segundo (90245-4752)
**PHONE**.................................213 254-5489
Alfred Fung, *CEO*
◆ **EMP:** 17 **EST:** 2015
**SALES (est):** 859.12K **Privately Held**
**Web:** www.fun-gi.com
**SIC: 3944** 7336 7389 7372 Electronic games and toys; Commercial art and graphic design; Business Activities at Non-Commercial Site; Prepackaged software

### (P-15750)
### GAMEFAM INC
777 S Alameda St Fl 2, Los Angeles (90021-1657)
**PHONE**.................................310 200-6623
Joseph Ferencz, *CEO*
**EMP:** 17 **EST:** 2019
**SALES (est):** 5.67MM **Privately Held**
**Web:** www.gamefam.com
**SIC: 3944** Electronic games and toys

### (P-15751)
### IMPERIAL TOY LLC (PA)
16641 Roscoe Pl, North Hills (91343-6104)
**PHONE**.................................818 536-6500
Peter Tiger, *Managing Member*
Arthur Hirsch, *
◆ **EMP:** 115 **EST:** 1969
**SQ FT:** 400,000
**SALES (est):** 25.12MM
**SALES (corp-wide):** 25.12MM **Privately Held**
**Web:** www.jaru.com
**SIC: 3944** Games, toys, and children's vehicles

### (P-15752)
### INSOMNIAC GAMES INC (PA)
2255 N Ontario St Ste 550, Burbank (91504-3120)
**PHONE**.................................818 729-2400
Theodore C Price, *Pr*
Alex Hastings, *VP*
Brian Hastings, *Sec*
**EMP:** 74 **EST:** 1994
**SALES (est):** 25.66MM

# 3944 - Games, Toys, And Children's Vehicles (P-15753)

**SALES (corp-wide):** 25.66MM **Privately Held**
Web: www.insomniac.games
SIC: **3944** Electronic games and toys

### (P-15753)
### INSOMNIAC GAMES INC
2207 Bridgepointe Pkwy, Foster City (94404-5060)
PHONE.................650 655-1633
Theodore C Price, *Pr*
**EMP:** 100
**SALES (corp-wide):** 25.66MM **Privately Held**
Web: www.insomniac.games
SIC: **3944** Electronic games and toys
PA: Insomniac Games, Inc.
   2255 N Ontario St Ste 550
   818 729-2400

### (P-15754)
### JADA GROUP INC
Also Called: Jada Toys
18521 Railroad St, City Of Industry (91748-1316)
PHONE.................626 810-8382
William Anthony Simons, *CEO*
Wai Han Ko, *
Manfred Duschl, *
◆ **EMP:** 70 **EST:** 1999
**SALES (est):** 23.52MM
**SALES (corp-wide):** 207.43MM **Privately Held**
Web: www.jadatoys.com
SIC: **3944** Games, toys, and children's vehicles
HQ: Simba-Dickie-Group Gmbh
   Werkstr. 1
   Furth BY 90765
   911976501

### (P-15755)
### JAKKS PACIFIC INC
Also Called: Flying Colors
21749 Baker Pkwy, Walnut (91789-5234)
PHONE.................909 594-7771
Michelle Tromp, *Brnch Mgr*
**EMP:** 30
Web: www.jakks.com
SIC: **3944** **5092** Games, toys, and children's vehicles; Toys, nec
PA: Jakks Pacific, Inc.
   2951 28th St

### (P-15756)
### JAKKS PACIFIC INC (PA)
Also Called: Jakks
2951 28th St, Santa Monica (90405-2961)
PHONE.................424 268-9444
Stephen G Berman, *Ch Bd*
Stephen G Berman, *Ch Bd*
John L Kimble, *Ex VP*
John J Mcgrath, *COO*
**EMP:** 66 **EST:** 1995
**SQ FT:** 65,858
**SALES (est):** 711.56MM **Publicly Held**
Web: www.jakks.com
SIC: **3944** Games, toys, and children's vehicles

### (P-15757)
### LEAPFROG ENTERPRISES INC (HQ)
2200 Powell St Ste 500, Emeryville (94608-1818)
PHONE.................510 420-5000
Nick Delany, *CEO*
William To, *
Alec Anderson, *
Linda Schwimmer, *

▲ **EMP:** 357 **EST:** 1995
**SALES (est):** 30.69MM **Privately Held**
Web: www.leapfrog.com
SIC: **3944** Games, toys, and children's vehicles
PA: Vtech Holdings Limited
   C/O Conyers Corporate Services
   (Bermuda) Limited

### (P-15758)
### LEARNING SQUARED INC
935 Benecia Ave, Sunnyvale (94085-2805)
PHONE.................650 567-9995
Andrew Butler, *CEO*
Thomas Boeckle, *
Katie Kirsch, *
**EMP:** 200 **EST:** 2014
**SQ FT:** 12,000
**SALES (est):** 10.11MM **Privately Held**
Web: www.squarepanda.com
SIC: **3944** Electronic toys

### (P-15759)
### MATTEL DIRECT IMPORT INC (HQ)
Also Called: Mattel
333 Continental Blvd, El Segundo (90245-5032)
PHONE.................310 252-2000
Kevin Farr, *CEO*
Bryan G Stockton, *Pr*
**EMP:** 48 **EST:** 2007
**SALES (est):** 3.96MM
**SALES (corp-wide):** 5.44B **Publicly Held**
SIC: **3944** **3942** **3949** Games, toys, and children's vehicles; Dolls, except stuffed toy animals; Sporting and athletic goods, nec
PA: Mattel, Inc.
   333 Continental Blvd
   310 252-2000

### (P-15760)
### MEGA BRANDS AMERICA INC (DH)
Also Called: Rose Art Industries
333 Continental Blvd, El Segundo (90245-5032)
PHONE.................949 727-9009
Marc Bertrand, *CEO*
Vic Bertrand, *
◆ **EMP:** 80 **EST:** 1923
**SALES (est):** 179.23MM
**SALES (corp-wide):** 5.44B **Publicly Held**
Web: support.megabrands.com
SIC: **3944** Blocks, toy
HQ: Mega Brands Inc.
   4505 Rue Hickmore
   Saint-Laurent QC H4T 1
   514 333-5555

### (P-15761)
### MOORES IDEAL PRODUCTS LLC
Also Called: M I P
830 W Golden Grove Way, Covina (91722-3257)
PHONE.................626 339-9007
Eustace Moore Junior, *Managing Member*
**EMP:** 20 **EST:** 1978
**SQ FT:** 8,600
**SALES (est):** 851.82K **Privately Held**
Web: www.miponline.com
SIC: **3944** Automobile and truck models, toy and hobby

### (P-15762)
### NINJA JUMP INC
3221 N San Fernando Rd, Los Angeles (90065-1414)

PHONE.................323 255-5418
Rouben Gourchounian, *Pr*
◆ **EMP:** 75 **EST:** 1984
**SQ FT:** 35,000
**SALES (est):** 5.23MM **Privately Held**
Web: www.ninjajump.com
SIC: **3944** Games, toys, and children's vehicles

### (P-15763)
### PH DIP INC
Also Called: Playhut, Inc.
18560 San Jose Ave, City Of Industry (91748-1365)
PHONE.................909 869-8083
Yu Zheng, *CEO*
▲ **EMP:** 20 **EST:** 1992
**SALES (est):** 4.99MM **Privately Held**
Web: www.basicfun.com
SIC: **3944** Games, toys, and children's vehicles
PA: Basic Fun, Inc.
   301 E Yamato Rd Ste 4200

### (P-15764)
### POCKET GEMS INC (PA)
Also Called: Pocket Gems
126 Post St Fl 3, San Francisco (94108-4704)
PHONE.................415 371-1333
Ben Liu, *CEO*
Daniel Terry, *Co-Worker*
**EMP:** 176 **EST:** 2009
**SALES (est):** 46.54MM **Privately Held**
Web: www.pocketgems.com
SIC: **3944** Electronic games and toys

### (P-15765)
### POOLMASTER INC (PA)
770 Del Paso Rd, Sacramento (95834-1117)
P.O. Box 340308 (95834-0308)
PHONE.................916 567-9800
Leon H Tager, *Pr*
Nora Davis, *VP*
Carol Tager, *Sec*
◆ **EMP:** 43 **EST:** 1959
**SQ FT:** 100,000
**SALES (est):** 8.81MM
**SALES (corp-wide):** 8.81MM **Privately Held**
Web: www.poolmaster.com
SIC: **3944** **5091** Games, toys, and children's vehicles; Sporting and recreation goods

### (P-15766)
### ROAD CHAMPS INC
22619 Pacific Coast Hwy Ste 250, Malibu (90265-5080)
PHONE.................310 456-7799
Stephen Berman, *Pr*
**EMP:** 150 **EST:** 1960
**SQ FT:** 51,000
**SALES (est):** 502.23K **Publicly Held**
SIC: **3944** Automobiles and trucks, toy
PA: Jakks Pacific, Inc.
   2951 28th St

### (P-15767)
### ROBOTO GAMES INC
72 E 3rd Ave, San Mateo (94401-4007)
PHONE.................650 380-5966
Curt Bererton, *Prin*
**EMP:** 24 **EST:** 2014
**SALES (est):** 1.73MM **Privately Held**
Web: www.robotogames.com
SIC: **3944** **7371** Video game machines, except coin-operated; Computer software development

### (P-15768)
### SHELCORE INC (PA)
Also Called: Shelcore Toys
7811 Lemona Ave, Van Nuys (91405-1139)
PHONE.................818 883-2400
Arnold Rubin, *Pr*
◆ **EMP:** 29 **EST:** 1975
**SQ FT:** 20,000
**SALES (est):** 61.17MM
**SALES (corp-wide):** 61.17MM **Privately Held**
Web: www.funrise.com
SIC: **3944** Blocks, toy

### (P-15769)
### SUN-MATE CORP
19730 Ventura Blvd Ste 18, Woodland Hills (91364-6304)
PHONE.................818 700-0572
Rami Ben-moshe, *Pr*
◆ **EMP:** 15 **EST:** 1985
**SQ FT:** 5,000
**SALES (est):** 517.48K **Privately Held**
Web: www.sun-mate.com
SIC: **3944** Electronic games and toys

### (P-15770)
### TOYMAX INTERNATIONAL INC (HQ)
22619 Pacific Coast Hwy, Malibu (90265-5054)
PHONE.................310 456-7799
Jack Friedman, *CEO*
Stephen G Berman, *
Joel M Bennett, *CFO*
◆ **EMP:** 56 **EST:** 1990
**SQ FT:** 30,000
**SALES (est):** 45.61MM **Publicly Held**
Web: jadehomeremodeling.website2.me
SIC: **3944** **5092** Games, toys, and children's vehicles; Toys and games
PA: Jakks Pacific, Inc.
   2951 28th St

### (P-15771)
### USAOPOLY INC
Also Called: Op Games, The
5999 Avenida Encinas Ste 150, Carlsbad (92008-4431)
PHONE.................760 431-5910
Dane S Chapin, *CEO*
Tom Nirschel, *
▲ **EMP:** 94 **EST:** 1994
**SQ FT:** 10,000
**SALES (est):** 17.94MM **Privately Held**
Web: www.theop.games
SIC: **3944** Board games, puzzles, and models, except electronic

## 3949 Sporting And Athletic Goods, Nec

### (P-15772)
### ABSOLUTE BOARD CO INC
4040 Calle Platino Ste 102, Oceanside (92056-5858)
P.O. Box 4098 (92056)
PHONE.................760 295-2201
Matt Logan, *CEO*
▲ **EMP:** 26 **EST:** 2011
**SALES (est):** 2.04MM **Privately Held**
Web: www.absoluteboardco.com
SIC: **3949** Skateboards

### (P-15773)
### ACUSHNET COMPANY
Also Called: Titleist
2819 Loker Ave E, Carlsbad (92010-6626)

PRODUCTS & SERVICES SECTION  3949 - Sporting And Athletic Goods, Nec (P-15795)

PHONE..................760 804-6500
John Worster, *Brnch Mgr*
**EMP:** 300
**Web:** www.titleist.com
**SIC: 3949** Shafts, golf club
**HQ:** Acushnet Company
333 Bridge St
Fairhaven MA 02719
508 979-2000

**(P-15774)**
**ADDADAY INC**
Also Called: Experience Lyric
12304 Santa Monica Blvd Ste 355, Los Angeles (90025-1542)
P.O. Box 163 (90274)
PHONE..................424 465-9106
Victor Yang, *CEO*
**EMP:** 20 **EST:** 2010
**SALES (est):** 6.9MM **Privately Held**
**Web:** www.experiencelyric.com
**SIC: 3949** 3634 Sporting and athletic goods, nec; Massage machines, electric, except for beauty/barber shops

**(P-15775)**
**ALDILA INC (HQ)**
1945 Kellogg Ave, Carlsbad (92008-6582)
PHONE..................858 513-1801
Peter R Mathewson, *Ch Bd*
Scott M Bier, *CAO*\*
▲ **EMP:** 15 **EST:** 1991
**SQ FT:** 125,000
**SALES (est):** 65.81MM **Privately Held**
**Web:** www.aldila.com
**SIC: 3949** 3297 Shafts, golf club; Graphite refractories: carbon bond or ceramic bond
**PA:** Mitsubishi Chemical Group Corporation
1-1-1, Marunouchi

**(P-15776)**
**ALDILA GOLF CORP**
13450 Stowe Dr, Poway (92064-6860)
PHONE..................858 513-1801
**EMP:** 104
**Web:** www.aldila.com
**SIC: 3949** Shafts, golf club
**HQ:** Aldila Golf Corp.
1945 Kellogg Ave
Carlsbad CA 92008

**(P-15777)**
**ALDILA GOLF CORP (DH)**
1945 Kellogg Ave, Carlsbad (92008-6582)
PHONE..................858 513-1801
Peter R Mathewson, *CEO*
Scott Bier, *\**
Sue-wei Yeh, *Contrlr*
▲ **EMP:** 78 **EST:** 1991
**SQ FT:** 52,156
**SALES (est):** 3.17MM **Privately Held**
**Web:** www.aldila.com
**SIC: 3949** Shafts, golf club
**HQ:** Aldila, Inc.
1945 Kellogg Ave
Carlsbad CA 92008
858 513-1801

**(P-15778)**
**AMERICAN UNDERWATER PRODUCTS (HQ)**
Also Called: Oceanic
2002 Davis St, San Leandro (94577-1211)
PHONE..................800 435-3483
Robert R Hollis, *CEO*
Paul Elsinga, *\**
◆ **EMP:** 93 **EST:** 1973
**SQ FT:** 74,000
**SALES (est):** 20.98MM **Privately Held**
**Web:** www.oceanicworldwide.com

**SIC: 3949** 5941 Sporting and athletic goods, nec; Skin diving, scuba equipment and supplies
**PA:** Australian Underwater Products Pty. Ltd.
4 Scotch Court

**(P-15779)**
**AMRON INTERNATIONAL INC (PA)**
Also Called: Amron
1380 Aspen Way, Vista (92081-8349)
PHONE..................760 208-6500
Debra L Ritchie, *CEO*
◆ **EMP:** 69 **EST:** 1979
**SQ FT:** 40,000
**SALES (est):** 10.62MM
**SALES (corp-wide):** 10.62MM **Privately Held**
**Web:** www.amronintl.com
**SIC: 3949** 5091 Skin diving equipment, scuba type; Diving equipment and supplies

**(P-15780)**
**ARROW SURF PRODUCTS (PA)**
1115 Thompson Ave Ste 7, Santa Cruz (95062-3253)
PHONE..................831 462-2791
Bob Pearson, *Owner*
**EMP:** 17 **EST:** 1975
**SQ FT:** 1,200
**SALES (est):** 752.34K
**SALES (corp-wide):** 752.34K **Privately Held**
**Web:** www.arrowsurfshop.com
**SIC: 3949** Surfboards

**(P-15781)**
**ASPHALT FABRIC AND ENGRG INC**
2683 Lime Ave, Signal Hill (90755-2718)
PHONE..................562 997-4129
Bill Goldsmith, *Pr*
Doug Coulter, *\**
Joe Salamone, *\**
**EMP:** 90 **EST:** 1998
**SQ FT:** 5,000
**SALES (est):** 1.29MM **Privately Held**
**Web:** www.afesports.com
**SIC: 3949** Sporting and athletic goods, nec

**(P-15782)**
**AVET INDUSTRIES INC**
Also Called: Avet Reels
9687 Topanga Canyon Pl, Chatsworth (91311-4118)
PHONE..................818 576-9895
Aruttyun Alajajyan, *Pr*
Sarkis Alajajyan, *VP*
**EMP:** 15 **EST:** 1989
**SQ FT:** 19,200
**SALES (est):** 1.97MM **Privately Held**
**Web:** www.avetreels.net
**SIC: 3949** Reels, fishing

**(P-15783)**
**AZA INDUSTRIES INC (PA)**
1410 Vantage Ct, Vista (92081-8509)
PHONE..................760 560-0440
David H Brown, *Pr*
Jim Passamonte, *\**
Bill Pierce, *\**
▲ **EMP:** 40 **EST:** 1977
**SQ FT:** 27,000
**SALES (est):** 600.58K **Privately Held**
**Web:** www.ca-tf.com
**SIC: 3949** Skateboards

**(P-15784)**
**BALANCED BODY INC (PA)**
5909 88th St, Sacramento (95828-1111)
PHONE..................916 388-2838
**TOLL FREE:** 800
◆ **EMP:** 16 **EST:** 1978
**SALES (est):** 6.67MM
**SALES (corp-wide):** 6.67MM **Privately Held**
**Web:** www.pilates.com
**SIC: 3949** Exercise equipment

**(P-15785)**
**BBS MANUFACTURING INC**
Also Called: Bbs
1905 Diamond St Ste A, San Marcos (92078-5185)
PHONE..................760 798-8011
Grant Burns, *CEO*
◆ **EMP:** 16 **EST:** 1996
**SQ FT:** 13,000
**SALES (est):** 5.63MM **Privately Held**
**Web:** www.bbsmfg.com
**SIC: 3949** Skateboards

**(P-15786)**
**BELL FOUNDRY CO (PA)**
5310 Southern Ave, South Gate (90280-3690)
P.O. Box 1070 (90280-1070)
PHONE..................323 564-5701
Cesar Capallini, *Pr*
Wanda De Wald, *\**
Dimitry Rabyy, *\**
▲ **EMP:** 50 **EST:** 1924
**SQ FT:** 140,000
**SALES (est):** 4.18MM
**SALES (corp-wide):** 4.18MM **Privately Held**
**Web:** www.bfco.com
**SIC: 3949** 3321 Dumbbells and other weightlifting equipment; Gray and ductile iron foundries

**(P-15787)**
**BELL SPORTS INC (HQ)**
Also Called: Easton Bell Sports
16752 Armstrong Ave, Irvine (92606-4912)
PHONE..................469 417-6600
Andrew Keegan, *CEO*
Jung Choi, *\**
◆ **EMP:** 75 **EST:** 1952
**SQ FT:** 27,197
**SALES (est):** 25.15MM
**SALES (corp-wide):** 2.75B **Privately Held**
**Web:** www.bellhelmets.com
**SIC: 3949** 3751 Helmets, athletic; Bicycles and related parts
**PA:** Vista Outdoor Inc.
1 Vista Way
763 433-1000

**(P-15788)**
**BLACK BOX DISTRIBUTION LLC**
371 2nd St Ste 1, Encinitas (92024-3524)
PHONE..................760 268-1174
James Thomas, *\**
Michelle Wenner, *\**
◆ **EMP:** 70 **EST:** 2009
**SALES (est):** 2.48MM **Privately Held**
**SIC: 3949** Skateboards

**(P-15789)**
**BOOST TREADMILLS LLC**
2155 Cornell St, Palo Alto (94306-1310)
PHONE..................650 424-1827
Thomas Allen, *Prin*
**EMP:** 16 **EST:** 2017
**SALES (est):** 1.49MM **Privately Held**
**Web:** www.boosttreadmills.com

**SIC: 3949** Treadmills

**(P-15790)**
**BOOSTED INC**
Also Called: Boosted Boards
400 Oyster Point Blvd Ste 229, South San Francisco (94080-1952)
PHONE..................650 933-5151
Sanjay Dastoor, *CEO*
**EMP:** 26 **EST:** 2012
**SALES (est):** 4.31MM **Privately Held**
**Web:** www.boostedboards.com
**SIC: 3949** Skateboards

**(P-15791)**
**BRAVO HIGHLINE LLC** ✪
3101 Ocean Park Blvd Ste 100, Santa Monica (90405-3022)
PHONE..................562 484-5100
Bart Thielen, *CEO*
Nicholas Schultz, *Managing Member*\*
Dinesh Mirchandani, *\**
**EMP:** 25 **EST:** 2023
**SALES (est):** 2.87MM **Privately Held**
**SIC: 3949** 3944 Skateboards; Scooters, children's

**(P-15792)**
**BRAVO SPORTS**
9043 Siempre Viva Rd, San Diego (92154-7662)
PHONE..................562 457-8916
**EMP:** 23
**SALES (corp-wide):** 28.11MM **Privately Held**
**Web:** www.bravosportscorp.com
**SIC: 3949** Sporting and athletic goods, nec
**HQ:** Bravo Sports
12801 Carmenita Rd
Santa Fe Springs CA 90670
562 484-5100

**(P-15793)**
**BRAVO SPORTS (HQ)**
12801 Carmenita Rd, Santa Fe Springs (90670-4805)
P.O. Box 2967 (90670)
PHONE..................562 484-5100
Nicholas R Schultz, *Pr*
◆ **EMP:** 80 **EST:** 1987
**SQ FT:** 100,000
**SALES (est):** 27.31MM
**SALES (corp-wide):** 28.11MM **Privately Held**
**Web:** www.bravosportscorp.com
**SIC: 3949** Sporting and athletic goods, nec
**PA:** Transom Bravo Holdings Corp.
12801 Carmenita Rd
562 484-5100

**(P-15794)**
**BRAVO SPORTS**
Also Called: Sector9
4370 Jutland Dr, San Diego (92117-3642)
PHONE..................858 408-0083
Derek Oneill, *CEO*
**EMP:** 23
**SALES (corp-wide):** 28.11MM **Privately Held**
**Web:** www.bravosportscorp.com
**SIC: 3949** Skateboards
**HQ:** Bravo Sports
12801 Carmenita Rd
Santa Fe Springs CA 90670
562 484-5100

**(P-15795)**
**C PREME LIMITED LLC**
Also Called: C-Preme
1250 E 223rd St, Carson (90745-4266)

(PA)=Parent Co (HQ)=Headquarters
✪ = New Business established in last 2 years

## 3949 - Sporting And Athletic Goods, Nec (P-15796)

**PHONE** ................ 310 355-0498
Ryan Ratner, *Managing Member*
Corey Ratner, *Managing Member*
▲ **EMP:** 21 **EST:** 2010
**SQ FT:** 40,000
**SALES (est):** 2.78MM
**SALES (corp-wide):** 2.75B **Privately Held**
Web: www.c-preme.com
**SIC: 3949** 5091 5571 5099 Skateboards; Bicycles; Motor scooters; Luggage
PA: Vista Outdoor Inc.
  1 Vista Way
  763 433-1000

### (P-15796)
### CALIFORNIA TRACK & ENGINEERING
4668 N Sonora Ave Ste 101, Fresno (93722-3970)
**PHONE** ................ 559 237-2590
Karol Fair, *Pr*
▲ **EMP:** 33 **EST:** 1981
**SQ FT:** 2,500
**SALES (est):** 10MM **Privately Held**
**SIC: 3949** 1629 Track and field athletic equipment; Athletic field construction

### (P-15797)
### CAMELBAK PRODUCTS LLC (HQ)
Also Called: Camelbak Products
2000 S Mcdowell Boulevard Ext Ste 200, Petaluma (94954-6901)
**PHONE** ................ 707 792-9700
Scott D Chaplin, *Managing Member*
Glenn Gross, *
Jody Brunner, *
Chris Strain, *
▲ **EMP:** 98 **EST:** 1989
**SQ FT:** 50,000
**SALES (est):** 36.76MM
**SALES (corp-wide):** 2.75B **Privately Held**
Web: www.camelbak.com
**SIC: 3949** Camping equipment and supplies
PA: Vista Outdoor Inc.
  1 Vista Way
  763 433-1000

### (P-15798)
### CASA DE HERMANDAD (PA)
Also Called: West Area Opportunity Center
1639 11th St, Santa Monica (90404-3727)
**PHONE** ................ 310 477-8272
David Abelar, *Pr*
**EMP:** 25 **EST:** 1970
**SALES (est):** 80.05K
**SALES (corp-wide):** 80.05K **Privately Held**
**SIC: 3949** Driving ranges, golf, electronic

### (P-15799)
### CHAPMN-WLTERS INTRCOASTAL CORP
Also Called: Cwic
141 Via Lampara, Rcho Sta Marg (92688-2954)
**PHONE** ................ 949 448-9940
Andrew De Camara, *Recvr*
Cindi A Walters, *Pr*
◆ **EMP:** 16 **EST:** 1996
**SQ FT:** 103,000
**SALES (est):** 1.17MM **Privately Held**
**SIC: 3949** Sporting and athletic goods, nec

### (P-15800)
### CONDOR OUTDOOR PRODUCTS INC (PA)
Also Called: Condor
5268 Rivergrade Rd, Baldwin Park (91706-1336)
**PHONE** ................ 626 358-3270
Spencer Tien, *Pr*
Neil Chen, *
◆ **EMP:** 38 **EST:** 1994
**SQ FT:** 11,000
**SALES (est):** 8.26MM
**SALES (corp-wide):** 8.26MM **Privately Held**
Web: www.condoroutdoor.com
**SIC: 3949** Sporting and athletic goods, nec

### (P-15801)
### CRAZY INDUSTRIES
Also Called: Savi Customs
8675 Avenida Costa Norte, San Diego (92154-6253)
**PHONE** ................ 619 270-9090
Jane Roe, *CEO*
Don Roe, *CFO*
**EMP:** 45 **EST:** 2018
**SALES (est):** 4.49MM **Privately Held**
Web: www.submfg.com
**SIC: 3949** 2339 2329 Sporting and athletic goods, nec; Sportswear, women's; Men's and boys' sportswear and athletic clothing

### (P-15802)
### DEUCE BRAND
3235 Hancock St Ste 7b, San Diego (92110-4420)
**PHONE** ................ 877 443-3823
Gary Michael Hughes, *Admn*
**EMP:** 18 **EST:** 2016
**SALES (est):** 326.66K **Privately Held**
Web: www.deucebrand.com
**SIC: 3949** Sporting and athletic goods, nec

### (P-15803)
### DIAMOND BASEBALL COMPANY INC
Also Called: Diamond Sports
121 Waterworks Way Ste 150, Irvine (92618-7719)
P.O. Box 55090 (92619-5090)
**PHONE** ................ 949 409-9200
Jay Hicks, *CEO*
Andrea Gordon, *
Robert W Ezell, *
◆ **EMP:** 23 **EST:** 1977
**SQ FT:** 120,000
**SALES (est):** 3.03MM **Privately Held**
Web: www.diamond-sports.com
**SIC: 3949** 5091 Baseball equipment and supplies, general; Athletic goods

### (P-15804)
### DIVING UNLIMITED INTL INC
Also Called: Diving Unlimited Int.
1148 Delevan Dr, San Diego (92102-2499)
**PHONE** ................ 619 236-1203
Susan Long, *CEO*
Richard Long, *
◆ **EMP:** 75 **EST:** 1963
**SQ FT:** 14,500
**SALES (est):** 3.62MM **Privately Held**
Web: www.divedui.com
**SIC: 3949** Skin diving equipment, scuba type

### (P-15805)
### EASTON HOCKEY INC
Also Called: Eastern Sports
3500 Willow Ln, Thousand Oaks (91361-4921)
**PHONE** ................ 818 782-6445
◆ **EMP:** 1500
Web: www.eastonhockey.com
**SIC: 3949** Sporting and athletic goods, nec

### (P-15806)
### EFGP INC
Also Called: E. Force Sports
1384 Poinsettia Ave Ste E, Vista (92081-8505)
**PHONE** ................ 760 692-3900
Ronald A Grimes, *Pr*
▲ **EMP:** 15 **EST:** 1988
**SALES (est):** 1.16MM **Privately Held**
**SIC: 3949** Racket sports equipment

### (P-15807)
### ERMICO ENTERPRISES INC
Also Called: Ermico
1111 17th St Ste B, San Francisco (94107-2406)
P.O. Box 885403 (94188-5403)
**PHONE** ................ 415 822-6776
Rebekah Engel, *Pr*
Gwynned Vitello, *
Linda Decay, *
▲ **EMP:** 100 **EST:** 1976
**SQ FT:** 19,000
**SALES (est):** 3.64MM **Privately Held**
**SIC: 3949** 3599 3365 3366 Skateboards; Machine shop, jobbing and repair; Aluminum foundries; Brass foundry, nec

### (P-15808)
### EVNROLL PUTTERS LLC
1817 Aston Ave Ste 101, Carlsbad (92008-7339)
**PHONE** ................ 321 277-1397
Guerin Rife, *Managing Member*
**EMP:** 16 **EST:** 2016
**SALES (est):** 4.01MM **Privately Held**
Web: www.evnroll.com
**SIC: 3949** Sporting and athletic goods, nec
PA: Creatz Inc.
  Rm A-407 Digital Empire

### (P-15809)
### EXACTACATOR INC (PA)
2237 Stagecoach Rd, Stockton (95215-7915)
P.O. Box 8501 (95208-0501)
**PHONE** ................ 209 464-8979
James G Nesbitt, *Pr*
John Nakashima, *VP*
Barbara Nesbitt, *Sec*
Shelley Holcomb, *Treas*
▲ **EMP:** 22 **EST:** 1983
**SQ FT:** 21,000
**SALES (est):** 2.16MM
**SALES (corp-wide):** 2.16MM **Privately Held**
Web: www.viseinserts.com
**SIC: 3949** Bowling equipment and supplies

### (P-15810)
### FASTHOUSE INC
29003 Avenue Sherman, Valencia (91355-4180)
**PHONE** ................ 661 775-5963
**EMP:** 18
**SALES (corp-wide):** 10.04MM **Privately Held**
Web: www.fasthouse.com
**SIC: 3949** Sporting and athletic goods, nec
PA: Fasthouse, Inc.
  28757 Industry Dr
  661 775-5963

### (P-15811)
### FASTHOUSE INC (PA)
28757 Industry Dr, Valencia (91355-5414)
**PHONE** ................ 661 775-5963
Kenneth Alexander, *CEO*
Dan Worrell, *Prin*
Jason Fonzy, *Prin*
**EMP:** 16 **EST:** 2013
**SALES (est):** 10.04MM
**SALES (corp-wide):** 10.04MM **Privately Held**
Web: www.fasthouse.com
**SIC: 3949** Team sports equipment

### (P-15812)
### FINIS INC (PA)
Also Called: Finis USA
5849 W Schulte Rd Ste 104, Tracy (95377-8135)
**PHONE** ................ 925 454-0111
John Mix, *CEO*
▲ **EMP:** 24 **EST:** 1993
**SALES (est):** 6.14MM
**SALES (corp-wide):** 6.14MM **Privately Held**
Web: www.finisswim.com
**SIC: 3949** Surfboards

### (P-15813)
### FITNESS WAREHOUSE LLC (PA)
Also Called: Hoist Fitness Systems
9990 Alesmith Ct Ste 130, San Diego (92126-4200)
**PHONE** ................ 858 578-7676
Jeffrey Partrick, *Pt*
◆ **EMP:** 30 **EST:** 1999
**SALES (est):** 4.65MM
**SALES (corp-wide):** 4.65MM **Privately Held**
Web: www.fitnesswarehouseusa.com
**SIC: 3949** Sporting and athletic goods, nec

### (P-15814)
### FUJIKURA COMPOSITE AMERICA INC
Also Called: Fujikuria Composits
1819 Aston Ave Ste 101, Carlsbad (92008-7338)
**PHONE** ................ 760 598-6060
Peter Sanchez, *Pr*
Kenji Morita, *CFO*
▲ **EMP:** 20 **EST:** 1994
**SALES (est):** 6.32MM **Privately Held**
Web: www.fujikuragolf.com
**SIC: 3949** Shafts, golf club
PA: Fujikura Composites Inc.
  3-5-7, Ariake

### (P-15815)
### FUTURE MOTION INC
Also Called: One Wheel
1201 Shaffer Rd Ste A, Santa Cruz (95060-5763)
**PHONE** ................ 650 814-8643
Kyle J Doerksen, *CEO*
**EMP:** 66 **EST:** 2013
**SALES (est):** 7.61MM **Privately Held**
Web: www.onewheel.com
**SIC: 3949** Skateboards

### (P-15816)
### GAMEBREAKER INC (PA)
31248 Oak Crest Dr Ste 210, Westlake Village (91361-4637)
**PHONE** ................ 818 224-7424
Michael Juels, *Pr*
Dina Juels, *Sec*
**EMP:** 20 **EST:** 2011
**SQ FT:** 5,000
**SALES (est):** 9.3MM
**SALES (corp-wide):** 9.3MM **Privately Held**
Web: www.gamebreaker.com
**SIC: 3949** 2329 2339 Guards: football, basketball, soccer, lacrosse, etc.; Men's and boys' athletic uniforms; Uniforms, athletic: women's, misses', and juniors'

## PRODUCTS & SERVICES SECTION
### 3949 - Sporting And Athletic Goods, Nec (P-15839)

**(P-15817)**
**GOLF SALES WEST INC**
Also Called: Golf Sales West
1901 Eastman Ave, Oxnard (93030-5171)
PHONE..................805 988-3363
▲ **EMP:** 50 **EST:** 1988
**SALES (est):** 2.7MM **Privately Held**
**Web:** www.golfsaleswest.com
**SIC: 3949** Bags, golf

**(P-15818)**
**GOLF SUPPLY HOUSE USA INC**
Also Called: Eagle One Golf Products
1340 N Jefferson St, Anaheim (92807-1614)
PHONE..................714 983-0050
◆ **EMP:** 70
**SIC: 3949** 5941 Golf equipment; Golf goods and equipment

**(P-15819)**
**GREENFIELDS OUTDOOR FITNES INC**
2617 W Woodland Dr, Anaheim (92801-2627)
PHONE..................888 315-9037
Samuel Mendelsohn, *CEO*
Aviv Avivshay, *Stockholder*
◆ **EMP:** 15 **EST:** 2010
**SALES (est):** 2.35MM **Privately Held**
**Web:** www.gfoutdoorfitness.com
**SIC: 3949** Gymnasium equipment

**(P-15820)**
**HEART RATE INC**
Also Called: Versaclimber
2619 Oak St, Santa Ana (92707-3720)
PHONE..................714 850-9716
Richard D Charnitski, *Pr*
Dan Charnitski, *
▲ **EMP:** 38 **EST:** 1978
**SQ FT:** 18,000
**SALES (est):** 75.04K **Privately Held**
**Web:** www.versaclimber.com
**SIC: 3949** Exercise equipment

**(P-15821)**
**HOBIE CAT COMPANY II LLC**
4925 Oceanside Blvd, Oceanside (92056-3099)
PHONE..................760 758-9100
**EMP:** 200 **EST:** 2021
**SALES (est):** 17.31MM **Privately Held**
**Web:** www.hobie.com
**SIC: 3949** Water sports equipment

**(P-15822)**
**HOIST FITNESS SYSTEMS INC**
Also Called: Hoist Fitness
11900 Community Rd, Poway (92064-7143)
PHONE..................858 578-7676
Jeffrey Partrick, *CEO*
Billy Kim, *
◆ **EMP:** 81 **EST:** 1977
**SQ FT:** 105,000
**SALES (est):** 8.36MM **Privately Held**
**Web:** www.hoistfitness.com
**SIC: 3949** 5941 Exercise equipment; Exercise equipment

**(P-15823)**
**HUPA INTERNATIONAL INC**
Also Called: Body Flex Sports
21717 Ferrero, Walnut (91789-5209)
PHONE..................909 598-9876
Bob Hsiung, *Pr*
▲ **EMP:** 21 **EST:** 1996
**SQ FT:** 30,000
**SALES (est):** 829.96K **Privately Held**
**Web:** www.hupa.net
**SIC: 3949** Exercise equipment

**(P-15824)**
**HYDRAPAK INC**
6605 San Leandro St, Oakland (94621-3317)
PHONE..................510 632-8318
Matthew Lyon, *CEO*
▲ **EMP:** 25 **EST:** 2001
**SALES (est):** 952.3K **Privately Held**
**Web:** www.hydrapak.com
**SIC: 3949** Sporting and athletic goods, nec

**(P-15825)**
**HYPER ICE INC (PA)**
Also Called: Hyperice
525 Technology Dr Ste 100, Irvine (92618-1389)
PHONE..................949 565-4994
Jim Huether, *CEO*
Robert Marton, *
▲ **EMP:** 44 **EST:** 2010
**SALES (est):** 13.68MM
**SALES (corp-wide):** 13.68MM **Privately Held**
**Web:** www.hyperice.com
**SIC: 3949** 5136 5621 5699 Sporting and athletic goods, nec; Sportswear, men's and boys'; Women's sportswear; Sports apparel

**(P-15826)**
**HYPERFLY INC**
8390 Miramar Pl Ste D, San Diego (92121-2104)
PHONE..................760 300-0909
Pascal Jean Pakter, *CEO*
Kerstin Pakter, *
Pascal Pakter, *
**EMP:** 25 **EST:** 2019
**SALES (est):** 832K **Privately Held**
**Web:** www.hyperfly.com
**SIC: 3949** Sporting and athletic goods, nec

**(P-15827)**
**I & I SPORTS SUPPLY COMPANY (PA)**
435 W Alondra Blvd, Gardena (90248-2424)
P.O. Box 4495 (92605-4495)
PHONE..................310 715-6800
Alan Iba, *Pr*
▲ **EMP:** 20 **EST:** 1984
**SALES (est):** 2.64MM
**SALES (corp-wide):** 2.64MM **Privately Held**
**Web:** www.iisports.com
**SIC: 3949** 5091 5941 Sporting and athletic goods, nec; Sporting and recreation goods; Martial arts equipment and supplies

**(P-15828)**
**IFIT INC**
2220 Almond Ave, Redlands (92374-2073)
PHONE..................909 335-2888
**EMP:** 1333
**SALES (corp-wide):** 1.75B **Privately Held**
**Web:** company.ifit.com
**SIC: 3949** Treadmills
**HQ:** Ifit Inc.
1500 S 1000 W
Logan UT 84321
435 750-5000

**(P-15829)**
**ILLAH SPORTS INC**
Also Called: Belding Golf Bag Company, The
1610 Fiske Pl, Oxnard (93033-1849)
PHONE..................805 240-7790

Brien Patermo, *CEO*
Steve Perrin, *
Jackie Perrin, *
▲ **EMP:** 50 **EST:** 2003
**SALES (est):** 934.49K **Privately Held**
**SIC: 3949** Sporting and athletic goods, nec

**(P-15830)**
**INDIAN INDUSTRIES INC**
Also Called: Escalade Sports
7756 Saint Andrews Ave Ste 115, San Diego (92154-8210)
P.O. Box 530960 (92153-0960)
PHONE..................800 467-1421
Daniel A Messmer, *Prin*
**EMP:** 29
**SALES (corp-wide):** 263.57MM **Publicly Held**
**Web:** www.escaladesports.com
**SIC: 3949** Ping-pong tables
**HQ:** Indian Industries Inc
817 Maxwell Ave
Evansville IN 47711
812 467-1200

**(P-15831)**
**IRON GRIP BARBELL COMPANY INC**
11377 Markon Dr, Garden Grove (92841-1402)
PHONE..................714 850-6900
Scott Frasco, *CEO*
Michael Rojas, *
Donna Lins, *Prin*
▼ **EMP:** 85 **EST:** 1993
**SALES (est):** 10.34MM **Privately Held**
**Web:** www.irongrip.com
**SIC: 3949** Exercise equipment

**(P-15832)**
**JOHN ROBERT ARD**
1930 Bacon St, San Diego (92107-2806)
PHONE..................619 326-0577
**EMP:** 15
**SALES (corp-wide):** 2.15MM **Privately Held**
**Web:** www.southcoast.com
**SIC: 3949** Surfboards
**PA:** Robert Ard John
5023 Newport Ave
619 223-7017

**(P-15833)**
**JOHNSON OUTDOORS INC**
Scuba Pro
1166 Fesler St Ste A, El Cajon (92020-1813)
PHONE..................619 402-1023
Joe Stella, *Brnch Mgr*
**EMP:** 96
**SALES (corp-wide):** 663.84MM **Publicly Held**
**Web:** scubapro.johnsonoutdoors.com
**SIC: 3949** 5091 Skin diving equipment, scuba type; Diving equipment and supplies
**PA:** Johnson Outdoors Inc.
555 Main St
262 631-6600

**(P-15834)**
**KEISER CORPORATION (PA)**
Also Called: Keiser Sports Health Equipment
2470 S Cherry Ave, Fresno (93706-5004)
PHONE..................559 256-8000
Dennis L Keiser, *CEO*
Randy Keiser, *
Gyl Keiser, *
Kathy Keiser, *
Portlinn Pangburn, *
◆ **EMP:** 85 **EST:** 1977

**SQ FT:** 100,000
**SALES (est):** 22.53MM
**SALES (corp-wide):** 22.53MM **Privately Held**
**Web:** www.keiser.com
**SIC: 3949** Exercise equipment

**(P-15835)**
**L A STEEL CRAFT PRODUCTS (PA)**
1975 Lincoln Ave, Pasadena (91103-1321)
P.O. Box 90365 (91109-0365)
PHONE..................626 798-7401
Beverly Holt, *Pr*
John C Gaudesi, *COO*
▲ **EMP:** 21 **EST:** 1951
**SQ FT:** 200,000
**SALES (est):** 1.06MM
**SALES (corp-wide):** 1.06MM **Privately Held**
**Web:** www.lasteelcraft.com
**SIC: 3949** Playground equipment

**(P-15836)**
**LIFEWARD CA INC**
Also Called: Alterg, Inc.
48368 Milmont Dr, Fremont (94538-7324)
PHONE..................510 270-5900
Larry Jasinski, *CEO*
Kevin Davidge, *
Gabriel Griego, *
Dev Mishra, *CMO**
Clement Leung, *
▲ **EMP:** 60 **EST:** 2004
**SQ FT:** 15,247
**SALES (est):** 12.99MM **Privately Held**
**Web:** www.alterg.com
**SIC: 3949** Lacrosse equipment and supplies, general
**HQ:** Rewalk Robotics, Inc.
200 Donald Lynch Blvd
Marlborough MA 01752
508 251-1154

**(P-15837)**
**LUCITE INTL PRTNR HOLDINGS INC**
MRC Composite Product
5441 Avenida Encinas Ste B, Carlsbad (92008-4412)
PHONE..................760 929-0001
Hikaro Shikashi, *VP*
**EMP:** 99
**SIC: 3949** Golf equipment
**PA:** Lucite International Partnership Holdings, Inc.
1403 Foulk Rd

**(P-15838)**
**MALBON GOLF LLC**
1740 Stanford St, Santa Monica (90404-4116)
PHONE..................323 433-4028
Stephen Malbon, *Pr*
**EMP:** 40 **EST:** 2016
**SALES (est):** 867.81K **Privately Held**
**Web:** www.malbongolf.com
**SIC: 3949** Golf equipment

**(P-15839)**
**MARTIN SPORTS INC (PA)**
Also Called: Martin Archery
1100 Glendon Ave Ste 920, Los Angeles (90024-3513)
PHONE..................509 529-2554
Rich Weatherford, *Prin*
Tracy Reiff, *
Richard Weatherford, *
Kevin Ma, *VP*
Tim Larkin, *

# 3949 - Sporting And Athletic Goods, Nec (P-15840)

▲ **EMP:** 21 **EST:** 2013
**SQ FT:** 28,000
**SALES (est):** 438.43K
**SALES (corp-wide):** 438.43K **Privately Held**
**SIC: 3949** Sporting and athletic goods, nec

### (P-15840)
**MELIN LLC**
10 Faraday, Irvine (92618-2714)
**PHONE**..............................323 489-3274
Hoang Tu, *Prin*
**EMP:** 41 **EST:** 2019
**SALES (est):** 2.64MM **Privately Held**
**Web:** www.melin.com
**SIC: 3949** Sporting and athletic goods, nec

### (P-15841)
**MISSION HOCKEY COMPANY (PA)**
12 Goodyear Ste 100, Irvine (92618-3764)
**PHONE**..............................949 585-9390
Michael Whan, *CEO*
Christopher Lynch, *
▲ **EMP:** 17 **EST:** 1994
**SQ FT:** 10,000
**SALES (est):** 1.97MM **Privately Held**
**Web:** inhaler.missionhockey.com
**SIC: 3949** Hockey equipment and supplies, general

### (P-15842)
**NHS INC**
Also Called: Santa Cruz Skateboards
104 Bronson St Ste 9, Santa Cruz (95062-3487)
P.O. Box 2718 (95063-2718)
**PHONE**..............................831 459-7800
Robert A Denike, *CEO*
Richard H Novak, *
Jeff Kendall, *CMO**
▲ **EMP:** 92 **EST:** 1972
**SQ FT:** 50,000
**SALES (est):** 24.38MM **Privately Held**
**Web:** www.nhs-inc.com
**SIC: 3949** 2329 Skateboards; Athletic clothing, except uniforms: men's, youths' and boys'

### (P-15843)
**NORBERTS ATHLETIC PRODUCTS INC**
354 W Gardena Blvd, Gardena (90248-2739)
P.O. Box 1890 (90733-1890)
**PHONE**..............................310 830-6672
Loren Dill, *Pr*
▲ **EMP:** 19 **EST:** 1977
**SQ FT:** 4,000
**SALES (est):** 2.91MM **Privately Held**
**Web:** www.norberts.com
**SIC: 3949** Sporting and athletic goods, nec

### (P-15844)
**ORCA ARMS LLC**
Also Called: Orca Arms
26500 Agoura Rd, Calabasas (91302-1952)
**PHONE**..............................858 586-0503
Hamid R Ray Akhavan, *Managing Member*
Ardeshir Akhavan, *
▲ **EMP:** 68 **EST:** 2012
**SQ FT:** 5,500
**SALES (est):** 380.42K **Privately Held**
**Web:** www.orcaarms.com
**SIC: 3949** 5099 Sporting and athletic goods, nec; Firearms and ammunition, except sporting

### (P-15845)
**RIP CURL INC**
193 Avenida La Pata, San Clemente (92673-6307)
**PHONE**..............................714 422-3617
**EMP:** 25
**Web:** www.ripcurl.com
**SIC: 3949** Surfboards
**HQ:** Rip Curl, Inc.
3030 Ariway Ave
Costa Mesa CA 92626

### (P-15846)
**RIP CURL INC (DH)**
Also Called: Rip Curl USA
3030 Airway Ave, Costa Mesa (92626-6036)
**PHONE**..............................714 422-3600
Kelly Gibson, *CEO*
Matt Szot, *
◆ **EMP:** 60 **EST:** 1992
**SALES (est):** 20.77MM **Privately Held**
**Web:** www.ripcurl.com
**SIC: 3949** Surfboards
**HQ:** Rip Curl International Pty Ltd
101 Surf Coast Hwy
Torquay VIC 3228

### (P-15847)
**ROSEN & ROSEN INDUSTRIES INC**
Also Called: R & R Industries
204 Avenida Fabricante, San Clemente (92672-7538)
**PHONE**..............................949 361-9238
Richard Rosen, *Pr*
Daniel Rosen, *
▲ **EMP:** 80 **EST:** 1979
**SQ FT:** 22,500
**SALES (est):** 4.15MM **Privately Held**
**Web:** www.rrind.com
**SIC: 3949** 7389 Sporting and athletic goods, nec; Embroidery advertising

### (P-15848)
**RPSZ CONSTRUCTION LLC**
1201 W 5th St Ste T340, Los Angeles (90017-1489)
**PHONE**..............................314 677-5831
Rick Platt, *Managing Member*
**EMP:** 104 **EST:** 2008
**SQ FT:** 3,500
**SALES (est):** 233.68K
**SALES (corp-wide):** 5.6MM **Privately Held**
**SIC: 3949** Trampolines and equipment
**PA:** Sky Zone, Llc
1201 W 5th St T-340
310 734-0300

### (P-15849)
**RUSTY SURFBOARDS INC (PA)**
Also Called: Rusty Surfboards
8495 Commerce Ave, San Diego (92121-2608)
**PHONE**..............................858 578-0414
Angela Preidendorfer, *Pr*
Angela Preisendorfer, *Pr*
◆ **EMP:** 15 **EST:** 1985
**SALES (est):** 921.5K
**SALES (corp-wide):** 921.5K **Privately Held**
**Web:** www.rustysurfboards.com
**SIC: 3949** 5941 Surfboards; Surfing equipment and supplies

### (P-15850)
**SAFER SPORTS INC**
Also Called: Light Helmets
5670 El Camino Real Ste B, Carlsbad (92008-7125)
**PHONE**..............................760 444-0082

Nick Esayian, *CEO*
Justin Bert, *
**EMP:** 30 **EST:** 2017
**SALES (est):** 2.07MM **Privately Held**
**Web:** www.lighthelmets.com
**SIC: 3949** Helmets, athletic

### (P-15851)
**SAINT NINE AMERICA INC**
10700 Norwalk Blvd, Santa Fe Springs (90670-3824)
**PHONE**..............................562 921-5300
Timothy Chae, *CEO*
Terry Kim, *
Max Kim, *
**EMP:** 40 **EST:** 2018
**SALES (est):** 619.71K **Privately Held**
**Web:** www.saintnineamerica.com
**SIC: 3949** Team sports equipment

### (P-15852)
**SBR SPORTS INC**
2806 Willis St, Santa Ana (92705-5714)
**PHONE**..............................800 620-4094
**EMP:** 19
**SALES (corp-wide):** 417.73K **Privately Held**
**Web:** www.sbrsportsinc.com
**SIC: 3949** Sporting and athletic goods, nec
**PA:** Sbr Sports, Inc.
2826 Willis St
800 620-4094

### (P-15853)
**SEIRUS INNOVATIVE ACC INC**
Also Called: Seirus Innovation
13975 Danielson St, Poway (92064-6889)
**PHONE**..............................858 513-1212
Michael Carey, *Pr*
Joseph H Edwards, *
Wendy Carey, *
Robert Murphy, *
▲ **EMP:** 65 **EST:** 1984
**SQ FT:** 11,000
**SALES (est):** 8.53MM **Privately Held**
**Web:** www.seirus.com
**SIC: 3949** Sporting and athletic goods, nec

### (P-15854)
**SHOCK DOCTOR INC**
Also Called: United Sports Brands
11488 Slater Ave, Fountain Valley (92708-5440)
**PHONE**..............................657 383-4400
**EMP:** 40
**Web:** www.shockdoctor.com
**SIC: 3949** Sporting and athletic goods, nec
**PA:** Doctor Shock Inc
11488 Slater Ave

### (P-15855)
**SHOCK DOCTOR INC (PA)**
Also Called: Shock Doctor Sports
11488 Slater Ave, Fountain Valley (92708-5440)
**PHONE**..............................800 233-6956
Philip Gyori, *CEO*
Kevin Johnson, *CFO*
▲ **EMP:** 82 **EST:** 2008
**SALES (est):** 74.86MM **Privately Held**
**Web:** www.shockdoctor.com
**SIC: 3949** Protective sporting equipment

### (P-15856)
**SKATE ONE CORP**
Also Called: Roller Bones
6860 Cortona Dr Ste B, Goleta (93117-3021)
**PHONE**..............................805 964-1330
George Powell, *Pr*

▲ **EMP:** 80 **EST:** 1976
**SALES (est):** 9.17MM **Privately Held**
**Web:** www.skateone.com
**SIC: 3949** Skateboards

### (P-15857)
**SKINTIGHT**
11740 San Vicente Blvd Ste 208, Los Angeles (90049-6610)
**PHONE**..............................310 829-4120
Leigh D Godfrey, *Prin*
**EMP:** 20 **EST:** 2012
**SALES (est):** 765.5K **Privately Held**
**Web:** www.skintightaesthetics.com
**SIC: 3949** Sporting and athletic goods, nec

### (P-15858)
**STANDARD SALES LLC (PA)**
Also Called: Stansport
2801 E 12th St, Los Angeles (90023-3621)
**PHONE**..............................323 269-0510
Max Wartnik, *Ch*
Victor Preisler, *
Eva Wartnik, *
◆ **EMP:** 35 **EST:** 1964
**SQ FT:** 100,000
**SALES (est):** 7.75MM
**SALES (corp-wide):** 7.75MM **Privately Held**
**Web:** www.stansport.com
**SIC: 3949** Camping equipment and supplies

### (P-15859)
**STAR TRAC HEALTH & FITNESS INC**
Also Called: Star Trac
14410 Myford Rd, Irvine (92606-1001)
Rural Route 300 (98662)
**PHONE**..............................714 669-1660
▲ **EMP:** 20
**Web:** www.corehandf.com
**SIC: 3949** Exercise equipment

### (P-15860)
**STAR TRAC STRENGTH INC**
Also Called: Star Trac Fitness
14410 Myford Rd, Irvine (92606-1001)
Rural Route 300 (98662)
**PHONE**..............................714 669-1660
▲ **EMP:** 405
**SIC: 3949** 5091 Exercise equipment; Exercise equipment

### (P-15861)
**SUBMERSIBLE SYSTEMS LLC**
7413 Slater Ave, Huntington Beach (92647-6228)
**PHONE**..............................714 842-6566
Anthony Buban, *Pr*
Christine Buban, *Sec*
▲ **EMP:** 15 **EST:** 1973
**SQ FT:** 12,000
**SALES (est):** 1.45MM **Privately Held**
**Web:** www.submersiblesystems.com
**SIC: 3949** Skin diving equipment, scuba type

### (P-15862)
**SURE GRIP INTERNATIONAL**
5519 Rawlings Ave, South Gate (90280-7495)
**PHONE**..............................562 923-0724
James Ball, *VP*
Ione L Ball, *
▲ **EMP:** 60 **EST:** 1937
**SQ FT:** 30,000
**SALES (est):** 4.61MM **Privately Held**
**Web:** www.suregrip.com
**SIC: 3949** Skates and parts, roller

▲ = Import ▼ = Export
◆ = Import/Export

# PRODUCTS & SERVICES SECTION
## 3952 - Lead Pencils And Art Goods (P-15885)

**(P-15863)**
**SURF TO SUMMIT INC**
Also Called: Photo Printing Pros
7234 Hollister Ave, Goleta (93117-2807)
PHONE.....................805 964-1896
▲ EMP: 18 EST: 1993
SALES (est): 1.9MM **Privately Held**
Web: www.surftosummit.com
SIC: 3949 Sporting and athletic goods, nec

**(P-15864)**
**TACTICOMBAT INC**
11640 Mcbean Dr, El Monte (91732-1105)
PHONE.....................626 315-4433
Daisy Chan, *Pr*
Tik Yan Tse, *CEO*
EMP: 19 EST: 2014
SQ FT: 2,500
SALES (est): 540.69K **Privately Held**
Web: www.tacticombat.com
SIC: 3949 2389 Golf equipment; Men's miscellaneous accessories

**(P-15865)**
**THOUSAND LLC**
915 Mateo St Ste 302, Los Angeles (90021-1786)
PHONE.....................310 745-0110
EMP: 38 EST: 2016
SALES (est): 4.8MM **Privately Held**
Web: www.explorethousand.com
SIC: 3949 Sporting and athletic goods, nec

**(P-15866)**
**TOPGOLF CALLAWAY BRANDS CORP (PA)**
2180 Rutherford Rd, Carlsbad (92008-7328)
PHONE.....................760 931-1771
Oliver G Brewer Iii, *Pr*
John F Lundgren, *
Erik J Anderson, *
Rebecca Fine, *CPO*
Brian P Lynch, *CLO*
◆ EMP: 349 EST: 1982
SALES (est): 4.28B
SALES (corp-wide): 4.28B **Publicly Held**
Web: prodpwa.callawaygolf.com
SIC: 3949 2329 2339 6794 Golf equipment; Men's and boys' sportswear and athletic clothing; Women's and misses' athletic clothing and sportswear; Patent buying, licensing, leasing

**(P-15867)**
**TOTAL GYM COMMERCIAL LLC**
100 Chesterfield Dr # G, Cardiff By The Sea (92007-1922)
PHONE.....................858 586-6080
▲ EMP: 18 EST: 2011
SALES (est): 1.34MM **Privately Held**
Web: www.totalgym.com
SIC: 3949 5091 Exercise equipment; Exercise equipment

**(P-15868)**
**TUFFSTUFF FITNESS INTL INC**
155 N Riverview Dr, Anaheim (92808-1225)
PHONE.....................909 629-1600
Richard M Reyes Junior, *Ch Bd*
Cammie Grider, *
◆ EMP: 66 EST: 1992
SALES (est): 12.82MM
SALES (corp-wide): 12.82MM **Privately Held**
Web: www.tuffstufffitness.com
SIC: 3949 Exercise equipment
PA: Brooks Industrial Marketplace
23401 Mount Ashland Ct
714 269-1689

**(P-15869)**
**TWIN PEAK INDUSTRIES INC**
Also Called: Jungle Jumps
12420 Montague St Ste E, Pacoima (91331-2140)
PHONE.....................800 259-5906
Edmond K Keshishian, *Pr*
Raffi Sepanian, *
EMP: 32 EST: 2008
SALES (est): 1.76MM **Privately Held**
SIC: 3949 3069 Playground equipment; Air-supported rubber structures

**(P-15870)**
**UKE CORPORATION**
Also Called: Underwater Kinetics
13400 Danielson St, Poway (92064-8830)
PHONE.....................858 513-9100
◆ EMP: 95 EST: 1971
SALES (est): 2.07MM **Privately Held**
Web: www.uwk.com
SIC: 3949 3648 3646 3161 Water sports equipment; Flashlights; Commercial lighting fixtures; Luggage

**(P-15871)**
**UNISEN INC**
Also Called: Star Trac
14410 Myford Rd, Irvine (92606-1001)
Rural Route 300 (98662)
PHONE.....................714 669-1660
◆ EMP: 20 EST: 1975
SALES (est): 2.2MM **Privately Held**
Web: www.corehandf.com
SIC: 3949 Exercise equipment

**(P-15872)**
**US BOWLING CORPORATION**
5480 Schaefer Ave, Chino (91710-6901)
PHONE.....................909 548-0644
David Frewing, *Pr*
Daroll L Frewing, *Prin*
Dolores Frewing, *Sec*
◆ EMP: 15 EST: 1994
SQ FT: 50,000
SALES (est): 2.65MM **Privately Held**
Web: www.usbowling.com
SIC: 3949 1799 Bowling alleys and accessories; Bowling alley installation

**(P-15873)**
**USA PRODUCTS GROUP (PA)**
Also Called: Progrip Cargo Control
1300 E Vine St, Lodi (95240-3148)
P.O. Box 1750 (95241-1750)
PHONE.....................209 334-1460
Stephen D Jackson, *Pr*
Raymond S Brown, *
▲ EMP: 30 EST: 1995
SALES (est): 4.25MM **Privately Held**
Web: www.usaprogrip.com
SIC: 3949 2399 Bags, golf; Seat covers, automobile

**(P-15874)**
**VISTA OUTDOOR INC**
Also Called: Brg Sports
5550 Scotts Valley Dr, Scotts Valley (95066-3438)
PHONE.....................831 461-7500
Mark Teixeira, *Brnch Mgr*
EMP: 32
SALES (corp-wide): 2.75B **Privately Held**
Web: www.vistaoutdoor.com
SIC: 3949 Bags, rosin
PA: Vista Outdoor Inc.
1 Vista Way
763 433-1000

**(P-15875)**
**WELCOME SKATEBOARDS INC**
26792 Vista Ter, Lake Forest (92630-8112)
PHONE.....................949 305-9200
Jason R Celaya, *Prin*
Kellen Matsufuji, *Prin*
EMP: 30 EST: 2014
SALES (est): 1.47MM **Privately Held**
Web: www.welcomeskateboards.com
SIC: 3949 Skateboards

**(P-15876)**
**WEST COAST TRENDS INC**
Also Called: Train Reaction
17811 Jamestown Ln, Huntington Beach (92647-7136)
PHONE.....................714 843-9288
Jeffrey C Herold, *CEO*
Vivienne Herold, *
▲ EMP: 50 EST: 1990
SQ FT: 26,000
SALES (est): 5.75MM **Privately Held**
Web: www.scheyden.com
SIC: 3949 Golf equipment

**(P-15877)**
**WESTERN GOLF CAR MFG INC**
Also Called: Western Golf Car Sales Co
69391 Dillon Rd, Desert Hot Springs (92241-8433)
PHONE.....................760 671-6691
Scott Stevens, *Pr*
Robert W Thomas, *
EMP: 55 EST: 1981
SQ FT: 60,000
SALES (est): 1.7MM **Privately Held**
SIC: 3949 3799 Sporting and athletic goods, nec; Golf carts, powered

**(P-15878)**
**WORLD CLASS CHEERLEADING INC**
20212 Hart St, Winnetka (91306-3520)
PHONE.....................877 923-2645
Akram Hemaidan, *CEO*
EMP: 33 EST: 2009
SALES (est): 1.73MM **Privately Held**
Web: www.worldclasscheerleading.com
SIC: 3949 Sporting and athletic goods, nec

**(P-15879)**
**XS SCUBA INC (PA)**
Also Called: Atlantic Diving Equipment
4040 W Chandler Ave, Santa Ana (92704-5202)
PHONE.....................714 424-0434
Daniel F Babcock, *Pr*
◆ EMP: 24 EST: 2002
SALES (est): 5.47MM
SALES (corp-wide): 5.47MM **Privately Held**
Web: www.xsscuba.com
SIC: 3949 5091 Skin diving equipment, scuba type; Diving equipment and supplies

**(P-15880)**
**ZONSON COMPANY INC**
3197 Lionshead Ave, Carlsbad (92010-4702)
PHONE.....................760 597-0338
Jeff Yearours, *VP*
▲ EMP: 26 EST: 2001
SALES (est): 1.96MM **Privately Held**
Web: www.zonson.com
SIC: 3949 Bags, golf

## 3951 Pens And Mechanical Pencils

**(P-15881)**
**HARTLEY COMPANY**
Also Called: Hartley-Racon
1987 Placentia Ave, Costa Mesa (92627-6265)
P.O. Box 10999 (92627-0999)
PHONE.....................949 646-9643
Ed Kuder, *Pr*
Mike Quinley, *VP*
▲ EMP: 22 EST: 1947
SQ FT: 75,000
SALES (est): 2.36MM **Privately Held**
Web: www.thehartleycompany.com
SIC: 3951 Cartridges, refill: ball point pens

## 3952 Lead Pencils And Art Goods

**(P-15882)**
**AARDVARK CLAY & SUPPLIES INC (PA)**
1400 E Pomona St, Santa Ana (92705-4858)
PHONE.....................714 541-4157
George Johnston, *Pr*
Daniel T Carreon, *
Richard Mac Pherson, *General Vice President*
K Douglas Pherson Mac, *Sec*
▲ EMP: 30 EST: 1972
SQ FT: 25,000
SALES (est): 5.34MM
SALES (corp-wide): 5.34MM **Privately Held**
Web: www.aardvarkclay.com
SIC: 3952 5945 Modeling clay; Arts and crafts supplies

**(P-15883)**
**AR-CE INC**
Also Called: Stretch Art
141 E 162nd St, Gardena (90248-2801)
PHONE.....................310 771-1960
Sarkis Cetinyan, *Pr*
Herman Artinian, *VP*
EMP: 15 EST: 1994
SQ FT: 6,000
SALES (est): 1.46MM **Privately Held**
Web: www.stretch-art.com
SIC: 3952 Lead pencils and art goods

**(P-15884)**
**CONVERSION TECHNOLOGY CO INC (PA)**
5360 N Commerce Ave, Moorpark (93021-1762)
PHONE.....................805 378-0033
Jim Newkirk, *Pr*
Russell Greenhouse, *
▲ EMP: 50 EST: 1994
SQ FT: 28,000
SALES (est): 15.86MM **Privately Held**
SIC: 3952 2893 2899 Ink, drawing: black and colored; Printing ink; Ink or writing fluids

**(P-15885)**
**DOSTAL STUDIO**
17 Woodland Ave, San Rafael (94901-5301)
PHONE.....................415 721-7080
Frank Dostal, *Owner*
EMP: 15 EST: 1990
SALES (est): 1.02MM **Privately Held**
Web: www.dostalstudio.com

# 3952 - Lead Pencils And Art Goods

SIC: 3952 Frames for artists' canvases

**(P-15886)**
**J F MCCAUGHIN CO**
2628 River Ave, Rosemead (91770-3302)
PHONE................626 573-3000
Jim Mallory, *Brnch Mgr*
EMP: 16
SALES (corp-wide): 982.03MM **Privately Held**
Web: www.paramelt.com
SIC: 3952 Wax, artists'
HQ: J. F. Mccaughin Co.
2817 Mccracken St
Norton Shores MI 49441
231 759-7304

**(P-15887)**
**SALIS INTERNATIONAL INC**
3921 Oceanic Dr Ste 802, Oceanside (92056-5857)
PHONE................303 384-3588
Lawrence R Salis, *Pr*
◆ EMP: 38 EST: 1934
SQ FT: 10,000
SALES (est): 2.22MM **Privately Held**
Web: www.docmartins.com
SIC: 3952 Water colors, artists'

**(P-15888)**
**WESTECH PRODUCTS INC (PA)**
Also Called: Westech Wax Products
1242 Enterprise Ct, Corona (92882-7125)
PHONE................951 279-4496
Lawrence Dahlin, *Pr*
Erik Dahlin, *
Barry Dahlin, *
▲ EMP: 24 EST: 1980
SQ FT: 31,000
SALES (est): 4.83MM
SALES (corp-wide): 4.83MM **Privately Held**
Web: www.westechwax.com
SIC: 3952 5169 Crayons: chalk, gypsum, charcoal, fusains, pastel, wax, etc.; Waxes, except petroleum

## 3953 Marking Devices

**(P-15889)**
**BRANDNEW INDUSTRIES INC**
375 Pine Ave Ste 22, Santa Barbara (93117-3725)
PHONE................805 964-8251
Sean David Clayton, *Pr*
EMP: 15 EST: 1991
SQ FT: 2,000
SALES (est): 949.69K **Privately Held**
Web: www.brandnew.net
SIC: 3953 Irons, marking or branding

**(P-15890)**
**HERO ARTS RUBBER STAMPS INC**
1200 Harbour Way S Ste 201, Richmond (94804-3638)
PHONE................510 232-4200
Aaron Leventhal, *CEO*
Jacqueline Leventhal, *
▲ EMP: 50 EST: 1974
SQ FT: 70,000
SALES (est): 2.22MM **Privately Held**
Web: www.heroarts.com
SIC: 3953 5945 Marking devices; Arts and crafts supplies

**(P-15891)**
**JOY PRODUCTS CALIFORNIA INC**
Also Called: Coastal Enterprises
17281 Mount Wynne Cir, Fountain Valley (92708-4107)
PHONE................714 437-7250
Shayne Perkins, *Pr*
Jay Kollins, *Off Mgr*
▲ EMP: 16 EST: 1981
SQ FT: 12,000
SALES (est): 1.41MM **Privately Held**
Web: www.coastalsportswear.com
SIC: 3953 2759 Screens, textile printing; Screen printing

**(P-15892)**
**SVEVIA USA INC**
Also Called: Roadmax Products
13643 5th St, Chino (91710-5168)
PHONE................909 559-4134
John Lucas, *Pr*
EMP: 15 EST: 2016
SALES (est): 2.66MM **Privately Held**
SIC: 3953 Stencils, painting and marking

## 3955 Carbon Paper And Inked Ribbons

**(P-15893)**
**CALIFORNIA RIBBON CARBN CO INC**
8420 Quinn St, Downey (90241-2624)
PHONE................323 724-9100
Robert J Picou, *CEO*
Robert J Picou, *Pr*
Clara Picou, *
Louis Titus, *
▲ EMP: 100 EST: 1939
SALES (est): 1.63MM **Privately Held**
SIC: 3955 Ribbons, inked: typewriter, adding machine, register, etc.

**(P-15894)**
**E ALKO INC**
Also Called: Laser Imaging International
8201 Woodley Ave, Van Nuys (91406-1231)
PHONE................818 587-9700
Eyal Alkoby, *Pr*
Eyal Alkoby, *CEO*
Beth Alkoby, *Prin*
▲ EMP: 39 EST: 1992
SQ FT: 45,000
SALES (est): 566.29K **Privately Held**
SIC: 3955 3861 Print cartridges for laser and other computer printers; Photographic equipment and supplies

**(P-15895)**
**ECMM SERVICES INC**
1320 Valley Vista Dr # 204, Diamond Bar (91765-3956)
PHONE................714 988-9388
Vincent Yang, *Pr*
Donald Sung, *
EMP: 250 EST: 2010
SALES (est): 5.1MM **Privately Held**
SIC: 3955 5045 Print cartridges for laser and other computer printers; Printers, computer
PA: Hon Hai Precision Industry Co., Ltd.
No. 2, Ziyou St.

**(P-15896)**
**GENERAL RIBBON CORP**
Also Called: G R C
5775 E Los Angeles Ave Ste 230, Chatsworth (91311)
PHONE................818 709-1234
Stephen R Morgan, *Pr*
Robert W Daggs, *
▲ EMP: 500 EST: 1946
SQ FT: 110,000
SALES (est): 993.96K **Privately Held**
Web: www.printgrc.com
SIC: 3955 3861 Ribbons, inked: typewriter, adding machine, register, etc.; Photographic equipment and supplies

**(P-15897)**
**LASER RECHARGE INC (PA)**
Also Called: Encompass
8250 Belvedere Ave Ste C, Sacramento (95826-4754)
PHONE................916 813-2717
Michael Mooney, *CEO*
Dave Michon, *Pr*
Shannon Mooney, *CFO*
EMP: 21 EST: 1990
SQ FT: 10,000
SALES (est): 4.05MM **Privately Held**
Web: www.encompass-mps.com
SIC: 3955 7699 5943 Print cartridges for laser and other computer printers; Office equipment and accessory customizing; Office forms and supplies

**(P-15898)**
**LASERCARE TECHNOLOGIES INC (PA)**
Also Called: Lasercare
14370 Myford Rd Ste 100, Irvine (92606-1015)
PHONE................310 202-4200
TOLL FREE: 800
Paul Wilhelm, *Pr*
▲ EMP: 34 EST: 1993
SALES (est): 2.06MM
SALES (corp-wide): 2.06MM **Privately Held**
Web: www.lasercare.com
SIC: 3955 7378 5734 Print cartridges for laser and other computer printers; Computer peripheral equipment repair and maintenance; Printers and plotters: computers

**(P-15899)**
**PLANET GREEN CARTRIDGES INC**
Also Called: Planet Green
20724 Lassen St, Chatsworth (91311-4507)
PHONE................818 725-2596
Sean Levi, *Pr*
Natalya Levi, *
◆ EMP: 84 EST: 2000
SQ FT: 29,699
SALES (est): 8.94MM **Privately Held**
Web: www.pginkjets.com
SIC: 3955 5093 Print cartridges for laser and other computer printers; Plastics scrap

**(P-15900)**
**RAYZIST PHOTOMASK INC (PA)**
Also Called: Honor Life
955 Park Center Dr, Vista (92081-8312)
PHONE................760 727-8561
Randy S Willis, *CEO*
▲ EMP: 54 EST: 1984
SQ FT: 28,000
SALES (est): 9.76MM
SALES (corp-wide): 9.76MM **Privately Held**
Web: www.rayzist.com
SIC: 3955 3281 3589 Stencil paper, gelatin or spirit process; Cut stone and stone products; Sandblasting equipment

**(P-15901)**
**SERCOMP LLC (PA)**
5401 Tech Cir Ste 200, Moorpark (93021-1713)
P.O. Box 92728 (91715-2728)
PHONE................805 299-0020
EMP: 89 EST: 2003
SQ FT: 67,000
SALES (est): 533.82K
SALES (corp-wide): 533.82K **Privately Held**
Web: www.sercomp.com
SIC: 3955 3577 Print cartridges for laser and other computer printers; Computer peripheral equipment, nec

**(P-15902)**
**US PRINT & TONER INC**
Also Called: National Copy Cartridge
14751 Franklin Ave Ste B, Tustin (92780-7272)
PHONE................619 562-6995
James Meyers, *Pr*
▲ EMP: 22 EST: 2011
SALES (est): 2.06MM **Privately Held**
SIC: 3955 Print cartridges for laser and other computer printers

**(P-15903)**
**VISION IMAGING SUPPLIES INC**
9540 Cozycroft Ave, Chatsworth (91311-5101)
PHONE................818 885-4515
Bernard Khachi, *CEO*
Raymond Khachi, *
▲ EMP: 40 EST: 2004
SALES (est): 1.22MM **Privately Held**
Web: www.vis-llc.com
SIC: 3955 Print cartridges for laser and other computer printers

## 3961 Costume Jewelry

**(P-15904)**
**BOB SIEMON DESIGNS INC**
3501 W Segerstrom Ave, Santa Ana (92704-6449)
PHONE................714 549-0678
▲ EMP: 95
Web: www.bobsiemon.com
SIC: 3961 3911 Costume jewelry, ex. precious metal and semiprecious stones; Jewelry, precious metal

**(P-15905)**
**LOUNGEFLY LLC**
Also Called: Lounge Fly
108 S Mayo Ave, Walnut (91789-3090)
PHONE................818 718-5600
Dale Schultz, *
▲ EMP: 25 EST: 1998
SALES (est): 5.52MM
SALES (corp-wide): 1.1B **Publicly Held**
Web: www.loungefly.com
SIC: 3961 Costume jewelry
PA: Funko, Inc.
2802 Wetmore Ave
425 783-3616

**(P-15906)**
**PINCRAFT INC**
Also Called: Pin Concepts
7933 Ajay Dr, Sun Valley (91352-5315)
PHONE................818 248-0077
Vahe Asatourian, *Pr*
▲ EMP: 27 EST: 1999
SALES (est): 2.37MM **Privately Held**
Web: www.pincraft.com

SIC: 3961 Pins (jewelry), except precious metal

## 3965 Fasteners, Buttons, Needles, And Pins

**(P-15907)**
**ALCOA FASTENING SYSTEMS**
11711 Arrow Rte, Rancho Cucamonga (91730-4902)
PHONE..................909 483-2333
EMP: 17 EST: 2014
SALES (est): 248.21K Privately Held
Web: www.alcoa.com
SIC: 3965 Fasteners

**(P-15908)**
**BECKMAN INDUSTRIES**
701 Del Norte Blvd Ste 205, Oxnard (93030-7978)
P.O. Box 2307 (91376-2307)
PHONE..................805 375-3003
Robert Becker, Pr
Danny Becker, VP
EMP: 16 EST: 1995
SQ FT: 19,248
SALES (est): 771.5K Privately Held
SIC: 3965 5072 Fasteners; Hardware

**(P-15909)**
**CATAME INC (PA)**
Also Called: Ucan Zippers
1930 Long Beach Ave, Los Angeles (90058-1020)
PHONE..................213 749-2610
Liz Lai, CEO
Liz H Lai, CEO
Paul Lai, CFO
Floyd Lai, Sec
▲ EMP: 17 EST: 1995
SQ FT: 50,000
SALES (est): 2.92MM
SALES (corp-wide): 2.92MM Privately Held
Web: www.ucanzippers.com
SIC: 3965 5131 Zipper; Zippers

**(P-15910)**
**GIST INC**
Also Called: Gist Silversmiths
4385 Pleasant Valley Rd, Placerville (95667-8430)
PHONE..................530 644-8000
Gary Gist, Pr
Jennifer Folsom, *
▲ EMP: 85 EST: 1977
SQ FT: 15,000
SALES (est): 4.47MM Privately Held
Web: www.gistsilversmiths.com
SIC: 3965 3911 Buckles and buckle parts; Jewelry apparel

**(P-15911)**
**HENWAY INC**
Also Called: Anatase Products
1314 Goodrick Dr, Tehachapi (93561-1508)
PHONE..................661 822-6873
David Benhan, VP
Scott D Baker, Sec
EMP: 18 EST: 1977
SQ FT: 18,500
SALES (est): 2MM Privately Held
Web: www.aircraftbolts.com
SIC: 3965 3452 Fasteners; Bolts, nuts, rivets, and washers

**(P-15912)**
**LABELTEX MILLS INC (PA)**
5301 S Santa Fe Ave, Vernon (90058-3519)
PHONE..................323 582-0228
Torag Pourshamtobi, CEO
Shahrokh Shamtobi, *
Ben Younessi, *
Babak Younessi, *
◆ EMP: 200 EST: 1994
SALES (est): 7.37MM Privately Held
Web: www.labeltexusa.com
SIC: 3965 2253 2241 Fasteners, buttons, needles, and pins; Collar and cuff sets, knit; Labels, woven

**(P-15913)**
**MATTHEW WARREN INC**
Also Called: Mw Compnnts - Anheim Ideal Fas
3850 E Miraloma Ave, Anaheim (92806-2108)
PHONE..................714 630-7840
Simon Newman, CEO
EMP: 50 EST: 2021
SALES (est): 556.23K Privately Held
SIC: 3965 Fasteners, buttons, needles, and pins

**(P-15914)**
**MORTON GRINDING INC**
Also Called: Morton Manufacturing
201 E Avenue K15, Lancaster (93535-4572)
PHONE..................661 298-0895
Yolanda A Morton, Ch Bd
Wallace Morton, *
John Morton, *
Patrick Dansby, *
EMP: 110 EST: 1967
SQ FT: 45,000
SALES (est): 15.62MM Privately Held
Web: www.mortonmanufacturing.com
SIC: 3965 3769 3452 Fasteners; Space vehicle equipment, nec; Bolts, nuts, rivets, and washers

**(P-15915)**
**PAIHO NORTH AMERICA CORP**
16051 El Prado Rd, Chino (91708-9144)
PHONE..................661 257-6611
Yi Ming Lin, Pr
Shu-ching Hsieh, CFO
▲ EMP: 22 EST: 2003
SQ FT: 52,000
SALES (est): 4.13MM Privately Held
Web: www.paiho-usa.com
SIC: 3965 Fasteners, hooks and eyes

**(P-15916)**
**ROSE LILLA INC**
1050 S Cypress St, La Habra (90631-6862)
PHONE..................888 519-8889
EMP: 29 EST: 2015
SALES (est): 796.15K Privately Held
Web: www.lillarose.com
SIC: 3965 Hairpins, except rubber

**(P-15917)**
**SPS TECHNOLOGIES LLC**
Also Called: Aerospace Fasteners Group
1224 E Warner Ave, Santa Ana (92705-5414)
PHONE..................714 545-9311
Mike Kleene, Brnch Mgr
EMP: 500
SQ FT: 40,000
SALES (corp-wide): 364.48B Publicly Held
Web: www.pccfasteners.com
SIC: 3965 3728 3452 3714 Fasteners; Aircraft parts and equipment, nec; Bolts, nuts, rivets, and washers; Motor vehicle parts and accessories
HQ: Sps Technologies, Llc
301 Highland Ave
Jenkintown PA 19046
215 572-3000

**(P-15918)**
**SPS TECHNOLOGIES LLC**
Cherry Aerospace Div
1224 E Warner Ave, Santa Ana (92705-5414)
PHONE..................714 371-1925
Michael Harhen, Brnch Mgr
EMP: 500
SALES (corp-wide): 364.48B Publicly Held
Web: www.pccfasteners.com
SIC: 3965 3452 Fasteners; Bolts, nuts, rivets, and washers
HQ: Sps Technologies, Llc
301 Highland Ave
Jenkintown PA 19046
215 572-3000

**(P-15919)**
**TOLEETO FASTENER INTERNATIONAL**
1580 Jayken Way, Chula Vista (91911-4644)
PHONE..................619 662-1355
David Deavenport, Pr
Tom V Oss, *
Sara Davenport, *
EMP: 26 EST: 1985
SQ FT: 10,000
SALES (est): 761.4K Privately Held
Web: www.tfifab.com
SIC: 3965 Fasteners

**(P-15920)**
**TOTAL CONCEPT ENTERPRISES INC**
3745 E Jensen Ave, Fresno (93725-1334)
PHONE..................559 485-8413
Liz Limoune, Pr
Carol Jacobs, VP
EMP: 17 EST: 2004
SQ FT: 18,000
SALES (est): 2.02MM Privately Held
Web: www.totalconceptent.com
SIC: 3965 5085 3842 Fasteners; Fasteners and fastening equipment; Abdominal supporters, braces, and trusses

**(P-15921)**
**TWO LADS INC (PA)**
5001 Hampton St, Vernon (90058-2133)
P.O. Box 58572 (90058-0572)
PHONE..................323 584-0064
Lee R Adams, Pr
David Scharf, *
▼ EMP: 30 EST: 1991
SQ FT: 6,300
SALES (est): 2.53MM Privately Held
Web: www.2lads.com
SIC: 3965 5131 2241 Buttons and parts; Buttons; Narrow fabric mills

**(P-15922)**
**WCBM COMPANY (PA)**
Also Called: West Coast Button Mfg Co
1812 W 135th St, Gardena (90249-2520)
PHONE..................323 262-3274
Keith Tanabe, CEO
Grace Kadoya, *
▲ EMP: 32 EST: 1976
SQ FT: 19,000
SALES (est): 471.86K
SALES (corp-wide): 471.86K Privately Held
SIC: 3965 Buttons and parts

**(P-15923)**
**WEST COAST AEROSPACE INC (PA)**
220 W E St, Wilmington (90744-5502)
PHONE..................310 518-3167
Kenneth L Wagner Junior, Pr
Thomas Lieb, *
▲ EMP: 90 EST: 1977
SQ FT: 7,200
SALES (est): 9.77MM
SALES (corp-wide): 9.77MM Privately Held
Web: www.westcoastaerospace.com
SIC: 3965 3452 Fasteners; Bolts, nuts, rivets, and washers

**(P-15924)**
**YKK (USA) INC**
Also Called: Y K K U S A
5001 E La Palma Ave, Anaheim (92807-1926)
PHONE..................714 701-1200
Mike Blunt, Mgr
EMP: 27
Web: www.ykkamericas.com
SIC: 3965 5131 Fasteners; Zippers
HQ: Ykk (U.S.A.) Inc.
1300 Cobb Industrial Dr
Marietta GA 30066
770 427-5521

## 3991 Brooms And Brushes

**(P-15925)**
**AMERICAN ROTARY BROOM CO INC**
688 New York Dr, Pomona (91768-3311)
PHONE..................909 629-9117
Joe Baeskens, Brnch Mgr
EMP: 23
SALES (corp-wide): 2.27MM Privately Held
Web: www.united-rotary.com
SIC: 3991 3711 4959 Brooms; Motor vehicles and car bodies; Sweeping service: road, airport, parking lot, etc.
PA: American Rotary Broom Co., Inc.
181 Pawnee St Ste B
760 591-4025

**(P-15926)**
**BRUSH RESEARCH MFG CO INC**
Also Called: Brm Manufacturing
4642 Floral Dr, Los Angeles (90022-1244)
PHONE..................323 261-2193
Tara L Rands, CEO
Robert Fowlie, *
Grant Fowlie, *
Heather Jones, *
▲ EMP: 130 EST: 1962
SALES (est): 21.15MM Privately Held
Web: www.brushresearch.com
SIC: 3991 Brushes, household or industrial

**(P-15927)**
**BUTLER HOME PRODUCTS LLC**
9409 Buffalo Ave, Rancho Cucamonga (91730-6012)
PHONE..................909 476-3884
Paul Anton, Brnch Mgr
EMP: 176
SALES (corp-wide): 642.04MM Privately Held
Web: www.cleanerhomeliving.com

# 3991 - Brooms And Brushes (P-15928)

SIC: **3991** 2392  Brooms; Mops, floor and dust
HQ: Butler Home Products, Llc
2 Cabot Rd Ste 102
Hudson MA 01749
508 597-8000

### (P-15928)
### EASY REACH SUPPLY  LLC
3737 Capitol Ave, City Of Industry  (90601-1732)
PHONE.................................601 582-7866
**EMP:** 26
**SALES (corp-wide):** 14.37MM **Privately Held**
Web: www.easyreachinc.com
SIC: **3991**  Brooms and brushes
HQ: Easy Reach Supply, Llc
32 Raspberry Ln
Hattiesburg MS 39402
601 582-7866

### (P-15929)
### FOAMPRO MFG  INC
Also Called: Foampro Manufacturing
1781 Langley Ave, Irvine  (92614-5621)
P.O. Box 18888  (92623-8888)
PHONE.................................949 252-0112
Gregory Isaac, *Ch Bd*
Chad Coil, *
▲ **EMP:** 80 **EST:** 1952
**SQ FT:** 25,000
**SALES (est):** 4.7MM **Privately Held**
Web: www.foampromfg.com
SIC: **3991**  Paint rollers

### (P-15930)
### GORDON BRUSH MFG CO  INC (PA)
3737 Capitol Ave, City Of Industry  (90601-1732)
PHONE.................................323 724-7777
**TOLL FREE:** 800
Kenneth L Rakusin, *Pr*
William E Loitz, *
▲ **EMP:** 20 **EST:** 1951
**SQ FT:** 51,600
**SALES (est):** 14.37MM
**SALES (corp-wide):** 14.37MM **Privately Held**
Web: www.gordonbrush.com
SIC: **3991**  Brushes, household or industrial

### (P-15931)
### KINGSOLVER  INC
Also Called: Supreme Enterprise
8417 Secura Way, Santa Fe Springs  (90670-2215)
P.O. Box 3106  (90670-0106)
PHONE.................................562 945-7590
Keith Kingsolver, *Pr*
Christina Kingsolver, *Sec*
▲ **EMP:** 19 **EST:** 1994
**SQ FT:** 22,000
**SALES (est):** 2.4MM **Privately Held**
SIC: **3991** 5199  Brooms; Broom, mop, and paint handles

### (P-15932)
### LAKIM INDUSTRIES INCORPORATED (PA)
Also Called: Quali-Tech Manufacturing
389 Rood Rd, Calexico  (92231-9763)
PHONE.................................310 637-8900
Song B Kim, *CEO*
▲ **EMP:** 20 **EST:** 1974
**SALES (est):** 5.16MM
**SALES (corp-wide):** 5.16MM **Privately Held**
Web: www.quali-tech.com

SIC: **3991**  Paint rollers

### (P-15933)
### WESTCOAST BRUSH MFG  INC
1330 Philadelphia St, Pomona  (91766-5563)
PHONE.................................909 627-7170
Heriberto Guerrero, *Pr*
Concepcion Guerrero, *VP*
▲ **EMP:** 22 **EST:** 1979
**SQ FT:** 20,000
**SALES (est):** 2.27MM **Privately Held**
Web: www.westcoastbrush.com
SIC: **3991**  Brushes, household or industrial

## 3993 Signs And Advertising Specialties

### (P-15934)
### 3S SIGN SERVICES INC
Also Called: P.S. Services
1320 N Red Gum St, Anaheim  (92806-1317)
PHONE.................................714 683-1120
Michael W Schmidt, *CEO*
**EMP:** 25 **EST:** 2018
**SALES (est):** 361.29K **Privately Held**
Web: www.psserv.com
SIC: **3993**  Signs and advertising specialties

### (P-15935)
### A PLUS SIGNS  LLC
4270 N Brawley Ave, Fresno  (93722)
PHONE.................................559 275-0700
Chris Pacheco, *Pr*
Jeff Ashlock, *
**EMP:** 47 **EST:** 1986
**SQ FT:** 12,000
**SALES (est):** 3.8MM **Privately Held**
Web: www.a-plussigns.com
SIC: **3993** 7389 2399  Electric signs; Sign painting and lettering shop; Banners, pennants, and flags

### (P-15936)
### AAHS ENTERPRISES INC
Also Called: Aahs Graphics Signs & Engrv
6600 Telegraph Rd, Commerce  (90040-3210)
PHONE.................................323 838-9130
Gurmeet Sawhney, *CEO*
**EMP:** 16 **EST:** 2005
**SALES (est):** 3.26MM **Privately Held**
Web: www.aahsigns.com
SIC: **3993**  Signs and advertising specialties

### (P-15937)
### AARROW SIGN SPINNERS
4312 Valeta St, San Diego  (92107-1510)
PHONE.................................510 200-7326
**EMP:** 17 **EST:** 2016
**SALES (est):** 729.92K **Privately Held**
Web: www.aarrowsignspinners.com
SIC: **3993**  Signs and advertising specialties

### (P-15938)
### ABSOLUTE SIGN  INC
Also Called: Absolute Sign
10655 Humbolt St, Los Alamitos  (90720-2447)
PHONE.................................562 592-5838
Patricia Scialampo, *Pr*
Gregory Benedict, *VP*
**EMP:** 15 **EST:** 1983
**SALES (est):** 2.35MM **Privately Held**
Web: www.absolutesign.com
SIC: **3993**  Electric signs

### (P-15939)
### ADTI MEDIA  LLC
Also Called: Advanced Digital Tech Intl
1257 Simpson Way, Escondido  (92029-1403)
PHONE.................................951 795-4446
◆ **EMP:** 36 **EST:** 2010
**SALES (est):** 1.71MM **Privately Held**
Web: www.adtimedia.com
SIC: **3993**  Signs and advertising specialties

### (P-15940)
### AINOR SIGNS  INC
5443 Stationers Way, Sacramento  (95842-1900)
PHONE.................................916 348-4370
Joseph Ainor, *Pr*
Catherine Bettencourt, *Sec*
**EMP:** 22 **EST:** 2006
**SQ FT:** 1,500
**SALES (est):** 2.45MM **Privately Held**
Web: www.ainorsigns.com
SIC: **3993**  Signs, not made in custom sign painting shops

### (P-15941)
### AMERICAN FLEET & RET GRAPHICS
Also Called: Amgraph
2091 Del Rio Way, Ontario  (91761-8038)
PHONE.................................909 937-7570
Kristin Stewart, *CEO*
Brian Stewart, *
**EMP:** 37 **EST:** 2006
**SALES (est):** 5.7MM **Privately Held**
Web: www.theamgraphgroup.com
SIC: **3993**  Signs and advertising specialties

### (P-15942)
### ARCHITECTURAL DESIGN SIGNS INC (PA)
Also Called: Ad/S Companies
1160 Railroad St, Corona  (92882-1835)
PHONE.................................951 278-0680
Sean L Solomon, *Pr*
Roberto Soltero Iii, *VP*
**EMP:** 95 **EST:** 1995
**SQ FT:** 630,000
**SALES (est):** 23.4MM **Privately Held**
Web: www.ad-s.com
SIC: **3993**  Signs and advertising specialties

### (P-15943)
### ARROW SIGN CO (PA)
Also Called: Arrow Sign Company
1051 46th Ave, Oakland  (94601)
PHONE.................................209 931-5522
Charles Sterne, *Pr*
**EMP:** 48 **EST:** 1958
**SQ FT:** 119,375
**SALES (est):** 9.52MM
**SALES (corp-wide):** 9.52MM **Privately Held**
Web: www.arrowsigncompany.com
SIC: **3993**  Electric signs

### (P-15944)
### ARROW SIGN CO
3133 N Ad Art Rd, Stockton  (95215-2217)
PHONE.................................209 931-7852
Chuck Sterne, *Brnch Mgr*
**EMP:** 27
**SALES (corp-wide):** 9.52MM **Privately Held**
Web: www.arrowsigncompany.com
SIC: **3993**  Electric signs
PA: Arrow Sign Co.
1051 46th Ave
209 931-5522

### (P-15945)
### ART SIGNWORKS INC
Also Called: Art Signworks
41785 Elm St, Murrieta  (92562)
PHONE.................................951 698-8484
Paul Williamson, *CEO*
Paul Williamson, *Pr*
Cheryl Burnette, *Prin*
Christie Valenzuela, *Prin*
**EMP:** 22 **EST:** 2005
**SQ FT:** 5,000
**SALES (est):** 2.32MM **Privately Held**
Web: www.artsignworks.com
SIC: **3993**  Signs and advertising specialties

### (P-15946)
### ATHLETIC SPORTS LLC
11327 Trade Center Dr Ste 330-335, Rancho Cordova  (95742-6238)
PHONE.................................310 709-3944
Ronnie Moers, *Managing Member*
**EMP:** 42 **EST:** 2020
**SALES (est):** 385.37K **Privately Held**
Web: www.athleticsigns.biz
SIC: **3993**  Signs and advertising specialties

### (P-15947)
### BEELINE GROUP  LLC
30941 San Clemente St, Hayward  (94544-7128)
P.O. Box 757  (64836)
PHONE.................................510 477-5400
Susan Terry, *Pr*
Jonathan Terry, *
**EMP:** 70 **EST:** 2014
**SALES (est):** 1.96MM **Privately Held**
Web: www.beelinegroup.com
SIC: **3993** 2542  Signs and advertising specialties; Fixtures: display, office, or store: except wood

### (P-15948)
### BK SIGNS  INC
1028 W Kirkwall Rd, Azusa  (91702-5126)
PHONE.................................626 334-5600
Brian Scott Kanner, *CEO*
**EMP:** 18 **EST:** 1992
**SQ FT:** 16,000
**SALES (est):** 742.99K **Privately Held**
Web: www.bksigns.com
SIC: **3993** 1731  Signs and advertising specialties; General electrical contractor

### (P-15949)
### BLAZER EXHIBITS & GRAPHICS INC
4227 Technology Dr, Fremont  (94538-6339)
PHONE.................................408 263-7000
David Graham, *CEO*
Loren Ellis, *Pr*
Susan Graham, *Treas*
Vanessa Ellis, *VP*
**EMP:** 15 **EST:** 1983
**SQ FT:** 20,000
**SALES (est):** 1.88MM **Privately Held**
Web: www.blazerexhibits.com
SIC: **3993**  Signs and advertising specialties

### (P-15950)
### BRIGHTSIGN LLC (PA)
983 University Ave Bldg A, Los Gatos  (95032-7637)
P.O. Box 320250  (95032-0104)
PHONE.................................408 852-9263
Jeffrey Hastings, *
▲ **EMP:** 79 **EST:** 2010
**SQ FT:** 19,362
**SALES (est):** 10.66MM **Privately Held**
Web: www.brightsign.biz

## 3993 - Signs And Advertising Specialties (P-15972)

SIC: 3993 Signs and advertising specialties

**(P-15951)**
**CAL-SIGN WHOLESALE INC**
2110 S Anne St, Santa Ana (92704-4409)
PHONE................................209 523-7446
Greg Johnson, *Pr*
Mark Johnson, *VP*
Roger Johnson, *Sec*
**EMP:** 17 **EST:** 1974
**SALES (est):** 593.07K **Privately Held**
Web: www.calsignwholesale.com
SIC: 3993 Electric signs

**(P-15952)**
**CALIFORNIA NEON PRODUCTS**
Also Called: C N P Signs & Graphics
9944 Blossom Valley Rd, El Cajon (92021-2203)
PHONE................................619 283-2191
Peter Mccarter, *CEO*
Robert Mccarter, *VP*
Richard Mccarter, *Sec*
**EMP:** 70 **EST:** 1939
**SALES (est):** 4.07MM **Privately Held**
Web: www.cnpsigns.com
SIC: 3993 1799 Electric signs; Sign installation and maintenance

**(P-15953)**
**CALIFORNIA SIGNS INC**
Also Called: CA Signs
10280 Glenoaks Blvd, Pacoima (91331-1604)
PHONE................................818 899-1888
Matthew Miller, *Pr*
Yvette Miller, *
**EMP:** 35 **EST:** 1962
**SQ FT:** 21,000
**SALES (est):** 4.63MM **Privately Held**
Web: www.casigns.com
SIC: 3993 Signs, not made in custom sign painting shops

**(P-15954)**
**CANZONE AND COMPANY**
Also Called: C & C Signs
661 W Villanova Rd, Ojai (93023-3859)
PHONE................................714 537-8175
Chris Canzone, *Pr*
Jessica Canzone, *VP*
**EMP:** 18 **EST:** 1985
**SALES (est):** 496.24K **Privately Held**
SIC: 3993 Signs, not made in custom sign painting shops

**(P-15955)**
**CELLOTAPE INC (HQ)**
39611 Eureka Dr, Newark (94560-4806)
PHONE................................510 651-5551
**TOLL FREE:** 888
Pete Offermann, *Ch Bd*
Eric Lomas, *
Nick Testanero, *
**EMP:** 102 **EST:** 1949
**SQ FT:** 55,000
**SALES (est):** 24.17MM **Privately Held**
Web: www.resourcelabel.com
SIC: 3993 2675 2672 2759 Signs and advertising specialties; Die-cut paper and board; Paper; coated and laminated, nec; Labels and seals: printing, nsk
PA: Resource Label Group, Llc
2550 Mridian Blvd Ste 370

**(P-15956)**
**CLEGG INDUSTRIES INC**
Also Called: Clegg Promo
19032 S Vermont Ave, Gardena (90248-4412)
PHONE................................310 225-3800
Timothy P Clegg, *CEO*
Kevin Clegg, *
Michael Bistocchi, *
Michael Amar, *
Los Angeles, *
▲ **EMP:** 175 **EST:** 1987
**SQ FT:** 31,000
**SALES (est):** 7.46MM **Privately Held**
SIC: 3993 3648 2542 Advertising novelties; Lighting equipment, nec; Partitions and fixtures, except wood

**(P-15957)**
**COAST SIGN INCORPORATED**
Also Called: Coast Sign Display
1500 W Embassy St, Anaheim (92802-1016)
PHONE................................714 520-9144
Afshan Alemi, *CEO*
S Charlie Alemi, *
Bonnie Metz, *
▲ **EMP:** 250 **EST:** 1964
**SQ FT:** 130,000
**SALES (est):** 27.64MM **Privately Held**
Web: www.coastsign.com
SIC: 3993 Signs, not made in custom sign painting shops

**(P-15958)**
**COASTAL CREATIVE**
13530 Los Coches Rd E, El Cajon (92021-2033)
PHONE................................858 866-6560
**EMP:** 15 **EST:** 2018
**SALES (est):** 511.7K **Privately Held**
Web: www.thecoastcreative.com
SIC: 3993 Signs and advertising specialties

**(P-15959)**
**CORNERSTONE DISPLAY GROUP INC**
Also Called: Cornerstone
28340 Avenue Crocker, Valencia (91355-1238)
PHONE................................661 705-1700
Tom Hester, *Prin*
▲ **EMP:** 45 **EST:** 1995
**SQ FT:** 20,000
**SALES (est):** 9.57MM **Privately Held**
Web: www.cornerstonedisplay.com
SIC: 3993 Advertising artwork

**(P-15960)**
**CORPORATE SIGN SYSTEMS INC**
2464 De La Cruz Blvd, Santa Clara (95050-2923)
PHONE................................408 292-1600
Danny Moran, *CEO*
**EMP:** 20 **EST:** 1961
**SQ FT:** 7,000
**SALES (est):** 4.97MM **Privately Held**
Web: www.corporatesigns.com
SIC: 3993 7389 Signs and advertising specialties; Sign painting and lettering shop

**(P-15961)**
**COWBOY DIRECT RESPONSE**
Also Called: Synergy Direct Response
130 E Alton Ave, Santa Ana (92707-4415)
PHONE................................714 824-3780
Cynthia Rogers, *CEO*
John T Rogers, *
Cynthia Rogers, *Pr*
**EMP:** 35 **EST:** 2004
**SQ FT:** 10,000
**SALES (est):** 4.53MM **Privately Held**
Web: www.synergydr.com

SIC: 3993 8999 2759 Advertising artwork; Advertising copy writing; Promotional printing

**(P-15962)**
**CRAIGO INVESTMENTS INC**
Also Called: Fastsigns
2745 W Shaw Ave Ste 120, Fresno (93711-3315)
PHONE................................559 222-9293
Robert Glenn Craigo, *CEO*
**EMP:** 17 **EST:** 2010
**SALES (est):** 1.98MM **Privately Held**
Web: www.fastsigns.com
SIC: 3993 Signs and advertising specialties

**(P-15963)**
**CUMMINGS RESOURCES LLC**
330 W Citrus St, Colton (92324-1417)
PHONE................................951 248-1130
**EMP:** 39
**SALES (corp-wide):** 691.84MM **Privately Held**
Web: www.cummingssigns.com
SIC: 3993 Signs and advertising specialties
HQ: Cummings Resources Llc
15 Century Blvd Ste 200
Nashville TN 37214

**(P-15964)**
**CUMMINGS RESOURCES LLC**
1495 Columbia Ave, Riverside (92507-2021)
PHONE................................951 248-1130
Jim Mole, *Manager*
**EMP:** 39
**SQ FT:** 50,000
**SALES (corp-wide):** 691.84MM **Privately Held**
Web: www.cummingssigns.com
SIC: 3993 Signs and advertising specialties
HQ: Cummings Resources Llc
15 Century Blvd Ste 200
Nashville TN 37214

**(P-15965)**
**DG-DISPLAYS LLC**
355 Parkside Dr, San Fernando (91340-3036)
PHONE................................877 358-5976
Zachary Blumenfeld, *
**EMP:** 30 **EST:** 2016
**SQ FT:** 25,000
**SALES (est):** 378.76K **Privately Held**
Web: shop.abex.com
SIC: 3993 Signs and advertising specialties

**(P-15966)**
**EDELMANN USA INC (DH)**
Also Called: Bert-Co. of Ontario CA
2150 S Parco Ave, Ontario (91761-5768)
P.O. Box 4150 (91761-1068)
PHONE................................323 669-5700
Constantin Karl Schuetz, *CEO*
**EMP:** 18 **EST:** 2016
**SALES:** 6.56MM
**SALES (corp-wide):** 370.8MM **Privately Held**
Web: www.edelmannusa.com
SIC: 3993 Signs and advertising specialties
HQ: Edelmann Gmbh
Steinheimer Str. 45
Heidenheim An Der Brenz BW 89518
73213400

**(P-15967)**
**ELRO MANUFACTURING COMPANY (PA)**
Also Called: Elro Sign Company
970 W 190th St, Torrance (90502-1000)
PHONE................................310 380-7444
Max R Rhodes, *CEO*
Frank J Rhodes, *VP*
**EMP:** 20 **EST:** 1948
**SALES (est):** 5.25MM
**SALES (corp-wide):** 5.25MM **Privately Held**
Web: www.elrosigns.com
SIC: 3993 Electric signs

**(P-15968)**
**ENCORE IMAGE INC**
303 W Main St, Ontario (91762-3843)
P.O. Box 9297 (91762-9297)
PHONE................................909 986-4632
Terry Wilkins, *CEO*
**EMP:** 27 **EST:** 2006
**SQ FT:** 30,000
**SALES (est):** 4.14MM
**SALES (corp-wide):** 9.86MM **Privately Held**
Web: www.encoreimage.com
SIC: 3993 1799 Electric signs; Sign installation and maintenance
PA: Encore Image Group, Inc.
1445 W Sepulveda Blvd
310 534-7500

**(P-15969)**
**ENCORE IMAGE GROUP INC (PA)**
Also Called: Encore Image
1445 Sepulveda Blvd, Torrance (90501-5004)
PHONE................................310 534-7500
Kozell Boren, *Ch Bd*
Tom Johnson, *
Tommy K Boren, *Prin*
▲ **EMP:** 90 **EST:** 1959
**SQ FT:** 70,000
**SALES (est):** 9.86MM
**SALES (corp-wide):** 9.86MM **Privately Held**
Web: www.encoreimagegroup.com
SIC: 3993 Electric signs

**(P-15970)**
**ENHANCE AMERICA INC**
3463 Grapevine St, Jurupa Valley (91752-3504)
PHONE................................951 361-3000
Jackson Ling, *Pr*
◆ **EMP:** 20 **EST:** 2002
**SALES (est):** 994.27K **Privately Held**
Web: www.enhanceamerica.com
SIC: 3993 Signs and advertising specialties

**(P-15971)**
**ERICSON OWENS ENTERPRISES**
Also Called: Speedpro East Bay
1734 Clement Ave, Alameda (94501-1205)
PHONE................................510 500-5491
Carrie Lee Ericson, *Prin*
**EMP:** 16 **EST:** 2015
**SALES (est):** 850.89K **Privately Held**
Web: www.speedpro.com
SIC: 3993 Signs and advertising specialties

**(P-15972)**
**EVANS MANUFACTURING LLC (HQ)**
Also Called: Evans Manufacturing, Inc.
7422 Chapman Ave, Garden Grove (92841-2106)
P.O. Box 5669 (92846-0669)
PHONE................................714 379-6100
Alan Vaught, *CEO*
▲ **EMP:** 185 **EST:** 1990
**SQ FT:** 17,000
**SALES (est):** 49.63MM

## 3993 - Signs And Advertising Specialties (P-15973)

**SALES (corp-wide):** 94.31MM **Privately Held**
**Web:** www.evans-mfg.com
**SIC:** 3993 3089 Signs and advertising specialties; Injection molding of plastics
**PA:** Hub Pen Company, Llc
1525 Washington St Ste 1
781 535-5500

**(P-15973)**
### EVEO INC
1160 Battery St Ste 275, San Francisco (94111-1247)
**PHONE**....................................415 749-6777
**EMP:** 100
**SIC:** 3993 Advertising artwork

**(P-15974)**
### EXITON INC
Also Called: Loren Electric Sign & Lighting
12226 Coast Dr, Whittier (90601)
**PHONE**....................................562 699-1122
Daniel Marc Lorenzon, *CEO*
Michelle Lornezon, *
**EMP:** 45 **EST:** 1996
**SQ FT:** 8,000
**SALES (est):** 6.78MM **Privately Held**
**Web:** www.lorenindustries.com
**SIC:** 3993 3648 1799 Electric signs; Outdoor lighting equipment; Sign installation and maintenance

**(P-15975)**
### EXPO-3 INTERNATIONAL INC
12350 Edison Way 60, Garden Grove (92841-2810)
**PHONE**....................................714 379-8383
Daniel J Mills, *Ch Bd*
Chris Smith, *Pr*
**EMP:** 21 **EST:** 1974
**SQ FT:** 60,000
**SALES (est):** 871.25K **Privately Held**
**Web:** www.expo3.com
**SIC:** 3993 Displays and cutouts, window and lobby

**(P-15976)**
### FAN FAVE INC
Also Called: Fanfave
10329 Dorset St, Rancho Cucamonga (91730-3067)
**PHONE**....................................909 975-4999
Gary Arnett, *CEO*
Jeff Arnett, *Pr*
**EMP:** 20 **EST:** 2012
**SQ FT:** 17,000
**SALES (est):** 2.49MM **Privately Held**
**Web:** www.fanfave.com
**SIC:** 3993 Advertising artwork

**(P-15977)**
### FEDERAL HEATH SIGN COMPANY LLC
3609 Ocean Ranch Blvd Ste 204, Oceanside (92056-8601)
**PHONE**....................................760 941-0715
Tim O'donald, *Brnch Mgr*
**EMP:** 120
**Web:** www.federalheath.com
**SIC:** 3993 Neon signs
**HQ:** Federal Heath Sign Company, Llc
1845 Prcnct Line Rd Ste 1
Hurst TX 76054

**(P-15978)**
### FEDERAL PRISON INDUSTRIES
Also Called: Unicor
3901 Klein Blvd, Lompoc (93436-2706)
**PHONE**....................................805 735-2771
Steve Southall, *Mgr*
**EMP:** 19
**Web:** www.bop.gov
**SIC:** 3993 2759 3315 2521 Signs and advertising specialties; Commercial printing, nec; Cable, steel: insulated or armored; Wood office furniture
**HQ:** Federal Prison Industries, Inc
320 Frst St N W Fncl Mgt
Washington DC 20534

**(P-15979)**
### FOVELL ENTERPRISES INC
Also Called: Southwest Sign Company
1852 Pomona Rd, Corona (92878-3277)
P.O. Box 6376 (92878-6376)
**PHONE**....................................951 734-6275
Jack Fovell, *CEO*
▲ **EMP:** 26 **EST:** 1991
**SQ FT:** 12,500
**SALES (est):** 2.45MM **Privately Held**
**Web:** www.southwestsign.com
**SIC:** 3993 Electric signs

**(P-15980)**
### FUSION SIGN & DESIGN INC
12226 Coast Dr, Whittier (90601-1607)
**PHONE**....................................562 946-7545
**EMP:** 26
**Web:** www.fusionsign.com
**SIC:** 3993 Electric signs
**PA:** Fusion Sign & Design, Inc.
680 Columbia Ave

**(P-15981)**
### FUSION SIGN & DESIGN INC (PA)
680 Columbia Ave, Riverside (92507)
**PHONE**....................................877 477-8777
Loren Hanson, *CEO*
Dave Haffter, *Prin*
▲ **EMP:** 17 **EST:** 2006
**SALES (est):** 7.43MM **Privately Held**
**Web:** www.fusionsign.com
**SIC:** 3993 Electric signs

**(P-15982)**
### GARNETT SIGNS LLC
Also Called: Garnett Sign Studio
48531 Warm Springs Blvd Ste 412, Fremont (94539-7793)
**PHONE**....................................650 871-9518
Stephen Savoy, *Pr*
**EMP:** 15 **EST:** 1946
**SALES (est):** 1.92MM **Privately Held**
**Web:** www.bestsigns.com
**SIC:** 3993 3479 Signs, not made in custom sign painting shops; Name plates: engraved, etched, etc.

**(P-15983)**
### GEORGE P JOHNSON COMPANY
18500 Crenshaw Blvd, Torrance (90504-5055)
**PHONE**....................................310 965-4300
Chris Meyer, *CEO*
**EMP:** 38
**SALES (corp-wide):** 281.93MM **Privately Held**
**Web:** www.gpj.com
**SIC:** 3993 Signs and advertising specialties
**HQ:** George P. Johnson Company
1914 Taylor Point Rd
Auburn Hills MI 48326
248 475-2500

**(P-15984)**
### GMPC LLC
Also Called: Big Accessories
1670 Corporate Cir Ste 100, Petaluma (94954-6947)
**PHONE**....................................707 766-1702
**EMP:** 27
**SALES (corp-wide):** 21.18MM **Privately Held**
**Web:** www.econscious.net
**SIC:** 3993 7336 Advertising novelties; Commercial art and graphic design
**PA:** Gmpc, Llc
1500 Olympic Blvd
310 392-4070

**(P-15985)**
### GPODISPLAY
7668 Las Positas Rd, Livermore (94551-8203)
**PHONE**....................................510 659-9855
**EMP:** 16 **EST:** 2019
**SALES (est):** 285.88K **Privately Held**
**Web:** www.gpodisplay.com
**SIC:** 3993 Signs and advertising specialties

**(P-15986)**
### ILLUMINATED CREATIONS INC
Also Called: Ellis and Ellis Sign
1111 Joellis Way, Sacramento (95815-3914)
**PHONE**....................................916 924-1936
Bret E Ellis, *CEO*
Sydney Ellis, *
Sharon Ellis, *
Brad Edward Ellis, *
**EMP:** 40 **EST:** 1975
**SQ FT:** 60,000
**SALES (est):** 4.92MM **Privately Held**
**Web:** www.ellissigns.com
**SIC:** 3993 Signs, not made in custom sign painting shops

**(P-15987)**
### INFINITY WATCH CORPORATION
Also Called: Iwcus
21078 Commerce Point Dr, Walnut (91789-3051)
**PHONE**....................................626 289-9878
Patrick Tam, *Pr*
Brenda Tam, *
▲ **EMP:** 25 **EST:** 1990
**SQ FT:** 12,000
**SALES (est):** 792.51K **Privately Held**
**Web:** www.infinitywatch.com
**SIC:** 3993 Signs and advertising specialties

**(P-15988)**
### INFLATABLE DESIGN GROUP INC
Also Called: Idg
1080 W Bradley Ave Ste B, El Cajon (92020-1500)
**PHONE**....................................619 596-6100
Shawn Mceachern, *
▲ **EMP:** 16 **EST:** 1996
**SQ FT:** 32,000
**SALES (est):** 875.86K **Privately Held**
**Web:** www.inflatabledesigngroup.com
**SIC:** 3993 Advertising novelties

**(P-15989)**
### INLAND SIGNS INC
Also Called: Inland Custom Manufacturing
1715 S Bon View Ave, Ontario (91761-4410)
**PHONE**....................................909 923-0006
Nthabeleng Maxwell Monese, *CEO*
**EMP:** 15 **EST:** 2002
**SQ FT:** 15,000
**SALES (est):** 4MM **Privately Held**
**Web:** www.inlandsigns.com
**SIC:** 3993 Electric signs

**(P-15990)**
### INTEGRTED SIGN ASSOC A CAL COR
Also Called: Integrated Sign Associates
1160 Pioneer Way Ste M, El Cajon (92020)
**PHONE**....................................619 579-2229
Aaron Coippinger, *Pr*
**EMP:** 30 **EST:** 1982
**SQ FT:** 15,000
**SALES (est):** 2.57MM **Privately Held**
**Web:** www.isasign.com
**SIC:** 3993 Neon signs

**(P-15991)**
### J S HCKLEY ARCHTCTRAL SGNAGE
1999 Alpine Way, Hayward (94545-1701)
**PHONE**....................................510 940-2608
John Hackley, *Pr*
**EMP:** 20 **EST:** 1981
**SQ FT:** 20,000
**SALES (est):** 424.44K **Privately Held**
**SIC:** 3993 Signs and advertising specialties

**(P-15992)**
### JAR VENTURES INC
Also Called: Sign-A-Rama
4351 Caterpillar Rd, Redding (96003-1423)
**PHONE**....................................530 224-9655
John Robbins, *Pr*
**EMP:** 18 **EST:** 2005
**SALES (est):** 1.07MM **Privately Held**
**Web:** www.signarama.com
**SIC:** 3993 Signs and advertising specialties

**(P-15993)**
### JEFF FRANK
Also Called: Northwest Signs
120 Encinal St, Santa Cruz (95060-2111)
**PHONE**....................................831 469-8208
Jeff Frank, *Owner*
**EMP:** 15 **EST:** 1987
**SQ FT:** 5,000
**SALES (est):** 1.21MM **Privately Held**
**Web:** www.northwestsigns.com
**SIC:** 3993 7349 Signs and advertising specialties; Lighting maintenance service

**(P-15994)**
### JOHN BISHOP DESIGN INC
731 N Main St, Orange (92868-1105)
**PHONE**....................................714 744-2300
John Bishop, *Pr*
Lisa Bishop, *
**EMP:** 38 **EST:** 1989
**SQ FT:** 1,000
**SALES (est):** 3.33MM **Privately Held**
**Web:** www.jb3d.com
**SIC:** 3993 Signs and advertising specialties

**(P-15995)**
### JOHNSON UNITED INC (PA)
Also Called: United Sign Systems
5201 Pentecost Dr, Modesto (95356-9271)
**PHONE**....................................209 543-1320
Darryl Johnson, *CEO*
Mike Noordewier, *
▼ **EMP:** 31 **EST:** 1967
**SQ FT:** 23,000
**SALES (est):** 6.22MM
**SALES (corp-wide):** 6.22MM **Privately Held**
**Web:** www.unitedsign.net
**SIC:** 3993 Signs and advertising specialties

**(P-15996)**
### JONES SIGN CO INC
Also Called: Ultrasigns Electrical Advg

## PRODUCTS & SERVICES SECTION
### 3993 - Signs And Advertising Specialties (P-16018)

9474 Chesapeake Dr Ste 902, San Diego (92123-1027)
PHONE..................................858 569-1400
John Mortensen, *Pr*
EMP: 134
SALES (corp-wide): 63.86MM **Privately Held**
Web: www.jonessign.com
SIC: 3993 Signs and advertising specialties
PA: Jones Sign Co., Inc.
1711 Scheuring Rd
920 983-6700

*(P-15997)*
**JSJ ELECTRICAL DISPLAY CORP**
340 Via Palo Linda, Fairfield (94534-1528)
PHONE..................................707 747-5595
Brian Schneider, *Pr*
Clayton Jensen, *VP*
Jeff Jensen, *Sec*
EMP: 18 EST: 1994
SALES (est): 2.23MM **Privately Held**
SIC: 3993 Neon signs

*(P-15998)*
**JUSTIPHER INC**
Also Called: Fastsigns
1248 W Winton Ave, Hayward (94545-1406)
PHONE..................................510 918-6800
Linda Fong, *Brnch Mgr*
EMP: 15
Web: www.fastsigns.com
SIC: 3993 Signs and advertising specialties
PA: Justipher, Inc.
325 5th St

*(P-15999)*
**K S DESIGNS INC**
Also Called: Cal West Designs
901 S Cypress St, La Habra (90631)
PHONE..................................562 929-3973
Robin Shelton, *Pr*
EMP: 32 EST: 1979
SALES (est): 2.96MM **Privately Held**
SIC: 3993 Displays and cutouts, window and lobby

*(P-16000)*
**LA6721 LLC**
1275 E 6th St, Los Angeles (90021-1209)
PHONE..................................323 484-4070
Maria Endoza, *Pr*
EMP: 15 EST: 2015
SALES (est): 6.92MM **Privately Held**
SIC: 3993 Signs and advertising specialties

*(P-16001)*
**LEOTEK ELECTRONICS USA LLC**
1955 Lundy Ave, San Jose (95131-1848)
PHONE..................................408 380-1788
James C Hwang, *CEO*
Chen-ho Wu, *Pr*
▲ EMP: 23 EST: 1996
SQ FT: 10,000
SALES (est): 14.25MM **Privately Held**
Web: www.leotek.com
SIC: 3993 5046 Electric signs; Signs, electrical
PA: Lite-On Technology Corporation
No. 392, Ruiguang Rd.,

*(P-16002)*
**MANERI SIGN CO INC**
2722 S Fairview St, Santa Ana (92704-5947)
PHONE..................................310 327-6261

Don Nicholas, *Pr*
EMP: 35 EST: 1980
SALES (est): 3.25MM
SALES (corp-wide): 48.27MM **Privately Held**
Web: www.statewidess.com
SIC: 3993 Signs and advertising specialties
PA: Traffic Solutions Corporation
4244 Mount Pleasant St Nw
949 553-8272

*(P-16003)*
**MARKETSHARE INC (PA)**
2001 Tarob Ct, Milpitas (95035-6825)
PHONE..................................408 262-0677
Frederick Wilhelm, *CEO*
John Lovell, *
EMP: 65 EST: 1987
SQ FT: 16,000
SALES (est): 10MM **Privately Held**
Web: www.marketshareonline.com
SIC: 3993 7312 Electric signs; Billboard advertising

*(P-16004)*
**MARTINELLI ENVMTL GRAPHICS**
1829 Egbert Ave, San Francisco (94124-2519)
PHONE..................................415 468-4000
Jack Martinelli, *Pr*
Patty Martinelli, *Sec*
EMP: 15 EST: 1988
SQ FT: 8,000
SALES (est): 3.64MM **Privately Held**
Web: www.martinelli-graphics.com
SIC: 3993 Electric signs

*(P-16005)*
**MAXWELL ALARM SCREEN MFG INC**
Also Called: Maxwell Sign and Decal Div
20327 Nordhoff St, Chatsworth (91311-6128)
PHONE..................................818 773-5533
Michael A Kagen, *CEO*
Patty Kagen, *
EMP: 28 EST: 1977
SQ FT: 28,000
SALES (est): 3.58MM **Privately Held**
Web: www.maxwellmfg.com
SIC: 3993 3442 Signs and advertising specialties; Screens, window, metal

*(P-16006)*
**MEDIA NATION ENTERPRISES LLC**
Also Called: Media Nation
25361 Commercentre Dr Ste 100, Lake Forest (92630-8822)
PHONE..................................714 371-9494
Navin Narang, *Brnch Mgr*
EMP: 21
SALES (corp-wide): 968.46K **Privately Held**
Web: www.medianationoutdoor.com
SIC: 3993 Signs and advertising specialties
PA: Media Nation Enterprises, Llc
15271 Barranca Pkwy
888 502-8222

*(P-16007)*
**MEDIA NATION ENTERPRISES LLC (PA)**
Also Called: Media Nation USA
15271 Barranca Pkwy, Irvine (92618-2201)
PHONE..................................888 502-8222
Navin D Narang, *Managing Member*
EMP: 24 EST: 2009
SALES (est): 968.46K

SALES (corp-wide): 968.46K **Privately Held**
Web: www.medianationoutdoor.com
SIC: 3993 5699 7371 Signs and advertising specialties; Customized clothing and apparel; Software programming applications

*(P-16008)*
**METAL ART OF CALIFORNIA INC (PA)**
Also Called: Sign Mart
640 N Cypress St, Orange (92867-6604)
PHONE..................................714 532-7100
Gene S Sobel, *Pr*
Calvin Larson, *
◆ EMP: 91 EST: 1974
SQ FT: 22,000
SALES (est): 19.07MM
SALES (corp-wide): 19.07MM **Privately Held**
Web: www.sign-mart.com
SIC: 3993 Signs and advertising specialties

*(P-16009)*
**MINA-TREE SIGNS INCORPORATED (PA)**
1233 E Ronald St, Stockton (95205-3331)
P.O. Box 8406 (95208-0406)
PHONE..................................209 941-2921
Harold Leroy Minatre, *Pr*
EMP: 22 EST: 1967
SALES (est): 2.34MM
SALES (corp-wide): 2.34MM **Privately Held**
Web: www.mina-treesigns.com
SIC: 3993 Electric signs

*(P-16010)*
**MMXVIII HOLDINGS INC**
20251 Sw Acacia St Ste 120, Newport Beach (92660-0768)
PHONE..................................800 672-3974
EMP: 24 EST: 2016
SQ FT: 7,500
SALES (est): 984.42K **Privately Held**
SIC: 3993 Signs and advertising specialties

*(P-16011)*
**MONARCH CORPORATION**
Also Called: The Sign Man
726 W Angus Ave Ste H, Orange (92868-1300)
PHONE..................................714 744-5098
Walter James Nelson Junior, *Pr*
Susan Nelson, *VP*
EMP: 16 EST: 1982
SQ FT: 5,000
SALES (est): 269.23K **Privately Held**
SIC: 3993 7812 Signs and advertising specialties; Motion picture and video production

*(P-16012)*
**MYERS & SONS HI-WAY SAFETY INC (PA)**
Also Called: Hi-Way Safety
13310 5th St, Chino (91710-5125)
P.O. Box 1030 (91708-1030)
PHONE..................................909 591-1781
TOLL FREE: 800
Michael Rodgers, *CEO*
Brandon Myer, *
▲ EMP: 80 EST: 1970
SQ FT: 36,400
SALES (est): 27.34MM
SALES (corp-wide): 27.34MM **Privately Held**
SIC: 3993 Signs, not made in custom sign painting shops

*(P-16013)*
**NATIONAL SIGN & MARKETING CORP**
Also Called: Visual Information Systems Co
13580 5th St, Chino (91710-5113)
P.O. Box 2409 (91710)
PHONE..................................909 591-4742
John J Kane, *Pr*
Jeffrey Fredrickson, *
EMP: 70 EST: 1997
SQ FT: 46,000
SALES (est): 9.42MM **Privately Held**
Web: www.nsmc.com
SIC: 3993 Neon signs

*(P-16014)*
**NEIMAN/HOELLER INC**
Also Called: Neiman & Company
6842 Valjean Ave, Van Nuys (91406-4712)
PHONE..................................818 781-8600
Harry J Neiman, *CEO*
Robert R Hoeller Iii, *Pr*
EMP: 56 EST: 1965
SQ FT: 17,000
SALES (est): 6.06MM **Privately Held**
Web: www.neimanandco.com
SIC: 3993 3646 Electric signs; Ornamental lighting fixtures, commercial

*(P-16015)*
**OPTEC DISPLAYS INC**
1700 S De Soto Pl Ste A, Ontario (91761-8060)
PHONE..................................866 924-5239
Jerry Luan, *CEO*
Shu-hwa Wu, *Sec*
◆ EMP: 64 EST: 1996
SALES (est): 21.51MM **Privately Held**
Web: www.optec.com
SIC: 3993 Signs and advertising specialties

*(P-16016)*
**ORANGE CNTY NAME PLATE CO INC**
13201 Arctic Cir, Santa Fe Springs (90670-5572)
P.O. Box 2764 (90670-0764)
PHONE..................................714 522-7693
Elias Rodriguez, *Pr*
Ben L Rodriguez, *
Sam Rodriguez, *
EMP: 85 EST: 1965
SQ FT: 31,000
SALES (est): 3.95MM **Privately Held**
Web: www.ocnameplates.com
SIC: 3993 Name plates: except engraved, etched, etc.: metal

*(P-16017)*
**OUTFORM GROUP INC**
1320 Performance Dr, Stockton (95206-4925)
PHONE..................................510 487-1122
Bruce Watson, *Pr*
EMP: 17
SALES (corp-wide): 77.61MM **Privately Held**
Web: www.cadaco.com
SIC: 3993 Displays and cutouts, window and lobby
PA: Outform Group, Inc.
4300 W 47th St
773 927-5000

*(P-16018)*
**PACIFIC NEON**
2939 Academy Way, Sacramento (95815-1802)
P.O. Box 15100 (95851-0100)

## 3993 - Signs And Advertising Specialties (P-16019)

PHONE..................................916 927-0527
Oleta Lambert, Ch Bd
John Drury, *
**EMP:** 40 **EST:** 1946
**SQ FT:** 65,000
**SALES (est):** 6.27MM **Privately Held**
**Web:** www.pacificneon.com
**SIC: 3993** 1799 7359 Electric signs; Sign installation and maintenance; Sign rental

### (P-16019)
**PARKOWORLD INC**
10314 Norris Ave Ste B, Pacoima (91331-2244)
PHONE..................................818 686-6900
Feredi Masihi, Pr
**EMP:** 15 **EST:** 2016
**SALES (est):** 1.96MM **Privately Held**
**Web:** www.parkoworld.com
**SIC: 3993** Signs and advertising specialties

### (P-16020)
**PD GROUP**
Also Called: Sign-A-Rama
41945 Boardwalk Ste L, Palm Desert (92211-9099)
PHONE..................................760 674-3028
Jeff Gracy, Pr
Terrance Flannagan, *
**EMP:** 22 **EST:** 1995
**SQ FT:** 11,500
**SALES (est):** 2.95MM **Privately Held**
**Web:** www.pdsignarama.com
**SIC: 3993** 7389 5999 Signs and advertising specialties; Sign painting and lettering shop ; Banners

### (P-16021)
**PRIMUS INC**
Also Called: Western Highway Products
17901 Jamestown Ln, Huntington Beach (92647-7138)
P.O. Box 534 (92648-0534)
PHONE..................................714 527-2261
Steve Ellsworth, Pr
Timothy M Riordan, *
▲ **EMP:** 80 **EST:** 1926
**SQ FT:** 120,000
**SALES (est):** 1.78MM **Privately Held**
**Web:** www.primus.us
**SIC: 3993** Signs, not made in custom sign painting shops

### (P-16022)
**PRIORITY ARCHTCTRAL GRPHICS IN**
Also Called: Sommer, Juliana Choy
1260 Egbert Ave, San Francisco (94124-3637)
PHONE..................................415 850-9836
Juliana Choy, Pr
**EMP:** 45 **EST:** 1995
**SQ FT:** 5,000
**SALES (est):** 7.27MM **Privately Held**
**Web:** www.prioritygraphics.com
**SIC: 3993** Signs and advertising specialties

### (P-16023)
**PRO-LITE INC**
Also Called: Advanced Products
3505 Cadillac Ave Ste D, Costa Mesa (92626-1464)
PHONE..................................714 668-9988
Kuo-fong Kaoh, Pr
◆ **EMP:** 17 **EST:** 1986
**SQ FT:** 7,200
**SALES (est):** 2.33MM **Privately Held**
**Web:** www.pro-lite.com
**SIC: 3993** Signs and advertising specialties

### (P-16024)
**QUIEL BROS ELC SIGN SVC CO INC**
272 S I St, San Bernardino (92410-2408)
PHONE..................................909 885-4476
Larry R Quiel, Pr
Raymond Quiel, *
Jerry Quiel, *
Gary Quiel, *
▲ **EMP:** 40 **EST:** 1962
**SQ FT:** 8,000
**SALES (est):** 470.21K **Privately Held**
**Web:** www.quielsigns.com
**SIC: 3993** 7353 1731 7629 Electric signs; Cranes and aerial lift equipment, rental or leasing; General electrical contractor; Electrical equipment repair, high voltage

### (P-16025)
**R&M DEESE INC**
Also Called: Electro-Tech's
1875 Sampson Ave, Corona (92879-6009)
P.O. Box 2317 (92878-2317)
PHONE..................................951 734-7342
Raymond Deese, Pr
Mary Deese, Sec
▲ **EMP:** 22 **EST:** 1976
**SQ FT:** 20,000
**SALES (est):** 5.29MM **Privately Held**
**Web:** www.electro-techs.net
**SIC: 3993** 3679 Signs and advertising specialties; Liquid crystal displays (LCD)

### (P-16026)
**RICHARDS NEON SHOP INC**
Also Called: RNS Channel Letters
4375 Prado Rd Ste 102, Corona (92878-7444)
PHONE..................................951 279-6767
Richard Pando, Pr
**EMP:** 24 **EST:** 1991
**SALES (est):** 2.35MM **Privately Held**
**Web:** www.rnsletters.com
**SIC: 3993** Electric signs

### (P-16027)
**ROSS NAME PLATE COMPANY**
2 Red Plum Cir, Monterey Park (91755-7486)
PHONE..................................323 725-6812
Michael Ross, Pr
**EMP:** 37 **EST:** 1957
**SQ FT:** 25,000
**SALES (est):** 3.43MM **Privately Held**
**Web:** www.rossnameplate.com
**SIC: 3993** 2754 Name plates: except engraved, etched, etc.: metal; Labels: gravure printing

### (P-16028)
**S2K GRAPHICS INC**
Also Called: S 2 K
4686 Industrial St, Simi Valley (93063-3413)
PHONE..................................818 885-3900
Dan C Pulos, CEO
Jack Wilson, Ch Bd
Dana Rosellini, Sec
**EMP:** 35 **EST:** 1989
**SALES (est):** 3.3MM **Privately Held**
**Web:** www.s2kgraphics.com
**SIC: 3993** 7532 2759 Signs and advertising specialties; Truck painting and lettering; Screen printing
**HQ:** Franke Usa Holding, Inc.
800 Aviation Pkwy
Smyrna TN 37167

### (P-16029)
**SAFEWAY SIGN COMPANY**
9875 Yucca Rd, Adelanto (92301-2282)
PHONE..................................760 246-7070
Michael F Moore, Pr
David C Moore, *
Andrea M Gutierrez, *
**EMP:** 49 **EST:** 1948
**SQ FT:** 60,000
**SALES (est):** 6.04MM **Privately Held**
**Web:** www.safewaysign.com
**SIC: 3993** Signs, not made in custom sign painting shops

### (P-16030)
**SAN DIEGO ELECTRIC SIGN INC**
Also Called: SD Electric Sign
1890 Cordell Ct Ste 105, El Cajon (92020-0913)
P.O. Box 103 (91908-0103)
PHONE..................................619 258-1775
Greg Ballard, Pr
Jayne Ballard, VP
Lelsie Crosby, Sec
**EMP:** 17 **EST:** 2001
**SALES (est):** 4.35MM **Privately Held**
**Web:** www.sdelectricsign.com
**SIC: 3993** Electric signs

### (P-16031)
**SANTA CLARITA SIGNS**
26330 Diamond Pl, Santa Clarita (91350-5820)
PHONE..................................661 291-1188
**EMP:** 23 **EST:** 2009
**SALES (est):** 302.69K **Privately Held**
**Web:** www.signalscv.com
**SIC: 3993** Signs and advertising specialties

### (P-16032)
**SCHEA HOLDINGS INC**
Also Called: Signgroup/Karman
9812 Independence Ave, Chatsworth (91311-4319)
PHONE..................................818 998-3636
Michael Schackne, Pr
Kathy Schackne, VP
**EMP:** 22 **EST:** 1993
**SQ FT:** 10,000
**SALES (est):** 2.28MM **Privately Held**
**Web:** www.sgksigns.net
**SIC: 3993** Electric signs

### (P-16033)
**SCOTT AG LLC**
1275 N Dutton Ave, Santa Rosa (95401-4663)
PHONE..................................707 545-4519
Jimmy D Burch, Prin
**EMP:** 22 **EST:** 2011
**SALES (est):** 4.25MM **Privately Held**
**Web:** www.scottag.com
**SIC: 3993** Signs and advertising specialties

### (P-16034)
**SHYE WEST INC (PA)**
Also Called: Imagine This
43 Corporate Park Ste 102, Irvine (92606)
PHONE..................................949 486-4598
Patrick Papaccio, Pr
Shawn Keep, *
▲ **EMP:** 27 **EST:** 1999
**SQ FT:** 6,000
**SALES (est):** 2.32MM
**SALES (corp-wide):** 2.32MM **Privately Held**
**Web:** www.imaginethis.com
**SIC: 3993** 5099 Advertising novelties; Novelties, durable

### (P-16035)
**SIGN DESIGNS INC**
Also Called: Macdonald Screen Print
204 Campus Way, Modesto (95350-5845)
P.O. Box 4590 (95352-4590)
PHONE..................................209 524-4484
David Johnston, Pr
Doug Smith, *
Pete Michelini, *
**EMP:** 44 **EST:** 1971
**SQ FT:** 35,000
**SALES (est):** 4.62MM **Privately Held**
**Web:** www.signdesigns.com
**SIC: 3993** Electric signs

### (P-16036)
**SIGN INDUSTRIES INC**
2101 Carrillo Privado, Ontario (91761-7600)
PHONE..................................909 930-0303
Maria Saavedra, Pr
Enrique Saavedra, *
▲ **EMP:** 30 **EST:** 1994
**SQ FT:** 4,500
**SALES (est):** 6.46MM **Privately Held**
**Web:** www.signindustries.tv
**SIC: 3993** Neon signs

### (P-16037)
**SIGN SPECIALISTS CORPORATION**
111 W Dyer Rd Ste F, Santa Ana (92707-3425)
PHONE..................................714 641-0064
Garrick Batt, CEO
**EMP:** 22 **EST:** 2001
**SALES (est):** 8.02MM **Privately Held**
**Web:** www.signspecialists.com
**SIC: 3993** Signs, not made in custom sign painting shops

### (P-16038)
**SIGN TECHNOLOGY INC**
Also Called: Signtech
1700 Enterprise Blvd Ste F, West Sacramento (95691-3474)
PHONE..................................916 372-1200
Michael Wilmer, CEO
**EMP:** 30 **EST:** 1979
**SQ FT:** 11,660
**SALES (est):** 4.39MM **Privately Held**
**Web:** www.signtechnology.com
**SIC: 3993** Signs, not made in custom sign painting shops

### (P-16039)
**SIGNAGE SOLUTIONS CORPORATION**
2231 S Dupont Dr, Anaheim (92806-6105)
PHONE..................................714 491-0299
Chris Deruyter, CEO
Jim Gledhill, *
**EMP:** 30 **EST:** 1990
**SQ FT:** 14,000
**SALES (est):** 4.2MM **Privately Held**
**Web:** www.signage-solutions.com
**SIC: 3993** 7389 Signs and advertising specialties; Sign painting and lettering shop

### (P-16040)
**SIGNRESOURCE LLC**
6135 District Blvd, Maywood (90270-3449)
PHONE..................................323 771-2098
**EMP:** 162
**Web:** www.signresource.com
**SIC: 3993** Signs and advertising specialties
**HQ:** Signresource, Llc
242 Industrial Pkwy
Jacksboro TN 37757
323 771-2098

## 3993 - Signs And Advertising Specialties (P-16061)

**(P-16041)**
**SIGNS AND SERVICES COMPANY**
10980 Boatman Ave, Stanton (90680-2602)
PHONE.................................714 761-8200
Jacob Deryuyter, *CEO*
Matt De Ruyter, *
**EMP:** 33 **EST:** 1986
**SQ FT:** 16,000
**SALES (est):** 4.61MM **Privately Held**
**Web:** www.signsandservicesco.com
**SIC: 3993** Signs, not made in custom sign painting shops

**(P-16042)**
**SIGNTECH ELECTRICAL ADVG INC**
Also Called: Signtech
4444 Federal Blvd, San Diego (92102-2505)
PHONE.................................619 527-6100
Harold E Schauer Junior, *CEO*
David E Schauer, *
Kimra Schauer, *
Art Navarro, *
Patty Soria, *
**EMP:** 120 **EST:** 1984
**SQ FT:** 25,000
**SALES (est):** 19.82MM **Privately Held**
**Web:** www.signtech.com
**SIC: 3993** 1799 Electric signs; Sign installation and maintenance

**(P-16043)**
**SIGNTRONIX INC**
Also Called: Gulf Development
1445 Sepulveda Blvd, Torrance (90501-5004)
PHONE.................................310 534-7500
▲ **EMP:** 100
**Web:** www.signtronix.com
**SIC: 3993** Signs and advertising specialties

**(P-16044)**
**SIMPLY DISPLAY**
12200 Los Nietos Rd, Santa Fe Springs (90670-2910)
P.O. Box 3691 (90274-9520)
PHONE.................................888 767-0676
Megan Barrett, *CEO*
▲ **EMP:** 24 **EST:** 2013
**SALES (est):** 766.51K **Privately Held**
**Web:** www.simplydisplays.com
**SIC: 3993** Signs and advertising specialties

**(P-16045)**
**STANDARDVISION LLC**
3370 N San Fernando Rd Ste 206, Los Angeles (90065-1437)
PHONE.................................323 222-3630
Alberto Garcia, *Prin*
Kevin Bartanian, *Prin*
Hs Moon, *Prin*
▲ **EMP:** 34 **EST:** 2007
**SQ FT:** 25,000
**SALES (est):** 11.09MM **Privately Held**
**Web:** www.standardvision.com
**SIC: 3993** 7336 Signs and advertising specialties; Commercial art and graphic design

**(P-16046)**
**STANFORD SIGN & AWNING INC (PA)**
2556 Faivre St, Chula Vista (91911-4604)
PHONE.................................619 423-6200
David Lesage, *Pr*
**EMP:** 50 **EST:** 1974
**SQ FT:** 35,000
**SALES (est):** 4.87MM
**SALES (corp-wide):** 4.87MM **Privately Held**
**Web:** www.stanfordsign.com
**SIC: 3993** 2394 Electric signs; Canvas awnings and canopies

**(P-16047)**
**STATEWIDE TRFFIC SFETY SGNS IN**
3049 S Golden State Frontage Rd, Fresno (93725-2312)
PHONE.................................559 291-8500
Aaron Blankenship, *Brnch Mgr*
**EMP:** 26
**SALES (corp-wide):** 539.72MM **Privately Held**
**Web:** www.statewidess.com
**SIC: 3993** Signs and advertising specialties
**HQ:** Statewide Traffic Safety And Signs, Inc.
2722 S Fairview St Fl 2
Santa Ana CA 92704
949 553-8272

**(P-16048)**
**STATEWIDE TRFFIC SFETY SGNS IN**
2722 S Fairview St, Santa Ana (92704-5947)
PHONE.................................714 468-1919
Don Nicholas, *Owner*
**EMP:** 26
**SALES (corp-wide):** 539.72MM **Privately Held**
**Web:** www.statewidess.com
**SIC: 3993** Signs and advertising specialties
**HQ:** Statewide Traffic Safety And Signs, Inc.
2722 S Fairview St Fl 2
Santa Ana CA 92704
949 553-8272

**(P-16049)**
**STATEWIDE TRFFIC SFETY SGNS IN**
6479 Eastside Rd, Redding (96001-5060)
PHONE.................................530 222-8023
Scott Lantum, *Brnch Mgr*
**EMP:** 26
**SALES (corp-wide):** 539.72MM **Privately Held**
**Web:** www.statewidess.com
**SIC: 3993** Signs and advertising specialties
**HQ:** Statewide Traffic Safety And Signs, Inc.
2722 S Fairview St Fl 2
Santa Ana CA 92704
949 553-8272

**(P-16050)**
**STATEWIDE TRFFIC SFETY SGNS IN**
40 S G St, Arcata (95521-6654)
PHONE.................................707 825-6927
**EMP:** 26
**SALES (corp-wide):** 539.72MM **Privately Held**
**Web:** www.statewidess.com
**SIC: 3993** Signs and advertising specialties
**HQ:** Statewide Traffic Safety And Signs, Inc.
2722 S Fairview St Fl 2
Santa Ana CA 92704
949 553-8272

**(P-16051)**
**STATEWIDE TRFFIC SFETY SGNS IN**
1100 Main St Ste 100, Irvine (92614-6737)
P.O. Box 5299 (92616-5299)
PHONE.................................949 553-8272
**EMP:** 26
**SALES (corp-wide):** 539.72MM **Privately Held**
**Web:** www.statewidess.com
**SIC: 3993** Signs and advertising specialties
**HQ:** Statewide Traffic Safety And Signs, Inc.
2722 S Fairview St Fl 2
Santa Ana CA 92704
949 553-8272

**(P-16052)**
**STOP-LOOK SIGN CO INTL INC**
Also Called: Stop Look Plastics Inc
401 Commercial Way, La Habra (90631-6168)
PHONE.................................562 690-7576
Larry Dobkin, *Pr*
Christine Dougherty, *VP*
Janet Dobkin, *Sec*
Mike Dougherty, *Treas*
▲ **EMP:** 15 **EST:** 1960
**SQ FT:** 8,000
**SALES (est):** 714.62K **Privately Held**
**SIC: 3993** Signs and advertising specialties

**(P-16053)**
**SUNSET SIGNS AND PRINTING INC**
Also Called: Contractor
2906 E Coronado St, Anaheim (92806-2501)
PHONE.................................714 255-9104
Tracy Eschenbrenner, *CEO*
**EMP:** 50 **EST:** 1992
**SALES (est):** 9.44MM **Privately Held**
**Web:** www.sunsetsignsoc.com
**SIC: 3993** Signs and advertising specialties

**(P-16054)**
**SUPERIOR SIGNS & INSTALLATION (PA)**
1700 W Anaheim St, Long Beach (90813)
PHONE.................................562 495-3808
Jim Sterk, *CEO*
Patti Skoglundadams, *
Doug Tokeshi, *
Stan Janocha, *
▲ **EMP:** 85 **EST:** 1962
**SQ FT:** 100,000
**SALES (est):** 24.66MM
**SALES (corp-wide):** 24.66MM **Privately Held**
**Web:** www.superiorsigns.com
**SIC: 3993** 7629 Electric signs; Electrical equipment repair services

**(P-16055)**
**SUPERSONIC ADS INC**
Also Called: Ironsource
17 Bluxome St, San Francisco (94107-1605)
PHONE.................................650 825-6010
Gil Shoham, *CEO*
**EMP:** 44 **EST:** 2011
**SALES (est):** 4.4MM **Privately Held**
**Web:** www.supersonic.com
**SIC: 3993** Advertising artwork

**(P-16056)**
**TDI SIGNS**
13158 Arctic Cir, Santa Fe Springs (90670-5508)
PHONE.................................562 436-5188
Arthur Rivas, *Pr*
**EMP:** 25 **EST:** 2003
**SALES (est):** 5.21MM **Privately Held**
**Web:** www.tdisigns.com
**SIC: 3993** Electric signs

**(P-16057)**
**TFN ARCHITECTURAL SIGNAGE INC (PA)**
Also Called: Third Floor North Company
527 Fee Ana St, Placentia (92870-6702)
PHONE.................................714 556-0990
Brian L Burnett, *Pr*
Ellen Vaughn, *
Teresa Burnett, *
Catherine Burnett, *Stockholder**
Jeff Burnett, *Stockholder**
**EMP:** 44 **EST:** 1980
**SALES (est):** 4.28MM
**SALES (corp-wide):** 4.28MM **Privately Held**
**Web:** www.thirdfloornorth.com
**SIC: 3993** Signs, not made in custom sign painting shops

**(P-16058)**
**THOMAS-SWAN SIGN COMPANY INC**
2717 Goodrick Ave, Richmond (94801-1109)
PHONE.................................415 621-1511
Allen E Thomas, *CEO*
Michael Roberts, *
Stacy Roberts, *
Donna Thomas, *
**EMP:** 35 **EST:** 1877
**SQ FT:** 40,000
**SALES (est):** 4.53MM **Privately Held**
**Web:** www.thomasswan.com
**SIC: 3993** Electric signs

**(P-16059)**
**TRADENET ENTERPRISE INC**
Also Called: Vantage Led
1580 Magnolia Ave, Corona (92879-2073)
PHONE.................................888 595-3956
Chris Ma, *CEO*
▲ **EMP:** 60 **EST:** 1997
**SALES (est):** 9.89MM **Privately Held**
**Web:** www.vantageled.com
**SIC: 3993** Electric signs

**(P-16060)**
**TRAFFIC CONTROL & SAFETY CORP**
13755 Blaisdell Pl, Poway (92064-6837)
PHONE.................................858 679-7292
David Nicholas, *Brnch Mgr*
**EMP:** 45
**Web:** www.statewidess.com
**SIC: 3993** 5088 7359 5082 Signs, not made in custom sign painting shops; Transportation equipment and supplies; Work zone traffic equipment (flags, cones, barrels, etc.); Contractor's materials
**PA:** Traffic Control And Safety Corporation
1100 Main St

**(P-16061)**
**UNIVERSAL CUSTOM DISPLAY**
Also Called: Universal Custom Design
9104 Elkmont Dr Ste 100, Elk Grove (95624-9724)
PHONE.................................916 714-2505
Daniel Hayes, *CEO*
Don Almeda, *
Charles Dickenson, *
Jeanne Hayes, *
▲ **EMP:** 175 **EST:** 1999
**SQ FT:** 120,000
**SALES (est):** 25.69MM **Privately Held**
**Web:** www.unicusdis.com
**SIC: 3993** 2541 Signs and advertising specialties; Display fixtures, wood

## 3993 - Signs And Advertising Specialties (P-16062)

**(P-16062)**
**VALLEY ENERPRISES INC**
18600 Van Buren Blvd, Riverside (92508-9111)
PHONE..................951 789-0843
EMP: 25 EST: 2011
SALES (est): 127.59K Privately Held
Web: www.vesigns.com
SIC: 3993 Signs and advertising specialties

**(P-16063)**
**VISIBLE GRAPHICS INC**
9736 Eton Ave, Chatsworth (91311-4305)
PHONE..................818 787-0477
Janine Kendall, CEO
Ken Kendall, CFO
EMP: 16 EST: 2002
SALES (est): 2.58MM Privately Held
Web: www.visiblegraphics.com
SIC: 3993 Signs and advertising specialties

**(P-16064)**
**VOMELA SPECIALTY COMPANY**
Corporate Identity Systems
1342 San Mateo Ave, South San Francisco (94080-6501)
PHONE..................650 877-8000
Robert Pietila, Brnch Mgr
EMP: 60
SALES (corp-wide): 258.06MM Privately Held
Web: www.vomela.com
SIC: 3993 2759 Signs and advertising specialties; Screen printing
PA: Vomela Specialty Company
845 Minnehaha Ave E
651 228-2200

**(P-16065)**
**WEIDNER ARCHTCTRAL SGNG/ HUSE S**
Also Called: Weidnerca
5001 24th St, Sacramento (95822-2201)
PHONE..................800 561-7446
Mark Douglas Copeland, Ch Bd
Mark Douglas Copeland, CEO
Edwin F Rick Weidner Iii, Pr
Kathy Weidner, *
Arie Korver, *
EMP: 58 EST: 1955
SQ FT: 20,450
SALES (est): 11.62MM Privately Held
Web: www.weidnerca.com
SIC: 3993 2759 7389 Signs and advertising specialties; Screen printing; Sign painting and lettering shop

**(P-16066)**
**WESTERN ELECTRICAL ADVG CO**
Also Called: Southwest Sign Systems
853 S Dogwood Rd, El Centro (92243-4606)
P.O. Box 587 (92244-0587)
PHONE..................760 352-0471
Dennis Berg, Pr
Vernon I Berg, *
Glenna L Berg, *
EMP: 25 EST: 1947
SALES (est): 635.31K Privately Held
SIC: 3993 1731 Electric signs; General electrical contractor

**(P-16067)**
**WESTERN SIGN COMPANY INC**
6221a Enterprise Dr Ste A, Diamond Springs (95619-9398)
PHONE..................916 933-3765
David Brazelton, Pr
Keith Wills, VP Sls
Todd Johnston, Product Vice President
Cindy Brazelton, Sec
EMP: 20 EST: 1959
SQ FT: 12,000
SALES (est): 4.98MM Privately Held
Web: www.westernsign.com
SIC: 3993 1799 Electric signs; Sign installation and maintenance

**(P-16068)**
**WESTERN SIGN SYSTEMS INC**
Also Called: Western Sign Systems
261 S Pacific St, San Marcos (92078-2429)
PHONE..................760 736-6070
David Lesage, Pr
EMP: 25 EST: 1993
SQ FT: 6,000
SALES (est): 2.21MM Privately Held
Web: www.western-sign.com
SIC: 3993 Signs and advertising specialties

**(P-16069)**
**WOLFPACK INC**
Also Called: Wolfpack Sign Group
2440 Grand Ave Ste B, Vista (92081-7829)
P.O. Box 3620 (92085-3620)
PHONE..................760 736-4500
Carolyn Wolf, CEO
Ryan Meyer, VP
Peter Wolf, Sec
EMP: 24 EST: 1995
SQ FT: 15,000
SALES (est): 2.86MM Privately Held
Web: www.wolfpackllc.com
SIC: 3993 Signs, not made in custom sign painting shops

**(P-16070)**
**YOUNG ELECTRIC SIGN COMPANY**
Also Called: Yesco
46750 Fremont Blvd Ste 101, Fremont (94538-6573)
PHONE..................510 877-7815
Kip Kitto, Brnch Mgr
EMP: 24
SALES (corp-wide): 498.12MM Privately Held
Web: www.yesco.com
SIC: 3993 Signs and advertising specialties
PA: Young Electric Sign Company Inc
2401 Foothill Dr
801 464-4600

**(P-16071)**
**YOUNG ELECTRIC SIGN COMPANY**
Also Called: Yesco
875 National Dr Ste 107, Sacramento (95834-1162)
PHONE..................916 419-8101
Rachel Williamson, Brnch Mgr
EMP: 38
SALES (corp-wide): 498.12MM Privately Held
Web: www.yesco.com
SIC: 3993 5999 1799 Electric signs; Awnings ; Sign installation and maintenance
PA: Young Electric Sign Company Inc
2401 Foothill Dr
801 464-4600

**(P-16072)**
**YOUNG ELECTRIC SIGN COMPANY**
Also Called: Yesco
10235 Bellegrave Ave, Jurupa Valley (91752-1919)
PHONE..................909 923-7668
Duane Wardle, Brnch Mgr
EMP: 203
SQ FT: 8,500
SALES (corp-wide): 498.12MM Privately Held
Web: www.yesco.com
SIC: 3993 1799 Electric signs; Sign installation and maintenance
PA: Young Electric Sign Company Inc
2401 Foothill Dr
801 464-4600

## 3995 Burial Caskets

**(P-16073)**
**UNIVERSAL MEDITECH INC**
1320 E Fortune Ave Ste 102, Fresno (93725-1958)
PHONE..................559 366-7798
Zhaoyan Wang, Pr
EMP: 45 EST: 2015
SALES (est): 2.53MM Privately Held
Web: www.universal-meditech.com
SIC: 3995 2835 Casket linings; Pregnancy test kits

## 3996 Hard Surface Floor Coverings, Nec

**(P-16074)**
**ALTRO USA INC**
Also Called: Compass Flooring
12648 Clark St, Santa Fe Springs (90670-3950)
PHONE..................562 944-8292
Al Boegh, Prin
EMP: 73
SALES (corp-wide): 216.3MM Privately Held
Web: www.altro.com
SIC: 3996 5023 Hard surface floor coverings, nec; Resilient floor coverings: tile or sheet
HQ: Altro Usa, Inc.
80 Industrial Way Suite 1
Wilmington MA 01887
800 377-5597

**(P-16075)**
**PARMA FLOORS INC**
2079 Hartog Dr, San Jose (95131-2215)
PHONE..................408 638-0247
Kaaveh Letafat, CEO
Chad Lopez, Prin
▲ EMP: 18 EST: 2013
SALES (est): 10MM Privately Held
Web: www.parmaflooring.com
SIC: 3996 Tile, floor: supported plastic

**(P-16076)**
**RAM BOARD INC**
27460 Avenue Scott Unit A, Valencia (91355-3472)
PHONE..................818 848-0400
◆ EMP: 30 EST: 2008
SALES (est): 5.19MM Privately Held
Web: www.ramboard.com
SIC: 3996 5023 Hard surface floor coverings, nec; Floor coverings

## 3999 Manufacturing Industries, Nec

**(P-16077)**
**4 D INDUSTRIES INC**
10550 Arno Rd, Galt (95632-8557)
PHONE..................209 745-0500
Brian Dongelmans, Prin
EMP: 16 EST: 2015
SALES (est): 3.06MM Privately Held
SIC: 3999 Manufacturing industries, nec

**(P-16078)**
**A & A STEPPING STONE MFG INC**
6325 Auburn Blvd, Citrus Heights (95621-5203)
PHONE..................916 723-1717
EMP: 16
SALES (corp-wide): 22.23MM Privately Held
Web: www.aasteppingstone.com
SIC: 3999 Atomizers, toiletry
PA: A & A Stepping Stone Mfg., Inc.
10291 Ophir Rd
530 885-7481

**(P-16079)**
**ABOVE & BEYOND BALLOONS INC**
Also Called: Above and Beyond
1 Wrigley, Irvine (92618-2711)
PHONE..................949 586-8470
Michael Chaklos, CEO
Karen Chaklos, *
▲ EMP: 44 EST: 2002
SALES (est): 4.31MM Privately Held
Web: www.advertisingballoons.com
SIC: 3999 Advertising display products

**(P-16080)**
**ACCURATE STAGING MFG INC (PA)**
13900 S Figueroa St, Los Angeles (90061-1028)
PHONE..................310 324-1040
Alfredo Gomez, CEO
Jose Cantu, *
EMP: 15 EST: 2001
SQ FT: 18,000
SALES: 4.32MM
SALES (corp-wide): 4.32MM Privately Held
Web: www.accuratestaging.com
SIC: 3999 Stage hardware and equipment, except lighting

**(P-16081)**
**ADVANCED BUILDING SYSTEMS INC**
11905 Regentview Ave, Downey (90241-5515)
PHONE..................818 652-4252
Alex Youssef, Pr
EMP: 20 EST: 2018
SALES (est): 1.42MM Privately Held
SIC: 3999 Manufacturing industries, nec

**(P-16082)**
**ADVANCED COSMETIC RES LABS INC**
Also Called: Acrl
20550 Prairie St, Chatsworth (91311-6006)
PHONE..................818 709-9945
Kitty Hunter, Pr
▲ EMP: 50 EST: 1994
SQ FT: 48,000
SALES (est): 10.05MM Privately Held
Web: www.advancedcosmeticresearchlaboratories.com
SIC: 3999 2844 Barber and beauty shop equipment; Perfumes, cosmetics and other toilet preparations

## PRODUCTS & SERVICES SECTION
### 3999 - Manufacturing Industries, Nec (P-16107)

**(P-16083)**
**AKON INCORPORATED**
Also Called: Akon
1828 Bering Dr, San Jose (95112-4212)
PHONE..................................408 432-8039
Surya Sareen, *Pr*
**EMP:** 60 **EST:** 1980
**SQ FT:** 35,000
**SALES (est):** 8.86MM **Privately Held**
Web: www.akoninc.com
**SIC: 3999** Slot machines

**(P-16084)**
**ALOHA BAY**
Also Called: Bright Lights Candle Company
16275 A Main St, Lower Lake (95457)
P.O. Box 539 (95457-0539)
PHONE..................................707 994-3267
Bernard S Burger, *CEO*
Roy Dixon, *
▲ **EMP:** 35 **EST:** 1992
**SQ FT:** 1,500
**SALES (est):** 965.22K **Privately Held**
Web: www.alohabay.com
**SIC: 3999** 5199 Candles; Candles

**(P-16085)**
**AMARETTO ORCHARDS LLC**
Also Called: Famoso Nut
32331 Famoso Woody Rd, Mc Farland (93250-9771)
PHONE..................................661 399-9697
◆ **EMP:** 20 **EST:** 1990
**SALES (est):** 2MM **Privately Held**
Web: www.famosonut.com
**SIC: 3999** 2068 Nut shells, grinding, from purchased nuts; Salted and roasted nuts and seeds

**(P-16086)**
**AMGEN MANUFACTURING LIMITED**
1 Amgen Center Dr, Newbury Park (91320-1799)
PHONE..................................787 656-2000
Victoria H Blatter, *Prin*
**EMP:** 34 **EST:** 2008
**SALES (est):** 10.71MM
**SALES (corp-wide):** 28.19B **Publicly Held**
Web: www.amgen.com
**SIC: 3999** Atomizers, toiletry
**PA:** Amgen Inc.
1 Amgen Center Dr
805 447-1000

**(P-16087)**
**AR INDUSTRIES**
730 E Edna Pl, Covina (91723-1408)
PHONE..................................626 332-8918
**EMP:** 15
**SALES (est):** 720.23K **Privately Held**
Web: www.anthonyrosaspaintingcontractor.com
**SIC: 3999** Manufacturing industries, nec

**(P-16088)**
**ARMINAK SOLUTIONS LLC**
475 N Sheridan St, Corona (92878)
PHONE..................................626 802-7332
Helga Arminak, *Pr*
**EMP:** 35 **EST:** 2019
**SALES (est):** 392.04K **Privately Held**
**SIC: 3999** Manufacturing industries, nec

**(P-16089)**
**ARTBOXX FRAMING INC**
Also Called: Intercontinental Art
555 W Victoria St, Compton (90220-5513)
PHONE..................................310 604-6933
**EMP:** 26
**SIC: 3999** 5999 Framed artwork; Art, picture frames, and decorations

**(P-16090)**
**ARTIFICIAL GRASS LIQUIDATORS**
Also Called: Agl
42505 Rio Nedo, Temecula (92590-3726)
PHONE..................................951 677-3377
Dillon Georgian, *Pr*
Vicky Hernandez, *Prin*
**EMP:** 30 **EST:** 2015
**SALES (est):** 473.22K **Privately Held**
Web: www.artificialgrassliquidators.com
**SIC: 3999** Grasses, artificial and preserved

**(P-16091)**
**ATA-BOY INC**
3171 Los Feliz Blvd Ste 205, Los Angeles (90039-1536)
PHONE..................................323 644-0117
Alan Cushman, *Pr*
Judy Albright, *
▲ **EMP:** 16 **EST:** 1986
**SQ FT:** 4,000
**SALES (est):** 475.44K **Privately Held**
Web: ata-boy.markettime.com
**SIC: 3999** 5947 Novelties, bric-a-brac, and hobby kits; Gift shop

**(P-16092)**
**BALSAM BRANDS INC (PA)**
Also Called: Balsam Hill
50 Woodside Plz Ste 111, Redwood City (94061-2500)
PHONE..................................877 442-2572
Thomas Harman, *CEO*
**EMP:** 70 **EST:** 2006
**SALES (est):** 44.35MM
**SALES (corp-wide):** 44.35MM **Privately Held**
Web: www.balsambrands.com
**SIC: 3999** Christmas trees, artificial

**(P-16093)**
**BCD INDUSTRIES CORP**
24298 Via Vargas Dr, Moreno Valley (92553-6231)
PHONE..................................760 927-8988
Juan Briseno, *Prin*
**EMP:** 15 **EST:** 2017
**SALES (est):** 2.16MM **Privately Held**
**SIC: 3999** Manufacturing industries, nec

**(P-16094)**
**BEACH HOUSE GROUP LLC**
Also Called: Beach House Group
222 N Pacific Coast Hwy Fl 10, El Segundo (90245-5615)
PHONE..................................310 356-6180
Paul James Brice, *Managing Member*
Lance Kalish, *
Shaun Neff, *
Ido Leffler, *
Sachin Harneja, *
**EMP:** 54 **EST:** 2014
**SALES (est):** 6.29MM **Privately Held**
Web: www.beachhousegrp.com
**SIC: 3999** Advertising display products

**(P-16095)**
**BEAUTY TENT INC**
1131 N Kenmore Ave Apt 6, Los Angeles (90029-1525)
PHONE..................................323 717-7131
Naira Harutyunyan, *Pr*
**EMP:** 25 **EST:** 2019
**SALES (est):** 735.9K **Privately Held**
Web: www.beautytent.com

**SIC: 3999** Hair curlers, designed for beauty parlors

**(P-16096)**
**BIL-JAX INC**
7438 Stanford Pl, Cupertino (95014-5815)
PHONE..................................408 446-2308
Dick Whittington, *Brnch Mgr*
**EMP:** 73
**SALES (corp-wide):** 1.22MM **Privately Held**
Web: www.biljax.com
**SIC: 3999** Stage hardware and equipment, except lighting
**HQ:** Bil-Jax, Inc.
125 Taylor Pkwy
Archbold OH 43502
419 445-8915

**(P-16097)**
**BLOOMIOS INC**
201 W Montecito St, Santa Barbara (93101-3824)
PHONE..................................805 222-6330
**EMP:** 30 **EST:** 2001
**SALES (est):** 6.08MM **Privately Held**
Web: www.bloomios.com
**SIC: 3999** 5159

**(P-16098)**
**BRIGHT GLOW CANDLE COMPANY INC (PA)**
Also Called: Bright Glow
20591 E Via Verde St, Covina (91724-3715)
PHONE..................................909 469-4733
Richard Alcedo, *Pr*
◆ **EMP:** 24 **EST:** 1990
**SALES (est):** 5.11MM
**SALES (corp-wide):** 5.11MM **Privately Held**
Web: www.brightglowcandle.com
**SIC: 3999** Candles

**(P-16099)**
**BRITE INDUSTRIES INC**
Also Called: Brite Labs
1746 13th St, Oakland (94607-1510)
PHONE..................................510 250-9330
Brian Brown, *CEO*
**EMP:** 96 **EST:** 2017
**SALES (est):** 1.47MM **Privately Held**
**SIC: 3999** 5159

**(P-16100)**
**BROTHERS OF INDUSTRY INC**
3891 N Ventura Ave Ste B1, Ventura (93001-1271)
PHONE..................................805 628-3545
Peter Hernandez, *Pr*
Andrew Hernandez, *Pr*
Kate Hernandez, *Pr*
Thomas Masker, *Pr*
**EMP:** 15 **EST:** 2017
**SALES (est):** 2MM **Privately Held**
Web: www.brothersofindustry.com
**SIC: 3999** Manufacturing industries, nec

**(P-16101)**
**BRYBRADAN INC**
Also Called: Mistic Products
191 E Jefferson Blvd, Los Angeles (90011-2330)
PHONE..................................323 230-8604
Raul Gonzalez, *Pr*
**EMP:** 15 **EST:** 2007
**SALES (est):** 525.63K **Privately Held**
**SIC: 3999** Candles

**(P-16102)**
**CAL AM MANUFACTURING CO INC**
1939 Friendship Dr Ste E, El Cajon (92020-1138)
P.O. Box 819 (91944-0819)
PHONE..................................800 992-0499
W Sidney Aitken, *CEO*
**EMP:** 16 **EST:** 1979
**SALES (est):** 1.84MM **Privately Held**
Web: www.calam.net
**SIC: 3999** Atomizers, toiletry

**(P-16103)**
**CAL CAT INDUSTRIES LLC**
2288 Geer Rd, Hughson (95326-9614)
PHONE..................................209 883-4890
Aaron Martella, *Prin*
**EMP:** 25 **EST:** 2014
**SALES (est):** 3.73MM **Privately Held**
**SIC: 3999** Manufacturing industries, nec

**(P-16104)**
**CALIFORNIA ACRYLIC INDS INC (HQ)**
Also Called: Cal Spas
1462 E 9th St, Pomona (91766-3833)
PHONE..................................909 623-8781
Casey Loyd, *CEO*
◆ **EMP:** 15 **EST:** 1981
**SQ FT:** 300,000
**SALES (est):** 2.93MM **Privately Held**
Web: www.californiaacrylicindustries.com
**SIC: 3999** 3949 Hot tubs; Billiard and pool equipment and supplies, general
**PA:** Lloyd's Material Supply Company, Inc.
1462 E 9th St

**(P-16105)**
**CALIFORNIA EXOTIC NOVLT LLC**
1455 E Francis St, Ontario (91761-8329)
P.O. Box 50400 (91761-1078)
PHONE..................................909 606-1950
Susan Colvin, *Managing Member*
Jackie White, *
▲ **EMP:** 88 **EST:** 1994
**SQ FT:** 66,000
**SALES (est):** 9.47MM **Privately Held**
Web: www.calexotics.com
**SIC: 3999** 5947 Novelties, bric-a-brac, and hobby kits; Novelties

**(P-16106)**
**CAMBRO MANUFACTURING COMPANY**
21558 Ferrero, City Of Industry (91789-5216)
PHONE..................................909 354-8962
**EMP:** 108
**SALES (corp-wide):** 307.89MM **Privately Held**
Web: www.cambro.com
**SIC: 3999** Barber and beauty shop equipment
**PA:** Cambro Manufacturing Company Inc
5801 Skylab Rd
714 848-1555

**(P-16107)**
**CANNALOGIC**
5404 Whitsett Ave # 219, Valley Village (91607-1615)
PHONE..................................619 458-0775
Jasmine Savoy, *Pr*
**EMP:** 17 **EST:** 2017
**SALES (est):** 174.05K **Privately Held**
**SIC: 3999** Manufacturing industries, nec

## 3999 - Manufacturing Industries, Nec (P-16108)

**(P-16108)**
**CARBERRY LLC (HQ)**
Also Called: Plus Products
17130 Muskrat Ave Ste B, Adelanto (92301-2473)
PHONE..................................800 564-0842
EMP: 24 EST: 2017
SQ FT: 12,000
SALES (est): 2.19MM
SALES (corp-wide): 2.19MM **Privately Held**
SIC: 3999 2064
; Chewing candy, not chewing gum
PA: Plus Products Holdings Inc.
340 S Lemon Ave Ste 9392
800 564-0842

**(P-16109)**
**CARBERRY LLC**
3645 Long Beach Blvd, Long Beach (90807-4018)
PHONE..................................562 264-5078
EMP: 24
SALES (corp-wide): 2.19MM **Privately Held**
SIC: 3999 2064
; Chewing candy, not chewing gum
HQ: Carberry Llc
17130 Muskrat Ave Ste B
Adelanto CA 92301
800 564-0842

**(P-16110)**
**CBD LIVING WATER**
1343 Versante Cir, Corona (92881-4192)
PHONE..................................800 940-3660
EMP: 25 EST: 2016
SALES (est): 1.66MM **Privately Held**
Web: www.cbdliving.com
SIC: 3999

**(P-16111)**
**CCL LABEL INC**
21481 8th St E, Sonoma (95476-9291)
PHONE..................................707 938-7800
EMP: 93
SALES (corp-wide): 4.84B **Privately Held**
Web: www.cclind.com
SIC: 3999 Barber and beauty shop equipment
HQ: Ccl Label, Inc.
161 Worcester Rd Ste 403
Framingham MA 01701
508 872-4511

**(P-16112)**
**CCS INDUSTRIES INC**
4125 W Noble Ave, Visalia (93277-1662)
PHONE..................................559 786-8489
Jeff Orchard, CEO
EMP: 15 EST: 2016
SALES (est): 292.91K **Privately Held**
SIC: 3999 Manufacturing industries, nec

**(P-16113)**
**CDM COMPANY INC**
Also Called: CDM
12 Corporate Plaza Dr Ste 200, Newport Beach (92660-7986)
PHONE..................................949 644-2820
Mitchell Jankins, CEO
▲ EMP: 23 EST: 1990
SQ FT: 7,000
SALES (est): 2.37MM **Privately Held**
Web: www.thecdmco.com
SIC: 3999 3944 8742 5112 Novelties, bric-a-brac, and hobby kits; Games, toys, and children's vehicles; Marketing consulting services; Pens and/or pencils

**(P-16114)**
**CECILIA TECH INC**
4290 E Brickell St Unit C, Ontario (91761-1560)
PHONE..................................818 533-9888
Chang Zhi Pan, Pr
Chang Zhi Pan, CEO
EMP: 15 EST: 2018
SALES (est): 1.06MM **Privately Held**
Web: www.ceciliatech.com
SIC: 3999 Barber and beauty shop equipment

**(P-16115)**
**CENTRAL VALLEY INDUSTRIES LLC**
20451 Mchenry Ave, Escalon (95320-9614)
P.O. Box 445 (95320-0445)
PHONE..................................209 838-8150
Phillip Lionudakis, Prin
EMP: 55 EST: 2012
SALES (est): 352.57K **Privately Held**
SIC: 3999 Manufacturing industries, nec

**(P-16116)**
**CHRIS PUTRIMAS**
1930 E Carson St Ste 102, Carson (90810-1246)
PHONE..................................877 434-1666
Chris Putrimas, Owner
EMP: 50
SALES (est): 575.93K **Privately Held**
SIC: 3999 Manufacturing industries, nec

**(P-16117)**
**CJ FOODS MFG BEAUMONT LLC**
415 Nicholas Rd, Beaumont (92223-2612)
PHONE..................................951 916-9300
Geon Il Lee, CEO
EMP: 71 EST: 2018
SALES (est): 20.76MM **Privately Held**
SIC: 3999 Chairs, hydraulic, barber and beauty shop
PA: Cj Cheiljedang Corporation
330 Dongho-Ro, Jung-Gu

**(P-16118)**
**CLAMP SWING PRICING CO INC**
8386 Capwell Dr, Oakland (94621-2114)
PHONE..................................510 567-1600
Benjamin Garfinkle, Pr
Wilma Garfinkle, *
◆ EMP: 30 EST: 1924
SQ FT: 47,000
SALES (est): 4.53MM **Privately Held**
Web: www.clampswing.com
SIC: 3999 Identification plates

**(P-16119)**
**CLAYBOURNE INDUSTRIES INC**
5055 Western Way, Perris (92571-7420)
P.O. Box 2231 (92516-2231)
PHONE..................................951 675-4508
Nicholas Ortega, Pr
EMP: 17 EST: 2017
SALES (est): 2.62MM **Privately Held**
Web: www.claybourneco.com
SIC: 3999

**(P-16120)**
**COMMERCE ON DEMAND LLC**
Also Called: Good Tree
7121 Telegraph Rd, Montebello (90640-6511)
PHONE..................................562 360-4819
Rashaan Everett, Managing Member
EMP: 60 EST: 2020
SALES (est): 10MM **Privately Held**
SIC: 3999 Manufacturing industries, nec

**(P-16121)**
**CORTECH INDUSTRIES LLC**
2850 Cordelia Rd Ste 160, Fairfield (94534-1618)
PHONE..................................818 267-8324
EMP: 20 EST: 2020
SALES (est): 1.25MM **Privately Held**
Web: www.cortechind.com
SIC: 3999 Manufacturing industries, nec

**(P-16122)**
**DARYLS PET SHOP**
115 S Center St, Redlands (92373-5134)
PHONE..................................909 793-1788
Leslie Triplette, Pr
EMP: 15 EST: 1975
SALES (est): 478.75K **Privately Held**
Web: www.darylspetshop.com
SIC: 3999 Pet supplies

**(P-16123)**
**DESTINATION AESTHETICS INC**
768 University Ave, Sacramento (95825-6703)
PHONE..................................916 844-4913
David Ferrera Doctor, Pr
EMP: 50 EST: 2011
SALES (est): 929.49K **Privately Held**
Web: www.destinationaesthetics.com
SIC: 3999 Barber and beauty shop equipment

**(P-16124)**
**DEVELOPLUS INC**
1575 Magnolia Ave, Corona (92879-2073)
PHONE..................................951 738-8595
Jeanne Nicodemus, CEO
Kiran Agrey, *
▲ EMP: 140 EST: 1990
SQ FT: 40,000
SALES (est): 21.74MM **Privately Held**
Web: www.developlus.com
SIC: 3999 5087 Hair and hair-based products
; Beauty parlor equipment and supplies

**(P-16125)**
**DKP DESIGNS INC**
110 Maryland St, El Segundo (90245-4115)
PHONE..................................310 322-6000
Deborah P Koppel, Pr
Brad Koppel, VP
▲ EMP: 15 EST: 1996
SQ FT: 4,000
SALES (est): 2.05MM **Privately Held**
Web: www.dkpdesigns.com
SIC: 3999 Advertising display products

**(P-16126)**
**DMA ENTERPRISES INC (PA)**
Also Called: Thermasol Steam Bath
2255 Union Pl, Simi Valley (93065-1661)
PHONE..................................805 520-2468
▲ EMP: 30 EST: 1989
SALES (est): 5.27MM **Privately Held**
SIC: 3999 3431 Hot tubs; Bathroom fixtures, including sinks

**(P-16127)**
**ECO-SHELL INC**
5230 Grange Rd, Corning (96021-9239)
PHONE..................................530 824-8794
Charles R Crain Junior, CEO
◆ EMP: 22 EST: 1996
SQ FT: 60,000
SALES (est): 1.51MM **Privately Held**
Web: www.ecoshell.com
SIC: 3999 Nut shells, grinding, from purchased nuts

**(P-16128)**
**FAMILY INDUSTRIES LLC**
2755 Fruitdale St, Los Angeles (90039-2814)
PHONE..................................619 306-1035
EMP: 17 EST: 2011
SALES (est): 305.35K **Privately Held**
Web: www.familyindustries.com
SIC: 3999 Barber and beauty shop equipment

**(P-16129)**
**FLAME AND WAX INC**
Also Called: Voluspa
2900 Mccabe Way, Irvine (92614-6239)
PHONE..................................949 752-4000
Troy C Arntsen, CEO
Troy C Arntsen, CEO
Traci Arntsen, *
▲ EMP: 134 EST: 2001
SALES (est): 18.59MM **Privately Held**
Web: www.voluspa.com
SIC: 3999 2844 Candles; Perfumes, cosmetics and other toilet preparations

**(P-16130)**
**FLORA GOLD CORPORATION (PA)** ✪
3165 Red Hill Ave Ste 201, Costa Mesa (92626-3417)
PHONE..................................949 252-1908
Laurie Holcomb, CEO
Marshall Minor, CFO
Judith Schvimmer, Sec
EMP: 586 EST: 2023
SALES (est): 90.96MM
SALES (corp-wide): 90.96MM **Privately Held**
SIC: 3999

**(P-16131)**
**FOLKMANIS INC**
1219 Park Ave, Emeryville (94608-3607)
PHONE..................................510 658-7677
Atis Folkmanis, Pr
Judy Folkmanis, *
▲ EMP: 40 EST: 1972
SALES (est): 1.41MM **Privately Held**
Web: www.folkmanis.com
SIC: 3999 3942 Puppets and marionettes; Dolls and stuffed toys

**(P-16132)**
**FOUNTAINHEAD INDUSTRIES**
700 N San Vicente Blvd Ste G410, West Hollywood (90069-5060)
PHONE..................................310 248-2444
Hal Kline, Pr
EMP: 20 EST: 2005
SALES (est): 1.13MM **Privately Held**
SIC: 3999 Chairs, hydraulic, barber and beauty shop

**(P-16133)**
**GARY W GRAY**
Also Called: Gray, Gary Phrmcist Cmplex Lab
1721 W Burrel Ave, Visalia (93291-4429)
P.O. Box 2522 (93279-2522)
PHONE..................................559 750-8462
Gary Gray, Owner
EMP: 18 EST: 2014
SALES (est): 948.24K **Privately Held**
SIC: 3999

# PRODUCTS & SERVICES SECTION
## 3999 - Manufacturing Industries, Nec (P-16155)

**(P-16134)**
**GEE MANUFACTURING INCORPORATED**
2200 S Golden State Blvd, Fowler (93625-9700)
P.O. Box P.O. Box 397 (93625-0397)
PHONE..................................559 834-2929
EMP: 35 EST: 1973
SALES (est): 2.99MM Privately Held
Web: www.geemanufacturing.com
SIC: 3999 3556 Bric-a-brac; Food products machinery

**(P-16135)**
**GENERAL WAX CO INC (PA)**
Also Called: General Wax & Candle Co
6863 Beck Ave, North Hollywood (91605-6206)
P.O. Box 9398 (91609-1398)
PHONE..................................818 765-5800
Carol Lazar, CEO
Mike Tapp, *
Colton Lazar, *
Keith Tapp, *
J C Edmond, *
◆ EMP: 85 EST: 1949
SQ FT: 120,000
SALES (est): 11.31MM
SALES (corp-wide): 11.31MM Privately Held
Web: www.generalwax.com
SIC: 3999 Candles

**(P-16136)**
**GLOBALUXE INC**
Also Called: Candle Crafters
405 Science Dr, Moorpark (93021-2093)
PHONE..................................805 583-4600
Michael Joseph Horn, CEO
▲ EMP: 20 EST: 2003
SALES (est): 2.43MM Privately Held
Web: www.aquiesse.com
SIC: 3999 5199 5999 Candles; Candles; Candle shops

**(P-16137)**
**GOLDEN SUPREME INC**
12304 Mccann Dr, Santa Fe Springs (90670-3333)
PHONE..................................562 903-1063
Ross Stillwagon, Pr
Fernando Fischbach, *
Ricardo J Fischbach, *
▲ EMP: 30 EST: 1990
SQ FT: 13,000
SALES (est): 956.66K Privately Held
Web: www.goldensupreme.com
SIC: 3999 5087 Hair curlers, designed for beauty parlors; Beauty parlor equipment and supplies

**(P-16138)**
**GOODIE CLOSETT LLC**
5255 Clayton Rd, Concord (94521-5283)
PHONE..................................980 895-0496
EMP: 18 EST: 2021
SALES (est): 239.39K Privately Held
SIC: 3999 7389 Candles; Business services, nec

**(P-16139)**
**GRENEKER LLC**
3110 E 12th St, Los Angeles (90023-3616)
PHONE..................................323 263-9000
EMP: 26 EST: 2021
SALES (est): 1.04MM Privately Held
Web: www.greneker.com
SIC: 3999 Manufacturing industries, nec

**(P-16140)**
**GUZZLER MANUFACTURING INC**
1510 Hayes Ave, Long Beach (90813-1126)
PHONE..................................562 436-0250
Mark Brockman, Mgr
EMP: 16
SALES (corp-wide): 1.72B Publicly Held
Web: www.fssolutionsgroup.com
SIC: 3999 Atomizers, toiletry
HQ: Guzzler Manufacturing, Inc.
8584 Borden Ave
Leeds AL 35094

**(P-16141)**
**H & H SPECIALTIES INC**
14850 Don Julian Rd Ste B, City Of Industry (91746-3122)
PHONE..................................626 575-0776
Reid Neslage, Owner
Mary Louise Higgins, *
EMP: 31 EST: 1967
SQ FT: 30,000
SALES (est): 3.55MM Privately Held
Web: www.hhspecialties.com
SIC: 3999 3625 Stage hardware and equipment, except lighting; Relays and industrial controls

**(P-16142)**
**HEMP INDUSTRIES**
3717 El Cajon Blvd, San Diego (92105-1004)
PHONE..................................619 458-9090
Brian S Gallagher, Owner
EMP: 25 EST: 2017
SALES (est): 236.26K Privately Held
Web: www.thehia.org
SIC: 3999 Manufacturing industries, nec

**(P-16143)**
**HERO INDUSTRIES INC**
1038 E Bastanchury Rd Ste 247, Fullerton (92835-2786)
PHONE..................................714 879-3900
EMP: 22 EST: 2015
SALES (est): 1.33MM Privately Held
Web: www.hero-industries.com
SIC: 3999 Manufacturing industries, nec

**(P-16144)**
**HEXODEN HOLDINGS INC (PA)**
1219 Linda Vista Dr, San Marcos (92078-3809)
PHONE..................................858 201-3412
Donna Razzoli, Pr
EMP: 89 EST: 2017
SALES (est): 299.72K
SALES (corp-wide): 299.72K Privately Held
SIC: 3999 Manufacturing industries, nec

**(P-16145)**
**HOGAN MFG INC (PA)**
1638 Main St, Escalon (95320-1722)
P.O. Box 398 (95320-0398)
PHONE..................................209 838-7323
Mark Hogan, CEO
Joe Debiasio, *
Zach Hogan, *
Tyler Lucas, *
Bernice Hogan, *
▲ EMP: 150 EST: 1944
SQ FT: 43,000
SALES (est): 38.38MM
SALES (corp-wide): 38.38MM Privately Held
Web: www.hoganmfg.com

SIC: 3999 3441 3443 1791 Wheelchair lifts; Fabricated structural metal; Fabricated plate work (boiler shop); Structural steel erection

**(P-16146)**
**HOGAN MFG INC**
19527 Mchenry Ave, Escalon (95320-9613)
PHONE..................................209 838-2400
EMP: 18
SALES (corp-wide): 38.38MM Privately Held
Web: www.hoganmfg.com
SIC: 3999 Wheelchair lifts
PA: Hogan Mfg., Inc.
1638 Main St
209 838-7323

**(P-16147)**
**HOGAN MFG INC**
Lift-U
1520 1st St, Escalon (95320-1703)
P.O. Box 398 (95320-0398)
PHONE..................................209 838-2400
Paul Riechmuth, Mgr
EMP: 107
SALES (corp-wide): 38.38MM Privately Held
Web: www.hoganmfg.com
SIC: 3999 3842 3714 3534 Wheelchair lifts; Surgical appliances and supplies; Motor vehicle parts and accessories; Elevators and moving stairways
PA: Hogan Mfg., Inc.
1638 Main St
209 838-7323

**(P-16148)**
**HOLIDAY FOLIAGE INC**
Also Called: Holiday Foliage
2592 Otay Center Dr, San Diego (92154-7611)
PHONE..................................619 661-9094
Kristine Vanzutphen, CEO
Juanita Keller, VP
William Vanzutphen Junior, CFO
▲ EMP: 38 EST: 1994
SQ FT: 18,000
SALES (est): 9.46MM Privately Held
Web: www.holidayfoliage.com
SIC: 3999 Artificial trees and flowers

**(P-16149)**
**HOUSE OF LASHES**
1565 Mcgaw Ave Ste C, Irvine (92614-5670)
P.O. Box 9016 (92728-9016)
PHONE..................................714 515-4162
▲ EMP: 28 EST: 2012
SALES (est): 3.89MM Privately Held
Web: www.houseoflashes.com
SIC: 3999 Wigs, including doll wigs, toupees, or wiglets

**(P-16150)**
**HUNTINGTON INGALLS INDUSTRIES**
9444 Balboa Ave Ste 400, San Diego (92123-4378)
PHONE..................................858 522-6000
EMP: 31 EST: 2011
SALES (est): 1.01MM Privately Held
Web: www.hii.com
SIC: 3999 Manufacturing industries, nec

**(P-16151)**
**INNOVATIVE CASEWORK MFG INC**
12261 Industry St, Garden Grove (92841-2815)
PHONE..................................714 890-9100
Valerie Perez, Prin
EMP: 25 EST: 2017
SALES (est): 217.84K Privately Held
SIC: 3999 Manufacturing industries, nec

**(P-16152)**
**INTEGRATED MFG SOLUTIONS LLC**
2590 Pioneer Ave Ste C, Vista (92081-8427)
PHONE..................................760 599-4300
Baophuong Nguyen, Pr
EMP: 24 EST: 2007
SQ FT: 2,000
SALES (est): 1.37MM Privately Held
Web: www.integratedmfg.net
SIC: 3999 Chairs, hydraulic, barber and beauty shop

**(P-16153)**
**J & A JEFFERY INC**
Also Called: Western Stabilization
395 Industrial Way Ste B, Dixon (95620-9787)
P.O. Box 1022 (95620-1022)
PHONE..................................707 678-0369
John Jordan, CEO
Judy Jeffery, *
Ashley Jeffery, *
EMP: 50 EST: 1988
SQ FT: 16,000
SALES (est): 5.76MM Privately Held
Web: www.wstabilization.com
SIC: 3999 0711 Grinding and pulverizing of materials, nec; Soil preparation services

**(P-16154)**
**JACUZZI BRANDS LLC**
Also Called: Sundance Spas
14525 Monte Vista Ave, Chino (91710-5721)
P.O. Box 2900 (91708-2900)
PHONE..................................909 606-1416
Diana Fox, Mgr
EMP: 41
SALES (corp-wide): 440.01K Privately Held
Web: www.jacuzzi.com
SIC: 3999 Hot tubs
HQ: Jacuzzi Brands Llc
17872 Gillette Ave Ste 300
Irvine CA 92614
909 606-1416

**(P-16155)**
**JOE BLASCO ENTERPRISES INC**
Also Called: Joe Blasco Cosmetics
1285 N Valdivia Way # A, Palm Springs (92262-5428)
PHONE..................................323 467-4949
Joseph D Blasco, Pr
▲ EMP: 38 EST: 1986
SQ FT: 13,788
SALES (est): 346.06K
SALES (corp-wide): 787.09K Privately Held
Web: www.joeblasco.com
SIC: 3999 7231 2844 Barber and beauty shop equipment; Cosmetology school; Perfumes, cosmetics and other toilet preparations
PA: Joe Blasco Make-Up Center West, Inc.
1285 N Valdivia Way # A
323 467-4949

(PA)=Parent Co (HQ)=Headquarters
✪ = New Business established in last 2 years

# 3999 - Manufacturing Industries, Nec (P-16156)

## PRODUCTS & SERVICES SECTION

**(P-16156)**
**JORGE ULLOA**
Also Called: Jem Unlimited Iron
3162 E La Palma Ave Ste F, Anaheim
(92806-2810)
PHONE..................................714 630-0499
Martha Ulloa, *Pr*
**EMP:** 18 **EST:** 2002
**SQ FT:** 4,000
**SALES (est):** 637.35K **Privately Held**
**SIC: 3999** Lawn ornaments

**(P-16157)**
**JUUL LABS INC (PA)**
Also Called: Juul Labs
560 20th St, San Francisco (94107)
PHONE..................................415 829-2336
K C Crosthwaite, *CEO*
Guy Cartwright, *
Elaine Paik, *
Josh Rafael, *CCO**
Joe Murillo, *CRO**
**EMP:** 194 **EST:** 2007
**SALES (est):** 473.82MM **Privately Held**
**Web:** www.juullabs.com
**SIC: 3999** Cigarette and cigar products and accessories

**(P-16158)**
**JUUL LABS INTERNATIONAL INC (HQ)**
560 20th St, San Francisco (94107-4344)
PHONE..................................415 829-2336
**EMP:** 356
**SALES (est):** 305.38K **Privately Held**
**Web:** www.juul.com
**SIC: 3999** Manufacturing industries, nec
**PA:** Juul Labs, Inc.
560 20th St

**(P-16159)**
**K31 ROAD ENGINEERING LLC**
Also Called: K31
1968 S Coast Hwy Pmb 593, Laguna Beach (92651-3681)
PHONE..................................305 928-1968
Rainer Piel, *CEO*
**EMP:** 35 **EST:** 2014
**SALES (est):** 212.55K **Privately Held**
**Web:** www.k31.org
**SIC: 3999** 5039 Manufacturing industries, nec; Construction materials, nec

**(P-16160)**
**K9 BALLISTICS INC**
708 Via Alondra, Camarillo (93012-8713)
PHONE..................................844 772-3125
Sean Farley, *CEO*
**EMP:** 16 **EST:** 2010
**SQ FT:** 20,000
**SALES (est):** 1.58MM **Privately Held**
**Web:** www.k9ballistics.com
**SIC: 3999** Pet supplies

**(P-16161)**
**KAIROS MANUFACTURING INC**
Also Called: Architectural Iron Works
201 Bridge St, San Luis Obispo (93401-5510)
PHONE..................................805 544-2216
**EMP:** 16 **EST:** 2017
**SALES (est):** 3.76MM **Privately Held**
**SIC: 3999** Manufacturing industries, nec

**(P-16162)**
**KIVA MANUFACTURING INC**
Also Called: Kiva Confections
445 Lesser St, Oakland (94601-4901)
PHONE..................................510 780-0777
Scott Palmer, *CEO*
**EMP:** 21 **EST:** 2019
**SALES (est):** 3.66MM **Privately Held**
**Web:** www.kivaconfections.com
**SIC: 3999**

**(P-16163)**
**KNT MANUFACTURING INC**
39760 Eureka Dr, Newark (94560-4808)
PHONE..................................510 896-1699
Keith Ngo, *CEO*
**EMP:** 60 **EST:** 2013
**SALES (est):** 7.83MM **Privately Held**
**Web:** www.kntmfg.com
**SIC: 3999** Barber and beauty shop equipment

**(P-16164)**
**KURZ TRANSFER PRODUCTS LP**
415 N Smith Ave, Corona (92878-4305)
PHONE..................................951 738-9521
Hastings Kurz, *Prin*
**EMP:** 65
**SALES (corp-wide):** 1B **Privately Held**
**Web:** www.kurzusa.com
**SIC: 3999** Atomizers, toiletry
**HQ:** Kurz Transfer Products, Lp
11836 Patterson Rd
Huntersville NC 28078
704 927-3700

**(P-16165)**
**L A HQ INC**
5363 Wilshire Blvd, Los Angeles (90036-4213)
PHONE..................................310 880-7433
Amiel Fonkou, *CEO*
**EMP:** 20 **EST:** 2018
**SALES (est):** 556.17K **Privately Held**
**SIC: 3999** Hair and hair-based products

**(P-16166)**
**LA SPAS INC**
1325 N Blue Gum St, Anaheim (92806-1750)
PHONE..................................714 630-1150
▲ **EMP:** 130
**Web:** www.maaxspas.com
**SIC: 3999** 5091 Hot tubs; Fitness equipment and supplies

**(P-16167)**
**LEARNING RESOURCES INC**
Also Called: Educational Insights
19700 S Vermont Ave, Torrance (90502-1100)
PHONE..................................800 995-4436
**EMP:** 20
**SALES (corp-wide):** 27.82MM **Privately Held**
**Web:** www.learningresources.com
**SIC: 3999** 3944 Education aids, devices and supplies; Games, toys, and children's vehicles
**PA:** Learning Resources, Inc.
380 N Fairway Dr
800 222-3909

**(P-16168)**
**LEOBEN COMPANY**
16692 Burke Ln, Huntington Beach (92647-4536)
PHONE..................................951 284-9653
Samir Tabikha, *Pr*
**EMP:** 26 **EST:** 2017
**SALES (est):** 3.65MM **Privately Held**
**Web:** www.leobenco.com

**(P-16169)**
**LEXOR INC**
7400 Hazard Ave, Westminster (92683-5031)
PHONE..................................714 444-4144
Marianna Magos, *CEO*
Christopher L Long, *
▲ **EMP:** 90 **EST:** 2007
**SALES (est):** 5.28MM **Privately Held**
**Web:** www.lexor.com
**SIC: 3999** Chairs, hydraulic, barber and beauty shop

**(P-16170)**
**LIVING TO 100 CLUB LLC**
4231 Balboa Ave Ste 316, San Diego (92117-5504)
PHONE..................................858 272-3992
**EMP:** 16 **EST:** 2018
**SALES (est):** 38.16K **Privately Held**
**Web:** www.livingto100.club
**SIC: 3999** Manufacturing industries, nec

**(P-16171)**
**LIXIT CORPORATION (PA)**
Also Called: Equitex
100 Coombs St, Napa (94559-3941)
P.O. Box 2580 (94558-0525)
PHONE..................................800 358-8254
Linda Parks, *Pr*
Laurie Corona, *
Elizabeth Dennis, *
Howard Pickens, *
▲ **EMP:** 67 **EST:** 1968
**SQ FT:** 50,000
**SALES (est):** 13.61MM
**SALES (corp-wide):** 13.61MM **Privately Held**
**Web:** www.lixit.com
**SIC: 3999** Pet supplies

**(P-16172)**
**LMS**
1462 E 9th St, Pomona (91766-3833)
PHONE..................................909 623-8781
George R Phillips Junior, *Admn*
**EMP:** 26 **EST:** 2016
**SALES (est):** 6.34MM **Privately Held**
**SIC: 3999** Manufacturing industries, nec

**(P-16173)**
**LUXSHARE-ICT INC**
480 N Mccarthy Blvd Ste 280, Milpitas (95035-5129)
PHONE..................................408 957-0535
Jerry Tsai, *CEO*
**EMP:** 70 **EST:** 2011
**SALES (est):** 10.73MM **Privately Held**
**Web:** www.luxshare-ict.com
**SIC: 3999** Manufacturing industries, nec
**HQ:** Luxshare-Ict Co., Ltd.
1f, No. 12, Lane 15, Minquan E. Rd., Sec. 6
Taipei City TAP 11406

**(P-16174)**
**MACRO INDUSTRIES INC**
14178 Albers Way, Chino (91710-6938)
PHONE..................................909 606-2218
Eric Zhang, *Prin*
**EMP:** 26 **EST:** 2019
**SALES (est):** 607.84K **Privately Held**
**Web:** www.macroindustries.com
**SIC: 3999** Manufacturing industries, nec

**(P-16175)**
**MACS LIFT GATE INC (PA)**
2801 E South St, Long Beach (90805-3736)
PHONE..................................562 529-3465
Michael Macdonald, *CEO*
Richard Mac Donald, *
Lawrence Mac Donald, *
Gerald J Donald Mac, *VP*
**EMP:** 24 **EST:** 1957
**SALES (est):** 5.03MM
**SALES (corp-wide):** 5.03MM **Privately Held**
**Web:** www.macsliftgate.com
**SIC: 3999** 5013 Wheelchair lifts; Motor vehicle supplies and new parts

**(P-16176)**
**MANUFACTUR**
411 S Main St Unit 422, Los Angeles (90013-1300)
PHONE..................................213 613-1246
Matthew Bowers, *Pr*
**EMP:** 20 **EST:** 2014
**SALES (est):** 2.03MM **Privately Held**
**Web:** www.manufactur.co
**SIC: 3999** Manufacturing industries, nec

**(P-16177)**
**MANUFACTURED SOLUTIONS LLC**
9601 Janice Cir, Villa Park (92861-2705)
PHONE..................................714 548-6915
Marcela Cortes, *Pr*
**EMP:** 40 **EST:** 2020
**SALES (est):** 2.21MM **Privately Held**
**SIC: 3999** 3444 Manufacturing industries, nec; Sheet metalwork

**(P-16178)**
**MARCH PRODUCTS INC**
Also Called: Astella
4645 Troy Ct, Jurupa Valley (92509-2003)
PHONE..................................909 622-4800
Yungcheng Ma, *Pr*
◆ **EMP:** 72 **EST:** 2001
**SQ FT:** 70,000
**SALES (est):** 17.5MM **Privately Held**
**Web:** www.californiaumbrella.com
**SIC: 3999** 2211 Umbrellas, garden or wagon ; Umbrella cloth, cotton

**(P-16179)**
**MCCALLS COUNTRY CANNING INC**
41735 Cherry St, Murrieta (92562-9186)
P.O. Box 1375 (92564-1375)
PHONE..................................951 461-2277
**EMP:** 15
**Web:** www.mccallscandles.com
**SIC: 3999** Candles

**(P-16180)**
**MEDICAL BRKTHRUGH MSSAGE CHIRS**
Also Called: Alicorns
24971 Avenue Stanford, Valencia (91355-1278)
PHONE..................................408 677-7702
Max Lun, *CEO*
**EMP:** 24 **EST:** 2016
**SALES (est):** 6.01MM **Privately Held**
**Web:** www.medicalbreakthrough.org
**SIC: 3999** Massage machines, electric: barber and beauty shops

## PRODUCTS & SERVICES SECTION
### 3999 - Manufacturing Industries, Nec (P-16204)

**(P-16181)**
**MERCADO LATINO INC**
Continental Candle Company
1420 W Walnut St, Compton (90220-5013)
PHONE.....................310 537-1062
EMP: 67
SALES (corp-wide): 32.57MM **Privately Held**
Web: www.continentalcandle.com
SIC: **3999** 3641 7699 3645 Candles; Electric lamps; Restaurant equipment repair; Residential lighting fixtures
PA: Mercado Latino, Inc.
245 Baldwin Park Blvd
626 333-6862

**(P-16182)**
**MERGE4 MFG INC**
6353 Glen Haven Rd, Soquel (95073-9745)
P.O. Box 1807 (95073-1807)
PHONE.....................831 239-5566
Cindi Busenhart, *Admn*
EMP: 30 EST: 2015
SALES (est): 3.07MM **Privately Held**
Web: www.merge4.com
SIC: **3999** Manufacturing industries, nec

**(P-16183)**
**MGR DESIGN INTERNATIONAL INC**
1950 Williams Dr, Oxnard (93036-2630)
PHONE.....................805 981-6400
Rony Haviv, *CEO*
◆ EMP: 200 EST: 2001
SQ FT: 80,000
SALES (est): 8.77MM **Privately Held**
Web: www.mgrdesign.com
SIC: **3999** Potpourri

**(P-16184)**
**MIDWAY GAMES WEST INC**
675 Sycamore Dr, Milpitas (95035-7458)
PHONE.....................408 434-3700
Dan Van Elderen, *Pr*
Dan Van Elderen, *Pr*
Mike Taylor, *
Mary Fujihara, *
Mark Pierce, *Senior Vice President Product Development*
EMP: 130 EST: 1972
SALES (est): 5.37MM **Privately Held**
SIC: **3999** 3944 Coin-operated amusement machines; Video game machines, except coin-operated

**(P-16185)**
**MOSAIC BRANDS INC**
Also Called: Hair ACC By Mia Minnelli
3266 Buskirk Ave, Pleasant Hill (94523-4315)
P.O. Box 585 (94507-0585)
PHONE.....................925 322-8700
Mia Minnelli, *Pr*
▲ EMP: 25 EST: 2000
SQ FT: 20,000
SALES (est): 1.4MM **Privately Held**
SIC: **3999** 3069 Hair and hair-based products; Rubber hair accessories

**(P-16186)**
**NANO FILTER INC**
22310 Bonita St, Carson (90745-4103)
PHONE.....................949 316-8866
Bennett Koo, *Pr*
EMP: 60 EST: 2020
SALES (est): 394.96K **Privately Held**
SIC: **3999** Manufacturing industries, nec

**(P-16187)**
**NEIGHBRHOOD BUS ADVRTSMENT LTD**
14752 Crenshaw Blvd, Gardena (90249-3602)
PHONE.....................442 300-1803
EMP: 26 EST: 2022
SALES (est): 437.13K **Privately Held**
SIC: **3999** Advertising display products

**(P-16188)**
**NEW DIMENSION ONE SPAS INC (DH)**
1819 Aston Ave Ste 105, Carlsbad (92008-7338)
P.O. Box 2600 (92051-2600)
PHONE.....................800 345-7727
Robert Hallam, *Pr*
Linda Hallam, *
Chris Theriot, *CIO*
Phil Sandner, *PROC*
Terry Hauser, *
◆ EMP: 160 EST: 1977
SQ FT: 125,000
SALES (est): 9.59MM
SALES (corp-wide): 440.01K **Privately Held**
Web: www.d1spas.com
SIC: **3999** 3088 Hot tubs; Plastics plumbing fixtures
HQ: Jacuzzi Brands Llc
17872 Gllette Ave Ste 300
Irvine CA 92614
909 606-1416

**(P-16189)**
**NORLAINE INC**
Also Called: Patina V
1449 W Industrial Park St, Covina (91722-3414)
PHONE.....................626 961-2471
◆ EMP: 200
Web: www.cnl-patina-v.com
SIC: **3999** Mannequins

**(P-16190)**
**OHAGIN MANUFACTURING COMPANY**
Also Called: O'Hagin Manufacturing
210 Classic Ct Ste 100, Rohnert Park (94928-1660)
PHONE.....................707 322-2402
David Mutter, *Pr*
EMP: 90 EST: 2018
SALES (est): 2.21MM **Privately Held**
Web: www.ohagin.com
SIC: **3999** Manufacturing industries, nec

**(P-16191)**
**ON PREMISE PRODUCTS INC**
8021 Wing Ave, El Cajon (92020-1245)
PHONE.....................619 562-1486
Michael Barnhill, *Pr*
EMP: 30 EST: 2018
SALES (est): 814.64K **Privately Held**
Web: www.onpremiseproducts.com
SIC: **3999** Manufacturing industries, nec

**(P-16192)**
**ORIGIN LLC**
119 E Graham Pl, Burbank (91502-2028)
PHONE.....................818 848-1648
▲ EMP: 35
SIC: **3999** Advertising display products

**(P-16193)**
**PACIFICA BEAUTY LLC**
Also Called: Pacifica International
1090 Eugenia Pl Ste 200, Carpinteria (93013-2011)
PHONE.....................844 332-8440
Brook Harvey Taylor, *CEO*
▲ EMP: 100 EST: 1997
SQ FT: 58,000
SALES (est): 9.74MM **Privately Held**
Web: www.pacificabeauty.com
SIC: **3999** 2844 Candles; Perfumes, cosmetics and other toilet preparations

**(P-16194)**
**PACMIN INCORPORATED (PA)**
Also Called: Pacific Miniatures
2021 Raymer Ave, Fullerton (92833-2664)
PHONE.....................714 447-4478
Frederick Ouweleen Junior, *Pr*
Flora Ouweleen, *
Daniel Ouweleen, *
▲ EMP: 91 EST: 1981
SQ FT: 35,400
SALES (est): 10.66MM
SALES (corp-wide): 10.66MM **Privately Held**
Web: www.pacmin.com
SIC: **3999** Models, general, except toy

**(P-16195)**
**PARADIGM CONTRACT MFG LLC**
5531 Belle Ave, Cypress (90630-4550)
PHONE.....................714 889-7074
Scott Penin, *Pt*
Faith Stancliff, *Pt*
EMP: 15 EST: 2006
SALES (est): 1.03MM **Privately Held**
SIC: **3999** Atomizers, toiletry

**(P-16196)**
**PAUL FERRANTE INC**
Also Called: Ferrante Paul Cstm Lmps & Shds
8464 Melrose Pl, West Hollywood (90069-5308)
PHONE.....................310 854-4412
Thomas Raynor, *Pr*
▲ EMP: 40 EST: 1962
SQ FT: 2,000
SALES (est): 2.48MM **Privately Held**
Web: www.paulferrante.com
SIC: **3999** 5099 3645 Shades, lamp or candle; Antiques; Residential lighting fixtures

**(P-16197)**
**PCI INDUSTRIES INC**
700 S Vail Ave, Montebello (90640-4954)
PHONE.....................323 889-6770
Jack Scilley, *Owner*
EMP: 27
SALES (corp-wide): 45.1MM **Privately Held**
Web: www.pottorff.com
SIC: **3999** Atomizers, toiletry
PA: Pci Industries, Inc.
5101 Blue Mound Rd
817 509-2300

**(P-16198)**
**PCI INDUSTRIES INC**
6490 Fleet St, Commerce (90040-1710)
PHONE.....................323 728-0004
Jim Turner, *Mgr*
EMP: 27
SALES (corp-wide): 45.1MM **Privately Held**
Web: www.pottorff.com
SIC: **3999** Atomizers, toiletry
PA: Pci Industries, Inc.
5101 Blue Mound Rd
817 509-2300

**(P-16199)**
**PENINSULA PACKAGING LLC (DH)**
1030 N Anderson Rd, Exeter (93221-9341)
PHONE.....................559 594-6813
▲ EMP: 70 EST: 2002
SALES (est): 33.23MM
SALES (corp-wide): 6.78B **Publicly Held**
Web: www.sonoco.com
SIC: **3999** 3085 Atomizers, toiletry; Plastics bottles
HQ: Sonoco Plastics, Inc.
1 N 2nd Ave
Hartsville SC 29550
843 383-7000

**(P-16200)**
**PERFECT CHOICE MFRS INC**
Also Called: West Coast Metal Stamping
17819 Gillette Ave, Irvine (92614-6501)
PHONE.....................714 792-0322
Kevin Price, *CEO*
EMP: 42 EST: 2021
SALES (est): 2.85MM **Privately Held**
SIC: **3999** Manufacturing industries, nec

**(P-16201)**
**PET PARTNERS INC (PA)**
Also Called: North American Pet Products
450 N Sheridan St, Corona (92878-4020)
PHONE.....................951 279-9888
Keith Bonner, *CEO*
Ronald Bonner, *
Gordan Thulemeyer, *
Gloria Bonner, *
▲ EMP: 170 EST: 1995
SQ FT: 120,000
SALES (est): 22.69MM **Privately Held**
Web: www.petpartners.org
SIC: **3999** Pet supplies

**(P-16202)**
**PF CANDLE CO**
2213 W Sunset Blvd, Los Angeles (90026-3053)
PHONE.....................323 284-8431
EMP: 22 EST: 2018
SALES (est): 239.94K **Privately Held**
Web: www.pfcandleco.com
SIC: **3999** Candles

**(P-16203)**
**PHIARO INCORPORATED**
9016 Research Dr, Irvine (92618-4215)
PHONE.....................949 727-1261
Takeichiro Iwasaki, *Pr*
▲ EMP: 32 EST: 1988
SQ FT: 35,000
SALES (est): 7.97MM **Privately Held**
Web: www.phiaro.jp
SIC: **3999** Models, general, except toy
PA: Phiaro Corporation, Inc.
8-2-3, Nobitome

**(P-16204)**
**PICNIC TIME INC**
Also Called: Beach State
5131 Maureen Ln, Moorpark (93021-1783)
PHONE.....................805 529-7400
Paul Cosaro, *CEO*
Gustavo Cosaro, *
◆ EMP: 77 EST: 1982
SQ FT: 20,000
SALES (est): 9.93MM **Privately Held**
Web: www.picnictime.com
SIC: **3999** 5199 Handles, handbag and luggage; Bags, baskets, and cases

## 3999 - Manufacturing Industries, Nec (P-16205)

**(P-16205)**
**PIERCO INCORPORATED**
680 Main St, Riverside (92501-1034)
PHONE..................................909 251-7100
Erik Flemming, CEO
EMP: 15 EST: 2015
SALES (est): 1.56MM Privately Held
Web: www.pierco.com
SIC: 3999 3089 Beekeepers' supplies; Air mattresses, plastics

**(P-16206)**
**POMMES FRITES CANDLE CO**
Also Called: Pf Candle Co
7300 E Slauson Ave, Commerce (90040-3627)
PHONE..................................213 488-2016
Kristen Pumphrey, CEO
Thomas Neuberger, *
EMP: 30 EST: 2014
SALES (est): 4.79MM Privately Held
Web: www.pfcandleco.com
SIC: 3999 5149 5199 5999 Candles; Flavorings and fragrances; Candles; Candle shops

**(P-16207)**
**POWERHOUSE ENGINEERING INC**
101 Industrial Way Ste 13, Belmont (94002-8207)
PHONE..................................650 226-3560
Carlo Bertocchini, Pr
EMP: 16 EST: 2007
SALES (est): 244.55K Privately Held
SIC: 3999 Manufacturing industries, nec

**(P-16208)**
**PRESERVED TREESCAPES INTERNATIONAL INC**
Also Called: Preserved Treescapes Intl
180 Vallecitos De Oro, San Marcos (92069-1435)
PHONE..................................760 631-6789
◆ EMP: 75
Web: www.treescapes.com
SIC: 3999 Artificial trees and flowers

**(P-16209)**
**PRIDE INDUSTRIES ONE INC**
Also Called: Pride Industries
10030 Foothills Blvd, Roseville (95747-7102)
P.O. Box 1200 (95677-7200)
PHONE..................................916 788-2100
Jeff Dern, CFO
Pete Berghuis, *
EMP: 4300 EST: 1997
SALES (est): 102.74MM
SALES (corp-wide): 279.83MM Privately Held
Web: www.prideindustries.com
SIC: 3999 Barber and beauty shop equipment
PA: Pride Industries
 10030 Foothills Blvd
 916 788-2100

**(P-16210)**
**PROCTER & GAMBLE MFG CO**
1415 L St, Sacramento (95814-3961)
PHONE..................................916 442-3135
▲ EMP: 26
SALES (corp-wide): 84.04B Publicly Held
Web: us.pg.com
SIC: 3999 Atomizers, toiletry
HQ: The Procter & Gamble Manufacturing Company
 1 Procter And Gamble Plz
 Cincinnati OH 45202
 513 983-1100

**(P-16211)**
**PRYSM INC (PA)**
Also Called: Prysm
513 Fairview Way, Milpitas (95035-3059)
PHONE..................................408 586-1127
Amit Jain, Pr
Tushar Kothari, *
Dana Corey, *
Jasbir Singh, *
Roger Hajjar, *
▲ EMP: 70 EST: 2005
SQ FT: 25,000
SALES (est): 26.47MM Privately Held
Web: www.prysmsystems.com
SIC: 3999 Advertising display products

**(P-16212)**
**QUALITY RESOURCES DIST LLC**
16254 Beaver Rd, Adelanto (92301-3906)
PHONE..................................510 378-6861
Wesley Staley, Managing Member
EMP: 21 EST: 2018
SALES (est): 429.14K Privately Held
SIC: 3999

**(P-16213)**
**REAPS COMPANY LLC**
Also Called: Caravan Distribution
1950 S Santa Fe Ave Ste 109, Los Angeles (90021-2935)
PHONE..................................212 256-1186
Michael Hurt, Owner
EMP: 21 EST: 2015
SALES (est): 1.5MM Privately Held
SIC: 3999

**(P-16214)**
**REDEFINED INDUSTRIES LLC**
9681 Business Center Dr Ste B, Rancho Cucamonga (91730-4579)
PHONE..................................909 991-9927
Ralph Vildosola, Prin
EMP: 20 EST: 2015
SALES (est): 166.67K Privately Held
SIC: 3999 Manufacturing industries, nec

**(P-16215)**
**REEL EFX INC**
5539 Riverton Ave, North Hollywood (91601-2816)
PHONE..................................818 762-1710
Jim Gill, Pr
Susan Gill, *
Rosy Romano, *
Susan Milliken, *
EMP: 25 EST: 1982
SQ FT: 34,000
SALES (est): 5.39MM Privately Held
Web: www.reelefx.com
SIC: 3999 Stage hardware and equipment, except lighting

**(P-16216)**
**RELAX MEDICAL SYSTEMS INC**
Also Called: RMS
3260 E Willow St, Signal Hill (90755-2309)
PHONE..................................800 405-7677
Leon Press, CEO
◆ EMP: 15 EST: 2000
SALES (est): 806.54K Privately Held
Web: www.relaxmedsyst.com
SIC: 3999 5083 5261 Hydroponic equipment; Hydroponic equipment and supplies; Hydroponic equipment and supplies

**(P-16217)**
**RESQ MANUFACTURING**
11430 White Rock Rd, Rancho Cordova (95742-6600)
PHONE..................................916 638-6786
Martin Szegedy, CEO
EMP: 45 EST: 2012
SALES (est): 5.16MM Privately Held
Web: www.resqmfg.com
SIC: 3999 Airplane models, except toy

**(P-16218)**
**RICON CORPORATION**
1135 Aviation Pl, San Fernando (91340-1460)
PHONE..................................818 267-3000
William Baldwin, Pr
◆ EMP: 135 EST: 1971
SQ FT: 225,000
SALES (est): 22.28MM Publicly Held
Web: www.riconcorp.com
SIC: 3999 Wheelchair lifts
PA: Westinghouse Air Brake Technologies Corporation
 30 Isabella St

**(P-16219)**
**RUKLI INC**
4150 Puente Ave, Baldwin Park (91706-3432)
PHONE..................................818 981-9137
Gregory Klibanov, CEO
EMP: 20 EST: 2017
SALES (est): 1.86MM Privately Held
SIC: 3999

**(P-16220)**
**SAVAGE INDUSTRIES**
48 Linda St, San Francisco (94110-1616)
PHONE..................................415 845-6264
Adam Savage, Prin
EMP: 32 EST: 2010
SALES (est): 491.29K Privately Held
Web: www.savageco.com
SIC: 3999 Manufacturing industries, nec

**(P-16221)**
**SAVI TECHNOLOGY HOLDINGS INC**
615 Tasman Dr, Sunnyvale (94089-1707)
PHONE..................................650 316-4950
▲ EMP: 330
Web: www.savi.com
SIC: 3999 3663 Identification tags, except paper; Radio and t.v. communications equipment

**(P-16222)**
**SC BLOOM NETWORK INC**
300 Pioneer St, Santa Cruz (95060-2176)
PHONE..................................415 650-8015
William Sump, CEO
Ryan Michaels, *
EMP: 27 EST: 2018
SALES (est): 2.32MM Privately Held
SIC: 3999 5159

**(P-16223)**
**SCAFCO CORPORATION**
Also Called: Scafco Steel Stud Mfg
2050 Farallon Dr, San Leandro (94577-6602)
PHONE..................................415 852-7974
EMP: 22
SALES (corp-wide): 29.47MM Privately Held
Web: www.scafco.com
SIC: 3999 Barber and beauty shop equipment
PA: Scafco Corporation
 2800 E Main Ave
 509 343-9000

**(P-16224)**
**SCAFCO CORPORATION**
2525 S Airport Way, Stockton (95206-3521)
PHONE..................................209 670-8053
Erick King, Brnch Mgr
EMP: 22
SALES (corp-wide): 29.47MM Privately Held
Web: www.scafco.com
SIC: 3999 Barber and beauty shop equipment
PA: Scafco Corporation
 2800 E Main Ave
 509 343-9000

**(P-16225)**
**SCRIPTO-TOKAI CORPORATION (HQ)**
2055 S Haven Ave, Ontario (91761-0736)
PHONE..................................909 930-5000
Tomoyuki Kurata, Pr
Tokiharu Murofushi, *
Fred Ashley, *
▲ EMP: 80 EST: 1923
SQ FT: 120,000
SALES (est): 3.88MM Privately Held
Web: www.calicobrands.com
SIC: 3999 3951 Cigarette lighters, except precious metal; Ball point pens and parts
PA: Tokai Corporation
 6-21-1, Nishishinjuku

**(P-16226)**
**SEGA HOLDINGS USA INC**
9737 Lurline Ave, Chatsworth (91311-4404)
PHONE..................................415 701-6000
◆ EMP: 1880
SIC: 3999 5045 Coin-operated amusement machines; Computers and accessories, personal and home entertainment

**(P-16227)**
**SGPS INC**
Also Called: Show Group Production Services
15823 S Main St, Gardena (90248-2548)
PHONE..................................310 538-4175
Barrie Owen, CEO
Katy Marx, *
EMP: 85 EST: 1991
SQ FT: 40,000
SALES (est): 8.99MM Privately Held
Web: www.sgpsshowrig.com
SIC: 3999 Theatrical scenery

**(P-16228)**
**SHAPELL INDUSTRIES**
1990 S Bundy Dr Ste 500, Los Angeles (90025-5245)
PHONE..................................323 655-7330
EMP: 19 EST: 2018
SALES (est): 595.62K Privately Held
Web: www.shapell.com
SIC: 3999 Manufacturing industries, nec

**(P-16229)**
**SILVESTRI STUDIO INC (PA)**
Also Called: Silvester California
8125 Beach St, Los Angeles (90001-3426)
P.O. Box P.O. Box 512198 (90061)
PHONE..................................323 277-4420
E Alain Levi, CEO
▲ EMP: 80 EST: 1934
SQ FT: 130,000
SALES (est): 4.61MM
SALES (corp-wide): 4.61MM Privately Held

Web: www.silvestricalifornia.com
SIC: 3999 2542 3993 Mannequins; Office and store showcases and display fixtures; Signs and advertising specialties

**(P-16230)**
**SMALL WNDERS HNDCRFTED MNTRES**
7033 Canoga Ave Ste 5, Canoga Park (91303-3118)
PHONE..............................818 703-7450
EMP: 15
SALES (est): 908.35K Privately Held
SIC: 3999 Miniatures

**(P-16231)**
**SNAPSHOT HAIR & EXTENSIONS LLC**
2892 N Bellflower Blvd, Long Beach (90815-1125)
PHONE..............................877 783-5658
EMP: 15 EST: 2021
SALES (est): 340K Privately Held
Web: www.snapshothair.com
SIC: 3999 Hair and hair-based products

**(P-16232)**
**SOCAL LABS LLC**
68739 Summit Dr, Cathedral City (92234-7349)
PHONE..............................813 857-5207
EMP: 16 EST: 2018
SALES (est): 576.59K Privately Held
Web: www.socallabs.org
SIC: 3999

**(P-16233)**
**SOCIAL BRANDS LLC**
6575 Simson St, Oakland (94605-2271)
PHONE..............................415 728-1761
Benjamin Seabury, Mgr
EMP: 20 EST: 2017
SALES (est): 288.49K Privately Held
SIC: 3999 Manufacturing industries, nec

**(P-16234)**
**SOFTUB INC (PA)**
24700 Avenue Rockefeller, Valencia (91355)
PHONE..............................858 602-1920
Liberte Chan, CEO
Tom Thornbury, *
▲ EMP: 85 EST: 1983
SALES (est): 27.1MM
SALES (corp-wide): 27.1MM Privately Held
Web: www.softub.com
SIC: 3999 Hot tubs

**(P-16235)**
**SONIYA VALLEY LLC**
Also Called: Sacramento Cash and Carry
1160 Tara Ct Ste A, Rocklin (95765-1224)
PHONE..............................916 221-4313
Abdul Hirani, Managing Member
EMP: 15 EST: 2013
SALES (est): 2.29MM Privately Held
SIC: 3999

**(P-16236)**
**SOTA EXTRACTS INC**
468 Yolanda Ave Ste 203, Santa Rosa (95404-6328)
PHONE..............................612 889-4049
Malcolm Smith, CEO
Travis Varpness, CFO
EMP: 19 EST: 2019
SALES (est): 1.64MM Privately Held
SIC: 3999

**(P-16237)**
**SPARKS EXHBITS ENVRNMENTS CORP**
Also Called: Sparks Los Angeles
3143 S La Cienega Blvd, Los Angeles (90016-3110)
PHONE..............................562 941-0101
EMP: 42
SALES (corp-wide): 1.56B Privately Held
Web: www.wearesparks.com
SIC: 3999 Advertising display products
HQ: Sparks Exhibits & Environments Pa Llc
2828 Charter Rd
Philadelphia PA 19154
215 676-1100

**(P-16238)**
**STANG INDUSTRIES INC**
Also Called: Stang Industrial Products
8778 Kimball Ave, Chino (91708-9613)
PHONE..............................914 479-9810
Charles Ronie, CEO
Abdul Kashif, CFO
◆ EMP: 19 EST: 1943
SALES (est): 4.84MM Privately Held
Web: www.stangindustries.com
SIC: 3999 3492 3561 Fire extinguishers, portable; Control valves, aircraft: hydraulic and pneumatic; Pumps and pumping equipment

**(P-16239)**
**STEELDECK INC**
13147 S Western Ave, Gardena (90249-1921)
PHONE..............................323 290-2100
Phil Parsons, Pr
Adrian Funnell, *
▲ EMP: 25 EST: 1993
SALES (est): 2.54MM Privately Held
Web: www.steeldeck.com
SIC: 3999 2541 2531 Stage hardware and equipment, except lighting; Partitions for floor attachment, prefabricated: wood; Theater furniture

**(P-16240)**
**SUBLIMATION INC**
Also Called: Sublime
2537 Willow St Unit 6, Oakland (94607-1723)
PHONE..............................888 994-2726
Matthew Hawkins, Interim Chief Executive Officer
Ahmer Iqbal, COO
EMP: 25 EST: 2016
SALES (est): 2.22MM
SALES (corp-wide): 2.46MM Privately Held
SIC: 3999 5159
PA: Harborside Inc.
66205 Paul Rd
888 994-2726

**(P-16241)**
**SUESS PROPERTIES INC**
18378 Atkins Rd, Lodi (95240)
P.O. Box 2680 (95241)
PHONE..............................209 334-2081
Calvin Suess, Pr
Virgil Suess, *
EMP: 18 EST: 2000
SQ FT: 225,000
SALES (est): 3.54MM Privately Held
Web: www.shellproinc.com
SIC: 3999 Nut shells, grinding, from purchased nuts

**(P-16242)**
**SUN BADGE CO**
2248 S Baker Ave, Ontario (91761-7710)
PHONE..............................909 930-1444
Rick Hamilton, Pr
Chris Hamilton, *
▲ EMP: 35 EST: 1957
SQ FT: 24,000
SALES (est): 3.53MM Privately Held
Web: www.sunbadgeorders.com
SIC: 3999 Badges, metal: policemen, firemen, etc.

**(P-16243)**
**SUN VALLEY FLORAL GROUP LLC**
3160 Upper Bay Rd, Arcata (95521-9690)
PHONE..............................707 826-8700
Lane Devries, CEO
▲ EMP: 750 EST: 2006
SALES (est): 11.35MM Privately Held
Web: www.tsvg.com
SIC: 3999 Flowers, artificial and preserved

**(P-16244)**
**SUNDANCE SPAS INC (DH)**
Also Called: Sundance Spas
17872 Gillette Ave Ste 300, Irvine (92614-6573)
PHONE..............................909 606-7733
David Jackson, CEO
Rich Strong, *
Jason Weintraub, *
◆ EMP: 73 EST: 1998
SALES (est): 18.65MM
SALES (corp-wide): 440.01K Privately Held
Web: www.sundancespas.com
SIC: 3999 1799 5999 Hot tubs; Swimming pool construction; Spas and hot tubs
HQ: Jacuzzi Brands Llc
17872 Gllette Ave Ste 300
Irvine CA 92614
909 606-1416

**(P-16245)**
**SUNDERSTORM LLC**
1146 N Central Ave, Glendale (91202-2506)
PHONE..............................818 605-6682
Cameron Clark, CEO
Keith Cich, Pr
EMP: 17 EST: 2015
SALES (est): 3.3MM Privately Held
Web: www.kanhatreats.com
SIC: 3999

**(P-16246)**
**SUNSTAR SPA COVERS INC (HQ)**
26074 Avenue Hall Ste 13, Valencia (91355-1240)
PHONE..............................858 602-1950
Tom Thornbury, Ch Bd
Edward Mcgarry, Pr
▲ EMP: 40 EST: 2000
SALES (est): 2.48MM
SALES (corp-wide): 27.1MM Privately Held
SIC: 3999 Hot tub and spa covers
PA: Softub, Inc.
24700 Ave Rockefeller
858 602-1920

**(P-16247)**
**SUPERIOR-STUDIO SPC INC**
2239 Yates Ave, Commerce (90040-1913)
PHONE..............................323 278-0100
TOLL FREE: 800
Jean-pierre Fournier, Pr
◆ EMP: 20 EST: 1995
SQ FT: 60,000
SALES (est): 757.14K Privately Held
Web: www.studiospecialties.ca
SIC: 3999 Advertising display products

**(P-16248)**
**T-REX PRODUCTS INCORPORATED**
7920 Airway Rd Ste A6, San Diego (92154-8311)
PHONE..............................619 482-4424
Alan Botterman, Pr
David Hanono, VP
▲ EMP: 15 EST: 1997
SQ FT: 14,000
SALES (est): 2.23MM Privately Held
Web: www.t-rexproducts.com
SIC: 3999 Pet supplies

**(P-16249)**
**TAG TOYS INC**
1810 S Acacia Ave, Compton (90220-4927)
PHONE..............................310 639-4566
Lawrence Mestyanek, CEO
Judy Mestyanek, *
EMP: 65 EST: 1976
SQ FT: 60,000
SALES (est): 4.71MM Privately Held
Web: www.tagtoys.com
SIC: 3999 8351 3944 Education aids, devices and supplies; Child day care services; Games, toys, and children's vehicles

**(P-16250)**
**TANDEM DESIGN INC**
Also Called: Tandem Exhibit
1916 W 144th St, Gardena (90249)
PHONE..............................714 978-7272
Maury Bonas, Pr
Susan Bonas, VP
EMP: 23 EST: 1975
SALES (est): 1.41MM Privately Held
Web: www.presentationmedia.com
SIC: 3999 Preparation of slides and exhibits

**(P-16251)**
**TECHNICAL MANUFACTURING W LLC**
24820 Avenue Tibbitts, Valencia (91355-3404)
PHONE..............................661 295-7226
EMP: 28 EST: 2010
SALES (est): 3.64MM Privately Held
Web: www.tmwmedical.com
SIC: 3999 Barber and beauty shop equipment

**(P-16252)**
**TECHNICAL REPS INTL INC**
Also Called: Scientific Hardware Systems
8525 Forest St Ste C, Gilroy (95020)
PHONE..............................408 848-8868
Scott Hagel, CEO
Scott Jay Hagel, Pr
EMP: 15 EST: 1981
SALES (est): 2.63MM Privately Held
Web: www.scientifichardware.com
SIC: 3999 1542 Atomizers, toiletry; Nonresidential construction, nec

**(P-16253)**
**TOPLINE MANUFACTURING INC**
7032 Alondra Blvd, Paramount (90723-3926)
PHONE..............................562 633-0605
Byungs Chae, CEO

# 3999 - Manufacturing Industries, Nec (P-16254)

**EMP:** 17 **EST:** 2020
**SALES (est):** 885.03K **Privately Held**
**Web:** www.toplinemfg.com
**SIC:** 3999 Manufacturing industries, nec

*(P-16254)*
**TOWER 26 INC**
8826 Bradley Ave Ste B, Sun Valley (91352-2703)
**PHONE**..................347 366-2706
Alexey Shkavrov, *CEO*
Eric Gersh, *
**EMP:** 30 **EST:** 2016
**SALES (est):** 741.78K **Privately Held**
**Web:** tower26official.com
**SIC:** 3999

*(P-16255)*
**TRANS FX INC**
Also Called: T F X
2361 Eastman Ave, Oxnard (93030-8136)
**PHONE**..................805 485-6110
Allen Pike, *Pr*
Rick Bordonaro, *Ex VP*
Hollis Hedrich, *Finance*
**EMP:** 15 **EST:** 1993
**SQ FT:** 25,000
**SALES (est):** 4.14MM **Privately Held**
**Web:** www.transfx.com
**SIC:** 3999 3711 7389 3812 Models, except toy; Automobile assembly, including specialty automobiles; Design services; Acceleration indicators and systems components, aerospace

*(P-16256)*
**TRAXX CORPORATION**
1201 E Lexington Ave, Pomona (91766-5520)
**PHONE**..................909 623-8032
Craig Silvers, *CEO*
Jon Hall, *
▲ **EMP:** 100 **EST:** 2007
**SQ FT:** 52,000
**SALES (est):** 2.33MM **Privately Held**
**Web:** www.traxxcorp.com
**SIC:** 3999 Carpet tackles

*(P-16257)*
**TRE MILANO LLC**
Also Called: Instyler
2730 Monterey St Ste 101, Torrance (90503-7230)
**PHONE**..................310 260-8888
▲ **EMP:** 38 **EST:** 2007
**SALES (est):** 2.12MM **Privately Held**
**Web:** www.instyler.com
**SIC:** 3999 Hair and hair-based products

*(P-16258)*
**TREESCAPES AND PLANT WORKS**
Also Called: International Treescapes
1248 Los Vallecitos Blvd, San Marcos (92069)
**PHONE**..................760 631-6789
**EMP:** 32 **EST:** 2021
**SALES (est):** 1.88MM **Privately Held**
**Web:** www.treescapes.com
**SIC:** 3999 Plants, artificial and preserved

*(P-16259)*
**TRICK OR TREAT STDIOS HLDNGS L**
1005 17th Ave, Santa Cruz (95062-3033)
**PHONE**..................831 713-9665
Christopher M Zephro, *Managing Member*
▲ **EMP:** 20 **EST:** 2013
**SQ FT:** 3,000

**SALES (est):** 831.51K **Privately Held**
**Web:** www.trickortreatstudios.com
**SIC:** 3999 7922 2389 Magic equipment, supplies, and props; Costume design, theatrical; Lodge costumes

*(P-16260)*
**TRNLWB LLC**
Also Called: Trinity Lighweight
17410 Lockwood Valley Rd, Frazier Park (93225-9318)
**PHONE**..................661 245-3736
**EMP:** 4900
**SALES (corp-wide):** 21.91MM **Privately Held**
**Web:** www.trinityesc.com
**SIC:** 3999 Barber and beauty shop equipment
**PA:** Trnlwb, Llc
1112 E Cpeland Rd Ste 500
800 581-3117

*(P-16261)*
**TTT INNOVATIONS LLC**
Also Called: TTT Innovations
20850 Plummer St, Chatsworth (91311-5004)
P.O. Box 86 (91365-0086)
**PHONE**..................818 201-8828
Thomas Bruggemann, *CEO*
**EMP:** 20 **EST:** 2016
**SALES (est):** 3.22MM **Privately Held**
**Web:** www.tomstumbletrimmer.com
**SIC:** 3999 Atomizers, toiletry

*(P-16262)*
**VAL USA MANUFACTURER INC**
1050 W Central Ave Ste A, Brea (92821-2200)
**PHONE**..................626 839-8069
Lijuan Zhen, *Mgr*
▲ **EMP:** 30 **EST:** 2014
**SALES (est):** 1.84MM **Privately Held**
**Web:** www.valcosmetics.com
**SIC:** 3999 Manufacturing industries, nec

*(P-16263)*
**VIRTUAL TECHNOLOGIES INC**
Also Called: Global V R
1380 Piper Dr, Milpitas (95035-6820)
**PHONE**..................408 597-3400
Ken Bayr, *Pr*
Frank Ballouz, *
Caryn Mical, *
Debbie Minardi, *
John Ray, *
◆ **EMP:** 50 **EST:** 1998
**SQ FT:** 60,000
**SALES (est):** 986.57K **Privately Held**
**SIC:** 3999 Coin-operated amusement machines

*(P-16264)*
**VITAVET LABS INC**
Also Called: Nuvet Labs
5717 Corsa Ave, Westlake Village (91362-4001)
**PHONE**..................818 865-2600
Blake Kirschbaum, *Pr*
Doctor Raymond Kirschbaum, *CFO*
▼ **EMP:** 20 **EST:** 1997
**SALES (est):** 2.73MM **Privately Held**
**Web:** www.nuvet.com
**SIC:** 3999 Pet supplies

*(P-16265)*
**VOLTA INDUSTRIES INC (DH)**
155 De Haro St, San Francisco (94103-5121)
**PHONE**..................415 583-3805

Scott Mercer, *Ch Bd*
Christopher Wendel, *Pr*
Francois P Chadwick, *CFO*
James S Degraw, *Chief*
**EMP:** 20 **EST:** 2010
**SALES (est):** 19.45MM
**SALES (corp-wide):** 316.62B **Privately Held**
**Web:** www.voltacharging.com
**SIC:** 3999 Barber and beauty shop equipment
**HQ:** Volta Inc.
155 De Haro St
San Francisco CA 94103
415 583-3805

*(P-16266)*
**W F F H INC**
Also Called: Hot Wire Foam Factory04
216 E Laurel Ave, Lompoc (93436-5364)
**PHONE**..................805 735-9255
David Natal, *CEO*
◆ **EMP:** 15 **EST:** 1991
**SQ FT:** 4,000
**SALES (est):** 1.81MM **Privately Held**
**Web:** www.hotwirefoamfactory.com
**SIC:** 3999 Manufacturing industries, nec

*(P-16267)*
**WALLY & PAT ENTERPRISES**
Also Called: Complete Aquatic Systems
13530 S Budlong Ave, Gardena (90247-2030)
**PHONE**..................310 532-2031
Shareen King, *Pr*
**EMP:** 48 **EST:** 2000
**SALES (est):** 4.72MM **Privately Held**
**Web:** www.completeaquaticsystems.com
**SIC:** 3999 Barber and beauty shop equipment

*(P-16268)*
**WATKINS MANUFACTURING CORP (HQ)**
Also Called: Watkins Wellness
1280 Park Center Dr, Vista (92081-8398)
**PHONE**..................760 598-6464
Vijaikrishna Teenarsipur, *CEO*
Christopher Peavey, *
◆ **EMP:** 127 **EST:** 1977
**SQ FT:** 430,000
**SALES (est):** 164.33MM
**SALES (corp-wide):** 7.97B **Publicly Held**
**Web:** www.hotspring.com
**SIC:** 3999 Hot tubs
**PA:** Masco Corporation
17450 College Pkwy
313 274-7400

*(P-16269)*
**WBT GROUP LLC**
Also Called: Wbt Industries
1401 S Shamrock Ave, Monrovia (91016-4246)
**PHONE**..................323 735-1201
▲ **EMP:** 40 **EST:** 2009
**SALES (est):** 4.44MM **Privately Held**
**Web:** www.wbtindustries.com
**SIC:** 3999 Buttons: Red Cross, union, identification

*(P-16270)*
**WHITESTONE INDUSTRIES INC**
4632 District Blvd, Bakersfield (93313-2316)
**PHONE**..................888 567-2234
Carlos Corado Garcia, *Admn*
**EMP:** 40 **EST:** 2015
**SALES (est):** 3.41MM **Privately Held**
**Web:** www.wsindustries.com

**SIC:** 3999 Manufacturing industries, nec

*(P-16271)*
**WHITLOCK INDUSTRIES INC**
Also Called: Whitlock Surfboards
609 Mission Ave, Oceanside (92054-2831)
**PHONE**..................760 231-9262
Cory Whitlock, *CEO*
Robert Whitlock, *Owner*
Cory Whitlock, *VP*
**EMP:** 17 **EST:** 2002
**SALES (est):** 975.43K **Privately Held**
**Web:** www.whitlocksurfexperience.com
**SIC:** 3999 3949 2759 7999 Manufacturing industries, nec; Sporting and athletic goods, nec; Screen printing; Amusement and recreation, nec

*(P-16272)*
**WOOD CANDLE WICK TECH INC**
Also Called: Makesy
9750 Irvine Blvd Ste 106, Irvine (92618-1676)
**PHONE**..................310 488-5885
Dayna Marie Decker, *CEO*
**EMP:** 66 **EST:** 2015
**SALES (est):** 6.38MM **Privately Held**
**SIC:** 3999 Candles

*(P-16273)*
**ZOO MED LABORATORIES INC**
3650 Sacramento Dr, San Luis Obispo (93401-7113)
**PHONE**..................805 542-9988
▲ **EMP:** 133 **EST:** 1977
**SALES (est):** 11.15MM **Privately Held**
**Web:** www.zoomed.com
**SIC:** 3999 5199 Pet supplies; Pets and pet supplies

## 4111 Local And Suburban Transit

*(P-16274)*
**FORREST GROUP LLC (PA)**
Also Called: Fly On My Jet
1422 N Curson Ave Apt 9, Los Angeles (90046-4037)
**PHONE**..................619 808-9798
Allen Forrest, *CEO*
**EMP:** 64 **EST:** 2016
**SALES (est):** 2.66MM
**SALES (corp-wide):** 2.66MM **Privately Held**
**Web:** www.tfgla.com
**SIC:** 4111 8742 7319 3532 Airport transportation; Food and beverage consultant; Display advertising service; Shuttle cars, underground

*(P-16275)*
**GLOCOL INC**
Also Called: Peoplesense
6541 Puerto Dr, Rancho Murieta (95683-9365)
**PHONE**..................650 224-2108
Ranju Verma, *Ex Dir*
Harsh Verma, *Prin*
**EMP:** 20 **EST:** 2003
**SALES (est):** 697.8K **Privately Held**
**Web:** www.glocol.net
**SIC:** 4111 7375 7371 7372 Local and suburban transit; Information retrieval services; Computer software systems analysis and design, custom; Business oriented computer software

## 4119 Local Passenger Transportation, Nec

**(P-16276)**
**AMERICAN MEDICAL RESPONSE INC**
1300 Illinois St, San Francisco (94107-3107)
PHONE..............................415 794-9204
Thomas Wagner, *CEO*
EMP: 250 EST: 1992
SALES (est): 1.55MM **Publicly Held**
SIC: 4119 7372 Ambulance service; Application computer software
HQ: Envision Healthcare Corporation
20 Burton Hlls Blvd Ste 5
Nashville TN 37215
615 787-2050

**(P-16277)**
**LEADER INDUSTRIES INC**
Also Called: Leader Emergency Vehicles
10941 Weaver Ave, South El Monte (91733-2752)
PHONE..............................626 575-0880
Gary Hunter, *Prin*
EMP: 160 EST: 2001
SALES (est): 16.12MM **Privately Held**
Web: www.leaderambulance.com
SIC: 4119 5046 3711 Ambulance service; Commercial equipment, nec; Motor vehicles and car bodies

## 4212 Local Trucking, Without Storage

**(P-16278)**
**CENTRAL VALLEY CONCRETE INC (PA)**
Also Called: Central Valley Trucking
3823 N State Highway 59, Merced (95348-9370)
PHONE..............................209 723-8846
Scott Neal, *CEO*
EMP: 150 EST: 1975
SQ FT: 2,000
SALES (est): 34.42MM
SALES (corp-wide): 34.42MM **Privately Held**
Web: www.centralvalleyconcrete.com
SIC: 4212 3273 Local trucking, without storage; Ready-mixed concrete

**(P-16279)**
**HANSON AGGRGTES MD-PACIFIC INC**
50 S Kellogg Ave, Goleta (93117-3417)
PHONE..............................805 967-2371
EMP: 18
SALES (corp-wide): 21.19B **Privately Held**
SIC: 4212 3281 Local trucking, without storage; Stone, quarrying and processing of own stone products
HQ: Hanson Aggregates Mid-Pacific, Inc.
12667 Alcosta Blvd # 400
San Ramon CA

**(P-16280)**
**MULECHAIN INC**
2901 W Coast Hwy Ste 200, Newport Beach (92663-4045)
PHONE..............................888 456-8881
Ralph Liu, *CEO*
EMP: 56 EST: 2017
SALES (est): 768.35K **Privately Held**
Web: www.mulechain.com

SIC: 4212 7372 Delivery service, vehicular; Application computer software

## 4215 Courier Services, Except By Air

**(P-16281)**
**NATIONAL LOGISTICS TEAM LLC**
21496 Main St, Grand Terrace (92313-5806)
P.O. Box 75 (92572-0075)
PHONE..............................951 369-5841
Eric Meza, *Managing Member*
EMP: 20 EST: 2013
SALES (est): 4.97MM **Privately Held**
Web: www.nlt-llc.com
SIC: 4215 2448 Package delivery, vehicular; Pallets, wood

## 4221 Farm Product Warehousing And Storage

**(P-16282)**
**HONEYVILLE INC**
11600 Dayton Dr, Rancho Cucamonga (91730-5525)
PHONE..............................909 980-9500
David Brown, *CEO*
EMP: 85
SALES (corp-wide): 188.43MM **Privately Held**
Web: www.honeyville.com
SIC: 4221 5153 2045 2041 Grain elevator, storage only; Grains; Prepared flour mixes and doughs; Flour and other grain mill products
PA: Honeyville, Inc.
1040 W 600 N
435 494-4193

## 4222 Refrigerated Warehousing And Storage

**(P-16283)**
**ECKERT COLD STORAGE COMPANY**
757 Moffat Blvd, Manteca (95336-5819)
PHONE..............................209 823-3181
Steve West, *Mgr*
EMP: 20
SALES (corp-wide): 141.5MM **Privately Held**
Web: www.eckertcs.com
SIC: 4222 2037 Storage, frozen or refrigerated goods; Frozen fruits and vegetables
PA: Eckert Cold Storage Company
905 Clough Rd
209 838-4040

**(P-16284)**
**MOUNTAIN WATER ICE COMPANY**
2843 Benet Rd, Oceanside (92058-1245)
PHONE..............................760 722-7611
Steven Gabriel, *Pr*
EMP: 26
SALES (corp-wide): 4.83MM **Privately Held**
Web: www.arcticglacier.com
SIC: 4222 2097 5999 Warehousing, cold storage or refrigerated; Block ice; Ice
PA: Mountain Water Ice Company Inc
17011 Central Ave
310 638-0321

**(P-16285)**
**PREMIER COLD STORAGE & PKG LLC**
1071 E 233rd St, Carson (90745-6206)
PHONE..............................949 444-8859
Steve Karo, *Pr*
EMP: 205 EST: 2022
SALES (est): 9.55MM **Privately Held**
SIC: 4222 3053 Warehousing, cold storage or refrigerated; Packing materials

## 4225 General Warehousing And Storage

**(P-16286)**
**ARB INC**
Also Called: Northern Division
1875 Loveridge Rd, Pittsburg (94565-4110)
P.O. Box 8189 (94565-8189)
PHONE..............................925 432-3649
Donnie Brown, *Brnch Mgr*
EMP: 410
Web: www.prim.com
SIC: 4225 1623 3444 General warehousing and storage; Pipeline construction, nsk; Sheet metalwork
HQ: Arb, Inc.
26000 Commercentre Dr
Lake Forest CA 92630
949 598-9242

**(P-16287)**
**CRYOMAX USA INC (HQ)**
127 N California Ave Ste B, City Of Industry (91744-4313)
PHONE..............................626 330-3388
Yen T Liu, *Pr*
James Ho, *CFO*
James Ting, *COO*
EMP: 17 EST: 2006
SQ FT: 55,000
SALES (est): 9.8MM **Privately Held**
Web: www.cryomaxcooling.com
SIC: 4225 3443 3714 General warehousing; Heat exchangers: coolers (after, inter), condensers, etc.; Radiators and radiator shells and cores, motor vehicle
PA: Cryomax Cooling System Corp.
No. 28, Gongqu Rd., Fangyuan Industrial Park

**(P-16288)**
**EDMUND A GRAY CO**
1901 Imperial St, Los Angeles (90021-2830)
PHONE..............................213 625-2725
Lawrence Gray Junior, *Brnch Mgr*
EMP: 35
SALES (corp-wide): 13.68MM **Privately Held**
Web: www.eagray.com
SIC: 4225 3498 General warehousing and storage; Pipe fittings, fabricated from purchased pipe
PA: Edmund A. Gray Co.
2277 E 15th St
213 625-0376

**(P-16289)**
**MULHOLLAND BROTHERS**
11840 Dorothy St Apt 301, Los Angeles (90049-7902)
PHONE..............................510 280-5485
John Holland, *Prin*
EMP: 49
SALES (corp-wide): 3.7MM **Privately Held**
Web: www.shopmulholland.com

SIC: 4225 3161 2512 General warehousing; Luggage; Upholstered household furniture
PA: Mulholland Brothers
1710 4th St
415 824-5995

**(P-16290)**
**ROYAL WESTLAKE ROOFING LLC**
Also Called: Lifetile
342 Roth Rd, Lathrop (95330-9029)
PHONE..............................209 983-1600
Norm Klingman, *Mgr*
EMP: 29
Web: www.westlakeroyalroofing.com
SIC: 4225 3272 2952 General warehousing and storage; Tile, precast terrazzo or concrete; Asphalt felts and coatings
HQ: Royal Westlake Roofing Llc
2801 Post Oak Blvd # 600
Houston TX 77056
800 658-8004

**(P-16291)**
**TOTAL WAREHOUSE INC**
Also Called: Total Warehouse
2895 E Miraloma Ave, Anaheim (92806-1804)
PHONE..............................714 332-3082
Boyd Kiefus, *CEO*
Dawn Koopmann, *
EMP: 119 EST: 2017
SALES (est): 2.23MM **Privately Held**
Web: www.totalwarehouse.com
SIC: 4225 7699 3537 5046 Miniwarehouse, warehousing; Industrial equipment services; Forklift trucks; Commercial equipment, nec

**(P-16292)**
**UNIFIED GROCERS INC**
Also Called: U W G Southern California Div
457 E Martin Luther King Jr Blvd, Los Angeles (90011-5650)
PHONE..............................323 232-6124
Maurice Ochua, *Brnch Mgr*
EMP: 150
Web: www.unfi.com
SIC: 4225 8742 2051 General warehousing and storage; Marketing consulting services; Bread, cake, and related products
HQ: Unfi Grocers Distribution, Inc.
2500 S Atlantic Blvd
Commerce CA 90040
323 264-5200

**(P-16293)**
**WILSONART LLC**
Also Called: Ralph Wilson Plastics
13911 Gannet St, Santa Fe Springs (90670-5326)
P.O. Box 2336 (90670-0336)
PHONE..............................562 921-7426
Carl Stephens, *Mgr*
EMP: 32
SQ FT: 72,000
SALES (corp-wide): 982.77MM **Privately Held**
Web: www.wilsonart.com
SIC: 4225 5162 3083 2891 General warehousing and storage; Plastics materials and basic shapes; Laminated plastics plate and sheet; Adhesives and sealants
HQ: Wilsonart Llc
2501 Wilsonart Dr
Temple TX 76504
254 207-7000

## 4226 Special Warehousing And Storage, Nec

**(P-16294)**
**PRIDE INDUSTRIES (PA)**
10030 Foothills Blvd, Roseville (95747-7102)
P.O. Box 1200 (95677)
PHONE.................................916 788-2100
TOLL FREE: 800
Jeffery Dern, *Pr*
Everett Crane, *
Tim Yamauchi, *
Peter Berghuis, *
Tina Oliveira, *
▲ **EMP:** 250 **EST:** 1966
**SQ FT:** 177,000
**SALES (est):** 279.83MM
**SALES (corp-wide):** 279.83MM **Privately Held**
Web: www.prideindustries.com
**SIC: 4226** 7349 3679  Special warehousing and storage, nec; Building maintenance services, nec; Electronic circuits

**(P-16295)**
**WOOD SPACE INDUSTRIES INC**
Also Called: Ariana Air Freight
429 W Levers Pl, Orange (92867-3620)
PHONE.................................714 996-4552
David E Reed, *Pr*
Gary Broyles, *Stockholder*
Jeff Horn, *Stockholder*
**EMP:** 18 **EST:** 1970
**SALES (est):** 868.39K **Privately Held**
Web: www.amexport.net
**SIC: 4226** 2441 4731 2449  Special warehousing and storage, nec; Nailed wood boxes and shook; Freight forwarding; Wood containers, nec

## 4491 Marine Cargo Handling

**(P-16296)**
**TOTAL INTERMODAL SERVICES INC (PA)**
7101 Jackson St, Paramount (90723-4836)
PHONE.................................562 427-6300
Amador Sanchez Junior, *Pr*
▲ **EMP:** 50 **EST:** 1991
**SALES (est):** 18.62MM **Privately Held**
Web: www.totalintermodal.com
**SIC: 4491** 4213 7534 4731  Marine cargo handling; Trucking, except local; Tire retreading and repair shops; Freight forwarding

## 4499 Water Transportation Services, Nec

**(P-16297)**
**BLUE OCEAN MARINE  LLC**
2060 Knoll Dr Ste 100, Ventura (93003-7391)
PHONE.................................805 658-2628
**EMP:** 30 **EST:** 2010
**SALES (est):** 512.99K **Privately Held**
**SIC: 4499** 1389 7359  Boat rental, commercial; Oil field services, nec; Equipment rental and leasing, nec

## 4581 Airports, Flying Fields, And Services

**(P-16298)**
**AIR 88  INC**
Also Called: Crownair Aviation
3753 John J Montgomery Dr, San Diego (92123-1751)
PHONE.................................858 277-1453
David Ryan, *Pr*
Laura Cagliero, *
**EMP:** 32 **EST:** 1951
**SQ FT:** 53,600
**SALES (est):** 2.54MM **Privately Held**
Web: www.crownairaviation.com
**SIC: 4581** 3829  Aircraft maintenance and repair services; Fuel system instruments, aircraft

**(P-16299)**
**AIRCRAFT REPAIR & OVERHAUL SVC (PA)**
Also Called: A R O Service
1186 N Grove St, Anaheim (92806-2109)
PHONE.................................714 630-9494
Thomas Haefele, *CEO*
Mark Haefele, *VP*
**EMP:** 20 **EST:** 1975
**SQ FT:** 90,000
**SALES (est):** 2.75MM
**SALES (corp-wide):** 2.75MM **Privately Held**
Web: www.aroservice.com
**SIC: 4581** 3728  Airports, flying fields, and services; Aircraft parts and equipment, nec

**(P-16300)**
**AVIATION REPAIR SOLUTIONS INC**
1480 Canal Ave, Long Beach (90813-1244)
PHONE.................................562 437-2825
James Meyer, *Pr*
**EMP:** 15 **EST:** 2005
**SQ FT:** 12,500
**SALES (est):** 2.39MM **Privately Held**
Web: www.aviation-repair.com
**SIC: 4581** 3471  Aircraft servicing and repairing; Electroplating and plating

**(P-16301)**
**PACIFIC OIL COOLER SERVICE INC**
1677 Curtiss Ct, La Verne (91750-5848)
PHONE.................................909 593-8400
Paul Saurenman Senior, *Pr*
Jan Saurenman, *Prin*
◆ **EMP:** 20 **EST:** 1988
**SALES (est):** 3.37MM **Privately Held**
Web: www.oilcoolers.com
**SIC: 4581** 3443  Aircraft servicing and repairing; Fabricated plate work (boiler shop)

**(P-16302)**
**PHS / MWA**
Also Called: Phs/Mwa Aviation Services
42374 Avenida Alvarado # A, Temecula (92590-3445)
PHONE.................................951 695-1008
Mary Bale, *CEO*
Bill Voetsch, *
**EMP:** 147 **EST:** 2003
**SALES (est):** 20.82MM **Publicly Held**
Web: www.wencor.com
**SIC: 4581** 3492 7629  Aircraft servicing and repairing; Control valves, aircraft: hydraulic and pneumatic; Electrical repair shops
**HQ:** Wencor Group, Llc
    416 Dividend Dr
    Peachtree City GA 30269
    678 490-0140

**(P-16303)**
**REPAIRTECH INTERNATIONAL INC**
Also Called: Repair Tech International
7850 Gloria Ave, Van Nuys (91406-1821)
PHONE.................................818 989-2681
Stanley H Bennett, *Pr*
Patricia J Bennett, *
**EMP:** 30 **EST:** 1978
**SALES (est):** 2.05MM **Privately Held**
Web: www.repairtechinternational.com
**SIC: 4581** 3721 3999  Aircraft servicing and repairing; Aircraft; Atomizers, toiletry

## 4724 Travel Agencies

**(P-16304)**
**IDS INC**
Also Called: IDS Technology
20300 Ventura Blvd Ste 200, Woodland Hills (91364-2448)
PHONE.................................866 297-5757
Nathan Morad, *CEO*
Alberto Gamez, *CMO*
John Ledo, *
Gary Kurtz, *Legal Counsel*
**EMP:** 97 **EST:** 2009
**SQ FT:** 9,000
**SALES (est):** 460.78K **Privately Held**
Web: www.idscontrols.com
**SIC: 4724** 7372  Travel agencies; Business oriented computer software

## 4725 Tour Operators

**(P-16305)**
**OLIVIA COMPANIES  LLC**
Also Called: Olivia Cruises & Resorts
434 Brannan St, San Francisco (94107-1816)
PHONE.................................415 962-5700
Judith Dlugacz, *Pr*
**EMP:** 31 **EST:** 1973
**SQ FT:** 9,000
**SALES (est):** 5.19MM **Privately Held**
Web: www.olivia.com
**SIC: 4725** 5961 3652  Arrangement of travel tour packages, wholesale; Record and/or tape (music or video) club, mail order; Master records or tapes, preparation of

## 4731 Freight Transportation Arrangement

**(P-16306)**
**AGILITY LOGISTICS CORP (DH)**
Also Called: Global Integrated Logistics
310 Commerce Ste 250, Irvine (92602-1399)
PHONE.................................714 617-6300
◆ **EMP:** 90 **EST:** 1973
**SALES (est):** 426.24MM
**SALES (corp-wide):** 21.99B **Privately Held**
Web: www.agility.com
**SIC: 4731** 7372 1381  Freight transportation arrangement; Prepackaged software; Drilling oil and gas wells
**HQ:** Agility Holdings, Inc.
    310 Commerce Ste 250
    Irvine CA 92602

**(P-16307)**
**MAPCARGO GLOBAL LOGISTICS (PA)**
2501 Santa Fe Ave, Redondo Beach (90278-1117)
PHONE.................................310 297-8300
Marek Adam Panasewicz, *Pr*
◆ **EMP:** 74 **EST:** 1990
**SQ FT:** 20,000
**SALES (est):** 38.58MM **Privately Held**
Web: www.mapcargo.com
**SIC: 4731** 2448  Domestic freight forwarding; Cargo containers, wood and wood with metal

**(P-16308)**
**RED ROCK PALLET COMPANY**
81153 Red Rock Rd, La Quinta (92253-9334)
P.O. Box 1231 (95763-1231)
PHONE.................................530 852-7744
Mark John Allen, *CEO*
**EMP:** 41 **EST:** 2008
**SQ FT:** 2,000
**SALES (est):** 950.46K **Privately Held**
Web: www.redrockcompany.com
**SIC: 4731** 2448  Freight transportation arrangement; Pallets, wood

## 4783 Packing And Crating

**(P-16309)**
**CHANDLER PACKAGING A TRANSPAK COMPANY**
Also Called: Fragile Handle With Care
7595 Raytheon Rd, San Diego (92111-1506)
P.O. Box 421110 (92142-1110)
PHONE.................................858 292-5674
**EMP:** 64
Web: www.chanpack.com
**SIC: 4783** 2449 3081 3086  Packing and crating; Wood containers, nec; Packing materials, plastics sheet; Packaging and shipping materials, foamed plastics

**(P-16310)**
**DIVERSIFIED LOGISTIC SVCS INC**
13033 Telegraph Rd, Santa Fe Springs (90670-4011)
PHONE.................................562 941-3600
Anthony Dellaquila, *Pr*
**EMP:** 22 **EST:** 2008
**SQ FT:** 11,000
**SALES (est):** 2.42MM **Privately Held**
Web: www.dlspro1.com
**SIC: 4783** 2449 1796 4214  Packing and crating; Rectangular boxes and crates, wood; Machine moving and rigging; Household goods moving and storage, local

**(P-16311)**
**WHALING PACKAGING CO**
21020 S Wilmington Ave, Carson (90810-1232)
P.O. Box 4547 (90749-4547)
PHONE.................................310 518-6021
Thomas Whaling, *Pr*
Michelle Whaling, *
**EMP:** 27 **EST:** 1978
**SQ FT:** 12,973
**SALES (est):** 4.61MM **Privately Held**
Web: www.whalingpackaging.com
**SIC: 4783** 2653 2441  Packing and crating; Corrugated and solid fiber boxes; Nailed wood boxes and shook

# PRODUCTS & SERVICES SECTION
## 4832 - Radio Broadcasting Stations (P-16328)

## 4785 Inspection And Fixed Facilities

### (P-16312)
**PACIFIC TOLL PROCESSING INC**
Also Called: P T P
24724 Wilmington Ave, Carson (90745-6127)
PHONE.................310 952-4992
Anthony Camasta, *Pr*
Anthony J Camasta, *
Mark Proner, *
**EMP:** 30 **EST:** 1999
**SQ FT:** 101,000
**SALES (est):** 5.3MM **Privately Held**
Web: www.pacifictoll.com
SIC: **4785** 3547 5051 Toll road operation; Steel rolling machinery; Steel

## 4812 Radiotelephone Communication

### (P-16313)
**3H COMMUNICATION SYSTEMS INC**
3 Winterbranch, Irvine (92604-4604)
PHONE.................949 529-1583
Purna Subedi, *CEO*
Michael Giarratano, *
**EMP:** 47 **EST:** 2014
**SALES (est):** 2.19MM **Privately Held**
Web: www.3hcommunicationsystems.com
SIC: **4812** 3663 3761 3812 Radiotelephone communication; Radio and t.v. communications equipment; Rockets, space and military, complete; Search and navigation equipment

### (P-16314)
**TRELLISWARE TECHNOLOGIES INC (HQ)**
10641 Scripps Summit Ct Ste 100, San Diego (92131-3918)
PHONE.................858 753-1600
Metin Bayram, *Pr*
Steve Fisher, *CFO*
Paul Konopka, *CCO*
Anna Kochka, *Pers/VP*
Matt Fallows, *Vice-President Global Business Development*
**EMP:** 115 **EST:** 2000
**SQ FT:** 46,000
**SALES (est):** 47.49MM
**SALES (corp-wide):** 4.28B **Publicly Held**
Web: www.trellisware.com
SIC: **4812** 4813 3663 Radiotelephone communication; Local and long distance telephone communications; Airborne radio communications equipment
PA: Viasat, Inc.
 6155 El Camino Real
 760 476-2200

## 4813 Telephone Communication, Except Radio

### (P-16315)
**8X8 INC (PA)**
Also Called: 8X8
675 Creekside Way, Campbell (95008)
PHONE.................408 727-1885
Samuel Wilson, *CEO*
Jaswinder Pal Singh, *Ch Bd*
Kevin Kraus, *CFO*
Hunter Middleton, *CPO*
Suzy Seandel, *CAO*
**EMP:** 454 **EST:** 1987
**SALES (est):** 743.94MM
**SALES (corp-wide):** 743.94MM **Publicly Held**
Web: www.8x8.com
SIC: **4813** 7372 Internet host services; Prepackaged software

### (P-16316)
**AUTOMTED MDIA PROC SLTIONS INC**
Also Called: Equilibrium
500 Tamal Plz Ste 520, Corte Madera (94925-1151)
PHONE.................415 332-4343
Sean Barger, *Bd of Dir*
**EMP:** 30 **EST:** 2004
**SALES (est):** 2.36MM **Privately Held**
Web: www.equilibrium.com
SIC: **4813** 7371 7373 7372 Internet host services; Computer software systems analysis and design, custom; Systems software development services; Business oriented computer software

### (P-16317)
**FORMAGRID INC (PA)**
Also Called: Airtable
799 Market St Fl 8, San Francisco (94103-2044)
PHONE.................415 200-2040
Howard Liu, *CEO*
Andrew Ofstad, *
**EMP:** 497 **EST:** 2013
**SQ FT:** 10,000
**SALES (est):** 80.94MM
**SALES (corp-wide):** 80.94MM **Privately Held**
Web: www.airtable.com
SIC: **4813** 7371 7372 7373 Proprietary online service networks; Computer software development and applications; Utility computer software; Systems software development services

### (P-16318)
**JYNORMUS LLC**
19800 Macarthur Blvd 3rd Fl, Irvine (92612-2421)
PHONE.................949 436-2112
**EMP:** 17 **EST:** 2006
**SQ FT:** 5,000
**SALES (est):** 244.86K **Privately Held**
SIC: **4813** 2741 Internet connectivity services; Racing forms and programs: publishing and printing

### (P-16319)
**KOS INC**
1205 N Miller St, Palo Alto (94303-3343)
PHONE.................650 231-2044
Schalal Habib, *CEO*
**EMP:** 25 **EST:** 2020
**SALES (est):** 2.61MM **Privately Held**
Web: www.kos-ai.com
SIC: **4813** 2834 Telephone communication, except radio; Pharmaceutical preparations

### (P-16320)
**NEXXEN GROUP LLC (PA)**
535 Mission St Fl 14, San Francisco (94105-3253)
PHONE.................425 279-1222
Amy Rosthstin, *Managing Member*
Yaniv Arvie, *
Sagi Niri, *
**EMP:** 67 **EST:** 2007
**SALES (est):** 22.86MM **Privately Held**
Web: www.rhythmone.com
SIC: **4813** 2741 7319 Online service providers; Internet publishing and broadcasting; Display advertising service

### (P-16321)
**PACIFIC BELL TELEPHONE COMPANY (HQ)**
Also Called: Pacbell
430 Bush St Fl 3, San Francisco (94108-3735)
PHONE.................415 542-9000
TOLL FREE: 800
Kenneth P Mcneely, *CEO*
Ray Wilkins Junior, *Pr*
▲ **EMP:** 2000 **EST:** 1906
**SQ FT:** 500,000
**SALES (est):** 214.02MM
**SALES (corp-wide):** 122.43B **Publicly Held**
Web: www.att.com
SIC: **4813** 2741 4822 Local and long distance telephone communications; Directories, telephone: publishing only, not printed on site; Telegraph and other communications
PA: At&T Inc.
 208 S Akard St
 210 821-4105

### (P-16322)
**SENDMAIL INC**
892 Ross Dr, Sunnyvale (94089-1443)
PHONE.................510 594-5400
Gregory S Olson, *Prin*
Sandy Abbott, *
Gregory Shapiro, *
Stephanie Nevin, *
Sherry Walden, *
**EMP:** 110 **EST:** 2013
**SQ FT:** 30,000
**SALES (est):** 3.92MM
**SALES (corp-wide):** 1.11B **Privately Held**
Web: www.proofpoint.com
SIC: **4813** 7371 7372 7373 Internet host services; Computer software development; Prepackaged software; Computer integrated systems design
HQ: Proofpoint, Inc.
 925 W Maude Ave
 Sunnyvale CA 94085
 408 517-4710

### (P-16323)
**TEMPO COMMUNICATIONS INC (PA)**
1390 Aspen Way, Vista (92081-8349)
PHONE.................800 642-2155
Jason Edward Butchko, *CEO*
John Parizek, *CFO*
David Collmann, *Prin*
**EMP:** 85 **EST:** 2019
**SALES (est):** 29.18MM
**SALES (corp-wide):** 29.18MM **Privately Held**
Web: www.tempocom.com
SIC: **4813** 3823 Telephone communication, except radio; Absorption analyzers: infrared, x-ray, etc.: industrial

### (P-16324)
**ULTRA COMMUNICATIONS INC**
990 Park Center Dr Ste H, Vista (92081-8352)
PHONE.................760 652-0011
Charles Kuznia, *Pr*
**EMP:** 44 **EST:** 2004
**SALES (est):** 2.44MM
**SALES (corp-wide):** 769.22MM **Privately Held**
Web: www.ultracomm-inc.com
SIC: **4813** 2653 Telephone communication, except radio; Corrugated and solid fiber boxes
PA: Samtec Inc
 520 Park E Blvd
 812 944-6733

### (P-16325)
**YUKEEP LLC**
4540 Kearny Villa Rd Ste 203, San Diego (92123-1577)
PHONE.................888 855-2568
**EMP:** 15 **EST:** 2012
**SALES (est):** 977.2K **Privately Held**
Web: www.yukeep.com
SIC: **4813** 3571 Online service providers; Electronic computers

## 4832 Radio Broadcasting Stations

### (P-16326)
**BUCK OWENS PRODUCTION CO INC (PA)**
Also Called: Kuzz FM
2800 Buck Owens Blvd, Bakersfield (93308-6314)
PHONE.................661 326-1011
Buck Owens Junior, *Pr*
Michael Owens, *VP*
**EMP:** 21 **EST:** 1966
**SQ FT:** 32,000
**SALES (est):** 4.47MM
**SALES (corp-wide):** 4.47MM **Privately Held**
Web: www.kuzz.com
SIC: **4832** 4833 2741 Radio broadcasting stations; Television broadcasting stations; Miscellaneous publishing

### (P-16327)
**KUIC INC**
Also Called: Kuic-FM
555 Mason St Ste 245, Vacaville (95688-4640)
PHONE.................707 446-0200
James Levitt, *Ch Bd*
John F Levitt, *
**EMP:** 130 **EST:** 1969
**SQ FT:** 4,200
**SALES (est):** 468.59K
**SALES (corp-wide):** 977.45K **Privately Held**
Web: www.kuic.com
SIC: **4832** 2711 Radio broadcasting stations; Newspapers
PA: Coast Radio Company, Inc.
 555 Mason St Ste 245
 707 446-0200

### (P-16328)
**NEW INSPIRATION BRDCSTG CO INC (HQ)**
4880 Santa Rosa Rd, Camarillo (93012-0948)
PHONE.................805 987-0400
Edward G Atsinger Iii, *CEO*
Stuart Epperson, *Ch Bd*
Evan Masyr, *VP*
Christopher Henderson, *VP*
David Evans, *NEW Business Development*
**EMP:** 30 **EST:** 1982
**SQ FT:** 40,000
**SALES (est):** 45.24MM
**SALES (corp-wide):** 266.97MM **Publicly Held**
SIC: **4832** 2731 Radio broadcasting stations; Book publishing

# 4833 - Television Broadcasting Stations (P-16329)

PA: Salem Media Group, Inc.
6400 N Belt Line Rd
805 987-0400

## 4833 Television Broadcasting Stations

**(P-16329)**
**AMERICAN MULTIMEDIA TV USA**
Also Called: Amtv USA
530 S Lake Ave Unit 368, Pasadena (91101-3515)
PHONE.................................626 466-1038
Jason Quin, *Pr*
EMP: 67 EST: 2004
SALES (est): 326.55K **Privately Held**
Web: www.amtvusa.tv
SIC: **4833** 7372 Television broadcasting stations; Application computer software

**(P-16330)**
**TWDC ENTERPRISES 18 CORP (HQ)**
Also Called: Disney Financial Services
500 S Buena Vista St, Burbank (91521-0001)
PHONE.................................818 560-1000
Robert Iger, *CEO*
Christine M Mccarthy, *V*
Alan N Braverman, *
Kevin A Mayer, *CSO*
M Jayne Parker, *Chief Human Resources Officer*
◆ EMP: 521 EST: 1925
SALES (est): 46.53B
SALES (corp-wide): 88.9B **Publicly Held**
Web: www.thewaltdisneycompany.com
SIC: **4833** 4841 7011 7996 Television broadcasting stations; Cable television services; Resort hotel; Amusement parks
PA: The Walt Disney Company
500 S Buena Vista St
818 560-1000

## 4841 Cable And Other Pay Television Services

**(P-16331)**
**CCO HOLDINGS LLC**
2684 N Tustin St, Orange (92865-2438)
PHONE.................................714 509-5861
EMP: 158
SALES (corp-wide): 54.61B **Publicly Held**
SIC: **4841** 3663 3651 Cable television services; Radio and t.v. communications equipment; Household audio and video equipment
HQ: Cco Holdings, Llc
400 Atlantic St
Stamford CT 06901
203 905-7801

**(P-16332)**
**CCO HOLDINGS LLC**
26827 Baseline St, Highland (92346-3059)
PHONE.................................909 742-8373
EMP: 158
SALES (corp-wide): 54.61B **Publicly Held**
SIC: **4841** 3663 3651 Cable television services; Radio and t.v. communications equipment; Household audio and video equipment
HQ: Cco Holdings, Llc
400 Atlantic St
Stamford CT 06901
203 905-7801

**(P-16333)**
**NETFLIX INC (PA)**
Also Called: Netflix
121 Albright Way, Los Gatos (95032-1801)
PHONE.................................408 540-3700
Ted Sarandos, *CCO*
Reed Hastings, *
Spencer Neumann, *CFO*
David Hyman, *CLO*
EMP: 166 EST: 1998
SALES (est): 33.72B **Publicly Held**
Web: www.netflix.com
SIC: **4841** 2741 Subscription television services; Internet publishing and broadcasting

## 4899 Communication Services, Nec

**(P-16334)**
**CALIX INC (PA)**
Also Called: CALIX
2777 Orchard Pkwy, San Jose (95134-2008)
PHONE.................................408 514-3000
Michael Weening, *Pr*
Carl Russo, *Ch Bd*
Cory Sindelar, *CAO*
J Matthew Collins, *COMMERCIAL*
Shane Eleniak, *Chief Product Officer*
◆ EMP: 911 EST: 1999
SALES (est): 1.04B
SALES (corp-wide): 1.04B **Publicly Held**
Web: www.calix.com
SIC: **4899** 7372 4813 Data communication services; Prepackaged software; Internet connectivity services

**(P-16335)**
**COMMUNICATIONS SUPPLY CORP**
6251 Knott Ave, Buena Park (90620-1010)
PHONE.................................714 670-7711
Michael Davis, *Genl Mgr*
EMP: 70
Web: www.wesco.com
SIC: **4899** 1731 3577 3357 Data communication services; Communications specialization; Computer peripheral equipment, nec; Nonferrous wiredrawing and insulating
HQ: Communications Supply Corp
225 W Stn Sq Dr Ste 700
Pittsburgh PA 15219
630 221-6400

**(P-16336)**
**CTEK INC**
2425 Golden Hill Rd Ste 106, Paso Robles (93446-7038)
PHONE.................................310 241-2973
Phil Sutter, *Pr*
EMP: 25 EST: 2003
SALES (est): 1.88MM
SALES (corp-wide): 444.85MM **Publicly Held**
Web: www.ctekproducts.com
SIC: **4899** 3661 Communication signal enhancement network services; Fiber optics communications equipment
PA: Digi International Inc.
9350 Exclsior Blvd Ste 70
952 912-3444

**(P-16337)**
**ITRON NETWORKED SOLUTIONS INC (HQ)**
230 W Tasman Dr, San Jose (95134-1714)
PHONE.................................669 770-4000
Thomas L Deitrich, *Pr*
Catriona M Fallon, *Sr VP*
Robert Farrow, *
Shannon M Votava, *Sec*
▲ EMP: 400 EST: 2002
SQ FT: 191,800
SALES (est): 51.3MM
SALES (corp-wide): 2.17B **Publicly Held**
Web: na.itron.com
SIC: **4899** 7372 Communication signal enhancement network services; Prepackaged software
PA: Itron, Inc.
2111 N Molter Rd
509 924-9900

**(P-16338)**
**MADE MEDIA LLC**
Also Called: Made Merch
2337 Roscomare Rd Ste 2302, Los Angeles (90077-1854)
PHONE.................................866 263-6233
Leamon Keishan Moseley, *CEO*
EMP: 25 EST: 2021
SALES (est): 589.72K **Privately Held**
SIC: **4899** 2741 2211 2389 Communication services, nec; Art copy: publishing and printing; Apparel and outerwear fabrics, cotton; Apparel and accessories, nec

**(P-16339)**
**MAXAR SPACE LLC (HQ)**
3875 Fabian Way, Palo Alto (94303)
PHONE.................................650 852-4000
John Celli, *Pr*
Bill Mccombe, *Sr VP*
David Bernstein, *
Richard Currier, *
Paul Estey, *
◆ EMP: 75 EST: 1892
SALES (est): 390.29MM
SALES (corp-wide): 1.6B **Privately Held**
Web: www.maxar.com
SIC: **4899** 3663 Satellite earth stations; Satellites, communications
PA: Maxar Technologies Inc.
1300 W 120th Ave
303 684-7660

**(P-16340)**
**OPLINK COMMUNICATIONS LLC (DH)**
Also Called: Oplink
46360 Fremont Blvd, Fremont (94538-6406)
PHONE.................................510 933-7200
Joseph Y Liu, *CEO*
Peter Lee, *Pr*
Shirley Yin, *Ex VP*
River Gong, *Executive Worldwide Sales Vice-President*
▲ EMP: 47 EST: 1995
SQ FT: 51,000
SALES (est): 14.71MM
SALES (corp-wide): 64.37B **Privately Held**
Web: www.oplink.com
SIC: **4899** 3661 Communication signal enhancement network services; Fiber optics communications equipment
HQ: Molex, Llc
2222 Wellington Ct
Lisle IL 60532
630 969-4550

**(P-16341)**
**SHIPSCIENCE LLC**
268 N Santa Cruz Ave, Los Gatos (95030-7228)
PHONE.................................800 303-6644
Anthony Robinson, *CEO*
EMP: 15 EST: 2017
SALES (est): 1.55MM **Privately Held**
Web: www.shipscience.com
SIC: **4899** 7372 Data communication services; Business oriented computer software

## 4911 Electric Services

**(P-16342)**
**COMBUSTION ASSOCIATES INC**
Also Called: Cai
555 Monica Cir, Corona (92878-5447)
PHONE.................................951 272-6999
Mukund Kavia, *Pr*
Kusum Kavia, *
Prajesh Kavia, *
▼ EMP: 50 EST: 1991
SQ FT: 40,000
SALES (est): 48.76MM **Privately Held**
Web: www.cai3.com
SIC: **4911** 3443 Fossil fuel electric power generation; Boiler and boiler shop work

**(P-16343)**
**LEEMAH ELECTRONICS INC**
Also Called: (415 Location)
1080 Samson St, San Francisco (94111-1308)
PHONE.................................415 394-1288
Jack Wang, *Mgr*
EMP: 105
SALES (corp-wide): 63.99MM **Privately Held**
Web: www.leemah.com
SIC: **4911** 3672 3669 3571 Electric services; Printed circuit boards; Intercommunication systems, electric; Electronic computers
HQ: Leemah Electronics, Inc.
155 S Hill Dr
Brisbane CA 94005

**(P-16344)**
**MAAS ENERGY WORKS LLC**
1730 South St, Redding (96001-1811)
PHONE.................................530 710-8545
Daryl Maas, *CEO*
EMP: 120 EST: 2010
SALES (est): 25.41MM **Privately Held**
Web: www.maasenergy.com
SIC: **4911** 3612 Electric services; Airport lighting transformers

**(P-16345)**
**MT POSO CGNRTION A CAL LTD PR**
10000 Stockdale Hwy Ste 100, Bakersfield (93311-3602)
PHONE.................................661 663-3155
Roger C Allred, *Genl Mgr*
EMP: 28 EST: 1986
SQ FT: 2,500
SALES (est): 9.65MM **Privately Held**
SIC: **4911** 1311 Generation, electric power; Crude petroleum production
HQ: Northern Star Generation Services, Llc
2929 Allen Pkwy
Houston TX 77019
713 580-6300

**(P-16346)**
**ORMAT TECHNOLOGIES INC**
855 Dogwood Rd, Heber (92249-9758)
PHONE.................................760 337-8872
Miki Juarez, *Brnch Mgr*
EMP: 44
Web: www.ormat.com

# PRODUCTS & SERVICES SECTION

**4953 - Refuse Systems (P-16366)**

SIC: **4911** 3621 3691 Electric services;
Power generators; Alkaline cell storage
batteries
PA: Ormat Technologies, Inc.
6140 Plumas St

*(P-16347)*
**PACIFIC GAS AND ELECTRIC CO**
Also Called: PG&e
2111 Hillcrest Ave, Antioch (94509-2862)
PHONE..............................925 779-7745
Mike Diaz, *Mgr*
**EMP:** 257
Web: www.pge.com
SIC: **4911** 4922 4924 1311 Distribution, electric power; Pipelines, natural gas; Natural gas distribution; Crude petroleum production
HQ: Pacific Gas And Electric Company
300 Lakeside Dr
Oakland CA 94612
415 973-7000

*(P-16348)*
**PACIFIC GAS AND ELECTRIC CO**
Also Called: PG&e
2180 Harrison St, San Francisco
(94110-1300)
PHONE..............................415 695-3513
Dave Bradley, *Brnch Mgr*
**EMP:** 291
Web: www.pge.com
SIC: **4911** 4922 4924 1311 Generation, electric power; Pipelines, natural gas; Natural gas distribution; Natural gas production
HQ: Pacific Gas And Electric Company
300 Lakeside Dr
Oakland CA 94612
415 973-7000

*(P-16349)*
**SERVITEK ELECTRIC INC**
Also Called: Servitek Electric Hawaii
618 Brea Canyon Rd Ste J, City Of Industry
(91789-3022)
PHONE..............................626 227-1650
Geoffrey Reyes, *Pr*
**EMP:** 20 **EST:** 2018
**SALES (est):** 641.61K **Privately Held**
Web: www.servitekelectric.com
SIC: **4911** 3612 Electric services; Voltage regulating transformers, electric power

## 4923 Gas Transmission And Distribution

*(P-16350)*
**CAPITOL AIR SYSTEMS INC**
4220 Duluth Ave Ste A, Rocklin
(95765-1408)
P.O. Box 1073 (95677-1073)
PHONE..............................916 259-1200
**EMP:** 28
Web: www.capitolair.com
SIC: **4923** 3563 7699 Gas transmission and distribution; Air and gas compressors including vacuum pumps; Compressor repair

## 4931 Electric And Other Services Combined

*(P-16351)*
**AMERICAN GREEN LIGHTS LLC**
Also Called: American Green Lights
10755 Scripps Poway Pkwy Ste 419, San Diego (92131-3924)

PHONE..............................858 547-8837
**EMP:** 25 **EST:** 2008
**SQ FT:** 25,000
**SALES (est):** 2.47MM **Privately Held**
Web: www.americangreenlights.com
SIC: **4931** 3648 3646 Electric and other services combined; Outdoor lighting equipment; Commercial lighting fixtures

## 4939 Combination Utilities, Nec

*(P-16352)*
**AAA UNDERGROUND INC**
3245 Elkhorn Blvd, North Highlands
(95660-3125)
PHONE..............................916 515-9348
Melvin Ortega, *Prin*
**EMP:** 17 **EST:** 2011
**SALES (est):** 2.75MM **Privately Held**
SIC: **4939** 1389 Combination utilities, nec; Pipe testing, oil field service

## 4941 Water Supply

*(P-16353)*
**AZULWORKS INC**
Also Called: Azul Works
1400 Egbert Ave, San Francisco
(94124-3222)
PHONE..............................415 558-1507
Sandra R Hernandez, *Pr*
Christopher Kahney, *
**EMP:** 103 **EST:** 2001
**SALES (est):** 2.69MM **Privately Held**
Web: www.azulworks.com
SIC: **4941** 1623 1389 1622 Water supply; Water, sewer, and utility lines; Construction, repair, and dismantling services; Tunnel construction

## 4952 Sewerage Systems

*(P-16354)*
**HADRONEX INC (PA)**
Also Called: Smartcover Systems
2110 Enterprise St, Escondido
(92029-2000)
PHONE..............................760 291-1980
David Drake, *Pr*
Gregory Quist, *CEO*
**EMP:** 33 **EST:** 2006
**SALES (est):** 36.59MM **Privately Held**
Web: www.smartcoversystems.com
SIC: **4952** 3594 Sewerage systems; Fluid power motors

## 4953 Refuse Systems

*(P-16355)*
**AGRI SERVICE INC**
2141 Oceanside Blvd, Oceanside
(92054-4405)
PHONE..............................760 295-6255
Mary Matava, *Pr*
Francesca San Diego, *
**EMP:** 24 **EST:** 1979
**SQ FT:** 1,700
**SALES (est):** 2.36MM **Privately Held**
Web: www.agriserviceinc.com
SIC: **4953** 2875 Recycling, waste materials; Potting soil, mixed

*(P-16356)*
**BRUNOS IRON & METAL LP**
3211 S Golden State Blvd, Fresno
(93725-2404)

PHONE..............................559 233-6543
Freda Tosi, *Pt*
▼ **EMP:** 25 **EST:** 1947
**SQ FT:** 3,528
**SALES (est):** 5.45MM **Privately Held**
Web: www.brunosrecycling.com
SIC: **4953** 5051 3441 5093 Recycling, waste materials; Aluminum bars, rods, ingots, sheets, pipes, plates, etc.; Fabricated structural metal; Metal scrap and waste materials

*(P-16357)*
**COUNTY QUARRY PRODUCTS**
5501 Imhoff Pl, Martinez (94553-4391)
PHONE..............................925 682-0707
Doug Foskett, *Pt*
Sonny Mc Dowell, *Pt*
**EMP:** 20 **EST:** 1986
**SQ FT:** 1,000
**SALES (est):** 2.06MM **Privately Held**
Web: www.countyquarryproducts.com
SIC: **4953** 5032 3272 2951 Recycling, waste materials; Brick, stone, and related material; Concrete products, nec; Asphalt paving mixtures and blocks

*(P-16358)*
**E J HARRISON & SONS INC**
Also Called: Harrison, E J & Sons Recycling
1589 Lirio Ave, Ventura (93004-3227)
PHONE..............................805 647-1414
**TOLL FREE:** 800
Ken Keys, *Genl Mgr*
**EMP:** 173
**SALES (corp-wide):** 24.61MM **Privately Held**
Web: www.ejharrison.com
SIC: **4953** 2611 Rubbish collection and disposal; Pulp mills
PA: E. J. Harrison & Sons, Inc.
5275 Colt St
805 647-1414

*(P-16359)*
**FIBRES INTERNATIONAL INC**
Also Called: Fibres Internation Recycling
88 Rowland Way Ste 300, Novato
(94945-5000)
PHONE..............................425 455-9811
Tony Rounds, *Genl Mgr*
**EMP:** 75
SIC: **4953** 4212 3341 3231 Refuse collection and disposal services; Local trucking, without storage; Secondary nonferrous metals; Products of purchased glass
PA: Fibres International, Inc.
88 Rowland Way Ste 300

*(P-16360)*
**NORTECH WASTE LLC**
Also Called: Nortech
219 Reward St, Nevada City (95959-2913)
P.O. Box 1748 (95648-1445)
PHONE..............................916 645-5230
Paul Szura, *Managing Member*
Jerry Jackson, *Managing Member*
Arthur A Daniels, *
Donald M Moriel, *
Michael J Sangiacomo, *
**EMP:** 120 **EST:** 1992
**SALES (est):** 8.86MM **Privately Held**
Web: www.nortechwaste.com
SIC: **4953** 3341 3312 3231 Sanitary landfill operation; Secondary nonferrous metals; Blast furnaces and steel mills; Products of purchased glass

*(P-16361)*
**R PLANET EARTH LLC**
3200 Fruitland Ave, Vernon (90058-3718)
PHONE..............................213 320-0601
**EMP:** 135 **EST:** 2013
**SALES (est):** 8.64MM **Privately Held**
Web: www.rplanetearth.com
SIC: **4953** 2611 Recycling, waste materials; Pulp mills, mechanical and recycling processing

*(P-16362)*
**RERUBBER LLC**
7372 Sonoma Creek Ct, Rancho Cucamonga (91739-1877)
PHONE..............................909 786-2811
▲ **EMP:** 19 **EST:** 2007
**SALES (est):** 1.77MM **Privately Held**
Web: www.rerubber.com
SIC: **4953** 3069 Recycling, waste materials; Type, rubber
PA: Enertech Solutions, Llc
30515 7th Ave

*(P-16363)*
**RIVER CITY WASTE RECYCLERS LLC (PA)**
8940 Elder Creek Rd, Sacramento
(95829-1031)
PHONE..............................916 383-5511
Bryan Wilson, *Managing Member*
**EMP:** 16 **EST:** 2011
**SALES (est):** 2.47MM
**SALES (corp-wide):** 2.47MM **Privately Held**
Web: www.rivercitymetalrecyclers.com
SIC: **4953** 3272 Recycling, waste materials; Concrete products, nec

*(P-16364)*
**SMC GREASE SPECIALIST INC**
1600 W Pellisier Rd, Colton (92324-3301)
P.O. Box 79200 (92877-0173)
PHONE..............................951 788-6042
Salvatore Coco, *Pr*
**EMP:** 27 **EST:** 2003
**SQ FT:** 2,500
**SALES (est):** 5.03MM **Privately Held**
Web: www.smcgrease.com
SIC: **4953** 2992 Recycling, waste materials; Oils and greases, blending and compounding

*(P-16365)*
**TALCO PLASTICS INC (PA)**
1000 W Rincon St, Corona (92878-9228)
PHONE..............................951 531-2000
John L Shedd Senior, *Ch*
John L Shedd Junior, *Pr*
Bob Shedd, *
Ron Petty, *
William O'grady, *VP*
**EMP:** 85 **EST:** 1972
**SQ FT:** 110,000
**SALES (est):** 25.65MM
**SALES (corp-wide):** 25.65MM **Privately Held**
Web: www.talcoplastics.com
SIC: **4953** 2821 Recycling, waste materials; Plastics materials and resins

*(P-16366)*
**VERDECO RECYCLING INC**
8685 Bowers Ave, South Gate
(90280-3317)
PHONE..............................323 537-4617
Robert Bindner, *CEO*
Alexander Delnik, *
Carmen Chivu, *
◆ **EMP:** 25 **EST:** 2011

# 4953 - Refuse Systems

**SALES (est):** 23.51MM
**SALES (corp-wide):** 1.4MM **Privately Held**
**Web:** www.verdecorecycling.com
**SIC: 4953** 3089 Recycling, waste materials; Plastics containers, except foam
**HQ:** Verdeco Recycling Holdings Llc
 8685 Bowers Ave
 South Gate CA 90280
 323 537-4617

**(P-16367)**
### VISIONS RECYCLING INC
Also Called: Visions Paint Recycling
4105 S Market Ct Ste A, Sacramento (95834-1215)
**PHONE** ................................. 916 564-9121
Jerry Noel, *CEO*
Jerry Noel, *Pr*
Marie Noel, *
▲ **EMP:** 42 **EST:** 2001
**SQ FT:** 47,000
**SALES (est):** 1.47MM **Privately Held**
**Web:** www.visionsqualitycoatings.com
**SIC: 4953** 2851 Recycling, waste materials; Paints and paint additives

## 4959 Sanitary Services, Nec

**(P-16368)**
### SUPERIOR EQUIPMENT COMPANY INC
2301 Napa Vallejo Hwy, Napa (94558-6242)
P.O. Box 10369 (94581-2369)
**PHONE** ................................. 707 256-3600
Jack Pagendarm, *Pr*
Kathleen Pagendarm, *
Nicolas Pagendarm, *
**EMP:** 28 **EST:** 1995
**SQ FT:** 4,300
**SALES (est):** 4.71MM **Privately Held**
**SIC: 4959** 5084 5093 7692 Sanitary services, nec; Compaction equipment; Metal scrap and waste materials; Welding repair

## 4971 Irrigation Systems

**(P-16369)**
### FRESNO VALVES & CASTINGS INC (PA)
7736 E Springfield Ave, Selma (93662-9408)
P.O. Box 40 (93662-0040)
**PHONE** ................................. 559 834-2511
Jeffery Showalter, *CEO*
Jeffery Showalter, *Pr*
Kevin Follansbee, *
Joni Roam, *
◆ **EMP:** 165 **EST:** 1952
**SALES (est):** 90.4MM
**SALES (corp-wide):** 90.4MM **Privately Held**
**Web:** www.fresnovalves.com
**SIC: 4971** 3491 3498 3441 Water distribution or supply systems for irrigation; Industrial valves; Fabricated pipe and fittings; Fabricated structural metal

**(P-16370)**
### HUNTER INDUSTRIES INCORPORATED (PA)
Also Called: Hunter
 1940 Diamond St, San Marcos (92078-5190)
**PHONE** ................................. 760 744-5240
Gregory R Hunter, *CEO*
Stephanie C Brownell, *

◆ **EMP:** 193 **EST:** 1993
**SQ FT:** 450,000
**SALES (est):** 423.39MM **Privately Held**
**Web:** www.hunterindustries.com
**SIC: 4971** 3089 Irrigation systems; Fittings for pipe, plastics

## 5012 Automobiles And Other Motor Vehicles

**(P-16371)**
### AMERICAN HONDA MOTOR CO INC (HQ)
Also Called: American Honda
 1919 Torrance Blvd, Torrance (90501-2746)
P.O. Box 2200 (90509-2200)
**PHONE** ................................. 310 783-2000
Noriya Kaihara, *CEO*
Lyle Shroyer, *VP*
Yuichi Shimizu, *Sec*
Mikio Himuro, *CFO*
◆ **EMP:** 2375 **EST:** 1959
**SALES (est):** 12.82B **Privately Held**
**Web:** www.honda.com
**SIC: 5012** 3732 Automobiles; Jet skis
**PA:** Honda Motor Co., Ltd.
 2-1-1, Minamioyama

**(P-16372)**
### MARATHON INDUSTRIES INC
Also Called: Marathon Truck Bodies
 20950 Centre Pointe Pkwy, Santa Clarita (91350-2975)
P.O. Box 800279 (91380-0279)
**PHONE** ................................. 661 286-1520
Chad Hess, *Pr*
Roger K Hess, *
Tom Garcia, *
**EMP:** 145 **EST:** 1993
**SALES (est):** 27.5MM **Privately Held**
**Web:** www.marathontruckbody.com
**SIC: 5012** 3713 Automobiles and other motor vehicles; Truck and bus bodies

## 5013 Motor Vehicle Supplies And New Parts

**(P-16373)**
### ASSOCIATED R V ENT INC
Also Called: All-Rite
 1500 Shelton Dr Frnt, Hollister (95023-2573)
**PHONE** ................................. 831 636-9566
Michael Zevar, *Pr*
Nancy Lopez, *
**EMP:** 45 **EST:** 1975
**SQ FT:** 20,000
**SALES (est):** 2.21MM **Privately Held**
**Web:** www.all-rite.com
**SIC: 5013** 3442 Automotive supplies and parts; Metal doors

**(P-16374)**
### AUTOMOTIVE IMPORTING MANUFACTURING INC (PA)
Also Called: Aim Mail Centers
 3920 Security Park Dr, Rancho Cordova (95742-6915)
P.O. Box 100 (95741-0100)
**PHONE** ................................. 916 985-8505
▲ **EMP:** 300 **EST:** 1967
**SALES (est):** 3.27MM
**SALES (corp-wide):** 3.27MM **Privately Held**
**Web:** www.aimpartsonline.com

**SIC: 5013** 3714 Automotive supplies and parts; Motor vehicle parts and accessories

**(P-16375)**
### B & A FRICTION MATERIALS INC
1164 Old Bayshore Hwy, San Jose (95112-2807)
**PHONE** ................................. 408 286-9200
**EMP:** 28
**Web:** www.bafriction.com
**SIC: 5013** 3714 Automotive brakes; Motor vehicle parts and accessories

**(P-16376)**
### BESTOP BAJA LLC
Also Called: Baja Designs
 2950 Norman Strasse Rd, San Marcos (92069-5946)
**PHONE** ................................. 760 560-2252
John Larson, *Managing Member*
▲ **EMP:** 115 **EST:** 1992
**SQ FT:** 14,000
**SALES (est):** 14.27MM
**SALES (corp-wide):** 91.9MM **Privately Held**
**Web:** www.bajadesigns.com
**SIC: 5013** 5571 3714 Motorcycle parts; Motorcycle parts and accessories; Motor vehicle electrical equipment
**PA:** Bestop, Inc.
 333 Centennial Pkwy Ste B
 303 464-2548

**(P-16377)**
### CLAUDES BUGGIES INC
Also Called: CB Performance Products
 1715 N Farmersville Blvd, Farmersville (93223-2302)
**PHONE** ................................. 559 733-8222
Richard A Tomlinson, *CEO*
Loretta Tomlinson, *Sec*
▲ **EMP:** 30 **EST:** 1959
**SQ FT:** 50,000
**SALES (est):** 4.88MM **Privately Held**
**Web:** www.cbperformance.com
**SIC: 5013** 3714 Automotive supplies and parts; Motor vehicle engines and parts

**(P-16378)**
### COMPETITION CLUTCH INC
1570 Lakeview Loop, Anaheim (92807-1819)
P.O. Box 380 (30012-0380)
**PHONE** ................................. 800 809-6598
Vaughn Christopher Jewell, *CEO*
Kimberly Mccool, *CFO*
Carla Oglesby, *Sec*
▲ **EMP:** 23 **EST:** 2003
**SALES (est):** 12.07MM
**SALES (corp-wide):** 12.07MM **Privately Held**
**Web:** www.competitionclutch.com
**SIC: 5013** 3568 Clutches; Clutches, except vehicular
**PA:** Wharton Automotive Group Inc.
 2590 N San Miguel Dr

**(P-16379)**
### DANA MOTORS INC (PA)
Also Called: Motor Warehouse
 901 Arden Way, Sacramento (95815-3201)
P.O. Box 15152 (95851-0152)
**PHONE** ................................. 916 920-0150
David A Kenmonth, *Pr*
**EMP:** 19 **EST:** 1959
**SQ FT:** 31,000
**SALES (est):** 4.59MM
**SALES (corp-wide):** 4.59MM **Privately Held**
**Web:** www.danamotorssac.com

**SIC: 5013** 3714 Automotive supplies and parts; Motor vehicle parts and accessories

**(P-16380)**
### DENSO PDTS & SVCS AMERICAS INC (DH)
Also Called: Dsca
 3900 Via Oro Ave, Long Beach (90810-1868)
**PHONE** ................................. 310 834-6352
Yoshihiko Yamada, *CEO*
Hirokatsu Yamashita, *Pr*
Roy Nakaue, *Ex V*
Peter Clotz, *VP Sls*
Eugene Stark, *VP Prd*
◆ **EMP:** 478 **EST:** 1971
**SQ FT:** 235,000
**SALES (est):** 221.87MM **Privately Held**
**Web:** www.densoautocare.com
**SIC: 5013** 7361 5075 3714 Automotive supplies and parts; Employment agencies; Warm air heating and air conditioning; Motor vehicle parts and accessories
**HQ:** Denso International America, Inc.
 24777 Denso Dr
 Southfield MI 48033
 248 350-7500

**(P-16381)**
### DNA SPECIALTY INC
200 W Artesia Blvd, Compton (90220-5500)
**PHONE** ................................. 310 767-4070
James Choi, *CEO*
▲ **EMP:** 90 **EST:** 1984
**SQ FT:** 80,000
**SALES (est):** 24.13MM **Privately Held**
**Web:** www.dnaspecialty.com
**SIC: 5013** 3714 Wheels, motor vehicle; Wheels, motor vehicle

**(P-16382)**
### EGGE MACHINE COMPANY INC (PA)
8403 Allport Ave, Santa Fe Springs (90670-2109)
**PHONE** ................................. 562 945-3419
Robert Egge, *Pr*
Kathy Weaver, *
Judy Egge, *
▲ **EMP:** 23 **EST:** 1915
**SQ FT:** 10,000
**SALES (est):** 5.16MM
**SALES (corp-wide):** 5.16MM **Privately Held**
**Web:** www.egge.com
**SIC: 5013** 3592 5531 Automotive supplies and parts; Valves; Automotive parts

**(P-16383)**
### EMPI INC
Also Called: Euro Motorparts Group
 301 E Orangethorpe Ave, Anaheim (92801-1032)
**PHONE** ................................. 714 446-9606
Peter Guile, *CEO*
Robert Keller, *
Todd Tyler, *
**EMP:** 89 **EST:** 2018
**SQ FT:** 127,000
**SALES (est):** 25.53MM **Privately Held**
**Web:** www.empius.com
**SIC: 5013** 3713 Automotive supplies and parts; Specialty motor vehicle bodies

**(P-16384)**
### FLEETPRIDE INC
1164 Old Bayshore Hwy, San Jose (95112-2807)
**PHONE** ................................. 408 286-9200
**EMP:** 28

Web: www.fleetpride.com
SIC: **5013** 3714  Automotive brakes; Motor vehicle parts and accessories
HQ: Fleetpride, Inc.
600 E Las Clnas Blvd Ste
Irving TX 75039
469 249-7500

### (P-16385)
### HIGHLINE AFTERMARKET LLC
Also Called: Atlantic Pacific Automotive
10385 San Sevaine Way Ste B, Jurupa Valley  (91752-3272)
PHONE.................................951 361-0331
Scott Hultman, *Mgr*
EMP: 57
SQ FT: 37,000
SALES (corp-wide): 741.18MM **Privately Held**
Web: www.highlinewarren.com
SIC: **5013** 6512 2992 3519  Automotive supplies and parts; Commercial and industrial building operation; Lubricating oils ; Parts and accessories, internal combustion engines
HQ: Highline Aftermarket, Llc
4500 Malone Rd
Memphis TN 38118

### (P-16386)
### INNOVATIVE METAL DESIGNS INC
12691 Monarch St, Garden Grove (92841-3918)
PHONE.................................714 799-6700
Carlos Danze, *CEO*
Marcelo Danze, *Pr*
▲ EMP: 20 EST: 1983
SQ FT: 6,000
SALES (est): 2.05MM **Privately Held**
Web: www.innovativemetals.com
SIC: **5013** 3841 3827  Motorcycle parts; Surgical and medical instruments; Optical instruments and lenses

### (P-16387)
### IPT INC
Also Called: Bad Habit Customs
150 Santa Fe Ave, Fresno  (93721-3035)
PHONE.................................559 266-6100
Jeremy A Thornton, *CEO*
EMP: 17 EST: 2015
SALES (est): 7.4MM **Privately Held**
Web: www.ironpanthertrailers.com
SIC: **5013** 3999  Automotive supplies and parts; Atomizers, toiletry

### (P-16388)
### MAXZONE VEHICLE LIGHTING CORP (HQ)
Also Called: Depo Auto Parts
15889 Slover Ave Unit A, Fontana (92337-7299)
PHONE.................................909 822-3288
Polo Hsu, *Pr*
◆ EMP: 50 EST: 1997
SQ FT: 32,000
SALES (est): 32.22MM **Privately Held**
Web: www.maxzone.com
SIC: **5013** 3714  Automotive supplies and parts; Motor vehicle electrical equipment
PA: Depo Auto Parts Ind. Co., Ltd.
No. 20-3, Nanshi Ln.

### (P-16389)
### PHOENIX WHEEL COMPANY INC
Also Called: Hre Performance Wheels
2611 Commerce Way Ste D, Vista (92081-8455)
PHONE.................................760 598-1960
Christian J Luhnow, *CEO*
Alan Peltier, *
Phillip Hillhouse, *
▲ EMP: 40 EST: 1993
SQ FT: 58,000
SALES (est): 17.47MM **Privately Held**
Web: www.hrewheels.com
SIC: **5013** 3714  Wheels, motor vehicle; Motor vehicle wheels and parts

### (P-16390)
### PREVOST CAR (US) INC
3384 De Forest Cir, Mira Loma (91752-3253)
PHONE.................................951 360-2550
Tim Willmuth, *Brnch Mgr*
EMP: 59
SALES (corp-wide): 119.84MM **Privately Held**
Web: www.prevostcar.com
SIC: **5013** 4173 5012 3711  Automotive supplies and parts; Maintenance facilities, buses; Busses; Buses, all types, assembly of
HQ: Prevost Car (Us) Inc.
7817 National Service Rd
Greensboro NC 27409
908 222-7211

### (P-16391)
### R1 CONCEPTS INC (PA)
Also Called: Zion Automotive Group
13140 Midway Pl, Cerritos  (90703-2233)
PHONE.................................714 777-2323
Phouc Martin Trinh, *Pr*
Thang Trinh, *COO*
◆ EMP: 25 EST: 2004
SALES (est): 22.47MM
SALES (corp-wide): 22.47MM **Privately Held**
Web: www.r1concepts.com
SIC: **5013** 3714  Automotive engines and engine parts; Motor vehicle brake systems and parts

### (P-16392)
### RALCO HOLDINGS INC (DH)
13861 Rosecrans Ave, Santa Fe Springs (90670-5207)
PHONE.................................949 440-5094
Michael Moore, *CEO*
EMP: 159 EST: 2009
SALES (est): 28.73MM **Privately Held**
SIC: **5013** 3751  Motorcycle parts; Motorcycle accessories
HQ: Velocity Pooling Vehicle, Llc
651 Canyon Drive Ste 100
Coppell TX

### (P-16393)
### RALLY HOLDINGS LLC
17771 Mitchell N, Irvine  (92614-6028)
PHONE.................................817 919-6833
EMP: 1151 EST: 2006
SALES (est): 3.08MM **Privately Held**
SIC: **5013** 3751  Motorcycle parts; Motorcycle accessories
HQ: Ralco Holdings, Inc.
13861 Rosecrans Ave
Santa Fe Springs CA 90670
949 440-5094

### (P-16394)
### RAMCAR BATTERIES INC
2700 Carrier Ave, Commerce  (90040-2572)
PHONE.................................323 726-1212
Clifford J Crowe, *CEO*
Jaime Agustines, *
◆ EMP: 42 EST: 1919
SQ FT: 90,000
SALES (est): 2.31MM **Privately Held**
Web: www.ramcarbattery.com
SIC: **5013** 3691  Automotive batteries; Lead acid batteries (storage batteries)

### (P-16395)
### RARE PARTS INC
Also Called: Auto Pride
621 Wilshire Ave, Stockton  (95203)
PHONE.................................209 948-6005
▲ EMP: 26 EST: 1981
SALES (est): 4.7MM **Privately Held**
Web: www.rareparts.com
SIC: **5013** 3714  Automotive supplies and parts; Motor vehicle parts and accessories

### (P-16396)
### REELS INC
Also Called: Mr Bug
301 E Orangethorpe Ave, Anaheim (92801-1032)
PHONE.................................714 446-9606
▲ EMP: 80 EST: 1971
SALES (est): 9.64MM **Privately Held**
Web: www.empius.com
SIC: **5013** 3714  Automotive supplies and parts; Motor vehicle parts and accessories

### (P-16397)
### SADDLEMEN CORPORATION
Also Called: Saddlemen
17801 S Susana Rd, Compton (90221-5411)
PHONE.................................310 638-1222
David Echert, *CEO*
▲ EMP: 140 EST: 1987
SQ FT: 20,000
SALES (est): 12.75MM **Privately Held**
Web: www.saddlemen.com
SIC: **5013** 3751  Motorcycle parts; Motorcycle accessories

### (P-16398)
### SCAT ENTERPRISES INC
1400 Kingsdale Ave Ste B, Redondo Beach  (90278-3983)
PHONE.................................310 370-5501
Philip T Lieb, *Pr*
Craig Schenasi, *
◆ EMP: 65 EST: 1967
SALES (est): 24.68MM **Privately Held**
Web: www.scatenterprises.com
SIC: **5013** 3714  Automotive supplies and parts; Motor vehicle parts and accessories

### (P-16399)
### SCOGGAN COMPANY INC (PA)
Also Called: Drive Line Service Sacramento
704 Houston St, West Sacramento (95691-2217)
PHONE.................................916 371-3984
James Scoggan, *Pr*
Elaine Scoggan, *
▲ EMP: 25 EST: 1971
SQ FT: 8,000
SALES (est): 9.05MM
SALES (corp-wide): 9.05MM **Privately Held**
Web: www.drive-lines.com
SIC: **5013** 3714 7539  Automotive supplies and parts; Drive shafts, motor vehicle; Automotive repair shops, nec

### (P-16400)
### SHRIN LLC
Also Called: Coverking
900 E Arlee Pl, Anaheim  (92805-5645)
P.O. Box 9860 (92812)
PHONE.................................714 850-0303
Narendra Gupta, *Managing Member*
◆ EMP: 100 EST: 1986
SQ FT: 90,000
SALES (est): 23.09MM **Privately Held**
Web: www.coverking.com
SIC: **5013** 3714  Automotive supplies and parts; Motor vehicle parts and accessories

### (P-16401)
### SOUND INVESTMENT GROUP
Also Called: Frsport.com
16402 Gothard St Ste E, Huntington Beach (92647-3647)
PHONE.................................714 515-4001
Dung T Nguyen, *CEO*
Donny Ton, *VP*
Lien Truong, *Sec*
EMP: 15 EST: 2004
SALES (est): 925.77K **Privately Held**
Web: www.frsport.com
SIC: **5013** 3465  Automotive supplies and parts; Body parts, automobile: stamped metal

### (P-16402)
### SPECIALTY INTERIOR MFG INC
Also Called: Sim Ideation
16751 Millikan Ave, Irvine  (92606-5009)
PHONE.................................714 296-8618
Courtney Tassie, *CEO*
EMP: 35 EST: 2012
SQ FT: 4,500
SALES (est): 1.98MM **Privately Held**
SIC: **5013** 2531  Automotive supplies and parts; Seats, aircraft

### (P-16403)
### SUPERWINCH LLC
Also Called: Superwinch
320 W Covina Blvd, San Dimas (91773-2907)
PHONE.................................800 323-2031
◆ EMP: 40 EST: 1970
SALES (est): 1.67MM **Privately Held**
Web: www.superwinch.com
SIC: **5013** 3531  Automotive supplies; Winches

### (P-16404)
### TOTAL IMPORT SOLUTIONS INC
Also Called: Nanoskin Car Care Products
14700 Radburn Ave, Santa Fe Springs (90670)
PHONE.................................562 691-6818
Jerry Heilian, *CEO*
Shengi Chang, *CFO*
▲ EMP: 15 EST: 2008
SQ FT: 31,000
SALES (est): 3.33MM **Privately Held**
Web: www.nanoskinusa.com
SIC: **5013** 3089  Automotive supplies; Automotive parts, plastic

### (P-16405)
### WABASH NATIONAL TRLR CTRS INC
16025 Slover Ave, Fontana  (92337-7368)
PHONE.................................765 771-5300
Joe Newfield, *Mgr*
EMP: 49
SALES (corp-wide): 2.54B **Publicly Held**
Web: www.onewabash.com
SIC: **5013** 5012 7539 3715  Motor vehicle supplies and new parts; Automobiles and other motor vehicles; Automotive repair shops, nec; Truck trailers
HQ: Wabash National Trailer Centers, Inc.
1000 Sagamore Pkwy S
Lafayette IN 47905
765 771-5300

## 5014 Tires And Tubes

**(P-16406)**
**AMCS INC**
Also Called: Aquamatic Cover Systems
200 Mayock Rd, Gilroy (95020-7029)
PHONE..................408 846-9274
TOLL FREE: 800
Harry Last, *CEO*
Tom Dankel, *
Barbara E Last, *
Debra Dankel, *
Robert Last, *
◆ EMP: 40 EST: 1980
SQ FT: 17,600
SALES (est): 8.57MM **Privately Held**
Web: www.aquamatic.com
SIC: **5014** 3069  Tire and tube repair materials; Sheeting, rubber or rubberized fabric

**(P-16407)**
**FLEET TIRE INC (PA)**
Also Called: Brannon Tire
3730 N Wilson Way, Stockton (95205-2437)
P.O. Box 1988 (95201-1988)
PHONE..................209 467-0154
Carey L Cumberlege, *Pr*
Craig Brannon, *
◆ EMP: 33 EST: 1984
SQ FT: 41,500
SALES (est): 20.44MM **Privately Held**
Web: www.brannontire.com
SIC: **5014** 5531 7538 7534  Automobile tires and tubes; Automotive tires; General automotive repair shops; Tire retreading and repair shops

**(P-16408)**
**GREENBALL CORP (PA)**
Also Called: Towmaster Tire & Wheel
222 S Harbor Blvd Ste 700, Anaheim (92805-3730)
PHONE..................714 782-3060
Chris S H Tsai, *CEO*
Jenny Tsai, *
◆ EMP: 50 EST: 1976
SQ FT: 80,000
SALES (est): 55.96MM
SALES (corp-wide): 55.96MM **Privately Held**
Web: www.greenballtires.com
SIC: **5014** 5013 3999  Automobile tires and tubes; Wheels, motor vehicle; Atomizers, toiletry

**(P-16409)**
**PETES ROAD SERVICE INC (PA)**
2230 E Orangethorpe Ave, Fullerton (92831-5329)
PHONE..................714 446-1207
▲ EMP: 55 EST: 1954
SALES (est): 51.31MM
SALES (corp-wide): 51.31MM **Privately Held**
Web: www.petesrs.com
SIC: **5014** 7534 7539  Tires and tubes; Tire retreading and repair shops; Wheel alignment, automotive

**(P-16410)**
**YOKOHAMA TIRE CORPORATION (DH)**
Also Called: Yokohama Tire USA
1 Macarthur Pl Ste 900, Santa Ana (92707)
P.O. Box 4550 (92834-4550)
PHONE..................714 870-3800
◆ EMP: 150 EST: 1969
SALES (est): 497.5MM **Privately Held**
Web: www.yokohamatruck.com
SIC: **5014** 3011  Automobile tires and tubes; Automobile tires, pneumatic
HQ: Yokohama Corporation Of North America
1 Macarthur Pl
Santa Ana CA 92707

## 5021 Furniture

**(P-16411)**
**BLUMENTHAL DISTRIBUTING INC (PA)**
Also Called: Office Star Products
1901 S Archibald Ave, Ontario (91761-8548)
P.O. Box 3520 (91761-0952)
PHONE..................909 930-2000
Richard Blumenthal, *CEO*
Richard Blumenthal, *Pr*
Rose Blumenthal, *Stockholder*
Jennifer Blumenthal, *
◆ EMP: 150 EST: 1983
SQ FT: 200,000
SALES (est): 49.22MM
SALES (corp-wide): 49.22MM **Privately Held**
Web: www.officestar.net
SIC: **5021** 2522  Office furniture, nec; Chairs, office: padded or plain: except wood

**(P-16412)**
**CAMBIUM BUSINESS GROUP INC (PA)**
Also Called: Fairmont Designs
6950 Noritsu Ave, Buena Park (90620-1311)
PHONE..................714 670-1171
George Tsai, *Ch*
Jason Liu, *
Kevin Fitzgerald, *
Mark Klingensmith, *
◆ EMP: 120 EST: 1984
SQ FT: 200,000
SALES (est): 22.56MM
SALES (corp-wide): 22.56MM **Privately Held**
Web: www.fairmontdesignshospitality.com
SIC: **5021** 2511  Household furniture; Wood household furniture

**(P-16413)**
**EMPIRE ENTERPRISES INC (PA)**
4264 Fulton Ave Ste 1, Studio City (91604-1802)
P.O. Box 1344 (91614-0344)
PHONE..................818 784-8918
William Landes, *Pr*
Wendy Landes, *VP*
Margie Clapper, *
EMP: 15 EST: 1982
SQ FT: 2,200
SALES (est): 214.94K
SALES (corp-wide): 214.94K **Privately Held**
SIC: **5021** 2731  Furniture; Books, publishing only

**(P-16414)**
**FURNITURE AMERICA CAL INC (PA)**
Also Called: Furniture of America
680 S Lemon Ave, City Of Industry (91789-2934)
PHONE..................866 923-8500
George Wells, *CEO*
Rocky Yang, *
Jean Chen, *
Jose Palacios, *
◆ EMP: 36 EST: 2005
SALES (est): 22.12MM **Privately Held**
Web: www.foagroup.com
SIC: **5021** 2512  Furniture; Upholstered household furniture

**(P-16415)**
**KIMLOR MILLS INC**
Also Called: Kimlor Innovative HM Fashions
18142 Blue Ridge Dr, Santa Ana (92705-2056)
PHONE..................803 531-2037
Wade Svicarovich, *Pr*
Matthew King, *
◆ EMP: 100 EST: 1980
SALES (est): 1.09MM **Privately Held**
Web: www.kimlor.com
SIC: **5021** 2392  Household furniture; Household furnishings, nec

**(P-16416)**
**LARRY FISHER & SONS LTD PARTNR**
5242 E Home Ave, Fresno (93727-2103)
PHONE..................559 252-2575
Larry Fisher, *Pt*
Jennifer Fisher, *Pt*
Sophia Fisher, *Pt*
▲ EMP: 19 EST: 1987
SQ FT: 10,000
SALES (est): 8.01MM **Privately Held**
Web: www.larryfisherandsons.com
SIC: **5021** 2542 3535  Racks; Racks, merchandise display or storage: except wood; Conveyors and conveying equipment

**(P-16417)**
**OFFICE MASTER INC**
Also Called: Om Smart Seating
1110 Mildred St, Ontario (91761-3512)
PHONE..................909 392-5678
◆ EMP: 60 EST: 1986
SALES (est): 11.16MM **Privately Held**
Web: www.omseating.com
SIC: **5021** 2522  Office furniture, nec; Benches, office: except wood

**(P-16418)**
**PHYLLIS MORRIS ORIGINALS (PA)**
Also Called: Morris, Phyllis
8772 Beverly Blvd, Los Angeles (90048-1804)
PHONE..................310 289-6868
Jamie Goller Adler, *Pr*
Nathan Goller, *Sec*
John Adler, *VP*
EMP: 16 EST: 1954
SQ FT: 27,000
SALES (est): 5.18MM
SALES (corp-wide): 5.18MM **Privately Held**
Web: www.phyllismorris.com
SIC: **5021** 2519 2511  Furniture; Fiberglass and plastic furniture; Wood household furniture

**(P-16419)**
**VIRCO INC (HQ)**
2027 Harpers Way, Torrance (90501-1524)
PHONE..................310 533-0474
Robert Virtue, *CEO*
Robert Dose, *
▼ EMP: 45 EST: 1998
SQ FT: 560,000
SALES (est): 20.3MM
SALES (corp-wide): 269.12MM **Publicly Held**
Web: www.virco.com
SIC: **5021** 2599  Furniture; Factory furniture and fixtures
PA: Virco Mfg. Corporation
2027 Harpers Way
310 533-0474

## 5023 Homefurnishings

**(P-16420)**
**AMERICAN FAUCET COATINGS CORP**
1333 Keystone Way, Vista (92081-8311)
PHONE..................760 598-5895
Susan E Butler, *Pr*
◆ EMP: 50 EST: 1993
SALES (est): 16MM **Privately Held**
Web: www.afccorp.net
SIC: **5023** 3432  Homefurnishings; Plumbing fixture fittings and trim

**(P-16421)**
**BUSTER AND PUNCH INC**
10844 Burbank Blvd, North Hollywood (91601-2519)
PHONE..................818 392-3827
David Schlocker, *CEO*
EMP: 25 EST: 2020
SALES (est): 2.34MM **Privately Held**
Web: www.busterandpunch.com
SIC: **5023** 5063 5719 3429  Homefurnishings; Lighting fixtures, residential; Lighting fixtures; Cabinet hardware

**(P-16422)**
**CLASSIC CONCEPTS INC (PA)**
Also Called: Classic Home
5200 Irwindale Ave Ste 120, Baldwin Park (91706-2010)
PHONE..................323 266-8993
Harpal Singh, *Pr*
Gita Singh, *VP*
Zaidi Bilgees, *Treas*
◆ EMP: 15 EST: 1984
SALES (est): 29.39MM **Privately Held**
Web: www.classichome.com
SIC: **5023** 2511 2512  Decorative home furnishings and supplies; Wood household furniture; Living room furniture: upholstered on wood frames

**(P-16423)**
**EV RAY INC**
6400 Variel Ave, Woodland Hills (91367-2577)
PHONE..................818 346-5381
Lee Brown, *Pr*
EMP: 50 EST: 1962
SQ FT: 22,000
SALES (est): 6.97MM **Privately Held**
Web: www.rayev.com
SIC: **5023** 2211 2591 2391  Draperies; Draperies and drapery fabrics, cotton; Drapery hardware and window blinds and shades; Curtains and draperies

**(P-16424)**
**FELLOW INDUSTRIES INC (PA)**
320 Florida St, San Francisco (94110-1411)
PHONE..................415 649-0361
Jacob Alan Miller, *CEO*
Omar Muakkassa, *CFO*
EMP: 17 EST: 2014
SALES (est): 8.2MM
SALES (corp-wide): 8.2MM **Privately Held**
Web: www.fellowproducts.com
SIC: **5023** 3639  Kitchen tools and utensils, nec; Major kitchen appliances, except refrigerators and stoves

# PRODUCTS & SERVICES SECTION

## 5031 - Lumber, Plywood, And Millwork (P-16445)

**(P-16425)**
**GALLEHER LLC (PA)**
Also Called: Galleher
9303 Greenleaf Ave, Santa Fe Springs (90670-3029)
PHONE..................562 944-8885
Sunil Palakodati, CEO
Rick Coates, Pr
David Burke, CFO
▲ EMP: 110 EST: 1937
SQ FT: 100,000
SALES (est): 356.59MM
SALES (corp-wide): 356.59MM Privately Held
Web: www.galleher.com
SIC: 5023 2426 Wood flooring; Hardwood dimension and flooring mills

**(P-16426)**
**GIBSON OVERSEAS INC (PA)**
Also Called: Gibson Homeware
2410 Yates Ave, Commerce (90040-1918)
PHONE..................323 832-8900
Sol Gabbay, CEO
Darioush Gabbay, *
Soloman Gabbay, *
◆ EMP: 475 EST: 1979
SQ FT: 850,000
SALES (est): 31.46MM
SALES (corp-wide): 31.46MM Privately Held
Web: www.gibsonusa.com
SIC: 5023 3269 2511 Glassware; Kitchen and table articles, coarse earthenware; Kitchen and dining room furniture

**(P-16427)**
**GTT INTERNATIONAL INC**
1615 Eastridge Ave, Riverside (92507-7111)
PHONE..................951 788-8729
Mohammed Arshad, Pr
Hafiz Ur Rahaman, *
▲ EMP: 35 EST: 1991
SALES (est): 1.89MM Privately Held
SIC: 5023 2258 Bedspreads; Lace and warp knit fabric mills

**(P-16428)**
**KATZIRS FLOOR & HM DESIGN INC (PA)**
Also Called: National Hrdwood Flrg Moulding
14959 Delano St, Van Nuys (91411-2123)
PHONE..................818 988-9663
Omer Katzir, CEO
Jeannette Katzir, *
▲ EMP: 22 EST: 1982
SQ FT: 19,270
SALES (est): 5.54MM
SALES (corp-wide): 5.54MM Privately Held
Web: www.nationalhardwood.com
SIC: 5023 2435 Wood flooring; Hardwood veneer and plywood

**(P-16429)**
**LOTUS & WINDOWARE INC (PA)**
Also Called: Lotus
14450 Yorba Ave, Chino (91710-5766)
PHONE..................909 606-8866
Charles Hartness, CEO
Donna David, CFO
◆ EMP: 17 EST: 1989
SQ FT: 40,000
SALES (est): 11.6MM Privately Held
Web: www.lotusblind.com
SIC: 5023 2591 Window covering parts and accessories; Window blinds

**(P-16430)**
**MEYER CORPORATION US**
Also Called: Faberware Div
2001 Meyer Way, Fairfield (94533-6802)
PHONE..................707 399-2100
Stuart Levine, Mgr
EMP: 38
Web: www.meyerus.com
SIC: 5023 3469 1541 5046 Kitchenware; Cooking ware, except porcelain enameled; Industrial buildings and warehouses; Commercial equipment, nec
HQ: Meyer Corporation, U.S.
1 Meyer Plz
Vallejo CA 94590
707 551-2800

**(P-16431)**
**NEXGRILL INDUSTRIES INC (PA)**
Also Called: Nexgrill Industries
14050 Laurelwood Pl, Chino (91710-5454)
PHONE..................909 598-8799
Sherman Lin, CEO
◆ EMP: 98 EST: 1993
SQ FT: 50,000
SALES (est): 22.45MM
SALES (corp-wide): 22.45MM Privately Held
Web: www.nexgrill.com
SIC: 5023 3631 Grills, barbecue; Barbecues, grills, and braziers (outdoor cooking)

**(P-16432)**
**OBERON DESIGN AND MFG LLC**
1076 Illinois St, San Francisco (94107-3120)
PHONE..................415 865-5440
▲ EMP: 23 EST: 1997
SALES (est): 1.79MM Privately Held
Web: www.oberondesign.net
SIC: 5023 5063 2519 Frames and framing, picture and mirror; Lighting fixtures; Household furniture, except wood or metal: upholstered

**(P-16433)**
**PACIFIC HERITG HM FASHION INC**
Also Called: Home Decor Wholesaler
901 Lawson St, City Of Industry (91748-1121)
PHONE..................909 598-5200
Meng Lan Liu, Pr
Frank Hsu, *
▲ EMP: 25 EST: 2002
SALES (est): 4.95MM Privately Held
SIC: 5023 2392 Window shades; Blankets, comforters and beddings

**(P-16434)**
**REU DISTRIBUTION LLC**
Also Called: Republic Floor
7227 Telegraph Rd, Montebello (90640-6512)
PHONE..................323 201-4200
Eliyahu Shuat, *
EMP: 700 EST: 2015
SALES (est): 3.42MM Privately Held
SIC: 5023 5211 2426 Wood flooring; Flooring, wood; Flooring, hardwood

**(P-16435)**
**SIDS CARPET BARN (PA)**
Also Called: Abbey Carpet
132 W 8th St, National City (91950-1197)
PHONE..................619 477-7000
Allan W Ziman, Pr
Allan W Ziman, Pr
Don Pasquill, *
Stacy B Ziman, *
Robert Wood, *
EMP: 24 EST: 1950
SQ FT: 7,800
SALES (est): 30.14MM
SALES (corp-wide): 30.14MM Privately Held
Web: www.sidscarpet.com
SIC: 5023 1771 5713 1389 Carpets; Flooring contractor; Carpets; Construction, repair, and dismantling services

**(P-16436)**
**THREE WISE MEN INC**
Also Called: Max Windsor Floors
11818 San Marino St Ste B, Rancho Cucamonga (91730-6015)
PHONE..................909 477-6698
▲ EMP: 20
Web: www.epochnetwork.com
SIC: 5023 3996 Wood flooring; Hard surface floor coverings, nec

**(P-16437)**
**UNIQUE CARPETS LTD**
7360 Jurupa Ave, Riverside (92504-1025)
PHONE..................951 352-8125
Bill D Graves, Pr
Robert L Binford, *
Martin Lopez, *
▲ EMP: 55 EST: 1985
SALES (est): 4.99MM Privately Held
Web: www.uniquecarpetsltd.com
SIC: 5023 2273 Carpets; Carpets and rugs

**(P-16438)**
**UNIVERSAL WOOD MOULDING INC (PA)**
Also Called: Universal Framing Products
21139 Centre Pointe Pkwy, Santa Clarita (91350-2994)
PHONE..................661 362-6262
Jon M Bromberg, CEO
Avi Feibenlatt, Ch Bd
Mark Gottlieb, *
▲ EMP: 50 EST: 1995
SALES (est): 24.32MM
SALES (corp-wide): 24.32MM Privately Held
Web: www.universalarquati.com
SIC: 5023 3999 Frames and framing, picture and mirror; Atomizers, toiletry

**(P-16439)**
**VENUS GROUP INC (PA)**
Also Called: Venus Textiles
25861 Wright, Foothill Ranch (92610-3504)
PHONE..................949 609-1299
Rajni D Patel, CEO
Aman Ullah, *
◆ EMP: 78 EST: 1971
SALES (est): 24.88MM
SALES (corp-wide): 24.88MM Privately Held
Web: www.venusgroup.com
SIC: 5023 2392 5719 Towels; Towels, fabric and nonwoven: made from purchased materials; Towels

**(P-16440)**
**VOGUE ENTERPRISE INC**
Also Called: Vogue Developement
1801 Kettering, Irvine (92614-5617)
PHONE..................949 833-9787
Douglas Wong, Pr
Jenny Wong, VP
▲ EMP: 15 EST: 1981
SQ FT: 24,000
SALES (est): 562.83K Privately Held
Web: www.voguewindows.com
SIC: 5023 2591 Venetian blinds; Venetian blinds

## 5031 Lumber, Plywood, And Millwork

**(P-16441)**
**ALL-COAST FOREST PRODUCTS INC (PA)**
250 Asti Rd, Cloverdale (95425)
P.O. Box 9 (95425-0009)
PHONE..................707 894-4281
EMP: 80 EST: 1975
SALES (est): 24.3MM
SALES (corp-wide): 24.3MM Privately Held
Web: www.all-coast.com
SIC: 5031 2421 Lumber: rough, dressed, and finished; Resawing lumber into smaller dimensions

**(P-16442)**
**BUILDERS FENCE COMPANY INC (PA)**
8937 San Fernando Rd, Sun Valley (91352-1410)
P.O. Box 125 (91353-0125)
PHONE..................818 768-5500
Marshall K Frankel, Pr
▲ EMP: 35 EST: 1959
SQ FT: 6,400
SALES (est): 48.82MM
SALES (corp-wide): 48.82MM Privately Held
Web: www.buildersfence.com
SIC: 5031 1799 3446 Fencing, wood; Ornamental metal work; Architectural metalwork

**(P-16443)**
**BUILDERS FIRSTSOURCE INC**
Also Called: Heritage One Door & Carpentry
4300 Jetway Ct, North Highlands (95660-5702)
PHONE..................916 481-5030
John Dutter, Brnch Mgr
EMP: 350
SALES (corp-wide): 17.1B Publicly Held
Web: www.bldr.com
SIC: 5031 2431 Doors and windows; Windows and window parts and trim, wood
PA: Builders Firstsource, Inc.
6031 Cnnection Dr Ste 400
214 880-3500

**(P-16444)**
**CAPITAL LUMBER COMPANY**
13480 Old Redwood Hwy, Healdsburg (95448)
P.O. Box 1396 (95448-1396)
PHONE..................707 433-7070
Jeff Howard, Prin
EMP: 27
SALES (corp-wide): 375MM Privately Held
Web: www.capital-lumber.com
SIC: 5031 2493 Lumber: rough, dressed, and finished; Reconstituted wood products
PA: Capital Lumber Company
2525 E Ariz Bltmore Cir S
602 381-0709

**(P-16445)**
**EXPO INDUSTRIES INC**
Also Called: Expo Builders Supply
7455 Carroll Rd, San Diego (92121-2303)
P.O. Box 711 (92121)
PHONE..................858 566-3110

## 5031 - Lumber, Plywood, And Millwork (P-16446)

EMP: 95
Web: www.expostucco.com
SIC: 5031 3299 Building materials, exterior; Stucco

**(P-16446)**
**HERITAGE ONE DOOR CRPENTRY LLC**
Also Called: Heritage One Door
4300 Jetway Ct, North Highlands (95660-5702)
P.O. Box 214609 (95821-0609)
PHONE..................................916 481-5030
Charles Gardemeyer, Managing Member
Geoff Hughes, *
John Dutter, *
John Ballou, *
Tyler Randolth, Installation Manager*
EMP: 86 EST: 2011
SQ FT: 80,000
SALES (est): 4.21MM
SALES (corp-wide): 30.55MM Privately Held
Web: www.allin1doors.com
SIC: 5031 2431 Doors and windows; Windows and window parts and trim, wood
PA: Heritage Interests, Llc
4300 Jetway Ct
916 481-5030

**(P-16447)**
**JAMES HARDIE BUILDING PDTS INC**
10901 Elm Ave, Fontana (92337-7327)
PHONE..................................909 355-6500
Bob Mussleman, Brnch Mgr
EMP: 53
Web: www.jameshardie.com
SIC: 5031 3272 Building materials, exterior; Areaways, basement window: concrete
HQ: James Hardie Building Products Inc.
303 E Wacker Dr
Chicago IL 60601
312 291-5072

**(P-16448)**
**MCDAVIS AND GUMBYS INC** ◆
Also Called: Fleetwood Windows and Doors
1 Fleetwood Way, Corona (92879-5101)
P.O. Box P.O. Box 1086 (92878-1086)
PHONE..................................800 736-7363
EMP: 250 EST: 2023
SALES (est): 25.59MM Publicly Held
Web: www.fleetwoodusa.com
SIC: 5031 3442 Doors and windows; Metal doors, sash, and trim
HQ: Masonite International Corporation
1242 E 5th Ave
Tampa FL 33605
813 877-2726

**(P-16449)**
**MEDALLION INDUSTRIES INC**
4771 Arroyo Vis Ste F, Livermore (94551-4847)
PHONE..................................925 449-9040
Jay Deyo, Brnch Mgr
EMP: 15
SALES (corp-wide): 503.44MM Privately Held
Web: www.medallionindustries.com
SIC: 5031 2431 2421 Windows; Millwork; Sawmills and planing mills, general
HQ: Medallion Industries, Inc.
3221 Nw Yeon Ave
Portland OR 97210
503 221-0170

**(P-16450)**
**MENDOCINO FOREST PDTS CO LLC**
Also Called: Sawmill
850 Kunzler Ranch Rd, Ukiah (95482-7294)
P.O. Box 996 (95482-0996)
PHONE..................................707 468-1431
Dean Kerstetter, Ex VP
EMP: 200
SALES (corp-wide): 134.91MM Privately Held
Web: www.mfp.com
SIC: 5031 2421 2499 Lumber: rough, dressed, and finished; Lumber: rough, dressed, and finished; Sawmills and planing mills, general; Fencing, docks, and other outdoor wood structural products
PA: Mendocino Forest Products Company Llc
3700 Old Redwood Hwy # 200
707 620-2961

**(P-16451)**
**MENDOCINO FOREST PDTS CO LLC (PA)**
Also Called: Mendocino
3700 Old Redwood Hwy Ste 200, Santa Rosa (95403-5739)
P.O. Box 390 (95418-0390)
PHONE..................................707 620-2961
Sandy Dean, CEO
Bob Mertz, CEO
John Russell, Pr
Jim Pelkey, CFO
EMP: 20 EST: 1998
SQ FT: 5,000
SALES (est): 134.91MM
SALES (corp-wide): 134.91MM Privately Held
Web: www.mfp.com
SIC: 5031 2421 Lumber: rough, dressed, and finished; Sawmills and planing mills, general

**(P-16452)**
**MENDOCINO FOREST PDTS CO LLC**
Also Called: Calpella Distribution Center
6375 N State St, Calpella (95418)
P.O. Box 336 (95418-0336)
PHONE..................................707 485-6800
Mike Benetti, Brnch Mgr
EMP: 53
SALES (corp-wide): 134.91MM Privately Held
Web: www.mfp.com
SIC: 5031 2421 Lumber: rough, dressed, and finished; Sawmills and planing mills, general
PA: Mendocino Forest Products Company Llc
3700 Old Redwood Hwy # 200
707 620-2961

**(P-16453)**
**MINTON DOOR COMPANY (PA)**
1150 Elko Dr, Sunnyvale (94089-2207)
PHONE..................................650 961-9800
Allen Minton, Pr
Richard Minton, VP
Nancy Minton, CFO
EMP: 23 EST: 1992
SQ FT: 100,000
SALES (est): 9.48MM Privately Held
Web: www.mintondoor.com
SIC: 5031 5072 3429 2431 Doors, nec; Hardware; Hardware, nec; Millwork

**(P-16454)**
**NICHOLS LUMBER & HARDWARE CO**
Also Called: Ace Hardware
13470 Dalewood St, Baldwin Park (91706-5883)
PHONE..................................626 960-4802
Judith A Nichols, Pr
Charles Nichols, *
EMP: 75 EST: 1958
SALES (est): 18.54MM Privately Held
Web: www.nicholslumber.com
SIC: 5031 5251 2421 Lumber: rough, dressed, and finished; Hardware stores; Sawmills and planing mills, general

**(P-16455)**
**PACIFIC COAST SUPPLY LLC**
Also Called: Pacific Supply
879 N Wright Rd, Santa Rosa (95407-6605)
PHONE..................................707 546-7317
Joe Burke, Mgr
EMP: 36
SALES (corp-wide): 1.21B Privately Held
Web: www.paccoastsupply.com
SIC: 5031 3275 1761 Lumber, plywood, and millwork; Wallboard, gypsum; Roofing contractor
HQ: Pacific Coast Supply, Llc
4290 Roseville Rd
North Highlands CA 95660
916 971-2301

**(P-16456)**
**POTTER ROEMER LLC (HQ)**
17451 Hurley St, City Of Industry (91744-5106)
P.O. Box 3527 (91744-0527)
PHONE..................................626 855-4890
Donald E Morris, Managing Member
▲ EMP: 22 EST: 1937
SQ FT: 110,000
SALES (est): 4.32MM
SALES (corp-wide): 99.75MM Privately Held
Web: www.potterroemer.com
SIC: 5031 3569 2542 Skylights, all materials; Firefighting and related equipment; Partitions and fixtures, except wood
PA: Acorn Engineering Company
15125 E Proctor Ave
800 488-8999

**(P-16457)**
**RELIABLE WHOLESALE LUMBER INC**
Also Called: Reliable Lumber and Hardware
1450 Citrus St, Riverside (92507-1608)
PHONE..................................951 300-2500
Robert Strutte, Brnch Mgr
EMP: 16
SALES (corp-wide): 92.3MM Privately Held
Web: www.reliablehardware.net
SIC: 5031 2421 Lumber: rough, dressed, and finished; Lumber: rough, sawed, or planed
PA: Reliable Wholesale Lumber, Inc.
7600 Redondo Cir
714 848-8222

**(P-16458)**
**RELIABLE WHOLESALE LUMBER INC (PA)**
7600 Redondo Cir, Huntington Beach (92648-1303)
P.O. Box 191 (92648-0191)
PHONE..................................714 848-8222

Jerome M Higman, Pr
Jerome M Higman, Pr
David Higman, *
Will Higman, *
Jerry Higman, Prin
EMP: 90 EST: 1970
SQ FT: 4,500
SALES (est): 92.3MM
SALES (corp-wide): 92.3MM Privately Held
Web: www.rwli.net
SIC: 5031 2421 Lumber: rough, dressed, and finished; Sawmills and planing mills, general

**(P-16459)**
**ROBERTS LUMBER SALES INC**
Also Called: Robert's Lumber
2661 S Lilac Ave, Bloomington (92316-3211)
PHONE..................................909 350-9164
Robert Cantero Junior, CEO
Lori Cantero, *
EMP: 57 EST: 1997
SALES (est): 9.09MM Privately Held
Web: www.robertslumbersales.com
SIC: 5031 2448 Lumber: rough, dressed, and finished; Wood pallets and skids

**(P-16460)**
**WEST WOOD PRODUCTS INC (PA)**
2943 E Las Hermanas St, Compton (90221-5508)
PHONE..................................310 631-8978
Golan Levy, Pr
Shrone Levy, VP
Orly Levy, Sec
▲ EMP: 18 EST: 1988
SQ FT: 91,000
SALES (est): 21.66MM Privately Held
Web: www.west-wood.net
SIC: 5031 2499 Lumber, plywood, and millwork; Decorative wood and woodwork

**(P-16461)**
**WESTSIDE BLDG SAN DIEGO LLC**
Also Called: Westside Building Materials
11620 Sorrento Valley Rd, San Diego (92121-1011)
PHONE..................................858 566-4343
Leana Aluria, Prin
Geraldine Peckham, *
Richard N Peckham, *
EMP: 48 EST: 2007
SALES (est): 9.64MM Privately Held
Web: www.westsidebmc.com
SIC: 5031 3299 Building materials, exterior; Mica products

---

## 5032 Brick, Stone, And Related Material

**(P-16462)**
**A TEICHERT & SON INC (HQ)**
Also Called: Teichert Construction
3500 American River Dr, Sacramento (95864-5802)
P.O. Box 15002 (95851)
PHONE..................................916 484-3011
Judson Riggs, CEO
Judson T Riggs, *
Kenneth A Kayser, TEICHERT CONSTRUCTION*
Dana M Davis, TEICHERT MATERIALS*
Narendra M Pathipati, *
▼ EMP: 34 EST: 1900
SALES (est): 798.78MM

# 5032 - Brick, Stone, And Related Material (P-16482)

SALES (corp-wide): 827.08MM **Privately Held**
Web: www.teichert.com
SIC: **5032** 3273 1611 1442 Brick, stone, and related material; Ready-mixed concrete; Highway and street construction; Construction sand and gravel
PA: Teichert, Inc.
5200 Franklin Dr Ste 115
916 484-3011

### (P-16463)
### ANTIOCH BUILDING MATERIALS CO (PA)
Also Called: A B M
1375 California Ave, Pittsburg (94565-4119)
P.O. Box 870 (94509-0086)
PHONE.................................925 432-0171
Niels Larsen, *CEO*
Susan Larsen, *
EMP: 24 EST: 1920
SQ FT: 4,000
SALES (est): 7.47MM
SALES (corp-wide): 7.47MM **Privately Held**
Web: www.antiochbuilding.com
SIC: **5032** 3273 Asphalt mixture; Ready-mixed concrete

### (P-16464)
### ATLAS CONSTRUCTION SUPPLY INC
7550 Stage Rd, Buena Park (90621-1224)
PHONE.................................714 441-9500
Pat Kelley, *Mgr*
EMP: 29
SALES (corp-wide): 49.08MM **Privately Held**
Web: www.atlasform.com
SIC: **5032** 5211 5082 3444 Concrete building products; Masonry materials and supplies; Contractor's materials; Concrete forms, sheet metal
PA: Atlas Construction Supply, Inc.
4640 Brinnell St
858 277-2100

### (P-16465)
### BEST CHEER STONE INC (PA)
3190 E Miraloma Ave, Anaheim (92806-1906)
PHONE.................................714 399-1588
Chung Lun Ko, *CEO*
Yanlin K Xu, *CFO*
▲ EMP: 22 EST: 2005
SALES (est): 25.71MM **Privately Held**
Web: www.bestcheerstone.com
SIC: **5032** 3281 Granite building stone; Stone, quarrying and processing of own stone products

### (P-16466)
### CEMEX CEMENT INC
1201 W Gladstone St, Azusa (91702-5142)
P.O. Box 575 (91702-0575)
PHONE.................................626 969-1747
Steve Hayes, *Mgr*
EMP: 168
SIC: **5032** 3273 3251 1411 Concrete mixtures; Ready-mixed concrete; Brick and structural clay tile; Dimension stone
HQ: Cemex Cement, Inc.
10100 Katy Fwy Ste 300
Houston TX 77043
713 650-6200

### (P-16467)
### CEMEX CNSTR MTLS PCF LLC
Also Called: Aggregate Clayton Quarry
515 Mitchell Canyon Rd, Clayton (94517-1529)
PHONE.................................925 672-4900
George J Allen, *Brnch Mgr*
EMP: 42
SIC: **5032** 3271 Cement; Concrete block and brick
HQ: Cemex Construction Materials Pacific, Llc
1501 Belvedere Rd
West Palm Beach FL 33406
561 833-5555

### (P-16468)
### CEMEX CONSTRUCTION MTLS INC (DH)
3990 Concours Ste 200, Ontario (91764-7971)
PHONE.................................909 974-5500
Deborah Sue Politte, *Pr*
Gilberto Perez, *
Thomas Edgeller, *
◆ EMP: 35 EST: 1990
SQ FT: 20,419
SALES (est): 9.17MM **Privately Held**
SIC: **5032** 1423 Cement; Crushed and broken granite
HQ: Cemex, Inc.
10100 Katy Fwy Ste 300
Houston TX 77043
713 650-6200

### (P-16469)
### CEMEX CORP
22101 W Sunset Ave, Los Banos (93635-9683)
PHONE.................................800 992-3639
EMP: 197
SIC: **5032** 3273 Cement; Ready-mixed concrete
HQ: Cemex Corp.
8888 E Rintree Dr Ste 205
Scottsdale AZ 85260
602 416-2600

### (P-16470)
### CEMEX CORP
808 Gilman St, Berkeley (94710-1422)
PHONE.................................800 992-3639
EMP: 197
SIC: **5032** 3273 Cement; Ready-mixed concrete
HQ: Cemex Corp.
8888 E Rintree Dr Ste 205
Scottsdale AZ 85260
602 416-2600

### (P-16471)
### CLARK - PACIFIC CORPORATION (PA)
Also Called: Clark Pacific
710 Riverpoint Ct Ste 100, West Sacramento (95605-1690)
PHONE.................................916 371-0305
Robert Clark, *Pr*
Don Clark, *
▲ EMP: 300 EST: 1966
SALES (est): 243.72MM
SALES (corp-wide): 243.72MM **Privately Held**
Web: www.clarkpacific.com
SIC: **5032** 3272 Brick, stone, and related material; Concrete products, precast, nec

### (P-16472)
### COAST ROCK PRODUCTS INC
1625 E Donovan Rd, Santa Maria (93454-2500)
P.O. Box 1280 (93456-1280)
PHONE.................................805 925-2505
Ron Root, *Pr*
Steve Will, *
John Will, *
George Hamel, *
EMP: 45 EST: 1955
SQ FT: 5,000
SALES (est): 437.09K **Privately Held**
SIC: **5032** 3273 3241 2951 Cement; Ready-mixed concrete; Cement, hydraulic; Asphalt paving mixtures and blocks

### (P-16473)
### CONCRETE TIE INDUSTRIES INC (PA)
Also Called: Concrete Tie
130 E Oris St, Compton (90222-2714)
P.O. Box 5406 (90224-5406)
PHONE.................................310 628-2328
Paul J Schoendienst, *Pr*
Steve Sim, *
EMP: 70 EST: 1981
SQ FT: 280,000
SALES (est): 2.75MM
SALES (corp-wide): 2.75MM **Privately Held**
SIC: **5032** 3452 Concrete and cinder building products; Bolts, nuts, rivets, and washers

### (P-16474)
### KRETUS GROUP INC (PA)
1129 N Patt St, Anaheim (92801-2568)
PHONE.................................714 738-6640
Ron Webber, *Pr*
EMP: 21 EST: 2005
SQ FT: 8,800
SALES (est): 5.5MM **Privately Held**
Web: www.jondon.com
SIC: **5032** 3569 Concrete building products; Assembly machines, non-metalworking

### (P-16475)
### L&W STONE CORPORATION (PA)
55 Independence Cir Ste 108, Chico (95973-4933)
EMP: 68 EST: 1996
SALES (est): 9.2MM **Privately Held**
Web: www.lwstone.com
SIC: **5032** 3281 Stone, crushed or broken; Stone, quarrying and processing of own stone products

### (P-16476)
### MARJAN STONE INC
2758 Via Orange Way, Spring Valley (91978-1744)
PHONE.................................619 825-6000
Hikmet Pauls, *CEO*
EMP: 25 EST: 2006
SQ FT: 1,600
SALES (est): 5.2MM **Privately Held**
Web: www.marjanstone.com
SIC: **5032** 3281 Granite building stone; Cut stone and stone products

### (P-16477)
### MILPITAS MATERIALS COMPANY
1125 N Milpitas Blvd, Milpitas (95035-3152)
P.O. Box 360003 (95036-0003)
PHONE.................................650 969-4401
Jon B Minnis, *Pr*
Val Fisher, *VP*
EMP: 20 EST: 1954
SQ FT: 1,000
SALES (est): 4.46MM **Privately Held**
Web: www.milpitasmaterials.com
SIC: **5032** 5211 3273 Concrete mixtures; Concrete and cinder block; Ready-mixed concrete

### (P-16478)
### NEW GENERATION ENGRG CNSTR INC
22815 Frampton Ave, Torrance (90501-5034)
PHONE.................................424 329-3950
Raul Ocegueda, *Pr*
EMP: 25 EST: 2016
SALES (est): 10.84MM **Privately Held**
Web: www.tngec.com
SIC: **5032** 1459 3317 3531 Brick, stone, and related material; Clays (common) quarrying; Steel pipe and tubes; Construction machinery

### (P-16479)
### PACIFIC CLAY PRODUCTS INC
14741 Lake St, Lake Elsinore (92530-1610)
PHONE.................................661 857-1401
Barry Coley, *Pr*
Kai Chin, *
Dale Kline, *
▲ EMP: 160 EST: 1930
SQ FT: 200,000
SALES (est): 20.81MM **Privately Held**
Web: www.pacificclay.com
SIC: **5032** 3251 Tile and clay products; Paving brick, clay

### (P-16480)
### PAREX USA INC
Alta Building Materials
111290 S Vallejo Ct, French Camp (95231)
P.O. Box 2399 (94614-0399)
PHONE.................................510 444-2497
Steve Horn, *Mgr*
EMP: 15
SQ FT: 66,000
Web: www.parexusa.com
SIC: **5032** 3299 Brick, stone, and related material; Stucco
HQ: Parex Usa, Inc.
2150 Eastridge Ave
Riverside CA 92507
714 778-2266

### (P-16481)
### PATRICK INDUSTRIES INC
Also Called: Custom Vinyls
13414 Slover Ave, Fontana (92337-6977)
PHONE.................................909 350-4440
Vince Fergan, *Brnch Mgr*
EMP: 41
SALES (corp-wide): 3.47B **Publicly Held**
Web: www.patrickind.com
SIC: **5032** 1799 2435 3083 Brick, stone, and related material; Building site preparation; Hardwood veneer and plywood; Laminated plastics plate and sheet
PA: Patrick Industries, Inc.
107 W Franklin St
574 294-7511

### (P-16482)
### RIVER CITY BUILDING SUPPLY INC
Also Called: Rcbs
801 Striker Ave, Sacramento (95834-1115)
P.O. Box 981298 (95798-1298)
PHONE.................................916 375-8322
EMP: 16
Web: www.rcbsusa.com
SIC: **5032** 3429 Brick, stone, and related material; Builders' hardware

# 5032 - Brick, Stone, And Related Material (P-16483)

## PRODUCTS & SERVICES SECTION

**(P-16483)**
**SACRAMENTO STUCCO CO**
Also Called: Western Blended Products
1550 Parkway Blvd, West Sacramento (95691-5009)
P.O. Box 981088 (95798-1088)
PHONE..................................916 372-7442
Lewis Winchell, *CEO*
Walter Rozewski, *
◆ **EMP:** 28 **EST:** 1930
**SQ FT:** 55,000
**SALES (est):** 9.13MM **Privately Held**
Web: www.sacramentostucco.com
**SIC:** 5032 2851 Stucco; Paints and allied products

**(P-16484)**
**SOUTHERNCARLSON INC**
801 Striker Ave, Sacramento (95834-1115)
PHONE..................................916 375-8322
Vinnie Villano, *Pr*
**EMP:** 16
Web: www.southerncarlson.com
**SIC:** 5032 3429 Brick, stone, and related material; Builders' hardware
**HQ:** Southerncarlson, Inc.
   10840 Harney St
   Omaha NE 68154

**(P-16485)**
**SYAR INDUSTRIES LLC (HQ)**
Also Called: Vallejo Building Materials
2301 Napa Vallejo Hwy, Napa (94558-6242)
P.O. Box 2540 (94558)
PHONE..................................707 252-8711
**EMP:** 37 **EST:** 1938
**SALES (est):** 40.47MM **Publicly Held**
Web: www.syarindustriesinc.com
**SIC:** 5032 2951 0762 7992 Aggregate; Asphalt and asphaltic paving mixtures (not from refineries); Vineyard management and maintenance services; Public golf courses
**PA:** Vulcan Materials Company
   1200 Urban Center Dr

**(P-16486)**
**TRIANGLE ROCK PRODUCT INC**
Also Called: Triangle Rock Products
22101 W Sunset Ave, Los Banos (93635-9683)
P.O. Box 1111 (93635-1111)
PHONE..................................209 826-5066
Don James, *Prin*
**EMP:** 240 **EST:** 1945
**SALES (est):** 2.75MM **Publicly Held**
**SIC:** 5032 3273 5211 Brick, stone, and related material; Ready-mixed concrete; Lumber and other building materials
**HQ:** Calmat Co.
   1200 Urban Center Dr
   Birmingham AL 35242
   818 553-8821

**(P-16487)**
**US TECHNICAL CERAMICS INC**
15400 Concord Cir, Morgan Hill (95037-5428)
PHONE..................................408 779-0303
Walt Carbonell, *CEO*
Joe Escobedo, *
▲ **EMP:** 40 **EST:** 1987
**SQ FT:** 30,000
**SALES (est):** 9.53MM **Privately Held**
Web: www.ustc.net
**SIC:** 5032 3677 3264 Ceramic construction materials, excluding refractory; Electronic coils and transformers; Porcelain electrical supplies

**(P-16488)**
**WHITEWATER ROCK & SUP CO INC**
58645 Old Highway 60, Whitewater (92282-7600)
PHONE..................................760 325-2747
Allan E Bankus Junior, *Pr*
Irene Bankus, *
▲ **EMP:** 31 **EST:** 1962
**SQ FT:** 4,500
**SALES (est):** 8.93MM **Privately Held**
Web: www.whitewater-rock.com
**SIC:** 5032 3281 Building stone; Stone, quarrying and processing of own stone products

## 5033 Roofing, Siding, And Insulation

**(P-16489)**
**CARLISLE CONSTRUCTION MTLS LLC**
Also Called: Western Insulfoam
5635 Schaefer Ave, Chino (91710-9048)
PHONE..................................909 591-7425
Tom Tartaglione, *Mgr*
**EMP:** 106
**SQ FT:** 45,464
**SALES (corp-wide):** 4.59B **Publicly Held**
Web: www.carlisleconstructionmaterials.com
**SIC:** 5033 3086 Insulation materials; Cups and plates, foamed plastics
**HQ:** Carlisle Construction Materials, Llc
   1285 Ritner Hwy
   Carlisle PA 17013

**(P-16490)**
**CARLISLE CONSTRUCTION MTLS LLC**
Also Called: Insulfoam
1155 Business Park Dr, Dixon (95620-4303)
PHONE..................................707 678-6900
Rick Canady, *Mgr*
**EMP:** 85
**SALES (corp-wide):** 4.59B **Publicly Held**
Web: www.carlisleconstructionmaterials.com
**SIC:** 5033 3086 Insulation materials; Plastics foam products
**HQ:** Carlisle Construction Materials, Llc
   1285 Ritner Hwy
   Carlisle PA 17013

**(P-16491)**
**INSUL-THERM INTERNATIONAL INC (PA)**
Also Called: Insul-Therm
6651 E 26th St, Commerce (90040-3215)
PHONE..................................323 728-0558
▲ **EMP:** 24 **EST:** 1982
**SALES (est):** 23.24MM
**SALES (corp-wide):** 23.24MM **Privately Held**
Web: www.insultherm.com
**SIC:** 5033 2899 3296 Insulation, thermal; Insulating compounds; Mineral wool

**(P-16492)**
**PACIFIC AWARD METALS INC**
Also Called: Gibraltar
10302 Birtcher Dr, Jurupa Valley (91752-1829)
PHONE..................................909 390-9880
Brian Lipke, *Brnch Mgr*
**EMP:** 55
**SALES (corp-wide):** 1.38B **Publicly Held**
Web: www.gibraltarbuildingproducts.com
**SIC:** 5033 2952 3444 Roofing and siding materials; Roofing materials; Sheet metalwork
**HQ:** Pacific Award Metals, Inc.
   1450 Virginia Ave
   Baldwin Park CA 91706
   626 814-4410

**(P-16493)**
**VALLEY METAL SUPPLY INC**
12950 Bradley Ave, Sylmar (91342-3829)
PHONE..................................818 837-6566
Douglas Kowalski, *Pr*
Alice Kowalski, *VP*
Coaudi Venegas, *Sec*
**EMP:** 15 **EST:** 1996
**SQ FT:** 12,000
**SALES (est):** 1MM **Privately Held**
Web: www.valleygutter.com
**SIC:** 5033 3444 1761 Roofing and siding materials; Metal roofing and roof drainage equipment; Roofing, siding, and sheetmetal work

## 5039 Construction Materials, Nec

**(P-16494)**
**GLASS & SASH INC (PA)**
425 Irwin St, San Rafael (94901-5112)
PHONE..................................415 456-2240
Fariborz Arfaian, *Pr*
Arlene Phillips, *Sec*
Tom Hess, *VP*
▲ **EMP:** 21 **EST:** 1958
**SQ FT:** 100,000
**SALES (est):** 5.62MM
**SALES (corp-wide):** 5.62MM **Privately Held**
Web: www.glassandsash.com
**SIC:** 5039 3231 5231 1793 Glass construction materials; Products of purchased glass; Glass; Glass and glazing work

**(P-16495)**
**SECURITY CONTRACTOR SVCS INC (PA)**
Also Called: S C S
5339 Jackson St, North Highlands (95660-5004)
PHONE..................................916 338-4200
Barry J Marrs, *CEO*
**EMP:** 60 **EST:** 1961
**SQ FT:** 50,000
**SALES (est):** 48.58MM
**SALES (corp-wide):** 48.58MM **Privately Held**
Web: www.scsfence.com
**SIC:** 5039 7359 3315 Wire fence, gates, and accessories; Equipment rental and leasing, nec; Steel wire and related products

**(P-16496)**
**ULTRAGLAS INC**
3392 Hampton Ct, Thousand Oaks (91362-1130)
PHONE..................................818 772-7744
Jane Skeeter, *Pr*
▼ **EMP:** 23 **EST:** 1972
**SALES (est):** 4.63MM **Privately Held**
Web: www.ultraglas.com
**SIC:** 5039 3231 3211 5231 Glass construction materials; Products of purchased glass; Flat glass; Glass, leaded or stained

**(P-16497)**
**VAN DUERR INDUSTRIES INC**
Also Called: Safe Path Products
21 Valley Ct, Chico (95973-0171)
PHONE..................................530 893-1596
Timothy Vanderheiden, *Pr*
▲ **EMP:** 20 **EST:** 2002
**SQ FT:** 2,600
**SALES (est):** 6.41MM **Privately Held**
Web: www.safepathproducts.com
**SIC:** 5039 5031 2822 Prefabricated structures; Lumber, plywood, and millwork; Acrylic rubbers, polyacrylate

## 5043 Photographic Equipment And Supplies

**(P-16498)**
**AAA IMAGING & SUPPLIES INC**
Also Called: AAA Imaging Solutions
2313 S Susan St, Santa Ana (92704-4420)
PHONE..................................714 431-0570
Robert G Noterman, *CEO*
Lou Burgess, *VP*
◆ **EMP:** 25 **EST:** 1998
**SALES (est):** 3.45MM **Privately Held**
Web: www.aaaimaging.com
**SIC:** 5043 3861 7699 Photographic processing equipment; Processing equipment, photographic; Photographic equipment repair

**(P-16499)**
**DIAKONT ADVANCED TECH INC**
Also Called: Diakont
1662 Ord Way, Oceanside (92056-1500)
PHONE..................................858 551-5551
Edward Petit De Mange, *CEO*
Mikhail Fedosovskiy, *
◆ **EMP:** 30 **EST:** 2011
**SALES (est):** 11.58MM **Privately Held**
Web: www.diakont.com
**SIC:** 5043 7389 3625 Photographic equipment and supplies; Patrol of electric transmission or gas lines; Actuators, industrial

**(P-16500)**
**UNINET IMAGING INC (PA)**
3308 W El Segundo Blvd, Hawthorne (90250-4824)
PHONE..................................424 675-3300
Nestor Saporiti, *CEO*
Claudia Saporiti, *
◆ **EMP:** 19 **EST:** 1997
**SALES (est):** 14.69MM **Privately Held**
Web: www.uninetimaging.com
**SIC:** 5043 3955 5084 Photographic equipment and supplies; Print cartridges for laser and other computer printers; Printing trades machinery, equipment, and supplies

## 5044 Office Equipment

**(P-16501)**
**CANON SOLUTIONS AMERICA INC**
Also Called: Canon
6435 Ventura Blvd Ste C007, Ventura (93003-7228)
PHONE..................................844 443-4636
Suzanne Alpizar, *Mgr*
**EMP:** 41
Web: csa.canon.com
**SIC:** 5044 7699 3861 Copying equipment; Photocopy machine repair; Photographic equipment and supplies
**HQ:** Canon Solutions America, Inc.
   One Canon Park

▲ = Import ▼ = Export
◆ = Import/Export

# 5045 - Computers, Peripherals, And Software (P-16520)

Melville NY 11747
631 330-5000

**(P-16502)**
**DOVE BUSINESS MACHINE INC**
Also Called: Semacon Business Machines
7430 Trade St, San Diego (92121-2410)
PHONE..................................858 638-0100
Mark Prager, *Owner*
▲ **EMP:** 15 **EST:** 2008
**SALES (est):** 1.99MM **Privately Held**
Web: www.semacon.com
**SIC: 5044** 3578 Office equipment; Coin counters

**(P-16503)**
**INTERNATIONAL BUS MCHS CORP**
Also Called: IBM
425 Market St, San Francisco (94105-2532)
PHONE..................................415 545-4747
Wirt Cook, *CEO*
**EMP:** 208
**SALES (corp-wide):** 61.86B **Publicly Held**
Web: community.ibm.com
**SIC: 5044** 5045 3571 Office equipment; Computers, peripherals, and software; Electronic computers
**PA:** International Business Machines Corporation
1 New Orchard Rd
914 499-1900

**(P-16504)**
**SHAMROCK OFFICE SOLUTIONS**
743 Ames Ave, Milpitas (95035-6319)
PHONE..................................408 791-6432
**EMP:** 16 **EST:** 2015
**SALES (est):** 432.86K **Privately Held**
Web: www.shamrockoffice.com
**SIC: 5044** 3579 Photocopy machines; Duplicating machines

## 5045 Computers, Peripherals, And Software

**(P-16505)**
**ALURATEK INC**
Also Called: Aluratek
15241 Barranca Pkwy, Irvine (92618-2201)
PHONE..................................866 580-1978
John P Wolikow, *CEO*
Akash Patel, *CFO*
Victor Wang, *Prin*
▲ **EMP:** 20 **EST:** 2006
**SQ FT:** 5,000
**SALES (est):** 4.62MM **Privately Held**
Web: www.aluratek.com
**SIC: 5045** 3651 Computers, peripherals, and software; Home entertainment equipment, electronic, nec

**(P-16506)**
**AMERICAN SCALE CO INC**
Also Called: Scales
21326 E Arrow Hwy, Covina (91724-1442)
P.O. Box 158 (91773-0158)
PHONE..................................800 773-7225
David William Eccles Iii, *CEO*
**EMP:** 24 **EST:** 1946
**SQ FT:** 4,150
**SALES (est):** 4.8MM **Privately Held**
Web: www.americanscale.com
**SIC: 5045** 3596 7699 Computers, peripherals, and software; Scales and balances, except laboratory; Scale repair service

**(P-16507)**
**AMETEK INC**
Also Called: Cognex
1288 San Luis Obispo St, Hayward (94544-7916)
PHONE..................................510 431-6718
Markku Jaaskelainen, *Brnch Mgr*
**EMP:** 45
**SALES (corp-wide):** 6.6B **Publicly Held**
Web: www.ametek.com
**SIC: 5045** 3829 3826 Computers, peripherals, and software; Measuring and controlling devices, nec; Analytical instruments
**PA:** Ametek, Inc.
1100 Cassatt Rd
610 647-2121

**(P-16508)**
**ASI COMPUTER TECHNOLOGIES INC (PA)**
Also Called: A S I
48289 Fremont Blvd, Fremont (94538-6510)
PHONE..................................510 226-8000
Christine Liang, *CEO*
Marcel Liang, *
Mae Gauss, *
◆ **EMP:** 50 **EST:** 1987
**SQ FT:** 155,000
**SALES (est):** 123.15MM
**SALES (corp-wide):** 123.15MM **Privately Held**
Web: www.asipartner.com
**SIC: 5045** 3577 Disk drives; Computer output to microfilm units

**(P-16509)**
**ASUS COMPUTER INTERNATIONAL**
48720 Kato Rd, Fremont (94538-7312)
PHONE..................................510 739-3777
Steve Chang, *CEO*
Ivan Hoe, *
Raymond Chen, *
▲ **EMP:** 130 **EST:** 1994
**SQ FT:** 13,000
**SALES (est):** 84.55MM **Privately Held**
Web: www.asus.com
**SIC: 5045** 3577 Computer peripheral equipment; Computer peripheral equipment, nec
**PA:** Asustek Computer Incorporation
No. 15, Li-Te Rd.

**(P-16510)**
**ATTIVO NETWORKS INC**
444 Castro St, Mountain View (94041-2017)
PHONE..................................510 623-1000
Tushar Kothari, *CEO*
Jilbert Washten, *
Ashok Shah, *
Tony Cole, *
**EMP:** 70 **EST:** 2011
**SALES (est):** 24.58MM
**SALES (corp-wide):** 621.15MM **Publicly Held**
Web: www.sentinelone.com
**SIC: 5045** 7371 7372 7373 Computers, peripherals, and software; Software programming applications; Prepackaged software; Systems software development services
**PA:** Sentinelone, Inc.
444 Castro St Ste 400
855 868-3733

**(P-16511)**
**AVATAR TECHNOLOGY INC**
339 Cheryl Ln, City Of Industry (91789-3003)
PHONE..................................909 598-7696
Juanito Pangalilingan, *CEO*
Toresa Lou, *
▲ **EMP:** 30 **EST:** 1999
**SQ FT:** 48,000
**SALES (est):** 1.48MM **Privately Held**
Web: www.v4me.com
**SIC: 5045** 3571 Computers, nec; Electronic computers

**(P-16512)**
**CABLE WHOLESALECOM INC (PA)**
1200 Voyager St, Livermore (94551-9498)
P.O. Box 11775 (94588-1775)
PHONE..................................925 455-0800
Shenrong Jiang, *Pr*
Michael Capone, *COO*
◆ **EMP:** 22 **EST:** 2000
**SQ FT:** 30,500
**SALES (est):** 12.37MM **Privately Held**
Web: www.cablewholesale.com
**SIC: 5045** 2298 Computer peripheral equipment; Cable, fiber

**(P-16513)**
**CHRONICLED INC**
Also Called: Chronicled
575 Mission St, San Francisco (94105)
PHONE..................................415 355-4681
Susanne Somerville, *CEO*
Ryan Orr, *Chief Development Officer*
Maurizio Greco, *
Abhishek Gutgutia, *Chief Product Officer*
Eric Garvin, *Head OF PHARMACEUTICAL SOLUTIONS*
**EMP:** 31 **EST:** 2014
**SALES (est):** 5.07MM **Privately Held**
Web: www.chronicled.com
**SIC: 5045** 7372 5734 Computer software; Application computer software; Software, business and non-game

**(P-16514)**
**CLIENTS & PROFITS INC**
Also Called: Working Computer
4755 Oceanside Blvd Ste 200, Oceanside (92056-3056)
PHONE..................................760 945-4334
Mark Robillard, *CEO*
Lisa Wagner, *
**EMP:** 15 **EST:** 1984
**SQ FT:** 2,500
**SALES (est):** 2.09MM **Privately Held**
Web: www.clientsandprofits.com
**SIC: 5045** 7371 7372 Computer software; Custom computer programming services; Prepackaged software

**(P-16515)**
**CREATIVE LABS INC (DH)**
2033 Gateway Pl Ste 500, San Jose (95110-3712)
PHONE..................................408 428-6600
Keh Long Ng, *CEO*
Craig Mchugh, *Pr*
◆ **EMP:** 200 **EST:** 1988
**SALES (est):** 14.28MM **Privately Held**
Web: us.creative.com
**SIC: 5045** 5734 3577 Computer peripheral equipment; Computer and software stores; Computer peripheral equipment, nec
**HQ:** Creative Holdings, Inc.
1900 Mccarthy Blvd # 103
Milpitas CA 95035

**(P-16516)**
**D-LINK SYSTEMS INCORPORATED**
Also Called: D - Link
14420 Myford Rd Ste 100, Irvine (92606-1019)
PHONE..................................714 885-6000
William Brown, *Pr*
▲ **EMP:** 164 **EST:** 1986
**SQ FT:** 120,000
**SALES (est):** 36.19MM **Privately Held**
Web: www.dlink.com
**SIC: 5045** 3577 Computers, nec; Computer peripheral equipment, nec
**PA:** D-Link Corporation
No. 289, Xinhu 3rd Rd.

**(P-16517)**
**DANE ELEC CORP USA (HQ)**
Also Called: Gigastone America
17520 Von Karman Ave, Irvine (92614-6208)
PHONE..................................949 450-2900
Michael Wang, *CEO*
◆ **EMP:** 32 **EST:** 1985
**SQ FT:** 25,000
**SALES (est):** 1MM **Privately Held**
Web: www.gigastone.com
**SIC: 5045** 3577 8731 Computer software; Computer peripheral equipment, nec; Computer (hardware) development
**PA:** Gigastone Corporation
4f, No. 166, Xinhu 2nd Rd.

**(P-16518)**
**DATA PHYSICS CORPORATION (PA)**
Also Called: Dp
1111 Spruce St, Riverside (92507-2429)
PHONE..................................408 437-0100
Sri R Welaratna, *CEO*
David C Snyder, *Ch*
Lisa Chisman, *Acctnt*
Kevin Mcintosh, *VP*
Thomas Reilly, *Dir*
▲ **EMP:** 15 **EST:** 1984
**SALES (est):** 17.07MM
**SALES (corp-wide):** 17.07MM **Privately Held**
Web: www.dataphysics.com
**SIC: 5045** 3672 7371 3577 Computer software; Wiring boards; Custom computer programming services; Computer peripheral equipment, nec

**(P-16519)**
**ELITEGROUP COMPUTER SYSTEMS HO**
Also Called: E C S-Elitegroup Cmpt Systems
6851 Mowry Ave, Newark (94560-4925)
PHONE..................................510 794-2952
Sam Tsai, *Pr*
Joseph Chang, *CFO*
Jon R Parsons, *Sec*
▲ **EMP:** 240 **EST:** 1999
**SQ FT:** 108,000
**SALES (est):** 4.36MM **Privately Held**
Web: www.ecsusa.com
**SIC: 5045** 3577 Computer peripheral equipment; Computer peripheral equipment, nec
**PA:** Hiyes International Co., Ltd.
7f., No.260, Dunhua N. Rd.,

**(P-16520)**
**ELOTEK SYSTEMS INC (PA)**
216 Avenida Fabricante Ste 112, San Clemente (92672-7559)
PHONE..................................949 366-4404

## 5045 - Computers, Peripherals, And Software (P-16521)

Michael Elovitz, *Pr*
Adam Elovitz, *VP*
David Elovitz, *VP*
Judith Elovitz, *VP*
**EMP:** 20 **EST:** 1981
**SQ FT:** 4,500
**SALES (est):** 4.98MM
**SALES (corp-wide):** 4.98MM **Privately Held**
Web: www.elotek.com
**SIC: 5045** 3825 Computers, nec; Instruments to measure electricity

### (P-16521)
### ENVISION PERIPHERALS INC (PA)
Also Called: E P I
490 N Mccarthy Blvd Ste 120, Milpitas (95035-5118)
**PHONE**..................510 770-9988
James Melendez, *CEO*
Tien Ming Ho, *
◆ **EMP:** 21 **EST:** 1998
**SALES (est):** 15.64MM
**SALES (corp-wide):** 15.64MM **Privately Held**
Web: www.aoc.com
**SIC: 5045** 3577 Computers and accessories, personal and home entertainment; Computer peripheral equipment, nec

### (P-16522)
### EPMWARE INC
333 W San Carlos St Ste 600, San Jose (95110-2726)
**PHONE**..................408 614-0442
Tony Kiratsous, *Managing Member*
Abhi Nerurkar, *
Deven Shah, *
**EMP:** 25 **EST:** 2013
**SALES (est):** 2.56MM **Privately Held**
Web: www.epmware.com
**SIC: 5045** 7372 Computer software; Business oriented computer software

### (P-16523)
### EXCLUSIVE NETWORKS USA INC
4038 Clipper Ct, Fremont (94538-6540)
**PHONE**..................408 943-9193
Olivier Breittmayer, *CEO*
James Zhi Fang Shen, *General Vice President*
◆ **EMP:** 29 **EST:** 1992
**SALES (est):** 84.24MM **Privately Held**
Web: www.exclusive-networks.com
**SIC: 5045** 3571 Computer peripheral equipment; Electronic computers

### (P-16524)
### GAR ENTERPRISES (PA)
Also Called: Kgs Electronics
418 E Live Oak Ave, Arcadia (91006)
**PHONE**..................626 574-1175
Nathan Sugimoto, *CEO*
Pastor Kazuo G Sugimoto, *Prin*
**EMP:** 70 **EST:** 1960
**SALES (est):** 23.35MM
**SALES (corp-wide):** 23.35MM **Privately Held**
Web: www.kgselectronics.com
**SIC: 5045** 3728 Anti-static equipment and devices; Aircraft assemblies, subassemblies, and parts, nec

### (P-16525)
### GENESIS COMPUTER SYSTEMS INC
4055 E La Palma Ave Ste C, Anaheim (92807-1750)
**PHONE**..................714 632-3648
Awaiz Akram, *Pr*
Shawn Dewan, *VP*
▼ **EMP:** 20 **EST:** 1994
**SQ FT:** 3,500
**SALES (est):** 4.74MM **Privately Held**
Web: www.usgenesis.com
**SIC: 5045** 3571 Computers, peripherals, and software; Electronic computers

### (P-16526)
### HITACHI SOLUTIONS AMERICA LTD (DH)
100 Spectrum Center Dr Ste 350, Irvine (92618-4967)
**PHONE**..................949 242-1300
Keiho Akiyama, *CEO*
▲ **EMP:** 30 **EST:** 1990
**SQ FT:** 12,000
**SALES (est):** 266.41MM **Privately Held**
Web: global.hitachi-solutions.com
**SIC: 5045** 7372 Computer software; Prepackaged software
HQ: Hitachi Solutions, Ltd.
  4-12-7, Higashishinagawa
  Shinagawa-Ku TKY 140-0

### (P-16527)
### HULA NETWORKS INC (PA)
929 Berryessa Rd Ste 10, San Jose (95133-1084)
**PHONE**..................866 485-2638
Joe Commendatore, *CEO*
Scott Hobin, *CFO*
Stephen Robinson, *Prin*
▲ **EMP:** 16 **EST:** 2002
**SALES (est):** 8.54MM
**SALES (corp-wide):** 8.54MM **Privately Held**
Web: www.hulanetworks.com
**SIC: 5045** 5065 3572 3577 Computers and accessories, personal and home entertainment; Electronic parts and equipment, nec; Computer storage devices; Computer peripheral equipment, nec

### (P-16528)
### HYPER PRODUCTS INC (DH)
Also Called: Hyper
46721 Fremont Blvd, Fremont (94538-6539)
**PHONE**..................714 765-5555
Mikel H Williams, *CEO*
Derek L Baker, *CFO*
▲ **EMP:** 15 **EST:** 2005
**SQ FT:** 6,000
**SALES (est):** 5.58MM **Publicly Held**
Web: www.hypershop.com
**SIC: 5045** 3577 7371 Computers and accessories, personal and home entertainment; Computer peripheral equipment, nec; Computer software development
HQ: Targus International Llc
  1211 N Miller St
  Anaheim CA 92806
  714 765-5555

### (P-16529)
### JAL AVIONET USA (HQ)
300 Continental Blvd # 190, El Segundo (90245-5045)
**PHONE**..................310 606-1000
◆ **EMP:** 30 **EST:** 1985
**SQ FT:** 13,375
**SALES (est):** 10.17MM **Privately Held**
Web: www.jalavionet.com

**SIC: 5045** 7372 5065 7377 Computer software; Prepackaged software; Communication equipment; Computer rental and leasing
PA: Japan Airlines Co.,Ltd.
  2-4-11, Higashishinagawa

### (P-16530)
### KINGSTON TECHNOLOGY COMPANY INC (HQ)
17600 Newhope St, Fountain Valley (92708-4298)
**PHONE**..................714 435-2600
◆ **EMP:** 780 **EST:** 1989
**SALES (est):** 418.24MM **Privately Held**
Web: www.kingston.com
**SIC: 5045** 3674 Computer peripheral equipment; Random access memory (RAM)
PA: Kingston Technology Corporation
  17600 Newhope St

### (P-16531)
### LITMUS AUTOMATION INC (PA)
2350 Mission College Blvd Ste 1020, Santa Clara (95054-1563)
**PHONE**..................765 418-7405
Vatsal Shah, *CEO*
Sacha Sawaya, *
John Younes, *
**EMP:** 73 **EST:** 2016
**SQ FT:** 3,500
**SALES (est):** 10.9MM
**SALES (corp-wide):** 10.9MM **Privately Held**
Web: www.litmus.io
**SIC: 5045** 7372 Computer software; Prepackaged software

### (P-16532)
### MICROLAND ELECTRONICS CORP (PA)
1883 Ringwood Ave, San Jose (95131-1721)
**PHONE**..................408 441-1688
Abraham Chen, *Pr*
▲ **EMP:** 40 **EST:** 1986
**SQ FT:** 40,000
**SALES (est):** 19.8MM
**SALES (corp-wide):** 19.8MM **Privately Held**
Web: www.microlandusa.com
**SIC: 5045** 3577 3572 3571 Computer peripheral equipment; Computer peripheral equipment, nec; Computer storage devices; Electronic computers

### (P-16533)
### MTC WORLDWIDE CORP
17837 Rowland St, City Of Industry (91748-1122)
**PHONE**..................626 839-6800
Roy Han, *CEO*
▲ **EMP:** 79 **EST:** 1989
**SQ FT:** 42,500
**SALES (est):** 2.76MM
**SALES (corp-wide):** 8.55MM **Privately Held**
Web: www.mtcusa.com
**SIC: 5045** 3577 Computer peripheral equipment; Computer peripheral equipment, nec
PA: Mtc Direct, Inc.
  17837 Rowland St
  626 839-6800

### (P-16534)
### NINJATECH AI
4410 El Camino Real Ste 100, Los Altos (94022-1049)
**PHONE**..................408 444-5101

Sam Naghshineh, *CEO*
Balak Pahlavan, *
**EMP:** 42 **EST:** 2022
**SALES (est):** 6.17MM **Privately Held**
**SIC: 5045** 2843 Computer software; Processing assistants

### (P-16535)
### NZXT INC (PA)
605 E Huntington Dr Ste 213, Monrovia (91016-6353)
**PHONE**..................626 385-8272
Johnny Chun Ju Hou, *CEO*
▲ **EMP:** 326 **EST:** 2015
**SALES (est):** 73.95MM
**SALES (corp-wide):** 73.95MM **Privately Held**
Web: www.nzxt.com
**SIC: 5045** 3571 7379 Computers, peripherals, and software; Computers, digital, analog or hybrid; Computer hardware requirements analysis

### (P-16536)
### PALAMIDA INC
215 2nd St Lbby 2, San Francisco (94105-3140)
**PHONE**..................415 777-9400
Mark E Tolliver, *CEO*
Jeff Luszcz, *
**EMP:** 40 **EST:** 2005
**SALES (est):** 3.61MM
**SALES (corp-wide):** 71.22MM **Privately Held**
Web: www.revenera.com
**SIC: 5045** 7372 Computer software; Application computer software
HQ: Flexera Software Llc
  300 Park Blvd Ste 400
  Itasca IL 60143

### (P-16537)
### PAYDARFAR INDUSTRIES INC
Also Called: Saratech
26054 Acero, Mission Viejo (92691-2768)
**PHONE**..................949 481-3267
Saeed Paydarfar Ph.d., *CEO*
**EMP:** 60 **EST:** 2002
**SQ FT:** 5,930
**SALES (est):** 22.86MM **Privately Held**
Web: www.saratech.com
**SIC: 5045** 8711 7372 7373 Computer software; Engineering services; Prepackaged software; Value-added resellers, computer systems

### (P-16538)
### PC SPECIALISTS INC (HQ)
Also Called: Technology Integration Group
11860 Community Rd Ste 160, Poway (92064-8888)
**PHONE**..................858 566-1900
**EMP:** 117 **EST:** 1983
**SALES (est):** 467.24MM
**SALES (corp-wide):** 1.97B **Privately Held**
Web: www.tig.com
**SIC: 5045** 3571 7371 Computers, peripherals, and software; Electronic computers; Custom computer programming services
PA: Converge Technology Solutions Corp
  161 Bay St Suite 2325
  416 360-3995

### (P-16539)
### PHIHONG USA CORP (HQ)
47800 Fremont Blvd, Fremont (94538-6551)
**PHONE**..................510 445-0100
Fei Hung Alex Lin, *Pr*

▲ = Import ▼ = Export
◆ = Import/Export

## PRODUCTS & SERVICES SECTION
## 5045 - Computers, Peripherals, And Software (P-16558)

▲ EMP: 58 EST: 1990
SQ FT: 33,000
SALES (est): 35.37MM Privately Held
Web: www.phihong.com
SIC: 5045 3572 Computer peripheral equipment; Computer disk and drum drives and components
PA: Phihong Technology Co., Ltd.
No.568, Fuxing 3rd Rd.

**(P-16540)**
**PREMIER SYSTEMS USA INC (PA)**
Also Called: Olloclip
16291 Gothard St, Huntington Beach (92647-3612)
PHONE.................................657 204-9861
Patrick O'neill, CEO
Anne O'neill, Opers Mgr
▲ EMP: 18 EST: 2010
SQ FT: 6,000
SALES (est): 4.29MM
SALES (corp-wide): 4.29MM Privately Held
SIC: 5045 3841 Computer peripheral equipment; Surgical and medical instruments

**(P-16541)**
**PRINTSAFE INC**
11895 Community Rd Ste B, Poway (92064-7125)
PHONE.................................858 748-8600
Thomas Hittle, CEO
Linda Hittle, *
EMP: 25 EST: 1988
SQ FT: 15,000
SALES (est): 4.98MM Privately Held
Web: www.printsafe.com
SIC: 5045 3953 5084 Printers, computer; Marking devices; Printing trades machinery, equipment, and supplies

**(P-16542)**
**QUARTIC SOLUTIONS LLC**
1427 Chalcedony St, San Diego (92109-2127)
PHONE.................................858 377-8470
Timo Luostarinen, Pr
Jodi Luostarinen, *
EMP: 35 EST: 2004
SALES (est): 2.28MM Privately Held
Web: www.quarticsolutions.com
SIC: 5045 7372 7389 7371 Computer software; Application computer software; Mapmaking services; Custom computer programming services

**(P-16543)**
**RAISE 3D INC**
Also Called: Raise 3d
43 Tesla, Irvine (92618-4603)
PHONE.................................888 963-9028
Hua Feng, CEO
Marc Franz, Ex VP
EMP: 15 EST: 2014
SQ FT: 12,000
SALES (est): 2.95MM Privately Held
Web: www.raise3d.com
SIC: 5045 5734 3999 8742 Printers, computer; Printers and plotters: computers; Advertising display products; Marketing consulting services
PA: Shanghai Fusion Tech Co., Ltd.
Room 402,403,404, No.68, 1688 Lane, Guoquan N. Road, Yangpu Dist

**(P-16544)**
**RASILIENT SYSTEMS INC (PA)**
3281 Kifer Rd, Santa Clara (95051-0826)
PHONE.................................408 730-2568
Sean Chang, CEO
◆ EMP: 39 EST: 2001
SALES (est): 10.46MM Privately Held
Web: www.rasilient.com
SIC: 5045 3572 Disk drives; Computer storage devices

**(P-16545)**
**RAVIG INC**
Also Called: Salient Global Technologies
510 Garcia Ave Ste E, Pittsburg (94565-7405)
PHONE.................................925 526-1234
Ravikanth Ganapavarapu, CEO
EMP: 60 EST: 1999
SQ FT: 34,000
SALES (est): 16.8MM
SALES (corp-wide): 26.34MM Privately Held
SIC: 5045 7373 3571 Computers, peripherals, and software; Systems software development services; Electronic computers
PA: Salient Global Technologies
11252 Leo Ln
925 526-1234

**(P-16546)**
**RIPPEY CORPORATION**
Also Called: ITW Rippey
5000 Hillsdale Cir, El Dorado Hills (95762-5706)
PHONE.................................916 939-4332
EMP: 70
Web: www.rippey.com
SIC: 5045 5065 3674 Computers, peripherals, and software; Electronic parts and equipment, nec; Semiconductor circuit networks

**(P-16547)**
**RIVERBED TECHNOLOGY LLC (HQ)**
275 Shoreline Dr Ste 350, Redwood City (94065-1446)
PHONE.................................415 247-8800
Dave Donatelli, CEO
Dan Smoot, *
Subbu Iyer, CMO*
Hansan Bae, *
John Tyler, *
▲ EMP: 70 EST: 2002
SALES (est): 342.73MM
SALES (corp-wide): 380MM Privately Held
Web: www.riverbed.com
SIC: 5045 3577 Computer software; Computer peripheral equipment, nec
PA: Vector Capital Management, L.P.
650 California St
415 293-5000

**(P-16548)**
**SIBLINGS INVESTMENT INC**
Also Called: Vantec Thermal Technologies
43951 Boscell Rd, Fremont (94538-5139)
PHONE.................................510 668-0368
Chin-che Huang, Pr
Sheena L Chang, *
▲ EMP: 25 EST: 1992
SQ FT: 12,000
SALES (est): 4.4MM Privately Held
Web: www.vantecusa.com
SIC: 5045 3577 Computer peripheral equipment; Computer peripheral equipment, nec

**(P-16549)**
**SOLID OAK SOFTWARE INC (PA)**
319 W Mission St, Santa Barbara (93101-2822)
P.O. Box 6826 (93160-6826)
PHONE.................................805 568-5415
Brian P Milburn Senior, Pr
Brian Milburn, *
Mark Kanter, *
EMP: 25 EST: 1990
SALES (est): 9.27MM Privately Held
Web: www.27labs.com
SIC: 5045 7372 Computer software; Prepackaged software

**(P-16550)**
**SOUTHLAND TECHNOLOGY INC**
8053 Vickers St, San Diego (92111-1917)
PHONE.................................858 694-0932
Grace Pedigo, CEO
Robert Pedigo, *
EMP: 65 EST: 2001
SQ FT: 16,000
SALES (est): 44.12MM Privately Held
Web: www.southlandtechnology.com
SIC: 5045 8748 7373 7379 Computer peripheral equipment; Systems engineering consultant, ex. computer or professional; Computer integrated systems design; Computer related maintenance services

**(P-16551)**
**SPIRENT COMMUNICATIONS INC (HQ)**
Also Called: Spirent Calabasas
27349 Agoura Rd, Calabasas (91301-2413)
PHONE.................................818 676-2300
Eric G Hutchinson, CEO
Bill Burns, *
▲ EMP: 350 EST: 1988
SALES (est): 474.73MM
SALES (corp-wide): 474.3MM Privately Held
Web: www.spirent.com
SIC: 5045 3663 3829 3825 Computers, peripherals, and software; Radio and t.v. communications equipment; Measuring and controlling devices, nec; Instruments to measure electricity
PA: Spirent Communications Plc
Origin One
129 376-7676

**(P-16552)**
**SQUARE ENIX INC**
999 N Pacific Coast Hwy Fl 3, El Segundo (90245-2731)
PHONE.................................310 846-0400
Mike Fischer, Pr
Clinton Foy, *
Koichiro Hyashi, *
▲ EMP: 110 EST: 1998
SALES (est): 24.13MM Privately Held
Web: www.square-enix.com
SIC: 5045 7372 Computer software; Publisher's computer software
HQ: Square Enix Of America Holdings, Inc.
999 N Pacific Coast Hwy # 3
El Segundo CA 90245

**(P-16553)**
**SYSPRO IMPACT SOFTWARE INC**
Also Called: Syspro
1735 Flight Way, Tustin (92782-1852)
PHONE.................................714 437-1000
Brian Stein, CEO
Joey Benadretti, *
Kristin Valentyn, CRO*
EMP: 200 EST: 1991
SALES (est): 23.5MM Privately Held
Web: us.syspro.com
SIC: 5045 7372 7371 Computer software; Prepackaged software; Custom computer programming services

**(P-16554)**
**T B B INC**
Also Called: Data Consultants
3586 N Hazel Ave, Fresno (93722-4912)
PHONE.................................559 222-4100
William Pardini, Pr
EMP: 15 EST: 1976
SQ FT: 16,000
SALES (est): 2.33MM Privately Held
Web: www.dataconsultants.com
SIC: 5045 7372 Computers, nec; Business oriented computer software

**(P-16555)**
**TEAC AMERICA INC (HQ)**
Also Called: Teac
10410 Pioneer Blvd, Santa Fe Springs (90670-8261)
PHONE.................................323 726-0303
Koichiro Nakamura, Pr
H Derek Davis, *
Patericia Wallace, *
Derek Davis, *
▲ EMP: 19 EST: 1967
SALES (est): 17.64MM Privately Held
Web: www.teac.co.jp
SIC: 5045 5064 5065 3651 Computer peripheral equipment; Electrical entertainment equipment; Magnetic recording tape; Household audio and video equipment
PA: Teac Corporation
1-47, Ochiai

**(P-16556)**
**TEAM RESEARCH INC**
Also Called: Team
1911 Hartog Dr, San Jose (95131-2213)
PHONE.................................408 452-8788
▲ EMP: 25 EST: 1992
SALES (est): 5.64MM Privately Held
Web: www.teamresearchinc.com
SIC: 5045 5043 3861 Computer peripheral equipment; Motion picture cameras, equipment, and supplies; Cameras and related equipment

**(P-16557)**
**TEAMSABLE INC**
1911 Hartog Dr, San Jose (95131-2213)
PHONE.................................408 452-8788
Tzuchiang Hsieh, CEO
EMP: 22 EST: 2018
SQ FT: 10,000
SALES (est): 1.83MM Privately Held
Web: www.teamsable.com
SIC: 5045 3861 5043 Computer peripheral equipment; Cameras and related equipment; Motion picture cameras, equipment, and supplies

**(P-16558)**
**TECHNOSYLVA INC (PA)**
7590 Fay Ave Ste 300, La Jolla (92037-4886)
PHONE.................................619 292-1935
Brian Spear, CEO
EMP: 18 EST: 2015
SALES (est): 2.45MM
SALES (corp-wide): 2.45MM Privately Held
Web: www.technosylva.com

# 5045 - Computers, Peripherals, And Software (P-16559)

*(P-16559)*
**TREND MICRO INCORPORATED**
Also Called: Deep Security
3031 Tisch Way, San Jose (95128-2584)
PHONE..................................408 257-1500
Dana L Testa, *Mgr*
**EMP:** 54
**Web:** www.trendmicro.com
**SIC:** 5045 7382 7372 Computer software; Security systems services; Prepackaged software
**HQ:** Trend Micro Incorporated
225 E John Crptr Fwy Ste
Irving TX 75062

*(P-16560)*
**TREND MICRO INCORPORATED**
10101 N De Anza Blvd, Cupertino (95014-2264)
PHONE..................................408 257-1500
Anrew Lai, *Brnch Mgr*
**EMP:** 285
**Web:** www.trendmicro.com
**SIC:** 5045 7382 7372 Computer software; Security systems services; Prepackaged software
**HQ:** Trend Micro Incorporated
225 E John Crptr Fwy Ste
Irving TX 75062

*(P-16561)*
**TRIVAD INC**
880 Mitten Rd Ste 107, Burlingame (94010-1309)
PHONE..................................650 286-1086
Jenna Lim, *CEO*
**EMP:** 230 **EST:** 2002
**SALES (est):** 29.81MM **Privately Held**
**Web:** www.trivad.com
**SIC:** 5045 7373 5734 3721 Computers, peripherals, and software; Computer integrated systems design; Computer and software stores; Airplanes, fixed or rotary wing

*(P-16562)*
**TWIN BRIDGES TECHNOLOGIES LLC**
Also Called: Crushvirus
30286 Oakbrook Rd, Hayward (94544-6670)
PHONE..................................707 591-4500
Seema Dhingra, *Managing Member*
**EMP:** 16 **EST:** 2016
**SALES (est):** 451.49K **Privately Held**
**Web:** www.crushvirus.com
**SIC:** 5045 7372 Computer software; Utility computer software

*(P-16563)*
**UBIQ SECURITY INC**
Also Called: Ubiq
4660 La Jolla Village Dr Ste 100, San Diego (92122-4604)
PHONE..................................888 434-6674
Wias Issa, *CEO*
Eric Tobias, *
Linda Eigner, *
**EMP:** 27 **EST:** 2012
**SALES (est):** 2.9MM **Privately Held**
**Web:** www.ubiqsecurity.com
**SIC:** 5045 7372 Computer software; Prepackaged software

*(P-16564)*
**VICARIOUS FPC INC**
Also Called: Vicarious
1320 Decoto Rd Ste 200, Union City (94587-3594)
PHONE..................................415 604-3278
David Scott Phoenix, *CEO*
**EMP:** 40 **EST:** 2010
**SALES (est):** 12.12MM **Privately Held**
**Web:** www.vicarious.com
**SIC:** 5045 3549 Computer software; Assembly machines, including robotic

## 5046 Commercial Equipment, Nec

*(P-16565)*
**AAMP OF FLORIDA INC**
Also Called: Aamp of America
7166 Bickmore Ave # 2, Chino (91708-9157)
PHONE..................................805 338-6800
◆ **EMP:** 50
**SALES (corp-wide):** 36.71MM **Privately Held**
**Web:** www.stingersolutions.com
**SIC:** 5046 3714 3629 Coin-operated equipment; Automotive wiring harness sets; Battery chargers, rectifying or nonrotating
**PA:** Aamp Of Florida, Inc.
15500 Lghtwave Dr Ste 202
727 572-9255

*(P-16566)*
**B & N INDUSTRIES INC (PA)**
15 Guittard Rd, Burlingame (94010-2203)
PHONE..................................650 593-4127
**TOLL FREE:** 800
Brad Somberg, *CEO*
Adam Brown, *
◆ **EMP:** 78 **EST:** 1975
**SQ FT:** 30,000
**SALES (est):** 19.16MM
**SALES (corp-wide):** 19.16MM **Privately Held**
**Web:** www.bnind.com
**SIC:** 5046 3089 2541 2542 Store fixtures and display equipment; Injection molded finished plastics products, nec; Wood partitions and fixtures; Office and store showcases and display fixtures

*(P-16567)*
**GEMCO DISPLAY AND STR FIXS LLC (PA)**
Also Called: Victory Display & Store Fixs
2640 E Del Amo Blvd, Compton (90221-6004)
PHONE..................................800 262-1126
**TOLL FREE:** 800
David Nutel, *Pr*
Fred Berman, *Ch Bd*
▲ **EMP:** 20 **EST:** 1999
**SALES (est):** 4.55MM **Privately Held**
**Web:** www.victorydisplay.com
**SIC:** 5046 3089 Store fixtures; Plastics processing

*(P-16568)*
**INNOVATIVE DISPLAYWORKS LLC (HQ)**
Also Called: I D W
8825 Boston Pl Ste 100, Rancho Cucamonga (91730-4922)
PHONE..................................909 447-8254
Leo Wills, *CEO*
Nathan W Linder, *
◆ **EMP:** 15 **EST:** 2000
**SQ FT:** 5,000
**SALES (est):** 26.42MM
**SALES (corp-wide):** 54.9MM **Privately Held**
**Web:** www.idw.global
**SIC:** 5046 3441 2541 5078 Display equipment, except refrigerated; Fabricated structural metal; Display fixtures, wood; Beverage coolers
**PA:** Oxford Financial Group, Ltd.
11711 N Meridian St # 600
317 843-5678

*(P-16569)*
**JUSTMAN PACKAGING & DISPLAY (PA)**
5819 Telegraph Rd, Commerce (90040-1515)
PHONE..................................323 728-8888
Morley Justman, *Pr*
Russell Justman, *VP*
Barbara Cabaret, *CFO*
▲ **EMP:** 65 **EST:** 1989
**SALES (est):** 25.37MM
**SALES (corp-wide):** 25.37MM **Privately Held**
**Web:** www.justmanpackaging.com
**SIC:** 5046 5113 2752 Display equipment, except refrigerated; Corrugated and solid fiber boxes; Commercial printing, lithographic

## 5047 Medical And Hospital Equipment

*(P-16570)*
**A PLUS INTERNATIONAL INC (PA)**
5138 Eucalyptus Ave, Chino (91710-9254)
PHONE..................................909 591-5168
Wayne Lin, *Pr*
David Lee, *VP*
◆ **EMP:** 73 **EST:** 1988
**SQ FT:** 150,000
**SALES (est):** 7.77MM
**SALES (corp-wide):** 7.77MM **Privately Held**
**Web:** www.aplusgroup.net
**SIC:** 5047 3842 Medical equipment and supplies; Surgical appliances and supplies

*(P-16571)*
**ALPHA IMAGING TECHNOLOGY**
16453 Old Valley Blvd, City Of Industry (91744-5541)
PHONE..................................626 330-0808
◆ **EMP:** 15
**SQ FT:** 25,000
**SALES (est):** 4MM **Privately Held**
**SIC:** 5047 3579 Medical equipment and supplies; Typing and word processing machines

*(P-16572)*
**ALPHA INNOTECH CORP**
3040 Oakmead Village Dr, Santa Clara (95051-0808)
PHONE..................................408 510-5500
Jason Novi, *Brnch Mgr*
**EMP:** 72
**SALES (corp-wide):** 1.16B **Publicly Held**
**Web:** www.proteinsimple.com
**SIC:** 5047 7372 Diagnostic equipment, medical; Prepackaged software
**HQ:** Alpha Innotech Corp.
81 Daggett Dr
San Jose CA 95134

*(P-16573)*
**AMERICAN MED & HOSP SUP CO INC**
Also Called: Am-Touch Dental
28703 Industry Dr, Valencia (91355-5414)
PHONE..................................661 294-1213
Harish Khetarpal, *CEO*
Roma Khetarpal, *
▲ **EMP:** 32 **EST:** 1987
**SQ FT:** 25,000
**SALES (est):** 9.27MM **Privately Held**
**Web:** www.amtouch.com
**SIC:** 5047 3843 3842 Medical equipment and supplies; Dental equipment and supplies; Surgical appliances and supplies

*(P-16574)*
**ATG - DESIGNING MOBILITY INC (DH)**
Also Called: Numotion
11075 Knott Ave Ste B, Cypress (90630-5150)
PHONE..................................562 921-0258
**TOLL FREE:** 800
Mike Swinford, *CEO*
**EMP:** 26 **EST:** 1996
**SQ FT:** 10,500
**SALES (est):** 9.69MM
**SALES (corp-wide):** 770.72MM **Privately Held**
**Web:** www.numotion.com
**SIC:** 5047 5999 3842 Medical equipment and supplies; Medical apparatus and supplies; Wheelchairs
**HQ:** Atg Holdings, Inc.
805 Brook St Ste 2
Rocky Hill CT 06067

*(P-16575)*
**AVENUE MEDICAL EQUIPMENT INC**
38062 Encanto Rd, Murrieta (92563-3208)
PHONE..................................949 680-7444
Myo Tun, *Pr*
**EMP:** 35 **EST:** 2015
**SALES (est):** 571.04K **Privately Held**
**Web:** www.avenueme.com
**SIC:** 5047 5021 3842 5048 Medical equipment and supplies; Furniture; Orthopedic appliances; Ophthalmic goods

*(P-16576)*
**BALT USA LLC**
Also Called: Blockade Medical
29 Parker Ste 100, Irvine (92618-1667)
PHONE..................................949 788-1443
David A Ferrera, *Pr*
**EMP:** 90 **EST:** 2011
**SQ FT:** 47,000
**SALES (est):** 37.79MM
**SALES (corp-wide):** 2.4MM **Privately Held**
**Web:** www.baltgroup.com
**SIC:** 5047 3841 Medical equipment and supplies; Surgical and medical instruments
**HQ:** Balt International
10 Rue De La Croix Vigneron
Montmorency IDF 95160
139894641

*(P-16577)*
**BIONIME USA CORPORATION**
1450 E Spruce St Ste B, Ontario (91761-8313)
PHONE..................................909 781-6969
Chun-mu Huang, *Prin*
Alex Wang, *
▲ **EMP:** 25 **EST:** 2008
**SALES (est):** 2.64MM **Privately Held**
**Web:** www.bionimeusa.com

# PRODUCTS & SERVICES SECTION

## 5049 - Professional Equipment, Nec (P-16598)

SIC: **5047** 2835 Diagnostic equipment, medical; In vitro diagnostics

**(P-16578)**
**CARLSBAD INTERNATIONAL EXPORT INC**
Also Called: Carlsbad Medical Supply
1954 Kellogg Ave, Carlsbad (92008-6581)
PHONE.............................760 438-5323
▲ **EMP:** 20
SIC: **5047** 3841 Medical equipment and supplies; Surgical and medical instruments

**(P-16579)**
**CRAMER-DECKER INDUSTRIES (PA)**
Also Called: Prorack Gas Products
1300 E Wakeham Ave Ste A, Santa Ana (92705-4145)
PHONE.............................714 566-3800
Ryan W Decker, *CEO*
Paul Cramer, *
Lorraine Cramer, *
Christine Decker, *
◆ **EMP:** 23 **EST:** 1980
**SQ FT:** 42,000
**SALES (est):** 9.24MM
**SALES (corp-wide):** 9.24MM **Privately Held**
Web: www.prorackgasproducts.com
SIC: **5047** 2813 Medical equipment and supplies; Oxygen, compressed or liquefied

**(P-16580)**
**DIGITAL DOC LLC**
4789 Golden Foothill Pkwy, El Dorado Hills (95762)
PHONE.............................916 941-8010
Don Berg, *Managing Member*
▲ **EMP:** 44 **EST:** 1998
**SALES (est):** 9.73MM **Privately Held**
Web: www.digi-doc.com
SIC: **5047** 3069 Medical equipment and supplies; Medical and laboratory rubber sundries and related products

**(P-16581)**
**DURASAFE INC**
Also Called: Life Guard Gloves
18999 Railroad St, City Of Industry (91748-1322)
PHONE.............................626 965-1588
Chih S Hung, *CEO*
Pai Hung, *CFO*
▲ **EMP:** 19 **EST:** 1988
**SQ FT:** 35,000
**SALES (est):** 2.16MM **Privately Held**
Web: www.lifeguardgloves.com
SIC: **5047** 3069 Medical equipment and supplies; Medical sundries, rubber

**(P-16582)**
**ELERS MEDICAL USA INC**
21707 Hawthorne Blvd Ste 206, Torrance (90503-7009)
PHONE.............................858 336-4900
Donald Mccormick, *Pr*
**EMP:** 20 **EST:** 2020
**SALES (est):** 1.08MM
**SALES (corp-wide):** 1.7MM **Privately Held**
SIC: **5047** 5999 3841 Medical equipment and supplies; Medical apparatus and supplies; Surgical and medical instruments
**PA:** Elers Medical Finland Oy
Niittytaival 13
207305010

**(P-16583)**
**HARDY DIAGNOSTICS (PA)**
1430 W Mccoy Ln, Santa Maria (93455-1005)
P.O. Box 645264 (45264-5264)
PHONE.............................805 346-2766
Jay R Hardy, *Pr*
Jeff Schroder, *
◆ **EMP:** 300 **EST:** 1980
**SQ FT:** 75,000
**SALES (est):** 95.87MM
**SALES (corp-wide):** 95.87MM **Privately Held**
Web: www.hardydiagnostics.com
SIC: **5047** 2836 Medical equipment and supplies; Agar culture media

**(P-16584)**
**KLM LABORATORIES INC**
Also Called: Klm Orthotic
28280 Alta Vista Ave, Valencia (91355-0958)
PHONE.............................661 295-2600
Kirk Marshall, *Pr*
Scott Marshall, *
Kent Marshall, *
**EMP:** 100 **EST:** 1974
**SQ FT:** 35,000
**SALES (est):** 4.57MM **Privately Held**
Web: www.klmlabstore.com
SIC: **5047** 3842 Medical laboratory equipment; Foot appliances, orthopedic

**(P-16585)**
**MOBILITY SOLUTIONS INC (PA)**
7895 Convoy Ct Ste 11, San Diego (92111-1215)
PHONE.............................858 278-0591
Martin Helsing, *Pr*
Richard Tuthill, *
▲ **EMP:** 25 **EST:** 1994
**SALES (est):** 17.43MM **Privately Held**
Web: www.mobility-solutions.com
SIC: **5047** 3842 Medical equipment and supplies; Wheelchairs

**(P-16586)**
**NOVA ORTHO-MED INC (PA)**
Also Called: Nova Medical Products
1470 Beachey Pl, Carson (90746-4002)
PHONE.............................310 352-3600
Sue Chen, *CEO*
Ronald Gaudiano, *
▲ **EMP:** 30 **EST:** 1993
**SQ FT:** 5,500
**SALES (est):** 22.67MM **Privately Held**
Web: www.novajoy.com
SIC: **5047** 3842 Medical equipment and supplies; Wheelchairs

**(P-16587)**
**PETER BRASSELER HOLDINGS LLC**
Also Called: Comet Medical
4837 Mcgrath St Ste J, Ventura (93003-8077)
PHONE.............................805 650-5209
Orlando Deleon, *Mgr*
**EMP:** 73
**SALES (corp-wide):** 22.1MM **Privately Held**
Web: www.brasselerusa.com
SIC: **5047** 3841 3843 Dental equipment and supplies; Surgical and medical instruments; Dental equipment
**PA:** Peter Brasseler Holdings, Llc
1 Brasseler Blvd
912 925-8525

**(P-16588)**
**PMB GROUP INC**
Also Called: Pmb Group
12778 Brookprinter Pl, Poway (92064-6810)
PHONE.............................619 690-7300
Fatih Buyuksonmez, *Pr*
▲ **EMP:** 17 **EST:** 2007
**SALES (est):** 4.18MM **Privately Held**
Web: www.conquerscientific.com
SIC: **5047** 3826 Medical laboratory equipment; Amino acid analyzers

**(P-16589)**
**SIGMA SUPPLY & DIST INC**
701 W Harvard St, Glendale (91204-1142)
PHONE.............................818 246-4624
Arthur Keshishyan, *CEO*
▲ **EMP:** 18 **EST:** 1998
**SQ FT:** 6,500
**SALES (est):** 4.49MM **Privately Held**
SIC: **5047** 3841 Medical equipment and supplies; Surgical and medical instruments

**(P-16590)**
**SUNRISE MEDICAL (US) LLC**
2842 N Business Park Ave, Fresno (93727-1328)
PHONE.............................559 292-2171
Thomas Babacan, *Pr*
Larry Jackson, *
▲ **EMP:** 28 **EST:** 2010
**SALES (est):** 2.69MM **Privately Held**
Web: www.sunrisemedical.com
SIC: **5047** 3842 Medical equipment and supplies; Wheelchairs

**(P-16591)**
**TOTAL HEALTH ENVIRONMENT LLC**
743 W Taft Ave, Orange (92865-4229)
PHONE.............................714 637-1010
**EMP:** 30 **EST:** 2014
**SALES (est):** 2.53MM **Privately Held**
Web: www.the-gsc.net
SIC: **5047** 3843 5021 Medical and hospital equipment; Dental equipment; Office furniture, nec

**(P-16592)**
**VERCITY PROTECT INC**
1625 El Paseo St, San Luis Obispo (93401-4674)
PHONE.............................917 689-0989
Charles Chen, *CEO*
**EMP:** 15 **EST:** 2020
**SALES (est):** 366.5K **Privately Held**
SIC: **5047** 3842 Industrial safety devices: first aid kits and masks; Gas masks

**(P-16593)**
**VISIONCARE DEVICES INC**
Also Called: Biotronics
6100 Bellevue Ln, Anderson (96007-4950)
PHONE.............................530 364-2271
Wayne Cook, *Pr*
**EMP:** 20 **EST:** 1990
**SQ FT:** 8,000
**SALES (est):** 4.53MM **Privately Held**
Web: www.visioncaredevices.com
SIC: **5047** 5048 3841 3851 Medical equipment and supplies; Ophthalmic goods ; Surgical and medical instruments; Ophthalmic goods

**(P-16594)**
**WALK VASCULAR LLC**
Also Called: Abbott Medical
3200 Lakeside Dr, Santa Clara (95054-2807)

PHONE.............................949 752-9642
Dave Look, *Managing Member*
**EMP:** 20 **EST:** 2010
**SALES (est):** 3.37MM
**SALES (corp-wide):** 40.11B **Publicly Held**
Web: www.cardiovascular.abbott
SIC: **5047** 3841 Medical equipment and supplies; Surgical and medical instruments
**PA:** Abbott Laboratories
100 Abbott Park Rd
224 667-6100

**(P-16595)**
**WEARLINQ INC**
1819 Polk St Pmb 148, San Francisco (94109-3003)
PHONE.............................650 785-8742
Konrad Morzkowski, *Pr*
**EMP:** 35 **EST:** 2019
**SALES (est):** 431.2K **Privately Held**
Web: www.wearlinq.com
SIC: **5047** 3841 Medical equipment and supplies; Surgical and medical instruments

## 5048 Ophthalmic Goods

**(P-16596)**
**NIDEK INCORPORATED**
2040 Corporate Ct, San Jose (95131-1753)
PHONE.............................800 223-9044
Hideo Ozawa, *Ch Bd*
Motoki Ozawa, *
◆ **EMP:** 25 **EST:** 1982
**SALES (est):** 18.98MM **Privately Held**
Web: usa.nidek.com
SIC: **5048** 8011 3845 3841 Optometric equipment and supplies; Offices and clinics of medical doctors; Electromedical equipment; Surgical and medical instruments
**PA:** Nidek Co.,Ltd.
34-14, Maehama, Hiroishicho

## 5049 Professional Equipment, Nec

**(P-16597)**
**ABB INC**
Also Called: ABB - Los Gatos Research
1960 Zanker Rd, San Jose (95112-4216)
P.O. Box 80065 (27623-0065)
PHONE.............................408 770-8968
Doug Baer, *Genl Mgr*
**EMP:** 223
Web: www.abb.com
SIC: **5049** 3826 Analytical instruments; Analytical instruments
**HQ:** Abb Inc.
305 Gregson Dr
Cary NC 27511

**(P-16598)**
**ABC SCHOOL EQUIPMENT INC**
Also Called: Platinum Visual Systems
1451 E 6th St, Corona (92879-1715)
PHONE.............................951 817-2200
Gary P Stell Junior, *CEO*
Thomas Mendez, *
**EMP:** 70 **EST:** 1964
**SQ FT:** 35,000
**SALES (est):** 1.7MM **Privately Held**
Web: www.abcse.com
SIC: **5049** 3861 2531 School supplies; Photographic equipment and supplies; Public building and related furniture

## 5049 - Professional Equipment, Nec (P-16599)

**(P-16599)**
**CPI INTERNATIONAL**
5580 Skylane Blvd, Santa Rosa (95403-1030)
PHONE..................707 521-6327
Ryan Vice, *CEO*
Joseph Phillips, *
▲ **EMP:** 70 **EST:** 1996
**SQ FT:** 20,000
**SALES (est):** 7.84MM **Privately Held**
Web: www.cpiinternational.com
**SIC: 5049** 3826  Analytical instruments; Analytical instruments

**(P-16600)**
**EXCEL SCIENTIFIC LLC**
18350 George Blvd, Victorville (92394-7930)
PHONE..................760 246-4545
Julie Cameron, *CEO*
▲ **EMP:** 21 **EST:** 2001
**SQ FT:** 27,000
**SALES (est):** 6.17MM **Privately Held**
Web: www.excelscientific.com
**SIC: 5049** 3821  Scientific and engineering equipment and supplies; Laboratory apparatus, except heating and measuring
**PA:** Vance Street Capital Llc
15304 W Sunset Blvd

**(P-16601)**
**INDIO PRODUCTS INC (PA)**
Also Called: Seven Sisters of New Orleans
12910 Mulberry Dr Unit A, Whittier (90602-3455)
PHONE..................323 720-1188
▲ **EMP:** 130 **EST:** 2010
**SALES (est):** 26.98MM
**SALES (corp-wide):** 26.98MM **Privately Held**
Web: www.indioproducts.com
**SIC: 5049** 3999  Religious supplies; Candles

**(P-16602)**
**MCBAIN SYSTEMS A CAL LTD PRTNR**
810 Lawrence Dr, Newbury Park (91320-2208)
PHONE..................805 581-6800
Michael Crump, *Pr*
▲ **EMP:** 20 **EST:** 1965
**SALES (est):** 2.05MM **Privately Held**
Web: www.mcbainsystems.com
**SIC: 5049** 3827 7699  Scientific and engineering equipment and supplies; Optical instruments and apparatus; Optical instrument repair

**(P-16603)**
**MOLECULAR BIOPRODUCTS SVC CORP (HQ)**
Also Called: Pgc Scientiifics
10636 Scripps Summit Ct Ste 130, San Diego (92131-3965)
PHONE..................858 875-7696
Paul Nowak, *Pr*
Ron Perkins, *CFO*
◆ **EMP:** 20 **EST:** 1988
**SALES (est):** 5.46MM **Privately Held**
**SIC: 5049** 3089 3821  Laboratory equipment, except medical or dental; Injection molded finished plastics products, nec; Laboratory apparatus and furniture
**PA:** Biotix Holdings, Inc.
10636 Scripps Summit Ct

**(P-16604)**
**REAGENT WORLD INC**
18401 Von Karman Ave, Irvine (92612-1542)
PHONE..................909 947-7779
Daniel Shen, *Pr*
**EMP:** 15 **EST:** 2007
**SALES (est):** 10.25MM **Privately Held**
Web: www.reagentworld.com
**SIC: 5049** 5169 2869 2899  Laboratory equipment, except medical or dental; Industrial chemicals; Industrial organic chemicals, nec; Fire retardant chemicals

**(P-16605)**
**TECHNICAL INSTR SAN FRANCISCO (PA)**
Also Called: Technical Instrument SF
1826 Rollins Rd Ste 100, Burlingame (94010-2215)
P.O. Box 2340  (94942-2340)
PHONE..................650 651-3000
Brian F Lundy, *CEO*
**EMP:** 29 **EST:** 1996
**SQ FT:** 11,000
**SALES (est):** 2.55MM **Privately Held**
**SIC: 5049** 3827  Optical goods; Optical instruments and lenses

## 5051 Metals Service Centers And Offices

**(P-16606)**
**AOC TECHNOLOGIES INC**
6900 Koll Center Pkwy Ste 401, Pleasanton (94566-3154)
PHONE..................925 875-0808
Gordon Gu, *Pr*
◆ **EMP:** 315 **EST:** 1999
**SALES (est):** 3.89MM **Privately Held**
Web: www.aoctech.com
**SIC: 5051** 3357  Metal wires, ties, cables, and screening; Fiber optic cable (insulated)

**(P-16607)**
**ARCHITECTURAL GL & ALUM CO INC (HQ)**
Also Called: Architectural Glass & Aluminum
6400 Brisa St, Livermore (94550-2550)
PHONE..................510 444-6100
Joseph Brescia, *CEO*
John Buckley, *
William Coll Junior, *VP*
▲ **EMP:** 155 **EST:** 1970
**SQ FT:** 33,000
**SALES (est):** 46.46MM
**SALES (corp-wide):** 60.63MM **Privately Held**
Web: www.aga-ca.com
**SIC: 5051** 1793 1791 3442  Aluminum bars, rods, ingots, sheets, pipes, plates, etc.; Glass and glazing work; Exterior wall system installation; Sash, door or window: metal
**PA:** Na Holding Corp.
4220 Angela Way
260 918-6041

**(P-16608)**
**BERGSEN INC**
12241 Florence Ave, Santa Fe Springs (90670-3805)
PHONE..................562 236-9787
Thomas Sharpe, *CEO*
◆ **EMP:** 25 **EST:** 1971
**SQ FT:** 27,000
**SALES (est):** 14MM **Privately Held**
Web: www.bergsen.com
**SIC: 5051** 3317  Steel; Boiler tubes (wrought)

**(P-16609)**
**CALIFORNIA STEEL SERVICES INC**
Also Called: California Steel Services
1212 S Mountain View Ave, San Bernardino (92408-3001)
PHONE..................909 796-2222
Parviz Razavian, *CEO*
**EMP:** 49 **EST:** 1983
**SQ FT:** 78,000
**SALES (est):** 22.09MM **Privately Held**
Web: www.calsteel.com
**SIC: 5051** 3444 3443  Steel; Sheet metalwork ; Fabricated plate work (boiler shop)

**(P-16610)**
**CAPITOL STEEL COMPANY**
1932 Auburn Blvd, Sacramento (95815-1910)
P.O. Box 215239  (95821-1239)
PHONE..................916 924-3195
Craig M Elowson, *Pr*
**EMP:** 19 **EST:** 1968
**SALES (est):** 7.4MM **Privately Held**
Web: www.capitolsteelcompany.com
**SIC: 5051** 5032 3444  Steel; Brick, stone, and related material; Concrete forms, sheet metal

**(P-16611)**
**CASTER TECHNOLOGY CORP (PA)**
11552 Markon Dr, Garden Grove (92841-1828)
PHONE..................714 893-6886
Karl Elles, *Pr*
David Elles, *VP*
Mark Tash, *CFO*
**EMP:** 17 **EST:** 1984
**SQ FT:** 17,100
**SALES (est):** 10.2MM
**SALES (corp-wide):** 10.2MM **Privately Held**
Web: www.labcasters.com
**SIC: 5051** 3562  Metals service centers and offices; Casters

**(P-16612)**
**CENTURY TUBES INC**
7910 Dunbrook Rd, San Diego (92126-4371)
PHONE..................858 586-0550
Christine Young, *Pr*
Conrad M Young, *VP*
▲ **EMP:** 22 **EST:** 1980
**SQ FT:** 10,000
**SALES (est):** 4.88MM **Privately Held**
Web: www.centurytubes.com
**SIC: 5051** 3312 3356 3351  Pipe and tubing, steel; Tubes, steel and iron; Nonferrous rolling and drawing, nec; Copper rolling and drawing

**(P-16613)**
**CKKM INC (PA)**
Also Called: Nova Steel Company
265 Radio Rd, Corona (92879-1725)
PHONE..................951 371-8484
Bernard Smokowski, *Pr*
Jacqueline Lowery, *
Mary Jo Thometz, *
**EMP:** 21 **EST:** 1991
**SQ FT:** 50,000
**SALES (est):** 22.16MM **Privately Held**
Web: www.adp-ca.com
**SIC: 5051** 3444  Steel; Pipe, sheet metal

**(P-16614)**
**CONQUEST INDUSTRIES INC**
12740 Lakeland Rd, Santa Fe Springs (90670-4633)
PHONE..................562 906-1111
▲ **EMP:** 25 **EST:** 1979
**SALES (est):** 2.99MM **Privately Held**
Web: www.conquestind.com
**SIC: 5051** 3559  Nonferrous metal sheets, bars, rods, etc., nec; Jewelers' machines

**(P-16615)**
**CONSOLDTED METAL FBRCTNG COINC**
2780 S Cherry Ave, Fresno  (93706-5424)
P.O. Box 12064  (93776-2064)
PHONE..................559 268-7887
Philip Alcorn, *Pr*
Deanna Alcorn, *
Scott Alcorn, *
Brent Alcorn, *
**EMP:** 30 **EST:** 1975
**SQ FT:** 40,080
**SALES (est):** 4.99MM **Privately Held**
**SIC: 5051** 3444 3441  Aluminum bars, rods, ingots, sheets, pipes, plates, etc.; Sheet metalwork; Fabricated structural metal

**(P-16616)**
**COONER SALES COMPANY LLC (PA)**
Also Called: Cooner Wire Company
9265 Owensmouth Ave, Chatsworth (91311-5854)
PHONE..................818 882-8311
Patrick G Weir, *Pr*
▲ **EMP:** 19 **EST:** 1957
**SQ FT:** 17,825
**SALES (est):** 9.68MM
**SALES (corp-wide):** 9.68MM **Privately Held**
Web: www.coonerwire.com
**SIC: 5051** 3679  Wire, nec; Harness assemblies, for electronic use: wire or cable

**(P-16617)**
**D P NICOLI INC**
266 Harbor Way, South San Francisco (94080-6816)
PHONE..................650 873-2999
Mike Welton, *Brnch Mgr*
**EMP:** 15
**SALES (corp-wide):** 10.66MM **Privately Held**
Web: www.dpnicoli.com
**SIC: 5051** 7359 3325  Steel; Equipment rental and leasing, nec; Steel foundries, nec
**PA:** D. P. Nicoli, Inc.
17888 Sw Mcewan Rd
503 692-6080

**(P-16618)**
**DANIEL GERARD WORLDWIDE INC**
Also Called: City Wire Cloth
13055 Jurupa Ave, Fontana  (92337-6982)
PHONE..................951 361-1111
**TOLL FREE:** 800
Todd Snelbaker, *Mgr*
**EMP:** 71
**SQ FT:** 50,000
**SALES (corp-wide):** 82.77MM **Privately Held**
Web: www.gerarddaniel.com
**SIC: 5051** 3496 3356 3315  Wire, nec; Mesh, made from purchased wire; Nonferrous rolling and drawing, nec; Steel wire and related products
**PA:** Gerard Daniel Worldwide, Inc.
150 Factory St

## PRODUCTS & SERVICES SECTION
## 5051 - Metals Service Centers And Offices (P-16636)

800 232-3332

**(P-16619)**
**ENDURA STEEL INC (HQ)**
Also Called: Smith Ironworks
17671 Bear Valley Rd, Hesperia (92345-4902)
PHONE..................760 244-9325
Jonathan D Hove, *Pr*
Robert E Hove, *Ch Bd*
Dan Such, *VP*
Lori A Clifton, *Sec*
EMP: 18 EST: 1972
SQ FT: 6,500
SALES (est): 3.33MM
SALES (corp-wide): 49.72MM **Privately Held**
Web: www.endura-steel.com
SIC: **5051** 3441 Steel; Fabricated structural metal
PA: Robar Enterprises, Inc.
17671 Bear Valley Rd
760 244-5456

**(P-16620)**
**GERLINGER FNDRY MCH WORKS INC**
Also Called: Gerlinger Steel & Supply Co
1510 Tanforan Ave, Woodland (95776-6109)
P.O. Box 992195 (96099-2195)
PHONE..................530 243-1053
Fred Gerlinger, *Brnch Mgr*
EMP: 17
SALES (corp-wide): 12.06MM **Privately Held**
Web: www.gerlinger.com
SIC: **5051** 5015 3441 Steel; Motor vehicle parts, used; Fabricated structural metal
PA: Gerlinger Foundry And Machine Works, Inc.
1527 Sacramento St
530 243-1053

**(P-16621)**
**JACK RUBIN & SONS INC (PA)**
13103 S Alameda St, Compton (90222-2898)
P.O. Box 3005 (90223-3005)
PHONE..................310 635-5407
Bruce Rubin, *CEO*
Phillip Mandel, *
Michael Rubin, *
▲ EMP: 25 EST: 1945
SQ FT: 30,000
SALES (est): 24.47MM
SALES (corp-wide): 24.47MM **Privately Held**
Web: www.wirerope.net
SIC: **5051** 3496 3999 Rope, wire (not insulated); Woven wire products, nec; Atomizers, toiletry

**(P-16622)**
**M-H IRONWORKS INC**
1000 S Seaward Ave, Ventura (93001-3735)
P.O. Box 58364 (90058-0364)
▲ EMP: 52 EST: 1947
SALES (est): 1.31MM **Privately Held**
SIC: **5051** 3312 Steel; Blast furnaces and steel mills

**(P-16623)**
**MCNICHOLS COMPANY**
Also Called: McNichols
14108 Arbor Pl, Cerritos (90703-2404)
PHONE..................562 921-3344
Pat Roche, *Mgr*
EMP: 17
SQ FT: 20,000
SALES (corp-wide): 191.36MM **Privately Held**
Web: www.mcnichols.com
SIC: **5051** 3496 3446 Steel; Wire cloth and woven wire products; Open flooring and grating for construction
PA: Mcnichols Company
2502 N Rocky Point Dr # 750
877 884-4653

**(P-16624)**
**MWS PRECISION WIRE INDS INC**
Also Called: Mws Wire Industries
3000 Camino Del Sol, Oxnard (93030)
PHONE..................818 991-8553
TOLL FREE: 888
Benjamin Konrad, *Pr*
Darrell H Friedman, *
Alan Friedman, *
Lois J Friedman, *
EMP: 52 EST: 1968
SQ FT: 32,000
SALES (est): 20.86MM **Privately Held**
Web: www.mwswire.com
SIC: **5051** 3351 3357 Copper sheets, plates, bars, rods, pipes, etc., nec; Wire, copper and copper alloy; Nonferrous wiredrawing and insulating

**(P-16625)**
**NEIGHBORHOOD STEEL LLC (HQ)**
Also Called: Maas-Hansen Steel
5555 Garden Grove Blvd Ste 250, Westminster (92683-8240)
P.O. Box 58307 (90058)
PHONE..................714 236-8700
Gary Stein, *Managing Member*
EMP: 30 EST: 2015
SALES (est): 8.11MM
SALES (corp-wide): 482.42MM **Privately Held**
Web: www.sss-steel.com
SIC: **5051** 3312 Steel; Blast furnaces and steel mills
PA: Triple-S Steel Holdings, Inc.
6000 Jensen Dr
713 697-7105

**(P-16626)**
**NORMAN INDUSTRIAL MTLS INC (PA)**
Also Called: Industrial Metal Supply Co
8300 San Fernando Rd, Sun Valley (91352-3222)
PHONE..................818 729-3333
TOLL FREE: 800
Eric Steinhauer, *CEO*
David Pace, *
David Berkey, *
Dave Cohen, *
▲ EMP: 125 EST: 1945
SQ FT: 70,000
SALES (est): 82.56MM
SALES (corp-wide): 82.56MM **Privately Held**
Web: www.industrialmetalsupply.com
SIC: **5051** 3441 3449 Metals service centers and offices; Fabricated structural metal; Miscellaneous metalwork

**(P-16627)**
**NORMAN INDUSTRIAL MTLS INC**
Also Called: Industrial Metal Supply Co
2481 Alton Pkwy, Irvine (92606-5030)
PHONE..................949 250-3343
Jerry Entin, *VP*
EMP: 41
SQ FT: 40,000
SALES (corp-wide): 150.06MM **Privately Held**
Web: www.industrialmetalsupply.com
SIC: **5051** 5099 3366 Steel; Brass goods; Bronze foundry, nec
PA: Norman Industrial Materials, Inc.
8300 San Fernando Rd
818 729-3333

**(P-16628)**
**PDM STEEL SERVICE CENTERS INC**
3500 Bassett St, Santa Clara (95054-2704)
P.O. Box 329 (95052-0329)
PHONE..................408 988-3000
John Norman, *Genl Mgr*
EMP: 21
SQ FT: 46,080
SALES (corp-wide): 14.81B **Publicly Held**
Web: www.pdmsteel.com
SIC: **5051** 3444 3272 Steel; Sheet metalwork; Concrete products, nec
HQ: Pdm Steel Service Centers, Inc.
3535 E Myrtle St
Stockton CA 95205
209 943-0513

**(P-16629)**
**PDM STEEL SERVICE CENTERS INC (HQ)**
Also Called: Specialty Steel Service
3535 E Myrtle St, Stockton (95205-4721)
PHONE..................209 943-0513
Derick Halecky, *Pr*
William Nixon, *VP Fin*
Joseph Anderson, *
Randy H Kearns, *
Brad Blickle, *
▲ EMP: 100 EST: 1954
SALES (est): 214.55MM
SALES (corp-wide): 14.81B **Publicly Held**
Web: www.pdmsteel.com
SIC: **5051** 3353 3354 Steel; Aluminum sheet and strip; Aluminum pipe and tube
PA: Reliance, Inc.
16100 N 71st St Ste 400
480 564-5700

**(P-16630)**
**RAMCAST ORNAMENTAL SUP CO INC**
Also Called: Ramcast Steel
1450 E Mission Blvd, Pomona (91766-2229)
PHONE..................909 469-4767
Ismael Ramirez, *Brnch Mgr*
EMP: 30
SQ FT: 5,478
SALES (corp-wide): 27.6MM **Privately Held**
Web: www.ramcaststeel.net
SIC: **5051** 3312 Steel; Stainless steel
PA: Ramcast Ornamental Supply Company, Inc.
2201 Firestone Blvd
323 585-1625

**(P-16631)**
**SACO ENTERPRISES INC**
Also Called: Pactech
2260 Trade Zone Blvd, San Jose (95131-1845)
PHONE..................408 526-9363
Aaron Chui, *CEO*
Aaron Chui, *Pr*
Sandy Cheng, *
◆ EMP: 35 EST: 2007
SQ FT: 8,000
SALES (est): 8.58MM **Privately Held**
Web: www.pactech-inc.com

SIC: **5051** 3678 3679 5065 Cable, wire; Electronic connectors; Electronic circuits; Electronic parts

**(P-16632)**
**SHAPCO INC (PA)**
1666 20th St Ste 100, Santa Monica (90404-3828)
PHONE..................310 264-1666
Leonard Shapiro, *Pr*
Leonard Shapiro, *Pr*
Bernard J Shapiro, *Ch Bd*
Jaime Gesundheidt, *VP*
Steve Teller, *VP*
◆ EMP: 15 EST: 1984
SQ FT: 7,598
SALES (est): 134.62MM
SALES (corp-wide): 134.62MM **Privately Held**
Web: www.shapco.com
SIC: **5051** 3317 6799 Iron and steel (ferrous) products; Steel pipe and tubes; Real estate investors, except property operators

**(P-16633)**
**STREUTER TECHNOLOGIES INC**
Also Called: Streuter Fastel Timtel
208 Avenida Fabricante Ste 200, San Clemente (92672-7536)
PHONE..................949 369-7676
Bart Streuter, *Pr*
Bart S Streuter, *Pr*
Brad Streuter, *VP*
▲ EMP: 18 EST: 2005
SQ FT: 13,000
SALES (est): 6.13MM **Privately Held**
Web: www.streuter.com
SIC: **5051** 2891 Ferrous metals; Adhesives and sealants

**(P-16634)**
**TOOL COMPONENTS INC (PA)**
Also Called: E-Z Lok Division
240 E Rosecrans Ave, Gardena (90248-1942)
P.O. Box 2069 (90247-0069)
PHONE..................310 323-5613
TOLL FREE: 800
▲ EMP: 38 EST: 1956
SALES (est): 21.33MM
SALES (corp-wide): 21.33MM **Privately Held**
Web: www.tciprecision.com
SIC: **5051** 3429 Aluminum bars, rods, ingots, sheets, pipes, plates, etc.; Metal fasteners

**(P-16635)**
**TOTTEN TUBES INC (PA)**
500 W Danlee St, Azusa (91702-2341)
PHONE..................626 812-0220
Tracy N Totten, *CEO*
David Totten, *
Linda Furse, *
Jeffrey Totten, *
EMP: 60 EST: 1955
SQ FT: 73,000
SALES (est): 48.57MM
SALES (corp-wide): 48.57MM **Privately Held**
Web: www.tottentubes.com
SIC: **5051** 3498 Pipe and tubing, steel; Coils, pipe; fabricated from purchased pipe

**(P-16636)**
**TRI-TECH METALS INC**
9039 Charles Smith Ave, Rancho Cucamonga (91730-5566)
PHONE..................909 948-1401
Sam Allen, *Pr*
Richard Lee Hiromoto, *CEO*

## 5051 - Metals Service Centers And Offices (P-16637)

Rock Hargus, *VP*
Sam Allen, *Sec*
Margo Beltran, *Treas*
**EMP:** 18 **EST:** 1998
**SQ FT:** 10,000
**SALES (est):** 5.2MM **Privately Held**
**Web:** www.tri-techmetals.com
**SIC:** 5051 3499 3291  Steel; Aerosol valves, metal; Steel wool

### (P-16637)
### VER SALES INC (PA)
2509 N Naomi St, Burbank  (91504-3236)
**PHONE**......................818 567-3000
**TOLL FREE:** 800
Gloria Ryan, *CEO*
James J Ryan, *CEO*
Craig Ryan, *VP*
Paul Ryan, *VP*
Patrick Ryan, *VP*
▲ **EMP:** 45 **EST:** 1972
**SQ FT:** 30,000
**SALES (est):** 24.36MM
**SALES (corp-wide):** 24.36MM **Privately Held**
**Web:** www.versales.com
**SIC:** 5051 5099 3357  Metal wires, ties, cables, and screening; Safety equipment and supplies; Nonferrous wiredrawing and insulating

## 5063 Electrical Apparatus And Equipment

### (P-16638)
### AAA ELECTRIC MOTOR SALES & SVC (PA)
1346 Venice Blvd, Los Angeles  (90006-5595)
**PHONE**......................213 749-2367
Brian A Maloney, *Pr*
Robert A Maloney, *Pr*
Nancy Maloney, *Sec*
**EMP:** 19 **EST:** 1971
**SQ FT:** 3,500
**SALES (est):** 14.63MM
**SALES (corp-wide):** 14.63MM **Privately Held**
**Web:** www.aaa-electric.net
**SIC:** 5063 7694  Motors, electric; Electric motor repair

### (P-16639)
### ADVANTAGE MANUFACTURING INC
Also Called: Electric Motors
616 S Santa Fe St, Santa Ana  (92705-4109)
**PHONE**......................714 505-1166
Lyann Courant, *CEO*
Michael Collins, *
◆ **EMP:** 30 **EST:** 1992
**SQ FT:** 25,000
**SALES (est):** 6.06MM **Privately Held**
**Web:** www.advantageman.com
**SIC:** 5063 5091 3621 5999  Motors, electric; Swimming pools, equipment and supplies; Motors, electric; Swimming pools, hot tubs, and sauna equipment and supplies

### (P-16640)
### AEE SOLAR INC (DH)
225 Bush St Ste 1400, San Francisco  (94104-4249)
**PHONE**......................800 777-6609
Mary Powell, *CEO*
Danny Abajian, *CFO*
Jeanna Steele, *Sec*
Edward Fenster, *Dir*
◆ **EMP:** 21 **EST:** 2003
**SQ FT:** 10,000
**SALES (est):** 36.12MM **Publicly Held**
**Web:** www.aeesolar.com
**SIC:** 5063 3645 1711  Generators; Residential lighting fixtures; Solar energy contractor
**HQ:** Sunrun South Llc
595 Market St Fl 29
San Francisco CA 94105
415 580-6900

### (P-16641)
### ALLIED ELECTRIC MOTOR SVC INC (PA)
4690 E Jensen Ave, Fresno  (93725-1603)
**PHONE**......................559 486-4222
Salvatore Rome, *Ch Bd*
Gail Mandal, *
Henry Mandal, *
Joyce Barnes, *
Sally Johnson, *
**EMP:** 55 **EST:** 1955
**SQ FT:** 100,000
**SALES (est):** 23.21MM
**SALES (corp-wide):** 23.21MM **Privately Held**
**Web:** pages.rexelusa.com
**SIC:** 5063 7694  Electrical supplies, nec; Electric motor repair

### (P-16642)
### APPLIMOTION INC
5915 Jetton Ln, Loomis  (95650-9594)
**PHONE**......................916 652-3118
▲ **EMP:** 69
**Web:** www.celeramotion.com
**SIC:** 5063 8711 3545  Motors, electric; Consulting engineer; Precision measuring tools

### (P-16643)
### AQ LIGHTING GROUP TEXAS INC
Also Called: Aq Lighting Group
28486 Westinghouse Pl Ste 120, Santa Clarita  (91355-0954)
**PHONE**......................818 534-5300
Cynthia Piana, *Pr*
Tom Piana, *
**EMP:** 25 **EST:** 2017
**SQ FT:** 16,000
**SALES (est):** 21MM **Privately Held**
**Web:** www.aqlightinggroup.com
**SIC:** 5063 3645 3612 2599  Light bulbs and related supplies; Light shades, metal; Distribution transformers, electric; Factory furniture and fixtures

### (P-16644)
### B&K PRECISION CORPORATION (PA)
22820 Savi Ranch Pkwy, Yorba Linda  (92887-4610)
**PHONE**......................714 921-9095
Victor Tolan, *CEO*
Linda Morton, *CFO*
▲ **EMP:** 21 **EST:** 1951
**SQ FT:** 17,000
**SALES (est):** 14.09MM **Privately Held**
**Web:** www.bkprecision.com
**SIC:** 5063 3599  Electrical apparatus and equipment; Machine shop, jobbing and repair

### (P-16645)
### BARTCO LIGHTING INC
5761 Research Dr, Huntington Beach  (92649-1616)
**PHONE**......................714 230-3200
Robert Barton, *CEO*
Dana B Mcke, *Ex VP*
Brian Labbe, *
▲ **EMP:** 70 **EST:** 1998
**SALES (est):** 23.98MM **Privately Held**
**Web:** www.bartcolighting.com
**SIC:** 5063 3648  Lighting fixtures, commercial and industrial; Airport lighting fixtures: runway approach, taxi, or ramp

### (P-16646)
### BRITHINEE ELECTRIC
620 S Rancho Ave, Colton  (92324-3243)
**PHONE**......................909 825-7971
Wallace P Brithinee, *Pr*
Donald P Brithinee, *VP*
**EMP:** 57 **EST:** 1963
**SALES (est):** 8.77MM **Privately Held**
**Web:** www.brithinee.com
**SIC:** 5063 7694  Motors, electric; Electric motor repair

### (P-16647)
### CABLECONN INDUSTRIES INC
Also Called: Cableconn
7198 Convoy Ct, San Diego  (92111-1019)
**PHONE**......................858 571-7111
Lisa Coffman, *Pr*
Roger Newman, *
Rod Coffman, *
**EMP:** 65 **EST:** 1991
**SQ FT:** 20,000
**SALES (est):** 22.72MM **Privately Held**
**Web:** www.cableconn.com
**SIC:** 5063 3678 3643  Building wire and cable ; Electronic connectors; Current-carrying wiring services

### (P-16648)
### CALIFORNIA BREAKERS INC (PA)
Also Called: Cbione
2490 Grand Ave, Vista  (92081-7804)
**PHONE**......................760 598-1528
Carlos Trevino, *CEO*
**EMP:** 22 **EST:** 1977
**SQ FT:** 18,000
**SALES (est):** 7MM
**SALES (corp-wide):** 7MM **Privately Held**
**Web:** www.cbione.com
**SIC:** 5063 1731 3823  Electrical supplies, nec ; Electric power systems contractors; Industrial process measurement equipment

### (P-16649)
### CITY ELECTRIC SUPPLY
360 Tesconi Cir, Santa Rosa  (95401-4677)
**PHONE**......................707 523-4600
Steve Acuri, *Mgr*
**EMP:** 22 **EST:** 2009
**SALES (est):** 8.44MM **Privately Held**
**Web:** ces-santarosa.portalced.com
**SIC:** 5063 3699 3634  Electrical supplies, nec ; Electrical equipment and supplies, nec; Electric housewares and fans

### (P-16650)
### EATON AEROSPACE LLC
Eaton Aerospace
4690 Colorado Blvd, Los Angeles  (90039-1106)
**PHONE**......................818 409-0200
Stephanie Stewart, *Brnch Mgr*
**EMP:** 256
**SQ FT:** 41,117
**SIC:** 5063 3492  Electrical apparatus and equipment; Fluid power valves and hose fittings
**HQ:** Eaton Aerospace Llc
1000 Eaton Blvd
Cleveland OH 44114
818 409-0200

### (P-16651)
### ELECTRIC MOTOR SHOP (PA)
Also Called: Electric Motor & Supply
253 Fulton St, Fresno  (93721-3164)
P.O. Box 446  (93709-0446)
**PHONE**......................559 233-1153
Richard M Caglia, *Pr*
Sally M Caglia, *
**EMP:** 24 **EST:** 1913
**SQ FT:** 7,500
**SALES (est):** 47.61MM
**SALES (corp-wide):** 47.61MM **Privately Held**
**Web:** www.electricmotorshop.com
**SIC:** 5063 1731 7694 7922  Motor controls, starters and relays; electric; Electrical work; Electric motor repair; Theatrical producers and services

### (P-16652)
### EXPO POWER SYSTEMS INC
Also Called: Enviroguard
5534 Olive St, Montclair  (91763-1649)
**PHONE**......................800 506-9884
Doug Frazier, *Pr*
**EMP:** 34 **EST:** 1993
**SQ FT:** 15,000
**SALES (est):** 18.79MM **Privately Held**
**Web:** www.enviroguard.com
**SIC:** 5063 3444  Batteries; Sheet metalwork

### (P-16653)
### FLIGHT LIGHT INC
2708 47th Ave, Sacramento  (95822-3806)
**PHONE**......................916 394-2800
**EMP:** 16 **EST:** 1993
**SALES (est):** 4.49MM **Privately Held**
**Web:** www.flightlight.com
**SIC:** 5063 3648  Lighting fixtures; Airport lighting fixtures: runway approach, taxi, or ramp

### (P-16654)
### HOCHIKI AMERICA CORPORATION (HQ)
Also Called: Hochiki
7051 Village Dr Ste 100, Buena Park  (90621-2262)
P.O. Box 514689  (90051-4689)
**PHONE**......................714 522-2246
Hisham Harake, *CEO*
Hiroshi Kamei, *VP*
Sunichi Shoji V Pes, *Prin*
Michel Nader, *Dir*
◆ **EMP:** 95 **EST:** 1972
**SQ FT:** 30,000
**SALES (est):** 48.18MM **Privately Held**
**Web:** www.hochikiamerica.com
**SIC:** 5063 3669  Fire alarm systems; Fire detection systems, electric
**PA:** Hochiki Corporation
2-10-43, Kamiosaki

### (P-16655)
### JME INC (PA)
Also Called: T M B
527 Park Ave, San Fernando  (91340-2557)
**PHONE**......................201 896-8600
Colin R Waters, *CEO*
Thomas M Bissett, *
◆ **EMP:** 80 **EST:** 1982
**SQ FT:** 34,000
**SALES (est):** 38.15MM
**SALES (corp-wide):** 38.15MM **Privately Held**
**Web:** www.tmb.com

# PRODUCTS & SERVICES SECTION
## 5063 - Electrical Apparatus And Equipment (P-16676)

SIC: 5063 3499 Lighting fittings and accessories; Aerosol valves, metal

**(P-16656)**
**KOFFLER ELEC MECH APPRTUS REPR**
Also Called: Koffler Electrical Mechanical
527 Whitney St, San Leandro (94577-1113)
PHONE..............................510 567-0630
Lari Koffler, *Pr*
Wayne Berner, *
Charles H Koffler, *
Michael Bucedi, *
Kerry Koffler, *
▲ EMP: 80 EST: 1994
SQ FT: 77,548
SALES (est): 23.38MM Privately Held
Web: www.koffler.com
SIC: 5063 7694 Motors, electric; Electric motor repair

**(P-16657)**
**LIGHTING TECHNOLOGIES INTL LLC**
13700 Live Oak Ave, Baldwin Park (91706-1319)
PHONE..............................626 480-0755
▲ EMP: 190 EST: 2016
SALES (est): 24.06MM Privately Held
Web: www.ltilighting.com
SIC: 5063 3648 Lighting fixtures; Lighting equipment, nec

**(P-16658)**
**LOS ANGELES LTG MFG CO INC**
Also Called: L A Lighting
10141 Olney St, El Monte (91731-2311)
PHONE..............................626 454-8300
William D Shapiro, *Pr*
Mieko Shapiro, *VP*
◆ EMP: 70 EST: 1988
SQ FT: 50,000
SALES (est): 22.27MM Privately Held
Web: www.lalighting.com
SIC: 5063 3646 Lighting fixtures; Ceiling systems, luminous

**(P-16659)**
**MAGNETIKA INC (PA)**
2041 W 139th St, Gardena (90249-2409)
PHONE..............................310 527-8100
Francis Ishida, *Pr*
Basil P Caloyeras, *
EMP: 80 EST: 1960
SQ FT: 40,000
SALES (est): 23.39MM
SALES (corp-wide): 23.39MM Privately Held
Web: www.magnetika.com
SIC: 5063 3612 Transformers, electric; Ballasts for lighting fixtures

**(P-16660)**
**MAIN ELECTRIC SUPPLY CO LLC**
8146 Byron Rd, Whittier (90606-2616)
PHONE..............................323 753-5131
Darrin Gunter, *Brnch Mgr*
EMP: 20
SALES (corp-wide): 464.19MM Privately Held
Web: www.mainelectricsupply.com
SIC: 5063 3699 Electrical supplies, nec; Electrical equipment and supplies, nec
PA: Main Electric Supply Company Llc
3600 W Segerstrom Ave
949 833-3052

**(P-16661)**
**MAIN ELECTRIC SUPPLY CO LLC**
1700 Morse Ave, Ventura (93003-5116)
PHONE..............................805 654-8600
Patrick Osullivan, *Mgr*
EMP: 25
SALES (corp-wide): 464.19MM Privately Held
Web: www.mainelectricsupply.com
SIC: 5063 3699 Electrical supplies, nec; Electrical equipment and supplies, nec
PA: Main Electric Supply Company Llc
3600 W Segerstrom Ave
949 833-3052

**(P-16662)**
**MAIN ELECTRIC SUPPLY CO LLC**
4674 Cardin St, San Diego (92111-1419)
PHONE..............................858 737-7000
Darryl Dalrymple, *Brnch Mgr*
EMP: 48
SALES (corp-wide): 464.19MM Privately Held
Web: www.mainelectricsupply.com
SIC: 5063 3699 Electrical supplies, nec; Electrical equipment and supplies, nec
PA: Main Electric Supply Company Llc
3600 W Segerstrom Ave
949 833-3052

**(P-16663)**
**MITRA FUTURE TECHNOLOGIES INC**
Also Called: Mitra Chem
1245 Terra Bella Ave, Mountain View (94043-1849)
PHONE..............................650 695-1245
Vivas Kumar, *CEO*
Chirranjeevi Gopal, *
Will Chueh, *
Melinda Berlant, *
EMP: 60 EST: 2021
SALES (est): 11.36MM Privately Held
Web: www.mitrachem.com
SIC: 5063 3356 Storage batteries, industrial; Battery metal

**(P-16664)**
**MPOWER ELECTRONICS INC (PA)**
2910 Scott Blvd, Santa Clara (95054-3312)
PHONE..............................408 320-1266
Hong Tao Sun, *Pr*
Peter Hsi, *
Weimin Cai, *
◆ EMP: 60 EST: 2018
SALES (est): 2.7MM
SALES (corp-wide): 2.7MM Privately Held
Web: www.mpowerinc.com
SIC: 5063 3829 3624 Fire alarm systems; Gas detectors; Carbon and graphite products

**(P-16665)**
**MULTIQUIP INC (DH)**
Also Called: Mq Power
6141 Katella Ave Ste 200, Cypress (90630-5202)
PHONE..............................310 537-3700
Robert J Graydon, *CEO*
James Henehan, *
◆ EMP: 300 EST: 1973
SALES (est): 214.36MM Privately Held
Web: www.multiquip.com

SIC: 5063 5082 3645 Generators; General construction machinery and equipment; Garden, patio, walkway and yard lighting fixtures: electric
HQ: Itochu International Inc.
1251 Ave Of The Amrcas Fl
New York NY 10020
212 818-8000

**(P-16666)**
**MURCAL INC**
Also Called: Murcal
41343 12th St W, Palmdale (93551-1442)
PHONE..............................661 272-4700
Robert J Murphy, *Pr*
John H Murphy, *
Essie Murphy, *Stockholder*
EMP: 26 EST: 1958
SQ FT: 20,000
SALES (est): 10.08MM Privately Held
Web: www.murcal.com
SIC: 5063 3621 3694 Motor controls, starters and relays: electric; Storage battery chargers, motor and engine generator type; Ignition apparatus, internal combustion engines

**(P-16667)**
**NORA LIGHTING INC**
6505 Gayhart St, Commerce (90040-2507)
PHONE..............................323 767-2600
Fred Farzan, *CEO*
Jill Farzan, *
Neda Farzan, *
◆ EMP: 144 EST: 1989
SQ FT: 150,000
SALES (est): 90MM Privately Held
Web: www.noralighting.com
SIC: 5063 3648 5719 Lighting fixtures; Lighting fixtures, except electric: residential; Lighting fixtures

**(P-16668)**
**ONESOURCE DISTRIBUTORS LLC**
2500 Bisso Ln Ste 100a, Concord (94520-4883)
P.O. Box 6226 (94520)
PHONE..............................925 827-9988
TOLL FREE: 800
Jess Paul, *Brnch Mgr*
EMP: 39
SQ FT: 10,000
SALES (corp-wide): 16.09MM Privately Held
Web: www.1sourcedist.com
SIC: 5063 5065 3625 Electrical supplies, nec; Electronic parts and equipment, nec; Motor control accessories, including overload relays
HQ: Onesource Distributors, Llc
3951 Oceanic Dr
Oceanside CA 92056
760 966-4500

**(P-16669)**
**PACIFIC POWER SYSTEMS INTEGRATION INC**
14729 Spring Ave, Santa Fe Springs (90670-5107)
PHONE..............................562 281-0500
EMP: 23
SIC: 5063 3826 Transformers, electric; Petroleum product analyzing apparatus

**(P-16670)**
**PLC IMPORTS INC**
Also Called: P L C Lighting
9667 Owensmouth Ave Ste 201, Chatsworth (91311-4819)
PHONE..............................818 349-1600
Daniel Gilardi, *Pr*
Robert Gilardi, *
▲ EMP: 25 EST: 1992
SALES (est): 4.63MM Privately Held
Web: www.plclighting.com
SIC: 5063 3646 Light bulbs and related supplies; Commercial lighting fixtures

**(P-16671)**
**QUANTUM AUTOMATION (PA)**
4400 E La Palma Ave, Anaheim (92807-1807)
P.O. Box 18687 (92817-8687)
PHONE..............................714 854-0800
Brian Gallogly, *Pr*
EMP: 35 EST: 1991
SQ FT: 11,000
SALES (est): 13.12MM Privately Held
Web: www.quantumautomation.com
SIC: 5063 3825 3613 Electrical apparatus and equipment; Electrical power measuring equipment; Control panels, electric

**(P-16672)**
**ROS ELECTRICAL SUP EQP CO LLC**
9529 Slauson Ave, Pico Rivera (90660-4749)
PHONE..............................562 695-9000
EMP: 20 EST: 2008
SALES (est): 2.74MM Privately Held
Web: www.rps-powersystems.com
SIC: 5063 3699 Electrical supplies, nec; Electrical equipment and supplies, nec

**(P-16673)**
**SLOAN ELECTRIC CORPORATION**
3520 Main St, San Diego (92113-3804)
PHONE..............................619 239-5174
EMP: 28 EST: 1985
SALES (est): 9.39MM Privately Held
Web: www.sloanelectric.com
SIC: 5063 7694 7629 Motor controls, starters and relays: electric; Electric motor repair; Generator repair

**(P-16674)**
**SUNCO LIGHTING INC**
27811 Hancock Pkwy Ste A, Valencia (91355-4187)
PHONE..............................844 334-9938
Sorush Tahour, *CEO*
EMP: 44 EST: 2014
SALES (est): 11.71MM Privately Held
Web: www.sunco.com
SIC: 5063 3699 Electrical supplies, nec; Electrical equipment and supplies, nec

**(P-16675)**
**UNS ELECTRIC INC**
6565 Valley View St, La Palma (90623-1060)
PHONE..............................714 690-3660
Irene Mitchell, *Prin*
EMP: 26
SALES (corp-wide): 8.38B Privately Held
Web: www.uesaz.com
SIC: 5063 3691 Storage batteries, industrial; Storage batteries
HQ: Uns Electric, Inc.
88 E Bradway Blvd Hqe 901
Tucson AZ 85701
928 681-8966

**(P-16676)**
**US ELECTRICAL SERVICES INC**
Also Called: Wiedenbach-Brown

# 5063 - Electrical Apparatus And Equipment (P-16677)

1501 E Orangethorpe Ave Ste 140, Fullerton (92831-5252)
PHONE..................714 982-1534
Scott King, Mgr
**EMP:** 28
**SALES (corp-wide):** 734.19MM **Privately Held**
Web: www.usesi.com
**SIC:** 5063 3645 Lighting fixtures; Residential lighting fixtures
**HQ:** U.S. Electrical Services, Inc.
  701 Middle St
  Middletown CT 06457

### (P-16677)
### VET NATIONAL INC
Also Called: Vet National Mail
3621 State St, Santa Barbara (93105-2521)
PHONE..................805 692-8487
Kevin Teel, Pr
Christopher Elsass, Prin
**EMP:** 20 **EST:** 1996
**SALES (est):** 3.91MM **Privately Held**
Web: www.vetnational.com
**SIC:** 5063 3088 3541 7331 Electrical apparatus and equipment; Plastics plumbing fixtures; Machine tools, metal cutting type; Mailing service

### (P-16678)
### WALTERS WHOLESALE ELECTRIC CO (HQ)
200 N Berry St, Brea (92821-3903)
PHONE..................714 784-1900
John L Walter, CEO
Bill Durkee, *
Roland Wood, *
Nancy Nielsen, *
▼ **EMP:** 50 **EST:** 1953
**SALES (est):** 374.7MM
**SALES (corp-wide):** 1.5B **Privately Held**
Web: www.walterswholesale.com
**SIC:** 5063 3699 1731 Wire and cable; Electronic training devices; Lighting contractor
**PA:** Consolidated Electrical Distributors, Inc.
  1920 Westridge Dr
  972 582-5300

### (P-16679)
### WAMCO INC (PA)
17752 Fitch, Irvine (92614-6303)
PHONE..................714 545-5560
Michael Matthews, CEO
Chris Matthews, Pr
Eric Lemay, VP
Michael Phillips, VP
Steve Dunkerken, CFO
▲ **EMP:** 19 **EST:** 1968
**SQ FT:** 30,000
**SALES (est):** 11.33MM
**SALES (corp-wide):** 11.33MM **Privately Held**
Web: www.wamcoinc.com
**SIC:** 5063 3647 5088 Electrical supplies, nec; Vehicular lighting equipment; Transportation equipment and supplies

### (P-16680)
### WESTERN LIGHTING INDS INC
Also Called: Orgatech Omegalux
12203 Magnolia Ave Ste 1, Riverside (92503-4890)
PHONE..................626 969-6820
Lawrence St Ives, CEO
▲ **EMP:** 22 **EST:** 1983
**SALES (est):** 5.34MM **Privately Held**

**SIC:** 5063 3646 Lighting fixtures; Fluorescent lighting fixtures, commercial

## 5064 Electrical Appliances, Television And Radio

### (P-16681)
### HARMAN-KARDON INCORPORATED
Also Called: Harman-Kardon
8500 Balboa Blvd, Northridge (91325-5802)
P.O. Box 2200 (91328-2200)
PHONE..................818 841-4600
Tom Mcloughlin, Pr
Chet Simon, VP Fin
▲ **EMP:** 275 **EST:** 1949
**SALES (est):** 5.83MM **Privately Held**
Web: www.harman.com
**SIC:** 5064 3651 High fidelity equipment; Household audio and video equipment
**HQ:** Harman International Industries Incorporated
  400 Atlantic St Fl 15
  Stamford CT 06901
  203 328-3500

### (P-16682)
### INFINITE NETWORKS INC
Also Called: Infinite Electric
457 E Mcglincy Ln Ste 1, Campbell (95008-4939)
PHONE..................408 796-7735
Sean Betti, Pr
Sean Betti, CEO
**EMP:** 30 **EST:** 1999
**SALES (est):** 1.55MM **Privately Held**
Web: www.infinitenetworksinc.com
**SIC:** 5064 1731 5063 3571 Electrical appliances, television and radio; Electrical work; Electrical apparatus and equipment; Electronic computers

### (P-16683)
### MEMOREX PRODUCTS INC
17777 Center Court Dr N Ste 800, Cerritos (90703-9320)
PHONE..................562 653-2800
Michael Golacinski, Pr
Allan Yap, *
Mae Higa, *
Kevin Mcdonnell, Sr VP
▲ **EMP:** 159 **EST:** 1993
**SQ FT:** 212,000
**SALES (est):** 7.95MM **Publicly Held**
**SIC:** 5064 5065 5045 3652 Electrical entertainment equipment; Radio and television equipment and parts; Computer peripheral equipment; Prerecorded records and tapes
**PA:** Glassbridge Enterprises, Inc.
  18 E 50th St Ste 700

### (P-16684)
### PIONEER NORTH AMERICA INC (DH)
970 W 190th St Ste 360, Torrance (90502-1069)
P.O. Box 1720 (90801-1720)
PHONE..................310 952-2000
Masao Kawabata, CEO
Kazunori Yamamoto, Pr
◆ **EMP:** 19 **EST:** 1978
**SQ FT:** 4,855
**SALES (est):** 66.82MM **Privately Held**
Web: www.pioneerelectronics.com
**SIC:** 5064 3651 High fidelity equipment; Household audio and video equipment
**HQ:** Pioneer Corporation
  2-28-8, Honkomagome

Bunkyo-Ku TKY 113-0

### (P-16685)
### PIONEER NORTH AMERICA INC
2050 W 190th St Ste 100, Torrance (90504-6229)
PHONE..................310 952-2000
**EMP:** 216
Web: www.pioneerelectronics.com
**SIC:** 5064 3651 High fidelity equipment; Household audio and video equipment
**HQ:** Pioneer North America, Inc.
  970 W 190th St Ste 360
  Torrance CA 90502
  310 952-2000

## 5065 Electronic Parts And Equipment, Nec

### (P-16686)
### ABX ENGINEERING INC
875 Stanton Rd, Burlingame (94010-1403)
PHONE..................650 552-2300
Paul Leininger Ii, CEO
**EMP:** 100 **EST:** 1980
**SQ FT:** 16,000
**SALES (est):** 23.07MM **Privately Held**
Web: www.abxengineering.com
**SIC:** 5065 7373 3672 Electronic parts; Turnkey vendors, computer systems; Printed circuit boards

### (P-16687)
### ACTIONTEC ELECTRONICS INC
590 Macara Ave, Sunnyvale (94085-2807)
PHONE..................408 752-7700
**EMP:** 66
Web: www.actiontec.com
**SIC:** 5065 5045 3571 Electronic parts and equipment, nec; Computers, peripherals, and software; Electronic computers
**PA:** Actiontec Electronics, Inc.
  2445 Augustine Dr Ste 501

### (P-16688)
### ADVANTEST AMERICA INC
3201 Scott Blvd, Santa Clara (95054-3008)
PHONE..................408 988-7700
**EMP:** 270
**SIC:** 5065 3825 Semiconductor devices; Instruments to measure electricity

### (P-16689)
### AIR ELECTRO INC (PA)
9452 De Soto Ave, Chatsworth (91311-4910)
P.O. Box 2231 (91313-2231)
PHONE..................818 407-5400
**EMP:** 104 **EST:** 1951
**SALES (est):** 24.47MM
**SALES (corp-wide):** 24.47MM **Privately Held**
Web: www.airelectro.com
**SIC:** 5065 3674 Electronic parts; Computer logic modules

### (P-16690)
### APPLIED WRLESS IDNTFCTONS GROU (PA)
Also Called: Awid
18300 Santa Sutter Blvd, Morgan Hill (95037-2841)
PHONE..................408 779-1929
Doctor Edward Liao, CEO
▲ **EMP:** 30 **EST:** 1997
**SQ FT:** 20,000
**SALES (est):** 10.2MM
**SALES (corp-wide):** 10.2MM **Privately Held**

Web: www.awid.com
**SIC:** 5065 3699 Security control equipment and systems; Security control equipment and systems

### (P-16691)
### AVAGO TECHNOLOGIES US INC (HQ)
Also Called: Avago Technologies
1320 Ridder Park Dr, San Jose (95131-2313)
P.O. Box 3643 (95055-3643)
PHONE..................800 433-8778
Hock Tan, Pr
Dick Chang, *
Douglas Bettinger, *
Jeff Henderson, *
Tze Siong Chong, *
▲ **EMP:** 400 **EST:** 2005
**SALES (est):** 1.41MM
**SALES (corp-wide):** 35.82B **Publicly Held**
Web: www.broadcom.com
**SIC:** 5065 3674 Semiconductor devices; Semiconductor diodes and rectifiers
**PA:** Broadcom Inc.
  3421 Hillview Ave
  650 427-6000

### (P-16692)
### BIP CORPORATION
2951 Norman Strasse Rd, San Marcos (92069-5933)
PHONE..................760 591-9822
Al Hatset, CEO
Nick Rahl, VP
▲ **EMP:** 19 **EST:** 1988
**SQ FT:** 3,000
**SALES (est):** 4.81MM **Privately Held**
Web: www.bipcorp.com
**SIC:** 5065 3663 Communication equipment; Radio and t.v. communications equipment

### (P-16693)
### CAL SOUTHERN SOUND IMAGE INC (PA)
Also Called: Sound Image
2425 Auto Park Way, Escondido (92029-1222)
PHONE..................760 737-3900
David R Shadoan, CEO
Ralph Wagner, *
**EMP:** 65 **EST:** 1984
**SQ FT:** 28,000
**SALES (est):** 49.52MM
**SALES (corp-wide):** 49.52MM **Privately Held**
Web: www.sound-image.com
**SIC:** 5065 3651 5064 Sound equipment, electronic; Speaker systems; Electrical appliances, television and radio

### (P-16694)
### CALRAD ELECTRONICS INC
819 N Highland Ave, Los Angeles (90038-3416)
PHONE..................323 465-2131
Robert Shupper, Pr
▲ **EMP:** 20 **EST:** 1939
**SALES (est):** 2.69MM **Privately Held**
Web: www.calrad.com
**SIC:** 5065 3678 3663 3661 Electronic parts; Electronic connectors; Radio and t.v. communications equipment; Telephone and telegraph apparatus

### (P-16695)
### CNET TECHNOLOGY CORPORATION
26291 Production Ave Ste 205, Hayward (94545)

# PRODUCTS & SERVICES SECTION
## 5065 - Electronic Parts And Equipment, Nec (P-16714)

PHONE..............................408 392-9966
▲ EMP: 250 EST: 1987
SQ FT: 50,000
SALES (est): 45.87MM Privately Held
Web: www.cnetusa.com
SIC: 5065 3661 3577 Communication equipment; Telephone and telegraph apparatus; Computer peripheral equipment, nec
PA: Kmc (Kuei Meng) International Inc.
8f-5, No. 425, Jhonghua Rd.

### (P-16696)
### COMBA TELECOM INC
568 Gibraltar Dr, Milpitas (95035-6315)
PHONE..............................408 526-0180
Tung Ling Fok, Pr
Bu Bin Long, VP
Chen Sui Yang, VP
Zhang Jin Yu Charles, VP
Luo Rui Bo, VP
EMP: 18 EST: 2005
SALES (est): 8.87MM Privately Held
Web: www.comba-telecom.com
SIC: 5065 3661 Telephone and telegraphic equipment; Telephones and telephone apparatus
HQ: Comba Telecom Systems Limited
Rm 611 6/F East Wing Hong Kong Science Park
Tai Po NT

### (P-16697)
### CYNERGY PROF SYSTEMS LLC
23187 La Cadena Dr Ste 102, Laguna Hills (92653)
PHONE..............................800 776-7978
Cynthia Mason, Pr
EMP: 30 EST: 2009
SALES (est): 34.81MM Privately Held
Web: www.cynergy.pro
SIC: 5065 7379 3663 3661 Communication equipment; Computer related maintenance services; Radio and t.v. communications equipment; Communication headgear, telephone

### (P-16698)
### DELTA AMERICA LTD (HQ)
Also Called: Delta Products
46101 Fremont Blvd, Fremont (94538-6468)
PHONE..............................510 668-5100
Ming H Huang, Pr
Yao Chou, Sec
◆ EMP: 130 EST: 1988
SALES (est): 465.66MM Privately Held
Web: www.delta-fan.com
SIC: 5065 3679 8731 Electronic parts and equipment, nec; Switches, stepping; Electronic research
PA: Delta Electronics, Inc.
No. 186, Ruey Kuang Road,

### (P-16699)
### DYNAMIC SECURITY TECH INC
28301 Industrial Blvd Ste B, Hayward (94545-4429)
PHONE..............................510 786-1121
Bryan Buenaventura, CEO
EMP: 24 EST: 2007
SALES (est): 5.94MM Privately Held
Web: www.dystinc.com
SIC: 5065 7382 3699 Security control equipment and systems; Security systems services; Security devices

### (P-16700)
### ELECTRONIC HARDWARE LIMITED (PA)
13257 Saticoy St, North Hollywood (91605-3486)
PHONE..............................818 982-6100
R E Vudrogivic, CEO
Richard Degn, Pr
EMP: 33 EST: 1973
SQ FT: 10,000
SALES (est): 1.67MM
SALES (corp-wide): 1.67MM Privately Held
Web: www.electronichardware.com
SIC: 5065 5072 3541 Electronic parts; Hardware; Machine tools, metal cutting type

### (P-16701)
### ENERPRO INC
99 Aero Camino, Goleta (93117-3822)
PHONE..............................805 683-2114
Thomas Bourbeau, Pr
Frank J Bourbeau, *
Ilse Bourbeau, *
Thomas Bourbeau, VP
◆ EMP: 25 EST: 1983
SQ FT: 27,000
SALES (est): 7.92MM Privately Held
Web: www.enerpro-inc.com
SIC: 5065 3699 Electronic parts and equipment, nec; Accelerating waveguide structures

### (P-16702)
### EVERFOCUS ELECTRONICS CORP (HQ)
324 W Blueridge Ave, Orange (92865-4202)
PHONE..............................626 844-8888
John Lee, Ch Bd
Alan Ying, *
James Weng, *
◆ EMP: 20 EST: 1996
SALES (est): 12.26MM Privately Held
Web: www.everfocus.com
SIC: 5065 3699 Security control equipment and systems; Security control equipment and systems
PA: Everfocus Electronics Corp.
2f, 8, Lane 270, Beishen Rd., Sec. 3

### (P-16703)
### GENERAL TRANSISTOR CORPORATION (PA)
Also Called: G T C
12449 Putnam St, Whittier (90602-1023)
PHONE..............................310 578-7344
Albert A Barrios, Pr
Ilan Israely, *
EMP: 30 EST: 1976
SALES (est): 9.06MM
SALES (corp-wide): 9.06MM Privately Held
Web: www.gtcelectronics.com
SIC: 5065 3674 Semiconductor devices; Semiconductor circuit networks

### (P-16704)
### HIGH TECH PET PRODUCTS
2111 Portola Rd # A, Ventura (93003-7723)
PHONE..............................805 644-1797
Nicholas Donge, Pr
▲ EMP: 60 EST: 1980
SALES (est): 4.4MM Privately Held
Web: www.hitecpet.com
SIC: 5065 2399 Electronic parts and equipment, nec; Pet collars, leashes, etc.: non-leather

### (P-16705)
### IMPACT COMPONENTS A CALIFORNIA LIMITED PARTNERSHIP
Also Called: Impact Components
6010 Cornerstone Ct W Ste 200, San Diego (92121-3746)
PHONE..............................858 634-4800
▲ EMP: 30 EST: 1897
SALES (est): 10.43MM Privately Held
SIC: 5065 3674 Electronic parts; Integrated circuits; semiconductor networks, etc.

### (P-16706)
### INTERNTIONAL TECH SYSTEMS CORP
Also Called: Itsco
10721 Walker St, Cypress (90630-4720)
PHONE..............................714 761-8886
Stanley Ning, Pr
▲ EMP: 48 EST: 1985
SQ FT: 40,000
SALES (est): 23.41MM Privately Held
Web: www.itsco.net
SIC: 5065 3578 Electronic parts and equipment, nec; Point-of-sale devices

### (P-16707)
### JAE ELECTRONICS INC (HQ)
142 Technology Dr Ste 100, Irvine (92618-2430)
PHONE..............................949 753-2600
Noriyuki Konishi, Pr
Shinjiro Ando, *
◆ EMP: 36 EST: 1977
SQ FT: 20,000
SALES (est): 154.52MM Privately Held
Web: www.jaeusa.com
SIC: 5065 3679 3829 3678 Connectors, electronic; Electronic circuits; Measuring and controlling devices, nec; Electronic connectors
PA: Japan Aviation Electronics Industry, Limited
1-21-1, Dogenzaka

### (P-16708)
### JAI INC
6800 Santa Teresa Blvd, San Jose (95119-1205)
PHONE..............................408 383-0300
Jorgen Andersen, Pr
Tomas Baek, *
Jimi Meshulam, *
▲ EMP: 29 EST: 1982
SQ FT: 35,000
SALES (est): 21.83MM
SALES (corp-wide): 45.06MM Privately Held
Web: www.jai.com
SIC: 5065 3663 Security control equipment and systems; Television broadcasting and communications equipment
HQ: Jai A/S
Valby Torvegade 17, Sal 1
Valby 2500
44578888

### (P-16709)
### JAMCOR CORPORATION (PA)
Also Called: S J S Products
6261 Angelo Ct, Loomis (95650-9565)
P.O. Box 90 (95650-0090)
PHONE..............................916 652-7713
William Mc Gillivray, Ch Bd
▲ EMP: 30 EST: 1931
SQ FT: 15,696
SALES (est): 5.17MM
SALES (corp-wide): 5.17MM Privately Held
Web: www.jamcorcorp.com

SIC: 5065 3469 3599 8711 Electronic parts; Electronic enclosures, stamped or pressed metal; Crankshafts and camshafts, machining; Engineering services

### (P-16710)
### JEI
Also Called: Jei
3087 Alhambra Dr, Cameron Park (95682-8849)
PHONE..............................530 677-3210
Jack Mahoney, CEO
Jack Mahoney, Pr
Steve Vodoklys, CFO
▲ EMP: 18 EST: 1959
SQ FT: 4,400
SALES (est): 2.39MM Privately Held
Web: www.jei-inc.com
SIC: 5065 3651 Electronic parts and equipment, nec; Recording machines, except dictation and telephone answering

### (P-16711)
### JRI INC
Also Called: J R Industries
31280 La Baya Dr, Westlake Village (91362-4005)
PHONE..............................818 706-2424
Craig Pfefferman, CEO
▲ EMP: 50 EST: 1987
SQ FT: 20,000
SALES (est): 9.03MM Privately Held
Web: www.jri.com
SIC: 5065 3679 Electronic parts; Harness assemblies, for electronic use: wire or cable

### (P-16712)
### KLEIN ELECTRONICS INC
Also Called: Klein Electronics
349 N Vinewood St, Escondido (92029-1338)
PHONE..............................760 781-3220
Richard Klein, Pr
▲ EMP: 26 EST: 1992
SQ FT: 13,700
SALES (est): 4.68MM Privately Held
Web: www.kleinelectronics.com
SIC: 5065 3663 Electronic parts and equipment, nec; Radio broadcasting and communications equipment

### (P-16713)
### KYCON INC
305 Digital Dr, Morgan Hill (95037-2878)
PHONE..............................408 494-0330
Kaya Erk, Pr
Carl Furumasu, *
▲ EMP: 50 EST: 1988
SQ FT: 25,000
SALES (est): 8.76MM Privately Held
Web: www.kycon.com
SIC: 5065 3678 Connectors, electronic; Electronic connectors

### (P-16714)
### LEMO USA INC
635 Park Ct, Rohnert Park (94928-7940)
P.O. Box 2408 (94927-2408)
PHONE..............................707 206-3700
Dinshaw Pohwala, CEO
EMP: 100 EST: 1972
SQ FT: 55,000
SALES (est): 28.65MM Privately Held
Web: www.lemo.com
SIC: 5065 3678 Connectors, electronic; Electronic connectors
HQ: Interlemo U.S.A. Inc.
635 Park Ct
Rohnert Park CA 94928

## 5065 - Electronic Parts And Equipment, Nec (P-16715)

**(P-16715)**
**LIGHTPOINTE COMMUNICATIONS INC**
Also Called: Lightpointe Wireless
8515 Arjons Dr Ste G, San Diego (92126-4358)
PHONE...................858 834-4083
Heinz A Willerbrand, *Ch Bd*
Lorian Sanders, *
▲ **EMP:** 25 **EST:** 2000
**SALES (est):** 2.97MM **Privately Held**
Web: www.lightpointe.com
**SIC: 5065** 3661 Communication equipment; Fiber optics communications equipment

**(P-16716)**
**LINKSYS USA INC**
121 Theory, Irvine (92617-3209)
PHONE...................949 270-8500
Jonathan Bettino, *CEO*
**EMP:** 100 **EST:** 2018
**SALES (est):** 24.82MM
**SALES (corp-wide):** 5.3B **Publicly Held**
Web: www.linksys.com
**SIC: 5065** 3577 Communication equipment; Data conversion equipment, media-to-media: computer
PA: Fortinet, Inc.
909 Kifer Rd
408 235-7700

**(P-16717)**
**MACRONIX AMERICA INC (HQ)**
Also Called: Mxic
680 N Mccarthy Blvd Ste 200, Milpitas (95035-5120)
PHONE...................408 262-8887
Arthur Yang, *CEO*
**EMP:** 53 **EST:** 1994
**SQ FT:** 20,000
**SALES (est):** 26.32MM **Privately Held**
Web: www.macronix.com
**SIC: 5065** 3674 Semiconductor devices; Semiconductors and related devices
PA: Macronix International Co., Ltd.
No.16, Li-Hsin Road, Hsinchu Science Park,

**(P-16718)**
**METRIC EQUIPMENT SALES INC**
Also Called: Microlease
25841 Industrial Blvd Ste 200, Hayward (94545-2991)
PHONE...................510 264-0887
TOLL FREE: 800
Nigel Brown, *CEO*
Mike Clark, *
David Sherve, *
Gordon Curwen, *
Nathan Hurst, *
**EMP:** 70 **EST:** 1992
**SQ FT:** 25,000
**SALES (est):** 22.86MM
**SALES (corp-wide):** 254.4MM **Privately Held**
Web: www.electrorent.com
**SIC: 5065** 5084 7359 3825 Electronic parts; Measuring and testing equipment, electrical; Electronic equipment rental, except computers; Instruments to measure electricity
HQ: Microlease Inc.
6060 Sepulveda Blvd
Van Nuys CA 91411
866 520-0200

**(P-16719)**
**MICRO-MECHANICS INC**
465 Woodview Ave, Morgan Hill (95037-2800)
PHONE...................408 779-2927
Christopher R Borch, *Pr*
**EMP:** 50 **EST:** 1997
**SQ FT:** 42,000
**SALES (est):** 24.27MM **Privately Held**
Web: www.micro-mechanics.com
**SIC: 5065** 3674 Semiconductor devices; Semiconductors and related devices
PA: Micro-Mechanics (Holdings) Ltd.
31 Kaki Bukit Place

**(P-16720)**
**MINIMATICS INC (PA)**
15500 Concord Cir, Morgan Hill (95037-7109)
PHONE...................650 969-5630
Walter Chew, *Pr*
Marjorie Chew, *
Charles R Fowler, *Stockholder*
**EMP:** 39 **EST:** 1973
**SALES (est):** 10.84MM
**SALES (corp-wide):** 10.84MM **Privately Held**
Web: www.minimatics.com
**SIC: 5065** 3599 Semiconductor devices; Machine shop, jobbing and repair

**(P-16721)**
**MITSUBISHI ELECTRIC US INC (DH)**
Also Called: Meus
5900 Katella Ave Ste A, Cypress (90630-5019)
P.O. Box 6007 (90630)
PHONE...................714 220-2500
Mike Corbo, *Pr*
Masahiro Oya, *
Mike Corbo, *Pr*
Jared Baker, *
Perry Pappous, *
◆ **EMP:** 200 **EST:** 2000
**SQ FT:** 10,400
**SALES (est):** 931.5MM **Privately Held**
Web: us.mitsubishielectric.com
**SIC: 5065** 3534 1796 3669 Electronic parts; Escalators, passenger and freight; Elevator installation and conversion; Visual communication systems
HQ: Mitsubishi Electric Us Holdings, Inc.
5900-A Katella Ave
Cypress CA 90630
714 220-2500

**(P-16722)**
**MOTOROLA MOBILITY LLC**
Also Called: Motorola
6450 Sequence Dr, San Diego (92121-4376)
PHONE...................858 455-1500
Rick Neal, *Brnch Mgr*
**EMP:** 73
**SQ FT:** 30,000
Web: www.motorola.com
**SIC: 5065** 3663 Communication equipment; Radio and t.v. communications equipment
HQ: Motorola Mobility Llc
222 W Mdse Mart Plz Ste 1
Chicago IL 60654

**(P-16723)**
**MOTORS & CONTROLS WHSE INC**
Also Called: Sabina Motors & Controls
1440 N Burton Pl, Anaheim (92806-1204)
PHONE...................714 956-0480
Vincent Tjelmeland, *Pr*
◆ **EMP:** 29 **EST:** 1969
**SQ FT:** 35,000
**SALES (est):** 6.93MM **Privately Held**
Web: www.sabinadrives.com
**SIC: 5065** 3621 Electronic parts; Motors, electric

**(P-16724)**
**MTROIZ INTERNATIONAL**
150 S Kenmore Ave, Los Angeles (90004-5603)
PHONE...................661 998-8013
Eun H Chae, *CEO*
Hong Chae, *
Stephen Banks, *
**EMP:** 32 **EST:** 2011
**SALES (est):** 1.24MM **Privately Held**
Web: www.mtroiz.com
**SIC: 5065** 2844 5023 5047 Communication equipment; Perfumes, cosmetics and other toilet preparations; Homefurnishings; Medical and hospital equipment

**(P-16725)**
**NETSOURCE TECHNOLOGY INC**
951 Calle Negocio Ste B, San Clemente (92673-6202)
PHONE...................949 713-0800
Gary B Munoz, *Pr*
Gary B Munoz, *Pr*
Lisa Quijada, *Mgr*
▲ **EMP:** 15 **EST:** 1997
**SQ FT:** 6,300
**SALES (est):** 4.77MM **Privately Held**
Web: www.nstechnology.com
**SIC: 5065** 3674 Electronic parts; Integrated circuits, semiconductor networks, etc.

**(P-16726)**
**NORTH AMERICAN VIDEO CORP (PA)**
Also Called: Navco Security Systems
1335 S Acacia Ave, Fullerton (92831-5315)
PHONE...................714 779-7499
Jason Oakley, *CEO*
William Augustus Groves, *
Margaret Groves, *
William Groves, *
Sharon Bryant, *
◆ **EMP:** 45 **EST:** 1975
**SALES (est):** 81.67MM
**SALES (corp-wide):** 81.67MM **Privately Held**
Web: www.navco.com
**SIC: 5065** 3812 Video equipment, electronic; Acceleration indicators and systems components, aerospace

**(P-16727)**
**ORANGE COUNTY COMPONENTS INC**
Also Called: O.C.components
3184 Airway Ave Ste C, Costa Mesa (92626-4619)
PHONE...................714 979-3597
Richard Hintermeyer, *CEO*
Pamela Hintermeyer, *Pr*
John J Hintermeyer, *Treas*
Marlene Gorke, *Sec*
▲ **EMP:** 15 **EST:** 1974
**SQ FT:** 6,000
**SALES (est):** 1.28MM **Privately Held**
**SIC: 5065** 3672 3679 Electronic parts and equipment, nec; Printed circuit boards; Harness assemblies, for electronic use: wire or cable

**(P-16728)**
**P C A ELECTRONICS INC**
16799 Schoenborn St, North Hills (91343-6194)
PHONE...................818 892-0761
Morris Weinberg, *Pr*
Benjamin Weinberg, *
**EMP:** 44 **EST:** 1949
**SQ FT:** 30,000
**SALES (est):** 5.82MM **Privately Held**
Web: www.pca.com
**SIC: 5065** 3674 Electronic parts; Semiconductors and related devices

**(P-16729)**
**PERILLO INDUSTRIES INC**
Also Called: Century Electronics
2150 Anchor Ct Ste A, Newbury Park (91320-1609)
PHONE...................805 498-9838
Mary Perillo, *Pr*
**EMP:** 50 **EST:** 1973
**SQ FT:** 20,000
**SALES (est):** 9.73MM **Privately Held**
Web: www.centuryelectronics.us
**SIC: 5065** 3679 Electronic parts and equipment, nec; Electronic loads and power supplies

**(P-16730)**
**QUANTIC M-WAVE**
82 W Cochran St Ste B, Simi Valley (93065-1618)
PHONE...................805 499-8825
Ken Boswell, *CEO*
Bonnie Murray, *Dir*
**EMP:** 18 **EST:** 1989
**SQ FT:** 6,600
**SALES (est):** 2.62MM **Privately Held**
Web: www.mwavedesign.com
**SIC: 5065** 3679 Electronic parts and equipment, nec; Microwave components

**(P-16731)**
**QUINSTAR TECHNOLOGY INC**
24085 Garnier St, Torrance (90505-5319)
PHONE...................310 320-1111
Leo Fong, *Pr*
John Kuno, *
▲ **EMP:** 72 **EST:** 1993
**SALES (est):** 23.14MM **Privately Held**
Web: www.quinstar.com
**SIC: 5065** 3671 Electronic parts and equipment, nec; Cathode ray tubes, including rebuilt

**(P-16732)**
**ROSE ELECTRONICS DISTRG CO LLC**
Also Called: Rose Batteries
2030 Ringwood Ave, San Jose (95131-1728)
PHONE...................408 943-0200
Itamar Frankenthal, *CEO*
▲ **EMP:** 34 **EST:** 1963
**SALES (est):** 10.19MM **Privately Held**
Web: www.rose-elec.com
**SIC: 5065** 3691 Electronic parts; Storage batteries
PA: Tropical Battery Company Limited
30 Automotive Parkway, Ferry Comercial Park

**(P-16733)**
**SAMSUNG INTERNATIONAL INC (DH)**
333 H St Ste 6000, Chula Vista (91910-5565)
PHONE...................619 671-6001
Byaong Gueon Jeon, *CEO*
Wonchul Song, *
Hak Seob Shim, *
◆ **EMP:** 50 **EST:** 1983
**SALES (est):** 14.95MM **Privately Held**
Web: www.samsung.com

**SIC: 5065** 3663 Mobile telephone equipment; Mobile communication equipment
**HQ:** Samsung Electronics America, Inc.
85 Challenger Rd
Ridgefield Park NJ 07660
201 229-4000

### (P-16734)
### SHINKO ELECTRIC AMERICA INC (DH)
2077 Gateway Pl Ste 250, San Jose (95110-1149)
PHONE..................................408 232-0499
Greg Bettencourt, *Pr*
▲ **EMP:** 20 **EST:** 1977
**SALES (est):** 35.21MM **Privately Held**
**Web:** www.shinko.co.jp
**SIC: 5065** 3674 Electronic parts and equipment, nec; Semiconductors and related devices
**HQ:** Shinko Electric Industries Co.,Ltd.
80, Oshimadamachi
Nagano NAG 381-2

### (P-16735)
### TAMURA CORPORATION OF AMERICA (HQ)
277 Rancheros Dr Ste 190, San Marcos (92069-2982)
PHONE..................................800 472-6624
Norihiko Nanjo, *CEO*
Junko Walker, *Sec*
Tony Shinonuma, *CFO*
Takatoshi Nakakariya, *Chief Operating Officer Sales*
▲ **EMP:** 26 **EST:** 1976
**SQ FT:** 10,801
**SALES (est):** 33.09MM **Privately Held**
**Web:** www.tamuracorp.com
**SIC: 5065** 5063 3677 Electronic parts; Electrical apparatus and equipment; Electronic coils and transformers
**PA:** Tamura Corporation
1-19-43, Higashioizumi

### (P-16736)
### TAPE SPECIALTY INC
Also Called: T S I
26017 Huntington Ln Ste C, Valencia (91355-1116)
PHONE..................................661 702-9030
Steve Feldman, *Pr*
Stu Feldman, *
Peggy James, *
▲ **EMP:** 28 **EST:** 1976
**SALES (est):** 4.76MM **Privately Held**
**Web:** www.tsidm.com
**SIC: 5065** 3652 7389 Magnetic recording tape; Magnetic tape (audio): prerecorded; Music and broadcasting services

### (P-16737)
### TPS AVIATION INC (PA)
1515 Crocker Ave, Hayward (94544-7038)
PHONE..................................510 475-1010
George Sozaburo Kujiraoka, *CEO*
◆ **EMP:** 100 **EST:** 1963
**SQ FT:** 58,700
**SALES (est):** 25.9MM
**SALES (corp-wide):** 25.9MM **Privately Held**
**Web:** www.tpsaviation.com
**SIC: 5065** 3728 3429 5088 Electronic parts; Aircraft parts and equipment, nec; Hardware, nec; Aircraft and parts, nec

### (P-16738)
### TRINET COMMUNICATIONS INC (PA)
6567 Brisa St, Livermore (94550-2519)
PHONE..................................925 294-1720
Jon J Fernandez, *Pr*
Jason Skeoch, *VP*
▲ **EMP:** 15 **EST:** 1990
**SQ FT:** 30,000
**SALES (est):** 1.33MM **Privately Held**
**SIC: 5065** 3661 Communication equipment; Telephone and telegraph apparatus

### (P-16739)
### TV EARS INC
2701 Via Orange Way Ste 1, Spring Valley (91978-1702)
PHONE..................................619 797-1600
George Dennis, *CEO*
Nancy Nelson, *
Steffens Meeks, *CPO*
▲ **EMP:** 30 **EST:** 1998
**SALES (est):** 9.56MM **Privately Held**
**Web:** www.tvears.com
**SIC: 5065** 3651 Sound equipment, electronic; Television receiving sets

### (P-16740)
### UNION TECHNOLOGY CORP
718 Monterey Pass Rd, Monterey Park (91754-3607)
PHONE..................................323 266-6871
David I Chu, *CEO*
Robert Boughrum, *
Raj Amin, *
Gary Koniow, *
Benha Choonhauri, *
◆ **EMP:** 50 **EST:** 1991
**SQ FT:** 21,800
**SALES (est):** 10.41MM **Privately Held**
**Web:** www.quanticutc.com
**SIC: 5065** 3675 Electronic parts; Electronic capacitors

### (P-16741)
### WATERFI LLC
4379 30th St Ste 2, San Diego (92104-1323)
PHONE..................................619 438-0058
Royce Nicholas, *Managing Member*
**EMP:** 18 **EST:** 2011
**SALES (est):** 864.46K **Privately Held**
**Web:** www.waterfi.com
**SIC: 5065** 2899 Electronic parts and equipment, nec; Waterproofing compounds

### (P-16742)
### WINBOND ELECTRONICS CORP AMER
2727 N 1st St, San Jose (95134-2029)
PHONE..................................408 943-6666
Yuan Mou Shu, *Prin*
▲ **EMP:** 60 **EST:** 1990
**SQ FT:** 50,000
**SALES (est):** 24.13MM **Privately Held**
**SIC: 5065** 8731 3674 Electronic parts; Commercial physical research; Semiconductors and related devices
**PA:** Winbond Electronics Corporation
No. 8, Keya 1st Rd.,

### (P-16743)
### WINCHESTER INTERCONNECT EC LLC
Also Called: Elrob LLC
12691 Monarch St, Garden Grove (92841-3918)
PHONE..................................714 230-6122
Arik Vrobel, *Pr*
Roberto Ortega, *Finance CTRL*
▲ **EMP:** 54 **EST:** 1960
**SQ FT:** 38,500
**SALES (est):** 98.57MM **Privately Held**
**Web:** www.el-comsystems.com
**SIC: 5065** 3679 3613 3643 Electronic parts; Harness assemblies, for electronic use: wire or cable; Switchgear and switchboard apparatus; Current-carrying wiring services
**HQ:** Winchester Interconnect Corporation
185 Plains Rd
Milford CT 06461

---

## 5072 Hardware

### (P-16744)
### ALLIED INTERNATIONAL LLC
Also Called: Allied International
28955 Avenue Sherman, Valencia (91355-5446)
PHONE..................................818 364-2333
Timothy Florian, *CEO*
Melissa Berninger, *
▲ **EMP:** 50 **EST:** 1962
**SQ FT:** 106,000
**SALES (est):** 14.87MM **Privately Held**
**Web:** www.alliedtools.com
**SIC: 5072** 3499 Hand tools; Stabilizing bars (cargo), metal

### (P-16745)
### AMERICAN KAL ENTERPRISES INC (PA)
Also Called: Pro America Premium Tools
4265 Puente Ave, Baldwin Park (91706-3420)
PHONE..................................626 338-7308
John Toshima, *Pr*
Mila Bierotte, *
▲ **EMP:** 90 **EST:** 1966
**SQ FT:** 32,000
**SALES (est):** 11.29MM
**SALES (corp-wide):** 11.29MM **Privately Held**
**SIC: 5072** 3546 3463 3462 Hand tools; Power-driven handtools; Nonferrous forgings; Iron and steel forgings

### (P-16746)
### B & B SPECIALTIES INC
G S Aerospace Division
4321 E La Palma Ave, Anaheim (92807-1887)
PHONE..................................714 985-3075
Tom Rutan, *Mgr*
**EMP:** 100
**SALES (corp-wide):** 22.69MM **Privately Held**
**Web:** www.bbspecialties.com
**SIC: 5072** 3429 Miscellaneous fasteners; Hardware, nec
**PA:** B & B Specialties, Inc.
4321 E La Palma Ave
714 985-3000

### (P-16747)
### BAY BOLT INC
4610 Malat St, Oakland (94601-4904)
PHONE..................................510 532-1188
Richard R Anderson, *Pr*
**EMP:** 15 **EST:** 1981
**SQ FT:** 30,000
**SALES (est):** 2.94MM **Privately Held**
**Web:** www.baybolt.com
**SIC: 5072** 5051 3452 Bolts; Steel; Bolts, nuts, rivets, and washers

### (P-16748)
### CHUAOLSON ENTERPRISES INC
1274 N Grove St, Anaheim (92806-2113)
P.O. Box 1240 (92871-1240)
PHONE..................................714 630-4751
Terry Olson, *CEO*
John Chua, *VP*
▲ **EMP:** 22 **EST:** 1984
**SQ FT:** 11,785
**SALES (est):** 2.02MM **Privately Held**
**SIC: 5072** 3429 Builders' hardware, nec; Hardware, nec

### (P-16749)
### CLARENDON SPECIALTY FAS INC
2180 Temple Ave, Long Beach (90804-1020)
PHONE..................................714 842-2603
Arnaud Zemmour, *Admn*
Michael Lang, *
Jeff Heywood, *
▲ **EMP:** 90 **EST:** 1985
**SQ FT:** 4,000
**SALES (est):** 23.06MM **Privately Held**
**Web:** www.clarendonsf.com
**SIC: 5072** 3444 Miscellaneous fasteners; Sheet metalwork

### (P-16750)
### CORONA CLIPPER INC
Also Called: Corona Tools
22440 Temescal Canyon Rd Ste 102, Corona (92883)
PHONE..................................800 847-7863
Thomas A Welke, *CEO*
Al Schulten, *
John Reisveck, *
John J Gordan, *
Eric Prendeville, *
◆ **EMP:** 86 **EST:** 1927
**SQ FT:** 85,000
**SALES (est):** 45.24MM
**SALES (corp-wide):** 26.64MM **Privately Held**
**Web:** www.coronatools.com
**SIC: 5072** 3524 Hand tools; Lawn and garden equipment
**PA:** Natt Tools Group Inc
460 Sherman Ave N
905 549-7433

### (P-16751)
### DH CASTER INTERNATIONAL INC
2260 S Haven Ave Ste C, Ontario (91761-0740)
PHONE..................................909 930-6400
Mary Lyn Baker, *CEO*
Richard J Baker, *Pr*
▲ **EMP:** 18 **EST:** 1996
**SQ FT:** 10,000
**SALES (est):** 2.63MM **Privately Held**
**Web:** www.dhcasters.com
**SIC: 5072** 3999 Hardware; Atomizers, toiletry

### (P-16752)
### E B BRADLEY CO (PA)
5602 Bickett St, Vernon (90058-2826)
P.O. Box 58548 (90058-0548)
PHONE..................................323 585-9917
Don Lorey, *Pr*
Scott Simons, *
Ramn Miramontes, *
David Jackson, *
▲ **EMP:** 48 **EST:** 1946
**SQ FT:** 45,000
**SALES (est):** 154.3MM
**SALES (corp-wide):** 154.3MM **Privately Held**
**Web:** www.ebbradley.com
**SIC: 5072** 2452 Hardware; Panels and sections, prefabricated, wood

# 5072 - Hardware

**(P-16753)**
**E B BRADLEY CO**
10903 Vanowen St, North Hollywood (91605-6408)
PHONE.................800 533-3030
Earl Bertrand Bradley, *Brnch Mgr*
**EMP:** 19
**SALES (corp-wide):** 154.3MM **Privately Held**
Web: www.ebbradley.com
**SIC:** 5072 2452 Hardware; Panels and sections, prefabricated, wood
**PA:** E. B. Bradley Co.
5602 Bickett St
323 585-9917

**(P-16754)**
**FASTENING SYSTEMS INTL**
Also Called: F S I
1206 E Macarthur St Ste 1, Sonoma (95476-3800)
PHONE.................707 935-1170
Roger Nikkel, *Pr*
Mark Herrand, *VP*
Kathryn Nikkel, *CFO*
Diane Nikkel, *Sec*
▲ **EMP:** 20 **EST:** 1983
**SALES (est):** 7.52MM **Privately Held**
Web: www.fsirivet.com
**SIC:** 5072 3429 Miscellaneous fasteners; Aircraft hardware

**(P-16755)**
**J MILANO CO INC**
910 W Charter Way, Stockton (95206-1104)
P.O. Box 688 (95201-0688)
PHONE.................209 944-0902
Gary L Milano, *Pr*
Gary L Milano, *Pr*
Don Milano, *VP*
▲ **EMP:** 18 **EST:** 1949
**SQ FT:** 9,000
**SALES (est):** 5.21MM **Privately Held**
**SIC:** 5072 3599 Hardware; Machine shop, jobbing and repair

**(P-16756)**
**LONG-LOK FASTENERS CORPORATION**
20531 Belshaw Ave, Carson (90746-3505)
PHONE.................424 213-4570
Sarah Melendez, *Brnch Mgr*
**EMP:** 19
**SALES (corp-wide):** 11.15MM **Privately Held**
Web: www.longlok.com
**SIC:** 5072 3452 5085 Bolts; Bolts, nuts, rivets, and washers; Fasteners, industrial: nuts, bolts, screws, etc.
**HQ:** Long-Lok Fasteners Corporation
14755 Preston Rd Ste 520
Dallas TX 75254
888 656-9450

**(P-16757)**
**MACPHERSON WSTN TL SUP CO LLC**
1160 N Tustin Ave, Anaheim (92807-1735)
PHONE.................714 666-4100
Jerry Gerardot, *Brnch Mgr*
**EMP:** 16
**SALES (corp-wide):** 28.85MM **Privately Held**
Web: www.westtool.com
**SIC:** 5072 3423 Hand tools; Hand and edge tools, nec
**PA:** Macpherson Western Tool & Supply Co. Llc
203 Lawrence Dr Ste D
925 443-8665

**(P-16758)**
**MONROE MAGNUS LLC (HQ)**
Also Called: Monroeone
1110 E Elm Ave, Fullerton (92831-5024)
PHONE.................714 771-2630
TOLL FREE: 800
Garrett Morelock, *CEO*
▲ **EMP:** 16 **EST:** 1978
**SALES (est):** 25.3MM
**SALES (corp-wide):** 25.3MM **Privately Held**
Web: www.monroeengineering.com
**SIC:** 5072 3562 Casters and glides; Casters
**PA:** Monroe Engineering Holdings, Llc
2990 Technology Dr
877 320-6907

**(P-16759)**
**PBB INC**
1311 E Philadelphia St, Ontario (91761-5719)
PHONE.................909 923-6250
Jeff Wood, *Pr*
R C Kung, *VP*
▲ **EMP:** 20 **EST:** 1987
**SQ FT:** 30,000
**SALES (est):** 4.34MM **Privately Held**
Web: www.pbbinc.com
**SIC:** 5072 3429 Builders' hardware, nec; Builders' hardware

**(P-16760)**
**PENN ELCOM INC (HQ)**
Also Called: Penn Elcom Hardware
7465 Lampson Ave, Garden Grove (92841-2903)
PHONE.................714 230-6200
Philip John Stratford, *CEO*
Roger Willems, *
◆ **EMP:** 35 **EST:** 1993
**SQ FT:** 28,000
**SALES (est):** 27MM **Privately Held**
Web: www.penn-elcom.com
**SIC:** 5072 3429 Hardware; Hardware, nec
**PA:** Penn Elcom Corporation
C/O Maples Corporate Services (Bvi) Limited

**(P-16761)**
**PENN ENGINEERING COMPONENTS**
29045 Avenue Penn, Valencia (91355-5426)
PHONE.................818 503-1511
Robert Washburn, *Pr*
Jane Washburn, *Sec*
Bill Down, *VP*
**EMP:** 20 **EST:** 1971
**SQ FT:** 10,500
**SALES (est):** 4.77MM **Privately Held**
Web: www.pennengineering.com
**SIC:** 5072 3679 Hardware; Microwave components

**(P-16762)**
**SHAMROCK SUPPLY COMPANY INC (PA)**
Also Called: Shamrock Companies, The
3366 E La Palma Ave, Anaheim (92806-2814)
PHONE.................714 575-1800
John J O'connor, *Co-Secretary*
Michael O'connor, *Pr*
▲ **EMP:** 52 **EST:** 1975
**SQ FT:** 45,000
**SALES (est):** 51.94MM
**SALES (corp-wide):** 51.94MM **Privately Held**
Web: www.shamrocksupply.com

**SIC:** 5072 5084 3842 Hand tools; Industrial machinery and equipment; Personal safety equipment

**(P-16763)**
**SUNCOAST POST-TENSION LTD**
Also Called: Suncoast Post
1528 E Cedar St, Ontario (91761-5761)
PHONE.................909 673-0490
Ken Douglas, *Mgr*
**EMP:** 19
Web: www.suncoast-pt.com
**SIC:** 5072 3316 3315 5211 Builders' hardware, nec; Cold finishing of steel shapes; Cable, steel: insulated or armored; Masonry materials and supplies
**HQ:** Suncoast Post-Tension, Ltd.
16825 Northchase Dr # 1100
Houston TX 77060
281 445-8886

**(P-16764)**
**UNBRAKO LLC**
11939 Woodruff Ave, Downey (90241-5601)
PHONE.................310 817-2400
Gary Bains, *CEO*
▲ **EMP:** 15 **EST:** 2012
**SQ FT:** 25,000
**SALES (est):** 2.6MM **Privately Held**
Web: www.unbrakousa.com
**SIC:** 5072 3399 3429 Bolts, nuts, and screws; Metal fasteners; Metal fasteners

## 5074 Plumbing And Hydronic Heating Supplies

**(P-16765)**
**CENTER STATE PIPE AND SUP CO**
2750 Cherokee Rd, Stockton (95205-2476)
P.O. Box 939 (95201-0939)
PHONE.................209 466-0871
Jeff Timbo, *Mgr*
**EMP:** 16
**SALES (corp-wide):** 4.5MM **Privately Held**
Web: www.buttespipe.com
**SIC:** 5074 5085 5963 5064 Plumbing and heating valves; Industrial fittings; Bottled water delivery; Water heaters, electric
**PA:** Center State Pipe And Supply Co.
1348 Mcwilliams Way
209 521-1151

**(P-16766)**
**EPS CORPORATE HOLDINGS INC**
12468 Lambert Rd, Whittier (90606-2710)
PHONE.................562 698-7774
Len Erickson, *Brnch Mgr*
**EMP:** 17
**SIC:** 5074 3498 Plumbing fittings and supplies; Pipe fittings, fabricated from purchased pipe
**HQ:** Eps Corporate Holdings, Inc.
3100 Dnald Dglas Loop Hng
Santa Monica CA 90405

**(P-16767)**
**GREEN CONVERGENCE (PA)**
Also Called: Sunpower By Green Convergence
28476 Westinghouse Pl, Valencia (91355-0929)
PHONE.................661 294-9495
Mark Clinton Figearo, *CEO*
Donald Schramm, *
Stacy Hitt, *

**EMP:** 52 **EST:** 2008
**SQ FT:** 6,000
**SALES (est):** 24.79MM
**SALES (corp-wide):** 24.79MM **Privately Held**
Web: www.greenconvergence.com
**SIC:** 5074 1711 2493 2621 Heating equipment and panels, solar; Solar energy contractor; Roofing board, unsaturated; Roofing felt stock

**(P-16768)**
**IRONRIDGE INC (DH)**
Also Called: Ironridge
28357 Industrial Blvd, Hayward (94545-4428)
PHONE.................800 227-9523
Sean Mcdonald, *CEO*
William Kim, *
Corey Geiger, *
Jim Clark, *
▲ **EMP:** 50 **EST:** 1998
**SQ FT:** 10,000
**SALES (est):** 56.58MM **Privately Held**
Web: www.ironridge.com
**SIC:** 5074 3433 Heating equipment and panels, solar; Solar heaters and collectors
**HQ:** Esdec, Inc.
976 Brady Ave Nw Ste 100
Atlanta GA 30318
404 512-0716

**(P-16769)**
**KEYLINE SALES INC**
9768 Firestone Blvd, Downey (90241-5510)
PHONE.................562 904-3910
Richard Banner, *Pr*
John Shaw, *
Mike Powers, *
**EMP:** 42 **EST:** 1974
**SQ FT:** 3,500
**SALES (est):** 9.77MM **Privately Held**
Web: www.keylinesales.com
**SIC:** 5074 3822 Plumbing fittings and supplies; Environmental controls

**(P-16770)**
**NANOSOLAR INC**
2434 Rock St Apt 14, Mountain View (94043-2671)
▲ **EMP:** 254
Web: www.nanosolar.com
**SIC:** 5074 3674 Plumbing and hydronic heating supplies; Solar cells

**(P-16771)**
**TA INDUSTRIES INC (HQ)**
Also Called: Truaire
11130 Bloomfield Ave, Santa Fe Springs (90670-4603)
P.O. Box 4448 (90670-1460)
PHONE.................562 466-1000
Yongki Yi, *Prin*
Elizabeth Yi, *VP*
▲ **EMP:** 17 **EST:** 1996
**SQ FT:** 86,000
**SALES (est):** 20.63MM
**SALES (corp-wide):** 792.84MM **Publicly Held**
Web: www.rectorseal.com
**SIC:** 5074 5075 3567 Heating equipment (hydronic); Air conditioning and ventilation equipment and supplies; Heating units and devices, industrial: electric
**PA:** Csw Industrials, Inc.
5420 Lyndon B Jhnson Fwy
214 884-3777

▲ = Import ▼ = Export
◆ = Import/Export

## PRODUCTS & SERVICES SECTION
## 5082 - Construction And Mining Machinery (P-16789)

**(P-16772)**
**WATERSTONE FAUCETS LLC**
Also Called: Waterstone Faucets
41180 Raintree Ct, Murrieta (92562-7020)
P.O. Box 1240 (92593-1240)
PHONE..................................951 304-0520
Christopher G Kuran, *Managing Member*
Steve Kliewer, *
Bob Santella, *
▲ **EMP:** 131 **EST:** 1999
**SQ FT:** 42,000
**SALES (est):** 23.78MM **Privately Held**
Web: www.waterstoneco.com
**SIC: 5074** 3432  Plumbing fittings and supplies; Faucets and spigots, metal and plastic

## 5075 Warm Air Heating And Air Conditioning

**(P-16773)**
**AC PRO INC (PA)**
Also Called: MSI Hvac
11700 Industry Ave, Fontana (92337-6934)
PHONE..................................951 360-7849
Dion Quinn, *CEO*
**EMP:** 250 **EST:** 1986
**SQ FT:** 80,000
**SALES (est):** 107.01MM
**SALES (corp-wide):** 107.01MM **Privately Held**
Web: www.acpro.com
**SIC: 5075** 3444  Air conditioning and ventilation equipment and supplies; Sheet metalwork

**(P-16774)**
**BIODEFENSOR CORPORATION**
13448 Manhasset Rd Ste 3, Apple Valley (92308-5799)
PHONE..................................888 899-2956
Jose Villalobos, *Pr*
**EMP:** 25 **EST:** 2018
**SALES (est):** 1.43MM **Privately Held**
Web: www.biodefensor.com
**SIC: 5075** 3564 3569 5013  Air filters; Filters: air: furnaces, air conditioning equipment, etc.; Filters; Filters, air and oil

**(P-16775)**
**CALIFORNIA HYDRONICS CORP (PA)**
Also Called: Columbia Hydronics Co.
2293 Tripaldi Way, Hayward (94545-5024)
P.O. Box 5049 (94540-5049)
PHONE..................................510 293-1993
Robert Polizzi, *CEO*
James A Attard, *
John Arthur, *
Kevin Mccloud, *Treas*
**EMP:** 50 **EST:** 1957
**SQ FT:** 50,000
**SALES (est):** 58.83MM
**SALES (corp-wide):** 58.83MM **Privately Held**
Web: www.chchydro.com
**SIC: 5075** 3585  Warm air heating equipment and supplies; Refrigeration and heating equipment

**(P-16776)**
**CFM EQUIPMENT DISTRIBUTORS INC (PA)**
1644 Main Ave Ste 1, Sacramento (95838-2409)
PHONE..................................916 447-7022
Andrew Barton, *CEO*
Chester Flint, *

Joe Souza, *
▲ **EMP:** 31 **EST:** 1984
**SQ FT:** 10,000
**SALES (est):** 25.35MM
**SALES (corp-wide):** 25.35MM **Privately Held**
Web: www.cfmequipment.com
**SIC: 5075** 3678 3999  Air conditioning equipment, except room units, nec; Electronic connectors; Atomizers, toiletry

**(P-16777)**
**DUST COLLECTOR SERVICES INC**
1280 N Sunshine Way, Anaheim (92806-1746)
PHONE..................................714 237-1690
**TOLL FREE:** 800
Timothy Schlentz, *Pr*
Jannie Schlentz, *VP*
Jeff Schlentz, *VP*
Gregory Schlentz, *VP*
**EMP:** 20 **EST:** 1994
**SQ FT:** 10,000
**SALES (est):** 10.06MM **Privately Held**
Web: www.dustcollectorservices.com
**SIC: 5075** 3564  Warm air heating and air conditioning; Purification and dust collection equipment

**(P-16778)**
**ESPECIAL T HVAC SHTMTL FTTNGS**
1239 E Franklin Ave, Pomona (91766-5450)
PHONE..................................909 869-9150
Gerardo Tavarez, *Pr*
Maria Tavarez, *
▲ **EMP:** 30 **EST:** 2001
**SQ FT:** 12,000
**SALES (est):** 10.99MM **Privately Held**
Web: www.especialt.com
**SIC: 5075** 3444  Air conditioning and ventilation equipment and supplies; Sheet metalwork

**(P-16779)**
**FLORENCE FILTER CORPORATION**
530 W Manville St, Compton (90220-5510)
PHONE..................................310 637-1137
Adrian M Anhood, *CEO*
Floriana A Anhood, *
Erika A Anhood, *
▲ **EMP:** 60 **EST:** 1971
**SQ FT:** 55,000
**SALES (est):** 11.25MM **Privately Held**
Web: www.florencefilter.com
**SIC: 5075** 3564 5211  Air filters; Filters: air: furnaces, air conditioning equipment, etc.; Lumber and other building materials

**(P-16780)**
**GEORGE T HALL CO INC (PA)**
Also Called: California Control Solutions
1605 E Gene Autry Way, Anaheim (92805-6730)
P.O. Box 25269 (92825-5269)
PHONE..................................909 825-9751
Charles Niemann, *Pr*
James Martin, *
Marlyn Niemann, *
▲ **EMP:** 30 **EST:** 1932
**SQ FT:** 15,000
**SALES (est):** 25.5MM
**SALES (corp-wide):** 25.5MM **Privately Held**
Web: www.georgethall.com

**SIC: 5075** 5085 3613  Warm air heating and air conditioning; Industrial supplies; Control panels, electric

**(P-16781)**
**HKF INC (PA)**
Also Called: Therm Pacific
5983 Smithway St, Commerce (90040-1607)
PHONE..................................323 225-1318
James P Hartfield, *Pr*
▲ **EMP:** 57 **EST:** 1990
**SALES (est):** 15.74MM
**SALES (corp-wide):** 15.74MM **Privately Held**
**SIC: 5075** 3873 5064 3567  Warm air heating and air conditioning; Watches, clocks, watchcases, and parts; Electrical appliances, television and radio; Industrial furnaces and ovens

**(P-16782)**
**INJEN TECHNOLOGY COMPANY LTD**
244 Pioneer Pl, Pomona (91768-3275)
PHONE..................................909 839-0706
Ron Delgado, *CEO*
▲ **EMP:** 30 **EST:** 1998
**SALES (est):** 17.42MM **Privately Held**
Web: www.injen.com
**SIC: 5075** 3714  Air filters; Filters: oil, fuel, and air, motor vehicle

**(P-16783)**
**PURE PROCESS FILTRATION INC**
Also Called: Ppf
11582 Markon Dr, Garden Grove (92841-1809)
PHONE..................................714 891-6527
Melinda Limas, *Pr*
Melinda James, *Pr*
Heather Stewart, *VP*
**EMP:** 17 **EST:** 2006
**SALES (est):** 5.91MM **Privately Held**
Web: www.pureprocessfiltration.com
**SIC: 5075** 3569 3599  Air filters; Filters; Air intake filters, internal combustion engine, except auto

## 5078 Refrigeration Equipment And Supplies

**(P-16784)**
**BRIO WATER TECHNOLOGY INC**
Also Called: Dtwusa
768 Turnbull Canyon Rd, Hacienda Heights (91745-1401)
PHONE..................................800 781-1680
Frank Melkonian, *CEO*
Gerard A Thompson, *Sec*
Arman Melkonian, *Dir*
▲ **EMP:** 30 **EST:** 2013
**SALES (est):** 15.45MM **Privately Held**
Web: www.dtwusa.com
**SIC: 5078** 3589  Drinking water coolers, mechanical; Water filters and softeners, household type

**(P-16785)**
**MARKET FIXTURES UNLIMITED INC (PA)**
13235 Woodruff Ave, Downey (90242-5096)
PHONE..................................562 803-5553
Randall Fitzpatrick, *Pr*
Gail Fitzpatrick, *VP*
Eunice Fitzpatrick, *Sec*

**EMP:** 15 **EST:** 1959
**SQ FT:** 14,000
**SALES (est):** 4.43MM
**SALES (corp-wide):** 4.43MM **Privately Held**
Web: www.marketfixturesunlimited.net
**SIC: 5078** 3231 5046  Refrigeration equipment and supplies; Doors, glass: made from purchased glass; Restaurant equipment and supplies, nec

**(P-16786)**
**PEPSI-COLA METRO BTLG CO INC**
Also Called: Pepsi-Cola
6659 Sycamore Canyon Blvd, Riverside (92507-0733)
PHONE..................................951 697-3200
Jerry Sime, *Mgr*
**EMP:** 26
**SALES (corp-wide):** 86.39B **Publicly Held**
Web: www.pepsico.com
**SIC: 5078** 2086 5149  Refrigerated beverage dispensers; Bottled and canned soft drinks; Soft drinks
**HQ:** Pepsi-Cola Metropolitan Bottling Company, Inc.
700 Anderson Hill Rd
Purchase NY 10577
914 767-6000

**(P-16787)**
**REFRIGERATION HDWR SUP CORP**
9255 Deering Ave, Chatsworth (91311-5804)
PHONE..................................800 537-8300
**TOLL FREE:** 800
Pamela Sylvester, *Brnch Mgr*
**EMP:** 52
**SALES (corp-wide):** 22.94MM **Privately Held**
Web: www.rhsparts.com
**SIC: 5078** 5722 3585 7699  Refrigeration equipment and supplies; Household appliance stores; Refrigeration and heating equipment; Restaurant equipment repair
**PA:** Refrigeration Hardware Supply Corporation
632 Foresight Cir
970 241-2800

## 5082 Construction And Mining Machinery

**(P-16788)**
**CAMERON WEST COAST INC**
Also Called: Cameron Surface Systems
4315 Yeager Way, Bakersfield (93313-2018)
▲ **EMP:** 90 **EST:** 1992
**SQ FT:** 48,000
**SALES (est):** 9.33MM **Publicly Held**
**SIC: 5082** 1389 7353  Oil field equipment; Oil field services, nec; Oil field equipment, rental or leasing
**HQ:** Cameron International Corporation
1333 West Loop S Ste 1700
Houston TX 77027

**(P-16789)**
**HERCA TELECOMM SERVICES INC**
Also Called: Herca Construction Services
18610 Beck St, Perris (92570-9185)
PHONE..................................951 940-5941
Hector R Castellon, *Pr*
Tracy Hertel, *
Raul Castellon, *

## 5082 - Construction And Mining Machinery (P-16790)

**PRODUCTS & SERVICES SECTION**

Alfredo Castellon, *
Alfonso Catellon, *
**EMP: 56 EST:** 2005
**SQ FT:** 67,900
**SALES (est):** 20.06MM Privately Held
Web: www.hercatelecomm.com
SIC: **5082** 1623 1731 3663  General construction machinery and equipment; Communication line and transmission tower construction; General electrical contractor; Antennas, transmitting and communications

### (P-16790)
**HULSEY CONTRACTING INC**
1370 Dodson Way, Riverside  (92507-2003)
PHONE.................................951 549-3665
Roberto Hulsey, *Prin*
Roberto Hulsey, *CEO*
**EMP:** 20 **EST:** 2012
**SALES (est):** 4.41MM Privately Held
Web: www.hulseycontracting.com
SIC: **5082** 2493 2851  General construction machinery and equipment; Insulation and roofing material, reconstituted wood; Polyurethane coatings

### (P-16791)
**JPL GLOBAL  LLC**
Also Called: Iq Power Tools
4635 Wade Ave, Perris (92571-7494)
P.O. Box 7449 (92552-7449)
PHONE.................................888 274-7744
Paul Guth, *Managing Member*
Scott Craft, *Genl Mgr*
▲ **EMP:** 23 **EST:** 2009
**SALES (est):** 5.16MM Privately Held
Web: www.iqpowertools.com
SIC: **5082** 1741 3541  Masonry equipment and supplies; Masonry and other stonework ; Machine tools, metal cutting type

### (P-16792)
**MALOOF NAMAN BUILDERS**
Also Called: Heavy Civil - Gen Engrg Cnstr
9614 Cozycroft Ave, Chatsworth (91311-5116)
PHONE.................................818 775-0040
Omar G Maloof, *Pr*
**EMP:** 52 **EST:** 2009
**SALES (est):** 2.2MM Privately Held
SIC: **5082** 3531 1629 8711  Road construction equipment; Road construction and maintenance machinery; Dams, waterways, docks, and other marine construction; Building construction consultant

### (P-16793)
**OAKCROFT ASSOCIATES  INC (PA)**
Also Called: American Assod Roofg Distrs
750 Monterey Pass Rd, Monterey Park (91754-3607)
P.O. Box 63309 (90063-0309)
PHONE.................................323 261-5122
James D Yundt, *Pr*
James S Yundt, *VP*
Joellen Yundt, *Sec*
John Carmack, *Dir*
Jonathan Yundt, *VP*
▲ **EMP:** 31 **EST:** 1950
**SQ FT:** 14,500
**SALES (est):** 13.82MM
**SALES (corp-wide):** 13.82MM Privately Held
Web: www.roofmaster.com
SIC: **5082** 3531 5199  General construction machinery and equipment; Roofing equipment; Broom, mop, and paint handles

### (P-16794)
**THOMPCO INC**
899 Mission Rock Rd, Santa Paula (93060-9800)
PHONE.................................805 933-8048
Dori Thompson, *Pr*
**EMP:** 27 **EST:** 2008
**SALES (est):** 3.25MM Privately Held
SIC: **5082** 1389  Oil field equipment; Oil and gas field services, nec

## 5083 Farm And Garden Machinery

### (P-16795)
**AMERICAN GRAPE HARVESTERS INC**
Also Called: Agh
5778 W Barstow Ave, Fresno  (93722-5024)
PHONE.................................559 277-7380
Tom M Thompson, *CEO*
▲ **EMP:** 22 **EST:** 1990
**SQ FT:** 30,000
**SALES (est):** 4.02MM Privately Held
Web: www.aghinc.com
SIC: **5083** 0722 3523 7699  Farm equipment parts and supplies; Grapes, machine harvesting services; Harvesters, fruit, vegetable, tobacco, etc.; Agricultural equipment repair services

### (P-16796)
**EURODRIP USA  INC**
7545 Carroll Rd, San Diego  (92121-2401)
PHONE.................................559 674-2670
Rowland Wilkinson, *CEO*
◆ **EMP:** 80 **EST:** 1996
**SALES (est):** 22.12MM Privately Held
Web: www.eurodripusa.com
SIC: **5083** 3084  Irrigation equipment; Plastics pipe
HQ: Rivulis A.V.E.G.E.
    Athinon - Lamias National Rd (55th Km), P.O. Box 34
    Oinofyta 32011

### (P-16797)
**EXACT CORP**
5143 Blue Gum Ave, Modesto (95358-9516)
PHONE.................................209 544-8600
Jonathan J Flora, *CEO*
▼ **EMP:** 45 **EST:** 1977
**SALES (est):** 23.74MM Privately Held
Web: www.exactcorp.com
SIC: **5083** 3523  Agricultural machinery and equipment; Cabs, tractors, and agricultural machinery

### (P-16798)
**FORTIER & FORTIER  INC**
Also Called: Reedley Irrigation & Supply
1260 S Buttonwillow Ave, Reedley (93654-9359)
P.O. Box 592 (93654-0592)
PHONE.................................559 638-5774
Paul Fortier, *CEO*
Mary E Fortier, *
Shelly Fortier, *
**EMP:** 34 **EST:** 1961
**SQ FT:** 6,500
**SALES (est):** 11.44MM Privately Held
Web: www.reedleyirrigation.com
SIC: **5083** 5261 5999 3272  Irrigation equipment; Retail nurseries and garden stores; Farm equipment and supplies; Pipe, concrete or lined with concrete

### (P-16799)
**JENSEN & PILEGARD (PA)**
Also Called: Jensen
1739 E Terrace Ave, Fresno (93703-1737)
PHONE.................................559 268-9221
Don J Pilegard, *Pr*
Chris Pilegard, *
**EMP:** 25 **EST:** 1952
**SQ FT:** 15,500
**SALES (est):** 8.49MM
**SALES (corp-wide):** 8.49MM Privately Held
Web: www.jensenandpilegard.com
SIC: **5082** 2048 5261  Farm equipment parts and supplies; Livestock feeds; Lawn and garden supplies

### (P-16800)
**NETAFIM IRRIGATION  INC (HQ)**
Also Called: Netafim USA
5470 E Home Ave, Fresno (93727-2107)
PHONE.................................559 453-6800
Igal Aisenberg, *Pr*
Lauri Hanover, *
Michael Dowgert, *
◆ **EMP:** 260 **EST:** 1965
**SQ FT:** 100,000
**SALES (est):** 51.06MM Privately Held
Web: www.netafimusa.com
SIC: **5083** 3523  Irrigation equipment; Irrigation equipment, self-propelled
PA: Netafim Ltd
    10 Hashalom Rd.

### (P-16801)
**SPEARS MANUFACTURING CO (PA)**
15853 Olden St, Rancho Cascades (91342-1293)
P.O. Box 9203 (91392-9203)
PHONE.................................818 364-1611
Robert Wayne Spears, *CEO*
Wayne Spears, *
Michael Valasquez, *General Vice President*
Ken Ruggles, *
◆ **EMP:** 134 **EST:** 1970
**SQ FT:** 119,088
**SALES (est):** 1.37B
**SALES (corp-wide):** 1.37B Privately Held
Web: www.spearsmanufacturing.com
SIC: **5083** 3494  Irrigation equipment; Valves and pipe fittings, nec

### (P-16802)
**URBAN FARMER STORE  INC (DH)**
2833 Vicente St, San Francisco (94116-2721)
PHONE.................................415 661-2204
Thomas Bressan, *CEO*
Adrian Smith, *Pr*
▲ **EMP:** 20 **EST:** 1983
**SQ FT:** 6,000
**SALES (est):** 10.18MM
**SALES (corp-wide):** 152.67B Publicly Held
Web: www.urbanfarmerstore.com
SIC: **5083** 3645  Irrigation equipment; Garden, patio, walkway and yard lighting fixtures: electric
HQ: Heritage Landscape Supply Group, Inc.
    7440 State Highway 121
    Mckinney TX 75070
    214 491-4149

### (P-16803)
**WESTSIDE EQUIPMENT CO (DH)**
Also Called: California Tomato Machinery
2500 W Industrial Ave, Madera (93637-5000)
P.O. Box 158 (95313-0158)
PHONE.................................209 856-4700
Daniel L Rodrick, *CEO*
Daniel Perez, *Ch Bd*
John Perez, *Sec*
▲ **EMP:** 19 **EST:** 2019
**SQ FT:** 14,000
**SALES (est):** 10.84MM Privately Held
Web: www.oxbo.com
SIC: **5083** 3559  Agricultural machinery and equipment; Foundry machinery and equipment
HQ: Oxbo International Corporation
    7275 Batavia Byron Rd
    Byron NY 14422
    585 548-2665

## 5084 Industrial Machinery And Equipment

### (P-16804)
**ACE HYDRAULIC SALES & SVC INC**
2901 Gibson St, Bakersfield (93308-6107)
P.O. Box 5097 (93388-5097)
PHONE.................................661 327-0571
Gary Chambers, *CEO*
Claus Bjorneboe, *VP*
**EMP:** 18 **EST:** 1976
**SQ FT:** 20,000
**SALES (est):** 4.81MM Privately Held
Web: www.acehydraulic.net
SIC: **5084** 7699 3561  Hydraulic systems equipment and supplies; Hydraulic equipment repair; Cylinders, pump

### (P-16805)
**AGGRESSIVE ENGINEERING CORP**
1235 N Knollwood Cir, Anaheim (92801-1382)
PHONE.................................714 995-8313
John L Bridges, *CEO*
Daniel M Bridges, *Pr*
Kathy Carter, *Contrlr*
**EMP:** 16 **EST:** 1968
**SQ FT:** 23,000
**SALES (est):** 4.86MM Privately Held
Web: www.aggrengr.com
SIC: **5084** 3544  Industrial machine parts; Special dies and tools

### (P-16806)
**AIRGAS SAFETY  INC**
Also Called: Airgas
2355 Workman Mill Rd, City Of Industry (90601-1459)
PHONE.................................562 699-5239
Olaya Rivera, *Brnch Mgr*
**EMP:** 21
**SALES (corp-wide):** 114.13MM Privately Held
Web: www.airgas.com
SIC: **5084** 5085 3561 3841  Safety equipment ; Welding supplies; Cylinders, pump; Surgical and medical instruments
HQ: Airgas Safety, Inc.
    2501 Green Ln
    Levittown PA 19057

### (P-16807)
**ALS GROUP INC**
Also Called: Capri Tools
1788 W 2nd St, Pomona (91766-1206)
PHONE.................................909 622-7555
Anderson Cheung, *CEO*
▲ **EMP:** 25 **EST:** 2005
**SALES (est):** 3.48MM Privately Held

# PRODUCTS & SERVICES SECTION
## 5084 - Industrial Machinery And Equipment (P-16826)

SIC: **5084** 3545 3546 3423 Pneumatic tools and equipment; Precision measuring tools; Power-driven handtools; Wrenches, hand tools

### (P-16808)
### CAL SOUTHERN PACKG EQP INC
Also Called: Scpe
4102 Valley Blvd, Walnut (91789-1404)
PHONE..................................909 598-3198
David Byrne, *Pr*
David Pagkalinawan, *VP*
EMP: 15 EST: 1994
SQ FT: 10,000
SALES (est): **5.47MM** Privately Held
Web: www.scpe.com
SIC: **5084** 3565 Packaging machinery and equipment; Packaging machinery

### (P-16809)
### CALIEXTRACTIONS LLC
8790 Fruitridge Rd, Sacramento (95826-9740)
PHONE..................................916 519-7649
EMP: 16 EST: 2014
SALES (est): **1.43MM** Privately Held
Web: www.caliextractions.com
SIC: **5084** 2992 Oil refining machinery, equipment, and supplies; Re-refining lubricating oils and greases, nec

### (P-16810)
### CENTERLINE INDUSTRIAL INC
2530 Southport Way Ste D, National City (91950-6676)
PHONE..................................858 505-0838
Joann Loehr, *Pr*
Richard Botkin, *Prin*
Jack Loehr, *Prin*
EMP: 29 EST: 1996
SQ FT: 15,000
SALES (est): **1.5MM** Privately Held
SIC: **5084** 3544 Machine tools and accessories; Special dies, tools, jigs, and fixtures

### (P-16811)
### CUMMINS WEST INC
Also Called: Cummins
14775 Wicks Blvd, San Leandro (94577-6717)
P.O. Box 3005 (47202-3005)
PHONE..................................510 351-6101
TOLL FREE: 800
▲ EMP: 325
Web: www.cumminswestinc.com
SIC: **5084** 7629 5063 3519 Engines and parts, diesel; Electrical repair shops; Electrical apparatus and equipment; Internal combustion engines, nec

### (P-16812)
### DIRECTED LIGHT INC
Also Called: Unitek Miyachi International
74 Bonaventura Dr, San Jose (95134-2123)
PHONE..................................408 321-8500
Mike Mccourt, *CEO*
Neil Bell, *
▲ EMP: 25 EST: 1983
SQ FT: 13,000
SALES (est): **4.59MM** Privately Held
Web: www.directedlight.com
SIC: **5084** 2759 7699 5072 Industrial machinery and equipment; Laser printing; Industrial machinery and equipment repair; Hardware

### (P-16813)
### DRILL COOL SYSTEMS INC (PA)
627 Williams St, Bakersfield (93305-5437)
PHONE..................................661 633-2665
Al Tom Champness, *CEO*
Tom Champness, *Pr*
▲ EMP: 19 EST: 1974
SQ FT: 10,000
SALES (est): **9.67MM**
SALES (corp-wide): **9.67MM** Privately Held
Web: www.drillcool.com
SIC: **5084** 1389 3533 Industrial machinery and equipment; Oil field services, nec; Oil and gas drilling rigs and equipment

### (P-16814)
### E & M ELECTRIC AND MCHY INC (PA)
Also Called: E&M
126 Mill St, Healdsburg (95448-4438)
PHONE..................................707 433-5578
Steven Edgar Deas, *CEO*
Paul Deas, *
◆ EMP: 50 EST: 1972
SQ FT: 25,000
SALES (est): **91.02MM**
SALES (corp-wide): **91.02MM** Privately Held
Web: www.eandm.com
SIC: **5084** 5999 5063 7694 Instruments and control equipment; Motors, electric; Motors, electric; Electric motor repair

### (P-16815)
### FRESNO OXGN WLDG SUPPLIERS INC (PA)
Also Called: Barnes Welding Supply
2825 S Elm Ave Ste 101, Fresno (93706-5460)
P.O. Box 1666 (93706)
PHONE..................................559 233-6684
Michael L Barnes, *CEO*
David Barnes, *
James Michael Mc Cann, *
▲ EMP: 30 EST: 1949
SQ FT: 5,000
SALES (est): **102.68MM**
SALES (corp-wide): **102.68MM** Privately Held
Web: www.barneswelding.com
SIC: **5084** 5169 3548 2813 Welding machinery and equipment; Industrial gases; Welding apparatus; Industrial gases

### (P-16816)
### GMW ASSOCIATES
951 Industrial Rd Ste D, San Carlos (94070-4154)
PHONE..................................650 802-8292
Brian J Richter, *Pr*
Ian J Walker, *VP*
Jocelyn Walker, *Sec*
Lalo Guitron, *VP*
Ben Hertzell, *VP*
▲ EMP: 18 EST: 1983
SQ FT: 13,000
SALES (est): **1.96MM** Privately Held
Web: www.gmw.com
SIC: **5084** 3823 Instruments and control equipment; Industrial process control instruments

### (P-16817)
### HITACHI AMERICA LTD (HQ)
Also Called: Hitachi
2535 Augustine Dr, Santa Clara (95054-3003)
PHONE..................................914 332-5800
◆ EMP: 125 EST: 1959
SALES (est): **517.81MM** Privately Held
Web: www.hitachi.us
SIC: **5084** 5065 3577 5063 Industrial machinery and equipment; Electronic parts and equipment, nec; Computer peripheral equipment, nec; Generators
PA: Hitachi, Ltd.
1-6-6, Marunouchi

### (P-16818)
### INDUSTRIAL DATA COMMUNICATIONS
Also Called: I D C
4000 Fruitvale Ave Ste 16, Bakersfield (93308-5176)
P.O. Box 287 (93651-0287)
PHONE..................................661 589-4477
Lisa Sanli, *CEO*
▲ EMP: 22 EST: 1989
SALES (est): **452.21K** Privately Held
Web: www.ese-corp.com
SIC: **5084** 7371 3663 Measuring and testing equipment, electrical; Custom computer programming services; Digital encoders

### (P-16819)
### INDUSTRIAL PARTS DEPOT LLC (HQ)
Also Called: Ipd
1550 Charles Willard St, Carson (90746-4039)
PHONE..................................310 530-1900
Michael Badar, *Pr*
Russell Kneipp, *Managing Member*
◆ EMP: 70 EST: 1955
SALES (est): **23.18MM**
SALES (corp-wide): **44.12MM** Privately Held
Web: www.ipdparts.com
SIC: **5084** 3519 Engines and parts, diesel; Parts and accessories, internal combustion engines
PA: Storm Industries, Inc.
970 W 190th St
310 534-5232

### (P-16820)
### JOHN TILLMAN COMPANY (DH)
1300 W Artesia Blvd, Compton (90220-5307)
PHONE..................................310 764-0110
Phillip Mcgreevy, *Pr*
▲ EMP: 100 EST: 1928
SQ FT: 25,000
SALES (est): **24.24MM**
SALES (corp-wide): **14.7B** Privately Held
Web: www.jtillman.com
SIC: **5084** 3842 3548 Safety equipment; Personal safety equipment; Welding apparatus
HQ: Bunzl Distribution Inc.
1 Cityplace Dr Ste 200
Saint Louis MO 63141

### (P-16821)
### JWC ENVIRONMENTAL INC (DH)
Also Called: Windjmmer Capitl Investors III
2850 Redhill Ave Ste 125, Santa Ana (92705-5541)
PHONE..................................949 833-3888
Ken Biele, *CEO*
Joe Ruiz, *CFO*
◆ EMP: 30 EST: 1989
SALES (est): **66.19MM** Privately Held
Web: www.jwce.com
SIC: **5084** 3589 Industrial machinery and equipment; Commercial cleaning equipment
HQ: Sulzer Management Ag
Neuwiesenstrasse 15
Winterthur ZH

### (P-16822)
### KAFCO SALES COMPANY
2300 E 37th St, Vernon (90058-1405)
P.O. Box 58563 (90058-0563)
PHONE..................................323 588-7141
Akira Urakawa, *CEO*
▲ EMP: 26 EST: 1978
SQ FT: 15,500
SALES (est): **4.54MM** Privately Held
Web: www.kafcosales.com
SIC: **5084** 3842 Safety equipment; Surgical appliances and supplies

### (P-16823)
### KECO INC
Also Called: Pump-A-Head
3475 Kurtz St, San Diego (92110-4430)
P.O. Box 80308 (92138-0308)
PHONE..................................619 298-3800
Anne Bleier, *Prin*
Anne Kenton Bleier, *Pr*
Andrew Bleier, *VP*
▼ EMP: 20 EST: 1954
SQ FT: 2,000
SALES (est): **6.74MM** Privately Held
Web: www.pumpahead.com
SIC: **5084** 3594 3561 3589 Pumps and pumping equipment, nec; Fluid power pumps; Pumps and pumping equipment; Sewage and water treatment equipment

### (P-16824)
### LAKOS CORPORATION (HQ)
Also Called: Lakos
1365 N Clovis Ave, Fresno (93727-2282)
P.O. Box 398936 (94139-8936)
PHONE..................................559 255-1601
Scott Marion, *CEO*
Eric Arneson, *
Brian Ketcham, *
Kathy Colby, *
◆ EMP: 48 EST: 1972
SQ FT: 100,000
SALES (est): **25.97MM**
SALES (corp-wide): **25.97MM** Privately Held
Web: www.lakos.com
SIC: **5084** 3491 Industrial machinery and equipment; Pressure valves and regulators, industrial
PA: Lakos Acquisition Holdco, Llc
1365 N Clovis Ave
559 255-1601

### (P-16825)
### MATHESON TRI-GAS INC
651 Solano Way, Pacheco (94553-1445)
PHONE..................................925 229-4350
Bill Picker, *Mgr*
EMP: 25
Web: www.mathesongas.com
SIC: **5084** 2813 Welding machinery and equipment; Nitrogen
HQ: Matheson Tri-Gas, Inc.
3 Mountainview Rd Ste 3 # 3
Warren NJ 07059
908 991-9200

### (P-16826)
### MAXON LIFT CORP (PA)
11921 Slauson Ave, Santa Fe Springs (90670-2221)
PHONE..................................562 464-0099
Casey Lugash, *Pr*
Brenda Leung, *VP Fin*
▲ EMP: 110 EST: 1957
SQ FT: 30,000
SALES (est): **66.93MM** Privately Held
Web: www.maxonlift.com

# 5084 - Industrial Machinery And Equipment (P-16827)

SIC: **5084** 3537 3534 Lift trucks and parts; Industrial trucks and tractors; Elevators and moving stairways

### (P-16827)
**MENKE MARKING DEVICES INC**
Also Called: Menke Marketing Devices
10440 Pioneer Blvd Ste 4, Santa Fe Springs (90670-5574)
P.O. Box 2986 (90670-0986)
PHONE.................................562 921-1380
Stephen Menke, *Pr*
EMP: 29 EST: 1943
SALES (est): 4.56MM **Privately Held**
Web: www.menkemarking.com
SIC: **5084** 3953 Industrial machinery and equipment; Marking devices

### (P-16828)
**MUTUAL LIQUID GAS & EQP CO INC (PA)**
Also Called: Mutual Propane
17117 S Broadway, Gardena (90248-3191)
PHONE.................................310 515-0553
Melvin Moore, *CEO*
Steve Moore, *
EMP: 30 EST: 1934
SQ FT: 3,100
SALES (est): 18.67MM
SALES (corp-wide): 18.67MM **Privately Held**
Web: www.mutualpropane.com
SIC: **5084** 3549 Propane conversion equipment; Metalworking machinery, nec

### (P-16829)
**NIDEC GENMARK AUTOMATION INC (DH)**
46723 Lakeview Blvd, Fremont (94538-6528)
PHONE.................................510 897-3400
Akihiro Suzuki, *CEO*
▼ EMP: 132 EST: 1985
SQ FT: 86,000
SALES (est): 19.6MM **Privately Held**
Web: www.genmarkautomation.com
SIC: **5084** 3674 Industrial machinery and equipment; Wafers (semiconductor devices)
HQ: Nidec Instruments Corporation
  5329, Shimosuwamachi
  Suwa-Gun NAG 393-0

### (P-16830)
**NORMONT HYDRAULIC SLS SVC INC**
Also Called: International Fluid Power Amer
43123 Business Park Dr, Temecula (92590-3628)
PHONE.................................951 676-2155
Denis Grierson, *CEO*
▲ EMP: 15 EST: 1979
SALES (est): 3.62MM **Privately Held**
Web: www.intlfpa.com
SIC: **5084** 3594 Pumps and pumping equipment, nec; Pumps, hydraulic power transfer

### (P-16831)
**OLIVER HEALTHCARE PACKAGING CO**
Also Called: Clean Cut Technologies
1145 N Ocean Cir, Anaheim (92806-1939)
PHONE.................................714 864-3500
Mike Benevento, *Pr*
EMP: 100
SALES (corp-wide): 2.26B **Privately Held**
Web: www.oliverhcp.com

SIC: **5084** 5199 3053 Processing and packaging equipment; Packaging materials; Packing materials
HQ: Oliver Healthcare Packaging Company
  445 6th St Nw
  Grand Rapids MI 49504
  833 465-4837

### (P-16832)
**OTIS ELEVATOR COMPANY**
470 Lakeside Dr Ste D, Sunnyvale (94085-4720)
PHONE.................................408 727-1231
Ed Persiclo, *Mgr*
EMP: 68
SQ FT: 2,500
SALES (corp-wide): 14.21B **Publicly Held**
Web: www.otis.com
SIC: **5084** 7699 3534 1796 Elevators; Elevators: inspection, service, and repair; Elevators and moving stairways; Installing building equipment
HQ: Otis Elevator Company
  1 Carrier Pl
  Farmington CT 06032
  860 674-3000

### (P-16833)
**OTIS ELEVATOR COMPANY**
3949 Viewridge Ave, San Diego (92123)
PHONE.................................858 560-5881
Brian Petler, *Mgr*
EMP: 57
SQ FT: 1,400
SALES (corp-wide): 14.21B **Publicly Held**
Web: www.otis.com
SIC: **5084** 5082 7699 3534 Elevators; General construction machinery and equipment; Door and window repair; Elevators and moving stairways
HQ: Otis Elevator Company
  1 Carrier Pl
  Farmington CT 06032
  860 674-3000

### (P-16834)
**POWERHOUSE DIESEL SERVICES INCORPORATED**
4700 E 2nd St, Benicia (94510-1012)
PHONE.................................707 747-6737
▲ EMP: 20
Web: www.powerhouseinc.com
SIC: **5084** 7699 3519 5983 Industrial machinery and equipment; Industrial machinery and equipment repair; Internal combustion engines, nec; Fuel oil dealers

### (P-16835)
**QUALLS STUD WELDING PDTS INC**
Also Called: Stud Welding Products
9459 Washburn Rd, Downey (90242-2912)
PHONE.................................562 923-7883
Robert Butcher, *Brnch Mgr*
EMP: 23
SALES (corp-wide): 12.92MM **Privately Held**
Web: www.studweldprod.com
SIC: **5084** 7692 1799 Welding machinery and equipment; Welding repair; Welding on site
PA: Quall's Stud Welding Products, Inc.
  7820 S 210th St Ste C103
  425 656-9787

### (P-16836)
**R & J MATERIAL HANDLING INC**
345 Adams Cir, Corona (92882-1896)
PHONE.................................951 735-0000
John Lessing Junior, *CEO*

John Lessing Junior, *Pr*
John Lessing Senior, *Pr*
Jason Lessing, *CFO*
EMP: 19 EST: 2006
SQ FT: 14,100
SALES (est): 4.55MM **Privately Held**
Web: www.rjforklift.com
SIC: **5084** 7692 Materials handling machinery; Welding repair

### (P-16837)
**RDM INDUSTRIES**
14310 Gannet St, La Mirada (90638-5221)
PHONE.................................714 690-0380
Jaz Manak, *CEO*
Jaz Manak, *Pr*
Dan Gilmore, *Stockholder**
◆ EMP: 28 EST: 2011
SALES (est): 5.16MM **Privately Held**
Web: www.rdmindustriesinc.com
SIC: **5084** 3565 5162 2671 Industrial machinery and equipment; Aerating machines, for beverages; Plastics materials, nec; Plastic film, coated or laminated for packaging

### (P-16838)
**RKI INSTRUMENTS INC (PA)**
Also Called: R K I
33248 Central Ave, Union City (94587-2010)
PHONE.................................510 441-5656
Robert Pellissier, *Pr*
Sandra Gallagher, *
▲ EMP: 35 EST: 1994
SQ FT: 10,000
SALES (est): 24.02MM **Privately Held**
Web: www.rkiinstruments.com
SIC: **5084** 3823 Industrial machinery and equipment; On-stream gas/liquid analysis instruments, industrial

### (P-16839)
**ROSE JOAQUIN INC**
Also Called: B & B Mfg Co
410 S Golden State Blvd, Turlock (95380-4959)
PHONE.................................209 632-0616
Joaquin A Rose, *Pr*
Michael A Rose, *VP*
David A Rose, *CFO*
EMP: 17 EST: 1936
SQ FT: 20,000
SALES (est): 4.91MM **Privately Held**
Web: www.bbmfgpower.com
SIC: **5084** 7692 3599 Hydraulic systems equipment and supplies; Welding repair; Machine shop, jobbing and repair

### (P-16840)
**SCHURMAN FINE PAPERS**
3333 Bristol St, Costa Mesa (92626-1873)
PHONE.................................714 549-0212
EMP: 26
SALES (corp-wide): 38.97MM **Privately Held**
Web: www.srgretail.com
SIC: **5084** 2621 Industrial machinery and equipment; Paper mills
PA: Schurman Fine Papers
  300 Oak Bluff Ln
  707 425-8006

### (P-16841)
**SHARP INDUSTRIES INC (PA)**
Also Called: Sharp
3501 Challenger St Fl 2, Torrance (90503-1697)
PHONE.................................310 370-5990
James Chen, *Ch Bd*

Nicholas Chen, *CEO*
George Lee, *Sr VP*
Roger Lee, *VP*
▲ EMP: 23 EST: 1976
SQ FT: 40,000
SALES (est): 10.21MM
SALES (corp-wide): 10.21MM **Privately Held**
Web: www.sharp-industries.com
SIC: **5084** 3542 Machine tools and accessories; Arbor presses

### (P-16842)
**SHIP & SHORE ENVIRONMENTAL INC**
2474 N Palm Dr, Signal Hill (90755-4007)
PHONE.................................562 997-0233
Anoosheh Mostafaei, *Pr*
Anu D Vij, *
▲ EMP: 38 EST: 2000
SQ FT: 4,000
SALES (est): 12.29MM **Privately Held**
Web: www.shipandshore.com
SIC: **5084** 3444 Pollution control equipment, air (environmental); Awnings and canopies

### (P-16843)
**SOUTHERN CAL HYDRLIC ENGRG COR**
Also Called: S C Hydraulic Engineering
1130 Columbia St, Brea (92821-2921)
PHONE.................................714 257-4800
Donna Perez, *Pr*
David Vedder, *
Manuel Perez, *
EMP: 40 EST: 1953
SQ FT: 65,000
SALES (est): 9.89MM **Privately Held**
Web: www.schydraulic.com
SIC: **5084** 3594 Pumps and pumping equipment, nec; Pumps, hydraulic power transfer

### (P-16844)
**STAINLESS STL FABRICATORS INC**
Also Called: Cook King
15120 Desman Rd, La Mirada (90638-5737)
PHONE.................................714 739-9904
Craig Miller, *Pr*
Dave Hart, *
Glenna Miller, *
Jennifer Arcos, *Prin*
EMP: 60 EST: 1985
SQ FT: 11,204
SALES (est): 8.35MM **Privately Held**
Web: www.ssfab.net
SIC: **5084** 3444 Industrial machinery and equipment; Restaurant sheet metalwork

### (P-16845)
**STATCO ENGRG & FABRICATORS LLC (DH)**
Also Called: Interstate Mnroe McHy Sups Div
7595 Reynolds Cir, Huntington Beach (92647)
PHONE.................................714 375-6300
Mark W Anderson, *Managing Member*
EMP: 20 EST: 1982
SQ FT: 11,000
SALES (est): 102.83MM **Privately Held**
Web: www.statco-engineering.com
SIC: **5084** 3556 Processing and packaging equipment; Food products machinery
HQ: Pro Mach, Inc.
  50 E Rvrcnter Blvd Ste 18
  Covington KY 41011
  513 831-8778

▲ = Import ▼ = Export
◆ = Import/Export

## PRODUCTS & SERVICES SECTION
## 5085 - Industrial Supplies (P-16864)

**(P-16846)**
**SURFACE PUMPS INC (PA)**
3301 Unicorn Rd, Bakersfield (93308-6852)
P.O. Box 5757 (93388-5757)
PHONE..................................661 393-1545
Steven J Durrett, *Pr*
David Cook, *
Marty Rushing, *
**EMP:** 51 **EST:** 1970
**SQ FT:** 14,000
**SALES (est):** 26.27MM
**SALES (corp-wide):** 26.27MM **Privately Held**
Web: www.surfacepumps.com
**SIC:** 5084 7699 8711 3519  Pumps and pumping equipment, nec; Pumps and pumping equipment repair; Engineering services; Parts and accessories, internal combustion engines

**(P-16847)**
**SVF FLOW CONTROLS INC**
5595 Fresca Dr, La Palma (90623-1006)
PHONE..................................562 802-2255
Wayne Ulanski, *Pr*
David Steel, *
Russell Stern, *Stockholder*
▲ **EMP:** 40 **EST:** 1993
**SQ FT:** 20,000
**SALES (est):** 9.72MM **Privately Held**
Web: www.svf.net
**SIC:** 5084 3491 3494 5085  Instruments and control equipment; Industrial valves; Valves and pipe fittings, nec; Valves and fittings

**(P-16848)**
**SWARCO MCCAIN INC (DH)**
2365 Oak Ridge Way, Vista (92081-8348)
PHONE..................................760 727-8100
Jimi Meshulam, *CEO*
Jo Ann Mills, *
▲ **EMP:** 250 **EST:** 1987
**SQ FT:** 6,700
**SALES (est):** 127MM
**SALES (corp-wide):** 2.67MM **Privately Held**
Web: www.mccain-inc.com
**SIC:** 5084 3444 3669  Industrial machinery and equipment; Sheet metalwork; Traffic signals, electric
HQ: Swarco Ag
  Blattenwaldweg 8
  Wattens 6112
  522458770

**(P-16849)**
**THE SERVICE WAREHOUSE INC**
Also Called: Service Warehouse, The
17819 S Figueroa St, Gardena (90248-4210)
P.O. Box 3459 (90247-7159)
PHONE..................................310 329-9110
**EMP:** 15 **EST:** 1985
**SALES (est):** 2.49MM **Privately Held**
Web: www.servicewarehouse.net
**SIC:** 5084 5072 3496 5251  Drilling bits; Bolts, nuts, and screws; Miscellaneous fabricated wire products; Hardware stores

**(P-16850)**
**TK ELEVATOR CORPORATION**
14400 Catalina St, San Leandro (94577-5516)
PHONE..................................510 476-1900
Ed Persico, *Mgr*
**EMP:** 208
**SALES (corp-wide):** 2.67MM **Privately Held**
Web: www.thyssenkruppelevator.com
**SIC:** 5084 1796 3534  Elevators; Elevator installation and conversion; Elevators and moving stairways
HQ: Tk Elevator Corporation
  788 Crcle 75 Pkwy Se Ste
  Atlanta GA 30339
  678 319-3240

**(P-16851)**
**TRI TOOL INC (HQ)**
3041 Sunrise Blvd, Rancho Cordova (95742-6502)
PHONE..................................916 288-6100
Christopher M Belle, *CEO*
George J Wernette Iii, *Pr*
Jerri Wernette, *
Chris Soriano, *
▲ **EMP:** 92 **EST:** 1972
**SQ FT:** 125,000
**SALES (est):** 33.53MM
**SALES (corp-wide):** 33.53MM **Privately Held**
Web: www.tritool.com
**SIC:** 5084 3548 3541  Industrial machinery and equipment; Welding apparatus; Pipe cutting and threading machines
PA: The Wernette Family Limited Partnership Of 1995
  3041 Sunrise Blvd
  916 288-6100

**(P-16852)**
**VALLEY POWER SYSTEMS INC**
Also Called: John Deere Authorized Dealer
2070 Farallon Dr, San Leandro (94577-6602)
PHONE..................................510 635-8991
Mickey Smith, *Brnch Mgr*
**EMP:** 28
**SALES (corp-wide):** 178.72MM **Privately Held**
Web: www.valleypowersystems.com
**SIC:** 5084 3531 5063  Engines and parts, diesel; Road construction and maintenance machinery; Generators
PA: Valley Power Systems, Inc.
  425 S Hacienda Blvd
  626 333-1243

**(P-16853)**
**VALTRA INC (PA)**
Also Called: Strong Hand Tools
8750 Pioneer Blvd, Santa Fe Springs (90670-2006)
PHONE..................................562 949-8625
Harry Hon Wong, *CEO*
▲ **EMP:** 24 **EST:** 1983
**SQ FT:** 24,000
**SALES (est):** 14.11MM
**SALES (corp-wide):** 14.11MM **Privately Held**
Web: lp.constantcontactpages.com
**SIC:** 5084 5085 3452 3429  Industrial machine parts; Industrial supplies; Bolts, nuts, rivets, and washers; Hardware, nec

**(P-16854)**
**VAUGHANS INDUSTRIAL REPAIR INC**
16224 Garfield Ave, Paramount (90723-4804)
P.O. Box 1898 (90723-1898)
PHONE..................................562 633-2660
Thomas Vaughan, *Pr*
Patricia Vaughan, *
David Newton, *
John L Smith, *
Keven Vaughan, *
**EMP:** 35 **EST:** 1978
**SQ FT:** 20,000
**SALES (est):** 7.48MM
**SALES (corp-wide):** 7.48MM **Privately Held**
Web: www.virc1.com
**SIC:** 5084 1711 3599  Oil refining machinery, equipment, and supplies; Mechanical contractor; Machine and other job shop work
PA: Vss Sales, Inc.
  16220 Garfield Ave
  562 630-0606

**(P-16855)**
**WASTECH CONTROLS & ENGRG LLC**
20600 Nordhoff St, Chatsworth (91311-6114)
PHONE..................................818 998-3500
Paul Nicolas, *Pr*
▲ **EMP:** 58 **EST:** 1987
**SQ FT:** 30,000
**SALES (est):** 24.8MM **Privately Held**
Web: www.wastechengineering.com
**SIC:** 5084 3561 3823 3559  Waste compactors; Pumps, domestic: water or sump; Industrial flow and liquid measuring instruments; Anodizing equipment

**(P-16856)**
**WCS DISTRIBUTING INC**
Also Called: Pro Spray Equipment
268 W Orange Show Ln, San Bernardino (92408-2037)
PHONE..................................909 888-2015
Steve Sykes, *Pr*
◆ **EMP:** 21 **EST:** 1990
**SQ FT:** 20,000
**SALES (est):** 8.16MM **Privately Held**
Web: www.wcsdistributinginc.com
**SIC:** 5084 3499 5083  Engines and transportation equipment; Nozzles, spray: aerosol, paint, or insecticide; Lawn machinery and equipment

**(P-16857)**
**WESTCOAST ROTOR INC**
119 W 154th St, Gardena (90248-2201)
PHONE..................................310 327-5050
**TOLL FREE:** 800
Vehan Mahdessian, *Pr*
Krikor Mahdessian, *CFO*
▲ **EMP:** 21 **EST:** 1982
**SQ FT:** 15,625
**SALES (est):** 4.7MM **Privately Held**
Web: www.westcoastrotor.com
**SIC:** 5084 3561  Pumps and pumping equipment, nec; Pumps and pumping equipment

**(P-16858)**
**WESTERN REFINING INC**
25225 Mission Blvd, Hayward (94544-2518)
PHONE..................................510 538-1679
**EMP:** 55
Web: www.wnr.com
**SIC:** 5084 2911  Metalworking machinery; Petroleum refining
HQ: Western Refining, Inc.
  212 N Clark Dr
  El Paso TX 79905

**(P-16859)**
**WESTERN REFINING INC**
22232 Wilmington Ave, Carson (90745-4308)
PHONE..................................310 834-1297
**EMP:** 55
Web: www.wnr.com
**SIC:** 5084 2911  Metalworking machinery; Petroleum refining
HQ: Western Refining, Inc.
  212 N Clark Dr
  El Paso TX 79905

**(P-16860)**
**WESTERN REFINING INC**
4357 E Cesar E Chavez Ave, Los Angeles (90022-1401)
PHONE..................................323 264-8500
**EMP:** 55
Web: www.wnr.com
**SIC:** 5084 2911  Metalworking machinery; Petroleum refining
HQ: Western Refining, Inc.
  212 N Clark Dr
  El Paso TX 79905

**(P-16861)**
**WESTERN REFINING INC**
1201 Baker St, Costa Mesa (92626-3916)
PHONE..................................714 708-2200
**EMP:** 55
Web: www.wnr.com
**SIC:** 5084 2911  Metalworking machinery; Petroleum refining
HQ: Western Refining, Inc.
  212 N Clark Dr
  El Paso TX 79905

## 5085 Industrial Supplies

**(P-16862)**
**ALCAN PACKG CAPSULES CAL LLC**
5425 Broadway St, American Canyon (94503-9678)
PHONE..................................707 257-6481
Richard Evans, *Pr*
Federick Catteau, *VP*
▲ **EMP:** 21 **EST:** 1982
**SQ FT:** 20,618
**SALES (est):** 9.3MM
**SALES (corp-wide):** 14.69B **Privately Held**
**SIC:** 5085 3466  Bottler supplies; Crowns and closures
HQ: Amcor European Holdings Pty Ltd
  L 11 60 City Rd
  Southbank VIC 3006

**(P-16863)**
**BAY STANDARD INC**
24485 Marsh Creek Rd, Brentwood (94513-4319)
P.O. Box 801 (94513-0801)
PHONE..................................925 634-1181
Gary W Landgraf, *Pr*
Karen Landgraf, *
Tom Landgraf, *
▲ **EMP:** 100 **EST:** 1966
**SALES (est):** 9.64MM **Privately Held**
Web: www.baystandard.com
**SIC:** 5085 3965  Fasteners and fastening equipment; Fasteners

**(P-16864)**
**BRIDGESTONE HOSEPOWER LLC**
Also Called: Hose Power USA
2865 Pellissier Pl, City Of Industry (90601-1512)
PHONE..................................562 699-9500
Alfonso Sanchez, *Genl Mgr*
**EMP:** 23
Web: www.hosepower.com
**SIC:** 5085 3492  Hose, belting, and packing; Hose and tube fittings and assemblies, hydraulic/pneumatic

## 5085 - Industrial Supplies (P-16865)

HQ: Bridgestone Hosepower, Llc
50 Industrial Loop Dr N
Orange Park FL 32073

**(P-16865)**
**CALIFORNIA INDUSTRIAL RBR CO (PA)**
2539 S Cherry Ave, Fresno (93706-5007)
**PHONE**..................559 268-7321
Larry T Cain Senior, *Pr*
Jeff T Brust, *CEO*
Carol Ann Cain, *Treas*
▲ **EMP:** 25 **EST:** 1958
**SQ FT:** 45,000
**SALES (est):** 60.31MM
**SALES (corp-wide):** 60.31MM **Privately Held**
Web: www.cir.net
SIC: **5085** 5999 3052 Hose, belting, and packing; Rubber stamps; Rubber and plastics hose and beltings

**(P-16866)**
**CARPENTER GROUP**
Also Called: American Rigging & Supply
2380 Main St, San Diego (92113-3643)
**PHONE**..................619 233-5625
Bruce Yoder, *Brnch Mgr*
**EMP:** 30
**SQ FT:** 10,000
**SALES (corp-wide):** 24.59MM **Privately Held**
Web: www.thecarpentergroup.com
SIC: **5085** 5084 3537 Industrial supplies; Industrial machinery and equipment; Industrial trucks and tractors
PA: The Carpenter Group
28800 Hesperian Blvd
415 285-1954

**(P-16867)**
**COFAN THERMAL INC**
Also Called: Cofan USA
46177 Warm Springs Blvd, Fremont (94539)
**PHONE**..................510 490-7533
Chang S Han, *Pr*
▲ **EMP:** 40 **EST:** 1994
**SALES (est):** 9.79MM **Privately Held**
Web: www.cofan-usa.com
SIC: **5085** 3444 3089 3672 Industrial supplies; Sheet metalwork; Injection molded finished plastics products, nec; Printed circuit boards

**(P-16868)**
**CONTINENTAL WESTERN CORP (PA)**
Also Called: C W C
2950 Merced St Ste 200, San Leandro (94577-5641)
P.O. Box 2418 (94577-0241)
**PHONE**..................510 352-3133
Frederick J Oshay, *Pr*
◆ **EMP:** 50 **EST:** 1957
**SQ FT:** 25,000
**SALES (est):** 40.48MM
**SALES (corp-wide):** 40.48MM **Privately Held**
Web: www.cwcglobal.com
SIC: **5085** 3069 Twine; Strapping, rubber

**(P-16869)**
**CUSTOM BUILDING PRODUCTS LLC**
1900 Norris Rd, Bakersfield (93308-2229)
**PHONE**..................661 393-0422
Kevin Odell, *Brnch Mgr*
**EMP:** 52

Web: www.custombuildingproducts.com
SIC: **5085** 5211 3531 Adhesives, tape and plasters; Masonry materials and supplies; Construction machinery
HQ: Custom Building Products Llc
7711 Center Ave Ste 500
Huntington Beach CA 92647
800 272-8786

**(P-16870)**
**DARCOID COMPANY OF CALIFORNIA**
Also Called: Darcoid Nor-Cal Seal
950 3rd St, Oakland (94607-2502)
**PHONE**..................510 836-2449
Robert M Loback, *CEO*
▲ **EMP:** 48 **EST:** 1945
**SQ FT:** 27,000
**SALES (est):** 22.01MM **Privately Held**
Web: www.darcoid.com
SIC: **5085** 3053 Rubber goods, mechanical; Gaskets, all materials

**(P-16871)**
**DELTA RUBBER CO INC**
2648 Teepee Dr, Stockton (95205-2419)
**PHONE**..................209 948-0511
▲ **EMP:** 80
SIC: **5085** 3535 3052 Rubber goods, mechanical; Conveyors and conveying equipment; Rubber and plastics hose and beltings

**(P-16872)**
**DHV INDUSTRIES INC**
3451 Pegasus Dr, Bakersfield (93308-6827)
**PHONE**..................661 392-8948
Tingchun Huang, *Pr*
◆ **EMP:** 52 **EST:** 1996
**SQ FT:** 180,000
**SALES (est):** 10.72MM **Privately Held**
Web: www.dhvindustries.com
SIC: **5085** 3491 Valves and fittings; Industrial valves

**(P-16873)**
**DUHIG AND CO INC**
Also Called: Duhig Stainless
5071 Telegraph Rd, Los Angeles (90022-4997)
P.O. Box 226966 (90022-0666)
◆ **EMP:** 48
Web: www.fergusonindustrial.com
SIC: **5085** 5051 3441 Valves and fittings; Pipe and tubing, steel; Fabricated structural metal

**(P-16874)**
**FASTENER DIST HOLDINGS LLC (HQ)**
Also Called: Stealth Aerospace
5200 Sheila St, Commerce (90040-3906)
**PHONE**..................213 620-9950
Scott Tucker, *Pr*
**EMP:** 86 **EST:** 2014
**SALES (est):** 399.16MM
**SALES (corp-wide):** 512.41MM **Privately Held**
Web: fdhaerostg.wpenginepowered.com
SIC: **5085** 3721 Fasteners, industrial: nuts, bolts, screws, etc.; Aircraft
PA: Fdh Aero, Llc
5200 Sheila St
213 620-9950

**(P-16875)**
**FASTENER TECHNOLOGY CORP**
7415 Fulton Ave, North Hollywood (91605-4116)

**PHONE**..................818 764-6467
Dennis Suedkamp, *CEO*
Thomas Boat, *
**EMP:** 125 **EST:** 1979
**SQ FT:** 24,000
**SALES (est):** 8.36MM
**SALES (corp-wide):** 123.82MM **Privately Held**
Web: www.ftc-usa.com
SIC: **5085** 3812 5251 Fasteners, industrial: nuts, bolts, screws, etc.; Aircraft/aerospace flight instruments and guidance systems; Tools
HQ: Avantus Aerospace, Inc.
29101 The Old Rd
Valencia CA 91355
661 295-8620

**(P-16876)**
**GRISWOLD INDUSTRIES**
Also Called: Griswald Industries
24100 Water Ave, Perris (92570-6738)
**PHONE**..................951 657-1718
Fred Zimmer, *Mgr*
**EMP:** 22
**SQ FT:** 25,000
**SALES (corp-wide):** 103.11MM **Privately Held**
Web: www.cla-val.com
SIC: **5085** 3494 Valves and fittings; Valves and pipe fittings, nec
PA: Griswold Industries
1701 Placentia Ave
949 722-4800

**(P-16877)**
**INDEX FASTENERS INC (PA)**
Also Called: Distribution
945 E Grevillea Ct, Ontario (91761-5612)
**PHONE**..................909 923-5002
Shane Bearly, *CEO*
▲ **EMP:** 19 **EST:** 1977
**SQ FT:** 30,000
**SALES (est):** 12.27MM
**SALES (corp-wide):** 12.27MM **Privately Held**
Web: www.indexfasteners.com
SIC: **5085** 2821 3081 Fasteners, industrial: nuts, bolts, screws, etc.; Plastics materials and resins; Plastics film and sheet

**(P-16878)**
**INDUSTRIAL CONT SVCS - CA N LL**
Also Called: Ics-CA North
749 Galleria Blvd, Roseville (95678-1331)
**PHONE**..................916 781-2775
Charles Veniez, *CEO*
Calvin G Lee, *Managing Member**
Gerald Butler, *
Kay Rykowski, *
Alain G Magnan, *
**EMP:** 52 **EST:** 1986
**SQ FT:** 10,000
**SALES (est):** 7.56MM
**SALES (corp-wide):** 3.82B **Privately Held**
SIC: **5085** 2655 Commercial containers; Fiber cans, drums, and similar products
HQ: Industrial Container Services Llc
375 Northridge Rd Ste 600
Atlanta GA 30350
407 930-4182

**(P-16879)**
**INDUSTRIAL VALCO INC (PA)**
3135 E Ana St, Compton (90221-5606)
**PHONE**..................310 635-0711
Rob C Raban, *Pr*
▲ **EMP:** 50 **EST:** 1983
**SQ FT:** 62,000

**SALES (est):** 18.07MM
**SALES (corp-wide):** 18.07MM **Privately Held**
Web: www.ivalco.com
SIC: **5085** 3498 Valves and fittings; Pipe fittings, fabricated from purchased pipe

**(P-16880)**
**LGG INDUSTRIAL INC**
Also Called: Valley Rubber & Gasket
10182 Croydon Way, Sacramento (95827-2102)
**PHONE**..................916 366-9340
Les A Shively, *CEO*
**EMP:** 98
**SALES (corp-wide):** 437.91MM **Privately Held**
Web: www.lggindustrial.com
SIC: **5085** 3053 3052 Hose, belting, and packing; Gaskets; packing and sealing devices; Rubber and plastics hose and beltings
PA: Lgg Industrial, Inc.
650 Washington Rd Ste 500
800 937-9070

**(P-16881)**
**LIBERTY SYNERGISTICS INC**
Also Called: Liberty Photo Products
1041 Calle Trepadora, San Clemente (92673-6204)
**PHONE**..................949 361-1100
▲ **EMP:** 55
Web: www.ivokenow.com
SIC: **5085** 3861 Industrial supplies; Photographic equipment and supplies

**(P-16882)**
**LINEAR INDUSTRIES LTD (PA)**
1850 Enterprise Way, Monrovia (91016-4271)
**PHONE**..................626 303-1130
Anthony Dell Angelica, *Pr*
Savonia Angelica, *
Jean Cade, *
▲ **EMP:** 36 **EST:** 1960
**SQ FT:** 45,000
**SALES (est):** 20.8MM
**SALES (corp-wide):** 20.8MM **Privately Held**
Web: www.linearindustries.com
SIC: **5085** 3625 5065 5072 Bearings; Positioning controls, electric; Electronic parts; Hardware

**(P-16883)**
**LORD & SONS INC (PA)**
430 E Trimble Rd, San Jose (95131)
**PHONE**..................408 293-4841
**EMP:** 20 **EST:** 1971
**SALES (est):** 47.02MM
**SALES (corp-wide):** 47.02MM **Privately Held**
Web: www.lordandsons.com
SIC: **5085** 5072 3429 Fasteners, industrial: nuts, bolts, screws, etc.; Hardware; Metal fasteners

**(P-16884)**
**MOTION INDUSTRIES INC**
Also Called: F & L Industrial Solutions
12550 Stowe Dr, Poway (92064-6804)
**PHONE**..................858 602-1500
Lori Lefeuvre, *Brnch Mgr*
**EMP:** 23
**SALES (corp-wide):** 23.09B **Publicly Held**
Web: www.fandl8020.com
SIC: **5085** 3355 Bearings; Extrusion ingot, aluminum: made in rolling mills
HQ: Motion Industries, Inc.
1605 Alton Rd

## 5085 - Industrial Supplies (P-16904)

Birmingham AL 35210
205 956-1122

**(P-16885)**
**NMC GROUP INC**
Also Called: Nylon Molding
300 E Cypress St, Brea (92821-4007)
PHONE..............................714 223-3525
Michael Johnson, Pr
Wolfgang Hombrecher, *
▲ EMP: 24 EST: 1972
SALES (est): 21.3MM
SALES (corp-wide): 7.94B **Publicly Held**
Web: www.kirkhill.com
SIC: **5085** 3089 Fasteners and fastening equipment; Injection molding of plastics
HQ: Ta Aerospace Co.
28065 Franklin Pkwy
Valencia CA 91355
661 775-1100

**(P-16886)**
**PACIFIC RUBBER & PACKING INC (PA)**
1160 Industrial Rd Ste 3, San Carlos (94070-4127)
PHONE..............................650 595-5888
Peter Burfield, Ch Bd
Ashley Burfield, *
Joyce Burfield, *
EMP: 27 EST: 1973
SQ FT: 12,000
SALES (est): 22.33MM
SALES (corp-wide): 22.33MM **Privately Held**
Web: www.pacificrubber.com
SIC: **5085** 3061 Rubber goods, mechanical; Mechanical rubber goods

**(P-16887)**
**PBM SUPPLY & MFG INC**
Also Called: P B M
324 Meyers St, Chico (95928-7175)
P.O. Box 3129 (95927-3129)
PHONE..............................530 345-1334
Barry S Jones, CEO
▲ EMP: 24 EST: 1969
SQ FT: 10,100
SALES (est): 15.07MM **Privately Held**
Web: www.pbmsprayers.com
SIC: **5085** 5191 3715 Industrial supplies; Farm supplies; Bus trailers, tractor type

**(P-16888)**
**PCBC HOLDCO INC**
12748 Florence Ave, Santa Fe Springs (90670-3906)
PHONE..............................562 944-9549
Robert Gardner, Pr
▲ EMP: 38 EST: 1989
SQ FT: 47,000
SALES (est): 7.99MM **Privately Held**
Web: www.pacificcoastbolt.com
SIC: **5085** 3965 3452 5072 Fasteners, industrial: nuts, bolts, screws, etc.; Fasteners; Bolts, nuts, rivets, and washers; Bolts, nuts, and screws

**(P-16889)**
**PINNACLE INDUSTRIAL SUPPLY INC (PA)**
1612 Pacific Rim Ct, San Diego (92154-7501)
PHONE..............................619 710-4255
Daniel Halecky, CEO
Brian Chin, Dir
EMP: 21 EST: 2002
SQ FT: 6,226
SALES (est): 1.64MM
SALES (corp-wide): 1.64MM **Privately Held**

Web: www.pinnacleca.com
SIC: **5085** 3312 3317 3494 Valves and fittings; Pipes, iron and steel; Pipes, seamless steel; Pipe fittings

**(P-16890)**
**RBC TRANSPORT DYNAMICS CORP**
3131 W Segerstrom Ave, Santa Ana (92704-5811)
PHONE..............................203 267-7001
Michael Harnett, Pr
▲ EMP: 185 EST: 1992
SQ FT: 75,000
SALES (est): 24.27MM
SALES (corp-wide): 1.56B **Publicly Held**
Web: www.rbcbearings.com
SIC: **5085** 3728 Bearings; Aircraft assemblies, subassemblies, and parts, nec
HQ: Roller Bearing Company Of America, Inc.
102 Willenbrock Rd
Oxford CT 06478
203 267-7001

**(P-16891)**
**REVCO INDUSTRIES INC (PA)**
Also Called: Black Stallion Industries
10747 Norwalk Blvd, Santa Fe Springs (90670-3823)
PHONE..............................562 777-1588
C Edward Chu, Ch Bd
Steve Hwang, *
Hong Brian Choi, *
Thomas Han, *
Jimmy Wu, *
◆ EMP: 28 EST: 1974
SQ FT: 24,000
SALES (est): 10.57MM
SALES (corp-wide): 10.57MM **Privately Held**
Web: www.revcoindustries.com
SIC: **5085** 5136 3842 Valves and fittings; Work clothing, men's and boys'; Personal safety equipment

**(P-16892)**
**SAN DIEGO SIGN COMPANY INC**
Also Called: Wholesale Displays
5960 Pascal Ct, Carlsbad (92008-8808)
PHONE..............................888 748-7446
Eric Steven Van Velzer, CEO
Vance Rodney Van Velzer, *
Eric Christopher Van Velzer, *
▲ EMP: 28 EST: 1963
SQ FT: 15,000
SALES (est): 9.69MM **Privately Held**
Web: www.sdsign.com
SIC: **5085** 3993 Signmaker equipment and supplies; Signs and advertising specialties

**(P-16893)**
**SAN JOAQUIN HYDRAULIC INC (PA)**
Also Called: North American Seal & Pkg Co
530 Van Ness Ave, Fresno (93721-2924)
PHONE..............................559 264-7325
Robert F Egan, Ch Bd
Lowell D Smith, Stockholder
▲ EMP: 15 EST: 1950
SQ FT: 40,000
SALES (est): 2.45MM
SALES (corp-wide): 2.45MM **Privately Held**
Web: www.centralsupply.com
SIC: **5085** 3053 5251 Industrial fittings; Gaskets; packing and sealing devices; Hardware stores

**(P-16894)**
**SAW DAILY SERVICE INC**
4481 Firestone Blvd, South Gate (90280-3320)
P.O. Box 3458 (92834-3458)
PHONE..............................323 564-1791
▲ EMP: 50
SIC: **5085** 7699 3546 Knives, industrial; Industrial machinery and equipment repair; Saws and sawing equipment

**(P-16895)**
**SEGUIN MREAU NAPA COPERAGE INC (PA)**
Also Called: Fine Northern Oak
151 Camino Dorado, Napa (94558-6213)
PHONE..............................707 252-3408
Magdeleine Allaume, CEO
Richard Kline, CFO
◆ EMP: 19 EST: 1992
SQ FT: 40,000
SALES (est): 10.65MM
SALES (corp-wide): 10.65MM **Privately Held**
Web: www.seguinmoreaunapa.com
SIC: **5085** 2449 Barrels, new or reconditioned; Barrels: wood, coopered

**(P-16896)**
**SHAR-CRAFT INC (PA)**
Also Called: Seal & Packing Supply
1103 33rd St, Bakersfield (93301-2121)
PHONE..............................661 324-4985
James L Craft, Pr
Chris Craft, VP
Sharon Craft, Sec
EMP: 22 EST: 1966
SQ FT: 14,000
SALES (est): 4.47MM
SALES (corp-wide): 4.47MM **Privately Held**
Web: www.sharcraftinc.com
SIC: **5085** 3599 3479 Packing, industrial; Machine shop, jobbing and repair; Coating of metals and formed products

**(P-16897)**
**STEWART SUPERIOR**
14487 Griffith St, San Leandro (94577-6701)
PHONE..............................510 346-9811
Jack Donnelly Junior, Pr
John Kuhr, VP
▲ EMP: 17 EST: 1885
SQ FT: 22,000
SALES (est): 3.75MM **Privately Held**
Web: www.stewartsuperior.com
SIC: **5085** 3953 Industrial supplies; Marking devices

**(P-16898)**
**SUNNYVALE FLUID SYS TECH INC (PA)**
Also Called: Swagelok Northern California
3393 W Warren Ave, Fremont (94538-6424)
PHONE..............................510 933-2500
Rod Fallow, CEO
EMP: 49 EST: 1956
SQ FT: 14,000
SALES (est): 22.56MM
SALES (corp-wide): 22.56MM **Privately Held**
Web: northerncal.swagelok.com
SIC: **5085** 3492 Valves and fittings; Fluid power valves and hose fittings

**(P-16899)**
**THALASINOS ENTERPRISES INC**
Also Called: T & T Enterprises
1220 Railroad St, Corona (92882-1837)
PHONE..............................951 340-0911
Brent Thalasinos, CEO
John Thalasinos, Ch Bd
Alison Siedler, VP
▲ EMP: 23 EST: 1993
SQ FT: 54,000
SALES (est): 8.83MM **Privately Held**
Web: www.ttenterprises.com
SIC: **5085** 3452 Fasteners, industrial: nuts, bolts, screws, etc.; Nuts, metal

**(P-16900)**
**TITAN NEWMAN INC (PA)**
Also Called: Newman Flange & Fitting Co
1649 L St, Newman (95360-1048)
P.O. Box 905 (95360-0905)
PHONE..............................209 862-2977
Samuel Liebelt, Pr
Helmut Liebelt, Treas
Penny Mello, BOARD
◆ EMP: 45 EST: 1974
SQ FT: 1,800
SALES (est): 5.72MM
SALES (corp-wide): 5.72MM **Privately Held**
Web: www.newmanflange.com
SIC: **5085** 3462 Valves and fittings; Aircraft forgings, ferrous

**(P-16901)**
**TONNAGE INDUSTRIAL LLC**
2130 W Cowles St, Long Beach (90813-1022)
PHONE..............................800 893-9681
EMP: 19 EST: 2018
SALES (est): 9.54MM **Privately Held**
Web: www.tonnageindustrial.com
SIC: **5085** 3312 5051 Industrial supplies; Bars and bar shapes, steel, hot-rolled; Structural shapes, iron or steel

**(P-16902)**
**TOOR KNIVES INC**
1488 Pioneer Way Ste 8, El Cajon (92020-1633)
PHONE..............................619 328-6118
Connor Alvin Toor, Pr
Saundra Wallace, Treas
Cameron Toor, Sec
EMP: 16 EST: 2016
SALES (est): 280K **Privately Held**
Web: www.toorknives.com
SIC: **5085** 3421 Knives, industrial; Knife blades and blanks

**(P-16903)**
**TRICO LEASING COMPANY LLC**
30154 Rhone Dr, Rancho Palos Verdes (90275-5736)
PHONE..............................877 259-9997
EMP: 52
SALES (corp-wide): 880.76K **Privately Held**
SIC: **5085** 3792 Commercial containers; Travel trailer chassis
PA: Trico Leasing Company, Llc
30154 Rhone Dr
877 259-9997

**(P-16904)**
**VALLEY RUBBER & GASKET COMPANY INC**
Also Called: Lewisgoetz -
10182 Croydon Way, Sacramento (95827-2102)

# 5085 - Industrial Supplies (P-16905)

PHONE..................916 369-8885
▲ EMP: 98
SIC: **5085** 3053 3052  Hose, belting, and packing; Gaskets; packing and sealing devices; Rubber and plastics hose and beltings

**(P-16905)**
**VAT INCORPORATED (DH)**
655 River Oaks Pkwy, San Jose (95134-1907)
PHONE..................800 935-1446
Andrew Witken, *Pr*
Robert Campbell, *Pr*
Simon Mansbridge, *Pr*
Brian J Darcy, *Treas*
▲ EMP: 20 EST: 1984
SALES (est): 24.58MM **Privately Held**
Web: www.vatvalve.com
SIC: **5085** 7699 3491  Valves and fittings; Valve repair, industrial; Industrial valves
HQ: Vat Holding Ag
Seelistrasse 1
Haag (Rheintal) SG 9469

**(P-16906)**
**WEST COAST AEROSPACE INC**
24224 Broad St, Carson (90745-6006)
PHONE..................310 518-0633
Ken Wagner, *Pr*
EMP: 18
SQ FT: 26,456
SALES (corp-wide): 9.77MM **Privately Held**
Web: www.westcoastaerospace.com
SIC: **5085** 3545 3541 3452  Fasteners, industrial: nuts, bolts, screws, etc.; Machine tool accessories; Machine tools, metal cutting type; Bolts, nuts, rivets, and washers
PA: West Coast Aerospace, Inc.
220 W E St
310 518-3167

**(P-16907)**
**WEST COAST PAPER COMPANY**
Also Called: Wcp Solutions
600 Sequoia Pacific Blvd, Sacramento (95811-0230)
PHONE..................916 599-1113
David Lewis, *Brnch Mgr*
EMP: 29
SALES (corp-wide): 337.75MM **Privately Held**
Web: www.wcpsolutions.com
SIC: **5085** 5169 5084 2677  Industrial supplies; Chemicals and allied products, nec; Packaging machinery and equipment; Envelopes
PA: West Coast Paper Company
6703 S 234th St Ste 120
253 850-1900

## 5087 Service Establishment Equipment

**(P-16908)**
**EXTENSIONS PLUS INC**
Also Called: Extensions Plus
5428 Reseda Blvd, Tarzana (91356-2606)
PHONE..................818 881-5611
Helene Stahl, *Pr*
EMP: 30 EST: 1994
SALES (est): 6.16MM **Privately Held**
Web: www.extensions-plus.com
SIC: **5087** 3999  Beauty parlor equipment and supplies; Hair and hair-based products

**(P-16909)**
**KAPLAN INDUS CAR WASH SUPS INC**
Also Called: Kaplan Industries Mfg
13875 Mica St, Santa Fe Springs (90670-5729)
PHONE..................562 921-5544
Everardo Llamas, *CEO*
Mert Ozkaya, *
EMP: 37 EST: 2006
SALES (est): 2.31MM **Privately Held**
SIC: **5087** 2841  Carwash equipment and supplies; Soap and other detergents

**(P-16910)**
**SWEIS INC (PA)**
20000 Mariner Ave, Torrance (90503-7140)
PHONE..................310 375-0558
Karl Sweis, *Pr*
Theresa Sweis, *
EMP: 70 EST: 2000
SALES (est): 23.12MM **Privately Held**
Web: www.sweisinc.com
SIC: **5087** 2844  Beauty parlor equipment and supplies; Hair preparations, including shampoos

**(P-16911)**
**WEST COAST BEAUTY SUPPLY CO**
5001 Industrial Way, Benicia (94510-1017)
PHONE..................707 748-4800
TOLL FREE: 800
▲ EMP: 1000
SIC: **5087** 3069  Beauty parlor equipment and supplies; Capes, vulcanized rubber or rubberized fabric

## 5088 Transportation Equipment And Supplies

**(P-16912)**
**AIR FRAME MFG & SUPPLY CO INC**
Also Called: Air Frame Mfg. & Supply Co.
26135 Technology Dr, Valencia (91355-1138)
PHONE..................661 257-7728
Yoshinobu Kawamura, *CEO*
Ray Wong, *
Howard Miyoshi, *
Yoshimi Sussan, *
▼ EMP: 35 EST: 1964
SQ FT: 30,000
SALES (est): 11.69MM **Privately Held**
Web: www.afmsupply.com
SIC: **5088** 3999 3728  Aircraft and parts, nec; Atomizers, toiletry; Accumulators, aircraft propeller

**(P-16913)**
**AIRCRAFT HARDWARE WEST**
Also Called: Ahw
2180 Temple Ave, Long Beach (90804-1020)
PHONE..................562 961-9324
Frank Ioffrida, *CEO*
Krista Wildermuth, *
▲ EMP: 30 EST: 2002
SQ FT: 15,000
SALES (est): 14.34MM **Privately Held**
Web: www.ahw-global.com
SIC: **5088** 3993 5072  Aircraft and parts, nec; Name plates: except engraved, etched, etc.: metal; Hardware

**(P-16914)**
**AM MACHINING INC**
Also Called: APV Manufacturing & Engrg Co
7422 Walnut Ave, Buena Park (90620-1762)
PHONE..................714 367-0830
Frank T Amador Junior, *Pr*
Jay Conlon, *Genl Mgr*
Stella Mermingez, *CFO*
EMP: 19 EST: 1993
SQ FT: 24,000
SALES (est): 5.57MM **Privately Held**
Web: www.apvmfg.com
SIC: **5088** 3541  Aeronautical equipment and supplies; Machine tool replacement & repair parts, metal cutting types

**(P-16915)**
**APICAL INDUSTRIES INC**
Also Called: Dart Aerospace
3030 Enterprise Ct Ste A, Vista (92081-8358)
PHONE..................760 724-5300
Alain Madore, *CEO*
EMP: 100 EST: 1995
SQ FT: 30,000
SALES (est): 21.75MM
SALES (corp-wide): 7.94B **Publicly Held**
Web: www.dartaerospace.com
SIC: **5088** 3728  Helicopter parts; Aircraft landing assemblies and brakes
HQ: Dart Aerospace Company
310-9900 Boul Cavendish
Saint-Laurent QC H4M 2
514 907-5959

**(P-16916)**
**BOEING STLLITE SYSTEMS INTL IN (HQ)**
Also Called: Boeing Company, The
2260 E Imperial Hwy, El Segundo (90245-3501)
P.O. Box 92919 (90009-2919)
PHONE..................310 364-4000
Randy Brinkley, *Pr*
Craig R Cooning, *
David Lillington, *
Danny Howard, *
▲ EMP: 40 EST: 1967
SALES (est): 106.54MM
SALES (corp-wide): 77.79B **Publicly Held**
Web: www.rvsatellite.com
SIC: **5088** 4899 3663  Aircraft and space vehicle supplies and parts; Satellite earth stations; Radio and t.v. communications equipment
PA: The Boeing Company
929 Long Bridge Dr
703 465-3500

**(P-16917)**
**COM DEV USA LLC**
2333 Utah Ave, El Segundo (90245-4818)
PHONE..................424 456-8000
EMP: 100
Web: www.comdev-usa.com
SIC: **5088** 3679  Aircraft equipment and supplies, nec; Microwave components

**(P-16918)**
**COMAV LLC (PA)**
18499 Phantom St Ste 17, Victorville (92394-7967)
PHONE..................760 523-5100
Craig Garrick, *Pr*
Jon Day, *CFO*
EMP: 47 EST: 2012
SQ FT: 58,732
SALES (est): 43.18MM
SALES (corp-wide): 43.18MM **Privately Held**
Web: www.comav.com
SIC: **5088** 4581 3599  Aircraft and parts, nec; Aircraft maintenance and repair services; Machine and other job shop work

**(P-16919)**
**DESSER TIRE & RUBBER CO LLC**
Also Called: Cee Baileys Aircraft Plastics
6900 W Acco St, Montebello (90640-5435)
PHONE..................323 837-1497
Brian Elliott, *Contrlr*
EMP: 30
SALES (corp-wide): 860.49MM **Publicly Held**
Web: www.vansaircrafttires.com
SIC: **5088** 3728  Aircraft and space vehicle supplies and parts; Aircraft parts and equipment, nec
HQ: Desser Tire & Rubber Co., Llc
6900 W Acco St
Montebello CA 90640
323 721-4900

**(P-16920)**
**ITOCHU AVIATION INC (DH)**
222 N Pacific Coast Hwy Ste 2200, El Segundo (90245-5629)
P.O. Box 997 (90245-0997)
PHONE..................310 640-2770
Naoya Osaki, *CEO*
Takehiko Yamada, *
▲ EMP: 25 EST: 1973
SALES (est): 43.62MM **Privately Held**
SIC: **5088** 3728  Aircraft and parts, nec; Aircraft parts and equipment, nec
HQ: Itochu International Inc.
1251 Ave Of The Amrcas Fl
New York NY 10020
212 818-8000

**(P-16921)**
**ONTIC ENGINEERING AND MFG INC (PA)**
20400 Plummer St, Chatsworth (91311-5372)
P.O. Box 2424 (91313)
PHONE..................818 678-6555
Gareth Hall, *CEO*
Peg Billson, *
Toby Richard Woolrych, *
Susan Coates Kroll, *
EMP: 95 EST: 1986
SQ FT: 54,000
SALES (est): 480.55MM
SALES (corp-wide): 480.55MM **Privately Held**
Web: www.ontic.com
SIC: **5088** 3728 3812 3563  Aircraft equipment and supplies, nec; Aircraft parts and equipment, nec; Search and navigation equipment; Air and gas compressors

**(P-16922)**
**PNI SENSOR CORPORATION**
2331 Circadian Way, Santa Rosa (95407-5437)
PHONE..................707 566-2260
◆ EMP: 23
Web: www.pnicorp.com
SIC: **5088** 3812  Navigation equipment and supplies; Compasses and accessories

**(P-16923)**
**PROPONENT INC (PA)**
Also Called: Proponent
3120 Enterprise St, Brea (92821-6236)
PHONE..................714 223-5400
Andrew Todhunter, *Pr*
Steven Frields, *

## PRODUCTS & SERVICES SECTION
### 5092 - Toys And Hobby Goods And Supplies (P-16942)

Corey Yarnell, *
▲ **EMP:** 175 **EST:** 1972
**SALES (est):** 127.06MM
**SALES (corp-wide):** 127.06MM **Privately Held**
**Web:** www.proponent.com
**SIC: 5088** 3728 Aircraft and parts, nec; Aircraft parts and equipment, nec

**(P-16924)**
### REGENT AEROSPACE CORPORATION (PA)
Also Called: Regent
28110 Harrison Pkwy, Valencia (91355-4109)
**PHONE**................................661 257-3000
Reza Soltanianzadeh, *CEO*
Reza Soltanian, *
Tim Garvin, *
▲ **EMP:** 200 **EST:** 1993
**SQ FT:** 90,000
**SALES (est):** 95.2MM **Privately Held**
**Web:** www.regentaerospace.com
**SIC: 5088** 3728 Aircraft and parts, nec; Aircraft parts and equipment, nec

**(P-16925)**
### STRECH PLASTICS INCORPORATED
900 John St Ste J, Banning (92220-6204)
**PHONE**................................951 922-2224
James M Strech, *CEO*
▲ **EMP:** 50 **EST:** 1974
**SQ FT:** 52,000
**SALES (est):** 10.21MM **Privately Held**
**Web:** www.strechplastics.com
**SIC: 5088** 3949 Golf carts; Sporting and athletic goods, nec

**(P-16926)**
### SUNDANCE CUSTOM GOLF CARTS INC
Also Called: Sundance Custom Golf Carts
1240 Vernon Way, El Cajon (92020-1839)
**PHONE**................................619 449-0822
Michael Matheny, *CEO*
**EMP:** 19 **EST:** 2010
**SALES (est):** 2.51MM **Privately Held**
**Web:** www.sundancegolfcars.com
**SIC: 5088** 3799 Golf carts; Golf carts, powered

**(P-16927)**
### SVENDSENS BOAT WORKS INC
Also Called: Svendsen Marine Distributing
2900 Main St Ste 1900, Alameda (94501-7265)
**PHONE**................................510 522-2886
▲ **EMP:** 70 **EST:** 1963
**SALES (est):** 9.32MM
**SALES (corp-wide):** 9.32MM **Privately Held**
**Web:** www.svendsens.com
**SIC: 5088** 5551 3732 Marine supplies; Marine supplies, nec; Sailboats, building and repairing
**PA:** Bay Maritime Corp
    2900 Main Street 2100
    510 337-9122

**(P-16928)**
### TELEDYNE RESON INC
5212 Verdugo Way, Camarillo (93012-8662)
**PHONE**................................805 964-6260
Robert Mehrabian, *CEO*
**EMP:** 33 **EST:** 1985
**SALES (est):** 5.4MM
**SALES (corp-wide):** 5.64B **Publicly Held**
**Web:** www.teledynemarine.com
**SIC: 5088** 3812 Navigation equipment and supplies; Sonar systems and equipment
**PA:** Teledyne Technologies Inc
    1049 Camino Dos Rios
    805 373-4545

**(P-16929)**
### THORNTON TECHNOLOGY CORP
Also Called: Thornton Technologies
2608 Temple Heights Dr, Oceanside (92056-3512)
**PHONE**................................760 471-9969
William S Thornton, *Prin*
**EMP:** 23
**SALES (corp-wide):** 4.59MM **Privately Held**
**Web:** www.thorntontech.com
**SIC: 5088** 4581 3812 Aircraft equipment and supplies, nec; Aircraft cleaning and janitorial service; Search and navigation equipment
**PA:** Thornton Technology Corp
    5410 Us Highway 2 W
    406 257-7223

**(P-16930)**
### UNITED AERONAUTICAL CORP
7360 Laurel Canyon Blvd, North Hollywood (91605-3710)
P.O. Box 7102 (91615-0102)
**PHONE**................................818 764-2102
Lawrence P Holt, *CEO*
Bradford T Beck, *
◆ **EMP:** 32 **EST:** 1988
**SQ FT:** 200,000
**SALES (est):** 14MM **Privately Held**
**Web:** www.unitedaero.com
**SIC: 5088** 3812 Aeronautical equipment and supplies; Search and navigation equipment

**(P-16931)**
### WILLIAMS AEROSPACE & MFG INC (DH)
999 Avenida Acaso, Camarillo (93012-8700)
**PHONE**................................805 586-8699
Greg Beason, *CEO*
Richard Drinkward, *
▲ **EMP:** 23 **EST:** 1982
**SQ FT:** 9,910
**SALES (est):** 9.03MM
**SALES (corp-wide):** 156.2MM **Privately Held**
**Web:** www.goallclear.com
**SIC: 5088** 3728 3724 Aircraft equipment and supplies, nec; Aircraft parts and equipment, nec; Aircraft engines and engine parts
**HQ:** Allclear Aerospace & Defense, Inc.
    15501 Sw 29th St Ste 101
    Miramar FL 33027
    954 239-7844

## 5091 Sporting And Recreation Goods

**(P-16932)**
### AQUA PERFORMANCE INC
Also Called: A.J. Metal Manufacturing
425 N Smith Ave, Corona (92880)
P.O. Box 370 (92878-0370)
**PHONE**................................951 340-2056
Sue Curi, *VP*
**EMP:** 34 **EST:** 1990
**SQ FT:** 20,000
**SALES (est):** 4.1MM **Privately Held**
**Web:** www.aquaperformance.com

**SIC: 5091** 3339 3444 Watersports equipment and supplies; Primary nonferrous metals, nec; Sheet metalwork

**(P-16933)**
### BODYKORE INC
7466 Orangewood Ave, Garden Grove (92841-1413)
**PHONE**................................949 325-3088
Leo Chang, *CEO*
**EMP:** 30 **EST:** 2020
**SALES (est):** 1MM **Privately Held**
**Web:** www.bodykore.com
**SIC: 5091** 5961 3949 5941 Fitness equipment and supplies; Fitness and sporting goods, mail order; Sporting and athletic goods, nec; Sporting goods and bicycle shops

**(P-16934)**
### EASTON BASEBALL / SOFTBALL INC
3500 Willow Ln, Thousand Oaks (91361-4921)
**PHONE**................................800 632-7866
Maria Easton, *Prin*
▲ **EMP:** 17 **EST:** 2014
**SALES (est):** 655.24K **Privately Held**
**Web:** easton.rawlings.com
**SIC: 5091** 3949 Sporting and recreation goods; Sporting and athletic goods, nec

**(P-16935)**
### FULL-SWING GOLF INC
1905 Aston Ave Ste 100, Carlsbad (92008-7393)
**PHONE**................................858 675-1100
▲ **EMP:** 30 **EST:** 1986
**SALES (est):** 51.31MM **Privately Held**
**Web:** www.fullswinggolf.com
**SIC: 5091** 3949 Golf equipment; Golf equipment

**(P-16936)**
### INTEX PROPERTIES S BAY CORP (PA)
4001 Via Oro Ave Ste 210, Long Beach (90810-1400)
**PHONE**................................310 549-5400
Tien P Zee, *Pr*
◆ **EMP:** 96 **EST:** 1970
**SQ FT:** 80,000
**SALES (est):** 91.03MM
**SALES (corp-wide):** 91.03MM **Privately Held**
**Web:** www.intexcorp.com
**SIC: 5091** 5092 5021 3081 Watersports equipment and supplies; Toys, nec; Waterbeds; Vinyl film and sheet

**(P-16937)**
### KAL-KUSTOM ENTERPRISES (PA)
43289 Osgood Rd, Fremont (94539-5657)
P.O. Box 1155 (94505-7155)
**PHONE**................................510 651-8400
Karl Koster, *Pr*
Jane Kiffel, *Sec*
**EMP:** 15 **EST:** 1964
**SQ FT:** 14,000
**SALES (est):** 9.94MM
**SALES (corp-wide):** 9.94MM **Privately Held**
**SIC: 5091** 3732 5012 Motorboats; Motorboats, inboard or outboard: building and repairing; Trailers for passenger vehicles

**(P-16938)**
### MARIN MOUNTAIN BIKES (PA)
1450 Technology Ln Ste 100, Petaluma (94954-6979)
**PHONE**................................415 382-6000
Robert F Buckley, *Ch Bd*
▲ **EMP:** 18 **EST:** 1986
**SQ FT:** 18,000
**SALES (est):** 8.28MM
**SALES (corp-wide):** 8.28MM **Privately Held**
**Web:** www.marinbikes.com
**SIC: 5091** 3751 Bicycles; Bicycles and related parts

**(P-16939)**
### POOL WATER PRODUCTS INC (PA)
17872 Mitchell N Ste 250, Irvine (92614-6004)
P.O. Box 17359 (92623-7359)
**PHONE**................................949 756-1666
Dean C Allred, *Pr*
Zelma Mabel Allred, *Ch Bd*
◆ **EMP:** 15 **EST:** 1964
**SQ FT:** 12,000
**SALES (est):** 116.42MM
**SALES (corp-wide):** 116.42MM **Privately Held**
**Web:** www.poolwaterproducts.com
**SIC: 5091** 2899 2812 Swimming pools, equipment and supplies; Chemical preparations, nec; Alkalies and chlorine

**(P-16940)**
### SUNWEST INDUSTRIES INC
Also Called: All-Safe Pool Fence & Covers
648 N Eckhoff St, Orange (92868-1004)
**PHONE**................................714 712-6233
Reed Hauge, *Pr*
Marsh Hauge, *Pr*
Helen Hauge, *Treas*
Reed Hauge, *Sec*
▲ **EMP:** 22 **EST:** 1992
**SQ FT:** 20,000
**SALES (est):** 2.06MM **Privately Held**
**Web:** www.allsafepool.com
**SIC: 5091** 1799 3446 5099 Swimming pools, equipment and supplies; Fence construction ; Fences, gates, posts, and flagpoles; Safety equipment and supplies

**(P-16941)**
### TEA FINANCIAL SERVICES
Also Called: Inland Sports Group
32100 Menifee Rd, Menifee (92584-9015)
**PHONE**................................951 301-8884
**EMP:** 20
**SIC: 5091** 2759 Sporting and recreation goods; Letterpress and screen printing

## 5092 Toys And Hobby Goods And Supplies

**(P-16942)**
### ANATEX ENTERPRISES INC
Also Called: Anatex
15911 Arminta St, Van Nuys (91406-1807)
**PHONE**................................818 908-1888
Fleur Chesler, *Pr*
Mark Chesler, *
▲ **EMP:** 25 **EST:** 1982
**SALES (est):** 1.52MM **Privately Held**
**Web:** www.anatex.com
**SIC: 5092** 3944 Toys, nec; Games, toys, and children's vehicles

# 5092 - Toys And Hobby Goods And Supplies (P-16943)

**(P-16943)**
**BANZAI**
2229 Barry Ave, Los Angeles (90064-1401)
PHONE..................................310 231-7292
Brian Dubinsky, *CEO*
**EMP:** 15 **EST:** 2005
**SALES (est):** 398.23K **Privately Held**
**SIC:** 5092 3949 Toys, nec; Water sports equipment

**(P-16944)**
**BIG TREE SALES INC**
11715 Clark St, Arcadia (91006)
PHONE..................................626 672-0048
Haibo Zheng, *Pr*
**EMP:** 15 **EST:** 2015
**SALES (est):** 1.01MM **Privately Held**
Web: www.bigtree-sales.com
**SIC:** 5092 3949 5199 Toys and games; Bags, rosin; Gifts and novelties

**(P-16945)**
**CAPCOM U S A INC (HQ)**
185 Berry St Ste 4800, San Francisco (94107-1726)
PHONE..................................650 350-6500
Koko Ishikawa, *Pr*
Rob Dyer, *
▲ **EMP:** 180 **EST:** 1985
**SALES (est):** 22.37MM **Privately Held**
Web: www.capcomusa.com
**SIC:** 5092 7993 7372 Video games; Arcades ; Prepackaged software
**PA:** Capcom Co., Ltd.
3-1-3, Uchihiranomachi, Chuo-Ku

**(P-16946)**
**CBB GROUP INC**
Also Called: Cbb Group
2747 S Malt Ave, Commerce (90040-3207)
PHONE..................................323 888-2800
◆ **EMP:** 16 **EST:** 1992
**SALES (est):** 2.46MM **Privately Held**
Web: www.cbbgroup.com
**SIC:** 5092 5099 3999 Toys and games; Brass goods; Atomizers, toiletry

**(P-16947)**
**CREATIVE BABY INC**
2222 Lee Ave, South El Monte (91733-2500)
PHONE..................................626 330-2289
Charles P C Hsieh, *CEO*
Bruce Hsieh, *VP*
Nancy Hsieh, *Sec*
Andy Hsieh, *Treas*
◆ **EMP:** 20 **EST:** 2013
**SALES (est):** 2.81MM **Privately Held**
Web: www.creativebabyinc.com
**SIC:** 5092 3999 Toys and hobby goods and supplies; Models, except toy

**(P-16948)**
**DESIGN INTERNATIONAL GROUP INC**
755 Epperson Dr, City Of Industry (91748-1335)
PHONE..................................626 369-2289
William Yeh, *Pr*
Julie Hwang, *
◆ **EMP:** 25 **EST:** 2003
**SALES (est):** 8.67MM **Privately Held**
Web: www.luckydig.com
**SIC:** 5092 5947 2678 Toys and hobby goods and supplies; Gifts and novelties; Stationery products

**(P-16949)**
**ME & MY BIG IDEAS LLC**
Also Called: Happy Planner, The
6261 Katella Ave Ste 150, Cypress (90630-5249)
PHONE..................................240 348-5240
Tom Shaw, *CEO*
Stephanie Rahmatulla, *
▲ **EMP:** 101 **EST:** 1998
**SALES (est):** 10.66MM **Privately Held**
Web: www.thehappyplanner.com
**SIC:** 5092 2678 Arts and crafts equipment and supplies; Notebooks: made from purchased paper

**(P-16950)**
**SEGA OF AMERICA INC (DH)**
140 Progress Ste 100, Irvine (92618-0338)
PHONE..................................949 788-0455
Shuji Utsumi, *CEO*
Mitsuhiro Tanaka, *
Jeffrey Shieh, *
▲ **EMP:** 45 **EST:** 1985
**SALES (est):** 44.58MM **Privately Held**
Web: www.sega.com
**SIC:** 5092 3999 Video games; Coin-operated amusement machines
**HQ:** Sega Corporation
1-1-1, Nishishinagawa
Shinagawa-Ku TKY 141-0

**(P-16951)**
**SMC PRODUCTS INC**
Also Called: Hpi Racing
22651 Lambert St Ste 105, Lake Forest (92630-1611)
PHONE..................................949 753-1099
▲ **EMP:** 68
**SIC:** 5092 3944 Toys and hobby goods and supplies; Electronic toys

**(P-16952)**
**ULTRA PRO INTERNATIONAL LLC**
Also Called: Jolly Roger Games
6049 E Slauson Ave, Commerce (90040-3007)
PHONE..................................323 890-2100
Sheldon Rosenberg, *Managing Member*
Marc Lieberman, *
Herman Lee, *
▲ **EMP:** 122 **EST:** 2011
**SALES (est):** 44.78MM **Privately Held**
Web: www.ultrapro.com
**SIC:** 5092 3944 Toys and hobby goods and supplies; Games, toys, and children's vehicles

**(P-16953)**
**VICTORY INTL GROUP LLC**
Also Called: M Z J
14748 Pipeline Ave Ste B, Chino Hills (91709-6024)
PHONE..................................949 407-5888
Dawson Fan, *Pr*
▲ **EMP:** 230 **EST:** 2001
**SQ FT:** 4,960
**SALES (est):** 896MM **Privately Held**
Web: www.victoryintlgroup.com
**SIC:** 5092 3843 2389 3842 Toys and hobby goods and supplies; Dental equipment and supplies; Hospital gowns; Respiratory protection equipment, personal

**(P-16954)**
**WHAM-O INC**
6301 Owensmouth Ave Ste 700, Woodland Hills (91367-2265)
PHONE..................................818 963-4200
Raylin Hsieh, *CEO*
Jeff Hsieh, *
Blake Wong, *
◆ **EMP:** 59 **EST:** 1997
**SALES (est):** 1.45MM **Privately Held**
Web: www.wham-o.com
**SIC:** 5092 5091 3944 3949 Toys and games; Surfing equipment and supplies; Toy trains, airplanes, and automobiles; Sporting and athletic goods, nec

## 5093 Scrap And Waste Materials

**(P-16955)**
**75S CORP**
Also Called: FMC Metals
800 E 62nd St, Los Angeles (90001-1506)
PHONE..................................323 234-7708
Kevin Armstrong, *CEO*
Octavio Cabrerra, *OK Vice President*
◆ **EMP:** 42 **EST:** 1959
**SALES (est):** 9.79MM **Privately Held**
Web: www.fmcmet.com
**SIC:** 5093 3341 Nonferrous metals scrap; Recovery and refining of nonferrous metals

**(P-16956)**
**ATLAS PACIFIC CORPORATION (PA)**
2803 Industrial Dr, Bloomington (92316-3249)
P.O. Box 726 (92324-0726)
PHONE..................................909 421-1200
Gregory Woolfson, *Pr*
▼ **EMP:** 25 **EST:** 1980
**SQ FT:** 10,000
**SALES (est):** 4.4MM
**SALES (corp-wide):** 4.4MM **Privately Held**
Web: www.atlaspacific.net
**SIC:** 5093 3341 3339 Nonferrous metals scrap; Brass smelting and refining (secondary); Zinc refining (primary), including slabs & dust

**(P-16957)**
**B & B PLASTICS RECYCLERS INC (PA)**
3040 N Locust Ave, Rialto (92377-3706)
PHONE..................................909 829-3606
Baltasar Mejia, *Pr*
Bacilio Mejia, *
**EMP:** 46 **EST:** 1998
**SQ FT:** 100,000
**SALES (est):** 7.67MM
**SALES (corp-wide):** 7.67MM **Privately Held**
Web: www.bbplasticsinc.com
**SIC:** 5093 2673 Plastics scrap; Bags: plastic, laminated, and coated

**(P-16958)**
**CEDARWOOD-YOUNG COMPANY**
Also Called: Allan Company
14618 Arrow Hwy, Baldwin Park (91706-1733)
PHONE..................................626 962-4047
Brett Weigand, *Brnch Mgr*
**EMP:** 55
**SQ FT:** 10,664
**SALES (corp-wide):** 252.16MM **Privately Held**
Web: www.allancompany.com
**SIC:** 5093 2611 Waste paper; Pulp mills
**PA:** Cedarwood-Young Company
14620 Joanbridge St
626 962-4047

**(P-16959)**
**GLOBAL PLASTICS INC**
145 Malbert St, Perris (92570-8624)
PHONE..................................951 657-5466
Nadim Salim Bahou, *Pr*
Patti Gilmour, *
▲ **EMP:** 120 **EST:** 1996
**SQ FT:** 55,000
**SALES (est):** 24.21MM **Privately Held**
Web: www.globalpetinc.com
**SIC:** 5093 4953 3053 Plastics scrap; Recycling, waste materials; Packing materials

**(P-16960)**
**GREENPATH RECOVERY WEST INC**
Also Called: Greenpath Recovery Recycl Svcs
330 W Citrus St Ste 250, Colton (92324-1422)
PHONE..................................909 954-0686
Joe Castro, *Pr*
**EMP:** 60 **EST:** 2012
**SQ FT:** 90,000
**SALES (est):** 4.38MM **Privately Held**
Web: www.greenpathrecovery.com
**SIC:** 5093 3089 2821 Scrap and waste materials; Plastics processing; Plastics materials and resins

**(P-16961)**
**PACIFIC STEEL INC**
1700 Cleveland Ave, National City (91950-4215)
PHONE..................................619 477-3925
Fernando Solorzano, *Pr*
**EMP:** 20 **EST:** 1981
**SQ FT:** 10,000
**SALES (est):** 5.88MM **Privately Held**
**SIC:** 5093 3317 Ferrous metal scrap and waste; Steel pipe and tubes
**HQ:** Compania Siderurgica De Guadalajara, S.A. De C.V.
Calz. Lazaro Cardenas No. 601
Guadalajara JAL 44470

**(P-16962)**
**SIMS GROUP USA CORPORATION**
Also Called: Sims/LMC Recyclers
1900 Monterey Hwy, San Jose (95112-6100)
PHONE..................................408 494-4242
Tom Sorci, *Mgr*
**EMP:** 20
Web: www.simsmm.com
**SIC:** 5093 4953 3231 Ferrous metal scrap and waste; Refuse systems; Products of purchased glass
**HQ:** Sims Group Usa Corporation
600 South 4th St
Richmond CA 94804
510 412-5300

**(P-16963)**
**STRATEGIC MATERIALS INC**
Container Recycl Aliance Div
3211 E 26th St, Vernon (90058-8007)
PHONE..................................323 415-0166
Dennis Hinson, *Brnch Mgr*
**EMP:** 19
**SALES (corp-wide):** 2.21B **Privately Held**
Web: www.smi.com
**SIC:** 5093 3231 Metal scrap and waste materials; Products of purchased glass
**HQ:** Strategic Materials, Inc.
17220 Katy Fwy Ste 150
Houston TX 77094

## PRODUCTS & SERVICES SECTION

**5099 - Durable Goods, Nec (P-16984)**

**(P-16964)**
**TST INC**
Standards Metals
2132 E Dominguez St, Long Beach (90810-1022)
PHONE...................310 835-0115
Andrew G Stein, CEO
**EMP:** 28
**SALES (corp-wide):** 53.72MM **Privately Held**
Web: www.tst-inc.com
**SIC:** 5093 3354 Metal scrap and waste materials; Aluminum extruded products
PA: Tst, Inc.
  13428 Benson Ave
  951 685-2155

**(P-16965)**
**TZENG LONG USA INC (PA)**
Also Called: Reynolds Paper Mill
2801 Vail Ave, Commerce (90040-2613)
PHONE...................323 722-5353
Bill Chang, Pr
Justine Chang, Sec
Jung Huai Chang, CEO
◆ **EMP:** 20 **EST:** 1982
**SQ FT:** 36,700
**SALES (est):** 12.91MM
**SALES (corp-wide):** 12.91MM **Privately Held**
Web: www.tzenglong.com
**SIC:** 5093 3565 Boxes, waste; Carton packing machines

---

### 5094 Jewelry And Precious Stones

**(P-16966)**
**C&C JEWELRY MFG INC**
323 W 8th St Fl 4, Los Angeles (90014-3109)
PHONE...................213 623-6800
Mikhail Chekhman, Pr
Robert Connolly, *
Dmitriy Moskalenko Ctrl, Prin
▲ **EMP:** 75 **EST:** 2001
**SQ FT:** 3,000
**SALES (est):** 28.36MM **Privately Held**
**SIC:** 5094 3915 Jewelry; Jewel preparing: instruments, tools, watches, and jewelry

**(P-16967)**
**GOLDEN STATE IMPORTS INTL INC (PA)**
Also Called: G S I
1101 Marina Village Pkwy Ste 201, Alameda (94501-6472)
P.O. Box 31088 (94604-7088)
PHONE...................510 995-1320
Jane Lai, Ch Bd
Jimmy Lai, Pr
Iling Chiang, Contrlr
▲ **EMP:** 19 **EST:** 1974
**SALES (est):** 2.26MM
**SALES (corp-wide):** 2.26MM **Privately Held**
**SIC:** 5094 2034 Clocks, watches, and parts; Dried and dehydrated fruits, vegetables and soup mixes

**(P-16968)**
**INDUSTRIAL STRENGTH CORP**
6115 Corte Del Cedro, Carlsbad (92011-1516)
PHONE...................760 795-1068
Jeffry D Lorenz, Pr
**EMP:** 17 **EST:** 1995
**SALES (est):** 3.75MM **Privately Held**
Web: www.isbodyjewelry.com
**SIC:** 5094 3961 3911 Jewelry; Costume jewelry; Jewelry, precious metal

**(P-16969)**
**MAURICE KRAIEM & COMPANY**
Also Called: Mk Luxury Group
228 S Beverly Dr, Beverly Hills (90212-3805)
PHONE...................213 629-0038
Moshe Kraiem, CEO
▲ **EMP:** 24 **EST:** 1978
**SALES (est):** 4.78MM **Privately Held**
Web: www.mkdiamonds.com
**SIC:** 5094 3911 Jewelry; Jewelry, precious metal

**(P-16970)**
**SIMON G JEWELRY INC**
Also Called: Zeghani
528 State St, Glendale (91203-1524)
PHONE...................818 500-8595
Zaven Ghanimian, CEO
Simon Ghanimian, *
Hratch Shahbazian, *
▲ **EMP:** 48 **EST:** 1994
**SQ FT:** 10,000
**SALES (est):** 9.85MM **Privately Held**
Web: www.simongjewelry.com
**SIC:** 5094 3911 Jewelry; Jewelry, precious metal

**(P-16971)**
**SIMON GOLUB & SONS INC (DH)**
Also Called: Lorenzo USA
514 Via De La Valle Ste 210, Solana Beach (92075-2717)
▲ **EMP:** 90 **EST:** 1923
**SQ FT:** 40,000
**SALES (est):** 4.37MM **Privately Held**
Web: www.portlandjewelrysupplies.com
**SIC:** 5094 3911 Jewelry; Jewelry, precious metal
HQ: Astral Holdings Inc
  5506 6th Ave S
  Seattle WA 98108

---

### 5099 Durable Goods, Nec

**(P-16972)**
**ACME SAFETY & SUPPLY CORP (PA)**
11478 Woodside Ave N, Santee (92071-4727)
PHONE...................619 299-5100
Candace Freidman, Pr
**EMP:** 15 **EST:** 1999
**SALES (est):** 4.8MM
**SALES (corp-wide):** 4.8MM **Privately Held**
Web: www.acmesafetysupply.com
**SIC:** 5099 3993 Safety equipment and supplies; Signs and advertising specialties

**(P-16973)**
**BURGETT INCORPORATED (PA)**
Also Called: Piano Disc
4111a N Freeway Blvd, Sacramento (95834-1209)
PHONE...................916 567-9999
Gary Burgett, CEO
Kirk Burgett, *
▲ **EMP:** 69 **EST:** 1977
**SQ FT:** 48,000
**SALES (est):** 5.01MM
**SALES (corp-wide):** 5.01MM **Privately Held**
Web: www.pianodiscremote.com
**SIC:** 5099 3429 3931 3651 Pianos; Piano hardware; Musical instruments; Household audio and video equipment

**(P-16974)**
**DENNIS FOLAND INC (PA)**
Also Called: Logo Expressions
1500 S Hellman Ave, Ontario (91761-7634)
P.O. Box 4591 (91761-0822)
PHONE...................909 930-9900
Dennis Foland, CEO
Beverly Foland, *
▲ **EMP:** 50 **EST:** 1979
**SQ FT:** 140,000
**SALES (est):** 23.66MM
**SALES (corp-wide):** 23.66MM **Privately Held**
Web: www.folandgroup.com
**SIC:** 5099 3944 Souvenirs; Games, toys, and children's vehicles

**(P-16975)**
**EASTMAN MUSIC COMPANY (PA)**
Also Called: Eastmans Guitars
2158 Pomona Blvd, Pomona (91768-3332)
PHONE...................909 868-1777
Saul Friedgood, CEO
Saul Friedgood, Pr
Qian Ni, *
▲ **EMP:** 40 **EST:** 2001
**SALES (est):** 24.14MM
**SALES (corp-wide):** 24.14MM **Privately Held**
Web: www.eastmanstrings.com
**SIC:** 5099 3931 Musical instruments; Accordions and parts

**(P-16976)**
**FT 2 INC**
1211 N Miller St, Anaheim (92806-1933)
PHONE...................714 765-5555
◆ **EMP:** 170
**SIC:** 5099 2393 3161 Carrying cases; Textile bags; Luggage

**(P-16977)**
**GENIUS PRODUCTS INC**
3301 Exposition Blvd Ste 100, Santa Monica (90404-5045)
PHONE...................310 453-1222
Trevor Drinkwater, Pr
Stephen K Bannon, *
Edward J Byrnes, *
▲ **EMP:** 222 **EST:** 2005
**SQ FT:** 40,520
**SALES (est):** 5.61MM **Privately Held**
Web: www.geniusproducts.com
**SIC:** 5099 3652 7819 Video and audio equipment; Prerecorded records and tapes; Video tape or disk reproduction

**(P-16978)**
**H2W**
Also Called: Iced Out Gear
7660 Alabama Ave, Canoga Park (91304-4902)
PHONE...................800 578-3088
Dan Gershon, CEO
Eric Liberman, Sec
David Levich, CFO
▲ **EMP:** 22 **EST:** 2002
**SQ FT:** 8,000
**SALES (est):** 9.69MM **Privately Held**
Web: www.noveltysunglasses.com
**SIC:** 5099 3052 Sunglasses; Air line or air brake hose, rubber or rubberized fabric

**(P-16979)**
**MADACO SAFETY PRODUCTS INC**
1313 N Grand Ave 249, Walnut (91789-1317)
PHONE...................909 614-1756
Frank Hsu, Pr
▲ **EMP:** 15 **EST:** 1997
**SQ FT:** 2,000
**SALES (est):** 656.2K **Privately Held**
Web: www.madaco.com
**SIC:** 5099 3841 Safety equipment and supplies; Surgical and medical instruments

**(P-16980)**
**MERIDIAN MOULDING INC**
330 Cessna Cir, Corona (92878-5009)
PHONE...................951 279-5220
George Noor, CEO
Mary Jo Elkareh, Sec
Najil Azzi, CFO
▲ **EMP:** 15 **EST:** 2001
**SQ FT:** 34,000
**SALES (est):** 2MM **Privately Held**
**SIC:** 5099 3089 Wood and wood by-products; Prefabricated plastics buildings

**(P-16981)**
**MIZARI ENTERPRISES INC (PA)**
5455 Wilshire Blvd Ste 1410, Los Angeles (90036-4201)
PHONE...................323 549-9400
Alon Mizrahi, CEO
**EMP:** 20 **EST:** 1997
**SQ FT:** 2,000
**SALES (est):** 1.96MM **Privately Held**
Web: www.mizari.com
**SIC:** 5099 3639 Video and audio equipment; Major kitchen appliances, except refrigerators and stoves

**(P-16982)**
**MONSTER INC (PA)**
Also Called: Monster Products
601 Gateway Blvd Ste 900, South San Francisco (94080)
P.O. Box 435 (94005)
PHONE...................415 840-2000
Noel Lee, Pr
Irene Baron, *
◆ **EMP:** 330 **EST:** 1978
**SQ FT:** 50,000
**SALES (est):** 26.91MM
**SALES (corp-wide):** 26.91MM **Privately Held**
Web: www.monsterstore.com
**SIC:** 5099 4841 3679 Video and audio equipment; Cable and other pay television services; Headphones, radio

**(P-16983)**
**OLIVET INTERNATIONAL INC (PA)**
11015 Hopkins St, Mira Loma (91752-3248)
PHONE...................951 681-8888
Sean Lin, Managing Member
Lydia Hsu, *
David Yu, *
Pei Te Lin, *
▲ **EMP:** 89 **EST:** 1984
**SQ FT:** 456,000
**SALES (est):** 172.9MM
**SALES (corp-wide):** 172.9MM **Privately Held**
Web: www.olivetintl.com
**SIC:** 5099 3161 Luggage; Luggage

**(P-16984)**
**PEL WHOLESALE INC**
Also Called: Jpc Wholesale
6818 Patterson Pass Rd # H, Livermore (94550-4230)
PHONE...................925 373-3628
Cindy Trinh, Managing Member
**EMP:** 20 **EST:** 2003

## 5099 - Durable Goods, Nec (P-16985)

SALES (est): 854.13K **Privately Held**
SIC: **5099** 3999 Durable goods, nec; Pet supplies

*(P-16985)*
### RGGD INC (PA)
Also Called: Crystal Art Gallery
4950 S Santa Fe Ave, Vernon (90058-2106)
PHONE..................323 581-6617
Randy Greenberg, *CEO*
Douglas Song, *
◆ **EMP:** 45 **EST:** 1994
**SQ FT:** 120,000
**SALES (est):** 23.59MM
**SALES (corp-wide):** 23.59MM **Privately Held**
Web: www.crystalartgallery.com
SIC: **5099** 3441 Wood and wood by-products ; Fabricated structural metal

*(P-16986)*
### ROLAND CORPORATION US (HQ)
5100 S Eastern Ave, Los Angeles (90040-2950)
P.O. Box 910921 (90091-0921)
PHONE..................323 890-3700
Christopher Bristol, *CEO*
Dennis M Houlihan, *
Mark S Malbon, *
Charles L Wright, *
Junpei Yamato, *
◆ **EMP:** 165 **EST:** 1953
**SQ FT:** 50,000
**SALES (est):** 49.39MM **Privately Held**
Web: www.roland.com
SIC: **5099** 5045 3931 Musical instruments; Computer peripheral equipment; Organs, all types: pipe, reed, hand, electronic, etc.
PA: Roland Corporation
2036-1, Hosoechonakagawa, Hamana-Ku

*(P-16987)*
### ROSEN ELECTRONICS LLC
Also Called: Rosen Electronics
2500 E Francis St, Ontario (91761-7730)
PHONE..................951 898-9808
W Thomas Clements, *Pr*
▲ **EMP:** 75 **EST:** 2003
**SALES (est):** 1.95MM **Privately Held**
Web: www.voxxelectronics.com
SIC: **5099** 3679 Video and audio equipment; Liquid crystal displays (LCD)

*(P-16988)*
### TAYLOR-LISTUG INC (PA)
Also Called: Taylor Guitars
1980 Gillespie Way, El Cajon (92020-1096)
PHONE..................619 258-1207
Kurt Listug, *CEO*
Robert Taylor, *
▲ **EMP:** 245 **EST:** 1968
**SQ FT:** 86,000
**SALES (est):** 39.74MM
**SALES (corp-wide):** 39.74MM **Privately Held**
Web: www.taylorguitars.com
SIC: **5099** 5736 3931 Musical instruments; Musical instrument stores; Guitars and parts, electric and nonelectric

*(P-16989)*
### YAMAHA CORPORATION OF AMERICA (HQ)
Also Called: Yamaha Music Corporation U S A
6600 Orangethorpe Ave, Buena Park (90620-1396)
PHONE..................714 522-9011
Hitoshi Fukutome, *CEO*
Terry Lewis, *
Brian Jemelian, *
◆ **EMP:** 300 **EST:** 1958
**SALES (est):** 427.4MM **Privately Held**
Web: usa.yamaha.com
SIC: **5099** 5065 5091 3931 Musical instruments; Sound equipment, electronic; Sporting and recreation goods; Musical instruments
PA: Yamaha Corporation
10-1, Nakazawacho, Chuo-Ku

---

## 5112 Stationery And Office Supplies

*(P-16990)*
### EMPIRE PAPER CORPORATION
Also Called: Baron
4930 Waterstone Dr, Roseville (95747-6385)
P.O. Box 24073 (94623-1073)
PHONE..................510 534-2700
Henry F Scarpelli, *Pr*
Matthew Meixell, *General Vice President*
**EMP:** 19 **EST:** 1963
**SQ FT:** 40,000
**SALES (est):** 849.04K **Privately Held**
Web: www.empirepaper.com
SIC: **5112** 2752 7389 2759 Office supplies, nec; Offset printing; Engraving service; Commercial printing, nec

*(P-16991)*
### GRAPHIC BUSINESS SOLUTIONS INC
Also Called: House of Magnets
1912 John Towers Ave, El Cajon (92020-1158)
PHONE..................619 258-4081
Gerald Rivaldi, *CEO*
Kenneth Hamilton, *
▲ **EMP:** 39 **EST:** 1994
**SQ FT:** 10,000
**SALES (est):** 16.89MM **Privately Held**
Web: www.gogbs.com
SIC: **5112** 2752 Business forms; Commercial printing, lithographic

*(P-16992)*
### PENTEL OF AMERICA LTD (DH)
2715 Columbia St, Torrance (90503-3861)
PHONE..................310 320-3831
Chotaro Koumi, *Pr*
Norikazu Hasegama, *
Nobuo Aihara, *CMO*
Toshiro Hemmi, *
◆ **EMP:** 132 **EST:** 1966
**SQ FT:** 46,000
**SALES (est):** 16.84MM **Privately Held**
Web: www.pentel.com
SIC: **5112** 3951 5199 3952 Pens and/or pencils; Pens and mechanical pencils; Artists' materials; Artists' materials, except pencils and leads
HQ: Pentel Co., Ltd.
7-2, Nihombashikoamicho
Chuo-Ku TKY 103-0

*(P-16993)*
### PRESTIGE GRAPHICS INC
9630 Ridgehaven Ct Ste B, San Diego (92123-5605)
PHONE..................858 560-8213
Mark Grantham, *Pr*
▲ **EMP:** 30 **EST:** 1988
**SALES (est):** 9.38MM **Privately Held**
SIC: **5112** 2752 Business forms; Offset printing
PA: Pgac Corp.
9630 Ridgehaven Crt Ste B

*(P-16994)*
### R R DONNELLEY & SONS COMPANY
Also Called: Moore Business Forms
40610 County Center Dr Ste 100, Temecula (92591-6021)
PHONE..................951 296-2890
Rick Budge, *Mgr*
**EMP:** 51
**SALES (corp-wide):** 15B **Privately Held**
Web: www.rrd.com
SIC: **5112** 2761 2752 Business forms; Manifold business forms; Color lithography
HQ: R. R. Donnelley & Sons Company
35 W Wacker Dr
Chicago IL 60601
312 326-8000

*(P-16995)*
### SYSTEM SUPPLY STATIONERY CORP
1251 E Walnut St, Carson (90746-1318)
PHONE..................310 223-0880
Enrico Ventura, *Pr*
▲ **EMP:** 18 **EST:** 1949
**SQ FT:** 30,000
**SALES (est):** 4.92MM **Privately Held**
Web: www.3scorp.com
SIC: **5112** 5021 2752 Office supplies, nec; Office furniture, nec; Billheads, lithographed

---

## 5113 Industrial And Personal Service Paper

*(P-16996)*
### ANDWIN CORPORATION (PA)
Also Called: Andwin Scientific
167 W Cochran St, Simi Valley (93065-6217)
P.O. Box 689 (91365-0689)
PHONE..................818 999-2828
Natalie Sarraf, *CEO*
Jesse Palaganas, *
▲ **EMP:** 62 **EST:** 1950
**SALES (est):** 59.75MM
**SALES (corp-wide):** 59.75MM **Privately Held**
Web: www.andwincorp.com
SIC: **5113** 5199 5087 5047 Shipping supplies ; Art goods and supplies; Janitors' supplies; Hospital equipment and furniture

*(P-16997)*
### CALIFORNIA BOX II
8949 Toronto Ave, Rancho Cucamonga (91730-5412)
PHONE..................909 944-9202
John Widera, *CEO*
Mackey Davis, *
**EMP:** 80 **EST:** 1990
**SQ FT:** 100,000
**SALES (est):** 5.68MM
**SALES (corp-wide):** 78.02MM **Privately Held**
Web: www.calbox.com
SIC: **5113** 2653 Corrugated and solid fiber boxes; Boxes, corrugated: made from purchased materials
PA: California Box Company
13901 Carmenita Rd
562 921-1223

*(P-16998)*
### CALPINE CONTAINERS INC (PA)
380 W Spruce Ave, Clovis (93611-8705)
PHONE..................559 519-7199
Sean Gallagher, *CEO*
▲ **EMP:** 15 **EST:** 1895
**SALES (est):** 101.19MM
**SALES (corp-wide):** 101.19MM **Privately Held**
Web: www.calpinecontainers.com
SIC: **5113** 5085 2441 2448 Corrugated and solid fiber boxes; Box shooks; Boxes, wood ; Pallets, wood

*(P-16999)*
### E & S PAPER CO
Also Called: Delta Packaging Products
14110 S Broadway, Los Angeles (90061-1019)
PHONE..................310 538-8700
TOLL FREE: 800
Spencer Pritkin, *Pr*
Richard Hemmer, *
Rosalind Pritikin, *
**EMP:** 28 **EST:** 1964
**SQ FT:** 21,000
**SALES (est):** 2.04MM **Privately Held**
Web: www.deltapackaging.com
SIC: **5113** 5085 2679 3086 Paperboard and products; Packing, industrial; Paperboard products, converted, nec; Packaging and shipping materials, foamed plastics

*(P-17000)*
### GEORGIA-PACIFIC LLC
Also Called: Georgia-Pacific
9206 Santa Fe Springs Rd, Santa Fe Springs (90670-2618)
PHONE..................562 861-6226
**EMP:** 275
**SALES (corp-wide):** 64.37B **Privately Held**
Web: www.gp.com
SIC: **5113** 2653 Corrugated and solid fiber boxes; Boxes, corrugated: made from purchased materials
HQ: Georgia-Pacific Llc
133 Peachtree St Nw
Atlanta GA 30303
404 652-4000

*(P-17001)*
### GOLDEN EYE MEDIA USA INC
Also Called: Lotus Trolley Bags
1000 Camino De Las Ondas, Carlsbad (92011-3402)
PHONE..................760 688-9962
Farzan Dehmoubed, *CEO*
◆ **EMP:** 17 **EST:** 2009
**SQ FT:** 2,000
**SALES (est):** 1.78MM **Privately Held**
Web: www.lotus-sustainables.com
SIC: **5113** 2394 Bags, paper and disposable plastic; Air cushions and mattresses, canvas

*(P-17002)*
### MAXCO SUPPLY INC (PA)
605 S Zediker Ave, Parlier (93648)
P.O. Box 814 (93648)
PHONE..................559 646-8449
Max Flaming, *Pr*
Robert Grote, *
David Bryant, *
▲ **EMP:** 45 **EST:** 1972
**SQ FT:** 8,500
**SALES (est):** 103.6MM
**SALES (corp-wide):** 103.6MM **Privately Held**
Web: www.maxcopackaging.com
SIC: **5113** 2436 3554 Shipping supplies; Softwood veneer and plywood; Box making machines, paper

# 5113 - Industrial And Personal Service Paper (P-17020)

**(P-17003)**
**OAK PAPER PRODUCTS CO LLC (PA)**
Also Called: Acorn Paper Products Co.
3686 E Olympic Blvd, Los Angeles (90023-3146)
P.O. Box 23965 (90023-0965)
PHONE..................323 268-0507
TOLL FREE: 800
David Weissberg, CEO
Max Weissberg, *
▲ EMP: 174 EST: 1959
SQ FT: 250,000
SALES (est): 49.97MM
SALES (corp-wide): 49.97MM Privately Held
Web: www.acorn-paper.com
SIC: 5113 5199 5087 2653  Shipping supplies; Packaging materials; Janitors' supplies; Corrugated and solid fiber boxes

**(P-17004)**
**ORORA PACKAGING SOLUTIONS (HQ)**
Also Called: Orora North America
6600 Valley View St, Buena Park (90620-1145)
PHONE..................714 562-6000
Kelly Barlow, Pr
David Conley, *
Lara Coons, *
◆ EMP: 100 EST: 1951
SQ FT: 300,000
SALES (est): 1.88B Privately Held
Web: www.ororapackagingsolutions.com
SIC: 5113 2653  Paper, wrapping or coarse, and products; Boxes, corrugated: made from purchased materials
PA: Orora Limited
    109 Burwood Rd

**(P-17005)**
**ORORA PACKAGING SOLUTIONS**
Also Called: Mpp Brea Div 6079
3200 Enterprise St, Brea (92821-6238)
PHONE..................714 984-2300
Carol Hortick, Mgr
EMP: 22
Web: www.ororagroup.com
SIC: 5113 2653  Paper, wrapping or coarse, and products; Boxes, corrugated: made from purchased materials
HQ: Orora Packaging Solutions
    6600 Valley View St
    Buena Park CA 90620
    714 562-6000

**(P-17006)**
**ORORA PACKAGING SOLUTIONS**
Also Called: Mpp San Diego Div 6064
664 N Twin Oaks Valley Rd, San Marcos (92069-1712)
PHONE..................760 510-7170
Scott Romagnoli, Mgr
EMP: 28
Web: www.ororapackagingsolutions.com
SIC: 5113 2653  Paper, wrapping or coarse, and products; Boxes, corrugated: made from purchased materials
HQ: Orora Packaging Solutions
    6600 Valley View St
    Buena Park CA 90620
    714 562-6000

**(P-17007)**
**ORORA PACKAGING SOLUTIONS**
Mpp Union City Div 6062
33463 Western Ave, Union City (94587-3201)
P.O. Box 60000 (94160-0001)
PHONE..................510 487-1211
Nafiz Korustan, Mgr
EMP: 34
Web: www.ororagroup.com
SIC: 5113 2653  Paper, wrapping or coarse, and products; Boxes, corrugated: made from purchased materials
HQ: Orora Packaging Solutions
    6600 Valley View St
    Buena Park CA 90620
    714 562-6000

**(P-17008)**
**ORORA PACKAGING SOLUTIONS**
Also Called: Landsberg Los Angeles Div 1001
1640 S Greenwood Ave, Montebello (90640-6538)
P.O. Box 800 (90640-0800)
PHONE..................323 832-2000
Jed Wockenfuss, Mgr
EMP: 168
Web: www.ororapackagingsolutions.com
SIC: 5113 2653  Paper, wrapping or coarse, and products; Boxes, corrugated: made from purchased materials
HQ: Orora Packaging Solutions
    6600 Valley View St
    Buena Park CA 90620
    714 562-6000

**(P-17009)**
**ORORA PACKAGING SOLUTIONS**
Also Called: Landsberg Orange Cnty Div 1025
7001 Village Dr Ste 155, Buena Park (90621-2276)
PHONE..................714 525-4900
Jerry Mejia, Mgr
EMP: 34
Web: www.ororapackagingsolutions.com
SIC: 5113 2653  Paper, wrapping or coarse, and products; Boxes, corrugated: made from purchased materials
HQ: Orora Packaging Solutions
    6600 Valley View St
    Buena Park CA 90620
    714 562-6000

**(P-17010)**
**ORORA PACKAGING SOLUTIONS**
Also Called: Mpp Fullerton Div 6061
1901 E Rosslynn Ave, Fullerton (92831-5141)
PHONE..................714 278-6000
Carol Hortick, Brnch Mgr
EMP: 53
Web: www.ororagroup.com
SIC: 5113 2653  Paper, wrapping or coarse, and products; Boxes, corrugated: made from purchased materials
HQ: Orora Packaging Solutions
    6600 Valley View St
    Buena Park CA 90620
    714 562-6000

**(P-17011)**
**ORORA PACKAGING SOLUTIONS**
Mpp Los Angeles Div 6060
3201 W Mission Rd, Alhambra (91803-1113)
PHONE..................626 284-9524
Marc Fenster, Mgr
EMP: 34
Web: www.ororapackagingsolutions.com
SIC: 5113 2653  Paper, wrapping or coarse, and products; Boxes, corrugated: made from purchased materials
HQ: Orora Packaging Solutions
    6600 Valley View St
    Buena Park CA 90620
    714 562-6000

**(P-17012)**
**ORORA PACKAGING SOLUTIONS**
Also Called: Landsberg Snta Brbara Div 1046
2146 Eastman Ave, Oxnard (93030-5168)
PHONE..................805 278-5040
Terry Mayfield, Mgr
EMP: 30
Web: www.ororapackagingsolutions.com
SIC: 5113 2653  Paper, wrapping or coarse, and products; Boxes, corrugated: made from purchased materials
HQ: Orora Packaging Solutions
    6600 Valley View St
    Buena Park CA 90620
    714 562-6000

**(P-17013)**
**ORORA PACKAGING SOLUTIONS**
Landsberg Sacramento Div 1020
1221 Tara Ct, Rocklin (95765-1200)
PHONE..................916 645-8100
Dan Davis, Brnch Mgr
EMP: 86
Web: www.ororapackagingsolutions.com
SIC: 5113 2653  Paper, wrapping or coarse, and products; Boxes, corrugated: made from purchased materials
HQ: Orora Packaging Solutions
    6600 Valley View St
    Buena Park CA 90620
    714 562-6000

**(P-17014)**
**ORORA PACKAGING SOLUTIONS**
Mpp San Jose Div 6066
8311 Central Ave, Newark (94560-3433)
PHONE..................510 896-4750
EMP: 15
Web: www.ororapackagingsolutions.com
SIC: 5113 2653  Paper, wrapping or coarse, and products; Boxes, corrugated: made from purchased materials
HQ: Orora Packaging Solutions
    6600 Valley View St
    Buena Park CA 90620
    714 562-6000

**(P-17015)**
**ORORA PACKAGING SOLUTIONS**
Also Called: Corru Kraft Fullerton Div 5068
1911 E Rosslynn Ave, Fullerton (92831-5141)
PHONE..................714 773-0124
Ron Crawford, Mgr
EMP: 18
Web: www.ororagroup.com
SIC: 5113 2653  Paper, wrapping or coarse, and products; Boxes, corrugated: made from purchased materials
HQ: Orora Packaging Solutions
    6600 Valley View St
    Buena Park CA 90620
    714 562-6000

**(P-17016)**
**ORORA PACKAGING SOLUTIONS**
Also Called: Corru Kraft Buena Pk Div 5058
6200 Caballero Blvd, Buena Park (90620-1124)
PHONE..................714 562-6002
Jim Wilczek, Brnch Mgr
EMP: 149
Web: www.ororacorrugated.com
SIC: 5113 2653  Paper, wrapping or coarse, and products; Boxes, corrugated: made from purchased materials
HQ: Orora Packaging Solutions
    6600 Valley View St
    Buena Park CA 90620
    714 562-6000

**(P-17017)**
**ORORA PACKAGING SOLUTIONS**
Also Called: Landsberg Flfilment Sltons Div
13397 Marlay Ave, Fontana (92337-6946)
PHONE..................909 770-5400
Jerry Mejia, Brnch Mgr
EMP: 53
Web: www.ororapackagingsolutions.com
SIC: 5113 2653  Paper, wrapping or coarse, and products; Boxes, corrugated: made from purchased materials
HQ: Orora Packaging Solutions
    6600 Valley View St
    Buena Park CA 90620
    714 562-6000

**(P-17018)**
**P&P INTERNATIONAL INC**
2014 2nd St, Selma (93662-3722)
PHONE..................559 891-9888
William A Spencer, Pr
▲ EMP: 20 EST: 2003
SALES (est): 5.43MM Privately Held
Web: www.usa-ppi.com
SIC: 5113 3221 5085  Cups, disposable plastic and paper; Water bottles, glass; Glass bottles

**(P-17019)**
**PACKAGING INNOVATORS LLC**
6850 Brisa St, Livermore (94550-2521)
P.O. Box 1110 (94551-1110)
PHONE..................925 371-2000
TOLL FREE: 800
William E Mazzocco, Pr
Beverly J Flynt, *
▲ EMP: 90 EST: 1975
SALES (est): 15.64MM
SALES (corp-wide): 792.6MM Privately Held
Web: www.goldenwestpackaging.com
SIC: 5113 2653 3993  Shipping supplies; Corrugated and solid fiber boxes; Signs and advertising specialties
PA: Golden West Packaging Group Llc
    15250 Don Julian Rd
    888 501-5893

**(P-17020)**
**PIONEER PACKING INC (PA)**
2430 S Grand Ave, Santa Ana (92705-5211)
PHONE..................714 540-9751
Michael S Blower, Pr
Ronald Scagliotti, *
▲ EMP: 26 EST: 1976
SQ FT: 170,000
SALES (est): 44.54MM
SALES (corp-wide): 44.54MM Privately Held
Web: www.pioneerpackinginc.com

# 5113 - Industrial And Personal Service Paper (P-17021)

## PRODUCTS & SERVICES SECTION

SIC: 5113 2653 Shipping supplies; Boxes, corrugated: made from purchased materials

**(P-17021)**
**SAMBRAILO PACKAGING**
1750 San Juan Rd, Aromas (95004-9027)
PHONE..................831 726-3210
Juan Garcia, *Mgr*
EMP: 45
SALES (corp-wide): 45.93MM **Privately Held**
Web: www.sambrailo.com
SIC: 5113 2657 Industrial and personal service paper; Folding paperboard boxes
PA: Sambrailo Packaging
    800 Walker St
    831 724-7581

**(P-17022)**
**SAN DIEGO DIE CUTTING INC**
3112 Moore St, San Diego (92110-4480)
PHONE..................619 297-4453
George Thomas Christian, *Pr*
James Roche, *
◆ EMP: 34 EST: 1956
SQ FT: 12,000
SALES (est): 9.96MM **Privately Held**
Web: www.sddiecutting.com
SIC: 5113 3554 7319 2759 Corrugated and solid fiber boxes; Special dies and tools; Display advertising service; Embossing on paper

**(P-17023)**
**STASHER INC**
Also Called: Modern-Twist
1310 63rd St, Emeryville (94608-2104)
PHONE..................510 531-2100
Kat Nouri, *CEO*
Katousha Nouri, *CEO*
EMP: 53 EST: 2015
SALES (est): 5.9MM **Privately Held**
Web: www.stasherbag.com
SIC: 5113 2656 Sanitary food containers; Frozen food containers: made from purchased material

**(P-17024)**
**T & W CONVERTERS INC**
15020 Marquardt Ave, Santa Fe Springs (90670-5704)
PHONE..................818 241-1707
Toni Hibbard, *Pr*
EMP: 16 EST: 1983
SQ FT: 12,500
SALES (est): 564.32K **Privately Held**
Web: www.qspac.com
SIC: 5113 2759 2675 2672 Pressure sensitive tape; Commercial printing, nec; Die-cut paper and board; Paper; coated and laminated, nec

**(P-17025)**
**VALLEY BOX CO INC**
10611 Prospect Ave, Santee (92071-4532)
PHONE..................619 449-2882
Robert Eschwege, *Pr*
EMP: 40 EST: 1966
SQ FT: 7,000
SALES (est): 1.83MM **Privately Held**
Web: www.valleybox.com
SIC: 5113 2448 2653 2449 Corrugated and solid fiber boxes; Cargo containers, wood; Corrugated and solid fiber boxes; Wood containers, nec

## 5122 Drugs, Proprietaries, And Sundries

**(P-17026)**
**ADVANCED PHRM SVCS INC**
Also Called: JBA Brands
11555 Monarch St Ste B, Garden Grove (92841-1814)
PHONE..................714 903-1006
Tracy Nguyen, *CEO*
Dennis Ngo, *CEO*
▲ EMP: 19 EST: 2005
SALES (est): 2.43MM **Privately Held**
SIC: 5122 2833 Pharmaceuticals; Medicinals and botanicals

**(P-17027)**
**BADASS BRAND INC**
Also Called: Badass Beard Care
8400 Moss Ct, Granite Bay (95746-7367)
PHONE..................916 990-3873
Charles Moyer, *CEO*
Charles Moyer, *Pr*
Ashley Moyer, *VP*
EMP: 20 EST: 2014
SALES (est): 3.12MM **Privately Held**
Web: www.badassbeardcare.com
SIC: 5122 2844 Cosmetics, perfumes, and hair products; Hair preparations, including shampoos

**(P-17028)**
**BAXTER HEALTHCARE CORPORATION**
1 Baxter Way Ste 100, Westlake Village (91362-3813)
PHONE..................805 372-3000
John Bacich, *Pr*
EMP: 127
SALES (corp-wide): 14.81B **Publicly Held**
Web: www.baxter.com
SIC: 5122 2834 2836 5047 Drugs, proprietaries, and sundries; Solutions, pharmaceutical; Biological products, except diagnostic; Medical equipment and supplies
HQ: Baxter Healthcare Corporation
    1 Baxter Pkwy
    Deerfield IL 60015
    224 948-2000

**(P-17029)**
**BEAUTY 21 COSMETICS INC**
Also Called: L A Girl
2021 S Archibald Ave, Ontario (91761-8535)
PHONE..................909 945-2220
Lan Jack Yu, *CEO*
Chafe Yu Trinh, *
Mahon So Yu, *
◆ EMP: 175 EST: 1985
SQ FT: 250,000
SALES (est): 49.52MM **Privately Held**
Web: www.lagirlusa.com
SIC: 5122 2844 Cosmetics; Perfumes, cosmetics and other toilet preparations

**(P-17030)**
**BRONDELL INC**
Also Called: Nebia
375 Alabama St Ste 200, San Francisco (94110-1966)
P.O. Box 470085 (94147-0085)
PHONE..................415 315-9000
David Samuel, *Ch*
Steven Scheer, *
Sara Adams, *
◆ EMP: 25 EST: 2003
SQ FT: 3,300
SALES (est): 13.96MM **Privately Held**
Web: www.brondell.com
SIC: 5122 2499 Toiletries; Seats, toilet

**(P-17031)**
**CHEMI-SOURCE INC**
Also Called: Metabolic Response Modifiers
2665 Vista Pacific Dr, Oceanside (92056-3500)
PHONE..................760 477-8177
Mark Olson, *CEO*
Rocky Palamara, *
Kristina Archuleta, *
▲ EMP: 38 EST: 1996
SQ FT: 24,000
SALES (est): 19.32MM **Privately Held**
Web: www.mrmnutrition.com
SIC: 5122 2833 5499 Vitamins and minerals; Medicinals and botanicals; Health and dietetic food stores

**(P-17032)**
**COLORESCIENCE INC**
2141 Palomar Airport Rd Ste 200, Carlsbad (92011-1425)
PHONE..................866 426-5673
Mary Fisher, *CEO*
Josie Juncal, *CCO*
Ted Ebel, *Chief Business Officer*
Steve P Loomis, *
▲ EMP: 111 EST: 2013
SQ FT: 15,000
SALES (est): 23.8MM **Privately Held**
Web: www.colorescience.com
SIC: 5122 2844 Cosmetics; Cosmetic preparations

**(P-17033)**
**COPAN DIAGNOSTICS INC (DH)**
26055 Jefferson Ave, Murrieta (92562-6983)
PHONE..................951 696-6957
Fabrizio Mazzocchi, *CEO*
Stefania Triva, *
Angelo Messa, *
◆ EMP: 18 EST: 1994
SQ FT: 28,000
SALES (est): 162.8MM **Privately Held**
Web: www.copanusa.com
SIC: 5122 5049 3826 Biologicals and allied products; Laboratory equipment, except medical or dental; Analytical instruments
HQ: Copan Italia Spa
    Via Francesco Perotti 10
    Brescia BS 25125
    030 268-7211

**(P-17034)**
**DAKO NORTH AMERICA INC**
6392 Via Real, Carpinteria (93013-2921)
P.O. Box 58059 (93013)
PHONE..................805 566-6655
◆ EMP: 325
SIC: 5122 3841 Biologicals and allied products; Diagnostic apparatus, medical

**(P-17035)**
**DANNE MONTAGUE KING CO (PA)**
Also Called: Dmk
10420 Pioneer Blvd, Santa Fe Springs (90670)
PHONE..................562 944-0230
Danne King, *Pr*
Randy Larsen, *
▲ EMP: 17 EST: 1996
SQ FT: 30,000
SALES (est): 10.38MM **Privately Held**
Web: www.dannemking.com

SIC: 5122 5999 2844 Cosmetics; Toiletries, cosmetics, and perfumes; Cosmetic preparations

**(P-17036)**
**DERM COSMETIC LABS INC (PA)**
Also Called: Derm Cosmetic Labs
6370 Altura Blvd, Buena Park (90620-1001)
PHONE..................714 562-8873
Loksarang D Hardas, *Pr*
▲ EMP: 22 EST: 1988
SQ FT: 60,000
SALES (est): 4.41MM
SALES (corp-wide): 4.41MM **Privately Held**
Web: www.lastotallyawesome.com
SIC: 5122 2844 Cosmetics, perfumes, and hair products; Cosmetic preparations

**(P-17037)**
**DHOUSE BRANDS INC**
Also Called: Comune
2301 E 7th St Ste F103, Los Angeles (90023-1037)
PHONE..................213 291-7576
John Inn, *CEO*
EMP: 20 EST: 2021
SALES (est): 455.97K **Privately Held**
SIC: 5122 2389 2339 2335 Cosmetics; Apparel and accessories, nec; Women's and misses' accessories; Women's, junior's, and misses' dresses

**(P-17038)**
**GLAMOUR INDUSTRIES CO (PA)**
Also Called: American International Inds
2220 Gaspar Ave, Los Angeles (90040-1516)
PHONE..................323 728-2999
Zvi Ryzman, *Pr*
Theresa Cooper, *Ex VP*
Charlie Loveless, *VP*
Betty Ryzman, *Sec*
EMP: 250 EST: 1971
SQ FT: 224,000
SALES (est): 47.77MM
SALES (corp-wide): 47.77MM **Privately Held**
Web: www.aiibeauty.com
SIC: 5122 2844 Cosmetics; Cosmetic preparations

**(P-17039)**
**GLOVES IN A BOTTLE INC**
3720 Park Pl, Montrose (91020-1623)
P.O. Box 615 (91021-0615)
PHONE..................818 248-9980
Dan Mueller, *Pr*
Wayne Weber, *Dir*
Olesja Mueller, *Sec*
Klaus Hilgers, *Dir*
▲ EMP: 20 EST: 1994
SQ FT: 4,000
SALES (est): 4.81MM **Privately Held**
Web: www.glovesinabottle.com
SIC: 5122 2844 5999 Cosmetics; Perfumes, cosmetics and other toilet preparations; Toiletries, cosmetics, and perfumes

**(P-17040)**
**JAPONESQUE LLC**
Also Called: Japonesque
12647 Alcosta Blvd Ste 375, San Ramon (94583-4774)
PHONE..................925 866-6670
Simon Worraker, *CEO*
▲ EMP: 80 EST: 2002
SALES (est): 23.37MM **Privately Held**
Web: www.japonesque.com

SIC: 5122 2844 Cosmetics; Cosmetic preparations

**(P-17041)**
**LIVING ECOLOGY**
240 Crouse Dr, Corona (92879-8093)
PHONE..................................951 371-4982
◆ EMP: 22 EST: 2015
SALES (est): 10.08MM **Privately Held**
Web: www.inwmfg.com
SIC: 5122 2048 Vitamins and minerals; Feed supplements

**(P-17042)**
**NATROL LLC**
9454 Jordan Ave, Chatsworth (91311-5813)
PHONE..................................818 739-6000
EMP: 36
SALES (corp-wide): 85.54MM **Privately Held**
Web: www.natrol.com
SIC: 5122 2099 Drugs, proprietaries, and sundries; Food preparations, nec
PA: Natrol Llc
  15233 Vntura Blvd Ste 900
  800 262-8765

**(P-17043)**
**ONCOR CORP**
Also Called: ONCOR CORP
13115 Barton Rd Ste G-H, Whittier (90605-2762)
PHONE..................................562 944-0230
Danne King, *Brnch Mgr*
EMP: 34
Web: www.dannemking.com
SIC: 5122 2844 Toilet preparations; Perfumes, cosmetics and other toilet preparations
PA: Danne Montague King Co
  10420 Pioneer Blvd

**(P-17044)**
**PLATINUM PERFORMANCE INC (HQ)**
90 Thomas Rd, Buellton (93427-9657)
P.O. Box 990 (93427-0990)
PHONE..................................800 553-2400
Mark J Herthel, *Pr*
EMP: 27 EST: 1996
SQ FT: 7,000
SALES (est): 23.45MM
SALES (corp-wide): 8.54B **Publicly Held**
Web: www.platinumperformance.com
SIC: 5122 2023 Vitamins and minerals; Dietary supplements, dairy and non-dairy based
PA: Zoetis Inc.
  10 Sylvan Way
  973 822-7000

**(P-17045)**
**PRESIDIO BRANDS INC (PA)**
Also Called: Every Man Jack
100 Shoreline Hwy Ste A200, Mill Valley (94941-3650)
PHONE..................................877 875-5225
Gerry Chesser, *CEO*
EMP: 46 EST: 2006
SQ FT: 2,200
SALES (est): 24.84MM
SALES (corp-wide): 24.84MM **Privately Held**
Web: www.presidiobrands.com
SIC: 5122 2844 Cosmetics, perfumes, and hair products; Cosmetic preparations

**(P-17046)**
**PRIMAL ELEMENTS INC**
Also Called: Primal Elements
18062 Redondo Cir, Huntington Beach (92648-1326)
PHONE..................................714 899-0757
Faith Freeman, *CEO*
Scott Freeman, *
▲ EMP: 99 EST: 1993
SQ FT: 56,500
SALES (est): 22.03MM **Privately Held**
Web: www.primalelements.com
SIC: 5122 2841 Cosmetics; Detergents, synthetic organic or inorganic alkaline

**(P-17047)**
**QYK BRANDS LLC**
12101 Western Ave, Garden Grove (92841-2914)
PHONE..................................833 795-7664
Rakesh Tammabattula, *CEO*
EMP: 189 EST: 2017
SALES (est): 20.76MM **Privately Held**
Web: www.qyk.us
SIC: 5122 2842 3842 2023 Pharmaceuticals; Disinfectants, household or industrial plant; Respiratory protection equipment, personal; Dietary supplements, dairy and non-dairy based

**(P-17048)**
**RUGBY LABORATORIES INC (DH)**
311 Bonnie Cir, Corona (92878-5182)
PHONE..................................951 270-1400
David C Hsia Ph.d., *Pr*
Michael E Boser, *
Chato Abad, *
Frederick Wilkinson, *
Michel J Feldman, *
EMP: 90 EST: 1961
SALES (est): 3.38MM
SALES (corp-wide): 226.83B **Publicly Held**
SIC: 5122 2834 Pharmaceuticals; Pharmaceutical preparations
HQ: The Harvard Drug Group L L C
  341 Mason Rd
  La Vergne TN 37086
  800 616-2471

**(P-17049)**
**SOS BEAUTY INC**
9100 Wilshire Blvd Ste 500w, Beverly Hills (90212-3445)
PHONE..................................424 285-1405
Dustin Cash, *CEO*
Charlene Valledor, *
EMP: 38 EST: 2017
SALES (est): 13.1MM **Privately Held**
Web: www.sosbty.com
SIC: 5122 3221 7389 3172 Cosmetics, perfumes, and hair products; Cosmetic jars, glass; Cosmetic kits, assembling and packaging; Cosmetic bags

**(P-17050)**
**SPA DE SOLEIL INC**
10443 Arminta St, Sun Valley (91352)
PHONE..................................818 504-3200
Rena Revivo, *CEO*
▲ EMP: 40 EST: 1994
Web: www.spadesoleil.com
SIC: 5122 2844 Cosmetics; Cosmetic preparations

**(P-17051)**
**SPECIALTY SALES LLC**
4672 E Drummond Ave, Fresno (93725-1601)
PHONE..................................559 862-6611
Matthew Nelson, *CEO*
Greg Alan Petersen, *Managing Member*
EMP: 54 EST: 1998
SALES (est): 16.95MM **Privately Held**
Web: www.hoofstrong.com
SIC: 5122 2869 4959 Animal medicines; Enzymes; Environmental cleanup services

**(P-17052)**
**STAR NAIL PRODUCTS INC**
Also Called: Star Nail International
29120 Avenue Paine, Valencia (91355-5402)
PHONE..................................661 257-3376
Tony Cuccio, *CEO*
Elaine Watson, *
Christina Jahn, *
Anthony Cuccio, *
Roberta Cuccio, *
◆ EMP: 55 EST: 1982
SQ FT: 14,000
SALES (est): 11.65MM **Privately Held**
Web: www.starnail.com
SIC: 5122 2844 7231 Cosmetics; Perfumes, cosmetics and other toilet preparations; Beauty shops

**(P-17053)**
**SV LABS CORPORATION (PA)**
Also Called: Sinclair & Valentine
480 Airport Blvd, Watsonville (95076-2002)
PHONE..................................831 722-9526
Graham Orriss, *CEO*
Jeffrey K Slaboden, *
Julie Ann Lemke, *
▲ EMP: 75 EST: 1979
SQ FT: 55,000
SALES (est): 111.37MM
SALES (corp-wide): 111.37MM **Privately Held**
Web: www.svlabs.com
SIC: 5122 2844 Cosmetics; Perfumes, cosmetics and other toilet preparations

**(P-17054)**
**VIVA LIFE SCIENCE INC**
350 Paularino Ave, Costa Mesa (92626-4616)
PHONE..................................949 645-6100
David Fan, *Pr*
EMP: 220 EST: 1987
SQ FT: 60,000
SALES (est): 2.43MM
SALES (corp-wide): 8.44MM **Privately Held**
Web: www.vivalife.com
SIC: 5122 2833 Vitamins and minerals; Medicinals and botanicals
PA: Westar Nutrition Corp.
  350 Paularino Ave
  949 645-6100

**(P-17055)**
**WECKERLE COSMETICS USA INC**
Also Called: Weckerle Cosmetic
525 Maple Ave, Torrance (90503-3905)
PHONE..................................310 328-7000
Thomas Weckerle, *Pr*
Petra Webersberger, *
▲ EMP: 35 EST: 1979
SQ FT: 20,000
SALES (est): 27.32MM
SALES (corp-wide): 90.77MM **Privately Held**
Web: www.weckerle.com
SIC: 5122 5084 2844 Cosmetics; Packaging machinery and equipment; Lipsticks
PA: Weckerle Holding Gmbh
  Holzhofstr. 26
  88192930

## 5131 Piece Goods And Notions

**(P-17056)**
**A W CHANG CORPORATION (PA)**
Also Called: Excalibur International
6945 Atlantic Ave, Long Beach (90805-1415)
PHONE..................................310 764-2000
William Chang, *CEO*
Abraham K Chang, *
William Chang, *VP*
▲ EMP: 27 EST: 1989
SQ FT: 12,000
SALES (est): 27.29MM **Privately Held**
SIC: 5131 5632 2211 Silk piece goods, woven; Apparel accessories; Apparel and outerwear fabrics, cotton

**(P-17057)**
**ALEXANDER HENRY FABRICS INC**
1550 Flower St, Glendale (91201-2356)
PHONE..................................818 562-8200
Marcus De Leon, *Pr*
Kim Dunn, *
EMP: 40 EST: 1992
SALES (est): 5.25MM **Privately Held**
Web: www.ahfabrics.com
SIC: 5131 2211 Cotton goods; Broadwoven fabric mills, cotton

**(P-17058)**
**AP UNLIMITED CORPORATION**
Also Called: American Plastic
1225 N Macarthur Dr Ste 200, Tracy (95376-2843)
PHONE..................................209 834-0287
Gary Grewal, *Pr*
◆ EMP: 15 EST: 1999
SQ FT: 18,000
SALES (est): 4.22MM **Privately Held**
Web: www.americanplastics.com
SIC: 5131 3965 Plastic piece goods, woven; Buckles and buckle parts

**(P-17059)**
**BLUE RIDGE HOME FASHIONS INC**
15761 Tapia St, Irwindale (91706-2177)
PHONE..................................626 960-6069
Ning He, *CEO*
Fred Buonocore, *
Jim England, *
◆ EMP: 39 EST: 1994
SALES (est): 9.44MM **Privately Held**
Web: www.blueridgehome.com
SIC: 5131 3999 2392 Textiles, woven, nec; Feathers and feather products; Blankets, comforters and beddings

**(P-17060)**
**CHARMING TRIM & PACKAGING**
5889 Rickenbacker Rd, Commerce (90040-3027)
PHONE..................................415 302-7021
Richard Ringeisen, *Pr*
Barry Chan, *
EMP: 1000 EST: 2011
SALES (est): 14.45MM **Privately Held**
Web: www.charmingtrim.com
SIC: 5131 3111 Trimmings, apparel; Garment leather

# 5131 - Piece Goods And Notions

**(P-17061)**
**CLOVER NEEDLECRAFT INC**
1441 S Carlos Ave, Ontario (91761-7676)
P.O. Box 3850 (91761-0981)
PHONE..................800 233-1703
Yasuhiro Okada, *Pr*
Tomoki Okada, *Sec*
Jan Carr, *VP*
Takayoshi Mukaigawa, *CFO*
▲ **EMP:** 21 **EST:** 1983
**SQ FT:** 17,000
**SALES (est):** 9.52MM **Privately Held**
Web: www.clover-usa.com
**SIC: 5131** 2284 2281 5949  Sewing supplies and notions; Sewing thread; Knitting yarn, spun; Knitting goods and supplies
PA: Clover Mfg.Co., Ltd.
3-15-5, Nakamichi, Higashinari-Ku

**(P-17062)**
**J ROBERT SCOTT INC (PA)**
722 N La Cienega Blvd, West Hollywood (90069-5086)
PHONE..................310 680-4300
Andrew Frumovitz, *CEO*
Sally Lewis, *
Nancy Preller, *
▲ **EMP:** 120 **EST:** 1972
**SALES (est):** 7.04MM
**SALES (corp-wide):** 7.04MM **Privately Held**
Web: www.jrobertscott.com
**SIC: 5131** 2512 2511  Textiles, woven, nec; Upholstered household furniture; Wood household furniture

**(P-17063)**
**MATRIX INTERNATIONAL TEX INC**
Also Called: Matrix
1363 S Bonnie Beach Pl, Commerce (90023-4001)
P.O. Box 23484 (90023)
PHONE..................323 582-9100
Kourosh Neman, *Prin*
Kourosh Neman, *CEO*
Chris Neman, *
Kevin Neman, *
Simin Neman, *
◆ **EMP:** 28 **EST:** 1997
**SQ FT:** 60,000
**SALES (est):** 8.62MM **Privately Held**
Web: www.matrixtextiles.com
**SIC: 5131** 2299  Broadwoven fabrics; Apparel filling: cotton waste, kapok, and related material

**(P-17064)**
**MOMENTUM TEXTILES LLC (PA)**
Also Called: Momentum Textiles Wallcovering
17811 Fitch, Irvine (92614-6001)
PHONE..................949 833-8886
David Krakoff, *CEO*
Joanne Corrao, *
◆ **EMP:** 40 **EST:** 1987
**SQ FT:** 20,000
**SALES (est):** 39.66MM
**SALES (corp-wide):** 39.66MM **Privately Held**
Web: www.momentumtextilesandwalls.com
**SIC: 5131** 2221  Upholstery fabrics, woven; Broadwoven fabric mills, manmade

**(P-17065)**
**MORGAN FABRICS CORPORATION (PA)**
Also Called: Morgan Fabrics
4265 Exchange Ave, Los Angeles (90058-2604)
P.O. Box 58523 (90058-0523)
PHONE..................323 583-9981
Arnold Gittelson, *Ch*
Michael Gittelson, *Pr*
Robert Gittelson, *VP*
Ken Yang, *CFO*
◆ **EMP:** 60 **EST:** 1956
**SQ FT:** 50,000
**SALES (est):** 15.58MM
**SALES (corp-wide):** 15.58MM **Privately Held**
Web: www.morgan-fabrics.com
**SIC: 5131** 2759  Textiles, woven, nec; Commercial printing, nec

**(P-17066)**
**RADIX TEXTILE INC**
Also Called: Radix
600 E Washington Blvd Ste C2, Los Angeles (90015-3739)
PHONE..................323 234-1667
Arad Shemirani, *CEO*
▲ **EMP:** 99 **EST:** 2007
**SALES (est):** 4.71MM **Privately Held**
**SIC: 5131** 2211  Piece goods and other fabrics; Broadwoven fabric mills, cotton

**(P-17067)**
**RDMM LEGACY INC**
Also Called: Fabri Cote
724 E 60th St, Los Angeles (90001-1013)
P.O. Box 1856 (90001-0856)
PHONE..................323 232-2147
▲ **EMP:** 30 **EST:** 1957
**SALES (est):** 2.28MM **Privately Held**
Web: www.fabricote.com
**SIC: 5131** 2295  Coated fabrics; Coated fabrics, not rubberized

**(P-17068)**
**ROMEX TEXTILES INC (PA)**
2454 E 27th St, Vernon (90058-1220)
PHONE..................213 749-9090
Shawn Binafard, *CEO*
▲ **EMP:** 39 **EST:** 1993
**SALES (est):** 10.54MM **Privately Held**
Web: www.romextex.com
**SIC: 5131** 2211  Textiles, woven, nec; Apparel and outerwear fabrics, cotton

**(P-17069)**
**SO TECH/SPCL OP TECH INC (PA)**
Also Called: Special Operations Tech
206 Star Of India Ln, Carson (90746-1418)
PHONE..................310 202-9007
James W Cragg V, *Pr*
▲ **EMP:** 32 **EST:** 1997
**SQ FT:** 12,000
**SALES (est):** 2.34MM
**SALES (corp-wide):** 2.34MM **Privately Held**
Web: www.sotechtactical.com
**SIC: 5131** 2396  Nylon piece goods, woven; Apparel findings and trimmings

**(P-17070)**
**SOFTLINE HOME FASHIONS INC**
13130 S Normandie Ave, Gardena (90249-2128)
PHONE..................310 630-4848
Jason Carr, *Pr*
Jason Carr, *CEO*
Rodney Carr, *Pr*
◆ **EMP:** 20 **EST:** 2000
**SALES (est):** 4.84MM **Privately Held**
Web: www.softlinehome.com
**SIC: 5131** 2391  Piece goods and other fabrics; Curtains and draperies

**(P-17071)**
**STEVEN LABEL CORPORATION (PA)**
11926 Burke St, Santa Fe Springs (90670-2546)
P.O. Box 3688 (90670-1688)
PHONE..................562 698-9971
▲ **EMP:** 119 **EST:** 1954
**SALES (est):** 25.94MM
**SALES (corp-wide):** 25.94MM **Privately Held**
Web: www.stevenlabel.com
**SIC: 5131** 3643  Labels; Electric switches

**(P-17072)**
**TALON INTERNATIONAL INC (PA)**
21900 Burbank Blvd Ste 101, Woodland Hills (91367-7419)
PHONE..................818 444-4100
Mark Dyne, *Ch Bd*
Larry Dyne, *Interim Chief Financial Officer*
Daniel Ryu, *CSO*
Gary Dyne, *Executive Global Sales Vice President*
Peter Vaz, *Area Vice President*
**EMP:** 122 **EST:** 1997
**SALES (est):** 15.41MM **Privately Held**
Web: www.taloninternational.com
**SIC: 5131** 3965  Sewing supplies and notions ; Zipper

## 5136 Men's And Boy's Clothing

**(P-17073)**
**ELIEL & CO**
Also Called: Eliel Cycling
2215 La Mirada Dr, Vista (92081-8828)
PHONE..................760 877-8469
Ryan Eliel Cady, *Pr*
**EMP:** 42 **EST:** 2014
**SALES (est):** 1.52MM **Privately Held**
Web: www.elielcycling.com
**SIC: 5136** 2389  Sportswear, men's and boys' ; Men's miscellaneous accessories

**(P-17074)**
**GONZALES PARK LLC**
Also Called: Fifth Sun
1811 Concord Ave Ste 200, Chico (95928-9208)
PHONE..................530 343-8725
Daniel Gonzales, *Managing Member*
▲ **EMP:** 192 **EST:** 1995
**SQ FT:** 26,000
**SALES (est):** 45.22MM
**SALES (corp-wide):** 638.25MM **Privately Held**
Web: www.5sun.com
**SIC: 5136** 2326 5699  Shirts, men's and boys' ; Men's and boy's work clothing; T-shirts, custom printed
HQ: Mad Engine Global, Llc
7 Studebaker
Irvine CA 92618
858 558-5270

**(P-17075)**
**HELMET HOUSE LLC (PA)**
Also Called: Tour Master
26855 Malibu Hills Rd, Calabasas Hills (91301-5100)
PHONE..................800 421-7247
Robert M Miller, *CEO*
Philip Bellomy, *
Randy Hutchings, *
◆ **EMP:** 84 **EST:** 1969
**SQ FT:** 80,000
**SALES (est):** 20.94MM
**SALES (corp-wide):** 20.94MM **Privately Held**
Web: www.helmethouse.com
**SIC: 5136** 3949 3751  Men's and boy's clothing; Helmets, athletic; Motorcycle accessories

**(P-17076)**
**KILAM INC**
Also Called: Kilam
47685 Lakeview Blvd, Fremont (94538-6544)
PHONE..................510 943-4040
Sunil Kilam, *Pr*
▼ **EMP:** 160 **EST:** 2006
**SALES (est):** 3.86MM **Privately Held**
Web: www.eastessence.com
**SIC: 5136** 5137 3842 5047  Apparel belts, men's and boys'; Apparel belts, women's and children's; Gloves, safety; Medical equipment and supplies

**(P-17077)**
**MICHAEL GERALD LTD**
Also Called: Mgl
7051 E Avenida De Santiago, Anaheim (92807-5130)
PHONE..................562 921-9611
Gerald Barnes, *CEO*
▲ **EMP:** 23 **EST:** 1983
**SALES (est):** 4.91MM **Privately Held**
**SIC: 5136** 2329 3999  Sweaters, men's and boys'; Men's and boys' sportswear and athletic clothing; Atomizers, toiletry

**(P-17078)**
**MURPHY HARTELIUS/M&H UNIFORMS (PA)**
Also Called: M & H Uniforms
845 Stanton Rd, Burlingame (94010-1403)
P.O. Box 4365 (94011-4365)
PHONE..................650 344-2997
Damian Murphy, *CEO*
Declan Murphy, *
**EMP:** 30 **EST:** 1960
**SALES (est):** 10MM
**SALES (corp-wide):** 10MM **Privately Held**
Web: www.mandhuniforms.com
**SIC: 5136** 5137 2339 2326  Uniforms, men's and boys'; Uniforms, women's and children's; Women's and misses' outerwear, nec; Men's and boy's work clothing

**(P-17079)**
**RRZ ENTERPRISES INC**
Also Called: Spectra Apparel
5521 Schaefer Ave, Chino (91710-9070)
PHONE..................714 683-2820
Rauf Gajiani, *Pr*
Mohammad Joorabchi, *COO*
**EMP:** 18 **EST:** 2011
**SQ FT:** 40,000
**SALES (est):** 796.88K **Privately Held**
**SIC: 5136** 5137 2253 2321  Men's and boy's clothing; Women's and children's clothing; T-shirts and tops, knit; Sport shirts, men's and boys': from purchased materials

**(P-17080)**
**SAYARI SHAHRZAD**
Also Called: Blue Bay Industries
4822 Aqueduct Ave, Encino (91436-1621)
PHONE..................310 903-6368
Shahrzad Sayari, *Owner*
**EMP:** 25 **EST:** 2017
**SALES (est):** 647.33K **Privately Held**

# PRODUCTS & SERVICES SECTION
## 5137 - Women's And Children's Clothing (P-17100)

SIC: 5136 2339 2329 5651 Men's and boys' sportswear and work clothing; Women's and misses' athletic clothing and sportswear ; Ski and snow clothing: men's and boys'; Unisex clothing stores

### (P-17081)
### SPORTEK INTERNATIONAL INC
Also Called: Sport Tek
2425 S Eastern Ave, Commerce (90040-1414)
PHONE..................213 239-6700
Joseph Hanasabzadeh, Pr
Manouchehr Satirian, VP
Ben Hanasabzadeh, CEO
◆ EMP: 18 EST: 2003
SQ FT: 50,000
SALES (est): 3.63MM Privately Held
Web: www.sportek.com
SIC: 5136 5137 2254 Sportswear, men's and boys'; Sportswear, women's and children's; Underwear, knit

### (P-17082)
### TEE TOP OF CALIFORNIA INC (PA)
Also Called: Procelebrity
11801 Goldring Rd, Arcadia (91006-5880)
PHONE..................626 303-1868
Herbert Huang, CEO
Frances Huang, Treas
Balentina Huang, VP Sls
◆ EMP: 20 EST: 1977
SQ FT: 2,000
SALES (est): 5.28MM
SALES (corp-wide): 5.28MM Privately Held
Web: www.goprocelebrity.com
SIC: 5136 2396 2395 Shirts, men's and boys' ; Automotive and apparel trimmings; Pleating and stitching

### (P-17083)
### URGENT GEAR INC
Also Called: Ug Storage
1955 E 48th St, Vernon (90058-2005)
PHONE..................213 741-9926
Babak Roofian, CEO
Soleiman Roofian, Pr
Ramin Roofian, VP
◆ EMP: 18 EST: 1982
SQ FT: 30,000
SALES (est): 2.91MM Privately Held
Web: www.urgentgear.com
SIC: 5136 2392 Men's and boy's clothing; Bags, garment storage: except paper or plastic film

### (P-17084)
### VANTAGE CUSTOM CLASSICS INC
Also Called: Vantage Apparel
1815 Ritchey St, Santa Ana (92705-5124)
PHONE..................714 755-1133
Patty Venny, Mgr
EMP: 117
SALES (corp-wide): 16.32MM Privately Held
Web: www.vantageapparel.com
SIC: 5136 2397 2395 Sportswear, men's and boys'; Schiffli machine embroideries; Pleating and stitching
PA: Vantage Custom Classics, Inc.
100 Vantage Dr
732 340-3000

## 5137 Women's And Children's Clothing

### (P-17085)
### 2253 APPAREL LLC (PA)
Also Called: Celebrity Pink
1708 Aeros Way, Montebello (90640-6504)
PHONE..................323 837-9800
Doron Kadosh, CEO
Benny Goldstein, *
David Kadosh, *
▲ EMP: 55 EST: 2004
SQ FT: 50,000
SALES (est): 20.12MM Privately Held
Web: www.celebpink.com
SIC: 5137 2211 2339 Women's and children's dresses, suits, skirts, and blouses ; Denims; Jeans: women's, misses', and juniors'

### (P-17086)
### DAMO TEXTILE INC
Also Called: Damo Clothing Company
12121 Wilshire Blvd Ste 1120, Los Angeles (90025-1164)
PHONE..................213 741-1323
James Min, CEO
Paul Eeahn, *
Edwin Min, *
▲ EMP: 40 EST: 1999
SALES (est): 8.59MM Privately Held
Web: www.damoclothing.com
SIC: 5137 3999 Women's and children's clothing; Atomizers, toiletry

### (P-17087)
### DC SHOES INC
Also Called: Quiksilver/Dc Shoes
11310 Cantu Galleano Ranch Rd, Mira Loma (91752-3717)
PHONE..................951 361-7712
EMP: 16
Web: www.dcshoes.com
SIC: 5137 5136 5139 2329 Women's and children's clothing; Men's and boy's clothing ; Footwear; Men's and boys' sportswear and athletic clothing
PA: Dc Shoes, Llc
5600 Argosy Ave Ste 100

### (P-17088)
### DG BRANDS INC
Also Called: Dreamgirl International
5548 Lindbergh Ln, Bell (90201-6410)
PHONE..................323 268-0220
▲ EMP: 55 EST: 1978
SALES (est): 8.84MM Privately Held
Web: www.dreamgirldirect.com
SIC: 5137 2389 2329 Lingerie; Costumes; Athletic clothing, except uniforms: men's, youths' and boys'

### (P-17089)
### DOUBLE ZERO INC (PA)
Also Called: Hyfve
5808 Wilmington Ave, Vernon (90058-3830)
PHONE..................323 234-6000
Hellen Lee, Pr
Denny Choi, VP
Bill Kim, CFO
▲ EMP: 15 EST: 2001
SALES (est): 2.51MM
SALES (corp-wide): 2.51MM Privately Held
Web: www.hyfve.com
SIC: 5137 5699 2339 Apparel belts, women's and children's; Designers, apparel ; Service apparel, washable: women's

### (P-17090)
### FINAL TOUCH APPAREL INC
Also Called: Final Touch Apparel
116 E 32nd St, Los Angeles (90011-1916)
PHONE..................323 484-9621
Mark Min Hyuk Kim, CEO
June Lim, *
▲ EMP: 25 EST: 2017
SQ FT: 16,000
SALES (est): 1.73MM Privately Held
Web: www.finaltouchapparel.com
SIC: 5137 2331 5632 Women's and children's clothing; Women's and misses' blouses and shirts; Apparel accessories

### (P-17091)
### FLIRT INC
Also Called: Belldini
141 E Jefferson Blvd, Los Angeles (90011-2330)
PHONE..................213 748-4442
▲ EMP: 20
Web: www.belldini.com
SIC: 5137 2339 Women's and children's sportswear and swimsuits; Sportswear, women's

### (P-17092)
### JOHNNY WAS LLC
395 Santa Monica Pl Ste 124, Santa Monica (90401-3477)
PHONE..................310 656-0600
Eli Levite, Brnch Mgr
EMP: 98
SALES (corp-wide): 1.57B Publicly Held
Web: www.johnnywas.com
SIC: 5137 2339 Women's and children's clothing; Women's and misses' accessories
HQ: Johnny Was, Llc
712 S Olive St
Los Angeles CA 90014
866 942-8806

### (P-17093)
### LA DYE & PRINT INC
13416 Estrella Ave, Gardena (90248-1513)
PHONE..................310 327-3200
George Chaghouri, CEO
EMP: 35 EST: 2011
SQ FT: 1,800
SALES (est): 5.4MM Privately Held
Web: www.ladyeandprint.com
SIC: 5137 2269 Women's and children's dresses, suits, skirts, and blouses; Linen fabrics: dyeing, finishing, and printing

### (P-17094)
### LILY BLEU INC
Also Called: Jessie & Jenna
1406 W 178th St, Gardena (90248-3202)
PHONE..................310 225-2522
Michael Weis, CEO
Barbara Cambilargiu, VP
▲ EMP: 20 EST: 2002
SQ FT: 8,700
SALES (est): 2.38MM Privately Held
Web: www.leahzawadzki.com
SIC: 5137 2339 Women's and children's clothing; Sportswear, women's

### (P-17095)
### LYMI INC (PA)
Also Called: Reformation
2263 E Vernon Ave, Vernon (90058-1631)
PHONE..................844 701-0139
Hali Borenstein, CEO
Jennifer Maclellan, *
Yael Alfalo, *
▲ EMP: 100 EST: 2013
SQ FT: 120,000
SALES (est): 97.11MM
SALES (corp-wide): 97.11MM Privately Held
Web: www.thereformation.com
SIC: 5137 2335 Women's and children's clothing; Women's, junior's, and misses' dresses

### (P-17096)
### NEW PRIDE CORPORATION
Also Called: Belinda
5101 Pacific Blvd, Vernon (90058-2217)
PHONE..................323 584-6608
Miran Byun, CEO
Ho Lee, Pr
EMP: 55 EST: 2007
SQ FT: 5,000
SALES (est): 4.76MM Privately Held
SIC: 5137 2331 Women's and children's clothing; Women's and misses' blouses and shirts

### (P-17097)
### PHOENIX TEXTILE INC (PA)
Also Called: Level 99
14600 S Broadway, Gardena (90248-1812)
PHONE..................310 715-7090
Cindy Change, CEO
Dominic Poon, CFO
◆ EMP: 87 EST: 1984
SQ FT: 39,000
SALES (est): 8.96MM
SALES (corp-wide): 8.96MM Privately Held
Web: www.level99jeans.com
SIC: 5137 2337 3144 Women's and children's accessories; Women's and misses' capes and jackets; Boots, canvas or leather: women's

### (P-17098)
### RUBY RIBBON INC
4607 Lakeview Canyon Rd Pmb 405, Westlake Village (91361-4028)
PHONE..................650 449-4470
Melyn Campbell, CEO
▲ EMP: 25 EST: 2012
SALES (est): 2.37MM Privately Held
Web: www.rubyribbon.com
SIC: 5137 5632 5699 2254 Underwear: women's, children's, and infants'; Lingerie and corsets (underwear); Sports apparel; Shorts, shirts, slips, and panties (underwear): knit

### (P-17099)
### RUNWAY LIQUIDATION LLC (HQ)
2761 Fruitland Ave, Vernon (90058-3607)
PHONE..................323 589-2224
Martine Melloul, *
Brian Fleming, *
Bernd Kroeber, *
◆ EMP: 75 EST: 1989
SQ FT: 500,000
SALES (est): 56.41MM
SALES (corp-wide): 122.83MM Privately Held
Web: www.bcbg.com
SIC: 5137 5621 2335 Women's and children's clothing; Women's clothing stores ; Women's, junior's, and misses' dresses
PA: Marquee Brands Llc
330 W 34th St Fl 15
212 203-8135

### (P-17100)
### SNOWMASS APPAREL INC (PA)
Also Called: County Clothing Company
15225 Alton Pkwy, Irvine (92618-2354)
PHONE..................949 788-0617

## 5137 - Women's And Children's Clothing (P-17101)

George Wong, *CEO*
Edmond Wong, *
Harry Yip, *
▲ **EMP:** 45 **EST:** 1984
**SALES (est):** 1.52MM
**SALES (corp-wide):** 1.52MM **Privately Held**
**SIC: 5137** 5136 2339 Women's and children's outerwear; Men's and boys' outerwear; Women's and misses' outerwear, nec

### (P-17101)
### SWATFAME INC (PA)
Also Called: Kut From The Kloth
16425 Gale Ave, City Of Industry (91745-1722)
**PHONE**.................................626 961-7928
Mitchell Quaranta, *CEO*
Jonathan Greenberg, *
Brian Min, *
Bruce Stern, *
▲ **EMP:** 290 **EST:** 1978
**SQ FT:** 233,000
**SALES (est):** 48.42MM
**SALES (corp-wide):** 48.42MM **Privately Held**
**Web:** www.swatfame.com
**SIC: 5137** 2211 2339 Dresses; Denims; Women's and misses' outerwear, nec

### (P-17102)
### TEEKI
1105 N Topanga Canyon Blvd, Topanga (90290-4233)
**PHONE**.................................323 835-6397
**EMP:** 17 **EST:** 2017
**SALES (est):** 449.2K **Privately Held**
**Web:** www.teeki.com
**SIC: 5137** 2389 Women's and children's clothing; Apparel and accessories, nec

### (P-17103)
### TEQUILA BLUES INC
Also Called: Lave Apparel
2475 Paseo De Las Americas # 1053, San Diego (92154-7255)
**PHONE**.................................310 526-8002
Odysseus Demetriadi, *CEO*
**EMP:** 15 **EST:** 2012
**SALES (est):** 2.69MM **Privately Held**
**Web:** www.laveapparel.com
**SIC: 5137** 5136 5047 3821 Apparel belts, women's and children's; Apparel belts, men's and boys'; Medical and hospital equipment; Incubators, laboratory

### (P-17104)
### THE TIMING INC
Also Called: Timing Fashion
2807 S Santa Fe Ave, Vernon (90058-1408)
**PHONE**.................................323 589-5577
Kevin Kim, *CEO*
Bowhan Kim, *
Alice Kang, *
◆ **EMP:** 40 **EST:** 1989
**SALES (est):** 4.93MM **Privately Held**
**Web:** www.timingfashion.com
**SIC: 5137** 2331 2335 2339 Women's and children's clothing; Women's and misses' blouses and shirts; Women's, junior's, and misses' dresses; Women's and misses' outerwear, nec

### (P-17105)
### THIRDLOVE INC
Also Called: Thirdlove
555 Market St Fl 13, San Francisco (94105-2806)
**PHONE**.................................415 692-0089
Heidi Zak, *CEO*
Jenny Oh, *CFO*
Phillip Spector, *
**EMP:** 230 **EST:** 2012
**SALES (est):** 46.19MM **Privately Held**
**Web:** www.thirdlove.com
**SIC: 5137** 2342 Underwear: women's, children's, and infants'; Brassieres

### (P-17106)
### TYR SPORT INC (HQ)
Also Called: T Y R
5559 Mcfadden Ave, Huntington Beach (92649-1317)
P.O. Box 1930 (92647-1930)
**PHONE**.................................714 897-0799
Matt Dilorenzo, *CEO*
◆ **EMP:** 17 **EST:** 1984
**SALES (est):** 48.54MM
**SALES (corp-wide):** 48.54MM **Privately Held**
**Web:** www.tyr.com
**SIC: 5137** 5136 5091 2329 Sportswear, women's and children's; Beachwear, men's and boys'; Sporting and recreation goods; Bathing suits and swimwear: men's and boys'
**PA:** Swimwear Anywhere, Inc.
   85 Sherwood Ave
   800 647-6335

---

## 5139 Footwear

### (P-17107)
### ACI INTERNATIONAL (PA)
844 Moraga Dr, Los Angeles (90049-1632)
**PHONE**.................................310 889-3400
Steven Jackson, *CEO*
David Mankowitz, *
Anna Liau, *
▲ **EMP:** 99 **EST:** 1952
**SQ FT:** 40,000
**SALES (est):** 23.7MM
**SALES (corp-wide):** 23.7MM **Privately Held**
**Web:** www.acifootwear.com
**SIC: 5139** 3021 Shoes; Rubber and plastics footwear

### (P-17108)
### ASICS AMERICA CORPORATION (HQ)
Also Called: Asics Tiger
7755 Irvine Center Dr Ste 400, Irvine (92618-2904)
**PHONE**.................................949 453-8888
Gene Mccarthy, *Pr*
Seiho Gohashi, *
Kenji Sakai, *
◆ **EMP:** 109 **EST:** 1973
**SALES (est):** 453.96MM **Privately Held**
**Web:** www.asics.com
**SIC: 5139** 5136 5137 2369 Footwear, athletic; Sportswear, men's and boys'; Sportswear, women's and children's; Girl's and children's outerwear, nec
**PA:** Asics Corporation
   7-1-1, Minatojimanakamachi, Chuo-Ku

### (P-17109)
### CAPE ROBBIN INC
1943 W Mission Blvd, Pomona (91766-1037)
**PHONE**.................................626 810-8080
Michael Chen, *CEO*
▲ **EMP:** 50 **EST:** 2011
**SQ FT:** 20,000
**SALES (est):** 4.33MM **Privately Held**
**Web:** www.caperobbin.com

**SIC: 5139** 3171 Shoes; Handbags, women's

### (P-17110)
### SKECHERS USA INC
Also Called: Skechers Factory Outlet 335
29800 Eucalyptus Ave, Moreno Valley (92555-6738)
**PHONE**.................................951 242-4307
Carlette Moore, *Mgr*
**EMP:** 49
**Web:** local.skechers.com
**SIC: 5139** 3021 Footwear; Shoes, rubber or plastic molded to fabric
**PA:** Skechers U.S.A., Inc.
   228 Manhattan Beach Blvd

### (P-17111)
### SOUTH CONE INC
Also Called: Reef
5935 Darwin Ct, Carlsbad (92008-7302)
**PHONE**.................................760 431-2300
Mike Jensen, *CEO*
Daniella Turenshine, *CFO*
◆ **EMP:** 120 **EST:** 1984
**SQ FT:** 37,583
**SALES (est):** 7.09MM
**SALES (corp-wide):** 10.45B **Publicly Held**
**Web:** www.reef.com
**SIC: 5139** 3144 3143 Shoes; Women's footwear, except athletic; Men's footwear, except athletic
**PA:** V.F. Corporation
   1551 Wewatta St
   720 778-4000

---

## 5141 Groceries, General Line

### (P-17112)
### AFC TRADING & WHOLESALE INC
Also Called: American Food Co
4738 Valley Blvd, Los Angeles (90032-3834)
**PHONE**.................................323 223-7738
Jackson K H Wu, *Pr*
◆ **EMP:** 20 **EST:** 1985
**SQ FT:** 20,000
**SALES (est):** 6.45MM **Privately Held**
**Web:** www.afcsoyfoods.com
**SIC: 5141** 2099 Food brokers; Tofu, except frozen desserts

### (P-17113)
### BROOKS RESTAURANT GROUP INC (PA)
Also Called: Dynaco Equipment Co
220 Five Cities Dr, Pismo Beach (93449-3004)
**PHONE**.................................559 485-8520
**EMP:** 35 **EST:** 1973
**SALES (est):** 23.06MM
**SALES (corp-wide):** 23.06MM **Privately Held**
**SIC: 5141** 5087 2011 5812 Groceries, general line; Restaurant supplies; Meat packing plants; Steak restaurant

### (P-17114)
### GOURMET FOODS INC (PA)
2910 E Harcourt St, Compton (90221-5502)
**PHONE**.................................310 632-3300
Marcel Lagnaz, *Managing Member*
Mitch Rosen, *Managing Member*
◆ **EMP:** 80 **EST:** 1986
**SQ FT:** 35,000
**SALES (est):** 21.76MM
**SALES (corp-wide):** 21.76MM **Privately Held**
**Web:** www.gourmetfoodsinc.com

**SIC: 5141** 5812 2099 Food brokers; Eating places; Food preparations, nec

### (P-17115)
### ICPK CORPORATION
Also Called: Hpp Food Services
1130 W C St, Wilmington (90744-5102)
**PHONE**.................................310 830-8020
**EMP:** 70
**SALES (corp-wide):** 17.78MM **Privately Held**
**Web:** www.hppfs.com
**SIC: 5141** 2035 Groceries, general line; Dressings, salad: raw and cooked (except dry mixes)
**PA:** Icpk Corporation
   16700 Valley View Ave # 170
   714 321-7025

### (P-17116)
### NONGSHIM AMERICA INC (HQ)
Also Called: Nongshim
12155 6th St, Rancho Cucamonga (91730-6115)
**PHONE**.................................909 481-3698
Dong Y Shin, *CEO*
Joon Park, *
Jongmin Chung, *
Chris Gepford, *
◆ **EMP:** 250 **EST:** 1994
**SALES (est):** 83.03MM **Privately Held**
**Web:** www.nongshimusa.com
**SIC: 5141** 2098 Food brokers; Noodles (e.g. egg, plain, and water), dry
**PA:** Nongshim Co., Ltd.
   112 Yeouidaebang-Ro, Dongjak-Gu

### (P-17117)
### OAKHURST INDUSTRIES INC
Also Called: Freund Baking Co
3265 Investment Blvd, Hayward (94545-3806)
**PHONE**.................................510 265-2400
Jim Freund, *Prin*
**EMP:** 130
**SQ FT:** 67,896
**Web:** www.crownbullionreceivership.com
**SIC: 5141** 2051 Groceries, general line; Bread, cake, and related products
**PA:** Oakhurst Industries, Inc.
   2050 S Tubeway Ave

### (P-17118)
### REAL MEX FOODS INC
Also Called: El Torito Franchising Company
5660 Katella Ave Ste 200, Cypress (90630-5059)
**PHONE**.................................714 523-0031
**EMP:** 100
**SIC: 5141** 5182 5087 2099 Food brokers; Wine and distilled beverages; Restaurant supplies; Food preparations, nec

### (P-17119)
### UNION SUP COMSY SOLUTIONS INC
2301 E Pacifica Pl, Rancho Dominguez (90220-6210)
**PHONE**.................................785 357-5005
Guy Steele, *CFO*
Kyle Deere, *
**EMP:** 323 **EST:** 2012
**SALES (est):** 18.19MM **Publicly Held**
**Web:** www.unionsupply.com
**SIC: 5141** 5661 2252 Food brokers; Footwear, athletic; Men's, boys', and girls' hosiery
**HQ:** Union Supply Group, Inc.
   2500 Regent Blvd Ste 100
   Dallas TX 75261

# PRODUCTS & SERVICES SECTION

## 5145 - Confectionery (P-17139)

**(P-17120)**
**US FOODS INC**
Also Called: Saladinos Foodservice
3325 W Figarden Dr, Fresno (93711-3909)
PHONE...................559 271-3700
Dave Flitman, *Brnch Mgr*
EMP: 559
Web: www.usfoods.com
SIC: **5141** 2099  Food brokers; Food preparations, nec
HQ: Us Foods, Inc.
9399 W Higgins Rd Ste 500
Rosemont IL 60018

**(P-17121)**
**US FOODS INC**
15155 Northam St, La Mirada (90638-5754)
P.O. Box 29283 (85038-9283)
PHONE...................714 670-3500
David Patterson, *Brnch Mgr*
EMP: 172
Web: www.usfoods.com
SIC: **5141** 5046 3556 2099  Food brokers; Commercial equipment, nec; Food products machinery; Food preparations, nec
HQ: Us Foods, Inc.
9399 W Higgins Rd Ste 500
Rosemont IL 60018

## 5142 Packaged Frozen Goods

**(P-17122)**
**JECKYS BEST INC**
Also Called: Jab Foods
26450 Summit Cir, Santa Clarita (91350-2991)
PHONE...................661 259-1313
Jecky Bicer, *Pr*
Eitay Bicer, *
▲ EMP: 30 EST: 1997
SQ FT: 25,000
SALES (est): 5.28MM **Privately Held**
Web: www.jabfoods.com
SIC: **5142** 2038  Bakery products, frozen; Frozen specialties, nec

**(P-17123)**
**LUNCH BUNCH CO**
Also Called: Lunch Bunch
4351 Melrose Ave, Los Angeles (90029-3542)
PHONE...................310 383-5233
Natasha Case, *CEO*
EMP: 16 EST: 2021
SALES (est): 1MM **Privately Held**
SIC: **5142** 8299 2656  Packaged frozen goods; Educational services; Sanitary food containers

**(P-17124)**
**WEI-CHUAN USA INC (PA)**
6655 Garfield Ave, Bell Gardens (90201-1807)
PHONE...................626 225-7168
Steve Lin, *Pr*
William Huang, *Treas*
Benny Chang, *Sec*
◆ EMP: 120 EST: 1972
SQ FT: 38,000
SALES (est): 92.64MM
SALES (corp-wide): 92.64MM **Privately Held**
Web: www.weichuanusa.com
SIC: **5142** 2038  Packaged frozen goods; Dinners, frozen and packaged

## 5143 Dairy Products, Except Dried Or Canned

**(P-17125)**
**CHALLENGE DAIRY PRODUCTS INC**
14970 Catalina St, San Leandro (94577-6614)
PHONE...................510 351-3600
Terry Bunk, *Brnch Mgr*
EMP: 15
SALES (corp-wide): 3.32B **Privately Held**
Web: www.challengedairy.com
SIC: **5143** 2023 2021 5149  Milk; Dry, condensed and evaporated dairy products; Creamery butter; Groceries and related products, nec
HQ: Challenge Dairy Products, Inc
6701 Donlon Way
Dublin CA 94568
925 828-6160

**(P-17126)**
**CLEMSON DISTRIBUTION INC (PA)**
20722 Currier Rd, City Of Industry (91789-2903)
PHONE...................909 595-2770
Rolando T Santos, *Pr*
Emeline Santos, *
▲ EMP: 23 EST: 1994
SQ FT: 32,000
SALES (est): 60.52MM
SALES (corp-wide): 60.52MM **Privately Held**
Web: www.clemsondistribution.com
SIC: **5143** 2013  Ice cream and ices; Prepared beef products, from purchased beef

**(P-17127)**
**CREMI MEX INC**
Also Called: Centro America Foods
14010 Live Oak Ave, Baldwin Park (91706-1340)
PHONE...................323 235-0004
Jose R Salinas, *CEO*
Guillermo Salinas, *Pr*
Juanita Salinas, *Sec*
Francisco Salinas, *Treas*
▲ EMP: 15 EST: 1998
SQ FT: 5,535
SALES (est): 6.8MM **Privately Held**
Web: www.cremimex.com
SIC: **5143** 2099  Cheese; Ready-to-eat meals, salads, and sandwiches

**(P-17128)**
**DREYERS GRND ICE CREAM HLDNGS (DH)**
590 Ygnacio Valley Rd, Walnut Creek (94596-1801)
PHONE...................510 652-8187
Michael T Mitchell, *CEO*
Steve Barbour, *
◆ EMP: 230 EST: 2002
SALES (est): 16.33MM
SALES (corp-wide): 2.67MM **Privately Held**
Web: www.dreyersgrandicecream.com
SIC: **5143** 5451 2024  Frozen dairy desserts; Ice cream (packaged); Ice cream and frozen deserts
HQ: Froneri International Limited
Richmond House
Northallerton DL7 9
167 742-3397

**(P-17129)**
**FOSTER DAIRY FARMS (PA)**
Also Called: Crystal Creamery
529 Kansas Ave, Modesto (95351-1515)
PHONE...................209 576-3400
Dennis Roberts, *Pr*
Mark Shaw, *
▼ EMP: 800 EST: 1958
SALES (est): 459.3MM
SALES (corp-wide): 459.3MM **Privately Held**
Web: www.crystalcreamery.com
SIC: **5143** 2026  Dairy products, except dried or canned; Fluid milk

**(P-17130)**
**FOSTER DAIRY PRODUCTS DISTRG (PA)**
529 Kansas Ave, Modesto (95351-1515)
PHONE...................209 576-3400
Jeff Foster, *Pr*
EMP: 25 EST: 1951
SALES (est): 4.55MM
SALES (corp-wide): 4.55MM **Privately Held**
SIC: **5143** 2026  Dairy products, except dried or canned; Fluid milk

**(P-17131)**
**HOKEY POKEY LLC**
Also Called: Hokey Pokey La
1235 24th St Unit 4, Santa Monica (90404-1329)
PHONE...................213 361-2503
Bharat Chalmers, *Managing Member*
EMP: 25 EST: 2022
SALES (est): 900K **Privately Held**
SIC: **5143** 5149 2024 7389  Frozen dairy desserts; Coffee and tea; Dairy based frozen desserts; Business services, nec

**(P-17132)**
**MCCONNELLS FINE ICE CREAMS LLC**
800 Del Norte Blvd, Oxnard (93030-8971)
PHONE...................805 963-8813
Briana Gray, *Managing Member*
Charlie Price, *Managing Member**
Michael Palmer, *Managing Member**
Eva Ein, *Managing Member**
EMP: 38 EST: 2011
SQ FT: 184,000
SALES (est): 20.28MM **Privately Held**
Web: www.mcconnells.com
SIC: **5143** 2024  Ice cream and ices; Ice cream, bulk

**(P-17133)**
**YOLO ICE & CREAMERY INC**
1462 Churchill Downs Ave, Woodland (95776-6113)
PHONE...................530 662-7337
David J Molinaro, *CEO*
EMP: 17 EST: 1960
SQ FT: 2,500
SALES (est): 4.53MM **Privately Held**
Web: www.yoloiceandcreamery.com
SIC: **5143** 2097  Dairy products, except dried or canned; Manufactured ice

## 5144 Poultry And Poultry Products

**(P-17134)**
**NULAID FOODS INC (PA)**
200 W 5th St, Ripon (95366-2793)
PHONE...................209 599-2121
David K Crockett, *Pr*
Scott Hennecke, *
EMP: 70 EST: 1963
SQ FT: 5,000
SALES (est): 20.66MM
SALES (corp-wide): 20.66MM **Privately Held**
Web: www.nulaid.com
SIC: **5144** 2047 2015 2023  Eggs; Dog food; Egg processing; Cream substitutes

**(P-17135)**
**SQUAB PRODUCERS CALIF INC**
409 Primo Way, Modesto (95358-5721)
PHONE...................209 537-4744
Robert Shipley, *Pr*
EMP: 55 EST: 1943
SQ FT: 11,000
SALES (est): 3.46MM **Privately Held**
Web: www.squab.com
SIC: **5144** 2015  Poultry: live, dressed or frozen (unpackaged); Poultry slaughtering and processing

**(P-17136)**
**SUNRISE FARMS LLC**
395 Liberty Rd, Petaluma (94952-2811)
PHONE...................707 778-6450
James Carlson, *Mgr*
Al Nissen, *
Richard Weber, *
Arnold Riebli, *
▲ EMP: 65 EST: 1966
SQ FT: 10,000
SALES (est): 9.96MM **Privately Held**
SIC: **5144** 2015  Eggs: cleaning, oil treating, packing, and grading; Poultry slaughtering and processing

## 5145 Confectionery

**(P-17137)**
**ALL NUTS AND SNACKS INC**
12910 San Fernando Rd, Sylmar (91342-3601)
PHONE...................818 367-5902
Gary Eshgian, *CEO*
Mehdi Vosogh, *COO*
EMP: 15 EST: 2011
SQ FT: 38,000
SALES (est): 1.6MM **Privately Held**
Web: www.americannuts.com
SIC: **5145** 2096  Nuts, salted or roasted; Cheese curls and puffs

**(P-17138)**
**AMERICAN NUTS LLC (HQ)**
12950 San Fernando Rd, Sylmar (91342-3601)
PHONE...................818 364-8855
Jim Duatte, *Pr*
Aamir Chinoy, *CFO*
Karrie Brooks Ctrl, *Prin*
EMP: 15 EST: 2018
SALES (est): 92.66MM
SALES (corp-wide): 132.47MM **Privately Held**
Web: www.americannuts.com
SIC: **5145** 2034  Nuts, salted or roasted; Dried and dehydrated fruits
PA: Gauge Capital Llc
1256 Main St Ste 256
682 334-5800

**(P-17139)**
**B B G MANAGEMENT GROUP (PA)**
Also Called: Granlund Candies
12164 California St, Yucaipa (92399-4333)
PHONE...................909 797-9581

## 5145 - Confectionery (P-17140)

R Scott Burkle, *Pr*
Margie Rogan, *
**EMP:** 50 **EST:** 1961
**SQ FT:** 10,000
**SALES (est):** 1.83MM
**SALES (corp-wide):** 1.83MM **Privately Held**
**SIC:** 5145 2064 Candy; Candy and other confectionery products

### (P-17140)
### BALANCE FOODS INC
5743 Smithway St Ste 103, Commerce (90040-1548)
**PHONE**..................323 838-5555
Florencia Cuetara, *CEO*
Theia D Ainlle Esq, *Sr VP*
**EMP:** 38 **EST:** 2014
**SALES (est):** 4.46MM **Privately Held**
**Web:** www.balancefoods.net
**SIC:** 5145 2096 Snack foods; Potato chips and similar snacks

### (P-17141)
### CARRIERE FAMILY FARMS LLC
1640 State Highway 45, Glenn (95943-9649)
**PHONE**..................530 934-8200
William David Carriere, *Managing Member*
**EMP:** 40 **EST:** 2016
**SALES (est):** 15.3MM **Privately Held**
**Web:** www.carrierefarms.com
**SIC:** 5145 0191 5159 3999 Nuts, salted or roasted; General farms, primarily crop; Nuts and nut by-products; Nut shells, grinding, from purchased nuts

### (P-17142)
### CENTURY SNACKS LLC
5560 E Slauson Ave, Commerce (90040-2921)
**PHONE**..................323 278-9578
Valerie Oswalt, *CEO*
David Lowe, *Ch*
Tiffany Obenchain, *VP*
Mel Deane, *Vice Chairman*
Stephen Famolaro, *CFO*
**EMP:** 330 **EST:** 1999
**SQ FT:** 280,000
**SALES (est):** 18.17MM
**SALES (corp-wide):** 118.93MM **Privately Held**
**Web:** www.centurysnacks.com
**SIC:** 5145 2064 Nuts, salted or roasted; Nuts, candy covered
**HQ:** Scncs, Llc
  5560 E Slauson Ave
  Commerce CA 90040
  323 278-9578

### (P-17143)
### ENERGY CLUB INC
Also Called: Energy Club
12950 Pierce St, Pacoima (91331-2526)
▲ **EMP:** 80 **EST:** 1984
**SALES (est):** 3.86MM
**SALES (corp-wide):** 5.29MM **Privately Held**
**SIC:** 5145 2099 Confectionery; Food preparations, nec
**PA:** Shackleton Equity Partners Llc
  4119 Guardian St
  310 733-5658

### (P-17144)
### FRITO-LAY NORTH AMERICA INC
Also Called: Frito-Lay
1500 Francisco St, Torrance (90501-1329)
**PHONE**..................310 224-5600

Dexter Matt, *Genl Mgr*
**EMP:** 15
**SQ FT:** 75,861
**SALES (corp-wide):** 86.39B **Publicly Held**
**Web:** www.fritolay.com
**SIC:** 5145 2099 2096 Snack foods; Food preparations, nec; Potato chips and similar snacks
**HQ:** Frito-Lay North America, Inc.
  7701 Legacy Dr
  Plano TX 75024

### (P-17145)
### FRITO-LAY NORTH AMERICA INC
Also Called: Frito-Lay
9846 4th St, Rancho Cucamonga (91730-5720)
**PHONE**..................909 941-6218
George Smith, *Mgr*
**EMP:** 44
**SALES (corp-wide):** 86.39B **Publicly Held**
**Web:** www.fritolay.com
**SIC:** 5145 2099 2096 Snack foods; Food preparations, nec; Potato chips and similar snacks
**HQ:** Frito-Lay North America, Inc.
  7701 Legacy Dr
  Plano TX 75024

### (P-17146)
### I LOVE BRACELETS INC
8940 Ellis Ave, Los Angeles (90034-3302)
**PHONE**..................310 839-5683
Marcia Miller, *Pr*
Jeremy Miller, *CFO*
**EMP:** 18 **EST:** 2002
**SQ FT:** 1,800
**SALES (est):** 321.33K **Privately Held**
**Web:** www.iloveaccessories.com
**SIC:** 5145 2064 Candy; Candy and other confectionery products

### (P-17147)
### JOS CANDIES LLC
2530 W 237th St, Torrance (90505-5217)
**PHONE**..................800 770-1946
Thomas King, *CEO*
Alex Schneider, *Pr*
David Choe, *CFO*
▲ **EMP:** 16 **EST:** 2012
**SALES (est):** 9.57MM **Privately Held**
**Web:** www.joscandies.com
**SIC:** 5145 2064 Candy; Candy and other confectionery products

### (P-17148)
### LAYMON CANDY CO INC
276 Commercial Rd, San Bernardino (92408-4149)
**PHONE**..................909 825-4408
Kenneth Laymon, *Pr*
Paul T Applen, *
▲ **EMP:** 27 **EST:** 1927
**SQ FT:** 43,000
**SALES (est):** 8.21MM **Privately Held**
**Web:** www.laymoncandy.com
**SIC:** 5145 2064 Candy; Candy and other confectionery products

### (P-17149)
### S&E GOURMET CUTS INC
Also Called: Country Archer Jerky
1055 E Cooley Ave, San Bernardino (92408-2819)
**PHONE**..................909 370-0155
Eugene Kang, *CEO*
Adam Razik, *
Susan Kang, *
**EMP:** 150 **EST:** 2011

**SALES (est):** 45.02MM **Privately Held**
**Web:** www.countryarcher.com
**SIC:** 5145 2013 Confectionery; Sausages and other prepared meats

### (P-17150)
### SUPERIOR NUT CO INC
5200 Valley Blvd, Los Angeles (90032-3929)
**PHONE**..................323 223-2431
Laura Rosen, *CEO*
Jacqueline Rosen, *Stockholder*
**EMP:** 18 **EST:** 1964
**SQ FT:** 22,000
**SALES (est):** 5.64MM **Privately Held**
**Web:** www.superiornutla.com
**SIC:** 5145 2068 Nuts, salted or roasted; Nuts: dried, dehydrated, salted or roasted

### (P-17151)
### TREE NUTS LLC
451 W F St, Turlock (95380-6079)
P.O. Box 1009 (95381-1009)
**PHONE**..................209 669-6400
◆ **EMP:** 40 **EST:** 2008
**SQ FT:** 50,000
**SALES (est):** 10.21MM **Privately Held**
**SIC:** 5145 2068 Nuts, salted or roasted; Salted and roasted nuts and seeds

### (P-17152)
### YOUBAR INC (PA)
445 Wilson Way, City Of Industry (91744-3935)
**PHONE**..................626 537-1851
Anthony Flynn, *CEO*
Anthony M Flynn, *
**EMP:** 53 **EST:** 2007
**SALES (est):** 30.25MM **Privately Held**
**Web:** www.youbars.com
**SIC:** 5145 5812 2064 Snack foods; Food bars; Granola and muesli, bars and clusters

## 5146 Fish And Seafoods

### (P-17153)
### BLUE RIVER SEAFOOD INC
Also Called: Joe Pucci & Sons Seafoods
25447 Industrial Blvd, Hayward (94545-2931)
**PHONE**..................510 300-6800
Chris Lam, *CEO*
▲ **EMP:** 53 **EST:** 1918
**SQ FT:** 53,000
**SALES (est):** 21.39MM **Privately Held**
**Web:** www.puccifoods.com
**SIC:** 5146 2092 Fish, fresh; Fresh or frozen packaged fish

### (P-17154)
### CAL RANCH INC
3201 Lance Dr, Stockton (95205-2441)
**PHONE**..................209 465-8999
Charles Doug, *VP*
**EMP:** 44
**SALES (corp-wide):** 8.27MM **Privately Held**
**Web:** www.calranchfood.com
**SIC:** 5146 2084 2092 2034 Seafoods; Wine cellars, bonded: engaged in blending wines ; Seafoods, frozen: prepared; Dried and dehydrated fruits
**PA:** Cal Ranch, Inc.
  4070 Nelson Ave Ste D
  925 429-2900

### (P-17155)
### CAL SOUTHERN SEAFOOD INC (PA)

125 Salinas Rd Ste 5b, Royal Oaks (95076-6706)
P.O. Box 939 (93441-0939)
**PHONE**..................805 698-8262
Pete J Guglielmo, *Pr*
Mike Salcedo, *Prin*
**EMP:** 25 **EST:** 2012
**SALES (est):** 11.07MM
**SALES (corp-wide):** 11.07MM **Privately Held**
**SIC:** 5146 2092 Seafoods; Seafoods, frozen: prepared

### (P-17156)
### EXCLUSIVE FRESH INC
165 Airport St, El Granada (94018-8044)
P.O. Box 308 (94018-0308)
**PHONE**..................650 728-7321
Philip Bruno, *CEO*
Greg Hampton, *
Margie Macdougall, *
**EMP:** 26 **EST:** 1993
**SQ FT:** 12,000
**SALES (est):** 5.41MM **Privately Held**
**Web:** www.exclusivefresh.com
**SIC:** 5146 2092 Seafoods; Fresh or frozen packaged fish

### (P-17157)
### H & T SEAFOOD INC
Also Called: Global Nature Foods
5598 Lindbergh Ln, Bell (90201-6410)
**PHONE**..................323 526-0888
Ivy N Tran, *CEO*
Thong Lu, *
◆ **EMP:** 41 **EST:** 1994
**SQ FT:** 120,000
**SALES (est):** 1.86MM **Privately Held**
**Web:** www.htseafood.com
**SIC:** 5146 2092 Fish and seafoods; Fresh or frozen fish or seafood chowders, soups, and stews

### (P-17158)
### PROSPECT ENTERPRISES INC (PA)
Also Called: American Fish and Seafood
625 Kohler St, Los Angeles (90021-1023)
**PHONE**..................213 599-5700
Ernest Y Doizaki, *Ch Bd*
Jack King, *
Paula Eberhardt, *
◆ **EMP:** 160 **EST:** 1947
**SQ FT:** 20,000
**SALES (est):** 47.37MM
**SALES (corp-wide):** 47.37MM **Privately Held**
**Web:** www.kansasmarine.com
**SIC:** 5146 2092 Fish, fresh; Fresh or frozen packaged fish

### (P-17159)
### TRI-UNION SEAFOODS LLC (DH)
Also Called: Chicken of Sea International
2150 E Grand Ave, El Segundo (90245-5024)
P.O. Box 85568 (92186-5568)
**PHONE**..................424 397-8556
Valentin Ramirez, *CEO*
Christie Fleming, *
Jim Cox, *
Ignatius Dharma, *
David E Roszmann, *
◆ **EMP:** 69 **EST:** 1996
**SQ FT:** 24,000
**SALES (est):** 139.17MM **Privately Held**
**SIC:** 5146 2091 Seafoods; Tuna fish: packaged in cans, jars, etc.
**HQ:** Thai Union North America, Inc.
  2150 E Grand Ave

## PRODUCTS & SERVICES SECTION
### 5149 - Groceries And Related Products, Nec (P-17179)

El Segundo CA 90245
424 397-8556

## 5147 Meats And Meat Products

**(P-17160)**
**AI FOODS CORPORATION (PA)**
1700 N Soto St, Los Angeles (90033-1127)
PHONE..................323 222-0827
Clarissa Takakawa, *CEO*
▲ **EMP:** 20 **EST:** 1995
**SALES (est):** 4.35MM
**SALES (corp-wide):** 4.35MM **Privately Held**
Web: www.aifoodscorp.com
**SIC:** 5147 2013 Meats, fresh; Cured meats, from purchased meat

**(P-17161)**
**EASTLAND CORPORATION**
Also Called: C & H Meat Company
3017 Bandini Blvd, Vernon (90058-4109)
PHONE..................323 261-5388
Young Yoo, *Pr*
Young Won, *
**EMP:** 23 **EST:** 1973
**SQ FT:** 10,000
**SALES (est):** 5.8MM **Privately Held**
Web: www.candhmeatco.com
**SIC:** 5147 2013 Meats, fresh; Cooked meats, from purchased meat

**(P-17162)**
**HEARTLAND MEAT COMPANY INC**
Also Called: H M C
3461 Main St, Chula Vista (91911-5828)
PHONE..................619 407-3668
**TOLL FREE:** 800
Joseph E Stidman, *CEO*
James Methey, *
Stephanie Stidman, *
**EMP:** 70 **EST:** 1971
**SQ FT:** 49,000
**SALES (est):** 23.07MM **Privately Held**
Web: www.heartlandmeat.com
**SIC:** 5147 2013 Meats, fresh; Sausages and other prepared meats

**(P-17163)**
**PONTRELLI & LARRICCHIA LTD**
Also Called: Pontrlli-Laricchia Sausage Mfg
6080 Malburg Way, Vernon (90058-3946)
PHONE..................323 583-6690
Dominic T Pontrelli, *Pt*
Vito Pontrelli, *Pt*
**EMP:** 21 **EST:** 1925
**SQ FT:** 20,000
**SALES (est):** 3.74MM **Privately Held**
Web: www.maestrosausage.com
**SIC:** 5147 2013 Meats and meat products; Sausages and other prepared meats

**(P-17164)**
**PRODUCERS MEAT AND PROV INC**
Also Called: Tarantino Wholesale Fd Distrs
7651 Saint Andrews Ave, San Diego (92154)
PHONE..................619 232-7593
Rose M Tarantino, *CEO*
▲ **EMP:** 35 **EST:** 1961
**SQ FT:** 10,000
**SALES (est):** 3.03MM **Privately Held**
**SIC:** 5147 2013 Meats, fresh; Sausages and other prepared meats

**(P-17165)**
**RANCHO FOODS INC**
2528 E 37th St, Vernon (90058-1725)
P.O. Box 58504 (90058-0504)
PHONE..................323 585-0503
Annette Mac Donald, *Pr*
John Mac Donald, *VP*
**EMP:** 100 **EST:** 1972
**SQ FT:** 26,000
**SALES (est):** 50.6MM **Privately Held**
Web: www.ranchofoods.com
**SIC:** 5147 2013 Meats, fresh; Sausages and other prepared meats

**(P-17166)**
**THREE SONS INC**
Also Called: Merit Day Food Service
5201 Industry Ave, Pico Rivera (90660-2505)
P.O. Box 6 (90660-0006)
PHONE..................562 801-4100
Michael Shannon Day, *CEO*
John Brenan, *
David Day, *Stockholder*
Mariellen Day, *Stockholder*
Michael Day, *Stockholder*
▲ **EMP:** 87 **EST:** 1975
**SQ FT:** 40,000
**SALES (est):** 21.35MM **Privately Held**
Web: www.americanmeatcompanies.com
**SIC:** 5147 2013 2011 Meats, cured or smoked; Sausages and other prepared meats; Meat packing plants

**(P-17167)**
**YOSEMITE MEAT COMPANY INC**
601 Zeff Rd, Modesto (95351-3942)
P.O. Box 31480 (95213-1480)
PHONE..................209 524-5117
Johnnie F Lau, *Pr*
Gay Lau, *
▲ **EMP:** 100 **EST:** 1974
**SQ FT:** 3,600
**SALES (est):** 19.55MM **Privately Held**
Web: www.yosemitemeat.com
**SIC:** 5147 2013 Meats, fresh; Bacon, side and sliced: from purchased meat

## 5148 Fresh Fruits And Vegetables

**(P-17168)**
**EVOLUTION FRESH INC**
Also Called: Evolution Juice
11655 Jersey Blvd Ste A, Rancho Cucamonga (91730-4903)
PHONE..................800 794-9986
Chris Bruzzo, *CEO*
Ricki Reves, *
▲ **EMP:** 180 **EST:** 2010
**SQ FT:** 70,000
**SALES (est):** 81.66MM
**SALES (corp-wide):** 562.6MM **Privately Held**
Web: www.evolutionfresh.com
**SIC:** 5148 2037 Fruits, fresh; Frozen fruits and vegetables
**HQ:** Wm. Bolthouse Farms, Inc.
7200 E Brundage Ln
Bakersfield CA 93307
800 467-4683

**(P-17169)**
**INDEX FRESH INC (PA)**
1250 Corona Pointe Ct Ste 401, Corona (92879-1781)
PHONE..................909 877-0999
**TOLL FREE:** 800
Dana L Thomas, *Pr*
Merrill Causey, *
Giovanni Cavaletto, *
◆ **EMP:** 52 **EST:** 1914
**SQ FT:** 40,000
**SALES (est):** 42.94MM
**SALES (corp-wide):** 42.94MM **Privately Held**
Web: www.indexfresh.com
**SIC:** 5148 2099 Fruits, fresh; Vegetables, peeled for the trade

**(P-17170)**
**LIBERTY PACKING COMPANY LLC (PA)**
Also Called: Morning Star Company The
724 Main St, Woodland (95695-3491)
PHONE..................209 826-7100
▲ **EMP:** 80 **EST:** 2001
**SALES (est):** 215.3MM
**SALES (corp-wide):** 215.3MM **Privately Held**
**SIC:** 5148 2033 Vegetables; Tomato products, packaged in cans, jars, etc.

**(P-17171)**
**SUNKIST GROWERS INC (PA)**
27770 Entertainment Dr, Valencia (91355-1091)
PHONE..................661 290-8900
Russell Hanlin Ii, *Pr*
Richard G French, *VP*
Michael Wootton, *Sr VP*
John Mc Guigan, *VP*
Russell L Hanlin Ii, *VP*
◆ **EMP:** 223 **EST:** 1893
**SQ FT:** 50,000
**SALES (est):** 81.32MM
**SALES (corp-wide):** 81.32MM **Privately Held**
Web: www.sunkist.com
**SIC:** 5148 2033 2037 2899 Fruits, fresh; Fruit juices: packaged in cans, jars, etc.; Fruit juice concentrates, frozen; Lemon oil (edible)

**(P-17172)**
**SUNKIST GROWERS INC**
11407 Avenue 144, Tipton (93272-9401)
P.O. Box 99 (93272-0099)
PHONE..................559 752-4256
John Ayers, *Mgr*
**EMP:** 18
**SALES (corp-wide):** 1.15B **Privately Held**
Web: www.sunkist.com
**SIC:** 5148 2033 Fruits, fresh; Canned fruits and specialties
**PA:** Sunkist Growers, Inc.
27770 Entertainment Dr
661 290-8900

**(P-17173)**
**VENTURA COUNTY LEMON COOP**
Also Called: Ventura Pacific Co
2620 Sakioka Dr, Oxnard (93030-5647)
P.O. Box 6986 (93031-6986)
PHONE..................805 385-3345
Donald Dames, *Pr*
Milton Daily, *Ch Bd*
James H Gill, *Sec*
Jim Waters, *Treas*
**EMP:** 80 **EST:** 1943
**SALES (est):** 14.18MM **Privately Held**
Web: www.venturapacific.com
**SIC:** 5148 4783 3999 Fruits, fresh; Containerization of goods for shipping; Fruits, artificial and preserved

## 5149 Groceries And Related Products, Nec

**(P-17174)**
**APP WHOLESALE LLC**
3686 E Olympic Blvd, Los Angeles (90023-3146)
PHONE..................323 980-8315
**EMP:** 500 **EST:** 2013
**SQ FT:** 220,000
**SALES (est):** 13.59MM **Privately Held**
Web: www.app-wholesale.com
**SIC:** 5149 2741 Specialty food items; Business service newsletters: publishing and printing

**(P-17175)**
**BAKEMARK USA LLC (PA)**
Also Called: Bakemark
7351 Crider Ave, Pico Rivera (90660-3705)
PHONE..................562 949-1054
Jim Parker, *Managing Member*
◆ **EMP:** 102 **EST:** 1928
**SQ FT:** 275,000
**SALES (est):** 563.73MM
**SALES (corp-wide):** 563.73MM **Privately Held**
Web: www.yourbakemark.com
**SIC:** 5149 2045 3556 2099 Bakery products; Flours and flour mixes, from purchased flour; Food products machinery; Food preparations, nec

**(P-17176)**
**BIZPACK LLC** ✪
17201 Daimler St, Irvine (92614-5508)
PHONE..................562 786-5159
Amjadkhan Pathan, *CEO*
**EMP:** 15 **EST:** 2023
**SALES (est):** 1.18MM **Privately Held**
**SIC:** 5149 2099 2086 Tea; Tea blending; Tea, iced: packaged in cans, bottles, etc.

**(P-17177)**
**BONAMI BAKING COMPANY INC**
380 E 10th St, Pittsburg (94565-2509)
PHONE..................925 473-9736
Magdiel F Cuellar, *Pr*
Tania Cuellar, *CFO*
**EMP:** 37 **EST:** 2011
**SALES (est):** 4.12MM **Privately Held**
**SIC:** 5149 2051 Bakery products; Bread, cake, and related products

**(P-17178)**
**CABO FOODS INC (PA)**
Also Called: Cabo Foods
301 Forest Ave, Laguna Beach (92651-2115)
PHONE..................949 463-2373
Brady Bunte, *Pr*
Jeffrey Kerr, *CEO*
**EMP:** 24 **EST:** 2003
**SALES (est):** 11.49MM
**SALES (corp-wide):** 11.49MM **Privately Held**
**SIC:** 5149 2086 2096 5145 Natural and organic foods; Carbonated beverages, nonalcoholic: pkged. in cans, bottles; Tortilla chips; Snack foods

**(P-17179)**
**CALIFORNIA BAKING COMPANY**
Also Called: California Bread Co.
681 Anita St, Chula Vista (91911-4663)
PHONE..................619 591-8289
Abraham Levy, *Pr*
**EMP:** 300 **EST:** 2002
**SALES (est):** 24.87MM **Privately Held**

## 5149 - Groceries And Related Products, Nec (P-17180)

Web: www.californiabaking.com
SIC: **5149** 2051 Bakery products; Sponge goods, bakery: except frozen

### (P-17180)
### CAPITOL DISTRIBUTION CO LLC (PA)
Also Called: Capitol Food Company
12836 Alondra Blvd, Cerritos (90703-2107)
PHONE..................562 404-4321
Douglas L Levi, *Managing Member*
John Levi, *
Douglas Jensen, *
▲ **EMP:** 36 **EST:** 1999
**SALES (est):** 139.39MM
**SALES (corp-wide):** 139.39MM **Privately Held**
Web: www.capitolfoodco.com
SIC: **5149** 2041 Bakery products; Biscuit dough

### (P-17181)
### CIBARIA INTERNATIONAL INC
705 Columbia Ave, Riverside (92507-2141)
PHONE..................951 823-8490
Kathy Griset, *Pr*
Karen Moore, *
▲ **EMP:** 30 **EST:** 1998
**SQ FT:** 55,000
**SALES (est):** 2.57MM **Privately Held**
Web: www.cibaria-intl.com
SIC: **5149** 2899 Cooking oils; Essential oils

### (P-17182)
### CJ AMERICA INC (HQ)
Also Called: C J Foods
300 S Grand Ave Ste 1100, Los Angeles (90071-3173)
PHONE..................213 338-2700
Hyunsoo Shin, *CEO*
Jae Kyung Jeon, *
◆ **EMP:** 54 **EST:** 1984
**SALES (est):** 485.8MM **Privately Held**
Web: www.cjamerica.com
SIC: **5149** 1541 3556 5169 Groceries and related products, nec; Food products manufacturing or packing plant construction; Food products machinery; Food additives and preservatives
PA: Cj Cheiljedang Corporation
  330 Dongho-Ro, Jung-Gu

### (P-17183)
### CLOVER-STORNETTA FARMS LLC (PA)
Also Called: Clover Sonoma
1800 S Mcdowell Boulevard Ext Ste 100, Petaluma (94954-6903)
P.O. Box 750369 (94975)
PHONE..................707 769-3282
TOLL FREE: 800
Marcus Benedetti, *Pr*
Dan Benedetti, *
Mike Keifer, *
Mkulima Britt, *
Gene Benedetti, *
**EMP:** 180 **EST:** 1977
**SQ FT:** 80,000
**SALES (est):** 62.21MM
**SALES (corp-wide):** 62.21MM **Privately Held**
Web: www.cloversonoma.com
SIC: **5149** 5143 2026 Juices; Dairy products, except dried or canned; Milk and cream, except fermented, cultured, and flavored

### (P-17184)
### COASTAL COCKTAILS INC (PA)
Also Called: Modern Gourmet Foods
1920 E Deere Ave Ste 100, Santa Ana (92705-5717)
PHONE..................949 250-8951
Boaz Shonfeld, *CEO*
William E Mote, *
▲ **EMP:** 35 **EST:** 2009
**SALES (est):** 39.55MM **Privately Held**
Web: www.coastalcocktails.com
SIC: **5149** 2086 Food gift baskets; Bottled and canned soft drinks

### (P-17185)
### CREATIVE ENERGY FOODS INC
9957 Medford Ave Ste 4, Oakland (94603-2360)
PHONE..................510 638-8668
Richard C Dwinell, *CEO*
Wesley Felton, *
George Jewell, *
Jacker Wong, *
◆ **EMP:** 95 **EST:** 1998
**SQ FT:** 105,000
**SALES (est):** 17.17MM **Privately Held**
Web: www.creativeenergyfoods.com
SIC: **5149** 2026 Health foods; Dips, sour cream based

### (P-17186)
### DEL MONTE FOODS INC (HQ)
Also Called: Del Monte Foods
205 N Wiget Ln, Walnut Creek (94598-2458)
PHONE..................925 949-2772
Greg Longstreet, *Pr*
Bibie Wu, *CMO*
Parag Schadeva, *
William Sawyers, *CCO*
◆ **EMP:** 125 **EST:** 2013
**SALES (est):** 784.65MM **Privately Held**
Web: www.delmontefoods.com
SIC: **5149** 2033 Groceries and related products, nec; Canned fruits and specialties
PA: Del Monte Pacific Limited
  17 Bukit Pasoh Road

### (P-17187)
### GOLD RUSH COFFEE
2626 Myrtle Ave, Eureka (95501)
P.O. Box 58 (95558)
PHONE..................707 442-2848
Karen Paff, *Owner*
**EMP:** 50 **EST:** 1984
**SALES (est):** 1.36MM **Privately Held**
Web: www.goldrushcoffee.com
SIC: **5149** 2095 5499 Coffee, green or roasted; Coffee roasting (except by wholesale grocers); Coffee

### (P-17188)
### GUAYAKI SSTNBLE RNFREST PDTS I (PA)
Also Called: Guayaki Yerba Mate
215 Rose Ave, Venice (90291-2567)
PHONE..................888 482-9254
Benjamin Mand, *CEO*
Steve Karr, *
Dave Karr, *
Alex Pryor, *
▲ **EMP:** 149 **EST:** 1999
**SALES (est):** 27.61MM
**SALES (corp-wide):** 27.61MM **Privately Held**
Web: www.guayaki.com
SIC: **5149** 2095 Beverages, except coffee and tea; Coffee extracts

### (P-17189)
### HARRIS FREEMAN & CO INC (PA)
Also Called: Harris Tea Company
3110 E Miraloma Ave, Anaheim (92806-1906)
PHONE..................714 765-7525
Anil J Shah, *CEO*
Kevin Shah, *
Meena Shah, *
◆ **EMP:** 500 **EST:** 1981
**SQ FT:** 58,000
**SALES (est):** 150K
**SALES (corp-wide):** 150K **Privately Held**
Web: www.harrisfreeman.com
SIC: **5149** 2099 Tea; Spices, including grinding

### (P-17190)
### JANS ENTERPRISES CORPORATION
Also Called: Wira Co
4181 Temple City Blvd Ste A, El Monte (91731-1030)
PHONE..................626 575-2000
Anthony Kartawinata, *Pr*
Nila Prawirawidjaja, *
◆ **EMP:** 25 **EST:** 1998
**SQ FT:** 50,000
**SALES (est):** 13.67MM **Privately Held**
Web: www.jansfood.com
SIC: **5149** 2026 2096 Specialty food items; Milk, ultra-high temperature (longlife); Potato chips and similar snacks

### (P-17191)
### KIDS HEALTHY FOODS LLC
2030 Main St Ste 1300, Irvine (92614-7220)
PHONE..................949 260-4950
Jeff Mcclelland, *CEO*
**EMP:** 25 **EST:** 2010
**SALES (est):** 9.64MM **Privately Held**
Web: www.kidshealthyfoods.com
SIC: **5149** 2099 Beverages, except coffee and tea; Tea blending

### (P-17192)
### KIKKOMAN SALES USA INC (HQ)
Also Called: Kikkoman
50 California St Ste 3600, San Francisco (94111-4760)
P.O. Box 420784 (94142-0784)
PHONE..................415 956-7750
Yuzaburo Mogi, *CEO*
Ken Saito, *
Michael Evans, *
Nakamura Mitsunodu, *
◆ **EMP:** 40 **EST:** 1957
**SQ FT:** 10,000
**SALES (est):** 40.06MM **Privately Held**
Web: www.kikkomanusa.com
SIC: **5149** 2035 Specialty food items; Pickles, sauces, and salad dressings
PA: Kikkoman Corporation
  2-1-1, Nishishimbashi

### (P-17193)
### LA TORTILLA FACTORY INC
3300 Westwind Blvd, Santa Rosa (95403-8273)
P.O. Box 763 (67107)
PHONE..................707 586-4000
Jeff D Ahlers, *CEO*
Carlos Tamayo, *
Willie Tamayo, *
David Trogdo, *
**EMP:** 310 **EST:** 1977
**SALES (est):** 64.02MM
**SALES (corp-wide):** 249.52MM **Privately Held**
Web: www.latortillafactory.com
SIC: **5149** 2051 Specialty food items; Bread, cake, and related products
PA: Flagship Food Group Llc
  2205 E Rvrside Dr Ste 200

208 383-9600

### (P-17194)
### LEE KUM KEE (USA) INC (DH)
Also Called: Lee's Kitchen
14841 Don Julian Rd, City Of Industry (91746-3110)
PHONE..................626 709-1888
Simon Wu, *CEO*
David H W Lee, *
◆ **EMP:** 44 **EST:** 1983
**SQ FT:** 50,000
**SALES (est):** 177.39MM **Privately Held**
Web: usa.lkk.com
SIC: **5149** 2099 2035 Sauces; Food preparations, nec; Pickles, sauces, and salad dressings
HQ: Lee Kum Kee International Holdings Limited
  Tai Po Indl Est
  Tai Po NT

### (P-17195)
### MANUFACTURING LOGISTICS INC
Also Called: Rising Dough Bakery
8135 Elder Creek Rd, Sacramento (95824-2307)
P.O. Box 633 (95763-0633)
PHONE..................916 387-9700
**EMP:** 20 **EST:** 1983
**SALES (est):** 784.21K **Privately Held**
SIC: **5149** 2053 2052 2051 Bakery products; Frozen bakery products, except bread; Cookies and crackers; Bread, cake, and related products

### (P-17196)
### MINH PHUNG INCORPORATED
Also Called: Banh Hoi Minh Phung
15216 Weststate St, Westminster (92683-6531)
PHONE..................714 379-0606
Chuyen Huynh, *Pr*
▲ **EMP:** 23 **EST:** 1996
**SALES (est):** 1.01MM **Privately Held**
SIC: **5149** 2098 Pasta and rice; Noodles (e.g. egg, plain, and water), dry

### (P-17197)
### MONDELEZ GLOBAL LLC
Also Called: Nabisco
5815 Clark St, Ontario (91761-3676)
PHONE..................909 605-0140
Botie Magee, *Brnch Mgr*
**EMP:** 51
Web: www.mondelezinternational.com
SIC: **5149** 2099 2052 Crackers, cookies, and bakery products; Food preparations, nec; Cookies and crackers
HQ: Mondelez Global Llc
  905 W Fulton Mkt Ste 200
  Chicago IL 60607
  847 943-4000

### (P-17198)
### MOUNTANOS BROTHERS COFFEE CO (PA)
Also Called: Mountanos Family Coffee & Tea
1331 Commerce St, Petaluma (94954-1426)
P.O. Box 927 (95470-0927)
PHONE..................707 774-8800
TOLL FREE: 800
Michael S Mountanos, *Pr*
◆ **EMP:** 45 **EST:** 1981
**SQ FT:** 24,000
**SALES (est):** 24.78MM
**SALES (corp-wide):** 24.78MM **Privately Held**

# PRODUCTS & SERVICES SECTION

## 5149 - Groceries And Related Products, Nec (P-17219)

Web: www.mfct.com
SIC: **5149** 0711 5812 2095  Coffee, green or roasted; Soil preparation services; Eating places; Roasted coffee

### (P-17199)
### NAWGAN PRODUCTS LLC
Also Called: Nawgan Beverages
34232 Pacific Coast Hwy Ste D, Dana Point (92629-3854)
PHONE..................................949 542-4425
**EMP:** 16 **EST:** 2007
**SALES (est):** 437.27K **Privately Held**
SIC: **5149** 2087  Beverages, except coffee and tea; Cordials, nonalcoholic

### (P-17200)
### NEW DESSERTS  LLC
Also Called: New Desserts, Inc.
5000 Fulton Dr, Fairfield  (94534-1677)
PHONE..................................415 780-6860
Michael Mendes, *CEO*
John Wohlgemuth, *
Leighton Mue, *
**EMP:** 71 **EST:** 1974
**SQ FT:** 73,500
**SALES (est):** 20.75MM
**SALES (corp-wide):** 228.96MM **Privately Held**
Web: www.justdesserts.com
SIC: **5149** 2024  Bakery products; Ice cream and frozen deserts
HQ: Rubicon Bakers Llc
  154 S 23rd St
  Richmond CA 94804
  510 779-3010

### (P-17201)
### NIITAKAYA USA  INC (PA)
1801 Aeros Way, Montebello  (90640-6505)
PHONE..................................323 720-5050
Katsutoshi Suda, *Pr*
Hideo Nakagawa, *
▲ **EMP:** 23 **EST:** 1981
**SQ FT:** 17,000
**SALES (est):** 9.17MM **Privately Held**
Web: www.niitakaya.com
SIC: **5149** 2099  Pickles, preserves, jellies, and jams; Food preparations, nec

### (P-17202)
### OLDE THOMPSON  LLC
2300 Celsius Ave, Oxnard  (93030-5372)
PHONE..................................805 983-0388
**EMP:** 22
**SALES (corp-wide):** 174.1MM **Privately Held**
Web: www.oldethompson.com
SIC: **5149** 2099  Groceries and related products, nec; Food preparations, nec
HQ: Olde Thompson, Llc
  3250 Camino Del Sol
  Oxnard CA 93030
  805 983-0388

### (P-17203)
### PASTA PICCININI  INC
950 N Fair Oaks Ave, Pasadena  (91103-3009)
PHONE..................................626 798-0841
Stefano Piccinini, *CEO*
▲ **EMP:** 37 **EST:** 1971
**SQ FT:** 30,000
**SALES (est):** 9.94MM **Privately Held**
Web: www.pastapiccinini.com
SIC: **5149** 5812 2045  Pasta and rice; Eating places; Biscuit dough, prepared: from purchased flour

### (P-17204)
### PEPSI-COLA METRO BTLG CO INC
Also Called: Pepsi-Cola
3029 Coffey Ln, Santa Rosa  (95403-2513)
PHONE..................................707 535-4560
Brad Pighin, *Genl Mgr*
**EMP:** 59
**SQ FT:** 32,000
**SALES (corp-wide):** 86.39B **Publicly Held**
Web: www.pepsico.com
SIC: **5149** 4225 2086  Soft drinks; General warehousing and storage; Bottled and canned soft drinks
HQ: Pepsi-Cola Metropolitan Bottling Company, Inc.
  700 Anderson Hill Rd
  Purchase NY 10577
  914 767-6000

### (P-17205)
### PF BAKERIES  LLC
Also Called: P-Tabun
1375 Fayette St, El Cajon  (92020-1512)
PHONE..................................858 263-4863
Elad Primosher Mbrprin, *Owner*
▲ **EMP:** 20 **EST:** 2013
**SALES (est):** 5.58MM **Privately Held**
Web: www.pfbakeries.com
SIC: **5149** 2051  Bakery products; Rolls, bread type: fresh or frozen

### (P-17206)
### QUALITY NATURALLY FOODS INC
Also Called: QUALITY NATURALLYU FOODS, INC.
17769 Railroad St, City Of Industry  (91748-1111)
PHONE..................................626 854-6363
**EMP:** 26
**SALES (corp-wide):** 20.26MM **Privately Held**
Web: www.qnfoods.com
SIC: **5149** 2099 2045  Bakery products; Food preparations, nec; Prepared flour mixes and doughs
PA: Quality Naturally Foods, Inc.
  18830 San Jose Ave
  626 854-6363

### (P-17207)
### QUALITY NATURALLY FOODS INC (PA)
Also Called: Yum Yum Donut Shop
18830 San Jose Ave, City Of Industry  (91748-1325)
PHONE..................................626 854-6363
◆ **EMP:** 24 **EST:** 1971
**SALES (est):** 20.26MM
**SALES (corp-wide):** 20.26MM **Privately Held**
Web: www.qnfoods.com
SIC: **5149** 2099 2045  Bakery products; Food preparations, nec; Prepared flour mixes and doughs

### (P-17208)
### REYES COCA-COLA BOTTLING LLC
Also Called: Coca-Cola
12925 Bradley Ave, Sylmar  (91342-3830)
PHONE..................................818 362-4307
Larry Campbell, *Brnch Mgr*
**EMP:** 62
**SALES (corp-wide):** 850.14MM **Privately Held**
Web: www.reyescocacola.com
SIC: **5149** 4225 2086  Soft drinks; General warehousing; Bottled and canned soft drinks
PA: Reyes Coca-Cola Bottling, L.L.C.
  3 Park Plz Ste 600
  213 744-8616

### (P-17209)
### ROCKVIEW DAIRIES  INC (PA)
Also Called: Motive Nation
7011 Stewart And Gray Rd, Downey  (90241-4347)
P.O. Box 668  (90241-0668)
PHONE..................................562 927-5511
Egbert Jim Degroot, *CEO*
Ted De Groot, *
Joe Valadez, *
◆ **EMP:** 188 **EST:** 1966
**SALES (est):** 42.13MM
**SALES (corp-wide):** 42.13MM **Privately Held**
Web: www.rockviewfarms.com
SIC: **5149** 5143 2026  Dried or canned foods; Milk; Fluid milk

### (P-17210)
### SABATER USA  INC
1904 1/2 E Dominguez St, Carson  (90810-1002)
PHONE..................................310 518-2227
Steven Brenneis, *Brnch Mgr*
**EMP:** 16
**SALES (corp-wide):** 8.6MM **Privately Held**
Web: www.sabaterglobal.com
SIC: **5149** 2099  Groceries and related products, nec; Food preparations, nec
PA: Sabater Usa, Inc.
  14824 S Main St
  310 518-2227

### (P-17211)
### SAN FRANCISCO HERB & NATURAL FOOD CO INC
Also Called: San Francisco Herb Tea & Spice
47444 Kato Rd, Fremont  (94538-7319)
PHONE..................................510 770-1215
◆ **EMP:** 85
Web: www.herbspicetea.com
SIC: **5149** 2833 2099  Tea; Medicinals and botanicals; Food preparations, nec

### (P-17212)
### SETTON PSTCHIO TERRA BELLA INC (HQ)
Also Called: Setton International Foods
9370 Road 234, Terra Bella  (93270-9226)
P.O. Box 11089  (93270-1089)
PHONE..................................559 535-6050
Joshua Setton, *Pr*
Morris Setton, *
▲ **EMP:** 16 **EST:** 1986
**SQ FT:** 133,000
**SALES (est):** 52.66MM
**SALES (corp-wide):** 60.13MM **Privately Held**
Web: www.settonfarms.com
SIC: **5149** 5145 0173 2068  Fruits, dried; Nuts, salted or roasted; Pistachio grove; Salted and roasted nuts and seeds
PA: Setton's International Foods, Inc.
  85 Austin Blvd
  631 543-8090

### (P-17213)
### SHAW BAKERS LLC (PA)
320b Shaw Rd, South San Francisco  (94080)
PHONE..................................650 273-1440
Nicolas Bernadi, *CEO*
Darrell Smith, *Managing Member*
**EMP:** 37 **EST:** 2015
**SALES (est):** 27.33MM
**SALES (corp-wide):** 27.33MM **Privately Held**
SIC: **5149** 5142 2053  Bakery products; Bakery products, frozen; Frozen bakery products, except bread

### (P-17214)
### SHAW BAKERS LLC
14490 Catalina St, San Leandro  (94577-5516)
PHONE..................................650 273-1440
**EMP:** 133
**SALES (corp-wide):** 27.33MM **Privately Held**
SIC: **5149** 5142 2053  Bakery products; Bakery products, frozen; Frozen bakery products, except bread
PA: Shaw Bakers Llc
  320b Shaw Rd
  650 273-1440

### (P-17215)
### SPECIALTY BAKING  INC
Also Called: Specialty Baking Co.
3134 Capelaw Ct, San Jose  (95135-1101)
PHONE..................................408 298-6950
Robert Murillo, *CEO*
Manual Escobar, *
Mark Murillo, *
Robert Murillo Junior, *Sec*
**EMP:** 70 **EST:** 1978
**SQ FT:** 10,000
**SALES (est):** 1.34MM **Privately Held**
Web: www.perfectdomain.com
SIC: **5149** 2051  Bakery products; Bread, cake, and related products

### (P-17216)
### SUGAR & RICE SARONI INC
Also Called: Saroni Total Food Ingredients
727 Kennedy St, Oakland  (94606-5327)
P.O. Box 1918  (94604-1918)
PHONE..................................510 261-9670
**EMP:** 36
SIC: **5149** 2079  Sugar, refined; Vegetable refined oils (except corn oil)

### (P-17217)
### SUN TEN LABS LIQUIDATION CO
9250 Jeronimo Rd, Irvine  (92618-1905)
PHONE..................................949 587-0509
Charleson C Hsu, *CEO*
▲ **EMP:** 18 **EST:** 1986
**SALES (est):** 2.51MM **Privately Held**
Web: www.sunten.com
SIC: **5149** 2834 2833  Spices and seasonings; Pharmaceutical preparations; Medicinals and botanicals

### (P-17218)
### SWEETENER PRODUCTS  INC (PA)
Also Called: Sweetener Products Company
2050 E 38th St, Vernon  (90058-1615)
P.O. Box 58426  (90058-0426)
PHONE..................................323 234-2200
Dale Jabour, *Pr*
**EMP:** 20 **EST:** 1923
**SALES (est):** 85.89MM
**SALES (corp-wide):** 85.89MM **Privately Held**
Web: www.sweetenerproducts.com
SIC: **5149** 2062  Groceries and related products, nec; Cane sugar refining

### (P-17219)
### SWELL COFFEE ROASTING CO LP

# 5149 - Groceries And Related Products, Nec (P-17220)

## PRODUCTS & SERVICES SECTION

Also Called: Swell Cafe, The
501 W Broadway Ste 290, San Diego (92101-8651)
PHONE................................619 504-9244
John Vallas, *CEO*
**EMP:** 20 **EST:** 2015
**SALES (est):** 1.7MM **Privately Held**
**SIC: 5149** 5046 8742 2095  Specialty food items; Commercial cooking and food service equipment; Restaurant and food services consultants; Roasted coffee

**(P-17220)**
**TOO GOOD GOURMET  INC (PA)**
Also Called: Too Good Gourmet
2380 Grant Ave, San Lorenzo (94580-1806)
PHONE................................510 317-8150
Amie G Watson, *CEO*
Jennifer Finley, *
Joe Waldrep, *
Liberty Smith, *
▲ **EMP:** 48 **EST:** 1998
**SQ FT:** 50,000
**SALES (est):** 23.58MM
**SALES (corp-wide):** 23.58MM **Privately Held**
Web: www.toogoodgourmet.com
**SIC: 5149** 5461 2052  Cookies; Cookies; Cookies

## 5153 Grain And Field Beans

**(P-17221)**
**RIVIANA FOODS INC**
Also Called: Inharvest
2870 Niagara Rd, Colusa (95932-0018)
P.O. Box 910 (95932-0910)
PHONE................................530 458-8512
Cruz Gonzalez, *Brnch Mgr*
**EMP:** 80
Web: www.riviana.com
**SIC: 5153** 5149 2099 2098  Grain and field beans; Rice, polished; Food preparations, nec; Macaroni and spaghetti
**HQ:** Riviana Foods Inc.
  2777 Allen Pkwy Ste 1500
  Houston TX 77019
  713 529-3251

## 5159 Farm-product Raw Materials, Nec

**(P-17222)**
**IMPERIAL WESTERN PRODUCTS INC A CALIFORNIA CORPORATION (HQ)**
86600 Avenue 54, Coachella (92236-3812)
P.O. Box 1110 (92236)
PHONE................................760 398-0815
▼ **EMP:** 50 **EST:** 1966
**SALES (est):** 86.81MM
**SALES (corp-wide):** 591.61MM **Privately Held**
Web: www.imperialwesternproducts.com
**SIC: 5159** 2841 2869  Cotton merchants and products; Glycerin, crude or refined: from fats; Industrial organic chemicals, nec
**PA:** Denali Water Solutions Llc
  3308 Bernice Ave
  479 498-0500

**(P-17223)**
**SOUTHWEST HIDE CO**
Also Called: Southwest Hide Co
925 Crows Landing Rd, Modesto (95351-5368)
P.O. Box 795 (95353-0795)
PHONE................................209 382-5633
Michael Girdner, *Mgr*
**EMP:** 40
**SALES (corp-wide):** 9.65MM **Privately Held**
Web: www.southwesthide.com
**SIC: 5159** 3111  Hides; Leather tanning and finishing
**PA:** Southwest Hide Co.
  9207 W Black Eagle Dr
  208 378-8000

## 5162 Plastics Materials And Basic Shapes

**(P-17224)**
**CIRRUS ENTERPRISES  LLC**
Also Called: E.V. Roberts
18027 Bishop Ave, Carson (90746-4019)
PHONE................................310 204-6159
Tracey H Cloud, *
▲ **EMP:** 52 **EST:** 1938
**SQ FT:** 26,000
**SALES (est):** 8.29MM **Privately Held**
Web: www.gracoroberts.com
**SIC: 5162** 2821 2891 5198  Plastics products, nec; Epoxy resins; Adhesives and sealants; Paints, varnishes, and supplies

**(P-17225)**
**COAST PLASTICS  INC**
4711 E Guasti Rd, Ontario (91761-8106)
PHONE................................626 812-9174
Matt Humphries, *Pr*
**EMP:** 21 **EST:** 1979
**SALES (est):** 3.79MM **Privately Held**
Web: www.coastplasticsinc.com
**SIC: 5162** 3089  Plastics materials, nec; Plastics processing

**(P-17226)**
**COATED FABRICS COMPANY (HQ)**
Also Called: Crystal Form
12658 Cisneros Ln, Santa Fe Springs (90670-3372)
P.O. Box 2222 (90670-0008)
PHONE................................562 298-1300
Jindas B Shah, *Ch Bd*
Eric Shah, *CEO*
Neil Shah, *CFO*
◆ **EMP:** 15 **EST:** 1966
**SQ FT:** 50,000
**SALES (est):** 27.7MM
**SALES (corp-wide):** 27.7MM **Privately Held**
Web: www.coatedfabrics.com
**SIC: 5162** 2339 5131  Plastics materials, nec ; Women's and misses' athletic clothing and sportswear; Coated fabrics
**PA:** Symbex Corporation
  12658 Cisneros Ln
  562 298-1300

**(P-17227)**
**CONSOLIDATED PLASTICS CORP (PA)**
Also Called: Paragon Plastics Co Div
14954 La Palma Dr, Chino (91710-9695)
PHONE................................909 393-8222
Jean Bouris, *Pr*
Gloria Jean Bouris, *
**EMP:** 50 **EST:** 1973
**SQ FT:** 45,000
**SALES (est):** 3.19MM
**SALES (corp-wide):** 3.19MM **Privately Held**
Web: www.planetplastics.com

**SIC: 5162** 3599  Plastics sheets and rods; Machine shop, jobbing and repair

**(P-17228)**
**MR PLASTICS**
844 Doolittle Dr, San Leandro (94577-1020)
PHONE................................510 895-0774
**TOLL FREE:** 800
Mike Adelson, *Pr*
▲ **EMP:** 25 **EST:** 1988
**SQ FT:** 24,000
**SALES (est):** 8.55MM **Privately Held**
Web: www.mr-plastics.com
**SIC: 5162** 2821 3089  Plastics sheets and rods; Acrylic resins; Plastics hardware and building products

**(P-17229)**
**ORANGE COUNTY INDUS PLAS INC (PA)**
Also Called: Ocip
4811 E La Palma Ave, Anaheim (92807-1954)
PHONE................................714 632-9450
Robert Robinson, *Pr*
▲ **EMP:** 25 **EST:** 1985
**SQ FT:** 70,198
**SALES (est):** 25.01MM
**SALES (corp-wide):** 25.01MM **Privately Held**
Web: www.ocip.com
**SIC: 5162** 2821  Plastics products, nec; Plastics materials and resins

**(P-17230)**
**PEAK TECHNOLOGY ENTPS INC**
Also Called: Peak Plastics
6951 Via Del Oro, San Jose (95119-1316)
PHONE................................408 748-1102
Sharon Woo Griffoul, *CEO*
Matt Griffoul, *
▼ **EMP:** 38 **EST:** 1999
**SQ FT:** 15,000
**SALES (est):** 9.11MM **Privately Held**
Web: www.peakfab.com
**SIC: 5162** 3089 3599  Plastics materials and basic shapes; Molding primary plastics; Hose, flexible metallic

**(P-17231)**
**PLASTIC SALES SOUTHERN INC**
Also Called: Plastic Sales
425 Havana Ave, Long Beach (90814-1928)
PHONE................................714 375-7900
James Quinn, *Pr*
**EMP:** 23 **EST:** 1980
**SALES (est):** 826.93K **Privately Held**
**SIC: 5162** 3089  Plastics sheets and rods; Injection molding of plastics

**(P-17232)**
**PLASTICS FAMILY HOLDINGS INC**
Also Called: Laird Plastics
12991 Marquardt Ave, Santa Fe Springs (90670-4828)
PHONE................................562 464-9929
**TOLL FREE:** 800
Anthony Durso, *Brnch Mgr*
**EMP:** 22
Web: www.lairdplastics.com
**SIC: 5162** 3089  Plastics materials, nec; Windows, plastics
**HQ:** Plastics Family Holdings, Inc.
  5800 Cmpus Cir Dr E Ste 1
  Irving TX 75063
  469 299-7000

**(P-17233)**
**PLASTIFAB SAN DIEGO**
12145 Paine St, Poway (92064-7124)
PHONE................................858 679-6600
Philip Staub, *Pt*
Robert M Lincoln, *Pt*
Richard E Donnelly, *Pt*
Mark Weinrich, *Pt*
**EMP:** 18 **EST:** 1986
**SQ FT:** 15,000
**SALES (est):** 5.45MM **Privately Held**
Web: www.plastifabsd.com
**SIC: 5162** 3089  Plastics sheets and rods; Plastics processing

**(P-17234)**
**REGAL-PIEDMONT PLASTICS LLC**
Also Called: Piedmont Plastics
17000 Valley View Ave, La Mirada (90638-5827)
P.O. Box 1274 (90308-1274)
PHONE................................562 404-4014
**TOLL FREE:** 800
Carlos Bennett, *Brnch Mgr*
**EMP:** 34
**SALES (corp-wide):** 201.65MM **Privately Held**
Web: www.piedmontplastics.com
**SIC: 5162** 2396 5169  Plastics sheets and rods; Furniture trimmings, fabric; Silicon lubricants
**HQ:** Regal-Piedmont Plastics, Llc
  5010 W W. T. Harris Blvd
  Charlotte NC 28269

**(P-17235)**
**S & W PLASTIC STORES  INC (PA)**
Also Called: S & W Plastics Supply
14270 Albers Way, Chino (91710-6940)
PHONE................................909 390-0090
William B Goldstein, *CEO*
David Goldstein, *
▲ **EMP:** 35 **EST:** 1964
**SQ FT:** 25,000
**SALES (est):** 2.61MM
**SALES (corp-wide):** 2.61MM **Privately Held**
Web: www.sandwplastics.com
**SIC: 5162** 5719 3089  Plastics products, nec; Housewares, nec; Plastics kitchenware, tableware, and houseware

**(P-17236)**
**TRANSCENDIA INC**
Also Called: Transilwrap Company
9000 9th St Ste 140, Rancho Cucamonga (91730-4499)
PHONE................................909 944-9981
Jorge Zaldivar, *Brnch Mgr*
**EMP:** 44
**SQ FT:** 41,400
**SALES (corp-wide):** 290.26MM **Privately Held**
Web: www.transcendia.com
**SIC: 5162** 3081 3089  Plastics materials and basic shapes; Unsupported plastics film and sheet; Plastics processing
**PA:** Transcendia, Inc.
  9201 W Belmont Ave
  847 678-1800

## 5169 Chemicals And Allied Products, Nec

**(P-17237)**
**ADVANTAGE CHEMICAL  LLC**

# PRODUCTS & SERVICES SECTION

## 5172 - Petroleum Products, Nec (P-17256)

27375 Via Industria, Temecula (92590-3699)
PHONE.................................951 225-4631
Mark Hottinger, *Ofcr*
Ben Olk Iii, *CEO*
**EMP:** 22 **EST:** 2010
**SQ FT:** 20,000
**SALES (est):** 1.03MM **Privately Held**
**Web:** www.advantagechemical.com
**SIC:** 5169 2842 Specialty cleaning and sanitation preparations; Sanitation preparations

### (P-17238)
### ALPHA DYNO NOBEL (PA)
Also Called: Alpha Explosives
3400 Nader Rd, Lincoln (95648)
PHONE.................................916 645-3377
Brad Langner, *CEO*
▲ **EMP:** 29 **EST:** 1906
**SQ FT:** 40,000
**SALES (est):** 24.67MM **Privately Held**
**Web:** www.alphaexplosives.com
**SIC:** 5169 2892 Explosives; Explosives

### (P-17239)
### CALWAX LLC (DH)
16511 Knott Ave, La Mirada (90638-6011)
PHONE.................................626 969-4334
John Paraszczak, *Managing Member*
▲ **EMP:** 37 **EST:** 1955
**SQ FT:** 40,000
**SALES (est):** 4.6MM **Privately Held**
**Web:** www.calwax.com
**SIC:** 5169 2842 Waxes, except petroleum; Waxes for wood, leather, and other materials
**HQ:** Remet Corporation
210 Commons Rd
Utica NY 13502
315 797-8700

### (P-17240)
### CHEMSIL SILICONES INC
21900 Marilla St, Chatsworth (91311-4129)
PHONE.................................818 700-0302
Williams S Patrick, *CEO*
Patrick S Williams, *
Bruce Mcdonald, *General Vice President*
Ian Cleminson, *
Tom Martin, *
◆ **EMP:** 26 **EST:** 2000
**SQ FT:** 32,789
**SALES (est):** 24.6MM
**SALES (corp-wide):** 1.95B **Publicly Held**
**Web:** www.chemsil.com
**SIC:** 5169 2869 Chemicals and allied products, nec; Silicones
**PA:** Innospec Inc.
8310 S Valley Hwy Ste 350
303 792-5554

### (P-17241)
### CHEROKEE CHEMICAL CO INC (PA)
Also Called: CCI
3540 E 26th St, Vernon (90058)
PHONE.................................323 265-1112
Da Criswell, *CEO*
**EMP:** 47 **EST:** 1964
**SQ FT:** 30,000
**SALES (est):** 28.76MM
**SALES (corp-wide):** 28.76MM **Privately Held**
**Web:** www.ccichemical.com
**SIC:** 5169 2842 2819 Specialty cleaning and sanitation preparations; Polishes and sanitation goods; Industrial inorganic chemicals, nec

### (P-17242)
### EMBEE PERFORMANCE LLC
Also Called: Embee Powder Coating
2100 Ritchey St, Santa Ana (92705-5134)
PHONE.................................714 540-1354
David Dahlberg, *Managing Member*
**EMP:** 20 **EST:** 2000
**SALES (est):** 2.26MM **Privately Held**
**Web:** www.embeeperformance.com
**SIC:** 5169 3471 Polishes, nec; Plating of metals or formed products

### (P-17243)
### ENVIRO TECH CHEMICAL SVCS INC (DH)
500 Winmoore Way, Modesto (95358-5750)
PHONE.................................209 581-9576
Michael S Harvey, *Pr*
Michael B Archibald, *
◆ **EMP:** 102 **EST:** 1991
**SQ FT:** 136,551
**SALES (est):** 29.82MM
**SALES (corp-wide):** 2.67MM **Privately Held**
**Web:** www.envirotech.com
**SIC:** 5169 2842 Industrial chemicals; Specialty cleaning
**HQ:** Arxada Ag
Lonzastrasse 2
Visp VS 3930

### (P-17244)
### ESE INC
Also Called: Ese
1163 E 12th St, Los Angeles (90021-2205)
PHONE.................................213 614-0102
David Kazemi, *CEO*
▲ **EMP:** 25 **EST:** 1993
**SALES (est):** 5MM **Privately Held**
**Web:** www.realklean.com
**SIC:** 5169 2841 5065 Alcohols and anti-freeze compounds; Soap and other detergents; Electronic parts and equipment, nec

### (P-17245)
### GEO DRILLING FLUIDS INC (PA)
Also Called: Industrial Minerals Company
1431 Union Ave, Bakersfield (93305-5732)
P.O. Box 1478 (93302-1478)
PHONE.................................661 325-5919
Jim Clifford, *Pr*
Dan Bauman, *
Bob French, *
Don Boulet, *
Tom Needham, *
▲ **EMP:** 30 **EST:** 1950
**SQ FT:** 7,500
**SALES (est):** 20.68MM
**SALES (corp-wide):** 20.68MM **Privately Held**
**Web:** www.geodf.com
**SIC:** 5169 1389 7389 Chemicals and allied products, nec; Servicing oil and gas wells; Grinding, precision: commercial or industrial

### (P-17246)
### HILL BROTHERS CHEMICAL COMPANY (PA)
Also Called: Hill Brothers Chemical
3000 E Birch St Ste 108, Brea (92821-6261)
PHONE.................................714 998-8800
Adam Hill, *Pr*
Matthew Thorne, *
Thomas F James, *
Kathryn J Waters, *
▲ **EMP:** 150 **EST:** 1935
**SALES (est):** 80.33MM
**SALES (corp-wide):** 80.33MM **Privately Held**
**Web:** www.hillbrothers.com
**SIC:** 5169 2819 Acids; Calcium chloride and hypochlorite

### (P-17247)
### NORMAN FOX & CO (PA)
Also Called: Norfox
14970 Don Julian Rd, City Of Industry (91746-3111)
PHONE.................................800 632-1777
Stephen Halpin, *CEO*
Bob Code, *
◆ **EMP:** 40 **EST:** 1971
**SQ FT:** 5,000
**SALES (est):** 30.33MM
**SALES (corp-wide):** 30.33MM **Privately Held**
**Web:** www.norfoxchem.com
**SIC:** 5169 2841 Chemicals and allied products, nec; Soap: granulated, liquid, cake, flaked, or chip

### (P-17248)
### NORMAN FOX & CO
5511 S Boyle Ave, Vernon (90058-3932)
P.O. Box 58727 (90058-0727)
PHONE.................................323 973-4900
Alex Kirby, *Brnch Mgr*
**EMP:** 23
**SALES (corp-wide):** 30.33MM **Privately Held**
**Web:** www.norfoxchem.com
**SIC:** 5169 2841 Industrial chemicals; Soap: granulated, liquid, cake, flaked, or chip
**PA:** Norman, Fox & Co.
14970 Don Julian Rd
800 632-1777

### (P-17249)
### SPECTRUM LABORATORY PDTS INC
Also Called: Spectrum Lab & Phrm Pdts
14422 S San Pedro St, Gardena (90248-2027)
PHONE.................................520 292-3103
Elizabeth Brown, *CEO*
**EMP:** 31
**SALES (corp-wide):** 100.56MM **Privately Held**
**Web:** www.spectrumchemical.com
**SIC:** 5169 2869 2819 Organic chemicals, synthetic; Laboratory chemicals, organic; Industrial inorganic chemicals, nec
**PA:** Spectrum Laboratory Products, Inc.
769 Jersey Ave
732 214-1300

### (P-17250)
### VALEANT BIOMEDICALS INC (DH)
1 Enterprise, Aliso Viejo (92656-2606)
PHONE.................................949 461-6000
Tim Tyson, *Pr*
**EMP:** 100 **EST:** 1983
**SQ FT:** 55,000
**SALES (est):** 7.34MM
**SALES (corp-wide):** 8.76B **Privately Held**
**SIC:** 5169 2835 8731 3826 Chemicals and allied products, nec; Diagnostic substances; Biotechnical research, commercial; Analytical instruments
**HQ:** Bausch Health Americas, Inc.
400 Somerset Corp Blvd
Bridgewater NJ 08807
908 927-1400

### (P-17251)
### VIJALL INC
Also Called: Chemtec Chemical Company
21900 Marilla St, Chatsworth (91311-4129)
PHONE.................................818 700-0071
Patrick S Williams, *Pr*
Bruce Mcdonald, *Pr*
Ian Cleminson, *
Tom Martin, *
David E Williams, *
▲ **EMP:** 26 **EST:** 1987
**SQ FT:** 32,789
**SALES (est):** 2.62MM
**SALES (corp-wide):** 1.95B **Publicly Held**
**Web:** www.chemteccc.com
**SIC:** 5169 2819 Industrial chemicals; Industrial inorganic chemicals, nec
**HQ:** Innospec Active Chemicals Llc
510 W Grimes Ave
High Point NC 27260
336 882-3308

## 5172 Petroleum Products, Nec

### (P-17252)
### CLIPPER OIL INC
Also Called: Clipper Oil Company
2488 Historic Decatur Rd, San Diego (92106)
PHONE.................................619 692-9701
Kenny Alameda, *Pr*
Kevin Alameda, *VP*
Sandi Myers, *Contrlr*
◆ **EMP:** 20 **EST:** 1985
**SALES (est):** 9.95MM **Privately Held**
**Web:** www.clipperoil.com
**SIC:** 5172 2873 5169 Diesel fuel; Anhydrous ammonia; Salts, industrial

### (P-17253)
### MARATHON PETROLEUM CORPORATION
Also Called: Martinez Refinery
150 Solano Way, Martinez (94553-1465)
PHONE.................................925 370-3290
Patty Deutsche, *Mgr*
**EMP:** 31
**Web:** www.marathonpetroleum.com
**SIC:** 5172 2911 Petroleum products, nec; Petroleum refining
**PA:** Marathon Petroleum Corporation
539 S Main St

### (P-17254)
### PREMIER FUEL DISTRIBUTORS INC
Also Called: Premier Fuel Delivery Service
156 E La Cadena Dr, Riverside (92507-8699)
PHONE.................................760 423-3610
Hugo Rodriguez, *CEO*
**EMP:** 150 **EST:** 2013
**SALES (est):** 19.06MM **Privately Held**
**SIC:** 5172 2869 Petroleum products, nec; Fuels

### (P-17255)
### REDWOOD COAST PETROLEUM INC
444 Yolanda Ave Ste A, Santa Rosa (95404-8090)
P.O. Box 428 (95402-0428)
PHONE.................................707 546-0766
**EMP:** 70
**Web:** www.flyersenergy.com
**SIC:** 5172 3569 Petroleum products, nec; Lubrication equipment, industrial

### (P-17256)
### TIODIZE CO INC
15701 Industry Ln, Huntington Beach (92649-1569)

# 5181 - Beer And Ale (P-17257)

## PRODUCTS & SERVICES SECTION

PHONE..................................714 898-4377
Thomas Adams, Pr
**EMP:** 48
**SALES (corp-wide):** 9.73MM **Privately Held**
Web: www.tiodize.com
**SIC:** 5172 3471 Lubricating oils and greases; Anodizing (plating) of metals or formed products
**PA:** Tiodize Co., Inc.
5858 Engineer Dr
714 898-4377

## 5181 Beer And Ale

### (P-17257)
### AUBURN ALEHOUSE LP
Also Called: Auburn Ale House
289 Washington St, Auburn (95603-5036)
PHONE..................................530 885-2537
Brian Ford, Owner
**EMP:** 40 **EST:** 2006
**SALES (est):** 8.44MM **Privately Held**
Web: www.auburnalehouse.com
**SIC:** 5181 2082 5921 5812 Beer and ale; Beer (alcoholic beverage); Wine and beer; American restaurant

### (P-17258)
### BENNY ENTERPRISES INC
Also Called: Quality Distributor
1100 N Johnson Ave Ste 110, El Cajon (92020-1917)
PHONE..................................619 592-4455
Raad Benny, CEO
**EMP:** 40 **EST:** 1994
**SQ FT:** 8,000
**SALES (est):** 9.79MM **Privately Held**
**SIC:** 5181 5141 5087 5015 Beer and ale; Groceries, general line; Cleaning and maintenance equipment and supplies; Automotive parts and supplies, used

### (P-17259)
### NOR-CAL BEVERAGE CO INC (PA)
2150 Stone Blvd, West Sacramento (95691-4049)
PHONE..................................916 372-0600
Shannon Deary-bell, Pr
Donald Deary, *
Grant Deary, *
Tim Deary, *
Mike Montroni, *
◆ **EMP:** 280 **EST:** 1937
**SQ FT:** 152,000
**SALES (est):** 53.99MM
**SALES (corp-wide):** 53.99MM **Privately Held**
Web: www.mannabev.com
**SIC:** 5181 2086 Beer and other fermented malt liquors; Soft drinks: packaged in cans, bottles, etc.

### (P-17260)
### T F LOUDERBACK INC
Also Called: Bay Area Beverage Company
700 National Ct, Richmond (94804-2008)
PHONE..................................510 965-6120
Thomas J Louderback, Pr
Ron Bishop, *
Todd Rovelstad, *
Michael J Marver Ctrl, Prin
◆ **EMP:** 102 **EST:** 1969
**SQ FT:** 65,000
**SALES (est):** 23.92MM **Privately Held**
Web: www.bayareabev.com

**SIC:** 5181 5149 2037 2033 Beer and other fermented malt liquors; Beverages, except coffee and tea; Frozen fruits and vegetables; Canned fruits and specialties

### (P-17261)
### VARNI BROTHERS CORPORATION (DH)
Also Called: Vbc Bottling Co.
400 Hosmer Ave, Modesto (95351-3999)
PHONE..................................209 521-1777
Brad Goist, CEO
Lila Ross, Sec
Shane Perkey, CFO
◆ **EMP:** 80 **EST:** 1960
**SQ FT:** 80,000
**SALES (est):** 30.86MM **Privately Held**
Web: www.vbcbottling.com
**SIC:** 5181 2086 5182 Beer and other fermented malt liquors; Bottled and canned soft drinks; Wine
**HQ:** Refresco Holding B.V.
Fascinatio Boulevard 270
Rotterdam ZH 3065
104405100

## 5182 Wine And Distilled Beverages

### (P-17262)
### BRONCO WINE COMPANY (PA)
Also Called: Classic Wines of California
6342 Bystrum Rd, Ceres (95307-6652)
P.O. Box P.O. Box 789 (95307-0789)
PHONE..................................209 538-3131
◆ **EMP:** 200 **EST:** 1973
**SALES (est):** 69.71MM
**SALES (corp-wide):** 69.71MM **Privately Held**
Web: www.broncowine.com
**SIC:** 5182 2084 Wine; Wines

### (P-17263)
### CUSHMAN WINERY CORPORATION
Also Called: Zaca Mesa Winery
6905 Foxen Canyon Rd, Los Olivos (93441-4530)
P.O. Box 899 (93441-0899)
PHONE..................................805 688-9339
Brook Williams, Pr
Susan English, *
▲ **EMP:** 31 **EST:** 1972
**SALES (est):** 10.58MM **Privately Held**
Web: www.zacamesa.com
**SIC:** 5182 2084 0172 Wine; Wines; Grapes

### (P-17264)
### DARCIE KENT WINERY LLC
Also Called: Almost Famous Wine Company
7000 Tesla Rd, Livermore (94550-9107)
PHONE..................................925 443-5368
David Kent, Managing Member
**EMP:** 20 **EST:** 2020
**SALES (est):** 1.12MM **Privately Held**
Web: www.darciekentvineyards.com
**SIC:** 5182 2084 Wine and distilled beverages; Wines, brandy, and brandy spirits

### (P-17265)
### FARM STREET DESIGNS INC
Also Called: Van's Gifts
2520 Mira Mar Ave, Long Beach (90815-1758)
PHONE..................................562 985-0026
Howard Colover, CEO
Reva Colover, *
▲ **EMP:** 33 **EST:** 1984

**SQ FT:** 39,000
**SALES (est):** 9.27MM **Privately Held**
**SIC:** 5182 2033 2035 5023 Wine; Tomato sauce: packaged in cans, jars, etc.; Dressings, salad: raw and cooked (except dry mixes); Kitchenware

### (P-17266)
### FRANK-LIN DISTILLERS PDTS LTD (PA)
2455 Huntington Dr, Fairfield (94533-9734)
PHONE..................................408 259-8900
Frank J Maestri, Pr
Michael Maestri, *
Vincent Maestri, *
Lindley Maestri, *
Michael Wasteney, *
◆ **EMP:** 110 **EST:** 1966
**SQ FT:** 54,216
**SALES (est):** 42.56MM
**SALES (corp-wide):** 42.56MM **Privately Held**
Web: www.frank-lin.com
**SIC:** 5182 2085 Wine; Distilled and blended liquors

### (P-17267)
### LUCAS & LEWELLEN VINEYARDS INC (PA)
Also Called: Lucas Lwllen Vnyrds Tasting Rm
1645 Copenhagen Dr, Solvang (93463-3742)
P.O. Box 648 (93440-0648)
PHONE..................................805 686-9336
Royce R Lewellen, Pr
Louis A Lucas, *
**EMP:** 25 **EST:** 1996
**SALES (est):** 9.3MM
**SALES (corp-wide):** 9.3MM **Privately Held**
Web: www.llwine.com
**SIC:** 5182 2084 Wine; Wines

## 5191 Farm Supplies

### (P-17268)
### BFG SUPPLY CO LLC
2552 Shenandoah Way, San Bernardino (92407-1845)
PHONE..................................909 591-0461
David C Daily, Pr
**EMP:** 190
**SALES (corp-wide):** 183.31MM **Privately Held**
Web: www.bfgsupply.com
**SIC:** 5191 2875 2449 5193 Insecticides; Potting soil, mixed; Wood containers, nec; Flowers and florists supplies
**PA:** Bfg Supply Co., Llc
14500 Kinsman Rd
800 883-0234

### (P-17269)
### BROMA APPLICATORS LLC
322 W J St, Brawley (92227-3116)
PHONE..................................760 351-0101
**EMP:** 20 **EST:** 1997
**SQ FT:** 1,200
**SALES (est):** 4.34MM **Privately Held**
**SIC:** 5191 2879 Pesticides; Fungicides, herbicides

### (P-17270)
### CORTEVA AGRISCIENCE LLC
901 Loveridge Rd, Pittsburg (94565-2811)
PHONE..................................925 432-5482
**EMP:** 197
**SALES (corp-wide):** 17.23B **Publicly Held**
Web: www.corteva.com

**SIC:** 5191 8731 0721 2879 Seeds and bulbs; Agricultural research; Crop protecting services; Insecticides and pesticides
**HQ:** Corteva Agriscience Llc
9330 Zionsville Rd
Indianapolis IN 46268

### (P-17271)
### E B STONE & SON INC
Also Called: Greenall
6111 Lambie Rd, Suisun City (94585-9789)
P.O. Box P.O Box 550 (94585)
PHONE..................................707 426-2500
Bradford Crandall Junior, CEO
Lynne Crandall, Sec
Brandi Palomo, CFO
**EMP:** 20 **EST:** 1918
**SQ FT:** 79,000
**SALES (est):** 12.66MM **Privately Held**
Web: www.ebstone.org
**SIC:** 5191 2873 2875 3423 Fertilizer and fertilizer materials; Nitrogenous fertilizers; Fertilizers, mixing only; Hand and edge tools, nec

### (P-17272)
### L A HEARNE COMPANY (PA)
512 Metz Rd, King City (93930-2503)
PHONE..................................831 385-5441
Francis Giudici, Pr
Dennis Hearne, *
Francis Giudici, Pr
Larry Hearne, *
Tim Hearne, *
◆ **EMP:** 70 **EST:** 1938
**SQ FT:** 220,000
**SALES (est):** 26.35MM
**SALES (corp-wide):** 26.35MM **Privately Held**
Web: www.hearneco.com
**SIC:** 5191 0723 5699 4214 Fertilizers and agricultural chemicals; Bean cleaning services; Western apparel; Local trucking with storage

### (P-17273)
### LEACH GRAIN & MILLING CO INC
8131 Pivot St, Downey (90241-4853)
PHONE..................................562 869-4451
Willis R Leach Senior, Pr
Roy Leach, *
Willis R Leach Junior, Sec
Bruce Leach, Stockholder*
**EMP:** 26 **EST:** 1934
**SQ FT:** 20,000
**SALES (est):** 5.24MM **Privately Held**
Web: www.leachgrain.com
**SIC:** 5191 2047 2048 Farm supplies; Dog and cat food; Bird food, prepared

### (P-17274)
### M CALOSSO & SON
1947 E Miner Ave, Stockton (95205-4543)
PHONE..................................209 466-8994
Susan Gay Calosso, Pr
Michael J Calosso, Sec
**EMP:** 34 **EST:** 1924
**SQ FT:** 48,500
**SALES (est):** 10.82MM **Privately Held**
Web: www.mcalossoandson.com
**SIC:** 5191 2441 5085 3993 Farm supplies; Boxes, wood; Box shooks; Signs and advertising specialties

### (P-17275)
### TREMONT GROUP INCORPORATED
Agriform Div
201 East St, Woodland (95776-3523)

PRODUCTS & SERVICES SECTION

5199 - Nondurable Goods, Nec (P-17295)

PHONE..................530 662-5442
Scott Mansell, *Mgr*
EMP: 23
SQ FT: 10,000
SALES (corp-wide): 236.82MM **Privately Held**
Web: www.growwest.com
SIC: **5191** 5261 2873 Chemicals, agricultural; Fertilizer; Nitrogenous fertilizers
HQ: The Tremont Group Incorporated
201 East St
Woodland CA 95776

## 5192 Books, Periodicals, And Newspapers

**(P-17276)**
**EL AVISO MAGAZINE**
4850 Gage Ave, Bell (90201-1409)
P.O. Box 3360 (90202-3360)
PHONE..................323 586-9199
Jose Zepeda, *CEO*
EMP: 37 EST: 1988
SALES (est): 616.68K **Privately Held**
Web: www.elaviso.com
SIC: **5192** 2721 Magazines; Magazines: publishing and printing

**(P-17277)**
**SAN JOAQUIN MAGAZINE**
1463 Moffat Blvd Ste 4, Manteca (95336-8952)
PHONE..................209 625-8313
Tony Zoccoli, *Prin*
EMP: 21 EST: 2013
SALES (est): 201.27K **Privately Held**
Web: www.sanjoaquinmagazine.com
SIC: **5192** 2741 2721 Magazines; Miscellaneous publishing; Periodicals, publishing only

## 5193 Flowers And Florists Supplies

**(P-17278)**
**ALTMAN SPECIALTY PLANTS LLC (PA)**
Also Called: Altman Plants
3742 Blue Bird Canyon Rd, Vista (92084-7432)
PHONE..................800 348-4881
Ken Altman, *CEO*
Deena Altman, *
▲ EMP: 800 EST: 1973
SQ FT: 4,000
SALES (est): 225.14MM
SALES (corp-wide): 225.14MM **Privately Held**
Web: www.altmanplants.com
SIC: **5193** 3999 Nursery stock; Atomizers, toiletry

**(P-17279)**
**CREATIVE PLANT DESIGN INC**
5895 Rue Ferrari, San Jose (95138-1857)
PHONE..................408 452-1444
Mary Mccormick, *Pr*
EMP: 17 EST: 1985
SALES (est): 4.56MM **Privately Held**
Web: www.creativeplant.com
SIC: **5193** 3999 7699 Flowers and nursery stock; Plants, artificial and preserved; Agricultural equipment repair services

**(P-17280)**
**JENNY SILKS INC**
Also Called: Jenny Silks
2101 S Grand Ave, Santa Ana (92705-5231)
PHONE..................714 597-7272
Jennifer Cheng, *Pr*
EMP: 17 EST: 1985
SALES (est): 939.29K **Privately Held**
Web: www.jennysilks.com
SIC: **5193** 3999 Flowers, fresh; Artificial flower arrangements

## 5198 Paints, Varnishes, And Supplies

**(P-17281)**
**BERG LACQUER CO (PA)**
Also Called: Pacific Coast Lacquer
3150 E Pico Blvd, Los Angeles (90023-3632)
PHONE..................323 261-8114
Sandra Berg, *Pr*
Robert O Berg, *
▲ EMP: 65 EST: 1934
SQ FT: 85,000
SALES (est): 5.22MM
SALES (corp-wide): 5.22MM **Privately Held**
SIC: **5198** 2851 Paints; Paints and paint additives

## 5199 Nondurable Goods, Nec

**(P-17282)**
**A B P INC**
Also Called: Scb Distributors
15608 New Century Dr, Gardena (90248-2129)
PHONE..................310 532-9400
Aaron Silverman, *Pr*
▲ EMP: 15 EST: 1989
SQ FT: 12,000
SALES (est): 4.15MM **Privately Held**
Web: www.scbdistributors.com
SIC: **5199** 2731 5192 Foil, aluminum: household; Book publishing; Books

**(P-17283)**
**AHI INVESTMENT INC (DH)**
Also Called: Linzer Products
675 Glenoaks Blvd, San Fernando (91340-1471)
P.O. Box 310 (91341-0310)
PHONE..................818 979-0030
Hisatoshi Ohtsuka, *Prin*
Mark Saji, *Ex VP*
Yuko Waki, *Prin*
◆ EMP: 25 EST: 1989
SQ FT: 75,000
SALES (est): 52.67MM **Privately Held**
Web: www.linzerproducts.com
SIC: **5199** 3991 Broom, mop, and paint handles; Paintbrushes
HQ: Ohtsuka Brush Mfg.Co., Ltd.
4-1, Yotsuya
Shinjuku-Ku TKY 160-0

**(P-17284)**
**ANNS TRADING COMPANY INC**
Also Called: Urban Concepts
5333 S Downey Rd, Vernon (90058-3725)
PHONE..................323 585-4702
Hyung Don Kim, *CEO*
Daniel Im, *
Mi H Kim, *Sec*
◆ EMP: 30 EST: 1981
SALES (est): 8.35MM **Privately Held**
Web: www.annstrading.com
SIC: **5199** 2335 Gifts and novelties; Women's, junior's, and misses' dresses

**(P-17285)**
**ARMANI TRADE LLC**
21255 Burbank Blvd Ste 120, Woodland Hills (91367-6669)
PHONE..................310 849-0067
Nader Abdollahi, *CEO*
EMP: 50 EST: 2018
SALES (est): 2.02MM **Privately Held**
SIC: **5199** 3699 General merchandise, nondurable; Electrical equipment and supplies, nec

**(P-17286)**
**BERNET INTERNATIONAL TRDG LLC (PA)**
12121 Wilshire Blvd Ste 1200, Los Angeles (90025-1168)
PHONE..................310 873-0300
Mervyn E Bernet, *CEO*
Kevin Bernet, *CFO*
Ryan Bernet, *Pr*
◆ EMP: 19 EST: 2003
SALES (est): 2.27MM
SALES (corp-wide): 2.27MM **Privately Held**
Web: www.bernetintl.com
SIC: **5199** 5023 5092 2299 Art goods and supplies; Homefurnishings; Toys and hobby goods and supplies; Fabrics: linen, jute, hemp, ramie

**(P-17287)**
**BIO HAZARD INC**
6019 Randolph St, Commerce (90040-3417)
PHONE..................213 625-2116
EMP: 36 EST: 2007
SALES (est): 4.15MM **Privately Held**
Web: www.biohazardinc.com
SIC: **5199** 3221 Smokers' supplies; Glass containers

**(P-17288)**
**BLISTERPAK INC**
Also Called: Blisterpak
3020 Supply Ave, Commerce (90040-2710)
PHONE..................323 728-5555
Steven C Mattis, *CEO*
▲ EMP: 20 EST: 1974
SQ FT: 15,000
SALES (est): 6.14MM **Privately Held**
Web: www.blisterpak.com
SIC: **5199** 3089 3069 Packaging materials; Air mattresses, plastics; Floor coverings, rubber

**(P-17289)**
**C SANDERS EMBLEMS LP**
26370 Diamond Pl Unit 506, Santa Clarita (91350-2986)
PHONE..................800 336-7467
Penelope Ledbetter, *Pt*
▲ EMP: 23 EST: 1959
SALES (est): 596.38K **Privately Held**
Web: www.csanders.net
SIC: **5199** 2395 Badges; Emblems, embroidered

**(P-17290)**
**CHUS PACKAGING SUPPLIES INC**
10011 Santa Fe Springs Rd, Santa Fe Springs (90670-2921)
PHONE..................562 944-6411
Pao Chang Chu, *CEO*
Julie Chieh Yu Chu, *Pr*
▲ EMP: 22 EST: 1985
SQ FT: 30,000
SALES (est): 12MM **Privately Held**
Web: www.chuspkg.com
SIC: **5199** 2653 Packaging materials; Boxes, corrugated: made from purchased materials

**(P-17291)**
**CORAL PORT LLC**
Also Called: Wholesale
1099 Vine St Ste 205, Sacramento (95811)
PHONE..................530 761-6400
Esat Malbelegi, *Managing Member*
EMP: 25 EST: 2016
SALES (est): 2.8MM **Privately Held**
Web: www.coralport.us
SIC: **5199** 3944 5063 5085 General merchandise, non-durable; Craft and hobby kits and sets; Batteries; Adhesives, tape and plasters

**(P-17292)**
**DAZPAK FLEXIBLE PACKAGING LLC**
Also Called: Dazpak Flexible Packaging
19310 San Jose Ave, City Of Industry (91748-1419)
PHONE..................909 598-7844
Howard H Applebaum, *Managing Member*
Art Rosen, *Managing Member*
▲ EMP: 15 EST: 1978
SQ FT: 11,000
SALES (est): 18.47MM **Privately Held**
Web: www.superior-bags.com
SIC: **5199** 2673 Packaging materials; Cellophane bags, unprinted: made from purchased materials

**(P-17293)**
**EMERALD PACKAGING INC**
Also Called: E P
33050 Western Ave, Union City (94587-2157)
PHONE..................510 429-5700
Kevin Kelly, *CEO*
James P Kelly Senior, *Ch Bd*
James M Kelly Junior, *Ex VP*
Maura Kelly Koberlein, *VP*
Mary Anne Lothrot, *Ex Sec*
▲ EMP: 250 EST: 1963
SQ FT: 80,000
SALES (est): 22.62MM **Privately Held**
Web: www.empack.com
SIC: **5199** 2673 Packaging materials; Food storage and frozen food bags, plastic

**(P-17294)**
**EUROW AND OREILLY CORP**
Also Called: Equine Comfort Products
51 Moreland Rd, Simi Valley (93065-1662)
PHONE..................800 747-7452
Donna O'reilly, *CEO*
Patrice Bonnefoi, *
◆ EMP: 32 EST: 2000
SQ FT: 60,000
SALES (est): 10.43MM **Privately Held**
Web: www.eurow.com
SIC: **5199** 2392 General merchandise, non-durable; Towels, dishcloths and dust cloths

**(P-17295)**
**EVE HAIR INC (PA)**
Also Called: Eve
3935 Paramount Blvd, Lakewood (90712-4100)
PHONE..................562 377-1020
Young Soo Cho, *Pr*
Young Soo Cho, *Pr*
Ed Pak, *
◆ EMP: 37 EST: 1990
SQ FT: 44,000
SALES (est): 1.63MM **Privately Held**
Web: www.evehairinc.com

## 5199 - Nondurable Goods, Nec (P-17296)

SIC: 5199 3999 Wigs; Hair and hair-based products

**(P-17296)**
**GAMUS LLC**
Also Called: GTS Distribution- Northern Cal
3286 Victor St, Santa Clara (95054-2317)
PHONE..................................408 441-0170
EMP: 43
Web: www.gtsdistribution.com
SIC: 5199 2754 Gifts and novelties; Cards, except greeting: gravure printing
PA: Gamus, Llc
2822 119th St Sw Ste B

**(P-17297)**
**HARV 81 USA INC**
531 Stone Rd, Benicia (94510-1113)
PHONE..................................707 746-0353
James W Herwatt, *CEO*
Jochen Michalski, *
Sofia Michalski, *
Miguel Mardel Correia, *
Antonio Correia, *
◆ EMP: 35 EST: 1981
SQ FT: 24,000
SALES (est): 26.17MM **Privately Held**
Web: www.corksupplygroup.com
SIC: 5199 2499 2448 Packaging materials; Corks, bottle; Pallets, wood

**(P-17298)**
**KATZKIN LEATHER INC (PA)**
6868 W Acco St, Montebello (90640-5441)
PHONE..................................323 725-1243
Brook Mayberry, *Pr*
Scott Briskie, *
▲ EMP: 200 EST: 1998
SQ FT: 50,000
SALES (est): 21.59MM
SALES (corp-wide): 21.59MM **Privately Held**
Web: www.katzkin.com
SIC: 5199 2531 Leather and cut stock; Seats, automobile

**(P-17299)**
**LEE-MAR AQUARIUM & PET SUPS**
Also Called: Lee Mar Aquarium & Pet Sups
2459 Dogwood Way, Vista (92081-8421)
PHONE..................................760 727-1300
Terran R Boyd, *Pr*
▲ EMP: 100 EST: 1971
SQ FT: 67,000
SALES (est): 10.08MM **Privately Held**
Web: www.petwholesaleusa.com
SIC: 5199 3999 Pet supplies; Pet supplies

**(P-17300)**
**MACK PACKAGING INC**
1239 Linda Vista Dr, San Marcos (92078-3809)
PHONE..................................760 752-3500
Kevin Mackinnon, *Pr*
EMP: 22 EST: 2009
SALES (est): 4.87MM **Privately Held**
Web: www.mackpacbranding.com
SIC: 5199 2759 Advertising specialties; Commercial printing, nec

**(P-17301)**
**MEG COMPANY INC (PA)**
Also Called: Grizzzly Clothing
1860 W 205th St, Torrance (90501-1526)
PHONE..................................310 372-8033
Yoshitsugu Matsuda, *Pr*
Megumi Adachi Matsuda, *Treas*
▲ EMP: 15 EST: 1989
SALES (est): 1.71MM **Privately Held**
Web: www.megcompany.com
SIC: 5199 5331 2387 2337 Variety store merchandise; Variety stores; Apparel belts; Women's and misses' capes and jackets

**(P-17302)**
**MODERN CANDLE CO INC**
Also Called: Modern Candles
12884 Bradley Ave, Sylmar (91342-3827)
PHONE..................................323 441-0104
Armik Pirijanian, *CEO*
Nora Pirijanian, *
▲ EMP: 45 EST: 1995
SALES (est): 11.5MM **Privately Held**
Web: www.moderncandle.com
SIC: 5199 3999 Candles; Candles

**(P-17303)**
**NIFTY PACKAGE CO INC**
175 S Cambridge St, Orange (92866-1634)
PHONE..................................714 863-6058
Michelle Hensley, *CEO*
EMP: 20 EST: 2015
SALES (est): 1.47MM **Privately Held**
Web: www.niftypackage.co
SIC: 5199 2679 5947 7299 Packaging materials; Gift wrap and novelties, paper; Gifts and novelties; Gift wrapping services

**(P-17304)**
**PCF GROUP LLC**
Also Called: Pacific Coast Foam
8585 Miramar Pl, San Diego (92121-2529)
PHONE..................................858 455-1274
EMP: 18 EST: 1995
SQ FT: 15,000
SALES (est): 1.66MM **Privately Held**
Web: www.pcfgroup.com
SIC: 5199 3086 Foams and rubber; Plastics foam products

**(P-17305)**
**POLYCELL PACKAGING CORPORATION**
12851 Midway Pl, Cerritos (90703-2141)
PHONE..................................562 483-6000
Chin Ching Hsu, *Pr*
▲ EMP: 35 EST: 1995
SALES (est): 11.82MM **Privately Held**
Web: www.polycellpkg.com
SIC: 5199 3089 Packaging materials; Blister or bubble formed packaging, plastics

**(P-17306)**
**PROFESSIONAL IMAGE INC**
10516 Sierra Estates Dr, Auburn (95602-9401)
PHONE..................................513 984-1111
◆ EMP: 16
SIC: 5199 2261 Advertising specialties; Screen printing of cotton broadwoven fabrics

**(P-17307)**
**REDBARN PET PRODUCTS INC (PA)**
Also Called: Redbarn Premium Pet Products
3229 E Spring St Ste 310, Long Beach (90806)
PHONE..................................562 495-7315
Jeff Baikie, *CEO*
Howard Bloxam, *
◆ EMP: 236 EST: 1994
SQ FT: 50,000
SALES (est): 39.4MM **Privately Held**
Web: www.redbarn.com
SIC: 5199 2047 Pet supplies; Dog and cat food

**(P-17308)**
**RENO JONES INC**
2373 N Watney Way, Fairfield (94533-6746)
PHONE..................................707 422-4300
▲ EMP: 48
SIC: 5199 5085 3221 Packaging materials; Glass bottles; Bottles for packing, bottling, and canning: glass

**(P-17309)**
**ROCKWELL ENTERPRISES INC**
20327 Regina Ave, Torrance (90503-2513)
PHONE..................................626 796-1511
Frank Giovinazzo, *Pr*
Akemi Giovinazzo, *Sec*
EMP: 20 EST: 1967
SALES (est): 571.25K **Privately Held**
Web: www.rockwellenterprises.com
SIC: 5199 3581 Maps and charts; Automatic vending machines

**(P-17310)**
**RYL INC**
2738 Supply Ave, Commerce (90040-2704)
PHONE..................................213 503-7968
James Lee, *CEO*
Ronald Lee, *
Sandra Lee, *
▲ EMP: 35 EST: 1996
SQ FT: 31,000
SALES (est): 5.33MM **Privately Held**
Web: www.colorglasstube.com
SIC: 5199 3221 General merchandise, non-durable; Glass containers

**(P-17311)**
**STRATOS MANUFACTURING LLC**
9885 Mesa Rim Rd Ste 112, San Diego (92121-2982)
PHONE..................................408 839-0054
Victor Berrio, *Pr*
Scott M Bryant, *CEO*
EMP: 15 EST: 2019
SALES (est): 768.05K **Privately Held**
SIC: 5199 3999 General merchandise, non-durable; Candles

**(P-17312)**
**VEGETABLE GROWERS SUPPLY CO (PA)**
Also Called: V G S
1360 Merrill St, Salinas (93901-4432)
P.O. Box 757 (93902-0757)
PHONE..................................831 759-4600
Ron Huff, *CEO*
William J Locke Iii, *Pr*
▲ EMP: 50 EST: 1948
SQ FT: 38,000
SALES (est): 57.43MM
SALES (corp-wide): 57.43MM **Privately Held**
Web: www.veggrow.com
SIC: 5199 2449 Packaging materials; Rectangular boxes and crates, wood

**(P-17313)**
**VICTORY FOAM INC (PA)**
3 Holland, Irvine (92618-2506)
PHONE..................................949 474-0690
Frank M Comerford, *CEO*
Myles Comerford, *
Helen Comerford, *
▲ EMP: 94 EST: 1982
SQ FT: 53,000
SALES (est): 24.15MM
SALES (corp-wide): 24.15MM **Privately Held**
Web: www.victoryfoam.com
SIC: 5199 3086 Packaging materials; Cups and plates, foamed plastics

**(P-17314)**
**VICTORY SPORTSWEAR INC**
Also Called: Victory Sportswear
2381 Buena Vista St, Duarte (91010-3301)
PHONE..................................866 308-0798
Victor Ju, *CEO*
Xiao Can Zhang, *CFO*
▲ EMP: 22 EST: 1999
SQ FT: 22,000
SALES (est): 2.38MM **Privately Held**
Web: www.victorysportswearinc.com
SIC: 5199 5949 2321 2326 Automobile fabrics; Knitting goods and supplies; Men's and boys' dress shirts; Men's and boy's work clothing

**(P-17315)**
**WALLYS NATURAL**
Also Called: Wally's Natural Products
11837 Kemper Rd Ste 5, Auburn (95603-9067)
P.O. Box 5275 (95604-5275)
PHONE..................................530 887-0396
Russell Shepard, *Pr*
▲ EMP: 21 EST: 1998
SQ FT: 1,600
SALES (est): 9.57MM **Privately Held**
Web: www.wallysnatural.com
SIC: 5199 3999 Candles; Candles

**(P-17316)**
**WAY TO BE DESIGNS LLC**
Also Called: Waytobe Prmtonal Pdts Uniforms
30987 San Clemente St, Hayward (94544-7128)
PHONE..................................510 476-6200
EMP: 38 EST: 1991
SALES (est): 9.16MM **Privately Held**
Web: www.waytobe.com
SIC: 5199 2389 7213 5699 Advertising specialties; Uniforms and vestments; Uniform supply; T-shirts, custom printed

**(P-17317)**
**WEST BAY IMPORTS INC**
Also Called: Euronext Hair Collection
7245 Oxford Way, Commerce (90040-3644)
PHONE..................................323 720-5777
Yong Kyu Yi, *CEO*
◆ EMP: 30 EST: 1981
SALES (est): 6.33MM **Privately Held**
Web: www.westbayinc.com
SIC: 5199 2389 Wigs; Masquerade costumes

**(P-17318)**
**WORLDWISE INC (DH)**
Also Called: Petwise
6 Hamilton Landing Ste 150, Novato (94949-8268)
P.O. Box 3360 (94903)
PHONE..................................415 721-7400
▲ EMP: 99 EST: 1991
SALES (est): 150MM
SALES (corp-wide): 1.22B **Privately Held**
Web: www.petwisebrands.com
SIC: 5199 3999 Pet supplies; Pet supplies
HQ: Alvarez & Marsal Capital, Llc
289 Greenwich Ave 2 Fl
Greenwich CT 06830
203 742-5880

# PRODUCTS & SERVICES SECTION
## 5211 - Lumber And Other Building Materials (P-17337)

## 5211 Lumber And Other Building Materials

**(P-17319)**
**A & A STEPPING STONE MFG INC (PA)**
10291 Ophir Rd, Newcastle (95658-9504)
PHONE..............................530 885-7481
Keith S Arellano, *Pr*
Diane Arellano, *
**EMP:** 25 **EST:** 1974
**SQ FT:** 3,740
**SALES (est):** 22.23MM
**SALES (corp-wide):** 22.23MM **Privately Held**
**Web:** www.aasteppingstone.com
**SIC:** 5211 3272 Concrete and cinder block; Precast terrazzo or concrete products

**(P-17320)**
**ACR SOLAR INTERNATIONAL CORP**
Also Called: Solarroofs.com
5840 Gibbons Dr Ste H, Carmichael (95608-6903)
PHONE..............................916 481-7200
Al Rich, *Pr*
Albert C Rich, *Pr*
Ashley Rich, *VP*
**EMP:** 20 **EST:** 1997
**SQ FT:** 7,500
**SALES (est):** 2.43MM **Privately Held**
**Web:** www.acrsolar.com
**SIC:** 5211 3433 1711 Solar heating equipment; Solar heaters and collectors; Solar energy contractor

**(P-17321)**
**ALKAL TILE INC (PA)**
Also Called: San Diego Marble & Tile
7946 Clairemont Mesa Blvd, San Diego (92111-1617)
PHONE..............................858 278-7828
Albert Goodman, *Pr*
Kalman Smith, *VP*
◆ **EMP:** 15 **EST:** 1989
**SQ FT:** 22,000
**SALES (est):** 5.24MM **Privately Held**
**Web:** www.sandiegomarbletile.com
**SIC:** 5211 5032 5023 5713 Brick; Brick, stone, and related material; Resilient floor coverings: tile or sheet; Floor tile

**(P-17322)**
**BIG CREEK LUMBER COMPANY (PA)**
3564 Highway 1, Davenport (95017-9706)
PHONE..............................831 457-5015
**TOLL FREE:** 800
Janet Webb, *Pr*
Dave Renkens, *
**EMP:** 100 **EST:** 1946
**SQ FT:** 3,000
**SALES (est):** 41.86MM
**SALES (corp-wide):** 41.86MM **Privately Held**
**Web:** www.bigcreeklumber.com
**SIC:** 5211 2421 Millwork and lumber; Sawmills and planing mills, general

**(P-17323)**
**BRACUT INTERNATIONAL CORP**
Also Called: Mill Yard
4949 West End Rd, Arcata (95521-9243)
PHONE..............................707 826-9850
**TOLL FREE:** 800
Laurie Mark, *Pr*
Tanka Chase, *VP*
**EMP:** 22 **EST:** 1972
**SALES (est):** 2.26MM **Privately Held**
**Web:** www.themillyard.biz
**SIC:** 5211 2421 Lumber products; Sawmills and planing mills, general

**(P-17324)**
**BUILDERS FIRSTSOURCE INC**
Also Called: BMC West Door Plant
4237 Murphy Rd, Modesto (95358-9702)
PHONE..............................209 545-0736
Joe Zuendel, *Brnch Mgr*
**EMP:** 16
**SQ FT:** 44,841
**SALES (corp-wide):** 17.1B **Publicly Held**
**Web:** www.bldr.com
**SIC:** 5211 2431 Lumber products; Doors and door parts and trim, wood
**PA:** Builders Firstsource, Inc.
6031 Cnnection Dr Ste 400
214 880-3500

**(P-17325)**
**BURGESS LUMBER (PA)**
3610 Copperhill Ln, Santa Rosa (95403-1090)
PHONE..............................707 542-5091
Orin Burgess, *CEO*
Andrew Lee Burgess, *Sec*
Warren A Burgess, *VP*
**EMP:** 15 **EST:** 1972
**SQ FT:** 1,500
**SALES (est):** 4.51MM
**SALES (corp-wide):** 4.51MM **Privately Held**
**Web:** www.goldenstatelumber.com
**SIC:** 5211 2421 Millwork and lumber; Resawing lumber into smaller dimensions

**(P-17326)**
**BURNETT SONS PLANING MILL LBR**
Also Called: Planing Mill & Lbr. Co.
214 11th St, Sacramento (95814-0893)
P.O. Box 1646 (95812-1646)
PHONE..............................916 442-0493
James Miller, *Ch Bd*
Fitz Miller, *
Simone Miller, *
**EMP:** 50 **EST:** 1869
**SQ FT:** 12,000
**SALES (est):** 4.59MM **Privately Held**
**Web:** www.burnett-sons.com
**SIC:** 5211 2434 2431 2421 Lumber and other building materials; Wood kitchen cabinets; Millwork; Sawmills and planing mills, general

**(P-17327)**
**DIXIELINE LUMBER COMPANY LLC (DH)**
Also Called: Dixieline Probuild
3250 Sports Arena Blvd, San Diego (92110-4588)
P.O. Box 85307 (92186-5307)
PHONE..............................619 224-4120
William S Cowling Ii, *Ch Bd*
Joe Laurence, *
Don Polich, *
▲ **EMP:** 55 **EST:** 1913
**SQ FT:** 12,000
**SALES (est):** 14.7MM
**SALES (corp-wide):** 17.1B **Publicly Held**
**Web:** www.dixieline.com
**SIC:** 5211 5251 2439 5072 Lumber and other building materials; Builders' hardware ; Trusses, wooden roof; Hardware
**HQ:** Lanoga Corporation
17946 Ne 65th St
Redmond WA 98052
425 883-4125

**(P-17328)**
**DIXIELINE LUMBER COMPANY LLC**
2625 Durahart St, Riverside (92507-2654)
PHONE..............................951 224-8491
**EMP:** 419
**SALES (corp-wide):** 17.1B **Publicly Held**
**Web:** www.dixieline.com
**SIC:** 5211 5251 2439 5072 Lumber and other building materials; Builders' hardware ; Trusses, wooden roof; Hardware
**HQ:** Dixieline Lumber Company Llc
3250 Sports Arena Blvd
San Diego CA 92110
619 224-4120

**(P-17329)**
**EMSER TILE LLC**
42092 Winchester Rd, Temecula (92590-4805)
PHONE..............................951 296-3671
Ed Combs, *Mgr*
**EMP:** 30
**SALES (corp-wide):** 273.97MM **Privately Held**
**Web:** www.emser.com
**SIC:** 5211 5032 5023 3272 Tile, ceramic; Tile and clay products; Floor coverings; Floor tile, precast terrazzo
**PA:** Emser Tile, Llc
8431 Santa Monica Blvd
323 650-2000

**(P-17330)**
**EMSER TILE LLC**
4546 Stine Rd, Bakersfield (93313-2300)
PHONE..............................661 837-4400
Ghodsian Sah, *Mgr*
**EMP:** 41
**SALES (corp-wide):** 273.97MM **Privately Held**
**Web:** www.emser.com
**SIC:** 5211 5032 3253 Tile, ceramic; Ceramic wall and floor tile, nec; Ceramic wall and floor tile
**PA:** Emser Tile, Llc
8431 Santa Monica Blvd
323 650-2000

**(P-17331)**
**G & G DOOR PRODUCTS INC**
7600 Stage Rd, Buena Park (90621-1226)
PHONE..............................714 228-2008
Bernie Gabel, *Pr*
Lynette Bleeker, *
Chad Gabel, *
Kathy Martens, *
**EMP:** 35 **EST:** 1995
**SQ FT:** 13,500
**SALES (est):** 6.52MM **Privately Held**
**Web:** www.ggdoor.net
**SIC:** 5211 3442 Doors, storm: wood or metal ; Metal doors, sash, and trim

**(P-17332)**
**GANAHL LUMBER COMPANY**
Also Called: Benjamin Moore Authorized Ret
150 W Blaine St, Corona (92878-4047)
P.O. Box 1326 (92878-1326)
PHONE..............................951 278-4000
Mark Ganahl, *Prin*
**EMP:** 67
**SALES (corp-wide):** 756.05MM **Privately Held**
**Web:** www.ganahllumber.com
**SIC:** 5211 2431 5031 1751 Millwork and lumber; Millwork; Lumber: rough, dressed, and finished; Window and door (prefabricated) installation
**PA:** Ganahl Lumber Company
1220 E Ball Rd
714 772-5444

**(P-17333)**
**HOLT LUMBER INC (PA)**
1916 S Cherry Ave, Fresno (93721-3398)
P.O. Box 1008 (93714-1008)
PHONE..............................559 233-3291
John W Holt Junior, *Pr*
Tom Powers, *
Jack Holt, *
**EMP:** 25 **EST:** 1960
**SQ FT:** 25,000
**SALES (est):** 3.42MM
**SALES (corp-wide):** 3.42MM **Privately Held**
**Web:** www.holtlumber.com
**SIC:** 5211 2439 Lumber and other building materials; Trusses, wooden roof

**(P-17334)**
**HOMER T HAYWARD LUMBER CO**
Also Called: Hayward Lumber Co
800 W Betteravia Rd, Santa Maria (93455-1125)
P.O. Box 7441 (93456-7441)
PHONE..............................805 928-8557
Rudy Lockhart, *Brnch Mgr*
**EMP:** 15
**SALES (corp-wide):** 98.48MM **Privately Held**
**Web:** www.haywardlumber.com
**SIC:** 5211 5999 5231 3444 Lumber products ; Plumbing and heating supplies; Glass; Concrete forms, sheet metal
**PA:** Homer T. Hayward Lumber Co.
2511 Garden Rd Ste A300
831 643-1900

**(P-17335)**
**INDUSTRIAL WOOD PRODUCTS INC**
5123 Brooks St, Montclair (91763-4806)
P.O. Box 3121 (91763-9221)
PHONE..............................909 625-1247
Jaime Ramirez, *Pr*
Lydia Ramrez, *VP*
**EMP:** 18 **EST:** 1984
**SALES (est):** 934.14K **Privately Held**
**SIC:** 5211 2448 2449 2441 Millwork and lumber; Pallets, wood; Rectangular boxes and crates, wood; Nailed wood boxes and shook

**(P-17336)**
**NOR-CAL OVERHEAD INC**
Also Called: Garage Doors
1799 Carpenter Rd Unit C, Oakley (94561-4005)
PHONE..............................925 240-5141
William Mcelmurry, *Pr*
William A Mcelmurry, *CEO*
**EMP:** 15 **EST:** 2003
**SALES (est):** 2.98MM **Privately Held**
**Web:** www.norcaloverheaddoor.com
**SIC:** 5211 3442 Garage doors, sale and installation; Garage doors, overhead: metal

**(P-17337)**
**NORTHERN CAL BLDG MTLS INC (PA)**
Also Called: Norcal Building Materials
1534 Copperhill Pkwy, Santa Rosa (95403-8200)
P.O. Box 751222 (94975-1222)
PHONE..............................707 546-9422
James B Hill, *Pr*
**EMP:** 20 **EST:** 1982
**SALES (est):** 1.12MM

---

(PA)=Parent Co (HQ)=Headquarters
◆ = New Business established in last 2 years

## 5211 - Lumber And Other Building Materials (P-17338)

SALES (corp-wide): 1.12MM **Privately Held**
Web: www.shamrockmaterials.com
SIC: 5211 3273 Lumber and other building materials; Ready-mixed concrete

### (P-17338)
### OKEEFFES INC
Also Called: Safti
220 S R St, Merced (95341-6833)
PHONE..................209 388-9072
William Keeffe, *Brnch Mgr*
EMP: 67
SALES (corp-wide): 26.33MM **Privately Held**
Web: www.safti.com
SIC: 5211 3444 3354 Lumber and other building materials; Sheet metalwork; Aluminum extruded products
PA: O'keeffe's, Inc.
100 N Hill Dr Ste 12
415 822-4222

### (P-17339)
### PARAGON INDUSTRIES INC (PA)
Also Called: Alysedwards
4285 N Golden State Blvd, Fresno (93722-6316)
P.O. Box 9697 (93793)
PHONE..................559 275-5000
Larry A Bedrosian, *CEO*
Janice Bedrosian, *
◆ EMP: 60 EST: 1974
SQ FT: 65,000
SALES (est): 251.57MM
SALES (corp-wide): 251.57MM **Privately Held**
Web: www.bedrosians.com
SIC: 5211 3281 3251 Tile, ceramic; Curbing, granite or stone; Brick and structural clay tile

### (P-17340)
### PARAGON INDUSTRIES II INC
Also Called: Paragon II Real Estate
4285 N Golden State Blvd, Fresno (93722-6316)
PHONE..................559 275-5000
Larry E Bedrosian, *Pr*
EMP: 57 EST: 2012
SALES (est): 4.83MM
SALES (corp-wide): 251.57MM **Privately Held**
SIC: 5211 3281 3251 Tile, ceramic; Curbing, granite or stone; Brick and structural clay tile
PA: Paragon Industries, Inc.
4285 N Golden State Blvd
559 275-5000

### (P-17341)
### PAREX USA INC
Also Called: La Habra Stucco
2150 Eastridge Ave, Riverside (92507-0720)
PHONE..................951 653-3549
Brian Carrier, *Mgr*
EMP: 33
Web: www.parexusa.com
SIC: 5211 3299 Lumber and other building materials; Stucco
HQ: Parex Usa, Inc.
2150 Eastridge Ave
Riverside CA 92507
714 778-2266

### (P-17342)
### PEGASUS SOLAR INC
Also Called: Pegasus Solar
506 W Ohio Ave, Richmond (94804-2040)
PHONE..................510 210-3797
Erich Stephan, *CEO*
EMP: 25 EST: 2012
SALES (est): 4.87MM **Privately Held**
Web: www.pegasussolar.com
SIC: 5211 3433 Solar heating equipment; Solar heaters and collectors

### (P-17343)
### SCOTT MILES
Also Called: R J Miles Co
Railroad & Oak St, Colfax (95713)
P.O. Box 758 (95713-0758)
PHONE..................530 346-2294
Scott Miles, *Owner*
EMP: 35 EST: 1945
SQ FT: 5,000
SALES (est): 683.23K **Privately Held**
SIC: 5211 3273 Sand and gravel; Ready-mixed concrete

### (P-17344)
### SEQUOIA STEEL AND SUPPLY CO
Also Called: Eagle Building Materials
1407 N Clark St, Fresno (93703-3615)
PHONE..................559 485-4100
Tom Graves, *Pr*
Carol Summers, *VP*
EMP: 15 EST: 1958
SQ FT: 12,000
SALES (est): 2.44MM **Privately Held**
SIC: 5211 5032 3299 Masonry materials and supplies; Stucco; Mica products

### (P-17345)
### SMI ARCHITECTURAL MILLWORK INC
Also Called: SMI Millwork
2116 W Chestnut Ave, Santa Ana (92703-4306)
PHONE..................714 567-0112
Robert Stolo, *Pr*
Karen Kawasaki, *
Timothy J Stolo, *
EMP: 35 EST: 1997
SQ FT: 1,500
SALES (est): 2MM **Privately Held**
Web: www.smimillwork.com
SIC: 5211 2431 Millwork and lumber; Millwork

### (P-17346)
### SUPERIOR READY MIX CONCRETE LP
Also Called: San Diego Ready Mix
9245 Camino Santa Fe, San Diego (92121-2201)
PHONE..................858 695-0666
J Frederickson, *Brnch Mgr*
EMP: 71
SALES (corp-wide): 205.26MM **Privately Held**
Web: www.superiorrm.com
SIC: 5211 3273 Concrete and cinder block; Ready-mixed concrete
PA: Superior Ready Mix Concrete L.P.
1564 Mission Rd
760 745-0556

### (P-17347)
### SWAN FENCE INCORPORATED
600 W Manville St, Compton (90220-5508)
PHONE..................310 669-8000
Shigehiro Hatake, *Pr*
Jun Ando, *
EMP: 25 EST: 1988
SQ FT: 50,000
SALES (est): 2.41MM **Privately Held**
Web: www.swanfence.com
SIC: 5211 3315 Fencing; Fence gates, posts, and fittings: steel
PA: Koiwa Kanaami Co., Ltd.
3-20-14, Nishiasakusa

## 5231 Paint, Glass, And Wallpaper Stores

### (P-17348)
### DUNN-EDWARDS CORPORATION (DH)
Also Called: Dunn-Dwrds Pints Wallcoverings
6119 E Washington Blvd, Commerce (90040-2436)
P.O. Box 30389 (90040)
PHONE..................888 337-2468
Karl Altergott, *Pr*
◆ EMP: 150 EST: 1925
SALES (est): 325.93MM **Privately Held**
Web: www.dunnedwards.com
SIC: 5231 2851 Paint; Lacquer: bases, dopes, thinner
HQ: Nippon Paint Holdings Co., Ltd.
2-1-2, Oyodokita, Ki-Ku
Osaka OSK 531-0

### (P-17349)
### OLDCASTLE BUILDINGENVELOPE INC
6850 Stevenson Blvd, Fremont (94538-2484)
PHONE..................510 651-2292
Barry Adams, *Brnch Mgr*
EMP: 155
SALES (corp-wide): 3.44B **Privately Held**
Web: www.obe.com
SIC: 5231 3231 Glass; Tempered glass: made from purchased glass
HQ: Oldcastle Buildingenvelope, Inc.
5005 Lyndon B Jhnson Fwy
Dallas TX 75244
214 273-3400

### (P-17350)
### SWARTZ GLASS CO INC (PA)
821 Lincoln Blvd, Venice (90291-2846)
PHONE..................310 392-0001
Raphael Swartz, *CEO*
Michael Swartz, *Treas*
Mark Swartz, *VP*
EMP: 18 EST: 1933
SQ FT: 2,500
SALES (est): 1.92MM
SALES (corp-wide): 1.92MM **Privately Held**
Web: www.swartzglassvenice.com
SIC: 5231 1793 7536 3231 Glass, leaded or stained; Glass and glazing work; Automotive glass replacement shops; Products of purchased glass

### (P-17351)
### VISTA PAINT CORPORATION (PA)
2020 E Orangethorpe Ave, Fullerton (92831-5327)
PHONE..................714 680-3800
Eddie R Fischer, *Pr*
Eddie R Fischer, *Pr*
Jerome Fischer, *
Joe Wittenberg, *Marketing*
▲ EMP: 150 EST: 1956
SQ FT: 140,000
SALES (est): 96.51MM
SALES (corp-wide): 96.51MM **Privately Held**
Web: www.vistapaint.com

SIC: 5231 2851 Paint; Paints and paint additives

## 5251 Hardware Stores

### (P-17352)
### CONSOLIDATED DEVICES INC (HQ)
Also Called: CDI Torque Products
19220 San Jose Ave, City Of Industry (91748-1417)
PHONE..................626 965-0668
Michael King, *Pr*
Gary Keefe, *
▲ EMP: 25 EST: 1968
SQ FT: 90,000
SALES (est): 9.26MM
SALES (corp-wide): 4.73B **Publicly Held**
Web: www.cditorque.com
SIC: 5251 3679 3625 5072 Tools; Transducers, electrical; Control equipment, electric; Hardware
PA: Snap-On Incorporated
2801 80th St
262 656-5200

### (P-17353)
### COORDNTED WIRE ROPE RGGING INC (HQ)
Also Called: Coordinated Companies
1707 E Anaheim St, Wilmington (90744-4706)
PHONE..................310 834-8535
Phlip T Gibson, *CEO*
Kristin Burgett, *VP*
▲ EMP: 20 EST: 1962
SQ FT: 8,640
SALES (est): 3.22MM
SALES (corp-wide): 6.74MM **Privately Held**
Web: www.coordinatedcompanies.com
SIC: 5251 2298 Hardware stores; Wire rope centers
PA: Coordinated Equipment Co.
1707 E Anaheim St
310 834-8535

### (P-17354)
### GEORGE L THROOP CO
Also Called: Do It Best
444 N Fair Oaks Ave, Pasadena (91103-3619)
P.O. Box 92405 (91109-2405)
PHONE..................626 796-0285
TOLL FREE: 800
Jeffrey Throop, *Pr*
George L Throop Iii, *VP*
Ann T Comey, *
▲ EMP: 32 EST: 1921
SQ FT: 10,500
SALES (est): 5.5MM **Privately Held**
Web: www.throop.com
SIC: 5251 3272 3273 Hardware stores; Concrete products, nec; Ready-mixed concrete

### (P-17355)
### HEALDSBURG LUMBER COMPANY INC
Also Called: Hlc
13534 Healdsburg Ave, Healdsburg (95448-9245)
P.O. Box 970 (95448-0970)
PHONE..................707 431-9663
Eric A Ziedrich, *CEO*
Janet Ziedrich, *
EMP: 90 EST: 1973
SALES (est): 23.13MM **Privately Held**
Web: www.healdsburglumber.com

▲ = Import  ▼ = Export
◆ = Import/Export

# PRODUCTS & SERVICES SECTION

## 5411 - Grocery Stores (P-17374)

SIC: 5251 5211 2431  Hardware stores; Lumber and other building materials; Millwork

### (P-17356)
### HERBERT RIZZARDINI
Also Called: Gateway Hardware
6259 Highway 178, Inyokern  (93527)
P.O. Box 1180  (93527-1180)
PHONE..............................760 377-4571
Herbert Rizzardini, *Owner*
EMP: 18 EST: 1987
SQ FT: 7,000
SALES (est): 800.62K **Privately Held**
SIC: 5251 2048  Hardware stores; Livestock feeds

### (P-17357)
### MORGAN & SLATES MFG & SUP INC (PA)
12918 Hanford Armona Rd, Hanford (93230-9023)
PHONE..............................559 582-4417
Leroy Morgan, *CEO*
Gloria Morgan, *Sec*
Brad Morgan, *VP*
EMP: 17 EST: 1973
SQ FT: 15,000
SALES (est): 4.83MM
SALES (corp-wide): 4.83MM **Privately Held**
Web: www.morganandslates.com
SIC: 5251 7692 3523  Hardware stores; Welding repair; Farm machinery and equipment

### (P-17358)
### ROCKLER COMPANIES INC
Also Called: Rockler Woodworking and Hdwr
1955 N Tustin St, Orange  (92865-4606)
PHONE..............................714 282-1157
Ann Rockler, *Pr*
EMP: 18
SALES (corp-wide): 105.5MM **Privately Held**
Web: www.rockler.com
SIC: 5251 5084 2499  Tools; Woodworking machinery; Decorative wood and woodwork
PA: Rockler Companies, Inc.
    4365 Willow Dr
    763 478-8201

### (P-17359)
### SMARTTHINGS INC (PA)
665 Clyde Ave, Mountain View (94043-2235)
PHONE..............................757 633-2308
Alex Hawkinson, *CEO*
Andrew Brooks, *COO*
Simon Seungmin Kim, *CFO*
James Stolp, *Sr VP*
Jeff Hagins, *Prin*
EMP: 18 EST: 2015
SALES (est): 13.41MM
SALES (corp-wide): 13.41MM **Privately Held**
Web: www.samsung.com
SIC: 5251 3567 3663  Door locks and lock sets; Electrical furnaces, ovens, & heating devices, exc.induction; Cameras, television

### (P-17360)
### WILLITTS EQP & ENGRG CO INC
Also Called: Water Well Solutions
30548 Road 196, Exeter  (93221-9773)
P.O. Box 1110  (93221-7110)
PHONE..............................559 594-5020
Ken Williams, *Pr*
Kenneth W Williams, *

Jean Jones, *

EMP: 36 EST: 1954
SALES (est): 5.2MM **Privately Held**
Web: www.willittspump.com
SIC: 5251 5999 7699 7694  Pumps and pumping equipment; Motors, electric; Pumps and pumping equipment repair; Electric motor repair

## 5261 Retail Nurseries And Garden Stores

### (P-17361)
### HELENA INDUSTRIES  LLC
Also Called: Rapids Warehousing
1075 S Vineland Ave, Kerman (93630-9246)
P.O. Box 305  (93630-0305)
PHONE..............................559 846-5303
Gerardo Salgado, *Manager*
EMP: 93
Web: www.helenaindustries.com
SIC: 5261 2875  Fertilizer; Compost
HQ: Helena Industries, Llc
    225 Schilling Blvd Ste 100
    Collierville TN 38017

### (P-17362)
### TREASURE GARDEN  INC (PA)
13401 Brooks Dr, Baldwin Park (91706-2294)
PHONE..............................626 814-0168
Oliver Ma, *Pr*
Margaret Chang, *
◆ EMP: 50 EST: 1984
SQ FT: 45,000
SALES (est): 23.25MM
SALES (corp-wide): 23.25MM **Privately Held**
Web: www.treasuregarden.com
SIC: 5261 2514  Retail nurseries and garden stores; Lawn furniture: metal

## 5311 Department Stores

### (P-17363)
### LADESSERTS INC
1433 E Gage Ave, Los Angeles (90001-1783)
PHONE..............................323 588-2522
EMP: 40
SALES (corp-wide): 10.98MM **Privately Held**
Web: www.theivyrestaurants.com
SIC: 5311 5137 2389  Department stores; Women's and children's clothing; Apparel for handicapped
PA: L.A.Desserts Inc.
    113 N Robertson Blvd
    310 274-8303

### (P-17364)
### WALMART INC
Also Called: Walmart
1601 S Lower Sacramento Rd Ste A, Lodi (95242)
PHONE..............................209 368-6658
EMP: 42
SALES (corp-wide): 648.13B **Publicly Held**
Web: www.walmart.com
SIC: 5311 2752  Department stores, discount ; Commercial printing, lithographic
PA: Walmart Inc.
    702 Sw 8th St
    479 273-4000

## 5411 Grocery Stores

### (P-17365)
### ALBECO INC
Also Called: Mollie Stone Market
270 Bon Air Ctr, Greenbrae  (94904-2416)
PHONE..............................415 461-1164
Jeffrey Lane, *Mgr*
EMP: 71
SALES (corp-wide): 57.83MM **Privately Held**
Web: www.starbucks.com
SIC: 5411 5921 5421 5431  Grocery stores, independent; Liquor stores; Meat markets, including freezer provisioners; Fruit stands or markets
PA: Albeco, Inc.
    150 Shrline Hwy Bldg D St
    415 289-5720

### (P-17366)
### ALBERTSONS LLC
Also Called: Albertsons 6514
8938 Trautwein Rd Ste A, Riverside (92508-9191)
PHONE..............................951 656-6603
Bill Brown, *Mgr*
EMP: 68
SALES (corp-wide): 79.24B **Publicly Held**
Web: local.albertsons.com
SIC: 5411 2051  Supermarkets, chain; Bread, cake, and related products
HQ: Albertson's Llc
    250 E Parkcenter Blvd
    Boise ID 83706
    208 395-6200

### (P-17367)
### ALBERTSONS LLC
Also Called: Albertsons 6798
30901 Riverside Dr, Lake Elsinore (92530-4934)
PHONE..............................951 245-4461
Brad Sharp, *Mgr*
EMP: 24
SALES (corp-wide): 79.24B **Publicly Held**
Web: www.starbucks.com
SIC: 5411 5992 2052 2051  Supermarkets, chain; Florists; Cookies and crackers; Bread, cake, and related products
HQ: Albertson's Llc
    250 E Parkcenter Blvd
    Boise ID 83706
    208 395-6200

### (P-17368)
### ARRIETTA INCORPORATED
Also Called: La Tolteca Mexican Foods
429 N Azusa Ave, Azusa  (91702-3442)
PHONE..............................626 334-0302
Benjamin E Arrietta, *Pr*
Jean Arrietta, *
Tim Arrietta, *
Ben D Arrietta, *
EMP: 33 EST: 1948
SQ FT: 19,000
SALES (est): 1.62MM **Privately Held**
Web: www.latoltecaazusa.com
SIC: 5411 2099 5812  Delicatessen stores; Tortillas, fresh or refrigerated; Mexican restaurant

### (P-17369)
### BEL AIR MART
Also Called: Bel Air Market 509
1039 Sunrise Ave, Roseville  (95661-7008)
PHONE..............................916 786-6101
EMP: 99
SALES (corp-wide): 2.33B **Privately Held**
Web: www.raleys.com
SIC: 5411 5992 5912 2051  Supermarkets, chain; Florists; Drug stores and proprietary stores; Bread, cake, and related products
HQ: Bel Air Mart
    500 W Capitol Ave
    West Sacramento CA

### (P-17370)
### BEL AIR MART
Also Called: Bel Air Market 501
6231 Fruitridge Rd, Sacramento (95820-5844)
PHONE..............................916 739-8647
Allen Kamura, *Mgr*
EMP: 101
SALES (corp-wide): 2.33B **Privately Held**
Web: www.raleys.com
SIC: 5411 2051 5461  Supermarkets, chain; Bread, cake, and related products; Retail bakeries
HQ: Bel Air Mart
    500 W Capitol Ave
    West Sacramento CA

### (P-17371)
### BEL AIR MART
Also Called: Bel Air Market 510
1540 W El Camino Ave, Sacramento (95833-1946)
PHONE..............................916 920-2493
Phil Canaday, *Mgr*
EMP: 99
SALES (corp-wide): 2.33B **Privately Held**
Web: www.raleys.com
SIC: 5411 5992 5912 2051  Supermarkets, chain; Florists; Drug stores and proprietary stores; Bread, cake, and related products
HQ: Bel Air Mart
    500 W Capitol Ave
    West Sacramento CA

### (P-17372)
### BEL AIR MART
Also Called: Bel Air Market 502
4320 Arden Way, Sacramento (95864-3103)
PHONE..............................916 972-0555
Gary Spencer, *Mgr*
EMP: 104
SALES (corp-wide): 2.33B **Privately Held**
Web: www.raleys.com
SIC: 5411 5912 2052 2051  Supermarkets, chain; Drug stores and proprietary stores; Cookies and crackers; Bread, cake, and related products
HQ: Bel Air Mart
    500 W Capitol Ave
    West Sacramento CA

### (P-17373)
### COUSINS FOODS  LLC
Also Called: Jericho Foods
2021 1st St, San Fernando  (91340-2611)
PHONE..............................818 767-3842
Zadi Janah, *CEO*
Moshe Sarid, *Managing Member*
EMP: 20 EST: 2011
SALES (est): 2.69MM **Privately Held**
Web: www.jerichofood.com
SIC: 5411 2035 1541  Grocery stores, independent; Dressings, salad: raw and cooked (except dry mixes); Food products manufacturing or packing plant construction

### (P-17374)
### DIANAS MEXICAN FOOD PDTS INC
Also Called: Labonita Diana's Mexican Food
300 E Sepulveda Blvd, Carson (90745-5923)

# 5411 - Grocery Stores (P-17375)

PHONE..................310 834-4886
Carlos Andres, *Mgr*
**EMP:** 44
**SQ FT:** 1,660
**SALES (corp-wide):** 23.78MM **Privately Held**
Web: www.dianas.net
**SIC:** 5411 2099 5812 Delicatessen stores; Food preparations, nec; Mexican restaurant
PA: Diana's Mexican Food Products, Inc.
16330 Pioneer Blvd
562 926-5802

**(P-17375)**
### DILLON COMPANIES INC
Also Called: Food 4 Less
4250 Van Buren Blvd, Riverside (92503-2602)
PHONE..................951 352-8353
Rocky Scmit, *Mgr*
**EMP:** 142
**SALES (corp-wide):** 150.04B **Publicly Held**
Web: www.dillons.com
**SIC:** 5411 2051 Supermarkets, chain; Bread, cake, and related products
HQ: Dillon Companies, Llc
2700 E 4th Ave
Hutchinson KS 67504
620 665-5511

**(P-17376)**
### DLA COLMENA INC
129 W Lake Ave, Watsonville (95076-4511)
PHONE..................831 724-4544
Manuel Gonzales, *Pr*
Andrean Gonzales, *
Connie Gonzales, *
**EMP:** 50 **EST:** 1978
**SQ FT:** 6,100
**SALES (est):** 4.67MM **Privately Held**
Web: www.dlacolmenacatering.com
**SIC:** 5411 2051 5812 Grocery stores, independent; Pastries, e.g. danish: except frozen; Delicatessen (eating places)

**(P-17377)**
### DOMINICS ORGNAL GNOVA DELI INC
Also Called: Ravioli Factory
1550 Trancas St, Napa (94558-2916)
PHONE..................707 253-8686
Dominic De Vincenzi, *Pr*
David De Vincenzi, *
**EMP:** 65 **EST:** 1966
**SQ FT:** 1,500
**SALES (est):** 2.15MM **Privately Held**
Web: www.genovadelinapa.com
**SIC:** 5411 2051 5921 Delicatessen stores; Bread, all types (white, wheat, rye, etc); fresh or frozen; Beer (packaged)

**(P-17378)**
### EL NOPALITO INC (PA)
Also Called: El Nopalito Mexican Food
560 Santa Fe Dr, Encinitas (92024-4640)
PHONE..................760 436-5775
Kia Garcia, *Pr*
Hilcias Garcia, *VP*
**EMP:** 20 **EST:** 1974
**SQ FT:** 4,000
**SALES (est):** 4.18MM
**SALES (corp-wide):** 4.18MM **Privately Held**
Web: www.el-nopalito.com
**SIC:** 5411 5812 2099 Grocery stores; Mexican restaurant; Tortillas, fresh or refrigerated

**(P-17379)**
### EL TIGRE INC
Also Called: El Tigre Warehouse 2
2909 Coronado Ave, San Diego (92154-2150)
PHONE..................619 429-8212
M Rodriguez, *Genl Mgr*
**EMP:** 108
**SALES (corp-wide):** 2.62MM **Privately Held**
**SIC:** 5411 2051 Grocery stores, independent; Bread, cake, and related products
PA: El Tigre, Inc.
1002 Mission Creek Rd
760 728-8800

**(P-17380)**
### GELSONS MARKETS
13455 Maxella Ave, Marina Del Rey (90292-5682)
PHONE..................310 306-3192
Romel Montero, *Genl Mgr*
**EMP:** 83
Web: www.gelsons.com
**SIC:** 5411 2051 5461 Supermarkets, chain; Bread, cake, and related products; Retail bakeries
HQ: Gelson's Markets
13833 Freeway Dr
Santa Fe Springs CA 90670
310 638-2842

**(P-17381)**
### ROF FERRARI LENDING 1 LLC
Also Called: A.G. Ferrari Foods
14234 Catalina St, San Leandro (94577-5512)
PHONE..................510 351-5520
▲ **EMP:** 190
**SIC:** 5411 5149 2032 Grocery stores; Natural and organic foods; Italian foods, nec: packaged in cans, jars, etc.

**(P-17382)**
### SAFEWAY INC
Also Called: Safeway
1200 Irving St Ste 2, San Francisco (94122-2121)
PHONE..................415 661-3220
John Bacho, *Mgr*
**EMP:** 5039
**SQ FT:** 36,999
**SALES (corp-wide):** 79.24B **Publicly Held**
Web: www.safeway.com
**SIC:** 5411 5912 2087 2051 Frozen food and freezer plans, except meat; Drug stores and proprietary stores; Flavoring extracts and syrups, nec; Bread, cake, and related products
HQ: Safeway Inc.
5918 Stoneridge Mall Rd
Pleasanton CA 94588
925 226-5000

**(P-17383)**
### SAMS ITALIAN DELI & MKT INC
Also Called: Sam's Super Market
2415 N 1st St, Fresno (93703-1202)
PHONE..................559 229-9333
Sam Mazeleano, *Pr*
Angelinas Mazeleano, *Pt*
**EMP:** 16 **EST:** 1979
**SQ FT:** 4,000
**SALES (est):** 2.18MM **Privately Held**
Web: www.samsitaliandeli.com
**SIC:** 5411 5921 2032 5812 Delicatessen stores; Wine and beer; Italian foods, nec: packaged in cans, jars, etc.; Delicatessen (eating places)

**(P-17384)**
### SAVE MART SUPERMARKETS DISC
Also Called: Foodmaxx
1330 Churn Creek Rd, Redding (96003-4087)
PHONE..................530 222-6740
Ray Prigmore, *Dir*
**EMP:** 104
**SALES (corp-wide):** 28.29B **Privately Held**
Web: www.thesavemartcompanies.com
**SIC:** 5411 5992 2051 Supermarkets, chain; Florists; Bread, cake, and related products
HQ: Save Mart Supermarkets Llc
1800 Standiford Ave
Modesto CA 95350
209 577-1600

**(P-17385)**
### STATER BROS MARKETS
10114 Adams Ave, Huntington Beach (92646-4907)
PHONE..................714 963-0949
Kevin Wagner, *Mgr*
**EMP:** 35
**SALES (corp-wide):** 1.5B **Privately Held**
Web: www.staterbros.com
**SIC:** 5411 5912 5992 2052 Supermarkets, chain; Drug stores; Florists; Cookies and crackers
HQ: Stater Bros. Markets
301 S Tippecanoe Ave
San Bernardino CA 92408
909 733-5000

**(P-17386)**
### STATER BROS MARKETS
1131 N State College Blvd, Anaheim (92806-2704)
PHONE..................714 991-5310
Scott Jefferson, *Mgr*
**EMP:** 35
**SALES (corp-wide):** 1.5B **Privately Held**
Web: www.staterbros.com
**SIC:** 5411 5912 5992 2051 Supermarkets, chain; Drug stores; Florists; Bread, cake, and related products
HQ: Stater Bros. Markets
301 S Tippecanoe Ave
San Bernardino CA 92408
909 733-5000

**(P-17387)**
### SUPER CENTER CONCEPTS INC
Also Called: Superior Warehouse
10211 Avalon Blvd, Los Angeles (90003-4819)
PHONE..................323 241-6789
Mat Kovacs, *Brnch Mgr*
**EMP:** 114
Web: www.superiorgrocers.com
**SIC:** 5411 2051 5812 5461 Supermarkets, independent; Bread, cake, and related products; Carry-out only (except pizza) restaurant; Retail bakeries
PA: Super Center Concepts, Inc.
15510 Carmenita Rd

**(P-17388)**
### SUPER CENTER CONCEPTS INC
Also Called: Superior Super Warehouse
7300 Atlantic Ave, Cudahy (90201-4305)
PHONE..................323 562-8980
Peter Buyn, *Brnch Mgr*
**EMP:** 114
Web: www.superiorgrocers.com
**SIC:** 5411 5421 2052 2051 Grocery stores, independent; Meat and fish markets; Cookies and crackers; Bread, cake, and related products

PA: Super Center Concepts, Inc.
15510 Carmenita Rd

**(P-17389)**
### VONS COMPANIES INC (DH)
Also Called: Pavilions
5918 Stoneridge Mall Rd, Pleasanton (94588-3229)
PHONE..................925 467-3000
Tom Keller, *Pr*
Harold Rudnick, *
David Bond, *
Melissa Plaisance, *
Jerry Tidwell, *
**EMP:** 900 **EST:** 1906
**SQ FT:** 244,000
**SALES (est):** 219.56MM
**SALES (corp-wide):** 79.24B **Publicly Held**
Web: www.albertsonscompanies.com
**SIC:** 5411 2026 2024 Supermarkets, chain; Fluid milk; Ice cream, packaged: molded, on sticks, etc.
HQ: Safeway Inc.
5918 Stoneridge Mall Rd
Pleasanton CA 94588
925 226-5000

**(P-17390)**
### VONS COMPANIES INC
Also Called: Vons 2030
25850 The Old Rd, Stevenson Ranch (91381-1710)
PHONE..................661 254-3570
Brian Flaherty, *Mgr*
**EMP:** 141
**SALES (corp-wide):** 79.24B **Publicly Held**
Web: local.vons.com
**SIC:** 5411 5912 2051 5461 Supermarkets, chain; Drug stores; Bread, cake, and related products; Retail bakeries
HQ: The Vons Companies Inc
5918 Stoneridge Mall Rd
Pleasanton CA 94588
925 467-3000

**(P-17391)**
### VONS COMPANIES INC
Also Called: Vons 2560
1758 W Grand Ave, Grover Beach (93433-2293)
PHONE..................805 481-2492
Jim Clark, *Mgr*
**EMP:** 161
**SALES (corp-wide):** 79.24B **Publicly Held**
Web: local.vons.com
**SIC:** 5411 5912 3556 Supermarkets, chain; Drug stores; Food products machinery
HQ: The Vons Companies Inc
5918 Stoneridge Mall Rd
Pleasanton CA 94588
925 467-3000

**(P-17392)**
### VONS COMPANIES INC
Also Called: Vons 2407
475 W Main St, Brawley (92227-2244)
PHONE..................760 351-3002
Frank Huerta, *Mgr*
**EMP:** 121
**SALES (corp-wide):** 79.24B **Publicly Held**
Web: www.vons.com
**SIC:** 5411 5912 2051 7384 Supermarkets, chain; Drug stores; Bread, cake, and related products; Photofinish laboratories
HQ: The Vons Companies Inc
5918 Stoneridge Mall Rd
Pleasanton CA 94588
925 467-3000

# PRODUCTS & SERVICES SECTION

## 5461 - Retail Bakeries (P-17411)

**(P-17393)**
**VONS COMPANIES INC**
Also Called: Vons 2124
7789 Foothill Blvd, Tujunga (91042-2195)
PHONE..................................818 353-4917
Kevin Micalles, *Mgr*
**EMP:** 121
**SQ FT:** 39,200
**SALES (corp-wide):** 79.24B **Publicly Held**
**Web:** local.vons.com
**SIC:** 5411 5912 5992 2051 Supermarkets, chain; Drug stores; Florists; Bread, cake, and related products
**HQ:** The Vons Companies Inc
  5918 Stoneridge Mall Rd
  Pleasanton CA 94588
  925 467-3000

**(P-17394)**
**VONS COMPANIES INC**
Also Called: Vons 2381
535 N Mckinley St, Corona (92879-1297)
PHONE..................................951 278-8284
Rick Williams, *Mgr*
**EMP:** 121
**SALES (corp-wide):** 79.24B **Publicly Held**
**Web:** local.vons.com
**SIC:** 5411 5912 2051 5461 Supermarkets, chain; Drug stores; Bread, cake, and related products; Retail bakeries
**HQ:** The Vons Companies Inc
  5918 Stoneridge Mall Rd
  Pleasanton CA 94588
  925 467-3000

**(P-17395)**
**VONS COMPANIES INC**
Also Called: Vons 2111
24160 Lyons Ave, Newhall (91321-2442)
PHONE..................................661 259-9214
Phil Nakamura, *Mgr*
**EMP:** 141
**SALES (corp-wide):** 79.24B **Publicly Held**
**Web:** www.vons.com
**SIC:** 5411 5912 2051 Supermarkets, chain; Drug stores; Bread, cake, and related products
**HQ:** The Vons Companies Inc
  5918 Stoneridge Mall Rd
  Pleasanton CA 94588
  925 467-3000

**(P-17396)**
**WORLD OIL MARKETING COMPANY (PA)**
9302 Garfield Ave, South Gate (90280-3805)
P.O. Box 1966 (90280-1966)
PHONE..................................562 928-0100
Robert S Roth, *Pr*
Florence Roth, *VP*
Steven Roth, *VP*
Richard Roth, *VP*
**EMP:** 20 **EST:** 1977
**SQ FT:** 60,000
**SALES (est):** 128.17MM
**SALES (corp-wide):** 128.17MM **Privately Held**
**Web:** www.worldoilcorp.com
**SIC:** 5411 2951 5541 4213 Convenience stores; Paving mixtures; Gasoline service stations; Liquid petroleum transport, non-local

### 5421 Meat And Fish Markets

**(P-17397)**
**SANTA ROSA SEAFOOD RETAIL INC**
946 Santa Rosa Ave, Santa Rosa (95404-5433)
PHONE..................................707 579-2085
Nick Svedise, *Pr*
Nick Speddise, *Pr*
**EMP:** 20 **EST:** 1983
**SALES (est):** 1.32MM **Privately Held**
**Web:** www.santarosaseafood.com
**SIC:** 5421 2092 5146 0913 Seafood markets; Seafoods, fresh: prepared; Seafoods; Crabs, catching of

### 5431 Fruit And Vegetable Markets

**(P-17398)**
**BROTHERS PRIDE PRODUCE INC (PA)**
Also Called: Sigona's Farmers Market
2345 Middlefield Rd, Redwood City (94063-2834)
PHONE..................................650 368-6993
Carmelo Sigona, *CEO*
John Sigona Junior, *Sec*
Paul Sigona, *
**EMP:** 30 **EST:** 1976
**SQ FT:** 10,000
**SALES (est):** 4.7MM
**SALES (corp-wide):** 4.7MM **Privately Held**
**Web:** www.sigonas.com
**SIC:** 5431 5411 5963 2034 Fruit stands or markets; Grocery stores, independent; Food services, direct sales; Fruits, dried or dehydrated, except freeze-dried

**(P-17399)**
**LINNS FRUIT BIN INC (PA)**
Also Called: Linn's Main Bin
2535 Village Ln Ste A, Cambria (93428-3428)
PHONE..................................805 927-1499
Maureen Linn, *Pr*
Renee Linn, *
John Linn, *
Aaron Linn, *
**EMP:** 35 **EST:** 1995
**SQ FT:** 16,000
**SALES (est):** 4.58MM
**SALES (corp-wide):** 4.58MM **Privately Held**
**Web:** www.linnsfruitbin.com
**SIC:** 5431 2053 5812 Fruit and vegetable markets; Frozen bakery products, except bread; Eating places

### 5441 Candy, Nut, And Confectionery Stores

**(P-17400)**
**DSD MERCHANDISERS LLC (DH)**
Also Called: Sweet Factory Express
6226 Industrial Way Ste A, Livermore (94551-9280)
P.O. Box 10008 (94588-0008)
PHONE..................................925 449-2044
Krishen Kotecha, *Genl Mgr*
Karrie Brooks Ctrl, *Prin*
**EMP:** 15 **EST:** 1996
**SQ FT:** 28,000
**SALES (est):** 9.34MM
**SALES (corp-wide):** 132.47MM **Privately Held**
**Web:** www.dsdmerchandisers.com
**SIC:** 5441 2068 2066 5153 Candy; Salted and roasted nuts and seeds; Chocolate and cocoa products; Grains
**HQ:** American Nuts, Llc
  12950 San Fernando Rd
  Sylmar CA 91342
  818 364-8855

**(P-17401)**
**GHIRARDELLI CHOCOLATE COMPANY (DH)**
Also Called: Ghirardelli
1111 139th Ave, San Leandro (94578-2616)
PHONE..................................510 483-6970
Martin Thompson, *CEO*
◆ **EMP:** 375 **EST:** 1852
**SQ FT:** 210,000
**SALES (est):** 137.91MM **Privately Held**
**Web:** www.ghirardelli.com
**SIC:** 5441 2066 5812 5149 Candy; Chocolate; Soda fountain; Chocolate
**HQ:** Lindt & Sprungli (Usa) Inc.
  One Fine Chocolate Pl
  Stratham NH 03885
  603 778-8100

**(P-17402)**
**GOURMET PLUS INC**
Also Called: Thatcher's Gourmet Popcorn
705 Bliss Ave, Pittsburg (94565-5005)
PHONE..................................415 643-9945
Abrahim Aboukhalil, *CEO*
Abrahim Aboukhalil, *Pr*
◆ **EMP:** 42 **EST:** 1983
**SALES (est):** 3.73MM **Privately Held**
**Web:** www.tgsp.com
**SIC:** 5441 2064 5145 Popcorn, including caramel corn; Breakfast bars; Popcorn and supplies

**(P-17403)**
**LEGENDARY FOODS LLC**
2601 Colorado Ave, Santa Monica (90404-3518)
PHONE..................................888 698-1708
Michael Veni, *
Nathan Tudhope, *
**EMP:** 48 **EST:** 2015
**SALES (est):** 63.33MM **Privately Held**
**Web:** www.eatlegendary.com
**SIC:** 5441 1541 2099 Candy; Food products manufacturing or packing plant construction; Food preparations, nec

**(P-17404)**
**LOGANS CANDIES**
125 W B St, Ontario (91762-3502)
PHONE..................................909 984-5410
Jerry Rowley, *Owner*
**EMP:** 16 **EST:** 1953
**SQ FT:** 2,800
**SALES (est):** 395.98K **Privately Held**
**Web:** www.loganscandies.com
**SIC:** 5441 2064 Candy; Candy and other confectionery products

**(P-17405)**
**MINTURN NUT CO INC**
8800 Minturn Rd, Le Grand (95333-9711)
PHONE..................................559 665-8500
Jeff Marchini, *CEO*
Kitt Kahl, *Brand President*
Brad Schnoor, *VP*
Henry Kelsey, *Contrlr*
◆ **EMP:** 20 **EST:** 1996
**SQ FT:** 75,000
**SALES (est):** 5.51MM **Privately Held**
**Web:** www.minturnnut.com
**SIC:** 5441 2096 Nuts; Cheese curls and puffs

**(P-17406)**
**YOSEMITE FARMS**
2341 N St, Merced (95340-3616)
PHONE..................................209 383-3411
Coleen Slacter, *Owner*
**EMP:** 22 **EST:** 1992
**SALES (est):** 434.98K **Privately Held**
**Web:** www.yosemitefarmcredit.com
**SIC:** 5441 2068 Nuts; Nuts: dried, dehydrated, salted or roasted

### 5461 Retail Bakeries

**(P-17407)**
**ANDRE-BOUDIN BAKERIES INC**
Also Called: Boudin Bakeries
619 Market St, San Francisco (94105-3301)
PHONE..................................415 283-1230
Stephen Floyd, *Mgr*
**EMP:** 38
**Web:** www.boudinbakery.com
**SIC:** 5461 2051 5812 Cakes; Bread, cake, and related products; Sandwiches and submarines shop
**HQ:** Andre-Boudin Bakeries, Inc.
  50 Francisco St Ste 200
  San Francisco CA 94133
  415 882-1849

**(P-17408)**
**CATHYS CREATIONS INC**
Also Called: Tastries Bakery
3665 Rosedale Hwy, Bakersfield (93308-6230)
PHONE..................................661 322-1110
Catharine M Miller, *Pr*
**EMP:** 16 **EST:** 2013
**SALES (est):** 1.04MM **Privately Held**
**Web:** www.tastriesbakery.com
**SIC:** 5461 2051 Cakes; Bread, cake, and related products

**(P-17409)**
**DUDLEYS BAKERY INC**
30218 Hwy 78, Santa Ysabel (92070-9733)
P.O. Box 67 (92070-0067)
PHONE..................................760 765-0488
Barry Burnye, *Mgr*
**EMP:** 38 **EST:** 1946
**SQ FT:** 6,000
**SALES (est):** 2.47MM **Privately Held**
**Web:** www.dudleysbakery.com
**SIC:** 5461 5149 2051 Bread; Bakery products; Bread, cake, and related products

**(P-17410)**
**EINSTEIN NOAH REST GROUP INC**
Also Called: Noah's
1521 Sloat Blvd, San Francisco (94132-1222)
PHONE..................................415 731-1700
Albert Puzon, *Genl Mgr*
**EMP:** 66
**Web:** www.bagelbrands.com
**SIC:** 5461 2051 2022 Bagels; Bagels, fresh or frozen; Spreads, cheese
**PA:** Einstein Noah Restaurant Group, Inc.
  555 Zang St Ste 300

**(P-17411)**
**EINSTEIN NOAH REST GROUP INC**
Also Called: Noah's Bagels
1067 El Camino Real, Redwood City (94063-1632)

# 5461 - Retail Bakeries (P-17412)

## PRODUCTS & SERVICES SECTION

PHONE..................650 299-9050
Antelop Tran, *Mgr*
**EMP:** 66
**Web:** www.bagelbrands.com
**SIC: 5461** 2051 2022 Bagels; Bagels, fresh or frozen; Spreads, cheese
**PA:** Einstein Noah Restaurant Group, Inc.
555 Zang St Ste 300

**(P-17412)**
**EVKII INC**
624 Garrison St Ste1-2, Oceanside (92054)
PHONE..................760 721-5200
Heath Squier, *CEO*
**EMP:** 40 **EST:** 1990
**SQ FT:** 35,000
**SALES (est):** 3.78MM **Privately Held**
**Web:** www.julianbakery.com
**SIC: 5461** 2053 2023 5149 Bread; Frozen bakery products, except bread; Dietary supplements, dairy and non-dairy based; Organic and diet food

**(P-17413)**
**JESSIE LORD BAKERY LLC**
Also Called: Jessie Lord
21100 S Western Ave, Torrance (90501-1705)
PHONE..................310 533-6010
Tracy Lee, *
▲ **EMP:** 50 **EST:** 2003
**SQ FT:** 130,000
**SALES (est):** 23.66MM **Privately Held**
**Web:** www.jessielordbakery.com
**SIC: 5461** 2051 Retail bakeries; Cakes, bakery; except frozen

**(P-17414)**
**KAYLAS CAKE CORPORATION**
1311 S Gilbert St, Fullerton (92833-4302)
PHONE..................714 869-1522
Kayla Lee, *CEO*
**EMP:** 30 **EST:** 2014
**SALES (est):** 476.26K **Privately Held**
**Web:** www.thekaylascake.com
**SIC: 5461** 5149 2024 Cakes; Bakery products; Ice cream and frozen deserts

**(P-17415)**
**LOS BAGELS INC (PA)**
1061 I St Ste 101, Arcata (95521-5517)
PHONE..................707 822-3150
Dennis Rael, *Pr*
Paul Hebb Junior, *VP*
Peter Jermyn, *Sec*
**EMP:** 21 **EST:** 1984
**SQ FT:** 1,500
**SALES (est):** 2.28MM **Privately Held**
**Web:** www.losbagels.com
**SIC: 5461** 2051 5149 Bagels; Bagels, fresh or frozen; Groceries and related products, nec

**(P-17416)**
**PACIFIC COOKIE COMPANY INC (PA)**
303 Potrero St Ste 40, Santa Cruz (95060-2719)
PHONE..................831 429-9709
Cara Pearson, *Pr*
Michele Pearson, *
Lawrence Pearson, *
**EMP:** 35 **EST:** 1980
**SQ FT:** 6,000
**SALES (est):** 1.86MM
**SALES (corp-wide):** 1.86MM **Privately Held**
**Web:** www.pacificcookie.com

**SIC: 5461** 5149 2053 2052 Cookies; Cookies; Frozen bakery products, except bread; Cookies and crackers

**(P-17417)**
**PORTOS BAKERY BURBANK INC**
Also Called: Portos Bakery & Cafe
3614 W Magnolia Blvd, Burbank (91505-2913)
PHONE..................818 846-9100
Raul R Porto, *CEO*
**EMP:** 50 **EST:** 2006
**SALES (est):** 10.63MM **Privately Held**
**Web:** www.portosbakery.com
**SIC: 5461** 2051 Cakes; Bread, cake, and related products

**(P-17418)**
**POSH BAKERY INC**
20488 Stevens Creek Blvd Ste 2010, Cupertino (95014-6807)
PHONE..................408 980-8451
Cherly Lee, *Pr*
Jeff Ottoveggio, *
▼ **EMP:** 120 **EST:** 2008
**SALES (est):** 5.17MM **Privately Held**
**Web:** www.theposhbakery.com
**SIC: 5461** 2051 Retail bakeries; Bagels, fresh or frozen

**(P-17419)**
**PURITAN BAKERY INC**
1624 E Carson St, Carson (90745-2599)
PHONE..................310 830-5451
Matthew R Grimes, *Pr*
John G Markulis, *
John John Markulis, *
**EMP:** 200 **EST:** 1940
**SQ FT:** 60,000
**SALES (est):** 24.2MM **Privately Held**
**Web:** www.puritanbakery.com
**SIC: 5461** 2051 Retail bakeries; Breads, rolls, and buns

**(P-17420)**
**SHENG-KEE OF CALIFORNIA INC**
201 S Hill Dr, Brisbane (94005-1204)
PHONE..................415 468-3800
Mark Kao, *Brnch Mgr*
▲ **EMP:** 61
**SALES (corp-wide):** 24.87MM **Privately Held**
**Web:** www.shengkee.com
**SIC: 5461** 2051 Cakes; Bread, cake, and related products
**PA:** Sheng-Kee Of California, Inc.
1941 Irving St
415 564-4800

**(P-17421)**
**SONORA BAKERY INC**
4484 Whittier Blvd, Los Angeles (90022-1534)
PHONE..................323 269-2253
Hector Oratowski, *Pr*
Theresa Oratowski, *
Dennis Oratowski, *
**EMP:** 30 **EST:** 1986
**SQ FT:** 6,000
**SALES (est):** 1MM **Privately Held**
**Web:** www.sonorabakery.com
**SIC: 5461** 2051 5812 Retail bakeries; Bread, cake, and related products; Caterers

**(P-17422)**
**WETZELS PRETZELS LLC**
Also Called: Store 3

525 Parkway Plz Unit 525, El Cajon (92020-2531)
PHONE..................619 588-1074
Linda Holm, *Genl Mgr*
**EMP:** 41
**SALES (corp-wide):** 11.08MM **Privately Held**
**Web:** www.wetzels.com
**SIC: 5461** 2099 Pretzels; Food preparations, nec
**HQ:** Wetzel's Pretzels, Llc
35 Hugus Alley Ste 300
Pasadena CA 91103

## 5499 Miscellaneous Food Stores

**(P-17423)**
**AHARONI & STEELE INC**
Also Called: Sante Specialty Foods
1855 Norman Ave, Santa Clara (95054-2029)
PHONE..................408 451-9585
Sara Tidhar, *Pr*
**EMP:** 18 **EST:** 2004
**SALES (est):** 2.75MM **Privately Held**
**Web:** www.santenuts.com
**SIC: 5499** 2068 Dried fruit; Salted and roasted nuts and seeds

**(P-17424)**
**CITY BEAN INC**
5051 W Jefferson Blvd, Los Angeles (90016-3940)
PHONE..................323 734-0828
Gary Salzer, *Pr*
**EMP:** 15 **EST:** 1991
**SQ FT:** 2,000
**SALES (est):** 733.23K **Privately Held**
**Web:** www.citybean.com
**SIC: 5499** 5149 2095 Coffee; Coffee, green or roasted; Coffee roasting (except by wholesale grocers)

**(P-17425)**
**COROMEGA COMPANY INC**
2525 Commerce Way, Vista (92081-8420)
P.O. Box 131135 (92013-1135)
PHONE..................760 599-6088
Frank Morley, *Pr*
Alice Chen, *
▲ **EMP:** 30 **EST:** 1999
**SALES (est):** 6.09MM **Privately Held**
**Web:** www.coromega.com
**SIC: 5499** 2099 Health foods; Food preparations, nec

**(P-17426)**
**HERB KAN COMPANY INC**
380 Encinal St Ste 100, Santa Cruz (95060-2178)
PHONE..................831 438-9450
Lise Groleau, *Pr*
▲ **EMP:** 17 **EST:** 1984
**SALES (est):** 2.5MM **Privately Held**
**Web:** www.kanherb.com
**SIC: 5499** 2833 Spices and herbs; Medicinals and botanicals

**(P-17427)**
**LA COSTA COFFEE ROASTING CO (PA)**
Also Called: COSTA COFFEE
6965 El Camino Real Ste 208, Carlsbad (92009-4113)
PHONE..................760 438-8160
Douglas Novak, *Prin*
Douglas Novak, *Mng Pt*
Paul Novak, *Pt*

Linda Novak, *Pt*
**EMP:** 25 **EST:** 1991
**SALES (est):** 823.01K **Privately Held**
**Web:** www.lacostacoffee.com
**SIC: 5499** 5149 2095 Coffee; Coffee, green or roasted; Coffee roasting (except by wholesale grocers)

**(P-17428)**
**LANGER JUICE COMPANY INC (PA)**
Also Called: Langers Juice
16195 Stephens St, City Of Industry (91745-1718)
PHONE..................626 336-3100
Bruce Langer, *CEO*
David Langer, *CFO*
◆ **EMP:** 154 **EST:** 1960
**SQ FT:** 140,000
**SALES (est):** 85.1MM
**SALES (corp-wide):** 85.1MM **Privately Held**
**Web:** www.langers.com
**SIC: 5499** 2033 Juices, fruit or vegetable; Vegetable juices: fresh

**(P-17429)**
**NAKED JUICE CO GLENDORA INC (HQ)**
1333 S Mayflower Ave Ste 100, Monrovia (91016-5265)
PHONE..................626 873-2600
Monty Sharma, *CEO*
Tom Hicks, *Pr*
Paul Travis, *VP Fin*
**EMP:** 50 **EST:** 1976
**SALES (est):** 3.44MM
**SALES (corp-wide):** 86.39B **Publicly Held**
**SIC: 5499** 2033 Juices, fruit or vegetable; Fruit juices: fresh
**PA:** Pepsico, Inc.
700 Anderson Hill Rd
914 253-2000

**(P-17430)**
**OLIVE PIT LLC**
2156 Solano St, Corning (96021-2713)
PHONE..................530 824-4667
Ron Craig, *Pr*
Bonnie Jackson, *Sec*
**EMP:** 15 **EST:** 1967
**SQ FT:** 2,500
**SALES (est):** 2.42MM **Privately Held**
**Web:** www.olivepit.com
**SIC: 5499** 5812 2033 Gourmet food stores; Delicatessen (eating places); Fruit juices: packaged in cans, jars, etc.

**(P-17431)**
**PEETS COFFEE INC (DH)**
Also Called: Peet's Coffee
1400 Park Ave, Emeryville (94608-3520)
P.O. Box 12509 (94712-3509)
PHONE..................510 594-2100
David Burwick, *Pr*
Gerald Baldwin, *
Patrick Odea, *
Shawn Conway, *
Tom Cawley, *
**EMP:** 75 **EST:** 1966
**SQ FT:** 60,000
**SALES (est):** 113.15MM
**SALES (corp-wide):** 2.67MM **Privately Held**
**Web:** www.peets.com
**SIC: 5499** 2095 5149 Coffee; Roasted coffee; Cat food
**HQ:** Peet's Coffee & Tea, Llc
1400 Park Ave
Emeryville CA 94608
510 594-2100

# PRODUCTS & SERVICES SECTION

## 5531 - Auto And Home Supply Stores (P-17451)

**(P-17432)**
**SUJA LIFE LLC (PA)**
Also Called: Suja Juice
3841 Ocean Ranch Blvd, Oceanside (92056-2694)
PHONE.................855 879-7852
Maria Stipp, CEO
James Brennan, Pr
▲ EMP: 48 EST: 2012
SALES (est): 59.64MM
SALES (corp-wide): 59.64MM Privately Held
Web: www.sujaorganic.com
SIC: 5499 2033 Juices, fruit or vegetable; Fruit juices: packaged in cans, jars, etc.

**(P-17433)**
**TEALOVE INC**
9810 Sierra Ave Ste A, Fontana (92335-6779)
PHONE.................714 408-8245
Elli Nguyen, CFO
EMP: 20 EST: 2018
SALES (est): 250K Privately Held
Web: tealove.smartonlineorder.com
SIC: 5499 2099 2086 5812 Tea; Tea blending; Tea, iced: packaged in cans, bottles, etc.; Coffee shop

**(P-17434)**
**TONE IT UP LLC**
1110 Manhattan Ave, Manhattan Beach (90266)
P.O. Box 323 (90245)
PHONE.................310 376-7645
Russell Sternlicht, CEO
Christine Sana, *
▲ EMP: 31 EST: 2009
SQ FT: 3,000
SALES (est): 6.03MM Privately Held
Web: my.toneitup.com
SIC: 5499 2099 5149 Health and dietetic food stores; Food preparations, nec; Groceries and related products, nec

**(P-17435)**
**VITA-HERB NUTRICEUTICALS INC**
172 E La Jolla St, Placentia (92870-7111)
PHONE.................714 632-3726
M Bing Baksh, CEO
▲ EMP: 35 EST: 1999
SQ FT: 11,000
SALES (est): 4.45MM Privately Held
Web: www.vhni.com
SIC: 5499 2834 Vitamin food stores; Pharmaceutical preparations

---

### 5511 New And Used Car Dealers

**(P-17436)**
**AL ASHER & SONS INC**
5301 Valley Blvd, Los Angeles (90032-3930)
PHONE.................800 896-2480
James A Asher, CEO
James A Asher, Pr
Robert L Asher, *
◆ EMP: 25 EST: 1914
SQ FT: 80,000
SALES (est): 3.55MM Privately Held
Web: www.alasher.com
SIC: 5511 7353 3531 Trucks, tractors, and trailers: new and used; Heavy construction equipment rental; Construction machinery

**(P-17437)**
**CADILLAC MOTOR DIV AREA**
30930 Russell Ranch Rd, Westlake Village (91362-7378)
PHONE.................805 373-9575
Mike Jackson, Mgr
EMP: 175 EST: 1955
SALES (est): 4.31MM Publicly Held
Web: www.cadillac.com
SIC: 5511 3711 Automobiles, new and used; Motor vehicles and car bodies
HQ: General Motors Llc
300 Rnaissance Ctr Ste L1
Detroit MI 48243

**(P-17438)**
**EMERGENCY VEHICLE GROUP INC**
Also Called: E V G
2883 E Coronado St Ste A, Anaheim (92806-2552)
PHONE.................714 238-0110
Travis Grinstead, Pr
EMP: 25 EST: 2005
SQ FT: 15,000
SALES (est): 2.41MM Privately Held
Web: www.evginc.net
SIC: 5511 5012 3569 5013 Trucks, tractors, and trailers: new and used; Ambulances; Firefighting apparatus; Motor vehicle supplies and new parts

**(P-17439)**
**GENERAL MOTORS LLC**
Also Called: General Motors
3050 Lomita Blvd Ste 237, Torrance (90505-5103)
PHONE.................313 556-5000
Nicholas Herron, Brnch Mgr
EMP: 25
Web: www.gm.com
SIC: 5511 3711 Automobiles, new and used; Automobile assembly, including specialty automobiles
HQ: General Motors Llc
300 Rnaissance Ctr Ste L1
Detroit MI 48243

**(P-17440)**
**MARK CHRISTOPHER CHEVROLET INC (PA)**
Also Called: Mark Christopher Hummer
2131 E Convention Center Way, Ontario (91764-4495)
PHONE.................909 321-5860
Chris Leggio, CEO
Shirley Leggid, *
Loretta Holtz, *
EMP: 132 EST: 1986
SQ FT: 15,000
SALES (est): 44.87MM
SALES (corp-wide): 44.87MM Privately Held
Web: www.markchristopher.com
SIC: 5511 5521 3714 Automobiles, new and used; Used car dealers; Motor vehicle parts and accessories

**(P-17441)**
**ROLLS-ROYCE CORPORATION**
7200 Earhart Rd, Oakland (94621-4511)
PHONE.................510 635-1500
Marion C Blakey, Pr
EMP: 500
SALES (corp-wide): 20.55B Privately Held
Web: www.rolls-roycemotorcars.com
SIC: 5511 3519 New and used car dealers; Jet propulsion engines
HQ: Rolls-Royce Corporation
450 S Meridian St
Indianapolis IN 46225

**(P-17442)**
**SUZUKI MOTOR OF AMERICA INC (HQ)**
Also Called: Suzuki USA
3251 E Imperial Hwy, Brea (92821-6795)
P.O. Box 1100 (92822-1100)
PHONE.................714 996-7040
Takeshi Hayasaki, Pr
Takuya Sato, *
◆ EMP: 250 EST: 2012
SALES (est): 96.42MM Privately Held
Web: www.suzuki.com
SIC: 5511 3519 3799 Automobiles, new and used; Outboard motors; Recreational vehicles
PA: Suzuki Motor Corporation
300, Takatsukacho, Chuo-Ku

**(P-17443)**
**TOYOTA LOGISTICS SERVICES INC (DH)**
19001 S Western Ave, Torrance (90501-1106)
PHONE.................310 468-4000
Randy Pflughaupt, CEO
Allen Decarr, *
Donald Esmond, *
◆ EMP: 176 EST: 1981
SQ FT: 600
SALES (est): 63.58MM Privately Held
Web: www.toyota.com
SIC: 5511 3711 Automobiles, new and used; Motor vehicles and car bodies
HQ: Toyota Motor Sales Usa Inc
6565 Hdqtr Dr Apt W1-3c
Plano TX 75024

**(P-17444)**
**WILSON CYCLES SPORTS CORP**
Also Called: CJ Wilson BMW Mtcyc Murrieta
26145 Jefferson Ave Ste 205, Murrieta (92562-9500)
PHONE.................951 894-5545
George Berta, Genl Mgr
Sarah Galin, Prin
EMP: 21 EST: 2015
SALES (est): 308.54K Privately Held
Web: www.bmwgroup.com
SIC: 5511 3751 7699 Automobiles, new and used; Motorcycle accessories; Motorcycle repair service

---

### 5531 Auto And Home Supply Stores

**(P-17445)**
**BERT WILLIAMS AND SONS INC**
525 Northbay Dr, Napa (94559-1425)
PHONE.................707 255-7003
Herbert L Williams, Pr
EMP: 36 EST: 1946
SQ FT: 8,400
SALES (est): 7.07MM Privately Held
Web: www.bertwilliamsandsons.com
SIC: 5531 5013 3714 Automotive parts; Truck parts and accessories; Motor vehicle parts and accessories

**(P-17446)**
**CARROLLS TIRE WAREHOUSE INC (PA)**
981 W Northgrand Ave, Porterville (93257-9529)
PHONE.................559 781-5040
EMP: 22 EST: 1973
SALES (est): 7.41MM
SALES (corp-wide): 7.41MM Privately Held
Web: www.carrollstire.com
SIC: 5531 7534 Automotive tires; Tire retreading and repair shops

**(P-17447)**
**CERTIFIED TIRE & SVC CTRS INC**
Also Called: Goodyear
23920 Alessandro Blvd Ste A, Moreno Valley (92553-8804)
PHONE.................951 656-6466
Victor Cervantes, Mgr
EMP: 36
SALES (corp-wide): 24.35MM Privately Held
Web: www.thetirechoice.com
SIC: 5531 7534 Automotive tires; Tire retreading and repair shops
PA: Certified Tire & Service Centers, Inc.
1875 Iowa Ave
951 369-0025

**(P-17448)**
**CHAMPION MOTOSPORTS INC (PA)**
Also Called: Champion Cooling Systems
32373 Corydon St, Lake Elsinore (92530-9604)
PHONE.................951 245-9464
Robert Cloke, CEO
Cid Martin, Pr
▲ EMP: 20 EST: 2008
SQ FT: 48,000
SALES (est): 4.54MM Privately Held
Web: www.championcooling.com
SIC: 5531 5013 3714 Automotive parts; Automotive supplies and parts; Radiators and radiator shells and cores, motor vehicle

**(P-17449)**
**DAPPER TIRE CO INC**
20380 Corsair Blvd, Hayward (94545-1025)
PHONE.................510 780-1616
Glen Ramirez, Mgr
EMP: 16
SALES (corp-wide): 20.07B Publicly Held
SIC: 5531 3714 3011 Automotive tires; Motor vehicle wheels and parts; Tires and inner tubes
HQ: Dapper Tire Co., Inc.
4025 Lockridge St
San Diego CA 92102
619 266-0200

**(P-17450)**
**DNA MOTOR INC**
Also Called: Dna Motoring
801 Sentous Ave, City Of Industry (91744-2543)
PHONE.................626 965-8898
Jia Jie Chen, CEO
◆ EMP: 40 EST: 2009
SALES (est): 7.14MM Privately Held
Web: www.dnamotoring.com
SIC: 5531 3714 Automotive parts; Motor vehicle parts and accessories

**(P-17451)**
**FREEDOM PRFMCE EXHAUST INC**
1255 Railroad St, Corona (92882-1838)
PHONE.................951 898-4733
Flora Arteaga, CEO
Martin Arteaga, *
EMP: 47 EST: 2006
SALES (est): 4.94MM Privately Held
Web: www.freedomperformexhaust.com

# 5531 - Auto And Home Supply Stores (P-17452)

SIC: 5531 3714 Speed shops, including race car supplies; Mufflers (exhaust), motor vehicle

### (P-17452)
### GRAND PRIX ROAD TRENDS INC (PA)
Also Called: Grand Prix Performance
1718 Newport Blvd, Costa Mesa (92627-3010)
PHONE..................................949 645-7022
Jerry Palanjian, *Pr*
EMP: 17 EST: 1972
SQ FT: 2,500
SALES (est): 4.93MM
SALES (corp-wide): 4.93MM **Privately Held**
Web: www.grandprixperformance.com
SIC: 5531 3312 Automotive tires; Wheels

### (P-17453)
### IH PARTS AMERICA INC
119 E Mcknight Way, Grass Valley (95949-9651)
PHONE..................................530 274-1795
Jeffery Ismail, *CEO*
EMP: 30 EST: 2004
SALES (est): 1.71MM **Privately Held**
Web: www.ihpartsamerica.com
SIC: 5531 2754 Automotive parts; Commercial printing, gravure

### (P-17454)
### KRACO ENTERPRISES LLC
505 E Euclid Ave, Compton (90222-2890)
PHONE..................................310 639-0666
◆ EMP: 164
Web: www.kraco.com
SIC: 5531 3069 5013 Automotive accessories; Hard rubber and molded rubber products; Motor vehicle supplies and new parts

### (P-17455)
### ORIGINAL PARTS GROUP INC (PA)
Also Called: Chevelle Classics Parts & ACC
1770 Saturn Way, Seal Beach (90740-5618)
PHONE..................................562 594-1000
David Harry Leonard, *Pr*
Anthony M Genty, *
▲ EMP: 84 EST: 1984
SQ FT: 100,000
SALES (est): 22.31MM
SALES (corp-wide): 22.31MM **Privately Held**
Web: www.opgi.com
SIC: 5531 3465 Automotive parts; Body parts, automobile: stamped metal

### (P-17456)
### PARKHOUSE TIRE SERVICE INC
Also Called: Parkhouse Tire
4660 Ruffner St, San Diego (92111-2220)
PHONE..................................858 565-8473
Janette Fox, *Mgr*
EMP: 39
SALES (corp-wide): 83.75MM **Privately Held**
Web: www.parkhousetire.com
SIC: 5531 5014 7534 Automotive tires; Tires and tubes; Tire retreading and repair shops
PA: Parkhouse Tire Service, Inc.
 6006 Shull St
 562 928-0421

### (P-17457)
### PARKHOUSE TIRE SERVICE INC (PA)
Also Called: Parkhouse Tire
6006 Shull St, Bell Gardens (90201-6237)
P.O. Box 2430 (90202)
PHONE..................................562 928-0421
◆ EMP: 75 EST: 1971
SALES (est): 83.75MM
SALES (corp-wide): 83.75MM **Privately Held**
Web: www.parkhousetire.com
SIC: 5531 5014 7534 Automotive tires; Automobile tires and tubes; Rebuilding and retreading tires

### (P-17458)
### PLASTICOLOR MOLDED PDTS INC (PA)
Also Called: Plasticolor
801 S Acacia Ave, Fullerton (92831-5398)
P.O. Box 6985 (92831)
PHONE..................................714 525-3880
Matthew Bagne, *CEO*
Shawn Diamond, *
Gayle Deflin, *
◆ EMP: 250 EST: 1971
SALES (est): 48.61MM
SALES (corp-wide): 48.61MM **Privately Held**
Web: www.plasticolorinc.com
SIC: 5531 3083 Automotive accessories; Plastics finished products, laminated

### (P-17459)
### POLAR SERVICE CENTER
4432 Winters Ave, Mcclellan (95652-2315)
PHONE..................................916 643-4689
EMP: 15 EST: 2014
SALES (est): 1.56MM **Privately Held**
Web: www.polarservicecenters.com
SIC: 5531 3542 5961 Truck equipment and parts; Mechanical (pneumatic or hydraulic) metal forming machines; Automotive supplies and equipment, mail order

### (P-17460)
### RAUDMANS CRAIG VICTORY CIRCLE
Also Called: Victory Circle Chassis & Parts
700 S Mount Vernon Ave Ste 100, Bakersfield (93307-2893)
PHONE..................................661 833-4600
Les Denherder, *Pr*
Craig Raudman, *Asst VP*
Susan Denherder, *VP*
EMP: 16 EST: 1995
SQ FT: 47,000
SALES (est): 457.83K **Privately Held**
Web: www.victorycircle.com
SIC: 5531 3799 Automotive parts; Recreational vehicles

### (P-17461)
### ROBERT JONES
Also Called: Big O Tires
742 S Main St, Sebastopol (95472-4275)
PHONE..................................707 829-9864
Robert Jones, *Pt*
Ronald Jones, *Pt*
Moses Ortiz, *Pt*
EMP: 15 EST: 1989
SALES (est): 802.17K **Privately Held**
Web: www.bigotires.com
SIC: 5531 7534 7539 5014 Automotive tires; Tire repair shop; Frame and front end repair services; Automobile tires and tubes

### (P-17462)
### RODRIGUEZ BROTHERS AUTO PARTS (PA)
812 N Anaheim Blvd, Anaheim (92805-1901)
PHONE..................................714 772-7278
Fermen Rodriguez, *Pt*
Ceasar Rodriguez, *Pt*
EMP: 15 EST: 1993
SALES (est): 1.6MM **Privately Held**
Web: www.rodriguezbrosautoparts.com
SIC: 5531 3599 Automotive parts; Machine shop, jobbing and repair

### (P-17463)
### SANTA MARIA TIRE INC (PA)
Also Called: SM Tire
2170 Hutton Rd Bldg A, Nipomo (93444-9717)
P.O. Box 6007 (93456-6007)
PHONE..................................805 347-4793
Craig Stephens, *Pr*
Brenee Stephens, *
C Kent Stephens, *
Cameron Stephens, *
Conrad Stephens Attorney, *Prin*
EMP: 75 EST: 1946
SALES (est): 20.64MM
SALES (corp-wide): 20.64MM **Privately Held**
Web: www.smtire.com
SIC: 5531 7534 Automotive tires; Rebuilding and retreading tires

### (P-17464)
### SOUTHERN CAL DISC TIRE CO INC
Also Called: Discount Tire
107 N El Camino Real, Encinitas (92024-2802)
PHONE..................................760 634-2202
Alan Brise, *Brnch Mgr*
EMP: 123
SALES (corp-wide): 3.69B **Privately Held**
Web: www.discounttire.com
SIC: 5531 7534 Automotive tires; Tire repair shop
HQ: Southern California Discount Tire Co., Inc.
 16100 N Grnway Hyden Loop
 Scottsdale AZ 85260
 602 996-0201

### (P-17465)
### SPECIALTY TRUCK PARTS INC (PA)
7700 Arroyo Cir, Gilroy (95020-7312)
P.O. Box 871 (95106-0871)
PHONE..................................408 998-7272
TOLL FREE: 800
Roger L Stanton, *Pr*
Roger L Stanton, *Pr*
Alvin B Davidson, *
Danny Green, *
Ron Lutz, *
EMP: 36 EST: 1923
SALES (est): 4.23MM
SALES (corp-wide): 4.23MM **Privately Held**
Web: www.specialtytruck.com
SIC: 5531 5511 5013 3713 Truck equipment and parts; Trucks, tractors, and trailers: new and used; Automotive supplies and parts; Truck and bus bodies

### (P-17466)
### TBC SHARED SERVICES LLC
742 S Main St, Sebastopol (95472-4275)
PHONE..................................707 829-9864
EMP: 2170
SIC: 5531 7534 Automotive tires; Tire retreading and repair shops

### (P-17467)
### TIRE CENTERS WEST LLC
12208 Industry Rd, Lakeside (92040-1747)
PHONE..................................619 596-8473
Tm Stocking, *Mgr*
EMP: 15
SALES (corp-wide): 1.95B **Privately Held**
Web: www.border-tire.com
SIC: 5531 5014 7534 1711 Automotive tires; Automobile tires and tubes; Rebuilding and retreading tires; Mechanical contractor
HQ: Tire Centers West, Llc
 1 Parkway S
 Greenville SC 29615
 864 458-5000

### (P-17468)
### VORSTEINER INC
Also Called: Nero
11621 Markon Dr, Garden Grove (92841-1810)
PHONE..................................714 379-4600
Seung Bum Nam, *CEO*
▲ EMP: 26 EST: 2008
SALES (est): 1.18MM **Privately Held**
Web: www.vorsteiner.com
SIC: 5531 3069 3089 Automotive parts; Rubber automotive products; Automotive parts, plastic

### (P-17469)
### XRP INC (PA)
5630 Imperial Hwy, South Gate (90280-7420)
PHONE..................................562 861-4765
David Barker, *CEO*
Debbie Singer, *Pr*
EMP: 19 EST: 1989
SQ FT: 25,000
SALES (est): 3.61MM **Privately Held**
Web: www.xrp.com
SIC: 5531 3714 Automotive parts; Fuel systems and parts, motor vehicle

## 5541 Gasoline Service Stations

### (P-17470)
### ATLANTIC RICHFIELD COMPANY (DH)
Also Called: A R C O
4 Centerpointe Dr, La Palma (90623-1015)
PHONE..................................800 333-3991
Robert A Malone, *Pr*
Ian Springett, *
▲ EMP: 2200 EST: 1870
SALES (est): 142.72MM
SALES (corp-wide): 171.22B **Privately Held**
Web: www.arco.com
SIC: 5541 1321 2911 Filling stations, gasoline; Natural gas liquids; Petroleum refining
HQ: Bp America Inc
 4101 Winfield Rd Ste 200
 Warrenville IL 60555
 214 210-4835

### (P-17471)
### CHEVRON CORPORATION
Also Called: Chevron
324 W El Segundo Blvd, El Segundo (90245-3635)
PHONE..................................310 615-5000
William Simok, *Ex Dir*

## PRODUCTS & SERVICES SECTION
### 5599 - Automotive Dealers, Nec (P-17489)

EMP: 812
SALES (corp-wide): 200.95B **Publicly Held**
Web: www.chevron.com
SIC: 5541 1311 1382 1321 Filling stations, gasoline; Crude petroleum production; Oil and gas exploration services; Natural gas liquids
PA: Chevron Corporation
5001 Exec Pkwy Ste 200
925 842-1000

**(P-17472)**
**CHEVRON USA INC (HQ)**
Also Called: Chevron
5001 Executive Pkwy Ste 200, San Ramon (94583-5006)
PHONE.................................925 842-1000
Michael K Mike Wirth, *Ch Bd*
Michael K Mike Wirth, *Ch*
D J O'reilly, *Ch*
P J Robertson, *
B J Koc, *
◆ EMP: 402 EST: 1922
SALES (est): 2.12B
SALES (corp-wide): 200.95B **Publicly Held**
Web: www.chevron.com
SIC: 5541 5983 2911 Filling stations, gasoline; Fuel oil dealers; Petroleum refining
PA: Chevron Corporation
5001 Exec Pkwy Ste 200
925 842-1000

**(P-17473)**
**CHEVRON USA INC**
Also Called: Chevron
5001 Executive Pkwy, San Ramon (94583-5006)
P.O. Box 6017 (94583-0717)
PHONE.................................925 842-0855
Kim Smith, *Brnch Mgr*
EMP: 100
SALES (corp-wide): 200.95B **Publicly Held**
Web: www.chevron.com
SIC: 5541 2911 Filling stations, gasoline; Petroleum refining
HQ: Chevron U.S.A. Inc.
5001 Exec Pkwy Ste 200
San Ramon CA 94583
925 842-1000

**(P-17474)**
**EVGO SERVICES LLC**
Also Called: Evgo Montgomery Co
11835 W Olympic Blvd Ste 900e, Los Angeles (90064-5088)
P.O. Box 642830 (90064-8287)
PHONE.................................310 954-2900
Cathy Zoi, *CEO*
Olga Shevorenkova, *
Ivo Steklac, *
EMP: 298 EST: 2010
SQ FT: 10,000
SALES (est): 37.36MM **Publicly Held**
Web: www.evgo.com
SIC: 5541 3694 Gasoline service stations; Automotive electrical equipment, nec
HQ: Evgo Inc.
11835 W Olympic Blvd Ste
Los Angeles CA 90064
877 494-3833

**(P-17475)**
**EXXON MOBIL CORPORATION**
Also Called: Exxon
12000 Calle Real, Goleta (93117-9708)
PHONE.................................805 961-4093
Bob Barnes, *Brnch Mgr*

EMP: 24
SALES (corp-wide): 344.58B **Publicly Held**
Web: corporate.exxonmobil.com
SIC: 5541 3533 Filling stations, gasoline; Oil and gas field machinery
PA: Exxon Mobil Corporation
22777 Sprngwoods Vlg Pkwy
972 940-6000

**(P-17476)**
**TEXACO INC (HQ)**
Also Called: Texaco
6001 Bollinger Canyon Rd, San Ramon (94583-2324)
PHONE.................................925 842-1000
David O'reilly, *Ch Bd*
Kari H Endries, *
◆ EMP: 800 EST: 1902
SQ FT: 110,000
SALES (est): 188.86MM
SALES (corp-wide): 200.95B **Publicly Held**
Web: www.texaco.com
SIC: 5541 5511 1321 4612 Filling stations, gasoline; Automobiles, new and used; Natural gas liquids production; Crude petroleum pipelines
PA: Chevron Corporation
5001 Exec Pkwy Ste 200
925 842-1000

**(P-17477)**
**TEXACO OVERSEAS HOLDINGS INC (DH)**
Also Called: Texaco
6001 Bollinger Canyon Rd, San Ramon (94583-2324)
PHONE.................................510 242-5357
John J O'connor, *Pr*
Michael H Rudy, *Sec*
Ira D Hall, *Treas*
▼ EMP: 15 EST: 1984
SALES (est): 13.57MM
SALES (corp-wide): 200.95B **Publicly Held**
Web: www.texaco.com
SIC: 5541 2911 Filling stations, gasoline; Petroleum refining
HQ: Texaco Inc.
6001 Bollinger Canyon Rd
San Ramon CA 94583
925 842-1000

**(P-17478)**
**VALERO ENERGY CORPORATION**
3400 E 2nd St, Benicia (94510-1005)
PHONE.................................707 745-7011
Don Wilson, *Mgr*
EMP: 450
SALES (corp-wide): 144.77B **Publicly Held**
Web: www.valero.com
SIC: 5541 2911 Filling stations, gasoline; Gas, refinery
PA: Valero Energy Corporation
1 Valero Way
210 345-2000

### 5551 Boat Dealers

**(P-17479)**
**COMMANDER BOATS**
Also Called: Commander Boats-Mira Loma Mar
4020 Tyler St, Riverside (92503-3402)
PHONE.................................951 273-0100
Shailendra H Singhal, *Owner*

EMP: 15 EST: 1984
SQ FT: 16,000
SALES (est): 159.88K **Privately Held**
Web: www.commanderboats.com
SIC: 5551 3732 Boat dealers; Boats, fiberglass; building and repairing

**(P-17480)**
**TOLLER ENTERPRISES INC (PA)**
Also Called: Electra Craft
2251 Townsgate Rd, Westlake Village (91361-2404)
PHONE.................................805 374-9455
Alex Toller, *Pr*
Cheryl Toller, *Sec*
EMP: 26 EST: 1979
SALES (est): 1.76MM
SALES (corp-wide): 1.76MM **Privately Held**
Web: www.electracraft.com
SIC: 5551 3732 Motor boat dealers; Boatbuilding and repairing

### 5571 Motorcycle Dealers

**(P-17481)**
**ARCH MOTORCYCLE COMPANY INC**
3216 W El Segundo Blvd, Hawthorne (90250-4823)
PHONE.................................970 443-1380
Gard Hollinger, *Prin*
EMP: 76 EST: 2012
SALES (est): 933.37K **Privately Held**
Web: www.archmotorcycle.com
SIC: 5571 3751 Motorcycles; Bicycles and related parts

**(P-17482)**
**JIM ONEAL DISTRIBUTING INC**
Also Called: O'Neal U S A
799 Camarillo Springs Rd, Camarillo (93012-9468)
PHONE.................................805 426-3300
Frank Kashare, *Pr*
▲ EMP: 40 EST: 1970
SALES (est): 5.36MM **Privately Held**
Web: www.oneal.com
SIC: 5571 3751 Motorcycle dealers; Motorcycles, bicycles and parts

**(P-17483)**
**OCELOT ENGINEERING INC**
Also Called: Chaparral Motorsports
555 S H St, San Bernardino (92410-3415)
PHONE.................................800 841-2960
David S Damron, *Pr*
James E Damron, *
Linda J Damron, *
◆ EMP: 160 EST: 1973
SALES (est): 15.79MM **Privately Held**
Web: www.chapmoto.com
SIC: 5571 5551 5013 3751 Motorcycles; Jet skis; Motorcycle parts; Motorcycle accessories

**(P-17484)**
**PRO CIRCUIT PRODUCTS INC (PA)**
Also Called: Pro Circuit Products & Racing
2771 Wardlow Rd, Corona (92882-2869)
PHONE.................................951 738-8050
Mitchell C Payton, *Prin*
◆ EMP: 20 EST: 1978
SALES (est): 4MM
SALES (corp-wide): 4MM **Privately Held**
Web: www.procircuit.com

SIC: 5571 3751 Motorcycle parts and accessories; Motorcycles and related parts

**(P-17485)**
**SR SHROEDER INC**
1150 N 1st St, Dixon (95620-3164)
P.O. Box 65 (95620-0065)
PHONE.................................707 693-8166
Diane Schroeder, *Pr*
Michelle Schroeder, *VP*
EMP: 18 EST: 1971
SALES (est): 1.22MM **Privately Held**
SIC: 5571 5012 3949 Motorcycle dealers; Automobiles and other motor vehicles; Water skiing equipment and supplies, except skis

**(P-17486)**
**ZERO MOTORCYCLES INC**
Also Called: Zero Motorcycles
380 El Pueblo Rd, Scotts Valley (95066-4212)
PHONE.................................831 438-3500
Sam Paschel, *CEO*
Curt Sacks, *
▲ EMP: 165 EST: 2008
SQ FT: 34,000
SALES (est): 47.77MM **Privately Held**
Web: www.zeromotorcycles.com
SIC: 5571 3751 Motorcycles; Motorcycles and related parts

### 5599 Automotive Dealers, Nec

**(P-17487)**
**CARSON TRAILER INC (PA)**
Also Called: Carson Trailer Sales
14831 S Maple Ave, Gardena (90248-1935)
PHONE.................................310 835-0876
William Modisette, *Pr*
EMP: 100 EST: 1991
SALES (est): 11.59MM **Privately Held**
Web: www.carsontrailer.com
SIC: 5599 3792 Utility trailers; Travel trailers and campers

**(P-17488)**
**PACIFIC BOAT TRAILERS INC (PA)**
Also Called: Pacific Boat Trailers
2855 Sampson Ave, Corona (92879-6126)
PHONE.................................909 902-0094
Roger Treichler, *VP*
Vicky Treichler, *VP*
EMP: 18 EST: 1986
SALES (est): 1.34MM
SALES (corp-wide): 1.34MM **Privately Held**
Web: www.pacifictrailers.com
SIC: 5599 3792 Utility trailers; Travel trailers and campers

**(P-17489)**
**PERFORMANCE TRAILER INC**
Also Called: Turnkey Industries
2901 Falcon Dr, Madera (93637-9287)
PHONE.................................559 673-6300
Kevin D Gerhardt Senior, *Pr*
Kevin Gerhardt, *
EMP: 25 EST: 1991
SQ FT: 24,000
SALES (est): 4.35MM **Privately Held**
Web: www.perftrlrs.com
SIC: 5599 3715 Utility trailers; Truck trailers

## 5621 Women's Clothing Stores

**(P-17490)**
**26 INTERNATIONAL INC (PA)**
Also Called: "the Jacket Club"
1500 Griffith Ave, Los Angeles (90021-2461)
PHONE..................213 745-4224
Mordechay Reuben, *CEO*
Frida Rouben, *CFO*
◆ **EMP:** 15 **EST:** 1997
**SQ FT:** 20,000
**SALES (est):** 2.31MM
**SALES (corp-wide):** 2.31MM **Privately Held**
Web: www.26international.com
SIC: 5621 5632 2339 Ready-to-wear apparel, women's; Women's accessory and specialty stores; Jackets, untailored: women's, misses', and juniors'

**(P-17491)**
**CHICOS FAS INC**
48400 Seminole Dr, Cabazon (92230-2125)
PHONE..................951 849-4069
**EMP:** 19
**SALES (corp-wide):** 2.14B **Privately Held**
Web: www.chicos.com
SIC: 5621 2337 2389 Women's specialty clothing stores; Women's and children's outerwear; Men's miscellaneous accessories
PA: Chico's Fas, Inc.
  11215 Metro Pkwy
  239 277-6200

**(P-17492)**
**COUNTRY CLUB FASHIONS INC**
Also Called: Theodore
6083 W Pico Blvd, Los Angeles (90035-2648)
PHONE..................323 965-2707
**EMP:** 45
Web: www.theodorebh.com
SIC: 5621 5611 2337 2331 Ready-to-wear apparel, women's; Clothing, sportswear, men's and boys'; Skirts, separate: women's, misses', and juniors'; Blouses, women's and juniors': made from purchased material

**(P-17493)**
**DAVIDS BRIDAL LLC**
Also Called: David's Bridal
1515 Springfield Dr Ste 100, Chico (95928-5996)
PHONE..................530 342-5914
Andrea Mckellips, *Brnch Mgr*
**EMP:** 15
**SALES (corp-wide):** 251.01MM **Publicly Held**
Web: www.davidsbridal.com
SIC: 5621 2335 Bridal shops; Wedding gowns and dresses
HQ: David's Bridal, Llc
  630 Allendale Rd Ste 250
  King Of Prussia PA 19406

**(P-17494)**
**LOLA BELLE BRANDS LLC**
629 S Palm Ave, Alhambra (91803-1424)
PHONE..................855 226-3526
**EMP:** 17 **EST:** 2017
**SALES (est):** 410.59K **Privately Held**
SIC: 5621 3999 Boutiques; Candles

**(P-17495)**
**NASTY GAL INC (HQ)**
2049 Century Park E Ste 3400, Los Angeles (90067-3101)
PHONE..................213 542-3436
Sheree Waterson, *CEO*
Bob Ross, *
◆ **EMP:** 23 **EST:** 2008
**SALES (est):** 9.47MM
**SALES (corp-wide):** 1.85B **Privately Held**
Web: www.nastygal.com
SIC: 5621 5139 2389 Ready-to-wear apparel, women's; Shoes; Academic vestments (caps and gowns)
PA: Boohoo Group Plc
  The Boohoo Group

**(P-17496)**
**SANCTUARY CLOTHING LLC (PA)**
Also Called: Sanctuary Clothing
3611 N San Fernando Blvd, Burbank (91505-1043)
PHONE..................818 505-0018
Kenneth Polanco, *Managing Member*
Debra Polanco, *Chief Creative Officer*
Elizabeth Fernando, *Contrlr*
**EMP:** 41 **EST:** 2008
**SALES (est):** 10.05MM
**SALES (corp-wide):** 10.05MM **Privately Held**
Web: www.sanctuaryclothing.com
SIC: 5621 5137 2211 Ready-to-wear apparel, women's; Women's and children's dresses, suits, skirts, and blouses; Apparel and outerwear fabrics, cotton

**(P-17497)**
**TOPSON DOWNS CALIFORNIA LLC (PA)**
Also Called: Topson Downs
3840 Watseka Ave, Culver City (90232-2633)
PHONE..................310 558-0300
Joe Wirht, *
Daniel Abramovitch, *
▲ **EMP:** 250 **EST:** 1971
**SQ FT:** 42,000
**SALES (est):** 45.02MM
**SALES (corp-wide):** 45.02MM **Privately Held**
Web: www.topsondowns.com
SIC: 5621 5136 2211 2221 Women's clothing stores; Shirts, men's and boys'; Apparel and outerwear fabrics, cotton; Apparel and outerwear fabric, manmade fiber or silk

**(P-17498)**
**YMI JEANSWEAR INC (PA)**
Also Called: Ymi Jeanswear
1155 S Boyle Ave, Los Angeles (90023-2109)
PHONE..................323 581-7700
David Vered, *CEO*
◆ **EMP:** 15 **EST:** 2000
**SALES (est):** 16.4MM
**SALES (corp-wide):** 16.4MM **Privately Held**
Web: www.ymijeans.com
SIC: 5621 2211 2339 Women's clothing stores; Denims; Jeans: women's, misses', and juniors'

## 5632 Women's Accessory And Specialty Stores

**(P-17499)**
**DARK GRDN UNIQUE CORSETRY INC**
Also Called: Dark Garden
321 Linden St, San Francisco (94102-5109)
PHONE..................415 431-7684
Autumn Adamme, *Pr*
Autumn Adamme, *CEO*
Monique Motil, *Pr*
**EMP:** 18 **EST:** 2010
**SALES (est):** 1.26MM **Privately Held**
Web: www.darkgarden.com
SIC: 5632 2341 Lingerie and corsets (underwear); Women's and children's underwear

**(P-17500)**
**IHEARTRAVES LLC**
240 S Loara St, Anaheim (92802-1020)
PHONE..................626 628-6482
Brian Lim, *CEO*
Scott Elliott, *Pr*
**EMP:** 19 **EST:** 2012
**SALES (est):** 2.37MM **Privately Held**
Web: www.iheartraves.com
SIC: 5632 2331 Apparel accessories; Women's and misses' blouses and shirts

**(P-17501)**
**VERA BRADLEY INC**
4525 La Jolla Village Dr, San Diego (92122-1215)
PHONE..................858 320-9020
**EMP:** 29
**SALES (corp-wide):** 470.79MM **Publicly Held**
Web: www.verabradley.com
SIC: 5632 5137 3171 Handbags; Purses; Handbags, women's
PA: Vera Bradley, Inc.
  12420 Stonebridge Rd
  877 708-8372

**(P-17502)**
**WEN U LUV LIQUIDATION LLC**
8383 Wilshire Blvd Ste 800, Beverly Hills (90211-2440)
PHONE..................323 456-8821
Alexander Compton, *Managing Member*
**EMP:** 25 **EST:** 2010
**SALES (est):** 165.82K **Privately Held**
SIC: 5632 2339 3911 5199 Handbags; Athletic clothing: women's, misses', and juniors'; Jewelry apparel; General merchandise, non-durable

## 5651 Family Clothing Stores

**(P-17503)**
**VIDA & CO**
353 Kearny St, San Francisco (94108-3246)
PHONE..................415 379-4325
Umaimah Mendhro, *CEO*
Alexandra Day Golden, *Prin*
Cameron Preston, *Prin*
**EMP:** 20 **EST:** 2014
**SALES (est):** 2.42MM **Privately Held**
Web: www.vida-studio.com
SIC: 5651 7389 2389 Family clothing stores; Styling of fashions, apparel, furniture, textiles, etc.; Men's miscellaneous accessories

## 5661 Shoe Stores

**(P-17504)**
**SKECHERS USA INC II**
228 Manhattan Beach Blvd Ste 200, Manhattan Beach (90266-5356)
PHONE..................800 746-3411
Robert Greenberg, *CEO*
David Weinberg, *
Philip Paccione, *
◆ **EMP:** 4000 **EST:** 1994
**SALES (est):** 5.63MM **Publicly Held**
Web: www.skechers.com
SIC: 5661 3021 Shoe stores; Shoes, rubber or plastic molded to fabric
PA: Skechers U.S.A., Inc.
  228 Manhattan Beach Blvd

**(P-17505)**
**VENTURA FEED AND PET SUPS INC**
Also Called: Wharf, The
980 E Front St, Ventura (93001-3017)
P.O. Box 1806 (93002-1806)
PHONE..................805 648-5035
Todd Butterbaugh, *CEO*
Darren Borgstedte, *
**EMP:** 42 **EST:** 1953
**SQ FT:** 13,000
**SALES (est):** 2.21MM **Privately Held**
Web: store.thewharfonline.com
SIC: 5661 3999 2048 5632 Shoe stores; Pet supplies; Prepared feeds, nec; Apparel accessories

## 5699 Miscellaneous Apparel And Accessories

**(P-17506)**
**511 INC (DH)**
Also Called: 5.11 Tactical Series
3150 Bristol St Ste 300, Costa Mesa (92626-3088)
PHONE..................866 451-1726
Francisco Morales, *CEO*
Dan Costa, *
John Wicks, *
James Mcginty, *CFO*
◆ **EMP:** 26 **EST:** 2003
**SQ FT:** 93,000
**SALES (est):** 97.95MM **Publicly Held**
Web: www.511tactical.com
SIC: 5699 2231 5139 2393 Uniforms; Apparel and outerwear broadwoven fabrics; Boots; Canvas bags
HQ: 5.11 Ta, Inc.
  4300 Spyres Way
  Modesto CA 95356
  209 527-4511

**(P-17507)**
**ADRENALINE LACROSSE INC**
24 21st St, San Diego (92102-3802)
PHONE..................888 768-8479
Alex Cade, *CEO*
Steve Sepeta, *
Parker Anger, *
Rory Doucette, *
Xander Ritz, *
**EMP:** 29 **EST:** 2012
**SALES (est):** 1.73MM **Privately Held**
Web: www.adrln.com
SIC: 5699 2389 Sports apparel; Men's miscellaneous accessories

# PRODUCTS & SERVICES SECTION
## 5713 - Floor Covering Stores (P-17527)

**(P-17508)**
**AMERICAN SOCCER COMPANY INC (PA)**
Also Called: Score Sports
726 E Anaheim St, Wilmington (90744-3635)
P.O. Box 3579 (90510-3579)
**PHONE**..................310 830-6161
Kevin Mahoney, *Pr*
◆ **EMP:** 127 **EST:** 1975
**SQ FT:** 30,000
**SALES (est):** 24.63MM
**SALES (corp-wide):** 24.63MM **Privately Held**
Web: www.scoresports.com
**SIC: 5699** 2329 2339 3949 Uniforms; Men's and boys' athletic uniforms; Uniforms, athletic: women's, misses', and juniors'; Sporting and athletic goods, nec

**(P-17509)**
**ATHLEISURE INC**
Also Called: Sun Diego
3126 Micaion Blvd Ste B, San Diego (92109)
**PHONE**..................858 866-0108
Graham Smith, *Brnch Mgr*
**EMP:** 23
**SALES (corp-wide):** 24.45MM **Privately Held**
Web: www.sundiego.com
**SIC: 5699** 5941 3021 Sports apparel; Water sport equipment; Shoes, rubber or plastic molded to fabric
**PA:** Athleisure, Inc.
1330 Specialty Dr Ste A1
760 734-3818

**(P-17510)**
**BOOT BARN INC**
101 S Broadway, Santa Maria (93454-5103)
**PHONE**..................805 614-9222
Kenneth J Meany, *Mgr*
**EMP:** 16
**SALES (corp-wide):** 1.67B **Publicly Held**
Web: www.bootbarn.com
**SIC: 5699** 5661 5139 3021 Western apparel; Shoe stores; Boots; Protective footwear, rubber or plastic
**HQ:** Boot Barn, Inc.
15345 Barranca Pkwy
Irvine CA 92618
714 288-8181

**(P-17511)**
**PATAGONIA WORKS (PA)**
259 W Santa Clara St, Ventura (93001-2545)
P.O. Box 150 (93002-0150)
**PHONE**..................805 643-8616
◆ **EMP:** 340 **EST:** 1966
**SALES (est):** 415.44MM
**SALES (corp-wide):** 415.44MM **Privately Held**
Web: www.patagonia.com
**SIC: 5699** 2339 2329 5961 Uniforms and work clothing; Sportswear, women's; Men's and boys' sportswear and athletic clothing; Catalog and mail-order houses

**(P-17512)**
**RDD ENTERPRISES INC**
Also Called: R D D USA Division
4638 E Washington Blvd, Commerce (90040-1026)
**PHONE**..................213 742-0666
Tony Lomeli, *Prin*
**EMP:** 16
**SALES (corp-wide):** 3.12MM **Privately Held**

Web: www.rddusa.com
**SIC: 5699** 2394 Military goods and regalia; Tents: made from purchased materials
**PA:** R.D.D. Enterprises, Inc.
4638 E Washington Blvd
213 742-0666

**(P-17513)**
**SAN DIEGO LEATHER INC**
Also Called: Leather.com
340 National City Blvd, National City (91950-1111)
**PHONE**..................619 477-2900
Mario P Estolano, *CEO*
Nancy Estolano, *CFO*
Tony Estolano, *Mgr*
**EMP:** 19 **EST:** 1969
**SQ FT:** 20,000
**SALES (est):** 842.05K **Privately Held**
Web: www.leather.com
**SIC: 5699** 2386 Leather garments; Pants, leather

**(P-17514)**
**TRIPLE AUGHT DESIGN LLC**
660 22nd St, San Francisco (94107-3119)
**PHONE**..................415 318-8252
Brett Eisenberg, *Managing Member*
Rex Chu, *
▲ **EMP:** 28 **EST:** 2010
**SALES (est):** 4.92MM **Privately Held**
Web: www.tripleaughtdesign.com
**SIC: 5699** 2253 5941 3161 Sports apparel; Jerseys, knit; Camping and backpacking equipment; Traveling bags

## 5712 Furniture Stores

**(P-17515)**
**BKM OFFICE ENVIRONMENTS INC (PA)**
Also Called: Steelcase Authorized Dealer
816 Via Alondra, Camarillo (93012-8045)
**PHONE**..................805 339-6388
Peter Sloan, *CEO*
Brenda Sloan, *Pr*
**EMP:** 19 **EST:** 2003
**SQ FT:** 10,000
**SALES (est):** 11.77MM
**SALES (corp-wide):** 11.77MM **Privately Held**
Web: www.bkmoe.com
**SIC: 5712** 1799 1761 2522 Office furniture; Office furniture installation; Roofing, siding, and sheetmetal work; Office furniture, except wood

**(P-17516)**
**BOYD FLOTATION INC**
Also Called: Boyd Specialty Sleep
7551 Cherry Ave, Fontana (92336-4276)
**PHONE**..................314 997-5222
Alfred Mayen, *Mgr*
**EMP:** 33
Web: www.boydsleep.com
**SIC: 5712** 2515 Mattresses; Mattresses and bedsprings
**PA:** Boyd Flotation, Inc.
2440 Adie Rd

**(P-17517)**
**BULL OUTDOOR PRODUCTS INC**
1011 E Pine St, Lodi (95240-3158)
**PHONE**..................909 770-8626
Mark Nureddine, *Pr*
◆ **EMP:** 50 **EST:** 1989
**SQ FT:** 25,000
**SALES (est):** 16.52MM **Privately Held**

Web: www.bullbbq.com
**SIC: 5712** 3631 Outdoor and garden furniture; Barbecues, grills, and braziers (outdoor cooking)

**(P-17518)**
**DIAMOND MATTRESS COMPANY INC (PA)**
Also Called: Diamond Mattress Nf
3112 E Las Hermanas St, Compton (90221-5513)
**PHONE**..................310 638-0363
Shaun Pennington, *Pr*
Breana Pennington, *
Brian Arnold, *
▲ **EMP:** 38 **EST:** 1955
**SQ FT:** 31,000
**SALES (est):** 33.46MM
**SALES (corp-wide):** 33.46MM **Privately Held**
Web: www.diamondmattress.com
**SIC: 5712** 2515 Mattresses; Bedsprings, assembled

**(P-17519)**
**FEIST CABINETS & WOODWORKS INC**
9930 Kent St, Elk Grove (95624-9400)
**PHONE**..................916 686-8230
Randall C Feist, *Pr*
Charles Feist, *VP*
Barbara Feist, *Treas*
Frank Feist, *Sec*
David Feist, *Asst VP*
**EMP:** 20 **EST:** 1987
**SQ FT:** 20,000
**SALES (est):** 2.98MM **Privately Held**
Web: www.feistcabinets.com
**SIC: 5712** 1751 2434 2431 Cabinet work, custom; Cabinet and finish carpentry; Wood kitchen cabinets; Millwork

**(P-17520)**
**FOAMORDERCOM INC**
3455 Collins Ave, Richmond (94806-2000)
**PHONE**..................415 503-1188
Michael Gorham, *Pr*
◆ **EMP:** 18 **EST:** 2001
**SQ FT:** 8,900
**SALES (est):** 2.48MM **Privately Held**
Web: www.foamorder.com
**SIC: 5712** 3086 Mattresses; Insulation or cushioning material, foamed plastics

**(P-17521)**
**KAISER FOUNDATION HOSPITALS**
Also Called: Kaiser Prmnnte Nat Fclties Svc
3355 E 26th St, Vernon (90058-4169)
**PHONE**..................323 264-4310
Jose Montero, *Prin*
**EMP:** 137
**SALES (corp-wide):** 70.8B **Privately Held**
Web: www.kaisercenter.com
**SIC: 5712** 2434 Cabinet work, custom; Vanities, bathroom: wood
**HQ:** Kaiser Foundation Hospitals Inc
1 Kaiser Plz
Oakland CA 94612
510 271-6611

**(P-17522)**
**MODERNICA INC (PA)**
Also Called: Modernica
2901 Saco St, Vernon (90058-1433)
**PHONE**..................323 826-1600
▲ **EMP:** 50 **EST:** 1990
**SALES (est):** 8.59MM **Privately Held**
Web: www.modernica.net

**SIC: 5712** 5021 2511 2512 Furniture stores; Furniture; Wood household furniture; Upholstered household furniture

**(P-17523)**
**PBK INTERNATIONAL LLC**
Also Called: Phatboykustomz
717 E Compton Blvd, Rancho Dominguez (90220-1103)
P.O. Box 40344 (90239-1344)
**PHONE**..................866 727-7195
Andrew Santana, *Mgr*
**EMP:** 20 **EST:** 2006
**SQ FT:** 20,000
**SALES (est):** 591.58K **Privately Held**
Web: www.pbkdecor.com
**SIC: 5712** 2519 Furniture stores; Furniture, household: glass, fiberglass, and plastic

**(P-17524)**
**ROYAL-PEDIC MATTRESS MFG LLC (PA)**
341 N Robertson Blvd, Beverly Hills (90211-1705)
**PHONE**..................310 278-9594
Martin E Kelemen, *Managing Member*
▲ **EMP:** 22 **EST:** 1946
**SQ FT:** 3,200
**SALES (est):** 1.63MM
**SALES (corp-wide):** 1.63MM **Privately Held**
Web: www.royalpedic.com
**SIC: 5712** 2515 Mattresses; Mattresses and bedsprings

## 5713 Floor Covering Stores

**(P-17525)**
**B & W TILE CO INC (PA)**
Also Called: B & W Tile Manufacturing
14600 S Western Ave, Gardena (90249-3399)
**PHONE**..................310 538-9579
Joe Logan, *VP*
Joseph Logan, *
Ralph Logan, *
▲ **EMP:** 35 **EST:** 1948
**SQ FT:** 32,000
**SALES (est):** 2.37MM
**SALES (corp-wide):** 2.37MM **Privately Held**
Web: www.bwtile.com
**SIC: 5713** 3253 Floor tile; Floor tile, ceramic

**(P-17526)**
**BLUE RIBBON DRAPERIES INC**
Also Called: Drapery Affair
7341 Adams St Ste A, Paramount (90723-4007)
**PHONE**..................562 425-4637
Roy Donald, *CEO*
Gene Donald, *Pr*
Delrose Donald, *Sec*
**EMP:** 24 **EST:** 1982
**SQ FT:** 9,000
**SALES (est):** 1.86MM **Privately Held**
Web: www.draperyaffairandfloorstore.com
**SIC: 5713** 2391 Floor covering stores; Cottage sets (curtains), made from purchased materials

**(P-17527)**
**FAIRPRICE ENTERPRISES INC**
Also Called: Fair Price Carpets
1070 Center St, Riverside (92507-1016)
**PHONE**..................951 684-8578
Kurt Ritz, *CEO*
Donovan Ritz, *

## 5713 - Floor Covering Stores (P-17528)

Marlene Ritz, *
**EMP:** 60 **EST:** 1957
**SQ FT:** 28,000
**SALES (est):** 4.68MM **Privately Held**
**Web:** www.fairpricecarpets.com
**SIC:** 5713 3281 2426 5032 Carpets; Granite, cut and shaped; Flooring, hardwood; Ceramic wall and floor tile, nec

### (P-17528)
### RM PARTNERS INC
Also Called: Sterling Carpets & Flooring
1439 S State College Blvd, Anaheim (92806-5718)
**PHONE**.................................714 765-5725
Richard Mandel, Pr
John Ernst, *
**EMP:** 40 **EST:** 1962
**SQ FT:** 16,000
**SALES (est):** 4.09MM **Privately Held**
**Web:** www.sterlingflooring.com
**SIC:** 5713 1752 2273 Carpets; Carpet laying; Dyeing and finishing of tufted rugs and carpets

## 5714 Drapery And Upholstery Stores

### (P-17529)
### SMITHS SHADE & LINOLEUM CO INC
6588 Federal Blvd, Lemon Grove (91945-1311)
P.O. Box 1488 (91946-1488)
**PHONE**.................................619 299-2228
Krista Neville, VP
Kristie Smith, Sec
Ralph Smith, Stockholder
**EMP:** 20 **EST:** 1934
**SQ FT:** 5,000
**SALES (est):** 2.22MM **Privately Held**
**Web:** www.smithshade.com
**SIC:** 5714 5023 2591 Curtains; Window furnishings; Shade, curtain, and drapery hardware

## 5719 Miscellaneous Homefurnishings

### (P-17530)
### AERO SHADE CO INC (PA)
Also Called: A-Z Industries Div
8404 W 3rd St, Los Angeles (90048-4112)
**PHONE**.................................323 938-2314
Jack Pitson, Pr
Mario Soulema, *
Shelly Soulema, *
**EMP:** 25 **EST:** 1942
**SQ FT:** 2,400
**SALES (est):** 2.34MM
**SALES (corp-wide):** 2.34MM **Privately Held**
**Web:** www.aeroshadeco.com
**SIC:** 5719 2591 5023 Window furnishings; Window shades; Window shades

### (P-17531)
### BEBE STUDIO INC
Also Called: B E B E
10250 Santa Monica Blvd Ste 6, Los Angeles (90067-6404)
**PHONE**.................................213 362-2323
Manny Mashouf, Pr
Gary Bosch, *
Marc So, *
▲ **EMP:** 150 **EST:** 2002
**SQ FT:** 46,685
**SALES (est):** 1.2MM **Publicly Held**
**SIC:** 5719 5621 5661 2339 Linens; Women's clothing stores; Women's shoes; Women's and misses' accessories
**HQ:** Bebe Stores, Inc.
400 Valley Dr
Brisbane CA 94005
415 715-3900

### (P-17532)
### BLACKTAG CORPORATION
505 N Tustin Ave Ste 243, Santa Ana (92705-3735)
**PHONE**.................................949 981-9063
Zhengyu Li, Pr
**EMP:** 15 **EST:** 2017
**SALES (est):** 338.21K **Privately Held**
**Web:** www.blacktaghw.com
**SIC:** 5719 5021 5023 2522 Window furnishings; Office furniture, nec; Homefurnishings; Office chairs, benches, and stools, except wood

### (P-17533)
### DACOR (DH)
14425 Clark Ave, City Of Industry (91745-1235)
P.O. Box 90070 (91715-0070)
**PHONE**.................................626 799-1000
Stanley Michael Joseph, Ch Bd
Charles J Huebner, *
Steve Joseph, *
Anthony B Joseph Iii, Prin
◆ **EMP:** 100 **EST:** 1965
**SQ FT:** 40,000
**SALES (est):** 29.68MM **Privately Held**
**Web:** www.dacor.com
**SIC:** 5719 3631 Kitchenware; Convection ovens, including portable: household
**HQ:** Samsung Electronics America, Inc.
85 Challenger Rd
Ridgefield Park NJ 07660
201 229-4000

### (P-17534)
### GOOD FELLAS INDUSTRIES INC
Also Called: G F I
4400 Bandini Blvd, Vernon (90058-4310)
P.O. Box 861657 (90086)
**PHONE**.................................323 924-9495
Judd A Shipper, CEO
◆ **EMP:** 85 **EST:** 1997
**SQ FT:** 40,000
**SALES (est):** 3.99MM **Privately Held**
**Web:** www.gfi-inc.net
**SIC:** 5719 1799 2591 Bedding (sheets, blankets, spreads, and pillows); Drapery track installation; Shade, curtain, and drapery hardware

### (P-17535)
### IMPRESSIONS VANITY COMPANY (PA)
17353 Derian Ave, Irvine (92614-5801)
**PHONE**.................................844 881-0790
Dong Kevin Choi, CEO
**EMP:** 29 **EST:** 2015
**SALES (est):** 3.29MM
**SALES (corp-wide):** 3.29MM **Privately Held**
**Web:** www.impressionsvanity.com
**SIC:** 5719 5063 2531 Mirrors; Lighting fixtures; Chairs, table and arm

### (P-17536)
### LA LINEN INC
1760 E 15th St, Los Angeles (90021-2716)
**PHONE**.................................213 745-4004
Danny Levy, CEO
**EMP:** 30 **EST:** 2010
**SQ FT:** 16,500

**SALES (est):** 2.4MM **Privately Held**
**Web:** www.lalinen.com
**SIC:** 5719 2392 2391 Linens; Tablecloths and table settings; Curtains and draperies

### (P-17537)
### LINEN SALVAGE ET CIE LLC
1073 Stearns Dr, Los Angeles (90035-2638)
**PHONE**.................................323 904-3100
Andrea Bernstein, Prin
**EMP:** 36 **EST:** 2018
**SALES (est):** 790.72K **Privately Held**
**Web:** www.linensalvage.com
**SIC:** 5719 2269 Linens; Linen fabrics: dyeing, finishing, and printing

### (P-17538)
### NORTH RANCH MANAGEMENT CORP
9754 Deering Ave, Chatsworth (91311-4301)
**PHONE**.................................800 410-2153
Richard Goldman, CEO
▲ **EMP:** 70 **EST:** 2000
**SALES (est):** 1.86MM **Privately Held**
**Web:** www.dreamproducts.com
**SIC:** 5719 3171 3172 4813 Housewares, nec; Women's handbags and purses; Wallets; Online service providers

### (P-17539)
### PRIORITY LIGHTING INC
77551 El Duna Ct Ste H, Palm Desert (92211-4147)
**PHONE**.................................800 709-1119
Daniel Hengstler, Managing Member
**EMP:** 18 **EST:** 2009
**SALES (est):** 2.25MM **Privately Held**
**Web:** www.prioritylighting.com
**SIC:** 5719 3648 5063 Lighting fixtures; Lighting equipment, nec; Lighting fittings and accessories

### (P-17540)
### SKYCO SHADING SYSTEMS INC
3411 W Fordham Ave, Santa Ana (92704-4422)
**PHONE**.................................714 708-3038
Davide Pesca, CEO
Davide Pesca, CEO
▲ **EMP:** 28 **EST:** 1994
**SQ FT:** 16,000
**SALES (est):** 4.57MM
**SALES (corp-wide):** 12.53MM **Privately Held**
**Web:** www.skycoshade.com
**SIC:** 5719 2431 Window furnishings; Millwork
**PA:** Pesca Holding Llc
2517 Manana Dr
469 423-9837

## 5722 Household Appliance Stores

### (P-17541)
### JOHNSTONE SUPPLY INC
Also Called: Johnson Contrls Authorized Dlr
8040 Slauson Ave, Montebello (90640-6620)
**PHONE**.................................323 722-2859
William J Salpaka, Pr
**EMP:** 70
**SALES (corp-wide):** 1.18B **Privately Held**
**Web:** www.johnstonesupply.com
**SIC:** 5722 3585 5075 Gas household appliances; Parts for heating, cooling, and refrigerating equipment; Warm air heating and air conditioning

**HQ:** Johnstone Supply, Llc
11632 Ne Ainsworth Cir
Portland OR 97220
503 256-3663

### (P-17542)
### PORTABLE CLERS SLS RENTALS INC
1250 Pacific Oaks Pl Ste 101, Escondido (92029-2908)
P.O. Box 460822 (92046-0822)
**PHONE**.................................760 747-9591
Mary Tennison, Pr
Don Tennison, VP
**EMP:** 18 **EST:** 1995
**SALES (est):** 792.22K **Privately Held**
**Web:** www.portablecoolers.com
**SIC:** 5722 3585 1711 Air conditioning room units, self-contained; Parts for heating, cooling, and refrigerating equipment; Heating and air conditioning contractors

## 5731 Radio, Television, And Electronic Stores

### (P-17543)
### MVINIX CORPORATION
1759 Mccarthy Blvd, Milpitas (95035-7416)
**PHONE**.................................408 321-9109
Daniel Tran, CEO
Huynh P Tan, *
**EMP:** 28 **EST:** 2008
**SALES (est):** 4.87MM **Privately Held**
**Web:** www.mvinix.com
**SIC:** 5731 3672 Consumer electronic equipment, nec; Printed circuit boards

### (P-17544)
### SATELLITE AV LLC
Also Called: Glorystar Satellite Systems
4021 Alvis Ct Ste 5, Rocklin (95677-4031)
**PHONE**.................................916 677-0720
Eugene Zaikin, Pt
Bred Kelly, Managing Member
Eugene Zaikin Managing, Prin
◆ **EMP:** 20 **EST:** 2004
**SQ FT:** 15,000
**SALES (est):** 2.5MM **Privately Held**
**Web:** www.satelliteav.com
**SIC:** 5731 3663 Antennas, satellite dish; Radio and t.v. communications equipment

### (P-17545)
### TEND INSIGHTS INC
46567 Fremont Blvd, Fremont (94538-6409)
**PHONE**.................................510 619-9289
Herman Yau, CEO
▲ **EMP:** 28 **EST:** 2008
**SQ FT:** 7,000
**SALES (est):** 1.42MM **Privately Held**
**Web:** www.tendinsights.com
**SIC:** 5731 7372 Video cameras and accessories; Prepackaged software

### (P-17546)
### VUDU INC
2901 Tasman Dr Ste 101, Santa Clara (95054-1136)
**PHONE**.................................408 492-1010
Neil Madden Ashe, CEO
Tony Miranz, *
Edward Lichty, *
Chris Watts, *
Prasanna Ganesan, *
**EMP:** 86 **EST:** 2005
**SALES (est):** 23.34MM
**SALES (corp-wide):** 121.57B **Publicly Held**

# PRODUCTS & SERVICES SECTION

**5812 - Eating Places (P-17564)**

Web: www.vudu.com
SIC: **5731** 3651  Television sets; Electronic kits for home assembly: radio, TV, phonograph
HQ: Fandango, Inc.
12200 W Olympic Blvd # 400
Los Angeles CA 90064
310 954-0278

## 5734 Computer And Software Stores

### (P-17547)
**COMPUTER PERFORMANCE INC**
Also Called: Digital Loggers
2695 Walsh Ave, Santa Clara  (95051-0920)
PHONE...................................408 330-5599
Martin Bodo, *Ch Bd*
Valerie Bodo, *
Jamal Keikha, *
▲ **EMP:** 35 **EST:** 1987
**SQ FT:** 42,000
**SALES (est):** 4.92MM **Privately Held**
Web: www.dlidirect.com
SIC: **5734** 5045 3572  Computer peripheral equipment; Computer peripheral equipment ; Computer disk and drum drives and components

### (P-17548)
**CONVERSICA  INC (PA)**
1730 S El Camino Real Ste 350, San Mateo  (94402-3078)
PHONE...................................650 290-7674
Jim Kaskade, *CEO*
Alex Terry, *
Sheryl Hawk, *
Jim Harriger, *
Jason Lund, *
**EMP:** 103 **EST:** 2007
**SALES (est):** 31.8MM
**SALES (corp-wide):** 31.8MM **Privately Held**
Web: www.conversica.com
SIC: **5734** 5045 7372  Software, business and non-game; Computer software; Business oriented computer software

### (P-17549)
**CORALTREE INC**
6920 Santa Teresa Blvd Ste 201, San Jose  (95119-1344)
PHONE...................................408 215-1441
Tiruvali Srinivasan, *CEO*
Tiruvali Srinivasan, *Pr*
**EMP:** 20 **EST:** 2009
**SALES (est):** 2.38MM **Privately Held**
Web: www.coraltreetech.com
SIC: **5734** 7372  Software, business and non-game; Prepackaged software

### (P-17550)
**DOME9 SECURITY  INC**
Also Called: Checkpoint Cloudguard Dome9
800 W El Camino Real Ste 100, Mountain View  (94040-2573)
PHONE...................................831 212-2353
Zohar Alon, *CEO*
**EMP:** 25 **EST:** 2011
**SALES (est):** 1.94MM
**SALES (corp-wide):** 894.19MM **Privately Held**
Web: www.checkpoint.com
SIC: **5734** 5045 7372 7382  Software, business and non-game; Computer software ; Business oriented computer software; Security systems services

HQ: Check Point Software Technologies Ltd.
5 Shlomo Kaplan
Tel Aviv-Jaffa 67891

### (P-17551)
**GOSECURE INC (PA)**
13220 Evening Creek Dr S Ste 107, San Diego  (92128-4103)
PHONE...................................301 442-3432
Neal Creighton, *CEO*
Neal Creighton, *Pr*
Robert J Mccullen, *Ofcr*
Richard Miller, *COO*
Thalia Gietzen, *CFO*
**EMP:** 178 **EST:** 2004
**SALES (est):** 22.51MM **Privately Held**
Web: www.gosecure.ai
SIC: **5734** 7382 7372 7373  Computer software and accessories; Protective devices, security; Publisher's computer software; Computer systems analysis and design

### (P-17552)
**GURUCUL SOLUTIONS  LLC**
222 N Pacific Coast Hwy Ste 1322, El Segundo  (90245-5629)
PHONE...................................213 291-6888
Saryu Nayyar, *
Jasen Meece, *
Nilesh Dherange, *
**EMP:** 74 **EST:** 2010
**SQ FT:** 4,360
**SALES (est):** 5.43MM **Privately Held**
Web: www.gurucul.com
SIC: **5734** 7372  Software, business and non-game; Publisher's computer software

### (P-17553)
**JAM CITY  INC (PA)**
Also Called: Social Gaming Network
3562 Eastham Dr, Culver City  (90232-2409)
PHONE...................................310 205-4800
**EMP:** 20 **EST:** 2007
**SQ FT:** 5,000
**SALES (est):** 59.07MM
**SALES (corp-wide):** 59.07MM **Privately Held**
Web: www.jamcity.com
SIC: **5734** 3944  Software, computer games; Games, toys, and children's vehicles

### (P-17554)
**KLEVERNESS INCORPORATED**
340 S Lemon Ave 2291, Walnut  (91789-2706)
PHONE...................................213 559-2480
Dan Nurko Elliot, *CEO*
Alex Fraind-dorfsman, *CFO*
**EMP:** 15 **EST:** 2017
**SALES (est):** 846.5K **Privately Held**
Web: hospitality.kleverness.com
SIC: **5734** 7372  Computer peripheral equipment; Application computer software

### (P-17555)
**NEW TECH SOLUTIONS  INC**
Also Called: NTS
4179 Business Center Dr, Fremont  (94538-6355)
PHONE...................................510 353-4070
Vijay Kumar, *CEO*
Rajesh Patel, *
**EMP:** 45 **EST:** 1997
**SQ FT:** 10,000
**SALES (est):** 537.84MM **Privately Held**
Web: www.newtechsolutions.com

SIC: **5734** 5045 7373 3571  Computer and software stores; Computers, peripherals, and software; Computer integrated systems design; Electronic computers

### (P-17556)
**PACTUM AI  INC (PA)**
Also Called: Pactum
800 W El Camino Real Ste 180, Mountain View  (94040-2586)
PHONE...................................669 289-9041
Martin Rand, *CEO*
Kaspar Korjus, *CPO*
**EMP:** 30 **EST:** 2019
**SALES (est):** 2.97MM
**SALES (corp-wide):** 2.97MM **Privately Held**
Web: www.pactum.com
SIC: **5734** 7372  Software, business and non-game; Business oriented computer software

### (P-17557)
**PCFS SOLUTIONS**
Also Called: Pcfs 2000
6353 El Cajon Blvd Ste 124, San Diego  (92115-2655)
PHONE...................................714 674-0009
Robert Cota, *Pr*
**EMP:** 28 **EST:** 1998
**SALES (est):** 837.59K **Privately Held**
Web: www.pcfssolutions.com
SIC: **5734** 2731  Computer software and accessories; Book publishing

### (P-17558)
**SAITECH INC**
42640 Christy St, Fremont  (94538-3135)
PHONE...................................510 440-0256
Vikram Mahajan, *CEO*
Vikram Mahajan, *Pr*
Sachin Sharma, *CFO*
▲ **EMP:** 18 **EST:** 2002
**SQ FT:** 9,000
**SALES (est):** 1.31MM **Privately Held**
Web: www.saitechincorporated.com
SIC: **5734** 7373 3572 5045  Computer peripheral equipment; Value-added resellers, computer systems; Computer storage devices; Computers, peripherals, and software

### (P-17559)
**TANGENT COMPUTER INC (PA)**
Also Called: Tanget Fastnet
191 Airport Blvd, Burlingame  (94010-2006)
PHONE...................................800 342-9388
Douglas James Monsour, *CEO*
Lannie H Tran, *CFO*
Maher M Zabaneh, *Sec*
**EMP:** 36 **EST:** 1989
**SQ FT:** 80,000
**SALES (est):** 24.79MM
**SALES (corp-wide):** 24.79MM **Privately Held**
Web: www.tangent.com
SIC: **5734** 3571  Computer and software stores; Personal computers (microcomputers)

### (P-17560)
**TINYCO INC**
225 Bush St Ste 1900, San Francisco  (94104-4292)
PHONE...................................415 644-8101
Saleman Ali, *CEO*
**EMP:** 125 **EST:** 2011
**SALES (est):** 2.42MM
**SALES (corp-wide):** 59.07MM **Privately Held**

SIC: **5734** 7372 7371  Software, computer games; Application computer software; Software programming applications
PA: Jam City, Inc.
3562 Eastham Dr
310 205-4800

## 5736 Musical Instrument Stores

### (P-17561)
**CARVIN CORP**
Also Called: Carvin Guitars & Pro Sound
16262 W Bernardo Dr, San Diego  (92127-1879)
PHONE...................................858 487-1600
Carson Kiesel, *CEO*
Carson L Kiesel, *
Jon Kiesel, *
Paul Kiesel, *
Mark Kiesel, *
◆ **EMP:** 179 **EST:** 1946
**SQ FT:** 82,000
**SALES (est):** 2.16MM **Privately Held**
Web: www.carvinaudio.com
SIC: **5736** 3931  Musical instrument stores; Guitars and parts, electric and nonelectric

### (P-17562)
**DEERING BANJO COMPANY  INC**
3733 Kenora Dr, Spring Valley  (91977-1206)
PHONE...................................619 464-8252
Charles Greg Deering, *Pr*
Janet Deering, *Sec*
▲ **EMP:** 40 **EST:** 1975
**SQ FT:** 18,000
**SALES (est):** 2.32MM **Privately Held**
Web: www.deeringbanjos.com
SIC: **5736** 3548  Musical instrument stores; Welding and cutting apparatus and accessories, nec

## 5812 Eating Places

### (P-17563)
**AIR FAYRE USA INC**
1720 W 135th St, Gardena  (90249-2508)
PHONE...................................310 808-1061
Stephen Yapp, *CEO*
Joe Golio, *
**EMP:** 200 **EST:** 2008
**SALES (est):** 24.56MM
**SALES (corp-wide):** 715.07K **Privately Held**
Web: www.airfayre.com
SIC: **5812** 2099  Caterers; Box lunches, for sale off premises
HQ: Journey Group Limited
One Bartholomew Close
London EC1A

### (P-17564)
**BELMONT BREWING COMPANY INC**
Also Called: B B C
25 39th Pl, Long Beach  (90803-2806)
PHONE...................................562 433-3891
David Hansen, *Pr*
David Lott, *
Jessica Bellows, *
**EMP:** 21 **EST:** 1989
**SQ FT:** 7,000
**SALES (est):** 1.07MM **Privately Held**
Web: www.belmontbrewing.com
SIC: **5812** 2082  American restaurant; Malt beverages

## 5812 - Eating Places (P-17565)

**(P-17565)**
**BREWERY ON HALF MOON BAY INC**
Also Called: Half Moon Bay Brewing Company
390 Capistrano Rd, Half Moon Bay (94019)
P.O. Box 879 (94018-0879)
PHONE..................................650 728-2739
Michael Laffen, *Pr*
Christine Mendonca, *
**EMP:** 140 **EST:** 2000
**SQ FT:** 12,000
**SALES (est):** 9.77MM **Privately Held**
Web: www.hmbbrewingco.com
**SIC: 5812** 2082 Chicken restaurant; Brewers' grain

**(P-17566)**
**BUCKHORN CAFE INC (PA)**
Also Called: Putah Creek Cafe
2 Main St, Winters (95694-1723)
PHONE..................................530 795-1319
John Pickerel, *Pr*
Laura Lucero, *Dir*
**EMP:** 70 **EST:** 1954
**SQ FT:** 7,000
**SALES (est):** 10.22MM
**SALES (corp-wide):** 10.22MM **Privately Held**
Web: www.buckhornsteakhouse.com
**SIC: 5812** 5813 2013 Cafe; Bar (drinking places); Smoked meats, from purchased meat

**(P-17567)**
**CAFE 21 GASLAMP INC**
Also Called: Cafe 21
2736 Adams Ave, San Diego (92116-1312)
PHONE..................................619 795-0721
Emran Javadov, *CEO*
**EMP:** 20 **EST:** 2011
**SALES (est):** 772.7K **Privately Held**
Web: www.cafe-21.com
**SIC: 5812** 2099 Cafe; Food preparations, nec

**(P-17568)**
**CALIMEX DELI**
711 1/2 S Kern Ave, Los Angeles (90022-2574)
PHONE..................................323 261-7271
Manuel Cortez, *Ch Bd*
Belen Medrano, *Prin*
Juan Cortez, *Prin*
**EMP:** 20 **EST:** 1994
**SQ FT:** 50,000
**SALES (est):** 236.74K **Privately Held**
Web: www.ordercalimexdeli.com
**SIC: 5812** 2051 Delicatessen (eating places); Bakery: wholesale or wholesale/retail combined

**(P-17569)**
**CASA LUPE INC (PA)**
Also Called: Casa Lupe Market & Restaurants
130 Magnolia St, Gridley (95948-2618)
P.O. Box 1230 (95948-1230)
PHONE..................................530 846-3218
Esther De La Torre, *Pr*
Lupe De La Torre, *
Luz Maria De La Torre, *
**EMP:** 55 **EST:** 1968
**SQ FT:** 11,000
**SALES (est):** 9.86MM
**SALES (corp-wide):** 9.86MM **Privately Held**
Web: casa-lupe-market.edan.io
**SIC: 5812** 5411 2099 Mexican restaurant; Grocery stores, independent; Tortillas, fresh or refrigerated

**(P-17570)**
**CASTLE IMPORTING INC**
14550 Miller Ave, Fontana (92336-1696)
PHONE..................................909 428-9200
Rosangela Borruso, *CEO*
Marc Zadra, *
Richard White, *
▲ **EMP:** 45 **EST:** 1989
**SALES (est):** 7.28MM **Privately Held**
Web: www.castleimporting.com
**SIC: 5812** 2022 Eating places; Processed cheese

**(P-17571)**
**CHEESECAKE FACTORY BAKERY INC**
26950 Agoura Rd, Calabasas Hills (91301-5335)
PHONE..................................818 871-3000
Keith T Carango, *CEO*
David Overton, *
Max Byfuglin, *
▲ **EMP:** 500 **EST:** 1972
**SQ FT:** 60,000
**SALES (est):** 27.64MM **Publicly Held**
Web: www.thecheesecakefactorybakery.com
**SIC: 5812** 2051 Eating places; Cakes, bakery: except frozen
**PA:** The Cheesecake Factory Incorporated
26901 Malibu Hills Rd

**(P-17572)**
**CHEESECAKE FACTORY INC (PA)**
Also Called: CHEESECAKE FACTORY, THE
26901 Malibu Hills Rd, Calabasas Hills (91301-5354)
PHONE..................................818 871-3000
David Overton, *Ch Bd*
David M Gordon, *Pr*
Matthew E Clark, *Ex VP*
Scarlett May, *Ex VP*
▲ **EMP:** 350 **EST:** 1972
**SQ FT:** 88,000
**SALES (est):** 3.44B **Publicly Held**
Web: www.thecheesecakefactory.com
**SIC: 5812** 2051 American restaurant; Cakes, bakery: except frozen

**(P-17573)**
**COSTEAUX FRENCH BAKERY INC**
Also Called: Costeaux French Bakery & Cafe
417 Healdsburg Ave, Healdsburg (95448-3814)
PHONE..................................707 433-1913
William Seppi, *CEO*
Karl Seppi, *
William Seppi, *VP*
**EMP:** 70 **EST:** 1959
**SQ FT:** 5,700
**SALES (est):** 5.65MM **Privately Held**
Web: www.costeaux.com
**SIC: 5812** 5461 2051 Cafe; Retail bakeries; Bakery: wholesale or wholesale/retail combined

**(P-17574)**
**COUNTER HOSPITALITY GROUP LLC**
Also Called: Heirloom
8398 N Fresno St Ste 101, Fresno (93720-1599)
PHONE..................................559 228-9735
**EMP:** 85 **EST:** 2019
**SALES (est):** 6.5MM **Privately Held**
Web: www.heirloom-eats.com

**SIC: 5812** 7372 American restaurant; Application computer software

**(P-17575)**
**DAD INVESTMENTS**
Also Called: Cater Tots Too
2929 Halladay St, Santa Ana (92705-5622)
PHONE..................................714 751-8500
Nadia Tayob, *Pr*
**EMP:** 22 **EST:** 2016
**SALES (est):** 654.77K **Privately Held**
**SIC: 5812** 2099 Caterers; Food preparations, nec

**(P-17576)**
**DICKEYS BARBECUE REST INC**
Also Called: Dickeys Barbecue Pit
17245 17th St, Tustin (92780-1974)
PHONE..................................714 602-3874
Roland Dickey, *Brnch Mgr*
**EMP:** 28
**SALES (corp-wide):** 94.85MM **Privately Held**
Web: www.dickeys.com
**SIC: 5812** 2033 Barbecue restaurant; Tomato products, packaged in cans, jars, etc.
**HQ:** Dickey's Barbecue Restaurants, Inc.
850 Cntral Pkwy E Ste 140
Plano TX 75074
972 248-9899

**(P-17577)**
**DREYERS GRAND ICE CREAM INC (DH)**
Also Called: Haagen-Dazs
590 Ygnacio Valley Rd Ste 300, Walnut Creek (94596-1801)
PHONE..................................510 594-9466
Kim Peddle Rguem, *CEO*
◆ **EMP:** 230 **EST:** 1928
**SQ FT:** 64,000
**SALES (est):** 369.46MM
**SALES (corp-wide):** 2.67MM **Privately Held**
Web: www.dreyersgrandicecream.com
**SIC: 5812** 2024 Ice cream stands or dairy bars; Ice cream and frozen deserts
**HQ:** Froneri International Limited
Richmond House
Northallerton DL7 9
167 742-3397

**(P-17578)**
**EINSTEIN NOAH REST GROUP INC**
Also Called: Einstein Brothers Bagels
170 Bon Air Ctr, Greenbrae (94904-2417)
PHONE..................................415 925-9971
Astid Ludlow, *Mgr*
**EMP:** 214
Web: www.noahs.com
**SIC: 5812** 2051 2022 Cafe; Bagels, fresh or frozen; Spreads, cheese
**PA:** Einstein Noah Restaurant Group, Inc.
555 Zang St Ste 300

**(P-17579)**
**FGR 1 LLC**
Also Called: Fresh Griller
3191 Red Hill Ave Ste 100, Costa Mesa (92626-3451)
PHONE..................................800 653-3517
Anand Gala, *Managing Member*
**EMP:** 40 **EST:** 2011
**SALES (est):** 219.34K **Privately Held**
**SIC: 5812** 7372 American restaurant; Application computer software

**(P-17580)**
**FLORENCE MEAT PACKING CO INC**
Also Called: F M P
9840 Everest St, Downey (90242-3114)
PHONE..................................562 401-0760
**EMP:** 35
**SIC: 5812** 2011 Eating places; Meat packing plants

**(P-17581)**
**GOTTS PARTNERS LP**
Also Called: Gott's Roadside
1344 Adams St, Saint Helena (94574-1938)
P.O. Box 1226 (94574-1179)
PHONE..................................415 213-2992
Clay Walker, *Pr*
**EMP:** 50 **EST:** 1999
**SALES (est):** 4.63MM **Privately Held**
Web: www.gotts.com
**SIC: 5812** 7372 Fast-food restaurant, chain; Application computer software

**(P-17582)**
**GRILLIN & CHILLIN INC**
Also Called: Grillin & Chillin Downtown
211 Donald Dr, Hollister (95023-6361)
PHONE..................................831 637-2337
Charles Patrick Frowein, *CEO*
**EMP:** 20 **EST:** 2013
**SALES (est):** 516.42K **Privately Held**
Web: www.831beer.com
**SIC: 5812** 5813 2082 Grills (eating places); Drinking places; Ale (alcoholic beverage)

**(P-17583)**
**HARVEST FOOD PRODUCTS CO INC**
710 Sandoval Way, Hayward (94544-7111)
PHONE..................................510 675-0383
Danny Kha, *Pr*
◆ **EMP:** 100 **EST:** 1981
**SQ FT:** 30,000
**SALES (est):** 17.7MM **Privately Held**
Web: www.harvestfoodproducts.com
**SIC: 5812** 2099 2038 Eating places; Food preparations, nec; Ethnic foods, nec, frozen

**(P-17584)**
**HUXTABLES KITCHEN INC**
Also Called: Huxtable's
2100 E 49th St, Vernon (90058-2825)
P.O. Box 2847 (90058)
PHONE..................................323 923-2900
▲ **EMP:** 100
Web: www.huxtables.com
**SIC: 5812** 2099 2015 2013 Eating places; Ready-to-eat meals, salads, and sandwiches; Poultry slaughtering and processing; Sausages and other prepared meats

**(P-17585)**
**IL FORNAIO (AMERICA) LLC (HQ)**
Also Called: IL Fornaio Cucina Italiana
770 Tamalpais Dr Ste 208, Corte Madera (94925-1795)
PHONE..................................415 945-0500
Mike Beatrice, *
Shaun Maki, *
Jun Kawai, *
▲ **EMP:** 35 **EST:** 1982
**SALES (est):** 114MM
**SALES (corp-wide):** 8.04B **Privately Held**
Web: www.ilfornaio.com
**SIC: 5812** 5813 5149 5461 Italian restaurant; Drinking places; Bakery products; Retail bakeries

## PRODUCTS & SERVICES SECTION
### 5812 - Eating Places (P-17606)

PA: Roark Capital Group Inc.
1180 Peachtree St Ne
404 591-5200

**(P-17586)**
**IL FORNAIO (AMERICA) LLC**
16932 Valley View Ave Ste A, La Mirada (90638-5826)
PHONE.................................714 752-7052
Luis Espinoza, *Brnch Mgr*
**EMP:** 140
**SALES (corp-wide):** 8.04B **Privately Held**
Web: www.ilfornaio.com
**SIC: 5812** 5813 5149 2051 Italian restaurant; Drinking places; Bakery products; Bread, cake, and related products
HQ: Il Fornaio (America) Llc
770 Tamalpais Dr Ste 208
Corte Madera CA 94925
415 945-0500

**(P-17587)**
**JIPCOB INC**
Also Called: John's Incredible Pizza Co
3709 Rosedale Hwy, Bakersfield (93308-6251)
PHONE.................................661 859-1111
John Parlet, *Pr*
Betty D Parlet, *
**EMP:** 180 **EST:** 1998
**SQ FT:** 26,000
**SALES (est):** 2.73MM **Privately Held**
**SIC: 5812** 2099 7993 5813 Italian restaurant; Salads, fresh or refrigerated; Video game arcade; Drinking places

**(P-17588)**
**JOES DWNTWN BREWRY & REST INC**
Also Called: Downtown Joe's
902 Main St, Napa (94559-3045)
PHONE.................................707 258-2337
Joe Peatman, *Pr*
**EMP:** 40 **EST:** 1994
**SQ FT:** 6,000
**SALES (est):** 2.05MM **Privately Held**
Web: www.downtownjoes.com
**SIC: 5812** 5813 2082 American restaurant; Drinking places; Malt beverages

**(P-17589)**
**JORODA INC (PA)**
Also Called: Sunrise Bistro
1559 Botelho Dr, Walnut Creek (94596-5102)
PHONE.................................925 930-0122
Cindy Gershen, *Pr*
**EMP:** 30 **EST:** 1980
**SQ FT:** 5,000
**SALES (est):** 2.45MM
**SALES (corp-wide):** 2.45MM **Privately Held**
Web: www.sunrisebistrocatering.com
**SIC: 5812** 2051 Caterers; Bakery: wholesale or wholesale/retail combined

**(P-17590)**
**KARL STRAUSS BREWING COMPANY**
40868 Winchester Rd, Temecula (92591-5521)
PHONE.................................951 225-7960
Steven Zeeb, *Genl Mgr*
**EMP:** 15
Web: www.karlstrauss.com
**SIC: 5812** 5181 2082 Grills (eating places); Beer and ale; Malt beverages
PA: Karl Strauss Brewing Company
5985 Santa Fe St

**(P-17591)**
**KING EXPRESS INC**
Also Called: King Ex Chinese Fd & Donut
12053 Vanowen St, North Hollywood (91605-5962)
PHONE.................................818 503-2772
Joel Lim, *Mgr*
**EMP:** 18 **EST:** 1993
**SALES (est):** 220.81K **Privately Held**
**SIC: 5812** 2051 Chinese restaurant; Doughnuts, except frozen

**(P-17592)**
**KING TACO RESTAURANT INC (PA)**
3421 E 14th St, Los Angeles (90023-3837)
PHONE.................................323 266-3585
Raul D Martinez, *CEO*
Raul O Martinez Senior, *Pr*
**EMP:** 65 **EST:** 1974
**SALES (est):** 25.69MM
**SALES (corp-wide):** 25.69MM **Privately Held**
Web: www.kingtaco.com
**SIC: 5812** 2099 Mexican restaurant; Food preparations, nec

**(P-17593)**
**KINGS HAWAIIAN BAKERY W INC (HQ)**
Also Called: Kings Hawaiian Bakery
1411 W 190th St, Gardena (90248-4324)
PHONE.................................310 533-3250
Mark Taira, *Pr*
Curtis Taira, *
Leatrice Taira, *
Vaughn Taira, *
Stella Taira, *
▲ **EMP:** 25 **EST:** 1950
**SALES (est):** 62.63MM
**SALES (corp-wide):** 153.92MM **Privately Held**
Web: www.kingshawaiian.com
**SIC: 5812** 5142 2051 Restaurant, family: independent; Bakery products, frozen; Bread, cake, and related products
PA: King's Hawaiian Holding Company, Inc.
19161 Harborgate Way
310 533-3250

**(P-17594)**
**KLATCH COFFEE INC (PA)**
Also Called: Coffee Klatch
9325 Feron Blvd, Rancho Cucamonga (91730-4516)
PHONE.................................909 981-4031
Mike Perry, *CEO*
Heather Perry, *VP*
Cindy Perry, *Sec*
**EMP:** 20 **EST:** 1993
**SQ FT:** 2,400
**SALES (est):** 4.36MM **Privately Held**
Web: shop.klatchcoffee.com
**SIC: 5812** 2095 Coffee shop; Coffee extracts

**(P-17595)**
**LAS GLONDRINAS MEXICAN FD PDTS (PA)**
27124 Paseo Espada Ste 803, San Juan Capistrano (92675-6787)
PHONE.................................949 240-3440
Arturo Galindo Junior, *Pr*
Maria Galindo, *Sec*
**EMP:** 18 **EST:** 1984
**SQ FT:** 3,000
**SALES (est):** 1.88MM
**SALES (corp-wide):** 1.88MM **Privately Held**
Web: www.lasgolondrinas.biz

**SIC: 5812** 2099 Mexican restaurant; Tortillas, fresh or refrigerated

**(P-17596)**
**LOFTY COFFEE INC**
97 N Coast Highway 101 Ste 101, Encinitas (92024-3282)
PHONE.................................760 230-6747
Eric Myers, *CEO*
**EMP:** 100 **EST:** 2011
**SALES (est):** 1.18MM **Privately Held**
Web: www.loftycoffee.com
**SIC: 5812** 2095 Coffee shop; Coffee roasting (except by wholesale grocers)

**(P-17597)**
**M & M BAKERY PRODUCTS INC**
Also Called: Maggiora Baking Co
1900 Garden Tract Rd, Richmond (94801-1219)
PHONE.................................510 235-0274
Dennis Maggiora, *Pr*
Margaret Maggiora, *
James Ghidella, *Stockholder*
Lisa Wilde, *Stockholder*
**EMP:** 80 **EST:** 1985
**SQ FT:** 35,000
**SALES (est):** 9.69MM **Privately Held**
Web: www.maggiorabaking.com
**SIC: 5812** 2051 Eating places; Bread, all types (white, wheat, rye, etc); fresh or frozen

**(P-17598)**
**MARIN BREWING COMPANY INC**
15 Rowland Way, Novato (94945-5001)
PHONE.................................415 461-4677
Brendon Moylan, *Genl Pt*
**EMP:** 18 **EST:** 1988
**SALES (est):** 934.52K **Privately Held**
Web: www.marinbrewing.com
**SIC: 5812** 2082 American restaurant; Beer (alcoholic beverage)

**(P-17599)**
**OGGIS PIZZA & BREWING COMPANY**
Also Called: Oggi's Sports Brewhouse Pizza
305 Encinitas Blvd, Encinitas (92024-3724)
PHONE.................................760 944-8170
Cherock Alcaser, *Pr*
**EMP:** 21 **EST:** 1998
**SQ FT:** 6,500
**SALES (est):** 1.14MM **Privately Held**
Web: www.oggis.com
**SIC: 5812** 2082 Pizzeria, chain; Beer (alcoholic beverage)

**(P-17600)**
**PBF & E LLC**
Also Called: Guelaguetza
3014 W Olympic Blvd, Los Angeles (90006-2516)
PHONE.................................213 427-0340
Bricia Lopez, *Managing Member*
**EMP:** 50 **EST:** 2000
**SALES (est):** 2.19MM **Privately Held**
Web: www.ilovemole.com
**SIC: 5812** 2087 Mexican restaurant; Cocktail mixes, nonalcoholic

**(P-17601)**
**PIE RISE LTD**
Also Called: Marie Callender's Pie Shops
29051 S Western Ave, Rancho Palos Verdes (90275-0806)
PHONE.................................310 832-4559
Jim Louder, *Pt*
John Turner, *Pt*
**EMP:** 50 **EST:** 1971

**SQ FT:** 5,000
**SALES (est):** 1.03MM **Privately Held**
Web: www.mariecallenders.com
**SIC: 5812** 2051 5461 Restaurant, family: chain; Pies, bakery: except frozen; Retail bakeries

**(P-17602)**
**QUETZAL GROUP INC**
Also Called: Quetzal
1234 Polk St, San Francisco (94109-5542)
PHONE.................................415 673-4181
Frederick L Charron, *CEO*
Wayne R Newman, *CFO*
**EMP:** 21 **EST:** 1997
**SQ FT:** 3,000
**SALES (est):** 407.57K **Privately Held**
**SIC: 5812** 2095 5499 5149 Coffee shop; Roasted coffee; Coffee; Cocoa

**(P-17603)**
**RAMISONS INC**
Pizza Press, The
1534 S Harbor Blvd, Anaheim (92802-2312)
PHONE.................................714 323-7134
Kiana Beuler, *Brnch Mgr*
**EMP:** 15
**SALES (corp-wide):** 13.94MM **Privately Held**
Web: www.thepizzapress.com
**SIC: 5812** 2064 Pizzeria, independent; Breakfast bars
PA: Ramisons, Inc.
1734 S Harbor Blvd
714 778-8111

**(P-17604)**
**SANCHEZ BUSINESS INC**
Also Called: Casa Sanchez
250 Napoleon St Ste M, San Francisco (94124-1040)
PHONE.................................415 282-2400
James Sanchez, *Pr*
George Sanchez, *
Martha Sanchez, *
Elizabeth Sanchez, *
**EMP:** 32 **EST:** 1986
**SQ FT:** 2,500
**SALES (est):** 364.13K **Privately Held**
Web: www.casasanchezsf.com
**SIC: 5812** 2032 Mexican restaurant; Tortillas: packaged in cans, jars, etc.

**(P-17605)**
**SNOWSHOE BREWING CO LLC (PA)**
Also Called: Snowshoe Brewing
2050 Hwy 4, Arnold (95223-9420)
P.O. Box 936 (95223-0936)
PHONE.................................209 795-2272
Jeannine Yarnell, *
Gregory Allen Obrien, *
**EMP:** 30 **EST:** 1995
**SQ FT:** 6,000
**SALES (est):** 2.2MM **Privately Held**
Web: www.snowshobrewing.com
**SIC: 5812** 2082 5813 Chicken restaurant; Malt beverages; Drinking places

**(P-17606)**
**ST FRANCIS MARINE CENTER**
Also Called: Ramp Restaurant, The
835 Terry A Francois Blvd, San Francisco (94158-2209)
PHONE.................................415 621-2876
Michael R Denman, *CEO*
Arvind Patel, *
**EMP:** 30 **EST:** 1984
**SQ FT:** 7,000

# 5812 - Eating Places (P-17607)

SALES (est): 3.85MM **Privately Held**
Web: www.sfboatworks.com
SIC: **5812** 4493 3732 7699  American restaurant; Boat yards, storage and incidental repair; Boatbuilding and repairing; Boat repair

### (P-17607)
### SUDWERK PRIVATBRAUEREI HUBSCH
Also Called: Sudwerk
2001 2nd St, Davis (95618-5474)
PHONE.................................530 756-2739
Ron Broward, *Pr*
**EMP:** 65 **EST:** 1989
**SQ FT:** 27,000
SALES (est): 2.28MM **Privately Held**
Web: www.sudwerkbrew.com
SIC: **5812** 5813 2082 5181  American restaurant; Beer garden (drinking places); Malt beverages; Beer and ale

### (P-17608)
### TS ENTERPRISES INC
Also Called: La Quinta Cliff House
78250 Highway 111, La Quinta (92253-2074)
PHONE.................................760 360-5991
David Potesta, *Brnch Mgr*
**EMP:** 23
SALES (corp-wide): 23.29MM **Privately Held**
Web: www.laquintacliffhouse.com
SIC: **5812** 5699 5261 2791  American restaurant; Custom tailor; Lawn and garden supplies; Typesetting
PA: T.S. Enterprises, Inc
   225 W Plaza St Ste 300
   858 720-2380

### (P-17609)
### UNIFIED NUTRIMEALS
5469 Ferguson Dr, Commerce (90022-5118)
PHONE.................................323 923-9335
Shabir Kashyap, *Pr*
Hugo Meza, *
Phil Chavez, *
**EMP:** 85 **EST:** 2005
SALES (est): 2.46MM **Privately Held**
Web: www.unifiednm.com
SIC: **5812** 2099  Contract food services; Ready-to-eat meals, salads, and sandwiches

### (P-17610)
### US DONUTS & YOGURT
11719 Whittier Blvd, Whittier (90601-3939)
PHONE.................................562 695-8867
Chhay Ny, *Owner*
Chhay Ny, *Prin*
**EMP:** 19 **EST:** 1996
SALES (est): 496.97K **Privately Held**
SIC: **5812** 2051  Ice cream stands or dairy bars; Doughnuts, except frozen

### (P-17611)
### VIE DE FRANCE YAMAZAKI INC
Also Called: Vie De France 108
3046 E 50th St, Vernon (90058-2918)
PHONE.................................323 582-1241
Driss Goulhiane, *Brnch Mgr*
**EMP:** 900
Web: www.viedefrance.com
SIC: **5812** 2051  Restaurant, family: chain; Breads, rolls, and buns
HQ: Vie De France Yamazaki, Inc.
   150 Linden Oaks
   Rochester NY 14625

### (P-17612)
### ZEEK MANAGEMENT GROUP LLC
Also Called: Darrow's New Orleans Grill
21720 Avalon Blvd Ste 102-B, Carson (90745-3301)
PHONE.................................424 570-0531
**EMP:** 15 **EST:** 2014
SALES (est): 565.2K **Privately Held**
SIC: **5812** 2035  Ice cream, soft drink and soda fountain stands; Dressings, salad: raw and cooked (except dry mixes)

## 5813 Drinking Places

### (P-17613)
### BELCHING BEAVER BREWERY
Also Called: Rocky Point RTD
1334 Rocky Point Dr, Oceanside (92056-5864)
PHONE.................................760 599-5832
Tom Vogel, *CEO*
▲ **EMP:** 145 **EST:** 2012
SALES (est): 3.65MM **Privately Held**
Web: www.belchingbeaver.com
SIC: **5813** 2082  Bars and lounges; Malt beverages

### (P-17614)
### BORDER X BREWING LLC
2181 Logan Ave, San Diego (92113-2203)
PHONE.................................619 501-0503
David Favela, *Prin*
Martin Favela, *
Marcelino Favela, *
Marcel Favela, *
Mike Fuller, *
**EMP:** 33 **EST:** 2012
SALES (est): 2.38MM **Privately Held**
Web: www.borderxbrewing.com
SIC: **5813** 2082  Bars and lounges; Ale (alcoholic beverage)

### (P-17615)
### CORONADO BREWING COMPANY INC (PA)
170 Orange Ave, Coronado (92118-1409)
PHONE.................................619 437-4452
Ron Chapman, *Pr*
Rick Chapman, *
**EMP:** 50 **EST:** 1996
**SQ FT:** 6,000
SALES (est): 10.5MM **Privately Held**
Web: www.coronadobrewing.com
SIC: **5813** 2082  Bars and lounges; Malt beverages

### (P-17616)
### EEL RIVER BREWING CO INC (PA)
1777 Alamar Way, Fortuna (95540-9548)
PHONE.................................707 725-2739
Ted Vivatson, *Pr*
Margaret Vivatson, *
**EMP:** 22 **EST:** 1995
**SQ FT:** 5,000
SALES (est): 3.64MM **Privately Held**
Web: www.eelriverbrewing.com
SIC: **5813** 5812 2082  Bars and lounges; Family restaurants; Beer (alcoholic beverage)

### (P-17617)
### EEL RIVER BREWING CO INC
Also Called: EEL RIVER BREWING CO INC
600 K Bridge St, Scotia (95565)
P.O. Box 155 (95565-0155)
PHONE.................................707 764-1772
Ted Vivatson, *Brnch Mgr*
**EMP:** 18
Web: www.eelriverbrewing.com
SIC: **5813** 2082  Beer garden (drinking places); Malt beverages
PA: Eel River Brewing Co., Inc.
   1777 Alamar Way

### (P-17618)
### HARLAND BREWING CO LLC
10115 Carroll Canyon Rd, San Diego (92131-1109)
PHONE.................................858 800-4566
Jeffrey Hansson, *Managing Member*
**EMP:** 34 **EST:** 2018
SALES (est): 3.05MM **Privately Held**
Web: www.harlandbeer.com
SIC: **5813** 2082  Bars and lounges; Beer (alcoholic beverage)

### (P-17619)
### HARMONIC BREWING LLC
7 Warriors Way, San Francisco (94158-2253)
PHONE.................................415 872-6817
Edward Gobbo, *Managing Member*
**EMP:** 16 **EST:** 2015
SALES (est): 833.52K **Privately Held**
Web: www.harmonicbrewing.com
SIC: **5813** 2082  Bars and lounges; Malt beverages

### (P-17620)
### KRIBI ENTERPRISES INC
Also Called: Business Management
322 Culver Blvd, Playa Del Rey (90293-7704)
PHONE.................................310 594-1222
Ferdinand Ndedi, *CEO*
**EMP:** 15 **EST:** 2021
SALES (est): 187.88K **Privately Held**
Web: www.kribienterprisesinc.com
SIC: **5813** 7922 5812 8731  Bars and lounges; Entertainment promotion; Restaurant, family: independent; Commercial physical research

### (P-17621)
### MAD RIVER BREWING COMPANY INC
101 Taylor Way, Blue Lake (95525-9724)
P.O. Box 767 (95525-0767)
PHONE.................................707 668-4151
Robert W Smith Junior, *Pr*
James Crowell, *
Charlie Jordan, *
Kelly Elliott, *
▼ **EMP:** 30 **EST:** 1988
**SQ FT:** 11,400
SALES (est): 69.9K **Privately Held**
Web: www.madriverbrewing.com
SIC: **5813** 2082  Bar (drinking places); Beer (alcoholic beverage)

### (P-17622)
### MISSION BREWERY INC
1441 L St, San Diego (92101-8967)
PHONE.................................619 818-7147
Daniel R Selis, *Pr*
▲ **EMP:** 29 **EST:** 2010
SALES (est): 3.88MM **Privately Held**
Web: www.missionbrewery.com
SIC: **5813** 5812 2082  Bars and lounges; Grills (eating places); Malt beverages

### (P-17623)
### SMITH RIVER BREWING COMPANY (PA)
Also Called: Seaquake Brewing
400 Front St, Crescent City (95531)
PHONE.................................707 465-4444
Matthew Wakefield, *CEO*
Kevin D Hartwick, *Pr*
**EMP:** 18 **EST:** 2015
SALES (est): 2.48MM
SALES (corp-wide): 2.48MM **Privately Held**
Web: www.seaquakebrewing.com
SIC: **5813** 2082  Bars and lounges; Ale (alcoholic beverage)

### (P-17624)
### STONE BREWING CO LLC (DH)
Also Called: Stone Brewing Co.
1999 Citracado Pkwy, Escondido (92029-4158)
PHONE.................................760 294-7866
▲ **EMP:** 24 **EST:** 1996
SALES (est): 175.4MM **Privately Held**
Web: www.stonebrewing.com
SIC: **5813** 2082  Bars and lounges; Ale (alcoholic beverage)
HQ: Sapporo Breweries Ltd.
   4-20-1, Ebisu
   Shibuya-Ku TKY 150-0

### (P-17625)
### TAVISTOCK RESTAURANTS LLC
Also Called: Alcatraz Brewing Company
20 City Blvd W Ste R1, Orange (92868-3116)
PHONE.................................714 939-8686
Jarred Creagan, *Mgr*
**EMP:** 150
SALES (corp-wide): 195.01MM **Privately Held**
Web: www.tavistockrestaurantcollection.com
SIC: **5813** 5812 2082  Bars and lounges; American restaurant; Malt beverages
PA: Tavistock Restaurants Llc
   6900 Tvstock Lkes Blvd St
   407 909-7101

## 5921 Liquor Stores

### (P-17626)
### DELEGAT USA INC
555 Mission St Ste 2625, San Francisco (94105-0922)
PHONE.................................415 538-7988
Jakov Nikola Delegat, *Ch Bd*
Alexandria Kimsey, *
▲ **EMP:** 50 **EST:** 2008
SALES (est): 1.46MM **Privately Held**
Web: www.delegat.com
SIC: **5921** 2084  Wine; Wines
HQ: Delegat Limited
   L 6, 10 Viaduct Harbour Avenue
   Auckland AUK 1010

### (P-17627)
### DR HOPS INC
2465 Bermuda Ave, San Leandro (94577)
PHONE.................................510 863-4522
Joshua Rood, *Prin*
**EMP:** 16 **EST:** 2015
SALES (est): 1.18MM **Privately Held**
Web: www.drhops.com
SIC: **5921** 2082  Liquor stores; Beer (alcoholic beverage)

### (P-17628)
### J FILIPPI VINTAGE CO (PA)
12467 Baseline Rd, Rancho Cucamonga (91739-9522)
PHONE.................................909 899-5755
Joseph P Filippi, *Pr*

# PRODUCTS & SERVICES SECTION

## 5944 - Jewelry Stores (P-17648)

Gino L Filippi, *VP*
James Filippi, *Stockholder*
▲ **EMP:** 16 **EST:** 1922
**SQ FT:** 50,000
**SALES (est):** 591.32K
**SALES (corp-wide):** 591.32K **Privately Held**
**SIC: 5921** 2084 Wine; Wines

### (P-17629)
### PEJU PRVNCE WNERY A CAL LTD PR
Also Called: Peju Province Winery
8466 Saint Helena Hwy, Rutherford (94573)
P.O. Box 478 (94573-0478)
**PHONE**..........................800 446-7358
Anthony Peju, *Pt*
Herta Peju, *
▲ **EMP:** 95 **EST:** 1983
**SQ FT:** 50,000
**SALES (est):** 5.46MM **Privately Held**
**Web:** www.peju.com
**SIC: 5921** 2084 Wine; Wines

### (P-17630)
### SUTTER HOME WINERY INC
303 Green Island Rd, Vallejo (94503-9637)
P.O. Box 248 (94574-0248)
**PHONE**..........................707 645-0661
Roger Trinchehero, *Owner*
**EMP:** 30
**SALES (corp-wide):** 188.11MM **Privately Held**
**Web:** www.tfewines.com
**SIC: 5921** 5182 2084 Wine; Wine; Wines
**PA:** Sutter Home Winery, Inc.
100 St Hlena Hwy S
707 963-3104

### (P-17631)
### V SATTUI WINERY
1111 White Ln, Saint Helena (94574-1599)
**PHONE**..........................707 963-7774
Tom Davies, *Pr*
Daryl Sattui, *
Rick Rosenbrand, *
Roumen Gadelev, *
Gordon Rickmart, *
▲ **EMP:** 65 **EST:** 1975
**SQ FT:** 20,000
**SALES (est):** 7.3MM **Privately Held**
**Web:** www.vsattui.com
**SIC: 5921** 5451 5947 5961 Wine; Cheese; Gift shop; General merchandise, mail order

## 5932 Used Merchandise Stores

### (P-17632)
### LABELS-R-US INC
Also Called: Label Shoppe, The
1121 Fullerton Rd, City Of Industry (91748-1232)
**PHONE**..........................626 333-4001
Rudolph Gaytan, *CEO*
**EMP:** 25 **EST:** 1991
**SQ FT:** 65,000
**SALES (est):** 2.58MM **Privately Held**
**Web:** www.labelsrus.com
**SIC: 5932** 2759 Used merchandise stores; Commercial printing, nec

## 5941 Sporting Goods And Bicycle Shops

### (P-17633)
### ECI WATER SKI PRODUCTS INC
Also Called: Skylon
224 Malbert St, Perris (92570-6279)
**PHONE**..........................951 940-9999
Tom Hellwig, *Pr*
Ronna Hellwig, *
**EMP:** 35 **EST:** 1984
**SALES (est):** 2.42MM **Privately Held**
**Web:** www.paradisesocal.com
**SIC: 5941** 3949 Water sport equipment; Water skiing equipment and supplies, except skis

### (P-17634)
### FOOTLOOSE INCORPORATED
Also Called: Footloose Sports
3043 Main St, Mammoth Lakes (93546-6075)
P.O. Box 1929 (93546-1929)
**PHONE**..........................760 934-2400
Silver Chesak, *Pr*
Zachary Yates, *
**EMP:** 35 **EST:** 1979
**SQ FT:** 15,000
**SALES (est):** 2.14MM **Privately Held**
**Web:** www.footloosesports.com
**SIC: 5941** 7999 3949 Skiing equipment; Bicycle rental; Snow skiing equipment and supplies, except skis

### (P-17635)
### PEDEGO LLC (PA)
Also Called: Pedego Electric Bikes
11230 Grace Ave, Fountain Valley (92708-5438)
**PHONE**..........................800 646-8604
Brian Stech, *CEO*
◆ **EMP:** 22 **EST:** 2008
**SALES (est):** 9.11MM **Privately Held**
**Web:** www.pedegoelectricbikes.com
**SIC: 5941** 3751 Bicycle and bicycle parts; Bicycles and related parts

### (P-17636)
### VICTORY ARCHERY
1945 Kellogg Ave, Carlsbad (92008-6582)
**PHONE**..........................866 934-6565
**EMP:** 18 **EST:** 2017
**SALES (est):** 313.8K **Privately Held**
**Web:** www.victoryarchery.com
**SIC: 5941** 3949 Archery supplies; Archery equipment, general

## 5942 Book Stores

### (P-17637)
### BNI PUBLICATIONS INC
Also Called: Building News
990 Park Center Dr Ste E, Vista (92081-8352)
**PHONE**..........................760 734-1113
William Mahoney, *Pr*
William Dennis Mahoney, *
Norman Peterson, *
Vincent Wilhelm, *
**EMP:** 38 **EST:** 1946
**SQ FT:** 2,000
**SALES (est):** 2.32MM **Privately Held**
**Web:** www.bnibooks.com
**SIC: 5942** 2731 8999 Book stores; Book publishing; Lecturing services

### (P-17638)
### KETAB CORPORATION
Also Called: Persian Bks Englsh-Prsian Bks
12701 Van Nuys Blvd Ste H, Pacoima (91331-7289)
**PHONE**..........................310 477-7477
Bijan Khalili, *CEO*
◆ **EMP:** 16 **EST:** 1981
**SQ FT:** 5,000
**SALES (est):** 466.39K **Privately Held**
**Web:** www.ketab.com
**SIC: 5942** 2741 Books, foreign; Directories, nec: publishing only, not printed on site

## 5943 Stationery Stores

### (P-17639)
### EC DESIGN LLC
Also Called: Erin Condren
4860 W 147th St, Hawthorne (90250-6706)
**PHONE**..........................310 220-2362
Eric Howard, *Pr*
**EMP:** 26
**SALES (corp-wide):** 76.59MM **Privately Held**
**Web:** www.erincondren.com
**SIC: 5943** 5049 5632 5331 Stationery stores; School supplies; Apparel accessories; Variety stores
**PA:** Ec Design Llc
201 W Howard Ln
512 676-4200

### (P-17640)
### RUSH BUSINESS FORMS INC
Also Called: Informs
3860 E Eagle Dr Ste A, Anaheim (92807-1706)
**PHONE**..........................714 630-5661
Louis John Katzman, *CEO*
David Flucht, *Pr*
John Katzman, *VP*
**EMP:** 22 **EST:** 1976
**SQ FT:** 10,000
**SALES (est):** 907.73K **Privately Held**
**Web:** rush-business-forms-inc-in-anaheim-ca.cityfos.com
**SIC: 5943** 3993 Office forms and supplies; Signs and advertising specialties

### (P-17641)
### SID-MAR INC
Also Called: Stationery Exchange
23303 La Palma Ave, Yorba Linda (92887-4773)
**PHONE**..........................213 626-8121
Brian Rosenblum, *CEO*
Craig Rosenblum, *
Darren Rosenblum, *
**EMP:** 18 **EST:** 1976
**SQ FT:** 14,000
**SALES (est):** 762.76K **Privately Held**
**Web:** www.bluespaceinteriors.com
**SIC: 5943** 2752 Office forms and supplies; Offset printing

### (P-17642)
### W B MASON CO INC
5911 E Washington Blvd, Commerce (90040-2412)
**PHONE**..........................888 926-2766
**EMP:** 27
**SALES (corp-wide):** 1.01B **Privately Held**
**Web:** www.wbmason.com
**SIC: 5943** 5712 2752 Office forms and supplies; Office furniture; Commercial printing, lithographic
**PA:** W. B. Mason Co., Inc.
59 Centre St
508 586-3434

### (P-17643)
### W B MASON CO INC
4100 Whipple Rd, Union City (94587-1522)
**PHONE**..........................888 926-2766
**EMP:** 27
**SALES (corp-wide):** 1.01B **Privately Held**
**Web:** www.wbmason.com
**SIC: 5943** 5712 2752 Office forms and supplies; Office furniture; Commercial printing, lithographic
**PA:** W. B. Mason Co., Inc.
59 Centre St
508 586-3434

### (P-17644)
### YEBO GROUP LLC
Also Called: Yebo Printing
2652 Dow Ave, Tustin (92780-7208)
**PHONE**..........................949 502-3317
Andrew Tosh, *Managing Member*
▲ **EMP:** 125 **EST:** 2008
**SALES (est):** 3.59MM **Privately Held**
**Web:** www.customboxesandpackaging.com
**SIC: 5943** 2652 3086 2752 Stationery stores; Boxes, newsboard, metal edged: made from purchased materials; Packaging and shipping materials, foamed plastics; Commercial printing, lithographic

## 5944 Jewelry Stores

### (P-17645)
### ENO BRANDS INC
Also Called: Alamo Rings
6481 Global Dr, Cypress (90630-5227)
**PHONE**..........................714 220-1318
Guey Miaw Tsao, *CEO*
Chun Tsao, *CFO*
Kevin Tsao, *Sec*
**EMP:** 24 **EST:** 2005
**SQ FT:** 5,000
**SALES (est):** 4.87MM **Privately Held**
**Web:** www.enobrands.com
**SIC: 5944** 5094 7389 5632 Jewelry stores; Jewelry; Design services; Costume jewelry

### (P-17646)
### JEWELERS TOUCH
2535 E Imperial Hwy, Brea (92821-6131)
**PHONE**..........................714 579-1616
Ken Rutz, *Pt*
Jana Rutz, *Pt*
**EMP:** 20 **EST:** 1992
**SALES (est):** 2.24MM **Privately Held**
**Web:** www.jewelerstouch.com
**SIC: 5944** 3915 Jewelry, precious stones and precious metals; Lapidary work and diamond cutting and polishing

### (P-17647)
### L & L DIAMOND CO
Also Called: Bony Levy
1801 Beverly Blvd, Los Angeles (90057-2501)
**PHONE**..........................213 622-5752
Bony Levy, *CEO*
**EMP:** 17 **EST:** 1986
**SALES (est):** 2.26MM **Privately Held**
**SIC: 5944** 3479 Jewelry stores; Engraving jewelry, silverware, or metal

### (P-17648)
### LUGANO DIAMONDS & JEWELRY INC (HQ)
545 Newport Center Dr, Newport Beach (92660-6937)
**PHONE**..........................949 625-7722
Mordechai Ferder, *CEO*
Joshua Gaynor, *
Idit Ferder, *
Stuart Winston, *CMO**
Scott Sussman, *
**EMP:** 76 **EST:** 2004

# 5944 - Jewelry Stores (P-17649)

SALES (est): 5.15MM **Publicly Held**
Web: www.luganodiamonds.com
SIC: **5944** 3911 Jewelry, precious stones and precious metals; Jewelry apparel
PA: Compass Diversified Holdings
    301 Riverside Ave Fl 2

### (P-17649)
### M & G JEWELERS INC
10823 Edison Ct, Rancho Cucamonga (91730-3868)
PHONE.................909 989-2929
Juan Guevara, *Pr*
Michael Insalago, *
EMP: 68 EST: 1991
SQ FT: 8,432
SALES (est): 9.97MM **Privately Held**
Web: www.mandgjewelers.com
SIC: **5944** 3911 7631 Jewelry, precious stones and precious metals; Jewelry, precious metal; Watch repair

### (P-17650)
### MONEX DEPOSIT A CAL LTD PARTNR
Also Called: Monex
4910 Birch St, Newport Beach (92660-8100)
PHONE.................800 444-8317
Mike Carabini, *Ltd Pt*
Louis E Carabini, *Pt*
EMP: 100 EST: 1987
SALES (est): 3.13MM **Privately Held**
SIC: **5944** 6722 3324 Jewelry, precious stones and precious metals; Management investment, open-end; Steel investment foundries

### (P-17651)
### S A TOP-U CORPORATION
1794 Illinois Ave, Perris (92571-9371)
PHONE.................951 916-4025
Hans Werner Wendel, *Ch*
Pia Wendel, *
◆ EMP: 27 EST: 1984
SQ FT: 20,000
SALES (est): 833.53K **Privately Held**
Web: www.rdit.com
SIC: **5944** 3993 Clock and watch stores; Signs and advertising specialties

## 5945 Hobby, Toy, And Game Shops

### (P-17652)
### SAILING INNOVATION (US) INC
17870 Castleton St Ste 220, City Of Industry (91748-1755)
PHONE.................626 965-6665
Steven Goldsmith, *CEO*
Valen Tong, *CFO*
Kiran Smith, *CMO*
EMP: 3187 EST: 2014
SALES (est): 380.18K **Privately Held**
SIC: **5945** 3651 Toys and games; Audio electronic systems

## 5946 Camera And Photographic Supply Stores

### (P-17653)
### FILMTOOLS INC (PA)
Also Called: Moviola Digital
1015 N Hollywood Way, Burbank (91505-2546)
PHONE.................323 467-1116
Joseph Paskal, *Pr*
Randy Paskal, *
Carl Nelson, *
Dana Newman, *
EMP: 50 EST: 1923
SQ FT: 30,000
SALES (est): 23.05MM
SALES (corp-wide): 23.05MM **Privately Held**
Web: www.filmtools.com
SIC: **5946** 5043 7819 3861 Photographic supplies; Motion picture equipment; Editing services, motion picture production; Photographic equipment and supplies

## 5947 Gift, Novelty, And Souvenir Shop

### (P-17654)
### ALIN PARTY SUPPLY CO
6493 Magnolia Ave, Riverside (92506-2409)
PHONE.................951 682-7441
Sherry Bauer, *Mgr*
EMP: 30
Web: www.alinpartysupply.com
SIC: **5947** 7389 2759 Party favors; Balloons, novelty and toy; Invitation and stationery printing and engraving
PA: Alin Party Supply Co.
    4139 Woodruff Ave

### (P-17655)
### CYBERBASKET INC
Also Called: Lucky You
2926 Main St, San Diego (92113-3730)
PHONE.................619 450-6700
Deborah A Roberts, *CEO*
EMP: 15 EST: 1997
SQ FT: 3,000
SALES (est): 1.92MM **Privately Held**
Web: www.luckyyougifts.com
SIC: **5947** 2052 5461 Gift shop; Cookies and crackers; Cookies

### (P-17656)
### VESUKI INC
Also Called: V R Gifts
1350 W Lambert Rd Ste A, Brea (92821-2886)
PHONE.................562 245-4000
Suru Manek, *Pr*
Kishorlal Manek, *VP*
▲ EMP: 18 EST: 1987
SALES (est): 2.38MM **Privately Held**
Web: www.vesuki.com
SIC: **5947** 3499 5199 5088 Greeting cards; Magnets, permanent: metallic; Gifts and novelties; Aeronautical equipment and supplies

## 5949 Sewing, Needlework, And Piece Goods

### (P-17657)
### ROBERT KAUFMAN CO INC (PA)
Also Called: Robert Kaufman Fabrics
129 W 132nd St, Los Angeles (90061-1619)
P.O. Box 59266 (90059-0266)
PHONE.................310 538-3482
Kenneth Kaufman, *CEO*
Harvey Kaufman, *
Alvin Kaufman, *
Joseph Kaufman, *
◆ EMP: 114 EST: 1942
SQ FT: 24,000
SALES (est): 59.89MM
SALES (corp-wide): 59.89MM **Privately Held**
Web: www.robertkaufman.com
SIC: **5949** 2299 Fabric stores piece goods; Linen fabrics

## 5961 Catalog And Mail-order Houses

### (P-17658)
### ADAPTIVE TECH GROUP INC
Also Called: Atm Fly-Ware
1635 E Burnett St, Signal Hill (90755-3603)
PHONE.................562 424-1100
Paul W Allen, *Pr*
▲ EMP: 20 EST: 1985
SALES (est): 4.64MM **Privately Held**
Web: www.adaptivetechnologiesgroup.com
SIC: **5961** 3651 Electronic kits and parts, mail order; Household audio equipment

### (P-17659)
### AL GLOBAL CORPORATION (HQ)
Also Called: Youngvity Essntial Lf Sciences
2400 Boswell Rd, Chula Vista (91914-3553)
PHONE.................619 934-3980
Stephan Wallach, *CEO*
William Andreoli, *Pr*
Michelle Wallach, *COO*
David Briskie, *CFO*
◆ EMP: 43 EST: 1996
SQ FT: 70,000
SALES (est): 18.66MM
SALES (corp-wide): 147.44MM **Publicly Held**
Web: www.youngevity.com
SIC: **5961** 2043 Catalog and mail-order houses; Cereal breakfast foods
PA: Youngevity International, Inc.
    2400 Boswell Rd
    619 934-3980

### (P-17660)
### BU RU LLC
Also Called: Shop Buru
826 E 3rd St, Los Angeles (90013-1820)
PHONE.................424 316-2878
Morgan Hutchinson, *Managing Member*
Brutt Hutchinson, *Managing Member*
EMP: 17 EST: 2013
SALES (est): 1.45MM **Privately Held**
SIC: **5961** 5621 2339 Electronic shopping; Women's clothing stores; Women's and misses' athletic clothing and sportswear

### (P-17661)
### CHRIS ALSTON CHASSISWORKS INC
11375 Sunrise Park Dr Ste 800, Rancho Cordova (95742-7209)
PHONE.................916 388-0288
EMP: 40 EST: 1987
SALES (est): 4.71MM **Privately Held**
Web: www.cachassisworks.com
SIC: **5961** 3711 7532 Automotive supplies and equipment, mail order; Chassis, motor vehicle; Body shop, automotive

### (P-17662)
### COLD STEEL INC (PA)
6060 Nicolle St, Ventura (93003-7600)
P.O. Box 535189 (75053-5189)
PHONE.................805 650-8481
Lynn C Thompson, *Pr*
▼ EMP: 18 EST: 1980
SQ FT: 7,000
SALES (est): 4.98MM
SALES (corp-wide): 4.98MM **Privately Held**
SIC: **5961** 3421 Catalog sales; Knives: butchers', hunting, pocket, etc.

### (P-17663)
### DR HAROLD KATZ LLC
Also Called: Therabreath
5802 Willoughby Ave, Los Angeles (90038-3012)
PHONE.................323 993-8320
▲ EMP: 16 EST: 2002
SQ FT: 1,800
SALES (est): 2.5MM **Privately Held**
Web: www.therabreath.com
SIC: **5961** 2844 Catalog and mail-order houses; Mouthwashes

### (P-17664)
### GOLD MINE NATURAL FOOD COMPANY
13200 Danielson St Ste A-1, Poway (92064-8823)
PHONE.................858 537-9830
Jean M Richardson, *CEO*
◆ EMP: 15 EST: 1985
SQ FT: 10,000
SALES (est): 2.18MM **Privately Held**
Web: www.goldminenaturalfood.com
SIC: **5961** 5141 5023 2099 Cheese, mail order; Groceries, general line; Kitchenware; Food preparations, nec

### (P-17665)
### HADLEY FRUIT ORCHARDS INC (PA)
48980 Seminole Dr, Cabazon (92230-2167)
P.O. Box 495 (92230-0495)
PHONE.................951 849-5255
Gerald Bench, *Pr*
John Taylor, *
Dennis Flint, *
James Taylor, *
Fred Bond, *
EMP: 35 EST: 1931
SALES (est): 1.01MM
SALES (corp-wide): 1.01MM **Privately Held**
Web: www.hadleyfruitorchards.com
SIC: **5961** 2034 5499 5441 Food, mail order; Fruits, dried or dehydrated, except freeze-dried; Dried fruit; Nuts

### (P-17666)
### LUTHIERS MERCANTILE INTL INC
Also Called: LMI
7975 Cameron Dr Ste 1600, Windsor (95492-8574)
PHONE.................707 433-1823
Duane Waterman, *Pr*
Natalie Swango, *CFO*
▲ EMP: 18 EST: 1994
SQ FT: 10,000
SALES (est): 923.46K **Privately Held**
Web: www.lmii.com
SIC: **5961** 2499 7389 Mail order house, nec; Carved and turned wood; Hand tool designers

### (P-17667)
### MELTON INTL TACKLE INC
1375 S State College Blvd, Anaheim (92806-5728)
PHONE.................714 978-9192
Tracy M Melton, *Pr*
◆ EMP: 28 EST: 1993
SALES (est): 2.47MM **Privately Held**
Web: www.meltontackle.com

## PRODUCTS & SERVICES SECTION

### 5999 - Miscellaneous Retail Stores, Nec (P-17687)

SIC: **5961** 5199 3949 5091  Fishing, hunting and camping equipment and supplies: by mail; Advertising specialties; Lures, fishing: artificial; Boat accessories and parts

**(P-17668)**
**MERQBIZ LLC**
300 Continental Blvd Ste 640, El Segundo (90245-5042)
PHONE.....................855 637-7249
John Fox, *
**EMP:** 35 **EST:** 2016
**SALES (est):** 2.29MM **Privately Held**
Web: www.voith.com
SIC: **5961** 3554  Electronic shopping; Paper industries machinery

**(P-17669)**
**PASSWORD ENTERPRISE INC**
3200 E 29th St, Long Beach (90806-2321)
P.O. Box 90729 (90809-0729)
PHONE.....................562 988-8889
Sophead Naing, *CEO*
Adam Chu, *
**EMP:** 25 **EST:** 2013
**SQ FT:** 32,000
**SALES (est):** 2.45MM **Privately Held**
Web: www.passwordmm.com
SIC: **5961** 3369  Automotive supplies and equipment, mail order; Aerospace castings, nonferrous: except aluminum

**(P-17670)**
**QUANTUM NETWORKS LLC**
3412 Garfield Ave, Commerce (90040-3104)
PHONE.....................212 993-5899
Jonathan Goldman, *Pr*
Eytan Wiener, *
**EMP:** 30 **EST:** 2008
**SALES (est):** 2.57MM **Privately Held**
Web: www.quantumnetworks.com
SIC: **5961** 5731 5065 3651  Computer equipment and electronics, mail order; Consumer electronic equipment, nec; Video equipment, electronic; Household audio and video equipment

**(P-17671)**
**QUILT IN A DAY INC**
1955 Diamond St, San Marcos (92078-5122)
PHONE.....................760 591-0929
TOLL FREE: 800
Eleanor A Burns, *CEO*
▲ **EMP:** 37 **EST:** 1979
**SQ FT:** 9,000
**SALES (est):** 4.45MM **Privately Held**
Web: www.quiltinaday.com
SIC: **5961** 5949 5192 2731  Books, mail order (except book clubs); Quilting materials and supplies; Books; Book publishing

**(P-17672)**
**RNBS CORPORATION**
Also Called: Rugged Notebooks
725 S Paseo Prado, Anaheim (92807-4949)
PHONE.....................714 998-1828
Alan Shad, *Pr*
**EMP:** 20 **EST:** 2000
**SALES (est):** 2.21MM **Privately Held**
Web: www.ruggednotebooks.com
SIC: **5961** 3571  Computers and peripheral equipment, mail order; Electronic computers

**(P-17673)**
**ROAD RUNNER SPORTS INC (PA)**
Also Called: Road Runner Sports
5549 Copley Dr, San Diego (92111-7904)
PHONE.....................858 974-4200
Michael Gotfredson, *CEO*
Scott Campbell, *
▲ **EMP:** 80 **EST:** 1987
**SQ FT:** 88,000
**SALES (est):** 136.68MM
**SALES (corp-wide):** 136.68MM **Privately Held**
Web: www.roadrunnersports.com
SIC: **5961** 3949 5661  Mail order house, nec; Sporting and athletic goods, nec; Footwear, athletic

**(P-17674)**
**RUGGABLE LLC**
17809 S Broadway, Gardena (90248-3541)
PHONE.....................310 295-0098
Nathan Baldwin, *CEO*
**EMP:** 378 **EST:** 2017
**SALES (est):** 51.95MM **Privately Held**
Web: www.ruggable.com
SIC: **5961** 2273  Electronic shopping; Rugs, hand and machine made

**(P-17675)**
**SPENCER FORREST INC**
Also Called: Toppik
11777 San Vicente Blvd Ste 650, Los Angeles (90049-5011)
▲ **EMP:** 25 **EST:** 1981
**SQ FT:** 3,000
**SALES (est):** 1.76MM **Privately Held**
Web: www.toppik.com
SIC: **5961** 3999  Cosmetics and perfumes, mail order; Hair and hair-based products

**(P-17676)**
**WESTATES INC**
Also Called: Westates Automotive Promotions
6800 Orangethorpe Ave Ste H, Buena Park (90620-1366)
PHONE.....................714 523-7600
Dale W Becker, *Pr*
Doug Pohl, *
Natalie Pohl, *
**EMP:** 29 **EST:** 1978
**SQ FT:** 12,900
**SALES (est):** 3.3MM **Privately Held**
Web: www.westates.net
SIC: **5961** 2752  Mail order house, nec; Offset printing

**(P-17677)**
**WORD FOR TODAY**
3232 W Macarthur Blvd # A, Santa Ana (92704-6802)
PHONE.....................714 825-9673
Charles W Smith, *Pr*
Jeff Smith, *
**EMP:** 39 **EST:** 1978
**SQ FT:** 19,000
**SALES (est):** 165.95K
**SALES (corp-wide):** 31.18MM **Privately Held**
Web: shop.twft.com
SIC: **5961** 2731 3652  Record and/or tape (music or video) club, mail order; Books, publishing only; Prerecorded records and tapes
PA: Calvary Chapel Of Costa Mesa 3800 S Fairview St 714 979-4422

### 5963 Direct Selling Establishments

**(P-17678)**
**BTG TEXTILES INC**
Also Called: Btg Textiles
710 Union St, Montebello (90640-6521)
PHONE.....................323 586-9488
Mohammed Alam, *CEO*
Yed Karim Raza, *
Nawarin Hasib, *
▲ **EMP:** 24 **EST:** 2011
**SALES (est):** 1.39MM **Privately Held**
Web: www.btgtextiles.com
SIC: **5963** 2299  Direct selling establishments ; Towels and towelings, linen and linen-and-cotton mixtures

**(P-17679)**
**ENAGIC USA INC (PA)**
4115 Spencer St, Torrance (90503-2419)
PHONE.....................310 542-7700
Hironari Oshiro, *Pr*
◆ **EMP:** 66 **EST:** 2003
**SALES (est):** 24.29MM
**SALES (corp-wide):** 24.29MM **Privately Held**
Web: www.enagic.com
SIC: **5963** 2086  Bottled water delivery; Mineral water, carbonated: packaged in cans, bottles, etc.

**(P-17680)**
**PERFORMANCE WATER PRODUCTS INC**
6902 Aragon Cir, Buena Park (90620-1118)
PHONE.....................714 736-0137
Kristopher Mecca, *Pr*
Kari Mecca, *Sec*
John Mecca, *VP*
Mike Mecca, *Dir*
Mat Mecca, *VP*
**EMP:** 17 **EST:** 1992
**SQ FT:** 51,000
**SALES (est):** 4.13MM **Privately Held**
Web: www.performancewater.com
SIC: **5963** 3589  Bottled water delivery; Water purification equipment, household type

**(P-17681)**
**STRATA USA LLC**
333 City Blvd W Fl 17, Orange (92868-5905)
PHONE.....................888 878-7282
**EMP:** 25 **EST:** 2014
**SALES (est):** 425.62K **Privately Held**
Web: www.strata-usa.com
SIC: **5963** 0175 5122 5047  Direct sales, telemarketing; Deciduous tree fruits; Medical rubber goods; Hospital equipment and furniture

### 5993 Tobacco Stores And Stands

**(P-17682)**
**VAPE CRAFT LLC**
2100 Palomar Airport Rd Ste 210, Carlsbad (92011-4405)
PHONE.....................760 295-7484
Ben Osmanson, *Managing Member*
**EMP:** 20 **EST:** 2019
**SALES (est):** 930.4K **Privately Held**
Web: www.vapecraftinc.com
SIC: **5993** 3999 5194 ; Cigarette and cigar products and accessories; Cigars

### 5994 News Dealers And Newsstands

**(P-17683)**
**HI-DESERT PUBLISHING COMPANY**
Also Called: Big Bear Grizzly & Big Bear Lf
42007 Fox Farm Rd Ste 3b, Big Bear Lake (92315-2192)
PHONE.....................909 866-3456
Gerald Wright, *Mgr*
**EMP:** 41
**SALES (corp-wide):** 21.91MM **Privately Held**
Web: www.hidesertstar.com
SIC: **5994** 2711  News dealers and newsstands; Newspapers
HQ: Hi-Desert Publishing Company 56445 29 Palms Hwy Yucca Valley CA 92284

### 5995 Optical Goods Stores

**(P-17684)**
**GUNNAR OPTIKS LLC**
2236 Rutherford Rd Ste 123, Carlsbad (92008-8836)
PHONE.....................858 769-2500
Joe Croft, *CEO*
◆ **EMP:** 20 **EST:** 2006
**SALES (est):** 4.26MM **Privately Held**
Web: www.gunnar.com
SIC: **5995** 3851  Optical goods stores; Ophthalmic goods

**(P-17685)**
**SOLVARI CORP**
Also Called: 7eye By Panoptx
2060 S Haven Ave, Ontario (91761-0735)
PHONE.....................909 509-8228
**EMP:** 22 **EST:** 2005
**SALES (est):** 223K **Privately Held**
Web: www.7eye.com
SIC: **5995** 3851  Eyeglasses, prescription; Contact lenses

### 5999 Miscellaneous Retail Stores, Nec

**(P-17686)**
**AAA FLAG & BANNER MFG CO INC (PA)**
Also Called: AAA Flag & Banner
8937 National Blvd, Los Angeles (90034-3307)
PHONE.....................310 836-3200
Howard S Furst, *Pr*
Susan Furst, *
▲ **EMP:** 150 **EST:** 1971
**SQ FT:** 4,000
**SALES (est):** 52.47MM
**SALES (corp-wide):** 52.47MM **Privately Held**
Web: www.a3visual.com
SIC: **5999** 2399  Flags; Banners, pennants, and flags

**(P-17687)**
**ALIGNMED INC**
Also Called: Alignmed
2691 Richter Ave, Irvine (92606-5125)
PHONE.....................866 987-5433
William Schultz, *Pr*
Eliana Schultz, *CFO*
▲ **EMP:** 18 **EST:** 2001
**SALES (est):** 4.35MM **Privately Held**

## 5999 - Miscellaneous Retail Stores, Nec (P-17688)

Web: www.alignmed.com
SIC: 5999 3842 Orthopedic and prosthesis applications; Braces, orthopedic

**(P-17688)**
**ARBONNE INTERNATIONAL LLC (DH)**
21 Technology Dr, Irvine (92618)
PHONE..................949 770-2610
Tyler Whitehead, CEO
Bernadette Chala, *
Amy Humfleet, *
Astrid Van-ruymbeke, CFO
Jen Orlando, GROWTH Innovation*
▲ EMP: 25 EST: 1984
SQ FT: 37,000
SALES (est): 89.85MM Privately Held
Web: www.arbonne.com
SIC: 5999 5961 5499 2834 Cosmetics; Cosmetics and perfumes, mail order; Vitamin food stores; Vitamin preparations
HQ: Groupe Rocher Operations
La Croix Des Archers
La Gacilly BRE 56200
299297474

**(P-17689)**
**ARBONNE INTERNATIONAL DIST INC**
9400 Jeronimo Rd, Irvine (92618-1907)
PHONE..................800 272-6663
Tyler Whitehead, CEO
EMP: 200 EST: 2006
SALES (est): 6.54MM Privately Held
SIC: 5999 5961 5499 2834 Cosmetics; Cosmetics and perfumes, mail order; Vitamin food stores; Vitamin preparations
HQ: Arbonne International, Llc
21 Technology Dr
Irvine CA 92618
949 770-2610

**(P-17690)**
**AT BATTERY COMPANY INC**
Also Called: Atbatt.com
28381 Constellation Rd Unit A, Valencia (91355)
PHONE..................661 775-2020
Young Lee, CEO
◆ EMP: 20 EST: 2000
SALES (est): 2.3MM Privately Held
Web: www.atbatt.com
SIC: 5999 5063 3691 Electronic parts and equipment; Batteries; Alkaline cell storage batteries

**(P-17691)**
**CALDESSO LLC**
Also Called: Therm Core Products
439 S Stoddard Ave, San Bernardino (92401-2025)
PHONE..................909 888-2882
Andrew Cameron, CEO
P Anthony Panico, *
▲ EMP: 65 EST: 2010
SQ FT: 23,500
SALES (est): 3.35MM Privately Held
SIC: 5999 3567 Hot tub and spa chemicals, equipment, and supplies; Heating units and devices, industrial: electric

**(P-17692)**
**CDM CORP**
Also Called: Rozge Cosmoceutical
7922 Haskell Ave, Van Nuys (91405)
P.O. Box P.O. Box 572643 (91357-2643)
PHONE..................818 787-4002
Mary Arshadi, Pr
▲ EMP: 15 EST: 2009
SQ FT: 30,000
SALES (est): 1.87MM Privately Held
Web: www.blak.com
SIC: 5999 2844 Toiletries, cosmetics, and perfumes; Cosmetic preparations

**(P-17693)**
**CINEMA SECRETS INC**
6639 Odessa Ave, Van Nuys (91406)
PHONE..................818 846-0579
Barbara Stein, Pr
Maurice Stein, *
Michael Stein, *
Daniel Stein, *
▲ EMP: 60 EST: 1985
SALES (est): 9.52MM Privately Held
Web: www.cinemasecrets.com
SIC: 5999 5699 2389 5122 Cosmetics; Costumes, masquerade or theatrical; Costumes; Cosmetics

**(P-17694)**
**CMC RESCUE INC**
Also Called: CMC
6740 Cortona Dr, Goleta (93117-5574)
PHONE..................805 562-9120
James A Frank, Ch
Richard M Phillips, *
Elizabeth Henry, *
▲ EMP: 65 EST: 1978
SQ FT: 23,000
SALES (est): 16.6MM Privately Held
Web: www.cmcpro.com
SIC: 5999 5099 3842 8299 Safety supplies and equipment; Safety equipment and supplies; Personal safety equipment; Educational services

**(P-17695)**
**COOKS COMMUNICATIONS CORP**
160 N Broadway St, Fresno (93701-1506)
PHONE..................559 233-8818
Robert D Cook, Pr
Peggy Cook, *
EMP: 27 EST: 1947
SQ FT: 16,000
SALES (est): 7.34MM Privately Held
Web: www.cookscom.com
SIC: 5999 7629 4812 5065 Telephone equipment and systems; Telephone set repair; Radiotelephone communication; Electronic parts and equipment, nec

**(P-17696)**
**COSMETIC LABORATORIES OF AMERICA LLC**
Also Called: Cosmetic Laboratories America
20245 Sunburst St, Chatsworth (91311-6219)
PHONE..................818 717-6140
▲ EMP: 400
SIC: 5999 5122 2844 2833 Cosmetics; Cosmetics; Perfumes, cosmetics and other toilet preparations; Medicinals and botanicals

**(P-17697)**
**COSMETIX WEST (PA)**
2305 Utah Ave, El Segundo (90245-4818)
PHONE..................310 726-3080
Ronald P Chavers, Pr
▲ EMP: 20 EST: 1993
SQ FT: 10,000
SALES (est): 15.91MM
SALES (corp-wide): 15.91MM Privately Held
Web: www.cosmetixwest.com
SIC: 5999 2844 Cosmetics; Bath salts

**(P-17698)**
**COUNTRY CONNECTION INC (PA)**
2805 Richter Ave, Oroville (95966-5917)
P.O. Box 1115 (95916-1115)
PHONE..................530 589-5176
Marc Hillier, Pr
◆ EMP: 15 EST: 2007
SQ FT: 20,000
SALES (est): 2.26MM Privately Held
Web: www.legacycooperages.com
SIC: 5999 2449 Alcoholic beverage making equipment and supplies; Planters and window boxes, wood

**(P-17699)**
**COWAY USA INC**
Also Called: Woongjin Coway USA Inc.
4221 Wilshire Blvd Ste 210, Los Angeles (90010-3501)
PHONE..................213 486-1600
Hong Rae Gim, Pr
Hosuk Yoon, *
▲ EMP: 39 EST: 2006
SQ FT: 4,200
SALES (est): 10.99MM Privately Held
Web: www.coway-usa.com
SIC: 5999 3564 Water purification equipment; Air purification equipment
PA: Coway Co., Ltd.
136-23 Yugumagoksa-Ro, Yugu-Eup

**(P-17700)**
**CREATION NETWORKS INC**
1001 Shary Cir Ste 1, Concord (94518-2419)
PHONE..................925 446-4332
Lisa Benson, Managing Member
Eric Benson, CEO
EMP: 19 EST: 2006
SALES (est): 540.24K Privately Held
Web: www.creationnetworks.net
SIC: 5999 1731 5065 5099 Audio-visual equipment and supplies; Computerized controls installation; Video equipment, electronic; Video and audio equipment

**(P-17701)**
**ELB US INC**
Also Called: Elb Global
4777 Bennett Dr Ste A, Livermore (94551-4860)
PHONE..................925 400-6175
Damian Bolton, Pr
▲ EMP: 42 EST: 2012
SALES (est): 42.53MM Privately Held
Web: www.elbglobal.com
SIC: 5999 2599 3651 8742 Audio-visual equipment and supplies; Factory furniture and fixtures; Audio electronic systems; Construction project management consultant

**(P-17702)**
**EVOQUA WATER TECHNOLOGIES LLC**
1441 E Washington Blvd, Los Angeles (90021-3039)
PHONE..................213 748-8511
Gary Cappeline, Interim Chief Executive Officer
EMP: 27
Web: www.evoqua.com
SIC: 5999 2899 Water purification equipment; Chemical preparations, nec
HQ: Evoqua Water Technologies Llc
210 6th Ave Ste 3300
Pittsburgh PA 15222
724 772-0044

**(P-17703)**
**EXCELLIGENCE LEARNING CORP (PA)**
20 Ryan Ranch Rd Ste 200, Monterey (93940-6439)
PHONE..................831 333-2000
Anupam Martins, CEO
Kelly Crampton, Prin
Dipak Golechha, Pr
Judith Mcguinn, COO
Kevin Kiper, Dir
▲ EMP: 50 EST: 2000
SQ FT: 27,000
SALES (est): 416.71MM
SALES (corp-wide): 416.71MM Privately Held
Web: www.excelligence.com
SIC: 5999 3944 Education aids, devices and supplies; Craft and hobby kits and sets

**(P-17704)**
**GEORGIA-PACIFIC LLC**
Also Called: Georgia-Pacific
15500 Valley View Ave, La Mirada (90638-5230)
P.O. Box 981953 (79998-1953)
PHONE..................562 926-8888
Sam Shah, Prin
EMP: 28
SALES (corp-wide): 64.37B Privately Held
Web: www.gp.com
SIC: 5999 5113 2653 3275 Alcoholic beverage making equipment and supplies; Corrugated and solid fiber boxes; Corrugated and solid fiber boxes; Gypsum products
HQ: Georgia-Pacific Llc
133 Peachtree St Nw
Atlanta GA 30303
404 652-4000

**(P-17705)**
**GRANDMA LUCYS LLC**
30432 Esperanza, Rcho Sta Marg (92688-2144)
PHONE..................949 206-8547
Eric Shook, Pt
Eric Shook, Managing Member
EMP: 19 EST: 1999
SALES (est): 2.21MM Privately Held
Web: www.grandmalucys.com
SIC: 5999 2047 Pets and pet supplies; Dog and cat food

**(P-17706)**
**GUARDIAN FIRE SERVICE INC**
Also Called: Guardian Fire & Safety
8248 W Doe Ave, Visalia (93291-9263)
PHONE..................559 651-0919
John Maly, Pr
EMP: 16 EST: 2010
SALES (est): 2.3MM Privately Held
Web: www.guardiansafety.com
SIC: 5999 1711 3842 Fire extinguishers; Fire sprinkler system installation; Personal safety equipment

**(P-17707)**
**HOWK WELL & EQUIPMENT CO INC**
Also Called: Howk Systems
1825 Yosemite Blvd, Modesto (95354-2905)
PHONE..................209 529-4110
Thomas R Weimer, Pr
EMP: 32 EST: 1985
SQ FT: 15,000
SALES (est): 4.78MM Privately Held
Web: www.howksystems.com

## PRODUCTS & SERVICES SECTION
### 6162 - Mortgage Bankers And Correspondents (P-17727)

SIC: 5999 1623 7699 5051 Farm equipment and supplies; Pumping station construction; Pumps and pumping equipment repair; Pipe and tubing, steel

**(P-17708)**
**INTELLIGENT BEAUTY LLC**
Also Called: Iq Cosmetics
2301 Rosecrans Ave Ste 5000, El Segundo (90245-4966)
PHONE..............................310 683-0940
▲ EMP: 550
Web: www.ibinc.com
SIC: 5999 2844 Cosmetics; Cosmetic preparations

**(P-17709)**
**JAFRA COSMETICS INTL INC (DH)**
Also Called: Jafra Cosmetics
1 Baxter Way Ste 150, Westlake Village (91362-3819)
PHONE..............................805 449-3000
Karalee Mora, *CEO*
Mauro Schnaidman, *
Stacy Wolf, *
Mark Funaki, *
James Christl, *
◆ EMP: 52 EST: 1956
SALES (est): 51.94MM Privately Held
Web: www.jafra.com
SIC: 5999 2844 Cosmetics; Perfumes, cosmetics and other toilet preparations
HQ: Betterware De Mexico, S.A.P.I. De C.V.
Cruce Carretera Gdl-Ameca-Huaxtla Km. 5
El Arenal JAL 45350

**(P-17710)**
**JON DAVLER INC**
9440 Gidley St, Temple City (91780-4211)
PHONE..............................626 941-6558
David J Sheen, *Pr*
Christina Yang, *
◆ EMP: 24 EST: 2001
SQ FT: 12,000
SALES (est): 3.04MM Privately Held
Web: www.jondavler.com
SIC: 5999 2844 Cosmetics; Perfumes, cosmetics and other toilet preparations

**(P-17711)**
**MADISON REED INC**
Also Called: Madison Reed Color Bar III
548 Market St, San Francisco (94104-5401)
PHONE..............................415 225-0872
Amy Erriatt, *CEO*
Eric Hutchinson, *
Heidi Doros, *CMO*
Jose Zuniga, *
Angela Jaskolski, *CRO*
▲ EMP: 31 EST: 2013
SALES (est): 16.86MM Privately Held
Web: www.madison-reed.com
SIC: 5999 2844 Hair care products; Hair coloring preparations

**(P-17712)**
**NATIONAL ADVANCED ENDOSCOPY DE**
22134 Sherman Way, Canoga Park (91303-1136)
PHONE..............................818 227-2720
Fawzia Dabiri, *CEO*
John Dawoodjee, *
EMP: 25 EST: 1994
SQ FT: 16,000
SALES (est): 2.64MM Privately Held
Web: www.aed.md

SIC: 5999 3841 5047 7629 Medical apparatus and supplies; Surgical and medical instruments; Medical and hospital equipment; Electrical repair shops

**(P-17713)**
**NICE NORTH AMERICA LLC (DH)**
5919 Sea Otter Pl Ste 100, Carlsbad (92010-6750)
P.O. Box 9003 (92008)
PHONE..............................760 438-7000
Emanuel Bertolini, *CEO*
Darren Learmonth, *
Senthoor Navaratnam, *Chief Product Officer*
◆ EMP: 200 EST: 1961
SQ FT: 32,000
SALES (est): 40.1MM
SALES (corp-wide): 865.12MM Privately Held
Web: na.niceforyou.com
SIC: 5999 3699 Alarm and safety equipment stores; Security control equipment and systems
HQ: Nice Spa
Via Callalta 1
Oderzo TV 31046

**(P-17714)**
**NINE STARS GROUP (USA) INC**
Also Called: Ninestars
1775 S Business Pkwy, Ontario (91761-8528)
PHONE..............................866 978-2778
Shiping Wang, *CEO*
▲ EMP: 15 EST: 2005
SALES (est): 2.51MM Privately Held
Web: www.ninestarsusa.com
SIC: 5999 3089 3999 Cleaning equipment and supplies; Tissue dispensers, plastics; Soap dispensers

**(P-17715)**
**OFFICIA IMAGING INC (PA)**
5636 Ruffin Rd, San Diego (92123-1317)
PHONE..............................858 348-0831
Todd Rogers, *Pr*
Cary Carlton, *
EMP: 24 EST: 1963
SALES (est): 9.97MM
SALES (corp-wide): 9.97MM Privately Held
Web: www.office1.com
SIC: 5999 5044 3861 Photocopy machines; Photocopy machines; Printing equipment, photographic

**(P-17716)**
**PETCO ANIMAL SUPS STORES INC**
Also Called: Petco
8161 Beverly Blvd, Los Angeles (90048-4514)
PHONE..............................323 852-1370
EMP: 15
SALES (corp-wide): 311.64K Privately Held
Web: stores.petco.com
SIC: 5999 5199 2048 Pets and pet supplies; Pet supplies; Prepared feeds, nec
HQ: Petco Animal Supplies Stores, Inc.
10850 Via Frontera
San Diego CA 92127

**(P-17717)**
**PNK ENTERPRISES INC**
Also Called: Anderson Trophy Company
12901 Saticoy St, North Hollywood (91605-3508)
PHONE..............................818 765-3770

Wesley Starnes, *Pr*
EMP: 21 EST: 1965
SALES (est): 788.18K Privately Held
Web: www.andersontrophy.com
SIC: 5999 3499 Trophies and plaques; Trophies, metal, except silver

**(P-17718)**
**RELIEF-MART INC**
Also Called: Selectabed
28505 Canwood St Ste C, Agoura Hills (91301-3207)
PHONE..............................805 379-4300
Rick T Swartzburg, *CEO*
Jim Swartzburg, *
▲ EMP: 42 EST: 2001
SQ FT: 36,000
SALES (est): 500K Privately Held
Web: www.reliefmart.com
SIC: 5999 2515 2392 Medical apparatus and supplies; Mattresses and foundations; Cushions and pillows

**(P-17719)**
**SCOPE ORTHTICS PROSTHETICS INC (DH)**
Also Called: Scope
7720 Cardinal Ct, San Diego (92123-3333)
PHONE..............................858 292-7448
Loren Saxton, *Pr*
Tony Di Santo, *
Kel Bergmann, *
EMP: 30 EST: 1982
SQ FT: 7,400
SALES (est): 9.35MM
SALES (corp-wide): 1.12B Privately Held
Web: www.scop.net
SIC: 5999 3842 Orthopedic and prosthesis applications; Prosthetic appliances
HQ: Hanger Prosthetics & Orthotics, Inc.
10910 Domain Dr Ste 300
Austin TX 78758
512 777-3800

**(P-17720)**
**SECURITY 20/20 INC**
Also Called: Security Pro USA
8543 Venice Blvd, Los Angeles (90034-2548)
PHONE..............................310 475-7780
Amnon Even, *CEO*
Galia Even, *Pr*
EMP: 15 EST: 1986
SQ FT: 2,600
SALES (est): 1.91MM Privately Held
Web: www.securityprousa.com
SIC: 5999 8748 3482 3812 Safety supplies and equipment; Safety training service; Small arms ammunition; Radar systems and equipment

**(P-17721)**
**SEXY HAIR CONCEPTS LLC**
21551 Prairie St, Chatsworth (91311-5831)
PHONE..............................818 435-0800
◆ EMP: 20 EST: 2001
SALES (est): 4.32MM
SALES (corp-wide): 23.39B Privately Held
Web: www.sexyhair.com
SIC: 5999 8331 3999 Hair care products; Skill training center; Hair and hair-based products
PA: Henkel Ag & Co. Kgaa
Henkelstr. 67
2117970

**(P-17722)**
**SMARTLABS INC**
Also Called: Smarthomepro
1621 Alton Pkwy Ste 100, Irvine (92606-4846)

PHONE..............................800 762-7846
Brian Taylor, *Interim Chief Executive Officer*
Rob Lilleness, *
◆ EMP: 85 EST: 1993
SQ FT: 59,230
SALES (est): 17.34MM Privately Held
Web: www.smartlabsinc.com
SIC: 5999 3822 Electronic parts and equipment; Environmental controls

**(P-17723)**
**SOUTHWEST BOULDER & STONE INC (PA)**
5002 2nd St, Fallbrook (92028-9790)
PHONE..............................760 451-3333
TOLL FREE: 800
Michelle S Mcleod, *Pr*
Michael O Mcleod, *Sec*
▲ EMP: 45 EST: 1996
SQ FT: 4,500
SALES (est): 26.38MM Privately Held
Web: www.southwestboulder.com
SIC: 5999 1422 Rock and stone specimens; Crushed and broken limestone

**(P-17724)**
**TANGERINE EXPRESS INC**
Also Called: Tangerine Office Systems
4870 Adohr Ln A, Camarillo (93012-8508)
PHONE..............................702 260-6650
▲ EMP: 20
SIC: 5999 2865 Photocopy machines; Color lakes or toners

**(P-17725)**
**TERADEK LLC**
8 Mason, Irvine (92618-2705)
PHONE..............................949 743-5780
EMP: 16 EST: 2008
SQ FT: 1,500
SALES (est): 14.91MM
SALES (corp-wide): 383.4MM Privately Held
Web: www.teradek.com
SIC: 5999 3663 5065 5047 Electronic parts and equipment; Television broadcasting and communications equipment; Video equipment, electronic; Medical equipment and supplies
PA: Videndum Plc
Bridge House
208 332-4600

**(P-17726)**
**WILSON TROPHY CO CALIFORNIA**
Also Called: Awards By Wilson
1724 Frienza Ave, Sacramento (95815-2710)
PHONE..............................916 927-9733
Gerald Loomis, *Pr*
Michelle Loomis, *VP*
▲ EMP: 17 EST: 1971
SQ FT: 12,500
SALES (est): 2.36MM Privately Held
Web: www.wilsontrophy.com
SIC: 5999 5094 3993 2396 Trophies and plaques; Trophies; Signs and advertising specialties; Automotive and apparel trimmings

---
### 6162 Mortgage Bankers And Correspondents
---

**(P-17727)**
**DECISION READY SOLUTIONS INC**
Also Called: Decision Ready

# 6163 - Loan Brokers (P-17728)

## PRODUCTS & SERVICES SECTION

400 Spectrum Center Dr Ste 2050, Irvine (92618-5024)
PHONE.................................949 400-1126
Ravi Ramanathan, *Pr*
Dan Mahler, *CSO\**
Claudia Sanchez, *\**
Tom Schmidt, *\**
**EMP:** 50 **EST:** 2011
**SALES (est):** 6MM **Privately Held**
Web: www.decisionreadysolutions.com
**SIC: 6162** 7371 7372 Mortgage bankers; Computer software systems analysis and design, custom; Business oriented computer software

## 6163 Loan Brokers

**(P-17728)**
**ROOSTIFY INC**
180 Howard St Ste 100, San Francisco (94105-6153)
PHONE.................................888 908-2470
Rajesh Bhat, *CEO*
Eric Amblard, *CFO*
Frank Gelbart, *CRO*
Syed Ijaz, *CCO*
**EMP:** 40 **EST:** 2016
**SALES (est):** 24.25MM
**SALES (corp-wide):** 1.64B **Privately Held**
Web: www.roostify.com
**SIC: 6163** 7372 Mortgage brokers arranging for loans, using money of others; Application computer software
**HQ:** Corelogic, Inc.
40 Pacifica Ste 900
Irvine CA 92618
866 873-3651

## 6211 Security Brokers And Dealers

**(P-17729)**
**GENSTAR CAPITAL LLC (PA)**
4 Embarcadero Ctr Ste 1900, San Francisco (94111-4191)
PHONE.................................415 834-2350
Richard Paterson, *Managing Member*
J Ryan Clark, *\**
Anthony J Salewski, *\**
Robert S Rutledge, *\**
▲ **EMP:** 35 **EST:** 1991
**SQ FT:** 10,000
**SALES (est):** 1.11B **Privately Held**
Web: www.gencap.com
**SIC: 6211** 3647 Investment firm, general brokerage; Vehicular lighting equipment

**(P-17730)**
**GORES GROUP LLC (PA)**
9800 Wilshire Blvd, Beverly Hills (90212-1804)
PHONE.................................310 209-3010
Alec Gores, *Managing Member*
Joseph Page, *\**
Vance Diggens, *\**
Frank Stefanik, *\**
**EMP:** 60 **EST:** 2003
**SALES (est):** 1.81B
**SALES (corp-wide):** 1.81B **Privately Held**
Web: www.gores.com
**SIC: 6211** 7372 5734 Investment firm, general brokerage; Prepackaged software; Computer software and accessories

## 6221 Commodity Contracts Brokers, Dealers

**(P-17731)**
**CABALLERO & SONS INC**
Also Called: Beyond Meat and Company
5753 E Santa Ana Canyon Rd Ste G-380, Anaheim (92807-3230)
PHONE.................................562 368-1644
Perpetua Duque-hata, *Pr*
Nathaniel Caballero, *\**
Marivet Caballero, *\**
**EMP:** 25 **EST:** 2017
**SQ FT:** 500
**SALES (est):** 7MM **Privately Held**
**SIC: 6221** 2392 5141 5149 Commodity traders, contracts; Cushions and pillows; Food brokers; Beverages, except coffee and tea

**(P-17732)**
**INVAPHARM INC (PA)**
1320 W Mission Blvd, Ontario (91762-4786)
PHONE.................................909 757-1818
Manu Patolia, *CEO*
Kalpesh Bodar, *Dir*
Nirmala Patolia, *Dir*
Mita Bodar, *Sec*
**EMP:** 26 **EST:** 2015
**SQ FT:** 60,000
**SALES (est):** 11.1MM
**SALES (corp-wide):** 11.1MM **Privately Held**
Web: www.invapharm.com
**SIC: 6221** 2023 Commodity brokers, contracts; Dietary supplements, dairy and non-dairy based

## 6282 Investment Advice

**(P-17733)**
**MARLIN EQUITY PARTNERS LLC (PA)**
1301 Manhattan Ave, Hermosa Beach (90254-3654)
PHONE.................................310 364-0100
David Mcgovern, *Managing Member*
Nick Kaiser, *\**
Peter Spasov, *\**
George Kase, *\**
Steve Johnson, *\**
**EMP:** 80 **EST:** 2005
**SALES (est):** 690.66MM **Privately Held**
Web: www.marlinequity.com
**SIC: 6282** 3661 Investment advisory service; Telephones and telephone apparatus

**(P-17734)**
**TARRANT CAPITAL IP LLC (PA)**
Also Called: Tpg Growth
345 California St Ste 3300, San Francisco (94104-2640)
PHONE.................................415 743-1500
**EMP:** 5490 **EST:** 2007
**SALES (est):** 91.69MM **Privately Held**
Web: www.tpg.com
**SIC: 6282** 7372 Manager of mutual funds, contract or fee basis; Prepackaged software

**(P-17735)**
**WEALTHFRONT CORPORATION**
261 Hamilton Ave Ste 10, Palo Alto (94301-2534)
PHONE.................................650 249-4258
David Fortunato, *CEO*
Andrew Rachleff, *\**
Alan Imberman, *\**
Julius Leiman-carbia, *Sec*
**EMP:** 25 **EST:** 2007
**SQ FT:** 3,000
**SALES (est):** 9.68MM **Privately Held**
Web: www.wealthfront.com
**SIC: 6282** 7372 Investment advisory service; Prepackaged software

## 6324 Hospital And Medical Service Plans

**(P-17736)**
**ALIGNMENT HEALTHCARE INC (PA)**
Also Called: ALIGNMENT HEALTH
1100 W Town And Country Rd Ste 1600, Orange (92868-4698)
PHONE.................................844 310-2247
John Kao, *CEO*
Joseph Konowiecki, *Ch Bd*
Thomas Freeman, *CFO*
Dinesh Kumar, *CMO*
Richard Cross, *Sr VP*
**EMP:** 71 **EST:** 2013
**SQ FT:** 89,000
**SALES (est):** 1.82B
**SALES (corp-wide):** 1.82B **Publicly Held**
Web: www.alignmenthealth.com
**SIC: 6324** 7372 Hospital and medical service plans; Prepackaged software

## 6411 Insurance Agents, Brokers, And Service

**(P-17737)**
**COLLECTIVEHEALTH INC (PA)**
Also Called: Collective Health
45 Fremont St Ste 1200, San Francisco (94105-2204)
PHONE.................................844 265-3288
Ali Diab, *CEO*
**EMP:** 172 **EST:** 2013
**SALES (est):** 61.59MM
**SALES (corp-wide):** 61.59MM **Privately Held**
Web: www.collectivehealth.com
**SIC: 6411** 7379 7372 Medical insurance claim processing, contract or fee basis; Online services technology consultants; Business oriented computer software

**(P-17738)**
**RUSS MIKE FINANCIAL TRAINING**
Also Called: Mike Russ School
8322 Clairemont Mesa Blvd, San Diego (92111-1317)
PHONE.................................800 724-5661
Michael Mitchel, *CFO*
Jessie Davis, *COO*
**EMP:** 15 **EST:** 1979
**SALES (est):** 522.62K **Privately Held**
Web: www.mikeruss.org
**SIC: 6411** 2621 Education services, insurance; Parchment, securities, and bank note papers

## 6512 Nonresidential Building Operators

**(P-17739)**
**THRIFTY OIL CO (PA)**
13116 Imperial Hwy, Santa Fe Springs (90670-4817)
PHONE.................................562 921-3581
Ted Orden, *Pr*
Dori Barber, *\**
Perry Freidrich, *\**
**EMP:** 18 **EST:** 1959
**SQ FT:** 1,624
**SALES (est):** 10.25MM
**SALES (corp-wide):** 10.25MM **Privately Held**
**SIC: 6512** 2911 6552 Nonresidential building operators; Petroleum refining; Subdividers and developers, nec

## 6531 Real Estate Agents And Managers

**(P-17740)**
**1370 REALTY CORP**
14545 Friar St, Van Nuys (91411-2397)
PHONE.................................818 817-0092
Kambiz Merabi, *Pr*
**EMP:** 17 **EST:** 1995
**SQ FT:** 16,400
**SALES (est):** 427.01K **Privately Held**
Web: www.1370realty.com
**SIC: 6531** 2451 Real estate agents and managers; Mobile buildings: for commercial use

**(P-17741)**
**CARLTON SENIOR LIVING INC (PA)**
Also Called: Intercontinental Services
4071 Port Chicago Hwy Ste 130, Concord (94520-1163)
PHONE.................................925 338-2434
Thomas Mcdonald, *Ch Bd*
Philp Scott, *\**
Ruby Mac Donald, *\**
**EMP:** 35 **EST:** 1982
**SALES (est):** 13.86MM
**SALES (corp-wide):** 13.86MM **Privately Held**
Web: www.carltonseniorliving.com
**SIC: 6531** 3732 6552 Real estate managers; Yachts, building and repairing; Subdividers and developers, nec

**(P-17742)**
**GOLDEN RAIN FOUNDATION (PA)**
Also Called: Rossmoor
1001 Golden Rain Rd, Walnut Creek (94595-2412)
P.O. Box 2070 (94595-0070)
PHONE.................................925 988-7700
Stephen Adams, *CEO*
**EMP:** 75 **EST:** 1963
**SQ FT:** 5,000
**SALES (est):** 24.44MM
**SALES (corp-wide):** 24.44MM **Privately Held**
Web: www.rossmoor.com
**SIC: 6531** 8011 2711 7997 Real estate managers; Offices and clinics of medical doctors; Newspapers; Golf club, membership

## 6719 Holding Companies, Nec

**(P-17743)**
**ASP HENRY HOLDINGS INC**
999 N Pacific Coast Hwy Ste 800, El Segundo (90245-2716)
PHONE.................................310 955-9200
Frank Ready, *CEO*
**EMP:** 600 **EST:** 2016
**SALES (corp-wide):** 4.59B **Publicly Held**

# PRODUCTS & SERVICES SECTION

## 6799 - Investors, Nec (P-17761)

SIC: **6719** 2952 Investment holding companies, except banks; Roof cement: asphalt, fibrous, or plastic
PA: Carlisle Companies Incorporated
16430 N Scttsdale Rd Ste
480 781-5000

### (P-17744)
### COADNA HOLDINGS INC
1020 Stewart Dr, Sunnyvale (94085-3914)
PHONE.............................408 736-1100
Jim Yuan, *Pr*
Irene Yum, *
Oliver Lu, *Chief Commercial Officer**
**EMP:** 80 **EST:** 2004
**SALES (corp-wide):** 4.71B **Publicly Held**
Web: www.coadna.com
SIC: **6719** 3661 Investment holding companies, except banks; Fiber optics communications equipment
PA: Coherent Corp.
375 Saxonburg Blvd
724 352-4455

### (P-17745)
### DESSER HOLDING COMPANY LLC (HQ)
Also Called: Desser Tire & Rubber Co.
6900 W Acco St, Montebello (90640-5435)
P.O. Box 1028 (90640-1028)
PHONE.............................323 721-4900
Christopher Lawler, *Ch*
Steven D Chlavin, *
Joseph Heinmiller, *
**EMP:** 30 **EST:** 2014
**SALES (est):** 40.92MM
**SALES (corp-wide):** 860.49MM **Publicly Held**
Web: www.desser.com
SIC: **6719** 3011 3691 Investment holding companies, except banks; Airplane tires, pneumatic; Batteries, rechargeable
PA: Vse Corporation
3361 Enterprise Way
950 430-6600

### (P-17746)
### GCM HOLDING CORPORATION
1350 Atlantic St, Union City (94587-2004)
PHONE.............................510 475-0404
Seamus Meagher, *Pr*
**EMP:** 300 **EST:** 2014
Web: www.gogcm.com
SIC: **6719** 8711 3444 3541 Investment holding companies, except banks; Machine tool design; Sheet metalwork; Machine tools, metal cutting type
PA: Avista Capital Holdings, L.P.
65 E 55th St Fl 18

### (P-17747)
### MILESTONE HOLDCO INC
901 Mariners Island Blvd, San Mateo (94404-1592)
PHONE.............................650 376-2300
Steve Lucas, *CEO*
**EMP:** 949 **EST:** 2016
**SALES (corp-wide):** 19.41B **Publicly Held**
SIC: **6719** 7371 7372 Investment holding companies, except banks; Custom computer programming services; Prepackaged software
HQ: Milestone Topco, Inc.
901 Mariners Island Blvd
San Mateo CA 94404
650 376-2300

### (P-17748)
### WILBUR CURTIS CO INC
6913 Acco St, Montebello (90640-5403)
PHONE.............................800 421-6150
Ray Peden, *CEO*
Michael A Curtis, *Ex VP*
Norman Fujitaki, *CFO*
Joe Laws, *COO*
Shubham Kumar, *Finance*
◆ **EMP:** 280 **EST:** 1941
**SQ FT:** 175,000
**SALES (corp-wide):** 2.67MM **Privately Held**
Web: www.wilburcurtis.com
SIC: **6719** 3589 Investment holding companies, except banks; Coffee brewing equipment
HQ: Groupe Seb Retailing
112 Che Du Moulin Carron
Ecully 69130

## 6722 Management Investment, Open-ended

### (P-17749)
### CLEARLAKE CAPITAL GROUP LP (PA)
233 Wilshire Blvd Ste 800, Santa Monica (90401-1207)
PHONE.............................310 400-8800
Behdad Eghbali, *Mng Pt*
Jose Feliciano, *Pt*
Paul Huber, *Pt*
Prashant Mehrotra, *Pt*
**EMP:** 258 **EST:** 2006
**SALES (est):** 3.89B **Privately Held**
Web: www.clearlake.com
SIC: **6722** 3694 3714 5013 Management investment, open-end; Engine electrical equipment; Motor vehicle parts and accessories; Automotive engines and engine parts

## 6726 Investment Offices, Nec

### (P-17750)
### CENTURY PK CAPITL PARTNERS LLC (PA)
880 Apollo St Ste 300, El Segundo (90245-4726)
PHONE.............................310 867-2210
Martin A Sarafa, *Managing Member*
**EMP:** 160 **EST:** 2004
**SALES (est):** 37.52MM **Privately Held**
Web: www.centuryparkcapital.com
SIC: **6726** 3569 3086 3448 Management investment funds, closed-end; Firefighting and related equipment; Carpet and rug cushions, foamed plastics; Ramps, prefabricated metal

## 6794 Patent Owners And Lessors

### (P-17751)
### ADVANCED FRESH CONCEPTS CORP (PA)
Also Called: A F C
19205 S Laurel Park Rd, Rancho Dominguez (90220)
PHONE.............................310 604-3630
Jeffery Seiler, *CEO*
◆ **EMP:** 25 **EST:** 1986
**SQ FT:** 60,000
**SALES (est):** 48.2MM
**SALES (corp-wide):** 48.2MM **Privately Held**
Web: www.afcsushi.com

SIC: **6794** 2032 2092 5141 Patent owners and lessors; Chinese foods, nec: packaged in cans, jars, etc.; Fresh or frozen packaged fish; Food brokers

## 6799 Investors, Nec

### (P-17752)
### AQM ACQUISITION CORP
Also Called: Finna Group
9567 Arrow Rte Ste E, Rancho Cucamonga (91730-4550)
PHONE.............................909 941-7776
Patrick Youssi, *Pr*
**EMP:** 15 **EST:** 2015
**SALES (est):** 2.04MM **Privately Held**
Web: www.finnasensors.com
SIC: **6799** 3829 Investors, nec; Measuring and controlling devices, nec

### (P-17753)
### FRANCISCO PARTNERS MGT LP (PA)
Also Called: Francisco Partners
1 Letterman Dr Ste 410, San Francisco (94129-1495)
PHONE.............................415 418-2900
Dipanjan Deb, *CEO*
David Golob, *CIO*
Tom Ludwig, *COO*
**EMP:** 177 **EST:** 1999
**SQ FT:** 15,000
**SALES (est):** 1.34B
**SALES (corp-wide):** 1.34B **Privately Held**
Web: www.franciscopartners.com
SIC: **6799** 7372 Venture capital companies; Application computer software

### (P-17754)
### GOLDEN GATE PRIVATE EQUITY INC (PA)
Also Called: Golden Gate Capital
1 Embarcadero Ctr Fl 39, San Francisco (94111-3714)
PHONE.............................415 983-2706
David Dominik, *Dir*
Jesse Rogers, *Dir*
Prescott Ashe, *Dir*
Ken Diekroeger, *Dir*
Stefan Kaluzny, *Dir*
**EMP:** 46 **EST:** 2000
**SQ FT:** 7,800
**SALES (est):** 81.93MM
**SALES (corp-wide):** 81.93MM **Privately Held**
Web: www.goldengatecap.com
SIC: **6799** 3534 Investors, nec; Elevators and moving stairways

### (P-17755)
### KDR HOLDING INC (PA)
47448 Fremont Blvd, Fremont (94538-6503)
PHONE.............................510 230-2777
James F Brear, *Pr*
**EMP:** 18 **EST:** 2015
**SALES (est):** 7.18MM
**SALES (corp-wide):** 7.18MM **Privately Held**
SIC: **6799** 7372 Investors, nec; Application computer software

### (P-17756)
### KLEINER PRKINS CFELD BYERS LLC (PA)
Also Called: Kpcb
2750 Sand Hill Rd, Menlo Park (94025-7020)
PHONE.............................650 233-2750
Frank Caufield, *Partner Emeritus*
John Doerr, *Ch*
Thomas J Perkins, *Genl Pt*
James Lally, *Genl Pt*
Joseph Lacob, *Genl Pt*
**EMP:** 25 **EST:** 1984
**SQ FT:** 11,000
**SALES (est):** 15.48MM
**SALES (corp-wide):** 15.48MM **Privately Held**
Web: www.kleinerperkins.com
SIC: **6799** 3691 Venture capital companies; Storage batteries

### (P-17757)
### MATSUSHITA INTERNATIONAL CORP (PA)
1141 Via Callejon, San Clemente (92673-6230)
PHONE.............................949 498-1000
Hiroyuki Matsushita, *Pr*
**EMP:** 80 **EST:** 1990
**SALES (est):** 21.11MM **Privately Held**
SIC: **6799** 3711 3714 Real estate investors, except property operators; Automobile assembly, including specialty automobiles; Motor vehicle parts and accessories

### (P-17758)
### TRANSOM CAPITAL GROUP LLC (PA)
10990 Wilshire Blvd Ste 440, Los Angeles (90024-3950)
PHONE.............................424 293-2818
Ken Firtel, *Managing Member*
**EMP:** 47 **EST:** 2007
**SALES (est):** 1.32B
**SALES (corp-wide):** 1.32B **Privately Held**
Web: www.transomcap.com
SIC: **6799** 5112 5943 3951 Investors, nec; Pens and/or pencils; Writing supplies; Fountain pens and fountain pen desk sets

### (P-17759)
### TRUE INVESTMENTS LLC (PA)
2260 University Dr, Newport Beach (92660-3319)
PHONE.............................949 258-9720
Alan True, *CEO*
**EMP:** 24 **EST:** 2012
**SALES (est):** 4.94MM
**SALES (corp-wide):** 4.94MM **Privately Held**
Web: www.twilatrue.com
SIC: **6799** 7372 Investors, nec; Application computer software

### (P-17760)
### TRUE INVESTMENTS LLC
6535 Caballero Blvd Unit B, Buena Park (90620-8106)
PHONE.............................949 258-9720
**EMP:** 26
**SALES (corp-wide):** 1.54MM **Privately Held**
Web: www.truefamilyenterprises.com
SIC: **6799** 7372 Investors, nec; Application computer software
PA: True Investments, Llc
2260 University Dr
949 258-9720

### (P-17761)
### XILINX INC (HQ)
Also Called: Xilinx
2100 Logic Dr, San Jose (95124-3400)
PHONE.............................408 559-7778
Lisa T Su, *Pr*
Devinder Kumar, *Ex VP*
Mark D Papermaster, *Ex VP*

# 7011 - Hotels And Motels (P-17762)

Darren Grasby, *CSO*
Harry A Wolin, *Corporate Secretary*
**EMP:** 1057 **EST:** 1990
**SQ FT:** 588,000
**SALES (est):** 3.15B
**SALES (corp-wide):** 22.68B **Publicly Held**
**Web:** www.xilinx.com
**SIC:** 6799 3674 7372  Venture capital companies; Microcircuits, integrated (semiconductor); Application computer software
**PA:** Advanced Micro Devices, Inc.
2485 Augustine Dr
408 749-4000

## 7011 Hotels And Motels

**(P-17762)**
**SUMMERWOOD WINERY & INN INC**
2175 Arbor Rd, Paso Robles (93446-8620)
**PHONE**..............................805 227-1365
Mark Uhalley, *Pr*
▲ **EMP:** 33 **EST:** 2002
**SALES (est):** 2.11MM **Privately Held**
**Web:** www.summerwoodwine.com
**SIC:** 7011 2084  Bed and breakfast inn; Wines

## 7033 Trailer Parks And Campsites

**(P-17763)**
**BURLINGAME INDUSTRIES INC (PA)**
Also Called: Eagle Roofing Products
3546 N Riverside Ave, Rialto (92377)
**PHONE**..............................909 355-7000
Robert C Burlingame, *Ch Bd*
Roger D Thompson, *Vice Chairman\**
Kevin C Burlingame, *
Seamus P Burlingame, *
William L Robinson, *
▲ **EMP:** 100 **EST:** 1969
**SQ FT:** 100,000
**SALES (est):** 54.45MM
**SALES (corp-wide):** 54.45MM **Privately Held**
**Web:** www.eagleroofing.com
**SIC:** 7033 0971 3559 3259  Campgrounds; Hunting preserve; Tile making machines; Roofing tile, clay

## 7212 Garment Pressing And Cleaners' Agents

**(P-17764)**
**FCSI INC**
Also Called: Alex's Dry Cleaning Valet
628 Lindaro St, San Rafael (94901-3936)
**PHONE**..............................415 457-8000
Alex Najafi, *Pr*
**EMP:** 29 **EST:** 2010
**SALES (est):** 3.6MM **Privately Held**
**Web:** www.alexdryclean.net
**SIC:** 7212 7372  Pickup station, laundry and drycleaning; Application computer software

**(P-17765)**
**PARK AVENUE CLEANERS INC**
2529 N Tracy Blvd, Tracy (95376-1768)
**PHONE**..............................209 832-3706
Gurtej Brar, *Pr*
**EMP:** 38 **EST:** 2007
**SALES (est):** 493.24K **Privately Held**
**Web:** www.parkavenuecleaners.co

**SIC:** 7212 3582  Laundry and drycleaner agents; Commercial laundry equipment

## 7213 Linen Supply

**(P-17766)**
**GBS LINENS INC (PA)**
Also Called: GBS Party Linens
305 N Muller St, Anaheim (92801-5445)
**PHONE**..............................714 778-6448
Pravin Mody, *Pr*
Sujata Mody, *
Ameer P Mody, *
Sudha Mody, *
▲ **EMP:** 100 **EST:** 1962
**SQ FT:** 57,000
**SALES (est):** 9.13MM
**SALES (corp-wide):** 9.13MM **Privately Held**
**Web:** www.gbslinens.com
**SIC:** 7213 2392 7211 5023  Linen supply; Household furnishings, nec; Power laundries, family and commercial; Homefurnishings

**(P-17767)**
**SOCAL AUTO SUPPLY INC**
21418 Osborne St, Canoga Park (91304-1520)
**PHONE**..............................302 360-8373
**EMP:** 46
**SIC:** 7213 2676  Towel supply; Towels, napkins, and tissue paper products
**PA:** Socal Auto Supply Inc
16192 Postal Hwy

## 7216 Drycleaning Plants, Except Rugs

**(P-17768)**
**AMERICAN WINDOW COVERING INC**
825 Williamson Ave, Fullerton (92832-2133)
P.O. Box 3518 (92834-3518)
**PHONE**..............................714 879-3880
Leland B Daniels, *Pr*
**EMP:** 18 **EST:** 1963
**SQ FT:** 2,400
**SALES (est):** 938.7K **Privately Held**
**Web:** www.awc-cwc.com
**SIC:** 7216 2391 5023  Drapery, curtain drycleaning; Draperies, plastic and textile: from purchased materials; Draperies

**(P-17769)**
**RICHARD C THURSTON**
Also Called: Eldon Drapery Cleaners
360 N Magnolia Ave, El Cajon (92020-3908)
**PHONE**..............................619 440-6165
**TOLL FREE:** 800
Richard Thurston, *Owner*
**EMP:** 15 **EST:** 1966
**SQ FT:** 3,000
**SALES (est):** 899.85K **Privately Held**
**Web:** www.eldonandcrystalcleaners.com
**SIC:** 7216 2211  Drapery, curtain drycleaning; Draperies and drapery fabrics, cotton

## 7218 Industrial Launderers

**(P-17770)**
**MAJOR GLOVES & SAFETY INC**
250 Turnbull Canyon Rd, City Of Industry (91745-1007)
**PHONE**..............................626 330-8022

Shu Wen Cheng, *CEO*
Kun Shan Ho, *CFO*
Kai Wen Cheng, *Sec*
Ken Ho, *Prin*
Flora Cheng, *Prin*
▲ **EMP:** 21 **EST:** 2005
**SQ FT:** 38,000
**SALES (est):** 1.05MM **Privately Held**
**Web:** www.mggloves.com
**SIC:** 7218 5099 5999 3842  Safety glove supply; Safety equipment and supplies; Safety supplies and equipment; Gloves, safety

## 7221 Photographic Studios, Portrait

**(P-17771)**
**CORBIS IMAGES LLC (PA)**
Also Called: Corbis
6060 Center Dr Ste 1000, Los Angeles (90045-8842)
**PHONE**..............................323 602-5700
**EMP:** 17 **EST:** 2005
**SALES (est):** 962.02K
**SALES (corp-wide):** 962.02K **Privately Held**
**Web:** www.corbisentertainment.com
**SIC:** 7221 7372  Photographic studios, portrait; Prepackaged software

## 7231 Beauty Shops

**(P-17772)**
**OGLEBY SISTERS SOAP**
1804 Garnet Ave, San Diego (92109-3352)
**PHONE**..............................212 518-1172
Linda Moncrief, *CEO*
**EMP:** 21 **EST:** 1985
**SALES (est):** 161.59K **Privately Held**
**Web:** www.oglebysisterssoap.com
**SIC:** 7231 2844  Beauty shops; Cosmetic preparations

## 7299 Miscellaneous Personal Services

**(P-17773)**
**JET FLEET INTERNATIONAL CORP**
Also Called: J F I
2370 Westwood Blvd Ste K, Los Angeles (90064-2150)
**PHONE**..............................310 440-3820
Finn Moller, *Pr*
Arcy Lariz, *
**EMP:** 28 **EST:** 2003
**SALES (est):** 1.06MM **Privately Held**
**Web:** www.jetfleetinternational.com
**SIC:** 7299 7363 2911 6361  Buyers' club; Pilot service, aviation; Jet fuels; Title insurance

**(P-17774)**
**LEAL VINEYARDS INC**
1978 Willow Springs Rd, Morgan Hill (95037-9426)
**PHONE**..............................408 778-1978
Geraldine Mercante, *Mgr*
**EMP:** 19 **EST:** 2015
**SALES (est):** 225.99K **Privately Held**
**Web:** www.liveloveleal.com
**SIC:** 7299 2084  Banquet hall facilities; Brandy and brandy spirits

**(P-17775)**
**SAFFRON & SAGE LLC**
2555 State St Ste 101, San Diego (92101-1315)
**PHONE**..............................619 933-2340
Cristin D Smith, *Managing Member*
**EMP:** 15 **EST:** 2014
**SALES (est):** 987.49K **Privately Held**
**Web:** www.saffronsageliving.com
**SIC:** 7299 8049 8011 2844  Massage parlor; Acupuncturist; Psychiatrists and psychoanalysts; Perfumes, cosmetics and other toilet preparations

**(P-17776)**
**WESTERN COSTUME CO (HQ)**
11041 Vanowen St, North Hollywood (91605-6314)
**PHONE**..............................818 760-0900
Eddie Marks, *Pr*
**EMP:** 48 **EST:** 1912
**SQ FT:** 150,000
**SALES (est):** 4.76MM **Privately Held**
**Web:** www.westerncostume.com
**SIC:** 7299 2389  Costume rental; Costumes
**PA:** Ahs Trinity Group, Inc.
11041 Vanowen St

## 7311 Advertising Agencies

**(P-17777)**
**COLOR AD INC**
18601 S Santa Fe Ave, Compton (90221-5901)
**PHONE**..............................310 632-5500
Daryl Oldencamp, *Pr*
**EMP:** 20 **EST:** 1994
**SQ FT:** 33,000
**SALES (est):** 2.13MM **Privately Held**
**Web:** www.gocolorad.com
**SIC:** 7311 2752  Advertising agencies; Commercial printing, lithographic

**(P-17778)**
**DG2 WORLDWIDE GROUP LLC**
Also Called: Dg2
12655 W Jefferson Blvd 4th Fl, Los Angeles (90066-7008)
**PHONE**..............................310 809-0899
Michael Lay, *Managing Member*
**EMP:** 22 **EST:** 2017
**SQ FT:** 10,000
**SALES (est):** 942.53K **Privately Held**
**SIC:** 7311 3577 8748  Advertising consultant; Data conversion equipment, media-to-media: computer; Agricultural consultant

**(P-17779)**
**KITARA MEDIA CORP (HQ)**
2010 Main St Ste 900, Irvine (92614-7215)
**EMP:** 15 **EST:** 2005
**SQ FT:** 12,235
**SALES (est):** 1.88MM
**SALES (corp-wide):** 16.91MM **Publicly Held**
**SIC:** 7311 7372  Advertising agencies; Prepackaged software
**PA:** Propel Media, Inc.
18565 Jamboree Rd Ste 200
949 251-0640

**(P-17780)**
**MARSHALL ADVERTISING AND DESIGN INC**
2729 Bristol St Ste 100, Costa Mesa (92626-7930)
**PHONE**..............................714 545-5757
**EMP:** 25
**Web:** www.marshallad.com

# PRODUCTS & SERVICES SECTION

## 7331 - Direct Mail Advertising Services (P-17800)

SIC: 7311 7336 2752 Advertising agencies; Commercial art and graphic design; Catalogs, lithographed

**(P-17781)**
**MOB SCENE LLC**
Also Called: Mob Scene Creative Productions
8447 Wilshire Blvd Ste 100, Beverly Hills (90211-3228)
PHONE..................323 648-7200
EMP: 135 EST: 2005
SALES (est): 8.47MM **Privately Held**
Web: www.mobscene.com
SIC: 7311 7929 3993 7812 Advertising consultant; Entertainment service; Advertising artwork; Television film production

**(P-17782)**
**QUAD/GRAPHICS INC**
Also Called: Sacramento Div
1201 Shore St, West Sacramento (95691-3510)
PHONE..................916 371-9500
Dan Coffee, Mgr
EMP: 27
SALES (corp-wide): 2.96B **Publicly Held**
Web: www.quad.com
SIC: 7311 2759 2752 Advertising agencies; Commercial printing, nec; Commercial printing, lithographic
PA: Quad/Graphics, Inc.
N61 W23044 Harry's Way
414 566-6000

**(P-17783)**
**SPORTS BOOSTERS INC (PA)**
9320 Chesapeake Dr Ste 118, San Diego (92123-1021)
PHONE..................888 541-5561
Charles Spindle, CEO
John Carreno, Pr
EMP: 15 EST: 2001
SQ FT: 2,800
SALES (est): 1.97MM
SALES (corp-wide): 1.97MM **Privately Held**
Web: www.sportsboosters.net
SIC: 7311 2759 Advertising agencies; Publication printing

## 7312 Outdoor Advertising Services

**(P-17784)**
**BRIMAD ENTERPRISES INC**
Also Called: Creative Outdoor Advertising
2900 Adams St Ste B16, Riverside (92504-4396)
PHONE..................951 354-8187
Eric Glaub, Pr
EMP: 15 EST: 1984
SQ FT: 10,000
SALES (est): 715.17K **Privately Held**
Web: www.coasigns.com
SIC: 7312 3993 Billboard advertising; Signs and advertising specialties

**(P-17785)**
**CLEAR CHANNEL OUTDOOR LLC**
555 12th St Ste 950, Oakland (94607-3689)
PHONE..................510 835-5900
EMP: 47
Web: www.clearchanneloutdoor.com
SIC: 7312 8611 3993 Billboard advertising; Business associations; Signs and advertising specialties
HQ: Clear Channel Outdoor, Llc
4830 N Loop 1604 W Ste 11
San Antonio TX 78249

**(P-17786)**
**OUTFRONT MEDIA LLC**
1731 Workman St, Los Angeles (90031-3334)
PHONE..................323 222-7171
Dennis Kuhl, Mgr
EMP: 27
SALES (corp-wide): 1.82B **Publicly Held**
Web: www.outfront.com
SIC: 7312 3993 Outdoor advertising services; Signs and advertising specialties
HQ: Outfront Media Llc
405 Lexington Ave Fl 14
New York NY 10174
212 297-6400

**(P-17787)**
**VOLTA CHARGING LLC**
155 De Haro St, San Francisco (94103-5121)
PHONE..................415 735-5169
Brandt Hastings, Pr
EMP: 70 EST: 2015
SQ FT: 8,250
SALES (est): 11.86MM
SALES (corp-wide): 316.62B **Privately Held**
Web: www.voltacharging.com
SIC: 7312 7694 Outdoor advertising services; Electric motor repair
HQ: Volta Industries, Inc.
155 De Haro St
San Francisco CA 94103
415 583-3805

## 7313 Radio, Television, Publisher Representatives

**(P-17788)**
**GRABIT INTERACTIVE INC**
Also Called: Kerv Interactive
14724 Ventura Blvd, Sherman Oaks (91403-3501)
PHONE..................844 472-2488
Gary Mittman, CEO
EMP: 34 EST: 2016
SALES (est): 681.8K **Privately Held**
Web: www.grabit.media
SIC: 7313 7372 Printed media advertising representatives; Application computer software

**(P-17789)**
**KARGO GLOBAL INC**
1437 4th St Ste 200, Santa Monica (90401-2377)
PHONE..................212 979-9000
Natalie Nelson, Brnch Mgr
EMP: 139
Web: www.kargo.com
SIC: 7313 7372 7374 Electronic media advertising representatives; Application computer software; Computer graphics service
PA: Kargo Global, Inc.
826 Broadway Fl 4

## 7319 Advertising, Nec

**(P-17790)**
**IMAGE OPTIONS (PA)**
Also Called: Image Options Painting & Dctg
80 Icon, Foothill Ranch (92610-3000)
PHONE..................949 586-7665
Barry Polan, CEO
Tim Bennett, Ch Bd
Brian Hite, Pr
Dave Brewer, VP
Barry Polan, CRO
EMP: 63 EST: 1999
SQ FT: 22,000
SALES (est): 24.71MM
SALES (corp-wide): 24.71MM **Privately Held**
Web: www.imageoptions.net
SIC: 7319 7336 2759 Display advertising service; Commercial art and graphic design; Commercial printing, nec

**(P-17791)**
**PANNONIA GROUP INC**
Also Called: Prolab Digital Imaging
5441 W 104th St, Los Angeles (90045-6011)
PHONE..................310 846-4496
Nicholas Urmossy, Pr
Julia Urmossy, Sec
EMP: 20 EST: 1989
SQ FT: 15,000
SALES (est): 3.45MM **Privately Held**
Web: www.prolabdigital.com
SIC: 7319 2752 Display advertising service; Offset and photolithographic printing

**(P-17792)**
**WEST COAST COUPON INC**
9400 Oso Ave, Chatsworth (91311-6020)
PHONE..................818 341-2400
Mark Fischer, Pr
Doug Rewers, *
EMP: 26 EST: 2004
SQ FT: 30,000
SALES (est): 1.38MM **Privately Held**
Web: www.westcoastcoupon.com
SIC: 7319 2731 5961 Coupon distribution; Books, publishing and printing; Computer software, mail order

## 7331 Direct Mail Advertising Services

**(P-17793)**
**ACE MAILING CORPORATION**
Also Called: Ace Mailing
2736 16th St, San Francisco (94103-4216)
PHONE..................415 863-4223
Royce Dyer, Pt
Gwendolyn Kaplan, *
Ron Ross, *
EMP: 38 EST: 1977
SQ FT: 12,000
SALES (est): 2.2MM **Privately Held**
Web: www.acemailingsf.com
SIC: 7331 2752 Mailing service; Commercial printing, lithographic

**(P-17794)**
**ADVANCED IMAGE DIRECT LLC**
Also Called: Fht Printing
1415 S Acacia Ave, Fullerton (92831-5317)
PHONE..................714 502-3900
Hugo Solorio, *
▲ EMP: 50 EST: 2008
SALES (est): 4.21MM
SALES (corp-wide): 29MM **Privately Held**
Web: www.advancedimagedirect.com
SIC: 7331 2752 Mailing service; Commercial printing, lithographic
PA: Real Estate Image, Inc.
1415 S Acacia Ave
714 502-3900

**(P-17795)**
**BUSINESS SERVICES NETWORK CORP**
1275 Fairfax Ave Ste 103, San Francisco (94124-1759)
PHONE..................415 282-8161
Harry Yue, Pr
Cindy Yue, *
▲ EMP: 72 EST: 1984
SQ FT: 31,120
SALES (est): 4.28MM **Privately Held**
Web: www.industry-business-network.org
SIC: 7331 2752 7374 Mailing service; Offset printing; Data processing service

**(P-17796)**
**CENTRAL VALLEY PRESORT INC**
Also Called: Presort Center, The
4215 S Dans St, Visalia (93277-7913)
PHONE..................559 906-2003
EMP: 85
Web: www.thepresort.com
SIC: 7331 2752 Mailing service; Promotional printing, lithographic

**(P-17797)**
**FINANCIAL STATEMENT SVCS INC (PA)**
Also Called: Fssi
3300 S Fairview St, Santa Ana (92704-7004)
PHONE..................714 436-3326
Jennifer Dietz, CEO
Jon Dietz, *
Karen Elsbury, *
Henry Perez, *
Dan Palmquist, *
EMP: 144 EST: 1984
SQ FT: 167,000
SALES (est): 31.62MM
SALES (corp-wide): 31.62MM **Privately Held**
Web: www.fssi-ca.com
SIC: 7331 7374 2759 Mailing service; Data processing and preparation; Laser printing

**(P-17798)**
**FULL/TECH SYSTEMS INC**
5525 Market St, San Diego (92114-2218)
PHONE..................619 297-0454
Donald Deblasio, Pr
EMP: 20 EST: 1996
SQ FT: 20,000
SALES (est): 2.27MM **Privately Held**
Web: www.fulltech.net
SIC: 7331 7374 2752 Mailing service; Data processing and preparation; Commercial printing, lithographic

**(P-17799)**
**GOODE PRINTING AND MAILING LLC**
Also Called: Goode Company, The
361 Blodgett St, Cotati (94931-8700)
PHONE..................707 588-8028
Michael Sanabria, CEO
William Goode, *
Laura Goode, *
Bryan Neill, *
Scott Worden, *
EMP: 44 EST: 2006
SALES (est): 2.7MM **Privately Held**
Web: www.almadenglobal.com
SIC: 7331 2759 2752 Mailing service; Commercial printing, nec; Commercial printing, lithographic

**(P-17800)**
**ORANGE COUNTY DIRECT MAIL INC**

# 7331 - Direct Mail Advertising Services (P-17801)

Also Called: Ocdm
2672 Dow Ave, Tustin (92780-7208)
PHONE...................714 444-4412
Mark Cretz, CEO
EMP: 45 EST: 1990
SQ FT: 35,000
SALES (est): 8.91MM Privately Held
Web: www.ocdm.com
SIC: 7331 7313 7389 2752 Mailing service; Printed media advertising representatives; Printers' services: folding, collating, etc.; Commercial printing, lithographic

**(P-17801)**
**PREMIER PRINT & MAIL INC**
Also Called: Tri-City Print & Mail
2615 Del Monte St, West Sacramento (95691-3809)
PHONE...................916 503-5300
Charles F Sievers Junior, Pr
EMP: 17 EST: 1993
SQ FT: 10,000
SALES (est): 495.13K Privately Held
Web: www.premierprint-mail.com
SIC: 7331 2752 Direct mail advertising services; Offset and photolithographic printing

**(P-17802)**
**PRESORT CENTER OF FRESNO LLC**
496 S Uruapan Way, Dinuba (93618-2719)
PHONE...................559 498-6151
EMP: 40 EST: 2015
SQ FT: 92,000
SALES (est): 2.97MM Privately Held
Web: www.thepresort.com
SIC: 7331 2759 Mailing service; Commercial printing, nec

**(P-17803)**
**REAL ESTATE IMAGE INC (PA)**
Also Called: Advanced Image Direct
1415 S Acacia Ave, Fullerton (92831-5317)
PHONE...................714 502-3900
Ty Mcmillin, Pr
Perry Wilson, *
Hugo Solorio, Product Vice President*
EMP: 150 EST: 1981
SQ FT: 136,000
SALES (est): 29MM
SALES (corp-wide): 29MM Privately Held
Web: www.advancedimagedirect.com
SIC: 7331 2752 Mailing service; Commercial printing, lithographic

## 7334 Photocopying And Duplicating Services

**(P-17804)**
**ALBERT MALDONADO**
Also Called: Mp Express
324 Lincoln Ave, Salinas (93901-2615)
PHONE...................831 758-9040
Albert Maldonado, Owner
EMP: 18 EST: 1980
SQ FT: 1,600
SALES (est): 2.3MM Privately Held
Web: www.myexpressprinter.com
SIC: 7334 2752 Photocopying and duplicating services; Offset printing

**(P-17805)**
**ALL-AMERICAN PRTG SVCS CORP (PA)**
1324 Rand St, Petaluma (94954-1138)
PHONE...................707 762-2500
Darren Keffury, Pr
Alan Brayton, *
EMP: 29 EST: 1990
SQ FT: 17,500
SALES (est): 6.55MM Privately Held
Web: www.allamericanprinting.com
SIC: 7334 2752 Photocopying and duplicating services; Offset printing

**(P-17806)**
**CONCORD DOCUMENT SERVICES INC (PA)**
1407 W 11th St, Los Angeles (90015-1227)
PHONE...................213 745-3175
Fernando B Flores, CEO
Hector Flores, *
EMP: 28 EST: 1996
SALES (est): 2.72MM
SALES (corp-wide): 2.72MM Privately Held
Web: www.concorddt.com
SIC: 7334 3577 Photocopying and duplicating services; Optical scanning devices

**(P-17807)**
**CP DOCUMENT TECHNOLOGIES LLC**
11835 W Olympic Blvd Ste 145, Los Angeles (90064-5001)
PHONE...................310 575-6640
Emily Go, Mgr
EMP: 50
SIC: 7334 2754 2759 Photocopying and duplicating services; Commercial printing, gravure; Commercial printing, nec
PA: Cp Document Technologies, Llc
800 W 6th St Ste 1400

**(P-17808)**
**CYBERCOPY INC (PA)**
2766 S La Cienega Blvd, Los Angeles (90034-2642)
P.O. Box 507 (90232-0507)
PHONE...................310 736-1001
Paul Fridrich, CEO
EMP: 17 EST: 1997
SALES (est): 4.8MM Privately Held
Web: www.cybercopyusa.com
SIC: 7334 2754 2741 2732 Blueprinting service; Commercial printing, gravure; Art copy and poster publishing; Book printing

**(P-17809)**
**DEL MAR BLUE PRINT CO INC**
2201 San Dieguito Dr Ste E, Del Mar (92014-2257)
PHONE...................858 755-5134
Michael Kraus, Pr
Kelly Kraus, VP
EMP: 18 EST: 1978
SQ FT: 4,000
SALES (est): 1.48MM Privately Held
Web: www.delmarblue.com
SIC: 7334 2752 Blueprinting service; Offset printing

**(P-17810)**
**DVS MEDIA SERVICES (PA)**
Also Called: D V S Mdia Srvces/Intelestream
2625 W Olive Ave, Burbank (91505-4526)
PHONE...................818 841-6750
Rick Appell, Managing Member
EMP: 46 EST: 2020
SALES (est): 5.91MM
SALES (corp-wide): 5.91MM Privately Held
SIC: 7334 2759 Photocopying and duplicating services; Commercial printing, nec

**(P-17811)**
**FAR WESTERN GRAPHICS INC**
Also Called: Denevi Digital
2642 Heritage Park Cir, San Jose (95132-2211)
PHONE...................408 481-9777
EMP: 65
Web: www.farwesterngraphics.com
SIC: 7334 2752 Photocopying and duplicating services; Offset printing

**(P-17812)**
**FRYES PRINTING INC**
1050 Lincoln Ave, Napa (94558-4914)
PHONE...................707 253-1114
Kevin Frye, Pr
EMP: 24 EST: 1981
SQ FT: 10,000
SALES (est): 2.18MM Privately Held
Web: www.fryesprinting.com
SIC: 7334 2752 Blueprinting service; Commercial printing, lithographic

**(P-17813)**
**GRAPHIC REPRODUCTION**
2327 Union St, Oakland (94607-2320)
PHONE...................510 268-9980
Dave Bethea, Brnch Mgr
EMP: 17
SIC: 7334 2759 3944 Blueprinting service; Commercial printing, nec; Board games, puzzles, and models, except electronic
PA: Graphic Reproduction
1381 Franquette Ave B1

**(P-17814)**
**MAINSTREET COMMUNICATION INC (PA)**
Also Called: PIP Printing
4093 Market St, Riverside (92501-3542)
PHONE...................951 682-2005
Justin Tracy, Pr
EMP: 15 EST: 1968
SQ FT: 5,500
SALES (est): 2.98MM
SALES (corp-wide): 2.98MM Privately Held
Web: www.printmystuff.com
SIC: 7334 2752 Photocopying and duplicating services; Offset printing

**(P-17815)**
**PACIFIC COPY AND PRINT**
9950 Horn Rd, Sacramento (95827-1905)
PHONE...................916 928-8434
Darren Herbert, Pr
Keith Lowe, VP
Corina Workman, Sec
EMP: 20 EST: 1991
SALES (est): 2.23MM Privately Held
Web: www.pacificcopy.com
SIC: 7334 2752 Blueprinting service; Commercial printing, lithographic

**(P-17816)**
**SPEEDWAY COPY SYSTEMS INC**
Also Called: Speedway Digital Printing
275 E L St, Benicia (94510-3238)
PHONE...................415 495-4330
Harry Newhall Junior, Pr
Gerard Burnett, *
Harry B Newhall Senior Stkldr, Prin
Carl Rubens Stkldr, Prin
EMP: 24 EST: 1969
SALES (est): 2.19MM Privately Held
Web: www.speedwayprinting.com
SIC: 7334 2752 Photocopying and duplicating services; Offset printing

**(P-17817)**
**THE ALTERNATIVE COPY SHOP INC**
3887 State St Ste 12, Santa Barbara (93105-3180)
PHONE...................805 569-2116
EMP: 52
SIC: 7334 2759 Photocopying and duplicating services; Commercial printing, nec

## 7335 Commercial Photography

**(P-17818)**
**ARC DOCUMENT SOLUTIONS INC (PA)**
Also Called: ARC DOCUMENT SOLUTIONS
12657 Alcosta Blvd Ste 200, San Ramon (94583-4433)
PHONE...................925 949-5100
Kumarakulasingam Suriyakumar, Prin
Kumarakulasingam Suriyakumar, Ch Bd
Dilantha Wijesuriya, Pr
Jorge Avalos, CFO
Tracey Luttrell, Corporate Counsel*
EMP: 146 EST: 1997
SALES (est): 281.2MM
SALES (corp-wide): 281.2MM Privately Held
Web: www.e-arc.com
SIC: 7335 7374 7372 7334 Photographic studio, commercial; Computer graphics service; Prepackaged software; Blueprinting service

**(P-17819)**
**ULTRAGRAPHICS INC**
2800 N Naomi St, Burbank (91504-2023)
PHONE...................818 295-3994
E Alexander Kilgo, CEO
Jon E Crossley, *
Nancy E Pasch Erlandsen, *
John T Crossley, *
EMP: 44 EST: 1980
SQ FT: 19,000
SALES (est): 1.66MM Privately Held
Web: www.ultragraphicsla.com
SIC: 7335 2752 Photographic studio, commercial; Offset printing

## 7336 Commercial Art And Graphic Design

**(P-17820)**
**ABC IMAGING OF WASHINGTON**
679 Bryant St, San Francisco (94107-1612)
PHONE...................415 869-1669
EMP: 23
SALES (corp-wide): 129.31MM Privately Held
Web: www.abcimaging.com
SIC: 7336 2759 Graphic arts and related design; Commercial printing, nec
PA: Abc Imaging Of Washington, Inc
5290 Shawnee Rd Ste 300
202 429-8870

**(P-17821)**
**BLACK ANCHOR SUPPLY CO LLC**
27636 Avenue Scott Ste A, Valencia (91355-3973)
PHONE...................661 309-1193
EMP: 18 EST: 2009
SALES (est): 1.1MM Privately Held
Web: www.blackanchorsupply.com

## PRODUCTS & SERVICES SECTION

## 7338 - Secretarial And Court Reporting (P-17842)

SIC: 7336 2759 Commercial art and graphic design; Screen printing

### (P-17822)
**CINNABAR**
4571 Electronics Pl, Los Angeles (90039-1007)
PHONE..............................818 842-8190
Jonathan Katz, *Pr*
EMP: 200 EST: 1982
SQ FT: 60,000
SALES (est): 21.6MM Privately Held
Web: www.cinnabar.com
SIC: 7336 3999 7819 Graphic arts and related design; Theatrical scenery; Sound effects and music production, motion picture

### (P-17823)
**CONCORD GRAPHIC ARTS INC**
Also Called: C G A
3270 Monument Way, Concord (94518-2406)
PHONE..............................925 682-9670
John J Yust, *Pr*
EMP: 21 EST: 1963
SQ FT: 11,000
SALES (est): 409.7K Privately Held
Web: www.concordgraphicarts.com
SIC: 7336 2752 Commercial art and graphic design; Offset printing

### (P-17824)
**CONSOLIDATED DESIGN WEST INC**
Also Called: Cdw
1345 S Lewis St, Anaheim (92805-6431)
PHONE..............................714 999-1476
Victor John Perrillo, *CEO*
▲ EMP: 50 EST: 1990
SQ FT: 7,500
SALES (est): 10.91MM Privately Held
Web: www.consolidateddesignwest.com
SIC: 7336 2754 Package design; Commercial printing, gravure

### (P-17825)
**DANDREA VSUAL CMMNCATIONS LLC**
Also Called: D'Andrea Graphics
6100 Gateway Dr, Cypress (90630-4840)
PHONE..............................714 947-8444
David D'andrea, *Managing Member*
▲ EMP: 80 EST: 2005
SQ FT: 25,000
SALES (est): 2.2MM Privately Held
Web: www.dandreavisual.com
SIC: 7336 2782 Graphic arts and related design; Account books

### (P-17826)
**DIGITAL DOMAIN MEDIA GROUP INC**
Also Called: Wyndcrest Dd Florida
12641 Beatrice St, Los Angeles (90066-7003)
EMP: 813
SIC: 7336 7812 7371 7372 Commercial art and graphic design; Non-theatrical motion picture production; Custom computer programming services; Business oriented computer software

### (P-17827)
**DIMENSIONAL SILK SCREEN INC**
Also Called: Dimensional Signs & Graphics
3750 Dalbergia St, San Diego (92113-3815)
PHONE..............................619 232-9100
Michael Tardy, *Pr*
EMP: 18 EST: 1972
SQ FT: 9,036
SALES (est): 823.76K Privately Held
Web: www.dimensionalsilkscreen.com
SIC: 7336 2396 Silk screen design; Automotive and apparel trimmings

### (P-17828)
**G3 ENTERPRISES INC**
Also Called: Label Division
2612 Crows Landing Rd, Modesto (95358-9400)
PHONE..............................209 341-5265
Tom Gallow, *Brnch Mgr*
EMP: 43
SALES (corp-wide): 74.57MM Privately Held
Web: www.g3enterprises.com
SIC: 7336 2752 Commercial art and graphic design; Commercial printing, lithographic
PA: G3 Enterprises, Inc.
502 E Whitmore Ave
209 499-9783

### (P-17829)
**GRAPHIC INK CORP**
Also Called: Graphic Ink and Graphic Ink
5382 Industrial Dr, Huntington Beach (92649-1517)
PHONE..............................714 901-2805
Vincent De La Torre, *Pr*
Jenny Lynn Quilico, *
EMP: 45 EST: 2005
SQ FT: 6,000
SALES (est): 2.39MM Privately Held
Web: www.graphicink.org
SIC: 7336 2262 Commercial art and graphic design; Finishing plants, manmade

### (P-17830)
**HOG INC**
Also Called: House of Graphics
9519 Rush St Ste A, South El Monte (91733-1556)
PHONE..............................626 279-5275
Michael Harada, *Pr*
EMP: 15 EST: 1975
SALES (est): 1.01MM Privately Held
Web: www.hogprinter.com
SIC: 7336 2752 Graphic arts and related design; Commercial printing, lithographic

### (P-17831)
**IDENTIGRAPHIX INC**
19866 Quiroz Ct, Walnut (91789-2828)
PHONE..............................909 468-4741
A Fred Mendoza, *Pr*
EMP: 25 EST: 1982
SQ FT: 17,000
SALES (est): 2.96MM Privately Held
Web: www.identigraphix.com
SIC: 7336 2396 Silk screen design; Automotive and apparel trimmings

### (P-17832)
**MEDIA PRINT SERVICES INC**
Also Called: Snap Pack Mail
10012 Del Almendra Dr, Oakdale (95361-9258)
PHONE..............................866 935-5077
Becky Gould, *Pr*
Marshall Gould, *Owner*
Kathy Royer, *VP*
Becky Mcginty, *VP*
EMP: 16 EST: 2005
SALES (est): 794.28K Privately Held
Web: www.snappackmail.com
SIC: 7336 2752 7389 Commercial art and graphic design; Commercial printing, lithographic; Business services, nec

### (P-17833)
**MOTIVATIONAL SYSTEMS INC (PA)**
2200 Cleveland Ave, National City (91950-6412)
PHONE..............................619 474-8246
Robert D Yound, *CEO*
David Cowan, *
Joe Jordan, *
Anthony Young, *
EMP: 100 EST: 1975
SQ FT: 50,000
SALES (est): 31.24MM
SALES (corp-wide): 31.24MM Privately Held
Web: www.motivational.com
SIC: 7336 3993 Graphic arts and related design; Signs and advertising specialties

### (P-17834)
**NEVER BORING DESIGN ASSOCIATES**
1016 14th St, Modesto (95354-1002)
PHONE..............................209 526-9136
David Boring, *Owner*
EMP: 25 EST: 1983
SQ FT: 2,500
SALES (est): 4.68MM Privately Held
Web: www.neverboring.com
SIC: 7336 3993 7311 Graphic arts and related design; Signs and advertising specialties; Advertising agencies

### (P-17835)
**ON TARGET MARKETING**
Also Called: Image Masters
429 Grogan Ave, Merced (95341-6401)
PHONE..............................209 723-1691
Tim O'neill, *CEO*
Tim O'neill, *Pr*
Marilyn O'neill, *VP*
EMP: 25 EST: 1988
SQ FT: 5,000
SALES (est): 6.07MM Privately Held
Web: www.imagemasters.com
SIC: 7336 2396 2759 7311 Graphic arts and related design; Screen printing on fabric articles; Promotional printing; Advertising consultant

### (P-17836)
**P5 GRAPHICS AND DISPLAYS INC**
625 Fee Ana St, Placentia (92870-6704)
PHONE..............................714 808-1645
Amit Patel, *Pr*
Kirit Ramani, *VP*
EMP: 21 EST: 2015
SALES (est): 4.41MM Privately Held
Web: www.p5graphics.net
SIC: 7336 2782 Graphic arts and related design; Account books

### (P-17837)
**PULP STUDIO INCORPORATED**
Also Called: CGB
2100 W 139th St, Gardena (90249-2412)
P.O. Box 16231 (90209-2231)
PHONE..............................310 815-4999
Bernard Lax, *CEO*
Lynda N Lax, *
▲ EMP: 60 EST: 1940
SQ FT: 36,000
SALES (est): 9.96MM Privately Held
Web: www.pulpstudio.com
SIC: 7336 3229 Commercial art and graphic design; Glass furnishings and accessories

### (P-17838)
**SALLINGERS SPCLTY SCRNPRINT EM**
1080 N Batavia St Ste L, Orange (92867-5540)
PHONE..............................714 532-6627
Larry Sallinger, *Mng Pt*
Pauline Sallinger, *Mng Pt*
EMP: 22 EST: 1993
SQ FT: 6,250
SALES (est): 720.6K Privately Held
SIC: 7336 2759 Silk screen design; Screen printing

### (P-17839)
**SESA INC (PA)**
Also Called: Signco
20391 Via Guadalupe, Yorba Linda (92887-3133)
PHONE..............................714 779-9700
Elaine M Roach, *CEO*
EMP: 23 EST: 1986
SQ FT: 18,000
SALES (est): 2.15MM
SALES (corp-wide): 2.15MM Privately Held
SIC: 7336 2759 3993 2396 Silk screen design; Screen printing; Signs and advertising specialties; Automotive and apparel trimmings

### (P-17840)
**STAR LINK COMPANY INC**
3300 Fujita St, Torrance (90505-4017)
PHONE..............................310 787-8299
Steven Chan, *Pr*
Heidi Chan, *VP*
EMP: 15 EST: 1988
SALES (est): 2.39MM Privately Held
Web: www.starlinkco.com
SIC: 7336 7374 2759 Graphic arts and related design; Service bureau, computer; Commercial printing, nec

### (P-17841)
**TREND DESIGN INC**
Also Called: Trend Graphics Screenprinting
1200 Lawrence Dr Ste 465, Newbury Park (91320-1342)
PHONE..............................805 498-0457
Steve Dilallo, *Pr*
Kim Di Lallo, *Sec*
Chris Kaul, *VP*
EMP: 17 EST: 1987
SQ FT: 3,000
SALES (est): 1.44MM Privately Held
SIC: 7336 2759 Silk screen design; Screen printing

## 7338 Secretarial And Court Reporting

### (P-17842)
**INFOSEND INC (PA)**
4240 E La Palma Ave, Anaheim (92807-1816)
PHONE..............................714 993-2690
Mahmood Rezai, *CEO*
Mahmood Rezai, *Pr*
Rusteen Rezai, *COO*
EMP: 49 EST: 1997
SALES (est): 132.63MM
SALES (corp-wide): 132.63MM Privately Held
Web: www.infosend.com

# 7342 - Disinfecting And Pest Control Services (P-17843)

SIC: **7338** 2732 2741 7389 Stenographic services; Pamphlets: printing only, not published on site; Business service newsletters: publishing and printing; Presorted mail service

## 7342 Disinfecting And Pest Control Services

### (P-17843)
**CARTWRIGHT TRMT PEST CTRL INC**
1376 Broadway, El Cajon (92021-5812)
P.O. Box 2398 (92021-0398)
PHONE....................619 442-9613
Michael Cartwright Ii, *CEO*
Michael Cartwright Senior, *VP*
Ben Cartwright, *
Willard Cartwright, *
**EMP:** 33 **EST:** 1962
**SQ FT:** 2,000
**SALES (est):** 2.49MM **Privately Held**
Web: www.cartwrightpest.com
SIC: **7342** 2879 Exterminating and fumigating ; Insecticides and pesticides

### (P-17844)
**CORKYS PEST CONTROL INC**
Also Called: Pro Pacific Pest Control
150 Vallecitos De Oro, San Marcos (92069-1435)
PHONE....................760 432-8801
Corky Mizer, *Pr*
▲ **EMP:** 60 **EST:** 1967
**SALES (est):** 9.35MM **Privately Held**
Web: www.corkyspest.com
SIC: **7342** 0782 2879 5211 Pest control in structures; Lawn and garden services; Insecticides and pesticides; Insulation material, building
HQ: Anticimex Inc.
106 Allen Rd Ste 310
Basking Ridge NJ 07920
800 618-2847

## 7349 Building Maintenance Services, Nec

### (P-17845)
**BREAKMART LLC**
Also Called: MD COMMERCIAL
4986 Lake Park Ct, Fallbrook (92028-7830)
PHONE....................760 310-2421
Decarlos Daniels, *CEO*
**EMP:** 15 **EST:** 2007
**SALES (est):** 606.3K **Privately Held**
Web: www.mdcommercialcleaning.com
SIC: **7349** 2676 Building maintenance services, nec; Sanitary paper products

### (P-17846)
**CERTIFIED WTR DMAGE RSTRTION E**
Also Called: Cwdre
5319 University Dr, Irvine (92612-2965)
PHONE....................800 417-1776
Cyrus Fatoure, *Pr*
**EMP:** 48 **EST:** 2016
**SALES (est):** 1.25MM **Privately Held**
SIC: **7349** 1389 6331 1521 Building maintenance services, nec; Construction, repair, and dismantling services; Property damage insurance; Repairing fire damage, single-family houses

### (P-17847)
**PREMIER FLOOR CARE INC (PA)**
5179 Lone Tree Way, Antioch (94531-8689)
PHONE....................925 679-4901
Cedric Moore, *Pr*
**EMP:** 23 **EST:** 2000
**SALES (est):** 5.22MM
**SALES (corp-wide):** 5.22MM **Privately Held**
Web: www.premierfloorcare.com
SIC: **7349** 3589 Janitorial service, contract basis; Commercial cleaning equipment

### (P-17848)
**PROPERTY CARE BUILDING SVC LLC**
126 La Porte St Ste F, Arcadia (91006-7190)
P.O. Box 661690 (91066-1690)
PHONE....................626 623-6420
Everardo Amezcua, *
Victoria Amezcua, *VP*
**EMP:** 26 **EST:** 2013
**SALES (est):** 5.03MM **Privately Held**
Web: www.propertycarebuildingservice.com
SIC: **7349** 2842 7342 Janitorial service, contract basis; Sanitation preparations, disinfectants and deodorants; Disinfecting services

### (P-17849)
**RESOURCE COLLECTION INC**
Also Called: Command Guard Services
3771 W 242nd St Ste 205, Torrance (90505-6566)
PHONE....................310 219-3272
Martin Benom, *Ch Bd*
Paula Benom, *
Marilyn Jacobson, *
Steven Jacobson, *
**EMP:** 29 **EST:** 1962
**SQ FT:** 15,000
**SALES (est):** 703.29K **Privately Held**
Web: www.resourcecollection.com
SIC: **7349** 7381 0782 3564 Air duct cleaning; Guard services; Lawn and garden services; Air cleaning systems

## 7353 Heavy Construction Equipment Rental

### (P-17850)
**CALIFRNIA SRVYING DRFTG SUP IN (PA)**
Also Called: CSDS
4733 Auburn Blvd, Sacramento (95841-3601)
PHONE....................916 344-0232
TOLL FREE: 800
Bruce Gandelman, *CEO*
Tom Cardenas, *
Mike Woodel, *
**EMP:** 49 **EST:** 1986
**SQ FT:** 17,500
**SALES (est):** 14.39MM
**SALES (corp-wide):** 14.39MM **Privately Held**
Web: www.csdsinc.com
SIC: **7353** 3993 5082 5045 Heavy construction equipment rental; Displays and cutouts, window and lobby; General construction machinery and equipment; Printers, computer

### (P-17851)
**FAIRFIELD RENTAL SERVICE INC**
Also Called: All Star Rentals
2525 Clay Bank Rd, Fairfield (94533-1656)
PHONE....................707 422-2270
Kenton De Vries, *Pr*
**EMP:** 16 **EST:** 1963
**SQ FT:** 12,000
**SALES (est):** 3.44MM **Privately Held**
Web: fairfield.allstarrents.com
SIC: **7353** 7359 3273 Heavy construction equipment rental; Rental store, general; Ready-mixed concrete

### (P-17852)
**KINGS OIL TOOLS INC (PA)**
2235 Spring St, Paso Robles (93446-1404)
PHONE....................805 238-9311
**EMP:** 30 **EST:** 1982
**SALES (est):** 11.13MM
**SALES (corp-wide):** 11.13MM **Privately Held**
Web: www.kingsoiltools.com
SIC: **7353** 1389 Oil field equipment, rental or leasing; Oil and gas wells: building, repairing and dismantling

### (P-17853)
**NATIONAL BUSINESS GROUP INC (PA)**
Also Called: National Tube & Steel
15319 Chatsworth St, Mission Hills (91345-2040)
PHONE....................818 221-6000
James Mooneyham, *Pr*
◆ **EMP:** 85 **EST:** 1985
**SQ FT:** 24,000
**SALES (est):** 16.88MM
**SALES (corp-wide):** 16.88MM **Privately Held**
Web: www.rentnational.com
SIC: **7353** 5039 7359 3496 Earth moving equipment, rental or leasing; Wire fence, gates, and accessories; Garage facility and tool rental; Fencing, made from purchased wire

## 7359 Equipment Rental And Leasing, Nec

### (P-17854)
**A & A PORTABLES INC**
201 Roscoe Rd, Modesto (95357-1828)
PHONE....................209 524-0401
Bill King, *CEO*
Michael King, *
**EMP:** 39 **EST:** 1960
**SQ FT:** 6,000
**SALES (est):** 935.1K **Privately Held**
Web: www.unitedsiteservices.com
SIC: **7359** 5082 3448 7699 Portable toilet rental; Contractor's materials; Prefabricated metal buildings and components; Septic tank cleaning service

### (P-17855)
**GOODWIN-COLE COMPANY INC**
8320 Belvedere Ave, Sacramento (95826-5902)
PHONE....................916 381-8888
TOLL FREE: 800
Roger B Gilleland, *Pr*
**EMP:** 20 **EST:** 1888
**SQ FT:** 17,000
**SALES (est):** 3.78MM **Privately Held**
Web: www.goodwincole.com
SIC: **7359** 2394 5999 2591 Tent and tarpaulin rental; Tents: made from purchased materials; Awnings; Drapery hardware and window blinds and shades

### (P-17856)
**J L FISHER INC**
1000 W Isabel St, Burbank (91506-1404)
PHONE....................818 846-8366
James L Fisher, *Pr*
Cary Clayton, *
▲ **EMP:** 60 **EST:** 1951
**SALES (est):** 5.28MM **Privately Held**
Web: www.jlfisher.com
SIC: **7359** 3861 3663 Equipment rental and leasing, nec; Motion picture apparatus and equipment; Radio and t.v. communications equipment

### (P-17857)
**MAGIC JUMP INC**
9165 Glenoaks Blvd, Sun Valley (91352-2612)
PHONE....................818 847-1313
TOLL FREE: 800
Andranik Bagumyan, *Pr*
Sam Bagumyan, *VP*
◆ **EMP:** 20 **EST:** 1996
**SQ FT:** 20,000
**SALES (est):** 4.25MM **Privately Held**
Web: www.magicjump.com
SIC: **7359** 3069 Party supplies rental services; Balloons, advertising and toy: rubber

### (P-17858)
**NATIONAL CNSTR RENTALS INC**
Also Called: National Construction Rental
1300 Business Center Dr, San Leandro (94577-2242)
PHONE....................510 563-4000
Marco Lopez, *Mgr*
**EMP:** 51
**SALES (corp-wide):** 323.59MM **Privately Held**
Web: www.rentnational.com
SIC: **7359** 3496 Portable toilet rental; Miscellaneous fabricated wire products
PA: National Construction Rentals, Inc.
15319 Chatsworth St
818 221-6000

### (P-17859)
**NORTHERN CALIFORNIA EQUIPMENT**
Also Called: Light Soda On Tap
1920 Ingalls St, San Francisco (94124-3301)
PHONE....................415 648-6262
Robert Shapiro, *Pr*
**EMP:** 24 **EST:** 1981
**SQ FT:** 6,000
**SALES (est):** 1.1MM **Privately Held**
SIC: **7359** 2087 7699 5078 Equipment rental and leasing, nec; Beverage bases, concentrates, syrups, powders and mixes; Restaurant equipment repair; Refrigerated beverage dispensers

### (P-17860)
**PANAVISION INC (PA)**
Also Called: Panavision Group
6101 Variel Ave, Woodland Hills (91367-3722)
PHONE....................818 316-1000
Ronald O Perelman, *Ch Bd*
Howard Gittis, *V Ch Bd*
Kimberly Snyder, *CEO*
William C Bevins, *Pr*
▲ **EMP:** 550 **EST:** 1990
**SQ FT:** 150,000
**SALES (est):** 160.24MM **Privately Held**
Web: www.panavision.com

**PRODUCTS & SERVICES SECTION**    **7371 - Custom Computer Programming Services (P-17879)**

SIC: **7359** 3861 3648 5063  Equipment rental and leasing, nec; Cameras and related equipment; Stage lighting equipment; Lighting fixtures

**(P-17861)**
**PORTER HIRE LTD**
Also Called: Heavy Equipment Rentals
13013 Temescal Canyon Rd, Corona (92883-8454)
PHONE..............................951 674-9999
◆ EMP: 46 EST: 1999
SALES (est): 11.55MM **Privately Held**
Web: www.porterrents.com
SIC: **7359** 5082 3523  Equipment rental and leasing, nec; Construction and mining machinery; Farm machinery and equipment
HQ: Porter Hire Limited
   1 Mark Porter Way, Burbush
   Hamilton WKO 3200

**(P-17862)**
**SKYVIEW AVIATION LLC**
5749 S Tracy Blvd, Tracy  (95377-8116)
PHONE..............................209 830-7666
Jay Vyas, Pr
Ricard Ortenheim, *
▼ EMP: 25 EST: 2002
SQ FT: 13,000
SALES (est): 3.41MM **Privately Held**
Web: www.skyviewaviation.com
SIC: **7359** 5599 3721 7699  Aircraft rental; Aircraft dealers; Aircraft; Aircraft and heavy equipment repair services

**(P-17863)**
**SOUNDBOKS INC**
1968 S Coast Hwy Pmb 2510, Laguna Beach  (92651-3681)
PHONE..............................310 774-0480
Jesper Theil Thomsen, CEO
Michael Winther, CFO
EMP: 15 EST: 2015
SALES (est): 1.78MM
SALES (corp-wide): 15.6MM **Privately Held**
Web: www.soundboks.com
SIC: **7359** 7819 1731 3651  Sound and lighting equipment rental; Sound effects and music production, motion picture; Sound equipment specialization; Sound reproducing equipment
PA: Soundboks Aps
   Esromgade 15,  Sal 11

**(P-17864)**
**SUNN AMERICA INC**
Also Called: Classe Party Rentals
10280 Indiana Ct, Rancho Cucamonga (91730-5332)
PHONE..............................909 944-5756
Vishnu Reddy, Pr
Saritha Reddy, *
Vishnu Reddy, CEO
Ronald Francis, *
EMP: 30 EST: 1999
SALES (est): 3.55MM **Privately Held**
Web: www.classeparty.com
SIC: **7359** 7299 3999  Party supplies rental services; Party planning service; Stage hardware and equipment, except lighting

**(P-17865)**
**WESTERN OILFIELDS SUPPLY CO (PA)**
Also Called: Rain For Rent
3404 State Rd, Bakersfield  (93308-4538)
P.O. Box 2248  (93303-2248)
PHONE..............................661 399-9124
Robert Lake, CEO

Maston Cunningham, CFO
▲ EMP: 150 EST: 1934
SQ FT: 57,000
SALES (est): 250.88MM
SALES (corp-wide): 250.88MM **Privately Held**
Web: www.rainforrent.com
SIC: **7359** 3523 5083  Equipment rental and leasing, nec; Farm machinery and equipment; Irrigation equipment

## 7363 Help Supply Services

**(P-17866)**
**BUTLER SERVICE GROUP  INC (HQ)**
3820 State St Ste A, Santa Barbara (93105-3182)
PHONE..............................201 891-5312
EMP: 100 EST: 1965
SQ FT: 82,000
SALES (est): 146.12MM
SALES (corp-wide): 242.14MM **Privately Held**
SIC: **7363** 8711 8748 3661  Engineering help service; Engineering services; Communications consulting; Telephone and telegraph apparatus
PA: Butler International, Inc.
   3820 State St Ste A
   805 882-2200

**(P-17867)**
**CARDINAL POINT CAPTAINS INC**
Also Called: Cardinal Point Captains
5005 Texas St Ste 104, San Diego (92108-3722)
PHONE..............................760 438-7361
Jordan E Cousino, CEO
Bill Green, CDO*
Heather Jenkins, ACCT AND CONTRACTS*
EMP: 56 EST: 2008
SQ FT: 2,633
SALES (est): 5.39MM **Privately Held**
Web: www.cpcperforms.com
SIC: **7363** 3812  Boat crew service; Search and navigation equipment

**(P-17868)**
**LANE SAFETY CO INC**
340 W Channel Rd Ste F, Benicia (94510-1160)
PHONE..............................707 746-4820
Marion Gizzi, Pr
EMP: 25 EST: 1991
SQ FT: 10,000
SALES (est): 899.22K **Privately Held**
Web: lanesafetycoinc.business.site
SIC: **7363** 3669  Help supply services; Transportation signaling devices

**(P-17869)**
**SHIFAMED  LLC**
590 Division St, Campbell  (95008-6906)
PHONE..............................408 364-1242
Omar Salahiah, Owner
EMP: 20 EST: 2010
SALES (est): 11.49MM **Privately Held**
Web: www.shifamed.com
SIC: **7363** 3841  Medical help service; Medical instruments and equipment, blood and bone work

**(P-17870)**
**THE MORNING STAR COMPANY (PA)**
724 Main St Ste 202, Woodland (95695-3491)

PHONE..............................530 666-6600
◆ EMP: 70 EST: 1970
SALES (est): 79.78MM
SALES (corp-wide): 79.78MM **Privately Held**
Web: www.morningstarco.com
SIC: **7363** 8741 4212 2033  Employee leasing service; Management services; Local trucking, without storage; Canned fruits and specialties

## 7371 Custom Computer Programming Services

**(P-17871)**
**3I INFOTECH INC**
Also Called: 3I INFOTECH INC
555 Chorro St Ste B, San Luis Obispo (93405-2398)
PHONE..............................805 544-8327
Mathew Philip, CFO
EMP: 45
Web: www.3i-infotech.com
SIC: **7371** 7372 7373 7379  Computer software development; Prepackaged software; Computer integrated systems design; Computer related consulting services
HQ: 3i Infotech Inc.
   110 Fieldcrest Ave Ste 25
   Edison NJ 08837

**(P-17872)**
**4D INC**
95 S Market St Ste 240, San Jose (95113-2311)
PHONE..............................408 557-4600
Laurent Ribardiere, CEO
Doris Beaulieu, *
Phillipe Berthault, *
EMP: 101 EST: 2000
SALES (est): 7.23MM
SALES (corp-wide): 937.39K **Privately Held**
Web: us.4d.com
SIC: **7371** 7372  Computer software development; Prepackaged software
HQ: 4d
   Parc Des Erables Batiment 4
   Le Pecq IDF 78230
   130539200

**(P-17873)**
**A R SANTEX LLC (PA)**
Also Called: Santex Group
6790 Embarcadero Ln Ste 100, Carlsbad (92011-3277)
PHONE..............................888 622-7098
Juan Santiago, CEO
Gabriela Fernandez, CFO
EMP: 39 EST: 1991
SALES (est): 4.31MM
SALES (corp-wide): 4.31MM **Privately Held**
Web: www.santexgroup.com
SIC: **7371** 7372 7373  Computer software systems analysis and design, custom; Business oriented computer software; Systems software development services

**(P-17874)**
**ABELISK  INC (PA)**
Also Called: Argos Software
7060 N Fresno St Ste 210, Fresno (93720-2984)
PHONE..............................559 227-1000
Alan R Thodey, Pr
EMP: 17 EST: 1979
SQ FT: 10,000

SALES (est): 2.45MM
SALES (corp-wide): 2.45MM **Privately Held**
Web: www.argosoftware.com
SIC: **7371** 7372  Computer software development; Prepackaged software

**(P-17875)**
**ACCESS SYSTEMS AMERICAS INC**
3965 Freedom Cir Ste 200, Santa Clara (95054-1293)
PHONE..............................408 400-3000
Kiyo Oishi, CEO
Michael Kelley, *
Jeanne Seeley, *
EMP: 23 EST: 2001
SQ FT: 71,000
SALES (est): 4.62MM **Privately Held**
Web: www.ipinfusion.com
SIC: **7371** 7372  Computer software development; Prepackaged software
PA: Access Co., Ltd.
   3, Kandaneribeicho

**(P-17876)**
**ADVANCED REALTIME SYSTEMS INC**
110 Conejo Cir, Palm Desert  (92260-0383)
PHONE..............................760 636-0444
Richard Roter, Pr
EMP: 15 EST: 1985
SALES (est): 906.51K **Privately Held**
Web: www.arsi.com
SIC: **7371** 7372 7373 7376  Computer software development; Prepackaged software; Computer integrated systems design; Computer facilities management

**(P-17877)**
**AECHELON TECHNOLOGY  INC (PA)**
611 Gateway Blvd Ste 300, South San Francisco  (94080)
PHONE..............................415 255-0120
Nacho Sanz-pastor, CEO
Luis Barcena, *
Chris Blumenthal, *
Bruce Johnson, *
▲ EMP: 147 EST: 1998
SALES (est): 17.05MM
SALES (corp-wide): 17.05MM **Privately Held**
Web: www.aechelon.com
SIC: **7371** 3571  Computer software development and applications; Electronic computers

**(P-17878)**
**ALGORITHMIC OBJECTIVE CORP**
Also Called: Algotive
8910 University Center Ln Ste 400, San Diego  (92122-1029)
PHONE..............................858 249-9580
Pablo Castillon, CEO
Pablo Antonio Castillon, *
EMP: 32 EST: 2019
SALES (est): 1.03MM **Privately Held**
Web: www.algotive.ai
SIC: **7371** 7372  Computer software development; Prepackaged software

**(P-17879)**
**ALLIANCEIT INC (PA)**
Also Called: Allianceit
6101 Bollinger Canyon Rd Ste 335g, San Ramon  (94583-5112)
PHONE..............................925 462-9787

## 7371 - Custom Computer Programming Services (P-17880)

Purushothama Polkampalli, *Pr*
**EMP:** 15 **EST:** 2011
**SALES (est):** 4.93MM **Privately Held**
Web: www.allianceit.com
**SIC: 7371** 8748 7379 7372 Computer software development; Systems engineering consultant, ex. computer or professional; Data processing consultant; Prepackaged software

### (P-17880)
### ANAMEX CORPORATION (PA)
250 S Peralta Way, Anaheim (92807-3618)
**PHONE**..............................714 779-7055
Cung Phan, *Pr*
**EMP:** 47 **EST:** 1986
**SQ FT:** 10,000
**SALES (est):** 2.29MM **Privately Held**
**SIC: 7371** 7372 8711 Computer software development; Prepackaged software; Electrical or electronic engineering

### (P-17881)
### APPLIED SPECTRAL IMAGING INC
Also Called: A S I
6160 Innovation Way, Carlsbad (92009-1728)
**PHONE**..............................760 929-2840
Limore Shiposh, *CEO*
Elizer Tokman, *CBH*
**EMP:** 18 **EST:** 1994
**SALES (est):** 4.5MM **Privately Held**
Web: www.spectral-imaging.com
**SIC: 7371** 3571 Computer software development and applications; Electronic computers
**PA:** Applied Spectral Imaging Ltd.
2 Hacarmel

### (P-17882)
### ASHUNYA INC
642 N Eckhoff St, Orange (92868-1004)
**PHONE**..............................714 385-1900
Melanie Merchant, *Prin*
**EMP:** 88 **EST:** 2001
**SALES (est):** 6.05MM **Privately Held**
Web: www.ashunya.com
**SIC: 7371** 7372 7373 Computer software development and applications; Application computer software; Office computer automation systems integration

### (P-17883)
### ASPIREZ INC
Also Called: Pegasus One
1440 N Harbor Blvd Ste 900, Fullerton (92835-4127)
**PHONE**..............................714 485-8104
Tushar Puri, *CEO*
**EMP:** 87 **EST:** 2010
**SALES (est):** 1.96MM **Privately Held**
**SIC: 7371** 7373 7379 7372 Custom computer programming services; Computer integrated systems design; Computer related maintenance services; Prepackaged software

### (P-17884)
### AUTOCLERK INC
1981 N Broadway Ste 430, Walnut Creek (94596-3829)
P.O. Box 398840 (94139-8840)
**PHONE**..............................925 284-1005
Gary Gibb, *Area President*
Gary Gibb, *Pr*
Edward Bear, *VP*
**EMP:** 16 **EST:** 1984
**SQ FT:** 2,500
**SALES (est):** 752.59K **Privately Held**
Web: www.autoclerk.com
**SIC: 7371** 7372 5734 Computer software development; Prepackaged software; Software, business and non-game

### (P-17885)
### BEA SYSTEMS INC (HQ)
2315 N 1st St, San Jose (95131-1010)
**PHONE**..............................650 506-7000
Alfred S Chuang, *Ch Bd*
Alfred S Chuang, *Ch Bd*
William Klein, *Executive Corporate Development Vice President*
Wai M Wong, *Product Vice President*
Mark T Carges, *Vice President Business*
**EMP:** 1000 **EST:** 1995
**SQ FT:** 236,000
**SALES:** 96.76MM
**SALES (corp-wide):** 52.96B **Publicly Held**
Web: www.bea.gov
**SIC: 7371** 7372 Computer software development; Prepackaged software
**PA:** Oracle Corporation
2300 Oracle Way
737 867-1000

### (P-17886)
### BELLROCK MEDIA INC (PA)
11500 W Olympic Blvd Ste 400, Los Angeles (90064-1525)
**PHONE**..............................310 315-2727
Peter Levin, *Pr*
**EMP:** 26 **EST:** 2005
**SALES (est):** 3.88MM **Privately Held**
**SIC: 7371** 3661 Software programming applications; Headsets, telephone

### (P-17887)
### BIG CART CORPORATION
16682 Millikan Ave, Irvine (92606-5008)
**PHONE**..............................949 250-7064
Chang Ho Lee, *CEO*
**EMP:** 19 **EST:** 2012
**SALES (est):** 1.18MM **Privately Held**
Web: www.bigcartcorp.com
**SIC: 7371** 3699 Computer software development and applications; Security devices

### (P-17888)
### BIOSERO (PA)
4770 Ruffner St, San Diego (92111-1520)
**PHONE**..............................858 880-7376
Thomas Gilman, *Pr*
Andrea Salazar, *
Tony Morand, *
Daniel Schumann, *
Ryan Bernhardt, *CCO*
▲ **EMP:** 33 **EST:** 2003
**SQ FT:** 6,000
**SALES (est):** 9.52MM
**SALES (corp-wide):** 9.52MM **Privately Held**
Web: www.biosero.com
**SIC: 7371** 3569 Computer software development and applications; Assembly machines, non-metalworking

### (P-17889)
### BIS COMPUTER SOLUTIONS INC (PA)
Also Called: Business Information Systems
5500 Alta Canyada Rd, La Canada Flintridge (91011-1610)
**PHONE**..............................818 248-4282
Miro J Macho, *Pr*
**EMP:** 25 **EST:** 1971
**SALES (est):** 5.18MM
**SALES (corp-wide):** 5.18MM **Privately Held**
Web: www.biscomputer.com
**SIC: 7371** 7379 5045 7372 Computer software development; Computer related consulting services; Computers, peripherals, and software; Prepackaged software

### (P-17890)
### BOULEVARD LABS INC
626 Wilshire Blvd Ste 410, Los Angeles (90005-3983)
**PHONE**..............................323 310-2093
Matthew Danna, *CEO*
**EMP:** 117 **EST:** 2016
**SALES (est):** 9.85MM **Privately Held**
Web: www.joinblvd.com
**SIC: 7371** 7389 7372 Computer software development and applications; Business Activities at Non-Commercial Site; Prepackaged software

### (P-17891)
### BRILLIO LLC
5201 Great America Pkwy Ste 100, Santa Clara (95054-1122)
**PHONE**..............................800 317-0575
**EMP:** 27
Web: www.brillio.com
**SIC: 7371** 7372 Computer software development; Prepackaged software
**HQ:** Brillio, Llc
399 Thornall St Ste 68
Edison NJ 08837
800 317-0575

### (P-17892)
### BUFFER INC (PA)
Also Called: Buffer
2443 Fillmore St # 380-7163, San Francisco (94115-1814)
**PHONE**..............................415 215-5571
Joel Gascoigne, *CEO*
**EMP:** 83 **EST:** 2011
**SALES (est):** 6.12MM
**SALES (corp-wide):** 6.12MM **Privately Held**
Web: www.buffer.com
**SIC: 7371** 7372 Software programming applications; Application computer software

### (P-17893)
### CA INC
Also Called: CA
10811 International Dr Uppr, Rancho Cordova (95670-7319)
**PHONE**..............................916 463-8500
King Gee, *Brnch Mgr*
**EMP:** 35
**SALES (corp-wide):** 35.82B **Publicly Held**
Web: www.broadcom.com
**SIC: 7371** 7372 Computer software development; Prepackaged software
**HQ:** Ca, Inc.
3421 Hillview Ave
Palo Alto CA 94304
800 225-5224

### (P-17894)
### CALLIDUS SOFTWARE INC (HQ)
Also Called: Calliduscloud
2700 Camino Ramon # 400, San Ramon (94583-5004)
**PHONE**..............................925 251-2200
Leslie Stretch, *Pr*
Roxanne Oulman, *
Jimmy Duan, *
Mary Ainsworth, *CPO*
Andres Botero, *CMO*
▲ **EMP:** 230 **EST:** 1996
**SALES:** 170.48MM
**SALES (corp-wide):** 33.92B **Privately Held**
Web: www.calliduscloud.com
**SIC: 7371** 7372 Custom computer programming services; Business oriented computer software
**PA:** Sap Se
Dietmar-Hopp-Allee 16
622 774-7474

### (P-17895)
### CHEQUE GUARD INC
512 S Verdugo Dr, Burbank (91502-2344)
**PHONE**..............................818 563-9335
Emil Ramzy, *Pr*
Alfred Ramzi, *
Louris Khalaf, *
**EMP:** 54 **EST:** 2002
**SQ FT:** 6,000
**SALES (est):** 2.52MM **Privately Held**
Web: www.cheque-guard.com
**SIC: 7371** 2893 Computer software development; Printing ink

### (P-17896)
### CHROMACODE INC
2330 Faraday Ave Ste 100, Carlsbad (92008-7244)
**PHONE**..............................442 244-4369
Mark Mcdonough, *CEO*
Mark Mcdonough, *CEO*
Alex Dickinson, *
Lynne Rollins, *
**EMP:** 27 **EST:** 2014
**SALES (est):** 8.45MM **Privately Held**
Web: www.chromacode.com
**SIC: 7371** 3841 8731 Computer software development; Diagnostic apparatus, medical ; Biological research

### (P-17897)
### CITRUSBYTE LLC
Also Called: Theorem LLC
21550 Oxnard St Ste 300 # 11, Woodland Hills (91367-7109)
**PHONE**..............................888 969-2983
William Jessup, *Managing Member*
**EMP:** 30 **EST:** 2015
**SALES (est):** 5.11MM **Privately Held**
Web: www.theoremone.co
**SIC: 7371** 7372 7373 Computer software development and applications; Business oriented computer software; Computer integrated systems design

### (P-17898)
### CLUSTRIX INC
699 Veterans Blvd, Redwood City (94063-1408)
**PHONE**..............................415 501-9560
Mike Azevedo, *CEO*
Robin Purohit, *
Aaron Passey, *
Mark Sarbiewski, *CMO*
Sergei Tsarev, *
**EMP:** 29 **EST:** 2006
**SALES (est):** 4.23MM
**SALES (corp-wide):** 10.05MM **Privately Held**
Web: www.mariadb.com
**SIC: 7371** 3577 Computer software development; Computer peripheral equipment, nec
**PA:** Mariadb Usa, Inc.
1900 Mccarthy Blvd
855 562-7423

### (P-17899)
### COMPUTER POWER SFTWR GROUP INC (PA)
Also Called: Cpsg

716 Figueroa St, Folsom (95630-2514)
PHONE..................916 985-4445
David M Saykally, *Pr*
**EMP:** 17 **EST:** 1992
**SQ FT:** 4,000
**SALES (est):** 8.87MM **Privately Held**
Web: www.cpsoftwaregroup.com
**SIC: 7371** 7372 Computer software development; Prepackaged software

### (P-17900)
### COMPUTRITION INC (HQ)
Also Called: Dfm Dietary Food Management
8521 Fallbrook Ave Ste 100, Canoga Park (91304-3236)
PHONE..................818 961-3999
Scott Saklad, *Pr*
Kim C Goldberg, *Marketing*
**EMP:** 60 **EST:** 1981
**SQ FT:** 16,763
**SALES (est):** 13.33MM
**SALES (corp-wide):** 8.41B **Privately Held**
Web: www.computrition.com
**SIC: 7371** 7372 Computer software development; Prepackaged software
**PA:** Constellation Software Inc
20 Adelaide St E Suite 1200
416 861-9677

### (P-17901)
### COUCHBASE INC (PA)
3250 Olcott St, Santa Clara (95054-3026)
PHONE..................650 417-7500
Matthew M Cain, *Pr*
Greg Henry, *Sr VP*
Margaret Chow, *CLO*
Bill Carey, *Corporate Vice President*
Huw Owen, *CRO*
**EMP:** 152 **EST:** 2008
**SQ FT:** 46,000
**SALES (est):** 180.04MM
**SALES (corp-wide):** 180.04MM **Publicly Held**
Web: www.couchbase.com
**SIC: 7371** 7372 Computer software development; Business oriented computer software

### (P-17902)
### CREATIVE DGTAL SYSTEMS INTGRTI
670 E Easy St, Simi Valley (93065-1808)
PHONE..................805 364-0555
Norman Lamarra, *CEO*
Anand Kelkar, *VP*
Luc Gravelle, *Sec*
Nancy Konysky, *Treas*
◆ **EMP:** 16 **EST:** 2006
**SQ FT:** 15,000
**SALES (est):** 4.27MM **Privately Held**
Web: www.cdsi-simi.com
**SIC: 7371** 3812 Computer software development; Defense systems and equipment

### (P-17903)
### CRESCENTONE INC (HQ)
200 Continental Blvd Fl 3, El Segundo (90245-4510)
PHONE..................310 563-7000
Chikara Ono, *CEO*
Jim Errington, *Ex VP*
Masahiro Cho, *CFO*
**EMP:** 150 **EST:** 1970
**SQ FT:** 53,000
**SALES (est):** 21.25MM
**SALES (corp-wide):** 8.41B **Privately Held**
Web: www.glovia.com
**SIC: 7371** 7372 Computer software development; Prepackaged software

**PA:** Constellation Software Inc
20 Adelaide St E Suite 1200
416 861-9677

### (P-17904)
### CUBIC TRNSP SYSTEMS INC (DH)
Also Called: Cubic
9233 Balboa Ave, San Diego (92123-1513)
P.O. Box 85587 (92186-5587)
PHONE..................858 268-3100
Stephen O Shewmaker, *CEO*
Walter C Zable, *
Raymond De Kozan, *
Steve Purcell, *
◆ **EMP:** 550 **EST:** 1950
**SALES (est):** 244.67MM
**SALES (corp-wide):** 1.48B **Privately Held**
Web: www.cubic.com
**SIC: 7371** 1731 3829 Custom computer programming services; Telephone and telephone equipment installation; Fare registers, for street cars, buses, etc.
**HQ:** Cubic Corporation
9233 Balboa Ave
San Diego CA 92123
858 277-6780

### (P-17905)
### CYBERDEFENDER CORPORATION
617 W 7th St Fl 10, Los Angeles (90017-3879)
PHONE..................323 449-0774
Kevin Harris, *Interim Chief Executive Officer*
Igor Barash, *COO*
**EMP:** 18 **EST:** 2003
**SALES (est):** 1.83MM **Privately Held**
Web: www.cyberdefender.com
**SIC: 7371** 7372 Custom computer programming services; Prepackaged software

### (P-17906)
### DATA PROCESSING DESIGN INC
Also Called: Goldfax
1409 Glenneyre St Ste B, Laguna Beach (92651-3171)
PHONE..................714 695-1000
Brendan Nolan, *CEO*
Tom Politowski, *
**EMP:** 31 **EST:** 1976
**SALES (est):** 3.13MM **Privately Held**
Web: www.egoldfax.com
**SIC: 7371** 7372 Computer software development; Prepackaged software

### (P-17907)
### DATASELF CORP
1200 Franklin Mall, Santa Clara (95050-4807)
PHONE..................888 910-9802
Joni Girardi, *CEO*
**EMP:** 20 **EST:** 2005
**SALES (est):** 2.36MM **Privately Held**
Web: www.dataself.com
**SIC: 7371** 7372 Software programming applications; Publisher's computer software

### (P-17908)
### DAZ SYSTEMS LLC
Also Called: Daz
1003 E 4th Pl Ste 800, Los Angeles (90013-2775)
PHONE..................310 640-1300
Walt Zipperman, *CEO*
Deborah Arnold, *
David Binkley, *
**EMP:** 375 **EST:** 1995
**SALES (est):** 14.39MM **Privately Held**

**SIC: 7371** 7372 Computer software development; Prepackaged software
**HQ:** Accenture Llp
500 W Madison St
Chicago IL 60661
312 693-5009

### (P-17909)
### DESIGN SCIENCE INC
444 W Ocean Blvd Ste 800, Long Beach (90802-4529)
PHONE..................562 442-4779
Paul Topping, *Pr*
**EMP:** 30 **EST:** 1986
**SALES (est):** 2.6MM **Privately Held**
Web: www.wiris.com
**SIC: 7371** 7379 7372 5045 Computer software development; Computer related consulting services; Prepackaged software; Computers, peripherals, and software

### (P-17910)
### DEVONWAY INC (DH)
601 California St Ste 615, San Francisco (94108-2811)
PHONE..................415 904-4000
Chris Moustakas, *Pr*
**EMP:** 21 **EST:** 2007
**SALES (est):** 4.65MM
**SALES (corp-wide):** 2.67MM **Privately Held**
Web: www.devonway.com
**SIC: 7371** 7372 Computer software development; Business oriented computer software
**HQ:** Ideagen Limited
Mere Way Ruddington Fields Business Park
Nottingham NOTTS NG11
162 969-9100

### (P-17911)
### DICOM SYSTEMS INC
1999 S Bascom Ave Ste 700, Campbell (95008-2205)
P.O. Box 923 (94528-0923)
PHONE..................415 684-8790
Dmitriy Tochilnik, *CEO*
Anna Koval, *
Tanya Wehr, *
Florent Saint-clair, *Ex VP*
**EMP:** 25 **EST:** 2008
**SALES (est):** 2.33MM **Privately Held**
Web: www.dcmsys.com
**SIC: 7371** 7372 Computer software development; Prepackaged software

### (P-17912)
### DISPLAYLINK CORP (HQ)
1251 Mckay Dr, San Jose (95131-1709)
PHONE..................650 838-0481
Graham Okeeffe, *CEO*
**EMP:** 16 **EST:** 2003
**SALES (est):** 3.44MM
**SALES (corp-wide):** 959.4MM **Publicly Held**
Web: www.synaptics.com
**SIC: 7371** 7372 Computer software development and applications; Prepackaged software
**PA:** Synaptics Incorporated
1109 Mckay Dr
408 904-1100

### (P-17913)
### DISTILLERY TECH INC
Also Called: Distillery
1500 Rosecrans Ave Ste 500, Manhattan Beach (90266-3771)
PHONE..................310 776-6234

Andrey Kudievskiy, *Pr*
**EMP:** 220 **EST:** 2012
**SALES (est):** 13.7MM **Privately Held**
Web: www.distillery.com
**SIC: 7371** 7372 7373 Computer software development; Application computer software; Computer systems analysis and design

### (P-17914)
### DREMIO CORPORATION (PA)
3970 Freedom Cir Ste 110, Santa Clara (95054)
PHONE..................408 882-3569
Sendur Sellakumar, *CEO*
Tomer Shiran, *
**EMP:** 24 **EST:** 2015
**SALES (est):** 14.93MM
**SALES (corp-wide):** 14.93MM **Privately Held**
Web: www.dremio.com
**SIC: 7371** 7372 Computer software development; Business oriented computer software

### (P-17915)
### DYNAMIC GRAPHICS INC (PA)
3697 Mt Diablo Blvd, Lafayette (94549-3747)
PHONE..................510 522-0700
Arthur Paradis, *Pr*
Tamara Paradis, *
**EMP:** 25 **EST:** 1969
**SALES (est):** 3.42MM
**SALES (corp-wide):** 3.42MM **Privately Held**
Web: www.dgi.com
**SIC: 7371** 7372 Computer software development; Prepackaged software

### (P-17916)
### EMILYKATE LLC
Also Called: Lifearound2angels
8336 Valdez Ave, Sacramento (95828-0938)
PHONE..................916 761-6261
Simon Leung, *Pt*
Ningzi Sun, *Pr*
**EMP:** 19 **EST:** 2017
**SALES (est):** 1.03MM **Privately Held**
**SIC: 7371** 2844 2841 2842 Computer software development and applications; Bath salts; Soap and other detergents; Disinfectants, household or industrial plant

### (P-17917)
### FALKONRY INC
10020 N De Anza Blvd Ste 200, Cupertino (95014-2213)
PHONE..................408 761-7108
Nikunj R Mehta, *CEO*
Nikunj R Mehta, *Pr*
Parveen Jain, *
Mark Gorenberg, *
**EMP:** 55 **EST:** 2013
**SALES (est):** 4.77MM **Privately Held**
Web: www.falkonry.com
**SIC: 7371** 7372 Software programming applications; Application computer software

### (P-17918)
### FASTLY INC (PA)
Also Called: FASTLY
475 Brannan St Ste 300, San Francisco (94107-5420)
P.O. Box 78266 (94107-8266)
PHONE..................844 432-7859
Todd Nightingale, *CEO*
David Hornik, *Ch Bd*
Ronald Kisling, *CFO*
**EMP:** 432 **EST:** 2011

## 7371 - Custom Computer Programming Services (P-17919)

SQ FT: 71,343
SALES (est): 505.99MM
SALES (corp-wide): 505.99MM **Publicly Held**
Web: www.fastly.com
SIC: **7371** 7372 Computer software development; Prepackaged software

### (P-17919)
### FATTAIL INC (HQ)
23586 Calabasas Rd Ste 102, Calabasas (91302-1322)
PHONE..................818 615-0380
Douglas Huntington, *CEO*
Barry Witkow, *
EMP: 30 EST: 2001
SQ FT: 3,500
SALES (est): 5.77MM
SALES (corp-wide): 5.77MM **Privately Held**
Web: www.fattail.com
SIC: **7371** 7372 Computer software development; Business oriented computer software
PA: Eventures International, Llc
23586 Clabasas Rd Ste 102

### (P-17920)
### FICTIV INC (PA)
48511 Warm Springs Blvd Ste 208, Fremont (94539-7746)
P.O. Box 14590 (94539-1090)
PHONE..................415 580-2509
David Evans, *CEO*
Nathan Evans, *
EMP: 119 EST: 2013
SQ FT: 1,000
SALES (est): 31.91MM
SALES (corp-wide): 31.91MM **Privately Held**
Web: www.fictiv.com
SIC: **7371** 3089 Computer software development; Air mattresses, plastics

### (P-17921)
### FICTO HOLDINGS LLC
Also Called: Ficto
1049 Havenhurst Dr Ste 236, West Hollywood (90046-6002)
PHONE..................424 250-2400
EMP: 17 EST: 2018
SALES (est): 3.33MM **Privately Held**
Web: www.ficto.tv
SIC: **7371** 2741 Computer software development and applications; Internet publishing and broadcasting

### (P-17922)
### FINANCIAL INFO NETWRK INC
Also Called: F I N
11164 Bertrand Ave, Granada Hills (91344-4005)
P.O. Box 7954 (91409-7954)
PHONE..................818 782-0331
Jerry Sears, *Pr*
EMP: 25 EST: 1969
SQ FT: 6,000
SALES (est): 1.7MM **Privately Held**
Web: www.fingps.com
SIC: **7371** 7372 Custom computer programming services; Prepackaged software

### (P-17923)
### FLEET DEVICE MANAGEMENT INC
548 Market St # 71434, San Francisco (94104-5401)
PHONE..................415 651-2575
EMP: 15 EST: 2020
SALES (est): 7.3MM **Privately Held**
Web: www.fleetdm.com
SIC: **7371** 8741 3577 Custom computer programming services; Management services; Computer peripheral equipment, nec

### (P-17924)
### FOREMAY INC (PA)
225 S Lake Ave Ste 300, Pasadena (91101-3009)
PHONE..................408 228-3468
Haining Fan, *CEO*
Tiffany Fan, *Pr*
EMP: 46 EST: 2002
SALES (est): 4.66MM **Privately Held**
Web: www.foremay.net
SIC: **7371** 7373 3572 Computer software systems analysis and design, custom; Computer systems analysis and design; Computer storage devices

### (P-17925)
### FULLCONTACT INC
Also Called: Mattermark
535 Mission St Fl 14, San Francisco (94105-3253)
PHONE..................415 366-6587
EMP: 22
SALES (corp-wide): 22.48MM **Privately Held**
Web: www.fullcontact.com
SIC: **7371** 7372 Computer software development; Application computer software
PA: Fullcontact Inc.
1615 Platte St Ste 3-163
888 330-6943

### (P-17926)
### HVANTAGE TECHNOLOGIES INC (PA)
22048 Sherman Way Ste 306, Canoga Park (91303-3011)
PHONE..................818 661-6301
Krishna Baderia, *CEO*
EMP: 79 EST: 2011
SALES (est): 4.62MM
SALES (corp-wide): 4.62MM **Privately Held**
Web: www.hvantagetechnologies.com
SIC: **7371** 8748 7372 7373 Computer software development; Systems engineering consultant, ex. computer or professional; Application computer software; Systems engineering, computer related

### (P-17927)
### HYLAND LLC
12919 Earhart Ave, Auburn (95602-9538)
PHONE..................440 788-5045
EMP: 15
SALES (corp-wide): 486.2MM **Privately Held**
Web: www.hyland.com
SIC: **7371** 7372 Computer software development; Prepackaged software
HQ: Hyland Llc
18103 W 106th St Ste 200
Olathe KS 66061
440 788-5045

### (P-17928)
### IMAGE-X ENTERPRISES INC
Also Called: Image X
6464 Hollister Ave Ste 7g, Goleta (93117-3110)
PHONE..................805 964-3535
Mohammed Shaikh, *Ch Bd*
EMP: 30 EST: 1989
SQ FT: 4,000
SALES (est): 1.12MM **Privately Held**
Web: www.imagexusa.com
SIC: **7371** 3577 Computer software development; Computer peripheral equipment, nec

### (P-17929)
### INNOSYS INCORPORATED
Also Called: Keyspan
1555 3rd Ave, Walnut Creek (94597-2604)
PHONE..................510 594-1034
Michael Ridenhour, *Pr*
Eric Welch, *
Vic Pectol, *
EMP: 30 EST: 1972
SQ FT: 10,000
SALES (est): 1.73MM **Privately Held**
Web: www.innosys.com
SIC: **7371** 3577 Computer software development; Computer peripheral equipment, nec

### (P-17930)
### INSTANT SYSTEMS INC
Also Called: Instantsys
447 King Ave, Fremont (94536-1516)
PHONE..................510 657-8100
Vipin K Chawla, *Pr*
Uzay Takaoglu, *
Mamta Chawla, *
▲ EMP: 90 EST: 2004
SALES (est): 4.66MM **Privately Held**
Web: www.instantsys.com
SIC: **7371** 7372 Custom computer programming services; Business oriented computer software

### (P-17931)
### INTAPP US INC (HQ)
Also Called: Intapp
3101 Park Blvd, Palo Alto (94306-2233)
PHONE..................650 852-0400
John Hall, *CEO*
Dan Tacone, *
Sanjeev Gandhi, *
Pat Archbold, *
Steve Robertson, *
EMP: 200 EST: 2005
SALES (est): 186.85MM
SALES (corp-wide): 430.52MM **Publicly Held**
Web: www.intapp.com
SIC: **7371** 7372 Computer software development and applications; Business oriented computer software
PA: Intapp, Inc.
3101 Park Blvd
650 852-0400

### (P-17932)
### INTEGEM
20432 Silverado Ave Ste 210, Cupertino (95014-4454)
PHONE..................408 459-0657
Eliza Du, *CEO*
EMP: 25 EST: 2015
SALES (est): 961.97K **Privately Held**
Web: www.integem.com
SIC: **7371** 8299 7372 Computer software development and applications; Educational services; Educational computer software

### (P-17933)
### INTELLISYNC CORPORATION
313 Fairchild Dr, Mountain View (94043-2215)
PHONE..................650 625-2185
Woodson Hobbs, *Pr*
Clyde Foster, *COO*
David Eichler, *CFO*
Robert Gerber, *CMO*
EMP: 456 EST: 1993
SQ FT: 33,821
SALES (est): 21.8MM
SALES (corp-wide): 24.19B **Privately Held**
SIC: **7371** 7372 Computer software development; Prepackaged software
PA: Nokia Oyj
Karakaari 7
104488000

### (P-17934)
### INTERNATIONAL BUS MCHS CORP
Also Called: IBM
555 Bailey Ave, San Jose (95141-1099)
PHONE..................408 463-2000
Lou Gerstner, *Mgr*
EMP: 1500
SALES (corp-wide): 61.86B **Publicly Held**
Web: www.ibm.com
SIC: **7371** 7372 5961 Computer software development; Prepackaged software; Catalog and mail-order houses
PA: International Business Machines Corporation
1 New Orchard Rd
914 499-1900

### (P-17935)
### INTERNATIONAL LOTTERY & TOTALIZATOR SYSTEMS INC
Also Called: Ilts California
2310 Cousteau Ct, Vista (92081-8346)
PHONE..................760 598-1655
EMP: 33
Web: www.ilts.com
SIC: **7371** 7372 3572 Custom computer programming services; Prepackaged software; Computer storage devices

### (P-17936)
### INTERNTNAL LTTERY TTLZTOR SYST
Also Called: Ilts Delaware
2310 Cousteau Ct, Vista (92081-8346)
PHONE..................760 598-1655
Theodore A Johnson, *
▲ EMP: 33 EST: 1999
SALES (est): 10.03MM **Privately Held**
Web: www.ilts.com
SIC: **7371** 7372 3572 Custom computer programming services; Prepackaged software; Computer storage devices
PA: Berjaya Lottery Management (Hk) Limited
5/F Manulife Place

### (P-17937)
### JAVANAN INC
Also Called: Javanan Magazine
24629 Calvert St, Woodland Hills (91367-1018)
PHONE..................310 741-0011
Mehdi Zokaei, *CEO*
EMP: 20 EST: 1991
SALES (est): 835.14K **Privately Held**
Web: www.javanan.com
SIC: **7371** 2721 Computer software development and applications; Magazines: publishing only, not printed on site

### (P-17938)
### KAIZEN TECHNOLOGY PARTNERS LLC
981 Mission St, San Francisco (94103-2912)
PHONE..................415 515-1909
Lori Jensen, *Pt*

# PRODUCTS & SERVICES SECTION
## 7371 - Custom Computer Programming Services (P-17958)

Dao Jensen, *Managing Member*
Arthur Chambers, *Managing Member*
**EMP:** 20 **EST:** 2013
**SALES (est):** 3.47MM **Privately Held**
**Web:** www.oakrocket.com
**SIC:** 7371 7372 8748 Computer software systems analysis and design, custom; Business oriented computer software; Systems engineering consultant, ex. computer or professional

### (P-17939)
### LADDER FINANCIAL INC
Also Called: Ladder
100 Forest Ave, Palo Alto (94301-1612)
P.O. Box 456 (94026-0456)
**PHONE**.................................844 533-7206
Jamie Hale, *Pr*
**EMP:** 35 **EST:** 2015
**SALES (est):** 14.1MM **Privately Held**
**Web:** www.ladderlife.com
**SIC:** 7371 7372 Computer software development and applications; Application computer software

### (P-17940)
### LAMBDA INC
Also Called: Lambda
2510 Zanker Rd, San Jose (95131-1127)
**PHONE**.................................650 741-0738
Stephen Balaban, *CEO*
Mitesh Agrawal, *
**EMP:** 130 **EST:** 2012
**SALES (est):** 31.53MM **Privately Held**
**Web:** www.lambdalabs.com
**SIC:** 7371 3571 7373 7377 Computer software development; Computers, digital, analog or hybrid; Computer systems analysis and design; Computer hardware rental or leasing, except finance leasing

### (P-17941)
### LAYLINE AUTOMATION
1005 Northgate Dr, San Rafael (94903-2500)
**PHONE**.................................415 758-0044
Hal Mccormack, *Pr*
**EMP:** 68 **EST:** 2013
**SALES (est):** 2.21MM **Privately Held**
**Web:** www.laylineautomation.com
**SIC:** 7371 8748 7372 Computer software systems analysis and design, custom; Telecommunications consultant; Utility computer software

### (P-17942)
### LOGILITY INC
4885 Greencraig Ln 200, San Diego (92123-1664)
**PHONE**.................................858 565-4238
**EMP:** 55
**SALES (corp-wide):** 102.52MM **Publicly Held**
**Web:** www.logility.com
**SIC:** 7371 7372 Computer software development; Prepackaged software
**HQ:** Logility, Inc.
470 E Paces Ferry Rd
Atlanta GA 30305
800 762-5207

### (P-17943)
### LUMEDX CORPORATION (PA)
555 12th St Ste 2060, Oakland (94607-3695)
P.O. Box 737096 (75373-7096)
**PHONE**.................................510 419-1000
Allyn Mc Auley, *Pr*
Laurel Shearer, *Ex VP*
**EMP:** 18 **EST:** 1984
**SQ FT:** 15,000
**SALES (est):** 8.98MM **Privately Held**
**Web:** www.lumedx.com
**SIC:** 7371 7372 Computer software development; Prepackaged software

### (P-17944)
### MAINTECH INCORPORATED
2401 N Glassell St, Orange (92865-2705)
P.O. Box 13500 (92857-8500)
**PHONE**.................................714 921-8000
Tony Donato, *VP*
**EMP:** 200
**SQ FT:** 1,200
**SALES (corp-wide):** 27.04MM **Privately Held**
**Web:** www.maintech.com
**SIC:** 7371 3577 Computer software systems analysis and design, custom; Computer peripheral equipment, nec
**PA:** Maintech, Incorporated
14 Commerce Dr Ste 200
973 330-3200

### (P-17945)
### MARKETO INC (HQ)
901 Mariners Island Blvd Ste 200, San Mateo (94404-1573)
**PHONE**.................................650 376-2303
Allison Blais, *CEO*
Keith San Felipe, *
Jonathan Vaas, *
**EMP:** 219 **EST:** 2006
**SQ FT:** 102,670
**SALES (corp-wide):** 19.41B **Publicly Held**
**SIC:** 7371 7372 Computer software development; Prepackaged software
**PA:** Adobe Inc.
345 Park Ave
408 536-6000

### (P-17946)
### MARVEL PARENT LLC (HQ)
1950 University Ave Ste 350, Palo Alto (94303-2286)
**PHONE**.................................650 321-4910
Scott E Landers, *Pr*
**EMP:** 54 **EST:** 2019
**SALES (est):** 127.56MM
**SALES (corp-wide):** 1.88MM **Privately Held**
**SIC:** 7371 7372 Custom computer programming services; Prepackaged software
**PA:** Hggc, Llc
1950 Univ Ave Ste 350
650 321-4910

### (P-17947)
### MEDIMIZER SOFTWARE
Also Called: Medimizer
9920 Pacific Heights Blvd Ste 150, San Diego (92121-4361)
**PHONE**.................................760 642-2000
Mark Woodruff, *Pr*
**EMP:** 20 **EST:** 2011
**SALES (est):** 1.58MM **Privately Held**
**Web:** www.medimizer.com
**SIC:** 7371 7372 Computer software development; Prepackaged software

### (P-17948)
### MERIDIANLINK INC (PA)
Also Called: Meridianlink
3560 Hyland Ave Ste 200, Costa Mesa (92626-1438)
**PHONE**.................................714 708-6950
Nicolaas Vlok, *CEO*
Edward H Mcdermott, *Non-Executive Chairman of the Board*
Laurence E Katz, *Pr*
Timothy Nguyen, *CSO*
Elias Olmeta, *CFO*
**EMP:** 58 **EST:** 1998
**SQ FT:** 19,838
**SALES (est):** 303.62MM
**SALES (corp-wide):** 303.62MM **Publicly Held**
**Web:** www.meridianlink.com
**SIC:** 7371 7372 Computer software development; Prepackaged software

### (P-17949)
### MINDSHARE DESIGN INC
Also Called: Savicom
475 14th St Ste 250, Oakland (94612-1833)
**PHONE**.................................510 904-6900
Meredith Crawford, *CEO*
**EMP:** 26 **EST:** 1996
**SQ FT:** 7,300
**SALES (est):** 749.19K **Privately Held**
**Web:** www.mindsharedesign.com
**SIC:** 7371 7336 7372 Custom computer programming services; Graphic arts and related design; Prepackaged software

### (P-17950)
### MINDSOURCE INC
995 Montague Expy Ste 121, Milpitas (95035-6827)
**PHONE**.................................650 314-6400
David Clark, *Pr*
Gabriel Meza, *
**EMP:** 55 **EST:** 1994
**SALES (est):** 5.42MM **Privately Held**
**Web:** www.mindsource.com
**SIC:** 7371 7372 Computer software development; Application computer software

### (P-17951)
### MODERN CAMPUS USA INC (PA)
1320 Flynn Rd Ste 100, Camarillo (93012-8745)
**PHONE**.................................805 484-9400
Brian Kibby, *CEO*
Tom Nalevanko, *
**EMP:** 60 **EST:** 1982
**SQ FT:** 6,600
**SALES (est):** 12.37MM
**SALES (corp-wide):** 12.37MM **Privately Held**
**Web:** www.moderncampus.com
**SIC:** 7371 7372 Computer software development; Prepackaged software

### (P-17952)
### MYEVALUATIONSCOM INC
11111 W Olympic Blvd Ste 401, Los Angeles (90064-1842)
**PHONE**.................................646 422-0554
David Melamed, *Ex Dir*
**EMP:** 25 **EST:** 2005
**SALES (est):** 1.69MM **Privately Held**
**Web:** www.myevaluations.com
**SIC:** 7371 7372 Computer software systems analysis and design, custom; Educational computer software

### (P-17953)
### NC AMERICA LLC ✪
400 Spectrum Center Dr Fl 18, Irvine (92618-5025)
**PHONE**.................................949 447-6287
Taekhun Kim, *CEO*
Taekhun Kim, *Managing Member*
Eunjung Kim, *
**EMP:** 26 **EST:** 2023
**SALES (est):** 1.12MM **Privately Held**
**SIC:** 7371 7372 Computer software development and applications; Prepackaged software

### (P-17954)
### NEURON FUEL INC
Also Called: Tynker
280 Hope St, Mountain View (94041-1308)
**PHONE**.................................408 537-3966
Krishna Vidati, *
**EMP:** 25 **EST:** 2011
**SALES (est):** 2.36MM **Privately Held**
**Web:** www.tynker.com
**SIC:** 7371 7372 Computer software development; Educational computer software

### (P-17955)
### NOVALOGIC INC
27489 Agoura Rd Ste 300, Agoura Hills (91301-2419)
**PHONE**.................................818 880-1997
John Garcia, *CEO*
David Seeholzer, *
John Butrovich, *
Kyle Freeman, *
**EMP:** 100 **EST:** 1985
**SALES (est):** 2.1MM **Privately Held**
**Web:** www.novalogic.com
**SIC:** 7371 5734 7372 Computer software development; Software, business and non-game; Prepackaged software

### (P-17956)
### OC ACQUISITION LLC (HQ)
500 Oracle Pkwy, Redwood City (94065-1677)
**PHONE**.................................650 506-7000
Dorian Daley, *Pr*
Eric Ball, *Treas*
**EMP:** 213 **EST:** 2011
**SALES (est):** 7.17B
**SALES (corp-wide):** 52.96B **Publicly Held**
**SIC:** 7371 7372 Computer software development; Business oriented computer software
**PA:** Oracle Corporation
2300 Oracle Way
737 867-1000

### (P-17957)
### OPSHUB INC
1000 Elwell Ct Ste 217, Palo Alto (94303-4306)
**PHONE**.................................650 701-1800
Sandeep Jain, *CEO*
**EMP:** 17 **EST:** 2010
**SALES (est):** 882.75K **Privately Held**
**Web:** www.opshub.com
**SIC:** 7371 7372 Computer software development; Prepackaged software

### (P-17958)
### OSISOFT LLC (DH)
Also Called: OSI Software
1600 Alvarado St, San Leandro (94577-2600)
**PHONE**.................................510 297-5800
Andrew Mccloskey, *CEO*
J Kennedy, *Prin*
▲ **EMP:** 418 **EST:** 1980
**SQ FT:** 55,000
**SALES (est):** 93.13MM
**SALES (corp-wide):** 82.05K **Privately Held**
**Web:** www.osisoft.com
**SIC:** 7371 7372 7373 Computer software development; Application computer software; Computer integrated systems design
**HQ:** Aveva Group Limited
High Cross

Cambridge CAMBS CB3 0

**(P-17959)**
**OTTERAI INC**
800 W El Camino Real Ste 170, Mountain View  (94040-2592)
PHONE..............................650 250-6322
Sam Liang, CEO
Yun Fu, *
EMP: 29 EST: 2016
SALES (est): 9.12MM Privately Held
Web: www.otter.ai
SIC: 7371 7372 7373  Computer software development and applications; Application computer software; Systems integration services

**(P-17960)**
**PACHAMA  INC**
2261 Market St Ste 4303, San Francisco (94114-1612)
PHONE..............................650 338-9394
Diego Saez Gil, CEO
EMP: 30 EST: 2018
SALES (est): 6.19MM Privately Held
Web: www.pachama.com
SIC: 7371 7372  Software programming applications; Application computer software

**(P-17961)**
**PARALLEL 6  INC (PA)**
1455 Frazee Rd Ste 900, San Diego (92108-4310)
PHONE..............................619 452-1750
Allan Camaisa, CEO
Adam Halbridge, *
EMP: 30 EST: 2009
SQ FT: 28,000
SALES (est): 3.19MM
SALES (corp-wide): 3.19MM Privately Held
Web: www.parallel6.com
SIC: 7371 7372  Computer software development; Business oriented computer software

**(P-17962)**
**PLATFORM SCIENCE  INC (PA)**
9560 Towne Centre Dr # 200, San Diego (92121)
PHONE..............................844 475-8724
John C Kennedy Iii, CEO
Chris Sultemeier, *
Greg Ivancich, *
Gerald Choung, CRO*
EMP: 140 EST: 2015
SALES (est): 27.19MM
SALES (corp-wide): 27.19MM Privately Held
Web: www.platformscience.com
SIC: 7371 7372  Custom computer programming services; Business oriented computer software

**(P-17963)**
**PRESTO  INC**
2472 Stapleton Ave, Imperial  (92251-9018)
PHONE..............................760 336-1455
Jong Soo Kang, CEO
EMP: 16 EST: 2012
SALES (est): 106.02K Privately Held
Web: www.presto.com
SIC: 7371 7372 7378  Computer software development and applications; Application computer software; Computer peripheral equipment repair and maintenance

**(P-17964)**
**PROCORE TECHNOLOGIES  INC (PA)**
6309 Carpinteria Ave, Carpinteria (93013-2924)
PHONE..............................866 477-6267
Craig F Courtemanche Junior, CEO
Howard Fu, CFO
Benjamin C Singer, CLO
Lawrence J Stack, CRO
Joy D Durling, CDO
EMP: 3386 EST: 2002
SQ FT: 176,000
SALES (est): 950.01MM
SALES (corp-wide): 950.01MM Publicly Held
Web: www.procore.com
SIC: 7371 7372  Computer software development; Prepackaged software

**(P-17965)**
**PROLIFICS TESTING INC**
24025 Park Sorrento Ste 405, Calabasas (91302-4018)
PHONE..............................925 485-9535
Danis Yadegar, Pr
Dale Lampson, VP
Rutesh Shah, VP
Armen Tekerian, VP
Claude Fenner, VP
EMP: 26 EST: 1988
SQ FT: 6,500
SALES (est): 1.9MM Privately Held
Web: www.prolifics.com
SIC: 7371 7372  Computer software development; Prepackaged software
HQ: Prolifics Application Services, Inc.
24025 Park Sorrento # 405
Calabasas CA 91302
646 201-4967

**(P-17966)**
**QUALYS  INC (PA)**
919 E Hillsdale Blvd Ste 400, Foster City (94404-4250)
PHONE..............................650 801-6100
Sumedh S Thakar, Pr
Jeffrey P Hank, *
Joo Mi Kim, CFO
Bruce K Posey, CLO
EMP: 2048 EST: 1999
SQ FT: 76,922
SALES (est): 554.46MM
SALES (corp-wide): 554.46MM Publicly Held
Web: www.qualys.com
SIC: 7371 7372  Custom computer programming services; Prepackaged software

**(P-17967)**
**QUANTCAST CORPORATION (PA)**
795 Folsom St Fl 5, San Francisco (94107-4226)
PHONE..............................800 293-5706
Konrad Feldman, Pr
Matthew Roberts, *
Michael Blum, *
Jag Duggal, *
Julio Pekarovic, *
EMP: 57 EST: 2005
SALES (est): 114.76MM Privately Held
Web: www.quantcast.com
SIC: 7371 7372  Computer software development and applications; Publisher's computer software

**(P-17968)**
**QUID  LLC**
3960 Freedom Cir Ste 200, Santa Clara (95054-1204)
PHONE..............................415 813-5300
Bob Goodson, CEO
Dan Buczaczer, CMO*
Sinohe Terrero, *
Saravanan Subbiah, *
Angela Bakker-lee, CSO
EMP: 125 EST: 2006
SALES (est): 24.83MM Privately Held
Web: www.quid.com
SIC: 7371 7372  Computer software development; Prepackaged software

**(P-17969)**
**RAPIDBIZAPPSCOM  LLC**
Also Called: Rapidbizapps
1525 Mccarthy Blvd Ste 1101, Milpitas (95035-7451)
PHONE..............................408 647-3050
Satish Penmetsa, CEO
Krishna Kunam, *
Hima Bindu Mudunuru, *
EMP: 16 EST: 2010
SQ FT: 500
SALES (est): 869.25K Privately Held
Web: www.rapidbizapps.com
SIC: 7371 7372 7373  Computer software development; Business oriented computer software; Systems software development services

**(P-17970)**
**REPLICON SOFTWARE INC**
Also Called: Replicon
1718 Waverley St, Palo Alto  (94301-3843)
PHONE..............................650 286-9200
Raj Narayanaswamy, CEO
Lakshmi Raj, *
Peter Kinash, *
Brent Sapiro, *
Suresh Kuppahally, *
EMP: 47 EST: 2006
SALES (est): 13.48MM Privately Held
Web: www.replicon.com
SIC: 7371 7372  Computer software development; Prepackaged software

**(P-17971)**
**RESONATE I INC (PA)**
90 Great Oaks Blvd Ste 205, San Jose (95119-1314)
PHONE..............................408 545-5500
Kishore Khandavalli, CEO
Peter R Watkins, *
Richard Hornstein, *
Christopher Marino, Corporate Vice President*
EMP: 160 EST: 1995
SQ FT: 38,000
SALES (est): 8.36MM Privately Held
Web: www.resonatenetworks.com
SIC: 7371 7372  Computer software development; Business oriented computer software

**(P-17972)**
**RETAIL PRO INTERNATIONAL LLC (HQ)**
Also Called: Retail Pro Software
400 Plaza Dr Ste 200, Folsom (95630-4746)
PHONE..............................916 605-7200
Kerry Lemos, CEO
William Colley, *
Kathleen Thompson, *
Shaff Kassam, *
Peter Latona, *
EMP: 61 EST: 1985
SQ FT: 7,500
SALES (est): 13.6MM Privately Held
Web: www.retailpro.com

SIC: 7371 7372  Computer software development; Prepackaged software
PA: Nayax Ltd
3 Arik Einstein

**(P-17973)**
**RISA TECH INC**
27442 Portola Pkwy Ste 200, Foothill Ranch (92610-2822)
PHONE..............................949 951-5815
Amber Freund, CEO
EMP: 22 EST: 2017
SALES (est): 4.63MM
SALES (corp-wide): 925.62MM Privately Held
Web: www.risa.com
SIC: 7371 7372  Computer software development; Prepackaged software
PA: Nemetschek Se
Konrad-Zuse-Platz 1
895404590

**(P-17974)**
**ROGUE GAMES  INC**
Also Called: Rogue Games
4056 Ventura Canyon Ave, Sherman Oaks (91423-4715)
PHONE..............................650 483-8008
Michael Delaet, Prin
Michael C Delaet, Mgr
EMP: 20 EST: 2017
SALES (est): 2.8MM Privately Held
Web: www.rogueco.com
SIC: 7371 2741  Computer software development and applications; Miscellaneous publishing

**(P-17975)**
**SCIFORMA CORPORATION**
600 B St Ste 300, San Diego  (92101-4505)
P.O. Box 9502 (95157-0502)
PHONE..............................408 899-0398
Yann Lebihan, CEO
Roger Meade, *
Charles Meade, *
Dan Karleskint, *
EMP: 28 EST: 2002
SALES (est): 4.86MM
SALES (corp-wide): 4.63MM Privately Held
Web: www.sciforma.com
SIC: 7371 7372  Computer software development; Prepackaged software
PA: Sciforma Holdco
9 Rue Ybry
178945570

**(P-17976)**
**SELECT DATA  INC**
Also Called: Select Data
4175 E La Palma Ave Ste 205, Anaheim (92807-1842)
PHONE..............................714 577-1000
Edward A Buckley, CEO
Pam Hernandez, *
Tawny Nichols, *
Ted A Schulte, *
Pete Poulis, *
EMP: 151 EST: 1991
SALES (est): 17.52MM Privately Held
Web: www.selectdata.com
SIC: 7371 7372  Computer code authors; Prepackaged software

**(P-17977)**
**SELECTIVA SYSTEMS INC**
2051 Junction Ave Ste 225, San Jose (95131-2114)
PHONE..............................408 297-1336
Milind Gokarn, CEO

# PRODUCTS & SERVICES SECTION
## 7371 - Custom Computer Programming Services (P-17997)

Milind Gokarn, *Pr*
Archana Gokarn, *
**EMP:** 92 **EST:** 1999
**SALES (est):** 1.57MM **Privately Held**
**Web:** www.selectiva.com
**SIC: 7371** 7372 Computer software systems analysis and design, custom; Publisher's computer software

**(P-17978)**
**SMART ERP SOLUTIONS INC (PA)**
3875 Hopyard Rd Ste 180, Pleasanton (94588-8505)
**PHONE**..................925 271-0200
Doris Wong, *CEO*
Ramesh B Panchagnula, *Pr*
Raghu Yelluru, *COO*
**EMP:** 35 **EST:** 2005
**SQ FT:** 6,000
**SALES (est):** 9.23MM
**SALES (corp-wide):** 9.23MM **Privately Held**
**Web:** www.smarterp.com
**SIC: 7371** 5734 7372 8742 Computer software development; Software, business and non-game; Prepackaged software; Management consulting services

**(P-17979)**
**SNAIL INC (PA)**
Also Called: SNAIL GAMES
12049 Jefferson Blvd, Culver City (90230-6219)
**PHONE**..................310 988-0643
Hai Shi, *CSO*
Heidy K Chow, *CFO*
Peter Kang, *OF Business Development Operations*
▲ **EMP:** 49 **EST:** 2009
**SQ FT:** 7,163
**SALES (est):** 60.9MM **Publicly Held**
**Web:** www.snail.com
**SIC: 7371** 5092 7372 Computer software development; Video games; Prepackaged software

**(P-17980)**
**SNAP INC (PA)**
Also Called: SNAPCHAT
3000 31st St Ste C, Santa Monica (90405-3046)
**PHONE**..................310 399-3339
Evan Spiegel, *CEO*
Michael Lynton, *
Derek Andersen, *CFO*
Robert Murphy, *
Rebecca Morrow, *CAO*
**EMP:** 520 **EST:** 2010
**SQ FT:** 718,000
**SALES (est):** 4.61B
**SALES (corp-wide):** 4.61B **Publicly Held**
**Web:** www.snap.com
**SIC: 7371** 7372 Computer software development and applications; Application computer software

**(P-17981)**
**SOLARTIS LLC**
Also Called: Solartis
1601 N Sepulveda Blvd Ste 606, Manhattan Beach (90266-5111)
**PHONE**..................310 251-4861
Siby Nidhiry, *
**EMP:** 26 **EST:** 2000
**SALES (est):** 2.46MM **Privately Held**
**Web:** www.solartis.com
**SIC: 7371** 7374 7372 Computer software development; Data processing and preparation; Business oriented computer software

**(P-17982)**
**STARTEL CORPORATION (PA)**
16 Goodyear B-125, Irvine (92618)
**PHONE**..................949 863-8700
William Lane, *Pr*
**EMP:** 60 **EST:** 1980
**SQ FT:** 27,000
**SALES (est):** 9.63MM
**SALES (corp-wide):** 9.63MM **Privately Held**
**Web:** www.startel.com
**SIC: 7371** 3661 Computer software development; Communication headgear, telephone

**(P-17983)**
**STRATCOM SYSTEMS INC**
Also Called: Sims Software
2701 Loker Ave W Ste 130, Carlsbad (92010-6637)
P.O. Box 607 (92075-0607)
**PHONE**..................858 481-9292
Michael Struttmann, *Pr*
**EMP:** 24 **EST:** 1983
**SQ FT:** 2,500
**SALES (est):** 3.15MM **Privately Held**
**Web:** www.simssoftware.com
**SIC: 7371** 7372 Computer software development; Prepackaged software

**(P-17984)**
**STREAMSETS INC**
1875 S Grant St Ste 810, San Mateo (94402-7048)
**PHONE**..................415 851-1018
Girish Pancha, *CEO*
**EMP:** 52 **EST:** 2014
**SALES (est):** 13.13MM
**SALES (corp-wide):** 61.86B **Publicly Held**
**Web:** www.streamsets.com
**SIC: 7371** 7372 Software programming applications; Business oriented computer software
**PA:** International Business Machines Corporation
1 New Orchard Rd
914 499-1900

**(P-17985)**
**TESLARATI LLC**
11040 Bollinger Canyon Rd Ste E879, San Ramon (94582-4969)
**PHONE**..................323 405-7657
**EMP:** 18 **EST:** 2016
**SALES (est):** 1.21MM **Privately Held**
**Web:** www.teslarati.com
**SIC: 7371** 2741 Computer software development and applications; Internet publishing and broadcasting

**(P-17986)**
**TOMITRIBE CORPORATION**
1519 6th St Apt 503, Santa Monica (90401-2532)
**PHONE**..................310 526-7676
David Blevins, *CEO*
Amelia Eiras, *COO*
**EMP:** 20 **EST:** 2012
**SALES (est):** 1.38MM **Privately Held**
**Web:** www.tomitribe.com
**SIC: 7371** 7372 8742 Computer software development; Prepackaged software; Programmed instruction service

**(P-17987)**
**TORR INDUSTRIES INC**
4564 Caterpillar Rd, Redding (96003-1418)
**PHONE**..................530 247-6909
Timothy Orr, *Prin*
**EMP:** 36 **EST:** 2007
**SALES (est):** 3.39MM **Privately Held**
**Web:** www.torrindustries.com
**SIC: 7371** 7692 Software programming applications; Welding repair

**(P-17988)**
**TOUCHTONE CORPORATION**
3151 Airway Ave Ste I3, Costa Mesa (92626-4624)
P.O. Box 5719 (92616-5719)
**PHONE**..................714 755-2810
Reza H Saraf, *Pr*
**EMP:** 20 **EST:** 1991
**SQ FT:** 5,000
**SALES (est):** 695.95K **Privately Held**
**Web:** www.touchtonecorp.com
**SIC: 7371** 7372 Computer software writing services; Prepackaged software

**(P-17989)**
**TRADE DESK INC (PA)**
Also Called: THETRADEDESK
42 N Chestnut St, Ventura (93001-2662)
**PHONE**..................805 585-3434
Jeff T Green, *Ch Bd*
Samantha Jacobson, *CSO*
Laura Schenkein, *CFO*
Jay R Grant, *CLO*
**EMP:** 271 **EST:** 2009
**SALES (est):** 1.95B
**SALES (corp-wide):** 1.95B **Publicly Held**
**Web:** www.thetradedesk.com
**SIC: 7371** 7372 Software programming applications; Prepackaged software

**(P-17990)**
**TUNGSTEN AUTOMATION CORP (PA)**
15211 Laguna Canyon Rd, Irvine (92618-3146)
**PHONE**..................949 783-1000
Reynolds Bish, *CEO*
Cort Townsend, *
Howard Dratler, *
Anthony Macciola, *
Grant Johnson, *
▼ **EMP:** 500 **EST:** 1985
**SQ FT:** 100,000
**SALES (est):** 289.38MM
**SALES (corp-wide):** 289.38MM **Privately Held**
**Web:** www.tungstenautomation.com
**SIC: 7371** 3577 Computer software development; Input/output equipment, computer

**(P-17991)**
**UDELV INC**
30516 Union City Blvd, Union City (94587-1518)
**PHONE**..................650 376-3785
Daniel Laury, *CEO*
**EMP:** 30 **EST:** 2016
**SALES (est):** 6.17MM **Privately Held**
**Web:** www.udelv.com
**SIC: 7371** 3711 Computer software development and applications; Motor vehicles and car bodies

**(P-17992)**
**UNITY SOFTWARE INC (PA)**
Also Called: UNITY
30 3rd St, San Francisco (94103-3104)
**PHONE**..................415 638-9950
Matthew S Bromberg, *Pr*
Roelof Botha, *Ch*
Mark Barrysmith, *Interim Chief Financial Officer*
Anirma Gupta, *CLO*
**EMP:** 255 **EST:** 2004
**SQ FT:** 86,000
**SALES (est):** 2.19B
**SALES (corp-wide):** 2.19B **Publicly Held**
**Web:** www.unity.com
**SIC: 7371** 7372 Computer software development; Prepackaged software

**(P-17993)**
**VERINT AMERICAS INC**
Blue Pumpkin
2250 Walsh Ave Ste 120, Santa Clara (95050-2514)
**PHONE**..................408 830-5400
Doron Aspitz, *Brnch Mgr*
**EMP:** 32
**Web:** www.verint.com
**SIC: 7371** 8742 7372 Computer software writers, freelance; Management consulting services; Prepackaged software
**HQ:** Verint Americas Inc.
225 Broadhollow Rd
Melville NY 11747

**(P-17994)**
**VOSSLOH SIGNALING LLC**
Also Called: Apex Rail Automation
12799 Loma Rica Dr, Grass Valley (95945-9552)
**PHONE**..................530 272-8194
David Ruskauff, *Pr*
**EMP:** 29 **EST:** 2020
**SALES (est):** 7.53MM **Privately Held**
**Web:** www.apexrailautomation.com
**SIC: 7371** 3679 Computer software systems analysis and design, custom; Electronic circuits

**(P-17995)**
**VYSHNAVI INFO TECH INDIA PRVAT**
2603 Camino Ramon Ste 200, San Ramon (94583-9137)
**PHONE**..................408 454-6218
Ravi H Krishnamurthy, *Ch*
**EMP:** 15 **EST:** 2008
**SALES (est):** 257.58K **Privately Held**
**SIC: 7371** 7372 7373 Computer software development and applications; Application computer software; Systems software development services

**(P-17996)**
**WAITWHILE INC**
548 Market St, San Francisco (94104-5401)
**PHONE**..................888 983-0869
Christoffer Klemming, *CEO*
Jonas Klemming, *
**EMP:** 50 **EST:** 2018
**SALES (est):** 2.23MM **Privately Held**
**Web:** www.waitwhile.com
**SIC: 7371** 7372 Computer software development and applications; Application computer software

**(P-17997)**
**WILLIAM STUCKY & ASSOC LLC**
6059 Sycamore Ter, Pleasanton (94566-3870)
**PHONE**..................415 788-2441
William Stucky, *Pr*
**EMP:** 20 **EST:** 1989
**SALES (est):** 2.74MM **Privately Held**
**Web:** www.stuckynet.com

# 7371 - Custom Computer Programming Services (P-17998)

SIC: 7371 7372 Computer software development; Business oriented computer software

**(P-17998)**
**WONDER WORKSHOP INC (PA)**
Also Called: Play-I
116c E 25th Ave, San Mateo (94403-2596)
P.O. Box 1520 (94030-5520)
PHONE.................................408 785-7981
Vikas Gupta, *CEO*
**EMP:** 30 **EST:** 2012
**SALES (est):** 4.97MM
**SALES (corp-wide):** 4.97MM **Privately Held**
Web: www.makewonder.com
SIC: 7371 3944 5092 5945 Computer software development and applications; Games, toys, and children's vehicles; Toys and hobby goods and supplies; Hobby, toy, and game shops

**(P-17999)**
**X1 DISCOVERY INC**
251 S Lake Ave Ste 800, Pasadena (91101-3052)
PHONE.................................877 999-1347
John Patzakis, *CEO*
**EMP:** 36 **EST:** 2011
**SQ FT:** 2,000
**SALES (est):** 6.75MM **Privately Held**
Web: www.x1.com
SIC: 7371 7372 Computer software development; Prepackaged software

**(P-18000)**
**XACTLY CORPORATION (HQ)**
221 Los Gatos Saratoga Rd, Los Gatos (95030-5308)
PHONE.................................408 977-3132
Christopher W Cabrera, *CEO*
L Evan Ellis Junior, *Pr*
Joseph C Consul, *
Elizabeth Salomon, *
Marc Gemassmer, *CSO**
**EMP:** 75 **EST:** 2005
**SALES (est):** 38.13MM
**SALES (corp-wide):** 55.01MM **Privately Held**
Web: www.xactlycorp.com
SIC: 7371 7372 Software programming applications; Prepackaged software
PA: Excalibur Parent, Llc
300 Park Ave Ste 1700
408 977-3132

**(P-18001)**
**ZOOVE LLC**
Also Called: Zoove Corp.
1901 S Bascom Ave Ste 400, Campbell (95008-2238)
PHONE.................................954 448-5442
Wes Hayden, *CEO*
**EMP:** 34 **EST:** 2004
**SALES (est):** 862.38K
**SALES (corp-wide):** 492.75MM **Privately Held**
Web: www.starstarmobile.com
SIC: 7371 7372 Custom computer programming services; Prepackaged software
HQ: Virtual Hold Technology Solutions, Llc
3875 Embassy Pkwy Ste 350
Akron OH 44333

**(P-18002)**
**ZSCALER INC (PA)**
Also Called: Zscaler
120 Holger Way, San Jose (95134-1376)
PHONE.................................408 533-0288
Jay Chaudhry, *Ch Bd*
Remo Canessa, *CFO*
Robert Schlossman, *CLO*
Adam Geller, *Chief Product Officer*
**EMP:** 3656 **EST:** 2007
**SQ FT:** 172,000
**SALES (est):** 2.17B **Publicly Held**
Web: www.zscaler.com
SIC: 7371 7372 Computer software development; Prepackaged software

## 7372 Prepackaged Software

**(P-18003)**
**1ON1 LLC**
8730 Wilshire Blvd Ste 350, Beverly Hills (90211-2716)
PHONE.................................310 998-7473
Susan Josephson, *Managing Member*
**EMP:** 50 **EST:** 2016
**SALES (est):** 3.36MM **Privately Held**
SIC: 7372 Application computer software

**(P-18004)**
**3BECOM INC (PA)**
Also Called: 3becom
2400 Lincoln Ave Ste 216, Altadena (91001-5425)
PHONE.................................818 726-0007
Bob Ntoya, *Pr*
Brian Jones, *COO*
Brennon Neff, *CFO*
Adam Gerber, *Prin*
Simon Wise, *Prin*
**EMP:** 15 **EST:** 2010
**SALES (est):** 2.11MM **Privately Held**
Web: www.3becom.com
SIC: 7372 Prepackaged software

**(P-18005)**
**42CRUNCH INC**
95 3rd St 2nd Fl, San Francisco (94103-3103)
PHONE.................................949 316-1173
**EMP:** 16 **EST:** 2018
**SALES (est):** 5.05MM **Privately Held**
Web: www.42crunch.com
SIC: 7372 Application computer software

**(P-18006)**
**42Q** ◊
60 E Plumeria Dr, San Jose (95134-2102)
PHONE.................................408 964-3222
**EMP:** 38 **EST:** 2023
**SALES (est):** 2.7MM **Privately Held**
Web: www.42-q.com
SIC: 7372 Prepackaged software

**(P-18007)**
**4D SIGHT INC**
2150 Shattuck Ave, Berkeley (94704-1345)
PHONE.................................415 425-1321
Erhan Ciris, *CEO*
Kivanc Alduran, *Chief of Staff*
**EMP:** 25 **EST:** 2020
**SALES (est):** 1.04MM **Privately Held**
Web: www.4dsight.com
SIC: 7372 Application computer software

**(P-18008)**
**ABAQUS INC**
972 N California Ave, Palo Alto (94303-3405)
PHONE.................................415 496-9436
Shailendra Jain, *CEO*
**EMP:** 40 **EST:** 2007
**SALES (est):** 3.64MM **Privately Held**
Web: www.allgeo.com

SIC: 7372 5734 Business oriented computer software; Software, business and non-game

**(P-18009)**
**ACCELA INC (PA)**
9110 Alcosta Blvd, San Ramon (94583-3853)
PHONE.................................925 659-3200
Noam Reininger, *CEO*
Ed Daihl, *
Maury Blackman, *
John Alves, *
Jeffrey Toung, *
**EMP:** 150 **EST:** 1979
**SALES (est):** 56.45MM **Privately Held**
Web: www.accela.com
SIC: 7372 Business oriented computer software

**(P-18010)**
**ACCELERANCE INC**
303 Twin Dolphin Dr Ste 600, Redwood City (94065-1497)
PHONE.................................650 472-3785
Stephan A Mezak, *Prin*
**EMP:** 52 **EST:** 2001
**SALES (est):** 1.11MM **Privately Held**
Web: www.accelerance.com
SIC: 7372 Prepackaged software

**(P-18011)**
**ACCOUNTMATE SOFTWARE CORP (PA)**
1445 Technology Ln Ste A5, Petaluma (94954-7613)
PHONE.................................707 774-7500
David Dierke, *Prin*
David Render, *
Tommy Tan, *
Donna Derosa, *
▲ **EMP:** 38 **EST:** 1984
**SQ FT:** 8,700
**SALES (est):** 4.91MM
**SALES (corp-wide):** 4.91MM **Privately Held**
Web: www.accountmate.com
SIC: 7372 Business oriented computer software

**(P-18012)**
**ACCRUALIFY INC**
333 S B St, San Mateo (94401-4019)
PHONE.................................650 437-7225
Benjamin Portusach, *CEO*
**EMP:** 28 **EST:** 2015
**SALES (est):** 3.5MM **Publicly Held**
Web: www.accrualify.com
SIC: 7372 Business oriented computer software
PA: Corpay, Inc.
3280 Pchtree Rd Ne Ste 24

**(P-18013)**
**ACTIANCE INC**
900 Veterans Blvd Ste 500, Redwood City (94063-1715)
PHONE.................................650 631-6300
**EMP:** 150
Web: www.smarsh.com
SIC: 7372 8742 Prepackaged software; Management consulting services

**(P-18014)**
**ACTIVISION BLIZZARD INC (HQ)**
Also Called: Activision Blizzard
2701 Olympic Blvd Bldg B, Santa Monica (90404-4183)
PHONE.................................310 255-2000
Brian G Kelly, *Ch Bd*
Armin Zerza, *CFO*
Brian Bulatao, *Chief*
Julie Hodges, *CPO*
Lulu Meservey, *Chief Communications Officer*
**EMP:** 333 **EST:** 1979
**SALES (est):** 7.53B
**SALES (corp-wide):** 245.12B **Publicly Held**
Web: www.activisionblizzard.com
SIC: 7372 Prepackaged software
PA: Microsoft Corporation
1 Microsoft Way
425 882-8080

**(P-18015)**
**ACTIVISION BLIZZARD INC**
Blizzard Entertainment
3 Blizzard, Irvine (92606)
P.O. Box 18979 (92623-8979)
PHONE.................................949 955-1380
Frank Pearce, *Prin*
**EMP:** 85
**SALES (corp-wide):** 245.12B **Publicly Held**
Web: www.activisionblizzard.com
SIC: 7372 Prepackaged software
HQ: Activision Blizzard, Inc.
2701 Olympic Blvd Bldg B
Santa Monica CA 90404
310 255-2000

**(P-18016)**
**ADAPTIVE INSIGHTS LLC (HQ)**
2300 Geng Rd Ste 100, Palo Alto (94303-3352)
PHONE.................................650 528-7500
Thomas F Bogan, *CEO*
Bhaskar Himatsingka, *Chief Product Officer**
Frederick M Gewant, *
Connie Dewitt, *
James D Johnson, *
**EMP:** 200 **EST:** 2003
**SALES (est):** 34.43MM **Publicly Held**
Web: www.adaptiveinsights.co.uk
SIC: 7372 Business oriented computer software
PA: Workday, Inc.
6110 Stoneridge Mall Rd

**(P-18017)**
**ADARA INC (PA)**
2625 Middlefield Rd Ste 827, Palo Alto (94306-2516)
PHONE.................................408 876-6360
Layton Han, *CEO*
Frank Teruel, *
Elizabeth Harz, *
Melissa Stein, *
Ellen Lee, *
**EMP:** 60 **EST:** 2005
**SALES (est):** 35.93MM
**SALES (corp-wide):** 35.93MM **Privately Held**
Web: www.adara.com
SIC: 7372 Business oriented computer software

**(P-18018)**
**ADEXA INC (PA)**
5777 W Century Blvd Ste 1100, Los Angeles (90045-5643)
PHONE.................................310 642-2100
Khosrow Cyrus Hadavi, *Ch*
Kameron Hadavi, *
Mario Disandro, *
Tim Field, *
John Hosford, *OF SVCS**
**EMP:** 50 **EST:** 1994
**SQ FT:** 31,000
**SALES (est):** 9.19MM **Privately Held**
Web: www.adexa.com

## 7372 - Prepackaged Software (P-18040)

SIC: 7372 Business oriented computer software

**(P-18019)**
**ADMI INC**
12300 Highland Estates Ln, San Martin (95046-9100)
PHONE...............................408 776-0060
Allen D Moyer, *Pr*
EMP: 52 EST: 2007
SALES (est): 4.63MM **Privately Held**
Web: www.admii.com
SIC: 7372 Operating systems computer software

**(P-18020)**
**ADOBE INC**
601 And 625 Townsend St, San Francisco (94103)
PHONE...............................415 832-2000
Les Schmidt, *VP*
EMP: 24
SALES (corp-wide): 19.41B **Publicly Held**
Web: www.adobe.com
SIC: 7372 Prepackaged software
PA: Adobe Inc.
345 Park Ave
408 536-6000

**(P-18021)**
**ADOBE INC**
321 Park Ave, San Jose (95110-2704)
PHONE...............................408 536-6000
EMP: 34
SALES (corp-wide): 19.41B **Publicly Held**
Web: www.adobe.com
SIC: 7372 Prepackaged software
PA: Adobe Inc.
345 Park Ave
408 536-6000

**(P-18022)**
**ADOBE INC (PA)**
345 Park Ave, San Jose (95110-2704)
PHONE...............................408 536-6000
Shantanu Narayen, *Ch Bd*
Daniel Durn, *Ex VP*
Scott Belsky, *Chief Product Officer*
Ann Lewnes, *CMO*
Dana Rao, *Corporate Secretary*
EMP: 600 EST: 1982
SQ FT: 1,100,000
SALES (est): 19.41B
SALES (corp-wide): 19.41B **Publicly Held**
Web: www.adobe.com
SIC: 7372 Prepackaged software

**(P-18023)**
**ADOBE MACROMEDIA SOFTWARE LLC (HQ)**
601 Townsend St, San Francisco (94103-5247)
PHONE...............................415 832-2000
▲ EMP: 58 EST: 1992
SQ FT: 210,000
SALES (est): 11.11MM
SALES (corp-wide): 19.41B **Publicly Held**
SIC: 7372 Prepackaged software
PA: Adobe Inc.
345 Park Ave
408 536-6000

**(P-18024)**
**ADVISOR SOFTWARE INC (PA)**
2185 N California Blvd Ste 290, Walnut Creek (94596-3540)
PHONE...............................925 299-7782
Andrew Rudd, *Ch*
Neal Ringquist, *
Greg Hutchings, *

Erik Jepson, *Chief Customer Officer**
David Cooper, *
EMP: 25 EST: 1995
SALES (est): 5.29MM **Privately Held**
Web: www.advisorpartners.com
SIC: 7372 Business oriented computer software

**(P-18025)**
**ADVISYS INC**
3 Corporate Park Ste 240, Irvine (92606-5163)
PHONE...............................949 250-0794
Kenneth Kerr, *CEO*
Richard M Kettley, *
Dane Parker, *
Gregg Janes, *
Sherelyn Kettley, *
EMP: 28 EST: 1979
SALES (est): 4.51MM **Privately Held**
Web: www.advisys.com
SIC: 7372 Application computer software

**(P-18026)**
**AFRESH TECHNOLOGIES INC**
33 New Montgomery St Ste 1100, San Francisco (94105-4527)
PHONE...............................415 651-5068
Matthew Schwartz, *CEO*
Nathan Fenner, *
Volodymyr Kuleshov, *
EMP: 100 EST: 2017
SQ FT: 1,400
SALES (est): 8.81MM **Privately Held**
Web: www.afresh.com
SIC: 7372 Business oriented computer software

**(P-18027)**
**AGENCYCOM LLC**
5353 Grosvenor Blvd, Los Angeles (90066-6913)
PHONE...............................415 817-3800
Chan Suh, *CEO*
Rob Elliott, *CFO*
EMP: 400 EST: 1995
SQ FT: 130,000
SALES (est): 2.47MM
SALES (corp-wide): 14.69B **Publicly Held**
SIC: 7372 Application computer software
PA: Omnicom Group Inc.
280 Park Ave
212 415-3600

**(P-18028)**
**AGILEPOINT INC (PA)**
1916 Old Middlefield Way Ste B, Mountain View (94043-2555)
PHONE...............................650 968-6789
Jesse Shiah, *Pr*
EMP: 82 EST: 2003
SQ FT: 2,000
SALES (est): 9.35MM
SALES (corp-wide): 9.35MM **Privately Held**
Web: www.agilepoint.com
SIC: 7372 Business oriented computer software

**(P-18029)**
**AGILOFT INC (PA)**
303 Twin Dolphin Dr, Redwood City (94065-1497)
P.O. Box 2574 (94546-0574)
PHONE...............................650 459-5637
Eric Laughlin, *CEO*
EMP: 73 EST: 1990
SQ FT: 3,200
SALES (est): 13.16MM **Privately Held**
Web: www.agiloft.com

SIC: 7372 Business oriented computer software

**(P-18030)**
**AHA LABS INC**
20 Gloria Cir, Menlo Park (94025)
PHONE...............................650 575-1425
Brian De Haaff, *CEO*
Christopher Waters, *
EMP: 100 EST: 2013
SALES (est): 5.74MM **Privately Held**
Web: www.aha.io
SIC: 7372 Business oriented computer software

**(P-18031)**
**AIRA TECH CORP**
Also Called: Aira Tech
3451 Via Montebello Ste 192 Pmb 214, Carlsbad (92009-8492)
PHONE...............................800 835-1934
Troy Otillio, *CEO*
EMP: 200 EST: 2015
SALES (est): 17.34MM **Privately Held**
Web: www.aira.io
SIC: 7372 Application computer software

**(P-18032)**
**AIRBASE INC (PA)**
548 Market St Ste 93249, San Francisco (94104-5401)
PHONE...............................415 625-6222
Thejo Kote, *CEO*
EMP: 32 EST: 2016
SALES (est): 18.14MM
SALES (corp-wide): 18.14MM **Privately Held**
Web: www.airbase-x.de
SIC: 7372 Application computer software

**(P-18033)**
**AKTANA INC (PA)**
207 Powell St Ste 700, San Francisco (94102-2231)
PHONE...............................888 616-2477
John Vitalie, *CEO*
David Ehrlich, *CEO*
EMP: 219 EST: 2008
SALES (est): 24.03MM **Privately Held**
Web: www.aktana.com
SIC: 7372 Prepackaged software

**(P-18034)**
**ALATION INC (PA)**
3 Lagoon Dr Ste 300, Redwood City (94065-1567)
P.O. Box 1216 (94064)
PHONE...............................650 779-4440
Satyen Sangani, *CEO*
Max Ochoa, *
Paul Sieben, *
Steve Kennedy, *CRO**
Bob Block Ccso, *Prin*
EMP: 483 EST: 2012
SALES (est): 37.71MM
SALES (corp-wide): 37.71MM **Privately Held**
Web: www.alation.com
SIC: 7372 Application computer software

**(P-18035)**
**ALERTENTERPRISE INC (PA)**
4350 Starboard Dr, Fremont (94538-6434)
PHONE...............................510 440-0840
Jasvir Gill, *CEO*
Kaval Kaur, *COO*
Mark Weatherford Ciso, *Prin*
EMP: 140 EST: 2007
SQ FT: 24,000
SALES (est): 14.67MM **Privately Held**

Web: www.alertenterprise.com
SIC: 7372 Prepackaged software

**(P-18036)**
**ALGOLIA INC (PA)**
Also Called: Seaurchin. Io.
301 Howard St Ste 300, San Francisco (94105-6620)
PHONE...............................415 366-9672
Nicolas Dessaigne, *CEO*
Ashley Stirrup, *CMO**
EMP: 49 EST: 2014
SALES (est): 10.7MM
SALES (corp-wide): 10.7MM **Privately Held**
Web: www.algolia.com
SIC: 7372 Prepackaged software

**(P-18037)**
**ALIENVAULT LLC (DH)**
1100 Park Pl Ste 300, San Mateo (94403-7108)
P.O. Box 25237 (94402-5237)
PHONE...............................650 713-3333
Barmak Meftah, *Pr*
Roger Thornton, *
J Alberto Yepez, *
Rita Selvaggi, *CMO**
Michael Biggee, *
EMP: 20 EST: 2009
SALES (est): 57.43MM
SALES (corp-wide): 122.43B **Publicly Held**
Web: cybersecurity.att.com
SIC: 7372 Business oriented computer software
HQ: Alienvault, Inc.
1100 Park Pl Ste 300
San Mateo CA 94403
650 713-3333

**(P-18038)**
**ALIVECOR INC (PA)**
Also Called: Alivecor
189 Bernardo Ave Ste 100, Mountain View (94043-5139)
PHONE...............................650 396-8650
Priya Abani, *CEO*
Jacqueline Shreibati, *Chief Medical Officer*
EMP: 22 EST: 2011
SALES (est): 12.33MM
SALES (corp-wide): 12.33MM **Privately Held**
Web: www.alivecor.com
SIC: 7372 Application computer software

**(P-18039)**
**ALL BLUE LABS INC**
Also Called: Series
548 Market St, San Francisco (94104-5401)
PHONE...............................707 492-5949
Daniel Lai, *Prin*
EMP: 30 EST: 2019
SALES (est): 4.13MM **Privately Held**
SIC: 7372 Prepackaged software

**(P-18040)**
**ALLDATA LLC**
9650 W Taron Dr Ste 100, Elk Grove (95757-8197)
PHONE...............................916 684-5200
Harry L Goldsmith, *
Bob Olsen, *
EMP: 400 EST: 1986
SQ FT: 35,000
SALES (est): 18.51MM
SALES (corp-wide): 18.49B **Publicly Held**
Web: www.alldata.com

## 7372 - Prepackaged Software (P-18041)

SIC: 7372 Business oriented computer software
PA: Autozone, Inc.
123 S Front St
901 495-6500

**(P-18041)**
**ALPHASTAR TECH SOLUTIONS LLC**
2601 Main St Ste 660, Irvine (92614-4257)
PHONE.....................562 961-7827
Frank Abdi, *CEO*
Frank Abdi, *Ch Bd*
Kay Matin, *Pr*
EMP: 18 EST: 1989
SQ FT: 3,800
SALES (est): 4.31MM **Privately Held**
Web: www.alphastarcorp.com
SIC: 7372 7371 3724 Prepackaged software; Computer software development; Research and development on aircraft engines and parts

**(P-18042)**
**ALTUMIND INC**
10620 Treena St Ste 230, San Diego (92131-1140)
PHONE.....................858 382-3956
Ali Naderi, *Managing Member*
EMP: 50 EST: 2021
SALES (est): 2.54MM **Privately Held**
Web: www.altumindtech.com
SIC: 7372 Application computer software

**(P-18043)**
**AMBIT SOFTWARE LLC**
138 W Avenida San Antonio, San Clemente (92672-4354)
PHONE.....................949 361-4070
EMP: 17 EST: 2013
SALES (est): 1.14MM **Privately Held**
Web: www.ambitsoftware.com
SIC: 7372 Prepackaged software

**(P-18044)**
**ANCORA SOFTWARE INC (PA)**
402 W Broadway Ste 400, San Diego (92101-3554)
PHONE.....................888 476-4839
Noel Flynn, *CEO*
Jane Christie, *COO*
David Pintsov, *COO*
Nick Bova, *VP*
EMP: 27 EST: 2015
SALES (est): 2.25MM
SALES (corp-wide): 2.25MM **Privately Held**
Web: www.ancorasoftware.com
SIC: 7372 Prepackaged software

**(P-18045)**
**ANDAPT INC**
950 S Bascom Ave Ste 3012, San Jose (95128-3539)
PHONE.....................408 931-4898
Kapil Shankar, *CEO*
EMP: 15 EST: 2015
SALES (est): 3.3MM **Privately Held**
Web: www.andapt.com
SIC: 7372 Prepackaged software

**(P-18046)**
**ANNEX PRO INC**
4100 W Alameda Ave Fl 3, Burbank (91505-4191)
PHONE.....................800 682-6639
Kerry Corlett, *CEO*
Kalinka Corlett, *Dir*
EMP: 20 EST: 2017
SALES (est): 12MM **Privately Held**
Web: www.annexpro.com
SIC: 7372 5734 8731 5946 Application computer software; Computer peripheral equipment; Computer (hardware) development; Camera and photographic supply stores

**(P-18047)**
**ANNOTATION UNLIMITED PBC**
548 Market St Ste 32444, San Francisco (94104-5401)
PHONE.....................415 295-5689
Daniel Whaley, *Pr*
Peg Fowler, *
EMP: 38 EST: 2019
SALES (est): 521.13K **Privately Held**
SIC: 7372 Educational computer software

**(P-18048)**
**APEX COMMUNICATIONS INC (DH)**
21700 Oxnard St Ste 1060, Woodland Hills (91367-7571)
PHONE.....................818 379-8400
Ben Levy, *Pr*
EMP: 15 EST: 1989
SQ FT: 7,500
SALES (est): 4.2MM
SALES (corp-wide): 335.89MM **Privately Held**
Web: www.apexvoice.com
SIC: 7372 Application computer software
HQ: Dialogic (Us) Inc.
216 Route 17 North # 301
Rochelle Park NJ 07662

**(P-18049)**
**APORETO INC**
10 Almaden Blvd Ste 400, San Jose (95113-2226)
PHONE.....................408 472-7648
Jason Schmitt, *CEO*
Sunil Sampat, *CRO*
Gregg Holzrichter, *CMO*
EMP: 57 EST: 2016
SALES (est): 2.94MM
SALES (corp-wide): 8.03B **Publicly Held**
SIC: 7372 Prepackaged software
PA: Palo Alto Networks Inc.
3000 Tannery Way
408 753-4000

**(P-18050)**
**APOTHEKA SYSTEMS INC**
14040 Panay Way, Marina Del Rey (90292-6697)
P.O. Box 1251 (90213-1251)
PHONE.....................844 777-4455
Dennis Maliani, *CEO*
EMP: 30 EST: 2018
SALES (est): 1.81MM **Privately Held**
Web: www.apotheka.co
SIC: 7372 Application computer software

**(P-18051)**
**APPCOLL INC**
325 Sharon Park Dr, Menlo Park (94025-6805)
PHONE.....................650 223-5460
Jeffrey J Cashen, *Prin*
EMP: 28 EST: 2010
SALES (est): 312.4K **Privately Held**
Web: www.appcoll.com
SIC: 7372 Prepackaged software

**(P-18052)**
**APPFOLIO INC**
Also Called: Mycase
2305 Historic Decatur Rd, San Diego (92106-6050)
PHONE.....................866 648-1536
Troy Alford, *Eng/Dir*
EMP: 162
SALES (corp-wide): 471.88MM **Publicly Held**
Web: www.appfolio.com
SIC: 7372 Prepackaged software
PA: Appfolio, Inc.
70 Castilian Dr
805 364-6093

**(P-18053)**
**APPFOLIO INC (PA)**
Also Called: Appfolio
70 Castilian Dr, Santa Barbara (93117-3027)
PHONE.....................805 364-6093
Jason Randall, *Pr*
Andreas Von Blottnitz, *
Jonathan Walker, *
Fay Sien Goon, *CFO*
Matt Mazza, *CLO*
EMP: 340 EST: 2006
SALES (est): 471.88MM
SALES (corp-wide): 471.88MM **Publicly Held**
Web: www.appfolio.com
SIC: 7372 Business oriented computer software

**(P-18054)**
**APPLIED BIOSYSTEMS LLC (DH)**
Also Called: Applied Biosystems
5791 Van Allen Way, Carlsbad (92008-7321)
▲ EMP: 120 EST: 1937
SQ FT: 51,000
SALES (est): 136.9MM
SALES (corp-wide): 42.86B **Publicly Held**
Web: www.thermofisher.com
SIC: 7372 3826 Prepackaged software; Gas chromatographic instruments
HQ: Life Technologies Corporation
5781 Van Allen Way
Carlsbad CA 92008
760 603-7200

**(P-18055)**
**APPLIED BUSINESS SOFTWARE INC**
Also Called: A B S
7755 Center Ave, Huntington Beach (92647-3007)
PHONE.....................562 426-2188
Jerry Delgado, *Pr*
Edimia Delgado, *Sec*
Gerardo Delgado, *VP*
Eddy Delgado, *VP*
Nelson Noahk, *Contrlr*
EMP: 35 EST: 1979
SALES (est): 3.88MM **Privately Held**
Web: www.themortgageoffice.com
SIC: 7372 5045 5734 Prepackaged software; Computers, peripherals, and software; Computer and software stores

**(P-18056)**
**APPLIED EXPERT SYSTEMS INC**
Also Called: AES
999 Commercial St Ste 201, Palo Alto (94303-4909)
P.O. Box 50927 (94303-0673)
PHONE.....................650 617-2400
Catherine H Liu, *Pr*
David Cheng, *
▲ EMP: 38 EST: 1991
SALES (est): 2.34MM **Privately Held**
Web: www.aesclever.com

**(P-18057)**
**APPLIED STATISTICS & MGT INC**
Also Called: Md-Staff
32848 Wolf Store Rd Ste A, Temecula (92592-8277)
P.O. Box 2738 (92593)
PHONE.....................951 699-4600
Nick Phan, *Pr*
Nickolaus Phan, *
EMP: 95 EST: 1982
SQ FT: 4,000
SALES (est): 9.29MM **Privately Held**
Web: www.mdstaff.com
SIC: 7372 7371 Prepackaged software; Computer software systems analysis and design, custom

**(P-18058)**
**APPLOVIN CORPORATION (PA)**
1100 Page Mill Rd, Palo Alto (94304-1047)
PHONE.....................800 839-9646
Adam Foroughi, *Ch Bd*
Matthew Stumpf, *CFO*
Katie Jansen, *CMO*
Victoria Valenzuela, *CLO*
EMP: 245 EST: 2011
SQ FT: 72,812
SALES (est): 3.28B **Publicly Held**
Web: www.applovin.com
SIC: 7372 Prepackaged software

**(P-18059)**
**APPORTO CORPORATION**
3558 Round Barn Blvd Ste 200, Santa Rosa (95403-1780)
P.O. Box 103081 (91189-0151)
PHONE.....................877 751-4081
Anthony Awaida, *CEO*
EMP: 35 EST: 2011
SALES (est): 5.35MM **Privately Held**
Web: www.apporto.com
SIC: 7372 Prepackaged software

**(P-18060)**
**APTIV DIGITAL LLC**
2160 Gold St, San Jose (95002-3700)
PHONE.....................818 295-6789
Neil Jones, *Pr*
EMP: 85 EST: 1996
SALES (est): 10.19MM
SALES (corp-wide): 388.79MM **Publicly Held**
SIC: 7372 Home entertainment computer software
HQ: Rovi Guides, Inc.
2233 N Ontario St Ste 100
Burbank CA 91504

**(P-18061)**
**ARABLE LABS INC**
51 Federal St Ste 301, San Francisco (94107-4150)
PHONE.....................510 992-4095
EMP: 66 EST: 2019
SALES (est): 8.86MM **Privately Held**
Web: www.arable.com
SIC: 7372 7376 Business oriented computer software; Computer facilities management

**(P-18062)**
**ARCARIS INC (PA)**
Also Called: Playvox
530 Lawrence Expy, Sunnyvale (94085-4014)
PHONE.....................415 854-3801
Louis Bucciarelli, *CEO*
Oscar Giraldo, *

## 7372 - Prepackaged Software (P-18085)

**EMP:** 247 **EST:** 2012
**SALES (est):** 9.07MM
**SALES (corp-wide):** 9.07MM **Privately Held**
**Web:** www.playvox.com
**SIC:** 7372 Prepackaged software

### (P-18063)
### ARCTIC WOLF NETWORKS INC
111 W Evelyn Ave Ste 115, Sunnyvale (94086-6131)
**PHONE**.................................888 272-8429
**EMP:** 114 **EST:** 2012
**SALES (est):** 7.3MM **Privately Held**
**Web:** www.arcticwolf.com
**SIC:** 7372 Business oriented computer software

### (P-18064)
### AREA 1 SECURITY INC
101 Townsend St, San Francisco (94107-1934)
**PHONE**.................................650 924-1637
Patrick Sweeney, *CEO*
Oren Falkowitz, *
Steve Pataky, *CRO*
**EMP:** 65 **EST:** 2014
**SALES (est):** 6.07MM **Privately Held**
**Web:** www.area1security.com
**SIC:** 7372 Prepackaged software

### (P-18065)
### ARIBA INC (DH)
3420 Hillview Ave, Palo Alto (94304-1355)
**PHONE**.................................650 849-4000
Alex Atzberger, *CEO*
Brad Brubaker, *
Marc Malone, *
**EMP:** 105 **EST:** 1996
**SQ FT:** 86,000
**SALES (est):** 204.35MM
**SALES (corp-wide):** 33.92B **Privately Held**
**Web:** www.ariba.com
**SIC:** 7372 Business oriented computer software
**HQ:** Sap America, Inc.
3999 West Chester Pike
Newtown Square PA 19073
610 661-1000

### (P-18066)
### ARTKIVE
16225 Huston St, Encino (91436-1323)
**PHONE**.................................310 975-9809
**EMP:** 41 **EST:** 2012
**SALES (est):** 1.32MM **Privately Held**
**Web:** www.artkiveapp.com
**SIC:** 7372 Prepackaged software

### (P-18067)
### ARXIS TECHNOLOGY INC
2468 Tapo Canyon Rd, Simi Valley (93063-2361)
**PHONE**.................................805 306-7890
Christopher L Hamilton, *CEO*
**EMP:** 21 **EST:** 1994
**SALES (est):** 4.25MM **Privately Held**
**Web:** www.rklesolutions.com
**SIC:** 7372 Prepackaged software

### (P-18068)
### ASCENDER SOFTWARE INC
8885 Rio San Diego Dr Ste 270, San Diego (92108-1624)
**PHONE**.................................877 561-7501
Theodore Kye, *Prin*
**EMP:** 214 **EST:** 2006
**SALES (est):** 1.12MM
**SALES (corp-wide):** 94.72MM **Privately Held**
**Web:** www.matrixmedicalnetwork.com
**SIC:** 7372 Prepackaged software
**PA:** Community Care Health Network, Llc
9201 E Mtn View Rd Ste 22
877 564-3627

### (P-18069)
### ASHBY INC
49 Geary St Ste 411, San Francisco (94108-5730)
**PHONE**.................................408 391-3578
Benjamin Encz, *CEO*
**EMP:** 38 **EST:** 2018
**SALES (est):** 9.03MM **Privately Held**
**Web:** www.ashbyhq.com
**SIC:** 7372 Prepackaged software

### (P-18070)
### ASTEA INTERNATIONAL INC
8 Hughes, Irvine (92618-2072)
**PHONE**.................................949 784-5000
Carl Smith, *Brnch Mgr*
**EMP:** 45
**SALES (corp-wide):** 496.72K **Privately Held**
**Web:** www.astea.com
**SIC:** 7372 Business oriented computer software
**HQ:** Astea International Inc.
300 Park Blvd Ste 350
Itasca IL 60143
888 437-4968

### (P-18071)
### ATELIERE CREATIVE TECH INC
315 S Beverly Dr Ste 315, Beverly Hills (90212-4309)
**PHONE**.................................800 921-4252
**EMP:** 25 **EST:** 2020
**SALES (est):** 1.32MM **Privately Held**
**Web:** www.ateliere.com
**SIC:** 7372 Application computer software

### (P-18072)
### ATLANTIS COMPUTING INC
900 Glenneyre St, Laguna Beach (92651-2707)
**PHONE**.................................650 917-9471
Jason Donahue, *Pr*
**EMP:** 35 **EST:** 2006
**SQ FT:** 5,000
**SALES (est):** 8.86MM **Privately Held**
**Web:** www.hiveio.com
**SIC:** 7372 Business oriented computer software

### (P-18073)
### ATLASSIAN US INC (DH)
Also Called: Atlassian
350 Bush St Fl 13, San Francisco (94104-2879)
**PHONE**.................................415 701-1110
Scott Farquhar, *CEO*
Doug Burgum, *
Jay Simons, *
Audra Eng, *
Daniel Freeman, *
**EMP:** 20 **EST:** 2005
**SALES (est):** 39.55MM **Privately Held**
**Web:** www.bitbucket.org
**SIC:** 7372 Business oriented computer software
**HQ:** Atlassian Pty Ltd
L 6 341 George St
Sydney NSW 2000

### (P-18074)
### ATOB ASSET VEHICLE I LLC
4 Embarcadero Ctr Ste 140, San Francisco (94111-4106)
**PHONE**.................................703 663-0658
**EMP:** 83 **EST:** 2021
**SALES (est):** 788.75K
**SALES (corp-wide):** 3.7MM **Privately Held**
**SIC:** 7372 Prepackaged software
**PA:** Celegans Labs, Inc.
4 Embarcadero Ctr # 1400
650 283-4882

### (P-18075)
### AUGMEDIX INC (PA)
111 Sutter St Fl 13, San Francisco (94104-4541)
**PHONE**.................................888 669-4885
Emmanuel Krakaris, *Pr*
Gerard Van Hamel Platerink, *Ch Bd*
Sandra Breber, *COO*
Paul Ginocchio, *CFO*
**EMP:** 128 **EST:** 2020
**SALES (est):** 44.85MM
**SALES (corp-wide):** 44.85MM **Privately Held**
**Web:** www.augmedix.com
**SIC:** 7372 Prepackaged software

### (P-18076)
### AURORA INNOVATION INC
Also Called: AURORA INNOVATION, INC.
77 Stillman St, San Francisco (94107-1309)
**PHONE**.................................646 725-4999
Christopher Paul Urmson, *CEO*
**EMP:** 283
**Web:** www.aurora.tech
**SIC:** 7372 Utility computer software
**HQ:** Aurora Operations, Inc.
50 33rd St
Pittsburgh PA 15201
888 583-9506

### (P-18077)
### AUTOCENE INC
2010 Crow Canyon Pl Ste 100, San Ramon (94583-1344)
**PHONE**.................................925 264-0045
Drake Beininger, *CEO*
**EMP:** 24 **EST:** 2006
**SALES (est):** 1.29MM **Privately Held**
**Web:** www.formverse.com
**SIC:** 7372 Application computer software

### (P-18078)
### AUTODESK INC (PA)
Also Called: Autodesk
1 Market St Ste 400, San Francisco (94105-1336)
**PHONE**.................................415 507-5000
Andrew Anagnost, *Pr*
Stacy J Smith, *Non-Executive Chairman of the Board*
Steve M Blum, *COO*
Deborah L Clifford, *Ex VP*
Pascal W Di Fronzo, *CLO*
◆ **EMP:** 400 **EST:** 1982
**SALES (est):** 4.39B
**SALES (corp-wide):** 4.39B **Publicly Held**
**Web:** www.autodesk.com
**SIC:** 7372 Prepackaged software

### (P-18079)
### AUTOGRID SYSTEMS INC (PA)
255 Shoreline Dr Ste 350, Redwood City (94065-1435)
**PHONE**.................................650 461-9038
Ruben Llanes, *CEO*
Quique Schwarz, *Chief Data Scientist*
Matthew Lee, *VP Fin*
**EMP:** 18 **EST:** 2010
**SALES (est):** 3.38MM **Privately Held**
**Web:** www.auto-grid.com
**SIC:** 7372 Business oriented computer software

### (P-18080)
### AVAST SOFTWARE INC (PA)
501 E Middlefield Rd, Mountain View (94043-4042)
**PHONE**.................................844 340-9251
Vincent Wayne Steckler, *CEO*
**EMP:** 76 **EST:** 2011
**SALES (est):** 14.18MM
**SALES (corp-wide):** 14.18MM **Privately Held**
**Web:** www.avast.com
**SIC:** 7372 Application computer software

### (P-18081)
### AVATIER CORPORATION (PA)
Also Called: Avatier
4733 Chabot Dr Ste 201, Pleasanton (94588-3971)
P.O. Box 12124 (94588-2124)
**PHONE**.................................925 217-5170
Nelson Cicchitto, *Ch*
Nelson A Cicchitto, *Ch*
**EMP:** 21 **EST:** 1995
**SQ FT:** 5,500
**SALES (est):** 9.96MM
**SALES (corp-wide):** 9.96MM **Privately Held**
**Web:** www.avatier.com
**SIC:** 7372 7373 Business oriented computer software; Systems software development services

### (P-18082)
### AVI NETWORKS INC (DH)
3401 Hillview Ave, Palo Alto (94304)
**PHONE**.................................408 628-1300
Amit Pandey, *CEO*
Murali Basavaiah, *
Guru Chahal, *
Mark Anderson, *
**EMP:** 28 **EST:** 2012
**SALES (est):** 5.79M
**SALES (corp-wide):** 35.82B **Publicly Held**
**Web:** www.avinetworks.com
**SIC:** 7372 Application computer software
**HQ:** Vmware Llc
3421 Hillview Ave
Palo Alto CA 94304
650 427-6000

### (P-18083)
### AVOCHATO INC
530 Howard St, Mill Valley (94941-3603)
**PHONE**.................................415 214-8977
**EMP:** 50 **EST:** 2019
**SALES (est):** 2.86MM **Privately Held**
**Web:** www.avochato.com
**SIC:** 7372 Prepackaged software

### (P-18084)
### AWAKE SECURITY LLC
5453 Great America Pkwy, Santa Clara (95054-3645)
**PHONE**.................................833 292-5348
Rahul Kashyap, *CEO*
**EMP:** 40 **EST:** 2014
**SALES (est):** 4.43MM **Privately Held**
**Web:** www.arista.com
**SIC:** 7372 Prepackaged software

### (P-18085)
### AXIA TECHNOLOGIES INC
Also Called: Axiamed
4183 State St, Santa Barbara (93110-1817)
**PHONE**.................................855 376-2942
Randal Clark, *Pr*
**EMP:** 21 **EST:** 2016

## 7372 - Prepackaged Software (P-18086)

SALES (est): 6.47MM
SALES (corp-wide): 171.91B **Publicly Held**
Web: business.bofa.com
SIC: **7372** Prepackaged software
HQ: Bank Of America, National Association
100 N Tryon St
Charlotte NC 28202
704 386-5681

### (P-18086)
### AXIOM ADVISORS & CONS INC (PA)
Also Called: Bargaining Hunter
4935 Hillsdale Cir, El Dorado Hills (95762-5707)
PHONE...............................800 818-3010
Dean Getz, *CEO*
EMP: 20 EST: 2001
SQ FT: 7,000
SALES (est): 787.02K
SALES (corp-wide): 787.02K **Privately Held**
SIC: **7372** Operating systems computer software

### (P-18087)
### AZUL SYSTEMS INC (PA)
385 Moffett Park Dr Ste 115, Sunnyvale (94089-1218)
PHONE...............................866 890-8951
Scott Sellers, *Pr*
Gil Tene, *
Peter Maloney, *
Ian Whiting, *CRO**
Andrew Savitz, *CMO**
EMP: 61 EST: 2002
SALES (est): 24.91MM
SALES (corp-wide): 24.91MM **Privately Held**
Web: www.azul.com
SIC: **7372** Operating systems computer software

### (P-18088)
### BADGER MAPS INC
539 Bdwy, San Francisco (94133-4521)
PHONE...............................415 592-5909
Steven Benson, *CEO*
EMP: 40 EST: 2012
SQ FT: 1,000
SALES (est): 4.73MM **Privately Held**
Web: www.badgermapping.com
SIC: **7372** Application computer software

### (P-18089)
### BADGEVILLE INC
805 Veterans Blvd Ste 307, Redwood City (94063-1737)
PHONE...............................650 323-6668
Jon Shalowitz, *Pr*
Stephanie Vinella, *
Karen Hsu, *
Roel Stalman, *
Andy Pederson, *
EMP: 20 EST: 2010
SALES (est): 2.08MM **Privately Held**
SIC: **7372** Prepackaged software

### (P-18090)
### BARCELONA MERGER SUB 3 LLC
3401 Hillview Ave, Palo Alto (94304-1320)
PHONE...............................650 427-5000
Raghu Raghuram, *CEO*
EMP: 38300 EST: 2022
SALES (est): 10.81MM
SALES (corp-wide): 35.82B **Publicly Held**
SIC: **7372** Prepackaged software
PA: Broadcom Inc.
3421 Hillview Ave
650 427-6000

### (P-18091)
### BARRA LLC (HQ)
Also Called: Msci Barra
2100 Milvia St, Berkeley (94704-1861)
PHONE...............................510 548-5442
Kamal Duggirala, *CEO*
Andrew Rudd, *Ch Bd*
Greg Stockett, *CFO*
Aamir Sheikh, *Pr*
▲ EMP: 280 EST: 1975
SQ FT: 35,000
SALES (est): 15.55MM **Publicly Held**
Web: www.holabarra.com
SIC: **7372** 8741 6282 Business oriented computer software; Financial management for business; Investment advisory service
PA: Msci Inc.
250 Greenwich St Fl 49

### (P-18092)
### BARRACUDA NETWORKS INC (PA)
Also Called: Barracuda
3175 Winchester Blvd, Campbell (95008-6557)
PHONE...............................408 342-5400
Hatem Naguib, *Pr*
William D Jenkins Junior, *Pr*
Joe Billante, *
Siroui Mushegian, *CIO**
EMP: 225 EST: 2003
SQ FT: 61,400
SALES (est): 418MM
SALES (corp-wide): 418MM **Privately Held**
Web: www.barracuda.com
SIC: **7372** 7373 Prepackaged software; Computer integrated systems design

### (P-18093)
### BASE CRM
1019 Market St Fl 1, San Francisco (94103-1637)
PHONE...............................773 796-6266
Uzi Shmilovici, *Prin*
EMP: 17 EST: 2013
SALES (est): 3.44MM **Privately Held**
Web: www.zendesk.com
SIC: **7372** Prepackaged software

### (P-18094)
### BEATS MUSIC LLC
235 2nd St, San Francisco (94105-3124)
PHONE...............................415 590-5104
Timothy Cook, *CEO*
EMP: 95 EST: 2012
SALES (est): 2.56MM
SALES (corp-wide): 391.04B **Publicly Held**
SIC: **7372** Prepackaged software
PA: Apple Inc.
1 Apple Park Way
408 996-1010

### (P-18095)
### BEAUTIFUL SLIDES INC
Also Called: Beautiful.ai
9836 Springfield St, Oakland (94603-2824)
PHONE...............................415 236-0955
Mitch Grasso, *CEO*
EMP: 30 EST: 2016
SALES (est): 7.1MM **Privately Held**
Web: www.beautiful.ai
SIC: **7372** Operating systems computer software

### (P-18096)
### BEE CONTENT DESIGN INC (PA)
450 Townsend St, San Francisco (94107-1510)
PHONE...............................888 962-4587
Massimo Arrigoni, *CEO*
EMP: 20 EST: 2011
SQ FT: 500
SALES (est): 7.63MM
SALES (corp-wide): 7.63MM **Privately Held**
Web: www.beefree.io
SIC: **7372** 7371 Operating systems computer software; Software programming applications

### (P-18097)
### BELKASOFT LLC
702 San Conrado Ter Unit 1, Sunnyvale (94085-2548)
PHONE...............................650 272-0384
Mikhail Pliskin, *
EMP: 35 EST: 2017
SALES (est): 1.51MM **Privately Held**
Web: www.belkasoft.com
SIC: **7372** 7389 5045 Application computer software; Business services, nec; Computers, peripherals, and software

### (P-18098)
### BENCHLING INC (PA)
680 Folsom St Ste 800, San Francisco (94107-2157)
PHONE...............................415 590-2798
Sajith Wickramasekara, *CEO*
EMP: 30 EST: 2012
SALES (est): 11.73MM
SALES (corp-wide): 11.73MM **Privately Held**
Web: www.benchling.com
SIC: **7372** Business oriented computer software

### (P-18099)
### BENCHMARKONE
5500 Bolsa Ave Ste 245, Huntington Beach (92649-1112)
PHONE...............................314 288-0399
Nicci Troiani, *Prin*
Donald Breckenridge, *CEO*
EMP: 16 EST: 2014
SALES (est): 300.41K **Privately Held**
Web: www.benchmarkone.com
SIC: **7372** Application computer software

### (P-18100)
### BENTO TECHNOLOGIES INC
Also Called: Bento Merge Enterprises
221 Main St Ste 1325, San Francisco (94105-1946)
P.O. Box 10929 (60610-0929)
PHONE...............................415 887-2028
Guido Schulz, *CEO*
Farhan Ahmad, *Ch Bd*
Sean Anderson, *CFO*
EMP: 28 EST: 2014
SQ FT: 2,628
SALES (est): 6.16MM **Privately Held**
Web: www.bentoforbusiness.com
SIC: **7372** Business oriented computer software

### (P-18101)
### BIG SWITCH NETWORKS LLC
5453 Great America Pkwy, Santa Clara (95054-3645)
PHONE...............................650 322-6510
Douglas Murray, *Pr*
Kyle Forster, *
Prashant Gandhi, *MGT AND STRAT**

Gregg Holzrichter, *CMO**
Shaun Page, *Worldwide Sales Vice President**
EMP: 180 EST: 2010
SALES (est): 12.51MM **Publicly Held**
Web: www.arista.com
SIC: **7372** Prepackaged software
PA: Arista Networks, Inc.
5453 Great America Pkwy

### (P-18102)
### BIGFIX INC
1480 64th St Ste 200, Emeryville (94608-1292)
PHONE...............................510 652-6700
EMP: 200
SIC: **7372** Prepackaged software

### (P-18103)
### BILL HOLDINGS INC (PA)
Also Called: BILL.COM
6220 America Center Dr Ste 100, San Jose (95002-2563)
P.O. Box 370 (95002)
PHONE...............................650 621-7700
Rene Lacerte, *Ch Bd*
John Rettig, *Pr*
Loren Padelford, *Chief Commercial Officer*
Raj Aji, *Chief Compliance Officer*
Sarah Acton, *CCO*
EMP: 249 EST: 2006
SQ FT: 138,000
SALES (est): 1.29B
SALES (corp-wide): 1.29B **Publicly Held**
Web: www.bill.com
SIC: **7372** Prepackaged software

### (P-18104)
### BILLCOM LLC (HQ)
Also Called: Bill
6220 America Center Dr Ste 100, San Jose (95002-2563)
P.O. Box 370 (95002-0370)
PHONE...............................650 353-3301
Rene Lacerte, *CEO*
Mark Orttung, *COO*
John Rettig, *CFO*
Irana Wasti, *CPO*
EMP: 140 EST: 2006
SALES (est): 84.38MM
SALES (corp-wide): 1.29B **Publicly Held**
Web: www.bill.com
SIC: **7372** Application computer software
PA: Bill Holdings, Inc.
6220 Amer Ctr Dr Ste 100
650 621-7700

### (P-18105)
### BINTI INC
1111 Broadway, Oakland (94607-4167)
PHONE...............................844 424-6844
Felicia Curcuru, *CEO*
EMP: 23 EST: 2014
SALES (est): 6.82MM **Privately Held**
Web: www.binti.com
SIC: **7372** 7389 Business oriented computer software; Business Activities at Non-Commercial Site

### (P-18106)
### BITZER MOBILE INC
4230 Leonard Stocking Dr, Santa Clara (95054-1777)
PHONE...............................866 603-8392
Naeem Zafar, *Pr*
Ali Ahmed, *
EMP: 24 EST: 2010
SQ FT: 2,000
SALES (est): 2.2MM
SALES (corp-wide): 52.96B **Publicly Held**

# PRODUCTS & SERVICES SECTION
## 7372 - Prepackaged Software (P-18126)

Web: www.oracle.com
**SIC: 7372** Business oriented computer software
**PA:** Oracle Corporation
2300 Oracle Way
737 867-1000

**(P-18107)**
### BIZ PERFORMANCE SOLUTIONS INC
Also Called: Bizps
840 Loma Vista St, Moss Beach (94038-9721)
**PHONE**..............................408 844-4284
David Mosher, *CEO*
Ken Matusow, *COO*
**EMP:** 15 **EST:** 2010
**SALES (est):** 1.49MM **Privately Held**
Web: www.bizps.com
**SIC: 7372** 8711 Application computer software; Consulting engineer

**(P-18108)**
### BLACKBERRY CORPORATION
331 Fairchild Dr, Mountain View (94043-2200)
**PHONE**..............................650 564-0016
**EMP:** 1568
**SALES (corp-wide):** 656MM **Privately Held**
Web: www.blackberry.com
**SIC: 7372** Prepackaged software
**HQ:** Blackberry Corporation
5030 Rvrside Dr Ste 200 B
Irving TX 75039
877 255-2377

**(P-18109)**
### BLACKLINE INC (PA)
Also Called: BLACKLINE
21300 Victory Blvd Fl 12, Woodland Hills (91367-7734)
**PHONE**..............................818 223-9008
Owen Ryan, *Ch Bd*
Mark Partin, *CFO*
Karole Morgan-prager, *Legal*
Mark Woodhams, *CRO*
**EMP:** 1557 **EST:** 2001
**SQ FT:** 89,000
**SALES (est):** 590MM
**SALES (corp-wide):** 590MM **Publicly Held**
Web: www.blackline.com
**SIC: 7372** Business oriented computer software

**(P-18110)**
### BLAMELESS INC
2261 Market St, San Francisco (94114-1612)
**PHONE**..............................650 563-7300
James Jim Goche, *CEO*
Ken Gavranovic, *
**EMP:** 42 **EST:** 2018
**SALES (est):** 6.23MM **Privately Held**
Web: www.blameless.com
**SIC: 7372** Prepackaged software

**(P-18111)**
### BLIND SQUIRREL GAMES INC
7545 Irvine Center Dr Ste 150, Irvine (92618-2935)
**PHONE**..............................714 460-0860
Bradford Hendricks, *CEO*
**EMP:** 23 **EST:** 2010
**SALES (est):** 11.07MM **Privately Held**
Web: www.blindsquirrelentertainment.com
**SIC: 7372** Home entertainment computer software

**(P-18112)**
### BLITZ ROCKS INC
750 B St Ste 3300, San Diego (92101-8188)
**PHONE**..............................310 883-5183
Mauricio Duran, *CEO*
**EMP:** 25 **EST:** 2016
**SALES (est):** 1.08MM
**SALES (corp-wide):** 4.2MM **Privately Held**
Web: www.blitzrocks.com
**SIC: 7372** Business oriented computer software
**PA:** Sieena, Inc.
600 B St Ste 300
310 455-6188

**(P-18113)**
### BLIZZARD ENTERTAINMENT INC (DH)
1 Blizzard, Irvine (92618-3628)
P.O. Box 18979 (92623-8979)
**PHONE**..............................949 955-1380
Mike Morhaime, *CEO*
Johanna Faries, *
Chris Metzen, *
Todd Pawlowski, *
Eric Roeder, *
▲ **EMP:** 85 **EST:** 2004
**SALES (est):** 155.37MM
**SALES (corp-wide):** 245.12B **Publicly Held**
Web: careers.blizzard.com
**SIC: 7372** 5734 7819 Prepackaged software; Software, computer games; Reproduction services, motion picture production
**HQ:** Activision Blizzard, Inc.
2701 Olympic Blvd Bldg B
Santa Monica CA 90404
310 255-2000

**(P-18114)**
### BLOCK INC (PA)
Also Called: BLOCK GROUP XYZ, THE
1955 Broadway Ste 600, Oakland (94612-2205)
**PHONE**..............................415 375-3176
Jack Dorsey, *Head*
Amrita Ahuja, *COO*
Chrysty Esperanza, *CLO*
Ajmere Dale, *CAO*
**EMP:** 50 **EST:** 2009
**SALES (est):** 21.92B **Publicly Held**
Web: www.block.xyz
**SIC: 7372** Prepackaged software

**(P-18115)**
### BLOCKFREIGHT INC
535 Mission St Fl 14, San Francisco (94105-3253)
**PHONE**..............................415 815-3924
Julian Smith, *CIO*
**EMP:** 20 **EST:** 2017
**SALES (est):** 1.3MM **Privately Held**
Web: www.blockfreight.com
**SIC: 7372** 7371 Business oriented computer software; Computer software development and applications

**(P-18116)**
### BLU BANYAN INC
1569 Solano Ave Ste 645, Berkeley (94707-2116)
**PHONE**..............................510 929-1070
Jan Marie Rippinggale, *Pr*
**EMP:** 30 **EST:** 2022
**SALES (est):** 4.75MM **Privately Held**
Web: www.blubanyan.com
**SIC: 7372** Business oriented computer software

**(P-18117)**
### BLUE COAT LLC
350 Ellis St, Mountain View (94043-2202)
**PHONE**..............................408 220-2200
Michael Fey, *Pr*
Stephen Trilling, *
Thomas Seifert, *
Scott Taylor, *
Amy Cappellanti-wolf, *Chief Human Resource Officer*
**EMP:** 1583 **EST:** 2015
**SALES (est):** 32.02MM
**SALES (corp-wide):** 3.81B **Publicly Held**
Web: www.broadcom.com
**SIC: 7372** Prepackaged software
**PA:** Gen Digital Inc.
60 E Rio Slado Pkwy Ste 1
650 527-8000

**(P-18118)**
### BLUE MARBLE REHAB INC
Also Called: Blue Marble Game Co
2400 Lincoln Ave, Altadena (91001-5425)
**PHONE**..............................626 296-6400
Sheryl Flynn, *CEO*
Sheryl Maureen Flynn, *CEO*
**EMP:** 15 **EST:** 2009
**SQ FT:** 60,000
**SALES (est):** 1.07MM **Privately Held**
Web: www.bluemarblegameco.com
**SIC: 7372** 5734 8731 Prepackaged software; Software, business and non-game; Biotechnical research, commercial

**(P-18119)**
### BLUESHIFT LABS INC
433 California St Ste 600, San Francisco (94130-1709)
**PHONE**..............................844 258-3735
Vijay Chittoor, *Pr*
Subramanyam Mallela, *
Mehul Shah, *
Tae Hea Nahm, *
Josh Francia, *CGO**
**EMP:** 176 **EST:** 2014
**SQ FT:** 5,000
**SALES (est):** 10.39MM **Privately Held**
Web: www.blueshift.com
**SIC: 7372** Business oriented computer software

**(P-18120)**
### BMC
300 Continental Blvd Ste 570, El Segundo (90245-5072)
**PHONE**..............................310 321-5555
Sean Allen, *CEO*
**EMP:** 37 **EST:** 2009
**SALES (est):** 190.6K **Privately Held**
Web: www.bmc.com
**SIC: 7372** Prepackaged software

**(P-18121)**
### BOOMERANG COMMERCE INC (PA)
2100 Geng Rd Ste 210, Palo Alto (94303-3307)
**PHONE**..............................602 459-2578
Gurushyam Hariharan, *CEO*
Abhimanyu Maheswari, *VP*
Jaya Jaware, *CFO*
**EMP:** 166 **EST:** 2012
**SALES (est):** 21MM
**SALES (corp-wide):** 21MM **Privately Held**
Web: www.commerceiq.ai
**SIC: 7372** Publisher's computer software

**(P-18122)**
### BOX INC (PA)
900 Jefferson Ave, Redwood City (94063-1837)
**PHONE**..............................877 729-4269
Aaron Levie, *CEO*
Bethany Mayer, *
Olivia Nottebohm, *COO*
Dylan Smith, *CFO*
Tricia Gellman, *CMO*
**EMP:** 441 **EST:** 2005
**SQ FT:** 340,000
**SALES (est):** 1.04B
**SALES (corp-wide):** 1.04B **Publicly Held**
Web: www.box.com
**SIC: 7372** Application computer software

**(P-18123)**
### BPOMS/HRO INC (HQ)
8175 E Kaiser Blvd # 100, Anaheim (92808-2214)
**PHONE**..............................714 974-2670
Patrick Dolan, *Ch Bd*
James Cortens, *COO*
Don Rutherford, *CFO*
**EMP:** 55 **EST:** 2008
**SQ FT:** 3,500
**SALES (est):** 3.33MM
**SALES (corp-wide):** 16.91MM **Privately Held**
**SIC: 7372** 7371 Prepackaged software; Custom computer programming services
**PA:** Bpo Management Services, Inc.
8175 E Kaiser Blvd 100
714 972-2670

**(P-18124)**
### BQE SOFTWARE INC
3825 Del Amo Blvd, Torrance (90503-2118)
**PHONE**..............................310 602-4020
Shafat Qazi, *CEO*
Austin Miller, *CMO**
**EMP:** 95 **EST:** 1995
**SQ FT:** 20,000
**SALES (est):** 12.55MM **Privately Held**
Web: www.bqe.com
**SIC: 7372** 5734 Application computer software; Software, business and non-game

**(P-18125)**
### BRAINCHIP INC (HQ)
23041 Avenida De La Carlota Ste 250, Laguna Hills (92653-1545)
**PHONE**..............................949 784-0040
Louis Dinardo, *CEO*
Ryan Benton, *CFO*
Steven Nguyen, *Asst Cont*
**EMP:** 15 **EST:** 2014
**SALES (est):** 9.06MM **Privately Held**
Web: www.brainchip.com
**SIC: 7372** Prepackaged software
**PA:** Brainchip Holdings Ltd
L 8 210 George Street

**(P-18126)**
### BRENDAN TECHNOLOGIES INC
1947 Camino Vida Roble Ste 103, Carlsbad (92008-6540)
**PHONE**..............................760 929-7500
John R Dunn Ii, *CEO*
George Dunn, *Sec*
Lowell W Giffhorn, *CFO*
▲ **EMP:** 15 **EST:** 1988
**SQ FT:** 3,988
**SALES (est):** 3.41MM **Privately Held**
Web: www.brendan.com
**SIC: 7372** Business oriented computer software

## 7372 - Prepackaged Software (P-18127)

**(P-18127)**
**BRIGHTIDEA INCORPORATED**
255 California St # 1100, San Francisco (94111-4927)
PHONE.................................415 814-1387
EMP: 25
SALES (corp-wide): 8.66MM **Privately Held**
SIC: 7372 Prepackaged software
PA: Brightidea Incorporated
   25 Pacific Ave
   415 814-3817

**(P-18128)**
**BRILLIANT WORLDWIDE INC**
550 Montgomery St Ste 800, San Francisco (94111-6548)
PHONE.................................650 468-2966
Suyeon Khim, *CEO*
EMP: 102 EST: 2012
SALES (est): 5.86MM **Privately Held**
Web: www.brilliant.org
SIC: 7372 Educational computer software

**(P-18129)**
**BROADLY INC**
548 Market St Ste 59118, San Francisco (94104-5401)
PHONE.................................510 400-6039
Mindy Lauck, *CEO*
EMP: 50 EST: 2014
SALES (est): 5.65MM
SALES (corp-wide): 25.86MM **Privately Held**
Web: www.broadly.com
SIC: 7372 Business oriented computer software
PA: Vendasta Technologies Inc
   410 22nd St E 15th Fl
   306 955-5512

**(P-18130)**
**BUGSNAG INC**
Also Called: Bugsnag
110 Sutter St Fl 10, San Francisco (94104-4027)
PHONE.................................415 484-8664
James Smith, *Prin*
James Smith, *CEO*
Simon Maynard, *
EMP: 45 EST: 2013
SALES (est): 2.02MM **Privately Held**
Web: www.bugsnag.com
SIC: 7372 Application computer software

**(P-18131)**
**BUOY LABS INC**
Also Called: Resideo Buoy
125 Mcpherson St, Santa Cruz (95060-5883)
PHONE.................................855 481-7112
Keri Waters, *CEO*
EMP: 16 EST: 2015
SALES (est): 2.33MM
SALES (corp-wide): 6.24B **Publicly Held**
Web: www.resideo.com
SIC: 7372 Prepackaged software
PA: Resideo Technologies, Inc.
   16100 N 71st St Ste 550
   480 573-5340

**(P-18132)**
**BUYERSROAD INC**
Also Called: Experience.com
2010 Crow Canyon Pl Ste 100, San Ramon (94583-1344)
PHONE.................................937 313-4466
Steven Scott Harris, *CEO*
Dave R Taylor, *CMO**
EMP: 50 EST: 2017
SALES (est): 4.54MM **Privately Held**
Web: www.experience.com
SIC: 7372 Prepackaged software

**(P-18133)**
**BUZZ SOLUTIONS INC**
119 University Ave, Palo Alto (94301-1629)
PHONE.................................949 637-7946
Kaitlyn Albertoli, *CEO*
Vikhyat Chaudhry, *COO*
EMP: 17 EST: 2017
SALES (est): 3.47MM **Privately Held**
Web: www.buzzsolutions.co
SIC: 7372 Utility computer software

**(P-18134)**
**C3 DELAWARE INC**
1300 Seaport Blvd Ste 500, Redwood City (94063-5592)
PHONE.................................650 503-2200
Patricia A House, *Owner*
EMP: 30 EST: 2013
SALES (est): 7.83MM **Privately Held**
Web: www.c3energy.com
SIC: 7372 Business oriented computer software

**(P-18135)**
**C3AI INC (PA)**
1400 Seaport Blvd Ste 100, Redwood City (94063-5594)
PHONE.................................650 503-2200
Thomas M Siebel, *Ch Bd*
Edward Y Abbo, *Pr*
Juho Parkkinen, *Sr VP*
Guy Wanger, *CAO*
EMP: 862 EST: 2009
SALES (est): 310.58MM **Publicly Held**
Web: www.c3.ai
SIC: 7372 Prepackaged software

**(P-18136)**
**CA INC**
Also Called: CA
3965 Freedom Cir Fl 6, Santa Clara (95054-1286)
PHONE.................................800 225-5224
EMP: 166
SALES (corp-wide): 35.82B **Publicly Held**
Web: www.broadcom.com
SIC: 7372 Business oriented computer software
HQ: Ca, Inc.
   3421 Hillview Ave
   Palo Alto CA 94304
   800 225-5224

**(P-18137)**
**CA INC (HQ)**
Also Called: CA
3421 Hillview Ave, Palo Alto (94304-1320)
PHONE.................................800 225-5224
Michael P Gregoire, *CEO*
Kieran J Mcgrath, *Ex VP*
Anthony Radesca, *CAO**
EMP: 1500 EST: 1974
SALES (est): 2.52B
SALES (corp-wide): 35.82B **Publicly Held**
Web: www.broadcom.com
SIC: 7372 8742 Business oriented computer software; Management consulting services
PA: Broadcom Inc.
   3421 Hillview Ave
   650 427-6000

**(P-18138)**
**CACHEFLOW INC**
195 Page Mill Rd Ste 111b, Palo Alto (94306-2072)
PHONE.................................818 659-1400
Sarika Garg, *CEO*
EMP: 20
SALES (est): 1.9MM **Privately Held**
SIC: 7372 Prepackaged software

**(P-18139)**
**CADENCE DESIGN SYSTEMS INC (PA)**
Also Called: CADENCE
2655 Seely Ave Bldg 5, San Jose (95134-1931)
PHONE.................................408 943-1234
Anirudh Devgan, *Pr*
John M Wall, *Sr VP*
Karna Nisewaner, *Corporate Vice President*
Neil Zaman, *CRO*
Thomas P Beckley, *Sr VP*
▲ EMP: 700 EST: 1982
SALES (est): 4.09B
SALES (corp-wide): 4.09B **Publicly Held**
Web: www.cadence.com
SIC: 7372 Prepackaged software

**(P-18140)**
**CALAMP CORP (PA)**
Also Called: Calamp
15635 Alton Pkwy Ste 250, Irvine (92618-7328)
PHONE.................................949 600-5600
Christopher R Adams, *Pr*
Henry J Maier, *Ch Bd*
Jikun Kim, *Sr VP*
Jeffrey Clark, *CPO*
◆ EMP: 101 EST: 1981
SQ FT: 23,000
SALES (est): 294.95MM
SALES (corp-wide): 294.95MM **Privately Held**
Web: www.calamp.com
SIC: 7372 Application computer software

**(P-18141)**
**CALEB ENTERPRISES INC**
5857 Owens Ave Ste 300, Carlsbad (92008-5507)
PHONE.................................760 683-8787
Matthew Menotti, *CEO*
EMP: 15 EST: 2019
SALES (est): 1.15MM **Privately Held**
Web: www.calebenterprisesinc.com
SIC: 7372 Prepackaged software

**(P-18142)**
**CALMCOM INC (PA)**
555 Bryant St Ste 262, Palo Alto (94301-1704)
PHONE.................................415 236-3012
David Ko, *CEO*
Alexander Tew, *Ofcr*
EMP: 27 EST: 2012
SALES (est): 11.4MM
SALES (corp-wide): 11.4MM **Privately Held**
Web: www.calm.com
SIC: 7372 Application computer software

**(P-18143)**
**CALYPTO DESIGN SYSTEMS INC**
2099 Gateway Pl Ste 550, San Jose (95110-1051)
PHONE.................................408 850-2300
Sanjiv Kaul, *Pr*
Chris Mausler, *CFO*
EMP: 20 EST: 2002
SALES (est): 2.37MM **Privately Held**
SIC: 7372 Prepackaged software

**(P-18144)**
**CAMBRIAN LAB INC**
Also Called: Software
7045 Corte Del Oro, Pleasanton (94566-5781)
PHONE.................................408 569-3744
Krishna Gorrepati, *Pr*
EMP: 15 EST: 2017
SALES (est): 1.97MM **Privately Held**
Web: www.cambrianlab.net
SIC: 7372 Prepackaged software

**(P-18145)**
**CANARY TECHNOLOGIES CORP**
275 Sacramento St, San Francisco (94105)
PHONE.................................415 578-1414
Satjot Sawhney, *CEO*
EMP: 22 EST: 2017
SALES (est): 2.52MM **Privately Held**
Web: www.canarytechnologies.com
SIC: 7372 Business oriented computer software

**(P-18146)**
**CANTO INC (PA)**
625 Market St Ste 600, San Francisco (94105-3308)
PHONE.................................415 495-6545
Jack Mcgannon, *CEO*
EMP: 55 EST: 2019
SALES (est): 9.33MM
SALES (corp-wide): 9.33MM **Privately Held**
Web: www.canto.com
SIC: 7372 Prepackaged software

**(P-18147)**
**CARE ZONE INC**
Also Called: Carezone
121 Capp St Ste 200, San Francisco (94110-1885)
P.O. Box 150 (94401)
PHONE.................................206 707-9127
Jonathan Schwartz, *CEO*
Walter Smith, *
EMP: 50 EST: 2010
SALES (est): 4.76MM **Privately Held**
Web: www.carezone.com
SIC: 7372 Application computer software

**(P-18148)**
**CARIDEN TECHNOLOGIES LLC**
840 W California Ave Ste 200, Sunnyvale (94086-4834)
PHONE.................................650 564-9200
EMP: 22
SIC: 7372 Prepackaged software

**(P-18149)**
**CASEMAKER INC**
1680 Civic Center Dr Frnt, Santa Clara (95050-4146)
PHONE.................................408 261-8265
Jui-long Liu, *Pr*
EMP: 15 EST: 1991
SQ FT: 11,000
SALES (est): 2.33MM **Privately Held**
Web: www.casemaker.com
SIC: 7372 7371 Application computer software; Custom computer programming services

**(P-18150)**
**CASPIO INC (PA)**
1286 Kifer Rd Ste 107, Sunnyvale (94086-5326)
PHONE.................................650 691-0900
Frank Zamani, *CEO*
Spring Babb, *

## 7372 - Prepackaged Software (P-18170)

**EMP:** 16 **EST:** 2000
**SALES (est):** 4.86MM
**SALES (corp-wide):** 4.86MM **Privately Held**
Web: www.caspio.com
SIC: 7372 Business oriented computer software

### (P-18151)
### CATALYST DEVELOPMENT CORP
56925 Yucca Trl, Yucca Valley (92284-7913)
**PHONE:** 760 228-9653
Cary Harwin, *Pr*
Mike Stefanik, *
**EMP:** 21 **EST:** 1995
**SALES (est):** 2.04MM **Privately Held**
Web: www.catalyst.com
SIC: 7372 Business oriented computer software

### (P-18152)
### CATAPULT COMMUNICATIONS CORP (DH)
26601 Agoura Rd, Calabasas (91302-1959)
**PHONE:** 818 871-1800
Richard A Karp, *Ch Bd*
David Mayfield, *Pr*
Chris Stephenson, *VP*
Barbara J Fairhurst, *VP Opers*
Terry Eastham, *SUPPORT*
▲ **EMP:** 37 **EST:** 1985
**SQ FT:** 39,000
**SALES (est):** 5.94MM
**SALES (corp-wide):** 5.46B **Publicly Held**
SIC: 7372 3661 Application computer software; Telephone and telegraph apparatus
HQ: Ixia
    26601 Agoura Rd
    Calabasas CA 91302
    818 871-1800

### (P-18153)
### CATO NETWORKS INC
3031 Tisch Way 110 Plz W, San Jose (95128)
**PHONE:** 646 975-9243
Shlomo Kramer, *CEO*
Steven Krausz, *VP*
Tomer Wald, *CFO*
**EMP:** 69 **EST:** 2015
**SALES (est):** 15.02MM **Privately Held**
Web: www.catonetworks.com
SIC: 7372 Application computer software
PA: Cato Networks Ltd
    2 Leonardo Da Vinci, Landmark Tower

### (P-18154)
### CCS INC
Also Called: Eliteprotek
11801 Pierce St Fl 2, Riverside (92505-4400)
**PHONE:** 888 256-8901
Lionel Mafouta, *Pr*
Pilar March, *VP*
**EMP:** 15 **EST:** 2006
**SALES (est):** 1.36MM **Privately Held**
SIC: 7372 Business oriented computer software

### (P-18155)
### CELIGO INC (PA)
1820 Gateway Dr Ste 260, Redwood City (94065-1561)
**PHONE:** 650 579-0210
Jan K Arendtsz, *CEO*
**EMP:** 20 **EST:** 2008
**SALES (est):** 19.9MM
**SALES (corp-wide):** 19.9MM **Privately Held**
Web: www.celigo.com
SIC: 7372 Business oriented computer software

### (P-18156)
### CENTRA SOFTWARE INC
Also Called: Field Sales Office
1840 Gateway Dr Fl 2, San Mateo (94404-4027)
**PHONE:** 650 378-1363
**EMP:** 30
**SALES (corp-wide):** 740.92MM **Privately Held**
SIC: 7372 7379 Business oriented computer software; Computer related consulting services
HQ: Centra Software Inc
    430 Bedford St Ste 220
    Lexington MA 02420

### (P-18157)
### CENTRL INC
257 Castro St Ste 215, Mountain View (94041-1287)
**PHONE:** 650 641-7092
Sanjeev Dheer, *CEO*
Chris Marino, *
Rupali Chopra, *
**EMP:** 33 **EST:** 2015
**SALES (est):** 2.87MM **Privately Held**
Web: www.centrl.ai
SIC: 7372 Application computer software

### (P-18158)
### CERTAIN INC (PA)
75 Hawthorne St Ste 550, San Francisco (94105-3901)
P.O. Box 2437 (94526-7437)
**PHONE:** 415 353-5330
Peter Micciche, *CEO*
Brian Bailard, *
**EMP:** 38 **EST:** 1994
**SALES (est):** 12.26MM
**SALES (corp-wide):** 12.26MM **Privately Held**
Web: www.certain.com
SIC: 7372 Prepackaged software

### (P-18159)
### CERTAIN SOFTWARE INC
75 Hawthorne St Ste 500, San Francisco (94105-3945)
**PHONE:** 415 353-5330
**EMP:** 30
Web: www.certain.com
SIC: 7372 5734 Prepackaged software; Software, business and non-game

### (P-18160)
### CERTEMY INC
14876 Raymer St Ste 200, Van Nuys (91405-1219)
**PHONE:** 866 907-4088
Zorik Gordon, *CEO*
Herman Berger, *CEO*
Oleg Shvarts, *Pr*
Shawn Cantor, *COO*
**EMP:** 18 **EST:** 2017
**SALES (est):** 3.94MM **Privately Held**
Web: www.certemy.com
SIC: 7372 7371 7379 Business oriented computer software; Custom computer programming services; Computer related services, nec

### (P-18161)
### CETAS INC
3260 Hillview Ave, Palo Alto (94304-1220)
**PHONE:** 847 530-5785
Lavanya Katla, *CEO*
**EMP:** 15 **EST:** 2018
**SALES (est):** 628.2K **Privately Held**
Web: www.cetascyber.com
SIC: 7372 Business oriented computer software

### (P-18162)
### CFORIA SOFTWARE LLC
Also Called: Cforia
4333 Park Terrace Dr Ste 201, Westlake Village (91361-5656)
**PHONE:** 818 871-9687
Karl Florida, *CEO*
Dave Mcintyre, *Pr*
Chris Caparon, *VP*
Joe Alie, *CFO*
**EMP:** 22 **EST:** 2001
**SALES (est):** 12.66MM **Privately Held**
Web: www.cforia.com
SIC: 7372 Business oriented computer software
PA: Highradius Corporation
    2107 Ctywest Blvd Ste 110

### (P-18163)
### CFS TAX SOFTWARE INC
Also Called: CFS Income Tax
1445 E Los Angeles Ave Ste 214, Simi Valley (93065-2828)
P.O. Box 941659 (93094-1659)
**PHONE:** 805 522-1157
Ted Sullivan, *Pr*
**EMP:** 22 **EST:** 1982
**SALES (est):** 4.35MM **Privately Held**
Web: www.taxtools.com
SIC: 7372 8721 Business oriented computer software; Accounting, auditing, and bookkeeping

### (P-18164)
### CHATMETER INC
225 Broadway Ste 2200, San Diego (92101-5011)
**PHONE:** 619 300-1050
Collin Holmes, *CEO*
John Fitzgerald, *
**EMP:** 80 **EST:** 2009
**SALES (est):** 11MM **Privately Held**
Web: www.chatmeter.com
SIC: 7372 Prepackaged software

### (P-18165)
### CHECK POINT SOFTWARE TECH INC (DH)
Also Called: Check Point Software
100 Oracle Pkwy, Redwood City (94065-1670)
**PHONE:** 800 429-4391
Gil Shwed, *CEO*
Roei Golan, *
Doctor Dorit Dor, *CPO*
Dan Yerushalmi, *CCO*
Peter Alexander, *CMO*
▲ **EMP:** 120 **EST:** 1996
**SALES (est):** 250.29MM
**SALES (corp-wide):** 894.19MM **Privately Held**
Web: www.checkpoint.com
SIC: 7372 Operating systems computer software
HQ: Check Point Software Technologies Ltd.
    5 Shlomo Kaplan
    Tel Aviv-Jaffa 67891

### (P-18166)
### CHEMSW INC
2480 Burskirk Ste 300, Pleasant Hill (94523)
**PHONE:** 707 864-0845
Brian Stafford, *Pr*
Patrick Spink, *VP*
**EMP:** 16 **EST:** 1991
**SQ FT:** 2,600
**SALES (est):** 1.89MM
**SALES (corp-wide):** 2.08B **Privately Held**
Web: www.chemsw.com
SIC: 7372 Prepackaged software
HQ: Dassault Systemes Biovia Corp.
    5005 Wateridge Vista Dr
    San Diego CA 92121

### (P-18167)
### CHOWNOW INC (PA)
3585 Hayden Ave, Culver City (90232-2412)
**PHONE:** 888 707-2469
Eric Jaffe, *Pr*
Stuart Hathaway, *
Andre Mancl, *
**EMP:** 70 **EST:** 2010
**SQ FT:** 25,000
**SALES (est):** 24.96MM
**SALES (corp-wide):** 24.96MM **Privately Held**
Web: www.chownow.com
SIC: 7372 Business oriented computer software

### (P-18168)
### CIPHERCLOUD INC (HQ)
2581 Junction Ave Ste 200, San Jose (95134-1923)
**PHONE:** 408 687-4350
James Dolce, *CEO*
Pravin Kothari, *
**EMP:** 90 **EST:** 2010
**SQ FT:** 21,800
**SALES (est):** 69.57MM **Privately Held**
Web: www.lookout.com
SIC: 7372 Business oriented computer software
PA: Lookout, Inc.
    60 State St

### (P-18169)
### CISCO SYSTEMS LLC (HQ)
Also Called: Cisco Systems
170 W Tasman Dr, San Jose (95134-1706)
**PHONE:** 650 989-6500
Scott Weiss, *CEO*
Bob Kavner, *Ch*
Craig Collins, *CFO*
Kelly Bodnar Battles, *VP*
**EMP:** 260 **EST:** 2000
**SALES (est):** 21.31MM
**SALES (corp-wide):** 53.8B **Publicly Held**
Web: www.cisco.com
SIC: 7372 5045 Prepackaged software; Computers, peripherals, and software
PA: Cisco Systems, Inc.
    170 W Tasman Dr
    408 526-4000

### (P-18170)
### CLARIFI TECHNOLOGIES INC ✪
424 2nd St Ste A, Davis (95616-4675)
**PHONE:** 866 997-2643
Matthew Berri, *CEO*
Matt Berri, *CEO*
Carrie Taylor, *COO*
Bettina Perry, *CFO*
**EMP:** 18 **EST:** 2023
**SALES (est):** 1.03MM **Privately Held**
Web: www.clarifi-tech.com
SIC: 7372 Application computer software

# 7372 - Prepackaged Software (P-18171)

**(P-18171)**
**CLASSY INC**
Also Called: Classy
350 10th Ave Ste 1300, San Diego
(92101-8703)
PHONE.................................619 961-1892
Chris Himes, *CEO*
**EMP:** 230 **EST:** 2006
**SALES (est):** 10.38MM
**SALES (corp-wide):** 23MM **Privately Held**
Web: www.classy.org
**SIC: 7372** Prepackaged software
PA: Gofundme Inc.
1010 Doyle St Ste 250
650 260-3436

**(P-18172)**
**CLEAR SKYE INC**
2340 Powell St Ste 325, Emeryville
(94608-1738)
PHONE.................................415 619-5001
John Milburn, *CEO*
Vahan Galachyan, *
**EMP:** 25 **EST:** 2015
**SALES (est):** 1.99MM **Privately Held**
Web: www.clearskye.com
**SIC: 7372** Prepackaged software

**(P-18173)**
**CLEARLAKE CAPITAL PARTNERS**
233 Wilshire Blvd Ste 800, Santa Monica
(90401-1207)
PHONE.................................310 400-8800
John A Mckenna Junior, *Pr*
**EMP:** 1832 **EST:** 2012
**SALES (est):** 3.88MM **Privately Held**
**SIC: 7372** Prepackaged software

**(P-18174)**
**CLIMATE CORPORATION (DH)**
Also Called: Climate Fieldview
201 3rd St Ste 1010, San Francisco
(94103-3129)
PHONE.................................415 363-0500
Mike Stern, *CEO*
Greg Smirin, *
Ranjeeta Singh, *CPO**
**EMP:** 64 **EST:** 2006
**SALES (est):** 63.9MM
**SALES (corp-wide):** 51.78B **Privately Held**
Web: www.climate.com
**SIC: 7372** 5045 Prepackaged software; Computer software
HQ: Monsanto Technology Llc.
800 N Lindbergh Blvd
Saint Louis MO 63167
314 694-1000

**(P-18175)**
**CLIOSOFT INC**
39500 Stevenson Pl Ste 110, Fremont
(94539-3102)
PHONE.................................510 790-4732
Srinath Anantharaman, *Pr*
▲ **EMP:** 15 **EST:** 1997
**SALES (est):** 2.72MM
**SALES (corp-wide):** 5.46B **Publicly Held**
Web: www.keysight.com
**SIC: 7372** Prepackaged software
PA: Keysight Technologies, Inc.
1400 Fountaingrove Pkwy
800 829-4444

**(P-18176)**
**CLONETAB INC**
1660 W Linne Rd Ste 214, Tracy
(95377-8027)
PHONE.................................209 292-5663
Hema Meka, *CEO*
Bharathi Meka, *
**EMP:** 39 **EST:** 2011
**SALES (est):** 932.41K **Privately Held**
Web: www.clonetab.com
**SIC: 7372** Prepackaged software

**(P-18177)**
**CLOUD SFTWR GROUP HOLDINGS INC**
7414 Hollister Ave Goleta, Los Angeles
(90074-0001)
PHONE.................................800 424-8749
**EMP:** 17
**SALES (corp-wide):** 4.38B **Privately Held**
**SIC: 7372** Prepackaged software
HQ: Cloud Software Group Holdings, Inc.
851 W Cypress Creek Rd
Fort Lauderdale FL 33309
954 267-3000

**(P-18178)**
**CLOUD SOFTWARE GROUP INC**
575 Market St, San Francisco
(94105-2854)
PHONE.................................415 344-0339
Vivek Ranadiv, *Brnch Mgr*
**EMP:** 15
**SALES (corp-wide):** 4.38B **Privately Held**
Web: www.tibco.com
**SIC: 7372** Prepackaged software
HQ: Cloud Software Group, Inc.
851 W Cypress Creek Rd
Fort Lauderdale FL 33309

**(P-18179)**
**CLOUD SOFTWARE GROUP FEDERAL**
Also Called: Tibco Software Federal, Inc.
4980 Great America Pkwy, Santa Clara
(95054-1200)
PHONE.................................703 208-3900
Richard L Mortin, *CEO*
Joseph Kijewski, *
**EMP:** 30 **EST:** 2010
**SALES (est):** 5.45MM
**SALES (corp-wide):** 4.38B **Privately Held**
**SIC: 7372** Application computer software
HQ: Cloud Software Group, Inc.
851 W Cypress Creek Rd
Fort Lauderdale FL 33309

**(P-18180)**
**CLOUD9 CHARTS INC**
1528 Webster St, Oakland (94612-3314)
PHONE.................................510 507-3661
Jay Gopalakrishn, *CEO*
Jay Gopalakrishnan, *CEO*
**EMP:** 15 **EST:** 2014
**SALES (est):** 1.16MM **Privately Held**
**SIC: 7372** Prepackaged software

**(P-18181)**
**CLOUDCAR INC**
2560 N 1st St Ste 100, San Jose
(95131-1041)
PHONE.................................650 946-1236
Philipp Popov, *CEO*
Bruce Leak, *COO*
Albert Jordan, *VP Prd*
**EMP:** 24 **EST:** 2010
**SALES (est):** 5.93MM **Privately Held**
Web: www.cloudcar.com
**SIC: 7372** Prepackaged software

**(P-18182)**
**CLOUDCOVER IOT INC (PA)**
Also Called: Cloudcover
14 Goodyear Ste 125b, Irvine (92618-3759)
PHONE.................................888 511-2022
Jeffrey Huggins, *CEO*
**EMP:** 35 **EST:** 2015
**SALES (est):** 14.71MM
**SALES (corp-wide):** 14.71MM **Privately Held**
Web: www.cloudcover.it
**SIC: 7372** 7379 7373 Prepackaged software; Computer related maintenance services; Systems engineering, computer related

**(P-18183)**
**CLOUDFILES TECHNOLOGIES INC**
38350 Fremont Blvd Ste 203, Fremont
(94536-6060)
PHONE.................................336 298-6575
Vishesh Singhal, *Pr*
**EMP:** 15 **EST:** 2021
**SALES (est):** 2.18MM **Privately Held**
**SIC: 7372** Prepackaged software

**(P-18184)**
**CLOUDFLARE INC (PA)**
Also Called: Cloudflare
101 Townsend St, San Francisco
(94107-1934)
PHONE.................................888 993-5273
Matthew Prince, *Ch Bd*
Michelle Zatlyn, *
Thomas Seifert, *CFO*
Douglas Kramer, *CLO*
**EMP:** 3346 **EST:** 2009
**SQ FT:** 112,000
**SALES (est):** 1.3B **Publicly Held**
Web: www.cloudflare.com
**SIC: 7372** 2741 7371 Prepackaged software; Internet publishing and broadcasting; Computer software development

**(P-18185)**
**CLOUDJEE INC**
Also Called: Cloudjee
1975 W El Camino Real # 30, Mountain View (94040-2274)
PHONE.................................866 660-6099
Samir Ghosh, *CEO*
**EMP:** 20 **EST:** 2012
**SQ FT:** 3,000
**SALES (est):** 590.96K **Privately Held**
Web: www.cloudjee.com
**SIC: 7372** 7371 Business oriented computer software; Computer software development

**(P-18186)**
**CLOUDSHIELD TECHNOLOGIES LLC**
212 Gibraltar Dr, Sunnyvale (94089-1324)
PHONE.................................408 331-6640
Randy Brumfield, *Sr VP*
Todd Beine, *
Timothy Laehy, *
**EMP:** 115 **EST:** 2000
**SQ FT:** 35,000
**SALES (est):** 2.11MM
**SALES (corp-wide):** 233.3MM **Privately Held**
**SIC: 7372** 8741 8742 Prepackaged software; Business management; Business management consultant
HQ: Lookingglass Cyber Solution, Inc.
1834 S Charles St
Baltimore MD 21230
703 351-1000

**(P-18187)**
**CLOUDSIMPLE INC**
1600 Amphitheatre Pkwy, Mountain View
(94043-1351)
PHONE.................................412 568-3487
Gururaj Pangal, *CEO*
**EMP:** 78 **EST:** 2016
**SALES (est):** 22.06MM
**SALES (corp-wide):** 307.39B **Publicly Held**
**SIC: 7372** Application computer software
HQ: Google Llc
1600 Amphitheatre Pkwy
Mountain View CA 94043
650 253-0000

**(P-18188)**
**CLOUDSODA INC ◆**
832 N Victory Blvd, Burbank (91502-1630)
PHONE.................................303 947-8661
Jack Fluor, *Pr*
Mark Zanotti, *CFO*
Tim Page, *Prin*
Bruce Lyon, *Prin*
John Zanotti, *Prin*
**EMP:** 19 **EST:** 2023
**SALES (est):** 1.41MM **Privately Held**
**SIC: 7372** Operating systems computer software

**(P-18189)**
**CLOUDVIRGA INC**
5291 California Ave Ste 300, Irvine
(92617-3221)
PHONE.................................949 799-2643
Daniel Akiva, *CEO*
Maria Moskver, *Legal**
**EMP:** 59 **EST:** 2015
**SALES (est):** 19.59MM
**SALES (corp-wide):** 2.26B **Publicly Held**
Web: www.cloudvirga.com
**SIC: 7372** Prepackaged software
PA: Stewart Information Services Corporation
1360 Post Oak Blvd Ste 10
713 625-8100

**(P-18190)**
**CLUB SPEED LLC (PA)**
300 Spectrum Center Dr, Irvine
(92618-4925)
PHONE.................................951 817-7073
Romir Bosu, *CEO*
Caleb Everett, *Pr*
Eric Novakovich, *Chief Strategy Officer*
**EMP:** 38 **EST:** 2007
**SALES (est):** 5.54MM
**SALES (corp-wide):** 5.54MM **Privately Held**
Web: www.clubspeed.com
**SIC: 7372** Prepackaged software

**(P-18191)**
**CODEFAST INC**
690 E Middlefield Rd, Mountain View
(94043-4010)
PHONE.................................408 687-4700
**EMP:** 22 **EST:** 2004
**SALES (est):** 1.03MM
**SALES (corp-wide):** 4.2B **Publicly Held**
**SIC: 7372** Business oriented computer software
HQ: Coverity Llc
185 Berry St Ste 6500
San Francisco CA 94107
415 321-5200

**(P-18192)**
**COLABO INC**
751 Laurel St Ste 840, San Carlos
(94070-3113)
PHONE.................................650 288-6649
Yoav Dembak, *CEO*
**EMP:** 34 **EST:** 2013
**SALES (est):** 2.29MM
**SALES (corp-wide):** 14.73MM **Privately Held**

# PRODUCTS & SERVICES SECTION

## 7372 - Prepackaged Software (P-18212)

Web: www.colabo.com
SIC: **7372** Prepackaged software
PA: Uniphore Technologies Inc.
    1001 Page Mill Rd Bldg 4
    650 352-5500

### (P-18193)
### COLLABRATIVE DRG DISCOVERY INC
Also Called: Molecular Databank
1633 Bayshore Hwy Ste 342, Burlingame (94010)
PHONE..................650 204-3084
Barry Bunin, *Pr*
EMP: 100 EST: 2004
SALES (est): 6.17MM **Privately Held**
Web: www.collaborativedrug.com
SIC: **7372** Prepackaged software

### (P-18194)
### COLORTOKENS INC (PA)
3590 N 1st St Ste 320, San Jose (95134-1812)
P.O. Box K (94087)
PHONE..................408 341-6030
Rajesh Parekh, *Pr*
Nitin Mehta, *Prin*
Vats Srivatsan, *
EMP: 50 EST: 2015
SALES (est): 5.38MM
SALES (corp-wide): 5.38MM **Privately Held**
Web: www.colortokens.com
SIC: **7372** Business oriented computer software

### (P-18195)
### COMPOSITE SOFTWARE LLC (DH)
755 Sycamore Dr, Milpitas (95035-7411)
PHONE..................800 553-6387
Jim Green, *CEO*
David Besemer, *
Jon Bode, *
EMP: 74 EST: 2002
SQ FT: 14,000
SALES (est): 12.9MM
SALES (corp-wide): 4.38B **Privately Held**
SIC: **7372** Prepackaged software
HQ: Cloud Software Group, Inc.
    851 W Cypress Creek Rd
    Fort Lauderdale FL 33309

### (P-18196)
### COMPUGROUP MEDICAL INC
25b Technology Dr Ste 200, Irvine (92618-2302)
PHONE..................949 789-0500
John Tangredi, *COO*
EMP: 37
SALES (corp-wide): 1.29B **Privately Held**
Web: www.cgm.com
SIC: **7372** Prepackaged software
HQ: Compugroup Medical, Inc.
    10901 Stonelake Blvd
    Austin TX 78759
    855 270-6700

### (P-18197)
### COMPULINK BUSINESS SYSTEMS INC (PA)
Also Called: Compulink Healthcare Solutions
1100 Business Center Cir, Newbury Park (91320-1124)
PHONE..................805 446-2050
Link Wilson, *Pr*
EMP: 117 EST: 1985
SQ FT: 15,000
SALES (est): 8.1MM
SALES (corp-wide): 8.1MM **Privately Held**
Web: www.compulinkadvantage.com
SIC: **7372** Business oriented computer software

### (P-18198)
### CONDECO SOFTWARE INC (DH)
2105 S Bascom Ave Ste 150, Campbell (95008-3276)
PHONE..................917 677-7600
Martin Brooker, *CEO*
EMP: 18 EST: 2010
SALES (est): 8.42MM **Privately Held**
Web: www.condecosoftware.com
SIC: **7372** Business oriented computer software
HQ: Eptura International Limited
    8th Floor Exchange Tower
    London E14 9
    207 001-2020

### (P-18199)
### CONFLUENT INC (PA)
899 W Evelyn Ave, Mountain View (94041-1225)
PHONE..................800 439-3207
Edward Jay Kreps, *Ch Bd*
Rohan Sivaram, *CFO*
Stephanie Buscemi, *CMO*
Kong Phan, *CAO*
EMP: 2137 EST: 2014
SQ FT: 75,475
SALES (est): 776.95MM
SALES (corp-wide): 776.95MM **Publicly Held**
Web: www.confluent.io
SIC: **7372** Application computer software

### (P-18200)
### CONSENSUS CLOUD SOLUTIONS INC (PA)
700 S Flower St Fl 15, Los Angeles (90017-4101)
PHONE..................323 860-9200
Scott Turicchi, *CEO*
John Nebergall, *COO*
Steve Emberland, *Contrlr*
James Malone, *CFO*
EMP: 65 EST: 2021
SALES (est): 362.56MM
SALES (corp-wide): 362.56MM **Publicly Held**
Web: www.consensus.com
SIC: **7372** Prepackaged software

### (P-18201)
### CONTRACT WRANGLER INC
400 Concar Dr, San Mateo (94402-2681)
PHONE..................408 472-6898
John Gengarella, *Admn*
John Gengarella, *CEO*
Harry Chip Register, *Ch*
Brian Ascher, *
Neil Peretz, *
EMP: 35 EST: 2016
SALES (est): 2.46MM **Privately Held**
Web: www.contractwrangler.com
SIC: **7372** Prepackaged software

### (P-18202)
### CONVERSIONPOINT HOLDINGS INC
840 Newport Center Dr Ste 450, Newport Beach (92660-6384)
PHONE..................888 706-6764
Robert Tallack, *Pr*
Don Walker Barrett Iii, *COO*
Raghu Kilambi, *CFO*
EMP: 85 EST: 2018
SALES (est): 812.26K **Privately Held**

### (P-18203)
### COPPER CRM INC (PA)
Also Called: Copper
2021 Fillmore St, San Francisco (94115-2708)
PHONE..................415 989-1477
Jonathan Lee, *CEO*
Jun Hu, *
Adrian Ivanov, *CRO**
Charles Ashworth, *CPO**
Chris Cheng, *
EMP: 18 EST: 2011
SALES (est): 10.31MM
SALES (corp-wide): 10.31MM **Privately Held**
Web: www.copper.com
SIC: **7372** Application computer software

### (P-18204)
### CORELIGHT INC
548 Market St, San Francisco (94104-5401)
P.O. Box 77799 (94104)
PHONE..................888 547-9497
Brian Dye, *CEO*
Russ Keefe, *CFO*
EMP: 65 EST: 2016
SALES (est): 3.17MM **Privately Held**
SIC: **7372** Operating systems computer software

### (P-18205)
### CORNERSTONE ONDEMAND INC (HQ)
Also Called: Cornerstone
1601 Cloverfield Blvd Ste 620s, Santa Monica (90404-4178)
PHONE..................310 752-0200
Himanshu Palsule, *CEO*
Scott Mcdermott, *Chief Accounting Officer*
Toya Del Valle, *Chief Customer Officer*
EMP: 247 EST: 1999
SQ FT: 94,000
SALES (est): 740.92MM
SALES (corp-wide): 740.92MM **Privately Held**
Web: www.cornerstoneondemand.com
SIC: **7372** Business oriented computer software
PA: Sunshine Software Holdings, Inc.
    1601 Cloverf Blvd Ste 62

### (P-18206)
### COUPA HOLDINGS LLC (PA)
1855 S Grant St Fl 4, San Mateo (94402-7034)
PHONE..................650 931-3200
Robert Bernshteyn, *Ch Bd*
EMP: 26 EST: 2022
SALES (est): 536.16MM
SALES (corp-wide): 536.16MM **Privately Held**
SIC: **7372** Business oriented computer software

### (P-18207)
### COUPA SOFTWARE INCORPORATED (HQ)
Also Called: Coupa
950 Tower Ln Ste 2000, Foster City (94404-4255)
PHONE..................650 931-3200
Leagh Turner, *CEO*
Anthony Tiscornia, *CFO*
Mark Riggs, *CCO*
Robert Glenn, *Executive Global Sales Vice President*
EMP: 128 EST: 2022
SQ FT: 69,220
SALES (est): 536.16MM
SALES (corp-wide): 536.16MM **Privately Held**
Web: www.coupa.com
SIC: **7372** Business oriented computer software
PA: Coupa Holdings, Llc
    1855 S Grant St
    650 931-3200

### (P-18208)
### COURSERA INC (PA)
Also Called: COURSERA
381 E Evelyn Ave, Mountain View (94041-1530)
PHONE..................650 963-9884
Jeffrey N Maggioncalda, *Pr*
Andrew Y Ng, *Non-Executive Chairman of the Board**
Kenneth R Hahn, *Sr VP*
Richard J Jacquet Junior, *CRO*
Alan B Cardenas, *Sr VP*
EMP: 925 EST: 2011
SALES (est): 523.76MM
SALES (corp-wide): 523.76MM **Publicly Held**
Web: www.coursera.org
SIC: **7372** Prepackaged software

### (P-18209)
### CREE8 INC ✪
2350 Keystone Dr, El Dorado Hills (95762-9543)
PHONE..................805 328-4204
Lisa Watts, *CEO*
EMP: 18 EST: 2023
SALES (est): 1.46MM **Privately Held**
Web: www.cree8.io
SIC: **7372** Prepackaged software

### (P-18210)
### CRERTIH INC
121 2nd St, San Francisco (94105-3608)
PHONE..................415 290-6603
Walter Ferguson, *CEO*
EMP: 23
SALES (est): 1.14MM **Privately Held**
SIC: **7372** Prepackaged software

### (P-18211)
### CROWDCIRCLE INC
Also Called: Healthcrowd
1810 Gateway Dr Ste 200, San Mateo (94404-4062)
PHONE..................206 853-7560
Neng Bing Doh, *CEO*
Nick Reutell, *Prin*
EMP: 50 EST: 2010
SALES (est): 4.95MM **Privately Held**
Web: www.mpulse.com
SIC: **7372** Prepackaged software

### (P-18212)
### CRYSTAL DYNAMICS INC (HQ)
2855 Campus Dr Ste 200, San Mateo (94403-2536)
PHONE..................650 421-7600
Philip Rogers, *CEO*
Robert Dyer, *Pr*
John Miller, *Executive Production*
John Horsley, *Executive Production*
Chris Hudson, *Dir Fin*
EMP: 36 EST: 1992
SALES (est): 26.87MM **Privately Held**
Web: www.crystaldynamics.com
SIC: **7372** Business oriented computer software
PA: Embracer Group Ab
    Tullhusgatan 1b

## 7372 - Prepackaged Software (P-18213)

**(P-18213)**
**CULTURE AMP INC (HQ)**
16501 Ventura Blvd Ste 400, Encino (91436-2067)
PHONE.................................415 326-8453
Didier Raoul Elzinga, *CEO*
Rodney James Hamilton, *
Douglas Mark English, *
**EMP:** 18 **EST:** 2013
**SALES (est):** 15.53MM **Privately Held**
Web: www.cultureamp.com
**SIC: 7372** Prepackaged software
**PA:** Culture Amp Pty Ltd
L 2 29 Stewart St

**(P-18214)**
**CUMULUS NETWORKS INC (HQ)**
Also Called: Cumulus Networks
185 E Dana St, Mountain View (94041-1507)
PHONE.................................650 383-6700
Jame Rivers, *CEO*
Reza Malekzadeh, *
Nolan Leake, *
Edward Leake, *
**EMP:** 124 **EST:** 2010
**SALES (est):** 7.95MM **Publicly Held**
Web: www.nvidia.com
**SIC: 7372** 7371 Publisher's computer software; Computer software development
**PA:** Nvidia Corporation
2788 San Tomas Expy

**(P-18215)**
**CURACUBBY INC**
2120 University Ave, Berkeley (94704-1026)
PHONE.................................415 200-3373
Rosauro Lugos, *Prin*
**EMP:** 54 **EST:** 2016
**SALES (est):** 4.42MM **Privately Held**
Web: www.curacubby.com
**SIC: 7372** Prepackaged software

**(P-18216)**
**CUREMETRIX INC**
402 W Broadway Ste 400, San Diego (92101-3554)
PHONE.................................858 333-5830
Kevin Harris, *Pr*
Kevin Harris, *CEO*
**EMP:** 20 **EST:** 2015
**SALES (est):** 3.4MM **Privately Held**
Web: www.curemetrix.com
**SIC: 7372** Application computer software

**(P-18217)**
**CXAPP INC ◆**
4 Palo Alto Sq Ste 200, Palo Alto (94306)
PHONE.................................650 575-4456
Khurram P Sheikh, *Interim Chief Financial Officer*
Khurram P Sheikh, *Interim Chief Financial Officer*
Leon Papkoff, *CPO*
**EMP:** 87 **EST:** 2023
**SALES (est):** 5.75MM
**SALES (corp-wide):** 5.75MM **Publicly Held**
Web: www.kins-tech.com
**SIC: 7372** Prepackaged software
**PA:** Kins Capital Llc
4 Palo Alto Sq Ste 200
650 575-4456

**(P-18218)**
**CYBERINC CORPORATION (HQ)**
Also Called: Aurionpro
4000 Executive Pkwy Ste 250, San Ramon (94583-4257)
PHONE.................................925 242-0777
Samir Shah, *CEO*
Nirav Shah, *COO*
Romi Randhawa, *CSO*
**EMP:** 30 **EST:** 2005
**SQ FT:** 3,000
**SALES (est):** 22.73MM **Privately Held**
Web: www.forcepoint.com
**SIC: 7372** 7371 Business oriented computer software; Custom computer programming services
**PA:** Aurionpro Solutions Limited
Synergia It Park, Plot No-R-270,

**(P-18219)**
**CYCLING 74 CORP**
433 Meder St, Santa Cruz (95060-2307)
PHONE.................................415 689-5777
**EMP:** 23 **EST:** 2018
**SALES (est):** 470.48K **Privately Held**
Web: www.cycling74.com
**SIC: 7372** Prepackaged software

**(P-18220)**
**CYLANCE INC (DH)**
3001 Bishop Dr Ste 400, San Ramon (94583-5005)
PHONE.................................949 375-3380
Stuart Mcclure, *CEO*
Daniel Doimo, *
Gregory Fitzgerald, *CMO*
Shane Shook, *Chief Knowledge*
Brady Berg, *
**EMP:** 87 **EST:** 2012
**SALES (est):** 200MM
**SALES (corp-wide):** 853MM **Privately Held**
Web: www.blackberry.com
**SIC: 7372** Application computer software
**HQ:** Blackberry Corporation
5030 Rvrside Dr Ste 200 B
Irving TX 75039
877 255-2377

**(P-18221)**
**D SOFTWARE INC**
Also Called: Zephyr
75 E Santa Clara St Fl 7, San Jose (95113-1826)
PHONE.................................415 795-7466
Scott Johnson, *CEO*
Robb Ellis, *CFO*
Hamesh Chawla, *CPO*
**EMP:** 21 **EST:** 2013
**SALES (est):** 4.87MM
**SALES (corp-wide):** 79.59MM **Privately Held**
Web: www.smartbear.com
**SIC: 7372** Business oriented computer software
**PA:** Smartbear Software Inc.
450 Artsan Way Ste 400 Fl
617 684-2600

**(P-18222)**
**D-WAVE QUANTUM INC**
2650 E Bayshore Rd, Palo Alto (94303-3211)
PHONE.................................604 630-1428
Alan Baratz, *Pr*
Steven M West, *
John M Markovich, *CFO*
Victoria Brydon, *PEOPLE & OPERATIONAL EXCELLENCE*
**EMP:** 200 **EST:** 1999
**SQ FT:** 6,000
**SALES (est):** 8.76MM **Privately Held**
**SIC: 7372** Prepackaged software

**(P-18223)**
**D3PUBLISHER OF AMERICA INC**
Also Called: D3 Go
15910 Ventura Blvd Ste 800, Encino (91436-2802)
PHONE.................................310 268-0820
Yoji Takenaka, *Pr*
Yuji Itoh, *Non-Executive Chairman of the Board*
Hidetaka Tachibana, *CFO*
**EMP:** 63 **EST:** 2004
**SQ FT:** 6,129
**SALES (est):** 18.5MM **Privately Held**
Web: www.d3go.com
**SIC: 7372** Home entertainment computer software
**HQ:** D3 Publisher Inc.
3-5-2, Kandakajicho
Chiyoda-Ku TKY 101-0

**(P-18224)**
**DACENSO INC**
Also Called: Exemptax
2030 Main St Ste 1300, Irvine (92614-7220)
PHONE.................................888 513-9367
Thomas Weiss, *CEO*
**EMP:** 20 **EST:** 2019
**SALES (est):** 3.02MM **Privately Held**
Web: www.exemptax.com
**SIC: 7372** Application computer software

**(P-18225)**
**DADO INC**
248 3rd St Ste 938, Oakland (94607-4375)
PHONE.................................866 704-7210
Jacob Olsen, *CEO*
**EMP:** 20 **EST:** 2018
**SALES (est):** 4.24MM **Privately Held**
Web: www.projectdado.com
**SIC: 7372** Publisher's computer software

**(P-18226)**
**DASSAULT SYSTEMES BIOVIA CORP (DH)**
Also Called: Biovia
5005 Wateridge Vista Dr, San Diego (92121-5780)
PHONE.................................858 799-5000
Max Carnecchia, *CEO*
Michael Piraino, *Ex VP*
Jason Gray, *Corporate Secretary*
Mathew Hahn, *Sr VP*
Judith Ohrn Hicks, *Senior Vice President Human Resources*
**EMP:** 43 **EST:** 1993
**SQ FT:** 68,436
**SALES (est):** 93.77MM
**SALES (corp-wide):** 2.08B **Privately Held**
Web: www.3ds.com
**SIC: 7372** Application computer software
**HQ:** 3ds Acquisition Corp.
175 Wyman St
Waltham MA 02451
781 810-5011

**(P-18227)**
**DATA APPOINTMENT**
6060 W Manchester Ave Ste 311, Los Angeles (90045-4200)
PHONE.................................310 979-3282
Nakita Muse, *Prin*
**EMP:** 20 **EST:** 2017
**SALES (est):** 683.66K **Privately Held**
Web: www.dataappointment.com
**SIC: 7372** Prepackaged software

**(P-18228)**
**DATAFOX INTELLIGENCE INC**
Also Called: Datafox
475 Sansome St Fl 15, San Francisco (94111-3166)
PHONE.................................415 969-2144
Bastiaan Janmaat, *CEO*
Michael Dorsey, *COO*
Benjamin Trombley, *Engr*
Alden Timme, *Engr*
**EMP:** 18 **EST:** 2013
**SALES (est):** 1.95MM **Privately Held**
**SIC: 7372** Business oriented computer software

**(P-18229)**
**DATAVISOR INC**
967 N Shoreline Blvd, Mountain View (94043-1932)
PHONE.................................408 331-9886
Yinglian Xie, *CEO*
Jon Sakoda, *
Fang Yu, *
Ron Bernal, *
**EMP:** 75 **EST:** 2014
**SALES (est):** 9.54MM **Privately Held**
Web: www.datavisor.com
**SIC: 7372** Business oriented computer software

**(P-18230)**
**DATERA INC**
2811 Mission College Blvd Fl 4, Santa Clara (95054-1884)
PHONE.................................844 432-8372
Guy Churchward, *CEO*
Marc Fleischmann, *
**EMP:** 36 **EST:** 2013
**SALES (est):** 6.84MM **Privately Held**
Web: www.datera.io
**SIC: 7372** Business oriented computer software

**(P-18231)**
**DAVE INC (PA)**
1265 S Cochran Ave, Los Angeles (90019-2846)
PHONE.................................844 857-3283
Jason Wilk, *Pr*
Kyle Beilman, *CFO*
**EMP:** 279 **EST:** 2015
**SQ FT:** 36,000
**SALES (est):** 259.09MM
**SALES (corp-wide):** 259.09MM **Publicly Held**
Web: www.dave.com
**SIC: 7372** 7389 Prepackaged software; Financial services

**(P-18232)**
**DCATALOG INC**
6250 Sagebrush Bend Way, San Diego (92130-6866)
PHONE.................................408 824-5648
Michael Raviv, *Pr*
**EMP:** 20 **EST:** 2012
**SALES (est):** 3.12MM **Privately Held**
Web: www.dcatalog.com
**SIC: 7372** Application computer software

**(P-18233)**
**DE NOVO SOFTWARE LLC**
207 N Sierra Madre Blvd # 1, Pasadena (91107-3302)
PHONE.................................213 814-1240
David Novo, *CEO*
**EMP:** 15 **EST:** 2003
**SALES (est):** 2.54MM
**SALES (corp-wide):** 201.3MM **Privately Held**

# PRODUCTS & SERVICES SECTION

**7372 - Prepackaged Software (P-18256)**

Web: www.denovosoftware.com
SIC: 7372 Prepackaged software
PA: Insightful Science Holdings, Llc
225 Franklin St
858 454-5577

**(P-18234)**
**DECISIONLOGIC LLC**
13500 Evening Creek Dr N Ste 600, San Diego (92128-8104)
PHONE..................................858 586-0202
David Evans, *Pr*
EMP: 23 EST: 2011
SALES (est): 2.34MM **Privately Held**
Web: www.decisionlogic.com
SIC: 7372 Business oriented computer software

**(P-18235)**
**DEEM INC (DH)**
1330 Broadway Fl 17, Oakland (94612-2537)
PHONE..................................415 590-8300
John Elieson, *Pr*
▲ EMP: 65 EST: 2001
SQ FT: 133,000
SALES (est): 42.91MM **Privately Held**
Web: www.deem.com
SIC: 7372 Prepackaged software
HQ: Travelport International Limited
Axis One Axis Park
Slough BERKS SL3 8
175 328-8000

**(P-18236)**
**DEEP LABS INC (PA)**
101 2nd St Ste 375, San Francisco (94105-3670)
PHONE..................................877 504-4544
Scott Edington, *CEO*
Tina Figueroa, *CPO**
EMP: 38 EST: 2016
SQ FT: 1,500
SALES (est): 3.17MM
SALES (corp-wide): 3.17MM **Privately Held**
Web: www.deep-labs.com
SIC: 7372 Business oriented computer software

**(P-18237)**
**DEMANDBASE INC (PA)**
222 2nd St 24th Fl, San Francisco (94105-3106)
PHONE..................................415 683-2660
Gabe Rogol, *CEO*
Umberto Milletti, *Research & Development*
Kelly V Hopping, *CMO*
John Eitel, *CSO*
Bryan Morris, *CFO*
EMP: 41 EST: 2005
SALES (est): 42.49MM **Privately Held**
Web: www.demandbase.com
SIC: 7372 Business oriented computer software

**(P-18238)**
**DEMANDWHIZ LLC**
4079 Middle Park Dr, San Jose (95135-1022)
PHONE..................................408 600-2720
Manish S, *Managing Member*
EMP: 100 EST: 2015
SALES (est): 1.82MM **Privately Held**
Web: www.demandwhiz.com
SIC: 7372 Prepackaged software

**(P-18239)**
**DENALI SOFTWARE INC (HQ)**
2655 Seely Ave, San Jose (95134-1931)
PHONE..................................408 943-1234
Sanjay Srivastava, *Pr*
R Mark Gogolewski, *
EMP: 36 EST: 1995
SQ FT: 10,000
SALES (est): 9.85MM
SALES (corp-wide): 4.09B **Publicly Held**
Web: www.denali.com
SIC: 7372 Application computer software
PA: Cadence Design Systems, Inc.
2655 Seely Ave Bldg 5
408 943-1234

**(P-18240)**
**DIGITAL ARBITRAGE DIST INC (PA)**
Also Called: Cloudbeds
3033 5th Ave Ste 100, San Diego (92103-5828)
PHONE..................................888 392-9478
Adam Harris, *CEO*
EMP: 30 EST: 2017
SALES (est): 7.7MM
SALES (corp-wide): 7.7MM **Privately Held**
Web: www.cloudbeds.com
SIC: 7372 Prepackaged software

**(P-18241)**
**DIGITS FINANCIAL INC**
1015 Fillmore St, San Francisco (94115-4709)
PHONE..................................814 634-4487
Katya Valadzko, *CEO*
EMP: 20 EST: 2018
SALES (est): 5.53MM **Privately Held**
Web: www.digits.com
SIC: 7372 Business oriented computer software

**(P-18242)**
**DINCLOUD INC**
27520 Hawthorne Blvd Ste 185, Rlng Hls Est (90274-3576)
PHONE..................................310 929-1101
Mark Briggs, *CEO*
Ali M Dincmo, *
Mike L Chase, *
EMP: 53 EST: 2011
SQ FT: 1,500
SALES (est): 10.4MM
SALES (corp-wide): 43.76MM **Privately Held**
Web: www.dincloud.com
SIC: 7372 Business oriented computer software
PA: Premier Bpo, Inc.
128 N 2nd St Ste 210
931 551-8888

**(P-18243)**
**DISCERNDX INC**
2478 Embarcadero Way, Palo Alto (94303-3313)
PHONE..................................909 319-9779
EMP: 16
SALES (est): 1.97MM **Privately Held**
Web: www.discerndx.com
SIC: 7372 Prepackaged software

**(P-18244)**
**DISRUPTIVE GAMES INC**
2030 Addison St Ste 610, Berkeley (94704-1147)
PHONE..................................310 922-6658
Jacob M Biegel, *CEO*
EMP: 42 EST: 2016
SALES (est): 2.1MM **Privately Held**
Web: www.disruptivegames.com
SIC: 7372 Prepackaged software

**(P-18245)**
**DISTRU CORP**
344 Thomas L Berkley Way, Oakland (94612-3577)
PHONE..................................603 630-0282
Jeffrey Blaine Hatab, *Prin*
EMP: 35 EST: 2016
SALES (est): 6.98MM **Privately Held**
Web: www.distru.com
SIC: 7372 Prepackaged software

**(P-18246)**
**DO DINE INC**
Also Called: Multani Logistics
24052 Mission Blvd, Hayward (94544-1017)
PHONE..................................510 583-7546
Bikramjit Singh, *CEO*
EMP: 15 EST: 2014
SQ FT: 5,000
SALES (est): 2.35MM **Privately Held**
Web: www.dodine.com
SIC: 7372 Business oriented computer software

**(P-18247)**
**DOCUSIGN INC (PA)**
Also Called: Docusign
221 Main St Ste 1550, San Francisco (94105-1947)
PHONE..................................415 489-4940
Allan Thygesen, *CEO*
Mary Agnes Wilderotter, *
Blake Grayson, *Ex VP*
James P Shaughnessy, *CLO*
Paula Hansen, *CRO*
EMP: 464 EST: 2003
SQ FT: 93,000
SALES (est): 2.76B
SALES (corp-wide): 2.76B **Publicly Held**
Web: www.docusign.com
SIC: 7372 Prepackaged software

**(P-18248)**
**DOMICO SOFTWARE**
1220 Oakland Blvd Ste 300, Walnut Creek (94596-8409)
PHONE..................................510 841-4155
Glenn Hunter, *Pr*
EMP: 15 EST: 1984
SQ FT: 4,000
SALES (est): 1.26MM **Privately Held**
Web: domicoblog.wordpress.com
SIC: 7372 7371 Prepackaged software; Custom computer programming services

**(P-18249)**
**DORADO NETWORK SYSTEMS CORP**
Also Called: Corelogic Dorado
40 Pacifica, Irvine (92618-7471)
PHONE..................................650 227-7300
Dain Ehring, *CEO*
Karen Camp, *
EMP: 140 EST: 1998
SALES (est): 9.64MM
SALES (corp-wide): 1.64B **Privately Held**
Web: www.corelogic.com
SIC: 7372 Application computer software
HQ: Corelogic, Inc.
40 Pacifica Ste 900
Irvine CA 92618
866 873-3651

**(P-18250)**
**DOUBLEDUTCH INC (DH)**
44 Tehama St Ste 504, San Francisco (94105-3110)
PHONE..................................800 748-9024
Lawrence Coburn, *CEO*
Brad Roberts, *CFO*
EMP: 94 EST: 1984
SALES (est): 12.59MM
SALES (corp-wide): 481.22MM **Privately Held**
Web: www.thedoubledutch.com
SIC: 7372 Application computer software
HQ: Cvent, Inc.
1765 Grnsboro Stn Pl Fl 7
Tysons Corner VA 22102
703 226-3500

**(P-18251)**
**DREAMSTART LABS INC**
2907 Shelter Island Dr Ste 105, San Diego (92106-2743)
PHONE..................................408 914-1234
Wes Wasson, *CEO*
EMP: 30 EST: 2016
SALES (est): 400K **Privately Held**
Web: www.dreamstartlabs.com
SIC: 7372 Application computer software

**(P-18252)**
**DRIVEAI INC**
365 Ravendale Dr, Mountain View (94043-5217)
P.O. Box 57 (94023)
PHONE..................................408 693-0765
Sameep Tandon, *CEO*
EMP: 150 EST: 15
SALES (est): 7.25MM **Privately Held**
SIC: 7372 Prepackaged software

**(P-18253)**
**DRIVER INC**
438 Shotwell St, San Francisco (94110-1914)
PHONE..................................415 999-4960
Will Polkinghorn, *CEO*
EMP: 85 EST: 2011
SALES (est): 5.32MM **Privately Held**
Web: www.driver.xyz
SIC: 7372 Educational computer software

**(P-18254)**
**DRIVESCALE INC**
1320 Hillview Dr, Menlo Park (94025-5513)
PHONE..................................408 849-4651
Gene Banman, *CEO*
Alvin Eugene Banman, *Prin*
Satya Nishtala, *Prin*
Denise Shiffman, *Chief Product Officer*
EMP: 19 EST: 2013
SALES (est): 2.7MM **Privately Held**
Web: www.drivescale.com
SIC: 7372 Application computer software

**(P-18255)**
**DRIZLY LLC (HQ)**
1725 3rd St, San Francisco (94158-2203)
PHONE..................................774 234-1033
Dara Khosrowshahi, *CEO*
EMP: 32 EST: 2012
SALES (est): 24.68MM
SALES (corp-wide): 37.28B **Publicly Held**
Web: www.drizly.com
SIC: 7372 7389 Application computer software; Business Activities at Non-Commercial Site
PA: Uber Technologies, Inc.
1725 3rd St
415 612-8582

**(P-18256)**
**DROPBOX INC (PA)**
Also Called: DROPBOX
1800 Owens St Ste 200, San Francisco (94158-2533)
PHONE..................................415 930-7766

## 7372 - Prepackaged Software (P-18257)

Andrew W Houston, *Ch Bd*
Timothy Regan, *CFO*
Bart E Volkmer, *CLO*
Eric Cox, *CCO*
**EMP:** 2105 **EST:** 2007
**SALES (est):** 2.5B **Publicly Held**
**Web:** www.dropbox.com
**SIC: 7372** Prepackaged software

### (P-18257)
### DRUVA INC
2051 Mission College Blvd, Santa Clara (95054-1519)
**PHONE**.................................650 241-3501
Jaspreet Singh, *CEO*
Mahesh Patel, *CFO*
Wynn White, *CMO*
Thorsten Freitag, *CRO*
Sherry Lowe, *CMO*
**EMP:** 58 **EST:** 2010
**SALES (est):** 24.14MM **Privately Held**
**Web:** www.druva.com
**SIC: 7372** Business oriented computer software
**PA:** Druva Software Private Limited
Muttha Chambers Ii, Level Vi

### (P-18258)
### DUDA MOBILE INC
577 College Ave, Palo Alto (94306-1433)
P.O. Box 60432 (94306-0432)
**PHONE**.................................855 790-0003
Itia Sadan, *CEO*
Sarah Carpenter, *CFO*
**EMP:** 161 **EST:** 2011
**SALES (est):** 2.12MM **Privately Held**
**Web:** www.duda.co
**SIC: 7372** Application computer software

### (P-18259)
### EAGLE TOPCO LP
18200 Von Karman Ave, Irvine (92612-1023)
**PHONE**.................................949 585-4329
**EMP:** 4000
**SIC: 7372** Business oriented computer software

### (P-18260)
### ECRIO INC
19925 Stevens Creek Blvd Ste 100, Cupertino (95014-2300)
**PHONE**.................................408 973-7290
Randy Granovetter, *CEO*
Nagesh Challa, *Chief Strategy Officer*
Tad Bogdan, *Ex VP*
Lina Martin, *VP Fin*
Ted Goldstein, *Chief Strategy Officer*
**EMP:** 90 **EST:** 1998
**SALES (est):** 7.13MM **Privately Held**
**Web:** www.ecrio.com
**SIC: 7372** Prepackaged software

### (P-18261)
### EDCAST LLC (DH)
4120 Dublin Blvd Ste 200, Dublin (94568-7759)
**PHONE**.................................844 833-2278
Karl Mehta, *CEO*
**EMP:** 47 **EST:** 2013
**SALES (est):** 15.17MM
**SALES (corp-wide):** 740.92MM **Privately Held**
**Web:** www.edcast.com
**SIC: 7372** Educational computer software
**HQ:** Cornerstone Ondemand, Inc.
1601 Clvrfeld Blvd Ste 62
Santa Monica CA 90404
310 752-0200

### (P-18262)
### EDGATE HOLDINGS INC
4655 Cass St, San Diego (92109-2813)
**PHONE**.................................858 712-9341
Peter Sibley, *CEO*
**EMP:** 32 **EST:** 2021
**SALES (est):** 1.45MM **Privately Held**
**Web:** www.edgate.com
**SIC: 7372** Educational computer software

### (P-18263)
### EDGEWAVE INC
4225 Executive Sq Ste 1600, La Jolla (92037-1487)
**PHONE**.................................800 782-3762
**EMP:** 100
**Web:** www.gosecure.ai
**SIC: 7372** Operating systems computer software

### (P-18264)
### EDUCATION ELEMENTS INC
101 Hickey Blvd Ste A # 526, South San Francisco (94080-1177)
**PHONE**.................................650 440-7860
Anthony Kim, *CEO*
Victoria Bernholz, *
**EMP:** 66 **EST:** 2010
**SALES (est):** 6.79MM **Privately Held**
**Web:** www.edelements.com
**SIC: 7372** Educational computer software

### (P-18265)
### EDVIN INC
976 Laurel Glen Dr, Palo Alto (94304-1322)
**PHONE**.................................415 800-4067
Prithviral Puttaraju, *Prin*
**EMP:** 20 **EST:** 2022
**SALES (est):** 1.33MM **Privately Held**
**SIC: 7372** Prepackaged software

### (P-18266)
### EFINIX INC (PA)
20400 Stevens Creek Blvd Ste 200, Cupertino (95014-2290)
**PHONE**.................................408 789-6917
Sammy Cheung, *CEO*
**EMP:** 31 **EST:** 2012
**SALES (est):** 9.35MM
**SALES (corp-wide):** 9.35MM **Privately Held**
**Web:** www.efinixinc.com
**SIC: 7372** Business oriented computer software

### (P-18267)
### EGAIN CORPORATION (PA)
Also Called: EGAIN
1252 Borregas Ave, Sunnyvale (94089-1309)
**PHONE**.................................408 636-4500
Ashutosh Roy, *Ch Bd*
Eric Smit, *CFO*
Promod Narang, *Sr VP*
**EMP:** 109 **EST:** 1997
**SQ FT:** 42,541
**SALES (est):** 92.8MM
**SALES (corp-wide):** 92.8MM **Publicly Held**
**Web:** www.egain.com
**SIC: 7372** 7371 Prepackaged software; Custom computer programming services

### (P-18268)
### EGL HOLDCO INC
18200 Von Karman Ave Ste 1000, Irvine (92612-1023)
**PHONE**.................................800 678-7423
**EMP:** 4000
**SIC: 7372** Prepackaged software

### (P-18269)
### EIGHTFOLD AI INC (PA)
2625 Augustine Dr 6th Fl, Santa Clara (95054-2956)
**PHONE**.................................650 265-7380
Ashutosh Garg, *CEO*
Chano Fernandez, *
Rupa Veerapuneni, *Dir*
**EMP:** 114 **EST:** 2016
**SALES (est):** 10.93MM
**SALES (corp-wide):** 10.93MM **Privately Held**
**Web:** www.eightfold.ai
**SIC: 7372** Prepackaged software

### (P-18270)
### EIS GROUP INC
4 Embarcadero Ctr Ste 3410, San Francisco (94111)
**PHONE**.................................415 402-2622
Alec Miloslavsky, *CEO*
Sergiy Synyanskyy, *
**EMP:** 128 **EST:** 2008
**SALES (est):** 22.6MM **Privately Held**
**Web:** www.eisgroup.com
**SIC: 7372** Business oriented computer software

### (P-18271)
### EKNOWLEDGE GROUP INC
160 W Foothill Pkwy Ste 105, Corona (92882-8545)
**PHONE**.................................951 256-4076
Scott Hildebrandt, *Pr*
**EMP:** 35 **EST:** 1999
**SALES (est):** 350.42K **Privately Held**
**SIC: 7372** Educational computer software

### (P-18272)
### ELECTRONIC ARTS INC (PA)
Also Called: EA
209 Redwood Shores Pkwy, Redwood City (94065-1175)
**PHONE**.................................650 628-1500
Andrew Wilson, *Ch Bd*
Laura Miele, *COO*
Mala Singh, *CPO*
Jacob J Schatz, *CLO*
Stuart Canfield, *Ex VP*
▲ **EMP:** 475 **EST:** 1982
**SALES (est):** 7.43B
**SALES (corp-wide):** 7.43B **Publicly Held**
**Web:** www.ea.com
**SIC: 7372** Home entertainment computer software

### (P-18273)
### ELECTRONIC CLEARING HOUSE INC (HQ)
730 Paseo Camarillo, Camarillo (93010-6064)
**PHONE**.................................805 419-8700
Charles J Harris, *Pr*
Alice L Cheung, *
Rick Slater, *
William Wied, *CIO**
Karl Asplund, *
**EMP:** 100 **EST:** 1981
**SQ FT:** 32,669
**SALES (est):** 2.42MM
**SALES (corp-wide):** 16.29B **Publicly Held**
**Web:** www.echo-inc.com
**SIC: 7372** Business oriented computer software
**PA:** Intuit Inc.
2700 Coast Ave
650 944-6000

### (P-18274)
### ELEKTA INC
101 Nicholson Ln, San Jose (95134)
**PHONE**.................................408 830-8000
**EMP:** 40
**SALES (corp-wide):** 1.62B **Privately Held**
**Web:** www.elekta.com
**SIC: 7372** 7373 Business oriented computer software; Computer integrated systems design
**HQ:** Elekta, Inc.
400 Perimeter Center Ter
Atlanta GA 30346
770 300-9725

### (P-18275)
### ELEVATE LABS LLC
1390 Market St Ste 200, San Francisco (94102-5404)
**PHONE**.................................415 875-9817
**EMP:** 22 **EST:** 2014
**SALES (est):** 2.35MM **Privately Held**
**Web:** www.elevateapp.com
**SIC: 7372** Application computer software

### (P-18276)
### ELLIPSIS HEALTH INC
118 2nd St, San Francisco (94105-3613)
**PHONE**.................................650 906-6117
Mainul I Mondal, *CEO*
Mainul Islam, *CEO*
**EMP:** 28 **EST:** 2013
**SALES (est):** 3.87MM **Privately Held**
**Web:** www.ellipsishealth.com
**SIC: 7372** Application computer software

### (P-18277)
### EMBODIED LABS INC
2112 Chestnut St Ste 135, Alhambra (91803-1401)
**PHONE**.................................323 421-7600
Thomas Leahy, *Admn*
Carrie Shaw, *CEO*
**EMP:** 20 **EST:** 2016
**SALES (est):** 2.29MM **Privately Held**
**Web:** www.embodiedlabs.com
**SIC: 7372** Educational computer software

### (P-18278)
### EMPOWER SOFTWARE TECH LLC
28999 Old Town Front St Ste 203, Temecula (92590-5806)
**PHONE**.................................951 672-6257
Thomas V Smith, *Pt*
**EMP:** 15 **EST:** 1998
**SALES (est):** 3.49MM **Privately Held**
**Web:** www.storagecommander.com
**SIC: 7372** Business oriented computer software

### (P-18279)
### ENABLE INTERNATIONAL INC
535 Mission St Fl 14, San Francisco (94105-3253)
**PHONE**.................................628 251-1057
Andrew William Butt, *CEO*
**EMP:** 24 **EST:** 2019
**SALES (est):** 7.35MM **Privately Held**
**Web:** www.enable.com
**SIC: 7372** Operating systems computer software

### (P-18280)
### ENABLENCE SYSTEMS INC (HQ)
Also Called: Pannaway
2933 Bayview Dr, Fremont (94538-6520)
**PHONE**.................................510 226-8900
Gary Davis, *Pr*

▲ = Import ▼ = Export
◆ = Import/Export

Robert Monaco, *COO*
Boris Grek, *VP*
▲ **EMP:** 72 **EST:** 2002
**SALES (est):** 5.42MM
**SALES (corp-wide):** 1.96MM **Privately Held**
**Web:** www.enablence.com
**SIC: 7372** Application computer software
**PA:** Enablence Technologies Inc
119-390 March Rd
613 656-2850

**(P-18281)**
### ENACT SYSTEMS INC
6200 Stoneridge Mall Rd Ste 300, Pleasanton (94588-3705)
**PHONE**..............510 828-2701
Deep Chakraborty, *CEO*
Matthew Cheney Board, *Ch*
Ryan Hamilton, *Ex VP*
Thomas King, *CFO*
Manish Anand, *Ex VP*
**EMP:** 19 **EST:** 2014
**SALES (est):** 5.1MM **Privately Held**
**Web:** www.enact.solar
**SIC: 7372** Business oriented computer software

**(P-18282)**
### ENGAGIO INC
181 2nd Ave Ste 200, San Mateo (94401-3816)
**PHONE**..............650 265-2264
Jon Miller, *CEO*
Heidi Bullock, *CMO\**
Cheryl Chavez, *Chief Product Officer\**
**EMP:** 50 **EST:** 2015
**SALES (est):** 4.61MM **Privately Held**
**Web:** www.demandbase.com
**SIC: 7372** Business oriented computer software
**PA:** Demandbase, Inc.
222 2nd St 24th Fl

**(P-18283)**
### ENTCO LLC
Also Called: Autonomy Interwoven
1140 Enterprise Way, Sunnyvale (94089-1412)
**PHONE**..............312 580-9100
**EMP:** 916
**SIC: 7372** Business oriented computer software

**(P-18284)**
### EOS SOFTWARE INC
10026 Crescent Rd, Cupertino (95014-1000)
**PHONE**..............408 439-2903
Mohit Doshi, *CEO*
**EMP:** 50 **EST:** 2004
**SQ FT:** 500
**SALES (est):** 1.89MM **Privately Held**
**Web:** www.eossoftware.com
**SIC: 7372** Business oriented computer software

**(P-18285)**
### EPICOR SOFTWARE CORPORATION
4120 Dublin Blvd Ste 300, Dublin (94568-7759)
**PHONE**..............949 585-4000
Pervez Qureshi, *Brnch Mgr*
**EMP:** 31
**Web:** www.epicor.com
**SIC: 7372** Prepackaged software
**PA:** Epicor Software Corporation
807 Las Cmas Pkwy Ste 400

**(P-18286)**
### EPIGNOSIS LLC
315 Montgomery St Fl 9, San Francisco (94104-1858)
**PHONE**..............646 797-2799
**EMP:** 37 **EST:** 2012
**SALES (est):** 3.47MM **Privately Held**
**Web:** www.epignosishq.com
**SIC: 7372** Application computer software

**(P-18287)**
### EPIRUS INC
19145 Gramercy Pl, Torrance (90501-1128)
P.O. Box 3927 (90277)
**PHONE**..............310 620-8678
Andy Lowery, *CEO*
Harry Marr, *\**
Joseph Lonsdale, *\**
John Tenet, *\**
Daniel Thompson, *\**
**EMP:** 26 **EST:** 2018
**SALES (est):** 1MM **Privately Held**
**Web:** www.epirusinc.com
**SIC: 7372** 7373 0781 1771 Prepackaged software; Computer integrated systems design; Landscape counseling and planning ; Stucco, gunite, and grouting contractors

**(P-18288)**
### EPODIUM INC
7020 Koll Center Pkwy Ste 127, Pleasanton (94566-3103)
**PHONE**..............925 621-0602
Romi Randhawa, *CEO*
**EMP:** 20 **EST:** 2017
**SALES (est):** 7.9MM **Privately Held**
**Web:** www.epodium.com
**SIC: 7372** Prepackaged software

**(P-18289)**
### EQUIMINE
Also Called: Propstream
26457 Rancho Pkwy S, Lake Forest (92630-8326)
**PHONE**..............877 204-9040
Brian Tepfer, *CEO*
**EMP:** 41 **EST:** 2006
**SALES (est):** 13.61MM
**SALES (corp-wide):** 2.26B **Publicly Held**
**Web:** www.propstream.com
**SIC: 7372** 3429 Business oriented computer software; Keys, locks, and related hardware
**PA:** Stewart Information Services Corporation
1360 Post Oak Blvd Ste 10
713 625-8100

**(P-18290)**
### ESMART SOURCE INC
Also Called: Rfid4u
5159 Commercial Cir Ste H, Concord (94520-8503)
P.O. Box 5366 (94524-0366)
**PHONE**..............408 739-3500
Sanjiv Dua, *CEO*
Anu Dua, *Dir*
**EMP:** 15 **EST:** 1999
**SALES (est):** 1.97MM **Privately Held**
**Web:** www.rfid4u.com
**SIC: 7372** 7373 Business oriented computer software; Local area network (LAN) systems integrator

**(P-18291)**
### ETECH-360 INC (PA)
Also Called: 360s2g
555 California St, San Francisco (94104-1503)
P.O. Box 7491 (92624)
**PHONE**..............714 900-3486
Isabelle Hughes, *CEO*
Douglas Carver, *\**
Amanda Gutierrez, *Senior Vice President Client Management\**
Devon Knittle, *\**
Pat Kyomoto, *\**
**EMP:** 551 **EST:** 2010
**SQ FT:** 8,000
**SALES (est):** 67.26MM
**SALES (corp-wide):** 67.26MM **Privately Held**
**Web:** www.360s2g.com
**SIC: 7372** 5045 7371 8243 Prepackaged software; Computers, peripherals, and software; Custom computer programming services; Data processing schools

**(P-18292)**
### ETURNS INC
19700 Fairchild Ste 290, Irvine (92612-2521)
**PHONE**..............949 265-2626
Richard Rockwell, *CEO*
**EMP:** 32 **EST:** 2010
**SALES (est):** 2.02MM **Privately Held**
**Web:** www.eturns.com
**SIC: 7372** 7371 Application computer software; Computer software development and applications

**(P-18293)**
### EVENTSCOM INC
Also Called: Bump.me
811 Prospect St, La Jolla (92037-4207)
P.O. Box 1209 (92038)
**PHONE**..............858 257-2300
Mitchell Thrower, *CEO*
Paul Brown, *CFO*
Stephen Partridge, *Sec*
**EMP:** 45 **EST:** 2009
**SALES (est):** 5.01MM **Privately Held**
**Web:** www.events.com
**SIC: 7372** Publisher's computer software

**(P-18294)**
### EVERBRIDGE INC (PA)
155 N Lake Ave Ste 900, Pasadena (91101-1849)
**PHONE**..............818 230-9700
David Wagner, *Pr*
Jaime Ellertson, *Ch Bd*
David Henshall, *Vice Chairman*
Robert Hughes, *Pr*
Patrick Brickley, *Sr VP*
**EMP:** 111 **EST:** 2002
**SQ FT:** 45,000
**SALES (est):** 448.79MM
**SALES (corp-wide):** 448.79MM **Privately Held**
**Web:** www.everbridge.com
**SIC: 7372** 4899 Prepackaged software; Data communication services

**(P-18295)**
### EVERLANCE INC
595 Pacific Ave Fl 4, San Francisco (94133-4685)
**PHONE**..............872 814-6308
Alexander Marlantes, *CEO*
Gabriel Garza, *\**
**EMP:** 68 **EST:** 2015
**SALES (est):** 5.04MM **Privately Held**
**Web:** www.everlance.com
**SIC: 7372** Business oriented computer software

**(P-18296)**
### EVOCATIVE INC
26 Centerpointe, La Palma (90623-1072)
**PHONE**..............888 365-2656
Patrick Rigney, *CEO*
Erin Mac Arthur, *\**
**EMP:** 75 **EST:** 1996
**SALES (est):** 15.96MM
**SALES (corp-wide):** 67.28MM **Privately Held**
**Web:** www.evocative.com
**SIC: 7372** Application computer software
**PA:** Evodc, Llc
26 Centerpointe Dr
888 365-2656

**(P-18297)**
### EVOLPHIN SOFTWARE INC
6101 Bollinger Canyon Rd Ste 324d, San Ramon (94583-5107)
**PHONE**..............888 386-4114
Brian Ahearn, *CEO*
**EMP:** 30 **EST:** 2010
**SALES (est):** 2.21MM **Privately Held**
**Web:** www.evolphin.com
**SIC: 7372** Business oriented computer software

**(P-18298)**
### EVOLUTION ROBOTICS INC
1055 E Colorado Blvd Ste 320, Pasadena (91106-2376)
**PHONE**..............626 993-3300
Paolo Pirjanian, *CEO*
Bill Gross, *\**
Doug Mcpherson, *Sec*
**EMP:** 18 **EST:** 2001
**SALES (est):** 4.33MM **Publicly Held**
**Web:** careers.evolution.com
**SIC: 7372** Application computer software
**PA:** Irobot Corporation
8 Crosby Dr

**(P-18299)**
### EVOLV TECHNOLOGY SOLUTIONS INC (PA)
580 Market St Ste 200, San Francisco (94104-5400)
**PHONE**..............415 444-9040
Michael Scharff, *CEO*
**EMP:** 30 **EST:** 2019
**SALES (est):** 4.32MM
**SALES (corp-wide):** 4.32MM **Privately Held**
**Web:** www.evolv.ai
**SIC: 7372** Prepackaged software

**(P-18300)**
### EXABLOX CORPORATION
1156 Sonora Ct, Sunnyvale (94086-5308)
**PHONE**..............408 773-8477
Douglas Brockett, *CEO*
Tad Hunt, *\**
Ramesh Iyer Balan, *\**
Shridar Subramanian, *CRO\**
Ezra Hookano, *\**
**EMP:** 50 **EST:** 2010
**SALES (est):** 2.23MM **Privately Held**
**SIC: 7372** Prepackaged software
**HQ:** Storagecraft Technology, Llc
6600 City West Pkwy
Eden Prairie MN 55344

**(P-18301)**
### EXACTTARGET LLC (HQ)
415 Mission St Fl 3, San Francisco (94105-2504)
**PHONE**..............415 901-7000
Sarah Dods, *Sec*
Joachim Wettermark, *Treas*
Darryl Yee, *VP*
**EMP:** 61 **EST:** 2000
**SQ FT:** 66,536

# 7372 - Prepackaged Software (P-18302)

SALES (est): 45.86MM
SALES (corp-wide): 34.86B **Publicly Held**
Web: www.salesforce.com
SIC: 7372 Business oriented computer software
PA: Salesforce, Inc.
415 Mission St Fl 3
415 901-7000

### (P-18302)
### EXACTUALS LLC
1100 Glendon Ave Fl 17, Los Angeles (90024-3588)
PHONE.....................310 689-7491
Michael Hurst, *CEO*
Bryan Walley, *COO*
Ilie Ardelean, *CPO*
EMP: 15 EST: 2012
SALES (est): 6.49MM
SALES (corp-wide): 41.52B **Privately Held**
Web: www.cnb.com
SIC: 7372 Prepackaged software
HQ: City National Bank
555 S Flower St 21st Flr
Los Angeles CA 90071
310 888-6000

### (P-18303)
### EXADEL INC (PA)
1255 Treat Blvd, Walnut Creek (94597-7968)
PHONE.....................925 363-9510
Fima Katz, *CEO*
Alex Kreymer, *COO*
EMP: 2654 EST: 1995
SALES (est): 99.03MM **Privately Held**
Web: www.exadel.com
SIC: 7372 Application computer software

### (P-18304)
### EXPANDABLE SOFTWARE INC (PA)
1762 Technology Dr Ste 118, San Jose (95110-1307)
PHONE.....................408 261-7880
Tony Nevshemal, *CEO*
Bob Swedroe, *CEO*
David Kearney, *Sec*
Gerald Lass, *VP*
Vern Marschke, *VP*
EMP: 40 EST: 1983
SALES (est): 4.25MM
SALES (corp-wide): 4.25MM **Privately Held**
Web: www.expandable.com
SIC: 7372 7371 Prepackaged software; Custom computer programming services

### (P-18305)
### FACEFIRST LLC ◊
31416 Agoura Rd Ste 250, Westlake Village (91361-5654)
PHONE.....................805 482-8428
EMP: 30 EST: 2023
SALES (est): 3.56MM **Privately Held**
SIC: 7372 Prepackaged software

### (P-18306)
### FACILITRON INC (PA)
485 Alberto Way Ste 210, Los Gatos (95032-5476)
PHONE.....................800 272-2962
Jeff Benjamin, *CEO*
EMP: 23 EST: 2014
SQ FT: 3,000
SALES (est): 4.96MM
SALES (corp-wide): 4.96MM **Privately Held**
Web: www.facilitron.com

SIC: 7372 Business oriented computer software

### (P-18307)
### FAIR ISAAC INTERNATIONAL CORP (HQ)
200 Smith Ranch Rd, San Rafael (94903-5551)
PHONE.....................415 446-6000
Thomas G Grudnowski, *Pr*
EMP: 600 EST: 1979
SALES (est): 14.79MM
SALES (corp-wide): 1.72B **Publicly Held**
Web: www.fico.com
SIC: 7372 Business oriented computer software
PA: Fair Isaac Corporation
5 W Mendenhall Ste 105
406 982-7276

### (P-18308)
### FIRST ADVNTAGE TLENT MGT SVCS
Also Called: Findly
98 Battery St Ste 400, San Francisco (94110-2404)
PHONE.....................415 446-3930
EMP: 18 EST: 2007
SQ FT: 4,000
SALES (est): 3.19MM **Privately Held**
SIC: 7372 Business oriented computer software

### (P-18309)
### FIRSTUP INC (PA)
1 Montgomery St Ste 2150, San Francisco (94104-5505)
PHONE.....................844 975-2533
Nicole Alvino, *CEO*
Gary Nakamura, *
Gregory Shove, *
Peter C Horan, *
Valerie Johnson, *
EMP: 391 EST: 2010
SALES (est): 39.13MM
SALES (corp-wide): 39.13MM **Privately Held**
Web: www.firstup.io
SIC: 7372 Business oriented computer software

### (P-18310)
### FITBOD INC
1655 Taraval St, San Francisco (94116-2353)
PHONE.....................415 727-6264
Allen Chen, *CEO*
EMP: 48 EST: 2013
SALES (est): 6.64MM **Privately Held**
Web: www.fitbod.me
SIC: 7372 Application computer software

### (P-18311)
### FITSTAR INC
80 Langton St, San Francisco (94103-3916)
PHONE.....................415 409-8348
Mike Maser, *CEO*
EMP: 1300 EST: 2004
SALES (est): 3.12MM
SALES (corp-wide): 307.39B **Publicly Held**
Web: www.fitstar.com
SIC: 7372 Application computer software
HQ: Fitbit Llc
199 Fremont St Fl 14
San Francisco CA 94105

### (P-18312)
### FIVE9 INC (PA)
3001 Bishop Dr Ste 350, San Ramon (94583-5005)
PHONE.....................925 201-2000
Rowan Trollope, *CEO*
Michael Burkland, *
Barry Zwarenstein, *CFO*
Daniel Burkland, *Pr*
Scott Welch, *CLOUD OPRS & PLATFORM ENGINEERING*
EMP: 2526 EST: 2001
SQ FT: 104,000
SALES (est): 910.49MM
SALES (corp-wide): 910.49MM **Publicly Held**
Web: www.five9.com
SIC: 7372 7374 Prepackaged software; Data processing and preparation

### (P-18313)
### FIVETRAN INC (PA)
405 14th St Ste 1100, Oakland (94612-2707)
PHONE.....................415 805-2799
George Fraser, *CEO*
Taylor Brown, *Prin*
Rachel Thornton, *CMO*
Scott Jones, *CRO*
Anjan Kundavaram, *Chief Product Officer*
EMP: 1192 EST: 2014
SALES (est): 200MM
SALES (corp-wide): 200MM **Privately Held**
Web: www.fivetran.com
SIC: 7372 Business oriented computer software

### (P-18314)
### FLASH CODE SOLUTIONS LLC
4727 Wilshire Blvd Ste 302, Los Angeles (90010-3806)
PHONE.....................800 633-7467
James B Davis, *Prin*
EMP: 17 EST: 2015
SQ FT: 2,600
SALES (est): 540.49K **Privately Held**
Web: www.flashcodesolutions.com
SIC: 7372 Application computer software

### (P-18315)
### FLIPCAUSE INC
101 Broadway Fl 3, Oakland (94607-3755)
PHONE.....................800 523-1950
Emerson Valiao, *CEO*
EMP: 15 EST: 2014
SALES (est): 5.74MM **Privately Held**
Web: www.flipcause.com
SIC: 7372 Prepackaged software

### (P-18316)
### FLOOR COVERING SOFT
221 E Walnut St Ste 110, Pasadena (91101-1554)
PHONE.....................626 683-9188
Steven Wang, *CEO*
▼ EMP: 25 EST: 2001
SQ FT: 2,500
SALES (est): 1.61MM **Privately Held**
Web: www.measuresquare.com
SIC: 7372 Prepackaged software

### (P-18317)
### FLYWHEEL SOFTWARE INC
816 Hamilton St, Redwood City (94063-1624)
PHONE.....................650 260-1700
Steve Humphreys, *CEO*
Mark Towfiq, *
Sachin Kansal, *

Brogan Keane, *
EMP: 35 EST: 2009
SALES (est): 4.12MM **Privately Held**
Web: www.upstartmobile.com
SIC: 7372 Business oriented computer software

### (P-18318)
### FOLIO3 SOFTWARE INC
1301 Shoreway Rd Ste 160, Belmont (94002-4158)
PHONE.....................650 802-8668
Peggy Chen, *Prin*
EMP: 51 EST: 2006
SALES (est): 2.27MM **Privately Held**
Web: www.folio3.com
SIC: 7372 Prepackaged software

### (P-18319)
### FORENSIC LOGIC INC
712 Bancroft Rd # 423, Walnut Creek (94598-1531)
PHONE.....................415 810-2114
Robert L Batty, *CEO*
EMP: 23 EST: 2003
SQ FT: 1,000
SALES (est): 3.35MM **Privately Held**
Web: www.soundthinking.com
SIC: 7372 Application computer software

### (P-18320)
### FORGE GLOBAL INC (HQ)
4 Embarcadero Ctr Ste 1500, San Francisco (94111)
PHONE.....................415 881-1612
Kelly Rodriques, *CEO*
Samvit Ramadurgam, *
Mark Lee, *
Jose Cobos, *CRO**
John-paul Teutonico, *CCO*
EMP: 126 EST: 2015
SALES (est): 15.58MM
SALES (corp-wide): 69.39MM **Publicly Held**
Web: www.forgeglobal.com
SIC: 7372 Business oriented computer software
PA: Forge Global Holdings, Inc.
4 Embarcadero Ctr Fl 15
415 881-1612

### (P-18321)
### FORGE GLOBAL HOLDINGS INC (PA)
Also Called: FORGE GLOBAL
4 Embarcadero Ctr Ste 1500, San Francisco (94111)
PHONE.....................415 881-1612
Kelly Rodriques, *CEO*
Mark Lee, *CFO*
Johnathan Short, *CLO*
Jennifer Phillips, *REVENUE GROWTH*
EMP: 212 EST: 2014
SQ FT: 21,800
SALES (est): 69.39MM
SALES (corp-wide): 69.39MM **Publicly Held**
Web: www.forgeglobal.com
SIC: 7372 Business oriented computer software

### (P-18322)
### FORMER NT CORP
1054 S De Anza Blvd Ste 202, San Jose (95129-3553)
PHONE.....................330 702-3070
EMP: 60
SIC: 7372 Business oriented computer software

## 7372 - Prepackaged Software (P-18344)

**(P-18323)**
**FORTEZZA IRIDIUM HOLDINGS INC**
150 California St, San Francisco (94111-4500)
PHONE..................................415 765-6500
Robert F Smith, *Pr*
**EMP:** 836 **EST:** 2006
**SALES (est):** 2.31MM **Privately Held**
**SIC:** 7372 Business oriented computer software
**PA:** Vista Equity Fund Ii Lp
150 California St Fl 19

**(P-18324)**
**FORWARD NETWORKS INC**
2390 Mission College Blvd # 401, Santa Clara (95054-1530)
PHONE..................................844 393-6389
David Erickson, *CEO*
Brandon Heller, *
Nikhil Ashok Handigol, *
Denis Maynard, *CRO*
**EMP:** 75 **EST:** 2013
**SALES (est):** 18.2MM **Privately Held**
Web: www.forwardnetworks.com
**SIC:** 7372 8748 Application computer software; Systems engineering consultant, ex. computer or professional

**(P-18325)**
**FOUNDATION 9 ENTERTAINMENT INC (PA)**
30211 Avenida De Las Bandera Ste 200, Rancho Santa Margari (92688-2159)
PHONE..................................949 698-1500
James N Hearn, *CEO*
John Goldman, *
David Mann, *
**EMP:** 200 **EST:** 2005
**SALES (est):** 14.55MM **Privately Held**
**SIC:** 7372 Home entertainment computer software

**(P-18326)**
**FOUNDATION INC**
Also Called: Foundation Ai
19800 Macarthur Blvd Ste 300, Irvine (92612-2421)
P.O. Box 344 (92655-0344)
PHONE..................................310 294-8955
Vivek Rao, *CEO*
Victor Gebhardt, *
Vamsi Kasivajjala, *
**EMP:** 38 **EST:** 2017
**SALES (est):** 6.96MM **Privately Held**
Web: www.foundationai.com
**SIC:** 7372 7371 Prepackaged software; Custom computer programming services

**(P-18327)**
**FOUNDSTONE INC**
27201 Puerta Real Ste 400, Mission Viejo (92691-8517)
PHONE..................................949 297-5600
George Kurtz, *CEO*
Stuart Mcclure, *Pr*
Gary Bahadur, *CIO**
Chris Prosise, *
William Chan, *Knowledge Management Vice-President**
**EMP:** 20 **EST:** 1999
**SQ FT:** 15,000
**SALES (est):** 2.79MM
**SALES (corp-wide):** 1.92B **Privately Held**
Web: www.trellix.com
**SIC:** 7372 Application computer software
**HQ:** Mcafee, Llc
6220 America Ctr Dr
San Jose CA 95002

**(P-18328)**
**FOXPASS INC**
10050 N Wolfe Rd Ste Sw2260, Cupertino (95014-2553)
PHONE..................................415 805-6350
Aren Sandersen, *Managing Member*
Aren Sandersen, *CEO*
**EMP:** 15 **EST:** 2015
**SALES (est):** 5.06MM
**SALES (corp-wide):** 75.64MM **Privately Held**
Web: www.foxpass.com
**SIC:** 7372 Prepackaged software
**PA:** Splashtop Inc.
10050 N Wlfe Rd Ste Sw2-S
408 861-1088

**(P-18329)**
**FRAMEHAWK INC**
650 Townsend St Ste 325, San Francisco (94103-6200)
PHONE..................................415 371-9110
**EMP:** 167 **EST:** 2010
**SALES (est):** 2.17MM
**SALES (corp-wide):** 4.38B **Privately Held**
**SIC:** 7372 Application computer software
**HQ:** Cloud Software Group Holdings, Inc.
851 W Cypress Creek Rd
Fort Lauderdale FL 33309
954 267-3000

**(P-18330)**
**FRANZ INC**
3685 Mt Diablo Blvd Ste 300, Lafayette (94549-6833)
PHONE..................................510 452-2000
Jans Aasman, *CEO*
Craig Norvell, *
Kevin Layer, *
John Foderar, *
**EMP:** 25 **EST:** 1984
**SQ FT:** 5,000
**SALES (est):** 4.43MM **Privately Held**
Web: www.franz.com
**SIC:** 7372 7371 Prepackaged software; Computer software development

**(P-18331)**
**FREEAGENT NETWORK INC**
307 Orchard City Dr, Campbell (95008-2931)
PHONE..................................650 880-3240
David Stephens, *CEO*
**EMP:** 20 **EST:** 2017
**SALES (est):** 1.47MM **Privately Held**
Web: www.freeagentcrm.com
**SIC:** 7372 Business oriented computer software

**(P-18332)**
**FREIGHTGATE INC**
Also Called: Edi Ideas
10055 Slater Ave Ste 231, Fountain Valley (92708-4722)
PHONE..................................714 799-2833
Martin Hubert, *Pr*
**EMP:** 32 **EST:** 2000
**SALES (est):** 4.64MM
**SALES (corp-wide):** 4.64MM **Privately Held**
Web: www.freightgate.com
**SIC:** 7372 7371 Application computer software; Computer software development and applications
**PA:** Edi Ideas Inc
16051 Springdale St # 111
714 841-2833

**(P-18333)**
**FRESHWORKS INC (PA)**
Also Called: FRESHWORKS
2950 S Delaware St Ste 201, San Mateo (94403-2578)
PHONE..................................650 513-0514
Dennis Woodside, *Pr*
Rathna Girish Mathrubootham, *Ch Bd*
Tyler Sloat, *CFO*
Mika Yamamoto, *CUSTOMER*
Pam Sergeeff, *CLO*
**EMP:** 37 **EST:** 2010
**SQ FT:** 20,000
**SALES (est):** 596.43MM
**SALES (corp-wide):** 596.43MM **Publicly Held**
Web: www.freshworks.com
**SIC:** 7372 Prepackaged software

**(P-18334)**
**FRONTAPP INC (PA)**
Also Called: Front
300 Montgomery St Ste 500, San Francisco (94104)
PHONE..................................415 680-3048
Mathilde Collin, *CEO*
Laurent Perrin, *
**EMP:** 68 **EST:** 2014
**SALES (est):** 5MM
**SALES (corp-wide):** 5MM **Privately Held**
Web: www.front.com
**SIC:** 7372 Application computer software

**(P-18335)**
**FRONTEGG INC**
2570 W El Camino Real Ste 440, Mountain View (94040-1338)
PHONE..................................408 734-6573
Sagi Rodin, *CEO*
**EMP:** 16 **EST:** 2021
**SALES (est):** 1.96MM **Privately Held**
**SIC:** 7372 Prepackaged software

**(P-18336)**
**FUJISOFT AMERICA INC**
1710 S Amphlett Blvd Ste 215, San Mateo (94402-2705)
PHONE..................................650 235-9422
James Prenton, *Admn*
**EMP:** 20
**SQ FT:** 2,700
Web: www.fsisb.co.jp
**SIC:** 7372 Prepackaged software
**HQ:** Fujisoft Service Bureau Incorporated
2-19-7, Kotobashi
Sumida-Ku TKY 130-0

**(P-18337)**
**FUTUR LLC**
1702 Olympic Blvd, Santa Monica (90404-3812)
PHONE..................................310 314-1618
Chris D.o.s., *CEO*
Greg Gunn, *CCO*
Matthew Encina, *CCO*
**EMP:** 28 **EST:** 2016
**SALES (est):** 4.48MM **Privately Held**
Web: www.thefutur.com
**SIC:** 7372 Educational computer software

**(P-18338)**
**FUZEBOX SOFTWARE CORPORATION (DH)**
Also Called: Fuzebox
150 Spear St Ste 900, San Francisco (94105-5118)
PHONE..................................415 692-4800
David Obrand, *CEO*
Charlie Newark-french, *Pr*
Mark Stubbs, *CFO*
Mary Pritchard, *Contrlr*
**EMP:** 22 **EST:** 2015
**SQ FT:** 16,000
**SALES (est):** 8.07MM
**SALES (corp-wide):** 743.94MM **Publicly Held**
**SIC:** 7372 Application computer software
**HQ:** Fuze, Inc.
675 Creekside Way
Campbell CA 95008

**(P-18339)**
**GAIKAI INC**
65 Enterprise, Aliso Viejo (92656-2705)
**EMP:** 51
Web: www.gaikai.com
**SIC:** 7372 Home entertainment computer software

**(P-18340)**
**GALLEY SOLUTIONS INC**
712 Archer St, San Diego (92109-1048)
P.O. Box 1051 (90294)
PHONE..................................818 636-1538
Ian Christopher, *CEO*
Benji Koltai, *Prin*
Matthew Ferguson, *Prin*
Jason Lazarski, *Prin*
Ashley Fontana, *Prin*
**EMP:** 17 **EST:** 2019
**SALES (est):** 3.98MM **Privately Held**
Web: www.galleysolutions.com
**SIC:** 7372 Prepackaged software

**(P-18341)**
**GAMEMINE LLC**
439 Carroll Canal, Venice (90291-4683)
PHONE..................................310 310-3105
Flaviu Rus, *Managing Member*
Daneil Starr, *
**EMP:** 35 **EST:** 2017
**SALES (est):** 3.5MM **Privately Held**
Web: www.gamemine.com
**SIC:** 7372 7389 Publisher's computer software; Business services, nec

**(P-18342)**
**GE DIGITAL LLC**
2700 Camino Ramon, San Ramon (94583-5004)
PHONE..................................925 242-6200
**EMP:** 262
**SALES (corp-wide):** 4.68B **Publicly Held**
Web: www.ge.com
**SIC:** 7372 Prepackaged software
**HQ:** Ge Digital Llc
58 S Charles St
Cambridge MA 02141
925 242-6200

**(P-18343)**
**GEARBOX PUBG SAN FRANCISCO INC**
100 Redwood Shores Pkwy Fl 2, Redwood City (94065-1226)
PHONE..................................650 590-7700
Yoon Im, *CEO*
**EMP:** 25 **EST:** 2022
**SALES (est):** 5.83MM **Privately Held**
Web: www.arcgames.com
**SIC:** 7372 Publisher's computer software

**(P-18344)**
**GENASYS INC (PA)**
Also Called: Genasys
16262 W Bernardo Dr, San Diego (92127-1879)
PHONE..................................858 676-1112
Richard S Danforth, *CEO*
Richard H Osgood Iii, *Ch Bd*

# 7372 - Prepackaged Software (P-18345)

Dennis D Klahn, *CFO*
◆ **EMP:** 91 **EST:** 1980
**SQ FT:** 55,766
**SALES (est):** 46.66MM
**SALES (corp-wide):** 46.66MM **Publicly Held**
**Web:** www.genasys.com
**SIC: 7372** 3651 Prepackaged software; Amplifiers: radio, public address, or musical instrument

### (P-18345)
### GENESYS CLOUD SERVICES INC (HQ)
Also Called: Genesys Telecom Labs
1302 El Camino Real Ste 300, Menlo Park (94025-4278)
**PHONE**.................................650 466-1100
Tony Bates, *Ch*
**EMP:** 450 **EST:** 1990
**SQ FT:** 156,000
**SALES (est):** 491.73MM
**SALES (corp-wide):** 241.26MM **Privately Held**
**Web:** www.genesys.com
**SIC: 7372** Business oriented computer software
**PA:** Permira Advisers Llp
80 Pall Mall
207 632-1000

### (P-18346)
### GEOPOGO
1335 Milvia St, Berkeley (94709-1934)
**PHONE**.................................510 918-7083
**EMP:** 46 **EST:** 2014
**SALES (est):** 2.71MM **Privately Held**
**Web:** www.geopogoar.com
**SIC: 7372** Prepackaged software

### (P-18347)
### GET SATISFACTION INC
1550 Bryant St Ste 350, San Francisco (94103-4854)
**PHONE**.................................877 339-3997
**EMP:** 20
**SIC: 7372** Prepackaged software

### (P-18348)
### GINSBERG HOLDCO INC
3300 Olcott St, Santa Clara (95054-3005)
**PHONE**.................................408 831-4000
Paul A Hooper, *CEO*
Rex S Jackson, *CFO*
Kim Decarlis, *CMO*
**EMP:** 500 **EST:** 2017
**SQ FT:** 105,600
**SALES (est):** 5.87MM **Privately Held**
**Web:** www.gigamon.com
**SIC: 7372** 3577 Prepackaged software; Computer peripheral equipment, nec

### (P-18349)
### GITLAB INC (PA)
Also Called: Gitlab
268 Bush St # 350, San Francisco (94104-3503)
**PHONE**.................................650 474-5175
Sytse Sijbrandij, *Ch Bd*
Brian Robins, *CFO*
Christopher Weber, *CRO*
Robin J Schulman, *CLO*
**EMP:** 18 **EST:** 2011
**SALES (est):** 579.91MM
**SALES (corp-wide):** 579.91MM **Publicly Held**
**Web:** about.gitlab.com
**SIC: 7372** Prepackaged software

### (P-18350)
### GLADIATOR CORPORATION
2882 Sand Hill Rd Ste 280, Menlo Park (94025-7057)
**PHONE**.................................650 233-2900
**EMP:** 338
**SIC: 7372** Prepackaged software

### (P-18351)
### GLASSLAB INC
209 Redwood Shores Pkwy, Redwood City (94065-1175)
**PHONE**.................................415 244-5584
Jessica Lindl, *Ex Dir*
Granetta Blevins, *
Michael John, *
Michelle Riconscente, *
**EMP:** 24 **EST:** 2014
**SALES (est):** 4.21MM **Privately Held**
**SIC: 7372** 8748 Educational computer software; Educational consultant

### (P-18352)
### GLOBAL CASH CARD INC
3972 Barranca Pkwy Ste J610, Irvine (92606-1204)
**PHONE**.................................949 751-0360
**EMP:** 165
**SIC: 7372** Business oriented computer software

### (P-18353)
### GLOBAL WAVE GROUP
26970 Aliso Viejo Pkwy, Aliso Viejo (92656-2621)
**PHONE**.................................949 916-9800
Zubin Mehta, *CEO*
Zubin Mehta, *Managing Member*
Rhett Rowe, *Senior Vice President Managing*
Randy M Ruckle, *Sr VP*
**EMP:** 42 **EST:** 2007
**SALES (est):** 2.11MM **Privately Held**
**Web:** www.globalwavegroup.com
**SIC: 7372** Prepackaged software

### (P-18354)
### GLYNTAI INC
Also Called: Wattzon
705 N Shoreline Blvd, Mountain View (94043-3208)
**PHONE**.................................650 386-6932
Martha Amram, *CEO*
**EMP:** 18 **EST:** 2008
**SALES (est):** 2.18MM **Privately Held**
**Web:** www.glynt.ai
**SIC: 7372** Application computer software

### (P-18355)
### GOALSR INC
933 Berryessa Rd Ste 10, San Jose (95133-1006)
**PHONE**.................................650 453-5844
Vidyadhar Handragal, *Pr*
Divya Krishnaswamy, *
**EMP:** 20 **EST:** 2014
**SALES (est):** 3.69MM **Privately Held**
**Web:** www.goalsr.com
**SIC: 7372** 7371 Application computer software; Computer software systems analysis and design, custom

### (P-18356)
### GOLINKS ENTERPRISES INC
Also Called: Go/Links
2558 Forest Ave, San Jose (95117-1117)
**PHONE**.................................562 715-4848
Jorge Zamora, *CEO*
George Samora, *
**EMP:** 75 **EST:** 2016
**SALES (est):** 6.34MM **Privately Held**
**Web:** www.golinks.io
**SIC: 7372** Application computer software

### (P-18357)
### GOOD TECHNOLOGY SOFTWARE INC
430 N Mary Ave Ste 200, Sunnyvale (94085-2923)
**PHONE**.................................408 212-7500
**EMP:** 600
**SIC: 7372** 3661 Prepackaged software; Telephones and telephone apparatus

### (P-18358)
### GOODRX INC (HQ)
2701 Olympic Blvd # A, Santa Monica (90404-4183)
**PHONE**.................................855 268-2822
Douglass Hirsch, *CEO*
Trevor Dezdek, *Dir*
**EMP:** 16 **EST:** 2011
**SALES (est):** 911.26K
**SALES (corp-wide):** 750.26MM **Publicly Held**
**Web:** www.goodrx.com
**SIC: 7372** Application computer software
**PA:** Goodrx Holdings, Inc.
2701 Olympic Blvd
855 268-2822

### (P-18359)
### GOOVER INC
440 N Wolfe Rd # E117, Sunnyvale (94085-3869)
**PHONE**.................................408 748-4333
Kyung Il Lee, *CEO*
**EMP:** 18 **EST:** 2022
**SALES (est):** 421.98K **Privately Held**
**SIC: 7372** Prepackaged software

### (P-18360)
### GOVERNMENTJOBSCOM INC
Also Called: Neogov
2120 Park Pl Ste 100, El Segundo (90245-4741)
**PHONE**.................................877 204-4442
Shane Evangelist, *CEO*
Alex Chun, *
David Eisler, *
**EMP:** 130 **EST:** 2000
**SQ FT:** 5,000
**SALES (est):** 23.8MM **Privately Held**
**Web:** www.neogov.com
**SIC: 7372** Prepackaged software

### (P-18361)
### GRAID TECHNOLOGY INC (PA)
5201 Great America Pkwy Ste 320, Santa Clara (95054-1140)
**PHONE**.................................669 258-8102
Tsung-lin Yu, *Prin*
**EMP:** 16 **EST:** 2020
**SALES (est):** 2.56MM
**SALES (corp-wide):** 2.56MM **Privately Held**
**Web:** www.graidtech.com
**SIC: 7372** Prepackaged software

### (P-18362)
### GREEN HILLS SOFTWARE LLC (HQ)
Also Called: Green Hills Software
30 W Sola St, Santa Barbara (93101-2599)
**PHONE**.................................805 965-6044
Daniel O Dowd, *CEO*
Daniel O'dowd, *CEO*
Jeffrey Hazarian, *

**EMP:** 105 **EST:** 1986
**SALES (est):** 41MM
**SALES (corp-wide):** 51.22MM **Privately Held**
**Web:** www.ghs.com
**SIC: 7372** Prepackaged software
**PA:** Ghs Holding Company
30 W Sola St
805 965-6044

### (P-18363)
### GREMLIN INC
Also Called: Gremlin Software, Inc.
440 N Barranca Ave Ste 3101, Walnut (91789)
**PHONE**.................................408 214-9885
Josh Leslie, *CEO*
Kolton Andrus, *
**EMP:** 80 **EST:** 2016
**SALES (est):** 9.57MM **Privately Held**
**Web:** www.gremlin.com
**SIC: 7372** 8742 Prepackaged software; Management consulting services

### (P-18364)
### GRID DYNAMICS HOLDINGS INC (PA)
5000 Executive Pkwy Ste 520, San Ramon (94583-4282)
**PHONE**.................................650 523-5000
Leonard Livschitz, *CEO*
Lloyd Carney, *Ch Bd*
Anil Doradla, *CFO*
Yury Gryzlov, *COO*
**EMP:** 27 **EST:** 2006
**SALES (est):** 312.91MM
**SALES (corp-wide):** 312.91MM **Publicly Held**
**Web:** www.griddynamics.com
**SIC: 7372** Prepackaged software

### (P-18365)
### GRIDGAIN SYSTEMS INC (PA)
1065 E Hillsdale Blvd Ste 410, Foster City (94404-1615)
**PHONE**.................................650 241-2281
Eoin O' Connor, *CEO*
Elena Schtein, *
Sarah Jadidi, *
**EMP:** 126 **EST:** 2010
**SALES (est):** 18.33MM
**SALES (corp-wide):** 18.33MM **Privately Held**
**Web:** www.gridgain.com
**SIC: 7372** Prepackaged software

### (P-18366)
### GRISLY MANOR LLC
Also Called: Grisly Studios
11799 Sebastian Way Ste 103, Rancho Cucamonga (91730-0708)
**PHONE**.................................714 482-8194
Michael Dykier, *CEO*
Pamela Dykier, *CEO*
Michael Dykier, *Contrlr*
Lawrence Dykier, *COO*
Stephen Dykier, *Dir Opers*
**EMP:** 15 **EST:** 2013
**SALES (est):** 2.63MM **Privately Held**
**Web:** www.grislymanorpdx.com
**SIC: 7372** 7812 7389 Home entertainment computer software; Audio-visual program production; Business Activities at Non-Commercial Site

### (P-18367)
### GROOVE LABS INC
660 4th St # 684, San Francisco (94107-1618)
**PHONE**.................................650 999-0200

# PRODUCTS & SERVICES SECTION
## 7372 - Prepackaged Software (P-18387)

Chris Rothstein, *CEO*
Michael Sutherland, *VP*
**EMP:** 68 **EST:** 2014
**SALES (est):** 5.66MM
**SALES (corp-wide):** 49.22MM **Privately Held**
**Web:** www.groove.co
**SIC: 7372** Application computer software
**PA:** Clari Inc.
1154 Sonora Ct
650 265-2111

### (P-18368)
### GUARDIAN ANALYTICS INC
2465 Latham St Ste 200, Mountain View (94040-4792)
**PHONE**..................................650 383-9200
Laurent Pacalin, *Pr*
Hue Harguindeguy, *CFO*
**EMP:** 27 **EST:** 2005
**SALES (est):** 4.91MM **Privately Held**
**Web:** www.niceactimize.com
**SIC: 7372** Prepackaged software

### (P-18369)
### GUAVUS INC (HQ)
2125 Zanker Rd, San Jose (95131-2109)
**PHONE**..................................650 243-3400
Anukool Lakhina, *CEO*
Ty Nam, *COO*
**EMP:** 50 **EST:** 2006
**SALES (est):** 9.93MM
**SALES (corp-wide):** 269.57MM **Privately Held**
**Web:** www.guavus.com
**SIC: 7372** 7371 Prepackaged software; Computer software development and applications
**PA:** Thales
4 Rue De La Verrerie
157778000

### (P-18370)
### GUIDANCE SOFTWARE INC (HQ)
1055 E Colorado Blvd Ste 400, Pasadena (91106-2375)
**PHONE**..................................626 229-9191
Patrick Dennis, *Pr*
Barry Plaga, *
Michael Harris, *CMO**
Alfredo Gomez, *Corporate Secretary**
**EMP:** 215 **EST:** 2006
**SQ FT:** 90,000
**SALES (est):** 51.33MM
**SALES (corp-wide):** 5.77B **Privately Held**
**Web:** www.opentext.com
**SIC: 7372** 3572 Business oriented computer software; Computer storage devices
**PA:** Open Text Corporation
275 Frank Tompa Dr
519 888-7111

### (P-18371)
### GUIDEWIRE SOFTWARE INC (PA)
Also Called: Guidewire
970 Park Pl Ste 200, San Mateo (94403-1907)
**PHONE**..................................650 357-9100
Mike Rosenbaum, *CEO*
Marcus S Ryu, *
Priscilla Hung, *Pr*
John Mullen, *CRO*
Jeff Cooper, *CFO*
**EMP:** 413 **EST:** 2001
**SQ FT:** 79,000
**SALES (est):** 980.5MM
**SALES (corp-wide):** 980.5MM **Publicly Held**
**Web:** www.guidewire.com
**SIC: 7372** Business oriented computer software

### (P-18372)
### GUILDED LLC
970 Park Pl, San Mateo (94403-1907)
**PHONE**..................................415 568-8186
David Baszucki, *CEO*
**EMP:** 17 **EST:** 2016
**SALES (est):** 4.52MM
**SALES (corp-wide):** 2.8B **Publicly Held**
**Web:** www.guilded.gg
**SIC: 7372** Prepackaged software
**PA:** Roblox Corporation
970 Park Pl
888 858-2569

### (P-18373)
### GUMGUM INC (PA)
2419 Michigan Ave Ste A, Santa Monica (90404-4009)
**PHONE**..................................310 260-9666
Ophir Taz, *CEO*
Phil Schraeder, *COO*
Patrick Gildea, *CFO*
Ben Plomion, *CGO*
**EMP:** 20 **EST:** 2007
**SALES (est):** 10.75MM
**SALES (corp-wide):** 10.75MM **Privately Held**
**Web:** www.gumgum.com
**SIC: 7372** Prepackaged software

### (P-18374)
### GUMGUM SPORTS INC
1314 7th St Fl 4, Santa Monica (90401-1608)
**PHONE**..................................310 400-0396
Brian Kim, *CEO*
**EMP:** 45 **EST:** 2021
**SALES (est):** 1.11MM **Privately Held**
**Web:** www.gumgum.com
**SIC: 7372** Business oriented computer software

### (P-18375)
### GUSTO INC (PA)
525 20th St, San Francisco (94107-4345)
**PHONE**..................................800 936-0383
Joshua D Reeves, *CEO*
Tomer London, *CPO*
Mike Dinsdale, *CFO*
Lexi Reese, *COO*
**EMP:** 250 **EST:** 2011
**SALES (est):** 101.28MM
**SALES (corp-wide):** 101.28MM **Privately Held**
**Web:** www.gusto.com
**SIC: 7372** Business oriented computer software

### (P-18376)
### HABEAS INC
779 E Evelyn Ave Ste 200, Mountain View (94041-1670)
**PHONE**..................................650 694-3300
Des Cahill, *CEO*
Don Kohn, *
Philip Smith, *
**EMP:** 45 **EST:** 2002
**SQ FT:** 14,000
**SALES (est):** 707K **Privately Held**
**SIC: 7372** Prepackaged software

### (P-18377)
### HAZELCAST INC (PA)
Also Called: Hazelcast
3000 El Camino Real, Palo Alto (94306-2100)
**PHONE**..................................650 521-5453
Kelly Herrell, *CEO*
Karen Smith, *CRO*
Tamzyn Furse, *CPO*
**EMP:** 41 **EST:** 2012
**SALES (est):** 10.6MM
**SALES (corp-wide):** 10.6MM **Privately Held**
**Web:** www.hazelcast.com
**SIC: 7372** 7371 Publisher's computer software; Computer software systems analysis and design, custom

### (P-18378)
### HEARSAY SYSTEMS INC (PA)
Also Called: Hearsay Social
600 Harrison St Ste 120, San Francisco (94107-1389)
**PHONE**..................................888 399-2280
Clara Shih, *CEO*
Michael H Lock, *
Caitlin Haberberger, *
William Salisbury, *
Mark Gilbert, *
**EMP:** 182 **EST:** 2009
**SALES (est):** 22.31MM
**SALES (corp-wide):** 22.31MM **Privately Held**
**Web:** www.hearsaysystems.com
**SIC: 7372** Publisher's computer software

### (P-18379)
### HEAT SOFTWARE USA INC
490 N Mccarthy Blvd Ste 100, Milpitas (95035-5118)
**PHONE**..................................408 601-2800
**EMP:** 258
**SIC: 7372** Prepackaged software

### (P-18380)
### HEAVYAI INC
95 3rd St, San Francisco (94103)
**PHONE**..................................415 997-2814
Jon Kondo, *CEO*
**EMP:** 90 **EST:** 2013
**SALES (est):** 7.96MM **Privately Held**
**Web:** www.heavy.ai
**SIC: 7372** Business oriented computer software

### (P-18381)
### HEIRLOOM COMPUTING INC (PA)
3000 Danville Blvd Ste 148, Alamo (94507-1574)
**PHONE**..................................510 709-7245
Gary Crook, *CEO*
Gary Crook, *Pr*
Kevin Moultrup, *COO*
Edward Abbati, *CFO*
**EMP:** 20 **EST:** 2010
**SALES (est):** 1.43MM
**SALES (corp-wide):** 1.43MM **Privately Held**
**Web:** www.heirloomcomputing.com
**SIC: 7372** Prepackaged software

### (P-18382)
### HEROKU INC
1 Market St Ste 300, San Francisco (94105-1315)
**PHONE**..................................650 704-6107
Tod Nielsen, *CEO*
**EMP:** 30 **EST:** 2007
**SALES (est):** 7.92MM
**SALES (corp-wide):** 34.86B **Publicly Held**
**Web:** www.heroku.com
**SIC: 7372** Application computer software
**PA:** Salesforce, Inc.
415 Mission St Fl 3
415 901-7000

### (P-18383)
### HIGHER ONE PAYMENTS INC
Also Called: Cashnet
80 Swan Way Ste 200, Oakland (94621-1439)
**PHONE**..................................510 769-9888
Dan Peterson, *Pr*
Greg Schuster, *Sr VP*
Chuck Haddock, *
**EMP:** 26 **EST:** 1983
**SQ FT:** 4,500
**SALES (est):** 2.21MM
**SALES (corp-wide):** 6.83MM **Privately Held**
**Web:** www.transactcampus.com
**SIC: 7372** Business oriented computer software
**HQ:** Transact Campus Payments, Inc.
18700 N Hayden Rd Ste 230
Scottsdale AZ 85255

### (P-18384)
### HIGHNOTE SOLUTIONS INC
Also Called: Highlabs
548 Market St # 46205, San Francisco (94104-5401)
**PHONE**..................................415 779-6275
Mark Choey, *CEO*
**EMP:** 15 **EST:** 2017
**SALES (est):** 5.17MM **Privately Held**
**Web:** www.highnote.io
**SIC: 7372** Application computer software

### (P-18385)
### HINT HEALTH INC (PA)
149 New Montgomery St Fl 4, San Francisco (94105-3739)
**PHONE**..................................415 854-6366
Zak Holdsworth, *CEO*
**EMP:** 29 **EST:** 2013
**SALES (est):** 5.83MM
**SALES (corp-wide):** 5.83MM **Privately Held**
**Web:** www.hint.com
**SIC: 7372** Application computer software

### (P-18386)
### HITACHI ENERGY USA INC
60 Spear St, San Francisco (94105-1506)
**PHONE**..................................415 527-2850
Greg Dukat, *Brnch Mgr*
**EMP:** 15
**SIC: 7372** Business oriented computer software
**HQ:** Hitachi Energy Usa Inc
901 Main Campus Dr
Raleigh NC 27606
919 856-2360

### (P-18387)
### HOLLYWOOD SOFTWARE INC
5000 Van Nuys Blvd Ste 300, Van Nuys (91403-1793)
**PHONE**..................................818 205-2121
Carol Dibattiste, *CEO*
Karl Anderson, *CFO*
Susan Wells, *Sr VP*
Kim Lockhart, *Sr VP*
Larry Mccourt, *Sr VP*
**EMP:** 46 **EST:** 1997
**SALES (est):** 3.2MM
**SALES (corp-wide):** 371.34MM **Publicly Held**
**Web:** www.comscore.com
**SIC: 7372** Business oriented computer software
**PA:** Comscore, Inc.
11950 Dmocracy Dr Ste 600

## 7372 - Prepackaged Software (P-18388)

703 438-2000

**(P-18388)**
**HOONUIT LLC (DH)**
Also Called: Atomic Training
150 Parkshore Dr, Folsom (95630-4710)
PHONE..................................320 631-5900
Paul Hesser, CEO
Lisa Barnett, *
Jon Blissenbach, *
Teseresa Giese, *
Shivani Stumpf, *
EMP: 45 EST: 2000
SALES (est): 18.16MM
SALES (corp-wide): 1.65B Privately Held
Web: www.infobase.com
SIC: 7372 Educational computer software
HQ: Powerschool Group Llc
150 Parkshore Dr
Folsom CA 95630
916 790-1509

**(P-18389)**
**HOOPLA SOFTWARE INC**
84 W Santa Clara St Ste 460, San Jose (95113-1815)
PHONE..................................408 498-9600
Michael Smalls, CEO
EMP: 38 EST: 2008
SALES (est): 1.87MM Privately Held
Web: www.hoopla.net
SIC: 7372 Application computer software

**(P-18390)**
**HORTONWORKS INC (DH)**
Also Called: Hortonworks
5470 Great America Pkwy, Santa Clara (95054-3644)
PHONE..................................408 916-4121
Scott Aronson, CRO
Amr Awadallah, Global Chief Technology Officer
Jim Frankola, *
Mick Hollison, CMO*
David Middler, CLO*
EMP: 725 EST: 2011
SQ FT: 92,000
SALES (est): 41.11MM
SALES (corp-wide): 496.12MM Privately Held
Web: www.cloudera.com
SIC: 7372 Application computer software
HQ: Cloudera, Inc.
5470 Great America Pkwy
Santa Clara CA 95054
650 362-0488

**(P-18391)**
**HOYLU INC**
Also Called: Hoylu La
6121 W Sunset Blvd, Los Angeles (90028-6442)
PHONE..................................213 440-2499
EMP: 34
SALES (corp-wide): 4.17MM Privately Held
Web: www.hoylu.com
SIC: 7372 Prepackaged software
PA: Hoylu, Inc.
11335 Ne 122nd Way # 105
877 554-6958

**(P-18392)**
**HPE ENTERPRISES LLC (HQ)**
6280 America Center Dr, San Jose (95002-2563)
PHONE..................................650 857-5817
EMP: 121 EST: 2015
SALES (est): 56.91MM
SALES (corp-wide): 29.14B Publicly Held
Web: www.hpe.com
SIC: 7372 7379 3572 Prepackaged software; Computer related maintenance services; Computer storage devices
PA: Hewlett Packard Enterprise Company
1701 E Mossy Oaks Rd
678 259-9860

**(P-18393)**
**HR CLOUD INC**
222 N Pacific Coast Hwy Ste 2000, El Segundo (90245-5614)
PHONE..................................510 909-1993
Damir Davidovic, CEO
EMP: 28 EST: 2016
SQ FT: 10,000
SALES (est): 3.82MM Privately Held
Web: www.hrcloud.com
SIC: 7372 Business oriented computer software

**(P-18394)**
**HUMANCONCEPTS LLC**
3 Harbor Dr Ste 200, Sausalito (94965-1491)
PHONE..................................650 581-2500
EMP: 40 EST: 2000
SQ FT: 6,500
SALES (est): 3.38MM
SALES (corp-wide): 740.92MM Privately Held
SIC: 7372 Application computer software
HQ: Saba Software, Inc.
4120 Dublin Blvd Ste 200
Dublin CA 94568
877 722-2101

**(P-18395)**
**HUMBL INC**
600 B St Ste 300, San Diego (92101-4505)
PHONE..................................786 738-9012
Brian Foote, Ch Bd
Jeffrey Hinshaw, Corporate Secretary
Michele Rivera, Global Vice President
EMP: 16 EST: 2000
SALES (est): 1.01MM Privately Held
SIC: 7372 Prepackaged software

**(P-18396)**
**HVR SOFTWARE USA INC**
44 Montgomery St Ste 3, San Francisco (94104-4618)
PHONE..................................415 489-3427
Anthony Brooks Williams, CEO
Kyle Klopfer, CFO
EMP: 62 EST: 2014
SALES (est): 2.39MM Privately Held
SIC: 7372 Business oriented computer software

**(P-18397)**
**I MANAGEPROPERTY INC**
Also Called: Peak Property Management Sftwr
1400 Shattuck Ave Ste 2, Berkeley (94709-1485)
PHONE..................................510 665-0665
Zorba Libeberman, Pr
Joesph Gaspardone, VP
EMP: 20 EST: 1994
SQ FT: 3,000
SALES (est): 648.93K Privately Held
Web: www.enterpret.com
SIC: 7372 Prepackaged software

**(P-18398)**
**IAMPLUS ELECTRONICS INC (PA)**
809 N Cahuenga Blvd, Los Angeles (90038-3703)
PHONE..................................323 210-3852
Will Adams, CEO
Phil Molyneux, *
Chandrasekar Rathakrishnan, *
Rosemary Peschken, *
EMP: 38 EST: 2013
SQ FT: 6,000
SALES (est): 9.1MM
SALES (corp-wide): 9.1MM Privately Held
Web: www.iamplus.com
SIC: 7372 Prepackaged software

**(P-18399)**
**ICE MORTGAGE TECHNOLOGY INC (HQ)**
Also Called: Ellie Mae
4420 Rosewood Dr Ste 500, Pleasanton (94588-3059)
PHONE..................................855 224-8572
Jonathan Corr, Pr
Dan Madden, *
Brian Brown, *
Joe Tyrrell, *
Cathleen Schreiner Gates, *
EMP: 318 EST: 1997
SQ FT: 280,680
SALES (est): 380.72MM
SALES (corp-wide): 7.99B Publicly Held
Web: www.icemortgagetechnology.com
SIC: 7372 7371 Prepackaged software; Computer software systems analysis and design, custom
PA: Intercontinental Exchange, Inc.
5660 New Nrthside Dr Fl 3
770 857-4700

**(P-18400)**
**IDENTIV INC**
1900 Carnegie Ave Ste B, Santa Ana (92705-5557)
PHONE..................................888 809-8880
Jason Hart, CEO
EMP: 52
Web: www.identiv.com
SIC: 7372 3669 Business oriented computer software; Burglar alarm apparatus, electric
PA: Identiv, Inc.
2201 Walnut Ave Ste 100

**(P-18401)**
**IFWE INC (DH)**
848 Battery St, San Francisco (94111-1504)
PHONE..................................415 946-1850
Dash Gopinath, CEO
Greg Tseng, *
Johann Schleier Smith, *
▼ EMP: 23 EST: 2005
SQ FT: 13,000
SALES (est): 9.79MM
SALES (corp-wide): 4.19B Privately Held
Web: www.tagged.com
SIC: 7372 Application computer software
HQ: The Meet Group Inc
100 Union Square Dr
New Hope PA 18938
215 862-1162

**(P-18402)**
**IGRAD LLC**
Also Called: Financial Fitness Group
2163 Newcastle Ave Ste 100, Cardiff By The Sea (92007)
PHONE..................................858 705-2917
Rob Labreche, Pr
EMP: 22 EST: 2009
SQ FT: 2,000
SALES (est): 2.55MM Privately Held
Web: www.igrad.com
SIC: 7372 Business oriented computer software
PA: Aztec Software, Llc
461 Headquarters Plz

**(P-18403)**
**ILLUMNATE EDUCATN HOLDINGS INC (PA)**
6531 Irvine Center Dr Ste 100, Irvine (92618-2146)
PHONE..................................949 656-3133
Christine Willig, CEO
Shawn Mahoney, Chief Product Officer*
Jane Snyder, CMO*
Dick Davidson, *
EMP: 28 EST: 2009
SALES (est): 9.91MM
SALES (corp-wide): 9.91MM Privately Held
Web: www.illuminateed.com
SIC: 7372 Educational computer software

**(P-18404)**
**IMAGEWARE SYSTEMS INC (PA)**
Also Called: IMAGEWARE SYSTEMS
11440 W Bernardo Ct Ste 300, San Diego (92127-1640)
PHONE..................................858 673-8600
Kristin Taylor, Pr
EMP: 16 EST: 1987
SALES (est): 3.47MM
SALES (corp-wide): 3.47MM Publicly Held
Web: www.imageware.io
SIC: 7372 3699 Business oriented computer software; Security control equipment and systems

**(P-18405)**
**IMPEX TECHNOLOGIES INC**
880 Apollo St Ste 315, El Segundo (90245-4783)
PHONE..................................310 320-0280
EMP: 15 EST: 1991
SALES (est): 38.96MM Privately Held
Web: www.impextechnologies.com
SIC: 7372 7373 Prepackaged software; Systems integration services

**(P-18406)**
**IMPLY DATA INC (PA)**
Also Called: Imply
1633 Bayshore Hwy Ste 232, Burlingame (94010-1533)
PHONE..................................415 685-8187
Fang Jin Yang, CEO
Gian Merlino, *
Anthony Russo, *
Juleen Konkel, *
EMP: 137 EST: 2015
SQ FT: 1,000
SALES (est): 10MM
SALES (corp-wide): 10MM Privately Held
Web: www.imply.io
SIC: 7372 Business oriented computer software

**(P-18407)**
**INBENTA TECHNOLOGIES INC (PA)**
440 N Wolfe Rd, Sunnyvale (94085-3869)
PHONE..................................408 213-8771
Jordi Torras, CEO
Chris Hancock, Contrlr
EMP: 20 EST: 2011
SALES (est): 5.23MM
SALES (corp-wide): 5.23MM Privately Held
Web: www.inbenta.com

## PRODUCTS & SERVICES SECTION
### 7372 - Prepackaged Software (P-18427)

SIC: 7372 Application computer software

**(P-18408)**
**INDIUM SOFTWARE INC**
10080 N Wolfe Rd Ste Sw3200, Cupertino (95014)
PHONE..............................408 501-8844
Harsha Nutalapati, *CEO*
Vijay Shankar Balaji, *
EMP: 61 EST: 2006
SALES (est): 11.63MM **Privately Held**
Web: www.indiumsoftware.com
SIC: 7372 Prepackaged software
HQ: Indium Software (India) Private Limited
41, Cathedral Road, Vds House, 2nd Floor,
Chennai TN 60008

**(P-18409)**
**INDIVIDUAL SOFTWARE INC**
3049 Independence Dr Ste E, Livermore (94551-7671)
PHONE..............................925 734-6767
Jo-I Hendrickson, *Pr*
Diane Dietzler, *
EMP: 48 EST: 1981
SALES (est): 9.84MM **Privately Held**
Web: www.individualsoftware.com
SIC: 7372 7371 Prepackaged software;
Custom computer programming services

**(P-18410)**
**INFOGRAM SOFTWARE INC**
633 Folsom St Fl 5, San Francisco (94107-3623)
PHONE..............................650 319-7291
Mikko Jarvenpaa, *CEO*
EMP: 25 EST: 2015
SALES (est): 1.78MM
SALES (corp-wide): 8.97MM **Privately Held**
Web: www.infogram.com
SIC: 7372 Application computer software
PA: Prezi, Inc.
101 Broadway 2nd Fl
415 398-8012

**(P-18411)**
**INFOR (US) LLC**
Also Called: Hansen Information Tech
11000 Olson Dr Ste 201, Rancho Cordova (95670-5642)
PHONE..............................916 921-0883
Charles Hansen, *Mgr*
EMP: 27
SALES (corp-wide): 64.37B **Privately Held**
Web: www.infor.com
SIC: 7372 Application computer software
HQ: Infor (Us), Llc
641 Ave Of The Americas
New York NY 10011
866 244-5479

**(P-18412)**
**INFOR PUBLIC SECTOR INC (DH)**
11092 Sun Center Dr, Rancho Cordova (95670-6109)
PHONE..............................916 921-0883
Charles Hansen, *CEO*
Mark Watts, *
Bob Benstead, *
EMP: 160 EST: 1983
SQ FT: 28,000
SALES (est): 11.57MM
SALES (corp-wide): 64.37B **Privately Held**
Web: www.infor.com
SIC: 7372 Application computer software
HQ: Infor (Us), Llc
641 Ave Of The Americas
New York NY 10011
866 244-5479

**(P-18413)**
**INFORM SOLUTION INCORPORATED**
201 Mentor Dr, Santa Barbara (93111-3337)
PHONE..............................805 879-6000
EMP: 20 EST: 1994
SALES (est): 2.12MM
SALES (corp-wide): 85.16B **Publicly Held**
SIC: 7372 Prepackaged software
HQ: Mentor Worldwide Llc
31 Technology Dr Ste 200
Irvine CA 92618
800 636-8678

**(P-18414)**
**INFORMATICA HOLDCO 2 INC**
2100 Seaport Blvd, Redwood City (94063-5596)
PHONE..............................650 385-5000
Amit Walia, *CEO*
EMP: 4897 EST: 2015
SALES (est): 3.24MM **Privately Held**
Web: www.informatica.com
SIC: 7372 Prepackaged software

**(P-18415)**
**INFORMATICA INC**
Also Called: INFORMATICA
2100 Seaport Blvd, Redwood City (94063-5596)
PHONE..............................650 385-5000
Amit Walia, *CEO*
Bruce Chizen, *
Eric Brown, *Ex VP*
Jitesh Ghai, *CPO*
John Schweitzer, *CRO*
EMP: 5000 EST: 1993
SQ FT: 290,000
SALES (est): 1.6B **Privately Held**
Web: www.informatica.com
SIC: 7372 Prepackaged software

**(P-18416)**
**INFORMATICA INTERNATIONAL INC (DH)**
2100 Seaport Blvd, Redwood City (94063-5596)
PHONE..............................650 385-5000
Sohaib Abbasi, *Pr*
EMP: 20 EST: 2005
SALES (est): 6.28MM
SALES (corp-wide): 241.26MM **Privately Held**
Web: www.informatica.com
SIC: 7372 Prepackaged software
HQ: Informatica Llc
2100 Seaport Blvd
Redwood City CA 94063

**(P-18417)**
**INFORMATICA LLC (DH)**
Also Called: Informatica LLC of Delaware
2100 Seaport Blvd, Redwood City (94063-5596)
PHONE..............................650 385-5000
Amit Walia, *CEO*
Bradford Lewis, *CLO**
Graeme Thompson, *CIO**
Erin Andre, *Chief Human Resource Officer**
Ansa Sekharan, *
EMP: 289 EST: 1999
SQ FT: 290,000
SALES (est): 1.51B
SALES (corp-wide): 220.02MM **Privately Held**
Web: www.informatica.com

SIC: 7372 Prepackaged software
HQ: Permira Advisers Llc
320 Park Ave Fl 28
New York NY 10022
212 386-7480

**(P-18418)**
**INFORMTION INTGRTION GROUP INC**
457 Palm Dr Ste 200, Glendale (91202-4339)
PHONE..............................818 956-3744
Alec Baghdasaryan, *Pr*
EMP: 17 EST: 1995
SALES (est): 3.84MM **Privately Held**
Web: www.iigservices.com
SIC: 7372 7371 Prepackaged software;
Computer software development

**(P-18419)**
**INKTOMI CORPORATION (HQ)**
701 First Ave, Sunnyvale (94089-1019)
PHONE..............................650 653-2800
David Peterschmidt, *Ch Bd*
David Peterschmidt, *Ch Bd*
Doctor Eric A Brewer, *Chief Scientist*
Randy Gottfried, *
EMP: 25 EST: 1996
SQ FT: 177,000
SALES (est): 4.4MM **Privately Held**
Web: www.robgeo.net
SIC: 7372 7371 Application computer
software; Custom computer programming services
PA: Altaba Inc.
140 E 45th St Fl 15

**(P-18420)**
**INMAGE SYSTEMS INC**
1065 La Avenida St, Mountain View (94043-1421)
PHONE..............................408 200-3840
Debbie Button, *CEO*
John Ferraro, *
Marty Bradford, *
EMP: 99 EST: 2001
SALES (est): 2.66MM
SALES (corp-wide): 245.12B **Publicly Held**
SIC: 7372 Business oriented computer software
PA: Microsoft Corporation
1 Microsoft Way
425 882-8080

**(P-18421)**
**INSTAGIS INC (PA)**
218 9th St, San Francisco (94103-3807)
PHONE..............................415 527-6636
Julian Garcia, *CEO*
Jean Coleman, *Prin*
EMP: 17 EST: 2013
SALES (est): 601.25K
SALES (corp-wide): 601.25K **Privately Held**
Web: www.instagis.com
SIC: 7372 7374 Prepackaged software; Data processing service

**(P-18422)**
**INSTRUMENTL INC**
440 N Barranca Ave, Covina (91723-1722)
PHONE..............................909 258-9291
Gauri Manglik, *CEO*
EMP: 36 EST: 2015
SALES (est): 1.39MM **Privately Held**
Web: www.instrumentl.com
SIC: 7372 Prepackaged software

**(P-18423)**
**INTEGRAL DEVELOPMENT CORP (PA)**
Also Called: Integral Engineering
380 Portage Ave, Palo Alto (94306-2244)
PHONE..............................650 424-4500
Harpal Sandhu, *CEO*
Sherry Chang, *
Vikas Srivastava, *
Jack Acosts, *
Tim Mahota, *
EMP: 50 EST: 1993
SALES (est): 17.27MM **Privately Held**
Web: www.integral.com
SIC: 7372 Business oriented computer software

**(P-18424)**
**INTEGRATED CHARTS INC**
Also Called: Tab32
915 Highland Pointe Dr Ste 250, Roseville (95765)
PHONE..............................855 698-2232
Kiltesh Patel, *CEO*
Daniel Masvidal, *Sr VP*
EMP: 23 EST: 2012
SALES (est): 1.95MM **Privately Held**
Web: www.tab32.com
SIC: 7372 7389 Business oriented computer software; Business Activities at Non-Commercial Site

**(P-18425)**
**INTEGRATEIO INC**
580 California St, San Francisco (94104-1000)
PHONE..............................888 884-6405
EMP: 36 EST: 2014
SALES (est): 2.74MM **Privately Held**
SIC: 7372 Application computer software

**(P-18426)**
**INTERACTIVE SOLUTIONS INC (DH)**
Also Called: Web Traffic School
283 4th St Ste 301, Oakland (94607-4320)
P.O. Box 209 (94604-0209)
PHONE..............................510 214-9002
Isaak Tsifrin, *CEO*
Gary Golduber, *
Gary Tsifrin, *
EMP: 67 EST: 1987
SQ FT: 14,000
SALES (est): 2.36MM
SALES (corp-wide): 1.21B **Privately Held**
SIC: 7372 Prepackaged software
HQ: Edriving Llc
1255 Treat Blvd Ste 300
Walnut Creek CA 94597
800 243-4008

**(P-18427)**
**INTERMDIA CLOUD CMMNCTIONS INC**
100 Mathilda Pl Ste 600, Sunnyvale (94086-6081)
PHONE..............................650 641-4000
Michael J Gold, *Pr*
Jason H Veldhuis, *CFO*
Jonathan S Mccormick, *CRO*
EMP: 1088 EST: 1993
SQ FT: 19,600
SALES (est): 310.27MM
SALES (corp-wide): 310.27MM **Privately Held**
Web: www.intermedia.com
SIC: 7372 Prepackaged software
PA: Ivy Parent Holdings, Llc
70 W Madison St Ste 4600

## 7372 - Prepackaged Software (P-18428)

312 895-1000

**(P-18428)**
**INTERSHOP COMMUNICATIONS INC**
461 2nd St Apt 151, San Francisco (94107-1498)
PHONE..................415 844-1500
Jochen Moll, *CEO*
Hans W Gutsch, *Treas*
Eckhard Pfeiffer, *Ch*
Peter Mark Droste, *Ch Bd*
Ralf Maennlein, *Ex Dir*
EMP: 20 EST: 1996
SQ FT: 2,700
SALES (est): 4.82MM
SALES (corp-wide): 41.29MM Privately Held
Web: www.intershop.com
SIC: 7372 7375 Prepackaged software; Information retrieval services
PA: Intershop Communications Ag
Steinweg 10
3641500

**(P-18429)**
**INTUIT FINANCING INC**
Also Called: Quickbooks Capital
2700 Coast Ave, Mountain View (94043-1140)
PHONE..................605 944-6000
Brad D Smith, *Pr*
EMP: 22 EST: 2013
SALES (est): 5.11MM
SALES (corp-wide): 16.29B Publicly Held
Web: quickbooks.intuit.com
SIC: 7372 Business oriented computer software
PA: Intuit Inc.
2700 Coast Ave
650 944-6000

**(P-18430)**
**INTUIT INC**
21650 Oxnard St Ste 2200, Woodland Hills (91367-7824)
PHONE..................818 436-7800
Michael Ermi, *Brnch Mgr*
EMP: 56
SALES (corp-wide): 16.29B Publicly Held
Web: www.intuit.com
SIC: 7372 Business oriented computer software
PA: Intuit Inc.
2700 Coast Ave
650 944-6000

**(P-18431)**
**INTUIT INC**
2650 Casey Ave, Mountain View (94043-1141)
P.O. Box 7850 (94039-7850)
PHONE..................650 944-6000
Stephen Bennett, *Pr*
EMP: 20
SALES (corp-wide): 16.29B Publicly Held
Web: www.intuit.com
SIC: 7372 Business oriented computer software
PA: Intuit Inc.
2700 Coast Ave
650 944-6000

**(P-18432)**
**INTUIT INC**
2535 Garcia Ave, Mountain View (94043-1111)
PHONE..................650 944-6000
Connie Berg, *Brnch Mgr*
EMP: 128

SALES (corp-wide): 16.29B Publicly Held
Web: www.intuit.com
SIC: 7372 Business oriented computer software
PA: Intuit Inc.
2700 Coast Ave
650 944-6000

**(P-18433)**
**INTUIT INC**
7535 Torrey Santa Fe Rd, San Diego (92129-5704)
PHONE..................858 780-2846
Brian Bequette, *Prin*
EMP: 313
SALES (corp-wide): 16.29B Publicly Held
Web: www.intuit.com
SIC: 7372 Business oriented computer software
PA: Intuit Inc.
2700 Coast Ave
650 944-6000

**(P-18434)**
**INTUIT INC**
180 Jefferson Dr, Menlo Park (94025-1115)
PHONE..................650 944-6000
Brad Smith, *Brnch Mgr*
EMP: 17
SALES (corp-wide): 16.29B Publicly Held
Web: www.intuit.com
SIC: 7372 Business oriented computer software
PA: Intuit Inc.
2700 Coast Ave
650 944-6000

**(P-18435)**
**INTUIT INC**
4760 Eastgate Mall, San Diego (92121-1970)
PHONE..................858 215-8000
Ron Hodge, *Brnch Mgr*
EMP: 20
SALES (corp-wide): 16.29B Publicly Held
Web: www.intuit.com
SIC: 7372 Business oriented computer software
PA: Intuit Inc.
2700 Coast Ave
650 944-6000

**(P-18436)**
**INTUIT INC**
Also Called: Turbotax
7545 Torrey Santa Fe Rd, San Diego (92129-5704)
PHONE..................858 215-8000
Jason Jackson, *Brnch Mgr*
EMP: 300
SALES (corp-wide): 16.29B Publicly Held
Web: www.intuit.com
SIC: 7372 Business oriented computer software
PA: Intuit Inc.
2700 Coast Ave
650 944-6000

**(P-18437)**
**INTUIT INC (PA)**
Also Called: Intuit
2700 Coast Ave, Mountain View (94043-1140)
P.O. Box 7850 (94039-7850)
PHONE..................650 944-6000
Sasan K Goodarzi, *Pr*
Scott Cook, *
Michelle M Clatterbuck, *Ex VP*
Kerry J Mclean, *Corporate Secretary*
Lara Balazs, *CMO*

EMP: 70 EST: 1983
SALES (est): 16.29B
SALES (corp-wide): 16.29B Publicly Held
Web: www.intuit.com
SIC: 7372 Prepackaged software

**(P-18438)**
**INVESTOPEDIA LLC**
555 12th St Ste 500, Oakland (94607-3699)
PHONE..................510 985-7400
David Siegel, *CEO*
EMP: 22 EST: 2013
SALES (est): 895.87K
SALES (corp-wide): 4.37B Publicly Held
Web: www.iac.com
SIC: 7372 Educational computer software
HQ: Iac Search, Llc
555 W 18th St
New York NY 10011
212 314-7300

**(P-18439)**
**INVISBLE PRTECTION SYSTEMS INC**
Also Called: Invisible Protection Svcs Inc
8847 S Halldale Ave, Los Angeles (90047-3428)
P.O. Box 452963 (90045-8541)
PHONE..................213 254-0463
Gregory Bryant, *CEO*
EMP: 20 EST: 2018
SALES (est): 1.04MM Privately Held
Web: www.ipsitech.com
SIC: 7372 Prepackaged software

**(P-18440)**
**INVOICE2GO LLC**
2317 Broadway St Fl 2, Redwood City (94063-1674)
PHONE..................650 300-5180
Mark Lenhard, *CEO*
Sean Deorsey, *
EMP: 100 EST: 2014
SALES (est): 4.9MM
SALES (corp-wide): 1.29B Publicly Held
Web: invoice.2go.com
SIC: 7372 Prepackaged software
HQ: Bill.Com, Llc
6220 America Center Dr # 100
San Jose CA 95002
650 353-3301

**(P-18441)**
**INVOTECH SYSTEMS INC**
20951 Burbank Blvd Ste B, Woodland Hills (91367-6696)
PHONE..................818 461-9800
Harvey Welles, *Pr*
EMP: 15 EST: 1991
SQ FT: 10,000
SALES (est): 2.89MM Privately Held
Web: www.invotech.com
SIC: 7372 Business oriented computer software

**(P-18442)**
**IPOLIPO INC**
Also Called: Jifflenow
440 N Wolfe Rd, Sunnyvale (94085-3869)
PHONE..................408 916-5290
Hari Shetty, *Pr*
Shekhar Kirani, *
Rajesh Setty, *
EMP: 75 EST: 2006
SALES (est): 1.62MM Privately Held
Web: www.jifflenow.com
SIC: 7372 Application computer software

**(P-18443)**
**IPR SOFTWARE INC**
Also Called: Ipr Software
16501 Ventura Blvd Ste 424, Encino (91436-2007)
PHONE..................310 499-0544
J D Bowles, *Pr*
James Madden Senior, *Treas*
EMP: 24 EST: 2000
SQ FT: 10,000
SALES (est): 1.69MM Privately Held
Web: www.iprsoftware.com
SIC: 7372 Application computer software

**(P-18444)**
**IPRAXA SOFTWARE & SERVICES**
663 Trousdale St, Oak Park (91377-4782)
PHONE..................800 459-7668
Nitesh Agarwal, *Admn*
EMP: 16 EST: 2014
SALES (est): 896.18K Privately Held
Web: www.ipraxa.com
SIC: 7372 Prepackaged software

**(P-18445)**
**IQMS LLC (HQ)**
2231 Wisteria Ln, Paso Robles (93446-9820)
PHONE..................805 227-1122
Gary Nemmers, *Pr*
Matt Ouska, *
Steve Bieszczat, *CMO**
Dan Vertachnik, *CRO**
Dan Radunz, *
EMP: 130 EST: 1989
SQ FT: 60,000
SALES (est): 15.94MM
SALES (corp-wide): 2.08B Privately Held
Web: www.iqms-erp-software.com
SIC: 7372 Prepackaged software
PA: Dassault Systemes
10 Rue Marcel Dassault
161626162

**(P-18446)**
**IRISLOGIC INC**
2336 Walsh Ave Ste F, Santa Clara (95051-1313)
PHONE..................408 855-8741
Nathan Sundeep, *CEO*
Maria D-cruz, *VP Opers*
Anoop Trivedi, *
EMP: 32 EST: 1998
SALES (est): 2.6MM Privately Held
Web: www.irislogic.com
SIC: 7372 7371 Prepackaged software; Custom computer programming services

**(P-18447)**
**ISOLUTECOM INC (PA)**
9 Northam Ave, Newbury Park (91320-3323)
PHONE..................805 498-6259
Byron Nutley, *Interim Chief Executive Officer*
Don Hyun, *
Thomas Mangle, *
Michael Brown, *
EMP: 50 EST: 1999
SALES (est): 1.75MM
SALES (corp-wide): 1.75MM Privately Held
SIC: 7372 Business oriented computer software

**(P-18448)**
**ISSIO SOLUTIONS INC**
1212 Broadway Plz Ste 1200, Walnut Creek (94596-5129)

## PRODUCTS & SERVICES SECTION
### 7372 - Prepackaged Software (P-18469)

P.O. Box 1683 (94549-1683)
PHONE.............................888 994-7746
Arne Brock Utne, *CEO*
**EMP:** 25 **EST:** 2011
**SALES (est):** 1.28MM **Privately Held**
Web: www.issio.com
**SIC: 7372** Business oriented computer software

**(P-18449)**
### ITC SFTWARE SLUTIONS GROUP LLC (PA)
Also Called: Itc Solutions & Services Group
201 Sandpointe Ave Ste 305, Santa Ana (92707-5778)
PHONE.............................877 248-2774
Del Husain, *CEO*
Ray Jandga, *Pr*
Guru Gurumoorthy, *VP*
**EMP:** 326 **EST:** 2008
**SQ FT:** 3,000
**SALES (est):** 22.21MM
**SALES (corp-wide):** 22.21MM **Privately Held**
Web: www.itcssg.com
**SIC: 7372** 7371 7373 Prepackaged software ; Computer software systems analysis and design, custom; Systems software development services

**(P-18450)**
### ITTAVI INC
Also Called: Supportpay
1100 La Avenida St Ste A, Mountain View (94043-1453)
PHONE.............................866 246-4408
Sheri Atwood, *CEO*
**EMP:** 25 **EST:** 2011
**SALES (est):** 1.78MM **Privately Held**
Web: www.supportpay.com
**SIC: 7372** 7373 7371 8748 Business oriented computer software; Systems software development services; Custom computer programming services; Systems engineering consultant, ex. computer or professional

**(P-18451)**
### IVANTI INC
150 Mathilda Pl Ste 302, Sunnyvale (94086-6012)
PHONE.............................408 343-8181
Scott Arnold, *Brnch Mgr*
**EMP:** 58
**SALES (corp-wide):** 521.05MM **Privately Held**
Web: www.ivanti.com
**SIC: 7372** Application computer software
**HQ:** Ivanti, Inc.
10377 S Jrdan Gtwy Ste 11
South Jordan UT 84095
801 208-1500

**(P-18452)**
### JACADA INC
Also Called: Jacada Autonomous Cx
1001 Page Mill Rd Ste 100, Palo Alto (94304-1073)
PHONE.............................770 352-1300
Gideon Hollander, *CEO*
Tzvia Broida, *
Guy Yair, *
Caroline Cronin, *
Dan Weil, *
**EMP:** 85 **EST:** 1991
**SALES (est):** 3.11MM
**SALES (corp-wide):** 14.73MM **Privately Held**
Web: www.uniphore.com

**SIC: 7372** Business oriented computer software
**PA:** Uniphore Technologies Inc.
1001 Page Mill Rd Bldg 4
650 352-5500

**(P-18453)**
### JAM CITY INC
2255 N Ontario St, Burbank (91504-3187)
PHONE.............................804 920-8760
Tiffany Van Decker, *Prin*
**EMP:** 74
**SALES (corp-wide):** 59.07MM **Privately Held**
Web: www.jamcity.com
**SIC: 7372** Prepackaged software
**PA:** Jam City, Inc.
3562 Eastham Dr
310 205-4800

**(P-18454)**
### JAUNT INC
Also Called: Jaunt Xr
951 Mariners Island Blvd Ste 500, San Mateo (94404-1589)
PHONE.............................650 618-6579
George Kliavkoff, *CEO*
Arthur Van Hoff, *
Fabrice Cantou, *
Jean-paul Colaco, *CRO*
**EMP:** 54 **EST:** 1999
**SALES (est):** 4.98MM **Privately Held**
Web: www.jauntxr.com
**SIC: 7372** 7371 Application computer software; Computer software development and applications

**(P-18455)**
### JEMSTEP INC
5150 El Camino Real Ste C20, Los Altos (94022-1550)
PHONE.............................650 966-6500
Kevin Cimring, *CEO*
Simon Roy, *Pr*
**EMP:** 20 **EST:** 2008
**SALES (est):** 1.86MM
**SALES (corp-wide):** 5.72B **Publicly Held**
Web: www.intelliflo.com
**SIC: 7372** Business oriented computer software
**HQ:** Invesco North American Holdings Inc
1555 Pchtree St Ne Ste 18
Atlanta GA 30309
404 892-0896

**(P-18456)**
### JFROG LTD (PA)
Also Called: JFROG
270 E Caribbean Dr, Sunnyvale (94089-1007)
PHONE.............................408 329-1540
Shlomi Ben Haim, *Ch Bd*
Jacob Shulman, *CFO*
Tali Notman, *CRO*
Frederic Simon, *Chief Data Scientist*
**EMP:** 1174 **EST:** 2008
**SQ FT:** 49,000
**SALES (est):** 349.89MM
**SALES (corp-wide):** 349.89MM **Publicly Held**
Web: www.jfrog.com
**SIC: 7372** Prepackaged software

**(P-18457)**
### JISEKI HEALTH INC
Also Called: Jiseki Health
10 Rollins Rd Ste 209, Millbrae (94030-3129)
PHONE.............................408 763-7264
Tushar Vasisht, *CEO*

Susan Bowen, *COO*
**EMP:** 22 **EST:** 2014
**SALES (est):** 2.22MM **Privately Held**
Web: www.jisekibenefits.com
**SIC: 7372** Business oriented computer software

**(P-18458)**
### JIVE SOFTWARE INC
735 Emerson St, Palo Alto (94301-2411)
PHONE.............................503 295-3700
**EMP:** 19 **EST:** 2019
**SALES (est):** 705.38K **Privately Held**
Web: www.jivesoftware.com
**SIC: 7372** Prepackaged software

**(P-18459)**
### JIVOX CORPORATION (HQ)
1810 Gateway Dr Ste 280, San Mateo (94404-4062)
PHONE.............................650 412-1125
Diaz Nesamoney, *Pr*
Leo Yen, *CFO*
**EMP:** 42 **EST:** 2007
**SALES (est):** 13.31MM **Privately Held**
Web: www.jivox.com
**SIC: 7372** Business oriented computer software
**PA:** Jivox Software India Private Limited
No 912, G K R Towers, 80 Feet Road

**(P-18460)**
### JOMU MIST INCORPORATED
Also Called: Myvr.com
309 Chapman Dr, Corte Madera (94925-1508)
PHONE.............................415 448-7273
Jonathan Murray, *CEO*
**EMP:** 24 **EST:** 2010
**SALES (est):** 1.17MM **Privately Held**
**SIC: 7372** 7389 Prepackaged software; Business services, nec

**(P-18461)**
### JOYCITY ANNEX INC
300 Spectrum Center Dr Ste 640, Irvine (92618-4990)
PHONE.............................949 892-0956
Yujin E Kim, *CEO*
**EMP:** 18 **EST:** 2017
**SALES (est):** 609.97K **Privately Held**
Web: corp.joycity.com
**SIC: 7372** Prepackaged software

**(P-18462)**
### JURNY INC
6600 W Sunset Blvd, Los Angeles (90028-7160)
PHONE.............................888 875-8769
Luca Zambello, *CEO*
**EMP:** 26 **EST:** 2018
**SALES (est):** 4.87MM **Privately Held**
Web: www.jurny.com
**SIC: 7372** Prepackaged software

**(P-18463)**
### JUSTENOUGH SOFTWARE CORP INC (HQ)
15440 Laguna Canyon Rd Ste 100, Irvine (92618-2139)
PHONE.............................949 706-5400
Malcolm Buxton, *Pr*
Robert Rackleff, *CFO*
**EMP:** 30 **EST:** 2001
**SALES (est):** 3.31MM
**SALES (corp-wide):** 28.94MM **Privately Held**
Web: www.justenoughsoftware.com

**SIC: 7372** Prepackaged software
**PA:** Mi9 Retail Inc.
1 Financial Plz Ste 601
888 326-8579

**(P-18464)**
### KAZUHM INC
6450 Lusk Blvd Ste E208, San Diego (92121-2756)
PHONE.............................858 771-3861
Tim O'neal, *CEO*
**EMP:** 20 **EST:** 2017
**SALES (est):** 947.17K **Privately Held**
Web: www.kazuhm.com
**SIC: 7372** Business oriented computer software

**(P-18465)**
### KERIO TECHNOLOGIES INC
111 W Saint John St Ste 1100, San Jose (95113-1107)
PHONE.............................409 880-7011
Jozef Belvon, *Dir*
**EMP:** 28 **EST:** 2017
**SALES (est):** 2.23MM **Privately Held**
Web: www.gfi.com
**SIC: 7372** Prepackaged software

**(P-18466)**
### KETERA TECHNOLOGIES INC (DH)
3055 Olin Ave Ste 2200, San Jose (95128-2066)
PHONE.............................408 572-9500
Steve Savignano, *CEO*
Tom Foody, *
Leslie Cedar, *
Chris Newton, *
Mike Gardner, *Product Vice President**
**EMP:** 30 **EST:** 2000
**SALES (est):** 4.37MM **Privately Held**
**SIC: 7372** Prepackaged software
**HQ:** Deem, Inc.
1330 Broadway Fl 17
Oakland CA 94612
415 590-8300

**(P-18467)**
### KEVALA INC
550 California St, San Francisco (94104-1010)
PHONE.............................415 712-7829
Aram Shumavon, *CEO*
**EMP:** 30 **EST:** 2016
**SALES (est):** 5.46MM **Privately Held**
Web: www.kevala.com
**SIC: 7372** Application computer software

**(P-18468)**
### KHAN ACADEMY INC
1200 Villa St Ste 200, Mountain View (94041-2922)
P.O. Box 1630 (94042-1630)
PHONE.............................650 336-5426
Salman Khan, *Ex Dir*
Shantanu Sinha, *
**EMP:** 85 **EST:** 2009
**SALES (est):** 53.23MM **Privately Held**
Web: www.khanacademy.org
**SIC: 7372** Educational computer software

**(P-18469)**
### KIBO SOFTWARE INC
617 2nd St, Petaluma (94952-5138)
PHONE.............................415 425-1833
**EMP:** 16
**SALES (corp-wide):** 91.29MM **Privately Held**
Web: www.kibocommerce.com

# 7372 - Prepackaged Software (P-18470)

**SIC: 7372** Prepackaged software
**PA:** Kibo Software, Inc.
1817 Braker Lane, Ste 200
707 780-1600

### (P-18470)
### KINGCOM(US) LLC (DH)
3100 Ocean Park Blvd, Santa Monica (90405-3032)
**PHONE**................................424 744-5697
**EMP:** 44 **EST:** 2016
**SALES (est):** 8.41MM
**SALES (corp-wide):** 245.12B **Publicly Held**
**SIC: 7372** Home entertainment computer software
**HQ:** Activision Blizzard, Inc.
2701 Olympic Blvd Bldg B
Santa Monica CA 90404
310 255-2000

### (P-18471)
### KINS CAPITAL LLC (PA)
4 Palo Alto Sq Ste 200, Palo Alto (94306-2122)
**PHONE**................................650 575-4456
Khurram P Sheikh, *Interim Chief Financial Officer*
Khurram P Sheikh, *Interim Chief Financial Officer*
**EMP:** 17 **EST:** 2020
**SALES (est):** 5.75MM
**SALES (corp-wide):** 5.75MM **Publicly Held**
**SIC: 7372** Prepackaged software

### (P-18472)
### KINTERA INC (HQ)
Also Called: Blackbaud Internet Solutions
9605 Scranton Rd Ste 200, San Diego (92121-1768)
**PHONE**................................858 795-3000
Marc E Chardon, *CEO*
Richard Labarbera, *
Alfred R Berkeley Iii, *Ch Bd*
Richard Davidson, *CFO*
**EMP:** 217 **EST:** 2000
**SQ FT:** 38,000
**SALES (est):** 14.11MM
**SALES (corp-wide):** 1.11B **Publicly Held**
**SIC: 7372** Business oriented computer software
**PA:** Blackbaud, Inc.
65 Fairchild St
843 216-6200

### (P-18473)
### KIVE COMPANY
Also Called: Artkive
15800 Arminta St, Van Nuys (91406-1918)
**PHONE**................................747 212-0337
Jedd Gold, *CEO*
**EMP:** 40 **EST:** 2018
**SALES (est):** 5.09MM **Privately Held**
**Web:** www.artkiveapp.com
**SIC: 7372** Prepackaged software

### (P-18474)
### KLENTYSOFT INC
440 N Barranca Ave # 2331, Covina (91723-1722)
**PHONE**................................707 518-9640
Vengat Krishnaraj, *CEO*
Praveen Kumar, *
Bhuvanesh Ram, *
**EMP:** 109 **EST:** 2015
**SALES (est):** 1.55MM **Privately Held**
**SIC: 7372** Business oriented computer software

### (P-18475)
### KLOOMA HOLDINGS INC
113 N San Vicente Blvd, Beverly Hills (90211-2303)
**PHONE**................................305 747-3315
Gary Merisier, *CEO*
**EMP:** 20 **EST:** 2017
**SALES (est):** 1.23MM **Privately Held**
**SIC: 7372** Application computer software

### (P-18476)
### KLOUDGIN INC (PA)
Also Called: Kloudgin
440 N Wolfe Rd, Sunnyvale (94085-3869)
**PHONE**................................704 904-4321
Vikram Takru, *CEO*
Dharmesh Sethi, *CFO*
**EMP:** 30 **EST:** 2010
**SALES (est):** 5.08MM
**SALES (corp-wide):** 5.08MM **Privately Held**
**Web:** www.kloudgin.com
**SIC: 7372** Business oriented computer software

### (P-18477)
### KLOUDSPOT INC
1285 Oakmead Pkwy, Sunnyvale (94085-4040)
**PHONE**................................800 709-2211
Ravi Akireddy, *CEO*
**EMP:** 80 **EST:** 2017
**SALES (est):** 2.61MM **Privately Held**
**Web:** www.kloudspot.com
**SIC: 7372** Prepackaged software

### (P-18478)
### KNO INC
2200 Mission College Blvd, Santa Clara (95054-1537)
**PHONE**................................408 844-8120
Ronald D Dickel, *CEO*
Babur Habib, *
**EMP:** 70 **EST:** 1998
**SQ FT:** 35,000
**SALES (est):** 22.7MM
**SALES (corp-wide):** 54.23B **Publicly Held**
**Web:** www.kno.com
**SIC: 7372** Educational computer software
**PA:** Intel Corporation
2200 Mission College Blvd
408 765-8080

### (P-18479)
### KOFAX LIMITED (PA)
15211 Laguna Canyon Rd, Irvine (92618-3146)
**PHONE**................................949 783-1000
Reynolds C Bish, *CEO*
Cort Townsend, *CFO*
**EMP:** 48 **EST:** 1985
**SQ FT:** 91,000
**SALES (est):** 75.49MM
**SALES (corp-wide):** 75.49MM **Privately Held**
**Web:** www.tungstenautomation.com
**SIC: 7372** Business oriented computer software

### (P-18480)
### KONAMI DIGITAL ENTRMT INC (DH)
Also Called: Konami
1 Konami Way, Hawthorne (90250-1144)
**PHONE**................................310 220-8100
Tomohiro Uesugi, *CEO*
Kazumi Kitaue, *
Takahiro Azuma, *
Chris Bartee, *
▲ **EMP:** 23 **EST:** 1996
**SALES (est):** 22.81MM **Privately Held**
**SIC: 7372** Home entertainment computer software
**HQ:** Konami Digital Entertainment Co., Ltd.
1-11-1, Ginza
Chuo-Ku TKY 104-0

### (P-18481)
### KRANEM CORPORATION
Also Called: Kranem
560 S Winchester Blvd Ste 500, San Jose (95128-2536)
**PHONE**................................650 319-6743
Ajay Batheja, *Ch Bd*
Edward Miller, *CFO*
Luigi Caramico, *Corporate Strategy Vice President*
**EMP:** 190 **EST:** 2002
**SALES (est):** 9.84MM **Privately Held**
**SIC: 7372** Business oriented computer software

### (P-18482)
### KYRIBA CORP (PA)
4435 Eastgate Mall Ste 200, San Diego (92121-1980)
**PHONE**................................858 210-3560
Melissa Di Donato, *Ch*
Edi Poloniato, *
Catherine Moore, *
Remy Dubois, *
Fabrice Lvy, *
**EMP:** 50 **EST:** 2000
**SALES (est):** 49.66MM
**SALES (corp-wide):** 49.66MM **Privately Held**
**Web:** www.kyriba.com
**SIC: 7372** Prepackaged software

### (P-18483)
### LABELBOX INC (PA)
Also Called: Labelbox
510 Treat Ave, San Francisco (94110-2014)
**PHONE**................................415 294-0791
Manu Sharma, *Pr*
Jackie Ricci, *
**EMP:** 18 **EST:** 2018
**SALES (est):** 6.34MM
**SALES (corp-wide):** 6.34MM **Privately Held**
**Web:** www.labelbox.com
**SIC: 7372** Prepackaged software

### (P-18484)
### LABELBOX INC
510 Treat Ave, San Francisco (94110-2014)
**PHONE**................................415 294-0791
Manu Sharma, *CEO*
**EMP:** 175 **EST:** 2018
**SALES (est):** 1.91MM **Privately Held**
**SIC: 7372** Prepackaged software

### (P-18485)
### LABS UPWEST
550 California Ave Ste 100, Palo Alto (94306-1401)
**PHONE**................................650 272-6529
Gil Ben-artzy, *Pt*
**EMP:** 16 **EST:** 2016
**SALES (est):** 4.87MM **Privately Held**
**Web:** www.upwest.vc
**SIC: 7372** Prepackaged software

### (P-18486)
### LASTLINE LLC (DH)
Also Called: Lastline, Inc.
3401 Hillview Ave, Palo Alto (94304)
**PHONE**................................877 671-3239
Hock Tan, *CEO*
**EMP:** 61 **EST:** 2009
**SALES (est):** 19.2MM
**SALES (corp-wide):** 35.82B **Publicly Held**
**Web:** www.vmware.com
**SIC: 7372** Prepackaged software
**HQ:** Vmware Llc
3421 Hillview Ave
Palo Alto CA 94304
650 427-6000

### (P-18487)
### LATTICE DATA INC
801 El Camino Real, Menlo Park (94025-4807)
**PHONE**................................650 800-7262
Andy Jacques, *CEO*
**EMP:** 20 **EST:** 2015
**SQ FT:** 5,700
**SALES (est):** 686.6K
**SALES (corp-wide):** 391.04B **Publicly Held**
**Web:** www.lattice.io
**SIC: 7372** Business oriented computer software
**PA:** Apple Inc.
1 Apple Park Way
408 996-1010

### (P-18488)
### LCPTRACKER INC
117 E Chapman Ave, Orange (92866-1401)
P.O. Box 187 (92856-6187)
**PHONE**................................714 669-0052
Mark Douglas, *CEO*
Mark Douglas, *Pr*
Loren Doll, *VP*
**EMP:** 20 **EST:** 1992
**SQ FT:** 1,500
**SALES (est):** 8.66MM **Privately Held**
**Web:** www.lcptracker.com
**SIC: 7372** Business oriented computer software

### (P-18489)
### LCR-DIXON CORPORATION
2048 Union St Apt 4, San Francisco (94123-4118)
P.O. Box 812 (21014-0812)
**PHONE**................................404 307-1695
Suzy Soo, *CEO*
Jeffrey Bleachler, *COO*
**EMP:** 17 **EST:** 2006
**SALES (est):** 1.34MM
**SALES (corp-wide):** 572.39MM **Publicly Held**
**Web:** www.vertexinc.com
**SIC: 7372** Application computer software
**PA:** Vertex, Inc.
2301 Renaissance Blvd
800 355-3500

### (P-18490)
### LEADCRUNCH INC (PA)
Also Called: Leadcrunch
750 B St Ste 1630, San Diego (92101-8131)
P.O. Box 712979 (92171-2979)
**PHONE**................................888 708-6649
Olin Hyde, *CEO*
David Toth, *Ch Bd*
Sanjit Singh, *COO*
**EMP:** 27 **EST:** 2018
**SALES (est):** 7.5MM
**SALES (corp-wide):** 7.5MM **Privately Held**
**Web:** www.getrev.ai
**SIC: 7372** Business oriented computer software

### (P-18491)
### LEADS360 LLC
207 Hindry Ave, Inglewood (90301-1519)

▲ = Import ▼ = Export
◆ = Import/Export

## PRODUCTS & SERVICES SECTION
### 7372 - Prepackaged Software (P-18512)

PHONE..................888 843-1777
Nick Hedges, *CEO*
Charles Chase, *
Jeff Solomon, *
Christopher Adams, *
Alan Lang, *
**EMP:** 30 **EST:** 2005
**SALES (est):** 2.33MM **Privately Held**
**SIC:** 7372 7371 Prepackaged software; Computer software development

*(P-18492)*
**LEAPFROG POWER INC (PA)**
Also Called: Leap
1700 Montgomery St Ste 200, San Francisco (94111-1021)
PHONE..................415 409-9783
Thomas Folker, *CEO*
**EMP:** 23 **EST:** 2017
**SALES (est):** 5.18MM
**SALES (corp-wide):** 5.18MM **Privately Held**
**Web:** www.leap.energy
**SIC:** 7372 Utility computer software

*(P-18493)*
**LEAPYEAR TECHNOLOGIES INC**
612 Howard St Ste 500, San Francisco (94105-3928)
PHONE..................510 542-9193
Colton Jang, *Admn*
Ishaan Nerurkar, *
Christopher Hockenbrocht, *
Richard Barber, *
Michael Theilmann, *
**EMP:** 50 **EST:** 2016
**SALES (est):** 5.07MM **Privately Held**
**Web:** www.leapyear.ai
**SIC:** 7372 Business oriented computer software

*(P-18494)*
**LEARNING EXPLORER INC**
924 Anacapa St Ste 4i, Santa Barbara (93101-2193)
PHONE..................888 909-9035
Mark Rankovic, *CEO*
**EMP:** 17 **EST:** 2021
**SALES (est):** 4.22MM **Privately Held**
**Web:** www.learningexplorer.com
**SIC:** 7372 Educational computer software

*(P-18495)*
**LEEYO SOFTWARE INC (HQ)**
Also Called: Leeyo
2841 Junction Ave Ste 201, San Jose (95134-1938)
PHONE..................408 988-5800
Jagan Reddy, *CEO*
Karthikeyan Ramamoorthy, *
Sudarsan Umashankar, *
Michael Compton, *
Jeffery Pickett, *
**EMP:** 41 **EST:** 2007
**SALES (est):** 4.65MM **Publicly Held**
**Web:** www.leeyo.com
**SIC:** 7372 Business oriented computer software
**PA:** Zuora, Inc.
101 Redwood Shores Pkwy

*(P-18496)*
**LIGHTSPEED SOFTWARE INC**
1800 19th St, Bakersfield (93301-4315)
PHONE..................661 716-7600
**EMP:** 18 **EST:** 2017
**SALES (est):** 1.83MM **Privately Held**
**SIC:** 7372 Prepackaged software

*(P-18497)*
**LIQUIDSPACE INC** ✪
2225 E Bayshore Rd # 200, Palo Alto (94303-3220)
PHONE..................855 254-7843
**EMP:** 22 **EST:** 2023
**SALES (est):** 3.81MM **Privately Held**
**SIC:** 7372 Prepackaged software

*(P-18498)*
**LIVEACTION INC (PA)**
901 Campisi Way Ste 222, Campbell (95008-2348)
PHONE..................888 881-1116
Steve Stuut, *CEO*
Dana Matsunaga, *
R Brooks Borcherding, *
Ulrica Menares, *
**EMP:** 28 **EST:** 2008
**SALES (est):** 57MM **Privately Held**
**Web:** www.liveaction.com
**SIC:** 7372 Business oriented computer software

*(P-18499)*
**LIVEOFFICE LLC**
Also Called: Advisorsquare
900 Corporate Pointe, Culver City (90230-7609)
PHONE..................877 253-2793
Matt Smith, *
Nikhil Menta, *
Jeffrey W Hausman, *
Matt Hardy, *
**EMP:** 29 **EST:** 2007
**SQ FT:** 15,000
**SALES (est):** 22.45MM
**SALES (corp-wide):** 3.81B **Publicly Held**
**Web:** www.liveoffice.com
**SIC:** 7372 Prepackaged software
**PA:** Gen Digital Inc.
60 E Rio Slado Pkwy Ste 1
650 527-8000

*(P-18500)*
**LOGINEXT SOLUTIONS INC (PA)**
Also Called: Loginext
5002 Spring Crest Ter, Fremont (94536-6525)
PHONE..................510 894-6225
Dhruvil Sanghvi, *CEO*
Manisha Raisinghani, *
**EMP:** 72 **EST:** 2017
**SALES (est):** 6.05MM
**SALES (corp-wide):** 6.05MM **Privately Held**
**Web:** www.loginextsolutions.com
**SIC:** 7372 7371 7379 8243 Prepackaged software; Computer software systems analysis and design, custom; Computer related consulting services; Software training, computer

*(P-18501)*
**LOOP AI LABS INC**
Also Called: Loop Ai Labs
404 Bryant St, San Francisco (94107-1303)
PHONE..................415 980-3655
Gianmauro Calafiore, *CEO*
Patrick Ehlen, *Chief Scientist*
**EMP:** 20 **EST:** 2012
**SALES (est):** 2.54MM **Privately Held**
**Web:** www.loop.ai
**SIC:** 7372 Business oriented computer software

*(P-18502)*
**LORE IO INC**
100 S Murphy Ave Ste 200, Sunnyvale (94086-6118)
PHONE..................408 256-1521
Digvijay Lamba, *CEO*
**EMP:** 25 **EST:** 2015
**SALES (est):** 1.02MM
**SALES (corp-wide):** 970MM **Privately Held**
**Web:** www.alteryx.com
**SIC:** 7372 Prepackaged software
**PA:** Alteryx, Inc.
3347 Michelson Dr Ste 400
888 836-4274

*(P-18503)*
**LOTUSFLARE INC**
2350 Mission College Blvd, Santa Clara (95054-1532)
PHONE..................626 695-5634
Surendra Gadodia, *CEO*
Nick Thakkar, *Dir*
**EMP:** 62 **EST:** 2012
**SALES (est):** 2.82MM **Privately Held**
**Web:** www.lotusflare.com
**SIC:** 7372 Business oriented computer software

*(P-18504)*
**LOYALTY JUGGERNAUT INC**
2100 Geng Rd Ste 210, Palo Alto (94303-3307)
PHONE..................650 283-5081
Shyam Shah, *CEO*
Shyam Shah, *Pr*
**EMP:** 263 **EST:** 2015
**SALES (est):** 10.96MM **Privately Held**
**Web:** www.lji.io
**SIC:** 7372 Prepackaged software

*(P-18505)*
**LPA INSURANCE AGENCY INC**
Also Called: Sat
3800 Watt Ave Ste 147, Sacramento (95821-2676)
PHONE..................916 286-7850
Michael Winkel, *Pr*
**EMP:** 100 **EST:** 1983
**SALES (est):** 2.22MM
**SALES (corp-wide):** 9.82B **Publicly Held**
**SIC:** 7372 Application computer software
**HQ:** Fis Capital Markets Us Llc
347 Riverside Ave
Jacksonville FL 32202
877 776-3706

*(P-18506)*
**LUMENOVA AI INC**
1419 Beaudry Blvd, 1419 Beaudry Blvd, Glendale (91208)
PHONE..................310 694-2461
Cosmin Andriescu, *Pr*
**EMP:** 25 **EST:** 2022
**SALES (est):** 1.03MM **Privately Held**
**SIC:** 7372 Prepackaged software

*(P-18507)*
**LUNA IMAGING INC**
2702 Media Center Dr, Los Angeles (90065-1733)
PHONE..................323 908-1400
Marlo Lee, *Pr*
James Lytras, *Mktg Dir*
Drake Zabriskie, *Eng/Dir*
David Larson, *S&M/Dir*
Lori Richmeier, *Genl Mgr*
**EMP:** 21 **EST:** 1993
**SQ FT:** 6,000
**SALES (est):** 615.64K **Privately Held**
**Web:** www.lunaimaging.com
**SIC:** 7372 7373 Publisher's computer software; Computer integrated systems design

*(P-18508)*
**LYNX SOFTWARE TECHNOLOGIES INC (PA)**
855 Embedded Way, San Jose (95138-1030)
PHONE..................408 979-3900
Inder Singh, *Ch*
Gurjot Singh, *
Will Keegan, *
Al Maillet, *CRO*
**EMP:** 52 **EST:** 1988
**SQ FT:** 30,000
**SALES (est):** 29.79MM
**SALES (corp-wide):** 29.79MM **Privately Held**
**Web:** www.lynx.com
**SIC:** 7372 Business oriented computer software

*(P-18509)*
**M NEXON INC**
Also Called: Nexon America
222 N Pacific Coast Hwy Ste 300, El Segundo (90245-5614)
PHONE..................213 858-5930
John Robinson, *CEO*
**EMP:** 25 **EST:** 2011
**SALES (est):** 5.8MM **Privately Held**
**Web:** www.nexon.com
**SIC:** 7372 5092 Application computer software; Video games
**PA:** Nexon Co., Ltd.
1-4-5, Roppongi

*(P-18510)*
**MACHINE ZONE LLC**
1900 S Norfolk St Ste 350, San Mateo (94403-1171)
PHONE..................650 320-1678
**EMP:** 26 **EST:** 2013
**SALES (est):** 8.79MM **Privately Held**
**Web:** www.mz.com
**SIC:** 7372 Publisher's computer software

*(P-18511)*
**MAGENTA BUYER LLC (HQ)**
Also Called: McAfee Enterprise
428 University Ave, Palo Alto (94301-1812)
PHONE..................650 935-9500
Gee Rittenhouse, *CEO*
William Chisholm, *Pr*
**EMP:** 34 **EST:** 2021
**SALES (est):** 20.41MM
**SALES (corp-wide):** 637.98MM **Privately Held**
**SIC:** 7372 Prepackaged software
**PA:** Symphony Technology Group, L.L.C.
428 University Ave
650 935-9500

*(P-18512)*
**MAGIC SOFTWARE ENTERPRISES INC**
530 Technology Dr Ste 100, Irvine (92618-1350)
P.O. Box 52020 (92619-2020)
PHONE..................949 250-1718
Eyal Karny, *CEO*
Glenn Johnson, *VP Mktg*
Fred Esquillo, *VP Fin*
Shimon Adimor, *Dir*
**EMP:** 20 **EST:** 1991
**SALES (est):** 9.86MM **Privately Held**
**Web:** www.magicsoftware.com
**SIC:** 7372 7379 7371 Prepackaged software; Computer related consulting services; Custom computer programming services
**PA:** Magic Software Enterprises Ltd.
1 Yahadut Canada

## 7372 - Prepackaged Software (P-18513)

**(P-18513)**
**MAGIC TOUCH SOFTWARE INTL**
950 Boardwalk Ste 200, San Marcos (92078-2600)
P.O. Box 142 (92079-0142)
PHONE.................................800 714-6490
Gary Bagheri, *CEO*
Gary Bagheri, *Pr*
George Peiov, *
**EMP:** 25 **EST:** 2007
**SQ FT:** 1,500
**SALES (est):** 1.22MM **Privately Held**
Web: www.magictouchsoftware.com
**SIC: 7372** Business oriented computer software

**(P-18514)**
**MAGNET SYSTEMS INC**
2300 Geng Rd Ste 100, Palo Alto (94303-3352)
P.O. Box 320805 (95032-0113)
PHONE.................................650 329-5904
Alfred Chuang, *CEO*
**EMP:** 24 **EST:** 2008
**SALES (est):** 518.97K **Privately Held**
Web: www.magnet.com
**SIC: 7372** Application computer software

**(P-18515)**
**MAGNIT LLC (PA)**
2635 Iron Point Rd Ste 270, Folsom (95630)
PHONE.................................516 437-3300
Teresa Carroll, *CEO*
**EMP:** 99 **EST:** 1992
**SALES (est):** 487.04MM **Privately Held**
Web: www.magnitglobal.com
**SIC: 7372** 8741 Application computer software; Personnel management

**(P-18516)**
**MAILBIRD INC**
2600 El Camino Real Ste 601, Palo Alto (94306-1717)
PHONE.................................650 830-9891
Sarah Lerche, *VP*
**EMP:** 15 **EST:** 2022
**SALES (est):** 2.04MM **Privately Held**
Web: www.getmailbird.com
**SIC: 7372** Application computer software

**(P-18517)**
**MALWAREBYTES INC (PA)**
Also Called: Malwarebytes
3979 Freedom Cir Fl 12, Santa Clara (95054-1256)
PHONE.................................408 852-4336
Marcin Kleczynski, *CEO*
Mark Harris, *
Bruce Harrison, *
Justin Dolly Ciso, *Prin*
Thomas R Fox, *
**EMP:** 301 **EST:** 2009
**SALES (est):** 59.58MM
**SALES (corp-wide):** 59.58MM **Privately Held**
Web: www.malwarebytes.com
**SIC: 7372** Prepackaged software

**(P-18518)**
**MANDIANT INC**
630 Alder Dr, Milpitas (95035-7435)
PHONE.................................408 321-6300
David G Dewalt, *Ch Bd*
**EMP:** 34
**SALES (corp-wide):** 307.39B **Publicly Held**
Web: www.trellix.com
**SIC: 7372** Prepackaged software
**HQ:** Mandiant, Inc.
11951 Freedom Dr Fl 6
Reston VA 20190

**(P-18519)**
**MANGOMINT INC**
10401 Venice Blvd 497, Los Angeles (90034-6491)
PHONE.................................310 496-8677
Daniel Lang, *CEO*
**EMP:** 40 **EST:** 2016
**SALES (est):** 7.41MM **Privately Held**
Web: www.mangomint.com
**SIC: 7372** 7371 Prepackaged software; Software programming applications

**(P-18520)**
**MANTICORE GAMES INC**
1390 Buckingham Way, Hillsborough (94010-7307)
PHONE.................................650 799-6145
Frederic Descamps, *Prin*
**EMP:** 25 **EST:** 2017
**SALES (est):** 2.9MM **Privately Held**
Web: www.manticoregames.com
**SIC: 7372** Prepackaged software

**(P-18521)**
**MARBLE SECURITY INC**
68 Willow Rd, Menlo Park (94025-3653)
PHONE.................................408 737-4300
David Jevans, *Ch Bd*
Stephen Ryan, *Sr VP*
**EMP:** 15 **EST:** 2005
**SQ FT:** 20,000
**SALES (est):** 4.65MM **Privately Held**
Web: www.marblesecurity.com
**SIC: 7372** Prepackaged software

**(P-18522)**
**MARQETA INC (PA)**
Also Called: Marqeta
180 Grand Ave Ste 600, Oakland (94612-3746)
PHONE.................................877 962-7738
Simon Khalaf, *CEO*
Judson Linville, *Ch Bd*
Michael Milotich, *CFO*
Randall Kern, *CPO*
Todd Pollak, *CRO*
**EMP:** 702 **EST:** 2010
**SQ FT:** 63,284
**SALES (est):** 676.17MM
**SALES (corp-wide):** 676.17MM **Publicly Held**
Web: www.marqeta.com
**SIC: 7372** Prepackaged software

**(P-18523)**
**MASTER OF CODE GLOBAL**
541 Jefferson Ave Ste 104, Redwood City (94063-1700)
PHONE.................................650 200-8490
Dmytro Hrytsenko, *Admn*
**EMP:** 48 **EST:** 2014
**SALES (est):** 1.44MM **Privately Held**
Web: www.masterofcode.com
**SIC: 7372** Prepackaged software

**(P-18524)**
**MATERIAL SECURITY INC**
33 New Montgomery St, San Francisco (94105-4506)
PHONE.................................408 649-9882
Ryan Noon, *CEO*
Ryan Seu, *Prin*
**EMP:** 52 **EST:** 2017
**SALES (est):** 1.1MM **Privately Held**
Web: www.material.security
**SIC: 7372** Business oriented computer software

**(P-18525)**
**MATTERPORT INC (PA)**
Also Called: MATTERPORT
352 E Java Dr, Sunnyvale (94089-1328)
PHONE.................................650 641-2241
R J Pittman, *Ch Bd*
James D Fay, *CFO*
Peter Presunka, *CAO*
Matthew Zinn, *CLO*
Jay Remley, *CRO*
**EMP:** 69 **EST:** 2011
**SQ FT:** 13,822
**SALES (est):** 157.75MM
**SALES (corp-wide):** 157.75MM **Publicly Held**
Web: www.matterport.com
**SIC: 7372** Prepackaged software

**(P-18526)**
**MAXXESS SYSTEMS INC (PA)**
135 S State College Blvd Ste 200, Brea (92821-5805)
PHONE.................................714 772-1000
Kevin Charles Daly, *CEO*
Nancy Islas, *Pr*
Joel Slutzky, *Ch*
**EMP:** 18 **EST:** 2003
**SALES (est):** 3.72MM **Privately Held**
Web: www.maxxess-systems.com
**SIC: 7372** Business oriented computer software

**(P-18527)**
**MCAFEE LLC (DH)**
6220 America Ctr Dr, San Jose (95002)
PHONE.................................888 847-8766
Peter Leav, *Pr*
Michael Berry, *
Terry Hicks, *
Sarah Decker, *CLO CCO*
▲ **EMP:** 96 **EST:** 1992
**SQ FT:** 208,000
**SALES (est):** 808.44MM
**SALES (corp-wide):** 1.92B **Privately Held**
Web: www.mcafee.com
**SIC: 7372** Application computer software
**HQ:** Mcafee Corp.
6220 America Ctr Dr
San Jose CA 95002
866 622-3911

**(P-18528)**
**MCAFEE CORP (HQ)**
6220 America Center Dr, San Jose (95002-2563)
PHONE.................................866 622-3911
Craig Boundy, *Pr*
Jennifer Biry, *COO*
Steve Grobman, *Ex VP*
Sarah Decker, *CLO*
**EMP:** 93 **EST:** 2017
**SQ FT:** 85,000
**SALES (est):** 1.92B
**SALES (corp-wide):** 1.92B **Privately Held**
Web: www.mcafee.com
**SIC: 7372** 7382 Prepackaged software; Security systems services
**PA:** Condor Bidco, Inc.
320 Park Ave Fl 28
866 622-3911

**(P-18529)**
**MCAFEE FINANCE 2 LLC**
2821 Mission College Blvd, Santa Clara (95054-1838)
P.O. Box 3128 (95002-3128)
PHONE.................................888 847-8766
**EMP:** 1881 **EST:** 2016
**SALES (est):** 2.11MM
**SALES (corp-wide):** 22.98MM **Privately Held**
**SIC: 7372** Prepackaged software
**HQ:** Mcafee Finance 1, Llc
2821 Mission College Blvd
Santa Clara CA 95054
888 847-8766

**(P-18530)**
**MCLOUD TCHNLGS (USA) INC**
Also Called: McLoud
580 California St, San Francisco (94104-1000)
PHONE.................................866 420-1781
Russ Mcmeekin, *CEO*
Michael Sicuro, *CFO*
Gino Lander, *Chief Growth Officer*
Darren Anderson, *VP Fin*
**EMP:** 15 **EST:** 2016
**SALES (est):** 2.62MM
**SALES (corp-wide):** 39.87MM **Privately Held**
Web: www.magcloud.com
**SIC: 7372** Business oriented computer software
**PA:** Mcloud Technologies Corp
550-510 Burrard St
866 420-1781

**(P-18531)**
**MEDALLIA INC (HQ)**
6220 Stoneridge Mall Rd Fl 2, Pleasanton (94588-3260)
PHONE.................................650 321-3000
Joe Tyrrell, *CEO*
Borge Hald, *CSO*
Roxanne M Oulman, *Ex VP*
Jimmy C Duan, *CCO*
Mikael J Ottosson, *Ex VP*
**EMP:** 145 **EST:** 2000
**SALES (est):** 492.75MM
**SALES (corp-wide):** 492.75MM **Privately Held**
Web: www.medallia.com
**SIC: 7372** 8732 Business oriented computer software; Market analysis, business, and economic research
**PA:** Medallia Parent, Lp
6220 Stnrdge Mall Rd Fl 2
650 321-3000

**(P-18532)**
**MEDATA LLC (HQ)**
5 Peters Canyon Rd Ste 250, Irvine (92606-1791)
PHONE.................................714 918-1310
Cy King, *CEO*
Tom Herndon, *
T Don Theis, *CSO*
Elizabeth King, *
Tori Henson, *
**EMP:** 51 **EST:** 1975
**SQ FT:** 17,192
**SALES (est):** 39.08MM **Privately Held**
Web: www.medata.com
**SIC: 7372** 6411 Business oriented computer software; Medical insurance claim processing, contract or fee basis
**PA:** Medrisk, Llc
2701 Renaissance Blvd

**(P-18533)**
**MEDEANALYTICS INC**
4160 Dublin Blvd Ste 200, Dublin (94568-7756)
PHONE.................................925 248-8118
**EMP:** 50
Web: www.medeanalytics.com
**SIC: 7372** Application computer software
**PA:** Medeanalytics, Inc.
501 W Prsdent Grge Bush H

# PRODUCTS & SERVICES SECTION
## 7372 - Prepackaged Software (P-18555)

**(P-18534)**
**MEDIA GOBBLER INC**
Also Called: Gobbler
6427 W Sunset Blvd, Los Angeles (90028-7314)
PHONE.................323 203-3222
Chris Kantrowitz, *CEO*
**EMP:** 15 **EST:** 2010
**SALES (est):** 2.78MM **Privately Held**
Web: www.gobbler.com
**SIC: 7372** Application computer software

**(P-18535)**
**MEDITAB SOFTWARE INC**
8795 Folsom Blvd Ste 205, Sacramento (95826-3721)
P.O. Box 255687 (95865-5687)
PHONE.................844 463-3482
Mike Patel, *Pr*
Kal Patel, *
**EMP:** 250 **EST:** 2002
**SQ FT:** 10,000
**SALES (est):** 18.36MM **Privately Held**
Web: www.meditab.com
**SIC: 7372** Business oriented computer software
**PA:** Meditab Software (India) Private Limited
Officeno. 219/A, 2nd Floor

**(P-18536)**
**MEDRICS CORP**
353 Sacramento St Ste 1820, San Francisco (94111-3620)
PHONE.................415 704-7404
Altug Ozdamar, *CEO*
**EMP:** 15 **EST:** 2018
**SALES (est):** 740.74K **Privately Held**
Web: www.medrics.net
**SIC: 7372** Application computer software

**(P-18537)**
**MEDRIO INC (PA)**
345 California St Ste 325, San Francisco (94104-2658)
PHONE.................415 963-3700
Nicole Latimer, *CEO*
Richard H Scheller, *
Nathan Weems, *
**EMP:** 100 **EST:** 2006
**SALES (est):** 20.24MM
**SALES (corp-wide):** 20.24MM **Privately Held**
Web: www.medrio.com
**SIC: 7372** Business oriented computer software

**(P-18538)**
**MEMORA HEALTH INC**
548 Market St, San Francisco (94104-5401)
PHONE.................480 335-7348
Manav Sevak, *CEO*
Divya Bhat, *Chief Product Officer**
Herman Ng, *
Nathan Leong, *
James Colbert, *CMO**
**EMP:** 62 **EST:** 2018
**SALES (est):** 2.91MM **Privately Held**
Web: www.memorahealth.com
**SIC: 7372** Publisher's computer software

**(P-18539)**
**MERIDIAN PROJECT SYSTEMS INC**
Also Called: Meridian Systems
1720 Prairie City Rd Ste 120, Folsom (95630-4044)
PHONE.................916 294-2000
**EMP:** 120
**SIC: 7372** Business oriented computer software

**(P-18540)**
**META PLATFORMS TECH LLC (HQ)**
Also Called: Oculus
1 Hacker Way, Menlo Park (94025-1456)
PHONE.................650 543-4800
Mark Zuckerberg, *Ch*
▲ **EMP:** 48 **EST:** 2014
**SALES (est):** 310.75MM
**SALES (corp-wide):** 134.9B **Publicly Held**
Web: www.meta.com
**SIC: 7372** 5731 Application computer software; Consumer electronic equipment, nec
**PA:** Meta Platforms, Inc.
1 Meta Way
650 543-4800

**(P-18541)**
**METRICSTREAM INC (PA)**
Also Called: Complianceonline
6201 America Center Dr Ste 240, San Jose (95002)
P.O. Box 246 (95002)
PHONE.................650 620-2955
Gaurav Kapoor, *
Prasad Sabbineni, *
Tony Caroll, *
**EMP:** 150 **EST:** 1999
**SALES (est):** 40.59MM **Privately Held**
Web: www.metricstream.com
**SIC: 7372** Application computer software

**(P-18542)**
**MICRO FOCUS (US) INC (DH)**
Also Called: Micro Focus
2440 Sand Hill Rd Ste 302, Menlo Park (94025)
PHONE.................301 838-5000
Stephen Murdoch, *CEO*
Kevin Loosemore, *Ofcr*
Chris Kennedy, *CFO*
Jon Hunter, *CRO*
**EMP:** 85 **EST:** 2001
**SQ FT:** 26,000
**SALES (est):** 209.36MM
**SALES (corp-wide):** 82.22MM **Privately Held**
Web: www.microfocus.com
**SIC: 7372** Business oriented computer software
**HQ:** Micro Focus International Limited
The Lawn
Newbury BERKS

**(P-18543)**
**MICRO FOCUS LLC**
Also Called: Micro Focus
6701 Koll Center Pkwy # 300, Pleasanton (94566-8061)
PHONE.................925 784-3242
**EMP:** 99
**SALES (corp-wide):** 88.51MM **Privately Held**
Web: www.microfocus.com
**SIC: 7372** Prepackaged software
**HQ:** Micro Focus Llc
2440 Sand Hill Rd Ste 302
Menlo Park CA 94025
650 645-3000

**(P-18544)**
**MICROSOFT CORPORATION**
Also Called: Microsoft
3 Park Plz Ste 1800, Irvine (92614-8541)
PHONE.................949 263-3000
Sandy Thomas, *Genl Mgr*
**EMP:** 25
**SALES (corp-wide):** 245.12B **Publicly Held**
Web: www.microsoft.com
**SIC: 7372** Application computer software
**PA:** Microsoft Corporation
1 Microsoft Way
425 882-8080

**(P-18545)**
**MILEIQ INC**
548 Market St, San Francisco (94104-5401)
PHONE.................415 528-7722
Daniel Bomze, *Ex Dir*
**EMP:** 57 **EST:** 2021
**SALES (est):** 6.38MM **Privately Held**
Web: www.mileiq.com
**SIC: 7372** Prepackaged software

**(P-18546)**
**MINDSHOW INC**
811 W 7th St Ste 500, Los Angeles (90017-3416)
PHONE.................213 531-0277
**EMP:** 51 **EST:** 2014
**SALES (est):** 4.49MM **Privately Held**
Web: www.mindshow.com
**SIC: 7372** Prepackaged software

**(P-18547)**
**MINDSNACKS INC**
1390 Market St Ste 200, San Francisco (94102-5404)
PHONE.................415 875-9817
Jesse Pickard, *CEO*
Aydin Senkut, *
Bryan Schreier, *
**EMP:** 30 **EST:** 2010
**SALES (est):** 3.4MM **Privately Held**
Web: www.elevateapp.com
**SIC: 7372** Application computer software

**(P-18548)**
**MINDTICKLE INC (PA)**
535 Mission St Fl 14, San Francisco (94105-3253)
PHONE.................973 400-1717
Krishna Depura, *CEO*
Jeff Santelices, *CRO*
**EMP:** 20 **EST:** 2011
**SALES (est):** 3.63MM
**SALES (corp-wide):** 3.63MM **Privately Held**
Web: www.mindtickle.com
**SIC: 7372** Business oriented computer software

**(P-18549)**
**MINT SOFTWARE INC**
280 Hope St, Mountain View (94041-1308)
P.O. Box 7850 (94039-7850)
PHONE.................650 944-6000
**EMP:** 53 **EST:** 2006
**SQ FT:** 5,000
**SALES (est):** 1.2MM
**SALES (corp-wide):** 16.29B **Publicly Held**
**SIC: 7372** Business oriented computer software
**PA:** Intuit Inc.
2700 Coast Ave
650 944-6000

**(P-18550)**
**MITEK SYSTEMS INC (PA)**
Also Called: Mitek
770 1st Ave Ste 425, San Diego (92101-6169)
PHONE.................619 269-6800
Scott Carter, *Ch Bd*
Scott Carter, *Non-Executive Chairman of the Board*
David Lyle, *Sr VP*
**EMP:** 100 **EST:** 1986
**SQ FT:** 29,000
**SALES (est):** 172.55MM
**SALES (corp-wide):** 172.55MM **Publicly Held**
Web: www.miteksystems.com
**SIC: 7372** Prepackaged software

**(P-18551)**
**MITRATECH HOLDINGS INC**
5900 Wilshire Blvd Ste 1500, Los Angeles (90036-5031)
PHONE.................323 964-0000
Jason Parkman, *CEO*
**EMP:** 125
**SALES (corp-wide):** 103.85MM **Privately Held**
Web: www.mitratech.com
**SIC: 7372** Business oriented computer software
**PA:** Mitratech Holdings, Inc.
5001 Plz On The Lk Ste 11
512 382-7322

**(P-18552)**
**MIXMODE INC**
111 W Michetlorena St Ste 300-A, Santa Barbara (93101-3095)
P.O. Box 92041 (93190-2041)
PHONE.................858 225-2352
John Keister, *CEO*
John Keister, *Pr*
Fred Wilmot, *
Mark Rotolo, *CRO**
Karen Buffo, *CMO**
**EMP:** 40 **EST:** 2012
**SALES (est):** 7.29MM **Privately Held**
Web: www.mixmode.ai
**SIC: 7372** Business oriented computer software

**(P-18553)**
**MLY TECHNIX CORP**
2005 De La Cruz Blvd Ste 180, Santa Clara (95050-3013)
PHONE.................650 384-1456
George Moser, *Prin*
Randy Linn, *Prin*
**EMP:** 26 **EST:** 2005
**SQ FT:** 6,000
**SALES (est):** 727.15K **Privately Held**
**SIC: 7372** Utility computer software

**(P-18554)**
**MOD2 INC**
Also Called: Mod 2
3317 S Broadway, Los Angeles (90007-4114)
PHONE.................213 747-8424
Javid Nia, *Pr*
**EMP:** 16 **EST:** 1992
**SQ FT:** 12,000
**SALES (est):** 2.29MM **Privately Held**
Web: www.mod2.com
**SIC: 7372** 7371 Business oriented computer software; Computer software systems analysis and design, custom

**(P-18555)**
**MODALITYAI INC**
149 New Montgomery St Fl 4, San Francisco (94105-3739)
PHONE.................415 200-8535
David Suendermann-oeft, *CEO*
Christiane Suendermann-oeft, *CFO*
David Fox, *Chief Business Officer*
Ira Shoulson, *Chief Medical Officer*

---

(PA)=Parent Co (HQ)=Headquarters
✪ = New Business established in last 2 years

## 7372 - Prepackaged Software (P-18556)

**EMP:** 18 **EST:** 2018
**SALES (est):** 1.01MM **Privately Held**
**SIC: 7372** Application computer software

### (P-18556)
### MODE ANALYTICS INC
Also Called: Mode
444 Castro St Ste 1000, Mountain View (94041-2070)
**PHONE**.............................415 271-7599
Gaurav Rewari, *CEO*
Bennett Stancil, *Sec*
**EMP:** 32 **EST:** 2013
**SALES (est):** 8.8MM
**SALES (corp-wide):** 91.15MM **Privately Held**
**Web:** www.mode.co
**SIC: 7372** Business oriented computer software
**PA:** Thoughtspot, Inc.
  444 Castro St Ste 1000
  800 508-7008

### (P-18557)
### MODEL MATCH INC
209 Avenida Fabricante Ste 150, San Clemente (92672-7546)
**PHONE**.............................949 525-9405
Kirk Waldfogel, *Prin*
Drew Waterhouse, *Prin*
Steve Rennie, *Prin*
Eric Levin, *Prin*
Eric Petersen, *Prin*
**EMP:** 18 **EST:** 2014
**SQ FT:** 3,400
**SALES (est):** 1.03MM **Privately Held**
**Web:** www.modelmatch.com
**SIC: 7372** Application computer software

### (P-18558)
### MOJO NETWORKS INC (HQ)
5453 Great America Pkwy, Santa Clara (95054-3645)
**PHONE**.............................650 961-1111
Rick Wilmer, *CEO*
Freddy Mangum, *CMO**
Faysal A Sohail, **
Mike Anthofer, **
**EMP:** 38 **EST:** 2003
**SALES (est):** 10.84MM **Publicly Held**
**Web:** www.arista.com
**SIC: 7372** Prepackaged software
**PA:** Arista Networks, Inc.
  5453 Great America Pkwy

### (P-18559)
### MONTAVISTA SOFTWARE LLC (DH)
2315 N 1st St 4th Fl, San Jose (95131-1010)
**PHONE**.............................408 572-8000
Art Landro, *Pr*
Sanjay Uppal, **
James Ready, **
Jason B Wacha, **
**EMP:** 100 **EST:** 1999
**SALES (est):** 8.67MM
**SALES (corp-wide):** 5.51B **Publicly Held**
**Web:** www.mvista.com
**SIC: 7372** Prepackaged software
**HQ:** Cavium, Llc
  5488 Marvell Ln
  Santa Clara CA 95054

### (P-18560)
### MOVEWORKS INC (PA)
1400 Terra Bella Ave, Mountain View (94043-3062)
**PHONE**.............................408 435-5100
Bhavin Shah, *CEO*
Vaibhav Nivargi, *Engr*
**EMP:** 36 **EST:** 2016
**SQ FT:** 818
**SALES (est):** 34.94MM
**SALES (corp-wide):** 34.94MM **Privately Held**
**Web:** www.moveworks.com
**SIC: 7372** 7371 Business oriented computer software; Custom computer programming services

### (P-18561)
### MSCSOFTWARE CORPORATION
5161 California Ave Ste 200, Irvine (92617-8002)
**PHONE**.............................714 540-8900
**EMP:** 855
**SALES (est):** 125.34MM **Privately Held**
**Web:** www.hexagon.com
**SIC: 7372** Business oriented computer software

### (P-18562)
### MULESOFT LLC
Also Called: Mulesoft, Inc.
415 Mission St Fl 3, San Francisco (94105-2504)
**PHONE**.............................800 596-4880
Greg Schott, *CEO*
Matt Langdon, *CFO*
Mark Dao, *Chief Product Officer*
**EMP:** 841 **EST:** 2006
**SQ FT:** 41,500
**SALES (est):** 11.47MM
**SALES (corp-wide):** 34.86B **Publicly Held**
**Web:** www.programmablecloud.com
**SIC: 7372** 7371 Prepackaged software; Computer software development
**PA:** Salesforce, Inc.
  415 Mission St Fl 3
  415 901-7000

### (P-18563)
### MURSION INC
2443 Fillmore St Pmb 515, San Francisco (94115-1814)
**PHONE**.............................415 746-9631
Mark Atkinson, *CEO*
Chris Laidley, **
**EMP:** 200 **EST:** 2014
**SQ FT:** 3,600
**SALES (est):** 24.5MM **Privately Held**
**Web:** www.mursion.com
**SIC: 7372** Educational computer software

### (P-18564)
### MUSICMATCH INC
16935 W Bernardo Dr Ste 270, San Diego (92127-1634)
**PHONE**.............................858 485-4300
Dennis Mudd, *CEO*
Peter Csathy, **
Gary Acord, **
Don Leigh, **
Chris Allen *Senior Vp Mkting Stragic Planning, Prin*
**EMP:** 140 **EST:** 1997
**SQ FT:** 20,000
**SALES (est):** 22.01MM **Privately Held**
**SIC: 7372** 5734 Prepackaged software; Software, business and non-game
**PA:** Altaba Inc.
  140 E 45th St Fl 15

### (P-18565)
### MUX INC (PA)
50 Beale St Fl 9, San Francisco (94105-1863)
**PHONE**.............................510 402-2257
Jonathan Dahl, *CEO*
Becca Axvig, *Pr*
**EMP:** 15 **EST:** 2015
**SALES (est):** 5.5MM
**SALES (corp-wide):** 5.5MM **Privately Held**
**Web:** www.mux.com
**SIC: 7372** Application computer software

### (P-18566)
### MY EYE MEDIA LLC
2211 N Hollywood Way, Burbank (91505-1113)
**PHONE**.............................818 559-7200
Michael Kadenacy, *Pr*
Rodd Feingold, *CFO*
**EMP:** 80 **EST:** 2004
**SQ FT:** 20,000
**SALES (est):** 10.29MM
**SALES (corp-wide):** 20.42MM **Privately Held**
**Web:** www.myeyemedia.com
**SIC: 7372** Business oriented computer software
**HQ:** Eurofins Product Testing Us Holdings, Inc.
  11720 N Creek Pkwy N Ste
  Bothell WA 98011
  800 383-0085

### (P-18567)
### MZLA TECHNOLOGIES CORPORATION
Also Called: Thunderbird
149 New Montgomery St Fl 4, San Francisco (94105-3739)
**PHONE**.............................650 903-0800
Mark Surman, *Ch Bd*
Mark Surman, *CEO*
Lisa Mccormack, *Dir Opers*
Zhilun Pang, **
**EMP:** 33 **EST:** 2019
**SALES (est):** 1.72MM
**SALES (corp-wide):** 30.69MM **Privately Held**
**Web:** www.thunderbird.net
**SIC: 7372** Prepackaged software
**PA:** Mozilla Foundation
  149 New Montgomery St
  650 903-0800

### (P-18568)
### NATIONWIDE TECHNOLOGIES INC
3684 W Uva Ln, San Bernardino (92407-1968)
**PHONE**.............................909 340-2770
Ajaydev Singh, *CEO*
Rares Sfetcu, **
**EMP:** 25 **EST:** 2019
**SALES (est):** 802.19K **Privately Held**
**SIC: 7372** 7389 Business oriented computer software; Business Activities at Non-Commercial Site

### (P-18569)
### NATIVE DATA INC
Also Called: Native
185 Berry St Ste 6850, San Francisco (94107-1798)
**PHONE**.............................855 466-9494
Matthew Mcnabb, *CEO*
David Kilcullen, *Ch Bd*
Steven Kashishian, *Dir*
**EMP:** 17 **EST:** 2014
**SALES (est):** 2.41MM **Privately Held**
**Web:** www.native.io
**SIC: 7372** 7371 Business oriented computer software; Computer software development and applications

### (P-18570)
### NAVIS LP
2001 Gateway Pl Ste 200, San Jose (95110-1056)
**PHONE**.............................408 512-2505
**EMP:** 102
**Web:** www.kaleris.com
**SIC: 7372** Prepackaged software
**PA:** Navis Lp
  3460 Prston Rdge Rd Ste 6

### (P-18571)
### NC4 SOLTRA LLC
21515 Hawthorne Blvd Ste 520, Torrance (90503-6501)
**PHONE**.............................408 489-5579
Tommy Mcdowell, *Managing Member*
**EMP:** 67 **EST:** 2016
**SALES (est):** 1.04MM
**SALES (corp-wide):** 9.82MM **Privately Held**
**SIC: 7372** Prepackaged software
**PA:** Celerium Inc.
  21515 Hawthorne Blvd # 520
  408 489-5579

### (P-18572)
### NCOUP INC (PA)
825 Corporate Way, Fremont (94539-6115)
**PHONE**.............................510 739-4010
John S Mcilwain, *Pr*
Kamar Aulakh, *COO*
**EMP:** 23 **EST:** 1994
**SALES (est):** 5.77MM **Privately Held**
**Web:** www.ncoup.com
**SIC: 7372** Publisher's computer software

### (P-18573)
### NET OPTICS INC
Also Called: Ixia
5301 Stevens Creek Blvd, Santa Clara (95051-7201)
**PHONE**.............................408 737-7777
Thomas B Miller, *CEO*
Robert Shaw, **
Burt Podbere, **
Nadine Matityahu, **
Dennis Omanoff, **
**EMP:** 85 **EST:** 1997
**SQ FT:** 39,000
**SALES (est):** 35.99MM
**SALES (corp-wide):** 5.46B **Publicly Held**
**SIC: 7372** Operating systems computer software
**HQ:** Ixia
  26601 Agoura Rd
  Calabasas CA 91302
  818 871-1800

### (P-18574)
### NETENSITY CORPORATION
1068 Balin Ct, Folsom (95630)
**PHONE**.............................855 222-8488
Adarsh Dattani, *CEO*
Adarsh P Dattani, **
**EMP:** 25 **EST:** 2010
**SALES (est):** 2.2MM **Privately Held**
**Web:** www.movegistics.com
**SIC: 7372** Business oriented computer software

### (P-18575)
### NETSARANG INC
4701 Patrick Henry Dr Bldg 22, Santa Clara (95054-1819)
**PHONE**.............................669 204-3301
Andrew Wonik Chang, *VP*
**EMP:** 15 **EST:** 2010
**SALES (est):** 177.78K **Privately Held**
**Web:** www.netsarang.com

## PRODUCTS & SERVICES SECTION
### 7372 - Prepackaged Software (P-18594)

SIC: 7372 Prepackaged software

**(P-18576)**
**NETSKOPE INC (PA)**
2445 Augustine Dr 3rd Fl, Santa Clara (95054-3032)
PHONE ................................ 800 979-6988
Sanjay Beri, *CEO*
Jason Clark, *CSO**
Lamont Orange Ciso, *Prin*
Andrew Del Matto, *
Jenefer Chin, *
EMP: 630 EST: 2012
SQ FT: 62,086
SALES (est): 450.09MM
SALES (corp-wide): 450.09MM **Privately Held**
Web: www.netskope.com
SIC: 7372 7371 Application computer software; Computer software development

**(P-18577)**
**NETSOL TECHNOLOGIES INC (PA)**
Also Called: NETSOL
16000 Ventura Blvd Ste 770, Encino (91436-2758)
PHONE ................................ 818 222-9195
Najeeb Ghauri, *Ch Bd*
Naeem Ghauri, *Pr*
Roger Almond, *CFO*
Erik Wagner, *CMO*
Patti L W Mcglasson, *Sr VP*
EMP: 86 EST: 1997
SQ FT: 2,400
SALES (est): 61.39MM
SALES (corp-wide): 61.39MM **Publicly Held**
Web: www.netsoltech.com
SIC: 7372 7373 7299 Business oriented computer software; Computer integrated systems design; Personal document and information services

**(P-18578)**
**NETSUITE INC (DH)**
Also Called: Oracle
2955 Campus Dr Ste 100, San Mateo (94403-2539)
PHONE ................................ 650 627-1000
Dorian Daley, *Pr*
Jim Mcgeever, *Ex VP*
Evan Goldberg, *
Jason Maynard, *
David Rodman, *
EMP: 892 EST: 1998
SQ FT: 165,000
SALES (est): 403.23B
SALES (corp-wide): 52.96B **Publicly Held**
Web: www.netsuite.com
SIC: 7372 Business oriented computer software
HQ: Oc Acquisition Llc
500 Oracle Parkway
Redwood City CA 94065
650 506-7000

**(P-18579)**
**NETWORK AUTOMATION INC**
3530 Wilshire Blvd Ste 1800, Los Angeles (90010-2335)
PHONE ................................ 213 738-1700
Dustin Snell, *CEO*
Graham Taylor, *
EMP: 50 EST: 2004
SQ FT: 9,000
SALES (est): 2.68MM
SALES (corp-wide): 1.88MM **Privately Held**
Web: www.fortra.com
SIC: 7372 Business oriented computer software
HQ: Fortra, Llc
11095 Viking Dr Ste 100
Eden Prairie MN 55344
952 933-0609

**(P-18580)**
**NETWRIX CORPORATION**
300 Spectrum Center Dr Ste 200, Irvine (92618-4987)
PHONE ................................ 888 638-9749
Steve Dickson, *Brnch Mgr*
EMP: 65
SALES (corp-wide): 942.12MM **Privately Held**
Web: www.netwrix.com
SIC: 7372 Prepackaged software
HQ: Netwrix Corporation
6160 Warren Pkwy Ste 100
Frisco TX 75034

**(P-18581)**
**NEW BI US GAMING LLC**
10920 Via Frontera Ste 420, San Diego (92127-1729)
PHONE ................................ 858 592-2472
Ian Bonner, *CEO*
Russell Schechter, *
Kimberly Armstrong, *
EMP: 92 EST: 2012
SALES (est): 2.05MM **Privately Held**
Web: www.vizexplorer.com
SIC: 7372 Prepackaged software

**(P-18582)**
**NEW GENERATION SOFTWARE INC**
Also Called: N G S
3835 N Freeway Blvd Ste 200, Sacramento (95834-1954)
PHONE ................................ 916 920-2200
Bernard B Gough, *CEO*
EMP: 45 EST: 1982
SQ FT: 10,000
SALES (est): 2.12MM **Privately Held**
Web: www.ngsi.com
SIC: 7372 Application computer software

**(P-18583)**
**NEW RELIC INC (HQ)**
188 Spear St Fl 11, San Francisco (94105)
PHONE ................................ 650 777-7600
William Staples, *CEO*
Lewis Cirne, *Non-Executive Chairman of the Board**
David Barter, *CFO*
Kristy Friedrichs, *COO*
Mark Dodds, *CRO*
EMP: 2474 EST: 2007
SQ FT: 73,000
SALES (est): 925.63MM
SALES (corp-wide): 925.63MM **Privately Held**
Web: www.newrelic.com
SIC: 7372 Prepackaged software
PA: Crewline Buyer, Inc.
188 Spear St Ste 1000
415 539-3008

**(P-18584)**
**NEXENTA BY DDN INC**
2025 Gateway Pl Ste 160, San Jose (95110-1059)
PHONE ................................ 408 791-3300
Tarkan Maner, *CEO*
EMP: 24 EST: 2019
SALES (est): 992.19K
SALES (corp-wide): 175.84MM **Privately Held**
Web: www.nexenta.com
SIC: 7372 Prepackaged software
PA: Datadirect Networks, Inc.
9351 Deering Ave
818 700-7600

**(P-18585)**
**NEXOGY INC**
10967 Via Frontera, San Diego (92127-1703)
PHONE ................................ 305 358-8952
Felipe Lahrssen, *VP*
EMP: 65 EST: 2005
SALES (est): 2.8MM
SALES (corp-wide): 31.62MM **Publicly Held**
Web: www.vervecloud.com
SIC: 7372 8741 Business oriented computer software; Management services
HQ: T3 Communications, Inc.
1610 Royal Palm Ave
Fort Myers FL 33901
239 333-0000

**(P-18586)**
**NEXTGEN HEALTHCARE INC (HQ)**
18111 Von Karman Ave Ste 600, Irvine (92612-7100)
PHONE ................................ 949 255-2600
David Sides, *Pr*
Jeffrey H Margolis, *Ch Bd*
James R Arnold Junior, *Ex VP*
Srinivas S Velamoor, *Chief Growth Vice President*
Mitchell L Waters, *Executive Commercial Vice President*
EMP: 475 EST: 1974
SALES (est): 653.17MM **Privately Held**
Web: www.nextgen.com
SIC: 7372 7373 Prepackaged software; Computer integrated systems design
PA: Thoma Bravo, L.P.
110 N Wacker Dr Fl 32

**(P-18587)**
**NEXTPATIENT INC**
655 Victoria St, San Francisco (94127-2836)
PHONE ................................ 617 504-4726
David Rodriguez, *CEO*
David Rodriguez, *Prin*
EMP: 25 EST: 2015
SALES (est): 3.93MM **Privately Held**
Web: www.nextpatient.co
SIC: 7372 Business oriented computer software

**(P-18588)**
**NEXTRACKER INC (PA)**
6200 Paseo Padre Pkwy, Fremont (94555-3601)
PHONE ................................ 510 270-2500
Daniel Shugar, *CEO*
William Watkins, *Ch Bd*
Howard Wenger, *Pr*
Charles Boynton, *CFO*
David P Bennett, *CAO*
EMP: 59 EST: 2013
SQ FT: 44,000
SALES (est): 2.5B
SALES (corp-wide): 2.5B **Publicly Held**
Web: www.nextracker.com
SIC: 7372 1711 Prepackaged software; Solar energy contractor

**(P-18589)**
**NEXTRACKER LLC (HQ)**
6200 Paseo Padre Pkwy, Fremont (94555-3601)
PHONE ................................ 510 270-2500
Daniel Shugar, *CEO*
Bruce Ledesma, *
Dave Bennett, *
Alex Au, *
Leah Schlesinger, *
◆ EMP: 126 EST: 2013
SQ FT: 30,000
SALES (est): 75.92MM
SALES (corp-wide): 2.5B **Publicly Held**
Web: www.nextracker.com
SIC: 7372 1711 Prepackaged software; Solar energy contractor
PA: Nextracker Inc.
6200 Paseo Padre Pkwy
510 270-2500

**(P-18590)**
**NEXTROLL INC (PA)**
Also Called: Adroll
201 California St Ste 500, San Francisco (94111-5028)
PHONE ................................ 415 236-3956
Roli Saxena, *CEO*
Aaron Bell, *CPO**
Peter Krivkovich, *
Sue Choe, *
Laura Zwahlen, *CRO**
EMP: 695 EST: 2006
SALES (est): 94.87MM
SALES (corp-wide): 94.87MM **Privately Held**
Web: www.nextroll.com
SIC: 7372 Prepackaged software

**(P-18591)**
**NGROK INC**
548 Market St Pmb 26741, San Francisco (94104-5401)
PHONE ................................ 415 323-4184
Alan Shreve, *CEO*
EMP: 80 EST: 2015
SALES (est): 13.52MM **Privately Held**
Web: www.ngrok.com
SIC: 7372 Application computer software

**(P-18592)**
**NILE AI INC**
15260 Ventura Blvd Ste 1410, Sherman Oaks (91403-5348)
PHONE ................................ 818 689-9107
Artin Davidian, *Admn*
EMP: 25 EST: 2020
SALES (est): 1.46MM
SALES (corp-wide): 1.04B **Privately Held**
SIC: 7372 Application computer software
HQ: Ucb Holdings, Inc.
1950 Lake Park Dr
Smyrna GA 30080
770 970-7500

**(P-18593)**
**NIS AMERICA INC**
4 Hutton Centre Dr Ste 650, Santa Ana (92707-8726)
PHONE ................................ 714 540-1122
Souhei Niikawa, *CEO*
Harusato Akenaga, *
Mitsuharu Hiraoka, *
Johanna Hirota, *
▲ EMP: 40 EST: 2003
SQ FT: 1,000
SALES (est): 8.83MM **Privately Held**
Web: www.nisamerica.com
SIC: 7372 Publisher's computer software

**(P-18594)**
**NIUM INC**
85 2nd St Fl 2, San Francisco (94105-3459)

## 7372 - Prepackaged Software (P-18595)

PHONE.................732 492-6908
Prajit Nanu, *CEO*
**EMP:** 42
**SALES (est):** 658.38K **Privately Held**
**Web:** www.nium.com
**SIC:** 7372 Prepackaged software

*(P-18595)*
### NOK NOK LABS INC
2890 Zanker Rd Ste 203, San Jose (95134-2118)
PHONE.................650 433-1300
Phil Dunkelberger, *CEO*
David Wiener, *VP*
**EMP:** 16 **EST:** 2011
**SALES (est):** 6.14MM **Privately Held**
**Web:** www.noknok.com
**SIC:** 7372 Business oriented computer software

*(P-18596)*
### NOMINUM INC
3355 Scott Blvd Fl 3, Santa Clara (95054-3127)
PHONE.................650 381-6000
Garry Messiana, *CEO*
Pete Wisowaty, *
Bob Verheecke, *
**EMP:** 126 **EST:** 1999
**SQ FT:** 15,000
**SALES (est):** 24.79MM
**SALES (corp-wide):** 3.81B **Publicly Held**
**SIC:** 7372 Prepackaged software
**PA:** Akamai Technologies, Inc.
145 Broadway
617 444-3000

*(P-18597)*
### NORTH BEAM INC
338 Main St Unit 32d, San Francisco (94105-2156)
PHONE.................860 940-4569
David Swenton, *CEO*
**EMP:** 36
**SALES (est):** 5.31MM **Privately Held**
**SIC:** 7372 7389 Prepackaged software; Business services, nec

*(P-18598)*
### NOVA MODULE LP
7901 Oakport St Ste 4250, Oakland (94621-2015)
PHONE.................415 323-0520
Basang Malunov, *Pt*
**EMP:** 45 **EST:** 2014
**SALES (est):** 3.16MM **Privately Held**
**Web:** www.novamodule.com
**SIC:** 7372 Prepackaged software

*(P-18599)*
### NOVASTOR CORPORATION (PA)
29209 Canwood St Ste 200, Agoura Hills (91301-1908)
PHONE.................805 579-6700
Peter Means, *Pr*
Martin Albert, *
**EMP:** 30 **EST:** 1987
**SQ FT:** 7,800
**SALES (est):** 4.17MM
**SALES (corp-wide):** 4.17MM **Privately Held**
**Web:** www.novastor.com
**SIC:** 7372 7371 5734 Business oriented computer software; Custom computer programming services; Software, business and non-game

*(P-18600)*
### NR2B RESEARCH INC
2121 S El Camino Real Ste 1000, San Mateo (94403-1864)
PHONE.................732 492-6908
Robert Hutter, *CEO*
Eric Garay, *
David Brevik, *
Bhavin Shah, *
**EMP:** 300 **EST:** 2005
**SQ FT:** 50,000
**SALES (est):** 7.27MM **Privately Held**
**SIC:** 7372 Publisher's computer software

*(P-18601)*
### NREACH ONLINE SERVICES INC
303 Twin Dolphin Dr Ste 6080, Redwood City (94065-1497)
PHONE.................425 301-9168
Mayank Singh, *Sr VP*
**EMP:** 400 **EST:** 2019
**SALES (est):** 40MM **Privately Held**
**SIC:** 7372 Prepackaged software

*(P-18602)*
### NTRUST INFOTECH INC
230 Commerce Ste 180, Irvine (92602-1336)
PHONE.................562 207-1600
Srikanth Ramachandran, *CEO*
**EMP:** 65 **EST:** 2003
**SALES (est):** 5.59MM **Privately Held**
**Web:** www.ntrustinfotech.com
**SIC:** 7372 Business oriented computer software; Computer software development and applications

*(P-18603)*
### NUMECENT INC
18565 Jamboree Rd, Irvine (92612-2532)
PHONE.................949 833-2800
Tom Lagatta, *CEO*
Osman Kent, *
Ed Corrente, *
Hildy Shandell, *
**EMP:** 30 **EST:** 2012
**SALES (est):** 4.43MM **Privately Held**
**Web:** www.numecent.com
**SIC:** 7372 Application computer software

*(P-18604)*
### NUMERICAL TECHNOLOGIES INC
70 W Plumeria Dr, San Jose (95134-2134)
PHONE.................408 919-1910
Naren Gupta, *Pr*
Yagyensh C Pati, *
William H Davidow, *
Richard Mora, *
**EMP:** 215 **EST:** 1995
**SQ FT:** 39,300
**SALES (est):** 3.62MM
**SALES (corp-wide):** 5.84B **Publicly Held**
**SIC:** 7372 7374 Business oriented computer software; Data processing and preparation
**PA:** Synopsys, Inc.
675 Almanor Ave
650 584-5000

*(P-18605)*
### NUTANIX INC (PA)
Also Called: Nutanix
1740 Technology Dr Ste 150, San Jose (95110-1348)
PHONE.................408 216-8360
Rajiv Ramaswami, *Pr*
Rukmini Sivaraman, *CFO*
David Sangster, *COO*
Tyler Wall, *CLO*
**EMP:** 623 **EST:** 2009
**SQ FT:** 333,000
**SALES (est):** 2.15B **Publicly Held**
**Web:** www.nutanix.com

**SIC:** 7372 7371 Prepackaged software; Computer software development

*(P-18606)*
### NUTSTAR SOFTWARE LLC
1460 W 18th St, Merced (95340-4403)
PHONE.................209 250-1324
Frank Ramos, *Pr*
**EMP:** 15 **EST:** 2012
**SALES (est):** 1.2MM **Privately Held**
**Web:** www.nutstar.net
**SIC:** 7372 Prepackaged software

*(P-18607)*
### NWP SERVICES CORPORATION (DH)
535 Anton Blvd Ste 1100, Costa Mesa (92626-7699)
P.O. Box 19661 (92623-9661)
PHONE.................949 253-2500
Ron Reed, *Pr*
Lana Reeve, *CLO**
Mike Haviken, *
**EMP:** 141 **EST:** 1995
**SQ FT:** 21,171
**SALES (est):** 37.12MM **Privately Held**
**Web:** www.mynwpsc.com
**SIC:** 7372 8721 Utility computer software; Billing and bookkeeping service
**HQ:** Realpage, Inc.
2201 Lakeside Blvd
Richardson TX 75082
972 820-3000

*(P-18608)*
### NXGN MANAGEMENT LLC
18111 Von Karman Ave Ste 600, Irvine (92612-0199)
PHONE.................949 255-2600
**EMP:** 45 **EST:** 2021
**SALES (est):** 11.23MM **Privately Held**
**Web:** www.nextgen.com
**SIC:** 7372 Prepackaged software
**HQ:** Nextgen Healthcare, Inc.
18111 Von Krman Ave Ste 6
Irvine CA 92612
949 255-2600

*(P-18609)*
### NYANSA INC
430 Cowper St Ste 250, Palo Alto (94301-1579)
PHONE.................650 446-7818
Abe Ankumah, *CEO*
Anand Srinivas, *
Daniel Kan, *
**EMP:** 45 **EST:** 2013
**SALES (est):** 2.49MM
**SALES (corp-wide):** 35.82B **Publicly Held**
**Web:** www.nyansa.com
**SIC:** 7372 Application computer software
**HQ:** Vmware Llc
3421 Hillview Ave
Palo Alto CA 94304
650 427-6000

*(P-18610)*
### OCCIDENTAL SYSTEMS INC
131a Stony Cir Ste 500, Santa Rosa (95401-9600)
PHONE.................800 902-4393
Kelly Clark, *CEO*
**EMP:** 15 **EST:** 2022
**SALES (est):** 630.9K **Privately Held**
**SIC:** 7372 Business oriented computer software

*(P-18611)*
### OCKAM INC
535 Mission St Fl 14, San Francisco (94105-3253)
PHONE.................415 407-3800
Matthew Gregory, *Pr*
Logan Gager, *COO*
**EMP:** 20 **EST:** 2017
**SALES (est):** 3.33MM **Privately Held**
**Web:** www.ockam.io
**SIC:** 7372 Prepackaged software

*(P-18612)*
### OEA INTERNATIONAL INCORPORATED
155 E Main Ave Ste 130, Morgan Hill (95037-7521)
PHONE.................408 778-6747
**FAX:** 408 778-6748
**EMP:** 25
**SALES (est):** 2MM **Privately Held**
**Web:** www.oea.com
**SIC:** 7372 Prepackaged software

*(P-18613)*
### OKERA INC
600 California St Fl 15, San Francisco (94108-2728)
PHONE.................415 741-3282
Nong Li, *CEO*
**EMP:** 55 **EST:** 2016
**SALES (est):** 3.92MM
**SALES (corp-wide):** 451.22MM **Privately Held**
**Web:** www.okera.com
**SIC:** 7372 Prepackaged software
**PA:** Databricks, Inc.
160 Spear St Fl 15
866 330-0121

*(P-18614)*
### OKTA INC (PA)
Also Called: OKTA
100 1st St Ste 600, San Francisco (94105-3513)
PHONE.................888 722-7871
Todd Mckinnon, *Ch Bd*
J Frederic Kerrest, *Executive Vice Chairman of the Board**
Brett Tighe, *CFO*
Shibu Ninan, *CAO*
Larissa Schwartz, *CLO*
**EMP:** 5530 **EST:** 2009
**SQ FT:** 285,996
**SALES (est):** 1.86B
**SALES (corp-wide):** 1.86B **Publicly Held**
**Web:** www.okta.com
**SIC:** 7372 7371 Prepackaged software; Software programming applications

*(P-18615)*
### OMNISSA LLC ◊
590 E Middlefield Rd, Mountain View (94043)
PHONE.................650 239-7600
Shanker Iyer, *CEO*
**EMP:** 3700 **EST:** 2024
**SALES (est):** 23.76MM
**SALES (corp-wide):** 35.82B **Publicly Held**
**SIC:** 7372 Prepackaged software
**PA:** Broadcom Inc.
3421 Hillview Ave
650 427-6000

*(P-18616)*
### OMNITRACS MIDCO LLC
9276 Scranton Rd Ste 200, San Diego (92121-7703)
PHONE.................858 651-5812
**EMP:** 30 **EST:** 2013

# PRODUCTS & SERVICES SECTION
## 7372 - Prepackaged Software (P-18638)

SALES (est): 2.64MM **Privately Held**
Web: www.omnitracs.com
SIC: 7372 Business oriented computer software

**(P-18617)**
**ON24 INC (PA)**
50 Beale St Fl 8, San Francisco (94105-1863)
PHONE.....................415 369-8000
Sharat Sharan, *Pr*
Steven Vattuone, *CFO*
James Blackie, *CRO*
Jayesh Sahasi, *Ex VP*
Steven Long, *CIO*
EMP: 366 EST: 1998
SQ FT: 31,182
SALES (est): 163.71MM
SALES (corp-wide): 163.71MM **Publicly Held**
Web: www.on24.com
SIC: 7372 Business oriented computer software

**(P-18618)**
**ONELOGIN INC (DH)**
848 Battery St, San Francisco (94111-1504)
PHONE.....................415 645-6830
Bradford Brooks, *CEO*
Bernard Huger, *CFO*
EMP: 175 EST: 2009
SQ FT: 44,461
SALES (est): 23.84MM
SALES (corp-wide): 647.68MM **Privately Held**
Web: www.onelogin.com
SIC: 7372 Prepackaged software
HQ: One Identity Llc
20 Enterprise Ste 100
Aliso Viejo CA 92656
949 754-8000

**(P-18619)**
**ONESIGNAL INC (PA)**
Also Called: Onesignal
201 S B St Ste 200, San Mateo (94401-4283)
PHONE.....................408 506-0701
George Deglin, *CEO*
George Deglin, *Pr*
Long Vo, *
EMP: 148 EST: 2011
SALES (est): 10.01MM
SALES (corp-wide): 10.01MM **Privately Held**
Web: www.onesignal.com
SIC: 7372 Business oriented computer software

**(P-18620)**
**ONTRAPORT INC**
2030 Alameda Padre Serra Ste 200, Santa Barbara (93103-1704)
PHONE.....................855 668-7276
Landon Ray, *CEO*
Lena Requist, *
EMP: 98 EST: 2006
SQ FT: 35,000
SALES (est): 20.78MM **Privately Held**
Web: www.ontraport.com
SIC: 7372 Business oriented computer software

**(P-18621)**
**ONVANTAGE INC**
3290 Freedom Cir # 200, Santa Clara (95054)
PHONE.....................408 562-3388
John Chang, *CEO*

David K Hunt, *
Edward J Tromczynski, *DIV**
Stanley Chin, *Corporate President**
Paul S Nestvold, *
EMP: 100 EST: 1991
SQ FT: 22,000
SALES (est): 5.35MM **Privately Held**
SIC: 7372 Prepackaged software

**(P-18622)**
**ONYMOS INC**
1600 El Camino Real, Menlo Park (94025-4119)
P.O. Box 351  (94002-0351)
PHONE.....................650 504-8037
Shivaguru Nathan, *CEO*
EMP: 40 EST: 2017
SALES (est): 4.62MM **Privately Held**
Web: www.onymos.com
SIC: 7372 Application computer software

**(P-18623)**
**OPEN SYSTEMS INC**
5250 Lankershim Blvd Ste 620, North Hollywood (91601-3186)
PHONE.....................317 566-6662
EMP: 46
SALES (corp-wide): 957.93MM **Privately Held**
Web: www.aptean.com
SIC: 7372 Business oriented computer software
HQ: Open Systems, Inc.
4325 Alexander Dr Ste 100
Alpharetta GA 30022
952 403-5700

**(P-18624)**
**OPENAI INC (PA)**
1960 Bryant St, San Francisco (94110-1409)
PHONE.....................650 387-6701
Sam Altman, *CEO*
Greg Brockman, *Pr*
Sarah Friar, *CFO*
Kevin Weil, *CPO*
EMP: 34 EST: 2015
SALES (est): 363.25MM
SALES (corp-wide): 363.25MM **Privately Held**
Web: www.openai.com
SIC: 7372 Prepackaged software

**(P-18625)**
**OPENTV INC**
Also Called: Nagra
275 Sacramento St, San Francisco (94111-3810)
PHONE.....................415 962-5000
EMP: 325
SIC: 7372 Prepackaged software

**(P-18626)**
**OPENWAVE MOBILITY INC (DH)**
303 Twin Dolphin Dr Ste 600, Redwood City (94065-1409)
PHONE.....................650 480-7200
John Paul Giere, *Pr*
Poh Sim Gan, *
EMP: 31 EST: 2012
SALES (est): 11.75MM
SALES (corp-wide): 6.45MM **Privately Held**
Web: www.enea.com
SIC: 7372 Prepackaged software
HQ: Enea Software Ab
Jan Stenbecks Torg 17
Kista 164 4
850714000

**(P-18627)**
**OPERA SOFTWARE INTERNATIONAL AS**
1875 S Grant St Ste 750, San Mateo (94402-2670)
PHONE.....................650 625-8470
EMP: 35
SIC: 7372 Application computer software

**(P-18628)**
**OPSCRUISE INC**
5255 Stevens Creek Blvd Ste 179, Santa Clara (95051-6664)
PHONE.....................916 204-4369
Scott Fulton, *CEO*
Aloke Guha, *
EMP: 30 EST: 2018
SALES (est): 5MM **Privately Held**
Web: www.virtana.com
SIC: 7372 Prepackaged software

**(P-18629)**
**OPTIMISCORP**
200 Mantua Rd, Pacific Palisades (90272-3349)
PHONE.....................310 230-2780
Alan Morelli, *CEO*
EMP: 60 EST: 2006
SALES (est): 3.45MM **Privately Held**
Web: www.optimiscorp.com
SIC: 7372 Business oriented computer software

**(P-18630)**
**OPTIMUM SOLUTIONS GROUP LLC**
419 Ponderosa Ct, Lafayette (94549-1812)
PHONE.....................415 954-7100
EMP: 17 EST: 1999
SQ FT: 3,300
SALES (est): 2.9MM
SALES (corp-wide): 1.34B **Privately Held**
Web: advisory.kpmg.us
SIC: 7372 7371 8243 7374 Prepackaged software; Computer software systems analysis and design, custom; Data processing schools; Computer graphics service
PA: Kpmg Llp
345 Park Ave
212 758-9700

**(P-18631)**
**OPTIWISE AI INC**
Also Called: Optiwise.ai
37298 Aleppo Dr, Newark (94560-3326)
PHONE.....................408 480-0482
Deepak Kumar Goyal, *CEO*
Ravinder P Singh, *Sec*
EMP: 16 EST: 2022
SALES (est): 1.61MM **Privately Held**
SIC: 7372 7371 Operating systems computer software; Computer software development and applications

**(P-18632)**
**ORACLE AMERICA INC**
4120 Network Cir, Santa Clara (95054-1778)
PHONE.....................408 276-3331
EMP: 150 EST: 1986
SALES (est): 7.08MM **Privately Held**
Web: www.jcp.org
SIC: 7372 Prepackaged software

**(P-18633)**
**ORACLE CORPORATION**
Also Called: Oracle
5805 Owens Dr, Pleasanton (94588-3939)

PHONE.....................877 767-2253
EMP: 36
SALES (corp-wide): 52.96B **Publicly Held**
Web: www.oracle.com
SIC: 7372 Business oriented computer software
PA: Oracle Corporation
2300 Oracle Way
737 867-1000

**(P-18634)**
**ORACLE CORPORATION**
Also Called: Oracle
1001 Sunset Blvd, Rocklin (95765-3702)
PHONE.....................916 315-3500
Chris Wilson, *Brnch Mgr*
EMP: 500
SALES (corp-wide): 52.96B **Publicly Held**
Web: www.oracle.com
SIC: 7372 7371 Business oriented computer software; Custom computer programming services
PA: Oracle Corporation
2300 Oracle Way
737 867-1000

**(P-18635)**
**ORACLE CORPORATION**
Also Called: Oracle
6020 West Oaks Blvd Ste 200, Rocklin (95765-5472)
PHONE.....................916 315-3500
James Kirkley, *Prin*
EMP: 47
SALES (corp-wide): 52.96B **Publicly Held**
Web: www.oracle.com
SIC: 7372 Prepackaged software
PA: Oracle Corporation
2300 Oracle Way
737 867-1000

**(P-18636)**
**ORACLE CORPORATION**
Also Called: Oracle
200 Oracle Pkwy, Redwood City (94065-1668)
PHONE.....................415 834-9731
Lisa Schwarz, *Dir*
EMP: 33
SALES (corp-wide): 52.96B **Publicly Held**
Web: www.oracle.com
SIC: 7372 Prepackaged software
PA: Oracle Corporation
2300 Oracle Way
737 867-1000

**(P-18637)**
**ORACLE CORPORATION**
Also Called: Oracle
1 Bolero, Mission Viejo (92692-5164)
PHONE.....................626 315-7513
Hemesh Surana, *Brnch Mgr*
EMP: 302
SALES (corp-wide): 52.96B **Publicly Held**
Web: www.oracle.com
SIC: 7372 Prepackaged software
PA: Oracle Corporation
2300 Oracle Way
737 867-1000

**(P-18638)**
**ORACLE CORPORATION**
Also Called: Oracle
3005 Bunker Hill Ln, Santa Clara (95054-1106)
PHONE.....................408 986-8800
EMP: 60
SALES (corp-wide): 52.96B **Publicly Held**
Web: www.oracle.com

## 7372 - Prepackaged Software (P-18639)

SIC: 7372 7379 8243 3571 Prepackaged software; Computer related consulting services; Software training, computer; Minicomputers
PA: Oracle Corporation
2300 Oracle Way
737 867-1000

**(P-18639)**
**ORACLE CORPORATION**
500 Oracle Pkwy, Redwood City (94065-1677)
PHONE..................650 506-7000
EMP: 22
SALES (corp-wide): 52.96B **Publicly Held**
Web: www.oracle.com
SIC: 7372 Prepackaged software
PA: Oracle Corporation
2300 Oracle Way
737 867-1000

**(P-18640)**
**ORACLE INTERNATIONAL CORP (HQ)**
500 Oracle Pkwy, Redwood City (94065)
PHONE..................650 506-7000
Dorian Daley, *CEO*
EMP: 19 EST: 2001
SALES (est): 4.4MM
SALES (corp-wide): 52.96B **Publicly Held**
SIC: 7372 Prepackaged software
PA: Oracle Corporation
2300 Oracle Way
737 867-1000

**(P-18641)**
**ORACLE JAPAN HOLDING INC (HQ)**
Also Called: Oracle
500 Oracle Pkwy, Redwood City (94065-1677)
PHONE..................650 506-7000
Safra A Catz, *CEO*
EMP: 52 EST: 1991
SALES (est): 16.66MM
SALES (corp-wide): 52.96B **Publicly Held**
Web: www.oracle.com
SIC: 7372 Prepackaged software
PA: Oracle Corporation
2300 Oracle Way
737 867-1000

**(P-18642)**
**ORACLE SYSTEMS CORPORATION**
Also Called: Oracle
301 Island Pkwy, Belmont (94002-4109)
PHONE..................650 654-7606
EMP: 21
SALES (corp-wide): 52.96B **Publicly Held**
SIC: 7372 Prepackaged software
HQ: Oracle Systems Corporation
500 Oracle Pkwy
Redwood City CA 94065

**(P-18643)**
**ORACLE SYSTEMS CORPORATION**
Also Called: Oracle
500 Oracle Pwky, San Mateo (94403)
PHONE..................650 506-6780
Sayekumar Arumugam, *Prin*
EMP: 16
SALES (corp-wide): 52.96B **Publicly Held**
SIC: 7372 Prepackaged software
HQ: Oracle Systems Corporation
500 Oracle Pkwy
Redwood City CA 94065

**(P-18644)**
**ORACLE SYSTEMS CORPORATION**
Also Called: Oracle
501 Island Pkwy, Belmont (94002-4153)
PHONE..................650 506-5062
Michael Rocha, *Brnch Mgr*
EMP: 19
SALES (corp-wide): 52.96B **Publicly Held**
Web: www.christianwimmer.at
SIC: 7372 Prepackaged software
HQ: Oracle Systems Corporation
500 Oracle Pkwy
Redwood City CA 94065

**(P-18645)**
**ORACLE SYSTEMS CORPORATION**
Also Called: Support Sales
300 Oracle Pkwy, Redwood City (94065-1667)
PHONE..................650 506-5887
Sam Mohamad, *VP*
EMP: 24
SALES (corp-wide): 52.96B **Publicly Held**
SIC: 7372 Prepackaged software
HQ: Oracle Systems Corporation
500 Oracle Pkwy
Redwood City CA 94065

**(P-18646)**
**ORACLE SYSTEMS CORPORATION**
Also Called: Oracle
5840 Owens Dr, Pleasanton (94588-3900)
PHONE..................925 694-3000
Apu Gupta, *Prin*
EMP: 27
SALES (corp-wide): 52.96B **Publicly Held**
Web: www.oracle.com
SIC: 7372 5734 Prepackaged software; Software, business and non-game
HQ: Oracle Systems Corporation
500 Oracle Pkwy
Redwood City CA 94065

**(P-18647)**
**ORACLE TALEO LLC (HQ)**
4140 Dublin Blvd Ste 400, Dublin (94568-7757)
PHONE..................925 452-3000
Dorian Daley, *Pr*
Eric Ball, *
Neil Hudspith, *Executive Worldwide Field Operations Vice President*
Guy Gauvin, *Executive Global Services Vice President*
Jason Blessing, *Senior Vice President Products*
EMP: 100 EST: 1999
SQ FT: 47,500
SALES (est): 18.33MM
SALES (corp-wide): 52.96B **Publicly Held**
Web: www.oracle.com
SIC: 7372 Business oriented computer software
PA: Oracle Corporation
2300 Oracle Way
737 867-1000

**(P-18648)**
**ORACLE USA INC**
500 Oracle Pkwy, Redwood City (94065-1677)
PHONE..................650 506-7000
EMP: 526
SIC: 7372 Prepackaged software

**(P-18649)**
**OSR ENTERPRISES INC**
1910 E Stowell Rd, Santa Maria (93454-8002)
P.O. Box 7200 (93456)
PHONE..................805 925-1831
James O Rice, *CEO*
Owen S Rice, *
Betty E Rice, *
EMP: 45 EST: 1937
SQ FT: 1,500
SALES (est): 11.09MM **Privately Held**
Web: www.osrenterprises.com
SIC: 7372 Publisher's computer software

**(P-18650)**
**OUTPUT INC**
3014 Worthen Ave, Los Angeles (90039-2830)
PHONE..................888 803-3175
Gregg Lehrmann, *CEO*
Gregg Lehrmann, *Pr*
Justin Calpito, *Asstg*
EMP: 18 EST: 2013
SALES (est): 8.77MM **Privately Held**
Web: www.output.com
SIC: 7372 Application computer software

**(P-18651)**
**OUTREACH CORPORATION**
Also Called: Sales & Marketing
600 California St Fl 7, San Francisco (94108-2731)
PHONE..................888 938-7356
EMP: 269
SALES (corp-wide): 101.15MM **Privately Held**
Web: www.outreach.io
SIC: 7372 Business oriented computer software
PA: Outreach Corporation
333 Elliott Ave W Ste 500
206 235-3672

**(P-18652)**
**PACSGEAR INC**
4309 Hacienda Dr Ste 500, Pleasanton (94588-2768)
PHONE..................925 225-6100
EMP: 51
SIC: 7372 Business oriented computer software

**(P-18653)**
**PALO ALTO NETWORKS INC (PA)**
3000 Tannery Way, Santa Clara (95054-2832)
PHONE..................408 753-4000
Nikesh Arora, *Ch Bd*
William Jenkins, *Pr*
Dipak Golechha, *Ex VP*
Josh Paul, *CAO*
EMP: 500 EST: 2005
SQ FT: 941,000
SALES (est): 8.03B
SALES (corp-wide): 8.03B **Publicly Held**
Web: www.paloaltonetworks.com
SIC: 7372 3577 Prepackaged software; Computer peripheral equipment, nec

**(P-18654)**
**PANDADOC INC**
400 Spear St Apt 217, San Francisco (94105-1697)
PHONE..................415 860-0176
Ena Zheng, *Brnch Mgr*
EMP: 24
SALES (corp-wide): 47MM **Privately Held**
Web: www.pandadoc.com

SIC: 7372 Business oriented computer software
PA: Pandadoc, Inc.
3739 Balboa St
415 779-0222

**(P-18655)**
**PANORAMIC SOFTWARE CORPORATION**
Also Called: Panosoft
9650 Research Dr, Irvine (92618-4666)
PHONE..................877 558-8526
Jeff Von Waldburg, *Pr*
EMP: 17 EST: 1990
SQ FT: 1,500
SALES (est): 1.55MM **Privately Held**
Web: www.panosoft.com
SIC: 7372 7371 Prepackaged software; Custom computer programming services

**(P-18656)**
**PAPAYA**
14140 Ventura Blvd Ste 209, Sherman Oaks (91423-2774)
PHONE..................310 740-6774
Dan Mintz, *Prin*
EMP: 35 EST: 2019
SALES (est): 3.92MM **Privately Held**
Web: www.papayaclothing.com
SIC: 7372 Prepackaged software

**(P-18657)**
**PARABLU INC**
38350 Fremont Blvd # 203, Fremont (94536-6060)
PHONE..................408 775-6571
EMP: 35
SALES (est): 3.09MM **Privately Held**
Web: www.parablu.com
SIC: 7372 Prepackaged software

**(P-18658)**
**PARALLEL MACHINES INC**
Also Called: Parallelm
2445 Augustine Dr Ste 150, Santa Clara (95054-3032)
PHONE..................669 467-2638
Sivan Metzger, *CEO*
Michal Kirshner, *CFO*
EMP: 15 EST: 2015
SALES (est): 2.45MM
SALES (corp-wide): 151.94MM **Privately Held**
Web: www.datarobot.com
SIC: 7372 Business oriented computer software
PA: Datarobot, Inc.
225 Franklin St Ste 1300
617 765-4500

**(P-18659)**
**PARENTSQUARE INC**
6144 Calle Real Ste 200a, Goleta (93117-2012)
PHONE..................888 496-3168
Sohit Wadhwa, *CEO*
Anupama Vaid, *Prin*
EMP: 65 EST: 2011
SALES (est): 5.71MM **Privately Held**
Web: www.parentsquare.com
SIC: 7372 Educational computer software

**(P-18660)**
**PATIENTPOP INC**
214 Wilshire Blvd, Santa Monica (90401-1202)
PHONE..................844 487-8399
Travis Schneider, *CEO*
Luke Kervin, *
David Mcneil, *Pr*

**PRODUCTS & SERVICES SECTION**

**7372 - Prepackaged Software (P-18680)**

Jason Gardner, *
Taylor Timmer, *
**EMP:** 51 **EST:** 2015
**SALES (est):** 5.59MM Privately Held
**Web:** www.tebra.com
**SIC: 7372** Business oriented computer software

**(P-18661)**
**PATRON SOLUTIONS LLC**
5171 California Ave Ste 200, Irvine (92617-3066)
**PHONE**..................................949 823-1700
Steve Shaw, *Owner*
**EMP:** 245 **EST:** 2015
**SALES (est):** 8.66MM Privately Held
**SIC: 7372** Application computer software

**(P-18662)**
**PAWLOYALTY SOFTWARE INC**
876 4th St E, Sonoma (95476-7116)
**PHONE**..................................866 594-6848
**EMP:** 18 **EST:** 2016
**SALES (est):** 370.71K Privately Held
**Web:** www.pawloyalty.com
**SIC: 7372** Business oriented computer software

**(P-18663)**
**PAXATA INC**
1800 Seaport Blvd # 1, Redwood City (94063-5543)
**PHONE**..................................650 542-7897
Prakasa Nanduri, *CEO*
David Brewster, *
Christopher Maddox, *
Nenshad Bardoliwalla, *
**EMP:** 90 **EST:** 2012
**SALES (est):** 5.08MM
**SALES (corp-wide):** 151.94MM Privately Held
**Web:** www.datarobot.com
**SIC: 7372** Business oriented computer software
**PA:** Datarobot, Inc.
    225 Franklin St Ste 1300
    617 765-4500

**(P-18664)**
**PAYJOY INC (PA)**
655 4th St, San Francisco (94107-1601)
**PHONE**..................................888 632-1922
Douglas Ricket, *CEO*
Deepak Murthy, *
Gib Lopez, *
Juan Castro-zumaeta, *VP Fin*
**EMP:** 36 **EST:** 2015
**SALES (est):** 10.2MM
**SALES (corp-wide):** 10.2MM Privately Held
**Web:** www.payjoy.com
**SIC: 7372** 7389 6141 Business oriented computer software; Financial services; Personal credit institutions

**(P-18665)**
**PAYLOCITY HOLDING CORPORATION**
2107 Livingston St, Oakland (94606-5218)
**PHONE**..................................847 956-4850
**EMP:** 940
**SALES (corp-wide):** 1.4B Publicly Held
**Web:** www.paylocity.com
**SIC: 7372** Prepackaged software
**PA:** Paylocity Holding Corporation
    1400 American Ln
    847 463-3200

**(P-18666)**
**PAZO INC**
505 Cento Ct, Pleasanton (94566-6329)
**PHONE**..................................786 786-1195
Sharjeel Ahmed, *CEO*
**EMP:** 22
**SALES (est):** 1.34MM Privately Held
**SIC: 7372** Prepackaged software

**(P-18667)**
**PDF SOLUTIONS INC (PA)**
Also Called: PDF SOLUTIONS
2858 De La Cruz Blvd, Santa Clara (95050-2619)
**PHONE**..................................408 280-7900
John K Kibarian, *Pr*
Adnan Raza, *Ex VP*
Kimon Michaels, *Ex VP*
**EMP:** 153 **EST:** 1992
**SQ FT:** 20,800
**SALES (est):** 165.84MM Publicly Held
**Web:** www.pdf.com
**SIC: 7372** 7371 Prepackaged software; Computer software development

**(P-18668)**
**PEOPLE CENTER INC**
Also Called: Rippling
430 California St, San Francisco (94104-1301)
**PHONE**..................................415 737-5780
Parker Conrad, *CEO*
Persona Sankaranarayana, *
Eisar Lipkovitz, *Chief Product Officer*
**EMP:** 50 **EST:** 2016
**SALES (est):** 30.55MM Privately Held
**Web:** www.rippling.com
**SIC: 7372** Business oriented computer software

**(P-18669)**
**PEOPLEADMIN INC (DH)**
150 Parkshore Dr, Folsom (95630-4710)
**PHONE**..................................877 637-5800
Jack Blaha, *CEO*
Ziad Sanous, *
Jimmy Kelly, *
**EMP:** 25 **EST:** 2000
**SALES (est):** 8.66MM
**SALES (corp-wide):** 1.65B Privately Held
**Web:** www.peopleadmin.com
**SIC: 7372** Business oriented computer software
**HQ:** Powerschool Group Llc
    150 Parkshore Dr
    Folsom CA 95630
    916 790-1509

**(P-18670)**
**PERFORMANCE MATTERS LLC (DH)**
150 Parkshore Dr, Folsom (95630-4710)
**PHONE**..................................801 453-0136
Adam J Klaber, *CEO*
Woody Dillaha, *Pr*
Jeanette Haren, *CPO*
**EMP:** 18 **EST:** 2000
**SALES (est):** 3.89MM
**SALES (corp-wide):** 1.65B Privately Held
**SIC: 7372** Educational computer software
**HQ:** Peopleadmin, Inc.
    150 Parkshore Dr
    Folsom CA 95630
    877 637-5800

**(P-18671)**
**PETADATA SOFTWARE LLC**
39159 Paseo Padre Pkwy Ste 116, Fremont (94538-1600)
**PHONE**..................................203 306-9949

Venkatasubramani Janardhan, *Prin*
**EMP:** 48 **EST:** 2015
**SALES (est):** 1.92MM Privately Held
**Web:** www.petadatasoftware.com
**SIC: 7372** Prepackaged software

**(P-18672)**
**PHANTOM CYBER CORPORATION**
2479 E Bayshore Rd Ste 185, Palo Alto (94303-3245)
**PHONE**..................................650 208-5151
Oliver Friedrichs, *CEO*
Tim Driscoll, *CFO*
**EMP:** 30 **EST:** 2014
**SALES (est):** 4.99MM
**SALES (corp-wide):** 53.8B Publicly Held
**Web:** www.splunk.com
**SIC: 7372** 7371 Prepackaged software; Computer software development and applications
**HQ:** Splunk Inc.
    270 Brannan St
    San Francisco CA 94107
    415 848-8400

**(P-18673)**
**PHOENIX TECHNOLOGIES LTD (HQ)**
150 S Los Robles Ave Ste 500, Pasadena (91101-2441)
**PHONE**..................................408 570-1000
Rich Geruson, *Pr*
Robb Warwick, *Prin*
Nick Kaiser, *Prin*
Vladimir Jacimovic, *Prin*
George Huang, *Prin*
◆ **EMP:** 20 **EST:** 1979
**SQ FT:** 47,000
**SALES (est):** 10.97MM Privately Held
**Web:** www.phoenix.com
**SIC: 7372** 6794 Prepackaged software; Patent owners and lessors
**PA:** Marlin Equity Partners, Llc
    1301 Manhattan Ave

**(P-18674)**
**PILOT SOFTWARE INC**
3410 Hillview Ave, Palo Alto (94304-1395)
**PHONE**..................................650 230-2830
Jonathan D Becher, *Pr*
**EMP:** 27 **EST:** 2002
**SQ FT:** 4,100
**SALES (est):** 2.84MM Privately Held
**SIC: 7372** Business oriented computer software

**(P-18675)**
**PIVOT3 INC**
614 Lighthouse Ave Ste C, Pacific Grove (93950-2680)
**PHONE**..................................512 807-2666
Bill Stover, *CEO*
Bill Galloway, *
Rance Poehler, *Global Sales Vice President*
John Spires, *OF STRATEGIES*
Carlo Garbagnati, *
**EMP:** 205 **EST:** 2002
**SALES (est):** 77MM Privately Held
**Web:** www.quantum.com
**SIC: 7372** Business oriented computer software

**(P-18676)**
**PLANET DDS INC (PA)**
Also Called: Planet DDS
17872 Gillette Ave Ste 250, Irvine (92614-6573)
**PHONE**..................................800 861-5098

Eric Giesecke, *CEO*
Stephen Fong, *CFO*
Matt Zelen, *COO*
**EMP:** 33 **EST:** 2004
**SALES (est):** 14.22MM
**SALES (corp-wide):** 14.22MM Privately Held
**Web:** www.planetdds.com
**SIC: 7372** Application computer software

**(P-18677)**
**PLANET FORWARD INC**
Also Called: Planet FWD
2443 Fillmore St, San Francisco (94115-1814)
**PHONE**..................................800 861-3787
Julia Collins, *CEO*
Julia Collins, *Pr*
Jourdan Clish, *Head OF BUS SERVICES*
**EMP:** 33 **EST:** 2019
**SALES (est):** 6.16MM Privately Held
**Web:** www.planetforward.org
**SIC: 7372** Business oriented computer software

**(P-18678)**
**PLANFUL INC (HQ)**
150 Spear St Ste 1850, San Francisco (94105-1564)
**PHONE**..................................650 249-7100
Grant Halloran, *CEO*
Ron Baden, *CRO*
Richard Ratkowski, *
Aravind Balakrishnan, *
John Perkins, *
**EMP:** 120 **EST:** 2000
**SALES (est):** 42.87MM Privately Held
**Web:** www.planful.com
**SIC: 7372** Application computer software
**PA:** Planful Software India Private Limited
    503 Model House

**(P-18679)**
**PLANGRID INC (HQ)**
Also Called: Loupe
2111 Mission St Ste 400, San Francisco (94110-6349)
P.O. Box 194087 (94119-4087)
**PHONE**..................................800 646-0796
Tracy Young, *CEO*
Linda Keala, *Chief Human Resource Officer*
Michael Galvin, *CFO*
**EMP:** 85 **EST:** 2011
**SQ FT:** 16,000
**SALES (est):** 16.07MM
**SALES (corp-wide):** 4.39B Publicly Held
**Web:** construction.autodesk.com
**SIC: 7372** Application computer software
**PA:** Autodesk, Inc.
    1 Market St Ste 400
    415 507-5000

**(P-18680)**
**PLAYFIRST INC**
160 Spear St Fl 13, San Francisco (94105-1546)
**PHONE**..................................415 738-4600
Mari Jean Baker, *CEO*
John R Welch, *Pr*
Becky Hughes, *VP*
Jim Wandrey, *CFO*
**EMP:** 186 **EST:** 2004
**SALES (est):** 2.43MM
**SALES (corp-wide):** 7.43B Publicly Held
**Web:** www.playfirst.com
**SIC: 7372** Prepackaged software
**HQ:** Glu Mobile Inc.
    209 Redwood Shores Pkwy
    Redwood City CA 94065
    415 800-6100

## 7372 - Prepackaged Software (P-18681)

**(P-18681)**
**PLUGG ME LNC**
18100 Von Karman Ave Ste 850, Irvine (92612-0169)
PHONE.................................949 705-4472
Clarissa Watkins, CEO
**EMP:** 25 **EST:** 2019
**SALES (est):** 1.06MM **Privately Held**
**SIC:** 7372 Application computer software

**(P-18682)**
**PLUSAI INC**
3315 Scott Blvd, Santa Clara (95054-3139)
PHONE.................................408 508-4758
David Wanqian Liu, CEO
**EMP:** 100 **EST:** 2016
**SALES (est):** 12.27MM **Privately Held**
Web: www.plus.ai
**SIC:** 7372 Application computer software

**(P-18683)**
**PLUTOSHIFT INC**
530 Lytton Ave Fl 2, Palo Alto (94301-1541)
PHONE.................................213 400-2104
Prateek Joshi, CEO
**EMP:** 18 **EST:** 2015
**SALES (est):** 2.34MM **Privately Held**
Web: www.plutoshift.com
**SIC:** 7372 Prepackaged software

**(P-18684)**
**POLARION SOFTWARE INC**
1001 Marina Village Pkwy Ste 403, Alameda (94501-6401)
PHONE.................................877 572-4005
Frank Schrder, CEO
George Briner, *
Stefano Rizzo, *
Nikolay Entin, *
Jiri Walek, *
**EMP:** 90 **EST:** 2005
**SALES (est):** 1.82MM **Privately Held**
Web: polarion.plm.automation.siemens.com
**SIC:** 7372 Prepackaged software

**(P-18685)**
**POPOUT INC (PA)**
Also Called: Shippo
731 Market St Ste 200, San Francisco (94103-2005)
PHONE.................................415 691-7447
Laura Behrens Wu, CEO
**EMP:** 81 **EST:** 2013
**SALES (est):** 17.83MM
**SALES (corp-wide):** 17.83MM **Privately Held**
Web: www.goshippo.com
**SIC:** 7372 Business oriented computer software

**(P-18686)**
**POPULUS TECHNOLOGIES INC**
Also Called: Populus
177 Post St Ste 200, San Francisco (94108-4700)
PHONE.................................415 364-8048
Regina Clewlow, CEO
Charles Hudson, Bd of Dir
**EMP:** 23 **EST:** 2017
**SALES (est):** 2.76MM **Privately Held**
Web: www.populus.ai
**SIC:** 7372 Prepackaged software

**(P-18687)**
**POSHMARK INC (HQ)**
203 Redwood Shores Pkwy Fl 8, Redwood City (94065-1198)
PHONE.................................650 262-4771
Manish Chandra, Pr
Rodrigo Brumana, *
John Mcdonald, COO
**EMP:** 17 **EST:** 2011
**SQ FT:** 75,876
**SALES (est):** 326.01MM **Privately Held**
Web: www.poshmark.com
**SIC:** 7372 5611 5621 Application computer software; Men's and boys' clothing stores; Women's clothing stores
**PA:** Naver Corporation
95 Jeongjail-Ro, Bundang-Gu

**(P-18688)**
**POSITON INC**
825 Oak Grove Ave Ste B401, Menlo Park (94025-4434)
PHONE.................................650 600-1924
Rabie Zahri, Prin
**EMP:** 15 **EST:** 2021
**SALES (est):** 2.79MM **Privately Held**
**SIC:** 7372 Prepackaged software

**(P-18689)**
**POWERSCHOOL GROUP LLC (HQ)**
150 Parkshore Dr, Folsom (95630-4710)
PHONE.................................916 790-1509
Hardeep Gulati, CEO
Mark Oldemeyer, *
Bryan Macdonald Csto, Prin
**EMP:** 106 **EST:** 2015
**SALES (est):** 265.14MM
**SALES (corp-wide):** 1.65B **Privately Held**
Web: www.powerschool.com
**SIC:** 7372 Prepackaged software
**PA:** Vista Equity Partners Management, Llc
401 Congress Ave Ste 3100
512 730-2400

**(P-18690)**
**POWERSCHOOL HOLDINGS INC (PA)**
150 Parkshore Dr, Folsom (95630-4710)
PHONE.................................877 873-1550
Hardeep Gulati, CEO
Eric Shander, Pr
**EMP:** 3236 **EST:** 2020
**SQ FT:** 36,138
**SALES (est):** 697.65MM
**SALES (corp-wide):** 697.65MM **Privately Held**
**SIC:** 7372 Prepackaged software

**(P-18691)**
**POWWOW INC**
71 Stevenson St Ste 400, San Francisco (94105-0908)
PHONE.................................877 800-4381
Jonathan Kaplan, CEO
**EMP:** 24 **EST:** 2012
**SALES (est):** 4.76MM **Privately Held**
Web: www.powwowmobile.com
**SIC:** 7372 Business oriented computer software
**PA:** Magic Software Enterprises Ltd.
1 Yahadut Canada

**(P-18692)**
**PRATA INC**
202 Bicknell Ave, Santa Monica (90405-2317)
PHONE.................................512 823-1002
Rajat Jain, CEO
**EMP:** 20 **EST:** 2020
**SALES (est):** 1.12MM **Privately Held**
**SIC:** 7372 Application computer software

**(P-18693)**
**PREDII INC**
2211 Park Blvd, Palo Alto (94306-1533)
PHONE.................................415 269-1146
Tilak Kasturi, CEO
**EMP:** 20 **EST:** 2013
**SALES (est):** 891.73K **Privately Held**
Web: www.predii.com
**SIC:** 7372 7389 Business oriented computer software; Business Activities at Non-Commercial Site

**(P-18694)**
**PREMISE DATA CORPORATION (PA)**
535 Mission St, San Francisco (94105-3225)
PHONE.................................415 419-8750
Maury Blackman, Pr
Brian Corey, COO
**EMP:** 19 **EST:** 2012
**SALES (est):** 14.9MM
**SALES (corp-wide):** 14.9MM **Privately Held**
Web: www.premise.com
**SIC:** 7372 5045 Application computer software; Computer software

**(P-18695)**
**PREY INC**
548 Market St, San Francisco (94104-5401)
PHONE.................................415 780-9090
Carlos Yaconi, CEO
**EMP:** 15 **EST:** 2013
**SALES (est):** 2.04MM **Privately Held**
Web: www.preyproject.com
**SIC:** 7372 Application computer software

**(P-18696)**
**PRISM SOFTWARE CORPORATION**
184 Technology Dr Ste 201, Irvine (92618-2401)
PHONE.................................949 855-3100
Carl S Von Bibra, Ch
David Ayres, *
Conrad Von Bibra, *
Michael Cheever, *
**EMP:** 25 **EST:** 1970
**SALES (est):** 5.04MM **Privately Held**
Web: www.prismsoftware.com
**SIC:** 7372 Publisher's computer software

**(P-18697)**
**PROCEDE SOFTWARE LP**
6815 Flanders Dr Ste 200, San Diego (92121-3914)
PHONE.................................858 450-4800
Peter Kneale, Genl Pt
Phillip Mossy, Pt
**EMP:** 20 **EST:** 2003
**SALES (est):** 4.48MM **Privately Held**
Web: www.procedesoftware.com
**SIC:** 7372 Business oriented computer software

**(P-18698)**
**PRODUCTPLAN LLC**
10 E Yanonali St Ste 2a, Santa Barbara (93101-1878)
P.O. Box 944 (93102-0944)
PHONE.................................805 618-2975
**EMP:** 20 **EST:** 2013
**SALES (est):** 2.67MM **Privately Held**
Web: www.productplan.com
**SIC:** 7372 Business oriented computer software

**(P-18699)**
**PROGRESS SOFTWARE CORPORATION**
800 W El Camino Real, Mountain View (94040-2567)
PHONE.................................650 341-7733
**EMP:** 68
**SALES (corp-wide):** 694.44MM **Publicly Held**
Web: www.progress.com
**SIC:** 7372 Application computer software
**PA:** Progress Software Corporation
15 Wayside Rd Ste 4
781 280-4000

**(P-18700)**
**PROJECTDISCOVERY INC**
548 Market St, San Francisco (94104-5401)
PHONE.................................510 681-4441
Rishiraj Sharma, CEO
**EMP:** 30
**SALES (est):** 5.34MM **Privately Held**
Web: www.projectdiscovery.io
**SIC:** 7372 Business oriented computer software

**(P-18701)**
**PROJECTORIS INC**
Also Called: Screenmeet.com
582 Market St Ste 1005, San Francisco (94104-5311)
PHONE.................................917 972-5553
Ben Lilienthal, Pr
Eugene Abovsky, Sec
**EMP:** 76 **EST:** 2015
**SALES (est):** 3.94MM **Privately Held**
Web: www.screenmeet.com
**SIC:** 7372 Prepackaged software

**(P-18702)**
**PROMENADE SOFTWARE INC**
16 Technology Dr Ste 100, Irvine (92618-2323)
PHONE.................................949 333-4634
Frances Cohen, CEO
Daniel Beard, Dir
Jeff Gable, Dir
**EMP:** 20 **EST:** 2013
**SALES (est):** 4.11MM **Privately Held**
Web: www.promenadesoftware.com
**SIC:** 7372 Prepackaged software

**(P-18703)**
**PROOFPOINT INC**
2216 Otoole Ave, San Jose (95131-1326)
PHONE.................................408 571-6400
**EMP:** 20
**SALES (corp-wide):** 1.11B **Privately Held**
Web: www.proofpoint.com
**SIC:** 7372 Prepackaged software
**HQ:** Proofpoint, Inc.
925 W Maude Ave
Sunnyvale CA 94085
408 517-4710

**(P-18704)**
**PROPERTYRADAR INC**
Also Called: Propertyradar.com
12242 Business Park Dr Ste 20, Truckee (96161-3327)
P.O. Box 837 (96160)
PHONE.................................530 550-8801
Sean O'toole, CEO
**EMP:** 50 **EST:** 2006
**SALES (est):** 2.52MM **Privately Held**
Web: www.propertyradar.com
**SIC:** 7372 Business oriented computer software

## PRODUCTS & SERVICES SECTION
### 7372 - Prepackaged Software (P-18725)

**(P-18705)**
**PROTAGONIST GAMES LLC**
10755 Scripps Poway Pkwy, San Diego (92131-3924)
PHONE..................512 785-4946
Anthony D Castoro, *Managing Member*
**EMP:** 20 **EST:** 2018
**SALES (est):** 3.52MM **Privately Held**
Web: www.protagonistgames.com
**SIC: 7372** 5734 Application computer software; Software, computer games

**(P-18706)**
**PROVENANCE TECHNOLOGIES INC**
Also Called: Fiant
650 California St Ste 07-126, San Francisco (94108)
PHONE..................415 796-6281
Richard Mark, *CEO*
**EMP:** 16 **EST:** 2018
**SALES (est):** 4.84MM **Privately Held**
Web: www.provenancetech.io
**SIC: 7372** Business oriented computer software

**(P-18707)**
**PROVIDE INC**
Also Called: Provide
268 Bush St # 2921, San Francisco (94104-3503)
PHONE..................877 341-0617
Daniel Titcomb, *CEO*
James Bachmeier, *COO*
Andrew Bennett, *CAO*
**EMP:** 39 **EST:** 2013
**SALES (est):** 5.33MM
**SALES (corp-wide):** 12.64B **Publicly Held**
Web: www.getprovide.com
**SIC: 7372** Prepackaged software
**PA:** Fifth Third Bancorp
 38 Fountain Square Plz
 800 972-3030

**(P-18708)**
**PURE STORAGE INC (PA)**
Also Called: Pure Storage
2555 Augustine Dr, Santa Clara (95054-3003)
PHONE..................800 379-7873
Charles Giancarlo, *Ch Bd*
Scott Dietzen, *V Ch Bd*
Kevan Krysler, *CFO*
John Colgrove Cvo, *Prin*
Ajay Singh, *CPO*
▲ **EMP:** 598 **EST:** 2009
**SALES (est):** 2.83B **Publicly Held**
Web: www.purestorage.com
**SIC: 7372** 3572 Prepackaged software; Computer storage devices

**(P-18709)**
**PVAI US OPCO INC**
4125 Hopyard Rd, Pleasanton (94588-8534)
PHONE..................703 929-6807
Eric Sandor, *CEO*
**EMP:** 26 **EST:** 2022
**SALES (est):** 890.81K **Privately Held**
**SIC: 7372** 7389 Business oriented computer software; Business services, nec

**(P-18710)**
**QAD INC**
6450 Via Real, Carpinteria (93013-2903)
PHONE..................805 684-6614
Mark Rasmussen, *Brnch Mgr*
**EMP:** 17
**SALES (corp-wide):** 307.87MM **Privately Held**
Web: www.qad.com
**SIC: 7372** Business oriented computer software
**HQ:** Qad Inc.
 101 Innovation Pl
 Santa Barbara CA 93108
 805 566-6000

**(P-18711)**
**QAD INC (HQ)**
Also Called: Qad
101 Innovation Pl, Santa Barbara (93108-2268)
PHONE..................805 566-6000
Anton Chilton, *CEO*
Peter R Van Cuylenburg, *
Pamela M Lopker, *
Daniel Lender, *Ex VP*
Kara Bellamy, *CAO*
**EMP:** 219 **EST:** 1979
**SALES (est):** 307.87MM
**SALES (corp-wide):** 307.87MM **Privately Held**
Web: www.qad.com
**SIC: 7372** Prepackaged software
**PA:** Qad Parent, Llc
 101 Innovation Pl
 805 566-6000

**(P-18712)**
**QDOS INC**
Also Called: Desksite
200 Spectrum Center Dr Ste 300, Irvine (92618-5003)
PHONE..................949 362-8888
Richard Gillam, *CEO*
Patricia Bender, *
**EMP:** 26 **EST:** 2003
**SQ FT:** 6,000
**SALES (est):** 3.24MM **Privately Held**
Web: www.directsportsnetwork.com
**SIC: 7372** 7812 7313 7922 Home entertainment computer software; Motion picture and video production; Radio, television, publisher representatives; Television program, including commercial producers

**(P-18713)**
**QED SOFTWARE LLC**
Also Called: Trinium Technologies
211 E Ocean Blvd, Long Beach (90802-4809)
PHONE..................310 214-3118
Michael Thomas, *CEO*
Barry Assadi, *
▲ **EMP:** 27 **EST:** 2001
**SALES (est):** 13.34MM **Privately Held**
Web: www.triniumtech.com
**SIC: 7372** Business oriented computer software
**PA:** Wisetech Global Limited
 U 3 72 O'riordan St

**(P-18714)**
**QUADROTECH SOLUTIONS INC (PA)**
Also Called: Quest
20 Enterprise, Aliso Viejo (92656-7104)
PHONE..................949 754-8000
Thomas Madsen, *CEO*
**EMP:** 25 **EST:** 2013
**SALES (est):** 10.31MM
**SALES (corp-wide):** 10.31MM **Privately Held**
Web: www.quest.com
**SIC: 7372** Application computer software

**(P-18715)**
**QUALER INC**
9477 Waples St, San Diego (92121-2937)
PHONE..................858 224-9516
Alex Spector, *CEO*
Darren Crochet, *
Ruslan Auvad, *
Michael Morozov Ce, *Prin*
**EMP:** 30 **EST:** 2018
**SALES (est):** 2.42MM **Privately Held**
Web: www.qualer.com
**SIC: 7372** Prepackaged software

**(P-18716)**
**QUALIO INC (PA)**
268 Bush St, San Francisco (94104-3503)
PHONE..................415 795-7331
Robert Fenton, *CEO*
**EMP:** 21 **EST:** 2016
**SALES (est):** 1.48MM
**SALES (corp-wide):** 1.48MM **Privately Held**
Web: www.qualio.com
**SIC: 7372** Prepackaged software

**(P-18717)**
**QUANTAL INTERNATIONAL INC**
455 Market St Ste 1200, San Francisco (94105-2441)
PHONE..................415 644-0754
Terry Marsh, *Pr*
Jeff Rogers, *
Paul Pfleiderer, *
Indro Fedrigo, *
**EMP:** 26 **EST:** 1992
**SQ FT:** 7,000
**SALES (est):** 2.15MM **Privately Held**
Web: www.quantal.com
**SIC: 7372** 6282 Business oriented computer software; Investment advisory service

**(P-18718)**
**QUANTMSHIFT COMMUNICATIONS INC**
Also Called: Vcom Solutions
12657 Alcosta Blvd, San Ramon (94583-4438)
PHONE..................800 804-8266
Matthew Mendenhall, *VP*
**EMP:** 16 **EST:** 1999
**SALES (est):** 6.72MM
**SALES (corp-wide):** 38.7MM **Privately Held**
Web: www.vcomsolutions.com
**SIC: 7372** Business oriented computer software
**PA:** Vcom Solutions, Inc.
 12657 Alcosta Blvd # 418
 925 244-1800

**(P-18719)**
**QUEST SOFTWARE INC**
Also Called: Cloud Automation Division
4 Polaris Way, Aliso Viejo (92656-7104)
PHONE..................949 754-8000
**EMP:** 80
**SALES (corp-wide):** 647.68MM **Privately Held**
Web: www.quest.com
**SIC: 7372** Prepackaged software
**PA:** Quest Software Inc.
 20 Enterprise Ste 100
 949 754-8000

**(P-18720)**
**QUESTIVITY INC**
1680 Civic Center Dr Ste 209, Santa Clara (95050-4660)
PHONE..................408 615-1781
Humayun Sohel, *Pr*
**EMP:** 15 **EST:** 1999
**SQ FT:** 1,180
**SALES (est):** 9.94MM **Privately Held**
Web: www.questivity.com
**SIC: 7372** 7361 Prepackaged software; Employment agencies

**(P-18721)**
**RADIANT LOGIC INC (HQ)**
818 5th Ave, San Rafael (94901-3262)
PHONE..................415 209-6800
Joe Sander, *CEO*
Justin Sollenne, *
**EMP:** 44 **EST:** 1995
**SQ FT:** 10,718
**SALES (est):** 37.9MM
**SALES (corp-wide):** 37.9MM **Privately Held**
Web: www.radiantlogic.com
**SIC: 7372** 8742 Prepackaged software; Management consulting services
**PA:** Moon Buyer, Inc.
 251 Little Falls Dr
 302 636-5401

**(P-18722)**
**RAILSTECH INC**
730 Arizona Ave, Santa Monica (90401-1702)
PHONE..................267 315-2998
Dov Marmor Coe, *Prin*
Dov Marmor, *CEO*
**EMP:** 23 **EST:** 2020
**SALES (est):** 2.43MM
**SALES (corp-wide):** 6.76MM **Privately Held**
**SIC: 7372** Business oriented computer software
**PA:** Railsbank Technology Limited
 1, Snowden Street
 239 431-1850

**(P-18723)**
**RATEGAIN ADARA INC**
2033 Gateway Pl 5th Fl, San Jose (95110-3709)
PHONE..................408 691-3603
Bahnu Chopra, *CEO*
**EMP:** 44 **EST:** 2022
**SALES (est):** 1.15MM **Privately Held**
**SIC: 7372** Prepackaged software

**(P-18724)**
**READ IT LATER INC**
Also Called: Pocket
233 Samsone St Ste 1200, San Francisco (94104-2300)
PHONE..................415 692-6111
Nathan Weiner, *CEO*
**EMP:** 34 **EST:** 2011
**SALES (est):** 4.74MM
**SALES (corp-wide):** 30.69MM **Privately Held**
Web: www.getpocket.com
**SIC: 7372** Application computer software
**HQ:** Mozilla Corporation
 149 New Mntgomery St Fl 4
 San Francisco CA 94105

**(P-18725)**
**REAL SOFTWARE SYSTEMS LLC (PA)**
21255 Burbank Blvd Ste 220, Woodland Hills (91367-6681)
P.O. Box 7046 (91365-7046)
PHONE..................818 313-8000
Kent Sahin, *Managing Member*
**EMP:** 50 **EST:** 1993
**SALES (est):** 9.03MM **Privately Held**
Web: www.rightsline.com

# 7372 - Prepackaged Software (P-18726)

SIC: 7372 Business oriented computer software

**(P-18726)**
**REALSCOUT INC**
480 Ellis St Ste 203, Mountain View (94043-2204)
PHONE...................................650 397-6500
Arthur Kaneko, *CEO*
Andrew S Flanchner, *Pr*
**EMP:** 15 **EST:** 2012
**SQ FT:** 500
**SALES (est):** 3.4MM **Privately Held**
Web: www.realscout.com
SIC: 7372 Business oriented computer software

**(P-18727)**
**RED GATE SOFTWARE INC**
144 W Colorado Blvd Ste 200, Pasadena (91105-1953)
PHONE...................................626 993-3949
Tom Curtis, *Pr*
**EMP:** 23 **EST:** 2011
**SQ FT:** 5,500
**SALES (est):** 5.54MM
**SALES (corp-wide):** 89.76MM **Privately Held**
Web: www.red-gate.com
SIC: 7372 Business oriented computer software
HQ: Red Gate Software Limited
   C Cavendish House
   Cambridge CAMBS CB4 0
   122 343-8500

**(P-18728)**
**RED HAT INC**
444 Castro St Ste 1200, Mountain View (94041-2050)
PHONE...................................650 567-9039
Alex Daly, *Mgr*
**EMP:** 21
**SALES (corp-wide):** 61.86B **Publicly Held**
Web: www.redhat.com
SIC: 7372 Operating systems computer software
HQ: Red Hat, Inc.
   100 E Davie St
   Raleigh NC 27601

**(P-18729)**
**REDSEAL INC**
1300 El Camino Real Ste 300, Menlo Park (94025-4211)
PHONE...................................408 641-2200
Gregory Enriquez, *CEO*
Bryan Barney, *
Bill Gadala, *
**EMP:** 145 **EST:** 2004
**SQ FT:** 6,500
**SALES (est):** 43.35MM **Privately Held**
Web: www.redseal.net
SIC: 7372 Prepackaged software

**(P-18730)**
**RELATIONAL CENTER**
2717 S Robertson Blvd Apt 1, Los Angeles (90034-2442)
PHONE...................................323 935-1807
Traci Bivens Davis, *Prin*
**EMP:** 47 **EST:** 2008
**SALES (est):** 1.14MM **Privately Held**
Web: www.relationalcenter.org
SIC: 7372 Prepackaged software

**(P-18731)**
**RELATIONALAI INC**
2120 University Ave, Berkeley (94704-1026)
PHONE...................................650 307-8776
Molham Aref, *Pr*
**EMP:** 62 **EST:** 2018
**SALES (est):** 5.18MM **Privately Held**
Web: www.relational.ai
SIC: 7372 Prepackaged software

**(P-18732)**
**REMEDLY INC**
407 Sansome St Fl 4, San Francisco (94111-3104)
PHONE...................................650 265-8449
Victor Gane, *Prin*
**EMP:** 20 **EST:** 2017
**SALES (est):** 2.2MM **Privately Held**
Web: www.remedly.com
SIC: 7372 Prepackaged software

**(P-18733)**
**REPLICANT SOLUTIONS INC**
1 Letterman Dr # 3500, San Francisco (94129-1494)
PHONE...................................415 854-3296
Gadi Shamia, *CEO*
Benjamin Gleitzman, *
**EMP:** 120 **EST:** 2017
**SALES (est):** 15.51MM **Privately Held**
Web: www.replicant.com
SIC: 7372 Application computer software

**(P-18734)**
**REPLICO CORPORATION**
18625 Sutter Blvd Ste 300, Morgan Hill (95037-2863)
PHONE...................................408 842-8600
**EMP:** 52
Web: www.replicocorp.com
SIC: 7372 Prepackaged software

**(P-18735)**
**REPUTATIONCOM INC (PA)**
6111 Bollinger Canyon Rd Ste 500, San Ramon (94583-5285)
PHONE...................................800 888-0924
Joe Burton, *CEO*
Joe Fuca, *
Jason Grier, *CCO*
Amir Jafari, *
Manish Balsara, *
**EMP:** 460 **EST:** 2006
**SQ FT:** 21,454
**SALES (est):** 45.68MM **Privately Held**
Web: www.reputation.com
SIC: 7372 7371 Business oriented computer software; Computer software development and applications

**(P-18736)**
**RETAIL SOLUTIONS INCORPORATED (HQ)**
Also Called: Retail Solutions
100 Century Center Ct Ste 800, San Jose (95112-4535)
PHONE...................................650 390-6100
Andrew Appel, *Pr*
**EMP:** 30 **EST:** 1997
**SALES (est):** 17.17MM
**SALES (corp-wide):** 420.86MM **Privately Held**
Web: www.retailsolutions.com
SIC: 7372 Business oriented computer software
PA: Circana, Llc
   203 N Lasalle St Ste 1500
   312 726-1221

**(P-18737)**
**RETAIL ZIPLINE INC (PA)**
2370 Market St Ste 436, San Francisco (94114-1696)
PHONE...................................510 390-4904
Melissa Wong, *CEO*
**EMP:** 82 **EST:** 2014
**SALES (est):** 7.43MM
**SALES (corp-wide):** 7.43MM **Privately Held**
Web: www.getzipline.com
SIC: 7372 Business oriented computer software

**(P-18738)**
**REVCO PRODUCTS**
7221 Acacia Ave, Garden Grove (92841-3908)
PHONE...................................714 891-6688
▲ **EMP:** 51 **EST:** 1977
**SALES (est):** 9.21MM **Privately Held**
Web: www.revcoproducts.com
SIC: 7372 Operating systems computer software

**(P-18739)**
**REVJET CORPORATION**
981 Industrial Rd Ste D, San Carlos (94070-4150)
PHONE...................................650 508-2215
Patrick Mcnenny, *VP*
David Mackay, *CRO*
**EMP:** 110 **EST:** 2017
**SALES (est):** 10.48MM **Privately Held**
Web: www.revjet.com
SIC: 7372 Application computer software

**(P-18740)**
**REVUP SOFTWARE INC**
101 Redwood Shores Pkwy Ste 125, Redwood City (94065-1176)
PHONE...................................415 231-2315
Steve Spinner, *CEO*
**EMP:** 15 **EST:** 2016
**SALES (est):** 3.44MM **Privately Held**
SIC: 7372 Prepackaged software

**(P-18741)**
**RIOT GAMES INC (DH)**
Also Called: Riot Games
12333 W Olympic Blvd, Los Angeles (90064-1021)
PHONE...................................310 207-1444
Nicolas Laurent, *CEO*
Marc Merrill, *
Dylan Jadeja, *
Mark Sottosanti, *
Daniel Chang, *
▲ **EMP:** 36 **EST:** 2006
**SALES (est):** 798.36MM **Privately Held**
Web: www.riotgames.com
SIC: 7372 5734 Prepackaged software; Software, computer games
HQ: Tencent Holdings Limited
   29/F Three Pacific Place
   Wan Chai HK

**(P-18742)**
**RIVAL IQ CORPORATION**
3945 Freedom Cir, Santa Clara (95054-1223)
PHONE...................................206 395-8572
John Clark, *CEO*
**EMP:** 19 **EST:** 2014
**SALES (est):** 2.35MM **Privately Held**
Web: www.rivaliq.com
SIC: 7372 Business oriented computer software

**(P-18743)**
**RIVERMEADOW SOFTWARE INC**
120 W Main St, Los Gatos (95030-6814)
PHONE...................................617 448-4990
Jim Jordan, *CEO*
**EMP:** 30 **EST:** 2013
**SALES (est):** 2.39MM **Privately Held**
Web: www.rivermeadow.com
SIC: 7372 Business oriented computer software

**(P-18744)**
**ROADZEN INC (PA)**
111 Anza Blvd Ste 109, Burlingame (94010-1918)
PHONE...................................650 414-3530
Rohan Malhotra, *CEO*
Steven Carlson, *Ch Bd*
Jean-noel Gallardo, *CFO*
Ankur Kamboj, *COO*
**EMP:** 360 **EST:** 2015
**SALES (est):** 46.72MM
**SALES (corp-wide):** 46.72MM **Publicly Held**
Web: www.vahannatech.com
SIC: 7372 Prepackaged software

**(P-18745)**
**ROBLOX CORPORATION (PA)**
Also Called: ROBLOX
970 Park Pl, San Mateo (94403-1907)
PHONE...................................888 858-2569
David Baszucki, *Pr*
Amy Rawlings, *CAO*
Manuel Bronstein, *CPO*
**EMP:** 2336 **EST:** 1989
**SQ FT:** 348,360
**SALES (est):** 2.8B
**SALES (corp-wide):** 2.8B **Publicly Held**
Web: www.roblox.com
SIC: 7372 Prepackaged software

**(P-18746)**
**ROVI CORPORATION**
2 Circle Star Way, San Carlos (94070-6200)
PHONE...................................408 562-8400
▲ **EMP:** 19
Web: www.rovicorp.com
SIC: 7372 Home entertainment computer software

**(P-18747)**
**RSA CONFERENCE LLC**
166 Geary St Ste 1500, San Francisco (94108-5628)
PHONE...................................415 707-2833
Hugh Thompson, *CEO*
**EMP:** 30 **EST:** 2019
**SALES (est):** 3MM **Privately Held**
Web: www.rsaconference.com
SIC: 7372 Prepackaged software

**(P-18748)**
**RYSIGO TECHNOLOGIES CORP (PA)**
119 Lyon St Apt A, San Francisco (94117-2291)
PHONE...................................408 621-9274
Suhail Maqsood, *Pr*
**EMP:** 18 **EST:** 2008
**SALES (est):** 1.37MM **Privately Held**
Web: www.rysigo.com
SIC: 7372 8748 7371 7373 Prepackaged software; Systems engineering consultant, ex. computer or professional; Custom computer programming services; Systems engineering, computer related

**(P-18749)**
**SABA SOFTWARE INC (DH)**
4120 Dublin Blvd Ste 200, Dublin (94568-7759)
PHONE...................................877 722-2101
Phil Saunders, *Pr*

## 7372 - Prepackaged Software (P-18769)

Jeff Lautenbach, *
Chirag Shah, *
Theresa Damato, *CMO**
Adam Weiss, *CAO**
**EMP:** 100 **EST:** 1997
**SQ FT:** 36,000
**SALES (est):** 81.68MM
**SALES (corp-wide):** 740.92MM **Privately Held**
Web: www.cornerstoneondemand.com
**SIC: 7372** 7371 Application computer software; Computer software development and applications
**HQ:** Cornerstone Ondemand, Inc.
1601 Clvrfeld Blvd Ste 62
Santa Monica CA 90404
310 752-0200

### (P-18750)
**SAFETYCHAIN SOFTWARE INC (PA)**
7599 Redwood Blvd Ste 205, Novato (94945-7706)
**PHONE**.............................415 233-9474
Walter Smith, *Prin*
**EMP:** 21 **EST:** 2012
**SALES (est):** 9.67MM
**SALES (corp-wide):** 9.67MM **Privately Held**
Web: www.safetychain.com
**SIC: 7372** Business oriented computer software

### (P-18751)
**SAGE SOFTWARE INC**
1380 Tartan Trail Rd, Burlingame (94010-7218)
**PHONE**.............................650 579-3628
Mau Chung Chang, *Brnch Mgr*
**EMP:** 18
**SALES (corp-wide):** 2.76B **Privately Held**
Web: www.sage.com
**SIC: 7372** Business oriented computer software
**HQ:** Sage Software, Inc.
271 17th St Nw Ste 1100
Atlanta GA 30363
866 996-7243

### (P-18752)
**SAGE SOFTWARE HOLDINGS INC (HQ)**
6561 Irvine Center Dr, Irvine (92618-2118)
**PHONE**.............................866 530-7243
Stev Swenson, *CEO*
Doug Meyer, *
Mack Lout, *
Stephen Kelly, *Prin*
Steve Hare, *Prin*
**EMP:** 400 **EST:** 2000
**SALES (est):** 870.22MM
**SALES (corp-wide):** 2.76B **Privately Held**
**SIC: 7372** 7371 Business oriented computer software; Custom computer programming services
**PA:** The Sage Group Plc.
C23 - 5 & 6 Cobalt Park Way
800 923-0344

### (P-18753)
**SALESCATCHER LLC**
Also Called: Salescatcher
1570 N Batavia St, Orange (92867-3507)
**PHONE**.............................714 376-6700
Augustin Gohil, *Managing Member*
**EMP:** 50 **EST:** 2009
**SALES (est):** 3.23MM **Privately Held**
Web: www.salescatcher.io
**SIC: 7372** Application computer software

### (P-18754)
**SALESFORCE INC (PA)**
Also Called: Salesforce
415 Mission St Fl 3, San Francisco (94105-2504)
**PHONE**.............................415 901-7000
Marc Benioff, *Ch Bd*
Brian Millham, *Pr*
Amy Weaver, *Pr*
Sabastian Niles, *CLO*
Miguel Milano, *CRO*
**EMP:** 600 **EST:** 1999
**SQ FT:** 900,000
**SALES (est):** 34.86B
**SALES (corp-wide):** 34.86B **Publicly Held**
Web: www.salesforce.com
**SIC: 7372** 7375 7371 7374 Business oriented computer software; Information retrieval services; Custom computer programming services; Data processing and preparation

### (P-18755)
**SALESFORCECOM INC**
Also Called: SALESFORCE.COM, INC.
1442 2nd St, Santa Monica (90401-2302)
**PHONE**.............................310 752-7000
Andy Demari, *Mgr*
**EMP:** 40
**SALES (corp-wide):** 34.86B **Publicly Held**
Web: www.salesforce.com
**SIC: 7372** Business oriented computer software
**PA:** Salesforce, Inc.
415 Mission St Fl 3
415 901-7000

### (P-18756)
**SALESFORCECOM LANDMARK**
1 Market St Ste 400, San Francisco (94105-1305)
**PHONE**.............................650 653-4500
Athanasia Charonis Attorney, *Prin*
**EMP:** 18 **EST:** 2018
**SALES (est):** 1.43MM **Privately Held**
Web: www.salesforce.com
**SIC: 7372** Business oriented computer software

### (P-18757)
**SALESFORCEORG LLC**
415 Mission St Fl 3, San Francisco (94105-2504)
**PHONE**.............................415 901-7000
Robert Acker, *CEO*
**EMP:** 429 **EST:** 2008
**SALES (est):** 11.5MM
**SALES (corp-wide):** 34.86B **Publicly Held**
Web: www.salesforce.org
**SIC: 7372** Business oriented computer software
**PA:** Salesforce, Inc.
415 Mission St Fl 3
415 901-7000

### (P-18758)
**SAP AMERICA INC**
Also Called: Sap AG
3410 Hillview Ave, Palo Alto (94304-1395)
**PHONE**.............................650 849-4000
John Schwarz, *CEO*
**EMP:** 28
**SALES (corp-wide):** 33.92B **Privately Held**
Web: www.sap.com
**SIC: 7372** Prepackaged software
**HQ:** Sap America, Inc.
3999 West Chester Pike
Newtown Square PA 19073
610 661-1000

### (P-18759)
**SAP LABS LLC (DH)**
3410 Hillview Ave, Palo Alto (94304-1395)
**PHONE**.............................650 849-4000
Hasso Plattner, *
Ben Frommherz, *
Eric Rubino, *
◆ **EMP:** 300 **EST:** 1996
**SQ FT:** 200,000
**SALES (est):** 60.62MM
**SALES (corp-wide):** 33.92B **Privately Held**
Web: www.sap.com
**SIC: 7372** Prepackaged software
**HQ:** Sap America, Inc.
3999 West Chester Pike
Newtown Square PA 19073
610 661-1000

### (P-18760)
**SASS LABS INC**
Also Called: Allyo
121 W Washington Ave Ste 212, Sunnyvale (94086-1107)
**PHONE**.............................404 731-7284
Ankit Somani, *Pr*
Sahil Sahni, *VP*
**EMP:** 20 **EST:** 2017
**SALES (est):** 2.18MM
**SALES (corp-wide):** 2.96B **Publicly Held**
**SIC: 7372** Application computer software
**HQ:** Hirevue, Inc.
10876 S Rver Front Pkwy S
South Jordan UT 84095
801 316-2910

### (P-18761)
**SAVEDAILY INC**
1503 S Coast Dr Ste 330, Costa Mesa (92626-1509)
**PHONE**.............................562 795-7500
**EMP:** 19
**SIC: 7372** Prepackaged software

### (P-18762)
**SAVIYNT INC (PA)**
1301 E El Segundo Blvd Ste D, El Segundo (90245-4303)
**PHONE**.............................310 641-1664
Sachin Nayyar, *CEO*
Paul Zolfaghari, *Pr*
Shankar Ganapathy, *COO*
James Jackson, *CFO*
**EMP:** 491 **EST:** 2011
**SQ FT:** 10,786
**SALES (est):** 79.73MM
**SALES (corp-wide):** 79.73MM **Privately Held**
Web: www.saviynt.com
**SIC: 7372** Prepackaged software

### (P-18763)
**SCHOOL INNOVATIONS ACHIEVEMENT (HQ)**
5200 Golden Foothill Pkwy, El Dorado Hills (95762-9610)
**PHONE**.............................800 487-9234
Aubrey R Davis, *CEO*
**EMP:** 50 **EST:** 2003
**SQ FT:** 25,000
**SALES (est):** 21.71MM
**SALES (corp-wide):** 28.67MM **Privately Held**
Web: www.sia-us.com
**SIC: 7372** 8742 Prepackaged software; Management consulting services
**PA:** Schoolstatus, Llc
800 Wodlands Pkwy Ste 107
601 620-0613

### (P-18764)
**SCIENTIFIC LEARNING CORP**
300 Frank H Ogawa Plz Ste 600, Oakland (94612-2056)
**PHONE**.............................510 444-3500
Louise Dube, *VP*
**EMP:** 48
**SALES (corp-wide):** 47.21MM **Privately Held**
Web: www.scilearn.com
**SIC: 7372** 7371 Prepackaged software; Computer software development
**HQ:** Scientific Learning Corporation
501 Grant St Ste 1075
Pittsburgh PA 15219

### (P-18765)
**SCOPE TECHNOLOGIES US INC (PA)**
Also Called: Scope AR
575 Market St Fl 4, San Francisco (94105-5818)
**PHONE**.............................855 207-2673
Scott Montgomerie, *CEO*
David Nedohin, *
**EMP:** 30 **EST:** 2014
**SALES (est):** 6.72MM
**SALES (corp-wide):** 6.72MM **Privately Held**
Web: www.scopear.com
**SIC: 7372** Application computer software

### (P-18766)
**SCOPELY INC (DH)**
3505 Hayden Ave, Culver City (90232-2412)
**PHONE**.............................323 400-6618
Tim Obrien, *CRO*
Roxane Lukas, *CPO*
**EMP:** 200 **EST:** 2011
**SALES (est):** 128.36MM **Privately Held**
Web: www.scopely.com
**SIC: 7372** Home entertainment computer software
**HQ:** Savvy Games Group
Office 2.14 B, 6th Floor, Kafd, King Fahad Road
Riyadh

### (P-18767)
**SCORELATE INC**
91301 Fairview Pl Ste 2, Agoura Hills (91301)
**PHONE**.............................818 602-9176
Sean Bar, *CEO*
**EMP:** 25
**SALES (est):** 441.68K **Privately Held**
**SIC: 7372** Business oriented computer software

### (P-18768)
**SCRY ANALYTICS INC (PA)**
Also Called: Scry Ai
2635 N 1st St Ste 200, San Jose (95131)
**PHONE**.............................408 740-8017
Alok Aggarwal, *Ch Bd*
Sangeeta Aggarwal, *Prin*
**EMP:** 50 **EST:** 2014
**SALES (est):** 2.89MM
**SALES (corp-wide):** 2.89MM **Privately Held**
Web: www.scryai.com
**SIC: 7372** Application computer software

### (P-18769)
**SCRY ANALYTICS INC**
Also Called: Scry Ai
12835 Pheasant Ridge Rd, Saratoga (95070-3756)
**PHONE**.............................408 740-8017

## 7372 - Prepackaged Software (P-18770)

Alok Aggarwal, *Ch Bd*
**EMP:** 260
**SALES (corp-wide):** 2.89MM **Privately Held**
**Web:** www.scryai.com
**SIC: 7372** Application computer software
**PA:** Scry Analytics, Inc.
2635 N 1st St Ste 200
408 740-8017

**(P-18770)**
**SE SOFTWARE INC**
3000 Olympic Blvd Bldg 4, Santa Monica (90404-5073)
P.O. Box 341469 (90034-9469)
**PHONE**..........................888 504-9876
Greg Hermanovic, *Pr*
Sean Lee, *Acctnt*
**EMP:** 15 **EST:** 1995
**SALES (est):** 734.57K **Privately Held**
**Web:** www.sidefx.com
**SIC: 7372** Prepackaged software

**(P-18771)**
**SEACLOUD SOFTWARE LLC**
Also Called: Daily Connect
2021 Fillmore St Pmb 9071, San Francisco (94115-2708)
**PHONE**..........................650 318-1172
Xavier Launay, *CEO*
**EMP:** 15 **EST:** 2009
**SALES (est):** 482.59K **Privately Held**
**Web:** en.dailyconnect.com
**SIC: 7372** Prepackaged software

**(P-18772)**
**SEAL SOFTWARE INCORPORATED (HQ)**
1990 N California Blvd Ste 500, Walnut Creek (94596-3743)
**PHONE**..........................650 938-7325
Ulf Zetterberg, *CEO*
David Gingell, *CMO*
Rich Bohne, *CRO*
Jim Wagner, *CSO*
**EMP:** 17 **EST:** 2013
**SALES (est):** 8.34MM
**SALES (corp-wide):** 2.76B **Publicly Held**
**Web:** www.apogeelegal.com
**SIC: 7372** Prepackaged software
**PA:** Docusign, Inc.
221 Main St Ste 1550
415 489-4940

**(P-18773)**
**SEAM LABS INC**
2948 20th St Ste 308-302, San Francisco (94110-2871)
**PHONE**..........................415 815-5509
Sy Bohy, *CEO*
Dawn Ho, *CPO*
**EMP:** 20 **EST:** 2019
**SALES (est):** 5.86MM **Privately Held**
**SIC: 7372** 7389 Prepackaged software; Business services, nec

**(P-18774)**
**SECPOD TECHNOLOGIES**
303 Twin Dolphin Dr Fl 6, Redwood City (94065-1497)
**PHONE**..........................405 385-9890
Chandrashekhar Basavanna, *CEO*
**EMP:** 40 **EST:** 2017
**SALES (est):** 3.25MM **Privately Held**
**Web:** www.sanernow.com
**SIC: 7372** Prepackaged software

**(P-18775)**
**SECURE COMPUTING CORPORATION (DH)**
3965 Freedom Cir # 4, Santa Clara (95054-1206)
**PHONE**..........................408 979-2020
Daniel Ryan, *Pr*
Richard Scott, *
Timothy J Steinkopf, *VP Opers*
Atri Chatterjee, *VP Mktg*
Michael J Gallagher, *Senior Vice President Product Development*
**EMP:** 40 **EST:** 1996
**SQ FT:** 10,895
**SALES (est):** 14.55MM
**SALES (corp-wide):** 1.92B **Privately Held**
**Web:** www.securecomputing.com
**SIC: 7372** Prepackaged software
**HQ:** Mcafee, Llc
6220 America Ctr Dr
San Jose CA 95002

**(P-18776)**
**SEISMIC SOFTWARE INC (HQ)**
12390 El Camino Real Ste 300, San Diego (92130-3162)
**PHONE**..........................714 404-7069
John Douglas Winter, *CEO*
**EMP:** 54 **EST:** 2010
**SALES (est):** 52.61MM
**SALES (corp-wide):** 151.4MM **Privately Held**
**Web:** www.seismic.com
**SIC: 7372** Prepackaged software
**PA:** Seismic Software Holdings, Inc.
11455 El Cmino Real Ste 3

**(P-18777)**
**SEMOTUS INC**
Also Called: Hiplink Software
20 S Santa Cruz Ave Ste 300, Los Gatos (95030)
**PHONE**..........................408 667-2046
Anthony Lapine, *Ch Bd*
Pamela Lapine, *Pr*
**EMP:** 20 **EST:** 2008
**SQ FT:** 4,000
**SALES (est):** 5.07MM **Privately Held**
**Web:** www.semotus.com
**SIC: 7372** 7371 8243 Prepackaged software ; Computer software systems analysis and design, custom; Operator training, computer

**(P-18778)**
**SENTINELONE INC (PA)**
Also Called: Sentinelone
444 Castro St Ste 400, Mountain View (94041-2053)
**PHONE**..........................855 868-3733
Tomer Weingarten, *Ch Bd*
Srivatsan Narayanan, *COO*
Keenan Conder, *CLO*
Sally Jenkins, *CMO*
**EMP:** 1893 **EST:** 2013
**SQ FT:** 10,000
**SALES (est):** 621.15MM
**SALES (corp-wide):** 621.15MM **Publicly Held**
**Web:** www.sentinelone.com
**SIC: 7372** 7382 Prepackaged software; Protective devices, security

**(P-18779)**
**SENTONS USA INC**
627 River Oaks Pkwy, San Jose (95134-1907)
**PHONE**..........................408 732-9000
Jess Lee, *Pr*
**EMP:** 24 **EST:** 2011
**SALES (est):** 2.47MM **Privately Held**
**Web:** www.sentons.com
**SIC: 7372** Prepackaged software

**(P-18780)**
**SEPASOFT INC**
1262 Hawks Flight Ct Ste 190, El Dorado Hills (95762-9803)
**PHONE**..........................916 939-1684
Thomas Andrew Hechtman, *Pr*
Roxanna Hechtman, *CFO*
**EMP:** 22 **EST:** 2003
**SQ FT:** 2,955
**SALES (est):** 1.17MM **Privately Held**
**Web:** www.sepasoft.com
**SIC: 7372** Prepackaged software

**(P-18781)**
**SEQUELAE INC**
101 W Bdwy Fl 9, San Diego (92101)
P.O. Box 431002 (92101)
**PHONE**..........................801 628-0256
Ken Ehlert, *CEO*
Lyle Parry, *
**EMP:** 80 **EST:** 2022
**SALES (est):** 1.95MM **Privately Held**
**SIC: 7372** Prepackaged software

**(P-18782)**
**SEQUENT SOFTWARE INC**
4699 Old Ironsides Dr Ste 470, Santa Clara (95054-1861)
**EMP:** 17 **EST:** 2010
**SALES (est):** 5.95MM **Privately Held**
**Web:** www.sequent.com
**SIC: 7372** Application computer software

**(P-18783)**
**SERRA SYSTEMS INC (HQ)**
126 Mill St, Healdsburg (95448-4438)
**PHONE**..........................707 433-5104
Paul Deas, *Pr*
Steven Deas, *VP*
Pamela Deas, *Sec*
**EMP:** 17 **EST:** 1984
**SQ FT:** 7,000
**SALES (est):** 2.36MM
**SALES (corp-wide):** 91.02MM **Privately Held**
**Web:** www.eandm.com
**SIC: 7372** Business oriented computer software
**PA:** E & M Electric And Machinery, Inc.
126 Mill St
707 433-5578

**(P-18784)**
**SERRALA AMERICAS INC**
17485 Monterey St Ste 201, Morgan Hill (95037-3674)
**PHONE**..........................650 655-3939
**EMP:** 88
**SALES (corp-wide):** 2.67MM **Privately Held**
**Web:** www.serrala.com
**SIC: 7372** Prepackaged software
**HQ:** Serrala Americas, Inc.
205 N Michigan Ave # 4110
Chicago IL 60601
312 620-1200

**(P-18785)**
**SERVICEAIDE INC (PA)**
2445 Augustine Dr Ste 150, Santa Clara (95054-3032)
**PHONE**..........................650 206-8988
Wai Wong, *CEO*
Wai Wong, *Pr*
Randall Tidwell, *CFO*
**EMP:** 58 **EST:** 2016
**SALES (est):** 23.99MM

**SALES (corp-wide):** 23.99MM **Privately Held**
**Web:** www.serviceaide.com
**SIC: 7372** Application computer software

**(P-18786)**
**SESAME SOFTWARE INC (PA)**
5201 Great America Pkwy Ste 320, Santa Clara (95054-1122)
**PHONE**..........................408 550-7999
Richard Banister, *CEO*
Richard D Banister, *Pr*
**EMP:** 22 **EST:** 1988
**SALES (est):** 3.33MM
**SALES (corp-wide):** 3.33MM **Privately Held**
**Web:** www.sesamesoftware.com
**SIC: 7372** Business oriented computer software

**(P-18787)**
**SHORTCUTS SOFTWARE INC**
7711 Center Ave Ste 550, Huntington Beach (92647-3075)
**PHONE**..........................714 622-6600
Rebecca Randall, *CEO*
Paul Tate, *
Malcom Raward, *
**EMP:** 30 **EST:** 2005
**SALES (est):** 5.47MM
**SALES (corp-wide):** 8.41B **Privately Held**
**Web:** www.shortcuts.net
**SIC: 7372** Business oriented computer software
**HQ:** Shortcuts Software Pty Ltd
L 2 South Tower 10 Browning St
South Brisbane QLD 4101

**(P-18788)**
**SHRED LABS LLC**
8033 W Sunset Blvd # 1112, Los Angeles (90046-2401)
**PHONE**..........................781 285-8622
**EMP:** 23 **EST:** 2018
**SALES (est):** 4.45MM **Privately Held**
**Web:** www.shred.app
**SIC: 7372** 7389 Application computer software; Business Activities at Non-Commercial Site

**(P-18789)**
**SIGHT MACHINE INC**
243 Vallejo St, San Francisco (94111)
**PHONE**..........................888 461-5739
Jon Sobel, *CEO*
Nathan Oostendorp, *
Keith Hartley, *CRO*
Kurt Demaagd, *Analytics Vice President*
Adam Taisch, *Vice-President Customer Development*
**EMP:** 60 **EST:** 2013
**SQ FT:** 6,500
**SALES (est):** 9.19MM **Privately Held**
**Web:** www.sightmachine.com
**SIC: 7372** Business oriented computer software

**(P-18790)**
**SIGNIFYD INC (PA)**
99 Almaden Blvd Ste 400, San Jose (95113-1604)
**PHONE**..........................866 220-1415
Rajesh Ramanand, *CEO*
Dan Strong, *CFO*
Danny Lorenzo, *CSO*
Indy Guha, *CMO*
Emily Mikailli, *People Operations*
**EMP:** 350 **EST:** 2011
**SALES (est):** 28.54MM
**SALES (corp-wide):** 28.54MM **Privately Held**

# PRODUCTS & SERVICES SECTION

**7372 - Prepackaged Software (P-18811)**

Web: www.signifyd.com
SIC: 7372  Prepackaged software

**(P-18791)**
**SIMPPLR INC (PA)**
3 Twin Dolphin Dr Ste 160, Redwood City (94065)
PHONE..............................650 396-2646
Dhiraj Sharma, *CEO*
Don Wight, *CRO*
EMP: 130 EST: 2014
SALES (est): 12.11MM
SALES (corp-wide): 12.11MM **Privately Held**
Web: www.simpplr.com
SIC: 7372  Business oriented computer software

**(P-18792)**
**SITECORE USA INC (DH)**
Also Called: Parent Is Sitecore USA Holding
44 Montgomery St Ste 3340, San Francisco (94104-4806)
PHONE..............................415 380-0600
EMP: 150 EST: 2009
SALES (est): 68.65MM
SALES (corp-wide): 2.67MM **Privately Held**
Web: www.sitecore.com
SIC: 7372  Business oriented computer software
HQ: Sitecore Corporation A/S
    Vester Farimagsgade 3, Sal 5
    Kobenhavn V 1606
    70236660

**(P-18793)**
**SKEDULO INC**
548 Market St Ste 80260, San Francisco (94104-5401)
PHONE..............................415 640-1997
EMP: 15 EST: 2017
SALES (est): 5.72MM **Privately Held**
Web: www.skedulo.com
SIC: 7372  Prepackaged software

**(P-18794)**
**SKUID INC**
2121 N California Blvd Ste 350, Walnut Creek (94596-7390)
PHONE..............................800 515-2535
EMP: 63
Web: www.skuid.com
SIC: 7372  Prepackaged software
HQ: Skuid, Inc.
    10800 Ne 8th St
    Bellevue WA 98004
    800 515-2535

**(P-18795)**
**SKY PARENT INC (PA)**
5470 Great America Pkwy, Santa Clara (95054-3644)
PHONE..............................650 362-0488
Robert Bearden, *CEO*
EMP: 17 EST: 2021
SQ FT: 92,000
SALES (est): 496.12MM
SALES (corp-wide): 496.12MM **Privately Held**
Web: www.cloudera.com
SIC: 7372  Prepackaged software

**(P-18796)**
**SLABS INC**
12555 W Jefferson Blvd, Los Angeles (90066-7032)
PHONE..............................424 289-0275
Iddris Sandu, *CEO*
EMP: 20 EST: 2022

SALES (est): 1.27MM **Privately Held**
SIC: 7372  Business oriented computer software

**(P-18797)**
**SLACK TECHNOLOGIES INC (HQ)**
Also Called: Slack
500 Howard St Ste 100, San Francisco (94105-3031)
PHONE..............................970 299-4848
Denise Dresser, *CEO*
Stewart Butterfield, *
Allen Shim, *CFO*
Tamar Yehoshua, *CPO*
Robert Frati, *SLS & CUSTOMER SUCCESS*
EMP: 279 EST: 2009
SQ FT: 228,998
SALES (est): 902.61MM
SALES (corp-wide): 34.86B **Publicly Held**
Web: www.slack.com
SIC: 7372  Business oriented computer software
PA: Salesforce, Inc.
    415 Mission St Fl 3
    415 901-7000

**(P-18798)**
**SMARSH INC**
Also Called: Actiance
900 Veterans Blvd Ste 500, Redwood City (94063-1715)
PHONE..............................650 631-6300
EMP: 150
SALES (corp-wide): 346.27MM **Privately Held**
Web: www.smarsh.com
SIC: 7372  8742  Prepackaged software; Management consulting services
HQ: Smarsh Inc.
    851 Sw 6th Ave Ste 800
    Portland OR 97204
    866 762-7741

**(P-18799)**
**SMART-TEK SERVICES INC (HQ)**
11838 Bernardo Plaza Ct Ste 250, San Diego (92128-2434)
PHONE..............................858 798-1644
Kelly Mowrey, *COO*
Bryan Bonar, *Interim Chief Executive Officer*
EMP: 17 EST: 2009
SQ FT: 2,000
SALES (est): 5.24MM
SALES (corp-wide): 6.44MM **Privately Held**
Web: www.smart-tekservices.com
SIC: 7372  Business oriented computer software
PA: Trucept, Inc.
    600 La Terraza Blvd
    866 798-1620

**(P-18800)**
**SMARTLOGIC SEMAPHORE INC**
Also Called: Smartlogic
111 N Market St Ste 365, San Jose (95113-1101)
PHONE..............................408 213-9500
Rupert Bentley, *Pr*
EMP: 150 EST: 2010
SALES (est): 4.78MM
SALES (corp-wide): 694.44MM **Publicly Held**
Web: www.progress.com
SIC: 7372  Business oriented computer software
HQ: Marklogic Corporation
    15 Wayside Rd

Burlington MA 01803
650 655-2300

**(P-18801)**
**SNAP INC**
579 Toyopa Dr, Pacific Palisades (90272-4470)
PHONE..............................310 745-0632
EMP: 95
SALES (corp-wide): 4.61B **Publicly Held**
Web: www.snap.com
SIC: 7372  Application computer software
PA: Snap Inc.
    3000 31st St
    310 399-3339

**(P-18802)**
**SNAPLOGIC INC (PA)**
1825 S Grant St Ste 550, San Mateo (94402)
PHONE..............................888 494-1570
Gaurav Dhillon, *CEO*
Ahsan Malik, *
James Markarian, *
David Downing, *CMO*
Dayle Hall, *CMO*
EMP: 136 EST: 2006
SALES (est): 20.06MM **Privately Held**
Web: www.snaplogic.com
SIC: 7372  Business oriented computer software

**(P-18803)**
**SNAPWIZ INC**
Also Called: Edulastic
39300 Civic Center Dr Ste 310, Fremont (94538-2338)
PHONE..............................510 328-3277
Madhu Narasa, *CEO*
Jeff Bork, *
Satish Kumar, *
EMP: 120 EST: 2010
SALES (est): 4.17MM **Privately Held**
Web: www.peardeck.com
SIC: 7372  Educational computer software

**(P-18804)**
**SNICKERDOODLE LABS INC**
3242 San Rivas Dr, San Jose (95148-2036)
PHONE..............................408 807-9426
Jonathan Padilla, *CEO*
EMP: 15
SALES (est): 2.8MM **Privately Held**
SIC: 7372  7389  Prepackaged software; Business services, nec

**(P-18805)**
**SOCKET MOBILE INC (PA)**
Also Called: SOCKET COMMUNICATIONS
40675 Encyclopedia Cir, Fremont (94538-2475)
PHONE..............................510 933-3000
Kevin J Mills, *Pr*
Charlie Bass, *
Leonard L Ott, *Ex VP*
Lynn Zhao, *
David A Holmes, *Chief Business Officer*
▲ EMP: 53 EST: 1992
SQ FT: 35,913
SALES (est): 17.03MM **Publicly Held**
Web: www.socketmobile.com
SIC: 7372  3575  Prepackaged software; Computer terminals, monitors and components

**(P-18806)**
**SOFTWARE DEVELOPMENT INC**
Also Called: Mi9
4900 Hopyard Rd, Pleasanton (94588-7100)

PHONE..............................925 847-8823
Michael Burge, *Pr*
EMP: 25 EST: 1979
SALES (est): 2.39MM
SALES (corp-wide): 161.29K **Privately Held**
Web: www.mi9retail.com
SIC: 7372  7379  Prepackaged software; Computer related consulting services
PA: Mi9 Business Intelligence Systems Inc
    301-245 Yorkland Blvd
    416 491-1483

**(P-18807)**
**SOFTWARE LICENSING CONSULTANTS**
Also Called: SLC
12030 Donner Pass Rd Ste 1, Truckee (96161-4989)
PHONE..............................925 371-1277
Edgardo Ramirez, *VP*
EMP: 35 EST: 2003
SALES (est): 3.49MM **Privately Held**
Web: slc.us.com
SIC: 7372  5087  Prepackaged software; Janitors' supplies

**(P-18808)**
**SOLARA HEALTH INC** ✪
50 Fox Hill Rd, Woodside (94062)
PHONE..............................650 270-4500
Randy Womack, *CEO*
EMP: 25 EST: 2023
SALES (est): 1.34MM **Privately Held**
SIC: 7372  7389  Prepackaged software; Business Activities at Non-Commercial Site

**(P-18809)**
**SOLIDCORE SYSTEMS INC (DH)**
3965 Freedom Cir, Santa Clara (95054-1206)
PHONE..............................408 387-8400
Anne Bonaparte, *Pr*
Rosen Sharma, *
Jay Vaishnav, *
David Walker Senior, *Worldwide Operations Vice President*
Bob Vieraitis, *
EMP: 100 EST: 2003
SQ FT: 2,000
SALES (est): 6.56MM
SALES (corp-wide): 1.92B **Privately Held**
SIC: 7372  Prepackaged software
HQ: Mcafee, Llc
    6220 America Ctr Dr
    San Jose CA 95002

**(P-18810)**
**SOLV ENERGY LLC**
Also Called: Swinerton Builders
16798 W Bernardo Dr, San Diego (92128-2850)
PHONE..............................858 622-4040
Danielle Hammersmith, *Mgr*
EMP: 236
Web: www.swinertonrenewable.com
SIC: 7372  Prepackaged software
HQ: Solv Energy, Llc
    16680 W Bernardo Dr
    San Diego CA 92127
    858 251-4888

**(P-18811)**
**SONENDO ACQUISITION CORP**
Also Called: Tdo Software, Inc.
6235 Lusk Blvd, San Diego (92121-2731)
PHONE..............................858 558-3696
Luiz Motta, *Genl Mgr*
EMP: 25 EST: 2004
SQ FT: 3,600

# 7372 - Prepackaged Software (P-18812)

**SALES (est):** 6.89MM
**SALES (corp-wide):** 300K **Privately Held**
**Web:** www.tdo4endo.com
**SIC: 7372** Prepackaged software
**HQ:** Societe Valsoft Inc
7405 Rte Transcanadienne Bureau 100
Saint-Laurent QC H4T 1
514 316-7647

### (P-18812)
### SONIC VR LLC
Also Called: Sonic Vr
225 Broadway Ste 650, San Diego (92101-5039)
**PHONE**..................................206 227-8585
Jason Riggs, *CEO*
Joy Lyons, *Engr*
David Carr, *Engr*
Jose Arjol Acebal, *COO*
**EMP:** 17 **EST:** 2015
**SQ FT:** 6,000
**SALES (est):** 372.94K **Privately Held**
**SIC: 7372** 8731 Application computer software; Commercial physical research

### (P-18813)
### SONY BIOTECHNOLOGY INC
1730 N 1st St 2nd Fl, San Jose (95112-4642)
**PHONE**..................................800 275-5963
James Graziadei, *Pr*
Narayan Prabhu, *
Peter Kim, *
**EMP:** 65 **EST:** 2003
**SALES (est):** 11.65MM **Privately Held**
**Web:** www.sonybiotechnology.com
**SIC: 7372** 3699 Prepackaged software; Laser systems and equipment
**HQ:** Sony Corporation Of America
25 Madison Ave Fl 27
New York NY 10010

### (P-18814)
### SOPACT INC
280 Chantecler Dr, Fremont (94539-4908)
**PHONE**..................................510 226-8535
Unmesh Sheth, *Admn*
**EMP:** 20 **EST:** 2015
**SALES (est):** 979.23K **Privately Held**
**Web:** www.sopact.com
**SIC: 7372** Prepackaged software

### (P-18815)
### SOUNDHOUND AI INC (PA)
Also Called: SOUNDHOUND
5400 Betsy Ross Dr, Santa Clara (95054-1101)
**PHONE**..................................408 441-3200
Keyvan Mohajer, *CEO*
Michael Zagorsek, *COO*
Nitesh Sharan, *CFO*
James Hom, *CPO*
**EMP:** 15 **EST:** 2005
**SALES (est):** 45.87MM
**SALES (corp-wide):** 45.87MM **Publicly Held**
**Web:** www.soundhound.com
**SIC: 7372** Prepackaged software

### (P-18816)
### SOUNDTHINKING INC (PA)
Also Called: SOUNDTHINKING
39300 Civic Center Dr Ste 300, Fremont (94538-2337)
**PHONE**..................................510 794-3100
Ralph A Clark, *Pr*
Pascal Levensohn, *Ch Bd*
Alan R Stewart, *CFO*
Nasim Golzadeh, *Sr VP*
Gary T Bunyard, *Sr VP*
**EMP:** 287 **EST:** 2001
**SALES (est):** 92.72MM **Publicly Held**
**Web:** www.soundthinking.com
**SIC: 7372** 7382 Prepackaged software; Security systems services

### (P-18817)
### SPACE TIME INSIGHT INC
1850 Gateway Dr Ste 125, San Mateo (94404-4082)
P.O. Box 729 (01740-0729)
**PHONE**..................................650 513-8550
Rob Schilling, *CEO*
William Tamblyn, *
Bryan Hughes, *
**EMP:** 47 **EST:** 2003
**SALES (est):** 12.59MM
**SALES (corp-wide):** 24.19B **Privately Held**
**SIC: 7372** Business oriented computer software
**PA:** Nokia Oyj
Karakaari 7
104488000

### (P-18818)
### SPARKCOGNITION INC (PA)
Also Called: Avathon
7901 Stoneridge Dr Ste 555, Pleasanton (94588)
**PHONE**..................................844 205-7173
Pervinder Johar, *CEO*
Sridhar Sudarsan, *
Doctor Bruce Porter, *CSO*
Niyati Kohler, *CSO**
**EMP:** 87 **EST:** 2013
**SALES (est):** 52.14MM
**SALES (corp-wide):** 52.14MM **Privately Held**
**Web:** www.sparkcognition.com
**SIC: 7372** Business oriented computer software

### (P-18819)
### SPARKTECH SOFTWARE LLC
1419 Beaudry Blvd, Glendale (91208-1707)
**PHONE**..................................818 330-9098
Cosmin Andriescu, *Prin*
**EMP:** 26 **EST:** 2010
**SALES (est):** 1.26MM **Privately Held**
**Web:** www.sparktechsoft.com
**SIC: 7372** Prepackaged software

### (P-18820)
### SPATIAL LABS INC
12555 W Jefferson Blvd Ste 220, Los Angeles (90066-7032)
**PHONE**..................................424 289-0275
Iddris Sandu, *CEO*
**EMP:** 32
**SALES (est):** 1.71MM **Privately Held**
**SIC: 7372** Prepackaged software

### (P-18821)
### SPEAKEASY TECH INC
525 Brannan St Ste 100, San Francisco (94107-1632)
**PHONE**..................................650 581-9701
**EMP:** 15
**SALES (est):** 406.28K **Privately Held**
**SIC: 7372** Prepackaged software

### (P-18822)
### SPECIALISTS IN CSTM SFTWR INC
2574 Wellesley Ave, Los Angeles (90064-2738)
**PHONE**..................................310 315-9660
Helen Russell, *Pr*
Melissa Vance, *
**EMP:** 27 **EST:** 1979
**SQ FT:** 2,400
**SALES (est):** 3.47MM **Privately Held**
**Web:** www.scs-mbs.com
**SIC: 7372** Prepackaged software

### (P-18823)
### SPIKES INC (PA)
Also Called: Spikes Security
4000 Executive Pkwy Ste 250, San Ramon (94583-4257)
**PHONE**..................................855 287-7453
Branden Spikes, *CEO*
Scott Alexander, *COO*
Scott Martin, *CCO*
Jed Katz, *Prin*
Greg Corona, *Prin*
**EMP:** 27 **EST:** 2012
**SQ FT:** 10,000
**SALES (est):** 774.12K
**SALES (corp-wide):** 774.12K **Privately Held**
**Web:** www.spikes.com
**SIC: 7372** Prepackaged software

### (P-18824)
### SPLUNK INC (HQ)
Also Called: Splunk
270 Brannan St, San Francisco (94107-2007)
**PHONE**..................................415 848-8400
Gary Steele, *Ex VP*
Scott Morgan, *CLO*
Sharyl Givens, *CPO*
Toni Pavlovich, *CCO*
Brian Roberts, *Sr VP*
**EMP:** 160 **EST:** 2003
**SQ FT:** 182,000
**SALES (est):** 3.65B
**SALES (corp-wide):** 53.8B **Publicly Held**
**Web:** www.splunk.com
**SIC: 7372** Prepackaged software
**PA:** Cisco Systems, Inc.
170 W Tasman Dr
408 526-4000

### (P-18825)
### SPOTON COMPUTING INC
Also Called: Stanza
548 Market St, San Francisco (94104-5401)
**PHONE**..................................650 293-7464
Smita Saxena, *CEO*
**EMP:** 28 **EST:** 2012
**SALES (est):** 3.82MM **Privately Held**
**Web:** www.spoton.com
**SIC: 7372** Business oriented computer software

### (P-18826)
### SPRING TECHNOLOGIES CORP
10170 Culver Blvd, Culver City (90232-3152)
**PHONE**..................................310 230-4000
Jonathan Finestone, *CEO*
**EMP:** 30 **EST:** 2022
**SALES (est):** 980.3K **Privately Held**
**SIC: 7372** Business oriented computer software

### (P-18827)
### SPRINGCOIN INC
4551 Glencoe Ave, Marina Del Rey (90292)
**PHONE**..................................310 494-6928
**EMP:** 20 **EST:** 2018
**SALES (est):** 1.22MM **Privately Held**
**Web:** www.springlabs.com
**SIC: 7372** Prepackaged software

### (P-18828)
### SQUELCH INC
3945 Freedom Cir Ste 560, Santa Clara (95054-1269)
**PHONE**..................................650 241-2700
Jayaram Bhat, *CEO*
Giorgina Gottlied, *
Ilan Raab, *
Dan Morris, *
Janette Schock, *
**EMP:** 30 **EST:** 2017
**SALES (est):** 2.31MM **Privately Held**
**Web:** www.squelch.io
**SIC: 7372** Application computer software

### (P-18829)
### SRA OSS INC
2114 Ringwood Ave, San Jose (95131-1715)
**PHONE**..................................408 855-8200
Rao Papolu, *Pr*
**EMP:** 52 **EST:** 2005
**SALES (est):** 3.6MM **Privately Held**
**Web:** www.sraoss.com
**SIC: 7372** Publisher's computer software
**HQ:** Software Research Associates, Inc.
2-32-8, Minamiikebukuro
Toshima-Ku TKY 171-0

### (P-18830)
### SRAX INC (PA)
1014 S Westlake Blvd # 14-299, Westlake Village (91361-3108)
**PHONE**..................................323 205-6109
Christopher Miglino, *Ch Bd*
**EMP:** 54 **EST:** 2009
**SALES (est):** 27.86MM
**SALES (corp-wide):** 27.86MM **Publicly Held**
**SIC: 7372** Prepackaged software

### (P-18831)
### STACKLA INC
548 Market St, San Francisco (94104-5401)
**PHONE**..................................415 789-3304
Damien Mahoney, *CEO*
Peter Cassaidy, *CPO**
**EMP:** 65 **EST:** 2014
**SALES (est):** 5.15MM **Privately Held**
**Web:** www.nosto.com
**SIC: 7372** Application computer software

### (P-18832)
### STACKWATCH INC
Also Called: Kubecost
315 Montgomery St Fl 9, San Francisco (94104-1858)
**PHONE**..................................301 202-4542
David W Brown, *Pr*
**EMP:** 32 **EST:** 2019
**SALES (est):** 5.17MM **Privately Held**
**Web:** www.kubecost.com
**SIC: 7372** Application computer software

### (P-18833)
### STALKER SOFTWARE INC
Also Called: Communigate Systems
6 Tara View Rd, Belvedere Tiburon (94920-1522)
**PHONE**..................................415 569-2280
Vladimir Butenko, *Pr*
**EMP:** 50 **EST:** 1993
**SALES (est):** 2.5MM **Privately Held**
**SIC: 7372** 7371 Prepackaged software; Custom computer programming services

## PRODUCTS & SERVICES SECTION
## 7372 - Prepackaged Software (P-18857)

**(P-18834)**
**STANDARD COGNITION CORP (PA)**
548 Market St # 96346, San Francisco (94104-5401)
PHONE.............................415 324-4156
Prena Patel, *Admn*
Jordan Fisher, *
Michael Suswal, *
Anthony Lutz, *
**EMP:** 27 **EST:** 2017
**SALES (est):** 10.04MM
**SALES (corp-wide):** 10.04MM **Privately Held**
Web: www.standard.ai
**SIC: 7372** Business oriented computer software

**(P-18835)**
**STEELWEDGE SOFTWARE INC**
3875 Hopyard Rd Ste 300, Pleasanton (94588-8527)
PHONE.............................925 460-1700
**EMP:** 70
Web: www.e2open.com
**SIC: 7372** Prepackaged software

**(P-18836)**
**STELLAR CYBER INC**
2590 N 1st St Ste 360, San Jose (95131-1057)
PHONE.............................408 548-0860
Changming Liu, *CEO*
Aimei Wei, *VP*
**EMP:** 100 **EST:** 2015
**SALES (est):** 13.46MM **Privately Held**
Web: www.stellarcyber.ai
**SIC: 7372** Business oriented computer software

**(P-18837)**
**STEP MOBILE INC**
Also Called: Step
380 Portage Ave, Palo Alto (94306-2244)
PHONE.............................203 913-9229
Cj Mcdonald, *CEO*
**EMP:** 35 **EST:** 2018
**SALES (est):** 6.4MM **Privately Held**
Web: www.step.com
**SIC: 7372** Application computer software

**(P-18838)**
**STORM8 INC**
Also Called: Storm8 Entertainment
2400 Bridge Pkwy Ste 2, Redwood City (94065-1166)
PHONE.............................650 596-8600
Perry Tam, *CEO*
Jeff Witt, *Pr*
Man Hay Tam, *VP*
**EMP:** 16 **EST:** 2009
**SALES (est):** 13.75MM **Privately Held**
Web: www.storm8.com
**SIC: 7372** Prepackaged software
**PA:** Stillfront Group Ab (Publ)
Kungsgatan 38

**(P-18839)**
**STRATEGIC INSIGHTS INC**
Also Called: Brightscope
9191 Towne Centre Dr Ste 401, San Diego (92122-1225)
PHONE.............................858 452-7500
**EMP:** 19
Web: www.issgovernance.com
**SIC: 7372** Business oriented computer software
**PA:** Strategic Insights, Inc.
805 3rd Ave

**(P-18840)**
**STRATEGY COMPANION CORP**
100 Pacifica Ste 220, Irvine (92618-7441)
PHONE.............................714 460-8398
Robert Sterling, *Pr*
**EMP:** 70 **EST:** 2006
**SALES (est):** 10.99MM **Privately Held**
Web: www.strategycompanion.com
**SIC: 7372** Prepackaged software
**PA:** Strategy Companion Corp.
Scotia Centre 4th Floor

**(P-18841)**
**STREET SMART LLC**
Also Called: Street Smart 247
100 N Pacific Coast Hwy, El Segundo (90245-4359)
PHONE.............................866 924-4644
Cicero Lucas, *CEO*
**EMP:** 27 **EST:** 2019
**SALES (est):** 1.44MM
**SALES (corp-wide):** 14.18MM **Privately Held**
Web: www.versaterm.com
**SIC: 7372** Prepackaged software
**HQ:** Fivepoint Payments Llc
204 Caughman Farm Ln # 201
Lexington SC 29072
803 951-2094

**(P-18842)**
**STROMASYS INC**
871 Marlborough Ave Ste 100, Riverside (92507-2131)
PHONE.............................919 239-8450
George Koukis, *Ch Bd*
John Prot, *
Chris Pavlou, *
Serge Pavoncello, *
**EMP:** 78 **EST:** 2008
**SALES (est):** 3.94MM
**SALES (corp-wide):** 600K **Privately Held**
Web: www.stromasys.com
**SIC: 7372** 5734 Operating systems computer software; Software, business and non-game
**HQ:** Stromasys Sa
Avenue Louis-Casal 18
GenCve GE 1209

**(P-18843)**
**STRYDER CORP (PA)**
Also Called: Handshake
225 Bush St Fl 12, San Francisco (94104-4254)
P.O. Box 40770 (94140-0770)
PHONE.............................415 981-8400
Garrett Lord, *Ch Bd*
Scott Ringwelski, *
Ben Christensen, *
Asif Makhani, *
**EMP:** 91 **EST:** 2014
**SALES (est):** 24.73MM
**SALES (corp-wide):** 24.73MM **Privately Held**
Web: www.joinhandshake.com
**SIC: 7372** 7371 7379 Educational computer software; Computer software development and applications; Computer related consulting services

**(P-18844)**
**SUBJECT TECHNOLOGIES INC**
Also Called: Subject
345 N Maple Dr, Beverly Hills (90210-3869)
PHONE.............................310 243-6484
Felix Ruano, *Prin*
**EMP:** 50 **EST:** 2020
**SALES (est):** 6.1MM **Privately Held**
Web: www.subject.com
**SIC: 7372** Educational computer software

**(P-18845)**
**SUBTLE MEDICAL INC**
883 Santa Cruz Ave Ste 205, Menlo Park (94025-4638)
PHONE.............................650 397-8709
Miriam Murase, *Pr*
Tao Zhang, *Dir*
**EMP:** 22 **EST:** 2017
**SALES (est):** 4.13MM **Privately Held**
Web: www.subtlemedical.com
**SIC: 7372** Prepackaged software

**(P-18846)**
**SUGARSYNC INC**
Also Called: Sharpcast
6922 Hollywood Blvd Ste 500, Los Angeles (90028-6125)
PHONE.............................650 571-5105
Laura Yecies, *Pr*
Peter Chantel, *
**EMP:** 30 **EST:** 2004
**SQ FT:** 11,000
**SALES (est):** 4.9MM **Privately Held**
Web: www.sugarsync.com
**SIC: 7372** Business oriented computer software

**(P-18847)**
**SUMOPTI**
742 Moreno Ave, Palo Alto (94303-3617)
PHONE.............................650 331-1126
Jay Goyal, *Pt*
Jay Goyal, *Owner*
**EMP:** 50 **EST:** 2007
**SQ FT:** 1,500
**SALES (est):** 684.63K **Privately Held**
Web: www.sumopti.com
**SIC: 7372** Business oriented computer software

**(P-18848)**
**SUNGARD TREASURY SYSTEMS INC**
Also Called: Sungard
23975 Park Sorrento Ste 100, Calabasas (91302-4010)
PHONE.............................818 223-2300
**EMP:** 250
**SIC: 7372** Prepackaged software

**(P-18849)**
**SUPERGIANT GAMES LLC**
521 Gough St, San Francisco (94102-4417)
PHONE.............................714 488-5642
David Edery, *Prin*
**EMP:** 32 **EST:** 2021
**SALES (est):** 3.79MM **Privately Held**
Web: www.supergiantgames.com
**SIC: 7372** Prepackaged software

**(P-18850)**
**SUPPORT TECHNOLOGIES INC**
1939 Deere Ave, Irvine (92606-4818)
PHONE.............................949 442-2957
Tayo Daramole, *Pr*
**EMP:** 15 **EST:** 1992
**SQ FT:** 2,000
**SALES (est):** 1.15MM **Privately Held**
Web: www.alexusinfo.com
**SIC: 7372** Prepackaged software

**(P-18851)**
**SWIFTCOMPLY US OPCO INC**
Also Called: Swiftcomply
6701 Koll Center Pkwy Ste 250, Pleasanton (94566-8061)
PHONE.............................650 430-4341
Michael O'dwyer, *CEO*
**EMP:** 17
**SALES (est):** 3.8MM **Privately Held**
Web: www.swiftcomply.com
**SIC: 7372** 7379 Prepackaged software; Data processing consultant
**PA:** Swiftcomply Us Opco, Inc.
405 E D St Ste D
800 761-4999

**(P-18852)**
**SWIFTLANE INC**
743 Clementina St, San Francisco (94103-3812)
PHONE.............................833 607-9438
Saurabh Bajaj, *CEO*
**EMP:** 16
**SALES (est):** 5.69MM **Privately Held**
Web: www.swiftlane.com
**SIC: 7372** Prepackaged software

**(P-18853)**
**SWIFTLY INC**
49 Stevenson St Ste 700, San Francisco (94105-2954)
PHONE.............................415 894-5223
Jonathan Simkin, *CEO*
**EMP:** 174 **EST:** 2014
**SALES (est):** 5.02MM **Privately Held**
Web: www.goswift.ly
**SIC: 7372** Application computer software

**(P-18854)**
**SWIFTSTACK INC (HQ)**
Also Called: Nvidia
423 Central Ave, Menlo Park (94025-2804)
PHONE.............................408 486-2000
Don Jaworski, *CEO*
Anders Tjernlund, *
**EMP:** 58 **EST:** 2011
**SALES (est):** 4.89MM **Publicly Held**
Web: www.nvidia.com
**SIC: 7372** Business oriented computer software
**PA:** Nvidia Corporation
2788 San Tomas Expy

**(P-18855)**
**SWITCHBOARD SOFTWARE INC**
268 Bush St, San Francisco (94104-3503)
PHONE.............................415 425-3660
**EMP:** 26 **EST:** 2019
**SALES (est):** 1.05MM **Privately Held**
Web: www.switchboard-software.com
**SIC: 7372** Prepackaged software

**(P-18856)**
**SWITCHBOARD SOFTWARE INC**
115 Sansome St Fl 7, San Francisco (94104-3601)
PHONE.............................415 506-9095
Kwek Ju-kay, *Admn*
**EMP:** 15 **EST:** 2015
**SALES (est):** 4.14MM **Privately Held**
Web: www.switchboard-software.com
**SIC: 7372** Prepackaged software

**(P-18857)**
**SYBASE INC (DH)**
Also Called: Sybase
One Sybase Dr, Dublin (94568-7976)
PHONE.............................925 236-5000
John S Chen, *Pr*
Jeffrey G Ross, *
Raj Nathan, *CMO*
Daniel R Carl, *General Vice President*
▲ **EMP:** 40 **EST:** 1984
**SQ FT:** 406,000
**SALES (est):** 21.13MM
**SALES (corp-wide):** 33.92B **Privately Held**

## 7372 - Prepackaged Software (P-18858)

Web: www.sybase.com
SIC: 7372 Prepackaged software
HQ: Sap America, Inc.
   3999 West Chester Pike
   Newtown Square PA 19073
   610 661-1000

**(P-18858)**
**SYNOPSYS INC (PA)**
Also Called: Synopsys
675 Almanor Ave, Sunnyvale (94085-2934)
PHONE..................................650 584-5000
Sassine Ghazi, *Pr*
Sassine Ghazi, *Pr*
Aart J De Geus, *
Shelagh Glaser, *CFO*
Richard Mahoney, *CRO*
EMP: 500 EST: 1986
SALES (est): 5.84B
SALES (corp-wide): 5.84B **Publicly Held**
Web: www.synopsys.com
SIC: 7372 7371 Prepackaged software; Computer software development

**(P-18859)**
**SYNPLICITY INC (HQ)**
690 E Middlefield Rd, Mountain View (94043-4010)
PHONE..................................650 584-5000
Gary Meyers, *Pr*
Alisa Yaffa, *SEC VP INTELLECTUAL PROPERTY*
John J Hanlon, *VP Fin*
Andrew Haines, *VP Mktg*
EMP: 160 EST: 1994
SQ FT: 66,212
SALES (est): 6.01MM
SALES (corp-wide): 5.84B **Publicly Held**
Web: www.synopsys.com
SIC: 7372 Prepackaged software
PA: Synopsys, Inc.
   675 Almanor Ave
   650 584-5000

**(P-18860)**
**SYSTEM1 INC (PA)**
4235 Redwood Ave, Los Angeles (90066-5605)
PHONE..................................310 924-6037
Michael Blend, *Ch Bd*
Paul Filsinger, *Pr*
Tridivesh Kidambi, *CFO*
Brian Coppola, *Chief Product Officer*
EMP: 400 EST: 2020
SALES (est): 401.97MM
SALES (corp-wide): 401.97MM **Publicly Held**
Web: www.system1.com
SIC: 7372 Business oriented computer software

**(P-18861)**
**TAGNOS INC**
555 W 5th St Fl 34, Los Angeles (90013-1051)
PHONE..................................949 305-0806
EMP: 26 EST: 2020
SALES (est): 4.94MM **Privately Held**
Web: www.tagnos.com
SIC: 7372 Prepackaged software

**(P-18862)**
**TALENA INC**
2860 Zanker Rd Ste 109, San Jose (95134-2119)
PHONE..................................408 649-6388
Justin Lau, *Admn*
EMP: 20 EST: 2013
SALES (est): 799.86K **Privately Held**

SIC: 7372 Prepackaged software

**(P-18863)**
**TALIX INC**
660 3rd St, San Francisco (94107-1927)
PHONE..................................628 220-3885
Dean Stephens, *CEO*
Ashmi Shah, *
Niraj Katwala, *
Abdo Abdo, *Chief Growth Officer*
Shahyan Currimbhoy, *CPO*
EMP: 59 EST: 2014
SALES (est): 9.45MM **Privately Held**
Web: www.talix.com
SIC: 7372 Application computer software
PA: Edifecs, Inc.
   1756 114th Ave Se

**(P-18864)**
**TANIUM INC**
Also Called: Kobe Protection Group
2100 Powell St 3rd Fl, Emeryville (94608-1892)
PHONE..................................510 704-0202
David Hindawi, *CEO*
Orion Hindawi, *
Eric Brown, *
Scott Rubin, *CMO*
Chris Bream, *
EMP: 804 EST: 2004
SALES (est): 57.11MM **Privately Held**
Web: www.tanium.com
SIC: 7372 Application computer software

**(P-18865)**
**TANKA INC**
303 Twin Dolphin Dr Ste 600, Redwood City (94065-1422)
PHONE..................................650 656-9560
Issac Lee, *Pr*
EMP: 80
SALES (est): 1.55MM **Privately Held**
SIC: 7372 Application computer software

**(P-18866)**
**TANOSHI INC**
505 14th St Ste 900, Oakland (94612-1406)
PHONE..................................949 677-5261
Bradley Wayne Johnston, *CEO*
EMP: 18 EST: 2017
SALES (est): 3.78MM **Privately Held**
Web: www.tanoshikidscomputers.com
SIC: 7372 Prepackaged software

**(P-18867)**
**TAPINGO INC (DH)**
Also Called: Tapingo
39 Stillman St, San Francisco (94107-1309)
PHONE..................................415 283-5222
Daniel Almog, *CEO*
EMP: 40 EST: 2012
SQ FT: 4,300
SALES (est): 4.26MM
SALES (corp-wide): 5.62B **Privately Held**
Web: onsite.grubhub.com
SIC: 7372 Prepackaged software
HQ: Grubhub Inc.
   111 W Wash St Ste 2100
   Chicago IL 60602
   877 585-7878

**(P-18868)**
**TEAMBRIDGE LLC** ◊
604 Mission St Fl 10, San Francisco (94105-3526)
PHONE..................................415 323-5571
Lawrence Goldstein, *CEO*
Arjun Vora, *
EMP: 25 EST: 2023
SALES (est): 753.43K **Privately Held**

SIC: 7372 Prepackaged software

**(P-18869)**
**TEAMOHANA INC**
2067 Golden Gate Ave, San Francisco (94115-4314)
PHONE..................................415 650-9767
Tushar Makhija, *CEO*
EMP: 20 EST: 2021
SALES (est): 5.03MM **Privately Held**
SIC: 7372 7389 Prepackaged software; Business services, nec

**(P-18870)**
**TEAMRADERIE INC**
171 Main St # 510, Los Altos (94022-2912)
PHONE..................................650 402-0030
EMP: 38
SALES (est): 7.13MM **Privately Held**
Web: www.teamraderie.com
SIC: 7372 Prepackaged software

**(P-18871)**
**TELESIGN HOLDINGS INC (HQ)**
13274 Fiji Way Ste 600, Marina Del Rey (90292-7293)
PHONE..................................310 740-9700
Ryan Disraeli, *CEO*
Philipp Gast, *
Tom Powledge, *Chief Product Officer*
Justin Hart, *
EMP: 30 EST: 2016
SALES (est): 53.8MM **Privately Held**
Web: www.telesign.com
SIC: 7372 Prepackaged software
PA: Belgacom International Carrier Services
   Boulevard Du Roi Albert Ii 27

**(P-18872)**
**TELLUS SOLUTIONS INC**
3080 Olcott St Ste D103, Santa Clara (95054-3268)
PHONE..................................408 850-2942
Sara Jain, *Pr*
Jinesh Jain, *
EMP: 38 EST: 2005
SALES (est): 4.76MM **Privately Held**
Web: www.tellussol.com
SIC: 7372 7371 7373 Prepackaged software; Custom computer programming services; Computer integrated systems design

**(P-18873)**
**TERADATA CORPORATION (PA)**
Also Called: TERADATA
17095 Via Del Campo, San Diego (92127-1711)
PHONE..................................866 548-8348
Stephen Mcmillan, *Pr*
Claire Bramley, *CFO*
Richard Petley, *CRO*
Kathleen Cullen-cote, *CPO*
Margaret Treese, *CLO*
EMP: 951 EST: 1979
SALES (est): 1.83B **Publicly Held**
Web: www.teradata.com
SIC: 7372 3572 7371 3571 Prepackaged software; Computer storage devices; Software programming applications; Mainframe computers

**(P-18874)**
**TESSITURA NETWORK INC**
2295 Fletcher Pkwy Ste 101, El Cajon (92020-2145)
PHONE..................................888 643-5778
Jack B Rubin, *Pr*
Jack B Rubin, *CEO*
Andrew Recinos, *Pr*

Laura Bowden, *
Ivan Medanic, *OF*
EMP: 198 EST: 2002
SALES (est): 52.16MM **Privately Held**
Web: www.tessitura.com
SIC: 7372 Prepackaged software

**(P-18875)**
**TEXICAN INC**
21031 Ventura Blvd Ste 1000, Woodland Hills (91364-2227)
PHONE..................................310 384-7000
Tony Reyna, *CEO*
EMP: 50 EST: 2013
SALES (est): 698.26K **Privately Held**
Web: www.texicaninc.com
SIC: 7372 Prepackaged software

**(P-18876)**
**TEXTEXPANDER INC**
Also Called: Previously Known As Smile Inc
548 Market St # 37453, San Francisco (94104-5401)
PHONE..................................510 289-4000
J D Mullin, *CEO*
Greg Scown, *CEO*
EMP: 20 EST: 2016
SALES (est): 5.6MM **Privately Held**
Web: www.smilesoftware.com
SIC: 7372 Application computer software

**(P-18877)**
**TFB GAMES INC** ◊
5401 Old Redwood Hwy Ste 109, Petaluma (94954-7133)
PHONE..................................707 582-0005
Paul Yan, *CEO*
Paul Yan, *Pr*
EMP: 45 EST: 2024
SALES (est): 1.26MM **Privately Held**
SIC: 7372 Application computer software

**(P-18878)**
**THEBRAIN TECHNOLOGIES LP**
11522 W Washington Blvd, Los Angeles (90066-5914)
PHONE..................................310 751-5000
Harlan Hugh, *Genl Pt*
Shelley Hayduk, *Pt*
EMP: 16 EST: 1996
SQ FT: 2,850
SALES (est): 1.03MM **Privately Held**
Web: www.thebrain.com
SIC: 7372 Business oriented computer software

**(P-18879)**
**THOUGHTSPOT INC (PA)**
444 Castro St Ste 1000, Mountain View (94041-2070)
PHONE..................................800 508-7008
Ketan Karkhanis, *CEO*
Ajeet Singh, *
Amit Prakash, *
EMP: 107 EST: 2012
SALES (est): 91.15MM
SALES (corp-wide): 91.15MM **Privately Held**
Web: www.thoughtspot.com
SIC: 7372 Business oriented computer software

**(P-18880)**
**THOUSANDEYES LLC (HQ)**
500 Terry A Francois Blvd, San Francisco (94158-2355)
PHONE..................................415 513-4526
Mohit Lad, *CEO*
Ricardo Oliviera, *
EMP: 73 EST: 2010

# PRODUCTS & SERVICES SECTION

## 7372 - Prepackaged Software (P-18902)

SALES (est): 20.49MM
SALES (corp-wide): 53.8B **Publicly Held**
Web: www.thousandeyes.com
SIC: **7372** Business oriented computer software
PA: Cisco Systems, Inc.
170 W Tasman Dr
408 526-4000

### (P-18881)
### THQ INC
Also Called: Thq San Diego
21900 Burbank Blvd, Woodland Hills (91367-6469)
PHONE..................818 591-1310
EMP: 1088
Web: www.thqnordic.com
SIC: **7372** Prepackaged software

### (P-18882)
### THRIO INC
5230 Las Virgenes Rd Ste 210, Calabasas (91302-3448)
PHONE..................858 299-7191
Edwin K Margulies, *CEO*
Rose M Sinicrope, *
Ran Ezerzer, *
EMP: 25 EST: 2017
SALES (est): 5.07MM **Privately Held**
Web: www.thrio.com
SIC: **7372** Prepackaged software
PA: Nextiva, Inc.
9451 E Via De Ventura

### (P-18883)
### THURSBY SOFTWARE SYSTEMS LLC
1900 Carnegie Ave, Santa Ana (92705-5557)
PHONE..................817 478-5070
William Thursby, *CEO*
EMP: 28 EST: 1986
SALES (est): 3.15MM **Publicly Held**
Web: shop.thursby.com
SIC: **7372** Prepackaged software
PA: Identiv, Inc.
2201 Walnut Ave Ste 100

### (P-18884)
### TI LIMITED LLC (PA)
20335 Ventura Blvd Ste 231-239, Woodland Hills (91364-2444)
PHONE..................323 877-5991
Alberto Gamez, *
EMP: 52 EST: 2016
SQ FT: 9,000
SALES (est): 2.44MM
SALES (corp-wide): 2.44MM **Privately Held**
SIC: **7372** 8748 Business oriented computer software; Business consulting, nec

### (P-18885)
### TIMEVALUE SOFTWARE
22 Mauchly, Irvine (92618-2306)
P.O. Box 50250 (92619-0250)
PHONE..................949 727-1800
Michael Applegate, *Pr*
Charles Miller, *
EMP: 25 EST: 1983
SQ FT: 18,000
SALES (est): 5.96MM **Privately Held**
Web: www.timevalue.com
SIC: **7372** 7371 Prepackaged software; Computer software development

### (P-18886)
### TOCA BOCA INC
848 Folsom St Ste 201, San Francisco (94107-1173)
PHONE..................415 352-9028
Bjorn Jeffery, *CEO*
EMP: 18 EST: 2011
SALES (est): 3.62MM
SALES (corp-wide): 1.9B **Privately Held**
Web: www.tocaboca.com
SIC: **7372** Application computer software
PA: Spin Master Corp
225 King St W Suite 200
416 364-6002

### (P-18887)
### TONKEAN INC
44 Montgomery St, San Francisco (94104-4602)
PHONE..................646 215-0493
Sagi Eliyahu, *CEO*
EMP: 100 EST: 2015
SALES (est): 8.69MM **Privately Held**
Web: www.tonkean.com
SIC: **7372** Business oriented computer software

### (P-18888)
### TOTALREWARDS SOFTWARE INC
2208 Plaza Dr Ste 100, Rocklin (95765-4418)
PHONE..................916 632-1000
Raymond Odonnell, *CEO*
EMP: 24 EST: 2006
SALES (est): 282.74K **Privately Held**
Web: www.totalrewardssoftware.com
SIC: **7372** Prepackaged software

### (P-18889)
### TRACKONOMY SYSTEMS INC (PA)
214 Devcon Dr, San Jose (95112-4210)
PHONE..................833 872-2566
Erik Volkerink, *CEO*
Ajay Khoche, *
Steve Roeser, *
Jake Medwell, *
Troy Ford, *
EMP: 263 EST: 2017
SALES (est): 49.68MM
SALES (corp-wide): 49.68MM **Privately Held**
Web: www.trackonomysystems.com
SIC: **7372** 7371 7377 3663 Prepackaged software; Computer software development and applications; Computer hardware rental or leasing, except finance leasing; Radio and t.v. communications equipment

### (P-18890)
### TRAFFIC MANAGEMENT PDTS INC
Also Called: Fivesixtwo Inc
4900 Airport Plaza Dr Ste 300, Long Beach (90815-1375)
PHONE..................800 763-3999
Jonathan E Spano, *CEO*
Ed Barrera, *
Christopher H Spano, *
EMP: 842 EST: 2015
SALES (est): 3.78MM **Privately Held**
SIC: **7372** Prepackaged software
PA: Traffic Management, Llc
4900 Arprt Plz Dr Ste 300

### (P-18891)
### TRAXERO NORTH AMERICA LLC
1730 E Holly Ave Ste 740, El Segundo (90245-4404)
PHONE..................423 497-1164
Mark Sedgley, *Managing Member*
EMP: 90 EST: 2020

SALES (est): 5.82MM **Privately Held**
SIC: **7372** Business oriented computer software

### (P-18892)
### TRION WORLDS INC
2400 Bridge Pkwy 100, Redwood City (94065-1166)
PHONE..................650 631-9800
EMP: 294
SIC: **7372** Home entertainment computer software

### (P-18893)
### TROV INC
1423 Broadway, Oakland (94612-2054)
PHONE..................925 478-5500
Scott Walchek, *CEO*
Michael Pearson, *Sec*
EMP: 21 EST: 2012
SALES (est): 2.75MM **Privately Held**
Web: www.trov.com
SIC: **7372** Application computer software

### (P-18894)
### TUBEMOGUL INC
1250 53rd St Ste 1, Emeryville (94608-2965)
PHONE..................510 653-0126
Brett Wilson, *Pr*
Ron Will, *
Robert Gatto, *
Keith Eadie, *CMO CSO**
Paul Joachim, *
EMP: 577 EST: 2007
SQ FT: 49,000
SALES (est): 119.14MM
SALES (corp-wide): 19.41B **Publicly Held**
SIC: **7372** Application computer software
PA: Adobe Inc.
345 Park Ave
408 536-6000

### (P-18895)
### TWILIO INC (PA)
Also Called: TWILIO
101 Spear St Fl 5, San Francisco (94105-1554)
PHONE..................415 390-2337
Khozema Shipchandler, *CEO*
Aidan Viggiano, *CFO*
Dana R Wagner, *CLO CCO*
Chris Koehler, *CMO*
EMP: 785 EST: 2008
SQ FT: 101,434
SALES (est): 4.15B
SALES (corp-wide): 4.15B **Publicly Held**
Web: www.twilio.com
SIC: **7372** Prepackaged software

### (P-18896)
### UJET INC (PA)
535 Mission St Fl 14, San Francisco (94105-2903)
PHONE..................855 242-8538
Anand Janefalkar, *CEO*
Kristin King, *CCO**
EMP: 17 EST: 2015
SALES (est): 11.61MM
SALES (corp-wide): 11.61MM **Privately Held**
Web: www.ujet.cx
SIC: **7372** Prepackaged software

### (P-18897)
### UNBROKEN STUDIOS LLC
2120 Park Pl Ste 110, El Segundo (90245-4741)
PHONE..................310 741-2670
Paul Ohanian, *CEO*

Anthony Scott, *
EMP: 80 EST: 2018
SALES (est): 8.64MM
SALES (corp-wide): 13.85MM **Privately Held**
Web: www.unbrokenstudios.com
SIC: **7372** Prepackaged software
PA: Pound Sand, Llc
2120 Park Pl Ste 110
310 741-2670

### (P-18898)
### UNCOUNTABLE INC (PA)
415 Brannan St, San Francisco (94107)
P.O. Box 77625 (94107)
PHONE..................650 208-5949
EMP: 15 EST: 2016
SALES (est): 2.87MM
SALES (corp-wide): 2.87MM **Privately Held**
Web: www.uncountable.com
SIC: **7372** Application computer software

### (P-18899)
### UNEEKOR INC
15770 Laguna Canyon Rd Ste 100, Irvine (92618-3187)
PHONE..................888 262-6498
Jey Ho Suk, *CEO*
Uinam Choi, *Sec*
EMP: 58 EST: 2018
SALES (est): 1.55MM **Privately Held**
Web: www.uneekor.com
SIC: **7372** Prepackaged software

### (P-18900)
### UNIFI SOFTWARE INC
1810 Gateway Dr Ste 380, San Mateo (94404-4063)
PHONE..................732 614-9522
Matt Mosman, *CEO*
Rob Carlson, *Pr*
Donald Carr, *Off Mgr*
Bill Serino, *CRO*
Intekhab Nazeer, *CFO*
EMP: 25 EST: 2015
SALES (est): 4.27MM **Privately Held**
SIC: **7372** Business oriented computer software

### (P-18901)
### UNLIMITED INNOVATIONS INC
Also Called: Cerecons
180 N Rverview Dr Ste 320, Anaheim (92808)
PHONE..................714 998-0866
FAX: 714 998-5641
EMP: 30
SQ FT: 5,000
SALES (est): 2.35MM
SALES (corp-wide): 12.81B **Privately Held**
Web: www.cerecons.com
SIC: **7372** Prepackaged software
HQ: Medecision, Inc.
550 E Swedesford Rd # 220
Wayne PA 19087
484 588-0102

### (P-18902)
### UNTANGLE HOLDINGS INC (PA)
Also Called: Untangle
25 Metro Dr Ste 210, San Jose (95110-1338)
PHONE..................408 598-4299
Scott Devens, *CEO*
Lori Booroojian, *CFO*
Dirk Morris, *Chief Product Officer*
EMP: 45 EST: 2016
SALES (est): 4.56MM
SALES (corp-wide): 4.56MM **Privately Held**

# 7372 - Prepackaged Software (P-18903)

**(P-18903)**
**UPGUARD INC (PA)**
723 N Shoreline Blvd, Mountain View (94043-3208)
PHONE..................................888 882-3223
Alan Sharp-paul, *CEO*
Mike Baukes, *
Vincent Chuang, *
**EMP:** 30 **EST:** 2012
**SQ FT:** 13,800
**SALES (est):** 10.39MM
**SALES (corp-wide):** 10.39MM **Privately Held**
**Web:** www.upguard.com
**SIC: 7372** Business oriented computer software

**(P-18904)**
**UPSTANDING LLC**
Also Called: Mobilityware
440 Exchange Ste 100, Irvine (92602-1390)
PHONE..................................949 788-9900
John Libby, *
**EMP:** 180 **EST:** 1990
**SQ FT:** 48,000
**SALES (est):** 5.02MM **Privately Held**
**Web:** www.mobilityware.com
**SIC: 7372** Business oriented computer software

**(P-18905)**
**UPTIMEAI INC**
611 Gateway Blvd, South San Francisco (94080-7017)
PHONE..................................415 935-1195
Jagadish Gattu, *CEO*
**EMP:** 25 **EST:** 2019
**SALES (est):** 1.09MM **Privately Held**
**Web:** www.uptimeai.com
**SIC: 7372** Business oriented computer software

**(P-18906)**
**USERTESTING INC (PA)**
Also Called: Usertesting
1484 Pollard Rd, Los Gatos (95032-1081)
PHONE..................................888 877-1882
Andy Macmillan, *Pr*
Mark Chamberlain, *
David Smith, *
**EMP:** 79 **EST:** 2007
**SALES (est):** 48.4MM
**SALES (corp-wide):** 48.4MM **Privately Held**
**Web:** www.usertesting.com
**SIC: 7372** Prepackaged software

**(P-18907)**
**VALDERA INC**
548 Market St Ste 85314, San Francisco (94104-5401)
PHONE..................................415 323-6646
**EMP:** 34 **EST:** 2020
**SALES (est):** 5.51MM **Privately Held**
**Web:** www.valdera.com
**SIC: 7372** Business oriented computer software

**(P-18908)**
**VALIANTICA INC (PA)**
9170 Irvine Center Dr, Irvine (92618-4614)
PHONE..................................408 694-3803
Peiwei Mi, *Pr*
**EMP:** 21 **EST:** 2007
**SALES (est):** 3.08MM **Privately Held**
**Web:** www.valiantica.com
**SIC: 7372** Business oriented computer software

**(P-18909)**
**VALUTICS INC**
34332 Eucalyptus Ter, Fremont (94555-1983)
PHONE..................................408 823-3597
Monica Singhai, *Pr*
**EMP:** 20 **EST:** 2017
**SALES (est):** 873.75K **Privately Held**
**Web:** www.valutics.com
**SIC: 7372** 8742 7379 8741 Prepackaged software; Management consulting services; Computer related consulting services; Financial management for business

**(P-18910)**
**VANTIQ INC (PA)**
1990 N California Blvd Ste 640, Walnut Creek (94596-3775)
PHONE..................................650 346-1114
Marty Sprinzen, *CEO*
Paul Butterworth, *
Miguel Nhuch, *CRO*
William Daniher, *
**EMP:** 36 **EST:** 2014
**SQ FT:** 3,500
**SALES (est):** 5.87MM
**SALES (corp-wide):** 5.87MM **Privately Held**
**Web:** www.vantiq.com
**SIC: 7372** Application computer software

**(P-18911)**
**VARMOUR NETWORKS INC (HQ)**
1825 S Grant St, San Mateo (94402-2672)
PHONE..................................650 564-5100
Matt Gyde, *CEO*
Marc Woolward, *EMEA*
Demetrios Lazarikos Chief Information, *Sec*
**EMP:** 23 **EST:** 2011
**SALES (est):** 17.82MM **Privately Held**
**Web:** www.varmour.com
**SIC: 7372** Prepackaged software
**PA:** Nightdragon Acquisition Corp.
101 2nd St Ste 1275
510 306-7780

**(P-18912)**
**VECTICE INC**
785 Market St Ste 700, San Francisco (94103-2014)
PHONE..................................650 399-0114
Cyril Brignone, *CEO*
**EMP:** 28 **EST:** 2020
**SALES (est):** 5.9MM **Privately Held**
**Web:** www.vectice.com
**SIC: 7372** Prepackaged software

**(P-18913)**
**VEEVA SYSTEMS INC (PA)**
Also Called: Veeva
4280 Hacienda Dr, Pleasanton (94588-2719)
PHONE..................................925 452-6500
Peter P Gassner, *CEO*
Gordon Ritter, *Non-Executive Chairman of the Board*
Thomas D Schwenger, *Pr*
E Nitsa Zuppas, *CMO*
Michele O'connor, *CAO*
**EMP:** 216 **EST:** 2007
**SALES (est):** 2.36B **Publicly Held**
**Web:** www.veeva.com
**SIC: 7372** 7371 7379 Prepackaged software; Software programming applications; Computer related consulting services

**(P-18914)**
**VELODYNE LLC (HQ)**
Also Called: Velodyne Lidar
5521 Hellyer Ave, San Jose (95138-1017)
PHONE..................................669 275-2251
Angus Pacala, *CEO*
**EMP:** 26 **EST:** 1983
**SQ FT:** 205,000
**SALES (est):** 39.46MM
**SALES (corp-wide):** 113.39MM **Privately Held**
**Web:** www.velodynelidar.com
**SIC: 7372** Prepackaged software
**PA:** Ouster, Inc.
350 Treat Ave
415 987-6972

**(P-18915)**
**VELTI INC**
Also Called: Velti USA
150 California St 10th Fl, San Francisco (94111-4500)
PHONE..................................
**EMP:** 58 **EST:** 2009
**SALES (est):** 1.83MM **Privately Held**
**SIC: 7372** Prepackaged software

**(P-18916)**
**VERANA HEALTH INC**
360 3rd St Ste 425, San Francisco (94107-2164)
PHONE..................................888 774-0077
Sujay Jadhav, *CEO*
Miki Kapoor, *
Marie-eve Piche, *CFO*
Matthew Roe, *Chief Medical Officer*
**EMP:** 200 **EST:** 2008
**SALES (est):** 18.19MM **Privately Held**
**Web:** www.veranahealth.com
**SIC: 7372** Prepackaged software

**(P-18917)**
**VERITAS SOFTWARE GLOBAL LLC**
1600 Plymouth St, Mountain View (94043-1203)
PHONE..................................650 335-8000
**EMP:** 19 **EST:** 1989
**SALES (est):** 449.66K **Privately Held**
**SIC: 7372** Prepackaged software

**(P-18918)**
**VEZA TECHNOLOGIES INC**
122 Lansberry Ct, Los Gatos (95032-4711)
PHONE..................................510 870-8692
Tarun Thakur, *CEO*
**EMP:** 140 **EST:** 2021
**SALES (est):** 9MM **Privately Held**
**Web:** www.veza.com
**SIC: 7372** Prepackaged software

**(P-18919)**
**VIDEOAMP INC (PA)**
12121 Bluff Creek Dr, Playa Vista (90094-2994)
PHONE..................................424 272-7774
Peter Liguori, *
Peter Bradbury Ccgo, *Prin*
Josh Hudgins, *CPO*
Sharon Lee, *Ex VP*
**EMP:** 86 **EST:** 2014
**SALES (est):** 36.08MM
**SALES (corp-wide):** 36.08MM **Privately Held**
**Web:** www.videoamp.com
**SIC: 7372** Prepackaged software

**(P-18920)**
**VINDICIA INC**
1000 Sansome St Ste 200, San Francisco (94111-1346)
PHONE..................................650 264-4700
Kris Nagel, *CEO*
Mark Elrod, *
Brett Thomas, *
**EMP:** 135 **EST:** 2003
**SALES (est):** 21.18MM
**SALES (corp-wide):** 4.89B **Privately Held**
**Web:** www.vindicia.com
**SIC: 7372** Business oriented computer software
**HQ:** Amdocs, Inc.
625 Mryvlle Cntre Dr Ste
Saint Louis MO 63141
314 212-7000

**(P-18921)**
**VINTELLUS INC**
19918 Wellington Ct, Saratoga (95070-3813)
PHONE..................................510 972-4710
Sivakumar Sundaresan, *CEO*
**EMP:** 16 **EST:** 2018
**SALES (est):** 347.68K **Privately Held**
**SIC: 7372** Business oriented computer software

**(P-18922)**
**VISIONARY VR INC**
409 N Plymouth Blvd, Los Angeles (90004-3001)
PHONE..................................323 868-7443
Gil Baron, *Prin*
**EMP:** 24 **EST:** 2014
**SALES (est):** 131.37K **Privately Held**
**Web:** www.visionaryvr.com
**SIC: 7372** Prepackaged software

**(P-18923)**
**VISUALON INC (PA)**
19925 Stevens Creek Blvd, Cupertino (95014-2384)
PHONE..................................408 645-6618
Andy Lin, *Pr*
Sean Torsney, *Senior Vice President Business Development*
**EMP:** 25 **EST:** 2003
**SALES (est):** 2.6MM **Privately Held**
**Web:** www.visualon.com
**SIC: 7372** Prepackaged software

**(P-18924)**
**VIV LABS INC**
665 Clyde Ave, Mountain View (94043-2235)
PHONE..................................650 268-9837
Dag Kittlaus, *CEO*
**EMP:** 23 **EST:** 2012
**SALES (est):** 2.34MM **Privately Held**
**SIC: 7372** Utility computer software
**PA:** Samsung Electronics Co., Ltd.
129 Samsung-Ro, Yeongtong-Gu

**(P-18925)**
**VMWARE LLC (HQ)**
Also Called: Vmware
3421 Hillview Ave, Palo Alto (94304-1320)
PHONE..................................650 427-6000
Hock Tan, *CEO*
Kirsten M Spears, *CFO*
▲ **EMP:** 846 **EST:** 1998
**SALES (est):** 13.35B
**SALES (corp-wide):** 35.82B **Publicly Held**
**Web:** www.vmware.com
**SIC: 7372** Prepackaged software
**PA:** Broadcom Inc.
3421 Hillview Ave
650 427-6000

## PRODUCTS & SERVICES SECTION
## 7372 - Prepackaged Software (P-18948)

**(P-18926)**
**VNOMIC INC**
Also Called: Vnomic
19925 Stevens Creek Blvd Ste 100, Cupertino (95014-2384)
PHONE...........................408 641-3810
Allen Bannon, *CEO*
Alle Bannon, *
Iris Chang, *
Derek Palma, *
**EMP:** 37 **EST:** 2009
**SALES (est):** 2.54MM **Privately Held**
Web: www.vnomic.com
**SIC: 7372** Business oriented computer software

**(P-18927)**
**WAGGL INC (PA)**
1750 Bridgeway Ste B103, Sausalito (94965-1900)
PHONE...........................415 399-9949
Michael Papay, *CEO*
**EMP:** 60 **EST:** 2014
**SALES (est):** 4.63MM
**SALES (corp-wide):** 4.63MM **Privately Held**
Web: www.waggl.com
**SIC: 7372** Application computer software

**(P-18928)**
**WATERSHED TECHNOLOGY INC (PA)**
360 9th St, San Francisco (94103-3809)
PHONE...........................650 561-5438
Taylor Francis, *Pr*
**EMP:** 88 **EST:** 2019
**SALES (est):** 1.87MM
**SALES (corp-wide):** 1.87MM **Privately Held**
Web: www.watershed.com
**SIC: 7372** Publisher's computer software

**(P-18929)**
**WEBEDOCTOR INC**
335 N Puente St Ste B, Brea (92821-5274)
PHONE...........................714 990-3999
Anwer Siddiqi, *CEO*
**EMP:** 18 **EST:** 1999
**SALES (est):** 1.54MM **Privately Held**
Web: www.webedoctor.com
**SIC: 7372** Application computer software

**(P-18930)**
**WEBMETRO**
Also Called: Multivest
160 Via Verde Ste 1, San Dimas (91773-3901)
PHONE...........................909 599-8885
**EMP:** 85
Web: www.perfectdomain.com
**SIC: 7372** 7311 Prepackaged software; Advertising agencies

**(P-18931)**
**WEBROOT INC**
Also Called: Advanced Technology Dev Ctr
1855 S Grant St Ste 100, San Mateo (94402-7017)
PHONE...........................650 292-6600
Dick Williams, *Brnch Mgr*
**EMP:** 44
**SALES (corp-wide):** 5.77B **Privately Held**
Web: www.webroot.com
**SIC: 7372** Prepackaged software
**HQ:** Webroot Inc.
385 Interlocken Cres # 800
Broomfield CO 80021
303 442-3813

**(P-18932)**
**WILDFIRE INTERACTIVE INC**
1600 Amphitheatre Pkwy, Mountain View (94043-1351)
PHONE...........................650 253-0000
**EMP:** 250
Web: marketingplatform.google.com
**SIC: 7372** Prepackaged software

**(P-18933)**
**WILDFLOWER HEALTH INC**
2443 Fillmore St # 380 Pmb 6499, San Francisco (94115-1814)
PHONE...........................415 430-7543
Leah Sparks, *Pr*
Leah Sparks, *CEO*
Kristin Begley, *CCO**
Kim Russell, *OF Finance**
**EMP:** 47 **EST:** 2012
**SALES (est):** 3.09MM **Privately Held**
Web: www.wildflowerhealth.com
**SIC: 7372** Application computer software

**(P-18934)**
**WILLOW TECHNOLOGY INC**
215 Cummins Ln, Mckinleyville (95519-9243)
PHONE...........................360 393-4962
Gary Clueit, *Pr*
Susan Clueit, *
Sarah Clueit, *
**EMP:** 30 **EST:** 1991
**SALES (est):** 2.43MM **Privately Held**
**SIC: 7372** Prepackaged software

**(P-18935)**
**WIND RIVER SYSTEMS INC (DH)**
Also Called: Wind River
500 Wind River Way, Alameda (94501-1162)
PHONE...........................510 748-4100
Bryan Leblanc, *CEO*
Sean Lamb, *
**EMP:** 600 **EST:** 1981
**SQ FT:** 273,000
**SALES (est):** 429.57MM **Privately Held**
Web: www.windriver.com
**SIC: 7372** 7373 Application computer software; Systems software development services
**HQ:** Wolfhound Holdings, Inc
5725 Innovation Dr
Troy MI

**(P-18936)**
**WIND RIVER SYSTEMS INC**
12770 High Bluff Dr Ste 300, San Diego (92130-3008)
PHONE...........................858 824-3100
Bryan Leblanc, *CEO*
**EMP:** 17
Web: www.windriver.com
**SIC: 7372** Prepackaged software
**HQ:** Wind River Systems, Inc.
500 Wind River Way
Alameda CA 94501
510 748-4100

**(P-18937)**
**WIREX SYSTEMS**
100 S Murphy Ave Ste 200, Sunnyvale (94086-6118)
PHONE...........................408 799-4498
Tomer Saban, *CEO*
**EMP:** 35 **EST:** 2015
**SALES (est):** 976.91K **Privately Held**
Web: www.wirexsystems.com
**SIC: 7372** Prepackaged software

**(P-18938)**
**WM TECHNOLOGY INC (PA)**
Also Called: WM TECHNOLOGY
41 Discovery, Irvine (92618-3150)
PHONE...........................646 699-3750
Douglas Francis, *Ex Ch Bd*
Mary Hoitt, *Interim Chief Financial Officer*
**EMP:** 26 **EST:** 2008
**SALES (est):** 215.53MM
**SALES (corp-wide):** 215.53MM **Publicly Held**
Web: www.weedmaps.com
**SIC: 7372** Prepackaged software

**(P-18939)**
**WME BI LLC**
17075 Camino, San Diego (92127)
PHONE...........................877 592-2472
**EMP:** 60 **EST:** 2012
**SALES (est):** 2.45MM **Privately Held**
**SIC: 7372** Operating systems computer software

**(P-18940)**
**WONDERWARE CORPORATION (DH)**
26561 Rancho Pkwy S, Lake Forest (92630-8301)
PHONE...........................949 727-3200
Rick Bullotta, *VP*
Brian Dibenedetto, *
Karen Hamilton, *
Peter Kent, *
Dave Pickett, *
**EMP:** 300 **EST:** 1993
**SQ FT:** 32,000
**SALES (est):** 13.82MM
**SALES (corp-wide):** 82.05K **Privately Held**
Web: www.wonderware.com
**SIC: 7372** Prepackaged software
**HQ:** Aveva Software, Llc
26561 Rancho Pkwy S
Lake Forest CA 92630

**(P-18941)**
**WORDSMART CORPORATION**
10025 Mesa Rim Rd, San Diego (92121-2913)
P.O. Box 366 (92038-0366)
**EMP:** 40 **EST:** 1990
**SQ FT:** 12,375
**SALES (est):** 2.12MM **Privately Held**
**SIC: 7372** Educational computer software

**(P-18942)**
**WORKBOARD INC (PA)**
487 Seaport Ct Ste 100, Redwood City (94063-2730)
PHONE...........................650 294-4480
Deidre Paknad, *CEO*
Diedre Paknad, *
Karim Damji, *
David Ginsburg, *Chief Customer Officer*
Stuart Crabb, *
**EMP:** 222 **EST:** 2013
**SALES (est):** 18.39MM
**SALES (corp-wide):** 18.39MM **Privately Held**
Web: www.workboard.com
**SIC: 7372** Business oriented computer software

**(P-18943)**
**WORKSPOT INC (PA)**
1999 S Bascom Ave Ste 1000, Campbell (95008-2206)
PHONE...........................888 426-8113
Brad Tompkins, *CEO*
Amitabh Sinha, *Chief Strategy Officer**
Ty Wang, *

Jervis Williams, *
Puneet Chawla, *
**EMP:** 25 **EST:** 2012
**SALES (est):** 18.15MM
**SALES (corp-wide):** 18.15MM **Privately Held**
Web: www.workspot.com
**SIC: 7372** Business oriented computer software

**(P-18944)**
**WOWYOW INC**
3919 30th St, San Diego (92104-3004)
PHONE...........................844 496-9969
Adam Boskovich, *CEO*
Mike Ramirez, *Pr*
**EMP:** 15 **EST:** 2015
**SALES (est):** 1.09MM **Privately Held**
Web: www.wowyow.com
**SIC: 7372** Prepackaged software

**(P-18945)**
**XCELMOBILITY INC**
Also Called: XCEL
2225 E Bayshore Rd Ste 200, Palo Alto (94303-3220)
PHONE...........................650 320-1728
Zhixiong Wei, *Ch Bd*
Li Ouyang, *CFO*
Ying Yang, *Corporate Secretary**
**EMP:** 98 **EST:** 2007
**SALES (est):** 1.67MM **Privately Held**
Web: www.xcelmobility.com
**SIC: 7372** 7999 Business oriented computer software; Gambling and lottery services

**(P-18946)**
**XLSOFT CORPORATION**
12 Mauchly Ste K, Irvine (92618-6304)
PHONE...........................949 453-2781
Mitsutoshi Watanabe, *Pr*
Nanako Watanabe, *CFO*
**EMP:** 15 **EST:** 1987
**SQ FT:** 7,000
**SALES (est):** 1.91MM **Privately Held**
Web: www.xlsoft.com
**SIC: 7372** 7371 Publisher's computer software; Custom computer programming services

**(P-18947)**
**XPERI INC (PA)**
2190 Gold St, San Jose (95002)
PHONE...........................408 519-9100
Jon E Kirchner, *CEO*
Robert Andersen, *CFO*
Murali Dharan, *Pr*
David C Habiger, *Ch*
**EMP:** 66 **EST:** 2019
**SALES (est):** 521.33MM
**SALES (corp-wide):** 521.33MM **Publicly Held**
Web: www.xperi.com
**SIC: 7372** Prepackaged software

**(P-18948)**
**XTIME INC**
1400 Bridge Pkwy Ste 200, Redwood City (94065-6130)
PHONE...........................650 508-4300
Neal East, *Pr*
Adam Galper, *
Jim Doehrman, *
**EMP:** 32 **EST:** 1999
**SQ FT:** 6,000
**SALES (est):** 9.46MM
**SALES (corp-wide):** 16.61B **Privately Held**
Web: www.xtime.com
**SIC: 7372** Prepackaged software
**HQ:** Cox Automotive, Inc.
6205 Pachtree Dunwoody Rd

Atlanta GA 30319
855 449-0010

**(P-18949)**
**YARDI KUBE INC**
Also Called: Wun
430 S Fairview Ave, Goleta (93117-3637)
PHONE.................805 699-2040
EMP: 52 EST: 2018
SALES (est): 5.52MM Privately Held
Web: www.yardikube.com
SIC: 7372 Prepackaged software

**(P-18950)**
**YOURPEOPLE INC (HQ)**
Also Called: Trinet Zenefits
50 Beale St Ste 1000, San Francisco (94105-1863)
PHONE.................888 249-3263
Jay Fulcher, CEO
Shaun Wiley, Sr VP
EMP: 50 EST: 2012
SALES (est): 24.19MM Publicly Held
Web: www.trinet.com
SIC: 7372 8741 6411 Business oriented computer software; Administrative management; Insurance brokers, nec
PA: Trinet Group, Inc.
1 Park Pl Ste 600

**(P-18951)**
**YUJA INC (PA)**
84 W Santa Clara St Ste 400, San Jose (95113-1820)
PHONE.................888 257-2278
Ajit Singh, Pr
Nathan Arora, Chief Business Officer*
EMP: 116 EST: 2013
SALES (est): 9.1MM
SALES (corp-wide): 9.1MM Privately Held
Web: www.yuja.com
SIC: 7372 Prepackaged software

**(P-18952)**
**ZENDESK INC (HQ)**
Also Called: Zendesk
181 Fremont St Fl 17, San Francisco (94105-2207)
PHONE.................415 418-7506
Tom Eggemeier, CEO
Jeffrey Titterton, *
Julie Swinney, *
Andrea Nieto, CPO*
EMP: 4741 EST: 2007
SQ FT: 108,000
SALES (est): 1.16B
SALES (corp-wide): 1.16B Privately Held
Web: www.zendesk.com
SIC: 7372 Business oriented computer software
PA: Zoro Bidco, Inc.
3000 Sand Hl Rd Bldg 1 St
650 681-4701

**(P-18953)**
**ZENTERA SYSTEMS INC**
1525 Mccarthy Blvd Ste 1104, Milpitas (95035-7451)
PHONE.................408 436-4811
Jaushin Lee, CEO
Mike Ichiriu, *
Belinda Shih, *
EMP: 25 EST: 2012
SQ FT: 2,834
SALES (est): 3.42MM Privately Held
Web: www.zentera.net
SIC: 7372 Business oriented computer software

**(P-18954)**
**ZERO GRAVITY LABS INC ◊**
548 Market St Pmb 33721, San Francisco (94104-5401)
PHONE.................707 653-6287
Michael Heinrich, CEO
EMP: 24 EST: 2023
SALES (est): 1.34MM Privately Held
SIC: 7372 Prepackaged software

**(P-18955)**
**ZINIO SYSTEMS INC**
114 Sansome St 4th Fl, San Francisco (94104-3803)
PHONE.................415 494-2700
Rusty Lewis, CEO
Richard A Maggiotto, *
Jeanniey Mullen, CMO*
Tom Nofziger, *
Michelle Bottomley, *
EMP: 75 EST: 2000
SALES (est): 9.48MM Privately Held
Web: www.racerxonline.com
SIC: 7372 Publisher's computer software

**(P-18956)**
**ZOOMIFIER CORPORATION (PA)**
Also Called: Fullfeel
8048 Golden Eagle Way, Pleasanton (94588-3119)
PHONE.................800 255-5303
Chetan Saiya, CEO
EMP: 400 EST: 2011
SALES (est): 1.78MM
SALES (corp-wide): 1.78MM Privately Held
Web: www.zoomifier.com
SIC: 7372 Business oriented computer software

**(P-18957)**
**ZUMEN INC**
340 S Lemon Ave Ste 3677, Walnut (91789-2706)
PHONE.................564 444-6964
EMP: 18 EST: 2019
SALES (est): 724.97K Privately Held
Web: www.zumen.com
SIC: 7372 Prepackaged software

**(P-18958)**
**ZUORA INC (PA)**
Also Called: Zuora
101 Redwood Shores Pkwy Ste 100, Redwood City (94065-6131)
PHONE.................
EMP: 300 EST: 2006
SQ FT: 100,000
SALES (est): 431.66MM Publicly Held
Web: www.zuora.com
SIC: 7372 Business oriented computer software

**(P-18959)**
**ZWIFT INC (PA)**
111 W Ocean Blvd Ste 1800, Long Beach (90802-7936)
PHONE.................855 469-9438
Eric Min, CEO
EMP: 281 EST: 2014
SALES (est): 26.51MM
SALES (corp-wide): 26.51MM Privately Held
Web: www.zwift.com
SIC: 7372 5961 Publisher's computer software; Fitness and sporting goods, mail order

## 7373 Computer Integrated Systems Design

**(P-18960)**
**AAE SYSTEMS INC**
445 S San Antonio Rd Ste 104, Los Altos (94022-3679)
P.O. Box 1088 (94023-1088)
PHONE.................408 732-1710
Javed Husain, Pr
EMP: 15 EST: 1984
SALES (est): 2.47MM Privately Held
Web: www.aaesys.com
SIC: 7373 3663 Turnkey vendors, computer systems; Radio and t.v. communications equipment

**(P-18961)**
**AARKI INC (PA)**
164 Townsend St Unit 3, San Francisco (94107-1990)
PHONE.................408 382-1180
Aman Sareen, CEO
Sid Bhatt, *
EMP: 94 EST: 2007
SALES (est): 9.86MM Privately Held
Web: www.aarki.com
SIC: 7373 7372 8742 7313 Systems software development services; Business oriented computer software; Marketing consulting services; Electronic media advertising representatives

**(P-18962)**
**ALTERYX INC (PA)**
Also Called: Alteryx
3347 Michelson Dr Ste 400, Irvine (92612-0691)
PHONE.................888 836-4274
Kevin Rubin, Interim Chief Executive Officer
Dean A Stoecker, *
Robert S Jones, Pr
Scott Davidson, COO
EMP: 25 EST: 1997
SQ FT: 180,000
SALES (est): 970MM
SALES (corp-wide): 970MM Privately Held
Web: www.alteryx.com
SIC: 7373 7372 Systems software development services; Prepackaged software

**(P-18963)**
**AT ROAD INC**
888 Tasman Dr, Milpitas (95035-7439)
PHONE.................510 668-1638
EMP: 582
SIC: 7373 7372 Systems integration services; Prepackaged software

**(P-18964)**
**BRILLIUS TECHNOLOGIES INC**
Also Called: Brillius
4305 Hacienda Dr, Pleasanton (94588-2743)
PHONE.................510 379-9027
Ram Danda, Pr
Prasha Ganga, *
EMP: 148 EST: 2013
SQ FT: 1,500
SALES (est): 16.32MM Privately Held
Web: www.brillius.com
SIC: 7373 7372 Systems engineering, computer related; Business oriented computer software

**(P-18965)**
**C 232 INC**
Also Called: Xenowulf
28486 Westinghouse Pl, Valencia (91355-0953)
PHONE.................818 731-1196
Elvis Sahakian, CEO
EMP: 18 EST: 2004
SQ FT: 3,000
SALES (est): 3.23MM Privately Held
Web: www.c232.com
SIC: 7373 3577 Systems engineering, computer related; Computer peripheral equipment, nec

**(P-18966)**
**CAPTIVA SOFTWARE CORPORATION (DH)**
10145 Pacific Heights Blvd, San Diego (92121-4234)
PHONE.................858 320-1000
Reynolds C Bish, Pr
Patrick L Edsell, *
Rick E Russo, CFO
Jim Nicol, Executive Product Development Vice President
Howard Dratler, OK Vice President
EMP: 80 EST: 1986
SQ FT: 25,000
SALES (est): 9.02MM Publicly Held
SIC: 7373 7372 Office computer automation systems integration; Prepackaged software
HQ: Emc Corporation
176 S St
Hopkinton MA 01748
508 435-1000

**(P-18967)**
**CAYLYM TECHNOLOGIES INTL LLC**
Also Called: Caylym Holdings
5340 E Home Ave, Fresno (93727-2104)
PHONE.................209 322-9596
John Kim, Managing Member
Michael Phillips, Legal Counsel
Richard Goddard, Managing Member
EMP: 21 EST: 2009
SQ FT: 2,000
SALES (est): 1.88MM Privately Held
Web: www.caylym.com
SIC: 7373 0851 2653 Computer systems analysis and design; Fire fighting services, forest; Boxes, corrugated: made from purchased materials

**(P-18968)**
**CHOUINARD & MYHRE INC**
655 Redwood Hwy Frontage Rd Ste 102, Mill Valley (94941-3034)
PHONE.................415 480-3636
Steve Giondomenica, Pr
Peter Bussi, COO
EMP: 30 EST: 1976
SQ FT: 4,000
SALES (est): 3.37MM Privately Held
SIC: 7373 7371 7372 Value-added resellers, computer systems; Computer software development; Prepackaged software
PA: Solutions-Ii, Inc.
8822 Ridgeline Blvd # 117

**(P-18969)**
**CLARITY DESIGN INC**
13000 Gregg St, Poway (92064-7151)
PHONE.................858 746-3500
Thomas H Lupfer, Pr
Robert Melucci, VP
◆ EMP: 17 EST: 1991
SALES (est): 3.84MM Privately Held
Web: www.claritydesign.com

**PRODUCTS & SERVICES SECTION**

**7373 - Computer Integrated Systems Design (P-18989)**

SIC: 7373 3672 Computer integrated systems design; Circuit boards, television and radio printed

**(P-18970)**
**CLINICOMP INTERNATIONAL INC (PA)**
9655 Towne Centre Dr, San Diego (92121-1964)
PHONE..................................858 546-8202
Chris Haudenschild, *CEO*
Eloisa Haudenschild, *CFO*
William Mcdonald, *Contrlr*
Jiao Fan Ph.d., *VP*
Kelley Malott, *VP*
EMP: 99 EST: 1983
SQ FT: 42,000
SALES (est): 21.96MM
SALES (corp-wide): 21.96MM **Privately Held**
Web: www.clinicomp.com
SIC: 7373 7371 3571 Systems software development services; Custom computer programming services; Electronic computers

**(P-18971)**
**EERO LLC**
660 3rd St, San Francisco (94107-1927)
PHONE..................................415 738-7972
Nick Weaver, *CEO*
EMP: 40 EST: 2014
SALES (est): 17.23MM **Publicly Held**
Web: www.eero.com
SIC: 7373 3669 5731 Computer integrated systems design; Intercommunication systems, electric; Consumer electronic equipment, nec
PA: Amazon.Com, Inc.
    410 Terry Ave N

**(P-18972)**
**ELECTRONIC ONLINE SYSTEMS INTERNATIONAL**
Also Called: E O S International
2292 Faraday Ave Frnt, Carlsbad (92008-7237)
PHONE..................................760 431-8400
EMP: 64 EST: 1981
SALES (est): 5.05MM **Privately Held**
SIC: 7373 7371 7372 Turnkey vendors, computer systems; Computer software development; Prepackaged software

**(P-18973)**
**EXTREME NETWORKS INC**
145 Rio Robles, San Jose (95134-1736)
PHONE..................................408 579-2800
EMP: 24
Web: www.extremenetworks.com
SIC: 7373 7372 Computer integrated systems design; Prepackaged software
PA: Extreme Networks, Inc.
    2121 Rdu Ctr Dr Ste 300

**(P-18974)**
**FILENET CORPORATION**
3565 Harbor Blvd, Costa Mesa (92626-1405)
PHONE..................................800 345-3638
EMP: 1695
SIC: 7373 7372 Computer integrated systems design; Business oriented computer software

**(P-18975)**
**FINSIX CORPORATION**
3565 Haven Ave Ste 1, Menlo Park (94025-1065)
P.O. Box 2224 (94026-2224)
PHONE..................................650 285-6400
Vanessa Green, *CEO*
Joseph Scarci, *
David Schaezler, *
Anthony Sagneri, *
Jim Kardarch, *
EMP: 30 EST: 2010
SALES (est): 2.04MM **Privately Held**
Web: www.finsix.com
SIC: 7373 3679 8731 Systems integration services; Electronic loads and power supplies; Electronic research

**(P-18976)**
**FRANCISCO PARTNERS GP III LP (HQ)**
Also Called: FP
1 Letterman Dr Bldg C, San Francisco (94129-2402)
PHONE..................................415 418-2900
Dipanjan Deb, *Mng Pt*
Chris Adams, *Pt*
Ben Ball, *Pt*
Neil Garfinkel, *Pt*
Peter Christodoulo, *Pt*
EMP: 60 EST: 2000
SALES (est): 17.08MM
SALES (corp-wide): 1.34B **Privately Held**
Web: www.franciscopartners.com
SIC: 7373 7372 Systems integration services; Prepackaged software
PA: Francisco Partners Management, L.P.
    1 Letterman Dr Ste 410
    415 418-2900

**(P-18977)**
**GBL SYSTEMS CORPORATION**
760 Paseo Camarillo Ste 401, Camarillo (93010-6002)
PHONE..................................805 987-4345
James Buscemi, *Pr*
EMP: 35 EST: 1990
SQ FT: 8,228
SALES (est): 7.46MM **Privately Held**
Web: www.gblsys.com
SIC: 7373 3559 Computer integrated systems design; Electronic component making machinery

**(P-18978)**
**GREENWAVE REALITY INC**
Also Called: Greenwave Systems
15420 Laguna Canyon Rd Ste 150, Irvine (92618-2128)
PHONE..................................714 805-9283
Martin Manniche, *CEO*
Peter Wilmar Christensen, *CFO*
Nate Williams, *Ex Dir*
Sharon Wang, *Ex VP*
Troy Pliska, *Sr VP*
▲ EMP: 20 EST: 2008
SALES (est): 4.39MM **Privately Held**
Web: www.greenwavesystems.com
SIC: 7373 7372 Systems software development services; Prepackaged software

**(P-18979)**
**GRIDBRIGHT INC**
Also Called: Gridbright
618 Oakshire Pl, Alamo (94507-2326)
P.O. Box 830 (94507-0830)
PHONE..................................925 899-9025
Alireza Vojdani, *CEO*
Stephen Callahan, *Sr VP*
EMP: 18 EST: 2013
SALES (est): 3.6MM
SALES (corp-wide): 196.94MM **Privately Held**
Web: www.gridbright.com
SIC: 7373 7372 7371 8711 Computer integrated systems design; Prepackaged software; Custom computer programming services; Engineering services
PA: Qualus Corp.
    4040 Rev Dr
    800 434-0415

**(P-18980)**
**INSIGNIA**
Also Called: Grande Vitesse Systems
390 Fremont St, San Francisco (94105-2316)
PHONE..................................415 777-0320
Jano Avanessian, *Pr*
Rene Young, *CFO*
Wendy Avanessian, *Stockholder*
EMP: 18 EST: 1987
SQ FT: 15,000
SALES (est): 853.33K **Privately Held**
Web: www.gvsnet.com
SIC: 7373 3572 5734 Systems integration services; Disk drives, computer; Computer and software stores

**(P-18981)**
**JUNIPER NETWORKS INC**
Also Called: Proof of Concept Poc Lab
1137 Innovation Way Bldg B, Sunnyvale (94089-1228)
PHONE..................................408 745-2000
Florin A Oprescu, *Prin*
EMP: 2000
Web: www.juniper.net
SIC: 7373 7372 Computer integrated systems design; Prepackaged software
PA: Juniper Networks, Inc.
    1133 Innovation Way

**(P-18982)**
**JUNIPER NETWORKS INTL LLC**
1133 Innovation Way, Sunnyvale (94089-1228)
PHONE..................................408 745-2000
Rami Rahim, *CEO*
EMP: 32 EST: 2016
SALES (est): 508.82K **Publicly Held**
Web: www.juniper.net
SIC: 7373 7372 Computer integrated systems design; Prepackaged software
PA: Juniper Networks, Inc.
    1133 Innovation Way

**(P-18983)**
**KETOS INC**
420 S Hillview Dr, Milpitas (95035-5464)
PHONE..................................408 550-2162
Meenakshi Sankaran, *CEO*
EMP: 55 EST: 2015
SALES (est): 2MM **Privately Held**
Web: www.ketos.co
SIC: 7373 3823 Computer integrated systems design; Process control instruments

**(P-18984)**
**LATTICE ENGINES INC (DH)**
1820 Gateway Dr Ste 200, San Mateo (94404-4059)
PHONE..................................877 460-0010
Bryan T Hipsher, *CEO*
Colleen Haley, *Sec*
EMP: 105 EST: 2010
SALES (est): 9.45MM
SALES (corp-wide): 2.31B **Publicly Held**
SIC: 7373 7372 Computer system selling services; Business oriented computer software
HQ: The Dun & Bradstreet Corporation
    5335 Gate Pkwy Ste 100
    Jacksonville FL 32256

**(P-18985)**
**LEADINGWAY CORPORATION (PA)**
Also Called: Leadingway Knowledge Systems
4199 Campus Dr Ste 550, Irvine (92612-4694)
PHONE..................................949 509-6589
James Li, *Pr*
Wei-wei Fang, *CFO*
EMP: 18 EST: 1991
SQ FT: 6,600
SALES (est): 453.88K **Privately Held**
SIC: 7373 7379 8742 7375 Systems software development services; Computer related consulting services; Management consulting services; Information retrieval services

**(P-18986)**
**MIRANTIS INC (PA)**
900 E Hamilton Ave Ste 650, Campbell (95008-0664)
PHONE..................................650 963-9828
Adrian Ionel, *CEO*
EMP: 15 EST: 2000
SALES (est): 24.66MM
SALES (corp-wide): 24.66MM **Privately Held**
Web: www.mirantis.com
SIC: 7373 3577 Computer integrated systems design; Computer peripheral equipment, nec

**(P-18987)**
**NORTHROP GRUMMAN SPACE & MISSION SYSTEMS CORP**
6379 San Ignacio Ave, San Jose (95119-1200)
PHONE..................................703 280-2900
◆ EMP: 12000
SIC: 7373 3663 3661 3812 Computer integrated systems design; Radio and t.v. communications equipment; Telephone and telegraph apparatus; Defense systems and equipment

**(P-18988)**
**QUEST SOFTWARE INC (PA)**
20 Enterprise Ste 100, Aliso Viejo (92656-7104)
PHONE..................................949 754-8000
Patrick Nichols, *CEO*
Carolyn Mccarthy, *CFO*
EMP: 600 EST: 1987
SQ FT: 170,000
SALES (est): 647.68MM
SALES (corp-wide): 647.68MM **Privately Held**
Web: www.quest.com
SIC: 7373 7379 7372 Computer integrated systems design; Computer related consulting services; Business oriented computer software

**(P-18989)**
**RAVENSWOOD SOLUTIONS INC (HQ)**
48371 Fremont Blvd Ste 105, Fremont (94538-6554)
PHONE..................................650 241-3661
Kipp Peppel, *CEO*
Kipp Peppel, *Pr*
John Prausa, *
Ernesto Lozano Junior, *Prin*
Peter Kuebler, *
EMP: 94 EST: 2015
SALES (est): 10.12MM

## 7373 - Computer Integrated Systems Design (P-18990)

SALES (corp-wide): 249.22MM Privately Held
Web: www.ravenswoodsolutions.com
SIC: 7373 7379 3679 8711  Systems engineering, computer related; Computer related maintenance services; Antennas, receiving; Engineering services
PA: Sri International
    333 Ravenswood Ave
    650 859-2000

**(P-18990)**
**RESULT GROUP INC**
2603 Main St Ste 710, Irvine (92614-4263)
PHONE..................480 777-7130
William Derick Robson, Pr
David Griffiths, *
EMP: 83 EST: 2003
SALES (est): 912.32K
SALES (corp-wide): 8.41B Privately Held
Web: www.rentalresult.com
SIC: 7373 7372  Systems software development services; Business oriented computer software
HQ: Wynne Systems, Inc.
    2601 Main St Ste 270
    Irvine CA 92614

**(P-18991)**
**SECOM INTERNATIONAL (PA)**
Also Called: Secom
15905 S Broadway, Gardena (90248-2405)
PHONE..................310 641-1290
Ted Burton, Pr
Terry Bixler, *
Linda Vose, *
EMP: 52 EST: 1978
SALES (est): 8.27MM
SALES (corp-wide): 8.27MM Privately Held
Web: www.spdprk.com
SIC: 7373 3446 3559 7371  Turnkey vendors, computer systems; Architectural metalwork; Parking facility equipment and supplies; Computer software systems analysis and design, custom

**(P-18992)**
**SINGTEL ENTERPRISE SEC US INC**
901 Marshall St Ste 125, Redwood City (94063-2026)
PHONE..................650 508-6800
Chang York Chye, CEO
EMP: 1610 EST: 2015
SALES (est): 20.78MM Privately Held
SIC: 7373 7372  Systems integration services; Prepackaged software
HQ: Singapore Telecommunications Limited
    10 Eunos Road 8
    Singapore 40860

**(P-18993)**
**SOURCE IT USA INC**
1150 S Olive St, Los Angeles (90015-2211)
PHONE..................714 318-4428
Peter Deralas, CEO
Peter Deralas, Pr
Fatana Deralas, VP
EMP: 22 EST: 2005
SALES (est): 1.8MM Privately Held
Web: www.sourceitusa.com
SIC: 7373 3577  Value-added resellers, computer systems; Computer peripheral equipment, nec

**(P-18994)**
**SURVIOS INC**
4501 Glencoe Ave, Marina Del Rey (90292-6372)
PHONE..................310 736-1503
Nathan Burba, CEO
EMP: 24 EST: 2013
SALES (est): 6.9MM Privately Held
Web: www.survios.com
SIC: 7373 7372  Computer integrated systems design; Prepackaged software

**(P-18995)**
**SYSTEM INTEGRATORS INC**
Also Called: Netlinx Publishing Solutions
1740 N Market Blvd, Sacramento (95834-1997)
PHONE..................916 830-2400
Paul Donlan, Pr
Allan Katzen, *
EMP: 180 EST: 1973
SQ FT: 70,000
SALES (est): 9.53MM
SALES (corp-wide): 355.83K Privately Held
SIC: 7373 7372 7371  Computer integrated systems design; Prepackaged software; Custom computer programming services
PA: Net-Linx Ag
    Kathe-Kollwitz-Ufer 76-79
    351318750

**(P-18996)**
**TRUEPOINT SOLUTIONS LLC (PA)**
3262 Penryn Rd Ste 100b, Loomis (95650)
PHONE..................916 259-1293
Bert Auburn, CEO
Keith Hobday, *
Robert Strouse, *
EMP: 29 EST: 2004
SQ FT: 1,800
SALES (est): 4.35MM Privately Held
Web: www.truepointsolutions.com
SIC: 7373 7372  Turnkey vendors, computer systems; Application computer software

**(P-18997)**
**UBIQUITI NETWORKS INC**
91 E Tasman Dr, San Jose (95134-1620)
PHONE..................408 942-3085
Robert J Pera, Ch
EMP: 81 EST: 2014
SALES (est): 5.46MM Publicly Held
SIC: 7373 5045 7372  Local area network (LAN) systems integrator; Computer software; Prepackaged software
PA: Ubiquiti Inc.
    685 3rd Ave Fl 27

**(P-18998)**
**URBAN INSIGHT INC**
3530 Wilshire Blvd Ste 1285, Los Angeles (90010-2328)
PHONE..................213 792-2000
Chris Steins, CEO
Abhijeet Chavan, COO
EMP: 54 EST: 1997
SQ FT: 4,000
SALES (est): 2.31MM Privately Held
Web: www.urbaninsight.com
SIC: 7373 7372 7371 8748  Computer integrated systems design; Business oriented computer software; Custom computer programming services; Systems engineering consultant, ex. computer or professional

**(P-18999)**
**WIPRO LLC**
Also Called: Wipro Technologies
425 National Ave Ste 200, Mountain View (94043-1399)
PHONE..................650 316-3555
Sridhar Ranasubbu, Fin Mgr
EMP: 45
Web: www.wipro.com
SIC: 7373 3571  Turnkey vendors, computer systems; Mainframe computers
HQ: Wipro, Llc
    300 Tri State Intl
    Lincolnshire IL 60069
    732 509-1502

**(P-19000)**
**WYTCOTE INC**
3 Park Plz Ste 480, Irvine (92614-2568)
PHONE..................877 472-5587
Frank Gomez, CEO
John Wilkerson, Pr
Bo Larsson, COO
EMP: 15 EST: 2016
SALES (est): 1.16MM Privately Held
Web: www.wytcote.com
SIC: 7373 3821 3826 3823  Systems integration services; Laboratory apparatus and furniture; Analytical instruments; Process control instruments

**(P-19001)**
**YANG-MING INTERNATIONAL CORP**
Also Called: Rackmountpro.com
595 Yorbita Rd, La Puente (91744-5956)
PHONE..................626 956-0100
Betty B Shou, Pr
Stephen Shou, *
◆ EMP: 25 EST: 1994
SQ FT: 10,000
SALES (est): 8.23MM Privately Held
Web: www.rackmountpro.com
SIC: 7373 3571  Systems integration services; Electronic computers

**(P-19002)**
**ZMICRO INC (PA)**
Also Called: Z Microsystems
9820 Summers Ridge Rd, San Diego (92121-3083)
PHONE..................858 831-7000
Jack Wade, CEO
John Howell, COO
Jason Wade, Pr
Rick Elliott, VP
Angi Smart, Contrlr
EMP: 57 EST: 1986
SQ FT: 36,800
SALES (est): 25.14MM
SALES (corp-wide): 25.14MM Privately Held
Web: www.zmicro.com
SIC: 7373 3577 3572  Computer integrated systems design; Computer peripheral equipment, nec; Computer storage devices

## 7374 Data Processing And Preparation

**(P-19003)**
**BAYTECH DIGITAL INC**
1798 Technology Dr Ste 178, San Jose (95110-1347)
PHONE..................408 533-8519
Howard Yeh, Pr
EMP: 24 EST: 2001
SQ FT: 5,000
SALES (est): 1.4MM Privately Held
Web: www.baytechwebdesign.com
SIC: 7374 7311 7336 2741  Computer graphics service; Advertising agencies; Commercial art and graphic design; Internet publishing and broadcasting

**(P-19004)**
**CASTLIGHT HEALTH INC (HQ)**
50 California St Ste 1800, San Francisco (94111-4602)
PHONE..................415 829-1400
Maeve O'meara, CEO
Will Bondurant, CFO
Richa Gupta, CPO
Dena Bravata, CMO
EMP: 93 EST: 2008
SQ FT: 31,000
SALES (est): 146.71MM
SALES (corp-wide): 147.15MM Privately Held
Web: www.mycastlighthealth.com
SIC: 7374 7372  Data processing and preparation; Prepackaged software
PA: Vera Whole Health, Inc
    1201 2nd Ave Ste 1400
    206 395-7870

**(P-19005)**
**CCH INCORPORATED**
2050 W 190th St, Torrance (90504-6228)
PHONE..................310 800-9800
EMP: 2178
SQ FT: 280,000
SALES (corp-wide): 6.07B Privately Held
Web: www.wolterskluwer.com
SIC: 7374 7372 7371  Data processing and preparation; Prepackaged software; Custom computer programming services
HQ: Cch Incorporated
    2700 Lake Cook Rd
    Riverwoods IL 60015
    847 267-7000

**(P-19006)**
**EXECUPRINT INC**
24963 Avenue Tibbitts, Santa Clarita (91355-3427)
PHONE..................818 993-8184
Amin Farag, Pr
Esther Farag, Prin
Bassem Farag, Prin
Michael Farag, Prin
EMP: 18 EST: 1975
SQ FT: 6,000
SALES (est): 4.88MM Privately Held
Web: www.execuprint.com
SIC: 7374 2752 2759  Computer graphics service; Offset printing; Commercial printing, nec

**(P-19007)**
**FORTINET INC (PA)**
Also Called: FORTINET
909 Kifer Rd, Sunnyvale (94086-5207)
PHONE..................408 235-7700
Ken Xie, Ch Bd
Michael Xie, Pr
Keith Jensen, CAO
John Whittle, Corporate Secretary
▲ EMP: 1367 EST: 2000
SQ FT: 395,000
SALES (est): 5.3B
SALES (corp-wide): 5.3B Publicly Held
Web: www.fortinet.com
SIC: 7374 3577  Data processing and preparation; Computer peripheral equipment, nec

**(P-19008)**
**HONK TECHNOLOGIES INC**
2251 Barry Ave, Los Angeles (90064-1401)
P.O. Box 910 (90078-0910)
PHONE..................800 979-3162
Corey Brundage, CEO
Dan Rosenthal, *
EMP: 151 EST: 2014

# PRODUCTS & SERVICES SECTION
## 7379 - Computer Related Services, Nec (P-19026)

SQ FT: 8,000
SALES (est): 75MM **Privately Held**
Web: www.honkforhelp.com
SIC: **7374** 7372 7371 Data processing and preparation; Business oriented computer software; Custom computer programming services

**(P-19009)**
**JASPERSOFT CORPORATION**
350 Rhode Island St Ste 250, San Francisco (94103-5187)
P.O. Box 77648 (94107-0648)
PHONE..............................415 348-2300
EMP: 175
SIC: **7374** 7372 7379 Computer graphics service; Business oriented computer software; Computer related consulting services

**(P-19010)**
**MAPLEBEAR INC (PA)**
Also Called: INSTACART
50 Beale St Ste 600, San Francisco (94105-1871)
PHONE..............................888 246-7822
Fidji Simo, *Ch Bd*
Emily Reuter, *CFO*
EMP: 3229 EST: 2012
SQ FT: 107,000
SALES (est): 3.04B
SALES (corp-wide): 3.04B **Publicly Held**
Web: www.instacart.com
SIC: **7374** 7372 7389 Data processing service; Publisher's computer software

**(P-19011)**
**MINDBODY INC (PA)**
Also Called: Mindbody
651 Tank Farm Rd, San Luis Obispo (93401-7062)
PHONE..............................877 755-4279
Richard Stollmeyer, *Ch Bd*
Josh Mccarter, *Pr*
Michael Mansbach, *
Brett White, *
Kimberly Lytikainen, *CLO**
EMP: 109 EST: 2001
SALES (est): 456.62MM **Privately Held**
Web: www.mindbodyonline.com
SIC: **7374** 7372 8741 Data processing and preparation; Business oriented computer software; Business management

**(P-19012)**
**RAZVI INC**
Also Called: Copy Rite
824 La Gonda Way, Danville (94526-1709)
PHONE..............................925 242-1200
Asad Razvi, *Pr*
EMP: 20 EST: 1985
SALES (est): 1.47MM **Privately Held**
Web: www.prestigeprinting.com
SIC: **7374** 2759 Computer graphics service; Commercial printing, nec

**(P-19013)**
**ROCKSTAR SAN DIEGO INC**
2200 Faraday Ave Ste 200, Carlsbad (92008-7233)
PHONE..............................760 929-0700
Allan Wasserman, *Pr*
EMP: 65 EST: 1984
SQ FT: 24,000
SALES (est): 6.89MM **Publicly Held**
SIC: **7374** 7372 Computer graphics service; Prepackaged software
PA: Take-Two Interactive Software, Inc.
  110 W 44th St

**(P-19014)**
**RUBRIK INC (PA)**
Also Called: Rubrik
3495 Deer Creek Rd, Palo Alto (94304-1316)
PHONE..............................844 478-2745
Bipul Sinha, *Ch Bd*
Kiran Choudary, *CFO*
Arvind Nithrakashyap, *
Brian Mccarthy, *CRO*
EMP: 2882 EST: 2013
SQ FT: 81,031
SALES (est): 627.89MM
SALES (corp-wide): 627.89MM **Publicly Held**
Web: www.rubrik.com
SIC: **7374** 7371 7372 Data processing and preparation; Computer software development and applications; Application computer software

**(P-19015)**
**ZYNGA INC (HQ)**
Also Called: Zynga
1200 Park Pl Ste 100, San Mateo (94403-1581)
PHONE..............................855 449-9642
Frank Gibeau, *Pr*
Gerard Griffin, *CFO*
Jeff Ryan, *CPO*
Phuong Y Phillips, *CLO*
Amy M Rawlings, *CAO*
EMP: 242 EST: 2007
SQ FT: 185,000
SALES (est): 2.8B **Publicly Held**
Web: www.zynga.com
SIC: **7374** 7372 Data processing and preparation; Application computer software
PA: Take-Two Interactive Software, Inc.
  110 W 44th St

## 7375 Information Retrieval Services

**(P-19016)**
**DIGITAL INSIGHT CORPORATION (HQ)**
Also Called: Intuit Financial Services
1300 Seaport Blvd Ste 300, Redwood City (94063-5591)
PHONE..............................818 879-1010
Jeffrey E Stiefler, *Pr*
Joseph M Mcdoniel, *Ex VP*
Robert R Surridge, *
Tom Shen, *
▲ EMP: 200 EST: 1997
SQ FT: 46,000
SALES (est): 21.17MM
SALES (corp-wide): 3.83B **Publicly Held**
Web: www.ncr.com
SIC: **7375** 7372 7371 Information retrieval services; Prepackaged software; Custom computer programming services
PA: Ncr Voyix Corporation
  864 Spring St Nw
  800 225-5627

**(P-19017)**
**ISN GLOBAL ENTERPRISES INC**
987 W Foothill Blvd Ste 200, Claremont (91711-3357)
P.O. Box 1391 (91711-1391)
PHONE..............................909 670-0601
Edgar Reece, *CEO*
Edgar Reece, *Pr*
Scott Miller, *VP*
J T Reece, *CIO*
James Lewis, *VP*
EMP: 15 EST: 1995

SQ FT: 1,500
SALES (est): 2.44MM **Privately Held**
Web: www.isnglobal.com
SIC: **7375** 5999 1731 3575 Information retrieval services; Hospital equipment and supplies; Telephone and telephone equipment installation; Computer terminals, monitors and components

**(P-19018)**
**SAGE SOFTWARE INC**
Sage
7595 Irvine Center Dr Ste 200, Irvine (92618-2957)
PHONE..............................949 753-1222
John Kang, *Brnch Mgr*
EMP: 52
SALES (corp-wide): 2.76B **Privately Held**
Web: na.sage.com
SIC: **7375** 7374 7372 3089 Information retrieval services; Data processing and preparation; Prepackaged software; Plastics processing
HQ: Sage Software, Inc.
  271 17th St Nw Ste 1100
  Atlanta GA 30363
  866 996-7243

## 7378 Computer Maintenance And Repair

**(P-19019)**
**ALCHEMY CAFE INC (PA)**
746 French Gulch Rd, Murphys (95247-9762)
PHONE..............................925 825-8400
Ken Eysel, *CEO*
Lorrie K Eysel, *
EMP: 25 EST: 1989
SQ FT: 11,000
SALES (est): 4.41MM **Privately Held**
Web: www.aristadoes.com
SIC: **7378** 3861 Computer peripheral equipment repair and maintenance; Photographic equipment and supplies

**(P-19020)**
**BCP SYSTEMS INC**
1560 S Sinclair St, Anaheim (92806-5933)
PHONE..............................714 202-3900
Carlos P Torres, *CEO*
William W Price, *
EMP: 60 EST: 1994
SALES (est): 16.5MM **Privately Held**
Web: www.bcpsystems.com
SIC: **7378** 3571 5063 Computer and data processing equipment repair/maintenance; Electronic computers; Electrical apparatus and equipment

**(P-19021)**
**QUEST INTL MONITOR SVC INC (PA)**
Also Called: Quest International
60 Parker 65, Irvine (92618-1604)
PHONE..............................949 581-9900
Shahnam Arshadi, *Pr*
Kamyar Katouzian, *
▲ EMP: 60 EST: 1985
SALES (est): 20.86MM
SALES (corp-wide): 20.86MM **Privately Held**
Web: www.questinc.com
SIC: **7378** 7379 7371 7373 Computer maintenance and repair; Computer related maintenance services; Custom computer programming services; Systems integration services

**(P-19022)**
**RAKWORX INC**
1 Mason, Irvine (92618-2514)
PHONE..............................949 215-1362
Yue Cong, *VP*
Zhiyong Ding, *
EMP: 150 EST: 2016
SALES (est): 1.56MM **Privately Held**
Web: www.rakworx.com
SIC: **7378** 3577 Computer and data processing equipment repair/maintenance; Data conversion equipment, media-to-media: computer

## 7379 Computer Related Services, Nec

**(P-19023)**
**A10 NETWORKS INC (PA)**
2300 Orchard Pkwy, San Jose (95131-1017)
PHONE..............................408 325-8668
Dhrupad Trivedi, *Ch Bd*
Karen Thomas, *Executive Worldwide Sales Vice-President*
Brian Becker, *CFO*
Scott Weber, *Corporate Secretary*
▲ EMP: 300 EST: 2004
SQ FT: 116,381
SALES (est): 251.7MM **Publicly Held**
Web: www.a10networks.com
SIC: **7379** 7372 Computer related maintenance services; Prepackaged software

**(P-19024)**
**ACT-ON SOFTWARE INC**
1620 E Roseville Pkwy Ste 200, Roseville (95661-3995)
PHONE..............................503 530-1555
EMP: 40
SALES (corp-wide): 1.82MM **Privately Held**
Web: www.act-on.com
SIC: **7379** 7372 Computer related maintenance services; Prepackaged software
HQ: Act-On Software, Inc.
  121 Sw Morrison St # 1600
  Portland OR 97204

**(P-19025)**
**AIMINSIGHT SOLUTIONS INC**
Also Called: A.I.M. Services
4127 Berryman Ave, Los Angeles (90066-5425)
PHONE..............................310 313-0047
Amjad Khanmohamed, *Pr*
Imtiaz Khanmohamed, *VP*
EMP: 15 EST: 2011
SALES (est): 1.24MM **Privately Held**
Web: www.aiminsight.com
SIC: **7379** 7371 8742 7372 Computer related consulting services; Computer software systems analysis and design, custom; Management consulting services; Business oriented computer software

**(P-19026)**
**ASANA INC (PA)**
Also Called: Asana
633 Folsom St Ste 100, San Francisco (94107-3600)
PHONE..............................415 525-3888
Dustin Moskovitz, *Ch Bd*
Sonalee Parekh, *CFO*
Anne Raimondi, *COO*
Eleanor Lacey, *Corporate Secretary*
EMP: 1764 EST: 2008

## 7379 - Computer Related Services, Nec (P-19027)

SQ FT: 88,000
SALES (est): 652.5MM
SALES (corp-wide): 652.5MM **Publicly Held**
Web: www.asana.com
SIC: **7379** 7372 Computer related consulting services; Prepackaged software

**(P-19027)**
**ASI NETWORKS INC**
19331 E Walnut Dr N, City Of Industry (91748-1436)
P.O. Box 867 (91773-0867)
PHONE..................................800 251-1336
Jeff Plumley, *Pr*
Pam Landers, *Prin*
Dean Nedelman, *Prin*
Richard Creed, *Prin*
EMP: 15 EST: 1997
SQ FT: 3,200
SALES (est): 9.03MM **Privately Held**
Web: www.asi-networks.com
SIC: **7379** 3825 Disk and diskette conversion service; Network analyzers

**(P-19028)**
**BEEWISE US INC**
3001 Bishop Dr Ste 300, San Ramon (94583-5005)
P.O. Box 767 (94583-5767)
PHONE..................................888 706-3907
EMP: 25 EST: 2020
SALES (est): 2.57MM **Privately Held**
SIC: **7379** 3523 Computer related maintenance services; Farm machinery and equipment

**(P-19029)**
**BERNARDO TECHNICAL SERVICES**
Also Called: Btsi
16885 W Bernardo Dr # 210, San Diego (92127-1618)
PHONE..................................858 779-9276
EMP: 18 EST: 2006
SQ FT: 2,300
SALES (est): 2.28MM **Privately Held**
Web: www.btsihq.com
SIC: **7379** 3399 Computer related consulting services; Laminating steel

**(P-19030)**
**BITSCOPIC INC**
10866 Wilshire Blvd Ste 400, Los Angeles (90024-4338)
PHONE..................................650 503-3120
Payam Etminani, *CEO*
EMP: 20 EST: 2012
SALES (est): 1.22MM **Privately Held**
Web: www.bitscopic.com
SIC: **7379** 7371 7372 7373 Computer related consulting services; Computer software writing services; Prepackaged software; Systems software development services

**(P-19031)**
**BLYTHECO INC (PA)**
530 Technology Dr Ste 100, Irvine (92618-1350)
PHONE..................................949 583-9500
Stephen P Blythe, *CEO*
Lori Seal, *
EMP: 45 EST: 1980
SALES (est): 9.61MM
SALES (corp-wide): 9.61MM **Privately Held**
Web: www.blytheco.com

SIC: **7379** 7372 7371 Computer related consulting services; Prepackaged software; Computer software systems analysis and design, custom

**(P-19032)**
**BOUGHTS INC**
5927 Balfour Ct, Carlsbad (92008-7375)
PHONE..................................619 895-7246
Amir Tafreshi, *Pr*
EMP: 30 EST: 2011
SALES (est): 777.69K **Privately Held**
SIC: **7379** 3842 Online services technology consultants; Respirators

**(P-19033)**
**BRANDCAST INC**
842 Folsom St, San Francisco (94107-1123)
PHONE..................................415 517-4772
Ashok Santhanam, *CEO*
Hayes Metzger, *
EMP: 30 EST: 2015
SALES (est): 2.34MM **Privately Held**
Web: www.timesites.com
SIC: **7379** 7372 Online services technology consultants; Business oriented computer software

**(P-19034)**
**CIPHERTRACE INC**
140 Victory Ln, Los Gatos (95030-5922)
PHONE..................................650 996-2142
David Jevans, *CEO*
Stephen Ryan, *COO*
EMP: 75 EST: 2015
SALES (est): 5.01MM
SALES (corp-wide): 25.1B **Publicly Held**
Web: www.ciphertrace.com
SIC: **7379** 8748 7372 7371 Computer related consulting services; Systems engineering consultant, ex. computer or professional; Application computer software; Custom computer programming services
PA: Mastercard Incorporated
2000 Purchase St
914 249-2000

**(P-19035)**
**ETHERWAN SYSTEMS INC**
2301 E Winston Rd, Anaheim (92806-5642)
P.O. Box 1048 (92781-1048)
PHONE..................................714 779-3800
Mitch Yang, *Pr*
▲ EMP: 100 EST: 1996
SQ FT: 5,000
SALES (est): 9.65MM
SALES (corp-wide): 3.74B **Privately Held**
Web: www.etherwan.com
SIC: **7379** 3577 Computer related maintenance services; Computer peripheral equipment, nec
HQ: Etherwan Systems, Inc.
8f, No. 2, Alley 6, Lane 235, Baoqiao Rd.
New Taipei City TAP 23102

**(P-19036)**
**GENERAL NETWORKS CORPORATION**
Also Called: Compass365
3524 Ocean View Blvd, Glendale (91208-1212)
PHONE..................................818 249-1962
Robert Todd Withers, *Pr*
Todd Withers, *
David Horwatt, *
Randall C Wise, *
Cort Baker, *
EMP: 60 EST: 1986

SQ FT: 3,600
SALES (est): 11.74MM **Privately Held**
Web: www.gennet.com
SIC: **7379** 5045 7372 Computer related consulting services; Terminals, computer; Prepackaged software

**(P-19037)**
**GLOBAL AUTOMATION INC (PA)**
Also Called: Dinostor
1388 Terra Bella Ave, Mountain View (94043-1836)
P.O. Box 1810 (94042-1810)
PHONE..................................650 316-5900
Srini Sankaran, *Pr*
▼ EMP: 27 EST: 1993
SQ FT: 6,000
SALES (est): 5.18MM **Privately Held**
Web: www.globalautomationinc.com
SIC: **7379** 7372 Computer related consulting services; Prepackaged software

**(P-19038)**
**GRISBY GAMING & TECH LLC** ◆
200 S Linden Ave Apt 5f, Rialto (92376-6210)
PHONE..................................415 463-8200
Don Juan Grisby, *Managing Member*
EMP: 20 EST: 2023
SALES (est): 441.9K **Privately Held**
SIC: **7379** 3577 Computer related consulting services; Computer peripheral equipment, nec

**(P-19039)**
**LEIDOS GOVERNMENT SERVICES INC**
500 N Via Val Verde, Montebello (90640-2358)
PHONE..................................323 721-6979
Nate Sadorian, *Brnch Mgr*
EMP: 146
SIC: **7379** 7372 Computer related consulting services; Prepackaged software
HQ: Leidos Government Services, Inc.
9737 Washingtonian Blvd
Gaithersburg MD 20878
856 486-5156

**(P-19040)**
**LIMSONS IT SERVICES LLC**
Also Called: Limsons
21255 Burbank Blvd Ste 120, Woodland Hills (91367-6669)
PHONE..................................323 988-5546
Pradeep Boddu, *CEO*
EMP: 21 EST: 2015
SALES (est): 1.03MM **Privately Held**
Web: www.limsons.com
SIC: **7379** 7372 Computer related consulting services; Prepackaged software

**(P-19041)**
**NTM CONSULTING SERVICES INC**
39300 Civic Center Dr Ste 250, Fremont (94538-2338)
PHONE..................................510 744-3901
Naji T Mourad, *CFO*
Najwa Mourad, *VP*
EMP: 20 EST: 1990
SALES (est): 956.09K **Privately Held**
Web: www.ntmcs.com
SIC: **7379** 7372 Online services technology consultants; Application computer software

**(P-19042)**
**ORACLE SYSTEMS CORPORATION (HQ)**
500 Oracle Pkwy, Redwood City (94065-1677)
PHONE..................................650 506-7000
Safra A Catz, *CEO*
Mark Hurd, *
Jeffrey O Henley, *
Mark V Hurd, *
Dorian Daley, *
EMP: 2300 EST: 1987
SQ FT: 2,200,000
SALES (est): 539.62MM
SALES (corp-wide): 52.96B **Publicly Held**
SIC: **7379** 8243 7372 Data processing consultant; Software training, computer; Business oriented computer software
PA: Oracle Corporation
2300 Oracle Way
737 867-1000

**(P-19043)**
**OSI DIGITAL INC (PA)**
26745 Malibu Hills Rd, Agoura Hills (91301-5355)
PHONE..................................818 992-2700
Kumar Yamani, *CEO*
Bob Ree, *
EMP: 40 EST: 1995
SALES (est): 24.49MM **Privately Held**
Web: www.osidigital.com
SIC: **7379** 7372 7371 8741 Online services technology consultants; Application computer software; Computer software development; Management services

**(P-19044)**
**SENSATA TECHNOLOGIES INC**
Also Called: BEI Industrial Encoders
1461 Lawrence Dr, Thousand Oaks (91320-1303)
PHONE..................................805 716-0322
Glenn Avolio, *Division Head*
EMP: 70
SALES (corp-wide): 4.05B **Privately Held**
Web: www.sensata.com
SIC: **7379** 3827 3663 Computer related maintenance services; Optical instruments and lenses; Radio and t.v. communications equipment
HQ: Sensata Technologies, Inc.
529 Pleasant St
Attleboro MA 02703

**(P-19045)**
**SERVICENOW INC (PA)**
Also Called: SERVICENOW
2225 Lawson Ln, Santa Clara (95054-3311)
PHONE..................................408 501-8550
William R Mcdermott, *CEO*
Frederic B Luddy, *
Gina Mastantuono, *CFO*
Chris Bedi, *Interim CAO*
EMP: 45 EST: 2004
SQ FT: 1,101,000
SALES (est): 8.97B **Publicly Held**
Web: www.servicenow.com
SIC: **7379** 7372 Computer related maintenance services; Prepackaged software

**(P-19046)**
**SOCAL TECHNOLOGIES LLC**
1305 Oakdale Ave, El Cajon (92021-8540)
PHONE..................................619 635-1128
Marwa Hasan Farhan, *CEO*
Saif Farhan, *Managing Member*
EMP: 23 EST: 2019
SALES (est): 344.62K **Privately Held**
Web: www.socal-technologies.com

## PRODUCTS & SERVICES SECTION

### 7383 - News Syndicates (P-19064)

SIC: 7379 1389 1799 1442 Computer related consulting services; Construction, repair, and dismantling services; Construction site cleanup; Construction sand mining

#### (P-19047)
**TIGERCONNECT INC (PA)**
2054 Broadway, Santa Monica (90404-2910)
PHONE.................310 401-1820
Jeffrey Evans, *CEO*
Sean Whiteley, *COO*
John Friedman, *Dir*
Herbert Madan, *Dir*
**EMP:** 58 **EST:** 2010
**SALES (est):** 20.92MM
**SALES (corp-wide):** 20.92MM **Privately Held**
Web: www.tigerconnect.com
SIC: 7379 7372 7373 Computer related maintenance services; Publisher's computer software; Computer systems analysis and design

#### (P-19048)
**TOM SAWYER SOFTWARE CORP (PA)**
1997 El Dorado Ave, Berkeley (94707-2441)
PHONE.................510 682-6313
Brendan P Madden, *CEO*
Joshua Feingold, *
**EMP:** 45 **EST:** 1991
**SQ FT:** 6,264
**SALES (est):** 8.25MM **Privately Held**
Web: www.tomsawyer.com
SIC: 7379 7371 7372 Computer related maintenance services; Computer software systems analysis and design, custom; Business oriented computer software

#### (P-19049)
**VERYS LLC**
Also Called: Verys
1251 E Dyer Rd Ste 210, Santa Ana (92705-5660)
PHONE.................949 423-3295
Christopher B Antonius, *CEO*
Mike Alan Zerkel, *Pr*
**EMP:** 125 **EST:** 2012
**SQ FT:** 15,500
**SALES (est):** 3.11MM
**SALES (corp-wide):** 332.34MM **Privately Held**
Web: www.verys.com
SIC: 7379 7371 7372 Online services technology consultants; Computer software development and applications; Application computer software
**PA:** West Monroe Partners, Llc
311 W Monroe St 14th Fl
312 602-4000

### 7381 Detective And Armored Car Services

#### (P-19050)
**GUARDSMARK LLC (DH)**
1551 N Tustin Ave Ste 650, Santa Ana (92705-8664)
PHONE.................714 619-9700
Steven S Jones, *CEO*
**EMP:** 101 **EST:** 2002
**SQ FT:** 32,107
**SALES (est):** 195.15MM
**SALES (corp-wide):** 12.86B **Privately Held**

SIC: 7381 8742 2721 Security guard service; Industry specialist consultants; Periodicals, publishing only
**HQ:** Universal Protection Service, Lp
450 Exchange
Irvine CA 92602
866 877-1965

### 7382 Security Systems Services

#### (P-19051)
**ACCURATE SECURITY PROS INC**
9919 Hibert St Ste D, San Diego (92131-1076)
PHONE.................858 271-1155
Gregory Parks, *CEO*
Gregory A Parks, *Pr*
**EMP:** 22 **EST:** 1983
**SQ FT:** 3,800
**SALES (est):** 2.8MM **Privately Held**
Web: www.accuratesecuritypros.com
SIC: 7382 3429 5065 5099 Security systems services; Door opening and closing devices, except electrical; Security control equipment and systems; Locks and lock sets

#### (P-19052)
**AUTONOMOUS DEFENSE TECH CORP**
Also Called: Swarm Aero
2889 W 5th St Ste 111, Oxnard (93030-6448)
PHONE.................805 616-2030
Daniel Goodman, *CEO*
Peter Kalogiannis, *
**EMP:** 32 **EST:** 2022
**SALES (est):** 5.6MM **Privately Held**
Web: www.swarm.aero
SIC: 7382 7371 3721 Security systems services; Software programming applications; Aircraft

#### (P-19053)
**DONE RIGHT SECURITY INC**
Also Called: Security Systems Installation
1260 Nimitz Ave Bldg 670, Vallejo (94592-1024)
PHONE.................510 621-7686
Brandon Newell, *CEO*
**EMP:** 20 **EST:** 2016
**SALES (est):** 5.46MM **Privately Held**
Web: www.donerightsecurity.com
SIC: 7382 1731 3446 Security systems services; Access control systems specialization; Gates, ornamental metal

#### (P-19054)
**ELITE INTRACTIVE SOLUTIONS INC**
1200 W 7th St Ste L1-180, Los Angeles (90017-6411)
PHONE.................310 740-5426
Aria Kozak, *Pr*
Jordan Lippel, *Chief Business Development Officer*
John Valdez, *Chief Business Development Officer*
Michael Zatulov, *
**EMP:** 32 **EST:** 2001
**SQ FT:** 8,000
**SALES (est):** 6.74MM **Privately Held**
Web: www.eliteisi.com

SIC: 7382 1731 3629 3669 Burglar alarm maintenance and monitoring; Electrical work; Electronic generation equipment; Visual communication systems

#### (P-19055)
**ENTERPRISE SECURITY INC (PA)**
Also Called: Enterprise Security Solutions
22860 Savi Ranch Pkwy, Yorba Linda (92887-4610)
PHONE.................714 630-9100
Samuel Troy Laughlin, *CEO*
Troy Laughlin, *
Daniel Steiner, *
Joseph Emens, *
**EMP:** 74 **EST:** 2000
**SALES (est):** 10.73MM **Privately Held**
Web: www.entersecurity.com
SIC: 7382 3699 3429 6211 Protective devices, security; Security devices; Security cable locking systems; Dealers, security

#### (P-19056)
**G4S JUSTICE SERVICES LLC**
Also Called: G4s Government Services
1290 N Hancock St Ste 103, Anaheim (92807-1925)
PHONE.................800 589-6003
**EMP:** 49 **EST:** 1995
**SALES (est):** 4.43MM
**SALES (corp-wide):** 94.13MM **Privately Held**
SIC: 7382 3669 Fire alarm maintenance and monitoring; Emergency alarms
**PA:** Sentinel Offender Services Llc
1220 N Simon Cir
949 453-1550

#### (P-19057)
**KESA INCORPORATED**
Also Called: Constrction Instlltion Mint Gr
960 E Discovery Ln, Anaheim (92801-1149)
PHONE.................714 956-2827
Nancy L Rojo, *Pr*
William B Morrill, *
**EMP:** 40 **EST:** 2003
**SALES (est):** 6.42MM **Privately Held**
Web: www.cimgroupinc.com
SIC: 7382 3577 Burglar alarm maintenance and monitoring; Computer peripheral equipment, nec

#### (P-19058)
**LOUROE ELECTRONICS INC**
6955 Valjean Ave, Van Nuys (91406-4716)
PHONE.................818 994-6498
Louis Weiss, *Pr*
Richard S Brent, *
Donald Schiffer, *
Pilar Frickey, *
Cameron Javdani, *
▼ **EMP:** 28 **EST:** 1979
**SQ FT:** 17,000
**SALES (est):** 6.55MM **Privately Held**
Web: www.louroe.com
SIC: 7382 3651 Burglar alarm maintenance and monitoring; Audio electronic systems

#### (P-19059)
**PELCO INC (HQ)**
Also Called: Pelco
625 W Alluvial Ave, Fresno (93711-5762)
PHONE.................559 292-1981
◆ **EMP:** 2100 **EST:** 1957
**SALES (est):** 73.28MM
**SALES (corp-wide):** 9.98B **Publicly Held**
Web: www.pelco.com

SIC: 7382 3663 Security systems services; Television closed circuit equipment
**PA:** Motorola Solutions, Inc.
500 W Monroe St Ste 4400
847 576-5000

#### (P-19060)
**REALDEFENSE LLC (PA)**
Also Called: PC Cleaner
150 S Los Robles Ave Ste 400, Pasadena (91101-2441)
PHONE.................801 895-7907
Gary Guseinov, *CEO*
Sean Whiteley, *Pr*
**EMP:** 30 **EST:** 2017
**SALES (est):** 74.63MM
**SALES (corp-wide):** 74.63MM **Privately Held**
Web: www.realdefen.se
SIC: 7382 7372 Security systems services; Prepackaged software

#### (P-19061)
**SAFESMART ACCESS INC**
13238 Florence Ave, Santa Fe Springs (90670-4510)
PHONE.................310 410-1525
**EMP:** 21 **EST:** 2017
**SALES (est):** 466.3K **Privately Held**
Web: www.safesmartaccess.com
SIC: 7382 3446 Security systems services; Ornamental metalwork

#### (P-19062)
**VIRTIS-US LLC (PA)**
Also Called: Virtis
11601 Wilshire Blvd 5th Fl, Los Angeles (90025-0509)
PHONE.................855 796-1457
Michelle Wilner, *CEO*
Michelle Wilner, *Managing Member*
**EMP:** 15 **EST:** 2016
**SQ FT:** 3,000
**SALES (est):** 1.85MM
**SALES (corp-wide):** 1.85MM **Privately Held**
Web: www.virtis-us.com
SIC: 7382 7371 7373 7372 Security systems services; Software programming applications; Computer integrated systems design; Prepackaged software

#### (P-19063)
**VONNIC INC**
16610 Gale Ave, City Of Industry (91745-1801)
PHONE.................626 964-2345
Kim Por Lin, *CEO*
Kitty Lam, *Sec*
▲ **EMP:** 23 **EST:** 2008
**SALES (est):** 2.48MM **Privately Held**
Web: www.vonnic.com
SIC: 7382 3861 Protective devices, security; Cameras and related equipment

### 7383 News Syndicates

#### (P-19064)
**THE COPLEY PRESS INC**
Also Called: Copley Newspapers
7776 Ivanhoe Ave, La Jolla (92037-4572)
P.O. Box 1530 (92038-1530)
PHONE.................858 454-0411
**EMP:** 4170
SIC: 7383 2711 7011 News syndicates; Newspapers, publishing and printing; Resort hotel

## 7389 Business Services, Nec

**(P-19065)**
**5 PALMS LLC**
800 S B St Fl 1, San Mateo (94401-4271)
PHONE.................650 457-0539
EMP: 212 EST: 2014
SALES (est): 2.38MM Privately Held
SIC: 7389 5083 3523
; Agricultural machinery and equipment; Farm machinery and equipment

**(P-19066)**
**A J PARENT COMPANY INC (PA)**
Also Called: Americas Printer.com
6910 Aragon Cir Ste 6, Buena Park (90620-8103)
PHONE.................714 521-1100
Arthur Parent, CEO
EMP: 88 EST: 1997
SALES (est): 6.67MM
SALES (corp-wide): 6.67MM Privately Held
Web: www.americasprinter.com
SIC: 7389 2752 Printers' services: folding, collating, etc.; Commercial printing, lithographic

**(P-19067)**
**A THREAD AHEAD INC**
1925 1st St, San Fernando (91340-2609)
P.O. Box 889 (91341-0889)
PHONE.................818 837-1984
Lori Banks, Pr
EMP: 20 EST: 2010
SALES (est): 1.21MM Privately Held
Web: www.athreadahead.com
SIC: 7389 2759 Advertising, promotional, and trade show services; Screen printing

**(P-19068)**
**AD ART INC (PA)**
Also Called: Ad Art Sign Company
150 Executive Park Blvd Ste 2100, San Francisco (94134-3364)
PHONE.................415 869-6460
Terry J Long, CEO
Robert Kiereczyk, *
Duane Contento, *
Doug Head, *
David Esajian, *
▲ EMP: 70 EST: 2003
SQ FT: 4,000
SALES (est): 28.96MM
SALES (corp-wide): 28.96MM Privately Held
Web: www.adart.com
SIC: 7389 7532 7812 3648 Interior design services; Exterior repair services; Video production; Decorative area lighting fixtures

**(P-19069)**
**ADVANSTAR COMMUNICATIONS INC**
2901 28th St Ste 100, Santa Monica (90405-2975)
PHONE.................310 857-7500
Danny Phillips, Mgr
EMP: 50
SALES (corp-wide): 3.98B Privately Held
Web: epay.advanstar.com
SIC: 7389 2721 7331 Trade show arrangement; Magazines: publishing only, not printed on site; Direct mail advertising services
HQ: Advanstar Communications Inc.
2501 Colorado Ave Ste 280
Santa Monica CA 90404
310 857-7500

**(P-19070)**
**ADVANSTAR COMMUNICATIONS INC (DH)**
Also Called: Advanstar Global
2501 Colorado Ave Ste 280, Santa Monica (90404-3754)
PHONE.................310 857-7500
◆ EMP: 177 EST: 1987
SALES (est): 21.62MM
SALES (corp-wide): 3.98B Privately Held
Web: epay.advanstar.com
SIC: 7389 2721 7331 Trade show arrangement; Magazines: publishing only, not printed on site; Direct mail advertising services
HQ: Ubm Limited
240 Blackfriars Road
London SE1 8

**(P-19071)**
**AMKOM DESIGN GROUP INC**
2598 Fortune Way Ste J, Vista (92081-8442)
PHONE.................760 295-1957
Ernest Kasparov, CEO
Shlaen Gregory, *
Greg Shlaen, *
Henry Belkin, *
EMP: 25 EST: 2016
SALES (est): 1.16MM Privately Held
Web: www.amkominc.com
SIC: 7389 3663 Design services; Radio and t.v. communications equipment

**(P-19072)**
**ASSAY TECHNOLOGY INC**
1382 Stealth St, Livermore (94551-9356)
PHONE.................925 461-8880
Charles Manning, CEO
Michael P Zagaris, *
Karina Abreckov, *
EMP: 24 EST: 1981
SQ FT: 17,000
SALES (est): 7.76MM Privately Held
Web: www.assaytech.com
SIC: 7389 3826 2899 2813 Inspection and testing services; Analytical instruments; Chemical preparations, nec; Industrial gases

**(P-19073)**
**AUTOCRIB INC**
2882 Dow Ave, Tustin (92780-7258)
PHONE.................714 274-0400
Stephen Pixley, CEO
▲ EMP: 150 EST: 1999
SQ FT: 58,000
SALES (est): 24.39MM
SALES (corp-wide): 4.73B Publicly Held
Web: www.autocrib.com
SIC: 7389 3581 Inventory computing service ; Automatic vending machines
PA: Snap-On Incorporated
2801 80th St
262 656-5200

**(P-19074)**
**BAER ENTERPRISES INC**
2513 Station Dr, Stockton (95215-7948)
PHONE.................209 390-0460
Dallas D Baer, CEO
EMP: 23 EST: 2011
SALES (est): 649.64K Privately Held
Web: www.baerenterprises.com
SIC: 7389 3577 2542 2653 Laminating service; Graphic displays, except graphic terminals; Racks, merchandise display or storage: except wood; Corrugated boxes, partitions, display items, sheets, and pad

**(P-19075)**
**BEAUMONT NIELSEN MARINE INC**
2420 Shelter Island Dr, San Diego (92106-3112)
P.O. Box 6633 (92166-0633)
PHONE.................619 223-2628
Don Beaumont, Pr
Thomas A Nielsen, *
EMP: 29 EST: 1979
SALES (est): 3.76MM Privately Held
Web: www.nielsenbeaumont.com
SIC: 7389 3732 Repossession service; Yachts, building and repairing

**(P-19076)**
**BENRICH SERVICE COMPANY INC (PA)**
3190 Airport Loop Dr Ste G, Costa Mesa (92626-3403)
PHONE.................714 241-0284
Peter W Bendheim, Pr
Redge Henn, *
EMP: 27 EST: 1958
SALES (est): 4.33MM
SALES (corp-wide): 4.33MM Privately Held
Web: www.benrichservice.com
SIC: 7389 3433 Water softener service; Heating equipment, except electric

**(P-19077)**
**BEST SIGNS INC (PA)**
1550 S Gene Autry Trl, Palm Springs (92264-3505)
PHONE.................760 320-3042
Jesse Cross, VP
Jim Cross, *
EMP: 26 EST: 1960
SQ FT: 6,000
SALES (est): 5.26MM
SALES (corp-wide): 5.26MM Privately Held
Web: www.bestsignsinc.com
SIC: 7389 3993 1799 Sign painting and lettering shop; Signs and advertising specialties; Sign installation and maintenance

**(P-19078)**
**BUSINESS PRINTING COMPANY INC**
Also Called: Express Printing Info MGT Co
9840 Prospect Ave, Santee (92071-4311)
PHONE.................858 453-2111
Bill Ball, Pt
Arthur Ball, Pt
Eric Ball, Pt
EMP: 15 EST: 1986
SALES (est): 857.38K Privately Held
Web: www.businessprintingco.com
SIC: 7389 5112 2791 2752 Printers' services: folding, collating, etc.; Stationery and office supplies; Typesetting; Commercial printing, lithographic

**(P-19079)**
**CANDLES BY HGBYG CORP**
1028 Market St, San Francisco (94102-4047)
PHONE.................415 655-9865
Alston Sheppard, CEO
EMP: 15
SALES (est): 254.7K Privately Held
SIC: 7389 3999 5199 Business Activities at Non-Commercial Site; Candles; Nondurable goods, nec

**(P-19080)**
**CAW COWIE INC (PA)**
Also Called: Colin Cowie Lifestyle
7 Ginger Root Ln, Rancho Palos Verdes (90275-5907)
PHONE.................212 396-9007
Colin Cowie, CEO
Stuart Brownstein, *
David Berke, *
EMP: 25 EST: 1994
SALES (est): 1.62MM
SALES (corp-wide): 1.62MM Privately Held
Web: www.rsclarkenergy.com
SIC: 7389 7299 5023 2731 Interior design services; Party planning service; Decorative home furnishings and supplies; Book publishing

**(P-19081)**
**CERAMIC DECORATING COMPANY INC**
4651 Sheila St, Commerce (90040-1003)
PHONE.................323 268-5135
Chad A Johnson, CEO
Burnell D Johnson, *
W Allan Johnson, *
Allan Johnson, *
EMP: 50 EST: 1934
SQ FT: 30,290
SALES (est): 2.57MM Privately Held
Web: www.ceramicdecoratingco.com
SIC: 7389 2396 Labeling bottles, cans, cartons, etc.; Automotive and apparel trimmings

**(P-19082)**
**CIRTECH INC**
Also Called: Apct Anaheim
250 E Emerson Ave, Orange (92865-3317)
PHONE.................714 921-0860
Brad Reese, Pr
Frank E Reese, *
EMP: 50 EST: 1965
SQ FT: 30,000
SALES (est): 6.05MM
SALES (corp-wide): 87.73MM Privately Held
Web: www.apct.com
SIC: 7389 3672 Printed circuitry graphic layout; Printed circuit boards
PA: Apct Holdings, Llc
3495 De La Cruz Blvd
408 727-6442

**(P-19083)**
**CONTRACT IT EXPERTS LLC**
17041 Miracle Ln, Riverside (92503-7307)
PHONE.................702 466-5022
EMP: 15 EST: 2008
SALES (est): 412.67K Privately Held
Web: www.citexperts.com
SIC: 7389 1731 7373 3699 Business Activities at Non-Commercial Site; Communications specialization; Local area network (LAN) systems integrator; Security control equipment and systems

**(P-19084)**
**CONTRACT LABELING SERVICE INC**
13885 Ramona Ave, Chino (91710-5426)
PHONE.................909 937-0344
Trevor Metcalf, CEO
Alexander Riff, *
Carolyn Johnson, *
▲ EMP: 48 EST: 1992
SALES (est): 4.06MM Privately Held
Web: www.contractlabel.com

## PRODUCTS & SERVICES SECTION

**7389 - Business Services, Nec (P-19105)**

SIC: 7389 3552 Packaging and labeling services; Silk screens for textile industry

### (P-19085)
**DECOR INTERIOR DESIGN INC**
21530 Sherman Way, Canoga Park (91303-1536)
PHONE.............................818 962-4800
Ronda Jackson, CEO
EMP: 21 EST: 2005
SALES (est): 2.74MM Privately Held
Web: www.designsbydecor.com
SIC: 7389 7349 1799 2521 Interior designer; Building and office cleaning services; Office furniture installation; Wood office furniture

### (P-19086)
**DEKRA-LITE INDUSTRIES INC**
Also Called: DI Imaging
3102 W Alton Ave, Santa Ana (92704-6817)
PHONE.............................714 436-0705
Jeffrey Lopez, CEO
▲ EMP: 80 EST: 1987
SQ FT: 30,000
SALES (est): 9.35MM Privately Held
Web: www.dekra-lite.com
SIC: 7389 5999 3999 Decoration service for special events; Art, picture frames, and decorations; Advertising curtains

### (P-19087)
**DIBA FASHIONS INC**
472 N Bowling Green Way, Los Angeles (90049-2820)
PHONE.............................323 232-3775
John Gir Daneshrad, Pr
Shahin Daneshrad, *
EMP: 70 EST: 1980
SQ FT: 22,400
SALES (est): 1.75MM Privately Held
SIC: 7389 2339 Sewing contractor; Women's and misses' outerwear, nec

### (P-19088)
**DYNOVAS INC**
Also Called: Dynovas
12250 Iavelli Way, Poway (92064-6818)
PHONE.............................508 717-7494
Quinn Mcallister, Pr
Robert Kolozs, Prin
EMP: 18 EST: 2020
SALES (est): 1.24MM Privately Held
Web: www.dynovas.com
SIC: 7389 3429 3769 3731 Business Activities at Non-Commercial Site; Aircraft hardware; Space vehicle equipment, nec; Dredges, building and repairing

### (P-19089)
**EAGLE MED PCKG STRLIZATION INC**
Also Called: Eagle Med Packg Sterilization
2921 Union Rd Ste A, Paso Robles (93446-7316)
P.O. Box 1228 (93447-1228)
PHONE.............................805 238-7401
Doyle Timmons, Pr
EMP: 35 EST: 1992
SQ FT: 10,000
SALES (est): 2.38MM Privately Held
Web: www.eaglemed.com
SIC: 7389 3841 Packaging and labeling services; Surgical and medical instruments

### (P-19090)
**ECONOLITE**
Also Called: Traffic Signal Maintenance
4120 Business Center Dr, Fremont (94538-6354)
PHONE.............................408 577-1733
Ron Hernandez, Off Mgr
EMP: 16 EST: 2012
SALES (est): 310.65K Privately Held
Web: www.econolite.com
SIC: 7389 3812 Flagging service (traffic control); Air traffic control systems and equipment, electronic

### (P-19091)
**FOCUS LANGUAGE INTL INC**
Also Called: Focus Interpreting
14450 Park Ave Ste 100, Victorville (92392-2901)
P.O. Box 634 (92856-6634)
PHONE.............................800 374-5444
Natalie Pena, CEO
Selim Cacao, Pr
Beatriz Resendiz, Coordtr
EMP: 18 EST: 2014
SALES (est): 532.52K Privately Held
Web: www.focusinterpreting.com
SIC: 7389 3652 Translation services; Prerecorded records and tapes

### (P-19092)
**FUTURE INNOVATIONS INC**
Also Called: Calwest Steel Detailing
4301 Hacienda Dr, Pleasanton (94588-2712)
PHONE.............................925 485-2000
Mark Frohnen, Pr
Robert Sprenkel, *
EMP: 44 EST: 1979
SALES (est): 1.83MM Privately Held
Web: www.cwsteeldetailing.com
SIC: 7389 8711 3441 Drafting service, except temporary help; Structural engineering; Fabricated structural metal

### (P-19093)
**GENERAL WATER SYSTEMS**
1525 E 6th St, Corona (92879-1716)
PHONE.............................951 278-8992
Tim Boylen, Pr
Tim Boylen, CEO
EMP: 17 EST: 2020
SALES (est): 1.25MM Privately Held
Web: www.gwslp.com
SIC: 7389 3585 3532 3589 Water softener service; Air conditioning equipment, complete; Feeders, ore and aggregate; Water treatment equipment, industrial

### (P-19094)
**GRANDALL DISTRIBUTING LLC**
321 El Bonito Ave, Glendale (91204)
PHONE.............................818 242-6640
Jose M Granda, Pr
Melisa J Granda, *
Joseph J Granda, *
Jessica J Granda, *
EMP: 30 EST: 1966
SQ FT: 18,000
SALES (est): 2.01MM Privately Held
Web: www.grandall.com
SIC: 7389 2844 Cosmetic kits, assembling and packaging; Cosmetic preparations

### (P-19095)
**GREAT WESTERN GRINDING INC**
15292 Bolsa Chica St, Huntington Beach (92649-1243)
PHONE.............................714 890-6592
Michael Del Medico, Pr
Revona Del Medico, VP
EMP: 15 EST: 1984
SQ FT: 8,000
SALES (est): 1.56MM Privately Held
Web: www.greatwesterngrinding.com
SIC: 7389 3812 3769 Grinding, precision: commercial or industrial; Search and navigation equipment; Space vehicle equipment, nec

### (P-19096)
**HYPER-TECH LLC**
2993 Yucca Dr, Santa Rosa Valley (93012-9252)
PHONE.............................805 988-2000
Mark Grant, Pt
Gaston M Grant, Pt
EMP: 18 EST: 2008
SALES (est): 1.18MM Privately Held
SIC: 7389 3499 Design, commercial and industrial; Machine bases, metal

### (P-19097)
**INTEGRATED VOTING SYSTEMS INC**
Also Called: Integrated Voting Solutions
496 S Uruapan Way, Dinuba (93618-2719)
PHONE.............................559 498-0281
Rebecca Kozlowski, Pr
EMP: 45 EST: 2015
SALES (est): 2.93MM Privately Held
Web: www.integravote.com
SIC: 7389 7331 8742 2741 Presorted mail service; Direct mail advertising services; Marketing consulting services; Business service newsletters: publishing and printing

### (P-19098)
**ISOVAC ENGINEERING INC**
614 Justin Ave, Glendale (91201-2327)
PHONE.............................818 552-6200
George R Neff, Pr
EMP: 25 EST: 1957
SALES (est): 2.44MM Privately Held
Web: www.isovac.com
SIC: 7389 3825 3829 3826 Inspection and testing services; Semiconductor test equipment; Measuring and controlling devices, nec; Analytical instruments

### (P-19099)
**JENCO PRODUCTIONS LLC (PA)**
401 S J St, San Bernardino (92410-2605)
PHONE.............................909 381-9453
Jennifer Imbriani, Pr
◆ EMP: 160 EST: 1995
SQ FT: 50,000
SALES (est): 24.08MM
SALES (corp-wide): 24.08MM Privately Held
Web: www.jencoproductions.com
SIC: 7389 2789 2653 7331 Packaging and labeling services; Bookbinding and related work; Boxes, corrugated: made from purchased materials; Mailing service

### (P-19100)
**JF FIXTURES & DESIGN LLC**
Also Called: Manufacturing/Distributrion
546 W Esther St, Long Beach (90813-1529)
PHONE.............................562 437-7466
Jaideep Ahluwalia, Managing Member
EMP: 15 EST: 2019
SALES (est): 842.27K Privately Held
Web: www.jffixtures.com
SIC: 7389 2542 2541 Design services; Office and store showcases and display fixtures; Store and office display cases and fixtures

### (P-19101)
**KOOS MANUFACTURING INC**
Also Called: Big Star
2741 Seminole Ave, South Gate (90280-5550)
PHONE.............................323 249-1000
U Yul Ku, CEO
John Hur, *
Nathan Aroonprapun, *
▲ EMP: 639 EST: 1985
SQ FT: 180,000
SALES (est): 23.78MM Privately Held
Web: www.koos.com
SIC: 7389 2325 2339 2369 Sewing contractor; Jeans: men's, youths', and boys'; Jeans: women's, misses', and juniors'; Jeans: girls', children's, and infants'

### (P-19102)
**KUKDONG APPAREL AMERICA INC**
17100 Pioneer Blvd Ste 230, Artesia (90701-2718)
▲ EMP: 20 EST: 1999
SQ FT: 5,000
SALES (est): 4.55MM Privately Held
Web: www.kd.co.kr
SIC: 7389 2386 Apparel designers, commercial; Garments, leather
PA: Kukdong Corporation
6, 7/F

### (P-19103)
**LA JOLLA GROUP INC (PA)**
Also Called: Ljg
14350 Myford Rd, Irvine (92606-1002)
PHONE.............................949 428-2800
Michael Pratt, CEO
▲ EMP: 421 EST: 1993
SALES (est): 38.41MM
SALES (corp-wide): 38.41MM Privately Held
Web: www.lajollagroup.com
SIC: 7389 6794 2326 Apparel designers, commercial; Copyright buying and licensing; Men's and boy's work clothing

### (P-19104)
**LESLIE HEAVY HAUL LLC**
Also Called: Leslie Heavy Haul
18971 Hess Ave, Sonora (95370-9724)
P.O. Box 4581 (95370-1581)
PHONE.............................209 840-1664
EMP: 25 EST: 2005
SALES (est): 2.26MM Privately Held
Web: www.leslieheavyhaul.com
SIC: 7389 2411 4213 8322 Business Activities at Non-Commercial Site; Timber, cut at logging camp; Heavy hauling, nec; Disaster service

### (P-19105)
**MANUFACTURING RESOURCE CORP**
Also Called: M R C
44853 Fremont Blvd, Fremont (94538-6318)
PHONE.............................510 438-9600
Bhavesh J Desai, Pr
Harshad Patel, *
EMP: 41 EST: 1994
SQ FT: 16,250
SALES (est): 999.32K
SALES (corp-wide): 1.79MM Privately Held
Web: www.m-r-c.com
SIC: 7389 3953 Packaging and labeling services; Stencils, painting and marking
PA: Emarcee Llc
45375 Onondaga Dr

## 7389 - Business Services, Nec (P-19106)

510 687-0153

**(P-19106)**
**MARINER SYSTEMS INC (PA)**
114 C Ave, Coronado (92118-1435)
PHONE..................305 266-7255
Carlos M Collazo, *Pr*
Carlos M Collazo, *Ch Bd*
Neil Park, *
**EMP:** 50 **EST:** 1982
**SALES (est):** 2.37MM
**SALES (corp-wide):** 2.37MM **Privately Held**
Web: www.carlocksmithcoronado.com
**SIC: 7389** 7374 7372 7371 Telephone services; Data processing service; Prepackaged software; Custom computer programming services

**(P-19107)**
**MVENTIX INC (PA)**
Also Called: Mventix
21600 Oxnard St Ste 1700, Woodland Hills (91367-4972)
PHONE..................818 337-3747
Kristian Beloff, *CEO*
Vesselin Kavrakov, *Research & Development*
Pavel Monev, *
**EMP:** 70 **EST:** 2004
**SQ FT:** 6,606
**SALES (est):** 2.71MM
**SALES (corp-wide):** 2.71MM **Privately Held**
Web: www.mventix.com
**SIC: 7389** 8732 7372 Advertising, promotional, and trade show services; Survey service: marketing, location, etc.; Business oriented computer software

**(P-19108)**
**N PHILANTHROPY LLC**
1132 E 12th St, Los Angeles (90021-2206)
PHONE..................213 278-0754
Yvonne Niami, *Managing Member*
**EMP:** 18 **EST:** 2013
**SALES (est):** 1.88MM **Privately Held**
**SIC: 7389** 2339 Textile and apparel services; Athletic clothing: women's, misses', and juniors'

**(P-19109)**
**NEW WAVE EMBROIDERY**
909 S Greenwood Ave Ste B, Montebello (90640-5836)
PHONE..................323 727-0076
Juan Vasquez, *Owner*
**EMP:** 15 **EST:** 1991
**SALES (est):** 145.28K **Privately Held**
**SIC: 7389** 2396 2395 Embroidery advertising ; Automotive and apparel trimmings; Pleating and stitching

**(P-19110)**
**NOR-CAL BEVERAGE CO INC**
Also Called: Norcal Beverage Co
1226 N Olive St, Anaheim (92801-2543)
PHONE..................714 526-8600
William Mcfarland, *Mgr*
**EMP:** 74
**SALES (corp-wide):** 53.99MM **Privately Held**
Web: www.mannabev.com
**SIC: 7389** 2033 Packaging and labeling services; Canned fruits and specialties
**PA:** Nor-Cal Beverage Co., Inc.
2150 Stone Blvd
916 372-0600

**(P-19111)**
**NSI GROUP LLC (PA)**
Also Called: Nsi - Natural Sourcing Intl
17031 Ventura Blvd, Encino (91316)
PHONE..................818 639-8335
**EMP:** 19 **EST:** 2013
**SQ FT:** 7,000
**SALES (est):** 6.24MM
**SALES (corp-wide):** 6.24MM **Privately Held**
Web: www.nsifood.com
**SIC: 7389** 2034 Packaging and labeling services; Dried and dehydrated fruits

**(P-19112)**
**OCS AMERICA INC (DH)**
Also Called: Ocs Bookstore
22912 Lockness Ave, Torrance (90501-5117)
PHONE..................310 417-0650
Yutaka Otake, *Ch Bd*
Susan Onuman, *
Takuya Hiraiwa, *
▲ **EMP:** 39 **EST:** 1972
**SALES (est):** 11.29MM **Privately Held**
Web: www.ocsworld.com
**SIC: 7389** 5192 2711 5942 Courier or messenger service; Newspapers; Newspapers: publishing only, not printed on site; Books, foreign
**HQ:** Overseas Courier Service Co., Ltd.
3-9-27, Tatsumi
Koto-Ku TKY 135-0

**(P-19113)**
**ORION GROUP WORLD LLC**
143 Seminary Dr Apt Q, Mill Valley (94941-6212)
PHONE..................415 602-5233
Ace Stojanovski, *Pr*
Monika Szczuka, *
**EMP:** 120 **EST:** 2017
**SALES (est):** 355.42K **Privately Held**
**SIC: 7389** 3812 3482 3489 Business Activities at Non-Commercial Site; Defense systems and equipment; Cartridges, 30 mm. and below; Rocket launchers

**(P-19114)**
**PACIFIC ASIAN ENTERPRISES INC (PA)**
Also Called: Nordhavn Yachts
25001 Dana Dr, Dana Point (92629-3005)
P.O. Box 874 (92629-0874)
PHONE..................949 496-4848
Dan Streech, *Pr*
Jeffrey Leishman, *Sec*
James Leishman, *CFO*
◆ **EMP:** 30 **EST:** 1978
**SQ FT:** 3,500
**SALES (est):** 8.01MM
**SALES (corp-wide):** 8.01MM **Privately Held**
Web: www.nordhavn.com
**SIC: 7389** 3732 Yacht brokers; Yachts, building and repairing

**(P-19115)**
**PACIFIC EMBROIDERY LLC**
Also Called: Pacific Embroidery
1189 N Kraemer Blvd, Anaheim (92806-1917)
PHONE..................714 630-4757
**EMP:** 15 **EST:** 1988
**SQ FT:** 3,600
**SALES (est):** 437.23K **Privately Held**
Web: www.pacificemb.com
**SIC: 7389** 2395 Sewing contractor; Pleating and stitching

**(P-19116)**
**PERFECT IMPRESSION INC**
Also Called: Perfect Banner, The
27111 Aliso Creek Rd Ste 145, Aliso Viejo (92656-3367)
PHONE..................949 305-0797
Suzie Abrahams, *Pr*
**EMP:** 28 **EST:** 2008
**SALES (est):** 899.3K **Privately Held**
Web: www.theperfectimpression.com
**SIC: 7389** 2395 Embroidery advertising; Embroidery and art needlework

**(P-19117)**
**PINNACLE SOLUTIONS INC**
Also Called: Acme Printing Co
1700 Mchenry Ave Ste 45, Modesto (95350-4309)
PHONE..................209 523-8300
Steven L Gold, *CEO*
Pinder Basi, *
Paul Draper, *Stockholder*
Robert A Vossoughi, *Prin*
**EMP:** 59 **EST:** 1983
**SQ FT:** 23,000
**SALES (est):** 2.36MM **Privately Held**
Web: www.dittosprint.com
**SIC: 7389** 8713 2752 Embroidery advertising ; Ariel digital imaging; Offset printing

**(P-19118)**
**QUINSTREET INC (PA)**
Also Called: QUINSTREET
950 Tower Ln Ste 600, Foster City (94404-4253)
PHONE..................650 578-7700
Douglas Valenti, *Ch Bd*
Nina Bhanap, *Technology*
Gregory Wong, *
Martin J Collins, *Legal*
Tim Stevens, *
**EMP:** 45 **EST:** 1999
**SQ FT:** 44,556
**SALES (est):** 613.51MM
**SALES (corp-wide):** 613.51MM **Publicly Held**
Web: www.quinstreet.com
**SIC: 7389** 7372 Advertising, promotional, and trade show services; Prepackaged software

**(P-19119)**
**RADIANT GRAPH INC**
3525 16th St, San Francisco (94114-1610)
PHONE..................857 928-3248
Anmol Madan, *CEO*
Geeta Nayyar, *Chief Medical Officer*
**EMP:** 20
**SALES (est):** 2.54MM **Privately Held**
**SIC: 7389** 7372 Business Activities at Non-Commercial Site; Prepackaged software

**(P-19120)**
**REASON FOUNDATION**
5737 Mesmer Ave, Los Angeles (90230-6316)
PHONE..................310 391-2245
David Nott, *Pr*
Mike Alissi, *
**EMP:** 35 **EST:** 1968
**SQ FT:** 6,300
**SALES (est):** 15.46MM **Privately Held**
Web: www.reason.org
**SIC: 7389** 2741 2721 Speakers' bureau; Newsletter publishing; Magazines: publishing and printing

**(P-19121)**
**REVERE DATA LLC**
1 California St Ste 1900, San Francisco (94111-5420)
PHONE..................415 782-0454
**EMP:** 40
**SALES (est):** 2.2MM
**SALES (corp-wide):** 1.13B **Publicly Held**
Web: www.reveredata.com
**SIC: 7389** 7372 Financial services; Business oriented computer software
**PA:** Factset Research Systems Inc.
601 Merritt 7
203 810-1000

**(P-19122)**
**ROBERTS CONTAINER CORPORATION**
Also Called: Roberts Cosmetics and Cntrs
9131 Oakdale Ave Ste 110, Chatsworth (91311-6503)
PHONE..................818 727-1700
Jacquelyn Irene Medina, *CEO*
◆ **EMP:** 22 **EST:** 1986
**SQ FT:** 28,000
**SALES (est):** 1.94MM **Privately Held**
Web: www.robertsbeauty.com
**SIC: 7389** 2844 Cosmetic kits, assembling and packaging; Bath salts

**(P-19123)**
**RUSH PCB INC**
500 Yosemite Dr Ste 106, Milpitas (95035-5467)
PHONE..................408 496-6013
Akber Roy, *CEO*
**EMP:** 20 **EST:** 2007
**SALES (est):** 7.76MM **Privately Held**
Web: www.rushpcb.com
**SIC: 7389** 3672 Business Activities at Non-Commercial Site; Printed circuit boards

**(P-19124)**
**RVL PACKAGING INC**
31330 Oak Crest Dr, Westlake Village (91361-4632)
PHONE..................818 735-5000
▼ **EMP:** 200
**SIC: 7389** 2396 2241 Packaging and labeling services; Automotive and apparel trimmings; Narrow fabric mills

**(P-19125)**
**SCILEX PHARMACEUTICALS INC (HQ)**
4955 Directors Pl Ste 100, San Diego (92121-3836)
PHONE..................949 441-2270
Anthony P Mack, *Pr*
Jiong Shao, *Ex VP*
**EMP:** 17 **EST:** 2012
**SQ FT:** 3,000
**SALES (est):** 4.1MM
**SALES (corp-wide):** 62.84MM **Publicly Held**
Web: www.scilexholding.com
**SIC: 7389** 5122 2834 Packaging and labeling services; Pharmaceuticals; Pharmaceutical preparations
**PA:** Sorrento Therapeutics, Inc.
4955 Directors Pl
858 203-4100

**(P-19126)**
**SCOTTXSCOTT INC**
3453 Union Pacific Ave, Los Angeles (90023-3834)
PHONE..................310 622-2775
Brandon J Scott, *CEO*
Sarah Scott, *
**EMP:** 24 **EST:** 2015
**SALES (est):** 1.12MM **Privately Held**
Web: www.scottxscott.com

## PRODUCTS & SERVICES SECTION
## 7389 - Business Services, Nec (P-19145)

SIC: 7389 2329 Apparel designers, commercial; Athletic clothing, except uniforms: men's, youths' and boys'

### (P-19127)
### SECURITY CLASSIFICATION INC
2339 Gold Meadow Way, Gold River (95670-4467)
PHONE.....................707 301-6052
Ted Golshanara, *Mgr*
Ted Golshanara, *CAO*
Harold Curtis, *Ch*
Andrea Curtis, *Managing Member*
Chyree Curtis, *Managing Member*
EMP: 35 EST: 2017
SALES (est): 666.01K **Privately Held**
SIC: 7389 7381 8741 6111 Automobile recovery service; Guard services; Financial management for business; Export/Import Bank

### (P-19128)
### SEDONA VENTURES INC (PA)
Also Called: Government Technology
100 Blue Ravine Rd, Folsom (95630-4509)
PHONE.....................916 932-1300
Dennis Mckenna, *CEO*
Dee Pearson, *VP*
Randall Mott, *CIO*
John Flynn, *VP*
EMP: 120 EST: 1984
SQ FT: 36,000
SALES (est): 4.94MM
SALES (corp-wide): 4.94MM **Privately Held**
Web: www.erepublic.com
SIC: 7389 2759 2721 Convention and show services; Publication printing; Periodicals

### (P-19129)
### SHERYL LOWE DESIGNS LLC
1187 Coast Village Rd Ste 156, Santa Barbara (93108-2737)
PHONE.....................805 969-1742
Sheryl Lowe, *CEO*
Jaden Levit, *CFO*
Jane Davis, *Dir*
EMP: 20 EST: 2010
SQ FT: 1,500
SALES (est): 1.38MM **Privately Held**
Web: www.sheryllowejewelry.com
SIC: 7389 3911 Design services; Jewelry apparel

### (P-19130)
### SIMPLE SCIENCE INC
1626 Ohms Way, Costa Mesa (92627-4329)
PHONE.....................949 335-1099
Christian Henderson, *Pr*
EMP: 40 EST: 2009
SALES (est): 5.67MM **Privately Held**
Web: www.simple.science
SIC: 7389 7812 7371 7311 Design services; Video production; Software programming applications; Advertising agencies

### (P-19131)
### SINECERA INC
Also Called: Crown Vly Precision Machining
5397 3rd St, Irwindale (91706-2085)
PHONE.....................626 962-1087
Donald Brown, *CEO*
Dale B Mikus, *CFO*
EMP: 80 EST: 1984
SQ FT: 10,500
SALES (est): 11.45MM
SALES (corp-wide): 93.1MM **Privately Held**
Web: www.crownprecision.com

SIC: 7389 3492 Grinding, precision: commercial or industrial; Control valves, aircraft: hydraulic and pneumatic
PA: H-D Advanced Manufacturing Company
2418 Greens Rd
346 219-0320

### (P-19132)
### SKDY OF SAN DIEGO INC
Also Called: Skyline Displays of San Diego
6455 Weathers Pl, San Diego (92121-2958)
PHONE.....................858 552-9033
John Lethert, *Pr*
Joseph Lethert, *VP*
EMP: 21 EST: 1986
SQ FT: 14,850
SALES (est): 2.46MM **Privately Held**
Web: www.skylinesandiego.com
SIC: 7389 3993 Trade show arrangement; Signs and advertising specialties

### (P-19133)
### SMART WORLD LLC
Also Called: Steri-Tek
48225 Lakeview Blvd, Fremont (94538-6519)
PHONE.....................510 933-9700
Larry Nichols, *CEO*
EMP: 49 EST: 2014
SQ FT: 3,600
SALES (est): 6.52MM **Privately Held**
Web: www.steri-tek.com
SIC: 7389 3841 Product sterilization service; Anesthesia apparatus

### (P-19134)
### SOCIAL JUNKY INC
7874 Palmetto Ave, Fontana (92336-2744)
PHONE.....................213 999-1275
Shannon Bryant, *CEO*
EMP: 43 EST: 2021
SALES (est): 232.91K **Privately Held**
SIC: 7389 2836 7929 Business Activities at Non-Commercial Site; Culture media; Entertainers and entertainment groups

### (P-19135)
### SUGAR FOODS LLC
9500 El Dorado Ave, Sun Valley (91352-1339)
PHONE.....................818 768-7900
Stephen Odell, *Pt*
EMP: 200
SALES (corp-wide): 677.96MM **Privately Held**
Web: www.sugarfoods.com
SIC: 7389 2099 2062 Packaging and labeling services; Food preparations, nec; Cane sugar refining
HQ: Sugar Foods Llc
3059 Townsgate Rd Ste 101
Westlake Village CA 91361
805 396-5000

### (P-19136)
### SUN LIGHT & POWER
1035 Folger Ave, Berkeley (94710-2819)
PHONE.....................510 845-2997
Gary Gerber, *CEO*
Gary Gerber, *Pr*
Eric Nyman, *
Blake Gleason, *
Patch Garcia, *
EMP: 75 EST: 1975
SQ FT: 10,000
SALES (est): 12.09MM **Privately Held**
Web: www.sunlightandpower.com

SIC: 7389 1796 3433 Design services; Power generating equipment installation; Solar heaters and collectors

### (P-19137)
### SURVEILLANCE SYSTEMS GROUP INC
Also Called: Corinthian Group
4193 Flat Rock Dr Ste 200, Riverside (92505-7113)
PHONE.....................877 687-3939
Claude Ammons, *CEO*
Claude Ammons, *Pr*
Kim Ammons, *Sec*
EMP: 15 EST: 2002
SALES (est): 839.63K **Privately Held**
Web: www.corinthian-group.com
SIC: 7389 1382 6411 8741 Personal investigation service; Aerial geophysical exploration, oil and gas; Inspection and investigation services, insurance; Business management

### (P-19138)
### TECHNOLOGY TRAINING CORP (PA)
Also Called: Avalon Communications
369 Van Ness Way Ste 735, Torrance (90501-6247)
P.O. Box 119 (90507-0119)
PHONE.....................310 320-8110
Hyman Silver, *CEO*
Steven Silver, *Pr*
Rick Hahn, *Sec*
EMP: 15 EST: 1974
SQ FT: 4,300
SALES (est): 4.84MM
SALES (corp-wide): 4.84MM **Privately Held**
Web: www.ttcus.com
SIC: 7389 8742 2741 Lecture bureau; Business management consultant; Technical manuals: publishing and printing

### (P-19139)
### THOUSAND OAKS PRTG & SPC INC
Also Called: T/O Printing
5334 Sterling Center Dr, Westlake Village (91361-4612)
PHONE.....................818 706-8330
Steve Mahr, *Pr*
▲ EMP: 140 EST: 1981
SQ FT: 60,000
SALES (est): 3.85MM
SALES (corp-wide): 15B **Privately Held**
Web: www.rrd.com
SIC: 7389 2752 Printing broker; Offset printing
HQ: Consolidated Graphics, Inc.
5858 Westheimer Rd # 200
Houston TX 77057

### (P-19140)
### UNIVERSAL MUSIC GROUP INC (HQ)
2220 Colorado Ave, Santa Monica (90404)
PHONE.....................310 865-0770
Lucian Grainge, *CEO*
Jeffrey Harleston, *
Philippe Flageul, *
Boyd Muir, *
▲ EMP: 100 EST: 1998
SALES (est): 455.88MM **Privately Held**
Web: www.universalmusic.com
SIC: 7389 2741 Music recording producer; Miscellaneous publishing
PA: Universal Music Group N.V.
S-Gravelandseweg 80

### (P-19141)
### V3 SYSTEMS SCRTYAUTOMATION INC
Also Called: V3 Systems
4925 Robert J Mathews Pkwy Ste 100, El Dorado Hills (95762-5700)
PHONE.....................916 543-1543
Adam Watts, *Pr*
Alexis Crayn, *Opers Mgr*
EMP: 20 EST: 2013
SALES (est): 864.33K **Privately Held**
Web: www.v3electric.com
SIC: 7389 5065 3699 Personal service agents, brokers, and bureaus; Security control equipment and systems; Security devices

### (P-19142)
### VOLCOM, LLC (HQ)
Also Called: Stone Entertainment
1740 Monrovia Ave, Costa Mesa (92627-4407)
PHONE.....................949 646-2175
Todd Hymel, *CEO*
Jason Steris, *
John W Fearnley, *
Tom D Ruiz, *
Ryan Immegart, *
EMP: 200 EST: 1991
SQ FT: 104,000
SALES (est): 134.77MM **Privately Held**
Web: www.volcom.com
SIC: 7389 2253 7822 5136 Design services; Bathing suits and swimwear, knit; Motion picture and tape distribution; Men's and boy's clothing
PA: Authentic Brands Group Llc
1411 Broadway Fl 21

### (P-19143)
### WET (PA)
Also Called: Wet Design
10847 Sherman Way, Sun Valley (91352-4829)
PHONE.....................818 769-6200
Mark W Fuller, *CEO*
Shemi Hart, *
Tania Avedissian, *
Helen Park, *
Maria Villamil, *
▲ EMP: 184 EST: 1983
SQ FT: 112,000
SALES (est): 47.23MM
SALES (corp-wide): 47.23MM **Privately Held**
Web: www.wetdesign.com
SIC: 7389 8711 3443 Design services; Engineering services; Metal parts

### (P-19144)
### WOLFGANG ENTERPRISE INC
Also Called: Fh Packaging
13977 The Merge St Unit B, Eastvale (92880-3860)
PHONE.....................951 848-7680
Gang Wu, *CEO*
EMP: 15 EST: 2014
SALES (est): 4.16MM **Privately Held**
Web: www.fhpkg.com
SIC: 7389 3221 5199 Packaging and labeling services; Glass containers; Packaging materials

### (P-19145)
### XO BABYPLUTO FADED PARADISE XO
3442 E 8th St, Los Angeles (90023-3025)
PHONE.....................650 750-5025
Brandon Aceituno, *CEO*
Brandon Aceituno, *Managing Member*

---

(PA)=Parent Co (HQ)=Headquarters
✪ = New Business established in last 2 years

# 7532 - Top And Body Repair And Paint Shops (P-19146)

**EMP:** 25 **EST:** 2019
**SALES (est):** 206.68K **Privately Held**
**SIC:** 7389 8641 8299 7372 Business Activities at Non-Commercial Site; Youth organizations; Music school; Educational computer software

## 7532 Top And Body Repair And Paint Shops

### (P-19146)
**ATC COLORS INC**
445 Lesser St, Oakland (94601-4901)
**PHONE**....................510 639-7337
Atc Colors, *CEO*
Hyo Song, *Managing Member*
**EMP:** 16 **EST:** 2010
**SALES (est):** 982.02K **Privately Held**
**Web:** www.atccolors.com
**SIC:** 7532 2851 5013 5231 Body shop, automotive; Paints and paint additives; Body repair or paint shop supplies, automotive; Paint

### (P-19147)
**METRO TRUCK BODY INC**
240 Citation Cir, Corona (92878-5022)
**PHONE**....................310 532-5570
Vincent Xavier Rigali, *CEO*
▲ **EMP:** 47 **EST:** 1968
**SQ FT:** 20,000
**SALES (est):** 2.68MM **Privately Held**
**Web:** www.metrotruckbody.com
**SIC:** 7532 3713 5012 5531 Body shop, automotive; Truck bodies (motor vehicles); Truck bodies; Truck equipment and parts

### (P-19148)
**SPORTSMOBILE WEST**
3631 S Bagley Ave, Fresno (93725-2441)
**PHONE**....................559 233-8267
Alan Feld, *Pr*
Liz Feld, *
▲ **EMP:** 49 **EST:** 1989
**SQ FT:** 60,000
**SALES (est):** 2.47MM **Privately Held**
**Web:** www.sportsmobile.com
**SIC:** 7532 3792 3716 Van conversion; Travel trailers and campers; Motor homes

### (P-19149)
**UNIVERSAL METAL PLATING (PA)**
626 1/2 S Gerhart Ave, Los Angeles (90022-3488)
**PHONE**....................626 969-7931
Jesus Martinez, *Pt*
**EMP:** 18 **EST:** 1978
**SALES (est):** 338.17K
**SALES (corp-wide):** 338.17K **Privately Held**
**Web:** www.universalplating.com
**SIC:** 7532 3471 Bump shops, automotive repair; Plating of metals or formed products

## 7534 Tire Retreading And Repair Shops

### (P-19150)
**AAA SIGNS INC**
Also Called: Total Tire Recycling
1644 Auburn Blvd, Sacramento (95815-1951)
**PHONE**....................916 568-3456
Gary Matranga, *Pr*
**EMP:** 54 **EST:** 1973
**SALES (est):** 1.66MM **Privately Held**
**Web:** www.aaacraneservices.com
**SIC:** 7534 7353 Tire retreading and repair shops; Cranes and aerial lift equipment, rental or leasing

### (P-19151)
**BRIDGESTONE AMERICAS**
Also Called: GCR Tires & Service 185
14521 Hawthorne Ave, Fontana (92335-2508)
**PHONE**....................909 770-8523
**EMP:** 32
**Web:** www.bridgestoneamericas.com
**SIC:** 7534 5531 Tire repair shop; Automotive tires
**HQ:** Bridgestone Americas Tire Operations, Llc
200 4th Ave S Ste 100
Nashville TN 37201
615 937-1000

### (P-19152)
**NEW PRIDE TIRE LLC (HQ)**
Also Called: Pacific Coast Retreaders
2900 Main St Bldg 137 Ste 201a, Alameda (94501-7522)
**PHONE**....................510 567-8800
Mohsen Ansari, *Pr*
◆ **EMP:** 23 **EST:** 1978
**SALES (est):** 3.07MM **Privately Held**
**Web:** www.newpridetire.com
**SIC:** 7534 Rebuilding and retreading tires
**PA:** Total Intermodal Services, Inc.
7101 Jackson St

### (P-19153)
**NEW PRIDE TIRE LLC**
1511 E Orangethorpe Ave Ste D, Fullerton (92831-5204)
**PHONE**....................310 631-7000
Edward Eunjong Kim, *Pr*
**EMP:** 50
**Web:** www.newpridetire.com
**SIC:** 7534 1799 Rebuilding and retreading tires; Antenna installation
**HQ:** New Pride Tire, Llc
2900 Main St Bldg 137
Alameda CA 94501
510 567-8800

### (P-19154)
**SCHER TIRE INC (PA)**
3863 Tyler St, Riverside (92503-3430)
**PHONE**....................951 343-3100
**EMP:** 20 **EST:** 1981
**SALES (est):** 12.51MM
**SALES (corp-wide):** 12.51MM **Privately Held**
**Web:** www.schertire.com
**SIC:** 7534 Tire retreading and repair shops

### (P-19155)
**TARULLI TIRE INC (PA)**
376 Broadway, Costa Mesa (92627-2344)
**PHONE**....................714 630-4722
Dan Tarulli, *CEO*
Rick Tarulli, *
**EMP:** 23 **EST:** 1979
**SQ FT:** 25,000
**SALES (est):** 1.55MM
**SALES (corp-wide):** 1.55MM **Privately Held**
**SIC:** 7534 5014 5531 Rebuilding and retreading tires; Tires and tubes; Automotive tires

### (P-19156)
**WAYNES TIRE INC (PA)**
895 Via Las Aguilas, Arroyo Grande (93420-1955)
P.O. Box 6150 (93456-6150)
**PHONE**....................805 928-2661
Robert L Miller, *CEO*
Russell Miller, *VP*
**EMP:** 15 **EST:** 1959
**SALES (est):** 2.37MM
**SALES (corp-wide):** 2.37MM **Privately Held**
**Web:** www.russellmillerproperties.com
**SIC:** 7534 5531 Tire recapping; Automotive tires

## 7537 Automotive Transmission Repair Shops

### (P-19157)
**H & A TRANSMISSIONS INC**
8727 Rochester Ave, Rancho Cucamonga (91730-4908)
P.O. Box 4378 (91729-4378)
**PHONE**....................909 941-9020
Gilbert H Dickason, *CEO*
Corina Dickason, *
▲ **EMP:** 26 **EST:** 1992
**SQ FT:** 3,500
**SALES (est):** 6.05MM **Privately Held**
**Web:** www.handatrans.com
**SIC:** 7537 3714 Automotive transmission repair shops; Axle housings and shafts, motor vehicle

## 7538 General Automotive Repair Shops

### (P-19158)
**10-8 RETROFIT INC**
415 W Main St, Ontario (91762-3845)
**PHONE**....................909 986-5551
Daniel Keenan, *Pr*
Jerry Keenan, *Prin*
**EMP:** 15 **EST:** 2000
**SQ FT:** 6,800
**SALES (est):** 2.19MM **Privately Held**
**Web:** www.10-8retrofit.com
**SIC:** 7538 3711 5087 General automotive repair shops; Ambulances (motor vehicles), assembly of; Service establishment equipment

### (P-19159)
**ALTEC INDUSTRIES INC**
Also Called: Pomona Service Center
2882 Pomona Blvd, Pomona (91768-3224)
**PHONE**....................909 444-0444
Rick Thompson, *Mgr*
**EMP:** 21
**SQ FT:** 13,240
**SALES (corp-wide):** 1.21B **Privately Held**
**Web:** www.altec.com
**SIC:** 7538 3713 3711 3531 General truck repair; Truck bodies and parts; Motor vehicles and car bodies; Construction machinery
**HQ:** Altec Industries, Inc.
210 Inverness Center Drv
Birmingham AL 35242
205 991-7733

### (P-19160)
**CENTRAL CALIFORNIA POWER**
19487 Broken Ct, Shafter (93263-3146)
P.O. Box 1934 (93303-1934)
**PHONE**....................661 589-2870
Rhoderick E Headley, *CEO*
Rhoderick E Headley, *Pr*
Blake Headley, *
**EMP:** 25 **EST:** 1982
**SQ FT:** 15,000
**SALES (est):** 8.8MM **Privately Held**
**Web:** www.gensets.com
**SIC:** 7538 7359 3569 Truck engine repair, except industrial; Equipment rental and leasing, nec; Gas generators

### (P-19161)
**NORTH VALLEY FLEET SVCS INC (PA)**
3115 Coke St, West Sacramento (95691-3003)
P.O. Box 980006 (95798-0006)
**PHONE**....................916 374-8850
Chan Sao Gi, *CEO*
**EMP:** 18 **EST:** 2004
**SALES (est):** 2.32MM
**SALES (corp-wide):** 2.32MM **Privately Held**
**Web:** www.nvisuzutrucks.com
**SIC:** 7538 3537 5012 3715 General truck repair; Industrial trucks and tractors; Trucks, commercial; Truck trailers

### (P-19162)
**SIEMENS MOBILITY INC**
5301 Price Ave, Mcclellan (95652-2401)
**PHONE**....................916 621-2700
Christopher Maynard, *Dist Vice President*
**EMP:** 100
**SALES (corp-wide):** 84.48B **Privately Held**
**Web:** www.siemens.com
**SIC:** 7538 3743 General truck repair; Train cars and equipment, freight or passenger
**HQ:** Siemens Mobility, Inc.
1 Penn Plz Ste 1100
New York NY 10119
212 672-4000

## 7539 Automotive Repair Shops, Nec

### (P-19163)
**AIRDRAULICS INC**
13261 Saticoy St, North Hollywood (91605-3401)
**PHONE**....................818 982-1400
Dan Tracey, *CEO*
Devin Tracey, *
**EMP:** 25 **EST:** 1986
**SQ FT:** 5,000
**SALES (est):** 5.83MM **Privately Held**
**Web:** www.airdraulicsinc.com
**SIC:** 7539 3599 5013 5084 Automotive repair shops, nec; Machine and other job shop work; Automotive servicing equipment; Industrial machinery and equipment

### (P-19164)
**JAMES MAGNA LTD**
Also Called: Northstar Engineering
8782 Lanyard Ct, Rancho Cucamonga (91730-0804)
**PHONE**....................909 391-2025
Mike Maedel, *CEO*
Gene Gregory, *VP*
◆ **EMP:** 17 **EST:** 1991
**SQ FT:** 19,696
**SALES (est):** 4MM **Privately Held**
**Web:** www.nsecal.com
**SIC:** 7539 3599 Fuel system repair, motor vehicle; Machine shop, jobbing and repair

## 7542 Carwashes

### (P-19165)
**EXECUTIVE AUTO RECONDITIONING**

* ▲ = Import ▼ = Export
◆ = Import/Export

# PRODUCTS & SERVICES SECTION

## 7692 - Welding Repair (P-19183)

Also Called: Dealership Auto Dtail Rstrtons
522 E Duarte Rd, Monrovia  (91016-4604)
P.O. Box 24  (90640-0033)
PHONE..................................626 416-3322
Miguel Alvarado, *CEO*
EMP: 45 EST: 2017
SALES (est): 468.96K **Privately Held**
SIC: 7542 7532 3842  Carwashes; Body shop, automotive; Cosmetic restorations

---

### 7549 Automotive Services, Nec

**(P-19166)**
**A-1 ALTERNATIVE FUEL SYSTEMS (PA)**
Also Called: A-1 Alternative Fuel Systems
2320 Stanislaus St, Fresno  (93721-1223)
PHONE..................................559 485-4427
Al Feijoo, *Pr*
Mark Gilio, *
EMP: 25 EST: 1988
SQ FT: 17,500
SALES (est): 4.33MM
SALES (corp-wide): 4.33MM **Privately Held**
Web: www.a1autoelectric.com
SIC: 7549 7538 3499  Fuel system conversion, automotive; Engine rebuilding: automotive; Ammunition boxes, metal

**(P-19167)**
**AMERICAN CRIER EQP TRLR SLS LL**
2285 E Date Ave, Fresno  (93706-5426)
PHONE..................................559 442-1500
TOLL FREE: 800
Tom Pistacchio, *Managing Member*
Phillip J Sweet, *
David Sweet, *
Dolores Pistacchio, *Managing Member*
Richard Hutchison Junior, *Managing Member*
EMP: 17 EST: 2011
SQ FT: 36,000
SALES (est): 640.39K **Privately Held**
Web: www.americancarrierequipment.com
SIC: 7549 3715  Trailer maintenance; Truck trailers

**(P-19168)**
**AUTO EX TOWING & RECOVERY LLC**
2594 Oakdale Ave, San Francisco  (94124-1520)
PHONE..................................415 846-2262
Vladimir Mikshansky, *Brnch Mgr*
EMP: 20
SALES (corp-wide): 2.52MM **Privately Held**
Web: www.moldremovalsanmateo.com
SIC: 7549 3715 3531 4212  Towing services; Truck trailers; Construction machinery; Local trucking, without storage
PA: Auto Express Towing & Recovery Llc
   270 Napoleon St
   415 407-8977

**(P-19169)**
**PRECISION AERIAL SERVICES INC**
2020 Lowell St, Rialto  (92377-3722)
PHONE..................................909 484-8259
Bill Payne Junior, *CEO*
Rachel Huston, *Vice Chairman*
EMP: 16 EST: 2012
SALES (est): 2.79MM **Privately Held**

Web: www.precisionaerialservices.com
SIC: 7549 7694  High performance auto repair and service; Electric motor repair

**(P-19170)**
**SINGER VEHICLE DESIGN LLC (PA)**
19500 S Vermont Ave, Torrance  (90502-1120)
PHONE..................................213 592-2728
Mazen Fawaz, *CEO*
Robert Peter Dickinson, *CPO*
Jason Grant, *CFO*
Jason Franklin, *COO*
EMP: 250 EST: 2009
SALES (est): 25.24MM
SALES (corp-wide): 25.24MM **Privately Held**
Web: www.singervehicledesign.com
SIC: 7549 3714  Automotive customizing services, nonfactory basis; Acceleration equipment, motor vehicle

---

### 7622 Radio And Television Repair

**(P-19171)**
**DISH FOR ALL  INC**
148 S Escondido Blvd, Escondido  (92025-4115)
PHONE..................................760 690-3869
Ahed Ihmud, *Pr*
Rania Abedel Whab, *
Mike Arfat, *
EMP: 30 EST: 2007
SQ FT: 4,000
SALES (est): 410.16K **Privately Held**
Web: www.dishforall.com
SIC: 7622 5731 3679  Radio and television receiver installation; Radio, television, and electronic stores; Antennas, satellite: household use

---

### 7623 Refrigeration Service And Repair

**(P-19172)**
**MRV SERVICE AIR  INC**
Also Called: Mrv Crane
937 High St, Delano  (93215-1704)
P.O. Box 535  (93216-0535)
PHONE..................................661 725-3400
Manuel Valdovinos, *Pr*
EMP: 18 EST: 2007
SQ FT: 7,200
SALES (est): 1.01MM **Privately Held**
Web: www.mrvserviceair.com
SIC: 7623 3444  Air conditioning repair; Sheet metalwork

---

### 7629 Electrical Repair Shops

**(P-19173)**
**5 STAR SERVICE  INC**
Also Called: E Appliance Repair and Hvac
18723 Via Princessa, Santa Clarita  (91387-4954)
PHONE..................................323 647-7777
Sardor Umrdinov, *CEO*
EMP: 50 EST: 2018
SALES (est): 324.78K **Privately Held**
SIC: 7629 1389  Electrical household appliance repair; Construction, repair, and dismantling services

**(P-19174)**
**AMERICAN ELC COMPONENTS INC**
4901 Fruitland Ave, Vernon  (90058-2728)
PHONE..................................323 771-4888
Raul Bauelos Senior, *Pr*
Antonio Camacho, *VP*
Victor M Banuelos, *Sec*
EMP: 15 EST: 1995
SALES (est): 3.27MM **Privately Held**
Web: www.aecinc1.com
SIC: 7629 3612  Electrical equipment repair services; Power transformers, electric

**(P-19175)**
**CPI ECONCO DIVISION**
Also Called: Econco Broadcast Service
1318 Commerce Ave, Woodland  (95776-5908)
PHONE..................................530 662-7553
◆ EMP: 73
Web: www.cpii.com
SIC: 7629 3671  Electrical repair shops; Vacuum tubes

**(P-19176)**
**PRO CIRCUITS MANUFACTURING INC** ✪
Also Called: Pro Circuits Mfg Inds
16464 Via Esprillo, San Diego  (92127-1702)
PHONE..................................858 899-4747
Jay Madhani, *CEO*
Jay G Madhani, *CEO*
Daljit K Dhindsa, *Pr*
EMP: 21 EST: 2023
SALES (est): 650.57K **Privately Held**
Web: www.pcmi-usa.com
SIC: 7629 3672 5961 3315  Electronic equipment repair; Printed circuit boards; Computer equipment and electronics, mail order; Wire and fabricated wire products

**(P-19177)**
**RUBEN & LEON  INC**
Also Called: Takyo Tyco
5002 Venice Blvd, Los Angeles  (90019-5308)
PHONE..................................323 937-4445
TOLL FREE: 800
Ruben Cielak, *Pr*
Leon Cielak, *VP*
EMP: 20 EST: 1983
SQ FT: 8,000
SALES (est): 2.22MM **Privately Held**
Web: www.tykosigns.com
SIC: 7629 5063 5719 3993  Electrical equipment repair services; Light bulbs and related supplies; Lighting, lamps, and accessories; Advertising artwork

**(P-19178)**
**SCHROFF  INC**
Also Called: Pentair Equipment Protection
7328 Trade St, San Diego  (92121-3435)
PHONE..................................858 740-2400
Robert Bradley, *Brnch Mgr*
EMP: 120
Web: schroff.nvent.com
SIC: 7629 3469  Telecommunication equipment repair (except telephones); Electronic enclosures, stamped or pressed metal
HQ: Schroff, Inc.
   170 Commerce Dr
   Warwick RI 02886
   763 204-7700

**(P-19179)**
**TELENET VOIP INC**
Also Called: Telenet
850 N Park View Dr, El Segundo  (90245-4914)
PHONE..................................310 253-9000
TOLL FREE: 800
Asghar Ghassemy, *Pr*
Nicol Payab, *
EMP: 65 EST: 1977
SQ FT: 11,000
SALES (est): 9.69MM **Privately Held**
Web: www.telenetvoip.com
SIC: 7629 7379 7382 3612  Telephone set repair; Computer related consulting services; Security systems services; Transmission and distribution voltage regulators

**(P-19180)**
**TESTEQUITY LLC (HQ)**
Also Called: Techni-Tools
6100 Condor Dr, Moorpark  (93021-2608)
PHONE..................................805 498-9933
Ruzz Frazee, *Pr*
Nick Hawtrey, *
Aftan Lorick, *
▲ EMP: 99 EST: 1971
SQ FT: 75,000
SALES (est): 163.89MM
SALES (corp-wide): 1.57B **Publicly Held**
Web: www.testequity.com
SIC: 7629 3825  Electrical equipment repair services; Test equipment for electronic and electrical circuits
PA: Distribution Solutions Group, Inc.
   301 Commerce St Ste 1700
   888 611-9888

---

### 7641 Reupholstery And Furniture Repair

**(P-19181)**
**GUYS PATIO INC**
Also Called: Patio Guys
845 N Elm St, Orange  (92867-7909)
PHONE..................................844 968-7485
Jan Vanderlinden, *Pr*
EMP: 25 EST: 1978
SALES (est): 1.42MM **Privately Held**
Web: www.patioguys.com
SIC: 7641 5712 5021 2514  Furniture repair and maintenance; Furniture stores; Outdoor and lawn furniture, nec; Metal household furniture

**(P-19182)**
**MOYES CUSTOM FURNITURE INC**
1884 Pomona Rd, Corona  (92878-3278)
PHONE..................................714 729-0234
Brian Moyes, *Pr*
Jane Moyes, *
David Moyes Secratry, *Prin*
EMP: 50 EST: 1961
SQ FT: 59,000
SALES (est): 1.72MM **Privately Held**
Web: www.moyesfurniture.com
SIC: 7641 2512  Reupholstery; Upholstered household furniture

---

### 7692 Welding Repair

**(P-19183)**
**B W PADILLA INC**
Also Called: Brian's Welding
197 Ryland St, San Jose  (95110-2241)
PHONE..................................408 275-9834
Brian Wade Padilla, *CEO*

# 7692 - Welding Repair (P-19184)

Diana Padilla, *
**EMP:** 24 **EST:** 1991
**SALES (est):** 2.33MM **Privately Held**
**Web:** www.brianswelding.com
**SIC: 7692** Welding repair

### (P-19184)
### BAXTER WLDG & FABRICATION LLC
Also Called: Baxter Welding
8 Dorr Ln, Oroville  (95966-3644)
**PHONE**.................................530 321-9216
**EMP:** 15 **EST:** 2012
**SALES (est):** 896.6K **Privately Held**
**SIC: 7692** 1799  Welding repair; Welding on site

### (P-19185)
### CAMERON WELDING SUPPLY (PA)
Also Called: Cameron Welding
11061 Dale Ave, Stanton  (90680-3206)
P.O. Box 266  (90680-0266)
**PHONE**.................................714 530-9353
Elizabeth Perry, CEO
Joseph Churilla, *
▲ **EMP:** 36 **EST:** 1963
**SQ FT:** 4,500
**SALES (est):** 6.19MM
**SALES (corp-wide):** 6.19MM **Privately Held**
**Web:** www.cameronwelding.com
**SIC: 7692** 5999  Welding repair; Welding supplies

### (P-19186)
### CLP INC (PA)
Also Called: Rick's Hitches & Welding
1546 E Main St, El Cajon  (92021-5901)
**PHONE**.................................619 444-3105
Richard Preston, Pr
Betty Preston, *
**EMP:** 30 **EST:** 1974
**SQ FT:** 23,500
**SALES (est):** 294.2K
**SALES (corp-wide):** 294.2K **Privately Held**
**Web:** www.cwclp.org
**SIC: 7692** 7533 7699  Welding repair; Muffler shop, sale or repair and installation; Recreational vehicle repair services

### (P-19187)
### COMPLETE WELDERS SUPPLY
1549 N Broadway Ave, Stockton  (95205-3044)
**PHONE**.................................209 462-3086
Michael Kowolski, Mgr
**EMP:** 16
**SALES (corp-wide):** 8.4MM **Privately Held**
**Web:** www.completewelderssupply.com
**SIC: 7692** Welding repair
**PA:** Complete Welders Supply
  101 Camino Dorado
  707 258-0885

### (P-19188)
### CW INDUSTRIES INC (PA)
1735 Santa Fe Ave, Long Beach  (90813-1242)
**PHONE**.................................562 432-5421
Craig Wildvank, Pr
**EMP:** 49 **EST:** 1979
**SQ FT:** 22,000
**SALES (est):** 7.8MM **Privately Held**
**Web:** www.cwindustries.us
**SIC: 7692** Welding repair

### (P-19189)
### DEANS CERTIFIED WELDING INC
27645 Commerce Center Dr, Temecula  (92590-2521)
**PHONE**.................................760 728-0292
Michael W Dean, Pr
Carolyn Dean, VP
Merle Geraths, Mgr
**EMP:** 19 **EST:** 1974
**SALES (est):** 2.49MM **Privately Held**
**Web:** www.deanswelding.com
**SIC: 7692** Welding repair

### (P-19190)
### DENTONIS WELDING WORKS INC (PA)
Also Called: Dentonis Spring and Suspension
801 S Airport Way, Stockton  (95205-6901)
**PHONE**.................................209 464-4930
David B Dentoni Ii, CEO
Dan Dentoni, *
Donna Dentoni, *
**EMP:** 45 **EST:** 1972
**SQ FT:** 1,000
**SALES (est):** 12.64MM
**SALES (corp-wide):** 12.64MM **Privately Held**
**Web:** www.dentoni.com
**SIC: 7692** 3599 5531 7539  Welding repair; Machine shop, jobbing and repair; Automotive parts; Automotive springs, rebuilding and repair

### (P-19191)
### DIP BRAZE INC
9131 De Garmo Ave, Sun Valley  (91352-2696)
**PHONE**.................................818 768-1555
Gail Brown, Pr
Robert Gebo, *
**EMP:** 19 **EST:** 1956
**SQ FT:** 10,500
**SALES (est):** 1.22MM **Privately Held**
**Web:** www.dipbraze.com
**SIC: 7692** 3398  Brazing; Metal heat treating

### (P-19192)
### FERGUSON WELDING SERVICE
1147 Atlantic St, Union City  (94587-2001)
**PHONE**.................................510 487-5906
Bob L Ferguson, Pr
**EMP:** 17 **EST:** 1974
**SALES (est):** 2.45MM **Privately Held**
**Web:** www.fergusonwelding.services
**SIC: 7692** Welding repair

### (P-19193)
### FINISHLINE CERTIFIED WELDING L
32082 Anna Marie Ln, Bonsall  (92003-3105)
**PHONE**.................................760 271-6364
**EMP:** 18 **EST:** 2016
**SALES (est):** 487.88K **Privately Held**
**Web:** www.finishlineweld.com
**SIC: 7692** Welding repair

### (P-19194)
### GALAXY BRAZING CO INC
10015 Freeman Ave, Santa Fe Springs  (90670-3405)
**PHONE**.................................562 946-9039
John Mc Gee, Pr
Donna Mc Gee, *
**EMP:** 16 **EST:** 1961
**SQ FT:** 13,144
**SALES (est):** 1.62MM **Privately Held**
**Web:** www.galaxybrazing.com
**SIC: 7692** 3398 1799  Brazing; Metal heat treating; Welding on site

### (P-19195)
### GLOBAL STEEL FABRICATORS INC
255 Demeter St, East Palo Alto  (94303-1304)
**PHONE**.................................650 321-9533
Johan Gidstedt, Pr
**EMP:** 15 **EST:** 2004
**SALES (est):** 1.03MM **Privately Held**
**Web:** www.globalsteelfab.com
**SIC: 7692** 1791  Welding repair; Structural steel erection

### (P-19196)
### HANSENS WELDING INC
358 W 168th St, Gardena  (90248-2733)
**PHONE**.................................310 329-6888
Gary D Hansen, CEO
Robert Hansen, *
Shauna Hansen, *
**EMP:** 25 **EST:** 1949
**SQ FT:** 26,000
**SALES (est):** 2.52MM **Privately Held**
**Web:** www.hansenswelding.com
**SIC: 7692** Welding repair

### (P-19197)
### HAYES WELDING INC (PA)
Also Called: Valew Welding & Fabrication
12522 Violet Rd, Adelanto  (92301-2704)
P.O. Box 310  (92301-0310)
**PHONE**.................................760 246-4878
Roger L Hayes, CEO
Velma D Hayes, *
Vernon L Hayes, *
▲ **EMP:** 91 **EST:** 1954
**SQ FT:** 45,000
**SALES (est):** 10.73MM
**SALES (corp-wide):** 10.73MM **Privately Held**
**Web:** www.valew.com
**SIC: 7692** 3465 3714 3713  Welding repair; Automotive stampings; Fuel systems and parts, motor vehicle; Truck and bus bodies

### (P-19198)
### HESTER FABRICATION INC
20876 Corsair Blvd, Hayward  (94545-1012)
**PHONE**.................................530 227-6867
Daniel Hester, Prin
**EMP:** 18 **EST:** 2014
**SALES (est):** 1.69MM **Privately Held**
**Web:** www.hesterfabrication.com
**SIC: 7692** Welding repair

### (P-19199)
### INTEGRATED MFG TECH INC
Also Called: INTEGRATED MANUFACTURING TECHNOLOGIES, INC.
1477 N Milpitas Blvd, Milpitas  (95035-3160)
**PHONE**.................................510 659-9770
Andy Luong, CEO
**EMP:** 28
**SIC: 7692** Welding repair
**HQ:** Integrated Manufacturing Technologies, Llc
  45473 Warm Springs Blvd
  Fremont CA 94539
  408 934-5879

### (P-19200)
### IRONMAN INC
20555 Superior St, Chatsworth  (91311-4418)
**PHONE**.................................818 341-0980
Joe Salem, CEO
Ziva Salem, *
Ben Salem, *
Tish Byrne, *
**EMP:** 25 **EST:** 1987
**SALES (est):** 4.49MM **Privately Held**
**Web:** www.ironmaninc.net
**SIC: 7692** Welding repair

### (P-19201)
### J AND D STL FBRICATION REPR LP
2360 Westgate Rd, Santa Maria  (93455-1046)
P.O. Box 5487  (93456-5487)
**PHONE**.................................805 928-9674
Joe Trevino, Pt
David Cox, Pt
**EMP:** 17 **EST:** 2018
**SALES (est):** 185.31K **Privately Held**
**Web:** www.jdfabandweld.com
**SIC: 7692** Welding repair

### (P-19202)
### J&K WELDING CO INC
6815 Foxtail Ct, Rancho Cucamonga  (91739-1577)
**PHONE**.................................909 226-1372
Kathleen Brugger, CEO
**EMP:** 20 **EST:** 1982
**SALES (est):** 348.54K **Privately Held**
**SIC: 7692** Welding repair

### (P-19203)
### JABIL SILVER CREEK INC (HQ)
4050 Technology Pl, Fremont  (94538-6362)
**PHONE**.................................669 255-2900
John P Wolfe, CEO
Rita Wolfe, *
▲ **EMP:** 85 **EST:** 1992
**SALES (est):** 29.7MM
**SALES (corp-wide):** 28.88B **Publicly Held**
**Web:** www.oakmontseniorliving.com
**SIC: 7692** 8711 3674 3317  Welding repair; Engineering services; Semiconductors and related devices; Steel pipe and tubes
**PA:** Jabil Inc.
  10800 Roosevelt Blvd N
  727 577-9749

### (P-19204)
### JETI INC
Also Called: Jet I
14578 Hawthorne Ave, Fontana  (92335-2507)
**PHONE**.................................909 357-2966
John Lowery, Pr
Jose Gradilla, VP
**EMP:** 17 **EST:** 1983
**SQ FT:** 10,000
**SALES (est):** 197.09K **Privately Held**
**Web:** www.jeti.com
**SIC: 7692** Welding repair

### (P-19205)
### JOBSITE STUD WELDING
9445 Washburn Rd, Downey  (90242-2912)
**PHONE**.................................855 885-7883
**EMP:** 40 **EST:** 2018
**SALES (est):** 774.23K **Privately Held**
**Web:** www.jobsitestud.com
**SIC: 7692** Welding repair

### (P-19206)
### JON STEEL ERECTORS INC
1431 S Gage St, San Bernardino  (92408-2835)
**PHONE**.................................909 799-0005
Octavio Arellano, Pr
**EMP:** 22 **EST:** 2005
**SALES (est):** 2.59MM **Privately Held**
**Web:** www.jonsteelinc.com

# PRODUCTS & SERVICES SECTION

## 7694 - Armature Rewinding Shops (P-19228)

SIC: **7692** 5082 1791 Welding repair; General construction machinery and equipment; Structural steel erection

### (P-19207)
**KNISLEY WELDING INC**
Also Called: Knisley Aircraft Exhaust
3450 Swetzer Rd, Loomis (95650-9581)
PHONE..................916 652-5891
Bill Knisley, *Pr*
Curtis Knisley, *VP*
**EMP:** 20 **EST:** 1975
**SQ FT:** 15,000
**SALES (est):** 2.66MM **Privately Held**
Web: www.knisleyexhaust.com
SIC: **7692** Welding repair

### (P-19208)
**MARTINS METAL FABRICATION & WELDING INC**
7260 Lewis Rd, Vacaville (95687-9451)
P.O. Box 1855 (95696-1855)
PHONE..................707 678-4117
**EMP:** 40 **EST:** 1972
**SALES (est):** 5.44MM **Privately Held**
Web: www.martinsmetalfab.com
SIC: **7692** Welding repair

### (P-19209)
**NEVADA HEAT TREATING LLC (PA)**
Also Called: California Brazing
37955 Central Ct Ste D, Newark (94560-3466)
PHONE..................510 790-2300
Richard T Penrose, *Dir*
Jeffrey A Ager, *
Ronald J Lustig, *
Richard T Penrose, *Sec*
◆ **EMP:** 37 **EST:** 2002
**SQ FT:** 45,000
**SALES (est):** 61.31MM
**SALES (corp-wide):** 61.31MM **Privately Held**
Web: www.vitessesys.com
SIC: **7692** 3398 3599 Brazing; Metal heat treating; Air intake filters, internal combustion engine, except auto

### (P-19210)
**RETTIG MACHINE INC**
301 Kansas St, Redlands (92373-8153)
P.O. Box 7460 (92375-0460)
PHONE..................909 793-7811
Franz A Rettig Senior, *Pr*
Robert A Rettig, *
Franz A Rettig Junior, *VP*
Susan L Rettig, *
**EMP:** 25 **EST:** 1952
**SQ FT:** 37,000
**SALES (est):** 2.19MM **Privately Held**
Web: www.rettigmachine.com
SIC: **7692** 3599 Welding repair; Machine shop, jobbing and repair

### (P-19211)
**RYLAND CUSTOM WELDING INC**
1815 Monterey Hwy, San Jose (95112-6117)
PHONE..................408 781-2509
Jose Gallegos, *CEO*
**EMP:** 19 **EST:** 2008
**SALES (est):** 1.49MM **Privately Held**
Web: www.rylandcustomwelding.com
SIC: **7692** Welding repair

### (P-19212)
**SANITARY STAINLESS WELDING INC**
2550 S East Ave Ste 101b, Fresno (93706-5121)
PHONE..................559 233-7116
James O Mosqueda, *Pr*
▲ **EMP:** 26 **EST:** 2004
**SALES (est):** 2.52MM
**SALES (corp-wide):** 30.63MM **Privately Held**
Web: www.sanitarystainless.com
SIC: **7692** Welding repair
PA: Dci, Inc.
600 54th Ave N
320 252-8200

### (P-19213)
**SHERRILL M CAMPBELL CORPORATION**
Also Called: Hcl Machine Works
15142 Merrill Ave, Dos Palos (93620-9458)
PHONE..................209 392-6103
**EMP:** 15 **EST:** 1947
**SALES (est):** 2.25MM **Privately Held**
Web: www.hclmachineworks.com
SIC: **7692** 3599 Welding repair; Machine shop, jobbing and repair

### (P-19214)
**SOUTHCOAST WELDING & MFG LLC**
2591 Faivre St Ste 1, Chula Vista (91911-7146)
PHONE..................619 429-1337
Patrick Shoup, *Pr*
Jay Parast, *
Leo Mathieu, *
**EMP:** 270 **EST:** 2004
**SQ FT:** 82,000
**SALES (est):** 44.01MM **Privately Held**
Web: www.southcoastwelding.net
SIC: **7692** Welding repair

### (P-19215)
**T L FABRICATIONS LP**
2921 E Coronado St, Anaheim (92806-2502)
PHONE..................562 802-3980
Ryan Kerrigan, *Pr*
Michael Hsu, *
▲ **EMP:** 60 **EST:** 1980
**SQ FT:** 30,000
**SALES (est):** 4.68MM **Privately Held**
SIC: **7692** Welding repair

### (P-19216)
**TC STEEL**
3700 Lakeville Hwy Ste 215, Petaluma (94954-7611)
PHONE..................707 773-2150
Tom Cleary, *Pr*
Kim Cleary, *
**EMP:** 21 **EST:** 1989
**SALES (est):** 507.63K **Privately Held**
Web: www.tcsteel.us
SIC: **7692** 3449 5051 7389 Welding repair; Miscellaneous metalwork; Structural shapes, iron or steel; Scrap steel cutting

### (P-19217)
**THOMAS WELDING & MACHINE INC**
1308 W 8th Ave, Chico (95926-3002)
PHONE..................530 893-8940
Thomas Danterman, *CEO*
Carolyn Sue Dauterman, *
**EMP:** 25 **EST:** 1970
**SQ FT:** 55,000
**SALES (est):** 3.08MM **Privately Held**
Web: www.thomaswelding.com
SIC: **7692** 5083 3599 Welding repair; Agricultural machinery and equipment; Machine shop, jobbing and repair

### (P-19218)
**TIKOS TANKS INC**
Also Called: Rte Welding
14561 Hawthorne Ave, Fontana (92335-2508)
PHONE..................951 757-8014
**EMP:** 18 **EST:** 2007
**SALES (est):** 2.95MM **Privately Held**
Web: www.rtewelding.com
SIC: **7692** Welding repair

### (P-19219)
**WELDLOGIC INC**
Also Called: Weldlogic Gas & Supply
2651 Lavery Ct, Newbury Park (91320-1502)
PHONE..................805 375-1670
Robert Elizarraz, *Pr*
Jack Froschauer, *
▲ **EMP:** 65 **EST:** 1980
**SQ FT:** 25,000
**SALES (est):** 9.89MM **Privately Held**
Web: www.weldlogic.com
SIC: **7692** Welding repair

### (P-19220)
**WEST COAST WELDING & CNSTR**
390 S Del Norte Blvd, Oxnard (93030-7914)
PHONE..................805 604-1222
Micheal Edward Barbey, *CEO*
Tamara Barbey, *CFO*
Stella Delgado, *Sec*
**EMP:** 18 **EST:** 2005
**SALES (est):** 641.72K **Privately Held**
SIC: **7692** Welding repair

### (P-19221)
**WEST COAST WLDG & PIPING INC**
Also Called: Pipline
760 W Hueneme Rd, Oxnard (93033-9013)
PHONE..................805 246-5841
Gabriel Nunez, *Managing Member*
Jose Vargas, *
Mike Barbey, *
**EMP:** 80 **EST:** 2018
**SALES (est):** 1.21MM **Privately Held**
Web: www.wcwpiping.com
SIC: **7692** Welding repair

### (P-19222)
**WYMORE INC**
697 S Dogwood Rd, El Centro (92243-4604)
P.O. Box 2618 (92244-2618)
PHONE..................760 352-2045
Marla Wymore Stilwell, *Pr*
Michael Mouser, *
Richard C Wymore, *
Thomas A Wymore, *
**EMP:** 30 **EST:** 1947
**SQ FT:** 25,200
**SALES (est):** 2.27MM **Privately Held**
Web: www.wymoreinc.com
SIC: **7692** 3599 5251 5085 Welding repair; Machine shop, jobbing and repair; Tools; Tools, nec

## 7694 Armature Rewinding Shops

### (P-19223)
**ARROW ELECTRIC MOTOR SERVICE**
645 Broadway St, Fresno (93721-2890)
PHONE..................559 266-0104
Larry Kragh, *Pr*
Geri Kragh, *Sec*
**EMP:** 19 **EST:** 1936
**SQ FT:** 25,000
**SALES (est):** 1.33MM **Privately Held**
Web: www.arrowelectricmotor.com
SIC: **7694** Electric motor repair

### (P-19224)
**AUL CORP (DH)**
1250 Main St Ste 300, Napa (94559-2622)
P.O. Box 830029 (35283-0029)
PHONE..................707 257-9700
Luis Nieves, *Pr*
**EMP:** 118 **EST:** 1989
**SQ FT:** 8,500
**SALES (est):** 2.29MM **Privately Held**
Web: www.aulcorp.com
SIC: **7694** 7549 Motor repair services; Automotive maintenance services
HQ: Protective Life Corporation
2801 Hwy 280 S
Birmingham AL 35223
205 268-1000

### (P-19225)
**BAKERSFIELD ELC MTR REPR INC**
Also Called: B E M R
121 W Sumner St, Bakersfield (93301-4137)
PHONE..................661 327-3583
Michael Wayne Langston, *Pr*
Jerry Endicott, *Pr*
Nina Endicott, *VP*
**EMP:** 16 **EST:** 1949
**SQ FT:** 12,350
**SALES (est):** 1.02MM **Privately Held**
Web: www.electricmotorworks.com
SIC: **7694** 5063 Rewinding services; Motors, electric

### (P-19226)
**E & L ELECTRIC**
12322 Los Nietos Rd, Santa Fe Springs (90670-2912)
PHONE..................562 903-9272
Mike Fitch, *Pr*
**EMP:** 17 **EST:** 1959
**SQ FT:** 10,000
**SALES (est):** 2.12MM **Privately Held**
Web: www.eandlelectric.com
SIC: **7694** 5063 Electric motor repair; Motors, electric

### (P-19227)
**EANDM**
126 Mill St, Healdsburg (95448-4438)
PHONE..................707 473-3137
Stephanie Clark, *Prin*
**EMP:** 27 **EST:** 2017
**SALES (est):** 1.85MM **Privately Held**
Web: www.eandm.com
SIC: **7694** Electric motor repair

### (P-19228)
**ELECTRIC MOTOR WORKS INC**
803 Inyo Street At 21st St, Bakersfield (93305-5127)
P.O. Box 3349 (93385-3349)

# 7694 - Armature Rewinding Shops (P-19229)

**PHONE**..................661 327-4271
L B Thomasl B Thomas, *CEO*
L B Thomasl B Thomas, *Pr*
Chuck Thomas, *VP*
**EMP:** 20 **EST:** 1939
**SQ FT:** 7,600
**SALES (est):** 2.29MM **Privately Held**
**Web:** www.electricmotorworks.com
**SIC: 7694** 5063 Electric motor repair; Motors, electric

### (P-19229)
### EURTON ELECTRIC COMPANY INC
9920 Painter Ave, Whittier (90605-2759)
P.O. Box 2113 (90670-0113)
**PHONE**..................562 946-4477
John Buchanan, *Pr*
Heather Buchanan, *
▲ **EMP:** 22 **EST:** 1973
**SQ FT:** 10,000
**SALES (est):** 2.36MM **Privately Held**
**Web:** www.eurtonelectric.com
**SIC: 7694** 5063 Rewinding services; Electrical supplies, nec

### (P-19230)
### GRECH MOTORS LLC (PA)
6915 Arlington Ave, Riverside (92504-1905)
**PHONE**..................951 688-8347
Edward P Grech, *Managing Member*
**EMP:** 25 **EST:** 2012
**SALES (est):** 24.57MM
**SALES (corp-wide):** 24.57MM **Privately Held**
**Web:** www.grechmotors.com
**SIC: 7694** Electric motor repair

### (P-19231)
### R A REED ELECTRIC COMPANY (PA)
Also Called: Reed Electric & Field Service
5503 S Boyle Ave, Vernon (90058-3932)
**PHONE**..................323 587-2284
John A Richard Junior, *Pr*
Dorothy J Richard, *
Alex Wong, *
**EMP:** 29 **EST:** 1929
**SQ FT:** 55,000
**SALES (est):** 6.22MM
**SALES (corp-wide):** 6.22MM **Privately Held**
**SIC: 7694** 5063 Electric motor repair; Motors, electric

### (P-19232)
### STANLEY ELECTRIC MOTOR CO INC
222 N Wilson Way, Stockton (95205-4506)
P.O. Box 5130 (95205-0130)
**PHONE**..................209 464-7321
Bradley Oneto, *Pr*
**EMP:** 27 **EST:** 1936
**SALES (est):** 2.2MM **Privately Held**
**SIC: 7694** 5063 Electric motor repair; Motors, electric

### (P-19233)
### SULZER ELCTR-MCHNCAL SVCS US I
620 S Rancho Ave, Colton (92324-3243)
**PHONE**..................909 825-7971
Gary Patton, *Brnch Mgr*
**EMP:** 50
**Web:** www.sulzer.com
**SIC: 7694** 5063 Electric motor repair; Motors, electric

**HQ:** Sulzer Electro-Mechanical Services (Us) Inc.
1910 Jasmine Dr
Pasadena TX 77503
713 473-3231

### (P-19234)
### SUPERIOR ELECTRIC MTR SVC INC
4622 Alcoa Ave, Vernon (90058-2416)
**PHONE**..................323 583-1040
Vicky Marachelian, *Pr*
Art Marachelian, *VP*
**EMP:** 18 **EST:** 1963
**SQ FT:** 12,000
**SALES (est):** 4.76MM **Privately Held**
**Web:** www.superiorelectricmotors.com
**SIC: 7694** 5063 Electric motor repair; Motors, electric

### (P-19235)
### VINCENT ELECTRIC COMPANY (PA)
Also Called: Vincent Electic Motor Company
8383 Baldwin St, Oakland (94621-1925)
**PHONE**..................510 639-4500
Ronald Vincent, *Ch Bd*
Thomas R Marvin, *
Sarah Beckwich, *
Nancy Vincent Marvin, *
**EMP:** 28 **EST:** 1932
**SQ FT:** 27,000
**SALES (est):** 3.33MM
**SALES (corp-wide):** 3.33MM **Privately Held**
**Web:** www.vincentelectric.com
**SIC: 7694** 5063 Electric motor repair; Motors, electric

### (P-19236)
### VISALIA ELECTRIC MOTOR SP INC
Also Called: Visalia Electric Motor Service
7515 W Sunnyview Ave, Visalia (93291-9602)
**PHONE**..................559 651-0606
Gene Quesnoy, *Pr*
**EMP:** 20 **EST:** 1945
**SQ FT:** 30,000
**SALES (est):** 951.3K **Publicly Held**
**Web:** www.electricmotorshop.com
**SIC: 7694** Electric motor repair
**HQ:** Magnetech Industrial Services, Inc.
800 Nave Rd Se
Massillon OH 44646
330 830-3500

### (P-19237)
### WRIGHTS SUPPLY INC
Also Called: Foothill Electric Motors
25838 Springbrook Ave, Santa Clarita (91350-2565)
**PHONE**..................661 254-8400
Steve Dalton, *Genl Mgr*
**EMP:** 22
**SALES (corp-wide):** 8.99MM **Privately Held**
**Web:** www.wrightssupply.com
**SIC: 7694** 7699 5999 5084 Electric motor repair; Pumps and pumping equipment repair; Engine and motor equipment and supplies; Water pumps (industrial)
**PA:** Wright's Supply, Inc.
640 Allen Ave
818 242-1418

## 7699 Repair Services, Nec

### (P-19238)
### ACTION CLEANING CORPORATION
1668 Newton Ave, San Diego (92113-1013)
**PHONE**..................619 233-1881
Roberto Victoria, *Pr*
**EMP:** 40 **EST:** 1982
**SALES (est):** 7.15MM **Privately Held**
**Web:** www.action-cleaning.com
**SIC: 7699** 4212 3732 Tank and boiler cleaning service; Hazardous waste transport ; Boatbuilding and repairing

### (P-19239)
### AEROWORX INC
Also Called: Aero Worx
2565 W 237th St, Torrance (90505-5216)
**PHONE**..................310 891-0300
Gary E Furlong, *Pr*
Carol Furlong, *
▼ **EMP:** 30 **EST:** 1999
**SQ FT:** 38,800
**SALES (est):** 5.02MM **Privately Held**
**Web:** www.aero-worx.com
**SIC: 7699** 3569 3492 3724 Industrial equipment services; Industrial shock absorbers; Control valves, aircraft: hydraulic and pneumatic; Pumps, aircraft engine

### (P-19240)
### ALLIED CRANE INC
855 N Parkside Dr, Pittsburg (94565-3734)
**PHONE**..................925 427-9200
David Costa, *CEO*
Sandy Cariel, *Acctnt*
Vanessa Surrell, *Admn*
**EMP:** 22 **EST:** 1977
**SQ FT:** 35,000
**SALES (est):** 4.78MM **Privately Held**
**Web:** www.alliedcrane.us
**SIC: 7699** 3536 Industrial machinery and equipment repair; Hoists, cranes, and monorails

### (P-19241)
### ALPHATECH GENERAL INC
Also Called: Ametek-Ameron
4750 Littlejohn St, Baldwin Park (91706-2274)
**PHONE**..................626 337-4640
**EMP:** 90
**SIC: 7699** 3812 Aircraft and heavy equipment repair services; Aircraft/ aerospace flight instruments and guidance systems

### (P-19242)
### AMERICAN COOLING TOWER INC (PA)
Also Called: American Cooling Tower
3130 W Harvard St, Santa Ana (92704-3937)
**PHONE**..................714 898-2436
Erik Johnson, *Pr*
**EMP:** 19 **EST:** 1990
**SQ FT:** 3,500
**SALES (est):** 6.53MM **Privately Held**
**Web:** www.americancoolingtower.com
**SIC: 7699** 3444 Tank repair and cleaning services; Cooling towers, sheet metal

### (P-19243)
### APPLIED FUSION LLC
1915 Republic Ave, San Leandro (94577-4220)
**PHONE**..................510 351-8314
**EMP:** 60 **EST:** 1972
**SALES (est):** 4.9MM **Privately Held**
**Web:** www.appliedfusionllc.com
**SIC: 7699** 3599 Metal reshaping and replating services; Machine and other job shop work

### (P-19244)
### B2 MACHINING LLC
4255 Business Center Dr, Fremont (94538-6357)
**PHONE**..................510 668-1360
Bryan Bach, *Managing Member*
**EMP:** 17 **EST:** 2014
**SQ FT:** 7,300
**SALES (est):** 2.87MM **Privately Held**
**Web:** www.b2machining.com
**SIC: 7699** 3449 Industrial machinery and equipment repair; Miscellaneous metalwork

### (P-19245)
### BRIDPORT ERIE AVIATION INC
Also Called: Amsafe Bridport
6900 Orangethorpe Ave, Buena Park (90620-1390)
**PHONE**..................714 634-8801
Sal Valle, *Genl Mgr*
Keith Mcconnell, *Pr*
Dennis Gilbert, *VP*
Harold Handelsman, *Sec*
Habib Enayetullah, *Treas*
**EMP:** 25 **EST:** 2000
**SALES (est):** 1.19MM **Privately Held**
**Web:** www.amsafebridport.com
**SIC: 7699** 7363 3728 Aircraft and heavy equipment repair services; Pilot service, aviation; Aircraft body and wing assemblies and parts

### (P-19246)
### BUILTWARE FABRICATION INC
Also Called: Ware Jared Construction
4569 Skyway Dr, Olivehurst (95961-7473)
**PHONE**..................530 634-0162
Jared Ware, *Pr*
Aubree Ware, *Sec*
**EMP:** 22 **EST:** 2005
**SQ FT:** 10,000
**SALES (est):** 10.24MM **Privately Held**
**Web:** www.builtwarefabrication.com
**SIC: 7699** 3441 1623 1799 Aircraft and heavy equipment repair services; Building components, structural steel; Pipe laying construction; Welding on site

### (P-19247)
### CALI FRAMING SUPPLIES LLC
Also Called: Cali Framing
20450 Plummer St, Chatsworth (91311-5372)
**PHONE**..................818 899-7777
Barry Kaufman, *Managing Member*
▲ **EMP:** 20 **EST:** 2009
**SALES (est):** 2.28MM **Privately Held**
**Web:** www.califraming.com
**SIC: 7699** 3999 Picture framing, custom; Framed artwork

### (P-19248)
### CARBIDE SAW AND TOOL INC
336 S Waterman Ave Ste P, San Bernardino (92408-1534)
**PHONE**..................909 884-9956
Mark Mackamul, *Dir*
Philip Mackamul, *Sec*
**EMP:** 15 **EST:** 1991
**SQ FT:** 2,500
**SALES (est):** 769.15K **Privately Held**
**Web:** www.carbidesawandtool.com

# PRODUCTS & SERVICES SECTION
## 7699 - Repair Services, Nec (P-19267)

SIC: **7699** 3545 3546 Knife, saw and tool sharpening and repair; Machine tool accessories; Saws and sawing equipment

### (P-19249)
### CHROMALLOY SAN DIEGO CORP
7007 Consolidated Way, San Diego (92121-2604)
PHONE.................858 877-2800
Armand F Lauzon Junior, *CEO*
Carlo Luzzatto, *
David G Albert, *
Michael Beffel, *
John Mckirdy, *VP*
EMP: 120 EST: 1986
SQ FT: 120,000
SALES (est): 16.69MM
SALES (corp-wide): 517.74MM **Privately Held**
Web: www.chromalloy.com
SIC: **7699** 3724 Aircraft and heavy equipment repair services; Aircraft engines and engine parts
HQ: Chromalloy American Llc
   330 Blaisdell Rd
   Orangeburg NY 10962
   845 230-7355

### (P-19250)
### CURTISS-WRIGHT CORPORATION
Also Called: Sgt Dresser-Rand
1675 Brandywine Ave Ste E, Chula Vista (91911-6064)
PHONE.................619 656-4740
Joshua Guedsse, *Service Center Manager*
EMP: 44
SALES (corp-wide): 2.85B **Publicly Held**
Web: www.curtisswright.com
SIC: **7699** 3731 Industrial machinery and equipment repair; Shipbuilding and repairing
PA: Curtiss-Wright Corporation
   130 Harbour Pl Dr Ste 300
   704 869-4600

### (P-19251)
### DK VALVE & SUPPLY INC
Also Called: DK Amans Valve & Supply
2385 E Artesia Blvd, Long Beach (90805-1707)
PHONE.................562 529-8400
David Kinzler, *CEO*
Eddie Kinzler, *Dir*
EMP: 22 EST: 1987
SALES (est): 2.36MM **Privately Held**
Web: www.dkamans.com
SIC: **7699** 3491 Valve repair, industrial; Industrial valves

### (P-19252)
### DON PEDRO PUMP LLC
Also Called: Don Pedro Pump
1930 S Walnut Rd, Turlock (95380-9219)
P.O. Box 1038 (95326-1038)
PHONE.................209 632-3161
Gary S Rossiter, *Pr*
Monica Rossiter, *VP*
EMP: 20 EST: 1938
SQ FT: 20,000
SALES (est): 3.86MM **Privately Held**
Web: www.donpedropump.com
SIC: **7699** 3561 Pumps and pumping equipment repair; Industrial pumps and parts

### (P-19253)
### DUCLOS LENSES INC
Also Called: Duclos Lenses
20222 Bahama St, Chatsworth (91311-6203)
PHONE.................818 773-0600
Paul Duclos, *Pr*
Michelle Duclos, *CFO*
EMP: 17 EST: 2013
SALES (est): 2.22MM **Privately Held**
Web: www.ducloslenses.com
SIC: **7699** 5731 3861 Camera repair shop; Video cameras and accessories; Lens shades, camera

### (P-19254)
### EDN AVIATION INC
6720 Valjean Ave, Van Nuys (91406-5818)
PHONE.................818 988-8826
Motti Kurzweil, *Pr*
EMP: 45 EST: 1987
SQ FT: 15,000
SALES (est): 4.07MM
SALES (corp-wide): 168.68MM **Privately Held**
Web: www.ednaviation.com
SIC: **7699** 3728 Aircraft and heavy equipment repair services; R and D by manuf., aircraft parts and auxiliary equipment
HQ: Velocity Aerospace Group, Inc.
   495 Lake Mirror Rd
   Atlanta GA 30349
   214 988-9898

### (P-19255)
### EISENBEISS INC
Also Called: Private
8440 Rovana Cir Ste 100, Sacramento (95828-2537)
PHONE.................916 262-7656
Valborg Burgholzer-kaiser, *CEO*
Valborg Burgholzer-kaiser, *Pr*
Andreas Pum, *CFO*
▲ EMP: 18 EST: 2011
SALES (est): 5.55MM **Privately Held**
Web: www.eisenbeiss.com
SIC: **7699** 3566 Industrial machinery and equipment repair; Gears, power transmission, except auto

### (P-19256)
### EVANS HYDRO INC
Also Called: Evans Hydro
18128 S Santa Fe Ave, Compton (90221-5517)
PHONE.................310 608-5801
James R Byrom, *Pr*
EMP: 28 EST: 1929
SQ FT: 16,000
SALES (est): 4.11MM
SALES (corp-wide): 90.74MM **Privately Held**
Web: www.hydroinc.com
SIC: **7699** 7694 5084 Pumps and pumping equipment repair; Armature rewinding shops; Pumps and pumping equipment, nec
PA: Hydro, Inc.
   834 W Madison St
   312 738-3000

### (P-19257)
### EXCEL PICTURE FRAMES INC
647 E 59th St, Los Angeles (90001-1001)
PHONE.................323 231-0244
Rafael Delgado, *CEO*
Antonio Delgado Senior, *Pr*
EMP: 50 EST: 1992
SALES (est): 2.37MM **Privately Held**
Web: www.excelimagegroup.com
SIC: **7699** 2791 Picture framing, custom; Photocomposition, for the printing trade

### (P-19258)
### FLUID TECH HYDRAULICS INC
8432 Tiogawoods Dr, Sacramento (95828-5046)
PHONE.................916 681-0888
Stephen A Sparks, *Pr*
EMP: 37 EST: 1989
SQ FT: 43,000
SALES (est): 4.05MM **Privately Held**
Web: www.fluidtechhydraulics.com
SIC: **7699** 5084 3599 Hydraulic equipment repair; Hydraulic systems equipment and supplies; Machine and other job shop work

### (P-19259)
### GENERAL CONVEYOR INC
Also Called: Cleveland Tramrail So Calif
13385 Estelle St, Corona (92879-1881)
PHONE.................951 734-3460
▼ EMP: 35
Web: tf.click.com.cn
SIC: **7699** 1796 3531 3536 Industrial machinery and equipment repair; Machinery installation; Backhoes, tractors, cranes, plows, and similar equipment; Hoists, cranes, and monorails

### (P-19260)
### GYMDOC INC
Also Called: Gym Doctors
3488 Arden Rd, Hayward (94545-3906)
PHONE.................510 886-4321
Daniel Daneshvar, *CEO*
EMP: 15 EST: 1991
SALES (est): 978.66K **Privately Held**
Web: www.gymdoc.com
SIC: **7699** 3949 Recreational sporting equipment repair services; Exercise equipment

### (P-19261)
### HAWKER PACIFIC AEROSPACE
11240 Sherman Way, Sun Valley (91352-4942)
PHONE.................818 765-6201
Bernd Riggers, *CEO*
Brian Carr, *
Troy Trower, *
◆ EMP: 355 EST: 1980
SQ FT: 193,000
SALES (est): 23.83MM
SALES (corp-wide): 38.52B **Privately Held**
Web: www.lufthansa-technik.com
SIC: **7699** 5088 3728 Hydraulic equipment repair; Aircraft and parts, nec; Aircraft parts and equipment, nec
HQ: Lufthansa Technik Ag
   Weg Beim Jager 193
   Hamburg HH 22335
   4050700

### (P-19262)
### HYDRALIC SYSTEMS CMPONENTS INC
Also Called: Rupe's Hydraulics Sales & Svc
725 N Twin Oaks Valley Rd, San Marcos (92069-1713)
PHONE.................760 744-9350
Patrick John Maluso, *CEO*
Stephanie Jennison, *
▲ EMP: 29 EST: 1977
SQ FT: 36,000
SALES (est): 5.12MM **Privately Held**
Web: www.rupeshydraulics.com
SIC: **7699** 5084 3559 Hydraulic equipment repair; Hydraulic systems equipment and supplies; Ammunition and explosives, loading machinery

### (P-19263)
### HYDRATECH LLC (HQ)
453 Pollasky Ave Ste 106, Clovis (93612-1178)
PHONE.................559 233-0876
Dave Ogden, *
▲ EMP: 84 EST: 1987
SALES (est): 5.32MM
SALES (corp-wide): 467.96MM **Privately Held**
Web: www.hydratechcylinders.com
SIC: **7699** 3593 Hydraulic equipment repair; Fluid power cylinders, hydraulic or pneumatic
PA: Ligon Industries, Llc
   1927 1st Ave N Fl 5
   205 322-3302

### (P-19264)
### INNOVATIVE EMERGENCY EQUIPMENT
1616 Marlborough Ave, Riverside (92507-2041)
PHONE.................951 222-2270
Sheri Kelley, *Prin*
EMP: 22 EST: 2016
SALES (est): 983.17K **Privately Held**
Web: www.idsmp.com
SIC: **7699** 3669 Repair services, nec; Sirens, electric: vehicle, marine, industrial, and air raid

### (P-19265)
### INTERFACE WELDING
20722 Belshaw Ave, Carson (90746-3510)
PHONE.................310 323-4944
A S Wadleigh, *Pr*
EMP: 20 EST: 1967
SQ FT: 12,000
SALES (est): 2.43MM **Privately Held**
Web: www.interfacewelding.com
SIC: **7699** 7692 3769 3728 Welding equipment repair; Welding repair; Space vehicle equipment, nec; Aircraft parts and equipment, nec

### (P-19266)
### KONE INC
1540 Scenic Ave # 100, Costa Mesa (92626-1408)
PHONE.................714 890-7080
Jeff Schultz, *Mgr*
EMP: 40
Web: www.kone.us
SIC: **7699** 3534 1796 Elevators: inspection, service, and repair; Elevators and moving stairways; Installing building equipment
HQ: Kone Inc.
   3333 Warrenville Rd
   Lisle IL 60532
   630 577-1650

### (P-19267)
### KONE INC
15021 Wicks Blvd, San Leandro (94577-6621)
PHONE.................510 351-5141
Drew Furman, *Brnch Mgr*
EMP: 96
Web: www.kone.us
SIC: **7699** 3534 1796 Elevators: inspection, service, and repair; Elevators and moving stairways; Installing building equipment
HQ: Kone Inc.
   3333 Warrenville Rd
   Lisle IL 60532
   630 577-1650

## 7699 - Repair Services, Nec (P-19268)

**(P-19268)**
**M TEK CORPORATION**
169 Borland Ave, Auburn (95603-4921)
PHONE..................................530 888-9609
Gordon Mason, *CEO*
**EMP:** 15 **EST:** 2005
**SALES (est):** 976.75K **Privately Held**
Web: www.mtekcorporation.com
**SIC:** 7699 3559 Industrial machinery and equipment repair; Semiconductor manufacturing machinery

**(P-19269)**
**MCKENNA BOILER WORKS INC**
2601 Industry St, Oceanside (92054-4808)
PHONE..................................323 221-1171
Howard Smith, *Pr*
Richard R Smith, *
James F Smith, *
**EMP:** 35 **EST:** 1921
**SALES (est):** 4.53MM **Privately Held**
Web: www.mckennaboiler.com
**SIC:** 7699 3823 Boiler repair shop; Boiler controls: industrial, power, and marine type

**(P-19270)**
**MKS INSTRUMENTS INC**
3625 Peterson Way, Santa Clara (95054-2809)
PHONE..................................408 750-0300
Bob Hays, *Mgr*
**EMP:** 21
**SQ FT:** 5,007
**SALES (corp-wide):** 3.62B **Publicly Held**
Web: www.mks.com
**SIC:** 7699 8741 3823 Ship boiler and tank cleaning and repair, contractors; Management services; Process control instruments
**PA:** Mks Instruments, Inc.
2 Tech Dr Ste 201
978 645-5500

**(P-19271)**
**NIACC-AVITECH TECHNOLOGIES INC (PA)**
245 W Dakota Ave, Clovis (93612-5608)
PHONE..................................559 291-2500
Jeff Andrews, *CEO*
Thomas S Irwin, *
Elizabeth R Letendre, *
**EMP:** 80 **EST:** 1983
**SALES (est):** 9.91MM
**SALES (corp-wide):** 9.91MM **Privately Held**
Web: www.heico.com
**SIC:** 7699 3471 Aircraft flight instrument repair; Plating of metals or formed products

**(P-19272)**
**O & S PROPERTIES INC (PA)**
1817 Chico Ave, South El Monte (91733)
P.O. Box 3246 (91733)
PHONE..................................626 579-1084
**TOLL FREE:** 800
Ozzie Levine, *Pr*
**EMP:** 80 **EST:** 1983
**SQ FT:** 200,000
**SALES (est):** 10.06MM
**SALES (corp-wide):** 10.06MM **Privately Held**
Web: www.tldrumco.com
**SIC:** 7699 4959 3412 Industrial equipment services; Sanitary services, nec; Metal barrels, drums, and pails

**(P-19273)**
**OMNI OPTICAL PRODUCTS INC**
22605 La Palma Ave Ste 505, Yorba Linda (92887-6713)
PHONE..................................714 692-1400
Jeffrey Frank, *Brnch Mgr*
**EMP:** 31
**SALES (corp-wide):** 1.9MM **Privately Held**
Web: www.omnisurvey.com
**SIC:** 7699 5048 3827 Photographic and optical goods equipment repair services; Optometric equipment and supplies; Optical instruments and lenses
**PA:** Omni Optical Products, Inc.
17282 Eastman
714 634-5700

**(P-19274)**
**PASSPORT TECHNOLOGY USA INC**
Also Called: Asai
400 N Brand Blvd Ste 800, Glendale (91203-2366)
PHONE..................................818 957-5471
Cleve Tzung, *CEO*
Scott Dowty, *
John Steely, *Chief Operations**
Paul Nielsen, *
Jason H King, *CRO**
**EMP:** 33 **EST:** 1997
**SQ FT:** 1,200
**SALES (est):** 1.55MM **Privately Held**
Web: www.passporttechnology.com
**SIC:** 7699 3578 6099 Automated teller machine (ATM) repair; Automatic teller machines (ATM); Automated teller machine (ATM) network

**(P-19275)**
**PEGGS COMPANY INC (PA)**
4851 Felspar St, Riverside (92509)
P.O. Box 907 (91752)
PHONE..................................800 242-8416
Brett Nelson, *Pr*
Chresten Revelle Nelson, *
John L Peggs, *
◆ **EMP:** 137 **EST:** 1964
**SQ FT:** 80,000
**SALES (est):** 32.15MM
**SALES (corp-wide):** 32.15MM **Privately Held**
Web: www.thepeggscompany.com
**SIC:** 7699 3496 5046 7359 Shopping cart repair; Miscellaneous fabricated wire products; Commercial equipment, nec; Equipment rental and leasing, nec

**(P-19276)**
**PORTER BOILER SERVICE INC**
1166 E 23rd St, Signal Hill (90755-3447)
PHONE..................................562 426-2528
George Hrebien, *Pr*
Nooshin Singhal, *
**EMP:** 25 **EST:** 1958
**SQ FT:** 5,000
**SALES (est):** 2.32MM **Privately Held**
Web: www.porterboiler.com
**SIC:** 7699 1711 3443 Boiler repair shop; Boiler maintenance contractor; Fabricated plate work (boiler shop)

**(P-19277)**
**R & S OVRHD DOORS SO-CAL INC**
Also Called: Door Doctor
1617 N Orangethorpe Way, Anaheim (92801-1228)
PHONE..................................714 680-0600
**TOLL FREE:** 800
David Fowler, *Pr*
**EMP:** 25 **EST:** 1991
**SALES (est):** 1.23MM **Privately Held**
Web: www.rsdoorsofsocal.com

**SIC:** 7699 1731 3446 1751 Door and window repair; Access control systems specialization; Gates, ornamental metal; Garage door, installation or erection

**(P-19278)**
**REDMAN EQUIPMENT & MFG CO**
19800 Normandie Ave, Torrance (90502-1182)
PHONE..................................310 329-1134
Gerald E Redman, *
Janelle Redman, *
▲ **EMP:** 48 **EST:** 1962
**SQ FT:** 8,000
**SALES (est):** 3.19MM
**SALES (corp-wide):** 12.58B **Publicly Held**
Web: www.redmaneq.com
**SIC:** 7699 3443 Boiler and heating repair services; Heat exchangers, condensers, and components
**HQ:** Ohmstede Ltd.
895 N Main St
Beaumont TX 77701
409 833-6375

**(P-19279)**
**SA CAMP PUMP COMPANY**
Also Called: SA Camp Pump and Drilling Co
17876 Zerker Rd, Bakersfield (93308-9221)
P.O. Box 82575 (93380-2575)
PHONE..................................661 399-2976
James S Camp, *Pr*
**EMP:** 60 **EST:** 1952
**SQ FT:** 10,000
**SALES (est):** 10.64MM
**SALES (corp-wide):** 22.14MM **Privately Held**
Web: www.sacampcompanies.com
**SIC:** 7699 3561 Agricultural equipment repair services; Pumps and pumping equipment
**PA:** S A Camp Companies
17876 Zerker Rd
661 399-4451

**(P-19280)**
**SAM SCHAFFER INC**
Also Called: Weld-It Co
3015 E Echo Hill Way, Orange (92867-1905)
PHONE..................................323 263-7524
Stephen Schaffer, *VP*
**EMP:** 43 **EST:** 1946
**SALES (est):** 2.5MM **Privately Held**
Web: www.welditco.com
**SIC:** 7699 3559 Industrial machinery and equipment repair; Petroleum refinery equipment

**(P-19281)**
**SECURITY CENTRAL INC**
Also Called: Reed Brothers Security
2950 Alvarado St Ste D, San Leandro (94577-5738)
PHONE..................................510 652-2477
Ronald Reed, *Pr*
Randall Reed, *
Michael Salk, *
**EMP:** 42 **EST:** 1990
**SQ FT:** 19,000
**SALES (est):** 4.81MM **Privately Held**
Web: www.reedbrotherssecurity.com
**SIC:** 7699 5099 3446 5999 Locksmith shop; Locks and lock sets; Fences or posts, ornamental iron or steel; Electronic parts and equipment

**(P-19282)**
**STAVROS ENTERPRISES INC**
Also Called: Facilitec West
681 Arrow Grand Cir, Covina (91722-2146)
PHONE..................................888 463-2293
Anthony Emanuel Stavros, *CEO*
**EMP:** 30 **EST:** 2006
**SALES (est):** 2.07MM **Privately Held**
Web: www.facilitecwest.com
**SIC:** 7699 3272 Cleaning services; Grease traps, concrete

**(P-19283)**
**SURVIVAL SYSTEMS INTL INC (PA)**
Also Called: Ssi
34140 Valley Center Rd, Valley Center (92082-6017)
P.O. Box 1855 (92082)
PHONE..................................760 749-6800
George Beatty, *CEO*
Mark Beatty, *
Colin Hooper, *
▲ **EMP:** 95 **EST:** 1968
**SQ FT:** 100,000
**SALES (est):** 20.08MM
**SALES (corp-wide):** 20.08MM **Privately Held**
Web: www.survivalsystemsinternational.com
**SIC:** 7699 3531 3086 Industrial equipment services; Winches; Plastics foam products

**(P-19284)**
**SWECO PRODUCTS INC (PA)**
Also Called: Sweco
8949 Colusa Hwy, Sutter (95982-9321)
P.O. Box 259 (95982-0259)
PHONE..................................530 673-8949
Maria Jesus Ziegenmeyer, *CEO*
Raymond Ziegenmeyer, *
Michael Ziegenmeyer, *
Bobby Ziegenmeyer, *
Joseph Ziegenmeyer, *
▲ **EMP:** 38 **EST:** 1946
**SQ FT:** 65,000
**SALES (est):** 4.24MM
**SALES (corp-wide):** 4.24MM **Privately Held**
Web: www.swecoproducts.com
**SIC:** 7699 3599 5082 Farm machinery repair; Custom machinery; Construction and mining machinery

**(P-19285)**
**TEAGUE CUSTOM MARINE INC**
28115 Avenue Stanford, Valencia (91355-1106)
PHONE..................................661 295-7000
Robert Teague, *Pr*
**EMP:** 17 **EST:** 1992
**SQ FT:** 30,000
**SALES (est):** 1.3MM **Privately Held**
Web: www.teaguecustommarine.com
**SIC:** 7699 5088 3732 7948 Boat repair; Marine crafts and supplies; Motorboats, inboard or outboard: building and repairing; Boat racing

**(P-19286)**
**THE GYRO HOUSE (PA)**
Also Called: T G H Aviation
2389 Rickenbacker Way, Auburn (95602-9537)
PHONE..................................530 823-6204
**EMP:** 19 **EST:** 1957
**SALES (est):** 4.43MM
**SALES (corp-wide):** 4.43MM **Privately Held**
Web: www.tghaviation.com

## PRODUCTS & SERVICES SECTION

### 7819 - Services Allied To Motion Pictures (P-19303)

SIC: 7699 3613 5599 5088  Precision instrument repair; Switchgear and switchboard apparatus; Aircraft instruments, equipment or parts; Aeronautical equipment and supplies

**(P-19287)**
**VENTEX CORP**
2153 Otoole Ave Ste 10, San Jose (95131-1331)
PHONE..............................408 436-2929
Brett Pearson, CEO
▲ EMP: 26 EST: 1994
SQ FT: 10,000
SALES (est): 2.47MM Privately Held
Web: www.ventexcorp.com
SIC: 7699 3559  Industrial machinery and equipment repair; Semiconductor manufacturing machinery

**(P-19288)**
**WCR INCORPORATED**
4636 E Drummond Ave, Fresno (93725-1601)
PHONE..............................559 266-8374
Jeff Simpson, Prin
EMP: 17
SQ FT: 12,656
SALES (corp-wide): 43.23MM Privately Held
Web: www.wcrhx.com
SIC: 7699 7629 3443  Metal reshaping and replating services; Electrical repair shops; Fabricated plate work (boiler shop)
PA: Wcr Incorporated
2377 Commerce Center Blvd B
937 223-0703

**(P-19289)**
**WESTERN PUMP INC (PA)**
Also Called: Competrol A Western Pump Co
3235 F St, San Diego (92102-3315)
PHONE..............................619 239-9988
Dennis Rethmeier, CEO
Ryan Rethmeier, *
Janice C Rethmeier, *
▲ EMP: 55 EST: 1988
SQ FT: 10,000
SALES (est): 22.99MM
SALES (corp-wide): 22.99MM Privately Held
Web: www.westernpump.com
SIC: 7699 5084 1799 3728  Tank repair and cleaning services; Petroleum industry machinery; Petroleum storage tanks, pumping and draining; Aircraft parts and equipment, nec

**(P-19290)**
**WHITING DOOR MFG CORP**
301 S Milliken Ave, Ontario (91761-7800)
PHONE..............................909 877-0120
Abdullah Eren, Brnch Mgr
EMP: 92
SQ FT: 5,400
SALES (corp-wide): 37.53MM Privately Held
Web: www.whitingdoor.com
SIC: 7699 3713 5531 5211  Door and window repair; Truck and bus bodies; Truck equipment and parts; Garage doors, sale and installation
PA: Whiting Door Mfg Corp
113 Cedar St
716 542-5427

**(P-19291)**
**WOODSIDE ELECTRONICS CORP**
Also Called: Weco
1311 Blue Grass Pl, Woodland (95776-5918)
PHONE..............................530 666-9190
▲ EMP: 92 EST: 1982
SALES (est): 21.55MM
SALES (corp-wide): 1.84B Privately Held
Web: www.wecotek.com
SIC: 7699 3523  Farm machinery repair; Farm machinery and equipment
HQ: Duravant Llc
3500 Lacey Rd Ste 290
Downers Grove IL 60515

**(P-19292)**
**WYND TECHNOLOGIES INC**
1037 S Claremont St, San Mateo (94402-1835)
PHONE..............................617 438-3694
Raymond Wu, CEO
EMP: 47 EST: 2014
SALES (est): 1.18MM Privately Held
Web: www.hellowynd.com
SIC: 7699 7371 3634  Cleaning services; Software programming applications; Personal electrical appliances

### 7812 Motion Picture And Video Production

**(P-19293)**
**AFRICAJUN LLC**
Also Called: Matrix
39874 Golfers Dr, Palmdale (93551-2982)
PHONE..............................310 403-1673
Charit Selico, CEO
EMP: 20 EST: 2017
SALES (est): 139.09K Privately Held
Web: www.africajun.com
SIC: 7812 8099 2099 8399  Television film production; Medical services organization; Seasonings and spices; Community development groups

**(P-19294)**
**FONCO CREATIVE SERVICES**
Also Called: Fonco Studios
1310 N San Fernando Rd, Los Angeles (90065-1237)
PHONE..............................415 254-5460
Phuong Davis, Owner
EMP: 38 EST: 1997
SALES (est): 991.07K Privately Held
Web: www.foncostudios.com
SIC: 7812 7819 7336 3999  Video production ; Equipment and prop rental, motion picture production; Commercial art and graphic design; Miniatures

**(P-19295)**
**PIXAR (DH)**
Also Called: Pixar Animation Studios
1200 Park Ave, Emeryville (94608-3677)
PHONE..............................510 922-3000
James W Morris, CEO
John Lasseter, Creative Vice President*
▲ EMP: 307 EST: 1985
SQ FT: 247,000
SALES (est): 65.34MM
SALES (corp-wide): 88.9B Publicly Held
Web: www.pixar.com
SIC: 7812 7372 7371  Cartoon motion picture production; Prepackaged software; Computer software development
HQ: Twdc Enterprises 18 Corp.
500 S Buena Vista St
Burbank CA 91521

**(P-19296)**
**SAINT JSEPH COMMUNICATIONS INC (PA)**
Also Called: Catholic Resource Center
1243 E Shamwood St, West Covina (91790-2348)
P.O. Box 720 (91793-0720)
PHONE..............................626 331-3549
Terry Barber, Pr
EMP: 25 EST: 1988
SALES (est): 2.46MM
SALES (corp-wide): 2.46MM Privately Held
Web: www.saintjoe.com
SIC: 7812 2741 7822  Motion picture and video production; Miscellaneous publishing; Motion picture and tape distribution

**(P-19297)**
**SONY MEDIA CLOUD SERVICES LLC**
10202 Washington Blvd, Culver City (90232-3119)
PHONE..............................877 683-9124
EMP: 50 EST: 2013
SALES (est): 294.4K Privately Held
Web: www.cloud19.com
SIC: 7812 7372  Video production; Business oriented computer software
PA: Sony Group Corporation
1-7-1, Konan

**(P-19298)**
**UNIVERSAL CY STDIOS PRDCTONS L (DH)**
Also Called: Nbcuniversal Television Dist
100 Universal City Plz, Universal City (91608-1085)
PHONE..............................818 777-1000
Ron Meyer, Pr
Maren Christensen, Ex VP
Kenneth L Kahrs, Ex VP
Lynn A Calpeter, Ex VP
Rick Finkelstein, Ex VP
▲ EMP: 25 EST: 2002
SALES (est): 38.1K
SALES (corp-wide): 121.57B Publicly Held
SIC: 7812 3652 2741 5947  Motion picture production and distribution; Phonograph records, prerecorded; Music, sheet: publishing and printing; Gift shop
HQ: Vivendi Universal Entertainment Lllp
30 Rockefeller Plaza
New York NY 10112
212 664-4444

**(P-19299)**
**UNIVERSAL STUDIOS COMPANY LLC (DH)**
100 Universal City Plz, North Hollywood (91608-1002)
PHONE..............................818 777-1000
Adam Fogelson, Ch
Donna Langley, *
Ron Meyer, *
Sean Gamble, *
▲ EMP: 720 EST: 1958
SQ FT: 100,000
SALES (est): 452.4MM
SALES (corp-wide): 121.57B Publicly Held
Web: www.universalstudioshollywood.com
SIC: 7812 3652 2741 5947  Motion picture production and distribution; Phonograph records, prerecorded; Music, sheet: publishing and printing; Gift shop
HQ: Nbcuniversal Media, Llc
30 Rockefeller Plz Fl 2
New York NY 10112

**(P-19300)**
**YOBS TECHNOLOGIES INC**
Also Called: Yobs
615 Childs Way Tro 370, Los Angeles (90089-0024)
PHONE..............................213 713-3825
Raphael Danilo, Pr
Federico Dubini, *
EMP: 50 EST: 2016
SALES (est): 383.47K Privately Held
Web: www.yobstech.com
SIC: 7812 8742 7389 3652  Educational motion picture production; Programmed instruction service; Business services, nec; Prerecorded records and tapes

### 7819 Services Allied To Motion Pictures

**(P-19301)**
**ALAN GORDON ENTERPRISES INC**
5625 Melrose Ave, Los Angeles (90038-3909)
PHONE..............................323 466-3561
Grant Loucks, Pr
Don Sahlein, *
◆ EMP: 24 EST: 1945
SQ FT: 15,000
SALES (est): 2.45MM Privately Held
Web: www.alangordon.com
SIC: 7819 3861  Equipment rental, motion picture; Photographic equipment and supplies

**(P-19302)**
**DTS INC (DH)**
5220 Las Virgenes Rd, Calabasas (91302-1064)
PHONE..............................818 436-1000
Jon E Kirchner, CEO
Melvin L Flanigan, *
Blake A Welcher, *
Kevin Doohan, CMO*
Kris M Graves, *
▲ EMP: 150 EST: 1990
SQ FT: 89,000
SALES (est): 29.43MM
SALES (corp-wide): 388.79MM Publicly Held
Web: www.dts.com
SIC: 7819 3651  Services allied to motion pictures; Household audio and video equipment
HQ: Adeia Holdings Inc.
3025 Orchard Pkwy
San Jose CA 95134
408 473-2500

**(P-19303)**
**PHORUS INC**
5220 Las Virgenes Rd, Calabasas (91302-1064)
PHONE..............................310 995-2521
Jon Kirchner, CEO
▲ EMP: 100 EST: 2012
SALES (est): 724.63K
SALES (corp-wide): 388.79MM Publicly Held
Web: www.phorus.com
SIC: 7819 3651  Services allied to motion pictures; Household audio and video equipment
HQ: Adeia Holdings Inc.
3025 Orchard Pkwy
San Jose CA 95134
408 473-2500

# 7819 - Services Allied To Motion Pictures (P-19304)

**PRODUCTS & SERVICES SECTION**

**(P-19304)**
**POINT 360**
1025 Sansome St, San Francisco (94111-1307)
PHONE...............................415 989-6245
**EMP:** 15
**SQ FT:** 19,000
**SALES (est):** 483.11K
**SALES (corp-wide):** 37.57MM **Publicly Held**
Web: www.point360.com
**SIC: 7819** 3652 Video tape or disk reproduction; Prerecorded records and tapes
**PA:** Point.360
   2701 Media Center Dr
   818 565-1400

## 7922 Theatrical Producers And Services

**(P-19305)**
**TICKETSCOM LLC (DH)**
2100 E Grand Ave Ste 600, El Segundo (90245)
PHONE...............................714 327-5400
Joe Choti, *CEO*
Joe Choti, *Pr*
Cristine Hurley, *CFO*
Curt Clausen, *Sec*
Larry D Witherspoon, *Pr*
**EMP:** 25 **EST:** 1995
**SALES (est):** 5.13MM
**SALES (corp-wide):** 4.71MM **Privately Held**
Web: www.tickets.com
**SIC: 7922** 7372 Ticket agency, theatrical; Application computer software
**HQ:** Mlb Advanced Media, L.P.
   1271 Ave Of The Americas
   New York NY 10020
   212 485-3444

## 7929 Entertainers And Entertainment Groups

**(P-19306)**
**SPECIAL EVENT AUDIO SVCS INC**
35889 Shetland Hls E, Fallbrook (92028-6519)
PHONE...............................800 518-9144
Mitchell J Grant, *CEO*
**EMP:** 24 **EST:** 2014
**SALES (est):** 3.88MM **Privately Held**
Web: www.seaspro.com
**SIC: 7929** 5099 3651 Orchestras or bands, nec; Video and audio equipment; Audio electronic systems

**(P-19307)**
**YANKA INDUSTRIES INC**
Also Called: Masterclass
660 4th St Ste 443, San Francisco (94107)
PHONE...............................855 981-8208
David Jeremy Rogier, *CEO*
Paul Bankhead, *Chief Product Officer*
**EMP:** 141 **EST:** 2012
**SALES (est):** 8.9MM **Privately Held**
Web: www.masterclass.com
**SIC: 7929** 7812 2721 Entertainment service; Video production; Periodicals

## 7948 Racing, Including Track Operation

**(P-19308)**
**NATIONAL HOT ROD ASSOCIATION (PA)**
Also Called: Nhra
140 Via Verde Ste 100, San Dimas (91773-5117)
P.O. Box 5555 (91740)
PHONE...............................626 914-4761
Wally Parks, *Dir*
Richard Wells, *
**EMP:** 200 **EST:** 1951
**SQ FT:** 30,000
**SALES (est):** 88.81MM
**SALES (corp-wide):** 88.81MM **Privately Held**
Web: www.nhra.com
**SIC: 7948** 2711 2741 Auto race track operation; Newspapers: publishing only, not printed on site; Miscellaneous publishing

## 7992 Public Golf Courses

**(P-19309)**
**CROCKETT & COINC (PA)**
Also Called: Bonita Golf Club
5120 Robinwood Rd Ste A22, Bonita (91902-1930)
P.O. Box 445 (91908-0445)
PHONE...............................619 267-6410
Phillip Crockett, *Pr*
James Crockett, *
Maryann Daly, *
**EMP:** 20 **EST:** 1961
**SQ FT:** 30,000
**SALES (est):** 2.09MM
**SALES (corp-wide):** 2.09MM **Privately Held**
Web: new.bonitagolf.net
**SIC: 7992** 5813 5812 3111 Public golf courses; Bar (drinking places); Eating places; Leather tanning and finishing

## 7993 Coin-operated Amusement Devices

**(P-19310)**
**PELICANTUNES INC**
3950 Valley Ave Ste A, Pleasanton (94566-4868)
PHONE...............................925 838-8484
**EMP:** 15 **EST:** 2012
**SALES (est):** 1.4MM **Privately Held**
Web: www.pelicantunes.com
**SIC: 7993** 5941 3944 Juke box; Pool and billiard tables; Darts and dart games

**(P-19311)**
**PLAYERS WEST AMUSEMENTS INC (PA)**
Also Called: Toy Barn
2360 Sturgis Rd Ste A, Oxnard (93030-8956)
PHONE...............................805 983-1400
Jack G Mann, *Pr*
▲ **EMP:** 38 **EST:** 1991
**SALES (est):** 784.54K **Privately Held**
Web: www.toybarn.com
**SIC: 7993** 5092 3942 Amusement machine rental, coin-operated; Toys and hobby goods and supplies; Dolls and stuffed toys

## 7997 Membership Sports And Recreation Clubs

**(P-19312)**
**AGI HOLDING CORP (PA)**
Also Called: Affinity Group
2575 Vista Del Mar Dr, Ventura (93001)
P.O. Box 6888 (80155)
PHONE...............................805 667-4100
Stephen Adams, *CEO*
Joe Mcadams, *Pr*
Mark Boggess, *
Michael Schneider, *
Mister Stephen Adams, *Prin*
◆ **EMP:** 52 **EST:** 1988
**SQ FT:** 74,000
**SALES (est):** 6.59MM
**SALES (corp-wide):** 6.59MM **Privately Held**
Web: www.goodsam.com
**SIC: 7997** 2741 Membership sports and recreation clubs; Directories, nec: publishing and printing

## 7999 Amusement And Recreation, Nec

**(P-19313)**
**CENTRAL VALLEY GAMING LLC**
Also Called: Turlock Poker Room
2321 W Main St Ste C, Turlock (95380-9485)
PHONE...............................209 668-1010
**EMP:** 25 **EST:** 2004
**SALES (est):** 841.89K **Privately Held**
Web: www.turlockpoker.com
**SIC: 7999** 3944 Gambling establishment; Poker chips

## 8011 Offices And Clinics Of Medical Doctors

**(P-19314)**
**ALEX A KHADAVI MD INC**
Also Called: Encino Drmtology Laser Med Ctr
16260 Ventura Blvd Ste 140, Encino (91436-2203)
PHONE...............................818 528-2500
Alex Khadavi, *Prin*
**EMP:** 20 **EST:** 2010
**SALES (est):** 848.86K **Privately Held**
**SIC: 8011** 2834 Dermatologist; Dermatologicals

**(P-19315)**
**COR MEDICA TECHNOLOGY**
Also Called: Cor Medica
188 Technology Dr Ste F, Irvine (92618-2459)
PHONE...............................949 353-4554
Fouad Ghaly, *CEO*
David Sestini, *
Rachel Everett, *
Robert Prestwood, *
Katalina Csoka, *
**EMP:** 26 **EST:** 2015
**SQ FT:** 2,200
**SALES (est):** 302.99K **Privately Held**
**SIC: 8011** 3841 Cardiologist and cardiovascular specialist; Diagnostic apparatus, medical

**(P-19316)**
**FOUR SEASONS SURGERY CENTERS**
1211 W 6th St, Ontario (91762-1103)
PHONE...............................909 933-6576
Andrea Amanda, *Prin*
**EMP:** 15 **EST:** 2004
**SALES (est):** 2.47MM **Privately Held**
Web: www.fssc.com
**SIC: 8011** 3842 Ambulatory surgical center; Grafts, artificial: for surgery

**(P-19317)**
**HEALTHTAP INC**
Also Called: Docphin
209 E Java Dr Unit 61987, Sunnyvale (94088-8020)
PHONE...............................650 268-9806
Bill Gossman, *CEO*
Jay Wohlgemuth, *CHO*
**EMP:** 66 **EST:** 2010
**SQ FT:** 16,000
**SALES (est):** 22.19MM **Privately Held**
Web: www.healthtap.com
**SIC: 8011** 7372 Group health association; Application computer software

**(P-19318)**
**INSITE DIGESTIVE HEALTH CARE**
21250 Hawthorne Blvd, Torrance (90503-5506)
PHONE...............................626 817-2900
Alaa Abousaif, *Brnch Mgr*
**EMP:** 42
**SALES (corp-wide):** 22.36MM **Privately Held**
Web: www.mygenesishealth.com
**SIC: 8011** 2834 General and family practice, physician/surgeon; Chlorination tablets and kits (water purification)
**PA:** Insite Digestive Health Care
   5525 Etiwanda Ave Ste 110
   818 437-8105

**(P-19319)**
**NEW SPIRIT NATURALS INC (PA)**
Also Called: Pentacare Skin Systems
615 W Allen Ave, San Dimas (91773-1447)
PHONE...............................909 592-4445
Larry Milam, *Pr*
◆ **EMP:** 20 **EST:** 1982
**SQ FT:** 25,000
**SALES (est):** 4.25MM
**SALES (corp-wide):** 4.25MM **Privately Held**
Web: www.newspirit.com
**SIC: 8011** 5122 2032 2844 Offices and clinics of medical doctors; Drugs, proprietaries, and sundries; Canned specialties; Shampoos, rinses, conditioners: hair

**(P-19320)**
**NEXTHEALTH WEST HOLLYWOOD INC**
24955 Pacific Coast Hwy Ste 203, Malibu (90265-4700)
PHONE...............................310 295-2075
Darshan Shah, *CEO*
Kevin Peake, *Pr*
**EMP:** 15 **EST:** 2015
**SALES (est):** 536.84K **Privately Held**
**SIC: 8011** 7372 Physicians' office, including specialists; Application computer software

**(P-19321)**
**SENTE INC**
701 Palomar Airport Rd Ste 300, Carlsbad (92011-1028)
PHONE...............................760 753-5400
Zubin Meshginpoosh, *Pr*

▲ = Import ▼ = Export
◆ = Import/Export

# 8099 - Health And Allied Services, Nec (P-19339)

Eglantine Proto, *VP Fin*
▲ **EMP:** 20 **EST:** 2007
**SALES (est):** 10MM **Privately Held**
**Web:** www.sentelabs.com
**SIC: 8011** 2834 Dermatologist; Dermatologicals

### (P-19322)
### T JOSEPH RAOOF MD INC
16133 Ventura Blvd Ste 340, Encino (91436-2428)
**PHONE**..................818 788-5060
Tooraj Joseph Raoof, *Pr*
**EMP:** 15 **EST:** 1989
**SQ FT:** 2,200
**SALES (est):** 1.16MM **Privately Held**
**Web:** www.drraoof.com
**SIC: 8011** 3444 5561 7631 Dermatologist; Sheet metalwork; Recreational vehicle parts and accessories; Jewelry repair services

## 8042 Offices And Clinics Of Optometrists

### (P-19323)
### JAMES G MEYERS & ASSOCIATES
Also Called: Eye Exam of California
4353 La Jolla Village Dr Ste 180, San Diego (92122-1259)
**PHONE**..................858 622-2165
Elliott Shapiro, *Owner*
**EMP:** 30
**SALES (corp-wide):** 4.18MM **Privately Held**
**Web:** www.shapirofamilyoptometry.com
**SIC: 8042** 3851 Offices and clinics of optometrists; Contact lenses
**PA:** James G Meyers & Associates
11700 Princeton Pike
513 671-0111

## 8062 General Medical And Surgical Hospitals

### (P-19324)
### CEDARS-SINAI MEDICAL CENTER
Anesthesiology Department
8700 Beverly Blvd Ste 8211, West Hollywood (90048-1804)
**PHONE**..................310 423-5841
Tom Pirscelac, *Admn*
**EMP:** 166
**SALES (corp-wide):** 4.66B **Privately Held**
**Web:** www.cedars-sinai.edu
**SIC: 8062** 3841 General medical and surgical hospitals; Anesthesia apparatus
**PA:** Cedars-Sinai Medical Center
8700 Beverly Blvd
310 423-3277

## 8071 Medical Laboratories

### (P-19325)
### BIORA THERAPEUTICS INC (PA)
Also Called: Biora Therapeutics
4330 La Jolla Village Dr Ste 300, San Diego (92122-6203)
P.O. Box 674425 (48267)
**PHONE**..................833 727-2841
Adi Mohanty, *CEO*
Jeffrey D Alter, *Ch Bd*
Eric Desparbes, *CFO*
Clarke Neumann, *Sr VP*
**EMP:** 22 **EST:** 2010
**SQ FT:** 25,800
**SALES (est):** 4K
**SALES (corp-wide):** 4K **Publicly Held**
**Web:** www.bioratherapeutics.com
**SIC: 8071** 8731 2834 Medical laboratories; Biotechnical research, commercial; Pharmaceutical preparations

### (P-19326)
### BIOTHERANOSTICS INC (HQ)
9640 Towne Centre Dr Ste 200, San Diego (92121-1987)
P.O. Box 749249 (90074-9249)
**PHONE**..................877 886-6739
Stephen P Macmillan, *Pr*
**EMP:** 40 **EST:** 1996
**SALES (est):** 24.64MM
**SALES (corp-wide):** 4.03B **Publicly Held**
**Web:** www.biotheranostics.com
**SIC: 8071** 2835 Medical laboratories; In vitro diagnostics
**PA:** Hologic, Inc.
250 Campus Dr
508 263-2900

### (P-19327)
### CARDIODX INC
3945 Freedom Cir Ste 560, Santa Clara (95054-1269)
**PHONE**..................650 475-2788
**EMP:** 146
**Web:** www.cardiodx.com
**SIC: 8071** 2834 Medical laboratories; Drugs acting on the cardiovascular system, except diagnostic

### (P-19328)
### MINARIS MEDICAL AMERICA INC
630 Clyde Ct, Mountain View (94043-2239)
**PHONE**..................650 961-5501
Mitsutaka Shimabe, *CEO*
Takashi Miyamoto, *
Kazuyoshi Tsunoda, *
Keiichi Takeda, *
**EMP:** 190 **EST:** 1982
**SQ FT:** 31,000
**SALES (est):** 20.29MM **Privately Held**
**Web:** www.minarismedical.com
**SIC: 8071** 2835 3821 Medical laboratories; In vitro diagnostics; Laboratory measuring apparatus

### (P-19329)
### POLYPEPTIDE LABORATORIES INC (DH)
365 Maple Ave, Torrance (90503-2602)
**PHONE**..................310 782-3569
Timothy Culbreth, *Pr*
Jane Salik, *
Michael Verlander, *
Nagana Goud, *
▲ **EMP:** 25 **EST:** 1996
**SQ FT:** 19,200
**SALES (est):** 34.69MM **Privately Held**
**Web:** www.polypeptide.com
**SIC: 8071** 2836 8731 2834 Medical laboratories; Biological products, except diagnostic; Biotechnical research, commercial; Pharmaceutical preparations
**HQ:** Polypeptide Group Ag
Neuhofstrasse 24
Baar ZG 6340

### (P-19330)
### PRODUCTION ENGINEERING & MCH
14955 Hilton Dr, Fontana (92336-2082)
P.O. Box 907 (91711-0907)
**PHONE**..................909 721-2455
Thomas Kearns, *Prin*
**EMP:** 21 **EST:** 2012
**SALES (est):** 1.27MM **Privately Held**
**Web:** www.pemmachining.com
**SIC: 8071** 3599 Medical laboratories; Machine shop, jobbing and repair

### (P-19331)
### QUEST DIAGNOSTICS INCORPORATED
Also Called: Quest Diagnostics
1165 S Dora St Ste A1, Ukiah (95482-6353)
**PHONE**..................707 462-7553
**EMP:** 17
**SALES (corp-wide):** 7.51B **Publicly Held**
**SIC: 8071** 2835 Medical laboratories; Diagnostic substances
**PA:** Quest Diagnostics Incorporated
500 Plaza Dr
973 520-2700

### (P-19332)
### UNCHAINED LABS (PA)
Also Called: Optim
4747 Willow Rd, Pleasanton (94588-2763)
**PHONE**..................925 587-9800
Tim Harness, *CEO*
Terry Salyer, *CCO*
Jason Novi, *
Will Lachnit, *
Scott Lockard, *
**EMP:** 140 **EST:** 2014
**SALES (est):** 78.22MM
**SALES (corp-wide):** 78.22MM **Privately Held**
**Web:** www.unchainedlabs.com
**SIC: 8071** 3826 Medical laboratories; Analytical instruments

### (P-19333)
### VERACYTE INC (PA)
Also Called: Veracyte
6000 Shoreline Ct Ste 300, South San Francisco (94080-7606)
**PHONE**..................650 243-6300
Marc Stapley, *CEO*
Robert S Epstein, *Ch Bd*
Rebecca Chambers, *CFO*
Annie Mcguire, *CPO*
Jonathan Wygant, *CAO*
**EMP:** 91 **EST:** 2006
**SQ FT:** 59,000
**SALES (est):** 361.05MM
**SALES (corp-wide):** 361.05MM **Publicly Held**
**Web:** www.veracyte.com
**SIC: 8071** 8733 2835 Medical laboratories; Medical research; Cytology and histology diagnostic agents

## 8072 Dental Laboratories

### (P-19334)
### POSCA BROTHERS DENTAL LAB INC
641 W Willow St, Long Beach (90806-2832)
**PHONE**..................562 427-1811
Alex Posca, *Pr*
Angel Jorge Posca, *
Yanette Posca, *
▲ **EMP:** 55 **EST:** 1965
**SQ FT:** 5,000
**SALES (est):** 2.33MM **Privately Held**
**Web:** www.poscabrothers.com
**SIC: 8072** 3843 Dental laboratories; Teeth, artificial (not made in dental laboratories)

## 8093 Specialty Outpatient Clinics, Nec

### (P-19335)
### ARC - IMPERIAL VALLEY
340 E 1st St, Calexico (92231-2732)
**PHONE**..................760 768-1944
Alex King, *Prin*
**EMP:** 42
**SALES (corp-wide):** 15.5MM **Privately Held**
**Web:** www.arciv.org
**SIC: 8093** 4783 2051 5812 Rehabilitation center, outpatient treatment; Packing goods for shipping; Bakery: wholesale or wholesale/retail combined; Delicatessen (eating places)
**PA:** Arc - Imperial Valley
298 E Ross Ave
760 352-0180

## 8099 Health And Allied Services, Nec

### (P-19336)
### HARBOR HEALTH SYSTEMS LLC
3501 Jamboree Rd Ste 540, Newport Beach (92660-2950)
P.O. Box 1145 (60009-1145)
**PHONE**..................949 273-7020
**EMP:** 506 **EST:** 2001
**SALES (est):** 1.27MM **Privately Held**
**Web:** www.harborhealthsytems.com
**SIC: 8099** 7372 Blood related health services; Business oriented computer software
**PA:** One Call Medical, Inc.
841 Prudential Dr Ste 204

### (P-19337)
### LIFESTREAM BLOOD BANK (PA)
Also Called: Lifestream
384 W Orange Show Rd, San Bernardino (92412)
P.O. Box 1429 (92402)
**PHONE**..................909 885-6503
Frederick B Axelrod, *CEO*
Joseph Dunn, *
Susan Marquez, *
**EMP:** 240 **EST:** 1951
**SQ FT:** 50,000
**SALES (est):** 66.4MM
**SALES (corp-wide):** 66.4MM **Privately Held**
**Web:** www.lstream.org
**SIC: 8099** 2836 Blood bank; Blood derivatives

### (P-19338)
### PROVISIO MEDICAL INC
10815 Rancho Bernardo Rd Ste 110, San Diego (92127-2187)
**PHONE**..................508 740-9940
Stephen Eric Ryan, *CEO*
**EMP:** 44 **EST:** 2014
**SALES (est):** 6.44MM **Privately Held**
**Web:** www.provisiomedical.com
**SIC: 8099** 3841 Medical services organization; Surgical and medical instruments

### (P-19339)
### TARGETED MEDICAL PHARMA INC

# 8111 - Legal Services (P-19340)

## PRODUCTS & SERVICES SECTION

2980 N Beverly Glen Cir Ste 100, Los Angeles (90077-1735)
PHONE.................310 474-9809
Marcus Charuvastra, CEO
EMP: 16 EST: 2003
SALES (est): 1.24MM
SALES (corp-wide): 5.73MM Privately Held
SIC: 8099 5912 2023 Nutrition services; Drug stores and proprietary stores; Dietary supplements, dairy and non-dairy based
PA: Targeted Medical Pharma, Inc.
2980 N Beverly Glen Cir # 301
310 474-9809

## 8111 Legal Services

### (P-19340)
**DEFENSE SPECIALISTS LLC**
Also Called: Defense Specialist, The
924 W Washington Blvd, Los Angeles (90015-3312)
P.O. Box 2266 (90251-2266)
PHONE.................818 270-7162
Emilio Pensado Junior, CEO
Elba Aguila, Prin
EMP: 55 EST: 2016
SALES (est): 376.61K Privately Held
Web: www.thedefensespecialist.com
SIC: 8111 7381 3812 7389 Legal services; Security guard service; Defense systems and equipment; Explosives recovery or extraction services

### (P-19341)
**WELLS MEDIA GROUP INC (PA)**
Also Called: Insurance Journal
3570 Camino Del Rio N Ste 100, San Diego (92108-1747)
PHONE.................619 584-1100
Mark Wells, Pr
EMP: 19 EST: 1923
SQ FT: 3,600
SALES (est): 4.57MM
SALES (corp-wide): 4.57MM Privately Held
Web: www.insurancejournal.com
SIC: 8111 2721 Legal services; Magazines: publishing and printing

## 8211 Elementary And Secondary Schools

### (P-19342)
**BLOOMBOARD INC**
Also Called: Bloomboard
430 Cowper St Ste 250, Palo Alto (94301-1579)
PHONE.................650 567-5656
EMP: 24
Web: www.bloomboard.com
SIC: 8211 7372 Private special education school; Educational computer software
PA: Bloomboard, Inc.
5401 Walnut St Ste 200

### (P-19343)
**CHRISTIAN EVANG CHRCHES AMER I**
Also Called: Patten Christian Schools
2433 Coolidge Ave, Oakland (94601-2630)
PHONE.................510 533-8300
Bebe Patten, Pr
Doctor Gary Moncher, Sec
Anna Jean Pyle, *
Gary Moncher, Pr
EMP: 45 EST: 1945
SQ FT: 25,000
SALES (est): 4.32MM Privately Held
Web: www.thecathedral.us
SIC: 8211 7922 8661 2711 Private combined elementary and secondary school; Television program, including commercial producers; Covenant and Evangelical Church; Newspapers: publishing only, not printed on site

### (P-19344)
**GARDEN GROVE UNIFIED SCHL DST**
Also Called: Alamitos Intermediate School
12381 Dale St, Garden Grove (92841-3219)
PHONE.................714 663-6101
Christina Pflughoft, Prin
EMP: 59
SALES (corp-wide): 994.66MM Privately Held
Web: www.ggusd.k12.ca.us
SIC: 8211 2731 Public junior high school; Book publishing
PA: Garden Grove Unified School District
10331 Stanford Ave
714 663-6000

### (P-19345)
**ROMAN CTHLIC DIOCESE OF ORANGE**
Also Called: Santa Mrgrita Cthlic High Schl
22062 Antonio Pkwy, Rcho Sta Marg (92688-1993)
PHONE.................949 766-6000
Mary B Dougherty, Prin
EMP: 200
SQ FT: 142,959
SALES (corp-wide): 92.62MM Privately Held
Web: www.smhs.org
SIC: 8211 2721 Catholic senior high school; Periodicals
PA: The Roman Catholic Diocese Of Orange
13280 Chapman Ave
714 282-3000

## 8231 Libraries

### (P-19346)
**PUBLIC LIBRARY OF SCIENCE (PA)**
1265 Battery St Ste 200, San Francisco (94111-6216)
PHONE.................415 624-1200
Alison Muddiit, CEO
Elizabeth Marincola, *
Kristina Martin, *
Vikas Thakker Cdoo, Prin
EMP: 162 EST: 2001
SALES (est): 34.99MM
SALES (corp-wide): 34.99MM Privately Held
Web: www.plos.org
SIC: 8231 2741 Public library; Miscellaneous publishing

### (P-19347)
**SAFARI BOOKS ONLINE LLC (PA)**
1003 Gravenstein Hwy N, Sebastopol (95472-2811)
PHONE.................707 827-7000
Laura Baldwin, *
EMP: 70 EST: 2001
SALES (est): 4.14MM Privately Held
Web: www.oreilly.com
SIC: 8231 2741 2731 Libraries; Internet publishing and broadcasting; Books, publishing only

## 8243 Data Processing Schools

### (P-19348)
**NEW HRZNS SRVING INDVDALS WITH (PA)**
Also Called: NEW HORIZONS CENTER & WORKSHOP
15725 Parthenia St, North Hills (91343-4913)
PHONE.................818 894-9301
Cynthia Kawa, CEO
▲ EMP: 100 EST: 1954
SQ FT: 60,000
SALES (est): 16.73MM
SALES (corp-wide): 16.73MM Privately Held
Web: www.newhorizons-sfv.org
SIC: 8243 2052 Software training, computer; Cookies

## 8249 Vocational Schools, Nec

### (P-19349)
**REAL ESTATE TRAINERS INC**
212 Towne Centre Pl Ste 100, Anaheim (92806)
PHONE.................800 282-2352
Jerry Mcharg, Pr
EMP: 35 EST: 1972
SQ FT: 17,000
SALES (est): 245.27K
SALES (corp-wide): 2.16MM Privately Held
Web: www.retrainersca.com
SIC: 8249 2721 Real estate and insurance school; Periodicals
PA: Universal Training Corporation
2121 S Twne Cntre Pl Ste
714 972-2211

## 8299 Schools And Educational Services

### (P-19350)
**EDUCATION TRAINING & RES ASSOC (PA)**
Also Called: ETR
5619 Scotts Valley Dr Ste 140, Scotts Valley (95066-3453)
PHONE.................831 438-4060
Vignetta Charles, CEO
Robert Keet, *
John Casken, *
Rosalind Alexander-kasperik, Sec
Robert Christensen, *
EMP: 51 EST: 1981
SALES (est): 20.8MM
SALES (corp-wide): 20.8MM Privately Held
Web: www.etr.org
SIC: 8299 2731 2741 Educational services; Pamphlets: publishing and printing; Miscellaneous publishing

### (P-19351)
**GREENWOOD HALL INC**
6230 Wilshire Blvd Ste 136, Los Angeles (90048-5126)
PHONE.................310 905-8300
John Hall, Ch Bd
Bill Bradfield, *
EMP: 111 EST: 1997
SALES (est): 4.28MM Privately Held
Web: www.answernet.com
SIC: 8299 8741 8742 7374 Educational services; Management services; Management consulting services; Data processing service

### (P-19352)
**LEARNING OVATIONS INC**
16 Coltrane Ct, Irvine (92617-4131)
PHONE.................734 904-1459
Jay Connor, CEO
Elliot Amiel, *
Alia Gates, *
Nick Voegeli, *
EMP: 28 EST: 2013
SALES (est): 6.68MM
SALES (corp-wide): 1.59B Publicly Held
Web: www.learningovations.com
SIC: 8299 7372 Educational services; Educational computer software
PA: Scholastic Corporation
557 Broadway
212 343-6100

### (P-19353)
**TAMANA CORPORATION**
Also Called: Kumon
455 Los Gatos Blvd Ste 10, Los Gatos (95032-5523)
PHONE.................408 358-0747
Uma Thontakudi, Owner
EMP: 15 EST: 2010
SALES (est): 145.7K Privately Held
Web: www.kumon.com
SIC: 8299 3672 Educational services; Printed circuit boards

## 8322 Individual And Family Services

### (P-19354)
**BRAILLE INSTITUTE AMERICA INC (PA)**
Also Called: BRAILLE INSTITUTE
741 N Vermont Ave, Los Angeles (90029-3594)
PHONE.................323 663-1111
Lester M Sussman, Ch Bd
Les Stocker, *
Peter Mindnich, *
Rezaur Rahman, *
EMP: 208 EST: 1919
SQ FT: 167,079
SALES (est): 29.58MM
SALES (corp-wide): 29.58MM Privately Held
Web: www.brailleinstitute.org
SIC: 8322 8231 2731 2759 Individual and family services; Specialized libraries; Textbooks: publishing and printing; Commercial printing, nec

### (P-19355)
**COVENANT COMMUNITY SVCS INC**
Also Called: C C S I
1700 N Chester Ave, Bakersfield (93308-2563)
PHONE.................661 829-6999
Randy Martin, CEO
EMP: 15 EST: 2003
SQ FT: 5,400
SALES (est): 1.75MM Privately Held
Web: www.covenantcs.net
SIC: 8322 2095 5149 8641 Child related social services; Coffee roasting (except by wholesale grocers); Coffee and tea; Youth organizations

## PRODUCTS & SERVICES SECTION
## 8711 - Engineering Services (P-19374)

**(P-19356)**
**DEAN L DAVIS MD**
Also Called: Mercy Hospital
2215 Truxtun Ave, Bakersfield
(93301-3602)
P.O. Box 119 (93302-0119)
PHONE..............................661 632-5000
Dean L Davis Md, *Owner*
**EMP:** 20 **EST:** 1996
**SALES (est):** 6.2MM **Privately Held**
**SIC:** 8322 3842 Community center; Gynecological supplies and appliances

**(P-19357)**
**ESSENCE OF AMERICA**
1855 1st Ave Ste 103, San Diego
(92101-2650)
P.O. Box 23682 (92193-3682)
PHONE..............................312 805-9365
Shannon Davis, *Pr*
**EMP:** 25 **EST:** 2011
**SALES (est):** 200K **Privately Held**
**SIC:** 8322 5812 2099 2599 Meal delivery program; Restaurant, family: independent; Syrups; Food wagons, restaurant

**(P-19358)**
**LOCAL FOODZ CALI INC**
Also Called: Boards On The Go
1552 Beach St Ste C, Emeryville
(94608-3525)
P.O. Box 307 (94522-0307)
PHONE..............................650 242-5651
Sandeep Rajbhandari, *CEO*
Jenifer Wohn, *COO*
**EMP:** 20 **EST:** 2014
**SALES (est):** 880.24K **Privately Held**
Web: www.localfoodz.co
**SIC:** 8322 5812 5963 1541 Meal delivery program; Caterers; Food service, mobile, except coffee-cart; Food products manufacturing or packing plant construction

**(P-19359)**
**SAN DEGO SECOND CHANCE PROGRAM**
6145 Imperial Ave, San Diego
(92114-4213)
PHONE..............................619 266-2506
Robert Coleman, *Ex Dir*
Scott Silverman, *
**EMP:** 35 **EST:** 1992
**SALES (est):** 3.92MM **Privately Held**
Web: www.secondchanceprogram.org
**SIC:** 8322 7361 3965 Social service center; Employment agencies; Fasteners, buttons, needles, and pins

**(P-19360)**
**SIERRA MOUNTAIN CNSTR INC**
Also Called: Sierra Mountain
13919 Mono Way, Sonora (95370-2807)
PHONE..............................209 928-1900
Douglas J Benton, *Pr*
**EMP:** 75 **EST:** 2003
**SALES (est):** 62.3MM **Privately Held**
Web: www.sierramtn.net
**SIC:** 8322 1389 Disaster service; Construction, repair, and dismantling services

### 8331 Job Training And Related Services

**(P-19361)**
**FONTANA RESOURCES AT WORK**
9460 Sierra Ave, Fontana (92335)
P.O. Box 848 (92334)
PHONE..............................909 428-3833
Joseph Varela, *Ex Dir*
**EMP:** 44 **EST:** 1965
**SQ FT:** 22,600
**SALES (est):** 1.73MM **Privately Held**
Web: www.industrial-support.org
**SIC:** 8331 3444 Vocational rehabilitation agency; Sheet metalwork

**(P-19362)**
**NAPA VALLEY PSI INC**
651 Trabajo Ln, Napa (94559-4258)
P.O. Box 600 (94559-0600)
PHONE..............................707 255-0177
Jeanne Fauquet, *Pr*
**EMP:** 80 **EST:** 1972
**SQ FT:** 43,800
**SALES (est):** 661.66K **Privately Held**
Web: www.napavalleypsi.org
**SIC:** 8331 2521 2511 Vocational rehabilitation agency; Filing cabinets (boxes), office: wood; Wood household furniture

**(P-19363)**
**VALLEY RESOURCE CENTER INC (PA)**
Also Called: Valley Resource Center
1285 N Santa Fe St, Hemet (92543-1823)
PHONE..............................951 766-8659
Lee Trisler, *CEO*
**EMP:** 50 **EST:** 1979
**SQ FT:** 80,000
**SALES (est):** 8.09MM
**SALES (corp-wide):** 8.09MM **Privately Held**
Web: www.weexceed.org
**SIC:** 8331 2389 Vocational training agency; Apparel for handicapped

### 8351 Child Day Care Services

**(P-19364)**
**SMART START EARLY CHILDHOOD**
101 Hazelmere Dr, Folsom (95630-5519)
PHONE..............................916 984-3800
**EMP:** 15
**SALES (corp-wide):** 655.16K **Privately Held**
**SIC:** 8351 3694 Child day care services; Ignition apparatus and distributors
**PA:** Smart Start Early Childhood Specialists, Inc.
3330 Chisom Trl
916 941-5304

### 8361 Residential Care

**(P-19365)**
**VINE VILLAGE INCORPORATED**
4059 Old Sonoma Rd, Napa (94559-9702)
P.O. Box 507 (94559-0507)
PHONE..............................707 255-4006
Micheal Kerson, *Ex Dir*
**EMP:** 20 **EST:** 1973
**SQ FT:** 6,500
**SALES (est):** 185.56K **Privately Held**
Web: www.vinevillage.org
**SIC:** 8361 8331 2099 Retarded home; Vocational training agency; Vinegar

### 8422 Botanical And Zoological Gardens

**(P-19366)**
**CALIFORNIA ACADEMY SCIENCES (PA)**
55 Music Concourse Dr, San Francisco
(94118-4503)
PHONE..............................415 379-8000
John Hafernik, *Pr*
Alison Brown, *
Jim Gohary, *
**EMP:** 635 **EST:** 1853
**SQ FT:** 410,000
**SALES (est):** 71.11MM
**SALES (corp-wide):** 71.11MM **Privately Held**
Web: www.calacademy.org
**SIC:** 8422 2721 8412 Aquarium; Periodicals, publishing only; Museums and art galleries

### 8661 Religious Organizations

**(P-19367)**
**ANANDA CHURCH OF SELF-REALZTN (PA)**
Also Called: EXPANDING LIGHT, THE
14618 Tyler Foote Rd Ste 146, Nevada City
(95959-9316)
PHONE..............................530 478-7560
John Novak, *Pr*
Cathy Parojinog, *
**EMP:** 80 **EST:** 1968
**SQ FT:** 25,000
**SALES (est):** 3.75MM
**SALES (corp-wide):** 3.75MM **Privately Held**
Web: www.ananda.org
**SIC:** 8661 8299 5942 2731 Religious organizations; Religious school; Books, religious; Books, publishing only

**(P-19368)**
**MORRIS CRULLO WORLD EVANGELISM (PA)**
875 Hotel Cir S # 2, San Diego
(92108-3406)
P.O. Box 85277 (92186-5277)
PHONE..............................858 277-2200
Reverend Morris Cerullo, *Pr*
Lynn Hodge, *
Teresa Cerullo, *
**EMP:** 77 **EST:** 1961
**SALES (est):** 9.56MM
**SALES (corp-wide):** 9.56MM **Privately Held**
Web: www.mcwe.com
**SIC:** 8661 2741 Churches, temples, and shrines; Miscellaneous publishing

**(P-19369)**
**NEIGHBORHOOD MENNONITE**
Also Called: Neighborhood Church
5505 W Riggin Ave, Visalia (93291-9084)
PHONE..............................559 732-9107
Pastor Forrest Jenan, *Prin*
Pastor Steve Harms, *Prin*
Pastor Kelly Thomas, *Prin*
**EMP:** 24 **EST:** 1950
**SALES (est):** 1.14MM **Privately Held**
Web: www.ncvisalia.com
**SIC:** 8661 7372 Miscellaneous denomination church; Application computer software

**(P-19370)**
**SAINT GERMAIN FOUNDATION (PA)**
Also Called: I AM Activity
1120 Stonehedge Dr, Dunsmuir (96025)
PHONE..............................530 235-2994
Barbara Arden, *Dir*
**EMP:** 15 **EST:** 1938
**SQ FT:** 7,500
**SALES (est):** 2.48MM
**SALES (corp-wide):** 2.48MM **Privately Held**
Web: www.saintgermainfoundation.org
**SIC:** 8661 2721 2731 Nonchurch religious organizations; Magazines: publishing only, not printed on site; Books, publishing only

**(P-19371)**
**SELF-REALIZATION FELLOWSHIP CH (PA)**
Also Called: Self Realization Fellowship
3880 San Rafael Ave, Los Angeles
(90065-3298)
PHONE..............................323 225-2471
Faye Wright, *Pr*
Mrinalini Mata, *
▲ **EMP:** 35 **EST:** 1935
**SALES (est):** 20.63MM
**SALES (corp-wide):** 20.63MM **Privately Held**
Web: www.yogananda.org
**SIC:** 8661 2741 Miscellaneous denomination church; Miscellaneous publishing

### 8699 Membership Organizations, Nec

**(P-19372)**
**ASTRONOMICAL SOC OF THE PCF**
Also Called: A S P
390 Ashton Ave, San Francisco
(94112-1722)
PHONE..............................415 337-1100
William A Gutsch Junior, *Pr*
Michael G Gibbs, *
Cathy Langridge, *
**EMP:** 26 **EST:** 1889
**SQ FT:** 10,000
**SALES (est):** 1.95MM **Privately Held**
Web: www.astrosociety.org
**SIC:** 8699 2721 Personal interest organization; Periodicals, publishing only

### 8711 Engineering Services

**(P-19373)**
**ACCUNEX INC**
Also Called: Accurate Electronics
20700 Lassen St, Chatsworth (91311-4507)
PHONE..............................818 882-5858
Farid Jadali, *Pr*
Roxana Coronado, *
▲ **EMP:** 50 **EST:** 1998
**SQ FT:** 25,000
**SALES (est):** 12.15MM **Privately Held**
Web: www.accurate-elec.com
**SIC:** 8711 3679 Engineering services; Electronic circuits

**(P-19374)**
**ACS ENGINEERING INC**
Also Called: Asce
33 Hammond Ste 209, Irvine (92618-1637)
PHONE..............................949 297-3777
Babak Kavoossi, *Pr*
Babak Kavoossi, *
**EMP:** 20 **EST:** 2011
**SQ FT:** 5,000
**SALES (est):** 2.54MM **Privately Held**
Web: www.acsengineering.net

## 8711 - Engineering Services (P-19375)

SIC: 8711 1731 3613 Consulting engineer; Electrical work; Control panels, electric

**(P-19375)**
**AHNTECH INC (PA)**
745 Distel Dr Ste 104, Los Altos (94022-1523)
PHONE..................650 861-3987
Eugene Ahn, *CEO*
Sam Ahn, *
Soo Myung Ahn, *Prin*
EMP: 70 EST: 1984
SALES (est): 8.15MM
SALES (corp-wide): 8.15MM **Privately Held**
Web: www.ahntech.com
SIC: 8711 3674 3679 3699 Engineering services; Semiconductors and related devices; Electronic circuits; Electronic training devices

**(P-19376)**
**AMP DISPLAY INC (PA)**
9856 6th St, Rancho Cucamonga (91730-5714)
P.O. Box 1735 (91729-1735)
PHONE..................909 980-1310
Jason Young, *Pr*
EMP: 21 EST: 1999
SQ FT: 12,000
SALES (est): 3.05MM
SALES (corp-wide): 3.05MM **Privately Held**
Web: www.ampdisplay.com
SIC: 8711 3679 Engineering services; Liquid crystal displays (LCD)

**(P-19377)**
**ANGKOR ENGINEERING INC**
36 Quail Run Cir Unit 100v, Salinas (93907-2351)
PHONE..................831 256-1015
Aurelio Sanchez L, *CEO*
EMP: 15 EST: 2020
SALES (est): 2.52MM **Privately Held**
SIC: 8711 1389 Engineering services; Construction, repair, and dismantling services

**(P-19378)**
**APEX ENERGY LLC (HQ)**
655 Deep Valley Dr Ste 310, Rllng Hls Est (90274-3605)
PHONE..................310 377-5579
Albert Bove Junior, *Pr*
◆ EMP: 17 EST: 2001
SQ FT: 900
SALES (est): 8.79MM
SALES (corp-wide): 96.85MM **Privately Held**
Web: www.apexenergyus.com
SIC: 8711 2865 5172 Engineering services; Cyclic organic crudes; Petroleum products, nec
PA: American Energy Partners, Inc.
645 Hamilton St
610 217-3275

**(P-19379)**
**APPLIED COMPANIES**
28020 Avenue Stanford, Santa Clarita (91355-1105)
P.O. Box 802078 (91380-2078)
PHONE..................661 257-0090
Mary Elizabeth Klinger, *CEO*
Joseph Klinger, *Development*
EMP: 50 EST: 1962
SQ FT: 58,000
SALES (est): 13.71MM **Privately Held**
Web: www.appliedcompanies.net

SIC: 8711 3585 3443 3621 Mechanical engineering; Ice making machinery; Cylinders, pressure: metal plate; Motors and generators

**(P-19380)**
**ARMADA ENGINEERING LLC**
21305 Itasca St, Chatsworth (91311-4929)
PHONE..................818 280-5138
Elliot Pollock, *CEO*
EMP: 15 EST: 2011
SALES (est): 1.76MM **Privately Held**
Web: www.armada-engineering.com
SIC: 8711 3799 Engineering services; Off-road automobiles, except recreational vehicles

**(P-19381)**
**BAS ENGINEERING INC**
11899 8th St, Rancho Cucamonga (91730-5501)
PHONE..................909 484-2575
Ajesh Bhakta, *Prin*
EMP: 18 EST: 2012
SALES (est): 1.07MM **Privately Held**
Web: basengineering.thebluebook.com
SIC: 8711 3312 Engineering services; Blast furnaces and steel mills

**(P-19382)**
**BAY-TEC ENGINEERING**
5130 Fulton Dr Ste X, Fairfield (94534)
PHONE..................714 257-1680
John Justus, *Pr*
Adam Beaddy, *
Alan Kelm, *
Rick Cavalli, *
EMP: 63 EST: 1983
SQ FT: 22,000
SALES (est): 1.61MM **Privately Held**
SIC: 8711 1731 3823 3829 Engineering services; Electronic controls installation; Process control instruments; Measuring and controlling devices, nec

**(P-19383)**
**BDG INNOVATIONS LLC (PA)**
6001 Outfall Cir, Sacramento (95828-1066)
PHONE..................855 725-9555
Jeremy Grosser, *
Jason Blum, *
EMP: 40 EST: 2016
SALES (est): 95.93MM
SALES (corp-wide): 95.93MM **Privately Held**
SIC: 8711 3699 Consulting engineer; Electrical equipment and supplies, nec

**(P-19384)**
**CONCEPT TECHNOLOGY INC (PA)**
895 Dove St 3rd Fl, Newport Beach (92660-2941)
PHONE..................949 854-7047
Mahesh P Badani, *Pr*
▲ EMP: 60 EST: 1981
SALES (est): 4.61MM
SALES (corp-wide): 4.61MM **Privately Held**
Web: m.conceptechnology.com
SIC: 8711 3599 8742 3825 Consulting engineer; Machine shop, jobbing and repair ; Management information systems consultant; Radio frequency measuring equipment

**(P-19385)**
**CORRPRO COMPANIES INC**
20991 Cabot Blvd, Hayward (94545-1155)
PHONE..................510 614-8800

Michelle Anderson, *Mgr*
EMP: 24
SALES (corp-wide): 1.48B **Privately Held**
Web: www.aegion.com
SIC: 8711 3699 1799 Engineering services; Electrical equipment and supplies, nec; Corrosion control installation
HQ: Corrpro Companies, Inc.
580 Goddard Ave
Chesterfield MO 63005
636 530-8000

**(P-19386)**
**CURRENT RENEWABLES ENGRG INC**
3600 Lime St, Riverside (92501-2971)
PHONE..................951 405-1733
Methode Maniraguha, *CEO*
EMP: 18 EST: 2018
SALES (est): 1.63MM **Privately Held**
Web: www.creng.co
SIC: 8711 5045 7372 Engineering services; Computer software; Business oriented computer software

**(P-19387)**
**CUSTOM BUILT MACHINERY INC**
Also Called: C B M
2614 S Hickory St, Santa Ana (92707-3714)
PHONE..................714 424-9250
Milan Chrena, *CEO*
Victor Escobedo, *
Milan Chrena, *Pr*
Pete Marloski, *Stockholder**
EMP: 25 EST: 1995
SQ FT: 11,000
SALES (est): 2.84MM **Privately Held**
SIC: 8711 3559 Engineering services; Pharmaceutical machinery

**(P-19388)**
**DB DESIGN GROUP INC**
48507 Milmont Dr, Fremont (94538-7336)
PHONE..................408 834-1400
Mark Stenholm, *Pr*
Rennie Bowers, *VP*
EMP: 23 EST: 1989
SQ FT: 25,155
SALES (est): 4.69MM **Privately Held**
Web: www.dbdesign.com
SIC: 8711 3469 Mechanical engineering; Machine parts, stamped or pressed metal
PA: Aem Holdings Ltd.
52 Serangoon North Avenue 4

**(P-19389)**
**DESIGNIT GLOBAL LLC**
Also Called: Designit Prototype
5935 Labath Ave, Rohnert Park (94928-2089)
PHONE..................707 584-4000
Larry Childs, *Managing Member*
Bob Lopes, *Genl Mgr*
EMP: 22 EST: 2004
SALES (est): 5.28MM **Privately Held**
Web: www.designitprototype.com
SIC: 8711 3441 Mechanical engineering; Fabricated structural metal

**(P-19390)**
**ELITE ENGINEERING CONTRS INC**
16619 S Broadway, Gardena (90248-2715)
PHONE..................310 465-8333
Brian Perazzolo, *CEO*
Jason M Metoyer, *Prin*
EMP: 20 EST: 2017

SALES (est): 5.16MM **Privately Held**
Web: www.eliteengineering.net
SIC: 8711 1771 1081 Engineering services; Stucco, gunite, and grouting contractors; Metal mining exploration and development services

**(P-19391)**
**EMBEE PROCESSING LLC**
Also Called: Embee Plating
2158 S Hathaway St, Santa Ana (92705-5249)
PHONE..................714 546-9842
Michael Coburn, *CEO*
Scott Chrisman, *
Derek Watson, *
▲ EMP: 385 EST: 1947
SQ FT: 100,000
SALES (est): 23.51MM **Privately Held**
Web: www.embee.com
SIC: 8711 3398 3479 8734 Aviation and/or aeronautical engineering; Shot peening (treating steel to reduce fatigue); Coating of metals and formed products; Metallurgical testing laboratory

**(P-19392)**
**ENCORE SEMI INC**
7310 Miramar Rd Ste 410, San Diego (92126-4226)
PHONE..................858 225-4993
Behrooz Abdi, *Ch Bd*
Olivier Lauvray, *
Angeline Trang Dof, *Prin*
EMP: 67 EST: 2011
SALES (est): 2.04MM **Privately Held**
Web: www.encoresemi.com
SIC: 8711 3674 Engineering services; Integrated circuits, semiconductor networks, etc.

**(P-19393)**
**ENTEK ADAPTIVE MTL HDLG LLC**
1921 Petra Ln, Placentia (92870-6749)
PHONE..................714 854-1300
Charles Nadolski, *CEO*
Richard Buschini, *VP*
EMP: 16 EST: 1996
SQ FT: 15,500
SALES (est): 5.4MM **Privately Held**
Web: www.aef-inc.com
SIC: 8711 3599 Engineering services; Machine and other job shop work
HQ: Entek Manufacturing Llc
200 Hansard Ave
Lebanon OR 97355
541 259-1068

**(P-19394)**
**FIRE PROTECTION GROUP AMER INC**
3712 W Jefferson Blvd, Los Angeles (90016-4208)
P.O. Box 180520 (90018-9682)
PHONE..................323 732-4200
George Saadian, *Pr*
Louise Tchaman, *
EMP: 40 EST: 1985
SQ FT: 20,000
SALES (est): 2.2MM **Privately Held**
Web: www.firesprinkler.com
SIC: 8711 1711 3569 1731 Fire protection engineering; Fire sprinkler system installation; Firefighting and related equipment; Fire detection and burglar alarm systems specialization

▲ = Import ▼ = Export
◆ = Import/Export

## PRODUCTS & SERVICES SECTION
### 8711 - Engineering Services (P-19414)

**(P-19395)**
**FORTEL TRAFFIC INC**
5310 E Hunter Ave, Anaheim (92807-2053)
PHONE...............................714 701-9800
Emery B Dyer, *Pr*
Jayne M Dyer, *Sec*
▼ **EMP:** 17 **EST:** 1995
**SQ FT:** 14,000
**SALES (est):** 3.84MM **Privately Held**
Web: www.forteltraffic.com
**SIC:** 8711 3669  Consulting engineer; Traffic signals, electric

**(P-19396)**
**GENER8 LLC (PA)**
2560 Junction Ave, San Jose (95134-1902)
PHONE...............................650 940-9898
Jerry Jurkiewicz, *CEO*
▲ **EMP:** 85 **EST:** 2002
**SALES (est):** 49.03MM
**SALES (corp-wide):** 49.03MM **Privately Held**
Web: www.gener8.net
**SIC:** 8711 3429  Engineering services; Locks or lock sets

**(P-19397)**
**HIKINO ASSOCIATES LLC**
Also Called: Intelesense Technologies
47865 Fremont Blvd, Fremont (94538-6506)
PHONE...............................408 781-1900
Kevin Montgomery, *CEO*
Carsten Mundt, *Ex VP*
**EMP:** 22 **EST:** 2005
**SQ FT:** 6,000
**SALES (est):** 1.86MM **Privately Held**
Web: www.iot.ai
**SIC:** 8711 3812 5999  Engineering services; Defense systems and equipment; Communication equipment

**(P-19398)**
**INLYTE ENERGY INC**
1933 Davis St Ste 281, San Leandro (94577)
PHONE...............................415 483-0608
Will Gent, *
Ben Kaun, *Chief Commercial Officer*
Roger Bull, *General*
**EMP:** 24 **EST:** 2021
**SALES (est):** 1.46MM **Privately Held**
**SIC:** 8711 3691  Energy conservation engineering; Storage batteries

**(P-19399)**
**INNOVATIVE LAB SOLUTIONS INC**
13200 Kirkham Way Ste 114, Poway (92064-7126)
P.O. Box 502907 (92150-2907)
PHONE...............................858 842-4127
Jeffrey Fulghum, *CEO*
Mary Fulghum, *Sec*
**EMP:** 16 **EST:** 2006
**SALES (est):** 2.63MM **Privately Held**
Web: www.ils-corp.com
**SIC:** 8711 8748 7629 3821  Consulting engineer; Telecommunications consultant; Telecommunication equipment repair (except telephones); Laboratory apparatus and furniture

**(P-19400)**
**KINEMETRICS INC (DH)**
222 Vista Ave, Pasadena (91107-3278)
PHONE...............................626 795-2220
Tadashi Jimbo, *CEO*
Melvin Lund, *
Ogie Kuraica, *
Ian Standley, *
Michelle Harrington, *
**EMP:** 59 **EST:** 1969
**SQ FT:** 50,000
**SALES (est):** 26.8MM **Privately Held**
Web: www.kinemetrics.com
**SIC:** 8711 3829  Engineering services; Seismographs
HQ: Oyo Corporation U.S.A.
245 N Carmelo Ave Ste 101
Pasadena CA 91107

**(P-19401)**
**KRATOS UNMNNED ARIAL SYSTEMS I (HQ)**
5381 Raley Blvd, Sacramento (95838-1701)
PHONE...............................916 991-1990
Eric M Demarco, *CEO*
Amy Fournier, *
Michel M Fournier, *
▲ **EMP:** 227 **EST:** 1963
**SQ FT:** 60,000
**SALES (est):** 30.71MM **Publicly Held**
Web: www.kratosdefense.com
**SIC:** 8711 3761  Engineering services; Guided missiles and space vehicles
PA: Kratos Defense & Security Solutions, Inc.
10680 Treena St Ste 600

**(P-19402)**
**LAMER STREET KREATIONS CORP**
Also Called: Calwest Mfg and Lsk Suspension
13815 Arrow Blvd, Fontana (92335-0255)
PHONE...............................909 305-4824
Aaron Rifkin, *Pr*
Aaron Riskin, *
Van Syverud, *
**EMP:** 25 **EST:** 2012
**SALES (est):** 5.98MM **Privately Held**
Web: www.lsksuspension.com
**SIC:** 8711 3499 3569  Sanitary engineers; Fire- or burglary-resistive products; Robots, assembly line: industrial and commercial

**(P-19403)**
**MEEDER EQUIPMENT COMPANY**
12323 6th St, Rancho Cucamonga (91739-9224)
PHONE...............................909 463-0600
David Flores, *Mgr*
**EMP:** 17
**SALES (corp-wide):** 16.99MM **Privately Held**
Web: www.meeder.com
**SIC:** 8711 3433 3824  Engineering services; Heating equipment, except electric; Fluid meters and counting devices
PA: Meeder Equipment Company
3495 S Maple Ave
559 485-0979

**(P-19404)**
**MELLINGER ENGINEERING INC**
20366 8th St E, Sonoma (95476-9601)
PHONE...............................707 935-1100
George Randolph Mellinger, *CEO*
Jana Kathleen Fiorito, *Sec*
Dana Beth Bacon, *CFO*
**EMP:** 18 **EST:** 2018
**SQ FT:** 27,000
**SALES (est):** 1.66MM **Privately Held**
Web: www.mellingerengineering.com
**SIC:** 8711 3491  Engineering services; Industrial valves

**(P-19405)**
**MICROWAVE APPLICATIONS GROUP**
Also Called: M A G
3030 Industrial Pkwy, Santa Maria (93455-1881)
PHONE...............................805 928-5711
Steven Van Dyke, *CEO*
Tom Janzen, *
Scott Mckechnie, *VP*
Robin Hopp, *
**EMP:** 26 **EST:** 1969
**SQ FT:** 22,000
**SALES (est):** 4.42MM **Privately Held**
Web: www.magsmx.com
**SIC:** 8711 3679  Engineering services; Microwave components

**(P-19406)**
**MODELO GROUP INC**
16751 Millikan Ave, Irvine (92606-5009)
PHONE...............................562 446-5091
Jose Vazquez, *CEO*
**EMP:** 25 **EST:** 2004
**SALES (est):** 1MM **Privately Held**
**SIC:** 8711 7373 3999  Engineering services; Computer-aided design (CAD) systems service; Barber and beauty shop equipment

**(P-19407)**
**MSM INDUSTRIES INC**
12660 Magnolia Ave, Riverside (92503-4636)
PHONE...............................951 735-0834
Darryl Clare, *Pr*
Peter Taylor, *
Craig Sparling, *
Carl Maas, *
**EMP:** 31 **EST:** 2002
**SALES (est):** 6.44MM **Privately Held**
Web: www.msm-ind.com
**SIC:** 8711 2891 2515  Engineering services; Epoxy adhesives; Mattresses, containing felt, foam rubber, urethane, etc.

**(P-19408)**
**ONCORE MANUFACTURING LLC (HQ)**
Also Called: Neo Tech
9340 Owensmouth Ave, Chatsworth (91311-6915)
PHONE...............................818 734-6500
Sudesh Arora, *Pr*
Laura Siegal, *
Kunal Sharma, *
David Brakenwagen Csmo, *Prin*
David Lane, *
▲ **EMP:** 700 **EST:** 2001
**SALES (est):** 146.23MM
**SALES (corp-wide):** 1.43B **Privately Held**
Web: www.neotech.com
**SIC:** 8711 3672  Electrical or electronic engineering; Printed circuit boards
PA: Natel Engineering Company, Llc
9340 Owensmouth Ave
818 495-8617

**(P-19409)**
**OPTOFIDELITY INC**
20863 Stevens Creek Blvd Ste 540, Cupertino (95014-2113)
PHONE...............................669 241-8383
Lasse Lepisto, *CEO*
**EMP:** 32 **EST:** 2017
**SALES (est):** 5.15MM **Privately Held**
Web: www.optofidelity.com
**SIC:** 8711 3827  Engineering services; Optical instruments and lenses

**(P-19410)**
**PANASONIC AVIONICS CORPORATION (DH)**
3347 Michelson Dr Ste 100, Irvine (92612-0661)
PHONE...............................949 672-2000
Kenneth W Sain, *CEO*
Seigo Tada, *
Jessica L Hodkinson, *
▲ **EMP:** 400 **EST:** 1990
**SQ FT:** 20,000
**SALES (est):** 925.13MM **Privately Held**
Web: www.panasonic.aero
**SIC:** 8711 3728  Aviation and/or aeronautical engineering; Aircraft parts and equipment, nec
HQ: Panasonic Corporation Of North America
Two Riverfront Plz Fl 7
Newark NJ 07102
201 348-7000

**(P-19411)**
**PROTOTYPE ENGINEERING AND MANUFACTURING INC**
140 E 162nd St, Gardena (90248-2802)
PHONE...............................310 532-6305
**EMP:** 24
Web: www.prototypeengineering.com
**SIC:** 8711 3825  Electrical or electronic engineering; Test equipment for electronic and electric measurement

**(P-19412)**
**PT SYSTEMS INC**
2350 Whitman Rd Ste B, Concord (94518-2541)
PHONE...............................925 676-0709
Peter Tchan, *Pr*
**EMP:** 16 **EST:** 1974
**SQ FT:** 30,000
**SALES (est):** 1.93MM **Privately Held**
Web: www.ptsystemsinc.com
**SIC:** 8711 7373 3823 3625  Electrical or electronic engineering; Computer integrated systems design; Process control instruments; Relays and industrial controls

**(P-19413)**
**PTEC SOLUTIONS INC (PA)**
48633 Warm Springs Blvd, Fremont (94539-7782)
PHONE...............................510 358-3578
Peter Pham, *CEO*
▲ **EMP:** 167 **EST:** 2010
**SQ FT:** 25,000
**SALES (est):** 23.69MM **Privately Held**
Web: www.ptecsolutions.com
**SIC:** 8711 3357 3599 3679  Engineering services; Fiber optic cable (insulated); Machine shop, jobbing and repair; Harness assemblies, for electronic use: wire or cable

**(P-19414)**
**RELIANT ENGRG & MFG SVCS INC**
Also Called: Reliant Ems
47366 Fremont Blvd, Fremont (94538-6501)
PHONE...............................510 252-1973
Kamran Honardoost, *Pr*
Tho Nguyen, *S&M/VP*
Bryan Sumoba, *QA*
Ali Alian, *Eng/Dir*
**EMP:** 22 **EST:** 2009
**SQ FT:** 10,000
**SALES (est):** 3.62MM **Privately Held**

# 8711 - Engineering Services (P-19415)

SIC: 8711 3841 3444 3824 Engineering services; Surgical and medical instruments; Sheet metalwork; Mechanical and electromechanical counters and devices

### (P-19415)
**ROCK WEST COMPOSITES INC**
7625 Panasonic Way, San Diego (92154-8204)
PHONE..................858 537-6260
James Gormican, *Brnch Mgr*
EMP: 25
Web: www.rockwestcomposites.com
SIC: 8711 3624 Engineering services; Carbon and graphite products
PA: Rock West Composites, Inc.
  7625 Panasonic Way

### (P-19416)
**SAIGON FABRICATION LTD**
Also Called: Fab-9
5750 Hellyer Ave Ste 20, San Jose (95138-1000)
PHONE..................408 693-2340
Anthony Viet Tran, *Pr*
Anthony Viet Tran, *CEO*
EMP: 25 EST: 2019
SALES (est): 7.85MM Privately Held
SIC: 8711 3672 Mechanical engineering; Printed circuit boards

### (P-19417)
**SAN DIEGO COMPOSITES INC**
9220 Activity Rd Ste 100, San Diego (92126-4420)
PHONE..................858 751-0450
Marc Duvall, *CEO*
Jeff Murphy, *
EMP: 70 EST: 2003
SQ FT: 70,000
SALES (est): 26.39MM
SALES (corp-wide): 189.21MM Privately Held
Web: www.appliedcomposites.com
SIC: 8711 8734 3761 3764 Consulting engineer; Testing laboratories; Guided missiles and space vehicles; Space propulsion units and parts
PA: Applied Composites Holdings, Llc
  25692 Atlantic Ocean Dr
  949 716-3511

### (P-19418)
**SCHILLING ROBOTICS LLC**
Also Called: Manufacturing Facility
201 Cousteau Pl, Davis (95618-5412)
PHONE..................530 753-6718
Tyler Schilling, *Mgr*
EMP: 49
SALES (corp-wide): 7.83B Privately Held
Web: www.technipfmc.com
SIC: 8711 3593 Engineering services; Fluid power cylinders and actuators
HQ: Schilling Robotics, Llc
  260 Cousteau Pl
  Davis CA 95618
  530 753-6718

### (P-19419)
**SCHILLING ROBOTICS LLC (DH)**
260 Cousteau Pl Ste 200, Davis (95618-5490)
PHONE..................530 753-6718
▲ EMP: 53 EST: 1985
SALES (est): 45.97MM
SALES (corp-wide): 7.83B Privately Held
Web: www.technipfmc.com
SIC: 8711 3593 Engineering services; Fluid power cylinders and actuators
HQ: Fmc Technologies, Inc.
  13460 Lockwood Rd
  Houston TX 77044
  281 591-4000

### (P-19420)
**SCICON TECHNOLOGIES CORP (PA)**
27525 Newhall Ranch Rd Ste 2, Valencia (91355-4003)
PHONE..................661 295-8630
Thomas J Bulger, *Pr*
Marie Bulger, *
▲ EMP: 50 EST: 1989
SQ FT: 25,000
SALES (est): 9.97MM Privately Held
Web: www.scicontech.com
SIC: 8711 3999 Mechanical engineering; Models, except toy

### (P-19421)
**SEP GROUP INC**
11374 Turtleback Ln, San Diego (92127-2009)
P.O. Box 270475 (92198-2475)
PHONE..................858 876-4621
Abtin Sepehri, *CEO*
EMP: 25 EST: 1998
SALES (est): 907.87K Privately Held
SIC: 8711 1611 1542 1389 Construction and civil engineering; General contractor, highway and street construction; Commercial and office building contractors; Construction, repair, and dismantling services

### (P-19422)
**SPEARMAN AEROSPACE INC**
9215 Greenleaf Ave, Santa Fe Springs (90670-3028)
PHONE..................714 523-4751
Urio Zanetti, *Pr*
EMP: 25 EST: 2013
SALES (est): 10MM Privately Held
Web: www.spearmanaerospace.com
SIC: 8711 3721 Aviation and/or aeronautical engineering; Aircraft

### (P-19423)
**SYSTEMS ENGINEERING & MGT CO (PA)**
Also Called: Semco
1430 Vantage Ct, Vista (92081-8568)
PHONE..................760 727-7800
William M Tincup, *Pr*
Doug Ocull, *
Michael Samuels, *
▼ EMP: 35 EST: 1982
SQ FT: 42,000
SALES (est): 14.14MM
SALES (corp-wide): 14.14MM Privately Held
Web: www.semco.com
SIC: 8711 3812 3825 3663 Consulting engineer; Search and navigation equipment; Instruments to measure electricity; Radio and t.v. communications equipment

### (P-19424)
**THERMAL ENGRG INTL USA INC (HQ)**
Also Called: Thermal Engineering
18000 Studebaker Rd Ste 400, Cerritos (90703-2691)
PHONE..................323 726-0641
Kenneth Murakoshi, *CEO*
Thomas Richardson, *
Micahel D Leclair, *
William J Ferguson Junior, *Law Vice President*
Scott Leeman, *
◆ EMP: 70 EST: 1969
SQ FT: 18,000
SALES (est): 43.84MM
SALES (corp-wide): 509.03MM Privately Held
Web: www.thermalengint.com
SIC: 8711 3443 Professional engineer; Air coolers, metal plate
PA: Babcock Power Inc.
  222 Rosewood Drive 3rd F
  978 646-3300

### (P-19425)
**THORPE TECHNOLOGIES INC (DH)**
449 W Allen Ave Ste 119, San Dimas (91773-1453)
PHONE..................562 903-8230
John E Allen, *Pr*
Thomas A Carpenter, *
EMP: 25 EST: 1988
SALES (est): 3.95MM
SALES (corp-wide): 45.32MM Privately Held
Web: www.thorpetech.com
SIC: 8711 3567 Engineering services; Industrial furnaces and ovens
HQ: Thorpe Holding Company
  9905 Painter Ave # D
  Whittier CA 90605

### (P-19426)
**TRENSOR LLC**
Also Called: Trensor
27051 Towne Centre Dr, Foothill Ranch (92610-2819)
PHONE..................949 379-6730
Scott Gilman, *Managing Member*
EMP: 15 EST: 2014
SALES (est): 2.52MM
SALES (corp-wide): 364.48B Publicly Held
Web: www.trensor.com
SIC: 8711 3829 Industrial engineers; Aircraft and motor vehicle measurement equipment
HQ: Marmon Holdings, Inc.
  181 W Madison St Ste 3900
  Chicago IL 60602
  312 372-9500

### (P-19427)
**TRINITY ENGINEERING**
583 Martin Ave, Rohnert Park (94928-2060)
PHONE..................707 585-2959
Bruce D Omholt, *CEO*
Michael Johnston, *
Denise R Palmer, *
Ronald R Milard, *
EMP: 16 EST: 1980
SQ FT: 18,000
SALES (est): 2.64MM Privately Held
Web: www.trinityengineering.com
SIC: 8711 2542 Designing: ship, boat, machine, and product; Fixtures: display, office, or store: except wood

### (P-19428)
**TRUST AUTOMATION INC**
125 Venture Dr Ste 110, San Luis Obispo (93401-9103)
PHONE..................805 544-0761
Ty Safreno, *CEO*
Trudie Safreno, *
Brett Keegan, *
Chuck Kass, *
Dave Rennie, *
▲ EMP: 65 EST: 1990
SQ FT: 100,000
SALES (est): 21.38MM Privately Held
Web: www.trustautomation.com
SIC: 8711 3812 3731 3621 Machine tool design; Antennas, radar or communications; Submersible marine robots, manned or unmanned; Generators for gas-electric or oil-electric vehicles

### (P-19429)
**UNITED INDUSTRIES GROUP INC**
Also Called: U I G
11 Rancho Cir, Lake Forest (92630-8324)
P.O. Box 8009 (92658-8009)
PHONE..................949 759-3200
James P Mansour, *Pr*
John Mensell, *
EMP: 26 EST: 1969
SQ FT: 10,000
SALES (est): 4.98MM Privately Held
Web: www.unitedind.com
SIC: 8711 3589 Engineering services; Water treatment equipment, industrial

### (P-19430)
**WEST COAST ENERGY SYSTEMS LLC (HQ)**
Also Called: Golden State Contractors
7100 Longe St Ste 300, Stockton (95206-3962)
PHONE..................209 870-1900
Pete Jacpof, *Pr*
EMP: 56 EST: 2020
SALES (est): 22.32MM Publicly Held
Web: www.gspowersolutions.com
SIC: 8711 3621 Engineering services; Power generators
PA: Generac Holdings Inc.
  S45 W29290 Hwy 59

## 8712 Architectural Services

### (P-19431)
**ARCHITECTURAL MTLS USA INC**
4025 Camino Del Rio S Ste 300, San Diego (92108-4108)
PHONE..................888 219-2126
Greg Romine, *CEO*
Serhan Emre, *
EMP: 70 EST: 1997
SALES (est): 2.39MM Privately Held
Web: www.architecturalmaterials.com
SIC: 8712 3999 3211 5039 Architectural engineering; Barber and beauty shop equipment; Construction glass; Prefabricated structures

### (P-19432)
**MEEHLEIS MODULAR BUILDINGS INC**
Also Called: Mmb
1303 E Lodi Ave, Lodi (95240-0840)
PHONE..................209 334-4637
EMP: 53 EST: 1984
SALES (est): 4.67MM Privately Held
Web: www.meehleis.com
SIC: 8712 1542 3448 2452 Architectural engineering; Commercial and office buildings, prefabricated erection; Prefabricated metal buildings and components; Prefabricated wood buildings

## 8721 Accounting, Auditing, And Bookkeeping

### (P-19433)
**INFINEON TECH AMERICAS CORP**

# PRODUCTS & SERVICES SECTION
## 8731 - Commercial Physical Research (P-19452)

Interntnal Rctfr/Ccunting Dept
222 Kansas St, El Segundo (90245-4315)
PHONE..................................310 726-8000
Michael Mcgee, *Mgr*
**EMP:** 699
**SALES (corp-wide):** 17.72B **Privately Held**
**Web:** www-blue.infineon.com
**SIC:** 8721 3674 Accounting, auditing, and bookkeeping; Semiconductors and related devices
**HQ:** Infineon Technologies Americas Corp.
101 N Pacific Coast Hwy
El Segundo CA 90245
310 726-8200

### (P-19434)
### SYMED CORPORATION
215 Gateway Rd W Ste 101, Napa (94558-7593)
P.O. Box 238 (94559-0238)
PHONE..................................707 255-3300
Arthur Roosa, *CEO*
**EMP:** 31 **EST:** 1990
**SQ FT:** 14,400
**SALES (est):** 4.04MM
**SALES (corp-wide):** 10.02MM **Privately Held**
**Web:** www.symed.net
**SIC:** 8721 7372 Billing and bookkeeping service; Prepackaged software
**PA:** Cosentus, Llc
300 Spectrum Center Dr # 1450
949 979-5627

### 8731 Commercial Physical Research

### (P-19435)
### ACCELIOT INC
16601 Gothard St Ste E, Huntington Beach (92647-4479)
PHONE..................................657 845-4250
Shawn Manesh, *CEO*
**EMP:** 15 **EST:** 2019
**SALES (est):** 15MM **Privately Held**
**Web:** www.acceliot.com
**SIC:** 8731 7372 Computer (hardware) development; Application computer software

### (P-19436)
### ADVANCED CELL DIAGNOSTICS INC
Also Called: Acd
7707 Gateway Blvd Ste 200, Newark (94560-1268)
PHONE..................................510 576-8800
Yuling Luo, *Pr*
Steve Chen, *COO*
Jessie Qian Wang, *CFO*
Tom Olenic, *CCO*
Rob Monroe, *CMO*
**EMP:** 90 **EST:** 2006
**SQ FT:** 2,500
**SALES (est):** 25.1MM
**SALES (corp-wide):** 1.16B **Publicly Held**
**SIC:** 8731 2835 Biotechnical research, commercial; Microbiology and virology diagnostic products
**PA:** Bio-Techne Corporation
614 Mckinley Pl Ne
612 379-8854

### (P-19437)
### AINOS INC (PA)
Also Called: VELDONA
8880 Rio San Diego Dr Ste 800, San Diego (92108-1642)
PHONE..................................858 869-2986
Chun-hsien Tsai, *Ch Bd*

Christopher Hsin-liang Lee, *CFO*
Lawrence K Lin, *Ofcr*
**EMP:** 46 **EST:** 1984
**SALES (est):** 122.11K
**SALES (corp-wide):** 122.11K **Publicly Held**
**Web:** www.amarbio.com
**SIC:** 8731 2834 Biotechnical research, commercial; Pharmaceutical preparations

### (P-19438)
### ALTO NEUROSCIENCE INC
650 Castro St Ste 450, Mountain View (94041-2026)
PHONE..................................650 200-0412
Amit Etkin, *Ch Bd*
Nicholas Smith, *CFO*
Adam Savitz, *CMO*
Erin Mcquade, *Chief*
Melissa Berman, *VP Fin*
**EMP:** 63 **EST:** 2019
**SQ FT:** 3,500
**Web:** www.altoneuroscience.com
**SIC:** 8731 2834 Biotechnical research, commercial; Pharmaceutical preparations

### (P-19439)
### ALZETA CORPORATION
1968 Hartog Dr, San Jose (95131-2200)
PHONE..................................408 727-8282
John D Sullivan, *Pr*
John E Kendall, *Ch Bd*
Stephen G Egli, *CFO*
Angela R Kendall, *Stockholder*
▲ **EMP:** 15 **EST:** 1982
**SALES (est):** 2.49MM **Privately Held**
**Web:** www.alzeta.com
**SIC:** 8731 3433 Energy research; Heating equipment, except electric

### (P-19440)
### AMT DATASOUTH CORP (PA)
Also Called: A M T
3222 Corte Malpaso, Camarillo (93012-8000)
PHONE..................................805 388-5799
Joseph E Eichberger, *Ch Bd*
James Nolan, *VP*
Chris Biggers, *VP*
◆ **EMP:** 20 **EST:** 1982
**SALES (est):** 9.91MM
**SALES (corp-wide):** 9.91MM **Privately Held**
**Web:** www.amtdatasouth.com
**SIC:** 8731 5045 7379 3577 Computer (hardware) development; Printers, computer ; Computer related maintenance services; Computer peripheral equipment, nec

### (P-19441)
### ANSUN BIOPHARMA INC
Also Called: Ansun
10045 Mesa Rim Rd, San Diego (92121-2913)
PHONE..................................858 452-2631
Nancy Chang, *CEO*
George Wang, *
Stanley Lewis, *CMO*
**EMP:** 25 **EST:** 2003
**SQ FT:** 12,000
**SALES (est):** 5.8MM **Privately Held**
**Web:** www.ansunbiopharma.com
**SIC:** 8731 2834 Biotechnical research, commercial; Druggists' preparations (pharmaceuticals)

### (P-19442)
### AQUANEERING LLC
Also Called: Aquaneering
340 Rancheros Dr Ste 180, San Marcos (92069-2980)

PHONE..................................858 578-2028
Sandeep Patel, *Managing Member*
**EMP:** 30 **EST:** 1984
**SALES (est):** 8.07MM **Privately Held**
**Web:** www.aquaneering.com
**SIC:** 8731 3589 Biotechnical research, commercial; Water filters and softeners, household type

### (P-19443)
### ASTERIAS BIOTHERAPEUTICS INC
Also Called: Asterias Biotherapeutics
1010 Atlantic Ave Ste 102, Alameda (94501-1258)
PHONE..................................510 456-3800
Michael H Mulroy, *Pr*
Katharine E Spink, *
Ryan D Chavez, *
Edward D Wirth Iii, *CMO*
**EMP:** 55 **EST:** 2012
**SALES (est):** 3.95MM **Publicly Held**
**Web:** www.asteriasbiotherapeutics.com
**SIC:** 8731 2836 Biotechnical research, commercial; Biological products, except diagnostic
**PA:** Lineage Cell Therapeutics, Inc.
2173 Salk Ave Ste 200

### (P-19444)
### BIO-VED PHARMACEUTICALS INC
1929 Otoole Way, San Jose (95131-2238)
PHONE..................................408 432-4020
Doctor Deepa Chitre, *CEO*
Deepa Chitre, *CEO*
Katki Sawant, *
**EMP:** 27 **EST:** 1994
**SQ FT:** 1,000
**SALES (est):** 839.23K **Privately Held**
**Web:** www.bioved.com
**SIC:** 8731 2834 Biotechnical research, commercial; Druggists' preparations (pharmaceuticals)

### (P-19445)
### BIODURO LLC (PA)
Also Called: Bioduro-Sundia
11011 Torreyana Rd, San Diego (92121-1104)
PHONE..................................858 529-6600
Kent M Payne, *CEO*
Teo Nee Chuan, *
**EMP:** 40 **EST:** 2005
**SALES (est):** 53.39MM **Privately Held**
**Web:** www.bioduro-sundia.com
**SIC:** 8731 2834 Biotechnical research, commercial; Medicines, capsuled or ampuled

### (P-19446)
### BIOQUIP PRODUCTS INC
2321 E Gladwick St, Rancho Dominguez (90220-6209)
PHONE..................................310 667-8800
▲ **EMP:** 30 **EST:** 1947
**SALES (est):** 2.65MM **Privately Held**
**Web:** www.bioquip.com
**SIC:** 8731 3821 Biological research; Laboratory apparatus and furniture

### (P-19447)
### BIOSPACE INC
Also Called: Inbody
13850 Cerritos Corporate Dr Ste C, Cerritos (90703-2467)
PHONE..................................323 932-6503
Ki Chul Cha, *Pr*
Hak Hee Yun, *
▲ **EMP:** 86 **EST:** 2000

**SQ FT:** 35,319
**SALES (est):** 18.64MM **Privately Held**
**Web:** www.inbody.com
**SIC:** 8731 3821 Energy research; Calibration tapes, for physical testing machines
**PA:** Shenzhen Longgang District Baolong Kangxing Fruit Firm
No.419-420, Chishi Gang Xiaoqu Tongfu Road, Longxin Community, B

### (P-19448)
### COI PHARMACEUTICALS INC
11099 N Torrey Pines Rd Ste 290, La Jolla (92037-1029)
PHONE..................................858 750-4700
Jay Lichter, *CEO*
**EMP:** 25 **EST:** 2013
**SALES (est):** 6.65MM **Privately Held**
**Web:** www.avalonbioventures.com
**SIC:** 8731 2834 Biological research; Pharmaceutical preparations

### (P-19449)
### DAY ONE BIOPHARMACEUTICALS INC (PA)
Also Called: DAY ONE
2000 Sierra Point Pkwy Ste 501, Brisbane (94005-1874)
PHONE..................................650 484-0899
Jeremy Bender, *Pr*
Garry Nicholson, *Non-Executive Chairman of the Board*
Charles York Ii, *COO*
Adam Dubow, *CCO*
Samuel Blackman, *Head Research & Development*
**EMP:** 28 **EST:** 2018
**SQ FT:** 12,000
**Web:** www.dayonebio.com
**SIC:** 8731 2834 Biotechnical research, commercial; Pharmaceutical preparations

### (P-19450)
### DEPOSITION SCIENCES INC
Also Called: D S I
3300 Coffey Ln, Santa Rosa (95403-1917)
PHONE..................................707 573-6700
Lee Bartolomei, *Pr*
Thomas Chambers, *
**EMP:** 96 **EST:** 1997
**SQ FT:** 8,400
**SALES (est):** 14.86MM **Publicly Held**
**Web:** www.depsci.com
**SIC:** 8731 3827 Industrial laboratory, except testing; Lens coating equipment
**PA:** Lockheed Martin Corporation
6801 Rockledge Dr

### (P-19451)
### DSM BIOMEDICAL INC
Also Called: Polymer Technology Group, The
2810 7th St, Berkeley (94710-2703)
PHONE..................................510 841-8800
**EMP:** 120
**Web:** www.dsm.com
**SIC:** 8731 2836 Commercial physical research; Biological products, except diagnostic

### (P-19452)
### FLUXERGY INC (PA)
Also Called: Carter Laboratories
30 Fairbanks, Irvine (92618-1623)
PHONE..................................949 305-4201
Tej Patel, *Pr*
Ryan Revilla, *
Jonathan Tu, *
**EMP:** 34 **EST:** 2013
**SALES (est):** 10.44MM

## 8731 - Commercial Physical Research (P-19453)

SALES (corp-wide): 10.44MM **Privately Held**
Web: www.fluxergy.com
SIC: **8731** 3841  Biotechnical research, commercial; Diagnostic apparatus, medical

### (P-19453)
### GENERAL ATOMICS
Also Called: General Atomics Energy Pdts
4949 Greencraig Ln, San Diego (92123-1675)
PHONE....................858 455-4000
Joel Ennis, *Genl Mgr*
EMP: 170
Web: www.ga.com
SIC: **8731** 7371 3823  Commercial physical research; Custom computer programming services; Process control instruments
HQ: General Atomics
3550 General Atomics Ct
San Diego CA 92121
858 455-2810

### (P-19454)
### GENTEX CORPORATION
Also Called: Western Operations
9859 7th St, Rancho Cucamonga (91730-5244)
PHONE....................909 481-7667
Robert Mccay, *Brnch Mgr*
EMP: 90
SALES (corp-wide): 106.5MM **Privately Held**
Web: www.gentexcorp.com
SIC: **8731** 3845 3841  Commercial research laboratory; Electromedical equipment; Surgical and medical instruments
PA: Gentex Corporation
324 Main St
570 282-3550

### (P-19455)
### GILEAD PALO ALTO  INC (HQ)
333 Lakeside Dr, Foster City (94404-1394)
PHONE....................650 384-8500
John C Martin, *Ch*
Louis Lange Ph.d., *Ch Bd*
John F Milligan, *Pr*
Daniel K Spiegelman, *Sr VP*
Brent K Blackburn Ph.d. Senior, *Drug Discovery Vice President*
EMP: 50 EST: 1987
SALES (est): 12.78MM
SALES (corp-wide): 27.12B **Publicly Held**
Web: www.gilead.com
SIC: **8731** 2834  Commercial physical research; Pharmaceutical preparations
PA: Gilead Sciences, Inc.
333 Lakeside Dr
650 574-3000

### (P-19456)
### INOVA DIAGNOSTICS  INC (HQ)
Also Called: Werfen
9900 Old Grove Rd, San Diego (92131-1638)
PHONE....................858 586-9900
Carlos Pascual, *CEO*
Javier Gomez, *
▲ EMP: 285 EST: 1987
SQ FT: 81,000
SALES (est): 37.29MM **Privately Held**
Web: www.werfen.com
SIC: **8731** 2835  Medical research, commercial; In vitro diagnostics
PA: Werfen S.A.
Plaza Europa, 21 - 23

### (P-19457)
### INTRI-PLEX TECHNOLOGIES INC
751 S Kellogg Ave, Goleta (93117-3806)
PHONE....................805 845-9600
David Dexter, *CEO*
EMP: 34 EST: 1989
SALES (est): 658.94K **Privately Held**
Web: www.intriplex.com
SIC: **8731** 3599  Commercial physical research; Machine shop, jobbing and repair

### (P-19458)
### ISE CORPORATION
Also Called: I S E
12302 Kerran St, Poway (92064-6884)
PHONE....................858 413-1720
▲ EMP: 140
SIC: **8731** 3621  Commercial physical research; Electric motor and generator parts

### (P-19459)
### KITE PHARMA  INC (HQ)
Also Called: Kite, A Gilead Company
2400 Broadway Ste 100, Santa Monica (90404-3058)
PHONE....................310 824-9999
Christi Shaw, *CEO*
Robin L Washington, *
Cindy Perettie, *
EMP: 92 EST: 2009
SQ FT: 20,000
SALES (est): 120.5MM
SALES (corp-wide): 27.12B **Publicly Held**
Web: www.kitepharma.com
SIC: **8731** 2836  Biotechnical research, commercial; Biological products, except diagnostic
PA: Gilead Sciences, Inc.
333 Lakeside Dr
650 574-3000

### (P-19460)
### LEIDOS  INC
Also Called: Reveal Imaging
2985 Scott St, Vista (92081-8339)
PHONE....................858 826-9090
EMP: 130
Web: www.leidos.com
SIC: **8731** 3829 3826  Commercial physical research; Measuring and controlling devices, nec; Analytical instruments
HQ: Leidos, Inc.
1750 Presidents St
Reston VA 20190
855 953-4367

### (P-19461)
### LEIDOS  INC
Also Called: Saic
Naval Air Station, San Diego (92135)
PHONE....................858 826-6000
EMP: 66
Web: www.leidos.com
SIC: **8731** 7373 8742 3679  Commercial physical research; Systems engineering, computer related; Training and development consultant; Recording and playback apparatus, including phonograph
HQ: Leidos, Inc.
1750 Presidents St
Reston VA 20190
855 953-4367

### (P-19462)
### LUIDIA  INC
591 W Hamilton Ave Ste 205, Campbell (95008-0566)
PHONE....................650 413-7500
C K Kim, *CEO*

▲ EMP: 47 EST: 2003
SALES (est): 8.3MM **Privately Held**
Web: www.lostarkfoundry.com
SIC: **8731** 3577  Electronic research; Computer peripheral equipment, nec

### (P-19463)
### LUMIATA  INC
Also Called: Medgle
489 S El Camino Real, San Mateo (94402-1727)
PHONE....................916 607-2442
Dilawar Syed, *CEO*
Miguel Alvarado, *
EMP: 34 EST: 2013
SALES (est): 3.76MM **Privately Held**
Web: www.somatus.com
SIC: **8731** 7372  Medical research, commercial; Application computer software

### (P-19464)
### M&B SCIENCES INC
4445 Eastgate Mall, San Diego (92121-1979)
PHONE....................858 812-8735
Eddilisa Martin, *CEO*
EMP: 20 EST: 2021
SALES (est): 1.28MM **Privately Held**
Web: www.mbsciences.com
SIC: **8731** 7372  Biotechnical research, commercial; Prepackaged software

### (P-19465)
### MAWI DNA TECHNOLOGIES  LLC
Also Called: Medical Device
1252 Quarry Ln, Pleasanton (94566-4756)
PHONE....................510 256-5186
Bassam El-fahmawi, *CEO*
Hycinth Ntchobo, *
EMP: 35 EST: 2013
SQ FT: 2,000
SALES (est): 2.31MM **Privately Held**
Web: www.mawidna.com
SIC: **8731** 5122 3841  Biotechnical research, commercial; Biologicals and allied products; Surgical instruments and apparatus

### (P-19466)
### MEMBRANE TECHNOLOGY & RES INC (PA)
Also Called: M T R
39630 Eureka Dr, Newark (94560-4805)
PHONE....................650 328-2228
Colin Bailey, *Ch*
Hans Wijmans, *
Meryl Rains, *
Richard W Baker, *
◆ EMP: 49 EST: 1982
SQ FT: 60,000
SALES (est): 17.92MM
SALES (corp-wide): 17.92MM **Privately Held**
Web: www.mtrinc.com
SIC: **8731** 3823  Commercial research laboratory; On-stream gas/liquid analysis instruments, industrial

### (P-19467)
### MERCURY MISSION SYSTEMS LLC
20701 Manhattan Pl, Torrance (90501-1829)
PHONE....................310 320-3088
Mark Bruington, *Brnch Mgr*
EMP: 22
SALES (corp-wide): 835.27MM **Publicly Held**
Web: www.mrcy.com

SIC: **8731** 3812 7299  Commercial research laboratory; Search and navigation equipment; Information services, consumer
HQ: Mercury Mission Systems, Llc
50 Minuteman Rd
Andover MA 01810
978 256-1300

### (P-19468)
### METAGENOMI  INC (PA)
Also Called: METAGENOMI
5959 Horton St Fl 7, Emeryville (94608-2120)
PHONE....................510 871-4880
Brian C Thomas, *CEO*
Juergen Eckhardt, *Ch Bd*
Jian Irish, *Pr*
Simon Harnest, *CIO*
Alan Brooks, *Sr VP*
EMP: 35 EST: 2016
SQ FT: 75,662
SALES (est): 17.2MM
SALES (corp-wide): 17.2MM **Publicly Held**
Web: www.metagenomi.co
SIC: **8731** 2834  Biotechnical research, commercial; Pharmaceutical preparations

### (P-19469)
### MOTECH AMERICAS LLC
Also Called: GE Energy
1300 Valley Vista Dr Ste 207, Diamond Bar (91765-3940)
PHONE....................302 451-7500
▲ EMP: 320
Web: www.motech-americas.com
SIC: **8731** 3674  Energy research; Solar cells

### (P-19470)
### OPTO-KNOWLEDGE SYSTEMS INC
Also Called: Optoknowledge
19805 Hamilton Ave, Torrance (90502-1341)
PHONE....................310 756-0520
Christopher Holmes Parker, *Prin*
Ilana Gat, *
Joel Gat, *
EMP: 29 EST: 1991
SQ FT: 14,000
SALES (est): 5.74MM **Privately Held**
Web: www.oksi.ai
SIC: **8731** 3827  Engineering laboratory, except testing; Optical instruments and lenses

### (P-19471)
### PADOMA WIND POWER  LLC (DH)
7777 Fay Ave Ste 200, La Jolla (92037-4324)
PHONE....................858 731-5001
Jan Paulin, *Pr*
Jan C Paulin, *Managing Member*
EMP: 15 EST: 2001
SALES (est): 1.28MM
SALES (corp-wide): 100.96B **Privately Held**
SIC: **8731** 3621  Energy research; Windmills, electric generating
HQ: Enel North America, Inc.
100 Brickstone Sq Ste 300
Andover MA 01810
978 681-1900

### (P-19472)
### REVEAL BIOSCIENCES  INC
80 Empire Dr, Lake Forest (92630-2244)
PHONE....................858 274-3663
Claire Weston, *Pr*

# PRODUCTS & SERVICES SECTION

## 8733 - Noncommercial Research Organizations (P-19491)

EMP: 25 EST: 2012
SALES (est): 2.24MM **Privately Held**
Web: www.revealbio.com
SIC: **8731** 2835  Biotechnical research, commercial; Cytology and histology diagnostic agents

### (P-19473)
### SEMINIS INC (DH)
2700 Camino Del Sol, Oxnard (93030-7967)
PHONE..................................805 485-7317
Bruno Ferrari, *Pr*
Oscar J Velasco Senior, *Area Vice President*
Charles E Green, *
Enrique Lopez, *
Jorge B Gutierrez, *
◆ EMP: 300 EST: 1995
SALES (est): 13.66MM
SALES (corp-wide): 51.78B **Privately Held**
Web: www.seminis.com
SIC: **8731** 8742 2099  Agricultural research; Productivity improvement consultant; Food preparations, nec
HQ: Monsanto Technology Llc.
800 N Lindbergh Blvd
Saint Louis MO 63167
314 694-1000

### (P-19474)
### SEMPRIUS INC
Also Called: Semprius
1100 La Avenida St Ste A, Mountain View (94043-1453)
EMP: 64 EST: 2005
SALES (est): 1.55MM **Privately Held**
SIC: **8731** 3674  Electronic research; Solar cells

### (P-19475)
### STELLARTECH RESEARCH CORP (PA)
560 Cottonwood Dr, Milpitas (95035-7403)
PHONE..................................408 331-3000
Roger Stern, *Pr*
Vincent Sullivan, *
Jerome Jackson, *
Jerry Smith, *
EMP: 109 EST: 1988
SQ FT: 68,000
SALES (est): 40MM **Privately Held**
Web: www.stellartec.com
SIC: **8731** 3841 8732 8733  Commercial physical research; Surgical and medical instruments; Sociological research; Physical research, noncommercial

### (P-19476)
### SYMYX TECHNOLOGIES INC
2804 Mission College Blvd Ste 240, Santa Clara (95054-1842)
PHONE..................................408 764-2000
EMP: 460
SIC: **8731** 7372  Commercial physical research; Business oriented computer software

### (P-19477)
### TAKARA BIO USA INC (DH)
Also Called: Clontech
2560 Orchard Pkwy, San Jose (95131-1033)
PHONE..................................650 919-7300
Carol Lou, *Pr*
EMP: 40 EST: 1984
SQ FT: 100,000
SALES (est): 95.62MM **Privately Held**
Web: www.takarabio.com

SIC: **8731** 2836  Biotechnical research, commercial; Biological products, except diagnostic
HQ: Takara Bio Inc.
7-4-38, Nojihigashi
Kusatsu SGA 525-0

### (P-19478)
### TANNER RESEARCH INC
Also Called: Little Green Forks
1851 Huntington Dr, Duarte (91010-2635)
PHONE..................................626 471-9700
EMP: 20 EST: 1988
SALES (est): 4.95MM **Privately Held**
Web: www.nusci.org
SIC: **8731** 5045 3549 7371  Computer (hardware) development; Computer software; Assembly machines, including robotic; Computer software development

### (P-19479)
### TAVIS CORPORATION
3636 State Highway 49 S, Mariposa (95338-9718)
PHONE..................................209 966-2027
John Tavis, *Ch Bd*
John A Tavis, *
Dina Lambert, *
Marty Kudela, *
EMP: 56 EST: 1969
SQ FT: 26,500
SALES (est): 8.62MM **Privately Held**
Web: www.taviscorp.com
SIC: **8731** 3679 3829  Commercial physical research; Transducers, electrical; Measuring and controlling devices, nec

### (P-19480)
### TEGILE SYSTEMS INC
7999 Gateway Blvd Ste 120, Newark (94560-1005)
PHONE..................................510 791-7900
Rohit Kshetrapal, *CEO*
Ian Edmundson, *
Rajesh Nair, *
Narayan Venkat, *CMO*
Michael Morgan, *
EMP: 130 EST: 2010
SQ FT: 6,500
SALES (est): 3.28MM **Privately Held**
Web: www.ddn.com
SIC: **8731** 3572  Computer (hardware) development; Computer storage devices

### (P-19481)
### UNITY BIOTECHNOLOGY INC
285 E Grand Ave, South San Francisco (94080-4804)
PHONE..................................650 416-1192
Anirvan Ghosh, *CEO*
Keith R Leonard Junior, *Ch Bd*
Lynne Sullivan, *CFO*
Jamie Dananberg, *CMO*
Alexander Nguyen, *Corporate Secretary*
EMP: 19 EST: 2009
SQ FT: 62,000
Web: www.unitybiotechnology.com
SIC: **8731** 2834  Medical research, commercial; Pharmaceutical preparations

### (P-19482)
### VERINATA HEALTH INC
Also Called: Illumina-Redwood City
200 Lincoln Centre Dr, Foster City (94404-1122)
PHONE..................................650 632-1680
Jeff Bird, *CEO*
Vance Vanier, *
EMP: 55 EST: 2002
SALES (est): 4.48MM

SALES (corp-wide): 4.5B **Publicly Held**
Web: www.illumina.com
SIC: **8731** 2835  Biotechnical research, commercial; Diagnostic substances
PA: Illumina, Inc.
5200 Illumina Way
858 202-4500

### (P-19483)
### WILDCAT DISCOVERY TECH INC
6255 Ferris Sq Ste A, San Diego (92121)
PHONE..................................858 550-1980
Mark Gresser, *CEO*
Mark Grasser, *Pr*
Steven Kaye, *Prin*
Jon Jacobs, *VP*
Laura Marion, *CFO*
EMP: 59 EST: 2006
SALES (est): 11.44MM **Privately Held**
Web: www.wildcatdiscovery.com
SIC: **8731** 2819  Biotechnical research, commercial; Industrial inorganic chemicals, nec

## 8732 Commercial Nonphysical Research

### (P-19484)
### MARKOV CORPORATION
Also Called: Level
1225 Magdalena Ct, Los Altos (94024-5205)
PHONE..................................650 207-9445
Lenard Spicer, *CEO*
EMP: 20 EST: 2016
SALES (est): 590.57K **Privately Held**
Web: www.smartprofitfx.com
SIC: **8732** 3634  Market analysis, business, and economic research; Housewares, excluding cooking appliances and utensils

### (P-19485)
### MEDALLIA PARENT LP (PA)
6220 Stoneridge Mall Rd Fl 2, Pleasanton (94588-3260)
PHONE..................................650 321-3000
Leslie Stretch, *CEO*
EMP: 66 EST: 2021
SALES (est): 492.75MM
SALES (corp-wide): 492.75MM **Privately Held**
SIC: **8732** 7372  Market analysis, business, and economic research; Business oriented computer software

### (P-19486)
### NITTO DENKO TECHNICAL CORP
Also Called: Nitto
501 Via Del Monte, Oceanside (92058-1251)
PHONE..................................760 435-7011
Kenji Matsumoto, *Pr*
EMP: 99 EST: 1985
SALES (est): 16.11MM **Privately Held**
Web: www.ndtcorp.com
SIC: **8732** 3089 3462  Research services, except laboratory; Automotive parts, plastic; Automotive and internal combustion engine forgings
PA: Nitto Denko Corporation
4-20, Ofukacho, Kita-Ku

### (P-19487)
### PACIFIC RES INST FOR PUB PLICY (PA)
1 Embarcadero Ctr, San Francisco (94111-3631)

PHONE..................................415 989-0833
Sally Pipes, *Pr*
Keith Chreston, *COO*
Christine Hughes, *VP*
Rowena Itchon, *VP*
EMP: 19 EST: 1979
SALES (est): 5.62MM
SALES (corp-wide): 5.62MM **Privately Held**
Web: www.pacificresearch.org
SIC: **8732** 2731  Economic research; Books, publishing only

### (P-19488)
### RAYDIANCE INC
1100 La Avenida St, Mountain View (94043-1452)
PHONE..................................408 764-4000
Richard Pierce, *CEO*
John H N Fisher, *
Mike Mielke, *CSO*
▼ EMP: 18 EST: 2003
SQ FT: 42,000
SALES (est): 925.68K **Privately Held**
SIC: **8732** 3826 3821  Research services, except laboratory; Laser scientific and engineering instruments; Laser beam alignment devices

### (P-19489)
### SHARETHIS INC (PA)
3000 El Camino Real Ste 5-150, Palo Alto (94306-2121)
PHONE..................................650 641-0191
Dana Hayes Junior, *CEO*
Tim Schigel, *Ch Bd*
Kurt Abrahamson, *Ofcr*
Matt Gallatin, *CFO*
Jonathan Gregg, *CRO*
EMP: 50 EST: 2004
SALES (est): 9.43MM
SALES (corp-wide): 9.43MM **Privately Held**
Web: www.sharethis.com
SIC: **8732** 7313 7372  Commercial nonphysical research; Electronic media advertising representatives; Prepackaged software

## 8733 Noncommercial Research Organizations

### (P-19490)
### ABBVIE STEMCENTRX LLC
Also Called: Abbvie
1000 Gateway Blvd, South San Francisco (94080-7028)
PHONE..................................415 298-9242
Brian Slingerland, *CEO*
Scott J Dylla, *
James N Strabridge, *
Julia Hong, *Prin*
EMP: 95 EST: 2008
SALES (est): 18.93MM
SALES (corp-wide): 54.32B **Publicly Held**
Web: www.abbvie.com
SIC: **8733** 2834  Medical research; Proprietary drug products
PA: Abbvie Inc.
1 N Waukegan Rd
847 932-7900

### (P-19491)
### AMERICAN REGENT INC
536 Vanguard Way, Brea (92821-3932)
PHONE..................................714 989-5058
Donald F Hodgson, *Brnch Mgr*
EMP: 40
Web: www.americanregent.com

## 8733 - Noncommercial Research Organizations (P-19492)

SIC: 8733 2834 Noncommercial research organizations; Pharmaceutical preparations
HQ: American Regent, Inc.
5 Ramsey Rd
Shirley NY 11967
631 924-4000

### (P-19492)
### DOMPE US INC
400 S El Camino Real Ste 400, San Mateo (94402-1741)
PHONE.................................833 366-7387
Eriona Gjinukaj, *CEO*
Giuseppe Andreano, *CFO*
Shannon Sullivan, *CCO*
EMP: 15 EST: 2013
SALES (est): 1.1MM Privately Held
Web: www.dompe.com
SIC: 8733 8732 2834 Medical research; Commercial nonphysical research; Pharmaceutical preparations

### (P-19493)
### DXTERITY DIAGNOSTICS INC (PA)
19500 S Rancho Way Ste 116, Compton (90220-6012)
PHONE.................................310 537-7857
Doctor Bob Terbrueggen, *CEO*
Bill Coty, *
Jim Healy, *
Aviva Jacobs, *
Brett Swansiger, *Chief Commercialization Officer*
EMP: 39 EST: 2006
SQ FT: 14,000
SALES (est): 8.45MM Privately Held
Web: www.dxterity.com
SIC: 8733 8071 2835 Medical research; Medical laboratories; Diagnostic substances

### (P-19494)
### GENENTECH INC (DH)
1 Dna Way Stop 258a, South San Francisco (94080-4990)
P.O. Box 4354 (97208-4354)
PHONE.................................650 225-1000
Ashley Magargee, *CEO*
Sean Johnston, *
Matteo Pietra, *
◆ EMP: 2000 EST: 1986
SALES (est): 1.2B Privately Held
Web: www.gene.com
SIC: 8733 2834 Medical research; Adrenal pharmaceutical preparations
HQ: Roche Holdings, Inc.
1 Dna Way
South San Francisco CA 94080
650 225-1000

### (P-19495)
### PERATON TECHNOLOGY SVCS INC
2750 Womble Rd Ste 202, San Diego (92106-6114)
PHONE.................................571 313-6000
John Curtis, *CEO*
EMP: 24
SQ FT: 10,000
SALES (corp-wide): 2.28B Privately Held
Web: www.perspecta.com
SIC: 8733 3812 7372 8711 Economic research, noncommercial; Defense systems and equipment; Application computer software; Professional engineer
HQ: Peraton Technology Services Inc.
12975 Worldgate Dr
Herndon VA 20170
571 313-6000

### (P-19496)
### SCIENCELL RESEARCH LABS INC
1610 Faraday Ave, Carlsbad (92008-7313)
PHONE.................................760 602-8549
James Shen, *Pr*
Yong Juan Yu, *
Jim Shen, *
EMP: 40 EST: 1990
SQ FT: 9,000
SALES (est): 5.76MM Privately Held
Web: www.sciencellonline.com
SIC: 8733 8731 2836 Medical research; Commercial physical research; Biological products, except diagnostic

### (P-19497)
### SINGULEX INC
Also Called: Singulex
1701 Harbor Bay Pkwy Ste 200, Alameda (94502-3014)
PHONE.................................510 995-9000
EMP: 260 EST: 1998
SALES (est): 24.31MM Privately Held
Web: www.singulex.com
SIC: 8733 8071 3841 Scientific research agency; Blood analysis laboratory; Diagnostic apparatus, medical

### (P-19498)
### VIACYTE INC
5580 Morehouse Dr Ste 100, San Diego (92121)
PHONE.................................858 455-3708
Paul K Laikind, *Pr*
Allan Robins, *VP*
Howard Foyt, *VP*
Anthony Gringeri, *Chief Development Officer*
EMP: 55 EST: 1999
SALES (est): 18.04MM Privately Held
Web: www.vrtx.com
SIC: 8733 2836 Medical research; Biological products, except diagnostic

### (P-19499)
### VIOPTIX INC
39655 Eureka Dr, Newark (94560-4806)
PHONE.................................510 226-5860
Larry C Heaton Ii, *Pr*
EMP: 18 EST: 1999
SQ FT: 11,000
SALES (est): 2.44MM Privately Held
Web: www.vioptix.com
SIC: 8733 3841 Medical research; Diagnostic apparatus, medical

## 8734 Testing Laboratories

### (P-19500)
### AIRCRAFT XRAY LABORATORIES INC
5216 Pacific Blvd, Huntington Park (90255-2595)
PHONE.................................323 587-4141
Gary G Newton, *CEO*
James Newton, *
Sandi Spelic, *
Justin Guzman, *
EMP: 80 EST: 1938
SQ FT: 60,000
SALES (est): 8.08MM Privately Held
Web: www.aircraftxray.com
SIC: 8734 7384 3471 Testing laboratories; Photograph developing and retouching; Plating and polishing

### (P-19501)
### CELLULAR LONGEVITY INC
Also Called: Loyal
548 Market St Pmb 26099, San Francisco (94104-5401)
PHONE.................................707 563-9236
EMP: 15 EST: 2019
SALES (est): 8.25MM Privately Held
Web: www.loyalfordogs.com
SIC: 8734 2834 Veterinary testing; Veterinary pharmaceutical preparations

### (P-19502)
### EUROFINS ENVMT TSTG NTHRN CAL
880 Riverside Pkwy, West Sacramento (95605-1500)
PHONE.................................916 373-5600
Roger Freize, *Mgr*
EMP: 41
SALES (corp-wide): 42.88MM Privately Held
Web: www.eurofinsus.com
SIC: 8734 8731 2899 Testing laboratories; Commercial physical research; Chemical preparations, nec
HQ: Eurofins Environment Testing Northern California, Llc
180 Blue Ravine Rd Ste B
Folsom CA 95630

### (P-19503)
### HAMPTON TDDER TCHNCAL SVCS INC
4571 State St, Montclair (91763-6129)
P.O. Box 2338 (91763-0838)
PHONE.................................909 628-1256
Matthew C Tedder Senior, *Pr*
EMP: 19 EST: 1972
SQ FT: 20,000
SALES (est): 2.38MM Privately Held
Web: www.httstesting.com
SIC: 8734 1731 1623 8711 Testing laboratories; Electrical work; Electric power line construction; Engineering services

### (P-19504)
### IDEAL AEROSMITH INC
155 Constitution Dr, Menlo Park (94025-1106)
PHONE.................................650 353-3641
Bill Meckfessel, *Brnch Mgr*
EMP: 15
SALES (corp-wide): 19.34MM Privately Held
Web: www.ideal-aerosmith.com
SIC: 8734 3826 3545 3494 Testing laboratories; Analytical instruments; Machine tool accessories; Valves and pipe fittings, nec
PA: Ideal Aerosmith, Inc.
3001 S Washington St
701 757-3400

### (P-19505)
### ISE LABS INC (DH)
46800 Bayside Pkwy, Fremont (94538-6592)
PHONE.................................510 687-2500
Tien Wu, *CEO*
Jeff Thompson, *
EMP: 200 EST: 1999
SQ FT: 69,000
SALES (est): 17.43MM Privately Held
Web: www.iselabs.com
SIC: 8734 3672 Calibration and certification; Printed circuit boards
HQ: Ase Test Limited
C/O: Allen & Gledhill Llp
Singapore 01898

### (P-19506)
### PPT GROUP CORP (HQ)
Also Called: Lansmont
17 Mandeville Ct, Monterey (93940-5745)
PHONE.................................831 655-6600
Dave Huntley, *Pr*
David Huntley, *
◆ EMP: 46 EST: 1971
SQ FT: 16,896
SALES (est): 17.95MM Privately Held
Web: www.lansmont.com
SIC: 8734 3829 Testing laboratories; Testing equipment: abrasion, shearing strength, etc.
PA: Battery Ventures, L.P.
1 Marina Park Dr Ste 1100

### (P-19507)
### SEMICONDUCTOR TECHNOLOGIES INC
3901 N 1st St, San Jose (95134-1506)
PHONE.................................408 240-7000
EMP: 360
SIC: 8734 3674 Testing laboratories; Semiconductors and related devices

### (P-19508)
### STERIGENICS US LLC
344 Bonnie Cir, Corona (92878-4374)
PHONE.................................951 340-0700
Skip Davis, *Brnch Mgr*
EMP: 16
SALES (corp-wide): 1.05B Publicly Held
Web: www.sterigenics.com
SIC: 8734 3821 Industrial sterilization service; Sterilizers
HQ: Sterigenics U.S., Llc
2015 Spring Rd Ste 650
Oak Brook IL 60523
630 928-1700

### (P-19509)
### TANDEX TEST LABS INC
15849 Business Center Dr, Irwindale (91706-2053)
PHONE.................................626 962-7166
Brian Peale, *Pr*
Charles T Goolsby, *
EMP: 49 EST: 1980
SQ FT: 15,000
SALES (est): 9.37MM Privately Held
Web: www.tandexlabs.com
SIC: 8734 3674 Testing laboratories; Hybrid integrated circuits

### (P-19510)
### UNITED MFG ASSEMBLY INC
44169 Fremont Blvd, Fremont (94538-6044)
PHONE.................................510 490-4680
Yonwen Chou, *Pr*
May Mah, *
Arlene Chou, *
EMP: 95 EST: 1987
SALES (est): 7.5MM Privately Held
Web: www.umai.com
SIC: 8734 3672 Testing laboratories; Printed circuit boards

### (P-19511)
### X-SCAN IMAGING CORPORATION
107 Bonaventura Dr, San Jose (95134-2106)
PHONE.................................408 432-9888
Chinlee Wang`, *Pr*
Chinlee Wang, *Pr*
EMP: 25 EST: 2006
SALES (est): 2.57MM Privately Held
Web: www.x-scanimaging.com

# PRODUCTS & SERVICES SECTION

## 8742 - Management Consulting Services (P-19532)

SIC: **8734** 3827 3829 X-ray inspection service, industrial; Optical test and inspection equipment; Thermometers and temperature sensors

## 8741 Management Services

**(P-19512)**
**CAELUS CORPORATION**
20472 Crescent Bay Dr Ste 100, Lake Forest (92630-8849)
P.O. Box 51865 (92619-1865)
PHONE..................................949 877-7170
Andre Afshar, *CEO*
**EMP: 25 EST:** 2017
**SALES (est):** 3.08MM **Privately Held**
SIC: **8741** 1389 1522 1542 Construction management; Construction, repair, and dismantling services; Residential construction, nec; Custom builders, non-residential

**(P-19513)**
**D I F GROUP INC**
Also Called: Manufacture
2201 Yates Ave, Commerce (90040-1913)
PHONE..................................323 231-8800
Angie Kim, *CEO*
**EMP: 23 EST:** 2010
**SALES (est):** 1.58MM **Privately Held**
SIC: **8741** 3161 Management services; Clothing and apparel carrying cases

**(P-19514)**
**DELTA ELECTRONICS AMERICAS LTD (DH)**
46101 Fremont Blvd, Fremont (94538-6468)
PHONE..................................510 668-5111
Austin Tseng, *CEO*
Chia-shien Chen, *CFO*
Chung-hsiu Yao, *Sec*
James Tang, *Dir*
Wilson Huang, *Dir*
◆ **EMP:** 100 **EST:** 1985
**SALES (est):** 462.92MM **Privately Held**
Web: www.delta-americas.com
SIC: **8741** 3577 5065 5063 Management services; Computer peripheral equipment, nec; Electronic parts and equipment, nec; Electrical apparatus and equipment
HQ: Delta America Ltd
46101 Fremont Blvd
Fremont CA 94538

**(P-19515)**
**ECH REAL ESTATE DEVELOPERS LLC**
4275 Executive Sq Ste 200, La Jolla (92037-1476)
PHONE..................................619 996-9269
Hector Vides, *Pr*
**EMP: 15 EST:** 2019
**SALES (est):** 706.37K **Privately Held**
SIC: **8741** 1389 1531 1711 Management services; Construction, repair, and dismantling services; Operative builders; Solar energy contractor

**(P-19516)**
**ENTEGRIS INC**
4175 Santa Fe Rd, San Luis Obispo (93401-8159)
PHONE..................................805 541-9299
**EMP:** 88
**SALES (corp-wide):** 3.52B **Publicly Held**
Web: www.entegris.com
SIC: **8741** 3674 Management services; Semiconductors and related devices

PA: Entegris, Inc.
129 Concord Rd
978 436-6500

**(P-19517)**
**GRIMMWAY ENTERPRISES INC**
Grimmway Fresh Processing
14141 Di Giorgio Rd, Arvin (93203-9518)
P.O. Box 81498 (93380-1498)
PHONE..................................661 854-6200
Jeff Meger, *Pr*
**EMP:** 193
**SALES (corp-wide):** 577.4MM **Privately Held**
Web: www.grimmway.com
SIC: **8741** 2099 2037 Management services; Food preparations, nec; Frozen fruits and vegetables
PA: Grimmway Enterprises, Inc.
12064 Buena Vista Blvd
800 301-3101

**(P-19518)**
**STITCH LABS INC**
1455 Market St Ste 600, San Francisco (94103-1332)
PHONE..................................415 323-0630
Brandon Levey, *CEO*
Jill Richards, *CMO*
**EMP:** 22 **EST:** 2011
**SALES (est):** 1.71MM **Privately Held**
Web: www.stitchlabs.com
SIC: **8741** 7372 Business management; Application computer software

## 8742 Management Consulting Services

**(P-19519)**
**ALAN B WHITSON COMPANY INC**
1507 W Alton Ave, Santa Ana (92704-7219)
P.O. Box 9229 (92728-9229)
PHONE..................................949 955-1200
Alan B Whitson, *Pr*
**EMP:** 750 **EST:** 1990
**SQ FT:** 18,000
**SALES (est):** 691.66K **Privately Held**
SIC: **8742** 1389 5411 Corporation organizing consultant; Servicing oil and gas wells; Convenience stores, chain

**(P-19520)**
**ANTHOS GROUP INC**
705 N Douglas St, El Segundo (90245-2830)
PHONE..................................888 778-2986
Shan Umer, *Pr*
**EMP:** 25 **EST:** 2019
**SALES (est):** 2.05MM **Privately Held**
Web: www.tidl.com
SIC: **8742** 5047 2834 6111 Manufacturing management consultant; Medical equipment and supplies; Pharmaceutical preparations; Export/Import Bank

**(P-19521)**
**AUNT RUBYS LLC**
1014 E Carson St, Long Beach (90807-3636)
PHONE..................................562 326-6783
Todd Dotson, *Prin*
**EMP:** 50 **EST:** 2017
**SALES (est):** 439.41K **Privately Held**
SIC: **8742** 7381 2771 8322 Corporation organizing consultant; Security guard service; Greeting cards; Adult day care center

**(P-19522)**
**BLUE SKY ELEARN LLC**
Also Called: Bluesky Broadcast
5405 Morehouse Dr Ste 340, San Diego (92121-4725)
PHONE..................................877 925-8375
Philip Forte, *CEO*
**EMP:** 20 **EST:** 2002
**SALES (est):** 7.36MM **Privately Held**
Web: www.blueskyelearn.com
SIC: **8742** 7389 7372 8299 Business planning and organizing services; Teleconferencing services; Educational computer software; Educational services

**(P-19523)**
**CENTRIC SOFTWARE INC (PA)**
Also Called: Centric
655 Campbell Technology Pkwy Ste 200, Campbell (95008-5062)
P.O. Box 111330 (95011)
PHONE..................................408 574-7802
Chris Groves, *Pr*
Ron Watson, *
Alice Gerbel, *
Fabrice Canonge, *
James Horne, *
**EMP:** 42 **EST:** 1989
**SQ FT:** 10,000
**SALES (est):** 23.06MM **Privately Held**
Web: www.centricsoftware.com
SIC: **8742** 7372 Management consulting services; Prepackaged software

**(P-19524)**
**CONCRETE WEST CONSTRUCTION INC**
1235 N Tustin Ave, Anaheim (92807-1603)
PHONE..................................949 448-9940
Amber Zamora, *Pr*
**EMP:** 18 **EST:** 2017
**SALES (est):** 2.38MM **Privately Held**
Web: www.concretewest.com
SIC: **8742** 1389 1542 5051 Construction project management consultant; Construction, repair, and dismantling services; Nonresidential construction, nec; Forms, concrete construction (steel)

**(P-19525)**
**CROWNE COLD STORAGE LLC**
786 Road 188, Delano (93215-9508)
PHONE..................................661 725-6458
Cliff Woolley, *Managing Member*
**EMP:** 50 **EST:** 2014
**SALES (est):** 2.33MM **Privately Held**
SIC: **8742** 2033 Business management consultant; Apple sauce: packaged in cans, jars, etc.

**(P-19526)**
**DAIKIN COMFORT TECH DIST INC**
2601 Teepee Dr, Stockton (95205-2421)
PHONE..................................209 946-9244
Don Carlson, *Mgr*
**EMP:** 299
Web: www.goodmanmfg.com
SIC: **8742** 5722 5075 3585 Industry specialist consultants; Air conditioning room units, self-contained; Air conditioning equipment, except room units, nec; Air conditioning equipment, complete
HQ: Daikin Comfort Technologies Distribution, Inc.
19001 Kermier Rd
Waller TX 77484
713 861-2500

**(P-19527)**
**DIVERSIFIED WATERSCAPES INC**
27324 Camino Capistrano Ste 213, Laguna Niguel (92677-1118)
PHONE..................................949 582-5414
Patrick Simmsgeiger, *Pr*
Maria Angel, *CFO*
**EMP:** 15 **EST:** 1988
**SQ FT:** 2,000
**SALES (est):** 2.35MM **Privately Held**
Web: www.dwiwater.com
SIC: **8742** 2842 Maintenance management consultant; Cleaning or polishing preparations, nec

**(P-19528)**
**EQUILIBRIUM MANAGEMENT LLC**
2443 Fillmore St Ste 345, San Francisco (94115-1814)
PHONE..................................415 516-2930
Gabriel Hulls, *Managing Member*
**EMP:** 25 **EST:** 2017
**SALES (est):** 513.44K **Privately Held**
SIC: **8742** 7372 Business planning and organizing services; Application computer software

**(P-19529)**
**HATCHBEAUTY AGENCY LLC (PA)**
355 S Grand Ave Ste 1450, Los Angeles (90071-3152)
PHONE..................................310 396-7070
Tracy Holland, *Managing Member*
◆ **EMP:** 30 **EST:** 2008
**SALES (est):** 9.89MM **Privately Held**
SIC: **8742** 2844 5122 Marketing consulting services; Perfumes, cosmetics and other toilet preparations; Cosmetics, perfumes, and hair products

**(P-19530)**
**INFORMATION FORECAST INC**
Also Called: Infocast
22144 Clarendon St Ste 280, Woodland Hills (91367-6321)
PHONE..................................818 888-4445
William A Meyer, *Pr*
Bill Meyer, *
Carin Ralph, *
**EMP:** 30 **EST:** 1986
**SALES (est):** 4.9MM **Privately Held**
Web: www.infocastinc.com
SIC: **8742** 2721 Public utilities consultant; Magazines: publishing only, not printed on site

**(P-19531)**
**INTERMOTIVE INC**
12840 Earhart Ave, Auburn (95602-9003)
PHONE..................................530 823-1048
Greg Schafer, *Pr*
Greg Schafer, *Pr*
Marc Ellison, *
**EMP:** 25 **EST:** 1996
**SQ FT:** 11,000
**SALES (est):** 12.03MM **Privately Held**
Web: www.intermotive.net
SIC: **8742** 3559 5531 8748 Training and development consultant; Automotive related machinery; Automotive accessories; Systems analysis or design

**(P-19532)**
**IRON HORSE VENTURES LLC**
Also Called: Iron Horse Interactive
6111 Bollinger Canyon Rd Ste 555, San Ramon (94583-5186)

## 8742 - Management Consulting Services (P-19533)

PHONE.................925 415-6141
Uzair Dada, *CEO*
**EMP:** 30 **EST:** 2001
**SALES (est):** 4.88MM **Privately Held**
**Web:** www.ironhorse.io
**SIC: 8742** 7372 Marketing consulting services; Business oriented computer software

### (P-19533)
### LTA RESEARCH & EXPLORATION LLC (PA)
642 N Pastoria Ave, Sunnyvale (94085-3521)
P.O. Box 2048 (94042-2048)
PHONE.................408 396-0577
Alan Weston, *CEO*
**EMP:** 77 **EST:** 2014
**SALES (est):** 45.41MM
**SALES (corp-wide):** 45.41MM **Privately Held**
**Web:** www.ltaresearch.com
**SIC: 8742** 3721 New products and services consultants; Research and development on aircraft by the manufacturer

### (P-19534)
### NAN MCKAY AND ASSOCIATES INC
1810 Gillespie Way Ste 202, El Cajon (92020-0920)
PHONE.................619 258-1855
Nan Mckay, *Pr*
James Mckay, *VP*
John Mckay, *CEO*
Raymond Adair, *
Dorian Jenkins, *
**EMP:** 58 **EST:** 1980
**SQ FT:** 14,000
**SALES (est):** 18.73MM **Privately Held**
**Web:** www.nanmckay.com
**SIC: 8742** 7371 2731 Training and development consultant; Computer software development; Textbooks: publishing and printing

### (P-19535)
### NATIONAL TOUR INTGRTED RSRCES
23141 Arroyo Vis Ste 100, Rcho Sta Marg (92688-2613)
PHONE.................949 215-6330
Johnny R Capels, *Pr*
**EMP:** 23 **EST:** 2009
**SQ FT:** 6,000
**SALES (est):** 2.24MM **Privately Held**
**Web:** www.nationaltourintegrated.com
**SIC: 8742** 3448 Marketing consulting services; Prefabricated metal buildings and components

### (P-19536)
### NISSAN NORTH AMERICA INC
18501 S Figueroa St, Gardena (90248-4504)
P.O. Box 2814 (90509-2814)
PHONE.................310 768-3700
Minoru Nakamura, *Pr*
**EMP:** 10350 **EST:** 1990
**SALES (est):** 5.12MM **Privately Held**
**SIC: 8742** 3711 5012 6159 Management consulting services; Motor vehicles and car bodies; Automobiles and other motor vehicles; Equipment and vehicle finance leasing companies
**PA:** Nissan Motor Co., Ltd.
    1-1-1, Takashima, Nishi-Ku

### (P-19537)
### RUBIK BUILT LLC
1004 Reno Ave, Modesto (95351-1127)
PHONE.................209 408-0626
Nicholas Whetstone, *Prin*
Tommy Phelen, *Prin*
Wayne Henry, *Prin*
**EMP:** 15 **EST:** 2018
**SALES (est):** 854.55K **Privately Held**
**Web:** www.rubikbuilt.com
**SIC: 8742** 2499 Management consulting services; Applicators, wood

### (P-19538)
### STONE CANYON INDS HOLDINGS LLC (PA)
1875 Century Park E Ste 320, Los Angeles (90067-2539)
PHONE.................424 316-2061
James Fordyce, *CEO*
Michael C Salvator, *COO*
Michael Neumann, *Pr*
**EMP:** 48 **EST:** 2018
**SALES (est):** 3.82B
**SALES (corp-wide):** 3.82B **Privately Held**
**Web:** www.scihinc.com
**SIC: 8742** 2899 Industrial consultant; Heat treating salts

### (P-19539)
### STRATEGIC CAPITAL INCORPORATED
Also Called: Pezzi King Vineyards
3225 W Dry Creek Rd, Healdsburg (95448-9724)
PHONE.................707 473-4310
James P Rowe Senior, *CEO*
Tom Rowe, *Pr*
**EMP:** 30 **EST:** 1982
**SQ FT:** 6,000
**SALES (est):** 3.72MM
**SALES (corp-wide):** 4.36MM **Privately Held**
**Web:** www.pezziking.com
**SIC: 8742** 6282 0172 2084 Marketing consulting services; Investment advisory service; Grapes; Wine cellars, bonded: engaged in blending wines
**PA:** Wilson Winery
    1960 Dry Creek Rd
    707 433-4355

### (P-19540)
### T G T ENTERPRISES INC
Also Called: Anderson
12650 Danielson Ct, Poway (92064-6822)
PHONE.................858 413-0300
Randy Dale, *CEO*
Scott Hopkins, *Ex VP*
Todd Stoker, *COO*
**EMP:** 145 **EST:** 1976
**SQ FT:** 77,000
**SALES (est):** 21.68MM **Privately Held**
**Web:** www.andersondd.com
**SIC: 8742** 2759 7311 Marketing consulting services; Commercial printing, nec; Advertising agencies

### (P-19541)
### TACNA INTERNATIONAL CORP
Also Called: Thermalflex
9255 Customhouse Plz Ste G, San Diego (92154-7636)
PHONE.................619 661-1261
Ross Baldwin, *CEO*
▲ **EMP:** 19 **EST:** 1984
**SQ FT:** 18,000
**SALES (est):** 7MM **Privately Held**
**Web:** www.tacna.net

### (P-19542)
### TECHNICAL MICRO CONS INC (PA)
Also Called: Technology Management Concepts
807 N Park View Dr Ste 150, El Segundo (90245-4932)
PHONE.................310 559-3982
Jennifer Harris, *Pr*
**EMP:** 25 **EST:** 1985
**SQ FT:** 3,000
**SALES (est):** 4.76MM
**SALES (corp-wide):** 4.76MM **Privately Held**
**Web:** www.abouttmc.com
**SIC: 8742** 7372 5734 Management information systems consultant; Prepackaged software; Software, business and non-game

### (P-19543)
### TELESTAR INTERNATIONAL CORP
Also Called: Telestar Material
5536 Balboa Blvd, Encino (91316-1505)
PHONE.................818 582-3018
Frank Liu, *Pr*
Charlie Fu, *
Karen Liu, *
**EMP:** 46 **EST:** 1976
**SALES (est):** 2.25MM **Privately Held**
**SIC: 8742** 3861 3663 Marketing consulting services; Photographic equipment and supplies; Antennas, transmitting and communications

### (P-19544)
### TOM PONTON INDUSTRIES INC
Also Called: Ponton Industries
22901 Savi Ranch Pkwy Ste B, Yorba Linda (92887-4615)
PHONE.................714 998-9073
Martin H Ponton, *Pr*
Carl Pino, *VP*
Karen Pettifer, *Sec*
**EMP:** 19 **EST:** 1972
**SALES (est):** 2.62MM **Privately Held**
**Web:** www.pontonind.com
**SIC: 8742** 3823 Industrial consultant; Absorption analyzers: infrared, x-ray, etc.: industrial

### (P-19545)
### TSMC NORTH AMERICA (HQ)
2851 Junction Ave, San Jose (95134-1910)
PHONE.................408 382-8000
Richard B Cassidy Ii, *CEO*
Rick Cassidy, *
Edward Ross, *
**EMP:** 359 **EST:** 1987
**SALES (est):** 56.33MM **Privately Held**
**SIC: 8742** 8711 5065 3674 Marketing consulting services; Consulting engineer; Electronic parts and equipment, nec; Semiconductor circuit networks
**PA:** Taiwan Semiconductor Manufacturing Company Limited
    No. 8, Li-Hsin Rd. 6, Hsinchu Science Park,

### (P-19546)
### WENTE BROS (PA)
Also Called: Wente Vineyards
5050 Arroyo Rd, Livermore (94550-9645)
PHONE.................925 456-2300
Jean Wente, *Ch Bd*
Eric P Wente, *
Carolyn Wente, *
Philip Wente, *
William Joslin, *
◆ **EMP:** 100 **EST:** 1900
**SQ FT:** 168,000
**SALES (est):** 47.28MM
**SALES (corp-wide):** 47.28MM **Privately Held**
**Web:** www.wentevineyards.com
**SIC: 8742** 2084 Restaurant and food services consultants; Wines

## 8743 Public Relations Services

### (P-19547)
### BEHR PROCESS SALES COMPANY
3000 S Main St Apt 84e, Santa Ana (92707-4225)
P.O. Box 1287 (92702-1287)
PHONE.................714 545-7101
Kevin Jaffe, *Pt*
John V Croul, *Pt*
**EMP:** 20 **EST:** 1969
**SQ FT:** 54,000
**SALES (est):** 2.56MM **Privately Held**
**Web:** www.behr.com
**SIC: 8743** 2851 5198 Sales promotion; Varnishes, nec; Paints, varnishes, and supplies

### (P-19548)
### CALIBRE INTERNATIONAL LLC
Also Called: High Caliber Line
6250 N Irwindale Ave, Irwindale (91702-3208)
PHONE.................626 969-4660
Catherine Oas, *
◆ **EMP:** 165 **EST:** 1998
**SQ FT:** 100,000
**SALES (est):** 23.2MM **Privately Held**
**Web:** www.highcaliberline.com
**SIC: 8743** 2759 Promotion service; Promotional printing

### (P-19549)
### COALITION TECHNOLOGIES LLC
445 S Figueroa St Ste 3100, Los Angeles (90071-1635)
PHONE.................310 827-3890
Joel Gross, *CEO*
**EMP:** 183 **EST:** 2009
**SALES (est):** 2.33MM **Privately Held**
**Web:** www.coalitiontechnologies.com
**SIC: 8743** 8243 7372 7371 Public relations services; Software training, computer; Business oriented computer software; Computer software development

### (P-19550)
### LEAGUE OF CALIFORNIA CITIES (PA)
Also Called: WESTERN CITY MAGAZINE
1400 K St Fl 4, Sacramento (95814-3916)
PHONE.................916 658-8200
Carolyn Coleman, *Ex Dir*
Norman Coppinger, *
**EMP:** 65 **EST:** 1932
**SQ FT:** 32,000
**SALES (est):** 434.94K
**SALES (corp-wide):** 434.94K **Privately Held**
**Web:** www.calcities.org
**SIC: 8743** 2721 Lobbyist; Magazines: publishing only, not printed on site

# PRODUCTS & SERVICES SECTION
## 8748 - Business Consulting, Nec (P-19570)

### 8744 Facilities Support Services

**(P-19551)**
**CAMSTON WRATHER LLC**
2856 Whiptail Loop, Carlsbad (92010-6708)
PHONE..............................858 525-9999
Dirk Wray, CEO
Aaron Kamenash, CIO*
Jason Price, *
EMP: 250 EST: 2014
SQ FT: 1,000
SALES (est): 5.85MM **Privately Held**
Web: www.camstonwrather.com
SIC: **8744** 8711 1629 1041 Environmental remediation; Mining engineer; Land reclamation; Placer gold mining

**(P-19552)**
**PONDER ENVIRONMENTAL SVCS INC**
19484 Broken Ct, Shafter (93263-3146)
PHONE..............................661 589-7771
Curtis Fox, Mgr
EMP: 25
SALES (corp-wide): 16.11MM **Privately Held**
Web: www.ponderenvironmentalservices.com
SIC: **8744** 4959 2899 Environmental remediation; Environmental cleanup services; Fuel tank or engine cleaning chemicals
PA: Ponder Environmental Services, Inc.
4563 E 2nd St
707 748-7775

**(P-19553)**
**ULTURA INC**
Also Called: Ultura
3605 Long Beach Blvd Ste 201, Long Beach (90807-4024)
PHONE..............................562 661-4999
EMP: 128
SIC: **8744** 3399 Environmental remediation; Iron ore recovery from open hearth slag

### 8748 Business Consulting, Nec

**(P-19554)**
**ADVANCED CORPORATE SVCS INC**
Also Called: ACS Cloud Partners
200 Pier Ave, Hermosa Beach (90254-3608)
PHONE..............................310 937-6848
Eric A Asquino, Pr
EMP: 20 EST: 2002
SALES (est): 2.14MM **Privately Held**
Web: www.acscp.com
SIC: **8748** 7372 Telecommunications consultant; Application computer software

**(P-19555)**
**BON SUISSE INC**
392 W Walnut Ave, Fullerton (92832-2351)
PHONE..............................714 578-0001
EMP: 30
Web: www.bonsuisse.com
SIC: **8748** 5149 2052 Agricultural consultant; Bakery products; Cones, ice cream
PA: Bon Suisse Inc.
11860 Cmnty Rd Ste 100

**(P-19556)**
**CWES INC**
Also Called: Califrnia Workforce Enrgy Svcs
3045 N Sunnyside Ave Ste 101, Fresno (93727-1300)
PHONE..............................559 346-1251
Michael Williams, Pr
EMP: 32 EST: 2001
SALES (est): 2.54MM **Privately Held**
Web: www.calwes.com
SIC: **8748** 1389 1521 Business consulting, nec; Construction, repair, and dismantling services; New construction, single-family houses

**(P-19557)**
**DAVINA DOUTHARD INC**
Also Called: Polishing The Professional
400 Corporate Pointe Ste 300, Culver City (90230-7620)
PHONE..............................310 540-5120
Davina Douthard, CEO
EMP: 15 EST: 1991
SQ FT: 1,600
SALES (est): 901.54K **Privately Held**
Web: polishingtheprofessional.davinadouthard.com
SIC: **8748** 8743 7361 2721 Business consulting, nec; Public relations services; Employment agencies; Magazines: publishing only, not printed on site

**(P-19558)**
**DOER MARINE OPERATIONS**
Also Called: Deep Ocean Exploration & RES
650 W Tower Ave, Alameda (94501-5047)
PHONE..............................510 530-9388
Liz Taylor, Pr
Sylvia Earle, VP
Josh Moser, CFO
▲ EMP: 20 EST: 1992
SQ FT: 36,000
SALES (est): 1.97MM **Privately Held**
Web: www.doermarine.com
SIC: **8748** 3731 Environmental consultant; Barges, building and repairing

**(P-19559)**
**F R O INC**
1607 Simpson St, Kingsburg (93631-1820)
PHONE..............................559 891-0237
Oscar F Ramos, Pr
EMP: 20 EST: 2000
SQ FT: 1,000
SALES (est): 4.65MM **Privately Held**
Web: www.ofrcorp.com
SIC: **8748** 3315 Agricultural consultant; Steel wire and related products

**(P-19560)**
**HQE SYSTEMS INC**
27348 Via Industria, Temecula (92590-3699)
PHONE..............................800 967-3036
Qais Alkurdi, CEO
Henry Hernandez, *
EMP: 65 EST: 2014
SALES (est): 16.2MM **Privately Held**
Web: www.hqesystems.com
SIC: **8748** 7629 3669 3571 Systems analysis and engineering consulting services; Telecommunication equipment repair (except telephones); Emergency alarms; Electronic computers

**(P-19561)**
**IACCESS TECHNOLOGIES INC (PA)**
1251 E Dyer Rd Ste 160, Santa Ana (92705-5655)
P.O. Box 53545 (92619-3545)
PHONE..............................714 922-9158
Hasan I Ramlaoui, CEO
Max Todorov, Dir Fin
EMP: 48 EST: 2003
SALES (est): 10.77MM
SALES (corp-wide): 10.77MM **Privately Held**
Web: www.iaccesstech.com
SIC: **8748** 3812 3699 3728 Business consulting, nec; Aircraft/aerospace flight instruments and guidance systems; Flight simulators (training aids), electronic; Refueling equipment for use in flight, airplane

**(P-19562)**
**IBASET INC (PA)**
26812 Vista Ter, Lake Forest (92630-8115)
PHONE..............................949 598-5200
Ladeira Poonian, Ch Bd
Naveen Poonian, *
Daniel De Haas, *
EMP: 34 EST: 2015
SQ FT: 28,000
SALES (est): 11.03MM
SALES (corp-wide): 11.03MM **Privately Held**
Web: www.ibaset.com
SIC: **8748** 7371 7372 Business consulting, nec; Custom computer programming services; Application computer software

**(P-19563)**
**INTEGRATED BLDG SOLUTIONS INC**
Also Called: Ibs
2000 Crow Canyon Pl Ste 440, San Ramon (94583-1383)
P.O. Box 2698 (94583-7698)
PHONE..............................925 244-1900
Eugene Gutkin, Pr
EMP: 15 EST: 1998
SALES (est): 2.41MM **Privately Held**
Web: www.ibismsi.com
SIC: **8748** 3822 1731 Energy conservation consultant; Building services monitoring controls, automatic; Energy management controls

**(P-19564)**
**KLH CONSULTING INCORPORATED**
2324 Bethards Dr, Santa Rosa (95405-8537)
PHONE..............................707 575-9986
Soni Lampert, CEO
Hub Lampert, *
EMP: 55 EST: 1978
SALES (est): 9.51MM **Privately Held**
Web: www.klhconsulting.com
SIC: **8748** 7371 7372 Systems engineering consultant, ex. computer or professional; Custom computer programming services; Business oriented computer software

**(P-19565)**
**LUSIVE DECOR**
Also Called: Luxe Light and Home
3400 Medford St, Los Angeles (90063-2530)
PHONE..............................323 227-9207
Jason Kai Cooper, CEO
EMP: 90 EST: 2006
SALES (est): 9.63MM **Privately Held**
Web: www.lusive.com
SIC: **8748** 3646 Lighting consultant; Ceiling systems, luminous

**(P-19566)**
**NETWORK SLTONS PRVIDER USA INC**
1240 Rosecrans Ave, Manhattan Beach (90266-2555)
PHONE..............................213 985-2173
Phillip Walker, CEO
EMP: 33 EST: 2011
SQ FT: 8,000
SALES (est): 1.89MM **Privately Held**
Web: www.networksolutionsprovider.com
SIC: **8748** 7379 3571 4813 Telecommunications consultant; Online services technology consultants; Computers, digital, analog or hybrid; Internet connectivity services

**(P-19567)**
**NOVATE SOLUTIONS INC (PA)**
Also Called: Novate Industrial Cnstr Svcs
2101 Stone Blvd Ste 210, West Sacramento (95691-4055)
P.O. Box 980936 (95798-0936)
PHONE..............................866 668-2830
Carlos Rogers, CEO
Carlos W Rogers, CEO
Tania Colderbank, COO
Brian Thomas, Pr
EMP: 21 EST: 2001
SQ FT: 3,000
SALES (est): 6.4MM
SALES (corp-wide): 6.4MM **Privately Held**
Web: www.novate.com
SIC: **8748** 8711 3613 8742 Systems engineering consultant, ex. computer or professional; Industrial engineers; Control panels, electric; Automation and robotics consultant

**(P-19568)**
**QUARTERWAVE CORP**
1500 Valley House Dr Ste 100, Rohnert Park (94928-4939)
PHONE..............................707 793-9105
Steven Price, CEO
EMP: 26 EST: 1987
SQ FT: 7,250
SALES (est): 2.61MM **Privately Held**
Web: www.quarterwave.com
SIC: **8748** 3663 3679 Telecommunications consultant; Amplifiers, RF power and IF; Microwave components

**(P-19569)**
**SANYO NORTH AMERICA CORP**
Also Called: Sanyo Fisher Company
2055 Sanyo Ave, San Diego (92154-6234)
PHONE..............................619 661-1134
◆ EMP: 400
SIC: **8748** 3632 Business consulting, nec; Household refrigerators and freezers

**(P-19570)**
**SIERRA MONOLITHICS INC (HQ)**
103 W Torrance Blvd, Redondo Beach (90277-3633)
PHONE..............................310 698-1000
Charles Harper, CEO
Javed Patel, Pr
Trevor Roots, CFO
EMP: 27 EST: 1986
SQ FT: 15,000
SALES (est): 4.63MM
SALES (corp-wide): 868.76MM **Publicly Held**
Web: www.jariettech.com
SIC: **8748** 8731 3812 Communications consulting; Electronic research; Radar systems and equipment

## 8748 - Business Consulting, Nec (P-19571)

PA: Semtech Corporation
200 Flynn Rd
805 498-2111

**(P-19571)**
**SITESERVER INC**
4514 Ish Dr, Simi Valley (93063-7666)
**PHONE**..................................805 579-7831
Mark Mcdonald, *Pr*
**EMP:** 15 **EST:** 2005
**SQ FT:** 4,000
**SALES (est):** 909.05K **Privately Held**
**Web:** www.siteserver.com
**SIC: 8748** 3674  Business consulting, nec; Hybrid integrated circuits

**(P-19572)**
**TRANSSIGHT LLC**
6200 Stoneridge Mall Rd Ste 300, Pleasanton (94588-3705)
**PHONE**..................................510 415-6301
Satinder Bhalla, *CEO*
Arvinder Bhalla, *
Satinder Bhalla, *Pr*
**EMP:** 35 **EST:** 2014
**SALES (est):** 8.36MM **Privately Held**
**Web:** www.transsight.com
**SIC: 8748** 8742 7371 7372  Systems engineering consultant, ex. computer or professional; Business management consultant; Computer software systems analysis and design, custom; Application computer software

**(P-19573)**
**TRICOPP INC (PA)**
Also Called: Cloudpaths
39899 Balentine Dr Ste 265, Newark (94560)
**PHONE**..................................925 520-5807
Subramaniam Koduvayur Ve, *Admn*
Sameer Ranabhor, *CEO*
Padman Ramankutty, *Ch Bd*
Jayashanker Paramasivam, *COO*
Latha Krishnamoorthy, *Dir*
**EMP:** 32 **EST:** 2017
**SALES (est):** 4.73MM
**SALES (corp-wide):** 4.73MM **Privately Held**
**Web:** www.cloudpaths.com
**SIC: 8748** 7372  Business consulting, nec; Application computer software

**(P-19574)**
**TRITON ENTERPRISES LLC**
5638 Wells Ln, San Ramon (94582-3079)
**PHONE**..................................925 230-8395
Lawrence Kodiyanplakkal, *Pt*
**EMP:** 20 **EST:** 2014
**SALES (est):** 429.92K **Privately Held**
**SIC: 8748** 2024  Business consulting, nec; Yogurt desserts, frozen

## 8999 Services, Nec

**(P-19575)**
**PACE LITHOGRAPHERS INC**
Also Called: Pace Marketing Communications
18030 Cortney Ct, City Of Industry (91748-1202)
**PHONE**..................................626 913-2108
Robert Bennitt, *Pr*
Robert Bennitt, *Pr*
Carl Bennitt Junior, *VP Opers*
Carl Bennitt Senior Sales, *Prin*
**EMP:** 35 **EST:** 1970
**SQ FT:** 27,000
**SALES (est):** 2.24MM **Privately Held**
**Web:** www.engagepace.com
**SIC: 8999** 2752  Communication services; Commercial printing, lithographic

## 9199 General Government, Nec

**(P-19576)**
**COUNTY OF ORANGE**
Also Called: Public Fclities Resources Dept
1300 S Grand Ave Ste B, Santa Ana (92705-4407)
**PHONE**..................................714 567-7444
Manny Apodaca, *Brnch Mgr*
**EMP:** 44
**SALES (corp-wide):** 5.63B **Privately Held**
**Web:** www.ocgov.com
**SIC: 9199** 2759  General government administration; Commercial printing, nec
PA: County Of Orange
400 W. Civic Center Dr
714 834-6200

## 9224 Fire Protection

**(P-19577)**
**CITY OF WOODLAND**
Also Called: Woodland Fire Department
1000 Lincoln Ave, Woodland (95695-4100)
**PHONE**..................................530 661-5860
Dan Belline, *Chief*
**EMP:** 30
**Web:** www.cityofwoodland.gov
**SIC: 9224** 3999  Fire department, not including volunteer; Badges, metal: policemen, firemen, etc.
PA: City Of Woodland
300 1st St
530 661-5830

# ALPHABETIC SECTION

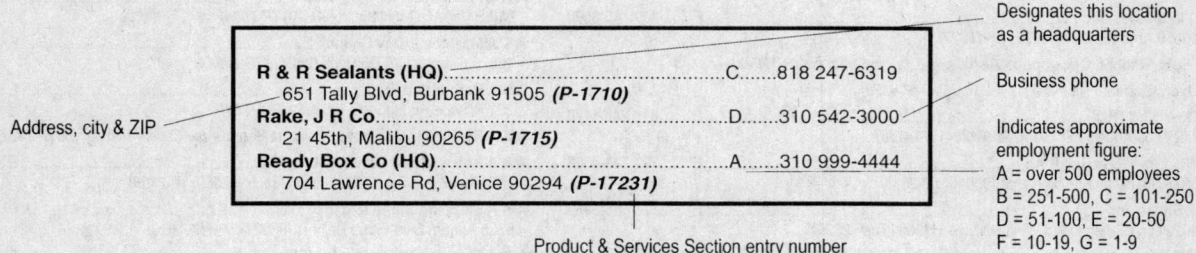

Address, city & ZIP → **R & R Sealants (HQ)** .................................................. C ...... 818 247-6319
651 Tally Blvd, Burbank 91505 *(P-1710)*
**Rake, J R Co** .................................................................. D ...... 310 542-3000
21 45th, Malibu 90265 *(P-1715)*
**Ready Box Co (HQ)** ......................................................... A ...... 310 999-4444
704 Lawrence Rd, Venice 90294 *(P-17231)*

Designates this location as a headquarters
Business phone
Indicates approximate employment figure:
A = over 500 employees
B = 251-500, C = 101-250
D = 51-100, E = 20-50
F = 10-19, G = 1-9

Product & Services Section entry number where full company information appears

*See footnotes for symbols and codes identification.*
- Companies listed alphabetically.
- Complete physical or mailing address.

---

**"the Jacket Club ", Los Angeles** *Also Called: 26 International Inc (P-17490)*
**(415 Location), San Francisco** *Also Called: Leemah Electronics Inc (P-16343)*
**(A Development Stage Company), Irvine** *Also Called: Voice Assist Inc (P-13119)*
**(A Development Stage Enterprise), Mountain View** *Also Called: Map Pharmaceuticals Inc (P-5542)*
**(An Exploration Stage Company), San Francisco** *Also Called: Colombia Energy Resources Inc (P-116)*
**(Former: Advanced Printed Circuit Technology), Santa Clara** *Also Called: Apct Inc (P-12055)*
**10 Day Parts Inc** ............................................................... E ...... 951 279-4810
20109 Paseo Del Prado Walnut (91789) *(P-6689)*
**10-8 Retrofit Inc** ............................................................... F ...... 909 986-5551
415 W Main St Ontario (91762) *(P-19158)*
**13 Stars** ........................................................................... F ...... 805 466-4086
5860 El Camino Real Ste G Atascadero (93422) *(P-4059)*
**1370 Realty Corp** ............................................................. F ...... 818 817-0092
14545 Friar St Van Nuys (91411) *(P-17740)*
**174 Power Global, Irvine** *Also Called: Hanwha Enrgy USA Holdings Corp (P-12460)*
**180 Snacks Inc** ................................................................. E ...... 714 238-1192
1173 N Armando St Anaheim (92806) *(P-1297)*
**1919 Investment Counsel LLC** ......................................... F ...... 415 500-6707
49 Stevenson St Ste 1075 San Francisco (94105) *(P-7090)*
**1le California Inc** .............................................................. E ...... 209 846-7541
3224 Mchenry Ave Ste F Modesto (95350) *(P-11512)*
**1on1 LLC** ......................................................................... E ...... 310 998-7473
8730 Wilshire Blvd Ste 350 Beverly Hills (90211) *(P-18003)*
**1perfectchoice** ................................................................. F ...... 909 594-8855
21908 Valley Blvd Walnut (91789) *(P-3731)*
**1st Century Builders Inc** .................................................. F ...... 818 254-7183
5737 Kanan Rd Agoura Hills (91301) *(P-342)*
**2.95 Guys, Poway** *Also Called: Smoothreads Inc (P-3018)*
**2100 Freedom Inc (HQ)** ................................................... D ...... 714 796-7000
625 N Grand Ave Santa Ana (92701) *(P-4060)*
**2253 Apparel LLC (PA)** .................................................... D ...... 323 837-9800
1708 Aeros Way Montebello (90640) *(P-17085)*
**24/7 Studio Equipment Inc** ............................................... F ...... 818 840-8247
3111 N Kenwood St Burbank (91505) *(P-11796)*
**26 International Inc (PA)** .................................................. F ...... 213 745-4224
1500 Griffith Ave Los Angeles (90021) *(P-17490)*
**2nd Gen Productions Inc** ................................................. F ...... 800 877-6282
400 El Sobrante Rd Corona (92879) *(P-5885)*
**2nd Source Wire & Cable, Walnut** *Also Called: 2nd Source Wire & Cable Inc (P-7602)*
**2nd Source Wire & Cable Inc** .......................................... D ...... 714 482-2866
20445 E Walnut Dr N Walnut (91789) *(P-7602)*
**3 Badge Beverage Corporation** ...................................... F ...... 707 343-1167
32 Patten St Sonoma (95476) *(P-1469)*
**3 Badge Enology, Sonoma** *Also Called: 3 Badge Beverage Corporation (P-1469)*
**3 D CAM, Chatsworth** *Also Called: 3d Cam Inc (P-6690)*
**3-D Precision Machine Inc** .............................................. E ...... 951 296-5449
42132 Remington Ave Temecula (92590) *(P-10639)*

**3-V Fastener Co Inc** ......................................................... D ...... 949 888-7700
630 E Lambert Rd Brea (92821) *(P-8740)*
**360s2g, San Francisco** *Also Called: Etech-360 Inc (P-18291)*
**365 Printing Inc** ................................................................ F ...... 714 752-6990
8475 Artesia Blvd Buena Park (90621) *(P-4498)*
**3becom, Altadena** *Also Called: 3becom Inc (P-18004)*
**3becom Inc (PA)** .............................................................. F ...... 818 726-0007
2400 Lincoln Ave Ste 216 Altadena (91001) *(P-18004)*
**3d Cam Inc** ...................................................................... E ...... 818 773-8777
9801 Variel Ave Chatsworth (91311) *(P-6690)*
**3d Instruments LLC** ........................................................ D ...... 714 399-9200
4990 E Hunter Ave Anaheim (92807) *(P-14380)*
**3d Machine Co Inc** .......................................................... E ...... 714 777-8985
4790 E Wesley Dr Anaheim (92807) *(P-10640)*
**3d Robotics Inc (PA)** ....................................................... D ...... 415 599-1404
1165 Miller Ave Berkeley (94708) *(P-13206)*
**3d/International Inc** ......................................................... C ...... 661 250-2020
20724 Centre Pointe Pkwy Unit 1 Santa Clarita (91350) *(P-5886)*
**3dcam International Corp** ................................................ F ...... 818 773-8777
9801 Variel Ave Chatsworth (91311) *(P-10641)*
**3dconnexion Inc** .............................................................. D ...... 510 713-6000
6505 Kaiser Dr Fremont (94555) *(P-10313)*
**3g Rebar Inc** .................................................................... F ...... 661 588-0294
6400 Price Way Bakersfield (93308) *(P-8690)*
**3h Communication Systems Inc** ..................................... E ...... 949 529-1583
3 Winterbranch Irvine (92604) *(P-16313)*
**3i Infotech Inc** .................................................................. E ...... 805 544-8327
555 Chorro St Ste B San Luis Obispo (93405) *(P-17871)*
**3I INFOTECH INC, San Luis Obispo** *Also Called: 3i Infotech Inc (P-17871)*
**3M, Monrovia** *Also Called: 3M Company (P-6479)*
**3M, Corona** *Also Called: 3M Company (P-7563)*
**3M Company** ................................................................... E ...... 626 358-0136
1601 S Shamrock Ave Monrovia (91016) *(P-6479)*
**3M Company** ................................................................... E ...... 951 737-3441
18750 Minnesota Rd Corona (92881) *(P-7563)*
**3M Company** ................................................................... B ...... 949 863-1360
2111 Mcgaw Ave Irvine (92614) *(P-15434)*
**3M Technical Ceramics Inc (HQ)** .................................... D ...... 949 862-9600
1922 Barranca Pkwy Irvine (92606) *(P-7584)*
**3M Technical Ceramics Inc** ............................................ E ...... 949 756-0642
17466 Daimler St Irvine (92614) *(P-7585)*
**3M Unitek, Monrovia** *Also Called: 3M Unitek Corporation (P-15435)*
**3M Unitek Corporation** ................................................... B ...... 626 445-7960
2724 Peck Rd Monrovia (91016) *(P-15435)*
**3m/Pharmaceuticals, Northridge** *Also Called: Kindeva Drug Delivery LP (P-5526)*
**3par Inc (HQ)** ................................................................... C ...... 510 445-1046
4209 Technology Dr Fremont (94538) *(P-10125)*
**3s Sign Services Inc** ....................................................... E ...... 714 683-1120
1320 N Red Gum St Anaheim (92806) *(P-15934)*

## ALPHABETIC SECTION

**3y Power Technology Inc** ............................................................. F ...... 949 450-0152
80 Bunsen Irvine (92618) *(P-12904)*

**4 D Industries Inc** ....................................................................... F ...... 209 745-0500
10550 Arno Rd Galt (95632) *(P-16077)*

**4 Flight, Rancho Cucamonga** Also Called: Safran Cabin Inc *(P-13943)*

**4 Over, Glendale** Also Called: 4 Over LLC *(P-4830)*

**4 Over LLC (HQ)** ........................................................................ E ...... 818 246-1170
1225 Los Angeles St Glendale (91204) *(P-4830)*

**4 What Its Worth Inc (PA)** ........................................................ E ...... 323 728-4503
5815 Smithway St Commerce (90040) *(P-2605)*

**402 Shoes Inc** ............................................................................ E ...... 323 655-5437
402 N La Cienega Blvd West Hollywood (90048) *(P-2826)*

**405 Cabinets & Stone, Fountain Valley** Also Called: Home Plus Group Inc *(P-3242)*

**418 Media, Los Angeles** Also Called: 418 Media LLC *(P-4357)*

**418 Media LLC** .......................................................................... E ...... 614 350-3960
1875 Century Park E Ste 370 Los Angeles (90067) *(P-4357)*

**42crunch Inc** ............................................................................. F ...... 949 316-1173
95 3rd St 2nd Fl San Francisco (94103) *(P-18005)*

**42q** .............................................................................................. E ...... 408 964-3222
60 E Plumeria Dr San Jose (95134) *(P-18006)*

**4505 Meats Inc** .......................................................................... E ...... 415 255-3094
548 Market St San Francisco (94104) *(P-2083)*

**478826 Limited** ......................................................................... E ...... 916 933-5280
5050 Hillsdale Cir El Dorado Hills (95762) *(P-10642)*

**4d Inc** .......................................................................................... C ...... 408 557-4600
95 S Market St Ste 240 San Jose (95113) *(P-17872)*

**4d Sight Inc** ............................................................................... E ...... 415 425-1321
2150 Shattuck Ave Berkeley (94704) *(P-18007)*

**4excelsior, Anaheim** Also Called: Excelsior Nutrition Inc *(P-5241)*

**4inkjets, Signal Hill** Also Called: Ld Products Inc *(P-3785)*

**4I Technologies Inc** .................................................................. A ...... 817 538-0974
325 Weakley St Calexico (92231) *(P-9761)*

**5 Palms LLC** ............................................................................. C ...... 650 457-0539
800 S B St Fl 1 San Mateo (94401) *(P-19065)*

**5 Star Service Inc** .................................................................... E ...... 323 647-7777
18723 Via Princessa Santa Clarita (91387) *(P-19173)*

**5.11 Tactical Series, Costa Mesa** Also Called: 511 Inc *(P-17506)*

**511 Inc (DH)** .............................................................................. E ...... 866 451-1726
3150 Bristol St Ste 300 Costa Mesa (92626) *(P-17506)*

**5e Boron Americas LLC** ......................................................... E ...... 442 292-2120
27555 Hector Rd Newberry Springs (92365) *(P-333)*

**5th Axis Inc (PA)** ...................................................................... C ...... 858 505-0432
7140 Engineer Rd San Diego (92111) *(P-10643)*

**6th Street Partners LLC** ......................................................... F ...... 213 377-5277
3950 W 6th St 201 Los Angeles (90020) *(P-3732)*

**7 Up, Stockton** Also Called: Varni Brothers Corporation *(P-1971)*

**7 Up / R C Bottling Co, Vernon** Also Called: American Bottling Company *(P-1859)*

**71yrs Inc (PA)** ........................................................................... D ...... 310 639-0390
6525 Flotilla St Commerce (90040) *(P-11982)*

**75s Corp** .................................................................................... E ...... 323 234-7708
800 E 62nd St Los Angeles (90001) *(P-16955)*

**7eye By Panoptx, Ontario** Also Called: Solvari Corp *(P-17685)*

**7x7, San Francisco** Also Called: Hartle Media Ventures LLC *(P-4262)*

**80Iv LLC** .................................................................................... E ...... 818 435-6613
15260 Ventura Blvd Ste 2230 Sherman Oaks (91403) *(P-4308)*

**860, Shameless, Hot Wire, Los Angeles** Also Called: JT Design Studio Inc *(P-2777)*

**88 Special Sweet Inc** .............................................................. D ...... 909 525-7055
10488 Hickson St El Monte (91731) *(P-4026)*

**89908 Inc** ................................................................................... E ...... 949 221-0003
15651 Mosher Ave Tustin (92780) *(P-13436)*

**89bio, San Francisco** Also Called: 89bio Inc *(P-5284)*

**89bio Inc** .................................................................................... D ...... 415 432-9270
655 Montgomery St Ste 1500 San Francisco (94111) *(P-5284)*

**8X8, Campbell** Also Called: 8x8 Inc *(P-16315)*

**8x8 Inc (PA)** .............................................................................. B ...... 408 727-1885
675 Creekside Way Campbell (95008) *(P-16315)*

**911 Restoration of San Diego, San Diego** Also Called: Demor Enterprises Inc *(P-561)*

**99 Ranch Market, Buena Park** Also Called: Tawa Supermarket Inc *(P-1049)*

**A & A Aerospace Inc** ............................................................... F ...... 562 901-6803
1987 W 16th St Long Beach (90813) *(P-13729)*

**A & A Electronic Assembly, San Fernando** Also Called: Signature Tech Group Inc *(P-13084)*

**A & A Fabrication & Polsg Corp** ........................................... F ...... 562 696-0441
610 S Vail Ave Montebello (90640) *(P-8084)*

**A & A Machine & Dev Co Inc** .................................................. F ...... 310 532-7706
16625 Gramercy Pl Gardena (90247) *(P-10644)*

**A & A Portables Inc** ................................................................. E ...... 209 524-0401
201 Roscoe Rd Modesto (95357) *(P-17854)*

**A & A Ready Mix Concrete, Newport Beach** Also Called: Lebata Inc *(P-7462)*

**A & A Ready Mixed Concrete Inc (PA)** ................................ E ...... 949 253-2800
4621 Teller Ave Ste 130 Newport Beach (92660) *(P-7399)*

**A & A Stepping Stone Mfg Inc** ............................................... F ...... 916 723-1717
6325 Auburn Blvd Citrus Heights (95621) *(P-16078)*

**A & A Stepping Stone Mfg Inc (PA)** ..................................... E ...... 530 885-7481
10291 Ophir Rd Newcastle (95658) *(P-17319)*

**A & B Aerospace Inc** .............................................................. E ...... 626 334-2976
612 S Ayon Ave Azusa (91702) *(P-10645)*

**A & B Die Casting Company Inc** ........................................... F ...... 877 708-0009
900 Alfred Nobel Dr Hercules (94547) *(P-7803)*

**A & B Diecasting, Hercules** Also Called: Benda Tool & Model Works Inc *(P-9607)*

**A & D Foam Products, Anaheim** Also Called: Dretloh Aircraft Supply Inc *(P-13826)*

**A & D Precision, Fremont** Also Called: A & D Precision Machining Inc *(P-10646)*

**A & D Precision Machining Inc** ............................................. E ...... 510 657-6781
4155 Business Center Dr Fremont (94538) *(P-10646)*

**A & D Precision Mfg Inc** ......................................................... E ...... 714 779-2714
4751 E Hunter Ave Anaheim (92807) *(P-10647)*

**A & D Rubber Products Co Inc (PA)** .................................... F ...... 209 941-0100
1438 Bourbon St Stockton (95204) *(P-6436)*

**A & E Anodizing** ....................................................................... F ...... 408 297-5910
652 Charles St Ste A San Jose (95112) *(P-8903)*

**A & J Industries Inc** ................................................................ F ...... 310 216-2170
1430 240th St Harbor City (90710) *(P-3322)*

**A & J Manufacturing, Harbor City** Also Called: A & J Industries Inc *(P-3322)*

**A & J Manufacturing Company** ............................................ E ...... 714 544-9570
70 Icon Foothill Ranch (92610) *(P-8813)*

**A & J Precision Sheetmetal Inc** ............................................ D ...... 408 885-9134
2233 Paragon Dr Ste A San Jose (95131) *(P-8357)*

**A & L Engineering, Hawthorne** Also Called: Acuna Dionisio Able *(P-10670)*

**A & L Ready Mix, Sonora** Also Called: L K Lehman Trucking *(P-7460)*

**A & M Electronics Inc** ............................................................. E ...... 661 257-3680
25018 Avenue Kearny Valencia (91355) *(P-12039)*

**A & M Engineering Inc** ........................................................... D ...... 626 813-2020
15854 Salvatiera St Irwindale (91706) *(P-10648)*

**A & M Printing, West Sacramento** Also Called: Leo Lam Inc *(P-4675)*

**A & R, Carson** Also Called: A & R Engineering Co Inc *(P-10649)*

**A & R Engineering Co Inc** ..................................................... D ...... 310 603-9060
1053 E Bedmar St Carson (90746) *(P-10649)*

**A & S Case Company Inc** ...................................................... E ...... 800 394-6181
5260 Vineland Ave North Hollywood (91601) *(P-3367)*

**A & S Mold and Die Corp** ....................................................... D ...... 818 341-5393
9705 Eton Ave Chatsworth (91311) *(P-6691)*

**A A A Furnace Company, San Jose** Also Called: Rando AAA Hvac Inc *(P-431)*

**A A A Partitions, Los Angeles** Also Called: King Wire Partitions Inc *(P-8702)*

**A A Cater Truck Mfg Co Inc** ................................................... E ...... 323 233-2343
750 E Slauson Ave Los Angeles (90011) *(P-3496)*

**A A Construction, Rialto** Also Called: Arnett Construction Inc *(P-543)*

**A A E Aerospace & Coml Tech, Huntington Beach** Also Called: American Automated Engrg Inc *(P-14108)*

**A A Label Inc (PA)** ................................................................... E ...... 925 803-5709
6958 Sierra Ct Dublin (94568) *(P-4027)*

**A A P, Gardena** Also Called: American Aircraft Products Inc *(P-8372)*

**A and G Inc (HQ)** ..................................................................... A ...... 714 765-0400
11296 Harrel St Jurupa Valley (91752) *(P-2606)*

**A and M Welding Inc** .............................................................. F ...... 310 329-2700
16935 S Broadway Gardena (90248) *(P-8085)*

**A B, Sylmar** Also Called: Advanced Bionics LLC *(P-15317)*

**A B & I, Fowler** Also Called: McWane Inc *(P-7678)*

**A B Boyd Co (PA)** .................................................................... E ...... 888 244-6931
5960 Inglewood Dr Ste 115 Pleasanton (94588) *(P-6480)*

**A B C Plastic Fabrication,, Chatsworth** Also Called: ABC Plastics Inc *(P-6580)*

# ALPHABETIC SECTION — Aa Leasing

A B C Restaurant Equipment Co, South El Monte *Also Called: Master Enterprises Inc* (P-8500)

A B M, Pittsburg *Also Called: Antioch Building Materials Co* (P-16463)

A B P Inc ..................................................................................... F ...... 310 532-9400
   15608 New Century Dr Gardena (90248) (P-17282)

A B S, Huntington Beach *Also Called: Applied Business Software Inc* (P-18055)

A Breast Pump and More, Carlsbad *Also Called: Hygeia II Medical Group Inc* (P-15545)

A C L, Santa Clara *Also Called: Advanced Component Labs Inc* (P-12277)

A C T, Ontario *Also Called: Aerospace and Coml Tooling Inc* (P-10690)

A C T, Fountain Valley *Also Called: Advanced Charging Tech LLC* (P-11358)

A Class Precision Inc ............................................................... F ...... 951 549-9706
   13395 Estelle St Corona (92879) (P-508)

A Commom Thread, Los Angeles *Also Called: Dda Holdings Inc* (P-2752)

A D A C Laboratories (inc) ...................................................... A ...... 408 321-9100
   3860 N 1st St San Jose (95134) (P-14837)

A Development Stage Company, Beverly Hills *Also Called: Stratos Renewables Corporation* (P-6161)

A Division Continental Can Co, Santa Ana *Also Called: Altium Packaging LP* (P-6619)

A E M, Hawthorne *Also Called: Nmsp Inc* (P-13547)

A F C, Rancho Dominguez *Also Called: Advanced Fresh Concepts Corp* (P-17751)

A F E Industries Inc (PA) ......................................................... F ...... 562 944-6889
   13233 Barton Cir Whittier (90605) (P-4831)

A Fab, Lake Forest *Also Called: American Deburring Inc* (P-10709)

A J Fasteners Inc ...................................................................... E ...... 714 630-1556
   2800 E Miraloma Ave Anaheim (92806) (P-8741)

A J Parent Company Inc (PA) ................................................. D ...... 714 521-1100
   6910 Aragon Cir Ste 6 Buena Park (90620) (P-19066)

A K M, San Jose *Also Called: Akm Semiconductor Inc* (P-12284)

A Lighting By Design, La Habra *Also Called: Albd Electric and Cable* (P-449)

A Lot To Say Inc ...................................................................... E ...... 877 366-8448
   1541 S Vineyard Ave Ontario (91761) (P-3021)

A M Cabinets Inc (PA) ............................................................. D ...... 310 532-1919
   239 E Gardena Blvd Gardena (90248) (P-3559)

A M I/Coast Magnetics Inc ...................................................... E ...... 323 936-6188
   5333 W Washington Blvd Los Angeles (90016) (P-12825)

A M T, Camarillo *Also Called: Amt Datasouth Corp* (P-19440)

A Media, El Segundo *Also Called: Sabot Publishing Inc* (P-4296)

A P S, Santa Clarita *Also Called: Applied Polytech Systems Inc* (P-3392)

A P Seedorff & Company Inc ................................................. F ...... 714 252-5330
   1338 N Knollwood Cir Anaheim (92801) (P-11303)

A P V Crepaco, Lake Forest *Also Called: SPX Flow Us LLC* (P-8339)

A Plus Custom Metal Supply Inc ........................................... F ...... 951 736-7900
   1891 1st St Norco (92860) (P-509)

A Plus Custom Shtmtl & Sup, Norco *Also Called: A Plus Custom Metal Supply Inc* (P-509)

A Plus International Inc (PA) ................................................. D ...... 909 591-5168
   5138 Eucalyptus Ave Chino (91710) (P-16570)

A Plus Label Inc ...................................................................... E ...... 714 229-9811
   3215 W Warner Ave Santa Ana (92704) (P-4028)

A Plus Signs LLC .................................................................... E ...... 559 275-0700
   4270 N Brawley Ave Fresno (93722) (P-15935)

A Q Pharmaceuticals Inc ........................................................ E ...... 714 903-1000
   11555 Monarch St Ste C Garden Grove (92841) (P-5285)

A R C O, La Palma *Also Called: Atlantic Richfield Company* (P-17470)

A R O Service, Anaheim *Also Called: Aircraft Repair & Overhaul Svc* (P-16299)

A R P, Ventura *Also Called: Automotive Racing Products Inc* (P-7977)

A R P, Santa Paula *Also Called: Automotive Racing Products Inc* (P-7978)

A R Santex LLC (PA) ............................................................... E ...... 888 622-7098
   6790 Embarcadero Ln Ste 100 Carlsbad (92011) (P-17873)

A Rudin Inc (PA) ...................................................................... D ...... 323 589-5547
   6062 Alcoa Ave Vernon (90058) (P-3464)

A Rudin Designs, Vernon *Also Called: A Rudin Inc* (P-3464)

A S I, Valencia *Also Called: Advanced Semiconductor Inc* (P-12278)

A S I, Valencia *Also Called: Asi Semiconductor Inc* (P-12335)

A S I, San Pablo *Also Called: Analytcal Scientific Instrs Inc* (P-14610)

A S I, Fremont *Also Called: Asi Computer Technologies Inc* (P-16508)

A S I, Carlsbad *Also Called: Applied Spectral Imaging Inc* (P-17881)

A S I American, Corona *Also Called: Spangler Industries Inc* (P-6539)

A S M P, Hayward *Also Called: Associated Screw Machine Pdts* (P-8717)

A S P, Irvine *Also Called: Advanced Sterlization* (P-14951)

A S P, San Francisco *Also Called: Astronomical Soc of The PCF* (P-19372)

A School Apparel, Burlingame *Also Called: School Apparel Inc* (P-2727)

A Shoc Beverage LLC ............................................................ E ...... 949 490-1612
   844 Production Pl Newport Beach (92663) (P-1117)

A Steris Company, Ontario *Also Called: Isomedix Operations Inc* (P-15366)

A T A, Paso Robles *Also Called: Applied Technologies Assoc Inc* (P-14844)

A T Parker Inc (PA) ................................................................. E ...... 818 755-1700
   10866 Chandler Blvd North Hollywood (91601) (P-13207)

A T S, Burbank *Also Called: Accratronics Seals LLC* (P-12907)

A T T, Orange *Also Called: Air Tube Transfer Systems Inc* (P-9479)

A Teichert & Son Inc (HQ) ..................................................... E ...... 916 484-3011
   3500 American River Dr Sacramento (95864) (P-16462)

A Thanks Million Inc .............................................................. F ...... 858 432-7744
   8195 Mercury Ct Ste 140 San Diego (92111) (P-2850)

A Thread Ahead Inc ............................................................... E ...... 818 837-1984
   1925 1st St San Fernando (91340) (P-19067)

A V Poles and Lighting Inc ..................................................... E ...... 661 945-2731
   43827 Division St Lancaster (93535) (P-11513)

A W Chang Corporation (PA) ................................................. E ...... 310 764-2000
   6945 Atlantic Ave Long Beach (90805) (P-17056)

A-1 Alternative Fuel Systems (PA) ........................................ E ...... 559 485-4427
   2320 Stanislaus St Fresno (93721) (P-19166)

A-1 Alternative Fuel Systems, Fresno *Also Called: A-1 Alternative Fuel Systems* (P-19166)

A-1 Enterprises Inc ................................................................ E ...... 714 630-3390
   2831 E La Cresta Ave Anaheim (92806) (P-552)

A-1 Fence, Anaheim *Also Called: A-1 Enterprises Inc* (P-552)

A-1 Grit Co, Riverside *Also Called: Newman Bros California Inc* (P-3164)

A-1 Jays Machining Inc (PA) ................................................. D ...... 408 262-1845
   2228 Oakland Rd San Jose (95131) (P-10653)

A-1 Machine Manufacturing Inc (PA) ................................... E ...... 408 727-0880
   490 Gianni St Santa Clara (95054) (P-10654)

A-1 Metal Products Inc ........................................................... E ...... 323 721-3334
   2707 Supply Ave Commerce (90040) (P-8358)

A-Aztec Rents & Sells Inc (PA) ............................................. C ...... 310 347-3010
   2665 Columbia St Torrance (90503) (P-2965)

A-Info Inc ................................................................................. E ...... 949 346-7326
   60 Tesla Irvine (92618) (P-13730)

A-List, Vernon *Also Called: Just For Wraps Inc* (P-2778)

A-W Engineering Company Inc ............................................ E ...... 562 945-1041
   8528 Dice Rd Santa Fe Springs (90670) (P-8814)

A-Z Industries Div, Los Angeles *Also Called: Aero Shade Co Inc* (P-17530)

A-Z Mfg Inc .............................................................................. E ...... 714 444-4446
   3101 W Segerstrom Ave Santa Ana (92704) (P-10655)

A.C.T., Sacramento *Also Called: Aluminum Coating Tech Inc* (P-8917)

A.G. Ferrari Foods, San Leandro *Also Called: Rof Ferrari Lending 1 LLC* (P-17381)

A.I.M. Services, Los Angeles *Also Called: Aiminsight Solutions Inc* (P-19025)

A.J. Metal Manufacturing, Corona *Also Called: Aqua Performance Inc* (P-16932)

A&A Concrete Supply, Newport Beach *Also Called: A & A Ready Mixed Concrete Inc* (P-7399)

A&A Fulfillment Center, Vernon *Also Called: A&A Global Imports LLC* (P-6692)

A&A Global Imports LLC (PA) .............................................. D ...... 888 315-2453
   1801 E 41st St Vernon (90058) (P-6692)

A&A Jewelry Supply, Los Angeles *Also Called: Adfa Incorporated* (P-9037)

A&A Metal Finishing Entps LLC ........................................... E ...... 916 442-1063
   8290 Alpine Ave Sacramento (95826) (P-8904)

A&G Machine Shop Inc .......................................................... E ...... 831 759-2261
   1352 Burton Ave Ste B Salinas (93901) (P-10650)

A&R Tarpaulins Inc ................................................................. E ...... 909 829-4444
   16246 Valley Blvd Fontana (92335) (P-2964)

A&T Precision, San Jose *Also Called: A&T Precision Machining Inc* (P-10651)

A&T Precision Machining Inc ............................................... F ...... 408 363-1198
   330 Piercy Rd San Jose (95138) (P-10651)

A&W Precision Machining Inc .............................................. F ...... 310 527-7242
   16320 S Main St Gardena (90248) (P-10652)

A10 Networks Inc (PA) ........................................................... B ...... 408 325-8668
   2300 Orchard Pkwy San Jose (95131) (P-19023)

A2, Sunnyvale *Also Called: Westak Inc* (P-12259)

A2z Color Graphics, Van Nuys *Also Called: Investment Enterprises Inc* (P-4900)

Aa Leasing, Los Angeles *Also Called: Vahe Enterprises Inc* (P-13434)

## ALPHABETIC SECTION

**AA Portable Power Corporation** ............................................. E ...... 510 525-2328
825 S 19th St Richmond (94804) *(P-13130)*

**AA Production Services Inc** ................................................ E ...... 530 982-0123
8032 County Road 61 Princeton (95970) *(P-150)*

**AAA Electric Motor Sales & Svc (PA)** ..................................... F ...... 213 749-2367
1346 Venice Blvd Los Angeles (90006) *(P-16638)*

**AAA Flag & Banner, Los Angeles** *Also Called: AAA Flag & Banner Mfg Co Inc (P-17686)*

**AAA Flag & Banner Mfg Co Inc (PA)** ....................................... C ...... 310 836-3200
8937 National Blvd Los Angeles (90034) *(P-17686)*

**AAA Imaging & Supplies Inc** ............................................... E ...... 714 431-0570
2313 S Susan St Santa Ana (92704) *(P-16498)*

**AAA Imaging Solutions, Santa Ana** *Also Called: AAA Imaging & Supplies Inc (P-16498)*

**AAA Pallet, Norco** *Also Called: AAA Pallet Recycling & Mfg Inc (P-3329)*

**AAA Pallet, Mentone** *Also Called: Power Pt Inc (P-9531)*

**AAA Pallet Recycling & Mfg Inc** ........................................... E ...... 951 681-7748
1346 Stirrup Way Norco (92860) *(P-3329)*

**AAA Plating & Inspection Inc** ............................................. D ...... 323 979-8930
424 E Dixon St Compton (90222) *(P-8905)*

**AAA Signs Inc** ............................................................ D ...... 916 568-3456
1644 Auburn Blvd Sacramento (95815) *(P-19150)*

**AAA Underground Inc** ...................................................... F ...... 916 515-9348
3245 Elkhorn Blvd North Highlands (95660) *(P-16352)*

**AAC, Irvine** *Also Called: American Audio Component Inc (P-12912)*

**AADI, Pacific Palisades** *Also Called: Aadi Bioscience Inc (P-5286)*

**Aadi Bioscience Inc (PA)** ................................................. E ...... 424 744-8055
17383 W Sunset Blvd Ste A250 Pacific Palisades (90272) *(P-5286)*

**Aae Systems Inc** .......................................................... F ...... 408 732-1710
445 S San Antonio Rd Ste 104 Los Altos (94022) *(P-18960)*

**Aahs Enterprises Inc** ..................................................... F ...... 323 838-9130
6600 Telegraph Rd Commerce (90040) *(P-15936)*

**Aahs Graphics Signs & Engrv, Commerce** *Also Called: Aahs Enterprises Inc (P-15936)*

**Aak USA Richmond Corp (DH)** ............................................... D ...... 510 233-7660
1145 Harbour Way S Richmond (94804) *(P-1391)*

**Aalba Dent Inc** ........................................................... F ...... 707 864-3334
5045 Fulton Dr Ste B Fairfield (94534) *(P-15436)*

**Aalto Scientific Ltd** ..................................................... E ...... 800 748-6674
1959 Kellogg Ave Carlsbad (92008) *(P-14939)*

**Aamp of America, Chino** *Also Called: Aamp of Florida Inc (P-16565)*

**Aamp of Florida Inc** ...................................................... E ...... 805 338-6800
7166 Bickmore Ave # 2 Chino (91708) *(P-16565)*

**Aap Division, Inglewood** *Also Called: Engineered Magnetics Inc (P-11370)*

**AAR Manufacturing Inc** .................................................... C ...... 714 634-8807
2220 E Cerritos Ave Anaheim (92806) *(P-8295)*

**Aard Industries Inc** ...................................................... E ...... 951 296-0844
42075 Avenida Alvarado Temecula (92590) *(P-9195)*

**Aard Spring & Stamping, Temecula** *Also Called: Aard Industries Inc (P-9195)*

**Aardvark Clay & Supplies Inc (PA)** ........................................ E ...... 714 541-4157
1400 E Pomona St Santa Ana (92705) *(P-15882)*

**Aaren Scientific Inc (DH)** ................................................ E ...... 909 937-1033
9010 Hellman Ave Rancho Cucamonga (91730) *(P-14758)*

**Aarki Inc (PA)** ........................................................... D ...... 408 382-1180
164 Townsend St Unit 3 San Francisco (94107) *(P-18961)*

**Aaron Corporation** ........................................................ C ...... 323 235-5959
2645 Industry Way Lynwood (90262) *(P-2730)*

**Aarrow Sign Spinners** ..................................................... F ...... 510 200-7326
4312 Valeta St San Diego (92107) *(P-15937)*

**Aasc, Stockton** *Also Called: Applied Arospc Structures Corp (P-13780)*

**Aavid California Design Center, San Jose** *Also Called: Aavid Thermalloy LLC (P-12905)*

**Aavid Thermalloy LLC** ..................................................... E ...... 408 522-8730
150 S 1st St Ste 200 San Jose (95113) *(P-12905)*

**Abacus Powder Coating** .................................................... E ...... 626 443-7556
1829 Tyler Ave South El Monte (91733) *(P-9034)*

**Abad Foam Inc** ............................................................ E ...... 714 994-2223
6560 Caballero Blvd Buena Park (90620) *(P-6618)*

**Abalquiga, Los Angeles** *Also Called: La Princesita Tortilleria Inc (P-2257)*

**Abaqus Inc** ............................................................... E ...... 415 496-9436
972 N California Ave Palo Alto (94303) *(P-18008)*

**Abaxis Inc (HQ)** .......................................................... C ...... 510 675-6500
3240 Whipple Rd Union City (94587) *(P-14838)*

**ABB - Los Gatos Research, San Jose** *Also Called: ABB Inc (P-16597)*

**ABB Enterprise Software Inc** .............................................. D ...... 213 743-4819
4600 Colorado Blvd Los Angeles (90039) *(P-12268)*

**ABB ENTERPRISE SOFTWARE INC., Los Angeles** *Also Called: ABB Enterprise Software Inc (P-12268)*

**ABB Inc** .................................................................. E ...... 510 987-7111
1321 Harbor Bay Pkwy Ste 101 Alameda (94502) *(P-11201)*

**ABB Inc** .................................................................. C ...... 408 770-8968
1960 Zanker Rd San Jose (95112) *(P-16597)*

**Abba Roller LLC (DH)** ..................................................... F ...... 909 947-1244
1351 E Philadelphia St Ontario (91761) *(P-6481)*

**Abbey Carpet, National City** *Also Called: Sids Carpet Barn (P-16435)*

**Abbott, Sunnyvale** *Also Called: St Jude Medical LLC (P-15267)*

**Abbott Diabetes Care, Alameda** *Also Called: Abbott Diabetes Care Sls Corp (P-5287)*

**Abbott Diabetes Care Inc (HQ)** ............................................ C ...... 855 632-8658
1360 S Loop Rd Alameda (94502) *(P-5727)*

**Abbott Diabetes Care Sls Corp** ............................................ D ...... 510 749-5400
1360 S Loop Rd Alameda (94502) *(P-5287)*

**Abbott Diagnostics Division, Santa Clara** *Also Called: Abbott Laboratories (P-14941)*

**Abbott Laboratories** ...................................................... E ...... 818 493-2388
15900 Valley View Ct Sylmar (91342) *(P-5288)*

**Abbott Laboratories** ...................................................... A ...... 408 845-3000
3200 Lakeside Dr Santa Clara (95054) *(P-14940)*

**Abbott Laboratories** ...................................................... B ...... 408 330-0057
4551 Great America Pkwy Santa Clara (95054) *(P-14941)*

**Abbott Medical, Santa Clara** *Also Called: Walk Vascular LLC (P-16594)*

**Abbott Nutrition** ......................................................... D ...... 707 399-1100
2302 Courage Dr Fairfield (94533) *(P-5289)*

**Abbott Nutrition Mfg Inc (HQ)** ............................................ C ...... 707 399-1100
2351 N Watney Way Ste C Fairfield (94533) *(P-5290)*

**Abbott Technologies Inc** .................................................. E ...... 818 504-0644
8203 Vineland Ave Sun Valley (91352) *(P-11202)*

**Abbott Vascular, Santa Clara** *Also Called: Abbott Laboratories (P-14940)*

**Abbott Vascular, Murrieta** *Also Called: Abbott Vascular Inc (P-14942)*

**Abbott Vascular Inc** ...................................................... B ...... 951 941-2400
26531 Ynez Rd Temecula (92591) *(P-5291)*

**Abbott Vascular Inc** ...................................................... A ...... 408 845-3186
30590 Cochise Cir Murrieta (92563) *(P-14942)*

**Abbott Vascular Inc** ...................................................... A ...... 951 914-2400
42301 Zevo Dr Ste D Temecula (92590) *(P-14943)*

**Abbott Vascular Inc (HQ)** ................................................. C ...... 408 845-3000
3200 Lakeside Dr Santa Clara (95054) *(P-14944)*

**Abbvie, South San Francisco** *Also Called: Abbvie Stemcentrx LLC (P-19490)*

**Abbvie Stemcentrx LLC** .................................................... D ...... 415 298-9242
1000 Gateway Blvd South San Francisco (94080) *(P-19490)*

**ABC - Clio Inc (HQ)** ...................................................... C ...... 805 968-1911
75 Aero Camino Goleta (93117) *(P-4309)*

**ABC Custom Wood Shutters Inc** ............................................. E ...... 949 595-0300
20561 Pascal Way Lake Forest (92630) *(P-3105)*

**ABC Imaging, Santa Fe Springs** *Also Called: ABC Imaging of Washington (P-4835)*

**ABC Imaging of Washington** ................................................ E ...... 949 419-3728
17240 Red Hill Ave Irvine (92614) *(P-4832)*

**ABC Imaging of Washington** ................................................ E ...... 202 429-8870
2327 Union St Oakland (94607) *(P-4833)*

**ABC Imaging of Washington** ................................................ E ...... 415 525-3874
832 Folsom St San Francisco (94107) *(P-4834)*

**ABC Imaging of Washington** ................................................ E ...... 562 375-7280
13573 Larwin Cir Santa Fe Springs (90670) *(P-4835)*

**ABC Imaging of Washington** ................................................ E ...... 415 869-1669
679 Bryant St San Francisco (94107) *(P-17820)*

**ABC Plastics Inc** ......................................................... F ...... 818 775-0065
9132 De Soto Ave Chatsworth (91311) *(P-6580)*

**ABC Printing, Milpitas** *Also Called: ABC Printing Inc (P-4499)*

**ABC Printing Inc** ......................................................... F ...... 408 263-1118
1090 S Milpitas Blvd Milpitas (95035) *(P-4499)*

**ABC School Equipment Inc** ................................................. D ...... 951 817-2200
1451 E 6th St Corona (92879) *(P-16598)*

**ABC Sheet Metal, Anaheim** *Also Called: Steeldyne Industries (P-8582)*

**ABC Sun Control LLC** ...................................................... F ...... 818 982-6989
7241 Ethel Ave North Hollywood (91605) *(P-2966)*

**ABC-Clio, Goleta** *Also Called: ABC - Clio Inc (P-4309)*

# ALPHABETIC SECTION

**Abco Laboratories Inc (PA)** .................................................. D ...... 707 432-2200
2450 S Watney Way Fairfield (94533) *(P-5292)*

**Abel Automatics LLC** ........................................................... E ...... 805 388-3721
165 N Aviador St Camarillo (93010) *(P-8713)*

**Abel Reels, Camarillo** *Also Called: Abel Automatics LLC (P-8713)*

**Abelisk Inc (PA)** ................................................................... F ...... 559 227-1000
7060 N Fresno St Ste 210 Fresno (93720) *(P-17874)*

**Aben, Chatsworth** *Also Called: Aben Machine Products Inc (P-10656)*

**Aben Machine Products Inc** ................................................. F ...... 818 960-4502
9550 Owensmouth Ave Chatsworth (91311) *(P-10656)*

**Aberdeen, Santa Fe Springs** *Also Called: Source Code LLC (P-10205)*

**Abex Display Systems Inc (PA)** .......................................... C ...... 800 537-0231
355 Parkside Dr San Fernando (91340) *(P-3817)*

**Abex Exhibit Systems, San Fernando** *Also Called: Abex Display Systems Inc (P-3817)*

**Abgb Designs Inc** ................................................................. F
6351 Regent St Ste 226 Huntington Park (90255) *(P-2652)*

**Ability, Carson** *Also Called: American Fruits & Flavors LLC (P-1982)*

**Abl Space Systems Company** ............................................. D ...... 424 321-6060
224 Oregon St El Segundo (90245) *(P-14076)*

**Ablacon Inc** ........................................................................... F ...... 303 955-5620
3350 Scott Blvd Santa Clara (95054) *(P-14945)*

**Able Card Corporation, Irwindale** *Also Called: Million Corporation (P-4923)*

**Able Design and Fabrication, Rancho Dominguez** *Also Called: Adf Incorporated (P-8615)*

**Able Industrial Products Inc (PA)** ........................................ E ...... 909 930-1585
2006 S Baker Ave Ontario (91761) *(P-6437)*

**Able Iron Works** .................................................................... E ...... 909 397-5300
222 Hershey St Pomona (91767) *(P-8086)*

**Able Sheet Metal Inc (PA)** .................................................... E ...... 323 269-2181
614 N Ford Blvd Los Angeles (90022) *(P-8359)*

**Able Wire Edm Inc** ................................................................ F ...... 714 255-1967
440 Atlas St Ste A Brea (92821) *(P-10657)*

**Above & Beyond Balloons Inc** ............................................. E ...... 949 586-8470
1 Wrigley Irvine (92618) *(P-16079)*

**Above and Beyond, Irvine** *Also Called: Above & Beyond Balloons Inc (P-16079)*

**Abracon** ................................................................................. F ...... 949 546-8000
30332 Esperanza Rcho Sta Marg (92688) *(P-12906)*

**Abrams Electronics Inc** ........................................................ F ...... 831 758-6400
420 W Market St Salinas (93901) *(P-11437)*

**Abraxis Bioscience LLC (DH)** .............................................. C ...... 800 564-0216
11755 Wilshire Blvd Fl 20 Los Angeles (90025) *(P-5293)*

**Abrisa Industrial Glass Inc (HQ)** ......................................... D ...... 805 525-4902
200 Hallock Dr Santa Paula (93060) *(P-14759)*

**Abrisa Technologies** ............................................................. D ...... 805 525-4902
200 Hallock Dr Santa Paula (93060) *(P-14760)*

**ABS By Allen Schwartz, Encino** *Also Called: Aquarius Rags LLC (P-2698)*

**ABS By Allen Schwartz LLC (HQ)** ....................................... E ...... 213 895-4400
15821 Ventura Blvd Ste 270 Encino (91436) *(P-2731)*

**Absinthe Group Inc** .............................................................. E ...... 530 823-8527
2043 Airpark Ct Ste 30 Auburn (95602) *(P-874)*

**Absolute Board Co Inc** ........................................................ E ...... 760 295-2201
4040 Calle Platino Ste 102 Oceanside (92056) *(P-15772)*

**Absolute EDM, Carlsbad** *Also Called: Diligent Solutions Inc (P-10812)*

**Absolute Graphic Tech USA Inc** ......................................... E ...... 909 597-1133
235 Jason Ct Corona (92879) *(P-11304)*

**Absolute Machine Inc** .......................................................... F ...... 530 242-6840
5020 Mountain Lakes Blvd Redding (96003) *(P-10658)*

**Absolute Packaging Inc** ...................................................... E ...... 714 630-3020
1201 N Miller St Anaheim (92806) *(P-3916)*

**Absolute Pro Music, Los Angeles** *Also Called: Absolute Usa Inc (P-11631)*

**Absolute Screenprint Inc** .................................................... C ...... 714 529-2120
333 Cliffwood Park St Brea (92821) *(P-3000)*

**Absolute Sign, Los Alamitos** *Also Called: Absolute Sign Inc (P-15938)*

**Absolute Sign Inc** ................................................................ F ...... 562 592-5838
10655 Humbolt St Los Alamitos (90720) *(P-15938)*

**Absolute Technologies, Anaheim** *Also Called: D & D Gear Incorporated (P-13819)*

**Absolute Usa Inc** ................................................................. E ...... 213 744-0044
1800 E Washington Blvd Los Angeles (90021) *(P-11631)*

**Abx Engineering Inc** ............................................................ D ...... 650 552-2300
875 Stanton Rd Burlingame (94010) *(P-16686)*

**AC Pro Inc (PA)** .................................................................... C ...... 951 360-7849
11700 Industry Ave Fontana (92337) *(P-16773)*

**AC Products Inc** ................................................................... E ...... 714 630-7311
9930 Painter Ave Whittier (90605) *(P-6215)*

**AC Propulsion Inc** ................................................................ E ...... 909 592-5399
441 Borrego Ct San Dimas (91773) *(P-11254)*

**AC Tech, Garden Grove** *Also Called: Advanced Chemistry & Technology Inc (P-6216)*

**AC&a Enterprises LLC (HQ)** ................................................ E ...... 949 716-3511
25671 Commercentre Dr Lake Forest (92630) *(P-13699)*

**Acacia Communications Inc** .............................................. D ...... 212 331-8417
2700 Zanker Rd Ste 160 San Jose (95134) *(P-12269)*

**Academic Cap & Gown, Chatsworth** *Also Called: Academic Ch Choir Gwns Mfg Inc (P-2887)*

**Academic Ch Choir Gwns Mfg Inc** ..................................... E ...... 818 886-8697
8944 Mason Ave Chatsworth (91311) *(P-2887)*

**ACADIA, San Diego** *Also Called: Acadia Pharmaceuticals Inc (P-5294)*

**Acadia Pharmaceuticals Inc (PA)** ....................................... A ...... 858 558-2871
12830 El Camino Real Ste 400 San Diego (92130) *(P-5294)*

**ACC Ca Inc (HQ)** ................................................................... F ...... 805 522-1646
2655 1st St Ste 210 Simi Valley (93065) *(P-6359)*

**ACC Precision Inc** ................................................................ F ...... 805 278-9801
321 Hearst Dr Oxnard (93030) *(P-10659)*

**Accel Manufacturing, Santa Clara** *Also Called: Accel Manufacturing Inc (P-9538)*

**Accel Manufacturing Inc** ..................................................... E ...... 408 727-5883
1709 Grant St Santa Clara (95050) *(P-9538)*

**Accela Inc (PA)** ..................................................................... C ...... 925 659-3200
9110 Alcosta Blvd San Ramon (94583) *(P-18009)*

**Accelerance Inc** .................................................................... D ...... 650 472-3785
303 Twin Dolphin Dr Ste 600 Redwood City (94065) *(P-18010)*

**Accelerated Memory Prod Inc** ............................................ E ...... 714 460-9800
1317 E Edinger Ave Santa Ana (92705) *(P-12270)*

**Acceliot Inc** ............................................................................ F ...... 657 845-4250
16601 Gothard St Ste E Huntington Beach (92647) *(P-19435)*

**Accent Awnings, Santa Ana** *Also Called: Accent Industries Inc (P-8250)*

**Accent Ceilings, City Of Industry** *Also Called: Adams-Campbell Company Ltd (P-8361)*

**Accent Industries Inc (PA)** .................................................. F ...... 714 708-1389
1600 E Saint Gertrude Pl Santa Ana (92705) *(P-8250)*

**Accent Plastics, Chino** *Also Called: Dacha Enterprises Inc (P-6791)*

**Acceptedcom LLC** ............................................................... E ...... 310 815-9553
2229 S Canfield Ave Los Angeles (90034) *(P-4358)*

**Acces I/O Products Inc** ....................................................... F ...... 858 550-9559
10623 Roselle St San Diego (92121) *(P-10314)*

**Access Biologicals, Vista** *Also Called: Grifols Usa LLC (P-5834)*

**Access Books** ....................................................................... C ...... 310 920-1694
1800 Century Park E Ste 600 Los Angeles (90067) *(P-4310)*

**Access Closure Inc** .............................................................. B ...... 408 610-6500
5452 Betsy Ross Dr Santa Clara (95054) *(P-14946)*

**Access Professional Inc** ...................................................... F ...... 858 571-4444
10225 Prospect Ave Ste A Santee (92071) *(P-8614)*

**Access Professional Systems, Santee** *Also Called: Access Professional Inc (P-8614)*

**Access Systems Inc** ............................................................ D ...... 916 941-8099
4947 Hillsdale Cir El Dorado Hills (95762) *(P-14602)*

**Access Systems Americas Inc** ........................................... E ...... 408 400-3000
3965 Freedom Cir Ste 200 Santa Clara (95054) *(P-17875)*

**Acclaim Lighting LLC** .......................................................... E ...... 323 213-4626
6122 S Eastern Ave Commerce (90040) *(P-11514)*

**Acclarent Inc** ......................................................................... B ...... 650 687-5888
31 Technology Dr Ste 200 Irvine (92618) *(P-14947)*

**Acco, Pasadena** *Also Called: Acco Engineered Systems Inc (P-402)*

**Acco Brands Corporation** ................................................... F ...... 650 572-2700
1350 Bayshore Hwy Ste 825 Burlingame (94010) *(P-10301)*

**Acco Brands USA LLC** ........................................................ D ...... 650 572-2700
1350 Bayshore Hwy Ste 825 Burlingame (94010) *(P-10302)*

**Acco Engineered Systems Inc** ........................................... E ...... 661 631-1975
3559 Landco Dr Ste B Bakersfield (93308) *(P-10476)*

**Acco Engineered Systems Inc (PA)** .................................. A ...... 818 244-6571
888 E Walnut St Pasadena (91101) *(P-402)*

**Accolade Pharma USA** ........................................................ E ...... 626 279-9699
13260 Temple Ave City Of Industry (91746) *(P-5295)*

**Accordion Networks Inc** ...................................................... E ...... 510 623-2876
990 Yakima Dr Fremont (94539) *(P-11747)*

**Accountmate Software Corp (PA)** ...................................... E ...... 707 774-7500
1445 Technology Ln Ste A5 Petaluma (94954) *(P-18011)*

# Accounts Payable — ALPHABETIC SECTION

**Accounts Payable, San Jose** *Also Called: Mellanox Technologies Inc (P-12556)*
**Accratronics Seals LLC** .................................................. D ...... 818 843-1500
2211 Kenmere Ave Burbank (91504) *(P-12907)*
**Accriva Dgnostics Holdings Inc (DH)** ......................... B ...... 858 404-8203
6260 Sequence Dr San Diego (92121) *(P-14948)*
**Accrualify Inc** ..................................................................... E ...... 650 437-7225
333 S B St San Mateo (94401) *(P-18012)*
**Accsys, Pleasanton** *Also Called: Accsys Technology Inc (P-13208)*
**Accsys Technology Inc** .................................................... E ...... 925 462-6949
1177 Quarry Ln Pleasanton (94566) *(P-13208)*
**Accu Machine Inc** ............................................................. E
440 Aldo Ave Santa Clara (95054) *(P-10660)*
**Accu-Blend Corporation** ................................................. F ...... 626 334-7744
364 Malbert St Perris (92570) *(P-6330)*
**Accu-Sembly Inc** .............................................................. D ...... 626 357-3447
1835 Huntington Dr Duarte (91010) *(P-12040)*
**Accu-Swiss Inc (PA)** ........................................................ F ...... 209 847-1016
544 Armstrong Way Oakdale (95361) *(P-8714)*
**Accu-Tech Laser Processing Inc** .................................. E ...... 760 744-6692
1175 Linda Vista Dr San Marcos (92078) *(P-10661)*
**Accudyne Engineering & Eqp, Bell** *Also Called: West Coast-Accudyne Inc (P-9592)*
**Accunex Inc** ....................................................................... E ...... 818 882-5858
20700 Lassen St Chatsworth (91311) *(P-19373)*
**Accurate, Newark** *Also Called: Accurate Tube Bending Inc (P-9245)*
**Accurate Air Engineering, Cerritos** *Also Called: Atlas Copco Compressors LLC (P-9957)*
**Accurate Always Inc** ....................................................... E ...... 650 728-9428
127 Ocean Blvd Half Moon Bay (94019) *(P-10126)*
**Accurate Circuit Engrg Inc** ............................................ D ...... 714 546-2162
3019 Kilson Dr Santa Ana (92707) *(P-12041)*
**Accurate Electronics, Chatsworth** *Also Called: Accunex Inc (P-19373)*
**Accurate Engineering Inc** ............................................... E ...... 818 768-3919
8710 Telfair Ave Sun Valley (91352) *(P-12042)*
**Accurate Grinding and Mfg Corp** .................................. E ...... 951 479-0909
807 E Parkridge Ave Corona (92879) *(P-13700)*
**Accurate Heating & Cooling Inc** ................................... E ...... 209 858-4125
3515 Yosemite Ave Lathrop (95330) *(P-8360)*
**Accurate Laminated Pdts Inc** ....................................... E ...... 714 632-2773
1826 Dawns Way Fullerton (92831) *(P-3212)*
**Accurate Manufacturing Company, Glendale** *Also Called: McCoppin Enterprises (P-10966)*
**Accurate Metal Products Inc** ......................................... F ...... 951 360-3594
4276 Campbell St Riverside (92509) *(P-8087)*
**Accurate Plating Company** ............................................ E ...... 323 268-8567
2811 Alcazar St Los Angeles (90033) *(P-8906)*
**Accurate Prfmce Machining Inc** ................................... E ...... 714 434-7811
2255 S Grand Ave Santa Ana (92705) *(P-10662)*
**Accurate Security Pros Inc** ........................................... E ...... 858 271-1155
9919 Hibert St Ste D San Diego (92131) *(P-19051)*
**Accurate Staging Mfg Inc (PA)** ..................................... F ...... 310 324-1040
13900 S Figueroa St Los Angeles (90061) *(P-16080)*
**Accurate Steel Treating Inc** .......................................... E ...... 562 927-6528
10008 Miller Way South Gate (90280) *(P-7873)*
**Accurate Technology, Anaheim** *Also Called: Gledhill/Lyons Inc (P-13851)*
**Accurate Technology Mfg, Sunnyvale** *Also Called: Accurate Technology Mfg Inc (P-10663)*
**Accurate Technology Mfg Inc** ....................................... D ...... 408 733-4344
930 Thompson Pl Sunnyvale (94085) *(P-10663)*
**Accurate Tube Bending Inc** .......................................... E ...... 510 790-6500
37770 Timber St Newark (94560) *(P-9245)*
**Accuride International Inc (PA)** .................................... E ...... 562 903-0200
12311 Shoemaker Ave Santa Fe Springs (90670) *(P-7972)*
**Accuryn Monitoring System, Hayward** *Also Called: Potrero Medical Inc (P-15228)*
**Accusplit (PA)** .................................................................. F ...... 925 290-1900
1262 Quarry Ln Ste B Pleasanton (94566) *(P-15673)*
**Accutek Packaging Equipment Co (PA)** ..................... E ...... 760 734-4177
2980 Scott St Vista (92081) *(P-10009)*
**Accuturn Corporation** ..................................................... E ...... 951 656-6621
7189 Old 215 Frontage Rd Ste 101 Moreno Valley (92553) *(P-14134)*
**Acd, Newark** *Also Called: Advanced Cell Diagnostics Inc (P-19436)*
**Acd LLC (DH)** ................................................................... E ...... 949 261-7533
2321 Pullman St Santa Ana (92705) *(P-8296)*
**Ace, Anaheim** *Also Called: Anaheim Custom Extruders Inc (P-6718)*
**Ace, Santa Ana** *Also Called: Accurate Circuit Engrg Inc (P-12041)*
**Ace Air Manufacturing** .................................................. F ...... 310 323-7246
1430 W 135th St Gardena (90249) *(P-10664)*
**Ace Boiler, Santa Ana** *Also Called: Ajax Boiler Inc (P-8298)*
**Ace Clearwater Enterprises Inc** ................................... E ...... 310 538-5380
1614 Kona Dr Compton (90220) *(P-9594)*
**Ace Clearwater Enterprises Inc (PA)** ......................... D ...... 310 323-2140
19815 Magellan Dr Torrance (90502) *(P-13731)*
**Ace Commercial Inc** ....................................................... E ...... 562 946-6664
10310 Pioneer Blvd Ste 1 Santa Fe Springs (90670) *(P-4500)*
**Ace Composites Inc** ....................................................... E ...... 530 743-1885
1394 Sky Harbor Dr Olivehurst (95961) *(P-6693)*
**Ace Creations LLC** .......................................................... F ...... 248 762-9679
2190 Grove St Apt 1 San Francisco (94117) *(P-5227)*
**Ace Hardware, Exeter** *Also Called: Exeter Mercantile Company (P-9353)*
**Ace Hardware, Baldwin Park** *Also Called: Nichols Lumber & Hardware Co (P-16454)*
**Ace Heaters LLC** ............................................................ E ...... 951 738-2230
130 Klug Cir Corona (92878) *(P-10477)*
**Ace Hydraulic Sales & Svc Inc** ..................................... F ...... 661 327-0571
2901 Gibson St Bakersfield (93308) *(P-16804)*
**Ace Industries Inc** .......................................................... E ...... 619 482-2700
195 Mace St Chula Vista (91911) *(P-10665)*
**Ace Machine Shop Inc** ................................................... D ...... 310 608-2277
11200 Wright Rd Lynwood (90262) *(P-10666)*
**Ace Mailing, San Francisco** *Also Called: Ace Mailing Corporation (P-17793)*
**Ace Mailing Corporation** ............................................... E ...... 415 863-4223
2736 16th St San Francisco (94103) *(P-17793)*
**Ace Products Enterprises Inc** ...................................... E ...... 707 765-1500
625 2nd St Petaluma (94952) *(P-7124)*
**Ace Products Group, Petaluma** *Also Called: Ace Products Enterprises Inc (P-7124)*
**Ace Sushi, Torrance** *Also Called: Asiana Cuisine Enterprises Inc (P-2132)*
**Ace Tube Bending** .......................................................... E ...... 949 362-2220
14 Journey Aliso Viejo (92656) *(P-10667)*
**Acer America, San Jose** *Also Called: Acer American Holdings Corp (P-10315)*
**Acer American Holdings Corp (DH)** ............................ F ...... 408 533-7700
1730 N 1st St Ste 400 San Jose (95112) *(P-10315)*
**Acg Ecopack, Ontario** *Also Called: Advanced Color Graphics (P-4504)*
**Achates Power Inc** .......................................................... D ...... 858 535-9920
4060 Sorrento Valley Blvd Ste A San Diego (92121) *(P-13437)*
**Achronix Semiconductor Corp (PA)** ............................ E ...... 408 889-4100
2903 Bunker Hill Ln Ste 200 Santa Clara (95054) *(P-12271)*
**Aci Alloys Inc** .................................................................. F ...... 408 259-7337
1458 Seareel Pl San Jose (95131) *(P-9035)*
**Aci International (PA)** .................................................... D ...... 310 889-3400
844 Moraga Dr Los Angeles (90049) *(P-17107)*
**Aci Medical LLC** .............................................................. E ...... 760 744-4400
1857 Diamond St Ste A San Marcos (92078) *(P-14949)*
**Acker Stone Industries Inc (DH)** .................................. E ...... 951 674-0047
13296 Temescal Canyon Rd Corona (92883) *(P-7306)*
**Acm Machining Inc (PA)** ................................................ E ...... 916 852-8600
11390 Gold Dredge Way Rancho Cordova (95742) *(P-10668)*
**Acm Machining Inc** ........................................................ E ...... 916 804-9489
240 State Highway 16 Unit 18 Plymouth (95669) *(P-10669)*
**Acm Research Inc (PA)** ................................................. C ...... 510 445-3700
42307 Osgood Rd Ste I Fremont (94539) *(P-10531)*
**Acme Auto Headlining, Long Beach** *Also Called: Acme Headlining Co (P-13438)*
**Acme Bag Co Inc (PA)** ................................................... F ...... 530 662-6130
440 N Pioneer Ave Ste 300 Woodland (95776) *(P-3989)*
**Acme Bread Co Div II, Berkeley** *Also Called: Doughtronics Inc (P-1188)*
**Acme Bread Company, Berkeley** *Also Called: Doughtronics Inc (P-1187)*
**Acme Cryogenics Inc** ..................................................... E ...... 805 981-4500
531 Sandy Cir Oxnard (93036) *(P-9823)*
**Acme Headlining Co** ....................................................... D ...... 562 432-0281
550 W 16th St Long Beach (90813) *(P-13438)*
**Acme Portable Machines Inc** ........................................ E ...... 626 610-1888
1330 Mountain View Cir Azusa (91702) *(P-10127)*
**Acme Press Inc** ............................................................... D ...... 925 682-1111
2312 Stanwell Dr Concord (94520) *(P-4501)*
**Acme Printing Co, Modesto** *Also Called: Pinnacle Solutions Inc (P-19117)*
**Acme Safety & Supply Corp (PA)** ................................ F ...... 619 299-5100
11478 Woodside Ave N Santee (92071) *(P-16972)*

## ALPHABETIC SECTION — Adam Nutrition Inc

Acme Scale, San Leandro *Also Called: Buran and Reed Inc (P-10637)*
Acme Tool Grinding Company, Santa Ana *Also Called: Connelly Machine Wks (P-10787)*
Acme United Corporation ............................................. E ...... 714 557-2001
   630 Young St Santa Ana (92705) *(P-3759)*
Acme Vial, Paso Robles *Also Called: Acme Vial & Glass Co (P-7181)*
Acme Vial & Glass Co ...................................................... E ...... 805 239-2666
   1601 Commerce Way Paso Robles (93446) *(P-7181)*
Acon Laboratories Inc (PA) ........................................... E ...... 858 875-8000
   9440 Carroll Park Dr San Diego (92121) *(P-5728)*
Acorn Engineering Company (PA) .............................. A ...... 800 488-8999
   15125 Proctor Ave City Of Industry (91746) *(P-6265)*
Acorn Newspaper Inc ..................................................... F ...... 818 706-0266
   29800 Agoura Rd Agoura Hills (91301) *(P-4061)*
Acorn Paper Products Co., Los Angeles *Also Called: Oak Paper Products Co LLC (P-17003)*
Acorn Publishing LLC ..................................................... F ...... 714 471-6973
   115 Quiet Pl Irvine (92602) *(P-4359)*
Acorn Vac, Chino *Also Called: Acornvac Inc (P-8045)*
Acorn-Gencon Plastics LLC ........................................ D ...... 909 591-8461
   13818 Oaks Ave Chino (91710) *(P-6694)*
Acornvac Inc ..................................................................... E ...... 909 902-1141
   13818 Oaks Ave Chino (91710) *(P-8045)*
Acosta Sheet Metal Mfg Co, San Jose *Also Called: Sal J Acsta Sheetmetal Mfg Inc (P-8565)*
Acousticfab LLC (DH) .................................................... D ...... 661 257-2242
   28150 Industry Dr Valencia (91355) *(P-9165)*
Acp Composites, Livermore *Also Called: Aerospace Composite Products (P-13750)*
Acp Noxtat Inc ................................................................. F ...... 714 547-5477
   1112 E Washington Ave Santa Ana (92701) *(P-5131)*
Acp Ventures ..................................................................... F ...... 925 297-0100
   3340 Mt Diablo Blvd Ste B Lafayette (94549) *(P-4502)*
Acpt, Huntington Beach *Also Called: Advanced Cmpsite Pdts Tech Inc (P-6696)*
ACR Solar International Corp ...................................... E ...... 916 481-7200
   5840 Gibbons Dr Ste H Carmichael (95608) *(P-17320)*
Acralight International, Santa Ana *Also Called: International Skylights (P-7174)*
Acrl, Chatsworth *Also Called: Advanced Cosmetic RES Labs Inc (P-16082)*
Acro Associates, Concord *Also Called: Acro Associates Inc (P-9142)*
Acro Associates Inc ....................................................... D ...... 925 676-8828
   1990 Olivera Rd Ste A Concord (94520) *(P-9142)*
Acroamatics Inc ............................................................... F ...... 805 967-9909
   125 Cremona Dr Ste 130 Goleta (93117) *(P-11797)*
Acrometrix Corporation ................................................. E ...... 707 746-8888
   46500 Kato Rd Fremont (94538) *(P-5729)*
Acromil LLC (HQ) ............................................................ C ...... 626 964-2522
   18421 Railroad St City Of Industry (91748) *(P-13732)*
Acromil LLC ...................................................................... D ...... 951 808-9929
   1168 Sherborn St Corona (92879) *(P-13733)*
Acromil Corporation (PA) ............................................. C ...... 626 964-2522
   18421 Railroad St City Of Industry (91748) *(P-13734)*
Acrontos Manufacturing Inc ........................................ E ...... 714 850-9133
   1641 E Saint Gertrude Pl Santa Ana (92705) *(P-8815)*
Acrylic Distribution, Sun Valley *Also Called: Acrylic Distribution Corp (P-3551)*
Acrylic Distribution Corp ............................................... E ...... 818 767-8448
   8421 Lankershim Blvd Sun Valley (91352) *(P-3551)*
ACS, Antioch *Also Called: Allied Container Systems Inc (P-8652)*
ACS Cloud Partners, Hermosa Beach *Also Called: Advanced Corporate Svcs Inc (P-19554)*
ACS Engineering Inc ..................................................... E ...... 949 297-3777
   33 Hammond Ste 209 Irvine (92618) *(P-19374)*
ACS Instrumentation Valves Inc ................................ D ...... 510 262-1880
   3065 Richmond Pkwy Ste 106 Richmond (94806) *(P-14381)*
Acsco Products Inc ........................................................ E ...... 818 953-2240
   313 N Lake St Burbank (91502) *(P-13439)*
Acss, Beaumont *Also Called: Anderson Chrnesky Strl Stl Inc (P-8096)*
Act Inc Dmand Kontrols Systems, Costa Mesa *Also Called: Advanced Cnsrvtion Tech Dist I (P-8058)*
Act-On Software Inc ...................................................... E ...... 503 530-1555
   1620 E Roseville Pkwy Ste 200 Roseville (95661) *(P-19024)*
Actavis LLC ...................................................................... D ...... 909 270-1400
   311 Bonnie Cir Corona (92878) *(P-5296)*
Actelion US Holding Company (HQ) ........................ E ...... 650 624-6900
   5000 Shoreline Ct Ste 200 South San Francisco (94080) *(P-5297)*
Actelis Networks, Fremont *Also Called: Actelis Networks Inc (P-11748)*

Actelis Networks Inc (PA) ............................................. E ...... 510 545-1045
   4039 Clipper Ct Fremont (94538) *(P-11748)*
Acti Corporation Inc ....................................................... E ...... 949 753-0352
   18 Technology Dr Ste 139 Irvine (92618) *(P-11632)*
Actiance, Redwood City *Also Called: Smarsh Inc (P-18798)*
Actiance Inc ...................................................................... C ...... 650 631-6300
   900 Veterans Blvd Ste 500 Redwood City (94063) *(P-18013)*
Action, Ontario *Also Called: Action Embroidery Corp (P-3022)*
Action Bag & Cover Inc ................................................. D ...... 714 965-7777
   18401 Mount Langley St Fountain Valley (92708) *(P-2953)*
Action Cleaning Corporation ....................................... E ...... 619 233-1881
   1668 Newton Ave San Diego (92113) *(P-19238)*
Action Embroidery Corp (PA) ..................................... C ...... 909 983-1359
   1315 Brooks St Ontario (91762) *(P-3022)*
Action Fire Fab & Supply Inc ...................................... E ...... 209 834-3460
   1600 W Linne Rd Tracy (95377) *(P-14839)*
Action Plastics, Santa Ana *Also Called: Smiths Action Plastics Inc (P-6686)*
Action Powder Coating LLC ........................................ F ...... 858 566-2288
   7949 Stromesa Ct Ste D San Diego (92126) *(P-9036)*
Action Stamping Inc ...................................................... E ...... 626 914-7466
   119 Explorer St Pomona (91768) *(P-8816)*
Actionpac Scales & Automation, Santa Paula *Also Called: Coastal Cnting Indus Scale Inc (P-9667)*
Actiontec Electronics Inc ............................................. D ...... 408 752-7700
   590 Macara Ave Sunnyvale (94085) *(P-16687)*
Active Radiator Supply, Santa Fe Springs *Also Called: M P N Inc (P-13534)*
Active Window Products ............................................... D ...... 323 245-5185
   5431 W San Fernando Rd Los Angeles (90039) *(P-8251)*
Activeapparel Inc (PA) ................................................... F ...... 951 361-0060
   11076 Venture Dr Jurupa Valley (91752) *(P-2607)*
Activeon Inc (PA) ............................................................. E ...... 858 798-3300
   10905 Technology Pl San Diego (92127) *(P-11633)*
Activision Blizzard, Santa Monica *Also Called: Activision Blizzard Inc (P-18014)*
Activision Blizzard Inc (HQ) ........................................ B ...... 310 255-2000
   2701 Olympic Blvd Bldg B Santa Monica (90404) *(P-18014)*
Activision Blizzard Inc .................................................. D ...... 949 955-1380
   3 Blizzard Irvine (92606) *(P-18015)*
Actron Manufacturing Inc ............................................ D ...... 951 371-0885
   1841 Railroad St Corona (92878) *(P-7973)*
Actsolar Inc ...................................................................... D ...... 408 721-5000
   2900 Semiconductor Dr Santa Clara (95051) *(P-12272)*
Actsyl, Los Angeles *Also Called: Xavier Group (P-6060)*
Actus Nutrition, Visalia *Also Called: Milk Specialties Company (P-5555)*
Acuantia Inc ...................................................................... F ...... 209 723-5000
   2651 Cooper Ave Merced (95348) *(P-5132)*
Acuantia Inc ..................................................................... E ...... 559 648-8235
   13375 11th Ave Hanford (93230) *(P-6695)*
Acufast Aircraft Products Inc ..................................... E ...... 818 365-7077
   12445 Gladstone Ave Sylmar (91342) *(P-13735)*
Acuity Brands Lighting Inc ......................................... E ...... 510 845-2760
   55 Harrison St Ste 200 Oakland (94607) *(P-11515)*
Acuity Brands Lighting Inc ......................................... E ...... 626 965-0711
   12281 Bradley Avenue City Of Industry (91748) *(P-11516)*
Acuna Dionisio Able ...................................................... F ...... 310 978-4741
   12629 Prairie Ave Hawthorne (90250) *(P-10670)*
Acuprint, Los Angeles *Also Called: Ink & Color Inc (P-4644)*
Acushnet Company ........................................................ B ...... 760 804-6500
   2819 Loker Ave E Carlsbad (92010) *(P-15773)*
Acutus Medical, Carlsbad *Also Called: Acutus Medical Inc (P-14950)*
Acutus Medical Inc ........................................................ C ...... 442 232-6080
   2210 Faraday Ave Ste 100 Carlsbad (92008) *(P-14950)*
Ad Art Inc (PA) ................................................................. D ...... 415 869-6460
   150 Executive Park Blvd Ste 2100 San Francisco (94134) *(P-19068)*
Ad Art Company, Los Angeles *Also Called: RJ Acquisition Corp (P-4954)*
Ad Art Sign Company, San Francisco *Also Called: Ad Art Inc (P-19068)*
Ad/S Companies, Corona *Also Called: Architectural Design Signs Inc (P-15942)*
Adac Medical Systems, San Jose *Also Called: A D A C Laboratories (inc) (P-14837)*
Adam Nutrition, Irvine *Also Called: International Vitamin Corp (P-5499)*
Adam Nutrition Inc .......................................................... C ...... 951 361-1120
   11010 Hopkins St Ste B Jurupa Valley (91752) *(P-5298)*

**Adams and Brooks Inc**                                                                      **ALPHABETIC SECTION**

**Adams and Brooks Inc** .................................................. C ...... 909 880-2305
4345 Hallmark Pkwy San Bernardino (92407) *(P-1298)*

**Adams Business Media, Palm Springs** *Also Called: Adams Trade Press LP (P-4225)*

**Adams Rite Aerospace, Fullerton** *Also Called: Zmp Aquisition Corporation (P-11357)*

**Adams Rite Aerospace Inc (DH)** ................................... D ...... 714 278-6500
4141 N Palm St Fullerton (92835) *(P-13736)*

**Adams Trade Press LP (PA)** .......................................... E ...... 760 318-7000
420 S Palm Canyon Dr Palm Springs (92262) *(P-4225)*

**Adams Winery LLC** ...................................................... E ...... 707 395-6126
9711 W Dry Creek Rd Healdsburg (95448) *(P-1470)*

**Adams-Campbell Company Ltd (PA)** ............................. D ...... 626 330-3425
15343 Proctor Ave City Of Industry (91745) *(P-8361)*

**Adapt Automation Inc** .................................................. E ...... 714 662-4454
1661 Palm St Ste A Santa Ana (92701) *(P-9733)*

**Adaptech Corporation** .................................................. F ...... 571 261-9823
301 Mission Ave Unit 505 Oceanside (92054) *(P-14485)*

**Adaptive Aerospace Corporation** ................................... E ...... 661 300-0616
501 Bailey Ave Tehachapi (93561) *(P-13737)*

**Adaptive Digital Systems Inc** ...................................... E ...... 949 955-3116
20322 Sw Acacia St Ste 200 Newport Beach (92660) *(P-11798)*

**Adaptive Insights LLC** ................................................. E ...... 408 656-4229
14 W Central Ave Los Gatos (95030) *(P-2581)*

**Adaptive Insights LLC (HQ)** ......................................... C ...... 650 528-7500
2300 Geng Rd Ste 100 Palo Alto (94303) *(P-18016)*

**Adaptive Tech Group Inc** ............................................. E ...... 562 424-1100
1635 E Burnett St Signal Hill (90755) *(P-17658)*

**Adaptive Technology, Oceanside** *Also Called: Adaptech Corporation (P-14485)*

**Adara Inc (PA)** ........................................................... D ...... 408 876-6360
2625 Middlefield Rd Ste 827 Palo Alto (94306) *(P-18017)*

**ADC Aerospace, Buena Park** *Also Called: Alloy Die Casting Co (P-7805)*

**Adco Manufacturing** .................................................... C ...... 559 875-5563
2170 Academy Ave Sanger (93657) *(P-10010)*

**Adcraft Labels, Anaheim** *Also Called: Adcraft Products Co Inc (P-4836)*

**Adcraft Products Co Inc** .............................................. E ...... 714 776-1230
1230 S Sherman St Anaheim (92805) *(P-4836)*

**Add-On Cmpt Peripherals Inc** ...................................... C ...... 949 546-8200
15775 Gateway Cir Tustin (92780) *(P-10316)*

**Add-On Cmpt Peripherals LLC** ..................................... D ...... 949 546-8200
15775 Gateway Cir Tustin (92780) *(P-10219)*

**Addaday Inc** ............................................................... E ...... 424 465-9106
12304 Santa Monica Blvd Ste 355 Los Angeles (90025) *(P-15774)*

**Addison Engineering, Santa Clara** *Also Called: Addison Technology Inc (P-12043)*

**Addison Technology Inc** .............................................. E ...... 408 749-1000
3350 Scott Blvd Santa Clara (95054) *(P-12043)*

**Addition Manufacturing Technologies CA Inc** ................. E ...... 760 597-5220
1391 Specialty Dr Ste A Vista (92081) *(P-9575)*

**Addon Networks, Tustin** *Also Called: Add-On Cmpt Peripherals LLC (P-10219)*

**Adel Park LLC** ............................................................ F ...... 510 620-9670
350 Carlson Blvd Richmond (94804) *(P-9403)*

**Adem LLC** .................................................................. E ...... 408 727-8955
1040 Di Giulio Ave Ste 160 Santa Clara (95050) *(P-10671)*

**Adept Fasteners Inc (PA)** ............................................ C ...... 661 257-6600
27949 Hancock Pkwy Valencia (91355) *(P-13738)*

**Adept Process Services Inc** ........................................ E ...... 619 434-3194
609 Anita St Chula Vista (91911) *(P-14026)*

**Adesto, San Jose** *Also Called: Adesto Technologies Corp (P-12273)*

**Adesto Technologies Corp (DH)** ................................... E ...... 408 400-0578
6024 Silver Creek Valley Rd San Jose (95138) *(P-12273)*

**Adex Electronics Inc** ................................................... F ...... 949 597-1772
3 Watson Irvine (92618) *(P-12274)*

**Adexa Inc (PA)** .......................................................... E ...... 310 642-2100
5777 W Century Blvd Ste 1100 Los Angeles (90045) *(P-18018)*

**Adeza Biomedical Corporation** ..................................... A ...... 408 745-6491
1240 Elko Dr Sunnyvale (94089) *(P-5730)*

**Adf Incorporated** ........................................................ E ...... 310 669-9700
1550 W Mahalo Pl Rancho Dominguez (90220) *(P-8615)*

**Adfa Incorporated** ....................................................... E ...... 213 627-8004
319 W 6th St Los Angeles (90014) *(P-9037)*

**Adhesves Sealants Coatings Div, Roseville** *Also Called: HB Fuller Company (P-6230)*

**ADI, Compton** *Also Called: American Dawn Inc (P-2541)*

**ADI, Valencia** *Also Called: Aerospace Dynamics Intl Inc (P-13753)*

**Adiana Inc** .................................................................. B ...... 650 421-2900
1240 Elko Dr Sunnyvale (94089) *(P-5299)*

**Adidas North America Inc** ........................................... F ...... 805 482-3475
950 Camarillo Center Dr Ste 956 Camarillo (93010) *(P-2608)*

**Adidas Outlet Store Camarillo, Camarillo** *Also Called: Adidas North America Inc (P-2608)*

**Adient Newark, Newark** *Also Called: Adient US LLC (P-13440)*

**Adient US LLC** ............................................................ E ...... 510 771-2300
6601 Overlake Pl Newark (94560) *(P-13440)*

**Adlink Technology, San Jose** *Also Called: Ampro Adlink Technology Inc (P-10136)*

**ADM, Lodi** *Also Called: Archer-Daniels-Midland Company (P-1053)*

**ADM Works, Santa Ana** *Also Called: Advanced Digital Mfg LLC (P-13739)*

**Admail West Inc** ......................................................... D ...... 916 554-5755
800 N 10th St Ste F Sacramento (95811) *(P-3899)*

**Admail-Express Inc** .................................................... E ...... 510 471-6200
31640 Hayman St Hayward (94544) *(P-4503)*

**Admi Inc** .................................................................... D ...... 408 776-0060
12300 Highland Estates Ln San Martin (95046) *(P-18019)*

**Adobe Inc** .................................................................. E ...... 415 832-2000
601 And 625 Townsend St San Francisco (94103) *(P-18020)*

**Adobe Inc** .................................................................. E ...... 408 536-6000
321 Park Ave San Jose (95110) *(P-18021)*

**Adobe Inc (PA)** .......................................................... A ...... 408 536-6000
345 Park Ave San Jose (95110) *(P-18022)*

**Adobe Macromedia Software LLC (HQ)** ........................ D ...... 415 832-2000
601 Townsend St San Francisco (94103) *(P-18023)*

**Adobe Road Winery** .................................................... F ...... 707 939-9099
6 Petaluma Blvd N Ste A1 Petaluma (94952) *(P-1471)*

**Adonis Inc** .................................................................. E ...... 951 432-3960
475 N Sheridan St Corona (92878) *(P-5939)*

**Adrenaline Lacrosse Inc** .............................................. E ...... 888 768-8479
24 21st St San Diego (92102) *(P-17507)*

**Adriennes Gourmet Foods** ........................................... D ...... 805 964-6848
849 Ward Dr Santa Barbara (93111) *(P-1257)*

**Adroll, San Francisco** *Also Called: Nextroll Inc (P-18590)*

**Adtech Optics, City Of Industry** *Also Called: Adtech Photonics Inc (P-12275)*

**Adtech Photonics Inc** .................................................. E ...... 626 956-1000
18007 Cortney Ct City Of Industry (91748) *(P-12275)*

**Adtek Inc** ................................................................... E ...... 209 634-0300
1460 Ellerd Dr Turlock (95380) *(P-8088)*

**Adti Media LLC** .......................................................... E ...... 951 795-4446
1257 Simpson Way Escondido (92029) *(P-15939)*

**Adult Video News, Chatsworth** *Also Called: Avn Media Network Inc (P-4312)*

**Aduro Gvax Inc** .......................................................... E ...... 510 848-4400
740 Heinz Ave Berkeley (94710) *(P-5300)*

**Advance Adapters Inc** ................................................. E ...... 805 238-7000
4320 Aerotech Center Way Paso Robles (93446) *(P-13441)*

**Advance Adapters LLC** ................................................ E ...... 805 238-7000
4320 Aerotech Center Way Paso Robles (93446) *(P-13442)*

**Advance Aqua Tanks, Los Angeles** *Also Called: Alan Lem & Co Inc (P-7210)*

**Advance Carbon Products Inc** ...................................... E ...... 510 293-5930
2036 National Ave Hayward (94545) *(P-11297)*

**Advance Elctro Polishing, Santa Clara** *Also Called: Process Stainless Lab Inc (P-8999)*

**Advance Fabrication, Gilroy** *Also Called: Advance Fabrication Inc (P-6482)*

**Advance Fabrication Inc** .............................................. E ...... 408 779-5424
370 Tomkins Ct Ste A Gilroy (95020) *(P-6482)*

**Advance Paper Box Company** ...................................... C ...... 323 750-2550
6100 S Gramercy Pl Los Angeles (90047) *(P-3818)*

**Advance Plastics, National City** *Also Called: B and P Plastics Inc (P-6731)*

**Advance Storage Products, Huntington Beach** *Also Called: JCM Industries Inc (P-3692)*

**Advance-Tech Plating Inc** ............................................ F ...... 714 630-7093
1061 N Grove St Anaheim (92806) *(P-8907)*

**Advanced Aircraft Seal, Riverside** *Also Called: Sphere Alliance Inc (P-5203)*

**Advanced Analogic Tech Inc** ........................................ E ...... 408 330-1400
2740 Zanker Rd San Jose (95134) *(P-12276)*

**Advanced Arm Dynamics (PA)** ..................................... E ...... 310 372-3050
123 W Torrance Blvd Ste 203 Redondo Beach (90277) *(P-15316)*

**Advanced Biohealing.com, San Diego** *Also Called: Shire Rgenerative Medicine Inc (P-5656)*

**Advanced Bionics LLC (HQ)** ........................................ B ...... 661 362-1400
12740 San Fernando Rd Sylmar (91342) *(P-15317)*

# ALPHABETIC SECTION — Advanced Transit Dynamics Inc

Advanced Bionics Corporation (HQ) .............. C ...... 661 362-1400
  28515 Westinghouse Pl Valencia (91355) *(P-15318)*
Advanced Building Systems Inc .................. E ...... 818 652-4252
  11905 Regentview Ave Downey (90241) *(P-16081)*
Advanced Cell Diagnostics Inc ................... D ...... 510 576-8800
  7707 Gateway Blvd Ste 200 Newark (94560) *(P-19436)*
Advanced Ceramic Technology .................... F ...... 714 538-2524
  803 W Angus Ave Orange (92868) *(P-10672)*
Advanced Charging Tech LLC ..................... E ...... 877 228-5922
  17260 Newhope St Fountain Valley (92708) *(P-11358)*
Advanced Chemical Technology ................... E ...... 800 527-9607
  3540 E 26th St Vernon (90058) *(P-5066)*
Advanced Chemical Technology, Vernon Also Called: Advanced Chemical Technology *(P-5066)*
Advanced Chemistry & Technology Inc ............ D ...... 714 373-8118
  7341 Anaconda Ave Garden Grove (92841) *(P-6216)*
Advanced Circuits Inc ........................... E ...... 818 345-1993
  17067 Cantara St Van Nuys (91406) *(P-12044)*
Advanced Circuits Inc ........................... C ...... 415 602-6834
  1602 Tacoma Way Redwood City (94063) *(P-12045)*
Advanced Clutch Technology Inc ................. E ...... 661 940-7555
  206 E Avenue K4 Lancaster (93535) *(P-13443)*
Advanced Cmpsite Pdts Tech Inc ................. E ...... 714 895-5544
  15602 Chemical Ln Huntington Beach (92649) *(P-6696)*
Advanced Cnsrvtion Tech Dist I .................. F ...... 714 668-1200
  3176 Pullman St Ste 119 Costa Mesa (92626) *(P-8058)*
Advanced Color Graphics ........................ D ...... 909 930-1500
  1921 S Business Pkwy Ontario (91761) *(P-4504)*
Advanced Component Labs Inc ................... E ...... 408 327-0200
  990 Richard Ave Ste 118 Santa Clara (95050) *(P-12277)*
Advanced Components Technology, Oakland Also Called: Mills Acquisition Corporation *(P-8512)*
Advanced Corporate Svcs Inc .................... E ...... 310 937-6848
  200 Pier Ave Hermosa Beach (90254) *(P-19554)*
Advanced Cosmetic RES Labs Inc ................. E ...... 818 709-9945
  20550 Prairie St Chatsworth (91311) *(P-16082)*
Advanced Cutting Tools Inc ..................... E ...... 714 842-9376
  17741 Metzler Ln Huntington Beach (92647) *(P-7942)*
Advanced Design Engrg & Mfg, Santa Clara Also Called: Adem LLC *(P-10671)*
Advanced Digital Mfg LLC ....................... E ...... 714 245-0536
  1343 E Wilshire Ave Santa Ana (92705) *(P-13739)*
Advanced Digital Tech Intl, Escondido Also Called: Adti Media LLC *(P-15939)*
Advanced Drainage Systems Inc .................. D ...... 559 674-4989
  1025 Commerce Dr Madera (93637) *(P-6595)*
Advanced Electromagnetics Inc .................. E ...... 619 449-9492
  1320 Air Wing Rd Ste 101 San Diego (92154) *(P-14382)*
Advanced Electronic Solutions, Irvine Also Called: Patric Communications Inc *(P-466)*
Advanced Engineering & EDM Inc ................. F ...... 858 679-6800
  13007 Kirkham Way Ste A Poway (92064) *(P-10673)*
Advanced Engineering and EDM ................... E ...... 858 679-6800
  13007 Kirkham Way Ste A Poway (92064) *(P-10674)*
Advanced Engrg Mlding Tech Inc .................. E ...... 888 264-0392
  6510 Box Springs Blvd Ste B Riverside (92507) *(P-6697)*
Advanced Equipment Corporation (PA) ............ E ...... 714 635-5350
  2401 W Commonwealth Ave Fullerton (92833) *(P-3679)*
Advanced Fabrication Technology LLC ............ D ...... 510 489-6218
  31154 San Benito St Hayward (94544) *(P-9038)*
Advanced Flow Engineering Inc (PA) ............. E ...... 951 493-7155
  252 Granite St Corona (92879) *(P-13444)*
Advanced Flow Engineering Inc .................. E ...... 951 493-7100
  1375 Sampson Ave Corona (92879) *(P-13445)*
Advanced Food Products, Visalia Also Called: AFP Advanced Food Products LLC *(P-847)*
Advanced Fresh Cncpts Frnchise ................. D ...... 310 604-3200
  19700 Mariner Ave Torrance (90503) *(P-2046)*
Advanced Fresh Concepts Corp (PA) .............. E ...... 310 604-3630
  19205 S Laurel Park Rd Rancho Dominguez (90220) *(P-17751)*
Advanced Grinding Incorporated ................. E ...... 510 536-3465
  812 49th Ave Oakland (94601) *(P-9039)*
Advanced Grund Systems Engrg L (HQ) ............ E ...... 562 906-9300
  10805 Painter Ave Santa Fe Springs (90670) *(P-13701)*
Advanced Helicopter Svs, Woodland Also Called: Dfc Inc *(P-13649)*

Advanced Hpc Inc ............................... F ...... 858 716-8262
  7879 Raytheon Rd San Diego (92111) *(P-10220)*
Advanced Image Direct, Fullerton Also Called: Real Estate Image Inc *(P-17803)*
Advanced Image Direct LLC ...................... E ...... 714 502-3900
  1415 S Acacia Ave Fullerton (92831) *(P-17794)*
Advanced Indus Ceramics LLC .................... E ...... 408 955-9990
  2449 Zanker Rd San Jose (95131) *(P-9824)*
Advanced Industrial Coatings, Stockton Also Called: Ahc Enterprises Inc *(P-9040)*
Advanced Industrial Services, Bakersfield Also Called: CL Knox Inc *(P-219)*
Advanced Innvtive Rcovery Tech, Lake Forest Also Called: Pura Naturals Inc *(P-6029)*
Advanced Innvtive Rcvery Tech (PA) .............. F ...... 949 273-8100
  23615 El Toro Rd Lake Forest (92630) *(P-3517)*
Advanced Innvtive Rcvery Tech .................. E ...... 949 273-8100
  3401 Space Center Ct Ste 811b Jurupa Valley (91752) *(P-3518)*
Advanced Instruments, Pomona Also Called: Analytical Industries Inc *(P-14387)*
Advanced Integration Tech, Hayward Also Called: Integrated Flow Systems LLC *(P-14424)*
Advanced Joining Technologies Inc .............. E ...... 949 756-8091
  3030 Red Hill Ave Santa Ana (92705) *(P-10675)*
Advanced Machining Tooling Inc ................. E ...... 858 486-9050
  13535 Danielson St Poway (92064) *(P-9595)*
Advanced Materials Inc (HQ) .................... E ...... 310 537-5444
  20211 S Susana Rd Compton (90221) *(P-6698)*
Advanced McHning Solutions Inc ................. E ...... 619 671-3055
  3523 Main St Ste 606 Chula Vista (91911) *(P-10676)*
Advanced McHning Tchniques Inc ................. E ...... 408 778-4500
  16205 Vineyard Blvd Morgan Hill (95037) *(P-10677)*
Advanced Metal Finishing LLC ................... E ...... 530 888-7772
  2130 March Rd Roseville (95747) *(P-8908)*
Advanced Metal Mfg Inc ......................... E ...... 805 322-4161
  49 Strathearn Pl Simi Valley (93065) *(P-8362)*
Advanced Mfg & Dev Inc ......................... C ...... 707 459-9451
  200 N Lenore Ave Willits (95490) *(P-8363)*
Advanced Micro Instruments Inc ................. E ...... 714 848-5533
  225 Paularino Ave Costa Mesa (92626) *(P-14840)*
Advanced Mold Technology Inc ................... F
  16507 Celadon Ct Chino Hills (91709) *(P-9596)*
Advanced Motion Controls, Camarillo Also Called: Barta - Schoenewald Inc *(P-11256)*
Advanced Mtls Joining Corp (PA) ................ E ...... 626 449-2696
  2858 E Walnut St Pasadena (91107) *(P-13740)*
Advanced Packaging Tech Amer, San Diego Also Called: Apta Group Inc *(P-12325)*
Advanced Pattern & Mold Inc .................... F ...... 909 930-3444
  1720 S Balboa Ave Ontario (91761) *(P-7704)*
Advanced Photonix, Camarillo Also Called: OSI Optoelectronics Inc *(P-12624)*
Advanced Phrm Svcs Inc ......................... F ...... 714 903-1006
  11555 Monarch St Ste B Garden Grove (92841) *(P-17026)*
Advanced Polymer Technologies LLC .............. E ...... 209 464-2701
  3837 Imperial Way Stockton (95215) *(P-6699)*
Advanced Precision Inc ......................... F ...... 909 591-4244
  13445 Yorba Ave Chino (91710) *(P-10678)*
Advanced Pressure Technology ................... D ...... 707 259-0102
  687 Technology Way Napa (94558) *(P-14383)*
Advanced Products, Costa Mesa Also Called: Pro-Lite Inc *(P-16023)*
Advanced Publishing Tech Inc ................... F ...... 818 557-3035
  1105 N Hollywood Way Burbank (91505) *(P-4360)*
Advanced Realtime Systems Inc .................. F ...... 760 636-0444
  110 Conejo Cir Palm Desert (92260) *(P-17876)*
Advanced Semiconductor Inc ..................... D ...... 818 982-1200
  24955 Avenue Kearny Valencia (91355) *(P-12278)*
Advanced Spectral Tech Inc ..................... F ...... 805 527-7657
  74 W Cochran St Ste A Simi Valley (93065) *(P-14761)*
Advanced Sterilization (HQ) .................... C ...... 800 595-0200
  33 Technology Dr Irvine (92618) *(P-14951)*
Advanced Structural Tech Inc ................... C ...... 805 204-9133
  950 Richmond Ave Oxnard (93030) *(P-8771)*
Advanced Tech Machining Inc .................... F ...... 661 257-2313
  28909 Avenue Williams Valencia (91355) *(P-10679)*
Advanced Technology Co, Pasadena Also Called: Advanced Mtls Joining Corp *(P-13740)*
Advanced Technology Dev Ctr, San Mateo Also Called: Webroot Inc *(P-18931)*
Advanced Transit Dynamics Inc .................. D ...... 510 619-8245
  3150 Corporate Pl Hayward (94545) *(P-13446)*

**Advanced Uv Inc (PA)** .......................................................... E ...... 562 407-0299
16350 Manning Way Cerritos (90703) *(P-10532)*

**Advanced Vision Science Inc** ............................................. E ...... 805 683-3851
5743 Thornwood Dr Goleta (93117) *(P-15593)*

**Advanced Vsual Image Dsign LLC** ................................... E ...... 951 279-2138
229 N Sherman Ave Irvine (92614) *(P-4505)*

**Advanced Waveguide Tech** ................................................ E ...... 949 297-3564
29 Musick Irvine (92618) *(P-12908)*

**Advanced Web Offset Inc** ................................................... D ...... 760 727-1700
2260 Oak Ridge Way Vista (92081) *(P-4837)*

**Advanstar Communications Inc** ........................................ F ...... 818 593-5000
6200 Canoga Ave Fl 3 Woodland Hills (91367) *(P-4226)*

**Advanstar Communications Inc** ........................................ D ...... 714 513-8400
2525 Main St Ste 300 Irvine (92614) *(P-4227)*

**Advanstar Communications Inc** ........................................ E ...... 310 857-7500
2901 28th St Ste 100 Santa Monica (90405) *(P-19069)*

**Advanstar Communications Inc (DH)** ............................... C ...... 310 857-7500
2501 Colorado Ave Ste 280 Santa Monica (90404) *(P-19070)*

**Advanstar Global, Santa Monica** *Also Called: Advanstar Communications Inc* *(P-19070)*

**Advantage Adhesives Inc** ................................................... E ...... 909 204-4990
1420 S Vintage Ave Ontario (91761) *(P-6217)*

**Advantage Backhoes, Blue Jay** *Also Called: Travis Snyder* *(P-9443)*

**Advantage Chemical LLC** .................................................... E ...... 951 225-4631
27375 Via Industria Temecula (92590) *(P-17237)*

**Advantage Engrg & Chemistry, Santa Ana** *Also Called: AEC Group Inc* *(P-13447)*

**Advantage Manufacturing Inc** ........................................... E ...... 714 505-1166
616 S Santa Fe St Santa Ana (92705) *(P-16639)*

**Advantage Metal Products Inc** .......................................... D ...... 925 667-2009
7855 Southfront Rd Livermore (94551) *(P-8364)*

**Advantage Truss Company LLC** ........................................ E ...... 831 635-0377
2025 San Juan Rd Hollister (95023) *(P-3290)*

**Advantest America Inc (HQ)** .............................................. D ...... 408 456-3600
3061 Zanker Rd San Jose (95134) *(P-12279)*

**Advantest America Inc** ....................................................... B ...... 408 988-7700
3201 Scott Blvd Santa Clara (95054) *(P-16688)*

**Advantest Test Solutions Inc** ............................................. D ...... 949 523-6900
26211 Enterprise Way Lake Forest (92630) *(P-12280)*

**Advertiser, The, Oakdale** *Also Called: Morris Publications* *(P-4163)*

**ADVERUM, Redwood City** *Also Called: Adverum Biotechnologies Inc* *(P-5786)*

**Adverum Biotechnologies Inc (PA)** .................................... D ...... 650 656-9323
100 Cardinal Way Redwood City (94063) *(P-5786)*

**Advexure LLC** ........................................................................ E ...... 920 917-9566
9281 Irvine Blvd Irvine (92618) *(P-15627)*

**Advisor Software Inc (PA)** .................................................. E ...... 925 299-7782
2185 N California Blvd Ste 290 Walnut Creek (94596) *(P-18024)*

**Advisorsquare, Culver City** *Also Called: Liveoffice LLC* *(P-18499)*

**Advisys Inc** ............................................................................ E ...... 949 250-0794
3 Corporate Park Ste 240 Irvine (92606) *(P-18025)*

**Advoque Group LLC** ............................................................ E ...... 408 560-2990
1030 Commercial St Ste 108 San Jose (95112) *(P-10680)*

**Adwest, Anaheim** *Also Called: Adwest Technologies Inc* *(P-9977)*

**Adwest Technologies Inc (HQ)** .......................................... E ...... 714 632-8595
4222 E La Palma Ave Anaheim (92807) *(P-9977)*

**AEC, Brea** *Also Called: Aerospace Engineering LLC* *(P-13755)*

**AEC - Able Engineering Company Inc** ............................. C ...... 805 685-2262
600 Pine Ave Goleta (93117) *(P-8089)*

**AEC Group Inc** ...................................................................... F ...... 714 444-1395
3600 W Carriage Dr Santa Ana (92704) *(P-13447)*

**Aechelon Technology Inc (PA)** .......................................... C ...... 415 255-0120
611 Gateway Blvd Ste 300 South San Francisco (94080) *(P-17877)*

**Aee Solar Inc (DH)** ............................................................... E ...... 800 777-6609
225 Bush St Ste 1400 San Francisco (94104) *(P-16640)*

**AEG Industries Inc** ............................................................... E ...... 707 575-0697
1219 Briggs Ave Santa Rosa (95401) *(P-13741)*

**Aegis Biodefense, San Diego** *Also Called: Aegis Life Inc* *(P-5301)*

**Aegis Life Inc** ........................................................................ E ...... 650 666-5287
3033 Science Park Rd Ste 270 San Diego (92121) *(P-5301)*

**Aehr Test, Fremont** *Also Called: Aehr Test Systems* *(P-14486)*

**Aehr Test Systems (PA)** ...................................................... D ...... 510 623-9400
400 Kato Ter Fremont (94539) *(P-14486)*

**Aem Components USA, San Diego** *Also Called: Aem Electronics (usa) Inc* *(P-12826)*

**Aem Electronics (usa) Inc (PA)** .......................................... F ...... 858 481-0210
6610 Cobra Way San Diego (92121) *(P-12826)*

**Aemetis Advnced Fels Keyes Inc** ...................................... E ...... 209 632-4511
4209 Jessup Rd Ceres (95307) *(P-6121)*

**Aemi, San Diego** *Also Called: Advanced Electromagnetics Inc* *(P-14382)*

**Aemi Holdings LLC** ............................................................. D ...... 858 481-0210
6610 Cobra Way San Diego (92121) *(P-11233)*

**AEP Span Inc** ........................................................................ E ...... 916 372-0933
2110 Enterprise Blvd West Sacramento (95691) *(P-510)*

**Aera Energy, Rio Vista** *Also Called: Dick Browns Technical Service* *(P-155)*

**Aera Energy LLC** .................................................................. A ...... 661 665-5000
10000 Ming Ave Bakersfield (93389) *(P-119)*

**Aera Energy LLC** .................................................................. C ...... 661 334-3100
19590 7th Standard Rd Mc Kittrick (93251) *(P-120)*

**Aera Energy Services Company (HQ)** .............................. A ...... 661 665-5000
10000 Ming Ave Bakersfield (93311) *(P-151)*

**Aera Energy Services Company** ...................................... C ...... 661 665-4400
59231 Main Camp Rd Mc Kittrick (93251) *(P-152)*

**Aera Energy Services Company** ...................................... D ...... 661 665-3200
29235 Highway 33 Maricopa (93252) *(P-153)*

**Aera Energy Services Company** ...................................... C ...... 559 935-7418
29010 Shell Rd Coalinga (93210) *(P-9453)*

**Aera Energy South Midway, Maricopa** *Also Called: Aera Energy Services Company* *(P-153)*

**Aereotech LLC** ...................................................................... F ...... 626 319-5394
4572 Fellows St Union City (94587) *(P-15512)*

**Aero ARC** ............................................................................... E ...... 310 324-3400
16634 S Figueroa St Gardena (90248) *(P-8365)*

**Aero Bending Company** ..................................................... D ...... 661 948-2363
560 Auto Center Dr Ste A Palmdale (93551) *(P-8366)*

**Aero Chip Inc** ....................................................................... E ...... 562 404-6300
13563 Freeway Dr Santa Fe Springs (90670) *(P-10681)*

**Aero Dynamic Machining Inc** ........................................... D ...... 714 379-1073
7472 Chapman Ave Garden Grove (92841) *(P-10682)*

**Aero Engineering, Valencia** *Also Called: Aero Engineering & Mfg Co LLC* *(P-13742)*

**Aero Engineering & Mfg Co LLC** ...................................... D ...... 661 295-0875
28217 Avenue Crocker Valencia (91355) *(P-13742)*

**Aero Industries LLC** ............................................................ B ...... 805 688-6734
139 Industrial Way Buellton (93427) *(P-10683)*

**Aero Mechanism Precision Inc** ........................................ E ...... 818 886-1855
21700 Marilla St Chatsworth (91311) *(P-10684)*

**Aero Pacific Corporation** ................................................... C ...... 714 961-9200
20445 E Walnut Dr N Walnut (91789) *(P-13743)*

**Aero Performance, Corona** *Also Called: Irwin Aviation Inc* *(P-13878)*

**Aero Precision Engineering** .............................................. E ...... 310 642-9747
11300 Hindry Ave Los Angeles (90045) *(P-8367)*

**Aero Products Co., Los Angeles** *Also Called: Coating Specialties Inc* *(P-13810)*

**Aero Sense Inc** .................................................................... F ...... 661 257-1608
26074 Avenue Hall Ste 18 Valencia (91355) *(P-13744)*

**Aero Shade Co Inc (PA)** ..................................................... E ...... 323 938-2314
8404 W 3rd St Los Angeles (90048) *(P-17530)*

**Aero Turbine Inc** ................................................................. D ...... 209 983-1112
6800 Lindbergh St Stockton (95206) *(P-9306)*

**Aero Worx, Torrance** *Also Called: Aeroworx Inc* *(P-19239)*

**Aero-Clssics Heat Trnsf Pdts I** .......................................... F ...... 909 596-1630
1677 Curtiss Ct La Verne (91750) *(P-8297)*

**Aero-Craft Hydraulics Inc** ................................................. E ...... 951 736-4690
392 N Smith Ave Corona (92878) *(P-13745)*

**Aero-Electric Connector Inc (PA)** .................................... B ...... 310 618-3737
2280 W 208th St Torrance (90501) *(P-11438)*

**Aero-k** .................................................................................. E ...... 626 350-5125
2040 E Dyer Rd Santa Ana (92705) *(P-10685)*

**Aero-Mechanical Engrg Inc** .............................................. F ...... 323 682-0961
5945 Engineer Dr Huntington Beach (92649) *(P-10686)*

**Aero-Nasch Aviation Inc** ................................................... F ...... 818 786-5480
6849 Hayvenhurst Ave Van Nuys (91406) *(P-13746)*

**Aeroantenna Technology Inc** ........................................... C ...... 818 993-3842
20732 Lassen St Chatsworth (91311) *(P-14135)*

**Aerocraft Heat Treating Co Inc** ........................................ D ...... 562 674-2400
15701 Minnesota Ave Paramount (90723) *(P-7874)*

**Aerodynamic Engineering Inc** .......................................... E ...... 714 891-2651
15495 Graham St Huntington Beach (92649) *(P-10687)*

# ALPHABETIC SECTION

**Aerodyne Prcsion Machining Inc** .................................................. E ...... 714 891-1311
5471 Argosy Ave Huntington Beach (92649) *(P-10688)*

**Aerofab Corporation** ...................................................................... F ...... 714 635-0902
4001 E Leaverton Ct Anaheim (92807) *(P-8090)*

**Aerofit LLC** ..................................................................................... C ...... 714 521-5060
1425 S Acacia Ave Fullerton (92831) *(P-9246)*

**Aeroflex Cupertino, Sunnyvale** *Also Called: Aeroflex High Speed Test Solutions Inc (P-14487)*

**Aeroflex High Speed Test Solutions Inc** ...................................... E ...... 516 694-6700
256 Gibraltar Dr Ste 110 Sunnyvale (94089) *(P-14487)*

**Aeroflex Incorporated** .................................................................... E ...... 800 843-1553
15375 Barranca Pkwy Ste F106 Irvine (92618) *(P-12281)*

**Aeroflite Enterprises Inc** ............................................................... D ...... 714 773-4251
261 Gemini Ave Brea (92821) *(P-12865)*

**Aerofoam Industries Inc** ................................................................ D ...... 951 245-4429
31855 Corydon St Lake Elsinore (92530) *(P-3612)*

**Aerojet Rcketdyne Holdings Inc (HQ)** .......................................... D ...... 310 252-8100
222 N Pacific Coast Hwy Ste 500 El Segundo (90245) *(P-14136)*

**Aerojet Rocketdyne, Canoga Park** *Also Called: Aerojet Rocketdyne De Inc (P-6122)*

**Aerojet Rocketdyne, Rancho Cordova** *Also Called: Aerojet Rocketdyne Inc (P-14101)*

**Aerojet Rocketdyne Inc** ................................................................. C ...... 916 355-4000
1180 Iron Point Rd Ste 350 Folsom (95630) *(P-13747)*

**Aerojet Rocketdyne Inc (DH)** ........................................................ A ...... 916 355-4000
2001 Aerojet Rd Rancho Cordova (95742) *(P-14101)*

**Aerojet Rocketdyne De Inc (DH)** .................................................. B ...... 818 586-1000
8900 De Soto Ave Canoga Park (91304) *(P-6122)*

**Aerojet Rocketdyne De Inc** ........................................................... C ...... 818 586-9629
8495 Carla Ln West Hills (91304) *(P-6123)*

**Aerojet Rocketdyne De Inc** ........................................................... C ...... 818 586-1000
9001 Lurline Ave Chatsworth (91311) *(P-6124)*

**Aerojet Rocketdyne De Inc** ........................................................... B ...... 818 586-1000
6633 Canoga Ave Canoga Park (91303) *(P-13702)*

**Aerojet Rocketdyne De Inc** ........................................................... A ...... 310 414-0110
222 N Pacific Coast Hwy Ste 50 El Segundo (90245) *(P-14137)*

**Aerol Co, Rancho Dominguez** *Also Called: Aerol Co Inc (P-7833)*

**Aerol Co Inc** .................................................................................... E ...... 310 762-2660
19560 S Rancho Way Rancho Dominguez (90220) *(P-7833)*

**Aeroliant Manufacturing Inc** ......................................................... E ...... 310 257-1903
1613 Lockness Pl Torrance (90501) *(P-10689)*

**Aerometals Inc** ............................................................................... C ...... 916 939-6888
3920 Sandstone Dr El Dorado Hills (95762) *(P-13748)*

**Aerontics Systems Arspc Strctr, San Diego** *Also Called: Northrop Grumman Systems Corp (P-14243)*

**Aeroshear Aviation Svcs Inc (PA)** ................................................ E ...... 818 779-1650
7701 Woodley Ave 200 Van Nuys (91406) *(P-13749)*

**Aerospace and Coml Tooling Inc** ................................................. F ...... 909 930-5780
1866 S Lake Pl Ontario (91761) *(P-10690)*

**Aerospace Composite Products (PA)** ......................................... F ...... 925 443-5900
78 Lindbergh Ave Livermore (94551) *(P-13750)*

**Aerospace Driven Tech Inc** .......................................................... F ...... 949 553-1606
2807 Catherine Way Santa Ana (92705) *(P-13751)*

**Aerospace Dynamics Intl Inc** ....................................................... B ...... 661 310-6986
25575 Rye Canyon Rd Santa Clarita (91355) *(P-13752)*

**Aerospace Dynamics Intl Inc (DH)** .............................................. C ...... 661 257-3535
25540 Rye Canyon Rd Valencia (91355) *(P-13753)*

**Aerospace Engineering LLC** ........................................................ E ...... 714 641-5884
2141 S Standard Ave Santa Ana (92707) *(P-13754)*

**Aerospace Engineering LLC (PA)** ................................................ D ...... 714 996-8178
2632 Saturn St Brea (92821) *(P-13755)*

**Aerospace Engrg Support Corp** .................................................. E ...... 310 297-4050
645 Hawaii St El Segundo (90245) *(P-13756)*

**Aerospace Fasteners Group, Santa Ana** *Also Called: SPS Technologies LLC (P-15917)*

**Aerospace Parts Holdings Inc** ..................................................... A ...... 949 877-3630
3150 E Miraloma Ave Anaheim (92806) *(P-13757)*

**Aerospace Service & Controls** .................................................... F ...... 818 833-0088
28402 Livingston Ave Valencia (91355) *(P-13758)*

**Aerospace Systems, Redondo Beach** *Also Called: Northrop Grumman Systems Corp (P-13682)*

**Aerotec Alloys Inc** ......................................................................... E ...... 562 809-1378
10632 Alondra Blvd Norwalk (90650) *(P-7804)*

**Aerotech News and Review Inc (PA)** .......................................... E ...... 661 945-5634
220 E Avenue K4 Ste 4 Lancaster (93535) *(P-4228)*

**Aerotech Precision Machining** ..................................................... F ...... 661 802-7185
42541 6th St E Ste 17 Lancaster (93535) *(P-10691)*

**Aerotek Inc** ..................................................................................... A ...... 805 604-3000
2751 Park View Ct Ste 221 Oxnard (93036) *(P-10692)*

**Aerovironment Inc** ......................................................................... E ...... 626 357-9983
1610 S Magnolia Ave Monrovia (91016) *(P-13626)*

**Aerovironment Inc** ......................................................................... E ...... 626 357-9983
222 E Huntington Dr Ste 118 Monrovia (91016) *(P-13627)*

**Aerovironment Inc** ......................................................................... E ...... 707 206-9372
1035 N Mcdowell Blvd Petaluma (94954) *(P-13628)*

**Aerovironment Inc** ......................................................................... E ...... 626 357-9983
825 S Myrtle Ave Monrovia (91016) *(P-13629)*

**Aerovironment Inc** ......................................................................... E ...... 805 520-8350
900 Innovators Way Simi Valley (93065) *(P-13630)*

**Aerowind Corporation** ................................................................... F ...... 619 569-1960
1959 John Towers Ave El Cajon (92020) *(P-14107)*

**Aeroworx Inc** .................................................................................. E ...... 310 891-0300
2565 W 237th St Torrance (90505) *(P-19239)*

**Aerwins Inc** .................................................................................... D ...... 808 892-6611
101 Jefferson Dr Fl 1 Menlo Park (94025) *(P-13759)*

**AES, Palo Alto** *Also Called: Applied Expert Systems Inc (P-18056)*

**Aethercomm Inc** ............................................................................. C ...... 760 208-6002
3205 Lionshead Ave Carlsbad (92010) *(P-11799)*

**AEVA, Mountain View** *Also Called: Aeva Technologies Inc (P-13448)*

**Aeva Technologies Inc (PA)** ......................................................... B ...... 650 481-7070
555 Ellis St Mountain View (94043) *(P-13448)*

**Aeye Inc (PA)** ................................................................................. F ...... 925 400-4366
4670 Willow Rd Ste 125 Pleasanton (94588) *(P-13449)*

**Afc Trading & Wholesale Inc** ....................................................... E ...... 323 223-7738
4738 Valley Blvd Los Angeles (90032) *(P-17112)*

**Afcfc, Torrance** *Also Called: Advanced Fresh Cncpts Frnchise (P-2046)*

**Afco, Alhambra** *Also Called: Alhambra Foundry Company Ltd (P-7674)*

**Afe Power, Corona** *Also Called: Advanced Flow Engineering Inc (P-13444)*

**Afe Power, Corona** *Also Called: Advanced Flow Engineering Inc (P-13445)*

**Aferin LLC** ....................................................................................... E ...... 562 903-1500
9808 Alburtis Ave Santa Fe Springs (90670) *(P-10221)*

**Affinity Group, Ventura** *Also Called: Agi Holding Corp (P-19312)*

**Affluent Living Publication, Anaheim** *Also Called: Affluent Target Marketing Inc (P-4229)*

**Affluent Target Marketing Inc** ...................................................... E ...... 714 446-6280
3855 E La Palma Ave Ste 250 Anaheim (92807) *(P-4229)*

**Affymetrix Inc** ................................................................................. D ...... 858 642-2058
5893 Oberlin Dr San Diego (92121) *(P-14603)*

**Affymetrix Inc** ................................................................................. E ...... 408 731-5000
3450 Central Expy Santa Clara (95051) *(P-14604)*

**Affymetrix Inc (HQ)** ....................................................................... C ...... 408 731-5000
428 Oakmead Pkwy Sunnyvale (94085) *(P-14605)*

**AFP, City Of Industry** *Also Called: Alum-A-Fold Pacific Inc (P-7726)*

**AFP Advanced Food Products LLC** ............................................ E ...... 559 651-1737
900 N Plaza Dr Visalia (93291) *(P-824)*

**AFP Advanced Food Products LLC** ............................................ D ...... 559 627-2070
1211 E Noble Ave Visalia (93292) *(P-847)*

**Afr Apparel International Inc** ....................................................... D ...... 818 773-5000
25365 Prado De La Felicidad Calabasas (91302) *(P-2827)*

**Afresh Technologies Inc** ............................................................... D ...... 415 651-5068
33 New Montgomery St Ste 1100 San Francisco (94105) *(P-18026)*

**Africajun LLC** ................................................................................. E ...... 310 403-1673
39874 Golfers Dr Palmdale (93551) *(P-19293)*

**AG Adriano Goldschmied Inc (PA)** .............................................. E ...... 323 357-1111
2741 Seminole Ave Ste A South Gate (90280) *(P-2585)*

**AG Industrial Mfg Inc** .................................................................... E ...... 209 369-1994
110 S Beckman Rd Lodi (95240) *(P-9334)*

**AG Jeans, South Gate** *Also Called: AG Adriano Goldschmied Inc (P-2585)*

**AG Machining Inc** .......................................................................... D ...... 805 531-9555
2401 W Almond Ave Madera (93637) *(P-8091)*

**AG Millworks, Ventura** *Also Called: Art Glass Etc Inc (P-3111)*

**AG Neovo Technology Corp** ......................................................... F ...... 408 321-8210
48501 Warm Springs Blvd Ste 114 Fremont (94539) *(P-10303)*

**Age Incorporated** .......................................................................... E ...... 562 483-7300
14831 Spring Ave Santa Fe Springs (90670) *(P-11234)*

**Agencycom LLC** ............................................................................ B ...... 415 817-3800
5353 Grosvenor Blvd Los Angeles (90066) *(P-18027)*

**Agents West Inc** .................................................................. E ...... 949 614-0293
6 Hughes Ste 210 Irvine (92618) *(P-13209)*

**Aggregate - Lapis Ind Sand/Mar, Marina** *Also Called: Cemex Cnstr Mtls PCF LLC (P-7254)*

**Aggregate -Eliot Quarry, Pleasanton** *Also Called: Cemex Cnstr Mtls PCF LLC (P-7420)*

**Aggregate Clayton Quarry, Clayton** *Also Called: Cemex Cnstr Mtls PCF LLC (P-16467)*

**Aggressive Engineering Corp** ............................................ F ...... 714 995-8313
1235 N Knollwood Cir Anaheim (92801) *(P-16805)*

**Agh, Fresno** *Also Called: American Grape Harvesters Inc (P-16795)*

**Agi Holding Corp (PA)** .......................................................... D ...... 805 667-4100
2575 Vista Del Mar Dr Ventura (93001) *(P-19312)*

**Agile Rf Inc** ........................................................................... E ...... 805 968-5159
93 Castilian Dr Santa Barbara (93117) *(P-12909)*

**Agilent, Santa Clara** *Also Called: Agilent Technologies Inc (P-14606)*

**Agilent Tech World Trade Inc (HQ)** ...................................... D ...... 408 345-8886
5301 Stevens Creek Blvd Santa Clara (95051) *(P-14488)*

**Agilent Technologies, Carpinteria** *Also Called: Agilent Technologies Inc (P-14493)*

**Agilent Technologies Inc** ..................................................... D ...... 916 985-7888
91 Blue Ravine Rd Folsom (95630) *(P-14489)*

**Agilent Technologies Inc** ..................................................... E ...... 805 566-6655
1170 Mark Ave Carpinteria (93013) *(P-14490)*

**Agilent Technologies Inc** ..................................................... D ...... 408 345-8886
5301 Stevens Creek Blvd Santa Clara (95051) *(P-14491)*

**Agilent Technologies Inc** ..................................................... D ...... 858 373-6300
11011 N Torrey Pines Rd La Jolla (92037) *(P-14492)*

**Agilent Technologies Inc** ..................................................... E ...... 805 566-1405
6392 Via Real Carpinteria (93013) *(P-14493)*

**Agilent Technologies Inc** ..................................................... F ...... 408 553-7777
3175 Bowers Ave Santa Clara (95054) *(P-14494)*

**Agilent Technologies Inc (PA)** ............................................. A ...... 800 227-9770
5301 Stevens Creek Blvd Santa Clara (95051) *(P-14606)*

**Agilepoint Inc (PA)** ............................................................... D ...... 650 968-6789
1916 Old Middlefield Way Ste B Mountain View (94043) *(P-18028)*

**Agilex Flavors & Fragrances, Commerce** *Also Called: Key Essentials Inc (P-2012)*

**Agility Fuel Systems LLC (DH)** ........................................... F ...... 949 236-5520
1815 Carnegie Ave Santa Ana (92705) *(P-13450)*

**Agility Logistics Corp (DH)** ................................................. D ...... 714 617-6300
310 Commerce Ste 250 Irvine (92602) *(P-16306)*

**Agiloft Inc (PA)** ...................................................................... D ...... 650 459-5637
303 Twin Dolphin Dr Redwood City (94065) *(P-18029)*

**Agl, Temecula** *Also Called: Artificial Grass Liquidators (P-16090)*

**Agnes Cove, Napa** *Also Called: Agnes Cove LLC (P-1472)*

**Agnes Cove LLC (PA)** .......................................................... E ...... 707 266-6899
50 Technology Ct Napa (94558) *(P-1472)*

**Agnetix Inc** ............................................................................ F ...... 833 246-3849
7965 Dunbrook Rd Ste I San Diego (92126) *(P-11517)*

**Agouron Pharmaceuticals Inc (HQ)** .................................... E ...... 858 622-3000
10777 Science Center Dr San Diego (92121) *(P-5302)*

**Agra Tech Inc** ........................................................................ F ...... 925 432-3399
2131 Piedmont Way Pittsburg (94565) *(P-8651)*

**Agreserves Inc** ..................................................................... E ...... 530 343-5365
6100 Wilson Landing Rd Chico (95973) *(P-35)*

**Agri Service Inc** ................................................................... E ...... 760 295-6255
2141 Oceanside Blvd Oceanside (92054) *(P-16355)*

**Agri Technovation Inc** ......................................................... C ...... 559 931-3332
516 Villa Ave Clovis (93612) *(P-6168)*

**Agribag Inc** ........................................................................... E ...... 510 533-2388
3925 Alameda Ave Oakland (94601) *(P-3960)*

**Agriculture Bag Manufacturing,, Oakland** *Also Called: Agriculture Bag Mfg USA Inc (P-2433)*

**Agriculture Bag Mfg USA Inc (PA)** ..................................... E ...... 510 632-5637
960 98th Ave Oakland (94603) *(P-2433)*

**Agrifim Irrigation Pdts Inc** .................................................. F ...... 559 443-6680
2855 S East Ave Fresno (93725) *(P-9335)*

**Agron Inc (PA)** ...................................................................... D ...... 310 473-7223
2440 S Sepulveda Blvd Ste 201 Los Angeles (90064) *(P-2840)*

**AGS Usa LLC** ........................................................................ C ...... 323 588-2200
1210 Rexford Ave Pasadena (91107) *(P-2697)*

**Agse, Santa Fe Springs** *Also Called: Advanced Grund Systems Engrg L (P-13701)*

**Agt, Corona** *Also Called: Absolute Graphic Tech USA Inc (P-11304)*

**Agua Dulce Vineyards LLC** ................................................. E ...... 661 268-7402
9640 Sierra Hwy Agua Dulce (91390) *(P-1473)*

**Agusa** ..................................................................................... E ...... 559 924-4785
1055 S 19th Ave Lemoore (93245) *(P-2120)*

**Aha Labs Inc** ......................................................................... D ...... 650 575-1425
20 Gloria Cir Menlo Park (94025) *(P-18030)*

**Aharoni & Steele Inc** ........................................................... F ...... 408 451-9585
1855 Norman Ave Santa Clara (95054) *(P-17423)*

**Ahc Enterprises Inc** ............................................................. D ...... 209 234-2700
950 Industrial Dr Stockton (95206) *(P-9040)*

**Ahead Magnetics Inc** .......................................................... D ...... 408 226-9800
6410 Via Del Oro San Jose (95119) *(P-12910)*

**Aheadtek, San Jose** *Also Called: Ahead Magnetics Inc (P-12910)*

**Ahf-Ducommun Incorporated (HQ)** .................................... C ...... 310 380-5390
268 E Gardena Blvd Gardena (90248) *(P-13760)*

**Ahi Investment Inc (DH)** ...................................................... E ...... 818 979-0030
675 Glenoaks Blvd San Fernando (91340) *(P-17283)*

**Ahlborn Companies, Santa Rosa** *Also Called: Ahlborn Fence & Steel Inc (P-553)*

**Ahlborn Fence & Steel Inc (PA)** .......................................... E ...... 707 573-0742
1230 Century Ct Santa Rosa (95403) *(P-553)*

**Ahlborn Structural Steel Inc** ............................................... E ...... 707 573-0742
1230 Century Ct Santa Rosa (95403) *(P-8092)*

**Ahntech Inc (PA)** .................................................................. D ...... 650 861-3987
745 Distel Dr Ste 104 Los Altos (94022) *(P-19375)*

**Ahs Trinity Group Inc (PA)** .................................................. E ...... 818 508-2105
11041 Vanowen St North Hollywood (91605) *(P-2888)*

**Ahw, Long Beach** *Also Called: Aircraft Hardware West (P-16913)*

**AI Foods Corporation (PA)** ................................................. E ...... 323 222-0827
1700 N Soto St Los Angeles (90033) *(P-17160)*

**Ai Industries, Redwood City** *Also Called: Ai Industries Inc (P-8909)*

**Ai Industries Inc (PA)** .......................................................... D ...... 650 366-4099
1725 E Bayshore Rd Ste 101 Redwood City (94063) *(P-8909)*

**Aibot US Operation Inc** ....................................................... E ...... 562 283-3286
2883 E Spring St Ste 200 Long Beach (90806) *(P-13631)*

**Aidells Sausage, San Lorenzo** *Also Called: Aidells Sausage Company Inc (P-628)*

**Aidells Sausage Company Inc** ........................................... A ...... 510 614-5450
2411 Baumann Ave San Lorenzo (94580) *(P-628)*

**Aii Beauty, Commerce** *Also Called: American Intl Inds Inc (P-5943)*

**Aim, Lodi** *Also Called: AG Industrial Mfg Inc (P-9334)*

**Aim Mail Centers, Woodland** *Also Called: American International Mfg Co (P-9338)*

**Aim Mail Centers, Rancho Cordova** *Also Called: Automotive Importing Manufacturing Inc (P-16374)*

**Aiminsight Solutions Inc** .................................................... F ...... 310 313-0047
4127 Berryman Ave Los Angeles (90066) *(P-19025)*

**Ainor Signs Inc** .................................................................... E ...... 916 348-4370
5443 Stationers Way Sacramento (95842) *(P-15940)*

**Ainos Inc (PA)** ...................................................................... E ...... 858 869-2986
8880 Rio San Diego Dr Ste 800 San Diego (92108) *(P-19437)*

**Aio Acquisition Inc (HQ)** ..................................................... D ...... 800 333-3795
3200 E Guasti Rd Ste 300 Ontario (91761) *(P-4361)*

**Air & Gas Tech Inc** .............................................................. E ...... 619 955-5980
11433 Woodside Ave Santee (92071) *(P-14027)*

**Air 88 Inc** ............................................................................... E ...... 858 277-1453
3753 John J Montgomery Dr San Diego (92123) *(P-16298)*

**Air Adhart Inc** ....................................................................... E ...... 951 698-4452
41549 Cherry St Murrieta (92562) *(P-12046)*

**Air Cabin Engineering Inc** .................................................. E ...... 714 637-4111
231 W Blueridge Ave Orange (92865) *(P-13761)*

**Air Combat Systems, Palmdale** *Also Called: Northrop Grumman Systems Corp (P-13680)*

**Air Components Inc** ............................................................ E ...... 909 980-8224
10235 Indiana Ct Rancho Cucamonga (91730) *(P-13762)*

**Air Electro Inc (PA)** .............................................................. C ...... 818 407-5400
9452 De Soto Ave Chatsworth (91311) *(P-16689)*

**Air Fayre USA Inc** ................................................................ C ...... 310 808-1061
1720 W 135th St Gardena (90249) *(P-17563)*

**Air Flow Research, Valencia** *Also Called: Air Flow Research Heads Inc (P-13451)*

**Air Flow Research Heads Inc** ............................................ E ...... 661 257-8124
28611 Industry Dr Valencia (91355) *(P-13451)*

**Air Frame Mfg & Supply Co Inc** ......................................... E ...... 661 257-7728
26135 Technology Dr Valencia (91355) *(P-16912)*

**Air Frame Mfg. & Supply Co., Valencia** *Also Called: Air Frame Mfg & Supply Co Inc (P-16912)*

**Air Gap International, Placentia** *Also Called: Altinex Inc (P-11804)*

# ALPHABETIC SECTION

**Air Liquid Healthcare** ............................................... E ...... 909 899-4633
12460 Arrow Rte Rancho Cucamonga (91739) *(P-5036)*

**Air Liquide Electronics US LP** ..................................... A ...... 310 549-7079
1502 W Anaheim St Wilmington (90744) *(P-5037)*

**Air Liquide Electronics US LP** ..................................... A ...... 559 685-2402
11754 Rd 120 Pixley (93256) *(P-5038)*

**Air Liquide Electronics US LP** ..................................... A ...... 510 624-4338
46401 Landing Pkwy Fremont (94538) *(P-5067)*

**Air Louvers Inc** ........................................................... E ...... 800 554-6077
6285 Randolph St Commerce (90040) *(P-8252)*

**Air Monitor Corporation (PA)** ....................................... D ...... 707 544-2706
1050 Hopper Ave Santa Rosa (95403) *(P-14384)*

**Air Products, Vernon** *Also Called: Evonik Corporation (P-6283)*

**Air Products, Torrance** *Also Called: Air Products and Chemicals Inc (P-6331)*

**Air Products and Chemicals Inc** .................................. D ...... 760 931-9555
1969 Palomar Oaks Way Carlsbad (92011) *(P-5039)*

**Air Products and Chemicals Inc** .................................. F ...... 310 212-2800
3700 W 190th St Torrance (90504) *(P-6331)*

**Air Protein Inc** ............................................................ E ...... 510 285-9097
2020 Williams St Ste B1 San Leandro (94577) *(P-2121)*

**Air Tube Transfer Systems Inc** .................................... F ...... 714 363-0700
715 N Cypress St Orange (92867) *(P-9479)*

**Air-Vol Block Inc** ......................................................... E ...... 805 543-1314
1 Suburban Rd San Luis Obispo (93401) *(P-7291)*

**Aira Tech, Carlsbad** *Also Called: Aira Tech Corp (P-18031)*

**Aira Tech Corp** ............................................................ C ...... 800 835-1934
3451 Via Montebello Ste 192 Pmb 214 Carlsbad (92009) *(P-18031)*

**Airbase Inc (PA)** .......................................................... E ...... 415 625-6222
548 Market St Ste 93249 San Francisco (94104) *(P-18032)*

**Airborne Components, Carson** *Also Called: Stanford Mu Corporation (P-14116)*

**Airborne Systems N Amer CA Inc** ................................ C ...... 714 662-1400
3100 W Segerstrom Ave Santa Ana (92704) *(P-3023)*

**Airborne Technologies, Camarillo** *Also Called: Airborne Technologies Inc (P-13763)*

**Airborne Technologies Inc** .......................................... C ...... 805 389-3700
999 Avenida Acaso Camarillo (93012) *(P-13763)*

**Aircarbon, Huntington Beach** *Also Called: Newlight Technologies Inc (P-6930)*

**Aircoat Inc** .................................................................. F ...... 310 527-2258
13405 S Broadway Los Angeles (90061) *(P-9041)*

**Aircraft Covers Inc** ..................................................... E ...... 408 738-3959
18850 Adams Ct Morgan Hill (95037) *(P-2967)*

**Aircraft Covers Inc (PA)** .............................................. E ...... 408 738-3959
18850 Adams Ct Morgan Hill (95037) *(P-2968)*

**Aircraft Hardware West** .............................................. E ...... 562 961-9324
2180 Temple Ave Long Beach (90804) *(P-16913)*

**Aircraft Hinge Inc** ...................................................... E ...... 661 257-3434
26074 Avenue Hall Ste 16 Valencia (91355) *(P-13764)*

**Aircraft Repair & Overhaul Svc (PA)** ........................... E ...... 714 630-9494
1186 N Grove St Anaheim (92806) *(P-16299)*

**Aircraft Xray Laboratories Inc** .................................... D ...... 323 587-4141
5216 Pacific Blvd Huntington Park (90255) *(P-19500)*

**Airdraulics Inc** ........................................................... E ...... 818 982-1400
13261 Saticoy St North Hollywood (91605) *(P-19163)*

**Airdyne Refrigeration, Cerritos** *Also Called: ARI Industries Inc (P-10482)*

**Airdyne Refrigeration, Cerritos** *Also Called: Refrigerator Manufacturers LLC (P-10513)*

**Aire Sheet Metal Inc** .................................................. E ...... 650 364-8081
1973 E Bayshore Rd Redwood City (94063) *(P-403)*

**Aireloom, Rancho Cucamonga** *Also Called: ES Kluft & Company Inc (P-3525)*

**AIRGAIN, San Diego** *Also Called: Airgain Inc (P-11800)*

**Airgain Inc (PA)** .......................................................... E ...... 760 579-0200
3611 Valley Centre Dr Ste 150 San Diego (92130) *(P-11800)*

**Airgard Inc (PA)** .......................................................... E ...... 408 573-0701
1755 Mccarthy Blvd Milpitas (95035) *(P-9978)*

**Airgas, Long Beach** *Also Called: Airgas Inc (P-5040)*

**Airgas, City Of Industry** *Also Called: Airgas Safety Inc (P-16806)*

**Airgas Inc** ................................................................... D ...... 510 429-4216
3737 Worsham Ave Long Beach (90808) *(P-5040)*

**Airgas Safety Inc** ........................................................ E ...... 562 699-5239
2355 Workman Mill Rd City Of Industry (90601) *(P-16806)*

**Airgas Usa LLC** ........................................................... E ...... 562 945-1383
8832 Dice Rd Santa Fe Springs (90670) *(P-5041)*

**Airgas Usa LLC** ........................................................... E ...... 562 906-8700
9756 Santa Fe Springs Rd Santa Fe Springs (90670) *(P-5042)*

**Airo Industries Company** ........................................... E ...... 818 838-1008
429 Jessie St San Fernando (91340) *(P-3613)*

**Airspace Systems Inc** ................................................ E ...... 415 226-7779
1933 Davis St Ste 229 San Leandro (94577) *(P-11305)*

**Airtable, San Francisco** *Also Called: Formagrid Inc (P-16317)*

**Airtech Advanced Mtls Group, Huntington Beach** *Also Called: Airtech International Inc (P-13765)*

**Airtech International Inc (PA)** .................................... C ...... 714 899-8100
5700 Skylab Rd Huntington Beach (92647) *(P-13765)*

**Airtronics Metal Products Inc (PA)** ............................ C ...... 408 977-7800
140 San Pedro Ave Morgan Hill (95037) *(P-8368)*

**Airx Utility Surveyors Inc (PA)** ................................... D ...... 760 480-2347
785 E Mission Rd # 100 San Marcos (92069) *(P-386)*

**Aisin, Stockton** *Also Called: Aisin Electronics Inc (P-13452)*

**Aisin Electronics Inc** .................................................. C ...... 209 983-4988
199 Frank West Cir Stockton (95206) *(P-13452)*

**Aisling Industries, Calexico** *Also Called: Creation Tech Calexico Inc (P-12083)*

**AITA Clutch Inc** .......................................................... E ...... 323 585-4140
960 S Santa Fe Ave Compton (90221) *(P-13453)*

**Aitech Defense Systems Inc** ...................................... D ...... 818 700-2000
19756 Prairie St Chatsworth (91311) *(P-13210)*

**Aitech Rugged Group Inc (PA)** ................................... E ...... 818 700-2000
19756 Prairie St Chatsworth (91311) *(P-13211)*

**Aivres Systems Inc (PA)** ............................................. E ...... 866 687-1430
615 N King Rd San Jose (95133) *(P-10128)*

**Aivres Systems Inc** .................................................... C ...... 510 400-7599
3347 Gateway Blvd Fremont (94538) *(P-10129)*

**Aivres Systems Inc** .................................................... C ...... 866 687-1430
1501 Mccarthy Blvd Milpitas (95035) *(P-10130)*

**Aixtron Inc** ................................................................. C ...... 669 228-3759
1700 Wyatt Dr Ste 15 Santa Clara (95054) *(P-12282)*

**Ajax - Untd Pttrns & Molds Inc** .................................. C ...... 510 476-8000
34585 7th St Union City (94587) *(P-6700)*

**Ajax Boiler Inc** ........................................................... D ...... 714 437-9050
2701 S Harbor Blvd Santa Ana (92704) *(P-8298)*

**Ajax Custom Manufacturing, Union City** *Also Called: Ajax - Untd Pttrns & Molds Inc (P-6700)*

**Ajax Forge Company (PA)** .......................................... F ...... 323 582-6307
1956 E 48th St Vernon (90058) *(P-8772)*

**Ajg Inc** ....................................................................... E ...... 323 346-0171
7220 E Slauson Ave Commerce (90040) *(P-2874)*

**Ajinomoto Althea Inc (HQ)** ......................................... E ...... 858 882-0123
11040 Roselle St San Diego (92121) *(P-14952)*

**Ajinomoto Bio-Pharma Services, San Diego** *Also Called: Ajinomoto Althea Inc (P-14952)*

**Ajinomoto Foods North Amer Inc** ............................... B ...... 510 293-1838
2395 American Ave Hayward (94545) *(P-1021)*

**Ajinomoto Foods North Amer Inc** ............................... C ...... 909 477-4700
4200 Concours Ste 100 Ontario (91764) *(P-1022)*

**Ajinomoto Foods North Amer Inc (DH)** ...................... D ...... 909 477-4700
4200 Concours Ste 100 Ontario (91764) *(P-1023)*

**AJW Construction** ..................................................... E ...... 510 568-2300
966 81st Ave Oakland (94621) *(P-6360)*

**AK Darcy, Costa Mesa** *Also Called: Darcy AK Corporation (P-10799)*

**AK Industries, Compton** *Also Called: Allan Kidd (P-11439)*

**AK Mak Bakeries Division, Sanger** *Also Called: Soojians Inc (P-1283)*

**Akash Winery & Vineyards LLC** .................................. F ...... 714 306-9966
39730 Calle Contento Temecula (92591) *(P-1474)*

**Akcea Therapeutics, Carlsbad** *Also Called: Akcea Therapeutics Inc (P-5303)*

**Akcea Therapeutics Inc (HQ)** ..................................... D ...... 617 207-0202
2850 Gazelle Ct Carlsbad (92010) *(P-5303)*

**Akeana Usa Inc** .......................................................... E ...... 408 332-3005
3131 Jay St Ste 210 Santa Clara (95054) *(P-12283)*

**Aker International Inc** ............................................... E ...... 619 423-5182
2248 Main St Ste 4 Chula Vista (91911) *(P-7152)*

**Aker Leather Products, Chula Vista** *Also Called: Aker International Inc (P-7152)*

**Akeso Health Sciences LLC** ........................................ F ...... 818 865-1046
822 Hampshire Rd Ste E Westlake Village (91361) *(P-5228)*

**Akido Printing Inc** ...................................................... F ...... 510 357-0238
2096 Merced St San Leandro (94577) *(P-4506)*

**Akm Semiconductor Inc** .................................................. E ...... 408 436-8580
1731 Technology Dr Ste 500 San Jose (95110) *(P-12284)*

**Akon, San Jose** *Also Called: Akon Incorporated (P-16083)*

**Akon Incorporated** ............................................................. D ...... 408 432-8039
1828 Bering Dr San Jose (95112) *(P-16083)*

**Akra Plastic Products Inc** ................................................. E ...... 909 930-1999
1504 E Cedar St Ontario (91761) *(P-6701)*

**Aks, Amy K Su, Garden Grove** *Also Called: Bodywaves Inc (P-2859)*

**Akt America Inc (HQ)** ........................................................ B ...... 408 563-5455
3101 Scott Blvd Bldg 91 Santa Clara (95054) *(P-12285)*

**Akt America Inc** ................................................................ B ...... 408 563-5455
1245 Walsh Ave Santa Clara (95050) *(P-12286)*

**Aktana Inc (PA)** ................................................................. C ...... 888 616-2477
207 Powell St Ste 700 San Francisco (94102) *(P-18033)*

**Akura Medical Inc** ............................................................. E ...... 408 560-2500
170 Knowles Dr Los Gatos (95032) *(P-14953)*

**Akzo Nobel Coatings Inc** .................................................. F ...... 510 562-8812
2100 Adams Ave San Leandro (94577) *(P-6066)*

**Al Asher & Sons Inc** .......................................................... E ...... 800 896-2480
5301 Valley Blvd Los Angeles (90032) *(P-17436)*

**Al Global Corporation (HQ)** .............................................. E ...... 619 934-3980
2400 Boswell Rd Chula Vista (91914) *(P-17659)*

**Al Industries, Santa Ana** *Also Called: Acrontos Manufacturing Inc (P-8815)*

**Al Johnson Company, Camarillo** *Also Called: Gc International Inc (P-11734)*

**Al Shellco LLC (HQ)** .......................................................... C ...... 570 296-6444
9330 Scranton Rd Ste 600 San Diego (92121) *(P-11634)*

**Alabama Metal Industries Corp** ........................................ E ...... 909 350-9280
11093 Beech Ave Fontana (92337) *(P-8616)*

**Alaco Ladder Company** .................................................... E ...... 909 591-7561
5167 G St Chino (91710) *(P-3409)*

**Alaco Ladder Company, Chino** *Also Called: B E & P Enterprises LLC (P-3411)*

**Alacritech, San Jose** *Also Called: Alacritech Inc (P-12287)*

**Alacritech Inc** ..................................................................... E ...... 408 867-3809
1995 N 1st St Ste 200 San Jose (95112) *(P-12287)*

**Alameda Construction Svcs Inc** ....................................... E ...... 310 635-3277
2528 E 125th St Compton (90222) *(P-307)*

**Alameda Newspapers Inc (DH)** ........................................ C ...... 510 783-6111
22533 Foothill Blvd Hayward (94541) *(P-4062)*

**Alameda Newspapers Inc** ................................................. C ...... 650 348-4321
1080 S Amphlett Blvd San Mateo (94402) *(P-4063)*

**Alamitos Intermediate School, Garden Grove** *Also Called: Garden Grove Unified Schl Dst (P-19344)*

**Alamo Rings, Cypress** *Also Called: Eno Brands Inc (P-17645)*

**Alan B Whitson Company Inc** ........................................... A ...... 949 955-1200
1507 W Alton Ave Santa Ana (92704) *(P-19519)*

**Alan Gordon Enterprises Inc** ............................................ E ...... 323 466-3561
5625 Melrose Ave Los Angeles (90038) *(P-19301)*

**Alan Johnson Prfmce Engrg Inc** ....................................... E ...... 805 922-1202
1097 Foxen Canyon Rd Santa Maria (93454) *(P-13335)*

**Alan Lem & Co Inc** ............................................................ F ...... 310 538-4282
515 W 130th St Los Angeles (90061) *(P-7210)*

**Alan Portable Buildings, Gardena** *Also Called: Alan Pre-Fab Building Corp (P-3390)*

**Alan Pre-Fab Building Corp** .............................................. F ...... 310 538-0333
17817 Evelyn Ave Gardena (90248) *(P-3390)*

**Alanic International Corp** ................................................. E ...... 855 525-2642
8730 Wilshire Blvd Ph Beverly Hills (90211) *(P-2540)*

**Alara Inc** ............................................................................. E ...... 510 315-5200
47505 Seabridge Dr Fremont (94538) *(P-15497)*

**Alard Machine Products, Gardena** *Also Called: GT Precision Inc (P-8724)*

**Alarin Aircraft Hinge Inc** ................................................... E ...... 323 725-1666
6231 Randolph St Commerce (90040) *(P-7974)*

**Alastin Skincare Inc** .......................................................... C ...... 844 858-7546
5999 Avenida Encinas Carlsbad (92008) *(P-5940)*

**Alation Inc (PA)** ................................................................. B ...... 650 779-4440
3 Lagoon Dr Ste 300 Redwood City (94065) *(P-18034)*

**Alatus Aerosystems (PA)** ................................................. E ...... 610 965-1630
9301 Mason Ave Chatsworth (91311) *(P-13766)*

**Alatus Aerosystems** .......................................................... D ...... 714 732-0559
9301 Mason Ave Chatsworth (91311) *(P-13767)*

**Alatus Aerosystems** .......................................................... D ...... 626 498-7376
9301 Mason Ave Chatsworth (91311) *(P-13768)*

**Albany Farms Inc** .............................................................. E ...... 213 330-6573
625 Fair Oaks Ave Ste 125 South Pasadena (91030) *(P-2122)*

**Albany Farms Inc (PA)** ..................................................... E ...... 877 832-8269
10680 W Pico Blvd Ste 230 Los Angeles (90064) *(P-2123)*

**Albd Electric and Cable** .................................................... D ...... 949 440-1216
1031 S Leslie St La Habra (90631) *(P-449)*

**Albeco Inc** .......................................................................... D ...... 415 461-1164
270 Bon Air Ctr Greenbrae (94904) *(P-17365)*

**Albers Dairy Equipment. Inc, Chino** *Also Called: Albers Mfg Co Inc (P-9336)*

**Albers Mfg Co Inc (PA)** ..................................................... E ...... 909 597-5537
14323 Albers Way Chino (91710) *(P-9336)*

**Albert Maldonado** .............................................................. F ...... 831 758-9040
324 Lincoln Ave Salinas (93901) *(P-17804)*

**Albertsons 6514, Riverside** *Also Called: Albertsons LLC (P-17366)*

**Albertsons 6798, Lake Elsinore** *Also Called: Albertsons LLC (P-17367)*

**Albertsons LLC** .................................................................. D ...... 951 656-6603
8938 Trautwein Rd Ste A Riverside (92508) *(P-17366)*

**Albertsons LLC** .................................................................. E ...... 951 245-4461
30901 Riverside Dr Lake Elsinore (92530) *(P-17367)*

**Alcan Packg Capsules Cal LLC** ........................................ E ...... 707 257-6481
5425 Broadway St American Canyon (94503) *(P-16862)*

**Alcast Mfg Inc** .................................................................... E ...... 310 542-3581
2910 Fisk Ln Redondo Beach (90278) *(P-7824)*

**Alcast Mfg Inc (PA)** ........................................................... E ...... 310 542-3581
7355 E Slauson Ave Commerce (90040) *(P-7834)*

**Alcatel-Lucent, Newbury Park** *Also Called: Nokia of America Corporation (P-11776)*

**Alcatel-Lucent Enterprise USA, Thousand Oaks** *Also Called: Ale USA Inc (P-11802)*

**Alcatel-Lucent USA Inc** ..................................................... D ...... 650 623-3300
777 E Middlefield Rd Mountain View (94043) *(P-11749)*

**ALCATEL-LUCENT USA INC., Mountain View** *Also Called: Alcatel-Lucent USA Inc (P-11749)*

**Alcatraz Brewing Company, Orange** *Also Called: Tavistock Restaurants LLC (P-17625)*

**Alchem Plastics Inc** .......................................................... C ...... 714 523-2260
14263 Gannet St La Mirada (90638) *(P-6581)*

**Alchemy Cafe Inc (PA)** ...................................................... E ...... 925 825-8400
746 French Gulch Rd Murphys (95247) *(P-19019)*

**Alco Designs** ...................................................................... F ...... 310 353-2300
15117 S Broadway Gardena (90248) *(P-3643)*

**Alco Designs, Gardena** *Also Called: Vege-Mist Inc (P-10525)*

**Alco Engrg & Tooling Corp** ............................................... E ...... 714 556-6060
3001 Oak St Santa Ana (92707) *(P-10693)*

**Alco Manufacturing Inc** ..................................................... F ...... 714 549-5007
207 E Alton Ave Santa Ana (92707) *(P-9597)*

**Alco Metal Fab, Santa Ana** *Also Called: Alco Engrg & Tooling Corp (P-10693)*

**Alco Plating Corp (PA)** ...................................................... E ...... 213 749-7561
1400 Long Beach Ave Los Angeles (90021) *(P-8910)*

**Alcoa Fastening Systems** ................................................. F ...... 909 483-2333
11711 Arrow Rte Rancho Cucamonga (91730) *(P-15907)*

**Alcon, Irvine** *Also Called: Alcon Lensx Inc (P-14954)*

**Alcon Lensx Inc (DH)** ........................................................ D ...... 949 753-1393
15800 Alton Pkwy Irvine (92618) *(P-14954)*

**Alcon Lighting Inc** ............................................................. E ...... 310 733-1248
2845 S Robertson Blvd Los Angeles (90034) *(P-11518)*

**Alcon Research Ltd** .......................................................... D ...... 949 387-2142
15800 Alton Pkwy Irvine (92618) *(P-14955)*

**ALCON RESEARCH, LTD., Irvine** *Also Called: Alcon Research Ltd (P-14955)*

**Alcon Surgical, Irvine** *Also Called: Alcon Vision LLC (P-14957)*

**Alcon Vision LLC** ............................................................... B ...... 949 753-6218
24514 Sunshine Dr Laguna Niguel (92677) *(P-14956)*

**Alcon Vision LLC** ............................................................... A ...... 949 753-6488
15800 Alton Pkwy Irvine (92618) *(P-14957)*

**Aldetec Inc** ......................................................................... E ...... 916 453-3382
3560 Business Dr Ste 100 Sacramento (95820) *(P-11801)*

**Aldila Inc (HQ)** ................................................................... F ...... 858 513-1801
1945 Kellogg Ave Carlsbad (92008) *(P-15775)*

**Aldila Golf Corp** ................................................................. C ...... 858 513-1801
13450 Stowe Dr Poway (92064) *(P-15776)*

**Aldila Golf Corp (DH)** ........................................................ D ...... 858 513-1801
1945 Kellogg Ave Carlsbad (92008) *(P-15777)*

**Aldila Materials Tech Corp (DH)** ...................................... E ...... 858 486-6970
13450 Stowe Dr Poway (92064) *(P-6264)*

## ALPHABETIC SECTION

**Ale USA Inc** .................................................................. A ...... 818 880-3500
2000 Corporate Center Dr Thousand Oaks (91320) *(P-11802)*

**Alector LLC** .................................................................. E ...... 415 231-5660
521 Cottonwood Dr Ste 112 Milpitas (95035) *(P-5304)*

**Alectro Inc** .................................................................. F ...... 909 590-9521
6770 Central Ave Ste B Riverside (92504) *(P-11203)*

**Aledon Inc** .................................................................. E ...... 415 898-0044
655 Irwin St Ste 1015 San Rafael (94901) *(P-6266)*

**Alegacy, Santa Fe Springs** *Also Called: Alegacy Fdsrvice Pdts Group In (P-3733)*

**Alegacy Fdsrvice Pdts Group In** .................................. D ...... 562 320-3100
12683 Corral Pl Santa Fe Springs (90670) *(P-3733)*

**Aleksandar Inc** .......................................................... F ...... 310 516-7700
1542 W 130th St Gardena (90249) *(P-486)*

**Alembic Inc** ............................................................... F ...... 707 523-2611
240 Classic Ct Rohnert Park (94928) *(P-15711)*

**Aleo, Santa Fe Springs** *Also Called: Aleo Lighting Inc (P-11485)*

**Aleo Lighting Inc** ...................................................... F ...... 877 358-8825
10988 Bloomfield Ave Santa Fe Springs (90670) *(P-11485)*

**Aleratec Inc** ............................................................... E
21722 Lassen St Chatsworth (91311) *(P-10131)*

**Alere Inc** .................................................................... D ...... 858 805-2000
9975 Summers Ridge Rd San Diego (92121) *(P-5731)*

**Alere Inc** .................................................................... F ...... 858 805-3810
5995 Pacific Center Blvd Ste 108 San Diego (92121) *(P-5732)*

**Alere of San Diego, San Diego** *Also Called: Alere Inc (P-5732)*

**Alere San Diego Inc** .................................................. B ...... 909 482-0840
829 Towne Center Dr Pomona (91767) *(P-5733)*

**Alere San Diego Inc (DH)** .......................................... D ...... 858 805-2000
9942 Mesa Rim Rd San Diego (92121) *(P-5734)*

**Alere San Diego Inc** .................................................. B ...... 858 805-2000
828 Towne Center Dr Pomona (91767) *(P-5735)*

**Alert Plating, Sun Valley** *Also Called: Alert Plating Company (P-8911)*

**Alert Plating Company** ............................................. E ...... 818 771-9304
9939 Glenoaks Blvd Sun Valley (91352) *(P-8911)*

**Alertenterprise Inc (PA)** ........................................... C ...... 510 440-0840
4350 Starboard Dr Fremont (94538) *(P-18035)*

**Alesmith Brewing Company, San Diego** *Also Called: Jdz Inc (P-1437)*

**Alex A Khadavi Md Inc** ............................................. E ...... 818 528-2500
16260 Ventura Blvd Ste 140 Encino (91436) *(P-19314)*

**Alex and Ani, Torrance** *Also Called: Alex and Ani LLC (P-15678)*

**Alex and Ani LLC** ..................................................... F ...... 310 214-3587
21540 Hawthorne Blvd Torrance (90503) *(P-15678)*

**Alex and Jane, Maywood** *Also Called: KSM Garment Inc (P-2676)*

**Alex's Dry Cleaning Valet, San Rafael** *Also Called: Fcsi Inc (P-17764)*

**Alexander Henry Fabrics Inc** ................................... E ...... 818 562-8200
1550 Flower St Glendale (91201) *(P-17057)*

**Alexander International Inc** .................................... E ...... 424 285-8080
150 S Rodeo Dr Ste 290 Beverly Hills (90212) *(P-1155)*

**Alexander Valley Gourmet LLC** ................................ E ...... 707 473-0116
256 Sutton Pl Santa Rosa (95407) *(P-2124)*

**Alexander Valley Vineyards, Healdsburg** *Also Called: AVV Winery Co LLC (P-1481)*

**Alexander Valley Winery, Healdsburg** *Also Called: Silver Oak Wine Cellars LLC (P-1748)*

**Alexs Tile Works Inc** ................................................ E ...... 805 967-5308
5920 Matthews St Goleta (93117) *(P-482)*

**Alexza Pharmaceuticals Inc (HQ)** ............................. E ...... 650 944-7000
6550 Dumbarton Cir Ste A Fremont (94555) *(P-5305)*

**Alfa Scientific Designs Inc** ....................................... D ...... 858 513-3888
13200 Gregg St Poway (92064) *(P-5736)*

**Alflex, Compton** *Also Called: Southwire Inc (P-7732)*

**Alfred Louie Incorporated** ...................................... E ...... 661 831-2520
4501 Shepard St Bakersfield (93313) *(P-2125)*

**Alfred Music Publishing, Van Nuys** *Also Called: The Full Void 2 Inc (P-4349)*

**Alfred's Machining, Plymouth** *Also Called: Acm Machining Inc (P-10669)*

**Alg Inc** ...................................................................... D ...... 424 258-8026
120 Broadway Ste 200 Santa Monica (90401) *(P-4362)*

**Alger International, Los Angeles** *Also Called: Alger-Triton Inc (P-11486)*

**Alger Precision Machining LLC** ............................... C ...... 909 986-4591
724 S Bon View Ave Ontario (91761) *(P-8715)*

**Alger-Triton Inc** ........................................................ E ...... 310 229-9500
5600 W Jefferson Blvd Los Angeles (90016) *(P-11486)*

**Algolia Inc (PA)** ......................................................... E ...... 415 366-9672
301 Howard St Ste 300 San Francisco (94105) *(P-18036)*

**Algonquin Power Sanger LLC** .................................. E ...... 559 875-0800
1125 Muscat Ave Sanger (93657) *(P-11204)*

**Algorithmic Objective Corp** ..................................... E ...... 858 249-9580
8910 University Center Ln Ste 400 San Diego (92122) *(P-17878)*

**Algotive, San Diego** *Also Called: Algorithmic Objective Corp (P-17878)*

**Alhambra Foundry Company Ltd** ............................ E ...... 626 289-4294
1147 S Meridian Ave Alhambra (91803) *(P-7674)*

**Alice G Fink-Painter, Santa Fe Springs** *Also Called: Spec Tool Company (P-13960)*

**Alicorns, Valencia** *Also Called: Medical Brkthrugh Mssage Chirs (P-16180)*

**Alien Technology LLC (PA)** ....................................... E ...... 408 782-3900
300 Piercy Rd San Jose (95138) *(P-11803)*

**Alienvault LLC (DH)** .................................................. E ...... 650 713-3333
1100 Park Pl Ste 300 San Mateo (94403) *(P-18037)*

**Align Aerospace LLC (PA)** ......................................... B ...... 818 727-7800
9401 De Soto Ave Chatsworth (91311) *(P-13769)*

**Align Precision - Anaheim Inc (DH)** ......................... D ...... 714 961-9200
7100 Belgrave Ave Garden Grove (92841) *(P-13770)*

**Alignmed, Irvine** *Also Called: Alignmed Inc (P-17687)*

**Alignmed Inc** ............................................................ F ...... 866 987-5433
2691 Richter Ave Irvine (92606) *(P-17687)*

**ALIGNMENT HEALTH, Orange** *Also Called: Alignment Healthcare Inc (P-17736)*

**Alignment Healthcare Inc (PA)** ................................ D ...... 844 310-2247
1100 W Town And Country Rd Ste 1600 Orange (92868) *(P-17736)*

**Aligos Therapeutics, South San Francisco** *Also Called: Aligos Therapeutics Inc (P-5787)*

**Aligos Therapeutics Inc (PA)** .................................... E ...... 800 466-6059
1 Corporate Dr Fl 2 South San Francisco (94080) *(P-5787)*

**Alin Party Supply Co** ................................................ E ...... 951 682-7441
6493 Magnolia Ave Riverside (92506) *(P-17654)*

**Aline Systems, Cerritos** *Also Called: Aline Systems Corporation (P-10011)*

**Aline Systems Corporation** ..................................... E ...... 562 229-9727
13844 Struikman Rd Cerritos (90703) *(P-10011)*

**Alion Energy, Richmond** *Also Called: Alion Energy Inc (P-12288)*

**Alion Energy Inc** ....................................................... D ...... 510 965-0868
2200 Central St # D Richmond (94801) *(P-12288)*

**Aliquantum International Inc** ................................. E ...... 909 773-0880
2009 S Parco Ave Ontario (91761) *(P-15737)*

**Alivecor, Mountain View** *Also Called: Alivecor Inc (P-18038)*

**Alivecor Inc (PA)** ....................................................... E ...... 650 396-8650
189 Bernardo Ave Ste 100 Mountain View (94043) *(P-18038)*

**Alj, Camarillo** *Also Called: Gc International Inc (P-7845)*

**Alkal Tile Inc (PA)** ..................................................... F ...... 858 278-7828
7946 Clairemont Mesa Blvd San Diego (92111) *(P-17321)*

**All 4-Pcb North America Inc** .................................... F ...... 866 734-9403
345 Mira Loma Ave Glendale (91204) *(P-10694)*

**All About Printing, Canoga Park** *Also Called: Barrys Printing Inc (P-4528)*

**All Access Apparel Inc (PA)** ...................................... C ...... 323 889-4300
1515 Gage Rd Montebello (90640) *(P-2851)*

**All Access Stging Prdctns Inc (PA)** ........................... E ...... 310 784-2464
1320 Storm Pkwy Torrance (90501) *(P-11578)*

**All American Label, Dublin** *Also Called: A A Label Inc (P-4027)*

**All American Pipe Bending, Santa Ana** *Also Called: Saf-T-Co Supply (P-11481)*

**All American Print Supply Co** .................................. E ...... 714 616-5834
17511 Valley View Ave Cerritos (90703) *(P-10317)*

**All American Racers Inc** .......................................... C ...... 714 540-1771
2334 S Broadway Santa Ana (92707) *(P-14052)*

**All Amrcan Injction Mlding Svc, Temecula** *Also Called: TST Molding LLC (P-7062)*

**All Bay Pallet Company Inc (PA)** .............................. E ...... 510 636-4131
24993 Tarman Ave Hayward (94544) *(P-3330)*

**All Blue Labs Inc** ...................................................... E ...... 707 492-5949
548 Market St San Francisco (94104) *(P-18039)*

**All Diameter Grinding Inc** ....................................... E ...... 714 744-1200
725 N Main St Orange (92868) *(P-10695)*

**All Fab Prcsion Sheetmetal Inc** ............................... D ...... 408 279-1099
1980 Senter Rd San Jose (95112) *(P-511)*

**All Good** ................................................................... E ...... 877 239-4667
1149 Market Ave Morro Bay (93442) *(P-5941)*

**All Good Pallets Inc** ................................................. E ...... 209 467-7000
1055 Diamond St Stockton (95205) *(P-3331)*

# All Manufacturers Inc

**ALPHABETIC SECTION**

All Manufacturers Inc .................................................................... C ...... 951 280-4200
   1831 Commerce St Ste 101 Corona (92878) *(P-14958)*

All Metals Inc (PA) ......................................................................... E ...... 408 200-7000
   705 Reed St Santa Clara (95050) *(P-7715)*

All Metals Processing of San Diego Inc ..................................... C ...... 714 828-8238
   8401 Standustrial St Stanton (90680) *(P-8912)*

All Mtals Proc Orange Cnty LLC .................................................. C ...... 714 828-8238
   8401 Standustrial St Stanton (90680) *(P-8913)*

All New Stamping Co ..................................................................... C ...... 626 443-8813
   10801 Lower Azusa Rd El Monte (91731) *(P-8817)*

All Nuts and Snacks Inc .................................................................. F ...... 818 367-5902
   12910 San Fernando Rd Sylmar (91342) *(P-17137)*

All One God Faith Inc ..................................................................... D ...... 760 599-4010
   1225 Park Center Dr Ste D Vista (92081) *(P-5870)*

All One God Faith Inc (PA) ........................................................... C ...... 844 937-2551
   1335 Park Center Dr Vista (92081) *(P-5871)*

All Out Inc ......................................................................................... E
   2121 S El Camino Real Ste B100 San Mateo (94403) *(P-4838)*

All Power Manufacturing Co ......................................................... C ...... 562 802-2640
   13141 Molette St Santa Fe Springs (90670) *(P-13771)*

All Quality & Services Inc (PA) .................................................... D ...... 510 249-5800
   47817 Fremont Blvd Fremont (94538) *(P-12047)*

All Risk Shield Inc ......................................................................... E ...... 866 991-7190
   1244 Pine St Ste 211 Paso Robles (93446) *(P-203)*

All Sensors Corporation ................................................................. E ...... 408 776-9434
   16035 Vineyard Blvd Morgan Hill (95037) *(P-12289)*

All Source Company Bldg Group ................................................. E ...... 858 586-0903
   10625 Scripps Ranch Blvd Ste D San Diego (92131) *(P-9042)*

All Star Precision ........................................................................... E ...... 909 944-8373
   8739 Lion St Rancho Cucamonga (91730) *(P-10696)*

All Star Rentals, Fairfield *Also Called: Fairfield Rental Service Inc (P-17851)*

All States Elc & Fire Alarm, San Francisco *Also Called: Carlos A Garcia (P-11987)*

All Strong Industry (usa) Inc (PA) ............................................... E ...... 909 598-6494
   326 Paseo Tesoro Walnut (91789) *(P-3715)*

All Swiss Turning ........................................................................... E ...... 818 466-3076
   7745 Alabama Ave Ste 13 Canoga Park (91304) *(P-10697)*

All Technology Machine, Irvine *Also Called: Lubrication Scientifics Inc (P-9158)*

All Weather Inc ............................................................................... D ...... 916 928-1000
   1065 National Dr Ste 1 Sacramento (95834) *(P-14841)*

All Weather Insulated Panels, Vacaville *Also Called: Pre-Insulated Metal Tech Inc (P-8680)*

All-American Prtg Svcs Corp (PA) .............................................. E ...... 707 762-2500
   1324 Rand St Petaluma (94954) *(P-17805)*

All-Battery.com, Fremont *Also Called: Tenergy Corporation (P-13153)*

All-Coast Forest Products Inc (PA) ............................................. D ...... 707 894-4281
   250 Asti Rd Cloverdale (95425) *(P-16441)*

All-In Machining LLC ..................................................................... F ...... 209 839-8672
   157 Sloan Ct Ste B Tracy (95304) *(P-10698)*

All-Power Plastcs Div Dial, Los Angeles *Also Called: Dial Industries Inc (P-6802)*

All-Rite, Hollister *Also Called: Associated R V Ent Inc (P-16373)*

All-Safe Pool Fence & Covers, Orange *Also Called: Sunwest Industries Inc (P-16940)*

All-Tech Machine & Engrg Inc .................................................... E ...... 510 353-2000
   2700 Prune Ave Fremont (94539) *(P-10699)*

All-Truss Inc ................................................................................... E ...... 707 938-5595
   22700 Bdwy Sonoma (95476) *(P-3291)*

All-Ways Metal Inc ........................................................................ E ...... 310 217-1177
   401 E Alondra Blvd Gardena (90248) *(P-8369)*

All-Weather Architectural Aluminum Inc ................................... D ...... 707 452-1600
   777 Aldridge Rd Vacaville (95688) *(P-3106)*

ALLAKOS, San Carlos *Also Called: Allakos Inc (P-5306)*

Allakos Inc ........................................................................................ C ...... 650 597-5002
   825 Industrial Rd Ste 500 San Carlos (94070) *(P-5306)*

Allan Aircraft Supply Co LLC ....................................................... E ...... 818 765-4992
   11643 Vanowen St North Hollywood (91605) *(P-9180)*

Allan Company, Baldwin Park *Also Called: Cedarwood-Young Company (P-16958)*

Allan Kidd ........................................................................................ E ...... 310 762-1600
   3115 E Las Hermanas St Compton (90221) *(P-11439)*

ALLBIRDS, San Francisco *Also Called: Allbirds Inc (P-2399)*

Allbirds Inc (PA) ............................................................................. C ...... 628 225-4848
   730 Montgomery St San Francisco (94111) *(P-2399)*

Allbirds Inc ....................................................................................... F ...... 415 469-1455
   57 Hotaling Pl San Francisco (94111) *(P-7094)*

Allbirds Inc ....................................................................................... F ...... 442 273-5519
   1923 Calle Barcelona Ste 136 Carlsbad (92009) *(P-7095)*

Allbirds Inc ....................................................................................... F ...... 628 266-0533
   1636 Redwood Hwy Corte Madera (94925) *(P-7096)*

Allbirds Inc ....................................................................................... F ...... 424 502-2383
   860 S Pacific Coast Hwy El Segundo (90245) *(P-7097)*

Allbirds Inc ....................................................................................... F ...... 626 344-2622
   77 W Colorado Blvd Pasadena (91105) *(P-7098)*

Allbirds Inc ....................................................................................... F ...... 949 942-1233
   1125 Newport Center Dr Newport Beach (92660) *(P-7099)*

Allbirds Inc ....................................................................................... F ...... 415 802-2800
   425 Hayes St San Francisco (94102) *(P-7100)*

Allbirds Inc ....................................................................................... F ...... 650 460-8040
   660 Stanford Shopping Ctr Palo Alto (94304) *(P-7101)*

Allbirds Inc ....................................................................................... F ...... 925 800-3331
   3228 Livermore Outlets Dr Ste 675 Livermore (94551) *(P-7102)*

Allbirds Inc ....................................................................................... F ...... 858 987-9533
   4301 La Jolla Village Dr Ste 2010 San Diego (92122) *(P-7103)*

Allbirds Inc ....................................................................................... F ...... 213 374-2354
   10250 Santa Monica Blvd Ste 1985 Los Angeles (90067) *(P-7104)*

Allbirds Inc ....................................................................................... F ...... 213 374-3533
   12833 Ventura Blvd Studio City (91604) *(P-7105)*

Allbirds Inc ....................................................................................... F ...... 424 295-9968
   1335 Abbot Kinney Blvd Venice (90291) *(P-7106)*

Allblack Co Inc ................................................................................ E ...... 562 946-2955
   8155 Byron Rd Whittier (90606) *(P-8914)*

Allclear Aerospace & Def Inc ....................................................... D ...... 805 446-2700
   1283 Flynn Rd Camarillo (93012) *(P-13772)*

Allclear Aerospace & Def Inc ....................................................... E ...... 619 660-6220
   757 Main St # 102 Chula Vista (91911) *(P-13773)*

Allclear Aerospace & Def Inc ....................................................... E ...... 954 239-7844
   2525 Collier Canyon Rd Livermore (94551) *(P-13774)*

Allclear Inc ....................................................................................... E ...... 424 316-1596
   200 N Pacific Coast Hwy Ste 1350 El Segundo (90245) *(P-13632)*

Alldata LLC ...................................................................................... B ...... 916 684-5200
   9650 W Taron Dr Ste 100 Elk Grove (95757) *(P-18040)*

Allegiance Supply Incorporated .................................................. E ...... 760 230-8018
   6354 Corte Del Abeto Ste D Carlsbad (92011) *(P-11750)*

Allegion Access Tech LLC ............................................................ E ...... 858 431-5940
   8380 Camino Santa Fe Ste 100 San Diego (92121) *(P-7943)*

Allegion Access Tech LLC ............................................................ E ...... 909 628-9272
   15750 Jurupa Ave Fontana (92337) *(P-7944)*

Allegion Access Tech LLC ............................................................ E ...... 209 221-4066
   1312 Dupont Ct Manteca (95336) *(P-7945)*

Allegro Copy & Print, Lafayette *Also Called: Acp Ventures (P-4502)*

Allen Mold Inc ................................................................................. F ...... 714 538-6517
   1100 W Katella Ave Ste N Orange (92867) *(P-6702)*

Allergan, Irvine *Also Called: Allergan Spclty Thrpeutics Inc (P-5308)*

Allergan Sales LLC (DH) ............................................................... A ...... 862 261-7000
   2525 Dupont Dr Irvine (92612) *(P-5307)*

Allergan Spclty Thrpeutics Inc ..................................................... A ...... 714 246-4500
   2525 Dupont Dr Irvine (92612) *(P-5308)*

Allergan Usa Inc (DH) .................................................................... D ...... 714 427-1900
   18581 Teller Ave Irvine (92612) *(P-5309)*

Allermed Laboratories Inc ............................................................ E ...... 858 292-1060
   7203 Convoy Ct San Diego (92111) *(P-5229)*

Allhealth ............................................................................................ E ...... 213 538-0762
   515 S Figueroa St Ste 1300 Los Angeles (90071) *(P-10132)*

Alliance Air Products Llc .............................................................. A ...... 619 664-0027
   9565 Heinrich Hertz Dr Ste 1 San Diego (92154) *(P-10478)*

Alliance Air Products Llc (DH) ..................................................... E ...... 619 428-9688
   2285 Michael Faraday Dr Ste 15 San Diego (92154) *(P-10479)*

Alliance Apparel Inc ...................................................................... E ...... 323 888-8900
   3422 Garfield Ave Commerce (90040) *(P-2653)*

Alliance Chemical & Envmtl ......................................................... F ...... 805 385-3330
   1721 Ives Ave Oxnard (93033) *(P-8915)*

Alliance Display & Packaging, Burbank *Also Called: Westrock Rkt LLC (P-3897)*

Alliance Fiber Optic Pdts Inc ....................................................... A ...... 408 736-6900
   840 N Mccarthy Blvd Milpitas (95035) *(P-7188)*

Alliance Finishing and Mfg, Oxnard *Also Called: Alliance Chemical & Envmtl (P-8915)*

Alliance Hose & Extrusions Inc ................................................... F ...... 714 202-8500
   533 W Collins Ave Orange (92867) *(P-6125)*

# ALPHABETIC SECTION — Alpha Research & Tech Inc

**Alliance Laundry Systems LLC** .................................................. E ...... 800 464-6866
162 Harbor Ct Pittsburg (94565) *(P-10473)*

**Alliance Medical Products Inc (DH)** ........................................... E ...... 949 768-4690
9342 Jeronimo Rd Irvine (92618) *(P-14959)*

**Alliance Medical Products Inc** .................................................. E ...... 949 664-9616
9292 Jeronimo Rd Irvine (92618) *(P-14960)*

**Alliance Metal Products Inc** ..................................................... C ...... 818 709-1204
20844 Plummer St Chatsworth (91311) *(P-8370)*

**Alliance Printing Assoc I** ......................................................... F ...... 562 594-7975
11807 Slauson Ave Santa Fe Springs (90670) *(P-4507)*

**Alliance Ready Mix Inc** ............................................................ E ...... 805 556-3015
310 James Way Ste 210 Pismo Beach (93449) *(P-7400)*

**Alliance Spacesystems, Los Alamitos** *Also Called: Vanguard Space Tech Inc (P-13985)*

**Alliance Spacesystems LLC** ..................................................... C ...... 714 226-1400
4398 Corporate Center Dr Los Alamitos (90720) *(P-11298)*

**Allianceit, San Ramon** *Also Called: Allianceit Inc (P-17879)*

**Allianceit Inc (PA)** ..................................................................... F ...... 925 462-9787
6101 Bollinger Canyon Rd Ste 335g San Ramon (94583) *(P-17879)*

**Alliant Tchsystems Oprtons LLC** .............................................. F ...... 818 887-8185
21250 Califa St Woodland Hills (91367) *(P-14138)*

**Alliant Tchsystems Oprtons LLC** .............................................. B ...... 818 887-8195
9401 Corbin Ave Northridge (91324) *(P-14139)*

**Alliant Tchsystems Oprtons LLC** .............................................. F ...... 408 513-3271
151 Martinvale Ln Ste 150 San Jose (95119) *(P-14140)*

**Alliant Tchsystems Oprtons LLC** .............................................. E ...... 818 887-8195
9401 Corbin Ave Northridge (91324) *(P-14141)*

**Allianz Sweeper Company** ....................................................... C
5405 Industrial Pkwy San Bernardino (92407) *(P-13336)*

**Allied Bio Medical, Ventura** *Also Called: Implantech Associates Inc (P-15361)*

**Allied Coatings Inc** ................................................................... F ...... 800 630-2375
795 North Ave Ste D Vista (92083) *(P-6067)*

**Allied Components Intl** ............................................................. E ...... 949 356-1780
19671 Descartes Foothill Ranch (92610) *(P-12827)*

**Allied Concrete and Supply Co** ................................................. E ...... 209 524-3177
440 Mitchell Rd Ste B Modesto (95354) *(P-7401)*

**Allied Container Systems Inc** ................................................... C ...... 925 944-7600
511 Wilbur Ave Ste B4 Antioch (94509) *(P-8652)*

**Allied Crane Inc** ........................................................................ E ...... 925 427-9200
855 N Parkside Dr Pittsburg (94565) *(P-19240)*

**Allied Electric Motor Svc Inc (PA)** ............................................. D ...... 559 486-4222
4690 E Jensen Ave Fresno (93725) *(P-16641)*

**Allied Engineering and Production Corporation** ........................ E ...... 510 522-1500
2421 Blanding Ave Alameda (94501) *(P-10700)*

**Allied Harbor Aerospace Fas, Corona** *Also Called: All Manufacturers Inc (P-14958)*

**Allied International, Valencia** *Also Called: Allied International LLC (P-16744)*

**Allied International LLC** ............................................................ E ...... 818 364-2333
28955 Avenue Sherman Valencia (91355) *(P-16744)*

**Allied Mdular Bldg Systems Inc (PA)** ....................................... E ...... 714 516-1188
642 W Nicolas Ave Orange (92868) *(P-8653)*

**Allied Mechanical Products, Ontario** *Also Called: Tower Industries Inc (P-11148)*

**Allied Mechanical Products, Ontario** *Also Called: Tower Mechanical Products Inc (P-14323)*

**Allied Signal Aerospace, Torrance** *Also Called: Alliedsignal Arospc Svc Corp (P-7857)*

**Allied Steel Co Inc** ................................................................... D ...... 951 241-7000
1027 Palmyrita Ave Riverside (92507) *(P-527)*

**Allied Telesis Inc** ..................................................................... D ...... 408 519-6700
468 S Abbott Ave Milpitas (95035) *(P-10318)*

**Allied Telesis Inc** ..................................................................... E ...... 408 519-8700
3041 Orchard Pkwy San Jose (95134) *(P-10319)*

**Allied West Paper Corp** ........................................................... D ...... 909 349-0710
11101 Etiwanda Ave Unit 100 Fontana (92337) *(P-3760)*

**Allied Wheel Components Inc** .................................................. E ...... 800 529-4335
12300 Edison Way Garden Grove (92841) *(P-13454)*

**Alliedsignal Arospc Svc Corp (HQ)** .......................................... D ...... 310 323-9500
2525 W 190th St Torrance (90504) *(P-7857)*

**Alling Iron Works, West Sacramento** *Also Called: Carter Group (P-8119)*

**Allison-Kaufman Co** ................................................................. D ...... 818 373-5100
7640 Haskell Ave Van Nuys (91406) *(P-15679)*

**ALLOGENE THERAPEUTICS, South San Francisco** *Also Called: Allogene Therapeutics Inc (P-5788)*

**Allogene Therapeutics Inc (PA)** ................................................ C ...... 650 457-2700
210 E Grand Ave South San Francisco (94080) *(P-5788)*

**Alloy Die Casting Co (PA)** ........................................................ C ...... 714 521-9800
6550 Caballero Blvd Buena Park (90620) *(P-7805)*

**Alloy Machining and Honing Inc** ............................................... F ...... 323 726-8248
2808 Supply Ave Commerce (90040) *(P-10701)*

**Alloy Metal Products, Livermore** *Also Called: Fred Matter Inc (P-10844)*

**Allstar Microelectronics Inc** ...................................................... F ...... 949 546-0888
30191 Avenida De Las Bandera Rancho Santa Margari (92688) *(P-10222)*

**Allstarshop.com, Rancho Santa Margari** *Also Called: Allstar Microelectronics Inc (P-10222)*

**Allstate Plastics LLC** ............................................................... F ...... 510 783-9600
1763 Sabre St Hayward (94545) *(P-6703)*

**Alltec Integrated Mfg Inc** .......................................................... E ...... 805 595-3500
2240 S Thornburg St Santa Maria (93455) *(P-6704)*

**Alltech Industries Inc** ............................................................... E ...... 323 450-2168
301 E Pomona Blvd Monterey Park (91755) *(P-450)*

**Allure Labs, Hayward** *Also Called: Allure Labs LLC (P-5942)*

**Allure Labs LLC** ....................................................................... D ...... 510 489-8896
30901 Wiegman Ct Hayward (94544) *(P-5942)*

**Allvia, Half Moon Bay** *Also Called: Allvia Inc (P-12290)*

**Allvia Inc** .................................................................................. E ...... 408 234-8778
445 Fairway Dr Half Moon Bay (94019) *(P-12290)*

**Ally Enterprises** ....................................................................... E ...... 661 412-9933
5001 E Commercecenter Dr Ste 260 Bakersfield (93309) *(P-204)*

**Allyo, Sunnyvale** *Also Called: Sass Labs Inc (P-18760)*

**Alma Rosa Winery Vineyards LLC** ........................................... E ...... 805 688-9090
1607 Mission Dr Ste 300 Solvang (93463) *(P-1475)*

**Almaden, Santa Clara** *Also Called: Almaden Press and Pubg LLC (P-4363)*

**Almaden Press and Pubg LLC (PA)** ........................................ C ...... 408 450-7910
2549 Scott Blvd Santa Clara (95050) *(P-4363)*

**Almost Famous Wine Company, Livermore** *Also Called: Darcie Kent Winery LLC (P-17264)*

**Alna Envelope Company, Pomona** *Also Called: Inland Envelope Company (P-4009)*

**Aloha, Fremont** *Also Called: Air Liquide Electronics US LP (P-5067)*

**Aloha Bay** ................................................................................ E ...... 707 994-3267
16275 A Main St Lower Lake (95457) *(P-16084)*

**Alor International Ltd** ............................................................... E ...... 858 454-0011
11722 Sorrento Valley Rd San Diego (92121) *(P-15680)*

**Alpargatas Usa Inc** .................................................................. E ...... 646 277-7171
513 Boccaccio Ave Venice (90291) *(P-7113)*

**Alpase, Chino** *Also Called: Tst Inc (P-7724)*

**Alpha & Omega Pavers, Calimesa** *Also Called: Paver Decor Masonry Inc (P-377)*

**Alpha and Omega Semicdtr Inc (HQ)** ...................................... E ...... 408 789-0008
475 Oakmead Pkwy Sunnyvale (94085) *(P-12291)*

**Alpha Aviation Components Inc (PA)** ...................................... E ...... 818 894-8801
16772 Schoenborn St North Hills (91343) *(P-10702)*

**Alpha Corporation of Tennessee** .............................................. C ...... 951 657-5161
19991 Seaton Ave Perris (92570) *(P-5133)*

**Alpha Dental of Utah Inc** ......................................................... E ...... 562 467-7759
12898 Towne Center Dr Cerritos (90703) *(P-15437)*

**Alpha Dyno Nobel (PA)** ........................................................... E ...... 916 645-3377
3400 Nader Rd Lincoln (95648) *(P-17238)*

**Alpha Ems Corporation** ........................................................... C ...... 510 498-8788
44193 S Grimmer Blvd Fremont (94538) *(P-12048)*

**Alpha Explosives, Lincoln** *Also Called: Alpha Dyno Nobel (P-17238)*

**Alpha Group US LLC** ............................................................... E ...... 844 303-8936
2100 E Grand Ave 5th Fl El Segundo (90245) *(P-6483)*

**Alpha Imaging Technology** ...................................................... F ...... 626 330-0808
16453 Old Valley Blvd City Of Industry (91744) *(P-16571)*

**Alpha Innotech Corp** ................................................................ D ...... 408 510-5500
3040 Oakmead Village Dr Santa Clara (95051) *(P-16572)*

**Alpha Machine Co, Capitola** *Also Called: Alpha Machine Company Inc (P-10703)*

**Alpha Machine Company Inc** ................................................... F ...... 831 462-7400
933 Chittenden Ln Ste A Capitola (95010) *(P-10703)*

**Alpha Materials Inc** .................................................................. E ...... 951 788-5150
6170 20th St Riverside (92509) *(P-7402)*

**Alpha Omega Swiss Inc** .......................................................... E ...... 714 692-8009
23305 La Palma Ave Yorba Linda (92887) *(P-8716)*

**Alpha Polishing Corporation (PA)** ............................................ D ...... 323 263-7593
1313 Mirasol St Los Angeles (90023) *(P-8916)*

**Alpha Printing & Graphics Inc** .................................................. E ...... 626 851-9800
12758 Schabarum Ave Irwindale (91706) *(P-4508)*

**Alpha Research & Tech Inc** ..................................................... D ...... 916 431-9340
5175 Hillsdale Cir Ste 100 El Dorado Hills (95762) *(P-10133)*

---

Employee Codes: A=Over 500 employees, B=251-500
C=101-250, D=51-100, E=20-50, F=10-19, G=1-9

## ALPHABETIC SECTION

**Alpha Technics Inc** .................................................................. C ...... 949 250-6578
24024 Humphries Rd Tecate (91980) *(P-14385)*

**Alpha Teknova Inc (PA)** .......................................................... D ...... 831 637-1100
2451 Bert Dr Hollister (95023) *(P-5789)*

**Alpha-Owens Corning, Perris** *Also Called: Alpha Corporation of Tennessee (P-5133)*

**Alphacoat Finishing LLC** ........................................................ E ...... 949 748-7796
9350 Cabot Dr San Diego (92126) *(P-9043)*

**Alphagem Bio Inc** .................................................................... E ...... 510 999-1153
4201 Business Center Dr Fremont (94538) *(P-6705)*

**AlphaGraphics, San Francisco** *Also Called: Integrated Digital Media (P-4652)*

**Alphastar Tech Solutions LLC** ................................................ F ...... 562 961-7827
2601 Main St Ste 660 Irvine (92614) *(P-18041)*

**ALPHATEC, Carlsbad** *Also Called: Alphatec Holdings Inc (P-14961)*

**Alphatec Holdings Inc (PA)** .................................................... B ...... 760 431-9286
1950 Camino Vida Roble Carlsbad (92008) *(P-14961)*

**Alphatec Spine Inc (HQ)** ......................................................... C ...... 760 431-9286
1950 Camino Vida Roble Carlsbad (92008) *(P-15319)*

**Alphatech General Inc** ............................................................ D ...... 626 337-4640
4750 Littlejohn St Baldwin Park (91706) *(P-19241)*

**Alphawave Semi Inc (HQ)** ....................................................... E ...... 408 240-5700
1730 N 1st St San Jose (95112) *(P-12292)*

**Alpine Biomed Corp** ................................................................ D ...... 650 802-0400
1501 Industrial Rd San Carlos (94070) *(P-14962)*

**Alpine Meats Inc** ..................................................................... E ...... 209 477-2691
9850 Lower Sacramento Rd Stockton (95210) *(P-629)*

**Alpine Pacific Nut Co Inc** ........................................................ E ...... 209 667-8688
6413 E Keyes Rd Hughson (95326) *(P-71)*

**Alpine Pacific Nut Co., Hughson** *Also Called: Alpine Pacific Nut Co Inc (P-71)*

**Alpine Truss LLC** ..................................................................... E ...... 209 345-0831
800 S State Highway 33 Patterson (95363) *(P-3292)*

**Alpinestars USA** ...................................................................... D ...... 310 891-0222
2780 W 237th St Torrance (90505) *(P-2654)*

**Alpinestars USA, Torrance** *Also Called: Alpinestars USA (P-2654)*

**Als Garden Art Inc (PA)** ........................................................... B ...... 909 424-0221
311 W Citrus St Colton (92324) *(P-7586)*

**Als Group Inc** .......................................................................... E ...... 909 622-7555
1788 W 2nd St Pomona (91766) *(P-16807)*

**Alstyle Apparel, Jurupa Valley** *Also Called: A and G Inc (P-2606)*

**Alstyle Apparel LLC** ................................................................ A ...... 714 765-0400
1501 E Cerritos Ave Anaheim (92805) *(P-2400)*

**Alta Devices Inc** ...................................................................... C ...... 408 988-8600
545 Oakmead Pkwy Sunnyvale (94085) *(P-12293)*

**Alta Manufacturing Inc** ........................................................... E ...... 510 668-1870
47650 Westinghouse Dr Fremont (94539) *(P-12049)*

**Alta Motors, Brisbane** *Also Called: Faster Faster Inc (P-13499)*

**Altaflex** ..................................................................................... D ...... 408 727-6614
336 Martin Ave Santa Clara (95050) *(P-12050)*

**Altair Lighting, Compton** *Also Called: Jimway Inc (P-11603)*

**Altair Technologies Inc** ............................................................ E ...... 650 508-8700
41970 Christy St Fremont (94538) *(P-9825)*

**Altamont Manufacturing Inc** ................................................... F ...... 925 371-5401
241 Rickenbacker Cir Livermore (94551) *(P-10704)*

**Altec Inc** .................................................................................. E ...... 661 679-4177
1127 Carrier Parkway Ave Bakersfield (93308) *(P-9404)*

**Altec Industries Inc** ................................................................. F ...... 707 678-0800
1450 N 1st St Dixon (95620) *(P-9405)*

**Altec Industries Inc** ................................................................. E ...... 707 678-0800
325 Industrial Way Dixon (95620) *(P-9406)*

**Altec Industries Inc** ................................................................. E ...... 909 444-0444
2882 Pomona Blvd Pomona (91768) *(P-19159)*

**Altera, San Jose** *Also Called: Altera Corporation (P-12294)*

**Altera Corporation (HQ)** .......................................................... C ...... 408 544-7000
101 Innovation Dr San Jose (95134) *(P-12294)*

**Alterg, Inc., Fremont** *Also Called: Lifeward Ca Inc (P-15836)*

**Alteryx, Irvine** *Also Called: Alteryx Inc (P-18962)*

**Alteryx Inc (PA)** ....................................................................... E ...... 888 836-4274
3347 Michelson Dr Ste 400 Irvine (92612) *(P-18962)*

**Altest, San Jose** *Also Called: Altest Corporation (P-10705)*

**Altest Corporation** .................................................................. E ...... 408 436-9900
898 Faulstich Ct San Jose (95112) *(P-10705)*

**Altierre Corporation** ................................................................ E ...... 408 435-7343
1980 Concourse Dr San Jose (95131) *(P-12295)*

**Altigen Communications Inc** .................................................. C ...... 408 597-9000
670 N Mccarthy Blvd Ste 200 Milpitas (95035) *(P-11751)*

**Altinex Inc** ............................................................................... E ...... 714 990-0877
500 S Jefferson St Placentia (92870) *(P-11804)*

**Altium Holdings LLC** ............................................................... A ...... 951 340-9390
12165 Madera Way Riverside (92503) *(P-6706)*

**Altium Packaging** .................................................................... D ...... 626 856-2100
4516 Azusa Canyon Rd Irwindale (91706) *(P-6707)*

**ALTIUM PACKAGING, Irwindale** *Also Called: Altium Packaging (P-6707)*

**Altium Packaging LLC** ............................................................. D ...... 310 952-8736
1500 E 223rd St Carson (90745) *(P-6606)*

**Altium Packaging LLC** ............................................................. E ...... 209 531-9180
1620 Gobel Way Modesto (95358) *(P-6607)*

**Altium Packaging LLC** ............................................................. D ...... 888 425-7343
1070 Samuelson St City Of Industry (91748) *(P-6708)*

**Altium Packaging LLC** ............................................................. D ...... 209 820-1700
75 W Valpico Rd Tracy (95376) *(P-6709)*

**Altium Packaging LP** ............................................................... E ...... 714 241-6640
1217 E Saint Gertrude Pl Santa Ana (92707) *(P-6619)*

**Altium Packaging LP** ............................................................... E ...... 909 590-7334
14312 Central Ave Chino (91710) *(P-6710)*

**Altman Plants, Vista** *Also Called: Altman Specialty Plants LLC (P-17278)*

**Altman Specialty Plants LLC (PA)** .......................................... A ...... 800 348-4881
3742 Blue Bird Canyon Rd Vista (92084) *(P-17278)*

**Alto Neuroscience Inc** ............................................................. D ...... 650 200-0412
650 Castro St Ste 450 Mountain View (94041) *(P-19438)*

**Altro Usa Inc** ............................................................................ D ...... 562 944-8292
12648 Clark St Santa Fe Springs (90670) *(P-16074)*

**Alts Tool & Machine Inc** .......................................................... D ...... 619 562-6653
10926 Woodside Ave N Santee (92071) *(P-10706)*

**Altumind Inc** ............................................................................ E ...... 858 382-3956
10620 Treena St Ste 230 San Diego (92131) *(P-18042)*

**Alturdyne Power Systems Inc** ................................................. E ...... 619 343-3204
1405 N Johnson Ave El Cajon (92020) *(P-9307)*

**Alum-A-Fold Pacific Inc** .......................................................... E ...... 562 699-4550
3730 Capitol Ave City Of Industry (90601) *(P-7726)*

**Alum-Alloy Co Inc** ................................................................... E ...... 909 986-0410
603 S Hope Ave Ontario (91761) *(P-8794)*

**Aluma USA Inc** ........................................................................ E ...... 707 545-9344
435 Tesconi Cir Santa Rosa (95401) *(P-15681)*

**Alumawall Inc** .......................................................................... D ...... 408 275-7165
1701 S 7th St Ste 9 San Jose (95112) *(P-8654)*

**Alumax Building Products, Sun City** *Also Called: Omnimax International LLC (P-8281)*

**Alumen-8, Oceanside** *Also Called: Amerillum LLC (P-11581)*

**Aluminum Casting Company, Ontario** *Also Called: Employee Owned PCF Cast Pdts I (P-7844)*

**Aluminum Coating Tech Inc** .................................................... E ...... 916 442-1063
8290 Alpine Ave Sacramento (95826) *(P-8917)*

**Aluminum Die Casting Co Inc** ................................................. D ...... 951 681-3900
10775 San Sevaine Way Jurupa Valley (91752) *(P-7806)*

**Aluminum Precision Pdts Inc (PA)** .......................................... A ...... 714 546-8125
3333 W Warner Ave Santa Ana (92704) *(P-7705)*

**Aluminum Tube Railings, Pomona** *Also Called: Atr Technologies Incorporated (P-8619)*

**Alumis Inc** ................................................................................ C ...... 650 231-6625
280 E Grand Ave South San Francisco (94080) *(P-5790)*

**Alumistar Inc** ........................................................................... E ...... 562 633-6673
520 S Palmetto Ave Ontario (91762) *(P-7835)*

**Aluratek, Irvine** *Also Called: Aluratek Inc (P-16505)*

**Aluratek** ................................................................................... E ...... 866 580-1978
15241 Barranca Pkwy Irvine (92618) *(P-16505)*

**Alva Manufacturing Inc** ........................................................... E ...... 714 237-0925
236 E Orangethorpe Ave Placentia (92870) *(P-13775)*

**Alvarado Manufacturing Co Inc** .............................................. C ...... 909 591-8431
12660 Colony Ct Chino (91710) *(P-14842)*

**Alvellan Inc** .............................................................................. E ...... 925 689-2421
1030 Shary Ct Concord (94518) *(P-10707)*

**Alx Oncology, South San Francisco** *Also Called: Alx Oncology Holdings Inc (P-5310)*

**Alx Oncology Holdings Inc (PA)** .............................................. D ...... 650 466-7125
323 Allerton Ave South San Francisco (94080) *(P-5310)*

**Alyn Industries Inc** .................................................................. D ...... 818 988-7696
16028 Arminta St Van Nuys (91406) *(P-12911)*

**Alysedwards, Fresno** *Also Called: Paragon Industries Inc (P-17339)*

**Alza Corporation (HQ)** ........................................................... A ...... 707 453-6400
700 Eubanks Dr Vacaville (95688) *(P-5311)*

**Alza Corporation** .................................................................... A ...... 650 564-5000
1010 Joaquin Rd Mountain View (94043) *(P-14607)*

**Alza Corporation** .................................................................... A ...... 707 453-6400
700 Eubanks Dr Vacaville (95688) *(P-14608)*

**Alza Pharmaceuticals, Vacaville** *Also Called: Alza Corporation (P-5311)*

**Alzeta Corporation** ................................................................. F ...... 408 727-8282
1968 Hartog Dr San Jose (95131) *(P-19439)*

**AM AND S MFG INC** ............................................................... E ...... 408 396-3027
1394 Tully Rd Ste 203-207 Pmb 213-215 San Jose (95122) *(P-9539)*

**AM Machining Inc** .................................................................. F ...... 714 367-0830
7422 Walnut Ave Buena Park (90620) *(P-16914)*

**AM Wax Inc** ........................................................................... F ...... 714 228-1999
625 The City Dr S Ste 325 Orange (92868) *(P-5887)*

**Am-Tek Engineering Inc** ........................................................ F ...... 909 673-1633
1180 E Francis St Ste C Ontario (91761) *(P-10708)*

**Am-Touch Dental, Valencia** *Also Called: American Med & Hosp Sup Co Inc (P-16573)*

**AM&s Mnufactruing Design Group, San Jose** *Also Called: AM AND S MFG INC (P-9539)*

**AMA Plastics** ......................................................................... B ...... 951 734-5600
1100 Citrus St Riverside (92507) *(P-6711)*

**Amada America Inc** .............................................................. D ...... 714 739-2111
100 S Puente St Brea (92821) *(P-9044)*

**Amada Weld Tech Inc (HQ)** .................................................. E ...... 626 303-5676
1820 S Myrtle Ave Monrovia (91016) *(P-9721)*

**Amada Weld Tech Inc** .......................................................... E ...... 626 303-5676
245 E El Norte St Monrovia (91016) *(P-14963)*

**Amag Technology Inc (DH)** ................................................... E ...... 310 518-2380
2205 W 126th St Ste B Hawthorne (90250) *(P-10320)*

**Amare Global LP** .................................................................. E ...... 888 898-8551
17872 Gillette Ave Ste 100 Irvine (92614) *(P-5312)*

**Amaretto Orchards LLC** ....................................................... E ...... 661 399-9697
32331 Famoso Woody Rd Mc Farland (93250) *(P-16085)*

**Amarillo Wind Machine LLC** ................................................. F ...... 559 592-4256
20513 Avenue 256 Exeter (93221) *(P-9337)*

**Amass Brands Inc** ................................................................ D ...... 619 204-2560
860 E Stowell Rd Santa Maria (93454) *(P-5230)*

**Amat** ..................................................................................... E ...... 408 563-5385
3101 Scott Blvd Santa Clara (95054) *(P-12296)*

**Amatix, Sun Valley** *Also Called: Marfred Industries (P-3866)*

**Amays Bakery & Noodle Co Inc (PA)** .................................... D ...... 213 626-2713
837 E Commercial St Los Angeles (90012) *(P-1258)*

**Amazing Facts Inc** ................................................................ D ...... 916 434-3880
1203 W Sunset Blvd Rocklin (95765) *(P-4311)*

**Amazing Facts Ministries, Rocklin** *Also Called: Amazing Facts Inc (P-4311)*

**Amazing Steel, Montclair** *Also Called: Mitchell Fabrication (P-8189)*

**Amazing Steel Company** ....................................................... E ...... 909 590-0393
4564 Mission Blvd Montclair (91763) *(P-8093)*

**Amazon Prsrvation Partners Inc** ........................................... E ...... 415 775-6355
1550 Leigh Ave San Jose (95125) *(P-875)*

**Ambarella, Santa Clara** *Also Called: Ambarella Inc (P-12297)*

**Ambarella Inc (PA)** ................................................................ A ...... 408 734-8888
3101 Jay St Santa Clara (95054) *(P-12297)*

**Amber, Danville** *Also Called: Amber Semiconductor Inc (P-12298)*

**Amber Chemical Inc** ............................................................. E ...... 661 325-2072
5201 Boylan St Bakersfield (93308) *(P-5068)*

**Amber Semiconductor Inc** .................................................... E ...... 510 364-4680
6400 Sierra Ct Ste F Danville (94506) *(P-12298)*

**Amber Steel Co., Rialto** *Also Called: H Wayne Lewis Inc (P-8698)*

**Amberwood Installation, San Jose** *Also Called: Amberwood Products Inc (P-3213)*

**Amberwood Products Inc** ..................................................... C ...... 408 938-1600
1555 S 7th St Bldg 7 San Jose (95112) *(P-3213)*

**Ambiance Apparel, Los Angeles** *Also Called: Ambiance USA Inc (P-2733)*

**Ambiance USA Inc** ................................................................ F ...... 323 587-0007
2465 E 23rd St Los Angeles (90058) *(P-2732)*

**Ambiance USA Inc (PA)** ........................................................ E ...... 323 587-0007
2415 E 15th St Los Angeles (90021) *(P-2733)*

**Ambiance USA Inc** ................................................................ F ...... 213 765-9600
930 Towne Ave Los Angeles (90021) *(P-2734)*

**AMBISOME, Foster City** *Also Called: Gilead Sciences Inc (P-5463)*

**Ambit Biosciences Corporation** ............................................. D ...... 858 334-2100
10201 Wateridge Cir Ste 200 San Diego (92121) *(P-5313)*

**Ambit Software LLC** .............................................................. F ...... 949 361-4070
138 W Avenida San Antonio San Clemente (92672) *(P-18043)*

**Ambr Inc (PA)** ........................................................................ E ...... 530 221-4759
1160 Industrial St Redding (96002) *(P-15738)*

**Ambrit Engineering Corporation** ............................................ D ...... 714 557-1074
2640 Halladay St Santa Ana (92705) *(P-9598)*

**Ambrit Industries Inc** ............................................................. E ...... 818 243-1224
432 Magnolia Ave Glendale (91204) *(P-9576)*

**Ambrx, La Jolla** *Also Called: Ambrx Biopharma Inc (P-5791)*

**Ambrx Inc (PA)** ...................................................................... D ...... 858 875-2400
10975 N Torrey Pines Rd Ste 100 La Jolla (92037) *(P-5314)*

**Ambrx Biopharma Inc** ........................................................... D ...... 858 875-2400
10975 N Torrey Pines Rd La Jolla (92037) *(P-5791)*

**AMC, Stanton** *Also Called: All Metals Processing of San Diego Inc (P-8912)*

**AMC Machining Inc** ............................................................... E ...... 805 238-5452
1540 Commerce Way Paso Robles (93446) *(P-8691)*

**Amcan Beverages Inc** ........................................................... D ...... 707 557-0500
1201 Commerce Blvd American Canyon (94503) *(P-1849)*

**Amcc Sales, Santa Clara** *Also Called: Applied Micro Circuits Corp (P-12322)*

**Amcor Flexibles Healthcare, American Canyon** *Also Called: Amcor Flexibles LLC (P-3921)*

**Amcor Flexibles Healthcare, Commerce** *Also Called: Amcor Flexibles LLC (P-3922)*

**Amcor Flexibles Healthcare, Yuba City** *Also Called: Amcor Flexibles LLC (P-4839)*

**Amcor Flexibles LLC** ............................................................. C ...... 707 257-6481
5425 Broadway St American Canyon (94503) *(P-3921)*

**Amcor Flexibles LLC** ............................................................. A ...... 323 721-6777
5416 Union Pacific Ave Commerce (90022) *(P-3922)*

**Amcor Flexibles LLC** ............................................................. D ...... 530 671-9000
800 N Walton Ave Yuba City (95993) *(P-4839)*

**Amcor Industries Inc** ............................................................. E ...... 323 585-2852
6131 Knott Ave Buena Park (90620) *(P-13455)*

**Amcor Manufacturing Inc** ...................................................... F ...... 209 581-9687
500 Winmoore Way Modesto (95358) *(P-5069)*

**AMCS** .................................................................................... F ...... 626 334-9160
125 N Aspan Ave Azusa (91702) *(P-9045)*

**Amcs Inc** ............................................................................... E ...... 408 846-9274
200 Mayock Rd Gilroy (95020) *(P-16406)*

**AMD Far East Ltd (HQ)** ......................................................... F ...... 408 749-4000
1 Amd Pl Sunnyvale (94085) *(P-12299)*

**AMD International Tech LLC** ................................................. E ...... 909 985-8300
1725 S Campus Ave Ontario (91761) *(P-8371)*

**Ameditech Inc** ....................................................................... C ...... 858 535-1968
9940 Mesa Rim Rd San Diego (92121) *(P-14964)*

**Amerex Company, Riverside** *Also Called: Nsa Holdings Inc (P-6939)*

**Amergence Technology Inc** .................................................. E ...... 909 859-8400
295 Brea Canyon Rd Walnut (91789) *(P-9826)*

**Ameri-Fax, Orange** *Also Called: Positive Concepts Inc (P-4046)*

**America Printing, Burlingame** *Also Called: Asia America Enterprise Inc (P-4517)*

**American & Efird LLC** ........................................................... F ...... 323 724-6884
6098 Rickenbacker Rd Commerce (90040) *(P-2524)*

**American Air Conditioning Co, Danville** *Also Called: Heathorn & Assoc Contrs Inc (P-423)*

**American Air Liquide Inc (DH)** ............................................... D ...... 510 624-4000
46409 Landing Pkwy Fremont (94538) *(P-5043)*

**American Aircraft Products Inc** .............................................. D ...... 310 532-7434
15411 S Broadway Gardena (90248) *(P-8372)*

**American Airframe Inc** .......................................................... E ...... 805 240-1608
1201 Vanguard Dr Oxnard (93033) *(P-13776)*

**American Apparel, Los Angeles** *Also Called: App Winddown LLC (P-2890)*

**American Arium** ..................................................................... E ...... 949 623-7090
17791 Fitch Irvine (92614) *(P-12300)*

**American Assod Roofg Distrs, Monterey Park** *Also Called: Oakcroft Associates Inc (P-16793)*

**American Audio Component Inc** ............................................ E ...... 909 596-3788
20 Fairbanks Ste 198 Irvine (92618) *(P-12912)*

**American Automated Engrg Inc** ............................................. C ...... 714 898-9951
5382 Argosy Ave Huntington Beach (92649) *(P-14108)*

## American Bath Factory — ALPHABETIC SECTION

**American Bath Factory, Corona** *Also Called: Le Elegant Bath Inc (P-6683)*
**American Beef Packers Inc** .................................................. C ...... 909 628-4888
   13677 Yorba Ave Chino (91710) *(P-91)*
**American Best Car Parts, Anaheim** *Also Called: American Fabrication Corp (P-13456)*
**American Bicycle Security Co, Santa Paula** *Also Called: Turtle Storage Ltd (P-3712)*
**American Bottling Company** ................................................. D ...... 951 341-7500
   1188 Mt Vernon Ave Riverside (92507) *(P-1850)*
**American Bottling Company** ................................................. D ...... 707 766-9750
   2210 S Mcdowell Boulevard Ext Petaluma (94954) *(P-1851)*
**American Bottling Company** ................................................. D ...... 707 462-8871
   100 Wabash Ave Ukiah (95482) *(P-1852)*
**American Bottling Company** ................................................. D ...... 661 323-7921
   230 E 18th St Bakersfield (93305) *(P-1853)*
**American Bottling Company** ................................................. D ...... 559 442-1553
   2012 S Pearl St Fresno (93721) *(P-1854)*
**American Bottling Company** ................................................. D ...... 707 840-9727
   1555 Heartwood Dr Mckinleyville (95519) *(P-1855)*
**American Bottling Company** ................................................. D ...... 818 898-1471
   1166 Arroyo St San Fernando (91340) *(P-1856)*
**American Bottling Company** ................................................. C ...... 714 974-8560
   1166 Arroyo St Orange (92865) *(P-1857)*
**American Bottling Company** ................................................. D ...... 805 928-1001
   618 Hanson Way Santa Maria (93458) *(P-1858)*
**American Bottling Company** ................................................. C ...... 323 268-7779
   3220 E 26th St Vernon (90058) *(P-1859)*
**American Bottling Company** ................................................. D ...... 916 929-3575
   2720 Land Ave Sacramento (95815) *(P-1860)*
**American Bottling Company** ................................................. D ...... 916 929-7777
   2670 Land Ave Sacramento (95815) *(P-1861)*
**American Bottling Company** ................................................. E ...... 831 632-0777
   11205 Commercial Pkwy Castroville (95012) *(P-1862)*
**American Bottling Company** ................................................. E ...... 925 251-3001
   6160 Stoneridge Mall Rd Ste 280 Pleasanton (94588) *(P-1863)*
**American Cabinet Works Inc** ................................................ E ...... 310 715-6815
   13518 S Normandie Ave Gardena (90249) *(P-3107)*
**American Carrier Systems** .................................................. F ...... 559 442-1500
   2285 E Date Ave Fresno (93706) *(P-13337)*
**American Casting Co, Hollister** *Also Called: Reed Manufacturing Inc (P-7695)*
**American Circuit Tech Inc (PA)** ............................................. E ...... 714 777-2480
   5330 E Hunter Ave Anaheim (92807) *(P-12051)*
**American City Bus Journals Inc** ........................................... C ...... 916 447-7661
   555 Capitol Mall Ste 200 Sacramento (95814) *(P-4064)*
**American Compaction Eqp Inc** .............................................. E ...... 949 661-2921
   29380 Hunco Way Lake Elsinore (92530) *(P-9407)*
**American Condenser, Gardena** *Also Called: American Condenser & Coil LLC (P-10480)*
**American Condenser & Coil LLC** ........................................... D ...... 310 327-8600
   1628 W 139th St Gardena (90249) *(P-10480)*
**American Consumer Products LLC** ....................................... D ...... 323 289-6610
   120 E 8th St Ste 908 Los Angeles (90014) *(P-6267)*
**American Cooling Tower, Santa Ana** *Also Called: American Cooling Tower Inc (P-19242)*
**American Cooling Tower Inc (PA)** ......................................... F ...... 714 898-2436
   3130 W Harvard St Santa Ana (92704) *(P-19242)*
**American Cover Design 26 Inc** ............................................. E ...... 323 582-8666
   2131 E 52nd St Vernon (90058) *(P-2508)*
**American Crier Eqp Trlr Sls LL** ............................................. F ...... 559 442-1500
   2285 E Date Ave Fresno (93706) *(P-19167)*
**American Custom Meats LLC** ............................................... D ...... 209 839-8800
   4276 N Tracy Blvd Tracy (95304) *(P-630)*
**American Dawn Inc (PA)** ..................................................... D ...... 800 821-2221
   401 W Artesia Blvd Compton (90220) *(P-2541)*
**American Deburring Inc** ..................................................... E ...... 949 457-9790
   20742 Linear Ln Lake Forest (92630) *(P-10709)*
**American Design Inc** ......................................................... F ...... 619 429-1995
   1672 Industrial Blvd Chula Vista (91911) *(P-6712)*
**American Designs, Los Angeles** *Also Called: Kesmor Associates (P-15695)*
**American Die Casting Inc** ................................................... E ...... 909 356-7768
   14576 Fontlee Ln Fontana (92335) *(P-7825)*
**American Elc Components Inc** ............................................. F ...... 323 771-4888
   4901 Fruitland Ave Vernon (90058) *(P-19174)*
**American Electronics, Carson** *Also Called: Ducommun Labarge Tech Inc (P-13832)*
**American Elements, Los Angeles** *Also Called: Merelex Corporation (P-5101)*

**American Etal Technology, Fremont** *Also Called: Axt Inc (P-12351)*
**American Etching & Mfg** ..................................................... E ...... 323 875-3910
   13730 Desmond St Pacoima (91331) *(P-9046)*
**American Fabrication, Bakersfield** *Also Called: Russell Fabrication Corp (P-9269)*
**American Fabrication Corp (PA)** ........................................... D ...... 714 632-1709
   2891 E Via Martens Anaheim (92806) *(P-13456)*
**American Faucet Coatings Corp** ........................................... E ...... 760 598-5895
   1333 Keystone Way Vista (92081) *(P-16420)*
**American Filter Company, Azusa** *Also Called: Water Filter Exchange Inc (P-10122)*
**American Fish and Seafood, Los Angeles** *Also Called: Prospect Enterprises Inc (P-17158)*
**American Fleet & Ret Graphics** ............................................ E ...... 909 937-7570
   2091 Del Rio Way Ontario (91761) *(P-15941)*
**American Foam & Packaging, Gardena** *Also Called: Amfoam Inc (P-6621)*
**American Foam Fiber & Sups Inc (PA)** ................................... E ...... 626 969-7268
   255 S 7th Ave Ste A City Of Industry (91746) *(P-2542)*
**American Food Co, Los Angeles** *Also Called: Afc Trading & Wholesale Inc (P-17112)*
**American Food Ingredients Inc** ............................................ E ...... 760 967-6287
   4021 Avenida De La Plata Ste 501 Oceanside (92056) *(P-943)*
**American Foothill Pubg Co Inc** ............................................. E ...... 818 352-7878
   10009 Commerce Ave Tujunga (91042) *(P-4840)*
**American Fruits & Flavors LLC (HQ)** ..................................... C ...... 818 899-9574
   10725 Sutter Ave Pacoima (91331) *(P-1978)*
**American Fruits & Flavors LLC** ............................................. E ...... 818 899-9574
   1527 Knowles Ave Los Angeles (90063) *(P-1979)*
**American Fruits & Flavors LLC** ............................................. E ...... 818 899-9574
   1565 Knowles Ave Los Angeles (90063) *(P-1980)*
**American Fruits & Flavors LLC** ............................................. D ...... 213 624-1831
   400 S Central Ave Los Angeles (90013) *(P-1981)*
**American Fruits & Flavors LLC** ............................................. D ...... 310 522-1844
   22560 Lucerne St Carson (90745) *(P-1982)*
**American Fruits & Flavors LLC** ............................................. E ...... 323 881-8321
   3001 Sierra Pine Ave Vernon (90058) *(P-1983)*
**American Fruits & Flavors LLC** ............................................. E ...... 909 291-2620
   9345 Santa Anita Ave Rancho Cucamonga (91730) *(P-1984)*
**American Fruits & Flavors LLC** ............................................. E ...... 562 320-2802
   13530 Rosecrans Ave Santa Fe Springs (90670) *(P-1985)*
**American Furniture Alliance, Corona** *Also Called: Widly Inc (P-3546)*
**American Garment Sewing, Pasadena** *Also Called: AGS Usa LLC (P-2697)*
**American General Tool Group** .............................................. E ...... 760 745-7993
   929 Poinsettia Ave Ste 101 Vista (92081) *(P-6404)*
**American Grape Harvesters Inc** ........................................... E ...... 559 277-7380
   5778 W Barstow Ave Fresno (93722) *(P-16795)*
**American Green Lights, San Diego** *Also Called: American Green Lights LLC (P-16351)*
**American Green Lights LLC** ................................................ E ...... 858 547-8837
   10755 Scripps Poway Pkwy Ste 419 San Diego (92131) *(P-16351)*
**American Grip Inc** ............................................................. E ...... 818 768-8922
   8468 Kewen Ave Sun Valley (91352) *(P-11579)*
**American Handgunner and Guns, Escondido** *Also Called: Publishers Development Corp (P-4290)*
**American Highway Technology, Modesto** *Also Called: Dayton Superior Corporation (P-9517)*
**American Histology Reagent Co, Lodi** *Also Called: American Mstr Tech Scntfc Inc (P-14965)*
**American Honda, Torrance** *Also Called: American Honda Motor Co Inc (P-16371)*
**American Honda Motor Co Inc (HQ)** ...................................... A ...... 310 783-2000
   1919 Torrance Blvd Torrance (90501) *(P-16371)*
**American Household Company, Los Angeles** *Also Called: Housewares International Inc (P-6859)*
**American HX Auto Trade Inc** ............................................... D ...... 909 484-1010
   4845 Via Del Cerro Yorba Linda (92887) *(P-13338)*
**American Industrial Manufacturing Services Inc** ..................... C ...... 951 698-3379
   41673 Corning Pl Murrieta (92562) *(P-13165)*
**American Industrial Partners LP** ........................................... A ...... 415 788-7354
   1 Maritime Plz Ste 1925 San Francisco (94111) *(P-9827)*
**American Integrity Corp** ..................................................... E ...... 760 247-1082
   13510 Central Rd Apple Valley (92308) *(P-6713)*
**American International Inds, Los Angeles** *Also Called: Glamour Industries Co (P-17038)*
**American International Mfg Co** ............................................ E ...... 530 666-2446
   1230 Fortna Ave Woodland (95776) *(P-9338)*
**American Intnl Inds Inc** ...................................................... A ...... 323 728-2999
   2220 Gaspar Ave Commerce (90040) *(P-5943)*
**American Kal Enterprises Inc (PA)** ....................................... D ...... 626 338-7308
   4265 Puente Ave Baldwin Park (91706) *(P-16745)*

## ALPHABETIC SECTION

**American Lab and Systems, Los Angeles** Also Called: Mjw Inc *(P-9931)*
**American Laminates Inc** ............................................. E ...... 209 869-2536
3142 Talbot Ave Riverbank (95367) *(P-6714)*
**American Licorice Company** ..................................... B ...... 510 487-5500
2477 Liston Way Union City (94587) *(P-1299)*
**American Liquid Packaging Systems Inc (PA)** .......... D ...... **408 524-7474**
440 N Wolfe Rd Sunnyvale (94085) *(P-5134)*
**American Lithium Energy Corp** ................................. F ...... 760 599-7388
2261 Rutherford Rd Carlsbad (92008) *(P-5070)*
**American Lithographers Inc** ..................................... D ...... 916 441-5392
1281 National Dr Sacramento (95834) *(P-4509)*
**American Mailing & Prtg Svc, Anaheim** Also Called: Sharon Havriluk *(P-5004)*
**American Marble, Vista** Also Called: Kammerer Enterprises Inc *(P-7540)*
**American Mechanical & Mfg Inc** ................................ F ...... 909 466-4713
10096 6th St Ste B Rancho Cucamonga (91730) *(P-8094)*
**American Mechanical & Mfg., Rancho Cucamonga** Also Called: American Mechanical & Mfg Inc *(P-8094)*
**American Med & Hosp Sup Co Inc** ............................ E ...... 661 294-1213
28703 Industry Dr Valencia (91355) *(P-16573)*
**American Med O & P Clinic Inc** ................................. E ...... 818 281-5747
4955 Van Nuys Blvd Sherman Oaks (91403) *(P-15320)*
**American Medical Bill Review, Redding** Also Called: Ambr Inc *(P-15738)*
**American Medical Response Inc** ............................... C ...... 415 794-9204
1300 Illinois St San Francisco (94107) *(P-16276)*
**American Metal, Pomona** Also Called: American Mtal Mfg Resource Inc *(P-13703)*
**American Metal Bearing Company** ............................ E ...... 714 892-5527
7191 Acacia Ave Garden Grove (92841) *(P-9948)*
**American Metal Filter Company** ................................ F ...... 619 628-1917
611 Marsat Ct Chula Vista (91911) *(P-9979)*
**American Modular Systems Inc** ................................ D ...... 209 825-1921
787 Spreckels Ave Manteca (95336) *(P-3391)*
**American Mstr Tech Scntfic Inc** ................................. C ...... 209 368-4031
1330 Thurman St Lodi (95240) *(P-14965)*
**American Mtal Mfg Resource Inc** .............................. E ...... 909 620-4500
1989 W Holt Ave Pomona (91768) *(P-13703)*
**American Multimedia TV USA** .................................... D ...... 626 466-1038
530 S Lake Ave Unit 368 Pasadena (91101) *(P-16329)*
**American Nail Plate Ltg Inc** ....................................... D ...... 909 982-1807
9044 Del Mar Ave Montclair (91763) *(P-11487)*
**American National Mfg Inc** ........................................ D ...... 951 273-7888
252 Mariah Cir Corona (92879) *(P-3519)*
**American Nuts LLC (HQ)** ........................................... F ...... **818 364-8855**
12950 San Fernando Rd Sylmar (91342) *(P-17138)*
**American Pacific Plastic Fabricators Inc** ................... F ...... 714 891-3191
7130 Fenwick Ln Westminster (92683) *(P-5135)*
**American Pallet & Lumber Inc** ................................... E ...... 209 847-6122
1001 Knox Rd Oakdale (95361) *(P-3332)*
**American PCF Prtrs College Inc** ................................ E ...... 949 250-3212
675 N Main St Orange (92868) *(P-4510)*
**American Peptide Company Inc** ................................ D ...... 408 733-7604
1271 Avenida Chelsea Vista (92081) *(P-5792)*
**American Plant Services Inc (PA)** ............................. E ...... **562 630-1773**
6242 N Paramount Blvd Long Beach (90805) *(P-7603)*
**American Plastic, Tracy** Also Called: AP Unlimited Corporation *(P-17058)*
**American Plastic Products Inc** .................................. D ...... 818 504-1073
9243 Glenoaks Blvd Sun Valley (91352) *(P-9599)*
**American Pneumatic Tools Inc** ................................. F ...... 562 204-1555
1000 S Grand Ave Santa Ana (92705) *(P-9577)*
**American Poly-Foam Company Inc** ........................... E ...... 510 786-3626
1455 Crocker Ave Hayward (94544) *(P-6620)*
**American Power Solutions Inc** .................................. E ...... 714 626-0300
14355 Industry Cir La Mirada (90638) *(P-11580)*
**American Precision Gear Co** ..................................... E ...... 650 627-8060
365 Foster City Blvd Foster City (94404) *(P-10038)*
**American Precision Hydraulics** ................................. E ...... 714 903-8610
5601 Research Dr Huntington Beach (92649) *(P-9578)*
**American Precision Sheet Metal, Chatsworth** Also Called: Keith E Archambeau Sr Inc *(P-8482)*
**American Precision Spring Corp** ............................... E ...... 408 986-1020
1513 Arbuckle Ct Santa Clara (95054) *(P-9196)*
**American Quality Tools, Riverside** Also Called: American Quality Tools Inc *(P-9659)*

**American Quality Tools Inc** ....................................... E ...... 951 280-4700
12650 Magnolia Ave Ste B Riverside (92503) *(P-9659)*
**American Quilting Company Inc** ............................... E ...... 323 233-2500
1540 Calzona St Los Angeles (90023) *(P-2988)*
**American Range Corporation** ................................... C ...... 818 897-0808
13592 Desmond St Pacoima (91331) *(P-8373)*
**American Ready Mix, Escondido** Also Called: Superior Ready Mix Concrete LP *(P-7508)*
**American Ready Mix Inc** ............................................ F ...... 760 446-4556
1141 W Graaf Ave Ridgecrest (93555) *(P-7403)*
**American Regent Inc** ................................................. E ...... 714 989-5058
536 Vanguard Way Brea (92821) *(P-19491)*
**American Reliance Inc** .............................................. E ...... 626 443-6818
789 N Fair Oaks Ave Pasadena (91103) *(P-10134)*
**American Rigging & Supply, San Diego** Also Called: Carpenter Group *(P-16866)*
**American Rim Supply Inc** ......................................... E ...... 760 431-3666
1955 Kellogg Ave Carlsbad (92008) *(P-13457)*
**American River Packaging, Madera** Also Called: Pk1 Inc *(P-3878)*
**American Rotary Broom Co Inc** ................................ E ...... 909 629-9117
688 New York Dr Pomona (91768) *(P-15925)*
**American Scale Co Inc** ............................................. E ...... 800 773-7225
21326 E Arrow Hwy Covina (91724) *(P-16506)*
**American Scence Tech As T Corp (PA)** ..................... C ...... **415 251-2800**
50 California St Fl 21 San Francisco (94111) *(P-13633)*
**American Scence Tech As T Corp** ............................. D ...... 310 773-1978
2372 Morse Ave Ste 571 Irvine (92614) *(P-13634)*
**American Security Products Co** ............................... C ...... 951 685-9680
11925 Pacific Ave Fontana (92337) *(P-9274)*
**American Sheet Metal, El Cajon** Also Called: Asm Construction Inc *(P-8383)*
**American Single Sheets, Redlands** Also Called: Continental Datalabel Inc *(P-4035)*
**American Soc Cmpsers Athors Pb** ............................ C ...... 323 883-1000
7920 W Sunset Blvd Ste 300 Los Angeles (90046) *(P-4364)*
**American Soccer Company Inc (PA)** ......................... C ...... **310 830-6161**
726 E Anaheim St Wilmington (90744) *(P-17508)*
**American Solar LLC** .................................................. E ...... 323 250-1307
8484 Wilshire Blvd Ste 630 Beverly Hills (90211) *(P-8059)*
**American Solar Advantage Inc** .................................. E ...... 877 765-2388
13348 Monte Vista Ave Chino (91710) *(P-12301)*
**American Spring Inc** ................................................. F ...... 310 324-2181
321 W 135th St Los Angeles (90061) *(P-9172)*
**American Steel & Stairways Inc** ................................ E ...... 408 848-2992
8525 Forest St Ste A Gilroy (95020) *(P-8617)*
**American Supply, Ontario** Also Called: Castillo Maritess *(P-2972)*
**American Traveler Inc** ............................................... E ...... 909 466-4000
9509 Feron Blvd Rancho Cucamonga (91730) *(P-7125)*
**American Trck Trlr Bdy Co Inc (PA)** .......................... E ...... **209 836-8985**
100 W Valpico Rd Ste D Tracy (95376) *(P-13400)*
**American Turn-Key Fabricators, Rancho Cucamonga** Also Called: Romeros Engineering Inc *(P-11087)*
**American Ultraviolet West Inc** .................................. E ...... 310 784-2930
23555 Telo Ave Torrance (90505) *(P-9480)*
**American Underwater Products (HQ)** ....................... D ...... **800 435-3483**
2002 Davis St San Leandro (94577) *(P-15778)*
**American Vanguard Corporation (PA)** ...................... D ...... **949 260-1200**
4695 Macarthur Ct Newport Beach (92660) *(P-6191)*
**American Window Covering Inc** ............................... F ...... 714 879-3880
825 Williamson Ave Fullerton (92832) *(P-17768)*
**American Wire Inc** .................................................... F ...... 909 884-9990
784 S Lugo Ave San Bernardino (92408) *(P-9209)*
**American Wire Sales, Rancho Dominguez** Also Called: Standard Wire & Cable Co *(P-7796)*
**American Woodmark Corporation** ............................ C ...... 916 851-7400
3146 Gold Camp Dr Rancho Cordova (95670) *(P-3214)*
**American Woodmark Corporation** ............................ B ...... 714 449-2200
400 E Orangethorpe Ave Anaheim (92801) *(P-3215)*
**American Yeast Corporation** .................................... E ...... 661 834-1050
5455 District Blvd Bakersfield (93313) *(P-2126)*
**American Zabin Intl Inc** ............................................ E ...... 213 746-3770
3933 S Hill St Los Angeles (90037) *(P-4841)*
**American Zinc Enterprises, Walnut** Also Called: Sea Shield Marine Products Inc *(P-7821)*
**Americas Best Beverage Inc** ..................................... E ...... 800 723-8808
600 50th Ave Oakland (94601) *(P-2066)*
**Americas Gold Inc** .................................................... E ...... 213 688-4904
650 S Hill St Ste 224 Los Angeles (90014) *(P-15682)*

**Americas Gold - Amrcas Damonds**  ALPHABETIC SECTION

Americas Gold - Amrcas Damonds, Los Angeles *Also Called: Americas Gold Inc (P-15682)*
Americas Printer.com, Buena Park *Also Called: A J Parent Company Inc (P-19066)*
Americas Regional Division, San Diego *Also Called: Synergy Health Ast LLC (P-15274)*
Americas Styrenics LLC ............................................................. D ...... 424 488-3757
  305 Crenshaw Blvd Torrance (90503) *(P-5136)*
Americawear, Commerce *Also Called: RDD Enterprises Inc (P-2564)*
Americh Corporation (PA) ........................................................ C ...... 818 982-1711
  13222 Saticoy St North Hollywood (91605) *(P-15321)*
Americhip, Gardena *Also Called: Americhip Inc (P-4511)*
Americhip Inc (PA) .................................................................... E ...... 310 323-3697
  19032 S Vermont Ave Gardena (90248) *(P-4511)*
Americon ................................................................................... F ...... 805 987-0412
  1690 Larkfield Ave Westlake Village (91362) *(P-3560)*
Americore, Hilmar *Also Called: Americore Inc (P-548)*
Americore Inc ............................................................................ D ...... 209 632-5679
  19705 August Ave Hilmar (95324) *(P-548)*
Ameriflex Inc ............................................................................. D ...... 951 737-5557
  2390 Railroad St Corona (92878) *(P-9247)*
Amerillum LLC .......................................................................... D ...... 760 727-7675
  3728 Maritime Way Oceanside (92056) *(P-11581)*
Amerimade Technology Inc ..................................................... E ...... 925 243-9090
  449 Mountain Vista Pkwy Livermore (94551) *(P-6715)*
Ameripec Inc ............................................................................. C ...... 714 690-9191
  6965 Aragon Cir Buena Park (90620) *(P-1864)*
Ameripharma, Orange *Also Called: Harpers Pharmacy Inc (P-5477)*
Ameripharma Specialty Phrm Div ........................................... E ...... 877 778-3773
  132 S Anita Dr Orange (92868) *(P-5315)*
Ameritex International, Los Angeles *Also Called: Amtex California Inc (P-2914)*
Ameron International Corp ...................................................... D ...... 805 524-0223
  1020 B St Fillmore (93015) *(P-7307)*
Ameron International Corp ...................................................... C ...... 425 258-2616
  1020 B St Fillmore (93015) *(P-7308)*
Ameron International Corp ...................................................... D ...... 209 836-5050
  10100 W Linne Rd Tracy (95377) *(P-9181)*
Ameron Protective Coatings, Fillmore *Also Called: Ameron International Corp (P-7308)*
Ames, Woodland *Also Called: Ames Fire Waterworks (P-11306)*
Ames Fire Waterworks .............................................................. D ...... 530 666-2493
  1485 Tanforan Ave Woodland (95776) *(P-11306)*
Ames Industrial, Los Angeles *Also Called: Ames Rubber Mfg Co Inc (P-6484)*
Ames Rubber Mfg Co Inc ......................................................... E ...... 818 240-9313
  4516 Brazil St Los Angeles (90039) *(P-6484)*
Ametek Inc ................................................................................ E ...... 510 431-6718
  1288 San Luis Obispo St Hayward (94544) *(P-16507)*
Ametek Ameron LLC (HQ) ..................................................... D ...... 626 856-0101
  4750 Littlejohn St Baldwin Park (91706) *(P-14386)*
Ametek HCC, Rosemead *Also Called: Hermetic Seal Corporation (P-12995)*
Ametek Programmable Power, San Diego *Also Called: Ametek Programmable Power Inc (P-14495)*
Ametek Programmable Power Inc (HQ) ................................ B ...... 858 450-0085
  9250 Brown Deer Rd San Diego (92121) *(P-14495)*
Ametek-Ameron, Baldwin Park *Also Called: Alphatech General Inc (P-19241)*
Amex Plating Incorporated ...................................................... E ...... 408 986-8222
  3333 Woodward Ave Santa Clara (95054) *(P-8918)*
AMF, Roseville *Also Called: Advanced Metal Finishing LLC (P-8908)*
AMF Anaheim LLC ................................................................... C ...... 714 363-9206
  2100 E Orangewood Ave Anaheim (92806) *(P-8374)*
AMF Pharma LLC ..................................................................... E ...... 909 930-9599
  1909 S Campus Ave Ontario (91761) *(P-5316)*
AMF Support Surfaces Inc (DH) ............................................. C ...... 951 549-6800
  1691 N Delilah St Corona (92879) *(P-3520)*
Amflex Plastics Incorporated .................................................. E ...... 760 643-1756
  4039 Calle Platino Ste G Oceanside (92056) *(P-6424)*
Amfoam Inc (PA) ...................................................................... E ...... 310 327-4003
  15110 S Broadway Gardena (90248) *(P-6621)*
AMG Employee Management Inc ........................................... F ...... 323 254-7448
  1220 S Central Ave Ste 203 Glendale (91204) *(P-15674)*
AMG Torrance LLC (DH) ........................................................ F ...... 310 515-2584
  5401 Business Dr Huntington Beach (92649) *(P-13777)*
Amgen, Thousand Oaks *Also Called: Amgen Inc (P-5793)*
Amgen Inc .................................................................................. C ...... 805 447-1000
  1840 De Havilland Dr Newbury Park (91320) *(P-5317)*

Amgen Inc (PA) ......................................................................... A ...... 805 447-1000
  1 Amgen Center Dr Thousand Oaks (91320) *(P-5793)*
Amgen Manufacturing Limited ............................................... E ...... 787 656-2000
  1 Amgen Center Dr Newbury Park (91320) *(P-16086)*
Amgen USA Inc (HQ) ............................................................... D ...... 805 447-1000
  1 Amgen Center Dr Thousand Oaks (91320) *(P-5318)*
Amgraph, Ontario *Also Called: American Fleet & Ret Graphics (P-15941)*
AMI, Costa Mesa *Also Called: Advanced Micro Instruments Inc (P-14840)*
Amiad Filtration Systems, Oxnard *Also Called: Amiad USA Inc (P-10534)*
Amiad USA Inc .......................................................................... E ...... 805 988-3323
  1251 Maulhardt Ave Oxnard (93030) *(P-10533)*
Amiad USA Inc .......................................................................... E ...... 805 988-3323
  1251 Maulhardt Ave Oxnard (93030) *(P-10534)*
Amico Fontana, Fontana *Also Called: Alabama Metal Industries Corp (P-8616)*
Aminco International USA Inc ................................................. D ...... 949 457-3261
  20571 Crescent Bay Dr Lake Forest (92630) *(P-15683)*
Amino Technologies (us) LLC (HQ) ....................................... E ...... 408 861-1400
  20863 Stevens Creek Blvd Ste 300 Cupertino (95014) *(P-11805)*
Amiri, Los Angeles *Also Called: Atelier Luxury Group LLC (P-3001)*
Amkom Design Group Inc ....................................................... E ...... 760 295-1957
  2598 Fortune Way Ste J Vista (92081) *(P-19071)*
Amlogic, Santa Clara *Also Called: Amlogic Inc (P-12302)*
Amlogic Inc ............................................................................... E ...... 408 850-9688
  2518 Mission College Blvd Ste 120 Santa Clara (95054) *(P-12302)*
AMO Usa Inc ............................................................................. C ...... 714 247-8200
  1700 E Saint Andrew Pl Santa Ana (92705) *(P-14966)*
Amonix Inc ................................................................................. C ...... 562 344-4750
  1709 Apollo Ct Seal Beach (90740) *(P-12303)*
Amoretti, Oxnard *Also Called: Noushig Inc (P-1230)*
AMP, Santa Ana *Also Called: Accelerated Memory Prod Inc (P-12270)*
AMP Display Inc (PA) ............................................................... E ...... 909 980-1310
  9856 6th St Rancho Cucamonga (91730) *(P-19376)*
AMP Plus Inc ............................................................................ D ...... 323 231-2600
  2042 E Vernon Ave Los Angeles (90058) *(P-11571)*
AMP Printing Inc ...................................................................... D ...... 925 556-9000
  6955 Sierra Ct Dublin (94568) *(P-4512)*
AMP Research, Tustin *Also Called: 89908 Inc (P-13436)*
AMP Research, Brea *Also Called: Lund Motion Products Inc (P-13532)*
Ampac Analytical, El Dorado Hills *Also Called: Ampac Fine Chemicals LLC (P-5319)*
Ampac Fine Chemicals LLC (DH) .......................................... D ...... 916 357-6880
  Highway 50 And Hazel Ave Rancho Cordova (95670) *(P-5071)*
Ampac Fine Chemicals LLC .................................................... B ...... 916 357-6221
  12295 Hartford St Rancho Cordova (95742) *(P-5072)*
Ampac Fine Chemicals LLC .................................................... B ...... 916 245-6500
  1100 Windfield Way El Dorado Hills (95762) *(P-5319)*
Ampac Usa Inc .......................................................................... E ...... 435 291-0961
  5255 State St 5275 Montclair (91763) *(P-10535)*
Ampere, Santa Clara *Also Called: Ampere Computing LLC (P-10135)*
Ampere Computing LLC .......................................................... E ...... 669 770-3700
  4655 Great America Pkwy Ste 601 Santa Clara (95054) *(P-10135)*
Ampersand Ice Cream LLC ..................................................... F ...... 559 264-8000
  3188 N Marks Ave Ste 110 Fresno (93722) *(P-791)*
Ampex Corporation .................................................................. C ...... 650 367-2011
  500 Broadway St Redwood City (94063) *(P-11806)*
Ampex Data Systems Corporation (HQ) ............................... D ...... 650 367-2011
  26460 Corporate Ave Hayward (94545) *(P-10223)*
AMPHASTAR, Rancho Cucamonga *Also Called: Amphastar Pharmaceuticals Inc (P-5320)*
Amphastar Pharmaceuticals Inc (PA) .................................... C ...... 909 980-9484
  11570 6th St Rancho Cucamonga (91730) *(P-5320)*
Amphenol DC Electronics Inc ................................................. B ...... 408 947-4500
  1870 Little Orchard St San Jose (95125) *(P-11440)*
Amphion, Rancho Cucamonga *Also Called: Executive Safe and SEC Corp (P-9286)*
Amplifier Technologies Inc (HQ) ............................................ E ...... 323 278-0001
  901 S Greenwood Ave Montebello (90640) *(P-11807)*
Amplitude, Milpitas *Also Called: Amplitude Laser Inc (P-14609)*
Amplitude Laser Inc (PA) ........................................................ E ...... 408 727-3240
  532 Gibraltar Dr Milpitas (95035) *(P-14609)*
AMpm Maintenance Corporation ............................................ E ...... 424 230-1300
  1010 E 14th St Los Angeles (90021) *(P-2543)*
Ampro Adlink Technology Inc ................................................. D ...... 408 360-0200
  6450 Via Del Oro San Jose (95119) *(P-10136)*

## ALPHABETIC SECTION

**Ampro Systems Inc** .................................................. E ...... 510 624-9000
2950 Merced St Ste 114 San Leandro (94577) *(P-12052)*

**Ampronix LLC** ........................................................... D ...... 949 273-8000
15 Whatney Irvine (92618) *(P-15513)*

**Amrapur Overseas Incorporated (PA)** ..................... E ...... 714 893-8808
1560 E 6th St Ste 101 Corona (92879) *(P-2544)*

**Amrel, Pasadena** *Also Called: American Reliance Inc (P-10134)*

**Amrep Inc** ................................................................ B ...... 770 422-2071
1555 S Cucamonga Ave Ontario (91761) *(P-5888)*

**Amrep Manufacturing Co LLC** ................................ B ...... 877 468-9278
1555 S Cucamonga Ave Ontario (91761) *(P-9828)*

**Amro Fabricating Corporation (PA)** ........................ C ...... 626 579-2200
1430 Amro Way South El Monte (91733) *(P-13778)*

**Amron, Vista** *Also Called: Amron International Inc (P-15779)*

**Amron International Inc (PA)** ................................. D ...... 760 208-6500
1380 Aspen Way Vista (92081) *(P-15779)*

**AMS, Manteca** *Also Called: American Modular Systems Inc (P-3391)*

**AMS Plastics Inc (PA)** ............................................. E ...... 619 713-2000
20109 Paseo Del Prado Walnut (91789) *(P-6716)*

**AMS Plastics Inc** ..................................................... B ...... 951 734-5600
1100 Citrus St Riverside (92507) *(P-6717)*

**Amsafe Bridport, Buena Park** *Also Called: Bridport Erie Aviation Inc (P-19245)*

**Amscan Inc** .............................................................. D ...... 714 972-2626
804 W Town & Country Rd Orange (92868) *(P-3912)*

**Amsco US Inc** .......................................................... C ...... 562 630-0333
15341 Texaco Ave Paramount (90723) *(P-12913)*

**Amscope, Irvine** *Also Called: United Scope LLC (P-14831)*

**Amsec, Fontana** *Also Called: American Security Products Co (P-9274)*

**Amt Datasouth Corp (PA)** ....................................... E ...... 805 388-5799
3222 Corte Malpaso Camarillo (93012) *(P-19440)*

**Amt Metal Fabricators Inc** ...................................... E ...... 510 236-1414
211 Parr Blvd Richmond (94801) *(P-8095)*

**Amtec Industries Inc** ............................................... E ...... 510 887-2289
7079 Commerce Cir Pleasanton (94588) *(P-11235)*

**Amtech Microelectronics Inc** ................................. E ...... 408 612-8888
485 Cochrane Cir Morgan Hill (95037) *(P-12053)*

**Amtek, Poway** *Also Called: United Security Products Inc (P-13322)*

**Amtex California Inc** ............................................... E ...... 323 859-2200
113 S Utah St Los Angeles (90033) *(P-2914)*

**Amtrend Corporation** ............................................... D ...... 714 630-2070
1458 Manhattan Ave Fullerton (92831) *(P-3644)*

**Amtv USA, Pasadena** *Also Called: American Multimedia TV USA (P-16329)*

**Amudan International, Oakland** *Also Called: Dura Chemicals Inc (P-6081)*

**Amvac Chemical Corporation (HQ)** ......................... E ...... 323 264-3910
4695 Macarthur Ct Ste 1200 Newport Beach (92660) *(P-6192)*

**Amwear USA Inc** ...................................................... E ...... 800 858-6755
250 Benjamin Dr Corona (92879) *(P-2556)*

**Amy Lacey Project** ................................................... E ...... 866 422-3568
1057 Village Ln Chico (95926) *(P-848)*

**Amylin Ohio LLC** ..................................................... A ...... 858 552-2200
9360 Towne Centre Dr San Diego (92121) *(P-5321)*

**Amyris, Emeryville** *Also Called: Amyris Inc (P-6126)*

**Amyris Inc (PA)** ........................................................ B ...... 510 450-0761
5885 Hollis St Ste 100 Emeryville (94608) *(P-6126)*

**Amys Kitchen Inc (PA)** ............................................. A ...... 707 578-7188
109 Kentucky St Petaluma (94952) *(P-1024)*

**Ana Global LLC (PA)** ............................................... D ...... 619 482-9990
2360 Marconi Ct San Diego (92154) *(P-3549)*

**Anaco Inc** ................................................................. C ...... 951 372-2732
311 Corporate Terrace Cir Corona (92879) *(P-10064)*

**Anacom Inc** .............................................................. E ...... 408 519-2062
11682 Vineyard Spring Ct Cupertino (95014) *(P-11808)*

**Anacom General Corporation** ................................. E ...... 714 774-8484
1240 S Claudina St Anaheim (92805) *(P-11635)*

**Anacom Medtek, Anaheim** *Also Called: Anacom General Corporation (P-11635)*

**Anacor Pharmaceuticals Inc** .................................. E ...... 650 543-7500
1060 E Meadow Cir Palo Alto (94303) *(P-5322)*

**Anaergia Services LLC** ........................................... E ...... 760 436-8870
705 Palomar Airport Rd Ste 200 Carlsbad (92011) *(P-392)*

**Anaerobe Systems** .................................................. E ...... 408 782-7557
15906 Concord Cir Morgan Hill (95037) *(P-5737)*

**Anaheim Automation Inc** ........................................ E ...... 714 992-6990
4985 E Landon Dr Anaheim (92807) *(P-11307)*

**Anaheim Custom Extruders Inc** ............................. E ...... 714 693-8508
1360 N Mccan St Anaheim (92806) *(P-6718)*

**Anaheim Extrusion Co Inc** ...................................... D ...... 714 630-3111
1330 N Kraemer Blvd Anaheim (92806) *(P-7735)*

**Anaheim Plant, Anaheim** *Also Called: Stepan Company (P-5205)*

**Anaheim Precision Mfg, Orange** *Also Called: APM Manufacturing (P-13779)*

**Anaheim Wire Products Inc** ................................... E ...... 714 563-8300
1009 E Vermont Ave Anaheim (92805) *(P-9210)*

**Anajet LLC** ............................................................... E ...... 714 662-3200
1100 Valencia Ave Tustin (92780) *(P-9762)*

**Analog, La Verne** *Also Called: Micro Analog Inc (P-12565)*

**Analog Bits Inc (HQ)** ................................................ F ...... 650 279-9323
945 Stewart Dr Sunnyvale (94085) *(P-12304)*

**Analog Devices Inc** ................................................. D ...... 408 428-2050
160 Rio Robles San Jose (95134) *(P-12305)*

**Analog Devices Inc** ................................................. C ...... 408 432-1900
160 Rio Robles San Jose (95134) *(P-12306)*

**Analog Devices Inc** ................................................. D ...... 408 727-9222
160 Rio Robles San Jose (95134) *(P-12307)*

**Analog Inference Inc** ............................................... E ...... 408 771-6413
2350 Mission College Blvd Ste 300 Santa Clara (95054) *(P-12308)*

**Analogix Semiconductor Inc (PA)** .......................... E ...... 408 988-8848
2350 Mission College Blvd Ste 1100 Santa Clara (95054) *(P-12309)*

**Analytcal Scientific Instrs Inc** ................................. E ...... 510 669-2250
3023 Research Dr San Pablo (94806) *(P-14610)*

**Analytic Endodontics, Orange** *Also Called: Sybron Dental Specialties Inc (P-15487)*

**Analytical Industries Inc** ......................................... E ...... 909 392-6900
2855 Metropolitan Pl Pomona (91767) *(P-14387)*

**Analytik Jena US LLC** .............................................. F ...... 781 376-9899
2066 W 11th St Upland (91786) *(P-14611)*

**Anamex Corporation (PA)** ....................................... E ...... 714 779-7055
250 S Peralta Way Anaheim (92807) *(P-17880)*

**Ananda Church of Self-Realztn (PA)** ...................... D ...... 530 478-7560
14618 Tyler Foote Rd Ste 146 Nevada City (95959) *(P-19367)*

**Anaplex Corporation** ............................................... E ...... 714 522-4481
15547 Garfield Ave Paramount (90723) *(P-8919)*

**ANAPTYSBIO, San Diego** *Also Called: Anaptysbio Inc (P-5323)*

**Anaptysbio Inc (PA)** ................................................. C ...... 858 362-6295
10770 Wateridge Cir Ste 210 San Diego (92121) *(P-5323)*

**Anasys Instruments Corp** ....................................... F ...... 805 730-3310
325 Chapala St Santa Barbara (93101) *(P-14612)*

**Anatase Products, Tehachapi** *Also Called: Henway Inc (P-15911)*

**Anatesco Inc** ............................................................ F ...... 661 399-6990
128 Bedford Way Bakersfield (93308) *(P-205)*

**Anatex, Van Nuys** *Also Called: Anatex Enterprises Inc (P-16942)*

**Anatex Enterprises Inc** ........................................... E ...... 818 908-1888
15911 Arminta St Van Nuys (91406) *(P-16942)*

**Anatometal LLC** ...................................................... E ...... 831 454-9880
165 Dubois St Santa Cruz (95060) *(P-15684)*

**Anatomic Global Inc** ............................................... C ...... 800 874-7237
1241 Old Temescal Rd Ste 103 Corona (92881) *(P-2921)*

**Anaya Brothers Cutting LLC** .................................. D ...... 323 582-5758
3130 Leonis Blvd Vernon (90058) *(P-2889)*

**Anc Technology Inc** ................................................ D ...... 805 530-3958
10195 Stockton Rd Moorpark (93021) *(P-12054)*

**Anchen Pharmaceuticals Inc** .................................. C ...... 949 639-8100
5 Goodyear Irvine (92618) *(P-5324)*

**Anchor Audio Inc** .................................................... D ...... 760 827-7100
5931 Darwin Ct Carlsbad (92008) *(P-11636)*

**Anchor Bay Technologies Inc** ................................. E ...... 888 651-1765
564 Crawford Dr Sunnyvale (94087) *(P-12310)*

**Anchor-41 Construction LLC** ................................. F ...... 559 740-7776
9301 W Airport Dr Ste A Visalia (93277) *(P-363)*

**Anchored Prints** ...................................................... E ...... 714 929-9317
1199 N Grove St Anaheim (92806) *(P-4513)*

**Ancient Harvest, Ukiah** *Also Called: Quinoa Corporation (P-1239)*

**Anco, San Bernardino** *Also Called: Anco International Inc (P-9182)*

**Anco International Inc** ............................................ E ...... 909 887-2521
19851 Cajon Blvd San Bernardino (92407) *(P-9182)*

**Ancora Heart Inc** .................................................................. E ...... 408 727-1105
  4001 Burton Dr Santa Clara (95054) *(P-14967)*
**Ancora Software Inc (PA)** ...................................................... E ...... 888 476-4839
  402 W Broadway Ste 400 San Diego (92101) *(P-18044)*
**Ancra International LLC** ........................................................ C ...... 626 765-4818
  601 S Vincent Ave Azusa (91702) *(P-9505)*
**Ancra International LLC (HQ)** ................................................ C ...... 626 765-4800
  601 S Vincent Ave Azusa (91702) *(P-9506)*
**Andanov Music, Burbank** *Also Called: Hollywood Records Inc (P-11735)*
**Andapt Inc** ............................................................................. F ...... 408 931-4898
  950 S Bascom Ave Ste 3012 San Jose (95128) *(P-18045)*
**Andari, El Monte** *Also Called: Andari Fashion Inc (P-2609)*
**Andari Fashion Inc** ................................................................ C ...... 626 575-2759
  9626 Telstar Ave El Monte (91731) *(P-2609)*
**Anderco Inc** ........................................................................... E ...... 714 446-9508
  540 Airpark Dr Fullerton (92833) *(P-3108)*
**Andersen Industries Inc** ........................................................ E ...... 760 246-8766
  17079 Muskrat Ave Adelanto (92301) *(P-13611)*
**Anderson, Poway** *Also Called: T G T Enterprises Inc (P-19540)*
**Anderson Chrnesky Strl Stl Inc** .............................................. D ...... 951 769-5700
  353 Risco Cir Beaumont (92223) *(P-8096)*
**Anderson La Inc** ................................................................... D ...... 323 460-4115
  3550 Tyburn St Los Angeles (90065) *(P-4514)*
**Anderson Logging Inc** .......................................................... D ...... 707 964-2770
  1296 N Main St Fort Bragg (95437) *(P-3041)*
**Anderson Moulds Incorporated** ............................................. F ...... 209 943-1145
  3131 E Anita St Stockton (95205) *(P-6719)*
**Anderson Printing, Los Angeles** *Also Called: Anderson La Inc (P-4514)*
**Anderson Trophy Company, North Hollywood** *Also Called: Pnk Enterprises Inc (P-17717)*
**Anderson Valley Brewing Inc** ................................................ E ...... 707 895-2337
  17700 Hwy 253 Boonville (95415) *(P-1412)*
**ANDERSON VALLEY BREWING COMPAN, Boonville** *Also Called: Anderson Valley Brewing Inc (P-1412)*
**Anderson's Carpet & Linoleum, Oakland** *Also Called: Linoleum Sales Co Inc (P-7175)*
**Andre-Boudin Bakeries Inc** ................................................... E ...... 925 935-4375
  67 Broadway Ln Walnut Creek (94596) *(P-1156)*
**Andre-Boudin Bakeries Inc** ................................................... E ...... 415 283-1230
  619 Market St San Francisco (94105) *(P-17407)*
**Andre-Boudin Bakeries Inc (HQ)** ........................................... E ...... 415 882-1849
  50 Francisco St Ste 200 San Francisco (94133) *(P-1157)*
**Andresen, Burlingame** *Also Called: Clic LLC (P-4554)*
**Andrew Alexander Inc** ........................................................... D ...... 323 752-0066
  1306 S Alameda St Compton (90221) *(P-7085)*
**Andrew LLC** .......................................................................... F ...... 909 270-9356
  17058 Lagos Dr Chino Hills (91709) *(P-1052)*
**Androp Packaging Inc** .......................................................... E ...... 909 605-8842
  4400 E Francis St Ontario (91761) *(P-3819)*
**Andrus Sheet Metal Inc** ........................................................ E ...... 510 232-8687
  5021 Seaport Ave Richmond (94804) *(P-8375)*
**Anduril Industries Inc (PA)** .................................................... A ...... 949 891-1607
  1400 Anduril Costa Mesa (92626) *(P-14142)*
**Anduril Industries Inc** ........................................................... E ...... 949 891-1607
  2910 S Tech Center Dr Santa Ana (92705) *(P-14143)*
**Andwin Corporation (PA)** ...................................................... D ...... 818 999-2828
  167 W Cochran St Simi Valley (93065) *(P-16996)*
**Andwin Scientific, Simi Valley** *Also Called: Andwin Corporation (P-16996)*
**Andy Anand Chocolates, Chino** *Also Called: Hira Paris Inc (P-1310)*
**Anemostat Products, Carson** *Also Called: Mestek Inc (P-10508)*
**Anettes Chocolate Factory Inc** .............................................. F ...... 707 252-4228
  1321 1st St Napa (94559) *(P-1300)*
**Angeleno Magazine, San Francisco** *Also Called: Modern Luxury Media LLC (P-4281)*
**Angell & Giroux Inc** ............................................................... D ...... 323 269-8596
  2727 Alcazar St Los Angeles (90033) *(P-3592)*
**Angelus Block Co Inc (PA)** .................................................... E ...... 714 637-8594
  11374 Tuxford St Sun Valley (91352) *(P-7292)*
**Angelus Machine Corp Intl** .................................................... E ...... 323 583-2171
  4900 Pacific Blvd Vernon (90058) *(P-9579)*
**Angioscore Inc** ...................................................................... C ...... 510 933-7900
  5055 Brandin Ct Fremont (94538) *(P-14968)*
**Angkor Engineering Inc** ........................................................ F ...... 831 256-1015
  36 Quail Run Cir Unit 100v Salinas (93907) *(P-19377)*

**Angular Machining Inc** .......................................................... E ...... 408 954-8326
  2040 Hartog Dr San Jose (95131) *(P-10710)*
**Anheuser-Busch, Santa Fe Springs** *Also Called: Anheuser-Busch LLC (P-1413)*
**Anheuser-Busch, San Diego** *Also Called: Anheuser-Busch LLC (P-1414)*
**Anheuser-Busch, Fairfield** *Also Called: Anheuser-Busch LLC (P-1415)*
**Anheuser-Busch, Pomona** *Also Called: Anheuser-Busch LLC (P-1416)*
**Anheuser-Busch, Carson** *Also Called: Anheuser-Busch LLC (P-1417)*
**Anheuser-Busch LLC** ........................................................... E ...... 562 699-3424
  12065 Pike St Santa Fe Springs (90670) *(P-1413)*
**Anheuser-Busch LLC** ........................................................... D ...... 858 581-7000
  5959 Santa Fe St San Diego (92109) *(P-1414)*
**Anheuser-Busch LLC** ........................................................... B ...... 707 429-7595
  3101 Busch Dr Fairfield (94534) *(P-1415)*
**Anheuser-Busch LLC** ........................................................... C ...... 951 782-3935
  2800 S Reservoir St Pomona (91766) *(P-1416)*
**Anheuser-Busch LLC** ........................................................... E ...... 310 761-4600
  20499 S Reeves Ave Carson (90810) *(P-1417)*
**Anillo Industries, Orange** *Also Called: Anillo Industries LLC (P-8742)*
**Anillo Industries, Orange** *Also Called: Hightower Plating & Mfg Co LLC (P-8970)*
**Anillo Industries LLC** ............................................................ E ...... 714 637-7000
  2090 N Glassell St Orange (92865) *(P-8742)*
**Animatics Corporation** .......................................................... E ...... 408 748-8721
  3200 Patrick Henry Dr Ste 110 Santa Clara (95054) *(P-11308)*
**Anita Gelato California Inc** .................................................... F ...... 818 987-4055
  18700 Ventura Blvd Tarzana (91356) *(P-792)*
**Anitas Mexican Foods Corp (PA)** .......................................... D ...... 909 884-8706
  3454 N Mike Daley Dr San Bernardino (92407) *(P-2084)*
**Anitas Mexican Foods Corp** .................................................. E ...... 909 884-8706
  3392 N Mike Daley Dr San Bernardino (92407) *(P-2085)*
**Anlin Window Systems, Clovis** *Also Called: Tollhouse Window Company (P-3199)*
**Anlin Windows & Doors** ........................................................ B ...... 800 287-7996
  1665 Tollhouse Rd Clovis (93611) *(P-8253)*
**Ann Lilli Corp (PA)** ................................................................ D ...... 415 482-9444
  1010 B St Ste 333 San Rafael (94901) *(P-2721)*
**Annex Pro Inc** ....................................................................... E ...... 800 682-6639
  4100 W Alameda Ave Fl 3 Burbank (91505) *(P-18046)*
**Annexon, Brisbane** *Also Called: Annexon Inc (P-5325)*
**Annexon Inc (PA)** .................................................................. D ...... 650 822-5500
  1400 Sierra Point Pkwy Ste 200 Brisbane (94005) *(P-5325)*
**Annieglass Inc (PA)** .............................................................. F ...... 831 761-2041
  310 Harvest Dr Watsonville (95076) *(P-7189)*
**Annies Inc (HQ)** .................................................................... D ...... 510 558-7500
  1610 5th St Berkeley (94710) *(P-2127)*
**Annotation Unlimited Pbc** ..................................................... E ...... 415 295-5689
  548 Market St Ste 32444 San Francisco (94104) *(P-18047)*
**Anns Trading Company Inc** ................................................. E ...... 323 585-4702
  5333 S Downey Rd Vernon (90058) *(P-17284)*
**Ano-Tech Metal Finishing, Clovis** *Also Called: Atmf Inc (P-8927)*
**Anodizing Industries Inc** ...................................................... E ...... 323 227-4916
  5222 Alhambra Ave Los Angeles (90032) *(P-8920)*
**Anodyne Inc** ......................................................................... E ...... 714 549-3321
  2230 S Susan St Santa Ana (92704) *(P-8921)*
**Anomalies International Inc** ................................................. D ...... 800 855-1113
  2833 Mission St Santa Cruz (95060) *(P-1865)*
**Anoroc, Compton** *Also Called: Anoroc Precision Shtmtl Inc (P-8376)*
**Anoroc Precision Shtmtl Inc** ................................................. E ...... 310 515-6015
  19122 S Santa Fe Ave Compton (90221) *(P-8376)*
**Anp Lighting, Montclair** *Also Called: American Nail Plate Ltg Inc (P-11487)*
**Anritsu Company (DH)** ......................................................... B ...... 800 267-4878
  490 Jarvis Dr Morgan Hill (95037) *(P-11809)*
**Anritsu Company, Morgan Hill** *Also Called: Anritsu US Holding Inc (P-14496)*
**Anritsu US Holding Inc (HQ)** ................................................ B ...... 408 778-2000
  490 Jarvis Dr Morgan Hill (95037) *(P-14496)*
**Anschutz Film Group LLC (HQ)** ........................................... E ...... 310 887-1000
  10201 W Pico Blvd # 52 Los Angeles (90064) *(P-15628)*
**Ansell Sndel Med Solutions LLC** .......................................... E ...... 818 534-2500
  9301 Oakdale Ave Ste 300 Chatsworth (91311) *(P-15322)*
**Ansun, San Diego** *Also Called: Ansun Biopharma Inc (P-19441)*
**Ansun Biopharma Inc** ........................................................... E ...... 858 452-2631
  10045 Mesa Rim Rd San Diego (92121) *(P-19441)*

# ALPHABETIC SECTION

**Antaeus Fashions Group Inc** .................................................. F ...... 626 452-0797
740 S 5th Ave City Of Industry (91746) *(P-2610)*

**Antaky Quilting Company, Los Angeles** *Also Called: American Quilting Company Inc (P-2988)*

**Antcom, Torrance** *Also Called: Antcom Corporation (P-11810)*

**Antcom Corporation** .................................................. E ...... 310 782-1076
367 Van Ness Way Ste 602 Torrance (90501) *(P-11810)*

**Antelope Valley Newspapers Inc** .................................................. E ...... 661 940-1000
44939 10th St W Lancaster (93534) *(P-4065)*

**Antelope Valley Press, Lancaster** *Also Called: Antelope Valley Newspapers Inc (P-4065)*

**Antex Knitting Mills, Los Angeles** *Also Called: Tenenblatt Corporation (P-2483)*

**Antex Knitting Mills, Los Angeles** *Also Called: Matchmaster Dyg & Finshg Inc (P-2504)*

**Antex Knitting Mills, Los Angeles** *Also Called: Guru Knits Inc (P-2667)*

**Anthony Inc (DH)** .................................................. A ...... 818 365-9451
12391 Montero Ave Sylmar (91342) *(P-10481)*

**Anthony California Inc (PA)** .................................................. E ...... 909 627-0351
14485 Monte Vista Ave Chino (91710) *(P-11488)*

**Anthony International, Sylmar** *Also Called: Anthony Inc (P-10481)*

**Anthony Leonardo Logging, Fortuna** *Also Called: Leonardo Logging and Cnstr Inc (P-3049)*

**Anthony Welded Products Inc (PA)** .................................................. E ...... 661 721-7211
1447 S Lexington St Delano (93215) *(P-9507)*

**Anthos Group Inc** .................................................. E ...... 888 778-2986
705 N Douglas St El Segundo (90245) *(P-19520)*

**Antibodies Incorporated** .................................................. F ...... 800 824-8540
25242 County Road 95 Davis (95616) *(P-5738)*

**Antica NAPA Valley, Napa** *Also Called: Antinori California (P-1476)*

**Antigen Discovery, Irvine** *Also Called: Immport Therapeutics Inc (P-15503)*

**Antinori California** .................................................. E ...... 707 265-8866
3149 Soda Canyon Rd Napa (94558) *(P-1476)*

**Antioch Building Materials Co (PA)** .................................................. E ...... 925 432-0171
1375 California Ave Pittsburg (94565) *(P-16463)*

**Antique Apparatus Company, Torrance** *Also Called: Rock-Ola Manufacturing Corp (P-11692)*

**Antonina's Bakery, Manteca** *Also Called: Pin Hsiao & Associates LLC (P-1238)*

**Antriabio Delaware Inc** .................................................. E ...... 303 222-2128
570 El Camino Real Redwood City (94063) *(P-5326)*

**Antrin Miniature Spc Inc** .................................................. F ...... 760 723-7605
342 Industrial Way Ste 201 Fallbrook (92028) *(P-10711)*

**Anvil Cases Inc** .................................................. C ...... 626 968-4100
1242 E Edna Pl Unit B Covina (91724) *(P-7126)*

**Anydata Corporation** .................................................. D ...... 949 900-6040
5405 Alton Pkwy Irvine (92604) *(P-11811)*

**Ao Sky Corporation** .................................................. E ...... 510 264-0402
20185 Skywest Dr Hayward (94541) *(P-14144)*

**Aoc LLC** .................................................. D ...... 951 657-5161
19991 Seaton Ave Perris (92570) *(P-2525)*

**AOC California Plant, Perris** *Also Called: Aoc LLC (P-2525)*

**AOC Technologies Inc** .................................................. B ...... 925 875-0808
6900 Koll Center Pkwy Ste 401 Pleasanton (94566) *(P-16606)*

**AOC USA, Pico Rivera** *Also Called: Lubricating Specialties Company (P-6398)*

**Aoclsc Inc** .................................................. E ...... 562 776-4000
3365 E Slauson Ave Vernon (90058) *(P-6386)*

**Aoclsc Inc** .................................................. C ...... 813 248-1988
8015 Paramount Blvd Pico Rivera (90660) *(P-6387)*

**Aocusa, Vernon** *Also Called: Aoclsc Inc (P-6386)*

**Aocusa, Pico Rivera** *Also Called: Aoclsc Inc (P-6387)*

**AOE International Inc** .................................................. E
20611 Belshaw Ave Carson (90746) *(P-5327)*

**Aos, Torrance** *Also Called: Finest Hour Holdings Inc (P-15347)*

**AP Parpro Inc** .................................................. E ...... 619 498-9004
2700 S Fairview St Santa Ana (92704) *(P-11309)*

**AP Precision Metals Inc** .................................................. E ...... 619 628-0003
1185 Park Center Dr Vista (92081) *(P-8377)*

**AP Tech, Napa** *Also Called: Advanced Pressure Technology (P-14383)*

**AP Unlimited Corporation** .................................................. F ...... 209 834-0287
1225 N Macarthur Dr Ste 200 Tracy (95376) *(P-17058)*

**Apct, Santa Clara** *Also Called: Apct Holdings LLC (P-12056)*

**Apct Inc (HQ)** .................................................. C ...... 408 727-6442
3495 De La Cruz Blvd Santa Clara (95054) *(P-12055)*

**Apct Anaheim, Orange** *Also Called: Cirtech Inc (P-19082)*

**Apct Holdings LLC (PA)** .................................................. C ...... 408 727-6442
3495 De La Cruz Blvd Santa Clara (95054) *(P-12056)*

**Apct Orange County, Placentia** *Also Called: Cartel Electronics LLC (P-12074)*

**Apct-Wallingford Inc** .................................................. E ...... 203 269-3311
3495 De La Cruz Blvd Santa Clara (95054) *(P-12057)*

**Apeel Sciences, Goleta** *Also Called: Apeel Technology Inc (P-73)*

**Apeel Technology Inc (PA)** .................................................. B ...... 805 203-0146
71 S Los Carneros Rd Goleta (93117) *(P-73)*

**Apem Inc (HQ)** .................................................. E ...... 978 372-1602
970 Park Center Dr Vista (92081) *(P-10321)*

**Apem Inc** .................................................. D ...... 760 598-2518
970 Park Center Dr Vista (92081) *(P-12914)*

**Aperia Technologies Inc (PA)** .................................................. D ...... 650 741-3231
3160 Corporate Pl Hayward (94545) *(P-9829)*

**Aperio, Vista** *Also Called: Leica Biosystems Imaging Inc (P-14683)*

**Apex Communications Inc (DH)** .................................................. F ...... 818 379-8400
21700 Oxnard St Ste 1060 Woodland Hills (91367) *(P-18048)*

**Apex Container Services, Commerce** *Also Called: Apex Drum Company Inc (P-3368)*

**Apex Conveyor Corp** .................................................. F ...... 951 304-7808
40001 Via Caseta Murrieta (92562) *(P-9481)*

**Apex Design Tech., Corona** *Also Called: Btl Machine (P-10755)*

**Apex Design Technology, Anaheim** *Also Called: Apex Technology Holdings Inc (P-14145)*

**Apex Die Corporation** .................................................. D ...... 650 592-6350
840 Cherry Ln San Carlos (94070) *(P-3995)*

**Apex Drum Company Inc** .................................................. F ...... 323 721-8994
6226 Ferguson Dr Commerce (90022) *(P-3368)*

**Apex Energy LLC (HQ)** .................................................. F ...... 310 377-5579
655 Deep Valley Dr Ste 310 Rllng Hls Est (90274) *(P-19378)*

**Apex Enterprises Inc** .................................................. E ...... 530 871-0723
461 Ophir Rd Oroville (95966) *(P-3042)*

**Apex Machining Inc** .................................................. E ...... 408 441-1335
1997 Hartog Dr San Jose (95131) *(P-10712)*

**Apex Medical Technologies Inc** .................................................. E ...... 858 535-0012
10064 Mesa Ridge Ct Ste 202 San Diego (92121) *(P-14969)*

**Apex Precision Technologies Inc** .................................................. E ...... 317 821-1000
23622 Calabasas Rd Ste 323 Calabasas (91302) *(P-13458)*

**Apex Rail Automation, Grass Valley** *Also Called: Vossloh Signaling LLC (P-17994)*

**Apex Technology Holdings Inc** .................................................. A ...... 321 270-3630
2850 E Coronado St Anaheim (92806) *(P-14145)*

**Apffels Coffee, Santa Fe Springs** *Also Called: Apffels Coffee Inc (P-2067)*

**Apffels Coffee Inc** .................................................. E ...... 562 309-0400
12115 Pacific St Santa Fe Springs (90670) *(P-2067)*

**Aphro-D LLC** .................................................. E ...... 201 574-1875
548 Market St San Francisco (94104) *(P-742)*

**API Marketing** .................................................. F ...... 916 632-1946
13020 Earhart Ave Auburn (95602) *(P-4515)*

**Apic Corporation** .................................................. D ...... 310 642-7975
5800 Uplander Way Culver City (90230) *(P-12311)*

**Apical Industries Inc** .................................................. D ...... 760 724-5300
3030 Enterprise Ct Ste A Vista (92081) *(P-16915)*

**APM Electronics USA, Santa Clara** *Also Called: Leadman Electronics USA Inc (P-10174)*

**APM Manufacturing** .................................................. C ...... 714 453-0100
341 W Blueridge Ave Orange (92865) *(P-13635)*

**APM Manufacturing (HQ)** .................................................. E ...... 714 453-0100
1738 N Neville St Orange (92865) *(P-13779)*

**Apogee Electronics, Santa Monica** *Also Called: Apogee Electronics Corporation (P-11637)*

**Apogee Electronics Corporation** .................................................. E ...... 310 584-9394
1715 Berkeley St Santa Monica (90404) *(P-11637)*

**Apogee Manufacturing** .................................................. F ...... 661 467-0440
28231 Avenue Crocker Ste 90 Valencia (91355) *(P-10713)*

**Apollo Manufacturing Services** .................................................. F ...... 858 271-8009
10360 Sorrento Valley Rd Ste A San Diego (92121) *(P-11359)*

**Apollo Metal Spinning Co Inc** .................................................. F ...... 562 634-5141
15315 Illinois Ave Paramount (90723) *(P-8807)*

**Apollo Printing & Graphics, Anaheim** *Also Called: Tajen Graphics Inc (P-4780)*

**Apollotek International Inc** .................................................. F ...... 800 787-1244
1702 Mcgaw Ave Irvine (92614) *(P-6268)*

**Apon Industries Corp** .................................................. C
10005 Marconi Dr Ste 2 San Diego (92154) *(P-6720)*

**Aporeto Inc** .................................................. D ...... 408 472-7648
10 Almaden Blvd Ste 400 San Jose (95113) *(P-18049)*

**Apotheka Systems Inc** .................................................. E ...... 844 777-4455
14040 Panay Way Marina Del Rey (90292) *(P-18050)*

## App Wholesale LLC — ALPHABETIC SECTION

**App Wholesale LLC** .......................................................... B ...... 323 980-8315
3686 E Olympic Blvd Los Angeles (90023) *(P-17174)*

**App Winddown LLC (HQ)** ................................................ C
747 Warehouse St Los Angeles (90021) *(P-2890)*

**Apparel House USA, Gardena** *Also Called: Stanzino Inc (P-2429)*

**Apparel Newsgroup, The, Los Angeles** *Also Called: Mnm Corporation (P-4279)*

**Apparel Prod Svcs Globl LLC** ........................................ E ...... 818 700-3700
8954 Lurline Ave Chatsworth (91311) *(P-2735)*

**Appcoll Inc** ........................................................................ E ...... 650 223-5460
325 Sharon Park Dr Menlo Park (94025) *(P-18051)*

**Apperson Inc (PA)** ............................................................ D ...... 562 356-3333
17315 Studebaker Rd Ste 211 Cerritos (90703) *(P-4987)*

**Appfolio, Santa Barbara** *Also Called: Appfolio Inc (P-18053)*

**Appfolio Inc** ...................................................................... C ...... 866 648-1536
2305 Historic Decatur Rd San Diego (92106) *(P-18052)*

**Appfolio Inc (PA)** .............................................................. B ...... 805 364-6093
70 Castilian Dr Santa Barbara (93117) *(P-18053)*

**Apple, Cupertino** *Also Called: Apple Inc (P-11812)*

**Apple Graphics Inc** .......................................................... E ...... 626 301-4287
3550 Tyburn St Los Angeles (90065) *(P-4516)*

**Apple Inc (PA)** ................................................................... A ...... 408 996-1010
1 Apple Park Way Cupertino (95014) *(P-11812)*

**Apple Paper Converting Inc** .......................................... E ...... 714 632-3195
3800 E Miraloma Ave Anaheim (92806) *(P-4029)*

**Applied Anodize Inc** ........................................................ F ...... 408 435-9191
622 Charcot Ave Ste D San Jose (95131) *(P-8922)*

**Applied Arospc Structures Corp (PA)** ........................... C ...... 209 982-0160
3437 S Airport Way Stockton (95206) *(P-13780)*

**Applied Biosystems, Pleasanton** *Also Called: Thermo Fisher Scientific Inc (P-14743)*

**Applied Biosystems, Carlsbad** *Also Called: Applied Biosystems LLC (P-18054)*

**Applied Biosystems Inc** .................................................. D ...... 800 327-3002
850 Lincoln Centre Dr Foster City (94404) *(P-14613)*

**Applied Biosystems LLC (DH)** ....................................... C
5791 Van Allen Way Carlsbad (92008) *(P-18054)*

**Applied Business Software Inc** .................................... E ...... 562 426-2188
7755 Center Ave Huntington Beach (92647) *(P-18055)*

**Applied Cardiac Systems Inc** ........................................ D ...... 949 855-9366
1 Hughes Ste A Irvine (92618) *(P-14970)*

**Applied Cells Inc** ............................................................. E ...... 800 960-3004
3350 Scott Blvd Bldg 6 Santa Clara (95054) *(P-14329)*

**Applied Ceramics, Fremont** *Also Called: Applied Ceramics Inc (P-12312)*

**Applied Ceramics Inc (PA)** ............................................. C ...... 510 249-9700
48630 Milmont Dr Fremont (94538) *(P-12312)*

**Applied Cmpsite Structures Inc (HQ)** .......................... D ...... 714 990-6300
1195 Columbia St Brea (92821) *(P-13781)*

**Applied Coatings & Linings** .......................................... E ...... 626 280-6354
3224 Rosemead Blvd El Monte (91731) *(P-9047)*

**Applied Companies** ......................................................... E ...... 661 257-0090
28020 Avenue Stanford Santa Clarita (91355) *(P-19379)*

**Applied Control Electronics** .......................................... E ...... 530 626-5181
5480 Merchant Cir Placerville (95667) *(P-11310)*

**Applied Expert Systems Inc** .......................................... E ...... 650 617-2400
999 Commercial St Ste 201 Palo Alto (94303) *(P-18056)*

**Applied Fusion LLC** ......................................................... D ...... 510 351-8314
1915 Republic Ave San Leandro (94577) *(P-19243)*

**Applied Instrument Tech Inc** ......................................... E ...... 909 204-3700
2121 Aviation Dr Upland (91786) *(P-14614)*

**Applied Manufacturing LLC** ........................................... A ...... 949 713-8000
22872 Avenida Empresa Rancho Santa Margari (92688) *(P-14971)*

**Applied Manufacturing Group** ....................................... E ...... 408 855-8857
941 George St Santa Clara (95054) *(P-12313)*

**APPLIED MATERIALS, Santa Clara** *Also Called: Applied Materials Inc (P-9830)*

**Applied Materials, Santa Clara** *Also Called: Applied Materials Inc (P-12314)*

**Applied Materials, Santa Clara** *Also Called: Applied Materials Inc (P-12315)*

**Applied Materials, Santa Clara** *Also Called: Applied Materials Inc (P-12316)*

**Applied Materials, Santa Clara** *Also Called: Applied Materials Inc (P-12317)*

**Applied Materials, Sunnyvale** *Also Called: Applied Materials Inc (P-12318)*

**Applied Materials, Santa Clara** *Also Called: Applied Materials Inc (P-12319)*

**Applied Materials, Santa Clara** *Also Called: Applied Materials (holdings) (P-12320)*

**Applied Materials, Santa Clara** *Also Called: Applied Mtls Asia-Pacific LLC (P-12323)*

**Applied Materials Inc (PA)** .............................................. A ...... 408 727-5555
3050 Bowers Ave Santa Clara (95054) *(P-9830)*

**Applied Materials Inc** ...................................................... E ...... 408 727-5555
3320 Scott Blvd Santa Clara (95054) *(P-12314)*

**Applied Materials Inc** ...................................................... E ...... 406 752-2107
1285 Walsh Ave Santa Clara (95050) *(P-12315)*

**Applied Materials Inc** ...................................................... D ...... 408 727-5555
3340 Scott Blvd Santa Clara (95054) *(P-12316)*

**Applied Materials Inc** ...................................................... E ...... 512 272-3692
3101 Scott Blvd Santa Clara (95054) *(P-12317)*

**Applied Materials Inc** ...................................................... E ...... 408 727-5555
974 E Arques Ave Bldg 81 Sunnyvale (94085) *(P-12318)*

**Applied Materials Inc** ...................................................... E ...... 408 727-5555
2821 Scott Blvd Bldg 17 Santa Clara (95050) *(P-12319)*

**Applied Materials (holdings) (HQ)** ................................ E ...... 408 727-5555
3050 Bowers Ave Santa Clara (95054) *(P-12320)*

**Applied Medical Corporation (PA)** ................................ C ...... 949 713-8000
22872 Avenida Empresa Rancho Santa Margari (92688) *(P-14972)*

**Applied Medical Dist Corp** ............................................. A ...... 949 713-8000
22872 Avenida Empresa Rcho Sta Marg (92688) *(P-14973)*

**Applied Medical Distribution, Rancho Santa Margari** *Also Called: Applied Medical Resources Corp (P-14975)*

**Applied Medical Resources** ........................................... D ...... 949 459-1042
30152 Esperanza Rcho Sta Marg (92688) *(P-14974)*

**Applied Medical Resources, Rancho Santa Margari** *Also Called: Applied Medical Corporation (P-14972)*

**Applied Medical Resources Corp (HQ)** ........................ E ...... 949 713-8000
22872 Avenida Empresa Rancho Santa Margari (92688) *(P-14975)*

**Applied Membranes Inc** ................................................. C ...... 760 727-3711
2450 Business Park Dr Vista (92081) *(P-10536)*

**Applied Micro Circuits Corp** .......................................... E ...... 408 523-1000
455 W Maude Ave Sunnyvale (94085) *(P-10224)*

**Applied Micro Circuits Corp (HQ)** ................................ C ...... 408 542-8600
4555 Great America Pkwy # 6 Santa Clara (95054) *(P-12321)*

**Applied Micro Circuits Corp** .......................................... E ...... 408 542-8600
4555 Great America Pkwy Ste 601 Santa Clara (95054) *(P-12322)*

**Applied Mlecular Evolution Inc (HQ)** ............................ E ...... 858 597-4990
10300 Campus Point Dr Ste 200 San Diego (92121) *(P-5328)*

**Applied Molecular Trnspt Inc** ........................................ D ...... 650 392-0420
325 Sharon Park Dr # 1001 Menlo Park (94025) *(P-5329)*

**Applied Mtls Asia-Pacific LLC (HQ)** .............................. C ...... 408 727-5555
3050 Bowers Ave Santa Clara (95054) *(P-12323)*

**Applied Orthopedic Design** ........................................... E ...... 805 481-3685
860 Oak Park Blvd Ste 101 Arroyo Grande (93420) *(P-15323)*

**Applied Photon Technology Inc** .................................... E ...... 510 780-9500
3346 Arden Rd Hayward (94545) *(P-11421)*

**Applied Physics Systems Inc (PA)** ............................... C ...... 650 965-0500
425 Clyde Ave Mountain View (94043) *(P-14843)*

**Applied Polytech Systems Inc** ...................................... E ...... 818 504-9261
26000 Springbrook Ave Ste 102 Santa Clarita (91350) *(P-3392)*

**Applied Powdercoat Inc** ................................................. E ...... 805 981-1991
3101 Camino Del Sol Oxnard (93030) *(P-9048)*

**Applied Silver Inc** ............................................................ E ...... 888 939-4747
26254 Eden Landing Rd Hayward (94545) *(P-3410)*

**Applied Spectral Imaging Inc** ........................................ F ...... 760 929-2840
6160 Innovation Way Carlsbad (92009) *(P-17881)*

**Applied Statistics & MGT Inc** ........................................ D ...... 951 699-4600
32848 Wolf Store Rd Ste A Temecula (92592) *(P-18057)*

**Applied Systems Engrg Inc** ........................................... F ...... 408 364-0500
2105 S Bascom Ave Ste 155 Campbell (95008) *(P-10322)*

**Applied Technologies Assoc Inc (HQ)** ......................... C ...... 805 239-9100
3025 Buena Vista Dr Paso Robles (93446) *(P-14844)*

**Applied Thin-Film Products (PA)** .................................. C ...... 510 661-4287
3620 Yale Way Fremont (94538) *(P-12324)*

**Applied Thin-Film Products** .......................................... F ...... 510 661-4287
3439 Edison Way Fremont (94538) *(P-12915)*

**Applied Thin-Film Products, Fremont** *Also Called: Dale Vishay Electronics LLC (P-12822)*

**Applied Wrless Idntfctons Grou (PA)** ........................... E ...... 408 779-1929
18300 Santa Sutter Blvd Morgan Hill (95037) *(P-16690)*

**Applimotion Inc** ............................................................... D ...... 916 652-3118
5915 Jetton Ln Loomis (95650) *(P-16642)*

# ALPHABETIC SECTION — ARCADIA INC.

**Applovin Corporation (PA)** ............................................................ C ...... 800 839-9646
1100 Page Mill Rd Palo Alto (94304) *(P-18058)*

**Apporto Corporation** ..................................................................... E ...... 877 751-4081
3558 Round Barn Blvd Ste 200 Santa Rosa (95403) *(P-18059)*

**Appro International Inc (DH)** ....................................................... D ...... 408 941-8100
220 Devcon Dr San Jose (95112) *(P-10225)*

**Approved Aeronautics LLC** ............................................................ E ...... 951 200-3730
9130 Pulsar Ct Corona (92883) *(P-13782)*

**APR Engineering Inc** ..................................................................... E ...... 562 983-3800
1812 W 9th St Long Beach (90813) *(P-13998)*

**Apricorn LLC** ................................................................................. E ...... 858 513-2000
12191 Kirkham Rd Poway (92064) *(P-10323)*

**APS Global, Chatsworth** *Also Called: Apparel Prod Svcs Globl LLC (P-2735)*

**APS Marine, Chula Vista** *Also Called: Adept Process Services Inc (P-14026)*

**APT, Santa Ana** *Also Called: American Pneumatic Tools Inc (P-9577)*

**APT Electronics, Anaheim** *Also Called: APT Electronics Inc (P-12058)*

**APT Electronics Inc** ....................................................................... C ...... 714 687-6760
241 N Crescent Way Anaheim (92801) *(P-12058)*

**APT Manufacturing LLC** ................................................................. F ...... 714 632-0040
2899 E Coronado St Ste E Anaheim (92806) *(P-9540)*

**APT Metal Fabricators Inc** ............................................................. E ...... 818 896-7478
11164 Bradley Ave Pacoima (91331) *(P-8818)*

**Apta Group Inc** .............................................................................. E ...... 619 710-8170
7580 Britannia Ct San Diego (92154) *(P-12325)*

**Aptco LLC (PA)** .............................................................................. D ...... 661 792-2107
31381 Pond Rd Bldg 2 Mc Farland (93250) *(P-5137)*

**Aptible Inc** .................................................................................... D ...... 866 296-5003
548 Market St San Francisco (94104) *(P-13212)*

**Aptina LLC** ..................................................................................... A ...... 408 660-2699
2660 Zanker Rd San Jose (95134) *(P-12326)*

**Aptina Imaging, San Jose** *Also Called: Aptina LLC (P-12326)*

**Aptiv Digital LLC** ............................................................................ D ...... 818 295-6789
2160 Gold St San Jose (95002) *(P-18060)*

**Aptiv Services Us LLC** ................................................................... B ...... 818 661-6667
5137 Clareton Dr Ste 220 Agoura Hills (91301) *(P-13459)*

**Aputure Imaging Industries** ........................................................... E ...... 626 295-6133
1715 N Gower St Los Angeles (90028) *(P-7190)*

**APV Manufacturing & Engrg Co, Buena Park** *Also Called: AM Machining Inc (P-16914)*

**Aq Lighting Group, Santa Clarita** *Also Called: Aq Lighting Group Texas Inc (P-16643)*

**Aq Lighting Group Texas Inc** ......................................................... E ...... 818 534-5300
28486 Westinghouse Pl Ste 120 Santa Clarita (91355) *(P-16643)*

**Aqi, Ontario** *Also Called: Aliquantum International Inc (P-15737)*

**Aqm Acquisition Corp** .................................................................... F ...... 909 941-7776
9567 Arrow Rte Ste E Rancho Cucamonga (91730) *(P-17752)*

**Aqs, Fremont** *Also Called: All Quality & Services Inc (P-12047)*

**Aqt Solar Inc** .................................................................................. E
1145 Sonora Ct Sunnyvale (94086) *(P-12327)*

**Aqua Measure Instrument Co** ........................................................ F ...... 909 941-7776
9567 Arrow Rte Ste E Rancho Cucamonga (91730) *(P-14845)*

**Aqua Performance Inc** ................................................................... E ...... 951 340-2056
425 N Smith Ave Corona (92880) *(P-16932)*

**Aqua Pro Properties Vii LP** ............................................................ B ...... 310 516-9911
2000 W 135th St Gardena (90249) *(P-9831)*

**Aqua Products Inc (DH)** ................................................................. E ...... 973 857-2700
2882 Whiptail Loop Ste 100 Carlsbad (92010) *(P-10537)*

**Aqua Sierra Controls Inc** ................................................................ F ...... 530 823-3241
1650 Industrial Dr Auburn (95603) *(P-14846)*

**Aquafine Corporation (HQ)** ............................................................ D ...... 661 257-4770
29010 Avenue Paine Valencia (91355) *(P-10538)*

**Aquahydrate Inc** ............................................................................ E ...... 310 559-5058
5870 W Jefferson Blvd Ste D Los Angeles (90016) *(P-1866)*

**Aquamar Inc** .................................................................................. C ...... 909 481-4700
10888 7th St Rancho Cucamonga (91730) *(P-2034)*

**Aquamatic Cover Systems, Gilroy** *Also Called: Amcs Inc (P-16406)*

**Aquamor LLC (PA)** ......................................................................... D ...... 951 541-9517
42188 Rio Nedo Temecula (92590) *(P-10539)*

**Aquaneering, San Marcos** *Also Called: Aquaneering LLC (P-19442)*

**Aquaneering LLC** ........................................................................... E ...... 858 578-2028
340 Rancheros Dr Ste 180 San Marcos (92069) *(P-19442)*

**Aquantia, Santa Clara** *Also Called: Aquantia Corp (P-12328)*

**Aquantia Corp (DH)** ....................................................................... E ...... 408 228-8300
5488 Marvell Ln Santa Clara (95054) *(P-12328)*

**Aquarian Coatings Corp** ................................................................. F ...... 714 632-0230
600 N Batavia St Orange (92868) *(P-8923)*

**Aquarius Rags LLC (PA)** ................................................................. D ...... 213 895-4400
15821 Ventura Blvd Ste 270 Encino (91436) *(P-2698)*

**Aquastar Pool Productions, Ventura** *Also Called: Aquastar Pool Products Inc (P-9914)*

**Aquastar Pool Products Inc** .......................................................... E ...... 877 768-2717
2340 Palma Dr Ste 104 Ventura (93003) *(P-9914)*

**Aquasyn LLC** .................................................................................. F ...... 818 350-0423
9525 Owensmouth Ave Ste E Chatsworth (91311) *(P-9143)*

**Aquatec International Inc** ............................................................. D ...... 949 225-2200
17422 Pullman St Irvine (92614) *(P-9915)*

**Aquatec Water Systems, Irvine** *Also Called: Aquatec International Inc (P-9915)*

**Aquatic Co** ..................................................................................... C ...... 714 993-1220
1700 N Delilah St Corona (92879) *(P-6673)*

**Aquatic Co** ..................................................................................... C ...... 714 993-1220
8101 E Kaiser Blvd Ste 200 Anaheim (92808) *(P-6674)*

**Aqueos Corporation** ....................................................................... C ...... 805 676-4330
2550 Eastman Ave Ventura (93003) *(P-9454)*

**Aqueos Corporation (PA)** ............................................................... E ...... 805 364-0570
418 Chapala St Ste E Santa Barbara (93101) *(P-9455)*

**Aqueous Technologies Corp** ........................................................... E ...... 909 944-7771
1678 N Maple St Corona (92878) *(P-10540)*

**AR Industries** ................................................................................. F ...... 626 332-8918
730 E Edna Pl Covina (91723) *(P-16087)*

**AR Tech Aerospace, Fontana** *Also Called: A&R Tarpaulins Inc (P-2964)*

**AR Wilson Quarry, Aromas** *Also Called: Granite Rock Co (P-313)*

**Ar-Ce Inc** ....................................................................................... F ...... 310 771-1960
141 E 162nd St Gardena (90248) *(P-15883)*

**Arable Labs Inc** ............................................................................. D ...... 510 992-4095
51 Federal St Ste 301 San Francisco (94107) *(P-18061)*

**Araca Merchandise LP** ................................................................... D ...... 818 743-5400
459 Park Ave San Fernando (91340) *(P-4842)*

**Aradigm, San Francisco** *Also Called: Aradigm Corporation (P-5330)*

**Aradigm Corporation** ..................................................................... E ...... 510 265-9000
1613 Lyon St San Francisco (94115) *(P-5330)*

**Aranda Tooling LLC** ........................................................................ D ...... 714 379-6565
13950 Yorba Ave Chino (91710) *(P-10714)*

**Arandas Tortilla Company Inc** ....................................................... F ...... 209 464-8675
1450 E Scotts Ave Stockton (95205) *(P-2128)*

**Arandas Tortilla Company Inc (PA)** ............................................... E ...... 209 464-8675
1318 E Scotts Ave Stockton (95205) *(P-2129)*

**Aras Power Technologies (PA)** ...................................................... F ...... 408 935-8877
371 Fairview Way Milpitas (95035) *(P-12828)*

**Arb Inc** ........................................................................................... B ...... 925 432-3649
1875 Loveridge Rd Pittsburg (94565) *(P-16286)*

**Arbiter Systems Incorporated (PA)** ............................................... E ...... 805 237-3831
1324 Vendels Cir Ste 121 Paso Robles (93446) *(P-14497)*

**Arbonne International LLC (DH)** ................................................... E ...... 949 770-2610
21 Technology Dr Irvine (92618) *(P-17688)*

**Arbonne International Dist Inc** ..................................................... C ...... 800 272-6663
9400 Jeronimo Rd Irvine (92618) *(P-17689)*

**Arbor Fence Inc** ............................................................................. E ...... 707 938-3133
22660 Broadway Sonoma (95476) *(P-8618)*

**ARC - Imperial Valley** .................................................................... E ...... 760 768-1944
340 E 1st St Calexico (92231) *(P-19335)*

**ARC Boat Company** ........................................................................ D ...... 877 272-2443
2261 Market St San Francisco (94114) *(P-14028)*

**ARC DOCUMENT SOLUTIONS, San Ramon** *Also Called: ARC Document Solutions Inc (P-17818)*

**ARC Document Solutions Inc (PA)** ................................................ C ...... 925 949-5100
12657 Alcosta Blvd Ste 200 San Ramon (94583) *(P-17818)*

**ARC Plastics Inc** ............................................................................ E ...... 562 802-3299
14010 Shoemaker Ave Norwalk (90650) *(P-6721)*

**ARC Products, San Diego** *Also Called: Ssco Manufacturing Inc (P-9731)*

**ARC Vineyards LLC** ........................................................................ E ...... 805 937-3901
5391 Presquile Dr Santa Maria (93455) *(P-1477)*

**Arcadia Inc** ..................................................................................... E ...... 916 375-1478
2324 Del Monte St West Sacramento (95691) *(P-7756)*

**ARCADIA INC., West Sacramento** *Also Called: Arcadia Inc (P-7756)*

**Arcadia Norcal, Los Angeles** *Also Called: Arcadia Products LLC (P-7757)*
**Arcadia Products LLC (HQ)**................................................................**C** ...... **323 771-9819**
2301 E Vernon Ave Los Angeles (90023) *(P-7757)*
**Arcaris Inc (PA)**................................................................................**C** ...... **415 854-3801**
530 Lawrence Expy Sunnyvale (94085) *(P-18062)*
**Arcbyt Inc (PA)**..................................................................................**F** ...... **415 449-4852**
548 Market St Pmb 39975 San Francisco (94104) *(P-9408)*
**ARCELLX, Redwood City** *Also Called: Arcellx Inc (P-5794)*
**Arcellx Inc**........................................................................................C ...... 240 327-0630
800 Bridge Pkwy Redwood City (94065) *(P-5794)*
**Arch Foods Inc**................................................................................E ...... 510 868-6000
610 85th Ave Oakland (94621) *(P-7935)*
**Arch Foods Inc (PA)**........................................................................F ...... 510 331-8352
25817 Clawiter Rd Hayward (94545) *(P-7936)*
**Arch Med Sltons - Escndido LLC**..................................................C ...... 760 432-9785
950 Borra Pl Escondido (92029) *(P-14976)*
**Arch Medical Solutions - Sonora LLC**..........................................D ...... 209 533-1033
20555 N Sunshine Rd Sonora (95370) *(P-12916)*
**Arch Motorcycle Company Inc**......................................................D ...... 970 443-1380
3216 W El Segundo Blvd Hawthorne (90250) *(P-17481)*
**ARCHER, San Jose** *Also Called: Archer Aviation Inc (P-13636)*
**Archer Aviation Inc (PA)**..................................................................**C** ...... **650 272-3233**
190 W Tasman Dr San Jose (95134) *(P-13636)*
**Archer Aviation Inc**........................................................................B ...... 650 272-3233
77 Rio Robles San Jose (95134) *(P-13637)*
**Archer Aviation Operating Corp**....................................................C ...... 650 272-3233
190 W Tasman Dr San Jose (95134) *(P-13638)*
**Archer-Daniels-Midland Company**..................................................F ...... 209 339-1252
350 N Guild Ave Lodi (95240) *(P-1053)*
**Archery Summit Winery**..................................................................F ...... 707 252-9777
5901 Silverado Trl Napa (94558) *(P-1478)*
**Archeyy & Friends LLC**..................................................................E ...... 703 579-7649
3630 Andrews Dr Apt 114 Pleasanton (94588) *(P-1091)*
**Archion, Glendora** *Also Called: Postvision Inc (P-10266)*
**Archipelago Inc**................................................................................C ...... 213 743-9200
1548 18th St Santa Monica (90404) *(P-5944)*
**Archipelago Botanicals, Santa Monica** *Also Called: Archipelago Inc (P-5944)*
**Architctral Coml Glzing Alum P, Morgan Hill** *Also Called: National Glass Systems Inc (P-541)*
**Architctral Fcdes Unlmited Inc**......................................................D ...... 408 846-5350
1346 The Alameda San Jose (95126) *(P-7309)*
**Architctral Mllwk Slutions Inc**........................................................F ...... 760 510-6440
2565 Progress St Vista (92081) *(P-3109)*
**Architctral Mllwk Snta Barbara**......................................................E ...... 805 965-7011
8 N Nopal St Santa Barbara (93103) *(P-3110)*
**Architectural Blomberg LLC**..........................................................E ...... 916 428-8060
1453 Blair Ave Sacramento (95822) *(P-8254)*
**Architectural Design Signs Inc (PA)**..............................................**D** ...... **951 278-0680**
1160 Railroad St Corona (92882) *(P-15942)*
**Architectural Enterprises Inc**........................................................E ...... 323 268-4000
5821 Randolph St Commerce (90040) *(P-8692)*
**Architectural GL & Alum Co Inc (HQ)**............................................**C** ...... **510 444-6100**
6400 Brisa St Livermore (94550) *(P-16607)*
**Architectural Glass & Aluminum, Livermore** *Also Called: Architectural GL & Alum Co Inc (P-16607)*
**Architectural Iron Works, San Luis Obispo** *Also Called: Kairos Manufacturing Inc (P-16161)*
**Architectural Mtls USA Inc**..............................................................D ...... 888 219-2126
4025 Camino Del Rio S Ste 300 San Diego (92108) *(P-19431)*
**Architectural Plastics Inc**..............................................................E ...... 707 765-9898
1299 N Mcdowell Blvd Petaluma (94954) *(P-6722)*
**Architectural Shtmtl Contr, Murrieta** *Also Called: Pgc Construction Inc (P-347)*
**Architectural Veneer Systems**......................................................F ...... 951 824-1079
2215 Via Cerro Jurupa Valley (92509) *(P-7310)*
**Architectural Window Shades, Pasadena** *Also Called: Roberson Construction (P-3726)*
**Architectural Wood Design Inc**......................................................E ...... 559 292-9104
5672 E Dayton Ave Fresno (93727) *(P-3216)*
**Architectural Woodworking Co**......................................................D ...... 626 570-4125
582 Monterey Pass Rd Monterey Park (91754) *(P-487)*
**Arconic Fastening Systems, Carson** *Also Called: Huck International Inc (P-8758)*
**Arconic Fastening Systems, City Of Industry** *Also Called: Valley-Todeco Inc (P-8770)*
**Arctic Glacier USA Inc**....................................................................C ...... 310 638-0321
17011 Central Ave Carson (90746) *(P-2106)*

**Arctic Glacier USA Inc**....................................................................E ...... 800 562-1990
8710 Park St Bellflower (90706) *(P-2107)*
**Arctic Semiconductor**....................................................................E ...... 408 712-3350
2216 Ringwood Ave San Jose (95131) *(P-11813)*
**Arctic Wolf Networks Inc**..............................................................C ...... 888 272-8429
111 W Evelyn Ave Ste 115 Sunnyvale (94086) *(P-18063)*
**ARCTURUS, San Diego** *Also Called: Arcturus Thrptics Holdings Inc (P-5331)*
**Arcturus Thrptics Holdings Inc (PA)**..............................................**E** ...... **858 900-2660**
10628 Science Center Dr Ste 250 San Diego (92121) *(P-5331)*
**Ardea Biosciences Inc**....................................................................E ...... 858 625-0787
9390 Towne Centre Dr Ste 100 San Diego (92121) *(P-5332)*
**Arden Engineering, Anaheim** *Also Called: Cadence Aerospace LLC (P-13800)*
**Arden Engineering Inc (DH)**..........................................................**E** ...... **949 877-3642**
3130 E Miraloma Ave Anaheim (92806) *(P-13783)*
**Arden Engineering Inc**....................................................................C ...... 714 998-6410
1878 N Main St Orange (92865) *(P-13784)*
**Arden Engineering Holdings Inc (DH)**..........................................**E** ...... **714 998-6410**
1878 N Main St Orange (92865) *(P-13785)*
**Ardent Mills, Stockton** *Also Called: Ardent Mills LLC (P-1056)*
**Ardent Mills LLC**..............................................................................E ...... 951 201-1170
2020 E Steel Rd Colton (92324) *(P-1054)*
**Ardent Mills LLC**..............................................................................E ...... 909 887-3407
19684 Cajon Blvd San Bernardino (92407) *(P-1055)*
**Ardent Mills LLC**..............................................................................F ...... 209 983-6551
3939 Producers Dr Stockton (95206) *(P-1056)*
**Ardent Systems Inc**........................................................................E ...... 408 526-0100
2040 Ringwood Ave San Jose (95131) *(P-12059)*
**Ardmore Home Design Inc (PA)**....................................................**E** ...... **626 803-7769**
918 S Stimson Ave City Of Industry (91745) *(P-3465)*
**Area 1 Security Inc**..........................................................................D ...... 650 924-1637
101 Townsend St San Francisco (94107) *(P-18064)*
**Arecont Vision LLC**........................................................................C ...... 818 937-0700
425 E Colorado St Fl 7 Glendale (91205) *(P-11360)*
**Arelac Inc**........................................................................................D ...... 669 267-6400
100 Great Oaks Blvd Ste 120 San Jose (95119) *(P-6218)*
**Aremac Associates Inc**..................................................................E ...... 626 303-8795
2004 S Myrtle Ave Monrovia (91016) *(P-10715)*
**Aremac Heat Treating Inc**..............................................................E ...... 626 333-3898
330 S 9th Ave City Of Industry (91746) *(P-7875)*
**Arete Associates (PA)**....................................................................**C** ...... **818 885-2200**
9301 Corbin Ave Ste 2000 Northridge (91324) *(P-14146)*
**Arete Associates, Northridge** *Also Called: Arete Associates (P-14146)*
**Arevalo Tortilleria Inc (PA)**............................................................**D** ...... **323 888-1711**
1537 W Mines Ave Montebello (90640) *(P-2130)*
**Arevalo Tortilleria Inc**....................................................................E ...... 323 888-1711
3033 Supply Ave Commerce (90040) *(P-2131)*
**Arga Cntrls A Unit Elctro Swtc, Rancho Cucamonga** *Also Called: Electro Switch Corp (P-12967)*
**Argee, Santee** *Also Called: Argee Mfg Co San Diego Inc (P-6723)*
**Argee Mfg Co San Diego Inc**..........................................................D ...... 619 449-5050
9550 Pathway St Santee (92071) *(P-6723)*
**Argen Corporation (PA)**..................................................................**C** ...... **858 455-7900**
8515 Miralani Dr San Diego (92126) *(P-7710)*
**Argo Spring Mfg Co Inc**..................................................................D ...... 800 252-2740
13930 Shoemaker Ave Norwalk (90650) *(P-9173)*
**Argon St Inc**....................................................................................E ...... 650 988-4700
329 Bernardo Ave Mountain View (94043) *(P-14147)*
**Argon St Inc**....................................................................................D ...... 703 270-6927
6696 Mesa Ridge Rd Ste A San Diego (92121) *(P-14148)*
**Argonaut**..........................................................................................E ...... 310 822-1629
5355 Mcconnell Ave Los Angeles (90066) *(P-4066)*
**Argos Software, Fresno** *Also Called: Abelisk Inc (P-17874)*
**Arguello Inc**......................................................................................E ...... 805 567-1632
17100 Calle Mariposa Reina Goleta (93117) *(P-168)*
**Argus Courier, Petaluma** *Also Called: St Louis Post-Dispatch LLC (P-4201)*
**ARI Industries Inc**..........................................................................D ...... 714 993-3700
17018 Edwards Rd Cerritos (90703) *(P-10482)*
**Aria Pharmaceuticals Inc**..............................................................F ...... 650 382-2605
265 Cambridge Ave Unit 60099 Palo Alto (94306) *(P-5333)*
**Aria Technologies Inc**....................................................................C ...... 925 447-7500
102 Wright Brothers Ave Livermore (94551) *(P-7771)*

# ALPHABETIC SECTION — ARS

**Ariana Air Freight, Orange** *Also Called: Wood Space Industries Inc (P-16295)*

**Ariat International Inc (HQ)** .................................................. A ...... 510 477-7000
1500 Alvarado St Ste 100 San Leandro (94577) *(P-7153)*

**Ariba Inc (DH)** ........................................................................ C ...... 650 849-4000
3420 Hillview Ave Palo Alto (94304) *(P-18065)*

**Aridis Pharmaceuticals Inc (PA)** ............................................ E ...... 408 385-1742
983 University Ave Bldg B Los Gatos (95032) *(P-5334)*

**Aries 33 LLC** ............................................................................ E ...... 310 355-8330
3400 S Main St Los Angeles (90007) *(P-2611)*

**Aries Beef LLC** ........................................................................ E ...... 818 526-4855
17 W Magnolia Blvd Burbank (91502) *(P-631)*

**Aries Prepared Beef Company** .............................................. F ...... 818 771-0181
11850 Sheldon St Sun Valley (91352) *(P-1092)*

**Aries Research Inc** .................................................................. E ...... 925 818-1078
46750 Fremont Blvd Ste 107 Fremont (94538) *(P-10324)*

**Aries Solutions, Fremont** *Also Called: Aries Research Inc (P-10324)*

**ARISTA, Santa Clara** *Also Called: Arista Networks Inc (P-10325)*

**Arista Networks Inc (PA)** ........................................................ D ...... 408 547-5500
5453 Great America Pkwy Santa Clara (95054) *(P-10325)*

**Aristikraft, Ontario** *Also Called: Masterbrand Cabinets LLC (P-3253)*

**Arium, Irvine** *Also Called: American Arium (P-12300)*

**Ariza Cheese Co Inc** ................................................................ E ...... 562 630-4144
7602 Jackson St Paramount (90723) *(P-708)*

**Ariza Global Foods Inc** ............................................................ E ...... 562 630-4144
7602 Jackson St Paramount (90723) *(P-709)*

**Arizona Portland Cement, Glendora** *Also Called: Calportland Company (P-7252)*

**Ark Animal Health Inc** ............................................................ E ...... 858 203-4100
4955 Directors Pl San Diego (92121) *(P-5795)*

**Arkema Coating Resins, Torrance** *Also Called: Arkema Inc (P-5029)*

**Arkema Inc** .............................................................................. E ...... 310 214-5327
19206 Hawthorne Blvd Torrance (90503) *(P-5029)*

**Arktura LLC (HQ)** .................................................................... E ...... 310 532-1050
966 Sandhill Ave Carson (90746) *(P-3552)*

**ARLO, Carlsbad** *Also Called: Arlo Technologies Inc (P-11638)*

**Arlo Technologies Inc (PA)** .................................................... D ...... 408 890-3900
2200 Faraday Ave Ste 150 Carlsbad (92008) *(P-11638)*

**Arlon Graphics LLC** ................................................................ C ...... 714 985-6300
200 Boysenberry Ln Placentia (92870) *(P-6551)*

**Arlon LLC** ................................................................................ C ...... 714 540-2811
2811 S Harbor Blvd Santa Ana (92704) *(P-6724)*

**Arm Inc** .................................................................................... A ...... 858 453-1900
5375 Mira Sorrento Pl Ste 540 San Diego (92121) *(P-12329)*

**Arm Inc (DH)** ............................................................................ B ...... 408 576-1500
120 Rose Orchard Way San Jose (95134) *(P-12330)*

**Armada Engineering LLC** ........................................................ F ...... 818 280-5138
21305 Itasca St Chatsworth (91311) *(P-19380)*

**Armani Trade LLC** .................................................................. E ...... 310 849-0067
21255 Burbank Blvd Ste 120 Woodland Hills (91367) *(P-17285)*

**Armanino Foods Distinction Inc** ............................................ E ...... 510 441-9300
5976 W Las Positas Blvd Ste 200 Pleasanton (94588) *(P-1025)*

**ARMATA PHARMACEUTICALS, Los Angeles** *Also Called: Armata Pharmaceuticals Inc (P-5796)*

**Armata Pharmaceuticals Inc (PA)** .......................................... E ...... 310 665-2928
5005 Mcconnell Ave Los Angeles (90066) *(P-5796)*

**Armen Living, Valencia** *Also Called: Legacy Commercial Holdings Inc (P-3447)*

**Arminak Solutions LLC** .......................................................... E ...... 626 802-7332
475 N Sheridan St Corona (92878) *(P-16088)*

**Armo, Redwood City** *Also Called: Armo Biosciences Inc (P-5335)*

**Armo Biosciences Inc** ............................................................ E ...... 650 779-5075
575 Chesapeake Dr Redwood City (94063) *(P-5335)*

**Armor Dermalogics LLC** ........................................................ E ...... 714 202-6424
9151 Atlanta Ave Unit 5864 Huntington Beach (92615) *(P-743)*

**Armorcast Products Company Inc** ........................................ E ...... 909 390-1365
500 S Dupont Ave Ontario (91761) *(P-6725)*

**Armorcast Products Company Inc (DH)** .............................. C ...... 818 982-3600
9140 Lurline Ave Chatsworth (91311) *(P-8378)*

**Armorstruxx LLC** .................................................................... E ...... 209 365-9400
850 Thurman St Lodi (95240) *(P-13786)*

**Armstrong Technology, Sunnyvale** *Also Called: Armstrong Technology Sv Inc (P-10716)*

**Armstrong Technology Sv Inc** ................................................ F ...... 408 734-4434
1271 Anvilwood Ave Sunnyvale (94089) *(P-10716)*

**Armstrong Technology Sv Inc** ................................................ F ...... 530 888-6262
12780 Earhart Ave Auburn (95602) *(P-10717)*

**Armstrong Technology SV Inc (PA)** ...................................... D ...... 408 734-4434
1121 Elko Dr Sunnyvale (94089) *(P-10718)*

**Armtec Countermeasures Co (DH)** ........................................ F ...... 760 398-0143
85901 Avenue 53 Coachella (92236) *(P-14149)*

**Armtec Defense Products Co (DH)** ........................................ B ...... 760 398-0143
85901 Avenue 53 Coachella (92236) *(P-9137)*

**Armtec Defense Technologies, Coachella** *Also Called: Armtec Defense Products Co (P-9137)*

**Army of Happy LLC** ................................................................ E ...... 704 517-9890
4580 Euclid Ave San Diego (92115) *(P-2582)*

**Arna Trading Inc (PA)** ............................................................ F ...... 760 940-2775
2892 S Santa Fe Ave Ste 109 San Marcos (92069) *(P-3754)*

**Arnaco Industrial Coatings** .................................................... E ...... 562 222-1022
8445 Warvale St Pico Rivera (90660) *(P-9049)*

**Arnco** ........................................................................................ E ...... 323 249-7500
5141 Firestone Pl South Gate (90280) *(P-5219)*

**Arnett Construction Inc** .......................................................... E ...... 909 421-7960
626 W 1st St Rialto (92376) *(P-543)*

**Arnies Supply Service Ltd (PA)** .............................................. E ...... 323 263-1696
1541 N Ditman Ave Los Angeles (90063) *(P-3333)*

**Arnold and Egan Mfg Co** ........................................................ E ...... 415 822-2700
1515 Griffith St San Francisco (94124) *(P-3645)*

**Arnold Magnetics, Camarillo** *Also Called: Arnold Magnetics Corporation (P-11205)*

**Arnold Magnetics Corporation** .............................................. D ...... 805 484-4221
841 Avenida Acaso Ste A Camarillo (93012) *(P-11205)*

**Arnold-Gonsalves Engrg Inc** .................................................. E ...... 909 465-1579
5731 Chino Ave Chino (91710) *(P-10719)*

**Arnolds Metal Finishing Inc** .................................................... D ...... 408 588-0079
805 Aldo Ave Ste 104 Santa Clara (95054) *(P-8924)*

**Aroma Housewares, San Diego** *Also Called: Mirama Enterprises Inc (P-11392)*

**Aron, Escalon** *Also Called: Caron Compactor Co (P-9414)*

**Arrhenius, Santa Clara** *Also Called: Prodigy Surface Tech Inc (P-9000)*

**Arrietta Incorporated** .............................................................. E ...... 626 334-0302
429 N Azusa Ave Azusa (91702) *(P-17368)*

**Arrive Technologies Inc** .......................................................... F ...... 916 715-9775
3693 Westchester Dr Roseville (95747) *(P-12331)*

**Arriver Holdco Inc** .................................................................. A ...... 858 587-1121
5775 Morehouse Dr San Diego (92121) *(P-13166)*

**Arrk North America Inc** .......................................................... C ...... 858 552-1587
4660 La Jolla Village Dr Ste 100 San Diego (92122) *(P-8379)*

**Arrow Electric Motor Service** ................................................ F ...... 559 266-0104
645 Broadway St Fresno (93721) *(P-19223)*

**Arrow Engineering** .................................................................. E ...... 626 960-2806
4946 Azusa Canyon Rd Irwindale (91706) *(P-10720)*

**Arrow Fence Co, Sacramento** *Also Called: Rowar Corporation (P-571)*

**Arrow Screw Products Inc** .................................................... E ...... 805 928-2269
941 W Mccoy Ln Santa Maria (93455) *(P-10721)*

**Arrow Sign Co (PA)** ................................................................ E ...... 209 931-5522
1051 46th Ave Oakland (94601) *(P-15943)*

**Arrow Sign Co** ........................................................................ E ...... 209 931-7852
3133 N Ad Art Rd Stockton (95215) *(P-15944)*

**Arrow Sign Company, Oakland** *Also Called: Arrow Sign Co (P-15943)*

**Arrow Surf Products (PA)** ...................................................... F ...... 831 462-2791
1115 Thompson Ave Ste 7 Santa Cruz (95062) *(P-15780)*

**Arrow Transit Mix** .................................................................. F ...... 661 945-7600
507 E Avenue L12 Lancaster (93535) *(P-7404)*

**Arrow Truck Bodies & Eqp Inc** .............................................. E ...... 909 947-3991
1639 S Campus Ave Ontario (91761) *(P-13401)*

**ARROWHEAD, Pasadena** *Also Called: Arrowhead Pharmaceuticals Inc (P-5337)*

**Arrowhead Pharmaceuticals Inc** ............................................ D ...... 626 304-3400
10102 Hoyt Park Dr San Diego (92131) *(P-5336)*

**Arrowhead Pharmaceuticals Inc (PA)** .................................. C ...... 626 304-3400
177 E Colorado Blvd Ste 700 Pasadena (91105) *(P-5337)*

**Arrowhead Products, Los Alamitos** *Also Called: Arrowhead Products Corporation (P-13787)*

**Arrowhead Products Corporation** ........................................ A ...... 714 822-2513
4411 Katella Ave Los Alamitos (90720) *(P-13787)*

**Arroyo Holdings Inc (PA)** ...................................................... F ...... 626 765-9340
898 N Fair Oaks Ave Pasadena (91103) *(P-8380)*

**ARS, Burbank** *Also Called: Hutchinson Arospc & Indust Inc (P-13859)*

**ARS Pharmaceuticals Inc (PA)**.................................................. E ...... 858 771-9307
  11682 El Camino Real Ste 120 San Diego (92130) *(P-5338)*
**Arsenic Inc** ............................................................................... F ...... 310 701-7559
  530 S Hewitt St Unit 119 Los Angeles (90013) *(P-4230)*
**Art, El Dorado Hills** *Also Called: Alpha Research & Tech Inc (P-10133)*
**Art Brand Studios LLC (PA)**............................................... E ...... 408 201-5000
  381 Cannery Row Monterey (93940) *(P-4365)*
**Art Glass Etc Inc** ................................................................ E ...... 805 644-4494
  3111 Golf Course Dr Ventura (93003) *(P-3111)*
**Art Mold Die Casting Inc** ..................................................D ...... 818 767-6464
  11872 Sheldon St Sun Valley (91352) *(P-9600)*
**Art of Entertainment, Monterey** *Also Called: Art Brand Studios LLC (P-4365)*
**Art Robbins Instruments LLC** ........................................ E ...... 408 734-8400
  1293 Mountain View Alviso Rd Ste D Sunnyvale (94089) *(P-14615)*
**Art Signworks, Murrieta** *Also Called: Art Signworks Inc (P-15945)*
**Art Signworks Inc** ................................................................ E ...... 951 698-8484
  41785 Elm St Murrieta (92562) *(P-15945)*
**Art19 LLC (DH)** .................................................................... E ...... 866 882-7819
  1999 Harrison St Ste 2675 Oakland (94612) *(P-4366)*
**Artboxx Framing Inc** .......................................................... E ...... 310 604-6933
  555 W Victoria St Compton (90220) *(P-16089)*
**Artcrafters Cabinets** .......................................................... E ...... 818 752-8960
  5446 Cleon Ave North Hollywood (91601) *(P-3217)*
**Arte De Mexico, North Hollywood** *Also Called: Arte De Mexico Inc (P-11519)*
**Arte De Mexico Inc (PA)** ..................................................D ...... 818 753-4559
  1000 Chestnut St Burbank (91506) *(P-3593)*
**Arte De Mexico Inc** ............................................................D ...... 818 753-4510
  5506 Riverton Ave North Hollywood (91601) *(P-11519)*
**Artehouse, San Rafael** *Also Called: One Bella Casa Inc (P-2942)*
**Arteris, Campbell** *Also Called: Arteris Holdings Inc (P-12333)*
**Arteris Inc (PA)** ....................................................................C ...... 408 470-7300
  900 E Hamilton Ave Ste 300 Campbell (95008) *(P-12332)*
**Arteris Holdings Inc** .......................................................... E ...... 408 470-7300
  591 W Hamilton Ave Ste 250 Campbell (95008) *(P-12333)*
**Artesa, Napa** *Also Called: Codorniu Napa Inc (P-1514)*
**Artesia Sawdust Products Inc** ........................................ E ...... 909 947-5983
  13434 S Ontario Ave Ontario (91761) *(P-3064)*
**Arthrex Inc** .......................................................................... F ...... 805 964-8104
  460 Ward Dr Ste C Santa Barbara (93111) *(P-14977)*
**Arthrex California Technology, Santa Barbara** *Also Called: Arthrex Inc (P-14977)*
**Arthrocare Corporation** .................................................... E ...... 408 736-0224
  680 Vaqueros Ave Sunnyvale (94085) *(P-14978)*
**Arthur Dogswell LLC (PA)**............................................... E ...... 888 559-8833
  11301 W Olympic Blvd Ste 520 Los Angeles (90064) *(P-1093)*
**Arthurmade Plastics Inc** ..................................................D ...... 323 721-7325
  2131 Garfield Ave City Of Commerce (90040) *(P-6726)*
**Artifacts International, Chula Vista** *Also Called: Califrnia Furn Collections Inc (P-3553)*
**Artificial Grass Liquidators** ............................................. E ...... 951 677-3377
  42505 Rio Nedo Temecula (92590) *(P-16090)*
**Artisan Brewers LLC** ........................................................ E ...... 510 567-4926
  1933 Davis St Ste 177 San Leandro (94577) *(P-1418)*
**Artisan House Inc** ............................................................. E ...... 818 767-7476
  8238 Lankershim Blvd North Hollywood (91605) *(P-9275)*
**ARTISAN HOUSE, INC, North Hollywood** *Also Called: Artisan House Inc (P-9275)*
**Artisan Nameplate Awards Corp** .................................... E ...... 714 556-6222
  2730 S Shannon St Santa Ana (92704) *(P-4843)*
**Artisan Screen Printing Inc** .............................................C ...... 626 815-2700
  1055 W 5th St Azusa (91702) *(P-4844)*
**Artisan Vehicle Systems Inc** ...........................................D ...... 805 402-6856
  742 Pancho Rd Camarillo (93012) *(P-13339)*
**Artisana, Oakland** *Also Called: Premier Organics (P-1363)*
**Artisans & Vines, Sonoma** *Also Called: Opal Moon Winery LLC (P-1697)*
**Artissimo Designs LLC (HQ)**........................................... E ...... 310 906-3700
  2100 E Grand Ave Ste 400 El Segundo (90245) *(P-4030)*
**Artiste Management Company, Los Olivos** *Also Called: Artiste Management Company LLC (P-1479)*
**Artiste Management Company LLC** ............................... F ...... 805 686-2626
  2948 Grand Ave Los Olivos (93441) *(P-1479)*
**Artistic Coverings, Cerritos** *Also Called: Sports Venue Padding Inc (P-6664)*
**Artistic Pltg & Met Finshg Inc** ......................................... E ...... 619 661-1691
  2801 E Miraloma Ave Anaheim (92806) *(P-8925)*

**Artistic Welding** ..................................................................D ...... 310 515-4922
  505 E Gardena Blvd Gardena (90248) *(P-8381)*
**Artistry In Motion Inc** ........................................................ E ...... 818 994-7388
  19411 Londelius St Northridge (91324) *(P-4031)*
**Artistry In Wood** ................................................................ F ...... 559 665-7171
  24350 Road 19 Chowchilla (93610) *(P-3734)*
**Artiva, Santa Fe Springs** *Also Called: Artiva USA Inc (P-11489)*
**Artiva, Chino** *Also Called: Artiva USA Inc (P-11490)*
**Artiva Biotherapeutics Inc** ...............................................D ...... 858 267-4467
  5505 Morehouse Dr Ste 100 San Diego (92121) *(P-5797)*
**Artiva USA Inc** .................................................................... E ...... 562 298-8968
  12866 Ann St Ste 1 Santa Fe Springs (90670) *(P-11489)*
**Artiva USA Inc (PA)**........................................................... E ...... 909 628-1388
  13901 Magnolia Ave Chino (91710) *(P-11490)*
**Artkive** .................................................................................. E ...... 310 975-9809
  16225 Huston St Encino (91436) *(P-18066)*
**Artkive, Van Nuys** *Also Called: Kive Company (P-18473)*
**Arto Brick / California Pavers** ......................................... E ...... 310 768-8500
  15209 S Broadway Gardena (90248) *(P-7264)*
**Arto Brick and Cal Pavers, Gardena** *Also Called: Arto Brick / California Pavers (P-7264)*
**Arts & Crafts Press, San Diego** *Also Called: Rush Press Inc (P-4757)*
**Arts Elegance Inc** .............................................................. E ...... 626 793-4794
  154 W Bellevue Dr Pasadena (91105) *(P-15685)*
**Arts Sheet Metal Mfg Inc** ..................................................D ...... 408 778-0606
  16075 Caputo Dr Morgan Hill (95037) *(P-8382)*
**Artsons Manufacturing Company** .................................. E ...... 323 773-3469
  11121 Garfield Ave South Gate (90280) *(P-7604)*
**Aruba Networks Inc** .......................................................... A ...... 408 227-4500
  1322 Crossman Ave Sunnyvale (94089) *(P-10326)*
**Aruba Networks Inc (HQ)**................................................. B ...... 408 941-4300
  6280 America Center Dr San Jose (95002) *(P-10327)*
**Aruba Networks Inc** .......................................................... A ...... 408 227-4500
  634 E Caribbean Dr Sunnyvale (94089) *(P-10328)*
**Aruba Networks Inc** .......................................................... A ...... 408 227-4500
  390 W Caribbean Dr Sunnyvale (94089) *(P-11814)*
**Aruba Networks Cafe, San Jose** *Also Called: Aruba Networks Inc (P-10327)*
**Arvato Services, Valencia** *Also Called: Bertelsmann Inc (P-4314)*
**Arvinyl Laminates LP** .......................................................D ...... 951 371-7800
  233 N Sherman Ave Corona (92882) *(P-6552)*
**Arxis Technology Inc** ........................................................ E ...... 805 306-7890
  2468 Tapo Canyon Rd Simi Valley (93063) *(P-18067)*
**Aryzta Sweet Life, Santa Ana** *Also Called: The Sweet Life Enterprises Inc (P-1065)*
**AS&t, San Francisco** *Also Called: American Scence Tech As T Corp (P-13633)*
**Asa, Oxnard** *Also Called: Advanced Structural Tech Inc (P-8771)*
**Asa Corporation** ................................................................ F ...... 530 305-3720
  3111 Sunset Blvd Ste V Rocklin (95677) *(P-14616)*
**Asa Power BDH Engrg & Cnstr, Chino** *Also Called: American Solar Advantage Inc (P-12301)*
**Asai, Glendale** *Also Called: Passport Technology Usa Inc (P-19274)*
**Asana, San Francisco** *Also Called: Asana Inc (P-19026)*
**Asana Inc (PA)**.................................................................... A ...... 415 525-3888
  633 Folsom St Ste 100 San Francisco (94107) *(P-19026)*
**Asante Technologies Inc (PA)**......................................... E ...... 408 435-8388
  2223 Oakland Rd San Jose (95131) *(P-10329)*
**ASC, Valencia** *Also Called: ASC Process Systems Inc (P-9832)*
**ASC Engineered Solutions LLC** .....................................D ...... 909 418-3233
  551 N Loop Dr Ontario (91761) *(P-9248)*
**ASC Engineered Solutions LLC** .....................................D ...... 800 766-0076
  2867 Vail Ave Commerce (90040) *(P-9249)*
**ASC Group Inc** .................................................................... B ...... 818 896-1101
  12243 Branford St Sun Valley (91352) *(P-12334)*
**ASC Process Systems Inc (PA)**.......................................C ...... 818 833-0088
  28402 Livingston Ave Valencia (91355) *(P-9832)*
**Ascap, Los Angeles** *Also Called: American Soc Cmpsers Athors Pb (P-4364)*
**Asce, Irvine** *Also Called: ACS Engineering Inc (P-19374)*
**Ascender Software Inc** .....................................................C ...... 877 561-7501
  8885 Rio San Diego Dr Ste 270 San Diego (92108) *(P-18068)*
**Ascent Aerospace** .............................................................D ...... 586 726-0500
  1395 S Lyon St Santa Ana (92705) *(P-14150)*
**Ascent Manufacturing LLC** .............................................. E ...... 714 540-6414
  2545 W Via Palma Anaheim (92801) *(P-8819)*

# ALPHABETIC SECTION
## Associated Screw Machine Pdts

**Asco Power Services Inc** ............................................. F ..... 714 283-4000
120 S Chaparral Ct Ste 200 Anaheim (92808) *(P-13213)*

**Asco Power Tech, Stockton** *Also Called: Asco Power Technologies LP (P-13214)*

**Asco Power Technologies LP** ..................................... C ..... 209 931-7700
3400 E Eight Mile Rd Ste B Stockton (95212) *(P-13214)*

**Asco Sintering Co** .......................................................... E ..... 323 725-3550
2750 Garfield Ave Commerce (90040) *(P-7975)*

**Asepco** ............................................................................ F
5002 Elester Dr San Jose (95124) *(P-9144)*

**Aseptic Technology, Yorba Linda** *Also Called: Aseptic Technology LLC (P-876)*

**Aseptic Technology LLC** .............................................. C ..... 714 694-0168
24855 Corbit Pl Yorba Linda (92887) *(P-876)*

**ASG, San Jose** *Also Called: Automated Solutions Group Inc (P-14354)*

**Ash & Violet, Commerce** *Also Called: Trixxi Clothing Company Inc (P-2720)*

**Ashby Inc** ........................................................................ E ..... 408 391-3578
49 Geary St Ste 411 San Francisco (94108) *(P-18069)*

**Ashera Motorsports, Brea** *Also Called: Hi Uriman Inc (P-13172)*

**Ashland Group LLC** ...................................................... F ..... 213 749-3709
11693 San Vicente Blvd Pmb 213 Los Angeles (90049) *(P-14498)*

**Ashtel Dental, Ontario** *Also Called: Ashtel Studios Inc (P-15498)*

**Ashtel Studios Inc** ........................................................ E ..... 909 434-0911
1610 E Philadelphia St Ontario (91761) *(P-15498)*

**Ashunya Inc** ................................................................... D ..... 714 385-1900
642 N Eckhoff St Orange (92868) *(P-17882)*

**Ashworth Inc** .................................................................. A ..... 760 438-6610
2765 Loker Ave W Carlsbad (92010) *(P-2612)*

**Ashworth Studio, Carlsbad** *Also Called: Ashworth Inc (P-2612)*

**Asi Computer Technologies Inc (PA)** ......................... E ..... 510 226-8000
48289 Fremont Blvd Fremont (94538) *(P-16508)*

**Asi Holdco Inc** ............................................................... E ..... 408 913-1300
780 Montague Expy Ste 508 San Jose (95131) *(P-11255)*

**Asi Networks Inc** .......................................................... F ..... 800 251-1336
19331 E Walnut Dr N City Of Industry (91748) *(P-19027)*

**Asi Semiconductor Inc** ................................................. E ..... 818 982-1200
24955 Avenue Kearny Valencia (91355) *(P-12335)*

**Asia America Enterprise Inc** ....................................... E ..... 650 348-2333
1321 N Carolan Ave Burlingame (94010) *(P-4517)*

**Asia Plastics Inc** ........................................................... E ..... 626 448-8100
9347 Rush St South El Monte (91733) *(P-3961)*

**Asia-Pacific California Inc (PA)** .................................. F ..... 323 318-2254
2121 W Mission Rd Ste 207 Alhambra (91803) *(P-4067)*

**Asia-Pacific California Inc** .......................................... E ..... 626 281-8500
1710 S Del Mar Ave San Gabriel (91776) *(P-4068)*

**Asiana Cuisine Enterprises Inc** .................................. A ..... 310 327-2223
22771 S Western Ave Ste 100 Torrance (90501) *(P-2132)*

**Asics America Corporation (HQ)** ............................... C ..... 949 453-8888
7755 Irvine Center Dr Ste 400 Irvine (92618) *(P-17108)*

**Asics Tiger, Irvine** *Also Called: Asics America Corporation (P-17108)*

**Asigma Corporation** ..................................................... F ..... 760 966-3103
2930 San Luis Rey Rd Oceanside (92058) *(P-10722)*

**Asl Print Fx, Napa** *Also Called: Asl Print Fx Ltd (P-4518)*

**Asl Print Fx Ltd** ............................................................. F ..... 707 927-3096
871 Latour Ct Napa (94558) *(P-4518)*

**Asm Construction Inc** ................................................. E ..... 619 449-1966
1947 John Towers Ave El Cajon (92020) *(P-8383)*

**Asm Precision Inc** ........................................................ F ..... 707 584-7950
613 Martin Ave Ste 106 Rohnert Park (94928) *(P-8384)*

**Asml Us Inc** ................................................................... B ..... 760 443-6244
1 Viper Way Ste A Vista (92081) *(P-9833)*

**Asml Us LLC** ................................................................. B ..... 858 385-6500
17075 Thornmint Ct San Diego (92127) *(P-9834)*

**ASML US, Inc., Vista** *Also Called: Asml Us Inc (P-9833)*

**Asp Henry Holdings Inc** .............................................. A ..... 310 955-9200
999 N Pacific Coast Hwy Ste 800 El Segundo (90245) *(P-17743)*

**ASPE Inc** ........................................................................ F ..... 951 296-2595
41658 Ivy St Ste 118 Murrieta (92562) *(P-4845)*

**Aspen Medical Products LLC** .................................... D ..... 949 681-0200
6481 Oak Cyn Irvine (92618) *(P-14979)*

**Asphalt Dr Inc** ............................................................... E ..... 661 437-5995
7440 Downing Ave Bakersfield (93308) *(P-6372)*

**Asphalt Fabric and Engrg Inc** ..................................... D ..... 562 997-4129
2683 Lime Ave Signal Hill (90755) *(P-15781)*

**Aspire Bakeries Holdco LLC (HQ)** ............................. C ..... 844 992-7747
6701 Center Dr W Ste 850 Los Angeles (90045) *(P-1259)*

**Aspire Bakeries LLC** .................................................... C ..... 209 469-4920
920 Shaw Rd Stockton (95215) *(P-1158)*

**Aspire Bakeries LLC (DH)** .......................................... C ..... 844 992-7747
6701 Center Dr W Ste 850 Los Angeles (90045) *(P-1260)*

**Aspire Bakeries LLC** .................................................... B ..... 818 904-8230
15963 Strathern St Van Nuys (91406) *(P-1261)*

**Aspire Bakeries LLC** .................................................... C ..... 714 478-4656
357 W Santa Ana Ave Bloomington (92316) *(P-1262)*

**Aspire Bakeries Midco LLC (DH)** ............................... F ..... 844 992-7747
6701 Center Dr W Ste 850 Los Angeles (90045) *(P-1263)*

**Aspirez Inc** ..................................................................... D ..... 714 485-8104
1440 N Harbor Blvd Ste 900 Fullerton (92835) *(P-17883)*

**Asrc Aerospace Corp** ................................................... B ..... 650 604-5946
Nasa Ames Research Center Mountain View (94035) *(P-14151)*

**ASRC AEROSPACE CORP, Mountain View** *Also Called: Asrc Aerospace Corp (P-14151)*

**Assa Abloy AB** ............................................................... A ..... 949 672-4003
19701 Da Vinci Lake Forest (92610) *(P-13156)*

**Assa Abloy ACC Door Cntrls Gro** ............................. D ..... 805 642-2600
4226 Transport St Ventura (93003) *(P-7976)*

**Assay Technology Inc** ................................................. E ..... 925 461-8880
1382 Stealth St Livermore (94551) *(P-19072)*

**ASSEMBLY, South San Francisco** *Also Called: Assembly Biosciences Inc (P-5339)*

**Assembly Automation, Duarte** *Also Called: Assembly Automation Industries (P-10723)*

**Assembly Automation Industries** .............................. E ..... 626 303-2777
1849 Business Center Dr Duarte (91010) *(P-10723)*

**Assembly Biosciences Inc** ......................................... D ..... 833 509-4583
2 Tower Pl Ste 700 # 2 South San Francisco (94080) *(P-5339)*

**Assembly Systems (PA)** .............................................. E ..... 408 395-5313
16595 Englewood Ave Los Gatos (95032) *(P-7946)*

**Associated Cnstr & Engrg Inc (PA)** ........................... E ..... 949 455-2682
23232 Peralta Dr Ste 206 Laguna Hills (92653) *(P-7311)*

**Associated Desert Newspaper (DH)** ......................... E ..... 760 337-3400
205 N 8th St El Centro (92243) *(P-4069)*

**Associated Desert Shoppers Inc (DH)** ..................... D ..... 760 346-1729
73400 Highway 111 Palm Desert (92260) *(P-4367)*

**Associated Electrics Inc (HQ)** ................................... F ..... 949 544-7500
21062 Bake Pkwy Ste 100 Lake Forest (92630) *(P-15739)*

**Associated Feed & Supply Co (PA)** .......................... F ..... 209 667-2708
5213 W Main St Turlock (95381) *(P-1118)*

**Associated Feed & Supply Co** ................................... C ..... 209 664-3323
4107 Avenue 360 Traver (93673) *(P-1119)*

**Associated Materials Inc** ............................................ A ..... 415 788-5111
1 Maritime Plz 12th Fl San Francisco (94111) *(P-6727)*

**Associated Microbreweries Inc** ................................. D ..... 858 587-2739
9675 Scranton Rd San Diego (92121) *(P-1419)*

**Associated Microbreweries Inc** ................................. D ..... 714 546-2739
901 S Coast Dr Ste A Costa Mesa (92626) *(P-1420)*

**Associated Microbreweries Inc (PA)** ........................ E ..... 858 273-2739
5985 Santa Fe St San Diego (92109) *(P-1421)*

**Associated Microbreweries Inc** ................................. D ..... 619 234-2739
1157 Columbia St San Diego (92101) *(P-1422)*

**Associated Plating Company** ..................................... E ..... 562 946-5525
9636 Ann St Santa Fe Springs (90670) *(P-8926)*

**Associated R V Ent Inc** ................................................ E ..... 831 636-9566
1500 Shelton Dr Frnt Hollister (95023) *(P-16373)*

**Associated Ready Mix Con Inc** .................................. D ..... 818 504-3100
8946 Bradley Ave Sun Valley (91352) *(P-7405)*

**Associated Ready Mix Concrete, Baldwin Park** *Also Called: Standard Concrete Products Inc (P-7502)*

**ASSOCIATED READY MIX CONCRETE, INC., Sun Valley** *Also Called: Associated Ready Mix Con Inc (P-7405)*

**Associated Ready Mixed Con Inc (PA)** ..................... E ..... 949 253-2800
4621 Teller Ave Ste 130 Newport Beach (92660) *(P-7406)*

**Associated Rebar Inc** .................................................. E ..... 831 758-1820
1095 Madison Ln Salinas (93907) *(P-8097)*

**Associated Screw Machine Pdts** ............................... E ..... 510 783-3831
23978 Connecticut St Ste A Hayward (94545) *(P-8717)*

Employee Codes: A=Over 500 employees, B=251-500
C=101-250, D=51-100, E=20-50, F=10-19, G=1-9

# Associated Students UCLA — ALPHABETIC SECTION

**Associated Students UCLA** .................................................. C ...... 310 825-2787
308 Westwood Plz Ste 118 Los Angeles (90095) *(P-4070)*

**Assocted McRbrwries Ltd A Cal** ........................................ E ...... 858 273-2739
5985 Santa Fe St San Diego (92109) *(P-1423)*

**Assocted Stdnts of The Univ CA** ....................................... D ...... 510 590-7874
112 Hearst Gym Rm 4520 Berkeley (94720) *(P-4368)*

**AST Enzymes** ........................................................................ F ...... 800 608-1688
4880 Murietta St Chino (91710) *(P-6127)*

**AST Sportswear Inc (PA)** .................................................... D ...... 714 223-2030
2701 E Imperial Hwy Brea (92821) *(P-2852)*

**Asta Construction, Rio Vista** *Also Called: Asta Construction Co Inc (P-154)*

**Asta Construction Co Inc (PA)** ........................................... E ...... 707 374-6472
1090 Saint Francis Way Rio Vista (94571) *(P-154)*

**Astea International Inc** ........................................................ E ...... 949 784-5000
8 Hughes Irvine (92618) *(P-18070)*

**Asteelflash California Inc** .................................................... A ...... 510 440-2840
4211 Starboard Dr Fremont (94538) *(P-12060)*

**Asteelflash Fremont, Milpitas** *Also Called: Asteelflash USA Corp (P-12061)*

**Asteelflash Group, Fremont** *Also Called: Asteelflash California Inc (P-12060)*

**Asteelflash USA Corp (DH)** ................................................. E ...... 510 440-2840
1940 Milmont Dr Milpitas (95035) *(P-12061)*

**Astella, Jurupa Valley** *Also Called: March Products Inc (P-16178)*

**Astellas Gene Therapies Inc (DH)** ..................................... E ...... 415 818-1001
480 Forbes Blvd South San Francisco (94080) *(P-5798)*

**Astellas Gene Therapies Inc** .............................................. D ...... 415 818-1001
201 Gateway Blvd South San Francisco (94080) *(P-5799)*

**Astellas Gene Therapies Inc** .............................................. E ...... 910 578-9806
528 Eccles Ave South San Francisco (94080) *(P-5800)*

**ASTERA LABS, Santa Clara** *Also Called: Astera Labs Inc (P-12336)*

**Astera Labs Inc (PA)** ........................................................... B ...... 408 337-9056
2901 Tasman Dr Ste 205 Santa Clara (95054) *(P-12336)*

**Asteres Inc (PA)** ................................................................... E ...... 858 777-8600
10650 Treena St Ste 105 San Diego (92131) *(P-10456)*

**Asterias Biotherapeutics, Alameda** *Also Called: Asterias Biotherapeutics Inc (P-19443)*

**Asterias Biotherapeutics Inc** .............................................. D ...... 510 456-3800
1010 Atlantic Ave Ste 102 Alameda (94501) *(P-19443)*

**Astex Pharmaceuticals Inc (DH)** ........................................ C ...... 925 560-0100
4420 Rosewood Dr Ste 200 Pleasanton (94588) *(P-5340)*

**Astor Manufacturing** ............................................................ E ...... 661 645-5585
779 Anita St Ste B Chula Vista (91911) *(P-13788)*

**Astra, Alameda** *Also Called: Astra Space Inc (P-14077)*

**Astra Space Inc (PA)** ........................................................... E ...... 866 278-7217
1900 Skyhawk St Alameda (94501) *(P-14077)*

**Astranis Space Tech Corp (PA)** .......................................... D ...... 408 829-1101
575 20th St San Francisco (94107) *(P-11815)*

**Astrazeneca LP** .................................................................... E ...... 650 634-0103
121 Oyster Point Blvd South San Francisco (94080) *(P-5341)*

**Astrazeneca Pharmaceuticals LP** ....................................... E ...... 650 305-2600
200 Cardinal Way Redwood City (94063) *(P-5342)*

**Astro Aluminum Treating Co** ............................................... D ...... 562 923-4344
11040 Palmer Ave South Gate (90280) *(P-7876)*

**Astro Chrome and Polsg Corp** ........................................... E ...... 818 781-1463
8136 Lankershim Blvd North Hollywood (91605) *(P-9050)*

**Astro Converters Inc (PA)** ................................................... E ...... 800 752-5003
2370 Oak Ridge Way Ste B Vista (92081) *(P-4007)*

**Astro Digital US Inc** ............................................................. D ...... 650 804-3210
3047 Orchard Pkwy Ste 20 San Jose (95134) *(P-14152)*

**Astro News, Lancaster** *Also Called: Aerotech News and Review Inc (P-4228)*

**Astro Packaging, Anaheim** *Also Called: Reliable Packaging Systems Inc (P-6243)*

**Astro Paper & Envelopes, Vista** *Also Called: Astro Converters Inc (P-4007)*

**Astro Seal Inc** ....................................................................... E ...... 951 787-6670
827 Palmyrita Ave Ste B Riverside (92507) *(P-12917)*

**Astro Spar Inc** ...................................................................... E ...... 626 839-7858
3130 E Miraloma Ave Anaheim (92806) *(P-13789)*

**Astrobotic Technology Inc** .................................................. D ...... 888 488-8455
1570 Sabovich St Mojave (93501) *(P-14078)*

**Astrochef LLC** ...................................................................... D ...... 213 627-9860
1111 Mateo St Los Angeles (90021) *(P-1026)*

**Astrologie California, Commerce** *Also Called: Ajg Inc (P-2874)*

**Astron Corporation** .............................................................. E ...... 949 458-7277
9 Autry Irvine (92618) *(P-12829)*

**Astronic** ................................................................................ C ...... 949 454-1180
2 Orion Aliso Viejo (92656) *(P-12062)*

**Astronics Company, Pasadena** *Also Called: Sabrin Corporation (P-13941)*

**Astronics Test Systems Inc (HQ)** ....................................... C ...... 800 722-2528
2652 Mcgaw Ave Irvine (92614) *(P-14499)*

**Astronomical Soc of The PCF** ............................................ E ...... 415 337-1100
390 Ashton Ave San Francisco (94112) *(P-19372)*

**Astrophysics Inc (PA)** .......................................................... C ...... 909 598-5488
21481 Ferrero City Of Industry (91789) *(P-15499)*

**Asturies Manufacturing Co Inc** ........................................... E ...... 951 270-1766
310 Cessna Cir Corona (92878) *(P-13790)*

**Asucla Publications, Los Angeles** *Also Called: Associated Students UCLA (P-4070)*

**Asus Computer International** .............................................. C ...... 510 739-3777
48720 Kato Rd Fremont (94538) *(P-16509)*

**Asv Wines, Delano** *Also Called: Asv Wines Inc (P-1480)*

**Asv Wines Inc (PA)** .............................................................. F ...... 661 792-3159
1998 Road 152 Delano (93215) *(P-1480)*

**Asylum Research, Santa Barbara** *Also Called: Oxford Instrs Asylum RES Inc (P-14700)*

**Asyst Technologies Inc** ....................................................... A ...... 408 329-6661
46897 Bayside Pkwy Fremont (94538) *(P-12337)*

**At Apollo Technologies LLC** ............................................... E ...... 949 888-0573
31441 Santa Margarita Pkwy Ste A219 Rcho Sta Marg (92688) *(P-6269)*

**At Battery Company Inc** ...................................................... E ...... 661 775-2020
28381 Constellation Rd Unit A Valencia (91355) *(P-17690)*

**At Road Inc** .......................................................................... A ...... 510 668-1638
888 Tasman Dr Milpitas (95035) *(P-18963)*

**Ata-Boy Inc** .......................................................................... F ...... 323 644-0117
3171 Los Feliz Blvd Ste 205 Los Angeles (90039) *(P-16091)*

**ATARA BIO, Thousand Oaks** *Also Called: Atara Biotherapeutics Inc (P-5801)*

**Atara Biotherapeutics Inc (PA)** ........................................... C ...... 805 623-4211
2380 Conejo Spectrum St Ste 200 Thousand Oaks (91320) *(P-5801)*

**Atari, San Jose** *Also Called: Jts Corporation (P-10249)*

**Atbatt.com, Valencia** *Also Called: At Battery Company Inc (P-17690)*

**Atc Colors Inc** ...................................................................... F ...... 510 639-7337
445 Lesser St Oakland (94601) *(P-19146)*

**Atco Rubber Products Inc** .................................................. F ...... 951 788-4345
3080 12th St Riverside (92507) *(P-8299)*

**Atco Rubber Products Inc** .................................................. D ...... 916 649-8690
1701 Diesel Dr Sacramento (95838) *(P-8385)*

**Atdynamics, Hayward** *Also Called: Advanced Transit Dynamics Inc (P-13446)*

**Atec Spine, Carlsbad** *Also Called: Alphatec Spine Inc (P-15319)*

**Atech Manufacturing, San Jose** *Also Called: T&S Manufacturing Tech LLC (P-8226)*

**Atelier Luxury Group LLC** .................................................. E ...... 310 751-2444
1330 Channing St Los Angeles (90021) *(P-3001)*

**Ateliere Creative Tech Inc** .................................................. E ...... 800 921-4252
315 S Beverly Dr Ste 315 Beverly Hills (90212) *(P-18071)*

**Ateliere Crtive Tech Hldg Corp** ........................................... E ...... 855 466-9696
315 S Beverly Dr Ste 315 Beverly Hills (90212) *(P-10330)*

**Atg - Designing Mobility Inc (DH)** ...................................... E ...... 562 921-0258
11075 Knott Ave Ste B Cypress (90630) *(P-16574)*

**Athanor Group Inc** ............................................................... E ...... 909 467-1205
921 E California St Ontario (91761) *(P-8718)*

**Athelas Inc** ........................................................................... E ...... 833 524-1318
1300 Terra Bella Ave Mountain View (94043) *(P-14980)*

**Athena Pick Your Fit, Tustin** *Also Called: Raj Manufacturing Inc (P-2803)*

**Athens Baking Company Inc** .............................................. F ...... 510 533-5705
1847 International Blvd Oakland (94606) *(P-1159)*

**Athens Baking Company Inc (PA)** ...................................... E ...... 559 324-8535
7080 N Whitney Ave Ste 103 Fresno (93720) *(P-1160)*

**Athleisure Inc** ....................................................................... E ...... 858 866-0108
3126 Micaion Blvd Ste B San Diego (92109) *(P-17509)*

**Athletic Sports LLC** ............................................................. E ...... 310 709-3944
11327 Trade Center Dr Ste 330-335 Rancho Cordova (95742) *(P-15946)*

**ATI Forged Products, Irvine** *Also Called: Chen-Tech Industries Inc (P-15041)*

**ATI Liquidating Inc** .............................................................. B ...... 831 438-2100
1150 Ringwood Ct San Jose (95131) *(P-9835)*

**ATI Windows, Riverside** *Also Called: San Joaquin Window Inc (P-8289)*

**Atia Vision Inc** ...................................................................... E ...... 408 805-0520
550 Division St Campbell (95008) *(P-14981)*

**Atieva Inc (HQ)** .................................................................... F ...... 510 648-3553
7373 Gateway Blvd Newark (94560) *(P-13340)*

Atk, San Diego *Also Called: Composite Optics Incorporated (P-14110)*
Atk Arspace Strctres Test Fclt, San Diego *Also Called: Atk Space Systems LLC (P-14160)*
Atk Launch Systems LLC ............................................................. B ...... 858 592-2509
  16707 Via Del Campo Ct San Diego (92127) *(P-14153)*
Atk Space Systems LLC ............................................................... C ...... 858 530-3047
  7130 Miramar Rd Ste 100b San Diego (92121) *(P-14154)*
Atk Space Systems LLC (DH) ........................................................ E ...... 323 722-0222
  6033 Bandini Blvd Commerce (90040) *(P-14155)*
Atk Space Systems LLC ............................................................... D ...... 858 621-5700
  7130 Miramar Rd Ste 100b San Diego (92121) *(P-14156)*
Atk Space Systems LLC ............................................................... D ...... 805 685-2262
  600 Pine Ave Goleta (93117) *(P-14157)*
Atk Space Systems LLC ............................................................... D ...... 310 343-3799
  1960 E Grand Ave Ste 1150 El Segundo (90245) *(P-14158)*
Atk Space Systems LLC ............................................................... D ...... 626 351-0205
  370 N Halstead St Pasadena (91107) *(P-14159)*
Atk Space Systems LLC ............................................................... C ...... 858 487-0970
  16707 Via Del Campo Ct San Diego (92127) *(P-14160)*
Atlantic Box & Carton Company, Pico Rivera *Also Called: Jkv Inc (P-3862)*
Atlantic Diving Equipment, Santa Ana *Also Called: Xs Scuba Inc (P-15879)*
Atlantic Pacific Automotive, Jurupa Valley *Also Called: Highline Aftermarket LLC (P-16385)*
Atlantic Representations Inc (PA) ................................................. E ...... 562 903-9550
  10018 Santa Fe Springs Rd Santa Fe Springs (90670) *(P-3497)*
Atlantic Richfield Company (DH) ................................................... A ...... 800 333-3991
  4 Centerpointe Dr La Palma (90623) *(P-17470)*
Atlantis Computing Inc ................................................................. E ...... 650 917-9471
  900 Glenneyre St Laguna Beach (92651) *(P-18072)*
Atlantis Seafood LLC .................................................................... D ...... 626 626-4900
  10501 Valley Blvd Ste 1820 El Monte (91731) *(P-2047)*
Atlas Carpet Mills Inc ................................................................... C ...... 323 724-7930
  3201 S Susan St Santa Ana (92704) *(P-2509)*
Atlas Construction Supply Inc ....................................................... E ...... 714 441-9500
  7550 Stage Rd Buena Park (90621) *(P-16464)*
Atlas Copco, Santa Maria *Also Called: Atlas Copco Mafi-Trench Co LLC (P-9980)*
Atlas Copco Compressors LLC ..................................................... E ...... 562 484-6370
  16207 Carmenita Rd Cerritos (90703) *(P-9957)*
Atlas Copco Mafi-Trench Co LLC (DH) ......................................... C ...... 805 928-5757
  3037 Industrial Pkwy Santa Maria (93455) *(P-9980)*
Atlas Foam Products ..................................................................... E ...... 818 837-3626
  12836 Arroyo St Sylmar (91342) *(P-6622)*
Atlas Galvanizing LLC .................................................................. E ...... 323 587-6247
  2639 Leonis Blvd Vernon (90058) *(P-9051)*
Atlas Lithium Corporation ............................................................. D ...... 833 661-7900
  433 N Camden Dr Ste 810 Beverly Hills (90210) *(P-337)*
Atlas Mechanical Inc (PA) ............................................................. D ...... 858 554-0700
  8260 Camino Santa Fe Ste B San Diego (92121) *(P-404)*
Atlas Pacific Corporation (PA) ...................................................... E ...... 909 421-1200
  2803 Industrial Dr Bloomington (92316) *(P-16956)*
Atlas Pacific Engineering Co ........................................................ E ...... 559 233-4500
  3115 S Willow Ave Fresno (93725) *(P-9778)*
Atlas Roofing Corporation ............................................................ E ...... 626 334-5358
  2335 Roll Dr Ste 4121 San Diego (92154) *(P-6623)*
Atlas Sheet Metal Inc ................................................................... F ...... 949 600-8787
  11614 Martens River Cir Fountain Valley (92708) *(P-8386)*
Atlas Specialties Corporation (PA) ............................................... E ...... 503 636-8182
  4337 Astoria St Sacramento (95838) *(P-7211)*
Atlas Survival Shelters LLC ......................................................... E ...... 323 727-7084
  7407 Telegraph Rd Montebello (90640) *(P-3498)*
Atlassian, San Francisco *Also Called: Atlassian Us Inc (P-18073)*
Atlassian Us Inc (DH) ................................................................... E ...... 415 701-1110
  350 Bush St Fl 13 San Francisco (94104) *(P-18073)*
Atm Fly-Ware, Signal Hill *Also Called: Adaptive Tech Group Inc (P-17658)*
Atmel Corporation ......................................................................... A ...... 408 735-9110
  1600 Technology Dr San Jose (95110) *(P-12338)*
Atmf Inc ......................................................................................... E ...... 559 299-6836
  807 Lincoln Ave Clovis (93612) *(P-8927)*
Atmospheric-Greenscreen, Los Angeles *Also Called: Greenscreen (P-96)*
Atob Asset Vehicle I LLC ............................................................. D ...... 703 663-0658
  4 Embarcadero Ctr Ste 140 San Francisco (94111) *(P-18074)*
Atomic Training, Folsom *Also Called: Hoonuit LLC (P-18388)*

Atomica Corp ................................................................................ C ...... 805 681-2807
  75 Robin Hill Rd Goleta (93117) *(P-12339)*
Atonarp Us Inc .............................................................................. E ...... 650 714-6290
  5960 Inglewood Dr Ste 100 Pleasanton (94588) *(P-14617)*
Atoria's Family Bakery, Gilroy *Also Called: Atorias Baking Company (P-1161)*
Atorias Baking Company ............................................................. E ...... 408 846-0876
  101 Leavesley Rd Gilroy (95020) *(P-1161)*
Atp, Fremont *Also Called: Applied Thin-Film Products (P-12324)*
Atp Clinical Research Inc ............................................................. F ...... 714 393-0787
  3151 Airway Ave Ste T3 Costa Mesa (92626) *(P-5343)*
Atp Electronics, San Jose *Also Called: Atp Electronics Inc (P-12340)*
Atp Electronics Inc ....................................................................... E ...... 408 732-5000
  2590 N 1st St Ste 150 San Jose (95131) *(P-12340)*
Atr Sales Inc ................................................................................. E ...... 714 432-8411
  110 E Garry Ave Santa Ana (92707) *(P-10065)*
Atr Technologies Incorporated ..................................................... F ...... 909 399-9724
  805 Towne Center Dr Pomona (91767) *(P-8619)*
Atra-Flex, Santa Ana *Also Called: Atr Sales Inc (P-10065)*
Atreca Inc ...................................................................................... C ...... 650 595-2595
  835 Industrial Rd Ste 400 San Carlos (94070) *(P-5802)*
Ats Products Inc (PA) ................................................................... E ...... 510 234-3173
  2785 Goodrick Ave Richmond (94801) *(P-6728)*
Ats Systems, Rancho Santa Margari *Also Called: Ats Workholding Llc (P-9660)*
Ats Tool Inc ................................................................................... E ...... 949 888-1744
  30222 Esperanza Rcho Sta Marg (92688) *(P-9601)*
Ats Workholding, Rcho Sta Marg *Also Called: Ats Tool Inc (P-9601)*
Ats Workholding Llc (PA) ............................................................. E ...... 800 321-1833
  30222 Esperanza Rancho Santa Margari (92688) *(P-9660)*
Attivo Networks Inc ...................................................................... D ...... 510 623-1000
  444 Castro St Mountain View (94041) *(P-16510)*
Attollo Engineering, Camarillo *Also Called: Attollo Engineering LLC (P-12341)*
Attollo Engineering LLC ............................................................... D ...... 805 384-8046
  160 Camino Ruiz Camarillo (93012) *(P-12341)*
Attralus Inc ................................................................................... E ...... 415 410-3268
  337 Beach Rd Ste C Burlingame (94010) *(P-5344)*
Atx Networks (san Diego) Corp (DH) ........................................... E ...... 858 546-5050
  2800 Whiptail Loop Ste 6 Carlsbad (92010) *(P-11816)*
Atx Networks San Diego, Carlsbad *Also Called: Atx Networks (san Diego) Corp (P-11816)*
Atxco Inc ....................................................................................... E ...... 650 334-2079
  3030 Bunker Hill St Ste 325 San Diego (92109) *(P-5345)*
ATYR PHARMA, San Diego *Also Called: Atyr Pharma Inc (P-5803)*
Atyr Pharma Inc (PA) ................................................................... D ...... 858 731-8389
  10240 Sorrento Valley Rd Ste 300 San Diego (92121) *(P-5803)*
Au Merrow Corporation ................................................................ F
  7210 Dominion Cir Commerce (90040) *(P-2655)*
Aubin Industries Inc ...................................................................... F ...... 800 324-0051
  23833 S Chrisman Rd Tracy (95304) *(P-6672)*
Auburn Ale House, Auburn *Also Called: Auburn Alehouse LP (P-17257)*
Auburn Alehouse LP ..................................................................... E ...... 530 885-2537
  289 Washington St Auburn (95603) *(P-17257)*
Auburn Printers and Mfg, Auburn *Also Called: API Marketing (P-4515)*
Auburn Trader Inc (DH) ................................................................ E ...... 530 888-7653
  1115 Grass Valley Hwy Auburn (95603) *(P-4071)*
Audentes, South San Francisco *Also Called: Astellas Gene Therapies Inc (P-5798)*
Audience Inc ................................................................................. B ...... 650 254-2800
  331 Fairchild Dr Mountain View (94043) *(P-12342)*
Audio Images, Irvine *Also Called: Henrys Adio Vsual Slutions Inc (P-11668)*
Audio Video Color Corporation (PA) ............................................ C ...... 424 213-7500
  17707 S Santa Fe Ave E Rncho Dmngz (90221) *(P-3923)*
Audio Visual MGT Solutions LLC ................................................. D ...... 707 254-3395
  3425 Solano Ave Napa (94558) *(P-11639)*
Auger Industries Inc ..................................................................... F ...... 714 577-9350
  390 E Crowther Ave Placentia (92870) *(P-10724)*
Augerscope Inc ............................................................................ E
  10375 Wilshire Blvd Apt 1b Los Angeles (90024) *(P-7947)*
Augmedix Inc (PA) ........................................................................ C ...... 888 669-4885
  111 Sutter St Fl 13 San Francisco (94104) *(P-18075)*
August Accessories, Thousand Oaks *Also Called: August Hat Company Inc (P-2841)*
August Hat Company Inc (PA) ..................................................... E ...... 805 983-4651
  2021 Calle Yucca Thousand Oaks (91360) *(P-2841)*

AUL Corp (DH) .................................................................... C ...... 707 257-9700
  1250 Main St Ste 300 Napa (94559) *(P-19224)*
Aunt Rubys LLC ................................................................. E ...... 562 326-6783
  1014 E Carson St Long Beach (90807) *(P-19521)*
Aurasound Inc ................................................................... D ...... 949 829-4000
  1801 E Edinger Ave Ste 190 Santa Ana (92705) *(P-11640)*
Aurident Incorporated ........................................................ E ...... 714 870-1851
  610 S State College Blvd Fullerton (92831) *(P-15438)*
Aurionpro, San Ramon *Also Called: Cyberinc Corporation (P-18218)*
Auris Health Inc (DH) ......................................................... C ...... 650 610-0750
  150 Shoreline Dr Redwood City (94065) *(P-14982)*
Aurora Innovation, Fairfield *Also Called: Aurora Innovations LLC (P-6169)*
Aurora Innovation Inc ........................................................ B ...... 646 725-4999
  77 Stillman St San Francisco (94107) *(P-18076)*
AURORA INNOVATION, INC., San Francisco *Also Called: Aurora Innovation Inc (P-18076)*
Aurora Innovations LLC ...................................................... C ...... 541 359-1580
  2225 Huntington Dr Fairfield (94533) *(P-6169)*
Aurora Networks Inc ......................................................... C ...... 408 428-9500
  2450 Walsh Ave Santa Clara (95051) *(P-7191)*
Auspex Pharmaceuticals Inc ................................................ E ...... 858 558-2400
  3333 N Torrey Pines Ct Ste 400 La Jolla (92037) *(P-5346)*
Aussie Bubs Inc ............................................................... E ...... 888 685-1508
  1390 Market St Ste 200 San Francisco (94102) *(P-744)*
Authors Press .................................................................. F ...... 925 698-2619
  1321 Buchanan Rd Pittsburg (94565) *(P-4369)*
Auto Doctor, Temecula *Also Called: Thompson Magnetics Inc (P-13109)*
Auto Edge Solutions, Pacoima *Also Called: Moc Products Company Inc (P-6310)*
Auto Ex Towing & Recovery LLC .......................................... E ...... 415 846-2262
  2594 Oakdale Ave San Francisco (94124) *(P-19168)*
Auto Motive Power Inc ...................................................... C ...... 800 894-7104
  11643 Telegraph Rd Santa Fe Springs (90670) *(P-13460)*
Auto Pride, Stockton *Also Called: Rare Parts Inc (P-16395)*
Auto Trend Products, Vernon *Also Called: Punch Press Products Inc (P-9644)*
Auto-Chlor System of Mid S LLC .......................................... D ...... 650 967-3085
  450 Ferguson Dr Mountain View (94043) *(P-10725)*
Auto-Chlor System Wash Inc .............................................. F ...... 818 376-0940
  16141 Hart St Van Nuys (91406) *(P-5889)*
Autocam Acquisition Inc ..................................................... E
  1209 San Luis Obispo St Hayward (94544) *(P-10726)*
Autocam California, Hayward *Also Called: Autocam Acquisition Inc (P-10726)*
Autocene Inc .................................................................. E ...... 925 264-0045
  2010 Crow Canyon Pl Ste 100 San Ramon (94583) *(P-18077)*
Autoclerk Inc .................................................................. F ...... 925 284-1005
  1981 N Broadway Ste 430 Walnut Creek (94596) *(P-17884)*
Autocrib Inc ................................................................... C ...... 714 274-0400
  2882 Dow Ave Tustin (92780) *(P-19073)*
Autodesk, San Francisco *Also Called: Autodesk Inc (P-18078)*
Autodesk Inc (PA) ............................................................ B ...... 415 507-5000
  1 Market St Ste 400 San Francisco (94105) *(P-18078)*
Autogrid Systems Inc (PA) ................................................. F ...... 650 461-9038
  255 Shoreline Dr Ste 350 Redwood City (94065) *(P-18079)*
Autoliv Inc ..................................................................... E ...... 619 661-0438
  9355 Airway Rd San Diego (92154) *(P-13461)*
Autoliv Akr Fcilty -Casa Whse, San Diego *Also Called: Autoliv Asp Inc (P-3024)*
Autoliv Asp Inc ............................................................... E ...... 619 662-8018
  9355 Airway Rd San Diego (92154) *(P-3024)*
Autoliv Safety Technology Inc ............................................ A ...... 619 662-8000
  2475 Paseo De Las Americas Ste A San Diego (92154) *(P-3025)*
Automated Bldg Components Inc ......................................... F ...... 559 485-8232
  4949 W Spruce Ave Fresno (93722) *(P-3293)*
Automated Solutions Group Inc ........................................... E ...... 408 432-0300
  2150 Bering Dr San Jose (95131) *(P-14354)*
Automatic Bar Controls Inc (HQ) .......................................... E ...... 707 448-5151
  2060 Cessna Dr #100 Vacaville (95688) *(P-10483)*
Automatic Control Engrg Corp ............................................. E ...... 510 293-6040
  5735 W Las Positas Blvd Ste 400 Pleasanton (94588) *(P-14847)*
Automation Plating Corporation ........................................... E ...... 323 245-4951
  927 Thompson Ave Glendale (91201) *(P-8928)*
Automax Styling Inc ......................................................... E ...... 951 530-1876
  16833 Krameria Ave Riverside (92504) *(P-13462)*

Automotive Importing Manufacturing Inc (PA) ........................... B ...... 916 985-8505
  3920 Security Park Dr Rancho Cordova (95742) *(P-16374)*
Automotive Racing Products Inc (PA) .................................... D ...... 805 339-2200
  1863 Eastman Ave Ventura (93003) *(P-7977)*
Automotive Racing Products Inc .......................................... D ...... 805 525-1497
  1760 E Lemonwood Dr Santa Paula (93060) *(P-7978)*
Automted Mdia Proc Sltions Inc ........................................... E ...... 415 332-4343
  500 Tamal Plz Ste 520 Corte Madera (94925) *(P-16316)*
Auton Motorized Systems, Valencia *Also Called: Virgil Walker Inc (P-8241)*
Autonomous Defense Tech Corp .......................................... E ...... 805 616-2030
  2889 W 5th St Ste 111 Oxnard (93030) *(P-19052)*
Autonomous Inc ............................................................. E ...... 844 949-3879
  21800 Opportunity Way Riverside (92518) *(P-3594)*
Autonomous Medical Devices Inc (PA) ................................... E ...... 657 660-6800
  3511 W Sunflower Ave Santa Ana (92704) *(P-14618)*
Autonomous Medical Devices Inc ......................................... E ...... 310 641-2700
  10524 S La Cienega Blvd Inglewood (90304) *(P-14619)*
Autonomy Interwoven, Sunnyvale *Also Called: Entco LLC (P-18283)*
Autopartsmarket, Norwalk *Also Called: Icarcover Inc (P-13516)*
Autosplice, San Diego *Also Called: Autosplice Parent Inc (P-11441)*
Autosplice Parent Inc (PA) .................................................. C ...... 858 535-0077
  10431 Wateridge Cir Ste 110 San Diego (92121) *(P-11441)*
Autostore Integrator, Valencia *Also Called: Sdi Industries Inc (P-9494)*
Autumn Press, Berkeley *Also Called: Autumn Press Inc (P-4519)*
Autumn Press Inc ............................................................ E ...... 510 654-4545
  945 Camelia St Berkeley (94710) *(P-4519)*
Auxin Solar Inc ............................................................... E ...... 408 225-4380
  6835 Via Del Oro San Jose (95119) *(P-12343)*
AV Now Inc ................................................................... E ...... 831 425-2500
  231 Technology Cir Scotts Valley (95066) *(P-11641)*
Ava James, Los Angeles *Also Called: C-Quest Inc (P-2659)*
Avago Technologies, San Jose *Also Called: Avago Technologies US Inc (P-16691)*
Avago Technologies US Inc ................................................ A ...... 408 433-4068
  1730 Fox Dr San Jose (95131) *(P-12344)*
Avago Technologies US Inc ................................................ A ...... 408 433-8000
  408 E Plumeria Dr San Jose (95134) *(P-12345)*
Avago Technologies US Inc (HQ) .......................................... B ...... 800 433-8778
  1320 Ridder Park Dr San Jose (95131) *(P-16691)*
Avail Medsystems Inc ....................................................... E ...... 650 772-1529
  2953 Bunker Hill Ln Ste 101 Santa Clara (95054) *(P-14983)*
Avails Medical Inc ........................................................... F ...... 650 427-0460
  1455 Adams Dr # 1288 Menlo Park (94025) *(P-14984)*
Avalanche Technology Inc ................................................. E ...... 510 438-0148
  3450 W Warren Ave Fremont (94538) *(P-12346)*
Avalon Apparel LLC ......................................................... D ...... 323 440-4344
  1901 W Center St Colton (92324) *(P-2699)*
Avalon Apparel LLC (PA) ................................................... C ...... 323 581-3511
  2520 W 6th St Los Angeles (90057) *(P-2700)*
Avalon Communications, Hawthorne *Also Called: Technology Training Corp (P-4782)*
Avalon Communications, Torrance *Also Called: Technology Training Corp (P-19138)*
Avalon Glass & Mirror, Carson *Also Called: Avalon Glass & Mirror Company (P-7212)*
Avalon Glass & Mirror Company .......................................... F ...... 323 321-8806
  642 Alondra Blvd Carson (90746) *(P-7212)*
Avalon Shutters Inc ......................................................... D ...... 909 937-4900
  3407 N Perris Blvd Perris (92571) *(P-3112)*
Avanir Pharmaceuticals Inc (DH) .......................................... D ...... 949 389-6700
  30 Enterprise Ste 200 Aliso Viejo (92656) *(P-5347)*
Avantec Manufacturing Inc ................................................. E ...... 714 532-6197
  1811 N Case St Orange (92865) *(P-12063)*
Avantec Vascular Corporation ............................................. E ...... 408 329-5400
  870 Hermosa Ave Sunnyvale (94085) *(P-14985)*
Avantier Inc ................................................................... D ...... 732 570-8800
  681 Garland Ave Apt 74 Sunnyvale (94086) *(P-14762)*
Avantis Medical Systems Inc .............................................. E ...... 408 733-1901
  2367 Bering Dr San Jose (95131) *(P-15514)*
Avantus Aerospace Inc ..................................................... E ...... 562 633-6626
  14957 Gwenchris Ct Paramount (90723) *(P-7979)*
Avantus Aerospace Inc (DH) ............................................... C ...... 661 295-8620
  29101 The Old Rd Valencia (91355) *(P-13791)*
Avanzato Technology Corp ................................................. E ...... 312 509-0506
  5335 Mcconnell Ave Los Angeles (90066) *(P-9836)*

# ALPHABETIC SECTION — Axiom Materials Inc

Avast Software Inc (PA) .................................................. D ...... 844 340-9251
   501 E Middlefield Rd Mountain View (94043) *(P-18080)*

Avatar Machine LLC .................................................... E ...... 714 434-2737
   18100 Mount Washington St Fountain Valley (92708) *(P-10727)*

Avatar Technology Inc ................................................. E ...... 909 598-7696
   339 Cheryl Ln City Of Industry (91789) *(P-16511)*

Avathon, Pleasanton *Also Called: Sparkcognition Inc (P-18818)*

Avatier, Pleasanton *Also Called: Avatier Corporation (P-18081)*

Avatier Corporation (PA) .............................................. E ...... 925 217-5170
   4733 Chabot Dr Ste 201 Pleasanton (94588) *(P-18081)*

AVD, Newport Beach *Also Called: American Vanguard Corporation (P-6191)*

Avenue Medical Equipment Inc ..................................... E ...... 949 680-7444
   38062 Encanto Rd Murrieta (92563) *(P-16575)*

Aveox Inc ................................................................... E ...... 805 915-0200
   2265 Ward Ave Ste A Simi Valley (93065) *(P-11361)*

Avery Dennison Corporation ......................................... B ...... 714 674-8500
   50 Pointe Dr Brea (92821) *(P-3942)*

Avery Dennison Corporation ......................................... C ...... 626 304-2000
   2900 Bradley St Pasadena (91107) *(P-3943)*

Avery Dennison Corporation ......................................... D ...... 909 987-4631
   11195 Eucalyptus St Rancho Cucamonga (91730) *(P-3944)*

Avery Dennison Foundation .......................................... E ...... 626 304-2000
   207 N Goode Ave Ste 500 Glendale (91203) *(P-3945)*

Avery Dennison Office Products Co Inc ......................... A
   50 Pointe Dr Brea (92821) *(P-4014)*

Avery Dnnson Ret Info Svcs LLC (HQ) ............................ D ...... 626 304-2000
   207 N Goode Ave Fl 6 Glendale (91203) *(P-4015)*

Avery Products Corporation .......................................... C ...... 619 671-1022
   6987 Calle De Linea Ste 101 San Diego (92154) *(P-4016)*

Avery Products Corporation (DH) ................................... C ...... 714 674-8500
   50 Pointe Dr Brea (92821) *(P-4017)*

Avet Industries Inc ..................................................... F ...... 818 576-9895
   9687 Topanga Canyon Pl Chatsworth (91311) *(P-15782)*

Avet Reels, Chatsworth *Also Called: Avet Industries Inc (P-15782)*

AVI Networks Inc (DH) ................................................ E ...... 408 628-1300
   3401 Hillview Ave Palo Alto (94304) *(P-18082)*

Aviate Enterprises Inc ................................................. E ...... 916 993-4000
   5844 Price Ave Mcclellan (95652) *(P-10484)*

Aviation Design Group Inc ........................................... E ...... 818 350-1900
   9060 Winnetka Ave Northridge (91324) *(P-13792)*

Aviation Equipment Processing, Costa Mesa *Also Called: Flare Group (P-13840)*

Aviation Repair Solutions Inc ....................................... F ...... 562 437-2825
   1480 Canal Ave Long Beach (90813) *(P-16300)*

Avibank, North Hollywood *Also Called: Avibank Mfg Inc (P-13793)*

Avibank Mfg Inc ........................................................ D ...... 661 257-2329
   25323 Rye Canyon Rd Valencia (91355) *(P-7980)*

Avibank Mfg Inc (DH) ................................................. C ...... 818 392-2100
   11500 Sherman Way North Hollywood (91605) *(P-13793)*

Avid, Norco *Also Called: Avid Idntification Systems Inc (P-12347)*

Avid, Burbank *Also Called: Avid Technology Inc (P-15630)*

AVID BIOSERVICES, Tustin *Also Called: Avid Bioservices Inc (P-5350)*

Avid Bioservices Inc ................................................... D ...... 714 508-6000
   14272 Franklin Ave Ste 115 Tustin (92780) *(P-5348)*

Avid Bioservices Inc ................................................... E ...... 714 508-6166
   14282 Franklin Ave Tustin (92780) *(P-5349)*

Avid Bioservices Inc (PA) ............................................ C ...... 714 508-6100
   14191 Myford Rd Tustin (92780) *(P-5350)*

Avid Idntification Systems Inc (PA) ................................ D ...... 951 371-7505
   3185 Hamner Ave Norco (92860) *(P-12347)*

Avid Ink, Irvine *Also Called: Advanced Vsual Image Dsign LLC (P-4505)*

Avid Systems Inc (DH) ................................................ C ...... 650 526-1600
   280 Bernardo Ave Mountain View (94043) *(P-11817)*

Avid Technology Inc ................................................... E ...... 510 486-8302
   2600 10th St Berkeley (94710) *(P-15629)*

Avid Technology Inc ................................................... D ...... 818 557-2520
   101 S 1st St Ste 200 Burbank (91502) *(P-15630)*

AVIDITY BIOSCIENCES, San Diego *Also Called: Avidity Biosciences Inc (P-5351)*

Avidity Biosciences Inc (PA) ........................................ E ...... 858 401-7900
   10578 Science Center Dr Ste 125 San Diego (92121) *(P-5351)*

Avient Colorants USA LLC ........................................... D ...... 909 606-1325
   14355 Ramona Ave Chino (91710) *(P-6128)*

Avient Corporation ..................................................... F ...... 310 513-7100
   2104 E 223rd St Carson (90810) *(P-5138)*

Avilas Garden Art (PA) ................................................ D ...... 909 350-4546
   14608 Merrill Ave Fontana (92335) *(P-7312)*

Avinger Inc ............................................................... D ...... 650 241-7900
   400 Chesapeake Dr Redwood City (94063) *(P-14986)*

Avion Graphics Inc .................................................... E ...... 949 472-0438
   27192 Burbank Foothill Ranch (92610) *(P-4520)*

Avis Roto Die Co ....................................................... E ...... 323 255-7070
   1560 N San Fernando Rd Los Angeles (90065) *(P-9602)*

Avista Technologies Inc .............................................. F ...... 760 744-0536
   140 Bosstick Blvd San Marcos (92069) *(P-6270)*

Avitex Inc (PA) .......................................................... C ...... 818 994-6487
   20362 Plummer St Chatsworth (91311) *(P-2401)*

Avn Media Network Inc ............................................... E ...... 818 718-5788
   9400 Penfield Ave Chatsworth (91311) *(P-4312)*

Avochato Inc ............................................................. E ...... 415 214-8977
   530 Howard St Mill Valley (94941) *(P-18083)*

Avogy Inc ................................................................. E ...... 408 684-5200
   677 River Oaks Pkwy San Jose (95134) *(P-12348)*

Avp Technology LLC .................................................. E ...... 510 683-0157
   4140 Business Center Dr Fremont (94538) *(P-10012)*

Avr Global Tech, Escondido *Also Called: Avr Global Technologies Inc (P-12918)*

Avr Global Technologies Inc (PA) .................................. C ...... 949 391-1180
   500 La Terraza Blvd Ste 150 Escondido (92025) *(P-12918)*

Avt Inc .................................................................... E ...... 951 737-1057
   341 Bonnie Cir Ste 102 Corona (92880) *(P-10469)*

AVV Winery Co LLC .................................................. E ...... 707 433-7209
   8644 Highway 128 Healdsburg (95448) *(P-1481)*

AVX Antenna, Inc., San Diego *Also Called: Kyocera AVX Cmpnnts San Dego I (P-11873)*

AVX Filters Corporation .............................................. D ...... 818 767-6770
   11144 Penrose St Sun Valley (91352) *(P-10075)*

AW Die Engraving Inc ................................................ E ...... 714 521-7910
   8550 Roland St Buena Park (90621) *(P-9603)*

Awake Security LLC .................................................. E ...... 833 292-5348
   5453 Great America Pkwy Santa Clara (95054) *(P-18084)*

Award Metals, Baldwin Park *Also Called: Pacific Award Metals Inc (P-8525)*

Award Metals, Jurupa Valley *Also Called: Pacific Award Metals Inc (P-8526)*

Awards By Wilson, Sacramento *Also Called: Wilson Trophy Co California (P-17726)*

Aware Products LLC .................................................. C ...... 818 206-6700
   9250 Mason Ave Chatsworth (91311) *(P-5945)*

Awbscqemgk Inc ....................................................... E ...... 408 988-8600
   545 Oakmead Pkwy Sunnyvale (94085) *(P-12349)*

Awesome Products Inc (PA) ........................................ C ...... 714 562-8873
   6370 Altura Blvd Buena Park (90620) *(P-5890)*

Aweta-Autoline Inc (DH) ............................................. E ...... 559 244-8340
   4516 E Citron Fresno (93725) *(P-9339)*

AWI, Sacramento *Also Called: All Weather Inc (P-14841)*

Awid, Morgan Hill *Also Called: Applied Wrless Idntfctons Grou (P-16690)*

Awnings.com, Cerritos *Also Called: Eide Industries Inc (P-2973)*

Awo, Vista *Also Called: Advanced Web Offset Inc (P-4837)*

Axelgaard, Fallbrook *Also Called: Axelgaard Manufacturing Co (P-15516)*

Axelgaard Manufacturing, Fallbrook *Also Called: Axelgaard Manufacturing Co (P-15515)*

Axelgaard Manufacturing Co ....................................... E ...... 760 723-7554
   329 W Aviation Rd Fallbrook (92028) *(P-15515)*

Axelgaard Manufacturing Co (PA) ................................. D ...... 760 723-7554
   520 Industrial Way Fallbrook (92028) *(P-15516)*

Axeon Water Technologies .......................................... D ...... 760 723-5417
   40980 County Center Dr Ste 100 Temecula (92591) *(P-10541)*

Axia Technologies Inc ................................................ E ...... 855 376-2942
   4183 State St Santa Barbara (93110) *(P-18085)*

Axiamed, Santa Barbara *Also Called: Axia Technologies Inc (P-18085)*

Axiom Advisors & Cons Inc (PA) ................................... E ...... 800 818-3010
   4935 Hillsdale Cir El Dorado Hills (95762) *(P-18086)*

Axiom Designs & Printing, Glendale *Also Called: Axiomprint Inc (P-4521)*

Axiom Industries Inc .................................................. E ...... 559 276-1310
   4202 W Sierra Madre Ave Fresno (93722) *(P-15324)*

Axiom Label & Packaging, Compton *Also Called: Resource Label Group LLC (P-4827)*

Axiom Label Group, Compton *Also Called: Kmr Label LLC (P-4823)*

Axiom Materials Inc ................................................... E ...... 949 623-4400
   2320 Pullman St Santa Ana (92705) *(P-6219)*

## ALPHABETIC SECTION

**Axiom Medical Incorporated** ............................................. E ...... 310 533-9020
19320 Van Ness Ave Torrance (90501) *(P-14987)*

**Axiomprint Inc** ........................................................................ F ...... 747 888-7777
4544 San Fernando Rd Ste 210 Glendale (91204) *(P-4521)*

**Axium Packaging LLC** ............................................................ A ...... 909 969-0766
5701 Clark St Ontario (91761) *(P-6729)*

**AXT, Fremont** *Also Called: Axt Inc (P-12350)*

**Axt Inc (PA)** ............................................................................ E ...... 510 438-4700
4281 Technology Dr Fremont (94538) *(P-12350)*

**Axt Inc** .................................................................................... B ...... 510 683-5900
4311 Solar Way Fremont (94538) *(P-12351)*

**Axt-Tongmei Inc** .................................................................... E ...... 510 438-4700
4281 Technology Dr Fremont (94538) *(P-12352)*

**Axxis Arms, Perris** *Also Called: Axxis Corporation (P-10728)*

**Axxis Corporation** .................................................................. E ...... 951 436-9921
1535 Nandina Ave Perris (92571) *(P-10728)*

**Axygen Inc (HQ)** .................................................................... D ...... 510 494-8900
33210 Central Ave Union City (94587) *(P-14620)*

**Axygen Scientific, Union City** *Also Called: Axygen Inc (P-14620)*

**Ayantra Inc** ............................................................................ F ...... 510 623-7526
47873 Fremont Blvd Fremont (94538) *(P-11752)*

**Ayar Labs Inc (PA)** ................................................................ D ...... 650 963-7200
695 River Oaks Pkwy San Jose (95134) *(P-10137)*

**Ayo Food, Delano** *Also Called: Ayo Foods LLC (P-825)*

**Ayo Foods LLC** ...................................................................... E ...... 661 345-5457
927 Main St Delano (93215) *(P-825)*

**AZ Displays Inc** ...................................................................... E ...... 949 831-5000
2410 Birch St Vista (92081) *(P-12919)*

**AZ Manufacturing, Santa Ana** *Also Called: A-Z Mfg Inc (P-10655)*

**Aza Industries Inc (PA)** .......................................................... E ...... 760 560-0440
1410 Vantage Ct Vista (92081) *(P-15783)*

**Azaa Investments Inc (PA)** .................................................... E ...... 858 569-8111
6602 Convoy Ct Ste 200 San Diego (92111) *(P-13341)*

**Azalea Systems Corp Inc** ...................................................... E ...... 951 547-5910
820 E Parkridge Ave Corona (92879) *(P-4522)*

**Azimuth Industrial Co Inc** ...................................................... E ...... 510 441-6000
30593 Union City Blvd Ste 110 Union City (94587) *(P-12353)*

**Azimuth Semiconductor Assembly, Union City** *Also Called: Azimuth Industrial Co Inc (P-12353)*

**Azitex Knitting Mills, Los Angeles** *Also Called: Azitex Trading Corp (P-2484)*

**Azitex Trading Corp** .............................................................. D ...... 213 745-7072
1850 E 15th St Los Angeles (90021) *(P-2484)*

**Azk Inc** .................................................................................... E ...... 510 724-9999
1990 San Pablo Ave Pinole (94564) *(P-5946)*

**Aztec Container, Vista** *Also Called: Aztec Technology Corporation (P-8098)*

**Aztec Manufacturing Inc (PA)** ................................................ E ...... 858 513-4350
13821 Danielson St Poway (92064) *(P-8743)*

**Aztec Perlite Company Inc** .................................................... F ...... 760 741-1733
1518 Simpson Way Escondido (92029) *(P-7564)*

**Aztec Technology Corporation (PA)** ...................................... E ...... 760 727-2300
2550 S Santa Fe Ave Vista (92084) *(P-8098)*

**Aztec Tents, Torrance** *Also Called: A-Aztec Rents & Sells Inc (P-2965)*

**Aztec Washer Company, Poway** *Also Called: Aztec Manufacturing Inc (P-8743)*

**Azul Systems Inc (PA)** .......................................................... D ...... 866 890-8951
385 Moffett Park Dr Ste 115 Sunnyvale (94089) *(P-18087)*

**Azul Works, San Francisco** *Also Called: Azulworks Inc (P-16353)*

**Azulworks Inc** ........................................................................ C ...... 415 558-1507
1400 Egbert Ave San Francisco (94124) *(P-16353)*

**Azuma Foods Internatl, Hayward** *Also Called: Azuma Foods Intl Inc USA (P-2048)*

**Azuma Foods Intl Inc USA (HQ)** .......................................... D ...... 510 782-1112
20201 Mack St Hayward (94545) *(P-2048)*

**Azumex Corp** .......................................................................... E ...... 619 710-8855
2320 Paseo De Las Americas San Diego (92154) *(P-1293)*

**Azure Microdynamics Inc** ...................................................... D ...... 949 699-3344
19652 Descartes Foothill Ranch (92610) *(P-10729)*

**Azusa Engineering Inc** .......................................................... F ...... 626 966-4071
1542 W Industrial Park St Covina (91722) *(P-13463)*

**Azusa Rock LLC** .................................................................... E ...... 619 440-2363
3605 Dehesa Rd El Cajon (92019) *(P-296)*

**Azusa Rock LLC** .................................................................... E ...... 209 826-5066
22101 W Sunset Ave Los Banos (93635) *(P-297)*

**B & A Friction Materials Inc** .................................................. E ...... 408 286-9200
1164 Old Bayshore Hwy San Jose (95112) *(P-16375)*

**B & B Battery (usa) Inc (PA)** ................................................ F ...... 323 278-1900
6415 Randolph St Commerce (90040) *(P-13157)*

**B & B Mfg Co, Turlock** *Also Called: Rose Joaquin Inc (P-16839)*

**B & B Pipe and Tool Co (PA)** ................................................ E ...... 562 424-0704
3035 Walnut Ave Long Beach (90807) *(P-206)*

**B & B Pipe and Tool Co** ........................................................ E ...... 661 323-8208
2301 Parker Ln Bakersfield (93308) *(P-10730)*

**B & B Plastics Inc** .................................................................. E ...... 909 829-3606
1892 W Casmalia St Rialto (92377) *(P-5139)*

**B & B Plastics Recyclers Inc (PA)** ........................................ E ...... 909 829-3606
3040 N Locust Ave Rialto (92377) *(P-16957)*

**B & B Specialties Inc (PA)** .................................................... D ...... 714 985-3000
4321 E La Palma Ave Anaheim (92807) *(P-7981)*

**B & B Specialties Inc** ............................................................ D ...... 714 985-3075
4321 E La Palma Ave Anaheim (92807) *(P-16746)*

**B & C Nutritional Products Inc** .............................................. D ...... 714 238-7225
2995 E Miraloma Ave Anaheim (92806) *(P-5231)*

**B & C Painting Solutions Inc** ................................................ E ...... 209 982-0422
107 Val Dervin Pkwy Stockton (95206) *(P-9052)*

**B & E Manufacturing Co Inc** .................................................. E ...... 714 898-2269
12151 Monarch St Garden Grove (92841) *(P-13794)*

**B & G Electronic Assembly Inc** ............................................ F ...... 909 608-2077
10350 Regis Ct Rancho Cucamonga (91730) *(P-12920)*

**B & G House of Printing, Gardena** *Also Called: Matsuda House Printing Inc (P-4691)*

**B & G Precision Inc** .............................................................. F ...... 510 438-9785
45450 Industrial Pl Ste 9 Fremont (94538) *(P-10731)*

**B & H Engineering Company, San Carlos** *Also Called: Begovic Industries Inc (P-10742)*

**B & H Labeling Systems, Ceres** *Also Called: B & H Manufacturing Co Inc (P-10013)*

**B & H Manufacturing Co Inc (PA)** ........................................ C ...... 209 537-5785
3461 Roeding Rd Ceres (95307) *(P-10013)*

**B & N Industries Inc (PA)** ...................................................... D ...... 650 593-4127
15 Guittard Rd Burlingame (94010) *(P-16566)*

**B & R Farms LLC** .................................................................. E ...... 831 637-9168
5280 Fairview Rd Hollister (95023) *(P-944)*

**B & S Plastics Inc** .................................................................. C ...... 805 981-0262
2200 Sturgis Rd Oxnard (93030) *(P-6730)*

**B & W Tile Co Inc (PA)** .......................................................... E ...... 310 538-9579
14600 S Western Ave Gardena (90249) *(P-17525)*

**B & W Tile Manufacturing, Gardena** *Also Called: B & W Tile Co Inc (P-17525)*

**B A L** ...................................................................................... D ...... 408 432-1980
1980 Lundy Ave San Jose (95131) *(P-4846)*

**B and F Solutions Inc** ............................................................ E ...... 530 343-5100
2377 Ivy St Chico (95928) *(P-10542)*

**B and P Plastics Inc** .............................................................. E ...... 619 477-1893
225 W 30th St National City (91950) *(P-6731)*

**B and Z Printing Inc** .............................................................. E ...... 714 892-2000
1300 E Wakeham Ave # B Santa Ana (92705) *(P-4523)*

**B B Blu, Los Angeles** *Also Called: Treivush Industries Inc (P-2818)*

**B B C, San Jose** *Also Called: Babbitt Bearing Co Inc (P-10735)*

**B B C, Long Beach** *Also Called: Belmont Brewing Company Inc (P-17564)*

**B B G Management Group (PA)** ............................................ E ...... 909 797-9581
12164 California St Yucaipa (92399) *(P-17139)*

**B Braun Medical, Irvine** *Also Called: B Braun Medical Inc (P-14989)*

**B Braun Medical Inc** .............................................................. C ...... 909 906-7575
1151 Mildred St Ste B Ontario (91761) *(P-14988)*

**B Braun Medical Inc** .............................................................. E ...... 949 660-3151
2206 Alton Pkwy Irvine (92606) *(P-14989)*

**B Braun Medical Inc** .............................................................. F ...... 949 660-2581
2488 Alton Pkwy Irvine (92606) *(P-14990)*

**B Braun Medical Inc** .............................................................. A ...... 610 691-5400
2525 Mcgaw Ave Irvine (92614) *(P-14991)*

**B C I, San Diego** *Also Called: Brehm Communications Inc (P-4537)*

**B C T, San Marcos** *Also Called: Business Cards Tomorrow (P-4538)*

**B D L, Orange** *Also Called: Belt Drives Ltd (P-14054)*

**B E & P Enterprises LLC (PA)** .............................................. E ...... 909 591-7561
5167 G St Chino (91710) *(P-3411)*

**B E B E, Los Angeles** *Also Called: Bebe Studio Inc (P-17531)*

**B E M R, Bakersfield** *Also Called: Bakersfield Elc Mtr Repr Inc (P-19225)*

B F, Riverside *Also Called: Brenner-Fiedler & Assoc Inc (P-14850)*

B F I Labels, Yorba Linda *Also Called: Beckers Fabrication Inc (P-3946)*

B Green, East Rancho Domingue *Also Called: International Tex Group Inc (P-2419)*

B J Bindery Inc ................................................................................ D ...... 714 835-7342
833 S Grand Ave Santa Ana (92705) *(P-5009)*

B M B, Rancho Cordova *Also Called: Bmb Metal Products Corporation (P-8392)*

B M S, Poway *Also Called: Broadcast Microwave Svcs LLC (P-11821)*

B Metal Fabrication Inc .................................................................. E ...... 650 615-7705
318 S Maple Ave South San Francisco (94080) *(P-8099)*

B P I Corp ......................................................................................... F ...... 408 988-7888
1208 Norman Ave Ste B Santa Clara (95054) *(P-10732)*

B P W, Santa Fe Springs *Also Called: Brown-Pacific Inc (P-7607)*

B R, San Jose *Also Called: B R Printers Inc (P-4524)*

B R & F Spray Inc ........................................................................... E ...... 408 988-7582
3380 De La Cruz Blvd Santa Clara (95054) *(P-9053)*

B R Printers Inc (PA) ....................................................................... D ...... 408 278-7711
665 Lenfest Rd San Jose (95133) *(P-4524)*

B S A, Fremont *Also Called: Ball Screws & Actuators Co Inc (P-10066)*

B Stephen Cooperage Inc ............................................................... F ...... 909 591-2929
10746 Vernon Ave Ontario (91762) *(P-7933)*

B T I, City Of Industry *Also Called: Battery Technology Inc (P-13131)*

B W Implement Co .......................................................................... E ...... 661 764-5254
288 W Front St Buttonwillow (93206) *(P-9340)*

B W Padilla Inc ................................................................................ E ...... 408 275-9834
197 Ryland St San Jose (95110) *(P-19183)*

B Young Enterprises Inc ................................................................. D ...... 858 748-0935
12254 Iavelli Way Poway (92064) *(P-3218)*

B-Bridge International Inc .............................................................. E ...... 408 252-6200
3350 Scott Blvd Bldg 29 Santa Clara (95054) *(P-5804)*

B-F Glass Inc .................................................................................. E ...... 559 221-4100
3603 W Gettysburg Ave Fresno (93722) *(P-554)*

B-K Lighting Inc .............................................................................. D ...... 559 438-5800
40429 Brickyard Dr Madera (93636) *(P-11491)*

B-K Mill and Fixtures Inc ................................................................ F ...... 510 713-8657
37523 Sycamore St Newark (94560) *(P-3219)*

B-Reel Films Inc .............................................................................. E ...... 917 388-3836
8383 Wilshire Blvd Ste 1000 Beverly Hills (90211) *(P-10138)*

B.R. Cohn Winery, Glen Ellen *Also Called: Vintage Wine Estates Inc CA (P-1815)*

B.T.i Tool Engineering, Santee *Also Called: T I B Inc (P-11134)*

B/E Aerospace Inc .......................................................................... C ...... 714 896-9001
7155 Fenwick Ln Westminster (92683) *(P-13795)*

B/E Aerospace Macrolink ............................................................... E ...... 714 777-8800
1500 N Kellogg Dr Anaheim (92807) *(P-13796)*

B&B Manufacturing Co (PA) ........................................................... C ...... 661 257-2161
27940 Beale Ct Santa Clarita (91355) *(P-10733)*

B&D Investment Partners Inc (PA) ................................................. E
20950 Centre Pointe Pkwy Santa Clarita (91350) *(P-5891)*

B&G Machine Shop, Bakersfield *Also Called: McCain & Mccain Inc (P-10965)*

B&K Precision Corporation (PA) .................................................... E ...... 714 921-9095
22820 Savi Ranch Pkwy Yorba Linda (92887) *(P-16644)*

B&R Mold Inc .................................................................................. F ...... 805 526-8665
4564 E Los Angeles Ave Ste C Simi Valley (93063) *(P-9604)*

B&W Custom Restaurant Eqp Inc .................................................. E ...... 714 578-0332
541 E Jamie Ave La Habra (90631) *(P-10543)*

B&Z Manufacturing Company Inc .................................................. E ...... 408 943-1117
1478 Seareel Ln San Jose (95131) *(P-10734)*

B2 Apparel Inc ................................................................................ F ...... 323 233-0044
219 E 32nd St Los Angeles (90011) *(P-2891)*

B2 Machining LLC .......................................................................... F ...... 510 668-1360
4255 Business Center Dr Fremont (94538) *(P-19244)*

Ba Holdings Inc (DH) ...................................................................... E ...... 951 684-5110
3016 Kansas Ave Bldg 1 Riverside (92507) *(P-8300)*

Baatz Enterprises Inc .................................................................... E ...... 323 660-4866
2223 W San Bernardino Rd West Covina (91790) *(P-13342)*

Bab Hydraulics, Fontana *Also Called: Bab Steering Hydraulics (P-13464)*

Bab Steering Hydraulics (PA) ........................................................ E ...... 208 573-4502
14554 Whittram Ave Fontana (92335) *(P-13464)*

Baba Small Batch LLC ................................................................... F ...... 805 439-2250
103 Santa Felicia Dr Goleta (93117) *(P-1027)*

Babbitt Bearing Co Inc ................................................................... E ...... 408 298-1101
1170 N 5th St San Jose (95112) *(P-10735)*

Babcock & Wilcox Company ......................................................... E ...... 707 259-1122
710 Airpark Rd Napa (94558) *(P-9308)*

Babcock and Wilcox, Napa *Also Called: Babcock & Wilcox Company (P-9308)*

Babcock Enterprises Inc ................................................................ E ...... 805 736-1455
5175 E Highway 246 Lompoc (93436) *(P-8)*

Babcock Vineyards, Lompoc *Also Called: Babcock Enterprises Inc (P-8)*

Baby Guess Inc .............................................................................. E ...... 213 765-3100
1444 S Alameda St Los Angeles (90021) *(P-2858)*

Babyfits LLC ................................................................................... E ...... 916 544-7018
3341 Mono Way Antelope (95843) *(P-7127)*

Babylon International LLC ............................................................. E ...... 323 433-4104
16520 Bake Pkwy Ste 230 Irvine (92618) *(P-2402)*

Babylon Printing Inc ...................................................................... E ...... 408 519-5000
15850 Concord Cir Ste B Morgan Hill (95037) *(P-4525)*

Bacchus Press Inc (PA) ................................................................. E ...... 510 420-5800
1287 66th St Emeryville (94608) *(P-4526)*

Bace Manufacturing Inc (HQ) ........................................................ A ...... 714 630-6002
3125 E Coronado St Anaheim (92806) *(P-6732)*

Bace Manufacturing Inc ................................................................. D ...... 510 657-5800
45581 Northport Loop W Fremont (94538) *(P-6733)*

Bachem, Torrance *Also Called: Bachem Bioscience Inc (P-5808)*

Bachem Americas Inc .................................................................... E ...... 424 347-5600
3131 Fujita St Torrance (90505) *(P-5352)*

Bachem Americas Inc .................................................................... E ...... 888 422-2436
1271 Avenida Chelsea Vista (92081) *(P-5353)*

Bachem Americas Inc (DH) ............................................................ E ...... 310 784-4440
3132 Kashiwa St Torrance (90505) *(P-5805)*

Bachem Americas Inc .................................................................... E ...... 310 784-4440
3152 Kashiwa St Torrance (90505) *(P-5806)*

Bachem Americas Inc .................................................................... E ...... 310 539-4171
3031 Fujita St Torrance (90505) *(P-5807)*

Bachem Bioscience Inc .................................................................. E ...... 310 784-7322
3132 Kashiwa St Torrance (90505) *(P-5808)*

Bachem California, Torrance *Also Called: Bachem Americas Inc (P-5805)*

Bachem Vista BSD, Vista *Also Called: Bachem Americas Inc (P-5353)*

Back Support Systems Inc ............................................................. F ...... 760 329-1472
1064 N E St San Bernardino (92410) *(P-6624)*

Bad Habit Customs, Fresno *Also Called: Ipt Inc (P-16387)*

Badass Beard Care, Granite Bay *Also Called: Badass Brand Inc (P-17027)*

Badass Brand Inc ........................................................................... E ...... 916 990-3873
8400 Moss Ct Granite Bay (95746) *(P-17027)*

Badger Maps Inc ............................................................................ E ...... 415 592-5909
539 Bdwy San Francisco (94133) *(P-18088)*

Badger Paperboard Cal LLC .......................................................... F ...... 657 529-0456
14657 Industry Cir La Mirada (90638) *(P-3924)*

Badgeville Inc ................................................................................. E ...... 650 323-6668
805 Veterans Blvd Ste 307 Redwood City (94063) *(P-18089)*

Bae Systems, San Diego *Also Called: Bae Systems Info Elctrnic Syst (P-14500)*

Bae Systems Imging Sltions Inc .................................................... D ...... 408 433-2500
1841 Zanker Rd Ste 50 San Jose (95112) *(P-12354)*

Bae Systems Info Elctrnic Syst ..................................................... A ...... 858 592-5000
10920 Technology Pl San Diego (92127) *(P-14500)*

Bae Systems Land Armaments LP ................................................ E ...... 619 455-0213
1650 Industrial Blvd Chula Vista (91911) *(P-14161)*

Bae Systems Land Armaments LP ................................................ D ...... 831 637-0356
900 John Smith Rd Hollister (95023) *(P-14162)*

Bae Systems Land Armaments LP ................................................ B ...... 408 289-0111
6331 San Ignacio Ave San Jose (95119) *(P-14163)*

Bae Systems National Security Solutions Inc .............................. A ...... 858 592-5000
10920 Technology Pl San Diego (92127) *(P-14501)*

Bae Systems San Dego Ship Repr ................................................ A ...... 619 238-1000
2205 Belt St San Diego (92113) *(P-13999)*

Bae Systems Tech Sltons Svcs I ................................................... D ...... 858 278-3042
9650 Chesapeake Dr San Diego (92123) *(P-14164)*

Baer Enterprises Inc ...................................................................... E ...... 209 390-0460
2513 Station Dr Stockton (95215) *(P-19074)*

Bagatelos Glass Systems Inc (PA) ................................................ E ...... 916 364-3600
2750 Redding Ave Sacramento (95820) *(P-539)*

Bagatlos Archtctral GL Systems, Sacramento *Also Called: Bagatelos Glass Systems Inc (P-539)*

Bagcraftpapercon III LLC ............................................................... C ...... 626 961-6766
515 Turnbull Canyon Rd City Of Industry (91745) *(P-3962)*

**Bagelry Inc (PA)** ............................................................... E ...... 831 429-8049
320 Cedar St Ste A Santa Cruz (95060) *(P-1162)*

**Baghouse and Indus Shtmtl Svcs, Corona** *Also Called: MS Industrial Shtmtl Inc (P-8516)*

**Bagmasters, Corona** *Also Called: CTA Manufacturing Inc (P-2956)*

**Baier Marine Company Inc** ................................................ E ...... 800 455-3917
2920 Airway Ave Costa Mesa (92626) *(P-7982)*

**Bailey Valve Inc** ................................................................. E ...... 559 434-2838
264 W Fallbrook Ave Ste 105 Fresno (93711) *(P-9145)*

**Baja Designs, San Marcos** *Also Called: Bestop Baja LLC (P-16376)*

**Bake R Us Inc** ..................................................................... F ...... 310 630-5873
2632 Wilshire Blvd Ste 463 Santa Monica (90403) *(P-1163)*

**Bake Usa Inc** ....................................................................... E ...... 415 629-8274
10250 Santa Monica Blvd Los Angeles (90067) *(P-1164)*

**Baked In The Sun** ............................................................... C ...... 760 591-9045
2560 Progress St Vista (92081) *(P-1165)*

**Bakell LLC** ............................................................................ D ...... 800 292-2137
824 Lytle St Redlands (92374) *(P-354)*

**Bakemark, Pico Rivera** *Also Called: Bakemark USA LLC (P-17175)*

**Bakemark USA LLC** ............................................................ E ...... 510 487-8188
32621 Central Ave Union City (94587) *(P-2133)*

**Bakemark USA LLC (PA)** ................................................... C ...... 562 949-1054
7351 Crider Ave Pico Rivera (90660) *(P-17175)*

**Baker Commodities Inc** ..................................................... E ...... 323 318-8260
3001 Sierra Pine Ave Vernon (90058) *(P-1376)*

**Baker Commodities Inc (PA)** ............................................ C ...... 323 268-2801
4020 Bandini Blvd Vernon (90058) *(P-1377)*

**Baker Commodities Inc** ..................................................... E ...... 559 237-4320
16801 W Jensen Ave Kerman (93630) *(P-1378)*

**Baker Commodities Inc** ..................................................... E ...... 559 686-4797
7480 Hanford Armona Rd Hanford (93230) *(P-1379)*

**Baker Furnace, Brea** *Also Called: Baker Furnace Inc (P-10046)*

**Baker Furnace Inc** .............................................................. F ...... 714 223-7262
2680 Orbiter St Brea (92821) *(P-10046)*

**Bakers Kneaded LLC** ......................................................... E ...... 310 819-8700
148 W 132nd St Ste D Los Angeles (90061) *(P-1166)*

**Bakersfield Elc Mtr Repr Inc** ............................................. E ...... 661 327-3583
121 W Sumner St Bakersfield (93301) *(P-19225)*

**Bakersfield Machine Co Inc** .............................................. D ...... 661 709-1992
5605 North Chester Ave Ext Bakersfield (93308) *(P-10736)*

**Bakery Depot Inc** ................................................................ F ...... 323 261-8388
4489 Bandini Blvd Vernon (90058) *(P-1167)*

**Bal Seal Engineering LLC (DH)** ........................................ C ...... 949 460-2100
19650 Pauling Foothill Ranch (92610) *(P-9197)*

**Balaji Trading Inc** ............................................................... D ...... 909 444-7999
4850 Eucalyptus Ave Chino (91710) *(P-11753)*

**Balance Foods Inc** ............................................................. E ...... 323 838-5555
5743 Smithway St Ste 103 Commerce (90040) *(P-17140)*

**Balanced Body Inc (PA)** .................................................... F ...... 916 388-2838
5909 88th St Sacramento (95828) *(P-15784)*

**Balboa Manufacturing Co LLC (PA)** ............................... E ...... 858 715-0060
4909 Murphy Canyon Rd Ste 310 San Diego (92123) *(P-2462)*

**Balboa Water Group LLC (HQ)** ........................................ D ...... 714 384-0384
3030 Airway Ave Ste B Costa Mesa (92626) *(P-11311)*

**Balda C Brewer Inc (DH)** ................................................... D ...... 909 212-0290
4501 E Wall St Ontario (91761) *(P-9605)*

**Balda HK Plastics Inc** ........................................................ E ...... 760 757-1100
3229 Roymar Rd Oceanside (92058) *(P-8719)*

**Balda Precision Inc (DH)** .................................................. D ...... 760 757-1100
3233 Roymar Rd Oceanside (92058) *(P-8720)*

**Baldwin Brass, Lake Forest** *Also Called: Baldwin Hardware Corporation (P-7983)*

**Baldwin Contracting Co Inc** .............................................. F ...... 209 460-3785
400 S Lincoln St Stockton (95203) *(P-308)*

**Baldwin Contracting Co Inc (DH)** .................................... E ...... 530 891-6555
1764 Skyway Chico (95928) *(P-373)*

**Baldwin Hardware Corporation (DH)** .............................. A ...... 949 672-4000
19701 Da Vinci Lake Forest (92610) *(P-7983)*

**Balita Media Inc** ................................................................. F ...... 818 552-4503
2629 Foothill Blvd La Crescenta (91214) *(P-4072)*

**Ball Corporation** ................................................................. B ...... 209 848-6500
300 Greger St Oakdale (95361) *(P-7918)*

**Ball Metal Beverage Cont Corp** ....................................... C ...... 707 437-7516
2400 Huntington Dr Fairfield (94533) *(P-7919)*

**Ball Screws & Actuators Co Inc (DH)** ............................. D ...... 510 770-5932
48767 Kato Rd Fremont (94538) *(P-10066)*

**Ball TEC, Los Angeles** *Also Called: Micro Surface Engr Inc (P-7908)*

**Ballard & Tighe Publishers, Brea** *Also Called: Educational Ideas Incorporated (P-4328)*

**Ballast Point Brewing Company, San Diego** *Also Called: Kings & Convicts Bp LLC (P-1441)*

**Balletto Vineyards, Santa Rosa** *Also Called: Laguna Oaks Vnyards Winery Inc (P-1659)*

**Balsam Brands Inc (PA)** .................................................... D ...... 877 442-2572
50 Woodside Plz Ste 111 Redwood City (94061) *(P-16092)*

**Balsam Hill, Redwood City** *Also Called: Balsam Brands Inc (P-16092)*

**Balt Usa LLC** ....................................................................... D ...... 949 788-1443
29 Parker Ste 100 Irvine (92618) *(P-16576)*

**Baltic Ltvian Unvrsal Elec LLC** ........................................ E ...... 818 879-5200
5706 Corsa Ave Westlake Village (91362) *(P-11642)*

**Baltimore Aircoil Company Inc** ........................................ C ...... 559 673-9231
15341 Road 28 1/2 Madera (93638) *(P-10485)*

**Bambacigno Steel Company** ............................................ E ...... 209 524-9681
4930 Mchenry Ave Modesto (95356) *(P-7605)*

**Bambeck Systems Inc (PA)** .............................................. F ...... 949 250-3100
1921 Carnegie Ave Ste 3a Santa Ana (92705) *(P-14388)*

**Bamford Equipment, Oroville** *Also Called: J W Bamford Inc (P-3047)*

**Banbury Precision, Santa Clara** *Also Called: B P I Corp (P-10732)*

**Bandai Nmco Toys Clictbles AME (DH)** ......................... D ...... 949 271-6000
23 Odyssey Irvine (92618) *(P-15740)*

**Bandel Mfg Inc** ................................................................... E ...... 818 246-7493
4459 Alger St Los Angeles (90039) *(P-8820)*

**Bandlock Corporation** ....................................................... D ...... 909 947-7500
1734 S Vineyard Ave Ontario (91761) *(P-6734)*

**Bandmerch LLC** ................................................................. E ...... 818 736-4800
3945 Freedom Cir Ste 560 Santa Clara (95054) *(P-3002)*

**Bandy Manufacturing LLC** ............................................... D ...... 818 846-9020
3420 N San Fernando Blvd Burbank (91504) *(P-13797)*

**Bang Printing, Palmdale** *Also Called: D & J Printing Inc (P-4581)*

**Banh Hoi Minh Phung, Westminster** *Also Called: Minh Phung Incorporated (P-17196)*

**Banks Power Products, Azusa** *Also Called: Gale Banks Engineering (P-9328)*

**Banner Mattress Inc** .......................................................... D ...... 909 835-4200
1501 E Cooley Dr Ste B Colton (92324) *(P-3521)*

**Banner Solutions, Anaheim** *Also Called: Mid-West Wholesale Hardware Co (P-8016)*

**Banzai** ................................................................................... F ...... 310 231-7292
2229 Barry Ave Los Angeles (90064) *(P-16943)*

**Bapko Metal Inc** ................................................................. D ...... 714 639-9380
721 S Parker St Ste 300 Orange (92868) *(P-528)*

**Bar Ale Inc (PA)** .................................................................. E ...... 530 473-3333
1011 5th St Williams (95987) *(P-1120)*

**Bar Code Specialties Inc** .................................................. E ...... 877 411-2633
12272 Monarch St Garden Grove (92841) *(P-10331)*

**Bar Manufacturing Inc** ...................................................... D ...... 916 939-0551
3921 Sandstone Dr Ste 1 El Dorado Hills (95762) *(P-12355)*

**Bar Media Inc** ..................................................................... F ...... 415 861-5019
44 Gough St Ste 302 San Francisco (94103) *(P-4073)*

**Bar None Inc** ....................................................................... F ...... 714 259-8450
1302 Santa Fe Dr Tustin (92780) *(P-1833)*

**Bar-S Foods Co** .................................................................. E ...... 408 941-9958
392 Railroad Ct Milpitas (95035) *(P-632)*

**Bar-S Foods Co** .................................................................. E ...... 323 589-3600
4919 Alcoa Ave Vernon (90058) *(P-633)*

**Bar-S Foods Co. Los Angeles, Vernon** *Also Called: Bar-S Foods Co (P-633)*

**Barber Welding and Mfg Co** ............................................. E ...... 562 928-2570
7171 Scout Ave Bell Gardens (90201) *(P-10737)*

**Barber-Webb Company Inc (PA)** ..................................... E ...... 541 488-4821
12912 Lakeland Rd Santa Fe Springs (90670) *(P-6735)*

**Barbosa Cabinets Inc** ....................................................... B ...... 209 836-2501
2020 E Grant Line Rd Tracy (95304) *(P-3220)*

**Barcelona Merger Sub 3 LLC** ........................................... A ...... 650 427-5000
3401 Hillview Ave Palo Alto (94304) *(P-18090)*

**Barco Uniforms Inc** ........................................................... B ...... 310 323-7315
350 W Rosecrans Ave Gardena (90248) *(P-2557)*

**Bardex Corporation (PA)** .................................................. D ...... 805 964-7747
6338 Lindmar Dr Goleta (93117) *(P-9456)*

**Bare Nothings Inc (PA)** ..................................................... E ...... 714 848-8532
17705 Sampson Ln Huntington Beach (92647) *(P-2736)*

## ALPHABETIC SECTION — Baxter Healthcare Corporation

**Barebottle Brewing Company Inc** .................... D ...... 415 926-8617
1525 Cortland Ave San Francisco (94110) *(P-1424)*

**Barefoot Cellars, Santa Rosa** Also Called: Grape Links Inc *(P-1600)*

**Bargaining Hunter, El Dorado Hills** Also Called: Axiom Advisors & Cons Inc *(P-18086)*

**Barkens Hardchrome Inc** .................... E ...... 310 632-2000
239 E Greenleaf Blvd Compton (90220) *(P-9837)*

**Barkerblue Inc** .................... E ...... 650 696-2100
363 N Amphlett Blvd San Mateo (94401) *(P-5016)*

**Barksdale Inc (DH)** .................... D ...... 323 583-6243
3211 Fruitland Ave Los Angeles (90058) *(P-14848)*

**Barlow and Sons Printing Inc** .................... F ...... 707 664-9773
481 Aaron St Cotati (94931) *(P-4527)*

**Barlow Printing, Cotati** Also Called: Barlow and Sons Printing Inc *(P-4527)*

**Barnes Plastics, Gardena** Also Called: Barnes Plastics Inc *(P-6736)*

**Barnes Plastics Inc** .................... E ...... 310 329-6301
18903 Anelo Ave Gardena (90248) *(P-6736)*

**Barnes Welding Supply, Fresno** Also Called: Fresno Oxgn Wldg Suppliers Inc *(P-16815)*

**Barnett Performance Products, Ventura** Also Called: Barnett Tool & Engineering *(P-14053)*

**Barnett Tool & Engineering** .................... D ...... 805 642-9435
2238 Palma Dr Ventura (93003) *(P-14053)*

**Barney & Co California LLC** .................... F ...... 559 442-1752
2925 S Elm Ave Ste 101 Fresno (93706) *(P-2134)*

**Baron, Roseville** Also Called: Empire Paper Corporation *(P-16990)*

**Baron Brand Spices, Fairfield** Also Called: Abco Laboratories Inc *(P-5292)*

**Baron Paper Company, Oceanside** Also Called: Triple D and DS *(P-4056)*

**Barra LLC (HQ)** .................... B ...... 510 548-5442
2100 Milvia St Berkeley (94704) *(P-18091)*

**Barracuda, Campbell** Also Called: Barracuda Networks Inc *(P-18092)*

**Barracuda Networks Inc (PA)** .................... C ...... 408 342-5400
3175 Winchester Blvd Campbell (95008) *(P-18092)*

**Barranca Diamond Products, Torrance** Also Called: Barranca Holdings Ltd *(P-9661)*

**Barranca Holdings Ltd** .................... C ...... 310 523-5867
22815 Frampton Ave Torrance (90501) *(P-9661)*

**Barrel Ten Qarter Cir Land Inc** .................... E ...... 209 538-3131
33 Harlow Ct Napa (94558) *(P-1482)*

**Barrette Outdoor Living Inc** .................... E ...... 800 336-2383
1151 Palmyrita Ave Riverside (92507) *(P-7637)*

**Barrot Corporation** .................... E ...... 949 852-1640
1881 Kaiser Ave Irvine (92614) *(P-9606)*

**Barry Avenue Plating Co Inc** .................... D ...... 310 478-0078
2210 Barry Ave Los Angeles (90064) *(P-8929)*

**Barry Callebaut USA LLC** .................... C ...... 707 642-8200
1175 Commerce Blvd Ste D American Canyon (94503) *(P-1337)*

**Barry Controls Aerospace, Burbank** Also Called: Hutchinson Arospc & Indust Inc *(P-6502)*

**Barrys Printing Inc** .................... E ...... 818 998-8600
9005 Eton Ave Ste D Canoga Park (91304) *(P-4528)*

**Barta - Schoenewald Inc (PA)** .................... C ...... 805 389-1935
3805 Calle Tecate Camarillo (93012) *(P-11256)*

**Bartco Lighting Inc** .................... D ...... 714 230-3200
5761 Research Dr Huntington Beach (92649) *(P-16645)*

**Bartholomew Park Winery, Sonoma** Also Called: Vineburg Wine Company Inc *(P-1813)*

**Barton Perreira LLC** .................... E ...... 949 305-5360
459 Wald Irvine (92618) *(P-15594)*

**Barzillai Manufacturing Co Inc** .................... F ...... 909 947-4200
1889 N Omalley Way Upland (91784) *(P-8387)*

**Bas Engineering Inc** .................... F ...... 909 484-2575
11899 8th St Rancho Cucamonga (91730) *(P-19381)*

**Basalite Building Products LLC** .................... C ...... 916 645-3341
601 7th St Lincoln (95648) *(P-7265)*

**Basalite Building Products LLC** .................... E ...... 209 833-3670
11888 W Linne Rd Tracy (95377) *(P-7293)*

**Basalite Building Products LLC (HQ)** .................... E ...... 707 678-1901
2150 Douglas Blvd Ste 260 Roseville (95661) *(P-7313)*

**Basalite-Tracy, Tracy** Also Called: Basalite Building Products LLC *(P-7293)*

**Basaw, North Hollywood** Also Called: Basaw Manufacturing Inc *(P-3324)*

**Basaw Manufacturing, North Hollywood** Also Called: Basaw Manufacturing Inc *(P-3323)*

**Basaw Manufacturing Inc (PA)** .................... E ...... 818 765-6650
11323 Hartland St North Hollywood (91605) *(P-3323)*

**Basaw Manufacturing Inc** .................... E ...... 818 765-6650
13340 Raymer North Hollywood (91605) *(P-3324)*

**Base Crm** .................... F ...... 773 796-6266
1019 Market St Fl 1 San Francisco (94103) *(P-18093)*

**Base Lite Corporation** .................... E ...... 909 444-2776
12260 Eastend Ave Chino (91710) *(P-11492)*

**Baselite, Chino** Also Called: Base Lite Corporation *(P-11492)*

**BASF Catalysts, Fremont** Also Called: BASF Catalysts LLC *(P-5073)*

**BASF Catalysts LLC** .................... A ...... 510 490-2150
46820 Fremont Blvd Fremont (94538) *(P-5073)*

**BASF Corporation** .................... C ...... 714 921-1430
138 E Meats Ave Orange (92865) *(P-6129)*

**BASF Corporation** .................... D ...... 510 796-9911
38403 Cherry St Newark (94560) *(P-6130)*

**BASF Corporation** .................... E ...... 714 521-6085
6700 8th St Buena Park (90620) *(P-6131)*

**BASF Enzymes LLC (DH)** .................... D ...... 858 431-8520
3550 John Hopkins Ct San Diego (92121) *(P-6132)*

**BASF Venture Capital Amer Inc** .................... E ...... 510 445-6140
46820 Fremont Blvd Fremont (94538) *(P-6133)*

**Basic American Inc (PA)** .................... D ...... 800 227-4050
1676 N California Blvd Ste 525 Walnut Creek (94596) *(P-945)*

**Basic American Foods, Walnut Creek** Also Called: Basic American Inc *(P-945)*

**Basic Electronics Inc** .................... E ...... 714 530-2400
11371 Monarch St Garden Grove (92841) *(P-12921)*

**Basic Energy Services Inc** .................... E ...... 661 588-3800
6710 Stewart Way Bakersfield (93308) *(P-207)*

**Basic Industries Intl Inc (PA)** .................... E ...... 951 226-1500
10850 Wilshire Blvd Ste 760 Los Angeles (90024) *(P-8301)*

**Basin Marine Inc** .................... E ...... 949 673-0360
829 Harbor Island Dr Ste A Newport Beach (92660) *(P-14029)*

**Basin Marine Shipyard, Newport Beach** Also Called: Basin Marine Inc *(P-14029)*

**Basmat Inc (PA)** .................... D ...... 310 325-2063
1531 240th St Harbor City (90710) *(P-8388)*

**Basque French Bakery, Fresno** Also Called: Fresno French Bread Bakery Inc *(P-1204)*

**Bassani Exhaust, Anaheim** Also Called: Bassani Manufacturing *(P-9250)*

**Bassani Manufacturing** .................... E ...... 714 630-1821
2900 E La Jolla St Anaheim (92806) *(P-9250)*

**Battery Technology Inc (PA)** .................... D ...... 626 336-6878
16651 E Johnson Dr City Of Industry (91745) *(P-13131)*

**Battery-Biz Inc** .................... D ...... 800 848-6782
1380 Flynn Rd Camarillo (93012) *(P-13167)*

**BATTERYSPACE.COM, Richmond** Also Called: AA Portable Power Corporation *(P-13130)*

**Batth Farms, Caruthers** Also Called: Batth Farms Inc *(P-36)*

**Batth Farms Inc** .................... D ...... 559 864-9421
5434 W Kamm Ave Caruthers (93609) *(P-36)*

**Bau Furniture Mfg Inc** .................... D ...... 949 643-2729
21 Kelly Ln Ladera Ranch (92694) *(P-3433)*

**Baugher Ranch Organics Inc** .................... E ...... 530 865-4015
7030 County Road 25 Orland (95963) *(P-37)*

**Baumann Engineering** .................... D ...... 909 621-4181
212 S Cambridge Ave Claremont (91711) *(P-10738)*

**Bausch & Lomb Surgical Div, Irvine** Also Called: Eyeonics Inc *(P-15601)*

**Bausch Health Americas Inc** .................... C ...... 707 793-2600
1330 Redwood Way Ste C Petaluma (94954) *(P-5354)*

**Bavarian Nordic Inc** .................... E ...... 919 600-1260
6275 Nancy Ridge Dr Ste 110 San Diego (92121) *(P-4018)*

**Baxalta US Inc** .................... A ...... 818 240-5600
4501 Colorado Blvd Los Angeles (90039) *(P-5355)*

**Baxalta US Inc** .................... A ...... 805 498-8664
1700 Rancho Conejo Blvd Thousand Oaks (91320) *(P-14992)*

**Baxano Inc** .................... E ...... 408 514-2200
655 River Oaks Pkwy San Jose (95134) *(P-14993)*

**Baxco Pharmaceutical Inc (PA)** .................... F ...... 626 610-7088
2393 Bateman Ave Irwindale (91010) *(P-5356)*

**Baxter Bioscience, Hayward** Also Called: Baxter Healthcare Corporation *(P-5809)*

**Baxter Healthcare Corporation** .................... D ...... 510 723-2000
21026 Alexander Ct Hayward (94545) *(P-5809)*

**Baxter Healthcare Corporation** .................... F ...... 949 250-2500
1402 Alton Pkwy Irvine (92606) *(P-14994)*

**Baxter Healthcare Corporation** .................... C ...... 949 474-6301
17511 Armstrong Ave Irvine (92614) *(P-14995)*

# Baxter Healthcare Corporation

**ALPHABETIC SECTION**

**Baxter Healthcare Corporation** ............................................. C ...... 805 372-3000
1 Baxter Way Ste 100 Westlake Village (91362) *(P-17028)*

**Baxter Medication Delivery, Irvine** *Also Called: Baxter Healthcare Corporation (P-14995)*

**Baxter Welding, Oroville** *Also Called: Baxter Wldg & Fabrication LLC (P-19184)*

**Baxter Wldg & Fabrication LLC** ............................................. F ...... 530 321-9216
8 Dorr Ln Oroville (95966) *(P-19184)*

**Bay Area Beverage Company, Richmond** *Also Called: T F Louderback Inc (P-17260)*

**Bay Area Circuits Inc** ............................................................. E ...... 510 933-9000
44358 Old Warm Springs Blvd Fremont (94538) *(P-12064)*

**Bay Area Indus Filtration Inc** ................................................ E ...... 510 562-6373
6355 Coliseum Way Oakland (94621) *(P-10076)*

**Bay Area Labels, San Jose** *Also Called: B A L (P-4846)*

**Bay Area Pallette Company, Antioch** *Also Called: Chep (usa) Inc (P-3334)*

**Bay Area Reporter, San Francisco** *Also Called: Bar Media Inc (P-4073)*

**Bay Associates Wire Tech Corp (DH)** ................................... E ...... 510 988-3800
46840 Lakeview Blvd Fremont (94538) *(P-2534)*

**Bay Bolt Inc** ........................................................................... F ...... 510 532-1188
4610 Malat St Oakland (94601) *(P-16747)*

**Bay Cities Container Corp (PA)** ............................................ D ...... 562 948-3751
5138 Industry Ave Pico Rivera (90660) *(P-3820)*

**Bay Cities Container Corp** ................................................... F ...... 562 302-2552
9206 Santa Fe Springs Rd Santa Fe Springs (90670) *(P-3821)*

**Bay Cities Container Corp** ................................................... E ...... 562 551-2946
9206 Santa Fe Springs Rd Santa Fe Springs (90670) *(P-3925)*

**Bay Cities Metal Products, Gardena** *Also Called: Bay Cities Tin Shop Inc (P-8389)*

**Bay Cities Packaging & Design, Pico Rivera** *Also Called: Bay Cities Container Corp (P-3820)*

**Bay Cities Tin Shop Inc** ........................................................ C ...... 310 660-0351
301 E Alondra Blvd Gardena (90248) *(P-8389)*

**Bay City Marine Inc (PA)** ...................................................... E ...... 619 477-3991
1625 Cleveland Ave National City (91950) *(P-8100)*

**Bay Elctrnic Spport Trnics Inc** ............................................. C ...... 408 432-3222
2090 Fortune Dr San Jose (95131) *(P-12065)*

**Bay Guardian Company** ....................................................... E ...... 415 255-3100
135 Micaicaippi St San Francisco (94107) *(P-4074)*

**Bay Precision Machining Inc** ............................................... F ...... 650 365-3010
815 Sweeney Ave Ste D Redwood City (94063) *(P-10739)*

**Bay Sheet Metal Inc** ............................................................. E ...... 619 401-9270
9343 Bond Ave Ste C El Cajon (92021) *(P-8390)*

**Bay Ship & Yacht Co (PA)** .................................................... C ...... 510 337-9122
2900 Main St Ste 2100 Alameda (94501) *(P-14000)*

**Bay Ship & Yacht Co., Alameda** *Also Called: Bay Ship & Yacht Co (P-14000)*

**Bay Standard Inc** ................................................................. D ...... 925 634-1181
24485 Marsh Creek Rd Brentwood (94513) *(P-16863)*

**Bay Standard Manufacturing Inc (PA)** ................................. E ...... 925 634-1181
24485 Marsh Creek Rd Brentwood (94513) *(P-8744)*

**Bay State Milling Company** ................................................. E ...... 530 666-6565
360 Hanson Way Woodland (95776) *(P-1057)*

**Bay-TEC Engineering** ........................................................... D ...... 714 257-1680
5130 Fulton Dr Ste X Fairfield (94534) *(P-19382)*

**Bayer Corporation** ............................................................... E ...... 412 777-2000
800 Dwight Way Berkeley (94710) *(P-5140)*

**Bayer Corporation** ............................................................... E ...... 408 406-8491
7025 Angelo Ln Gilroy (95020) *(P-5357)*

**Bayer Corporation** ............................................................... D ...... 510 705-5000
820 Parker Berkeley (94710) *(P-14996)*

**Bayer Diabetes Care, Sunnyvale** *Also Called: Bayer Healthcare LLC (P-5361)*

**Bayer Healthcare LLC** ......................................................... C ...... 510 597-6150
5885 Hollis St Emeryville (94608) *(P-5358)*

**Bayer Healthcare LLC** ......................................................... C ...... 510 705-7545
800 Dwight Way Berkeley (94710) *(P-5359)*

**Bayer Healthcare LLC** ......................................................... D ...... 510 705-4421
747 Grayson St Berkeley (94710) *(P-5360)*

**Bayer Healthcare LLC** ......................................................... E ...... 408 499-0606
510 Oakmead Pkwy Sunnyvale (94085) *(P-5361)*

**Bayfab Metals Inc** ............................................................... E ...... 510 568-8950
870 Doolittle Dr San Leandro (94577) *(P-8255)*

**Bayless Manufacturing LLC** ............................................... C ...... 661 257-3373
26140 Avenue Hall Valencia (91355) *(P-10740)*

**Bayshore Lights, San Francisco** *Also Called: Ijk & Co Inc (P-13249)*

**Bayspec, San Jose** *Also Called: Bayspec Inc (P-14621)*

**Bayspec Inc** ......................................................................... E ...... 408 512-5928
1101 Mckay Dr San Jose (95131) *(P-14621)*

**Baytech Digital Inc** .............................................................. E ...... 408 533-8519
1798 Technology Dr Ste 178 San Jose (95110) *(P-19003)*

**Bayview Plastic Solutions Inc** ............................................. E ...... 510 360-0001
43651 S Grimmer Blvd Fremont (94538) *(P-6737)*

**Baywa R.E., Irvine** *Also Called: Baywa RE Operation Svcs LLC (P-405)*

**Baywa R.E.renewable Energy, Irvine** *Also Called: Baywa RE Solar Projects LLC (P-12357)*

**Baywa RE Epc LLC** ............................................................. E ...... 949 398-3915
17901 Von Karman Ave Ste 1050 Irvine (92614) *(P-12356)*

**Baywa RE Operation Svcs LLC** ........................................... E ...... 949 398-3915
18575 Jamboree Rd Ste 850 Irvine (92612) *(P-405)*

**Baywa RE Solar Projects LLC (DH)** .................................... F ...... 949 398-3915
18575 Jamboree Rd Ste 850 Irvine (92612) *(P-12357)*

**Baywood Cellars Inc** ........................................................... E ...... 415 606-4640
5573 W Woodbridge Rd Lodi (95242) *(P-1483)*

**Bazz Houston Co, Garden Grove** *Also Called: Houston Bazz Co (P-8850)*

**Bb Apparel, Los Angeles** *Also Called: B2 Apparel Inc (P-2891)*

**Bb Co Inc** ............................................................................. E ...... 213 550-1158
1753 E 21st St Los Angeles (90058) *(P-2737)*

**Bbe Sound Inc (PA)** ............................................................. E ...... 714 897-6766
2548 Fender Ave Fullerton (92831) *(P-15712)*

**Bbeautiful LLC** ..................................................................... E ...... 626 610-2332
1361 Mountain View Cir Azusa (91702) *(P-5947)*

**Bbm Fairway Inc (PA)** .......................................................... C
3520 Challenger St Torrance (90503) *(P-4231)*

**Bbs, San Marcos** *Also Called: Bbs Manufacturing Inc (P-15785)*

**Bbs Manufacturing Inc** ........................................................ F ...... 760 798-8011
1905 Diamond St Ste A San Marcos (92078) *(P-15785)*

**Bcc Dissolution Inc** ............................................................. E ...... 323 583-3444
2929 S Santa Fe Ave Los Angeles (90058) *(P-9251)*

**Bcd Food Inc** ....................................................................... E ...... 310 323-1200
320 W Carob St Compton (90220) *(P-2135)*

**Bcd Industries Corp** ............................................................ F ...... 760 927-8988
24298 Via Vargas Dr Moreno Valley (92553) *(P-16093)*

**Bcp Systems Inc** ................................................................. D ...... 714 202-3900
1560 S Sinclair St Anaheim (92806) *(P-19020)*

**Bd Carefusion, San Diego** *Also Called: Carefusion Corporation (P-15524)*

**Bdc Distribution Center, Redlands** *Also Called: Becton Dickinson and Company (P-14625)*

**Bdc Epoxy Systems Inc** ...................................................... E ...... 562 944-6177
12903 Sunshine Ave Santa Fe Springs (90670) *(P-5141)*

**Bdfco Inc** ............................................................................. D ...... 714 228-2900
1926 Kauai Dr Costa Mesa (92626) *(P-11983)*

**Bdg Innovations LLC (PA)** .................................................. E ...... 855 725-9555
6001 Outfall Cir Sacramento (95828) *(P-19383)*

**BDR Industries Inc** .............................................................. E ...... 818 341-2112
9700 Owensmouth Ave Lbby Chatsworth (91311) *(P-10332)*

**Be Beauty, Garden Grove** *Also Called: Cali Chem Inc (P-5952)*

**Be Bop Clothing** ................................................................... B ...... 323 846-0121
5833 Avalon Blvd Los Angeles (90003) *(P-2738)*

**Bea Systems Inc (HQ)** ......................................................... A ...... 650 506-7000
2315 N 1st St San Jose (95131) *(P-17885)*

**Beach House Group, El Segundo** *Also Called: Beach House Group LLC (P-16094)*

**Beach House Group LLC** .................................................... D ...... 310 356-6180
222 N Pacific Coast Hwy Fl 10 El Segundo (90245) *(P-16094)*

**Beach News, Encinitas** *Also Called: Coast News Inc (P-4095)*

**Beach Paving Inc** ................................................................ F ...... 714 978-2414
749 N Poplar St Orange (92868) *(P-519)*

**Beach Reporter, Rllng Hls Est** *Also Called: National Media Inc (P-4167)*

**Beach Reporter, The, Hermosa Beach** *Also Called: National Media Inc (P-4166)*

**Beach State, Moorpark** *Also Called: Picnic Time Inc (P-16204)*

**Beacon Manufacturing Inc** ................................................. E ...... 714 529-0980
1000 Beacon St Brea (92821) *(P-5232)*

**Beale Afb, Beale Afb** *Also Called: Military Advantage Inc (P-2561)*

**Beale Air Force Base, Marysville** *Also Called: Hf Group Inc (P-10093)*

**Beall Trailers of California Inc** ............................................. E ...... 209 669-7151
1301 South Ave Turlock (95380) *(P-13612)*

**Beam Global (PA)** ................................................................ C ...... 858 799-4583
5660 Eastgate Dr San Diego (92121) *(P-12358)*

**Beam On Technology Corporation** ..................................... E ...... 408 982-0161
317 Brokaw Rd Santa Clara (95050) *(P-10077)*

# ALPHABETIC SECTION — BELAGIO ENTERPRISES INC

**Beam Wine Estates, Healdsburg** *Also Called: Constltition Brnds US Oprtons I (P-1517)*

**Beamreach Solar, Milpitas** *Also Called: Beamreach Solar Inc (P-12359)*

**Beamreach Solar Inc** .............................................................. E ...... 408 240-3800
1530 Mccarthy Blvd Milpitas (95035) *(P-12359)*

**Bear Creek Winery, Lodi** *Also Called: Goldstone Land Company LLC (P-1599)*

**Bear State Kitchen, Los Angeles** *Also Called: Jackson Manufacturing LLC (P-896)*

**Bear State Water Heating LLC** ............................................ F ...... 951 269-3753
43234 Business Park Dr Ste 105 Temecula (92590) *(P-14355)*

**Bears For Humanity Inc** ........................................................ E ...... 866 325-1668
841 Ocean View Ave San Mateo (94401) *(P-6134)*

**Bearsaver, Ontario** *Also Called: Compumeric Engineering Inc (P-8413)*

**Beats By Dre, Culver City** *Also Called: Beats Electronics LLC (P-11643)*

**Beats Electronics LLC** ........................................................... B ...... 424 326-4679
8600 Hayden Pl Culver City (90232) *(P-11643)*

**Beats Music LLC** .................................................................... D ...... 415 590-5104
235 2nd St San Francisco (94105) *(P-18094)*

**Beaulieu Vineyard, Rutherford** *Also Called: Treasury Wine Estates Americas (P-1848)*

**Beaumont Juice LLC** ............................................................. D ...... 951 769-7171
550 B St Beaumont (92223) *(P-877)*

**Beaumont Nielsen Marine Inc** .............................................. E ...... 619 223-2628
2420 Shelter Island Dr San Diego (92106) *(P-19075)*

**Beautiful Slides Inc** ............................................................... E ...... 415 236-0955
9836 Springfield St Oakland (94603) *(P-18095)*

**Beautiful.ai, Oakland** *Also Called: Beautiful Slides Inc (P-18095)*

**Beauty & Health International** .............................................. E ...... 714 903-9730
7541 Anthony Ave Garden Grove (92841) *(P-5362)*

**Beauty 21 Cosmetics Inc** ....................................................... C ...... 909 945-2220
2021 S Archibald Ave Ontario (91761) *(P-17029)*

**Beauty Craft Furniture Corp** ................................................. E ...... 916 428-2238
3316 51st Ave Sacramento (95823) *(P-3434)*

**Beauty Health Company (PA)** ............................................... B ...... 800 603-4996
2165 E Spring St Long Beach (90806) *(P-14997)*

**Beauty Tent Inc** ...................................................................... E ...... 323 717-7131
1131 N Kenmore Ave Apt 6 Los Angeles (90029) *(P-16095)*

**Bebe Studio Inc** ..................................................................... C ...... 213 362-2323
10250 Santa Monica Blvd Ste 6 Los Angeles (90067) *(P-17531)*

**Beber Inc** ................................................................................ E ...... 530 487-8676
144 Meyers St Ste 140 Chico (95928) *(P-826)*

**Beber Almond Milk, Chico** *Also Called: Beber Inc (P-826)*

**Bebop Sensors Inc** ................................................................ E ...... 503 875-4990
970 Miller Ave Berkeley (94708) *(P-2532)*

**Becca, Anaheim** *Also Called: The Lunada Bay Corporation (P-2866)*

**Bechler Cams Inc** .................................................................. F ...... 714 774-5150
1313 S State College Pkwy Anaheim (92806) *(P-10741)*

**Becker Automotive Design USA, Oxnard** *Also Called: Becker Automotive Designs Inc (P-13343)*

**Becker Automotive Designs Inc** ........................................... E ...... 805 487-5227
1711 Ives Ave Oxnard (93033) *(P-13343)*

**Becker Specialty Corporation** ............................................... D ...... 909 356-1095
15310 Arrow Blvd Fontana (92335) *(P-12830)*

**Beckers Fabrication Inc** ........................................................ E ...... 714 692-1600
22465 La Palma Ave Yorba Linda (92887) *(P-3946)*

**Beckman Coulter Inc** ............................................................. C ...... 760 438-9151
2470 Faraday Ave Carlsbad (92010) *(P-14622)*

**Beckman Coulter Inc** ............................................................. C ...... 818 970-2161
250 S Kraemer Blvd Brea (92821) *(P-14998)*

**Beckman Coulter Inc (HQ)** .................................................... A ...... 714 993-5321
250 S Kraemer Blvd Brea (92821) *(P-14623)*

**Beckman Industries** .............................................................. F ...... 805 375-3003
701 Del Norte Blvd Ste 205 Oxnard (93030) *(P-15908)*

**Beckman Instruments Inc** ..................................................... D ...... 626 309-0110
8733 Scott St Rosemead (91770) *(P-14624)*

**Beckmann's Bakery, Santa Cruz** *Also Called: Beckmanns Old World Bakery Ltd (P-1168)*

**Beckmanns Old World Bakery Ltd** ....................................... D ...... 831 423-9242
1053 17th Ave Santa Cruz (95062) *(P-1168)*

**Beco Baby Carrier, Costa Mesa** *Also Called: Caperon Designs Inc (P-15743)*

**Becton Dickinson and Company** ......................................... D ...... 909 748-7300
2200 W San Bernardino Ave Redlands (92374) *(P-14625)*

**Becton Dickinson and Company** ......................................... D ...... 734 812-5271
86 Montecito Vista Dr San Jose (95111) *(P-14999)*

**Becton Dickinson and Company** ......................................... A ...... 734 812-5271
155 N Mccarthy Blvd Milpitas (95035) *(P-15000)*

**Becton Dickinson and Company** ......................................... D ...... 888 876-4287
3750 Torrey View Ct San Diego (92130) *(P-15001)*

**Becton Dickinson and Company** ......................................... B ...... 408 432-9475
2350 Qume Dr San Jose (95131) *(P-15002)*

**Becton Dickinson and Company** ......................................... E ...... 858 617-2000
3750 Torrey View Ct San Diego (92130) *(P-15003)*

**Bed Time Originals, El Segundo** *Also Called: Lambs & Ivy Inc (P-2935)*

**Bedrosian's Tile, Sylmar** *Also Called: Paragon Industries Inc (P-484)*

**Bee Content Design Inc (PA)** ................................................ E ...... 888 962-4587
450 Townsend St San Francisco (94107) *(P-18096)*

**Bee Wire & Cable Inc** ............................................................ E ...... 909 923-5800
2850 E Spruce St Ontario (91761) *(P-7772)*

**Beef Jerky Factory, Colton** *Also Called: Hawa Corporation (P-646)*

**Beef Packers Inc** .................................................................... B ...... 559 268-5586
3115 S Fig Ave Fresno (93706) *(P-582)*

**Beeline Group LLC** ................................................................ D ...... 510 477-5400
30941 San Clemente St Hayward (94544) *(P-15947)*

**Beemak Plastics LLC** ............................................................ D ...... 800 421-4393
1515 S Harris Ct Anaheim (92806) *(P-6738)*

**Beemak-Idl Display Products, Anaheim** *Also Called: Beemak Plastics LLC (P-6738)*

**Beer Beer & More Beer, Pittsburg** *Also Called: Moreflavor Inc (P-1449)*

**Beewise US Inc** ...................................................................... E ...... 888 706-3907
3001 Bishop Dr Ste 300 San Ramon (94583) *(P-19028)*

**Bega, Carpinteria** *Also Called: Bega North America Inc (P-11582)*

**Bega North America Inc** ........................................................ D ...... 805 684-0533
1000 Bega Way Carpinteria (93013) *(P-11582)*

**Begovic Industries Inc** .......................................................... E ...... 650 594-2861
1725 Old County Rd San Carlos (94070) *(P-10742)*

**Behr Holdings, Santa Ana** *Also Called: Behr Sales Inc (P-6070)*

**Behr Holdings Corporation (HQ)** .......................................... E ...... 714 545-7101
3400 W Segerstrom Ave Santa Ana (92704) *(P-6068)*

**Behr Paint Company, Santa Ana** *Also Called: Behr Process LLC (P-6069)*

**Behr Process LLC (DH)** ......................................................... A ...... 714 545-7101
1801 E Saint Andrew Pl Santa Ana (92705) *(P-6069)*

**Behr Process Sales Company** .............................................. E ...... 714 545-7101
3000 S Main St Apt 84e Santa Ana (92707) *(P-19547)*

**Behr Sales Inc (HQ)** ............................................................... C ...... 714 545-7101
3400 W Segerstrom Ave Santa Ana (92704) *(P-6070)*

**BEI Industrial Encoders, Thousand Oaks** *Also Called: Carros Sensors Systems Co LLC (P-14856)*

**BEI Industrial Encoders, Thousand Oaks** *Also Called: Sensata Technologies Inc (P-19044)*

**BEI North America LLC (DH)** ................................................ C ...... 805 716-0642
1461 Lawrence Dr Thousand Oaks (91320) *(P-14849)*

**Beigene Usa Inc** ..................................................................... B ...... 619 733-1842
1900 Powell St Ste 500 Emeryville (94608) *(P-5233)*

**Beigene Usa Inc** ..................................................................... B ...... 877 828-5568
1840 Gateway Dr Fl 3 San Mateo (94404) *(P-5363)*

**Bel Air Market 501, Sacramento** *Also Called: Bel Air Mart (P-17370)*

**Bel Air Market 502, Sacramento** *Also Called: Bel Air Mart (P-17372)*

**Bel Air Market 509, Roseville** *Also Called: Bel Air Mart (P-17369)*

**Bel Air Market 510, Sacramento** *Also Called: Bel Air Mart (P-17371)*

**Bel Air Mart** ............................................................................ D ...... 916 786-6101
1039 Sunrise Ave Roseville (95661) *(P-17369)*

**Bel Air Mart** ............................................................................ C ...... 916 739-8647
6231 Fruitridge Rd Sacramento (95820) *(P-17370)*

**Bel Air Mart** ............................................................................ D ...... 916 920-2493
1540 W El Camino Ave Sacramento (95833) *(P-17371)*

**Bel Air Mart** ............................................................................ C ...... 916 972-0555
4320 Arden Way Sacramento (95864) *(P-17372)*

**Bel Aire Displays** ................................................................... D ...... 510 232-5100
506 W Ohio Ave Richmond (94804) *(P-4847)*

**Bel Power Solutions Inc (HQ)** .............................................. D ...... 866 513-2839
2390 Walsh Ave Santa Clara (95051) *(P-12831)*

**Bel-Air Cases, Ontario** *Also Called: California Quality Plas Inc (P-6758)*

**Bel-Air Machining Co** ............................................................ F ...... 714 953-6616
151 E Columbine Ave Santa Ana (92707) *(P-10743)*

**Belagio Enterprises Inc** ......................................................... E ...... 323 731-6934
3737 Ross St Vernon (90058) *(P-2403)*

**Belching Beaver Brewery** ........................................... C ...... 760 599-5832
1334 Rocky Point Dr Oceanside (92056) *(P-17613)*

**Belco Cabinets Inc** .................................................... F ...... 209 334-5437
1109 Black Diamond Way Lodi (95240) *(P-8256)*

**Belco Packaging Systems Inc** ................................. E ...... 626 357-9566
910 S Mountain Ave Monrovia (91016) *(P-10014)*

**Belden Inc** .................................................................. A ...... 310 639-9473
1048 E Burgrove St Carson (90746) *(P-7773)*

**Belding Golf Bag Company, The, Oxnard** *Also Called: Illah Sports Inc (P-15829)*

**Belhome Inc** ............................................................... E ...... 310 618-8437
560 Alaska Ave Torrance (90503) *(P-9722)*

**Belinda, Vernon** *Also Called: New Pride Corporation (P-17096)*

**Belkasoft LLC** ............................................................ E ...... 650 272-0384
702 San Conrado Ter Unit 1 Sunnyvale (94085) *(P-18097)*

**Belkin, El Segundo** *Also Called: Belkin Inc (P-11644)*

**Belkin Inc** .................................................................... A ...... 800 223-5546
555 S Aviation Blvd El Segundo (90245) *(P-11644)*

**Belkin Components, El Segundo** *Also Called: Belkin International Inc (P-10333)*

**Belkin International Inc (DH)** .................................. B ...... 310 751-5100
555 S Aviation Blvd Ste 180 El Segundo (90245) *(P-10333)*

**Bell Bros Steel Inc** ..................................................... F ...... 951 784-0903
1510 Palmyrita Ave Riverside (92507) *(P-8101)*

**Bell Foundry Co (PA)** ............................................... E ...... 323 564-5701
5310 Southern Ave South Gate (90280) *(P-15786)*

**Bell Powder Coating Inc** .......................................... F ...... 805 658-2233
4747 Mcgrath St Ventura (93003) *(P-9054)*

**Bell Sports Inc (HQ)** ................................................. D ...... 469 417-6600
16752 Armstrong Ave Irvine (92606) *(P-15787)*

**Bell-Carter Foods Inc** ............................................... C ...... 559 568-1650
20497 Avenue 184 Strathmore (93267) *(P-878)*

**Bell-Carter Foods Inc** ............................................... E ...... 209 549-5939
4207 Finch Rd Modesto (95357) *(P-879)*

**Bell-Carter Foods LLC** ............................................. B ...... 530 528-4820
1012 2nd St Corning (96021) *(P-975)*

**BELL-CARTER FOODS, INC., Strathmore** *Also Called: Bell-Carter Foods Inc (P-878)*

**Bell-Carter Olive Company, Walnut Creek** *Also Called: Bell-Carter Olive Packing Co (P-880)*

**Bell-Carter Olive Packing Co (PA)** ......................... C ...... 209 549-5939
590 Ygnacio Valley Rd Ste 300 Walnut Creek (94596) *(P-880)*

**Bell-Carter Packaging, Modesto** *Also Called: Bell-Carter Foods Inc (P-879)*

**Bella Sun Luci, Chico** *Also Called: Mooney Farms (P-84)*

**Bella Union Winery, Saint Helena** *Also Called: FN Cellars LLC (P-1573)*

**Bella Viva Orchards Inc** ........................................... E ...... 209 883-9015
7030 Hughson Ave Hughson (95326) *(P-53)*

**Belldini, Los Angeles** *Also Called: Flirt Inc (P-17091)*

**Bellingham Marine Inds Inc** .................................... E ...... 707 678-2385
8810 Sparling Ln Dixon (95620) *(P-393)*

**Bellissimo Distribution LLC** .................................... E ...... 760 292-9100
1389 Park Center Dr Vista (92081) *(P-849)*

**Bellou Publishing, San Jose** *Also Called: Times Media Incorporated (P-4212)*

**Bellows Mfg & RES Inc** ............................................ E ...... 818 838-1333
864 Arroyo St San Fernando (91340) *(P-8102)*

**Bellrock Media Inc (PA)** ........................................... E ...... 310 315-2727
11500 W Olympic Blvd Ste 400 Los Angeles (90064) *(P-17886)*

**Belmont Brewing Company Inc** ............................. E ...... 562 433-3891
25 39th Pl Long Beach (90803) *(P-17564)*

**Belport Company Inc (PA)** ..................................... F ...... 805 484-1051
4825 Calle Alto Camarillo (93012) *(P-15439)*

**Belt Drives Ltd** .......................................................... E ...... 714 693-1313
1959 N Main St Orange (92865) *(P-14054)*

**Bema Electronic Mfg Inc** ......................................... D ...... 510 490-7770
4545 Cushing Pkwy Fremont (94538) *(P-12066)*

**Bemco Inc (PA)** ......................................................... E ...... 805 583-4970
2255 Union Pl Simi Valley (93065) *(P-14626)*

**Beme International LLC** .......................................... F ...... 858 751-0580
7333 Ronson Rd San Diego (92111) *(P-2922)*

**Ben Franklin Press, Napa** *Also Called: Ben Franklin Press & Label Co (P-4529)*

**Ben Franklin Press & Label Co** .............................. E ...... 707 253-8250
480 Technology Way Napa (94558) *(P-4529)*

**Bench 2 Bench Technologies, Fullerton** *Also Called: Winonics Inc (P-12263)*

**Benchling Inc (PA)** ................................................... E ...... 415 590-2798
680 Folsom St Ste 800 San Francisco (94107) *(P-18098)*

**Benchmark, Moorpark** *Also Called: Benchmark Elec Mfg Sltions Mrpa (P-12068)*

**Benchmark Elec Mfg Sltions Inc (HQ)** ................. D ...... 805 222-1303
5550 Hellyer Ave San Jose (95138) *(P-12067)*

**Benchmark Elec Mfg Sltions Mrpa** ....................... A ...... 805 532-2800
200 Science Dr Moorpark (93021) *(P-12068)*

**Benchmark Elec Phoenix Inc** .................................. B ...... 619 397-2402
1659 Gailes Blvd San Diego (92154) *(P-12069)*

**Benchmark Electronics Inc** ..................................... E ...... 510 360-2800
42701 Christy St Fremont (94538) *(P-12070)*

**Benchmark Electronics Inc** ..................................... E ...... 925 363-1151
2301 Arnold Industrial Way Ste G Concord (94520) *(P-12071)*

**Benchmark Secure Technology, Santa Ana** *Also Called: Secure Comm Systems Inc (P-11942)*

**Benchmark Thermal, Grass Valley** *Also Called: Manufacturers Coml Fin LLC (P-8071)*

**Benchmark Thermal Corporation** ......................... D ...... 530 477-5011
13185 Nevada City Ave Grass Valley (95945) *(P-8060)*

**Benchmarkone** .......................................................... F ...... 314 288-0399
5500 Bolsa Ave Ste 245 Huntington Beach (92649) *(P-18099)*

**Bend-Tek Inc (PA)** .................................................... E ...... 714 210-8966
2205 S Yale St Santa Ana (92704) *(P-8391)*

**Benda Tool & Model Works Inc** ............................ E ...... 510 741-3170
900 Alfred Nobel Dr Hercules (94547) *(P-9607)*

**Bender Ccp Inc (PA)** ................................................ C ...... 323 232-2371
2150 E 37th St Vernon (90058) *(P-10744)*

**Bender Ccp Inc** ......................................................... E ...... 619 232-5719
757 Main St Unit 102 Chula Vista (91911) *(P-10745)*

**Bender Ready Mix Inc** ............................................. E ...... 714 560-0744
516 S Santa Fe St Santa Ana (92705) *(P-7407)*

**Bender Ready Mix Concrete, Santa Ana** *Also Called: Bender Ready Mix Inc (P-7407)*

**Bender US, Vernon** *Also Called: Bender Ccp Inc (P-10744)*

**Bendick Precision Inc** .............................................. F ...... 626 445-0217
56 La Porte St Arcadia (91006) *(P-10746)*

**Bendpak Inc (PA)** ..................................................... C ...... 805 933-9970
30440 Agoura Rd Agoura Hills (91301) *(P-9838)*

**Beneficial AG Services, Ontario** *Also Called: Circle Green Inc (P-6140)*

**Benevolence Food Products LLC** ........................ E ...... 888 832-3738
2761 Saturn St Ste D Brea (92821) *(P-2136)*

**Benicia Fabrication & Mch Inc** .............................. C ...... 707 745-8111
101 E Channel Rd Benicia (94510) *(P-8302)*

**Benicia Herald, Benicia** *Also Called: Gibson Printing & Pubg Inc (P-4122)*

**Benjamin Moore Authorized Ret, Corona** *Also Called: Ganahl Lumber Company (P-17332)*

**Bennett & Bennett Inc** ............................................. E ...... 559 582-9336
955 S Commerce Way Lemoore (93245) *(P-406)*

**Bennett Bnnett Irrgtion System, Lemoore** *Also Called: Bennett & Bennett Inc (P-406)*

**Bennett's Bakery, Sacramento** *Also Called: Bennetts Baking Company (P-1285)*

**Bennetts Baking Company** ..................................... F ...... 916 481-3349
2530 Tesla Way Sacramento (95825) *(P-1285)*

**Benny Enterprises Inc** ............................................. E ...... 619 592-4455
1100 N Johnson Ave Ste 110 El Cajon (92020) *(P-17258)*

**Benrich Service Company Inc (PA)** ...................... E ...... 714 241-0284
3190 Airport Loop Dr Ste G Costa Mesa (92626) *(P-19076)*

**Bent Manufacturing Co Inc** .................................... D ...... 714 842-0600
17311 Nichols Ln Huntington Beach (92647) *(P-6739)*

**Bent Manufacturing Company, Huntington Beach** *Also Called: Bent Manufacturing Co Inc (P-6739)*

**Bentec Medical** ......................................................... D ...... 530 406-3333
1380 E Beamer St Woodland (95776) *(P-15004)*

**Bentec Medical Opco LLC** ..................................... E ...... 530 406-3333
1380 E Beamer St Woodland (95776) *(P-15005)*

**Bentek Corporation** .................................................. D ...... 408 954-9600
1991 Senter Rd San Jose (95112) *(P-12922)*

**Bentek Solar, San Jose** *Also Called: Bentek Corporation (P-12922)*

**Bentley Mills, City Of Industry** *Also Called: Bentley Mills Inc (P-2510)*

**Bentley Mills Inc (PA)** .............................................. C ...... 626 333-4585
14641 Don Julian Rd City Of Industry (91746) *(P-2510)*

**Bento Merge Enterprises, San Francisco** *Also Called: Bento Technologies Inc (P-18100)*

**Bento Technologies Inc** .......................................... E ...... 415 887-2028
221 Main St Ste 1325 San Francisco (94105) *(P-18100)*

**Benton Enterprises LLC** .......................................... E ...... 559 664-0800
18252 Avenue 20 Madera (93637) *(P-38)*

**Benziger Family Winery, Glen Ellen** *Also Called: Bfw Associates LLC (P-1485)*

## ALPHABETIC SECTION

**Beonca Machine Inc** .................................................................. F ...... 909 392-9991
  1680 Curtiss Ct La Verne (91750) *(P-10747)*
**Beranek LLC** ........................................................................... E ...... 310 328-9094
  2340 W 205th St Torrance (90501) *(P-10748)*
**Berber Food Manufacturing LLC** ............................................. C ...... 510 553-0444
  10115 Iron Rock Way Ste 1 Elk Grove (95624) *(P-2137)*
**Berenice 2 AM Corp** ................................................................ E ...... 858 255-8693
  8008 Girard Ave Ste 150 La Jolla (92037) *(P-793)*
**Berg Lacquer Co (PA)** ............................................................. D ...... 323 261-8114
  3150 E Pico Blvd Los Angeles (90023) *(P-17281)*
**Bergandi Machinery Company, Ontario** *Also Called: Bmci Inc (P-9734)*
**Berger Steel Corporation** ........................................................ E ...... 916 640-8778
  4728 Kilzer Ave # 692 Mcclellan (95652) *(P-8103)*
**Bergin Screen Prtg & Etching** ................................................. E ...... 707 224-0111
  451 Technology Way Napa (94558) *(P-4530)*
**Bergsen Inc** ............................................................................. E ...... 562 236-9787
  12241 Florence Ave Santa Fe Springs (90670) *(P-16608)*
**Bericap, Ontario** *Also Called: Bericap LLC (P-6740)*
**Bericap LLC** ............................................................................ D ...... 909 390-5518
  1671 Champagne Ave Ste B Ontario (91761) *(P-6740)*
**Beringer, Napa** *Also Called: Treasury Wine Estates Americas (P-1793)*
**Beringer Vineyards, Saint Helena** *Also Called: Treasury Wine Estates Americas (P-1799)*
**Berkeley Farms LLC** ................................................................ B ...... 510 265-8600
  17637 E Valley Blvd City Of Industry (91744) *(P-827)*
**Berkeley Forge & Tool, Berkeley** *Also Called: Bierwith Forge & Tool Inc (P-8773)*
**Berkeley Mills, Berkeley** *Also Called: Berkeley Mllwk & Furn Co Inc (P-3435)*
**Berkeley Mllwk & Furn Co Inc** ................................................. E ...... 510 549-2854
  2830 7th St Berkeley (94710) *(P-3435)*
**Berkeleyside LLC** .................................................................... E ...... 510 671-0380
  2120 University Ave Berkeley (94704) *(P-4075)*
**Berlin Food & Lab Equipment Co** ........................................... E ...... 650 589-4231
  43 S Linden Ave South San Francisco (94080) *(P-14330)*
**Bermad Inc (PA)** ...................................................................... E ...... 877 577-4283
  3816 S Willow Ave Ste 101 Fresno (93725) *(P-9183)*
**Bermad Control Valves, Fresno** *Also Called: Bermad Inc (P-9183)*
**Bermingham Cntrls Inc A Cal Co (PA)** ..................................... E ...... 562 860-0463
  11144 Business Cir Cerritos (90703) *(P-9146)*
**Bernardo Technical Services** .................................................. F ...... 858 779-9276
  16885 W Bernardo Dr # 210 San Diego (92127) *(P-19029)*
**Bernardo Winery Inc (PA)** ....................................................... F ...... 858 487-1866
  13330 Paseo Del Verano Norte San Diego (92128) *(P-1484)*
**Bernell Hydraulics Inc (PA)** ..................................................... E ...... 909 899-1751
  8821 Etiwanda Ave Rancho Cucamonga (91739) *(P-10630)*
**Bernet International Trdg LLC (PA)** ........................................ F ...... 310 873-0300
  12121 Wilshire Blvd Ste 1200 Los Angeles (90025) *(P-17286)*
**Berney-Karp Inc** ...................................................................... D ...... 323 260-7122
  3350 E 26th St Vernon (90058) *(P-7286)*
**Bernhardt and Bernhardt Inc** ................................................... E ...... 714 544-0708
  14771 Myford Rd Ste D Tustin (92780) *(P-9541)*
**Berns Bros Inc** ......................................................................... F ...... 562 437-0471
  1250 W 17th St Long Beach (90813) *(P-10749)*
**Berrett-Koehler Publishers Inc (PA)** ........................................ F ...... 510 817-2277
  1333 Broadway Ste 1000 Oakland (94612) *(P-4313)*
**Berri Pro Inc** ............................................................................ F ...... 781 929-8288
  840 Apollo St Ste 100 El Segundo (90245) *(P-1986)*
**Berry Global Inc** ...................................................................... D ...... 714 777-5200
  4875 E Hunter Ave Anaheim (92807) *(P-6741)*
**Berry Global Inc** ...................................................................... C ...... 909 465-9055
  14000 Monte Vista Ave Chino (91710) *(P-6742)*
**Berry Global Films LLC** .......................................................... C ...... 909 517-2872
  14000 Monte Vista Ave Chino (91710) *(P-6553)*
**Berry Petroleum Company LLC** ............................................. D ...... 661 255-6066
  25121 Sierra Hwy Newhall (91321) *(P-121)*
**Berry Petroleum Company LLC** ............................................. D ...... 661 769-8820
  28700 Hovey Hills Rd Taft (93268) *(P-122)*
**Berry Petroleum Company LLC (HQ)** .................................... E ...... 661 616-3900
  11117 River Run Blvd Bakersfield (93311) *(P-123)*
**Bert Williams and Sons Inc** .................................................... E ...... 707 255-7003
  525 Northbay Dr Napa (94559) *(P-17445)*
**Bert-Co, Ontario** *Also Called: Bert-Co Industries Inc (P-4531)*
**Bert-Co Industries Inc** ............................................................. C ...... 323 669-5700
  2150 S Parco Ave Ontario (91761) *(P-4531)*

**Bert-Co. of Ontario CA, Ontario** *Also Called: Edelmann Usa Inc (P-15966)*
**Bertelsmann Inc** ...................................................................... A ...... 661 702-2700
  29011 Commerce Center Dr Valencia (91355) *(P-4314)*
**Bertram Capital, Foster City** *Also Called: Bertram Capital Management LLC (P-9542)*
**Bertram Capital Management LLC (PA)** ................................ C ...... 650 358-5000
  950 Tower Ln Ste 1000 Foster City (94404) *(P-9542)*
**Best Buy Imports, Vernon** *Also Called: Makabi 26 Inc (P-6901)*
**Best Cheer Stone Inc (PA)** ..................................................... E ...... 714 399-1588
  3190 E Miraloma Ave Anaheim (92806) *(P-16465)*
**Best Data Products Inc** .......................................................... D ...... 818 534-1414
  7801 Alabama Ave Canoga Park (91304) *(P-10334)*
**Best Express Foods Inc** ......................................................... B ...... 209 465-5540
  2651 S Airport Way Stockton (95206) *(P-1169)*
**Best Formulations, City Of Industry** *Also Called: Best Formulations LLC (P-2139)*
**Best Formulations LLC** ........................................................... C ...... 626 912-9998
  938 Radecki Ct City Of Industry (91748) *(P-2138)*
**Best Formulations LLC (HQ)** .................................................. E ...... 626 912-9998
  17758 Rowland St City Of Industry (91748) *(P-2139)*
**Best Formulations LLC** ........................................................... C ...... 626 912-9998
  17775 Rowland St City Of Industry (91748) *(P-5364)*
**Best Redwood, San Diego** *Also Called: Rtmex Inc (P-3102)*
**Best Roll-Up Door Inc** ............................................................. E ...... 562 802-2233
  13202 Arctic Cir Santa Fe Springs (90670) *(P-8257)*
**Best Sanitizers Inc** .................................................................. D ...... 530 265-1800
  310 Providence Mine Rd Ste 120 Nevada City (95959) *(P-5892)*
**Best Signs Inc (PA)** ................................................................. E ...... 760 320-3042
  1550 S Gene Autry Trl Palm Springs (92264) *(P-19077)*
**Best Slip Cover Company, Studio City** *Also Called: Harmony Infinite Inc (P-3743)*
**Best Way Marble, Los Angeles** *Also Called: Best-Way Marble & Tile Co Inc (P-7534)*
**Best- In- West** ......................................................................... E ...... 909 947-6507
  2279 Eagle Glen Pkwy Ste 112 Corona (92883) *(P-2989)*
**Best-In-West Emblem Co, Corona** *Also Called: Best- In- West (P-2989)*
**Best-Way Marble & Tile Co Inc** .............................................. E ...... 323 266-6794
  5037 Telegraph Rd Los Angeles (90022) *(P-7534)*
**Bestek Manufacturing Inc** ...................................................... E ...... 408 321-8834
  675 Sycamore Dr # 170 Milpitas (95035) *(P-10335)*
**Bestforms Inc** ......................................................................... E ...... 805 388-0503
  1135 Avenida Acaso Camarillo (93012) *(P-4988)*
**Bestop Baja LLC** .................................................................... C ...... 760 560-2252
  2950 Norman Strasse Rd San Marcos (92069) *(P-16376)*
**Bestpack Packaging Systems, Ontario** *Also Called: Future Commodities Intl Inc (P-10018)*
**Bestronics, San Jose** *Also Called: Bay Elctrnc Spport Trnics Inc (P-12065)*
**Bestronics Holdings Inc (PA)** ................................................. E ...... 408 385-7777
  2090 Fortune Dr San Jose (95131) *(P-12815)*
**Bestsio LLC** ............................................................................ F ...... 626 841-8543
  1230 Santa Anita Ave Ste D South El Monte (91733) *(P-15686)*
**Bestway Foods, Valencia** *Also Called: Bestway Sandwiches Inc (P-1170)*
**Bestway Sandwiches Inc (PA)** ............................................... E ...... 818 361-1800
  28209 Avenue Stanford Valencia (91355) *(P-1170)*
**Beta Bionics Inc** ..................................................................... E ...... 949 297-6635
  11 Hughes Irvine (92618) *(P-15517)*
**Beta Offshore, Long Beach** *Also Called: Beta Operating Company LLC (P-124)*
**Beta Operating Company LLC** .............................................. D ...... 562 628-1526
  111 W Ocean Blvd Long Beach (90802) *(P-124)*
**Betensh LLC** ........................................................................... F ...... 626 841-8543
  1230 Santa Anita Ave Ste D South El Monte (91733) *(P-15675)*
**Better Bakery Co, Ventura** *Also Called: Better Bakery LLC (P-1264)*
**Better Bakery LLC** .................................................................. C ...... 661 294-9882
  444 E Santa Clara St Ventura (93001) *(P-1264)*
**Better Bar Manufacturing LLC** ............................................... E ...... 951 525-3111
  6975 Arlington Ave Riverside (92503) *(P-745)*
**Better Beverages Inc (PA)** ..................................................... E ...... 562 924-8321
  10624 Midway Ave Cerritos (90703) *(P-1987)*
**Better Built Truss Inc** ............................................................. E ...... 209 869-4545
  251 E 4th St Ripon (95366) *(P-3294)*
**Better Cleaning Systems Inc** ................................................. E ...... 559 673-5700
  1122 Maple St Madera (93637) *(P-11415)*
**Better Meat Co** ....................................................................... F ...... 916 893-8777
  2939 Promenade St Ste 100 West Sacramento (95691) *(P-2140)*
**Better Mens Clothes, Los Angeles** *Also Called: Hirsh Inc (P-238)*

**Better Nutritionals LLC**          **ALPHABETIC SECTION**

Better Nutritionals LLC (PA) .................................................. D ...... 310 356-9019
   3390 Horseless Carriage Dr Norco (92860) *(P-746)*
Better Nutritionals LLC .......................................................... E ...... 310 356-9019
   17120 S Figueroa St Ste B Gardena (90248) *(P-747)*
Better Nutritionals LLC .......................................................... D ...... 310 356-9019
   3380 Horseless Carriage Rd Norco (92860) *(P-748)*
Better Nutritionals LLC .......................................................... D ...... 310 356-9019
   3350 Horseless Carriage Rd Norco (92860) *(P-749)*
Better Therapeutics Inc (PA) .................................................. F ...... 415 887-2311
   548 Market St # 49404 San Francisco (94104) *(P-5365)*
Better Therapeutics Opco Inc ................................................. F ...... 415 887-2311
   548 Market St # 49404 San Francisco (94104) *(P-5366)*
Betts Company (PA) .............................................................. D ...... 559 498-3304
   2843 S Maple Ave Fresno (93725) *(P-9198)*
Betts Company ..................................................................... E ...... 909 427-9988
   10007 Elm Ave Fontana (92335) *(P-9199)*
Betts Spring Manufacturing, Fresno *Also Called: Betts Company (P-9198)*
Betts Truck Parts, Fontana *Also Called: Betts Company (P-9199)*
Beveled Edge Inc .................................................................. F ...... 408 467-9900
   1740 Junction Ave Ste D San Jose (95112) *(P-7213)*
Beveragefactory.com, San Diego *Also Called: Cydea Inc (P-1523)*
Beverages & More Inc ........................................................... C ...... 949 643-3020
   28011 Greenfield Dr Laguna Niguel (92677) *(P-1867)*
Beverly Furniture, Pomona *Also Called: Rbf Lifestyle Holdings LLC (P-3585)*
Beverly Hillcrest Oil Corp ....................................................... F ...... 949 598-7300
   27241 Burbank El Toro (92610) *(P-125)*
Bevmo, Laguna Niguel *Also Called: Beverages & More Inc (P-1867)*
Bevpack, Van Nuys *Also Called: Power Brands Consulting LLC (P-1454)*
Bey-Berk International (PA) .................................................... E ...... 818 773-7534
   9145 Deering Ave Chatsworth (91311) *(P-9276)*
BEYOND MEAT, El Segundo *Also Called: Beyond Meat Inc (P-1028)*
Beyond Meat Inc (PA) ............................................................ E ...... 866 756-4112
   888 N Douglas St Ste 100 El Segundo (90245) *(P-1028)*
Beyond Meat and Company, Anaheim *Also Called: Caballero & Sons Inc (P-17731)*
Beyond Nature Company, Carson *Also Called: Teaaroma Inc (P-1368)*
Beyondgreen, Santa Ana *Also Called: Beyondgreen Biotech Inc (P-4848)*
Beyondgreen Biotech Inc ....................................................... F ...... 800 983-7221
   1202 E Wakeham Ave Santa Ana (92705) *(P-4848)*
Bezel, San Luis Obispo *Also Called: Phase 2 Cellars LLC (P-1707)*
BF Suma Pharmaceuticals Inc ................................................ D ...... 626 285-8366
   5001 Earle Ave Rosemead (91770) *(P-5367)*
Bfg Supply Co LLC ................................................................ C ...... 909 591-0461
   2552 Shenandoah Way San Bernardino (92407) *(P-17268)*
Bfp, Brea *Also Called: Benevolence Food Products LLC (P-2136)*
Bfw Associates LLC (HQ) ...................................................... E ...... 707 935-3000
   1883 London Ranch Rd Glen Ellen (95442) *(P-1485)*
Bh-Tech Inc .......................................................................... A ...... 858 694-0900
   5425 Oberlin Dr Ste 207 San Diego (92121) *(P-6743)*
Bhc Industries, Compton *Also Called: Barkens Hardchrome Inc (P-9837)*
BHC Industries Inc ................................................................ E ...... 310 632-2000
   239 E Greenleaf Blvd Compton (90220) *(P-8930)*
Bhu Food, San Diego *Also Called: Lauras Orgnal Bston Brwnies In (P-1221)*
Bi Nutraceuticals Inc ............................................................. C ...... 310 669-2100
   2384 E Pacifica Pl Rancho Dominguez (90220) *(P-1988)*
Bi Technologies Corporation (HQ) .......................................... B ...... 714 447-2300
   120 S State College Blvd Ste 175 Brea (92821) *(P-12923)*
Bi-Search International Inc .................................................... E ...... 714 258-4500
   17550 Gillette Ave Irvine (92614) *(P-12924)*
Biagro Western Sales Inc ...................................................... E ...... 559 635-4784
   35803 Road 132 Visalia (93292) *(P-6193)*
Bianchi Orchard Systems Inc ................................................. C ...... 530 846-5625
   1221 Independence Pl Gridley (95948) *(P-9341)*
Bien Air, Irvine *Also Called: Bien Air Usa Inc (P-15440)*
Bien Air Usa Inc ................................................................... D ...... 949 477-6050
   8861 Research Dr Ste 100 Irvine (92618) *(P-15440)*
Bierwith Forge & Tool Inc ..................................................... D ...... 510 526-5034
   1331 Eastshore Hwy Berkeley (94710) *(P-8773)*
Big 5 Electronics Inc ............................................................. E ...... 562 941-4669
   13452 Alondra Blvd Cerritos (90703) *(P-11645)*
Big Accessories, Petaluma *Also Called: Gmpc LLC (P-15984)*

Big Basin Foods, Aptos *Also Called: Tradin Organics USA LLC (P-2376)*
Big Bear Bowling Barn Inc ..................................................... E ...... 909 878-2695
   40625 Big Bear Blvd Big Bear Lake (92315) *(P-555)*
Big Bear Grizzly & Big Bear Lf, Big Bear Lake *Also Called: Hi-Desert Publishing Company (P-17683)*
Big Brand Tire & Service ....................................................... D ...... 951 679-6266
   26920 Newport Rd Menifee (92584) *(P-6405)*
Big Brand Tire & Svc - Menifee, Menifee *Also Called: Big Brand Tire & Service (P-6405)*
Big Cart Corporation ............................................................. F ...... 949 250-7064
   16682 Millikan Ave Irvine (92606) *(P-17887)*
Big Creek Lumber Company (PA) ........................................... D ...... 831 457-5015
   3564 Highway 1 Davenport (95017) *(P-17322)*
BIG Enterprises .................................................................... E ...... 626 448-1449
   9702 Rush St El Monte (91733) *(P-8655)*
Big Five Electronics, Cerritos *Also Called: Big 5 Electronics Inc (P-11645)*
Big Heart Pet Brands Inc (HQ) ............................................... B ...... 415 247-3000
   1 Maritime Plz Fl 2 San Francisco (94111) *(P-1094)*
Big Hill Log & Rd Bldg Co Inc (PA) ........................................ E ...... 530 673-4155
   680 Sutter St Yuba City (95991) *(P-3043)*
Big Horn Wealth Management Inc ......................................... D ...... 951 273-7900
   2577 Research Dr Corona (92882) *(P-4532)*
Big Nickel, Palm Desert *Also Called: Daniels Inc (P-4387)*
Big O Tires, Sebastopol *Also Called: Robert Jones (P-17461)*
Big Star, South Gate *Also Called: Koos Manufacturing Inc (P-19101)*
Big Strike, Los Angeles *Also Called: Tlmf Inc (P-2717)*
Big Switch Networks LLC ...................................................... C ...... 650 322-6510
   5453 Great America Pkwy Santa Clara (95054) *(P-18101)*
Big T Industries, Lake Forest *Also Called: Big Train Inc (P-794)*
Big Train Inc ......................................................................... C ...... 949 340-8800
   25392 Commercentre Dr Lake Forest (92630) *(P-794)*
Big Tree Furniture & Inds Inc (PA) ......................................... E ...... 310 894-7500
   760 S Vail Ave Montebello (90640) *(P-3436)*
Big Tree Sales Inc ................................................................. F ...... 626 672-0048
   11715 Clark St Arcadia (91006) *(P-16944)*
Bigband Networks Inc ........................................................... B ...... 650 995-5000
   475 Broadway St Redwood City (94063) *(P-11818)*
Bigfix Inc ............................................................................. C ...... 510 652-6700
   1480 64th St Ste 200 Emeryville (94608) *(P-18102)*
Bigfogg Inc (PA) ................................................................... F ...... 951 587-2460
   30818 Wealth St Murrieta (92563) *(P-10486)*
Bil-Jax Inc ............................................................................ D ...... 408 446-2308
   7438 Stanford Pl Cupertino (95014) *(P-16096)*
Bill, San Jose *Also Called: Billcom LLC (P-18104)*
Bill Holdings Inc (PA) ........................................................... C ...... 650 621-7700
   6220 America Center Dr Ste 100 San Jose (95002) *(P-18103)*
BILL.COM, San Jose *Also Called: Bill Holdings Inc (P-18103)*
Billcom LLC (HQ) .................................................................. C ...... 650 353-3301
   6220 America Center Dr Ste 100 San Jose (95002) *(P-18104)*
Billington Welding & Mfg Inc ................................................. D ...... 209 526-0846
   1442 N Emerald Ave Modesto (95351) *(P-9779)*
Bimbo Bakeries Usa Inc ........................................................ F ...... 209 825-8647
   2007 N Main St Manteca (95336) *(P-1171)*
Bimbo Bakeries Usa Inc ........................................................ F ...... 323 720-6099
   480 S Vail Ave Montebello (90640) *(P-1172)*
Bimbo Bakeries USA, Inc, Manteca *Also Called: Bimbo Bakeries Usa Inc (P-1171)*
Bimbo Bakeries USA, Inc, Montebello *Also Called: Bimbo Bakeries Usa Inc (P-1172)*
Bimeda Inc ........................................................................... C ...... 626 815-1680
   5539 Ayon Ave Irwindale (91706) *(P-5368)*
Binder Metal Products Inc ..................................................... D ...... 800 233-0896
   14909 S Broadway Gardena (90248) *(P-8821)*
Bindi North America Inc ........................................................ F ...... 562 531-4301
   14502 Garfield Ave Paramount (90723) *(P-795)*
Bingo Publishers Incorporated ............................................... E ...... 949 581-5410
   24881 Alicia Pkwy Ste E Laguna Hills (92653) *(P-4370)*
Binti Inc ............................................................................... E ...... 844 424-6844
   1111 Broadway Oakland (94607) *(P-18105)*
Bio Creative Enterprises (PA) ................................................ F ...... 714 352-3600
   350 Kalmus Dr Costa Mesa (92626) *(P-5948)*
Bio Creative Labs, Costa Mesa *Also Called: Bio Creative Enterprises (P-5948)*
Bio Hazard Inc ..................................................................... E ...... 213 625-2116
   6019 Randolph St Commerce (90040) *(P-17287)*

## ALPHABETIC SECTION

**Bio-Medical Devices Inc** .................................................... E ...... 949 752-9642
17171 Daimler St Irvine (92614) *(P-15006)*

**Bio-Medical Devices Intl Inc** ............................................. E ...... 949 752-9642
17171 Daimler St Irvine (92614) *(P-15007)*

**Bio-Nutraceuticals Inc (PA)** ............................................. F ...... 818 727-0246
21820 Marilla St Chatsworth (91311) *(P-5369)*

**Bio-Nutritional RES Group Inc** ........................................ C ...... 714 427-6990
6 Morgan Ste 100 Irvine (92618) *(P-750)*

**Bio-RAD, Hercules** *Also Called: Bio-RAD Laboratories Inc (P-14632)*

**Bio-RAD Export LLC (HQ)** ................................................ F ...... 510 724-7000
1000 Alfred Nobel Dr Hercules (94547) *(P-15518)*

**Bio-RAD Laboratories Inc** ................................................ C ...... 949 598-1200
9500 Jeronimo Rd Irvine (92618) *(P-5234)*

**Bio-RAD Laboratories Inc** ................................................ E ...... 510 232-7000
3110 Regatta Ave Richmond (94804) *(P-14627)*

**Bio-RAD Laboratories Inc** ................................................ C ...... 510 741-1000
2000 Alfred Nobel Dr Hercules (94547) *(P-14628)*

**Bio-RAD Laboratories Inc** ................................................ C ...... 510 232-7000
2000 Alfred Nobel Dr Hercules (94547) *(P-14629)*

**Bio-RAD Laboratories Inc** ................................................ F ...... 510 741-6999
2000 Alfred Nobel Dr Hercules (94547) *(P-14630)*

**Bio-RAD Laboratories Inc** ................................................ E ...... 510 741-6709
4000 Alfred Nobel Dr Hercules (94547) *(P-14631)*

**Bio-RAD Laboratories Inc (PA)** ........................................ A ...... 510 724-7000
1000 Alfred Nobel Dr Hercules (94547) *(P-14632)*

**Bio-RAD Laboratories Inc** ................................................ A ...... 510 741-6916
225 Linus Pauling Dr Stop 225-101 Hercules (94547) *(P-14633)*

**Bio-RAD Labs, Richmond** *Also Called: Bio-RAD Laboratories Inc (P-14627)*

**Bio-Ved Pharmaceuticals Inc** .......................................... E ...... 408 432-4020
1929 Otoole Way San Jose (95131) *(P-19444)*

**BIOAGE, Richmond** *Also Called: Bioage Labs Inc (P-5370)*

**Bioage Labs Inc** ................................................................ D ...... 510 806-1445
1445 S 50th St Ste A Richmond (94804) *(P-5370)*

**Bioatla Inc** .......................................................................... D ...... 858 558-0708
11085 Torreyana Rd San Diego (92121) *(P-5810)*

**Biocare Medical LLC (PA)** .............................................. C ...... 925 603-8000
60 Berry Dr Pacheco (94553) *(P-5739)*

**Biocell Laboratories Inc** ................................................. E ...... 310 537-3300
2001 E University Dr Rancho Dominguez (90220) *(P-5740)*

**Biocentury Inc (PA)** ......................................................... F ...... 650 595-5333
1235 Radio Rd Ste 100 Redwood City (94065) *(P-4076)*

**Biocheck Inc (HQ)** ........................................................... F ...... 650 573-1968
425 Eccles Ave South San Francisco (94080) *(P-15008)*

**Biocompare, San Francisco** *Also Called: Comparenetworks Inc (P-4382)*

**Biodefensor Corporation** ............................................... E ...... 888 899-2956
13448 Manhasset Rd Ste 3 Apple Valley (92308) *(P-16774)*

**Biodot Inc (HQ)** ................................................................ D ...... 949 440-3685
2852 Alton Pkwy Irvine (92606) *(P-14389)*

**Bioduro LLC (PA)** ............................................................. E ...... 858 529-6600
11011 Torreyana Rd San Diego (92121) *(P-19445)*

**Bioduro-Sundia, San Diego** *Also Called: Bioduro LLC (P-19445)*

**Biofilm Inc** ......................................................................... D ...... 760 727-9030
3225 Executive Rdg Vista (92081) *(P-15009)*

**Biogeneral Inc** .................................................................. E ...... 858 453-4451
9925 Mesa Rim Rd San Diego (92121) *(P-15010)*

**Biogenex, Fremont** *Also Called: Biogenex Laboratories (P-15011)*

**Biogenex Laboratories (PA)** .......................................... E ...... 510 824-1400
48810 Kato Rd Ste 200 Fremont (94538) *(P-15011)*

**Biointellisense Inc** ........................................................... E ...... 650 481-8140
570 El Camino Real Ste 200 Redwood City (94063) *(P-15519)*

**Bioject Inc** ......................................................................... E ...... 503 692-8001
6769 Mesa Ridge Rd Ste 99 San Diego (92121) *(P-15012)*

**BIOLASE, Lake Forest** *Also Called: Biolase Inc (P-15442)*

**Biolase Inc** ........................................................................ D ...... 949 361-1200
4225 Prado Rd Ste 102 Corona (92880) *(P-15441)*

**Biolase Inc (PA)** ................................................................ D
27042 Towne Centre Dr Ste 270 Lake Forest (92610) *(P-15442)*

**Biolog Inc (PA)** .................................................................. E ...... 800 284-4949
21124 Cabot Blvd Hayward (94545) *(P-14634)*

**BIOMARIN, San Rafael** *Also Called: Biomarin Pharmaceutical Inc (P-5371)*

**Biomarin Pharmaceutical Inc (PA)** ................................ B ...... 415 506-6700
770 Lindaro St San Rafael (94901) *(P-5371)*

**Biomea Fusion, Redwood City** *Also Called: Biomea Fusion Inc (P-5372)*

**Biomea Fusion Inc (PA)** .................................................. E ...... 650 980-9099
900 Middlefield Rd Ste 4 Redwood City (94063) *(P-5372)*

**Biomed California Inc** ..................................................... E ...... 310 665-1121
721 S Glasgow Ave Ste C Inglewood (90301) *(P-5373)*

**Biomed Industries Inc (PA)** ............................................ F ...... 800 824-5135
2570 N 1st St Fl 2 San Jose (95131) *(P-5374)*

**BIOMERICA, Irvine** *Also Called: Biomerica Inc (P-5741)*

**Biomerica Inc (PA)** ........................................................... F ...... 949 645-2111
17571 Von Karman Ave Irvine (92614) *(P-5741)*

**Biomerics Imp, Fairfield** *Also Called: Biomerics Imp Indus Hldngs LLC (P-6744)*

**Biomerics Imp Indus Hldngs LLC** ................................ D ...... 707 863-4900
4900 Fulton Dr Fairfield (94534) *(P-6744)*

**Biomet Inc** ......................................................................... E ...... 949 453-3200
181 Technology Dr Irvine (92618) *(P-15325)*

**Bionano Genomics, San Diego** *Also Called: Bionano Genomics Inc (P-14635)*

**Bionano Genomics Inc (PA)** ........................................... D ...... 858 888-7600
9540 Towne Centre Dr Ste 100 San Diego (92121) *(P-14635)*

**Bioness Inc** ........................................................................ C ...... 661 362-4850
25103 Rye Canyon Loop Valencia (91355) *(P-15520)*

**Bionime USA Corporation** ............................................. E ...... 909 781-6969
1450 E Spruce St Ste B Ontario (91761) *(P-16577)*

**Biopac Systems Inc** ......................................................... E ...... 805 685-0066
42 Aero Camino Goleta (93117) *(P-14636)*

**Biopharmaceutical RES Co LLC** .................................. E ...... 704 905-8703
11045 Commercial Pkwy Castroville (95012) *(P-5375)*

**Bioplate Inc** ....................................................................... E ...... 310 815-2100
570 S Melrose St Placentia (92870) *(P-15013)*

**Bioq Pharma Incorporated (PA)** .................................... F ...... 415 336-6496
1325 Howard St San Francisco (94103) *(P-5376)*

**Bioquip Products Inc** ...................................................... E ...... 310 667-8800
2321 E Gladwick St Rancho Dominguez (90220) *(P-19446)*

**Biora Therapeutics, San Diego** *Also Called: Biora Therapeutics Inc (P-19325)*

**Biora Therapeutics Inc (PA)** .......................................... E ...... 833 727-2841
4330 La Jolla Village Dr Ste 300 San Diego (92122) *(P-19325)*

**Bioray Inc** ........................................................................... F ...... 949 305-7454
10 Mason Ste 150 Irvine (92618) *(P-751)*

**Biorx Laboratories, Commerce** *Also Called: Biorx Pharmaceuticals Inc (P-5377)*

**Biorx Pharmaceuticals Inc** ............................................. E ...... 323 725-3100
6320 Chalet Dr Commerce (90040) *(P-5377)*

**Bioscience Research Reagents, Temecula** *Also Called: EMD Millipore Corporation (P-5826)*

**Bioseal** ............................................................................... E ...... 714 528-4695
167 W Orangethorpe Ave Placentia (92870) *(P-15014)*

**Biosearch Technologies Inc (HQ)** ................................. E ...... 415 883-8400
2199 S Mcdowell Boulevard Ext Petaluma (94954) *(P-5811)*

**Biosense Webster Inc (HQ)** ............................................ C ...... 909 839-8500
31 Technology Dr Ste 200 Irvine (92618) *(P-15521)*

**Biosero (PA)** ...................................................................... E ...... 858 880-7376
4770 Ruffner St San Diego (92111) *(P-17888)*

**Bioserv Corporation** ........................................................ E ...... 917 817-1326
9380 Judicial Dr San Diego (92121) *(P-5742)*

**Bioserve, San Diego** *Also Called: Bioserv Corporation (P-5742)*

**Biosource International Inc** ........................................... E ...... 805 659-5759
5791 Van Allen Way Carlsbad (92008) *(P-5743)*

**Biospace Inc** ..................................................................... D ...... 323 932-6503
13850 Cerritos Corporate Dr Ste C Cerritos (90703) *(P-19447)*

**Biotheranostics Inc (HQ)** ................................................ E ...... 877 886-6739
9640 Towne Centre Dr Ste 200 San Diego (92121) *(P-19326)*

**Biotherm Hydronic Inc** .................................................... F ...... 707 794-9660
476 Primero Ct Cotati (94931) *(P-8061)*

**Biotix** ................................................................................... E ...... 858 875-5479
6995 Calle De Linea Ste 106 San Diego (92154) *(P-355)*

**Biotix (HQ)** ......................................................................... F ...... 858 875-7696
10636 Scripps Summit Ct Ste 130 San Diego (92131) *(P-6135)*

**Biotone Professional Products, San Diego** *Also Called: Natural Thoughts Incorporated (P-6010)*

**Biotricity Inc** ...................................................................... E ...... 650 832-1626
275 Shoreline Dr Ste 150 Redwood City (94065) *(P-15015)*

**Biotronics, Anderson** *Also Called: Visioncare Devices Inc (P-16593)*

**Biovail Technologies Ltd** ................................................ D ...... 703 995-2400
1 Enterprise Aliso Viejo (92656) *(P-5378)*

**Biovia, San Diego** *Also Called: Dassault Systemes Biovia Corp (P-18226)*
**BIP Corporation** ............................................................................. F ...... 760 591-9822
2951 Norman Strasse Rd San Marcos (92069) *(P-16692)*
**Birchwood Lighting Inc** ................................................................. E ...... 714 550-7118
3340 E La Palma Ave Anaheim (92806) *(P-11583)*
**Bird B Gone LLC** ............................................................................ D ...... 949 472-3122
1921 E Edinger Ave Santa Ana (92705) *(P-6577)*
**Bird of Paradise Renewables, La Mirada** *Also Called: Bop Renewables Inc (P-170)*
**Birdeye Inc (PA)** .............................................................................. E ...... 800 561-3357
2479 E Bayshore Rd Ste 188 Palo Alto (94303) *(P-4371)*
**Birdwell Beach Britches, Irvine** *Also Called: Birdwell Enterprises Inc (P-2613)*
**Birdwell Enterprises Inc** ............................................................... E ...... 714 557-7040
8801 Research Dr Irvine (92618) *(P-2613)*
**Birmingham Fastener & Sup Inc** ................................................. E ...... 562 944-9549
12748 Florence Ave Santa Fe Springs (90670) *(P-7984)*
**Birns, Oxnard** *Also Called: Birns Oceanographics Inc (P-11584)*
**Birns Oceanographics Inc** ............................................................ F ...... 805 487-5393
1720 Fiske Pl Oxnard (93033) *(P-11584)*
**Bis Computer Solutions Inc (PA)** ................................................ E ...... 818 248-4282
5500 Alta Canyada Rd La Canada Flintridge (91011) *(P-17889)*
**Biscomerica Corp** ........................................................................... B ...... 909 877-5997
565 West Slover Ave Rialto (92377) *(P-1265)*
**Biscotti and Kate Mack, Oakland** *Also Called: Mack & Reiss Inc (P-2864)*
**Bish Inc** ............................................................................................ E ...... 619 660-6220
2820 Via Orange Way Ste G Spring Valley (91978) *(P-13798)*
**Bishop-Wisecarver Corporation (PA)** ......................................... D ...... 925 439-8272
2104 Martin Way Pittsburg (94565) *(P-9277)*
**Bitchin Inc (PA)** .............................................................................. E ...... 760 224-7447
6211 Yarrow Dr Ste C Carlsbad (92011) *(P-2141)*
**Bitchin Sauce, Carlsbad** *Also Called: Bitchin Inc (P-2141)*
**Bitchin Sauce LLC** ......................................................................... D ...... 737 248-2446
4509 Adams St Carlsbad (92008) *(P-2142)*
**Bitchin' Sauce, Carlsbad** *Also Called: Bitchin Sauce LLC (P-2142)*
**Bitmax LLC (PA)** ............................................................................ E ...... 323 978-7878
6255 W Sunset Blvd Ste 1515 Los Angeles (90028) *(P-11984)*
**Bitscopic Inc** .................................................................................. E ...... 650 503-3120
10866 Wilshire Blvd Ste 400 Los Angeles (90024) *(P-19030)*
**Bittree Incorporated** ...................................................................... E ...... 818 500-8142
600 W Elk Ave Glendale (91204) *(P-11819)*
**Bitzer Mobile Inc** ............................................................................ E ...... 866 603-8392
4230 Leonard Stocking Dr Santa Clara (95054) *(P-18106)*
**Bivar, Irvine** *Also Called: Bivar Inc (P-12925)*
**Bivar Inc** ......................................................................................... E ...... 949 951-8808
4 Thomas Irvine (92618) *(P-12925)*
**Bivouac Ciderworks, San Diego** *Also Called: Rising Tide Bottleworks LLC (P-2337)*
**BIW Connector Systems, Irvine** *Also Called: ITT Cannon LLC (P-11326)*
**Bixolon America Inc** ...................................................................... E ...... 858 764-4580
2575 W 237th St Torrance (90505) *(P-10336)*
**Biz Performance Solutions Inc** ................................................... F ...... 408 844-4284
840 Loma Vista St Moss Beach (94038) *(P-18107)*
**Bizlink Technology Inc (HQ)** ........................................................ D ...... 510 252-0786
47211 Bayside Pkwy Fremont (94538) *(P-11442)*
**Bizpack LLC** ................................................................................... F ...... 562 786-5159
17201 Daimler St Irvine (92614) *(P-17176)*
**Bizps, Moss Beach** *Also Called: Biz Performance Solutions Inc (P-18107)*
**BJ Liquidation Inc** ......................................................................... D ...... 626 961-7221
428 Turnbull Canyon Rd City Of Industry (91745) *(P-3466)*
**Bjb Enterprises Inc** ....................................................................... E ...... 714 734-8450
14791 Franklin Ave Tustin (92780) *(P-5142)*
**BJS&t Enterprises Inc** ................................................................... E ...... 619 448-7795
1702 N Magnolia Ave El Cajon (92020) *(P-9055)*
**BK Signs Inc** .................................................................................. F ...... 626 334-5600
1028 W Kirkwall Rd Azusa (91702) *(P-15948)*
**BKM Office Environments Inc (PA)** ............................................ F ...... 805 339-6388
816 Via Alondra Camarillo (93012) *(P-17515)*
**Black & Decker, El Toro** *Also Called: Black & Decker Corporation (P-9709)*
**Black & Decker Corporation** ....................................................... E ...... 949 672-4000
19701 Da Vinci El Toro (92610) *(P-9709)*
**Black Anchor Supply Co LLC** ..................................................... F ...... 661 309-1193
27636 Avenue Scott Ste A Valencia (91355) *(P-17821)*

**Black Box Distribution LLC** ......................................................... D ...... 760 268-1174
371 2nd St Ste 1 Encinitas (92024) *(P-15788)*
**Black Box Project LLC** ................................................................. E ...... 626 356-1302
87 E Green St Ste 210 Pasadena (91105) *(P-15741)*
**Black Diamond Blade Company (PA)** ........................................ E ...... 800 949-9014
234 E O St Colton (92324) *(P-9409)*
**Black Diamond Video Inc** ............................................................. D ...... 510 439-4500
503 Canal Blvd Richmond (94804) *(P-10337)*
**Black Gold Pump & Supply Inc** .................................................. F ...... 323 298-0077
2459 Lewis Ave Signal Hill (90755) *(P-208)*
**Black N Gold, Paramount** *Also Called: Kum Kang Trading USA Inc (P-6001)*
**Black Oxide, Anaheim** *Also Called: Black Oxide Industries Inc (P-8931)*
**Black Oxide Industries Inc** .......................................................... E ...... 714 870-9610
1745 N Orangethorpe Park Ste A Anaheim (92801) *(P-8931)*
**Black Point Products Inc** ............................................................. E ...... 510 232-7723
650 Central Ave Alameda (94501) *(P-11754)*
**Black Series Campers, City Of Industry** *Also Called: Blackseries Campers Inc (P-13613)*
**Black Stallion Industries, Santa Fe Springs** *Also Called: Revco Industries Inc (P-16891)*
**Blackbaud Internet Solutions, San Diego** *Also Called: Kintera Inc (P-18472)*
**Blackberry Corporation** ............................................................... A ...... 650 564-0016
331 Fairchild Dr Mountain View (94043) *(P-18108)*
**Blackburn Alton Invstments LLC** ................................................ E ...... 714 731-2000
700 E Alton Ave Santa Ana (92705) *(P-4849)*
**BLACKLINE, Woodland Hills** *Also Called: Blackline Inc (P-18109)*
**Blackline Inc (PA)** .......................................................................... A ...... 818 223-9008
21300 Victory Blvd Fl 12 Woodland Hills (91367) *(P-18109)*
**Blackline Manufacturing, Chico** *Also Called: Mtech Inc (P-6925)*
**Blackseries Campers Inc** ............................................................. E ...... 833 822-6737
19501 E Walnut Dr S City Of Industry (91748) *(P-13613)*
**Blacktag Corporation** .................................................................... F ...... 949 981-9063
505 N Tustin Ave Ste 243 Santa Ana (92705) *(P-17532)*
**Blackthorn Therapeutics Inc** ....................................................... E ...... 510 828-4062
780 Brannan St San Francisco (94103) *(P-5379)*
**Blackwing, Stockton** *Also Called: California Cedar Products Co (P-3413)*
**Blade Therapeutics Inc** ................................................................ E ...... 650 334-2079
181 28th Ave San Francisco (94121) *(P-5380)*
**Blaize Inc** ........................................................................................ B ...... 916 347-0050
4659 Golden Foothill Pkwy El Dorado Hills (95762) *(P-12360)*
**Blameless Inc** ................................................................................ E ...... 650 563-7300
2261 Market St San Francisco (94114) *(P-18110)*
**Blankstylcom Vision Sport Mtrs, Irvine** *Also Called: Cnm Marketing Inc (P-4860)*
**Blazer Exhibits & Graphics Inc** .................................................. F ...... 408 263-7000
4227 Technology Dr Fremont (94538) *(P-15949)*
**Blc Wc Inc (PA)** .............................................................................. C ...... 562 926-1452
13260 Moore St Cerritos (90703) *(P-4850)*
**Blc Wc Inc** ...................................................................................... E ...... 510 489-5400
2900 Faber St Union City (94587) *(P-10015)*
**Bleau Consulting Inc (PA)** ........................................................... D ...... 619 263-5550
555 Raven St San Diego (92102) *(P-3561)*
**Blenders Eyewear, San Diego** *Also Called: Blenders Eyewear LLC (P-15595)*
**Blenders Eyewear LLC** ................................................................. D ...... 858 490-2178
4683 Cass St San Diego (92109) *(P-15595)*
**Blentech Corporation** ................................................................... D ...... 707 523-5949
2899 Dowd Dr Santa Rosa (95407) *(P-9780)*
**Blind Squirrel Games Inc** ............................................................ E ...... 714 460-0860
7545 Irvine Center Dr Ste 150 Irvine (92618) *(P-18111)*
**Bliss Holdings LLC** ....................................................................... E ...... 626 506-8696
745 S Vinewood St Escondido (92029) *(P-11585)*
**Blissera Corp** ................................................................................. F ...... 844 960-4141
101 Jefferson Dr Menlo Park (94025) *(P-9469)*
**Blisslights Inc** ............................................................................... E ...... 888 868-4603
2449 Cades Way Vista (92081) *(P-13215)*
**Blisslights LLC** .............................................................................. F ...... 888 868-4603
2449 Cades Way Vista (92081) *(P-11586)*
**Blisterpak, Commerce** *Also Called: Blisterpak Inc (P-17288)*
**Blisterpak Inc** ................................................................................. E ...... 323 728-5555
3020 Supply Ave Commerce (90040) *(P-17288)*
**Blitz Rocks Inc** .............................................................................. E ...... 310 883-5183
750 B St Ste 3300 San Diego (92101) *(P-18112)*
**Blizzard Entertainment Inc (DH)** ................................................. D ...... 949 955-1380
1 Blizzard Irvine (92618) *(P-18113)*

## ALPHABETIC SECTION — Bmp

**Blk International LLC** ............................................................. E ...... 424 282-3443
12410 Clark St Santa Fe Springs (90670) *(P-1868)*

**Block Inc (PA)** ....................................................................... E ...... 415 375-3176
1955 Broadway Ste 600 Oakland (94612) *(P-18114)*

**BLOCK GROUP XYZ, THE, Oakland** *Also Called: Block Inc (P-18114)*

**Block Tops Inc (PA)** ............................................................ E ...... 714 978-5080
1321 S Sunkist St Anaheim (92806) *(P-3646)*

**Blockade Medical, Irvine** *Also Called: Balt Usa LLC (P-16576)*

**Blockfreight Inc** .................................................................. E ...... 415 815-3924
535 Mission St Fl 14 San Francisco (94105) *(P-18115)*

**Blomberg Building Materials (PA)** ..................................... D ...... 916 428-8060
1453 Blair Ave Sacramento (95822) *(P-8258)*

**Blomberg Window Systems, Sacramento** *Also Called: Architectural Blomberg LLC (P-8254)*

**Blomberg Window Systems, Sacramento** *Also Called: Blomberg Building Materials (P-8258)*

**Blommer Chocolate Company Cal** ................................... C ...... 510 471-4300
1515 Pacific St Union City (94587) *(P-1338)*

**Bloom Designs Corp** .......................................................... F ...... 949 250-4929
3347 Michelson Dr Ste 100 Irvine (92612) *(P-7128)*

**BLOOM ENERGY, San Jose** *Also Called: Bloom Energy Corporation (P-12361)*

**Bloom Energy Corporation (PA)** ......................................... B ...... 408 543-1500
4353 N 1st St San Jose (95134) *(P-12361)*

**Bloomboard, Palo Alto** *Also Called: Bloomboard Inc (P-19342)*

**Bloomboard Inc** ................................................................. E ...... 650 567-5656
430 Cowper St Ste 250 Palo Alto (94301) *(P-19342)*

**Bloomers Metal Stampings Inc** ........................................ E ...... 661 257-2955
28615 Braxton Ave Valencia (91355) *(P-8822)*

**Bloomfield Bakers** ............................................................. A ...... 626 610-2253
10711 Bloomfield St Los Alamitos (90720) *(P-1266)*

**Bloomfield Bakers, Los Alamitos** *Also Called: Bloomfield Bakers (P-1266)*

**Bloomfield Food Inc** .......................................................... E ...... 714 779-7273
4740 E Hunter Ave Anaheim (92807) *(P-583)*

**Bloomios Inc** ...................................................................... E ...... 805 222-6330
201 W Montecito St Santa Barbara (93101) *(P-16097)*

**Bloomlife Inc** ...................................................................... E ...... 415 215-4251
181 2nd St San Francisco (94105) *(P-15016)*

**Blossom Valley Foods Inc** ................................................. E ...... 408 848-5520
20 Casey Ln Gilroy (95020) *(P-1989)*

**Blow Molded Products, Riverside** *Also Called: Plastic Technologies Inc (P-6963)*

**Blow Molded Products Inc** ................................................ E ...... 951 360-6055
4720 Felspar St Riverside (92509) *(P-6745)*

**Blower-Dempsay Corporation (PA)** .................................... C ...... 714 481-3800
4042 W Garry Ave Santa Ana (92704) *(P-3822)*

**Bltee LLC** ............................................................................ E ...... 213 802-1736
7101 Telegraph Rd Montebello (90640) *(P-2656)*

**Blu Banyan Inc** ................................................................... E ...... 510 929-1070
1569 Solano Ave Ste 645 Berkeley (94707) *(P-18116)*

**Blu Heaven, Commerce** *Also Called: Alliance Apparel Inc (P-2653)*

**Blue Bay Industries, Encino** *Also Called: Sayari Shahrzad (P-17080)*

**Blue Berry Health Care, Arcadia** *Also Called: Motomotion USA Corporation (P-3098)*

**Blue Cedar Networks Inc** .................................................. E ...... 415 329-0401
325 Pacific Ave Fl 1 San Francisco (94111) *(P-10338)*

**Blue Circle Corp** ................................................................. F ...... 562 531-2711
7520 Monroe St Paramount (90723) *(P-8745)*

**Blue Coat, Fremont** *Also Called: Mitac Information Systems Corp (P-10184)*

**Blue Coat LLC** .................................................................... A ...... 408 220-2200
350 Ellis St Mountain View (94043) *(P-18117)*

**Blue Desert International Inc** ............................................ D ...... 951 273-7575
510 N Sheridan St Ste A Corona (92878) *(P-10544)*

**Blue Diamond, Turlock** *Also Called: Blue Diamond Growers (P-2144)*

**Blue Diamond Growers** ..................................................... C ...... 209 545-6221
4800 Sisk Rd Modesto (95356) *(P-74)*

**Blue Diamond Growers** ..................................................... C ...... 916 446-8464
1701 C St Sacramento (95811) *(P-2143)*

**Blue Diamond Growers** ..................................................... C ...... 209 604-1501
1300 N Washington Rd Turlock (95380) *(P-2144)*

**Blue Marble Game Co, Altadena** *Also Called: Blue Marble Rehab Inc (P-18118)*

**Blue Marble Rehab Inc** ...................................................... F ...... 626 296-6400
2400 Lincoln Ave Altadena (91001) *(P-18118)*

**Blue Microphone, Westlake Village** *Also Called: Baltic Ltvian Unvrsal Elec LLC (P-11642)*

**Blue Mountain Minerals, Columbia** *Also Called: Portola Minerals Company (P-301)*

**Blue Nalu Inc** ...................................................................... E ...... 858 703-8703
6060 Nancy Ridge Dr Ste 100 San Diego (92121) *(P-2049)*

**Blue Ocean Marine LLC** ..................................................... E ...... 805 658-2628
2060 Knoll Dr Ste 100 Ventura (93003) *(P-16297)*

**Blue Pacific Flavors Inc** ..................................................... E ...... 626 934-0099
1354 Marion Ct City Of Industry (91745) *(P-1990)*

**Blue Planet Energy Solutions** ............................................ F ...... 858 947-0100
4370 La Jolla Village Dr Ste 660 San Diego (92122) *(P-11520)*

**Blue Ribbon Cont & Display Inc** ....................................... E ...... 562 944-1217
5450 Dobbs Ave Buena Park (90621) *(P-3823)*

**Blue Ribbon Draperies Inc** ................................................ E ...... 562 425-4637
7341 Adams St Ste A Paramount (90723) *(P-17526)*

**Blue Ridge Home Fashions Inc** ......................................... E ...... 626 960-6069
15761 Tapia St Irwindale (91706) *(P-17059)*

**Blue River Seafood Inc** ...................................................... D ...... 510 300-6800
25447 Industrial Blvd Hayward (94545) *(P-17153)*

**Blue River Technology Inc** ................................................. D ...... 408 733-2583
3303 Scott Blvd Santa Clara (95054) *(P-9342)*

**Blue Sea Resources Inc** .................................................... E ...... 530 666-1442
1400 Churchill Downs Ave Ste A Woodland (95776) *(P-14118)*

**Blue Sky Elearn LLC** .......................................................... E ...... 877 925-8375
5405 Morehouse Dr Ste 340 San Diego (92121) *(P-19522)*

**Blue Sky Research Incorporated (PA)** ............................... E ...... 408 941-6068
510 Alder Dr Milpitas (95035) *(P-14763)*

**Blue Sphere Inc** ................................................................. E ...... 714 953-7555
10869 Portal Dr Los Alamitos (90720) *(P-2558)*

**Blue Squirrel Inc** ................................................................ D ...... 858 268-0717
8295 Aero Pl San Diego (92123) *(P-11985)*

**Blue Star Education, Garden Grove** *Also Called: Teacher Created Resources Inc (P-4347)*

**Blue Star Steel Inc** ............................................................. E ...... 619 448-5520
12122 Industry Rd Lakeside (92040) *(P-8104)*

**Blue Tees Enterprises LLC** ................................................ E ...... 949 702-0564
1990 N California Blvd Ste 20 Pmb 1111 Walnut Creek (94596) *(P-4851)*

**Blue-White Industries Ltd (PA)** ......................................... D ...... 714 893-8529
5300 Business Dr Huntington Beach (92649) *(P-14473)*

**Bluearc Corporation** .......................................................... B ...... 408 576-6600
50 Rio Robles San Jose (95134) *(P-10226)*

**Bluefield Associates Inc** .................................................... E ...... 909 476-6027
5430 Brooks St Montclair (91763) *(P-5949)*

**Bluelab Corporation Usa Inc** ............................................. E ...... 909 599-1940
437 S Cataract Ave San Dimas (91773) *(P-10078)*

**Bluenalu, San Diego** *Also Called: Blue Nalu Inc (P-2049)*

**Bluescope Buildings N Amer Inc** ...................................... C ...... 559 651-5300
7440 W Doe Ave Visalia (93291) *(P-8656)*

**Blueshift Labs Inc** .............................................................. C ...... 844 258-3735
433 California St Ste 600 San Francisco (94130) *(P-18119)*

**Bluesky Broadcast, San Diego** *Also Called: Blue Sky Elearn LLC (P-19522)*

**Blum Construction Co Inc** ................................................. F ...... 408 629-3740
404 Umbarger Rd Ste A San Jose (95111) *(P-8259)*

**Blumenthal Distributing Inc (PA)** ...................................... C ...... 909 930-2000
1901 S Archibald Ave Ontario (91761) *(P-16411)*

**Bluprint Clothing Corp** ....................................................... D ...... 323 780-4347
4851 S Santa Fe Ave Vernon (90058) *(P-2657)*

**Blurb Inc** ............................................................................. E ...... 415 364-6300
580 California St Fl 3 San Francisco (94104) *(P-4315)*

**Blythe Energy Inc** .............................................................. F ...... 760 922-9950
385 N Buck Blvd Blythe (92225) *(P-148)*

**Blytheco Inc (PA)** ............................................................... E ...... 949 583-9500
530 Technology Dr Ste 100 Irvine (92618) *(P-19031)*

**Bm Extrusion Inc** ............................................................... E ...... 951 782-9020
1575 Omaha Ct Riverside (92507) *(P-6746)*

**Bmb Metal Products Corporation** ..................................... E ...... 916 631-9120
11460 Elks Cir Rancho Cordova (95742) *(P-8392)*

**BMC** .................................................................................... E ...... 310 321-5555
300 Continental Blvd Ste 570 El Segundo (90245) *(P-18120)*

**BMC Industries, Bakersfield** *Also Called: Bakersfield Machine Co Inc (P-10736)*

**BMC West Door Plant, Modesto** *Also Called: Builders Firstsource Inc (P-17324)*

**Bmci Inc** ............................................................................. E ...... 951 361-8000
1689 S Parco Ave Ontario (91761) *(P-9734)*

**Bmi, Temecula** *Also Called: Bomatic Inc (P-6748)*

**Bmp, Riverside** *Also Called: Blow Molded Products Inc (P-6745)*

**BMW of Palm Springs** ......................................................... D ...... 760 324-7071
3737 E Palm Canyon Dr Palm Springs (92264) *(P-9662)*

**BMw Precision Machining Inc** ............................................. E ...... 760 439-6813
2379 Industry St Oceanside (92054) *(P-10750)*

**Bni, Chatsworth** *Also Called: Bio-Nutraceuticals Inc (P-5369)*

**Bni Publications Inc** ......................................................... E ...... 760 734-1113
990 Park Center Dr Ste E Vista (92081) *(P-17637)*

**Bnk Petroleum (us) Inc** ..................................................... E ...... 805 484-3613
925 Broadbeck Dr Ste 220 Newbury Park (91320) *(P-169)*

**Bnl Technologies Inc** ........................................................ E ...... 310 320-7272
22301 S Western Ave Ste 101 Torrance (90501) *(P-10227)*

**Bnle Berg Holdings, Santa Clara** *Also Called: Bnle Berg Holdings LLC (P-10751)*

**Bnle Berg Holdings LLC** .................................................... D ...... 408 727-2374
408 Aldo Ave Santa Clara (95054) *(P-10751)*

**Bo Dean A Crh Company, Santa Rosa** *Also Called: Bo Dean Co Inc (P-293)*

**Bo Dean Co Inc (DH)** ........................................................ E ...... 707 576-8205
1060 N Dutton Ave Santa Rosa (95401) *(P-293)*

**BOa Inc** .............................................................................. E ...... 714 256-8960
580 W Lambert Rd Ste L Brea (92821) *(P-2614)*

**Boardriders Wholesale LLC** .............................................. E ...... 949 916-3060
6201 Oak Cyn Ste 100 Irvine (92618) *(P-2739)*

**Boards On The Go, Emeryville** *Also Called: Local Foodz Cali Inc (P-19358)*

**Boardwalk Solutions, Gardena** *Also Called: Ocean Direct LLC (P-2059)*

**Boatyard-Channel Islands, The, Oxnard** *Also Called: Tbyci LLC (P-14045)*

**Bob Siemon Designs Inc** ................................................... D ...... 714 549-0678
3501 W Segerstrom Ave Santa Ana (92704) *(P-15904)*

**Bobboi Natural Gelato, La Jolla** *Also Called: Berenice 2 AM Corp (P-793)*

**Bobby Salazar Corporate, Fowler** *Also Called: Bobby Slzars Mxcan Fd Pdts Inc (P-850)*

**Bobby Slzars Mxcan Fd Pdts Inc (PA)** .............................. E ...... 559 834-4787
2810 San Antonio Dr Fowler (93625) *(P-850)*

**Bobit Business Media Inc** ................................................. C ...... 310 533-2400
21250 Hawthorne Blvd Ste 360 Torrance (90503) *(P-4232)*

**Bobrick Washroom Equipment Inc (HQ)** ........................... D ...... 818 764-1000
6901 Tujunga Ave North Hollywood (91605) *(P-3680)*

**Bobster Eyewear, San Diego** *Also Called: Balboa Manufacturing Co LLC (P-2462)*

**Bocchi Laboratories, Santa Clarita** *Also Called: Bright Innovation Labs (P-5951)*

**Body Flex Sports, Walnut** *Also Called: Hupa International Inc (P-15823)*

**Body Glove, Hollywood** *Also Called: Body Glove International LLC (P-2615)*

**Body Glove International LLC** ........................................... E ...... 310 374-3441
6255 W Sunset Blvd Ste 650 Hollywood (90028) *(P-2615)*

**Bodycote Thermal Proc Inc** ............................................... E ...... 310 604-8000
515 W Apra St Ste A Rancho Dominguez (90220) *(P-7877)*

**Bodycote Thermal Proc Inc** ............................................... E ...... 714 893-6561
7474 Garden Grove Blvd Westminster (92683) *(P-7878)*

**Bodycote Thermal Proc Inc** ............................................... E ...... 510 492-4200
4240 Technology Dr Fremont (94538) *(P-7879)*

**Bodycote Thermal Proc Inc** ............................................... E ...... 562 946-1717
9921 Romandel Ave Santa Fe Springs (90670) *(P-7880)*

**Bodycote Thermal Proc Inc** ............................................... D ...... 323 583-1231
3370 Benedict Way Huntington Park (90255) *(P-8932)*

**Bodycote Usa Inc** ............................................................. A ...... 323 264-0111
2900 S Sunol Dr Vernon (90058) *(P-7881)*

**Bodykore Inc** ..................................................................... E ...... 949 325-3088
7466 Orangewood Ave Garden Grove (92841) *(P-16933)*

**Bodywaves Inc (PA)** .......................................................... E ...... 714 898-9900
12362 Knott St Garden Grove (92841) *(P-2859)*

**Boeger, Placerville** *Also Called: Boeger Winery Inc (P-1486)*

**Boeger Winery Inc** ............................................................ E ...... 530 622-8094
1709 Carson Rd Placerville (95667) *(P-1486)*

**Boehrnger Inglheim Fremont Inc (DH)** ............................... C ...... 510 608-6500
6397 Kaiser Dr Fremont (94555) *(P-5381)*

**Boeing** ................................................................................. E ...... 949 623-2222
15320 Barranca Pkwy Irvine (92618) *(P-13639)*

**Boeing, El Segundo** *Also Called: Boeing Satellite Systems Inc (P-11820)*

**Boeing, Fairfield** *Also Called: Boeing Arospc Operations Inc (P-13640)*

**Boeing, Carson** *Also Called: Boeing Company (P-13641)*

**Boeing, San Diego** *Also Called: Boeing Company (P-13642)*

**Boeing, Long Beach** *Also Called: Boeing Company (P-13643)*

**Boeing, Long Beach** *Also Called: Boeing Company (P-13644)*

**Boeing, El Segundo** *Also Called: Boeing Satellite Systems Inc (P-13646)*

**Boeing, Huntington Beach** *Also Called: Boeing Company (P-14079)*

**Boeing Arospc Operations Inc** .......................................... E ...... 707 437-3175
640 E St Fairfield (94535) *(P-13640)*

**Boeing Company** ............................................................... C ...... 310 522-2809
2220 E Carson St Carson (90810) *(P-13641)*

**Boeing Company** ............................................................... A ...... 619 545-8382
Bldg-1454 Receiving San Diego (92135) *(P-13642)*

**Boeing Company** ............................................................... A ...... 562 496-1000
4000 N Lakewood Blvd Long Beach (90808) *(P-13643)*

**Boeing Company** ............................................................... A ...... 562 593-5511
4060 N Lakewood Blvd Long Beach (90808) *(P-13644)*

**Boeing Company** ............................................................... B ...... 714 896-3311
14441 Astronautics Ln Huntington Beach (92647) *(P-14079)*

**Boeing Company, The, El Segundo** *Also Called: Boeing Stllite Systems Intl In (P-16916)*

**Boeing Intllctual Prprty Lcnsi** ............................................. C ...... 562 797-2020
14441 Astronautics Ln Huntington Beach (92647) *(P-13645)*

**Boeing Satellite Systems Inc (HQ)** .................................... E ...... 310 791-7450
900 N Pacific Coast Hwy El Segundo (90245) *(P-11820)*

**Boeing Satellite Systems Inc** ............................................. A ...... 310 568-2735
2300 E Imperial Hwy El Segundo (90245) *(P-13646)*

**Boeing Stllite Systems Intl In (HQ)** .................................... E ...... 310 364-4000
2260 E Imperial Hwy El Segundo (90245) *(P-16916)*

**Boghosian Raisin Pkg Co Inc** ............................................ E ...... 559 834-5348
726 S 8th St Fowler (93625) *(P-75)*

**Boise Cascade, Lathrop** *Also Called: Boise Cascade Company (P-3762)*

**Boise Cascade Company** .................................................. F ...... 310 815-2200
3221 Hutchison Ave Los Angeles (90034) *(P-3761)*

**Boise Cascade Company** .................................................. C ...... 209 983-4114
12030 S Harlan Rd Lathrop (95330) *(P-3762)*

**Bojer Inc** ............................................................................ E ...... 626 334-1711
177 S Peckham Rd Azusa (91702) *(P-2923)*

**Bok Modern LLC** ............................................................... E ...... 415 749-6500
912 Irwin St San Rafael (94901) *(P-8105)*

**Bold Data Technology Inc** ................................................. E ...... 510 490-8296
47540 Seabridge Dr Fremont (94538) *(P-10139)*

**Bolero Inds Inc A Cal Corp** ................................................ E ...... 562 693-3000
11850 Burke St Santa Fe Springs (90670) *(P-6747)*

**Bolero Plastics, Santa Fe Springs** *Also Called: Bolero Inds Inc A Cal Corp (P-6747)*

**BOLT BIOTHERAPEUTICS, Redwood City** *Also Called: Bolt Biotherapeutics Inc (P-5382)*

**Bolt Biotherapeutics Inc** .................................................... D ...... 650 665-9295
900 Chesapeake Dr Redwood City (94063) *(P-5382)*

**Bolt Brewery, La Mesa** *Also Called: Prost LLC (P-1455)*

**Bolt Medical Inc** ................................................................ D ...... 949 287-3207
2131 Faraday Ave Carlsbad (92008) *(P-15017)*

**Bolthouse Farms, Bakersfield** *Also Called: Wm Bolthouse Farms Inc (P-1020)*

**Bomatic Inc (DH)** ............................................................... E ...... 909 947-3900
43225 Business Park Dr Temecula (92590) *(P-6748)*

**Bomatic Inc** ....................................................................... D ...... 909 947-3900
2181 E Francis St Ontario (91761) *(P-6749)*

**Bon Suisse Inc** .................................................................. E ...... 714 578-0001
392 W Walnut Ave Fullerton (92832) *(P-19555)*

**Bonami Baking Company Inc** ............................................ E ...... 925 473-9736
380 E 10th St Pittsburg (94565) *(P-17177)*

**Bond Manufacturing Co Inc (PA)** ...................................... D ...... 866 771-2663
2516 Verne Roberts Cir Ste H3 Antioch (94509) *(P-7314)*

**Bonded Fiberloft Inc** .......................................................... B ...... 323 726-7820
2748 Tanager Ave Commerce (90040) *(P-2404)*

**Bonded Window Coverings Inc** ......................................... E ...... 858 576-8400
7831 Ostrow St San Diego (92111) *(P-3716)*

**Bondline Elctrnic Adhsive Corp** ......................................... E ...... 408 830-9200
777 N Pastoria Ave Sunnyvale (94085) *(P-6220)*

**Bonert's Slice of Pie, Santa Ana** *Also Called: Bonerts Incorporated (P-1286)*

**Bonerts Incorporated** ......................................................... E ...... 714 540-3535
3144 W Adams St Santa Ana (92704) *(P-1286)*

**Bonita Golf Club, Bonita** *Also Called: Crockett & Coinc (P-19309)*

**Bonny Doon Winery Inc** .................................................... F ...... 831 425-3625
328 Ingalls St Santa Cruz (95060) *(P-1487)*

**Bony Levy, Los Angeles** *Also Called: L & L Diamond Co (P-17647)*

**Boochcraft, Chula Vista** *Also Called: Boochery Inc (P-1834)*

## ALPHABETIC SECTION — Braga Fresh Foods LLC

**Boochery Inc** .................................................. D ...... 619 207-0530
684 Anita St Ste F Chula Vista (91911) *(P-1834)*

**Book Binders, Los Angeles** *Also Called: Kater-Crafts Incorporated (P-5012)*

**Book Buddy Digital Media Inc** ........................ E ...... 510 226-9074
42982 Osgood Rd Fremont (94539) *(P-4316)*

**Boom Industrial Inc** ....................................... D ...... 909 495-3555
2010 Wright Ave La Verne (91750) *(P-9839)*

**Boomerang Commerce Inc (PA)** .................... C ...... 602 459-2578
2100 Geng Rd Ste 210 Palo Alto (94303) *(P-18121)*

**Boone Printing & Graphics Inc** ..................... D ...... 805 683-2349
70 S Kellogg Ave Ste 8 Goleta (93117) *(P-4533)*

**Boost Treadmills LLC** .................................... F ...... 650 424-1827
2155 Cornell St Palo Alto (94306) *(P-15789)*

**Boosted Inc** .................................................... E ...... 650 933-5151
400 Oyster Point Blvd Ste 229 South San Francisco (94080) *(P-15790)*

**Boosted Boards, South San Francisco** *Also Called: Boosted Inc (P-15790)*

**Boot Barn Inc** ................................................. F ...... 805 614-9222
101 S Broadway Santa Maria (93454) *(P-17510)*

**Boozak Inc** ..................................................... E ...... 951 245-6045
508 Chaney St Ste A Lake Elsinore (92530) *(P-8393)*

**Bop Renewables Inc** ..................................... F ...... 714 418-4420
14111 La Gloria St La Mirada (90638) *(P-170)*

**Bordeaux, Vernon** *Also Called: Heather By Bordeaux Inc (P-2764)*

**Borden Lighting** ............................................. E ...... 510 357-0171
2355 Verna Ct San Leandro (94577) *(P-11521)*

**Borden Manufacturing** ................................... E ...... 530 347-6642
3314 Pacific Trail Cottonwood (96022) *(P-9580)*

**Border X Brewing LLC** ................................... E ...... 619 501-0503
2181 Logan Ave San Diego (92113) *(P-17614)*

**Borga, Fowler** *Also Called: Borga Stl Bldngs Cmponents Inc (P-8658)*

**Borga Inc** ....................................................... E ...... 559 834-5375
300 W Peach St Fowler (93625) *(P-8657)*

**Borga Stl Bldngs Cmponents Inc** ................. D ...... 559 834-5375
300 W Peach St Fowler (93625) *(P-8658)*

**Borin Manufacturing Inc** ................................ E ...... 310 822-1000
5741 Buckingham Pkwy Ste B Culver City (90230) *(P-9916)*

**Borla Performance, Oxnard** *Also Called: Borla Performance Inds Inc (P-13465)*

**Borla Performance Inds Inc (PA)** .................. C ...... 805 986-8600
701 Arcturus Ave Oxnard (93033) *(P-13465)*

**Borodian Inc (PA)** .......................................... F ...... 323 225-0500
2428 Dallas St Los Angeles (90031) *(P-3647)*

**Borrmann Metal Center** ................................. E ...... 951 367-1510
12790 Holly St Riverside (92509) *(P-7606)*

**Boss, Commerce** *Also Called: Norstar Office Products Inc (P-3576)*

**Boss Litho Inc** ................................................ E ...... 626 912-7088
1544 Hauser Blvd Los Angeles (90019) *(P-4534)*

**Bostik Inc** ....................................................... E ...... 951 296-6425
27460 Bostik Ct Temecula (92590) *(P-6221)*

**Boston Scientific - Valencia, Valencia** *Also Called: Boston Scientific Corporation (P-15018)*

**Boston Scientific Corporation** ....................... E ...... 800 678-2575
25155 Rye Canyon Loop Valencia (91355) *(P-15018)*

**Boston Scntfc Nrmdlation Corp (HQ)** ........... B ...... 661 949-4310
25155 Rye Canyon Loop Valencia (91355) *(P-15326)*

**Botanas Mexico Inc** ....................................... F ...... 626 279-1512
11122 Rush St South El Monte (91733) *(P-2145)*

**Botanx LLC** .................................................... E ...... 714 854-1601
3357 E Miraloma Ave Ste 156 Anaheim (92806) *(P-5950)*

**Bottaia Wines LP** ........................................... E ...... 951 252-1799
35601 Rancho California Rd Temecula (92591) *(P-1488)*

**Bottle Coatings, Sun Valley** *Also Called: Sundial Powder Coatings Inc (P-9127)*

**Bottlemate Inc (PA)** ....................................... E ...... 323 887-9009
2095 Leo Ave Commerce (90040) *(P-6750)*

**Bottling Group LLC** ........................................ A ...... 914 767-6000
3440 S East Ave Fresno (93725) *(P-1869)*

**Bottling Group LLC** ........................................ A ...... 510 781-3723
29000 Hesperian Blvd Hayward (94545) *(P-1870)*

**Bottling Group LLC** ........................................ A ...... 559 485-5050
1150 E North Ave Fresno (93725) *(P-1871)*

**Bottling Group LLC** ........................................ D ...... 951 697-3200
6659 Sycamore Canyon Blvd Riverside (92507) *(P-1872)*

**Bouchaine Vineyards Inc** ............................... F ...... 707 252-9065
1075 Buchli Station Rd Napa (94559) *(P-1489)*

**Bouchaine Wineary, Napa** *Also Called: Bouchaine Vineyards Inc (P-1489)*

**Boudin Bakeries, San Francisco** *Also Called: Andre-Boudin Bakeries Inc (P-17407)*

**Boudin Sourdough Bakery & Cafe, San Francisco** *Also Called: Andre-Boudin Bakeries Inc (P-1157)*

**Boudraux Prcsion McHining Corp** ................. E ...... 714 894-4523
11762 Western Ave Ste G Stanton (90680) *(P-10752)*

**Boughts Inc** .................................................... E ...... 619 895-7246
5927 Balfour Ct Carlsbad (92008) *(P-19032)*

**Boulevard Labs Inc** ....................................... C ...... 323 310-2093
626 Wilshire Blvd Ste 410 Los Angeles (90005) *(P-17890)*

**Boundary Bend Inc** ........................................ E ...... 844 626-2726
455 Harter Ave Woodland (95776) *(P-1392)*

**Boundary Bend Olives, Woodland** *Also Called: Boundary Bend Inc (P-1392)*

**Bourns, Riverside** *Also Called: Bourns Inc (P-12832)*

**Bourns Inc (PA)** ............................................. C ...... 951 781-5500
1200 Columbia Ave Riverside (92507) *(P-12832)*

**Bourns Inc** ..................................................... E ...... 951 781-5690
1200 Columbia Ave Riverside (92507) *(P-14502)*

**Bowman Pipeline Contractors, Bakersfield** *Also Called: Southwest Contractors (P-389)*

**Bowman Plating Co Inc** ................................. C ...... 310 639-4343
2631 E 126th St Compton (90222) *(P-8933)*

**Bowman-Field Inc** .......................................... D ...... 310 638-8519
2800 Martin Luther King Jr Blvd Lynwood (90262) *(P-8934)*

**Box Inc (PA)** ................................................... B ...... 877 729-4269
900 Jefferson Ave Redwood City (94063) *(P-18122)*

**Box Co Inc** ..................................................... F ...... 619 661-8090
7575 Britannia Park Pl San Diego (92154) *(P-4535)*

**Boxes R Us Inc** .............................................. D ...... 626 820-5410
15051 Don Julian Rd City Of Industry (91746) *(P-3824)*

**Boyd, Pleasanton** *Also Called: LTI Holdings Inc (P-5221)*

**Boyd, Pleasanton** *Also Called: A B Boyd Co (P-6480)*

**Boyd Chatsworth Inc** ..................................... D ...... 818 998-1477
9959 Canoga Ave Chatsworth (91311) *(P-15327)*

**Boyd Coddington Wheels, La Habra** *Also Called: NRG Motorsports Inc (P-13551)*

**Boyd Construction, Yorba Linda** *Also Called: Boyd Corporation (P-8106)*

**Boyd Corporation (HQ)** .................................. D ...... 209 236-1111
5960 Inglewood Dr Ste 125 Pleasanton (94588) *(P-6222)*

**Boyd Corporation (PA)** .................................. E ...... 714 533-2375
5832 Ohio St Yorba Linda (92886) *(P-8106)*

**Boyd Flotation Inc** ......................................... E ...... 314 997-5222
7551 Cherry Ave Fontana (92336) *(P-17516)*

**Boyd Gmn Inc** ................................................ C ...... 408 435-1666
2095 Otoole Ave San Jose (95131) *(P-4032)*

**Boyd Lighting, Sausalito** *Also Called: Boyd Lighting Fixture Company (P-11522)*

**Boyd Lighting Fixture Company (PA)** ............ E ...... 415 778-4300
200a Harbor Dr Sausalito (94965) *(P-11522)*

**Boyd Specialties LLC** .................................... D ...... 909 219-5120
1016 E Cooley Dr Ste N Colton (92324) *(P-634)*

**Boyd Specialty Sleep, Fontana** *Also Called: Boyd Flotation Inc (P-17516)*

**Boyer Inc** ....................................................... E ...... 831 724-0123
105 Thompson Rd Watsonville (95076) *(P-6170)*

**BP, San Diego** *Also Called: Qualcomm Technologies Inc (P-12661)*

**Bpi Records, Commerce** *Also Called: Bridge Publications Inc (P-4317)*

**Bpoms/Hro Inc (HQ)** ...................................... D ...... 714 974-2670
8175 E Kaiser Blvd # 100 Anaheim (92808) *(P-18123)*

**BQE Software Inc** .......................................... D ...... 310 602-4020
3825 Del Amo Blvd Torrance (90503) *(P-18124)*

**Bracut International Corp** .............................. E ...... 707 826-9850
4949 West End Rd Arcata (95521) *(P-17323)*

**Bradford Soap Mexico Inc** ............................. B ...... 760 768-4539
1778 Zinetta Rd Ste G Calexico (92231) *(P-5872)*

**Bradley Manufacturing Co Inc** ....................... E ...... 562 923-5556
9368 Stewart And Gray Rd Downey (90241) *(P-6751)*

**Bradley Tanks Inc** ......................................... E ...... 925 831-3562
301 Durham Ct Danville (94526) *(P-14124)*

**Bradley's Plastic Bag Co, Downey** *Also Called: Bradley Manufacturing Co Inc (P-6751)*

**Braga Fresh Foods Inc (PA)** .......................... E ...... 831 756-7614
121 Spreckels Blvd Bldg 10 Salinas (93962) *(P-2146)*

**Braga Fresh Foods LLC** ................................ A ...... 831 751-5573
180 Katherine St Gonzales (93926) *(P-2147)*

Braga Fresh Foods Gonzales, Gonzales *Also Called: Braga Fresh Foods LLC (P-2147)*

Bragel International Inc .................................................................. E ...... 909 598-8808
3383 Pomona Blvd Pomona (91768) *(P-2836)*

Braid Logistics, Mountain View *Also Called: Hansen Medical Inc (P-15104)*

BRAILLE INSTITUTE, Los Angeles *Also Called: Braille Institute America Inc (P-19354)*

Braille Institute America Inc (PA) ................................................. C ...... 323 663-1111
741 N Vermont Ave Los Angeles (90029) *(P-19354)*

Brainchip Inc (HQ) ............................................................................ F ...... 949 784-0040
23041 Avenida De La Carlota Ste 250 Laguna Hills (92653) *(P-18125)*

Brainstormproducts LLC ................................................................ E ...... 760 871-1135
1011 S Andreasen Dr Ste 100 Escondido (92029) *(P-15742)*

Branan Medical Corporation (PA) ................................................ E ...... 949 598-7166
9940 Mesa Rim Rd San Diego (92121) *(P-15019)*

Brand Marinade, San Leandro *Also Called: Brand Marinade Holdings LLC (P-4852)*

Brand Marinade Holdings LLC ..................................................... F ...... 510 435-2002
717 Whitney St San Leandro (94577) *(P-4852)*

Brandcast Inc .................................................................................... E ...... 415 517-4772
842 Folsom St San Francisco (94107) *(P-19033)*

Brandelli Arts Inc ............................................................................. E ...... 714 537-0969
1250 Shaws Flat Rd Sonora (95370) *(P-7587)*

Brandmd Skin Care, Chatsworth *Also Called: Samuel Raoof (P-6033)*

Brandnew Industries Inc ................................................................. F ...... 805 964-8251
375 Pine Ave Ste 22 Santa Barbara (93117) *(P-15889)*

Brands Republic Inc ........................................................................ E ...... 302 401-1195
10333 Rush St South El Monte (91733) *(P-11400)*

Brandt Consolidated Inc ................................................................. C ...... 559 499-2100
3654 S Willow Ave Fresno (93725) *(P-6185)*

Brandt Electronics Inc ..................................................................... E ...... 408 240-0004
1971 Tarob Ct Milpitas (95035) *(P-12926)*

Brannon Tire, Stockton *Also Called: Fleet Tire Inc (P-16407)*

Brantner and Associates Inc (DH) ................................................ C ...... 619 456-6827
1700 Gillespie Way El Cajon (92020) *(P-12866)*

Brantner Holding LLC (HQ) ............................................................ F ...... 650 361-5292
501 Oakside Ave Redwood City (94063) *(P-12867)*

Brassington Caseworks ................................................................. F ...... 619 442-7277
1035 Pioneer Way Ste 150 El Cajon (92020) *(P-3221)*

Brasstech Inc .................................................................................... C ...... 714 796-9278
1301 E Wilshire Ave Santa Ana (92705) *(P-8046)*

Brasstech Inc (HQ) .......................................................................... C ...... 949 417-5207
2001 Carnegie Ave Santa Ana (92705) *(P-8047)*

Brava, Pomona *Also Called: Bragel International Inc (P-2836)*

Brava Home Inc ............................................................................... E ...... 855 276-6767
2211 Warm Springs Ct Fremont (94539) *(P-11401)*

Brava Oven, Fremont *Also Called: Brava Home Inc (P-11401)*

Bravo Fono, Palo Alto *Also Called: Fono Unlimited (P-801)*

Bravo Highline LLC .......................................................................... E ...... 562 484-5100
3101 Ocean Park Blvd Ste 100 Santa Monica (90405) *(P-15791)*

Bravo Sign & Design Inc ................................................................ F ...... 714 284-0500
520 S Central Park Ave E Anaheim (92802) *(P-556)*

Bravo Sports ..................................................................................... E ...... 562 457-8916
9043 Siempre Viva Rd San Diego (92154) *(P-15792)*

Bravo Sports (HQ) ........................................................................... D ...... 562 484-5100
12801 Carmenita Rd Santa Fe Springs (90670) *(P-15793)*

Bravo Sports ..................................................................................... E ...... 858 408-0083
4370 Jutland Dr San Diego (92117) *(P-15794)*

Bravo Support, Los Angeles *Also Called: S Bravo Systems Inc (P-8333)*

Brax Company Inc .......................................................................... E ...... 760 749-2209
31248 Valley Center Rd Valley Center (92082) *(P-526)*

Braxton Caribbean Mfg Co Inc ..................................................... D ...... 714 508-3570
2641 Walnut Ave Tustin (92780) *(P-8823)*

Brea Canon Oil Co Inc .................................................................... F ...... 310 326-4002
18000 Studebaker Rd Cerritos (90703) *(P-126)*

Bread Bar, El Segundo *Also Called: El Segundo Bread Bar LLC (P-1191)*

Bread Srsly LLC ............................................................................... F ...... 646 244-9553
3310 Peralta St Oakland (94608) *(P-1173)*

Breakaway Press Inc ...................................................................... E ...... 818 727-7388
9620 Topanga Canyon Pl Ste A Chatsworth (91311) *(P-4536)*

Breakmart LLC ................................................................................. F ...... 760 310-2421
4986 Lake Park Ct Fallbrook (92028) *(P-17845)*

Breathe Technologies Inc .............................................................. E ...... 949 988-7700
15091 Bake Pkwy Irvine (92618) *(P-15328)*

Bree Engineering Corp ................................................................... E ...... 760 510-4950
1750 Marilyn Ln San Marcos (92069) *(P-12927)*

Breeze Air Conditioning LLC ......................................................... D ...... 760 346-0855
75145 Saint Charles Pl Ste A Palm Desert (92211) *(P-407)*

Breg Inc (HQ) .................................................................................... C ...... 760 599-3000
2382 Faraday Ave Ste 300 Carlsbad (92008) *(P-15020)*

Brehm Communications Inc (PA) ................................................. E ...... 858 451-6200
16644 W Bernardo Dr Ste 300 San Diego (92127) *(P-4537)*

Breitburn Energy Holdings LLC .................................................... E ...... 213 225-5900
707 Wilshire Blvd Ste 4600 Los Angeles (90017) *(P-171)*

Breitburn Energy Partners LP ....................................................... A ...... 213 225-5900
707 Wilshire Blvd Ste 4600 Los Angeles (90017) *(P-127)*

Breitburn GP LLC ............................................................................. E ...... 213 225-5900
707 Wilshire Blvd Ste 4600 Los Angeles (90017) *(P-128)*

Brek Manufacturing Co .................................................................. C ...... 310 329-7638
1513 W 132nd St Gardena (90249) *(P-10753)*

Brelyon Inc ........................................................................................ E ...... 650 246-9426
930 Park Pl San Mateo (94403) *(P-10140)*

Brendan Technologies Inc ............................................................. F ...... 760 929-7500
1947 Camino Vida Roble Ste 103 Carlsbad (92008) *(P-18126)*

Brenner-Fiedler & Assoc Inc (PA) ................................................ E ...... 562 404-2721
4059 Flat Rock Dr Riverside (92505) *(P-14850)*

Brent-Wood Products Inc .............................................................. E ...... 800 400-7335
17071 Hercules St Hesperia (92345) *(P-3412)*

Brentwood Appliances Inc ............................................................. E ...... 323 266-4600
3088 E 46th St Vernon (90058) *(P-11416)*

Brentwood Home LLC (PA) ........................................................... C ...... 562 949-3759
621 Burning Tree Rd Fullerton (92833) *(P-3522)*

Brentwood Originals, Long Beach *Also Called: Brentwood Originals Inc (P-2924)*

Brentwood Originals Inc (PA) ....................................................... E ...... 310 637-6804
3780 Kilroy Airport Way Ste 540 Long Beach (90806) *(P-2924)*

Brentwood Press & Pubg Co LLC ................................................ E ...... 925 516-4757
248 Oak St Brentwood (94513) *(P-4077)*

Brentwood Yellow Pages, Brentwood *Also Called: Brentwood Press & Pubg Co LLC (P-4077)*

Bretkeri Corporation ....................................................................... E ...... 858 292-4919
8316 Clairemont Mesa Blvd Ste 105 San Diego (92111) *(P-4853)*

Breville, Torrance *Also Called: Breville Usa Inc (P-11417)*

Breville Usa Inc ................................................................................ E ...... 310 755-3000
19400 S Western Ave Torrance (90501) *(P-11417)*

Brew Building, Fort Bragg *Also Called: North Coast Brewing Co Inc (P-1450)*

Brewery On Half Moon Bay Inc ................................................... C ...... 650 728-2739
390 Capistrano Rd Half Moon Bay (94019) *(P-17565)*

Brg Sports, Scotts Valley *Also Called: Vista Outdoor Inc (P-15874)*

Brian Guy Electric Ltg Svcs Co, Moorpark *Also Called: Insparation Inc (P-5994)*

Brian's Welding, San Jose *Also Called: B W Padilla Inc (P-19183)*

Brice Tool & Stamping Inc ............................................................. F ...... 714 630-6400
1170 N Van Horne Way Anaheim (92806) *(P-8824)*

Bridge Metals, Los Angeles *Also Called: Zia Aamir (P-8249)*

Bridge Publications Inc (PA) ......................................................... E ...... 323 888-6200
5600 E Olympic Blvd Commerce (90022) *(P-4317)*

BRIDGEBIO, Palo Alto *Also Called: Bridgebio Pharma Inc (P-5383)*

Bridgebio Pharma Inc (PA) ............................................................ C ...... 650 391-9740
3160 Porter Dr Ste 250 Palo Alto (94304) *(P-5383)*

Bridgene Biosciences Inc .............................................................. E ...... 626 632-3188
75 Nicholson Ln San Jose (95134) *(P-5384)*

Bridgestone Americas .................................................................... E ...... 909 770-8523
14521 Hawthorne Ave Fontana (92335) *(P-19151)*

Bridgestone Americas Inc ............................................................. E ...... 858 874-3109
3690 Murphy Canyon Rd San Diego (92123) *(P-6406)*

Bridgestone Hosepower LLC ........................................................ E ...... 562 699-9500
2865 Pellissier Pl City Of Industry (90601) *(P-16864)*

Bridgewave Communications Inc ................................................ E ...... 408 567-6900
17034 Camino San Bernardo San Diego (92127) *(P-7774)*

Bridport Erie Aviation Inc ............................................................... E ...... 714 634-8801
6900 Orangethorpe Ave Buena Park (90620) *(P-19245)*

Bright Glow, Covina *Also Called: Bright Glow Candle Company Inc (P-16098)*

Bright Glow Candle Company Inc (PA) ....................................... E ...... 909 469-4733
20591 E Via Verde St Covina (91724) *(P-16098)*

Bright Innovation Labs .................................................................... E ...... 661 252-3807
26421 Ruether Ave Santa Clarita (91350) *(P-5951)*

**Bright Lights Candle Company, Lower Lake** *Also Called: Aloha Bay (P-16084)*
**Bright Machines Inc (PA)** ............................................................ B ...... 415 867-4402
2445 16th St San Francisco (94103) *(P-9735)*
**Bright People Foods Inc (PA)** ..................................................... E ...... 530 669-6870
1640 Tide Ct Woodland (95776) *(P-2148)*
**Brightidea Incorporated** ............................................................... E ...... 415 814-1387
255 California St # 1100 San Francisco (94111) *(P-18127)*
**Brightscope, San Diego** *Also Called: Strategic Insights Inc (P-18839)*
**Brightsign LLC (PA)** ..................................................................... D ...... 408 852-9263
983 University Ave Bldg A Los Gatos (95032) *(P-15950)*
**Brightwater Medical Inc** .............................................................. F ...... 951 290-3410
42580 Rio Nedo Temecula (92590) *(P-15021)*
**Briles Aerospace LLC** ................................................................ D ...... 424 320-3817
1559 W 135th St Gardena (90249) *(P-8746)*
**Brilliant AV, Costa Mesa** *Also Called: Walin Group Inc (P-10120)*
**Brilliant Earth Group Inc (PA)** ..................................................... A ...... 800 691-0952
300 Grant Ave Fl 3 San Francisco (94108) *(P-15687)*
**Brilliant Home Technology Inc** .................................................... D ...... 855 650-0940
28 E 3rd Ave San Mateo (94401) *(P-11236)*
**Brilliant Solutions, Irvine** *Also Called: Meguiars Inc (P-5916)*
**Brilliant Worldwide Inc** ................................................................ C ...... 650 468-2966
550 Montgomery St Ste 800 San Francisco (94111) *(P-18128)*
**Brillio LLC** ................................................................................... E ...... 800 317-0575
5201 Great America Pkwy Ste 100 Santa Clara (95054) *(P-17891)*
**Brillius, Pleasanton** *Also Called: Brillius Technologies Inc (P-18964)*
**Brillius Technologies Inc** ............................................................. C ...... 510 379-9027
4305 Hacienda Dr Pleasanton (94588) *(P-18964)*
**Brimad Enterprises Inc** .............................................................. F ...... 951 354-8187
2900 Adams St Ste B16 Riverside (92504) *(P-17784)*
**Brimes International, San Diego** *Also Called: Cali Resources Inc (P-12931)*
**Bring Rokk LLC** .......................................................................... F ...... 714 904-2243
1275 N Manassero St Anaheim (92807) *(P-2591)*
**Brio Water Technology Inc** ......................................................... E ...... 800 781-1680
768 Turnbull Canyon Rd Hacienda Heights (91745) *(P-16784)*
**Bristol Farms (HQ)** ...................................................................... D ...... 310 233-4700
915 E 230th St Carson (90745) *(P-2149)*
**Bristol Industries LLC** ................................................................. C ...... 714 990-4121
630 E Lambert Rd Brea (92821) *(P-8747)*
**Bristol Management Svcs Inc** ..................................................... F ...... 714 267-7346
4621 Teller Ave Ste 130 Newport Beach (92660) *(P-3763)*
**Bristol Omega Inc** ....................................................................... E ...... 909 794-6862
9441 Opal Ave Ste 2 Mentone (92359) *(P-3648)*
**Bristol-Myers Squibb, Redwood City** *Also Called: Bristol-Myers Squibb Company (P-5385)*
**Bristol-Myers Squibb Company** ................................................. D ...... 800 332-2056
700 Bay Rd Redwood City (94063) *(P-5385)*
**Bristolite, Santa Ana** *Also Called: Sundown Liquidating Corp (P-7178)*
**Britcan Inc** .................................................................................. E ...... 760 722-2300
3809 Ocean Ranch Blvd Ste 110 Oceanside (92056) *(P-3681)*
**Brite Industries Inc** .................................................................... D ...... 510 250-9330
1746 13th St Oakland (94607) *(P-16099)*
**Brite Labs, Oakland** *Also Called: Brite Industries Inc (P-16099)*
**Brite Vue Div, Visalia** *Also Called: Kawneer Company Inc (P-8632)*
**Britelab Inc** ................................................................................. D ...... 650 961-0691
6341 San Ignacio Ave San Jose (95119) *(P-14474)*
**Britex, San Jose** *Also Called: Britelab Inc (P-14474)*
**Brithinee Electric** ........................................................................ D ...... 909 825-7971
620 S Rancho Ave Colton (92324) *(P-16646)*
**Britz Fertilizers Inc** ..................................................................... E ...... 559 582-0942
12498 11th Ave Hanford (93230) *(P-9343)*
**Brix Group Inc** ............................................................................ E ...... 559 457-4750
80 Van Ness Ave Fresno (93721) *(P-13216)*
**Brixen & Sons Inc** ....................................................................... E ...... 714 566-1444
2100 S Fairview St Santa Ana (92704) *(P-4854)*
**Brm Manufacturing, Los Angeles** *Also Called: Brush Research Mfg Co Inc (P-15926)*
**Broach Masters Inc** .................................................................... E ...... 530 885-1939
2160 Precision Pl Auburn (95603) *(P-9663)*
**Broadata Communications Inc** ................................................... E ...... 310 530-1416
2545 W 237th St Ste K Torrance (90505) *(P-7775)*
**Broadcast Microwave Svcs LLC (PA)** ......................................... C ...... 858 391-3050
13475 Danielson St Ste 130 Poway (92064) *(P-11821)*

**Broadcom, Palo Alto** *Also Called: Broadcom Inc (P-12368)*
**Broadcom, Santa Clara** *Also Called: Netlogic Microsystems LLC (P-12601)*
**Broadcom Corporation** ............................................................... E ...... 707 792-9000
1465 N Mcdowell Blvd Ste 140 Petaluma (94954) *(P-12362)*
**Broadcom Corporation** ............................................................... C ...... 949 926-5000
15101 Alton Pkwy Irvine (92618) *(P-12363)*
**Broadcom Corporation** ............................................................... E ...... 714 376-5029
15191 Alton Pkwy Irvine (92618) *(P-12364)*
**Broadcom Corporation** ............................................................... E ...... 408 922-7000
250 Innovation Dr San Jose (95134) *(P-12365)*
**Broadcom Corporation (HQ)** ...................................................... B ...... 408 433-8000
1320 Ridder Park Dr San Jose (95131) *(P-12366)*
**Broadcom Corporation** ............................................................... C ...... 858 385-8800
16340 W Bernardo Dr Bldg A San Diego (92127) *(P-12367)*
**Broadcom Inc (PA)** ..................................................................... A ...... 650 427-6000
3421 Hillview Ave Palo Alto (94304) *(P-12368)*
**Broadcom Inc** ............................................................................. F ...... 650 427-6000
1730 Fox Dr San Jose (95131) *(P-12369)*
**Broadcom Limited Bldg 2, Irvine** *Also Called: Broadcom Corporation (P-12364)*
**Broadcom Technologies Inc (HQ)** .............................................. D ...... 408 433-8000
1320 Ridder Park Dr San Jose (95131) *(P-12370)*
**Broadley-James Corporation (PA)** ............................................. D ...... 949 829-5555
19 Thomas Irvine (92618) *(P-14637)*
**Broadlight Inc** .............................................................................. E ...... 408 982-4210
2901 Tasman Dr Ste 218 Santa Clara (95054) *(P-12371)*
**Broadly Inc** ................................................................................. E ...... 510 400-6039
548 Market St Ste 59118 San Francisco (94104) *(P-18129)*
**Broadway AC Htg & Shtmtl** ........................................................ E ...... 818 781-1477
7855 Burnet Ave Van Nuys (91405) *(P-8394)*
**Broadway Sheet Metal, Van Nuys** *Also Called: Broadway AC Htg & Shtmtl (P-8394)*
**Broadway Sheet Metal & Mfg, South San Francisco** *Also Called: Fonco Inc (P-514)*
**Brocade Cmmnctions Systems LLC (DH)** .................................. A ...... 408 333-8000
3421 Hillview Ave Palo Alto (94304) *(P-10339)*
**Brochure Holders 4u, Santa Ana** *Also Called: Clear-Ad Inc (P-6776)*
**Broco, Ontario** *Also Called: Broco Inc (P-9723)*
**Broco Inc** .................................................................................... E ...... 909 483-3222
400 S Rockefeller Ave Ontario (91761) *(P-9723)*
**Broderick General Engineering** .................................................. D ...... 707 996-7809
21750 8th St E Ste B Sonoma (95476) *(P-9410)*
**Broma Applicators LLC** ............................................................. E ...... 760 351-0101
322 W J St Brawley (92227) *(P-17269)*
**Bromack, Los Angeles** *Also Called: LA Cabinet & Millwork Inc (P-3663)*
**Bromack Company** ..................................................................... E ...... 323 227-5000
3005 Humboldt St Los Angeles (90031) *(P-3222)*
**Bronco Wine Company (PA)** ...................................................... C ...... 209 538-3131
6342 Bystrum Rd Ceres (95307) *(P-17262)*
**Brondell Inc** ................................................................................ E ...... 415 315-9000
375 Alabama St Ste 200 San Francisco (94110) *(P-17030)*
**Bronze-Way Plating Corporation (PA)** ....................................... E ...... 323 266-6933
3301 E 14th St Los Angeles (90023) *(P-8935)*
**Brook & Whittle Limited** .............................................................. E ...... 714 634-3466
1177 N Grove St Anaheim (92806) *(P-4855)*
**Brookcrest By Culligan, Sacramento** *Also Called: Waterco of Central States Inc (P-1972)*
**Brooks Automation Us LLC** ....................................................... E ...... 510 661-5132
46702 Bayside Pkwy Fremont (94538) *(P-9840)*
**Brooks Restaurant Group Inc (PA)** ............................................ E ...... 559 485-8520
220 Five Cities Dr Pismo Beach (93449) *(P-17113)*
**Brothers Desserts, Santa Ana** *Also Called: Brothers Intl Desserts (P-796)*
**Brothers Intl Desserts (PA)** ........................................................ C ...... 949 655-0080
3400 W Segerstrom Ave Santa Ana (92704) *(P-796)*
**Brothers Machine & Tool Inc** ..................................................... E ...... 951 361-9454
11095 Inland Ave Jurupa Valley (91752) *(P-9581)*
**Brothers Machine & Tool Inc (PA)** ............................................. F ...... 951 361-2909
11098 Inland Ave Jurupa Valley (91752) *(P-10754)*
**Brothers Machine & Toolinc., Jurupa Valley** *Also Called: Brothers Machine & Tool Inc (P-10754)*
**Brothers of Industry Inc** ............................................................. F ...... 805 628-3545
3891 N Ventura Ave Ste B1 Ventura (93001) *(P-16100)*
**Brothers Pride Produce Inc (PA)** ............................................... E ...... 650 368-6993
2345 Middlefield Rd Redwood City (94063) *(P-17398)*

**Brotherwise Games**        **ALPHABETIC SECTION**

**Brotherwise Games, Hawthorne** *Also Called: Marina Graphic Center Inc (P-4689)*

**Brown Hnycutt Truss Systems In** ............................................. F ...... 760 244-8887
16775 Smoke Tree St Hesperia (92345) *(P-3295)*

**Brown-Pacific Inc** .................................................................. E ...... 562 921-3471
13639 Bora Dr Santa Fe Springs (90670) *(P-7607)*

**Brownie Baker Inc** ................................................................. D ...... 559 277-7070
4870 W Jacquelyn Ave Fresno (93722) *(P-1267)*

**Browntrout, El Segundo** *Also Called: Browntrout Publishers Inc (P-4372)*

**Browntrout Publishers Inc (PA)** ............................................... E ...... 424 290-6122
201 Continental Blvd Ste 200 El Segundo (90245) *(P-4372)*

**Brownwood Furniture Inc** ...................................................... C ...... 909 945-5613
9805 6th St Ste 104 Rancho Cucamonga (91730) *(P-3437)*

**Bruce's Custom Covers, Morgan Hill** *Also Called: Aircraft Covers Inc (P-2967)*

**Bruce's Custom Covers, Morgan Hill** *Also Called: Aircraft Covers Inc (P-2968)*

**Brud Inc** ............................................................................... F ...... 310 806-2283
837 N Spring St Ste 101 Los Angeles (90012) *(P-4373)*

**Bruin Biometrics LLC** ............................................................ F ...... 310 268-9494
10877 Wilshire Blvd Ste 1600 Los Angeles (90024) *(P-15022)*

**Bruker Cellular Analysis Inc (HQ)** ........................................... C ...... 510 858-2855
5858 Horton St Ste 320 Emeryville (94608) *(P-14638)*

**Bruker Corporation** ............................................................... F ...... 510 683-4300
61 Daggett Dr San Jose (95134) *(P-14639)*

**Bruker Corporation** ............................................................... F ...... 805 388-3326
3601 Calle Tecate Ste C Camarillo (93012) *(P-14640)*

**Bruker Nano Inc** ................................................................... E ...... 408 230-7164
70 Bonaventura Dr San Jose (95134) *(P-14641)*

**Bruker-Michrom Inc** .............................................................. E ...... 530 888-6498
61 Daggett Dr San Jose (95134) *(P-14390)*

**Brunos Iron & Metal LP** ........................................................ F ...... 559 233-6543
3211 S Golden State Blvd Fresno (93725) *(P-16356)*

**Brunton Enterprises Inc** ........................................................ C ...... 562 945-0013
8815 Sorensen Ave Santa Fe Springs (90670) *(P-8107)*

**Brush Research Mfg Co Inc** .................................................. C ...... 323 261-2193
4642 Floral Dr Los Angeles (90022) *(P-15926)*

**Bryant Rubber Corp (PA)** ...................................................... E ...... 310 530-2530
1580 W Carson St Long Beach (90810) *(P-6438)*

**Bryant Rubber Corp** ............................................................. C ...... 310 530-2530
1083 W 251st St. Bellflower (90706) *(P-6439)*

**Brybradan Inc** ...................................................................... F ...... 323 230-8604
191 E Jefferson Blvd Los Angeles (90011) *(P-16101)*

**Brydenscot Metal Products Inc** ............................................. F ...... 909 799-0088
1299 Riverview Dr San Bernardino (92408) *(P-8395)*

**Bryr LLC** ............................................................................. F ...... 415 374-7323
2331 3rd St San Francisco (94107) *(P-7114)*

**Bryr Studio, San Francisco** *Also Called: Bryr LLC (P-7114)*

**Bsmi, Brentwood** *Also Called: Bay Standard Manufacturing Inc (P-8744)*

**Bsr, Berkeley** *Also Called: Assocted Stdnts of The Univ CA (P-4368)*

**Btg Textiles, Montebello** *Also Called: Btg Textiles Inc (P-17678)*

**Btg Textiles Inc** .................................................................... E ...... 323 586-9488
710 Union St Montebello (90640) *(P-17678)*

**Btl Machine** ......................................................................... D ...... 951 808-9929
1168 Sherborn St Corona (92879) *(P-10755)*

**BTS Trading Inc** ................................................................... E ...... 213 800-6755
2052 E Vernon Ave Vernon (90058) *(P-2405)*

**Btsi, San Diego** *Also Called: Bernardo Technical Services (P-19029)*

**Bu LLC** ................................................................................ F ...... 951 277-7470
9073 Pulsar Ct Ste A Corona (92883) *(P-1425)*

**Bu Ru LLC** .......................................................................... F ...... 424 316-2878
826 E 3rd St Los Angeles (90013) *(P-17660)*

**Bubbie's Bagel Scooper, Gardena** *Also Called: Independent Ink Inc (P-6295)*

**Bubblegum USA, Los Angeles** *Also Called: Komex International Inc (P-2675)*

**Bubbles Baking Company** ..................................................... E ...... 818 786-1700
15215 Keswick St Van Nuys (91405) *(P-1174)*

**Bubbles Baking Company, Van Nuys** *Also Called: Danish Baking Co Inc (P-1179)*

**Buchbinder, Jay Industries, Compton** *Also Called: Jbi LLC (P-3505)*

**Buck Owens Production Co Inc (PA)** ..................................... E ...... 661 326-1011
2800 Buck Owens Blvd Bakersfield (93308) *(P-16326)*

**Buckhorn Cafe Inc (PA)** ........................................................ D ...... 530 795-1319
2 Main St Winters (95694) *(P-17566)*

**Buddha Teas, Carlsbad** *Also Called: Living Wellness Partners LLC (P-2267)*

**Buddy Bar Casting LLC** ........................................................ C ...... 562 861-9664
10801 Sessler St South Gate (90280) *(P-7836)*

**Buddy Homes 355, Woodland** *Also Called: Skyline Homes Inc (P-3389)*

**Budget Enterprises Llc** ......................................................... E ...... 949 697-9544
23042 Mill Creek Dr Laguna Hills (92653) *(P-7164)*

**Buds Ice Cream San Francisco, City Of Industry** *Also Called: Berkeley Farms LLC (P-827)*

**Buena Park Tool, Huntington Beach** *Also Called: Buena Park Tool & Engrg Inc (P-10756)*

**Buena Park Tool & Engrg Inc** ................................................ F ...... 714 843-6215
7661 Windfield Dr Huntington Beach (92647) *(P-10756)*

**Buff and Shine Mfg Inc** ........................................................ E ...... 310 886-5111
2139 E Del Amo Blvd Rancho Dominguez (90220) *(P-7551)*

**Buffalo Bills Brewery, Hayward** *Also Called: Steinbeck Brewing Company (P-1460)*

**Buffer, San Francisco** *Also Called: Buffer Inc (P-17892)*

**Buffer Inc (PA)** ..................................................................... D ...... 415 215-5571
2443 Fillmore St # 380-7163 San Francisco (94115) *(P-17892)*

**Bug-A-Salt, Santa Monica** *Also Called: Skell Inc (P-6207)*

**Buggy Whip Inc** ................................................................... F ...... 760 789-3230
3245 Production Ave Oceanside (92058) *(P-9411)*

**Bugsnag, San Francisco** *Also Called: Bugsnag Inc (P-18130)*

**Bugsnag Inc** ........................................................................ E ...... 415 484-8664
110 Sutter St Fl 10 San Francisco (94104) *(P-18130)*

**Build Your Own Garment, Dublin** *Also Called: Print Ink LLC (P-4943)*

**Builders Concrete Inc (DH)** .................................................. E ...... 559 225-3667
3664 W Ashlan Ave Fresno (93722) *(P-7408)*

**Builders Fence Company Inc (PA)** ........................................ E ...... 818 768-5500
8937 San Fernando Rd Sun Valley (91352) *(P-16442)*

**Builders Firstsource Inc** ....................................................... B ...... 916 481-5030
4300 Jetway Ct North Highlands (95660) *(P-16443)*

**Builders Firstsource Inc** ....................................................... F ...... 209 545-0736
4237 Murphy Rd Modesto (95358) *(P-17324)*

**Building Electronic Contrls Inc (PA)** ..................................... E ...... 909 305-1600
2246 Lindsay Way Glendora (91740) *(P-451)*

**Building News, Vista** *Also Called: Bni Publications Inc (P-17637)*

**Builtware Fabrication Inc** ..................................................... E ...... 530 634-0162
4569 Skyway Dr Olivehurst (95961) *(P-19246)*

**Buk Optics Inc** .................................................................... E ...... 714 384-9620
3600 W Moore Ave Santa Ana (92704) *(P-14764)*

**Bull Outdoor Products Inc** ................................................... E ...... 909 770-8626
1011 E Pine St Lodi (95240) *(P-17517)*

**Bullseye Leak Detection Inc** ................................................. E ...... 916 760-8944
4015 Seaport Blvd West Sacramento (95691) *(P-10757)*

**Bumble Bee Foods LLC** ....................................................... E ...... 562 483-7474
13100 Arctic Cir Santa Fe Springs (90670) *(P-2035)*

**Bumble Bee Foods LLC (HQ)** ............................................... F ...... 800 800-8572
280 10th Ave San Diego (92101) *(P-2036)*

**Bumble Bee Seafoods LP** .................................................... C ...... 858 715-4000
280 10th Ave San Diego (92101) *(P-2037)*

**Bump.me, La Jolla** *Also Called: Eventscom Inc (P-18293)*

**Bunge North America, Modesto** *Also Called: Bunge Oils Inc (P-1393)*

**Bunge Oils Inc** ..................................................................... C ...... 209 574-9981
436 S Mcclure Rd Modesto (95357) *(P-1393)*

**Bunker Corp (PA)** ................................................................ D ...... 949 361-3935
1131 Via Callejon San Clemente (92673) *(P-13466)*

**Bunzl Agrclture Group Chstrfel, Oxnard** *Also Called: Cool-Pak LLC (P-6780)*

**Buoy Labs Inc** ..................................................................... F ...... 855 481-7112
125 Mcpherson St Santa Cruz (95060) *(P-18131)*

**Buran and Reed Inc (PA)** ..................................................... E ...... 888 638-5040
1801 Adams Ave San Leandro (94577) *(P-10637)*

**Burbank Leader, Glendale** *Also Called: California Community News LLC (P-4081)*

**Burbank Steel Treating Inc** .................................................. E ...... 818 842-0975
415 S Varney St Burbank (91502) *(P-7882)*

**Burgess Cellars Inc** ............................................................. E ...... 707 963-4766
1108 Deer Park Rd Saint Helena (94574) *(P-1490)*

**Burgess Lumber** .................................................................. E ...... 707 485-8072
8800 West Rd Redwood Valley (95470) *(P-3065)*

**Burgess Lumber (PA)** .......................................................... F ...... 707 542-5091
3610 Copperhill Ln Santa Rosa (95403) *(P-17325)*

**Burgett Incorporated (PA)** ................................................... D ...... 916 567-9999
4111a N Freeway Blvd Sacramento (95834) *(P-16973)*

**Burke Industries Delaware Inc (HQ)** ..................................... C ...... 408 297-3500
2250 S 10th St San Jose (95112) *(P-6485)*

## ALPHABETIC SECTION — C M C Steel Fabricators Inc

Burlingame Industries Inc .................................................. C ..... 909 355-7000
2352 N Locust Ave Rialto (92377) *(P-7588)*

Burlingame Industries Inc (PA) ........................................... D ..... 909 355-7000
3546 N Riverside Ave Rialto (92377) *(P-17763)*

Burnett & Son Meat Co Inc .................................................. D ..... 626 357-2165
1420 S Myrtle Ave Monrovia (91016) *(P-584)*

Burnett Fine Foods, Monrovia Also Called: Burnett & Son Meat Co Inc *(P-584)*

Burnett Sons Planing Mill Lbr ............................................. E ..... 916 442-0493
214 11th St Sacramento (95814) *(P-17326)*

Burning Torch Inc ............................................................... E ..... 323 733-7700
1738 Cordova St Los Angeles (90007) *(P-2740)*

Burns Environmental Svcs Inc ............................................. E ..... 800 577-4009
19360 Rinaldi St Ste 381 Northridge (91326) *(P-5893)*

Burtech Family Wines, San Luis Obispo Also Called: Chamisal Vineyards LLC *(P-1501)*

Burton James, City Of Industry Also Called: BJ Liquidation Inc *(P-3466)*

Bushman Products, Torrance Also Called: Momentum Management LLC *(P-6516)*

Business Cards Tomorrow .................................................. F ..... 760 471-2012
546 S Pacific St Ste 104 San Marcos (92078) *(P-4538)*

Business Extension Bureau Ltd ........................................... F ..... 650 737-5700
500 S Airport Blvd South San Francisco (94080) *(P-4233)*

Business Information Systems, La Canada Flintridge Also Called: Bis Computer Solutions Inc *(P-17889)*

Business Journal ............................................................... E ..... 559 490-3400
1315 Van Ness Ave Ste 200 Fresno (93721) *(P-4234)*

Business Jrnl Publications Inc ............................................ A ..... 408 295-3800
125 S Market St Ste 1100 # 11 San Jose (95113) *(P-4078)*

Business Jrnl Publications Inc ............................................ E ..... 415 989-2522
275 Battery St Ste 250 San Francisco (94111) *(P-4079)*

Business Management, Playa Del Rey Also Called: Kribi Enterprises Inc *(P-17620)*

Business Point Impressions, Concord Also Called: Hnc Printing Services LLC *(P-4633)*

Business Printing Company Inc .......................................... F ..... 858 453-2111
9840 Prospect Ave Santee (92071) *(P-19078)*

Business Services Network Corp ........................................ D ..... 415 282-8161
1275 Fairfax Ave Ste 103 San Francisco (94124) *(P-17795)*

Buslink Media, Baldwin Park Also Called: Global Silicon Electronics Inc *(P-10239)*

Busseto Foods, Fresno Also Called: Fratelli Beretta Usa Inc *(P-641)*

Busseto Foods, Fresno Also Called: Fratelli Beretta Usa Inc *(P-642)*

Buster and Punch Inc ......................................................... E ..... 818 392-3827
10844 Burbank Blvd North Hollywood (91601) *(P-16421)*

Butler Inc .......................................................................... F ..... 310 323-3114
2140 S Dupont Dr Anaheim (92806) *(P-8748)*

Butler Home Products LLC ................................................ C ..... 909 476-3884
9409 Buffalo Ave Rancho Cucamonga (91730) *(P-15927)*

Butler Manufacturing, Visalia Also Called: Bluescope Buildings N Amer Inc *(P-8656)*

Butler Service Group Inc (HQ) ........................................... D ..... 201 891-5312
3820 State St Ste A Santa Barbara (93105) *(P-17866)*

Butte Sand and Gravel ....................................................... E ..... 530 755-0225
10373 S Butte Rd Sutter (95982) *(P-309)*

Butte Steel & Fabrication Inc ............................................. E
13290 Contractors Dr Chico (95973) *(P-8108)*

Buxcon Sheetmetal Inc ...................................................... F ..... 619 937-0001
11222 Woodside Ave N Santee (92071) *(P-8396)*

Buyersroad Inc .................................................................. E ..... 937 313-4466
2010 Crow Canyon Pl Ste 100 San Ramon (94583) *(P-18132)*

Buzz Solutions Inc ............................................................. F ..... 949 637-7946
119 University Ave Palo Alto (94301) *(P-18133)*

Bvi International Inc .......................................................... E ..... 661 834-1775
4301 Yeager Way Bakersfield (93313) *(P-9147)*

Bwm, Modesto Also Called: Billington Welding & Mfg Inc *(P-9779)*

Bwsc LLC .......................................................................... E ..... 424 353-1767
1 Winemaster Way Ste D Lodi (95240) *(P-1491)*

By Quest LLC .................................................................... F ..... 209 234-0202
2518 Boeing Way Stockton (95206) *(P-4856)*

Byd Motors LLC (DH) ........................................................ E ..... 213 748-3980
888 E Walnut St Fl 2 Pasadena (91101) *(P-13467)*

Byer California .................................................................. C ..... 323 780-7615
1201 Rio Vista Ave Los Angeles (90023) *(P-2463)*

Byer California (PA) .......................................................... A ..... 415 626-7844
66 Potrero Ave San Francisco (94103) *(P-2658)*

Byrnes & Kiefer Co ............................................................ D ..... 714 554-4000
501 Airpark Dr Fullerton (92833) *(P-1991)*

Byte, Santa Monica Also Called: Straight Smile LLC *(P-15485)*

Byton North America Corp ................................................. C ..... 408 966-5078
4201 Burton Dr Santa Clara (95054) *(P-13344)*

C & C Signs, Ojai Also Called: Canzone and Company *(P-15954)*

C & D Aerospace, Garden Grove Also Called: Safran Cabin Inc *(P-13951)*

C & D Semiconductor Svcs Inc (PA) .................................... D ..... 408 383-1888
1110 Ringwood Ct San Jose (95131) *(P-12372)*

C & F Foods Inc ................................................................. B ..... 626 723-1000
12400 Wilshire Blvd Ste 1180 Los Angeles (90025) *(P-2150)*

C & G Mercury Plastics, Sylmar Also Called: C & G Plastics *(P-6752)*

C & G Plastics ................................................................... E ..... 818 837-3773
12729 Foothill Blvd Sylmar (91342) *(P-6752)*

C & H Enterprises, Fremont Also Called: Colleen & Herb Enterprises Inc *(P-10784)*

C & H Machine Inc ............................................................. D ..... 760 746-6459
943 S Andreasen Dr Escondido (92029) *(P-10758)*

C & H Meat Company, Vernon Also Called: Eastland Corporation *(P-17161)*

C & H Testing Service Inc (PA) ........................................... E ..... 661 589-4030
6224 Price Way Bakersfield (93308) *(P-209)*

C & J Food, Oakland Also Called: CJ United Food Corporation *(P-3913)*

C & J Industries, Santa Fe Springs Also Called: Custom Steel Fabrication Inc *(P-8128)*

C & J Metal Prducts, Paramount Also Called: Jeffrey Fabrication LLC *(P-8478)*

C & K Johnson Industries Inc ............................................. E ..... 707 822-7687
1061 Samoa Blvd Arcata (95521) *(P-8397)*

C & L Graphics Inc ............................................................ F ..... 818 785-8310
16461 Sherman Way Van Nuys (91406) *(P-4539)*

C & M Manufacturing, Santee Also Called: C&M Manufacturing Company Inc *(P-6578)*

C & P Microsystems, Petaluma Also Called: Colter & Peterson Microsystems *(P-14395)*

C & R Molds Inc ................................................................. E ..... 805 658-7098
2737 Palma Dr Ventura (93003) *(P-6753)*

C & S Assembly Inc ............................................................ F ..... 866 779-8939
1150 N Armando St Anaheim (92806) *(P-12928)*

C & S Plastics .................................................................... F ..... 818 896-2489
18209 Chatsworth St Porter Ranch (91326) *(P-6754)*

C 232 Inc ........................................................................... F ..... 818 731-1196
28486 Westinghouse Pl Valencia (91355) *(P-18965)*

C A Buchen Corp ................................................................ E ..... 818 767-5408
9231 Glenoaks Blvd Sun Valley (91352) *(P-8109)*

C A Schroeder Inc (PA) ...................................................... E ..... 818 365-9561
1318 1st St San Fernando (91340) *(P-7573)*

C B M, Santa Ana Also Called: Custom Built Machinery Inc *(P-19387)*

C B S, San Marcos Also Called: Winchster Intrcnnect CM CA Inc *(P-7800)*

C B Sheets Inc ................................................................... E ..... 562 921-1223
13901 Carmenita Rd Santa Fe Springs (90670) *(P-3825)*

C Brewer Company, Ontario Also Called: Balda C Brewer Inc *(P-9605)*

C C I, Orange Also Called: Coastal Component Inds Inc *(P-12942)*

C C M P, Anaheim Also Called: Copper Clad Mltilayer Pdts Inc *(P-12082)*

C C S I, Bakersfield Also Called: Covenant Community Svcs Inc *(P-19355)*

C Ceronix Incorporated ..................................................... E ..... 530 886-6400
13350 New Airport Rd Auburn (95602) *(P-15631)*

C D S, Canyon Country Also Called: Commercial Display Systems LLC *(P-10490)*

C D Video, Santa Ana Also Called: CD Video Manufacturing Inc *(P-13193)*

C Enterprises, Inc., San Diego Also Called: Exce LP *(P-10366)*

C F W Research & Dev Co ................................................... F ..... 805 489-8750
338 S 4th St Grover Beach (93433) *(P-7725)*

C G A, Concord Also Called: Concord Graphic Arts Inc *(P-17823)*

C G Systems LLC .............................................................. E ..... 714 632-8882
1470 N Hundley St Anaheim (92806) *(P-452)*

C I W, Pittsburg Also Called: Concord Iron Works Inc *(P-8123)*

C J Foods, Los Angeles Also Called: CJ America Inc *(P-17182)*

C J Instruments Incorporated ............................................ E ..... 818 996-4131
Canoga Park (91304) *(P-14851)*

C L E, Downey Also Called: Can Lines Engineering Inc *(P-10016)*

C L Hann Industries Inc ..................................................... F ..... 408 293-4800
7200 Alexander St Gilroy (95020) *(P-10759)*

C M Automotive Systems Inc (PA) ..................................... E ..... 909 869-7912
5646 W Mission Blvd Ontario (91762) *(P-9958)*

C M C, Ontario Also Called: California Mfg Cabinetry Inc *(P-3649)*

C M C Steel Fabricators Inc .............................................. E ..... 909 899-9993
1455 Auto Center Dr Ste 200 Ontario (91761) *(P-9211)*

---

Employee Codes: A=Over 500 employees, B=251-500
C=101-250, D=51-100, E=20-50, F=10-19, G=1-9

# C M I
## ALPHABETIC SECTION

**C M I, Corona** *Also Called: Corona Magnetics Inc (P-12835)*

**C M P, San Leandro** *Also Called: Peggy S Lane Inc (P-6684)*

**C Magazine, Santa Monica** *Also Called: C Publishing LLC (P-4374)*

**C Mondavi & Family (PA)** ............................................................. D ...... 707 967-2200
2800 Main St Saint Helena (94574) *(P-1492)*

**C N P Signs & Graphics, El Cajon** *Also Called: California Neon Products (P-15952)*

**C P I, Simi Valley** *Also Called: Chatsworth Products Inc (P-9279)*

**C P Shades, Sausalito** *Also Called: C P Shades Inc (P-2741)*

**C P Shades Inc (PA)** .................................................................... F ...... 415 331-4581
403 Coloma St Sausalito (94965) *(P-2741)*

**C Preme Limited LLC** .................................................................. E ...... 310 355-0498
1250 E 223rd St Carson (90745) *(P-15795)*

**C Publishing LLC** ........................................................................ E ...... 310 393-3800
1543 7th St Ste 202 Santa Monica (90401) *(P-4374)*

**C R Laurence Co Inc (HQ)** .......................................................... B ...... 323 588-1281
2503 E Vernon Ave Los Angeles (90058) *(P-13468)*

**C R M, Newport Beach** *Also Called: Crm Co LLC (P-6472)*

**C S Bio Co** ................................................................................... D ...... 650 322-1111
20 Kelly Ct Ste 127 Menlo Park (94025) *(P-5744)*

**C S C, Garden Grove** *Also Called: Container Supply Company Incorporated (P-7920)*

**C S C, Poway** *Also Called: Advanced Machining Tooling Inc (P-9595)*

**C S Dash Cover Inc** .................................................................... F ...... 562 790-8300
14020 Paramount Blvd Paramount (90723) *(P-3003)*

**C S I, Santa Ana** *Also Called: Color Science Inc (P-6119)*

**C S L, Santa Clara** *Also Called: Nxedge Csl LLC (P-8989)*

**C S S, Bakersfield** *Also Called: Construction Specialty Svc Inc (P-387)*

**C S T, Thousand Oaks** *Also Called: Custom Sensors & Tech Inc (P-12952)*

**C S T I, San Jose** *Also Called: Chemical Safety Technology Inc (P-6773)*

**C Sanders Emblems LP** ............................................................. E ...... 800 336-7467
26370 Diamond Pl Unit 506 Santa Clarita (91350) *(P-17289)*

**C T L Printing Inds Inc** ............................................................... E ...... 714 635-2980
1741 W Lincoln Ave Ste A Anaheim (92801) *(P-4857)*

**C T R, Healdsburg** *Also Called: Martin Group Inc (P-3420)*

**C W C, San Leandro** *Also Called: Continental Western Corp (P-16868)*

**C W Cole & Company Inc** .......................................................... E ...... 626 443-2473
2560 Rosemead Blvd South El Monte (91733) *(P-11523)*

**C Wolfe Industries Inc** ............................................................... E ...... 626 443-7185
14420 Marquardt Ave Santa Fe Springs (90670) *(P-8825)*

**C-Cure, Huntington Beach** *Also Called: Custom Building Products LLC (P-6224)*

**C-Cure, Ontario** *Also Called: Western States Wholesale Inc (P-7304)*

**C-Pak Industries Inc** .................................................................. E ...... 909 880-6017
4925 Hallmark Pkwy San Bernardino (92407) *(P-6755)*

**C-Preme, Carson** *Also Called: C Preme Limited LLC (P-15795)*

**C-Quest Inc** ................................................................................ E ...... 323 980-1400
1439 S Herbert Ave Los Angeles (90023) *(P-2659)*

**C-Thru Sunrooms, Ontario** *Also Called: Stell Industries Inc (P-8686)*

**C.A.R ENTERPRISES, INC., Hesperia** *Also Called: CAr Enterprises Inc (P-10457)*

**C.A.R ENTERPRISES, INC., Moreno Valley** *Also Called: CAr Enterprises Inc (P-10458)*

**C&C Aerol Machining, South Gate** *Also Called: Precision Forging Dies Inc (P-9641)*

**C&C Building Automation Co Inc** ............................................... E ...... 650 292-7450
23520 Foley St Hayward (94545) *(P-14852)*

**C&C Jewelry Mfg Inc** .................................................................. D ...... 213 623-6800
323 W 8th St Fl 4 Los Angeles (90014) *(P-16966)*

**C&D Aerodesign, San Diego** *Also Called: Safran Cabin Inc (P-13946)*

**C&D Precision Machining, San Jose** *Also Called: C & D Semiconductor Svcs Inc (P-12372)*

**C&D Zodiac Aerospace** .............................................................. E ...... 714 891-0683
7330 Lincoln Way Garden Grove (92841) *(P-13799)*

**C&F Wire Products, Stanton** *Also Called: Stecher Enterprises Inc (P-9207)*

**C&H Sugar, Crockett** *Also Called: C&H Sugar Company Inc (P-1295)*

**C&H Sugar Company Inc** ........................................................... A ...... 510 787-2121
830 Loring Ave Crockett (94525) *(P-1295)*

**C&J Well Services LLC** .............................................................. A ...... 661 589-5220
3752 Allen Rd Bakersfield (93314) *(P-210)*

**C&K Form Fabrication Inc** ......................................................... E ...... 909 825-1882
370 N 9th St Colton (92324) *(P-8693)*

**C&M Manufacturing Company Inc (PA)** .................................... E ...... **619 449-7200**
9640b Mission Gorge Rd Ste 165 Santee (92071) *(P-6578)*

**C&O Manufacturing Company Inc** ............................................. D ...... 562 692-7525
9640 Beverly Rd Pico Rivera (90660) *(P-8398)*

**C&T Publishing Inc** .................................................................... E ...... 925 677-0377
1651 Challenge Dr Concord (94520) *(P-4375)*

**C3 Delaware Inc** ......................................................................... E ...... 650 503-2200
1300 Seaport Blvd Ste 500 Redwood City (94063) *(P-18134)*

**C3AI INC (PA)** ............................................................................. A ...... 650 503-2200
1400 Seaport Blvd Ste 100 Redwood City (94063) *(P-18135)*

**C4 Litho LLC** .............................................................................. E ...... 714 259-1073
27020 Daisy Cir Yorba Linda (92887) *(P-4540)*

**CA, South San Francisco** *Also Called: Ca Inc (P-12373)*

**CA, Roseville** *Also Called: Ca Inc (P-12374)*

**CA, Rancho Cordova** *Also Called: Ca Inc (P-17893)*

**CA, Santa Clara** *Also Called: Ca Inc (P-18136)*

**CA, Palo Alto** *Also Called: Ca Inc (P-18137)*

**Ca Inc** ......................................................................................... E ...... 650 534-9000
6000 Shoreline Ct Ste 300 South San Francisco (94080) *(P-12373)*

**Ca Inc** ......................................................................................... E ...... 800 405-5540
3013 Douglas Blvd Ste 120 Roseville (95661) *(P-12374)*

**Ca Inc** ......................................................................................... E ...... 916 463-8500
10811 International Dr Uppr Rancho Cordova (95670) *(P-17893)*

**Ca Inc** ......................................................................................... C ...... 800 225-5224
3965 Freedom Cir Fl 6 Santa Clara (95054) *(P-18136)*

**Ca Inc (HQ)** ................................................................................. A ...... **800 225-5224**
3421 Hillview Ave Palo Alto (94304) *(P-18137)*

**CA Creamery Holdings LLC** ....................................................... E ...... 270 861-5956
21750 8th St E Sonoma (95476) *(P-2086)*

**CA Signs, Pacoima** *Also Called: California Signs Inc (P-15953)*

**Ca75 Atk, San Diego** *Also Called: Northrop Grmman Innvtion Syste (P-14230)*

**Caballero & Sons Inc** ................................................................. E ...... 562 368-1644
5753 E Santa Ana Canyon Rd Ste G-380 Anaheim (92807) *(P-17731)*

**Caban Systems Inc** .................................................................... E ...... 831 245-1608
858 Stanton Rd Burlingame (94010) *(P-13132)*

**Cabinet Manufacturing, Ramona** *Also Called: Millwork Company Inc (P-3159)*

**Cabinets 2000 LLC** .................................................................... C ...... 562 868-0909
11100 Firestone Blvd Norwalk (90650) *(P-3223)*

**Cabinets By Prcision Works Inc** ............................................... E ...... 760 342-1133
81101 Indio Blvd Ste D22 Indio (92201) *(P-3224)*

**Cabinets Galore Oc, San Diego** *Also Called: Cabinets Glore Orange Cnty Inc (P-3066)*

**Cabinets Glore Orange Cnty Inc** .............................................. E ...... 858 586-0555
9279 Cabot Dr Ste D San Diego (92126) *(P-3066)*

**Cabinets R US** ........................................................................... E ...... 562 483-6886
1240 N Fee Ana St Anaheim (92807) *(P-3225)*

**Cable Connection Inc** ............................................................... D ...... 510 249-9000
1035 Mission Ct Fremont (94539) *(P-11443)*

**Cable Moore Inc (PA)** ................................................................ E ...... **510 436-8000**
4700 Coliseum Way Oakland (94601) *(P-9212)*

**Cable Wholesalecom Inc (PA)** .................................................. E ...... **925 455-0800**
1200 Voyager St Livermore (94551) *(P-16512)*

**Cable-Cisco, Hayward** *Also Called: Carpenter Group (P-9499)*

**Cableconn, San Diego** *Also Called: Cableconn Industries Inc (P-16647)*

**Cableconn Industries Inc** ......................................................... D ...... 858 571-7111
7198 Convoy Ct San Diego (92111) *(P-16647)*

**Cablesys LLC** ............................................................................ E ...... 562 356-3222
1270 N Hancock St Anaheim (92807) *(P-7776)*

**Cabo Foods, Laguna Beach** *Also Called: Cabo Foods Inc (P-17178)*

**Cabo Foods Inc (PA)** ................................................................. E ...... 949 463-2373
301 Forest Ave Laguna Beach (92651) *(P-17178)*

**Cabrac Inc** ................................................................................. E ...... 818 834-0177
13250 Paxton St Pacoima (91331) *(P-8826)*

**Cache Creek Foods LLC** ........................................................... D ...... 530 662-1764
411 N Pioneer Ave Woodland (95776) *(P-2151)*

**Cacheflow Inc** ............................................................................ E ...... 818 659-1400
195 Page Mill Rd Ste 111b Palo Alto (94306) *(P-18138)*

**Caci Photonics LLC** .................................................................. C ...... 408 560-3500
120 Knowles Dr Los Gatos (95032) *(P-14165)*

**Caco-Pacific Corporation (PA)** ................................................. C ...... **626 331-3361**
813 N Cummings Rd Covina (91724) *(P-9608)*

**Cad Works Inc** .......................................................................... E ...... 626 336-5491
16366 E Valley Blvd La Puente (91744) *(P-8110)*

**Cade Co, San Jose** *Also Called: Cade Corporation (P-6271)*

**Cade Corporation** ..................................................................... D ...... 310 539-2508
100 Lewis St San Jose (95112) *(P-6271)*

# ALPHABETIC SECTION

**Calaveras Materials Inc**

**CADENCE, San Jose** *Also Called: Cadence Design Systems Inc (P-18139)*
**Cadence Aerospace, Anaheim** *Also Called: Aerospace Parts Holdings Inc (P-13757)*
**Cadence Aerospace LLC (HQ)**.................................................. D ...... 949 877-3630
 3150 E Miraloma Ave Anaheim (92806) *(P-13800)*
**Cadence Aerospace LLC** ........................................................... F ...... 425 353-0405
 3130 E Miraloma Ave Anaheim (92806) *(P-13801)*
**Cadence Design Systems Inc (PA)**........................................... A ...... 408 943-1234
 2655 Seely Ave Bldg 5 San Jose (95134) *(P-18139)*
**Cadence Gourmet LLC (PA)**..................................................... F ...... 951 444-9269
 155 Klug Cir Corona (92878) *(P-2152)*
**Cadence Gourmet Involve Foods, Corona** *Also Called: Cadence Gourmet LLC (P-2152)*
**Cadillac Motor Div Area** ............................................................ C ...... 805 373-9575
 30930 Russell Ranch Rd Westlake Village (91362) *(P-17437)*
**Caelus Corporation** .................................................................... E ...... 949 877-7170
 20472 Crescent Bay Dr Ste 100 Lake Forest (92630) *(P-19512)*
**Caelux Corporation** ................................................................... E ...... 626 502-7033
 404 N Halstead St Pasadena (91107) *(P-12375)*
**Caer Inc** ....................................................................................... E ...... 415 879-9864
 8070 Melrose Ave Los Angeles (90046) *(P-851)*
**Caes Mission Systems LLC** ..................................................... E ...... 858 812-7300
 4820 Eastgate Mall Ste 200 San Diego (92121) *(P-12929)*
**Caes Systems LLC** ................................................................... B ...... 408 624-3000
 5300 Hellyer Ave San Jose (95138) *(P-14166)*
**Caes Systems LLC** ................................................................... C ...... 858 560-1301
 9404 Chesapeake Dr San Diego (92123) *(P-14167)*
**Caesar Hardware Intl Ltd** ......................................................... E ...... 800 306-3829
 4985 Hallmark Pkwy San Bernardino (92407) *(P-7985)*
**Cafe 21, San Diego** *Also Called: Cafe 21 Gaslamp Inc (P-17567)*
**Cafe 21 Gaslamp Inc** ................................................................ E ...... 619 795-0721
 2736 Adams Ave San Diego (92116) *(P-17567)*
**Cafe Champagne, Temecula** *Also Called: Thornton Winery (P-1784)*
**Cafe Niebaum Coppola, San Francisco** *Also Called: Niebam-Cppola Estate Winery LP (P-1691)*
**Caffe DAmore Inc** ...................................................................... C
 1916 S Tubeway Ave Commerce (90040) *(P-2068)*
**Cafvina Coffee & Tea, Garden Grove** *Also Called: Quoc Viet Foods (P-2330)*
**Cageco Inc** .................................................................................. E ...... 800 605-4859
 16225 Beaver Rd Adelanto (92301) *(P-9344)*
**Cai, Orange** *Also Called: Califrnia Anlytical Instrs Inc (P-14392)*
**Cai, Corona** *Also Called: Combustion Associates Inc (P-16342)*
**Caitac Garment Processing Inc** ............................................... B ...... 310 217-9888
 14725 S Broadway Gardena (90248) *(P-2489)*
**Cakebread Cellar Vineyards, Rutherford** *Also Called: Cakebread Cellars (P-1493)*
**Cakebread Cellars** .................................................................... D ...... 707 963-5221
 8300 Saint Helena Hwy Rutherford (94573) *(P-1493)*
**Cal AM Manufacturing Co Inc** ................................................. F ...... 800 992-0499
 1939 Friendship Dr Ste E El Cajon (92020) *(P-16102)*
**Cal Cat Industries LLC** ............................................................ E ...... 209 883-4890
 2288 Geer Rd Hughson (95326) *(P-16103)*
**Cal Central Catering Trailers, Modesto** *Also Called: Golden Valley & Associates Inc (P-9522)*
**Cal Electro-Coatings Inc** .......................................................... E ...... 510 849-4075
 893 Carleton St Berkeley (94710) *(P-8936)*
**Cal LLC Powerflex Systems** .................................................... E ...... 650 469-3392
 15445 Innovation Dr San Diego (92128) *(P-11257)*
**Cal Pac Sheet Metal, Santa Ana** *Also Called: Cal Pac Sheet Metal Inc (P-8399)*
**Cal Pac Sheet Metal Inc** ........................................................... E ...... 714 979-2733
 2720 S Main St Ste B Santa Ana (92707) *(P-8399)*
**Cal Pipe Manufacturing Inc (PA)**............................................. E ...... 562 803-4388
 12160 Woodruff Ave Downey (90241) *(P-9252)*
**Cal Plate (PA)** ............................................................................. D ...... 562 403-3000
 17110 Jersey Ave Artesia (90701) *(P-9763)*
**Cal Ranch Inc** ............................................................................. E ...... 209 465-8999
 3201 Lance Dr Stockton (95205) *(P-17154)*
**Cal Ranch Inc (PA)** .................................................................... E ...... 925 429-2900
 4070 Nelson Ave Ste D Concord (94520) *(P-946)*
**Cal Ranch Wines, Concord** *Also Called: Cal Ranch Inc (P-946)*
**Cal Sheets LLC** .......................................................................... D ...... 209 234-3300
 1212 Performance Dr Stockton (95206) *(P-3826)*
**Cal Simba Inc (PA)** .................................................................... E ...... 805 240-1177
 1283 Flynn Rd Camarillo (93012) *(P-15707)*

**Cal Southern Braiding Inc** ........................................................ D ...... 562 927-5531
 7450 Scout Ave Bell Gardens (90201) *(P-12930)*
**Cal Southern Graphics Corp (HQ)**.......................................... D ...... 310 559-3600
 9655 De Soto Ave Chatsworth (91311) *(P-4541)*
**Cal Southern Packg Eqp Inc** ................................................... F ...... 909 598-3198
 4102 Valley Blvd Walnut (91789) *(P-16808)*
**Cal Southern Seafood Inc (PA)**............................................... E ...... 805 698-8262
 125 Salinas Rd Ste 5b Royal Oaks (95076) *(P-17155)*
**Cal Southern Sound Image Inc (PA)**...................................... D ...... 760 737-3900
 2425 Auto Park Way Escondido (92029) *(P-16693)*
**Cal Spas, Pomona** *Also Called: California Acrylic Inds Inc (P-16104)*
**Cal State Rubber, Santa Fe Springs** *Also Called: Duro Roller Company Inc (P-6489)*
**Cal State Site Services** ............................................................ E ...... 800 499-5757
 4518 Industrial St Simi Valley (93063) *(P-7638)*
**Cal Tape & Label, Anaheim** *Also Called: C T L Printing Inds Inc (P-4857)*
**Cal Tech Precision Inc** ............................................................. D ...... 714 992-4130
 1830 N Lemon St Anaheim (92801) *(P-13802)*
**Cal Treehouse Almonds LLC (PA)**.......................................... E ...... 559 757-5020
 6914 Road 160 Earlimart (93219) *(P-1348)*
**Cal Vsta Erosion Ctrl Pdts LLC** .............................................. E ...... 530 476-0706
 459 Country Rd 99w Arbuckle (95912) *(P-9412)*
**Cal West Designs, La Habra** *Also Called: K S Designs Inc (P-15999)*
**Cal Yuba Investments, Olivehurst** *Also Called: Yuba Rver Mlding Mill Work Inc (P-3211)*
**Cal-Asia Truss Inc** .................................................................... E ...... 916 685-5648
 10547 E Stockton Blvd Elk Grove (95624) *(P-3296)*
**Cal-Aurum, Huntington Beach** *Also Called: Cal-Aurum Industries (P-8937)*
**Cal-Aurum Industries** ............................................................... E ...... 714 898-0996
 15632 Container Ln Huntington Beach (92649) *(P-8937)*
**Cal-AZ Sales & Marketing, Placentia** *Also Called: Fruth Custom Plastics Inc (P-6834)*
**Cal-Coast Manufacturing Inc** .................................................. F ...... 209 634-9026
 424 S Tegner Rd Turlock (95380) *(P-8400)*
**Cal-Coast Pkg & Crating Inc** ................................................... E ...... 310 518-7215
 2040 E 220th St Carson (90810) *(P-3325)*
**Cal-Comp Electronics (usa) Co Ltd** ....................................... B ...... 858 587-6900
 9877 Waples St San Diego (92121) *(P-11312)*
**Cal-Comp USA (san Diego) Inc** .............................................. C ...... 858 587-6900
 1940 Camino Vida Roble Carlsbad (92008) *(P-12072)*
**Cal-Craft Design Intl Inc** .......................................................... F
 1615 Riverview Dr Ste A San Bernardino (92408) *(P-9664)*
**Cal-Draulics, Corona** *Also Called: Johnson Caldraul Inc (P-13882)*
**Cal-India Foods International** .................................................. E ...... 909 613-1660
 13591 Yorba Ave Chino (91710) *(P-6136)*
**Cal-June Inc (PA)**....................................................................... E ...... 323 877-4164
 5238 Vineland Ave North Hollywood (91601) *(P-7986)*
**Cal-Mil, Oceanside** *Also Called: Cal-Mil Plastic Products Inc (P-6756)*
**Cal-Mil Plastic Products Inc (PA)**........................................... E ...... 800 321-9069
 4079 Calle Platino Oceanside (92056) *(P-6756)*
**Cal-Monarch, Corona** *Also Called: California Wire Products Corp (P-9213)*
**Cal-Pac Chemical Co Inc** ........................................................ F ...... 323 585-2178
 6231 Maywood Ave Huntington Park (90255) *(P-5074)*
**Cal-Quake Construction Inc** ................................................... E ...... 323 931-2969
 636 N Formosa Ave Los Angeles (90036) *(P-211)*
**Cal-Sign Wholesale Inc** ........................................................... F ...... 209 523-7446
 2110 S Anne St Santa Ana (92704) *(P-15951)*
**Cal-Tron Corporation** ............................................................... E ...... 760 873-8491
 2290 Dixon Ln Bishop (93514) *(P-6757)*
**Cal-Tron Plating Inc** ................................................................. E ...... 562 945-1181
 11919 Rivera Rd Santa Fe Springs (90670) *(P-8938)*
**Cal-Weld Inc** ............................................................................... C ...... 510 226-0100
 4308 Solar Way Fremont (94538) *(P-9278)*
**Cala Action Inc** .......................................................................... E ...... 213 272-9759
 2440 Troy Ave South El Monte (91733) *(P-2406)*
**Cala Health Inc** .......................................................................... D ...... 415 890-3961
 1800 Gateway Dr Ste 120 San Mateo (94404) *(P-15522)*
**Calamp, Irvine** *Also Called: Calamp Corp (P-18140)*
**Calamp Corp (PA)** ..................................................................... C ...... 949 600-5600
 15635 Alton Pkwy Ste 250 Irvine (92618) *(P-18140)*
**Calaveras Materials Inc** ............................................................ E ...... 209 634-4931
 1301 Fulkerth Rd Turlock (95380) *(P-7409)*
**Calaveras Materials Inc (HQ)**................................................... E ...... 209 883-0448
 1100 Lowe Rd Hughson (95326) *(P-7410)*

# Calavo — ALPHABETIC SECTION

**Calavo, Santa Paula** Also Called: Calavo Growers Inc *(P-2153)*
**Calavo Growers Inc (PA)** ............................................................. D ...... 805 525-1245
1141 Cummings Rd Ste A Santa Paula (93060) *(P-2153)*
**Calbee America Incorporated** ..................................................... D ...... 559 661-4845
17577 Road 24 Madera (93638) *(P-2087)*
**Calbiotech Export Inc** .................................................................. E ...... 619 660-6162
1935 Cordell Ct El Cajon (92020) *(P-15023)*
**Calcareous Vineyard LLC** ........................................................... F ...... 805 239-0289
3430 Peachy Canyon Rd Paso Robles (93446) *(P-1494)*
**Calchef Foods LLC (HQ)** ............................................................. E ...... 888 638-7083
4221 E Mariposa Rd Ste B Stockton (95215) *(P-976)*
**Calcraft Company, Rialto** Also Called: Calcraft Corporation *(P-8111)*
**Calcraft Corporation** .................................................................... F ...... 909 879-2900
1426 S Willow Ave Rialto (92376) *(P-8111)*
**Calculex** ......................................................................................... E ...... 707 578-2307
131 Stony Cir Ste 500a Santa Rosa (95401) *(P-12868)*
**Caldera Medical Inc (PA)** ............................................................ D ...... 818 879-6555
4360 Park Terrace Dr Ste 140 Westlake Village (91361) *(P-15024)*
**Caldesso LLC** ............................................................................... D ...... 909 888-2882
439 S Stoddard Ave San Bernardino (92401) *(P-17691)*
**Caldigit Inc** .................................................................................... F ...... 714 572-6668
1941 E Miraloma Ave Ste B Placentia (92870) *(P-10228)*
**Caldwell Vineyard LLC** ................................................................ F ...... 707 255-1294
169 Kreuzer Ln Napa (94559) *(P-1495)*
**Caldwell Winery, Napa** Also Called: Caldwell Vineyard LLC *(P-1495)*
**Caldyn, Chatsworth** Also Called: California Dynamics Corp *(P-14853)*
**Caleb Enterprises Inc** .................................................................. F ...... 760 683-8787
5857 Owens Ave Ste 300 Carlsbad (92008) *(P-18141)*
**Calera Corporation** ...................................................................... E
11500 Dolan Road Moss Landing Moss Landing (95039) *(P-6137)*
**Calgren Renewable Fuels, Pixley** Also Called: Gfp Ethanol LLC *(P-6147)*
**Cali Chem Inc** ............................................................................... E ...... 714 265-3740
14271 Corporate Dr Ste B Garden Grove (92843) *(P-5952)*
**Cali Framing, Chatsworth** Also Called: Cali Framing Supplies LLC *(P-19247)*
**Cali Framing Supplies LLC** ......................................................... E ...... 818 899-7777
20450 Plummer St Chatsworth (91311) *(P-19247)*
**Cali Resources Inc** ....................................................................... E ...... 619 661-5741
2310 Michael Faraday Dr San Diego (92154) *(P-12931)*
**Cali-Fame Los Angeles Inc** ......................................................... D ...... 310 747-5263
20934 S Santa Fe Ave Carson (90810) *(P-2842)*
**Cali'flour Foods, Chico** Also Called: Amy Lacey Project *(P-848)*
**Calibre International LLC** ............................................................ C ...... 626 969-4660
6250 N Irwindale Ave Irwindale (91702) *(P-19548)*
**Calidad Inc** .................................................................................... E ...... 909 947-3937
1730 S Balboa Ave Ontario (91761) *(P-7837)*
**Calient Technologies, Goleta** Also Called: Calient Technologies Inc *(P-11755)*
**Calient Technologies Inc (PA)** .................................................... E ...... 805 695-4800
120 Cremona Dr Ste 160 Goleta (93117) *(P-11755)*
**Caliextractions LLC** ..................................................................... F ...... 916 519-7649
8790 Fruitridge Rd Sacramento (95826) *(P-16809)*
**California Academy Sciences (PA)** ............................................ A ...... 415 379-8000
55 Music Concourse Dr San Francisco (94118) *(P-19366)*
**California Acrylic Inds Inc (HQ)** .................................................. F ...... 909 623-8781
1462 E 9th St Pomona (91766) *(P-16104)*
**California Acti, Irvine** Also Called: Acti Corporation Inc *(P-11632)*
**California Air Conveying Corp** ................................................... F ...... 562 531-4570
16260 Minnesota Ave Paramount (90723) *(P-549)*
**California Air Tools Inc** ............................................................... E ...... 619 407-7905
8560 Siempre Viva Rd San Diego (92154) *(P-9710)*
**California Almond Growers Exch, Sacramento** Also Called: Diamond Blue Growers *(P-2183)*
**California Amforge, Azusa** Also Called: California Amforge Corporation *(P-7608)*
**California Amforge Corporation** ................................................ C ...... 626 334-4931
750 N Vernon Ave Azusa (91702) *(P-7608)*
**California Bag, Woodland** Also Called: Acme Bag Co Inc *(P-3989)*
**California Baking Company** ........................................................ B ...... 619 591-8289
681 Anita St Chula Vista (91911) *(P-17179)*
**California Blue Apparel Inc** ........................................................ E ...... 213 745-5400
245 W 28th St Los Angeles (90007) *(P-2701)*
**California Bottling Company** ...................................................... E ...... 916 772-1000
8250 Industrial Ave Roseville (95678) *(P-1873)*

**California Box Company (PA)** ..................................................... D ...... 562 921-1223
13901 Carmenita Rd Santa Fe Springs (90670) *(P-3827)*
**California Box II** ........................................................................... D ...... 909 944-9202
8949 Toronto Ave Rancho Cucamonga (91730) *(P-16997)*
**California Brazing, Newark** Also Called: Nevada Heat Treating LLC *(P-19209)*
**California Bread Co., Chula Vista** Also Called: California Baking Company *(P-17179)*
**California Breakers Inc (PA)** ....................................................... E ...... 760 598-1528
2490 Grand Ave Vista (92081) *(P-16648)*
**California Cab & Store Fix** .......................................................... E ...... 916 386-1340
8472 Carbide Ct Sacramento (95828) *(P-3113)*
**California Cabinet & Storage, Sacramento** Also Called: California Cabinet & Str Fixs *(P-3226)*
**California Cabinet & Str Fixs** ...................................................... E ...... 916 681-0901
8472 Carbide Ct Sacramento (95828) *(P-3226)*
**California Candy, South El Monte** Also Called: California Snack Foods Inc *(P-1301)*
**California Cascade Industries** .................................................... C ...... 916 736-3353
7512 14th Ave Sacramento (95820) *(P-3401)*
**California Cedar Products Co (PA)** ............................................ E ...... 209 932-5002
2385 Arch Airport Rd Ste 500 Stockton (95206) *(P-3413)*
**California Chassis Inc** ................................................................. C ...... 714 666-8511
3356 E La Palma Ave Anaheim (92806) *(P-8401)*
**California Churros Corporation** .................................................. B ...... 909 370-4777
751 Via Lata Colton (92324) *(P-1175)*
**California Classics, Santa Clarita** Also Called: California Millworks Corp *(P-3114)*
**California Combining Corp** ......................................................... E ...... 323 589-5727
5607 S Santa Fe Ave Vernon (90058) *(P-2526)*
**California Commercial Asp LLC** ................................................. F ...... 858 513-0611
4211 Ponderosa Ave Ste C San Diego (92123) *(P-7411)*
**California Community News LLC (DH)** ..................................... B ...... 626 388-1017
2000 E 8th St Los Angeles (90021) *(P-4080)*
**California Community News LLC** .............................................. D ...... 818 843-8700
221 N Brand Blvd Fl 2 Glendale (91203) *(P-4081)*
**California Concentrate Company** .............................................. E ...... 209 334-9112
18678 N Highway 99 Acampo (95220) *(P-998)*
**California Control Solutions, Anaheim** Also Called: George T Hall Co Inc *(P-16780)*
**California Costume Int'l, Los Angeles** Also Called: Califrnia Cstume Cllctions Inc *(P-2892)*
**California Countertop Inc (PA)** .................................................. F ...... 619 460-0205
7811 Alvarado Rd La Mesa (91942) *(P-557)*
**California Cstm Frt & Flavors, Irwindale** Also Called: Califrnia Cstm Frits Flvors LL *(P-1992)*
**California Custom Proc LLC** ...................................................... E ...... 559 416-5122
3211 Aviation Dr Madera (93637) *(P-356)*
**California Dairies Inc** .................................................................. C ...... 209 656-1942
475 S Tegner Rd Turlock (95380) *(P-704)*
**California Dairies Inc (PA)** ......................................................... D ...... 559 625-2200
2000 N Plaza Dr Visalia (93291) *(P-828)*
**California Dairies Inc** .................................................................. D ...... 559 233-5154
755 F St Fresno (93706) *(P-829)*
**California Dairies Inc** .................................................................. D ...... 562 809-2595
11709 Artesia Blvd Artesia (90701) *(P-830)*
**California Dept Wtr Resources** .................................................. E ...... 916 651-9203
901 P St Lbby Sacramento (95814) *(P-14391)*
**California Die Casting Inc** .......................................................... E ...... 909 947-9947
1820 S Grove Ave Ontario (91761) *(P-7826)*
**California Digital Inc (PA)** .......................................................... D ...... 310 217-0500
6 Saddleback Rd Rolling Hills (90274) *(P-10340)*
**California Door, Morgan Hill** Also Called: California Kit Cab Door Corp *(P-3227)*
**California Dynamics Corp (PA)** ................................................. E ...... 323 223-3882
20500 Prairie St Chatsworth (91311) *(P-14853)*
**California Dynasty, Los Angeles** Also Called: MGT Industries Inc *(P-2791)*
**California Exotic Novlt LLC** ....................................................... D ...... 909 606-1950
1455 E Francis St Ontario (91761) *(P-16105)*
**California Family Foods LLC** ..................................................... D ...... 530 476-3326
6550 Struckmeyer Rd Arbuckle (95912) *(P-1072)*
**California Faucets Inc** ................................................................ E ...... 657 400-1639
5231 Argosy Ave Huntington Beach (92649) *(P-8048)*
**California Faucets Inc (PA)** ....................................................... E ...... 800 822-8855
5271 Argosy Ave Huntington Beach (92649) *(P-8049)*
**California Fiber Drum Co, Merced** Also Called: Mauser Usa LLC *(P-3906)*
**California Fine Wire Co (PA)** ..................................................... E ...... 805 489-5144
338 S 4th St Grover Beach (93433) *(P-7777)*
**California Flexrake Corp** ............................................................ E ...... 626 443-4026
9620 Gidley St Temple City (91780) *(P-7948)*

California Fruit Basket, Sanger *Also Called: Melkonian Enterprises Inc (P-957)*
California Gasket and Rbr Corp (PA) .................................................... E ...... 714 202-8500
   533 W Collins Ave Orange (92867) *(P-6486)*
California Gate Entry Systems, Anaheim *Also Called: C G Systems LLC (P-452)*
California Glass & Mirror Div, Santa Ana *Also Called: Twed-Dells Inc (P-7245)*
California Graphics, Chatsworth *Also Called: Cal Southern Graphics Corp (P-4541)*
California Heritage Mills Inc .................................................................. E ...... 530 438-2100
   15 Comet Ln Maxwell (95955) *(P-1073)*
California House, Sacramento *Also Called: Beauty Craft Furniture Corp (P-3434)*
California Hydroforming Co Inc ............................................................ F ...... 626 912-0036
   850 Lawson St City Of Industry (91748) *(P-8402)*
California Hydronics Corp (PA) ............................................................ E ...... 510 293-1993
   2293 Tripaldi Way Hayward (94545) *(P-16775)*
California Industrial, Eastvale *Also Called: Califrnia Indus Rfrgn Mchs Inc (P-10487)*
California Industrial Fabrics ................................................................. E ...... 619 661-7166
   2325 Marconi Ct San Diego (92154) *(P-2443)*
California Industrial Rbr Co (PA) ......................................................... E ...... 559 268-7321
   2539 S Cherry Ave Fresno (93706) *(P-16865)*
California Insulated Wire & ................................................................. D ...... 818 569-4930
   3050 N California St Burbank (91504) *(P-7778)*
California Interfill Inc ............................................................................. F ...... 951 351-2619
   8178 Mar Vista Ct Riverside (92504) *(P-5953)*
California Kit Cab Door Corp (PA) ....................................................... D ...... 408 782-5700
   610 Jarvis Dr Morgan Hill (95037) *(P-3227)*
California Lithographers, Concord *Also Called: Acme Press Inc (P-4501)*
California Machine Specialties, Chino *Also Called: Young Machine Inc (P-11198)*
California Metal, Cerritos *Also Called: California Metal & Supply Inc (P-8303)*
California Metal & Supply Inc .............................................................. F ...... 800 707-6061
   14020 Bolsa Ln Cerritos (90703) *(P-8303)*
California Mfg & Engrg Co LLC ........................................................... C ...... 559 842-1500
   1401 S Madera Ave Kerman (93630) *(P-9413)*
California Mfg Cabinetry Inc ................................................................ F ...... 909 930-3632
   1474 E Francis St Ontario (91761) *(P-3649)*
California Millworks Corp ..................................................................... E ...... 661 294-2345
   27772 Avenue Scott Santa Clarita (91355) *(P-3114)*
California Natural Products ................................................................. B ...... 209 858-2525
   1250 Lathrop Rd Lathrop (95330) *(P-2154)*
California Neon Products .................................................................... D ...... 619 283-2191
   9944 Blossom Valley Rd El Cajon (92021) *(P-15952)*
California New Foods LLC .................................................................. E ...... 831 444-1872
   1101 Roosevelt St Monterey (93940) *(P-2155)*
California Newspaper Service, Los Angeles *Also Called: California Newsppr Svc Bur Inc (P-4084)*
California Newspapers Inc .................................................................. A ...... 415 883-8600
   150 Alameda Del Prado Novato (94949) *(P-4082)*
California Newspapers Partnr (PA) ..................................................... E ...... 408 920-5333
   4 N 2nd St Ste 700 San Jose (95113) *(P-4083)*
California Newsppr Svc Bur Inc .......................................................... F ...... 213 229-5500
   915 E 1st St Los Angeles (90012) *(P-4084)*
California Nuggets Inc ......................................................................... E ...... 209 599-7131
   23073 S Frederick Rd Ripon (95366) *(P-2088)*
California Offset Printers Inc (PA) ....................................................... D ...... 818 291-1100
   5075 Brooks St Montclair (91763) *(P-4542)*
California Oils, Richmond *Also Called: Aak USA Richmond Corp (P-1391)*
California Olive and Vine LLC ............................................................. F ...... 530 763-7921
   1670 Poole Blvd Yuba City (95993) *(P-1394)*
California Olive Ranch Inc (PA) .......................................................... D ...... 530 846-8000
   265 Airpark Blvd Ste 200 Chico (95973) *(P-1395)*
California Pak Intl Inc ........................................................................... E ...... 310 223-2500
   17706 S Main St Gardena (90248) *(P-11206)*
California Paperboard, Santa Clara *Also Called: Caraustar Industries Inc (P-3901)*
California PCF Trdg Co II Inc .............................................................. F ...... 951 218-8253
   1320 Riverview Dr San Bernardino (92408) *(P-9508)*
California Performance Packg ............................................................ D ...... 909 390-4422
   33200 Lewis St Union City (94587) *(P-6625)*
California Plasteck, Ontario *Also Called: Paramount Panels Inc (P-6950)*
California Plastics, Riverside *Also Called: Altium Holdings LLC (P-6706)*
California Plastix Inc ............................................................................ E ...... 909 629-8288
   1319 E 3rd St Pomona (91766) *(P-3963)*
California Portland Cement, Mojave *Also Called: Calportland Company (P-7249)*

California Poultry, Los Angeles *Also Called: Western Supreme Inc (P-702)*
California Premium Incentives, Lake Forest *Also Called: Aminco International USA Inc (P-15683)*
California Quality Plas Inc ................................................................... E ...... 909 930-5667
   2104 S Cucamonga Ave Ontario (91761) *(P-6758)*
California Resources Corp (PA) .......................................................... D ...... 888 848-4754
   1 World Trade Ctr Ste 1500 Long Beach (90831) *(P-129)*
California Resources Corp .................................................................. D ...... 661 395-8000
   5000 Stockdale Hwy Bakersfield (93309) *(P-172)*
California Resources Prod Corp ......................................................... E ...... 661 869-8000
   4900 W Lokern Rd Mc Kittrick (93251) *(P-130)*
California Resources Prod Corp (HQ) ................................................ C ...... 661 869-8000
   27200 Tourney Rd Ste 200 Santa Clarita (91355) *(P-131)*
California Respiratory Care ................................................................. D ...... 818 379-9999
   16055 Ventura Blvd # 715 Encino (91436) *(P-6272)*
California Ribbon Carbn Co Inc .......................................................... D ...... 323 724-9100
   8420 Quinn St Downey (90241) *(P-15893)*
California Royale LLC ......................................................................... E ...... 209 874-1866
   5043 N Montpelier Rd Denair (95316) *(P-76)*
California Scents LLC .......................................................................... F
   18850 Von Karman Ave Ste 200 Irvine (92612) *(P-5894)*
California Screw Products Corp .......................................................... D ...... 562 633-6626
   14950 Gwenchris Ct Paramount (90723) *(P-7987)*
California Sensor Corporation ............................................................. E ...... 760 438-0525
   2075 Corte Del Nogal Ste P Carlsbad (92011) *(P-14854)*
California Sheet Metal, El Cajon *Also Called: California Shtmtl Works Inc (P-357)*
California Shtmtl Works Inc ................................................................. D ...... 619 562-7010
   1020 N Marshall Ave El Cajon (92020) *(P-357)*
California Signs Inc ............................................................................. E ...... 818 899-1888
   10280 Glenoaks Blvd Pacoima (91331) *(P-15953)*
California Silica Products LLC ............................................................ D ...... 909 947-0028
   12808 Rancho Rd Adelanto (92301) *(P-5075)*
California Snack Foods Inc ................................................................. E ...... 626 444-4508
   2131 Tyler Ave South El Monte (91733) *(P-1301)*
California Specialty Farms, Los Angeles *Also Called: Worldwide Specialties Inc (P-2392)*
California Spirits Company LLC .......................................................... E ...... 619 677-7066
   2946 Norman Strasse Rd San Marcos (92069) *(P-1874)*
California Steel Inds Inc (HQ) ............................................................. C ...... 909 350-6300
   14000 San Bernardino Ave Fontana (92335) *(P-7609)*
California Steel Inds Inc ...................................................................... B ...... 909 350-6300
   1 California Steel Way Fontana (92335) *(P-7661)*
California Steel Services, San Bernardino *Also Called: California Steel Services Inc (P-16609)*
California Steel Services Inc ............................................................... E ...... 909 796-2222
   1212 S Mountain View Ave San Bernardino (92408) *(P-16609)*
California Stl Fabricators Inc ............................................................... F ...... 209 566-0629
   1120 Reno Ave Modesto (95351) *(P-8112)*
California Sugars LLC ......................................................................... E ...... 800 333-9666
   1465 Tanforan Ave Woodland (95776) *(P-1294)*
California Sulphur Company ............................................................... E ...... 562 437-0768
   2250 E Pacific Coast Hwy Wilmington (90744) *(P-5076)*
California Sun Rooms, Rancho Cordova *Also Called: Califrnia Cstm Snroms Ptio Cve (P-558)*
California Supertrucks Inc ................................................................... F ...... 951 656-2903
   14385 Veterans Way Moreno Valley (92553) *(P-13402)*
California Tiny House, Fresno *Also Called: California Tiny House Inc (P-3381)*
California Tiny House Inc .................................................................... F ...... 559 316-4500
   3337 W Sussex Way Fresno (93722) *(P-3381)*
California Tomato Machinery, Madera *Also Called: Westside Equipment Co (P-16803)*
California Tool & Die, Azusa *Also Called: Mc William & Son Inc (P-8863)*
California Tool & Engineering, Jurupa Valley *Also Called: Cte California Tl & Engrg Inc (P-9672)*
California Track & Engineering ........................................................... E ...... 559 237-2590
   4668 N Sonora Ave Ste 101 Fresno (93722) *(P-15796)*
California Trusframe LLC .................................................................... C ...... 559 876-3630
   1144 Commerce Way Sanger (93657) *(P-3297)*
California Trusframe LLC .................................................................... C ...... 951 657-7491
   23447 Cajalco Rd Perris (92570) *(P-3298)*
California Trusframe LLC .................................................................... C ...... 209 883-8000
   2800 Tully Rd Hughson (95326) *(P-3299)*
California Trusframe LLC (HQ) ........................................................... D ...... 951 350-4880
   23665 Cajalco Rd Perris (92570) *(P-3300)*
California Truss Company (PA) ........................................................... D ...... 951 657-7491
   23665 Cajalco Rd Perris (92570) *(P-3301)*

**California Truss Company** ......................................................... C ...... 209 883-8000
2800 Tully Rd Hughson (95326) *(P-3302)*

**California Wine Company** ............................................................ E ...... 707 603-2203
2785 Napa Valley Corporate Dr Napa (94558) *(P-9)*

**California Wire Products Corp** ..................................................... E ...... 951 371-7730
1316 Railroad St Corona (92882) *(P-9213)*

**California Wood Cstm Solutions (PA)** ......................................... F ...... 909 364-2440
4857 Schaefer Ave Chino (91710) *(P-3115)*

**California Woodworking Inc** ......................................................... E ...... 805 982-9090
1726 Ives Ave Oxnard (93033) *(P-3228)*

**Californian, The, San Diego** *Also Called: North County Times (P-4172)*

**Califrnia Anlytical Instrs Inc** ........................................................ D ...... 714 974-5560
1312 W Grove Ave Orange (92865) *(P-14392)*

**Califrnia Citrus Producers Inc** .................................................... D ...... 559 562-5169
525 E Lindmore St Lindsay (93247) *(P-999)*

**Califrnia Cstm Frts Flvors LL (PA)** .............................................. E ...... 626 736-4130
15800 Tapia St Irwindale (91706) *(P-1992)*

**Califrnia Cstm Snroms Ptio Cve** ................................................. F ...... 800 834-3211
3160 Gold Valley Dr Ste 300 Rancho Cordova (95742) *(P-558)*

**Califrnia Cstume Cllctions Inc (PA)** ............................................ B ...... 323 262-8383
210 S Anderson St Los Angeles (90033) *(P-2892)*

**Califrnia Dluxe Wndows Inds In (PA)** ......................................... E ...... 818 349-5566
20735 Superior St Chatsworth (91311) *(P-3116)*

**Califrnia Dsgners Chice Cstm C** ................................................ E ...... 805 987-5820
547 Constitution Ave Ste F Camarillo (93012) *(P-3229)*

**Califrnia Furn Collections Inc** ..................................................... C ...... 619 621-2455
150 Reed Ct Ste A Chula Vista (91911) *(P-3553)*

**Califrnia Indus Rfrgn Mchs Inc** .................................................... F ...... 951 361-0040
3197 Cornerstone Dr Eastvale (91752) *(P-10487)*

**Califrnia Mantel Fireplace Inc (PA)** ............................................ E ...... 916 925-5775
4141 N Freeway Blvd Sacramento (95834) *(P-3117)*

**Califrnia Nutritional Pdts Inc** ...................................................... D ...... 760 625-3884
64405 Lincoln St Mecca (92254) *(P-1069)*

**Califrnia Nwspapers Ltd Partnr (DH)** ......................................... B ...... 626 962-8811
605 E Huntington Dr Ste 100 Monrovia (91016) *(P-4085)*

**Califrnia Nwspapers Ltd Partnr** .................................................. B ...... 909 987-6397
3200 E Guasti Rd Ste 100 Ontario (91761) *(P-4086)*

**Califrnia Nwspapers Ltd Partnr** .................................................. B ...... 909 793-3221
19 E Citrus Ave Ste 102 Redlands (92373) *(P-4087)*

**Califrnia Nwspapers Ltd Partnr** .................................................. B ...... 530 877-4413
5399 Clark Rd Paradise (95969) *(P-4088)*

**Califrnia Prcast Stone Mfg Inc** .................................................... F ...... 951 657-7913
1796 Karen Ct Hemet (92545) *(P-7315)*

**Califrnia Prtland Cem Dispatch, Vernon** *Also Called: Calportland Company (P-7413)*

**Califrnia Rcrtion Instllations, Corona** *Also Called: Playmax Surfacing Inc (P-6522)*

**Califrnia Rsrces Elk Hills LLC** ..................................................... B ...... 661 412-0000
27200 Tourney Rd Ste 200 Santa Clarita (91355) *(P-173)*

**Califrnia Srvying Drftg Sup In (PA)** ............................................. E ...... 916 344-0232
4733 Auburn Blvd Sacramento (95841) *(P-17850)*

**Califrnia Trade Converters Inc** ................................................... E ...... 818 899-1455
9816 Variel Ave Chatsworth (91311) *(P-3800)*

**Califrnia Workforce Enrgy Svcs, Fresno** *Also Called: Cwes Inc (P-19556)*

**Calimex Deli** ................................................................................. E ...... 323 261-7271
711 1/2 S Kern Ave Los Angeles (90022) *(P-17568)*

**CALIX, San Jose** *Also Called: Calix Inc (P-16334)*

**Calix Inc (PA)** ............................................................................... A ...... 408 514-3000
2777 Orchard Pkwy San Jose (95134) *(P-16334)*

**Callaway Vineyard & Winery** ....................................................... D ...... 951 676-4001
32720 Rancho California Rd Temecula (92591) *(P-1496)*

**Callidus Software Inc (HQ)** ......................................................... C ...... 925 251-2200
2700 Camino Ramon # 400 San Ramon (94583) *(P-17894)*

**Calliduscloud, San Ramon** *Also Called: Callidus Software Inc (P-17894)*

**Callisto Media Inc** ....................................................................... C ...... 510 253-0500
1955 Broadway # 400 Oakland (94612) *(P-4318)*

**Calmar Laser, Inc., Palo Alto** *Also Called: Calmar Optcom Inc (P-11756)*

**Calmar Optcom Inc** ..................................................................... E ...... 408 733-7800
951 Commercial St Palo Alto (94303) *(P-11756)*

**Calmat Co** .................................................................................... B ...... 661 858-2673
16101 Hwy 156 Maricopa (93252) *(P-298)*

**Calmax Technology Inc** ............................................................... F ...... 408 506-2035
558 Laurelwood Rd Santa Clara (95054) *(P-10760)*

**Calmax Technology Inc** .............................................................. E ...... 408 513-2139
526 Laurelwood Rd Santa Clara (95054) *(P-10761)*

**Calmax Technology Inc (PA)** ...................................................... E ...... 408 748-8660
3491 Lafayette St Santa Clara (95054) *(P-10762)*

**Calmcom Inc (PA)** ....................................................................... E ...... 415 236-3012
555 Bryant St Ste 262 Palo Alto (94301) *(P-18142)*

**Calmex Fireplace Eqp Mfg Inc** ................................................... E ...... 716 645-2901
13629 Talc St Santa Fe Springs (90670) *(P-7988)*

**Calmex Fireplace Equip Mfg, Santa Fe Springs** *Also Called: Calmex Fireplace Eqp Mfg Inc (P-7988)*

**Calmont Engrg & Elec Corp (PA)** ............................................... E ...... 714 549-0336
420 E Alton Ave Santa Ana (92707) *(P-7779)*

**Calmont Wire & Cable, Santa Ana** *Also Called: Calmont Engrg & Elec Corp (P-7779)*

**Calnetix Technologies LLC (HQ)** ................................................ D ...... 562 293-1660
16323 Shoemaker Ave Cerritos (90703) *(P-11258)*

**Calnrg Operating LLC (PA)** ........................................................ E ...... 805 477-9805
1536 Eastman Ave Ventura (93003) *(P-132)*

**Calogic (PA)** ................................................................................ E ...... 510 656-2900
237 Whitney Pl Fremont (94539) *(P-14503)*

**Calpack Foods LLC** .................................................................... E ...... 310 320-0141
22625 S Western Ave Torrance (90501) *(P-9781)*

**Calpaco Papers Inc (PA)** ............................................................ C ...... 323 767-2800
3155 Universe Dr Jurupa Valley (91752) *(P-4033)*

**Calpak Usa Inc** ............................................................................ E ...... 310 937-7335
13748 Prairie Ave Hawthorne (90250) *(P-12073)*

**Calpella Distribution Center, Calpella** *Also Called: Mendocino Forest Pdts Co LLC (P-16452)*

**Calpico Inc** ................................................................................... E ...... 650 588-2241
1387 San Mateo Ave South San Francisco (94080) *(P-11444)*

**Calpine Containers Inc (PA)** ....................................................... F ...... 559 519-7199
380 W Spruce Ave Clovis (93611) *(P-16998)*

**Calpipe Industries LLC** ............................................................... E ...... 562 803-4388
923 Calpipe Rd Santa Paula (93060) *(P-7610)*

**Calpipe Security Bollards, Downey** *Also Called: Cal Pipe Manufacturing Inc (P-9252)*

**Calplant I LLC** ............................................................................. E ...... 530 361-0003
6101 State Hwy 162 Willows (95988) *(P-3406)*

**Calplant I Holdco LLC (PA)** ........................................................ E ...... 530 570-0542
6101 State Hwy 162 Willows (95988) *(P-3407)*

**Calportland** .................................................................................. D ...... 760 343-3403
2025 E Financial Way Glendora (91741) *(P-7412)*

**Calportland Company** ................................................................. C ...... 661 824-2401
9350 Oak Creek Rd Mojave (93501) *(P-7249)*

**Calportland Company** ................................................................. D ...... 760 245-5321
19409 National Trails Hwy Oro Grande (92368) *(P-7250)*

**Calportland Company** ................................................................. E ...... 209 469-0109
2201 W Washington St Ste 6 Stockton (95203) *(P-7251)*

**Calportland Company (DH)** ........................................................ D ...... 626 852-6200
2025 E Financial Way Glendora (91741) *(P-7252)*

**Calportland Company** ................................................................. F ...... 800 272-1891
1862 E 27th St Vernon (90058) *(P-7413)*

**Calportland Company** ................................................................. F ...... 626 334-3226
1030 W Gladstone St Azusa (91702) *(P-7414)*

**Calrad Electronics Inc** ................................................................. E ...... 323 465-2131
819 N Highland Ave Los Angeles (90038) *(P-16694)*

**Calsak Plastics, Rancho Dominguez** *Also Called: Plastics Family Holdings Inc (P-6965)*

**Calsense, Carlsbad** *Also Called: California Sensor Corporation (P-14854)*

**Calstar Systems Group Inc** ......................................................... E ...... 818 922-2000
6345 Balboa Blvd Ste 105 Encino (91316) *(P-13217)*

**Calva Products LLC (PA)** ........................................................... E ...... 800 328-9680
4351 E Winery Rd Acampo (95220) *(P-1121)*

**Calva Products Co Inc** ................................................................ E ...... 209 339-1516
4351 E Winery Rd Acampo (95220) *(P-1122)*

**Calvillo Construction Corp** .......................................................... E ...... 310 985-3911
1133 Brooks St Ste C Ontario (91762) *(P-343)*

**Calwax LLC (DH)** ........................................................................ E ...... 626 969-4334
16511 Knott Ave La Mirada (90638) *(P-17239)*

**Calwest Galvanizing, Carson** *Also Called: Calwest Galvanizing Corp (P-9056)*

**Calwest Galvanizing Corp** .......................................................... F ...... 310 549-2200
2226 E Dominguez St Carson (90810) *(P-9056)*

**Calwest Mfg and Lsk Suspension, Fontana** *Also Called: Lamer Street Kreations Corp (P-19402)*

**Calwest Steel Detailing, Pleasanton** *Also Called: Future Innovations Inc (P-19092)*

# ALPHABETIC SECTION                                              Canyon Products Corporation

Calypto Design Systems  Inc ............................................ E ...... 408 850-2300
  2099 Gateway Pl Ste 550 San Jose (95110) *(P-18143)*
Calysta  Inc (PA)............................................................. F ...... 650 492-6880
  1900 Alameda De Las Pulgas Ste 200 San Mateo (94403) *(P-6138)*
CAM, Fullerton *Also Called: Consolidated Aerospace Mfg LLC (P-14172)*
Camar Aircraft Parts Co .................................................. E ...... 805 389-8944
  743 Flynn Rd Camarillo (93012) *(P-13803)*
Camar Aircraft Parts Company, Camarillo *Also Called: Camar Aircraft Parts Co (P-13803)*
Cambium Business Group  Inc (PA)................................ C ...... 714 670-1171
  6950 Noritsu Ave Buena Park (90620) *(P-16412)*
Camblin Steel Service Inc .............................................. D ...... 916 644-1300
  548 Gibson Dr Ste 150 Roseville (95678) *(P-8694)*
Cambrian Lab Inc ........................................................... F ...... 408 569-3744
  7045 Corte Del Oro Pleasanton (94566) *(P-18144)*
Cambridge Equities  LP ................................................. E ...... 858 350-2300
  9922 Jefferson Blvd Culver City (90232) *(P-5812)*
Cambro, Huntington Beach *Also Called: Cambro Manufacturing Company (P-6760)*
Cambro Manufacturing, Huntington Beach *Also Called: Cambro Manufacturing Company (P-6761)*
Cambro Manufacturing Company .................................. B ...... 714 848-1555
  7601 Clay Ave Huntington Beach (92648) *(P-6759)*
Cambro Manufacturing Company (PA)........................... B ...... 714 848-1555
  5801 Skylab Rd Huntington Beach (92647) *(P-6760)*
Cambro Manufacturing Company .................................. D ...... 714 848-1555
  5801 Skylab Rd Huntington Beach (92647) *(P-6761)*
Cambro Manufacturing Company .................................. C ...... 909 354-8962
  21558 Ferrero City Of Industry (91789) *(P-16106)*
Camelbak Products, Petaluma *Also Called: Camelbak Products  LLC (P-15797)*
Camelbak Products  LLC (HQ)....................................... D ...... 707 792-9700
  2000 S Mcdowell Boulevard Ext Ste 200 Petaluma (94954) *(P-15797)*
Cameo Crafts, Sonoma *Also Called: Cameo Sonoma Limited (P-4034)*
Cameo Sonoma Limited ................................................. D ...... 707 935-0202
  21684 8th St E Ste 700 Sonoma (95476) *(P-4034)*
Cameo Technologies Inc ................................................ E ...... 949 672-7000
  20511 Lake Forest Dr Lake Forest (92630) *(P-10229)*
Camera Ready Cars, Fountain Valley *Also Called: Gaffoglio Fmly Mtlcrafters Inc (P-7222)*
Cameron International Corp ........................................... E ...... 707 752-8800
  535 Getty Ct Ste A Benicia (94510) *(P-9457)*
Cameron Surface Systems, Bakersfield *Also Called: Cameron West Coast Inc (P-16788)*
Cameron Technologies Us  LLC ..................................... E ...... 562 222-8440
  4040 Capitol Ave Whittier (90601) *(P-14393)*
Cameron Welding, Stanton *Also Called: Cameron Welding Supply (P-19185)*
Cameron Welding Supply (PA)....................................... E ...... 714 530-9353
  11061 Dale Ave Stanton (90680) *(P-19185)*
Cameron West Coast Inc ................................................ D
  4315 Yeager Way Bakersfield (93313) *(P-16788)*
Cameron's Measurement Systems, Whittier *Also Called: Cameron Technologies Us  LLC (P-14393)*
Cameroncompany, Petaluma *Also Called: Robert W Cameron & Co  Inc (P-4343)*
Camfil Farr Inc ................................................................ E ...... 973 616-7300
  3625 Del Amo Blvd Ste 260 Torrance (90503) *(P-9981)*
Camfil Usa Inc ................................................................ E ...... 559 992-5118
  500 Industrial Ave Corcoran (93212) *(P-9982)*
Camino Real Foods  Inc (PA)......................................... C ...... 323 585-6599
  2638 E Vernon Ave Los Angeles (90058) *(P-2156)*
Camino Real Kitchens, Los Angeles *Also Called: Camino Real Foods  Inc (P-2156)*
Camisasca Automotive Mfg Inc ...................................... E ...... 949 452-0195
  20341 Hermana Cir Lake Forest (92630) *(P-8827)*
Camisasca Automotive Mfg Inc (PA).............................. E ...... 949 452-0195
  20352 Hermana Cir Lake Forest (92630) *(P-8828)*
Camp Smidgemore  Inc (DH)......................................... E ...... 323 634-0333
  3641 10th Ave Los Angeles (90018) *(P-2742)*
Campbell Certified  Inc .................................................. E ...... 760 722-9353
  1629 Ord Way Oceanside (92056) *(P-8113)*
Campbell Engineering, Lake Forest *Also Called: Campbell Engineering Inc (P-9665)*
Campbell Engineering Inc .............................................. E ...... 949 859-3306
  20412 Barents Sea Cir Lake Forest (92630) *(P-9665)*
Campbell Grinding  Inc .................................................. F ...... 209 339-8838
  1003 E Vine St Lodi (95240) *(P-10763)*
Campbell Membrane Tech Inc ........................................ E ...... 619 938-2481
  1168 N Johnson Ave El Cajon (92020) *(P-10079)*

Camper Packaging  LLC ................................................ F ...... 562 239-6167
  13208 Arctic Cir Santa Fe Springs (90670) *(P-752)*
Campos Family Vineyards, Byron *Also Called: Campos Vineyards LLC (P-1497)*
Campos Vineyards LLC .................................................. E ...... 925 308-7963
  3501 Byer Rd Byron (94514) *(P-1497)*
Campus Images, Anaheim *Also Called: University Frames  Inc (P-3429)*
Camston Wrather LLC .................................................... C ...... 858 525-9999
  2856 Whiptail Loop Carlsbad (92010) *(P-19551)*
Camtech, Irvine *Also Called: Computer Assisted Mfg Tech LLC (P-10785)*
Can Lines Engineering  Inc (PA).................................... D ...... 562 861-2996
  9839 Downey Norwalk Rd Downey (90241) *(P-10016)*
Canaan Company, Fresno *Also Called: DV Kap  Inc (P-2928)*
Canadas Finest Foods  Inc ............................................ D ...... 951 296-1040
  26090 Ynez Rd Temecula (92591) *(P-1000)*
Canari, San Marcos *Also Called: Leemarc Industries  LLC (P-2630)*
Canary Communications  Inc ......................................... F ...... 408 365-0609
  6040 Hellyer Ave Ste 150 San Jose (95138) *(P-11822)*
Canary Medical USA LLC ............................................... D ...... 760 448-5066
  2710 Loker Ave W Ste 350 Carlsbad (92010) *(P-15025)*
Canary Technologies Corp ............................................. E ...... 415 578-1414
  275 Sacramento St San Francisco (94105) *(P-18145)*
Candela Renewables  LLC ............................................ E ...... 415 515-9627
  500 Sansome St Ste 500 San Francisco (94111) *(P-8062)*
Candle Crafters, Moorpark *Also Called: Globaluxe  Inc (P-16136)*
Candle Lamp Holdings  LLC ......................................... B ...... 951 682-9600
  949 S Coast Dr Ste 650 Costa Mesa (92626) *(P-11422)*
Candles By Hgbyg Corp ................................................. F ...... 415 655-9865
  1028 Market St San Francisco (94102) *(P-19079)*
Candlewick-Porterville, Porterville *Also Called: Tdg Operations  LLC (P-2523)*
Canine Caviar, Riverside *Also Called: Canine Caviar Pet Foods  Inc (P-1123)*
Canine Caviar Pet Foods  Inc ........................................ E ...... 714 223-1800
  4131 Tigris Way Riverside (92503) *(P-1123)*
Canine Caviar Pet Foods De Inc .................................... F ...... 714 223-1800
  4131 Tigris Way Riverside (92503) *(P-1095)*
Cannalogic ..................................................................... F ...... 619 458-0775
  5404 Whitsett Ave # 219 Valley Village (91607) *(P-16107)*
Cannery Seafood of Pacific LLC .................................... F ...... 949 566-0060
  3010 Lafayette Rd Newport Beach (92663) *(P-2038)*
Cannon Gasket Inc .......................................................... E ...... 909 355-1547
  7784 Edison Ave Fontana (92336) *(P-6440)*
Canoga Perkins Corporation (HQ).................................. D ...... 818 718-6300
  20600 Prairie St Chatsworth (91311) *(P-11986)*
Canon, Ventura *Also Called: Canon Solutions America  Inc (P-16501)*
Canon Solutions America  Inc ....................................... E ...... 844 443-4636
  6435 Ventura Blvd Ste C007 Ventura (93003) *(P-16501)*
Canoo, Torrance *Also Called: Canoo Inc (P-13469)*
Canoo Inc (PA)................................................................ E ...... 424 271-2144
  19951 Mariner Ave Torrance (90503) *(P-13469)*
Cantare Foods  Inc ......................................................... E
  900 Glenneyre St Laguna Beach (92651) *(P-2157)*
Canterbury Designs  Inc ................................................ E ...... 323 936-7111
  6195 Maywood Ave Huntington Park (90255) *(P-8620)*
Canterbury International, Huntington Park *Also Called: Canterbury Designs  Inc (P-8620)*
Canto  Inc (PA)................................................................ D ...... 415 495-6545
  625 Market St Ste 600 San Francisco (94105) *(P-18146)*
Canvas Concepts, San Diego *Also Called: Masterpiece Artist Canvas  LLC (P-2422)*
Canvas Concepts  Inc .................................................... E ...... 619 424-3428
  649 Anita St Ste A2 Chula Vista (91911) *(P-2969)*
Canvas Specialty  Inc .................................................... E
  1309 S Eastern Ave Commerce (90040) *(P-2970)*
Canyon Composites Incorporated .................................. E ...... 714 991-8181
  1548 N Gemini Pl Anaheim (92801) *(P-13804)*
Canyon Engineering Pdts Inc ......................................... D ...... 661 294-0084
  28909 Avenue Williams Valencia (91355) *(P-13805)*
Canyon Graphics  Inc .................................................... D ...... 858 646-0444
  3738 Ruffin Rd San Diego (92123) *(P-3118)*
Canyon Plastics  LLC .................................................... D ...... 800 350-6325
  28455 Livingston Ave Valencia (91355) *(P-6762)*
Canyon Products Corporation ........................................ E ...... 916 361-1687
  10173 Croydon Way Ste 1 Sacramento (95827) *(P-15329)*

**Canyon Road Winery, Napa** *Also Called: Geyser Peak Winery (P-1586)*

**Canyon Rock & Asphalt, San Diego** *Also Called: Superior Ready Mix Concrete LP (P-7506)*

**Canyon Rock Co Inc** .................................................. E ...... 707 887-2207
7525 Hwy 116 Forestville (95436) *(P-310)*

**Canyon Steel Fabricators Inc** .................................. E ...... 951 683-2352
4280 Patterson Ave Perris (92571) *(P-8114)*

**Canzone and Company** ............................................. F ...... 714 537-8175
661 W Villanova Rd Ojai (93023) *(P-15954)*

**Capax Technologies Inc** .......................................... E ...... 661 257-7666
24842 Avenue Tibbitts Valencia (91355) *(P-11362)*

**Capcom U S A Inc (HQ)** ............................................ C ...... 650 350-6500
185 Berry St Ste 4800 San Francisco (94107) *(P-16945)*

**Cape Robbin Inc** ....................................................... E ...... 626 810-8080
1943 W Mission Blvd Pomona (91766) *(P-17109)*

**Capella Photonics Inc** ............................................. E ...... 408 360-4240
1100 La Avenida St Ste A Mountain View (94043) *(P-13192)*

**Capella Space Corp** ................................................. D ...... 650 334-7734
438 Shotwell St San Francisco (94110) *(P-14168)*

**Caperon Designs Inc** ............................................... F ...... 714 552-3201
1733 Monrovia Ave Ste N Costa Mesa (92627) *(P-15743)*

**Capillary Biomedical Inc** ......................................... E ...... 949 317-1701
2 Wrigley Ste 101 Irvine (92618) *(P-14642)*

**Capital Brands Distribution L (PA)** ......................... D ...... 800 523-5993
11601 Wilshire Blvd Ste 2300 Los Angeles (90025) *(P-11402)*

**Capital Cooking, Carson** *Also Called: Capital Cooking Equipment Inc (P-8063)*

**Capital Cooking Equipment Inc** ............................... E ...... 562 903-1168
1025 E Bedmar St Carson (90746) *(P-8063)*

**Capital Corrugated and Carton, Sacramento** *Also Called: Capital Corrugated LLC (P-3828)*

**Capital Corrugated LLC** ........................................... D ...... 916 388-7848
8333 24th Ave Sacramento (95826) *(P-3828)*

**Capital Lumber Company** ........................................ E ...... 707 433-7070
13480 Old Redwood Hwy Healdsburg (95448) *(P-16444)*

**Capital Ready Mix Inc** .............................................. E ...... 818 771-1122
11311 Pendleton St Sun Valley (91352) *(P-7415)*

**Capital Westward, Cerritos** *Also Called: Bermingham Cntrls Inc A Cal Co (P-9146)*

**Capitol Air Systems Inc** ........................................... E ...... 916 259-1200
4220 Duluth Ave Ste A Rocklin (95765) *(P-16350)*

**Capitol Components, Sacramento** *Also Called: Capitol Store Fixtures (P-3562)*

**Capitol Distribution Co LLC (PA)** ............................ E ...... 562 404-4321
12836 Alondra Blvd Cerritos (90703) *(P-17180)*

**Capitol Food Company, Cerritos** *Also Called: Capitol Distribution Co LLC (P-17180)*

**Capitol Iron Works Inc** ............................................. E ...... 916 381-1554
7009 Power Inn Rd Sacramento (95828) *(P-8115)*

**Capitol Steel Company** ............................................ F ...... 916 924-3195
1932 Auburn Blvd Sacramento (95815) *(P-16610)*

**Capitol Steel Fabricators Inc** .................................. E ...... 323 721-5460
3522 Greenwood Ave Commerce (90040) *(P-8116)*

**Capitol Steel Products** ............................................ E ...... 916 383-3368
6331 Power Inn Rd Ste B Sacramento (95824) *(P-8117)*

**Capitol Store Fixtures** ............................................. E ...... 916 646-9096
4220 Pell Dr Ste C Sacramento (95838) *(P-3562)*

**Capitol-Emi Music Inc** ............................................. A ...... 323 462-6252
1750b Vine St Los Angeles (90028) *(P-11723)*

**Caplugs, Rancho Dominguez** *Also Called: Caplugs Inc (P-6763)*

**Caplugs Inc** .............................................................. D ...... 310 537-2300
18704 S Ferris Pl Rancho Dominguez (90220) *(P-6763)*

**Capna Fabrication** .................................................... E ...... 888 416-6777
9801 Independence Ave Chatsworth (91311) *(P-9782)*

**Capna Systems, Chatsworth** *Also Called: Capna Fabrication (P-9782)*

**Capnia Inc** ................................................................ E ...... 650 213-8444
1101 Chess Dr Foster City (94404) *(P-5386)*

**Capo Industries Division, El Cajon** *Also Called: Senior Operations LLC (P-11107)*

**Capri Tools, Pomona** *Also Called: Als Group Inc (P-16807)*

**Capricor** .................................................................... E ...... 310 423-2104
8700 Beverly Blvd West Hollywood (90048) *(P-5387)*

**Capricor, San Diego** *Also Called: Capricor Therapeutics Inc (P-5388)*

**Capricor Therapeutics Inc (PA)** ............................... F ...... 858 727-1755
10865 Road To The Cure Ste 150 San Diego (92121) *(P-5388)*

**Capsida Biotherapeutics Inc (PA)** ........................... E ...... 805 410-2673
3075 Townsgate Rd Westlake Village (91361) *(P-5813)*

**Capstone, Van Nuys** *Also Called: Capstone Dstr Spport Svcs Corp (P-9309)*

**Capstone Dstr Spport Svcs Corp (PA)** .................... C ...... 818 734-5300
16640 Stagg St Van Nuys (91406) *(P-9309)*

**Capstone Fire Management Inc (PA)** ...................... E ...... 760 839-2290
2240 Auto Park Way Escondido (92029) *(P-10080)*

**Capsule Manufacturing Inc** ..................................... D ...... 949 245-4151
1399 N Miller St Anaheim (92806) *(P-212)*

**Capsule Mfg, Anaheim** *Also Called: Capsule Manufacturing Inc (P-212)*

**Captek Midco Inc** ..................................................... D ...... 760 734-6800
2710 Progress St Vista (92081) *(P-5389)*

**Captek Pharma, La Mirada** *Also Called: Captek Softgel Intl Inc (P-5391)*

**Captek Softgel Intl Inc (DH)** ..................................... B ...... 562 921-9511
16218 Arthur St Cerritos (90703) *(P-5390)*

**Captek Softgel Intl Inc** ............................................. E ...... 657 325-0412
14535 Industry Cir La Mirada (90638) *(P-5391)*

**Captiva Software Corporation (DH)** ........................ D ...... 858 320-1000
10145 Pacific Heights Blvd San Diego (92121) *(P-18966)*

**Captivate Brands Usa Inc** ........................................ F ...... 949 229-8927
19781 Pauling Foothill Ranch (92610) *(P-11386)*

**Captive Plastics LLC** ............................................... D ...... 209 858-9188
601 Nestle Way Ste A Lathrop (95330) *(P-6764)*

**Captive-Aire Systems Inc** ........................................ E ...... 310 876-8505
1123 Washington Ave Santa Monica (90403) *(P-8403)*

**Captive-Aire Systems Inc** ........................................ C ...... 530 351-7150
6856 Lockheed Dr Redding (96002) *(P-8404)*

**CAr Enterprises Inc** ................................................. E ...... 760 947-6411
13100 Main St Hesperia (92345) *(P-10457)*

**CAr Enterprises Inc** ................................................. F ...... 951 413-6262
12301 Heacock St Moreno Valley (92557) *(P-10458)*

**Car Sound Exhaust System Inc** ............................... C ...... 949 888-1625
1901 Corporate Centre Dr Oceanside (92056) *(P-5077)*

**Car Sound Exhaust System Inc (PA)** ...................... E ...... 949 858-5900
1901 Corporate Ctr Oceanside (92056) *(P-13470)*

**Car Sound Exhaust System Inc** ............................... E ...... 949 858-5900
30142 Avenida De Las Bandera Rcho Sta Marg (92688) *(P-13471)*

**Car Sound Exhaust System Inc** ............................... E ...... 949 858-5900
23201 Antonio Pkwy Rcho Sta Marg (92688) *(P-13472)*

**Caracal Enterprises LLC** .......................................... E ...... 707 773-3373
1260 Holm Rd Ste A Petaluma (94954) *(P-10470)*

**Caran Precision Engineering & Manufacturing Corp (PA)** ........ D ...... 714 447-5400
2830 Orbiter St Brea (92821) *(P-8829)*

**Carando Technologies Inc** ....................................... E ...... 209 948-6500
345 N Harrison St Stockton (95203) *(P-9582)*

**Caraustar Industries Inc** ......................................... E ...... 951 685-5544
4502 E Airport Dr Ontario (91761) *(P-3801)*

**Caraustar Industries Inc** ......................................... E ...... 209 464-6590
800b W Church St Stockton (95203) *(P-3900)*

**Caraustar Industries Inc** ......................................... D ...... 408 845-7600
525 Mathew St Santa Clara (95050) *(P-3901)*

**Caravan Canopy, Cerritos** *Also Called: Caravan Canopy Intl Inc (P-2971)*

**Caravan Canopy Intl Inc** .......................................... D ...... 714 367-3000
17510-17512 Studebaker Rd Cerritos (90703) *(P-2971)*

**Caravan Distribution, Los Angeles** *Also Called: Reaps Company LLC (P-16213)*

**Carberry LLC (HQ)** ................................................... E ...... 800 564-0842
17130 Muskrat Ave Ste B Adelanto (92301) *(P-16108)*

**Carberry LLC** ........................................................... E ...... 562 264-5078
3645 Long Beach Blvd Long Beach (90807) *(P-16109)*

**Carbide Saw and Tool Inc** ....................................... F ...... 909 884-9956
336 S Waterman Ave Ste P San Bernardino (92408) *(P-19248)*

**Carbomer Inc** ........................................................... D ...... 858 552-0992
6324 Ferris Sq Ste B San Diego (92121) *(P-5078)*

**Carbon Inc (PA)** ...................................................... C ...... 650 285-6307
1089 Mills Way Redwood City (94063) *(P-10341)*

**Carbon 38 Inc** .......................................................... D ...... 888 723-5838
2866 Westbrook Ave Los Angeles (90046) *(P-2743)*

**Carbon Activated Corporation (PA)** ........................ E ...... 310 885-4555
2250 S Central Ave Compton (90220) *(P-5079)*

**Carbon By Design LLC** ............................................ D ...... 760 643-1300
1491 Poinsettia Ave Ste 136 Vista (92081) *(P-13806)*

**Carbon California Company LLC** ............................ E ...... 805 933-1901
270 Quail Ct Ste 201 Santa Paula (93060) *(P-133)*

## ALPHABETIC SECTION

**Carbon3d, Redwood City** *Also Called: Carbon Inc (P-10341)*
**Carbro Company, Lawndale** *Also Called: Curry Company LLC (P-9673)*
**Cardenas Markets LLC** .................................................................. C ...... 909 923-7426
1621 E Francis St Ontario (91761) *(P-1029)*
**Cardeon Corporation** ....................................................................... E ...... 408 253-3319
10161 Bubb Rd Cupertino (95014) *(P-15026)*
**Cardic Machine Products Inc** ......................................................... F ...... 310 884-3400
17000 Keegan Ave Carson (90746) *(P-10764)*
**CARDIFF ONCOLOGY, San Diego** *Also Called: Cardiff Oncology Inc (P-5392)*
**Cardiff Oncology Inc** ....................................................................... E ...... 858 952-7570
11055 Flintkote Ave San Diego (92121) *(P-5392)*
**Cardinal C G, Moreno Valley** *Also Called: Cardinal Glass Industries Inc (P-7165)*
**Cardinal Cg Company, Galt** *Also Called: Cardinal Glass Industries Inc (P-7166)*
**Cardinal CT Company, Dixon** *Also Called: Cardinal Glass Industries Inc (P-7214)*
**Cardinal Glass Industries Inc** ........................................................ C ...... 951 485-9007
24100 Cardinal Ave Moreno Valley (92551) *(P-7165)*
**Cardinal Glass Industries Inc** ........................................................ C ...... 209 744-8940
680 Industrial Dr Galt (95632) *(P-7166)*
**Cardinal Glass Industries Inc** ........................................................ C ...... 323 319-0070
1320 Business Park Dr Dixon (95620) *(P-7214)*
**Cardinal Health 245 Henrico Co, Santa Clara** *Also Called: Access Closure Inc (P-14946)*
**Cardinal Health 414 LLC** ................................................................ E ...... 714 572-9900
640 S Jefferson St Placentia (92870) *(P-5393)*
**Cardinal Industrial Finishes (PA)** ................................................... D ...... 626 444-9274
1329 Potrero Ave Ca South El Monte (91733) *(P-6071)*
**Cardinal Paint and Powder Inc** ...................................................... C ...... 626 937-6767
15010 Don Julian Rd City Of Industry (91746) *(P-6072)*
**Cardinal Paint and Powder Inc** ...................................................... D ...... 408 452-8522
890 Commercial St San Jose (95112) *(P-6073)*
**Cardinal Paint and Powder Inc** ...................................................... D ...... 626 444-9274
1329 Potrero Ave South El Monte (91733) *(P-6074)*
**Cardinal Point Captains, San Diego** *Also Called: Cardinal Point Captains Inc (P-17867)*
**Cardinal Point Captains Inc** .......................................................... D ...... 760 438-7361
5005 Texas St Ste 104 San Diego (92108) *(P-17867)*
**Cardiodx Inc** ..................................................................................... C ...... 650 475-2788
3945 Freedom Cir Ste 560 Santa Clara (95054) *(P-19327)*
**Cardiovascular Systems, Tustin** *Also Called: Terumo Americas Holding Inc (P-14732)*
**Cardiva Medical Inc** ........................................................................ C ...... 408 470-7100
1615 Wyatt Dr Santa Clara (95054) *(P-15027)*
**Cardona Manufacturing Corp** ........................................................ E ...... 818 841-8358
1869 N Victory Pl Burbank (91504) *(P-13807)*
**Care Fusion Products, San Diego** *Also Called: Becton Dickinson and Company (P-15001)*
**Care Innovations LLC** .................................................................... E ...... 800 450-0970
950 Iron Point Rd Ste 160 Folsom (95630) *(P-15523)*
**Care Zone Inc** .................................................................................. E ...... 206 707-9127
121 Capp St Ste 200 San Francisco (94110) *(P-18147)*
**Career Tech Circuit Services, Chatsworth** *Also Called: Circuit Services Llc (P-12078)*
**Carefusion 207 Inc** ......................................................................... B ...... 760 778-7200
1100 Bird Center Dr Palm Springs (92262) *(P-15028)*
**Carefusion 213 LLC (DH)** .............................................................. B ...... 800 523-0502
3750 Torrey View Ct San Diego (92130) *(P-15029)*
**Carefusion Corporation** .................................................................. D ...... 858 617-4271
10020 Pacific Mesa Blvd Bldg A San Diego (92121) *(P-15030)*
**Carefusion Corporation** .................................................................. D ...... 760 778-7200
1100 Bird Center Dr Palm Springs (92262) *(P-15031)*
**Carefusion Corporation** .................................................................. D ...... 800 231-2466
22745 Savi Ranch Pkwy Yorba Linda (92887) *(P-15032)*
**Carefusion Corporation (HQ)** ........................................................ B ...... 858 617-2000
3750 Torrey View Ct San Diego (92130) *(P-15524)*
**Carefusion Solutions LLC (DH)** .................................................... A ...... 858 617-2100
3750 Torrey View Ct San Diego (92130) *(P-15033)*
**Careismatic Brands LLC (DH)** ..................................................... C ...... 818 671-2128
15301 Ventura Blvd Sherman Oaks (91403) *(P-7107)*
**Careismatic Group II Inc (HQ)** ..................................................... F ...... 818 671-2100
1119 Colorado Ave Santa Monica (90401) *(P-7108)*
**Careismatic Group Inc (PA)** .......................................................... F ...... 818 671-2100
15301 Ventura Blvd Sherman Oaks (91403) *(P-7109)*
**Careray USA, Santa Clara** *Also Called: Compass Innovations Inc (P-6554)*
**Carezone, San Francisco** *Also Called: Care Zone Inc (P-18147)*
**Cargill, Fullerton** *Also Called: Cargill Incorporated (P-5235)*

**Cargill Incorporated** ........................................................................ E ...... 714 449-6708
600 N Gilbert St Fullerton (92833) *(P-5235)*
**Cargill Flour Milling Division, San Bernardino** *Also Called: Ardent Mills LLC (P-1055)*
**Cargill Meat Solutions Corp** ........................................................... E ...... 562 345-5240
13034 Excelsior Dr Norwalk (90650) *(P-585)*
**Cargill Meat Solutions Corp** ........................................................... D ...... 559 875-2232
2350 Academy Ave Sanger (93657) *(P-586)*
**Cargill Meat Solutions Corp** ........................................................... A ...... 559 268-5586
3115 S Fig Ave Fresno (93706) *(P-587)*
**Cargill Meat Solutions Corp** ........................................................... D ...... 909 476-3120
10602 N Trademark Pkwy Ste 500 Rancho Cucamonga (91730) *(P-588)*
**Cargill Meat Solutions Corp** ........................................................... C ...... 515 735-9800
3501 E Vernon Ave Vernon (90058) *(P-2158)*
**Cargo Therapeutics Inc** .................................................................. C ...... 650 499-8950
835 Industrial Rd Ste 400 San Carlos (94070) *(P-5814)*
**CARIBOU BIOSCIENCES, Berkeley** *Also Called: Caribou Biosciences Inc (P-5815)*
**Caribou Biosciences Inc** ................................................................ C ...... 510 982-6030
2929 7th St Ste 105 Berkeley (94710) *(P-5815)*
**Cariden Technologies LLC** ............................................................ E ...... 650 564-9200
840 W California Ave Ste 200 Sunnyvale (94086) *(P-18148)*
**Cariloha, Rancho Cucamonga** *Also Called: South Bay International Inc (P-3540)*
**Carl Zeiss Meditec Inc** ................................................................... B ...... 650 871-4747
607 N Mccarthy Blvd Milpitas (95035) *(P-14765)*
**Carl Zeiss Meditec Inc (DH)** ......................................................... E ...... 925 557-4100
5300 Central Pkwy Dublin (94568) *(P-14766)*
**Carl Zeiss Meditec Prod LLC** ........................................................ D ...... 877 644-4657
1040 S Vintage Ave Ste A Ontario (91761) *(P-14767)*
**Carl Zeiss Meditec,, Rancho Cucamonga** *Also Called: Aaren Scientific Inc (P-14758)*
**Carl Zeiss Ophthalmic Systems** .................................................... F ...... 925 557-4100
5300 Central Pkwy Dublin (94568) *(P-14768)*
**Carl Ziss X-Ray Microscopy Inc** .................................................... D ...... 925 701-3600
5300 Central Pkwy Dublin (94568) *(P-15500)*
**Carla Senter** ..................................................................................... F ...... 310 366-7295
515 E Alondra Blvd Gardena (90248) *(P-8405)*
**Carley (PA)** ....................................................................................... C ...... 310 325-8474
1502 W 228th St Torrance (90501) *(P-7192)*
**Carlisle Construction Mtls LLC** ...................................................... C ...... 909 591-7425
5635 Schaefer Ave Chino (91710) *(P-16489)*
**Carlisle Construction Mtls LLC** ...................................................... D ...... 707 678-6900
1155 Business Park Dr Dixon (95620) *(P-16490)*
**Carlos A Garcia** ............................................................................... D ...... 888 410-1648
582 Market St Ste 204 San Francisco (94104) *(P-11987)*
**Carlsbad International Export Inc** .................................................. E ...... 760 438-5323
1954 Kellogg Ave Carlsbad (92008) *(P-16578)*
**Carlsbad Medical Supply, Carlsbad** *Also Called: Carlsbad International Export Inc (P-16578)*
**Carlsbad Tech, Carlsbad** *Also Called: Carlsbad Technology Inc (P-5394)*
**Carlsbad Tech, Carlsbad** *Also Called: Carlsbad Technology Inc (P-5395)*
**Carlsbad Technology Inc (DH)** ..................................................... E ...... 760 431-8284
5922 Farnsworth Ct Ste 101 Carlsbad (92008) *(P-5394)*
**Carlsbad Technology Inc** ............................................................... D ...... 760 431-8284
5923 Balfour Ct Carlsbad (92008) *(P-5395)*
**Carlsmed Inc** .................................................................................... F ...... 760 766-1923
1800 Aston Ave Ste 100 Carlsbad (92008) *(P-15034)*
**Carlson Wireless, Eureka** *Also Called: Carlson Wireless Tech Inc (P-11823)*
**Carlson Wireless Tech Inc** ............................................................. F ...... 707 443-0100
3134 Jacobs Ave Ste C Eureka (95501) *(P-11823)*
**Carlstar Group LLC** ........................................................................ C ...... 909 829-1703
10730 Production Ave Fontana (92337) *(P-13473)*
**Carlton Forge Works, Paramount** *Also Called: Carlton Forge Works LLC (P-8795)*
**Carlton Forge Works LLC** .............................................................. B ...... 562 633-1131
7743 Adams St Paramount (90723) *(P-8795)*
**Carlton Senior Living Inc (PA)** ...................................................... E ...... 925 338-2434
4071 Port Chicago Hwy Ste 130 Concord (94520) *(P-17741)*
**Carmel Food Group Inc** .................................................................. E ...... 510 471-4889
31128 San Clemente St Hayward (94544) *(P-2159)*
**Carmi Flavors, Commerce** *Also Called: Carmi Flvr & Fragrance Co Inc (P-1993)*
**Carmi Flvr & Fragrance Co Inc (PA)** ........................................... E ...... 323 888-9240
6030 Scott Way Commerce (90040) *(P-1993)*
**Carmot Therapeutics Inc** ................................................................ F ...... 888 402-4674
740 Heinz Ave Berkeley (94710) *(P-5396)*

**Carneros Vintners Inc**     **ALPHABETIC SECTION**

**Carneros Vintners Inc** ................................................... F ...... 707 933-9349
   4202 Stage Gulch Rd Sonoma (95476) *(P-72)*

**Carnevale & Lohr Inc** ..................................................... E ...... 562 927-8311
   6521 Clara St Bell Gardens (90201) *(P-7535)*

**Caro Nut, Fresno** *Also Called: Caro Nut Company (P-1349)*

**Caro Nut Company** ........................................................ C ...... 559 475-5471
   2904 S Angus Ave Ste 106 Fresno (93725) *(P-947)*

**Caro Nut Company (HQ)** ............................................... E ...... 559 475-5400
   2885 S Cherry Ave Fresno (93706) *(P-1349)*

**Carol Anderson Inc (PA)** ............................................... E ...... 310 638-3333
   18700 S Laurel Park Rd Rancho Dominguez (90220) *(P-2702)*

**Carol Anderson By Invitation, Rancho Dominguez** *Also Called: Carol Anderson Inc (P-2702)*

**Carol Cole Company** ..................................................... C ...... 888 360-9171
   1325 Sycamore Ave Ste A Vista (92081) *(P-15035)*

**Carol Wior Inc** ................................................................ E ...... 562 927-0052
   7533 Garfield Ave Bell (90201) *(P-2744)*

**Carolense Entrmt Group LLC** ....................................... D ...... 405 493-1120
   506 S Spring St Los Angeles (90013) *(P-15632)*

**Carolina Lquid Chmistries Corp** .................................. E ...... 336 722-8910
   510 W Central Ave Ste C Brea (92821) *(P-15036)*

**Caroline Chu Inc** ........................................................... E ...... 415 279-2358
   288 Evelyn Way San Francisco (94127) *(P-5954)*

**Caron Compactor Co** ................................................... E ...... 800 448-8236
   1204 Ullrey Ave Escalon (95320) *(P-9414)*

**Carousel USA, Fontana** *Also Called: JE Thomson & Company LLC (P-9526)*

**Carpenter Co** ................................................................. E ...... 951 354-7550
   7809 Lincoln Ave Riverside (92504) *(P-6626)*

**Carpenter Co** ................................................................. D ...... 209 982-4800
   17100 S Harlan Rd Lathrop (95330) *(P-6627)*

**Carpenter E R Co, Riverside** *Also Called: Carpenter Co (P-6626)*

**Carpenter Group (PA)** ................................................... E ...... 415 285-1954
   28800 Hesperian Blvd Hayward (94545) *(P-9499)*

**Carpenter Group** ........................................................... E ...... 619 233-5625
   2380 Main St San Diego (92113) *(P-16866)*

**Carpentry Millwork, Fresno** *Also Called: Architectural Wood Design Inc (P-3216)*

**Carpet Wagon-Glendale Inc (PA)** ................................. F ...... 818 937-9545
   3614 San Fernando Rd Glendale (91204) *(P-3230)*

**Carr Corporation (PA)** ................................................... E ...... 310 587-1113
   1547 11th St Santa Monica (90401) *(P-15501)*

**Carr Management Inc** .................................................. D ...... 951 277-4800
   22324 Temescal Canyon Rd Corona (92883) *(P-6765)*

**Carriage Carpet Mills, Cypress** *Also Called: Shaw Industries Group Inc (P-2520)*

**Carriere Family Farms LLC** ......................................... E ...... 530 934-8200
   1640 State Highway 45 Glenn (95943) *(P-17141)*

**Carris Reels California Inc (HQ)** .................................. E ...... 802 733-9111
   2100 W Almond Ave Madera (93637) *(P-3414)*

**Carroll Metal Works Inc** .............................................. D ...... 619 477-9125
   740 W 16th St National City (91950) *(P-8118)*

**Carrolls Tire Warehouse Inc (PA)** ................................ E ...... 559 781-5040
   981 W Northgrand Ave Porterville (93257) *(P-17446)*

**Carros Americas, Inc., Westlake Village** *Also Called: Carros Sensors Americas LLC (P-12932)*

**Carros Sensors Americas LLC** .................................... C ...... 805 267-7176
   2945 Townsgate Rd Ste 200 Westlake Village (91361) *(P-12932)*

**Carros Sensors Systems Co LLC** ................................ B ...... 925 979-4400
   355 Lennon Ln Walnut Creek (94598) *(P-14855)*

**Carros Sensors Systems Co LLC (DH)** ....................... C ...... 805 968-0782
   1461 Lawrence Dr Thousand Oaks (91320) *(P-14856)*

**Carson Industries LLC** ................................................ A ...... 951 788-9720
   2434 Rubidoux Blvd Riverside (92509) *(P-6766)*

**Carson Trailer Inc (PA)** ............................................... D ...... 310 835-0876
   14831 S Maple Ave Gardena (90248) *(P-17487)*

**Carson Trailer Sales, Gardena** *Also Called: Carson Trailer Inc (P-17487)*

**Carson's Coatings, Galt** *Also Called: Carsons Coatings Inc (P-8830)*

**Carsons Coatings Inc** .................................................. E ...... 209 745-2387
   550 Industrial Dr Ste 200 Galt (95632) *(P-8830)*

**Cartel Electronics LLC** ................................................ D ...... 714 993-0270
   1900 Petra Ln Ste C Placentia (92870) *(P-12074)*

**Cartel Industries, Irvine** *Also Called: Cartel Industries LLC (P-8406)*

**Cartel Industries LLC** .................................................. E ...... 949 474-3200
   17152 Armstrong Ave Irvine (92614) *(P-8406)*

**Carter Group (PA)** ......................................................... E ...... 916 373-0148
   3709 Seaport Blvd West Sacramento (95691) *(P-8119)*

**Carter Laboratories, Irvine** *Also Called: Fluxergy Inc (P-19452)*

**Carters Metal Fabricators Inc** ...................................... E ...... 626 815-4225
   935 W 5th St Azusa (91702) *(P-3595)*

**Carton Design, Pico Rivera** *Also Called: CD Container Inc (P-3829)*

**Carttronics LLC (HQ)** ................................................... E ...... 888 696-2278
   90 Icon Foothill Ranch (92610) *(P-13218)*

**Cartwright Trmt Pest Ctrl Inc** ...................................... E ...... 619 442-9613
   1376 Broadway El Cajon (92021) *(P-17843)*

**Caruthers Raisin Pkg Co Inc (PA)** ............................... D ...... 559 864-9448
   12797 S Elm Ave Caruthers (93609) *(P-948)*

**Carvin Corp** ................................................................... C ...... 858 487-1600
   16262 W Bernardo Dr San Diego (92127) *(P-17561)*

**Carvin Guitars & Pro Sound, San Diego** *Also Called: Carvin Corp (P-17561)*

**Cas Medical Systems Inc (HQ)** ................................... D ...... 203 488-6056
   1 Edwards Way Irvine (92614) *(P-15037)*

**Casa De Hermandad (PA)** ........................................... E ...... 310 477-8272
   1639 11th St Santa Monica (90404) *(P-15798)*

**Casa Herrera Inc (PA)** .................................................. D ...... 909 392-3930
   2655 Pine St Pomona (91767) *(P-9783)*

**Casa Lupe Inc (PA)** ...................................................... D ...... 530 846-3218
   130 Magnolia St Gridley (95948) *(P-17569)*

**Casa Lupe Market & Restaurants, Gridley** *Also Called: Casa Lupe Inc (P-17569)*

**Casa Sanchez, San Francisco** *Also Called: Sanchez Business Inc (P-17604)*

**Casa Sanchez Foods, Hayward** *Also Called: Fante Inc (P-2090)*

**Cascade Comfort Service Inc** ..................................... E ...... 530 365-5350
   5203 Industrial Way Anderson (96007) *(P-408)*

**Cascade Pump Company** ............................................ D ...... 562 946-1414
   10107 Norwalk Blvd Santa Fe Springs (90670) *(P-9917)*

**Cascade Thermal Solutions LLC (PA)** ........................ E ...... 619 562-8852
   1890 Cordell Ct Ste 102 El Cajon (92020) *(P-409)*

**Casco Mfg, San Fernando** *Also Called: C A Schroeder Inc (P-7573)*

**Case Club, Anaheim** *Also Called: Foam Plastics & Rbr Pdts Corp (P-6638)*

**Casemaker Inc** .............................................................. F ...... 408 261-8265
   1680 Civic Center Dr Frnt Santa Clara (95050) *(P-18149)*

**Caseworx, Redlands** *Also Called: Caseworx Inc (P-3563)*

**Caseworx Inc (PA)** ....................................................... E ...... 909 799-8550
   1130 Research Dr Redlands (92374) *(P-3563)*

**Casey Printing Inc** ....................................................... E ...... 831 385-3221
   398 E San Antonio Dr King City (93930) *(P-4543)*

**Cashnet, Oakland** *Also Called: Higher One Payments Inc (P-18383)*

**Casing Specialties Inc** ................................................. E ...... 661 399-5522
   12454 Snow Rd Bakersfield (93314) *(P-213)*

**Caspers, San Leandro** *Also Called: Spar Sausage Co (P-668)*

**Caspio Inc (PA)** ............................................................. F ...... 650 691-0900
   1286 Kifer Rd Ste 107 Sunnyvale (94086) *(P-18150)*

**Cast Partner Inc** ........................................................... E ...... 323 876-9000
   4658 W Washington Blvd Los Angeles (90016) *(P-7858)*

**Cast Parts Inc (HQ)** ..................................................... C ...... 909 595-2252
   4200 Valley Blvd Walnut (91789) *(P-7683)*

**Cast Parts Inc** ............................................................... C ...... 626 937-3444
   16800 Chestnut St City Of Industry (91748) *(P-7684)*

**Cast-Rite Corporation** .................................................. D ...... 310 532-2080
   515 E Airline Way Gardena (90248) *(P-9609)*

**Cast-Rite International Inc (PA)** .................................. D ...... 310 532-2080
   515 E Airline Way Gardena (90248) *(P-7859)*

**Castaic Truck Stop Inc** ................................................ E ...... 661 295-1374
   31611 Castaic Rd Castaic (91384) *(P-6332)*

**Castello Diamorosa, Calistoga** *Also Called: Villa Amorosa (P-1810)*

**Caster Technology Corp (PA)** ..................................... F ...... 714 893-6886
   11552 Markon Dr Garden Grove (92841) *(P-16611)*

**Castillo Maritess** .......................................................... F ...... 949 216-0468
   1490 S Vineyard Ave Ste G Ontario (91761) *(P-2972)*

**Castle Importing Inc** .................................................... E ...... 909 428-9200
   14550 Miller Ave Fontana (92336) *(P-17570)*

**Castle Industries Inc of California** ............................. E ...... 909 390-0899
   4056 Easy St El Monte (91731) *(P-8407)*

**Castle Press** .................................................................. E ...... 800 794-0858
   1128 N Gilbert St Anaheim (92801) *(P-5017)*

## ALPHABETIC SECTION — CDM Corp

**Castle Rock Spring Water Co** .................................................. E ...... 530 678-4444
4121 Dunsmuir Ave Dunsmuir (96025) *(P-1875)*

**Castlelite Block LLC (PA)** ........................................................ F ...... 707 678-3465
8615 Robben Rd Dixon (95620) *(P-7294)*

**Castlight Health Inc (HQ)** ........................................................ D ...... 415 829-1400
50 California St Ste 1800 San Francisco (94111) *(P-19004)*

**Castro Construction LLC** ........................................................ E ...... 689 220-9145
18375 Ventura Blvd Tarzana (91356) *(P-214)*

**Casualway Home & Garden, Oxnard** *Also Called: Casualway Usa LLC (P-3499)*

**Casualway Usa LLC** ................................................................. D ...... 805 660-7408
1623 Lola Way Oxnard (93030) *(P-3499)*

**Catalent Pharma Solutions Inc** .................................................. C ...... 858 805-6383
7330 Carroll Rd Ste 200 San Diego (92121) *(P-5397)*

**Catalent Pharma Solutions Inc** .................................................. D ...... 877 587-1835
8926 Ware Ct San Diego (92121) *(P-5398)*

**Catalina Carpet Mills Inc (PA)** .................................................. E ...... 562 926-5811
14418 Best Ave Santa Fe Springs (90670) *(P-2511)*

**Catalina Home, Santa Fe Springs** *Also Called: Catalina Carpet Mills Inc (P-2511)*

**Catalina Pacific Concrete** ........................................................ E ...... 310 532-4600
19030 Normandie Ave Torrance (90502) *(P-7416)*

**Catalina Pacific Concrete, Azusa** *Also Called: Calportland Company (P-7414)*

**Catalina Yachts Inc (PA)** ........................................................... E ...... 818 884-7700
2259 Ward Ave Simi Valley (93065) *(P-14030)*

**Catalyst Development Corp** ..................................................... E ...... 760 228-9653
56925 Yucca Trl Yucca Valley (92284) *(P-18151)*

**Catalytic Solutions Inc (HQ)** ..................................................... E ...... 805 486-4649
1700 Fiske Pl Oxnard (93033) *(P-14356)*

**Catame Inc (PA)** ....................................................................... F ...... 213 749-2610
1930 Long Beach Ave Los Angeles (90058) *(P-15909)*

**Catapult Communications Corp (DH)** ....................................... E ...... 818 871-1800
26601 Agoura Rd Calabasas (91302) *(P-18152)*

**Catawba County Schools, Camarillo** *Also Called: Microsemi Communications Inc (P-12569)*

**Cater Tots Too, Santa Ana** *Also Called: DAd Investments (P-17575)*

**Caterpillar Authorized Dealer, Imperial** *Also Called: Empire Southwest LLC (P-9421)*

**Catholic Resource Center, West Covina** *Also Called: Saint Jseph Communications Inc (P-19296)*

**Cathy Ireland Home, Chino** *Also Called: Omnia Leather Motion Inc (P-2941)*

**Cathys Creations Inc** ............................................................... F ...... 661 322-1110
3665 Rosedale Hwy Bakersfield (93308) *(P-17408)*

**Cato Networks Inc** ................................................................... D ...... 646 975-9243
3031 Tisch Way 110 Plz W San Jose (95128) *(P-18153)*

**Catridge Return Center, Calexico** *Also Called: 4I Technologies Inc (P-9761)*

**Cattaneo Bros, San Luis Obispo** *Also Called: Cattaneo Bros Inc (P-635)*

**Cattaneo Bros Inc** .................................................................... E ...... 805 543-7188
769 Caudill St San Luis Obispo (93401) *(P-635)*

**Cavallo & Cavallo Inc** ............................................................... F ...... 909 428-6994
14955 Hilton Dr Fontana (92336) *(P-10765)*

**Cavanaugh Machine Works Inc** ................................................ E ...... 562 437-1126
1540 Santa Fe Ave Long Beach (90813) *(P-10766)*

**Cavco Industries Inc** ................................................................ E ...... 951 688-5353
7007 Jurupa Ave Riverside (92504) *(P-3382)*

**Caviar Affair LLC** ...................................................................... E ...... 415 235-4169
637 Homer Ave Palo Alto (94301) *(P-4235)*

**Cavins Oil Well Tools, Signal Hill** *Also Called: Dawson Enterprises (P-9460)*

**Cavium LLC (DH)** ..................................................................... E ...... 408 222-2500
5488 Marvell Ln Santa Clara (95054) *(P-12376)*

**Cavium Networks Intl Inc** ......................................................... D ...... 650 625-7000
2315 N 1st St San Jose (95131) *(P-12377)*

**Cavli Inc** .................................................................................. E ...... 650 605-8166
99 Almaden Blvd Ste 600 San Jose (95113) *(P-12378)*

**Cavotec Dabico US Inc** ............................................................. E ...... 714 947-0005
5665 Corporate Ave Cypress (90630) *(P-13808)*

**Cavotec Inet, Cypress** *Also Called: Cavotec US Holdings Inc (P-9448)*

**Cavotec Inet US Inc** .................................................................. D ...... 714 947-0005
5665 Corporate Ave Cypress (90630) *(P-9415)*

**Cavotec US Holdings Inc (HQ)** .................................................. F ...... 714 545-7900
5665 Corporate Ave Cypress (90630) *(P-9448)*

**CAW Cowie Inc (PA)** ................................................................ E ...... 212 396-9007
7 Ginger Root Ln Rancho Palos Verdes (90275) *(P-19080)*

**Caylym Holdings, Fresno** *Also Called: Caylym Technologies Intl LLC (P-18967)*

**Caylym Technologies Intl LLC** .................................................. E ...... 209 322-9596
5340 E Home Ave Fresno (93727) *(P-18967)*

**Caymus Vineyards** ................................................................... E ...... 707 963-4204
8700 Conn Creek Rd Rutherford (94573) *(P-1498)*

**CB Performance Products, Farmersville** *Also Called: Claudes Buggies Inc (P-16377)*

**Cbb Group, Commerce** *Also Called: Cbb Group Inc (P-16946)*

**Cbb Group Inc** ......................................................................... F ...... 323 888-2800
2747 S Malt Ave Commerce (90040) *(P-16946)*

**Cbc Steel Buildings LLC** .......................................................... C ...... 209 858-2425
1700 E Louise Ave Lathrop (95330) *(P-8659)*

**Cbd Living Water** ..................................................................... E ...... 800 940-3660
1343 Versante Cir Corona (92881) *(P-16110)*

**Cbec, San Diego** *Also Called: Clear Blue Energy Corp (P-11587)*

**Cbione, Vista** *Also Called: California Breakers Inc (P-16648)*

**Cbj LP** ...................................................................................... E ...... 323 549-5225
11150 Santa Monica Blvd Los Angeles (90025) *(P-4236)*

**Cbj LP** ...................................................................................... D ...... 818 676-1750
11150 Santa Monica Blvd Ste 350 Los Angeles (90025) *(P-4237)*

**Cbj LP** ...................................................................................... E ...... 949 833-8373
18500 Von Karman Ave Ste 150 Irvine (92612) *(P-4238)*

**Cbj LP** ...................................................................................... E ...... 858 277-6359
4909 Murphy Canyon Rd Ste 200 San Diego (92123) *(P-4239)*

**CBS Fasteners LLC** .................................................................. E ...... 714 779-6368
1345 N Brasher St Anaheim (92807) *(P-8749)*

**Ccd, Ceres** *Also Called: Craftsman Cutting Dies Inc (P-7949)*

**Ccd, Los Angeles** *Also Called: ITI Electro-Optic Corporation (P-14425)*

**Cce** .......................................................................................... E ...... 213 744-8909
1334 S Central Ave Los Angeles (90021) *(P-1876)*

**CCH Incorporated** .................................................................... A ...... 310 800-9800
2050 W 190th St Torrance (90504) *(P-19005)*

**CCI, Vernon** *Also Called: Cherokee Chemical Co Inc (P-17241)*

**CCI Industries Inc (PA)** ............................................................ E ...... 714 662-3879
350 Fischer Ave Ste A Costa Mesa (92626) *(P-6767)*

**CCL Label Inc** .......................................................................... D ...... 909 608-2655
576 College Commerce Way Upland (91786) *(P-4858)*

**CCL Label Inc** .......................................................................... D ...... 707 938-7800
21481 8th St E Sonoma (95476) *(P-16111)*

**CCL Label (delaware) Inc** ........................................................ B ...... 909 608-2260
576 College Commerce Way Upland (91786) *(P-4859)*

**CCL Tube Inc (HQ)** .................................................................. D ...... 310 635-4444
2250 E 220th St Carson (90810) *(P-6768)*

**CCM Assembly & Mfg Inc (PA)** ................................................. E ...... 760 560-1310
2275 Michael Faraday Dr Ste 6 San Diego (92154) *(P-12933)*

**CCM Enterprises (PA)** .............................................................. D ...... 619 562-2605
10848 Wheatlands Ave Santee (92071) *(P-3650)*

**Cco Holdings LLC** .................................................................... C ...... 714 509-5861
2684 N Tustin St Orange (92865) *(P-16331)*

**Cco Holdings LLC** .................................................................... C ...... 909 742-8273
26827 Baseline St Highland (92346) *(P-16332)*

**Ccoi Gate & Fence, Aromas** *Also Called: Gregory Patterson (P-8627)*

**Ccpu, San Diego** *Also Called: Continuous Computing Corp (P-10144)*

**CCS Composites, Fairfield** *Also Called: Yla Inc (P-7601)*

**CCS Inc** ................................................................................... F ...... 888 256-8901
11801 Pierce St Fl 2 Riverside (92505) *(P-18154)*

**CCS Industries Inc** ................................................................... F ...... 559 786-8489
4125 W Noble Ave Visalia (93277) *(P-16112)*

**Ccsd, San Diego** *Also Called: Cal-Comp Electronics (usa) Co Ltd (P-11312)*

**CD Container Inc** ..................................................................... D ...... 562 948-1910
7343 Paramount Blvd Pico Rivera (90660) *(P-3829)*

**CD Digital, Rancho Cucamonga** *Also Called: Digital Flex Media Inc (P-11727)*

**CD Video Manufacturing Inc** .................................................... D ...... 714 265-0770
12650 Westminster Ave Santa Ana (92706) *(P-13193)*

**CDI, San Diego** *Also Called: Century Design Inc (P-9666)*

**CDI, Irvine** *Also Called: Concept Development Llc (P-12081)*

**CDI Torque Products, City Of Industry** *Also Called: Consolidated Devices Inc (P-17352)*

**CDM, Newport Beach** *Also Called: CDM Company Inc (P-16113)*

**CDM Company Inc** ................................................................... E ...... 949 644-2820
12 Corporate Plaza Dr Ste 200 Newport Beach (92660) *(P-16113)*

**CDM Corp** ................................................................................ F ...... 818 787-4002
7922 Haskell Ave Van Nuys (91405) *(P-17692)*

**Cdr Graphics Inc**                                                                               **ALPHABETIC SECTION**

**Cdr Graphics Inc (PA)** .................................................. E ...... 310 474-7600
  1207 E Washington Blvd Los Angeles (90021) *(P-4544)*
**Cds California LLC** ...................................................... F ...... 818 766-5000
  3330 Cahuenga Blvd W Ste 200 Los Angeles (90068) *(P-15633)*
**CDS Engineering Inc** ................................................... C ...... 510 252-2100
  40725 Encyclopedia Cir Fremont (94538) *(P-10767)*
**Cds Leopold, Fremont** *Also Called: CDS Engineering Inc (P-10767)*
**Cdti, Oxnard** *Also Called: Cdti Advanced Materials Inc (P-5080)*
**Cdti Advanced Materials Inc (PA)** ................................ E ...... 805 639-9458
  1641 Fiske Pl Oxnard (93033) *(P-5080)*
**Cdw, Anaheim** *Also Called: Consolidated Design West Inc (P-17824)*
**Cecilia Tech Inc** ........................................................... F ...... 818 533-9888
  4290 E Brickell St Unit C Ontario (91761) *(P-16114)*
**Ceco, Oxnard** *Also Called: Component Equipment Co Inc (P-12871)*
**Cedar Knoll Vineyards Inc** ........................................... E ...... 707 226-5587
  4029 Hagen Rd Napa (94558) *(P-1499)*
**Cedar Valley Manufacturing Inc** ................................... C ...... 831 636-8110
  943 San Felipe Rd Hollister (95023) *(P-3104)*
**Cedarlane Foods, Carson** *Also Called: Cedarlane Natural Foods Inc (P-2160)*
**Cedarlane Natural Foods Inc (PA)** ............................... D ...... 310 886-7720
  717 E Artesia Blvd Ste A Carson (90746) *(P-2160)*
**Cedars-Sinai Medical Center** ...................................... C ...... 310 423-5841
  8700 Beverly Blvd Ste 8211 West Hollywood (90048) *(P-19324)*
**Cedarwood-Young Company** ....................................... D ...... 626 962-4047
  14618 Arrow Hwy Baldwin Park (91706) *(P-16958)*
**Cee Baileys Aircraft Plastics, Montebello** *Also Called: Desser Tire & Rubber Co LLC (P-16919)*
**Celebration West Inc** ................................................... C
  2505 N Shirk Rd Visalia (93291) *(P-4545)*
**Celebrity Pink, Montebello** *Also Called: 2253 Apparel LLC (P-17085)*
**Celestial Lighting, Santa Fe Springs** *Also Called: Shimada Enterprises Inc (P-11622)*
**Celestica, San Jose** *Also Called: Celestica Inc (P-13219)*
**Celestica Aerospace Tech Corp** ................................... C ...... 512 310-7540
  895 S Rockefeller Ave Ste 102 Ontario (91761) *(P-12075)*
**Celestica Inc** ............................................................... D ...... 408 727-0880
  40725 Encyclopedia Cir Fremont (94538) *(P-8408)*
**Celestica Inc** ............................................................... E ...... 416 448-5800
  5325 Hellyer Ave San Jose (95138) *(P-13219)*
**Celestica LLC** ............................................................. D ...... 760 357-4880
  280 Campillo St Ste G Calexico (92231) *(P-11445)*
**Celestica LLC** ............................................................. C ...... 408 574-6000
  5325 Hellyer Ave San Jose (95138) *(P-12379)*
**Celestica LLC** ............................................................. C ...... 510 770-5100
  49235 Milmont Dr Fremont (94538) *(P-12934)*
**Celestica-Aerospace, Ontario** *Also Called: Celestica Aerospace Tech Corp (P-12075)*
**Celgene Corporation** ................................................... E ...... 858 795-4961
  10300 Campus Point Dr Ste 100 San Diego (92121) *(P-5399)*
**Celgene Signal Research, San Diego** *Also Called: Celgene Corporation (P-5399)*
**Celigo Inc (PA)** ............................................................ E ...... 650 579-0210
  1820 Gateway Dr Ste 260 Redwood City (94065) *(P-18155)*
**Celite Corporation** ....................................................... F ...... 805 736-1221
  2500 San Miguelito Rd Lompoc (93436) *(P-5081)*
**Cell Design Labs Inc** ................................................... E ...... 510 398-0501
  5858 Horton St Ste 240 Emeryville (94608) *(P-5400)*
**Cell Marque Corporation** ............................................. E ...... 916 746-8900
  6600 Sierra College Blvd Rocklin (95677) *(P-5745)*
**Cellar 360, Sonoma** *Also Called: Treasury Wine Estates Americas (P-1794)*
**Cellarpro Cooling Systems, Petaluma** *Also Called: Planet One Products Inc (P-3669)*
**Cellink Corporation (PA)** .............................................. D ...... 650 799-3018
  610 Quarry Rd San Carlos (94070) *(P-12935)*
**Cellmobility Inc** ............................................................ E ...... 510 549-3300
  808 Gilman St Berkeley (94710) *(P-7907)*
**Cello Jeans, Commerce** *Also Called: Hidden Jeans Inc (P-2418)*
**Cellotape Inc (HQ)** ...................................................... C ...... 510 651-5551
  39611 Eureka Dr Newark (94560) *(P-15955)*
**Cellphone-Mate Inc** ..................................................... D ...... 510 770-0469
  48346 Milmont Dr Fremont (94538) *(P-11824)*
**Celltheon, Union City** *Also Called: Celltheon Corporation (P-5401)*
**Celltheon Corporation** ................................................. F ...... 650 743-3672
  32980 Alvarado Niles Rd Ste 826 Union City (94587) *(P-5401)*

**Cellu-Con Inc** .............................................................. E ...... 559 568-0190
  19994 Meredith Dr Strathmore (93267) *(P-6194)*
**Cellular Longevity Inc** ................................................. F ...... 707 563-9236
  548 Market St Pmb 26099 San Francisco (94104) *(P-19501)*
**Cellulo Co Division, Fresno** *Also Called: Gusmer Enterprises Inc (P-10092)*
**Cem, Santee** *Also Called: Air & Gas Tech Inc (P-14027)*
**Cemco, Pittsburg** *Also Called: Cemco LLC (P-8660)*
**Cemco LLC (DH)** ......................................................... D ...... 800 775-2362
  13191 Crossroads Pkwy N Ste 325 City Of Industry (91746) *(P-8409)*
**Cemco LLC** ................................................................. D ...... 925 473-9340
  1001a Pittsburg Antioch Hwy Pittsburg (94565) *(P-8660)*
**Cemco Steel, City Of Industry** *Also Called: Cemco LLC (P-8409)*
**Cemex** ........................................................................ D ...... 916 941-2800
  5180 Golden Foothill Pkwy Ste 200 El Dorado Hills (95762) *(P-7417)*
**Cemex, Pleasanton** *Also Called: RMC Pacific Materials LLC (P-7263)*
**Cemex, Fresno** *Also Called: Cemex Materials LLC (P-7430)*
**Cemex Inc** ................................................................... D ...... 916 941-2999
  2365 Iron Point Rd Folsom (95630) *(P-7418)*
**Cemex California Cement LLC** ................................... B ...... 760 381-7616
  5050 83rd St Sacramento (95826) *(P-7253)*
**Cemex Cement Inc** ..................................................... C ...... 760 381-7616
  25220 Black Mountain Quarry Rd Apple Valley (92307) *(P-7419)*
**Cemex Cement Inc** ..................................................... C ...... 626 969-1747
  1201 W Gladstone St Azusa (91702) *(P-16466)*
**Cemex Cnstr Mtls PCF LLC** ........................................ E ...... 831 883-3701
  100 Lapis Rd Marina (93933) *(P-7254)*
**Cemex Cnstr Mtls PCF LLC** ........................................ E ...... 800 992-3639
  4132 Cordelia Rd Suisun City (94585) *(P-7316)*
**Cemex Cnstr Mtls PCF LLC** ........................................ E ...... 925 846-2824
  1544 Stanley Blvd Pleasanton (94566) *(P-7420)*
**Cemex Cnstr Mtls PCF LLC** ........................................ E ...... 707 422-2520
  1601 Cement Hill Rd Fairfield (94533) *(P-7421)*
**Cemex Cnstr Mtls PCF LLC** ........................................ F ...... 909 335-3105
  8203 Alabama Ave Highland (92346) *(P-7422)*
**Cemex Cnstr Mtls PCF LLC** ........................................ E ...... 855 292-8453
  900 Whipple Rd Union City (94587) *(P-7423)*
**Cemex Cnstr Mtls PCF LLC** ........................................ E ...... 855 292-8453
  1290 E Turner Rd Lodi (95240) *(P-7424)*
**Cemex Cnstr Mtls PCF LLC** ........................................ E ...... 925 672-4900
  515 Mitchell Canyon Rd Clayton (94517) *(P-16467)*
**Cemex Construction Mtls Inc (DH)** .............................. E ...... 909 974-5500
  3990 Concours Ste 200 Ontario (91764) *(P-16468)*
**Cemex Corp** ................................................................ C ...... 800 992-3639
  22101 W Sunset Ave Los Banos (93635) *(P-16469)*
**Cemex Corp** ................................................................ C ...... 800 992-3639
  808 Gilman St Berkeley (94710) *(P-16470)*
**Cemex Materials LLC** ................................................. C ...... 831 883-3700
  100 Lapis Rd Marina (93933) *(P-7425)*
**Cemex Materials LLC** ................................................. D ...... 707 678-4311
  7059 Tremont Rd Dixon (95620) *(P-7426)*
**Cemex Materials LLC** ................................................. E ...... 855 292-8453
  1645 Stanley Blvd Pleasanton (94566) *(P-7427)*
**Cemex Materials LLC** ................................................. C ...... 510 234-3616
  401 Wright Ave Richmond (94804) *(P-7428)*
**Cemex Materials LLC** ................................................. C ...... 707 255-3035
  385 Tower Rd Napa (94558) *(P-7429)*
**Cemex Materials LLC** ................................................. D ...... 559 275-2241
  4150 N Brawley Ave Fresno (93722) *(P-7430)*
**Cemex Materials LLC** ................................................. D ...... 909 825-1500
  1205 S Rancho Ave Colton (92324) *(P-7431)*
**Cemex USA Inc** ........................................................... F ...... 909 974-5500
  4120 Jurupa St Ste 202 Ontario (91761) *(P-7432)*
**Cemtrol Inc** ................................................................. F ...... 714 666-6606
  3035 E La Jolla St Anaheim (92806) *(P-10141)*
**Cencal Cnc Inc** ........................................................... E ...... 559 897-8706
  2491 Simpson St Kingsburg (93631) *(P-10768)*
**Cencal Foods LLC** ...................................................... F ...... 559 341-5742
  1828 E Hedges Ave Fresno (93703) *(P-678)*
**Cencal Recycling LLC** ................................................. F ...... 209 546-8000
  501 Port Road 22 Stockton (95203) *(P-3755)*
**Center For Clbrtive Classroom** ................................... D ...... 510 533-0213
  1001 Marina Village Pkwy Ste 110 Alameda (94501) *(P-4319)*

# ALPHABETIC SECTION — Certance LLC

**Center Line Performance Wheels, Newport Beach** *Also Called: Center Line Wheel Corporation (P-13474)*

**Center Line Wheel Corporation** .......................................... F ..... 562 921-9637
23 Corporate Plaza Dr Ste 150 Newport Beach (92660) *(P-13474)*

**Center of Media Justice** ....................................................... E ..... 510 698-3800
1300 Clay St Ste 600 Oakland (94612) *(P-4376)*

**Center State Pipe and Sup Co** ............................................. F ..... 209 466-0871
2750 Cherokee Rd Stockton (95205) *(P-16765)*

**Centerline Industrial Inc** ........................................................ E ..... 858 505-0838
2530 Southport Way Ste D National City (91950) *(P-16810)*

**Centerpoint Mfg Co Inc** ......................................................... E ..... 818 842-2147
2625 N San Fernando Blvd Burbank (91504) *(P-10769)*

**Centon, Aliso Viejo** *Also Called: Centon Electronics Inc (P-10230)*

**Centon Electronics Inc (PA)** ................................................. D ..... 949 855-9111
27 Journey Ste 100 Aliso Viejo (92656) *(P-10230)*

**Centra Software Inc** .............................................................. E ..... 650 378-1363
1840 Gateway Dr Fl 2 San Mateo (94404) *(P-18156)*

**Central Blower Co** ................................................................. E ..... 626 330-3182
3427 Pomona Blvd Pomona (91768) *(P-9983)*

**Central Business Forms Inc** ................................................. E ..... 650 548-0918
289 Foster City Blvd Ste B Foster City (94404) *(P-4546)*

**Central Cal Almond Grwers Assn (PA)** ................................. E ..... 559 846-5377
8325 S Madera Ave Kerman (93630) *(P-77)*

**Central Cal Metals, Fresno** *Also Called: Robert J Alandt & Sons (P-8212)*

**Central California Baking Co** ................................................ C ..... 559 592-2270
701 Industrial Dr Ca Exeter (93221) *(P-1176)*

**Central California Cnstr Inc** .................................................. E ..... 661 978-8230
7221 Downing Ave Bakersfield (93308) *(P-215)*

**Central California Cont Mfg** .................................................. E ..... 559 665-7611
800 Commerce Dr Chowchilla (93610) *(P-6769)*

**Central California Power** ....................................................... E ..... 661 589-2870
19487 Broken Ct Shafter (93263) *(P-19160)*

**Central Coast Agriculture Inc (PA)** ....................................... E ..... 805 694-8594
8701 Santa Rosa Rd Buellton (93427) *(P-54)*

**Central Coast Printing, San Luis Obispo** *Also Called: David B Anderson (P-4584)*

**Central Coast Wine Services, Santa Maria** *Also Called: Central Coast Wine Warehouse (P-1500)*

**Central Coast Wine Warehouse (PA)** ................................... F ..... 805 928-9210
2717 Aviation Way Ste 101 Santa Maria (93455) *(P-1500)*

**Central Concrete Supply Co Inc (DH)** .................................. D ..... 408 293-6272
755 Stockton Ave San Jose (95126) *(P-7433)*

**Central Plastics and Mfg, Tracy** *Also Called: Mother Lode Plas Molding Inc (P-6924)*

**Central Precast Concrete Inc** ................................................ E ..... 925 417-6854
3500 Boulder St Pleasanton (94566) *(P-7317)*

**Central Printing Group, Foster City** *Also Called: Central Business Forms Inc (P-4546)*

**Central Tech Inc** .................................................................... E ..... 408 955-0919
2271 Ringwood Ave San Jose (95131) *(P-13220)*

**Central Tent, Santa Clarita** *Also Called: Frametent Inc (P-2974)*

**Central Valley AG Grinding LLC (PA)** ................................... C ..... 209 869-1721
5509 Langworth Rd Oakdale (95361) *(P-78)*

**Central Valley Concrete Inc** ................................................. E ..... 209 667-0161
4200 Lester Rd Denair (95316) *(P-410)*

**Central Valley Concrete Inc (PA)** ......................................... C ..... 209 723-8846
3823 N State Highway 59 Merced (95348) *(P-16278)*

**Central Valley Gaming LLC** .................................................. E ..... 209 668-1010
2321 W Main St Ste C Turlock (95380) *(P-19313)*

**Central Valley Industries LLC** .............................................. D ..... 209 838-8150
20451 Mchenry Ave Escalon (95320) *(P-16115)*

**Central Valley Meat Co Inc (PA)** .......................................... C ..... 559 583-9624
10431 8 3/4 Ave Hanford (93230) *(P-589)*

**Central Valley Presort Inc** .................................................... D ..... 559 906-2003
4215 S Dans St Visalia (93277) *(P-17796)*

**Central Valley Tank of Cal** .................................................... F ..... 559 456-3500
4752 E Carmen Ave Fresno (93703) *(P-8304)*

**Central Valley Trucking, Merced** *Also Called: Central Valley Concrete Inc (P-16278)*

**Central Valley Truss** ............................................................. F ..... 707 963-3622
1804 Soscol Ave Ste 205 Napa (94559) *(P-3303)*

**Central Vly Assembly Packg Inc** .......................................... E ..... 559 486-4260
5515 E Lamona Ave # 103 Fresno (93727) *(P-8050)*

**Centric, Campbell** *Also Called: Centric Software Inc (P-19523)*

**Centric Brands Inc** ................................................................ E ..... 951 797-5077
48650 Seminole Dr Ste 170 Cabazon (92230) *(P-2407)*

**Centric Brands Inc** ................................................................ E ..... 760 603-8520
5630 Paseo Del Norte Ste 144 Carlsbad (92008) *(P-2408)*

**Centric Brands Inc** ................................................................ F ..... 323 837-3700
1500 N El Centro Ave Ste 150 Los Angeles (90025) *(P-2409)*

**CENTRIC BRANDS INC., Carlsbad** *Also Called: Centric Brands Inc (P-2408)*

**Centric Software Inc (PA)** ..................................................... E ..... 408 574-7802
655 Campbell Technology Pkwy Ste 200 Campbell (95008) *(P-19523)*

**Centrifuge-Systems LLC** ....................................................... C ..... 209 583-3753
825 Performance Dr Stockton (95206) *(P-10081)*

**Centrisys/Cnp West, Stockton** *Also Called: Centrifuge-Systems LLC (P-10081)*

**Centrl Inc** ............................................................................... E ..... 650 641-7092
257 Castro St Ste 215 Mountain View (94041) *(P-18157)*

**Centro America Foods, Baldwin Park** *Also Called: Cremi Mex Inc (P-17127)*

**Centron Industries Inc** .......................................................... E ..... 310 324-6443
441 W Victoria St Gardena (90248) *(P-11825)*

**Centurion, Merced** *Also Called: Fineline Industries Inc (P-14033)*

**Centurum Information Tech Inc** ............................................ E ..... 619 224-1100
4250 Pacific Hwy Ste 105 San Diego (92110) *(P-7780)*

**Century Blinds Inc** ................................................................ D ..... 951 734-3762
300 S Promenade Ave Corona (92879) *(P-3717)*

**Century Design Inc** ............................................................... F ..... 858 292-1212
7485 Trade St Ste A San Diego (92121) *(P-9666)*

**Century Electronics, Newbury Park** *Also Called: Perillo Industries Inc (P-16729)*

**Century Pallets, Lynwood** *Also Called: Roger R Caruso Enterprises Inc (P-3358)*

**Century Parts Inc** .................................................................. F ..... 310 328-0281
913 W 223rd St Torrance (90502) *(P-10770)*

**Century Pk Capitl Partners LLC (PA)** ................................... C ..... 310 867-2210
880 Apollo St Ste 300 El Segundo (90245) *(P-17750)*

**Century Precision Engrg Inc** ................................................ E ..... 310 538-0015
2141 W 139th St Gardena (90249) *(P-10771)*

**Century Snacks LLC** ............................................................. B ..... 323 278-9578
5560 E Slauson Ave Commerce (90040) *(P-17142)*

**Century Spring, Commerce** *Also Called: Matthew Warren Inc (P-9202)*

**Century Stereo, San Jose** *Also Called: New Century Audio / Video Inc (P-11682)*

**Century Tubes Inc** ................................................................. E ..... 858 586-0550
7910 Dunbrook Rd San Diego (92126) *(P-16612)*

**Century Wire & Cable Inc** ..................................................... D ..... 800 999-5566
5701 S Eastern Ave Commerce (90040) *(P-7781)*

**Cepheid (HQ)** ........................................................................ A ..... 408 541-4191
904 E Caribbean Dr Sunnyvale (94089) *(P-14643)*

**Cepton Inc (PA)** .................................................................... F ..... 408 459-7579
399 W Trimble Rd San Jose (95131) *(P-13475)*

**Cepton Technologies Inc** ...................................................... C ..... 408 493-6246
399 W Trimble Rd San Jose (95131) *(P-13476)*

**Cera Inc** ................................................................................ E ..... 626 814-2688
14180 Live Oak Ave Ste I Baldwin Park (91706) *(P-14331)*

**Ceradyne Esk LLC** ................................................................ E ..... 714 549-0421
3169 Red Hill Ave M Costa Mesa (92626) *(P-7589)*

**Ceramic Decorating Company Inc** ....................................... E ..... 323 268-5135
4651 Sheila St Commerce (90040) *(P-19081)*

**Ceramic Tech Inc** .................................................................. E ..... 510 252-8500
46211 Research Ave Fremont (94539) *(P-10772)*

**Ceratizit Los Angeles LLC** .................................................... D ..... 310 464-8050
11312 Sunrise Gold Cir Rancho Cordova (95742) *(P-9543)*

**Cerecons, Anaheim** *Also Called: Unlimited Innovations Inc (P-18901)*

**Cerexa** ................................................................................... F ..... 510 285-9200
2100 Franklin St Ste 900 Oakland (94612) *(P-5402)*

**Cerk Beverage, El Segundo** *Also Called: Hemilane Inc (P-1839)*

**Cernex Inc** ............................................................................. F ..... 408 541-9226
1710 Zanker Rd Ste 103 San Jose (95112) *(P-12936)*

**Certain Inc (PA)** .................................................................... E ..... 415 353-5330
75 Hawthorne St Ste 550 San Francisco (94105) *(P-18158)*

**Certain Software Inc** ............................................................. E ..... 415 353-5330
75 Hawthorne St Ste 500 San Francisco (94105) *(P-18159)*

**Certainteed LLC** .................................................................... D ..... 510 490-0890
6400 Stevenson Blvd Fremont (94538) *(P-6373)*

**Certainteed LLC** .................................................................... D ..... 559 665-4831
17775 Avenue 23 1/2 Chowchilla (93610) *(P-7574)*

**Certance LLC (HQ)** ............................................................... B ..... 949 856-7800
141 Innovation Dr Irvine (92617) *(P-10231)*

**Certemy Inc** ......................................................................... F ...... 866 907-4088
14876 Raymer St Ste 200 Van Nuys (91405) *(P-18160)*

**Certified Ad Services** .......................................................... C ...... 559 233-1891
909 W Nielsen Ave Fresno (93706) *(P-4547)*

**Certified Alloy Products Inc** ............................................... C ...... 562 595-6621
3245 Cherry Ave Long Beach (90807) *(P-7716)*

**Certified Archtctral Fbrction, Los Angeles** *Also Called: Certified Enameling Inc (P-9057)*

**Certified Enameling Inc (PA)** ............................................. D ...... 323 264-4403
3342 Emery St Los Angeles (90023) *(P-9057)*

**Certified Meat Products Inc** ............................................... D ...... 559 256-1433
4586 E Commerce Ave Fresno (93725) *(P-590)*

**Certified Stainless Svc Inc** ................................................. D ...... 209 356-3300
441 Business Park Way Atwater (95301) *(P-8305)*

**Certified Stainless Svc Inc (PA)** ......................................... E ...... 209 537-4747
2704 Railroad Ave Ceres (95307) *(P-8306)*

**Certified Stainless Svc Inc** ................................................. D ...... 209 537-4747
581 Industry Way Atwater (95301) *(P-8307)*

**Certified Steel Treating Corp** ............................................. E ...... 323 583-8711
2454 E 58th St Vernon (90058) *(P-8939)*

**Certified Thermoplastics Inc** .............................................. E ...... 661 222-3006
26381 Ferry Ct Santa Clarita (91350) *(P-6770)*

**Certified Thermoplastics LLC, Santa Clarita** *Also Called: Certified Thermoplastics Inc (P-6770)*

**Certified Tire & Svc Ctrs Inc** ............................................... E ...... 951 656-6466
23920 Alessandro Blvd Ste A Moreno Valley (92553) *(P-17447)*

**Certified Wtr Dmage Rstrtion E** ........................................... E ...... 800 417-1776
5319 University Dr Irvine (92612) *(P-17846)*

**Certis USA LLC** .................................................................... E ...... 661 758-8471
720 5th St Wasco (93280) *(P-6195)*

**Cerus Corporation (PA)** ...................................................... C ...... 925 288-6000
1220 Concord Ave Ste 600 Concord (94520) *(P-5816)*

**CESCA THERAPEUTICS, Rancho Cordova** *Also Called: Thermogenesis Holdings Inc (P-15283)*

**Cessna Scrmnto Ctation Svc Ctr, Sacramento** *Also Called: Textron Aviation Inc (P-13695)*

**Cetas Inc** ............................................................................. F ...... 847 530-5785
3260 Hillview Ave Palo Alto (94304) *(P-18161)*

**Ceterix Orthopaedics, Fremont** *Also Called: Ceterix Orthopaedics Inc (P-15038)*

**Ceterix Orthopaedics Inc** .................................................... E ...... 650 241-1748
6500 Kaiser Dr Ste 120 Fremont (94555) *(P-15038)*

**Ceva Development Inc (HQ)** ............................................... F ...... 650 417-7900
1174 Castro St Ste 275 Mountain View (94040) *(P-12380)*

**Cevians LLC (PA)** ................................................................. D ...... 714 619-5135
3193 Red Hill Ave Costa Mesa (92626) *(P-7167)*

**Cexi, Oxnard** *Also Called: Cryogenic Experts Inc (P-9845)*

**CF&b Manufacturing Inc** ..................................................... E ...... 714 744-8361
1700 Barcelona Cir Placentia (92870) *(P-3964)*

**Cfarms Inc** .......................................................................... E ...... 916 375-3000
1244 E Beamer St Woodland (95776) *(P-2161)*

**Cfarms Inc (PA)** ................................................................... E ...... 916 375-3000
1330 N Dutton Ave Ste 100 Santa Rosa (95401) *(P-2162)*

**CFI Holdings Corp** .............................................................. F ...... 909 595-2252
4200 Valley Blvd Pomona (91765) *(P-7685)*

**Cfkba Inc** ............................................................................. E ...... 650 302-6331
508 2nd Ave Redwood City (94063) *(P-7782)*

**Cfkba Inc (PA)** ..................................................................... E ...... 650 847-3900
150 Jefferson Dr Menlo Park (94025) *(P-7783)*

**Cflute Corp** .......................................................................... C ...... 562 404-6221
13220 Molette St Santa Fe Springs (90670) *(P-3830)*

**CFM Equipment Distributors Inc (PA)** ............................... E ...... 916 447-7022
1644 Main Ave Ste 1 Sacramento (95838) *(P-16776)*

**Cforia, Westlake Village** *Also Called: Cforia Software LLC (P-18162)*

**Cforia Software LLC** .......................................................... E ...... 818 871-9687
4333 Park Terrace Dr Ste 201 Westlake Village (91361) *(P-18162)*

**CFS, Apple Valley** *Also Called: Consolidated Frt Systems LLC (P-9509)*

**CFS Income Tax, Simi Valley** *Also Called: CFS Tax Software Inc (P-18163)*

**CFS Tax Software Inc** ......................................................... E ...... 805 522-1157
1445 E Los Angeles Ave Ste 214 Simi Valley (93065) *(P-18163)*

**Cfw Precision Metal Components, Grover Beach** *Also Called: C F W Research & Dev Co (P-7725)*

**Cfwf Inc** ................................................................................ C ...... 310 221-6280
842 Flint Ave Wilmington (90744) *(P-2050)*

**Cg Financial LLC** ................................................................. F ...... 619 656-2919
7020 Alamitos Ave Ste B San Diego (92154) *(P-852)*

**CG ONCOLOGY, Irvine** *Also Called: Cg Oncology Inc (P-5817)*

**Cg Oncology Inc** ................................................................. D ...... 949 409-3700
400 Spectrum Center Dr Ste 2040 Irvine (92618) *(P-5817)*

**Cg Roxane LLC** ................................................................... F ...... 530 225-1260
1400 Marys Dr Weed (96094) *(P-1877)*

**Cg Roxane Shasta, Weed** *Also Called: Cg Roxane LLC (P-1877)*

**CGB, Gardena** *Also Called: Pulp Studio Incorporated (P-17837)*

**Cgm Inc** ................................................................................ E ...... 818 609-7088
19611 Ventura Blvd Ste 211 Tarzana (91356) *(P-15709)*

**Cgm Findings, Tarzana** *Also Called: Cgm Inc (P-15709)*

**Cgpc America Corporation** ................................................. E ...... 951 332-4100
4 Latitude Way Unit 108 Corona (92881) *(P-5143)*

**CH Laboratories Inc (PA)** .................................................... E ...... 310 516-8273
1243 W 130th St Gardena (90247) *(P-5403)*

**Ch Products, Vista** *Also Called: Apem Inc (P-12914)*

**Cha Industries Inc** ............................................................... E ...... 510 683-8554
250 S Vasco Rd Livermore (94551) *(P-9841)*

**Cha Vacuum Technology, Livermore** *Also Called: Cha Industries Inc (P-9841)*

**Chaco Flaco Drinks, Jurupa Valley** *Also Called: Levecke LLC (P-1668)*

**Chad, Anaheim** *Also Called: Chad Industries Incorporated (P-12076)*

**Chad Industries Incorporated** ............................................. E ...... 714 938-0080
1565 S Sinclair St Anaheim (92806) *(P-12076)*

**Challenge Dairy Products Inc** ............................................. F ...... 510 351-3600
14970 Catalina St San Leandro (94577) *(P-17125)*

**Chalone Vineyard, Healdsburg** *Also Called: Treasury Chateau & Estates (P-1790)*

**Cham-Cal Engineering Co** ................................................... D ...... 714 898-9721
12722 Western Ave Garden Grove (92841) *(P-7215)*

**Chameleon Beverage Company Inc (PA)** ........................... D ...... 323 724-8223
6444 E 26th St Commerce (90040) *(P-1878)*

**Chameleon Books & Journals, Gilroy** *Also Called: Chameleon Like Inc (P-4998)*

**Chameleon Like Inc** ............................................................. D ...... 408 847-3661
345 Kishimura Dr Gilroy (95020) *(P-4998)*

**Chamisal Vineyards LLC** .................................................... F ...... 866 808-9463
7525 Orcutt Rd San Luis Obispo (93401) *(P-1501)*

**Champ Co, Campbell** *Also Called: Consoldted Hnge Mnfctured Pdts (P-10789)*

**Champion Cooling Systems, Lake Elsinore** *Also Called: Champion Motosports Inc (P-17448)*

**Champion Home Builders Inc** ............................................. C ...... 951 256-4617
299 N Smith Ave Corona (92878) *(P-344)*

**Champion Industrial Contrs Inc (PA)** ................................. E ...... 209 524-6601
1420 Coldwell Ave Modesto (95350) *(P-411)*

**Champion Industrial Contrs Inc** ......................................... E ...... 209 579-5478
451 Tully Rd Modesto (95350) *(P-412)*

**Champion Installs Inc** ......................................................... F ...... 916 627-0929
11075 Jeff Brian Ln Wilton (95693) *(P-3231)*

**Champion Motosports Inc (PA)** .......................................... E ...... 951 245-9464
32373 Corydon St Lake Elsinore (92530) *(P-17448)*

**Championx LLC** ................................................................... E ...... 661 834-0454
6321 District Blvd Bakersfield (93313) *(P-5082)*

**Chancellor Oil Tools Inc** ..................................................... E ...... 661 324-2213
3521 Gulf St Bakersfield (93308) *(P-9458)*

**Chandler Aggregates Inc (PA)** ............................................ E ...... 951 277-1341
24867 Maitri Rd Corona (92883) *(P-294)*

**Chandler Packaging A Transpak Company** ....................... D ...... 858 292-5674
7595 Raytheon Rd San Diego (92111) *(P-16309)*

**Channel Medsystems Inc** ................................................... E ...... 603 318-5084
2919 7th St Berkeley (94710) *(P-15039)*

**Channel Technologies Group, Santa Barbara** *Also Called: International Tranducer Corp (P-14538)*

**Channel Technologies Group LLC** ..................................... A
879 Ward Dr Santa Barbara (93111) *(P-14169)*

**Channel Vision Technology, Laguna Hills** *Also Called: Djh Enterprises (P-11842)*

**Chaparral Blend, Paso Robles** *Also Called: Halter Winery LLC (P-1610)*

**Chaparral Motorsports, San Bernardino** *Also Called: Ocelot Engineering Inc (P-17483)*

**Chapman Cbc LLC** ............................................................... E ...... 844 855-2337
123 N Cypress St Orange (92866) *(P-1426)*

**Chapmn-Wlters Intrcoastal Corp** ........................................ F ...... 949 448-9940
141 Via Lampara Rcho Sta Marg (92688) *(P-15799)*

**Chappellet Vineyard** ............................................................ D ...... 707 286-4219
1581 Sage Canyon Rd Saint Helena (94574) *(P-1502)*

## ALPHABETIC SECTION — Chester Paul Company

Chappellet Winery Inc (PA) .................................... E ...... 707 286-4219
  1581 Sage Canyon Rd Saint Helena (94574) *(P-1503)*
Charades, Walnut  *Also Called: Diamond Collection LLC (P-2897)*
Charades LLC .................................................... C ...... 626 435-0077
  20579 Valley Blvd Walnut (91789) *(P-2893)*
Chargepoint Inc (HQ) ........................................... C ...... 408 841-4500
  240 E Hacienda Ave Campbell (95008) *(P-11363)*
Chargie LLC ..................................................... E ...... 310 621-0024
  3947 Landmark St Culver City (90232) *(P-11259)*
Charging Tree Corporation ...................................... F ...... 559 760-5473
  35788 Highway 41 Coarsegold (93614) *(P-216)*
Charles Gemeiner Cabinets ...................................... F ...... 323 299-8696
  3225 Exposition Pl Los Angeles (90018) *(P-3119)*
Charles Komar & Sons Inc ....................................... B ...... 951 934-1377
  11850 Riverside Dr Jurupa Valley (91752) *(P-2828)*
Charles Krug Winery, Saint Helena  *Also Called: C Mondavi & Family (P-1492)*
Charles Meisner Inc ............................................ E ...... 909 946-8216
  201 Sierra Pl Ste A Upland (91786) *(P-9610)*
Charlies Specialties Inc ....................................... D ...... 724 346-2350
  501 Airpark Dr Fullerton (92833) *(P-1268)*
Charmaine Plastics Inc ......................................... D ...... 714 630-8117
  2941 E La Jolla St Anaheim (92806) *(P-6771)*
Charman Manufacturing Inc ...................................... F ...... 213 489-7000
  5681 S Downey Rd Vernon (90058) *(P-7662)*
Charming Trim & Packaging ...................................... A ...... 415 302-7021
  5889 Rickenbacker Rd Commerce (90040) *(P-17060)*
Chart, San Jose  *Also Called: Cryotech International Inc (P-9253)*
Chart Sequal Technologies Inc .................................. D ...... 858 202-3100
  12230 World Trade Dr Ste 100 San Diego (92128) *(P-15040)*
Chase-Durer Ltd (PA) ........................................... F ...... 310 550-7280
  8455 Fountain Ave Unit 515 West Hollywood (90069) *(P-15676)*
Chateau Diana LLC (PA) ......................................... F ...... 707 433-6992
  6195 Dry Creek Rd Healdsburg (95448) *(P-1504)*
Chateau Masson LLC ............................................. E ...... 408 741-7002
  14831 Pierce Rd Saratoga (95070) *(P-1505)*
Chateau Montelena LLC .......................................... E ...... 707 942-5105
  1429 Tubbs Ln Calistoga (94515) *(P-1506)*
Chateau Montelena Winery, Calistoga  *Also Called: Chateau Montelena LLC (P-1506)*
Chateau Woltner, Angwin  *Also Called: Ladera Winery LLC (P-1656)*
Chatmeter Inc .................................................. D ...... 619 300-1050
  225 Broadway Ste 2200 San Diego (92101) *(P-18164)*
Chatsworth Products Inc (PA) ................................... E ...... 818 735-6100
  4175 Guardian St Simi Valley (93063) *(P-9279)*
Chavers Gasket Corporation ..................................... E ...... 949 472-8118
  23325 Del Lago Dr Laguna Hills (92653) *(P-6441)*
Chawk Technology Intl Inc (PA) ................................. D ...... 510 330-5299
  31033 Huntwood Ave Hayward (94544) *(P-6772)*
Chay & Harris Pntg Contrs Inc .................................. E ...... 650 966-1472
  2520 Wyandotte St Ste E Mountain View (94043) *(P-443)*
CHE Precision Inc .............................................. E ...... 805 499-8885
  2586 Calcite Cir Newbury Park (91320) *(P-10773)*
Checchi Enterprises Inc ........................................ F ...... 530 378-1207
  19849 Riverside Ave Anderson (96007) *(P-4548)*
Check It Out, Los Angeles  *Also Called: Nexxen Apparel Inc (P-2795)*
Check Point Software, Redwood City  *Also Called: Check Point Software Tech Inc (P-18165)*
Check Point Software Tech Inc (DH) ............................. C ...... 800 429-4391
  100 Oracle Pkwy Redwood City (94065) *(P-18165)*
Checkpoint Cloudguard Dome9, Mountain View  *Also Called: Dome9 Security Inc (P-17550)*
Checkworks Inc ................................................. D ...... 626 333-1444
  315 Cloverleaf Dr Ste J Baldwin Park (91706) *(P-4999)*
Cheek Machine Corp ............................................. E ...... 714 279-9486
  1312 S Allec St Anaheim (92805) *(P-10774)*
Cheesecake Factory Bakery Inc .................................. B ...... 818 871-3000
  26950 Agoura Rd Calabasas Hills (91301) *(P-17571)*
Cheesecake Factory Inc (PA) .................................... B ...... 818 871-3000
  26901 Malibu Hills Rd Calabasas Hills (91301) *(P-17572)*
CHEESECAKE FACTORY, THE, Calabasas Hills  *Also Called: Cheesecake Factory Inc (P-17572)*
Chef Merito Inc ................................................ F ...... 818 781-0470
  15355 Raymer St Van Nuys (91406) *(P-2163)*
Chef Merito LLC (PA) ........................................... E ...... 818 787-0100
  7915 Sepulveda Blvd Van Nuys (91405) *(P-2164)*
Chef Merito, Inc., Van Nuys  *Also Called: Chef Merito Inc (P-2163)*
Chefmaster ..................................................... E ...... 714 554-4000
  501 Airpark Dr Fullerton (92833) *(P-2165)*
Chefsattraction ................................................ E ...... 310 800-3778
  3400 Cottage Way Sacramento (95825) *(P-2166)*
Chem Arrow Corp ................................................ E ...... 626 358-2255
  13643 Live Oak Ln Irwindale (91706) *(P-6388)*
Chem-Mark of Orange County, Cerritos  *Also Called: Better Beverages Inc (P-1987)*
Chem-Tronics, El Cajon  *Also Called: GKN Aerospace Chem-Tronics Inc (P-13709)*
Chemat Technology Inc .......................................... E ...... 818 727-9786
  9036 Winnetka Ave Northridge (91324) *(P-14332)*
Chemat Vision, Northridge  *Also Called: Chemat Technology Inc (P-14332)*
Chemco Products Company, Paramount  *Also Called: LMC Enterprises (P-5913)*
Chemcraft Coatings Technology Inc .............................. D ...... 530 894-3585
  311 Otterson Dr Ste 60 Chico (95928) *(P-6075)*
Chemdiv Inc .................................................... E ...... 858 794-4860
  12730 High Bluff Dr San Diego (92130) *(P-6273)*
Chemeor Inc .................................................... E ...... 626 966-3808
  727 Arrow Grand Cir Covina (91722) *(P-5935)*
Chemetall Oakite, Fremont  *Also Called: Chemetall US Inc (P-5895)*
Chemetall US Inc ............................................... E ...... 408 387-5340
  46716 Lakeview Blvd Fremont (94538) *(P-5895)*
Chemetry, Moss Landing  *Also Called: Calera Corporation (P-6137)*
Chemi-Source Inc ............................................... E ...... 760 477-8177
  2665 Vista Pacific Dr Oceanside (92056) *(P-17031)*
Chemical Diversity Labs, San Diego  *Also Called: Chemdiv Inc (P-6273)*
Chemical Guys, Torrance  *Also Called: Smart LLC (P-7030)*
Chemical Methods Assoc LLC (DH) ................................ E ...... 714 898-8781
  17707 Valley View Ave Cerritos (90703) *(P-10545)*
Chemical Safety Technology Inc ................................. E ...... 408 263-0984
  2461 Autumnvale Dr San Jose (95131) *(P-6773)*
Chemical Systems Div, San Jose  *Also Called: Rtx Corporation (P-13721)*
Chemical Technologies Intl Inc ................................. F ...... 916 638-1315
  2747 Mercantile Dr Ste 200 Rancho Cordova (95742) *(P-10546)*
Chemlogics Group LLC ........................................... E ...... 805 591-3314
  7305 Morro Rd Ste 200 Atascadero (93422) *(P-6139)*
Chemocentryx Inc (HQ) .......................................... E ...... 650 210-2900
  750 Gateway Blvd South San Francisco (94080) *(P-5404)*
Chempartner Inc ................................................ E ...... 215 720-6650
  280 Utah Ave Ste 100 South San Francisco (94080) *(P-5405)*
Chemseal, Pacoima  *Also Called: Flamemaster Corporation (P-6228)*
Chemsil Silicones Inc .......................................... E ...... 818 700-0302
  21900 Marilla St Chatsworth (91311) *(P-17240)*
Chemsw Inc ..................................................... F ...... 707 864-0845
  2480 Burskirk Ste 300 Pleasant Hill (94523) *(P-18166)*
Chemtainer Industries, Compton  *Also Called: County Plastics Corp (P-6783)*
Chemtec Chemical Company, Chatsworth  *Also Called: Vijall Inc (P-17251)*
Chemtex International, Sunnyvale  *Also Called: American Liquid Packaging Systems Inc (P-5134)*
Chemtool Incorporated .......................................... C ...... 661 823-7190
  1300 Goodrick Dr Tehachapi (93561) *(P-6389)*
Chemtrade Chemicals US LLC ..................................... D ...... 510 232-7193
  525 Castro St Richmond (94801) *(P-5083)*
Chemtreat Inc .................................................. D ...... 804 935-2000
  8885 Rehco Rd San Diego (92121) *(P-6274)*
Chemtrol, Santa Barbara  *Also Called: Santa Barbara Control Systems (P-14454)*
Chen-Tech Industries Inc (DH) .................................. E ...... 949 855-6716
  9 Wrigley Irvine (92618) *(P-15041)*
Chenbro Micom (usa) Inc ........................................ E ...... 909 937-0100
  2800 Jurupa St Ontario (91761) *(P-10232)*
Chep (usa) Inc ................................................. F ...... 925 234-4970
  2276 Wilbur Ln Antioch (94509) *(P-3334)*
Cheque Guard Inc ............................................... D ...... 818 563-9335
  512 S Verdugo Dr Burbank (91502) *(P-17895)*
Cherokee Chemical Co Inc (PA) .................................. E ...... 323 265-1112
  3540 E 26th St Vernon (90058) *(P-17241)*
Cherokee Uniform, Sherman Oaks  *Also Called: Careismatic Brands LLC (P-7107)*
Cherokee Uniforms, Sherman Oaks  *Also Called: Strategic Distribution L P (P-2603)*
Chester Paul Company, Anaheim  *Also Called: Welbilt Fdsrvice Companies LLC (P-10527)*

Employee Codes: A=Over 500 employees, B=251-500
C=101-250, D=51-100, E=20-50, F=10-19, G=1-9

## Chevelle Classics Parts & ACC — ALPHABETIC SECTION

Chevelle Classics Parts & ACC, Seal Beach *Also Called: Original Parts Group Inc (P-17455)*

Chevron, San Ramon *Also Called: Chevron Corporation (P-6333)*

Chevron, Richmond *Also Called: Chevron USA Inc (P-6335)*

Chevron, El Segundo *Also Called: Chevron Corporation (P-17471)*

Chevron, San Ramon *Also Called: Chevron USA Inc (P-17472)*

Chevron, San Ramon *Also Called: Chevron USA Inc (P-17473)*

Chevron Corporation (PA) ............................................................. A ...... 925 842-1000
   5001 Executive Pkwy Ste 200 San Ramon (94583) *(P-6333)*

Chevron Corporation ..................................................................... A ...... 310 615-5000
   324 W El Segundo Blvd El Segundo (90245) *(P-17471)*

Chevron Energy Solutions Co, San Francisco *Also Called: Chevron Energy Solutions LP (P-14357)*

Chevron Energy Solutions LP ........................................................ B ...... 415 894-4188
   345 California St Fl 18 San Francisco (94104) *(P-14357)*

Chevron Global Energy Inc (HQ) ................................................... D ...... 925 842-1000
   5001 Executive Pkwy San Ramon (94583) *(P-6334)*

Chevron Global Lubricants, San Ramon *Also Called: Chevron Global Energy Inc (P-6334)*

Chevron Mining Inc ........................................................................ C ...... 760 856-7625
   67750 Bailey Rd Mountain Pass (92366) *(P-111)*

Chevron Oronite, San Ramon *Also Called: Chevron Oronite Company LLC (P-6275)*

Chevron Oronite Company LLC ..................................................... B ...... 925 842-1000
   100 Chevron Way Richmond (94801) *(P-5144)*

Chevron Oronite Company LLC (DH) ............................................ E ...... 713 954-6060
   5001 Executive Pkwy San Ramon (94583) *(P-6275)*

Chevron Phillips Chem Co LP ....................................................... E ...... 909 420-5500
   5001 Executive Pkwy San Ramon (94583) *(P-5145)*

Chevron USA Inc ........................................................................... D ...... 510 242-3000
   841 Chevron Way Frnt Richmond (94801) *(P-6335)*

Chevron USA Inc (HQ) .................................................................. B ...... 925 842-1000
   5001 Executive Pkwy Ste 200 San Ramon (94583) *(P-17472)*

Chevron USA Inc ........................................................................... D ...... 925 842-0855
   5001 Executive Pkwy San Ramon (94583) *(P-17473)*

Chicago Brothers, Vernon *Also Called: Overhill Farms Inc (P-2308)*

Chick Publications Inc .................................................................. E ...... 909 987-0771
   8780 Archibald Ave Rancho Cucamonga (91730) *(P-4320)*

Chicken of Sea International, El Segundo *Also Called: Tri-Union Seafoods LLC (P-17159)*

Chicken Rnch Economic Dev Corp ............................................... E ...... 209 984-9066
   16929 Chicken Ranch Rd Jamestown (95327) *(P-4089)*

Chico Community Publishing (PA) ................................................. E ...... 530 894-2300
   603 Orange St Chico (95928) *(P-4090)*

Chico Community Publishing ........................................................ C ...... 916 498-1234
   3925 Power Inn Rd Sacramento (95826) *(P-4091)*

Chico Enterprise Record, Chico *Also Called: Gatehouse Media LLC (P-4120)*

Chico Site, Chico *Also Called: Truroots LLC (P-2380)*

Chicobag, Chico *Also Called: Chicoeco Inc (P-2954)*

Chicoeco Inc .................................................................................. E ...... 530 342-4426
   747 Fortress St Chico (95973) *(P-2954)*

Chicos Fas Inc .............................................................................. F ...... 951 849-4069
   48400 Seminole Dr Cabazon (92230) *(P-17491)*

Chili's, Santa Maria *Also Called: Impo International LLC (P-7116)*

Chilicon Power LLC (PA) .............................................................. E ...... 310 800-1396
   15415 W Sunset Blvd Ste 102 Pacific Palisades (90272) *(P-14504)*

China Custom Manufacturing Ltd .................................................. A ...... 510 979-1920
   44843 Fremont Blvd Fremont (94538) *(P-6774)*

China Pac Sheet Metal Mfg, Los Angeles *Also Called: China Pacific Inc (P-364)*

China Pacific Inc .......................................................................... F ...... 323 222-9580
   1777 N Main St Los Angeles (90031) *(P-364)*

China Press, The, Alhambra *Also Called: Asia-Pacific California Inc (P-4067)*

Chinese Consumer Yellow Pages, Fremont *Also Called: Chinese Overseas Mktg Svc Corp (P-4378)*

Chinese Consumer Yellow Pages, Rosemead *Also Called: Chinese Overseas Mktg Svc Corp (P-4379)*

Chinese Overseas Mktg Svc Corp ................................................. E ...... 510 476-0880
   33420 Alvarado Niles Rd Union City (94587) *(P-4377)*

Chinese Overseas Mktg Svc Corp ................................................. E ...... 626 280-8588
   46292 Warm Springs Blvd Unit 614 Fremont (94539) *(P-4378)*

Chinese Overseas Mktg Svc Corp (PA) ........................................ D ...... 626 280-8588
   3940 Rosemead Blvd Rosemead (91770) *(P-4379)*

Chinese Times, San Francisco *Also Called: Gum Sun Times Inc (P-4124)*

Chip-Makers Tooling Supply Inc .................................................... F ...... 562 698-5840
   33867 Petunia St Murrieta (92563) *(P-9611)*

Chipmasters Manufacturing, Azusa *Also Called: Chipmasters Manufacturing Inc (P-10775)*

Chipmasters Manufacturing Inc (PA) ............................................. F ...... 626 804-8178
   798 N Coney Ave Azusa (91702) *(P-10775)*

Chipton-Ross Inc .......................................................................... D ...... 310 414-7800
   420 Culver Blvd Playa Del Rey (90293) *(P-13647)*

Chlor Alkali Products & Vinyls, Santa Fe Springs *Also Called: Olin Chlor Alkali Logistics (P-5034)*

Chlor Alkali Products & Vinyls, Tracy *Also Called: Olin Chlor Alkali Logistics (P-5035)*

Chocolates A La Carte Inc ........................................................... C ...... 661 257-3700
   24836 Avenue Rockefeller Valencia (91355) *(P-1302)*

Chocolates and Health, La Verne *Also Called: Vitawest Nutraceuticals Inc (P-787)*

Choice Lithographics, Buena Park *Also Called: Cyu Lithographics Inc (P-4580)*

Chooljian & Sons Inc (PA) ............................................................. E ...... 559 888-2031
   5287 S Del Rey Ave Del Rey (93616) *(P-79)*

Chooljian & Sons Inc .................................................................... E ...... 559 888-2031
   Del Rey Ave Del Rey (93616) *(P-9784)*

Choon Inc (PA) .............................................................................. E ...... 213 225-2500
   1443 E 4th St Los Angeles (90033) *(P-2703)*

Choose Manufacturing Co LLC ..................................................... E ...... 714 327-1698
   24 Passion Flower Irvine (92618) *(P-12077)*

Chouinard & Myhre Inc ................................................................. E ...... 415 480-3636
   655 Redwood Hwy Frontage Rd Ste 102 Mill Valley (94941) *(P-18968)*

Chownow Inc (PA) ........................................................................ D ...... 888 707-2469
   3585 Hayden Ave Culver City (90232) *(P-18167)*

Chris Alston Chassisworks Inc ..................................................... E ...... 916 388-0288
   11375 Sunrise Park Dr Ste 800 Rancho Cordova (95742) *(P-17661)*

Chris Putrimas ............................................................................... E ...... 877 434-1666
   1930 E Carson St Ste 102 Carson (90810) *(P-16116)*

Chrislie Formulations, Azusa *Also Called: Bbeautiful LLC (P-5947)*

Christian Evang Chrches Amer I ................................................... E ...... 510 533-8300
   2433 Coolidge Ave Oakland (94601) *(P-19343)*

Christie Digital Systems Inc (HQ) .................................................. D ...... 714 236-8610
   10550 Camden Dr Cypress (90630) *(P-15634)*

Christie Medical Holdings Inc ....................................................... E ...... 714 236-8610
   10550 Camden Dr Cypress (90630) *(P-15525)*

Christy Vault Company (PA) ......................................................... E ...... 650 994-1378
   1000 Collins Ave Colma (94014) *(P-7318)*

Chroma Systems Solutions Inc (HQ) ............................................ E ...... 949 297-4848
   19772 Pauling Foothill Ranch (92610) *(P-14505)*

Chroma Systems Solutions Inc .................................................... E ...... 949 600-6400
   25612 Commercentre Dr Lake Forest (92630) *(P-14506)*

Chromacode Inc ............................................................................ E ...... 442 244-4369
   2330 Faraday Ave Ste 100 Carlsbad (92008) *(P-17896)*

Chromadex, Los Angeles *Also Called: Chromadex Corporation (P-5236)*

Chromadex Corporation (PA) ........................................................ E ...... 310 388-6706
   10900 Wilshire Blvd Ste 600 Los Angeles (90024) *(P-5236)*

Chromagraphics, Santa Rosa *Also Called: Graphic Enterprises Inc (P-4623)*

Chromal Plating & Grinding, Los Angeles *Also Called: Chromal Plating Company (P-8940)*

Chromal Plating Company ............................................................ E ...... 323 222-0119
   1748 Workman St Los Angeles (90031) *(P-8940)*

Chromalloy Component Svcs Inc .................................................. E ...... 858 877-2800
   7007 Consolidated Way San Diego (92121) *(P-13704)*

Chromalloy Gas Turbine LLC ........................................................ D ...... 760 768-3723
   1749 Stergios Rd Ste 2 Calexico (92231) *(P-13705)*

Chromalloy San Diego Corp ......................................................... C ...... 858 877-2800
   7007 Consolidated Way San Diego (92121) *(P-19249)*

Chromalloy Southwest, Calexico *Also Called: Chromalloy Gas Turbine LLC (P-13705)*

Chromatic Inc Lithographers ......................................................... E ...... 818 242-5785
   127 Concord St Glendale (91203) *(P-4549)*

Chromcraft Rvngton Douglas Ind (PA) .......................................... F ...... 909 930-9891
   1011 S Grove Ave Ontario (91761) *(P-3467)*

Chrome Hearts, Los Angeles *Also Called: Chrome Hearts LLC (P-2875)*

Chrome Hearts LLC (PA) .............................................................. E ...... 323 957-7544
   915 N Mansfield Ave Los Angeles (90038) *(P-2875)*

Chrome Nickel Plating, Lynwood *Also Called: Bowman-Field Inc (P-8934)*

Chrome Tech Inc ........................................................................... C ...... 714 543-4092
   2310 Cape Cod Way Santa Ana (92703) *(P-8941)*

Chromologic, Monrovia *Also Called: Chromologic LLC (P-15042)*

# ALPHABETIC SECTION

**Chromologic LLC** .................................................................. E ...... 626 381-9974
1225 S Shamrock Ave Monrovia (91016) *(P-15042)*

**Chronicle Books LLC (HQ)** ................................................... D ...... 415 537-4200
680 2nd St San Francisco (94107) *(P-4321)*

**Chronicled, San Francisco** *Also Called: Chronicled Inc (P-16513)*

**Chronicled Inc** ....................................................................... E ...... 415 355-4681
575 Mission St San Francisco (94105) *(P-16513)*

**Chronomite Laboratories Inc** ............................................... E ...... 310 534-2300
17451 Hurley St City Of Industry (91744) *(P-14358)*

**Chrontel Inc (PA)** .................................................................. D ...... 408 383-9328
2210 Otoole Ave Ste 100 San Jose (95131) *(P-12381)*

**Chua & Sons Co Inc** ............................................................. E ...... 323 588-8044
3300 E 50th St Vernon (90058) *(P-2451)*

**Chuaolson Enterprises Inc** ................................................... E ...... 714 630-4751
1274 N Grove St Anaheim (92806) *(P-16748)*

**Chubby Gorilla Inc (PA)** ........................................................ E ...... 844 365-5218
4320 N Harbor Blvd Fullerton (92835) *(P-6775)*

**Chup Corporation** ................................................................ F ...... 949 455-0676
2990 Airway Ave Ste A Costa Mesa (92626) *(P-4550)*

**Church & Dwight Co Inc** ...................................................... E ...... 559 661-2790
31266 Avenue 12 Madera (93638) *(P-5030)*

**Church & Dwight Co Inc** ...................................................... F ...... 609 613-1551
17486 Nisqualli Rd Victorville (92395) *(P-5873)*

**Churm Publishing Inc (PA)** .................................................. E ...... 714 796-7000
1451 Quail St Ste 201 Newport Beach (92660) *(P-4092)*

**Chus Packaging Supplies Inc** ............................................... E ...... 562 944-6411
10011 Santa Fe Springs Rd Santa Fe Springs (90670) *(P-17290)*

**Ci, Mather** *Also Called: Construction Innovations LLC (P-13225)*

**Ciao, Camarillo** *Also Called: Ciao Wireless Inc (P-12937)*

**Ciao Wireless Inc** ................................................................. D ...... 805 389-3224
4000 Via Pescador Camarillo (93012) *(P-12937)*

**Ciasons Industrial Inc** .......................................................... E ...... 714 259-0838
1615 Boyd St Santa Ana (92705) *(P-6442)*

**Cibaria International Inc** ...................................................... E ...... 951 823-8490
705 Columbia Ave Riverside (92507) *(P-17181)*

**Cibus, San Diego** *Also Called: Cibus Inc (P-6196)*

**Cibus Inc** .............................................................................. C ...... 858 450-0008
6455 Nancy Ridge Dr San Diego (92121) *(P-6196)*

**Cicon Engineering Inc (PA)** .................................................. C ...... 818 909-6060
6633 Odessa Ave Van Nuys (91406) *(P-12938)*

**CIDARA THERAPEUTICS, San Diego** *Also Called: Cidara Therapeutics Inc (P-5818)*

**Cidara Therapeutics Inc (PA)** ............................................... D ...... 858 752-6170
6310 Nancy Ridge Dr Ste 101 San Diego (92121) *(P-5818)*

**Cii, Santee** *Also Called: Compucraft Industries Inc (P-13814)*

**Cilajet LLC** ........................................................................... E ...... 310 320-8000
16425 Ishida Ave Gardena (90248) *(P-5896)*

**Cim Services, Compton** *Also Called: Circle Industrial Mfg Corp (P-10047)*

**Cimc Intermodal Equipment, South Gate** *Also Called: Cimc Intermodal Equipment LLC (P-13614)*

**Cimc Intermodal Equipment LLC (HQ)** ................................. D ...... 562 904-8600
10530 Sessler St South Gate (90280) *(P-13614)*

**Cincinnati Div, San Jose** *Also Called: Sumco USA Sales Corporation (P-12740)*

**Cinder Block LLC** ................................................................. F ...... 510 957-1333
2220 W Winton Ave Hayward (94545) *(P-2490)*

**Cinema Secrets Inc** .............................................................. D ...... 818 846-0579
6639 Odessa Ave Van Nuys (91406) *(P-17693)*

**Cinnabar** .............................................................................. C ...... 818 842-8190
4571 Electronics Pl Los Angeles (90039) *(P-17822)*

**Cinton LLC** ........................................................................... E ...... 714 961-8808
620 Richfield Rd Placentia (92870) *(P-3947)*

**Ciphercloud Inc (HQ)** ........................................................... D ...... 408 687-4350
2581 Junction Ave Ste 200 San Jose (95134) *(P-18168)*

**Ciphertex LLC** ...................................................................... F ...... 818 773-8989
9301 Jordan Ave Ste 105a Chatsworth (91311) *(P-10342)*

**Ciphertex Data Security, Chatsworth** *Also Called: Ciphertex LLC (P-10342)*

**Ciphertrace Inc** .................................................................... D ...... 650 996-2142
140 Victory Ln Los Gatos (95030) *(P-19034)*

**Circle Green Inc** ................................................................... F ...... 909 930-0200
8271 Chino Ave Ontario (91761) *(P-6140)*

**Circle Industrial Mfg Corp (PA)** ............................................. E ...... 310 638-5101
1613 W El Segundo Blvd Compton (90222) *(P-10047)*

**Circle W Enterprises Inc** ....................................................... E ...... 661 257-2400
27737 Avenue Hopkins Valencia (91355) *(P-9214)*

**Circor Aerospace Inc (DH)** ................................................... C ...... 951 270-6200
2301 Wardlow Cir Corona (92878) *(P-9148)*

**Circuit Assembly Corp (PA)** .................................................. F ...... 949 855-7887
6 Autry Ste 150 Irvine (92618) *(P-12869)*

**Circuit Services Llc** ............................................................. E ...... 818 701-5391
9134 Independence Ave Chatsworth (91311) *(P-12078)*

**Circus Ice Cream, Santa Clara** *Also Called: Wonder Ice Cream Inc (P-821)*

**Cirexx International Inc (PA)** ................................................ C ...... 408 988-3980
791 Nuttman St Santa Clara (95054) *(P-12079)*

**Cirrus Enterprises LLC** ......................................................... D ...... 310 204-6159
18027 Bishop Ave Carson (90746) *(P-17224)*

**Cirtec Medical Corp** ............................................................. D ...... 408 395-0443
101b Cooper Ct Los Gatos (95032) *(P-15043)*

**Cirtech Inc** ........................................................................... E ...... 714 921-0860
250 E Emerson Ave Orange (92865) *(P-19082)*

**Cisco & Brothers Designs, Pasadena** *Also Called: Cisco Bros Corp (P-3468)*

**Cisco Bros Corp (PA)** ........................................................... C ...... 323 778-8612
474 S Arroyo Pkwy Pasadena (91105) *(P-3468)*

**Cisco Systems, Milpitas** *Also Called: Cisco Systems Inc (P-10343)*

**Cisco Systems, San Jose** *Also Called: Cisco Systems Inc (P-10345)*

**Cisco Systems, Pleasanton** *Also Called: Cisco Systems Inc (P-10346)*

**Cisco Systems, San Francisco** *Also Called: Cisco Systems Inc (P-10347)*

**Cisco Systems, San Jose** *Also Called: Cisco Systems LLC (P-18169)*

**Cisco Systems Inc** ............................................................... D ...... 408 526-6200
755 Sycamore Dr Milpitas (95035) *(P-10343)*

**Cisco Systems Inc** ............................................................... E ...... 408 216-3440
3675 Cisco Way San Jose (95134) *(P-10344)*

**Cisco Systems Inc (PA)** ....................................................... A ...... 408 526-4000
170 W Tasman Dr San Jose (95134) *(P-10345)*

**Cisco Systems Inc** ............................................................... E ...... 925 225-2111
4464 Willow Rd Ste 102 Pleasanton (94588) *(P-10346)*

**Cisco Systems Inc** ............................................................... E ...... 415 845-8008
85 2nd St Ste 710 San Francisco (94105) *(P-10347)*

**Cisco Systems LLC (HQ)** ..................................................... B ...... 650 989-6500
170 W Tasman Dr San Jose (95134) *(P-18169)*

**Citala US Inc** ........................................................................ E ...... 408 745-8500
1277 Reamwood Ave Sunnyvale (94089) *(P-12939)*

**Citation Press** ...................................................................... D ...... 408 957-9900
2050 Junction Ave San Jose (95131) *(P-4551)*

**Citizens of Humanity LLC (PA)** ............................................. C ...... 323 923-1240
5715 Bickett St Huntington Park (90255) *(P-2745)*

**Citrogene Inc** ....................................................................... F ...... 408 930-5070
2528 Qume Dr Ste 6 San Jose (95131) *(P-10776)*

**Citrusbyte LLC** ..................................................................... E ...... 888 969-2983
21550 Oxnard St Ste 300 # 11 Woodland Hills (91367) *(P-17897)*

**City Baking Company** .......................................................... D ...... 650 332-8730
1373 Lowrie Ave South San Francisco (94080) *(P-1177)*

**City Bean Inc** ....................................................................... F ...... 323 734-0828
5051 W Jefferson Blvd Los Angeles (90016) *(P-17424)*

**City Electric Supply** ............................................................. E ...... 707 523-4600
360 Tesconi Cir Santa Rosa (95401) *(P-16649)*

**City News Group Inc** ........................................................... E ...... 909 370-1200
22797 Barton Rd Grand Terrace (92313) *(P-4093)*

**City of Delano** ..................................................................... E ...... 661 721-3352
1107 Lytle Ave Delano (93215) *(P-10547)*

**City of Industry, Chino** *Also Called: Balaji Trading Inc (P-11753)*

**City of Riverside** .................................................................. C ...... 951 351-6140
5950 Acorn St Riverside (92504) *(P-10548)*

**City of San Diego** ................................................................ C ...... 619 758-2310
2392 Kincaid Rd San Diego (92101) *(P-14644)*

**City of Santa Monica** ........................................................... C ...... 310 826-6712
1228 S Bundy Dr Los Angeles (90025) *(P-10549)*

**City of Stockton** .................................................................. C ...... 209 937-8339
22 E Weber Ave Ste 301 Stockton (95202) *(P-3614)*

**City of Woodland** ................................................................ E ...... 530 661-5860
1000 Lincoln Ave Woodland (95695) *(P-19577)*

**City Paper Box Co** ............................................................... F ...... 323 231-5990
652 E 61st St Los Angeles (90001) *(P-3831)*

**City Snta Mnica Wtr Trtmnt Pla, Los Angeles** *Also Called: City of Santa Monica (P-10549)*

City Steel Heat Treating, Orange  *Also Called: Thermal-Vac Technology Inc (P-7902)*
City Triangles, Los Angeles  *Also Called: Jodi Kristopher LLC (P-2706)*
City Wire Cloth, Fontana  *Also Called: Daniel Gerard Worldwide Inc (P-16618)*
CJ Advisors Inc .................................................................. E ...... 714 956-3388
  6900 8th St Buena Park (90620) *(P-10777)*
CJ America, La Palma  *Also Called: CJ Foods Inc (P-2167)*
CJ America Inc (HQ) ............................................................ D ...... 213 338-2700
  300 S Grand Ave Ste 1100 Los Angeles (90071) *(P-17182)*
CJ Berry Well Services MGT LLC ........................................ A ...... 661 589-5220
  3752 Allen Rd Bakersfield (93314) *(P-217)*
CJ Foods Inc (HQ) ................................................................ D ...... 714 367-7200
  4 Centerpointe Dr Ste 100 La Palma (90623) *(P-2167)*
CJ Foods Mfg Beaumont LLC .............................................. D ...... 951 916-9300
  415 Nicholas Rd Beaumont (92223) *(P-16117)*
CJ Products Inc .................................................................... F ...... 760 444-4217
  310 Via Vera Cruz Ste 211 San Marcos (92078) *(P-2925)*
CJ United Food Corporation (PA) ......................................... F ...... 510 895-6868
  155 98th Ave Oakland (94603) *(P-3913)*
CJ Wilson BMW Mtcyc Murrieta, Murrieta  *Also Called: Wilson Cycles Sports Corp (P-17444)*
CJd Construction Svcs Inc ................................................... E ...... 626 335-1116
  503 E Route 66 Glendora (91740) *(P-218)*
Cji Process Systems Inc ...................................................... D ...... 562 777-0614
  12000 Clark St Santa Fe Springs (90670) *(P-8308)*
CK Manufacturing & Trading Inc .......................................... E ...... 949 529-3400
  3 Holland Irvine (92618) *(P-3651)*
CK Technologies Inc (PA) .................................................... F ...... 805 987-4801
  3629 Vista Mercado Camarillo (93012) *(P-14394)*
Ckkm Inc (PA) ...................................................................... E ...... 951 371-8484
  265 Radio Rd Corona (92879) *(P-16613)*
Cks Solution Incorporated .................................................... E ...... 714 292-6307
  556 Vanguard Way Ste C Brea (92821) *(P-12940)*
Ckt, Camarillo  *Also Called: CK Technologies Inc (P-14394)*
CL Knox Inc ......................................................................... D ...... 661 837-0477
  34933 Imperial Ave Bakersfield (93308) *(P-219)*
CL Solutions LLC ................................................................ D ...... 714 597-6499
  1900 S Susan St Santa Ana (92704) *(P-7168)*
Cla-Val Co, Costa Mesa  *Also Called: Griswold Industries (P-7847)*
Clamp Swing Pricing Co Inc ................................................. E ...... 510 567-1600
  8386 Capwell Dr Oakland (94621) *(P-16118)*
Clamshell Buildings, Oxnard  *Also Called: Clamshell Structures Inc (P-8661)*
Clamshell Structures Inc ...................................................... F ...... 805 988-1340
  300 Graves Ave Ste B Oxnard (93030) *(P-8661)*
Clara Foods Co .................................................................... F ...... 650 733-4015
  1 Tower Pl Fl 8 South San Francisco (94080) *(P-949)*
Claremont Courier Inc .......................................................... F ...... 909 621-4761
  114 Olive St Claremont (91711) *(P-4094)*
Clarendon Specialty Fas Inc ................................................ D ...... 714 842-2603
  2180 Temple Ave Long Beach (90804) *(P-16749)*
Clariant Corporation ............................................................. E ...... 909 825-1793
  926 S 8th St Colton (92324) *(P-3948)*
Clariant Corporation ............................................................. F ...... 562 322-6647
  3355 Olive Ave Signal Hill (90755) *(P-6141)*
Clarifi Technologies Inc ........................................................ F ...... 866 997-2643
  424 2nd St Ste A Davis (95616) *(P-18170)*
Clarios LLC .......................................................................... E ...... 951 222-0284
  2100 Chicago Ave Riverside (92507) *(P-3615)*
Clarios LLC .......................................................................... E ...... 510 783-4000
  3526 Breakwater Ct Bldg E Hayward (94545) *(P-3616)*
Clarios LLC .......................................................................... E ...... 805 522-5555
  4100 Guardian St Simi Valley (93063) *(P-3617)*
Clarios LLC .......................................................................... E ...... 760 200-5225
  39312 Leopard St Ste A Palm Desert (92211) *(P-3618)*
Clarios LLC .......................................................................... D ...... 916 294-8866
  103 Woodmere Rd Ste 110 Folsom (95630) *(P-3619)*
Clarios LLC .......................................................................... E ...... 408 346-9984
  2200 Mis Santa Clara (95054) *(P-13133)*
Clariphy Communications Inc (DH) ..................................... D ...... 949 861-3074
  15485 Sand Canyon Ave Irvine (92618) *(P-12382)*
Clarity Design Inc ................................................................ F ...... 858 746-3500
  13000 Gregg St Poway (92064) *(P-18969)*
Clark - Pacific Corporation ................................................... E ...... 626 962-8755
  9367 Holly Rd Adelanto (92301) *(P-7319)*
Clark - Pacific Corporation ................................................... E ...... 909 823-1433
  4684 Ontario Mills Pkwy Ste 200 Ontario (91764) *(P-7320)*
Clark - Pacific Corporation (PA) ........................................... B ...... 916 371-0305
  710 Riverpoint Ct Ste 100 West Sacramento (95605) *(P-16471)*
Clark Bros Inc ...................................................................... D ...... 209 392-6144
  745 Broadway St Fresno (93721) *(P-394)*
Clark Pacific, West Sacramento  *Also Called: Clark - Pacific Corporation (P-16471)*
Clark Steel Fabricators Inc .................................................. E ...... 619 390-1502
  12610 Vigilante Rd Lakeside (92040) *(P-8621)*
Clarkdietrich Building Systems, Riverside  *Also Called: Clarkwestern Dietrich Building (P-8410)*
Clarkwestern Dietrich Building ............................................ E ...... 951 360-3500
  6510 General Rd Riverside (92509) *(P-8410)*
Clarmil Manufacturing Corp (PA) ......................................... E ...... 510 476-0700
  30865 San Clemente St Hayward (94544) *(P-2168)*
Clarus Therapeutics Inc ....................................................... F ...... 847 562-4300
  355 S Grand Ave Los Angeles (90071) *(P-5819)*
Clary Corporation ................................................................ E ...... 626 359-4486
  150 E Huntington Dr Monrovia (91016) *(P-12941)*
Class a Powdercoat Inc ....................................................... E ...... 916 681-7474
  7506 Henrietta Dr Sacramento (95822) *(P-9058)*
Classe Party Rentals, Rancho Cucamonga  *Also Called: Sunn America Inc (P-17864)*
Classic Concepts Inc (PA) ................................................... F ...... 323 266-8993
  5200 Irwindale Ave Ste 120 Baldwin Park (91706) *(P-16422)*
Classic Containers Inc ........................................................ B ...... 909 930-3610
  1700 S Hellman Ave Ontario (91761) *(P-6608)*
Classic Home, Baldwin Park  *Also Called: Classic Concepts Inc (P-16422)*
Classic Innovations, Cloverdale  *Also Called: Classic Mill & Cabinet LLC (P-3232)*
Classic Litho & Design Inc .................................................. E ...... 310 224-5200
  340 Maple Ave Torrance (90503) *(P-4552)*
Classic Mill & Cabinet LLC .................................................. E ...... 707 894-9800
  590 Santana Dr Cloverdale (95425) *(P-3232)*
Classic Salads LLC ............................................................ E ...... 831 763-4520
  525 Old Natividad Rd Salinas (93908) *(P-2169)*
Classic Tents ....................................................................... E ...... 310 328-5060
  19119 S Reyes Ave Compton (90221) *(P-10488)*
Classic Tents, Compton  *Also Called: Classic Tents (P-10488)*
Classic Wines of California, Ceres  *Also Called: Bronco Wine Company (P-17262)*
Classic Wire Cut Company Inc ............................................ C ...... 661 257-0558
  28210 Constellation Rd Valencia (91355) *(P-10778)*
Classy, San Diego  *Also Called: Classy Inc (P-18171)*
Classy Inc ............................................................................ C ...... 619 961-1892
  350 10th Ave Ste 1300 San Diego (92101) *(P-18171)*
Claudes Buggies Inc ........................................................... E ...... 559 733-8222
  1715 N Farmersville Blvd Farmersville (93223) *(P-16377)*
Clausen Meat Company Inc ................................................ E ...... 209 667-8690
  19455 W Clausen Rd Turlock (95380) *(P-591)*
CLAVE, San Clemente  *Also Called: Icu Medical Inc (P-15111)*
Clay Corona Company (PA) ................................................ E ...... 951 277-2667
  22079 Knabe Rd Corona (92883) *(P-365)*
Clayborn Lab, Truckee  *Also Called: Horvath Holdings Inc (P-2453)*
Claybourne Industries Inc .................................................... F ...... 951 675-4508
  5055 Western Way Perris (92571) *(P-16119)*
Clayton Industries, City Of Industry  *Also Called: Clayton Manufacturing Company (P-10082)*
Clayton Manufacturing Company (PA) ................................ C ...... 626 443-9381
  17477 Hurley St City Of Industry (91744) *(P-10082)*
Clayton Manufacturing Inc (HQ) .......................................... D ...... 626 443-9381
  17477 Hurley St City Of Industry (91744) *(P-10083)*
CLC Work Gear, Commerce  *Also Called: Custom Leathercraft Mfg LLC (P-7154)*
Clean 360, Oakland  *Also Called: Roots Community Health Center (P-5881)*
Clean America Inc ............................................................... F ...... 800 336-2946
  1400 Pioneer St Brea (92821) *(P-13221)*
Clean Cut Technologies, Anaheim  *Also Called: Oliver Healthcare Packaging Co (P-16831)*
Clean Cut Technologies LLC ............................................... D ...... 714 864-3500
  1145 N Ocean Cir Anaheim (92806) *(P-6628)*
Clean Water Stores Inc ....................................................... F ...... 888 600-5426
  2806 Soquel Ave Ste A Santa Cruz (95062) *(P-1879)*
Clean Water Technology Inc (HQ) ....................................... E ...... 310 380-4648
  13008 S Western Ave Gardena (90249) *(P-10550)*
Clean Wave Management Inc ............................................. E ...... 949 370-0740
  1291 Puerta Del Sol San Clemente (92673) *(P-9949)*

## ALPHABETIC SECTION

**Cleanroom Film & Bags, Placentia** *Also Called: CF&b Manufacturing Inc (P-3964)*
**Cleantek Electric Inc** ............................................................................. E ...... 424 400-3315
   403 W 21st St San Pedro (90731) *(P-453)*
**Clear Blue Energy Corp** ....................................................................... D ...... 858 451-1549
   17150 Via Del Campo Ste 203 San Diego (92127) *(P-11587)*
**Clear Channel Outdoor LLC** ................................................................ E ...... 510 835-5900
   555 12th St Ste 950 Oakland (94607) *(P-17785)*
**Clear Channel Radio Sales, Los Angeles** *Also Called: Katz Millennium Sls & Mktg Inc (P-11871)*
**Clear Image Printing Inc** ...................................................................... E ...... 818 547-4684
   12744 San Fernando Rd Sylmar (91342) *(P-4553)*
**Clear Power Innovations Co, Diamond Bar** *Also Called: Prime Wire & Cable Inc (P-7793)*
**Clear Sign & Design Inc** ....................................................................... F ...... 760 736-8111
   170 Navajo St San Marcos (92078) *(P-559)*
**Clear Skye Inc** ...................................................................................... E ...... 415 619-5001
   2340 Powell St Ste 325 Emeryville (94608) *(P-18172)*
**Clear View LLC** .................................................................................... F ...... 408 271-2734
   1650 Las Plumas Ave Ste A San Jose (95133) *(P-8260)*
**Clear-Ad Inc** ......................................................................................... E ...... 866 627-9718
   2410 W 3rd St Santa Ana (92703) *(P-6776)*
**Clear-Com Communications, Alameda** *Also Called: Clear-Com LLC (P-11826)*
**Clear-Com LLC (HQ)** ............................................................................ A ...... 510 337-6600
   1301 Marina Village Pkwy Ste 105 Alameda (94501) *(P-11826)*
**Clearedge Power Inc** ........................................................................... C ...... 877 257-3343
   920 Thompson Pl 100 Sunnyvale (94085) *(P-11364)*
**Clearedge Solutions Inc** ...................................................................... E ...... 408 434-5984
   1020 Rock Ave San Jose (95131) *(P-7193)*
**Clearflow, Irvine** *Also Called: Clearflow Inc (P-15044)*
**Clearflow Inc (PA)** ................................................................................ E ...... 714 916-5010
   16 Technology Dr Ste 150 Irvine (92618) *(P-15044)*
**Clearlake Capital Group LP (PA)** ........................................................ B ...... 310 400-8800
   233 Wilshire Blvd Ste 800 Santa Monica (90401) *(P-17749)*
**Clearlake Capital Partners** .................................................................. A ...... 310 400-8800
   233 Wilshire Blvd Ste 800 Santa Monica (90401) *(P-18173)*
**Clearly Filtered Inc** .............................................................................. E ...... 877 876-2740
   23121 Antonio Pkwy Rcho Sta Marg (92688) *(P-10551)*
**Clearpathgps, Santa Barbara** *Also Called: Clearpathgps LLC (P-12870)*
**Clearpathgps LLC** ................................................................................ E ...... 805 979-3442
   3463 State St # 494 Santa Barbara (93105) *(P-12870)*
**Clearpoint Neuro Inc (PA)** ................................................................... D ...... 949 900-6833
   120 S Sierra Ave Ste 100 Solana Beach (92075) *(P-15045)*
**Clearwell Systems Inc** ......................................................................... C ...... 877 253-2793
   350 Ellis St Mountain View (94043) *(P-12383)*
**Cleasby Manufacturing Co Inc (PA)** ................................................... E ...... 415 822-6565
   1414 Bancroft Ave San Francisco (94124) *(P-9416)*
**Cleatech LLC** ....................................................................................... E ...... 714 754-6668
   2106 N Glassell St Orange (92865) *(P-14333)*
**Clegg Industries Inc** ............................................................................ C ...... 310 225-3800
   19032 S Vermont Ave Gardena (90248) *(P-15956)*
**Clegg Promo, Gardena** *Also Called: Clegg Industries Inc (P-15956)*
**Clemson Distribution Inc (PA)** ............................................................ E ...... 909 595-2770
   20722 Currier Rd City Of Industry (91789) *(P-17126)*
**Clerprem USA Corp** ............................................................................. E ...... 415 856-9001
   1330 Del Paso Rd Ste 300 Sacramento (95834) *(P-3620)*
**Cleughs Frozen Foods Inc** .................................................................. E
   6571 Altura Blvd Ste 200 Buena Park (90620) *(P-1001)*
**Cleveland Tramrail So Calif, Corona** *Also Called: General Conveyor Inc (P-19259)*
**Clic LLC** ................................................................................................ E ...... 415 421-2900
   855 Stanton Rd Ste 300 Burlingame (94010) *(P-4554)*
**Clients & Profits Inc** ............................................................................ F ...... 760 945-4334
   4755 Oceanside Blvd Ste 200 Oceanside (92056) *(P-16514)*
**Clif Bar & Company LLC (HQ)** ............................................................ C ...... 510 596-6300
   1451 66th St Emeryville (94608) *(P-1303)*
**Cliff Lede Vineyards, Yountville** *Also Called: Twin Peaks Winery Inc (P-1806)*
**Cliffdale Manufacturing LLC** ............................................................... C ...... 818 341-3344
   20409 Prairie St Chatsworth (91311) *(P-14109)*
**Climate Corporation (DH)** ................................................................... D ...... 415 363-0500
   201 3rd St Ste 1010 San Francisco (94103) *(P-18174)*
**Climate Fieldview, San Francisco** *Also Called: Climate Corporation (P-18174)*
**Clincapture** ........................................................................................... E ...... 408 412-7256
   1428 Bush St San Francisco (94109) *(P-11724)*

**Cline Cellars Inc (PA)** ........................................................................... E ...... 707 940-4000
   24737 Arnold Dr Sonoma (95476) *(P-1507)*
**Cline Cellars Winery, Sonoma** *Also Called: Cline Cellars Inc (P-1507)*
**Clinicomp International Inc (PA)** ........................................................ D ...... 858 546-8202
   9655 Towne Centre Dr San Diego (92121) *(P-18970)*
**Cliniqa, San Marcos** *Also Called: Cliniqa Corporation (P-5820)*
**Cliniqa Corporation (HQ)** .................................................................... E ...... 760 744-1900
   495 Enterprise St San Marcos (92078) *(P-5820)*
**Cliniqa Corporation** ............................................................................. D ...... 760 744-1900
   258 La Moree Rd San Marcos (92078) *(P-5821)*
**Cliosoft Inc** ........................................................................................... F ...... 510 790-4732
   39500 Stevenson Pl Ste 110 Fremont (94539) *(P-18175)*
**Clip Health, Fremont** *Also Called: Luminostics Inc (P-15156)*
**Cliphouse, Pomona** *Also Called: Solo Clip Inc (P-15617)*
**Clipper Oil Inc** ...................................................................................... E ...... 619 692-9701
   2488 Historic Decatur Rd San Diego (92106) *(P-17252)*
**Clipper Oil Company, San Diego** *Also Called: Clipper Oil Inc (P-17252)*
**Clipper Windpower, Carpinteria** *Also Called: Clipper Windpower PLC (P-9310)*
**Clipper Windpower PLC** ..................................................................... A ...... 805 690-3275
   6305 Carpinteria Ave Ste 300 Carpinteria (93013) *(P-9310)*
**Clique Brands Inc** ................................................................................ E ...... 310 623-6916
   750 N San Vicente Blvd Ste 800 West Hollywood (90069) *(P-4240)*
**Clonetab Inc** ......................................................................................... E ...... 209 292-5663
   1660 W Linne Rd Ste 214 Tracy (95377) *(P-18176)*
**Clontech, San Jose** *Also Called: Takara Bio Usa Inc (P-19477)*
**Clorox, Pleasanton** *Also Called: Clorox Company (P-5897)*
**CLOROX, Oakland** *Also Called: Clorox Company (P-5898)*
**Clorox, Redlands** *Also Called: Clorox Manufacturing Company (P-5899)*
**Clorox, Oakland** *Also Called: Clorox Manufacturing Company (P-5900)*
**Clorox, Fairfield** *Also Called: Clorox Manufacturing Company (P-5901)*
**Clorox, Oakland** *Also Called: Clorox Services Company (P-5902)*
**Clorox, Oakland** *Also Called: Clorox International Company (P-6197)*
**Clorox Company** .................................................................................. F ...... 925 368-6000
   4900 Johnson Dr Pleasanton (94588) *(P-5897)*
**Clorox Company (PA)** .......................................................................... A ...... 510 271-7000
   1221 Broadway Oakland (94612) *(P-5898)*
**Clorox International Company (HQ)** .................................................. D ...... 510 271-7000
   1221 Broadway Fl 13 Oakland (94612) *(P-6197)*
**Clorox Manufacturing Company** ........................................................ E ...... 909 307-2756
   2300 W San Bernardino Ave Redlands (92374) *(P-5899)*
**Clorox Manufacturing Company (HQ)** ............................................... C ...... 510 271-7000
   1221 Bdwy Oakland (94612) *(P-5900)*
**Clorox Manufacturing Company** ........................................................ C ...... 707 437-1051
   2600 Huntington Dr Fairfield (94533) *(P-5901)*
**Clorox Services Company (HQ)** ......................................................... D ...... 510 271-7000
   1221 Broadway Oakland (94612) *(P-5902)*
**Clos De La Tech LLC** .......................................................................... E ...... 650 722-3038
   1000 Fern Hollow Rd La Honda (94020) *(P-1508)*
**Clos Du Bois Wines Inc** ...................................................................... F ...... 707 857-1651
   19410 Geyserville Ave Geyserville (95441) *(P-1509)*
**Clos Du Val Wine Company Ltd** ........................................................ E ...... 707 259-2200
   5330 Silverado Trl Napa (94558) *(P-1510)*
**Clos La Chance Wines Inc** ................................................................. E ...... 408 686-1050
   1 Hummingbird Ln San Martin (95046) *(P-1511)*
**Clos Lachance Wines LLC** ................................................................. F ...... 408 686-1050
   1 Hummingbird Ln San Martin (95046) *(P-1512)*
**Closet World, The, City Of Industry** *Also Called: Home Organizers Inc (P-494)*
**Clothing Illustrated Inc (PA)** ............................................................... E ...... 213 403-9950
   836 Traction Ave Los Angeles (90013) *(P-2746)*
**Clothng/Pparel/Uniform/ppe Mfg, Vernon** *Also Called: David Grment Ctng Fsing Svc In (P-2751)*
**Cloud Automation Division, Aliso Viejo** *Also Called: Quest Software Inc (P-18719)*
**Cloud B Inc** ........................................................................................... E ...... 310 781-3833
   150 W Walnut St Ste 100 Gardena (90248) *(P-15728)*
**Cloud Nine Comforts, Los Angeles** *Also Called: Universal Cushion Company Inc (P-2951)*
**Cloud Sftwr Group Holdings Inc** ........................................................ F ...... 800 424-8749
   7414 Hollister Ave Goleta Los Angeles (90074) *(P-18177)*
**Cloud Software Group Inc** .................................................................. F ...... 415 344-0339
   575 Market St San Francisco (94105) *(P-18178)*

**Cloud Software Group Federal** ................................... E ...... 703 208-3900
4980 Great America Pkwy Santa Clara (95054) *(P-18179)*

**Cloud9 Charts Inc** ................................................. F ...... 510 507-3661
1528 Webster St Oakland (94612) *(P-18180)*

**Cloudbeds, San Diego** *Also Called: Digital Arbitrage Dist Inc (P-18240)*

**Cloudcar Inc** ...................................................... E ...... 650 946-1236
2560 N 1st St Ste 100 San Jose (95131) *(P-18181)*

**Cloudcover, Irvine** *Also Called: Cloudcover Iot Inc (P-18182)*

**Cloudcover Iot Inc (PA)** ........................................ E ...... 888 511-2022
14 Goodyear Ste 125b Irvine (92618) *(P-18182)*

**Cloudfiles Technologies Inc** ................................... F ...... 336 298-6575
38350 Fremont Blvd Ste 203 Fremont (94536) *(P-18183)*

**Cloudflare, San Francisco** *Also Called: Cloudflare Inc (P-18184)*

**Cloudflare Inc (PA)** ............................................. A ...... 888 993-5273
101 Townsend St San Francisco (94107) *(P-18184)*

**Cloudjee, Mountain View** *Also Called: Cloudjee Inc (P-18185)*

**Cloudjee Inc** ..................................................... E ...... 866 660-6099
1975 W El Camino Real # 30 Mountain View (94040) *(P-18185)*

**Cloudpaths, Newark** *Also Called: Tricopp Inc (P-19573)*

**Cloudshield Technologies LLC** ................................. C ...... 408 331-6640
212 Gibraltar Dr Sunnyvale (94089) *(P-18186)*

**Cloudsimple Inc** ................................................. D ...... 412 568-3487
1600 Amphitheatre Pkwy Mountain View (94043) *(P-18187)*

**Cloudsoda Inc** ................................................... F ...... 303 947-8661
832 N Victory Blvd Burbank (91502) *(P-18188)*

**Cloudvirga Inc** .................................................. D ...... 949 799-2643
5291 California Ave Ste 300 Irvine (92617) *(P-18189)*

**Clougherty Packing LLC (DH)** .................................. B ...... 323 583-4621
3049 E Vernon Ave Los Angeles (90058) *(P-592)*

**Clover Envmtl Solutions LLC** ................................... E ...... 760 357-9277
315 Weakley St Bldg 3 Calexico (92231) *(P-15635)*

**Clover Imaging, Calexico** *Also Called: Clover Envmtl Solutions LLC (P-15635)*

**Clover Needlecraft Inc** ......................................... E ...... 800 233-1703
1441 S Carlos Ave Ontario (91761) *(P-17061)*

**Clover Network Inc** ............................................. D ...... 650 210-7888
415 N Mathilda Ave Sunnyvale (94085) *(P-10459)*

**Clover Sonoma, Petaluma** *Also Called: Clover-Stornetta Farms LLC (P-17183)*

**Clover-Stornetta Farms LLC (PA)** .............................. C ...... 707 769-3282
1800 S Mcdowell Boulevard Ext Ste 100 Petaluma (94954) *(P-17183)*

**Cloverdale Ready Mix, Cloverdale** *Also Called: Ebac Investments Inc (P-7442)*

**Clovis Independent, Sacramento** *Also Called: El Dorado Newspapers (P-4109)*

**CLP Inc (PA)** ..................................................... E ...... 619 444-3105
1546 E Main St El Cajon (92021) *(P-19186)*

**Club Speed LLC (PA)** ............................................ E ...... 951 817-7073
300 Spectrum Center Dr Irvine (92618) *(P-18190)*

**Clue Clothing Corp** ............................................. F ...... 323 277-4500
2325 E 55th St Vernon (90058) *(P-2747)*

**Clustrix Inc** ..................................................... E ...... 415 501-9560
699 Veterans Blvd Redwood City (94063) *(P-17898)*

**Clw Foods LLC** .................................................. F ...... 323 432-4600
3425 E Vernon Ave Vernon (90058) *(P-2170)*

**CM Brewing Technologies LLC** .................................. F ...... 888 391-9990
42245 Remington Ave Temecula (92590) *(P-10552)*

**CM Construction Services Inc (PA)** ............................ E ...... 559 735-9556
8300 W Doe Ave Visalia (93291) *(P-366)*

**CM Machine Inc** ................................................. F ...... 951 654-6019
560 S Grand Ave San Jacinto (92582) *(P-10779)*

**CM Manufacturing Inc** .......................................... C ...... 408 284-7200
6321 San Ignacio Ave San Jose (95119) *(P-12384)*

**CMA Dish Machines, Cerritos** *Also Called: Chemical Methods Assoc LLC (P-10545)*

**Cmblu Energy Inc** ............................................... E ...... 650 272-8804
621 2nd St Ste A Petaluma (94952) *(P-174)*

**CMC, Goleta** *Also Called: CMC Rescue Inc (P-17694)*

**CMC Rescue Inc** ................................................. D ...... 805 562-9120
6740 Cortona Dr Goleta (93117) *(P-17694)*

**CMC Steel California, San Bernardino** *Also Called: Tamco (P-7630)*

**CMC Steel Us LLC** ............................................... E ...... 909 646-7827
5425 Industrial Pkwy San Bernardino (92407) *(P-8695)*

**CMH Records Inc** ................................................ E ...... 323 663-8098
2898 Rowena Ave Ste 201 Los Angeles (90039) *(P-11725)*

**CMI, Hughson** *Also Called: Calaveras Materials Inc (P-7410)*

**CMI, Irvine** *Also Called: Cooper Microelectronics Inc (P-12391)*

**CMI, San Clemente** *Also Called: Composite Manufacturing Inc (P-15047)*

**CMI Integrated Tech Inc** ........................................ E
11250 Playa Ct Culver City (90230) *(P-11260)*

**Cmk Manufacturing LLC** ......................................... E
10375 Wilshire Blvd Apt 2h Los Angeles (90024) *(P-2444)*

**CMr Marketing and RES Inc** .................................... B ...... 559 499-2100
3594 E Wawona Ave Fresno (93725) *(P-6198)*

**CMS Products LLC** .............................................. E ...... 714 424-5520
29620 Skyline Dr Tehachapi (93561) *(P-10348)*

**Cmt Sheet Metal** ................................................ F ...... 949 679-9868
22732 Granite Way Ste C Laguna Hills (92653) *(P-8309)*

**Cmy Image Corporation** ......................................... F ...... 510 516-6668
33268 Central Ave Union City (94587) *(P-4555)*

**CN Publishing Group, Irvine** *Also Called: Cycle News Inc (P-4100)*

**Cnc Machining Inc** .............................................. F ...... 805 681-8855
510 S Fairview Ave Goleta (93117) *(P-10780)*

**Cnc Noodle Corporation** ........................................ F ...... 510 732-1318
1787 Sabre St Hayward (94545) *(P-2171)*

**Cnet Technology Corporation** .................................. C ...... 408 392-9966
26291 Production Ave Ste 205 Hayward (94545) *(P-16695)*

**Cnex Labs Inc (PA)** ............................................. E ...... 408 695-1045
2390 Bering Dr San Jose (95131) *(P-12385)*

**Cni Mfg Inc** ..................................................... F ...... 626 962-6646
15627 Arrow Hwy Irwindale (91706) *(P-10781)*

**Cnm Marketing Inc** .............................................. F ...... 866 792-5265
2392 Morse Ave Unit 120 Irvine (92614) *(P-4860)*

**Co-West Commodities, San Bernardino** *Also Called: Park West Enterprises Inc (P-1388)*

**Coachworks Holdings Inc** ....................................... F ...... 951 684-9585
1863 Service Ct Riverside (92507) *(P-13345)*

**Coadna Holdings Inc** ............................................ D ...... 408 736-1100
1020 Stewart Dr Sunnyvale (94085) *(P-17744)*

**Coadna Photonics Inc (HQ)** .................................... D ...... 408 736-1100
1012 Stewart Dr Sunnyvale (94085) *(P-11757)*

**Coalition Technologies LLC** .................................... C ...... 310 827-3890
445 S Figueroa St Ste 3100 Los Angeles (90071) *(P-19549)*

**Coast Aerospace, Placentia** *Also Called: Coast Aerospace Mfg Inc (P-9612)*

**Coast Aerospace Mfg Inc** ....................................... E ...... 714 893-8066
950 Richfield Rd Placentia (92870) *(P-9612)*

**Coast Autonomous Inc (PA)** .................................... E ...... 626 838-2469
23 E Colorado Blvd Ste 203 Pasadena (91105) *(P-13477)*

**Coast Composites LLC** .......................................... E ...... 949 455-0665
7 Burroughs Irvine (92618) *(P-10782)*

**Coast Composites LLC (PA)** .................................... D ...... 949 455-0665
5 Burroughs Irvine (92618) *(P-13809)*

**Coast Creative Nameplates, Monte Sereno** *Also Called: Coast Engraving Companies Inc (P-5023)*

**Coast Custom Cable, Carson** *Also Called: Belden Inc (P-7773)*

**Coast Engraving Companies Inc** ................................ E ...... 408 297-2555
18220 Bancroft Ave Monte Sereno (95030) *(P-5023)*

**Coast Flagstone Co** ............................................. D ...... 310 829-4010
1810 Colorado Ave Santa Monica (90404) *(P-7536)*

**Coast Index 965, Newbury Park** *Also Called: Coast Index Co Inc (P-4019)*

**Coast Index Co Inc** ............................................. D ...... 805 499-6844
850 Lawrence Dr Newbury Park (91320) *(P-4019)*

**Coast Iron & Steel Co** .......................................... E ...... 562 946-4421
12300 Lakeland Rd Santa Fe Springs (90670) *(P-529)*

**Coast Label Company, Fountain Valley** *Also Called: Moreland Manufacturing Inc (P-4924)*

**Coast Magnetics, Los Angeles** *Also Called: A M I/Coast Magnetics Inc (P-12825)*

**Coast News Inc** .................................................. D ...... 760 436-9737
531 Encinitas Blvd Ste 204 Encinitas (92024) *(P-4095)*

**Coast Packing Company** ........................................ D ...... 323 277-7700
3275 E Vernon Ave Vernon (90058) *(P-1396)*

**Coast Plastics Inc** .............................................. E ...... 626 812-9174
4711 E Guasti Rd Ontario (91761) *(P-17225)*

**Coast Plating Inc (PA)** ......................................... E ...... 323 770-0240
128 W 154th St Gardena (90248) *(P-8942)*

**Coast Rock Products Inc** ....................................... E ...... 805 925-2505
1625 E Donovan Rd Santa Maria (93454) *(P-16472)*

# ALPHABETIC SECTION

**Coast Seafoods Company** .................................................. D ...... 707 442-2947
25 Waterfront Dr Eureka (95501) *(P-2039)*

**Coast Sheet Metal Inc** .......................................................... E ...... 949 645-2224
990 W 17th St Costa Mesa (92627) *(P-8411)*

**Coast Sign Display, Anaheim** *Also Called: Coast Sign Incorporated (P-15957)*

**Coast Sign Incorporated** ..................................................... C ...... 714 520-9144
1500 W Embassy St Anaheim (92802) *(P-15957)*

**Coast Specialty, Redondo Beach** *Also Called: Coast Specialty Printing Co (P-4556)*

**Coast Specialty Printing Co** ................................................. E ...... 626 359-2451
403 S Gertruda Ave Redondo Beach (90277) *(P-4556)*

**Coast To Coast Circuits Inc (PA)** ......................................... E ...... 714 891-9441
5331 Mcfadden Ave Huntington Beach (92649) *(P-12080)*

**Coast To Coast Met Finshg Corp** ......................................... E ...... 626 282-2122
401 S Raymond Ave Alhambra (91803) *(P-8943)*

**Coast Wire & Plastic Tech LLC** ........................................... A ...... 310 639-9473
1048 E Burgrove St Carson (90746) *(P-13222)*

**Coast/A C M, Torrance** *Also Called: Coast/Dvnced Chip Mgnetics Inc (P-12833)*

**Coast/Dvnced Chip Mgnetics Inc** ......................................... F ...... 310 370-8188
4225 Spencer St Torrance (90503) *(P-12833)*

**Coastal Circuit, Redwood City** *Also Called: Advanced Circuits Inc (P-12045)*

**Coastal Cnting Indus Scale Inc** ............................................. E ...... 805 487-0403
270 Quail Ct Ste 100 Santa Paula (93060) *(P-9667)*

**Coastal Cocktails Inc (PA)** ................................................... E ...... 949 250-8751
1920 E Deere Ave Ste 100 Santa Ana (92705) *(P-17184)*

**Coastal Component Inds Inc** ................................................ E ...... 714 685-6677
133 E Bristol Ln Orange (92865) *(P-12942)*

**Coastal Connections** ............................................................ E ...... 805 644-5051
2085 Sperry Ave Ste B Ventura (93003) *(P-11758)*

**Coastal Creative** .................................................................. F ...... 858 866-6560
13530 Los Coches Rd E El Cajon (92021) *(P-15958)*

**Coastal Enterprises** ............................................................. E ...... 714 771-4969
1925 W Collins Ave Orange (92867) *(P-5146)*

**Coastal Enterprises, Fountain Valley** *Also Called: Joy Products California Inc (P-15891)*

**Coastal Enterprises Company, Orange** *Also Called: Coastal Enterprises (P-5146)*

**Coastal Tag & Label Inc** ....................................................... D ...... 562 946-4318
13233 Barton Cir Whittier (90605) *(P-4861)*

**Coastal Vineyard Services LLC** ........................................... E ...... 805 441-4465
120 Callie Ct Arroyo Grande (93420) *(P-1513)*

**Coastal Wood Products, City Of Industry** *Also Called: McConnell Cabinets Inc (P-3254)*

**Coastline High Prfmce Ctngs Lt** ........................................... F ...... 714 372-3263
7181 Orangewood Ave Garden Grove (92841) *(P-11827)*

**Coastline International** ......................................................... C ...... 888 748-7177
1207 Bangor St San Diego (92106) *(P-15526)*

**Coastline Metal Finishing Corp** ............................................. D ...... 714 895-9099
7061 Patterson Dr Garden Grove (92841) *(P-8944)*

**Coated Fabrics Company (HQ)** ............................................ F ...... 562 298-1300
12658 Cisneros Ln Santa Fe Springs (90670) *(P-17226)*

**Coatinc United States Inc** .................................................... E ...... 619 638-7261
325 W Washington St Ste 2340 San Diego (92103) *(P-6276)*

**Coating Specialties Inc** ........................................................ F ...... 310 639-6900
815 E Rosecrans Ave Los Angeles (90059) *(P-13810)*

**Coatings Resource, Huntington Beach** *Also Called: Laird Coatings Corporation (P-6092)*

**Cobalt Ai, San Francisco** *Also Called: Cobalt Robotics Inc (P-10142)*

**Cobalt Robotics Inc** .............................................................. D ...... 650 781-3623
526 2nd St San Francisco (94107) *(P-10142)*

**Cobblestone Fruit** ................................................................. C ...... 559 524-1005
730 N Oliver Ave Sanger (93657) *(P-881)*

**Cobel Technologies Inc** ........................................................ F ...... 626 332-2100
822 N Grand Ave Covina (91724) *(P-11237)*

**Cobham, San Diego** *Also Called: Remec Defense & Space Inc (P-14292)*

**Cobham Satcom, Concord** *Also Called: Seatel Inc (P-11941)*

**Coc Inc, Los Angeles** *Also Called: Colon Manufacturing Inc (P-2660)*

**Coca-Cola, Ontario** *Also Called: Coca-Cola Company (P-1880)*

**Coca-Cola, American Canyon** *Also Called: Coca-Cola Company American Cyn (P-1881)*

**Coca-Cola, Irvine** *Also Called: Reyes Coca-Cola Bottling LLC (P-1932)*

**Coca-Cola, San Jose** *Also Called: Reyes Coca-Cola Bottling LLC (P-1934)*

**Coca-Cola, Downey** *Also Called: Reyes Coca-Cola Bottling LLC (P-1935)*

**Coca-Cola, San Leandro** *Also Called: Reyes Coca-Cola Bottling LLC (P-1936)*

**Coca-Cola, Fresno** *Also Called: Reyes Coca-Cola Bottling LLC (P-1937)*

**Coca-Cola, Ventura** *Also Called: Reyes Coca-Cola Bottling LLC (P-1938)*

**Coca-Cola, Sacramento** *Also Called: Reyes Coca-Cola Bottling LLC (P-1939)*

**Coca-Cola, Coachella** *Also Called: Reyes Coca-Cola Bottling LLC (P-1940)*

**Coca-Cola, Santa Maria** *Also Called: Reyes Coca-Cola Bottling LLC (P-1941)*

**Coca-Cola, Salinas** *Also Called: Reyes Coca-Cola Bottling LLC (P-1942)*

**Coca-Cola, Fontana** *Also Called: Reyes Coca-Cola Bottling LLC (P-1943)*

**Coca-Cola, Santa Maria** *Also Called: Reyes Coca-Cola Bottling LLC (P-1944)*

**Coca-Cola, Redding** *Also Called: Reyes Coca-Cola Bottling LLC (P-1946)*

**Coca-Cola, San Diego** *Also Called: Reyes Coca-Cola Bottling LLC (P-1947)*

**Coca-Cola, Marysville** *Also Called: Reyes Coca-Cola Bottling LLC (P-1949)*

**Coca-Cola, Orange** *Also Called: Reyes Coca-Cola Bottling LLC (P-1950)*

**Coca-Cola, Los Angeles** *Also Called: Reyes Coca-Cola Bottling LLC (P-1952)*

**Coca-Cola, San Ramon** *Also Called: Reyes Coca-Cola Bottling LLC (P-1953)*

**Coca-Cola, Victorville** *Also Called: Reyes Coca-Cola Bottling LLC (P-1954)*

**Coca-Cola, El Centro** *Also Called: Reyes Coca-Cola Bottling LLC (P-1955)*

**Coca-Cola, Sacramento** *Also Called: Sacramento Coca-Cola Btlg Inc (P-1957)*

**Coca-Cola, Modesto** *Also Called: Sacramento Coca-Cola Btlg Inc (P-1958)*

**Coca-Cola, Santa Maria** *Also Called: Tognazzini Beverage Service (P-1968)*

**Coca-Cola, Sylmar** *Also Called: Reyes Coca-Cola Bottling LLC (P-17208)*

**Coca-Cola Company** ............................................................ D ...... 909 975-5200
1650 S Vintage Ave Ontario (91761) *(P-1880)*

**Coca-Cola Company American Cyn** ..................................... E ...... 707 556-1220
1201 Commerce Blvd American Canyon (94503) *(P-1881)*

**Cod USA Inc** ......................................................................... E ...... 949 381-7367
25954 Commercentre Dr Lake Forest (92630) *(P-3621)*

**Coda Energy, Glendale** *Also Called: Coda Energy Holdings LLC (P-13223)*

**Coda Energy Holdings LLC** .................................................. F ...... 626 775-3900
111 N Artsakh Ave Ste 300 Glendale (91206) *(P-13223)*

**Codan Mexico, San Diego** *Also Called: Eleanor Rigby Leather Co (P-7155)*

**Codan US, Santa Ana** *Also Called: Codan US Corporation (P-6777)*

**Codan US Corporation** .......................................................... D ...... 714 545-2111
3501 W Sunflower Ave Santa Ana (92704) *(P-6777)*

**Code-In-Motion LLC** ............................................................. F ...... 949 361-2633
1307 Calle Avanzado San Clemente (92673) *(P-10084)*

**Codefast Inc** ......................................................................... E ...... 408 687-4700
690 E Middlefield Rd Mountain View (94043) *(P-18191)*

**Codexis, Redwood City** *Also Called: Codexis Inc (P-5084)*

**Codexis Inc (PA)** ................................................................... C ...... 650 421-8100
200 Penobscot Dr Redwood City (94063) *(P-5084)*

**Codorniu Napa Inc** ............................................................... E ...... 707 254-2148
1345 Henry Rd Napa (94559) *(P-1514)*

**Cody Cylinder Service LLC** .................................................. E ...... 951 786-3650
1393 Dodson Way Ste A Riverside (92507) *(P-10783)*

**Coe, Live Oak** *Also Called: Coe Orchard Equipment Inc (P-9345)*

**Coe Orchard Equipment Inc** ................................................. A ...... 530 695-5121
3453 Riviera Rd Live Oak (95953) *(P-9345)*

**Coen Company Inc (DH)** ...................................................... E ...... 650 522-2100
951 Mariners Island Blvd San Mateo (94404) *(P-8064)*

**Cofan Thermal Inc** ................................................................ E ...... 510 490-7533
46177 Warm Springs Blvd Fremont (94539) *(P-16867)*

**Cofan USA, Fremont** *Also Called: Cofan Thermal Inc (P-16867)*

**Coffee Klatch, Rancho Cucamonga** *Also Called: Klatch Coffee Inc (P-17594)*

**Cognella Inc** .......................................................................... D ...... 858 552-1120
320 S Cedros Ave Ste 400 Solana Beach (92075) *(P-4380)*

**Cognex, Hayward** *Also Called: Ametek Inc (P-16507)*

**Coherent, Santa Clara** *Also Called: Coherent Inc (P-14645)*

**Coherent Inc (HQ)** ................................................................ A ...... 408 764-4000
5100 Patrick Henry Dr Santa Clara (95054) *(P-14645)*

**Coherent Aerospace & Def Inc** ............................................. D ...... 714 247-7100
14192 Chambers Rd Tustin (92780) *(P-14769)*

**Coherent Aerospace & Defense Inc (HQ)** ............................ C ...... 951 926-2994
36570 Briggs Rd Murrieta (92563) *(P-14170)*

**Coherent Asia Inc (HQ)** ........................................................ C ...... 408 764-4000
5100 Patrick Henry Dr Santa Clara (95054) *(P-12943)*

**Coherent Auburn Group, The, Santa Clara** *Also Called: Coherent Corp (P-13224)*

**Coherent Corp** ...................................................................... E ...... 408 764-4000
5100 Patrick Henry Dr Santa Clara (95054) *(P-13224)*

**Coherent Tios Inc** ................................................................. E ...... 510 964-5600
4040 Lakeside Dr Richmond (94806) *(P-14646)*

## COHERUS BIOSCIENCES · ALPHABETIC SECTION

**COHERUS BIOSCIENCES, Redwood City** *Also Called: Coherus Biosciences Inc (P-5822)*
Coherus Biosciences Inc (PA) ................................................. C ...... 650 649-3530
  333 Twin Dolphin Dr Ste 600 Redwood City (94065) *(P-5822)*
**COHU, Poway** *Also Called: Cohu Inc (P-14507)*
Cohu Inc (PA) ................................................................. C ...... 858 848-8100
  12367 Crosthwaite Cir Poway (92064) *(P-14507)*
Cohu Interface Solutions LLC (HQ) ....................................... D ...... 858 848-8000
  12367 Crosthwaite Cir Poway (92064) *(P-14508)*
Coi Ceramics Inc .............................................................. E ...... 858 621-5700
  7130 Miramar Rd Ste 100b San Diego (92121) *(P-13811)*
Coi Pharmaceuticals Inc ..................................................... 858 750-4700
  11099 N Torrey Pines Rd Ste 290 La Jolla (92037) *(P-19448)*
Coi Rubber Products Inc .................................................... B ...... 626 965-9966
  19255 San Jose Ave Unit D-1 City Of Industry (91748) *(P-6487)*
**Coic, San Diego** *Also Called: Coi Ceramics Inc (P-13811)*
Coil Winding Specialist Inc ................................................. F ...... 714 279-9010
  353 W Grove Ave Orange (92865) *(P-12834)*
Colabo Inc ....................................................................... E ...... 650 288-6649
  751 Laurel St Ste 840 San Carlos (94070) *(P-18192)*
Colbi Technologies Inc ...................................................... E ...... 714 505-9544
  13891 Newport Ave Ste 150 Tustin (92780) *(P-4381)*
Colbrit Manufacturing Co Inc .............................................. E ...... 818 709-3608
  9666 Owensmouth Ave Ste G Chatsworth (91311) *(P-9613)*
Cold Creek Compost Inc ..................................................... F ...... 707 485-5966
  6000 E Side Potter Valley Rd Ukiah (95482) *(P-6186)*
Cold Steel Inc (PA) ............................................................ F ...... 805 650-8481
  6060 Nicolle St Ventura (93003) *(P-17662)*
Cold Storage Manufacturing Inc ......................................... E ...... 510 476-1700
  740 Bradford Way Union City (94587) *(P-10489)*
Cole Instrument Corp ........................................................ D ...... 714 556-3100
  2650 S Croddy Way Santa Ana (92704) *(P-11261)*
**Cole Lighting, South El Monte** *Also Called: C W Cole & Company Inc (P-11523)*
Colfax International .......................................................... E ...... 408 730-2275
  2805 Bowers Ave Ste 230 Santa Clara (95051) *(P-10143)*
**Colin Cowie Lifestyle, Rancho Palos Verdes** *Also Called: CAW Cowie Inc (P-19080)*
Collabrative DRG Discovery Inc .......................................... D ...... 650 204-3084
  1633 Bayshore Hwy Ste 342 Burlingame (94010) *(P-18193)*
**Collective Health, San Francisco** *Also Called: Collectivehealth Inc (P-17737)*
Collectivehealth Inc (PA) .................................................... C ...... 844 265-3288
  45 Fremont St Ste 1200 San Francisco (94105) *(P-17737)*
Colleen & Herb Enterprises Inc .......................................... C ...... 510 226-6083
  46939 Bayside Pkwy Fremont (94538) *(P-10784)*
Collicutt Energy Services Inc .............................................. C ...... 562 944-4413
  12349 Hawkins St Santa Fe Springs (90670) *(P-8051)*
Collins Aerospace ............................................................. E ...... 951 351-5659
  8200 Arlington Ave Riverside (92503) *(P-13812)*
**Collins Aerospace, Fairfield** *Also Called: Rockwell Collins Inc (P-13936)*
**Collins Aerospace, Chula Vista** *Also Called: Rohr Inc (P-13939)*
**Collins Company, Ontario** *Also Called: Warren Collins and Assoc Inc (P-401)*
Collins Pine Company ....................................................... E ...... 530 258-2111
  500 Main St Chester (96020) *(P-3067)*
Collins Pine Company ....................................................... D ...... 530 258-2131
  540 Main St Chester (96020) *(P-3068)*
**Collins Technologies, Brea** *Also Called: Curtiss-Wright Flow Ctrl Corp (P-9153)*
Collotype Labels USA Inc (DH) ........................................... C ...... 707 603-2500
  21 Executive Way Napa (94558) *(P-4862)*
Colmol Inc ....................................................................... E ...... 858 693-7575
  8517 Production Ave San Diego (92121) *(P-4863)*
Colombia Energy Resources Inc ......................................... C
  1 Embarcadero Ctr Ste 500 San Francisco (94111) *(P-116)*
Colon Manufacturing Inc (PA) ............................................ F ...... 213 749-6149
  1100 S San Pedro St Ste 0-08 Los Angeles (90015) *(P-2660)*
**Colonel Lee's Enterprises, Vernon** *Also Called: T & T Foods Inc (P-871)*
Colonial Enterprises Inc .................................................... E ...... 909 822-8700
  690 Knox St Ste 200 Torrance (90502) *(P-5955)*
**Colonial Home Textiles, Corona** *Also Called: Amrapur Overseas Incorporated (P-2544)*
Colonnas Shipyard West LLC ............................................. E ...... 757 545-2414
  2890 Faivre St Ste 150 Chula Vista (91911) *(P-14001)*
Color Inc ......................................................................... E ...... 818 240-1350
  1600 Flower St Glendale (91201) *(P-4557)*

Color Ad Inc .................................................................... E ...... 310 632-5500
  18601 S Santa Fe Ave Compton (90221) *(P-17777)*
**Color Digit, Costa Mesa** *Also Called: Chup Corporation (P-4550)*
Color Fx Inc .................................................................... E ...... 877 763-7671
  8000 Haskell Ave Van Nuys (91406) *(P-4558)*
**Color ME Cotton, Los Angeles** *Also Called: Jd/Cmc Inc (P-2772)*
Color Science Inc ............................................................. E ...... 714 434-1033
  1230 E Glenwood Pl Santa Ana (92707) *(P-6119)*
**Color Tech Commercial Printing, Lake Forest** *Also Called: Universal Printing Svcs Inc (P-4798)*
Color West Inc ................................................................. C ...... 818 840-8881
  2228 N Hollywood Way Burbank (91505) *(P-4559)*
**Color West Printing & Packg, Burbank** *Also Called: Color West Inc (P-4559)*
**Colorama Paints, Los Angeles** *Also Called: Ennis Traffic Safety Solutions (P-6083)*
Colorcom Inc ................................................................... F ...... 323 246-4640
  2437 S Eastern Ave Commerce (90040) *(P-4560)*
Colorescience Inc ............................................................ C ...... 866 426-5673
  2141 Palomar Airport Rd Ste 200 Carlsbad (92011) *(P-17032)*
Colorfx Inc ...................................................................... E ...... 818 767-7671
  11050 Randall St Sun Valley (91352) *(P-4561)*
**Colorgraphics, Los Angeles** *Also Called: Madisn/Grham Clor Graphics Inc (P-4685)*
Colormax Industries Inc (PA) ............................................. E ...... 213 748-6600
  1627 Paloma St Los Angeles (90021) *(P-2410)*
**Colornet Press, Van Nuys** *Also Called: Niknejad Inc (P-4706)*
Colortokens Inc (PA) ........................................................ E ...... 408 341-6030
  3590 N 1st St Ste 320 San Jose (95134) *(P-18194)*
Colour Concepts Inc ......................................................... C
  1225 Los Angeles St Glendale (91204) *(P-4562)*
Colter & Peterson Microsystems ........................................ E ...... 707 776-4500
  1260 Holm Rd Ste C Petaluma (94954) *(P-14395)*
**Colton Truck Terminal Garage, Colton** *Also Called: Erf Enterprises Inc (P-13411)*
Columbia Aluminum Products LLC .................................... D ...... 323 728-7361
  1150 W Rincon St Corona (92878) *(P-8120)*
Columbia Cosmetics Mfrs Inc (PA) ..................................... D ...... 510 562-5900
  1661 Timothy Dr San Leandro (94577) *(P-5956)*
**Columbia Hydronics Co., Hayward** *Also Called: California Hydronics Corp (P-16775)*
**Columbia Products Co, Irvine** *Also Called: Columbia Sanitary Products Inc (P-8052)*
Columbia Sanitary Products Inc ........................................ E ...... 949 474-0777
  1622 Browning Irvine (92606) *(P-8052)*
Columbia Showcase & Cab Co Inc ...................................... C ...... 818 765-9710
  11034 Sherman Way Ste A Sun Valley (91352) *(P-3652)*
Columbia Steel Inc ........................................................... D ...... 909 874-8840
  2175 N Linden Ave Rialto (92377) *(P-8121)*
Columbus Foods LLC ........................................................ B ...... 510 921-3400
  30977 San Antonio St Hayward (94544) *(P-593)*
Columbus Manufacturing Inc (HQ) ..................................... D ...... 510 921-3423
  30977 San Antonio St Hayward (94544) *(P-636)*
**Colvin-Friedman, Petaluma** *Also Called: Colvin-Friedman LLC (P-6778)*
Colvin-Friedman LLC ........................................................ E ...... 707 769-4488
  1311 Commerce St Petaluma (94954) *(P-6778)*
Com Dev Usa LLC ............................................................. D ...... 424 456-8000
  2333 Utah Ave El Segundo (90245) *(P-16917)*
Comac America Corporation ............................................. E ...... 760 616-9614
  4350 Von Karman Ave Ste 400 Newport Beach (92660) *(P-13648)*
Comav LLC (PA) ............................................................... E ...... 760 523-5100
  18499 Phantom St Ste 17 Victorville (92394) *(P-16918)*
Comba Telecom Inc ......................................................... F ...... 408 526-0180
  568 Gibraltar Dr Milpitas (95035) *(P-16696)*
Combimatrix Corporation (HQ) .......................................... E ...... 949 753-0624
  310 Goddard Ste 150 Irvine (92618) *(P-14647)*
Combustion Associates Inc .............................................. E ...... 951 272-6999
  555 Monica Cir Corona (92878) *(P-16342)*
Comco Inc ...................................................................... E ...... 818 333-8500
  2151 N Lincoln St Burbank (91504) *(P-10553)*
**Comet Medical, Ventura** *Also Called: Peter Brasseler Holdings LLC (P-16587)*
Comet Technologies USA Inc ............................................ C ...... 408 325-8770
  541 E Trimble Rd San Jose (95131) *(P-14857)*
Comexposium US LLC ...................................................... F ...... 310 598-1376
  5455 Wilshire Blvd Ste 1150 Los Angeles (90036) *(P-10349)*
Comfort Industries Inc ..................................................... E ...... 562 692-8288
  301 W Las Tunas Dr San Gabriel (91776) *(P-2445)*

# ALPHABETIC SECTION — Compucraft Industries Inc

**Command Guard Services, Torrance** *Also Called: Resource Collection Inc (P-17849)*

**Commander Boats** ................................................................. F ...... 951 273-0100
4020 Tyler St Riverside (92503) *(P-17479)*

**Commander Boats-Mira Loma Mar, Riverside** *Also Called: Commander Boats (P-17479)*

**Commander Packaging West Inc** ........................................... E ...... 714 921-9350
602 S Rockefeller Ave Ste D Ontario (91761) *(P-3832)*

**Commerce, Commerce** *Also Called: Alarin Aircraft Hinge Inc (P-7974)*

**Commerce Ave Meat, Fresno** *Also Called: Certified Meat Products Inc (P-590)*

**Commerce Coating Services Inc** ........................................... D ...... 310 345-1979
20725 S Western Ave Ste 144 Torrance (90501) *(P-6076)*

**Commerce On Demand LLC** .................................................. D ...... 562 360-4819
7121 Telegraph Rd Montebello (90640) *(P-16120)*

**Commerce Printing Services** .................................................. D ...... 916 442-8100
322 N 12th St Sacramento (95811) *(P-4563)*

**Commercial Casework Inc (PA)** .............................................. D ...... 510 657-7933
41780 Christy St Fremont (94538) *(P-3120)*

**Commercial Cstm Sting Uphl Inc** ........................................... D ...... 714 850-0520
12601 Western Ave Garden Grove (92841) *(P-3735)*

**Commercial Display Systems LLC** ......................................... E ...... 818 361-8160
17341 Sierra Hwy Canyon Country (91351) *(P-10490)*

**Commercial Intr Resources Inc** .............................................. D ...... 562 926-5885
6077 Rickenbacker Rd Commerce (90040) *(P-3469)*

**Commercial Lbr & Pallet Co Inc (PA)** ..................................... C ...... 626 968-0631
135 Long Ln City Of Industry (91746) *(P-3335)*

**Commercial Manufacturing** ..................................................... E ...... 559 237-1855
2432 S East Ave Fresno (93706) *(P-9785)*

**Commercial Metal Forming, Orange** *Also Called: Commercial Metal Forming Inc (P-8310)*

**Commercial Metal Forming Inc** .............................................. E ...... 714 532-6321
341 W Collins Ave Orange (92867) *(P-8310)*

**Commercial Shtmtl Works Inc** ................................................ E ...... 213 748-7321
1800 S San Pedro St Los Angeles (90015) *(P-8122)*

**Commercial Truck Eqp Co LLC** .............................................. D ...... 562 803-4466
12351 Bellflower Blvd Downey (90242) *(P-13403)*

**Commercial Truck Equipment Co, Downey** *Also Called: Commercial Truck Eqp Co LLC (P-13403)*

**Commodity Resource Envmtl Inc** ........................................... E ...... 661 824-2416
11847 United St Mojave (93501) *(P-7711)*

**Commodity Rsource Enviromental, Mojave** *Also Called: Commodity Resource Envmtl Inc (P-7711)*

**Commodity Sales Co** .............................................................. C ...... 323 980-5463
517 S Clarence St Los Angeles (90033) *(P-679)*

**Common Collabs LLC (PA)** ................................................... F ...... 714 519-3245
1820 E Walnut Ave Fullerton (92831) *(P-1994)*

**Commonpath LLC** .................................................................. F ...... 858 922-8116
5963 Olivas Park Dr Ste F Ventura (93003) *(P-7216)*

**Commscope** ............................................................................ E ...... 408 952-2454
3839 Spinnaker Ct Fremont (94538) *(P-11828)*

**Commscope** ............................................................................ F ...... 650 265-4200
350 W Java Dr Sunnyvale (94089) *(P-11829)*

**Communction Systms-Wst/Lnkabit, San Diego** *Also Called: L3 Technologies Inc (P-11875)*

**Communication Services Ctr Inc** ............................................ E ...... 415 252-1600
1099 Mariposa St San Francisco (94107) *(P-4564)*

**Communications & Pwr Inds LLC** .......................................... C ...... 650 846-3494
811 Hansen Way Palo Alto (94304) *(P-11830)*

**Communications & Pwr Inds LLC** .......................................... A ...... 650 846-3729
811 Hansen Way Palo Alto (94304) *(P-11831)*

**Communications & Pwr Inds LLC** .......................................... F ...... 650 846-2900
6385 San Ignacio Ave San Jose (95119) *(P-11832)*

**Communications & Pwr Inds LLC** .......................................... D ...... 650 846-2900
811 Hansen Way Palo Alto (94304) *(P-11833)*

**Communications & Pwr Inds LLC** .......................................... D ...... 530 662-7553
1318 Commerce Ave Woodland (95776) *(P-12028)*

**Communications & Pwr Inds LLC (HQ)** ................................. A ...... 650 846-2900
811 Hansen Way Palo Alto (94304) *(P-12029)*

**Communications Supply Corp** ................................................ D ...... 714 670-7711
6251 Knott Ave Buena Park (90620) *(P-16335)*

**Communigate Systems, Belvedere Tiburon** *Also Called: Stalker Software Inc (P-18833)*

**Community Media Corporation** .............................................. E ...... 657 337-0200
19100 Crest Ave Apt 26 Castro Valley (94546) *(P-4096)*

**Community Media Corporation (PA)** ...................................... E ...... 714 220-0292
15005 S Vermont Ave Gardena (90247) *(P-4097)*

**Community Printers Inc** .......................................................... E ...... 831 426-4682
1827 Soquel Ave Santa Cruz (95062) *(P-4565)*

**Compaction American, Lake Elsinore** *Also Called: American Compaction Eqp Inc (P-9407)*

**Compactor Management Co LLC** .......................................... E ...... 510 623-2323
32420 Central Ave Union City (94587) *(P-8412)*

**Compactor Management Company, Union City** *Also Called: Compactor Management Co LLC (P-8412)*

**Compandsave, Union City** *Also Called: Cmy Image Corporation (P-4555)*

**Companion Medical Inc** .......................................................... D ...... 858 522-0252
11011 Via Frontera Ste D San Diego (92127) *(P-15046)*

**Comparenetworks Inc (PA)** .................................................... D ...... 518 238-6617
164 Townsend St Unit 2 San Francisco (94107) *(P-4382)*

**Compass Components Inc (PA)** ............................................. C ...... 510 656-4700
48133 Warm Springs Blvd Fremont (94539) *(P-12944)*

**Compass Equipment Inc (PA)** ................................................ E ...... 530 533-7284
4688 Pacific Heights Rd Oroville (95965) *(P-9482)*

**Compass Flooring, Santa Fe Springs** *Also Called: Altro Usa Inc (P-16074)*

**Compass Innovations Inc** ....................................................... C ...... 408 418-3985
2352 Walsh Ave Santa Clara (95051) *(P-6554)*

**Compass Manufacturing Service, Fremont** *Also Called: Compass Components Inc (P-12944)*

**Compass Water Solutions Inc (HQ)** ....................................... E ...... 949 222-5777
15542 Mosher Ave Tustin (92780) *(P-10554)*

**Compass365, Glendale** *Also Called: General Networks Corporation (P-19036)*

**Compatico Inc** ......................................................................... E ...... 616 940-1772
1901 S Archibald Ave Ontario (91761) *(P-3653)*

**Competition Clutch Inc** ........................................................... E ...... 800 809-6598
1570 Lakeview Loop Anaheim (92807) *(P-16378)*

**Competrol A Western Pump Co, San Diego** *Also Called: Western Pump Inc (P-19289)*

**Complete Aquatic Systems, Gardena** *Also Called: Wally & Pat Enterprises (P-16267)*

**Complete Clothing Company (PA)** ......................................... E ...... 213 892-1188
4950 E 49th St Vernon (90058) *(P-2704)*

**Complete Truck Body Repair Inc** ............................................ E ...... 323 445-2675
1217 N Alameda St Compton (90222) *(P-13404)*

**Complete Welders Supply** ..................................................... F ...... 209 462-3086
1549 N Broadway Ave Stockton (95205) *(P-19187)*

**Compliance Poster, Monrovia** *Also Called: Global Compliance Inc (P-4403)*

**Complianceonline, San Jose** *Also Called: Metricstream Inc (P-18541)*

**Complyright Dist Svcs Inc** ...................................................... E ...... 805 981-0992
3451 Jupiter Ct Oxnard (93030) *(P-4989)*

**Component Equipment Coinc** ................................................ E ...... 805 988-8004
3050 Camino Del Sol Oxnard (93030) *(P-12871)*

**Component Surfaces Inc** ........................................................ F ...... 858 513-3656
11880 Community Rd Ste 380 Poway (92064) *(P-8945)*

**Composite Manufacturing Inc** ................................................ E ...... 949 361-7580
970 Calle Amanecer Ste D San Clemente (92673) *(P-15047)*

**Composite Optics Incorporated** ............................................. A ...... 937 490-4145
7130 Miramar Rd Ste 100b San Diego (92121) *(P-14110)*

**Composite Software LLC (DH)** ............................................... D ...... 800 553-6387
755 Sycamore Dr Milpitas (95035) *(P-18195)*

**Composite Support and Sltns In** ............................................. F ...... 310 514-3162
767 W Channel St San Pedro (90731) *(P-3902)*

**Composite Technology Corp** .................................................. C ...... 949 428-8500
2026 Mcgaw Ave Irvine (92614) *(P-11365)*

**Composite Technology Intl, Sacramento** *Also Called: Composite Technology Intl Inc (P-3121)*

**Composite Technology Intl Inc** ............................................... D ...... 916 551-1850
622 20th St Sacramento (95811) *(P-3121)*

**Composites Horizons LLC (DH)** ............................................ C ...... 626 331-0861
1629 W Industrial Park St Covina (91722) *(P-5147)*

**Composites Horizons LLC** ..................................................... E ...... 626 331-0861
1471 W Industrial Park St Covina (91722) *(P-13813)*

**Compound Focus Inc** ............................................................. E ...... 650 228-1400
385 Oyster Point Blvd Ste 1 South San Francisco (94080) *(P-220)*

**Comppro, San Diego** *Also Called: Rf Industries Ltd (P-12895)*

**Compu Aire Inc** ....................................................................... C ...... 562 945-8971
8167 Byron Rd Whittier (90606) *(P-10491)*

**Compu-Tech Lumber Products Inc** ........................................ E ...... 707 437-6683
1980 Huntington Ct Fairfield (94533) *(P-3304)*

**Compucase Corporation** ........................................................ A ...... 626 336-6588
16720 Chestnut St Ste C City Of Industry (91748) *(P-10233)*

**Compucraft Industries Inc** ...................................................... E ...... 619 448-0787
8787 Olive Ln Santee (92071) *(P-13814)*

**Compugroup Medical Inc** ............................................................ E ...... 949 789-0500
25b Technology Dr Ste 200 Irvine (92618) *(P-18196)*

**Compulink Business Systems Inc (PA)** ................................. C ...... 805 446-2050
1100 Business Center Cir Newbury Park (91320) *(P-18197)*

**Compulink Healthcare Solutions, Newbury Park** *Also Called: Compulink Business Systems Inc (P-18197)*

**Compumeric Engineering Inc** ............................................... E ...... 909 605-7666
1390 S Milliken Ave Ontario (91761) *(P-8413)*

**Computational Systems Inc** ................................................. D ...... 661 832-5306
4301 Resnik Ct Bakersfield (93313) *(P-14396)*

**Computer Assisted Mfg Tech LLC** ........................................ E ...... 949 263-8911
8710 Research Dr 8750 Irvine (92618) *(P-10785)*

**Computer Intgrted McHining Inc** .......................................... E ...... 619 596-9246
10940 Wheatlands Ave Santee (92071) *(P-10786)*

**Computer Metal Products Corp** ............................................ D ...... 805 520-6966
370 E Easy St Simi Valley (93065) *(P-8414)*

**Computer Performance Inc** .................................................. E ...... 408 330-5599
2695 Walsh Ave Santa Clara (95051) *(P-17547)*

**Computer Plastics** ................................................................ E ...... 510 785-3600
1914 National Ave Hayward (94545) *(P-9614)*

**Computer Power Sftwr Group Inc (PA)** ................................ F ...... 916 985-4445
716 Figueroa St Folsom (95630) *(P-17899)*

**Computer Service Company** ................................................ E ...... 951 738-1444
210 N Delilah St Corona (92879) *(P-11988)*

**Computer-Nozzles, Irwindale** *Also Called: Cni Mfg Inc (P-10781)*

**Computerized Security Systems, Costa Mesa** *Also Called: Winfield Locks Inc (P-8038)*

**Computrition Inc (HQ)** ........................................................... D ...... 818 961-3999
8521 Fallbrook Ave Ste 100 Canoga Park (91304) *(P-17900)*

**Compuvac Industries Inc** ...................................................... F ...... 949 574-5085
18381 Mount Langley St Fountain Valley (92708) *(P-9959)*

**Comstock Publishing Inc** ...................................................... F ...... 916 364-1000
2335 American River Dr Ste 301 Sacramento (95825) *(P-4241)*

**Comstock's Magazine, Sacramento** *Also Called: Comstock Publishing Inc (P-4241)*

**Comtech Stllite Ntwrk Tech Inc** ............................................. C ...... 408 213-3000
3550 Bassett St Santa Clara (95054) *(P-11834)*

**Comtech Xicom Technology, Santa Clara** *Also Called: Comtech Stllite Ntwrk Tech Inc (P-11834)*

**Comune, Los Angeles** *Also Called: Dhouse Brands Inc (P-17037)*

**Con-Cise Contact Lens Co, Alameda** *Also Called: Lens C-C Inc (P-15606)*

**Con-Fab California Corporation (PA)** .................................... D ...... 209 249-4700
1910 Lathrop Rd Lathrop (95330) *(P-7321)*

**Con-Tech Plastics, Brea** *Also Called: Ramtec Associates Inc (P-6993)*

**Conamco SA De CV** .............................................................. D ...... 760 586-4356
3008 Palm Hill Dr Vista (92084) *(P-15443)*

**Concannon Vineyard, Livermore** *Also Called: Tesla Vineyards Lp (P-1778)*

**Concealed Carrier LLC** ......................................................... E ...... 916 530-6205
11315 Sunrise Gold Cir Ste F Rancho Cordova (95742) *(P-9138)*

**Concentric Analgesics Inc** .................................................... E ...... 415 771-5129
1824 Jackson St Apt A San Francisco (94109) *(P-5406)*

**Concept Development Llc** .................................................... E ...... 949 623-8000
1881 Langley Ave Irvine (92614) *(P-12081)*

**Concept Packaging Group, Ontario** *Also Called: Southland Container Corp (P-3889)*

**Concept Part Solutions Inc** ................................................... E ...... 408 748-1244
2047 Zanker Rd San Jose (95131) *(P-9668)*

**Concept Systems Mfg Inc** .................................................... E ...... 408 855-8595
2047 Zanker Rd San Jose (95131) *(P-12386)*

**Concept Technology Inc (PA)** ............................................... D ...... 949 854-7047
895 Dove St 3rd Fl Newport Beach (92660) *(P-19384)*

**Concepts & Wood, Huntington Park** *Also Called: Plycraft Industries Inc (P-3287)*

**Concise Fabricators, San Diego** *Also Called: Concise Fabricators Inc (P-8415)*

**Concise Fabricators Inc** ....................................................... E ...... 520 746-3226
7550 Panasonic Way San Diego (92154) *(P-8415)*

**CONCISYS** ............................................................................ E ...... 858 292-5888
5452 Oberlin Dr San Diego (92121) *(P-14509)*

**Concord Document Services Inc (PA)** .................................. E ...... 213 745-3175
1407 W 11th St Los Angeles (90015) *(P-17806)*

**Concord Graphic Arts Inc** ..................................................... E ...... 925 682-9670
3270 Monument Way Concord (94518) *(P-17823)*

**Concord Iron Works Inc** ....................................................... E ...... 925 432-0136
1 Leslie Dr Pittsburg (94565) *(P-8123)*

**Concord Sheet Metal, Pittsburg** *Also Called: Levmar Inc (P-8486)*

**Concrete Inc (DH)** ................................................................. D ...... 209 933-6999
400 S Lincoln St Stockton (95203) *(P-7434)*

**Concrete Holding Co Cal Inc** ................................................ A ...... 818 788-4228
15821 Ventura Blvd Ste 475 Encino (91436) *(P-7435)*

**Concrete Ready Mix Inc** ....................................................... E ...... 408 224-2452
33 Hillsdale Ave San Jose (95136) *(P-7436)*

**Concrete Tie, Compton** *Also Called: Concrete Tie Industries Inc (P-16473)*

**Concrete Tie Industries Inc (PA)** .......................................... D ...... 310 628-2328
130 E Oris St Compton (90222) *(P-16473)*

**Concrete West Construction Inc** .......................................... F ...... 949 448-9940
1235 N Tustin Ave Anaheim (92807) *(P-19524)*

**Concurrent Holdings LLC** ..................................................... A ...... 310 473-3065
11150 Santa Monica Blvd Ste 825 Los Angeles (90025) *(P-11366)*

**Condeco Software Inc (DH)** .................................................. F ...... 917 677-7600
2105 S Bascom Ave Ste 150 Campbell (95008) *(P-18198)*

**Condition Monitoring Services, Nipomo** *Also Called: Condition Monitoring Svcs LLC (P-14648)*

**Condition Monitoring Svcs LLC** ............................................ E ...... 888 359-3277
855 San Ysidro Ln Nipomo (93444) *(P-14648)*

**Condor, Baldwin Park** *Also Called: Condor Outdoor Products Inc (P-15800)*

**Condor Outdoor Products Inc (PA)** ....................................... E ...... 626 358-3270
5268 Rivergrade Rd Baldwin Park (91706) *(P-15800)*

**Condor Pacific Industries Inc (PA)** ........................................ E ...... 818 889-2150
905 Rancho Conejo Blvd Newbury Park (91320) *(P-14171)*

**Condor Reliability Svcs Inc** .................................................. E ...... 408 486-9600
3400 De La Cruz Blvd Santa Clara (95054) *(P-12387)*

**Conductive, Rcho Sta Marg** *Also Called: Standard Cable Usa Inc (P-9233)*

**Conejo Valley Air, Newbury Park** *Also Called: Conejo Valley Heating & AC Inc (P-413)*

**Conejo Valley Heating & AC Inc** ........................................... F ...... 833 538-9810
2639 Lavery Ct Ste 7 Newbury Park (91320) *(P-413)*

**Conesco Industries, Riverside** *Also Called: Doka USA Ltd (P-8434)*

**Conesys Inc** .......................................................................... D ...... 310 212-0065
548 Amapola Ave Torrance (90501) *(P-12872)*

**Conetech Custom Services LLC** ........................................... E ...... 707 823-2404
2191 Laguna Rd Santa Rosa (95401) *(P-1515)*

**Conexant Holdings Inc** ......................................................... A ...... 415 983-2706
4000 Macarthur Blvd Newport Beach (92660) *(P-12388)*

**Conexant Systems LLC (HQ)** ............................................... E ...... 949 483-4600
1901 Main St Ste 300 Irvine (92614) *(P-12389)*

**Confab, Lathrop** *Also Called: Con-Fab California Corporation (P-7321)*

**Confab, Van Nuys** *Also Called: Consolidated Fabricators Corp (P-8311)*

**Confluent Inc (PA)** ................................................................. A ...... 800 439-3207
899 W Evelyn Ave Mountain View (94041) *(P-18199)*

**Confluent Medical Tech Inc** .................................................. E ...... 510 683-2000
47533 Westinghouse Dr Fremont (94539) *(P-5407)*

**Confluent Medical Tech Inc** .................................................. E ...... 510 683-2000
47600 Westinghouse Dr Fremont (94539) *(P-15048)*

**Confluent Medical Tech Inc** .................................................. C ...... 949 448-7056
27752 El Lazo Laguna Niguel (92677) *(P-15049)*

**Confluent Medical Tech Inc** .................................................. D ...... 949 448-7056
27721 La Paz Rd Laguna Niguel (92677) *(P-15050)*

**Congatec Inc** ........................................................................ E ...... 858 457-2600
6262 Ferris Sq San Diego (92121) *(P-10350)*

**Conglas, Bakersfield** *Also Called: Consolidated Fibrgls Pdts Co (P-7575)*

**Conklin & Conklin Incorporated** ........................................... E ...... 510 489-5500
34101 7th St Union City (94587) *(P-8750)*

**Conleys Greenhouse Mfg & Sales, Montclair** *Also Called: John L Conley Inc (P-8671)*

**Connectec Company Inc (PA)** ............................................... D ...... 949 252-1077
1701 Reynolds Ave Irvine (92614) *(P-11446)*

**Connected Trnsp Prtners Sthern** .......................................... E ...... 510 542-5446
1035 22nd Ave Unit 19 Oakland (94606) *(P-4566)*

**Connell Processing Inc (PA)** ................................................. E ...... 818 845-7661
3094 N Avon St Burbank (91504) *(P-8946)*

**Connelly Machine Wks** ......................................................... E ...... 714 558-6855
420 N Terminal St Santa Ana (92701) *(P-10787)*

**Conners Oro-Cal Mfg Co** ...................................................... F ...... 530 533-5065
1720 Bird St Oroville (95965) *(P-15688)*

**Conor Medsystems LLC** ....................................................... E
1003 Hamilton Ct Menlo Park (94025) *(P-15527)*

# ALPHABETIC SECTION — Control Air Conditioning Corporation

**Conquer Nation Inc** .................................................................. C ...... 310 651-5555
2651 E 12th St Los Angeles (90023) *(P-2894)*

**Conquer Nation Staffing, Los Angeles** *Also Called: Conquer Nation Inc (P-2894)*

**Conquest Industries Inc** .................................................................. E ...... 562 906-1111
12740 Lakeland Rd Santa Fe Springs (90670) *(P-16614)*

**Conquip Inc** .................................................................................... D ...... 916 379-8200
11255 Pyrites Way Ste 100 Gold River (95670) *(P-10788)*

**Consensus Cloud Solutions Inc (PA)** .......................................... D ...... 323 860-9200
700 S Flower St Fl 15 Los Angeles (90017) *(P-18200)*

**Consoldted Hnge Mnfctured Pdts** ................................................ F ...... 408 379-6550
1150b Dell Ave Campbell (95008) *(P-10789)*

**Consoldted Metal Fbrctng Coinc** ................................................. E ...... 559 268-7887
2780 S Cherry Ave Fresno (93706) *(P-16615)*

**Consoldted Precision Pdts Corp** ................................................. D ...... 805 488-6451
705 Industrial Way Port Hueneme (93041) *(P-7838)*

**Consoldted Precision Pdts Corp** ................................................. D ...... 909 595-2252
4200 West Valley Blvd Pomona (91769) *(P-7839)*

**Consolidated Aerospace Mfg LLC** ............................................... D ...... 714 989-2802
630 E Lambert Rd Brea (92821) *(P-7989)*

**Consolidated Aerospace Mfg LLC (HQ)** ...................................... E ...... 714 989-2797
1425 S Acacia Ave Fullerton (92831) *(P-14172)*

**Consolidated Aircraft Coatings, Riverside** *Also Called: Poly-Fiber Inc (P-6101)*

**Consolidated Color Corporation** .................................................. E ...... 562 420-7714
12316 Carson St Hawaiian Gardens (90716) *(P-6077)*

**Consolidated Design West, Baldwin Park** *Also Called: Western Converting Spc Inc (P-4982)*

**Consolidated Design West Inc** ..................................................... E ...... 714 999-1476
1345 S Lewis St Anaheim (92805) *(P-17824)*

**Consolidated Devices Inc (HQ)** ................................................... E ...... 626 965-0668
19220 San Jose Ave City Of Industry (91748) *(P-17352)*

**Consolidated Eagle Press Inc** ...................................................... E ...... 916 383-7850
2629 5th St Sacramento (95818) *(P-4864)*

**Consolidated Fabricators Corp (PA)** ........................................... C ...... 800 635-8335
14620 Arminta St Van Nuys (91402) *(P-8311)*

**Consolidated Fibrgls Pdts Co** ...................................................... D ...... 661 323-6026
3801 Standard St Bakersfield (93308) *(P-7575)*

**Consolidated Foundries, Pomona** *Also Called: CFI Holdings Corp (P-7685)*

**Consolidated Foundries Inc** ......................................................... C ...... 323 773-2363
8333 Wilcox Ave Cudahy (90201) *(P-7840)*

**Consolidated Frt Systems LLC** .................................................... E ...... 310 424-9924
24407 Shoshone Rd Apple Valley (92307) *(P-9509)*

**Consolidated Graphics Inc** ........................................................... C ...... 323 460-4115
3550 Tyburn St Los Angeles (90065) *(P-4865)*

**Consolidated Plastics Corp (PA)** ................................................. E ...... 909 393-8222
14954 La Palma Dr Chino (91710) *(P-17227)*

**Consolidated Printers Inc** ............................................................. E ...... 510 843-8524
2459 Radley Ct Hayward (94545) *(P-4356)*

**Constlltion Brnds US Oprations, Geyserville** *Also Called: Clos Du Bois Wines Inc (P-1509)*

**Constlltion Brnds US Oprtons I** ................................................... E ...... 707 467-4840
2399 N State St Ukiah (95482) *(P-1516)*

**Constlltion Brnds US Oprtons I** ................................................... E ...... 707 433-8268
349 Healdsburg Ave Healdsburg (95448) *(P-1517)*

**Constrction Instlltion Mint Gr, Anaheim** *Also Called: Kesa Incorporated (P-19057)*

**Construction, Loomis** *Also Called: Sierra Trim Inc (P-501)*

**Construction Electrical Pdts, Livermore** *Also Called: R K Larrabee Company Inc (P-11282)*

**Construction Innovations LLC** ..................................................... C ...... 855 725-9555
10630 Mather Blvd Ste 200 Mather (95655) *(P-13225)*

**Construction Specialty Svc Inc** ................................................... D ...... 661 864-7573
4550 Buck Owens Blvd Bakersfield (93308) *(P-387)*

**Contadina Foods, Woodland** *Also Called: Pacific Coast Producers (P-916)*

**Container Graphics Corp** .............................................................. D ...... 209 577-0181
1137 Graphics Dr Modesto (95351) *(P-9764)*

**Container Options** ........................................................................ F ...... 909 478-0045
1493 E San Bernardino Ave San Bernardino (92408) *(P-6779)*

**Container Supply Company Incorporated** ................................... C ...... 714 892-8321
12571 Western Ave Garden Grove (92841) *(P-7920)*

**Containment Consultants Inc** ...................................................... F ...... 408 848-6998
110 Old Gilroy St Gilroy (95020) *(P-8312)*

**Contech Solutions Incorporated** .................................................. E ...... 510 357-7900
631 Montague St San Leandro (94577) *(P-12390)*

**Contemporary Bath.com, City Of Industry** *Also Called: Tonusa LLC (P-3274)*

**Contessa Premium Foods, Vernon** *Also Called: F I O Imports Inc (P-2195)*

**Context Engineering Co** ............................................................... E ...... 408 748-9112
6805 Silacci Way Gilroy (95020) *(P-8831)*

**Continental Acrylics, Compton** *Also Called: Plaskolite West LLC (P-5187)*

**Continental Bdr Specialty Corp (PA)** ........................................... C ...... 310 324-8227
407 W Compton Blvd Gardena (90248) *(P-5000)*

**Continental Coatings Inc** ............................................................. F ...... 909 355-1200
10938 Beech Ave Fontana (92337) *(P-6078)*

**Continental Colorcraft, Monterey Park** *Also Called: Graphic Color Systems Inc (P-4622)*

**Continental Controls Corp** ........................................................... E ...... 858 453-9880
7710 Kenamar Ct San Diego (92121) *(P-14397)*

**Continental Data Graphics, Rancho Cucamonga** *Also Called: Continental Graphics Corp (P-4569)*

**Continental Data Graphics, Long Beach** *Also Called: Continental Graphics Corp (P-4570)*

**Continental Data Graphics, El Segundo** *Also Called: Continental Graphics Corp (P-4571)*

**Continental Datalabel Inc** ............................................................ F ...... 909 307-3600
211 Business Center Ct Redlands (92373) *(P-4035)*

**Continental Engineering Svcs, San Diego** *Also Called: Continental Graphics Corp (P-4567)*

**Continental Forge Company LLC** ................................................. D ...... 310 603-1014
412 E El Segundo Blvd Compton (90222) *(P-8796)*

**Continental Graphics Corp** .......................................................... D ...... 858 552-6520
6910 Carroll Rd San Diego (92121) *(P-4567)*

**Continental Graphics Corp** .......................................................... D ...... 714 827-1752
4060 N Lakewood Blvd Bldg 801 Long Beach (90808) *(P-4568)*

**Continental Graphics Corp** .......................................................... D ...... 909 758-9800
9302 Pittsburgh Ave Ste 100 Rancho Cucamonga (91730) *(P-4569)*

**Continental Graphics Corp** .......................................................... D ...... 714 503-4200
4000 N Lakewood Blvd Long Beach (90808) *(P-4570)*

**Continental Graphics Corp** .......................................................... D ...... 310 662-2307
222 N Pacific Coast Hwy Ste 300 El Segundo (90245) *(P-4571)*

**Continental Heat Treating Inc** ..................................................... D ...... 562 944-8808
10643 Norwalk Blvd Santa Fe Springs (90670) *(P-7883)*

**Continental Industries, Anaheim** *Also Called: International West Inc (P-8476)*

**Continental Maritime Inds Inc** ..................................................... B ...... 619 234-8851
1995 Bay Front St San Diego (92113) *(P-14002)*

**Continental Marketing, City Of Industry** *Also Called: Continental Marketing Svc Inc (P-2955)*

**Continental Marketing Svc Inc** .................................................... F ...... 626 626-8888
15381 Proctor Ave City Of Industry (91745) *(P-2955)*

**Continental Vitamin Co Inc** ......................................................... D ...... 323 581-0176
4510 S Boyle Ave Vernon (90058) *(P-5408)*

**Continental Western Corp (PA)** ................................................... E ...... 510 352-3133
2950 Merced St Ste 200 San Leandro (94577) *(P-16868)*

**Continential Data Graphics, Long Beach** *Also Called: Continental Graphics Corp (P-4568)*

**Continuous Computing Corp** ....................................................... C ...... 858 882-8800
10431 Wateridge Cir Ste 110 San Diego (92121) *(P-10144)*

**Contixo Inc** ................................................................................... E ...... 909 465-5668
13947 Central Ave Chino (91710) *(P-4020)*

**Contra Costa Metal Fabricators, Oakland** *Also Called: Monterey Mechanical Co (P-426)*

**Contra Costa Newspapers Inc (DH)** ............................................ A ...... 925 935-2525
175 Lennon Ln Ste 100 Walnut Creek (94598) *(P-4098)*

**Contra Costa Newspapers Inc** ..................................................... D ...... 510 758-8400
4301 Lakeside Dr San Pablo (94806) *(P-4099)*

**Contra Costa Times, Walnut Creek** *Also Called: Contra Costa Newspapers Inc (P-4098)*

**Contract Furn & Ancillary Pdts, Commerce** *Also Called: 71yrs Inc (P-11982)*

**Contract IT Experts LLC** ............................................................... F ...... 702 466-5022
17041 Miracle Ln Riverside (92503) *(P-19083)*

**Contract Labeling Service Inc** ..................................................... E ...... 909 937-0344
13885 Ramona Ave Chino (91710) *(P-19084)*

**Contract Manufacturing, Anaheim** *Also Called: Konark Silicone Tech Inc (P-6890)*

**Contract Metal Products Inc** ........................................................ E ...... 510 979-0000
6451 W Schulte Rd Ste 110 Tracy (95377) *(P-8416)*

**Contract Resources, Commerce** *Also Called: Commercial Intr Resources Inc (P-3469)*

**Contract Wrangler Inc** .................................................................. E ...... 408 472-6898
400 Concar Dr San Mateo (94402) *(P-18201)*

**Contractor, Anaheim** *Also Called: Sunset Signs and Printing Inc (P-16053)*

**Contractors Wardrobe, Valencia** *Also Called: Contractors Wardrobe Inc (P-3122)*

**Contractors Wardrobe Inc (PA)** ................................................... C ...... 661 257-1177
26121 Avenue Hall Valencia (91355) *(P-3122)*

**Control Air Conditioning Corporation** .......................................... B ...... 714 777-8600
5200 E La Palma Ave Anaheim (92807) *(P-414)*

**Control Switches Intl Inc** — 2425 Mira Mar Ave Long Beach (90815) *(P-11313)* ........ E ...... 562 498-7331

**Control Systems Intl Inc** — 35 Parker Irvine (92618) *(P-9459)* ........ D ...... 949 238-4150

**Controlmyspa, Costa Mesa** *Also Called: Balboa Water Group LLC (P-11311)*

**Controlomatic Inc** — 12146 Charles Dr Ste 7-8 Grass Valley (95945) *(P-11262)* ........ E ...... 530 205-4520

**Convergent Laser Technologies, Alameda** *Also Called: Xintec Corporation (P-15309)*

**Conversica Inc (PA)** — 1730 S El Camino Real Ste 350 San Mateo (94402) *(P-17548)* ........ C ...... 650 290-7674

**Conversion Technology Co Inc (PA)** — 5360 N Commerce Ave Moorpark (93021) *(P-15884)* ........ E ...... 805 378-0033

**Conversionpoint Holdings Inc** — 840 Newport Center Dr Ste 450 Newport Beach (92660) *(P-18202)* ........ D ...... 888 706-6764

**Convertly, San Jose** *Also Called: Medianews Group Inc (P-4157)*

**Conveyor Concepts, Los Angeles** *Also Called: Machine Building Spc Inc (P-9804)*

**Conveyor Mfg & Svc Inc** — 771 Marylind Ave Claremont (91711) *(P-9483)* ........ F ...... 909 621-0406

**Conveyor Service & Electric** — 9550 Ann St Santa Fe Springs (90670) *(P-9484)* ........ E ...... 562 777-1221

**Conxtech Inc** — 6600 Koll Center Pkwy Ste 210 Pleasanton (94566) *(P-8124)* ........ C ...... 510 264-9111

**Cook and Cook Incorporated** — 1000 E Elm Ave Fullerton (92831) *(P-8313)* ........ E ...... 714 680-6669

**Cook Concrete Products Inc** — 5461 Eastside Rd Redding (96001) *(P-7322)* ........ E ...... 530 243-2562

**Cook Induction Heating Co Inc** — 4925 Slauson Ave Maywood (90270) *(P-7884)* ........ E ...... 323 560-1327

**Cook Induction Heating Co., Maywood** *Also Called: Cook Induction Heating Co Inc (P-7884)*

**Cook King, La Mirada** *Also Called: Stainless Stl Fabricators Inc (P-16844)*

**Cookie Lovers, Vernon** *Also Called: Interntnal Desserts Delicacies (P-1277)*

**Cooks Communications Corp** — 160 N Broadway St Fresno (93701) *(P-17695)* ........ E ...... 559 233-8818

**Cool Curtain CCI, Costa Mesa** *Also Called: CCI Industries Inc (P-6767)*

**Cool Things, Santa Ana** *Also Called: Ecoolthing Corp (P-9283)*

**Cool-Pak LLC** — 401 N Rice Ave Oxnard (93030) *(P-6780)* ........ D ...... 805 981-2434

**Coola LLC** — 6023 Innovation Way Ste 110 Carlsbad (92009) *(P-5957)* ........ D ...... 760 940-2125

**Coola Sunblock** — 1726 Ord Way Oceanside (92056) *(P-5958)* ........ F ...... 760 940-2125

**Coola Suncare, Carlsbad** *Also Called: Coola LLC (P-5957)*

**Coolhaus, Culver City** *Also Called: Farchitecture Bb LLC (P-800)*

**Cooling Source Inc** — 2021 Las Positas Ct Ste 101 Livermore (94551) *(P-7807)* ........ C ...... 925 292-1293

**Cooljet Systems, Placentia** *Also Called: Mkt Innovations (P-10988)*

**Coolsculpting, Pleasanton** *Also Called: Zeltiq Aesthetics Inc (P-15315)*

**Coolsculpting By Allergan, Livermore** *Also Called: Zeltiq Aesthetics Inc (P-15314)*

**Coolssculpting, Dublin** *Also Called: Zeltiq Aesthetics Inc (P-15312)*

**Cooltec Refrigeration Corp** — 1250 E Franklin Ave Unit B Pomona (91766) *(P-10492)* ........ E ...... 909 865-2229

**Cooner Sales Company LLC (PA)** — 9265 Owensmouth Ave Chatsworth (91311) *(P-16616)* ........ F ...... 818 882-8311

**Cooner Wire Company, Chatsworth** *Also Called: Cooner Sales Company LLC (P-16616)*

**Coop, Irvine** *Also Called: Coop Home Goods LLC (P-2926)*

**Coop Home Goods LLC** — 9 Executive Cir Irvine (92614) *(P-2926)* ........ E ...... 888 316-1886

**COOPER, San Ramon** *Also Called: Cooper Companies Inc (P-15596)*

**Cooper Bussmann LLC** — 5735 W Las Positas Blvd Ste 100 Pleasanton (94588) *(P-11367)* ........ C ...... 925 924-8500

**Cooper Bussmann-Automotive, Pleasanton** *Also Called: Cooper Bussmann LLC (P-11367)*

**Cooper Companies Inc (PA)** — 6101 Bollinger Canyon Rd Ste 500 San Ramon (94583) *(P-15596)* ........ C ...... 925 460-3600

**Cooper Crouse-Hinds LLC** — 3350 Enterprise Dr Bloomington (92316) *(P-13226)* ........ E ...... 951 241-8766

**Cooper Interconnect, Bloomington** *Also Called: Cooper Crouse-Hinds LLC (P-13226)*

**Cooper Interconnect Inc (DH)** — 750 W Ventura Blvd Camarillo (93010) *(P-12873)* ........ F ...... 805 484-0543

**Cooper Interconnect Inc** — 13039 Crossroads Pkwy S City Of Industry (91746) *(P-12945)* ........ D ...... 617 389-7080

**Cooper Lighting, Bloomington** *Also Called: Cooper Lighting LLC (P-11588)*

**Cooper Lighting LLC** — 3350 Enterprise Dr Bloomington (92316) *(P-11588)* ........ B ...... 909 605-6615

**Cooper Medical Inc (HQ)** — 6140 Stoneridge Mall Rd Ste 590 Pleasanton (94588) *(P-15051)* ........ E ...... 925 460-3600

**Cooper Microelectronics Inc** — 1671 Reynolds Ave Irvine (92614) *(P-12391)* ........ E ...... 949 553-8352

**Coopervision Inc** — 6101 Bollinger Canyon Rd # 500 San Ramon (94583) *(P-15597)* ........ C ...... 925 251-6600

**Coopervision Inc** — 5870 Stoneridge Dr Ste 1 Pleasanton (94588) *(P-15598)* ........ D ...... 925 251-2032

**Coordinated Companies, Wilmington** *Also Called: Coordnted Wire Rope Rgging Inc (P-17353)*

**Coordnted Wire Rope Rgging Inc (HQ)** — 1707 E Anaheim St Wilmington (90744) *(P-17353)* ........ E ...... 310 834-8535

**Cop Communications, Montclair** *Also Called: California Offset Printers Inc (P-4542)*

**Cop Shopper, San Diego** *Also Called: Krasnes Inc (P-2881)*

**Copan Diagnostics Inc (DH)** — 26055 Jefferson Ave Murrieta (92562) *(P-17033)* ........ F ...... 951 696-6957

**Coplan & Coplan Inc** — 2270 Camino Vida Roble Ste H Carlsbad (92011) *(P-9669)* ........ E ...... 760 268-0583

**Copley Newspapers, La Jolla** *Also Called: The Copley Press Inc (P-19064)*

**Copp Industrial Mfg Inc** — 5510 Brooks St Montclair (91763) *(P-13815)* ........ E ...... 909 593-7448

**Copper, San Francisco** *Also Called: Copper Crm Inc (P-18203)*

**Copper Clad Mltilayer Pdts Inc** — 1150 N Hawk Cir Anaheim (92807) *(P-12082)* ........ E ...... 714 237-1388

**Copper Crm Inc (PA)** — 2021 Fillmore St San Francisco (94115) *(P-18203)* ........ F ...... 415 989-1477

**Copper Harbor Company Inc** — 2300 Davis St San Leandro (94577) *(P-6277)* ........ F ...... 510 639-4670

**Copy 2 Copy, San Diego** *Also Called: Mody Entrepreneurs Inc (P-4698)*

**Copy Rite, Danville** *Also Called: Razvi Inc (P-19012)*

**Copy Solutions Inc** — 919 S Fremont Ave Ste 398 Alhambra (91803) *(P-4572)* ........ E ...... 323 307-0900

**Copymat, San Francisco** *Also Called: Digital Mania Inc (P-4589)*

**Cor Medica, Irvine** *Also Called: Cor Medica Technology (P-19315)*

**Cor Medica Technology** — 188 Technology Dr Ste F Irvine (92618) *(P-19315)* ........ E ...... 949 353-4554

**Cor Therapeutics Inc** — 256 E Grand Ave South San Francisco (94080) *(P-5409)* ........ B ...... 650 244-6800

**Coral Port LLC** — 1099 Vine St Ste 205 Sacramento (95811) *(P-17291)* ........ E ...... 530 761-6400

**Coraltree Inc** — 6920 Santa Teresa Blvd Ste 201 San Jose (95119) *(P-17549)* ........ E ...... 408 215-1441

**Corbell Products, Bloomington** *Also Called: Westco Industries Inc (P-8245)*

**Corbett Vineyards LLC** — 2195 Corbett Canyon Rd Arroyo Grande (93420) *(P-1518)* ........ E ...... 805 782-9463

**Corbion Biotech Inc (HQ)** — 1 Tower Pl Ste 600 South San Francisco (94080) *(P-2172)* ........ E ...... 650 780-4777

**Corbis, Los Angeles** *Also Called: Corbis Images LLC (P-17771)*

**Corbis Images LLC (PA)** — 6060 Center Dr Ste 1000 Los Angeles (90045) *(P-17771)* ........ F ...... 323 602-5700

**CORCEPT, Redwood City** *Also Called: Corcept Therapeutics Inc (P-5410)*

**Corcept Therapeutics Inc (PA)** — 101 Redwood Shores Pkwy Redwood City (94065) *(P-5410)* ........ C ...... 650 327-3270

**Cordis Corporation** — 5452 Betsy Ross Dr Santa Clara (95054) *(P-15052)* ........ C ...... 408 273-3700

**Cordova Industries, Sylmar** *Also Called: International Academy of Fin (P-6148)*

**Core Brands LLC** — 1800 S Mcdowell Boulevard Ext Petaluma (94954) *(P-11207)* ........ D ...... 707 283-5900

**Core System, San Jose** *Also Called: Innovion LLC (P-12487)*

**Core Systems, Poway** *Also Called: Rugged Systems Inc (P-10200)*

**Core Systems LLC** — 2121 Zanker Rd San Jose (95131) *(P-12392)* ........ E ...... 510 933-2300

**Coredux USA LLC** — 6721 Cobra Way San Diego (92121) *(P-10790)* ........ D ...... 858 642-0713

**Corelight Inc** — 548 Market St San Francisco (94104) *(P-18204)* ........ D ...... 888 547-9497

**Corelis Inc** — 13100 Alondra Blvd Ste 102 Cerritos (90703) *(P-12946)* ........ E ...... 562 926-6727

# ALPHABETIC SECTION — Cosmobeauti Labs & Mfg Inc

**Corelogic Dorado, Irvine** *Also Called: Dorado Network Systems Corp (P-18249)*

**Corenco, Vernon** *Also Called: Baker Commodities Inc (P-1377)*

**Coreshell Technologies Inc** .................................... E ...... 415 265-4887
2625 Alcatraz Ave # 314 Berkeley (94705) *(P-13158)*

**Coreslab Structures La Inc** .................................... C ...... 951 943-9119
150 W Placentia Ave Perris (92571) *(P-7323)*

**Coretex USA Inc** .................................... F ...... 877 247-8725
15110 Avenue Of Science Ste 100 San Diego (92128) *(P-14173)*

**Corinthian Group, Riverside** *Also Called: Surveillance Systems Group Inc (P-19137)*

**Cork Supply USA Inc** .................................... D ...... 707 746-0353
531 Stone Rd Benicia (94510) *(P-3415)*

**Corkys Pest Control Inc** .................................... D ...... 760 432-8801
150 Vallecitos De Oro San Marcos (92069) *(P-17844)*

**Corn Maiden Foods Inc** .................................... D ...... 310 784-0400
24201 Frampton Ave Harbor City (90710) *(P-853)*

**Corn Products Development Inc (HQ)** .................................... E ...... 209 982-1920
1021 Industrial Dr Stockton (95206) *(P-1089)*

**Corn Products-Stockton Plant, Stockton** *Also Called: Ingredion Incorporated (P-1090)*

**Corneagen LLC** .................................... F ...... 786 992-2688
2019 Artisan Way Apt 312 Chula Vista (91915) *(P-15053)*

**Cornerstone, Valencia** *Also Called: Cornerstone Display Group Inc (P-15959)*

**Cornerstone, Santa Monica** *Also Called: Cornerstone Ondemand Inc (P-18205)*

**Cornerstone Display Group Inc** .................................... E ...... 661 705-1700
28340 Avenue Crocker Valencia (91355) *(P-15959)*

**Cornerstone Ondemand Inc (HQ)** .................................... C ...... 310 752-0200
1601 Cloverfield Blvd Ste 620s Santa Monica (90404) *(P-18205)*

**Corningware Corelle & More, Riverside** *Also Called: Snapware Corporation (P-7031)*

**Cornucopia Tool & Plastics Inc** .................................... E ...... 805 238-7660
448 Sherwood Rd Paso Robles (93446) *(P-6781)*

**Coromega Company Inc** .................................... E ...... 760 599-6088
2525 Commerce Way Vista (92081) *(P-17425)*

**Coron-Rnge Fods Intrmdate Hldn, Fullerton** *Also Called: Vanlaw Food Products Inc (P-997)*

**Corona Clipper Inc** .................................... D ...... 800 847-7863
22440 Temescal Canyon Rd Ste 102 Corona (92883) *(P-16750)*

**Corona Magnetics Inc** .................................... C ...... 951 735-7558
201 Corporate Terrace St Corona (92879) *(P-12835)*

**Corona Millworks Company (PA)** .................................... D ...... 909 606-3288
5572 Edison Ave Chino (91710) *(P-3233)*

**Corona Tools, Corona** *Also Called: Corona Clipper Inc (P-16750)*

**Coronado Brewing Company Inc (PA)** .................................... E ...... 619 437-4452
170 Orange Ave Coronado (92118) *(P-17615)*

**Coronado Leather Co Inc** .................................... F ...... 619 238-0265
1961 Main St San Diego (92113) *(P-2876)*

**Coronado Manufacturing LLC** .................................... E ...... 818 768-5010
8991 Glenoaks Blvd Sun Valley (91352) *(P-13816)*

**Coronado Stone Products, Perris** *Also Called: Creative Stone Mfg Inc (P-7324)*

**Coronet Concrete Products Inc (PA)** .................................... E ...... 760 398-2441
83801 Avenue 45 Indio (92201) *(P-7437)*

**Coronet Lighting, Beverly Hills** *Also Called: Dasol Inc (P-11423)*

**Corporate Graphics & Printing** .................................... F ...... 805 529-5333
335 Science Dr Moorpark (93021) *(P-4573)*

**Corporate Graphics Intl Inc** .................................... D ...... 323 826-3440
4909 Alcoa Ave Vernon (90058) *(P-4574)*

**Corporate Graphics West, Vernon** *Also Called: Corporate Graphics Intl Inc (P-4574)*

**Corporate Impressions La Inc** .................................... E ...... 818 761-9295
10742 Burbank Blvd North Hollywood (91601) *(P-4866)*

**Corporate Sign Systems Inc** .................................... E ...... 408 292-1600
2464 De La Cruz Blvd Santa Clara (95050) *(P-15960)*

**Correa Pallet Inc (PA)** .................................... E ...... 559 757-1790
13036 Avenue 76 Pixley (93256) *(P-3336)*

**Corrpro Companies Inc** .................................... E ...... 562 944-1636
23309 La Palma Ave Yorba Linda (92887) *(P-7703)*

**Corrpro Companies Inc** .................................... E ...... 510 614-8800
20991 Cabot Blvd Hayward (94545) *(P-19385)*

**Corru Kraft Buena Pk Div 5058, Buena Park** *Also Called: Orora Packaging Solutions (P-17016)*

**Corru Kraft Fullerton Div 5068, Fullerton** *Also Called: Orora Packaging Solutions (P-17015)*

**Corru-Kraft IV** .................................... F ...... 714 773-0124
1911 E Rosslynn Ave Fullerton (92831) *(P-3833)*

**Corrugados De Baja California** .................................... A ...... 619 662-8672
2475 Paseo De Las A San Diego (92154) *(P-3834)*

**Corrugated Packaging Pdts Inc** .................................... F ...... 650 615-9180
21615 Hesperian Blvd Ste B Hayward (94541) *(P-3835)*

**Corrwood Containers** .................................... E ...... 559 651-0335
7182 Rasmussen Ave Visalia (93291) *(P-3369)*

**CORSAIR, Milpitas** *Also Called: Corsair Gaming Inc (P-10352)*

**Corsair, Milpitas** *Also Called: Corsair Memory Inc (P-12393)*

**Corsair Components Inc** .................................... A ...... 510 657-8747
47100 Bayside Pkwy Fremont (94538) *(P-10351)*

**Corsair Elec Connectors Inc** .................................... C ...... 949 833-0273
17100 Murphy Ave Irvine (92614) *(P-12874)*

**Corsair Gaming Inc (HQ)** .................................... E ...... 510 657-8747
115 N Mccarthy Blvd Milpitas (95035) *(P-10352)*

**Corsair Memory Inc (DH)** .................................... C ...... 510 657-8747
115 N Mccarthy Blvd Milpitas (95035) *(P-12393)*

**Corte Custom Case, San Jacinto** *Also Called: Wallace Wood Products (P-3677)*

**Cortec Precision Shtmtl Inc (PA)** .................................... C ...... 408 278-8540
2231 Will Wool Dr San Jose (95112) *(P-8417)*

**Cortech Industries LLC** .................................... E ...... 818 267-8324
2850 Cordelia Rd Ste 160 Fairfield (94534) *(P-16121)*

**Corteva Agriscience LLC** .................................... C ...... 925 432-5482
901 Loveridge Rd Pittsburg (94565) *(P-17270)*

**Cortex Inc** .................................... E ...... 916 501-7214
3350 Scott Blvd Ste 37b Santa Clara (95054) *(P-15054)*

**Cortexyme, South San Francisco** *Also Called: Quince Therapeutics Inc (P-5857)*

**Cortez Pallets Service Inc (PA)** .................................... F ...... 626 961-9891
14739 Proctor Ave La Puente (91746) *(P-3337)*

**Cortina Systems Inc (DH)** .................................... C ...... 408 481-2300
2953 Bunker Hill Ln Ste 300 Santa Clara (95054) *(P-12394)*

**CORVUS PHARMACEUTICALS, Burlingame** *Also Called: Corvus Pharmaceuticals Inc (P-5411)*

**Corvus Pharmaceuticals Inc** .................................... E ...... 650 900-4520
863 Mitten Rd Ste 102 Burlingame (94010) *(P-5411)*

**Corwin Press Inc** .................................... D ...... 805 499-9734
2455 Teller Rd Newbury Park (91320) *(P-4383)*

**Corza Medical Inc** .................................... F ...... 619 671-0276
2001 Sanyo Ave San Diego (92154) *(P-15055)*

**Cosasco Inc** .................................... D ...... 562 949-0123
11841 Smith Ave Santa Fe Springs (90670) *(P-14398)*

**Cosco Fire Protection Inc** .................................... D ...... 925 455-2751
7455 Longard Rd Livermore (94551) *(P-454)*

**Cosco Home & Office Products, Ontario** *Also Called: Dorel Juvenile Group Inc (P-6810)*

**Cosentino Signature Wineries** .................................... E ...... 707 921-2809
7415 St Helena Hwy Yountville (94599) *(P-1519)*

**Cosentino Winery, Yountville** *Also Called: Cosentino Signature Wineries (P-1519)*

**Cosmedx Science Inc** .................................... E ...... 951 371-0509
3550 Vine St Ste 210 Riverside (92507) *(P-5412)*

**Cosmetic Enterprises Ltd** .................................... F ...... 818 896-5355
12848 Pierce St Pacoima (91331) *(P-5959)*

**Cosmetic Group Usa Inc** .................................... C ...... 818 767-2889
12708 Branford St Pacoima (91331) *(P-5960)*

**Cosmetic Laboratories America, Chatsworth** *Also Called: Cosmetic Laboratories of America LLC (P-17696)*

**Cosmetic Laboratories of America LLC** .................................... B ...... 818 717-6140
20245 Sunburst St Chatsworth (91311) *(P-17696)*

**Cosmetic Laboratories-America, Chatsworth** *Also Called: Kdc/One Chatsworth Inc (P-5998)*

**Cosmetic Technologies LLC** .................................... D ...... 805 376-9960
2585 Azurite Cir Newbury Park (91320) *(P-5961)*

**Cosmetix West (PA)** .................................... E ...... 310 726-3080
2305 Utah Ave El Segundo (90245) *(P-17697)*

**Cosmic Plastics Inc (PA)** .................................... F ...... 661 257-3274
28410 Industry Dr Valencia (91355) *(P-5148)*

**Cosmo Beauty Lab & Mfg, San Dimas** *Also Called: Cosmobeauti Labs & Mfg Inc (P-5963)*

**Cosmo Fiber Corporation (PA)** .................................... E ...... 626 256-6098
1802 Santo Domingo Ave Duarte (91010) *(P-4867)*

**Cosmo Import & Export LLC** .................................... E ...... 916 209-5500
3771 Channel Dr West Sacramento (95691) *(P-3500)*

**Cosmo International Corp** .................................... D ...... 310 271-1100
9200 W Sunset Blvd Ste 401 West Hollywood (90069) *(P-5962)*

**Cosmo International Fragrances, West Hollywood** *Also Called: Cosmo International Corp (P-5962)*

**Cosmobeauti Labs & Mfg Inc** .................................... F ...... 909 971-9832
480 E Arrow Hwy San Dimas (91773) *(P-5963)*

**Cosmodyne LLC** .................................................................. E ...... 562 795-5990
3010 Old Ranch Pkwy Ste 300 Seal Beach (90740) *(P-9842)*

**Cosmos Food Co Inc** .............................................................. E ...... 323 221-9142
17501 Mondino Dr Rowland Heights (91748) *(P-2173)*

**Cosrich Group Inc** ................................................................. E ...... 818 686-2500
12243 Branford St Sun Valley (91352) *(P-5964)*

**COSTA COFFEE, Carlsbad** *Also Called: La Costa Coffee Roasting Co (P-17427)*

**Costal Brands, Manteca** *Also Called: Delicato Vineyards LLC (P-1535)*

**Costeaux French Bakery Inc** ............................................... D ...... 707 433-1913
417 Healdsburg Ave Healdsburg (95448) *(P-17573)*

**Costeaux French Bakery & Cafe, Healdsburg** *Also Called: Costeaux French Bakery Inc (P-17573)*

**Cosway Company Inc** ............................................................ F ...... 310 527-9135
14805 S Maple Ave Gardena (90248) *(P-5965)*

**Cosway Company Inc (PA)** .................................................. E ...... 310 900-4100
20633 S Fordyce Ave Carson (90810) *(P-5966)*

**Cosway Company Inc** ............................................................ F ...... 310 609-3352
20488 S Reeves Ave Carson (90810) *(P-5967)*

**Cothera Biopharma Inc** ....................................................... E ...... 510 364-1930
1960 Noel Dr Los Altos (94024) *(P-5413)*

**Cots Journal Magazine, San Clemente** *Also Called: R T C Group (P-4292)*

**Cottage Bakery Inc** .............................................................. B ...... 209 334-3616
1831 S Stockton St Lodi (95240) *(P-1178)*

**Cotterman Company, Bakersfield** *Also Called: Material Control Inc (P-9293)*

**Cotton Links LLC** ................................................................. E ...... 714 444-4700
2990 Grace Ln Costa Mesa (92626) *(P-2570)*

**Couchbase Inc (PA)** .............................................................. C ...... 650 417-7500
3250 Olcott St Santa Clara (95054) *(P-17901)*

**Cougar Biotechnology Inc** .................................................. D ...... 310 943-8040
10990 Wilshire Blvd Ste 1200 Los Angeles (90024) *(P-5414)*

**Coulter Forge Technology Inc** ............................................ F ...... 510 420-3500
1494 67th St Emeryville (94608) *(P-8774)*

**Coulter Steel and Forge, Emeryville** *Also Called: Coulter Forge Technology Inc (P-8774)*

**Count Machinery Co, Escondido** *Also Called: Count Numbering Machine Inc (P-9765)*

**Count Numbering Machine Inc** ........................................... E ...... 760 739-9357
2128 Auto Park Way Escondido (92029) *(P-9765)*

**Counter Hospitality Group LLC** ........................................... D ...... 559 228-9735
8398 N Fresno St Ste 101 Fresno (93720) *(P-17574)*

**Counter Santana Row LP** ..................................................... E ...... 408 610-1362
3055 Olin Ave San Jose (95128) *(P-7091)*

**Countertop** ............................................................................ E ...... 323 788-3591
230 W Avenue 26 Unit 256 Los Angeles (90031) *(P-2174)*

**Countess Walewska, The, Geyserville** *Also Called: Francis Coppola Winery LLC (P-1577)*

**Country Almanac, Menlo Park** *Also Called: Embarcadero Media (P-4110)*

**Country Almanac, Palo Alto** *Also Called: Embarcadero Media (P-4111)*

**Country Archer Jerky, San Bernardino** *Also Called: S&E Gourmet Cuts Inc (P-17149)*

**Country Club Fashions Inc** ................................................. E ...... 323 965-2707
6083 W Pico Blvd Los Angeles (90035) *(P-17492)*

**Country Connection Inc (PA)** ............................................... F ...... 530 589-5176
2805 Richter Ave Oroville (95966) *(P-17698)*

**Country Plastics Inc** ............................................................. F ...... 559 597-2556
32501 Road 228 Woodlake (93286) *(P-6782)*

**Countryman Associates, Menlo Park** *Also Called: Countryman Associates Inc (P-11646)*

**Countryman Associates Inc** ................................................. F ...... 650 364-9988
195 Constitution Dr Menlo Park (94025) *(P-11646)*

**County Clothing Company, Irvine** *Also Called: Snowmass Apparel Inc (P-17100)*

**County of Alameda** ............................................................... E ...... 510 272-6964
1225 Fallon St Ste G1 Oakland (94612) *(P-14475)*

**County of Los Angeles** ........................................................ E ...... 310 456-8014
3637 Winter Canyon Rd Malibu (90265) *(P-9417)*

**County of Los Angeles** ........................................................ E ...... 626 968-3312
14959 Proctor Ave La Puente (91746) *(P-9418)*

**County of NAPA** .................................................................... E ...... 707 259-8620
804 1st St Napa (94559) *(P-14399)*

**County of Orange** ................................................................. E ...... 714 567-7444
1300 S Grand Ave Ste B Santa Ana (92705) *(P-19576)*

**County Plastics Corp** ............................................................ E ...... 310 635-5400
135 E Stanley St Compton (90220) *(P-6783)*

**County Quarry Products** ...................................................... E ...... 925 682-0707
5501 Imhoff Pl Martinez (94553) *(P-16357)*

**Coupa, Foster City** *Also Called: Coupa Software Incorporated (P-18207)*

**Coupa Holdings LLC (PA)** ..................................................... E ...... 650 931-3200
1855 S Grant St Fl 4 San Mateo (94402) *(P-18206)*

**Coupa Software Incorporated (HQ)** ..................................... C ...... 650 931-3200
950 Tower Ln Ste 2000 Foster City (94404) *(P-18207)*

**Courage Production LLC** ...................................................... D ...... 707 422-6300
2475 Courage Dr Fairfield (94533) *(P-637)*

**COURSERA, Mountain View** *Also Called: Coursera Inc (P-18208)*

**Coursera Inc (PA)** .................................................................. A ...... 650 963-9884
381 E Evelyn Ave Mountain View (94041) *(P-18208)*

**Court Galvanizing Inc** ........................................................... F ...... 707 448-4848
4937 Allison Pkwy Vacaville (95688) *(P-9059)*

**Courtside Cellars LLC (PA)** .................................................. E ...... 805 782-0500
4910 Edna Rd San Luis Obispo (93401) *(P-1520)*

**Courtside Cellars LLC** ........................................................... F ...... 805 467-2882
2425 Mission St San Miguel (93451) *(P-1521)*

**Cousins Foods LLC** ............................................................... E ...... 818 767-3842
2021 1st St San Fernando (91340) *(P-17373)*

**Covalent Cbd, San Diego** *Also Called: Green Star Labs Inc (P-5244)*

**Covenant Community Svcs Inc** ............................................ F ...... 661 829-6999
1700 N Chester Ave Bakersfield (93308) *(P-19355)*

**Coveris, Ontario** *Also Called: Transcontinental US LLC (P-3986)*

**Coverking, Anaheim** *Also Called: Shrin LLC (P-16400)*

**Covidien** ................................................................................. F ...... 909 605-6572
4651 E Francis St Ontario (91761) *(P-15056)*

**Covidien, Fremont** *Also Called: Covidien Holding Inc (P-15059)*

**Covidien, Costa Mesa** *Also Called: Newport Medical Instrs Inc (P-15205)*

**Covidien Holding Inc** ............................................................ C ...... 408 585-7700
3062 Bunker Hill Ln Santa Clara (95054) *(P-15057)*

**Covidien Holding Inc** ............................................................ C ...... 760 603-5020
2101 Faraday Ave Carlsbad (92008) *(P-15058)*

**Covidien Holding Inc** ............................................................ C ...... 510 456-1500
6531 Dumbarton Cir Fremont (94555) *(P-15059)*

**Covidien Holding Inc** ............................................................ C ...... 619 690-8500
2475 Paseo De Las Americas Ste A San Diego (92154) *(P-15060)*

**Covidien Kenmex, San Diego** *Also Called: Covidien Holding Inc (P-15060)*

**Covidien LP** ............................................................................ C ...... 949 837-3700
9775 Toledo Way Irvine (92618) *(P-15061)*

**Coway Usa Inc** ....................................................................... E ...... 213 486-1600
4221 Wilshire Blvd Ste 210 Los Angeles (90010) *(P-17699)*

**Cowboy Direct Response** ..................................................... E ...... 714 824-3780
130 E Alton Ave Santa Ana (92707) *(P-15961)*

**Cowelco** .................................................................................. E ...... 562 432-5766
1634 W 14th St Long Beach (90813) *(P-8418)*

**Cowelco Steel Contractors, Long Beach** *Also Called: Cowelco (P-8418)*

**Coy Industries Inc** ................................................................ D ...... 310 603-2970
2970 E Maria St E Rncho Dmngz (90221) *(P-8419)*

**Coyle Reproductions Inc (PA)** .............................................. C ...... 866 269-5373
2850 Orbiter St Brea (92821) *(P-4575)*

**Cozad Trailer Sales LLC** ...................................................... D ...... 209 931-3000
4907 E Waterloo Rd Stockton (95215) *(P-13615)*

**Cozzia USA LLC (HQ)** ............................................................ F ...... 626 667-2272
861 S Oak Park Rd Covina (91724) *(P-13227)*

**CP Document Technologies LLC** ......................................... E ...... 310 575-6640
11835 W Olympic Blvd Ste 145 Los Angeles (90064) *(P-17807)*

**CP Kelco, San Diego** *Also Called: CP Kelco US Inc (P-332)*

**CP Kelco US Inc** .................................................................... E ...... 619 595-5000
2025 Harbor Dr San Diego (92113) *(P-332)*

**CP Kelco US Inc** .................................................................... E ...... 619 652-5326
2031 E Belt St San Diego (92113) *(P-6278)*

**CP Manufacturing, San Diego** *Also Called: CP Manufacturing Inc (P-9843)*

**CP Manufacturing Inc (HQ)** .................................................. C ...... 619 477-3175
6795 Calle De Linea San Diego (92154) *(P-9843)*

**Cp-Carrillo Inc** ...................................................................... E ...... 949 567-9000
17401 Armstrong Ave Irvine (92614) *(P-10620)*

**Cp-Carrillo Inc (DH)** .............................................................. C ...... 949 567-9000
1902 Mcgaw Ave Irvine (92614) *(P-10621)*

**Cpacket Networks Inc** ........................................................... E ...... 650 969-9500
480 N Mccarthy Blvd Ste 100 Milpitas (95035) *(P-10353)*

**Cpaperless LLC** ..................................................................... E ...... 949 510-3365
605 1/2 Orchid Ave Corona Del Mar (92625) *(P-11726)*

## ALPHABETIC SECTION

CPC Fabrication Inc .................................................................. F ...... 714 549-2426
   2904 Oak St Santa Ana (92707) *(P-8420)*

Cpd Industries ........................................................................ E ...... 909 465-5596
   4665 State St Montclair (91763) *(P-6784)*

CPI, Palo Alto *Also Called: Communications & Pwr Inds LLC (P-11831)*

CPI, Palo Alto *Also Called: Communications & Pwr Inds LLC (P-12029)*

CPI Econco Division ................................................................ D ...... 530 662-7553
   1318 Commerce Ave Woodland (95776) *(P-19175)*

CPI International ..................................................................... D ...... 707 521-6327
   5580 Skylane Blvd Santa Rosa (95403) *(P-16599)*

CPI International Holding Corp ............................................... F ...... 650 846-2900
   811 Hansen Way Palo Alto (94304) *(P-12947)*

CPI Malibu Division ................................................................. D ...... 805 383-1829
   3623 Old Conejo Rd Ste 205 Newbury Park (91320) *(P-11835)*

CPI Satcom & Antenna Tech Inc ............................................ D ...... 408 955-1900
   2205 Fortune Dr San Jose (95131) *(P-11836)*

CPI Satcom & Antenna Tech Inc ............................................ C ...... 310 539-6704
   3111 Fujita St Torrance (90505) *(P-11837)*

Cpk Manufacturing Inc ........................................................... F ...... 408 971-4019
   2188 Del Franco St Ste 70 San Jose (95131) *(P-10791)*

Cpp - Pomona, Pomona *Also Called: Consoldted Precision Pdts Corp (P-7839)*

Cpp Cudahy, Cudahy *Also Called: Consolidated Foundries Inc (P-7840)*

Cpp Inc .................................................................................. F ...... 650 969-8901
   185 N Wolfe Rd Sunnyvale (94086) *(P-4322)*

Cpp Rancho Cucamonga, Rancho Cucamonga *Also Called: Pac-Rancho Inc (P-7693)*

Cpp-Azusa, Azusa *Also Called: Magparts (P-7848)*

Cpp-City of Industry, City Of Industry *Also Called: Cast Parts Inc (P-7684)*

Cpp-Pomona, Walnut *Also Called: Cast Parts Inc (P-7683)*

Cpp-Port Hueneme, Port Hueneme *Also Called: Pac Foundries Inc (P-7856)*

Cpp/Belwin Inc ....................................................................... D ...... 818 891-5999
   16320 Roscoe Blvd Ste 100 Van Nuys (91406) *(P-4323)*

Cpsg, Folsom *Also Called: Computer Power Sftwr Group Inc (P-17899)*

Cq Press Fairfax Co, Thousand Oaks *Also Called: Sage Publications Inc (P-4345)*

Cr & A Custom, Los Angeles *Also Called: CR & A Custom Apparel Inc (P-4868)*

CR & A Custom Apparel Inc ................................................... E ...... 213 749-4440
   312 W Pico Blvd Los Angeles (90015) *(P-4868)*

Cr Print, Westlake Village *Also Called: Earth Print Inc (P-4599)*

Craft, San Diego *Also Called: Elco Rfrgn Solutions LLC (P-10497)*

Craft Labor & Support Svcs LLC ............................................ C ...... 619 336-9977
   1545 Tidelands Ave Ste C National City (91950) *(P-14003)*

Craftech, Anaheim *Also Called: Sp Craftech I LLC (P-7036)*

Craftech Metal Forming Inc ................................................... E ...... 951 940-6444
   24100 Water Ave Ste B Perris (92570) *(P-8125)*

Craftsman Cutting Dies Inc (PA) ............................................ E ...... 714 776-8995
   1992 Rockefeller Dr Ceres (95307) *(P-7949)*

Craftsman Unity LLC ............................................................. C ...... 714 776-8995
   2273 E Via Burton Anaheim (92806) *(P-7950)*

Crafttech, Anaheim *Also Called: Charmaine Plastics Inc (P-6771)*

Craftwood Industries Inc ........................................................ E ...... 616 796-1209
   222 Shelbourne Irvine (92620) *(P-3596)*

Craig Kackert Design Tech, Simi Valley *Also Called: Jaxx Manufacturing Inc (P-13013)*

Craig Manufacturing Company (PA) ....................................... D ...... 323 726-7355
   8129 Slauson Ave Montebello (90640) *(P-13478)*

Craig Tools Inc ....................................................................... E ...... 310 322-0614
   142 Lomita St El Segundo (90245) *(P-9670)*

Craigo Investments Inc .......................................................... F ...... 559 222-9293
   2745 W Shaw Ave Ste 120 Fresno (93711) *(P-15962)*

Crain Cutter Company Inc ...................................................... D ...... 408 946-6100
   1155 Wrigley Way Milpitas (95035) *(P-7990)*

Cramer-Decker Industries (PA) .............................................. E ...... 714 566-3800
   1300 E Wakeham Ave Ste A Santa Ana (92705) *(P-16579)*

Crane Aerospace Inc ............................................................. D ...... 818 526-2600
   3000 Winona Ave Burbank (91504) *(P-13817)*

Crane Co ................................................................................ C ...... 562 426-2531
   3201 Walnut Ave Long Beach (90755) *(P-9166)*

Crane Co ................................................................................ E ...... 707 748-7166
   3948 Teal Ct Benicia (94510) *(P-12948)*

CRANE CO., Long Beach *Also Called: Crane Co (P-9166)*

Crane Instrmnttion Smpling Inc .............................................. D ...... 951 270-6200
   2301 Wardlow Cir Corona (92878) *(P-9149)*

Crane Valves Services Division, Benicia *Also Called: Crane Co (P-12948)*

Crane, John, Santa Fe Springs *Also Called: John Crane Inc (P-7569)*

Craneveyor Corp (PA) ............................................................ D ...... 626 442-1524
   1524 Potrero Ave El Monte (91733) *(P-9500)*

Craneworks Southwest Inc .................................................... F ...... 760 735-9793
   1312 E Barham Dr San Marcos (92078) *(P-9510)*

Crate Modular Inc .................................................................. D ...... 310 405-0829
   3025 E Dominguez St Carson (90810) *(P-8662)*

Cratex, Encinitas *Also Called: Cratex Manufacturing Co Inc (P-7552)*

Cratex Manufacturing Co Inc ................................................. D ...... 760 942-2877
   328 Encinitas Blvd Ste 200 Encinitas (92024) *(P-7552)*

Crave Foods, Los Angeles *Also Called: Crave Foods Inc (P-1030)*

Crave Foods Inc ..................................................................... E ...... 562 900-7272
   2043 Imperial St Los Angeles (90021) *(P-1030)*

Crawford Associates ............................................................. E ...... 760 922-6804
   2635 E Chanslor Way Blythe (92225) *(P-520)*

Cray Cluster Solutions, San Jose *Also Called: Appro International Inc (P-10225)*

Crazy Industries .................................................................... E ...... 619 270-9090
   8675 Avenida Costa Norte San Diego (92154) *(P-15801)*

Crazy Maple Studio Inc (PA) .................................................. E ...... 972 757-1283
   1277 Borregas Ave Ste C Sunnyvale (94089) *(P-4384)*

CRC Services LLC ................................................................ F ...... 888 848-4754
   27200 Tourney Rd Ste 200 Santa Clarita (91355) *(P-175)*

Crd Mfg Inc ............................................................................ E ...... 714 871-3300
   615 Fee Ana St Placentia (92870) *(P-7991)*

Creation Networks Inc ........................................................... E ...... 925 446-4332
   1001 Shary Cir Ste 1 Concord (94518) *(P-17700)*

Creation Tech Calexico Inc (HQ) ............................................ E
   1778 Zinetta Rd Ste F Calexico (92231) *(P-12083)*

Creative Accents ................................................................... E ...... 760 373-1222
   6294 Curtis Pl California City (93505) *(P-2512)*

Creative Age Publications Inc ................................................ E ...... 818 782-7328
   15975 High Knoll Rd Encino (91436) *(P-4242)*

Creative Baby Inc .................................................................. E ...... 626 330-2289
   2222 Lee Ave South El Monte (91733) *(P-16947)*

Creative Costuming & Designs, Huntington Beach *Also Called: Creative Costuming Designs Inc (P-2411)*

Creative Costuming Designs Inc ............................................ E ...... 714 895-0982
   15402 Electronic Ln Huntington Beach (92649) *(P-2411)*

Creative Design Industries ..................................................... C ...... 619 710-2525
   2587 Otay Center Dr San Diego (92154) *(P-2571)*

Creative Dgtal Systems Intgrti ............................................... F ...... 805 364-0555
   670 E Easy St Simi Valley (93065) *(P-17902)*

Creative Energy Foods Inc .................................................... D ...... 510 638-8668
   9957 Medford Ave Ste 4 Oakland (94603) *(P-17185)*

Creative Foods LLC .............................................................. E ...... 858 748-0070
   12622 Poway Rd # A Poway (92064) *(P-2175)*

Creative Graphic Services, Santa Clarita *Also Called: Living Way Industries Inc (P-4681)*

Creative Impressions Inc ....................................................... F ...... 714 521-4441
   7697 9th St Buena Park (90621) *(P-6555)*

Creative Inflatables, South El Monte *Also Called: Promotonal Design Concepts Inc (P-6528)*

Creative Labs Inc (DH) .......................................................... C ...... 408 428-6600
   2033 Gateway Pl Ste 500 San Jose (95110) *(P-16515)*

Creative Machine Technology, Corona *Also Called: Cremach Tech Inc (P-9544)*

Creative Machine Technology, Corona *Also Called: Cremach Tech Inc (P-9545)*

Creative Mfg Solutions Inc ..................................................... E ...... 408 327-0600
   18400 Sutter Blvd Morgan Hill (95037) *(P-8421)*

Creative Outdoor Advertising, Riverside *Also Called: Brimad Enterprises Inc (P-17784)*

Creative Outdoor Distrs USA, Lake Forest *Also Called: Cod USA Inc (P-3621)*

Creative Pathways Inc ........................................................... E ...... 310 530-1965
   20815 Higgins Ct Torrance (90501) *(P-9724)*

Creative Plant Design Inc ...................................................... F ...... 408 452-1444
   5895 Rue Ferrari San Jose (95138) *(P-17279)*

Creative Press, Anaheim *Also Called: Creative Press LLC (P-4577)*

Creative Press LLC ............................................................... E ...... 714 774-5060
   1600 E Ball Rd Anaheim (92805) *(P-4576)*

Creative Press LLC (PA) ........................................................ E ...... 714 774-5060
   1350 S Caldwell Cir Anaheim (92805) *(P-4577)*

Creative Stone Mfg Inc (PA) .................................................. C ...... 800 847-8663
   342 W Perry St Perris (92571) *(P-7324)*

# Creative Teaching Press Inc — ALPHABETIC SECTION

**Creative Teaching Press Inc (PA)** ............................................. D ...... 714 799-2100
11145 Knott Ave Cypress (90630) *(P-4324)*

**Creative Wood Products Inc** .................................................. C ...... 510 635-5399
900 77th Ave Oakland (94621) *(P-3564)*

**Cred-Corp, Jamestown** *Also Called: Chicken Rnch Economic Dev Corp (P-4089)*

**Credence Id LLC** ............................................................... E ...... 888 243-5452
2335 Broadway Ste 100 Oakland (94612) *(P-11838)*

**Credence Medsystems Inc** .................................................. E ...... 844 263-3797
1430 Obrien Dr Ste D Menlo Park (94025) *(P-15062)*

**Credo, San Jose** *Also Called: Credo Semiconductor Inc (P-12395)*

**Credo Semiconductor Inc** ................................................... D ...... 408 906-8557
110 Rio Robles Fl 1 San Jose (95134) *(P-12395)*

**Cree8 Inc** ......................................................................... F ...... 805 328-4204
2350 Keystone Dr El Dorado Hills (95762) *(P-18209)*

**Cremach Tech Inc (DH)** ..................................................... E ...... 951 735-3194
369 Meyer Cir Corona (92879) *(P-9544)*

**Cremach Tech Inc** ............................................................. C ...... 951 735-3194
400 E Parkridge Ave Corona (92879) *(P-9545)*

**Cremi Mex Inc** .................................................................. F ...... 323 235-0004
14010 Live Oak Ave Baldwin Park (91706) *(P-17127)*

**Crenshaw Die and Mfg Corp** ............................................... D ...... 949 475-5505
7432 Prince Dr Huntington Beach (92647) *(P-9615)*

**Crertih Inc** ........................................................................ E ...... 415 290-6603
121 2nd St San Francisco (94105) *(P-18210)*

**Crescent Inc** ..................................................................... E ...... 714 992-6030
670 S Jefferson St Placentia (92870) *(P-4578)*

**Crescentone Inc (HQ)** ........................................................ C ...... 310 563-7000
200 Continental Blvd Fl 3 El Segundo (90245) *(P-17903)*

**Cresco Manufacturing Inc** .................................................. E ...... 714 525-2326
1614 N Orangethorpe Way Anaheim (92801) *(P-10792)*

**Crescomfg.com, Anaheim** *Also Called: Cresco Manufacturing Inc (P-10792)*

**Crest Coating Inc** ............................................................. D ...... 714 635-7090
1361 S Allec St Anaheim (92805) *(P-9060)*

**Crestec Los Angeles, Long Beach** *Also Called: Crestec Usa Inc (P-4579)*

**Crestec Usa Inc** ................................................................ E ...... 310 327-9000
2410 Mira Mar Ave Long Beach (90815) *(P-4579)*

**Crestmark Millwork Inc** ..................................................... E ...... 707 822-4034
5640 West End Rd Arcata (95521) *(P-3123)*

**Crestone LLC** ................................................................... E ...... 323 588-8857
2511 S Alameda St Vernon (90058) *(P-2661)*

**Cretex Med Cmpnent DVC Tech In** ..................................... C ...... 831 462-1141
2840 Research Park Dr Ste 160 Soquel (95073) *(P-6785)*

**Creu LLC** ......................................................................... E ...... 909 483-4888
12750 Baltic Ct Rancho Cucamonga (91739) *(P-6786)*

**Crew Knitwear LLC** .......................................................... D ...... 323 526-3888
2155 E 7th St Ste 125 Los Angeles (90023) *(P-2464)*

**Crew Knitwear LLC (PA)** ................................................... D ...... 323 526-3888
660 S Myers St Los Angeles (90023) *(P-2748)*

**Cri 2000 LP (PA)** .............................................................. E ...... 619 542-1975
2245 San Diego Ave Ste 125 San Diego (92110) *(P-3416)*

**Cri Sub 1 (DH)** ................................................................. E ...... 310 537-1657
1715 S Anderson Ave Compton (90220) *(P-3565)*

**Cricket Company LLC** ....................................................... E ...... 415 475-4150
68 Leveroni Ct Ste 200 Novato (94949) *(P-6488)*

**CRIMSON, Napa** *Also Called: Crimson Wine Group Ltd (P-1522)*

**Crimson Resource Management, Bakersfield** *Also Called: Delta Trading LP (P-6361)*

**Crimson Wine Group Ltd (PA)** ........................................... C ...... 800 486-0503
5901 Silverado Trl Napa (94558) *(P-1522)*

**CRINETICS, San Diego** *Also Called: Crinetics Pharmaceuticals Inc (P-5415)*

**Crinetics Pharmaceuticals Inc (PA)** .................................... D ...... 858 450-6464
6055 Lusk Blvd San Diego (92121) *(P-5415)*

**Crislu Corp** ...................................................................... E ...... 310 322-3444
20916 Higgins Ct Torrance (90501) *(P-15689)*

**Crissair Inc** ...................................................................... C ...... 661 367-3300
28909 Avenue Williams Valencia (91355) *(P-10631)*

**Crist Group Inc** ................................................................ E ...... 530 661-0700
1324 E Beamer St Woodland (95776) *(P-9844)*

**Cristal Materials Inc** ......................................................... F ...... 323 855-1688
6825 Mckinley Ave Los Angeles (90001) *(P-3523)*

**Cristek, Anaheim** *Also Called: Cristek Interconnects LLC (P-12875)*

**Cristek Interconnects LLC (DH)** ......................................... C ...... 714 696-5200
5395 E Hunter Ave Anaheim (92807) *(P-12875)*

**Criterion Machine Works** ................................................... E
765 W 16th St Costa Mesa (92627) *(P-9671)*

**Criticalpoint Capital LLC** ................................................... D ...... 909 987-9533
9433 Hyssop Dr Rancho Cucamonga (91730) *(P-5220)*

**Criveller California Corp** .................................................... F ...... 707 431-2211
185 Grant Ave Healdsburg (95448) *(P-9786)*

**Crl, Los Angeles** *Also Called: C R Laurence Co Inc (P-13468)*

**Crm Co LLC (PA)** ............................................................. F ...... 949 263-9100
1301 Dove St Ste 940 Newport Beach (92660) *(P-6472)*

**Crm of America LLC (PA)** .................................................. F ...... 949 263-9100
1301 Dove St Ste 940 Newport Beach (92660) *(P-6407)*

**Crockett & Coinc (PA)** ...................................................... E ...... 619 267-6410
5120 Robinwood Rd Ste A22 Bonita (91902) *(P-19309)*

**Crockett Graphics Inc (PA)** ............................................... D ...... 805 987-8577
980 Avenida Acaso Camarillo (93012) *(P-3836)*

**Crosby Fruit Products, Fontana** *Also Called: Refresco Beverages US Inc (P-921)*

**Crosno Construction Inc** .................................................. E ...... 805 343-7437
819 Sheridan Rd Arroyo Grande (93420) *(P-8126)*

**Crossbar Inc** .................................................................... E ...... 408 884-0281
2055 Laurelwood Rd Santa Clara (95054) *(P-12396)*

**Crossfield Products Corp (PA)** .......................................... E ...... 310 886-9100
3000 E Harcourt St Compton (90221) *(P-5149)*

**Crossport Mocean** ........................................................... F ...... 949 646-1701
1611 Babcock St Newport Beach (92663) *(P-2559)*

**Crowdcircle Inc** ................................................................ E ...... 206 853-7560
1810 Gateway Dr Ste 200 San Mateo (94404) *(P-18211)*

**Crower Cams, San Diego** *Also Called: Crower Engrg & Sls Co Inc (P-13479)*

**Crower Engrg & Sls Co Inc** .............................................. D ...... 619 661-6477
6180 Business Center Ct San Diego (92154) *(P-13479)*

**Crown Carton Company Inc** ............................................. E ...... 323 582-3053
1820 E 48th Pl Vernon (90058) *(P-3837)*

**Crown Citrus Company Inc** .............................................. F ...... 760 348-9755
407 S Industrial Ave Calipatria (92233) *(P-1002)*

**Crown Discount Tools, Sylmar** *Also Called: TMW Corporation (P-13975)*

**Crown Equipment Corporation** ......................................... F ...... 559 585-8000
1355 E Fontana Ave Ste 102 Fresno (93725) *(P-9511)*

**Crown Equipment Corporation** ......................................... E ...... 626 968-0556
1300 Palomares St La Verne (91750) *(P-9512)*

**Crown Equipment Corporation** ......................................... D ...... 909 923-8357
4250 Greystone Dr Ontario (91761) *(P-9513)*

**Crown Equipment Corporation** ......................................... E ...... 510 471-7272
1400 Crocker Ave Hayward (94544) *(P-9514)*

**Crown Equipment Corporation** ......................................... E ...... 916 373-8980
1420 Enterprise Blvd West Sacramento (95691) *(P-9515)*

**Crown Equipment Corporation** ......................................... D ...... 310 952-6600
4061 Via Oro Ave Long Beach (90810) *(P-9516)*

**Crown Fashion, Los Angeles** *Also Called: Grand West Inc (P-2472)*

**Crown Lift Trucks, Fresno** *Also Called: Crown Equipment Corporation (P-9511)*

**Crown Lift Trucks, La Verne** *Also Called: Crown Equipment Corporation (P-9512)*

**Crown Lift Trucks, Ontario** *Also Called: Crown Equipment Corporation (P-9513)*

**Crown Lift Trucks, Hayward** *Also Called: Crown Equipment Corporation (P-9514)*

**Crown Lift Trucks, West Sacramento** *Also Called: Crown Equipment Corporation (P-9515)*

**Crown Lift Trucks, Long Beach** *Also Called: Crown Equipment Corporation (P-9516)*

**Crown Mfg Co Inc** ........................................................... E ...... 510 742-8800
37625 Sycamore St Newark (94560) *(P-6787)*

**Crown Micro, Fremont** *Also Called: Bold Data Technology Inc (P-10139)*

**Crown Paper Converting, Ontario** *Also Called: Crown Paper Converting Inc (P-3764)*

**Crown Paper Converting Inc** ............................................ E ...... 909 923-5226
1380 S Bon View Ave Ontario (91761) *(P-3764)*

**Crown Poly Inc** ................................................................ C ...... 323 585-5522
5700 Bickett St Huntington Park (90255) *(P-3965)*

**Crown Printers, San Bernardino** *Also Called: Shorett Printing Inc (P-4960)*

**Crown Products Inc** ......................................................... E ...... 760 471-1188
177 Newport Dr Ste A San Marcos (92069) *(P-8422)*

**Crown Sheet Metal & Skylights, Burlingame** *Also Called: Crown Shtmtl & Skylights Inc (P-512)*

**Crown Shtmtl & Skylights Inc** .......................................... E ...... 415 467-5008
855 Stanton Rd Burlingame (94010) *(P-512)*

**Crown Steel, San Marcos** *Also Called: Crown Products Inc (P-8422)*

**Crown Technical Systems (PA)** ........................................ C ...... 951 332-4170
13470 Philadelphia Ave Fontana (92337) *(P-11238)*

## ALPHABETIC SECTION — Culinary International LLC

Crown Vly Precision Machining, Irwindale *Also Called: Sinecera Inc (P-19131)*
Crownair Aviation, San Diego *Also Called: Air 88 Inc (P-16298)*
Crowne Cold Storage LLC .................................................. E ...... 661 725-6458
   786 Road 188 Delano (93215) *(P-19525)*
Crowntonka California Inc .................................................. E ...... 909 230-6720
   6514 E 26th St Commerce (90040) *(P-10493)*
Crucial Power Products ...................................................... F ...... 323 721-5017
   14000 S Broadway Los Angeles (90061) *(P-12949)*
Crumbl Cookies .................................................................... D ...... 949 519-0791
   23702 El Toro Rd Ste B Lake Forest (92630) *(P-1269)*
Crush Master Grinding Corp ............................................. E ...... 909 595-2249
   755 Penarth Ave Walnut (91789) *(P-10793)*
Crushvirus, Hayward *Also Called: Twin Bridges Technologies LLC (P-16562)*
Crydom Inc (DH) ................................................................. E ...... 619 210-1590
   2320 Paseo De Las Americas Ste 201 San Diego (92154) *(P-11314)*
Cryogenic Experts, Oxnard *Also Called: Acme Cryogenics Inc (P-9823)*
Cryogenic Experts Inc ........................................................ E ...... 805 981-4500
   531 Sandy Cir Oxnard (93036) *(P-9845)*
Cryogenic Industries, Murrieta *Also Called: Hexco International (P-9864)*
Cryogenic Industries Inc ................................................... E ...... 714 568-0201
   1326 N Santiago St Santa Ana (92701) *(P-9846)*
Cryogenic Industries Inc ................................................... C ...... 951 677-2060
   25720 Jefferson Ave Murrieta (92562) *(P-11403)*
Cryomax USA Inc (HQ) ....................................................... F ...... 626 330-3388
   127 N California Ave Ste B City Of Industry (91744) *(P-16287)*
Cryoport Systems LLC (HQ) ............................................ F ...... 949 470-2300
   19000 Macarthur Blvd Ste 800 Irvine (92612) *(P-9847)*
Cryostar USA, Whittier *Also Called: Messer LLC (P-5054)*
Cryostar USA LLC ............................................................... D ...... 562 903-1290
   13117 Meyer Rd Whittier (90605) *(P-9918)*
Cryotech International Inc ................................................ E ...... 408 371-3303
   161 Baypointe Pkwy San Jose (95134) *(P-9253)*
Cryowest Inc ........................................................................ E ...... 831 786-9721
   25 Hangar Way Watsonville (95076) *(P-8314)*
Cryoworks Inc ..................................................................... D ...... 951 360-0920
   3309 Grapevine St Mira Loma (91752) *(P-9254)*
Cryptic Studios Inc ............................................................ D ...... 408 399-1969
   980 University Ave Los Gatos (95032) *(P-15744)*
Cryst Mark Inc A Swan Techno C .................................. E ...... 818 240-7520
   613 Justin Ave Glendale (91201) *(P-9848)*
Crystal, Riverside *Also Called: Crystal PCF Win & Door Sys LLC (P-8261)*
Crystal Art Gallery, Vernon *Also Called: Rggd Inc (P-16985)*
Crystal Blue Inc .................................................................. E ...... 510 783-5888
   236 S Puente Dr Tracy (95391) *(P-9280)*
Crystal Castle, Pomona *Also Called: Golden Grove Trading Inc (P-4883)*
Crystal Cream & Butter Co (HQ) ................................... D ...... 916 444-7200
   8340 Belvedere Ave Sacramento (95826) *(P-831)*
Crystal Creamery, Modesto *Also Called: Foster Dairy Farms (P-17129)*
Crystal Dynamics Inc (HQ) .............................................. E ...... 650 421-7600
   2855 Campus Dr Ste 200 San Mateo (94403) *(P-18212)*
Crystal Engineering Corp ................................................. E ...... 805 595-5477
   708 Fiero Ln Ste 9 San Luis Obispo (93401) *(P-14400)*
Crystal Form, Santa Fe Springs *Also Called: Coated Fabrics Company (P-17226)*
Crystal Geyser Water Company (DH) ........................... E ...... 888 424-1977
   501 Washington St Calistoga (94515) *(P-1882)*
Crystal Geyser Water Company ..................................... E ...... 661 323-6296
   1233 E California Ave Bakersfield (93307) *(P-1883)*
Crystal Geyser Water Company ..................................... E ...... 661 321-0896
   2351 E Brundage Ln Ste A Bakersfield (93307) *(P-1884)*
Crystal Mark, Glendale *Also Called: Cryst Mark Inc A Swan Techno C (P-9848)*
Crystal PCF Win & Door Sys LLC ................................. C ...... 951 779-9300
   1850 Atlanta Ave Riverside (92507) *(P-8261)*
Crystal Technology, Fremont *Also Called: Gooch & Housego Palo Alto LLC (P-12988)*
Crystal Tip, Irvine *Also Called: Westside Resources Inc (P-15495)*
Cs Electronics, Irvine *Also Called: Cs Systems Inc (P-10354)*
Cs Systems Inc ................................................................... E ...... 949 475-9100
   16781 Noyes Ave Irvine (92606) *(P-10354)*
CSDS, Sacramento *Also Called: Califrnia Srvying Drftg Sup In (P-17850)*
Csi, Santa Clarita *Also Called: Custom Suppression Inc (P-12837)*

Csi Technologies Inc ......................................................... F ...... 760 682-2222
   2540 Fortune Way Vista (92081) *(P-12816)*
CSM Metal Fabricating & Engrg, Los Angeles *Also Called: Commercial Shtmtl Works Inc (P-8122)*
Csr Technology Inc (DH) .................................................. E ...... 408 523-6500
   1060 Rincon Cir San Jose (95131) *(P-12950)*
CTA Fixtures Inc ................................................................. D ...... 909 390-6744
   5721 Santa Ana St Ste B Ontario (91761) *(P-3682)*
CTA Manufacturing Inc ..................................................... E ...... 951 280-2400
   1160 California Ave Corona (92881) *(P-2956)*
Ctbla Inc ................................................................................ D ...... 323 276-1933
   1740 Albion St Los Angeles (90031) *(P-13405)*
Ctc Global, Irvine *Also Called: Ctc Global Corporation (P-11447)*
Ctc Global Corporation (PA) ........................................... C ...... 949 428-8500
   2026 Mcgaw Ave Irvine (92614) *(P-11447)*
Ctd Machines Inc ............................................................... F ...... 213 689-4455
   7355 E Slauson Ave Commerce (90040) *(P-9546)*
Cte California TI & Engrg Inc .......................................... E
   7801 Bolero Dr Jurupa Valley (92509) *(P-9672)*
Ctek Inc ................................................................................. E ...... 310 241-2973
   2425 Golden Hill Rd Ste 106 Paso Robles (93446) *(P-16336)*
Ctf, Perris *Also Called: California Trusframe LLC (P-3300)*
Ctg, Santa Barbara *Also Called: Channel Technologies Group LLC (P-14169)*
CTI, Rancho Cordova *Also Called: Chemical Technologies Intl Inc (P-10546)*
CTI Foods Azusa LLC ...................................................... C ...... 626 633-1609
   1120 W Foothill Blvd Azusa (91702) *(P-638)*
Cti-Controltech, San Ramon *Also Called: Cti-Controltech Inc (P-11315)*
Cti-Controltech Inc ............................................................ F ...... 925 208-4250
   22 Beta Ct San Ramon (94583) *(P-11315)*
Ctr America ......................................................................... F ...... 323 332-1417
   530 Technology Dr Ste 100 Irvine (92618) *(P-6788)*
CTS, San Jose *Also Called: CTS Corporation (P-12084)*
CTS Cement Manufacturing Co, Los Angeles *Also Called: CTS Cement Manufacturing Corp (P-6223)*
CTS Cement Manufacturing Corp ................................. E ...... 310 472-4004
   2077 Linda Flora Dr Los Angeles (90077) *(P-6223)*
CTS Cement Manufacturing Corp (PA) ....................... E ...... 714 379-8260
   12442 Knott St Garden Grove (92841) *(P-7255)*
CTS Corporation ................................................................. F ...... 408 955-9001
   2271 Ringwood Ave San Jose (95131) *(P-12084)*
CTS Electronics Manufacturing Solutions (santa Clara) Inc ........ B ...... 408 754-9800
   5550 Hellyer Ave San Jose (95138) *(P-10145)*
CTT Inc., San Jose *Also Called: Kratos Microwave Inc (P-11872)*
Ctu Precast, Olivehurst *Also Called: Precast Con Tech Unlimited LLC (P-7373)*
Cubic, San Diego *Also Called: Cubic Corporation (P-14174)*
Cubic, San Diego *Also Called: Cubic Trnsp Systems Inc (P-17904)*
Cubic Corporation (HQ) .................................................... A ...... 858 277-6780
   9233 Balboa Ave San Diego (92123) *(P-14174)*
Cubic Defense Applications Inc .................................... A ...... 858 277-6780
   4285 Ponderosa Ave San Diego (92123) *(P-13228)*
Cubic Defense Applications Inc (DH) .......................... A ...... 858 776-5664
   9233 Balboa Ave San Diego (92123) *(P-13229)*
Cubic Defense Applications Inc .................................... C ...... 858 505-2870
   9233 Balboa Ave San Diego (92123) *(P-13230)*
Cubic Ground Training, San Diego *Also Called: Cubic Defense Applications Inc (P-13229)*
Cubic Transportation System, Concord *Also Called: Cubic Trnsp Systems Inc (P-14858)*
Cubic Trnsp Systems Inc ................................................ E ...... 925 348-9163
   1800 Sutter St Ste 900 Concord (94520) *(P-14858)*
Cubic Trnsp Systems Inc (DH) ...................................... A ...... 858 268-3100
   9233 Balboa Ave San Diego (92123) *(P-17904)*
Cudoform Inc., Camarillo *Also Called: Cudoquanta Photonics Inc (P-8832)*
Cudoquanta Photonics Inc .............................................. F ...... 805 617-0818
   802 Calle Plano Camarillo (93012) *(P-8832)*
Culinary Brands Inc (PA) ................................................. E ...... 626 289-3000
   3280 E 44th St Vernon (90058) *(P-1031)*
Culinary Farms, Santa Rosa *Also Called: Cfarms Inc (P-2162)*
Culinary Farms Inc ............................................................ E ...... 916 375-3000
   1244 E Beamer St Woodland (95776) *(P-950)*
Culinary International LLC (PA) .................................... C ...... 626 289-3000
   3280 E 44th St Vernon (90058) *(P-2176)*

# Culinary Specialties

**ALPHABETIC SECTION**

**Culinary Specialties, San Marcos** *Also Called: Culinary Specialties Inc (P-2177)*
**Culinary Specialties Inc** ............................................................. D ...... 760 744-8220
1231 Linda Vista Dr San Marcos (92078) *(P-2177)*
**Cult/Cvlt LLC** ............................................................................... E ...... 714 435-2858
1555 E Saint Gertrude Pl Santa Ana (92705) *(P-14055)*
**Culture AMP Inc (HQ)** ................................................................. F ...... 415 326-8453
16501 Ventura Blvd Ste 400 Encino (91436) *(P-18213)*
**Cultured Stone Corporation (PA)** .............................................. A ...... 707 255-1727
Hwy 29 & Tower Rd Napa (94559) *(P-7325)*
**Cummings Resources LLC** ........................................................ E ...... 951 248-1130
330 W Citrus St Colton (92324) *(P-15963)*
**Cummings Resources LLC** ........................................................ E ...... 951 248-1130
1495 Columbia Ave Riverside (92507) *(P-15964)*
**Cummings Transportation, Bakersfield** *Also Called: Cummings Vacuum Service Inc (P-221)*
**Cummings Vacuum Service Inc** ................................................ D ...... 661 746-1786
112 El Paso Rd Bakersfield (93314) *(P-221)*
**Cummins, Bloomington** *Also Called: Cummins Pacific LLC (P-9322)*
**Cummins, Fresno** *Also Called: Cummins Pacific LLC (P-9323)*
**Cummins, Irvine** *Also Called: Cummins Pacific LLC (P-9324)*
**Cummins, El Cajon** *Also Called: Cummins Pacific LLC (P-9325)*
**Cummins, Ventura** *Also Called: Cummins Pacific LLC (P-9326)*
**Cummins, Arcata** *Also Called: Cummins Pacific LLC (P-13480)*
**Cummins, San Leandro** *Also Called: Cummins West Inc (P-16811)*
**Cummins Aerospace, Anaheim** *Also Called: Cummins Aerospace LLC (P-14175)*
**Cummins Aerospace LLC (PA)** .................................................. E ...... 714 879-2800
2320 E Orangethorpe Ave Anaheim (92806) *(P-14175)*
**Cummins Pacific LLC** ................................................................. F ...... 909 877-0433
3061 S Riverside Ave Bloomington (92316) *(P-9322)*
**Cummins Pacific LLC** ................................................................ E ...... 559 277-6760
2755 S Cherry Ave Fresno (93706) *(P-9323)*
**Cummins Pacific LLC (HQ)** ....................................................... D ...... 949 253-6000
1939 Deere Ave Irvine (92606) *(P-9324)*
**Cummins Pacific LLC** ................................................................ F ...... 619 593-3093
310 N Johnson Ave El Cajon (92020) *(P-9325)*
**Cummins Pacific LLC** ................................................................ F ...... 805 644-7281
3958 Transport St Ventura (93003) *(P-9326)*
**Cummins Pacific LLC** ................................................................ E ...... 707 822-7392
5150 Boyd Rd Arcata (95521) *(P-13480)*
**Cummins West Inc** ..................................................................... B ...... 510 351-6101
14775 Wicks Blvd San Leandro (94577) *(P-16811)*
**Cumulus Networks, Mountain View** *Also Called: Cumulus Networks Inc (P-18214)*
**Cumulus Networks Inc (HQ)** ..................................................... C ...... 650 383-6700
185 E Dana St Mountain View (94041) *(P-18214)*
**Cunico Corporation** ................................................................... E ...... 562 733-4600
1910 W 16th St Long Beach (90813) *(P-9255)*
**Cupix America Inc** ..................................................................... D ...... 650 785-2122
3003 N 1st St San Jose (95134) *(P-4869)*
**Curacubby Inc** ............................................................................ D ...... 415 200-3373
2120 University Ave Berkeley (94704) *(P-18215)*
**Curae Pharma360 Inc** ................................................................ E ...... 415 951-8700
49 Stevenson St Ste 1100 San Francisco (94105) *(P-5416)*
**Curation Foods Inc (HQ)** ........................................................... D ...... 800 454-1355
2811 Airpark Dr Santa Maria (93455) *(P-2178)*
**Cure Apparel Llc** ........................................................................ F ...... 562 927-7460
3338 S Malt Ave Commerce (90040) *(P-2662)*
**Curemetrix Inc** ............................................................................ E ...... 858 333-5830
402 W Broadway Ste 400 San Diego (92101) *(P-18216)*
**Curio Home Goods, Van Nuys** *Also Called: Munchkin Inc (P-6610)*
**CURRAN ENGINEERING COMPANY I** ..................................... E ...... 800 643-6353
28727 Industry Dr Valencia (91355) *(P-8622)*
**Current Renewables Engrg Inc** ................................................ F ...... 951 405-1733
3600 Lime St Riverside (92501) *(P-19386)*
**Current Ways Inc** ....................................................................... F ...... 619 596-3984
10221 Buena Vista Ave Santee (92071) *(P-11368)*
**Currie Acquisitions LLC** ........................................................... E ...... 805 915-4900
3850 Royal Ave Ste A Simi Valley (93063) *(P-14056)*
**Currie Enterprises** ..................................................................... D ...... 714 528-6957
382 N Smith Ave Corona (92878) *(P-13481)*
**Currie Technologies, Simi Valley** *Also Called: Currie Acquisitions LLC (P-14056)*
**Curry Company LLC** ................................................................. E ...... 310 643-8400
15724 Condon Ave Lawndale (90260) *(P-9673)*

**Curtco Media Group** .................................................................. F ...... 310 589-7700
29160 Heathercliff Rd Fl 1 Malibu (90265) *(P-4243)*
**Curtco Robb Media LLC (PA)** ................................................... E ...... 310 589-7700
29160 Heathercliff Rd Ste 200 Malibu (90265) *(P-4244)*
**Curtis Industries, Visalia** *Also Called: Powers Holdings Inc (P-13064)*
**Curtis Winery, Los Olivos** *Also Called: Firestone Vineyard LP (P-1569)*
**Curtiss-Wrght Cntrls Elctrnic (DH)** .......................................... C ...... 661 257-4430
28965 Avenue Penn Santa Clarita (91355) *(P-11316)*
**Curtiss-Wrght Cntrls Elctrnic, Santa Clarita** *Also Called: Curtiss-Wrght Cntrls Elctrnic (P-11316)*
**Curtiss-Wrght Cntrls Intgrted** ................................................... D ...... 714 982-1860
210 Ranger Ave Brea (92821) *(P-15330)*
**Curtiss-Wrght Nclear Div Enrte, Brea** *Also Called: Curtiss-Wright Flow Ctrl Corp (P-9154)*
**Curtiss-Wright Controls Inc** ..................................................... E ...... 818 503-0998
6940 Farmdale Ave North Hollywood (91605) *(P-13818)*
**Curtiss-Wright Corporation** ..................................................... D ...... 661 257-4430
28965 Avenue Penn Santa Clarita (91355) *(P-9150)*
**Curtiss-Wright Corporation** ..................................................... D ...... 619 482-3405
1675 Brandywine Ave Ste F Chula Vista (91911) *(P-9151)*
**Curtiss-Wright Corporation** ..................................................... E ...... 619 656-4740
1675 Brandywine Ave Ste E Chula Vista (91911) *(P-19250)*
**Curtiss-Wright Flow Control** .................................................... C ...... 626 851-3100
28965 Avenue Penn Valencia (91355) *(P-9152)*
**Curtiss-Wright Flow Ctrl Corp** ................................................. E ...... 949 271-7500
2950 E Birch St Brea (92821) *(P-9153)*
**Curtiss-Wright Flow Ctrl Corp** ................................................. D ...... 714 528-2301
260 Ranger Ave Brea (92821) *(P-9154)*
**Curtiss-Wright Flow Ctrl Corp (DH)** ........................................ D ...... 714 528-1365
2950 E Birch St Brea (92821) *(P-9184)*
**Curtiss-Wright Surfc Tech LLC** ................................................ F ...... 714 546-4160
2151 S Hathaway St Santa Ana (92705) *(P-7885)*
**Cushman Winery Corporation** ................................................. E ...... 805 688-9339
6905 Foxen Canyon Rd Los Olivos (93441) *(P-17263)*
**Custom Alloy Light Metals, City Of Industry** *Also Called: Custom Alloy Sales Inc (P-7717)*
**Custom Alloy Sales Inc (PA)** .................................................... F ...... 626 369-3641
13181 Crossroads Pkwy N Ste 440 City Of Industry (91746) *(P-7717)*
**Custom Almonds** ....................................................................... E ...... 559 346-8212
7014 Road 160 Earlimart (93219) *(P-1350)*
**Custom Aviation Supply, Chatsworth** *Also Called: Custom Control Sensors LLC (P-11239)*
**Custom Building Products Inc** ................................................. E ...... 209 983-8322
3525 Zephyr Ct Stockton (95206) *(P-9419)*
**Custom Building Products LLC (DH)** ..................................... D ...... 800 272-8786
7711 Center Ave Ste 500 Huntington Beach (92647) *(P-6224)*
**Custom Building Products LLC** .............................................. C ...... 323 582-0846
6511 Salt Lake Ave Bell (90201) *(P-6225)*
**Custom Building Products LLC** .............................................. D ...... 661 393-0422
1900 Norris Rd Bakersfield (93308) *(P-16869)*
**Custom Building Products, Inc., Stockton** *Also Called: Custom Building Products Inc (P-9419)*
**Custom Built Machinery Inc** ..................................................... E ...... 714 424-9250
2614 S Hickory St Santa Ana (92707) *(P-19387)*
**Custom Carbon Composite Creations Inc** ............................ E ...... 209 845-2930
693 Hi Tech Pkwy Oakdale (95361) *(P-15331)*
**Custom Characters Inc** ............................................................. F ...... 818 507-5940
621 Thompson Ave Glendale (91201) *(P-2895)*
**Custom Chemical Formulators, Santa Fe Springs** *Also Called: Morgan Gallacher Inc (P-5917)*
**Custom Cmpstes Fbrgls Fbrction, Olivehurst** *Also Called: Ace Composites Inc (P-6693)*
**Custom Coils Inc** ....................................................................... F ...... 707 752-8633
4000 Industrial Way Benicia (94510) *(P-12836)*
**Custom Control Sensors Inc** ................................................... F ...... 818 341-4610
21111 Plummer St Chatsworth (91311) *(P-11317)*
**Custom Control Sensors LLC (PA)** ......................................... C ...... 818 341-4610
21111 Plummer St Chatsworth (91311) *(P-11239)*
**Custom Crushing Industries Inc** ............................................. E ...... 530 842-5544
2409 E Oberlin Rd Yreka (96097) *(P-112)*
**Custom Engineering Plastics, San Diego** *Also Called: Custom Engineering Plastics LP (P-6789)*
**Custom Engineering Plastics LP** ............................................. F ...... 858 452-0961
8558 Miramar Pl San Diego (92121) *(P-6789)*
**Custom Fibreglass Mfg Co** ...................................................... C ...... 562 432-5454
1711 Harbor Ave Long Beach (90813) *(P-14119)*

# ALPHABETIC SECTION

Custom Flavors, San Clemente *Also Called: Custom Ingredients Inc (P-1995)*
Custom Foods, Santa Fe Springs *Also Called: J & J Processing Inc (P-2010)*
Custom Furniture Designs, LLC, Chino *Also Called: Royal Custom Designs LLC (P-3488)*
Custom Hardtops, Long Beach *Also Called: Custom Fibreglass Mfg Co (P-14119)*
Custom Home Accessories, Rancho Cordova *Also Called: Penfield Products Inc (P-8535)*
Custom Industries Inc .................................................................. E ...... 714 779-9101
  1371 N Miller St Anaheim (92806) *(P-7217)*
Custom Ingredients Inc (PA) ........................................................ E ...... 949 276-7995
  160 Calle Iglesia Ste 102 San Clemente (92672) *(P-1995)*
Custom Iron Corporation ............................................................. F ...... 949 939-4379
  26895 Aliso Creek Rd Ste B787 Aliso Viejo (92656) *(P-8127)*
Custom Label, Hayward *Also Called: Custom Label & Decal LLC (P-4870)*
Custom Label & Decal LLC .......................................................... E ...... 510 876-0000
  3392 Investment Blvd Hayward (94545) *(P-4870)*
Custom Leathercraft Mfg LLC ..................................................... D
  5701 S Eastern Ave Commerce (90040) *(P-7154)*
Custom Line Shower Door Co, Sacramento *Also Called: Atlas Specialties Corporation (P-7211)*
Custom Logos Inc ........................................................................ E ...... 858 277-1886
  7889 Clairemont Mesa Blvd San Diego (92111) *(P-2491)*
Custom Magnetics Cal Inc .......................................................... E ...... 909 620-3877
  15142 Vista Del Rio Ave Chino (91710) *(P-11208)*
Custom Micro Machining Inc ..................................................... E ...... 510 651-9434
  365 Reed St Santa Clara (95050) *(P-10794)*
Custom Molded Devices, Simi Valley *Also Called: Poly-Tainer Inc (P-6614)*
Custom Packaging Design, Montclair *Also Called: Cpd Industries (P-6784)*
Custom Pad and Partition Inc .................................................... D ...... 408 970-9711
  1100 Richard Ave Santa Clara (95050) *(P-3838)*
Custom Paper Products LP ........................................................ D ...... 510 352-6880
  2360 Teagarden St San Leandro (94577) *(P-3814)*
Custom Pipe & Fabrication Inc (HQ) ......................................... D ...... 800 553-3058
  10560 Fern Ave Stanton (90680) *(P-9256)*
Custom Quilting Inc .................................................................... E ...... 714 731-7271
  2832 Walnut Ave Ste D Tustin (92780) *(P-2927)*
Custom Sensors & Tech Inc ........................................................ B ...... 805 716-0322
  2475 Paseo De Las Americas San Diego (92154) *(P-12951)*
Custom Sensors & Tech Inc (HQ) ............................................... A ...... 805 716-0322
  1461 Lawrence Dr Thousand Oaks (91320) *(P-12952)*
Custom Steel Fabrication Inc ..................................................... F ...... 562 907-2777
  11966 Rivera Rd Santa Fe Springs (90670) *(P-8128)*
Custom Suppression Inc ............................................................ F ...... 818 718-1040
  26470 Ruether Ave Ste 106 Santa Clarita (91350) *(P-12837)*
Custom Truck One Source LP .................................................... E ...... 316 627-2608
  4500 State Rd Bakersfield (93308) *(P-13406)*
Custom Vinyls, Fontana *Also Called: Patrick Industries Inc (P-16481)*
Custom Wood Products, Parlier *Also Called: John Daniel Gonzalez (P-3372)*
Customfab Inc ............................................................................. C ...... 714 891-9119
  7345 Orangewood Ave Garden Grove (92841) *(P-7086)*
Cut and Sew Co Inc .................................................................... C ...... 714 981-7244
  1939 S Susan St Santa Ana (92704) *(P-2465)*
Cut Loose (PA) ............................................................................. D ...... 415 822-2031
  101 Williams Ave San Francisco (94124) *(P-2749)*
CUTERA, Brisbane *Also Called: Cutera Inc (P-15528)*
Cutera Inc (PA) ............................................................................ C ...... 415 657-5500
  3240 Bayshore Blvd Brisbane (94005) *(P-15528)*
Cutie Pie Snack Pies, Lathrop *Also Called: Horizon Snack Foods Inc (P-1287)*
Cutter Lumber Products ............................................................. E ...... 209 982-4477
  4004 S El Dorado St Stockton (95206) *(P-3338)*
Cutting Edge Creative LLC ......................................................... D ...... 562 907-7007
  9944 Flower St Bellflower (90706) *(P-3683)*
Cutting Edge Machining Inc (PA) ............................................... E ...... 408 738-8677
  1331 Old County Rd Belmont (94002) *(P-10795)*
Cutting Edge Supply, Colton *Also Called: Black Diamond Blade Company (P-9409)*
Cutwater Spirits LLC (HQ) .......................................................... D ...... 858 672-3848
  9750 Distribution Ave San Diego (92121) *(P-6279)*
Cv Ingenuity Corp ....................................................................... E ...... 508 261-8000
  6531 Dumbarton Cir Fremont (94555) *(P-14334)*
Cv Sciences Inc (PA) ................................................................... E ...... 866 290-2157
  9530 Padgett St Ste 107 San Diego (92126) *(P-5417)*
Cvag, Oakdale *Also Called: Central Valley AG Grinding LLC (P-78)*

Cvc Specialties, Vernon *Also Called: Continental Vitamin Co Inc (P-5408)*
Cvc Technologies Inc .................................................................. E ...... 909 355-0311
  10861 Business Dr Fontana (92337) *(P-10017)*
Cw Industries Inc (PA) ................................................................ E ...... 562 432-5421
  1735 Santa Fe Ave Long Beach (90813) *(P-19188)*
Cwdre, Irvine *Also Called: Certified Wtr Dmage Rstrtion E (P-17846)*
Cwes Inc ...................................................................................... E ...... 559 346-1251
  3045 N Sunnyside Ave Ste 101 Fresno (93727) *(P-19556)*
Cwi Steel Technologies Corporation ......................................... E ...... 949 476-7600
  2415 Campus Dr Ste 100 Irvine (92612) *(P-7697)*
Cwic, Rcho Sta Marg *Also Called: Chapmn-Wlters Intrcoastal Corp (P-15799)*
Cwp Cabinets Inc ........................................................................ C ...... 760 246-4530
  15447 Anacapa Rd Ste 102 Victorville (92392) *(P-488)*
Cwr Labs, Milpitas *Also Called: Cpacket Networks Inc (P-10353)*
Cws, Orange *Also Called: Coil Winding Specialist Inc (P-12834)*
CWT, Gardena *Also Called: Clean Water Technology Inc (P-10550)*
Cxapp Inc ..................................................................................... D ...... 650 575-4456
  4 Palo Alto Sq Ste 200 Palo Alto (94306) *(P-18217)*
Cy Truss ....................................................................................... E ...... 559 888-2160
  10715 E American Ave Del Rey (93616) *(P-3305)*
Cyantek Corporation .................................................................. E
  3055 Osgood Ct Fremont (94539) *(P-6280)*
Cyber Medical Imaging Inc ........................................................ E ...... 888 937-9729
  11300 W Olympic Blvd Ste 710 Los Angeles (90064) *(P-15444)*
Cyber Press, Santa Clara *Also Called: Nss Enterprises (P-4708)*
Cyberbasket Inc .......................................................................... F ...... 619 450-6700
  2926 Main St San Diego (92113) *(P-17655)*
Cybercopy Inc (PA) ..................................................................... F ...... 310 736-1001
  2766 S La Cienega Blvd Los Angeles (90034) *(P-17808)*
Cyberdata Corporation .............................................................. E ...... 831 373-2601
  3 Justin Ct Monterey (93940) *(P-10355)*
Cyberdefender Corporation ...................................................... F ...... 323 449-0774
  617 W 7th St Fl 10 Los Angeles (90017) *(P-17905)*
Cyberinc Corporation (HQ) ........................................................ E ...... 925 242-0777
  4000 Executive Pkwy Ste 250 San Ramon (94583) *(P-18218)*
Cybernet Manufacturing Inc ..................................................... A ...... 949 600-8000
  5 Holland Ste 201 Irvine (92618) *(P-10146)*
Cycle News Inc (PA) .................................................................... E ...... 949 863-7082
  17771 Mitchell N Irvine (92614) *(P-4100)*
Cycling 74 Corp ........................................................................... E ...... 415 689-5777
  433 Meder St Santa Cruz (95060) *(P-18219)*
Cydea Inc ..................................................................................... E ...... 800 710-9939
  8510 Miralani Dr San Diego (92126) *(P-1523)*
Cydwoq Inc .................................................................................. E ...... 818 848-8307
  2102 Kenmere Ave Burbank (91504) *(P-7092)*
Cygnet Stampng & Fabrictng Inc (PA) ....................................... E ...... 818 240-7574
  613 Justin Ave Glendale (91201) *(P-8833)*
Cylance Inc (DH) ......................................................................... D ...... 949 375-3380
  3001 Bishop Dr Ste 400 San Ramon (94583) *(P-18220)*
Cylinder Division, Corona *Also Called: Parker-Hannifin Corporation (P-10634)*
Cymabay Therapeutics Inc (PA) ................................................. D ...... 650 574-3000
  333 Lakeside Dr Foster City (94404) *(P-5418)*
Cymbiotika LLC (PA) ................................................................... E ...... 770 910-4945
  5825 Oberlin Dr Ste 5 San Diego (92121) *(P-5419)*
Cymbiotika LLC ........................................................................... D ...... 949 652-8177
  8885 Rehco Rd San Diego (92121) *(P-5420)*
Cymer LLC (HQ) .......................................................................... A ...... 858 385-7300
  17075 Thornmint Ct San Diego (92127) *(P-13231)*
Cynergy Prof Systems LLC ......................................................... E ...... 800 776-7978
  23187 La Cadena Dr Ste 102 Laguna Hills (92653) *(P-16697)*
CYNGN, Menlo Park *Also Called: Cyngn Inc (P-13346)*
Cyngn Inc (PA) ............................................................................. D ...... 650 924-5905
  1015 Obrien Dr Menlo Park (94025) *(P-13346)*
Cyp Online Inc ............................................................................. F ...... 510 516-6589
  4500 Great America Pkwy Ste 93 Santa Clara (95054) *(P-4385)*
Cypress, San Jose *Also Called: Cypress Semiconductor Corp (P-12397)*
Cypress Envirosystems Inc ........................................................ E ...... 800 544-5411
  5883 Rue Ferrari Ste 100 San Jose (95119) *(P-14359)*
Cypress Grove Chevre Inc ......................................................... D ...... 707 825-1100
  1330 Q St Arcata (95521) *(P-710)*

**Cypress Magazines Inc** ............................................................ F ...... 858 503-7572
  5715 Kearny Villa Rd Ste 107 San Diego (92123) *(P-4245)*

**Cypress Semiconductor Corp (HQ)** ...................................... A ...... 408 943-2600
  198 Champion Ct San Jose (95134) *(P-12397)*

**Cypress Semiconductor Intl Inc (DH)** .................................. E ...... 408 943-2600
  4001 N 1st St San Jose (95134) *(P-12398)*

**Cytec, Anaheim** *Also Called: Cytec Engineered Materials Inc (P-5150)*

**Cytec Engineered Materials Inc** ............................................ E ...... 714 632-8444
  1191 N Hawk Cir Anaheim (92807) *(P-5150)*

**Cytec Engineered Materials Inc** ............................................ C ...... 714 630-9400
  645 N Cypress St Orange (92867) *(P-6281)*

**Cytec Engineered Materials Inc** ............................................ C ...... 714 632-1174
  1440 N Kraemer Blvd Anaheim (92806) *(P-7841)*

**Cytec Solvay Group** ............................................................... F ...... 714 630-9400
  1440 N Kraemer Blvd Anaheim (92806) *(P-5085)*

**Cytek Biosciences Inc (PA)** ................................................... B ...... 510 657-0102
  47215 Lakeview Blvd Fremont (94538) *(P-14649)*

**CYTOKINETICS, South San Francisco** *Also Called: Cytokinetics Incorporated (P-5421)*

**Cytokinetics Incorporated (PA)** ............................................. B ...... 650 624-3000
  350 Oyster Point Blvd South San Francisco (94080) *(P-5421)*

**CYTOMX THERAPEUTICS, South San Francisco** *Also Called: Cytomx Therapeutics Inc (P-5422)*

**Cytomx Therapeutics Inc** ....................................................... C ...... 650 515-3185
  151 Oyster Point Blvd Ste 400 South San Francisco (94080) *(P-5422)*

**Cytosport Inc** ........................................................................... C ...... 707 751-3942
  1340 Treat Blvd Ste 350 Walnut Creek (94597) *(P-753)*

**Cyu Lithographics Inc** ............................................................ E ...... 888 878-9898
  6951 Oran Cir Buena Park (90621) *(P-4580)*

**Czinger Vehicles, Torrance** *Also Called: Czv Inc (P-13347)*

**Czv Inc** ..................................................................................... D ...... 424 603-1450
  19601 Hamilton Ave Torrance (90502) *(P-13347)*

**D - Link, Irvine** *Also Called: D-Link Systems Incorporated (P-16516)*

**D & D Cbnets - Svage Dsgns Inc** .......................................... E ...... 530 634-9713
  1478 Sky Harbor Dr Olivehurst (95961) *(P-3234)*

**D & D Cremations Service, Vernon** *Also Called: D & D Services Inc (P-1380)*

**D & D Gear Incorporated** ........................................................ C ...... 714 692-6570
  4890 E La Palma Ave Anaheim (92807) *(P-13819)*

**D & D Services Inc** ................................................................. E ...... 323 261-4176
  4105 Bandini Blvd Vernon (90058) *(P-1380)*

**D & H Mfg Co** ........................................................................... C ...... 510 770-5100
  49235 Milmont Dr Fremont (94538) *(P-10796)*

**D & J Printing Inc** ................................................................... D ...... 661 265-1995
  600 W Technology Dr Palmdale (93551) *(P-4581)*

**D & K Engineering (HQ)** .......................................................... C ...... 760 840-2214
  16990 Goldentop Rd San Diego (92127) *(P-14476)*

**D & M Steel Inc** ....................................................................... E ...... 818 896-2070
  13020 Pierce St Pacoima (91331) *(P-8129)*

**D & R Screen Printing Inc** ...................................................... E ...... 562 458-6443
  7314 Pierce Ave Whittier (90602) *(P-4582)*

**D & T Fiberglass Inc** ............................................................... E ...... 916 383-9012
  8900 Osage Ave Sacramento (95828) *(P-6790)*

**D A C, Carpinteria** *Also Called: Dac International Inc (P-9547)*

**D A C, Carpinteria** *Also Called: Development Associates Contrls (P-9548)*

**D and J Marketing Inc** ............................................................ E ...... 310 538-1583
  580 W 184th St Gardena (90248) *(P-3004)*

**D D Office Products Inc** ......................................................... F ...... 323 582-3400
  5025 Hampton St Los Angeles (90058) *(P-3765)*

**D D Wire Co Inc (PA)** .............................................................. E ...... 626 442-0459
  4335 Temple City Blvd Temple City (91780) *(P-8130)*

**D Davis Enterprise, Davis** *Also Called: McNaughton Newspapers (P-4155)*

**D E I, Chino Hills** *Also Called: Dynamic Enterprises Inc (P-10817)*

**D F Stauffer Biscuit Co Inc** .................................................... E ...... 714 546-6855
  4041 W Garry Ave Santa Ana (92704) *(P-1270)*

**D G A Machine Shop Inc** ........................................................ F ...... 951 354-2113
  5825 Ordway St Riverside (92504) *(P-10797)*

**D G A Mch Sp Blnchard Grinding, Riverside** *Also Called: D G A Machine Shop Inc (P-10797)*

**D I F Group Inc** ........................................................................ E ...... 323 231-8800
  2201 Yates Ave Commerce (90040) *(P-19513)*

**D K Environmental, Vernon** *Also Called: Demenno/Kerdoon Holdings (P-6390)*

**D L B Pallets (PA)** .................................................................... F ...... 951 360-9896
  4510 Rutile St Riverside (92509) *(P-3339)*

**D Mills Grnding Machining Inc** .............................................. C ...... 951 697-6847
  1738 N Neville St Orange (92865) *(P-10798)*

**D P I, Porterville** *Also Called: Distributors Processing Inc (P-1998)*

**D P Nicoli Inc** ........................................................................... F ...... 650 873-2999
  266 Harbor Way South San Francisco (94080) *(P-16617)*

**D S I, Santa Rosa** *Also Called: Deposition Sciences Inc (P-19450)*

**D Software Inc** ......................................................................... E ...... 415 795-7466
  75 E Santa Clara St Fl 7 San Jose (95113) *(P-18221)*

**D V S Mdia Srvces/Intelestream, Burbank** *Also Called: Dvs Media Services (P-17810)*

**D W Mack Co Inc** ..................................................................... E ...... 626 969-1817
  900 W 8th St Azusa (91702) *(P-6443)*

**D X Communications Inc** ....................................................... E ...... 323 256-3000
  8160 Van Nuys Blvd Panorama City (91402) *(P-11839)*

**D-K-P Inc** .................................................................................. F ...... 559 266-2695
  275 N Marks Ave Fresno (93706) *(P-9347)*

**D-Link Systems Incorporated** ............................................... C ...... 714 885-6000
  14420 Myford Rd Ste 100 Irvine (92606) *(P-16516)*

**D-Mac Inc** ................................................................................. E ...... 714 808-3918
  1105 E Discovery Ln Anaheim (92801) *(P-3383)*

**D-Tech Optoelectronics Inc** ................................................... E ...... 626 956-1100
  18052 Rowland St City Of Industry (91748) *(P-11989)*

**D-Tek Manufacturing** .............................................................. E ...... 408 588-1574
  3245 Woodward Ave Santa Clara (95054) *(P-12399)*

**D-Wave Quantum Inc** .............................................................. C ...... 604 630-1428
  2650 E Bayshore Rd Palo Alto (94303) *(P-18222)*

**D. Zelinsky & Sons Inc, Oakland** *Also Called: Dz-Fdt LLC (P-444)*

**D.F. Industries, Chino** *Also Called: Dick Farrell Industries Inc (P-10048)*

**D'Ambrosio Bros, Sunnyvale** *Also Called: Fullfillment Systems Inc (P-643)*

**D'Andrea Graphics, Cypress** *Also Called: DAndrea Vsual Cmmncations LLC (P-17825)*

**D&A Metal Fabrication Inc** ..................................................... F ...... 818 780-8231
  16129 Runnymede St Van Nuys (91406) *(P-8131)*

**D&H Manufacturing, Fremont** *Also Called: Celestica LLC (P-12934)*

**D&M Manufacturing Co LLC** .................................................. F ...... 559 834-4668
  5400 S Villa Ave Fresno (93725) *(P-9346)*

**D3 Go, Encino** *Also Called: D3publisher of America Inc (P-18223)*

**D3publisher of America Inc** ................................................... D ...... 310 268-0820
  15910 Ventura Blvd Ste 800 Encino (91436) *(P-18223)*

**Dab Inc** ..................................................................................... D ...... 562 623-4773
  13415 Marquardt Ave Santa Fe Springs (90670) *(P-11493)*

**Dac Heating and AC** ................................................................ F ...... 661 441-2787
  190 Sierra Ct Ste B3 Palmdale (93550) *(P-415)*

**Dac Heating and Air, Palmdale** *Also Called: Dac Heating and AC (P-415)*

**Dac International Inc** .............................................................. E ...... 805 684-8307
  6390 Rose Ln Carpinteria (93013) *(P-9547)*

**Dacenso Inc** ............................................................................. E ...... 888 513-9367
  2030 Main St Ste 1300 Irvine (92614) *(P-18224)*

**Dacha Enterprises Inc (HQ)** ................................................... E ...... 951 273-7777
  13948 Mountain Ave Chino (91710) *(P-6791)*

**Dacha Enterprises Inc** ............................................................ D ...... 951 273-7777
  1915 Elise Cir Corona (92879) *(P-6792)*

**Dacor (DH)** ................................................................................ D ...... 626 799-1000
  14425 Clark Ave City Of Industry (91745) *(P-17533)*

**DAd Investments** ..................................................................... E ...... 714 751-8500
  2929 Halladay St Santa Ana (92705) *(P-2179)*

**DAd Investments** ..................................................................... E ...... 714 751-8500
  2929 Halladay St Santa Ana (92705) *(P-17575)*

**Dado Inc** ................................................................................... E ...... 866 704-7210
  248 3rd St Ste 938 Oakland (94607) *(P-18225)*

**Dae Shin Usa Inc** ..................................................................... D ...... 714 578-8900
  610 N Gilbert St Fullerton (92833) *(P-2434)*

**Dae-IL Usa Inc** ......................................................................... F ...... 562 422-4046
  5712 Cherry Ave Long Beach (90805) *(P-8947)*

**Daico Industries Inc** ................................................................ D ...... 310 507-3242
  1070 E 233rd St Carson (90745) *(P-12953)*

**Daikin Comfort Tech Dist Inc** ................................................ B ...... 209 946-9244
  2601 Teepee Dr Stockton (95205) *(P-19526)*

**Daikin Comfort Tech Mfg LP** .................................................. B ...... 510 265-1212
  3018 Alvarado St Ste C San Leandro (94577) *(P-10494)*

**Daikin Comfort Tech Mfg LP** .................................................. B ...... 760 955-7770
  15024 Anacapa Rd Victorville (92392) *(P-10495)*

## ALPHABETIC SECTION

DAILY CALIFORNIAN, Berkeley *Also Called: Indepndent Brkley Stdnt Pubg I (P-4133)*
Daily Connect, San Francisco *Also Called: Seacloud Software LLC (P-18771)*
Daily Journal Corporation (PA) ............................................. D ...... 213 229-5300
   915 E 1st St Los Angeles (90012) *(P-4101)*
Daily News, The, Whittier *Also Called: Pasadena Newspapers Inc (P-4179)*
Daily Republic, Fairfield *Also Called: McNaughton Newspapers Inc (P-4156)*
Daily Transcript, Laguna Niguel *Also Called: San Diego Daily Transcript (P-3795)*
Dailymedia Inc (PA) ............................................................ F ...... 541 821-5207
   8 E Figueroa St Ste 220 Santa Barbara (93101) *(P-4102)*
Dairy Farmers America Inc ................................................. E ...... 209 667-9627
   600 Trade Way Turlock (95380) *(P-711)*
Dairy Farmers America Inc ................................................. E ...... 805 653-0042
   4375 N Ventura Ave Ventura (93001) *(P-832)*
Daisy Publishing Company Inc ............................................ D ...... 661 295-1910
   25233 Anza Dr Santa Clarita (91355) *(P-4386)*
Dakine Equipment LLC ....................................................... E ...... 424 276-3618
   19400 Harborgate Way Torrance (90501) *(P-2750)*
Dako North America Inc ..................................................... B ...... 805 566-6655
   6392 Via Real Carpinteria (93013) *(P-17034)*
Dakota AG Welding, Modesto *Also Called: Jackrabbit (P-9362)*
Dakota AG Welding, Ripon *Also Called: Jackrabbit (P-9363)*
Dakota Press Inc ................................................................. F ...... 510 895-1300
   14400 Doolittle Dr San Leandro (94577) *(P-4583)*
Dale Brisco Inc .................................................................... F ...... 559 834-5926
   2132 S Temperance Ave Fowler (93625) *(P-8423)*
Dale Vishay Electronics LLC ............................................... E ...... 510 661-4287
   3620 Yale Way Fremont (94538) *(P-12822)*
Dallas Electronics Inc .......................................................... E ...... 831 457-3610
   2151 Delaware Ave Ste A Santa Cruz (95060) *(P-12085)*
Damac, Costa Mesa *Also Called: Bdfco Inc (P-11983)*
Damar Plastics, El Cajon *Also Called: Damar Plastics Manufacturing Inc (P-6793)*
Damar Plastics Manufacturing Inc ...................................... E ...... 619 283-2300
   1035 Pioneer Way Ste 160 El Cajon (92020) *(P-6793)*
Dameron Alloy Foundries (PA) ............................................ D ...... 310 631-5165
   6330 Gateway Dr Ste B Cypress (90630) *(P-7698)*
Damo Clothing Company, Los Angeles *Also Called: Damo Textile Inc (P-17086)*
Damo Textile Inc ................................................................. E ...... 213 741-1323
   12121 Wilshire Blvd Ste 1120 Los Angeles (90025) *(P-17086)*
Dan Gurneys All Amercn Racers, Santa Ana *Also Called: All American Racers Inc (P-14052)*
Dan-Loc Bolt & Gasket, Carson *Also Called: Dan-Loc Group LLC (P-6444)*
Dan-Loc Group LLC ............................................................ D ...... 310 538-2822
   20444 Tillman Ave Carson (90746) *(P-6444)*
Dana Creath Designs Ltd ................................................... E ...... 714 662-0111
   3030 Kilson Dr Santa Ana (92707) *(P-11589)*
Dana Estates Inc (PA) ........................................................ E ...... 707 963-4365
   1500 Whitehall Ln Saint Helena (94574) *(P-1524)*
Dana Innovations (PA) ........................................................ C ...... 949 492-7777
   991 Calle Amanecer San Clemente (92673) *(P-11647)*
Dana Motors Inc (PA) ......................................................... F ...... 916 920-0150
   901 Arden Way Sacramento (95815) *(P-16379)*
Danchuk Manufacturing Inc ............................................... D ...... 714 540-4363
   3211 Halladay St Santa Ana (92705) *(P-13482)*
Danco, Ontario *Also Called: Danco Anodizing Inc (P-8948)*
Danco Anodizing Inc .......................................................... C ...... 909 923-0562
   1750 E Monticello Ct Ontario (91761) *(P-8948)*
Danco Anodizing Inc (PA) .................................................. E ...... 626 445-3303
   44 La Porte St Arcadia (91006) *(P-8949)*
Danco Machine, Santa Clara *Also Called: P M S D Inc (P-11020)*
Danco Metal Surfacing, Arcadia *Also Called: Danco Anodizing Inc (P-8949)*
Danco Valve Company ....................................................... E ...... 562 925-2588
   15230 Lakewood Blvd Bellflower (90706) *(P-9155)*
DAndrea Vsual Cmmncations LLC .................................... D ...... 714 947-8444
   6100 Gateway Dr Cypress (90630) *(P-17825)*
Dane Elec Corp USA (HQ) .................................................. E ...... 949 450-2900
   17520 Von Karman Ave Irvine (92614) *(P-16517)*
Daniel Gerard Worldwide Inc ............................................. D ...... 951 361-1111
   13055 Jurupa Ave Fontana (92337) *(P-16618)*
Daniel Loria Novartis .......................................................... E ...... 510 655-8729
   4560 Horton St Emeryville (94608) *(P-5423)*
Daniel Rainn, Commerce *Also Called: Au Merrow Corporation (P-2655)*

Daniels Inc (PA) .................................................................. E ...... 801 621-3355
   74745 Leslie Ave Palm Desert (92260) *(P-4387)*
Danisco US Inc (HQ) ........................................................... C ...... 650 846-7500
   925 Page Mill Rd Palo Alto (94304) *(P-5746)*
Danish Baking Co Inc ......................................................... D ...... 818 786-1700
   15215 Keswick St Van Nuys (91405) *(P-1179)*
Danmer Custom Shutters, Van Nuys *Also Called: Danmer Inc (P-3124)*
Danmer Inc .......................................................................... C ...... 516 670-5125
   8000 Woodley Ave Van Nuys (91406) *(P-3124)*
Danne Montague King Co (PA) .......................................... F ...... 562 944-0230
   10420 Pioneer Blvd Santa Fe Springs (90670) *(P-17035)*
Danoc Embroidery, Sacramento *Also Called: Danoc Manufacturing Corp (P-2722)*
Danoc Manufacturing Corp ................................................ F ...... 916 455-2876
   6015 Power Inn Rd Ste A Sacramento (95824) *(P-2722)*
Danone Us LLC .................................................................. E ...... 949 474-9670
   3500 Barranca Pkwy Ste 240 Irvine (92606) *(P-797)*
Danrich Welding Co Inc ..................................................... E ...... 562 634-4811
   155 N Eucla Ave San Dimas (91773) *(P-8424)*
Dansereau Health Products ............................................... E ...... 951 549-1400
   1581 Commerce St Corona (92878) *(P-15445)*
Dantel Inc ............................................................................ E ...... 559 292-1111
   4210 N Brawley Ave # 108 Fresno (93722) *(P-11759)*
Danville, Carlsbad *Also Called: Danville Materials LLC (P-15446)*
Danville Materials LLC (HQ) ............................................... F ...... 760 743-7744
   2875 Loker Ave E Carlsbad (92010) *(P-15446)*
Danville Materials LLC ....................................................... E ...... 714 399-0334
   4020 E Leaverton Ct Anaheim (92807) *(P-15447)*
Danza Del Sol Winery Inc .................................................. E ...... 951 302-6363
   39050 De Portola Rd Temecula (92592) *(P-1525)*
Daou Vineyards, Paso Robles *Also Called: Daou Vineyards LLC (P-1526)*
Daou Vineyards LLC ........................................................... E ...... 805 226-5460
   2740 Hidden Mountain Rd Paso Robles (93446) *(P-1526)*
Dapper Tire Co Inc ............................................................. F ...... 510 780-1616
   20380 Corsair Blvd Hayward (94545) *(P-17449)*
Dar-Ken Inc ......................................................................... E ...... 760 246-4010
   10515 Rancho Rd Adelanto (92301) *(P-6445)*
Darcie Kent Vineyards LLC ................................................ E ...... 925 243-9040
   4590 Tesla Rd Livermore (94550) *(P-1527)*
Darcie Kent Winery LLC .................................................... E ...... 925 443-5368
   7000 Tesla Rd Livermore (94550) *(P-17264)*
Darcoid Company of California .......................................... E ...... 510 836-2449
   950 3rd St Oakland (94607) *(P-16870)*
Darcoid Nor-Cal Seal, Oakland *Also Called: Darcoid Company of California (P-16870)*
Darcy AK Corporation ........................................................ F ...... 949 650-5566
   1760 Monrovia Ave Ste A22 Costa Mesa (92627) *(P-10799)*
Darfield Industries Inc (PA) ................................................ F ...... 818 247-8350
   4626 Sperry St Los Angeles (90039) *(P-7736)*
Darioush Khaledi Winery LLC ............................................ E ...... 707 257-2345
   4240 Silverado Trl Napa (94558) *(P-1528)*
Dark Garden, San Francisco *Also Called: Dark Grdn Unique Corsetry Inc (P-17499)*
Dark Grdn Unique Corsetry Inc ......................................... F ...... 415 431-7684
   321 Linden St San Francisco (94102) *(P-17499)*
Darko Precision Inc ............................................................ D ...... 408 988-6133
   470 Gianni St Santa Clara (95054) *(P-10800)*
Darling Ingredients Inc ....................................................... E ...... 559 268-5325
   795 W Belgravia Ave Fresno (93706) *(P-1381)*
Darling Ingredients Inc ....................................................... E ...... 323 583-6311
   2626 E 25th St Los Angeles (90058) *(P-1382)*
Darling Ingredients Inc ....................................................... E ...... 415 647-4890
   429 Amador St Pier 92 San Francisco (94124) *(P-1383)*
Darling Ingredients Inc ....................................................... E ...... 209 667-9153
   11946 Carpenter Rd Crows Landing (95313) *(P-1384)*
Darmark Corporation .......................................................... D ...... 858 679-3970
   13225 Gregg St Poway (92064) *(P-10801)*
Darnell-Rose Inc ................................................................. E ...... 626 912-1688
   1205 Via Roma Colton (92324) *(P-7992)*
Darrow's New Orleans Grill, Carson *Also Called: Zeek Management Group LLC (P-17612)*
Dart Aerospace, Vista *Also Called: Apical Industries Inc (P-16915)*
Dart Container Corp Calif, Lodi *Also Called: Dart Container Corp California (P-6630)*
Dart Container Corp California (PA) .................................. B ...... 951 735-8115
   150 S Maple Center Corona (92880) *(P-6629)*

**Dart Container Corp California** .................................................. D ...... 209 333-8088
  1400 E Victor Rd Lodi (95240) *(P-6630)*

**Daryls Pet Shop** ........................................................................ F ...... 909 793-1788
  115 S Center St Redlands (92373) *(P-16122)*

**Dasco Engineering Corp** ......................................................... C ...... 310 326-2277
  24747 Crenshaw Blvd Torrance (90505) *(P-13820)*

**Dasol Inc** ................................................................................... C ...... 310 327-6700
  9004 Meredith Pl Beverly Hills (90210) *(P-11423)*

**Dassault Systemes Biovia Corp (DH)** ..................................... **E ...... 858 799-5000**
  5005 Wateridge Vista Dr San Diego (92121) *(P-18226)*

**Data Aire Inc (HQ)** ................................................................... **D ...... 800 347-2473**
  230 W Blueridge Ave Orange (92865) *(P-10496)*

**Data Appointment** .................................................................. E ...... 310 979-3282
  6060 W Manchester Ave Ste 311 Los Angeles (90045) *(P-18227)*

**Data Consultants, Fresno** *Also Called: T B B Inc (P-16554)*

**Data Device Corporation** ........................................................ E ...... 858 503-3300
  13000 Gregg St Ste C Poway (92064) *(P-12400)*

**Data Display Products, El Segundo** *Also Called: Display Products Inc (P-12404)*

**Data Physics Corporation (PA)** ............................................... **F ...... 408 437-0100**
  1111 Spruce St Riverside (92507) *(P-16518)*

**Data Processing Design Inc** .................................................... E ...... 714 695-1000
  1409 Glenneyre St Ste B Laguna Beach (92651) *(P-17906)*

**Datafox, San Francisco** *Also Called: Datafox Intelligence Inc (P-18228)*

**Datafox Intelligence Inc** .......................................................... F ...... 415 969-2144
  475 Sansome St Fl 15 San Francisco (94111) *(P-18228)*

**Dataself Corp** ........................................................................... E ...... 888 910-9802
  1200 Franklin Mall Santa Clara (95050) *(P-17907)*

**Datatronic Distribution Inc** ..................................................... F
  28151 Us Highway 74 Romoland (92585) *(P-11209)*

**Datatronics, Menifee** *Also Called: Datatronics Romoland Inc (P-11210)*

**Datatronics Romoland Inc** ...................................................... D ...... 951 928-7700
  28151 Us Highway 74 Menifee (92585) *(P-11210)*

**Datavisor Inc** ............................................................................ D ...... 408 331-9886
  967 N Shoreline Blvd Mountain View (94043) *(P-18229)*

**Datera Inc** ................................................................................. E ...... 844 432-8372
  2811 Mission College Blvd Fl 4 Santa Clara (95054) *(P-18230)*

**Datron Advanced Tech Inc** ..................................................... C ...... 805 579-2966
  200 W Los Angeles Ave Simi Valley (93065) *(P-13821)*

**Dauntless Industries Inc** ......................................................... E ...... 626 966-4494
  806 N Grand Ave Covina (91724) *(P-9616)*

**Dauntless Molds, Covina** *Also Called: Dauntless Industries Inc (P-9616)*

**Davberta Inc** ............................................................................. D ...... 408 453-3272
  181 E Tasman Dr Ste 20 San Jose (95134) *(P-12954)*

**Dave Inc (PA)** ............................................................................ **B ...... 844 857-3283**
  1265 S Cochran Ave Los Angeles (90019) *(P-18231)*

**Dave J Mendrin Inc** ................................................................. F ...... 559 352-1700
  4876 W Athens Ave Fresno (93722) *(P-10)*

**Dave Whipple Sheet Metal Inc** ............................................... E ...... 619 562-6962
  1077 N Cuyamaca St El Cajon (92020) *(P-8425)*

**Dave's Baking Goods, Santa Monica** *Also Called: Bake R Us Inc (P-1163)*

**Davero Farms & Winery LLC** .................................................. F ...... 707 431-8000
  766 Westside Rd Healdsburg (95448) *(P-1529)*

**David B Anderson** ................................................................... E ...... 805 489-0661
  174 Suburban Rd Ste 100 San Luis Obispo (93401) *(P-4584)*

**David Bruce Winery Inc** .......................................................... F ...... 408 354-4214
  21439 Bear Creek Rd Los Gatos (95033) *(P-1530)*

**David Engineering & Manufacturing Inc** ............................... E ...... 951 735-5200
  1230 Quarry St Corona (92879) *(P-9617)*

**David Engineering & Mfg, Corona** *Also Called: David Engineering & Mfg Inc (P-8834)*

**David Engineering & Mfg Inc** ................................................. E ...... 951 735-5200
  1230 Quarry St Corona (92879) *(P-8834)*

**David Grment Ctng Fsing Svc In** ............................................ E ...... 323 216-1574
  5008 S Boyle Ave Vernon (90058) *(P-2751)*

**David H Fell & Co Inc (PA)** ...................................................... **E ...... 323 722-9992**
  6009 Bandini Blvd Los Angeles (90040) *(P-7718)*

**David Haid** ............................................................................... E ...... 323 752-8096
  8619 Crocker St Los Angeles (90003) *(P-3736)*

**David James LLC** .................................................................... E ...... 925 817-9215
  21660 8th St E Ste A Sonoma (95476) *(P-1531)*

**David Kopf Instruments** .......................................................... E ...... 818 352-3274
  7324 Elmo St Tujunga (91042) *(P-15063)*

**David Schnur Assoc** ................................................................ E ...... 650 363-8797
  1755 E Bayshore Rd Ste 8b Redwood City (94063) *(P-6794)*

**David's Bridal, Chico** *Also Called: Davids Bridal LLC (P-17493)*

**Davids Bridal LLC** .................................................................... F ...... 530 342-5914
  1515 Springfield Dr Ste 100 Chico (95928) *(P-17493)*

**Davids Natural Toothpaste Inc** ............................................... E ...... 949 933-1185
  33360 Zeiders Rd Ste 106 Menifee (92584) *(P-5968)*

**Davidson Enterprises Inc** ........................................................ E ...... 661 325-2145
  3223 Brittan St Bakersfield (93308) *(P-560)*

**Davidson Optronics Inc** .......................................................... E ...... 626 962-5181
  9087 Arrow Rte Ste 180 Rancho Cucamonga (91730) *(P-14859)*

**Davina Douthard Inc** .............................................................. F ...... 310 540-5120
  400 Corporate Pointe Ste 300 Culver City (90230) *(P-19557)*

**Davis California Industries, North Hollywood** *Also Called: Davis California Industries Ltd (P-8426)*

**Davis California Industries Ltd** .............................................. E ...... 818 980-6178
  11323 Hartland St North Hollywood (91605) *(P-8426)*

**Davis Instruments Corporation** ............................................. D ...... 510 732-9229
  3465 Diablo Ave Hayward (94545) *(P-14176)*

**Davis Machine Shop Inc** ......................................................... E ...... 530 696-2577
  15805 Central St Meridian (95957) *(P-9348)*

**Davis Wire Corporation (HQ)** ................................................. **C ...... 626 969-7651**
  5555 Irwindale Ave Irwindale (91706) *(P-7639)*

**Davison Iron Works Inc** ........................................................... E ...... 916 381-2121
  8845 Elder Creek Rd Ste A Sacramento (95828) *(P-8132)*

**Dawn Bakery Service Center, Union City** *Also Called: Dawn Food Products Inc (P-1180)*

**Dawn Food Products Inc** ........................................................ E ...... 510 487-9007
  2845 Faber St Union City (94587) *(P-1180)*

**Dawn Food Products Inc** ........................................................ C ...... 714 258-1223
  15601 Mosher Ave Ste 230 Tustin (92780) *(P-1181)*

**Dawn Food Products Inc** ........................................................ E ...... 517 789-4400
  2455 Tenaya Dr Modesto (95354) *(P-1271)*

**Dawn Sign Press Inc** ............................................................... E ...... 858 625-0600
  6130 Nancy Ridge Dr San Diego (92121) *(P-4325)*

**Dawson Enterprises (PA)** ........................................................ **E ...... 562 424-8564**
  2853 Cherry Ave Signal Hill (90755) *(P-9460)*

**DAY ONE, Brisbane** *Also Called: Day One Biopharmaceuticals Inc (P-19449)*

**Day One Biopharmaceuticals Inc (PA)** .................................. **E ...... 650 484-0899**
  2000 Sierra Point Pkwy Ste 501 Brisbane (94005) *(P-19449)*

**Day Star Industries** ................................................................. F ...... 562 926-8800
  13727 Excelsior Dr Santa Fe Springs (90670) *(P-3125)*

**Day-Glo, Cudahy** *Also Called: Day-Glo Color Corp (P-5061)*

**Day-Glo Color Corp** ................................................................ F ...... 323 560-2000
  4615 Ardine St Cudahy (90201) *(P-5061)*

**Daylight Defense LLC** ............................................................. C ...... 858 432-7500
  16465 Via Esprillo Ste 100 San Diego (92127) *(P-15529)*

**Daylight Solutions Inc (DH)** .................................................... **C ...... 858 432-7500**
  16465 Via Esprillo Ste 100 San Diego (92127) *(P-12401)*

**Daystar Technologies Inc** ....................................................... D ...... 408 582-7100
  1010 S Milpitas Blvd Milpitas (95035) *(P-12402)*

**Dayton Rogers of California Inc** ............................................. C ...... 763 784-7714
  13630 Saticoy St Van Nuys (91402) *(P-8835)*

**Dayton Superior Corporation** ................................................ E ...... 951 782-9517
  6001 20th St Riverside (92509) *(P-7640)*

**Dayton Superior Corporation** ................................................ E ...... 209 869-1201
  5300 Claus Rd Ste 7 Modesto (95357) *(P-9517)*

**Daz, Los Angeles** *Also Called: Daz Systems LLC (P-17908)*

**Daz Inc** ..................................................................................... F ...... 949 724-8800
  2500 White Rd Ste B Irvine (92614) *(P-6582)*

**Daz Systems LLC** .................................................................... B ...... 310 640-1300
  1003 E 4th Pl Ste 800 Los Angeles (90013) *(P-17908)*

**Dazpak Flexible Packaging, City Of Industry** *Also Called: Signature Flexible Packg LLC (P-6246)*

**Dazpak Flexible Packaging, Irvine** *Also Called: Signature Flexible Packg LLC (P-6247)*

**Dazpak Flexible Packaging, City Of Industry** *Also Called: Dazpak Flexible Packaging LLC (P-17292)*

**Dazpak Flexible Packaging LLC** ............................................. F ...... 909 598-7844
  19310 San Jose Ave City Of Industry (91748) *(P-17292)*

**Db Building Fasteners, Ontario** *Also Called: Db Building Fasteners Inc (P-8696)*

**Db Building Fasteners Inc (PA)** .............................................. **F ...... 909 581-6740**
  5555 E Gibralter Ontario (91764) *(P-8696)*

# ALPHABETIC SECTION — Defoe Furniture

**Db Control Corp (HQ)** .................................................. D ...... 510 656-2325
1120 Auburn St Fremont (94538) *(P-14510)*

**Db Design Group Inc** .................................................... E ...... 408 834-1400
48507 Milmont Dr Fremont (94538) *(P-19388)*

**Dbi, Cypress** *Also Called: Hilti US Manufacturing Inc (P-7969)*

**DC, Huntington Beach** *Also Called: DC Shoes LLC (P-2616)*

**DC Electronics, San Jose** *Also Called: Amphenol DC Electronics Inc (P-11440)*

**DC Electronics Inc** ........................................................ E ...... 408 947-4500
1870 Little Orchard St San Jose (95125) *(P-11448)*

**DC Locker Inc** ................................................................ F ...... 909 480-0066
160 Commerce Way Walnut (91789) *(P-3684)*

**DC Partners Inc (PA)** .................................................... E ...... 714 558-9444
1356 N Santiago St Santa Ana (92701) *(P-7842)*

**DC Shoes Inc** ................................................................ F ...... 951 361-7712
11310 Cantu Galleano Ranch Rd Mira Loma (91752) *(P-17087)*

**DC Shoes LLC (PA)** ...................................................... D ...... 714 889-4206
5600 Argosy Ave Ste 100 Huntington Beach (92649) *(P-2616)*

**DC Valve Mfg & Precision Mchs, Morgan Hill** *Also Called: Dcpm Inc (P-10802)*

**Dcatalog Inc** .................................................................. E ...... 408 824-5648
6250 Sagebrush Bend Way San Diego (92130) *(P-18232)*

**Dcc General Engrg Contrs Inc** .................................... D ...... 760 480-7400
2180 Meyers Ave Escondido (92029) *(P-7326)*

**Dcec Holdings Inc** ........................................................ C ...... 562 802-3488
13259 166th St Cerritos (90703) *(P-11387)*

**Dcg Systems, Fremont** *Also Called: Fei Efa Inc (P-14665)*

**DCI Hollow Metal On Demand, Fontana** *Also Called: Door Components Inc (P-8262)*

**Dcii North America LLC (HQ)** ...................................... E ...... 714 817-7000
200 S Kraemer Blvd Bldg E Brea (92821) *(P-15448)*

**Dcl, Ontario** *Also Called: Discopylabs (P-11729)*

**Dcor, Oxnard** *Also Called: Dcor LLC (P-176)*

**Dcor LLC (PA)** .............................................................. D ...... 805 535-2000
1000 Town Center Dr Fl 6 Oxnard (93036) *(P-176)*

**Dcpm Inc** ...................................................................... E ...... 408 928-2510
885 Jarvis Dr Morgan Hill (95037) *(P-10802)*

**Dcx-Chol Enterprises Inc** ............................................ F ...... 310 516-1692
12831 S Figueroa St Los Angeles (90061) *(P-12030)*

**Dcx-Chol Enterprises Inc (PA)** .................................... D ...... 310 516-1692
12831 S Figueroa St Los Angeles (90061) *(P-12955)*

**Dda Holdings Inc** .......................................................... E ...... 213 624-5200
834 S Broadway Ste 600 Los Angeles (90014) *(P-2752)*

**Ddh Enterprise Inc (PA)** .............................................. D ...... 760 599-0171
2220 Oak Ridge Way Vista (92081) *(P-11449)*

**DDS, Hayward** *Also Called: Detention Device Systems (P-10809)*

**De Anza Manufacturing Svcs Inc** ................................ D ...... 408 734-2020
1271 Reamwood Ave Sunnyvale (94089) *(P-12956)*

**De Berns Company, Long Beach** *Also Called: Berns Bros Inc (P-10749)*

**De La Calle Co (PA)** .................................................... F ...... 650 465-0093
5701 W Adams Blvd Los Angeles (90016) *(P-1996)*

**De La Cruz Lath and Plaster Co** .................................. F ...... 209 368-8658
3480 Carpenter Rd Stockton (95215) *(P-521)*

**De Leon Enterprises, Sun Valley** *Also Called: De Leon Entps Elec Spclist Inc (P-12086)*

**De Leon Entps Elec Spclist Inc** .................................... E ...... 818 252-6690
11934 Allegheny St Sun Valley (91352) *(P-12086)*

**De Menno-Kerdoon Trading Co (HQ)** .......................... C ...... 310 537-7100
2000 N Alameda St Compton (90222) *(P-6336)*

**De Nora Water Technologies LLC** .............................. F ...... 310 618-9700
1230 Rosecrans Ave Ste 300 Manhattan Beach (90266) *(P-10555)*

**De Novo Software LLC** ................................................ F ...... 213 814-1240
207 N Sierra Madre Blvd # 1 Pasadena (91107) *(P-18233)*

**De Soto Clothing Inc** .................................................... F ...... 858 578-6672
7584 Trade St San Diego (92121) *(P-2753)*

**De Soto Sport, San Diego** *Also Called: De Soto Clothing Inc (P-2753)*

**De Vries International Inc (PA)** .................................. E ...... 949 252-1212
17671 Armstrong Ave Irvine (92614) *(P-222)*

**Dealership Auto Dtail Rstrtons, Monrovia** *Also Called: Executive Auto Reconditioning (P-19165)*

**Dean Distributors Inc** .................................................. E ...... 323 587-8147
5015 Hallmark Pkwy San Bernardino (92407) *(P-2180)*

**Dean Hesketh Company Inc** ........................................ E ...... 714 236-2138
2551 W La Palma Ave Anaheim (92801) *(P-4871)*

**Dean L Davis MD** .......................................................... E ...... 661 632-5000
2215 Truxtun Ave Bakersfield (93301) *(P-19356)*

**Dean Socal LLC** ............................................................ C ...... 951 734-3950
17637 E Valley Blvd City Of Industry (91744) *(P-833)*

**Deans Certified Welding Inc** ........................................ F ...... 760 728-0292
27645 Commerce Center Dr Temecula (92590) *(P-19189)*

**Dearly Beloved Wines, Ripon** *Also Called: McManis Family Vineyards Inc (P-1676)*

**Dec, Santa Ana** *Also Called: Dynasty Electronic Company LLC (P-12088)*

**Deca International Corp** .............................................. E ...... 714 367-5900
10700 Norwalk Blvd Santa Fe Springs (90670) *(P-14177)*

**Decatur Electronics Inc (DH)** ...................................... D ...... 888 428-4315
15890 Bernardo Center Dr San Diego (92127) *(P-14178)*

**Decatur Electronics Inc** .............................................. F ...... 619 596-1925
10729 Wheatlands Ave Ste C Santee (92071) *(P-14179)*

**Decco Castings Inc (PA)** .............................................. F ...... 619 444-9437
1596 Pioneer Way El Cajon (92020) *(P-7860)*

**Decco Castings Inc** ...................................................... E ...... 818 416-0068
1410 Hill St El Cajon (92020) *(P-7861)*

**Decco US Post-Harvest Inc (HQ)** ................................ F ...... 800 221-0925
1713 S California Ave Monrovia (91016) *(P-6199)*

**Deccofelt Corporation** .................................................. E ...... 626 963-8511
555 S Vermont Ave Glendora (91741) *(P-2545)*

**Decision Medical, Poway** *Also Called: Decision Sciences Med Co LLC (P-15530)*

**Decision Ready, Irvine** *Also Called: Decision Ready Solutions Inc (P-17727)*

**Decision Ready Solutions Inc** .................................... E ...... 949 400-1126
400 Spectrum Center Dr Ste 2050 Irvine (92618) *(P-17727)*

**Decision Sciences Med Co LLC** .................................. E ...... 858 602-1600
12345 First American Way Ste 100 Poway (92064) *(P-15530)*

**Decisionlogic LLC** ........................................................ E ...... 858 586-0202
13500 Evening Creek Dr N Ste 600 San Diego (92128) *(P-18234)*

**Deck West Inc** .............................................................. E ...... 209 939-9700
1900 Sanguinetti Ln Stockton (95205) *(P-8427)*

**DECKERS, Goleta** *Also Called: Deckers Outdoor Corporation (P-2896)*

**Deckers Outdoor Corporation (PA)** ............................ A ...... 805 967-7611
250 Coromar Dr Goleta (93117) *(P-2896)*

**Deco Enterprises Inc** .................................................. D ...... 323 726-2575
2917 Vail Ave Commerce (90040) *(P-11524)*

**Deco Lighting, Commerce** *Also Called: Deco Enterprises Inc (P-11524)*

**Decor Interior Design Inc** ............................................ E ...... 818 962-4800
21530 Sherman Way Canoga Park (91303) *(P-19085)*

**Decore-Ative Spc NC LLC (PA)** .................................... A ...... 626 254-9191
2772 Peck Rd Monrovia (91016) *(P-3126)*

**Decore-Ative Spc NC LLC** ............................................ C ...... 626 960-7731
4414 Azusa Canyon Rd Irwindale (91706) *(P-3127)*

**Decore-Ative Spc NC LLC** ............................................ C ...... 916 686-4700
104 Gate Eats Stock Blvd Elk Grove (95624) *(P-3128)*

**Decra, Corona** *Also Called: Decra Roofing Systems Inc (P-8428)*

**Decra Roofing Systems Inc (DH)** ................................ D ...... 951 272-8180
1230 Railroad St Corona (92882) *(P-8428)*

**Dedon Inc** .................................................................... F ...... 310 388-4721
8687 Melrose Ave Ste B188 West Hollywood (90069) *(P-3438)*

**Dee Engineering Inc** .................................................... E ...... 909 947-5616
6918 Ed Perkic St Riverside (92504) *(P-13483)*

**Deem Inc (DH)** .............................................................. D ...... 415 590-8300
1330 Broadway Fl 17 Oakland (94612) *(P-18235)*

**Deep Labs Inc (PA)** ...................................................... E ...... 877 504-4544
101 2nd St Ste 375 San Francisco (94105) *(P-18236)*

**Deep Ocean Engineering Inc** ...................................... F ...... 408 436-1102
2261 Fortune Dr San Jose (95131) *(P-14031)*

**Deep Ocean Exploration & RES, Alameda** *Also Called: Doer Marine Operations (P-19558)*

**Deep Security, San Jose** *Also Called: Trend Micro Incorporated (P-16559)*

**Deepsea Power & Light Inc** ........................................ E ...... 858 576-1261
4033 Ruffin Rd San Diego (92123) *(P-11590)*

**Deering Banjo Company Inc** ........................................ E ...... 619 464-8252
3733 Kenora Dr Spring Valley (91977) *(P-17562)*

**Defense Solutions, Santa Clarita** *Also Called: Curtiss-Wright Corporation (P-9150)*

**Defense Specialist, The, Los Angeles** *Also Called: Defense Specialists LLC (P-19340)*

**Defense Specialists LLC** .............................................. D ...... 818 270-7162
924 W Washington Blvd Los Angeles (90015) *(P-19340)*

**Defoe Furniture, San Bernardino** *Also Called: Defoe Furniture For Kids Inc (P-3622)*

**Defoe Furniture For Kids  Inc**  ............................................................ ALPHABETIC SECTION

**Defoe Furniture For Kids  Inc** ............................................................... F ...... 909 947-4459
  723 W Mill St San Bernardino (92410) *(P-3622)*
**Dei Headquarters  Inc** ......................................................................... B ...... 760 598-6200
  3002 Wintergreen Dr Carlsbad (92008) *(P-11990)*
**Dei Holdings  Inc  (HQ)** ........................................................................ E ...... 760 598-6200
  5541 Fermi Ct Carlsbad (92008) *(P-11991)*
**Dek Industry  Inc** ................................................................................. C ...... 909 941-8810
  807 Palmyrita Ave Riverside (92507) *(P-9849)*
**Dekra-Lite Industries Inc** .................................................................... D ...... 714 436-0705
  3102 W Alton Ave Santa Ana (92704) *(P-19086)*
**Del Castillo Foods  Inc** ........................................................................ E ...... 209 369-2877
  2346 Maggio Cir Lodi (95240) *(P-2181)*
**Del Dotto, Napa** *Also Called: Del Dotto Vineyards (P-1534)*
**Del Dotto Vineyards** ............................................................................ E ...... 707 603-1084
  1445 Saint Helena Hwy S Saint Helena (94574) *(P-1532)*
**Del Dotto Vineyards** ............................................................................ E ...... 707 963-2134
  1055 Atlas Peak Rd Napa (94558) *(P-1533)*
**Del Dotto Vineyards** ............................................................................ D ...... 707 963-2134
  540 Technology Way Napa (94558) *(P-1534)*
**Del Mar Blue Print Co  Inc** .................................................................. F ...... 858 755-5134
  2201 San Dieguito Dr Ste E Del Mar (92014) *(P-17809)*
**Del Mar Die Casting Co, Gardena** *Also Called: Del Mar Industries (P-7827)*
**Del Mar Food Products Corp** .............................................................. D ...... 831 722-3516
  1720 Beach Rd Watsonville (95076) *(P-882)*
**Del Mar Industries  (PA)** ...................................................................... D ...... 323 321-0600
  12901 S Western Ave Gardena (90249) *(P-7827)*
**Del Monte Foods, Hanford** *Also Called: Del Monte Foods  Inc (P-883)*
**Del Monte Foods, Modesto** *Also Called: Del Monte Foods  Inc (P-884)*
**Del Monte Foods, Kingsburg** *Also Called: Del Monte Foods  Inc (P-885)*
**Del Monte Foods, Walnut Creek** *Also Called: Del Monte Foods  Inc (P-17186)*
**Del Monte Foods Inc** ............................................................................ D ...... 559 639-6160
  10652 Jackson Ave Hanford (93230) *(P-883)*
**Del Monte Foods Inc** ............................................................................ D ...... 209 548-5509
  4000 Yosemite Blvd Modesto (95357) *(P-884)*
**Del Monte Foods  Inc** .......................................................................... F ...... 559 419-9214
  1509 Draper St Ste A Kingsburg (93631) *(P-885)*
**Del Monte Foods  Inc  (HQ)** ................................................................. C ...... 925 949-2772
  205 N Wiget Ln Walnut Creek (94598) *(P-17186)*
**Del Ray Packaging, Del Rey** *Also Called: Chooljian & Sons Inc (P-9784)*
**Del Real  LLC  (PA)** .............................................................................. D ...... 951 681-0395
  11041 Inland Ave Jurupa Valley (91752) *(P-1032)*
**Del Real Foods, Jurupa Valley** *Also Called: Del Real LLC (P-1032)*
**Del Rey Packing Co, Del Rey** *Also Called: Chooljian & Sons Inc (P-79)*
**Del West Engineering  Inc  (PA)** .......................................................... C ...... 661 295-5700
  28128 Livingston Ave Valencia (91355) *(P-13484)*
**Del West USA, Valencia** *Also Called: Del West Engineering  Inc (P-13484)*
**Delafield Corporation  (PA)** ................................................................. C ...... 626 303-0740
  1520 Flower Ave Duarte (91010) *(P-10803)*
**Delafield Fluid Technology, Duarte** *Also Called: Delafield Corporation (P-10803)*
**Delafoil Holdings Inc  (PA)** .................................................................. C ...... 949 752-4580
  18500 Von Karman Ave Ste 450 Irvine (92612) *(P-8429)*
**Delallo Italian Foods, Oroville** *Also Called: George Delallo Company  Inc (P-891)*
**Delamo Manufacturing  Inc** ................................................................. D ...... 323 936-3566
  7171 Telegraph Rd Montebello (90640) *(P-6795)*
**Delano Growers Grape Products** ........................................................ D ...... 661 725-3255
  32351 Bassett Ave Delano (93215) *(P-1997)*
**Delano Waste Water Treatment, Delano** *Also Called: City of Delano (P-10547)*
**Delaware Ancra Intl LLC, Azusa** *Also Called: Ancra International LLC (P-9506)*
**Delaware Systems Technology, San Bernardino** *Also Called: Systems Technology Inc (P-10032)*
**Delectus Winery, Saint Helena** *Also Called: Vintage Wine Estates Inc CA (P-1816)*
**Delegat Usa Inc** ................................................................................... E ...... 415 538-7988
  555 Mission St Ste 2625 San Francisco (94105) *(P-17626)*
**Delfin Design & Mfg Inc** ...................................................................... E ...... 949 888-4644
  15672 Producer Ln Huntington Beach (92649) *(P-6796)*
**Delicato Vineyards  LLC  (PA)** ............................................................. C ...... 209 824-3600
  12001 S Highway 99 Manteca (95336) *(P-1535)*
**Delicato Vineyards  LLC** ..................................................................... E ...... 707 265-1700
  455 Devlin Rd Ste 201 Napa (94558) *(P-1536)*
**Delkin Devices, Poway** *Also Called: Delkin Devices Inc (P-10356)*

**Delkin Devices Inc  (PA)** ...................................................................... D ...... 858 391-1234
  13350 Kirkham Way Poway (92064) *(P-10356)*
**Della Robbia  Inc** ................................................................................. E ...... 951 372-9199
  796 E Harrison St Corona (92879) *(P-3524)*
**Dellarise, Pasadena** *Also Called: Pak Group LLC (P-1281)*
**Dellarobbia Inc  (PA)** ........................................................................... E ...... 949 251-9532
  119 Waterworks Way Irvine (92618) *(P-3470)*
**Delong Manufacturing Co  Inc** ............................................................ F ...... 408 727-3348
  967 Parker Ct Santa Clara (95050) *(P-10804)*
**Delori Foods, City Of Industry** *Also Called: Delori-Nutifood Products  Inc (P-2182)*
**Delori-Nutifood Products  Inc** ............................................................. E ...... 626 965-3006
  17043 Green Dr City Of Industry (91745) *(P-2182)*
**Delphi Control Systems  Inc** ............................................................... F ...... 909 593-8099
  2806 Metropolitan Pl Pomona (91767) *(P-14401)*
**Delphi Display Systems  Inc** ............................................................... D ...... 714 825-3400
  3550 Hyland Ave Costa Mesa (92626) *(P-10357)*
**Delphon Industries  LLC  (PA)** ............................................................. C ...... 510 576-2220
  31398 Huntwood Ave Hayward (94544) *(P-6797)*
**Delstar Holding Corp** .......................................................................... E ...... 619 258-1503
  9225 Isaac St Santee (92071) *(P-6556)*
**Delstar Technologies  Inc** ................................................................... E ...... 619 258-1503
  1306 Fayette St El Cajon (92020) *(P-6557)*
**Delt Industries  Inc** .............................................................................. F ...... 805 579-0213
  90 W Easy St Ste 2 Simi Valley (93065) *(P-7862)*
**Delta America Ltd  (HQ)** ...................................................................... C ...... 510 668-5100
  46101 Fremont Blvd Fremont (94538) *(P-16698)*
**Delta Design  Inc** ................................................................................. B ...... 858 848-8000
  12367 Crosthwaite Cir Poway (92064) *(P-10085)*
**Delta Design (littleton)  Inc** ................................................................. A ...... 858 848-8100
  12367 Crosthwaite Cir Poway (92064) *(P-14511)*
**Delta Electronics Americas Ltd  (DH)** ................................................. D ...... 510 668-5111
  46101 Fremont Blvd Fremont (94538) *(P-19514)*
**Delta Fabrication  Inc** .......................................................................... D ...... 818 407-4000
  9600 De Soto Ave Chatsworth (91311) *(P-10805)*
**Delta Galil USA Inc** ............................................................................. B ...... 213 488-4859
  777 S Alameda St Fl 3 Los Angeles (90021) *(P-2829)*
**Delta Group Electronics, San Diego** *Also Called: Delta Group Electronics  Inc (P-12957)*
**Delta Group Electronics  Inc** .............................................................. D ...... 858 569-1681
  10180 Scripps Ranch Blvd San Diego (92131) *(P-12957)*
**Delta Hi-Tech** ....................................................................................... C ...... 818 407-4000
  9600 De Soto Ave Chatsworth (91311) *(P-10806)*
**Delta Ironworks, Salinas** *Also Called: Delta Ironworks  Inc (P-8623)*
**Delta Ironworks  Inc** ............................................................................ F ...... 831 663-1190
  15420 Meridian Rd Salinas (93907) *(P-8623)*
**Delta Machine, San Jose** *Also Called: Delta Matrix  Inc (P-10807)*
**Delta Matrix  Inc** .................................................................................. E ...... 408 955-9140
  2180 Oakland Rd San Jose (95131) *(P-10807)*
**Delta Microwave LLC** ......................................................................... D ...... 805 751-1100
  300 Del Norte Blvd Oxnard (93030) *(P-12958)*
**Delta Pacific Activewear  Inc** .............................................................. D ...... 714 871-9281
  331 S Hale Ave Fullerton (92831) *(P-2466)*
**Delta Pacific Products, Union City** *Also Called: Delta Yimin Technologies  Inc (P-6798)*
**Delta Packaging Products, Los Angeles** *Also Called: E & S Paper Co (P-16999)*
**Delta Print Group  LLC** ....................................................................... E ...... 916 928-0801
  4251 Gateway Park Blvd Sacramento (95834) *(P-4585)*
**Delta Printing Solutions  Inc** .............................................................. C ...... 661 257-0584
  28210 Avenue Stanford Valencia (91355) *(P-4586)*
**Delta Products, Fremont** *Also Called: Delta America Ltd (P-16698)*
**Delta Rubber Co Inc** ........................................................................... D ...... 209 948-0511
  2648 Teepee Dr Stockton (95205) *(P-16871)*
**Delta Specialties  Inc** .......................................................................... F ...... 209 937-9650
  1374 E Turner Rd Ste A Lodi (95240) *(P-540)*
**Delta Tau Data Systems Inc Cal  (HQ)** ............................................... C ...... 818 998-2095
  21314 Lassen St Chatsworth (91311) *(P-10086)*
**Delta Trading  LP** ................................................................................ E ...... 661 834-5560
  17731 Millux Rd Bakersfield (93311) *(P-6361)*
**Delta Ultraviolet Corporation** ............................................................. F ...... 310 323-6400
  1535 W Rosecrans Ave Gardena (90249) *(P-11424)*
**Delta Web Printing  Inc** ....................................................................... E ...... 916 375-0044
  4251 Gateway Park Blvd Sacramento (95834) *(P-4872)*
**Delta Web Printing & Bindery, Sacramento** *Also Called: Delta Web Printing  Inc (P-4872)*

# ALPHABETIC SECTION

**Delta Yimin Technologies Inc** ............................................. E ...... 510 487-4411
33170 Central Ave Union City (94587) *(P-6798)*

**Deltatrak, Pleasanton** *Also Called: Deltatrak Inc (P-14861)*

**Deltatrak Inc** ............................................................................... E ...... 209 579-5343
1236 Doker Dr Modesto (95351) *(P-14860)*

**Deltatrak Inc (PA)** ..................................................................... E ...... 925 249-2250
6801 Koll Center Pkwy # 120 Pleasanton (94566) *(P-14861)*

**Deltronic Corporation** ............................................................. D ...... 714 545-5800
3900 W Segerstrom Ave Santa Ana (92704) *(P-14770)*

**Deluxe Building Products, Pomona** *Also Called: Wcs Equipment Holdings LLC (P-7700)*

**Deluxe Pckges An Amcor Flexble, Yuba City** *Also Called: Paperboard Packaging Corp (P-3933)*

**Demand Cnc, Irvine** *Also Called: Synventive Engineering Inc (P-9589)*

**Demandbase Inc (PA)** ............................................................. E ...... 415 683-2660
222 2nd St 24th Fl San Francisco (94105) *(P-18237)*

**Demandwhiz LLC** ..................................................................... D ...... 408 600-2720
4079 Middle Park Dr San Jose (95135) *(P-18238)*

**Demeine Estates LLC** ............................................................. E ...... 707 531-7838
1380 Main St Ste 200 Saint Helena (94574) *(P-1537)*

**Demenno Kerdoon** .................................................................. F ...... 310 537-7100
2000 N Alameda St Compton (90222) *(P-177)*

**Demenno-Kerdoon, South Gate** *Also Called: Demenno/Kerdoon Holdings (P-6391)*

**Demenno/Kerdoon Holdings** ................................................. E ...... 323 268-3387
3650 E 26th St Vernon (90058) *(P-6390)*

**Demenno/Kerdoon Holdings (DH)** ........................................ D ...... 562 231-1550
9302 Garfield Ave South Gate (90280) *(P-6391)*

**Demor Enterprises Inc** ........................................................... E ...... 858 625-0003
4174 Sorrento Valley Blvd Ste H San Diego (92121) *(P-561)*

**Demtech Services Inc** ............................................................. E ...... 530 621-3200
6414 Capitol Ave Diamond Springs (95619) *(P-6799)*

**Den-Mat Corporation (DH)** .................................................... B ...... 805 922-8491
236 S Bdwy Orcutt (93455) *(P-5969)*

**Den-Mat Corporation** .............................................................. C ...... 800 445-0345
21515 Vanowen St Ste 200 Canoga Park (91303) *(P-5970)*

**Denali Software Inc (HQ)** ....................................................... E ...... 408 943-1234
2655 Seely Ave San Jose (95134) *(P-18239)*

**DENALI THERAPEUTICS, South San Francisco** *Also Called: Denali Therapeutics Inc (P-5823)*

**Denali Therapeutics Inc (PA)** ................................................ B ...... 650 866-8548
161 Oyster Point Blvd South San Francisco (94080) *(P-5823)*

**Denbeste Manufacturing Inc** ................................................ E ...... 707 838-1407
820 Den Beste Ct Windsor (95492) *(P-13407)*

**Dendreon Pharmaceuticals LLC (HQ)** ................................ E ...... 562 252-7500
1700 Saturn Way Seal Beach (90740) *(P-5424)*

**Denevi Digital, San Jose** *Also Called: Far Western Graphics Inc (P-17811)*

**Denim-Tech LLC** ..................................................................... D ...... 323 277-8998
375 E 2nd St Apt 604 Los Angeles (90012) *(P-10474)*

**Denmac Industries Inc** ........................................................... E ...... 562 634-2714
7616 Rosecrans Ave Paramount (90723) *(P-9061)*

**Dennis Bolton Enterprises Inc** ............................................. F ...... 818 982-1800
7285 Coldwater Canyon Ave North Hollywood (91605) *(P-4587)*

**Dennis DiGiorgio** .................................................................... E ...... 714 408-7527
333 City Blvd W Ste 1700 Orange (92868) *(P-7218)*

**Dennis Foland Inc (PA)** .......................................................... E ...... 909 930-9900
1500 S Hellman Ave Ontario (91761) *(P-16974)*

**Dennison Division, Brea** *Also Called: Avery Dennison Office Products Co Inc (P-4014)*

**Dennison Inc** ............................................................................ E ...... 626 965-8917
17901 Railroad St City Of Industry (91748) *(P-8624)*

**Denny Bar Company LLC** ...................................................... E ...... 530 467-5115
511 Main St Etna (96027) *(P-1835)*

**Denovo, Baldwin Park** *Also Called: Denovo Dental Inc (P-15449)*

**Denovo Dental Inc** .................................................................. E ...... 626 480-0182
5130 Commerce Dr Baldwin Park (91706) *(P-15449)*

**Denron Inc** ................................................................................ B ...... 408 435-8588
2135 Ringwood Ave San Jose (95131) *(P-12959)*

**Denso Pdts & Svcs Americas Inc** ........................................ C ...... 951 698-3379
41673 Corning Pl Murrieta (92562) *(P-13485)*

**Denso Pdts & Svcs Americas Inc (DH)** .............................. B ...... 310 834-6352
3900 Via Oro Ave Long Beach (90810) *(P-16380)*

**Denso Wireless Systems America Inc** .............................. C ...... 760 734-4600
2251 Rutherford Rd # 100 Carlsbad (92008) *(P-11840)*

**Dentis, Cypress** *Also Called: Dentis USA Corporation (P-15450)*

**Dentis USA Corporation** ........................................................ E ...... 323 677-4363
11095 Knott Ave Ste B Cypress (90630) *(P-15450)*

**Dentists Supply Company** .................................................... F ...... 888 253-1223
1201 K St Ste 740 Sacramento (95814) *(P-15451)*

**Dentonis Spring and Suspension, Stockton** *Also Called: Dentonis Welding Works Inc (P-19190)*

**Dentonis Welding Works Inc (PA)** ....................................... E ...... 209 464-4930
801 S Airport Way Stockton (95205) *(P-19190)*

**Denttio Inc** ................................................................................ F ...... 323 254-1000
116 N Maryland Ave Ste 125 Glendale (91206) *(P-15452)*

**Dependable Furniture Mfg Co, San Francisco** *Also Called: Van Sark Inc (P-3494)*

**Dependable Precision Mfg Inc** ............................................. F ...... 209 369-1055
1111 S Stockton St Ste A Lodi (95240) *(P-8430)*

**Depo Auto Parts, Fontana** *Also Called: Maxzone Vehicle Lighting Corp (P-16388)*

**Deposition Sciences Inc** ........................................................ D ...... 707 573-6700
3300 Coffey Ln Santa Rosa (95403) *(P-19450)*

**Depuy, San Diego** *Also Called: Medical Device Bus Svcs Inc (P-15374)*

**Derek and Constance Lee Corp (PA)** .................................. D ...... 909 595-8831
19355 San Jose Ave City Of Industry (91748) *(P-639)*

**Derm Cosmetic Labs, Buena Park** *Also Called: Derm Cosmetic Labs Inc (P-17036)*

**Derm Cosmetic Labs Inc (PA)** .............................................. E ...... 714 562-8873
6370 Altura Blvd Buena Park (90620) *(P-17036)*

**Dermal Group, The, Carson** *Also Called: Dermalogica LLC (P-5971)*

**Dermalogica LLC (HQ)** .......................................................... C ...... 310 900-4000
1535 Beachey Pl Carson (90746) *(P-5971)*

**Dermira Inc** ............................................................................... B ...... 650 421-7200
275 Middlefield Rd Ste 150 Menlo Park (94025) *(P-5425)*

**Dermtech Inc (PA)** ................................................................... C ...... 866 450-4223
12340 El Camino Real San Diego (92130) *(P-5747)*

**Derosa Enterprises Inc** .......................................................... F ...... 760 743-5500
15935 Spring Oaks Rd Spc 1 El Cajon (92021) *(P-8431)*

**Desco, Chino** *Also Called: Desco Industries Inc (P-11369)*

**Desco Industries Inc (PA)** ..................................................... D ...... 909 627-8178
3651 Walnut Ave Chino (91710) *(P-11369)*

**Desco Manufacturing Company (PA)** ................................. F ...... 949 858-7400
23031 Arroyo Vis Ste A Rcho Sta Marg (92688) *(P-10808)*

**Deseret Farms of California, Chico** *Also Called: Agreserves Inc (P-35)*

**Desert Block Co Inc** ............................................................... E ...... 661 824-2624
11374 Tuxford St Sun Valley (91352) *(P-6362)*

**Desert Brand, City Of Industry** *Also Called: Hill Brothers Chemical Company (P-5032)*

**Desert Grafics, Palm Springs** *Also Called: Desert Publications Inc (P-4246)*

**Desert Publications Inc (PA)** ................................................ E ...... 760 325-2333
303 N Indian Canyon Dr Palm Springs (92262) *(P-4246)*

**Desert Redi Mix, Indio** *Also Called: Coronet Concrete Products Inc (P-7437)*

**Desert Sun Publishing Co (DH)** ........................................... C ...... 760 322-8889
750 N Gene Autry Trl Palm Springs (92262) *(P-4103)*

**Desert Sun The, Palm Springs** *Also Called: Desert Sun Publishing Co (P-4103)*

**Design Engineering, Simi Valley** *Also Called: Infinity Precision Inc (P-10884)*

**Design International Group Inc** ........................................... E ...... 626 369-2289
755 Epperson Dr City Of Industry (91748) *(P-16948)*

**Design Knit Inc** ........................................................................ E ...... 213 742-1234
1636 Staunton Ave Los Angeles (90021) *(P-2467)*

**Design Octaves** ....................................................................... E ...... 831 464-8500
2701 Research Park Dr Soquel (95073) *(P-6800)*

**Design Printing, Los Angeles** *Also Called: Red Brick Corporation (P-4751)*

**Design Rite XI, Rancho Cordova** *Also Called: Promax Tools LP (P-9563)*

**Design Science Inc** ................................................................. E ...... 562 442-4779
444 W Ocean Blvd Ste 800 Long Beach (90802) *(P-17909)*

**Design Synthesis Inc** ............................................................. E ...... 858 271-8480
9855 Black Mountain Rd San Diego (92126) *(P-3129)*

**DESIGN THERAPEUTICS, Carlsbad** *Also Called: Design Therapeutics Inc (P-5426)*

**Design Therapeutics Inc** ....................................................... C ...... 858 293-4900
6005 Hidden Valley Rd Ste 110 Carlsbad (92011) *(P-5426)*

**Design Todays Inc (PA)** ......................................................... E ...... 213 745-3091
11707 Cetona Way Porter Ranch (91326) *(P-2754)*

**Design West Technologies Inc** ............................................ D ...... 714 731-0201
2701 Dow Ave Tustin (92780) *(P-6801)*

**Design Woodworking Inc (PA)** ............................................. E ...... 209 334-6674
709 N Sacramento St Lodi (95240) *(P-3130)*

**Designed MBL Systems Inds Inc** ......................................... F ...... 209 892-6298
800 S State Highway 33 Patterson (95363) *(P-367)*

**Designed Metal Connections Inc**     ALPHABETIC SECTION

Designed Metal Connections Inc .................................................. E ...... 310 323-6200
623 E Artesia Blvd Carson (90746) *(P-8721)*

Designed Metal Connections Inc (DH) ........................................ B ...... 310 323-6200
14800 S Figueroa St Gardena (90248) *(P-13822)*

Designit Global LLC ....................................................................... E ...... 707 584-4000
5935 Labath Ave Rohnert Park (94928) *(P-19389)*

Designit Prototype, Rohnert Park *Also Called: Designit Global LLC (P-19389)*

Deskless.ai, Santa Clara *Also Called: Innowi Inc (P-10167)*

Deskmakers Inc ............................................................................. E ...... 323 264-2260
6525 Flotilla St Commerce (90040) *(P-3566)*

Desksite, Irvine *Also Called: Qdos Inc (P-18712)*

Desmond Ventures Inc ................................................................. C ...... 949 474-0400
17451 Von Karman Ave Irvine (92614) *(P-6226)*

Desotec US LLC ............................................................................ E ...... 530 527-2664
11711 Reading Rd Red Bluff (96080) *(P-8315)*

Desser Holding Company LLC (HQ) ......................................... E ...... 323 721-4900
6900 W Acco St Montebello (90640) *(P-17745)*

Desser Tire & Rubber Co, Montebello *Also Called: Desser Tire & Rubber Co LLC (P-6408)*

Desser Tire & Rubber Co LLC ...................................................... E ...... 323 837-1497
6900 W Acco St Montebello (90640) *(P-16919)*

Desser Tire & Rubber Co LLC (DH) ............................................ E ...... 323 721-4900
6900 W Acco St Montebello (90640) *(P-6408)*

Desser Tire & Rubber Co., Montebello *Also Called: Desser Holding Company LLC (P-17745)*

Desserts On Us Inc ....................................................................... F ...... 707 822-0160
57 Belle Falor Ct Arcata (95521) *(P-1182)*

Destefano Design Group, Sacramento *Also Called: John C Destefano (P-3244)*

Destination Aesthetics Inc ........................................................... E ...... 916 844-4913
768 University Ave Sacramento (95825) *(P-16123)*

Destiny Tool, Morgan Hill *Also Called: Step Tools Unlimited Inc (P-9701)*

Detention Device Systems ........................................................... E ...... 510 783-0771
25545 Seaboard Ln Hayward (94545) *(P-10809)*

Detoronics Corp ............................................................................. E ...... 626 579-7130
13071 Rosecrans Ave Santa Fe Springs (90670) *(P-12876)*

Detroit Diesel Corporation ........................................................... D ...... 562 929-7016
10645 Studebaker Rd 2nd Fl Downey (90241) *(P-9327)*

Deuce Brand .................................................................................. F ...... 877 443-3823
3235 Hancock St Ste 7b San Diego (92110) *(P-15802)*

Deva, Tustin *Also Called: Distribution Electrnics Vlued (P-13232)*

Devax Inc ........................................................................................ E ...... 949 461-0450
13900 Alton Pkwy Ste 125 Irvine (92618) *(P-15064)*

Developers General Contracting ................................................ F ...... 949 351-7872
10 Hughes Irvine (92618) *(P-562)*

Developlus Inc ............................................................................... C ...... 951 738-8595
1575 Magnolia Ave Corona (92879) *(P-16124)*

Development Associates Contrls ............................................... E ...... 805 684-8307
6390 Rose Ln Carpinteria (93013) *(P-9548)*

Devincenzi Metal Products Inc ................................................... D ...... 650 692-5800
1809 Castenada Dr Burlingame (94010) *(P-8432)*

Devonway Inc (DH) ....................................................................... E ...... 415 904-4000
601 California St Ste 615 San Francisco (94108) *(P-17910)*

Deweyl Tool Co Inc ....................................................................... E ...... 707 765-5779
959 Transport Way Petaluma (94954) *(P-9674)*

Dex Liquidating Co ....................................................................... E ...... 650 364-9975
900 Saginaw Dr Redwood City (94063) *(P-15065)*

Dex-O-Tex Division, Compton *Also Called: Crossfield Products Corp (P-5149)*

Dexcom, San Diego *Also Called: Dexcom Inc (P-15066)*

Dexcom Inc (PA) ............................................................................ A ...... 858 200-0200
6340 Sequence Dr San Diego (92121) *(P-15066)*

Dexerials America Corporation (HQ) ......................................... E ...... 770 945-3845
215 Satellite Blvd Ne Ste 400 Santa Clara (95054) *(P-14477)*

Dext Company, Santa Monica *Also Called: Reconserve Inc (P-1145)*

Dext Company of Maryland (DH) ............................................... E ...... 310 458-1574
2811 Wilshire Blvd Ste 410 Santa Monica (90403) *(P-1124)*

Dexta Corporation ......................................................................... D ...... 707 255-2454
957 Enterprise Way Napa (94558) *(P-15453)*

Dexter Axle Company ................................................................... D ...... 760 744-1610
135 Sunshine Ln San Marcos (92069) *(P-13616)*

Dfc Inc (PA) .................................................................................... D ...... 530 669-7115
17986 County Road 94b Woodland (95695) *(P-13649)*

Dfine Inc (HQ) ................................................................................ E ...... 408 321-9999
3047 Orchard Pkwy San Jose (95134) *(P-15067)*

Dfm Dietary Food Management, Canoga Park *Also Called: Computrition Inc (P-17900)*

Dfndr Armor, Camarillo *Also Called: Engense Inc (P-7612)*

Dfv Wines, Napa *Also Called: Delicato Vineyards LLC (P-1536)*

Dg Brands Inc ................................................................................ D ...... 323 268-0220
5548 Lindbergh Ln Bell (90201) *(P-17088)*

Dg Engineering Corp (PA) ........................................................... E ...... 818 364-9024
13326 Ralston Ave Sylmar (91342) *(P-14180)*

Dg Mountz Associates, San Jose *Also Called: Mountz Inc (P-14437)*

DG Performance Spc Inc ............................................................. D ...... 714 961-8850
4100 E La Palma Ave Anaheim (92807) *(P-14129)*

Dg-Displays LLC ........................................................................... E ...... 877 358-5976
355 Parkside Dr San Fernando (91340) *(P-15965)*

Dg2, Los Angeles *Also Called: Dg2 Worldwide Group LLC (P-17778)*

Dg2 Worldwide Group LLC ......................................................... E ...... 310 809-0899
12655 W Jefferson Blvd 4th Fl Los Angeles (90066) *(P-17778)*

Dgl Holdings Inc ............................................................................ E ...... 714 630-7840
3850 E Miraloma Ave Anaheim (92806) *(P-8751)*

DH Caster International Inc ........................................................ F ...... 909 930-6400
2260 S Haven Ave Ste C Ontario (91761) *(P-16751)*

Dha America Inc ............................................................................ D ...... 858 925-3246
5403 Harvest Run Dr San Diego (92130) *(P-9215)*

Dharma Mudranalaya (PA) .......................................................... E ...... 707 847-3380
35788 Hauser Bridge Rd Cazadero (95421) *(P-4326)*

Dharma Publishing, Cazadero *Also Called: Dharma Mudranalaya (P-4326)*

Dhouse Brands Inc ........................................................................ E ...... 213 291-7576
2301 E 7th St Ste F103 Los Angeles (90023) *(P-17037)*

Dhv Industries Inc ......................................................................... D ...... 661 392-8948
3451 Pegasus Dr Bakersfield (93308) *(P-16872)*

Diab Holdings Inc .......................................................................... E ...... 408 598-2241
830 Stewart Dr Sunnyvale (94085) *(P-6631)*

Diablo Clinical Research Inc ....................................................... E ...... 925 930-7267
2255 Ygnacio Valley Rd Ste M Walnut Creek (94598) *(P-5427)*

Diablo Country Magazine Inc ..................................................... E ...... 925 943-1111
2520 Camino Diablo Walnut Creek (94597) *(P-4247)*

Diablo Custom Publishing, Walnut Creek *Also Called: Diablo Country Magazine Inc (P-4247)*

Diadexus Inc .................................................................................. E ...... 650 246-6400
349 Oyster Point Blvd South San Francisco (94080) *(P-5748)*

Diageo North America Inc ........................................................... E ...... 415 835-7300
1160 Battery St Ste 30 San Francisco (94111) *(P-1538)*

Diageo North America Inc ........................................................... E ...... 925 520-3116
6130 Stoneridge Mall Rd Ste 250 Pleasanton (94588) *(P-1836)*

Diageo North America Inc ........................................................... E ...... 650 329-3220
151 Commonwealth Dr Menlo Park (94025) *(P-1837)*

DIAGEO NORTH AMERICA INC., Pleasanton *Also Called: Diageo North America Inc (P-1836)*

DIAGEO NORTH AMERICA INC., Menlo Park *Also Called: Diageo North America Inc (P-1837)*

Diagnostic Solutions Intl LLC ..................................................... F ...... 909 930-3600
2580 E Philadelphia St Ste C Ontario (91761) *(P-13823)*

Diagnostixx of California Corp .................................................... E ...... 909 482-0840
829 Towne Center Dr Pomona (91767) *(P-15068)*

Diagnstic Intrvntonal Crdiolgy, Santa Clara *Also Called: Intuitive Surgical Inc (P-15129)*

Diakont, Oceanside *Also Called: Diakont Advanced Tech Inc (P-16499)*

Diakont Advanced Tech Inc ........................................................ E ...... 858 551-5551
1662 Ord Way Oceanside (92056) *(P-16499)*

Dial Industries Inc ......................................................................... D ...... 323 263-6878
3616 Noakes St Los Angeles (90023) *(P-6802)*

Dial Industries Inc (PA) ................................................................ D ...... 323 263-6878
3628 Noakes St Los Angeles (90023) *(P-6803)*

Dial Precision Inc .......................................................................... D ...... 760 947-3557
17235 Darwin Ave Hesperia (92345) *(P-10810)*

Diality Inc ........................................................................................ D ...... 949 916-5851
181 Technology Dr Ste 150 Irvine (92618) *(P-15069)*

Dialog Semiconductor, San Jose *Also Called: Iwatt Inc (P-12506)*

Diamante Worldwide Inc ............................................................. F ...... 714 822-7458
387 Magnolia Ave Ste 103 Corona (92879) *(P-3718)*

Diamanti Inc (PA) .......................................................................... E ...... 408 645-5111
111 N Market St Ste 800 San Jose (95113) *(P-10304)*

Diamon Fusion, Irvine *Also Called: Diamon Fusion Intl Inc (P-6282)*

Diamon Fusion Intl Inc ................................................................. F ...... 949 388-8000
9361 Irvine Blvd Irvine (92618) *(P-6282)*

Diamond Baseball Company Inc ................................................ E ...... 949 409-9300
121 Waterworks Way Ste 150 Irvine (92618) *(P-15803)*

# ALPHABETIC SECTION — Dimensions In Screen Printing

**Diamond Blue Growers (PA)** ............................................. A ...... 800 987-2329
1802 C St Sacramento (95811) *(P-2183)*

**Diamond Collection LLC** ................................................. E ...... 626 435-0077
20579 Valley Blvd Walnut (91789) *(P-2897)*

**Diamond Creek Vineyard** ................................................ F ...... 707 942-6926
1500 Diamond Mountain Rd Calistoga (94515) *(P-1539)*

**Diamond Crystal Brands Inc** ............................................ E ...... 559 651-7782
8700 W Doe Ave Visalia (93291) *(P-2184)*

**Diamond Crystal Brands-Hormel, Visalia** *Also Called: Diamond Crystal Brands Inc (P-2184)*

**Diamond Foods LLC (PA)** ............................................... A ...... 209 467-6000
1050 Diamond St Stockton (95205) *(P-1351)*

**Diamond Gloves** ........................................................ E ...... 714 667-0506
1100 S Linwood Ave Ste A Santa Ana (92705) *(P-15332)*

**Diamond Ground Products Inc** ........................................... E ...... 805 498-3837
2651 Lavery Ct Newbury Park (91320) *(P-9725)*

**Diamond Mattress Company Inc (PA)** .................................... E ...... 310 638-0363
3112 E Las Hermanas St Compton (90221) *(P-17518)*

**Diamond Mattress Nf, Compton** *Also Called: Diamond Mattress Company Inc (P-17518)*

**Diamond Multimedia, Canoga Park** *Also Called: Best Data Products Inc (P-10334)*

**Diamond of California, Stockton** *Also Called: Diamond Foods LLC (P-1351)*

**Diamond Sports, Irvine** *Also Called: Diamond Baseball Company Inc (P-15803)*

**Diamond Tool and Die Inc** .............................................. E ...... 510 534-7050
508 29th Ave Oakland (94601) *(P-10811)*

**Diamond Wipes, Chino** *Also Called: Diamond Wipes Intl Inc (P-5974)*

**Diamond Wipes Intl Inc** ................................................ C ...... 909 230-9888
4200 E Mission Blvd Ontario (91761) *(P-5972)*

**Diamond Wipes Intl Inc** ................................................ D ...... 909 230-9888
13775 Ramona Ave Chino (91710) *(P-5973)*

**Diamond Wipes Intl Inc (PA)** ........................................... D ...... 909 230-9888
4651 Schaefer Ave Chino (91710) *(P-5974)*

**Diana Did-It Designs Inc** .............................................. E ...... 970 226-5062
20579 Valley Blvd Walnut (91789) *(P-2898)*

**Diana Fruit Co Inc** .................................................... D ...... 408 727-9631
651 Mathew St Santa Clara (95050) *(P-886)*

**Dianas Mexican Food Pdts Inc (PA)** .................................... E ...... 562 926-5802
16330 Pioneer Blvd Norwalk (90650) *(P-2185)*

**Dianas Mexican Food Pdts Inc** ......................................... D ...... 626 444-0555
2905 Durfee Ave El Monte (91732) *(P-2186)*

**Dianas Mexican Food Pdts Inc** ......................................... E ...... 310 834-4886
300 E Sepulveda Blvd Carson (90745) *(P-17374)*

**Diasorin Molecular LLC** ................................................ C ...... 562 240-6500
11331 Valley View St Cypress (90630) *(P-5749)*

**Diatomaceous Earth.com, Santa Barbara** *Also Called: Esperer Webstores LLC (P-755)*

**Diba Fashions Inc** ..................................................... D ...... 323 232-3775
472 N Bowling Green Way Los Angeles (90049) *(P-19087)*

**Dibella, Oceanside** *Also Called: Dibella Baking Company Inc (P-1272)*

**Dibella Baking Company Inc** ............................................ D ...... 951 797-4144
3524 Seagate Way Ste 110 Oceanside (92056) *(P-1272)*

**Dicalite, Burney** *Also Called: Dicalite Minerals LLC (P-7565)*

**Dicalite Minerals LLC (HQ)** ............................................ E ...... 530 335-5451
36994 Summit Lake Rd Burney (96013) *(P-7565)*

**Dicaperl Corporation (DH)** ............................................. D ...... 610 667-6640
23705 Crenshaw Blvd Ste 101 Torrance (90505) *(P-338)*

**Dicar Inc** ............................................................. E ...... 408 295-1106
1285 Alma Ct San Jose (95112) *(P-7784)*

**Dick Browns Technical Service** ......................................... F ...... 707 374-2133
553 Airport Rd Ste B Rio Vista (94571) *(P-155)*

**Dick Farrell Industries Inc** ........................................... F ...... 909 613-9424
5071 Lindsay Ct Chino (91710) *(P-10048)*

**Dick Howells Hole Drlg Svc Inc** ........................................ F ...... 562 633-9898
2579 E 67th St Long Beach (90805) *(P-156)*

**Dicken Enterprises Inc** ................................................ E ...... 760 246-7733
22060 Bear Valley Rd Apple Valley (92308) *(P-10049)*

**Dickeys Barbecue Pit, Tustin** *Also Called: Dickeys Barbecue Rest Inc (P-17576)*

**Dickeys Barbecue Rest Inc** ............................................. E ...... 714 602-3874
17245 17th St Tustin (92780) *(P-17576)*

**Dicom Systems Inc** ..................................................... E ...... 415 684-8790
1999 S Bascom Ave Ste 700 Campbell (95008) *(P-17911)*

**Dicon Fiberoptics Inc** ................................................. B ...... 510 620-5000
1689 Regatta Blvd Richmond (94804) *(P-12960)*

**Die and Tool Products Inc** ............................................. F ...... 415 822-2888
1842 Sabre St Hayward (94545) *(P-8836)*

**Die Shop** .............................................................. F ...... 562 630-4400
7302 Adams St Paramount (90723) *(P-9618)*

**Diego & Son Printing Inc** .............................................. F ...... 619 233-5373
2277 National Ave San Diego (92113) *(P-4588)*

**Dig Corporation** ....................................................... E ...... 760 727-0914
1210 Activity Dr Vista (92081) *(P-9349)*

**Digicom Electronics, Oakland** *Also Called: Digicom Electronics Inc (P-12087)*

**Digicom Electronics Inc** ............................................... E ...... 510 639-7003
7799 Pardee Ln Oakland (94621) *(P-12087)*

**Digilens, Sunnyvale** *Also Called: Digilens Inc (P-14771)*

**Digilens Inc** .......................................................... E ...... 408 734-0219
1276 Hammerwood Ave Sunnyvale (94089) *(P-14771)*

**Digital Arbitrage Dist Inc (PA)** ....................................... E ...... 888 392-9478
3033 5th Ave Ste 100 San Diego (92103) *(P-18240)*

**Digital Doc LLC** ....................................................... E ...... 916 941-8010
4789 Golden Foothill Pkwy El Dorado Hills (95762) *(P-16580)*

**Digital Domain Media Group Inc** ........................................ A
12641 Beatrice St Los Angeles (90066) *(P-17826)*

**Digital Dynamics Inc** .................................................. E ...... 831 438-4444
5 Victor Sq Scotts Valley (95066) *(P-14402)*

**DIGITAL FIRST MEDIA, San Jose** *Also Called: San Jose Mercury-News LLC (P-4189)*

**Digital Flex Media Inc** ................................................ D ...... 909 484-8440
11150 White Birch Dr Rancho Cucamonga (91730) *(P-11727)*

**Digital Force Technologies, San Diego** *Also Called: Raytheon Dgital Force Tech LLC (P-14291)*

**Digital Insight Corporation (HQ)** ...................................... C ...... 818 879-1010
1300 Seaport Blvd Ste 300 Redwood City (94063) *(P-19016)*

**Digital Label Solutions LLC** ........................................... E ...... 714 982-5000
1177 N Grove St Anaheim (92806) *(P-4036)*

**Digital Loggers, Santa Clara** *Also Called: Computer Performance Inc (P-17547)*

**Digital Mania Inc** ..................................................... E ...... 415 896-0500
455 Market St Ste 180 San Francisco (94105) *(P-4589)*

**Digital Periph Solutions Inc** .......................................... E ...... 714 998-3440
160 S Old Springs Rd Ste 220 Anaheim (92808) *(P-11648)*

**Digital Power, Milpitas** *Also Called: Digital Power Corporation (P-12961)*

**Digital Power Corporation (HQ)** ........................................ E ...... 510 657-2635
1635 S Main St Milpitas (95035) *(P-12961)*

**Digital Printing Systems Inc (PA)** ..................................... D ...... 626 815-1888
2350 Panorama Ter Los Angeles (90039) *(P-4590)*

**Digital Prototype Systems Inc** ......................................... E ...... 559 454-1600
4955 E Yale Ave Fresno (93727) *(P-11841)*

**Digital Room Holdings Inc (HQ)** ........................................ D ...... 310 575-4440
8000 Haskell Ave Van Nuys (91406) *(P-4873)*

**Digital Signal Power Mfg, San Bernardino** *Also Called: DSPM Inc (P-12838)*

**Digital Storm, Gilroy** *Also Called: Hanaps Enterprises (P-10375)*

**Digital Supercolor Inc** ................................................ D ...... 949 622-0010
Irvine (92606) *(P-4591)*

**Digital Surgery Systems Inc** ........................................... E ...... 805 978-5400
125 Cremona Dr Pmb 110 Goleta (93117) *(P-15070)*

**Digitalpro Inc** ........................................................ D ...... 858 874-7750
13257 Kirkham Way Poway (92064) *(P-4592)*

**Digitran, Rancho Cucamonga** *Also Called: Electro Switch Corp (P-11240)*

**Digits Financial Inc** .................................................. E ...... 814 634-4487
1015 Fillmore St San Francisco (94115) *(P-18241)*

**Digivision Inc** ........................................................ E ...... 858 530-0100
9830 Summers Ridge Rd San Diego (92121) *(P-14403)*

**Dilco Industrial Inc** .................................................. F ...... 714 998-5266
205 E Bristol Ln Orange (92865) *(P-9750)*

**Diligent Solutions Inc** ................................................ E ...... 760 814-8960
3240 Grey Hawk Ct Carlsbad (92010) *(P-10812)*

**Dillon Companies Inc** .................................................. C ...... 951 352-8353
4250 Van Buren Blvd Riverside (92503) *(P-17375)*

**Dimaxx Technologies LLC** ............................................... F ...... 530 888-1942
11842 Kemper Rd Auburn (95603) *(P-14772)*

**Dimensional Signs & Graphics, San Diego** *Also Called: Dimensional Silk Screen Inc (P-17827)*

**Dimensional Silk Screen Inc** ........................................... F ...... 619 232-9100
3750 Dalbergia St San Diego (92113) *(P-17827)*

**Dimensions In Screen Printing, Irvine** *Also Called: Tomorrows Look Inc (P-2497)*

# Dimensions Unlimited

**ALPHABETIC SECTION**

**Dimensions Unlimited, Vallejo** *Also Called: Jbe Inc (P-3659)*
**Dimic Steel Tech Inc** ............................................................. E ...... 909 946-6767
145 N 8th Ave Upland (91786) *(P-8433)*
**Dinan Engineering Inc** ........................................................... E ...... 408 779-8584
865 Jarvis Dr Morgan Hill (95037) *(P-13486)*
**Dincloud Inc** ............................................................................. D ...... 310 929-1101
27520 Hawthorne Blvd Ste 185 Rllng Hls Est (90274) *(P-18242)*
**Ding Sticks, Huntington Beach** *Also Called: Sandra Gruca (P-13572)*
**Dinostor, Mountain View** *Also Called: Global Automation Inc (P-19037)*
**Dinsmore & Associates LLC** ................................................ F ...... 714 641-7111
1681 Kettering Irvine (92614) *(P-6558)*
**Dionex Corporation** ............................................................... F ...... 408 737-0700
501 Mercury Dr Sunnyvale (94085) *(P-14650)*
**Dionex Corporation (HQ)** ...................................................... B ...... 408 737-0700
1228 Titan Way Ste 1002 Sunnyvale (94085) *(P-14651)*
**Dioz Group, The, Beverly Hills** *Also Called: Alanic International Corp (P-2540)*
**Dip Braze Inc** ........................................................................... F ...... 818 768-1555
9131 De Garmo Ave Sun Valley (91352) *(P-19191)*
**Direct Chemicals, Huntington Beach** *Also Called: Home & Body Company (P-6292)*
**Direct Drive Systems Inc** ...................................................... D ...... 714 872-5500
621 Burning Tree Rd Fullerton (92833) *(P-11263)*
**Direct Mail Center, San Francisco** *Also Called: Communication Services Ctr Inc (P-4564)*
**Directed Light Inc** .................................................................. E ...... 408 321-8500
74 Bonaventura Dr San Jose (95134) *(P-16812)*
**Disc Replicator Inc** ................................................................ E ...... 909 385-0118
21137 Commerce Point Dr Walnut (91789) *(P-11728)*
**Discera Inc** ............................................................................... F
950 Tower Ln Ste 700 Foster City (94404) *(P-12403)*
**Discerndx Inc** .......................................................................... F ...... 909 319-9779
2478 Embarcadero Way Palo Alto (94303) *(P-18243)*
**Discopylabs** .............................................................................. E ...... 909 390-3800
4455 E Philadelphia St Ontario (91761) *(P-11729)*
**Discount Tire, Encinitas** *Also Called: Southern Cal Disc Tire Co Inc (P-17464)*
**Discounted Wheel Warehouse, Santa Ana** *Also Called: Wheel and Tire Club Inc (P-7634)*
**Disguise Inc (HQ)** ................................................................... D ...... 858 391-3600
12120 Kear Pl Poway (92064) *(P-2899)*
**Dish For All Inc** ...................................................................... E ...... 760 690-3869
148 S Escondido Blvd Escondido (92025) *(P-19171)*
**Disney, Anaheim** *Also Called: Walt Dsney Imgnring RES Dev In (P-2913)*
**Disney Book Group LLC (DH)** ............................................. E ...... 818 560-1000
500 S Buena Vista St Burbank (91521) *(P-4327)*
**Disney Editions, Burbank** *Also Called: Disney Publishing Worldwide (P-4248)*
**Disney Financial Services, Burbank** *Also Called: Twdc Enterprises 18 Corp (P-16330)*
**Disney Publishing Worldwide (DH)** ................................... D ...... 212 633-4400
500 S Buena Vista St Burbank (91521) *(P-4248)*
**Disorderly Kids, Los Angeles** *Also Called: Avalon Apparel LLC (P-2700)*
**Dispensing Dynamics Intl Inc (PA)** .................................... D ...... 626 961-3691
1940 Diamond St San Marcos (92078) *(P-6804)*
**Display Fabrication Group Inc** ............................................ E ...... 714 373-2100
1231 N Miller St Ste 100 Anaheim (92806) *(P-3026)*
**Display Products Inc** ............................................................. E ...... 310 640-0442
445 S Douglas St El Segundo (90245) *(P-12404)*
**Display Supply Chain Cons LLC** ......................................... F ...... 512 577-3672
1237 Muirlands Vista Way La Jolla (92037) *(P-3654)*
**Displaylink Corp (HQ)** ........................................................... F ...... 650 838-0481
1251 Mckay Dr San Jose (95131) *(P-17912)*
**Disposable Waste System, Santa Ana** *Also Called: Jwc Environmental Inc (P-10569)*
**Disruptive Games Inc** ........................................................... E ...... 310 922-6658
2030 Addison St Ste 610 Berkeley (94704) *(P-18244)*
**Distillery, Manhattan Beach** *Also Called: Distillery Tech Inc (P-17913)*
**Distillery Tech Inc** ................................................................. C ...... 310 776-6234
1500 Rosecrans Ave Ste 500 Manhattan Beach (90266) *(P-17913)*
**Distinct Indulgence Inc** ........................................................ E ...... 818 546-1700
5018 Lante St Baldwin Park (91706) *(P-1183)*
**Distinctive Inds Texas Inc** ................................................... E ...... 512 491-3500
10618 Shoemaker Ave Santa Fe Springs (90670) *(P-2877)*
**Distinctive Inds Texas Inc** ................................................... E ...... 323 889-5766
9419 Ann St Santa Fe Springs (90670) *(P-2878)*
**Distinctive Industries** ........................................................... B ...... 800 421-9777
10618 Shoemaker Ave Santa Fe Springs (90670) *(P-3005)*

**Distinctive Plastics Inc** ......................................................... D ...... 760 599-9100
1385 Decision St Vista (92081) *(P-6805)*
**Distribution, Ontario** *Also Called: Index Fasteners Inc (P-16877)*
**Distribution Electrnics Vlued** .............................................. E ...... 714 368-1717
2651 Dow Ave Tustin (92780) *(P-13232)*
**Distributors Processing Inc** ................................................. F ...... 559 781-0297
17656 Avenue 168 Porterville (93257) *(P-1998)*
**Distro Worldwide LLC** .......................................................... E ...... 818 849-0953
3400 S Main St Los Angeles (90007) *(P-2572)*
**Distru Corp** .............................................................................. E ...... 603 630-0282
344 Thomas L Berkley Way Oakland (94612) *(P-18245)*
**Ditech Networks Inc (DH)** ................................................... E ...... 408 883-3636
3099 N 1st St San Jose (95134) *(P-11760)*
**Diverse Optics Inc** ................................................................. E ...... 909 593-9330
10339 Dorset St Rancho Cucamonga (91730) *(P-6806)*
**Diversified Nano Solutions Corp** ....................................... E ...... 858 924-1013
12140 Community Rd Poway (92064) *(P-6253)*
**Diversfied Tchncal Systems Inc (HQ)** ............................... E ...... 562 493-0158
1720 Apollo Ct Seal Beach (90740) *(P-14512)*
**Diversified Logistic Svcs Inc** ............................................... E ...... 562 941-3600
13033 Telegraph Rd Santa Fe Springs (90670) *(P-16310)*
**Diversified Mfg Cal Inc, Vista** *Also Called: Router Works Inc (P-11092)*
**Diversified Minerals Inc** ....................................................... E ...... 805 247-1069
1100 Mountain View Ave Ste F Oxnard (93030) *(P-7438)*
**Diversified Plastics Inc** ........................................................ E ...... 760 598-5333
1333 Keystone Way Vista (92081) *(P-6807)*
**Diversified Printers Inc** ........................................................ D ...... 714 994-3400
12834 Maxwell Dr Tustin (92782) *(P-4388)*
**Diversified Silicone, Santa Fe Springs** *Also Called: Rogers Corporation (P-6534)*
**Diversified Tool & Die** .......................................................... E ...... 760 598-9100
2585 Birch St Vista (92081) *(P-8837)*
**Diversified Trading Corp** ..................................................... F ...... 714 237-9995
1640 E Miraloma Ave Placentia (92870) *(P-7993)*
**Diversified Waterscapes Inc** ............................................... F ...... 949 582-5414
27324 Camino Capistrano Ste 213 Laguna Niguel (92677) *(P-19527)*
**Divine Pasta Company** ......................................................... E ...... 818 559-7440
140 W Providencia Ave Burbank (91502) *(P-2187)*
**Divine Pasta Company, Burbank** *Also Called: Palermo Family LP (P-2312)*
**Diving Unlimited Int., San Diego** *Also Called: Diving Unlimited Intl Inc (P-15804)*
**Diving Unlimited Intl Inc** ..................................................... D ...... 619 236-1203
1148 Delevan Dr San Diego (92102) *(P-15804)*
**Dixieline Lumber Company LLC (DH)** ............................... D ...... 619 224-4120
3250 Sports Arena Blvd San Diego (92110) *(P-17327)*
**Dixieline Lumber Company LLC** ........................................ B ...... 951 224-8491
2625 Durahart St Riverside (92507) *(P-17328)*
**Dixieline Probuild, San Diego** *Also Called: Dixieline Lumber Company LLC (P-17327)*
**Diy Co** ....................................................................................... F ...... 844 564-6349
3360 20th St San Francisco (94110) *(P-13233)*
**Diy Drones, Berkeley** *Also Called: 3d Robotics Inc (P-13206)*
**DJ Grey Company Inc** .......................................................... F ...... 707 431-2779
455 Allan Ct Healdsburg (95448) *(P-12962)*
**Djh Enterprises** ...................................................................... E ...... 714 424-6500
23011 Moulton Pkwy Ste B6 Laguna Hills (92653) *(P-11842)*
**Dji Service LLC** ...................................................................... F ...... 818 235-0788
17301 Edwards Rd Cerritos (90703) *(P-13824)*
**Dji Technology Inc** ................................................................ D ...... 818 235-0789
17301 Edwards Rd Cerritos (90703) *(P-15636)*
**DJM Suspension, Gardena** *Also Called: D and J Marketing Inc (P-3004)*
**Djo LLC (HQ)** .......................................................................... D ...... 800 321-9549
5919 Sea Otter Pl Ste 200 Carlsbad (92010) *(P-15333)*
**Djo Holdings LLC (DH)** ......................................................... E ...... 760 727-1280
1430 Decision St Vista (92081) *(P-15334)*
**DK, Los Angeles** *Also Called: Design Knit Inc (P-2467)*
**DK Amans Valve & Supply, Long Beach** *Also Called: DK Valve & Supply Inc (P-19251)*
**DK Valve & Supply Inc** ......................................................... E ...... 562 529-8400
2385 E Artesia Blvd Long Beach (90805) *(P-19251)*
**Dkp Designs Inc** .................................................................... F ...... 310 322-6000
110 Maryland St El Segundo (90245) *(P-16125)*
**Dkw Precision Machining Inc** ............................................. E ...... 209 824-7899
17731 Ideal Pkwy Manteca (95336) *(P-10813)*

## ALPHABETIC SECTION — Don Vito Ozuna Food Corp

**DL Horton Enterprises Inc** ............................................................. D ...... 323 777-1700
  12705 Daphne Ave Hawthorne (90250) *(P-10814)*
**Dl Imaging, Santa Ana** *Also Called: Dekra-Lite Industries Inc (P-19086)*
**DLa Colmena Inc** ........................................................................... E ...... 831 724-4544
  129 W Lake Ave Watsonville (95076) *(P-17376)*
**Dm Luxury LLC** .............................................................................. C ...... 858 366-9721
  875 Prospect St Ste 300 La Jolla (92037) *(P-4874)*
**DMA Enterprises Inc (PA)** ............................................................ E ...... 805 520-2468
  2255 Union Pl Simi Valley (93065) *(P-16126)*
**Dmbm LLC** ..................................................................................... E ...... 714 321-6032
  2445 E 12th St Ste C Los Angeles (90021) *(P-2755)*
**DMC, Carson** *Also Called: Designed Metal Connections Inc (P-8721)*
**DMC Power Inc (PA)** ..................................................................... E ...... 310 323-1616
  623 E Artesia Blvd Carson (90746) *(P-11450)*
**Dmf Inc** ........................................................................................... D ...... 323 934-7779
  1118 E 223rd St Unit 1 Carson (90745) *(P-11494)*
**Dmf Lighting, Carson** *Also Called: Dmf Inc (P-11494)*
**Dmg Mori Digital Tech Lab Corp** .................................................. D ...... 530 746-7400
  3601 Faraday Ave Davis (95618) *(P-9675)*
**Dmg Mori Manufacturing USA Inc (HQ)** ..................................... D ...... 530 746-7400
  3601 Faraday Ave Davis (95618) *(P-9549)*
**Dmg Mori Manufacturing USA Inc** ............................................... D ...... 530 746-3140
  3601 Faraday Ave Davis (95618) *(P-9550)*
**Dmi Ready Mix, Oxnard** *Also Called: Diversified Minerals Inc (P-7438)*
**Dmk, Santa Fe Springs** *Also Called: Danne Montague King Co (P-17035)*
**Dn Tanks Inc** .................................................................................. C ...... 619 440-8181
  351 Cypress Ln El Cajon (92020) *(P-14125)*
**Dna Motor Inc** ................................................................................ E ...... 626 965-8898
  801 Sentous Ave City Of Industry (91744) *(P-17450)*
**Dna Motoring, City Of Industry** *Also Called: Dna Motor Inc (P-17450)*
**Dna Script Inc** ................................................................................ E ...... 650 457-0844
  2001 Junipero Serra Blvd Ste 400 Daly City (94014) *(P-14652)*
**Dna Specialty Inc** .......................................................................... D ...... 310 767-4070
  200 W Artesia Blvd Compton (90220) *(P-16381)*
**DNam Apparel Industries LLC** ..................................................... E ...... 323 859-0114
  4938 Triggs St Commerce (90022) *(P-2756)*
**Dnatrix Inc** ...................................................................................... E ...... 832 930-2401
  2659 State St # 100 Carlsbad (92008) *(P-5824)*
**Dnf Controls, Northridge** *Also Called: Universal Ctrl Solutions Corp (P-11354)*
**Dnib Unwind Inc** ........................................................................... C ...... 213 617-2717
  333 S Grand Ave Ste 4070 Los Angeles (90071) *(P-5428)*
**Dns Electronics, Santa Clara** *Also Called: Screen Spe Usa LLC (P-9898)*
**Do Dine Inc** .................................................................................... F ...... 510 583-7546
  24052 Mission Blvd Hayward (94544) *(P-18246)*
**Do It American Mfg Company LLC** ............................................. F ...... 951 254-9204
  137 Vander St Corona (92878) *(P-9281)*
**Do It Best, Pasadena** *Also Called: George L Throop Co (P-17354)*
**Dobake Bakeries Inc** .................................................................... D ...... 510 834-3134
  810 81st Ave Oakland (94621) *(P-1184)*
**Docphin, Sunnyvale** *Also Called: Healthtap Inc (P-19317)*
**Document Capture Technologies Inc** ......................................... E ...... 408 436-9888
  41332 Christy St Fremont (94538) *(P-10358)*
**Document Proc Solutions Inc** ..................................................... E ...... 925 839-1182
  535 Main St Ste 317 Martinez (94553) *(P-3766)*
**Documotion Research Inc** ........................................................... F ...... 714 662-3800
  2020 S Eastwood Ave Santa Ana (92705) *(P-4593)*
**Docupak Inc** .................................................................................. F ...... 714 670-7944
  1702 Edinger Ave Tustin (92780) *(P-5001)*
**Docusign, San Francisco** *Also Called: Docusign Inc (P-18247)*
**Docusign Inc (PA)** ........................................................................ B ...... 415 489-4940
  221 Main St Ste 1550 San Francisco (94105) *(P-18247)*
**DOE & Ingalls Cal Oper LLC** ....................................................... E ...... 951 801-7175
  1060 Citrus St Riverside (92507) *(P-14653)*
**Doer Marine Operations** .............................................................. E ...... 510 530-9388
  650 W Tower Ave Alameda (94501) *(P-19558)*
**Dogswell, Los Angeles** *Also Called: Arthur Dogswell LLC (P-1093)*
**Doh Quest LLC** ............................................................................. E ...... 213 651-3441
  8939 S Sepulveda Blvd Ste 102 Los Angeles (90045) *(P-2617)*
**Doi Venture, Rancho Cucamonga** *Also Called: Davidson Optronics Inc (P-14859)*
**Doka USA Ltd** ................................................................................ E ...... 951 509-0023
  6901 Central Ave Riverside (92504) *(P-8434)*

**Dolby, San Francisco** *Also Called: Dolby Laboratories Inc (P-11652)*
**Dolby Laboratories Inc** ................................................................. C ...... 415 645-5000
  999 Brannan St San Francisco (94103) *(P-11649)*
**Dolby Laboratories Inc** ................................................................. E ...... 408 730-5543
  432 Lakeside Dr Sunnyvale (94085) *(P-11650)*
**Dolby Laboratories Inc** ................................................................. E ...... 818 562-1101
  1020 Chestnut St Burbank (91506) *(P-11651)*
**Dolby Laboratories Inc (PA)** ........................................................ B ...... 415 558-0200
  1275 Market St Fl 15 San Francisco (94103) *(P-11652)*
**Dolby Laboratories Inc** ................................................................. E ...... 415 715-2500
  175 S Hill Dr Brisbane (94005) *(P-11843)*
**Dolby Labs, Brisbane** *Also Called: Dolby Laboratories Inc (P-11843)*
**Dolby Labs Licensing Corp** ......................................................... C ...... 415 558-0200
  1275 Market St Fl 15 San Francisco (94103) *(P-11653)*
**Dolce Dolci LLC** ............................................................................ F ...... 818 343-8400
  16745 Saticoy St Ste 112 Van Nuys (91406) *(P-798)*
**Dole, Monterey** *Also Called: Dole Fresh Vegetables Inc (P-2188)*
**Dole Food, Salinas** *Also Called: Dole Food Company Inc (P-44)*
**Dole Food Company Inc** .............................................................. F ...... 831 422-8871
  639 Sanborn Pl Salinas (93901) *(P-44)*
**Dole Fresh Vegetables Inc (HQ)** ................................................. C ...... 831 422-8871
  2959 Salinas Hwy Monterey (93940) *(P-2188)*
**Dole Holding Company LLC** ....................................................... A ...... 818 879-6600
  1 Dole Dr Westlake Village (91362) *(P-45)*
**Dole Packaged Foods LLC (HQ)** ................................................ A ...... 800 232-8888
  1 Baxter Way Westlake Village (91362) *(P-1003)*
**Dole Packaged Foods LLC** ......................................................... C ...... 559 875-3354
  1117 K St Sanger (93657) *(P-1004)*
**Dolex Dollar Express Inc** ............................................................. F ...... 818 982-2852
  12727 Sherman Way North Hollywood (91605) *(P-4389)*
**Dollar Shave Club Inc (HQ)** ........................................................ C ...... 310 975-8528
  13335 Maxella Ave Marina Del Rey (90292) *(P-9551)*
**Dolores Canning Co Inc** .............................................................. E ...... 323 263-9155
  1020 N Eastern Ave Los Angeles (90063) *(P-854)*
**Dolphin Medical Inc (HQ)** ............................................................ D ...... 800 448-6506
  12525 Chadron Ave Hawthorne (90250) *(P-15531)*
**Dolphin Technology Inc** ............................................................... E ...... 408 392-0012
  333 W Santa Clara St Ste 920 San Jose (95113) *(P-12405)*
**Domaine Carneros Ltd** ................................................................. D ...... 707 257-0101
  1240 Duhig Rd Napa (94559) *(P-11)*
**Domaine Chandon Inc (DH)** ....................................................... D ...... 707 944-8844
  1 California Dr Yountville (94599) *(P-1540)*
**Dome Printing & Packaging LLC (HQ)** ...................................... E ...... 800 343-3139
  2031 Dome Ln Mcclellan (95652) *(P-4594)*
**Dome9 Security Inc** ...................................................................... E ...... 831 212-2353
  800 W El Camino Real Ste 100 Mountain View (94040) *(P-17550)*
**Domico Software** .......................................................................... F ...... 510 841-4155
  1220 Oakland Blvd Ste 300 Walnut Creek (94596) *(P-18248)*
**Dominics Orgnal Gnova Deli Inc** ................................................. D ...... 707 253-8686
  1550 Trancas St Napa (94558) *(P-17377)*
**Domino Plastics Mfg Inc** ............................................................. E ...... 661 396-3744
  601 Gateway Ct Bakersfield (93307) *(P-6808)*
**Dominus Estate Corporation** ...................................................... F ...... 707 944-8954
  2570 Napa Nook Rd Yountville (94599) *(P-1541)*
**Dompe US Inc** ............................................................................... F ...... 833 366-7387
  400 S El Camino Real Ste 400 San Mateo (94402) *(P-19492)*
**Domries Enterprises Inc** ............................................................. E ...... 559 485-4306
  12281 Road 29 Madera (93638) *(P-9350)*
**Don Alderson Associates Inc** ..................................................... E ...... 310 837-5141
  3327 La Cienega Pl Los Angeles (90016) *(P-3554)*
**Don Francisco Cheese, Modesto** *Also Called: Rizo-Lopez Foods Inc (P-730)*
**Don Lee Farms, Inglewood** *Also Called: Goodman Food Products Inc (P-2222)*
**Don Miguel Foods, Orange** *Also Called: Don Miguel Mexican Foods Inc (P-1033)*
**Don Miguel Mexican Foods Inc (HQ)** ......................................... E ...... 714 385-4500
  333 S Anita Dr Ste 1000 Orange (92868) *(P-1033)*
**Don Pedro Pump, Turlock** *Also Called: Don Pedro Pump LLC (P-19252)*
**Don Pedro Pump LLC** .................................................................. E ...... 209 632-3161
  1930 S Walnut Rd Turlock (95380) *(P-19252)*
**Don Sbstani Sons Intl Wine Ngc** ................................................ E ...... 707 337-1961
  520 Airpark Rd Napa (94558) *(P-1542)*
**Don Vito Ozuna Food Corp** ......................................................... E ...... 408 465-2010
  180 Cochrane Cir Morgan Hill (95037) *(P-2089)*

**Donal Machine Inc** .................................................................................. E ...... 707 763-6625
591 N Mcdowell Blvd Petaluma (94954) *(P-10815)*

**Donaldson Company Inc** ......................................................................... E ...... 661 295-0800
26235 Technology Dr Valencia (91355) *(P-13487)*

**Doncasters Gce Integrated, Chula Vista** *Also Called: Integrated Energy Technologies Inc*
*(P-9951)*

**Donco & Sons Inc** .................................................................................... E ...... 714 779-0099
2871 E Blue Star St Anaheim (92806) *(P-455)*

**Donco Associates & Sons, Anaheim** *Also Called: Donco & Sons Inc (P-455)*

**Done Right Security Inc** .......................................................................... E ...... 510 621-7686
1260 Nimitz Ave Bldg 670 Vallejo (94592) *(P-19053)*

**Donoco Industries Inc** ............................................................................. E ...... 714 893-7889
5642 Research Dr Ste B Huntington Beach (92649) *(P-7194)*

**Donsuemor Inc** ........................................................................................ D ...... 888 420-4441
2080 N Loop Rd Alameda (94502) *(P-1185)*

**Dool Fna Inc** ............................................................................................. C ...... 562 483-4100
16624 Edwards Rd Cerritos (90703) *(P-2435)*

**Door Components Inc** ............................................................................. C ...... 909 770-5700
7980 Redwood Ave Fontana (92336) *(P-8262)*

**Door Doctor, Anaheim** *Also Called: R & S Ovrhd Doors So-Cal Inc (P-19277)*

**Doorking, Inglewood** *Also Called: Doorking Inc (P-13234)*

**Doorking Inc (PA)** ..................................................................................... C ...... 310 645-0023
120 S Glasgow Ave Inglewood (90301) *(P-13234)*

**Dorado Network Systems Corp** .............................................................. C ...... 650 227-7300
40 Pacifica Irvine (92618) *(P-18249)*

**Dorado Pkg, North Hollywood** *Also Called: Corporate Impressions La Inc (P-4866)*

**Dorco Electronics Inc** .............................................................................. F ...... 562 623-1133
13540 Larwin Cir Santa Fe Springs (90670) *(P-3903)*

**Dorco Fiberglass Products, Santa Fe Springs** *Also Called: Dorco Electronics Inc (P-3903)*

**Dorel Home Furnishings Inc** ................................................................... D ...... 909 390-5705
5400 Shea Center Dr Ontario (91761) *(P-3439)*

**Dorel Juvenile Group Inc** ........................................................................ C ...... 909 428-0295
9950 Calabash Ave Fontana (92335) *(P-6809)*

**Dorel Juvenile Group Inc** ........................................................................ C ...... 909 390-5705
5400 Shea Center Dr Ontario (91761) *(P-6810)*

**Doremi, Burbank** *Also Called: Doremi Labs Inc (P-11654)*

**Doremi Labs, Burbank** *Also Called: Dolby Laboratories Inc (P-11651)*

**Doremi Labs Inc** ...................................................................................... E ...... 818 562-1101
1020 Chestnut St Burbank (91506) *(P-11654)*

**Doringer Manufacturing Co Inc** ............................................................... F ...... 310 366-7766
13400 Estrella Ave Gardena (90248) *(P-9552)*

**Dorris Lumber and Moulding Co (PA)** ................................................... D ...... 916 452-7531
3453 Ramona Ave Ste 5 Sacramento (95826) *(P-3131)*

**Dose Medical Corporation** ...................................................................... F ...... 949 367-9600
229 Avenida Fabricante San Clemente (92672) *(P-15071)*

**Dostal Studio** ............................................................................................ F ...... 415 721-7080
17 Woodland Ave San Rafael (94901) *(P-15885)*

**DOT Blue Safes Corporation** .................................................................. E ...... 909 445-8888
2707 N Garey Ave Pomona (91767) *(P-9282)*

**DOT Corp** ................................................................................................. F ...... 714 708-5960
1801 S Standard Ave Santa Ana (92707) *(P-4595)*

**DOT Printer Inc (PA)** ............................................................................... D ...... 949 474-1100
2424 Mcgaw Ave Irvine (92614) *(P-4596)*

**Double K Industries, Chatsworth** *Also Called: Invelop Inc (P-9360)*

**Double Zero Inc (PA)** ............................................................................... F ...... 323 234-6000
5808 Wilmington Ave Vernon (90058) *(P-17089)*

**Doubleco Incorporated** ............................................................................ D ...... 909 481-0799
9444 9th St Rancho Cucamonga (91730) *(P-8752)*

**Doubledutch Inc (DH)** .............................................................................. D ...... 800 748-9024
44 Tehama St Ste 504 San Francisco (94105) *(P-18250)*

**Douce De France** ..................................................................................... F ...... 650 369-9644
686 Brdwy St Redwood City (94063) *(P-1186)*

**Doug Mockett & Company Inc** ................................................................ D ...... 310 318-2491
1915 Abalone Ave Torrance (90501) *(P-3440)*

**Doughpro, Perris** *Also Called: Stearns Product Dev Corp (P-10117)*

**Doughtronics Inc (PA)** ............................................................................. E ...... 510 524-1327
1601 San Pablo Ave Berkeley (94702) *(P-1187)*

**Doughtronics Inc** ...................................................................................... E ...... 510 843-2978
2730 9th St Berkeley (94710) *(P-1188)*

**Douglas Casual Living, Ontario** *Also Called: Chromcraft Rvngton Douglas Ind (P-3467)*

**Douglas Furniture of California LLC** ....................................................... A ...... 310 749-0003
809 Tyburn Rd Palos Verdes Estates (90274) *(P-3501)*

**Douglas Technologies Group Inc** ........................................................... E ...... 760 758-5560
42092 Winchester Rd Ste B Temecula (92590) *(P-13488)*

**Douglas Wheel, Temecula** *Also Called: Douglas Technologies Group Inc (P-13488)*

**Douglass Truck Bodies Inc** ..................................................................... E ...... 661 327-0258
231 21st St Bakersfield (93301) *(P-13408)*

**Doval Industries Inc** ................................................................................. D ...... 323 226-0335
3961 N Mission Rd Los Angeles (90031) *(P-7994)*

**Doval Industries Co, Los Angeles** *Also Called: Doval Industries Inc (P-7994)*

**Dove Business Machine Inc** ................................................................... F ...... 858 638-0100
7430 Trade St San Diego (92121) *(P-16502)*

**Dow Chemical Company** ......................................................................... D ...... 510 786-0100
25500 Whitesell St Hayward (94545) *(P-5151)*

**Dow Company Foundation** ..................................................................... C ...... 909 476-4127
11266 Jersey Blvd Rancho Cucamonga (91730) *(P-5152)*

**Dow Hydraulic Systems Inc** .................................................................... D ...... 909 596-6602
2895 Metropolitan Pl Pomona (91767) *(P-10816)*

**Dow Jones, San Francisco** *Also Called: Dow Jones & Company Inc (P-4104)*

**Dow Jones & Company Inc** ..................................................................... E ...... 415 765-6131
201 California St Ste 1350 San Francisco (94111) *(P-4104)*

**Dow Jones Lmg Stockton** ....................................................................... C ...... 209 943-6397
530 E Market St Stockton (95202) *(P-4105)*

**Dow Pharmaceutical Sciences Inc** .......................................................... C ...... 707 793-2600
1330 Redwood Way Ste C Petaluma (94954) *(P-14654)*

**Dow-Elco Inc** ............................................................................................ E ...... 323 723-1288
1313 W Olympic Blvd Montebello (90640) *(P-11211)*

**Dow-Key Microwave, Ventura** *Also Called: Dow-Key Microwave Corporation (P-11318)*

**Dow-Key Microwave Corporation** ........................................................... C ...... 805 650-0260
4822 Mcgrath St Ventura (93003) *(P-11318)*

**Dowdys Sales and Services Inc** ............................................................. F ...... 559 688-6973
15185 Avenue 224 Tulare (93274) *(P-9351)*

**Dowell Schlumberger, Bakersfield** *Also Called: Schlumberger Technology Corp (P-275)*

**Down River, Stockton** *Also Called: Signode Industrial Group LLC (P-4050)*

**Downey Grinding Co** ................................................................................ E ...... 562 803-5556
12323 Bellflower Blvd Downey (90242) *(P-9553)*

**Downhole Stabilization Inc** ...................................................................... E ...... 661 631-1044
3515 Thomas Way Bakersfield (93308) *(P-9461)*

**Downtown Joe's, Napa** *Also Called: Joes Dwntwn Brewry & Rest Inc (P-17588)*

**Dp, Riverside** *Also Called: Data Physics Corporation (P-16518)*

**Dpa Components International, Simi Valley** *Also Called: Dpa Labs Inc (P-12406)*

**Dpa Labs Inc** ............................................................................................ E ...... 805 581-9200
2251 Ward Ave Simi Valley (93065) *(P-12406)*

**Dpi Direct, Poway** *Also Called: Digitalpro Inc (P-4592)*

**DPI Labs Inc** ............................................................................................. E ...... 909 392-5777
1350 Arrow Hwy La Verne (91750) *(P-13825)*

**Dpp 2020 Inc (DH)** ................................................................................... E ...... 951 845-3161
533 E Third St Beaumont (92223) *(P-6811)*

**Dps Telecom, Fresno** *Also Called: Digital Prototype Systems Inc (P-11841)*

**Dpss Lasers Inc** ....................................................................................... E ...... 408 988-4300
2525 Walsh Ave Santa Clara (95051) *(P-13235)*

**Dr Earth Inc** .............................................................................................. F ...... 707 448-4676
4021 Devon Ct Vacaville (95688) *(P-6171)*

**Dr Harold Katz LLC** ................................................................................. F ...... 323 993-8320
5802 Willoughby Ave Los Angeles (90038) *(P-17663)*

**Dr Heater USA, Burlingame** *Also Called: Tlm International Inc (P-11420)*

**Dr Hops Inc** .............................................................................................. F ...... 510 863-4522
2465 Bermuda Ave San Leandro (94577) *(P-17627)*

**Dr McDougall's Right Foods, Woodland** *Also Called: Bright People Foods Inc (P-2148)*

**Dr Pepper Snapple Group, Riverside** *Also Called: American Bottling Company (P-1850)*

**Dr Pepper/Seven Up Inc** .......................................................................... F ...... 707 545-7797
1901 Russell Ave Santa Rosa (95403) *(P-1885)*

**Dr Smoothie Brands LLC** ........................................................................ E ...... 714 449-9787
1730 Raymer Ave Fullerton (92833) *(P-1999)*

**Dr Smoothie Enterprises LLC** ................................................................. E ...... 714 449-9787
1730 Raymer Ave Fullerton (92833) *(P-2000)*

**Dr Squatch LLC** ....................................................................................... C ...... 631 229-7068
4065 Glencoe Ave Apt 300b Marina Del Rey (90292) *(P-5975)*

**Dr. Bronners Magic Soaps, Vista** *Also Called: All One God Faith Inc (P-5870)*

**Dr. Bronners Magic Soaps, Vista** *Also Called: All One God Faith Inc (P-5871)*

## ALPHABETIC SECTION — Ducommun Aerostructures Inc

Dr. Fresh, La Palma *Also Called: Ranir LLC (P-5627)*

Dragon Alliance, San Clemente *Also Called: Dragon Alliance Inc (P-15599)*

Dragon Alliance Inc ............................................. E ...... 760 931-4900
971 Calle Amanecer San Clemente (92673) *(P-15599)*

Dragon Herbs, Los Angeles *Also Called: Ron Teeguarden Enterprises Inc (P-5267)*

Drake's Brewing Company, San Leandro *Also Called: Artisan Brewers LLC (P-1418)*

Drapery Affair, Paramount *Also Called: Blue Ribbon Draperies Inc (P-17526)*

Dreambig Semiconductor Inc ............................... D ...... 408 839-1232
2860 Zanker Rd Ste 210 San Jose (95134) *(P-12407)*

Dreamctchers Empwerment Netwrk ...................... E ...... 707 558-1775
2201 Tuolumne St Vallejo (94589) *(P-12963)*

Dreamfields California LLC ................................. B ...... 310 691-9739
65000 Two Bunch Palms Trl Desert Hot Springs (92240) *(P-3926)*

Dreamgear LLC .................................................. E ...... 310 222-5522
20001 S Western Ave Torrance (90501) *(P-15745)*

Dreamgirl International, Bell *Also Called: Dg Brands Inc (P-17088)*

Dreamhome Remodeling and Bldrs, San Jose *Also Called: Eli Kiselman (P-226)*

Dreamstart Labs Inc ........................................... E ...... 408 914-1234
2907 Shelter Island Dr Ste 105 San Diego (92106) *(P-18251)*

Drees Wood Products Inc ................................... D ...... 562 633-7337
14020 Orange Ave Paramount (90723) *(P-3235)*

Dremio Corporation (PA) ..................................... E ...... 408 882-3569
3970 Freedom Cir Ste 110 Santa Clara (95054) *(P-17914)*

Dresser-Rand Company ...................................... E ...... 310 223-0600
18502 Dominguez Hill Dr Rancho Dominguez (90220) *(P-9960)*

Dretloh Aircraft Supply Inc .................................. F ...... 714 632-6982
2830 E La Cresta Ave Anaheim (92806) *(P-13826)*

Dreyers Grand Ice Cream Inc (DH) ....................... C ...... 510 594-9466
590 Ygnacio Valley Rd Ste 300 Walnut Creek (94596) *(P-17577)*

Dreyers Grnd Ice Cream Hldngs (DH) .................... C ...... 510 652-8187
590 Ygnacio Valley Rd Walnut Creek (94596) *(P-17128)*

Dri Clean & Restoration ...................................... E ...... 559 292-1100
2918 N Blackstone Ave Fresno (93703) *(P-223)*

Drill Cool Systems Inc (PA) ................................. F ...... 661 633-2665
627 Williams St Bakersfield (93305) *(P-16813)*

Drilling & Trenching Sup Inc (PA) ......................... F ...... 510 895-1650
1458 Mariani Ct Tracy (95376) *(P-9676)*

Drilling World, Tracy *Also Called: Drilling & Trenching Sup Inc (P-9676)*

Drillmec Inc ...................................................... D ...... 281 885-0777
8140 Rosecrans Ave Paramount (90723) *(P-178)*

Drinkpak LLC .................................................... A ...... 833 376-5725
21375 Needham Ranch Pkwy Santa Clarita (91321) *(P-1886)*

Drip Research Technology Svcs, San Diego *Also Called: DRTS Enterprises Ltd (P-9352)*

Driscoll Inc ....................................................... E ...... 619 226-2500
2500 Shelter Island Dr San Diego (92106) *(P-14032)*

Driscoll Boat Works, San Diego *Also Called: Driscoll Inc (P-14032)*

Drive Devilbiss Healthcare, Rialto *Also Called: Medical Depot Inc (P-15166)*

Drive Greenlane, Santa Monica *Also Called: Greenlane Infrastructure LLC (P-13171)*

Drive Line Service Sacramento, West Sacramento *Also Called: Scoggan Company Inc (P-16399)*

Driveai Inc ........................................................ C ...... 408 693-0765
365 Ravendale Dr Mountain View (94043) *(P-18252)*

Driven Technologies, Santa Ana *Also Called: Aerospace Driven Tech Inc (P-13751)*

Driver Inc ......................................................... D ...... 415 999-4960
438 Shotwell St San Francisco (94110) *(P-18253)*

Drivescale Inc ................................................... F ...... 408 849-4651
1320 Hillview Dr Menlo Park (94025) *(P-18254)*

Driveshaftpro .................................................... E ...... 714 893-4585
7532 Anthony Ave Garden Grove (92841) *(F-13489)*

Drizly LLC (HQ) ................................................. E ...... 774 234-1033
1725 3rd St San Francisco (94158) *(P-18255)*

DROPBOX, San Francisco *Also Called: Dropbox Inc (P-18256)*

Dropbox Inc (PA) ............................................... A ...... 415 930-7766
1800 Owens St Ste 200 San Francisco (94158) *(P-18256)*

Drs Daylight Defense, San Diego *Also Called: Daylight Defense LLC (P-15529)*

Drs Daylight Solutions, San Diego *Also Called: Daylight Solutions Inc (P-12401)*

Drs Network & Imaging Systems, Cypress *Also Called: Drs Ntwork Imaging Systems LLC (P-12408)*

Drs Ntwork Imaging Systems LLC ......................... D ...... 714 220-3800
10600 Valley View St Cypress (90630) *(P-12408)*

Drs Own Inc (PA) ............................................... E ...... 760 804-0751
5923 Farnsworth Ct Carlsbad (92008) *(P-15335)*

Drsd Inc ........................................................... E ...... 408 230-7164
90 Bonaventura Dr San Jose (95134) *(P-14655)*

DRTS Enterprises Ltd ......................................... E ...... 858 270-7244
7979 Stromesa Ct Ste A San Diego (92126) *(P-9352)*

Druva Inc ......................................................... D ...... 650 241-3501
2051 Mission College Blvd Santa Clara (95054) *(P-18257)*

Dry Creek Vineyard, Healdsburg *Also Called: Dry Creek Vineyard Inc (P-1543)*

Dry Creek Vineyard Inc ....................................... E ...... 707 433-1000
3770 Lambert Bridge Rd Healdsburg (95448) *(P-1543)*

Dry Farm Wines LLC (PA) ................................... E ...... 707 944-1500
2114 W Park Ave Napa (94558) *(P-1544)*

Dry Launch Light Co, Livermore *Also Called: Sierra Design Mfg Inc (P-11575)*

Dry Vac Environmental Inc (PA) ........................... E ...... 707 374-7500
864 Saint Francis Way Rio Vista (94571) *(P-14656)*

Drywater Inc ..................................................... E ...... 844 434-0829
3901 Westerly Pl Ste 111 Newport Beach (92660) *(P-2001)*

Ds Fibertech Corp .............................................. E ...... 619 562-7001
11015 Mission Park Ct Santee (92071) *(P-10050)*

Ds Services of America Inc ................................. F ...... 323 551-5724
1449 N Avenue 46 Los Angeles (90041) *(P-1887)*

DSA Phototech LLC ............................................ E ...... 866 868-1602
2321 E Gladwick St Rancho Dominguez (90220) *(P-11525)*

DSA Signage, Rancho Dominguez *Also Called: DSA Phototech LLC (P-11525)*

Dsca, Long Beach *Also Called: Denso Pdts & Svcs Americas Inc (P-16380)*

DSD Merchandisers LLC (DH) .............................. F ...... 925 449-2044
6226 Industrial Way Ste A Livermore (94551) *(P-17400)*

DSM Biomedical Inc ........................................... C ...... 510 841-8800
2810 7th St Berkeley (94710) *(P-19451)*

DSM&t Co Inc ................................................... C ...... 909 357-7960
10609 Business Dr Fontana (92337) *(P-13168)*

Dsp Group, San Jose *Also Called: Dsp Group Inc (P-12409)*

Dsp Group Inc (HQ) ............................................ D ...... 408 986-4300
2055 Gateway Pl Ste 480 San Jose (95110) *(P-12409)*

Dsp Winner Inc .................................................. F ...... 858 336-9471
1641 W Main St Ste 222 Alhambra (91801) *(P-11388)*

DSPM Inc ......................................................... E ...... 714 970-2304
439 S Stoddard Ave San Bernardino (92401) *(P-12838)*

Dst Controls, Benicia *Also Called: Dusouth Industries (P-14405)*

DT Mattson Enterprises Inc .................................. E ...... 951 849-9781
201 W Lincoln St Banning (92220) *(P-15746)*

Dt123 (PA) ........................................................ E ...... 213 488-1230
13035 Hartsook St Sherman Oaks (91423) *(P-5018)*

DTE Stockton LLC .............................................. E ...... 209 467-3838
2526 W Washington St Stockton (95203) *(P-224)*

DTL Mori Seiki, Davis *Also Called: Dmg Mori Digital Tech Lab Corp (P-9675)*

DTL Research & Technical Ctr, Davis *Also Called: Dmg Mori Manufacturing USA Inc (P-9549)*

Dts Inc (DH) ...................................................... C ...... 818 436-1000
5220 Las Virgenes Rd Calabasas (91302) *(P-19302)*

Dtwusa, Hacienda Heights *Also Called: Brio Water Technology Inc (P-16784)*

Dtx, Corona *Also Called: Dart Container Corp California (P-6629)*

Duckback Acquisition Corp .................................. E ...... 530 343-3261
2644 Hegan Ln Chico (95928) *(P-6079)*

Duckback Products, Chico *Also Called: Duckback Acquisition Corp (P-6079)*

Duckhorn Wine Company (DH) ............................. E ...... 707 963-7108
1000 Lodi Ln Saint Helena (94574) *(P-1545)*

Duclos Lenses, Chatsworth *Also Called: Duclos Lenses Inc (P-19253)*

Duclos Lenses Inc .............................................. F ...... 818 773-0600
20222 Bahama St Chatsworth (91311) *(P-19253)*

DUCOMMUN, Costa Mesa *Also Called: Ducommun Incorporated (P-13831)*

Ducommun Aerostructures Inc (HQ) ...................... B ...... 310 380-5390
600 Anton Blvd Ste 1100 Costa Mesa (92626) *(P-13706)*

Ducommun Aerostructures Inc .............................. C ...... 714 637-4401
1885 N Batavia St Orange (92865) *(P-13707)*

Ducommun Aerostructures Inc .............................. E ...... 626 358-3211
801 Royal Oaks Dr Monrovia (91016) *(P-13827)*

Ducommun Aerostructures Inc .............................. E ...... 760 246-4191
4001 El Mirage Rd Adelanto (92301) *(P-13828)*

Ducommun Aerostructures Inc .............................. C ...... 310 513-7200
23301 Wilmington Ave Carson (90745) *(P-13829)*

**Ducommun Arostructures-Gardena, Gardena** *Also Called: Ahf-Ducommun Incorporated* ***(P-13760)***
**Ducommun Incorporated** .......... E ...... 626 358-3211
801 Royal Oaks Dr Monrovia (91016) ***(P-13830)***
**Ducommun Incorporated (PA)** .......... **C ...... 657 335-3665**
600 Anton Blvd Ste 1100 Costa Mesa (92626) ***(P-13831)***
**Ducommun Labarge Tech Inc (HQ)** .......... **C ...... 310 513-7200**
23301 Wilmington Ave Carson (90745) ***(P-13832)***
**Duda Mobile Inc** .......... C ...... 855 790-0003
577 College Ave Palo Alto (94306) ***(P-18258)***
**Dudes Brewing Company** .......... E ...... 424 271-2915
1840 W 208th St Somis (93066) ***(P-1427)***
**Dudleys Bakery Inc** .......... E ...... 760 765-0488
30218 Hwy 78 Santa Ysabel (92070) ***(P-17409)***
**Duds By Dudes, San Diego** *Also Called: Duds By Dudes LLC* ***(P-3006)***
**Duds By Dudes LLC** .......... F ...... 858 442-5613
7855 Ostrow St Ste A San Diego (92111) ***(P-3006)***
**Duel Systems Inc** .......... F ...... 408 453-9500
2025 Gateway Pl Ste 235 San Jose (95110) ***(P-12877)***
**Duhig and Co Inc** .......... E
5071 Telegraph Rd Los Angeles (90022) ***(P-16873)***
**Duhig Stainless, Los Angeles** *Also Called: Duhig and Co Inc* ***(P-16873)***
**Duke Empirical, Morgan Hill** *Also Called: Duke Empirical Inc* ***(P-15072)***
**Duke Empirical Inc** .......... D ...... 831 420-1104
18705 Madrone Pkwy Morgan Hill (95037) ***(P-15072)***
**Duke Scientific Corporation** .......... D ...... 650 424-1177
46360 Fremont Blvd Fremont (94538) ***(P-14657)***
**Dumbarton Quarry Associates (PA)** .......... **F ...... 510 793-8861**
2000 Scott Creek Rd Milpitas (95035) ***(P-299)***
**Dumont Printing Inc** .......... E ...... 559 485-6311
1333 G St Fresno (93706) ***(P-4597)***
**Dumont Printing & Mailing, Fresno** *Also Called: Dumont Printing Inc* ***(P-4597)***
**Duncan Bolt Co** .......... F ...... 909 581-6740
5555 E Gibralter Ontario (91764) ***(P-8753)***
**Duncan Carter Corporation (PA)** .......... **D ...... 805 964-9749**
5427 Hollister Ave Santa Barbara (93111) ***(P-15713)***
**Duncan Enterprises (PA)** .......... **C ...... 559 291-4444**
555 E Serena Ave Fresno (93720) ***(P-6080)***
**Duncan McIntosh Company Inc (PA)** .......... **E ...... 949 660-6150**
18475 Bandilier Cir Fountain Valley (92708) ***(P-4249)***
**Dunkel Bros. Machinery Moving, La Mirada** *Also Called: MEI Rigging & Crating LLC* ***(P-9875)***
**Dunlop, Benicia** *Also Called: Dunlop Manufacturing Inc* ***(P-15714)***
**Dunlop Manufacturing Inc (PA)** .......... **D ...... 707 745-2722**
150 Industrial Way Benicia (94510) ***(P-15714)***
**Dunn-Dwrds Pints Wallcoverings, Commerce** *Also Called: Dunn-Edwards Corporation* ***(P-17348)***
**Dunn-Edwards Corporation (DH)** .......... **C ...... 888 337-2468**
6119 E Washington Blvd Commerce (90040) ***(P-17348)***
**Dunnewood Vineyards, Ukiah** *Also Called: Constlltion Brnds US Oprtons I* ***(P-1516)***
**Dupaco Inc** .......... E ...... 760 758-4550
4144 Avenida De La Plata Ste B Oceanside (92056) ***(P-15073)***
**Dupont De Nemours Inc** .......... E ...... 408 419-4491
965 W Maude Ave Sunnyvale (94085) ***(P-5086)***
**Dupont Slcon Vly Innvation Ctr, Sunnyvale** *Also Called: Dupont De Nemours Inc* ***(P-5086)***
**Dupree Inc** .......... E ...... 909 597-4889
14395 Ramona Ave Chino (91710) ***(P-8754)***
**Dur-Red Products** .......... E ...... 323 771-9000
5634 Costa Dr Chino Hills (91709) ***(P-8435)***
**Dura Chemicals Inc (PA)** .......... **E ...... 510 658-1987**
1901 Harrison St Ste 1100 Oakland (94612) ***(P-6081)***
**Dura Coat Products Inc (PA)** .......... **D ...... 951 341-6500**
5361 Via Ricardo Riverside (92509) ***(P-9062)***
**Dura Technologies Inc** .......... C ...... 909 877-8477
2720 S Willow Ave Ste A Bloomington (92316) ***(P-6082)***
**Durabag Company Inc** .......... D ...... 714 259-8811
1432 Santa Fe Dr Tustin (92780) ***(P-3966)***
**Durable Coating Inc** .......... F ...... 805 299-8850
28716 Garnet Canyon Dr Santa Clarita (91390) ***(P-9063)***
**Duracite, Fairfield** *Also Called: Halabi Inc* ***(P-7539)***
**Duraco Express, Walnut** *Also Called: Essentra International LLC* ***(P-6227)***
**Duracold Refrigeration Mfg LLC** .......... E ...... 626 358-1710
1551 S Primrose Ave Monrovia (91016) ***(P-8663)***
**Duralum, Ontario** *Also Called: Duralum Products Inc* ***(P-7758)***
**Duralum Products Inc** .......... F ...... 951 736-4500
551 N Loop Dr Ontario (91761) ***(P-7758)***
**Duramar Interior Surfaces, Irvine** *Also Called: Daz Inc* ***(P-6582)***
**Duramax Building Products, Montebello** *Also Called: US Polymers Inc* ***(P-7066)***
**Duraplex Inc** .......... F ...... 714 538-1335
1005 W Hoover Ave Orange (92867) ***(P-6812)***
**Durasafe Inc** .......... F ...... 626 965-1588
18999 Railroad St City Of Industry (91748) ***(P-16581)***
**Duray, Vernon** *Also Called: J F Duncan Industries Inc* ***(P-10567)***
**Durkan Patterned Carpets Inc** .......... C ...... 310 838-2898
3633 Lenawee Ave # 120 Los Angeles (90016) ***(P-2513)***
**Duro Corporation** .......... F
918 Canada Ct City Of Industry (91748) ***(P-11389)***
**Duro Roller Company Inc** .......... F ...... 562 944-8856
13006 Park St Santa Fe Springs (90670) ***(P-6489)***
**Duro-Flex Rubber Products Inc** .......... E ...... 562 946-5533
13215 Lakeland Rd Santa Fe Springs (90670) ***(P-6490)***
**Duro-Sense Corporation** .......... F ...... 310 533-6877
869 Sandhill Ave Carson (90746) ***(P-14404)***
**Durston Manufacturing Company** .......... F ...... 909 593-1506
1395 Palomares St La Verne (91750) ***(P-7951)***
**Dusouth Industries** .......... E ...... 707 745-5117
651 Stone Rd Benicia (94510) ***(P-14405)***
**Dust Collector Services Inc** .......... E ...... 714 237-1690
1280 N Sunshine Way Anaheim (92806) ***(P-16777)***
**Dust Networks Inc** .......... E ...... 510 400-2900
32990 Alvarado Niles Rd Ste 910 Union City (94587) ***(P-12410)***
**Dutchman Doors, Tracy** *Also Called: Hand Crfted Dutchman Doors Inc* ***(P-3143)***
**Dutek Incorporated** .......... E ...... 760 566-8888
2228 Oak Ridge Way Vista (92081) ***(P-13236)***
**Dutra Group (PA)** .......... **D ...... 415 258-6876**
2350 Kerner Blvd Ste 200 San Rafael (94901) ***(P-395)***
**Dutra Group, The, San Rafael** *Also Called: Dutra Group* ***(P-395)***
**Dutra Materials, San Rafael** *Also Called: San Rafael Rock Quarry Inc* ***(P-305)***
**Dutra Materials, Richmond** *Also Called: San Rafael Rock Quarry Inc* ***(P-6370)***
**Dux Dental Products, Orange** *Also Called: Dux Industries Inc* ***(P-15454)***
**Dux Industries Inc** .......... D ...... 805 488-1122
1717 W Collins Ave Orange (92867) ***(P-15454)***
**DV Kap Inc** .......... E ...... 559 435-5575
426 W Bedford Ave Fresno (93711) ***(P-2928)***
**Dvdo, Sunnyvale** *Also Called: Anchor Bay Technologies Inc* ***(P-12310)***
**Dvele Inc** .......... E ...... 909 796-2561
25525 Redlands Blvd Loma Linda (92354) ***(P-3384)***
**Dvele Inc (PA)** .......... **F ...... 805 323-3711**
5521 La Jolla Blvd La Jolla (92037) ***(P-3393)***
**Dvele Omega Corporation** .......... D ...... 909 796-2561
25525 Redlands Blvd Loma Linda (92354) ***(P-3385)***
**Dvs Media Services (PA)** .......... **E ...... 818 841-6750**
2625 W Olive Ave Burbank (91505) ***(P-17810)***
**Dw and Bb Consulting Inc** .......... D ...... 818 896-9899
11381 Bradley Ave Pacoima (91331) ***(P-14111)***
**Dwa Alminum Composites USA Inc** .......... E ...... 818 998-1504
21100 Superior St Chatsworth (91311) ***(P-7843)***
**Dwa Aluminum Composites, Chatsworth** *Also Called: Dwa Composite Specialties Inc* ***(P-7737)***
**Dwa Composite Specialties Inc** .......... F ...... 818 885-8654
21100 Superior St Chatsworth (91311) ***(P-7737)***
**Dwaynes Engineering & Cnstr** .......... E ...... 661 762-7261
3559 Addie Ave Fellows (93224) ***(P-225)***
**Dwell, San Francisco** *Also Called: Dwell Life Inc* ***(P-4250)***
**Dwell Life Inc (PA)** .......... **E ...... 415 373-5100**
595 Pacific Ave Fl 4 San Francisco (94133) ***(P-4250)***
**Dwell Life Inc** .......... F ...... 212 382-2010
548 Market St San Francisco (94104) ***(P-4390)***
**Dwell Records, Los Angeles** *Also Called: CMH Records Inc* ***(P-11725)***
**Dwell Store The, San Francisco** *Also Called: Dwell Life Inc* ***(P-4390)***
**Dwi Enterprises** .......... E ...... 714 842-2236
11081 Winners Cir Ste 100 Los Alamitos (90720) ***(P-11655)***

## ALPHABETIC SECTION

**Dx Radio Systems Inc** ............................................................. F ..... 818 252-6700
10941 Pendleton St Sun Valley (91352) *(P-11844)*

**Dxterity Diagnostics Inc (PA)** ................................................ E ..... 310 537-7857
19500 S Rancho Way Ste 116 Compton (90220) *(P-19493)*

**Dyk, El Cajon** *Also Called: Dn Tanks Inc (P-14125)*

**Dyk Incorporated (HQ)** .......................................................... E ..... 619 440-8181
351 Cypress Ln El Cajon (92020) *(P-14126)*

**Dyk Prestressed Tanks, El Cajon** *Also Called: Dyk Incorporated (P-14126)*

**Dynabook Americas Inc (HQ)** ................................................ B ..... 949 583-3000
5241 California Ave Ste 100 Irvine (92617) *(P-10147)*

**Dynacast LLC** ......................................................................... C ..... 949 707-1211
25952 Commercentre Dr Lake Forest (92630) *(P-7828)*

**Dynacast, LLC, Lake Forest** *Also Called: Dynacast LLC (P-7828)*

**Dynaco Equipment Co, Pismo Beach** *Also Called: Brooks Restaurant Group Inc (P-17113)*

**Dynaflex Products (PA)** ......................................................... D ..... 323 724-1555
6466 Gayhart St Commerce (90040) *(P-13409)*

**Dynalloy Inc** ............................................................................ E ..... 714 436-1206
2801 Mcgaw Ave Irvine (92614) *(P-12964)*

**Dynamation Research Inc** ..................................................... F ..... 909 864-2310
2301 Pontius Ave Los Angeles (90064) *(P-13833)*

**Dynamet Incorporated** ........................................................... E ..... 714 375-3150
16052 Beach Blvd Ste 221 Huntington Beach (92647) *(P-7762)*

**Dynamex Corporation** ............................................................ E ..... 310 329-0399
155 E Albertoni St Carson (90746) *(P-2535)*

**Dynamic Chiropractic, Huntington Beach** *Also Called: Maxwell Petersen Associates (P-4277)*

**Dynamic Cooking Systems Inc** ............................................. A ..... 714 372-7000
695 Town Center Dr Ste 180 Costa Mesa (92626) *(P-10556)*

**Dynamic Digital Displays, Rancho Cordova** *Also Called: Project Sutter Holdings LLC (P-11619)*

**Dynamic Enterprises Inc** ....................................................... E ..... 562 944-0271
2081 Rancho Hills Dr Chino Hills (91709) *(P-10817)*

**Dynamic Fabrication Inc** ....................................................... E ..... 714 662-2440
890 Mariner St Brea (92821) *(P-13834)*

**Dynamic Graphics Inc (PA)** .................................................. E ..... 510 522-0700
3697 Mt Diablo Blvd Lafayette (94549) *(P-17915)*

**Dynamic Intgrted Solutions LLC** .......................................... E ..... 408 727-3400
1710 Fortune Dr San Jose (95131) *(P-12411)*

**Dynamic Intgrted Solutions LLC (PA)** ................................. F ..... 408 727-3400
3964 Rivermark Plz Ste 104 Santa Clara (95054) *(P-12412)*

**Dynamic Resources Inc** ........................................................ D ..... 619 268-3070
7894 Dagget St Ste 202e San Diego (92111) *(P-3767)*

**Dynamic Sciences Intl Inc** .................................................... E ..... 818 226-6262
9400 Lurline Ave Unit B Chatsworth (91311) *(P-11845)*

**Dynamic Security Tech Inc** ................................................... E ..... 510 786-1121
28301 Industrial Blvd Ste B Hayward (94545) *(P-16699)*

**Dynamic Vision Inc** ................................................................ E ..... 858 877-6200
550 Seagaze Dr Apt 32 Oceanside (92054) *(P-11730)*

**Dynamic Woodworks Inc** ...................................................... F ..... 562 483-8400
3509 Crooked Creek Dr Diamond Bar (91765) *(P-3132)*

**Dynamics O&P, Los Angeles** *Also Called: Dynamics Orthtics Prsthtics In (P-15336)*

**Dynamics Orthtics Prsthtics In** ............................................. E ..... 213 383-9212
1830 W Olympic Blvd Ste 123 Los Angeles (90006) *(P-15336)*

**Dynamo Aviation Inc** ............................................................. D ..... 818 785-9561
9601 Mason Ave # A Chatsworth (91311) *(P-8436)*

**Dynasty Electronic Company LLC** ....................................... D ..... 714 550-1197
1790 E Mcfadden Ave Ste 105 Santa Ana (92705) *(P-12088)*

**Dynatect Ro-Lab Inc** .............................................................. E ..... 262 786-1500
8830 W Linne Rd Tracy (95304) *(P-6473)*

**Dynatrac Products LLC** ........................................................ E ..... 714 596-4461
7392 Count Cir Huntington Beach (92647) *(P-13490)*

**Dynatrac Products Co Inc** .................................................... F ..... 714 596-4461
7392 Count Cir Huntington Beach (92647) *(P-13491)*

**Dynavax Technologies Corp (PA)** ........................................ D ..... 510 848-5100
2100 Powell St 7th Fl Emeryville (94608) *(P-5825)*

**Dynovas, Poway** *Also Called: Dynovas Inc (P-19088)*

**Dynovas Inc** ............................................................................ F ..... 508 717-7494
12250 Iavelli Way Poway (92064) *(P-19088)*

**Dytran Instruments Inc** ......................................................... C ..... 818 700-7818
21592 Marilla St Chatsworth (91311) *(P-12965)*

**Dz-Fdt LLC** .............................................................................. E ..... 510 215-5253
5301 Adeline St Oakland (94608) *(P-444)*

**E & B Ntrral Resources MGT Corp** ...................................... E ..... 661 766-2501
1848 Perkins Rd New Cuyama (93254) *(P-179)*

**E & B Ntrral Resources Mgt Corp (PA)** ............................... D ..... 661 387-8500
1608 Norris Rd Bakersfield (93308) *(P-180)*

**E & E TOA Corporation** ......................................................... F
11450 Sheldon St Sun Valley (91352) *(P-12878)*

**E & F Plas Fbrction Spcialists, San Jose** *Also Called: E & F Plastics Inc (P-6813)*

**E & F Plastics Inc** .................................................................. E ..... 408 226-6672
2742 Aiello Dr San Jose (95111) *(P-6813)*

**E & J Gallo Winery** ................................................................ F ..... 707 431-5400
11447 Old Redwood Hwy Healdsburg (95448) *(P-12)*

**E & J Gallo Winery (PA)** ....................................................... A ..... 209 341-3111
600 Yosemite Blvd Modesto (95354) *(P-1546)*

**E & J Gallo Winery** ................................................................ C ..... 559 458-0807
5610 E Olive Ave Fresno (93727) *(P-1547)*

**E & J Gallo Winery** ................................................................ E ..... 707 431-1946
3387 Dry Creek Rd Healdsburg (95448) *(P-1548)*

**E & J Gallo Winery** ................................................................ E ..... 209 341-3111
2101 Yosemite Blvd Modesto (95354) *(P-1549)*

**E & J Gallo Winery** ................................................................ D ..... 209 394-6200
18000 River Rd Livingston (95334) *(P-1550)*

**E & L Electric** ......................................................................... F ..... 562 903-9272
12322 Los Nietos Rd Santa Fe Springs (90670) *(P-19226)*

**E & M Electric and McHy Inc (PA)** ....................................... E ..... 707 433-5578
126 Mill St Healdsburg (95448) *(P-16814)*

**E & S Paper Co** ...................................................................... E ..... 310 538-8700
14110 S Broadway Los Angeles (90061) *(P-16999)*

**E & S Precision Machine Inc** ................................................ E ..... 209 545-6161
4631 Enterprise Way Modesto (95356) *(P-10818)*

**E Alko Inc** ................................................................................ E ..... 818 587-9700
8201 Woodley Ave Van Nuys (91406) *(P-15894)*

**E Appliance Repair and Hvac, Santa Clarita** *Also Called: 5 Star Service Inc (P-19173)*

**E B Bradley Co (PA)** .............................................................. E ..... 323 585-9917
5602 Bickett St Vernon (90058) *(P-16752)*

**E B Bradley Co** ...................................................................... F ..... 800 533-3030
10903 Vanowen St North Hollywood (91605) *(P-16753)*

**E B Stone & Son Inc** ............................................................. E ..... 707 426-2500
6111 Lambie Rd Suisun City (94585) *(P-17271)*

**E C S-Elitegroup Cmpt Systems, Newark** *Also Called: Elitegroup Computer Systems Ho (P-16519)*

**E D Q Inc** ................................................................................. E ..... 714 546-6010
2920 Halladay St Santa Ana (92705) *(P-14406)*

**E J Harrison & Sons Inc** ....................................................... C ..... 805 647-1414
1589 Lirio Ave Ventura (93004) *(P-16358)*

**E J Lauren LLC** ...................................................................... E ..... 562 803-1113
2690 Pellissier Pl City Of Industry (90601) *(P-3471)*

**E K C Technology/Burmar Chem, Hayward** *Also Called: Ekc Technology Inc (P-5089)*

**E M C, Moreno Valley** *Also Called: Envirnmntal Mlding Cncepts LLC (P-6491)*

**E M D, Los Angeles** *Also Called: Capitol-Emi Music Inc (P-11723)*

**E M E Inc** ................................................................................. C ..... 310 639-1621
500 E Pine St Compton (90222) *(P-8950)*

**E M S, Santa Ana** *Also Called: Sandberg Industries Inc (P-13081)*

**E O C, Compton** *Also Called: Cri Sub 1 (P-3565)*

**E O I, Walnut** *Also Called: Excellence Opto Inc (P-11572)*

**E O S International, Carlsbad** *Also Called: Electronic Online Systems International (P-18972)*

**E P, Union City** *Also Called: Emerald Packaging Inc (P-17293)*

**E P I, Milpitas** *Also Called: Envision Peripherals Inc (P-16521)*

**E P S Products, Palm Springs** *Also Called: Xy Corp Inc (P-9593)*

**E R C Company, E Rncho Dmngz** *Also Called: Coy Industries Inc (P-8419)*

**E R G International, Oxnard** *Also Called: Ergonom Corporation (P-3739)*

**E S T, Carlsbad** *Also Called: Electro Surface Tech Inc (P-12089)*

**E Sales, Garden Grove** *Also Called: Elasco Inc (P-5155)*

**E V G, Anaheim** *Also Called: Emergency Vehicle Group Inc (P-17438)*

**E Vasquez Distributors Inc** .................................................. E ..... 805 487-8458
4524 E Pleasant Valley Rd Oxnard (93033) *(P-3340)*

**E Z Buy & E Z Sell Recycl Corp (DH)** ................................. C ..... 310 886-7808
4954 Van Nuys Blvd Ste 201 Sherman Oaks (91403) *(P-4106)*

**E-Band Communications LLC** .............................................. E ..... 858 408-0660
82 Coromar Dr Goleta (93117) *(P-11846)*

# ALPHABETIC SECTION

**E-Fab Inc** .................................................................... E ...... 408 727-5218
1075 Richard Ave Santa Clara (95050) *(P-9064)*

**E-M Manufacturing Inc** ................................................ F ...... 209 825-1800
1290 Dupont Ct Manteca (95336) *(P-8437)*

**E-Scepter, City Of Industry** *Also Called: Sceptre Inc (P-13083)*

**E-Z Haul Ready Mix Inc** ............................................... E ...... 559 233-6603
1538 N Blackstone Ave Fresno (93703) *(P-7439)*

**E-Z Lok Division, Gardena** *Also Called: Tool Components Inc (P-16634)*

**E-Z Mix Inc (PA)** ........................................................... E ...... 818 768-0568
11450 Tuxford St Sun Valley (91352) *(P-7440)*

**E-Z-Hook Test Products Div, Baldwin Park** *Also Called: Tektest Inc (P-12901)*

**E. Force Sports, Vista** *Also Called: Efgp Inc (P-15806)*

**E.V. Roberts, Carson** *Also Called: Cirrus Enterprises LLC (P-17224)*

**E/G Electro-Graph, Vista** *Also Called: Plansee USA LLC (P-12633)*

**E&M, Healdsburg** *Also Called: E & M Electric and McHy Inc (P-16814)*

**E&S Precision Machine, Hayward** *Also Called: Therm-X of California Inc (P-14934)*

**E2e Mfg LLC** ................................................................. E ...... 925 862-2057
3500 Yale Way Fremont (94538) *(P-8838)*

**EA, Redwood City** *Also Called: Electronic Arts Inc (P-18272)*

**Ea Sports, Redwood City** *Also Called: Electronic Arts Redwood LLC (P-13194)*

**Eagle Access Ctrl Systems Inc** .................................... E ...... 818 837-7900
12953 Foothill Blvd Sylmar (91342) *(P-11319)*

**Eagle Building Materials, Fresno** *Also Called: Sequoia Steel and Supply Co (P-17344)*

**Eagle Dominion Energy Corp** ...................................... E ...... 270 366-4817
3020 W Olive Ave Burbank (91505) *(P-181)*

**Eagle Dominion Trust, Burbank** *Also Called: Eagle Dominion Energy Corp (P-181)*

**Eagle Graphics Inc (PA)** ............................................... F ...... 714 978-2200
1430 W Katella Ave Orange (92867) *(P-4598)*

**Eagle Labs, Rancho Cucamonga** *Also Called: Eagle Labs LLC (P-15074)*

**Eagle Labs LLC** ............................................................. D ...... 909 481-0011
10201a Trademark St Ste A Rancho Cucamonga (91730) *(P-15074)*

**Eagle Med Packg Sterilization, Paso Robles** *Also Called: Eagle Med Pckg Strlization Inc (P-19089)*

**Eagle Med Pckg Strlization Inc** ................................... E ...... 805 238-7401
2921 Union Rd Ste A Paso Robles (93446) *(P-19089)*

**Eagle Mold Technologies Inc** ...................................... E ...... 858 530-0888
12330 Crosthwaite Cir Poway (92064) *(P-6814)*

**Eagle One Golf Products, Anaheim** *Also Called: Golf Supply House Usa Inc (P-15818)*

**Eagle Press, Sacramento** *Also Called: Consolidated Eagle Press Inc (P-4864)*

**Eagle Print Dynamics, Orange** *Also Called: Eagle Graphics Inc (P-4598)*

**Eagle Rock Incorporated** ............................................. F ...... 530 623-4444
40029 La Grange Rd Junction City (96048) *(P-9420)*

**Eagle Roofing Products, Rialto** *Also Called: Burlingame Industries Inc (P-17763)*

**Eagle Roofing Products Co, Rialto** *Also Called: Burlingame Industries Inc (P-7588)*

**Eagle Roofing Products Fla LLC** .................................. F ...... 909 822-6000
3546 N Riverside Ave Rialto (92377) *(P-7273)*

**Eagle Tech Manufacturing Inc** .................................... E ...... 831 768-7467
841 Walker St Watsonville (95076) *(P-14407)*

**Eagle Topco LP** ............................................................ A ...... 949 585-4329
18200 Von Karman Ave Irvine (92612) *(P-18259)*

**Eagleware Manufacturing Co Inc** ............................... E ...... 562 320-3100
12683 Corral Pl Santa Fe Springs (90670) *(P-8839)*

**Eandm** .......................................................................... E ...... 707 473-3137
126 Mill St Healdsburg (95448) *(P-19227)*

**Eargo Inc (PA)** ............................................................... D ...... 650 351-7700
2665 N 1st St Ste 300 San Jose (95134) *(P-15337)*

**Early Childhood Resources, San Diego** *Also Called: Ecr4kids LP (P-3623)*

**Early Morning Inc** ........................................................ E ...... 916 871-9005
2180 Golden Centre Ln Ste 100 Gold River (95670) *(P-3737)*

**Earth Island LLC (HQ)** .................................................. E ...... 818 725-2820
9201 Owensmouth Ave Chatsworth (91311) *(P-2189)*

**Earth Print Inc** .............................................................. F ...... 818 879-6050
31115 Via Colinas Ste 301 Westlake Village (91362) *(P-4599)*

**Earthbound Farm LLC (PA)** .......................................... A ...... 831 623-7880
1721 San Juan Hwy San Juan Bautista (95045) *(P-80)*

**Earthlite, Vista** *Also Called: Earthlite LLC (P-3502)*

**Earthlite LLC (DH)** ........................................................ D ...... 760 599-1112
990 Joshua Way Vista (92081) *(P-3502)*

**Earthquake Audio Products, Hayward** *Also Called: Earthquake Sound Corporation (P-11656)*

**Earthquake Sound Corporation** .................................. F ...... 510 732-1000
2727 Mccone Ave Hayward (94545) *(P-11656)*

**Earthrise Nutritionals LLC** ........................................... E ...... 760 348-5027
113 E Hoober Rd Calipatria (92233) *(P-2190)*

**Earthrise Nutritionals LLC (HQ)** .................................. E ...... 949 623-0980
3333 Michelson Dr Ste 300 Irvine (92612) *(P-5429)*

**Earthwise Bag Company Inc** ....................................... F ...... 818 396-5025
207 N Goode Ave Ste 340 Glendale (91203) *(P-3967)*

**Eascare Products USA, Fresno** *Also Called: McGrayel Company (P-6308)*

**East Bay Express, Oakland** *Also Called: East Bay Publishing LLC (P-4107)*

**East Bay Fixture Company** ......................................... E ...... 510 652-4421
941 Aileen St Oakland (94608) *(P-3402)*

**East Bay Machine and Shtmtl, Concord** *Also Called: Alvellan Inc (P-10707)*

**East Bay Publishing LLC** .............................................. F ...... 510 879-3708
318 Harrison St Ste 302 Oakland (94607) *(P-4107)*

**East Bay Tire Co** .......................................................... F ...... 707 747-5613
4961 Park Rd Benicia (94510) *(P-6409)*

**East Cast Repr Fabrication LLC** .................................. E ...... 619 591-9577
280 Trousdale Dr Ste E Chula Vista (91910) *(P-8133)*

**East Electronics, Fremont** *Also Called: Myntahl Corporation (P-13043)*

**East Penn Manufacturing** .......................................... F ...... 619 660-0016
2709 Via Orange Way Ste B Spring Valley (91978) *(P-13134)*

**East Private Holdings II LLC (PA)** ................................ E ...... 650 357-3500
6750 Dumbarton Cir Fremont (94555) *(P-4875)*

**East Shore Garment Company LLC** ............................ E ...... 323 923-4454
3250 E Olympic Blvd Los Angeles (90023) *(P-2412)*

**East West Tea Company LLC** ..................................... C ...... 310 275-9891
1616 Preuss Rd Los Angeles (90035) *(P-1070)*

**Eastern Sports, Thousand Oaks** *Also Called: Easton Hockey Inc (P-15805)*

**Eastland Corporation** ................................................. E ...... 323 261-5388
3017 Bandini Blvd Vernon (90058) *(P-17161)*

**Eastman Music Company (PA)** ................................... E ...... 909 868-1777
2158 Pomona Blvd Pomona (91768) *(P-16975)*

**Eastmans Guitars, Pomona** *Also Called: Eastman Music Company (P-16975)*

**Easton Baseball / Softball Inc** ..................................... F ...... 800 632-7866
3500 Willow Ln Thousand Oaks (91361) *(P-16934)*

**Easton Bell Sports, Irvine** *Also Called: Bell Sports Inc (P-15787)*

**Easton Hockey Inc** ...................................................... A ...... 818 782-6445
3500 Willow Ln Thousand Oaks (91361) *(P-15805)*

**Eastwest Clothing Inc (PA)** ......................................... F ...... 323 980-1177
40 E Verdugo Ave Burbank (91502) *(P-2663)*

**Eastwest Container Group Inc** ................................... E ...... 626 523-1523
5521 Schaefer Ave Chino (91710) *(P-3802)*

**Easy Ad Magazine, San Luis Obispo** *Also Called: M G A Investment Co Inc (P-4430)*

**Easy Reach Supply LLC** ............................................... E ...... 601 582-7866
3737 Capitol Ave City Of Industry (90601) *(P-15928)*

**Easyflex, Santa Ana** *Also Called: Easyflex Inc (P-7611)*

**Easyflex Inc** .................................................................. E ...... 888 577-8999
2700 N Main St Ste 800 Santa Ana (92705) *(P-7611)*

**Eat Just Inc (PA)** ........................................................... D ...... 844 423-6637
1145 Atlantic Ave Alameda (94501) *(P-977)*

**Eat Like A Woman, Burbank** *Also Called: Staness Jonekos Entps Inc (P-2360)*

**Eatgud, Los Angeles** *Also Called: Pensieve Foods (P-2319)*

**Eaton, Irvine** *Also Called: Eaton Aerospace LLC (P-14181)*

**Eaton Aerospace LLC** ................................................. E ...... 949 452-9500
9650 Jeronimo Rd Irvine (92618) *(P-14181)*

**Eaton Aerospace LLC** ................................................. B ...... 818 409-0200
4690 Colorado Blvd Los Angeles (90039) *(P-16650)*

**Eaton Corporation** ...................................................... F ...... 714 272-4700
9650 Jeronimo Rd Irvine (92618) *(P-13835)*

**Eaton Electrical Inc** ..................................................... C ...... 951 685-5788
13201 Dahlia St Fontana (92337) *(P-11320)*

**Ebac Investments Inc (PA)** .......................................... E ...... 707 781-9000
181 Lynch Creek Way Petaluma (94954) *(P-7441)*

**Ebac Investments Inc** .................................................. F ...... 707 894-4425
Levee Rd Cloverdale (95425) *(P-7442)*

**Ebac Investments Inc** .................................................. E ...... 707 792-4695
8150 Gravenstein Hwy Cotati (94931) *(P-7443)*

**Ebac Investments Inc** .................................................. E ...... 415 455-1575
548 Du Bois St San Rafael (94901) *(P-7444)*

## ALPHABETIC SECTION — Edison Opto USA Corporation

**Ebara, Sacramento** *Also Called: Ebara Technologies Inc (P-9961)*
**Ebara Mixers Inc** .................................................................. E ...... 760 246-3430
 9351 Industrial Way Adelanto (92301) *(P-9787)*
**Ebara Technologies Inc (DH)** ................................................ D ...... 916 920-5451
 51 Main Ave Sacramento (95838) *(P-9961)*
**Ebatts.com, Camarillo** *Also Called: Battery-Biz Inc (P-13167)*
**Eberine Enterprises Inc** ......................................................... E ...... 323 587-1111
 3360 Fruitland Ave Los Angeles (90058) *(P-2069)*
**Ebr Systems Inc (PA)** ............................................................ F ...... 408 720-1906
 480 Oakmead Pkwy Sunnyvale (94085) *(P-15532)*
**Ebus Inc** ................................................................................ F ...... 562 904-3474
 9250 Washburn Rd Downey (90242) *(P-13410)*
**EC Design LLC** ...................................................................... E ...... 310 220-2362
 4860 W 147th St Hawthorne (90250) *(P-17639)*
**Eca, Brea** *Also Called: Energy Cnvrsion Applctions Inc (P-11212)*
**Eca Medical Instruments (DH)** ............................................. E ...... 805 376-2509
 1107 Tourmaline Dr Newbury Park (91320) *(P-15075)*
**ECB Corp (PA)** ..................................................................... D ...... 714 385-8900
 6400 Artesia Blvd Buena Park (90620) *(P-416)*
**ECB Corp** ............................................................................. E ...... 916 492-8900
 1650 Parkway Blvd West Sacramento (95691) *(P-8438)*
**Ech Real Estate Developers LLC** ......................................... F ...... 619 996-9269
 4275 Executive Sq Ste 200 La Jolla (92037) *(P-19515)*
**Echelon Corporation (DH)** .................................................... D ...... 408 938-5200
 6024 Silver Creek Valley Rd San Jose (95138) *(P-14513)*
**Echelon Fine Printing, Vernon** *Also Called: The Ligature Inc (P-4784)*
**Echo Labs** ............................................................................. E ...... 650 561-3446
 235 Alma St Palo Alto (94301) *(P-10148)*
**Eci Fuel Systems, Upland** *Also Called: Exhaust Center Inc (P-8448)*
**Eci Water Ski Products Inc** .................................................. E ...... 951 940-9999
 224 Malbert St Perris (92570) *(P-17633)*
**Eckert Cold Storage Company (PA)** ..................................... B ...... 209 838-4040
 905 Clough Rd Escalon (95320) *(P-1005)*
**Eckert Cold Storage Company** ............................................. E ...... 209 823-3181
 757 Moffat Blvd Manteca (95336) *(P-16283)*
**Eckert Zegler Isotope Pdts Inc** ............................................. E ...... 661 309-1010
 1800 N Keystone St Burbank (91504) *(P-14862)*
**Eckert Zegler Isotope Pdts Inc (HQ)** .................................... E ...... 661 309-1010
 24937 Avenue Tibbitts Valencia (91355) *(P-14863)*
**Ecko Print & Packaging, Ontario** *Also Called: Ecko Products Group LLC (P-3839)*
**Ecko Products Group LLC** ................................................... E ...... 909 628-5678
 740 S Milliken Ave Ste C Ontario (91761) *(P-3839)*
**Eclectic Printing & Design LLC** ........................................... F ...... 714 528-8040
 1030 Ortega Way Ste A Placentia (92870) *(P-4876)*
**Eclipse Metal Fabrication Inc** .............................................. E ...... 650 298-8731
 17700 Shideler Pkwy Lathrop (95330) *(P-8439)*
**Eclipse Prtg & Graphics LLC** ............................................... E ...... 909 390-2452
 9145 Milliken Ave Rancho Cucamonga (91730) *(P-4600)*
**Ecliptek Inc** .......................................................................... F ...... 714 433-1200
 24422 Avenida De La Carlota Ste 290 Laguna Hills (92653) *(P-12966)*
**Eclypse International Corp (PA)** ........................................... F ...... 951 371-8008
 341 S Maple St Corona (92878) *(P-14514)*
**Ecmd Inc** .............................................................................. C ...... 530 741-0769
 4722 Skyway Dr Marysville (95901) *(P-3133)*
**Ecmd Inc** .............................................................................. E ...... 909 980-1775
 10863 Jersey Blvd 100 Rancho Cucamonga (91730) *(P-3134)*
**Ecmm Services Inc** .............................................................. C ...... 714 988-9388
 1320 Valley Vista Dr # 204 Diamond Bar (91765) *(P-15895)*
**Eco Sensors, Newark** *Also Called: Kwj Engineering Inc (P-14891)*
**Eco Services Operations Corp** ............................................. E ...... 925 313-8224
 100 Mococo Rd Martinez (94553) *(P-5087)*
**Eco Services Operations Corp** ............................................. D ...... 310 885-6719
 20720 S Wilmington Ave Long Beach (90810) *(P-5088)*
**Eco-Shell Inc** ........................................................................ E ...... 530 824-8794
 5230 Grange Rd Corning (96021) *(P-16127)*
**Ecoatm LLC** ......................................................................... E ...... 858 255-4111
 900 Dana Dr Redding (96003) *(P-12031)*
**Ecoatm LLC (DH)** ................................................................. C ...... 858 999-3200
 10121 Barnes Canyon Rd San Diego (92121) *(P-12032)*
**Ecolink Intelligent Tech Inc** ................................................. E ...... 855 432-6546
 2055 Corte Del Nogal Carlsbad (92011) *(P-11657)*

**Ecomicron Inc** ...................................................................... F ...... 408 526-1020
 2161 Otoole Ave Ste 30 San Jose (95131) *(P-12413)*
**Econ-O-Plate Inc** ................................................................. F ...... 310 342-5900
 5731 W Slauson Ave Ste 175 Culver City (90230) *(P-4601)*
**Econco Broadcast Service, Woodland** *Also Called: CPI Econco Division (P-19175)*
**Econocold Refrigerators, Cerritos** *Also Called: Refrigerator Manufacturers Inc (P-11399)*
**Econoday Inc** ....................................................................... F ...... 925 299-5350
 3730 Mt Diablo Blvd Ste 340 Lafayette (94549) *(P-4391)*
**Econolite** ............................................................................. F ...... 408 577-1733
 4120 Business Center Dr Fremont (94538) *(P-19090)*
**Econolite Control Products Inc (PA)** ................................... C ...... 714 630-3700
 1250 N Tustin Ave Anaheim (92807) *(P-11992)*
**Economy Plastics, Santa Cruz** *Also Called: K&R Products Inc (P-6879)*
**Ecoolthing Corp** .................................................................. E ...... 714 368-4791
 1321 E Saint Gertrude Pl Ste A Santa Ana (92705) *(P-9283)*
**Ecosmart Technologies Inc** ................................................. E ...... 770 667-0006
 1585 W Mission Blvd Pomona (91766) *(P-6200)*
**Ecotality Inc** ........................................................................ C ...... 415 992-3000
 1 Montgomery St Ste 2525 San Francisco (94104) *(P-13237)*
**Ecowater Systems, Vista** *Also Called: Yanchewski & Wardell Entps Inc (P-10615)*
**Ecowise Inc** ......................................................................... E ...... 626 759-3997
 13538 Excelsior Dr Unit B Santa Fe Springs (90670) *(P-5153)*
**Ecr4kids LP** ........................................................................ E ...... 619 323-2005
 5630 Kearny Mesa Rd Ste B San Diego (92111) *(P-3623)*
**Ecrio Inc** .............................................................................. D ...... 408 973-7290
 19925 Stevens Creek Blvd Ste 100 Cupertino (95014) *(P-18260)*
**Ecs Refining, Santa Clara** *Also Called: All Metals Inc (P-7715)*
**Ect News Network Inc** ........................................................ F ...... 818 461-9700
 16133 Ventura Blvd Ste 700 Encino (91436) *(P-4392)*
**Ectron Corporation** ............................................................. E ...... 858 278-0600
 9340 Hazard Way Ste B2 San Diego (92123) *(P-11847)*
**Ed & Don's Candies, Burlingame** *Also Called: Ed & Dons of Hawaii Inc (P-1304)*
**Ed & Dons of Hawaii Inc** .................................................... D ...... 808 423-8200
 1555 Bayshore Hwy Burlingame (94010) *(P-1304)*
**Ed Hardy, Commerce** *Also Called: DNam Apparel Industries LLC (P-2756)*
**Ed Stiglic** ............................................................................ F ...... 760 744-7239
 1125 Linda Vista Dr Ste 110 San Marcos (92078) *(P-10819)*
**Edcast LLC (DH)** ................................................................. E ...... 844 833-2278
 4120 Dublin Blvd Ste 200 Dublin (94568) *(P-18261)*
**Edco Plastics Inc** ................................................................ E ...... 714 772-1986
 2110 E Winston Rd Anaheim (92806) *(P-6815)*
**Edelbrock LLC** .................................................................... E ...... 310 781-2290
 501 Amapola Ave Torrance (90501) *(P-13492)*
**Edelbrock Foundry Corp** ..................................................... E ...... 951 654-6677
 1320 S Buena Vista St San Jacinto (92583) *(P-7808)*
**Edelmann Usa Inc (DH)** ...................................................... F ...... 323 669-5700
 2150 S Parco Ave Ontario (91761) *(P-15966)*
**Edelstein Printing Co** .......................................................... E ...... 510 352-7890
 2725 Miller St San Leandro (94577) *(P-4602)*
**Eden Beauty Concepts Inc** .................................................. E ...... 760 330-9941
 5876 Owens Ave Ste 200 Carlsbad (92008) *(P-5976)*
**Edeniq Inc** ........................................................................... D ...... 559 302-1777
 6910 W Pershing Ct Visalia (93291) *(P-6142)*
**Edgate Holdings Inc** ........................................................... E ...... 858 712-9341
 4655 Cass St San Diego (92109) *(P-18262)*
**Edge Autonomy Slo LLC** ..................................................... E ...... 805 544-0932
 831 Buckley Rd San Luis Obispo (93401) *(P-14182)*
**Edge Solutions Consulting Inc (PA)** .................................... E ...... 818 591-3500
 5126 Clareton Dr Ste 160 Agoura Hills (91301) *(P-10149)*
**Edge Systems, Long Beach** *Also Called: Hydrafacial LLC (P-15108)*
**Edge Theory Labs, Carlsbad** *Also Called: Edge Theory Labs Inc (P-6675)*
**Edge Theory Labs Inc** ......................................................... F ...... 858 358-5386
 5825 Avenida Encinas Ste 109 Carlsbad (92008) *(P-6675)*
**Edgeq, Santa Clara** *Also Called: EdgeQ Inc (P-12414)*
**EdgeQ Inc** ........................................................................... E ...... 408 209-0368
 2550 Great America Way Ste 125 Santa Clara (95054) *(P-12414)*
**Edgewave Inc** ...................................................................... D ...... 800 782-3762
 4225 Executive Sq Ste 1600 La Jolla (92037) *(P-18263)*
**Edi Ideas, Fountain Valley** *Also Called: Freightgate Inc (P-18332)*
**Edison Opto USA Corporation** ............................................ E ...... 909 284-9710
 1809 Excise Ave Ste 201 Ontario (91761) *(P-12415)*

**Edison Price Lighting Inc (PA)** .................................................. C ...... 718 685-0700
5424 E Slauson Ave Commerce (90040) *(P-11526)*

**Edisonfuture Inc (HQ)** ............................................................... F ...... 408 919-8000
4677 Old Ironsides Dr Ste 190 Santa Clara (95054) *(P-13348)*

**EDM Performance Accessories, Brea** *Also Called: Clean America Inc (P-13221)*

**Edmeades Estate Winery, Geyserville** *Also Called: Edmeades LLC (P-1551)*

**Edmeades LLC** ............................................................................ E ...... 707 895-3232
18700 Geyserville Ave Geyserville (95441) *(P-1551)*

**Edmund A Gray Co (PA)** ........................................................... D ...... 213 625-0376
2277 E 15th St Los Angeles (90021) *(P-9257)*

**Edmund A Gray Co** .................................................................... E ...... 213 625-2725
1901 Imperial St Los Angeles (90021) *(P-16288)*

**Edmund Kim International Inc (PA)** ........................................ E ...... 310 604-1100
2880 E Ana St Compton (90221) *(P-2618)*

**EDN Aviation Inc** ........................................................................ E ...... 818 988-8826
6720 Valjean Ave Van Nuys (91406) *(P-19254)*

**Edner Corporation** ..................................................................... F ...... 925 831-1248
528 Oakshire Pl Alamo (94507) *(P-1189)*

**Edo Communications and Countermeasures Systems Inc** ........ D ...... 818 464-2475
7821 Orion Ave Van Nuys (91406) *(P-14183)*

**Edris Plastics Mfg Inc** ............................................................... E ...... 323 581-7000
4560 Pacific Blvd Vernon (90058) *(P-6816)*

**Edro Engineering LLC (DH)** ..................................................... E ...... 909 594-5751
20500 Carrey Rd Walnut (91789) *(P-9619)*

**Edt, Irvine** *Also Called: Emerging Display Technologies Corporation (P-12971)*

**Education Elements Inc** ............................................................ D ...... 650 440-7860
101 Hickey Blvd Ste A # 526 South San Francisco (94080) *(P-18264)*

**Education Training & RES Assoc (PA)** .................................. D ...... 831 438-4060
5619 Scotts Valley Dr Ste 140 Scotts Valley (95066) *(P-19350)*

**Educational Ideas Incorporated** ................................................ E ...... 714 990-4332
950 W Central Ave Brea (92821) *(P-4328)*

**Educational Insights, Torrance** *Also Called: Learning Resources Inc (P-16167)*

**Edulastic, Fremont** *Also Called: Snapwiz Inc (P-18803)*

**Edvin Inc** ..................................................................................... E ...... 415 800-4067
976 Laurel Glen Dr Palo Alto (94304) *(P-18265)*

**EDWARDS, Irvine** *Also Called: Edwards Lifesciences Corp (P-15340)*

**Edwards, Irvine** *Also Called: Edwards Lifesciences US Inc (P-15533)*

**Edwards Assoc Cmmnications Inc (PA)** ................................ C ...... 805 658-2626
2277 Knoll Dr Ste A Ventura (93003) *(P-3949)*

**Edwards Label, Ventura** *Also Called: Edwards Assoc Cmmnications Inc (P-3949)*

**Edwards Life Sciences Cardio V, Irvine** *Also Called: Edwards Lifesciences Corp (P-15338)*

**Edwards Lifesciences Corp** ..................................................... C ...... 949 250-2500
17221 Red Hill Ave Irvine (92614) *(P-15338)*

**Edwards Lifesciences Corp** ..................................................... F ...... 949 250-3522
1402 Alton Pkwy Irvine (92606) *(P-15339)*

**Edwards Lifesciences Corp (PA)** ............................................ A ...... 949 250-2500
1 Edwards Way Irvine (92614) *(P-15340)*

**Edwards Lifesciences Corp** ..................................................... E ...... 949 553-0611
1212 Alton Pkwy Irvine (92606) *(P-15341)*

**Edwards Lifesciences LLC (HQ)** ............................................. A ...... 949 250-2500
1 Edwards Way Irvine (92614) *(P-5430)*

**Edwards Lifesciences US Inc (HQ)** ........................................ D ...... 949 250-2500
1 Edwards Way Irvine (92614) *(P-15533)*

**Edys Grand Ice Cream** .............................................................. A ...... 510 652-8187
5929 College Ave Oakland (94618) *(P-799)*

**Eeco Switch, Brea** *Also Called: Transico Inc (P-13111)*

**Eeg 3 LLC (DH)** ........................................................................... C
6080 Center Dr Ste 1200 Los Angeles (90045) *(P-11848)*

**Eel River Brewing Co Inc (PA)** ................................................. E ...... 707 725-2739
1777 Alamar Way Fortuna (95540) *(P-17616)*

**Eel River Brewing Co Inc** .......................................................... F ...... 707 764-1772
600 K Bridge St Scotia (95565) *(P-17617)*

**EEL RIVER BREWING CO INC, Scotia** *Also Called: Eel River Brewing Co Inc (P-17617)*

**Eema Industries Inc** .................................................................... E ...... 323 904-0200
5461 W Jefferson Blvd Los Angeles (90016) *(P-11591)*

**Eero LLC** ...................................................................................... E ...... 415 738-7972
660 3rd St San Francisco (94107) *(P-18971)*

**Eevelle LLC** ................................................................................. E ...... 760 434-2231
5928 Balfour Ct Carlsbad (92008) *(P-3027)*

**Eew Holdings Inc** ........................................................................ E ...... 916 685-1855
10149 Iron Rock Way Elk Grove (95624) *(P-3135)*

**Eezer Products Inc** ..................................................................... E ...... 559 255-4140
4734 E Home Ave Fresno (93703) *(P-5154)*

**Efaxcom (DH)** .............................................................................. D ...... 323 817-3207
6922 Hollywood Blvd Fl 5 Los Angeles (90028) *(P-10359)*

**Efaxcom** ....................................................................................... E ...... 805 692-0064
5385 Hollister Ave Ste 208 Santa Barbara (93111) *(P-10360)*

**Eff Aero, Stockton** *Also Called: Wkf (friedman Enterprises Inc (P-13728)*

**Efgp Inc** ........................................................................................ F ...... 760 692-3900
1384 Poinsettia Ave Ste E Vista (92081) *(P-15806)*

**Efinix Inc (PA)** ............................................................................. E ...... 408 789-6917
20400 Stevens Creek Blvd Ste 200 Cupertino (95014) *(P-18266)*

**EGAIN, Sunnyvale** *Also Called: Egain Corporation (P-18267)*

**Egain Corporation (PA)** ............................................................. C ...... 408 636-4500
1252 Borregas Ave Sunnyvale (94089) *(P-18267)*

**Egge Machine Company Inc (PA)** ............................................ E ...... 562 945-3419
8403 Allport Ave Santa Fe Springs (90670) *(P-16382)*

**Egl Holdco Inc** ............................................................................. A ...... 800 678-7423
18200 Von Karman Ave Ste 1000 Irvine (92612) *(P-18268)*

**Ego One LLC** ............................................................................... F ...... 707 253-1615
1285 Dealy Ln Napa (94559) *(P-1552)*

**Egr Incorporated (DH)** ............................................................... E ...... 800 757-7075
4000 Greystone Dr Ontario (91761) *(P-13493)*

**EH Suda Inc (PA)** ........................................................................ F ...... 650 622-9700
1811 Jefferson Ave Redwood City (94062) *(P-10820)*

**EH Suda Inc** ................................................................................. E ...... 530 778-9830
210 Texas Ave Lewiston (96052) *(P-10821)*

**Ehlers Estate, Saint Helena** *Also Called: New Vavin Inc (P-1688)*

**Ehmcke Sheet Metal Corp** ......................................................... D ...... 619 477-6484
840 W 19th St National City (91950) *(P-513)*

**Ei Corp** ......................................................................................... E ...... 530 274-1240
13355 Grass Valley Ave Ste A Grass Valley (95945) *(P-11658)*

**Eibach Inc** .................................................................................... D ...... 951 256-8300
264 Mariah Cir Corona (92879) *(P-9174)*

**Eibach Springs, Inc., Corona** *Also Called: Eibach Inc (P-9174)*

**Eide Industries Inc** ..................................................................... D ...... 562 402-8335
16215 Piuma Ave Cerritos (90703) *(P-2973)*

**Eightfold Ai Inc (PA)** .................................................................. C ...... 650 265-7380
2625 Augustine Dr 6th Fl Santa Clara (95054) *(P-18269)*

**Einstein Brothers Bagels, Greenbrae** *Also Called: Einstein Noah Rest Group Inc (P-17578)*

**Einstein Noah Rest Group Inc** ................................................. C ...... 714 847-4609
16304 Beach Blvd Westminster (92683) *(P-712)*

**Einstein Noah Rest Group Inc** ................................................. C ...... 408 358-5895
15996 Los Gatos Blvd Los Gatos (95032) *(P-713)*

**Einstein Noah Rest Group Inc** ................................................. D ...... 415 731-1700
1521 Sloat Blvd San Francisco (94132) *(P-17410)*

**Einstein Noah Rest Group Inc** ................................................. D ...... 650 299-9050
1067 El Camino Real Redwood City (94063) *(P-17411)*

**Einstein Noah Rest Group Inc** ................................................. C ...... 415 925-9971
170 Bon Air Ctr Greenbrae (94904) *(P-17578)*

**Eis Group Inc** .............................................................................. C ...... 415 402-2622
4 Embarcadero Ctr Ste 3410 San Francisco (94111) *(P-18270)*

**Eisel Enterprises Inc** ................................................................. E ...... 714 993-1706
714 Fee Ana St Placentia (92870) *(P-7327)*

**Eisenbeiss Inc** ............................................................................. F ...... 916 262-7656
8440 Rovana Cir Ste 100 Sacramento (95828) *(P-19255)*

**Ejay Filtration Inc** ....................................................................... E ...... 951 683-0805
3036 Durahart St Riverside (92507) *(P-9216)*

**Ejays Machine Co Inc** ................................................................ E ...... 714 879-0558
1108 E Valencia Dr Fullerton (92831) *(P-10822)*

**Ejl, City Of Industry** *Also Called: E J Lauren LLC (P-3471)*

**Ekc Technology Inc (HQ)** .......................................................... C ...... 510 784-9105
2520 Barrington Ct Hayward (94545) *(P-5089)*

**Eknowledge Group Inc** ............................................................... E ...... 951 256-4076
160 W Foothill Pkwy Ste 105 Corona (92882) *(P-18271)*

**Eko Devices, Emeryville** *Also Called: Eko Health Inc (P-15534)*

**Eko Health Inc** ............................................................................. D ...... 844 356-3384
2100 Powell St 3rd Fl Emeryville (94608) *(P-15534)*

**Ekso Bionics, San Rafael** *Also Called: Ekso Bionics Inc (P-9850)*

**Ekso Bionics Inc (PA)** ............................................................... E ...... 510 984-1761
101 Glacier Pt Ste A San Rafael (94901) *(P-9850)*

**Ekso Bionics Holdings Inc** ........................................................ D ...... 510 984-1761
101 Glacier Pt Ste A San Rafael (94901) *(P-15342)*

## ALPHABETIC SECTION

**El Aviso Magazine** ............................................................ E ...... 323 586-9199
4850 Gage Ave Bell (90201) *(P-17276)*

**El Camino Machine & Wldg LLC (PA)** ............................... E ...... 831 758-8309
296 El Camino Real S Salinas (93901) *(P-10823)*

**El Clasificado (PA)** ............................................................ E ...... 323 837-4095
11205 Imperial Hwy Norwalk (90650) *(P-4108)*

**El Dorado Molds LLC** ....................................................... F ...... 916 635-4558
2691 Mercantile Dr Rancho Cordova (95742) *(P-6817)*

**El Dorado Newspapers (DH)** ............................................. C ...... 916 321-1826
2100 Q St Sacramento (95816) *(P-4109)*

**El Dorado Truss Co Inc** ..................................................... E ...... 530 622-1264
300 Industrial Dr Placerville (95667) *(P-3306)*

**El Gallito Market Inc** ........................................................ E ...... 626 442-1190
12242 Valley Blvd El Monte (91732) *(P-2191)*

**El Indio Mexican Restaurant, San Diego** *Also Called: El Indio Shops Incorporated (P-754)*

**El Indio Shops Incorporated** ............................................ D ...... 619 299-0333
3695 India St San Diego (92103) *(P-754)*

**El Latino Newspaper, Chula Vista** *Also Called: Latina & Associates Inc (P-4147)*

**El Metate Inc** .................................................................... C ...... 949 646-9362
817 W 19th St Costa Mesa (92627) *(P-1190)*

**El Metate Market, Costa Mesa** *Also Called: El Metate Inc (P-1190)*

**El Nopalito Inc (PA)** .......................................................... E ...... 760 436-5775
560 Santa Fe Dr Encinitas (92024) *(P-17378)*

**El Nopalito Mexican Food, Encinitas** *Also Called: El Nopalito Inc (P-17378)*

**El Segundo Bread Bar LLC** ............................................... E ...... 310 615-9898
701 E El Segundo Blvd El Segundo (90245) *(P-1191)*

**El Super Leon Pnchin Sncks Inc** ....................................... E ...... 619 426-2968
2545 Britannia Blvd Ste A San Diego (92154) *(P-1305)*

**El Tigre Inc** ....................................................................... C ...... 619 429-8212
2909 Coronado Ave San Diego (92154) *(P-17379)*

**El Tigre Warehouse 2, San Diego** *Also Called: El Tigre Inc (P-17379)*

**El Torito Franchising Company, Cypress** *Also Called: Real Mex Foods Inc (P-17118)*

**Elasco Inc** ........................................................................ D ...... 714 373-4767
11377 Markon Dr Garden Grove (92841) *(P-5155)*

**Elasco Urethane Inc** ......................................................... E ...... 714 895-7031
11377 Markon Dr Garden Grove (92841) *(P-5156)*

**Elation Lighting Inc** .......................................................... D ...... 323 582-3322
6122 S Eastern Ave Commerce (90040) *(P-11592)*

**Elation Professional, Commerce** *Also Called: Elation Lighting Inc (P-11592)*

**Elb Global, Livermore** *Also Called: Elb US Inc (P-17701)*

**Elb US Inc** ........................................................................ E ...... 925 400-6175
4777 Bennett Dr Ste A Livermore (94551) *(P-17701)*

**Elba Company, San Dimas** *Also Called: Elba Jewelry Inc (P-15690)*

**Elba Jewelry Inc** ............................................................... F ...... 909 394-5803
910 N Amelia Ave San Dimas (91773) *(P-15690)*

**Elco Lighting, Los Angeles** *Also Called: AMP Plus Inc (P-11571)*

**Elco Rfrgn Solutions LLC** .................................................. A ...... 858 888-9447
2554 Commercial St San Diego (92113) *(P-10497)*

**Elcon Inc** .......................................................................... E ...... 408 292-7800
1009 Timothy Dr San Jose (95133) *(P-10824)*

**Elcon Precision LLC** ........................................................ D ...... 408 292-7800
1009 Timothy Dr San Jose (95133) *(P-9677)*

**Eldon Drapery Cleaners, El Cajon** *Also Called: Richard C Thurston (P-17769)*

**Eldorado Stone LLC (DH)** ................................................. E ...... 800 925-1491
3817 Ocean Ranch Blvd Oceanside (92056) *(P-7328)*

**Eldorado Usa LLC** ............................................................ F ...... 925 285-4572
1405 Stonewood Pl Concord (94520) *(P-1397)*

**Eldridge Products Inc** ...................................................... E ...... 831 648-7777
465 Reservation Rd Marina (93933) *(P-14408)*

**Eleanor Rigby Leather Co** ................................................ D ...... 619 356-5590
4660 La Jolla Village Dr Ste 500 Pmb 50054 San Diego (92122) *(P-7155)*

**Elecraft Incorporated** ....................................................... E ...... 831 763-4211
125 Westridge Dr Watsonville (95076) *(P-14515)*

**Electra Craft, Westlake Village** *Also Called: Toller Enterprises Inc (P-17480)*

**Electrasem Corp** .............................................................. D ...... 951 371-6140
372 Elizabeth Ln Corona (92878) *(P-14360)*

**Electric, San Clemente** *Also Called: Electric Visual Evolution LLC (P-15600)*

**Electric Designs, Gardena** *Also Called: Gloria Lance Inc (P-2666)*

**Electric Gate Store Inc** ..................................................... C ...... 818 504-2300
15342 Chatsworth St Mission Hills (91345) *(P-13238)*

**Electric Innovations Inc** ................................................... D ...... 530 222-3366
3711 Meadow View Dr Ste 100 Redding (96002) *(P-456)*

**Electric Motor & Supply, Fresno** *Also Called: Electric Motor Shop (P-16651)*

**Electric Motor Shop (PA)** .................................................. E ...... 559 233-1153
253 Fulton St Fresno (93721) *(P-16651)*

**Electric Motor Works Inc** ................................................. E ...... 661 327-4271
803 Inyo Street At 21st St Bakersfield (93305) *(P-19228)*

**Electric Motors, Santa Ana** *Also Called: Advantage Manufacturing Inc (P-16639)*

**Electric Solidus LLC** ......................................................... E ...... 917 692-7764
26565 Agoura Rd Ste 200 Calabasas (91302) *(P-4393)*

**Electric Vehicles International LLC** .................................. E ...... 209 939-0405
1627 Army Ct Ste 1 Stockton (95206) *(P-13349)*

**Electric Visual Evolution LLC (PA)** ................................... E ...... 949 940-9125
950 Calle Amanecer Ste 101 San Clemente (92673) *(P-15600)*

**Electrical Products Division, Fontana** *Also Called: Southwire Inc (P-7733)*

**Electrical Products Rep, Irvine** *Also Called: Agents West Inc (P-13209)*

**Electrical Rebuilders Sls Inc** ............................................. D ...... 323 249-7545
7603 Willow Glen Rd Los Angeles (90046) *(P-13169)*

**Electro Adapter Inc** .......................................................... D ...... 818 998-1198
20640 Nordhoff St Chatsworth (91311) *(P-11451)*

**Electro Kinetics Division, Simi Valley** *Also Called: Pacific Scientific Company (P-14278)*

**Electro Machine & Engrg Co, Compton** *Also Called: E M E Inc (P-8950)*

**Electro Star Indus Coating Inc** ......................................... F ...... 530 527-5400
1945 Airport Blvd Red Bluff (96080) *(P-9065)*

**Electro Star Powder Coatings, Red Bluff** *Also Called: Electro Star Indus Coating Inc (P-9065)*

**Electro Surface Tech Inc** .................................................. E ...... 760 431-8306
2281 Las Palmas Dr # 101 Carlsbad (92011) *(P-12089)*

**Electro Switch Corp** ......................................................... D ...... 909 581-0855
10410 Trademark St Rancho Cucamonga (91730) *(P-11240)*

**Electro Switch Corp** ......................................................... E ...... 909 581-0855
10410 Trademark St Rancho Cucamonga (91730) *(P-12967)*

**Electro Tech Coatings Inc** ................................................ E ...... 760 746-0292
836 Rancheros Dr Ste A San Marcos (92069) *(P-9066)*

**Electro Tech Powder Coating, San Marcos** *Also Called: Electro Tech Coatings Inc (P-9066)*

**Electro-Comm, Burbank** *Also Called: Y B S Enterprises Inc (P-11795)*

**Electro-Optical Industries LLC** ......................................... E ...... 805 964-6701
859 Ward Dr Santa Barbara (93111) *(P-14773)*

**Electro-Plating Spc Inc** .................................................... E ...... 510 786-1881
2436 American Ave Hayward (94545) *(P-8951)*

**Electro-Tech Machining Div, Long Beach** *Also Called: Kbr Inc (P-11299)*

**Electro-Tech Products, Glendora** *Also Called: Electro-Tech Products Inc (P-12968)*

**Electro-Tech Products Inc** ............................................... E ...... 909 592-1434
2001 E Gladstone St Ste A Glendora (91740) *(P-12968)*

**Electro-Tech's, Corona** *Also Called: R&M Deese Inc (P-16025)*

**Electrochem Solutions LLC** ............................................. E ...... 510 476-1840
32500 Central Ave Union City (94587) *(P-8952)*

**Electrocube Inc (PA)** ........................................................ E ...... 909 595-1821
3366 Pomona Blvd Pomona (91768) *(P-12969)*

**Electrode Technologies Inc** ............................................. E ...... 714 549-3771
3110 W Harvard St Ste 14 Santa Ana (92704) *(P-8953)*

**Electrofilm Mfg Co LLC** .................................................... D ...... 661 257-2242
28150 Industry Dr Valencia (91355) *(P-9167)*

**Electrolift, San Bernardino** *Also Called: California PCF Trdg Co II Inc (P-9508)*

**Electrolizing Inc** ............................................................... E ...... 213 749-7876
1947 Hooper Ave Los Angeles (90011) *(P-8954)*

**Electrolurgy Inc** ................................................................ D ...... 949 250-4494
1121 Duryea Ave Irvine (92614) *(P-8955)*

**Electromatic** .................................................................... F ...... 562 623-9993
14025 Stage Rd Santa Fe Springs (90670) *(P-8956)*

**Electromax Inc** ................................................................. E ...... 408 428-9474
1960 Concourse Dr San Jose (95131) *(P-12090)*

**Electron Devices, Torrance** *Also Called: Stellant Systems Inc (P-14310)*

**Electronic Arts Inc (PA)** .................................................... B ...... 650 628-1500
209 Redwood Shores Pkwy Redwood City (94065) *(P-18272)*

**Electronic Arts Redwood LLC** .......................................... A ...... 650 628-1500
209 Redwood Shores Pkwy Redwood City (94065) *(P-13194)*

**Electronic Chrome Grinding Inc** ...................................... E ...... 562 946-6711
9128 Dice Rd Santa Fe Springs (90670) *(P-8957)*

**Electronic Clearing House Inc (HQ)** ................................. D ...... 805 419-8700
730 Paseo Camarillo Camarillo (93010) *(P-18273)*

## Electronic Hardware Limited — ALPHABETIC SECTION

**Electronic Hardware Limited (PA)** .......... E ...... 818 982-6100
13257 Saticoy St North Hollywood (91605) *(P-16700)*

**Electronic Online Systems International** .......... D ...... 760 431-8400
2292 Faraday Ave Frnt Carlsbad (92008) *(P-18972)*

**Electronic Precision Spc Inc** .......... E ...... 714 256-8950
545 Mercury Ln Brea (92821) *(P-8958)*

**Electronic Prtg Solutions LLC** .......... E ...... 858 576-3000
4879 Ronson Ct Ste C San Diego (92111) *(P-4877)*

**Electronic Source Company, Van Nuys** *Also Called: Alyn Industries Inc (P-12911)*

**Electronic Surfc Mounted Inds** .......... E ...... 858 455-1710
6731 Cobra Way San Diego (92121) *(P-12091)*

**Electronic Systems Co Esco, Sunnyvale** *Also Called: Northrop Grumman Systems Corp (P-14267)*

**Electronic Waveform Lab Inc** .......... E ...... 714 843-0463
5702 Bolsa Ave Huntington Beach (92649) *(P-15076)*

**Electrotek Corporation** .......... C ...... 414 762-1390
1108 W Evelyn Ave Sunnyvale (94086) *(P-12092)*

**Elegance Upholstery Inc** .......... F ...... 562 698-2584
11803 Slauson Ave Unit A Ontario (91762) *(P-3738)*

**Elekta Inc** .......... E ...... 408 830-8000
101 Nicholson Ln San Jose (95134) *(P-18274)*

**Element Anheim Rsort Cnvntion, Anaheim** *Also Called: Singod Investors Vi LLC (P-5117)*

**Element Controls Corp** .......... F ...... 323 727-2737
2917 Vail Ave Commerce (90040) *(P-11527)*

**Element Materials Tech Anaheim, Anaheim** *Also Called: Preferred Testing Labs Inc (P-12192)*

**Element Santa Clara, Santa Clara** *Also Called: Mission Park Hotel LP (P-5102)*

**Element Six Tech US Corp** .......... F ...... 408 986-8184
3901 Burton Dr Santa Clara (95054) *(P-5090)*

**Elementis Specialties Inc** .......... D ...... 760 257-9112
31763 Mountain View Rd Newberry Springs (92365) *(P-5091)*

**Elements Food Group Inc** .......... D ...... 909 983-2011
5560 Brooks St Montclair (91763) *(P-1273)*

**Elements Manufacturing Inc** .......... E ...... 831 421-9440
115 Harvey West Blvd Ste C Santa Cruz (95060) *(P-3236)*

**Elers Medical Usa Inc** .......... E ...... 858 336-4900
21707 Hawthorne Blvd Ste 206 Torrance (90503) *(P-16582)*

**Elevate Labs LLC** .......... E ...... 415 875-9817
1390 Market St Ste 200 San Francisco (94102) *(P-18275)*

**Elevator Controls Company LLC** .......... D ...... 916 428-1708
6150 Warehouse Way Sacramento (95826) *(P-11321)*

**Elevator Industries Inc** .......... F ...... 916 921-1495
110 Main Ave Sacramento (95838) *(P-9470)*

**Elevator Research & Mfg Co** .......... F ...... 213 746-1914
1417 Elwood St Los Angeles (90021) *(P-9471)*

**Eli Kiselman** .......... E ...... 832 886-3743
98 N 1st St Unit 725 San Jose (95113) *(P-226)*

**Eliel & Co** .......... E ...... 760 877-8469
2215 La Mirada Dr Vista (92081) *(P-17073)*

**Eliel Cycling, Vista** *Also Called: Eliel & Co (P-17073)*

**Eligius Manufacturing Inc** .......... E ...... 408 437-0337
1177 N 15th St San Jose (95112) *(P-8134)*

**Eligius Manufacturing & Cnstr, San Jose** *Also Called: Eligius Manufacturing Inc (P-8134)*

**Elisid Magazine** .......... E ...... 619 990-9999
1485 Spruce St Riverside (92507) *(P-4251)*

**Elisity Inc** .......... F ...... 408 839-3971
6203 San Ignacio Ave Ste 110 San Jose (95119) *(P-10361)*

**Elite 4 Print Inc** .......... E ...... 310 366-1344
851 E Walnut St Carson (90746) *(P-4603)*

**Elite E/M Inc** .......... E ...... 408 988-3505
340 Martin Ave Santa Clara (95050) *(P-8440)*

**Elite Engineering and Mfg LLC** .......... E ...... 408 988-3505
340 Martin Ave Santa Clara (95050) *(P-8316)*

**Elite Engineering Contrs Inc** .......... E ...... 310 465-8333
16619 S Broadway Gardena (90248) *(P-19390)*

**Elite Intractive Solutions Inc** .......... E ...... 310 740-5426
1200 W 7th St Ste L1-180 Los Angeles (90017) *(P-19054)*

**Elite Leather LLC** .......... D ...... 909 548-8600
1620 5th Ave Ste 400 San Diego (92101) *(P-3472)*

**Elite Lighting** .......... C ...... 323 888-1973
5424 E Slauson Ave Commerce (90040) *(P-11593)*

**Elite Lighting, Commerce** *Also Called: Elite Lighting (P-11593)*

**Elite Metal Finishing, Oceanside** *Also Called: Rose Manufacturing Group Inc (P-9006)*

**Elite Metal Finishing LLC (PA)** .......... C ...... 805 983-4320
540 Spectrum Cir Oxnard (93030) *(P-8959)*

**Elite Mfg Corp** .......... C ...... 888 354-8356
12143 Altamar Pl Santa Fe Springs (90670) *(P-3597)*

**Elite Modern, Santa Fe Springs** *Also Called: Elite Mfg Corp (P-3597)*

**Elite Ready-Mix LLC** .......... E ...... 916 366-4627
6790 Bradshaw Rd Sacramento (95829) *(P-7445)*

**Elite Screens Inc** .......... E ...... 877 511-1211
12282 Knott St Garden Grove (92841) *(P-15637)*

**Elite Service Experts Inc (PA)** .......... E ...... 916 568-1400
819 Striker Ave Sacramento (95834) *(P-9851)*

**Elite Shutters & Shadings Inc** .......... F ...... 209 825-1400
2343 W Yosemite Ave Manteca (95337) *(P-8263)*

**Elite Stone Group Inc** .......... E ...... 909 629-6988
1205 S Dupont Ave Ontario (91761) *(P-3237)*

**Elitegroup Cmpt Systems Inc** .......... C ...... 510 226-7333
6851 Mowry Ave Newark (94560) *(P-10362)*

**Elitegroup Computer Systems Ho** .......... C ...... 510 794-2952
6851 Mowry Ave Newark (94560) *(P-16519)*

**Eliteprotek, Riverside** *Also Called: CCS Inc (P-18154)*

**Elitra Pharmaceuticals** .......... D ...... 858 410-3030
3510 Dunhill St Ste A San Diego (92121) *(P-5431)*

**Elixir Industries** .......... D ...... 949 860-5000
24800 Chrisanta Dr Ste 210 Mission Viejo (92691) *(P-8840)*

**Elixir Medical Corporation** .......... F ...... 408 636-2000
920 N Mccarthy Blvd Milpitas (95035) *(P-15077)*

**Elizabeth Headrick** .......... F ...... 530 247-8000
7194 Bridge St Anderson (96007) *(P-3044)*

**Elizabeth Shutters, Colton** *Also Called: Elizabeth Shutters Inc (P-8264)*

**Elizabeth Shutters Inc** .......... E ...... 909 825-1531
525 S Rancho Ave Colton (92324) *(P-8264)*

**Elk, Shafter** *Also Called: Elk Corporation of Texas (P-7329)*

**Elk Corporation of Texas** .......... C ...... 661 391-3900
6200 Zerker Rd Shafter (93263) *(P-7329)*

**Elk Grove Milling Inc** .......... E ...... 916 684-2056
8320 Eschinger Rd Elk Grove (95757) *(P-1125)*

**Elk Ridge Almonds, Madera** *Also Called: Benton Enterprises LLC (P-38)*

**Ellensburg Lamb Company Inc** .......... D ...... 707 678-3091
7390 Rio Dixon Rd Dixon (95620) *(P-594)*

**Ellensburg Lamb Company Inc (HQ)** .......... F ...... 530 758-3091
2530 River Plaza Dr Ste 200 Sacramento (95833) *(P-595)*

**Ellie Mae, Pleasanton** *Also Called: Ice Mortgage Technology Inc (P-18399)*

**Elliott Company** .......... E ...... 916 920-5451
51 Main Ave Sacramento (95838) *(P-9919)*

**Elliott Company** .......... F ...... 707 665-5307
6014 Bloomfield Rd Petaluma (94952) *(P-9962)*

**Elliotts Designs Inc** .......... E ...... 310 631-4931
2473 E Rancho Del Amo Pl Compton (90220) *(P-3503)*

**Ellipsis Health Inc** .......... E ...... 650 906-6117
118 2nd St San Francisco (94105) *(P-18276)*

**Ellis and Ellis Sign, Sacramento** *Also Called: Illuminated Creations Inc (P-15986)*

**Ellison Educational Eqp Inc (PA)** .......... E ...... 949 598-8822
25671 Commercentre Dr Lake Forest (92630) *(P-9759)*

**Elliston Vineyards Inc** .......... D ...... 925 862-2377
463 Kilkare Rd Sunol (94586) *(P-1553)*

**Elm System Inc** .......... F ...... 408 694-2750
11622 El Camino Real Ste 100 San Diego (92130) *(P-13195)*

**Elma Bustronic Corp** .......... E ...... 510 490-7388
44350 S Grimmer Blvd Fremont (94538) *(P-12093)*

**Elma Electronic Inc (HQ)** .......... C ...... 510 656-3400
44350 S Grimmer Blvd Fremont (94538) *(P-10150)*

**Elmco & Assoc (HQ)** .......... F ...... 916 383-0110
11225 Trade Center Dr Ste 100 Rancho Cordova (95742) *(P-6676)*

**Elotek Systems Inc (PA)** .......... E ...... 949 366-4404
216 Avenida Fabricante Ste 112 San Clemente (92672) *(P-16520)*

**Elro Manufacturing Company (PA)** .......... E ...... 310 380-7444
970 W 190th St Torrance (90502) *(P-15967)*

**Elro Sign Company, Torrance** *Also Called: Elro Manufacturing Company (P-15967)*

**Elrob LLC, Garden Grove** *Also Called: Winchester Interconnect EC LLC (P-16743)*

## ALPHABETIC SECTION

**Elsevier, San Diego** *Also Called: Elsevier Inc (P-4395)*
**Elsevier Academic Press, San Diego** *Also Called: Elsevier Inc (P-4394)*
Elsevier Inc .................................................................... E ...... 619 231-6616
  525 B St San Diego (92101) *(P-4394)*
Elsevier Inc .................................................................... D ...... 619 231-6616
  10620 Treena St San Diego (92131) *(P-4395)*
**Eltron International, Agoura Hills** *Also Called: Zebra Technologies Corporation (P-10454)*
**Elum, San Diego** *Also Called: Elum Designs Inc (P-4604)*
Elum Designs Inc .......................................................... E ...... 858 650-3586
  8969 Kenamar Dr Ste 113 San Diego (92121) *(P-4604)*
Elve Inc .......................................................................... F ...... 734 846-2705
  1440 Drew Ave Ste 150 Davis (95618) *(P-11849)*
Elwin Inc ........................................................................ E ...... 714 752-6962
  6910 8th St Buena Park (90620) *(P-3719)*
Ely Co Inc ...................................................................... E ...... 310 539-5831
  3046 Kashiwa St Torrance (90505) *(P-10825)*
**Elysium, Anaheim** *Also Called: Elysium Tiles Inc (P-7267)*
Elysium Jennings LLC ................................................. C ...... 661 679-1700
  1600 Norris Rd Bakersfield (93308) *(P-157)*
Elysium Tiles Inc .......................................................... F ...... 714 991-7885
  1180 N Anaheim Blvd Anaheim (92801) *(P-7267)*
Elyte Inc ......................................................................... F ...... 661 832-1000
  4516 District Blvd Bakersfield (93313) *(P-9067)*
**Ema, City Of Industry** *Also Called: Engineering Model Assoc Inc (P-6820)*
Emagin Corporation ..................................................... E ...... 408 327-8500
  3140 De La Cruz Blvd Santa Clara (95054) *(P-12416)*
Emagin Corporation ..................................................... E ...... 845 838-7989
  3080 Olcott St Ste C100 Santa Clara (95054) *(P-12417)*
Emazing Lights LLC .................................................... F ...... 626 628-6482
  240 S Loara St Anaheim (92802) *(P-11594)*
Embarcadero Media ...................................................... E ...... 650 854-2626
  3525 Alameda De Las Pulgas Menlo Park (94025) *(P-4110)*
Embarcadero Media (PA) ............................................ D ...... **650 964-6300**
  450 Cambridge Ave Palo Alto (94306) *(P-4111)*
Embedded Designs Inc ................................................. E ...... 858 673-6050
  16120 W Bernardo Dr Ste A San Diego (92127) *(P-14409)*
Embedded Systems Inc ................................................ E ...... 805 624-6030
  2250a Union Pl Simi Valley (93065) *(P-11322)*
Embee Performance LLC ............................................. E ...... 714 540-1354
  2100 Ritchey St Santa Ana (92705) *(P-17242)*
**Embee Plating, Santa Ana** *Also Called: Embee Processing LLC (P-19391)*
**Embee Powder Coating, Santa Ana** *Also Called: Embee Performance LLC (P-17242)*
Embee Processing LLC ................................................ B ...... 714 546-9842
  2158 S Hathaway St Santa Ana (92705) *(P-19391)*
Embodied Labs Inc ...................................................... E ...... 323 421-7600
  2112 Chestnut St Ste 135 Alhambra (91803) *(P-18277)*
EMC Corporation ......................................................... E ...... 408 646-4406
  No Physicla Address Santa Clara (95054) *(P-10234)*
EMC Corporation ......................................................... C ...... 925 600-6800
  6801 Koll Center Pkwy Pleasanton (94566) *(P-10235)*
EMC Water LLC ........................................................... D ...... 209 616-6963
  4114 S Airport Way Stockton (95206) *(P-8040)*
Emco High Voltage Corporation ................................ D ...... 209 267-1630
  1 Emco Ct Sutter Creek (95685) *(P-12970)*
Emcor Facilities Services Inc ...................................... C ...... 949 475-6020
  2 Cromwell Irvine (92618) *(P-14478)*
**Emcore, Alhambra** *Also Called: Emcore Corporation (P-12419)*
Emcore Corporation .................................................... C ...... 925 979-4500
  2700 Systron Dr Concord (94518) *(P-12418)*
Emcore Corporation (PA) ........................................... C ...... **626 293-3400**
  2015 Chestnut St Alhambra (91803) *(P-12419)*
EMD Millipore Corporation ........................................ D ...... 951 676-8080
  28820 Single Oak Dr Temecula (92590) *(P-5826)*
EMD Millipore Corporation ........................................ E ...... 510 576-1367
  25801 Industrial Blvd Ste B Hayward (94545) *(P-14658)*
EMD Millipore Corporation ........................................ E ...... 760 788-9692
  26578 Old Julian Hwy Ramona (92065) *(P-14659)*
EMD Millipore Corporation ........................................ D ...... 951 676-8080
  28835 Single Oak Dr Temecula (92590) *(P-14660)*
**Eme Fan & Motor, La Verne** *Also Called: Sunon Inc (P-10000)*

Eme Technologies Inc .................................................. E ...... 408 720-8817
  3485 Victor St Santa Clara (95054) *(P-10826)*
Emed Technologies Corporation (PA) ....................... F ...... **916 932-0071**
  1262 Hawks Flight Ct Ste 200 El Dorado Hills (95762) *(P-15078)*
Emerald Kingdom Greenhouse LLC .......................... F ...... 530 241-5670
  1593 Beltline Rd Redding (96003) *(P-8664)*
Emerald Packaging Inc ................................................ C ...... 510 429-5700
  33050 Western Ave Union City (94587) *(P-17293)*
Emerald X LLC ............................................................. E ...... 949 226-5754
  31910 Del Obispo St Ste 200 San Juan Capistrano (92675) *(P-4252)*
Emergency Vehicle Group Inc .................................... E ...... 714 238-0110
  2883 E Coronado St Ste A Anaheim (92806) *(P-17438)*
Emergent Group Inc (DH) .......................................... D ...... **818 394-2800**
  10939 Pendleton St Sun Valley (91352) *(P-15343)*
Emerging Display Technologies Corporation (HQ) ... F ...... **949 296-8300**
  390 Goddard Irvine (92618) *(P-12971)*
**Emeritus Vineyards, Sebastopol** *Also Called: Goldridgepinotcom LLC (P-1598)*
Emerzian Woodworking Inc ........................................ E ...... 559 292-2448
  2555 N Argyle Ave Fresno (93727) *(P-3238)*
Emg Inc .......................................................................... D ...... 707 525-9941
  675 Aviation Blvd Ste B Santa Rosa (95403) *(P-15715)*
EMI Solutions LLC ...................................................... E ...... 949 206-9960
  13805 Alton Pkwy Ste B Irvine (92618) *(P-12972)*
**Emile's Table Wines, Morgan Hill** *Also Called: Guglielmo Emilo Winery Inc (P-16)*
Emilio Guglielmo Winery Inc ..................................... F ...... 408 779-2145
  1480 E Main Ave Morgan Hill (95037) *(P-1554)*
Emilykate LLC .............................................................. F ...... 916 761-6261
  8336 Valdez Ave Sacramento (95828) *(P-17916)*
**Emkay Mfg., Redwood City** *Also Called: Bay Precision Machining Inc (P-10739)*
Emp Connectors Inc .................................................... E ...... 310 533-6799
  2280 W 208th St Torrance (90501) *(P-11452)*
Empi Inc ......................................................................... D ...... 714 446-9606
  301 E Orangethorpe Ave Anaheim (92801) *(P-16383)*
Empire Container Corporation ................................... D ...... 310 537-8190
  1161 E Walnut St Carson (90746) *(P-3840)*
Empire Enterprises Inc (PA) ...................................... F ...... **818 784-8918**
  4264 Fulton Ave Ste 1 Studio City (91604) *(P-16413)*
**Empire Milling, Empire** *Also Called: Modesto Milling Inc (P-1137)*
Empire Paper Corporation .......................................... F ...... 510 534-2700
  4930 Waterstone Dr Roseville (95747) *(P-16990)*
Empire Products Inc .................................................... D ...... 909 399-3355
  5061 Brooks St Montclair (91763) *(P-8065)*
Empire Sheet Metal Inc ............................................... F ...... 909 923-2927
  1215 S Bon View Ave Ontario (91761) *(P-8441)*
Empire Shower Doors Inc ........................................... E ...... 707 773-2898
  1217 N Mcdowell Blvd Petaluma (94954) *(P-7219)*
Empire Southwest LLC ............................................... E ...... 760 545-6200
  3393 Us Highway 86 Imperial (92251) *(P-9421)*
Empire West Inc .......................................................... E ...... 707 823-1190
  9270 Graton Rd Graton (95444) *(P-6818)*
**Empire West Plastics, Graton** *Also Called: Empire West Inc (P-6818)*
Empirical Systems Arospc Inc (PA) .......................... C ...... **805 474-5900**
  3580 Sueldo St San Luis Obispo (93401) *(P-13650)*
Employee Owned PCF Cast Pdts I ............................ E ...... 562 633-6673
  520 S Palmetto Ave Ontario (91762) *(P-7844)*
Employer Defense Group ............................................ E ...... 949 200-0137
  2390 E Orangewood Ave Ste 520 Anaheim (92806) *(P-14184)*
**Employment Screening Resources, San Rafael** *Also Called: Aledon Inc (P-6266)*
**Empower Rf, Inglewood** *Also Called: Empower Rf Systems Inc (P-11850)*
Empower Rf Systems Inc (PA) ................................... D ...... **310 412-8100**
  316 W Florence Ave Inglewood (90301) *(P-11850)*
Empower Software Tech LLC ..................................... F ...... 951 672-6257
  28999 Old Town Front St Ste 203 Temecula (92590) *(P-18278)*
EMR Final Ctrl US Holdg Corp .................................. F ...... 858 740-2471
  7328 Trade St San Diego (92121) *(P-9920)*
Emser Tile LLC ............................................................. E ...... 951 296-3671
  42092 Winchester Rd Temecula (92590) *(P-17329)*
Emser Tile LLC ............................................................. E ...... 661 837-4400
  4546 Stine Rd Bakersfield (93313) *(P-17330)*
Emsolutions Inc ............................................................ E ...... 510 668-1118
  2152 Zanker Rd San Jose (95131) *(P-12094)*

**Emtec Engineering** .................................................................. F ...... 408 779-5800
  16840 Joleen Way Ste F1 Morgan Hill (95037) *(P-8442)*
**Emulex Corporation (DH)** ........................................................ C
  5300 California Ave Irvine (92617) *(P-10363)*
**Enable International Inc** ........................................................ E ...... 628 251-1057
  535 Mission St Fl 14 San Francisco (94105) *(P-18279)*
**Enablence Systems Inc (HQ)** ............................................... D ...... 510 226-8900
  2933 Bayview Dr Fremont (94538) *(P-18280)*
**Enablence USA Components Inc** ........................................ D ...... 510 226-8900
  2933 Bayview Dr Fremont (94538) *(P-11761)*
**Enact Systems Inc** ................................................................. F ...... 510 828-2701
  6200 Stoneridge Mall Rd Ste 300 Pleasanton (94588) *(P-18281)*
**Enagic Usa Inc (PA)** ............................................................. D ...... 310 542-7700
  4115 Spencer St Torrance (90503) *(P-17679)*
**Enaqua (DH)** ........................................................................... F ...... 760 599-2644
  1350 Specialty Dr Ste D Vista (92081) *(P-10557)*
**Enchannel Medical Ltd** ........................................................ E ...... 949 694-6802
  555 Corporate Dr Ste 165 Ladera Ranch (92694) *(P-15079)*
**Encino Drmtology Laser Med Ctr, Encino** *Also Called: Alex A Khadavi Md Inc (P-19314)*
**Encompass, Sacramento** *Also Called: Laser Recharge Inc (P-15897)*
**Encore Cases Inc** .................................................................. E ...... 818 768-8803
  8600 Tamarack Ave Sun Valley (91352) *(P-7129)*
**Encore Image, Torrance** *Also Called: Encore Image Group Inc (P-15969)*
**Encore Image Inc** .................................................................. E ...... 909 986-4632
  303 W Main St Ontario (91762) *(P-15968)*
**Encore Image Group Inc (PA)** ............................................. D ...... 310 534-7500
  1445 Sepulveda Blvd Torrance (90501) *(P-15969)*
**Encore Industries** .................................................................. E ...... 408 416-0501
  597 Brennan St San Jose (95131) *(P-8443)*
**Encore Plastics, Huntington Beach** *Also Called: Donoco Industries Inc (P-7194)*
**Encore Seats Inc** ................................................................... E ...... 949 559-0930
  5511 Skylab Rd Huntington Beach (92647) *(P-13836)*
**Encore Semi Inc** .................................................................... D ...... 858 225-4993
  7310 Miramar Rd Ste 410 San Diego (92126) *(P-19392)*
**Encorr Sheets LLC** ............................................................... E ...... 626 523-4661
  5171 E Francis St Ontario (91761) *(P-4037)*
**Encrypted Access Corporation** ........................................... C ...... 714 371-4125
  1730 Redhill Ave Irvine (92697) *(P-10364)*
**Endeavor Homes Inc** ............................................................ E ...... 530 534-0300
  655 Cal Oak Rd Oroville (95965) *(P-9422)*
**Enderle Fuel Injection** .......................................................... E ...... 805 526-3838
  1830 Voyager Ave Simi Valley (93063) *(P-13494)*
**Endologix, Irvine** *Also Called: Endologix Inc (P-15080)*
**Endologix Inc (PA)** ................................................................ C ...... 949 595-7200
  2 Musick Irvine (92618) *(P-15080)*
**Endologix Canada LLC** ....................................................... D ...... 949 595-7200
  2 Musick Irvine (92618) *(P-15081)*
**Endpak Packaging Inc** ......................................................... D ...... 562 801-0281
  9101 Perkins St Pico Rivera (90660) *(P-3990)*
**Endress & Hauser Conducta Inc** ........................................ E ...... 800 835-5474
  4123 E La Palma Ave St200 Anaheim (92807) *(P-14661)*
**Endress+hser Optcal Analis Inc** ......................................... E ...... 909 477-2329
  11027 Arrow Rte Rancho Cucamonga (91730) *(P-14662)*
**Endresshauser Conducta, Anaheim** *Also Called: Endress & Hauser Conducta Inc (P-14661)*
**Endrun Technologies LLC** .................................................. F ...... 707 573-8633
  2270 Northpoint Pkwy Santa Rosa (95407) *(P-14335)*
**Endura Steel Inc (HQ)** .......................................................... F ...... 760 244-9325
  17671 Bear Valley Rd Hesperia (92345) *(P-16619)*
**Enduratex, Corona** *Also Called: Cgpc America Corporation (P-5143)*
**Endurequest Corporation** .................................................... E ...... 559 783-9220
  1813 Thunderbolt Dr Porterville (93257) *(P-6819)*
**Energetic Lighting, Chino** *Also Called: Yankon Industries Inc (P-11570)*
**ENERGOUS, San Jose** *Also Called: Energous Corporation (P-11851)*
**Energous Corporation** ......................................................... E ...... 408 963-0200
  3590 N 1st St Ste 210 San Jose (95134) *(P-11851)*
**Energy Absorption Systems Inc** ........................................ C ...... 916 645-8181
  3617 Cincinnati Ave Rocklin (95765) *(P-9284)*
**ENERGY ABSORPTION SYSTEMS, INC., Rocklin** *Also Called: Energy Absorption Systems Inc (P-9284)*
**Energy Club, Pacoima** *Also Called: Energy Club Inc (P-17143)*
**Energy Club Inc** ..................................................................... D
  12950 Pierce St Pacoima (91331) *(P-17143)*
**Energy Cnvrsion Applctions Inc** ........................................ F ...... 714 256-2166
  582 Explorer St Brea (92821) *(P-11212)*
**Energy Link Indus Svcs Inc** ................................................ E ...... 661 765-4444
  11439 S Enos Ln Bakersfield (93311) *(P-10827)*
**ENERGY RECOVERY, San Leandro** *Also Called: Energy Recovery Inc (P-9852)*
**Energy Recovery Inc (PA)** ................................................... B ...... 510 483-7370
  1717 Doolittle Dr San Leandro (94577) *(P-9852)*
**Energy Solutions (us) LLC** .................................................. B ...... 310 669-5300
  20851 S Santa Fe Ave Long Beach (90810) *(P-5092)*
**Energy Suspension, San Clemente** *Also Called: Bunker Corp (P-13466)*
**Energy Systems, Stockton** *Also Called: ES West Coast LLC (P-11265)*
**Energy Vault Inc (HQ)** .......................................................... E ...... 805 852-0000
  4360 Park Terrace Dr Ste 100 Westlake Village (91361) *(P-13135)*
**Enerpro Inc** ............................................................................. E ...... 805 683-2114
  99 Aero Camino Goleta (93117) *(P-16701)*
**Enersponse Inc** ..................................................................... E ...... 949 829-3901
  1148 Manhattan Ave Manhattan Beach (90266) *(P-14516)*
**Enersys** ................................................................................... E ...... 510 887-8080
  30069 Ahern Ave Union City (94587) *(P-13136)*
**Enersys** ................................................................................... E ...... 909 464-8251
  5580 Edison Ave Chino (91710) *(P-13137)*
**Enertron Technologies Inc** .................................................. E ...... 800 537-7649
  3525 Del Mar Heights Rd San Diego (92130) *(P-11528)*
**Enervenue Inc** ........................................................................ C ...... 408 664-0355
  3500 Gateway Blvd Fremont (94538) *(P-12420)*
**Enevate, Irvine** *Also Called: Enevate Corporation (P-13138)*
**Enevate Corporation** ............................................................ D ...... 949 243-0399
  101 Theory Ste 200 Irvine (92617) *(P-13138)*
**Enfabrica Corporation** ......................................................... E ...... 650 206-8533
  295 Bernardo Ave Ste 200 Mountain View (94043) *(P-12421)*
**Engagio Inc** ............................................................................ E ...... 650 265-2264
  181 2nd Ave Ste 200 San Mateo (94401) *(P-18282)*
**Engel & Gray Inc** ................................................................... E ...... 805 925-2771
  745 W Betteravia Rd Ste A Santa Maria (93455) *(P-227)*
**Engense Inc** ........................................................................... F ...... 805 484-8317
  2255 Pleasant Valley Rd Ste G Camarillo (93012) *(P-7612)*
**Engine World LLC** ................................................................ E ...... 510 653-4444
  1487 67th St Emeryville (94608) *(P-13495)*
**Engineered Food Systems** .................................................. E ...... 714 921-9913
  2490 Anselmo Dr Corona (92879) *(P-10558)*
**Engineered Lighting Products, El Monte** *Also Called: R W Swarens Associates Inc (P-11554)*
**Engineered Machinery Group Inc** ...................................... F ...... 909 579-0088
  1042 N Mountain Ave Ste B561 Upland (91786) *(P-9717)*
**Engineered Magnetics Inc** .................................................. E ...... 310 649-9000
  10524 S La Cienega Blvd Inglewood (90304) *(P-11370)*
**Engineered Well Svc Intl Inc** ............................................... F ...... 866 913-6283
  3120 Standard St Bakersfield (93308) *(P-228)*
**Engineering Jk Aerospace & Def** ...................................... E ...... 714 499-9092
  23231 La Palma Ave Yorba Linda (92887) *(P-13837)*
**Engineering Model Assoc Inc (PA)** ................................... E ...... 626 912-7011
  1020 Wallace Way City Of Industry (91748) *(P-6820)*
**Enhance America Inc** ........................................................... E ...... 951 361-3000
  3463 Grapevine St Jurupa Valley (91752) *(P-15970)*
**Enhanced Vision Systems Inc (HQ)** .................................. D ...... 800 440-9476
  15301 Springdale St Huntington Beach (92649) *(P-14774)*
**Enjoy Haircare, Oceanside** *Also Called: USP Inc (P-6052)*
**Enkeboll Design, Carson** *Also Called: The Enkeboll Co (P-3198)*
**Enlighted Inc** .......................................................................... D ...... 650 964-1094
  46897 Bayside Pkwy Fremont (94538) *(P-11529)*
**Enlink Geoenergy Services Inc** ......................................... E ...... 424 242-1200
  2630 Homestead Pl Rancho Dominguez (90220) *(P-10498)*
**Ennis Traffic Safety Solutions** ............................................ E ...... 323 758-1147
  6624 Stanford Ave Los Angeles (90001) *(P-6083)*
**Enniss Inc** ............................................................................... E ...... 619 561-1101
  12535 Vigilante Rd Lakeside (92040) *(P-311)*
**Eno Brands Inc** ...................................................................... E ...... 714 220-1318
  6481 Global Dr Cypress (90630) *(P-17645)*
**ENOVIX, Fremont** *Also Called: Enovix Corporation (P-13159)*
**Enovix Corporation (PA)** ..................................................... D ...... 510 695-2350
  3501 W Warren Ave Fremont (94538) *(P-13159)*

## ALPHABETIC SECTION

**Enovix Operations Inc** .......... C ...... 510 695-2399
3501 W Warren Ave Fremont (94538) *(P-13160)*

**Enphase Energy, Fremont** *Also Called: Enphase Energy Inc (P-12422)*

**Enphase Energy Inc (PA)** .......... A ...... 707 774-7000
47281 Bayside Pkwy Fremont (94538) *(P-12422)*

**Enpower Greentech Inc** .......... E ...... 916 220-6060
333 W San Carlos St San Jose (95110) *(P-13139)*

**Enrich Enterprises Inc** .......... E ...... 310 515-5055
3925 E Vernon St Long Beach (90815) *(P-2990)*

**Ensemble Communications Inc** .......... C ...... 858 458-1400
2223 Avenida De La Playa La Jolla (92037) *(P-11852)*

**Ensign US Drlg Cal Inc (HQ)** .......... E ...... 661 589-0111
7001 Charity Ave Bakersfield (93308) *(P-9554)*

**Ensign-Bickford Arospc Def Co** .......... C ...... 805 292-4000
14370 White Sage Rd Moorpark (93021) *(P-14185)*

**Enstrom Mold & Engineering Inc** .......... F ...... 760 744-1880
235 Trade St San Marcos (92078) *(P-9620)*

**Ensurge Micropower Inc** .......... D ...... 408 503-7300
2581 Junction Ave San Jose (95134) *(P-12973)*

**Entco LLC** .......... A ...... 312 580-9100
1140 Enterprise Way Sunnyvale (94089) *(P-18283)*

**Entech Instruments Inc** .......... E ...... 805 527-5939
2207 Agate Ct Simi Valley (93065) *(P-14663)*

**Entegris Inc** .......... D ...... 805 541-9299
4175 Santa Fe Rd San Luis Obispo (93401) *(P-19516)*

**Entegris Gp Inc** .......... C ...... 805 541-9299
4175 Santa Fe Rd San Luis Obispo (93401) *(P-10087)*

**Entek Adaptive Mtl Hdlg LLC** .......... F ...... 714 854-1300
1921 Petra Ln Placentia (92870) *(P-19393)*

**Entekra LLC** .......... D ...... 209 624-1630
945 E Whitmore Ave Modesto (95358) *(P-3394)*

**Enterprise Security Inc (PA)** .......... D ...... 714 630-9100
22860 Savi Ranch Pkwy Yorba Linda (92887) *(P-19055)*

**Enterprise Security Solutions, Yorba Linda** *Also Called: Enterprise Security Inc (P-19055)*

**Enterprise Svcs Asia PCF Corp** .......... E ...... 650 857-1501
3000 Hanover St Palo Alto (94304) *(P-10151)*

**Enterprise Vineyards Inc** .......... E ...... 707 996-6513
16600 Norrbom Rd Sonoma (95476) *(P-1555)*

**Enterprises Industries Inc** .......... C ...... 818 989-6103
7500 Tyrone Ave Van Nuys (91405) *(P-8841)*

**Entexs Corporation** .......... F ...... 888 960-3689
3720 Trade Way Ste A Cameron Park (95682) *(P-6143)*

**Entos Pharmaceuticals Inc** .......... F ...... 800 727-0884
3040 Science Park Rd San Diego (92121) *(P-5432)*

**Entrance Tech, El Monte** *Also Called: Santoshi Corporation (P-9010)*

**Entrepeneur Magazine, Santa Ana** *Also Called: Entrepreneur Media LLC (P-4253)*

**Entrepreneur Media LLC (PA)** .......... D ...... 949 261-2325
1651 E 4th St Ste 125 Santa Ana (92701) *(P-4253)*

**Envelopments Inc** .......... E ...... 714 569-3300
13091 Sandhurst Pl Santa Ana (92705) *(P-3768)*

**Envia Systems Inc** .......... E ...... 510 509-1367
7979 Gateway Blvd Ste 101 Newark (94560) *(P-13239)*

**Envion LLC** .......... D ...... 818 217-2500
14724 Ventura Blvd Fl 200 Sherman Oaks (91403) *(P-9984)*

**Envirnmental Catalyst Tech LLC** .......... E ...... 949 459-3870
3937 Ocean Ranch Blvd Oceanside (92056) *(P-5093)*

**Envirnmntal Cmpliance Pros Inc** .......... E ...... 916 953-9006
2701 Del Paso Rd Ste 130-704 Sacramento (95835) *(P-5903)*

**Envirnmntal Mlding Cncepts LLC** .......... F ...... 951 214-6596
14050 Day St Moreno Valley (92553) *(P-6491)*

**Envirnmntal Systems Inc Nthrn (PA)** .......... D ...... 408 980-1711
3353 De La Cruz Blvd Santa Clara (95054) *(P-417)*

**Enviro Tech Chemical Svcs Inc (DH)** .......... C ...... 209 581-9576
500 Winmoore Way Modesto (95358) *(P-17243)*

**Envirocare International Inc** .......... E ...... 707 638-6800
507 Green Island Rd American Canyon (94503) *(P-9985)*

**Envirochem Technologies, Atascadero** *Also Called: Chemlogics Group LLC (P-6139)*

**Envirofabrics, Los Angeles** *Also Called: Roshan Trading Inc (P-2449)*

**Enviroguard, Montclair** *Also Called: Expo Power Systems Inc (P-16652)*

**Envirokinetics Inc (PA)** .......... F ...... 909 621-7599
101 S Milliken Ave Ontario (91761) *(P-9853)*

**Environmental Sampling Sup Inc** .......... D ...... 510 465-4988
640 143rd Ave San Leandro (94578) *(P-6821)*

**Environmental Science US LLC** .......... C ...... 800 331-2867
890 Embarcadero Dr West Sacramento (95605) *(P-5433)*

**Enviroplex Inc** .......... D ...... 209 466-8000
4777 Carpenter Rd Stockton (95215) *(P-8665)*

**Envision Peripherals Inc (PA)** .......... E ...... 510 770-9988
490 N Mccarthy Blvd Ste 120 Milpitas (95035) *(P-16521)*

**Envision Plastics, Chino** *Also Called: Envision Plastics Industries LLC (P-6822)*

**Envision Plastics Industries LLC** .......... E ...... 909 590-7334
14312 Central Ave Chino (91710) *(P-6822)*

**ENVISTA, Brea** *Also Called: Envista Holdings Corporation (P-15455)*

**Envista Holdings Corporation (PA)** .......... D ...... 714 817-7000
200 S Kraemer Blvd Bldg E Brea (92821) *(P-15455)*

**Envu, West Sacramento** *Also Called: Environmental Science US LLC (P-5433)*

**Envveno Medical Corporation** .......... E ...... 949 261-2900
70 Doppler Irvine (92618) *(P-15082)*

**Enzyme Corporation** .......... E ...... 415 638-9595
340 S Lemon Ave Walnut (91789) *(P-6144)*

**Eo Products, San Rafael** *Also Called: Small World Trading Co (P-6038)*

**Eos, Paso Robles** *Also Called: Eos Estate Winery (P-1556)*

**Eos Estate Winery** .......... E ...... 805 239-2562
2300 Airport Rd Paso Robles (93446) *(P-1556)*

**Eos Software Inc** .......... E ...... 408 439-2903
10026 Crescent Rd Cupertino (95014) *(P-18284)*

**Ep Holdings Inc** .......... E ...... 949 713-4600
30442 Esperanza Rcho Sta Marg (92688) *(P-10236)*

**Ep Memory, Rcho Sta Marg** *Also Called: Ep Holdings Inc (P-10236)*

**Epac Flexible Packaging, Chino** *Also Called: Epac Los Angeles LLC (P-4605)*

**Epac Los Angeles LLC** .......... F ...... 844 623-8603
5475 Daniels St Chino (91710) *(P-4605)*

**Epac Technologies Inc (PA)** .......... C ...... 510 317-7979
2561 Grant Ave San Leandro (94579) *(P-4606)*

**EPC Power Corp (PA)** .......... C ...... 858 748-5590
13250 Gregg St Ste A2 Poway (92064) *(P-11371)*

**Epe Industries Usa Inc (HQ)** .......... F ...... 800 315-0336
17835 Newhope St Ste G Fountain Valley (92708) *(P-6632)*

**Epe USA, Fountain Valley** *Also Called: Epe Industries Usa Inc (P-6632)*

**Epic Plastics, Roseville** *Also Called: Basalite Building Products LLC (P-7313)*

**Epic Sheet Metal Inc** .......... F ...... 714 679-5917
1720 Industrial Ave Norco (92860) *(P-8444)*

**Epic Technologies LLC** .......... A ...... 908 707-4085
9340 Owensmouth Ave Chatsworth (91311) *(P-11762)*

**Epica Medical Innovations LLC** .......... E ...... 949 238-6323
901 Calle Amanecer Ste 150 San Clemente (92673) *(P-15083)*

**Epicor Software Corporation** .......... E ...... 949 585-4000
4120 Dublin Blvd Ste 300 Dublin (94568) *(P-18285)*

**Epicuren Discovery** .......... D ...... 949 588-5807
31 Journey Ste 100 Aliso Viejo (92656) *(P-5750)*

**Epignosis LLC** .......... E ...... 646 797-2799
315 Montgomery St Fl 9 San Francisco (94104) *(P-18286)*

**Epilogue and Arrested, Los Angeles** *Also Called: Rhapsody Clothing Inc (P-2804)*

**Epirus Inc** .......... E ...... 310 620-8678
19145 Gramercy Pl Torrance (90501) *(P-18287)*

**Epl, Commerce** *Also Called: Edison Price Lighting Inc (P-11526)*

**Eplastics, San Diego** *Also Called: Plastics Family Holdings Inc (P-6566)*

**Epmar Corporation** .......... E ...... 562 946-8781
9930 Painter Ave Whittier (90605) *(P-6084)*

**Epmware Inc** .......... E ...... 408 614-0442
333 W San Carlos St Ste 600 San Jose (95110) *(P-16522)*

**Epoca Yocool, South Gate** *Also Called: Win Soon Inc (P-846)*

**Epoch International Entps Inc (PA)** .......... E ...... 510 556-1225
2383 Bering Dr San Jose (95131) *(P-9854)*

**Epoch Times Los Angeles** .......... F ...... 626 401-1828
9550 Flair Dr El Monte (91731) *(P-4112)*

**Epodium Inc** .......... E ...... 925 621-0602
7020 Koll Center Pkwy Ste 127 Pleasanton (94566) *(P-18288)*

**Eppig Brewing, Vista** *Also Called: J&L Eppig Brewing LLC (P-1436)*

**Eps Corporate Holdings Inc (DH)** .......... F ...... 310 204-7238
3100 Donald Douglas Loop N Hngr 3 Santa Monica (90405) *(P-9258)*

## ALPHABETIC SECTION

**Eps Corporate Holdings Inc** .................................................. F ...... 562 698-7774
  12468 Lambert Rd Whittier (90606) *(P-16766)*

**Epson America Inc (DH)** .................................................. A ...... 800 463-7766
  3131 Katella Ave Los Alamitos (90720) *(P-10365)*

**Epson Electronics America Inc (DH)** .................................. E ...... 408 922-0200
  3131 Katella Ave Los Alamitos (90720) *(P-12423)*

**Epworth Morehouse Cowles, Chino** *Also Called: Morehouse-Cowles LLC (P-9878)*

**Eqrx, Redwood City** *Also Called: Eqrx Inc (P-5434)*

**Eqrx Inc (HQ)** .................................................................. D ...... 617 315-2255
  700 Saginaw Dr Redwood City (94063) *(P-5434)*

**Equal Exchange Inc** .......................................................... D ...... 619 335-6259
  2920 Norman Strasse Rd San Marcos (92069) *(P-2070)*

**Equilibrium, Corte Madera** *Also Called: Automted Mdia Proc Sltions Inc (P-16316)*

**Equilibrium Management LLC** ........................................... E ...... 415 516-2930
  2443 Fillmore St Ste 345 San Francisco (94115) *(P-19528)*

**Equillium Inc (PA)** ............................................................ E ...... 858 412-5302
  2223 Avenida De La Playa Ste 105 La Jolla (92037) *(P-5435)*

**Equimine** ......................................................................... E ...... 877 204-9040
  26457 Rancho Pkwy S Lake Forest (92630) *(P-18289)*

**Equine Comfort Products, Simi Valley** *Also Called: Eurow and OReilly Corp (P-17294)*

**Equinox Construction, Union City** *Also Called: Equinox Millworks Inc (P-3136)*

**Equinox Millworks Inc** ...................................................... E ...... 510 946-9729
  1440 Whipple Rd Union City (94587) *(P-3136)*

**Equipment & Tool Institute, Irvine** *Also Called: Innova Electronics Corporation (P-13519)*

**Equipment Design & Mfg Inc** ........................................... D ...... 909 594-2229
  119 Explorer St Pomona (91768) *(P-8445)*

**Equitex, Napa** *Also Called: Lixit Corporation (P-16171)*

**Equus Products Inc** .......................................................... E ...... 714 424-6779
  17352 Von Karman Ave Irvine (92614) *(P-14517)*

**ERA Products Inc** ............................................................. F ...... 310 324-4908
  1130 Benedict Canyon Dr Beverly Hills (90210) *(P-3624)*

**Erasca Inc** ....................................................................... C ...... 858 465-6511
  10835 Road To The Cure Ste 140 San Diego (92121) *(P-5436)*

**Erba Organics, Chatsworth** *Also Called: Erbaviva Inc (P-5237)*

**Erbaviva Inc** .................................................................... E ...... 818 998-7112
  19831 Nordhoff Pl Ste 116 Chatsworth (91311) *(P-5237)*

**ERC Concepts Co Inc** ....................................................... F ...... 408 734-5345
  1255 Birchwood Dr Sunnyvale (94089) *(P-10828)*

**Ereplacements LLC** ......................................................... E ...... 714 361-2652
  16885 W Bernardo Dr Ste 370 San Diego (92127) *(P-13140)*

**Erf Enterprises Inc** .......................................................... F ...... 909 825-4080
  863 E Valley Blvd Colton (92324) *(P-13411)*

**Erg International, Oxnard** *Also Called: Ergonom Corporation (P-3740)*

**Ergocraft Contract Solutions** ........................................... E
  6055 E Washington Blvd Ste 500 Commerce (90040) *(P-3598)*

**Ergocraft Office Furniture, Commerce** *Also Called: Ergocraft Contract Solutions (P-3598)*

**Ergonom Corporation (PA)** ............................................. D ...... 805 981-9978
  361 Bernoulli Cir Oxnard (93030) *(P-3739)*

**Ergonom Corporation** ..................................................... D ...... 805 981-9978
  390 Lombard St Oxnard (93030) *(P-3740)*

**Ergononmic Comfort Design Inc** .................................... F ...... 951 277-1558
  9140 Stellar Ct Ste B Corona (92883) *(P-3599)*

**Ericson Owens Enterprises** ............................................. F ...... 510 500-5491
  1734 Clement Ave Alameda (94501) *(P-15971)*

**Eridan Communications Inc (PA)** .................................... E ...... 650 492-0657
  400 W California Ave Sunnyvale (94086) *(P-14518)*

**Erika Records Inc** ............................................................ E ...... 714 228-5420
  6300 Caballero Blvd Buena Park (90620) *(P-11731)*

**Erin Condren, Hawthorne** *Also Called: EC Design LLC (P-17639)*

**Ermico, San Francisco** *Also Called: Ermico Enterprises Inc (P-15807)*

**Ermico Enterprises Inc** .................................................... D ...... 415 822-6776
  1111 17th St Ste B San Francisco (94107) *(P-15807)*

**Ernie Ball, San Luis Obispo** *Also Called: Ernie Ball Inc (P-15716)*

**Ernie Ball Inc (PA)** ........................................................... E ...... 805 544-7726
  4117 Earthwood Ln San Luis Obispo (93401) *(P-15716)*

**Ernst Publishing Co, Half Moon Bay** *Also Called: Ucc Guide Inc (P-4485)*

**Eroad Inc** ........................................................................ D ...... 503 305-2255
  15110 Avenue Of Science Ste 100 San Diego (92128) *(P-11264)*

**Erp, Rancho Dominguez** *Also Called: Expanded Rubber & Plastics Corp (P-6823)*

**Erp Power LLC (PA)** ........................................................ F ...... 805 517-1300
  2625 Townsgate Rd Westlake Village (91361) *(P-14519)*

**ES Kluft & Company Inc (DH)** ......................................... C ...... 909 373-4211
  11096 Jersey Blvd Ste 101 Rancho Cucamonga (91730) *(P-3525)*

**Es Operating Co** .............................................................. F
  19200 Stevens Creek Blvd Ste 200 Cupertino (95014) *(P-6145)*

**ES West Coast LLC** ......................................................... E ...... 209 870-1900
  7100 Longe St Ste 300 Stockton (95206) *(P-11265)*

**Esaero, San Luis Obispo** *Also Called: Empirical Systems Arospc Inc (P-13650)*

**Escalade Sports, San Diego** *Also Called: Indian Industries Inc (P-15830)*

**Escalon Premier Brands Inc** ............................................ D ...... 209 838-7341
  1905 Mchenry Ave Escalon (95320) *(P-887)*

**Escape Communications Inc** .......................................... F ...... 310 997-1300
  2790 Skypark Dr Ste 203 Torrance (90505) *(P-11853)*

**Esco Industries Inc** ......................................................... F ...... 951 782-2130
  1755 Iowa Ave Bldg A Riverside (92507) *(P-8775)*

**Esco Technologies Inc** .................................................... E ...... 805 604-3875
  501 Del Norte Blvd Oxnard (93030) *(P-11993)*

**Escort Health, City Of Industry** *Also Called: Health One Pharmaceutical Inc (P-5478)*

**Ese, El Segundo** *Also Called: Mod-Electronics Inc (P-15677)*

**Ese, Los Angeles** *Also Called: ESE INC (P-17244)*

**ESE INC** ........................................................................... E ...... 213 614-0102
  1163 E 12th St Los Angeles (90021) *(P-17244)*

**Esi Motion, Simi Valley** *Also Called: Embedded Systems Inc (P-11322)*

**Esign Emcee, Moorpark** *Also Called: Topaz Systems Inc (P-10445)*

**Esilicon Corporation (DH)** ............................................... C
  2130 Gold St Ste 100 San Jose (95002) *(P-12424)*

**Esionic, Cupertino** *Also Called: Es Operating Co (P-6145)*

**Eska Inc** .......................................................................... E ...... 323 846-3700
  1370 Mirasol St Los Angeles (90023) *(P-2757)*

**Esl Power Systems Inc** .................................................... D ...... 800 922-4188
  2800 Palisades Dr Corona (92878) *(P-11453)*

**ESM Aerospace Inc** ......................................................... E ...... 818 841-3653
  1203 W Isabel St Burbank (91506) *(P-8446)*

**Esmart Source Inc** .......................................................... F ...... 408 739-3500
  5159 Commercial Cir Ste H Concord (94520) *(P-18290)*

**Esmi, San Diego** *Also Called: Electronic Surfc Mounted Inds (P-12091)*

**Esmond Natural Inc** ........................................................ E ...... 626 337-1588
  5316 Irwindale Ave Irwindale (91706) *(P-5238)*

**Especial T Hvac Shtmtl Fttngs** ........................................ E ...... 909 869-9150
  1239 E Franklin Ave Pomona (91766) *(P-16778)*

**Especializados Del Aire, San Diego** *Also Called: Alliance Air Products Llc (P-10479)*

**Esperanto Technologies Inc (PA)** ................................... D ...... 650 319-7357
  800 W El Camino Real Ste 410 Mountain View (94040) *(P-12425)*

**Esperanto.ai, Mountain View** *Also Called: Esperanto Technologies Inc (P-12425)*

**Esperanzas Tortilleria** ..................................................... E ...... 760 743-5908
  750 Rock Springs Rd Escondido (92025) *(P-2192)*

**Esperer Webstores LLC** ................................................... F ...... 805 880-1900
  3820 State St Ste B Santa Barbara (93105) *(P-755)*

**Ess Technology, San Jose** *Also Called: Ess Technology Holdings Inc (P-12426)*

**Ess Technology Holdings Inc (HQ)** .................................. E ...... 408 643-8818
  109 Bonaventura Dr San Jose (95134) *(P-12426)*

**Essai Inc (DH)** ................................................................. E ...... 510 580-1700
  48580 Kato Rd Fremont (94538) *(P-14520)*

**Essence of America** ........................................................ E ...... 312 805-9365
  1855 1st Ave Ste 103 San Diego (92101) *(P-19357)*

**Essence Printing Inc (PA)** ............................................... E ...... 650 952-5072
  270 Oyster Point Blvd South San Francisco (94080) *(P-4607)*

**Essential Pharmaceutical Corp** ...................................... E ...... 909 623-4565
  1906 W Holt Ave Pomona (91768) *(P-5437)*

**Essentra International LLC** ............................................. A ...... 708 315-7498
  21303 Ferrero Walnut (91789) *(P-6227)*

**Essex Electronics Inc** ...................................................... E ...... 805 684-7601
  1130 Mark Ave Carpinteria (93013) *(P-12427)*

**Essex Industries, Huntington Beach** *Also Called: Momeni Engineering LLC (P-10991)*

**Esslinger Engineering Inc** ............................................... E ...... 909 539-0544
  5946 Freedom Dr Chino (91710) *(P-13496)*

**Estam, Los Angeles** *Also Called: Orbita Corp (P-2871)*

**Estech Digital, Los Angeles** *Also Called: Techture Inc (P-4477)*

**Esterline Mason, Rancho Cascades** *Also Called: Janco Corporation (P-13010)*

**Esterline Technologies Corp** .......................................... F ...... 805 238-2840
  1740 Commerce Way Paso Robles (93446) *(P-13838)*

## ALPHABETIC SECTION — Everett Graphics Inc

Et Water Systems LLC .................................................. E ...... 415 945-9383
384 Bel Marin Keys Blvd Ste 145 Novato (94949) *(P-14864)*

Eta Compute Inc ........................................................... E ...... 650 255-1293
182 S Murphy Ave Sunnyvale (94086) *(P-14521)*

Etagen, Menlo Park *Also Called: Mainspring Energy Inc (P-8780)*

Etech-360 Inc (PA) ........................................................ A ...... 714 900-3486
555 California St San Francisco (94104) *(P-18291)*

Eternity Floors, Pacoima *Also Called: LA Hardwood Flooring Inc (P-3096)*

Etherwan Systems Inc ................................................. D ...... 714 779-3800
2301 E Winston Rd Anaheim (92806) *(P-19035)*

Ethicon Endo - Surgery, Redwood City *Also Called: Ethicon Inc (P-15344)*

Ethicon Inc ..................................................................... C ...... 650 306-7900
700 Bay Rd Redwood City (94063) *(P-15344)*

Ethicon Inc ..................................................................... B ...... 949 581-5799
33 Technology Dr Irvine (92618) *(P-15345)*

Ethos Seafood Group LLC ......................................... D ...... 312 858-3474
18531 S Broadwick St Rancho Dominguez (90220) *(P-2051)*

Ethosenergy Field Services LLC (DH) ...................... E ...... 310 639-3523
10455 Slusher Dr # 12 Santa Fe Springs (90670) *(P-229)*

Eti, Fields Landing *Also Called: Rock Springs Industries Inc (P-5195)*

Eti B Si Professional, Commerce *Also Called: Eti Sound Systems Inc (P-11659)*

Eti Partners IV LLC ....................................................... E ...... 949 273-4990
901 Washington Blvd Ste 208 Marina Del Rey (90292) *(P-12095)*

Eti Sound Systems Inc ................................................ E ...... 323 835-6660
5300 Harbor St Commerce (90040) *(P-11659)*

Eti Systems .................................................................... D ...... 310 684-3664
1800 Century Park E Ste 600 Los Angeles (90067) *(P-14410)*

ETM Teledyne, Newark *Also Called: Teledyne Etm Inc (P-11962)*

Etnies, Lake Forest *Also Called: Sole Technology Inc (P-7123)*

Eton Corporation .......................................................... E ...... 650 903-3866
1015 Corporation Way Palo Alto (94303) *(P-13240)*

ETR, Scotts Valley *Also Called: Education Training & RES Assoc (P-19350)*

Etrade 24 Inc ................................................................ E ...... 818 712-0574
16600 Calneva Dr Encino (91436) *(P-2546)*

Etro USA Incorporated ................................................ E ...... 310 248-2855
9501 Wilshire Blvd Beverly Hills (90212) *(P-2664)*

Ets Express, Oxnard *Also Called: Ets Express LLC (P-9068)*

Ets Express LLC (DH) ................................................. E ...... 805 278-7771
420 Lombard St Oxnard (93030) *(P-9068)*

Etude Wines, Napa *Also Called: Treasury Wine Estates Americas (P-1798)*

Eturns Inc ...................................................................... E ...... 949 265-2626
19700 Fairchild Ste 290 Irvine (92612) *(P-18292)*

Eubanks Engineering Co (PA) ................................... E ...... 909 483-2456
1921 S Quaker Ridge Pl Ontario (91761) *(P-9736)*

Eufora, Carlsbad *Also Called: Eden Beauty Concepts Inc (P-5976)*

Eugenus Inc (HQ) ........................................................ D ...... 669 235-8244
677 River Oaks Pkwy San Jose (95134) *(P-14522)*

Euhomy LLC ................................................................. E ...... 213 265-5081
1230 Santa Anita Ave South El Monte (91733) *(P-6410)*

Euphonix Inc (DH) ........................................................ D ...... 650 526-1600
280 Bernardo Ave Mountain View (94043) *(P-11854)*

Eureka, Willows *Also Called: Calplant I LLC (P-3406)*

Eureka Times-Standard, Eureka *Also Called: Pasadena Newspapers Inc (P-4181)*

Euri Lighting, Torrance *Also Called: Irtronix Inc (P-11425)*

Euro Coffee, Los Angeles *Also Called: Eberine Enterprises Inc (P-2069)*

Euro Motorparts Group, Anaheim *Also Called: Empi Inc (P-16383)*

Eurobizusa Inc ............................................................. F ...... 626 793-0032
572 E Green St Ste 301 Pasadena (91101) *(P-1557)*

Eurocraft Archtectural Met Inc .................................... E ...... 323 771-1323
5619 Watcher St Bell Gardens (90201) *(P-8625)*

Eurodrip USA Inc ......................................................... D ...... 559 674-2670
7545 Carroll Rd San Diego (92121) *(P-16796)*

Eurofins Envmt Tstg Nthrn Cal ................................... E ...... 916 373-5600
880 Riverside Pkwy West Sacramento (95605) *(P-19502)*

Euroline Steel Windows .............................................. D ...... 877 590-2741
22600 Savi Ranch Pkwy Ste E Yorba Linda (92887) *(P-8265)*

Euroline Steel Windows & Doors, Yorba Linda *Also Called: Euroline Steel Windows (P-8265)*

Euronext Hair Collection, Commerce *Also Called: West Bay Imports Inc (P-17317)*

Europa Village, Temecula *Also Called: Europa Village LLC (P-1558)*

Europa Village LLC ...................................................... C ...... 951 506-1818
33475 La Serena Way Temecula (92591) *(P-1558)*

European Paving Designs Inc ................................... D ...... 408 283-5230
1474 Berger Dr San Jose (95112) *(P-445)*

European Rolling Shutters, San Jose *Also Called: Blum Construction Co Inc (P-8259)*

European Wholesale Counter ..................................... C ...... 619 562-0565
10051 Prospect Ave Santee (92071) *(P-3655)*

Eurostampa California LLC ......................................... E ...... 707 927-4848
1315 Airport Blvd Ste A Napa (94558) *(P-4821)*

Eurotec Seating, La Habra *Also Called: Orbo Corporation (P-3636)*

Eurotec Seating Incorporated ..................................... E ...... 562 806-6171
1000 S Euclid St La Habra (90631) *(P-3625)*

Eurotech Luxury Shower Doors, Laguna Hills *Also Called: Eurotech Showers Inc (P-6677)*

Eurotech Showers Inc ................................................. E ...... 949 716-4099
23552 Commerce Center Dr Ste B Laguna Hills (92653) *(P-6677)*

Eurow and OReilly Corp ............................................. E ...... 800 747-7452
51 Moreland Rd Simi Valley (93065) *(P-17294)*

Eurton Electric Company Inc ...................................... E ...... 562 946-4477
9920 Painter Ave Whittier (90605) *(P-19229)*

Eurus Energy America Corp (DH) ............................. F ...... 858 638-7115
9255 Towne Centre Dr Ste 840 San Diego (92121) *(P-11266)*

Euv Tech, Martinez *Also Called: Euv Tech Inc (P-14664)*

Euv Tech Inc ................................................................. D ...... 925 229-4388
2830 Howe Rd Ste A Martinez (94553) *(P-14664)*

Ev Charging Solutions Inc .......................................... D ...... 866 300-3827
11800 Clark St Arcadia (91006) *(P-13170)*

Ev R Inc ......................................................................... E ...... 323 312-5400
3400 Slauson Ave Maywood (90270) *(P-2758)*

Ev Ray Inc .................................................................... E ...... 818 346-5381
6400 Variel Ave Woodland Hills (91367) *(P-16423)*

Ev3 Neurovascular, Irvine *Also Called: Micro Therapeutics Inc (P-15188)*

Eva Franco Inc ............................................................. F ...... 213 746-4776
1509 Mission St South Pasadena (91030) *(P-2723)*

Evan-Moor Corporation (HQ) ..................................... E ...... 831 649-5901
18 Lower Ragsdale Dr Monterey (93940) *(P-4329)*

Evan-Moor Educational Publr, Monterey *Also Called: Evan-Moor Corporation (P-4329)*

Evans Hydro, Compton *Also Called: Evans Hydro Inc (P-19256)*

Evans Hydro Inc ........................................................... E ...... 310 608-5801
18128 S Santa Fe Ave Compton (90221) *(P-19256)*

Evans Industries Inc ................................................... D ...... 626 912-1688
17915 Railroad St City Of Industry (91748) *(P-9285)*

Evans Manufacturing LLC (HQ) ................................ C ...... 714 379-6100
7422 Chapman Ave Garden Grove (92841) *(P-15972)*

Evans Manufacturing, Inc., Garden Grove *Also Called: Evans Manufacturing LLC (P-15972)*

Evans Medical, El Dorado Hills *Also Called: Emed Technologies Corporation (P-15078)*

Evans Walker Inc ......................................................... E ...... 951 784-7223
2304 Fleetwood Dr Riverside (92509) *(P-13497)*

Evans, Walker Racing, Riverside *Also Called: Evans Walker Inc (P-13497)*

Evapco Inc .................................................................... D ...... 559 673-2207
1900 W Almond Ave Madera (93637) *(P-10499)*

Evapco West, Madera *Also Called: Evapco Inc (P-10499)*

Eve, Lakewood *Also Called: Eve Hair Inc (P-17295)*

Eve Hair Inc (PA) .......................................................... E ...... 562 377-1020
3935 Paramount Blvd Lakewood (90712) *(P-17295)*

Eventscom Inc .............................................................. E ...... 858 257-2300
811 Prospect St La Jolla (92037) *(P-18293)*

Eveo Inc ........................................................................ D ...... 415 749-6777
1160 Battery St Ste 275 San Francisco (94111) *(P-15973)*

Ever Blue, Los Angeles *Also Called: California Blue Apparel Inc (P-2701)*

Ever-Pac, Riverside *Also Called: Jmc Closing Co LLC (P-10910)*

Everactive Inc .............................................................. D ...... 517 256-0679
2150 Paragon Dr San Jose (95131) *(P-14523)*

Everbrands Inc ............................................................. E ...... 855 595-2999
11791 Monarch St Garden Grove (92841) *(P-5977)*

Everbridge Inc (PA) ..................................................... C ...... 818 230-9700
155 N Lake Ave Ste 900 Pasadena (91101) *(P-18294)*

Everest Group USA Inc ............................................... E ...... 909 923-1818
2030 S Carlos Ave Ontario (91761) *(P-7952)*

Everett Graphics Inc .................................................... D ...... 510 577-6777
7300 Edgewater Dr Oakland (94621) *(P-3917)*

Everfilt
ALPHABETIC SECTION

**Everfilt, Jurupa Valley** *Also Called: Puri Tech Inc* ***(P-10593)***

**Everfocus Electronics Corp (HQ)** ........................ **E ...... 626 844-8888**
324 W Blueridge Ave Orange (92865) ***(P-16702)***

**Evergreen Environmental Svcs, Gardena** *Also Called: Evergreen Oil Inc* ***(P-6393)***

**Evergreen Holdings Inc** ........................ C ...... 949 757-7770
18952 Macarthur Blvd Ste 410 Irvine (92612) ***(P-6392)***

**Evergreen Industries Inc (DH)** ........................ **D ...... 323 583-1331**
2254 E 49th St Vernon (90058) ***(P-14336)***

**Evergreen Licensing, Agoura Hills** *Also Called: Evergreen Licensing LLC* ***(P-5239)***

**Evergreen Licensing LLC** ........................ F ...... 844 270-2700
5737 Kanan Rd Agoura Hills (91301) ***(P-5239)***

**Evergreen Lighting, Pomona** *Also Called: Yawitz Inc* ***(P-11510)***

**Evergreen Oil Inc (HQ)** ........................ **E ...... 949 757-7770**
18025 S Broadway Gardena (90248) ***(P-6393)***

**Evergreen Paper and Energy LLC (PA)** ........................ **D ...... 802 357-1003**
353 Rio Del Oro Ln Sacramento (95825) ***(P-3756)***

**Evergreen Scientific, Vernon** *Also Called: Evergreen Industries Inc* ***(P-14336)***

**Evergreen-Energy, Sacramento** *Also Called: Evergreen Paper and Energy LLC* ***(P-3756)***

**Everidge Inc** ........................ E ...... 909 605-6419
8886 White Oak Ave Rancho Cucamonga (91730) ***(P-10500)***

**Everlance Inc** ........................ D ...... 872 814-6308
595 Pacific Ave Fl 4 San Francisco (94133) ***(P-18295)***

**Everleigh, Los Angeles** *Also Called: J Heyri Inc* ***(P-2671)***

**Everson Spice Company Inc** ........................ E ...... 562 595-4785
2667 Gundry Ave Long Beach (90755) ***(P-2193)***

**Every Man Jack, Mill Valley** *Also Called: Presidio Brands Inc* ***(P-17045)***

**Everybody World LLC** ........................ F ...... 213 305-9450
5718 S Santa Fe Ave Vernon (90058) ***(P-2413)***

**Everybody.world, Vernon** *Also Called: Everybody World LLC* ***(P-2413)***

**Everytable, Los Angeles** *Also Called: Everytable Pbc* ***(P-2194)***

**Everytable Pbc** ........................ E ...... 323 296-0311
3650 W Martin Luther King Jr Blvd Los Angeles (90008) ***(P-2194)***

**Evgo Montgomery Co, Los Angeles** *Also Called: Evgo Services LLC* ***(P-17474)***

**Evgo Services LLC** ........................ B ...... 310 954-2900
11835 W Olympic Blvd Ste 900e Los Angeles (90064) ***(P-17474)***

**Evkii Inc** ........................ E ...... 760 721-5200
624 Garrison St Ste1-2 Oceanside (92054) ***(P-17412)***

**Evnroll Putters LLC** ........................ F ...... 321 277-1397
1817 Aston Ave Ste 101 Carlsbad (92008) ***(P-15808)***

**Evocative Inc** ........................ D ...... 888 365-2656
26 Centerpointe Dr La Palma (90623) ***(P-18296)***

**Evolife Scientific Llc** ........................ E ...... 888 750-0310
3150 Long Beach Blvd Long Beach (90807) ***(P-5240)***

**Evolphin Software Inc** ........................ E ...... 888 386-4114
6101 Bollinger Canyon Rd Ste 324d San Ramon (94583) ***(P-18297)***

**EVOLUS, Newport Beach** *Also Called: Evolus Inc* ***(P-5438)***

**Evolus Inc (PA)** ........................ **C ...... 949 284-4555**
520 Newport Center Dr Ste 1200 Newport Beach (92660) ***(P-5438)***

**Evolution Design Lab Inc** ........................ E ...... 626 960-8388
144 W Colorado Blvd Pasadena (91105) ***(P-7115)***

**Evolution Fresh Inc** ........................ C ...... 800 794-9986
11655 Jersey Blvd Ste A Rancho Cucamonga (91730) ***(P-17168)***

**Evolution Industries, Walnut** *Also Called: Crush Master Grinding Corp* ***(P-10793)***

**Evolution Juice, Rancho Cucamonga** *Also Called: Evolution Fresh Inc* ***(P-17168)***

**Evolution Robotics Inc** ........................ F ...... 626 993-3300
1055 E Colorado Blvd Ste 320 Pasadena (91106) ***(P-18298)***

**Evolv Surfaces Inc** ........................ C ...... 415 767-4600
825 Potter St Berkeley (94710) ***(P-3685)***

**Evolv Technology Solutions Inc (PA)** ........................ **E ...... 415 444-9040**
580 Market St Ste 200 San Francisco (94104) ***(P-18299)***

**Evolve Dental Technologies Inc** ........................ F ...... 949 713-0909
5 Vanderbilt Irvine (92618) ***(P-15456)***

**Evolve Manufacturing Tech Inc** ........................ D ...... 510 690-8959
47300 Bayside Pkwy Fremont (94538) ***(P-15084)***

**Evome Medical Technologies Inc (PA)** ........................ **F ...... 800 760-6826**
3330 Caminito Daniella Del Mar (92014) ***(P-15085)***

**Evonik Corporation** ........................ D ...... 323 264-0311
3305 E 26th St Vernon (90058) ***(P-6283)***

**Evoqua Water Technologies LLC** ........................ E ...... 707 747-9600
6160 Egret Ct Benicia (94510) ***(P-11372)***

**Evoqua Water Technologies LLC** ........................ E ...... 213 748-8511
1441 E Washington Blvd Los Angeles (90021) ***(P-17702)***

**Evoralight, Costa Mesa** *Also Called: Flexfire Leds Inc* ***(P-11532)***

**Evy of California Inc** ........................ C ...... 213 746-4647
2042 Garfield Ave Commerce (90040) ***(P-2853)***

**Ew Corprtion Indus Fabricators (PA)** ........................ **D ...... 760 337-0020**
1002 E Main St El Centro (92243) ***(P-8135)***

**Exablox Corporation** ........................ E ...... 408 773-8477
1156 Sonora Ct Sunnyvale (94086) ***(P-18300)***

**Exact Corp** ........................ E ...... 209 544-8600
5143 Blue Gum Ave Modesto (95358) ***(P-16797)***

**Exactacator Inc (PA)** ........................ **E ...... 209 464-8979**
2237 Stagecoach Rd Stockton (95215) ***(P-15809)***

**Exacttarget LLC (HQ)** ........................ **D ...... 415 901-7000**
415 Mission St Fl 3 San Francisco (94105) ***(P-18301)***

**Exactuals LLC** ........................ F ...... 310 689-7491
1100 Glendon Ave Fl 17 Los Angeles (90024) ***(P-18302)***

**Exadel Inc (PA)** ........................ **A ...... 925 363-9510**
1255 Treat Blvd Walnut Creek (94597) ***(P-18303)***

**Exalt Communications Inc** ........................ D ...... 408 688-0200
530 Division St Campbell (95008) ***(P-11855)***

**Exam Room Supply LLC** ........................ F ...... 805 298-3631
2419 Harbor Blvd Unit 126 Ventura (93001) ***(P-15535)***

**Exar, San Jose** *Also Called: Exar Corporation* ***(P-12428)***

**Exar Corporation (HQ)** ........................ **E ...... 669 265-6100**
1060 Rincon Cir San Jose (95131) ***(P-12428)***

**Exatron Inc** ........................ E ...... 408 629-7600
2842 Aiello Dr San Jose (95111) ***(P-14524)***

**Excalibur Extrusion Inc** ........................ E ...... 714 528-8834
110 E Crowther Ave Placentia (92870) ***(P-6596)***

**Excalibur International, Long Beach** *Also Called: A W Chang Corporation* ***(P-17056)***

**Excalibur Well Services Corp** ........................ C ...... 661 589-5338
22034 Rosedale Hwy Bakersfield (93314) ***(P-158)***

**Exce LP** ........................ D ...... 858 549-6340
16868 Via Del Campo Ct Ste 200 San Diego (92127) ***(P-10366)***

**Excel Bridge Manufacturing Co., Santa Fe Springs** *Also Called: Excel Sheet Metal Inc* ***(P-8447)***

**Excel Cabinets Inc** ........................ E ...... 951 279-4545
225 Jason Ct Corona (92879) ***(P-3239)***

**Excel Cnc Machining Inc** ........................ E ...... 408 970-9460
3185 De La Cruz Blvd Santa Clara (95054) ***(P-10829)***

**Excel Machining, Santa Clara** *Also Called: Excel Cnc Machining Inc* ***(P-10829)***

**Excel Manufacturing Inc** ........................ E ...... 661 257-1900
20409 Prairie St Chatsworth (91311) ***(P-10830)***

**Excel Picture Frames Inc** ........................ E ...... 323 231-0244
647 E 59th St Los Angeles (90001) ***(P-19257)***

**Excel Precision, Santa Clara** *Also Called: Excel Precision Corp USA* ***(P-14525)***

**Excel Precision Corp USA** ........................ E ...... 408 727-4260
3350 Scott Blvd Bldg 62 Santa Clara (95054) ***(P-14525)***

**Excel Scientific LLC** ........................ E ...... 760 246-4545
18350 George Blvd Victorville (92394) ***(P-16600)***

**Excel Sheet Metal Inc (PA)** ........................ **D ...... 562 944-0701**
12001 Shoemaker Ave Santa Fe Springs (90670) ***(P-8447)***

**Excelitas Tech Illumination, Pleasanton** *Also Called: Excelitas Technologies Corp* ***(P-11596)***

**Excelitas Technologies Corp** ........................ C ...... 510 979-6500
6701 Koll Center Pkwy Unit 400 Pleasanton (94566) ***(P-11595)***

**Excelitas Technologies Corp** ........................ E ...... 510 979-6500
6701 Koll Center Pkwy # 400 Pleasanton (94566) ***(P-11596)***

**Excellence Magazine Inc** ........................ F ...... 415 382-0582
42 Digital Dr Ste 5 Novato (94949) ***(P-4254)***

**Excellence Opto Inc (PA)** ........................ **E ...... 909 468-0550**
21858 Garcia Ln Walnut (91789) ***(P-11572)***

**Excelligence Learning Corp (PA)** ........................ **E ...... 831 333-2000**
20 Ryan Ranch Rd Ste 200 Monterey (93940) ***(P-17703)***

**Excelline Food Products LLC** ........................ E ...... 818 701-7710
833 N Hollywood Way Burbank (91505) ***(P-1034)***

**Excello Circuits Inc** ........................ D ...... 714 993-0560
5330 E Hunter Ave Anaheim (92807) ***(P-12096)***

**Excellon Acquisition LLC (HQ)** ........................ **E ...... 310 668-7700**
16130 Gundry Ave Paramount (90723) ***(P-9855)***

**Excellon Automation Co, Paramount** *Also Called: Excellon Acquisition LLC* ***(P-9855)***

## ALPHABETIC SECTION — F I O Imports Inc

Excellos Incorporated .................................................. E ...... 619 400-8235
　1155 Island Ave San Diego (92101) *(P-5827)*
Excelpro Inc (PA) ........................................................ F ...... 323 415-8544
　1630 Amapola Ave Torrance (90501) *(P-714)*
Excelsior Construction, Tulare *Also Called: Excelsior Metals LLC (P-8136)*
Excelsior Metals LLC ................................................. E ...... 559 346-0932
　795 E Levin Ave Tulare (93274) *(P-8136)*
Excelsior Nutrition Inc ................................................ D ...... 657 999-5188
　1206 N Miller St Unit D Anaheim (92806) *(P-5241)*
Exclusive Fresh Inc ................................................... E ...... 650 728-7321
　165 Airport St El Granada (94018) *(P-17156)*
Exclusive Networks Usa Inc ...................................... E ...... 408 943-9193
　4038 Clipper Ct Fremont (94538) *(P-16523)*
Execuprint Inc ............................................................. F ...... 818 993-8184
　24963 Avenue Tibbitts Santa Clarita (91355) *(P-19006)*
Executive Auto Reconditioning .................................. E ...... 626 416-3322
　522 E Duarte Rd Monrovia (91016) *(P-19165)*
Executive Safe and SEC Corp .................................. E ...... 909 947-7020
　10722 Edison Ct Rancho Cucamonga (91730) *(P-9286)*
EXELIXIS, Alameda *Also Called: Exelixis Inc (P-5828)*
Exelixis Inc (PA) ........................................................ D ...... 650 837-7000
　1851 Harbor Bay Pkwy Alameda (94502) *(P-5828)*
Exelixis Inc ................................................................. B ...... 650 837-7000
　1851 Harbor Bay Pkwy Alameda (94502) *(P-14479)*
Exemplis LLC .............................................................. C ...... 714 995-4800
　6280 Artesia Blvd Buena Park (90620) *(P-3600)*
Exemplis LLC .............................................................. E ...... 714 898-5500
　6280 Artesia Blvd Buena Park (90620) *(P-3601)*
Exemplis LLC (PA) .................................................... E ...... 714 995-4800
　6415 Katella Ave Cypress (90630) *(P-3602)*
Exemptax, Irvine *Also Called: Dacenso Inc (P-18224)*
Exeter Mercantile Company ....................................... F ...... 559 592-2121
　258 E Pine St Exeter (93221) *(P-9353)*
Exhaust Center Inc .................................................... F ...... 951 685-8602
　1794 W 11th St Upland (91786) *(P-8448)*
Exhaust Tech, Commerce *Also Called: Dynaflex Products (P-13409)*
Exigent Sensors LLC ................................................. E ...... 949 439-1321
　11441 Markon Dr Garden Grove (92841) *(P-11994)*
Exit Light Co Inc ........................................................ F ...... 877 352-3948
　3170 Scott St Vista (92081) *(P-11530)*
Exiton Inc .................................................................... E ...... 562 699-1122
　12226 Coast Dr Whittier (90601) *(P-15974)*
Exo Imaging Inc ......................................................... C ...... 833 633-8396
　4201 Burton Dr Santa Clara (95054) *(P-15536)*
Expand Machinery LLC ............................................. F ...... 818 349-9166
　20869 Plummer St Chatsworth (91311) *(P-10831)*
Expand Toolroom Solutions, Chatsworth *Also Called: Expand Machinery LLC (P-10831)*
Expandable Software Inc (PA) .................................. E ...... 408 261-7880
　1762 Technology Dr Ste 118 San Jose (95110) *(P-18304)*
Expanded Rubber & Plastics Corp ........................... E ...... 310 324-6692
　19200 S Laurel Park Rd Rancho Dominguez (90220) *(P-6823)*
EXPANDING LIGHT, THE, Nevada City *Also Called: Ananda Church of Self-Realztn (P-19367)*
Expedite Precision Works Inc ................................... E ...... 408 573-9600
　931 Berryessa Rd San Jose (95133) *(P-10832)*
Experience Lyric, Los Angeles *Also Called: Addaday Inc (P-15774)*
Experience.com, San Ramon *Also Called: Buyersroad Inc (P-18132)*
Expert Assembly Services Inc .................................. E ...... 714 258-8880
　14312 Chambers Rd Ste B Tustin (92780) *(P-12097)*
Expert Ems, Tustin *Also Called: Expert Assembly Services Inc (P-12097)*
Expert Semiconductor Tech Inc ................................ E ...... 831 439-9300
　10 Victor Sq Ste 100 Scotts Valley (95066) *(P-12429)*
Expertech, Scotts Valley *Also Called: Expert Semiconductor Tech Inc (P-12429)*
Exploding Kittens LLC ............................................... E ...... 310 788-8699
　101 S La Brea Ave Ste A Los Angeles (90036) *(P-15747)*
Exploramed Nc7 LLC ................................................. C ...... 650 559-5805
　1975 W El Camino Real Ste 306 Mountain View (94040) *(P-15537)*
Expo Builders Supply, San Diego *Also Called: Expo Industries Inc (P-16445)*
Expo Dyeing & Finishing Inc .................................... C ...... 714 220-9583
　8898 Los Coyotes Ct Unit 320 Buena Park (90621) *(P-2502)*
Expo Industries Inc ................................................... D ...... 858 566-3110
　7455 Carroll Rd San Diego (92121) *(P-16445)*
Expo Power Systems Inc .......................................... E ...... 800 506-9884
　5534 Olive St Montclair (91763) *(P-16652)*
Expo-3 International Inc ............................................. E ...... 714 379-8383
　12350 Edison Way 60 Garden Grove (92841) *(P-15975)*
Express, San Diego *Also Called: Express Business Systems Inc (P-4878)*
Express Business Systems Inc ................................ E ...... 858 549-9828
　9155 Trade Pl San Diego (92126) *(P-4878)*
Express Container Inc ............................................... E ...... 909 798-3857
　5450 Dodds Ave Buena Park (90621) *(P-3841)*
Express Die Supply Inc ............................................. E ...... 562 903-1700
　10020 Freeman Ave Santa Fe Springs (90670) *(P-9621)*
Express Manufacturing Inc (PA) ................................ B ...... 714 979-2228
　3519 W Warner Ave Santa Ana (92704) *(P-12974)*
Express Press ............................................................. E ...... 424 228-2261
　12021 Jefferson Blvd Culver City (90230) *(P-4396)*
Express Printing Info MGT Co, Santee *Also Called: Business Printing Company Inc (P-19078)*
Expression Systems LLC (PA) .................................. E ...... 877 877-7421
　2537 2nd St Davis (95618) *(P-5829)*
Expro Manufacturing Corporation .............................. E ...... 323 415-8544
　2800 Ayers Ave Vernon (90058) *(P-855)*
Exrox Inc ..................................................................... E ...... 213 536-5290
　535 Ceres Ave Los Angeles (90013) *(P-6492)*
Extensions Plus, Tarzana *Also Called: Extensions Plus Inc (P-16908)*
Extensions Plus Inc ................................................... E ...... 818 881-5611
　5428 Reseda Blvd Tarzana (91356) *(P-16908)*
Extreme Group Holdings LLC ................................... F ...... 310 899-3200
　1531 14th St Santa Monica (90404) *(P-11732)*
Extreme Networks Inc ............................................... E ...... 408 579-2800
　145 Rio Robles San Jose (95134) *(P-18973)*
Extreme Precision Inc ............................................... F ...... 408 275-8365
　7855 Prestwick Cir San Jose (95135) *(P-10833)*
Extreme Production Music, Santa Monica *Also Called: Extreme Group Holdings LLC (P-11732)*
Extreme Reach, Burbank *Also Called: Extreme Reach Inc (P-4397)*
Extreme Reach Inc .................................................... E ...... 818 588-3635
　1048 N Lake St Burbank (91502) *(P-4397)*
Extron Electronics, Anaheim *Also Called: Rgb Systems Inc (P-10429)*
Extrumed Inc (DH) ..................................................... E ...... 951 547-7400
　547 Trm Cir Corona (92879) *(P-6824)*
Exxel Outdoors Inc .................................................... C ...... 626 369-7278
　343 Baldwin Park Blvd City Of Industry (91746) *(P-3028)*
Exxon, Goleta *Also Called: Exxon Mobil Corporation (P-17475)*
Exxon Mbil - Rfnery Dist Plant .................................. F ...... 323 586-5329
　2619 E 37th St Vernon (90058) *(P-6337)*
Exxon Mobil Corporation ........................................... E ...... 805 961-4093
　12000 Calle Real Goleta (93117) *(P-17475)*
Eye Exam of California, San Diego *Also Called: James G Meyers & Associates (P-19323)*
Eye-Fi Inc ................................................................... E ...... 650 969-3162
　967 N Shoreline Blvd Mountain View (94043) *(P-10237)*
Eyeonics Inc ............................................................... E ...... 949 788-6000
　32 Discovery Irvine (92618) *(P-15601)*
Eyeshadow, Los Angeles *Also Called: Stony Apparel Corp (P-2689)*
EZ Lube LLC .............................................................. D ...... 951 766-1996
　532 W Florida Ave Hemet (92543) *(P-6394)*
Ezaki Glico, Irvine *Also Called: Ezaki Glico USA Corporation (P-1306)*
Ezaki Glico USA Corporation .................................... F ...... 949 251-0144
　18022 Cowan Ste 110 Irvine (92614) *(P-1306)*
Ezchip Semiconductor Inc ......................................... E ...... 408 520-3700
　2700 Zanker Rd San Jose (95134) *(P-10152)*
F & L Industrial Solutions, Poway *Also Called: Motion Industries Inc (P-16884)*
F & L Tls Precision Machining, Corona *Also Called: F & L Tools Corporation (P-10834)*
F & L Tools Corporation ............................................ F ...... 951 279-1555
　245 Jason Ct Corona (92879) *(P-10834)*
F C I, San Marcos *Also Called: Fluid Components Intl LLC (P-14412)*
F G S Packing Services, Exeter *Also Called: Fruit Growers Supply Company (P-3844)*
F Gavina & Sons Inc ................................................. B ...... 323 582-0671
　2700 Fruitland Ave Vernon (90058) *(P-2071)*
F I N, Granada Hills *Also Called: Financial Info Netwrk Inc (P-17922)*
F I O Imports Inc ....................................................... C ...... 323 263-5100
　5980 Alcoa Ave Vernon (90058) *(P-2195)*

F I T, Compton *Also Called: Fastener Innovation Tech Inc (P-8722)*
F Korbel & Bros (PA) .................................................................. C ...... 707 824-7000
13250 River Rd Guerneville (95446) *(P-1559)*
F M H, Irvine *Also Called: Fmh Aerospace Corp (P-13844)*
F M I, Santa Ana *Also Called: Flexible Manufacturing LLC (P-12879)*
F M P, Downey *Also Called: Florence Meat Packing Co Inc (P-17580)*
F R O Inc .................................................................................... E ...... 559 891-0237
1607 Simpson St Kingsburg (93631) *(P-19559)*
F S I, Sonoma *Also Called: Fastening Systems Intl (P-16754)*
F T B & Son Inc ........................................................................ E ...... 714 891-8003
11551 Markon Dr Garden Grove (92841) *(P-8449)*
F T I, Long Beach *Also Called: Fundamental Tech Intl Inc (P-14415)*
F-J-E Inc .................................................................................... E ...... 562 437-7466
546 W Esther St Long Beach (90813) *(P-3656)*
F-P Press, Union City *Also Called: Fricke-Parks Press Inc (P-4617)*
Fab Services West Inc ............................................................ D ...... 909 350-7500
10007 Elm Ave Fontana (92335) *(P-8697)*
Fab-9, San Jose *Also Called: Saigon Fabrication Ltd (P-19416)*
Fabco Holdings Inc ................................................................. A ...... 925 454-9500
151 Lawrence Dr Livermore (94551) *(P-13498)*
Fabco Steel Fabrication Inc .................................................. E ...... 909 350-1535
14688 San Bernardino Ave Fontana (92335) *(P-8137)*
Fabcon, Santa Ana *Also Called: Fabrication Concepts Corporation (P-8450)*
Fabcon, Valencia *Also Called: Bayless Manufacturing LLC (P-10740)*
Faber Enterprises Inc ............................................................ C ...... 310 323-6200
14800 S Figueroa St Gardena (90248) *(P-9168)*
Faberware Div, Fairfield *Also Called: Meyer Corporation US (P-16430)*
Fabfad LLC .............................................................................. F ...... 213 488-0456
1901 E 7th Pl Los Angeles (90021) *(P-4879)*
Fabnet, Anaheim *Also Called: Fabrication Network Inc (P-8451)*
Fabri Cote, Los Angeles *Also Called: Rdmm Legacy Inc (P-17067)*
Fabri-Tech Components Inc ................................................. F ...... 510 249-2000
576 Sycamore Dr Milpitas (95035) *(P-12975)*
Fabric8labs Inc ....................................................................... D ...... 858 215-1142
11075 Roselle St San Diego (92121) *(P-9766)*
Fabrica Fine Carpet, Santa Ana *Also Called: Fabrica International Inc (P-2514)*
Fabrica International Inc ....................................................... C ...... 949 261-7181
3201 S Susan St Santa Ana (92704) *(P-2514)*
Fabricast Inc (PA) .................................................................. E ...... 626 443-3247
2517 Seaman Ave South El Monte (91733) *(P-12976)*
Fabricated Components Corp .............................................. C ...... 714 974-8590
130 W Bristol Ln Orange (92865) *(P-12098)*
Fabricated Extrusion Co LLC (PA) ...................................... E ...... 209 529-9200
2331 Hoover Ave Modesto (95354) *(P-6825)*
Fabricated Glass Spc Inc ...................................................... E ...... 707 429-6160
2350 S Watney Way Ste E Fairfield (94533) *(P-7220)*
Fabrication Concepts Corporation ....................................... C ...... 714 881-2000
1800 E Saint Andrew Pl Santa Ana (92705) *(P-8450)*
Fabrication Network Inc ....................................................... F ...... 714 393-5282
5410 E La Palma Ave Anaheim (92807) *(P-8451)*
Fabrication Tech Inds Inc ..................................................... D ...... 619 477-4141
2200 Haffley Ave National City (91950) *(P-8138)*
Fabricator, Santa Rosa *Also Called: Sonoma Stainless Inc (P-8336)*
Fabricmate, Ventura *Also Called: Fabricmate Systems Inc (P-2436)*
Fabricmate Systems Inc ....................................................... E ...... 805 642-7470
2781 Golf Course Dr Unit A Ventura (93003) *(P-2436)*
Fabrinet West, Santa Clara *Also Called: Fabrinet West Inc (P-12099)*
Fabrinet West Inc .................................................................. D ...... 408 748-0900
4900 Patrick Henry Dr Santa Clara (95054) *(P-12099)*
Fabrique Delices, Hayward *Also Called: Sapar Usa Inc (P-665)*
Fabritec Structures, Tustin *Also Called: Shade Structures Inc (P-8569)*
Fabtex Inc ................................................................................ C ...... 714 538-0877
615 S State College Blvd Fullerton (92831) *(P-2437)*
Fabtron, Redwood City *Also Called: EH Suda Inc (P-10820)*
Fabtron, Lewiston *Also Called: EH Suda Inc (P-10821)*
Fabtronics Inc ......................................................................... E ...... 626 962-3293
5026 Calmview Ave Baldwin Park (91706) *(P-8452)*
Facefirst LLC ........................................................................... E ...... 805 482-8428
31416 Agoura Rd Ste 250 Westlake Village (91361) *(P-18305)*

Facilitec West, Covina *Also Called: Stavros Enterprises Inc (P-19282)*
Facilitron Inc (PA) .................................................................. E ...... 800 272-2962
485 Alberto Way Ste 210 Los Gatos (95032) *(P-18306)*
Facility Maintenance & Cnstr, Sacramento *Also Called: Triamid Cnstr Centl Cal Inc (P-353)*
Facility Makers Inc ................................................................ E ...... 714 544-1702
345 W Freedom Ave Orange (92865) *(P-8453)*
Factory One Studio Inc ......................................................... D ...... 323 752-1670
6700 Avalon Blvd Ste 101 Los Angeles (90003) *(P-2414)*
Factory Pipe LLC ................................................................... E ...... 707 463-1322
1307 Masonite Rd Ukiah (95482) *(P-14057)*
Factory Pipe Products, Ukiah *Also Called: Factory Pipe LLC (P-14057)*
Factory Showroom Exchange, Los Angeles *Also Called: Sofa U Love LLC (P-3490)*
Factory Technologies Inc ...................................................... E ...... 209 248-8420
627 Bitritto Ct Ste A Modesto (95356) *(P-11241)*
Factron Test Fixtures, Poway *Also Called: Cohu Interface Solutions LLC (P-14508)*
Fafco Inc (PA) ......................................................................... E ...... 530 332-2100
435 Otterson Dr Chico (95928) *(P-8066)*
Fair Isaac International Corp (HQ) ...................................... A ...... 415 446-6000
200 Smith Ranch Rd San Rafael (94903) *(P-18307)*
Fair Price Carpets, Riverside *Also Called: Fairprice Enterprises Inc (P-17527)*
Fairchild Semicdtr Intl Inc (HQ) ........................................... B ...... 408 822-2000
1272 Borregas Ave Sunnyvale (94089) *(P-12430)*
Fairfield Rental Service Inc .................................................. F ...... 707 422-2270
2525 Clay Bank Rd Fairfield (94533) *(P-17851)*
Fairmont Designs, Buena Park *Also Called: Cambium Business Group Inc (P-16412)*
Fairprice Enterprises Inc ....................................................... D ...... 951 684-8578
1070 Center St Riverside (92507) *(P-17527)*
Fairway Injection Molds Inc ................................................ D ...... 909 595-2201
20109 Paseo Del Prado Walnut (91789) *(P-9622)*
Fairwinds Estate Winery LLC .............................................. F ...... 707 341-5300
4550 Silverado Trl Calistoga (94515) *(P-1560)*
Falcon Trading Company Inc .............................................. C ...... 831 786-7000
423 Salinas Rd Royal Oaks (95076) *(P-2196)*
Falcon Waterfree Tech LLC (HQ) ........................................ E ...... 310 209-7250
2255 Barry Ave Los Angeles (90064) *(P-6493)*
Falkner Winery Inc ................................................................ D ...... 951 676-6741
40620 Calle Contento Temecula (92591) *(P-1561)*
Falkonry Inc ............................................................................ D ...... 408 761-7108
10020 N De Anza Blvd Ste 200 Cupertino (95014) *(P-17917)*
Fallbrook Bonsall Village News, Temecula *Also Called: Village News Inc (P-4217)*
Fallbrook Industries Inc ........................................................ E ...... 760 728-7229
323 Industrial Way Ste 1 Fallbrook (92028) *(P-8842)*
Falltech, Compton *Also Called: Andrew Alexander Inc (P-7085)*
Fam LLC (PA) .......................................................................... D ...... 323 888-7755
5553 Bandini Blvd B Bell (90201) *(P-2446)*
Fam Brands, Bell *Also Called: Fam LLC (P-2446)*
Family Industries LLC ........................................................... F ...... 619 306-1035
2755 Fruitdale St Los Angeles (90039) *(P-16128)*
Family Loompya Corporation ............................................... E ...... 619 477-2125
2626 Southport Way Ste F National City (91950) *(P-2197)*
Family Vineyards, Healdsburg *Also Called: Seghesio Wineries Inc (P-1744)*
Famoso Nut, Mc Farland *Also Called: Amaretto Orchards LLC (P-16085)*
Fan Fave Inc ........................................................................... E ...... 909 975-4999
10329 Dorset St Rancho Cucamonga (91730) *(P-15976)*
Fanboys Window Factory Inc (PA) ..................................... E ...... 626 280-8787
1250 S Johnson Dr City Of Industry (91745) *(P-8266)*
Fanfave, Rancho Cucamonga *Also Called: Fan Fave Inc (P-15976)*
Fantasia Distribution Inc ....................................................... F ...... 714 817-8300
2400 E Katella Ave Ste 800 Anaheim (92806) *(P-2398)*
Fantasia Hookah Tobacco, Anaheim *Also Called: Fantasia Distribution Inc (P-2398)*
Fantasy Activewear Inc (PA) ................................................ E ...... 213 705-4111
5383 Alcoa Ave Vernon (90058) *(P-2468)*
Fantasy Activewear Inc ........................................................ F ...... 714 751-0137
3420 W Maywood Ave Santa Ana (92704) *(P-2592)*
Fantasy Cookie Company, Sylmar *Also Called: Fantasy Cookie Corporation (P-1274)*
Fantasy Cookie Corporation (PA) ........................................ E ...... 818 361-6901
12322 Gladstone Ave Sylmar (91342) *(P-1274)*
Fantasy Dyeing & Finishing Inc .......................................... E ...... 323 983-9988
5383 Alcoa Ave Vernon (90058) *(P-2469)*
Fantasy Manufacturing, Vernon *Also Called: Fantasy Activewear Inc (P-2468)*

## ALPHABETIC SECTION — Fellow Industries Inc

Fante Inc (PA) .................................................................... E ...... 650 697-7525
  2898 W Winton Ave Hayward (94545) *(P-2090)*

Fantom Drives, Torrance *Also Called: Bnl Technologies Inc (P-10227)*

Fanuc America Corporation ............................................... D ...... 949 595-2700
  25951 Commercentre Dr Lake Forest (92630) *(P-9856)*

Fanuc Robotics West, Lake Forest *Also Called: Fanuc America Corporation (P-9856)*

Far Niente, Oakville *Also Called: FN Cellars LLC (P-1572)*

Far Niente Wine Estates, Oakville *Also Called: Far Niente Winery Inc (P-1562)*

Far Niente Winery Inc ........................................................ D ...... 707 944-2861
  1350 Acacia Dr Oakville (94562) *(P-1562)*

Far Out Toys Inc ................................................................. E ...... 310 480-7554
  300 N Pacific Coast Hwy Ste 1050 El Segundo (90245) *(P-15729)*

Far West Meats, Highland *Also Called: Raemica Inc (P-662)*

Far West Rice Inc .............................................................. E ...... 530 891-1339
  3455 Nelson Rd Nelson (95958) *(P-1074)*

Far West Technology Inc ................................................... F ...... 805 964-3615
  330 S Kellogg Ave Ste B Goleta (93117) *(P-14865)*

Far Western Graphics Inc ................................................. D ...... 408 481-9777
  2642 Heritage Park Cir San Jose (95132) *(P-17811)*

Farallon Brands Inc (PA) ................................................... E ...... 510 550-4299
  33300 Central Ave Union City (94587) *(P-15748)*

Farasis Energy Usa Inc ..................................................... D ...... 510 732-6600
  21363 Cabot Blvd Hayward (94545) *(P-11267)*

Farchitecture Bb LLC ........................................................ E ...... 917 701-2777
  8588 Washington Blvd Culver City (90232) *(P-800)*

Farley Interlocking Pav Stones, Palm Desert *Also Called: Farley Paving Stone Co Inc (P-7330)*

Farley Paving Stone Co Inc .............................................. D ...... 760 773-3960
  39301 Badger St Palm Desert (92211) *(P-7330)*

Farm Street Designs Inc ................................................... E ...... 562 985-0026
  2520 Mira Mar Ave Long Beach (90815) *(P-17265)*

Farmdale, San Bernardino *Also Called: Farmdale Creamery LLC (P-834)*

Farmdale Creamery LLC ................................................... D ...... 909 888-4938
  1049 W Base Line St San Bernardino (92411) *(P-834)*

Farmers Rice Cooperative ................................................ E ...... 530 439-2244
  4937 Hwy 45 Colusa (95932) *(P-81)*

Farmers Rice Cooperative (PA) ........................................ E ...... 916 923-5100
  2566 River Plaza Dr Sacramento (95833) *(P-1075)*

Farmers Rice Cooperative ................................................ D ...... 530 666-1691
  845 Kentucky Ave Woodland (95695) *(P-1076)*

Farmers Rice Cooperative ................................................ D ...... 916 373-5500
  2224 Industrial Blvd West Sacramento (95691) *(P-1077)*

Farmers Rice Cooperative ................................................ D ...... 530 666-1691
  845 Kentucky Ave Woodland (95695) *(P-1078)*

Farrell Brothers Holding Corp ........................................... F ...... 714 630-3417
  1137 N Armando St Anaheim (92806) *(P-10835)*

Farstone Technology Inc .................................................. C ...... 949 336-4321
  184 Technology Dr Ste 205 Irvine (92618) *(P-13196)*

Farwest Trading, Turlock *Also Called: Associated Feed & Supply Co (P-1118)*

Fashiongo ......................................................................... E ...... 213 745-2667
  2250 Maple Ave Los Angeles (90011) *(P-2583)*

Fast Track Energy Drink LLc ............................................ E ...... 310 281-2045
  8447 Wilshire Blvd Ste 401 Beverly Hills (90211) *(P-1888)*

Fastec Imaging Corporation .............................................. E ...... 858 592-2342
  17150 Via Del Campo Ste 301 San Diego (92127) *(P-15638)*

Fastener Dist Holdings LLC .............................................. E ...... 213 620-9950
  5200 Sheila St Commerce (90040) *(P-13651)*

Fastener Dist Holdings LLC (HQ) ..................................... D ...... 213 620-9950
  5200 Sheila St Commerce (90040) *(P-16874)*

Fastener Innovation Tech Inc ............................................ D ...... 310 538-1111
  19300 S Susana Rd Compton (90221) *(P-8722)*

Fastener Technology Corp ................................................ C ...... 818 764-6467
  7415 Fulton Ave North Hollywood (91605) *(P-16875)*

Fastening Systems Intl ..................................................... E ...... 707 935-1170
  1206 E Macarthur St Ste 1 Sonoma (95476) *(P-16754)*

Faster Faster Inc ............................................................... E ...... 323 839-0654
  185 Valley Dr Brisbane (94005) *(P-13499)*

Fasthouse Inc .................................................................... F ...... 661 775-5963
  29003 Avenue Sherman Valencia (91355) *(P-15810)*

Fasthouse Inc (PA) ............................................................ F ...... 661 775-5963
  28757 Industry Dr Valencia (91355) *(P-15811)*

FASTLY, San Francisco *Also Called: Fastly Inc (P-17918)*

Fastly Inc (PA) ................................................................... B ...... 844 432-7859
  475 Brannan St Ste 300 San Francisco (94107) *(P-17918)*

Fastrak Manufacturing, San Jose *Also Called: Fastrak Manufacturing Svcs Inc (P-12977)*

Fastrak Manufacturing Svcs Inc ....................................... E ...... 408 298-6414
  1275 Alma Ct San Jose (95112) *(P-12977)*

Fastramp, Fremont *Also Called: Stats Chippac Test Svcs Inc (P-12735)*

Fastsigns, Fresno *Also Called: Craigo Investments Inc (P-15962)*

Fastsigns, Hayward *Also Called: Justipher Inc (P-15998)*

Fattail Inc (HQ) .................................................................. E ...... 818 615-0380
  23586 Calabasas Rd Ste 102 Calabasas (91302) *(P-17919)*

Fazeli Vineyards LLC ........................................................ F ...... 951 303-3366
  37320 De Portola Rd Temecula (92592) *(P-1563)*

Fcp Inc (PA) ....................................................................... D ...... 951 678-4571
  23100 Wildomar Trl Wildomar (92595) *(P-8666)*

Fcp Inc .............................................................................. F ...... 805 684-1117
  4125 Market St Ste 14 Ventura (93003) *(P-8667)*

Fcsi Inc .............................................................................. E ...... 415 457-8000
  628 Lindaro St San Rafael (94901) *(P-17764)*

Fdh Aero, Commerce *Also Called: Fastener Dist Holdings LLC (P-13651)*

FDS Manufacturing Company (PA) .................................. D ...... 909 591-1733
  2200 S Reservoir St Pomona (91766) *(P-4038)*

FDS Manufacturing Company Svcs, Pomona *Also Called: Federated Diversified Sls Inc (P-3927)*

Fear of God LLC ............................................................... D ...... 213 235-7985
  558 S Alameda St Los Angeles (90013) *(P-2619)*

Feather Publishing Company Inc (PA) ............................. E ...... 530 283-0800
  287 Lawrence St Quincy (95971) *(P-4113)*

Feather River Bulletin, Quincy *Also Called: Feather Publishing Company Inc (P-4113)*

Featherock Inc (PA) .......................................................... F ...... 818 882-3888
  20219 Bahama St Chatsworth (91311) *(P-339)*

Feathersoft Inc .................................................................. E ...... 925 230-0740
  600 N Mountain Ave Ste C100 Upland (91786) *(P-11733)*

Federal Heath Sign Company LLC ................................... C ...... 760 941-0715
  3609 Ocean Ranch Blvd Ste 204 Oceanside (92056) *(P-15977)*

Federal Industries Inc ....................................................... E ...... 310 297-4040
  645 Hawaii St El Segundo (90245) *(P-9185)*

Federal Manufacturing Corp ............................................. E ...... 818 341-9825
  9825 De Soto Ave Chatsworth (91311) *(P-8755)*

Federal Prison Industries ................................................. F ...... 805 735-2771
  3901 Klein Blvd Lompoc (93436) *(P-15978)*

Federated Diversified Sls Inc ............................................ D ...... 909 591-1733
  2200 S Reservoir St Pomona (91766) *(P-3927)*

Federated Media Publishing LLC ..................................... C ...... 415 332-6955
  350 Sansome St Ste 925 San Francisco (94104) *(P-4398)*

Feemster Co Inc ................................................................ E ...... 909 621-9772
  119 Yale Ave Claremont (91711) *(P-1192)*

Feeney Inc ......................................................................... E ...... 510 893-9473
  2603 Union St Oakland (94607) *(P-9217)*

Feeney Wire Rope & Rigging, Oakland *Also Called: Feeney Inc (P-9217)*

Fei Efa Inc (DH) ................................................................. D ...... 510 897-6800
  3400 W Warren Ave Fremont (94538) *(P-14665)*

Feihe International Inc (PA) .............................................. A ...... 626 757-8885
  2275 Huntington Dr Pmb 278 San Marino (91108) *(P-756)*

Feist Cabinets & Woodworks Inc ..................................... E ...... 916 686-8230
  9930 Kent St Elk Grove (95624) *(P-17519)*

Feit Electric, Pico Rivera *Also Called: Feit Electric Company Inc (P-11495)*

Feit Electric Company Inc (PA) ........................................ C ...... 562 463-2852
  4901 Gregg Rd Pico Rivera (90660) *(P-11495)*

Fel Wines, Yountville *Also Called: Lady Family Wines (P-1657)*

Felbro, Los Angeles *Also Called: Felbro Food Products Inc (P-2002)*

Felbro Inc .......................................................................... C ...... 323 263-8686
  3666 E Olympic Blvd Los Angeles (90023) *(P-3686)*

Felbro Food Products Inc ................................................. E ...... 323 936-5266
  5700 W Adams Blvd Los Angeles (90016) *(P-2002)*

Felix Schoeller North Amer Inc ........................................ E ...... 315 298-8425
  1260 N Lakeview Ave Anaheim (92807) *(P-3950)*

Fellow, Venice *Also Called: Fellow Industries Inc (P-11404)*

Fellow Industries Inc ........................................................ E ...... 415 649-0361
  1342 1/2 Abbot Kinney Blvd Venice (90291) *(P-11404)*

**Fellow Industries Inc**          **ALPHABETIC SECTION**

Fellow Industries Inc (PA) .................................................. F ...... 415 649-0361
   320 Florida St San Francisco (94110) *(P-16424)*

Fema Electronics Corporation .................................................. E ...... 714 825-0140
   22 Corporate Park Irvine (92606) *(P-12978)*

Fenchem, Chino *Also Called: Fenchem Inc (P-757)*

Fenchem Inc (HQ) .................................................. E ...... 909 597-8880
   15308 El Prado Rd Bldg 8 Chino (91710) *(P-757)*

Fender Musical Instrs Corp .................................................. A ...... 480 596-9690
   311 Cessna Cir Corona (92878) *(P-15717)*

Fenico Precision Castings Inc .................................................. D ...... 562 634-5000
   7805 Madison St Paramount (90723) *(P-7863)*

Feral Productions LLC .................................................. E ...... 510 791-5392
   1935 N Macarthur Dr Tracy (95376) *(P-10836)*

Ferco Color Inc (PA) .................................................. E ...... 909 930-0773
   5498 Vine St Chino (91710) *(P-5157)*

Ferco Plastic Products, Chino *Also Called: Ferco Color Inc (P-5157)*

Ferguson Welding Service .................................................. F ...... 510 487-5906
   1147 Atlantic St Union City (94587) *(P-19192)*

Fernqvist Labeling Solutions, Mountain View *Also Called: Fernqvist Retail Systems Inc (P-4822)*

Fernqvist Retail Systems Inc (DH) .................................................. F ...... 650 428-0330
   2544 Leghorn St Mountain View (94043) *(P-4822)*

Ferra Aerospace Inc .................................................. 918 787-2220
   940 E Orangethorpe Ave Ste A Anaheim (92801) *(P-13839)*

Ferraco Inc (HQ) .................................................. E ...... 562 988-2414
   2933 Long Beach Blvd Long Beach (90806) *(P-15346)*

Ferrante Paul Cstm Lmps & Shds, West Hollywood *Also Called: Paul Ferrante Inc (P-16196)*

Ferrar-Crano Vnyrds Winery LLC (PA) .................................................. D ...... 707 433-6700
   8761 Dry Creek Rd Healdsburg (95448) *(P-1564)*

Ferrari-Carano Winery, Healdsburg *Also Called: Ferrar-Crano Vnyrds Winery LLC (P-1564)*

Ferrosaur Inc .................................................. E ...... 530 246-7843
   4821 Mountain Lakes Blvd Redding (96003) *(P-8139)*

Ferrotec (usa) Corporation (HQ) .................................................. D ...... 408 964-7700
   566 Exchange Ct Livermore (94550) *(P-10067)*

Ferrotec (usa) Corporation .................................................. E ...... 408 362-1000
   5830 Hellyer Ave San Jose (95138) *(P-12431)*

Fetish Group Inc (PA) .................................................. E ...... 323 587-7873
   1013 S Los Angeles St Ste 700 Los Angeles (90015) *(P-2620)*

Fetters U.S.A., San Francisco *Also Called: Mr S Leather (P-2882)*

Fetzer Vineyards (HQ) .................................................. C ...... 707 744-1250
   12901 Old River Rd Hopland (95449) *(P-1565)*

Fgr 1 LLC .................................................. E ...... 800 653-3517
   3191 Red Hill Ave Ste 100 Costa Mesa (92626) *(P-17579)*

Fgs Packing Services, Valencia *Also Called: Fruit Growers Supply Company (P-3843)*

Fgs-Wi LLC .................................................. E ...... 909 467-8300
   5401 Jurupa St Ontario (91761) *(P-4608)*

Fh Packaging, Eastvale *Also Called: Wolfgang Enterprise Inc (P-19144)*

Fhc, South Gate *Also Called: Frameless Hardware Company LLC (P-7996)*

Fht Printing, Fullerton *Also Called: Advanced Image Direct LLC (P-17794)*

Fi, El Segundo *Also Called: Federal Industries Inc (P-9185)*

Fiant, San Francisco *Also Called: Provenance Technologies Inc (P-18706)*

Fiber Care Baths Inc .................................................. B ...... 760 246-0019
   9832 Yucca Rd Ste A Adelanto (92301) *(P-6678)*

Fiber Optic Cable Shop, Richmond *Also Called: Support Systems Intl Corp (P-13095)*

Fiberlite Centrifuge LLC .................................................. D ...... 408 492-1109
   422 Aldo Ave Santa Clara (95054) *(P-14666)*

Fiberoptic Systems Inc .................................................. E ...... 805 579-6600
   60 Moreland Rd Ste A Simi Valley (93065) *(P-7785)*

Fibreform Electronics Inc .................................................. E ...... 714 898-9641
   5341 Argosy Ave Huntington Beach (92649) *(P-10837)*

Fibreform Precision Machining, Huntington Beach *Also Called: Fibreform Electronics Inc (P-10837)*

Fibres Internation Recycling, Novato *Also Called: Fibres International Inc (P-16359)*

Fibres International Inc .................................................. D ...... 425 455-9811
   88 Rowland Way Ste 300 Novato (94945) *(P-16359)*

FIBROGEN, San Francisco *Also Called: Fibrogen Inc (P-5439)*

Fibrogen Inc (PA) .................................................. C ...... 415 978-1200
   350 Bay St Ste 100 San Francisco (94133) *(P-5439)*

Fictiv Inc (PA) .................................................. C ...... 415 580-2509
   48511 Warm Springs Blvd Ste 208 Fremont (94539) *(P-17920)*

Ficto, West Hollywood *Also Called: Ficto Holdings LLC (P-17921)*

Ficto Holdings LLC .................................................. F ...... 424 250-2400
   1049 Havenhurst Dr Ste 236 West Hollywood (90046) *(P-17921)*

Field Manufacturing Corp (PA) .................................................. E ...... 310 781-9292
   1751 Torrance Blvd Ste N Torrance (90501) *(P-3687)*

Field Sales Office, San Mateo *Also Called: Centra Software Inc (P-18156)*

Field Time Target Training LLC .................................................. E ...... 714 677-2841
   8230 Electric Ave Stanton (90680) *(P-9134)*

Fieldpiece, Orange *Also Called: Fieldpiece Instruments Inc (P-14526)*

Fieldpiece Instruments Inc (PA) .................................................. E ...... 714 634-1844
   1636 W Collins Ave Orange (92867) *(P-14526)*

Fiesta Concession, Vernon *Also Called: Mahar Manufacturing Corp (P-15731)*

Fiesta Mexican Foods Inc .................................................. E ...... 760 344-3580
   979 G St Brawley (92227) *(P-1193)*

Fife Metal Fabricating Inc .................................................. F ...... 530 243-4696
   2305 Radio Ln Redding (96001) *(P-8140)*

Fifth Sun, Chico *Also Called: Gonzales Park LLC (P-17074)*

Figs, Santa Monica *Also Called: Figs Inc (P-2593)*

Figs Inc .................................................. B ...... 424 300-8330
   2834 Colorado Ave Ste 100 Santa Monica (90404) *(P-2593)*

Figure 8, Torrance *Also Called: Nothing To Wear Inc (P-2685)*

Figure Ai Inc .................................................. E ...... 716 830-0904
   1247 Elko Dr Sunnyvale (94089) *(P-10088)*

Filenet Corporation .................................................. A ...... 800 345-3638
   3565 Harbor Blvd Costa Mesa (92626) *(P-18974)*

Filmetrics Inc (HQ) .................................................. E ...... 858 573-9300
   10655 Roselle St Ste 200 San Diego (92121) *(P-14667)*

Filmtools Inc (PA) .................................................. E ...... 323 467-1116
   1015 N Hollywood Way Burbank (91505) *(P-17653)*

Filtec, Torrance *Also Called: Industrial Dynamics Co Ltd (P-9867)*

Filter Concepts Incorporated .................................................. E ...... 714 545-7003
   22895 Eastpark Dr Yorba Linda (92887) *(P-12839)*

Filter Pump Industries, Sun Valley *Also Called: Penguin Pumps Incorporated (P-9933)*

Filtration Group LLC .................................................. C ...... 707 525-8633
   498 Aviation Blvd Santa Rosa (95403) *(P-9986)*

Final Touch Apparel, Los Angeles *Also Called: Final Touch Apparel Inc (P-17090)*

Final Touch Apparel Inc .................................................. E ...... 323 484-9621
   116 E 32nd St Los Angeles (90011) *(P-17090)*

Finance Department, Hercules *Also Called: Bio-RAD Laboratories Inc (P-14633)*

Financial Fitness Group, Cardiff By The Sea *Also Called: Igrad LLC (P-18402)*

Financial Info Netwrk Inc .................................................. E ...... 818 782-0331
   11164 Bertrand Ave Granada Hills (91344) *(P-17922)*

Financial Statement Svcs Inc (PA) .................................................. C ...... 714 436-3326
   3300 S Fairview St Santa Ana (92704) *(P-17797)*

Findly, San Francisco *Also Called: First Advntage Tlent MGT Svcs (P-18308)*

Fine Chemicals Holdings Corp .................................................. A ...... 916 357-6880
   Hazel Ave Hwy 50 Bldg 05019 Rancho Cordova (95741) *(P-5440)*

Fine Line Circuits & Tech Inc .................................................. E ...... 714 529-2942
   594 Apollo St Ste A Brea (92821) *(P-12100)*

Fine Magazine .................................................. F ...... 858 261-0963
   905 1/2 Crest Rd Del Mar (92014) *(P-4255)*

Fine Mexican Food Products Inc .................................................. F ...... 714 476-7104
   7025 Old 215 Frontage Rd Moreno Valley (92553) *(P-2198)*

Fine Northern Oak, Napa *Also Called: Seguin Mreau NAPA Coperage Inc (P-16895)*

Fine Pitch, Irwindale *Also Called: Fine Ptch Elctrnic Assmbly LLC (P-12101)*

Fine Ptch Elctrnic Assmbly LLC .................................................. E ...... 626 337-2800
   5106 Azusa Canyon Rd Irwindale (91706) *(P-12101)*

Fine Quality Metal, Long Beach *Also Called: Fine Quality Metal Finshg Inc (P-8960)*

Fine Quality Metal Finshg Inc .................................................. F ...... 562 983-7425
   1640 Daisy Ave Long Beach (90813) *(P-8960)*

Fineline Architectural Mllwk, Costa Mesa *Also Called: Fineline Woodworking Inc (P-3137)*

Fineline Carpentry Inc .................................................. E ...... 650 592-2442
   1297 Old County Rd Belmont (94002) *(P-3240)*

Fineline Industries Inc (PA) .................................................. D ...... 209 384-0255
   2047 Grogan Ave Merced (95341) *(P-14033)*

Fineline Settings LLC .................................................. E ...... 845 369-6100
   2041 S Turner Ave Unit 30 Ontario (91761) *(P-3914)*

Fineline Woodworking Inc .................................................. D ...... 714 540-5468
   1139 Baker St Costa Mesa (92626) *(P-3137)*

## ALPHABETIC SECTION

**Finelite, Union City** *Also Called: Finelite Inc (P-11531)*
**Finelite Inc (PA)**..................................................................... C ...... 510 441-1100
  30500 Whipple Rd Union City (94587) *(P-11531)*
**Finesse, South Pasadena** *Also Called: Finesse Apparel Inc (P-2759)*
**Finesse Apparel Inc** ................................................................ E ...... 213 747-7077
  815 Fairview Ave Unit 101 South Pasadena (91030) *(P-2759)*
**Finest Hour Holdings Inc** ...................................................... E ...... 310 533-9966
  3203 Kashiwa St Torrance (90505) *(P-15347)*
**Finis LLC** ................................................................................ D ...... 949 250-4929
  3347 Michelson Dr Ste 100 Irvine (92612) *(P-10367)*
**Finis Inc (PA)** .......................................................................... E ...... 925 454-0111
  5849 W Schulte Rd Ste 104 Tracy (95377) *(P-15812)*
**Finis USA, Tracy** *Also Called: Finis Inc (P-15812)*
**Finisar, San Jose** *Also Called: Finisar Corporation (P-11763)*
**Finisar Corporation (HQ)** ...................................................... E ...... 408 548-1000
  1830 Bering Dr San Jose (95112) *(P-11763)*
**Finisar Corporation** .............................................................. F ...... 408 548-1000
  41762 Christy St Fremont (94538) *(P-12432)*
**Finishing Touch Millwork, Carlsbad** *Also Called: Finishing Touch Moulding Inc (P-3241)*
**Finishing Touch Moulding Inc** ............................................. D ...... 760 444-1019
  6190 Corte Del Cedro Carlsbad (92011) *(P-3241)*
**Finishline Certified Welding L** ............................................. F ...... 760 271-6364
  32082 Anna Marie Ln Bonsall (92003) *(P-19193)*
**Finna Group, Rancho Cucamonga** *Also Called: Aqm Acquisition Corp (P-17752)*
**Finsix Corporation** ................................................................ E ...... 650 285-6400
  3565 Haven Ave Ste 1 Menlo Park (94025) *(P-18975)*
**Fior Di Sole LLC (PA)** ............................................................ E ...... 707 259-1477
  2511 Napa Valley Corporate Dr Napa (94558) *(P-1566)*
**Fior Di Sole LLC** .................................................................... E ...... 707 492-3506
  504 Devlin Rd Napa (94558) *(P-1567)*
**Fior Di Sole LLC** .................................................................... E ...... 707 204-8268
  2515 Napa Valley Corporate Dr Napa (94558) *(P-1568)*
**Fior Di Sole 504 Devlin, Napa** *Also Called: Fior Di Sole LLC (P-1567)*
**Fiore Di Pasta Inc** ................................................................. D ...... 559 457-0431
  4776 E Jensen Ave Fresno (93725) *(P-2199)*
**Fiore Stone Inc** ..................................................................... E ...... 909 424-0221
  1814 Commercenter W Ste E San Bernardino (92408) *(P-7331)*
**Firan Tech Group USA Corp (HQ)** ....................................... D ...... 818 407-4024
  20750 Marilla St Chatsworth (91311) *(P-14186)*
**Fire & Gas Detection Tech Inc** ............................................ F ...... 714 671-8500
  2570 E Cerritos Ave Anaheim (92806) *(P-14866)*
**Fire Protection Group Amer Inc** .......................................... E ...... 323 732-4200
  3712 W Jefferson Blvd Los Angeles (90016) *(P-19394)*
**Fireblast, Murrieta** *Also Called: Fireblast Global Inc (P-10089)*
**Fireblast Global Inc** .............................................................. E ...... 951 277-8319
  41633 Eastman Dr Murrieta (92562) *(P-10089)*
**Firebrand Pbc** ....................................................................... D ...... 510 594-9213
  707 W Tower Ave Alameda (94501) *(P-1194)*
**Firebrand Media LLC** ........................................................... E ...... 949 715-4100
  900 Glenneyre St Laguna Beach (92651) *(P-4609)*
**Firequick Products Inc** ........................................................ F ...... 760 371-4279
  1137 Red Rock Inyokern Rd Inyokern (93527) *(P-10090)*
**Firestone Cmplete Auto Care 79, San Diego** *Also Called: Bridgestone Americas Inc (P-6406)*
**Firestone Vineyard LP** ......................................................... D ...... 805 688-3940
  5000 Zaca Station Rd Los Olivos (93441) *(P-1569)*
**Firestone Walker Inc** ............................................................ D ...... 805 226-8514
  1332 Vendels Cir Paso Robles (93446) *(P-1428)*
**Firestone Walker Inc** ............................................................ D ...... 805 254-4205
  620 Mcmurray Rd Buellton (93427) *(P-1429)*
**Firestone Walker Inc (PA)** .................................................... C ...... 805 225-5911
  1400 Ramada Dr Paso Robles (93446) *(P-1430)*
**Firestone Walker Brewing Co, Buellton** *Also Called: Firestone Walker Inc (P-1429)*
**Firestone Walker Brewing Co, Paso Robles** *Also Called: Firestone Walker Inc (P-1430)*
**Firestone Walker Brewing Co, Penn Valley** *Also Called: Firestone Walker LLC (P-1431)*
**Firestone Walker LLC** .......................................................... D ...... 805 225-5911
  10130 Commercial Ave Penn Valley (95946) *(P-1431)*
**Firetide, Campbell** *Also Called: Firetide Inc (P-10368)*
**Firetide Inc (DH)** ................................................................... E ...... 408 399-7771
  2105 S Bascom Ave Ste 220 Campbell (95008) *(P-10368)*
**Firmenich** ............................................................................... D ...... 714 535-2771
  424 S Atchison St Anaheim (92805) *(P-6146)*

**Firmenich, Anaheim** *Also Called: Firmenich Incorporated (P-6285)*
**Firmenich Incorporated** ....................................................... D ...... 858 646-8323
  10636 Scripps Summit Ct San Diego (92131) *(P-6284)*
**Firmenich Incorporated** ....................................................... C ...... 714 535-2871
  424 S Atchison St Anaheim (92805) *(P-6285)*
**First Advntage Tlent MGT Svcs** .......................................... F ...... 415 446-3930
  98 Battery St Ste 400 San Francisco (94110) *(P-18308)*
**First Class Foods, Hawthorne** *Also Called: Firstclass Foods - Trojan Inc (P-596)*
**First Class Packaging Inc** ................................................... E ...... 619 579-7166
  280 Cypress Ln Ste D El Cajon (92020) *(P-3370)*
**First Energy Services Inc** ................................................... E ...... 661 387-1972
  1031 Carrier Parkway Ave Bakersfield (93308) *(P-230)*
**First Finish Inc** ..................................................................... E ...... 310 631-6717
  11126 Wright Rd Lynwood (90262) *(P-2415)*
**First Impressions Printing Inc** ............................................ E ...... 510 784-0811
  25030 Viking St Hayward (94545) *(P-4610)*
**First Legal Network** ............................................................. C ...... 213 250-1111
  1517 Beverly Blvd Los Angeles (90026) *(P-14527)*
**First Person Inc** .................................................................... F ...... 609 760-0040
  611 N Brand Blvd Ste 1300 Glendale (91203) *(P-5441)*
**First Person Group, Glendale** *Also Called: First Person Inc (P-5441)*
**First Tactical, Modesto** *Also Called: First Tactical LLC (P-2560)*
**First Tactical LLC** ................................................................ A ...... 209 482-7255
  496 E Whitmore Ave Bldg 4 Modesto (95358) *(P-2560)*
**Firstclass Foods - Trojan Inc** .............................................. C ...... 310 676-2500
  12500 Inglewood Ave Hawthorne (90250) *(P-596)*
**Firstup Inc (PA)** ..................................................................... B ...... 844 975-2533
  1 Montgomery St Ste 2150 San Francisco (94104) *(P-18309)*
**Fisa, Laguna Beach** *Also Called: Flavor Infusion LLC (P-2005)*
**Fischer Cstm Cmmunications Inc (PA)** .............................. E ...... 310 303-3300
  19220 Normandie Ave Unit B Torrance (90502) *(P-14528)*
**Fischer Mold Incorporated** .................................................. D ...... 951 279-1140
  393 Meyer Cir Corona (92879) *(P-6826)*
**Fish Bowl, Woodland Hills** *Also Called: Second Generation Inc (P-2806)*
**Fish House Foods Inc** ......................................................... C ...... 760 597-1270
  1263 Linda Vista Dr San Marcos (92078) *(P-2052)*
**Fisher & Paykel, Costa Mesa** *Also Called: Dynamic Cooking Systems Inc (P-10556)*
**Fisher & Paykel Appliances Inc (DH)** ................................. E ...... 949 790-8900
  695 Town Center Dr Ste 180 Costa Mesa (92626) *(P-11418)*
**Fisher Nut Company, Modesto** *Also Called: Pacific Holdings 137 Company (P-2310)*
**Fisher Printing Inc (PA)** ....................................................... C ...... 714 998-9200
  2257 N Pacific St Orange (92865) *(P-4611)*
**Fishermans Pride Prcessors Inc** ........................................ B ...... 323 232-1980
  4510 S Alameda St Vernon (90058) *(P-2053)*
**Fisica Applied Tech Inc** ....................................................... C ...... 650 326-9500
  150 Constitution Dr Menlo Park (94025) *(P-11856)*
**Fisker, La Palma** *Also Called: Fisker Group Inc (P-13351)*
**Fisker, La Palma** *Also Called: Fisker Inc (P-13352)*
**Fisker Automotive Inc** ......................................................... D
  3080 Airway Ave Costa Mesa (92626) *(P-13350)*
**Fisker Group Inc (HQ)** .......................................................... A ...... 833 434-7537
  14 Centerpointe Dr La Palma (90623) *(P-13351)*
**Fisker Inc (PA)** ...................................................................... E ...... 833 434-7537
  14 Centerpointe Dr La Palma (90623) *(P-13352)*
**Fit-Line Inc** ............................................................................ E ...... 714 549-9091
  2901 S Tech Center Dr Santa Ana (92705) *(P-6827)*
**Fit-Line Global, Santa Ana** *Also Called: Fit-Line Inc (P-6827)*
**Fitbit, San Francisco** *Also Called: Fitbit LLC (P-14868)*
**Fitbit LLC** .............................................................................. C ...... 415 513-1000
  15255 Innovation Dr Ste 200 San Diego (92128) *(P-14867)*
**Fitbit LLC (DH)** ..................................................................... C ...... 415 513-1000
  199 Fremont St Fl 14 San Francisco (94105) *(P-14868)*
**Fitbod Inc** .............................................................................. E ...... 415 727-6264
  1655 Taraval St San Francisco (94116) *(P-18310)*
**Fitness Warehouse LLC (PA)** ............................................. E ...... 858 578-7676
  9990 Alesmith Ct Ste 130 San Diego (92126) *(P-15813)*
**Fitparts, Gardena** *Also Called: Getpart La Inc (P-6841)*
**Fitstar Inc** ............................................................................. A ...... 415 409-8348
  80 Langton St San Francisco (94103) *(P-18311)*
**Fittings That Fit Inc** .............................................................. F ...... 909 248-2808
  4628 Mission Blvd Montclair (91763) *(P-9218)*

**Fitzgerald Formliners**     ALPHABETIC SECTION

**Fitzgerald Formliners, Santa Ana** *Also Called: Prime Forming & Cnstr Sups Inc (P-7375)*
**Five Prime, South San Francisco** *Also Called: Five Prime Therapeutics Inc (P-5442)*
**Five Prime Therapeutics Inc** .................................................. D ...... 415 365-5600
   750 Gateway Blvd South San Francisco (94080) *(P-5442)*
**Five Star Food Containers Inc** ................................................ D ...... 626 437-6219
   250 Eastgate Rd Barstow (92311) *(P-6633)*
**Five Star Gourmet Foods Inc (PA)**............................................ C ...... 909 390-0032
   3880 Ebony St Ontario (91761) *(P-2200)*
**Five Star Lumber Company LLC (PA)** ....................................... E ...... 510 795-7204
   6899 Smith Ave Newark (94560) *(P-3341)*
**Five Star Pallet Co, Newark** *Also Called: Five Star Lumber Company LLC (P-3341)*
**Five9 Inc (PA)**......................................................................... A ...... 925 201-2000
   3001 Bishop Dr Ste 350 San Ramon (94583) *(P-18312)*
**Fivesixtwo Inc, Long Beach** *Also Called: Traffic Management Pdts Inc (P-18890)*
**Fivetran Inc (PA)**..................................................................... A ...... 415 805-2799
   405 14th St Ste 1100 Oakland (94612) *(P-18313)*
**Flame and Wax Inc** ................................................................ C ...... 949 752-4000
   2900 Mccabe Way Irvine (92614) *(P-16129)*
**Flame-Spray Inc** ..................................................................... E ...... 619 283-2007
   4674 Alvarado Canyon Rd San Diego (92120) *(P-9069)*
**Flamemaster Corporation** ...................................................... E ...... 818 890-1401
   13576 Desmond St Pacoima (91331) *(P-6228)*
**Flare Group** ............................................................................ E ...... 714 549-0202
   1571 Macarthur Blvd Costa Mesa (92626) *(P-8961)*
**Flare Group** ............................................................................ E ...... 714 850-2080
   1571 Macarthur Blvd Costa Mesa (92626) *(P-13840)*
**Flash Code Solutions LLC** ..................................................... F ...... 800 633-7467
   4727 Wilshire Blvd Ste 302 Los Angeles (90010) *(P-18314)*
**Flat Planet Inc** ....................................................................... E ...... 888 656-6872
   618 Hampton Dr Venice (90291) *(P-9857)*
**Flaunt Magazine** .................................................................... F ...... 323 836-1044
   1418 N Highland Ave Los Angeles (90028) *(P-4256)*
**Flavor Factory Inc** ................................................................. F ...... 951 273-9877
   2058 2nd St Norco (92860) *(P-2003)*
**Flavor House Inc** ................................................................... E ...... 760 246-9131
   16378 Koala Rd Adelanto (92301) *(P-2004)*
**Flavor Infusion LLC** ............................................................... E ...... 949 715-4369
   332 Forest Ave Ste 19 Laguna Beach (92651) *(P-2005)*
**Flavor Producers, West Hills** *Also Called: Flavor Producers LLC (P-2006)*
**Flavor Producers LLC (PA)** .................................................... E ...... 661 257-3400
   8521 Fallbrook Ave Ste 380 West Hills (91304) *(P-2006)*
**Fleenor Company Inc (PA)** .................................................... E ...... 800 433-2531
   2225 Harbor Bay Pkwy Alameda (94502) *(P-4039)*
**Fleenor Paper Company, Alameda** *Also Called: Fleenor Company Inc (P-4039)*
**Fleet Device Management Inc** ............................................... F ...... 415 651-2575
   548 Market St # 71434 San Francisco (94104) *(P-17923)*
**Fleet Management Solutions Inc** ........................................... E ...... 800 500-6009
   310 Commerce Ste 100 Irvine (92602) *(P-11857)*
**Fleet Tire Inc (PA)** ................................................................. E ...... 209 467-0154
   3730 N Wilson Way Stockton (95205) *(P-16407)*
**Fleetpride Inc** ........................................................................ E ...... 408 286-9200
   1164 Old Bayshore Hwy San Jose (95112) *(P-16384)*
**Fleetwood Continental Inc** .................................................... D ...... 310 609-1477
   19451 S Susana Rd Compton (90221) *(P-7852)*
**Fleetwood Fibre LLC** ............................................................. C ...... 626 968-8503
   15250 Don Julian Rd City Of Industry (91745) *(P-3842)*
**Fleetwood Fibre Pkg & Graphics, City Of Industry** *Also Called: Fleetwood Fibre LLC (P-3842)*
**Fleetwood Homes, Riverside** *Also Called: Cavco Industries Inc (P-3382)*
**Fleetwood Homes, Riverside** *Also Called: Fleetwood Homes California Inc (P-3386)*
**Fleetwood Homes California Inc (DH)**.................................... C ...... 951 351-2494
   7007 Jurupa Ave Riverside (92504) *(P-3386)*
**Fleetwood Travel Trlrs Ind Inc (DH)** ...................................... C ...... 951 354-3000
   3125 Myers St Riverside (92503) *(P-14120)*
**Fleetwood Windows and Doors, Corona** *Also Called: McDavis and Gumbys Inc (P-16448)*
**Fleischmanns Vinegar Company Inc (DH)** ............................ E ...... 562 483-4619
   12604 Hiddencreek Way Ste A Cerritos (90703) *(P-2201)*
**Fleming Metal Fabricators** .................................................... E ...... 323 723-8203
   874 Camino De Los Mares San Clemente (92673) *(P-13412)*
**Fletcher Bldg Holdings USA Inc (DH)**.................................... D ...... 951 272-8180
   1230 Railroad St Corona (92882) *(P-8454)*

**Fletcher Coating, Orange** *Also Called: Fletcher Coating Co (P-9070)*
**Fletcher Coating Co** .............................................................. E ...... 714 637-4763
   426 W Fletcher Ave Orange (92865) *(P-9070)*
**Flex, San Jose** *Also Called: Flextronics Intl USA Inc (P-12115)*
**Flex, San Jose** *Also Called: Flextronics Logistics USA Inc (P-12117)*
**Flex Company** ....................................................................... E ...... 424 209-2711
   318 Lincoln Blvd Ste 204 Venice (90291) *(P-6494)*
**Flex Interconnect Tech Inc** ................................................... E ...... 408 956-8204
   1603 Watson Ct Milpitas (95035) *(P-12102)*
**Flex Interconnect Technologies, Milpitas** *Also Called: Flex Interconnect Tech Inc (P-12102)*
**Flex Logix Technologies, Mountain View** *Also Called: Flex Logix Technologies Inc (P-12433)*
**Flex Logix Technologies Inc** ................................................. D ...... 650 867-2904
   2465 Latham St Ste 100 Mountain View (94040) *(P-12433)*
**Flex Products Inc** ................................................................. C ...... 707 525-9200
   1402 Mariner Way Santa Rosa (95407) *(P-14775)*
**Flexco Inc** .............................................................................. E ...... 562 927-2525
   6855 Suva St Bell Gardens (90201) *(P-13841)*
**Flexcon Company Inc** ........................................................... E ...... 909 465-0408
   12840 Reservoir St Chino (91710) *(P-6559)*
**Flexfire Leds Inc** .................................................................. E ...... 925 273-9080
   3554 Business Park Dr Ste F Costa Mesa (92626) *(P-11532)*
**Flexfirm Holdings LLC** .......................................................... F ...... 323 283-1173
   2300 Chico Ave El Monte (91733) *(P-2527)*
**Flexi-Liner, Chino** *Also Called: Liner Technologies Inc (P-6896)*
**Flexible Manufacturing LLC** ................................................. D ...... 714 259-7996
   1719 S Grand Ave Santa Ana (92705) *(P-12879)*
**Flexible Metal Inc** ................................................................. C ...... 734 516-3017
   1685 Brandywine Ave Chula Vista (91911) *(P-9259)*
**Flexible Video Systems, Marina Del Rey** *Also Called: Sewer Rodding Equipment Co (P-10599)*
**Flexicare Incorporated** .......................................................... E ...... 949 450-9999
   15281 Barranca Pkwy Ste D Irvine (92618) *(P-15538)*
**Flexline Incorporated** ............................................................ E ...... 562 921-4141
   3727 S Meyler St San Pedro (90731) *(P-5024)*
**Flexrake, Temple City** *Also Called: California Flexrake Corp (P-7948)*
**Flextronics America LLC** ...................................................... C ...... 512 425-4129
   6201 America Center Dr Alviso (95002) *(P-12103)*
**Flextronics America LLC** ...................................................... C ...... 408 576-7156
   777 Gibraltar Dr Milpitas (95035) *(P-12104)*
**Flextronics Ap LLC (DH)**....................................................... C ...... 408 576-7000
   6201 America Center Dr Alviso (95002) *(P-12979)*
**Flextronics Global Services, Milpitas** *Also Called: Flextronics Intl USA Inc (P-12116)*
**Flextronics Intl PA Inc** .......................................................... F ...... 408 577-2489
   677 Gibraltar Dr Milpitas (95035) *(P-12105)*
**Flextronics Intl USA Inc** ....................................................... D ...... 408 576-7492
   727 Gibraltar Dr Milpitas (95035) *(P-12106)*
**Flextronics Intl USA Inc** ....................................................... B ...... 408 576-7000
   260 S Milpitas Blvd Bldg 15 Milpitas (95035) *(P-12107)*
**Flextronics Intl USA Inc** ....................................................... C ...... 510 814-7000
   927 Gibraltar Dr Milpitas (95035) *(P-12108)*
**Flextronics Intl USA Inc** ....................................................... E ...... 408 678-3268
   1177 Gibraltar Dr Bldg 9 Milpitas (95035) *(P-12109)*
**Flextronics Intl USA Inc** ....................................................... C ...... 408 577-4874
   777 Gibraltar Dr Milpitas (95035) *(P-12110)*
**Flextronics Intl USA Inc** ....................................................... C ...... 408 576-7044
   1077 Gibraltar Dr Milpitas (95035) *(P-12111)*
**Flextronics Intl USA Inc** ....................................................... C ...... 408 576-7076
   847 Gibraltar Dr Milpitas (95035) *(P-12112)*
**Flextronics Intl USA Inc** ....................................................... B ...... 408 577-2262
   925 Lightpost Way Morgan Hill (95037) *(P-12113)*
**Flextronics Intl USA Inc** ....................................................... A ...... 408 576-7000
   6201 America Center Dr San Jose (95002) *(P-12114)*
**Flextronics Intl USA Inc (HQ)**............................................... A ...... 408 576-7000
   6201 America Center Dr San Jose (95002) *(P-12115)*
**Flextronics Intl USA Inc** ....................................................... C ...... 408 576-6769
   890 Yosemite Dr Milpitas (95035) *(P-12116)*
**Flextronics Logistics USA Inc (DH)**...................................... D ...... 408 576-7000
   6201 America Center Dr Fl 6 San Jose (95101) *(P-12117)*
**Flextronics Semiconductor (DH)**........................................... E ...... 408 576-7000
   2241 Lundy Ave Bldg 2 San Jose (95131) *(P-12434)*
**Flight Environments Inc** ....................................................... E
   570 Linne Rd Ste 100 Paso Robles (93446) *(P-13842)*

# ALPHABETIC SECTION
## Foam Molders and Specialties

Flight Light Inc .................................................................... F ...... 916 394-2800
  2708 47th Ave Sacramento (95822) *(P-16653)*
Flight Line Products Inc ...................................................... E ...... 661 775-8366
  28732 Witherspoon Pkwy Valencia (91355) *(P-13843)*
Flight Microwave Corporation ............................................. E ...... 310 607-9819
  410 S Douglas St El Segundo (90245) *(P-9858)*
Flight Suits .......................................................................... D ...... 619 440-2700
  1900 Weld Blvd Ste 140 El Cajon (92020) *(P-2879)*
Flightways Manufacturing, Valencia *Also Called: Flight Line Products Inc (P-13843)*
Flipcause Inc ...................................................................... F ...... 800 523-1950
  101 Broadway Fl 3 Oakland (94607) *(P-18315)*
Flirt Inc ................................................................................ E ...... 213 748-4442
  141 E Jefferson Blvd Los Angeles (90011) *(P-17091)*
Flo Dynamics, Compton *Also Called: Norco Industries Inc (P-10102)*
Flo Kino Inc ........................................................................ C ...... 818 767-6528
  2840 N Hollywood Way Burbank (91505) *(P-11533)*
Flo Stor Engineering Inc (PA) ............................................. E ...... 510 887-7179
  21371 Cabot Blvd Hayward (94545) *(P-9485)*
Flo-Kem, Compton *Also Called: LMC Enterprises (P-5914)*
Flo-Kem Inc ........................................................................ E ...... 310 632-7124
  19402 S Susana Rd Compton (90221) *(P-5904)*
Flo-Mac Inc ......................................................................... F ...... 323 583-8751
  1846 E 60th St Los Angeles (90001) *(P-9260)*
Flood Ctrl Wtr Cnservation Dst, Napa *Also Called: County of NAPA (P-14399)*
Flood Ranch Company ....................................................... E ...... 805 937-3616
  6600 Foxen Canyon Rd Santa Maria (93454) *(P-1570)*
Floor Covering Soft ............................................................ E ...... 626 683-9188
  221 E Walnut St Ste 110 Pasadena (91101) *(P-18316)*
Floor Seal Technology Inc (PA) .......................................... E ...... 408 436-8181
  1566 S 7th St San Jose (95112) *(P-504)*
Flora Gold Corporation (PA) ............................................... A ...... 949 252-1908
  3165 Red Hill Ave Ste 201 Costa Mesa (92626) *(P-16130)*
Flora Springs Wine Company ............................................. F ...... 707 963-5711
  677 Saint Helena Hwy S Saint Helena (94574) *(P-1571)*
Floral Gift HM Decor Intl Inc ............................................... E ...... 818 849-8832
  3200 Golf Course Dr Ste B Ventura (93003) *(P-47)*
Florence & New Itln Art Co Inc .......................................... E ...... 510 785-9674
  27735 Industrial Blvd Hayward (94545) *(P-7332)*
Florence Filter Corporation ................................................ D ...... 310 637-1137
  530 W Manville St Compton (90220) *(P-16779)*
Florence Meat Packing Co Inc ........................................... E ...... 562 401-0760
  9840 Everest St Downey (90242) *(P-17580)*
Flores Family Development (HQ) ....................................... E ...... 559 661-4171
  2851 Falcon Dr Madera (93637) *(P-6679)*
Florian Industries Inc ......................................................... F ...... 415 330-9000
  151 Industrial Way Brisbane (94005) *(P-8141)*
Flory Industries (PA) ........................................................... D ...... 209 545-1167
  4737 Toomes Rd Salida (95368) *(P-9354)*
Flostor, Hayward *Also Called: Flo Stor Engineering Inc (P-9485)*
Flotron ................................................................................. E ...... 760 727-2700
  2630 Progress St Vista (92081) *(P-9623)*
Flow Dynamics Inc .............................................................. F ...... 909 930-5522
  1215 E Acacia St Ste 104 Ontario (91761) *(P-7613)*
Flowers Bakeries Sls Socal LLC ........................................ E ...... 702 281-4797
  10625 Poplar Ave Fontana (92337) *(P-1195)*
Flowers Baking Co Modesto LLC ...................................... F ...... 209 526-5512
  906 N Carpenter Rd Modesto (95351) *(P-1196)*
Flowers Baking Co Modesto LLC (HQ) .............................. D ...... 209 857-4600
  736 Mariposa Rd Modesto (95354) *(P-1197)*
Flowers Bkg Co Henderson LLC ....................................... D ...... 818 884-8970
  21540 Blythe St Canoga Park (91304) *(P-1198)*
Flowers Bkg Co Henderson LLC ....................................... D ...... 310 695-9846
  3800 W Century Blvd Inglewood (90303) *(P-1199)*
Flowers Bkg Co Henderson LLC ....................................... D ...... 702 281-4797
  7311 Doig Dr Garden Grove (92841) *(P-1200)*
Flowline Inc ........................................................................ E ...... 562 598-3015
  10500 Humbolt St Los Alamitos (90720) *(P-14869)*
Flowline Liquid Intelligence, Los Alamitos *Also Called: Flowline Inc (P-14869)*
Flowmaster Inc ................................................................... D ...... 707 544-4761
  100 Stony Point Rd Ste 125 Santa Rosa (95401) *(P-13500)*
Flowmetrics Inc .................................................................. F ...... 818 407-3420
  9201 Independence Ave Chatsworth (91311) *(P-14411)*

Flowserve Corporation ....................................................... B ...... 323 584-1890
  2300 E Vernon Ave Stop 76 Vernon (90058) *(P-9921)*
Flowserve Corporation ....................................................... D ...... 310 667-4220
  1909 E Cashdan St Compton (90220) *(P-9922)*
Flowserve Corporation ....................................................... F ...... 707 748-4900
  6077 Egret Ct Benicia (94510) *(P-9923)*
Flowserve Corporation ....................................................... D ...... 951 296-2464
  27455 Tierra Alta Way Ste C Temecula (92590) *(P-9924)*
Fluid Components Intl LLC (DH) ........................................ F ...... 760 744-6950
  1755 La Costa Meadows Dr San Marcos (92078) *(P-14412)*
Fluid Line Technology Corp ............................................... E ...... 818 998-8848
  4590 Ish Dr Simi Valley (93063) *(P-15086)*
Fluid Tech Hydraulics Inc .................................................. E ...... 916 681-0888
  8432 Tiogawoods Dr Sacramento (95828) *(P-19258)*
Fluidlogic, El Segundo *Also Called: Rainmaker Solutions Inc (P-6428)*
Fluidmaster Inc (PA) ........................................................... D ...... 949 728-2000
  30800 Rancho Viejo Rd San Juan Capistrano (92675) *(P-6828)*
Fluidra North America LLC (HQ) ........................................ D ...... 760 599-9600
  2882 Whiptail Loop Ste 100 Carlsbad (92010) *(P-10559)*
Fluidra Usa LLC (PA) .......................................................... E ...... 904 378-0999
  2882 Whiptail Loop Ste 100 Carlsbad (92010) *(P-10560)*
Fluorescent Supply Co Inc ................................................ F ...... 909 948-8878
  9120 Center Ave Rancho Cucamonga (91730) *(P-11534)*
Flux Power Holdings Inc (PA) ............................................ C ...... 877 505-3589
  2685 S Melrose Dr Vista (92081) *(P-13141)*
Fluxergy Inc ........................................................................ F ...... 949 305-4201
  15 Musick Irvine (92618) *(P-15087)*
Fluxergy Inc ........................................................................ F ...... 949 305-4201
  13766 Alton Pkwy Irvine (92618) *(P-15088)*
Fluxergy Inc (PA) ................................................................ E ...... 949 305-4201
  30 Fairbanks Irvine (92618) *(P-19452)*
Fluxion, Oakland *Also Called: Fluxion Biosciences Inc (P-15089)*
Fluxion Biosciences Inc ..................................................... E ...... 650 241-4577
  1407 E 20th St Oakland (94607) *(P-15089)*
Fly On My Jet, Los Angeles *Also Called: Forrest Group LLC (P-16274)*
Flyer Defense LLC ............................................................. D ...... 310 324-5650
  151 W 135th St Los Angeles (90061) *(P-13353)*
Flying Colors, Walnut *Also Called: Jakks Pacific Inc (P-15755)*
Flying Machine Factory, Compton *Also Called: Fmf Racing (P-14058)*
Flyleaf Windows Inc ........................................................... E ...... 925 344-1181
  11040 Bollinger Canyon Rd E-407 San Ramon (94582) *(P-7221)*
Flynt, Larry Publishing, Beverly Hills *Also Called: L F P Inc (P-4270)*
Flywheel Software Inc ........................................................ E ...... 650 260-1700
  816 Hamilton St Redwood City (94063) *(P-18317)*
FM Industries, Fremont *Also Called: FM Industries Inc (P-10838)*
FM Industries Inc (DH) ...................................................... C ...... 510 668-1900
  221 E Warren Ave Fremont (94539) *(P-10838)*
FMC Metals, Los Angeles *Also Called: 75s Corp (P-16955)*
FMC Technologies Inc ....................................................... E ...... 530 753-6718
  260 Cousteau Pl Davis (95618) *(P-9462)*
Fmf Racing .......................................................................... C ...... 310 631-4363
  18033 S Santa Fe Ave Compton (90221) *(P-14058)*
Fmh Aerospace Corp .......................................................... D ...... 714 751-1000
  17072 Daimler St Irvine (92614) *(P-13844)*
FMI, Chula Vista *Also Called: Flexible Metal Inc (P-9259)*
FN Cellars LLC ................................................................... F ...... 707 944-2861
  1350 Acacia Dr Oakville (94562) *(P-1572)*
FN Cellars LLC ................................................................... F ...... 707 967-9600
  1695 Saint Helena Hwy S Saint Helena (94574) *(P-1573)*
Fnc Medical Corporation .................................................... E ...... 805 644-7576
  6000 Leland St Ventura (93003) *(P-5978)*
Foam Concepts Inc ............................................................. E ...... 714 693-1037
  4729 E Wesley Dr Anaheim (92807) *(P-6634)*
Foam Depot, City Of Industry *Also Called: American Foam Fiber & Sups Inc (P-2542)*
Foam Factory Inc ................................................................ E ...... 310 603-9808
  17515 S Santa Fe Ave Compton (90221) *(P-6635)*
Foam Molders and Specialties (PA) ................................... E ...... 562 924-7757
  11110 Business Cir Cerritos (90703) *(P-6636)*
Foam Molders and Specialties ........................................... E ...... 562 924-7757
  20004 State Rd Cerritos (90703) *(P-6637)*

**Foam Plastics & Rbr Pdts Corp** .................................................. F ...... 714 779-0990
4765 E Bryson St Anaheim (92807) *(P-6638)*
**Foam Specialties, Cerritos** *Also Called: Foam Molders and Specialties (P-6636)*
**Foam-Craft Inc** ............................................................................ C ...... 714 459-9971
2441 Cypress Way Fullerton (92831) *(P-6639)*
**Foamex, San Bernardino** *Also Called: Foamex LP (P-6640)*
**Foamex LP** ................................................................................. E ...... 909 824-8981
1400 E Victoria Ave San Bernardino (92408) *(P-6640)*
**Foamordercom Inc** .................................................................... F ...... 415 503-1188
3455 Collins Ave Richmond (94806) *(P-17520)*
**Foampro Manufacturing, Irvine** *Also Called: Foampro Mfg Inc (P-15929)*
**Foampro Mfg Inc** ....................................................................... D ...... 949 252-0112
1781 Langley Ave Irvine (92614) *(P-15929)*
**Focus Industries Inc** ................................................................. D ...... 949 830-1350
25301 Commercentre Dr Lake Forest (92630) *(P-11535)*
**Focus Interpreting, Victorville** *Also Called: Focus Language Intl Inc (P-19091)*
**Focus Landscape, Lake Forest** *Also Called: Focus Industries Inc (P-11535)*
**Focus Language Intl Inc** ........................................................... F ...... 800 374-5444
14450 Park Ave Ste 100 Victorville (92392) *(P-19091)*
**Focus One Home, Corona** *Also Called: Della Robbia Inc (P-3524)*
**Foggy Dog LLC** ......................................................................... F ...... 415 993-1130
3360 20th St Ste A San Francisco (94110) *(P-7156)*
**Foh Group Inc (PA)** ................................................................... E
6255 W Sunset Blvd Ste 2212 Los Angeles (90028) *(P-2837)*
**Foldimate Inc** ............................................................................. E ...... 805 876-4418
879 White Pine Ct Oak Park (91377) *(P-11405)*
**Folding Cartons, Camarillo** *Also Called: Crockett Graphics Inc (P-3836)*
**Foley Fmly Wines Holdings Inc** ................................................ D ...... 805 450-7225
90 Easy St Buellton (93427) *(P-1574)*
**Folgergraphics Inc** .................................................................... E ...... 510 293-2294
21093 Forbes Ave Hayward (94545) *(P-5019)*
**Folio3 Software Inc** .................................................................. D ...... 650 802-8668
1301 Shoreway Rd Ste 160 Belmont (94002) *(P-18318)*
**Folkmanis Inc** ............................................................................ E ...... 510 658-7677
1219 Park Ave Emeryville (94608) *(P-16131)*
**Follow Your Heart, Chatsworth** *Also Called: Earth Island LLC (P-2189)*
**Folsom Ready Mix Inc (HQ)** ..................................................... F ...... 916 851-8300
3401 Fitzgerald Rd Rancho Cordova (95742) *(P-7446)*
**Fonco Inc** ................................................................................... F ...... 650 873-4585
133 Starlite St South San Francisco (94080) *(P-514)*
**Fonco Creative Services** .......................................................... E ...... 415 254-5460
1310 N San Fernando Rd Los Angeles (90065) *(P-19294)*
**Fonco Studios, Los Angeles** *Also Called: Fonco Creative Services (P-19294)*
**Fonegear LLC** ............................................................................ F ...... 909 627-7999
13953 Ramona Ave Chino (91710) *(P-11764)*
**Fong Brothers Printing Inc (PA)** ............................................... C ...... 415 467-1050
320 Valley Dr Brisbane (94005) *(P-4612)*
**Fong Engineering Enterprise** ................................................... E ...... 909 598-8835
166 University Pkwy Pomona (91768) *(P-12980)*
**Fong Fong Prtrs Lthgrphers Inc** ............................................... E ...... 916 739-1313
3009 65th St Sacramento (95820) *(P-4613)*
**Fono Unlimited (PA)** ................................................................. E ...... 650 322-4664
99 Stanford Shopping Ctr Palo Alto (94304) *(P-801)*
**Fontana Paper Mills Inc** ........................................................... D ...... 909 823-4100
13733 Valley Blvd Fontana (92335) *(P-6374)*
**Fontana Resources At Work** .................................................... E ...... 909 428-3833
9460 Sierra Ave Fontana (92335) *(P-19361)*
**Fontana Steel, Ontario** *Also Called: C M C Steel Fabricators Inc (P-9211)*
**Food & Bev Innovations LLC** ................................................... F ...... 888 491-3772
1801 Century Park E Ste 1420 Los Angeles (90067) *(P-9788)*
**Food 4 Less, Riverside** *Also Called: Dillon Companies Inc (P-17375)*
**Food and Beverage, Fresno** *Also Called: Fury Hot Chicken LLC (P-3742)*
**Food For Life Baking Co Inc (PA)** ............................................ D ...... 951 279-5090
2991 Doherty St Corona (92879) *(P-1201)*
**Food Pharma, Santa Fe Springs** *Also Called: Food Technology and Design LLC (P-1307)*
**Food Processing Equipment Co, Santa Fe Springs** *Also Called: FPec Corporation A Cal Corp (P-9791)*
**Food Technology and Design LLC (PA)** ................................... E ...... 562 944-7821
10012 Painter Ave Santa Fe Springs (90670) *(P-1307)*
**Foodbeast Inc** ............................................................................ F ...... 949 344-2634
220 E 4th St Ste 202 Santa Ana (92701) *(P-4399)*

**Foodmaxx, Redding** *Also Called: Save Mart Supermarkets Disc (P-17384)*
**Foodology LLC** .......................................................................... D ...... 818 252-1888
8920 Norris Ave Sun Valley (91352) *(P-2202)*
**Foods On Fly LLC** ..................................................................... E ...... 858 404-0642
7004 Carroll Rd San Diego (92121) *(P-2203)*
**Foodtools Consolidated Inc (PA)** ............................................ E ...... 805 962-8383
315 Laguna St Santa Barbara (93101) *(P-9789)*
**Fooma America Inc** .................................................................. E ...... 310 921-0717
12735 Stanhill Dr La Mirada (90638) *(P-9737)*
**Foot In Motion Inc** .................................................................... F ...... 312 752-0990
2239 Business Way Riverside (92501) *(P-15348)*
**Foote Axle & Forge LLC** ........................................................... E ...... 323 268-4151
250 W Duarte Rd Ste A Monrovia (91016) *(P-13501)*
**Foothill Electric Motors, Santa Clarita** *Also Called: Wrights Supply Inc (P-19237)*
**Foothill Vctonal Opportunities, Pasadena** *Also Called: Fvo Solutions Inc (P-9073)*
**Foothills Advertiser, Exeter** *Also Called: Foothills Sun-Gazette (P-4114)*
**Foothills Sun-Gazette** ............................................................... E ...... 559 592-3171
120 Ne St Exeter (93221) *(P-4114)*
**Footloose Incorporated** ........................................................... E ...... 760 934-2400
3043 Main St Mammoth Lakes (93546) *(P-17634)*
**Footloose Sports, Mammoth Lakes** *Also Called: Footloose Incorporated (P-17634)*
**Foppiano Vineyards, Healdsburg** *Also Called: L Foppiano Wine Co (P-1654)*
**Forager Project, San Francisco** *Also Called: Forager Project LLC (P-1006)*
**Forager Project LLC (PA)** ......................................................... D ...... 855 729-5253
235 Montgomery St Ste 420 San Francisco (94104) *(P-1006)*
**Forbes Industries Div** ............................................................... C ...... 909 923-4559
1933 E Locust St Ontario (91761) *(P-3741)*
**Force Protection Systems, Van Nuys** *Also Called: Edo Communications and Countermeasures Systems Inc (P-14183)*
**Ford Logging Inc** ...................................................................... F ...... 707 840-9442
1225 Central Ave Ste 11 Mckinleyville (95519) *(P-3045)*
**Fordon Grind Industries, Torrance** *Also Called: Aerioliant Manufacturing Inc (P-10689)*
**Foreal Spectrum Inc** ................................................................. E ...... 408 923-1675
2370 Qume Dr Ste A San Jose (95131) *(P-14776)*
**Forecast 3d, Carlsbad** *Also Called: Product Slingshot Inc (P-9643)*
**Foremay Inc (PA)** ...................................................................... E ...... 408 228-3468
225 S Lake Ave Ste 300 Pasadena (91101) *(P-17924)*
**Foremost Spring & Mfg, Santa Fe Springs** *Also Called: Foremost Spring Company Inc (P-9200)*
**Foremost Spring Company Inc** ................................................ F ...... 562 923-0791
11876 Burke St Santa Fe Springs (90670) *(P-9200)*
**Forensic Logic Inc** .................................................................... E ...... 415 810-2114
712 Bancroft Rd # 423 Walnut Creek (94598) *(P-18319)*
**Foresee Orthopedic Product, Oakdale** *Also Called: Custom Carbon Composite Creations Inc (P-15331)*
**Foreseeson Custom Displays Inc (PA)** .................................... E ...... 714 300-0540
2210 E Winston Rd Anaheim (92806) *(P-10369)*
**Forespar, Rcho Sta Marg** *Also Called: Light Composite Corporation (P-8010)*
**Forespar Products Corp** ........................................................... D ...... 949 858-8820
22322 Gilberto Rancho Santa Margari (92688) *(P-7995)*
**Forest Investment Group Inc** .................................................. F ...... 415 459-2330
83 Hamilton Dr Ste 100 Novato (94949) *(P-4614)*
**Forever Rich International LLC** ............................................... E ...... 310 867-4723
14622 Ventura Blvd Sherman Oaks (91403) *(P-758)*
**FORGE GLOBAL, San Francisco** *Also Called: Forge Global Holdings Inc (P-18321)*
**Forge Global Inc (HQ)** .............................................................. C ...... 415 881-1612
4 Embarcadero Ctr Ste 1500 San Francisco (94111) *(P-18320)*
**Forge Global Holdings Inc** ...................................................... C ...... 415 881-1612
4 Embarcadero Ctr Ste 1500 San Francisco (94111) *(P-18321)*
**Forged Metals Inc** .................................................................... C ...... 909 350-9260
10685 Beech Ave Fontana (92337) *(P-8776)*
**Forgiato, Sun Valley** *Also Called: Forgiato Inc (P-13502)*
**Forgiato Inc** ............................................................................... D ...... 818 771-9779
11915 Wicks St Sun Valley (91352) *(P-13502)*
**Form & Fusion Mfg Inc (PA)** .................................................... E ...... 916 638-8576
11261 Trade Center Dr Rancho Cordova (95742) *(P-8843)*
**Form Grind Corporation** .......................................................... E ...... 949 858-7000
30062 Aventura Rcho Sta Marg (92688) *(P-10839)*
**Form Products, Rcho Sta Marg** *Also Called: Form Grind Corporation (P-10839)*
**Formagrid Inc (PA)** ................................................................... B ...... 415 200-2040
799 Market St Fl 8 San Francisco (94103) *(P-16317)*

# ALPHABETIC SECTION — Foundry Networks Inc

**Formed Lighting, Chatsworth** *Also Called: Lf Illumination LLC (P-11543)*

**Former Luna Subsidiary Inc (HQ)** .................................................. D ...... 805 987-0146
Camarillo (93012) *(P-12435)*

**Former Nt Corp** ............................................................................... D ...... 330 702-3070
1054 S De Anza Blvd Ste 202 San Jose (95129) *(P-18322)*

**Formex LLC** ..................................................................................... E ...... 858 529-6600
9601 Jeronimo Rd Irvine (92618) *(P-5443)*

**FORMFACTOR, Livermore** *Also Called: Formfactor Inc (P-12436)*

**Formfactor Inc (PA)** ........................................................................ C ...... 925 290-4000
7005 Southfront Rd Livermore (94551) *(P-12436)*

**Formosa Meat Company Inc** .......................................................... E ...... 909 987-0470
10646 Fulton Ct Rancho Cucamonga (91730) *(P-640)*

**Forms and Surfaces Inc** ................................................................. D ...... 805 684-8626
6395 Cindy Ln Carpinteria (93013) *(P-8626)*

**Forms and Surfaces Company LLC** .............................................. C ...... 805 684-8626
6395 Cindy Ln Carpinteria (93013) *(P-7333)*

**Formula Plastics Inc** ...................................................................... B ...... 866 307-1362
451 Tecate Rd Ste 2b Tecate (91980) *(P-6829)*

**Formulation Technology Inc** ........................................................ E ...... 209 847-0331
571 Armstrong Way Oakdale (95361) *(P-5444)*

**Forrest Group LLC (PA)** ................................................................. D ...... 619 808-9798
1422 N Curson Ave Apt 9 Los Angeles (90046) *(P-16274)*

**Forrest Machining LLC** .................................................................. C ...... 661 257-0231
27756 Avenue Mentry Valencia (91355) *(P-13845)*

**Forrestmachining.com, Valencia** *Also Called: Forrest Machining LLC (P-13845)*

**Fort Bragg Advocate-News, Ukiah** *Also Called: Gatehouse Media LLC (P-4118)*

**Fort Ord Works Inc** ........................................................................ E ...... 831 275-1294
791 Neeson Rd Marina (93933) *(P-14187)*

**Fortel Traffic Inc** ............................................................................ F ...... 714 701-9800
5310 E Hunter Ave Anaheim (92807) *(P-19395)*

**Fortemedia Inc (PA)** ....................................................................... E ...... 408 716-8028
2150 Gold St Ste 250 San Jose (95002) *(P-12437)*

**Fortera, San Jose** *Also Called: Arelac Inc (P-6218)*

**Forterra Inc** ..................................................................................... F ...... 559 221-2070
8050 N Palm Ave Ste 300 Fresno (93711) *(P-7334)*

**Forterra Pipe & Precast LLC** ......................................................... E ...... 951 523-7039
26380 Palomar Rd Sun City (92585) *(P-7335)*

**Forterra Pipe & Precast LLC** ......................................................... E ...... 858 715-5600
9229 Harris Plant Rd San Diego (92145) *(P-7336)*

**Forterra Pipe & Precast LLC** ......................................................... D ...... 916 379-9695
7020 Tokay Ave Sacramento (95828) *(P-7337)*

**Fortezza Iridium Holdings Inc** ..................................................... A ...... 415 765-6500
150 California St San Francisco (94111) *(P-18323)*

**Fortier & Fortier Inc** ...................................................................... E ...... 559 638-5774
1260 S Buttonwillow Ave Reedley (93654) *(P-16798)*

**FORTINET, Sunnyvale** *Also Called: Fortinet Inc (P-19007)*

**Fortinet Inc (PA)** ............................................................................. A ...... 408 235-7700
909 Kifer Rd Sunnyvale (94086) *(P-19007)*

**Fortis Solutions Group LLC** .......................................................... D ...... 800 388-1990
1870 Wardrobe Ave Merced (95341) *(P-4880)*

**Fortner Eng & Mfg Inc** .................................................................... E ...... 818 240-7740
2927 N Ontario St Burbank (91504) *(P-10840)*

**Fortrend Engineering Corp (PA)** ................................................... E ...... 408 734-9311
2220 Otoole Ave San Jose (95131) *(P-14413)*

**Fortress Inc** .................................................................................... E ...... 909 593-8600
1721 Wright Ave La Verne (91750) *(P-3567)*

**Fortune Brands Windows Inc** ...................................................... C ...... 707 446-7600
2019 E Monte Vista Ave Vacaville (95688) *(P-6830)*

**Fortune Casuals LLC (PA)** ............................................................. D ...... 310 733-2100
10119 Jefferson Blvd Culver City (90232) *(P-2665)*

**Fortune Manufacturing Inc** ........................................................... E ...... 909 591-1547
13849 Magnolia Ave Chino (91710) *(P-10841)*

**Fortune Swimwear LLC (HQ)** ......................................................... E ...... 310 733-2130
2340 E Olympic Blvd Ste A Los Angeles (90021) *(P-2470)*

**Forty Seven, Foster City** *Also Called: Forty Seven Inc (P-5445)*

**Forty Seven Inc (HQ)** ...................................................................... E ...... 650 352-4150
333 Lakeside Dr Foster City (94404) *(P-5445)*

**Forty Seven Inc** .............................................................................. E ...... 650 352-4150
1661 Page Mill Rd Ste C Palo Alto (94304) *(P-5446)*

**Forward** ........................................................................................... E ...... 310 962-2522
13020 Pacific Promenade Los Angeles (90094) *(P-10068)*

**Forward Networks Inc** ................................................................... D ...... 844 393-6389
2390 Mission College Blvd # 401 Santa Clara (95054) *(P-18324)*

**Foss Maritime Company** ............................................................... F ...... 562 437-6098
49 W Pier D St Long Beach (90802) *(P-8142)*

**FOSS MARITIME COMPANY, Long Beach** *Also Called: Foss Maritime Company (P-8142)*

**Foster Dairy Farms (PA)** ................................................................ A ...... 209 576-3400
529 Kansas Ave Modesto (95351) *(P-17129)*

**Foster Dairy Products Distrg (PA)** ............................................... E ...... 209 576-3400
529 Kansas Ave Modesto (95351) *(P-17130)*

**Foster Farms, Porterville** *Also Called: Foster Farms LLC (P-61)*

**Foster Farms, Waterford** *Also Called: Foster Poultry Farms (P-683)*

**Foster Farms, Livingston** *Also Called: Foster Poultry Farms (P-684)*

**Foster Farms, Fresno** *Also Called: Foster Poultry Farms (P-688)*

**Foster Farms LLC** ........................................................................... D ...... 559 793-5501
770 N Plano St Porterville (93257) *(P-61)*

**Foster Farms LLC** ........................................................................... E ...... 559 897-1081
1900 Kern St Kingsburg (93631) *(P-680)*

**Foster Farms LLC** ........................................................................... E ...... 209 948-0129
1111 Navy Dr Stockton (95206) *(P-681)*

**Foster Farms LLC** ........................................................................... E ...... 559 443-2750
2222 S East Ave Fresno (93721) *(P-682)*

**Foster Farms LLC (HQ)** .................................................................. D ...... 209 394-7901
1000 Davis St Livingston (95334) *(P-62)*

**Foster Poultry Farms** ..................................................................... B ...... 209 394-7901
1307 Ellenwood Rd Waterford (95386) *(P-683)*

**Foster Poultry Farms** ..................................................................... A ...... 209 394-7901
1333 Swan St Livingston (95334) *(P-684)*

**Foster Poultry Farms** ..................................................................... C ...... 209 394-7901
843 Davis St Unit 1p Livingston (95334) *(P-685)*

**Foster Poultry Farms** ..................................................................... D ...... 209 668-5922
1033 S Center St Turlock (95380) *(P-686)*

**Foster Poultry Farms** ..................................................................... B ...... 310 223-1499
1805 N Santa Fe Ave Compton (90221) *(P-687)*

**Foster Poultry Farms** ..................................................................... A ...... 559 442-3771
2960 S Cherry Ave Fresno (93706) *(P-688)*

**Foster Poultry Farms** ..................................................................... B ...... 559 265-2000
900 W Belgravia Ave Fresno (93706) *(P-689)*

**Foster Poultry Farms** ..................................................................... C ...... 559 793-5501
770 N Plano St Porterville (93257) *(P-690)*

**Foster Poultry Farms** ..................................................................... C ...... 209 394-7950
221 Stefani Ave Livingston (95334) *(P-1126)*

**Foster Poultry Farms, Livingston** *Also Called: Foster Poultry Farms (P-685)*

**FOSTER POULTRY FARMS, Compton** *Also Called: Foster Poultry Farms (P-687)*

**FOSTER POULTRY FARMS, Fresno** *Also Called: Foster Poultry Farms (P-689)*

**FOSTER POULTRY FARMS, Porterville** *Also Called: Foster Poultry Farms (P-690)*

**FOSTER POULTRY FARMS, Livingston** *Also Called: Foster Poultry Farms (P-1126)*

**Foster Poultry Farms LLC** ............................................................. B ...... 209 394-7901
834 Davis St Livingston (95334) *(P-68)*

**Foster Poultry Farms LLC (PA)** ..................................................... C ...... 209 394-7901
1000 Davis St Livingston (95334) *(P-691)*

**Foster Print, Santa Ana** *Also Called: Blackburn Alton Invstments LLC (P-4849)*

**Foster Printing Company Inc** ....................................................... F ...... 714 731-2000
700 E Alton Ave Santa Ana (92705) *(P-4615)*

**Foster Sand & Gravel, Corona** *Also Called: Werner Corporation (P-7521)*

**Foster Turkey Live Haul, Turlock** *Also Called: Foster Poultry Farms (P-686)*

**Fotis and Son Imports Inc (PA)** ..................................................... E ...... 714 894-9022
15451 Electronic Ln Huntington Beach (92649) *(P-9790)*

**Found Image Press Inc** ................................................................. F ...... 619 282-3452
5151 Santa Fe St San Diego (92109) *(P-4995)*

**Foundation 9 Entertainment Inc (PA)** .......................................... C ...... 949 698-1500
30211 Avenida De Las Bandera Ste 200 Rancho Santa Margari (92688) *(P-18325)*

**Foundation Ai, Irvine** *Also Called: Foundation Inc (P-18326)*

**Foundation For Nat Progress** ....................................................... E ...... 415 321-1700
222 Sutter St Ste 600 San Francisco (94108) *(P-4257)*

**Foundation Inc** ............................................................................... E ...... 310 294-8955
19800 Macarthur Blvd Ste 300 Irvine (92612) *(P-18326)*

**Foundry Med Innovations Inc** ...................................................... F ...... 888 445-2333
1965 Kellogg Ave Carlsbad (92008) *(P-15090)*

**Foundry Networks Inc** ................................................................... A ...... 408 207-1700
1745 Technology Dr San Jose (95110) *(P-10370)*

**Foundry Service & Supplies Inc** ........ E ...... 909 284-5000
2029 S Parco Ave Ontario (91761) ***(P-7590)***

**Foundstone Inc** ........ E ...... 949 297-5600
27201 Puerta Real Ste 400 Mission Viejo (92691) ***(P-18327)***

**Fountainhead Industries** ........ E ...... 310 248-2444
700 N San Vicente Blvd Ste G410 West Hollywood (90069) ***(P-16132)***

**Four D Metal Finishing** ........ E ...... 408 730-5722
1065 Memorex Dr Santa Clara (95050) ***(P-8962)***

**Four In One Company, San Jose** *Also Called: Lee Brothers Inc* ***(P-982)***

**Four Seasons Design Inc (PA)** ........ **E ...... 619 761-5151**
2451 Britannia Blvd San Diego (92154) ***(P-3007)***

**Four Seasons Hummus Inc** ........ F ...... 305 409-0449
11030 Randall St Sun Valley (91352) ***(P-2204)***

**Four Seasons Surgery Centers** ........ F ...... 909 933-6576
1211 W 6th St Ontario (91762) ***(P-19316)***

**Four Star Chemical, Los Angeles** *Also Called: Starco Enterprises Inc* ***(P-9901)***

**Fovell Enterprises Inc** ........ E ...... 951 734-6275
1852 Pomona Rd Corona (92878) ***(P-15979)***

**Foveon Inc** ........ E ...... 408 855-6800
2249 Zanker Rd San Jose (95131) ***(P-12438)***

**Fox Barrel Cider Company Inc** ........ E ...... 530 346-9699
1213 S Auburn St Ste A Colfax (95713) ***(P-1575)***

**Fox Electronics, Laguna Hills** *Also Called: Fox Enterprises LLC* ***(P-12981)***

**Fox Enterprises LLC (HQ)** ........ **E ...... 239 693-0099**
24422 Avenida De La Carlota Ste 290 Laguna Hills (92653) ***(P-12981)***

**Fox Factory Inc** ........ E ...... 831 274-6545
200 El Pueblo Rd Scotts Valley (95066) ***(P-13503)***

**Fox Marble & Granite, Berkeley** *Also Called: Evolv Surfaces Inc* ***(P-3685)***

**Fox Thermal Instruments Inc** ........ E ...... 831 384-4300
399 Reservation Rd Marina (93933) ***(P-14414)***

**Foxconn Electronics Inc** ........ E ...... 714 988-9230
105 S Puente St Brea (92821) ***(P-6831)***

**Foxen Canyon Winery & Vineyard, Santa Maria** *Also Called: Foxen Vineyard Inc* ***(P-1576)***

**Foxen Vineyard Inc** ........ E ...... 805 937-4251
7600 Foxen Canyon Rd Santa Maria (93454) ***(P-1576)***

**Foxfury Lighting Solution, Oceanside** *Also Called: Foxfury LLC* ***(P-11597)***

**Foxfury LLC** ........ E ...... 760 945-4231
3544 Seagate Way Oceanside (92056) ***(P-11597)***

**Foxlink International Inc (HQ)** ........ **E ...... 714 256-1777**
3010 Saturn St Ste 200 Brea (92821) ***(P-11454)***

**Foxpass Inc** ........ F ...... 415 805-6350
10050 N Wolfe Rd Ste Sw2260 Cupertino (95014) ***(P-18328)***

**FP, San Francisco** *Also Called: Francisco Partners GP III LP* ***(P-18976)***

**Fpc Inc** ........ E ...... 323 468-5778
1017 N Las Palmas Ave Los Angeles (90038) ***(P-15639)***

**FPec Corporation A Cal Corp (PA)** ........ **F ...... 562 802-3727**
13623 Pumice St Santa Fe Springs (90670) ***(P-9791)***

**Fragile Handle With Care, San Diego** *Also Called: Chandler Packaging A Transpak Company* ***(P-16309)***

**Fralock, Fremont** *Also Called: Ceramic Tech Inc* ***(P-10772)***

**Fralock, Milpitas** *Also Called: Lenthor Engineering Inc* ***(P-12153)***

**Fralock, Valencia** *Also Called: Lockwood Industries LLC* ***(P-12533)***

**Framehawk Inc** ........ C ...... 415 371-9110
650 Townsend St Ste 325 San Francisco (94103) ***(P-18329)***

**Frameless Hardware Company LLC** ........ E ...... 888 295-4531
4361 Firestone Blvd South Gate (90280) ***(P-7996)***

**Frametent Inc** ........ E ...... 661 290-3375
26480 Summit Cir Santa Clarita (91350) ***(P-2974)***

**Franchise Services Inc (PA)** ........ **E ...... 949 348-5400**
26722 Plaza Mission Viejo (92691) ***(P-4616)***

**Franchise Update Inc** ........ F ...... 408 402-5681
6489 Camden Ave Ste 204 San Jose (95120) ***(P-4258)***

**Franchise Update Media Group, San Jose** *Also Called: Franchise Update Inc* ***(P-4258)***

**Francis Coppola Winery LLC** ........ E ...... 707 857-1400
300 Via Archimedes Geyserville (95441) ***(P-1577)***

**Francis Ford Coppola Winery, Geyserville** *Also Called: Francis Ford Cppola Prsnts LLC* ***(P-1578)***

**Francis Ford Cppola Prsnts LLC** ........ E ...... 707 251-3200
300 Via Archimedes Geyserville (95441) ***(P-1578)***

**Franciscan Vineyards Inc., Saint Helena** *Also Called: Tpwc Inc* ***(P-1787)***

**Francisco Partners, San Francisco** *Also Called: Francisco Partners MGT LP* ***(P-17753)***

**Francisco Partners GP III LP (HQ)** ........ **D ...... 415 418-2900**
1 Letterman Dr Bldg C San Francisco (94129) ***(P-18976)***

**Francisco Partners MGT LP (PA)** ........ **C ...... 415 418-2900**
1 Letterman Dr Ste 410 San Francisco (94129) ***(P-17753)***

**Frank M Booth Inc** ........ D ...... 650 871-8292
251 Michelle Ct South San Francisco (94080) ***(P-418)***

**Frank Russell Inc** ........ F ...... 661 324-5575
341 Pacific Ave Shafter (93263) ***(P-10842)***

**Frank-Lin Distillers Pdts Ltd (PA)** ........ **C ...... 408 259-8900**
2455 Huntington Dr Fairfield (94533) ***(P-17266)***

**Frankies Bikinis, Venice** *Also Called: Frankies Bikinis LLC* ***(P-2860)***

**Frankies Bikinis LLC** ........ E ...... 323 354-4133
4030 Del Rey Ave Venice (90292) ***(P-2860)***

**Franklin Logging, Burney** *Also Called: Shasta Green Inc* ***(P-3055)***

**Franklin Wireless, San Diego** *Also Called: Franklin Wireless Corp* ***(P-11765)***

**Franklin Wireless Corp** ........ D ...... 858 623-0000
3940 Ruffin Rd Ste C San Diego (92123) ***(P-11765)***

**Franklins Inds San Diego Inc** ........ E ...... 858 486-9399
12135 Dearborn Pl Poway (92064) ***(P-10843)***

**Franklinwh Energy Storage Inc** ........ F ...... 888 837-2655
1731 Technology Dr Ste 530 San Jose (95110) ***(P-13142)***

**Frantz Wholesale Nursery LLC** ........ E ...... 209 874-1459
12161 Delaware Rd Hickman (95323) ***(P-48)***

**Franz Family Bakeries, Los Angeles** *Also Called: United States Bakery* ***(P-1249)***

**Franz Inc** ........ E ...... 510 452-2000
3685 Mt Diablo Blvd Ste 300 Lafayette (94549) ***(P-18330)***

**Frase Enterprises** ........ E ...... 510 856-3600
2261 Carion Ct Pittsburg (94565) ***(P-11479)***

**Fratelli Beretta Usa Inc** ........ E ...... 559 237-9591
1090 W Church Ave Fresno (93706) ***(P-641)***

**Fratelli Beretta Usa Inc** ........ E ...... 201 438-0723
1351 N Crystal Ave Fresno (93728) ***(P-642)***

**Frazee Industries Inc** ........ A ...... 858 626-3600
6625 Miramar Rd San Diego (92121) ***(P-6085)***

**Frazee Paint & Wallcovering, San Diego** *Also Called: Frazee Industries Inc* ***(P-6085)***

**Frazier Aviation Inc** ........ E ...... 818 898-1998
445 N Fox St San Fernando (91340) ***(P-13846)***

**Frc, Sacramento** *Also Called: Farmers Rice Cooperative* ***(P-1075)***

**Freal, Emeryville** *Also Called: FReal Foods LLC* ***(P-759)***

**FReal Foods LLC** ........ D ...... 800 483-3218
2100 Powell St Ste 700 Emeryville (94608) ***(P-759)***

**Fred Matter Inc** ........ E ...... 925 371-1234
7801 Las Positas Rd Livermore (94551) ***(P-10844)***

**Fred R Rippy Inc** ........ E ...... 562 698-9801
12450 Whittier Blvd Whittier (90602) ***(P-8844)***

**Frederick Pump Company, Valley Center** *Also Called: Brax Company Inc* ***(P-526)***

**Fredericks.com, Los Angeles** *Also Called: Foh Group Inc* ***(P-2837)***

**Freds Foods Inc** ........ F ...... 707 639-9438
2300 S Watney Way Ste J Fairfield (94533) ***(P-1275)***

**Free Hot Water, San Jose** *Also Called: Gemtech Sales Corp* ***(P-8067)***

**Freeagent Network Inc** ........ E ...... 650 880-3240
307 Orchard City Dr Campbell (95008) ***(P-18331)***

**Freeberg Indus Fbrication Corp** ........ D ...... 760 737-7614
2874 Progress Pl Escondido (92029) ***(P-8143)***

**Freeberg Industrial, Escondido** *Also Called: Freeberg Indus Fbrication Corp* ***(P-8143)***

**Freedom Communications Inc** ........ A ...... 714 796-7000
625 N Grand Ave Santa Ana (92701) ***(P-4115)***

**Freedom Designs Inc** ........ C ...... 805 582-0077
2241 N Madera Rd Simi Valley (93065) ***(P-15349)***

**Freedom Newspapers, Santa Ana** *Also Called: Freedom Communications Inc* ***(P-4115)***

**Freedom of Press Foundation** ........ F ...... 510 995-0780
601 Van Ness Ave Ste E731 San Francisco (94102) ***(P-4259)***

**Freedom Photonics LLC** ........ E ...... 805 967-4900
41 Aero Camino Santa Barbara (93117) ***(P-13241)***

**Freedom Prfmce Exhaust Inc** ........ E ...... 951 898-4733
1255 Railroad St Corona (92882) ***(P-17451)***

**Freenome Inc** ........ A ...... 650 446-6630
279 E Grand Ave South San Francisco (94080) ***(P-5751)***

**Freeport Bakery Inc** ........ E ...... 916 442-4256
2966 Freeport Blvd Sacramento (95818) ***(P-1202)***

**Freeport-Mcmoran Oil & Gas LLC** .................................................. E ...... 805 567-1601
  760 W Hueneme Rd Oxnard (93033) *(P-182)*
**Freeport-Mcmoran Oil & Gas LLC** .................................................. E ...... 661 768-4831
  3252 W Crocker Springs Rd Fellows (93224) *(P-183)*
**Freeport-Mcmoran Oil & Gas LLC** .................................................. C ...... 661 322-7600
  1200 Discovery Dr Ste 500 Bakersfield (93309) *(P-184)*
**Freeport-Mcmoran Oil & Gas LLC** .................................................. F ...... 805 567-1667
  17100 Calle Mariposa Reina Goleta (93117) *(P-185)*
**Freeport-Mcmoran Oil & Gas LLC** .................................................. C ...... 323 298-2200
  5640 S Fairfax Ave Los Angeles (90056) *(P-186)*
**Freestyle Cinemas Rentals, Los Angeles** *Also Called: Freestyle Filmworks LLC (P-15640)*
**Freestyle Filmworks LLC** ............................................................... F ...... 818 660-2888
  1518 Talmadge St Los Angeles (90027) *(P-15640)*
**Freetech Plastics Inc** ..................................................................... E ...... 510 651-9996
  2211 Warm Springs Ct Fremont (94539) *(P-6832)*
**Freewire Technologies Inc (PA)** ..................................................... E ...... 415 779-5515
  7200 Gateway Blvd Newark (94560) *(P-11268)*
**Freightgate Inc** .............................................................................. E ...... 714 799-2833
  10055 Slater Ave Ste 231 Fountain Valley (92708) *(P-18332)*
**Freixenet Sonoma Caves Inc** ........................................................ E ...... 707 996-4981
  23555 Arnold Dr Sonoma (95476) *(P-1579)*
**Fremarc Designs, City Of Industry** *Also Called: Fremarc Industries Inc (P-3441)*
**Fremarc Industries Inc (PA)** .......................................................... D ...... 626 965-0802
  18810 San Jose Ave City Of Industry (91748) *(P-3441)*
**Fremont Office, Irvine** *Also Called: Western Digital Corporation (P-10296)*
**Fremont Package Express** ............................................................ F ...... 916 541-1812
  734 Still Breeze Way Sacramento (95831) *(P-9518)*
**French Tradition Inc (PA)** .............................................................. F ...... 310 719-9977
  2413 Moreton St Torrance (90505) *(P-3442)*
**Freschi Air Systems Inc** ................................................................ D ...... 925 827-9761
  715 Fulton Shipyard Rd Antioch (94509) *(P-419)*
**Freschi Service Experts, Antioch** *Also Called: Freschi Air Systems Inc (P-419)*
**Fresenius Med Care Hldngs Inc** .................................................... F ...... 888 373-1470
  4040 Nelson Ave Concord (94520) *(P-15091)*
**Fresh & Ready, San Fernando** *Also Called: Lehman Foods Inc (P-2263)*
**Fresh & Ready Foods LLC (PA)** .................................................... D ...... 818 837-7600
  1145 Arroyo St Ste B San Fernando (91340) *(P-2205)*
**Fresh Express, Salinas** *Also Called: Fresh Express Inc (P-2206)*
**Fresh Express Inc** ......................................................................... D ...... 831 770-7600
  900 E Blanco Rd Salinas (93901) *(P-2206)*
**Fresh Griller, Costa Mesa** *Also Called: Fgr 1 LLC (P-17579)*
**Fresh Packing Corporation** ........................................................... E ...... 213 612-0136
  4333 S Maywood Ave Vernon (90058) *(P-856)*
**Fresh Start Bakeries, Stockton** *Also Called: Aspire Bakeries LLC (P-1158)*
**Fresh Start Bakeries Inc** ............................................................... A ...... 714 256-8900
  145 S State College Blvd Ste 200 Brea (92821) *(P-1203)*
**Fresh Start Bakeries N Amer, Brea** *Also Called: Fresh Start Bakeries Inc (P-1203)*
**Fresh Venture Foods LLC** ............................................................. C ...... 805 928-3374
  1205 Craig Dr Santa Maria (93458) *(P-9792)*
**Freshrealm Inc (PA)** ...................................................................... C ...... 800 264-1297
  1330 Calle Avanzado San Clemente (92673) *(P-2207)*
**Freshrealm Inc** .............................................................................. B ...... 888 278-4349
  3151 Regatta Ave Pmb B60 Richmond (94804) *(P-2208)*
**Freshrealm Inc** .............................................................................. B ...... 800 264-1297
  2900 N Macarthur Dr Unit 300 Tracy (95376) *(P-2209)*
**Freshsource North Inc** .................................................................. F ...... 805 878-6567
  16478 Beach Blvd # 391 Westminster (92683) *(P-888)*
**FRESHWORKS, San Mateo** *Also Called: Freshworks Inc (P-18333)*
**Freshworks Inc (PA)** ..................................................................... E ...... 650 513-0514
  2950 S Delaware St Ste 201 San Mateo (94403) *(P-18333)*
**FRESNO "D", Fresno** *Also Called: Fresno Distributing Co (P-11660)*
**Fresno Business Journal, Fresno** *Also Called: Business Journal (P-4234)*
**Fresno Distributing Co** .................................................................. E ...... 559 442-8800
  2055 E Mckinley Ave Fresno (93703) *(P-11660)*
**Fresno Fab-Tech Inc** ..................................................................... E ...... 559 875-9800
  1035 K St Sanger (93657) *(P-8144)*
**Fresno French Bread Bakery Inc** .................................................. E ...... 559 268-7088
  2625 Inyo St Fresno (93721) *(P-1204)*
**Fresno Glass Plant, Fresno** *Also Called: Vitro Flat Glass LLC (P-7180)*
**Fresno Meat Company, Fresno** *Also Called: Beef Packers Inc (P-582)*

**Fresno Oxgn Wldg Suppliers Inc (PA)** ............................................ E ...... 559 233-6684
  2825 S Elm Ave Ste 101 Fresno (93706) *(P-16815)*
**Fresno Paper Express, Fresno** *Also Called: Paper Pulp & Film (P-4045)*
**Fresno Precision Plastics Inc** ........................................................ D ...... 916 689-5284
  8456 Carbide Ct Sacramento (95828) *(P-6833)*
**Fresno Rack & Shelving Inc** ......................................................... E ...... 559 275-7225
  711 N Armstrong Ave Ste 107 Fresno (93727) *(P-3688)*
**Fresno Shower Door and Mirror, Fresno** *Also Called: B-F Glass Inc (P-554)*
**Fresno Valves & Castings Inc (PA)** ............................................... C ...... 559 834-2511
  7736 E Springfield Ave Selma (93662) *(P-16369)*
**Freudenberg Medical LLC** ............................................................ C ...... 626 814-9684
  5050 Rivergrade Rd Baldwin Park (91706) *(P-15092)*
**Freudenberg Medical LLC** ............................................................ D ...... 805 576-5308
  6385 Rose Ln Ste A Carpinteria (93013) *(P-15350)*
**Freudenberg Medical LLC** ............................................................ E ...... 805 684-3304
  1009 Cindy Ln Carpinteria (93013) *(P-15351)*
**Freudenberg Medical LLC (DH)** .................................................... C ...... 805 684-3304
  1110 Mark Ave Carpinteria (93013) *(P-15352)*
**Freudenberg-Nok General Partnr** ................................................. C ...... 714 834-0602
  2041 E Wilshire Ave Santa Ana (92705) *(P-6446)*
**Freund Baking Co, Hayward** *Also Called: Oakhurst Industries Inc (P-17117)*
**Fricke-Parks Press Inc** .................................................................. E ...... 510 489-6543
  33250 Transit Ave Union City (94587) *(P-4617)*
**Friday Flier, Canyon Lake** *Also Called: Golding Publications (P-5020)*
**Fringe Studio LLC** ......................................................................... E ...... 310 390-9900
  6029 W Slauson Ave Culver City (90230) *(P-3769)*
**Frisco Baking Company, Los Angeles** *Also Called: Frisco Baking Company Inc (P-1205)*
**Frisco Baking Company Inc** ......................................................... C ...... 323 225-6111
  621 W Avenue 26 Los Angeles (90065) *(P-1205)*
**Frito-Lay, Manteca** *Also Called: Frito-Lay North America Inc (P-2091)*
**Frito-Lay, Bloomington** *Also Called: Frito-Lay North America Inc (P-2092)*
**Frito-Lay, Modesto** *Also Called: Frito-Lay North America Inc (P-2093)*
**Frito-Lay, Torrance** *Also Called: Frito-Lay North America Inc (P-17144)*
**Frito-Lay, Rancho Cucamonga** *Also Called: Frito-Lay North America Inc (P-17145)*
**Frito-Lay North America Inc** ......................................................... F ...... 209 824-3700
  1190 Spreckels Rd Manteca (95336) *(P-2091)*
**Frito-Lay North America Inc** ......................................................... F ...... 909 877-0902
  635 W Valley Blvd Bloomington (92316) *(P-2092)*
**Frito-Lay North America Inc** ......................................................... B ...... 209 544-5400
  600 Garner Rd Modesto (95357) *(P-2093)*
**Frito-Lay North America Inc** ......................................................... F ...... 310 224-5600
  1500 Francisco St Torrance (90501) *(P-17144)*
**Frito-Lay North America Inc** ......................................................... E ...... 909 941-6218
  9846 4th St Rancho Cucamonga (91730) *(P-17145)*
**Frogs Leap Winery** ........................................................................ E ...... 707 963-4704
  8815 Conn Creek Rd Rutherford (94573) *(P-1580)*
**Front, San Francisco** *Also Called: Frontapp Inc (P-18334)*
**Frontage Laboratories Inc** ............................................................. F ...... 510 626-9993
  3825 Bay Center Pl Hayward (94545) *(P-5447)*
**Frontapp Inc (PA)** .......................................................................... D ...... 415 680-3048
  300 Montgomery St Ste 500 San Francisco (94104) *(P-18334)*
**Frontegg Inc** .................................................................................. F ...... 408 734-6573
  2570 W El Camino Real Ste 440 Mountain View (94040) *(P-18335)*
**Frontgrade Technologies LLC** ....................................................... D ...... 714 870-2420
  577 Burning Tree Rd Fullerton (92833) *(P-14188)*
**Frontier Electronics Corp** ............................................................... F ...... 805 522-9998
  667 Cochran St Simi Valley (93065) *(P-12840)*
**Frontier Engrg & Mfg Tech Inc (PA)** .............................................. E ...... 310 767-1227
  800 W 16th St Long Beach (90813) *(P-10845)*
**Frontier Medicines Corporation (PA)** ............................................ E ...... 650 457-1005
  151 Oyster Point Blvd Fl 2 South San Francisco (94080) *(P-5448)*
**Frontier Semiconductor (PA)** ........................................................ E ...... 408 432-8338
  165 Topaz St Milpitas (95035) *(P-12439)*
**Frontier Technologies, Long Beach** *Also Called: Frontier Engrg & Mfg Tech Inc (P-10845)*
**Frozen Bakery, Lodi** *Also Called: Cottage Bakery Inc (P-1178)*
**Frozen Bean Inc** ............................................................................ E ...... 855 837-6936
  9238 Bally Ct Rancho Cucamonga (91730) *(P-2007)*
**Frsport.com, Huntington Beach** *Also Called: Sound Investment Group (P-16401)*
**Fruit Growers Supply Company (PA)** ........................................... E ...... 888 997-4855
  27770 Entertainment Dr Ste 120 Valencia (91355) *(P-3843)*

**Fruit Growers Supply Company**

**ALPHABETIC SECTION**

**Fruit Growers Supply Company** ............................................... F ...... 559 592-6550
674 E Myer Ave Exeter (93221) *(P-3844)*

**Fruitridge Prtg Lithograph Inc (PA)** ......................................... E ...... 916 452-9213
3258 Stockton Blvd Sacramento (95820) *(P-4618)*

**Fruth Custom Plastics Inc** ...................................................... D ...... 714 993-9955
701 Richfield Rd Placentia (92870) *(P-6834)*

**Frutstix Company, San Diego** *Also Called: Von Hoppen Ice Cream (P-818)*

**Fry Reglet Corporation (PA)** .................................................... D ...... 800 237-9773
14013 Marquardt Ave Santa Fe Springs (90670) *(P-7738)*

**Fryes Printing Inc** ................................................................... E ...... 707 253-1114
1050 Lincoln Ave Napa (94558) *(P-17812)*

**Fs - Precision Tech Co LLC** ................................................... D ...... 310 638-0595
3025 E Victoria St Compton (90221) *(P-7864)*

**Fsc, Rancho Cucamonga** *Also Called: Fluorescent Supply Co Inc (P-11534)*

**FSI Coating Technologies Inc** ................................................. E ...... 949 540-1140
45 Parker Ste 100 Irvine (92618) *(P-6086)*

**Fsm, Milpitas** *Also Called: Frontier Semiconductor (P-12439)*

**Fssi, Santa Ana** *Also Called: Financial Statement Svcs Inc (P-17797)*

**Fst Design Build Concrete, San Jose** *Also Called: Floor Seal Technology Inc (P-504)*

**Ft 2 Inc** ................................................................................. C ...... 714 765-5555
1211 N Miller St Anaheim (92806) *(P-16976)*

**Ft Textiles, Fullerton** *Also Called: Fabtex Inc (P-2437)*

**Ft3 Tactical, Stanton** *Also Called: Field Time Target Training LLC (P-9134)*

**Ftg Aerospace Inc (DH)** ......................................................... E ...... 818 407-4024
20740 Marilla St Chatsworth (91311) *(P-7829)*

**Ftg Circuits Inc (DH)** ............................................................. D ...... 818 407-4024
20750 Marilla St Chatsworth (91311) *(P-12118)*

**Ftr Associates Inc** .................................................................. E ...... 562 945-7504
11862 Burke St Santa Fe Springs (90670) *(P-8845)*

**Fuel Total Systems California Corporation** ............................. E
18231 Murphy Pkwy Lathrop (95330) *(P-6495)*

**Fuji Food Products Inc (PA)** ................................................... D ...... 562 404-2590
14420 Bloomfield Ave Santa Fe Springs (90670) *(P-2210)*

**Fuji Food Products Inc** ........................................................... C ...... 619 268-3118
8660 Miramar Rd Ste N San Diego (92126) *(P-2211)*

**Fuji Natural Foods Inc (HQ)** ................................................... D ...... 909 947-1008
13500 S Hamner Ave Ontario (91761) *(P-2212)*

**Fuji Xerox, Palo Alto** *Also Called: Xerox International Partners (P-9777)*

**Fujifilm Dimatix Inc (DH)** ....................................................... D ...... 408 565-9150
2250 Martin Ave Santa Clara (95050) *(P-10371)*

**Fujifilm Dsynth Btchnlgies Cal** ................................................ E ...... 914 789-8100
2430 Conejo Spectrum St Thousand Oaks (91320) *(P-5830)*

**Fujifilm Dsynth Btchnlgies USA** .............................................. C ...... 805 699-5579
2430 Conejo Spectrum St Thousand Oaks (91320) *(P-5831)*

**Fujifilm Irvine Scientific Inc (DH)** ............................................ E ...... 949 261-7800
1830 E Warner Ave Santa Ana (92705) *(P-5832)*

**Fujifilm Rcrding Media USA Inc** .............................................. D ...... 310 536-0800
6200 Phyllis Dr Cypress (90630) *(P-15641)*

**Fujifilm Ultra Pure Sltons Inc (DH)** .......................................... E ...... 831 632-2120
11225 Commercial Pkwy Castroville (95012) *(P-6286)*

**Fujikura Composite America Inc** ............................................. E ...... 760 598-6060
1819 Aston Ave Ste 101 Carlsbad (92008) *(P-15814)*

**Fujikuria Composits, Carlsbad** *Also Called: Fujikura Composite America Inc (P-15814)*

**Fujisoft America Inc** ............................................................... E ...... 650 235-9422
1710 S Amphlett Blvd Ste 215 San Mateo (94402) *(P-18336)*

**Fujitsu Management Services of America Inc** ........................ C ...... 408 746-6000
1250 E Arques Ave Sunnyvale (94085) *(P-10372)*

**Fujitsu Software, Sunnyvale** *Also Called: Fujitsu Management Services of America Inc (P-10372)*

**Fulcrum Microsystems Inc** ..................................................... D ...... 818 871-8100
26630 Agoura Rd Calabasas (91302) *(P-12440)*

**Fulghum Fibres, Los Angeles** *Also Called: Fulghum Fibres Inc (P-3069)*

**Fulghum Fibres Inc (HQ)** ....................................................... F ...... 706 651-1000
333 S Grand Ave Ste 4100 Los Angeles (90071) *(P-3069)*

**Fulham Co Inc** ....................................................................... E ...... 323 779-2980
12705 S Van Ness Ave Hawthorne (90250) *(P-11213)*

**Full Circle Brewing Co Ltd LLC** .............................................. F ...... 559 264-6323
620 F St Fresno (93704) *(P-1432)*

**Full-Swing Golf Inc** ................................................................ E ...... 858 675-1100
1905 Aston Ave Ste 100 Carlsbad (92008) *(P-16935)*

**Full/Tech Systems Inc** ............................................................ E ...... 619 297-0454
5525 Market St San Diego (92114) *(P-17798)*

**Fullbloom Baking Company Inc** .............................................. D ...... 510 456-3638
6500 Overlake Pl Newark (94560) *(P-1206)*

**Fullcontact Inc** ....................................................................... E ...... 415 366-6587
535 Mission St Fl 14 San Francisco (94105) *(P-17925)*

**Fullfeel, Pleasanton** *Also Called: Zoomifier Corporation (P-18956)*

**Fullfillment Systems Inc** ......................................................... E ...... 408 745-7675
1228 Reamwood Ave Sunnyvale (94089) *(P-643)*

**Fullfillment Systems Inc (PA)** ................................................. D ...... 408 745-7675
1228 Reamwood Ave Sunnyvale (94089) *(P-644)*

**Fun Flex, Big Bear Lake** *Also Called: Big Bear Bowling Barn Inc (P-555)*

**Fun Furnishings, La Verne** *Also Called: G & M Mattress and Foam Corporation (P-3526)*

**Fun Properties Inc** .................................................................. D ...... 310 787-4500
2645 Maricopa St Torrance (90503) *(P-7953)*

**Fun-GI, El Segundo** *Also Called: Fun-GI Games LLC (P-15749)*

**Fun-GI Games LLC** ............................................................... F ...... 213 254-5489
880 Apollo St Ste 229 El Segundo (90245) *(P-15749)*

**Funai Corporation Inc (DH)** .................................................... E ...... 310 787-3000
12489 Lakeland Rd Santa Fe Springs (90670) *(P-11661)*

**Funai Corporation Inc** ............................................................ D ...... 201 727-4560
19900 Van Ness Ave Torrance (90501) *(P-11662)*

**Funai Electric Co., Torrance** *Also Called: Funai Corporation Inc (P-11662)*

**Fundamental Tech Intl Inc** ...................................................... E ...... 562 595-0661
2900 E 29th St Long Beach (90806) *(P-14415)*

**Fundex Investment Group, San Francisco** *Also Called: Fundx Investment Group LLC (P-4400)*

**Fundx Investment Group LLC** ................................................ F ...... 415 986-7979
101 Montgomery St Ste 2400 San Francisco (94104) *(P-4400)*

**Fungs Village Inc** ................................................................... E ...... 323 881-1600
5339 E Washington Blvd Commerce (90040) *(P-2113)*

**Funway Snack Foods, Signal Hill** *Also Called: Jnr Confection Specialty Corp (P-1315)*

**Fur Accents LLC** .................................................................... F ...... 714 403-5286
349 W Grove Ave Orange (92865) *(P-2870)*

**Furman, Petaluma** *Also Called: Core Brands LLC (P-11207)*

**Furnace Super Heros Inc** ....................................................... F ...... 714 238-9009
920 S Placentia Ave Ste A Placentia (92870) *(P-10051)*

**Furniture America Cal Inc (PA)** .............................................. E ...... 866 923-8500
680 S Lemon Ave City Of Industry (91789) *(P-16414)*

**Furniture of America, City Of Industry** *Also Called: Furniture America Cal Inc (P-16414)*

**Furniture Solutions Inc** ........................................................... E ...... 714 666-0424
1347 N Blue Gum St Anaheim (92806) *(P-3568)*

**Furniture Technics Inc** ........................................................... E ...... 562 802-0261
2900 Supply Ave Commerce (90040) *(P-3443)*

**Furniture Techniques, Commerce** *Also Called: Furniture Technics Inc (P-3443)*

**Furniture Technologies Inc** .................................................... E ...... 760 246-9180
17227 Columbus St Adelanto (92301) *(P-3092)*

**Furst, Marina Del Rey** *Also Called: Lf Sportswear Inc (P-2679)*

**Fury Hot Chicken LLC** ........................................................... F ...... 559 944-8061
3035 E Malaga Ave Fresno (93725) *(P-3742)*

**Fusion Biotec LLC** ................................................................. E ...... 949 264-3437
160 S Cypress St Ste 400 Orange (92866) *(P-15093)*

**Fusion Coatings Inc** ............................................................... F ...... 925 443-8083
6589 Las Positas Rd Livermore (94551) *(P-9071)*

**Fusion Finish LLC** ................................................................. F ...... 562 619-1189
2527 Ximeno Ave Long Beach (90815) *(P-9072)*

**Fusion Food Factory** ............................................................. E ...... 858 578-8001
8980 Crestmar Pt San Diego (92121) *(P-1207)*

**Fusion Product Mfg Inc** ......................................................... D ...... 619 819-5521
24024 Humphries Rd Bldg 1 Tecate (91980) *(P-9624)*

**Fusion Sign & Design Inc** ..................................................... E ...... 562 946-7545
12226 Coast Dr Whittier (90601) *(P-15980)*

**Fusion Sign & Design Inc (PA)** .............................................. F ...... 877 477-8777
680 Columbia Ave Riverside (92507) *(P-15981)*

**Futek Advanced Sensor Tech, Irvine** *Also Called: Futek Advanced Sensor Tech Inc (P-14416)*

**Futek Advanced Sensor Tech Inc** ........................................... C ...... 949 465-0900
10 Thomas Irvine (92618) *(P-14416)*

**Futur LLC** .............................................................................. E ...... 310 314-1618
1702 Olympic Blvd Santa Monica (90404) *(P-18337)*

**Futurama, San Mateo** *Also Called: Bears For Humanity Inc (P-6134)*

## ALPHABETIC SECTION — Gallagher & Burk

**Future Commodities Intl Inc** ............................................. E ...... 888 588-2378
1425 S Campus Ave Ontario (91761) *(P-10018)*

**Future Foam, Fullerton** *Also Called: Future Foam Inc (P-6641)*

**Future Foam Inc** ............................................................... C ...... 714 459-9971
2441 Cypress Way Fullerton (92831) *(P-6641)*

**Future Foam Inc** ............................................................... F ...... 209 832-1886
1050 E Grant Line Rd Ste 100 Tracy (95304) *(P-6642)*

**Future Foam Inc** ............................................................... E ...... 714 871-2344
2451 Cypress Way Fullerton (92831) *(P-6643)*

**Future Innovations Inc** ..................................................... E ...... 925 485-2000
4301 Hacienda Dr Pleasanton (94588) *(P-19092)*

**Future Motion Inc** ............................................................ D ...... 650 814-8643
1201 Shaffer Rd Ste A Santa Cruz (95060) *(P-15815)*

**Future Tech Metals Inc** ................................................... E ...... 951 781-4801
719 Palmyrita Ave Riverside (92507) *(P-10846)*

**Futurestitch Inc** ............................................................... F ...... 760 707-2003
144 Avenida Serra San Clemente (92672) *(P-2471)*

**Futuristics Machine Inc** .................................................. E ...... 858 450-0644
7014 Carroll Rd San Diego (92121) *(P-10847)*

**Fuzebox, San Francisco** *Also Called: Fuzebox Software Corporation (P-18338)*

**Fuzebox Software Corporation (DH)** .............................. E ...... 415 692-4800
150 Spear St Ste 900 San Francisco (94105) *(P-18338)*

**Fvo Solutions Inc** ............................................................ D ...... 626 449-0218
789 N Fair Oaks Ave Pasadena (91103) *(P-9073)*

**Fxc Corporation** ............................................................. D ...... 714 557-8032
3050 Red Hill Ave Costa Mesa (92626) *(P-3029)*

**Fxc Corporation (PA)** ..................................................... E ...... 714 556-7400
3050 Red Hill Ave Costa Mesa (92626) *(P-7997)*

**Fxp Technologies, Brea** *Also Called: S&B Industry Inc (P-7017)*

**Fziomed Inc (PA)** ............................................................ E ...... 805 546-0610
231 Bonetti Dr San Luis Obispo (93401) *(P-15094)*

**G - L Veneer Co Inc (PA)** ............................................... D ...... 323 582-5203
2224 E Slauson Ave Huntington Park (90255) *(P-3284)*

**G & G Door Products Inc** ............................................... E ...... 714 228-2008
7600 Stage Rd Buena Park (90621) *(P-17331)*

**G & G Foods, Santa Rosa** *Also Called: G&G Specialty Foods Inc (P-715)*

**G & G Quality Case Co Inc** ............................................ D ...... 323 233-2482
2025 E 25th St Vernon (90058) *(P-7130)*

**G & I Industries, Baldwin Park** *Also Called: G & I Islas Industries Inc (P-9793)*

**G & I Islas Industries Inc (PA)** ........................................ E ...... 626 960-5020
12860 Schabarum Ave Baldwin Park (91706) *(P-9793)*

**G & L Musical Instruments, Fullerton** *Also Called: Bbe Sound Inc (P-15712)*

**G & M Mattress and Foam Corporation** ......................... D ...... 909 593-1000
1943 N White Ave La Verne (91750) *(P-3526)*

**G A Systems, Orange** *Also Called: SA Serving Lines Inc (P-8563)*

**G A Systems Inc** ............................................................. F ...... 714 848-7529
226 W Carleton Ave Orange (92867) *(P-10561)*

**G and H Vineyards, Rutherford** *Also Called: Grgich Hills Cellar (P-1602)*

**G B Remanufacturing Inc** ............................................... D ...... 562 272-7333
2040 E Cherry Industrial Cir Long Beach (90805) *(P-6835)*

**G C Pallets Inc** ................................................................ E ...... 909 357-8515
5490 26th St Riverside (92509) *(P-3342)*

**G C S, Torrance** *Also Called: Global Comm Semiconductors LLC (P-12447)*

**G D M Electronic Assembly Inc** ..................................... D ...... 408 945-4100
740 S Milpitas Blvd Milpitas (95035) *(P-11455)*

**G Debbas Chocolatier Inc** .............................................. E ...... 559 294-2071
5877 E Brown Ave Fresno (93727) *(P-1339)*

**G E Aviation, Victorville** *Also Called: General Electric Company (P-13665)*

**G F Cole Corporation (PA)** ............................................. F ...... 310 320-0601
21735 S Western Ave Torrance (90501) *(P-6447)*

**G F I, Vernon** *Also Called: Good Fellas Industries Inc (P-17534)*

**G Girl Clothing, Vernon** *Also Called: LAT LLC (P-2785)*

**G Hartley Inc** ................................................................... E ...... 707 523-3513
3224 Dutton Ave Santa Rosa (95407) *(P-368)*

**G Kagan and Sons Inc (PA)** ........................................... E ...... 323 583-1400
3957 S Hill St Los Angeles (90037) *(P-2416)*

**G L Mezzetta Inc** ............................................................ D ...... 707 648-1050
2200 Larkspur Landing Cir Larkspur (94939) *(P-889)*

**G L Mezzetta Inc (PA)** .................................................... C ...... 707 648-1050
105 Mezzetta Ct American Canyon (94503) *(P-890)*

**G M I, Anaheim** *Also Called: Gear Manufacturing Inc (P-13847)*

**G M Quartz, Oakland** *Also Called: GM Associates Inc (P-12987)*

**G M S, Carlsbad** *Also Called: Global Microwave Systems Inc (P-11858)*

**G P Manufacturing Inc** ................................................... F ...... 714 974-0288
541 W Briardale Ave Orange (92865) *(P-10848)*

**G R C, Chatsworth** *Also Called: General Ribbon Corp (P-15896)*

**G R Leonard & Co Inc** .................................................... E ...... 847 797-8101
181 N Vermont Ave Glendora (91741) *(P-4401)*

**G S I, Alameda** *Also Called: Golden State Imports Intl Inc (P-16967)*

**G T C, Whittier** *Also Called: General Transistor Corporation (P-16703)*

**G T Water Products Inc** .................................................. F ...... 805 529-2900
5239 N Commerce Ave Moorpark (93021) *(P-8053)*

**G V Industries Inc** ........................................................... E ...... 619 474-3013
1346 Cleveland Ave National City (91950) *(P-10849)*

**G-2 Graphic Service Inc** ................................................. D ...... 818 623-3100
5510 Cleon Ave North Hollywood (91601) *(P-4881)*

**G-G Distribution & Dev Co Inc** ....................................... C ...... 661 257-5700
28545 Livingston Ave Valencia (91355) *(P-9186)*

**G-M Enterprises, Corona** *Also Called: Jhawar Industries LLC (P-10055)*

**G.I.M.S., San Francisco** *Also Called: Galindo Instlltion Mvg Svcs In (P-3689)*

**G/G Industries, Valencia** *Also Called: G-G Distribution & Dev Co Inc (P-9186)*

**G&G Specialty Foods Inc** ............................................... C
322 Bellevue Ave Santa Rosa (95407) *(P-715)*

**G2 Microsystems Inc** ..................................................... E ...... 408 879-2614
1999 S Baston Ave Campbell (95008) *(P-12119)*

**G3 Enterprises Inc** ......................................................... E ...... 209 341-5265
2612 Crows Landing Rd Modesto (95358) *(P-17828)*

**G3 Virtus Solutions Inc** .................................................. E ...... 323 724-6771
12850 Florence Ave Santa Fe Springs (90670) *(P-11269)*

**G4s Government Services, Anaheim** *Also Called: G4s Justice Services LLC (P-19056)*

**G4s Justice Services LLC** ............................................. E ...... 800 589-6003
1290 N Hancock St Ste 103 Anaheim (92807) *(P-19056)*

**Ga-Asi, Poway** *Also Called: General Atmics Arntcal Systems (P-13660)*

**Gabriel Container (PA)** ................................................... C ...... 562 699-1051
8844 Millergrove Dr Santa Fe Springs (90670) *(P-3845)*

**Gaffoglio Fmly Mtlcrafters Inc (PA)** ................................ C ...... 714 444-2000
11161 Slater Ave Fountain Valley (92708) *(P-7222)*

**Gaikai Inc** ........................................................................ D
65 Enterprise Aliso Viejo (92656) *(P-18339)*

**Gail Materials Inc** ........................................................... E ...... 951 667-6106
10060 Dawson Canyon Rd Corona (92883) *(P-312)*

**Gaines Manufacturing Inc** ............................................. E ...... 858 486-7100
12200 Kirkham Rd Poway (92064) *(P-8455)*

**Gainey Vineyard** ............................................................. E ...... 805 688-0558
3950 E Highway 246 Santa Ynez (93460) *(P-1581)*

**Gainspan Corp** ............................................................... E ...... 408 627-6500
125 S Market St Ste 400 San Jose (95113) *(P-12441)*

**Galactic Co LLC (DH)** .................................................... E ...... 661 824-6600
1700 Flight Way Ste 400 Tustin (92782) *(P-14080)*

**Galassos Bakery (PA)** .................................................... C ...... 951 360-1211
10820 San Sevaine Way Mira Loma (91752) *(P-1208)*

**Galaxy Bearing Company, Valencia** *Also Called: Galaxy Die and Engineering Inc (P-7853)*

**Galaxy Brazing Co Inc** ................................................... F ...... 562 946-9039
10015 Freeman Ave Santa Fe Springs (90670) *(P-19194)*

**Galaxy Desserts** ............................................................. C ...... 510 439-3160
1100 Marina Way S Ste D Richmond (94804) *(P-1209)*

**Galaxy Die and Engineering Inc** .................................... E ...... 661 775-9301
24910 Avenue Tibbitts Valencia (91355) *(P-7853)*

**Galaxy Medical Inc** ......................................................... E ...... 510 847-5189
3200 Bridge Pkwy Ste 100 Redwood City (94065) *(P-15095)*

**Gale Banks Engineering** ................................................. C ...... 626 969-9600
546 S Duggan Ave Azusa (91702) *(P-9328)*

**Galgon Industries Inc** ..................................................... E ...... 510 792-8211
37399 Centralmont Pl Fremont (94536) *(P-8723)*

**Galil, Rocklin** *Also Called: Galil Motion Control Inc (P-14417)*

**Galil Motion Control Inc** ................................................. E ...... 800 377-6329
270 Technology Way Rocklin (95765) *(P-14417)*

**Galindo Instlltion Mvg Svcs In** ........................................ F ...... 415 861-4230
2901 Mariposa St Ste 3 San Francisco (94110) *(P-3689)*

**Gallagher & Burk, Dublin** *Also Called: Oliver De Silva Inc (P-303)*

## ALPHABETIC SECTION

Gallagher Properties Inc (PA) ............................................. E ...... 510 261-0466
344 High St Oakland (94601) *(P-544)*

Gallagher Rental Inc ............................................. E ...... 714 690-1559
15701 Heron Ave La Mirada (90638) *(P-11598)*

Galleher, Santa Fe Springs *Also Called: Galleher LLC (P-16425)*

Galleher LLC (PA) ............................................. C ...... 562 944-8885
9303 Greenleaf Ave Santa Fe Springs (90670) *(P-16425)*

Galley Solutions Inc ............................................. F ...... 818 636-1538
712 Archer St San Diego (92109) *(P-18340)*

Gallien Technology Inc (PA) ............................................. D ...... 209 234-7300
2234 Industrial Dr Stockton (95206) *(P-11663)*

Galliien Krueger, Stockton *Also Called: Gallien Technology Inc (P-11663)*

Gallo Glass Company (HQ) ............................................. A ...... 209 341-3710
605 S Santa Cruz Ave Modesto (95354) *(P-7182)*

Gallo Os Sonoma, Healdsburg *Also Called: E & J Gallo Winery (P-1548)*

Gallo Sales Company Inc (DH) ............................................. C ...... 510 476-5000
30825 Wiegman Rd Hayward (94544) *(P-1582)*

Gallo Vineyards Inc ............................................. C ...... 209 394-6281
5595 Creston Rd Paso Robles (93446) *(P-1583)*

Galt, San Diego *Also Called: Global A Lgistics Training Inc (P-14194)*

Galt Herald, Galt *Also Called: Herburger Publications Inc (P-4128)*

Galt Steel Foundry, Lodi *Also Called: Lodi Iron Works Inc (P-7677)*

Galtech Computer Corporation ............................................. E ...... 805 376-1060
501 Flynn Rd Camarillo (93012) *(P-3569)*

Galtech International, Camarillo *Also Called: Galtech Computer Corporation (P-3569)*

Galvanize Therapeutics Inc (PA) ............................................. F ...... 628 800-1154
3200 Bridge Pkwy Ste 100 Redwood City (94065) *(P-15096)*

Gambol Industries Inc ............................................. E ...... 562 901-2470
1880 Century Park E Ste 950 Los Angeles (90067) *(P-14034)*

Gamco, North Hollywood *Also Called: Bobrick Washroom Equipment Inc (P-3680)*

Gamdan Optics Inc ............................................. F ...... 669 214-2100
1751 Fortune Dr Ste J San Jose (95131) *(P-14777)*

Game Insight Publishing ............................................. E ...... 415 412-5064
211 Gough St Ste 116 San Francisco (94102) *(P-4402)*

Gamebreaker Inc (PA) ............................................. E ...... 818 224-7424
31248 Oak Crest Dr Ste 210 Westlake Village (91361) *(P-15816)*

Gamefam Inc ............................................. F ...... 310 200-6623
777 S Alameda St Fl 2 Los Angeles (90021) *(P-15750)*

Gamemine LLC ............................................. E ...... 310 310-3105
439 Carroll Canal Venice (90291) *(P-18341)*

Gamma, Vernon *Also Called: Rotax Incorporated (P-2805)*

Gamma Aerospace LLC ............................................. E ...... 310 532-4480
1461 S Balboa Ave Ontario (91761) *(P-10850)*

Gamma Scientific Inc ............................................. E ...... 858 635-9008
9925 Carroll Canyon Rd San Diego (92131) *(P-14870)*

Gamus LLC ............................................. E ...... 408 441-0170
3286 Victor St Santa Clara (95054) *(P-17296)*

Ganahl Lumber Company ............................................. D ...... 951 278-4000
150 W Blaine St Corona (92878) *(P-17332)*

Gannett Stllite Info Ntwrk LLC ............................................. F ...... 310 846-5870
6060 Center Dr Los Angeles (90045) *(P-4116)*

Gans Digital, Los Angeles *Also Called: Gans Ink and Supply Co Inc (P-6254)*

Gans Ink and Supply Co Inc (PA) ............................................. E ...... 323 264-2200
1441 Boyd St Los Angeles (90033) *(P-6254)*

Gantner Instruments Inc ............................................. E ...... 888 512-5788
402 W Broadway Ste 400 San Diego (92101) *(P-14871)*

Gar Bennett LLC ............................................. E ...... 559 582-9336
955 S Commerce Way Lemoore (93245) *(P-420)*

Gar Enterprises ............................................. E ...... 909 985-4575
1396 W 9th St Upland (91786) *(P-12982)*

Gar Enterprises (PA) ............................................. D ...... 626 574-1175
418 E Live Oak Ave Arcadia (91006) *(P-16524)*

Gar Laboratories Inc ............................................. C ...... 951 788-0700
1844 Massachusetts Ave Riverside (92507) *(P-5979)*

Garabedian Bros Inc (PA) ............................................. E ...... 559 268-5014
2543 S Orange Ave Fresno (93725) *(P-10851)*

Garage Cabinet Warehouse Inc (PA) ............................................. E ...... 916 638-0123
2700 Mercantile Dr Ste 800 Rancho Cordova (95742) *(P-489)*

Garage Champs, Sacramento *Also Called: Hironaka Promotions LLC (P-4892)*

Garage Doors, Oakley *Also Called: Nor-Cal Overhead Inc (P-17336)*

Garage Doors Incorporated ............................................. F ...... 408 293-7443
147 Martha St San Jose (95112) *(P-3138)*

Garage Equipment Supply Inc ............................................. F ...... 805 530-0027
16000 Ventura Blvd Ste 1000 Encino (91436) *(P-9859)*

Garcia Pallet, Fresno *Also Called: Garcias Pallets Inc (P-3343)*

Garcias Pallets Inc ............................................. E ...... 559 485-8182
4125 S Golden State Blvd Fresno (93725) *(P-3343)*

Gard Inc ............................................. E ...... 714 738-5891
524 E Walnut Ave Fullerton (92832) *(P-8456)*

Garden Grove Unified Schl Dst ............................................. D ...... 714 663-6101
12381 Dale St Garden Grove (92841) *(P-19344)*

Garden Pals Inc ............................................. E ...... 909 605-0200
3632 E Moonlight St Unit 91 Ontario (91761) *(P-7954)*

Gardena Valley News Inc ............................................. E ...... 310 329-6351
15005 S Vermont Ave Gardena (90247) *(P-4117)*

Gardner Family Ltd Partnership ............................................. E ...... 559 675-8149
300 Commerce Dr Madera (93637) *(P-7998)*

Gardner Systems Inc ............................................. F ...... 714 668-9018
17891 Georgetown Ln Huntington Beach (92647) *(P-14337)*

Garlic Company (PA) ............................................. D ...... 661 393-4212
18602 Zerker Rd Shafter (93263) *(P-2)*

Garmin International Inc ............................................. B ...... 909 444-5000
135 S State College Blvd Ste 110 Brea (92821) *(P-14189)*

Garmon Corporation ............................................. F ...... 951 296-6308
43350 Business Park Dr Unit 2 Temecula (92590) *(P-1096)*

Garmon Corporation ............................................. F ...... 951 296-6308
27497 Via Industria Temecula (92590) *(P-1097)*

Garmon Corporation ............................................. F ...... 951 296-6308
27503 Via Industria Unit Q2 Temecula (92590) *(P-1098)*

Garmon Corporation ............................................. F ...... 951 296-6308
41995 Remington Ave Temecula (92590) *(P-1099)*

Garmon Corporation (PA) ............................................. D ...... 888 628-8783
27461 Via Industria Temecula (92590) *(P-1127)*

Garner Holt Productions, Redlands *Also Called: Garner Holt Productions Inc (P-10153)*

Garner Holt Productions Inc ............................................. E ...... 909 799-3030
1255 Research Dr Redlands (92374) *(P-10153)*

Garner Products Inc ............................................. F ...... 916 784-0200
10620 Industrial Ave Ste 100 Roseville (95678) *(P-14190)*

Garnett Sign Studio, Fremont *Also Called: Garnett Signs LLC (P-15982)*

Garnett Signs LLC ............................................. F ...... 650 871-9518
48531 Warm Springs Blvd Ste 412 Fremont (94539) *(P-15982)*

Garratt-Callahan Company (PA) ............................................. D ...... 650 697-5811
50 Ingold Rd Burlingame (94010) *(P-6287)*

Garre Vineyard and Winery Inc ............................................. E ...... 925 371-8200
7986 Tesla Rd Livermore (94550) *(P-1584)*

Garrett Moulding Company Inc ............................................. E ...... 831 426-2020
200 Coral St Santa Cruz (95060) *(P-3417)*

Garrett Precision Inc ............................................. F ...... 949 855-9710
25082 La Suen Rd Laguna Hills (92653) *(P-10852)*

Garrett Transportation I Inc (HQ) ............................................. E ...... 973 455-2000
2525 W 190th St Torrance (90504) *(P-13708)*

Garrison Manufacturing Inc ............................................. E ...... 714 549-4880
3320 S Yale St Santa Ana (92704) *(P-13504)*

Garvey Nut & Candy, Pico Rivera *Also Called: Genesis Foods Corporation (P-1308)*

Gary Bale Redi-Mix Con Inc ............................................. D ...... 949 786-9441
16131 Construction Cir W Irvine (92606) *(P-7447)*

Gary Berke Mscp Prosthetics ............................................. F ...... 650 570-5861
2001 Winward Way San Mateo (94404) *(P-15353)*

Gary Doupnik Manufacturing Inc ............................................. E ...... 916 652-9291
3237 Rippey Rd Loomis (95650) *(P-3395)*

GARY MANUFACTURING, National City *Also Called: Gmi Inc (P-2957)*

Gary Manufacturing Inc ............................................. E ...... 619 429-4479
2626 Southport Way Ste E National City (91950) *(P-6836)*

Gary W Gray ............................................. F ...... 559 750-8462
1721 W Burrel Ave Visalia (93291) *(P-16133)*

Gasket Associates LP (PA) ............................................. F ...... 310 217-5630
10816 Kurt St Sylmar (91342) *(P-6448)*

Gasket Manufacturing Co ............................................. E ...... 310 217-5600
8427 Secura Way Santa Fe Springs (90670) *(P-6449)*

Gasket Manufacturing Engrg Inc ............................................. F ...... 310 217-5600
8427 Secura Way Santa Fe Springs (90670) *(P-8846)*

# ALPHABETIC SECTION — Gemperle Enterprises

Gasket Specialties Inc (PA) .................................................. E ...... 510 547-7955
  1143 Marina Way S Richmond (94804) *(P-6450)*
Gasketfab Division, Lakewood  Also Called: Industrial Gasket and Sup Co *(P-6453)*
Gatan Inc (HQ) ................................................................. E ...... **925 463-0200**
  5794 W Las Positas Blvd Pleasanton (94588) *(P-14668)*
Gatan International Inc ..................................................... E ...... 925 463-0200
  5794a W Las Positas Blvd Pleasanton (94588) *(P-14669)*
Gatc Ghq, Rancho Dominguez  Also Called: Global Agri-Trade *(P-1371)*
Gate Bioscience Inc ........................................................... E ...... 650 241-8057
  2000 Sierra Point Pkwy Ste 200 Brisbane (94005) *(P-5752)*
Gatehouse Media LLC ....................................................... E ...... 707 964-5642
  617 S State St Ukiah (95482) *(P-4118)*
Gatehouse Media LLC ....................................................... E ...... 530 842-5777
  309 S Broadway St Yreka (96097) *(P-4119)*
Gatehouse Media LLC ....................................................... C ...... 530 891-1234
  400 E Park Ave Chico (95928) *(P-4120)*
Gatehouse Media LLC ....................................................... E ...... 760 241-7744
  13891 Park Ave Victorville (92392) *(P-4121)*
Gatekeeper Systems Inc (PA) ............................................. D ...... **888 808-9433**
  90 Icon Foothill Ranch (92610) *(P-13242)*
Gateway, Poway  Also Called: Gateway Inc *(P-10154)*
Gateway, Irvine  Also Called: Gateway Inc *(P-10155)*
Gateway Inc ....................................................................... E ...... 858 451-9933
  12750 Gateway Park Rd # 124 Poway (92064) *(P-10154)*
Gateway Inc (DH) ............................................................... C ...... **949 471-7000**
  7565 Irvine Center Dr Ste 150 Irvine (92618) *(P-10155)*
Gateway Genomics LLC .................................................... D ...... 858 886-7250
  11436 Sorrento Valley Rd San Diego (92121) *(P-5753)*
Gateway Hardware, Inyokern  Also Called: Herbert Rizzardini *(P-17356)*
Gateway Manufacturing LLC ............................................. E ...... 949 471-7000
  7565 Irvine Center Dr Irvine (92618) *(P-10305)*
Gateway Mattress Co Inc .................................................. D ...... 323 725-1923
  624 S Vail Ave Montebello (90640) *(P-3527)*
Gateway Precision Inc ...................................................... E ...... 408 942-8849
  480 Vista Way Milpitas (95035) *(P-10853)*
Gateway US Retail Inc ....................................................... E ...... 949 471-7000
  7565 Irvine Center Dr Irvine (92618) *(P-10156)*
Gauss Surgical Inc ............................................................ E ...... 650 919-4683
  4085 Campbell Ave Ste 200 Menlo Park (94025) *(P-15354)*
Gavia, Vernon  Also Called: F Gavina & Sons Inc *(P-2071)*
Gavial Engineering & Mfg, Santa Maria  Also Called: Gavial Holdings Inc *(P-12983)*
Gavial Engineering & Mfg Inc ............................................ E ...... 805 614-0060
  1435 W Mccoy Ln Santa Maria (93455) *(P-12120)*
Gavial Holdings Inc (PA) .................................................... F ...... **805 614-0060**
  1435 W Mc Coy Lane Santa Maria (93455) *(P-12983)*
Gaylord's Meat Co, Fullerton  Also Called: Gaylords HRI Meats *(P-597)*
Gaylords HRI Meats ........................................................... F ...... 714 526-2278
  1100 E Ash Ave Ste C Fullerton (92831) *(P-597)*
Gaytan Foods LLC ............................................................. D ...... 626 330-4553
  15430 Proctor Ave City Of Industry (91745) *(P-645)*
Gaze USA Inc .................................................................... E ...... 213 622-0022
  2011 E 25th St Vernon (90058) *(P-2760)*
Gb Sport Sf LLC ................................................................ E ...... 415 863-6171
  200 Potrero Ave San Francisco (94103) *(P-2880)*
GBF Enterprises Inc .......................................................... E ...... 714 979-7131
  2709 Halladay St Santa Ana (92705) *(P-10854)*
Gbl Systems Corporation .................................................. E ...... 805 987-4345
  760 Paseo Camarillo Ste 401 Camarillo (93010) *(P-18977)*
Gbm, Alhambra  Also Called: Gracing Brand Management Inc *(P-2861)*
GBS Linens Inc (PA) .......................................................... D ...... **714 778-6448**
  305 N Muller St Anaheim (92801) *(P-17766)*
GBS Party Linens, Anaheim  Also Called: GBS Linens Inc *(P-17766)*
Gbt, South San Francisco  Also Called: Global Blood Therapeutics Inc *(P-5465)*
Gc International Inc (PA) .................................................... E ...... **805 389-4631**
  4671 Calle Carga Camarillo (93012) *(P-7845)*
Gc International Inc ........................................................... E ...... 805 389-4631
  4671 Calle Carga Camarillo (93012) *(P-11734)*
GCI, San Diego  Also Called: Goto California Inc *(P-11664)*
Gcm Holding Corporation ................................................. B ...... 510 475-0404
  1350 Atlantic St Union City (94587) *(P-17746)*

Gcm Medical & Oem Inc (PA) ............................................ D ...... **510 475-0404**
  1350 Atlantic St Union City (94587) *(P-8457)*
Gcn Supply LLC ................................................................ E ...... 909 643-4603
  9070 Bridgeport Pl Rancho Cucamonga (91730) *(P-8668)*
GCR Tires & Service 185, Fontana  Also Called: Bridgestone Americas *(P-19151)*
Gcx Corporation (DH) ........................................................ D ...... **707 773-1100**
  3875 Cypress Dr Petaluma (94954) *(P-7999)*
Gdca Inc ............................................................................ E ...... 925 456-9900
  1799 Portola Ave Ste 1 Livermore (94551) *(P-10373)*
Gdm Electronic & Medical, Milpitas  Also Called: G D M Electronic Assembly Inc *(P-11455)*
Gdsi, San Jose  Also Called: Grinding & Dicing Services Inc *(P-12455)*
GE Digital LLC ................................................................... B ...... 925 242-6200
  2700 Camino Ramon San Ramon (94583) *(P-18342)*
GE Energy, Diamond Bar  Also Called: Motech Americas LLC *(P-19469)*
GE Renewables North Amer LLC ...................................... C ...... 661 823-6423
  13681 Chantico Rd Tehachapi (93561) *(P-9311)*
GE Vallecitos Nuclear Center, Sunol  Also Called: Ge-Hitachi Nuclear Energy *(P-5094)*
GE Water & Process Tech, Avila Beach  Also Called: Veolia Wts Usa Inc *(P-6328)*
Ge-Hitachi Nuclear Energy ................................................ D ...... 925 862-4382
  6705 Vallecitos Rd Sunol (94586) *(P-5094)*
Gea Farm Technologies Inc ............................................... E ...... 559 497-5074
  2717 S 4th St Fresno (93725) *(P-5905)*
Gear Manufacturing Inc .................................................... E ...... 714 792-2895
  3701 E Miraloma Ave Anaheim (92806) *(P-13847)*
Gear Technology, Rancho Cucamonga  Also Called: Marino Enterprises Inc *(P-13898)*
Gear Vendors, El Cajon  Also Called: Gear Vendors Inc *(P-13505)*
Gear Vendors Inc .............................................................. E ...... 619 562-0060
  1717 N Magnolia Ave El Cajon (92020) *(P-13505)*
Gearbox Pubg San Francisco Inc ...................................... E ...... 650 590-7700
  100 Redwood Shores Pkwy Fl 2 Redwood City (94065) *(P-18343)*
Gearment, Huntington Beach  Also Called: Gearment Inc *(P-2503)*
Gearment Inc (PA) ............................................................. C ...... **866 236-5476**
  14801 Able Ln Ste 102 Huntington Beach (92647) *(P-2503)*
Gedney Foods Company .................................................. C ...... 952 448-2612
  12243 Branford St Sun Valley (91352) *(P-978)*
Gee Manufacturing Incorporated ..................................... E ...... 559 834-2929
  2200 S Golden State Blvd Fowler (93625) *(P-16134)*
Geeriraj Inc ....................................................................... E ...... 760 244-6149
  7042 Santa Fe Ave E Ste A1 Hesperia (92345) *(P-12121)*
Gefen LLC .......................................................................... E ...... 818 772-9100
  1800 S Mcdowell Boulevard Ext Petaluma (94954) *(P-13243)*
Gehr Group, Commerce  Also Called: Gehr Industries Inc *(P-7786)*
Gehr Industries Inc (HQ) ................................................... C ...... **323 728-5558**
  5701 S Eastern Ave Commerce (90040) *(P-7786)*
Geiger Manufacturing Inc ................................................. F ...... 209 464-7746
  1110 E Scotts Ave Stockton (95205) *(P-10855)*
Geiger Plastics Inc ............................................................ E ...... 310 327-9926
  16150 S Maple Ave # A Gardena (90248) *(P-6837)*
Gekkeikan Sake (usa) Inc ................................................. E ...... 916 985-3111
  1136 Sibley St Folsom (95630) *(P-1585)*
Gel Industries Inc ............................................................. C ...... 714 639-8191
  810 N Lemon St Orange (92867) *(P-8797)*
Gelateria Naia, Hercules  Also Called: Naia Inc *(P-813)*
Gelsons Markets ............................................................... D ...... 310 306-3192
  13455 Maxella Ave Marina Del Rey (90292) *(P-17380)*
Geltman Industries, Vernon  Also Called: Rezex Corporation *(P-2507)*
Gem Tech Jewelry Corporation ........................................ E ...... 213 623-2222
  3250 W Olympic Blvd Ste 207 Los Angeles (90006) *(P-15691)*
Gemco Display and Str Fixs LLC (PA) ............................... E ...... **800 262-1126**
  2640 E Del Amo Blvd Compton (90221) *(P-16567)*
Gemini Film & Bag Inc (PA) ............................................... E ...... **323 582-0901**
  3574 Fruitland Ave Maywood (90270) *(P-6838)*
Gemini GEL Llc .................................................................. E ...... 323 651-0513
  8365 Melrose Ave Los Angeles (90069) *(P-5025)*
Gemini Industries Inc ....................................................... D ...... 949 250-4011
  2311 Pullman St Santa Ana (92705) *(P-7719)*
Gemini Mfg & Engrg Inc .................................................... E ...... 714 999-0010
  1020 E Vermont Ave Anaheim (92805) *(P-9625)*
Gemini Plastics, Maywood  Also Called: Gemini Film & Bag Inc *(P-6838)*
Gemperle Enterprises ....................................................... D ...... 209 667-2651
  10218 Lander Ave Turlock (95380) *(P-63)*

**Gemperle Farms, Turlock** *Also Called: Gemperle Enterprises (P-63)*
**Gemsa Enterprises LLC** .................................................... E ...... 714 521-1736
14370 Gannet St La Mirada (90638) *(P-1398)*
**Gemsa Oils, La Mirada** *Also Called: Gemsa Enterprises LLC (P-1398)*
**Gemtech Inds Good Earth Mfg** .................................................... E ...... 714 848-2517
2737 S Garnsey St Santa Ana (92707) *(P-9074)*
**Gemtech International, Santa Ana** *Also Called: Gemtech Inds Good Earth Mfg (P-9074)*
**Gemtech Sales Corp** .................................................... E ...... 408 432-9900
2146 Bering Dr San Jose (95131) *(P-8067)*
**Gen Digital Inc** .................................................... E ...... 781 530-2200
380 Ellis St Mountain View (94043) *(P-12442)*
**Gen Labs Inc (PA)** .................................................... C ...... 909 591-8451
5568 Schaefer Ave Chino (91710) *(P-5906)*
**Gen-Probe Incorporated** .................................................... D ...... 858 410-8000
10210 Genetic Center Dr San Diego (92121) *(P-5754)*
**Gen-Probe Sales & Service Inc** .................................................... E ...... 858 410-8000
10210 Genetic Center Dr San Diego (92121) *(P-15539)*
**Genalyte Inc (PA)** .................................................... F ...... 858 956-1200
6620 Mesa Ridge Rd Ste 100 San Diego (92121) *(P-15097)*
**Genasys, San Diego** *Also Called: Genasys Inc (P-18344)*
**Genasys Inc (PA)** .................................................... D ...... 858 676-1112
16262 W Bernardo Dr San Diego (92127) *(P-18344)*
**Genbody America LLC** .................................................... E ...... 949 561-0664
3420 De Forest Cir Jurupa Valley (91752) *(P-15098)*
**Genencor International, Palo Alto** *Also Called: Danisco US Inc (P-5746)*
**Genentech, South San Francisco** *Also Called: Genentech Inc (P-5451)*
**Genentech Inc** .................................................... A ...... 650 467-0810
501 Dna Way South San Francisco (94080) *(P-5449)*
**Genentech Inc** .................................................... A ...... 760 231-2440
1 Antibody Way Oceanside (92056) *(P-5450)*
**Genentech Inc** .................................................... A ...... 650 225-1000
640 Forbes Blvd # B9 South San Francisco (94080) *(P-5451)*
**Genentech Inc** .................................................... E ...... 707 454-1000
1000 New Horizons Way Vacaville (95688) *(P-5452)*
**Genentech Inc** .................................................... A ...... 650 438-2626
340 Point San Bruno Blvd South San Francisco (94080) *(P-5453)*
**Genentech Inc (DH)** .................................................... A ...... 650 225-1000
1 Dna Way Stop 258a South San Francisco (94080) *(P-19494)*
**Genentech Usa Inc** .................................................... A ...... 650 225-1000
1 Dna Way South San Francisco (94080) *(P-5454)*
**Gener8 LLC (PA)** .................................................... D ...... 650 940-9898
2560 Junction Ave San Jose (95134) *(P-19396)*
**General Atmics Arntcal Systems** .................................................... C ...... 858 455-3358
11906 Tech Center Ct Poway (92064) *(P-13652)*
**General Atmics Arntcal Systems** .................................................... B ...... 858 964-6700
13330 Evening Creek Dr N San Diego (92128) *(P-13653)*
**General Atmics Arntcal Systems** .................................................... B ...... 858 312-4247
13550 Stowe Dr Poway (92064) *(P-13654)*
**General Atmics Arntcal Systems** .................................................... C ...... 858 455-3000
12220 Parkway Centre Dr Poway (92064) *(P-13655)*
**General Atmics Arntcal Systems** .................................................... A ...... 858 762-6700
16761 Via Del Campo Ct San Diego (92127) *(P-13656)*
**General Atmics Arntcal Systems** .................................................... C ...... 858 312-2810
14102 Stowe Dr Ste A47 Poway (92064) *(P-13657)*
**General Atmics Arntcal Systems** .................................................... B ...... 858 455-2810
3550 General Atomics Ct San Diego (92121) *(P-13658)*
**General Atmics Arntcal Systems** .................................................... B ...... 858 762-6700
12365 Crosthwaite Cir Poway (92064) *(P-13659)*
**General Atmics Arntcal Systems (DH)** .................................................... B ...... 858 312-2810
14200 Kirkham Way Poway (92064) *(P-13660)*
**General Atomic Aeron** .................................................... C ...... 858 455-4560
14040 Danielson St Poway (92064) *(P-13661)*
**General Atomic Aeron** .................................................... C ...... 858 312-3428
13950 Stowe Dr Poway (92064) *(P-13662)*
**General Atomic Aeron** .................................................... C ...... 760 388-8208
73 El Mirage Airport Rd Ste B Adelanto (92301) *(P-13663)*
**General Atomic Aeron** .................................................... B ...... 858 312-2543
14115 Stowe Dr Poway (92064) *(P-13664)*
**General Atomics** .................................................... C ...... 858 455-4000
4949 Greencraig Ln San Diego (92123) *(P-19453)*
**General Atomics, San Diego** *Also Called: General Atmics Arntcal Systems (P-13658)*

**General Atomics, Adelanto** *Also Called: General Atomic Aeron (P-13663)*
**General Atomics Electronic Systems Inc** .................................................... B ...... 858 522-8495
4949 Greencraig Ln San Diego (92123) *(P-12817)*
**General Atomics Energy Pdts, San Diego** *Also Called: General Atomics (P-19453)*
**General Coatings, Fresno** *Also Called: Walton Industries Inc (P-6117)*
**General Container** .................................................... D ...... 714 562-8700
235 Radio Rd Corona (92879) *(P-3846)*
**General Conveyor Inc** .................................................... E ...... 951 734-3460
13385 Estelle St Corona (92879) *(P-19259)*
**General Dynamics Mission** .................................................... C ...... 619 671-5400
7603 Saint Andrews Ave Ste H San Diego (92154) *(P-11323)*
**General Dynamics Mission** .................................................... B ...... 408 908-7300
2688 Orchard Pkwy San Jose (95134) *(P-11995)*
**GENERAL DYNAMICS OTS (CALIFORNIA), INC., San Diego** *Also Called: General Dynamics Ots Cal Inc (P-13848)*
**General Dynamics Ots Cal Inc** .................................................... C ...... 619 671-5411
7603 Saint Andrews Ave Ste H San Diego (92154) *(P-13848)*
**General Dynmics Mssion Systems** .................................................... D ...... 650 966-2000
100 Ferguson Dr Mountain View (94043) *(P-10157)*
**General Dynmics Ots Ncvlle Inc (DH)** .................................................... D ...... 707 473-9200
511 Grove St Healdsburg (95448) *(P-13849)*
**General Dynmics Ots Ncvlle Inc** .................................................... D ...... 916 355-7700
105 Lake Forest Way Folsom (95630) *(P-14191)*
**General Elec Assembly Inc** .................................................... E ...... 408 980-8819
1525 Atteberry Ln San Jose (95131) *(P-12122)*
**General Electric Company** .................................................... E ...... 760 530-5200
18000 Phantom St Victorville (92394) *(P-13665)*
**General Forming Corporation** .................................................... E ...... 310 326-0624
640 Alaska Ave Torrance (90503) *(P-14192)*
**General Foundry Service Corp** .................................................... D ...... 510 297-5040
1390 Business Center Pl San Leandro (94577) *(P-7846)*
**General Graphic Chem Co Inc** .................................................... F ...... 510 879-7010
729 Fulton Shipyard Rd Ste A2 Antioch (94509) *(P-6288)*
**General Grinding, La Mirada** *Also Called: General Grinding & Mfg Co LLC (P-10627)*
**General Grinding Inc** .................................................... E ...... 510 261-5557
801 51st Ave Oakland (94601) *(P-10856)*
**General Grinding & Mfg Co LLC** .................................................... F ...... 562 921-7033
15100 Valley View Ave La Mirada (90638) *(P-10627)*
**General Hydroponics, Sebastopol** *Also Called: General Hydroponics Inc (P-6187)*
**General Hydroponics Inc** .................................................... D ...... 707 824-9376
3789 Vine Hill Rd Sebastopol (95472) *(P-6187)*
**General Industrial Repair** .................................................... E ...... 323 278-0873
6865 Washington Blvd Montebello (90640) *(P-10857)*
**General Linear Systems Inc** .................................................... F ...... 714 994-4822
4332 Artesia Ave Fullerton (92833) *(P-12841)*
**General Mills, Carson** *Also Called: General Mills Inc (P-835)*
**General Mills, Vernon** *Also Called: General Mills Inc (P-1058)*
**General Mills Inc** .................................................... D ...... 310 605-6108
1055 Sandhill Ave Carson (90746) *(P-835)*
**General Mills Inc** .................................................... E ...... 323 584-3433
4309 Fruitland Ave Vernon (90058) *(P-1058)*
**General Monitors Inc (DH)** .................................................... C ...... 949 581-4464
16782 Von Karman Ave Ste 14 Irvine (92606) *(P-11996)*
**General Motors, Torrance** *Also Called: General Motors LLC (P-17439)*
**General Motors LLC** .................................................... E ...... 313 556-5000
3050 Lomita Blvd Ste 237 Torrance (90505) *(P-17439)*
**General Networks Corporation** .................................................... D ...... 818 249-1962
3524 Ocean View Blvd Glendale (91208) *(P-19036)*
**General Newsprint, Placentia** *Also Called: General Rewinding Inc (P-5010)*
**General Photonics, Chino** *Also Called: General Photonics Corp (P-11766)*
**General Photonics Corp** .................................................... D ...... 909 590-5473
14351 Pipeline Ave Chino (91710) *(P-11766)*
**General Plastics, Sun Valley** *Also Called: Plastic Services and Products (P-6651)*
**General Plating, Los Angeles** *Also Called: Alpha Polishing Corporation (P-8916)*
**General Power Systems, Anaheim** *Also Called: General Power Systems Inc (P-12984)*
**General Power Systems Inc** .................................................... E ...... 714 956-9321
955 E Ball Rd Anaheim (92805) *(P-12984)*
**General Radar Corp (PA)** .................................................... F ...... 650 304-9033
616 Mountain View Ave Belmont (94002) *(P-14193)*
**General Rewinding Inc** .................................................... E ...... 714 776-5561
888 W Crowther Ave Placentia (92870) *(P-5010)*

# ALPHABETIC SECTION — Geyser Peak Winery

**General Ribbon Corp** .......................................................... B ...... 818 709-1234
5775 E Los Angeles Ave Ste 230 Chatsworth (91311) *(P-15896)*

**General Sealants** .................................................................. C ...... 626 961-0211
300 Turnbull Canyon Rd City Of Industry (91745) *(P-6229)*

**General Surgical Innovations** ............................................. F ...... 408 863-2500
10460 Bubb Rd Cupertino (95014) *(P-15099)*

**General Switchgear Inc** ...................................................... E
14729 Spring Ave Santa Fe Springs (90670) *(P-11242)*

**General Transistor Corporation (PA)** ................................ E ...... 310 578-7344
12449 Putnam St Whittier (90602) *(P-16703)*

**General Truss Company Inc** ................................................ F ...... 916 388-9300
6947 Power Inn Rd Sacramento (95828) *(P-3307)*

**General Veneer Mfg Co** ...................................................... E ...... 323 564-2661
8652 Otis St South Gate (90280) *(P-3285)*

**General Water Systems** ...................................................... F ...... 951 278-8992
1525 E 6th St Corona (92879) *(P-19093)*

**General Wax & Candle Co, North Hollywood** *Also Called: General Wax Co Inc (P-16135)*

**General Wax Co Inc (PA)** .................................................... D ...... 818 765-5800
6863 Beck Ave North Hollywood (91605) *(P-16135)*

**General Window Corporation** ............................................. C ...... 510 487-1122
30526 San Antonio St Hayward (94544) *(P-6839)*

**Generis Holdings LP (PA)** ................................................... C ...... 661 366-7209
7200 E Brundage Ln Bakersfield (93307) *(P-5)*

**Genes Plating Works Inc (PA)** ............................................ E ...... 323 269-8748
3498 E 14th St Los Angeles (90023) *(P-8963)*

**Genesis 2000, La Puente** *Also Called: Genesis Tc Inc (P-3473)*

**Genesis Computer Systems Inc** ........................................... E ...... 714 632-3648
4055 E La Palma Ave Ste C Anaheim (92807) *(P-16525)*

**Genesis Foods Corporation** ................................................ D ...... 323 890-5890
8825 Mercury Ln Pico Rivera (90660) *(P-1308)*

**Genesis Tc Inc** ...................................................................... E ...... 626 968-4455
524 Hofgaarden St La Puente (91744) *(P-3473)*

**Genesys Cloud Services Inc (HQ)** ...................................... B ...... 650 466-1100
1302 El Camino Real Ste 300 Menlo Park (94025) *(P-18345)*

**Genesys Telecom Labs, Menlo Park** *Also Called: Genesys Cloud Services Inc (P-18345)*

**Genetronics Inc** .................................................................... E ...... 858 597-6006
11494 Sorrento Valley Rd Ste A San Diego (92121) *(P-14338)*

**Genetronics Inc** .................................................................... E ...... 858 410-3112
10480 Wateridge Cir San Diego (92121) *(P-5455)*

**Genius Products Inc** ............................................................ C ...... 310 453-1222
3301 Exposition Blvd Ste 100 Santa Monica (90404) *(P-16977)*

**Genius Products Nt Inc** ....................................................... C ...... 510 671-0219
556 N Diamond Bar Blvd Ste 101 Diamond Bar (91765) *(P-1889)*

**Genmark, Carlsbad** *Also Called: Genmark Diagnostics Inc (P-15100)*

**Genmark Diagnostics Inc (DH)** ........................................... A ...... 760 448-4300
5964 La Place Ct Ste 100 Carlsbad (92008) *(P-15100)*

**Genomics Inst of Nvrtis RES FN** ........................................ D ...... 858 812-1805
10675 John J Hopkins Dr San Diego (92121) *(P-5456)*

**Genstar Capital LLC (PA)** .................................................... E ...... 415 834-2350
4 Embarcadero Ctr Ste 1900 San Francisco (94111) *(P-17729)*

**Gentec Manufacturing Inc** .................................................. F ...... 408 432-6220
2241 Ringwood Ave San Jose (95131) *(P-10858)*

**Gentex Corporation** ............................................................. D ...... 909 481-7667
9859 7th St Rancho Cucamonga (91730) *(P-19454)*

**Genuine Parts Distributors, Ontario** *Also Called: Tracy Industries Inc (P-9332)*

**Genvivo Inc** .......................................................................... E ...... 626 441-6695
1981 E Locust St Ontario (91761) *(P-5457)*

**Genzyme Corporation** ......................................................... D ...... 626 471-9922
655 E Huntington Dr Monrovia (91016) *(P-5458)*

**Genzyme Genetics, Monrovia** *Also Called: Genzyme Corporation (P-5458)*

**Geo, San Jose** *Also Called: Geo Semiconductor Inc (P-12443)*

**Geo Drilling Fluids Inc (PA)** ................................................ E ...... 661 325-5919
1431 Union Ave Bakersfield (93305) *(P-17245)*

**Geo Guidance Drilling Svcs Inc (PA)** ................................ E ...... 661 833-9999
200 Old Yard Dr Bakersfield (93307) *(P-159)*

**Geo M Martin Company (PA)** ............................................. D ...... 510 652-2200
1250 67th St Emeryville (94608) *(P-9760)*

**Geo Plastics** ......................................................................... E ...... 323 277-8106
2200 E 52nd St Vernon (90058) *(P-6840)*

**Geo Semiconductor Inc (PA)** ............................................... F ...... 408 638-0400
181 Metro Dr San Jose (95110) *(P-12443)*

**Geolabs Westlake Village, Newbury Park** *Also Called: R & R Services Corporation (P-6532)*

**Geometrics Inc** .................................................................... D ...... 408 428-4244
2190 Fortune Dr San Jose (95131) *(P-14872)*

**Geoplanter, Santa Rosa** *Also Called: Rbd Online Inc (P-7289)*

**Geopogo** ............................................................................... E ...... 510 918-7083
1335 Milvia St Berkeley (94709) *(P-18346)*

**Georg Fischer Signet LLC** ................................................... D ...... 626 571-2770
5462 Irwindale Ave Ste A Baldwin Park (91706) *(P-14418)*

**George Delallo Company Inc** .............................................. F ...... 530 533-3303
1800 Idora St Oroville (95966) *(P-891)*

**George Fischer Inc (HQ)** ..................................................... C ...... 626 571-2770
5462 Irwindale Ave Ste A Baldwin Park (91706) *(P-10859)*

**George Industries (HQ)** ...................................................... E ...... 323 264-6660
4116 Whiteside St Los Angeles (90063) *(P-8964)*

**George Jue Mfg Co Inc** ....................................................... D ...... 562 634-8181
8140 Rosecrans Ave Paramount (90723) *(P-9711)*

**George L Throop Co** ............................................................ E ...... 626 796-0285
444 N Fair Oaks Ave Pasadena (91103) *(P-17354)*

**George M Robinson & Co (PA)** ........................................... E ...... 510 632-7017
1461 Atteberry Ln San Jose (95131) *(P-421)*

**George P Johnson Company** ............................................... E ...... 310 965-4300
18500 Crenshaw Blvd Torrance (90504) *(P-15983)*

**George Reed Inc (HQ)** ........................................................ E ...... 877 823-2305
140 Empire Ave Modesto (95354) *(P-522)*

**George T Hall Co Inc (PA)** .................................................. E ...... 909 825-9751
1605 E Gene Autry Way Anaheim (92805) *(P-16780)*

**George Verhoeven Grain Inc (PA)** ..................................... F ...... 909 605-1531
301 E 6th St Hanford (93230) *(P-1128)*

**Georgia-Pacific, San Leandro** *Also Called: Georgia-Pacific LLC (P-3770)*
**Georgia-Pacific, Antioch** *Also Called: Georgia-Pacific LLC (P-7524)*
**Georgia-Pacific, Santa Fe Springs** *Also Called: Georgia-Pacific LLC (P-17000)*
**Georgia-Pacific, La Mirada** *Also Called: Georgia-Pacific LLC (P-17704)*

**Georgia-Pacific LLC** ............................................................ E ...... 510 483-7580
1988 Marina Blvd San Leandro (94577) *(P-3770)*

**Georgia-Pacific LLC** ............................................................ D ...... 209 522-5201
2400 Lapham Dr Modesto (95354) *(P-3847)*

**Georgia-Pacific LLC** ............................................................ D ...... 559 674-4685
24600 Avenue 13 Madera (93637) *(P-3848)*

**Georgia-Pacific LLC** ............................................................ D ...... 925 757-2870
801 Minaker Dr Antioch (94509) *(P-7524)*

**Georgia-Pacific LLC** ............................................................ B ...... 562 861-6226
9206 Santa Fe Springs Rd Santa Fe Springs (90670) *(P-17000)*

**Georgia-Pacific LLC** ............................................................ E ...... 562 926-8888
15500 Valley View Ave La Mirada (90638) *(P-17704)*

**Gerdau Ameristeel, San Bernardino** *Also Called: CMC Steel Us LLC (P-8695)*
**Gerdau Rancho Cucamonga, Newport Beach** *Also Called: Tamco (P-8712)*

**Gerhardt Gear Co Inc** .......................................................... E ...... 818 842-6700
133 E Santa Anita Ave Burbank (91502) *(P-13506)*

**Gerlinger Fndry Mch Works Inc (PA)** ................................ E ...... 530 243-1053
1527 Sacramento St Redding (96001) *(P-8145)*

**Gerlinger Fndry Mch Works Inc** ......................................... F ...... 530 243-1053
1510 Tanforan Ave Woodland (95776) *(P-16620)*

**Gerlinger Steel & Supply Co, Woodland** *Also Called: Gerlinger Fndry Mch Works Inc (P-16620)*
**Gerlinger Steel & Supply Co., Redding** *Also Called: Gerlinger Fndry Mch Works Inc (P-8145)*
**German Machine Products, Gardena** *Also Called: German Machined Products Inc (P-10860)*

**German Machined Products Inc** ......................................... E ...... 310 532-4480
1415 W 178th St Gardena (90248) *(P-10860)*

**GERON, Foster City** *Also Called: Geron Corporation (P-5459)*

**Geron Corporation (PA)** ...................................................... C ...... 650 473-7700
919 E Hillsdale Blvd Ste 250 Foster City (94404) *(P-5459)*

**Get Engineering, El Cajon** *Also Called: Get Engineering Corp (P-14419)*

**Get Engineering Corp** .......................................................... F ...... 619 443-8295
9350 Bond Ave El Cajon (92021) *(P-14419)*

**Get Primped, Los Angeles** *Also Called: Distro Worldwide LLC (P-2572)*

**Get Satisfaction Inc** ............................................................. E ...... 877 339-3997
1550 Bryant St Ste 350 San Francisco (94103) *(P-18347)*

**Getpart La Inc** ...................................................................... E ...... 424 331-9599
13705 Cimarron Ave Gardena (90249) *(P-6841)*

**Geyser Peak Winery** ............................................................ E ...... 707 857-9463
1300 1st St Ste 368 Napa (94559) *(P-1586)*

Gff Inc .................................................................................... D ...... 323 232-6255
  145 Willow Ave City Of Industry (91746) *(P-979)*

Gfi Poultry LLC (PA) ........................................................... E
  2495 W Shaw Ave Ste 102 Fresno (93711) *(P-692)*

Gfp Ethanol  LLC ............................................................... E ...... 559 757-3850
  11704 Road 120 Pixley (93256) *(P-6147)*

GGF Marble & Supply Inc ................................................ E ...... 925 676-8385
  1375 Franquette Ave Ste F Concord (94520) *(P-7537)*

Ggtw LLC .......................................................................... E ...... 619 423-3388
  1470 Bay Blvd Chula Vista (91911) *(P-6289)*

Gh Foods Ca LLC (DH) .................................................. B ...... 916 844-1140
  8425 Carbide Ct Sacramento (95828) *(P-2213)*

Ghangor Cloud Inc .......................................................... D ...... 408 713-3303
  2001 Gateway Pl Ste 710 San Jose (95110) *(P-13244)*

Ghirardelli, San Leandro Also Called: Ghirardelli Chocolate Company *(P-17401)*

Ghirardelli Chocolate Company (DH) ............................. B ...... 510 483-6970
  1111 139th Ave San Leandro (94578) *(P-17401)*

Ghiringhlli Spcialty Foods Inc ......................................... C ...... 707 561-7670
  101 Benicia Rd Vallejo (94590) *(P-2214)*

Giannini Garden Ornaments Inc ..................................... E ...... 650 873-4493
  225 Shaw Rd South San Francisco (94080) *(P-7338)*

Giant Mgllan Tlscope Orgnztion, Pasadena Also Called: Gmto Corporation *(P-14778)*

Giant Teddy, Anaheim Also Called: Raykorvay Inc *(P-15734)*

Gibbs Plastic & Rubber  LLC ......................................... F ...... 707 746-7300
  3959 Teal Ct Benicia (94510) *(P-6496)*

Gibo/Kodama Chairs, Garden Grove Also Called: Intra Storage Systems Inc *(P-9289)*

Gibraltar, Jurupa Valley Also Called: Pacific Award Metals  Inc *(P-16492)*

Gibraltar Plastic Pdts Corp ............................................. E ...... 818 365-9318
  12885 Foothill Blvd Sylmar (91342) *(P-6842)*

Gibson & Barnes, El Cajon Also Called: Flight Suits *(P-2879)*

Gibson & Schaefer Inc (PA) ........................................... E ...... 619 352-3535
  1126 Rock Wood Rd Heber (92249) *(P-7448)*

Gibson Exhaust Systems, Corona Also Called: Gibson Performance Corporation *(P-13507)*

Gibson Homeware, Commerce Also Called: Gibson Overseas  Inc *(P-16426)*

Gibson Overseas Inc (PA) .............................................. B ...... 323 832-8900
  2410 Yates Ave Commerce (90040) *(P-16426)*

Gibson Performance Corporation ................................... D ...... 951 372-1220
  1270 Webb Cir Corona (92879) *(P-13507)*

Gibson Printing & Pubg Inc ............................................. E ...... 707 745-0733
  820 1st St Benicia (94510) *(P-4122)*

Gibson Wine Company .................................................... E ...... 559 875-2505
  1720 Academy Ave Sanger (93657) *(P-1587)*

Giddens Industries Inc (DH) ........................................... C
  3130 E Miraloma Ave Anaheim (92806) *(P-13850)*

Gifts International  Inc .................................................... F ...... 909 854-3977
  5620 Villa Mar Pl Malibu (90265) *(P-9287)*

Gigamat Technologies  Inc ............................................. F ...... 510 770-8008
  47358 Fremont Blvd Fremont (94538) *(P-12444)*

Gigamem  LLC ................................................................ F ...... 949 461-9999
  9 Spectrum Pointe Dr Lake Forest (92630) *(P-10238)*

Gigamon Inc (HQ) .......................................................... D ...... 408 831-4000
  3300 Olcott St Santa Clara (95054) *(P-10374)*

Gigastone America, Irvine Also Called: Dane Elec Corp USA *(P-16517)*

Gigatera Communications ............................................... D ...... 714 515-1100
  1413 Vista Del Mar Dr Fullerton (92831) *(P-12985)*

Gigpeak  Inc (DH) ........................................................... C ...... 408 546-3316
  6024 Silver Creek Valley Rd San Jose (95138) *(P-12445)*

Gilbert Martin Wdwkg Co Inc (PA) .................................. E ...... 800 268-5669
  2345 Britannia Blvd San Diego (92154) *(P-3550)*

Gilbert Spray Coat, Santa Clara Also Called: Gilbert Spray Coat  Inc *(P-9075)*

Gilbert Spray Coat  Inc ................................................... F ...... 408 988-0747
  300 Laurelwood Rd Santa Clara (95054) *(P-9075)*

Gildan USA Inc ................................................................ E ...... 909 485-1475
  28200 Highway 189 Lake Arrowhead (92352) *(P-2457)*

GILDAN USA INC., Lake Arrowhead Also Called: Gildan USA Inc *(P-2457)*

Gilead Palo Alto  Inc ....................................................... C ...... 760 945-7701
  4049 Avenida De La Plata Oceanside (92056) *(P-5460)*

Gilead Palo Alto  Inc ....................................................... C ...... 909 394-4000
  550 Cliffside Dr San Dimas (91773) *(P-5461)*

Gilead Palo Alto  Inc (HQ) .............................................. E ...... 650 384-8500
  333 Lakeside Dr Foster City (94404) *(P-19455)*

Gilead Sciences  Inc ...................................................... D ...... 650 522-2771
  1800 Wheeler St La Verne (91750) *(P-5462)*

Gilead Sciences  Inc (PA) .............................................. B ...... 650 574-3000
  333 Lakeside Dr Foster City (94404) *(P-5463)*

Gilead Sciences  Inc ...................................................... F ...... 909 394-4000
  650 Cliffside Dr San Dimas (91773) *(P-5464)*

Gilead Scientist, San Dimas Also Called: Gilead Palo Alto  Inc *(P-5461)*

Gill Corporation (PA) ...................................................... C ...... 626 443-6094
  4056 Easy St El Monte (91731) *(P-6843)*

Gilli Inc ........................................................................... F ...... 213 744-9808
  1100 S San Pedro St Ste C07 Los Angeles (90015) *(P-2900)*

Gillig LLC (HQ) .............................................................. C ...... 510 264-5000
  451 Discovery Dr Livermore (94551) *(P-13413)*

Gilwin Company ............................................................. E ...... 209 522-9775
  2354 Lapham Dr Modesto (95354) *(P-8267)*

Gingi Pak, Camarillo Also Called: Belport Company  Inc *(P-15439)*

Gino Corporation ............................................................ E ...... 323 234-7979
  555 E Jefferson Blvd Los Angeles (90011) *(P-2573)*

Ginsberg Holdco Inc ...................................................... B ...... 408 831-4000
  3300 Olcott St Santa Clara (95054) *(P-18348)*

Giorgio's Pizza House, Sunnyvale Also Called: Fullfillment Systems Inc *(P-644)*

Giorgios Restaurant Italiano ........................................... E ...... 415 925-0808
  99 Rock Rd Greenbrae (94904) *(P-857)*

Giovanni Cosmetics  Inc ................................................. D ...... 310 952-9960
  2064 E University Dr Rancho Dominguez (90220) *(P-5980)*

Giovanni Hair Care & Cosmetics, Rancho Dominguez Also Called: Giovanni Cosmetics  Inc *(P-5980)*

Girard Food Service, City Of Industry Also Called: Gff Inc *(P-979)*

Gist  Inc ......................................................................... D ...... 530 644-8000
  4385 Pleasant Valley Rd Placerville (95667) *(P-15910)*

Gist Silversmiths, Placerville Also Called: Gist Inc *(P-15910)*

Gitlab, San Francisco Also Called: Gitlab Inc *(P-18349)*

Gitlab Inc (PA) ............................................................... F ...... 650 474-5175
  268 Bush St # 350 San Francisco (94104) *(P-18349)*

Giuliano-Pagano Corporation ......................................... D ...... 310 537-7700
  1264 E Walnut St Carson (90746) *(P-1210)*

Giuliano's Bakery, Carson Also Called: Giuliano-Pagano Corporation *(P-1210)*

Giumarra Vineyards Corporation (PA) ............................ B ...... 661 395-7000
  11220 Edison Hwy Edison (93220) *(P-13)*

Giumarra Vineyards Corporation .................................... C ...... 661 395-7000
  11220 Edison Hwy Bakersfield (93307) *(P-1588)*

Giustos Specialty Foods  LLC (PA) ................................ E ...... 650 873-6566
  344 Littlefield Ave South San Francisco (94080) *(P-1059)*

Given Imaging Los Angeles LLC .................................... C ...... 310 641-8492
  5860 Uplander Way Culver City (90230) *(P-15540)*

Giving Keys Inc ............................................................. E ...... 213 935-8791
  836 Traction Ave Los Angeles (90013) *(P-15692)*

GK Foods  Inc ................................................................ E ...... 760 752-5230
  133 Mata Way Ste 101 San Marcos (92069) *(P-1060)*

GKN Aerospace .............................................................. D ...... 714 653-7531
  12122 Western Ave Garden Grove (92841) *(P-13666)*

GKN Aerospace Camarillo Inc ........................................ F ...... 805 383-6684
  3030 Redhll Ave Santa Ana (92705) *(P-8458)*

GKN Aerospace Chem-Tronics Inc (DH) ........................ A ...... 619 258-5000
  1150 W Bradley Ave El Cajon (92020) *(P-13709)*

GKN Arspace Trnsprncy Systems .................................. B ...... 714 893-7531
  12122 Western Ave Garden Grove (92841) *(P-6844)*

GL Woodworking  Inc ..................................................... D ...... 949 515-2192
  14341 Franklin Ave Tustin (92780) *(P-3139)*

Glacier Foods Division, Westlake Village Also Called: Dole Packaged Foods  LLC *(P-1003)*

Glacier Foods Division, Sanger Also Called: Dole Packaged Foods LLC *(P-1004)*

Glacier Ice Company, Elk Grove Also Called: Glacier Valley Ice Company LP *(P-2108)*

Glacier Valley Ice Company LP (PA) .............................. E ...... 916 394-2939
  8580 Laguna Station Rd Elk Grove (95758) *(P-2108)*

Glad, Oakland Also Called: Glad Products Company *(P-6560)*

Glad Products Company (HQ) ....................................... C ...... 510 271-7000
  1221 Broadway Ste A Oakland (94612) *(P-6560)*

Gladding McBean, Lincoln Also Called: Basalite Building Products LLC *(P-7265)*

Gladding McBean, Lincoln Also Called: Pabco Building Products  LLC *(P-7275)*

Gladiator Corporation ..................................................... B ...... 650 233-2900
  2882 Sand Hill Rd Ste 280 Menlo Park (94025) *(P-18350)*

# ALPHABETIC SECTION

**Glam and Glits Nail Design Inc** .................................................. D ...... 661 393-4800
  8700 Swigert Ct Unit 209 Bakersfield (93311) *(P-5981)*
**Glamour Industries Co (PA)**.......................................................... C ...... 323 728-2999
  2220 Gaspar Ave Los Angeles (90040) *(P-17038)*
**Glas Werk Inc** ................................................................................ E ...... 949 766-1296
  29710 Avenida De Las Bandera Rancho Santa Margari (92688) *(P-7195)*
**Glaspro, Santa Fe Springs** *Also Called: GP Merger Sub Inc (P-7225)*
**Glass & Sash Inc (PA)**.................................................................. E ...... 415 456-2240
  425 Irwin St San Rafael (94901) *(P-16494)*
**Glass Fab Tempering Sv, Tracy** *Also Called: Glassfab Tempering Svcs Inc (P-7169)*
**Glass Jar Inc** ................................................................................. D ...... 831 427-9946
  125 Beach St Santa Cruz (95060) *(P-802)*
**Glass Jar Inc (PA)** ........................................................................ E ...... 831 227-2247
  913 Cedar St Santa Cruz (95060) *(P-803)*
**Glassfab Tempering Svcs Inc (PA)**............................................. D ...... 209 229-1060
  8690 W Linne Rd Tracy (95304) *(P-7169)*
**Glasslab Inc** .................................................................................. E ...... 415 244-5584
  209 Redwood Shores Pkwy Redwood City (94065) *(P-18351)*
**Glassplax** ...................................................................................... F ...... 951 677-4800
  26605 Madison Ave Murrieta (92562) *(P-7223)*
**Glasswerks Group, South Gate** *Also Called: Glasswerks La Inc (P-7224)*
**Glasswerks La Inc (HQ)**............................................................... B ...... 888 789-7810
  8600 Rheem Ave South Gate (90280) *(P-7224)*
**Glastar, Canoga Park** *Also Called: Glastar Corporation (P-9860)*
**Glastar Corporation** ..................................................................... E ...... 818 341-0301
  8425 Canoga Ave Canoga Park (91304) *(P-9860)*
**Glaukos Corporation (PA)**............................................................ C ...... 949 367-9600
  1 Glaukos Way Aliso Viejo (92656) *(P-15101)*
**Glazier Steel, Hayward** *Also Called: Glazier Steel Inc (P-8146)*
**Glazier Steel Inc** ........................................................................... D ...... 510 471-5300
  650 Sandoval Way Hayward (94544) *(P-8146)*
**Gleason Industrial Pdts Inc** .......................................................... 574 533-1141
  10474 Santa Monica Blvd Ste 400 Los Angeles (90025) *(P-9519)*
**Gleason Industries** ....................................................................... D ...... 800 488-3471
  1277 Santa Anita Ct Woodland (95776) *(P-4040)*
**Gledhill/Lyons Inc** ......................................................................... E ...... 714 502-0274
  1521 N Placentia Ave Anaheim (92806) *(P-13851)*
**Glen - Mac Swiss Co** .................................................................... E ...... 310 978-4555
  12848 Weber Way Hawthorne (90250) *(P-12880)*
**Glenair Inc (PA)**............................................................................. B ...... 818 247-6000
  1211 Air Way Glendale (91201) *(P-11456)*
**Glendee Corp (PA)**....................................................................... E ...... 805 523-2422
  5390 Gabbert Rd Moorpark (93021) *(P-10861)*
**Glendee Corp** ............................................................................... E ...... 805 523-2422
  5151 N Commerce Ave Moorpark (93021) *(P-10862)*
**Glenoaks Food Inc** ...................................................................... E ...... 818 768-9091
  11030 Randall St Sun Valley (91352) *(P-693)*
**Glentek Inc** ................................................................................... D ...... 310 322-3026
  208 Standard St El Segundo (90245) *(P-11270)*
**Glf Integrated Power Inc** ............................................................. F ...... 408 239-4326
  4500 Great America Pkwy Rm 1045 Santa Clara (95054) *(P-12446)*
**Glide-Write, Milpitas** *Also Called: Marburg Technology Inc (P-10407)*
**Glimmerglass, Santa Clara** *Also Called: Glimmerglass Networks Inc (P-12986)*
**Glimmerglass Networks Inc** ....................................................... E ...... 510 780-1800
  3945 Freedom Cir Ste 560 Santa Clara (95054) *(P-12986)*
**Global A Lgistics Training Inc** .................................................... E ...... 760 688-0365
  3860 Calle Fortunada Ste 100 San Diego (92123) *(P-14194)*
**Global Aerospace Tech Corp** ..................................................... E ...... 818 407-5600
  29077 Avenue Penn Valencia (91355) *(P-13852)*
**Global Aerostructures** ................................................................. F ...... 909 987-4888
  10291 Trademark St Ste C Rancho Cucamonga (91730) *(P-13853)*
**Global Agri-Trade (PA)**................................................................. E ...... 562 320-8550
  15500 S Avalon Blvd Rancho Dominguez (90220) *(P-1371)*
**Global Automation Inc (PA)**........................................................ E ...... 650 316-5900
  1388 Terra Bella Ave Mountain View (94043) *(P-19037)*
**Global Blood Therapeutics Inc (HQ)**.......................................... B ...... 650 741-7700
  181 Oyster Point Blvd South San Francisco (94080) *(P-5465)*
**Global Cash Card Inc** .................................................................. C ...... 949 751-0360
  3972 Barranca Pkwy Ste J610 Irvine (92606) *(P-18352)*
**Global Casuals Inc** ...................................................................... E ...... 310 817-2828
  18505 S Broadway Gardena (90248) *(P-2621)*

**Global Comm Semiconductors LLC** .......................................... E ...... 310 530-7274
  23155 Kashiwa Ct Torrance (90505) *(P-12447)*
**Global Compliance Inc** ............................................................... E ...... 626 303-6855
  438 W Chestnut Ave Ste A Monrovia (91016) *(P-4403)*
**Global Contract Manufacturing, Union City** *Also Called: Gcm Medical & Oem Inc (P-8457)*
**Global Diversified Inds Inc (PA)**................................................. F ...... 559 665-5800
  450 Commerce Ave Atwater (95301) *(P-3396)*
**Global Elastomeric Pdts Inc** ....................................................... D ...... 661 831-5380
  5551 District Blvd Bakersfield (93313) *(P-9463)*
**Global Environmental Pdts Inc** .................................................. D ...... 909 713-1600
  5405 Industrial Pkwy San Bernardino (92407) *(P-13354)*
**Global Equipment Rental Co, Dixon** *Also Called: Global Rental Co Inc (P-9423)*
**Global Equipment Services, San Jose** *Also Called: Kimball Electronics Ind Inc (P-12149)*
**Global Fabricators, Shafter** *Also Called: McM Fabricators Inc (P-8179)*
**Global Impact Inv Partners LLC** ................................................. E ...... 310 592-2000
  1410 Westwood Blvd Apt 260 Los Angeles (90024) *(P-1211)*
**Global Integrated Logistics, Irvine** *Also Called: Agility Logistics Corp (P-16306)*
**GLOBAL LAB SUPPLY, Orange** *Also Called: Cleatech LLC (P-14333)*
**Global Link Sourcing Inc** ............................................................ D ...... 951 698-1977
  41690 Corporate Center Ct Murrieta (92562) *(P-3928)*
**Global Metal Solutions Inc** ......................................................... E ...... 949 872-2995
  2150 Mcgaw Ave Irvine (92614) *(P-8965)*
**Global Microwave Systems Inc** .................................................. E ...... 760 496-0046
  1916 Palomar Oaks Way Ste 100 Carlsbad (92008) *(P-11858)*
**Global Modular Inc (HQ)**............................................................. E ...... 209 676-8029
  450 Commerce Ave Atwater (95301) *(P-8669)*
**Global Motorsport Parts Inc** ...................................................... D ...... 408 778-0500
  15750 Vineyard Blvd Ste 100 Morgan Hill (95037) *(P-14059)*
**Global Nature Foods, Bell** *Also Called: H & T Seafood Inc (P-17157)*
**Global Packaging Solutions Inc** ................................................. B ...... 619 710-2661
  6259 Progressive Dr Ste 200 San Diego (92154) *(P-3849)*
**Global Pcci (gpc) (PA)**.................................................................. C ...... 757 637-9000
  2465 Campus Dr Ste 100 Irvine (92612) *(P-8847)*
**Global Plastics Inc** ....................................................................... C ...... 951 657-5466
  145 Malbert St Perris (92570) *(P-16959)*
**Global Plating Inc** ........................................................................ E ...... 510 659-8764
  44620 S Grimmer Blvd Fremont (94538) *(P-8966)*
**Global Precision Manufacturing, Grass Valley** *Also Called: Taylor Investments LLC (P-9976)*
**Global Printing Sourcing & Dev, San Rafael** *Also Called: Goff Investment Group LLC (P-4406)*
**Global Publishing Inc** .................................................................. E
  4415 Technology Dr Fremont (94538) *(P-4404)*
**Global Rental Co Inc** ................................................................... C ...... 707 693-2520
  325 Industrial Way Dixon (95620) *(P-9423)*
**Global Silicon Electronics Inc** .................................................... E ...... 626 336-1888
  440 Cloverleaf Dr Baldwin Park (91706) *(P-10239)*
**Global Specialties Direct, West Sacramento** *Also Called: Global Steel Products Corp (P-3690)*
**Global Steel Fabricators Inc** ....................................................... F ...... 650 321-9533
  255 Demeter St East Palo Alto (94303) *(P-19195)*
**Global Steel Products Corp** ....................................................... E ...... 510 652-2060
  1030 Riverside Pkwy West Sacramento (95605) *(P-3690)*
**Global Sweeping Solutions, San Bernardino** *Also Called: Global Environmental Pdts Inc (P-13354)*
**Global Testing Corporation** ........................................................ D ...... 408 745-0718
  225 Pamela Dr Apt 205 Mountain View (94040) *(P-12448)*
**Global Truss, Vernon** *Also Called: Global Truss America LLC (P-7739)*
**Global Truss America LLC** ......................................................... D ...... 323 415-6225
  4295 Charter St Vernon (90058) *(P-7739)*
**Global V R, Milpitas** *Also Called: Virtual Technologies Inc (P-16263)*
**Global Wave Group** ..................................................................... E ...... 949 916-9800
  26970 Aliso Viejo Pkwy Aliso Viejo (92656) *(P-18353)*
**Global Wine Group** ...................................................................... E ...... 209 340-8500
  3750 E Woodbridge Rd Acampo (95220) *(P-1589)*
**Globalfoundries Dresden** ........................................................... A ...... 408 462-3900
  1050 E Arques Ave Sunnyvale (94085) *(P-12449)*
**Globalfoundries US 2 LLC** .......................................................... E ...... 408 462-3900
  2600 Great America Way Santa Clara (95054) *(P-12450)*
**Globalfoundries US Inc** ............................................................... A ...... 971 285-7461
  2600 Great America Way Santa Clara (95054) *(P-12451)*
**Globalfoundries US Inc** ............................................................... B ...... 408 462-3900
  1278 Reamwood Ave Sunnyvale (94089) *(P-12452)*

## ALPHABETIC SECTION

**Globalridge LLC** ..................................................... F ...... 800 225-4345
865 Parallel Dr Lakeport (95453) *(P-5242)*

**Globalux Lighting LLC** ............................................ F ...... 909 591-7506
773 S Benson Ave Ontario (91762) *(P-11496)*

**Globaluxe Inc** ......................................................... E ...... 805 583-4600
405 Science Dr Moorpark (93021) *(P-16136)*

**Globe Iron Foundry Inc** .......................................... D ...... 323 723-8983
5649 Randolph St Commerce (90040) *(P-7675)*

**Globe Plastics, Chino** *Also Called: PRC Composites LLC (P-6975)*

**Glocol Inc** ............................................................... E ...... 650 224-2108
6541 Puerto Dr Rancho Murieta (95683) *(P-16275)*

**Gloria Ferrer Winery, Sonoma** *Also Called: Freixenet Sonoma Caves Inc (P-1579)*

**Gloria Lance Inc (PA)** ............................................. D ...... 310 767-4400
15616 S Broadway Gardena (90248) *(P-2666)*

**Gloriann Farms Inc** ................................................ C ...... 209 221-7121
11104 W Tracy Blvd Tracy (95304) *(P-6644)*

**Glorystar Satellite Systems, Rocklin** *Also Called: Satellite Av LLC (P-17544)*

**Gloves In A Bottle Inc** ............................................ E ...... 818 248-9980
3720 Park Pl Montrose (91020) *(P-17039)*

**Glp German Light Products Inc** ............................. F ...... 818 767-8899
16170 Stagg St Van Nuys (91406) *(P-12453)*

**GLS US Freight Inc** ................................................ E ...... 909 627-2538
3561 Philadelphia St Chino (91710) *(P-4405)*

**Gluten Free Foods Mfg LLC (PA)** ........................... F ...... 909 823-8230
5010 Eucalyptus Ave Chino (91710) *(P-2215)*

**Glyntai Inc** ............................................................. F ...... 650 386-6932
705 N Shoreline Blvd Mountain View (94043) *(P-18354)*

**Glysens Incorporated** ............................................. E ...... 858 638-7708
3931 Sorrento Valley Blvd Ste 110 San Diego (92121) *(P-15102)*

**GM Associates Inc** ................................................. D ...... 510 430-0806
9824 Kitty Ln Oakland (94603) *(P-12987)*

**Gma Cover Corp** .................................................... C
1170 Somera Rd Los Angeles (90077) *(P-2975)*

**GMI, La Jolla** *Also Called: Groundmetrics Inc (P-232)*

**Gmi Inc** .................................................................. E ...... 619 429-4479
2626 Southport Way Ste E National City (91950) *(P-2957)*

**Gmic Vineyards LLC** .............................................. E ...... 707 996-3860
18596 Lomita Ave Sonoma (95476) *(P-1590)*

**Gmp Laboratories America Inc (PA)** ...................... D ...... 714 630-2467
2931 E La Jolla St Anaheim (92806) *(P-5466)*

**Gmp Labratories of America, Anaheim** *Also Called: Gmp Laboratories America Inc (P-5466)*

**Gmpc LLC** .............................................................. E ...... 707 766-1702
1670 Corporate Cir Ste 100 Petaluma (94954) *(P-15984)*

**Gms Elevator Services, San Dimas** *Also Called: Gms Elevator Services Inc (P-9472)*

**Gms Elevator Services Inc** .................................... E ...... 909 599-3904
401 Borrego Ct San Dimas (91773) *(P-9472)*

**Gmto Corporation** ................................................. D ...... 626 204-0500
300 N Lake Ave Fl 14 Pasadena (91101) *(P-14778)*

**Gmw Associates** .................................................... E ...... 650 802-8292
955 Industrial Rd San Carlos (94070) *(P-14873)*

**Gmw Associates** .................................................... F ...... 650 802-8292
951 Industrial Rd Ste D San Carlos (94070) *(P-16816)*

**GNB Corporation** ................................................... D ...... 916 395-3003
3200 Dwight Rd Ste 100 Elk Grove (95758) *(P-9555)*

**GNB Vacuum Excellence Defined, Elk Grove** *Also Called: GNB Corporation (P-9555)*

**GO Pallets Inc** ....................................................... F ...... 909 823-4663
15642 Slover Ave Fontana (92337) *(P-3344)*

**Go Sales.us, West Covina** *Also Called: Ola Nation LLC (P-2712)*

**Go/Links, San Jose** *Also Called: Golinks Enterprises Inc (P-18356)*

**Go2zero Strategies LLC** ........................................ F ...... 626 840-1850
6625 N Calle Eva Miranda Ste A Irwindale (91702) *(P-3757)*

**Goalsr Inc** .............................................................. E ...... 650 453-5844
933 Berryessa Rd Ste 10 San Jose (95133) *(P-18355)*

**Gobble, Morgan Hill** *Also Called: Gobble Inc (P-2216)*

**Gobble Inc** ............................................................. C ...... 650 847-1258
18675 Madrone Pkwy Morgan Hill (95037) *(P-2216)*

**Gobbler, Los Angeles** *Also Called: Media Gobbler Inc (P-18534)*

**Goff Investment Group LLC** .................................. E ...... 415 456-2934
135 3rd St Ste 150 San Rafael (94901) *(P-4406)*

**Gohz Inc** ................................................................ E ...... 800 603-1219
23555 Golden Springs Dr Ste K1 Diamond Bar (91765) *(P-11271)*

**Gold Coast Baking Company LLC** ......................... E ...... 714 545-2253
1590 E Saint Gertrude Pl Santa Ana (92705) *(P-1212)*

**Gold Coast Baking Company LLC** ......................... F ...... 818 575-7280
21160 Califa St Woodland Hills (91367) *(P-1213)*

**Gold Coast Baking Company LLC (PA)** ................. D ...... 818 575-7280
21250 Califa St Ste 104 Woodland Hills (91367) *(P-1214)*

**Gold Coast Ingredients Inc** .................................... D ...... 323 724-8935
2429 Yates Ave Commerce (90040) *(P-2217)*

**Gold Coast Sunwear, San Marcos** *Also Called: Peter Grimm Ltd (P-2849)*

**Gold Crest Industries Inc** ...................................... E ...... 909 930-9069
1018 E Acacia St Ontario (91761) *(P-2958)*

**Gold Medal Press, Dublin** *Also Called: AMP Printing Inc (P-4512)*

**Gold Mine Natural Food Company** ........................ F ...... 858 537-9830
13200 Danielson St Ste A-1 Poway (92064) *(P-17664)*

**Gold Peak Industries (north America) Inc** ............. E ...... 858 674-6099
11245 W Bernardo Ct Ste 104 San Diego (92127) *(P-13143)*

**Gold Prospectors Assn Amer, Murrieta** *Also Called: Gold Prospectors Assn Amer LLC (P-4260)*

**Gold Prospectors Assn Amer LLC** ........................ D ...... 951 699-4749
25819 Jefferson Ave Ste 110 Murrieta (92562) *(P-4260)*

**Gold River Mills LLC (PA)** ..................................... E ...... 530 661-1923
1620 E Kentucky Ave Woodland (95776) *(P-1079)*

**Gold Rush Coffee** .................................................. E ...... 707 442-2848
2626 Myrtle Ave Eureka (95501) *(P-17187)*

**Gold Star Foods, Dixon** *Also Called: Gold Star Foods Inc (P-2218)*

**Gold Star Foods Inc** .............................................. E ...... 909 843-9600
1000 Vaughn Rd Dixon (95620) *(P-2218)*

**Gold Star Foods Inc (HQ)** ..................................... D ...... 909 843-9600
3781 E Airport Dr Ontario (91761) *(P-2219)*

**Gold Star Painting, Modesto** *Also Called: R & M Painting Inc (P-448)*

**Gold Technologies Inc** .......................................... E ...... 408 321-9568
1648 Mabury Rd Ste A San Jose (95133) *(P-11457)*

**Goldak Inc** ............................................................. E ...... 818 240-2666
15835 Monte St Ste 104 Sylmar (91342) *(P-14195)*

**Golden Altos Corporation** ..................................... E ...... 408 956-1010
44061 Old Warm Springs Blvd Fremont (94538) *(P-14529)*

**Golden Applexx Co Inc** ......................................... F ...... 909 594-9788
19805 Harrison Ave Walnut (91789) *(P-4882)*

**Golden Bear Packaging Inc** ................................... E ...... 925 455-4283
6645 Las Positas Rd Livermore (94551) *(P-3850)*

**Golden Bear Sportswear, San Francisco** *Also Called: Gb Sport Sf LLC (P-2880)*

**Golden Bolt LLC** .................................................... E ...... 818 626-8261
9361 Canoga Ave Chatsworth (91311) *(P-8756)*

**Golden By-Products Inc** ........................................ D ...... 209 668-4855
13000 Newport Rd Ballico (95303) *(P-9861)*

**Golden Empire Con Pdts Inc** ................................. D ...... 661 833-4490
8261 Mccutchen Rd Bakersfield (93311) *(P-7339)*

**Golden Eye Media Usa Inc** .................................... F ...... 760 688-9962
1000 Camino De Las Ondas Carlsbad (92011) *(P-17001)*

**Golden Gate Capital, San Francisco** *Also Called: Golden Gate Private Equity Inc (P-17754)*

**Golden Gate Freightliner Inc** ................................. B ...... 559 486-4310
2727 E Central Ave Fresno (93725) *(P-9520)*

**Golden Gate Private Equity Inc (PA)** ..................... E ...... 415 983-2706
1 Embarcadero Ctr Fl 39 San Francisco (94111) *(P-17754)*

**Golden Gate Steel Inc** ........................................... F ...... 310 638-0855
19826 S Alameda St Compton (90221) *(P-8147)*

**Golden Gate Truck Center, Fresno** *Also Called: Golden Gate Freightliner Inc (P-9520)*

**Golden Grove Trading Inc** ..................................... F ...... 909 718-8000
468 S Humane Way Pomona (91766) *(P-4883)*

**Golden Island Jerky Co Inc, Rancho Cucamonga** *Also Called: Tfi of California Inc (P-674)*

**Golden Kraft Inc** .................................................... B ...... 562 926-8888
15500 Valley View Ave La Mirada (90638) *(P-4041)*

**Golden Mattress Co Inc** ........................................ D ...... 323 887-1888
11680 Wright Rd Lynwood (90262) *(P-3528)*

**Golden Pacific, Pomona** *Also Called: Travelers Choice Travelware (P-7143)*

**Golden Pacific Seafoods Inc** ................................. E ...... 714 589-8888
700 S Raymond Ave Fullerton (92831) *(P-9794)*

**Golden Plastics Corporation** ................................. F ...... 510 569-6465
8465 Baldwin St Oakland (94621) *(P-6845)*

**Golden Queen Mining Co LLC** ............................... C ...... 661 824-4300
2818 Silver Queen Rd Mojave (93501) *(P-103)*

# ALPHABETIC SECTION — Goodles

**Golden Rain Foundation (PA)** .......................................................... D ...... 925 988-7700
1001 Golden Rain Rd Walnut Creek (94595) *(P-17742)*

**Golden Rule Bindery Inc** ................................................................. E ...... 760 471-2013
221 Townsite Dr Vista (92084) *(P-5011)*

**Golden Rule Packaging, Vista** *Also Called: Golden Rule Bindery Inc (P-5011)*

**Golden Specialty Foods LLC** .......................................................... E ...... 562 802-2537
14605 Best Ave Norwalk (90650) *(P-2220)*

**Golden State Assembly Inc** ............................................................ C ...... 510 226-8155
18220 Butterfield Blvd Morgan Hill (95037) *(P-7727)*

**Golden State Assembly Inc (PA)** .................................................... C ...... 510 226-8155
47823 Westinghouse Dr Fremont (94539) *(P-7728)*

**Golden State Contractors, Stockton** *Also Called: West Coast Energy Systems LLC (P-19430)*

**Golden State Drilling Inc** ................................................................ D ...... 661 589-0730
3500 Fruitvale Ave Bakersfield (93308) *(P-160)*

**Golden State Engineering Inc** ........................................................ C ...... 562 634-3125
15338 Garfield Ave Paramount (90723) *(P-9738)*

**Golden State Fire Appratus Inc** ...................................................... F ...... 916 330-1638
7400 Reese Rd Sacramento (95828) *(P-13355)*

**Golden State Foods, Irvine** *Also Called: Golden State Foods Corp (P-2008)*

**Golden State Foods Corp** ............................................................... B ...... 626 465-7500
640 S 6th Ave City Of Industry (91746) *(P-1035)*

**Golden State Foods Corp (PA)** ....................................................... E ...... 949 247-8000
18301 Von Karman Ave Ste 1100 Irvine (92612) *(P-2008)*

**Golden State Graphics, Carlsbad** *Also Called: Gsg Printing Inc (P-4625)*

**Golden State Imports Intl Inc (PA)** .................................................. F ...... 510 995-1320
1101 Marina Village Pkwy Ste 201 Alameda (94501) *(P-16967)*

**Golden State Mixing Inc** ................................................................. E ...... 209 632-3656
415 D St Turlock (95380) *(P-836)*

**Golden State Trck Trlr Repr In** ........................................................ E ...... 888 881-8825
1354 Dayton St Salinas (93901) *(P-9521)*

**Golden State Vintners** .................................................................... E ...... 559 266-6548
7409 W Central Ave Fresno (93706) *(P-14)*

**Golden State Vintners (PA)** ............................................................ F ...... 707 254-4900
4596 S Tracy Blvd Tracy (95377) *(P-1591)*

**Golden State Vintners** .................................................................... E ...... 831 678-3991
1777 Metz Rd Soledad (93960) *(P-1592)*

**Golden State Vintners** .................................................................... E ...... 707 553-6480
1175 Commerce Blvd Vallejo (94503) *(P-1593)*

**Golden State Vintners** .................................................................... E ...... 707 254-1985
1075 Golden Gate Dr Napa (94558) *(P-1594)*

**Golden State Winery, Fresno** *Also Called: Golden State Vintners (P-14)*

**Golden Supreme Inc** ....................................................................... E ...... 562 903-1063
12304 Mccann Dr Santa Fe Springs (90670) *(P-16137)*

**Golden Temple, Los Angeles** *Also Called: East West Tea Company LLC (P-1070)*

**Golden Valley & Associates Inc** ...................................................... E ...... 209 549-1549
3511 Finch Rd # A Modesto (95357) *(P-9522)*

**Golden Valley Dairy Products** ......................................................... E ...... 559 687-1188
1025 E Bardsley Ave Tulare (93274) *(P-716)*

**Golden Valley Industries Inc** ........................................................... E ...... 209 939-3370
960 Lone Palm Ave Modesto (95351) *(P-598)*

**Golden Vly Grape Jice Wine LLC (PA)** .......................................... E ...... 559 661-4657
11770 Road 27 1/2 Madera (93637) *(P-1595)*

**Golden Vly Grape Jice Wine LLC** ................................................... E ...... 559 661-4657
11770 Road 27 And Half Madera (93637) *(P-1596)*

**Golden W Ppr Converting Corp** ...................................................... E ...... 510 317-0646
2480 Grant Ave San Lorenzo (94580) *(P-3918)*

**Golden West Envelope Corp** .......................................................... E ...... 510 452-5419
1009 Morton St Alameda (94501) *(P-4008)*

**Golden West Food Group Inc (PA)** ................................................. E ...... 888 807-3663
4401 S Downey Rd Vernon (90058) *(P-599)*

**Golden West Machine Inc** .............................................................. E ...... 562 903-1111
9930 Jordan Cir Santa Fe Springs (90670) *(P-10863)*

**Golden West Packg Group LLC (PA)** ............................................. B ...... 888 501-5893
15250 Don Julian Rd City Of Industry (91745) *(P-3851)*

**Golden West Refining Company** .................................................... F ...... 562 921-3581
13116 Imperial Hwy Santa Fe Springs (90670) *(P-6338)*

**Golden West Shutters, Lake Forest** *Also Called: ABC Custom Wood Shutters Inc (P-3105)*

**Golden West Technology** ............................................................... D ...... 714 738-3775
1180 E Valencia Dr Fullerton (92831) *(P-12123)*

**Goldencorr Sheets LLC** .................................................................. C ...... 626 369-6446
13890 Nelson Ave City Of Industry (91746) *(P-3852)*

**Goldeneye, Saint Helena** *Also Called: Duckhorn Wine Company (P-1545)*

**Goldenwood Truss Corporation** ...................................................... D ...... 805 659-2520
11032 Nardo St Ventura (93004) *(P-3308)*

**Goldfax, Laguna Beach** *Also Called: Data Processing Design Inc (P-17906)*

**Goldfire Corporation** ........................................................................ F ...... 510 354-3666
4882 Davenport Pl Fremont (94538) *(P-490)*

**Goldilocks, Hayward** *Also Called: Clarmil Manufacturing Corp (P-2168)*

**Goldilocks Bakeshop and Rest, Hayward** *Also Called: Goldilocks Corporation Calif (P-1215)*

**Goldilocks Corporation Calif (PA)** ................................................... E ...... 510 476-0700
30865 San Clemente St Hayward (94544) *(P-1215)*

**Golding Publications** ....................................................................... F ...... 951 244-1966
31558 Railroad Canyon Rd Canyon Lake (92587) *(P-5020)*

**Goldline Brands Inc** ........................................................................ E ...... 818 319-7038
7449 Fairplay Rd Somerset (95684) *(P-1597)*

**Goldridgepinotcom LLC** .................................................................. D ...... 707 823-4464
2500 Gravenstein Hwy N Sebastopol (95472) *(P-1598)*

**Goldsign, Huntington Park** *Also Called: Citizens of Humanity LLC (P-2745)*

**Goldstar Asphalt Products, Perris** *Also Called: Npg Inc (P-6366)*

**Goldstar Asphalt Products Inc** ........................................................ E ...... 951 940-1610
1354 Jet Way Perris (92571) *(P-6363)*

**Goldstone Land Company LLC** ...................................................... E ...... 209 368-3113
11900 Furry Rd Lodi (95240) *(P-1599)*

**Goldtec USA, San Jose** *Also Called: Gold Technologies Inc (P-11457)*

**Golet Wine Estates, Napa** *Also Called: Clos Du Val Wine Company Ltd (P-1510)*

**Golf Buddy, Santa Fe Springs** *Also Called: Deca International Corp (P-14177)*

**Golf Sales West, Oxnard** *Also Called: Golf Sales West Inc (P-15817)*

**Golf Sales West Inc** ........................................................................ E ...... 805 988-3363
1901 Eastman Ave Oxnard (93030) *(P-15817)*

**Golf Supply House Usa Inc** ............................................................. D ...... 714 983-0050
1340 N Jefferson St Anaheim (92807) *(P-15818)*

**Golinks Enterprises Inc** ................................................................... D ...... 562 715-4848
2558 Forest Ave San Jose (95117) *(P-18356)*

**Gomen Furniture Mfg Inc** ................................................................ E ...... 310 635-4894
11612 Wright Rd Lynwood (90262) *(P-3474)*

**Gonzales Park LLC** ......................................................................... C ...... 530 343-8725
1811 Concord Ave Ste 200 Chico (95928) *(P-17074)*

**Gonzalez Feliciano** .......................................................................... F ...... 909 236-1372
1583 E Grand Ave Pomona (91766) *(P-3140)*

**Gonzalez Pallets Inc (PA)** ............................................................... E ...... 408 999-0280
1261 Yard Ct San Jose (95133) *(P-3345)*

**Gooch & Housego Palo Alto LLC (HQ)** .......................................... E ...... 650 856-7911
44247 Nobel Dr Fremont (94538) *(P-12988)*

**Gooch and Housego Cal LLC** ......................................................... D ...... 805 529-3324
5390 Kazuko Ct Moorpark (93021) *(P-14779)*

**Good American LLC (PA)** ............................................................... E ...... 213 357-5100
1601 Vine St Los Angeles (90028) *(P-2761)*

**Good Culture LLC** ........................................................................... E ...... 949 545-9945
22 Corporate Park Irvine (92606) *(P-837)*

**Good Feet, Carlsbad** *Also Called: Drs Own Inc (P-15335)*

**Good Fellas Industries Inc** ............................................................... D ...... 323 924-9495
4400 Bandini Blvd Vernon (90058) *(P-17534)*

**Good Technology Software Inc** ....................................................... A ...... 408 212-7500
430 N Mary Ave Ste 200 Sunnyvale (94085) *(P-18357)*

**Good Tree, Montebello** *Also Called: Commerce On Demand LLC (P-16120)*

**Good View Future Group Inc** .......................................................... F ...... 408 834-5698
277 S B St San Mateo (94401) *(P-2221)*

**Good Worldwide LLC** ...................................................................... E ...... 323 206-6495
6380 Wilshire Blvd # 15 Los Angeles (90048) *(P-4407)*

**Good-West Rubber Corp (PA)** ........................................................ C ...... 909 987-1774
9615 Feron Blvd Rancho Cucamonga (91730) *(P-6497)*

**Goode Company, The, Cotati** *Also Called: Goode Printing and Mailing LLC (P-17799)*

**Goode Printing and Mailing LLC** ..................................................... E ...... 707 588-8028
361 Blodgett St Cotati (94931) *(P-17799)*

**Gooder Foods Inc** ........................................................................... E ...... 773 541-4108
415 River St Ste A Santa Cruz (95060) *(P-2114)*

**Goodfor LLC** .................................................................................... F ...... 833 488-3489
5927 Balfour Ct Ste 206 Carlsbad (92008) *(P-12842)*

**Goodie Closett LLC** ........................................................................ F ...... 980 895-0496
5255 Clayton Rd Concord (94521) *(P-16138)*

**Goodles, Santa Cruz** *Also Called: Gooder Foods Inc (P-2114)*

**Goodman Food Products Inc (PA)** ............................................. C ...... 310 674-3180
200 E Beach Ave Fl 1 Inglewood (90302) *(P-2222)*

**Goodrich, Fairfield** *Also Called: Universal Propulsion Co Inc (P-13984)*

**Goodrich Corporation** .......................................................... C ...... 714 984-1461
3355 E La Palma Ave Anaheim (92806) *(P-13854)*

**Goodrich Corporation** .......................................................... D ...... 562 944-4441
9920 Freeman Ave Santa Fe Springs (90670) *(P-13855)*

**Goodrich Corporation** .......................................................... F ...... 530 788-9214
5801 C St # 200 Beale Afb (95903) *(P-13856)*

**Goodrich Rconnaissance Systems, Beale Afb** *Also Called: Goodrich Corporation (P-13856)*

**Goodrx Inc (HQ)** ................................................................. F ...... 855 268-2822
2701 Olympic Blvd # A Santa Monica (90404) *(P-18358)*

**Goodwest Linings & Coatings, Rancho Cucamonga** *Also Called: Goodwest Rubber Linings Inc (P-6498)*

**Goodwest Rubber Linings Inc** ................................................ E ...... 888 499-0085
8814 Industrial Ln Rancho Cucamonga (91730) *(P-6498)*

**Goodwin Ammonia Company LLC (PA)** .................................... F ...... 714 894-0531
12361 Monarch St Garden Grove (92841) *(P-5874)*

**Goodwin Ammonia Company LLC** ........................................... D ...... 714 894-0531
12361 Monarch St Garden Grove (92841) *(P-5875)*

**Goodwin-Cole Company Inc** ................................................... E ...... 916 381-8888
8320 Belvedere Ave Sacramento (95826) *(P-17855)*

**Goodyear, Moreno Valley** *Also Called: Certified Tire & Svc Ctrs Inc (P-17447)*

**Goodyear Rbr Co Southern Cal, Rancho Cucamonga** *Also Called: Good-West Rubber Corp (P-6497)*

**Goover Inc** ......................................................................... F ...... 408 748-4333
440 N Wolfe Rd # E117 Sunnyvale (94085) *(P-18359)*

**Gopro, San Mateo** *Also Called: Gopro Inc (P-15642)*

**Gopro Inc (PA)** ................................................................... B ...... 650 332-7600
3025 Clearview Way San Mateo (94402) *(P-15642)*

**Gordon Biersch Brewing Company (PA)** ................................... F ...... 408 278-1008
357 E Taylor St San Jose (95112) *(P-1433)*

**Gordon Biersch Brewing Company, San Jose** *Also Called: Gordon Biersch Brewing Company (P-1433)*

**Gordon Brush Mfg Co Inc (PA)** ............................................... E ...... 323 724-7777
3737 Capitol Ave City Of Industry (90601) *(P-15930)*

**Gores Group LLC (PA)** ......................................................... D ...... 310 209-3010
9800 Wilshire Blvd Beverly Hills (90212) *(P-17730)*

**Gores Radio Holdings LLC** .................................................... D ...... 310 209-3010
10877 Wilshire Blvd Ste 1805 Los Angeles (90024) *(P-13245)*

**Gorilla Automotive Products, Buena Park** *Also Called: Amcor Industries Inc (P-13455)*

**Gorilla Circuits (PA)** ............................................................ C ...... 408 294-9897
1445 Oakland Rd San Jose (95112) *(P-12124)*

**Gorlitz Sewer & Drain Inc** .................................................... E ...... 562 944-3060
10132 Norwalk Blvd Santa Fe Springs (90670) *(P-10562)*

**Gorman Catalog Printing Inc** ................................................. E
492 Koller St San Francisco (94110) *(P-4619)*

**Gorman Manufacturing Company Inc (PA)** ............................... C ...... 650 555-0000
492 Koller St San Francisco (94110) *(P-4620)*

**Gosecure Inc (PA)** .............................................................. C ...... 301 442-3432
13220 Evening Creek Dr S Ste 107 San Diego (92128) *(P-17551)*

**Gossamer Bio Inc (PA)** ........................................................ C ...... 858 684-1300
3013 Science Park Rd Ste 200 San Diego (92121) *(P-5467)*

**Goto California Inc (HQ)** ...................................................... F ...... 619 691-8722
6120 Business Center Ct Ste F200 San Diego (92154) *(P-11664)*

**Gotprint.com, Burbank** *Also Called: Printograph Inc (P-4736)*

**Gott's Roadside, Saint Helena** *Also Called: Gotts Partners LP (P-17581)*

**Gotts Partners LP** ............................................................... E ...... 415 213-2992
1344 Adams St Saint Helena (94574) *(P-17581)*

**Gould & Bass Company Inc** .................................................. E ...... 909 623-6793
1431 W 2nd St Pomona (91766) *(P-14530)*

**Gourmet Coffee Warehouse Inc (PA)** ..................................... E ...... 323 871-8930
920 N Formosa Ave Los Angeles (90046) *(P-2072)*

**Gourmet Electronics Ltd** ...................................................... E ...... 408 467-1100
1805 Junction Ave San Jose (95131) *(P-12989)*

**Gourmet Foods Inc (PA)** ..................................................... D ...... 310 632-3300
2910 E Harcourt St Compton (90221) *(P-17114)*

**Gourmet Plus Inc** ............................................................... E ...... 415 643-9945
705 Bliss Ave Pittsburg (94565) *(P-17402)*

**Government Technology, Folsom** *Also Called: Sedona Ventures Inc (P-19128)*

**Governmentjobscom Inc** ...................................................... C ...... 877 204-4442
2120 Park Pl Ste 100 El Segundo (90245) *(P-18360)*

**Goyard Miami LLC** .............................................................. C ...... 415 398-1110
345 Powell St San Francisco (94102) *(P-7131)*

**GP Batteries, San Diego** *Also Called: Gold Peak Industries (north America) Inc (P-13143)*

**GP Color Imaging Group, North Hollywood** *Also Called: Wes Go Inc (P-4981)*

**GP Merger Sub Inc** ............................................................. D ...... 562 946-7722
9401 Ann St Santa Fe Springs (90670) *(P-7225)*

**GPA Printing CA LLC (PA)** .................................................... F ...... 818 237-9771
9655 De Soto Ave Chatsworth (91311) *(P-4621)*

**Gpc, Irvine** *Also Called: Global Pcci (gpc) (P-8847)*

**GPde Slva Spces Incrporation (PA)** ....................................... D ...... 562 407-2643
8531 Loch Lomond Dr Pico Rivera (90660) *(P-2223)*

**Gpodisplay** ....................................................................... F ...... 510 659-9855
7668 Las Positas Rd Livermore (94551) *(P-15985)*

**Gps Associates Inc** ............................................................ E ...... 949 408-3162
1803 Carnegie Ave Santa Ana (92705) *(P-5907)*

**Grabit Interactive Inc** ......................................................... E ...... 844 472-2488
14724 Ventura Blvd Sherman Oaks (91403) *(P-17788)*

**Grace Communications Inc (PA)** ........................................... E ...... 213 628-4384
210 S Spring St Los Angeles (90012) *(P-4123)*

**Grace Dvson Discovery Sciences, Hesperia** *Also Called: W R Grace & Co-Conn (P-14754)*

**Gracek Jewelry, Newport Coast** *Also Called: Krystal Ventures LLC (P-15696)*

**Gracing Brand Management Inc** ........................................... B ...... 626 297-2472
1108 W Valley Blvb Ste 660 Alhambra (91803) *(P-2861)*

**Graco Childrens Products Inc** ............................................... B ...... 770 418-7200
17182 Nevada St Victorville (92394) *(P-3504)*

**Gradient, San Francisco** *Also Called: Treau Inc (P-10522)*

**Graffiti Shield Inc** .............................................................. E ...... 714 575-1100
2940 E La Palma Ave Ste D Anaheim (92806) *(P-6561)*

**Grafico Inc** ....................................................................... F ...... 562 832-7601
15326 Cornet St Santa Fe Springs (90670) *(P-5026)*

**Graham Webb International Inc (HQ)** .................................... D ...... 760 918-3600
6109 De Soto Ave Woodland Hills (91367) *(P-5982)*

**Graid Technology Inc (PA)** .................................................. F ...... 669 258-8102
5201 Great America Pkwy Ste 320 Santa Clara (95054) *(P-18361)*

**Grail Inc (PA)** ................................................................... C ...... 833 694-2553
1525a Obrien Dr Menlo Park (94025) *(P-5468)*

**Granatelli Motor Sports Inc** ................................................. E ...... 805 486-6644
1000 Yarnell Pl Oxnard (93033) *(P-13508)*

**Granberg International, Pittsburg** *Also Called: Granberg Pump and Meter Ltd (P-9712)*

**Granberg Pump and Meter Ltd** ............................................. F ...... 707 562-2099
1051 Los Medanos St Pittsburg (94565) *(P-9712)*

**Grand General, Rancho Dominguez** *Also Called: Grand General Accessories LLC (P-11214)*

**Grand General Accessories LLC** ............................................ E ...... 310 631-2589
1965 E Vista Bella Way Rancho Dominguez (90220) *(P-11214)*

**Grand Prix Performance, Costa Mesa** *Also Called: Grand Prix Road Trends Inc (P-17452)*

**Grand Prix Road Trends Inc (PA)** .......................................... F ...... 949 645-7022
1718 Newport Blvd Costa Mesa (92627) *(P-17452)*

**Grand Textile, Cerritos** *Also Called: Dool Fna Inc (P-2435)*

**Grand West Inc (PA)** .......................................................... E ...... 323 235-2700
1441 E Adams Blvd Los Angeles (90011) *(P-2472)*

**Grandall Distributing LLC** ................................................... E ...... 818 242-6640
321 El Bonito Ave Glendale (91204) *(P-19094)*

**Grande Vitesse Systems, San Francisco** *Also Called: Insignia (P-18980)*

**Grandma Lucys LLC** ........................................................... F ...... 949 206-8547
30432 Esperanza Rcho Sta Marg (92688) *(P-17705)*

**Grandville Llc** ................................................................... F ...... 213 382-3878
1670 Cordova St Los Angeles (90007) *(P-1276)*

**GRANITE, Watsonville** *Also Called: Granite Construction Inc (P-385)*

**Granite Construction Inc** ..................................................... B ...... 831 724-1011
585 W Beach St Watsonville (95076) *(P-385)*

**Granite Gold Inc** ................................................................ D ...... 858 499-8933
12780 Danielson Ct Ste A Poway (92064) *(P-5908)*

**Granite Rock Co** ................................................................ E ...... 831 768-2300
Quarry Rd Aromas (95004) *(P-313)*

**Granite Rock Co** ................................................................ D ...... 831 392-3700
1755 Del Monte Blvd Seaside (93955) *(P-7449)*

**Granite Rock Company (PA)** ................................................ D ...... 831 768-2000
350 Technology Dr Watsonville (95076) *(P-314)*

**Granite Rock Company** ....................................................... D ...... 650 482-3800
365 Blomquist St Redwood City (94063) *(P-6364)*

# ALPHABETIC SECTION  
## Greenshine New Energy LLC

**Granitize Aviation Intl, South Gate** *Also Called: Granitize Products Inc (P-5909)*
**Granitize Products Inc** .................................................. D ...... 562 923-5438
11022 Vulcan St South Gate (90280) *(P-5909)*

**Granlund Candies, Yucaipa** *Also Called: B B G Management Group (P-17139)*

**Grant Piston Rings, Anaheim** *Also Called: Rtr Industries LLC (P-10625)*

**Grape Links Inc** ............................................................... E ...... 707 524-8000
420 Aviation Blvd Ste 106 Santa Rosa (95403) *(P-1600)*

**Grapeseed Wines, Geyserville** *Also Called: J Pedroncelli Winery Inc (P-1625)*

**Graphic Business Solutions Inc** .................................... E ...... 619 258-4081
1912 John Towers Ave El Cajon (92020) *(P-16991)*

**Graphic Center, Sacramento** *Also Called: Terry Grimes Graphic Center of Sacramento Inc (P-4783)*

**Graphic Color Systems Inc** ........................................... D ...... 323 283-3000
1166 W Garvey Ave Monterey Park (91754) *(P-4622)*

**Graphic Enterprises Inc** ................................................. E ...... 707 528-2644
440 Tesconi Cir Santa Rosa (95401) *(P-4623)*

**Graphic Film Group LLC (PA)** ...................................... F ...... 310 887-6330
1901 Avenue Of The Stars Los Angeles (90067) *(P-4261)*

**Graphic Ink Corp** ............................................................ E ...... 714 901-2805
5382 Industrial Dr Huntington Beach (92649) *(P-17829)*

**Graphic Ink and Graphic Ink, Huntington Beach** *Also Called: Graphic Ink Corp (P-17829)*

**Graphic Lab Inc** .............................................................. E ...... 858 437-9100
1263 Pioneer Way El Cajon (92020) *(P-4884)*

**Graphic Packaging Intl LLC** .......................................... C ...... 530 533-1058
525 Airport Pkwy Oroville (95965) *(P-4885)*

**Graphic Prints Inc** .......................................................... E ...... 310 870-1239
904 Silver Spur Rd Ste 415 Rolling Hills Estate (90274) *(P-3008)*

**Graphic Reproduction** ................................................... F ...... 510 268-9980
2327 Union St Oakland (94607) *(P-17813)*

**Graphic Research Inc** .................................................... E ...... 818 886-7340
3339 Durham Ct Burbank (91504) *(P-12125)*

**Graphic Sportswear LLC** ............................................... D ...... 415 206-7200
173 Utah Ave South San Francisco (94080) *(P-4886)*

**Graphic Trends Incorporated** ....................................... E ...... 562 531-2339
7301 Adams St Paramount (90723) *(P-4887)*

**Graphic Visions Inc** ....................................................... E ...... 818 845-8393
7119 Fair Ave North Hollywood (91605) *(P-4624)*

**Graphics 2000 LLC** ........................................................ D ...... 714 879-1188
1600 E Valencia Dr Fullerton (92831) *(P-4888)*

**Graphics Microsystems LLC (DH)** ................................ D
484 Oakmead Pkwy Sunnyvale (94085) *(P-9767)*

**Graphics One, Sunnyvale** *Also Called: Prism Inks (P-6260)*

**Graphics United, Covina** *Also Called: Shift Calendars Inc (P-4762)*

**Graphiq LLC** .................................................................... C ...... 805 335-2433
101a Innovation Pl Santa Barbara (93108) *(P-4408)*

**Graphtec, Irvine** *Also Called: Graphtec America Inc (P-14420)*

**Graphtec America Inc (DH)** ........................................... E ...... 949 770-6010
17462 Armstrong Ave Irvine (92614) *(P-14420)*

**Grass Valley Inc (HQ)** .................................................... D ...... 530 265-1000
310 Providence Mine Rd Nevada City (95959) *(P-11859)*

**Grass Valley Usa LLC (PA)** ........................................... B ...... 800 547-8949
310 Providence Mine Rd Ste 200 Nevada City (95959) *(P-11767)*

**Grating Pacific Inc (PA)** ................................................. E ...... 562 598-4314
3651 Sausalito St Los Alamitos (90720) *(P-8148)*

**Gray, Gary Phrmcst Cmplex Lab, Visalia** *Also Called: Gary W Gray (P-16133)*

**Grayd-A Prcsion Met Fbricators** .................................. E ...... 562 944-8951
13233 Florence Ave Santa Fe Springs (90670) *(P-8459)*

**Graysix Company** .......................................................... E ...... 510 845-5936
2427 4th St Berkeley (94710) *(P-8460)*

**Grayson Service Inc** ...................................................... F ...... 661 589-5444
1845 Greeley Rd Bakersfield (93314) *(P-231)*

**Great Amercn Seafood Import Co, Carson** *Also Called: Southwind Foods LLC (P-2043)*

**Great American Packaging** ........................................... E ...... 323 582-2247
4361 S Soto St Vernon (90058) *(P-3968)*

**Great American Wineries Inc** ........................................ E ...... 831 920-4736
2511 Garden Rd Ste B100 Monterey (93940) *(P-1601)*

**Great Eastern Entertainment Co** .................................. E ...... 310 638-5058
610 W Carob St Compton (90220) *(P-4409)*

**Great Pacific Elbow LLC** ............................................... E ...... 909 606-5551
13900 Sycamore Way Chino (91710) *(P-8461)*

**Great Pacific Elbow Company, Chino** *Also Called: Great Pacific Elbow LLC (P-8461)*

**Great Pacific Patagonia, Ventura** *Also Called: Patagonia Inc (P-2636)*

**Great River Food, City Of Industry** *Also Called: Derek and Constance Lee Corp (P-639)*

**Great Spaces USA, Merced** *Also Called: Olde World Corporation (P-3666)*

**Great Wall International Corp** ....................................... F ...... 626 457-1022
617 S Raymond Ave Alhambra (91803) *(P-7538)*

**Great Western Grinding Inc** .......................................... F ...... 714 890-6592
15292 Bolsa Chica St Huntington Beach (92649) *(P-19095)*

**Great Western Malting Co** ............................................ D ...... 360 991-0888
995 Joshua Way Ste B Vista (92081) *(P-1468)*

**Great Western Packaging LLC** .................................... D ...... 818 464-3800
8230 Haskell Ave 8240 Van Nuys (91406) *(P-4889)*

**Greatbatch Medical, San Diego** *Also Called: Integer Holdings Corporation (P-15120)*

**Grech Motors LLC (PA)** ................................................. E ...... 951 688-8347
6915 Arlington Ave Riverside (92504) *(P-19230)*

**Greco and Sons, Vista** *Also Called: Bellissimo Distribution LLC (P-849)*

**Gredes Corporation** ....................................................... E ...... 714 262-9150
15615 Alton Pkwy Ste 450 Irvine (92618) *(P-13509)*

**Green Circuits Inc** .......................................................... C ...... 408 526-1700
1130 Ringwood Ct San Jose (95131) *(P-12126)*

**Green Convergence (PA)** .............................................. D ...... 661 294-9495
28476 Westinghouse Pl Valencia (91355) *(P-16767)*

**Green Dragon, Los Angeles** *Also Called: Cmk Manufacturing LLC (P-2444)*

**Green Dragon Caregivers Inc** ....................................... F ...... 818 997-1368
7236 Varna Ave North Hollywood (91605) *(P-5243)*

**Green Hills Software, Santa Barbara** *Also Called: Green Hills Software LLC (P-18362)*

**Green Hills Software LLC (HQ)** .................................... C ...... 805 965-6044
30 W Sola St Santa Barbara (93101) *(P-18362)*

**Green Room Oc, Santa Ana** *Also Called: Outer Rebel Inc (P-2907)*

**Green Rubber-Kennedy Ag LP (PA)** ............................. E ...... 831 753-6100
1310 Dayton St Salinas (93901) *(P-6645)*

**Green Spot Packaging Inc** ............................................ E ...... 909 625-8771
100 S Cambridge Ave Claremont (91711) *(P-1890)*

**Green Spot USA, Claremont** *Also Called: Green Spot Packaging Inc (P-1890)*

**Green Star Labs Inc** ...................................................... E ...... 619 489-9020
4075 Ruffin Rd San Diego (92123) *(P-5244)*

**Green Valley Foods Product** ........................................ F ...... 760 964-1105
25684 Community Blvd Barstow (92311) *(P-717)*

**Greenall, Suisun City** *Also Called: E B Stone & Son Inc (P-17271)*

**Greenball Corp (PA)** ...................................................... E ...... 714 782-3060
222 S Harbor Blvd Ste 700 Anaheim (92805) *(P-16408)*

**Greenbox Art and Culture, San Diego** *Also Called: No Boundaries Inc (P-4707)*

**Greenbroz Inc** ................................................................. F ...... 844 379-8746
955 Vernon Way El Cajon (92020) *(P-9355)*

**Greene & Company** ....................................................... E ...... 212 203-1107
9465 Wilshire Blvd Ste 820 Beverly Hills (90212) *(P-15693)*

**Greene Group Industries, Oceanside** *Also Called: Southwest Greene Intl Inc (P-8889)*

**Greener Printer, Richmond** *Also Called: Tulip Pubg & Graphics Inc (P-4792)*

**Greenfields Outdoor Fitnes Inc** .................................... F ...... 888 315-9037
2617 W Woodland Dr Anaheim (92801) *(P-15819)*

**Greenheck Fan Corporation** ......................................... D ...... 916 643-4616
3034 Peacekeeper Way Mcclellan (95652) *(P-9987)*

**Greenheck Fan Corporation** ......................................... D ...... 916 626-3400
170 Cyber Ct Rocklin (95765) *(P-9988)*

**Greenkraft Inc** ................................................................. F ...... 714 545-7777
2530 S Birch St Santa Ana (92707) *(P-13356)*

**Greenlane Infrastructure LLC** ...................................... E ...... 503 839-8116
3101 Ocean Park Blvd Ste 100 Santa Monica (90405) *(P-13171)*

**Greenliant Systems Inc** ................................................. C ...... 408 217-7400
3970 Freedom Cir Ste 100 Santa Clara (95054) *(P-12454)*

**Greenpath Recovery Recycl Svcs, Colton** *Also Called: Greenpath Recovery West Inc (P-16960)*

**Greenpath Recovery West Inc** ..................................... D ...... 909 954-0686
330 W Citrus St Ste 250 Colton (92324) *(P-16960)*

**Greenpower Motor Company Inc** ................................. D ...... 909 308-0960
8885 Haven Ave Ste 200 Rancho Cucamonga (91730) *(P-13357)*

**Greenscreen** ................................................................... E ...... 310 837-0526
725 S Figueroa St Ste 1825 Los Angeles (90017) *(P-96)*

**Greenshine New Energy LLC** ....................................... D ...... 949 609-9636
23661 Birtcher Dr Lake Forest (92630) *(P-11599)*

**Greenvolts Inc** .................................................................. D ...... 415 963-4030
19200 Stevens Creek Blvd Ste 200 Cupertino (95014) *(P-8068)*

**Greenwaste Recovery LLC** .................................................. E ...... 408 283-4800
610 E Gish Rd San Jose (95112) *(P-6846)*

**Greenwave Reality Inc** ........................................................ E ...... 714 805-9283
15420 Laguna Canyon Rd Ste 150 Irvine (92618) *(P-18978)*

**Greenwave Systems, Irvine** *Also Called: Greenwave Reality Inc (P-18978)*

**Greenwich Biosciences LLC (DH)** ....................................... E ...... 760 795-2200
5750 Fleet St Ste 200 Carlsbad (92008) *(P-5469)*

**Greenwich Biosciences, Inc., Carlsbad** *Also Called: Greenwich Biosciences LLC (P-5469)*

**Greenwood Hall Inc** .............................................................. C ...... 310 905-8300
6230 Wilshire Blvd Ste 136 Los Angeles (90048) *(P-19351)*

**Grefco Dicaperl, Torrance** *Also Called: Dicaperl Corporation (P-338)*

**Gregory Patterson** ................................................................ E ...... 831 636-1015
2960 San Juan Rd Aromas (95004) *(P-8627)*

**Greif Inc** ................................................................................ E ...... 323 724-7500
6001 S Eastern Ave Commerce (90040) *(P-3371)*

**Greif Inc** ................................................................................ D ...... 209 383-4396
2400 Cooper Ave Merced (95348) *(P-3904)*

**Greif Inc** ................................................................................ D ...... 408 779-2161
235 San Pedro Ave Morgan Hill (95037) *(P-3905)*

**Greif Inc** ................................................................................ D ...... 909 350-2112
8250 Almeria Ave Fontana (92335) *(P-7934)*

**Greiner Heating & AC, Dixon** *Also Called: Greiner Heating Air & Elc Inc (P-422)*

**Greiner Heating Air & Elc Inc** ............................................... E ...... 707 678-1784
8235 Pedrick Rd Dixon (95620) *(P-422)*

**Greka, Santa Maria** *Also Called: Greka Integrated Inc (P-187)*

**Greka Integrated Inc** ............................................................ C ...... 805 347-8700
1700 Sinton Rd Santa Maria (93458) *(P-187)*

**Gremlin Inc** ........................................................................... D ...... 408 214-9885
440 N Barranca Ave Ste 3101 Walnut (91789) *(P-18363)*

**Gremlin Software, Inc., Walnut** *Also Called: Gremlin Inc (P-18363)*

**Greneker LLC** ....................................................................... E ...... 323 263-9000
3110 E 12th St Los Angeles (90023) *(P-16139)*

**Greneker Solutions, Los Angeles** *Also Called: Pacific Manufacturing MGT Inc (P-3700)*

**Gresean Industries Inc** ......................................................... E
6320 Caballero Blvd Buena Park (90620) *(P-491)*

**Grey Studio, Los Angeles** *Also Called: Grey Studio Inc (P-2417)*

**Grey Studio Inc** .................................................................... F ...... 323 780-8111
629 S Clarence St Los Angeles (90023) *(P-2417)*

**Grgich Hills Cellar** ................................................................. E ...... 707 963-2784
1829 St Helena Hwy Rutherford (94573) *(P-1602)*

**Grid Dynamics Holdings Inc (PA)** ........................................ E ...... 650 523-5000
5000 Executive Pkwy Ste 520 San Ramon (94583) *(P-18364)*

**Gridbright, Alamo** *Also Called: Gridbright Inc (P-18979)*

**Gridbright Inc** ....................................................................... F ...... 925 899-9025
618 Oakshire Pl Alamo (94507) *(P-18979)*

**Gridgain Systems Inc (PA)** ................................................... C ...... 650 241-2281
1065 E Hillsdale Blvd Ste 410 Foster City (94404) *(P-18365)*

**Griff Industries Inc** ................................................................ F ...... 661 728-0111
4515 Runway Dr Lancaster (93536) *(P-6847)*

**Grifols Biologicals LLC (DH)** ................................................ D ...... 323 225-2221
5555 Valley Blvd Los Angeles (90032) *(P-5833)*

**Grifols Usa LLC** ................................................................... D ...... 760 931-8444
995 Park Center Dr Vista (92081) *(P-5834)*

**Grillin & Chillin Inc** ................................................................ E ...... 831 637-2337
211 Donald Dr Hollister (95023) *(P-17582)*

**Grillin & Chillin Downtown, Hollister** *Also Called: Grillin & Chillin Inc (P-17582)*

**Grimaud Farms California Inc (DH)** ..................................... E ...... 209 466-3200
1320 S Aurora St Ste A Stockton (95206) *(P-694)*

**Grimmway Enterprises Inc** ................................................... C ...... 661 854-6200
14141 Di Giorgio Rd Arvin (93203) *(P-19517)*

**Grinding & Dicing Services Inc** ............................................ E ...... 408 451-2000
925 Berryessa Rd San Jose (95133) *(P-12455)*

**Grindstone Wines LLC** ......................................................... E ...... 530 393-2162
130 Cortina School Rd Arbuckle (95912) *(P-1603)*

**Grinnell LLC** ......................................................................... C ...... 707 578-3212
3077 Wiljan Ct Ste B Santa Rosa (95407) *(P-10091)*

**Grisby Gaming & Tech LLC** ................................................. E ...... 415 463-8200
200 S Linden Ave Apt 5f Rialto (92376) *(P-19038)*

**Grisly Manor LLC** ................................................................. F ...... 714 482-8194
11799 Sebastian Way Ste 103 Rancho Cucamonga (91730) *(P-18366)*

**Grisly Studios, Rancho Cucamonga** *Also Called: Grisly Manor LLC (P-18366)*

**Griswald Industries, Perris** *Also Called: Griswold Industries (P-16876)*

**Griswold Controls, Irvine** *Also Called: Griswold Controls LLC (P-9187)*

**Griswold Controls LLC (PA)** ................................................. D ...... 949 559-6000
1700 Barranca Pkwy Irvine (92606) *(P-9187)*

**Griswold Industries (PA)** ...................................................... B ...... 949 722-4800
1701 Placentia Ave Costa Mesa (92627) *(P-7847)*

**Griswold Industries** .............................................................. E ...... 951 657-1718
24100 Water Ave Perris (92570) *(P-16876)*

**Griswold Pump Company** .................................................... E ...... 909 422-1700
22069 Van Buren St Grand Terrace (92313) *(P-9925)*

**Gritstone, Emeryville** *Also Called: Gritstone Bio Inc (P-5835)*

**Gritstone Bio Inc (PA)** .......................................................... C ...... 510 871-6100
5959 Horton St Ste 300 Emeryville (94608) *(P-5835)*

**Grizzzly Clothing, Torrance** *Also Called: Meg Company Inc (P-17301)*

**Gro-Power Inc** ...................................................................... E ...... 909 393-3744
15065 Telephone Ave Chino (91710) *(P-6172)*

**Groove Labs Inc** ................................................................... D ...... 650 999-0200
660 4th St # 684 San Francisco (94107) *(P-18367)*

**Groskopf Warehouse & Logistics** ........................................ E ...... 707 939-3100
20580 8th St E Sonoma (95476) *(P-1604)*

**Grossi Fabrication Inc** .......................................................... F ...... 209 883-2817
3200 Tully Rd Hughson (95326) *(P-9219)*

**Groth Vineyards and Winery** ............................................... E ...... 707 944-0290
750 Oakville Cross Rd Oakville (94562) *(P-15)*

**Ground Control Business MGT (DH)** ................................... E ...... 310 315-6200
2049 Century Park E Ste 1400 Los Angeles (90067) *(P-2438)*

**Ground Control Inc** .............................................................. E ...... 415 508-8589
1485 Bay Shore Blvd Ste 451 San Francisco (94124) *(P-11860)*

**Ground Fueling, Irvine** *Also Called: Eaton Corporation (P-13835)*

**Ground Hog Inc** ................................................................... E ...... 909 478-5700
1470 Victoria Ct San Bernardino (92408) *(P-9424)*

**Groundmetrics Inc** ............................................................... F ...... 619 786-8023
7514 Girard Ave Ste 1306 La Jolla (92037) *(P-232)*

**Groundwork Coffee, North Hollywood** *Also Called: Groundwork Coffee Roasters LLC (P-2073)*

**Groundwork Coffee Company, Los Angeles** *Also Called: Gourmet Coffee Warehouse Inc (P-2072)*

**Groundwork Coffee Roasters LLC** ...................................... C ...... 818 506-6020
5457 Cleon Ave North Hollywood (91601) *(P-2073)*

**Group Five, Whittier** *Also Called: Russ Bassett Corp (P-3454)*

**Group H Engineering** .......................................................... E ...... 818 999-0999
2030 Vista Ave Sierra Madre (91024) *(P-233)*

**Group Manufacturing Svcs Inc (PA)** ................................... D ...... 408 436-1040
1928 Hartog Dr San Jose (95131) *(P-8462)*

**Group Manufacturing Svcs Inc** ........................................... F ...... 916 858-3270
2751 Mercantile Dr Ste 900 Rancho Cordova (95742) *(P-8463)*

**Grover Manufacturing, South El Monte** *Also Called: Grover Smith Mfg Corp (P-9926)*

**Grover Products Co** ............................................................ D ...... 323 263-9981
3424 E Olympic Blvd Los Angeles (90023) *(P-13510)*

**Grover Smith Mfg Corp** ....................................................... E ...... 323 724-3444
9717 Factorial Way South El Monte (91733) *(P-9926)*

**Grow More Inc** .................................................................... D ...... 310 515-1700
15600 New Century Dr Gardena (90248) *(P-6201)*

**Grow West LLC** ................................................................... E ...... 707 678-5542
7235 Tremont Rd Dixon (95620) *(P-6173)*

**Growers Ice Co** ................................................................... E ...... 831 424-5781
1124 Abbott St Salinas (93901) *(P-2109)*

**Growest Inc (PA)** ................................................................ F ...... 951 638-1000
1660 Chicago Ave Ste M11 Riverside (92507) *(P-1605)*

**Growest Development, Riverside** *Also Called: Growest Inc (P-1605)*

**Grubb & Nadler Inc** ............................................................. E ...... 760 728-0040
1719 Rainbow Valley Blvd Fallbrook (92028) *(P-113)*

**Grubb & Nadler Inc (PA)** ..................................................... E ...... 415 694-6441
1634 Jerrold Ave San Francisco (94124) *(P-114)*

**Gruber Systems Inc** ............................................................ E ...... 661 257-0464
29071 The Old Rd Valencia (91355) *(P-9626)*

**Gruma Corporation** ............................................................. B ...... 323 803-1400
5505 E Olympic Blvd Commerce (90022) *(P-2094)*

## ALPHABETIC SECTION — Gyrfalcon Technology Inc

Gruma Corporation .................................................................. D ...... 909 980-3566
    11559 Jersey Blvd Ste A Rancho Cucamonga (91730) *(P-2095)*

Gruma Corporation .................................................................. D ...... 559 498-7820
    2849 E Edgar Ave Fresno (93706) *(P-2224)*

Grundfos Pumps Manufacturing Corporation (DH) .............. C ...... 559 292-8000
    5900 E Shields Ave Fresno (93727) *(P-9927)*

Grupo Flor Corporation ........................................................... D ...... 559 940-1070
    514 Work St Salinas (93901) *(P-3)*

GS Cosmeceutical Usa Inc ..................................................... D ...... 925 371-5000
    131 Pullman St Livermore (94551) *(P-5983)*

Gsg Printing Inc (PA) ............................................................... E ...... 760 752-9500
    2304 Faraday Ave Carlsbad (92008) *(P-4625)*

Gsi Technology Inc (PA) .......................................................... D ...... 408 331-8800
    1213 Elko Dr Sunnyvale (94089) *(P-12456)*

Gsl, Sacramento Also Called: Gsl Fine Lithographers *(P-4626)*

Gsl Fine Lithographers ............................................................ E ...... 916 231-1410
    1281 National Dr Sacramento (95834) *(P-4626)*

Gsl Tech Inc ............................................................................ F ...... 877 572-9617
    172 W Pomona Ave Monrovia (91016) *(P-760)*

Gsms Inc (PA) ......................................................................... E ...... 805 477-9866
    5187 Camino Ruiz Camarillo (93012) *(P-5470)*

Gsp Metal Finishing Inc ........................................................... E ...... 818 744-1328
    16520 S Figueroa St Gardena (90248) *(P-8967)*

Gst Industries, Inc., Northridge Also Called: Aviation Design Group Inc *(P-13792)*

GT Precision Inc ...................................................................... C ...... 310 323-4374
    1629 W 132nd St Gardena (90249) *(P-8724)*

GT Styling Corp ....................................................................... E ...... 714 644-9214
    2830 E Via Martens Anaheim (92806) *(P-6848)*

Gtran Inc (PA) .......................................................................... E ...... 805 445-4500
    829 Flynn Rd Camarillo (93012) *(P-12990)*

GTS Distribution- Northern Cal, Santa Clara Also Called: Gamus LLC *(P-17296)*

Gts Living Foods LLC ............................................................. E ...... 323 581-7787
    4646 Hampton St Vernon (90058) *(P-1891)*

Gts Living Foods LLC (PA) ..................................................... A ...... 323 581-7787
    4415 Bandini Blvd Vernon (90058) *(P-1892)*

Gtt International Inc ................................................................. E ...... 951 788-8729
    1615 Eastridge Ave Riverside (92507) *(P-16427)*

Gu ............................................................................................ E ...... 510 527-4664
    1204 10th St Berkeley (94710) *(P-5471)*

Gu Pure Performing Energy, Berkeley Also Called: Sports Street Marketing A California Limited Partnership *(P-2025)*

Guadalupe Associates Inc (PA) .............................................. F ...... 415 387-2324
    1348 10th Ave San Francisco (94122) *(P-4410)*

Guardian Analytics Inc ............................................................ E ...... 650 383-9200
    2465 Latham St Ste 200 Mountain View (94040) *(P-18368)*

Guardian Fire & Safety, Visalia Also Called: Guardian Fire Service Inc *(P-17706)*

Guardian Fire Service Inc ........................................................ F ...... 559 651-0919
    8248 W Doe Ave Visalia (93291) *(P-17706)*

Guardian Industries LLC ......................................................... B ...... 559 891-8867
    11535 E Mountain View Ave Kingsburg (93631) *(P-7170)*

Guardian Phrm Southern Cal LLC .......................................... F ...... 858 652-6900
    10121 Carroll Canyon Rd San Diego (92131) *(P-7340)*

Guardian-Kingsburg, Kingsburg Also Called: Guardian Industries LLC *(P-7170)*

Guardsmark LLC (DH) ........................................................... C ...... 714 619-9700
    1551 N Tustin Ave Ste 650 Santa Ana (92705) *(P-19050)*

Guavus Inc (HQ) ...................................................................... E ...... 650 243-3400
    2125 Zanker Rd San Jose (95131) *(P-18369)*

Guayaki Sstnble Rnfrest Pdts I (PA) ....................................... C ...... 888 482-9254
    215 Rose Ave Venice (90291) *(P-17188)*

Guayaki Yerba Mate, Venice Also Called: Guayaki Sstnble Rnfrest Pdts I *(P-17188)*

Guckenheimer Enterprises Inc ................................................ D ...... 760 414-3659
    4010 Ocean Ranch Blvd Oceanside (92056) *(P-5472)*

Guelaguetza, Los Angeles Also Called: Pbf & E LLC *(P-17600)*

Guess, Los Angeles Also Called: Guess Inc *(P-2830)*

Guess, Los Angeles Also Called: Baby Guess Inc *(P-2858)*

Guess Inc (PA) ........................................................................ A ...... 213 765-3100
    1444 S Alameda St Los Angeles (90021) *(P-2830)*

Guglielmo Emilo Winery Inc ................................................... F ...... 408 779-2145
    1480 E Main Ave Morgan Hill (95037) *(P-16)*

Guhring Inc .............................................................................. E ...... 714 841-3582
    15581 Computer Ln Huntington Beach (92649) *(P-9678)*

Guidance Software Inc (HQ) .................................................. C ...... 626 229-9191
    1055 E Colorado Blvd Ste 400 Pasadena (91106) *(P-18370)*

Guidant Sales LLC ................................................................. A ...... 650 965-2634
    825 E Middlefield Rd Mountain View (94043) *(P-15103)*

Guided Wave Inc., Rancho Cordova Also Called: Process Insghts - Gded Wave In *(P-14706)*

Guidetech Inc ......................................................................... E ...... 408 733-6555
    774 Charcot Ave San Jose (95131) *(P-14531)*

Guidewire, San Mateo Also Called: Guidewire Software Inc *(P-18371)*

Guidewire Software Inc (PA) .................................................. B ...... 650 357-9100
    970 Park Pl Ste 200 San Mateo (94403) *(P-18371)*

Guilded LLC .......................................................................... F ...... 415 568-8186
    970 Park Pl San Mateo (94403) *(P-18372)*

Guittard Chocolate Holdings Co ............................................. C ...... 650 697-4427
    10 Guittard Rd Burlingame (94010) *(P-1340)*

Gulf Development, Torrance Also Called: Signtronix Inc *(P-16043)*

Gulf Enterprises, Canoga Park Also Called: Mercury Magnetics Inc *(P-12848)*

Gulfstream, Van Nuys Also Called: Gulfstream Aerospace Corp GA *(P-13667)*

Gulfstream Aerospace Corp GA ............................................ B ...... 805 236-5755
    16644 Roscoe Blvd Van Nuys (91406) *(P-13667)*

Gulfstream Aerospace Corp GA ............................................ A ...... 562 420-1818
    4150 E Donald Douglas Dr Long Beach (90808) *(P-13668)*

Gulfstream Aerospace Corp GA ............................................ C ...... 562 907-9300
    9818 Mina Ave Whittier (90605) *(P-13669)*

Gum Sun Times Inc (PA) ........................................................ F ...... 415 379-6788
    625 Kearny St San Francisco (94108) *(P-4124)*

Gumgum Inc (PA) ................................................................... E ...... 310 260-9666
    2419 Michigan Ave Ste A Santa Monica (90404) *(P-18373)*

Gumgum Sports Inc ............................................................... E ...... 310 400-0396
    1314 7th St Fl 4 Santa Monica (90401) *(P-18374)*

Gund Company Inc ................................................................ F ...... 909 890-9300
    4701 E Airport Dr Ontario (91761) *(P-11480)*

Gunjoy Inc ............................................................................... E ...... 714 289-0055
    22895 Eastpark Dr Yorba Linda (92887) *(P-12991)*

Gunnar Lllp ............................................................................. F ...... 281 690-0322
    3600 Pegasus Dr Bakersfield (93308) *(P-161)*

Gunnar Optiks LLC ................................................................ E ...... 858 769-2500
    2236 Rutherford Rd Ste 123 Carlsbad (92008) *(P-17684)*

Guru Knits Inc ........................................................................ D ...... 323 235-9424
    225 W 38th St Los Angeles (90037) *(P-2667)*

Gurucul Solutions LLC .......................................................... D ...... 213 291-6888
    222 N Pacific Coast Hwy Ste 1322 El Segundo (90245) *(P-17552)*

GUSB Inc ............................................................................... F ...... 323 233-0044
    219 E 32nd St Los Angeles (90011) *(P-2668)*

Gusmer Enterprises Inc ......................................................... E ...... 866 213-1131
    2200 Northpoint Pkwy Santa Rosa (95407) *(P-6290)*

Gusmer Enterprises Inc ......................................................... E ...... 908 301-1811
    81 M St Fresno (93721) *(P-10092)*

Guss Automation LLC ........................................................... F ...... 559 897-0245
    2545 Simpson St Kingsburg (93631) *(P-9356)*

Gusto Inc (PA) ........................................................................ C ...... 800 936-0383
    525 20th St San Francisco (94107) *(P-18375)*

Guys Patio Inc ........................................................................ E ...... 844 968-7485
    845 N Elm St Orange (92867) *(P-19181)*

Guzik Technical Enterprises (PA) ........................................... E ...... 650 625-8000
    2443 Wyandotte St Mountain View (94043) *(P-13246)*

Guzzler Manufacturing Inc ..................................................... F ...... 562 436-0250
    1510 Hayes Ave Long Beach (90813) *(P-16140)*

GW Reed Printing Inc ............................................................ E ...... 909 947-0599
    4071 Greystone Dr Ontario (91761) *(P-4627)*

Gw Stone, Alhambra Also Called: Great Wall International Corp *(P-7538)*

Gwla Acquisition Corp (PA) ................................................... F ...... 323 789-7800
    8600 Rheem Ave South Gate (90280) *(P-7171)*

Gym Doctors, Hayward Also Called: Gymdoc Inc *(P-19260)*

Gymdoc Inc ............................................................................ F ...... 510 886-4321
    3488 Arden Rd Hayward (94545) *(P-19260)*

Gypsy 05 Inc .......................................................................... E ...... 323 265-2700
    3200 Union Pacific Ave Los Angeles (90023) *(P-2762)*

Gyre Therapeutics Inc (PA) ................................................... B ...... 650 266-8674
    12730 High Bluff Dr Ste 250 San Diego (92130) *(P-5473)*

Gyrfalcon Technology Inc (PA) ............................................. E ...... 408 944-9219
    1900 Mccarthy Blvd Ste 412 Milpitas (95035) *(P-12457)*

---

Employee Codes: A=Over 500 employees, B=251-500 C=101-250, D=51-100, E=20-50, F=10-19, G=1-9

**H & A Transmissions Inc** .................................................. E ...... 909 941-9020
  8727 Rochester Ave Rancho Cucamonga (91730) *(P-19157)*
**H & H Manufacturing, Pomona** Also Called: Holland & Herring Mfg Inc *(P-10875)*
**H & H Specialties Inc** ......................................................... E ...... 626 575-0776
  14850 Don Julian Rd Ste B City Of Industry (91746) *(P-16141)*
**H & L Forge Company, Montebello** Also Called: H & L Tooth Company *(P-9425)*
**H & L Tooth Company (PA)** ................................................. D ...... 323 721-5146
  1540 S Greenwood Ave Montebello (90640) *(P-9425)*
**H & T Seafood Inc** .............................................................. E ...... 323 526-0888
  5598 Lindbergh Ln Bell (90201) *(P-17157)*
**H A I, Placentia** Also Called: Hai Advnced Mtl Spcialists Inc *(P-9076)*
**H Co Computer Products (PA)** ............................................. E ...... 949 833-3222
  16812 Hale Ave Irvine (92606) *(P-10240)*
**H De V LLC** ......................................................................... E ...... 541 386-9119
  588 Trancas St Napa (94558) *(P-1606)*
**H J Harkins Company Inc** .................................................. E ...... 805 929-1333
  1400 W Grand Ave Ste F Grover Beach (93433) *(P-5474)*
**H K Prcision Turning Machining, Oceanside** Also Called: Balda HK Plastics Inc *(P-8719)*
**H Lima Company Inc** ......................................................... E ...... 209 239-6787
  704 E Yosemite Ave Manteca (95336) *(P-340)*
**H M C, Chula Vista** Also Called: Heartland Meat Company Inc *(P-17162)*
**H M Electronics Inc** ........................................................... E ...... 858 535-6139
  2848 Whiptail Loop Carlsbad (92010) *(P-11997)*
**H M F, Anaheim** Also Called: Hitech Metal Fabrication Corp *(P-8151)*
**H M T, Madera** Also Called: Horn Machine Tools Inc *(P-9583)*
**H Roberts Construction** ..................................................... D ...... 562 590-4825
  2165 W Gaylord St Long Beach (90813) *(P-8670)*
**H Wayne Lewis Inc** ............................................................ E ...... 909 874-2213
  312 S Willow Ave Rialto (92376) *(P-8698)*
**H-Square Corporation** ........................................................ E ...... 408 982-9108
  3100 Patrick Henry Dr Santa Clara (95054) *(P-12458)*
**H. M. ELECTRONICS, INC., Carlsbad** Also Called: H M Electronics Inc *(P-11997)*
**H&Gbygiselleco** ................................................................... F ...... 415 829-3867
  626 Mission Bay Blvd N Apt 114 San Francisco (94158) *(P-98)*
**H2 Co, Santa Clara** Also Called: H-Square Corporation *(P-12458)*
**H2o Audio, San Diego** Also Called: X-1 Audio Inc *(P-11721)*
**H2o Plus LLC (PA)** ............................................................. D ...... 800 242-2284
  111 Sutter St Fl 22 San Francisco (94104) *(P-5984)*
**H2scan Corporation (PA)** .................................................... E ...... 661 775-9575
  27215 Turnberry Ln Unit A Valencia (91355) *(P-14874)*
**H2u Technologies Inc** ........................................................ E ...... 626 344-0505
  20360 Plummer St Chatsworth (91311) *(P-5044)*
**H2v By Burke Williams, Inglewood** Also Called: Hunter Vaughan LLC *(P-5990)*
**H2w** .................................................................................... E ...... 800 578-3088
  7660 Alabama Ave Canoga Park (91304) *(P-16978)*
**H2w Technologies Inc** ........................................................ F ...... 661 291-1620
  26380 Ferry Ct Santa Clarita (91350) *(P-11324)*
**HA Rider & Sons Inc** .......................................................... E ...... 831 722-3882
  2482 Freedom Blvd Watsonville (95076) *(P-1893)*
**Haagen-Dazs, Walnut Creek** Also Called: Dreyers Grand Ice Cream Inc *(P-17577)*
**Haas Automation Inc (PA)** .................................................. A ...... 805 278-1800
  2800 Sturgis Rd Oxnard (93030) *(P-9556)*
**Habeas Inc** ......................................................................... E ...... 650 694-3300
  779 E Evelyn Ave Ste 200 Mountain View (94041) *(P-18376)*
**Habit Homes, Bellflower** Also Called: Kevin White *(P-4142)*
**Hackett Industries Inc** ....................................................... E ...... 209 955-8220
  4445 E Fremont St Stockton (95215) *(P-9795)*
**Hadley Fruit Orchards Inc (PA)** ........................................... E ...... 951 849-5255
  48980 Seminole Dr Cabazon (92230) *(P-17665)*
**Hadrian, Torrance** Also Called: Hadrian Automation Inc *(P-11861)*
**Hadrian Automation Inc** .................................................... D ...... 503 807-4490
  19501 S Western Ave Torrance (90502) *(P-11861)*
**Hadronex Inc (PA)** ............................................................. E ...... 760 291-1980
  2110 Enterprise St Escondido (92029) *(P-16354)*
**Hagadone Directories Inc** .................................................. C ...... 707 444-0255
  555 H St Ste E Eureka (95501) *(P-4411)*
**Hagafen Cellars Inc** ........................................................... F ...... 707 252-0781
  4160 Silverado Trl Napa (94558) *(P-1607)*
**Hagen-Renaker Inc (PA)** .................................................... D ...... 909 599-2341
  914 W Cienega Ave San Dimas (91773) *(P-7287)*

**Hai Advnced Mtl Spcialists Inc** ........................................... F ...... 714 414-0575
  1600 E Miraloma Ave Placentia (92870) *(P-9076)*
**Haig Precision Mfg Corp** .................................................... D ...... 408 378-4920
  3616 Snell Ave San Jose (95136) *(P-10864)*
**Haigs Delicacies LLC** ........................................................ E ...... 510 782-6285
  25673 Nickel Pl Hayward (94545) *(P-2225)*
**Hain Celestial Group Inc** ................................................... C ...... 323 859-0553
  5630 Rickenbacker Rd Bell (90201) *(P-5985)*
**Hair ACC By Mia Minnelli, Pleasant Hill** Also Called: Mosaic Brands Inc *(P-16185)*
**Haisch Construction Co Inc** ............................................... F ...... 530 378-6800
  1800 S Barney Rd Anderson (96007) *(P-3309)*
**Hakes Sash & Door Inc** ..................................................... C ...... 951 674-2414
  31945 Corydon St Lake Elsinore (92530) *(P-492)*
**Halabi Inc (PA)** ................................................................... C ...... 707 402-1600
  4447 Green Valley Rd Fairfield (94534) *(P-7539)*
**Halcore Group Inc** ............................................................. E ...... 626 575-0880
  10941 Weaver Ave South El Monte (91733) *(P-13358)*
**Haleon US LP** ..................................................................... D ...... 559 650-1550
  2020 E Vine Ave Fresno (93706) *(P-5475)*
**Hales Engineering Coinc** ................................................... E
  18 Wood Rd Camarillo (93010) *(P-10865)*
**Halex Corporation (DH)** .................................................... E ...... 909 629-6219
  4200 Santa Ana St Ste A Ontario (91761) *(P-7955)*
**Haley Bros, Riverside** Also Called: T M Cobb Company *(P-3194)*
**Haley Bros Inc** ................................................................... C ...... 800 854-5951
  1575 Riverview Dr San Bernardino (92408) *(P-3141)*
**Haley Bros Inc (HQ)** .......................................................... D ...... 714 670-2112
  6291 Orangethorpe Ave Buena Park (90620) *(P-3142)*
**Haley Brothers, Stockton** Also Called: T M Cobb Company *(P-3195)*
**Haley Indus Ctings Linings Inc** ......................................... E ...... 323 588-8086
  2919 Tanager Ave Commerce (90040) *(P-9077)*
**Half Moon Bay Brewing Company, Half Moon Bay** Also Called: Brewery On Half Moon Bay Inc *(P-17565)*
**Half Moon Bay Review, Half Moon Bay** Also Called: Wick Communications Co *(P-4222)*
**Haliburton International Foods Inc** ................................... B ...... 909 428-8520
  3855 Jurupa St Ontario (91761) *(P-2226)*
**Halio Inc (PA)** .................................................................... D ...... 650 416-5200
  3945 Freedom Cir Santa Clara (95054) *(P-7226)*
**Hall Associates Racg Pdts Inc** ............................................ F ...... 310 326-4111
  2711 Plaza Del Amo Ste 503 Torrance (90503) *(P-14130)*
**Hall Wines LLC** ................................................................. E ...... 707 967-2626
  401 Saint Helena Hwy S Saint Helena (94574) *(P-1608)*
**Halliburton Company** ........................................................ D ...... 661 393-8111
  34722 7th Standard Rd Bakersfield (93314) *(P-234)*
**Halliburton Legal** ............................................................... E ...... 415 955-1155
  315 Bay St San Francisco (94133) *(P-235)*
**Hallmark Floors, Ontario** Also Called: Hallmark Home Interiors Inc *(P-3093)*
**Hallmark Home Interiors Inc (PA)** ..................................... F ...... 909 947-7736
  2360 S Archibald Ave Ontario (91761) *(P-3093)*
**Hallmark Lighting, Commerce** Also Called: Hallmark Lighting LLC *(P-11536)*
**Hallmark Lighting LLC** ...................................................... D ...... 818 885-5010
  1945 S Tubeway Ave Commerce (90040) *(P-11536)*
**Hallmark Metals Inc** .......................................................... E ...... 626 335-1263
  600 W Foothill Blvd Glendora (91741) *(P-8464)*
**Hallmark Southwest, Loma Linda** Also Called: Dvele Omega Corporation *(P-3385)*
**Hallsten Corporation** ......................................................... E ...... 916 331-7211
  6944 34th St North Highlands (95660) *(P-8149)*
**Halo Neuro Inc** .................................................................. F ...... 415 851-3338
  735 Market St Fl 4 San Francisco (94103) *(P-15541)*
**Halo Neuroscience, San Francisco** Also Called: Halo Neuro Inc *(P-15541)*
**HALOZYME, San Diego** Also Called: Halozyme Therapeutics Inc *(P-5836)*
**Halozyme Therapeutics Inc (PA)** ....................................... D ...... 858 794-8889
  12390 El Camino Real San Diego (92130) *(P-5836)*
**Halsteel Inc (DH)** ............................................................... E ...... 909 937-1001
  4190 Santa Ana St Ste A Ontario (91761) *(P-7641)*
**Halter Properties LLC** ....................................................... F ...... 805 226-9455
  8910 Adelaida Rd Paso Robles (93446) *(P-1609)*
**Halter Ranch Vineyard, Paso Robles** Also Called: Halter Properties LLC *(P-1609)*
**Halter Winery LLC (PA)** ..................................................... E ...... 805 226-9455
  8910 Adelaida Rd Paso Robles (93446) *(P-1610)*

## ALPHABETIC SECTION — Harkham Industries Inc

**Hamby Corporation** ............................................. E ...... 661 257-1924
27704 Avenue Scott Valencia (91355) *(P-12127)*

**Hamilton Metalcraft Inc** ..................................... E ...... 626 795-4811
848 N Fair Oaks Ave Pasadena (91103) *(P-8465)*

**Hamilton Sundstrand Corp** ................................. C ...... 909 593-5300
960 Overland Ct San Dimas (91773) *(P-14670)*

**Hamilton Sundstrand Spc Systms** ...................... D ...... 909 288-5300
960 Overland Ct San Dimas (91773) *(P-14875)*

**Hammitt Inc** ........................................................ D ...... 310 292-5200
2101 Pacific Coast Hwy Hermosa Beach (90254) *(P-7132)*

**Hammon Plating Corporation** ............................. E ...... 650 494-2691
890 Commercial St Palo Alto (94303) *(P-8968)*

**Hammond Enterprises Inc** .................................. E ...... 925 432-3537
1911 Tarob Ct Milpitas (95035) *(P-10866)*

**Hammond Inc Which Will Do Bus** ....................... E ...... 925 381-5392
404 S Coast Hwy Oceanside (92054) *(P-1838)*

**Hamo Construction** ............................................. E ...... 818 415-3334
3650 Altura Ave La Crescenta (91214) *(P-236)*

**Hampton Products Intl Corp (PA)** ....................... C ...... 800 562-5625
50 Icon Foothill Ranch (92610) *(P-8000)*

**Hampton Tdder Tchncal Svcs Inc** ....................... F ...... 909 628-1256
4571 State St Montclair (91763) *(P-19503)*

**Hamrock Inc** ....................................................... C ...... 562 944-0255
3019 Wilshire Blvd Santa Monica (90403) *(P-7642)*

**Hana Group Ops LLC** ........................................ E ...... 628 280-9401
5919 3rd St San Francisco (94124) *(P-2227)*

**Hanaps Enterprises** ............................................ D ...... 669 235-3810
8100 Camino Arroyo Gilroy (95020) *(P-10375)*

**Hancor Inc** .......................................................... D ...... 661 366-1520
140 Vineland Rd Bakersfield (93307) *(P-6597)*

**Hand Biomechanics Lab Inc** ............................... F ...... 916 923-5073
77 Scripps Dr Ste 104 Sacramento (95825) *(P-15355)*

**Hand Crfted Dutchman Doors Inc** ...................... E ...... 209 833-7378
770 Stonebridge Dr Tracy (95376) *(P-3143)*

**Handbill Printers, Corona** *Also Called: Azalea Systems Corp Inc (P-4522)*

**Handbill Printers, Corona** *Also Called: Handbill Printers LP (P-4628)*

**Handbill Printers LP** ........................................... E ...... 951 547-5910
820 E Parkridge Ave Corona (92879) *(P-4628)*

**Handle Inc** .......................................................... E ...... 650 863-6113
580 Howard St Unit 404 San Francisco (94105) *(P-3418)*

**Handpiece Parts & Products Inc** ........................ E ...... 714 997-4331
707 W Angus Ave Orange (92868) *(P-15457)*

**Handshake, San Francisco** *Also Called: Stryder Corp (P-18843)*

**Hane and Hane Inc** ............................................ E ...... 408 292-2140
303 Piercy Rd San Jose (95138) *(P-8969)*

**Hanergy Holding (america) LLC (HQ)** ................ D ...... 650 288-3722
1350 Bayshore Hwy Ste 825 Burlingame (94010) *(P-12459)*

**Hanford Ready-Mix Inc** ...................................... E ...... 916 405-1918
9800 Kent St Elk Grove (95624) *(P-7450)*

**Hanford Sentinel Inc** .......................................... B ...... 559 582-0471
300 W 6th St Hanford (93230) *(P-4125)*

**Hangar 1, Fullerton** *Also Called: Common Collabs LLC (P-1994)*

**Hanger Prsthtics Orthtics W In (HQ)** .................. E ...... 714 961-2112
4155 E La Palma Ave Ste 400 Anaheim (92807) *(P-15356)*

**Hanger Prsthtics Orthtics W In** ........................... D ...... 213 250-7850
1127 Wilshire Blvd Ste 310 Los Angeles (90017) *(P-15357)*

**Hanley Wood Media Inc (HQ)** ............................ E ...... 202 736-3300
4000 Macarthur Blvd Ste 400 Newport Beach (92660) *(P-4412)*

**Hanmar LLC (PA)** .............................................. E ...... 818 890-2802
11441 Bradley Ave Pacoima (91331) *(P-8848)*

**Hanna Fuji Sushi, Santa Fe Springs** *Also Called: Nikko Enterprise Corporation (P-2058)*

**Hannah Industries Inc** ........................................ F ...... 714 939-7873
401 S Santa Fe St Santa Ana (92705) *(P-10563)*

**Hannahmax Baking Inc** ...................................... C ...... 310 380-6778
14601 S Main St Gardena (90248) *(P-1216)*

**Hannan Products Corp (PA)** .............................. F ...... 951 735-1587
9106 Pulsar Ct Ste C Corona (92883) *(P-10019)*

**Hannspree North America Inc** ........................... D ...... 909 992-5025
13223 Black Mountain Rd San Diego (92129) *(P-12992)*

**Hanover Accessories Corp** ................................ C
6049 E Slauson Ave Commerce (90040) *(P-5002)*

**Hansen Bros Enterprises (PA)** ........................... D ...... 530 273-3100
11727 La Barr Meadows Rd Grass Valley (95949) *(P-315)*

**Hansen Engineering Co** ..................................... D ...... 310 534-3870
24020 Frampton Ave Harbor City (90710) *(P-10867)*

**Hansen Engineering Co** ..................................... E ...... 310 534-3870
24050 Frampton Ave Harbor City (90710) *(P-13857)*

**Hansen Information Tech, Rancho Cordova** *Also Called: Infor (us) LLC (P-18411)*

**Hansen Medical Inc** ........................................... C ...... 650 404-5800
800 E Middlefield Rd Mountain View (94043) *(P-15104)*

**Hansens Welding Inc** ......................................... E ...... 310 329-6888
358 W 168th St Gardena (90248) *(P-19196)*

**Hanson Aggrgtes Md-Pacific Inc** ........................ F ...... 925 862-2236
7999 Athenour Way Sunol (94586) *(P-7451)*

**Hanson Aggrgtes Md-Pacific Inc** ........................ F ...... 510 526-1611
699 Virginia St Berkeley (94710) *(P-7452)*

**Hanson Aggrgtes Md-Pacific Inc** ........................ F ...... 805 967-2371
50 S Kellogg Ave Goleta (93117) *(P-16279)*

**Hanson Lab Solutions LLC** ................................ E ...... 805 498-3121
747 Calle Plano Camarillo (93012) *(P-14339)*

**Hanson Roof Tile Inc** ......................................... B ...... 888 509-4787
10651 Elm Ave Fontana (92337) *(P-7341)*

**Hanson Tank, Los Angeles** *Also Called: Roy E Hanson Jr Mfg (P-8331)*

**Hanson Truss Inc** .............................................. B ...... 909 591-9256
13950 Yorba Ave Chino (91710) *(P-3310)*

**Hantronix Inc** ..................................................... E ...... 408 252-1100
10080 Bubb Rd Cupertino (95014) *(P-9862)*

**Hanwha Enrgy USA Holdings Corp (HQ)** ........... E ...... 949 748-5996
400 Spectrum Center Dr Ste 1400 Irvine (92618) *(P-12460)*

**Hanwha Q Cells Usa Inc** ................................... E ...... 706 671-3077
300 Spectrum Center Dr Ste 500 Irvine (92618) *(P-12461)*

**Hanzell Vineyards, Sonoma** *Also Called: Gmic Vineyards LLC (P-1590)*

**Happy Doughnuts, Oakland** *Also Called: Dobake Bakeries Inc (P-1184)*

**Happy Planner, The, Cypress** *Also Called: ME & My Big Ideas LLC (P-16949)*

**Harari Inc (PA)** ................................................... E ...... 323 734-5302
9646 Brighton Way Los Angeles (90016) *(P-2669)*

**Harbinger Motors Inc** ......................................... C ...... 714 684-1067
12821 Knott St Ste A Garden Grove (92841) *(P-13359)*

**Harbor Electronics Inc (PA)** ............................... C ...... 408 988-6544
3021 Kenneth St Santa Clara (95054) *(P-12128)*

**Harbor Furniture Mfg Inc (PA)** ........................... E ...... 323 636-1201
15817 Whitepost Ln La Mirada (90638) *(P-3475)*

**Harbor Green Grain LP** ..................................... E ...... 310 991-8089
13181 Crossroads Pkwy N Ste 200 City Of Industry (91746) *(P-1129)*

**Harbor Health Systems LLC** .............................. A ...... 949 273-7020
3501 Jamboree Rd Ste 540 Newport Beach (92660) *(P-19336)*

**Harbor House, La Mirada** *Also Called: Harbor Furniture Mfg Inc (P-3475)*

**Harbor Ready Mix, San Carlos** *Also Called: Norcal Materials Inc (P-7481)*

**Harbor Truck Bodies Inc** ................................... D ...... 714 996-0411
255 Voyager Ave Brea (92821) *(P-13414)*

**Harbor Truck Body, Brea** *Also Called: Harbor Truck Bodies Inc (P-13414)*

**Harcon Precision Metals Inc** ............................. E ...... 619 423-5544
1790 Dornoch Ct Chula Vista (91910) *(P-9426)*

**Harcourt Trade Publishers, San Diego** *Also Called: Houghton Mifflin Harcourt Pubg (P-4332)*

**Hardcraft Industries Inc** .................................... D ...... 408 432-8340
2221 Ringwood Ave San Jose (95131) *(P-8466)*

**Harding Containers Intl Inc** ............................... F ...... 310 549-7272
4000 Santa Fe Ave Long Beach (90810) *(P-3346)*

**Hardwood Flrg Liquidators Inc (PA)** .................. D ...... 323 201-4200
7227 Telegraph Rd Montebello (90640) *(P-3094)*

**Hardy & Harper Inc** ........................................... C ...... 714 444-1851
32 Rancho Cir Lake Forest (92630) *(P-374)*

**Hardy Diagnostics (PA)** ..................................... B ...... 805 346-2766
1430 W Mccoy Ln Santa Maria (93455) *(P-16583)*

**Hardy Frames Inc** ............................................. D ...... 951 245-9525
250 Klug Cir Corona (92878) *(P-7614)*

**Hardy Process Solutions** .................................. E ...... 858 278-2900
10075 Mesa Rim Rd San Diego (92121) *(P-14421)*

**Hardy Process Solutions, San Diego** *Also Called: Hardy Process Solutions (P-14421)*

**Harkham Industries Inc (PA)** ............................. E ...... 323 586-4600
857 S San Pedro St Ste 300 Los Angeles (90014) *(P-2670)*

Harkness Enterprises Inc ........................................................ D ...... 831 462-1141
    2840 Research Park Dr Ste 160 Soquel (95073) *(P-6849)*
Harland Brewing Co  LLC ..................................................... E ...... 858 800-4566
    10115 Carroll Canyon Rd San Diego (92131) *(P-17618)*
Harman Envelopes, North Hollywood *Also Called: Harman Press Inc (P-4629)*
Harman Press Inc ................................................................... E ...... 818 432-0570
    6840 Vineland Ave North Hollywood (91605) *(P-4629)*
Harman Professional, Northridge *Also Called: Harman Professional  Inc (P-11667)*
Harman Professional  Inc ...................................................... C ...... 951 242-2927
    24950 Grove View Rd Moreno Valley (92551) *(P-11665)*
Harman Professional  Inc ...................................................... C ...... 844 776-4899
    14780 Bar Harbor Rd Fontana (92336) *(P-11666)*
Harman Professional  Inc (DH) .............................................. B ...... 818 893-8411
    8500 Balboa Blvd Northridge (91329) *(P-11667)*
Harman-Kardon, Northridge *Also Called: Harman-Kardon  Incorporated (P-16681)*
Harman-Kardon  Incorporated ............................................... B ...... 818 841-4600
    8500 Balboa Blvd Northridge (91325) *(P-16681)*
Harmless Harvest, Oakland *Also Called: Harmless Harvest  Inc (P-2228)*
Harmless Harvest  Inc ............................................................ E ...... 347 688-6286
    1814 Franklin St Ste 1000 Oakland (94612) *(P-2228)*
HARMONIC, San Jose *Also Called: Harmonic Inc (P-11862)*
Harmonic Brewing LLC .......................................................... F ...... 415 872-6817
    7 Warriors Way San Francisco (94158) *(P-17619)*
Harmonic Drive LLC ............................................................... E ...... 800 921-3332
    333 W San Carlos St Ste 1070 San Jose (95110) *(P-10039)*
Harmonic Inc (PA) .................................................................. D ...... 408 542-2500
    2590 Orchard Pkwy San Jose (95131) *(P-11862)*
Harmony Foods  LLC (PA) .................................................... B ...... 831 457-3200
    2200 Delaware Ave Santa Cruz (95060) *(P-5476)*
Harmony Infinite Inc ............................................................... F
    12918 Bloomfield St Studio City (91604) *(P-3743)*
Harold Smith & Son  Inc ......................................................... E ...... 707 963-7977
    800 Crane Ave Saint Helena (94574) *(P-396)*
Harper & Two  Inc (PA) .......................................................... F ...... 562 424-3030
    2937 Cherry Ave Signal Hill (90755) *(P-12993)*
Harpers Pharmacy  Inc .......................................................... C ...... 877 778-3773
    132 S Anita Dr Ste 210 Orange (92868) *(P-5477)*
Harrell Holdings (PA) ............................................................. C ...... 661 322-5627
    1707 Eye St Ste 102 Bakersfield (93301) *(P-4126)*
Harrington & Sons Inc ........................................................... E ...... 951 674-0998
    590 Crane St Lake Elsinore (92530) *(P-7591)*
Harris, Van Nuys *Also Called: L3harris Technologies  Inc (P-14205)*
Harris, Los Angeles *Also Called: L3harris Technologies  Inc (P-14206)*
Harris & Bruno International, Roseville *Also Called: Harris & Bruno Machine Co Inc (P-9768)*
Harris & Bruno Machine Co Inc (PA)................................... D ...... 916 781-7676
    8555 Washington Blvd Roseville (95678) *(P-9768)*
Harris Farms Inc (PA)............................................................ C ...... 559 884-2435
    29475 Fresno Coalinga Rd Coalinga (93210) *(P-55)*
Harris Freeman & Co  Inc (PA) ............................................. B ...... 714 765-7525
    3110 E Miraloma Ave Anaheim (92806) *(P-17189)*
Harris Industries  Inc (PA)...................................................... E ...... 714 898-8048
    5181 Argosy Ave Huntington Beach (92649) *(P-3951)*
Harris Organs  Inc .................................................................. E ...... 562 693-3442
    7047 Comstock Ave Whittier (90602) *(P-15718)*
Harris Ranch Beef Co, Coalinga *Also Called: Harris Farms Inc (P-55)*
Harris Ranch Beef Company ................................................ A ...... 559 896-3081
    16277 S Mccall Ave Selma (93662) *(P-600)*
Harris Tea Company, Anaheim *Also Called: Harris Freeman & Co Inc (P-17189)*
Harris' Precision Products, Whittier *Also Called: Harris Organs Inc (P-15718)*
Harrison, E J & Sons Recycling, Ventura *Also Called: E J Harrison & Sons  Inc (P-16358)*
Harry's Dye & Wash, Anaheim *Also Called: Harrys Dye and Wash  Inc (P-2492)*
Harrys Dye and Wash  Inc ..................................................... E ...... 714 446-0300
    1015 E Orangethorpe Ave Anaheim (92801) *(P-2492)*
Hart & Cooley  Inc .................................................................. E ...... 951 332-5132
    10855 Philadelphia Ave Ste B Jurupa Valley (91752) *(P-8628)*
HART & COOLEY, INC., Jurupa Valley *Also Called: Hart & Cooley  Inc (P-8628)*
Hartle Media Ventures LLC ................................................... F ...... 415 362-7797
    680 2nd St San Francisco (94107) *(P-4262)*
Hartley Company .................................................................... E ...... 949 646-9643
    1987 Placentia Ave Costa Mesa (92627) *(P-15881)*

Hartley-Racon, Costa Mesa *Also Called: Hartley Company (P-15881)*
Hartman Slicer Div, Santa Fe Springs *Also Called: United Bakery Equipment Co Inc (P-10034)*
Hartmark Cab Design & Mfg Inc .......................................... E ...... 909 591-9153
    3575 Grapevine St Jurupa Valley (91752) *(P-563)*
Hartmark Cabinet Design, Jurupa Valley *Also Called: Hartmark Cab Design & Mfg Inc (P-563)*
Hartwell Corporation (DH) ..................................................... C ...... 714 993-4200
    900 Richfield Rd Placentia (92870) *(P-8001)*
Hartzell Aerospace, Valencia *Also Called: Electrofilm Mfg Co LLC (P-9167)*
Harv 81 Usa  Inc ..................................................................... E ...... 707 746-0353
    531 Stone Rd Benicia (94510) *(P-17297)*
Harvard Card Systems, City Of Industry *Also Called: Harvard Label LLC (P-3771)*
Harvard Label LLC ................................................................. C ...... 626 333-8881
    111 Baldwin Park Blvd City Of Industry (91746) *(P-3771)*
Harvest Container Company ................................................. E ...... 559 562-1394
    24476 Road 216 Lindsay (93247) *(P-3853)*
Harvest Farms  Inc ................................................................. D ...... 661 945-3636
    45000 Yucca Ave Lancaster (93534) *(P-1036)*
Harvest Food Products Co Inc ............................................. D ...... 510 675-0383
    710 Sandoval Way Hayward (94544) *(P-17583)*
Harvest Pack  Inc ................................................................... F ...... 888 727-7225
    12336 Lower Azusa Rd Arcadia (91006) *(P-3915)*
Harvest Printing Company, Anderson *Also Called: Checchi Enterprises  Inc (P-4548)*
Harvest Thermal  Inc .............................................................. F ...... 408 597-7152
    663 Coventry Rd Kensington (94707) *(P-10501)*
Harwil, Oxnard *Also Called: Harwil Precision Products (P-12994)*
Harwil Precision Products ..................................................... E ...... 805 988-6800
    541 Kinetic Dr Oxnard (93030) *(P-12994)*
Harwood Products .................................................................. C ...... 707 984-1601
    Branscomb Rd Branscomb (95417) *(P-3144)*
Hasa Inc (PA)........................................................................... D ...... 661 259-5848
    23119 Drayton St Saugus (91350) *(P-5031)*
Hasbro, Burbank *Also Called: Hasbro  Inc (P-15730)*
Hasbro  Inc .............................................................................. F ...... 818 478-4320
    3333 W Empire Ave Burbank (91504) *(P-15730)*
Hasco, Placentia *Also Called: Hartwell Corporation (P-8001)*
Haskel International  LLC (HQ)............................................. C ...... 818 843-4000
    100 E Graham Pl Burbank (91502) *(P-9928)*
Haskon, Div of, Brea *Also Called: Kirkhill Inc (P-6456)*
Hatchbeauty Agency  LLC (PA) ........................................... E ...... 310 396-7070
    355 S Grand Ave Ste 1450 Los Angeles (90071) *(P-19529)*
Hathaway LLC ......................................................................... E ...... 661 393-2004
    4205 Atlas Ct Bakersfield (93308) *(P-134)*
Haus Beverage  Inc ................................................................ E ...... 503 939-5298
    1377 Grove St Ste D Healdsburg (95448) *(P-1611)*
Hauslane Inc ............................................................................ F ...... 800 929-0168
    222 Harris Ct South San Francisco (94080) *(P-8467)*
Havaianas, Venice *Also Called: Alpargatas Usa  Inc (P-7113)*
Havuni LLC .............................................................................. E ...... 917 428-1183
    2701 S Harcourt Ave Los Angeles (90016) *(P-2901)*
Hawa Corporation (PA).......................................................... F ...... 909 825-8882
    125 E Laurel St Colton (92324) *(P-646)*
Hawk Crest, Napa *Also Called: Stags Leap Wine Cellars  LLC (P-1760)*
Hawker Pacific Aerospace .................................................... B ...... 818 765-6201
    11240 Sherman Way Sun Valley (91352) *(P-19261)*
Hawkeye Acquisition  Inc ....................................................... D ...... 415 249-2362
    201 Mission St Fl 12 San Francisco (94105) *(P-4330)*
Hawthorne Hydroponics LLC ................................................ E ...... 800 221-1760
    2877 Giffen Ave Santa Rosa (95407) *(P-6174)*
Hayes Valley Wine, San Martin *Also Called: Clos Lachance Wines  LLC (P-1512)*
Hayes Welding  Inc (PA) ....................................................... D ...... 760 246-4878
    12522 Violet Rd Adelanto (92301) *(P-19197)*
Haymarket Worldwide Inc ..................................................... E ...... 949 417-6700
    17030 Red Hill Ave Irvine (92614) *(P-4263)*
Haynes Publications, Westlake Village *Also Called: Odcombe Press (nashville) (P-4711)*
Hayward Lumber Co, Santa Maria *Also Called: Homer T Hayward Lumber Co (P-17334)*
Hayward Plant, Hayward *Also Called: Teikuro Corporation (P-9021)*
Hayward Quartz Technology Inc .......................................... C ...... 510 657-9605
    1700 Corporate Way Fremont (94539) *(P-12462)*
Hazel Clothes, Vernon *Also Called: Crestone  LLC (P-2661)*

## ALPHABETIC SECTION — Heller Seasoning

**Hazelcast, Palo Alto** *Also Called: Hazelcast Inc (P-18377)*

**Hazelcast Inc (PA)**..................................................E ...... 650 521-5453
3000 El Camino Real Palo Alto (94306) *(P-18377)*

**Haztech Systems Inc** ...............................................E ...... 209 966-8088
4996 Gold Leaf Dr Mariposa (95338) *(P-6120)*

**HB Fuller Company** .................................................E ...... 916 787-6000
10500 Industrial Ave Roseville (95678) *(P-6230)*

**HB Products LLC** ....................................................E ...... 714 799-6967
5671 Engineer Dr Huntington Beach (92649) *(P-4890)*

**Hbe Rental, Grass Valley** *Also Called: Hansen Bros Enterprises (P-315)*

**Hbno, Chico** *Also Called: IL Helth Buty Natural Oils Inc (P-6294)*

**Hc West LLC** ............................................................B ...... 858 277-3473
7130 Convoy Ct San Diego (92111) *(P-13247)*

**HCC Industries Leasing Inc (HQ)**.............................F ...... 626 443-8933
4232 Temple City Blvd Rosemead (91770) *(P-14422)*

**Hci, San Marcos** *Also Called: Hughes Circuits Inc (P-12130)*

**Hcl Machine Works, Dos Palos** *Also Called: Sherrill M Campbell Corporation (P-19213)*

**Hco Holding II Corporation** .....................................A ...... 310 955-9200
999 N Pacific Coast Hwy Ste 800 El Segundo (90245) *(P-6375)*

**Hd Window Fashions Inc (DH)** ................................B ...... 213 749-6333
1818 Oak St Los Angeles (90015) *(P-3720)*

**Hdp Holdings, San Diego** *Also Called: Wd-40 Company (P-6358)*

**Hdz Brothers Inc** .....................................................E ...... 714 953-4010
1924 E Mcfadden Ave Santa Ana (92705) *(P-6451)*

**Headmaster Inc (PA)**...............................................F ...... 714 556-5244
3000 S Croddy Way Santa Ana (92704) *(P-2843)*

**Headrick Logging, Anderson** *Also Called: Elizabeth Headrick (P-3044)*

**Headwaters Incorporated** ........................................E ...... 909 627-9066
1345 Philadelphia St Pomona (91766) *(P-7342)*

**Headway Technologies Inc** .....................................A ...... 408 934-5300
682 S Hillview Dr Milpitas (95035) *(P-10241)*

**Healdsburg Lumber Company Inc** ...........................D ...... 707 431-9663
13534 Healdsburg Ave Healdsburg (95448) *(P-17355)*

**Healdsburg Wine Co., Saint Helena** *Also Called: Raymond Vineyard & Cellar Inc (P-25)*

**Health One Pharmaceutical Inc** ...............................F ...... 626 279-9699
13260 Temple Ave City Of Industry (91746) *(P-5478)*

**Healthcrowd, San Mateo** *Also Called: Crowdcircle Inc (P-18211)*

**Healthtap Inc** ...........................................................D ...... 650 268-9806
209 E Java Dr Unit 61987 Sunnyvale (94088) *(P-19317)*

**Healthy Times Inc** ....................................................F ...... 858 513-1550
225 Broadway Ste 450 San Diego (92101) *(P-2229)*

**Healthy Tmes Ntral Pdts For Ch, San Diego** *Also Called: Healthy Times Inc (P-2229)*

**Hearsay Social, San Francisco** *Also Called: Hearsay Systems Inc (P-18378)*

**Hearsay Systems Inc (PA)**.......................................C ...... 888 399-2280
600 Harrison St Ste 120 San Francisco (94107) *(P-18378)*

**Hearst Communications Inc** ....................................E ...... 415 537-4200
680 2nd St San Francisco (94107) *(P-4127)*

**Heart Rate Inc** .........................................................E ...... 714 850-9716
2619 Oak St Santa Ana (92707) *(P-15820)*

**Heartland Farms, City Of Industry** *Also Called: Sbm Dairies Inc (P-1959)*

**Heartland Harvest** ...................................................F ...... 619 729-1604
1174 Pierre Way El Cajon (92021) *(P-2230)*

**Heartland Label Printers LLC** .................................A ...... 909 243-7151
9817 7th St Ste 703 Rancho Cucamonga (91730) *(P-4891)*

**Heartland Meat Company Inc** .................................D ...... 619 407-3668
3461 Main St Chula Vista (91911) *(P-17162)*

**Hearts Delight** .........................................................E ...... 805 648-7123
4035 N Ventura Ave Ventura (93001) *(P-2763)*

**Heat Press Nation** ...................................................E ...... 800 215-0894
2300 E Walnut Ave Fullerton (92831) *(P-4413)*

**Heat Software USA Inc** ............................................B ...... 408 601-2800
490 N Mccarthy Blvd Ste 100 Milpitas (95035) *(P-18379)*

**Heatech, Placentia** *Also Called: Furnace Super Heros Inc (P-10051)*

**Heater Designs Inc** ..................................................E ...... 909 421-0971
2211 S Vista Ave Bloomington (92316) *(P-10052)*

**Heath Ceramics Ltd** .................................................E ...... 415 361-5552
2900 18th St San Francisco (94110) *(P-7288)*

**Heath Ceramics Ltd (PA)**.........................................D ...... 415 332-3732
400 Gate 5 Rd Sausalito (94965) *(P-7268)*

**Heather By Bordeaux Inc** ........................................E ...... 213 622-0555
5983 Malburg Way Vernon (90058) *(P-2764)*

**Heatherfield Foods Inc** ............................................E ...... 877 460-3060
1150 Brooks St Ontario (91762) *(P-601)*

**Heathorn & Assoc Contrs Inc** ..................................E ...... 510 351-7578
500 Old Farm Rd Danville (94526) *(P-423)*

**Heatshield Products Inc** ..........................................E ...... 760 751-0441
1040 S Andreasen Dr Ste 110 Escondido (92029) *(P-13511)*

**Heatwave Labs Inc** ..................................................F ...... 831 722-9081
195 Aviation Way Ste 100 Watsonville (95076) *(P-12033)*

**Heavy Civil - Gen Engrg Cnstr, Chatsworth** *Also Called: Maloof Naman Builders (P-16792)*

**Heavy Duty Trucking, Irvine** *Also Called: HIC Corporation (P-4264)*

**Heavy Equipment Rentals, Corona** *Also Called: Porter Hire Ltd (P-17861)*

**Heavy Metal Steel, San Diego** *Also Called: Heavy Metal Steel Company Inc (P-530)*

**Heavy Metal Steel Company Inc** ..............................E ...... 858 433-4800
12130 Lomica Dr San Diego (92128) *(P-530)*

**Heavyai Inc** ..............................................................D ...... 415 997-2814
95 3rd St San Francisco (94103) *(P-18380)*

**Heco Inc** ..................................................................F ...... 916 372-5411
2350 Del Monte St West Sacramento (95691) *(P-10040)*

**Heco-Pacific Manufacturing Inc** ...............................E ...... 510 487-1155
1510 Pacific St Union City (94587) *(P-9486)*

**Hedman Hedders, Whittier** *Also Called: Hedman Manufacturing (P-13512)*

**Hedman Manufacturing (PA)**....................................E ...... 562 204-1031
12438 Putnam St Whittier (90602) *(P-13512)*

**Hee Environmental Engineering LLC** ......................E ...... 760 530-1409
16605 Koala Rd Adelanto (92301) *(P-6850)*

**Hehr International Inc** ..............................................C ...... 323 663-1261
Los Angeles (90039) *(P-8268)*

**Hehr International Polymers, Los Angeles** *Also Called: Hehr International Inc (P-8268)*

**HEIDELBERG MATERIALS SOUTHWEST AGG LLC, Chula Vista** *Also Called: Heidelberg Mtls Sthwest Agg LL (P-7453)*

**HEIDELBERG MATERIALS SOUTHWEST AGG LLC, Pala** *Also Called: Heidelberg Mtls Sthwest Agg LL (P-7454)*

**Heidelberg Mtls Sthwest Agg LL** .............................E ...... 619 425-0290
5330 Main St Chula Vista (91911) *(P-7453)*

**Heidelberg Mtls Sthwest Agg LL** .............................F ...... 877 642-6766
10331 Highway 76 Pala (92059) *(P-7454)*

**Heighten America Inc** ..............................................E ...... 209 845-0455
1144 Post Rd Oakdale (95361) *(P-10868)*

**Heighten Manfacturing, Oakdale** *Also Called: Heighten America Inc (P-10868)*

**Heinzen Manufacturing Inc** ......................................D ...... 408 842-7233
405 Mayock Rd Gilroy (95020) *(P-9796)*

**Heinzen Manufacturing Intl, Gilroy** *Also Called: Heinzen Manufacturing Inc (P-9796)*

**Heirloom, Fresno** *Also Called: Counter Hospitality Group LLC (P-17574)*

**Heirloom Computing Inc (PA)**..................................E ...... 510 709-7245
3000 Danville Blvd Ste 148 Alamo (94507) *(P-18381)*

**Helados La Tapatia Inc** ............................................E ...... 559 441-1105
4495 W Shaw Ave Fresno (93722) *(P-804)*

**Helena Industries LLC** ............................................D ...... 559 846-5303
1075 S Vineland Ave Kerman (93630) *(P-17361)*

**Helendale Lckheed Plant Prtcti, Helendale** *Also Called: Lockheed Martin Corporation (P-14215)*

**Helica Biosystems Inc** .............................................F ...... 714 578-7830
3310 W Macarthur Blvd Santa Ana (92704) *(P-5755)*

**Helical Products, Santa Maria** *Also Called: Matthew Warren Inc (P-9177)*

**Helical Products Company Inc** ................................C ...... 805 928-3851
901 W Mccoy Ln Santa Maria (93455) *(P-10069)*

**Helicopter Tech Co Ltd Partnr** .................................E ...... 310 523-2750
12902 S Broadway Los Angeles (90061) *(P-13858)*

**Helicopter Technology Company, Los Angeles** *Also Called: Helicopter Tech Co Ltd Partnr (P-13858)*

**Heliospace Corporation** ...........................................E ...... 415 385-6803
2448 6th St Berkeley (94710) *(P-14112)*

**Heliotrope Technologies Inc** .....................................F ...... 510 871-3980
850 Marina Village Pkwy Ste 102 Alameda (94501) *(P-7172)*

**Helistrand Inc** ..........................................................E ...... 805 963-4518
707 E Yanonali St Santa Barbara (93103) *(P-7787)*

**Helitek Company Ltd** ...............................................E ...... 510 933-7688
4033 Clipper Ct Fremont (94538) *(P-12463)*

**Helix Medical, Carpinteria** *Also Called: Freudenberg Medical LLC (P-15352)*

**Heller Seasoning, Modesto** *Also Called: Newly Weds Foods Inc (P-2296)*

**Hellman Properties LLC** ............................................. F ...... 562 431-6022
711 First St Seal Beach (90740) *(P-135)*

**Hellwig Products Company Inc** ............................... D ...... 559 734-7451
16237 Avenue 296 Visalia (93292) *(P-13513)*

**Helmet House LLC (PA)** ........................................... D ...... 800 421-7247
26855 Malibu Hills Rd Calabasas Hills (91301) *(P-17075)*

**Hely & Weber Orthopedic, Santa Paula** *Also Called: Weber Orthopedic LP (P-15429)*

**Hemet Ready Mix, Hemet** *Also Called: Superior Ready Mix Concrete LP (P-7511)*

**Hemilane Inc** ............................................................... F ...... 424 277-1134
909 E El Segundo Blvd El Segundo (90245) *(P-1839)*

**Hemlock Hat Company** ............................................. 888 490-6440
2793 Loker Ave W Carlsbad (92010) *(P-2844)*

**Hemostat Laboratories Inc (PA)** .............................. E ...... 707 678-9594
515 Industrial Way Dixon (95620) *(P-5837)*

**Hemosure Inc** ............................................................ E ...... 888 436-6787
5358 Irwindale Ave Baldwin Park (91706) *(P-6291)*

**Hemp Industries** ....................................................... E ...... 619 458-9090
3717 El Cajon Blvd San Diego (92105) *(P-16142)*

**Hempacco Co Inc (HQ)** ............................................. F ...... 619 779-0715
9925 Airway Rd San Diego (92154) *(P-2394)*

**Henkel Chemical Management LLC** ........................ C ...... 888 943-6535
14000 Jamboree Rd Irvine (92606) *(P-6231)*

**Henkel Electronic Mtls LLC, Irvine** *Also Called: Henkel Chemical Management LLC (P-6231)*

**Henkel US Operations Corp** ..................................... E ...... 818 435-0889
21551 Prairie St Chatsworth (91311) *(P-5936)*

**Henkel US Operations Corp** ..................................... C ...... 562 297-6840
20021 S Susana Rd Compton (90221) *(P-5937)*

**Henkel US Operations Corp** ..................................... E ...... 203 655-8911
12155 Paine Pl Poway (92064) *(P-5986)*

**Henkel US Operations Corp** ..................................... E ...... 626 321-4100
5800 Bristol Pkwy Culver City (90230) *(P-5987)*

**Henkel US Operations Corp** ..................................... D ...... 626 968-6511
15051 Don Julian Rd City Of Industry (91746) *(P-6232)*

**Henlius USA Inc** ........................................................ C ...... 510 445-0305
430 N Mccarthy Blvd Milpitas (95035) *(P-5245)*

**Henry Building Products, El Segundo** *Also Called: Henry Company LLC (P-6376)*

**Henry Company LLC (HQ)** ........................................ D ...... 310 955-9200
999 N Pacific Coast Hwy Ste 800 El Segundo (90245) *(P-6376)*

**Henry Machine Inc** ................................................... F
2316 La Mirada Dr Vista (92081) *(P-10869)*

**Henry Schein Orthodontics, Carlsbad** *Also Called: Ortho Organizers Inc (P-15471)*

**Henrys Adio Vsual Slutions Inc** ............................... E ...... 714 258-7238
18002 Cowan Irvine (92614) *(P-11668)*

**Henway Inc** ............................................................... F ...... 661 822-6873
1314 Goodrick Dr Tehachapi (93561) *(P-15911)*

**Hepa Corporation** ..................................................... D ...... 714 630-5700
3071 E Coronado St Anaheim (92806) *(P-9989)*

**Hera Technologies LLC** ............................................ E ...... 951 751-6191
1055 E Francis St Ontario (91761) *(P-10870)*

**Heraeus Medical Components LLC** ......................... D ...... 925 798-4080
4090 Nelson Ave Concord (94520) *(P-9175)*

**Heraeus Prcous Mtls N Amer LLC (DH)** .................. C ...... 562 921-7464
15524 Carmenita Rd Santa Fe Springs (90670) *(P-7720)*

**Herald Printing Ltd** ................................................... F ...... 805 647-1870
3536 Aliso Canyon Rd Santa Paula (93060) *(P-4630)*

**Herb KAn Company Inc** ............................................ F ...... 831 438-9450
380 Encinal St Ste 100 Santa Cruz (95060) *(P-17426)*

**Herbalife Manufacturing LLC (DH)** ......................... E ...... 866 866-4744
800 W Olympic Blvd Ste 406 Los Angeles (90015) *(P-2009)*

**Herbert Rizzardini** .................................................... F ...... 760 377-4571
6259 Highway 178 Inyokern (93527) *(P-17356)*

**Herburger Publications Inc (PA)** ............................ D ...... 916 685-5533
604 N Lincoln Way Galt (95632) *(P-4128)*

**Herca Construction Services, Perris** *Also Called: Herca Telecomm Services Inc (P-16789)*

**Herca Telecomm Services Inc** ................................. D ...... 951 940-5941
18610 Beck St Perris (92570) *(P-16789)*

**Herdell Prtg & Lithography Inc** ............................... F ...... 707 963-3634
340 Mccormick St Saint Helena (94574) *(P-4631)*

**Heritage Container Inc** ............................................ 951 360-1900
4777 Felspar St Riverside (92509) *(P-3854)*

**Heritage Distributing Company** ............................. E ...... 626 333-9526
425 S 9th Ave City Of Industry (91746) *(P-761)*

**Heritage Distributing Company (PA)** ..................... E ...... 323 838-1225
5743 Smithway St Ste 105 Commerce (90040) *(P-838)*

**Heritage Foods, Santa Ana** *Also Called: Stremicks Heritage Foods LLC (P-845)*

**Heritage Interests LLC (PA)** .................................... D ...... 916 481-5030
4300 Jetway Ct North Highlands (95660) *(P-493)*

**Heritage Leather Company Inc** .............................. E ...... 323 983-0420
4011 E 52nd St Maywood (90270) *(P-7087)*

**Heritage One Door, North Highlands** *Also Called: Heritage One Door Crpentry LLC (P-16446)*

**Heritage One Door & Carpentry, North Highlands** *Also Called: Builders Firstsource Inc (P-16443)*

**Heritage One Door Crpentry LLC** ........................... D ...... 916 481-5030
4300 Jetway Ct North Highlands (95660) *(P-16446)*

**Heritage Paper Co (HQ)** .......................................... D ...... 714 540-9737
2400 S Grand Ave Santa Ana (92705) *(P-3855)*

**Heritage Paper Co, Livermore** *Also Called: Heritage Paper LLC (P-3856)*

**Heritage Paper LLC (PA)** ......................................... C ...... 925 449-1148
6850 Brisa St Livermore (94550) *(P-3856)*

**Herman Engineering & Mfg Inc** .............................. F ...... 909 483-1631
4501 E Airport Dr Ste B Ontario (91761) *(P-6851)*

**Hermetic Seal Corporation (DH)** ............................ C ...... 626 443-8931
4232 Temple City Blvd Rosemead (91770) *(P-12995)*

**Hermetics Material Solutions, Santa Ana** *Also Called: IJ Research Inc (P-12997)*

**Hero Arts Rubber Stamps Inc** ................................. E ...... 510 232-4200
1200 Harbour Way S Ste 201 Richmond (94804) *(P-15890)*

**Hero Industries Inc** .................................................. E ...... 714 879-3900
1038 E Bastanchury Rd Ste 247 Fullerton (92835) *(P-16143)*

**Heroku Inc** ................................................................ E ...... 650 704-6107
1 Market St Ste 300 San Francisco (94105) *(P-18382)*

**Heron Innovators Inc** .............................................. F ...... 916 408-6601
10624 Industrial Ave Roseville (95678) *(P-397)*

**HERON THERAPEUTICS, San Diego** *Also Called: Heron Therapeutics Inc (P-5479)*

**Heron Therapeutics Inc (PA)** .................................. C ...... 858 251-4400
4242 Campus Point Ct Ste 200 San Diego (92121) *(P-5479)*

**Herotek Inc (PA)** ...................................................... E ...... 408 941-8399
155 Baytech Dr San Jose (95134) *(P-11863)*

**Herrick Corporation (PA)** ........................................ E ...... 209 956-4751
3003 E Hammer Ln Stockton (95212) *(P-8150)*

**Hertz Entertainment Services, Burbank** *Also Called: 24/7 Studio Equipment Inc (P-11796)*

**Herzog Wine Cellars, Oxnard** *Also Called: Royal Wine Corporation (P-1733)*

**Hesperia Holding Inc** .............................................. D ...... 760 244-8787
9780 E Ave Hesperia (92345) *(P-3311)*

**Hesperia Unified School Dst** .................................. D ...... 760 948-1051
11176 G Ave Hesperia (92345) *(P-2231)*

**Hesperia Usd Food Service, Hesperia** *Also Called: Hesperia Unified School Dst (P-2231)*

**Hesperian Health Guides (PA)** ............................... E ...... 510 845-1447
2860 Telegraph Ave Oakland (94609) *(P-4331)*

**Hess Collection Import Co, Napa** *Also Called: Hess Collection Winery (P-1613)*

**Hess Collection Winery** .......................................... D ...... 707 255-1144
1166 Commerce Blvd American Canyon (94503) *(P-1612)*

**Hess Collection Winery (DH)** ................................. E ...... 707 255-1144
4411 Redwood Rd Napa (94558) *(P-1613)*

**Hesse Mechatronics Inc** ......................................... E ...... 657 720-1233
3002 Dow Ave Ste 308 Tustin (92780) *(P-9863)*

**Hestan Commercial Corporation** .......................... C ...... 714 869-2380
3375 E La Palma Ave Anaheim (92806) *(P-11419)*

**Hester Fabrication Inc** ............................................ F ...... 530 227-6867
20876 Corsair Blvd Hayward (94545) *(P-19198)*

**Hewlett-Packard Entps LLC (PA)** ........................... F ...... 650 687-5817
3000 Hanover St Palo Alto (94304) *(P-10158)*

**Hexagon Agility Inc** ................................................ E ...... 949 236-5520
3335 Susan St Ste 100 Costa Mesa (92626) *(P-149)*

**Hexagon Mfg Intelligence Inc** ............................... D ...... 760 994-1401
3536 Seagate Way Ste 100 Oceanside (92056) *(P-14532)*

**Hexco International** ............................................... C ...... 951 677-2081
25720 Jefferson Ave Murrieta (92562) *(P-9864)*

**Hexoden Holdings Inc (PA)** .................................... D ...... 858 201-3412
1219 Linda Vista Dr San Marcos (92078) *(P-16144)*

**Hexpol Compounding CA Inc (DH)** ........................ D ...... 626 961-0311
2500 E Thompson St Long Beach (90805) *(P-6499)*

**Hf Group Inc** ............................................................ F ...... 530 788-0288
5801 C St Marysville (95903) *(P-10093)*

# ALPHABETIC SECTION — Hilti US Manufacturing Inc

**Hf Group Inc (PA)** ............................................................ E ...... 310 605-0755
203 W Artesia Blvd Compton (90220) *(P-15643)*

**Hgc Holdings Inc** ............................................................. E ...... 323 567-2226
3303 Martin Luther King Jr Blvd Lynwood (90262) *(P-1309)*

**Hgst Inc (DH)** .................................................................. C ...... 408 717-6000
5601 Great Oaks Pkwy San Jose (95119) *(P-10242)*

**Hhb Holdings Inc** ............................................................. C ...... 510 489-8100
2600 Central Ave Ste E Union City (94587) *(P-7561)*

**Hhi, Lake Forest** *Also Called: Assa Abloy AB (P-13156)*

**HI Rel Connectors Inc** ...................................................... B ...... 909 626-1820
760 Wharton Dr Claremont (91711) *(P-11458)*

**HI Relblity McRelectronics Inc** .......................................... D ...... 408 764-5500
1804 Mccarthy Blvd Milpitas (95035) *(P-12464)*

**HI Tech Electronic Mfg Corp** ............................................. D ...... 858 657-0908
1938 Avenida Del Oro Oceanside (92056) *(P-12129)*

**HI Tech Fire Apparatus, Oakdale** *Also Called: Hi-Tech Emergency Vehicle Service Inc (P-13360)*

**HI Tech Honeycomb Inc** .................................................... C ...... 858 974-1600
9355 Ruffin Ct San Diego (92123) *(P-8849)*

**Hi-Craft Metal Products** ................................................... E ...... 310 323-6949
606 W 184th St Gardena (90248) *(P-8468)*

**Hi-Desert Publishing Company** ......................................... E ...... 909 795-8145
35154 Yucaipa Blvd Yucaipa (92399) *(P-4129)*

**Hi-Desert Publishing Company (HQ)** ................................. D ...... 760 365-3315
56445 29 Palms Hwy Yucca Valley (92284) *(P-4130)*

**Hi-Desert Publishing Company** ......................................... E ...... 909 336-3555
28200 Highway 189 Bldg O-1 Lake Arrowhead (92352) *(P-4131)*

**Hi-Desert Publishing Company** ......................................... E ...... 909 866-3456
42007 Fox Farm Rd Ste 3b Big Bear Lake (92315) *(P-17683)*

**Hi-Grade Materials Co** ..................................................... D ...... 661 533-3100
6500 E Avenue T Littlerock (93543) *(P-7455)*

**Hi-Lite Manufacturing Co Inc** ........................................... D ...... 909 465-1999
13450 Monte Vista Ave Chino (91710) *(P-11537)*

**Hi-Plas, Mira Loma** *Also Called: Highland Plastics Inc (P-6853)*

**Hi-Precision Grinding, Santa Ana** *Also Called: Deltronic Corporation (P-14770)*

**Hi-Rel Plastics & Molding Corp** ........................................ E ...... 951 354-0258
7575 Jurupa Ave Riverside (92504) *(P-6852)*

**Hi-Shear Corporation (DH)** .............................................. A ...... 310 326-8110
2600 Skypark Dr Torrance (90505) *(P-8757)*

**Hi-Tech Emergency Vehicle Service Inc** ............................ E ...... 209 847-3042
444 Greger St Oakdale (95361) *(P-13360)*

**Hi-Tech Engineering, Camarillo** *Also Called: Hte Acquisition LLC (P-10877)*

**Hi-Tech Iron Works, Commerce** *Also Called: Architectural Enterprises Inc (P-8692)*

**Hi-Tech Labels Incorporated** ............................................ E ...... 714 670-2150
8530 Roland St Buena Park (90621) *(P-10871)*

**Hi-Tech Products, Buena Park** *Also Called: Hi-Tech Labels Incorporated (P-10871)*

**Hi-Torque Publications, Santa Clarita** *Also Called: Daisy Publishing Company Inc (P-4386)*

**Hi-Way Safety, Chino** *Also Called: Myers & Sons Hi-Way Safety Inc (P-16012)*

**Hiatus, Los Angeles** *Also Called: Crew Knitwear LLC (P-2748)*

**Hibernia Woolen Mills, Manhattan Beach** *Also Called: Stanton Carpet Corp (P-2521)*

**HIC Corporation (PA)** ....................................................... F ...... 949 261-1636
38 Executive Park Ste 300 Irvine (92614) *(P-4264)*

**Hid Global Corporation** .................................................... D ...... 949 732-2000
15370 Barranca Pkwy Irvine (92618) *(P-14533)*

**Hid Global Corporation** .................................................... F ...... 949 466-9508
53 Discovery Irvine (92618) *(P-14534)*

**Hidden Jeans Inc** ............................................................. E ...... 213 746-4223
7210 Dominion Cir Commerce (90040) *(P-2418)*

**High Caliber Line, Irwindale** *Also Called: Calibre International LLC (P-19548)*

**High Camp Home, Truckee** *Also Called: Recycled Spaces Inc (P-3557)*

**High Connection Density Inc** ............................................ E ...... 408 743-9700
542 Gibraltar Dr Milpitas (95035) *(P-12881)*

**High Country Water, Roseville** *Also Called: California Bottling Company (P-1873)*

**High Performance Seals, Garden Grove** *Also Called: Saint-Gobain Prfmce Plas Corp (P-5199)*

**High Prcsion Grnding McHning I** ...................................... F ...... 619 440-0303
1130 Pioneer Way El Cajon (92020) *(P-10872)*

**High Road Craft Ice Cream Inc (PA)** ................................ E ...... 678 701-7623
12243 Branford St Sun Valley (91352) *(P-805)*

**High Sierra Electronics, Grass Valley** *Also Called: Slouber Enterprises Inc (P-14720)*

**High Tech Pet Products** ................................................... D ...... 805 644-1797
2111 Portola Rd # A Ventura (93003) *(P-16704)*

**High Tek Usa Inc** ............................................................. F ...... 800 504-7120
12420 Gold Flake Ct Rancho Cordova (95742) *(P-3969)*

**Highball Signal Inc** .......................................................... E ...... 310 961-1122
6767 Di Carlo Pl Rancho Cucamonga (91739) *(P-11998)*

**Higher Ground LLC (PA)** .................................................. F ...... 650 322-3958
2595 E Bayshore Rd Ste 200 Palo Alto (94303) *(P-11864)*

**Higher One Payments Inc** ................................................ E ...... 510 769-9888
80 Swan Way Ste 200 Oakland (94621) *(P-18383)*

**Highlabs, San Francisco** *Also Called: Highnote Solutions Inc (P-18384)*

**Highland Lumber Sales Inc** .............................................. E ...... 714 778-2293
300 E Santa Ana St Anaheim (92805) *(P-3145)*

**Highland Plastics Inc** ...................................................... C ...... 951 360-9587
3650 Dulles Dr Mira Loma (91752) *(P-6853)*

**Highland Technology** ...................................................... E ...... 415 551-1700
650 Potrero Ave San Francisco (94110) *(P-14876)*

**Highlander Harvesting Aid, Gonzales** *Also Called: Ramsay Highlander Inc (P-9378)*

**Highline Aftermarket LLC** ............................................... D ...... 951 361-0331
10385 San Sevaine Way Ste B Jurupa Valley (91752) *(P-16385)*

**Highmark, Huntington Beach** *Also Called: Highmark Smart Reliable Seating Inc (P-3603)*

**Highmark Smart Reliable Seating Inc** .............................. C ...... 714 903-2257
5559 Mcfadden Ave Huntington Beach (92649) *(P-3603)*

**Highnote Solutions Inc** .................................................... F ...... 415 779-6275
548 Market St # 46205 San Francisco (94104) *(P-18384)*

**Highpoint Technologies Inc** ............................................. E ...... 408 942-5800
41650 Christy St Fremont (94538) *(P-10243)*

**Hightower Metal Products LLC** ....................................... D ...... 714 637-7000
2090 N Glassell St Orange (92865) *(P-9627)*

**Hightower Plating & Mfg Co LLC** ..................................... E ...... 714 637-9110
2090 N Glassell St Orange (92865) *(P-8970)*

**Highway Safety Control, Napa** *Also Called: Radiator Specialty Company (P-6319)*

**Highways Magazine, Oxnard** *Also Called: TI Enterprises LLC (P-4301)*

**Hii San Diego Shipyard Inc** .............................................. B ...... 619 234-8851
1995 Bay Front St San Diego (92101) *(P-14004)*

**Hikino Associates LLC** .................................................... E ...... 408 781-1900
47865 Fremont Blvd Fremont (94538) *(P-19397)*

**Hikma Pharmaceuticals USA Inc** ..................................... E ...... 760 683-0901
2325 Camino Vida Roble Ste B Carlsbad (92011) *(P-5480)*

**Hilfiker Pipe Co** ............................................................... E ...... 707 443-5091
1902 Hilfiker Ln Eureka (95503) *(P-7343)*

**Hilfiker Retaining Walls, Eureka** *Also Called: Hilfiker Pipe Co (P-7343)*

**Hill Brothers Chemical, Brea** *Also Called: Hill Brothers Chemical Company (P-17246)*

**Hill Brothers Chemical Company** .................................... F ...... 626 333-2251
15017 Clark Ave City Of Industry (91745) *(P-5032)*

**Hill Brothers Chemical Company (PA)** ............................ C ...... 714 998-8800
3000 E Birch St Ste 108 Brea (92821) *(P-17246)*

**Hill Manufacturing Company LLC** ................................... E ...... 408 988-4744
3363 Edward Ave Santa Clara (95054) *(P-8469)*

**Hillcor Distribution Inc** ................................................... F ...... 626 960-8789
5100 Commerce Dr Baldwin Park (91706) *(P-6854)*

**Hiller Companies LLC** .................................................... E ...... 858 899-5008
7070 Convoy Ct San Diego (92111) *(P-7854)*

**Hiller Marine, San Diego** *Also Called: Hiller Companies LLC (P-7854)*

**Hilliard Bruce Vineyards LLC (PA)** .................................. F ...... 805 736-5366
2097 Vineyard View Ln Lompoc (93436) *(P-1614)*

**Hills Wldg & Engrg Contr Inc** .......................................... D ...... 661 746-5400
22038 Stockdale Hwy Bakersfield (93314) *(P-237)*

**Hillside Capital Inc** ......................................................... C ...... 650 367-2011
6222 Fallbrook Ave Woodland Hills (91367) *(P-11865)*

**Hillside Farms Corporation** ............................................ F ...... 888 846-9653
16330 Bake Pkwy Irvine (92618) *(P-1100)*

**Hilmar Cheese Company Inc** .......................................... B ...... 209 667-6076
3600 W Canal Dr Turlock (95380) *(P-718)*

**Hilmar Cheese Company Inc (PA)** .................................. B ...... 209 667-6076
8901 Lander Ave Hilmar (95324) *(P-719)*

**Hilmar Whey Protein Inc (PA)** ......................................... E ...... 209 667-6076
9001 Lander Ave Hilmar (95324) *(P-762)*

**Hilmar Whey Protein Inc** ................................................ B ...... 209 667-6076
8901 Lander Ave Hilmar (95324) *(P-763)*

**HILMAR WHEY PROTEIN INC, Hilmar** *Also Called: Hilmar Whey Protein Inc (P-763)*

**Hilti US Manufacturing Inc** ............................................. E ...... 714 230-7410
6601 Darin Way Cypress (90630) *(P-7969)*

---

Employee Codes: A=Over 500 employees, B=251-500
C=101-250, D=51-100, E=20-50, F=10-19, G=1-9

**Hilz Cable Assemblies Inc** ............................................. F ...... 951 245-0499
31889 Corydon St Ste 110 Lake Elsinore (92530) *(P-14877)*

**Himco National Inc** ..................................................... F ...... 323 231-9104
120 E 33rd St Los Angeles (90011) *(P-457)*

**Himco Security Products, Los Angeles** *Also Called: Himco National Inc (P-457)*

**Hims Inc (HQ)** ............................................................. E ...... 415 851-0195
2269 Chestnut St # 523 San Francisco (94123) *(P-5988)*

**Hims & Hers, San Francisco** *Also Called: Hims Inc (P-5988)*

**Hims & Hers Health Inc (PA)** ..................................... E ...... 415 851-0195
2269 Chestnut St # 523 San Francisco (94123) *(P-5481)*

**Hinoichi Tofu, Garden Grove** *Also Called: House Foods America Corp (P-2233)*

**Hint Inc** .................................................................... C ...... 415 513-4051
625 Market St Ste 1000 San Francisco (94105) *(P-1894)*

**Hint Health Inc (PA)** ................................................. E ...... 415 854-6366
149 New Montgomery St Fl 4 San Francisco (94105) *(P-18385)*

**Hintex** ...................................................................... F ...... 320 400-0009
1230 S Glendale Ave Glendale (91205) *(P-7344)*

**Hip Hop Royalty, Santa Ana** *Also Called: Tailgate Printing Inc (P-4779)*

**Hiplink Software, Los Gatos** *Also Called: Semotus Inc (P-18777)*

**Hira Paris Inc** ........................................................... C ...... 909 634-3900
3811 Schaefer Ave Ste B Chino (91710) *(P-1310)*

**Hire Elegance** .......................................................... F ...... 858 740-7862
8333 Arjons Dr Ste E San Diego (92126) *(P-3744)*

**Hirel Connectors, Claremont** *Also Called: HI Rel Connectors Inc (P-11458)*

**Hirok Inc** .................................................................. E ...... 619 713-5066
5644 Kearny Mesa Rd Ste H San Diego (92111) *(P-9427)*

**Hironaka Promotions LLC** ......................................... E ...... 916 631-8470
2608 R St Sacramento (95816) *(P-4892)*

**Hironori Ramen Factory, Cerritos** *Also Called: Hny Ramen Inc (P-9797)*

**Hirsch Winery LLC** .................................................. F ...... 707 847-3001
57 Front St Healdsburg (95448) *(P-1615)*

**Hirsh Inc** .................................................................. E ...... 213 622-9441
860 S Los Angeles St # 900 Los Angeles (90014) *(P-238)*

**His Industries Inc** .................................................... E ...... 949 383-4308
1202 W Shelley Ct Orange (92868) *(P-10020)*

**Historynet, Beverly Hills** *Also Called: World History Group LLC (P-4307)*

**Hitachi, Santa Clara** *Also Called: Hitachi America Ltd (P-16817)*

**Hitachi America Ltd (HQ)** ......................................... C ...... 914 332-5800
2535 Augustine Dr Santa Clara (95054) *(P-16817)*

**Hitachi Astemo Americas Inc** ................................... B ...... 951 340-0702
1235 Graphite Dr Corona (92881) *(P-13514)*

**Hitachi Automotive Systems** ..................................... D ...... 310 212-0200
6200 Gateway Dr Cypress (90630) *(P-11272)*

**Hitachi Energy USA Inc** ............................................ F ...... 415 527-2850
60 Spear St San Francisco (94105) *(P-18386)*

**Hitachi Prticle Engrg Svcs Inc (DH)** ......................... E ...... 215 619-4920
1177 Quarry Ln Ste A Pleasanton (94566) *(P-14878)*

**Hitachi Solutions America Ltd (DH)** ......................... E ...... 949 242-1300
100 Spectrum Center Dr Ste 350 Irvine (92618) *(P-16526)*

**Hitachi Vantara Corporation (DH)** ............................ B ...... 858 225-2095
2535 Augustine Dr Santa Clara (95054) *(P-10244)*

**Hitech Metal Fabrication Corp** ................................ D ...... 714 635-3505
1705 S Claudina Way Anaheim (92805) *(P-8151)*

**Hitem, Oceanside** *Also Called: HI Tech Electronic Mfg Corp (P-12129)*

**Hitex Dyeing & Finishing Inc** ................................... E ...... 626 363-0160
355 Vineland Ave City Of Industry (91746) *(P-3030)*

**Hitt Companies** ....................................................... E ...... 714 979-1405
3231 W Macarthur Blvd Santa Ana (92704) *(P-6500)*

**Hitt Marking Devices I D Tech, Santa Ana** *Also Called: Hitt Companies (P-6500)*

**Hixson Metal Finishing** ............................................ D ...... 800 900-9798
829 Production Pl Newport Beach (92663) *(P-8971)*

**Hizco Truck Body, Los Angeles** *Also Called: A A Cater Truck Mfg Co Inc (P-3496)*

**HJS Graphics** .......................................................... F ...... 818 782-5490
3533 Old Conejo Rd Ste 104 Newbury Park (91320) *(P-4632)*

**HK Canning Inc (PA)** ............................................... E ...... 805 652-1392
130 N Garden St Ventura (93001) *(P-892)*

**HK Precision Turning Machining, Oceanside** *Also Called: Balda Precision Inc (P-8720)*

**Hkf Inc (PA)** ............................................................. D ...... 323 225-1318
5983 Smithway St Commerce (90040) *(P-16781)*

**Hl Uriman Inc (HQ)** .................................................. F ...... 714 257-2080
650 N Puente St Brea (92821) *(P-13172)*

**Hlc, Healdsburg** *Also Called: Healdsburg Lumber Company Inc (P-17355)*

**HMC Display, Madera** *Also Called: Gardner Family Ltd Partnership (P-7998)*

**Hmclause Inc (DH)** ................................................. C ...... 800 320-4672
260 Cousteau Pl Ste 210 Davis (95618) *(P-49)*

**HMcompany** ........................................................... F ...... 805 650-2651
4464 Mcgrath St Ste 111 Ventura (93003) *(P-10873)*

**Hmr Building Systems LLC** .................................... D ...... 951 749-4700
620 Newport Center Dr Fl 12 Newport Beach (92660) *(P-3070)*

**Hnc Parent Inc (PA)** ............................................... D ...... 310 955-9200
999 N Pacific Coast Hwy Ste 800 El Segundo (90245) *(P-6377)*

**Hnc Printing Services LLC** ..................................... F ...... 925 771-2080
2490 Arnold Industrial Way Ste B Concord (94520) *(P-4633)*

**Hny Ramen Inc** ...................................................... F ...... 626 586-7209
17109 Edwards Rd Cerritos (90703) *(P-9797)*

**Hobie Cat Company (PA)** ....................................... C ...... 760 758-9100
4925 Oceanside Blvd Oceanside (92056) *(P-14035)*

**Hobie Cat Company II LLC** .................................... C ...... 760 758-9100
4925 Oceanside Blvd Oceanside (92056) *(P-15821)*

**Hochiki, Buena Park** *Also Called: Hochiki America Corporation (P-16654)*

**Hochiki America Corporation (HQ)** ........................ D ...... 714 522-2246
7051 Village Dr Ste 100 Buena Park (90621) *(P-16654)*

**Hodge Products Inc** ............................................... E ...... 800 778-2217
7365 Mission Gorge Rd Ste F San Diego (92120) *(P-8002)*

**Hoefner Corporation** .............................................. E ...... 626 443-3258
9722 Rush St South El Monte (91733) *(P-10874)*

**Hoffman Plastic Compounds Inc** ........................... D ...... 323 636-3346
16616 Garfield Ave Paramount (90723) *(P-5158)*

**Hoffy, Vernon** *Also Called: Square H Brands Inc (P-669)*

**Hofmann Company, Walnut Creek** *Also Called: Hofmann Construction Co (P-350)*

**Hofmann Construction Co (PA)** ............................. E ...... 925 478-2000
3000 Oak Rd Ste 300 Walnut Creek (94597) *(P-350)*

**Hog Inc** .................................................................. F ...... 626 279-5275
9519 Rush St Ste A South El Monte (91733) *(P-17830)*

**Hogan Co Inc** ........................................................ E ...... 909 421-0245
2741 S Lilac Ave Bloomington (92316) *(P-7643)*

**Hogan Mfg Inc (PA)** ............................................... C ...... 209 838-7323
1638 Main St Escalon (95320) *(P-16145)*

**Hogan Mfg Inc** ....................................................... F ...... 209 838-2400
19527 Mchenry Ave Escalon (95320) *(P-16146)*

**Hogan Mfg Inc** ....................................................... C ...... 209 838-2400
1520 1st St Escalon (95320) *(P-16147)*

**Hogue Bros Inc** ...................................................... E ...... 805 239-1440
550 Linne Rd Paso Robles (93446) *(P-3095)*

**Hogue Grips, Paso Robles** *Also Called: Hogue Bros Inc (P-3095)*

**Hoist Fitness, Poway** *Also Called: Hoist Fitness Systems Inc (P-15822)*

**Hoist Fitness Systems, San Diego** *Also Called: Fitness Warehouse LLC (P-15813)*

**Hoist Fitness Systems Inc** ..................................... D ...... 858 578-7676
11900 Community Rd Poway (92064) *(P-15822)*

**Hokey Pokey La, Santa Monica** *Also Called: Hokey Pokey LLC (P-17131)*

**Hokey Pokey LLC** ................................................. E ...... 213 361-2503
1235 24th St Unit 4 Santa Monica (90404) *(P-17131)*

**Holcim Solutions & Pdts US LLC** .......................... E ...... 714 898-0025
12271 Monarch St Garden Grove (92841) *(P-5159)*

**Holdrite, Poway** *Also Called: Securus Inc (P-8645)*

**Holguin & Holguin Inc** ........................................... E ...... 626 815-0168
968 W Foothill Blvd Azusa (91702) *(P-3626)*

**Holiday Foliage, San Diego** *Also Called: Holiday Foliage Inc (P-16148)*

**Holiday Foliage Inc** ............................................... E ...... 619 661-9094
2592 Otay Center Dr San Diego (92154) *(P-16148)*

**Holiday Transportation, Van Nuys** *Also Called: Rwh Inc (P-7495)*

**Holland & Herring Mfg Inc** .................................... E ...... 909 469-4700
661 E Monterey Ave Pomona (91767) *(P-10875)*

**Holland Electronics, Ventura** *Also Called: Holland Electronics LLC (P-12882)*

**Holland Electronics LLC** ....................................... E ...... 888 628-5411
2935 Golf Course Dr Ventura (93003) *(P-12882)*

**Holliday Trucking Inc (PA)** .................................... D ...... 909 982-1553
1401 N Benson Ave Upland (91786) *(P-7456)*

**Holliday Trucking Inc** ............................................ D ...... 888 273-2200
2300 W Base Line St San Bernardino (92410) *(P-7457)*

**Hollister Incorporated** .......................................... F ...... 805 845-4785
5276 Hollister Ave Ste 45 Santa Barbara (93111) *(P-15105)*

**Hollister Landscape Supply Inc** .................................................. D ...... 831 636-8750
 2410 San Juan Rd Hollister (95023) *(P-7458)*

**Holly Yashi Inc** ........................................................................... D ...... 707 822-0389
 1300 9th St Arcata (95521) *(P-15694)*

**Hollywood Bed & Spring Mfg, Commerce** *Also Called: Hollywood Bed Spring Mfg Inc (P-8003)*

**Hollywood Bed Spring Mfg Inc (PA)** ........................................... D ...... 323 887-9500
 5959 Corvette St Commerce (90040) *(P-8003)*

**Hollywood Chairs (PA)** .............................................................. E ...... 760 471-6600
 120 W Grand Ave Ste 102 Escondido (92025) *(P-3444)*

**Hollywood Records Inc** ............................................................. E ...... 818 560-5670
 500 S Buena Vista St Burbank (91521) *(P-11735)*

**Hollywood Ribbon Industries Inc** .............................................. B ...... 323 266-0670
 9000 Rochester Ave Rancho Cucamonga (91730) *(P-2452)*

**Hollywood Software Inc** ............................................................ E ...... 818 205-2121
 5000 Van Nuys Blvd Ste 300 Van Nuys (91403) *(P-18387)*

**Hologic Inc** ................................................................................. E ...... 408 745-0975
 1240 Elko Dr Sunnyvale (94089) *(P-15502)*

**Hologic Inc** ................................................................................. C ...... 858 410-8000
 10210 Genetic Center Dr San Diego (92121) *(P-15542)*

**Hologic Inc** ................................................................................. E ...... 858 410-8792
 9393 Waples St San Diego (92121) *(P-15543)*

**Holophane Corporation** ............................................................. A ...... 510 540-0156
 2231 4th St Berkeley (94710) *(P-11538)*

**Holt Integrated Circuits, Aliso Viejo** *Also Called: W G Holt Inc (P-12799)*

**Holt Lumber Inc (PA)** .................................................................. E ...... 559 233-3291
 1916 S Cherry Ave Fresno (93721) *(P-17333)*

**Holt Tool & Machine Inc** ........................................................... E ...... 650 364-2547
 2909 Middlefield Rd Redwood City (94063) *(P-7615)*

**Holy High Wines, Fremont** *Also Called: Jaton Corporation (P-12146)*

**Holz Rubber Company Inc** ......................................................... C ...... 209 368-7171
 1129 S Sacramento St Lodi (95240) *(P-6501)*

**Home & Body Company (PA)** ..................................................... B ...... 714 842-8000
 5800 Skylab Rd Huntington Beach (92647) *(P-6292)*

**Home Brew Mart Inc** .................................................................. B ...... 858 790-6900
 9045 Carroll Way San Diego (92121) *(P-1434)*

**Home Concepts Products Inc** .................................................... E ...... 866 981-0500
 4199 Bandini Blvd Vernon (90058) *(P-6855)*

**Home Decor Wholesaler, City Of Industry** *Also Called: Pacific Heritg HM Fashion Inc (P-16433)*

**Home Factories Inc (HQ)** ............................................................ F ...... 209 745-3001
 225 Elm Ave Galt (95632) *(P-3397)*

**Home Organizers Inc** ................................................................. A ...... 562 699-9945
 3860 Capitol Ave City Of Industry (90601) *(P-494)*

**Home Plus Group Inc** ................................................................. F ...... 714 500-3855
 18315 Mount Baldy Cir Fountain Valley (92708) *(P-3242)*

**Home-Flex, Valencia** *Also Called: Valencia Pipe Company (P-6605)*

**Homegrown Naturals, Berkeley** *Also Called: Annies Inc (P-2127)*

**Homer T Hayward Lumber Co** ................................................... F ...... 805 928-8557
 800 W Betteravia Rd Santa Maria (93455) *(P-17334)*

**Homes & Land of Ventura** ......................................................... E ...... 805 644-9816
 2193 Portola Rd Ventura (93003) *(P-4132)*

**Homestead Sheet Metal** ............................................................ E ...... 619 469-4373
 9031 Memory Ln Spring Valley (91977) *(P-8152)*

**Hone Maxwell LLP** ..................................................................... F ...... 415 765-1754
 3465 Camino Del Rio S Ste 400 San Diego (92108) *(P-7553)*

**HONEST, Los Angeles** *Also Called: Honest Company Inc (P-2831)*

**Honest Company Inc (PA)** .......................................................... C ...... 310 917-9199
 12130 Millennium Ste 500 Los Angeles (90094) *(P-2831)*

**Honest Kitchen Inc** ..................................................................... D ...... 619 544-0018
 1785 Hancock St Ste 100 San Diego (92110) *(P-1101)*

**Honey Bennetts Farm** ................................................................ E ...... 805 521-1375
 3176 Honey Ln Fillmore (93015) *(P-2232)*

**Honey Isabells Inc** ...................................................................... E ...... 800 708-8485
 539 N Glenoaks Blvd Ste 207b Burbank (91502) *(P-69)*

**Honey Punch, Los Angeles** *Also Called: Klk Forte Industry Inc (P-2781)*

**Honeybee Robotics LLC** ............................................................ D ...... 303 774-7613
 2408 Lincoln Ave Altadena (91001) *(P-10094)*

**Honeybee Robotics LLC** ............................................................ D ...... 510 207-4555
 398 W Washington Blvd Ste 200 Pasadena (91103) *(P-10095)*

**Honeydew Apparel Group Inc** ................................................... F ...... 818 717-9751
 20830 Dearborn St Chatsworth (91311) *(P-2832)*

**Honeyville Inc** ............................................................................. D ...... 909 980-9500
 11600 Dayton Dr Rancho Cucamonga (91730) *(P-16282)*

**Honeywell, Santa Clara** *Also Called: Honeywell International Inc (P-5095)*

**Honeywell, Torrance** *Also Called: Honeywell International Inc (P-13710)*

**Honeywell, Calexico** *Also Called: Honeywell International Inc (P-13711)*

**Honeywell, San Diego** *Also Called: Honeywell International Inc (P-14361)*

**Honeywell Authorized Dealer, San Diego** *Also Called: Atlas Mechanical Inc (P-404)*

**Honeywell Authorized Dealer, Anaheim** *Also Called: Control Air Conditioning Corporation (P-414)*

**Honeywell Authorized Dealer, Santa Clara** *Also Called: Envirnmntal Systems Inc Nthrn (P-417)*

**Honeywell Authorized Dealer, Santa Fe Springs** *Also Called: Western Allied Corporation (P-442)*

**Honeywell International Inc** ...................................................... D ...... 408 962-2000
 3500 Garrett Dr Santa Clara (95054) *(P-5095)*

**Honeywell International Inc** ...................................................... A ...... 310 323-9500
 2525 W 190th St Torrance (90504) *(P-13710)*

**Honeywell International Inc** ...................................................... F ...... 760 312-5300
 233 Paulin Ave Box 8500 Calexico (92231) *(P-13711)*

**Honeywell International Inc** ...................................................... C ...... 619 671-5612
 2055 Dublin Dr San Diego (92154) *(P-14361)*

**Honeywell Safety Pdts USA Inc** ................................................. C ...... 619 661-8383
 7828 Waterville Rd San Diego (92154) *(P-13712)*

**Honeywell SEC Americas LLC** ................................................... D ...... 949 737-7800
 2955 Red Hill Ave Ste 100 Costa Mesa (92626) *(P-11999)*

**Hongfa America Inc** ................................................................... E ...... 714 669-2888
 20381 Hermana Cir Lake Forest (92630) *(P-11325)*

**Honig Cellars, Rutherford** *Also Called: Honig Vineyard and Winery LLC (P-17)*

**Honig Vineyard and Winery LLC** ............................................... E ...... 707 963-5618
 850 Rutherford Rd Rutherford (94573) *(P-17)*

**Honk Technologies Inc** .............................................................. C ...... 800 979-3162
 2251 Barry Ave Los Angeles (90064) *(P-19008)*

**Honor Life, Vista** *Also Called: Rayzist Photomask Inc (P-15900)*

**Honor Plastics, Pomona** *Also Called: Performnce Engineered Pdts Inc (P-6954)*

**Honulua Surf Co, Irvine** *Also Called: Veezee Inc (P-2694)*

**Hood Container Corporation** .................................................... F ...... 818 848-1648
 25014 Avenue Kearny Santa Clarita (91355) *(P-3857)*

**Hood Manufacturing Inc** ........................................................... D ...... 714 979-7681
 2621 S Birch St Santa Ana (92707) *(P-6856)*

**Hook It Up** .................................................................................. E ...... 714 600-0100
 1513 S Grand Ave Santa Ana (92705) *(P-2395)*

**Hook or Crook Cellars, Lodi** *Also Called: Baywood Cellars Inc (P-1483)*

**Hoonuit LLC (DH)** ...................................................................... E ...... 320 631-5900
 150 Parkshore Dr Folsom (95630) *(P-18388)*

**Hoopa Forest Industries** ........................................................... E ...... 530 625-4281
 778 Marshall Ln Hoopa (95546) *(P-3046)*

**Hoopla Software Inc** .................................................................. E ...... 408 498-9600
 84 W Santa Clara St Ste 460 San Jose (95113) *(P-18389)*

**Hoosier Inc** .................................................................................. D ...... 951 272-3070
 1152 California Ave Corona (92881) *(P-6857)*

**Hoover Containers Inc** ............................................................... D ...... 909 444-9454
 19570 San Jose Ave City Of Industry (91748) *(P-3858)*

**Hoover Treated Wood Pdts Inc** ................................................. E ...... 661 833-0429
 5601 District Blvd Bakersfield (93313) *(P-3403)*

**Hoover Treated Wood Pdts Plant, Bakersfield** *Also Called: Hoover Treated Wood Pdts Inc (P-3403)*

**Hope Plastics Co Inc** .................................................................. E ...... 818 769-5560
 5353 Strohm Ave North Hollywood (91601) *(P-6858)*

**Hopkins Labratory Co, Irwindale** *Also Called: Esmond Natural Inc (P-5238)*

**Hopscotch Press Inc** .................................................................. E ...... 510 548-0400
 21 Orinda Way Ste C428 Orinda (94563) *(P-4414)*

**Horiba Americas Holding Inc (HQ)** ............................................ A ...... 949 250-4811
 9755 Research Dr Irvine (92618) *(P-14671)*

**Horiba Automotive Test Systems, Irvine** *Also Called: Horiba Instruments Inc (P-14672)*

**Horiba Instruments Inc (DH)** ..................................................... C ...... 949 250-4811
 9755 Research Dr Irvine (92618) *(P-14672)*

**Horiba Instruments Inc** ............................................................. D ...... 408 730-4772
 430 Indio Way Sunnyvale (94085) *(P-14879)*

**Horiba International Corp** ......................................................... A ...... 949 250-4811
 9755 Research Dr Irvine (92618) *(P-14880)*

**Horiba Semiconductor, Sunnyvale** *Also Called: Horiba/Stec Incorporated (P-14881)*
**Horiba/Stec Incorporated** .................................. D ...... 408 730-4772
  430 Indio Way Sunnyvale (94085) *(P-14881)*
**Horizon Snack Foods Inc** ................................... D ...... 925 373-7700
  197 Darcy Pkwy Lathrop (95330) *(P-1287)*
**Horizon Surgical Systems, Malibu** *Also Called: Horizon Surgical Systems Inc (P-15358)*
**Horizon Surgical Systems Inc** ............................ F ...... 310 876-2460
  22619 Pacific Coast Hwy Ste C280 Malibu (90265) *(P-15358)*
**Horizon Well Logging Inc** .................................. E ...... 805 733-0972
  711 Saint Andrews Way Lompoc (93436) *(P-239)*
**Hormel, Stockton** *Also Called: Hormel Foods Corporation (P-602)*
**Hormel, Irvine** *Also Called: Hormel Foods Corp Svcs LLC (P-647)*
**Hormel, Fresno** *Also Called: Hormel Foods Corporation (P-1352)*
**Hormel Foods Corp Svcs LLC** ............................ E ...... 949 753-5350
  2 Venture Ste 250 Irvine (92618) *(P-647)*
**Hormel Foods Corporation** ................................. D ...... 800 523-4635
  3656 Perlman Dr Stockton (95206) *(P-602)*
**Hormel Foods Corporation** ................................. E ...... 559 237-9206
  4343 E Florence Ave Fresno (93725) *(P-1352)*
**Horn Machine Tools Inc (PA)** ............................. E ...... 559 431-4131
  40455 Brickyard Dr Ste 101 Madera (93636) *(P-9583)*
**Hortonworks, Santa Clara** *Also Called: Hortonworks Inc (P-18390)*
**Hortonworks Inc (DH)** ........................................ A ...... 408 916-4121
  5470 Great America Pkwy Santa Clara (95054) *(P-18390)*
**Horvath Holdings Inc** ........................................ F ...... 530 587-4700
  12755 Rainbow Dr Truckee (96161) *(P-2453)*
**Hose Power USA, City Of Industry** *Also Called: Bridgestone Hosepower LLC (P-16864)*
**Hospital Systems Inc** ........................................ D ...... 925 427-7800
  750 Garcia Ave Pittsburg (94565) *(P-15544)*
**Hospitality Wood Products Inc** ........................... F ...... 562 806-5564
  7206 E Gage Ave Commerce (90040) *(P-3146)*
**Hot Shoppe Design, San Clemente** *Also Called: Hot Shoppe Designs Inc (P-2622)*
**Hot Shoppe Designs Inc** .................................... F ...... 949 487-2828
  1323 Calle Avanzado San Clemente (92673) *(P-2622)*
**Hot Wire Foam Factory04, Lompoc** *Also Called: W F F H Inc (P-16266)*
**Hotlix (PA)** ...................................................... E ...... 805 473-0596
  966 Griffin St Grover Beach (93433) *(P-1311)*
**Hotlix Candy, Grover Beach** *Also Called: Hotlix (P-1311)*
**Houghton Mifflin Harcourt Pubg** .......................... E ...... 617 351-5000
  525 B St Ste 1900 San Diego (92101) *(P-4332)*
**House Foods America Corp (HQ)** ........................ E ...... 714 901-4350
  7351 Orangewood Ave Garden Grove (92841) *(P-2233)*
**House of Bagels Inc (PA)** .................................. F ...... 650 595-4700
  1007 Washington St San Carlos (94070) *(P-1217)*
**House of Graphics, South El Monte** *Also Called: Hog Inc (P-17830)*
**House of Lashes** .............................................. E ...... 714 515-4162
  1565 Mcgaw Ave Ste C Irvine (92614) *(P-16149)*
**House of Magnets, El Cajon** *Also Called: Graphic Business Solutions Inc (P-16991)*
**House of Printing Inc** ........................................ E ...... 626 793-7034
  3336 E Colorado Blvd Pasadena (91107) *(P-4634)*
**Housewares International Inc** ............................. E ...... 323 581-3000
  1933 S Broadway Ste 867 Los Angeles (90007) *(P-6859)*
**Houston Bazz Co** .............................................. D ...... 714 898-2666
  12700 Western Ave Garden Grove (92841) *(P-8850)*
**Houston Fearless 76, Compton** *Also Called: Hf Group Inc (P-15643)*
**Houston Ontic Inc** ............................................ F ...... 818 678-6555
  20400 Plummer St Chatsworth (91311) *(P-10876)*
**Howell Drilling, Long Beach** *Also Called: Dick Howells Hole Drlg Svc Inc (P-156)*
**Howk Systems, Modesto** *Also Called: Howk Well & Equipment Co Inc (P-17707)*
**Howk Well & Equipment Co Inc** .......................... E ...... 209 529-4110
  1825 Yosemite Blvd Modesto (95354) *(P-17707)*
**Howmedica Osteonics Corp** ............................... C ...... 800 621-6104
  6885 Flanders Dr Ste G San Diego (92121) *(P-15359)*
**Howmet Aerospace Inc** ..................................... B ...... 212 836-2674
  3016 Lomita Blvd Torrance (90505) *(P-7706)*
**Howmet Aerospace Inc** ..................................... C ...... 323 728-3901
  1550 Gage Rd Montebello (90640) *(P-7729)*
**Howmet Aerospace Inc, Montebello** *Also Called: Howmet Aerospace Inc (P-7729)*
**Howmet Corporation** ......................................... A ...... 310 847-8152
  900 E Watson Center Rd Carson (90745) *(P-7686)*

**Howmet Globl Fstning Systems I** ........................ D ...... 714 871-1550
  800 S State College Blvd Fullerton (92831) *(P-7687)*
**Hoya Corporation** ............................................ E ...... 858 309-6050
  4255 Ruffin Rd San Diego (92123) *(P-14780)*
**Hoya Corporation** ............................................ E ...... 209 579-7739
  1400 Carpenter Ln Modesto (95351) *(P-15602)*
**Hoya Holdings Inc** ........................................... C ...... 626 739-5200
  425 E Huntington Dr Monrovia (91016) *(P-14781)*
**Hoya Holdings Inc (HQ)** .................................... C ...... 408 654-2300
  820 N Mccarthy Blvd Ste 220 Milpitas (95035) *(P-15644)*
**Hoya Optical Inc (PA)** ....................................... D ...... 209 579-7739
  1400 Carpenter Ln Modesto (95351) *(P-15603)*
**Hoya San Diego, San Diego** *Also Called: Hoya Corporation (P-14780)*
**Hoya Surgical Optics Inc** .................................. F ...... 909 680-3900
  110 Progress Irvine (92618) *(P-15106)*
**Hoylu Inc** ........................................................ E ...... 213 440-2499
  6121 W Sunset Blvd Los Angeles (90028) *(P-18391)*
**Hoylu La, Los Angeles** *Also Called: Hoylu Inc (P-18391)*
**HP, Palo Alto** *Also Called: Enterprise Svcs Asia PCF Corp (P-10151)*
**HP, Palo Alto** *Also Called: HP Inc (P-10161)*
**HP, San Diego** *Also Called: HP Inc (P-10162)*
**HP, Palo Alto** *Also Called: HP Inc (P-10163)*
**Hp Inc** ............................................................ D ...... 415 979-3700
  303 2nd St Ste S500 San Francisco (94107) *(P-10159)*
**HP Hewlett Packard Group LLC** ......................... F ...... 650 857-1501
  1501 Page Mill Rd Palo Alto (94304) *(P-10160)*
**HP Hood LLC** .................................................. B ...... 916 379-9266
  8340 Belvedere Ave Sacramento (95826) *(P-839)*
**HP Inc (PA)** .................................................... A ...... 650 857-1501
  1501 Page Mill Rd Palo Alto (94304) *(P-10161)*
**HP Inc** ............................................................ B ...... 858 924-5117
  16399 W Bernardo Dr Bldg 61 San Diego (92127) *(P-10162)*
**HP Inc** ............................................................ F ...... 650 857-1501
  3495 Deer Creek Rd Palo Alto (94304) *(P-10163)*
**HP It Services Incorporated** .............................. E ...... 714 844-7737
  1506 W Flower Ave Fullerton (92833) *(P-10376)*
**HP Water Systems Inc** ..................................... E ...... 559 268-4751
  9338 W Whites Bridge Ave Fresno (93706) *(P-9929)*
**Hpcwire, San Diego** *Also Called: Tabor Communications Inc (P-4475)*
**Hpe Enterprises LLC (HQ)** ................................ C ...... 650 857-5817
  6280 America Center Dr San Jose (95002) *(P-18392)*
**Hpi Cylinders, Santa Fe Springs** *Also Called: Hydraulic Pneumatic Inc (P-10628)*
**Hpi Liquidations Inc** ......................................... C ...... 858 391-7302
  13100 Danielson St Poway (92064) *(P-3859)*
**Hpi Racing, Lake Forest** *Also Called: SMC Products Inc (P-16951)*
**Hpl Contract Inc** .............................................. F ...... 209 892-1717
  525 Baldwin Rd Patterson (95363) *(P-3570)*
**Hpp Food Services, Wilmington** *Also Called: Icpk Corporation (P-17115)*
**Hqe Systems Inc** ............................................. D ...... 800 967-3036
  27348 Via Industria Temecula (92590) *(P-19560)*
**Hr, Lodi** *Also Called: Holz Rubber Company Inc (P-6501)*
**Hr Cloud Inc** ................................................... E ...... 510 909-1993
  222 N Pacific Coast Hwy Ste 2000 El Segundo (90245) *(P-18393)*
**Hre Performance Wheels, Vista** *Also Called: Phoenix Wheel Company Inc (P-16389)*
**Hrk Pet Food Products Inc** ................................ F ...... 818 897-2521
  12924 Pierce St Pacoima (91331) *(P-1130)*
**Hsb Holdings Inc** ............................................. E ...... 951 214-6590
  14050 Day St Moreno Valley (92553) *(P-6411)*
**Hsi Mechanical Inc** .......................................... E ...... 209 408-0183
  1013 N Emerald Ave Modesto (95351) *(P-8470)*
**Hsiao & Montano Inc** ....................................... E ...... 626 588-2528
  809 W Santa Anita Ave San Gabriel (91776) *(P-7133)*
**Hsssi, San Dimas** *Also Called: Hamilton Sundstrand Spc Systms (P-14875)*
**Ht Multinational Inc** ......................................... E ...... 909 325-8582
  501 W Foothill Blvd Azusa (91702) *(P-13515)*
**Hte Acquisition LLC** ......................................... E ...... 805 987-0520
  4610 Calle Quetzal Camarillo (93012) *(P-10877)*
**Hti Turnkey Manufacturing Svcs** ........................ E ...... 408 955-0807
  2200 Zanker Rd Ste A San Jose (95131) *(P-12996)*
**Htl Manufacturing Div, Simi Valley** *Also Called: Meggitt Safety Systems Inc (P-13908)*

## ALPHABETIC SECTION

Hts Division, Lake Elsinore *Also Called: Mercury Metal Die & Ltr Co Inc (P-9092)*
Huawei Device USA Inc .................................................................. C ...... 408 306-7171
 345 E Middlefield Rd Mountain View (94043) *(P-11866)*
Huck International Inc .................................................................... C ...... 310 830-8200
 900 E Watson Center Rd Carson (90745) *(P-8758)*
Hudson Printing, Carlsbad *Also Called: Hudson Printing Inc (P-4893)*
Hudson Printing Inc ....................................................................... E ...... 760 602-1260
 2780 Loker Ave W Carlsbad (92010) *(P-4893)*
Hudson Wines LLC ........................................................................ F ...... 707 255-1345
 5398 Sonoma Hwy Napa (94559) *(P-1616)*
Hughes Bros Aircrafters Inc .......................................................... E ...... 323 773-4541
 11010 Garfield Pl South Gate (90280) *(P-9628)*
Hughes Circuits Inc (PA).................................................................D ...... 760 744-0300
 546 S Pacific St San Marcos (92078) *(P-12130)*
Hughes Circuits Inc ........................................................................ C ...... 760 744-0300
 540 S Pacific St San Marcos (92078) *(P-12131)*
Hughson Nut Inc (DH).....................................................................D ...... 209 883-0403
 1825 Verduga Rd Hughson (95326) *(P-1353)*
Hughson Nut Inc ............................................................................ C ...... 209 394-6005
 11173 Mercedes Ave Livingston (95334) *(P-2234)*
Hugo Venture Solutions Corp ........................................................ E ...... 805 684-0935
 6325 Carpinteria Ave Carpinteria (93013) *(P-10878)*
Huhtamaki Inc ................................................................................ C ...... 323 269-0151
 4209 Noakes St Commerce (90023) *(P-6646)*
Hula Networks Inc (PA)................................................................... F ...... 866 485-2638
 929 Berryessa Rd Ste 10 San Jose (95133) *(P-16527)*
Hulsey Contracting Inc .................................................................. E ...... 951 549-3665
 1370 Dodson Way Riverside (92507) *(P-16790)*
Human Dsgns Prsthtic Orthtic L, Long Beach *Also Called: Ferraco Inc (P-15346)*
Human Resources, Anaheim *Also Called: L3harris Interstate Elec Corp (P-14546)*
Humanconcepts LLC ..................................................................... E ...... 650 581-2500
 3 Harbor Dr Ste 200 Sausalito (94965) *(P-18394)*
Humbl Inc ....................................................................................... F ...... 786 738-9012
 600 B St Ste 300 San Diego (92101) *(P-18395)*
Humboldt Creamery Association, Fortuna *Also Called: Humboldt Creamery LLC (P-764)*
Humboldt Creamery LLC ............................................................... C ...... 209 576-3400
 572 Fernbridge Dr Fortuna (95540) *(P-764)*
Hummus Guy, The, Torrance *Also Called: Thg Brands Inc (P-2373)*
Huneeus Vintners LLC (PA)............................................................ F ...... 707 286-2724
 1224 Adams St Ste B Saint Helena (94574) *(P-1617)*
Hunniface LLC ............................................................................... F ...... 424 966-0281
 9350 Wilshire Blvd Ste 203 Beverly Hills (90212) *(P-5989)*
Hunt Electronic, Rancho Cucamonga *Also Called: Hunt Electronic Usa Inc (P-13248)*
Hunt Electronic Usa Inc ................................................................. F ...... 909 987-6999
 11790 Jersey Blvd Rancho Cucamonga (91730) *(P-13248)*
Hunter, San Marcos *Also Called: Hunter Industries Incorporated (P-16370)*
Hunter Douglas Inc ........................................................................ B ...... 858 679-7500
 9900 Gidley St El Monte (91731) *(P-3721)*
Hunter Industries Incorporated .................................................... E ...... 559 347-0816
 3950 N Chestnut Ave Ste 101 Fresno (93726) *(P-9357)*
Hunter Industries Incorporated (PA)............................................. C ...... 760 744-5240
 1940 Diamond St San Marcos (92078) *(P-16370)*
Hunter Vaughan LLC ..................................................................... C ...... 626 534-7050
 450 N Oak St Inglewood (90302) *(P-5990)*
Huntington Beach Machining, Huntington Beach *Also Called: Madsen Products Incorporated (P-10954)*
Huntington Industries Inc ............................................................. C ...... 323 772-5575
 12520 Chadron Ave Hawthorne (90250) *(P-3476)*
Huntington Ingalls Industries ....................................................... E ...... 858 522-6000
 9444 Balboa Ave Ste 400 San Diego (92123) *(P-16150)*
Huntington Mechanical Labs, Grass Valley *Also Called: Huntington Mechanical Labs Inc (P-9963)*
Huntington Mechanical Labs Inc .................................................. E ...... 530 273-9533
 13355 Nevada City Ave Grass Valley (95945) *(P-9963)*
Huntsman, Los Angeles *Also Called: Huntsman Advanced Materials AM (P-5160)*
Huntsman Advanced Materials AM .............................................. C ...... 818 265-7221
 5121 W San Fernando Rd Los Angeles (90039) *(P-5160)*
Huntsman Advnced Mtls Amrcas L ............................................... E ...... 818 265-7302
 4541 Electronics Pl Los Angeles (90039) *(P-5161)*
Hupa International Inc .................................................................. E ...... 909 598-9876
 21717 Ferrero Walnut (91789) *(P-15823)*

Hurley, Costa Mesa *Also Called: Hurley International LLC (P-2623)*
Hurley International LLC (PA)........................................................ C ...... 855 655-2515
 3080 Bristol St Costa Mesa (92626) *(P-2623)*
Hurst International, Chatsworth *Also Called: Labeling Hurst Systems LLC (P-4910)*
Husch Vineyards Inc (PA).............................................................. E ...... 707 895-3216
 4400 Highway 128 Philo (95466) *(P-1618)*
Husks Unlimited (PA)..................................................................... E ...... 619 476-8301
 9925 Airway Rd # C San Diego (92154) *(P-2235)*
Husky Injction Mlding Systems .................................................... E ...... 805 523-9593
 5245 Maureen Ln Moorpark (93021) *(P-6860)*
Husky Injction Mlding Systems ....................................................D ...... 714 545-8200
 3505 Cadillac Ave Ste N4 Costa Mesa (92626) *(P-6861)*
Hussmann Corporation ................................................................. B ...... 909 590-4910
 13770 Ramona Ave Chino (91710) *(P-10502)*
Hutchinson Arospc & Indust Inc ................................................... C ...... 818 843-1000
 4510 W Vanowen St Burbank (91505) *(P-6502)*
Hutchinson Arospc & Indust Inc ................................................... C ...... 818 843-1000
 4510 W Vanowen St Burbank (91505) *(P-13859)*
Hutchinson Seal Corporation (DH)................................................ C ...... 248 375-4190
 11634 Patton Rd Downey (90241) *(P-6452)*
Huxtable's, Vernon *Also Called: Huxtables Kitchen Inc (P-17584)*
Huxtables Kitchen Inc ...................................................................D ...... 323 923-2900
 2100 E 49th St Vernon (90058) *(P-17584)*
Huy Fong Foods Inc ....................................................................... E ...... 626 286-8328
 4800 Azusa Canyon Rd Irwindale (91706) *(P-893)*
Hvantage Technologies Inc (PA)....................................................D ...... 818 661-6301
 22048 Sherman Way Ste 306 Canoga Park (91303) *(P-17926)*
Hvr Software Usa Inc ....................................................................D ...... 415 489-3427
 44 Montgomery St Ste 3 San Francisco (94104) *(P-18396)*
Hwe Mechanical, Bakersfield *Also Called: Hills Wldg & Engrg Contr Inc (P-237)*
Hyatt Die Cast and Engineering Corporation - South (PA)..........D ...... 714 826-7550
 4656 Lincoln Ave Cypress (90630) *(P-7809)*
Hyatt Die Cast Engrg Corp - S ...................................................... E ...... 714 622-2131
 12250 Industry St Garden Grove (92841) *(P-7810)*
Hyatt Die Cast Engrg Corp - S ...................................................... E ...... 408 523-7000
 1250 Kifer Rd Sunnyvale (94086) *(P-7811)*
Hyatt Die Casting, Sunnyvale *Also Called: Hyatt Die Cast Engrg Corp - S (P-7811)*
Hybond Inc ..................................................................................... F ...... 760 746-7105
 330 State Pl Escondido (92029) *(P-12132)*
Hycor, Garden Grove *Also Called: Hycor Biomedical LLC (P-15107)*
Hycor Biomedical LLC ................................................................... C ...... 714 933-3000
 7272 Chapman Ave Ste A Garden Grove (92841) *(P-15107)*
Hyde, Vernon *Also Called: Streets Ahead Inc (P-2885)*
Hydra-Electric Company (PA)........................................................ C ...... 818 843-6211
 3151 N Kenwood St Burbank (91505) *(P-11243)*
Hydrafacial Company, The, Long Beach *Also Called: Hydrafacial LLC (P-15109)*
Hydrafacial LLC ............................................................................. E ...... 562 391-2052
 3600 E Burnett St Long Beach (90815) *(P-15108)*
Hydrafacial LLC (HQ)..................................................................... C ...... 800 603-4996
 3600 E Burnett St Long Beach (90815) *(P-15109)*
Hydraflow ....................................................................................... B ...... 714 773-2600
 1881 W Malvern Ave Fullerton (92833) *(P-13860)*
Hydraflow, Fullerton *Also Called: Hydraflow (P-13860)*
Hydralic Systems Cmponents Inc ................................................ E ...... 760 744-9350
 725 N Twin Oaks Valley Rd San Marcos (92069) *(P-19262)*
Hydranautics (DH)......................................................................... B ...... 760 901-2500
 401 Jones Rd Oceanside (92058) *(P-6293)*
Hydrapak Inc .................................................................................. E ...... 510 632-8318
 6605 San Leandro St Oakland (94621) *(P-15824)*
Hydratech LLC (HQ).......................................................................D ...... 559 233-0876
 453 Pollasky Ave Ste 106 Clovis (93612) *(P-19263)*
Hydraulic Pneumatic Inc ............................................................... F ...... 562 926-1122
 13766 Milroy Pl Santa Fe Springs (90670) *(P-10628)*
Hydraulic Shop Inc ........................................................................ E ...... 909 875-9336
 2753 S Vista Ave Bloomington (92316) *(P-9523)*
Hydraulics International Inc (PA).................................................. B ...... 818 998-1231
 20961 Knapp St Chatsworth (91311) *(P-13861)*
Hydraulics International Inc .......................................................... E ...... 818 998-1236
 9000 Mason Ave Chatsworth (91311) *(P-13862)*
Hydraulics International Inc .......................................................... E ...... 818 998-1231
 9261 Independence Ave Chatsworth (91311) *(P-13863)*

## Hydro Components and Tech — ALPHABETIC SECTION

**Hydro Components and Tech, Vista** *Also Called: Hydrocomponents & Tech Inc (P-10564)*
**Hydro Extrusion Usa LLC** ............................................................. B ...... 626 964-3411
   18111 Railroad St City Of Industry (91748) *(P-7740)*
**Hydro Quip, Corona** *Also Called: Blue Desert International Inc (P-10544)*
**Hydro Systems Inc (PA)** ............................................................... D ...... 661 775-0686
   29132 Avenue Paine Valencia (91355) *(P-8041)*
**Hydro-Aire Inc (HQ)** .................................................................... C ...... 818 526-2600
   3000 Winona Ave Burbank (91504) *(P-13864)*
**Hydro-Aire Aerospace Corp** ........................................................ C ...... 818 526-2600
   3000 Winona Ave Burbank (91504) *(P-13865)*
**Hydrochempsc, Bakersfield** *Also Called: PSC Industrial Outsourcing LP (P-271)*
**Hydrocomponents & Tech Inc** .................................................... F ...... 760 598-0189
   1175 Park Center Dr Ste H Vista (92081) *(P-10564)*
**Hydrodex LLC** ............................................................................. E ...... 800 218-8813
   31225 La Baya Dr Westlake Village (91362) *(P-10565)*
**Hydrofarm LLC (HQ)** ................................................................... E ...... 707 765-9990
   1304 Southpoint Blvd Ste 200 Petaluma (94954) *(P-11600)*
**Hydrofarm LLC** ............................................................................ D ...... 707 765-9990
   2225 Huntington Dr Fairfield (94533) *(P-11601)*
**Hydroform USA Incorporated** .................................................... C ...... 310 632-6353
   2848 E 208th St Carson (90810) *(P-13866)*
**Hydromach Inc** ........................................................................... E ...... 818 341-0915
   20400 Prairie St Chatsworth (91311) *(P-14113)*
**Hydropoint, Petaluma** *Also Called: Hydropoint Data Systems Inc (P-9358)*
**Hydropoint Data Systems Inc** .................................................... E ...... 707 769-9696
   1720 Corporate Cir Petaluma (94954) *(P-9358)*
**Hyfve, Vernon** *Also Called: Double Zero Inc (P-17089)*
**Hygeia II Medical Group Inc** ....................................................... E ...... 714 515-7571
   6241 Yarrow Dr Ste A Carlsbad (92011) *(P-15545)*
**Hygenia, Camarillo** *Also Called: Medical Packaging Corporation (P-15376)*
**Hygieia Biological Labs** ............................................................. E ...... 530 661-1442
   1240 Commerce Ave Ste B Woodland (95776) *(P-5838)*
**Hyland LLC** .................................................................................. F ...... 440 788-5045
   12919 Earhart Ave Auburn (95602) *(P-17927)*
**Hyland's Homeopathic, Los Angeles** *Also Called: Hylands Consumer Health Inc (P-5482)*
**Hylands Consumer Health Inc (PA)** ........................................... B ...... 310 768-0700
   13301 S Main St Los Angeles (90061) *(P-5482)*
**Hylete, San Diego** *Also Called: Hylete Inc (P-2765)*
**Hylete Inc** ..................................................................................... E ...... 858 225-8998
   11622 El Camino Real Ste 100 San Diego (92130) *(P-2765)*
**Hyper, Fremont** *Also Called: Hyper Products Inc (P-16528)*
**Hyper Ice Inc (PA)** ....................................................................... E ...... 949 565-4994
   525 Technology Dr Ste 100 Irvine (92618) *(P-15825)*
**Hyper Products Inc (DH)** ............................................................ F ...... 714 765-5555
   46721 Fremont Blvd Fremont (94538) *(P-16528)*
**Hyper-Tech LLC** .......................................................................... F ...... 805 988-2000
   2993 Yucca Dr Santa Rosa Valley (93012) *(P-19096)*
**Hyperbaric Technologies Inc** .................................................... D ...... 619 336-2022
   3224 Hoover Ave National City (91950) *(P-15546)*
**Hyperfly Inc** ................................................................................. E ...... 760 300-0909
   8390 Miramar Pl Ste D San Diego (92121) *(P-15826)*
**Hyperice, Irvine** *Also Called: Hyper Ice Inc (P-15825)*
**Hyperion Books For Children, Burbank** *Also Called: Disney Book Group LLC (P-4327)*
**Hyperion Motors LLC** ................................................................ E ...... 714 363-5858
   1032 W Taft Ave Orange (92865) *(P-10632)*
**Hyponex Corporation** ................................................................ C ...... 909 597-2811
   12273 Brown Ave Jurupa Valley (92509) *(P-6175)*
**Hyponex Corporation** ................................................................ E ...... 209 887-3845
   23390 E Flood Rd Linden (95236) *(P-6176)*
**Hyspan, Chula Vista** *Also Called: Hyspan Precision Products Inc (P-10070)*
**Hyspan Precision Products Inc (PA)** ........................................ D ...... 619 421-1355
   1685 Brandywine Ave Chula Vista (91911) *(P-10070)*
**Hytek R&D Inc (PA)** .................................................................... E ...... 408 761-5266
   2044 Corporate Ct Milpitas (95035) *(P-12133)*
**Hytron Mfg Co Inc** ...................................................................... E ...... 714 903-6701
   15582 Chemical Ln Huntington Beach (92649) *(P-10879)*
**Hyundai Rotem USA Corporation** ............................................. F ...... 215 227-6836
   12750 Center Court Dr S Cerritos (90703) *(P-14049)*
**Hyundai Translead (HQ)** ............................................................ D ...... 619 574-1500
   8880 Rio San Diego Dr Ste 600 San Diego (92108) *(P-8317)*

**I & A Inc** ........................................................................................ E ...... 408 432-8340
   2221 Ringwood Ave San Jose (95131) *(P-8471)*
**I & I Sports Supply Company (PA)** ............................................ E ...... 310 715-6800
   435 W Alondra Blvd Gardena (90248) *(P-15827)*
**I A D S, Palmdale** *Also Called: Teletronics Technology Corp (P-14318)*
**I AM Activity, Dunsmuir** *Also Called: Saint Germain Foundation (P-19370)*
**I and E Cabinets Inc** .................................................................. E ...... 818 933-6480
   14660 Raymer St Van Nuys (91405) *(P-3243)*
**I C C, Anaheim** *Also Called: Interntnal Cnnctors Cable Corp (P-11772)*
**I C S, Ventura** *Also Called: Instrument Control Services (P-240)*
**I Copy Inc** .................................................................................... E ...... 562 921-0202
   11266 Monarch St Ste B Garden Grove (92841) *(P-10880)*
**I D Brand LLC** ............................................................................. E ...... 949 422-7057
   3185 Airway Ave Ste A Costa Mesa (92626) *(P-3009)*
**I D C, Bakersfield** *Also Called: Industrial Data Communications (P-16818)*
**I D W, Rancho Cucamonga** *Also Called: Innovative Displayworks LLC (P-16568)*
**I G M, Fresno** *Also Called: Integrated Grain & Milling Inc (P-1131)*
**I G S Inc** ....................................................................................... F ...... 408 733-4621
   916 E California Ave Sunnyvale (94085) *(P-7173)*
**I Love Bracelets Inc** .................................................................. F ...... 310 839-5683
   8940 Ellis Ave Los Angeles (90034) *(P-17146)*
**I M T Precision Inc** .................................................................... E ...... 510 324-8926
   31902 Hayman St Hayward (94544) *(P-10881)*
**I Manageproperty Inc** ................................................................ E ...... 510 665-0665
   1400 Shattuck Ave Ste 2 Berkeley (94709) *(P-18397)*
**I P, Chatsworth** *Also Called: International Precision Inc (P-10889)*
**I P E, Norco** *Also Called: Industrial Process Eqp Inc (P-10054)*
**I S E, Poway** *Also Called: ISE Corporation (P-19458)*
**I V C, Newport Beach** *Also Called: International Vitamin Corporat (P-5500)*
**I-Coat Company LLC** ................................................................ E ...... 562 941-9989
   12020 Mora Dr Ste 2 Santa Fe Springs (90670) *(P-14782)*
**I-Flow LLC** .................................................................................. A ...... 800 448-3569
   43 Discovery Ste 100 Irvine (92618) *(P-15110)*
**I.V. League Medical, Camarillo** *Also Called: Western Mfg & Distrg LLC (P-14075)*
**I/O Magic Corporation** .............................................................. E ...... 949 707-4800
   4 Marconi Irvine (92618) *(P-10164)*
**I/Omagic Corporation (PA)** ...................................................... E ...... 949 707-4800
   20512 Crescent Bay Dr Lake Forest (92630) *(P-10245)*
**I2a Technologies Inc** ................................................................. E ...... 510 770-0322
   3399 W Warren Ave Fremont (94538) *(P-12465)*
**I2k LLC** ........................................................................................ E ...... 626 788-0247
   748 N Mckeever Ave Azusa (91702) *(P-3745)*
**I2k Defense, Azusa** *Also Called: I2k LLC (P-3745)*
**Iaccess Technologies Inc (PA)** ................................................ E ...... 714 922-9158
   1251 E Dyer Rd Ste 160 Santa Ana (92705) *(P-19561)*
**IaMplus LLC** ............................................................................... D ...... 323 210-3852
   809 N Cahuenga Blvd Los Angeles (90038) *(P-11373)*
**IaMplus Electronics Inc (PA)** .................................................... E ...... 323 210-3852
   809 N Cahuenga Blvd Los Angeles (90038) *(P-18398)*
**Ibaset Inc (PA)** ............................................................................ E ...... 949 598-5200
   26812 Vista Ter Lake Forest (92630) *(P-19562)*
**Ibe Digital, Garden Grove** *Also Called: I Copy Inc (P-10880)*
**Ibg Holdings Inc** ......................................................................... E ...... 661 702-8680
   24841 Avenue Tibbitts Valencia (91355) *(P-5991)*
**IBM, Glendale** *Also Called: International Bus Mchs Corp (P-10169)*
**IBM, San Francisco** *Also Called: International Bus Mchs Corp (P-16503)*
**IBM, San Jose** *Also Called: International Bus Mchs Corp (P-17934)*
**Ibs, San Ramon** *Also Called: Integrated Bldg Solutions Inc (P-19563)*
**IC Ink Image Co Inc** ................................................................... E ...... 209 931-3040
   4627 E Fremont St Stockton (95215) *(P-4894)*
**Ic Sensors Inc** ............................................................................ C ...... 510 498-1570
   45738 Northport Loop W Fremont (94538) *(P-12466)*
**Icarcover Inc** .............................................................................. E ...... 714 469-7759
   15529 Blackburn Ave Norwalk (90650) *(P-13516)*
**Ice Management Systems Inc** .................................................. E ...... 951 676-2751
   27449 Colt Ct Temecula (92590) *(P-13867)*
**Ice Mortgage Technology Inc (HQ)** .......................................... B ...... 855 224-8572
   4420 Rosewood Dr Ste 500 Pleasanton (94588) *(P-18399)*
**Ice Splash, San Jose** *Also Called: Siplast Inc (P-6384)*

## ALPHABETIC SECTION — ILLUMINA

**Iced Out Gear, Canoga Park** *Also Called: H2w (P-16978)*

**Ichia USA Inc** ............................................................................. D ...... 619 482-2222
509 Telegraph Canyon Rd Chula Vista (91910) *(P-12467)*

**Ichor, Fremont** *Also Called: Ichor Holdings Ltd (P-12468)*

**Ichor Holdings Ltd (PA)** ............................................................ D ...... 510 897-5200
3185 Laurelview Ct Fremont (94538) *(P-12468)*

**Ichor Systems Inc** .................................................................... D ...... 510 226-0100
4308 Solar Way Fremont (94538) *(P-12469)*

**Ichor Systems Inc** .................................................................... E ...... 510 226-0100
4302 Solar Way Fremont (94538) *(P-12470)*

**Ichor Systems Inc (HQ)** ............................................................ E ...... 510 897-5200
3185 Laurelview Ct Fremont (94538) *(P-12471)*

**ICI Architectural Millwork Inc** ................................................. F ...... 323 759-4993
14059 Garfield Ave Paramount (90723) *(P-3147)*

**ICO Rally, Palo Alto** *Also Called: Insulation Sources Inc (P-13000)*

**Icon Aircraft Inc (PA)** ................................................................ D ...... 707 564-4000
2141 Icon Way Vacaville (95688) *(P-13868)*

**Icon Apparel Group LLC** ........................................................... E ...... 916 372-4266
2989 Promenade St Ste 100 West Sacramento (95691) *(P-2447)*

**Iconn Inc** ................................................................................... D ...... 800 286-6742
8909 Irvine Center Dr Irvine (92618) *(P-11244)*

**Iconn Engineering LLC** ............................................................ E ...... 714 696-8826
6882 Preakness Dr Huntington Beach (92648) *(P-9201)*

**Iconn Technologies, Irvine** *Also Called: Iconn Inc (P-11244)*

**ICP West, Buena Park** *Also Called: Interntional Color Posters Inc (P-4899)*

**Icpk Corporation** ...................................................................... D ...... 310 830-8020
1130 W C St Wilmington (90744) *(P-17115)*

**Ics-CA North, Roseville** *Also Called: Industrial Cont Svcs - CA N LL (P-16878)*

**Icu Medical Inc (PA)** ................................................................. A ...... 949 366-2183
951 Calle Amanecer San Clemente (92673) *(P-15111)*

**Icu Medical Inc** ........................................................................ D ...... 408 284-7064
5729 Fontanoso Way San Jose (95138) *(P-15112)*

**ID Matters LLC** ........................................................................ E ...... 323 822-4800
7060 Hollywood Blvd 8th Fl Los Angeles (90028) *(P-4265)*

**ID Supply** .................................................................................. E ...... 949 287-9200
3183 Red Hill Ave Costa Mesa (92626) *(P-4895)*

**ID&c, Brea** *Also Called: Avery Products Corporation (P-4017)*

**Ida Classic Inc (PA)** .................................................................. C ...... 818 773-9042
9530 De Soto Ave Chatsworth (91311) *(P-5992)*

**IDB Holdings Inc (DH)** .............................................................. F ...... 909 390-5624
601 S Rockefeller Ave Ontario (91761) *(P-720)*

**Idea Tooling and Engrg Inc** ...................................................... D ...... 310 608-7488
13915 S Main St Los Angeles (90061) *(P-9629)*

**Ideal Aerosmith Inc** .................................................................. F ...... 650 353-3641
155 Constitution Dr Menlo Park (94025) *(P-19504)*

**Ideal Envmtl Pdts & Svcs, Gilroy** *Also Called: Containment Consultants Inc (P-8312)*

**Ideal Mattress Company Inc** .................................................... E ...... 619 595-0003
1901 Main St San Diego (92113) *(P-3529)*

**Ideal Printing Company** ........................................................... E ...... 626 964-2019
17855 Maclaren St City Of Industry (91744) *(P-4635)*

**Ideal Products Inc** ................................................................... E ...... 951 727-8600
4025 Garner Rd Riverside (92501) *(P-3657)*

**IDEAYA BIOSCIENCES, South San Francisco** *Also Called: Ideaya Biosciences Inc (P-5483)*

**Ideaya Biosciences Inc (PA)** .................................................... D ...... 650 443-6209
7000 Shoreline Ct Ste 350 South San Francisco (94080) *(P-5483)*

**Ideaya Biosciences Inc** ........................................................... D ...... 650 534-3568
5000 Shoreline Ct Ste 300 South San Francisco (94080) *(P-5484)*

**Idemia America Corp** ............................................................... C ...... 310 884-7900
3150 E Ana St Compton (90221) *(P-6862)*

**Identigraphix Inc** ..................................................................... E ...... 909 468-4741
19866 Quiroz Ct Walnut (91789) *(P-17831)*

**IDENTIV, Fremont** *Also Called: Identiv Inc (P-10377)*

**Identiv Inc (PA)** ........................................................................ D ...... 949 250-8888
2201 Walnut Ave Ste 100 Fremont (94538) *(P-10377)*

**Identiv Inc** ............................................................................... D ...... 888 809-8880
1900 Carnegie Ave Ste B Santa Ana (92705) *(P-18400)*

**Ideon, Buena Park** *Also Called: Exemplis LLC (P-3601)*

**Idex Health & Science LLC (HQ)** ............................................. D ...... 707 588-2000
600 Park Ct Rohnert Park (94928) *(P-14340)*

**Idex Health & Science LLC** ..................................................... C ...... 760 438-2131
2051 Palomar Airport Rd Ste 200 Carlsbad (92011) *(P-14783)*

**Idg, El Cajon** *Also Called: Inflatable Design Group Inc (P-15988)*

**Idg Consumer & Smb Inc (DH)** ................................................. C ...... 415 243-0500
501 2nd St San Francisco (94107) *(P-4266)*

**IDS Inc** ...................................................................................... D ...... 866 297-5757
20300 Ventura Blvd Ste 200 Woodland Hills (91364) *(P-16304)*

**IDS Technology, Woodland Hills** *Also Called: IDS Inc (P-16304)*

**Idt Telecomm Data, San Rafael** *Also Called: Installtion Dgtal Trnsmssons I (P-565)*

**Idx Los Angeles LLC** ................................................................ C ...... 909 212-8333
5005 E Philadelphia St Ontario (91761) *(P-3691)*

**Iee, Sylmar** *Also Called: Industrial Elctrnic Engners In (P-10380)*

**If Copack LLC** .......................................................................... E ...... 559 875-3354
1912 Industrial Way Sanger (93657) *(P-858)*

**If Holding Inc (PA)** .................................................................... D ...... 559 875-3354
1912 Industrial Way Sanger (93657) *(P-2236)*

**Ifco Systems Us LLC** ............................................................... D ...... 909 484-4332
8950 Rochester Ave Ste 150 Rancho Cucamonga (91730) *(P-3347)*

**Ifiber Optix Inc** ......................................................................... E ...... 714 665-9796
14450 Chambers Rd Tustin (92780) *(P-7196)*

**Ifit Inc** ....................................................................................... A ...... 909 335-2888
2220 Almond Ave Redlands (92374) *(P-15828)*

**Ifwe Inc (DH)** ............................................................................ E ...... 415 946-1850
848 Battery St San Francisco (94111) *(P-18401)*

**Igencia Biotherapeutics Inc** .................................................... E ...... 650 231-4320
863 Mitten Rd Ste 102 Burlingame (94010) *(P-5485)*

**Igenomix Usa Inc** ..................................................................... E ...... 818 919-1657
383 Van Ness Ave Ste 1605 Torrance (90501) *(P-15113)*

**Igm Biosciences Inc** ................................................................. C ...... 650 965-7873
325 E Middlefield Rd Mountain View (94043) *(P-5839)*

**Ignatius Press, San Francisco** *Also Called: Guadalupe Associates Inc (P-4410)*

**Ignyta, South San Francisco** *Also Called: Ignyta Inc (P-5486)*

**Ignyta Inc (DH)** ......................................................................... D ...... 858 255-5959
1 Dna Way South San Francisco (94080) *(P-5486)*

**Igrad LLC** ................................................................................. E ...... 858 705-2917
2163 Newcastle Ave Ste 100 Cardiff By The Sea (92007) *(P-18402)*

**Igraphics (PA)** .......................................................................... E ...... 530 273-2200
165 Spring Hill Dr Grass Valley (95945) *(P-4896)*

**Ih Parts America Inc** ................................................................ E ...... 530 274-1795
119 E Mcknight Way Grass Valley (95949) *(P-17453)*

**Iheartraves LLC** ...................................................................... F ...... 626 628-6482
240 S Loara St Anaheim (92802) *(P-17500)*

**Ii-VI Aerospace & Defense Inc, Murrieta** *Also Called: Coherent Aerospace & Defense Inc (P-14170)*

**IJ Research Inc** ........................................................................ E ...... 714 546-8522
2919 S Tech Center Dr Santa Ana (92705) *(P-12997)*

**Ijk & Co Inc** ............................................................................... E ...... 415 826-8899
225 Industrial St San Francisco (94124) *(P-13249)*

**Ikanos Communications Inc (DH)** .......................................... F ...... 858 587-1121
5775 Morehouse Dr San Diego (92121) *(P-12472)*

**Ikhana Aircraft Services, Murrieta** *Also Called: Ikhana Group LLC (P-13869)*

**Ikhana Group LLC** ................................................................... C ...... 951 600-0009
37260 Sky Canyon Dr Hngr 20 Murrieta (92563) *(P-13869)*

**Ikonick LLC** .............................................................................. E ...... 516 680-7765
705 W 9th St Apt 1404 Los Angeles (90015) *(P-4636)*

**IL Fornaio (america) LLC (HQ)** ................................................ E ...... 415 945-0500
770 Tamalpais Dr Ste 208 Corte Madera (94925) *(P-17585)*

**IL Fornaio (america) LLC** ........................................................ C ...... 714 752-7052
16932 Valley View Ave Ste A La Mirada (90638) *(P-17586)*

**IL Fornaio Cucina Italiana, Corte Madera** *Also Called: IL Fornaio (america) LLC (P-17585)*

**IL Helth Buty Natural Oils Inc** ................................................. E ...... 530 399-3782
2644 Hegan Ln Chico (95928) *(P-6294)*

**Ilco Industries, Compton** *Also Called: Ilco Industries Inc (P-9261)*

**Ilco Industries Inc** ................................................................... E ...... 310 631-8655
1308 W Mahalo Pl Compton (90220) *(P-9261)*

**Illah Sports Inc** ........................................................................ E ...... 805 240-7790
1610 Fiske Pl Oxnard (93033) *(P-15829)*

**Illinois Tool Works Inc** ............................................................ D ...... 916 939-4332
5000 Hillsdale Cir El Dorado Hills (95762) *(P-12473)*

**Illume Agriculture LLC** ............................................................ C ...... 661 587-5198
9100 Ming Ave Ste 200 Bakersfield (93311) *(P-92)*

**ILLUMINA, San Diego** *Also Called: Illumina Inc (P-14674)*

**Illumina Inc** .................................................................... F ...... 800 809-4566
9885 Towne Centre Dr San Diego (92121) *(P-14673)*

**Illumina Inc (PA)** ............................................................ B ...... 858 202-4500
5200 Illumina Way San Diego (92122) *(P-14674)*

**Illumina Inc** .................................................................... E ...... 510 670-9300
25861 Industrial Blvd Hayward (94545) *(P-14675)*

**Illumina-Redwood City, Foster City** *Also Called: Verinata Health Inc (P-19482)*

**Illuminated Creations Inc** ............................................... E ...... 916 924-1936
1111 Joellis Way Sacramento (95815) *(P-15986)*

**Illumnate Educatn Holdings Inc (PA)** .............................. E ...... 949 656-3133
6531 Irvine Center Dr Ste 100 Irvine (92618) *(P-18403)*

**Ilovetocreate A Duncan Entps, Fresno** *Also Called: Duncan Enterprises (P-6080)*

**Ilts California, Vista** *Also Called: International Lottery & Totalizator Systems Inc (P-17935)*

**Ilts Delaware, Vista** *Also Called: Interntnal Lttery Ttlztor Syst (P-17936)*

**Image Apparel For Business Inc** ..................................... E ...... 714 541-5247
1618 E Edinger Ave Santa Ana (92705) *(P-2594)*

**Image Masters, Merced** *Also Called: On Target Marketing (P-17835)*

**Image Options (PA)** ........................................................ D ...... 949 586-7665
80 Icon Foothill Ranch (92610) *(P-17790)*

**Image Options Painting & Dctg, Foothill Ranch** *Also Called: Image Options (P-17790)*

**Image Solutions, Torrance** *Also Called: Image Solutions Apparel Inc (P-2595)*

**Image Solutions Apparel Inc** ........................................... C ...... 310 464-8991
19571 Magellan Dr Torrance (90502) *(P-2595)*

**Image Technology, Palo Alto** *Also Called: Suss McRtec Prcsion Phtmask In (P-15668)*

**Image X, Goleta** *Also Called: Image-X Enterprises Inc (P-17928)*

**Image-X Enterprises Inc** ................................................. E ...... 805 964-3535
6464 Hollister Ave Ste 7g Goleta (93117) *(P-17928)*

**Imagegrid Inc** ................................................................. E ...... 949 852-1000
5010 Campus Dr Newport Beach (92660) *(P-14882)*

**Imagemover Inc** ............................................................. F ...... 818 485-8840
13031 Bradley Ave Sylmar (91342) *(P-4637)*

**IMAGEWARE SYSTEMS, San Diego** *Also Called: Imageware Systems Inc (P-18404)*

**Imageware Systems Inc (PA)** .......................................... F ...... 858 673-8600
11440 W Bernardo Ct Ste 300 San Diego (92127) *(P-18404)*

**Imagex Inc** ..................................................................... F ...... 925 474-8100
5990 Stoneridge Dr Ste 112 Pleasanton (94588) *(P-4638)*

**Imagic** ............................................................................ D ...... 818 333-1670
2810 N Lima St Burbank (91504) *(P-4639)*

**Imagine This, Irvine** *Also Called: Shye West Inc (P-16034)*

**IMC Networks Corp (PA)** ................................................ E ...... 949 465-3000
25531 Commercentre Dr Ste 200 Lake Forest (92630) *(P-10306)*

**Imcsd, San Diego** *Also Called: Integrated Microwave Corp (P-13001)*

**Imdex Technology Usa LLC** ............................................ E ...... 805 540-2017
179 Cross St San Luis Obispo (93401) *(P-14883)*

**Imerys Filtration Minerals Inc (DH)** ................................. E ...... 805 562-0200
1732 N 1st St Ste 450 San Jose (95112) *(P-7566)*

**Imerys Minerals California Inc (HQ)** ................................ D ...... 805 736-1221
2500 San Miguelito Rd Lompoc (93436) *(P-341)*

**Imerys Talc America Inc (DH)** ......................................... B
1732 N 1st St Ste 450 San Jose (95112) *(P-7567)*

**IMG, Livermore** *Also Called: IMG Companies LLC (P-10882)*

**IMG Altair LLC** ................................................................ D ...... 650 508-8700
41970 Christy St Fremont (94538) *(P-9865)*

**IMG Companies LLC (HQ)** .............................................. D ...... 925 273-1100
225 Mountain Vista Pkwy Livermore (94551) *(P-10882)*

**IMI CCI, Rcho Sta Marg** *Also Called: IMI Critical Engineering LLC (P-9156)*

**IMI Critical Engineering LLC (DH)** .................................. B ...... 949 858-1877
22591 Avenida Empresa Rcho Sta Marg (92688) *(P-9156)*

**Imidomics Inc** ................................................................. F ...... 415 652-4963
1000 4th St Ste 500 San Rafael (94901) *(P-5487)*

**Immortal Masks Inc** ........................................................ E ...... 909 599-5391
261 W Allen Ave San Dimas (91773) *(P-2902)*

**Immotion Vr Ltd** .............................................................. E ...... 818 813-3923
1067 Gayley Ave Los Angeles (90024) *(P-10883)*

**Immport Therapeutics Inc** ............................................... F ...... 949 679-4068
1 Technology Dr Ste E309 Irvine (92618) *(P-15503)*

**Immunalysis, Pomona** *Also Called: Alere San Diego Inc (P-5733)*

**Immunalysis, Pomona** *Also Called: Diagnostixx of California Corp (P-15068)*

**IMMUNITYBIO, San Diego** *Also Called: Immunitybio Inc (P-5840)*

**Immunitybio Inc (PA)** ...................................................... D ...... 844 696-5235
3530 John Hopkins Ct San Diego (92121) *(P-5840)*

**Immunoscience LLC** ....................................................... D ...... 925 400-6055
6780 Sierra Ct Ste M Dublin (94568) *(P-5756)*

**Impac International, Ontario** *Also Called: LLC Walker West (P-3696)*

**Impact Bearing, San Clemente** *Also Called: Clean Wave Management Inc (P-9949)*

**Impact Components, San Diego** *Also Called: Impact Components A California Limited Partnership (P-16705)*

**Impact Components A California Limited Partnership** ..... E ...... 858 634-4800
6010 Cornerstone Ct W Ste 200 San Diego (92121) *(P-16705)*

**Impact Creative LLC** ....................................................... F ...... 831 824-9660
155 Dubois St Ste G Santa Cruz (95060) *(P-4640)*

**Impact LLC** ..................................................................... E ...... 714 546-6000
7121 Magnolia Ave Riverside (92504) *(P-12998)*

**Impact Printing & Graphics** ............................................. E ...... 909 614-1678
15150 Sierra Bonita Ln Chino (91710) *(P-4641)*

**Impact Project Management Inc** ..................................... F ...... 760 747-6616
2872 S Santa Fe Ave San Marcos (92069) *(P-12134)*

**Impact-O-Graph Devices, Chatsworth** *Also Called: log Products LLC (P-12503)*

**Impax Laboratories LLC** ................................................. E ...... 510 240-6000
30831 Huntwood Ave Hayward (94544) *(P-5488)*

**Impax Laboratories LLC (DH)** ......................................... A
30831 Huntwood Ave Hayward (94544) *(P-5489)*

**Impax Laboratories LLC** ................................................. D ...... 510 240-6000
31047 Genstar Rd Hayward (94544) *(P-5490)*

**Impax Laboratories Usa LLC** .......................................... E ...... 510 240-6000
30831 Huntwood Ave Hayward (94544) *(P-5491)*

**Impco, Santa Ana** *Also Called: Impco Technologies Inc (P-13517)*

**Impco Technologies Inc (HQ)** ......................................... C ...... 714 656-1200
3030 S Susan St Santa Ana (92704) *(P-13517)*

**Impedimed Inc (HQ)** ....................................................... E ...... 760 585-2100
5900 Pasteur Ct Ste 125 Carlsbad (92008) *(P-15114)*

**Imperative Care Inc (PA)** ................................................ B ...... 669 228-3814
1359 Dell Ave Campbell (95008) *(P-15360)*

**Imperfect Foods Inc (HQ)** ............................................... D ...... 510 595-6683
351 Cheryl Ln Walnut (91789) *(P-2237)*

**Imperfect Produce, Walnut** *Also Called: Imperfect Foods Inc (P-2237)*

**Imperial Cal Products Inc** ............................................... E ...... 714 990-9100
425 Apollo St Brea (92821) *(P-8851)*

**Imperial Coml Cooking Eqp, Corona** *Also Called: Spenuzza Inc (P-10603)*

**Imperial Garment Inds Inc** .............................................. F ...... 510 834-7771
831 International Blvd Oakland (94606) *(P-2862)*

**Imperial Marking Systems, Cerritos** *Also Called: Blc Wc Inc (P-4850)*

**Imperial Pipe Services LLC** ............................................ E ...... 951 682-3307
1666 20th St Santa Monica (90404) *(P-7663)*

**Imperial Printers (PA)** ..................................................... F ...... 760 352-4374
430 W Main St El Centro (92243) *(P-4642)*

**Imperial Printers Rocket Copy, El Centro** *Also Called: Imperial Printers (P-4642)*

**Imperial Rubber Products Inc** ......................................... E ...... 909 393-0528
5691 Gates St Chino (91710) *(P-9769)*

**Imperial System, Union City** *Also Called: Blc Wc Inc (P-10015)*

**Imperial Toy LLC (PA)** .................................................... C ...... 818 536-6500
16641 Roscoe Pl North Hills (91343) *(P-15751)*

**Imperial Trade Bindery Inc** ............................................. E ...... 916 443-6142
300 N 12th St Sacramento (95811) *(P-3996)*

**Imperial Valley Foods Inc** ............................................... B ...... 760 203-1896
1961 Buchanan Ave Calexico (92231) *(P-1007)*

**Imperial Valley Press, El Centro** *Also Called: Associated Desert Newspaper (P-4069)*

**Imperial Western Products Inc A California Corporation (HQ)** ..... E ...... 760 398-0815
86600 Avenue 54 Coachella (92236) *(P-17222)*

**Imperials Sand Dunes, Brea** *Also Called: Worldwide Envmtl Pdts Inc (P-14470)*

**Impex Technologies Inc** .................................................. F ...... 310 320-0280
880 Apollo St Ste 315 El Segundo (90245) *(P-18405)*

**Implant Direct, Thousand Oaks** *Also Called: Implant Direct Sybron Mfg LLC (P-15459)*

**Implant Direct Sybron Intl LLC (HQ)** ............................... D ...... 818 444-3000
3050 E Hillcrest Dr Ste 100 Westlake Village (91362) *(P-15458)*

**Implant Direct Sybron Mfg LLC** ...................................... C ...... 818 444-3300
3050 E Hillcrest Dr Thousand Oaks (91362) *(P-15459)*

**Implantech Associates Inc** .............................................. E ...... 805 289-1665
6025 Nicolle St Ste B Ventura (93003) *(P-15361)*

# ALPHABETIC SECTION
## Industrial Electrical Company

**Implus LLC** .................................................................................. E ...... 408 796-7739
1610 Dell Ave Ste S Campbell (95008) *(P-6415)*

**Imply, Burlingame** *Also Called: Imply Data Inc (P-18406)*

**Imply Data Inc (PA)** ..................................................................... C ...... 415 685-8187
1633 Bayshore Hwy Ste 232 Burlingame (94010) *(P-18406)*

**Impo International LLC** ............................................................... E ...... 805 922-7753
3510 Black Rd Santa Maria (93455) *(P-7116)*

**Import, Vernon** *Also Called: Brentwood Appliances Inc (P-11416)*

**Impossible Aerospace Corp** ........................................................ F ...... 707 293-9367
1709 Junction Ct San Jose (95112) *(P-13670)*

**Impossible Foods Inc (PA)** ......................................................... C ...... 650 461-4385
400 Saginaw Dr Redwood City (94063) *(P-2238)*

**Impresa Aerospace LLC** ............................................................. C ...... 310 354-1200
344 W 157th St Gardena (90248) *(P-13870)*

**Impress Communications LLC** .................................................. D ...... 818 701-8800
9320 Lurline Ave Chatsworth (91311) *(P-4643)*

**Impressions Vanity Company (PA)** ............................................ E ...... 844 881-0790
17353 Derian Ave Irvine (92614) *(P-17535)*

**Imprimisrx, Carlsbad** *Also Called: Imprimisrx LLC (P-5492)*

**Imprimisrx LLC** ........................................................................... D ...... 844 446-6979
1000 Aviara Dr Ste 220 Carlsbad (92011) *(P-5492)*

**Imprimus Labels and Packaging, Long Beach** *Also Called: Western Shield Acquisitions LLC (P-4829)*

**Imprint Energy Inc** ...................................................................... E ...... 510 847-7027
1320 Harbor Bay Pkwy Ste 110 Alameda (94502) *(P-13161)*

**Impulse Amusement, Sun Valley** *Also Called: Impulse Industries Inc (P-10471)*

**Impulse Enterprise** ..................................................................... F ...... 858 565-7050
9855 Carroll Canyon Rd San Diego (92131) *(P-11459)*

**Impulse Industries Inc** ................................................................ E ...... 818 767-4258
9281 Borden Ave Sun Valley (91352) *(P-10471)*

**Impulse Space Inc** ...................................................................... E ...... 949 315-5540
2651 Manhattan Beach Blvd Redondo Beach (90278) *(P-14081)*

**IMS, South El Monte** *Also Called: Interntnal Mdction Systems Ltd (P-5501)*

**IMS, Chula Vista** *Also Called: Integrated Marine Services Inc (P-14005)*

**IMS Products Inc** ........................................................................ F ...... 951 653-7720
700 S Hathaway St Banning (92220) *(P-14060)*

**IMS-Ess, Temecula** *Also Called: Ice Management Systems Inc (P-13867)*

**IMT Analytical, Goleta** *Also Called: Atomica Corp (P-12339)*

**IMT-Stason Laboratories, Irvine** *Also Called: Stason Pharmaceuticals Inc (P-5675)*

**Imtec Acculine LLC** ..................................................................... E ...... 510 770-1800
48625 Warm Springs Blvd Fremont (94539) *(P-9866)*

**Imtec Biomedical Inc** .................................................................. F ...... 619 316-1207
13193 Polvera Ave San Diego (92128) *(P-15115)*

**In Win Development USA Inc** ..................................................... E ...... 909 348-0588
188 Brea Canyon Rd Walnut (91789) *(P-10246)*

**In-Line Construction, Ramona** *Also Called: In-Line Fence & Railing Co Inc (P-564)*

**In-Line Fence & Railing Co Inc** .................................................. E ...... 760 789-0282
1307 Walnut St Ramona (92065) *(P-564)*

**Inaba Foods (usa) Inc** ................................................................. F ...... 310 818-2270
19191 S Vermont Ave Ste 1050 Torrance (90502) *(P-1102)*

**Inapac Technology Inc** ............................................................... E ...... 408 746-0614
46848 Lakeview Blvd Fremont (94538) *(P-12474)*

**Inari, Irvine** *Also Called: Inari Medical Inc (P-15116)*

**Inari Medical Inc (PA)** ................................................................. A ...... 877 927-4747
6001 Oak Cyn Ste 100 Irvine (92618) *(P-15116)*

**Inbenta Technologies Inc (PA)** ................................................... E ...... 408 213-8771
440 N Wolfe Rd Sunnyvale (94085) *(P-18407)*

**Inbody, Cerritos** *Also Called: Biospace Inc (P-19447)*

**Inc Polycarbon, Valencia** *Also Called: Sgl Technic LLC (P-7571)*

**Inca One Corporation** ................................................................. E ...... 310 808-0001
1632 1/2 W 134th St Gardena (90249) *(P-12818)*

**Incal Technology Inc** .................................................................. E ...... 510 657-8405
46420 Fremont Blvd Fremont (94538) *(P-10378)*

**Incarda Therapeutics, Newark** *Also Called: Incarda Therapeutics Inc (P-5493)*

**Incarda Therapeutics Inc** ........................................................... E ...... 510 422-5522
39899 Balentine Dr Ste 185 Newark (94560) *(P-5493)*

**Incipio Group, Irvine** *Also Called: Incipio Technologies Inc (P-10379)*

**Incipio Technologies Inc (PA)** .................................................... E ...... 888 893-1638
190 Newport Ctr Dr Ste 150 Irvine (92612) *(P-10379)*

**Inclinator of California, San Fernando** *Also Called: TL Shield & Associates Inc (P-9477)*

**Incotec, Mojave** *Also Called: Innovative Coatings Technology Corporation (P-9080)*

**Indel Engineering Inc** ................................................................. E ...... 562 594-0995
6400 E Marina Dr Long Beach (90803) *(P-14036)*

**Independent, Santa Barbara** *Also Called: Santa Barbara Independent Inc (P-4191)*

**Independent Energy Solutions Inc** ............................................ E ...... 760 752-9706
663 S Rancho Santa Fe Rd Ste 682 San Marcos (92078) *(P-8069)*

**Independent Forge Company** .................................................... E ...... 714 997-7337
692 N Batavia St Orange (92868) *(P-8777)*

**Independent Ink Inc (PA)** ............................................................ F ...... 310 523-4657
13700 Gramercy Pl Gardena (90249) *(P-6295)*

**Indepndent Brkley Stdnt Pubg I** ................................................. E ...... 510 548-8300
2483 Hearst Ave Berkeley (94709) *(P-4133)*

**Indepndent Flr Tstg Insptn Inc** ................................................... F ...... 925 676-7682
1390 Willow Pass Rd Ste 1010 Concord (94520) *(P-7345)*

**Index Fasteners Inc (PA)** ............................................................ F ...... 909 923-5002
945 E Grevillea Ct Ontario (91761) *(P-16877)*

**Index Fresh Inc (PA)** ................................................................... D ...... 909 877-0999
1250 Corona Pointe Ct Ste 401 Corona (92879) *(P-17169)*

**India Tea Importers, Commerce** *Also Called: Interntional Tea Importers Inc (P-2240)*

**India-West Publications Inc (PA)** .............................................. E ...... 510 383-1140
933 Macarthur Blvd San Leandro (94577) *(P-4134)*

**Indian Industries Inc** .................................................................. E ...... 800 467-1421
7756 Saint Andrews Ave Ste 115 San Diego (92154) *(P-15830)*

**Indian Summer, Rancho Cucamonga** *Also Called: Mizkan America Inc (P-2282)*

**INDIE, Aliso Viejo** *Also Called: Indie Semiconductor Inc (P-12475)*

**Indie Semiconductor Inc (PA)** ................................................... E ...... 949 608-0854
32 Journey Ste 100 Aliso Viejo (92656) *(P-12475)*

**Indie Source** ................................................................................. E ...... 424 200-2027
940 Venice Blvd Venice (90291) *(P-2596)*

**Indigo America Inc** ..................................................................... D ...... 650 857-1501
1501 Page Mill Rd Palo Alto (94304) *(P-10165)*

**Indio Products Inc** ...................................................................... E ...... 323 720-9117
5331 E Slauson Ave Commerce (90040) *(P-6296)*

**Indio Products Inc (PA)** .............................................................. C ...... 323 720-1188
12910 Mulberry Dr Unit A Whittier (90602) *(P-16601)*

**Indium Software Inc** ................................................................... D ...... 408 501-8844
10080 N Wolfe Rd Ste Sw3200 Cupertino (95014) *(P-18408)*

**Individual Software Inc** ............................................................... E ...... 925 734-6767
3049 Independence Dr Ste E Livermore (94551) *(P-18409)*

**Indorama Vntres Sstnble Sltion** ................................................. E ...... 951 727-8318
11591 Etiwanda Ave Fontana (92337) *(P-5162)*

**Indtec Corporation** ..................................................................... E ...... 831 582-9388
3348 Paul Davis Dr Ste 109 Marina (93933) *(P-12135)*

**Indu-Electric North Amer Inc (PA)** ............................................ E ...... 310 578-2144
27756 Avenue Hopkins Valencia (91355) *(P-10071)*

**Induction Technology Corp** ....................................................... E ...... 760 246-7333
22060 Bear Valley Rd Apple Valley (92308) *(P-10053)*

**Induspac California Inc** .............................................................. E ...... 909 390-4422
1550 Champagne Ave Ontario (91761) *(P-5163)*

**Induspac California Inc (HQ)** ..................................................... F ...... 510 324-3626
38505 Cherry St Newark (94560) *(P-5164)*

**Industrial Coatings Division, Huntington Beach** *Also Called: PPG Industries Inc (P-6103)*

**Industrial Components Div, Simi Valley** *Also Called: Rexnord Industries LLC (P-9814)*

**Industrial Cont Svcs - CA N LL** ................................................. D ...... 916 781-2775
749 Galleria Blvd Roseville (95678) *(P-16878)*

**Industrial Data Communications** ............................................... E ...... 661 589-4477
4000 Fruitvale Ave Ste 16 Bakersfield (93308) *(P-16818)*

**Industrial Design Products Inc** .................................................. E ...... 909 468-0693
2700 Pomona Blvd Pomona (91768) *(P-9524)*

**Industrial Dynamics Co Ltd (PA)** ............................................... C ...... 310 325-5633
3100 Fujita St Torrance (90505) *(P-9867)*

**Industrial Elctrnic Engners In** ................................................... D ...... 818 787-0311
13170 Telfair Ave Sylmar (91342) *(P-10380)*

**Industrial Elctrnic Systems In (PA)** ........................................... E ...... 916 638-1000
3250 Monier Cir Ste F Rancho Cordova (95742) *(P-458)*

**Industrial Electric Mfg, Fremont** *Also Called: New Iem LLC (P-11247)*

**Industrial Electric Mfg Inc** .......................................................... C ...... 510 656-1600
48205 Warm Springs Blvd Fremont (94539) *(P-11245)*

**Industrial Electrical Co, Fresno** *Also Called: Modesto Industrial Elec Co Inc (P-462)*

**Industrial Electrical Company, Modesto** *Also Called: Modesto Industrial Electrical Co Inc (P-463)*

**Industrial Fire Sprnklr Co Inc**

Industrial Fire Sprnklr Co Inc .................................................. E ...... 619 266-6030
  3845 Imperial Ave San Diego (92113) *(P-10096)*
Industrial Gasket and Sup Co ................................................. E ...... 310 530-1771
  2702 Dashwood St Lakewood (90712) *(P-6453)*
Industrial Glass Products Inc ................................................. F ...... 323 526-7125
  4229 Union Pacific Ave Los Angeles (90023) *(P-7227)*
Industrial Glass Service, Sunnyvale *Also Called: I G S Inc (P-7173)*
Industrial Metal Finishing Inc ................................................. F ...... 714 628-8808
  1941 Petra Ln Placentia (92870) *(P-8972)*
Industrial Metal Supply Co, Sun Valley *Also Called: Norman Industrial Mtls Inc (P-16626)*
Industrial Metal Supply Co, Irvine *Also Called: Norman Industrial Mtls Inc (P-16627)*
Industrial Minerals Company, Bakersfield *Also Called: Geo Drilling Fluids Inc (P-17245)*
Industrial Parts Depot LLC (HQ) ........................................... D ...... 310 530-1900
  1550 Charles Willard St Carson (90746) *(P-16819)*
Industrial Process Eqp Inc ..................................................... F ...... 714 447-0171
  1700 Industrial Ave Norco (92860) *(P-10054)*
Industrial Sprockets Gears Inc ............................................... E ...... 323 233-7221
  13650 Rosecrans Ave Santa Fe Springs (90670) *(P-10072)*
Industrial Strength Corp ......................................................... F ...... 760 795-1068
  6115 Corte Del Cedro Carlsbad (92011) *(P-16968)*
Industrial Tctnics Brings Corp (DH) ...................................... C ...... 310 537-3750
  18301 S Santa Fe Ave E Rncho Dmngz (90221) *(P-9950)*
Industrial Tools Inc ................................................................ E ...... 805 483-1111
  1800 Avenue Of The Stars Los Angeles (90067) *(P-9868)*
Industrial Tube Company, Valencia *Also Called: Industrial Tube Company LLC (P-9169)*
Industrial Tube Company LLC ............................................... D ...... 661 295-4000
  28150 Industry Dr Valencia (91355) *(P-9169)*
Industrial Valco Inc (PA) ......................................................... E ...... 310 635-0711
  3135 E Ana St Compton (90221) *(P-16879)*
Industrial Welding, Redding *Also Called: Ferrosaur Inc (P-8139)*
Industrial Wood Products Inc ................................................ F ...... 909 625-1247
  5123 Brooks St Montclair (91763) *(P-17335)*
Industry Threadworks .............................................................. E ...... 858 265-6177
  8902 Activity Rd Ste C San Diego (92126) *(P-2493)*
Indyme Solutions LLC ............................................................ E ...... 858 268-0717
  8295 Aero Pl Ste 260 San Diego (92123) *(P-12000)*
Ineoquest, Nevada City *Also Called: Ineoquest Technologies Inc (P-14535)*
Ineoquest Technologies Inc (HQ) .......................................... F ...... 508 339-2497
  848 Gold Flat Rd Nevada City (95959) *(P-14535)*
Ineos, Carson *Also Called: Ineos Polypropylene LLC (P-5166)*
Ineos Composites Us LLC .................................................... D ...... 323 767-1300
  6608 E 26th St Los Angeles (90040) *(P-5165)*
Ineos Polypropylene LLC ....................................................... C ...... 310 847-8523
  2384 E 223rd St Carson (90810) *(P-5166)*
Inertech, Monterey Park *Also Called: Inertech Supply Inc (P-6454)*
Inertech Supply Inc ................................................................ D ...... 626 282-2000
  641 Monterey Pass Rd Monterey Park (91754) *(P-6454)*
Inet, Cypress *Also Called: Inet Airport Systems Inc (P-13871)*
Inet Airport Systems Inc ......................................................... E ...... 714 888-2700
  5665 Corporate Ave Cypress (90630) *(P-13871)*
Inevit Inc ................................................................................. C ...... 650 298-6001
  541 Jefferson Ave Ste 100 Redwood City (94063) *(P-13144)*
Infab LLC ............................................................................... D ...... 805 987-5255
  1040 Avenida Acaso Camarillo (93012) *(P-15362)*
Infineon Tech Americas Corp ................................................ A ...... 951 375-6008
  41915 Business Park Dr Temecula (92590) *(P-10381)*
Infineon Tech Americas Corp ................................................ E ...... 310 726-8000
  233 Kansas St El Segundo (90245) *(P-12476)*
Infineon Tech Americas Corp ................................................ A ...... 866 951-9519
  198 Champion Ct San Jose (95134) *(P-12477)*
Infineon Tech Americas Corp ................................................ C ...... 310 252-7116
  1521 E Grand Ave El Segundo (90245) *(P-12478)*
Infineon Tech Americas Corp (HQ) ....................................... A ...... 310 726-8200
  101 N Pacific Coast Hwy El Segundo (90245) *(P-12479)*
Infineon Tech Americas Corp ................................................ A ...... 310 726-8000
  222 Kansas St El Segundo (90245) *(P-19433)*
Infineon Tech N Amer Corp (DH) .......................................... B ...... 866 951-9519
  198 Champion Ct San Jose (95134) *(P-12480)*
Infineon Tech N Amer Corp ................................................... C ...... 919 768-0315
  30805 Santana St Hayward (94544) *(P-12481)*

Infineon Tech US Holdco Inc (HQ) ........................................ D ...... 866 951-9519
  198 Champion Ct San Jose (95134) *(P-12482)*
Infineon Technologies ............................................................ F ...... 408 779-2367
  18225 Serene Dr Morgan Hill (95037) *(P-12483)*
Infineon Technologies AG, San Jose *Also Called: Infineon Tech US Holdco Inc (P-12482)*
Infinera, San Jose *Also Called: Infinera Corporation (P-11768)*
Infinera Corporation (PA) ....................................................... B ...... 408 572-5200
  6373 San Ignacio Ave San Jose (95119) *(P-11768)*
Infinera International Corp (HQ) ............................................. F ...... 408 572-5200
  6373 San Ignacio Ave San Jose (95119) *(P-11769)*
Infinera Optical Networks Inc (HQ) ........................................ E ...... 630 798-8800
  6373 San Ignacio Ave San Jose (95119) *(P-11770)*
Infineta Systems Inc .............................................................. E ...... 408 514-6650
  1100 La Avenida St Ste A Mountain View (94043) *(P-10382)*
Infinite Electric, Campbell *Also Called: Infinite Networks Inc (P-16682)*
Infinite Electronics Inc (HQ) ................................................... E ...... 949 261-1920
  17792 Fitch Irvine (92614) *(P-12999)*
Infinite Electronics Intl Inc (DH) ............................................. D ...... 949 261-1920
  17792 Fitch Irvine (92614) *(P-12883)*
Infinite Electronics Intl Inc ..................................................... F ...... 949 261-1920
  17802 Fitch Irvine (92614) *(P-12884)*
Infinite Networks Inc .............................................................. E ...... 408 796-7735
  457 E Mcglincy Ln Ste 1 Campbell (95008) *(P-16682)*
Infinite Optics Inc ................................................................... E ...... 714 557-2299
  1712 Newport Cir Ste F Santa Ana (92705) *(P-14784)*
Infinite Rabbit Holes, Pasadena *Also Called: Black Box Project LLC (P-15741)*
Infinity Aerospace Inc (PA) .................................................... E ...... 818 998-9811
  9060 Winnetka Ave Northridge (91324) *(P-13872)*
Infinity Kitchen Products Inc ................................................. F ...... 562 806-5771
  7750 Scout Ave Bell Gardens (90201) *(P-8472)*
Infinity Precision Inc .............................................................. E ...... 818 727-0504
  730 E Easy St Simi Valley (93065) *(P-10884)*
Infinity Stainless Products, Bell Gardens *Also Called: Infinity Kitchen Products Inc (P-8472)*
Infinity Watch Corporation ..................................................... E ...... 626 289-9878
  21078 Commerce Point Dr Walnut (91789) *(P-15987)*
Infinity Yacht Sales, San Diego *Also Called: Infinity Yachts Inc (P-14037)*
Infinity Yachts Inc .................................................................. F ...... 619 431-1194
  1450 Harbor Island Dr Ste 208 San Diego (92101) *(P-14037)*
Inflatable Design Group Inc .................................................. F ...... 619 596-6100
  1080 W Bradley Ave Ste B El Cajon (92020) *(P-15988)*
Inflight Entrmt & Connectivity, Irvine *Also Called: Thales Avionics Inc (P-13971)*
Inflight Warning Systems Inc ................................................ F ...... 714 993-9394
  3940 Prospect Ave Ste P Yorba Linda (92886) *(P-13873)*
Infocast, Woodland Hills *Also Called: Information Forecast Inc (P-19530)*
Infocus Cnc Machining Inc .................................................... E ...... 714 979-1253
  11245 Young River Ave Fountain Valley (92708) *(P-10885)*
Infocus Jupiter, Hayward *Also Called: Jupiter Systems Inc (P-10307)*
Infogram Software Inc ........................................................... E ...... 650 319-7291
  633 Folsom St Fl 5 San Francisco (94107) *(P-18410)*
Infoimage, Brisbane *Also Called: Infoimage of California Inc (P-4897)*
Infoimage of California Inc (PA) ............................................ D ...... 650 473-6388
  175 S Hill Dr Brisbane (94005) *(P-4897)*
Infor (us) LLC ........................................................................ E ...... 916 921-0883
  11000 Olson Dr Ste 201 Rancho Cordova (95670) *(P-18411)*
Infor Public Sector Inc (DH) .................................................. C ...... 916 921-0883
  11092 Sun Center Dr Rancho Cordova (95670) *(P-18412)*
Inform Solution Incorporated ................................................. E ...... 805 879-6000
  201 Mentor Dr Santa Barbara (93111) *(P-18413)*
Informa Business Media Inc .................................................. E ...... 949 252-1146
  16815 Von Karman Ave # 150 Irvine (92606) *(P-4415)*
INFORMATICA, Redwood City *Also Called: Informatica Inc (P-18415)*
Informatica Holdco 2 Inc ........................................................ A ...... 650 385-5000
  2100 Seaport Blvd Redwood City (94063) *(P-18414)*
Informatica Inc ....................................................................... A ...... 650 385-5000
  2100 Seaport Blvd Redwood City (94063) *(P-18415)*
Informatica International Inc (DH) ......................................... E ...... 650 385-5000
  2100 Seaport Blvd Redwood City (94063) *(P-18416)*
Informatica LLC (DH) ............................................................ B ...... 650 385-5000
  2100 Seaport Blvd Redwood City (94063) *(P-18417)*
Informatica LLC of Delaware, Redwood City *Also Called: Informatica LLC (P-18417)*

## ALPHABETIC SECTION — Innovative Casework Mfg Inc

**Information Forecast Inc** .................................................. E ...... 818 888-4445
22144 Clarendon St Ste 280 Woodland Hills (91367) *(P-19530)*

**Informs, Anaheim** *Also Called: Rush Business Forms Inc (P-17640)*

**Informtion Intgrtion Group Inc** ........................................ F ...... 818 956-3744
457 Palm Dr Ste 200 Glendale (91202) *(P-18418)*

**Infosend Inc (PA)** ............................................................. E ...... 714 993-2690
4240 E La Palma Ave Anaheim (92807) *(P-17842)*

**Infoworld, San Francisco** *Also Called: Infoworld Media Group Inc (P-4267)*

**Infoworld Media Group Inc (DH)** ..................................... D ...... 415 243-4344
501 2nd St Ste 500 San Francisco (94107) *(P-4267)*

**Infrared Dynamics Inc** ..................................................... E ...... 714 572-4050
3830 Prospect Ave Yorba Linda (92886) *(P-8070)*

**Infrastructureworld LLC** .................................................. E ...... 415 699-1543
377 Margarita Dr San Rafael (94901) *(P-14676)*

**Infratab** ............................................................................ E ...... 805 986-8880
4347 Raytheon Rd Unit 6 Oxnard (93033) *(P-5841)*

**Ingalls Conveyors Inc** ...................................................... E ...... 323 837-9900
1005 W Olympic Blvd Montebello (90640) *(P-9487)*

**Ingenu, San Diego** *Also Called: Ingenu Inc (P-11867)*

**Ingenu Inc (PA)** ................................................................ E ...... 858 201-6000
10301 Meanley Dr San Diego (92131) *(P-11867)*

**Ingenue Inc** ...................................................................... D ...... 323 726-8084
1111 W Olympic Blvd Montebello (90640) *(P-695)*

**Ingersoll-Rand, City Of Industry** *Also Called: Trane Technologies Company LLC (P-9944)*

**Ingla Rubber Products, Bellflower** *Also Called: Bryant Rubber Corp (P-6439)*

**Inglenook** ......................................................................... D ...... 707 968-1100
1991 St Helena Hwy Rutherford (94573) *(P-1619)*

**Ingomar Packing Company LLC (PA)** .............................. D ...... 209 826-9494
9950 S Ingomar Grade Los Banos (93635) *(P-894)*

**Ingrasys Technology USA Inc** ........................................... D ...... 970 301-5069
1768 Automation Pkwy San Jose (95131) *(P-14536)*

**Ingredients By Nature LLC** .............................................. F ...... 909 230-6200
5555 Brooks St Montclair (91763) *(P-2239)*

**Ingredion Incorporated** ..................................................... D ...... 209 982-1920
1021 Industrial Dr Stockton (95206) *(P-1090)*

**Ingrooves, San Francisco** *Also Called: Isolation Network Inc (P-11669)*

**Inharvest, Colusa** *Also Called: Riviana Foods Inc (P-17221)*

**Inhealth Technologies** ...................................................... E ...... 800 477-5969
1110 Mark Ave Carpinteria (93013) *(P-15363)*

**Inhibrx, La Jolla** *Also Called: Inhibrx Inc (P-5842)*

**Inhibrx Inc (HQ)** ................................................................ C ...... 858 795-4220
11025 N Torrey Pines Rd Ste 200 La Jolla (92037) *(P-5842)*

**Initiative Food Company, Sanger** *Also Called: If Holding Inc (P-2236)*

**Initiative Foods, Sanger** *Also Called: If Copack LLC (P-858)*

**Initiative Foods LLC** ........................................................ C ...... 559 875-3354
1912 Industrial Way Sanger (93657) *(P-859)*

**Initium Aerospace LLC** .................................................... F ...... 818 324-3684
4255 Ruffin Rd Ste 100 San Diego (92123) *(P-7688)*

**Injen Technology Company Ltd** ....................................... E ...... 909 839-0706
244 Pioneer Pl Pomona (91768) *(P-16782)*

**Ink & Color Inc** ................................................................. E ...... 310 280-6060
5920 Bowcroft St Los Angeles (90016) *(P-4644)*

**Ink Fx Corporation** ........................................................... E ...... 909 673-1950
513 S La Serena Dr Covina (91723) *(P-4898)*

**Ink Solutions LLC** ............................................................. F ...... 323 726-8100
5928 Garfield Ave Commerce (90040) *(P-6255)*

**Ink Spot Inc** ...................................................................... E ...... 626 338-4500
9737 Bell Ranch Dr Santa Fe Springs (90670) *(P-4645)*

**Ink Spots, Montclair** *Also Called: Thomas Burt (P-4786)*

**Ink Systems Inc (PA)** ........................................................ D ...... 323 720-4000
2311 S Eastern Ave Commerce (90040) *(P-6256)*

**Inkitt Inc** ............................................................................ E ...... 978 844-1074
50 Francisco St Ste 100 San Francisco (94133) *(P-4416)*

**Inkovation Inc** ................................................................... F ...... 800 465-4174
13659 Excelsior Dr Santa Fe Springs (90670) *(P-4646)*

**Inkspace Imaging Inc** ....................................................... F ...... 925 425-7410
5635 W Las Positas Blvd Ste 403-404 Pleasanton (94588) *(P-15547)*

**Inktomi Corporation (HQ)** ................................................. E ...... 650 653-2800
701 First Ave Sunnyvale (94089) *(P-18419)*

**Inkwright LLC** ................................................................... E ...... 714 892-3300
5822 Research Dr Huntington Beach (92649) *(P-4647)*

**Inland Cold Storage** ......................................................... E ...... 951 369-0230
2356 Fleetwood Dr Riverside (92509) *(P-2054)*

**Inland Custom Manufacturing, Ontario** *Also Called: Inland Signs Inc (P-15989)*

**Inland Empire Drv Line Svc Inc (PA)** ............................... F ...... 909 390-3030
4035 E Guasti Rd Ste 301 Ontario (91761) *(P-13518)*

**Inland Empire Foods Inc (PA)** .......................................... E ...... 951 682-8222
5425 Wilson St Riverside (92509) *(P-951)*

**Inland Empire Magazine, Temecula** *Also Called: Inland Empire Media Group Inc (P-4268)*

**Inland Empire Media Group Inc** ....................................... E ...... 951 682-3026
36095 Monte De Oro Rd Temecula (92592) *(P-4268)*

**Inland Envelope Company** ............................................... D ...... 909 622-2016
150 N Park Ave Pomona (91768) *(P-4009)*

**Inland Group, Anaheim** *Also Called: Inland Litho LLC (P-4648)*

**Inland Litho LLC** ............................................................... D ...... 714 993-6000
4305 E La Palma Ave Anaheim (92807) *(P-4648)*

**Inland Marine Industries Inc (PA)** .................................... C ...... 510 785-8555
3245 Depot Rd Hayward (94545) *(P-8473)*

**Inland Metal Technologies, Hayward** *Also Called: Inland Marine Industries Inc (P-8473)*

**Inland Pacific Coatings Inc** .............................................. E ...... 909 822-0594
3556 Lytle Creek Rd Lytle Creek (92358) *(P-9078)*

**Inland Powder Coating Corp** ............................................ C ...... 909 947-1122
1656 S Bon View Ave Ste F Ontario (91761) *(P-9079)*

**Inland Signs Inc** ................................................................ F ...... 909 923-0006
1715 S Bon View Ave Ontario (91761) *(P-15989)*

**Inland Sports Group, Menifee** *Also Called: Tea Financial Services (P-16941)*

**Inland Truss Inc (PA)** ........................................................ D ...... 951 300-1758
275 W Rider St Perris (92571) *(P-3312)*

**Inland Valley Daily Bulletin, Monrovia** *Also Called: Califrnia Nwspapers Ltd Partnr (P-4085)*

**Inland Valley Daily Bulletin, Ontario** *Also Called: Califrnia Nwspapers Ltd Partnr (P-4086)*

**Inline Plastics Inc** ............................................................. E ...... 909 923-1033
1950 S Baker Ave Ontario (91761) *(P-6863)*

**Inlyte Energy Inc** .............................................................. E ...... 415 483-0608
1933 Davis St Ste 281 San Leandro (94577) *(P-19398)*

**Inmage Systems Inc** ......................................................... D ...... 408 200-3840
1065 La Avenida St Mountain View (94043) *(P-18420)*

**Inneos LLC** ....................................................................... E ...... 925 226-0138
4255 Hopyard Rd Pleasanton (94588) *(P-14785)*

**Inners Tasks LLC** .............................................................. E ...... 951 225-9696
27708 Jefferson Ave Ste 201 Temecula (92590) *(P-10166)*

**Innerstep BSE** ................................................................... D ...... 831 461-5600
4742 Scotts Valley Dr Scotts Valley (95066) *(P-12136)*

**Inno Tech Manufacturing Inc** ........................................... F ...... 858 565-4556
10109 Carroll Canyon Rd San Diego (92131) *(P-10886)*

**Innocoll Biotherapeutics NA** ............................................ D ...... 484 406-5200
5163 Lakeview Canyon Rd Westlake Village (91362) *(P-5494)*

**Innocor West LLC** ............................................................ A ...... 909 307-3737
300 S Tippecanoe Ave 310 San Bernardino (92408) *(P-6503)*

**Innodisk Usa Corporation** ................................................ E ...... 510 770-9421
42996 Osgood Rd Fremont (94539) *(P-12484)*

**Innogrit Corporation** ......................................................... E ...... 408 785-3678
1735 Technology Dr Ste 600 San Jose (95110) *(P-12485)*

**Innophase, San Diego** *Also Called: Innophase Inc (P-12486)*

**Innophase Inc** ................................................................... D ...... 619 541-8280
5880 Oberlin Dr Ste 600 San Diego (92121) *(P-12486)*

**Innosys Incorporated** ........................................................ E ...... 510 594-1034
1555 3rd Ave Walnut Creek (94597) *(P-17929)*

**Innov8v, Irvine** *Also Called: Innovative Tech & Engrg Inc (P-10383)*

**Innova Electronics Corporation** ....................................... E ...... 714 241-6800
17352 Von Karman Ave Irvine (92614) *(P-13519)*

**Innovalight Inc** .................................................................. E ...... 408 419-4400
965 W Maude Ave Sunnyvale (94085) *(P-11602)*

**Innovated Solutions Inc** .................................................... F ...... 949 222-1088
7201 Garden Grove Blvd Ste C Garden Grove (92841) *(P-9869)*

**Innovation Brewworks** ...................................................... F ...... 909 979-6197
3650 W Temple Ave Ste 100 Pomona (91768) *(P-1435)*

**Innovative Biosciences Corp** ............................................ E ...... 760 603-0772
1849 Diamond St San Marcos (92078) *(P-5993)*

**Innovative Body Science, San Marcos** *Also Called: Innovative Biosciences Corp (P-5993)*

**Innovative Casework Mfg Inc** ........................................... E ...... 714 890-9100
12261 Industry St Garden Grove (92841) *(P-16151)*

Innovative Coatings Technology Corporation ........................... C ...... 661 824-8101
  1347 Poole St 106 Mojave (93501) *(P-9080)*
Innovative Displayworks LLC (HQ) ........................................... F ...... 909 447-8254
  8825 Boston Pl Ste 100 Rancho Cucamonga (91730) *(P-16568)*
Innovative Emergency Equipment ............................................. E ...... 951 222-2270
  1616 Marlborough Ave Riverside (92507) *(P-19264)*
Innovative Emergency Equipment, Riverside *Also Called: Innovtive Dsign Shtmtl Pdts In (P-8475)*
Innovative Healthcare Svcs LLC .................................................. E ...... 909 280-0559
  2108 N St Ste 8083 Sacramento (95816) *(P-6297)*
Innovative Integration Inc ............................................................ E ...... 805 520-3300
  741 Flynn Rd Camarillo (93012) *(P-14423)*
Innovative Lab Solutions Inc ........................................................ F ...... 858 842-4127
  13200 Kirkham Way Ste 114 Poway (92064) *(P-19399)*
Innovative Machining Inc ............................................................. E ...... 408 262-2270
  845 Yosemite Way Milpitas (95035) *(P-10887)*
Innovative Metal Designs Inc ....................................................... E ...... 714 799-6700
  12691 Monarch St Garden Grove (92841) *(P-16386)*
Innovative Metal Inds Inc ............................................................. D ...... 909 796-6200
  1330 Riverview Dr San Bernardino (92408) *(P-8699)*
Innovative Metal Products Inc ...................................................... F ...... 760 734-1010
  2443 Cades Way Ste 200 Vista (92081) *(P-8474)*
Innovative Stamping Inc .............................................................. E ...... 310 537-6996
  2068 E Gladwick St Compton (90220) *(P-8852)*
Innovative Steel Structures, Modesto *Also Called: JR Daniels Commercial Bldrs (P-8701)*
Innovative Systems, Compton *Also Called: Innovative Stamping Inc (P-8852)*
Innovative Tech & Engrg Inc ........................................................ E ...... 949 955-2501
  2691 Richter Ave Ste 124 Irvine (92606) *(P-10383)*
Innovativetek Inc .......................................................................... F ...... 909 981-3401
  1271 W 9th St Upland (91786) *(P-13250)*
Innovion LLC (HQ) ....................................................................... D ...... 408 501-9140
  2121 Zanker Rd San Jose (95131) *(P-12487)*
INNOVIVA, Burlingame *Also Called: Innoviva Inc (P-5495)*
Innoviva Inc (PA) .......................................................................... F ...... 650 238-9600
  1350 Bayshore Hwy Ste 400 Burlingame (94010) *(P-5495)*
Innovive LLC (PA) ........................................................................ E ...... 858 309-6620
  10019 Waples Ct San Diego (92121) *(P-9220)*
Innovtive Dsign Shtmtl Pdts In ..................................................... F ...... 951 222-2270
  616 Marlborough Ave Unit S-1 Riverside (92507) *(P-8475)*
Innovtive Rttional Molding Inc ...................................................... E ...... 559 673-4764
  2300 W Pecan Ave Madera (93637) *(P-6864)*
Innowi Inc ..................................................................................... E ...... 408 609-9404
  3240 Scott Blvd Santa Clara (95054) *(P-10167)*
Ino-Tech Laser Processing Inc .................................................... E ...... 408 262-1845
  1060 Commercial St Ste 101 San Jose (95112) *(P-13251)*
INOGEN, Goleta *Also Called: Inogen Inc (P-15117)*
Inogen Inc (PA) ............................................................................ C ...... 805 562-0500
  859 Ward Dr Ste 200 Goleta (93111) *(P-15117)*
Inova Diagnostics Inc ................................................................... C ...... 858 586-9900
  9889 Willow Creek Rd San Diego (92131) *(P-5496)*
Inova Diagnostics Inc ................................................................... C ...... 858 586-9900
  9675 Businesspark Ave San Diego (92131) *(P-5757)*
Inova Diagnostics Inc (HQ) .......................................................... B ...... 858 586-9900
  9900 Old Grove Rd San Diego (92131) *(P-19456)*
Inova Labs Inc .............................................................................. D ...... 866 647-0691
  9001 Spectrum Center Blvd Ste 200 San Diego (92123) *(P-15118)*
Inovati .......................................................................................... E ...... 805 571-8384
  1522 Cook Pl Goleta (93117) *(P-9081)*
Inovativ Inc ................................................................................... E ...... 626 969-5300
  1500 W Mckinley St Azusa (91702) *(P-7707)*
Inovit Inc ....................................................................................... F ...... 626 444-4775
  5120 Commerce Dr Baldwin Park (91706) *(P-13520)*
Inphenix Inc .................................................................................. E ...... 925 606-8809
  250 N Mines Rd Livermore (94551) *(P-12488)*
Inphi, San Jose *Also Called: Inphi Corporation (P-12489)*
Inphi Corporation (HQ) ................................................................. C
  110 Rio Robles San Jose (95134) *(P-12489)*
Inphi International Pte Ltd ............................................................ E ...... 805 719-2300
  112 S Lakeview Canyon Rd Ste 100 Westlake Village (91362) *(P-12490)*
Input/Output Technology Inc ........................................................ E ...... 661 257-1000
  28415 Industry Dr Ste 520 Valencia (91355) *(P-10384)*

Inscopix Inc .................................................................................. C ...... 650 600-3886
  1212 Terra Bella Ave Ste 200 Mountain View (94043) *(P-14786)*
Inseat Solutions LLC ................................................................... E ...... 562 447-1780
  1871 Wright Ave La Verne (91750) *(P-11406)*
Inside East Sacramento .............................................................. F ...... 916 443-5087
  625 33rd St Sacramento (95816) *(P-4417)*
Insight Editions, San Rafael *Also Called: Insight Editions LP (P-4333)*
Insight Editions LP ....................................................................... D ...... 415 526-1370
  800 A St San Rafael (94901) *(P-4333)*
Insight Manufacturing Services, Rancho Cordova *Also Called: Kaiser Enterprises Inc (P-9263)*
Insight Mfg Services, Murphys *Also Called: Kaiser Enterprises Inc (P-9264)*
Insignia ........................................................................................ F ...... 415 777-0320
  390 Fremont St San Francisco (94105) *(P-18980)*
Insite Digestive Health Care ........................................................ E ...... 626 817-2900
  21250 Hawthorne Blvd Torrance (90503) *(P-19318)*
Insomniac Games Inc (PA) .......................................................... D ...... 818 729-2400
  2255 N Ontario St Ste 550 Burbank (91504) *(P-15752)*
Insomniac Games Inc .................................................................. D ...... 650 655-1633
  2207 Bridgepointe Pkwy Foster City (94404) *(P-15753)*
Insound Medical Inc ..................................................................... E ...... 510 792-4000
  47257 Fremont Blvd Fremont (94538) *(P-15119)*
Insparation Inc ............................................................................. E ...... 805 553-0820
  11950 Hertz Ave Moorpark (93021) *(P-5994)*
Inspira, Vernon *Also Called: Offline Inc (P-2600)*
Inspired Flight, San Luis Obispo *Also Called: Inspired Flight Tech Inc (P-8004)*
Inspired Flight Tech Inc ............................................................... E ...... 805 776-3640
  225 Suburban Rd Ste A San Luis Obispo (93401) *(P-8004)*
Inspur US R&D Technology Ctr, Fremont *Also Called: Aivres Systems Inc (P-10129)*
Insta Graphic Systems, Cerritos *Also Called: Insta-Lettering Machine Co (P-2473)*
Insta-Lettering Machine Co (PA) ................................................. D ...... 562 404-3000
  13925 166th St Cerritos (90703) *(P-2473)*
INSTACART, San Francisco *Also Called: Maplebear Inc (P-19010)*
Instacure Healing Products ......................................................... E ...... 818 222-9600
  235 N Moorpark Rd Unit 2022 Thousand Oaks (91360) *(P-5497)*
Instagis Inc (PA) .......................................................................... F ...... 415 527-6636
  218 9th St San Francisco (94103) *(P-18421)*
Installtion Dgtal Trnsmssons I ..................................................... F ...... 415 226-0020
  517 Jacoby St Ste C San Rafael (94901) *(P-565)*
Instant Algae, Campbell *Also Called: Reed Mariculture Inc (P-1146)*
Instant Systems Inc ..................................................................... D ...... 510 657-8100
  447 King Ave Fremont (94536) *(P-17930)*
Instant Tuck Inc ............................................................................ E ...... 310 955-8824
  9663 Santa Monica Blvd Beverly Hills (90210) *(P-2929)*
Instant Web LLC .......................................................................... C ...... 562 658-2020
  7300 Flores St Downey (90242) *(P-4649)*
Instantsys, Fremont *Also Called: Instant Systems Inc (P-17930)*
Institutional Real Estate Inc (PA) ................................................. E ...... 925 933-4040
  1475 N Broadway Ste 300 Walnut Creek (94596) *(P-4418)*
Instrument Bearing Factory USA ................................................. E ...... 818 989-5052
  19360 Rinaldi St Northridge (91326) *(P-8759)*
Instrument Control Services ........................................................ E ...... 805 642-1999
  6085 King Dr Unit 100 Ventura (93003) *(P-240)*
Instrumentl Inc ............................................................................. E ...... 909 258-9291
  440 N Barranca Ave Covina (91723) *(P-18422)*
Instruments Incorporated ............................................................. E ...... 858 571-1111
  7263 Engineer Rd Ste G San Diego (92111) *(P-13252)*
Instyler, Torrance *Also Called: Tre Milano LLC (P-16257)*
Insua Graphics Incorporated ....................................................... E ...... 818 767-7007
  9121 Glenoaks Blvd Sun Valley (91352) *(P-4650)*
Insul-Therm, Commerce *Also Called: Insul-Therm International Inc (P-16491)*
Insul-Therm International Inc (PA) ............................................... E ...... 323 728-0558
  6651 E 26th St Commerce (90040) *(P-16491)*
Insulation Sources Inc (PA) ......................................................... E ...... 650 856-8378
  2575 E Bayshore Rd Palo Alto (94303) *(P-13000)*
Insulfoam, Dixon *Also Called: Carlisle Construction Mtls LLC (P-16490)*
Insultech, Santa Ana *Also Called: Insultech LLC (P-6298)*
Insultech LLC (PA) ...................................................................... E ...... 714 384-0506
  3530 W Garry Ave Santa Ana (92704) *(P-6298)*
Insurance Journal, San Diego *Also Called: Wells Media Group Inc (P-19341)*

# ALPHABETIC SECTION — Intercontinental Art

**Intake Screens Inc** ............................................................ F ...... 916 665-2727
8417 River Rd Sacramento (95832) *(P-8153)*

**Intapp, Palo Alto** *Also Called: Intapp Us Inc (P-17931)*

**Intapp Us Inc (HQ)** ........................................................... C ...... 650 852-0400
3101 Park Blvd Palo Alto (94306) *(P-17931)*

**Integem** ............................................................................ E ...... 408 459-0657
20432 Silverado Ave Ste 210 Cupertino (95014) *(P-17932)*

**Integenx, Pleasanton** *Also Called: Integenx Inc (P-14677)*

**Integenx Inc (HQ)** ............................................................. D ...... 925 701-3400
5720 Stoneridge Dr Ste 300 Pleasanton (94588) *(P-14677)*

**Integer Holdings Corporation** ........................................... E ...... 619 498-9448
8830 Siempre Viva Rd Ste 100 San Diego (92101) *(P-15120)*

**Integra Devices, Irvine** *Also Called: Xidas Inc (P-13127)*

**Integra Lfscnces Holdings Corp** ....................................... E ...... 609 529-9748
5955 Pacific Center Blvd San Diego (92121) *(P-15121)*

**Integra Lifesciences, Carlsbad** *Also Called: Seaspine Inc (P-15402)*

**Integra Tech Silicon Vly LLC (DH)** ................................... C ...... 408 618-8700
1635 Mccarthy Blvd Milpitas (95035) *(P-12491)*

**Integra Technologies Inc** .................................................. E ...... 310 606-0855
321 Coral Cir El Segundo (90245) *(P-12492)*

**Integral Aerospace LLC** .................................................. C ...... 949 250-3123
2040 E Dyer Rd Santa Ana (92705) *(P-13874)*

**Integral Development Corp (PA)** ..................................... E ...... 650 424-4500
380 Portage Ave Palo Alto (94306) *(P-18423)*

**Integral Engineering, Palo Alto** *Also Called: Integral Development Corp (P-18423)*

**Integrated Bldg Solutions Inc** ........................................... F ...... 925 244-1900
2000 Crow Canyon Pl Ste 440 San Ramon (94583) *(P-19563)*

**Integrated Charts Inc** ....................................................... E ...... 855 698-2232
915 Highland Pointe Dr Ste 250 Roseville (95765) *(P-18424)*

**Integrated Communications Inc** ....................................... E ...... 310 851-8066
208 N Broadway Santa Ana (92701) *(P-4651)*

**Integrated Digital Media** .................................................. F ...... 415 627-8310
14 Avila St San Francisco (94123) *(P-4652)*

**Integrated Energy Technologies Inc** ................................ C ...... 619 421-1151
1478 Santa Sierra Dr Chula Vista (91913) *(P-9951)*

**Integrated Flow Systems LLC (HQ)** ................................ D ...... 510 659-4900
26462 Corporate Ave Hayward (94545) *(P-14424)*

**Integrated Food Service, Gardena** *Also Called: Lets Do Lunch (P-2264)*

**Integrated Grain & Milling Inc** .......................................... E ...... 559 443-6500
7910 N Ingram Ave Ste 101 Fresno (93711) *(P-1131)*

**Integrated Magnetics, Culver City** *Also Called: Magnet Sales & Mfg Co Inc (P-7284)*

**Integrated Magnetics Inc** ................................................. E ...... 310 391-7213
11250 Playa Ct Culver City (90230) *(P-11273)*

**INTEGRATED MANUFACTURING TECHNOLOGIES, INC., Milpitas** *Also Called: Integrated Mfg Tech Inc (P-19199)*

**Integrated Marine Services Inc** ........................................ D ...... 619 429-0300
2320 Main St Chula Vista (91911) *(P-14005)*

**Integrated Mfg Solutions LLC** .......................................... E ...... 760 599-4300
2590 Pioneer Ave Ste C Vista (92081) *(P-16152)*

**Integrated Mfg Tech Inc** ................................................... E ...... 510 659-9770
1477 N Milpitas Blvd Milpitas (95035) *(P-19199)*

**Integrated Microwave Corp** ............................................. D ...... 858 259-2600
11353 Sorrento Valley Rd San Diego (92121) *(P-13001)*

**Integrated Optical Svcs Corp** ........................................... E ...... 408 982-9510
3270 Keller St Ste 102 Santa Clara (95054) *(P-6087)*

**Integrated Polymer Solutions, Long Beach** *Also Called: Sanders Inds Holdings Inc (P-5200)*

**Integrated Sign Associates, El Cajon** *Also Called: Integrted Sign Assoc A Cal Cor (P-15990)*

**Integrated Solutions, Garden Grove** *Also Called: Innovated Solutions Inc (P-9869)*

**Integrated Tech Group Inc (PA)** ....................................... E ...... 310 391-7213
11250 Playa Ct Culver City (90230) *(P-9288)*

**Integrated Technical Services, Anaheim** *Also Called: L3harris Interstate Elec Corp (P-14544)*

**Integrated Voting Solutions, Dinuba** *Also Called: Integrated Voting Systems Inc (P-19097)*

**Integrated Voting Systems Inc** ......................................... E ...... 559 498-0281
496 S Uruapan Way Dinuba (93618) *(P-19097)*

**Integrateio Inc** .................................................................. 888 884-6405
580 California St San Francisco (94104) *(P-18425)*

**Integris Composites Inc (DH)** .......................................... E ...... 740 928-0326
120 Cremona Dr Ste 130 Goleta (93117) *(P-9135)*

**Integrity Bottles LLC** ........................................................ F ...... 847 922-0920
9225 Carlton Hills Blvd Ste 2 Santee (92071) *(P-7197)*

**Integrity Municipal Systems, Poway** *Also Called: Integrity Municpl Systems LLC (P-10566)*

**Integrity Municpl Systems LLC** ........................................ F ...... 858 486-1620
13135 Danielson St Ste 204 Poway (92064) *(P-10566)*

**Integrted Crygnic Slutions LLC** ........................................ E ...... 951 234-0899
2835 Progress Pl Escondido (92029) *(P-9870)*

**Integrted Sign Assoc A Cal Cor** ....................................... E ...... 619 579-2229
1160 Pioneer Way Ste M El Cajon (92020) *(P-15990)*

**Integrted Silicon Solution Inc (PA)** .................................. B ...... 408 969-6600
1623 Buckeye Dr Milpitas (95035) *(P-12493)*

**Intel, Santa Clara** *Also Called: Intel Corporation (P-10386)*

**Intel, San Jose** *Also Called: Intel Corporation (P-10387)*

**Intel, Santa Clara** *Also Called: Intel Technologies Inc (P-10389)*

**Intel Corp Prfit Shring Rtrmen** .......................................... E ...... 408 765-8080
2200 Mission College Blvd Santa Clara (95054) *(P-10385)*

**Intel Corporation** .............................................................. C ...... 408 425-8398
2300 Mission College Blvd Santa Clara (95054) *(P-10386)*

**Intel Corporation** .............................................................. A ...... 408 544-7000
101 Innovation Dr Bldg 1 San Jose (95134) *(P-10387)*

**Intel Corporation (PA)** ...................................................... A ...... 408 765-8080
2200 Mission College Blvd Santa Clara (95054) *(P-12494)*

**Intel Semiconductor (us) LLC (HQ)** ................................. E ...... 408 765-8080
2200 Mission College Blvd Santa Clara (95054) *(P-12495)*

**Intel Services LLC (HQ)** .................................................. F ...... 408 765-8080
2200 Mission College Blvd Sc4-203 Santa Clara (95054) *(P-10388)*

**Intel Technologies Inc (HQ)** ............................................. F ...... 408 765-8080
2200 Mission College Blvd Santa Clara (95054) *(P-10389)*

**Intelesense Technologies, Fremont** *Also Called: Hikino Associates LLC (P-19397)*

**Intellgard Inventory Solutions, San Diego** *Also Called: Intelliguard Group LLC (P-14884)*

**Intelligent Beauty LLC** ..................................................... A ...... 310 683-0940
2301 Rosecrans Ave Ste 5000 El Segundo (90245) *(P-17708)*

**Intelligent Blends LLC** ..................................................... E ...... 858 888-7937
5330 Eastgate Mall San Diego (92121) *(P-1071)*

**Intelligent Cmpt Solutions Inc (PA)** ................................. E ...... 818 998-5805
8968 Fullbright Ave Chatsworth (91311) *(P-14537)*

**Intelligent Energy Inc** ...................................................... E ...... 562 997-3600
1731 Technology Dr Ste 755 San Jose (95110) *(P-8005)*

**Intelligent Photonics, San Francisco** *Also Called: Invuity Inc (P-15131)*

**Intelligent Quartz Solutions, Fremont** *Also Called: Imtec Acculine LLC (P-9866)*

**Intelligent Storage Solution** ............................................. F ...... 408 428-0105
2073 Otoole Ave San Jose (95131) *(P-10247)*

**Intelligent Technologies LLC** ........................................... C ...... 858 458-1500
9454 Waples St San Diego (92121) *(P-11374)*

**Intelliguard Group LLC** .................................................... E ...... 760 448-9500
12220 World Trade Dr Ste 210 San Diego (92128) *(P-14884)*

**Intellisense Systems Inc** .................................................. C ...... 310 320-1827
21041 S Western Ave Torrance (90501) *(P-14196)*

**Intellisync Corporation** ..................................................... B ...... 650 625-2185
313 Fairchild Dr Mountain View (94043) *(P-17933)*

**Intematix Corporation** ...................................................... F ...... 925 631-9005
351 Rheem Blvd Moraga (94556) *(P-11771)*

**Intematix Corporation (PA)** .............................................. D ...... 510 933-3300
46410 Fremont Blvd Fremont (94538) *(P-14362)*

**Intense Lighting LLC** ....................................................... D ...... 714 630-9877
3340 E La Palma Ave Anaheim (92806) *(P-11539)*

**Inter-City Manufacturing Inc** ............................................. E ...... 831 899-3636
507 Redwood Ave Seaside (93955) *(P-10888)*

**Inter-City Printing Co Inc** ................................................. F ...... 510 451-4775
614 Madison St Oakland (94607) *(P-4653)*

**Interactive Display Solutions, Irvine** *Also Called: Interctive Dsplay Slutions Inc (P-13003)*

**Interactive Solutions Inc (DH)** ......................................... D ...... 510 214-9002
283 4th St Ste 301 Oakland (94607) *(P-18426)*

**Intercom, Los Angeles** *Also Called: Ashland Group LLC (P-14498)*

**Interconnect Solutions Co LLC (PA)** ............................... D ...... 714 556-7007
17595 Mount Herrmann St Fountain Valley (92708) *(P-11375)*

**Interconnect Solutions Co LLC** ....................................... D ...... 661 295-0020
25358 Avenue Stanford Valencia (91355) *(P-13002)*

**Interconnect Systems Intl LLC (DH)** ............................... D ...... 805 482-2870
741 Flynn Rd Camarillo (93012) *(P-12496)*

**Interconnect Systems, Inc., Camarillo** *Also Called: Interconnect Systems Intl LLC (P-12496)*

**Intercontinental Art, Compton** *Also Called: Artboxx Framing Inc (P-16089)*

---

Employee Codes: A=Over 500 employees, B=251-500
C=101-250, D=51-100, E=20-50, F=10-19, G=1-9

# Intercontinental Services

## ALPHABETIC SECTION

**Intercontinental Services, Concord** *Also Called: Carlton Senior Living Inc (P-17741)*
**Intercive Dsplay Slutions Inc** .................................................. E ...... 949 727-1959
 490 Wald Irvine (92618) *(P-13003)*
**Interdigital Inc** .................................................. D ...... 858 210-4800
 9276 Scranton Rd Ste 300 San Diego (92121) *(P-11868)*
**INTERDIGITAL, INC., San Diego** *Also Called: Interdigital Inc (P-11868)*
**Interface Associates, Laguna Niguel** *Also Called: Confluent Medical Tech Inc (P-15049)*
**Interface Associates Inc** .................................................. C ...... 949 448-7056
 27721 La Paz Rd Laguna Niguel (92677) *(P-15122)*
**Interface Catheter Solutions, Laguna Niguel** *Also Called: Interface Associates Inc (P-15122)*
**Interface Masters Tech Inc** .................................................. E ...... 408 676-1086
 48430 Lakeview Blvd Fremont (94538) *(P-13004)*
**Interface Welding** .................................................. E ...... 310 323-4944
 20722 Belshaw Ave Carson (90746) *(P-19265)*
**Interfaceflor LLC** .................................................. D ...... 213 741-2139
 1111 S Grand Ave Ste 103 Los Angeles (90015) *(P-2515)*
**Intergen Inc** .................................................. F ...... 408 245-2737
 1145 Tasman Dr Sunnyvale (94089) *(P-13253)*
**Interglobal Waste MGT Inc** .................................................. D ...... 805 388-1588
 820 Calle Plano Camarillo (93012) *(P-14678)*
**Interlink Inc** .................................................. E ...... 714 905-7700
 3845 E Coronado St Anaheim (92807) *(P-4654)*
**Interlog Construction, Anaheim** *Also Called: Interlog Corporation (P-13005)*
**Interlog Corporation** .................................................. E ...... 714 529-7808
 1295 N Knollwood Cir Anaheim (92801) *(P-13005)*
**Intermdia Cloud Cmmnctions Inc** .................................................. A ...... 650 641-4000
 100 Mathilda Pl Ste 600 Sunnyvale (94086) *(P-18427)*
**Intermolecular, San Jose** *Also Called: Intermolecular Inc (P-12497)*
**Intermolecular Inc (HQ)** .................................................. F ...... 408 582-5700
 3011 N 1st St San Jose (95134) *(P-12497)*
**Intermolecular Inc** .................................................. D ...... 408 416-2300
 2865 Zanker Rd San Jose (95134) *(P-13254)*
**Intermotive Inc** .................................................. E ...... 530 823-1048
 12840 Earhart Ave Auburn (95602) *(P-19531)*
**Intermune Inc (DH)** .................................................. C ...... 415 466-4383
 1 Dna Way South San Francisco (94080) *(P-5498)*
**International Academy of Fin (PA)** .................................................. E ...... 818 361-7724
 13177 Foothill Blvd Sylmar (91342) *(P-6148)*
**International Bus Mchs Corp** .................................................. E ...... 714 472-2237
 600 Anton Blvd Ste 400 Costa Mesa (92626) *(P-10168)*
**International Bus Mchs Corp** .................................................. A ...... 818 553-8100
 400 N Brand Blvd Fl 7 Glendale (91203) *(P-10169)*
**International Bus Mchs Corp** .................................................. C ...... 415 545-4747
 425 Market St San Francisco (94105) *(P-16503)*
**International Bus Mchs Corp** .................................................. A ...... 408 463-2000
 555 Bailey Ave San Jose (95141) *(P-17934)*
**International Cases & Mfg Inc (PA)** .................................................. E ...... 559 253-4111
 2541 N Fowler Ave Fresno (93727) *(P-7134)*
**International Co-Packing Co, Fresno** *Also Called: Lidestri Foods Inc (P-2266)*
**International Coatings, Cerritos** *Also Called: International Coatings Co Inc (P-6233)*
**International Coatings Co Inc (PA)** .................................................. E ...... 562 926-1010
 13929 166th St Cerritos (90703) *(P-6233)*
**International Component Tech, Santa Ana** *Also Called: Nivek Industries Inc (P-11466)*
**International Consulting Unltd** .................................................. E ...... 714 449-3318
 13045 Park St Santa Fe Springs (90670) *(P-7664)*
**International Daily News Inc (PA)** .................................................. E ...... 323 265-1317
 870 Monterey Pass Rd Monterey Park (91754) *(P-4135)*
**International Die Casting Inc** .................................................. E ...... 310 324-2278
 515 E Airline Way Gardena (90248) *(P-7865)*
**International E-Z Up Inc (PA)** .................................................. D ...... 800 742-3363
 1900 2nd St Norco (92860) *(P-2976)*
**International Fluid Power Amer, Temecula** *Also Called: Normont Hydraulic Sls Svc Inc (P-16830)*
**International Glace Inc (PA)** .................................................. E ...... 559 385-7675
 4067 W Shaw Ave Fresno (93722) *(P-1312)*
**International Group Inc** .................................................. D ...... 510 232-8704
 102 Cutting Blvd Richmond (94804) *(P-6339)*
**International Hort Tech LLC** .................................................. E ...... 831 637-1800
 150 Acquistapace Rd Hollister (95023) *(P-9359)*
**International Iron Products, San Diego** *Also Called: Price Industries Inc (P-7622)*

**International Lottery & Totalizator Systems Inc** .................................................. E ...... 760 598-1655
 2310 Cousteau Ct Vista (92081) *(P-17935)*
**International Mfg Tech Inc (DH)** .................................................. D ...... 619 544-7741
 2798 Harbor Dr San Diego (92113) *(P-7616)*
**International Paper, Fremont** *Also Called: International Paper Company (P-3772)*
**International Paper, Exeter** *Also Called: International Paper Company (P-3774)*
**International Paper, Elk Grove** *Also Called: International Paper Company (P-3775)*
**International Paper, Camarillo** *Also Called: International Paper Company (P-3776)*
**International Paper, Compton** *Also Called: International Paper Company (P-3777)*
**International Paper, Sanger** *Also Called: International Paper Company (P-3778)*
**International Paper, Salinas** *Also Called: International Paper Company (P-3779)*
**International Paper, Gilroy** *Also Called: International Paper Company (P-3780)*
**International Paper, Santa Fe Springs** *Also Called: International Paper Company (P-3782)*
**International Paper, Carson** *Also Called: International Paper Company (P-3783)*
**International Paper, Gilroy** *Also Called: International Paper Company (P-3784)*
**International Paper, Ontario** *Also Called: New-Indy Containerboard LLC (P-3787)*
**International Paper, Modesto** *Also Called: International Paper Company (P-3803)*
**International Paper, Santa Fe Springs** *Also Called: International Paper Company (P-3860)*
**International Paper Company** .................................................. D ...... 510 490-5887
 42305 Albrae St Fremont (94538) *(P-3772)*
**International Paper Company** .................................................. C ...... 714 776-6060
 601 E Ball Rd Anaheim (92805) *(P-3773)*
**International Paper Company** .................................................. D ...... 559 592-7279
 1111 N Anderson Rd Exeter (93221) *(P-3774)*
**International Paper Company** .................................................. D ...... 916 685-9000
 10268 Waterman Rd Elk Grove (95624) *(P-3775)*
**International Paper Company** .................................................. E ...... 805 933-4347
 2000 Pleasant Valley Rd Camarillo (93010) *(P-3776)*
**International Paper Company** .................................................. E ...... 310 639-2310
 19615 S Susana Rd Compton (90221) *(P-3777)*
**International Paper Company** .................................................. D ...... 559 875-3311
 1000 Muscat Ave Sanger (93657) *(P-3778)*
**International Paper Company** .................................................. E ...... 831 755-2100
 1345 Harkins Rd Salinas (93901) *(P-3779)*
**International Paper Company** .................................................. C ...... 408 847-6400
 6400 Jamieson Way Gilroy (95020) *(P-3780)*
**International Paper Company** .................................................. D ...... 916 371-4634
 1714 Cebrian St West Sacramento (95691) *(P-3781)*
**International Paper Company** .................................................. D ...... 562 692-9465
 9211 Norwalk Blvd Santa Fe Springs (90670) *(P-3782)*
**International Paper Company** .................................................. D ...... 310 549-5525
 1350 E 223rd St Carson (90745) *(P-3783)*
**International Paper Company** .................................................. E ...... 408 846-2060
 6791 Alexander St Gilroy (95020) *(P-3784)*
**International Paper Company** .................................................. C ...... 209 526-4700
 660 Mariposa Rd Modesto (95354) *(P-3803)*
**International Paper Company** .................................................. E ...... 323 946-6100
 11211 Greenstone Ave Santa Fe Springs (90670) *(P-3860)*
**International Plating Svc LLC (PA)** .................................................. E ...... 619 454-2135
 4045 Bonita Rd Ste 309 Bonita (91902) *(P-8973)*
**International Precision Inc** .................................................. F ...... 818 882-3933
 9526 Vassar Ave Chatsworth (91311) *(P-10889)*
**International Processing Corp (DH)** .................................................. E ...... 310 458-1574
 233 Wilshire Blvd Ste 310 Santa Monica (90401) *(P-1132)*
**International RES Dev Corp Nev (PA)** .................................................. F ...... 858 488-9900
 5212 Chelsea St La Jolla (92037) *(P-13173)*
**International Rite-Way Pdts, Ontario** *Also Called: AMD International Tech LLC (P-8371)*
**International Rubber Pdts Inc (HQ)** .................................................. D ...... 909 947-1244
 1035 Calle Amanecer San Clemente (92673) *(P-6504)*
**International Seal Company, Santa Ana** *Also Called: Freudenberg-Nok General Partnr (P-6446)*
**International Sensor Tech** .................................................. E ...... 949 452-9000
 3 Whatney Ste 100 Irvine (92618) *(P-14885)*
**International Skylights** .................................................. C ...... 800 325-4355
 1831 Ritchey St Santa Ana (92705) *(P-7174)*
**International Technidyne Corp (DH)** .................................................. C ...... 858 263-2300
 6260 Sequence Dr San Diego (92121) *(P-15123)*
**International Tex Group Inc** .................................................. F ...... 310 667-9030
 3097 E Ana St East Rancho Domingue (90221) *(P-2419)*
**International Tranducer Corp** .................................................. C ...... 805 683-2575
 869 Ward Dr Santa Barbara (93111) *(P-14538)*

# ALPHABETIC SECTION — Invensys Climate Controls

International Treescapes, San Marcos  *Also Called: Treescapes and Plant Works (P-16258)*
International Vitamin Corp ................................................. C ...... 949 664-5500
  1 Park Plz Ste 800 Irvine (92614)  *(P-5499)*
International Vitamin Corporat (PA) ..................................... D ...... 949 664-5500
  4695 Macarthur Ct Ste 1400 Newport Beach (92660)  *(P-5500)*
International West  Inc ........................................................ E ...... 714 632-9190
  1025 N Armando St Anaheim (92806)  *(P-8476)*
International Wind  Inc (PA) ................................................ E ...... 562 240-3963
  137 N Joy St Corona (92879)  *(P-13713)*
International Wood Industries, Turlock  *Also Called: International Wood Industries Inc (P-3071)*
International Wood Industries Inc ....................................... E ...... 209 632-3300
  250 D St Turlock (95380)  *(P-3071)*
International Wood Products, San Diego  *Also Called: Jeld-Wen  Inc (P-3150)*
Internet Machines Corporation (PA) .................................... D ...... 818 575-2100
  30501 Agoura Rd Ste 203 Agoura Hills (91301)  *(P-10390)*
Interntional Color Posters Inc ............................................. E ...... 949 768-1005
  8081 Orangethorpe Ave Buena Park (90621)  *(P-4899)*
Interntional Horticulture Tech, Hollister  *Also Called: International Hort Tech LLC (P-9359)*
Interntional Photo Plates Corp ............................................ E ...... 805 496-5031
  2641 Townsgate Rd Ste 100 Westlake Village (91361)  *(P-8974)*
Interntional Tea Importers Inc (PA) .................................... E ...... 562 801-9600
  2140 Davie Ave Commerce (90040)  *(P-2240)*
Interntional Tech Systems Corp .......................................... E ...... 714 761-8886
  10721 Walker St Cypress (90630)  *(P-16706)*
Interntnal Cnnctors Cable Corp .......................................... C ...... 888 275-4422
  1270 N Hancock St Anaheim (92807)  *(P-11772)*
Interntnal Desserts Delicacies (PA) .................................... F ...... 818 549-0056
  4700 District Blvd Vernon (90058)  *(P-1277)*
Interntnal Lttery Ttlztor Syst ............................................... E ...... 760 598-1655
  2310 Cousteau Ct Vista (92081)  *(P-17936)*
Interntnal Mdction Systems Ltd .......................................... A ...... 626 442-6757
  1886 Santa Anita Ave South El Monte (91733)  *(P-5501)*
Interntnal Mtllrgical Svcs LLC ............................................. F ...... 310 645-7300
  6371 Arizona Cir Los Angeles (90045)  *(P-7886)*
Interntnal Ntrtn Wllness Hldng, Corona  *Also Called: Inw Living Ecology Opco LLC (P-1313)*
Interntnal Ptro Pdts Addtves I ............................................ F ...... 925 556-5530
  7600 Dublin Blvd Ste 240 Dublin (94568)  *(P-6395)*
Interntnal Window-Northern Cal, Hayward  *Also Called: General Window Corporation (P-6839)*
Interntonal Thermoproducts Div, Santee  *Also Called: Ds Fibertech Corp (P-10050)*
Interocean Industries  Inc .................................................... E ...... 858 292-0808
  9201 Isaac St Ste C Santee (92071)  *(P-14197)*
Interocean Systems, Santee  *Also Called: Interocean Industries  Inc (P-14197)*
Interocean Systems  LLC .................................................... E ...... 858 565-8400
  9201 Isaac St Ste C Santee (92071)  *(P-14198)*
Interpore Cross Intl Inc (DH) .............................................. D ...... 949 453-3200
  181 Technology Dr Irvine (92618)  *(P-15364)*
Interscan Corporation .......................................................... E ...... 805 823-8301
  4590 Ish Dr Ste 110 Simi Valley (93063)  *(P-14480)*
Intersect Ent  Inc ................................................................. B ...... 650 641-2100
  1555 Adams Dr Menlo Park (94025)  *(P-15124)*
Intershop Communications Inc ........................................... E ...... 415 844-1500
  461 2nd St Apt 151 San Francisco (94107)  *(P-18428)*
Intersil Communications LLC ............................................. A ...... 408 432-8888
  1001 Murphy Ranch Rd Milpitas (95035)  *(P-12498)*
Intersil Techwell, South San Francisco  *Also Called: Renesas Electronics Amer Inc (P-12674)*
Interspace Battery  Inc (PA) ............................................... E ...... 626 813-1234
  2009 W San Bernardino Rd West Covina (91790)  *(P-7763)*
Interstate Meat Co  Inc ........................................................ E ...... 323 838-9400
  6114 Scott Way Commerce (90040)  *(P-9798)*
Interstate Mnroe McHy Sups Div, Huntington Beach  *Also Called: Statco Engrg & Fabricators LLC (P-16845)*
Interstate Steel Center Co Inc ............................................ E ...... 323 583-0855
  7001 S Alameda St Los Angeles (90001)  *(P-7617)*
Intertrade Industries Ltd ..................................................... D ...... 714 894-5566
  14600 Hoover St Westminster (92683)  *(P-6865)*
Interventional Spine  Inc .................................................... F ...... 949 472-0006
  30 Fairbanks Ste 100 Irvine (92618)  *(P-15125)*
Intevac  Inc ......................................................................... F ...... 408 986-9888
  3560 Bassett St Santa Clara (95054)  *(P-9871)*
Intevac Photonics  Inc (PA) ................................................ D ...... 408 986-9888
  3560 Bassett St Santa Clara (95054)  *(P-14787)*

Intevac Photonics  Inc ......................................................... E ...... 760 476-0339
  5909 Sea Lion Pl Ste A Carlsbad (92010)  *(P-14788)*
Intevac Vision Systems, Carlsbad  *Also Called: Intevac Photonics  Inc (P-14788)*
Intex Properties S Bay Corp (PA) ...................................... D ...... 310 549-5400
  4001 Via Oro Ave Ste 210 Long Beach (90810)  *(P-16936)*
Intexforms Inc .................................................................... D ...... 916 388-9933
  9293 Beatty Dr Sacramento (95826)  *(P-7592)*
Intimo Industry, Vernon  *Also Called: Pjy  LLC (P-2424)*
Intra Aerospace LLC .......................................................... E ...... 909 476-0343
  10671 Civic Center Dr Rancho Cucamonga (91730)  *(P-10890)*
Intra Storage Systems Inc .................................................. E ...... 714 373-2346
  7100 Honold Cir Garden Grove (92841)  *(P-9289)*
Intri-Plex Technologies  Inc (HQ) ....................................... C ...... 805 683-3414
  751 S Kellogg Ave Goleta (93117)  *(P-10891)*
Intri-Plex Technologies  Inc ................................................ E ...... 805 845-9600
  751 S Kellogg Ave Goleta (93117)  *(P-19457)*
Intricast Company Incorporated ......................................... E ...... 408 988-6200
  2160 Walsh Ave Santa Clara (95050)  *(P-7866)*
Intuit, Mountain View  *Also Called: Intuit Inc (P-18437)*
Intuit Financial Services, Redwood City  *Also Called: Digital Insight Corporation (P-19016)*
Intuit Financing Inc ............................................................ E ...... 605 944-6000
  2700 Coast Ave Mountain View (94043)  *(P-18429)*
Intuit Inc ............................................................................. D ...... 818 436-7800
  21650 Oxnard St Ste 2200 Woodland Hills (91367)  *(P-18430)*
Intuit Inc ............................................................................. E ...... 650 944-6000
  2650 Casey Ave Mountain View (94043)  *(P-18431)*
Intuit Inc ............................................................................. C ...... 650 944-6000
  2535 Garcia Ave Mountain View (94043)  *(P-18432)*
Intuit Inc ............................................................................. B ...... 858 780-2846
  7535 Torrey Santa Fe Rd San Diego (92129)  *(P-18433)*
Intuit Inc ............................................................................. F ...... 650 944-6000
  180 Jefferson Dr Menlo Park (94025)  *(P-18434)*
Intuit Inc ............................................................................. E ...... 858 215-8000
  4760 Eastgate Mall San Diego (92121)  *(P-18435)*
Intuit Inc ............................................................................. B ...... 858 215-8000
  7545 Torrey Santa Fe Rd San Diego (92129)  *(P-18436)*
Intuit Inc (PA) .................................................................... D ...... 650 944-6000
  2700 Coast Ave Mountain View (94043)  *(P-18437)*
Intuitive Srgcal Oprations Inc (HQ) .................................... E ...... 408 523-2100
  1020 Kifer Rd Sunnyvale (94086)  *(P-15126)*
INTUITIVE SURGICAL, Sunnyvale  *Also Called: Intuitive Surgical  Inc (P-15365)*
Intuitive Surgical  Inc ......................................................... E ...... 408 523-4000
  1266 Kifer Rd Bldg 101 Sunnyvale (94086)  *(P-15127)*
Intuitive Surgical  Inc ......................................................... E ...... 408 523-7314
  1250 Kifer Rd Sunnyvale (94086)  *(P-15128)*
Intuitive Surgical  Inc ......................................................... F ...... 408 523-7579
  3410 Central Expy Santa Clara (95051)  *(P-15129)*
Intuitive Surgical  Inc (PA) ................................................. C ...... 408 523-2100
  1020 Kifer Rd Sunnyvale (94086)  *(P-15365)*
Intuity Medical  Inc ............................................................. D ...... 408 530-1700
  3500 W Warren Ave Fremont (94538)  *(P-15130)*
Invapharm  Inc (PA) ........................................................... E ...... 909 757-1818
  1320 W Mission Blvd Ontario (91762)  *(P-17732)*
Invecas, San Jose  *Also Called: Invecas  Inc (P-12499)*
Invecas Inc (HQ) ................................................................ E ...... 408 758-5636
  2655 Seely Ave San Jose (95134)  *(P-12499)*
Inveco Inc ........................................................................... E ...... 949 378-3850
  440 Fair Dr Ste 200 Costa Mesa (92626)  *(P-8975)*
Invelop Inc ......................................................................... E ...... 818 772-2887
  9711 Mason Ave Chatsworth (91311)  *(P-9360)*
Invenios, Santa Barbara  *Also Called: Picosys Incorporated (P-9689)*
Invenios  LLC ..................................................................... D ...... 805 962-3333
  320 N Nopal St Santa Barbara (93103)  *(P-7228)*
Invenlux Corporation .......................................................... E ...... 626 277-4163
  168 Mason Way Ste B5 City Of Industry (91746)  *(P-12500)*
Invensas Corporation ......................................................... F ...... 408 324-5100
  3025 Orchard Pkwy San Jose (95134)  *(P-12501)*
Invensense, San Jose  *Also Called: Invensense  Inc (P-14199)*
Invensense Inc (HQ) .......................................................... C ...... 408 501-2200
  1745 Technology Dr Ste 200 San Jose (95110)  *(P-14199)*
Invensys Climate Controls, Long Beach  *Also Called: Schneider Elc Buildings LLC (P-13303)*

**Inverse Solutions Inc** ..................................................... E ...... 925 931-9500
3922 Valley Ave Ste A Pleasanton (94566) *(P-10892)*

**Investment Enterprises Inc (PA)** ........................................ E ...... 818 464-3800
8230 Haskell Ave Ste 8240 Van Nuys (91406) *(P-4900)*

**Investopedia LLC** ............................................................. E ...... 510 985-7400
555 12th St Ste 500 Oakland (94607) *(P-18438)*

**Investors Business Daily Inc (HQ)** ..................................... C ...... 800 831-2525
5900 Wilshire Blvd Ste 2950 Los Angeles (90036) *(P-4136)*

**Invisble Prtection Systems Inc** ........................................... E ...... 213 254-0463
8847 S Halldale Ave Los Angeles (90047) *(P-18439)*

**Invisible Protection Svcs Inc, Los Angeles** Also Called: Invisble Prtection Systems Inc *(P-18439)*

**Invitrogen Corp** .................................................................. F ...... 760 476-7055
1600 Faraday Ave Carlsbad (92008) *(P-14679)*

**Invitrogen Ip Holdings Inc** .................................................. D ...... 760 603-7200
5791 Van Allen Way Carlsbad (92008) *(P-14680)*

**Invoice2go LLC** .................................................................. D ...... 650 300-5180
2317 Broadway St Fl 2 Redwood City (94063) *(P-18440)*

**Invotech Systems Inc** .......................................................... F ...... 818 461-9800
20951 Burbank Blvd Ste B Woodland Hills (91367) *(P-18441)*

**Invuity Inc** ........................................................................... C ...... 415 665-2100
444 De Haro St Ste 110 San Francisco (94107) *(P-15131)*

**Inw Living Ecology Opco LLC (DH)** ................................... E ...... 951 371-4982
240 Crouse Dr Corona (92879) *(P-1313)*

**Inwesco Incorporated (HQ)** ................................................ D ...... 626 334-7115
746 N Coney Ave Azusa (91702) *(P-7644)*

**INX Digital Intl, San Leandro** Also Called: INX International Ink Co *(P-6258)*

**INX International Ink Co** ..................................................... F ...... 630 382-1800
16700 Valley View Ave Ste 275 La Mirada (90638) *(P-6257)*

**INX International Ink Co** ..................................................... E ...... 510 895-8001
2125 Williams St San Leandro (94577) *(P-6258)*

**INX International Ink Co** ..................................................... F ...... 707 693-2990
1000 Business Park Dr Dixon (95620) *(P-6259)*

**INX International Ink Co** ..................................................... E ...... 562 404-5664
13821 Marquardt Ave Santa Fe Springs (90670) *(P-6299)*

**INX INTERNATIONAL INK CO, La Mirada** Also Called: INX International Ink Co *(P-6257)*

**INX Prints Inc** ..................................................................... D ...... 949 660-9190
1802 Kettering Irvine (92614) *(P-2499)*

**Inyoag LLC** ......................................................................... E ...... 775 427-8345
13 Utah Dr Darwin (93522) *(P-107)*

**Io Semiconductor Incorporated** ......................................... E ...... 858 362-4074
4795 Eastgate Mall San Diego (92121) *(P-12502)*

**Iog Products LLC** ............................................................... F ...... 818 350-5070
9737 Lurline Ave Chatsworth (91311) *(P-12503)*

**IONIS, Carlsbad** Also Called: Ionis Pharmaceuticals Inc *(P-5503)*

**Ionis Pharmaceuticals Inc** .................................................. D ...... 760 931-9200
1896 Rutherford Rd Carlsbad (92008) *(P-5502)*

**Ionis Pharmaceuticals Inc (PA)** ........................................... A ...... 760 931-9200
2855 Gazelle Ct Carlsbad (92010) *(P-5503)*

**Ionis Pharmaceuticals Inc** .................................................. C ...... 760 603-3567
2282 Faraday Ave Carlsbad (92008) *(P-5504)*

**Ionis Pharmaceuticals Inc** .................................................. F ...... 760 603-2631
1767 Avenida Segovia Oceanside (92056) *(P-5505)*

**Ios Optics, Santa Clara** Also Called: Integrated Optical Svcs Corp *(P-6087)*

**Iosafe Inc** ............................................................................ F ...... 888 984-6723
10600 Industrial Ave Ste 120 Roseville (95678) *(P-10248)*

**Iosemi, San Diego** Also Called: Io Semiconductor Incorporated *(P-12502)*

**Iovance Biotherapeutics Inc (PA)** ....................................... B ...... 650 260-7120
825 Industrial Rd Fl 4 San Carlos (94070) *(P-5506)*

**Ip Corporation** .................................................................... E ...... 323 757-1801
12335 S Van Ness Ave Hawthorne (90250) *(P-5167)*

**Ipac, Dublin** Also Called: Interntnal Ptro Pdts Addtves I *(P-6395)*

**Ipac Inc** ............................................................................... F ...... 925 556-5530
7600 Dublin Blvd Ste 240 Dublin (94568) *(P-6396)*

**IPC Cal Flex Inc** .................................................................. E ...... 714 952-0373
13337 South St # 307 Cerritos (90703) *(P-12137)*

**Ipd, Carson** Also Called: Industrial Parts Depot LLC *(P-16819)*

**Ipolipo Inc** ........................................................................... D ...... 408 916-5290
440 N Wolfe Rd Sunnyvale (94085) *(P-18442)*

**Ipr Software, Encino** Also Called: Ipr Software Inc *(P-18443)*

**Ipr Software Inc** .................................................................. E ...... 310 499-0544
16501 Ventura Blvd Ste 424 Encino (91436) *(P-18443)*

**Ipraxa Software & Services** ................................................ F ...... 800 459-7668
663 Trousdale St Oak Park (91377) *(P-18444)*

**Ips Corporation (HQ)** .......................................................... C ...... 310 898-3300
455 W Victoria St Compton (90220) *(P-6234)*

**Ips Group Inc (PA)** .............................................................. E ...... 858 404-0607
7737 Kenamar Ct San Diego (92121) *(P-14481)*

**Ips Industries Inc** ................................................................ D ...... 562 623-2555
12641 166th St Cerritos (90703) *(P-6866)*

**Ipt Holding Inc (PA)** ............................................................ F ...... 805 683-3414
751 S Kellogg Ave Goleta (93117) *(P-8853)*

**Ipt Inc** .................................................................................. F ...... 559 266-6100
150 Santa Fe Ave Fresno (93721) *(P-16387)*

**Iq Cosmetics, El Segundo** Also Called: Intelligent Beauty LLC *(P-17708)*

**Iq Power Tools, Perris** Also Called: Jpl Global LLC *(P-16791)*

**Iq-Analog Corporation** ....................................................... E ...... 858 200-0388
12348 High Bluff Dr Ste 110 San Diego (92130) *(P-12504)*

**Iqair North America Inc** ...................................................... E ...... 877 715-4247
14351 Firestone Blvd La Mirada (90638) *(P-9990)*

**Iqd Frequency Products Inc** ............................................... E ...... 408 250-1435
592 N Tercero Cir Palm Springs (92262) *(P-13006)*

**Iqms LLC (HQ)** .................................................................... C ...... 805 227-1122
2231 Wisteria Ln Paso Robles (93446) *(P-18445)*

**Irca Group USA LLC** .......................................................... D ...... 678 679-3292
33063 Western Ave Union City (94587) *(P-1341)*

**Ircamera LLC** ...................................................................... E ...... 805 965-9650
30 S Calle Cesar Chavez Santa Barbara (93103) *(P-14789)*

**IRD, La Jolla** Also Called: International RES Dev Corp Nev *(P-13173)*

**IRD Acquisitions LLC** ......................................................... F ...... 530 210-2966
12810 Earhart Ave Auburn (95602) *(P-15604)*

**Irhythm Technologies Inc (PA)** ........................................... E ...... 415 632-5700
699 8th St Ste 600 San Francisco (94103) *(P-15132)*

**IRIDEX, Mountain View** Also Called: Iridex Corporation *(P-15548)*

**Iridex Corporation (PA)** ...................................................... C ...... 650 940-4700
1212 Terra Bella Ave Mountain View (94043) *(P-15548)*

**Iris Group Inc** ...................................................................... C ...... 760 431-1103
1675 Faraday Ave Carlsbad (92008) *(P-4901)*

**Irish Interiors Inc (HQ)** ........................................................ C ...... 949 559-0930
5511 Skylab Rd Ste 101 Huntington Beach (92647) *(P-13875)*

**Irish Interiors Inc** ................................................................ C ...... 562 344-1700
5511 Skylab Rd Ste 101 Huntington Beach (92647) *(P-13876)*

**Irish Interiors Holdings Inc** ................................................ E ...... 949 559-0930
1729 Apollo Ct Seal Beach (90740) *(P-13877)*

**IRISH INTERIORS HOLDINGS, INC., Seal Beach** Also Called: Irish Interiors Holdings Inc *(P-13877)*

**Irish International** ............................................................... C ...... 949 559-0930
5511 Skylab Rd Huntington Beach (92647) *(P-13714)*

**Irislogic Inc** ......................................................................... E ...... 408 855-8741
2336 Walsh Ave Ste F Santa Clara (95051) *(P-18446)*

**IRM, Madera** Also Called: Innovtive Rttional Molding Inc *(P-6864)*

**Iron Beds of America, Los Angeles** Also Called: Wesley Allen Inc *(P-3516)*

**Iron Dog Fabrication Inc** .................................................... F ...... 707 579-7831
3450 Regional Pkwy Ste E Santa Rosa (95403) *(P-8154)*

**Iron Grip Barbell Company Inc** .......................................... D ...... 714 850-6900
11377 Markon Dr Garden Grove (92841) *(P-15831)*

**Iron Horse Interactive, San Ramon** Also Called: Iron Horse Ventures LLC *(P-19532)*

**Iron Horse Ventures LLC** ................................................... E ...... 925 415-6141
6111 Bollinger Canyon Rd Ste 555 San Ramon (94583) *(P-19532)*

**Iron Horse Vineyards** ......................................................... E ...... 707 887-1909
9786 Ross Station Rd Sebastopol (95472) *(P-1620)*

**Ironies** .................................................................................. E ...... 510 644-2100
2200 Central St Ste D Richmond (94801) *(P-3571)*

**Ironman Inc** ......................................................................... E ...... 818 341-0980
20555 Superior St Chatsworth (91311) *(P-19200)*

**Ironridge, Hayward** Also Called: Ironridge Inc *(P-16768)*

**Ironridge Inc (DH)** ............................................................... E ...... 800 227-9523
28357 Industrial Blvd Hayward (94545) *(P-16768)*

**Ironsource, San Francisco** Also Called: Supersonic ADS Inc *(P-16055)*

**Ironwood Electric Inc** ......................................................... E ...... 714 630-2350
13 Ashton Mission Viejo (92692) *(P-13255)*

**Ironwood Fabrication Inc** ................................................... F ...... 714 576-7320
761 Monroe Way Placentia (92870) *(P-8778)*

## ALPHABETIC SECTION

**Ironwood Packaging LLC** .................................................. E ...... 909 581-0077
8975 Cottage Ave Rancho Cucamonga (91730) *(P-3929)*

**Irp, San Clemente** *Also Called: International Rubber Pdts Inc (P-6504)*

**Irritec Usa Inc** ....................................................................... D ...... 559 275-8825
1420 N Irritec Way Fresno (93703) *(P-9361)*

**Irrometer Company Inc** ...................................................... F ...... 951 682-9505
1425 Palmyrita Ave Riverside (92507) *(P-14886)*

**Irtronix Inc** .......................................................................... E ...... 310 787-1100
20900 Normandie Ave Bldg B Torrance (90502) *(P-11425)*

**Irvine Biomedical Inc** ......................................................... C ...... 949 851-3053
2375 Morse Ave Irvine (92614) *(P-15133)*

**Irvine Electronics LLC** ...................................................... D ...... 949 250-0315
1601 Alton Pkwy Ste A Irvine (92606) *(P-12138)*

**Irvine Electronics Inc, Irvine** *Also Called: Irvine Electronics LLC (P-12138)*

**Irvine Scientific, Santa Ana** *Also Called: Fujifilm Irvine Scientific Inc (P-5832)*

**Irvine Sensors, Costa Mesa** *Also Called: Isc8 Inc (P-13256)*

**Irvine Sensors Corporation** ................................................ E ...... 714 444-8700
3000 Airway Ave Ste A1 Costa Mesa (92626) *(P-12505)*

**Irwin Aviation Inc** ............................................................... E ...... 951 372-9555
225 Airport Cir Corona (92878) *(P-13878)*

**Isabell's Honey Farm, Burbank** *Also Called: Honey Isabells Inc (P-69)*

**Isabelle Handbag Inc** ......................................................... E ...... 323 277-9888
3155 Bandini Blvd Unit A Vernon (90058) *(P-7145)*

**Isc8 Inc** ............................................................................... E ...... 714 549-8211
151 Kalmus Dr Ste A203 Costa Mesa (92626) *(P-13256)*

**ISE Corporation** .................................................................. C ...... 858 413-1720
12302 Kerran St Poway (92064) *(P-19458)*

**ISE Labs Inc (DH)** ............................................................. C ...... 510 687-2500
46800 Bayside Pkwy Fremont (94538) *(P-19505)*

**Isec Incorporated** ............................................................... C ...... 858 279-9085
5735 Kearny Villa Rd Ste 105 San Diego (92123) *(P-14341)*

**Isiqalo LLC** ......................................................................... B ...... 714 683-2820
5610 Daniels St Chino (91710) *(P-2474)*

**Island Powder Coating** ...................................................... E ...... 626 279-2460
1830 Tyler Ave South El Monte (91733) *(P-9082)*

**Island Products, Buena Park** *Also Called: Island Snacks Inc (P-1314)*

**Island Snacks Inc** ............................................................... E ...... 714 994-1228
7650 Stage Rd Buena Park (90621) *(P-1314)*

**Island View Outfitters, Goleta** *Also Called: Island View Print Works Inc (P-4902)*

**Island View Print Works Inc** .............................................. E ...... 805 845-1333
6565 Trigo Rd Ste A Goleta (93117) *(P-4902)*

**Isn Global Enterprises Inc** ................................................. F ...... 909 670-0601
987 W Foothill Blvd Ste 200 Claremont (91711) *(P-19017)*

**Isolatek International, San Bernardino** *Also Called: Usmpc Buyer Inc (P-7583)*

**Isolation Network Inc (PA)** ................................................ D ...... 818 212-2600
55 Francisco St Ste 350 San Francisco (94133) *(P-11669)*

**Isolink Inc** ........................................................................... E ...... 408 946-1968
880 Yosemite Way Milpitas (95035) *(P-13007)*

**Isolutecom Inc (PA)** ........................................................... E ...... 805 498-6259
9 Northam Ave Newbury Park (91320) *(P-18447)*

**Isomedia LLC** ..................................................................... E ...... 510 668-1656
43297 Osgood Rd Fremont (94539) *(P-11736)*

**Isomedix Operations Inc** .................................................... E ...... 909 390-9942
1000 Sarah Pl Ontario (91761) *(P-15366)*

**Isomedix Operations Inc** .................................................... D ...... 951 694-9340
43425 Business Park Dr Temecula (92590) *(P-15367)*

**Isotope Products Lab, Valencia** *Also Called: Eckert Zegler Isotope Pdts Inc (P-14863)*

**Isound, Torrance** *Also Called: Dreamgear LLC (P-15745)*

**Isovac Engineering Inc** ...................................................... E ...... 818 552-6200
614 Justin Ave Glendale (91201) *(P-19098)*

**Isp Granule Products Inc** .................................................. C ...... 209 274-2930
1900 Hwy 104 Ione (95640) *(P-7568)*

**Issac, Tustin** *Also Called: Trellborg Sling Sltions US Inc (P-15287)*

**Issac Medical Inc** ............................................................... B ...... 805 239-4284
2761 Walnut Ave Tustin (92780) *(P-15134)*

**Issio Solutions Inc** ............................................................. E ...... 888 994-7746
1212 Broadway Plz Ste 1200 Walnut Creek (94596) *(P-18448)*

**Issuu Inc (PA)** .................................................................... E ...... 844 477-8800
131 Lytton Ave Palo Alto (94301) *(P-4419)*

**Ista Pharmaceuticals Inc** ................................................... B ...... 949 788-6000
50 Technology Dr Irvine (92618) *(P-5507)*

**Istarusa Group** .................................................................... E ...... 888 989-1189
727 Phillips Rowland Heights (91748) *(P-10170)*

**ISU Petasys Corp** .............................................................. D ...... 818 833-5800
12930 Bradley Ave Sylmar (91342) *(P-12139)*

**It Campus, Vernon** *Also Called: It Jeans Inc (P-2766)*

**It Concepts LLC** ................................................................ F ...... 925 401-0010
1244 Quarry Ln Ste B Pleasanton (94566) *(P-14790)*

**It Jeans Inc** ........................................................................ E ...... 323 588-2156
2425 E 38th St Vernon (90058) *(P-2766)*

**It's Delish, North Hollywood** *Also Called: Mave Enterprises Inc (P-1320)*

**Italix Company Inc** ............................................................. F ...... 408 988-2487
120 Mast St Ste A Morgan Hill (95037) *(P-9083)*

**Itc, San Diego** *Also Called: International Technidyne Corp (P-15123)*

**Itc Nexus Holding Company, San Diego** *Also Called: Accriva Dgnostics Holdings Inc (P-14948)*

**Itc Sftware Slutions Group LLC (PA)** ................................ B ...... 877 248-2774
201 Sandpointe Ave Ste 305 Santa Ana (92707) *(P-18449)*

**Itc Solutions & Services Group, Santa Ana** *Also Called: Itc Sftware Slutions Group LLC (P-18449)*

**Itech, San Diego** *Also Called: Intelligent Technologies LLC (P-11374)*

**Iteris Inc** ............................................................................. F ...... 510 540-7647
2150 Shattuck Ave Ste 175 Berkeley (94704) *(P-12001)*

**ITI Electro-Optic Corporation (PA)** ................................... E ...... 310 445-8900
11500 W Olympic Blvd 400 Los Angeles (90064) *(P-14425)*

**ITI Electro-Optic Corporation** ............................................ E ...... 310 312-4526
1500 Olympia Blvd Ste 400 Los Angeles (90021) *(P-14426)*

**Itochu Aviation Inc (DH)** .................................................... E ...... 310 640-2770
222 N Pacific Coast Hwy Ste 2200 El Segundo (90245) *(P-16920)*

**Itouchless Housewares Pdts Inc** ...................................... E ...... 650 578-0578
777 Mariners Island Blvd Ste 125 San Mateo (94404) *(P-6867)*

**Itron Networked Solutions Inc (HQ)** ................................. B ...... 669 770-4000
230 W Tasman Dr San Jose (95134) *(P-16337)*

**Itsco, Cypress** *Also Called: Interntional Tech Systems Corp (P-16706)*

**Itsj Group Inc** .................................................................... E ...... 408 609-6392
148 E Brokaw Rd San Jose (95112) *(P-10893)*

**ITT Aerospace Controls LLC (HQ)** ................................... D ...... 315 568-7258
28150 Industry Dr Valencia (91355) *(P-13879)*

**ITT Aerospace Controls LLC** ............................................ B ...... 661 295-4000
28150 Industry Dr Valencia (91355) *(P-13880)*

**ITT Cannon LLC** ................................................................ C ...... 714 557-4700
56 Technology Dr Irvine (92618) *(P-11326)*

**ITT LLC** ............................................................................... D ...... 562 908-4144
3951 Capitol Ave City Of Industry (90601) *(P-11327)*

**ITT LLC** ............................................................................... C ...... 707 523-2300
500 Tesconi Cir Santa Rosa (95401) *(P-11328)*

**Ittavi Inc** .............................................................................. E ...... 866 246-4408
1100 La Avenida St Ste A Mountain View (94043) *(P-18450)*

**Ituner Networks Corporation** ............................................. F ...... 510 573-0783
44244 Fremont Blvd Fremont (94538) *(P-10391)*

**ITW Alpine, Sacramento** *Also Called: ITW Blding Cmponents Group Inc (P-8318)*

**ITW Blding Cmponents Group Inc** .................................... E ...... 916 387-0116
8801 Folsom Blvd Ste 107 Sacramento (95826) *(P-8318)*

**ITW Rippey, El Dorado Hills** *Also Called: Rippey Corporation (P-16546)*

**ITW Space Bag, San Diego** *Also Called: New West Products Inc (P-6928)*

**Ivanti Inc** ............................................................................. D ...... 408 343-8181
150 Mathilda Pl Ste 302 Sunnyvale (94086) *(P-18451)*

**Ivantis Inc (PA)** .................................................................. F ...... 949 600-9650
201 Technology Dr Irvine (92618) *(P-15135)*

**Ivar's Displays, Ontario** *Also Called: Ivars Display (P-3658)*

**Ivars Display (PA)** .............................................................. D ...... 909 923-2761
2314 E Locust Ct Ontario (91761) *(P-3658)*

**Ivc Inc** ................................................................................. F ...... 215 671-1400
4695 Macarthur Ct Ste 1400 Newport Beach (92660) *(P-5508)*

**Ives Bay, Napa** *Also Called: Ives Bay LLC (P-1621)*

**Ives Bay LLC (PA)** ............................................................. E ...... 707 266-6899
50 Technology Ct Napa (94558) *(P-1621)*

**Ivigen, Torrance** *Also Called: Igenomix Usa Inc (P-15113)*

**Ivu Traffic Technologies Inc** .............................................. F ...... 415 655-2200
2612 8th St Ste A Berkeley (94710) *(P-13521)*

**Iwatt Inc (DH)** ..................................................................... E ...... 408 374-4200
6024 Silver Creek Valley Rd San Jose (95138) *(P-12506)*

# ALPHABETIC SECTION

Iwco Direct - Downey, Downey *Also Called: Instant Web LLC (P-4649)*
Iwcus, Walnut *Also Called: Infinity Watch Corporation (P-15987)*
Iwerks Entertainment Inc ................................................................. D ...... 661 678-1800
   25040 Avenue Tibbitts Ste F Valencia (91355) *(P-13257)*
Iworks, Commerce *Also Called: Iworks Us Inc (P-11426)*
Iworks Us Inc ............................................................................... D ...... 323 278-8363
   2501 S Malt Ave Commerce (90040) *(P-11426)*
Iws Predictive Technologies, Yorba Linda *Also Called: Inflight Warning Systems Inc (P-13873)*
Ixi Technology, Yorba Linda *Also Called: Ixi Technology Inc (P-10171)*
Ixi Technology Inc .......................................................................... E ...... 714 221-5000
   22705 Savi Ranch Pkwy Ste 200 Yorba Linda (92887) *(P-10171)*
Ixia (HQ) ........................................................................................ C ...... 818 871-1800
   26601 Agoura Rd Calabasas (91302) *(P-14539)*
Ixia ................................................................................................ E ...... 818 871-1800
   26701 Agoura Rd Calabasas (91302) *(P-14540)*
Ixia, Santa Clara *Also Called: Net Optics Inc (P-18573)*
Ixia Communications, Calabasas *Also Called: Ixia (P-14540)*
Ixys LLC (HQ) ............................................................................... D ...... 408 457-9000
   1590 Buckeye Dr Milpitas (95035) *(P-12507)*
Ixys Intgrted Crcits Div AV In ........................................................ A ...... 949 831-4622
   145 Columbia Aliso Viejo (92656) *(P-12508)*
Ixys Long Beach Inc (DH) ............................................................. E ...... 562 296-6584
   2500 Mira Mar Ave Long Beach (90815) *(P-12509)*
Izabel Karcher, Owner, Clovis *Also Called: Karcher Design (P-8008)*
Izola, San Diego *Also Called: Tallgrass Pictures LLC (P-1246)*
J-TECH ......................................................................................... C ...... 310 533-6700
   548 Amapola Ave Torrance (90501) *(P-12885)*
J & A Jeffery Inc ............................................................................ E ...... 707 678-0369
   395 Industrial Way Ste B Dixon (95620) *(P-16153)*
J & C Custom Cabinets Inc .......................................................... F ...... 916 638-3400
   11451 Elks Cir Rancho Cordova (95742) *(P-3572)*
J & D Laboratories Inc ................................................................. B ...... 760 734-6800
   2710 Progress St Vista (92081) *(P-5246)*
J & F Design Inc .......................................................................... D ...... 323 526-4444
   2042 Garfield Ave Commerce (90040) *(P-2767)*
J & F Machine Inc ........................................................................ E ...... 714 527-3499
   6401 Global Dr Cypress (90630) *(P-10894)*
J & H Production ........................................................................... E ...... 323 261-6600
   4481 S Santa Fe Ave Vernon (90058) *(P-3010)*
J & J Processing Inc .................................................................... E ...... 562 926-2333
   14715 Anson Ave Santa Fe Springs (90670) *(P-2010)*
J & J Quality Door Inc .................................................................. E ...... 209 948-5013
   1233 E Ronald St Stockton (95205) *(P-3148)*
J & J Snack Foods Corp Cal (HQ) ................................................ D ...... 323 581-0171
   5353 S Downey Rd Los Angeles (90058) *(P-1278)*
J & L Cstm Plstic Extrsons Inc ..................................................... E ...... 626 442-0711
   850 Lawson St City Of Industry (91748) *(P-6868)*
J & M Products Inc ....................................................................... D ...... 818 837-0205
   1647 Truman St San Fernando (91340) *(P-8006)*
J & M Richman Corporation ......................................................... E ...... 800 422-9646
   1501 Beach St Montebello (90640) *(P-2991)*
J & R Bottling and Distributing Inc ............................................... E ...... 323 724-4076
   1130 S Vail Ave Montebello (90640) *(P-1895)*
J & R Concrete Products Inc ....................................................... E ...... 951 943-5855
   440 W Markham St Perris (92571) *(P-7346)*
J & R Machine Works ................................................................... E ...... 661 945-8826
   45420 60th St W Lancaster (93536) *(P-10895)*
J & S Inc ....................................................................................... E ...... 310 719-7144
   229 E Gardena Blvd Gardena (90248) *(P-10896)*
J A English II Inc ........................................................................... E ...... 760 598-5333
   1333 Keystone Way Vista (92081) *(P-6869)*
J A-Co Machine Works LLC ........................................................ E ...... 877 429-8175
   4 Carbonero Way Scotts Valley (95066) *(P-10897)*
J and D Stl Fbrication Repr LP .................................................... F ...... 805 928-9674
   2360 Westgate Rd Santa Maria (93455) *(P-19201)*
J and K Manufacturing Inc ........................................................... E ...... 562 630-8417
   14701 Garfield Ave Paramount (90723) *(P-10898)*
J and L Industries, El Segundo *Also Called: Aerospace Engrg Support Corp (P-13756)*
J B Enterprises, Sacramento *Also Called: John Boyd Enterprises Inc (P-13522)*

J B Precision, Campbell *Also Called: Jessee Brothers Machine Sp Inc (P-10907)*
J B Tool Inc .................................................................................. F ...... 714 993-7173
   350 E Orangethorpe Ave Ste 6 Placentia (92870) *(P-10899)*
J B3d, Orange *Also Called: John Bishop Design Inc (P-15994)*
J C Ford Company (HQ) ............................................................... E ...... 714 871-7361
   901 S Leslie St La Habra (90631) *(P-9799)*
J C Precision, Rancho Cucamonga *Also Called: JCPM Inc (P-10905)*
J C Trimming Company Inc ......................................................... D ...... 323 235-4458
   3800 S Hill St Los Angeles (90037) *(P-2705)*
J Deluca Fish Company Inc ........................................................ E ...... 310 221-6500
   505 E Harry Bridges Blvd Wilmington (90744) *(P-2055)*
J F Duncan Industries Inc (PA) ................................................... D ...... 562 862-4269
   4380 Ayers Ave Vernon (90058) *(P-10567)*
J F I, Los Angeles *Also Called: Jet Fleet International Corp (P-17773)*
J F McCaughin Co ........................................................................ F ...... 626 573-3000
   2628 River Ave Rosemead (91770) *(P-15886)*
J Filippi Vintage Co (PA) .............................................................. F ...... 909 899-5755
   12467 Baseline Rd Rancho Cucamonga (91739) *(P-17628)*
J H Textiles Inc ............................................................................. E ...... 323 585-4124
   2301 E 55th St Vernon (90058) *(P-2547)*
J Hellman Frozen Foods Inc (PA) ............................................... E ...... 213 243-9105
   1601 E Olympic Blvd Ste 200 Los Angeles (90021) *(P-1008)*
J Heyri Inc .................................................................................... E ...... 323 588-1234
   219 E 32nd St Los Angeles (90011) *(P-2671)*
J I Machine Company Inc ............................................................ E ...... 858 695-1787
   9720 Distribution Ave San Diego (92121) *(P-10900)*
J J Foil Company Inc ................................................................... E ...... 714 998-9920
   1734 W Sequoia Ave Orange (92868) *(P-3997)*
J L Cooper Electronics Inc .......................................................... E ...... 310 322-9990
   142 Arena St El Segundo (90245) *(P-13008)*
J L F/Lone Meadow, San Diego *Also Called: J L Furnishings LLC (P-3627)*
J L Fisher Inc ............................................................................... D ...... 818 846-8366
   1000 W Isabel St Burbank (91506) *(P-17856)*
J L Furnishings LLC ..................................................................... B ...... 310 605-6600
   1620 5th Ave Ste 400 San Diego (92101) *(P-3627)*
J L M C Inc ................................................................................... E ...... 909 947-2980
   1944 S Bon View Ave Ontario (91761) *(P-8155)*
J L Precision Sheet Metal, San Jose *Also Called: Laptalo Enterprises Inc (P-8484)*
J L Shepherd and Assoc Inc ........................................................ E ...... 818 898-2361
   1010 Arroyo St San Fernando (91340) *(P-14887)*
J Lohr Viney, San Jose *Also Called: J Lohr Winery Corporation (P-1623)*
J Lohr Warehouse, San Jose *Also Called: J Lohr Winery Corporation (P-1624)*
J Lohr Winery Corporation ........................................................... E ...... 805 239-8900
   6169 Airport Rd Paso Robles (93446) *(P-1622)*
J Lohr Winery Corporation (PA) ................................................... E ...... 408 288-5057
   1000 Lenzen Ave San Jose (95126) *(P-1623)*
J Lohr Winery Corporation ........................................................... E ...... 408 293-1345
   1935 S 10th St San Jose (95112) *(P-1624)*
J M I, Union City *Also Called: Jenson Mechanical Inc (P-10906)*
J M Smucker Company ................................................................ E ...... 805 487-5483
   800 Commercial Ave Oxnard (93030) *(P-895)*
J Manufacturing, Grass Valley *Also Called: Vossloh Signaling Usa Inc (P-8793)*
J Milano Co Inc ............................................................................ E ...... 209 944-0902
   910 W Charter Way Stockton (95206) *(P-16755)*
J Miller Canvas LLC .................................................................... E ...... 714 641-0052
   2429 S Birch St Santa Ana (92707) *(P-2528)*
J Miller Co Inc .............................................................................. E ...... 818 837-0181
   11537 Bradley Ave San Fernando (91340) *(P-6455)*
J P B Jewelry Box Co, Los Angeles *Also Called: Borodian Inc (P-3647)*
J P Graphics Inc .......................................................................... E ...... 408 235-8821
   3310 Woodward Ave Santa Clara (95054) *(P-4655)*
J P L, Fresno *Also Called: J P Lamborn Co (P-10503)*
J P Lamborn Co (PA) ................................................................... E ...... 559 650-2120
   3663 E Wawona Ave Fresno (93725) *(P-10503)*
J P Sportswear, Lynwood *Also Called: Aaron Corporation (P-2730)*
J Pedroncelli Winery Inc .............................................................. E ...... 707 857-3531
   1220 Canyon Rd Geyserville (95441) *(P-1625)*
J R Industries, Westlake Village *Also Called: Jri Inc (P-16711)*
J R Scientific, Woodland *Also Called: Mediatech Inc (P-5549)*
J R Scientific, Woodland *Also Called: Mediatech Inc (P-5848)*

## ALPHABETIC SECTION — Jain Farm Fresh Foods Inc

J Robert Scott Inc (PA) .......................................................... C ...... 310 680-4300
722 N La Cienega Blvd West Hollywood (90069) *(P-17062)*

J Roberts Design, La Mirada *Also Called: M3 Products Inc (P-3697)*

J S Hckley Archtctral Sgnage .................................................... E ...... 510 940-2608
1999 Alpine Way Hayward (94545) *(P-15991)*

J Summitt Inc ..................................................................... F ...... 562 236-5744
13834 Bettencourt St Cerritos (90703) *(P-3149)*

J T Walker Industries Inc ........................................................ A ...... 909 481-1909
9322 Hyssop Dr Rancho Cucamonga (91730) *(P-8269)*

J Talley Corporation (PA) ......................................................... D ...... 951 654-2123
989 W 7th St San Jacinto (92582) *(P-8629)*

J Vineyards & Winery, Healdsburg *Also Called: E & J Gallo Winery (P-12)*

J Vineyards & Winery LP .......................................................... D ...... 707 431-5400
11447 Old Redwood Hwy Healdsburg (95448) *(P-18)*

J W Bamford Inc .................................................................. F ...... 530 533-0732
4288 State Highway 70 Oroville (95965) *(P-3047)*

J W Floor Covering Inc ........................................................... C ...... 858 444-1214
3401 Enterprise Ave Hayward (94545) *(P-2241)*

J-M Manufacturing Company Inc .................................................... E ...... 559 651-2100
7501 W Goshen Ave Visalia (93291) *(P-5168)*

J-M Manufacturing Company Inc .................................................... E ...... 951 657-7400
23711 Rider St Perris (92570) *(P-5169)*

J-M Manufacturing Company Inc .................................................... D ...... 909 822-3009
10990 Hemlock Ave Fontana (92337) *(P-5170)*

J-M Manufacturing Company Inc .................................................... D ...... 209 982-1500
1051 Sperry Rd Stockton (95206) *(P-5171)*

J-M Manufacturing Company Inc (PA) ............................................... C ...... 310 693-8200
5200 W Century Blvd Los Angeles (90045) *(P-6598)*

J-Mark Company, Vista *Also Called: J-Mark Manufacturing Inc (P-8854)*

J-Mark Manufacturing Inc ......................................................... E ...... 760 727-6956
2480 Coral St Vista (92081) *(P-8854)*

J.L. Haley, Rancho Cordova *Also Called: Vander-Bend Manufacturing Inc (P-11169)*

J&D 2050 Wardrobe Inc A California Corporation ................................... C ...... 209 384-1000
2050 Wardrobe Ave Merced (95341) *(P-4903)*

J&E Conveyor Services, Lake Elsinore *Also Called: Jose Perez (P-9488)*

J&K Welding Co Inc ............................................................... E ...... 909 226-1372
6815 Foxtail Ct Rancho Cucamonga (91739) *(P-19202)*

J&L Eppig Brewing LLC ............................................................ F ...... 760 295-2009
1347 Keystone Way Ste C Vista (92081) *(P-1436)*

J&M Manufacturing Inc ............................................................ E ...... 707 795-8223
430 Aaron St Cotati (94931) *(P-13009)*

J&N Engineering Inc .............................................................. E ...... 408 680-1810
1310 N 4th St San Jose (95112) *(P-9557)*

J&R Taylor Brothers Assoc Inc .................................................... D ...... 626 334-9301
16321 Arrow Hwy Irwindale (91706) *(P-1103)*

J&S Goodwin Inc (HQ) ............................................................. D ...... 714 956-4040
5753 E Santa Ana Canyon Rd Ste G-355 Anaheim (92807) *(P-9525)*

J&S Machine Works, Sylmar *Also Called: Kay & James Inc (P-10922)*

J2 Llc ............................................................................ F ...... 760 930-1738
2251 Faraday Ave Ste A Carlsbad (92008) *(P-2624)*

J2 Global Communications, Santa Barbara *Also Called: Efaxcom (P-10360)*

J2m Test Solutions Inc ........................................................... D ...... 571 333-0291
13225 Gregg St Poway (92064) *(P-14541)*

Jab Foods, Santa Clarita *Also Called: Jeckys Best Inc (P-17122)*

Jabil, San Jose *Also Called: Jabil Inc (P-12141)*

Jabil Chad Automation, Anaheim *Also Called: Jabil Inc (P-12143)*

Jabil Circuit, San Jose *Also Called: Jabil Inc (P-12145)*

Jabil Inc ......................................................................... C ...... 510 353-1000
4050 Technology Pl Fremont (94538) *(P-12140)*

Jabil Inc ......................................................................... D ...... 408 361-3200
1925 Lundy Ave San Jose (95131) *(P-12141)*

Jabil Inc ......................................................................... C ...... 408 360-3475
6375 San Ignacio Ave San Jose (95119) *(P-12142)*

Jabil Inc ......................................................................... E ...... 714 938-0080
1565 S Sinclair St Anaheim (92806) *(P-12143)*

Jabil Inc ......................................................................... E ...... 925 447-2000
122 Lindbergh Ave Livermore (94551) *(P-12144)*

Jabil Inc ......................................................................... B ...... 408 361-3200
30 Great Oaks Blvd San Jose (95119) *(P-12145)*

Jabil Silver Creek Inc (HQ) ...................................................... D ...... 669 255-2900
4050 Technology Pl Fremont (94538) *(P-19203)*

Jacada Autonomous Cx, Palo Alto *Also Called: Jacada Inc (P-18452)*

Jacada Inc ....................................................................... D ...... 770 352-1300
1001 Page Mill Rd Ste 100 Palo Alto (94304) *(P-18452)*

Jack Rubin & Sons Inc (PA) ....................................................... E ...... 310 635-5407
13103 S Alameda St Compton (90222) *(P-16621)*

Jackrabbit ....................................................................... F ...... 209 521-9325
1318 Dakota Ave Modesto (95358) *(P-9362)*

Jackrabbit (PA) .................................................................. D ...... 209 599-6118
471 Industrial Ave Ripon (95366) *(P-9363)*

JACKSAM CORP BLACKOUT, Newport Beach *Also Called: Jacksam Corporation (P-10021)*

Jacksam Corporation ............................................................. E ...... 800 605-3580
4440 Von Karman Ave Ste 220 Newport Beach (92660) *(P-10021)*

Jackson Engineering Co Inc ...................................................... E ...... 818 886-9567
9411 Winnetka Ave # A Chatsworth (91311) *(P-11215)*

Jackson Family Farms LLC ........................................................ F ...... 707 836-2047
5660 Skylane Blvd Santa Rosa (95403) *(P-1626)*

Jackson Family Wines Inc ........................................................ E ...... 707 836-2035
1190 Kittyhawk Blvd Santa Rosa (95403) *(P-1627)*

Jackson Family Wines Inc (PA) ................................................... D ...... 707 544-4000
425 Aviation Blvd Santa Rosa (95403) *(P-1628)*

Jackson Manufacturing LLC ....................................................... F ...... 213 399-9300
3515 W Washington Blvd Los Angeles (90018) *(P-896)*

Jackson-Mitchell Inc (PA) ....................................................... E ...... 209 667-0786
1240 South Ave Turlock (95380) *(P-840)*

Jaco Engineering ................................................................ E ...... 714 991-1680
879 S East St Anaheim (92805) *(P-10901)*

Jaco Machine Works, Scotts Valley *Also Called: J A-Co Machine Works LLC (P-10897)*

Jacobson Plastics Inc ........................................................... D ...... 562 433-4911
1401 Freeman Ave Long Beach (90804) *(P-6870)*

Jacquard Products, Healdsburg *Also Called: Rupert Gibbon & Spider Inc (P-6111)*

Jacuzzi Brands LLC .............................................................. E ...... 909 606-1416
14525 Monte Vista Ave Chino (91710) *(P-16154)*

Jacuzzi Family Vineyards LLC .................................................... F ...... 707 931-7500
24724 Arnold Dr Sonoma (95476) *(P-1629)*

Jacuzzi Family Winery, Sonoma *Also Called: Jacuzzi Family Vineyards LLC (P-1629)*

Jacuzzi Inc (DH) ................................................................ C ...... 909 606-7733
17872 Gillette Ave Ste 300 Irvine (92614) *(P-10568)*

Jacuzzi Outdoor Products, Irvine *Also Called: Jacuzzi Inc (P-10568)*

Jacuzzi Products Co (DH) ........................................................ C ...... 909 606-1416
13925 City Center Dr Ste 200 Chino Hills (91709) *(P-6680)*

Jacuzzi Products Co ............................................................. B ...... 909 548-7732
14525 Monte Vista Ave Chino (91710) *(P-6681)*

Jada Group Inc .................................................................. D ...... 626 810-8382
18521 Railroad St City Of Industry (91748) *(P-15754)*

Jada Toys, City Of Industry *Also Called: Jada Group Inc (P-15754)*

Jada Vineyards & Winery ......................................................... F ...... 805 226-4200
5620 Vineyard Dr Paso Robles (93446) *(P-1630)*

Jade Products, Brea *Also Called: Jade Range LLC (P-11390)*

Jade Range LLC .................................................................. C ...... 714 961-2400
2650 Orbiter St Brea (92821) *(P-11390)*

Jadra Inc ....................................................................... D ...... 916 921-3399
4600 Beloit Dr Sacramento (95838) *(P-6871)*

Jae Electronics Inc (HQ) ........................................................ E ...... 949 753-2600
142 Technology Dr Ste 100 Irvine (92618) *(P-16707)*

Jaffa Precision Engrg Inc ....................................................... F ...... 951 278-8797
12117 Madera Way Riverside (92503) *(P-10902)*

Jafra Cosmetics, Westlake Village *Also Called: Jafra Cosmetics Intl Inc (P-17709)*

Jafra Cosmetics Intl Inc (DH) ................................................... D ...... 805 449-3000
1 Baxter Way Ste 150 Westlake Village (91362) *(P-17709)*

JAGUAR ANIMAL HEALTH, San Francisco *Also Called: Jaguar Health Inc (P-5509)*

Jaguar Energy LLC (PA) .......................................................... E ...... 949 706-7060
2404 Colony Plz Newport Beach (92660) *(P-241)*

Jaguar Health Inc (PA) .......................................................... E ...... 415 371-8300
200 Pine St Fl 4 San Francisco (94104) *(P-5509)*

Jai Inc ......................................................................... E ...... 408 383-0300
6800 Santa Teresa Blvd San Jose (95119) *(P-16708)*

Jaime Enterprise Group .......................................................... F ...... 619 454-7681
3200 Paseo Village Way San Diego (92130) *(P-351)*

Jain Farm Fresh Foods Inc (DH) .................................................. E ...... 541 481-2522
2525 Cooper Ave Merced (95348) *(P-952)*

## ALPHABETIC SECTION

Jain Irrigation Inc .................................................................. F ...... 315 782-1170
  7545 Carroll Rd San Diego (92121) *(P-6425)*
Jakks, Santa Monica *Also Called: Jakks Pacific Inc (P-15756)*
Jakks Pacific Inc .................................................................. E ...... 909 594-7771
  21749 Baker Pkwy Walnut (91789) *(P-15755)*
Jakks Pacific Inc (PA) ........................................................... D ...... 424 268-9444
  2951 28th St Santa Monica (90405) *(P-15756)*
Jal Avionet USA (HQ) ........................................................... E ...... 310 606-1000
  300 Continental Blvd # 190 El Segundo (90245) *(P-16529)*
Jam City Inc (PA) .................................................................. E ...... 310 205-4800
  3562 Eastham Dr Culver City (90232) *(P-17553)*
Jam City Inc ......................................................................... D ...... 804 920-8760
  2255 N Ontario St Burbank (91504) *(P-18453)*
Jamcor Corporation (PA) ...................................................... E ...... 916 652-7713
  6261 Angelo Ct Loomis (95650) *(P-16709)*
JAMES ALLYN INC ................................................................ F
  6575 Trinity Ct Ste B Dublin (94568) *(P-4656)*
James G Meyers & Associates ............................................. E ...... 858 622-2165
  4353 La Jolla Village Dr Ste 180 San Diego (92122) *(P-19323)*
James Hardie Building Pdts Inc .......................................... D ...... 949 348-1800
  26300 La Alameda Ste 400 Mission Viejo (92691) *(P-7256)*
James Hardie Building Pdts Inc .......................................... D ...... 909 355-6500
  10901 Elm Ave Fontana (92337) *(P-16447)*
James Hardie Trading Co Inc ............................................. C ...... 949 582-2378
  26300 La Alameda Ste 400 Mission Viejo (92691) *(P-6378)*
James Jones Company ......................................................... A ...... 909 418-2558
  1470 S Vintage Ave Ontario (91761) *(P-9157)*
James L Hall Co Incorporated ............................................ D ...... 707 544-2436
  218 Roberts Ave Santa Rosa (95401) *(P-12843)*
James Litho, Rancho Cucamonga *Also Called: Eclipse Prtg & Graphics LLC (P-4600)*
James Magna Ltd .................................................................. F ...... 909 391-2025
  8782 Lanyard Ct Rancho Cucamonga (91730) *(P-19164)*
James Stout ........................................................................... E ...... 408 988-8582
  481 Gianni St Santa Clara (95054) *(P-10903)*
James Tobin Cellars Inc ....................................................... E ...... 805 239-2204
  8950 Union Rd Paso Robles (93446) *(P-1631)*
Jampro Antennas Inc (PA) .................................................... E ...... 916 383-1177
  6340 Sky Creek Dr Sacramento (95828) *(P-11869)*
Jan-Al Cases, Los Angeles *Also Called: Jan-Al Innerprizes Inc (P-7135)*
Jan-Al Innerprizes Inc .......................................................... E ...... 323 260-7212
  3339 Union Pacific Ave Los Angeles (90023) *(P-7135)*
Jan-Kens Enameling Company Inc ...................................... E ...... 626 358-1849
  715 E Cypress Ave Monrovia (91016) *(P-9084)*
Janco Airless Center, Berkeley *Also Called: Janco Chemical Corporation (P-6088)*
Janco Chemical Corporation ............................................... E ...... 510 527-9770
  1235 5th St Berkeley (94710) *(P-6088)*
Janco Corporation ................................................................ C ...... 818 361-3366
  13955 Balboa Blvd Rancho Cascades (91342) *(P-13010)*
Jandy Pool Products, Carlsbad *Also Called: Zodiac Pool Systems LLC (P-10619)*
Jane Nextgen Inc .................................................................. F ...... 415 722-2226
  400 29th St Ste 105 Oakland (94609) *(P-5758)*
Janin ...................................................................................... C ...... 323 564-0995
  10031 Hunt Ave South Gate (90280) *(P-2768)*
Jano Graphics, Oxnard *Also Called: National Graphics LLC (P-4703)*
Jans Enterprises Corporation ............................................. E ...... 626 575-2000
  4181 Temple City Blvd Ste A El Monte (91731) *(P-17190)*
Jansen Ornamental Supply Co ............................................ E ...... 626 442-0271
  10926 Schmidt Rd El Monte (91733) *(P-8630)*
Janssen Biopharma Inc ........................................................ E ...... 650 452-0210
  1600 Sierra Point Pkwy Brisbane (94005) *(P-5510)*
Janssen Biopharma Inc ........................................................ E ...... 650 635-5500
  260 E Grand Ave South San Francisco (94080) *(P-5511)*
Janssen Research & Dev LLC .............................................. C ...... 858 450-2000
  3210 Merryfield Row San Diego (92121) *(P-5512)*
Janus International Group LLC ........................................... F ...... 714 503-6120
  2535 W La Palma Ave Anaheim (92801) *(P-8270)*
JANUX, San Diego *Also Called: Janux Therapeutics Inc (P-5513)*
Janux Therapeutics Inc ........................................................ D ...... 858 751-4493
  10955 Vista Sorrento Pkwy Ste 200 San Diego (92130) *(P-5513)*
Japanese Weekend Inc (PA) ................................................ E ...... 415 621-0555
  496 S Airport Blvd South San Francisco (94080) *(P-2769)*

Japonesque, San Ramon *Also Called: Japonesque LLC (P-17040)*
Japonesque LLC ................................................................... D ...... 925 866-6670
  12647 Alcosta Blvd Ste 375 San Ramon (94583) *(P-17040)*
Jar Ventures Inc ................................................................... F ...... 530 224-9655
  4351 Caterpillar Rd Redding (96003) *(P-15992)*
Jariet Technologies Inc ........................................................ E ...... 310 698-1000
  103 W Torrance Blvd Redondo Beach (90277) *(P-14200)*
Jarrow Industries LLC (PA) .................................................. D ...... 562 906-1919
  12246 Hawkins St Santa Fe Springs (90670) *(P-5514)*
Jarrow Industries LLC .......................................................... E ...... 562 631-9330
  12342 Hawkins St Santa Fe Springs (90670) *(P-5515)*
Jarrow Industries LLC .......................................................... E ...... 562 631-9330
  10226 Palm Dr Santa Fe Springs (90670) *(P-5516)*
Jarrow Industries LLC .......................................................... E ...... 562 631-9330
  12328 Hawkins St Santa Fe Springs (90670) *(P-5517)*
Jarvis ..................................................................................... E ...... 707 255-5280
  2970 Monticello Rd Napa (94558) *(P-1632)*
Jarvis Manufacturing Inc ..................................................... F ...... 408 226-2600
  210 Hillsdale Ave San Jose (95136) *(P-10904)*
Jarvis Winery, Napa *Also Called: Jarvis (P-1632)*
Jason Incorporated .............................................................. E ...... 562 921-9821
  13006 Philadelphia St Ste 305 Whittier (90601) *(P-7554)*
Jason Markk Inc (PA) ........................................................... E ...... 213 687-7060
  15325 Blackburn Ave Norwalk (90650) *(P-5910)*
Jason Tool and Engineering Inc .......................................... E ...... 714 895-5067
  7101 Honold Cir Garden Grove (92841) *(P-6872)*
Jason's Natural, Bell *Also Called: Hain Celestial Group Inc (P-5985)*
Jasper Electronics ................................................................ E ...... 714 917-0749
  1580 N Kellogg Dr Anaheim (92807) *(P-13011)*
Jasper Therapeutics Inc (PA) ............................................... F ...... 650 549-1400
  2200 Bridge Pkwy Ste 102 Redwood City (94065) *(P-5843)*
Jaspersoft Corporation ........................................................ C ...... 415 348-2300
  350 Rhode Island St Ste 250 San Francisco (94103) *(P-19009)*
Jaton Corporation ................................................................ E ...... 510 933-8888
  47677 Lakeview Blvd Fremont (94538) *(P-12146)*
Jaunt Inc ............................................................................... D ...... 650 618-6579
  951 Mariners Island Blvd Ste 500 San Mateo (94404) *(P-18454)*
Jaunt Xr, San Mateo *Also Called: Jaunt Inc (P-18454)*
Javad Ems Inc ....................................................................... D ...... 408 770-1700
  900 Rock Ave San Jose (95131) *(P-13012)*
Javanan Inc .......................................................................... E ...... 310 741-0011
  24629 Calvert St Woodland Hills (91367) *(P-17937)*
Javanan Magazine, Woodland Hills *Also Called: Javanan Inc (P-17937)*
Javo Beverage Company Inc ............................................... D ...... 760 560-5286
  1311 Specialty Dr Vista (92081) *(P-2011)*
Jaxx Manufacturing Inc ....................................................... E ...... 805 526-4979
  1912 Angus Ave Simi Valley (93063) *(P-13013)*
Jaya Apparel Group LLC ...................................................... F ...... 323 584-3500
  2761 Fruitland Ave Vernon (90058) *(P-2770)*
Jaya Apparel Group LLC (PA) .............................................. D ...... 323 584-3500
  2761 Fruitland Ave Fl 2 Los Angeles (90058) *(P-2771)*
Jayco/Mmi Inc ...................................................................... E ...... 951 738-2000
  1351 Pico St Corona (92881) *(P-13014)*
Jayone Foods Inc .................................................................. E ...... 562 633-7400
  7212 Alondra Blvd Paramount (90723) *(P-2242)*
Jazz Pharmaceuticals Inc .................................................... C ...... 650 496-3777
  3180 Porter Dr Palo Alto (94304) *(P-5518)*
Jazz Pharmaceuticals Inc (HQ) ............................................ F ...... 650 496-3777
  3170 Porter Dr Palo Alto (94304) *(P-5519)*
Jazz Semiconductor, Newport Beach *Also Called: Newport Fab LLC (P-12602)*
JB Brananne Inc ................................................................... E ...... 949 215-7704
  6 Orchard Lake Forest (92630) *(P-6873)*
JB Plastics Inc ...................................................................... E ...... 714 541-8500
  1921 E Edinger Ave Santa Ana (92705) *(P-6874)*
JB&a Distribution, San Rafael *Also Called: Jeff Burgess & Associates Inc (P-11670)*
JBA Brands, Garden Grove *Also Called: Advanced Phrm Svcs Inc (P-17026)*
Jbb Inc .................................................................................. E ...... 888 538-9287
  492 W Meats Ave Orange (92865) *(P-13258)*
Jbe Inc .................................................................................. F ...... 707 552-6800
  1080 Nimitz Ave Ste 400 Vallejo (94592) *(P-3659)*
Jbi LLC .................................................................................. E ...... 310 537-2910
  18521 S Santa Fe Ave Compton (90221) *(P-3505)*

## ALPHABETIC SECTION

Jbi LLC (PA) .................................................................. C ...... 310 886-8034
  2650 E El Presidio St Long Beach (90810) *(P-3746)*
Jbi Interiors, Long Beach *Also Called: Jbi LLC (P-3746)*
Jbr Inc (PA) .................................................................... C ...... 916 258-8000
  1731 Aviation Blvd Lincoln (95648) *(P-2243)*
Jbs Case Ready, Riverside *Also Called: Swift Beef Company (P-672)*
Jbt Food Tech Madera, Madera *Also Called: John Bean Technologies Corp (P-9801)*
JBW Precision Inc ......................................................... E ...... 805 499-1973
  2650 Lavery Ct Newbury Park (91320) *(P-8477)*
JC Ford, La Habra *Also Called: J C Ford Company (P-9799)*
JC Industries, Los Angeles *Also Called: J C Trimming Company Inc (P-2705)*
JC Metal Specialists Inc .............................................. E ...... 415 822-3878
  2708 Ingalls St San Francisco (94124) *(P-8156)*
JC Metal Specialists Inc (PA) ..................................... E ...... 650 827-1618
  238 Michelle Ct South San Francisco (94080) *(P-8157)*
JC Supply & Manufacturing, Ontario *Also Called: Lightcap Industries Inc (P-8170)*
JC Supply & Manufacturing, Diamond Bar *Also Called: Simplex Supplies Inc (P-8216)*
JC Window Fashions, Whittier *Also Called: JC Window Fashions Inc (P-3722)*
JC Window Fashions Inc ............................................. E ...... 909 364-8888
  2438 Peck Rd Whittier (90601) *(P-3722)*
Jc's Pie Pops, Chatsworth *Also Called: We The Pie People LLC (P-820)*
Jci Jones Chemicals Inc ............................................. E ...... 310 523-1629
  1401 Del Amo Blvd Torrance (90501) *(P-5033)*
Jci Metal Products (PA) ............................................... D ...... 619 229-8206
  6540 Federal Blvd Lemon Grove (91945) *(P-8158)*
Jck Legacy Company (HQ) ......................................... D ...... 916 321-1844
  1601 Alhambra Blvd Ste 100 Sacramento (95816) *(P-4137)*
JCM Industries Inc (PA) .............................................. E ...... 714 902-9000
  15302 Pipeline Ln Huntington Beach (92649) *(P-3692)*
JCPM Inc ......................................................................... E ...... 909 484-9040
  8576 Red Oak St Rancho Cucamonga (91730) *(P-10905)*
Jcr Aircraft Deburring LLC ........................................ D ...... 714 870-4427
  221 Foundation Ave La Habra (90631) *(P-8976)*
Jcr Deburring, La Habra *Also Called: Jcr Aircraft Deburring LLC (P-8976)*
JD Processing Inc ........................................................ E ...... 714 972-8161
  2220 Cape Cod Way Santa Ana (92703) *(P-8977)*
Jd/Cmc Inc ..................................................................... E ...... 818 767-2260
  2834 E 11th St Los Angeles (90023) *(P-2772)*
Jdh Pacific Inc (PA) ...................................................... E ...... 562 926-8088
  1818 E Orangethorpe Ave Fullerton (92831) *(P-7676)*
Jdi Distribution, Redlands *Also Called: Bakell LLC (P-354)*
Jdsu, San Jose *Also Called: Viavi Solutions Inc (P-12788)*
Jdz Inc ............................................................................. D ...... 858 549-9888
  9990 Alesmith Ct San Diego (92126) *(P-1437)*
JE Rich Company .......................................................... E ...... 909 464-1872
  7225 Edison Ave Ontario (91762) *(P-1104)*
JE Thomson & Company LLC ................................... F ...... 626 334-7190
  15206 Ceres Ave Fontana (92335) *(P-9526)*
Jean-Claude Bsset Wines USA Inc .......................... F ...... 707 963-6903
  124 Matheson St Healdsburg (95448) *(P-1633)*
Jean-Claude Bsset Wines USA Inc .......................... E ...... 800 926-1266
  18000 Old Winery Rd Sonoma (95476) *(P-1634)*
Jeannine's Bakery, Santa Barbara *Also Called: Jeannines Bkg Co Santa Barbara (P-1218)*
Jeannines Bkg Co Santa Barbara (PA) .................... F ...... 805 687-8701
  3607 State St Santa Barbara (93105) *(P-1218)*
Jeb Holdings Corp ....................................................... E ...... 951 296-9900
  42033 Rio Nedo Temecula (92590) *(P-7788)*
Jeb-Phi Inc .................................................................... F ...... 562 861-0863
  10417 Lakewood Blvd Downey (90241) *(P-4657)*
Jeckys Best Inc ............................................................ E ...... 661 259-1313
  26450 Summit Cir Santa Clarita (91350) *(P-17122)*
Jeff Burgess & Associates Inc (DH) ........................ E ...... 415 256-2800
  1050 Northgate Dr Ste 200 San Rafael (94903) *(P-11670)*
Jeff Frank ...................................................................... F ...... 831 469-8208
  120 Encinal St Santa Cruz (95060) *(P-15993)*
Jeffco Painting & Coating Inc .................................. D ...... 707 562-1900
  1260 Railroad Ave Vallejo (94592) *(P-446)*
Jeffrey Fabrication LLC ............................................. E ...... 562 634-3101
  6323 Alondra Blvd Paramount (90723) *(P-8478)*
JEI .................................................................................... F ...... 530 677-3210
  3087 Alhambra Dr Cameron Park (95682) *(P-16710)*

Jei, Cameron Park *Also Called: JEI (P-16710)*
Jeld-Wen Inc ................................................................. C ...... 800 468-3667
  3760 Convoy St Ste 111 San Diego (92111) *(P-3150)*
Jeld-Wen Inc ................................................................. C ...... 916 782-4900
  3901 Cincinnati Ave Rocklin (95765) *(P-3151)*
Jelenko, San Diego *Also Called: Argen Corporation (P-7710)*
Jellco Container Inc .................................................... D ...... 714 666-2728
  1151 N Tustin Ave Anaheim (92807) *(P-3861)*
Jellypop, Pasadena *Also Called: Evolution Design Lab Inc (P-7115)*
Jem Unlimited Iron, Anaheim *Also Called: Jorge Ulloa (P-16156)*
Jem-Hd Co Inc .............................................................. E ...... 619 710-1443
  10030 Via De La Amistad Ste F San Diego (92154) *(P-6875)*
Jemstep Inc ................................................................... E ...... 650 966-6500
  5150 El Camino Real Ste C20 Los Altos (94022) *(P-18455)*
Jenco Productions LLC (PA) .................................... C ...... 909 381-9453
  401 S J St San Bernardino (92410) *(P-19099)*
Jeneric/Pentron Incorporated (HQ) ........................ C ...... 203 265-7397
  1717 W Collins Ave Orange (92867) *(P-15460)*
Jennings, San Jose *Also Called: Jennings Technology Co LLC (P-12819)*
Jennings Technology Co LLC (DH) ........................ D ...... 408 292-4025
  970 Mclaughlin Ave San Jose (95122) *(P-12819)*
Jenny Silks, Santa Ana *Also Called: Jenny Silks Inc (P-17280)*
Jenny Silks Inc ............................................................. F ...... 714 597-7272
  2101 S Grand Ave Santa Ana (92705) *(P-17280)*
Jenoptik Optical Systems LLC ................................ E ...... 510 676-0019
  39300 Civic Center Dr Ste 240 Fremont (94538) *(P-14791)*
Jensen, Fresno *Also Called: Jensen & Pilegard (P-16799)*
Jensen & Pilegard (PA) .............................................. E ...... 559 268-9221
  1739 E Terrace Ave Fresno (93703) *(P-16799)*
Jensen Enterprises Inc ............................................. B ...... 909 357-7264
  14221 San Bernardino Ave Fontana (92335) *(P-7347)*
Jensen Enterprises Inc ............................................. E ...... 530 865-4277
  7210 State Highway 32 Orland (95963) *(P-7348)*
Jensen Precast, Fontana *Also Called: Jensen Enterprises Inc (P-7347)*
Jenson Mechanical Inc ............................................. E ...... 510 429-8078
  32420 Central Ave Union City (94587) *(P-10906)*
Jepson Vineyard Ltd .................................................. F ...... 707 468-8936
  10400 S Highway 101 Ukiah (95482) *(P-1635)*
Jepson Vnyrds-Wnery-Distillery, Ukiah *Also Called: Jepson Vineyard Ltd (P-1635)*
Jeremiahs Pick Coffee Company ............................ F ...... 415 206-9900
  1495 Evans Ave San Francisco (94124) *(P-2074)*
Jericho Foods, San Fernando *Also Called: Cousins Foods LLC (P-17373)*
Jerry Leigh Entertainment AP, Van Nuys *Also Called: Leigh Jerry California Inc (P-2856)*
Jerry Melton & Sons Cnstr, Taft *Also Called: Jerry Melton & Sons Cnstr Inc (P-242)*
Jerry Melton & Sons Cnstr Inc ................................. D ...... 661 765-5546
  100 Jamison Ln Taft (93268) *(P-242)*
Jessee Brothers Machine Sp Inc ............................ F ...... 408 866-1755
  1640 Dell Ave Campbell (95008) *(P-10907)*
Jessica McClintock Inc (PA) ..................................... C ...... 415 553-8200
  2307 Bdwy St San Francisco (94115) *(P-2854)*
Jessie & Jenna, Gardena *Also Called: Lily Bleu Inc (P-17094)*
Jessie Lord, Torrance *Also Called: Jessie Lord Bakery LLC (P-17413)*
Jessie Lord Bakery LLC ............................................ E ...... 310 533-6010
  21100 S Western Ave Torrance (90501) *(P-17413)*
Jessup Cellars Inc ...................................................... F ...... 707 944-8523
  6740 Washington St Yountville (94599) *(P-1636)*
Jet Air Fbo LLC ........................................................... E ...... 619 448-5991
  681 Kenney St El Cajon (92020) *(P-13881)*
Jet Cutting Solutions Inc .......................................... E ...... 909 948-2424
  10853 Bell Ct Rancho Cucamonga (91730) *(P-10908)*
Jet Fleet International Corp ..................................... E ...... 310 440-3820
  2370 Westwood Blvd Ste K Los Angeles (90064) *(P-17773)*
Jet I, Fontana *Also Called: Jeti Inc (P-19204)*
Jet Plastics (PA) .......................................................... E ...... 323 268-6706
  941 N Eastern Ave Los Angeles (90063) *(P-6876)*
Jet Products, San Diego *Also Called: Senior Operations LLC (P-11108)*
Jetfax, Los Angeles *Also Called: Efaxcom (P-10359)*
Jeti Inc ........................................................................... F ...... 909 357-2966
  14578 Hawthorne Ave Fontana (92335) *(P-19204)*

**Jetronics Company**            ALPHABETIC SECTION

Jetronics Company, Santa Rosa *Also Called: James L Hall Co Incorporated (P-12843)*
Jetstream Communications Inc ............................................................... D ...... 408 361-7000
   5400 Hellyer Ave San Jose (95138) *(P-11773)*
Jetzero Inc (PA) ............................................................................................ E ...... 949 474-8222
   4150 E Donald Douglas Dr Long Beach (90808) *(P-13671)*
Jewelers Touch ............................................................................................ E ...... 714 579-1616
   2535 E Imperial Hwy Brea (92821) *(P-17646)*
Jewish Journal, The, Los Angeles *Also Called: Tribe Mdia Corp A Cal Nnprfit (P-4214)*
Jf Fixtures & Design, Long Beach *Also Called: F-J-E Inc (P-3656)*
Jf Fixtures & Design LLC ........................................................................... F ...... 562 437-7466
   546 W Esther St Long Beach (90813) *(P-19100)*
Jfc International Vineyards, Sanger *Also Called: Gibson Wine Company (P-1587)*
Jfcmirin Inc, Hollister *Also Called: Ozeki Sake (usa) Inc (P-1702)*
Jff Uniforms, Torrance *Also Called: Just For Fun Inc (P-2575)*
JFROG, Sunnyvale *Also Called: Jfrog Ltd (P-18456)*
Jfrog Ltd (PA) .............................................................................................. A ...... 408 329-1540
   270 E Caribbean Dr Sunnyvale (94089) *(P-18456)*
JG Plastics Group LLC .............................................................................. E ...... 714 751-4266
   335 Fischer Ave Costa Mesa (92626) *(P-6877)*
Jh Biotech, Ventura *Also Called: Jh Biotech Inc (P-6188)*
Jh Biotech Inc (PA) ..................................................................................... E ...... 805 650-8933
   4951 Olivas Park Dr Ventura (93003) *(P-6188)*
Jh Design Group ......................................................................................... D ...... 213 747-5700
   940 W Washington Blvd Los Angeles (90015) *(P-2625)*
Jhawar Industries LLC .............................................................................. E ...... 951 340-4646
   525 Klug Cir Corona (92878) *(P-10055)*
Jhc Materials Inc ........................................................................................ E ...... 916 645-3870
   601 7th St Lincoln (95648) *(P-7349)*
JIC Industrial Co Inc ................................................................................. E ...... 408 935-9880
   978 Hanson Ct Milpitas (95035) *(P-13015)*
Jifco Inc (PA) .............................................................................................. E ...... 925 449-4665
   571 Exchange Ct Livermore (94550) *(P-9262)*
Jifco Fabricated Piping, Livermore *Also Called: Jifco Inc (P-9262)*
Jifflenow, Sunnyvale *Also Called: Ipolipo Inc (P-18442)*
Jigsaw Data Corporation .......................................................................... E ...... 650 235-8400
   900 Concar Dr San Mateo (94402) *(P-4420)*
Jihwaja Rice Bakery, Los Angeles *Also Called: Grandville Llc (P-1276)*
Jim Little Raymonds Print Shop, Fremont *Also Called: Raymonds Little Print Shop Inc (P-4749)*
Jim ONeal Distributing Inc ...................................................................... E ...... 805 426-3300
   799 Camarillo Springs Rd Camarillo (93012) *(P-17482)*
Jim-Buoy, North Hollywood *Also Called: Cal-June Inc (P-7986)*
Jim's Machining, Camarillo *Also Called: Thiessen Products Inc (P-11142)*
Jimenes Food Inc ....................................................................................... E ...... 562 602-2505
   7046 Jackson St Paramount (90723) *(P-2244)*
Jimenez Mexican Foods Inc ................................................................... E ...... 951 351-0102
   20343 Harvill Ave Perris (92570) *(P-860)*
Jimway Inc .................................................................................................. D ...... 310 886-3718
   20101 S Santa Fe Ave Compton (90221) *(P-11603)*
Jinkosolar (us) Inc ..................................................................................... E ...... 415 402-0502
   1901 S Bascom Ave Campbell (95008) *(P-12510)*
Jipcob Inc .................................................................................................... C ...... 661 859-1111
   3709 Rosedale Hwy Bakersfield (93308) *(P-17587)*
Jireh Semiconductor Inc ......................................................................... E
   475 Oakmead Pkwy Sunnyvale (94085) *(P-12511)*
Jiseki Health, Millbrae *Also Called: Jiseki Health Inc (P-18457)*
Jiseki Health Inc ........................................................................................ E ...... 408 763-7264
   10 Rollins Rd Ste 209 Millbrae (94030) *(P-18457)*
JIT Manufacturing Inc .............................................................................. E ...... 805 238-5000
   1610 Commerce Way Paso Robles (93446) *(P-15136)*
Jive Software Inc ....................................................................................... F ...... 503 295-3700
   735 Emerson St Palo Alto (94301) *(P-18458)*
Jivox Corporation (HQ) ............................................................................ E ...... 650 412-1125
   1810 Gateway Dr Ste 280 San Mateo (94404) *(P-18459)*
Jj Acquisitions LLC .................................................................................. E ...... 818 772-0100
   8501 Fallbrook Ave Ste 370 West Hills (91304) *(P-6505)*
Jjs Mae Inc (PA) ......................................................................................... D ...... 415 255-7047
   1812 Harrison St San Francisco (94103) *(P-2773)*
JKL Components Corporation ............................................................... E ...... 818 896-0019
   13343 Paxton St Pacoima (91331) *(P-11573)*

Jkv Inc ......................................................................................................... E ...... 562 948-3000
   8343 Loch Lomond Dr Pico Rivera (90660) *(P-3862)*
Jl Design Enterprises Inc ....................................................................... D ...... 714 479-0240
   37407 Industry Way Murrieta (92563) *(P-2574)*
JL Haley Enterprises Inc ........................................................................ C ...... 916 631-6375
   3510 Luyung Dr Rancho Cordova (95742) *(P-10909)*
Jl Racing.com, Murrieta *Also Called: Jl Design Enterprises Inc (P-2574)*
Jla Home, Fremont *Also Called: Jla Home Inc (P-2930)*
Jla Home Inc .............................................................................................. E ...... 510 490-9788
   45875 Northport Loop E Fremont (94538) *(P-2930)*
Jlcooper, El Segundo *Also Called: J L Cooper Electronics Inc (P-13008)*
Jlg Industries Inc ...................................................................................... E ...... 951 358-1915
   7820 Lincoln Ave Riverside (92504) *(P-9428)*
Jlg Serviceplus, Riverside *Also Called: Jlg Industries Inc (P-9428)*
JLJ Rebar Extreme Inc ............................................................................ E ...... 909 381-9177
   1532 Wall Ave San Bernardino (92404) *(P-8700)*
JM Eagle, Perris *Also Called: J-M Manufacturing Company Inc (P-5169)*
JM Eagle, Los Angeles *Also Called: J-M Manufacturing Company Inc (P-6598)*
JM Eagle, Los Angeles *Also Called: Pw Eagle Inc (P-6601)*
JM Huber Corporation ............................................................................. D ...... 209 549-9771
   700 Kiernan Ave Ste D Modesto (95356) *(P-5096)*
JM Huber Micropowders Inc ................................................................. E ...... 714 994-7855
   16024 Phoebe Ave La Mirada (90638) *(P-5097)*
Jmc Closing Co LLC ................................................................................ E ...... 951 278-9900
   1499 Palmyrita Ave Riverside (92507) *(P-10910)*
Jme Inc (PA) .............................................................................................. D ...... 201 896-8600
   527 Park Ave San Fernando (91340) *(P-16655)*
Jmg Machine Inc ....................................................................................... E ...... 714 522-6221
   17037 Industry Pl La Mirada (90638) *(P-10911)*
Jmmca Inc (PA) ......................................................................................... D ...... 619 448-2711
   850 W Bradley Ave El Cajon (92020) *(P-8779)*
Jmw Truss and Components, San Diego *Also Called: Trademark Construction Co Inc (P-13190)*
JNJ Apparel Inc ......................................................................................... E ...... 323 584-9700
   18788 Fairfield Rd Porter Ranch (91326) *(P-2774)*
Jnr Confection Specialty Corp .............................................................. F
   2399 Walnut Ave Signal Hill (90755) *(P-1315)*
Jns Industries, Eastvale *Also Called: Jns Industries Inc (P-10912)*
Jns Industries Inc .................................................................................... F ...... 909 923-8334
   5120 Hamner Ave Eastvale (91752) *(P-10912)*
Jo's Candies, Torrance *Also Called: Manhattan Confectioners Inc (P-1318)*
Jobbers Meat Packing Co LLC ............................................................. C ...... 323 585-6328
   3336 Fruitland Ave Vernon (90058) *(P-603)*
Jobsite Stud Welding ............................................................................... E ...... 855 885-7883
   9445 Washburn Rd Downey (90242) *(P-19205)*
Joby Aero Inc (HQ) ................................................................................... A ...... 831 426-3733
   333 Encinal St Santa Cruz (95060) *(P-13672)*
Joby Aviation Inc (PA) ............................................................................. B ...... 831 201-6006
   333 Encinal St Santa Cruz (95060) *(P-13673)*
Jodi Kristopher LLC (PA) ........................................................................ D ...... 323 890-8000
   1950 Naomi Ave Los Angeles (90011) *(P-2706)*
Jody of California, Los Angeles *Also Called: Private Brand Mdsg Corp (P-2713)*
Joe Blasco Cosmetics, Palm Springs *Also Called: Joe Blasco Enterprises Inc (P-16155)*
Joe Blasco Enterprises Inc ................................................................... E ...... 323 467-4949
   1285 N Valdivia Way # A Palm Springs (92262) *(P-16155)*
Joe Pucci & Sons Seafoods, Hayward *Also Called: Blue River Seafood Inc (P-17153)*
Joe Wells Enterprises Inc ...................................................................... E
   1500 S Sunkist St Ste D Anaheim (92806) *(P-2626)*
Joe's Dsert Hlls Prmium Otlets, Cabazon *Also Called: Centric Brands Inc (P-2407)*
Joe's Jeans, Los Angeles *Also Called: Centric Brands Inc (P-2409)*
Joes Dwntwn Brewry & Rest Inc ......................................................... E ...... 707 258-2337
   902 Main St Napa (94559) *(P-17588)*
Joes Plastics, Vernon *Also Called: Joes Plastics Inc (P-5172)*
Joes Plastics Inc ...................................................................................... E ...... 323 771-8433
   5725 District Blvd Vernon (90058) *(P-5172)*
Johanson Technology Inc ..................................................................... C ...... 805 575-0124
   4001 Calle Tecate Camarillo (93012) *(P-12820)*
Johasee Rebar, Corona *Also Called: Johasee Rebar Inc (P-8159)*
Johasee Rebar Inc .................................................................................. E ...... 661 589-0972
   26365 Earthmover Cir Corona (92883) *(P-8159)*

## ALPHABETIC SECTION

**John B Sanfilippo & Son  Inc** .................................................. B ...... 209 854-2455
29241 Cottonwood Rd Gustine (95322) *(P-1354)*

**John Bean Technologies Corp** .................................................. D ...... 951 222-2300
1660 Iowa Ave Ste 100 Riverside (92507) *(P-9800)*

**John Bean Technologies Corp** .................................................. C ...... 559 661-3200
2300 W Industrial Ave Madera (93637) *(P-9801)*

**John Bishop Design  Inc** ............................................................. E ...... 714 744-2300
731 N Main St Orange (92868) *(P-15994)*

**John Boyd Enterprises  Inc (PA)**............................................... C ...... 916 381-4790
8401 Specialty Cir Sacramento (95828) *(P-13522)*

**John C Destefano** ........................................................................ E ...... 916 276-4056
7325 Reese Rd Sacramento (95828) *(P-3244)*

**John Crane Inc** ............................................................................. F ...... 562 802-2555
12760 Florence Ave Santa Fe Springs (90670) *(P-7569)*

**John Currie Performance Group** .............................................. E ...... 714 367-1580
1592 Jenks Dr Corona (92878) *(P-9872)*

**John Daniel Gonzalez** ................................................................. E ...... 559 646-6621
13458 E Industrial Dr Parlier (93648) *(P-3372)*

**John Deere Authorized Dealer, San Leandro** *Also Called: Valley Power Systems  Inc (P-16852)*

**John Deere Water, San Diego** *Also Called: Rivulis Irrigation Inc (P-9380)*

**John Fitzpatrick & Sons** ............................................................. E ...... 530 241-3216
1480 Beltline Rd Redding (96003) *(P-1896)*

**John L Conley  Inc** ...................................................................... D ...... 909 627-0981
4344 Mission Blvd Montclair (91763) *(P-8671)*

**John List Corporation** ................................................................ E ...... 818 882-7848
9732 Cozycroft Ave Chatsworth (91311) *(P-9718)*

**John M Phillips  LLC** .................................................................. E ...... 661 327-3118
2800 Gibson St Bakersfield (93308) *(P-243)*

**John M Phillips Oil Field Eqp, Bakersfield** *Also Called: John M Phillips  LLC (P-243)*

**John Robert Ard** .......................................................................... F ...... 619 326-0577
1930 Bacon St San Diego (92107) *(P-15832)*

**JOHN TILLMAN COMPANY (DH)**............................................ D ...... 310 764-0110
1300 W Artesia Blvd Compton (90220) *(P-16820)*

**John Wheeler Logging  Inc** ....................................................... C ...... 530 527-2993
13570 State Highway 36 E Red Bluff (96080) *(P-3048)*

**John's Formica Shop, Santa Rosa** *Also Called: Johns Formica  Inc (P-3693)*

**John's Incredible Pizza Co, Bakersfield** *Also Called: Jipcob  Inc (P-17587)*

**Johnny Was  LLC** ........................................................................ D ...... 310 656-0600
395 Santa Monica Pl Ste 124 Santa Monica (90401) *(P-17092)*

**Johnny Was Showroom, Los Angeles** *Also Called: Jwc Studio  Inc (P-2707)*

**Johns Formica  Inc** ..................................................................... E ...... 707 544-8585
2439 Piner Rd Santa Rosa (95403) *(P-3693)*

**Johns Manville Corporation** ...................................................... D ...... 323 568-2220
4301 Firestone Blvd South Gate (90280) *(P-7576)*

**Johns Manville Corporation** ...................................................... D ...... 530 934-6243
5916 County Road 49 Willows (95988) *(P-7577)*

**Johnson & Johnson** .................................................................... D ...... 650 237-4878
3509 Langdon Cmn Fremont (94538) *(P-4002)*

**Johnson & Johnson** .................................................................... E ...... 650 903-4800
365 Ravendale Dr Mountain View (94043) *(P-15368)*

**Johnson & Johnson** .................................................................... B ...... 909 839-8650
15715 Arrow Hwy Irwindale (91706) *(P-15369)*

**Johnson & Johnson, Mountain View** *Also Called: Johnson & Johnson (P-15368)*

**Johnson & Johnson Vision, Milpitas** *Also Called: Johnson Jhnson Srgcal Vsion In (P-15549)*

**Johnson & Johnson Vision, Irvine** *Also Called: Johnson Jhnson Srgcal Vsion In (P-15549)*

**Johnson Caldraul Inc** .................................................................. E ...... 951 340-1067
220 N Delilah St Ste 101 Corona (92879) *(P-13882)*

**Johnson Cntrls Fire Prtction L** .................................................. C ...... 858 633-9100
3568 Ruffin Rd San Diego (92123) *(P-12002)*

**Johnson Contrls Authorized Dlr, Pleasanton** *Also Called: Automatic Control Engrg Corp (P-14847)*

**Johnson Contrls Authorized Dlr, Montebello** *Also Called: Johnstone Supply  Inc (P-17541)*

**Johnson Controls, Riverside** *Also Called: Clarios LLC (P-3615)*

**Johnson Controls, Hayward** *Also Called: Clarios  LLC (P-3616)*

**Johnson Controls, Simi Valley** *Also Called: Clarios  LLC (P-3617)*

**Johnson Controls, Palm Desert** *Also Called: Clarios  LLC (P-3618)*

**Johnson Controls, Folsom** *Also Called: Clarios  LLC (P-3619)*

**Johnson Controls, Cypress** *Also Called: Johnson Controls  Inc (P-3628)*

**Johnson Controls, Whittier** *Also Called: Johnson Controls  Inc (P-3629)*

**Johnson Controls, Santa Rosa** *Also Called: Johnson Controls  Inc (P-3630)*

**Johnson Controls, Bakersfield** *Also Called: Johnson Controls Inc (P-3631)*

**Johnson Controls, Santa Clara** *Also Called: Clarios  LLC (P-13133)*

**Johnson Controls  Inc** ................................................................ C ...... 562 594-3200
5770 Warland Dr Ste A Cypress (90630) *(P-3628)*

**Johnson Controls  Inc** ................................................................ E ...... 562 698-8301
12393 Slauson Ave Whittier (90606) *(P-3629)*

**Johnson Controls  Inc** ................................................................ E ...... 707 546-3042
2226 Northpoint Pkwy Santa Rosa (95407) *(P-3630)*

**Johnson Controls Inc** .................................................................. F ...... 661 862-5706
1828 34th St #c Bakersfield (93301) *(P-3631)*

**Johnson doc Enterprises** ........................................................... E ...... 818 764-1543
11933 Vose St North Hollywood (91605) *(P-6506)*

**Johnson Industries, Arcata** *Also Called: C & K Johnson Industries Inc (P-8397)*

**Johnson Jhnson Srgcal Vsion In** .............................................. B ...... 408 273-4100
510 Cottonwood Dr Milpitas (95035) *(P-15137)*

**Johnson Jhnson Srgcal Vsion In (HQ)**................................... B ...... 949 581-5799
31 Technology Dr Bldg 29a Irvine (92618) *(P-15549)*

**Johnson Laminating Coating Inc** .............................................. D ...... 310 635-4929
20631 Annalee Ave Carson (90746) *(P-6583)*

**Johnson Manufacturing  Inc** ..................................................... E ...... 714 903-0393
15201 Connector Ln Huntington Beach (92649) *(P-10913)*

**Johnson Matthey Inc** ................................................................... C ...... 858 716-2400
12205 World Trade Dr San Diego (92128) *(P-7721)*

**Johnson Matthey Inc** ................................................................... D ...... 408 727-2221
1070 Commercial St Ste 110 San Jose (95112) *(P-15138)*

**Johnson Outdoors  Inc** ............................................................... D ...... 619 402-1023
1166 Fesler St Ste A El Cajon (92020) *(P-15833)*

**Johnson Precision Products LLC** ............................................. F ...... 714 824-6971
1308 E Wakeham Ave Santa Ana (92705) *(P-10914)*

**Johnson Racing, Santa Maria** *Also Called: Alan Johnson Prfmce Engrg Inc (P-13335)*

**Johnson United  Inc (PA)**.......................................................... E ...... 209 543-1320
5201 Pentecost Dr Modesto (95356) *(P-15995)*

**Johnson Wilshire Inc** .................................................................. E ...... 562 777-0088
17343 Freedom Way City Of Industry (91748) *(P-15370)*

**Johnston International Corporation** ........................................ E ...... 714 542-4487
14272 Chambers Rd Tustin (92780) *(P-10097)*

**Johnstone Supply  Inc** ............................................................... D ...... 323 722-2859
8040 Slauson Ave Montebello (90640) *(P-17541)*

**Johnstons Trading Post  Inc** .................................................... E ...... 530 661-6152
11 N Pioneer Ave Woodland (95776) *(P-3373)*

**Joico Laboratories  Inc** .............................................................. E ...... 626 321-4100
5800 Bristol Pkwy Culver City (90230) *(P-5995)*

**Joimax  Inc** .................................................................................... E ...... 949 859-3472
140 Technology Dr Ste 150 Irvine (92618) *(P-15139)*

**Jolly Roger Games, Commerce** *Also Called: Ultra Pro International LLC (P-16952)*

**Jolyn Clothing Company   LLC** ................................................. E ...... 714 794-2149
16390 Pacific Coast Hwy Ste 201 Huntington Beach (92649) *(P-2775)*

**Jomar Table Linens Inc** .............................................................. D ...... 909 390-1444
4000 E Airport Dr Ste A Ontario (91761) *(P-2931)*

**Jomu Mist Incorporated** ............................................................. E ...... 415 448-7273
309 Chapman Dr Corte Madera (94925) *(P-18460)*

**Jon Brooks  Inc (PA)**................................................................... D ...... 626 330-0631
14400 Lomitas Ave City Of Industry (91746) *(P-7570)*

**Jon Davler  Inc** ............................................................................ E ...... 626 941-6558
9440 Gidley St Temple City (91780) *(P-17710)*

**Jon Steel Erectors  Inc** .............................................................. E ...... 909 799-0005
1431 S Gage St San Bernardino (92408) *(P-19206)*

**Jonathan Engnred Slutions Corp (HQ)**.................................. E ...... 714 665-4400
250 Commerce Ste 100 Irvine (92618) *(P-8007)*

**Jonathan Martin, Los Angeles** *Also Called: Harkham Industries  Inc (P-2670)*

**Jondo  Ltd (HQ)**........................................................................... D ...... 714 279-2300
22700 Savi Ranch Pkwy Yorba Linda (92887) *(P-15645)*

**Jonel Engineering** ........................................................................ E ...... 714 879-2360
500 E Walnut Ave Fullerton (92832) *(P-10638)*

**Jones Chemicals, Torrance** *Also Called: Jci Jones Chemicals  Inc (P-5033)*

**Jones Sign Co  Inc** ...................................................................... C ...... 858 569-1400
9474 Chesapeake Dr Ste 902 San Diego (92123) *(P-15996)*

**Jonna Corporation  Inc** .............................................................. E ...... 408 297-7910
348 Phelan Ave San Jose (95112) *(P-8319)*

**Joong-Ang Daily News Cal Inc** ................................................. D ...... 858 573-1111
7750 Dagget St Ste 208 San Diego (92111) *(P-4138)*

**Joong-Ang Daily News Cal Inc** ................................ D ...... 510 487-3333
23575 Cabot Blvd Ste 201 Hayward (94545) *(P-4139)*

**Joong-Ang Daily News Cal Inc, Los Angeles** *Also Called: Joongangilbo Usa Inc (P-4140)*

**JOONG-ANG DAILY NEWS CALIFORNIA, INC., San Diego** *Also Called: Joong-Ang Daily News Cal Inc (P-4138)*

**JOONG-ANG DAILY NEWS CALIFORNIA, INC., Hayward** *Also Called: Joong-Ang Daily News Cal Inc (P-4139)*

**Joongangilbo Usa Inc (DH)** .................................. C ...... 213 368-2512
690 Wilshire Pl Los Angeles (90005) *(P-4140)*

**Jordahl USA Inc** ..................................................... E ...... 866 332-6687
34420 Gateway Dr Palm Desert (92211) *(P-8479)*

**Jordan Vineyard & Winery, Healdsburg** *Also Called: Jvw Corporation (P-1643)*

**Jordan Vineyard & Winery LP** ............................... D ...... 707 431-5250
1474 Alexander Valley Rd Healdsburg (95448) *(P-1637)*

**Jorge Ulloa** ............................................................. F ...... 714 630-0499
3162 E La Palma Ave Ste F Anaheim (92806) *(P-16156)*

**Joroda Inc (PA)** ..................................................... E ...... 925 930-0122
1559 Botelho Dr Walnut Creek (94596) *(P-17589)*

**Jos Candies LLC** .................................................. F ...... 800 770-1946
2530 W 237th St Torrance (90505) *(P-17147)*

**Jose Garcia Astorga** ............................................. E ...... 559 500-9338
26820 Hansen Rd Tracy (95377) *(P-3348)*

**Jose Perez** ............................................................ E ...... 920 318-6527
41403 Stork Ct Lake Elsinore (92532) *(P-9488)*

**Joseph Company Intl Inc** ...................................... E
1711 Langley Ave Irvine (92614) *(P-7921)*

**Joseph Gallo Cheese Company LP** ..................... C ...... 209 394-7984
10561 State Highway 140 Atwater (95301) *(P-721)*

**Joseph Gallo Farms, Atwater** *Also Called: Joseph Gallo Cheese Company LP (P-721)*

**Joseph Manufacturing Co Inc** .............................. D ...... 626 334-1471
411 N Aerojet Dr Azusa (91702) *(P-3632)*

**Joseph Phelps Vineyards, Saint Helena** *Also Called: Stone Bridge Cellars Inc (P-1764)*

**Joseph Phelps Vineyards LLC** ............................. E ...... 707 967-3717
1625 Freestone Flat Rd Sebastopol (95472) *(P-1638)*

**Joseph Phelps Vineyards LLC (DH)** ................... E ...... 707 963-2745
200 Taplin Rd Saint Helena (94574) *(P-1639)*

**Joslyn Sunbank Company LLC** ........................... B ...... 805 238-2840
1740 Commerce Way Paso Robles (93446) *(P-12886)*

**Joullian Vineyards Ltd** .......................................... E ...... 831 659-8100
2 Village Dr Ste A Carmel Valley (93924) *(P-1640)*

**Journeyworks Publishing** ..................................... F ...... 831 423-1400
763 Chestnut St Santa Cruz (95060) *(P-4421)*

**Jowett Garments Factory Inc** ............................... E ...... 626 350-0515
10359 Rush St South El Monte (91733) *(P-2776)*

**Jowett Group, South El Monte** *Also Called: Jowett Garments Factory Inc (P-2776)*

**Joy Products California Inc** ................................. F ...... 714 437-7250
17281 Mount Wynne Cir Fountain Valley (92708) *(P-15891)*

**Joy Signal Technology LLC** ................................. E ...... 530 891-3551
1020 Marauder St Ste A Chico (95973) *(P-11460)*

**Joybird, Los Angeles** *Also Called: Stitch Industries Inc (P-3492)*

**Joycity Annex Inc** ................................................. F ...... 949 892-0956
300 Spectrum Center Dr Ste 640 Irvine (92618) *(P-18461)*

**Joyfull Cheese Co., South San Francisco** *Also Called: Raison DEtre Bakery LLC (P-2101)*

**JP, Santa Clara** *Also Called: J P Graphics Inc (P-4655)*

**JP Graphics, Los Gatos** *Also Called: Tscg Ventures Inc (P-4791)*

**JP Gunite Inc** ......................................................... E ...... 619 938-0228
9458 New Colt Ct El Cajon (92021) *(P-7459)*

**JP Products LLC** .................................................. E ...... 310 237-6237
2054 Davie Ave Commerce (90040) *(P-3445)*

**Jpc Wholesale, Livermore** *Also Called: Pel Wholesale Inc (P-16984)*

**Jpl Global LLC** ...................................................... E ...... 888 274-7744
4635 Wade Ave Perris (92571) *(P-16791)*

**JR Daniels Commercial Bldrs** .............................. F ...... 209 545-6040
907 Maze Blvd Modesto (95351) *(P-8701)*

**Jr Grease Services Inc** ........................................ E ...... 323 318-2096
5900 S Eastern Ave Ste 150 Commerce (90040) *(P-1385)*

**JR Machine Company Inc** .................................... E ...... 562 903-9477
13245 Florence Ave Santa Fe Springs (90670) *(P-10915)*

**JR Simplot Company** ........................................... E ...... 209 941-4456
4863 Carpenter Rd Stockton (95215) *(P-1009)*

**JR Stephens Company** ......................................... E ...... 707 825-0100
5208 Boyd Rd Arcata (95521) *(P-3245)*

**Jri Inc** ..................................................................... E ...... 818 706-2424
31280 La Baya Dr Westlake Village (91362) *(P-16711)*

**Js Apparel Inc** ....................................................... D ...... 310 631-6333
1751 E Del Amo Blvd Carson (90746) *(P-2627)*

**Js Trucking, Turlock** *Also Called: Js Trucking Inc (P-9527)*

**Js Trucking Inc** ..................................................... E ...... 209 252-0007
2930 Geer Rd Turlock (95382) *(P-9527)*

**Jsdu, Santa Rosa** *Also Called: Viavi Solutions Inc (P-13326)*

**Jsj Electrical Display Corp** .................................. F ...... 707 747-5595
340 Via Palo Linda Fairfield (94534) *(P-15997)*

**Jsl Foods Inc (PA)** ............................................... D ...... 323 223-2484
3550 Pasadena Ave Los Angeles (90031) *(P-2245)*

**Jsn Industries Inc** ................................................ D ...... 949 458-0050
9700 Jeronimo Rd Irvine (92618) *(P-6878)*

**Jsn Packaging Products Inc** ............................... D ...... 949 458-0050
9700 Jeronimo Rd Irvine (92618) *(P-6579)*

**Jsr Micro Inc (DH)** ................................................ C ...... 408 543-8800
1280 N Mathilda Ave Sunnyvale (94089) *(P-6149)*

**JT Design Studio Inc (PA)** ................................... E ...... 213 891-1500
860 S Los Angeles St Ste 912 Los Angeles (90014) *(P-2777)*

**Jts Corporation** .................................................... A ...... 408 468-1800
166 Baypointe Pkwy San Jose (95134) *(P-10249)*

**Jts Modular Inc** ..................................................... E ...... 661 835-9270
7001 Mcdivitt Dr Ste B Bakersfield (93313) *(P-8672)*

**Juanita F Wade** ...................................................... E ...... 310 519-1208
435 N Harbor Blvd Ste B1 San Pedro (90731) *(P-3031)*

**Juanitas Foods** ..................................................... C ...... 310 834-5339
645 George De La Torre Jr Ave Wilmington (90744) *(P-861)*

**Judco Manufacturing Inc (PA)** ............................. C ...... 310 534-0959
1429 240th St Harbor City (90710) *(P-11461)*

**Judith Von Hopf Inc** .............................................. E ...... 909 481-1884
1525 W 13th St Ste H Upland (91786) *(P-3660)*

**Judson Studios Inc** .............................................. E ...... 323 255-0131
200 S Avenue 66 Los Angeles (90042) *(P-7229)*

**Judy Ann, Culver City** *Also Called: Fortune Casuals LLC (P-2665)*

**Judy Ann of California Inc** ................................... C ...... 213 623-9233
1936 Mateo St Los Angeles (90021) *(P-2672)*

**Judy O Productions Inc** ....................................... E ...... 323 938-8513
4858 W Pico Blvd Ste 331 Los Angeles (90019) *(P-4334)*

**Judy's Candy Company, Berkeley** *Also Called: Shelton Inc (P-1344)*

**Juengermann Inc** .................................................. E ...... 805 644-7165
1899 Palma Dr Ste A Ventura (93003) *(P-9176)*

**Juice Division, Pacoima** *Also Called: American Fruits & Flavors LLC (P-1978)*

**Juicy Couture Inc** ................................................. C ...... 888 824-8826
1580 Jesse St Los Angeles (90021) *(P-2439)*

**Juicy Whip Inc** ....................................................... E ...... 909 392-7500
1668 Curtiss Ct La Verne (91750) *(P-9802)*

**Julians Foods LLC** ............................................... E ...... 760 583-9358
3021 Industry St Oceanside (92054) *(P-1219)*

**Jumper Media, La Jolla** *Also Called: Jumper Media LLC (P-4422)*

**Jumper Media LLC** ............................................... D ...... 831 333-6202
1719 Alta La Jolla Dr La Jolla (92037) *(P-4422)*

**Jungle Jumps, Pacoima** *Also Called: Twin Peak Industries Inc (P-15869)*

**Jungotv LLC** .......................................................... D ...... 650 207-6227
1800 Vine St Los Angeles (90028) *(P-4423)*

**Junior Steel Co** ..................................................... E ...... 310 856-6868
134 W 168th St Gardena (90248) *(P-8160)*

**JUNIPER NETWORKS, Sunnyvale** *Also Called: Juniper Networks Inc (P-10392)*

**Juniper Networks Inc (PA)** ................................... A ...... 408 745-2000
1133 Innovation Way Sunnyvale (94089) *(P-10392)*

**Juniper Networks Inc** .......................................... A ...... 408 745-2000
1137 Innovation Way Bldg B Sunnyvale (94089) *(P-18981)*

**Juniper Networks Intl LLC** ................................... E ...... 408 745-2000
1133 Innovation Way Sunnyvale (94089) *(P-18982)*

**Jupiter Systems Inc** ............................................. E ...... 510 675-1000
31015 Huntwood Ave Hayward (94544) *(P-10307)*

**Jurny Inc** ................................................................ E ...... 888 875-8769
6600 W Sunset Blvd Los Angeles (90028) *(P-18462)*

**Just Egg, Alameda** *Also Called: Eat Just Inc (P-977)*

## ALPHABETIC SECTION

Just For Fun Inc .................................................. E ...... 310 320-1327
  557 Van Ness Ave Torrance (90501) *(P-2575)*
Just For Wraps Inc (PA) ......................................... C ...... 213 239-0503
  4871 S Santa Fe Ave Vernon (90058) *(P-2778)*
Just Tomatoes Inc ................................................ E ...... 209 894-5371
  2103 W Hamilton Rd Westley (95387) *(P-82)*
Justenough Software Corp Inc (HQ) .............................. E ...... 949 706-5400
  15440 Laguna Canyon Rd Ste 100 Irvine (92618) *(P-18463)*
Justfoodfordogs LLC (PA) ........................................ F ...... 949 722-3647
  1787 Flight Way Tustin (92782) *(P-1105)*
Justice Bros Dist Co Inc ........................................ E ...... 626 359-9174
  2734 Huntington Dr Duarte (91010) *(P-5938)*
Justice Bros-J B Car Care Pdts, Duarte *Also Called: Justice Bros Dist Co Inc (P-5938)*
Justified Performance LLC ....................................... F ...... 916 771-8994
  1111 W Sunset Blvd Rocklin (95765) *(P-8161)*
Justin, El Monte *Also Called: Justin Inc (P-11216)*
Justin Inc ...................................................... E ...... 626 444-4516
  2663 Lee Ave El Monte (91733) *(P-11216)*
Justin Vineyards & Winery LLC ................................... F ...... 805 238-6932
  2265 Wisteria Ln Paso Robles (93446) *(P-1641)*
Justin Vineyards & Winery LLC ................................... F ...... 805 591-3260
  6050 Westside Rd Healdsburg (95448) *(P-1642)*
Justipher Inc ................................................... E ...... 510 918-6800
  1248 W Winton Ave Hayward (94545) *(P-15998)*
Justman Packaging & Display (PA) ................................ D ...... 323 728-8888
  5819 Telegraph Rd Commerce (90040) *(P-16569)*
Juul Labs, San Francisco *Also Called: Juul Labs Inc (P-16157)*
Juul Labs Inc (PA) .............................................. C ...... 415 829-2336
  560 20th St San Francisco (94107) *(P-16157)*
Juul Labs International Inc (HQ) ................................ B ...... 415 829-2336
  560 20th St San Francisco (94107) *(P-16158)*
Jvr Sheetmetal Fabrication Inc .................................. E ...... 714 841-2464
  7101 Patterson Dr Garden Grove (92841) *(P-13674)*
Jvw Corporation ................................................. D ...... 707 431-5250
  1474 Alexander Valley Rd Healdsburg (95448) *(P-1643)*
JW Molding Inc .................................................. F ...... 805 499-2682
  2523 Calcite Cir Newbury Park (91320) *(P-9630)*
Jwc Environmental Inc ........................................... D ...... 714 662-5829
  2600 S Garnsey St Santa Ana (92707) *(P-10569)*
Jwc Environmental Inc (DH) ...................................... E ...... 949 833-3888
  2850 Redhill Ave Ste 125 Santa Ana (92705) *(P-16821)*
Jwc Studio Inc (PA) ............................................. E ...... 323 231-8222
  2423 E 23rd St Los Angeles (90058) *(P-2707)*
JWP Manufacturing LLC ........................................... E ...... 408 970-0641
  3500 De La Cruz Blvd Santa Clara (95054) *(P-10916)*
Jynormus LLC .................................................... F ...... 949 436-2112
  19800 Macarthur Blvd 3rd Fl Irvine (92612) *(P-16318)*
K & D Contracting, Diamond Bar *Also Called: Dynamic Woodworks Inc (P-3132)*
K & D Graphics .................................................. E ...... 714 639-8900
  1432 N Main St Ste C Orange (92867) *(P-3998)*
K & D Graphics Prtg & Packg, Orange *Also Called: K & D Graphics (P-3998)*
K & E Inc ....................................................... F ...... 310 675-3309
  3906 W 139th St Hawthorne (90250) *(P-13883)*
K & G Latirovian Inc ............................................ D ...... 818 319-2862
  11182 Penrose St Sun Valley (91352) *(P-13523)*
K & J Wire Products Corp ........................................ E ...... 714 816-0360
  1220 N Lance Ln Anaheim (92806) *(P-8631)*
K & L Shutters, Bellflower *Also Called: Kl Decorator Sales (P-3152)*
K & N Engineering Inc (PA) ...................................... A ...... 951 826-4000
  1455 Citrus St Riverside (92507) *(P-14061)*
K & S Enterprises, Adelanto *Also Called: Dar-Ken Inc (P-6445)*
K & Z Cabinet Co Inc ............................................ D ...... 909 947-3567
  1450 S Grove Ave Ontario (91761) *(P-3246)*
K 2 Diamond, Torrance *Also Called: Kuz & Kirb (P-7970)*
K A McNair Brewing Co LLC ....................................... E ...... 858 254-3238
  3038 University Ave San Diego (92104) *(P-1438)*
K B Socks Inc (DH) .............................................. D ...... 310 670-3235
  550 N Oak St Inglewood (90302) *(P-2458)*
K Bell, Inglewood *Also Called: K B Socks Inc (P-2458)*
K C Restoration Co Inc .......................................... E ...... 310 280-0597
  1514 W 130th St Gardena (90249) *(P-244)*

K I C, San Diego *Also Called: Embedded Designs Inc (P-14409)*
K L Electronic Inc .............................................. E ...... 714 751-5611
  3083 S Harbor Blvd Santa Ana (92704) *(P-12147)*
K M I, Dana Point *Also Called: Kanstul Musical Instrs Inc (P-15719)*
K Mars, Van Nuys *Also Called: Kazak-Mars Inc (P-15605)*
K P Graphics, Stockton *Also Called: Kp LLC (P-4666)*
K P I, Fremont *Also Called: Knightsbridge Plastics Inc (P-6889)*
K S Designs Inc ................................................. E ...... 562 929-3973
  901 S Cypress St La Habra (90631) *(P-15999)*
K Squared Metals, Lake Elsinore *Also Called: Boozak Inc (P-8393)*
K Too ........................................................... E ...... 213 747-7766
  800 E 12th St Ste 117 Los Angeles (90021) *(P-2673)*
K Tube Technologies, Poway *Also Called: K-Tube Corporation (P-7665)*
K-1 Packaging Group ............................................. C ...... 626 964-9384
  2001 W Mission Blvd Pomona (91766) *(P-4658)*
K-1 Packaging Group, Pomona *Also Called: K-1 Packaging Group (P-4658)*
K-1 Packaging Group LLC (PA) .................................... D ...... 626 964-9384
  17989 Arenth Ave City Of Industry (91748) *(P-4659)*
K-Fab, Santa Clara *Also Called: P M S D Inc (P-11021)*
K-Jack Engineering Co Inc ....................................... D ...... 310 327-8389
  5672 Buckingham Dr Huntington Beach (92649) *(P-3694)*
K-Max Health Products Corp ...................................... F ...... 909 455-0158
  1468 E Mission Blvd Pomona (91766) *(P-5520)*
K-P Engineering Corp ............................................ E ...... 714 545-7045
  2614 Rousselle St Santa Ana (92707) *(P-10917)*
K-Swiss, Glendale *Also Called: K-Swiss Inc (P-6416)*
K-Swiss Inc (DH) ................................................ E ...... 323 675-2700
  101 N Brand Blvd Ste 1700 Glendale (91203) *(P-6416)*
K-Swiss Inc ..................................................... E ...... 951 361-7501
  12450 Philadelphia Ave Eastvale (91752) *(P-6417)*
K-Swiss Sales Corp .............................................. C ...... 323 675-2700
  101 N Brand Blvd Glendale (91203) *(P-6418)*
K-Tech Machine Inc .............................................. C ...... 800 274-9424
  1377 Armorlite Dr San Marcos (92069) *(P-10918)*
K-Tek, Vista *Also Called: M Klemme Technology Corp (P-11672)*
K-Too, Los Angeles *Also Called: K Too (P-2673)*
K-Tube Corporation .............................................. D ...... 858 513-9229
  13400 Kirkham Way Frnt Poway (92064) *(P-7665)*
K-V Engineering Inc ............................................. D ...... 714 229-9977
  2411 W 1st St Santa Ana (92703) *(P-9558)*
K.G.S.electronics, Upland *Also Called: Gar Enterprises (P-12982)*
K&N, Riverside *Also Called: K & N Engineering Inc (P-14061)*
K&R Products Inc ................................................ E ...... 208 935-8824
  370 Encinal St Ste 200 Santa Cruz (95060) *(P-6879)*
K2 Pure Solutions, Pittsburg *Also Called: K2 Pure Solutions Nocal LP (P-6300)*
K2 Pure Solutions Nocal LP ...................................... D ...... 713 249-8057
  950 Loveridge Rd Pittsburg (94565) *(P-6300)*
K31, Laguna Beach *Also Called: K31 Road Engineering LLC (P-16159)*
K31 Road Engineering LLC ........................................ E ...... 305 928-1968
  1968 S Coast Hwy Pmb 593 Laguna Beach (92651) *(P-16159)*
K9 Ballistics Inc ............................................... F ...... 844 772-3125
  708 Via Alondra Camarillo (93012) *(P-16160)*
Kaar Drect Mail Flfillment LLC .................................. E ...... 619 382-3670
  1225 Exposition Way Ste 160 San Diego (92154) *(P-4141)*
Kadan Consultants Incorporated .................................. F ...... 562 988-1165
  5662 Research Dr Huntington Beach (92649) *(P-10919)*
Kafco Sales Company ............................................. E ...... 323 588-7141
  2300 E 37th St Vernon (90058) *(P-16822)*
Kaga (usa) Inc .................................................. E ...... 714 540-2697
  2620 S Susan St Santa Ana (92704) *(P-8855)*
Kagan Trim Center, Los Angeles *Also Called: G Kagan and Sons Inc (P-2416)*
Kagome Inc (HQ) ................................................. E ...... 209 826-8850
  333 Johnson Rd Los Banos (93635) *(P-897)*
Kahgo Truck Parts, Sun Valley *Also Called: K & G Latirovian Inc (P-13523)*
Kai Pharmaceuticals Inc ......................................... E ...... 650 328-9164
  1120 Veterans Blvd South San Francisco (94080) *(P-5521)*
Kai USA Ltd ..................................................... E ...... 323 589-2600
  6031 Malburg Way Vernon (90058) *(P-7937)*
Kainalu Blue Inc ................................................ E ...... 760 806-6400
  4675 North Ave Oceanside (92056) *(P-7578)*

**Kainos Dental Technologies LLC (PA)**................E ...... 800 331-4834
2975 Treat Blvd Bldg D Concord (94518) *(P-15140)*

**Kairos Manufacturing Inc**................F ...... 805 544-2216
201 Bridge St San Luis Obispo (93401) *(P-16161)*

**Kaise Perma San Franc Medic Ce**................E ...... 415 833-2000
2425 Geary Blvd San Francisco (94115) *(P-15371)*

**Kaiser Aerospace & Electronics Corporation**................A ...... 949 250-1015
2701 Orchard Pkwy Ste 100 San Jose (95134) *(P-13884)*

**Kaiser Air Conditioning, Oxnard** *Also Called: Kaiser Air Conditioning and Sheet Metal Inc (P-515)*

**Kaiser Air Conditioning and Sheet Metal Inc**................E ...... 805 988-1800
600 Pacific Ave Oxnard (93030) *(P-515)*

**Kaiser Aluminum Corporation**................D ...... 323 726-8011
6250 Bandini Blvd Commerce (90040) *(P-7741)*

**Kaiser Aluminum Intl Corp**................D ...... 949 614-1740
6177 Sunal Blvd Pleasanton (94566) *(P-7708)*

**Kaiser Enterprises Inc**................E ...... 916 203-9797
11375 Sunrise Park Dr Ste 500 Rancho Cordova (95742) *(P-9263)*

**Kaiser Enterprises Inc (PA)**................E ...... 209 728-2091
798 Murphys Creek Rd Murphys (95247) *(P-9264)*

**Kaiser Foundation Hospitals**................C ...... 323 264-4310
3355 E 26th St Vernon (90058) *(P-17521)*

**Kaiser Prmnnte Nat Fclties Svc, Vernon** *Also Called: Kaiser Foundation Hospitals (P-17521)*

**Kaizen Technology Partners LLC**................E ...... 415 515-1909
981 Mission St San Francisco (94103) *(P-17938)*

**Kakuichi America Inc**................D ...... 310 539-1590
23540 Telo Ave Torrance (90505) *(P-6599)*

**Kal Plastics, Vernon** *Also Called: Tom York Enterprises Inc (P-7055)*

**Kal-Cameron Manufacturing Corp (HQ)**................D ...... 626 338-7308
4265 Puente Ave Baldwin Park (91706) *(P-7956)*

**Kal-Kustom Enterprises (PA)**................F ...... 510 651-8400
43289 Osgood Rd Fremont (94539) *(P-16937)*

**Kalap Inc**................F ...... 818 332-6916
401 N Brand Blvd Ste 814 Glendale (91203) *(P-15646)*

**Kalila Medical Inc**................E ...... 408 819-5175
1400 Dell Ave Ste C Campbell (95008) *(P-14888)*

**Kalman Manufacturing Inc**................E ...... 408 776-7664
780 Jarvis Dr Ste 150 Morgan Hill (95037) *(P-10920)*

**Kama Sutra, Moorpark** *Also Called: Kamsut Incorporated (P-5996)*

**Kama-Tech Corporation**................F ...... 619 421-7858
3451 Main St Ste 109 Chula Vista (91911) *(P-14792)*

**Kamet, Milpitas** *Also Called: Khuus Inc (P-10926)*

**Kamm Industries Inc**................E ...... 800 317-6253
43352 Business Park Dr Temecula (92590) *(P-3011)*

**Kammerer Enterprises Inc**................D ...... 760 560-0550
1280 N Melrose Dr Vista (92083) *(P-7540)*

**Kamper Fabrication Inc**................E ...... 209 599-7137
20107 N Ripon Rd Ripon (95366) *(P-9364)*

**Kamsut Incorporated**................E ...... 805 495-7479
5260 Kazuko Ct Moorpark (93021) *(P-5996)*

**Kanan Baking Company, Woodland Hills** *Also Called: Gold Coast Baking Company LLC (P-1214)*

**Kandy Kiss of California Inc**................D
14761 Califa St Van Nuys (91411) *(P-2674)*

**Kanex**................E ...... 714 332-1681
9377 Haven Ave Rancho Cucamonga (91730) *(P-13259)*

**Kanstul Musical Instrs Inc**................E ...... 714 563-1000
23772 Perth Bay Dana Point (92629) *(P-15719)*

**Kap Manufacturing Inc**................E ...... 909 599-2525
327 W Allen Ave San Dimas (91773) *(P-10921)*

**Kap Medical**................E ...... 951 340-4360
1395 Pico St Corona (92881) *(P-14889)*

**Kapan - Kent Company Inc**................E ...... 760 631-1716
3540 Seagate Way Ste 100 Oceanside (92056) *(P-3012)*

**Kaplan Indus Car Wash Sups Inc**................E ...... 562 921-5544
13875 Mica St Santa Fe Springs (90670) *(P-16909)*

**Kaplan Industries Mfg, Santa Fe Springs** *Also Called: Kaplan Indus Car Wash Sups Inc (P-16909)*

**Kapsch Trafficcom Usa Inc**................C ...... 925 225-1600
4256 Hacienda Dr Ste 100 Pleasanton (94588) *(P-11329)*

**Kar Ice Service Inc (PA)**................F ...... 760 256-2648
2521 Solar Way Barstow (92311) *(P-2110)*

**KARAT, Chino** *Also Called: Karat Packaging Inc (P-6880)*

**Karat Packaging Inc (PA)**................E ...... 626 965-8882
6185 Kimball Ave Chino (91708) *(P-6880)*

**Karbide Inc**................E ...... 951 354-0900
12650 Magnolia Ave Ste B Riverside (92503) *(P-9679)*

**Karcher Design**................D ...... 253 220-8244
235 W Paul Ave Clovis (93612) *(P-8008)*

**Karel Manufacturing, Calexico** *Also Called: Lorenz Inc (P-13268)*

**Karem Aircraft Inc**................E ...... 949 859-4444
1 Capital Dr Lake Forest (92630) *(P-13885)*

**Kargo Global Inc**................C ...... 212 979-9000
1437 4th St Ste 200 Santa Monica (90401) *(P-17789)*

**Kargo Master Inc**................E ...... 916 638-8703
11261 Trade Center Dr Rancho Cordova (95742) *(P-8480)*

**Kargo Technologies Corp**................E ...... 312 925-1565
424 9th St San Francisco (94103) *(P-14006)*

**Karl Storz Endscpy-America Inc (HQ)**................C ...... 424 218-8100
2151 E Grand Ave El Segundo (90245) *(P-15141)*

**Karl Storz Endscpy-America Inc**................D ...... 800 964-5563
1 N Los Carneros Dr Goleta (93117) *(P-15142)*

**Karl Storz Imaging Inc (HQ)**................B ...... 805 968-5563
1 S Los Carneros Rd Goleta (93117) *(P-14890)*

**Karl Storz Imaging Inc**................E ...... 805 968-5563
32 Aero Camino Goleta (93117) *(P-15143)*

**Karl Storz Intgrated Solutions, El Segundo** *Also Called: Karl Storz Endscpy-America Inc (P-15141)*

**Karl Strauss Brewery & Rest, San Diego** *Also Called: Associated Microbreweries Inc (P-1422)*

**Karl Strauss Brewery Garden, San Diego** *Also Called: Associated Microbreweries Inc (P-1421)*

**Karl Strauss Brewing Company**................F ...... 213 228-2739
600 Wilshire Blvd Ste 100 Los Angeles (90017) *(P-1439)*

**Karl Strauss Brewing Company (PA)**................E ...... 858 273-2739
5985 Santa Fe St San Diego (92109) *(P-1440)*

**Karl Strauss Brewing Company**................F ...... 951 225-7960
40868 Winchester Rd Temecula (92591) *(P-17590)*

**Karl Strauss Brewing Company, San Diego** *Also Called: Associated McRbrwries Ltd A Cal (P-1423)*

**Karma Automotive LLC**................A ...... 855 565-2762
9950 Jeronimo Rd Irvine (92618) *(P-13361)*

**Karman Missile & Space Systems, South El Monte** *Also Called: Amro Fabricating Corporation (P-13778)*

**Karoun Cheese, San Fernando** *Also Called: Karoun Dairies Inc (P-722)*

**Karoun Dairies Inc (PA)**................E ...... 818 767-7000
13023 Arroyo St San Fernando (91340) *(P-722)*

**Kartos Therapeutics Inc**................D ...... 650 542-0130
275 Shoreline Dr Ste 100 Redwood City (94065) *(P-5522)*

**Kas Engineering Inc (PA)**................E ...... 310 450-8925
1714 14th St Santa Monica (90404) *(P-6881)*

**Kasco Fab Inc**................D ...... 559 442-1018
4529 S Chestnut Ave Lowr Fresno (93725) *(P-8162)*

**Kashiyama-Usa Inc**................F ...... 510 979-0070
3765 Yale Way Fremont (94538) *(P-14681)*

**Kaslen Textiles, Vernon** *Also Called: Kaslen Textiles LLC (P-2529)*

**Kaslen Textiles LLC**................F ...... 323 588-7700
2140 E 51st St Vernon (90058) *(P-2529)*

**Katadyn Desalination LLC**................E ...... 415 526-2780
2220 S Mcdowell Boulevard Ext Petaluma (94954) *(P-11407)*

**Katch Inc**................E ...... 626 369-0958
520 Hofgaarden St City Of Industry (91744) *(P-8163)*

**Kate Farms Inc**................C ...... 805 845-2446
101 Innovation Pl Santa Barbara (93108) *(P-2246)*

**Kate Smrvlle Skin Hlth Experts, El Segundo** *Also Called: Kate Somerville Skincare LLC (P-5523)*

**Kate Somerville Skincare LLC (HQ)**................D ...... 323 655-7546
2121 Park Pl Ste 100 El Segundo (90245) *(P-5523)*

**Kateeva Inc (PA)**................C ...... 800 385-7802
7015 Gateway Blvd Newark (94560) *(P-11870)*

**Kater-Crafts Incorporated**................E ...... 562 692-0665
3205 Weldon Ave Los Angeles (90065) *(P-5012)*

**Katz Millennium Sls & Mktg Inc**................C ...... 323 966-5066
5700 Wilshire Blvd Ste 100 Los Angeles (90036) *(P-11871)*

ALPHABETIC SECTION
Kennfoods Usa LLC

**Katzirs Floor & HM Design Inc (PA)** ........ E ...... 818 988-9663
14959 Delano St Van Nuys (91411) ***(P-16428)***
**Katzkin Leather Inc (PA)** ........ C ...... 323 725-1243
6868 W Acco St Montebello (90640) ***(P-17298)***
**Kaufman Building & MGT Inc** ........ F ...... 707 732-3770
1834 Soscol Ave Ste C Napa (94559) ***(P-316)***
**Kautz Vineyards Inc** ........ E ...... 209 369-1911
6111 E Armstrong Rd Lodi (95240) ***(P-1644)***
**Kavlico Corporation (DH)** ........ A ...... 805 523-2000
1461 Lawrence Dr Thousand Oaks (91320) ***(P-13016)***
**Kawasaki Micro Elec Amer, San Jose** *Also Called: Megachips Technology America Corporation* ***(P-12555)***
**Kaweah Container Inc (HQ)** ........ E ...... 559 651-7846
7101 Avenue 304 Visalia (93291) ***(P-3863)***
**Kawneer Company Inc** ........ D ...... 951 410-4779
925 Marlborough Ave Riverside (92507) ***(P-8271)***
**Kawneer Company Inc** ........ C ...... 559 651-4000
7200 W Doe Ave Visalia (93291) ***(P-8632)***
**Kay & James Inc** ........ D ...... 818 998-0357
14062 Balboa Blvd Sylmar (91342) ***(P-10922)***
**Kay Chesterfield Inc** ........ F ...... 510 533-5565
3109 Adeline St Emeryville (94608) ***(P-3477)***
**Kaye Sandy Enterprises Inc** ........ E ...... 650 961-5334
344 Alameda De Las Pulgas Redwood City (94062) ***(P-14038)***
**Kaylas Cake Corporation** ........ E ...... 714 869-1522
1311 S Gilbert St Fullerton (92833) ***(P-17414)***
**Kayo Clothing Company, Lynwood** *Also Called: Kayo of California* ***(P-2779)***
**Kayo of California (PA)** ........ E ...... 323 233-6107
11854 Alameda St Lynwood (90262) ***(P-2779)***
**Kazak-Mars Inc** ........ E ...... 818 375-1033
16430 Vanowen St Van Nuys (91406) ***(P-15605)***
**Kazuhm Inc** ........ E ...... 858 771-3861
6450 Lusk Blvd Ste E208 San Diego (92121) ***(P-18464)***
**KB Delta Inc** ........ E ...... 310 530-1539
3155 Fujita St Torrance (90505) ***(P-8856)***
**KB Delta Comprsr Valve Parts, Torrance** *Also Called: KB Delta Inc* ***(P-8856)***
**KB Sheetmetal Fabrication Inc** ........ E ...... 714 979-1780
17371 Mount Wynne Cir # B Fountain Valley (92708) ***(P-8481)***
**KB Wines LLC** ........ F ...... 707 823-7430
220 Morris St Sebastopol (95472) ***(P-1645)***
**Kba Engineering LLC** ........ D ...... 661 323-0487
2157 Mohawk St Bakersfield (93308) ***(P-9464)***
**Kbr Inc** ........ E ...... 562 436-9281
2000 W Gaylord St Long Beach (90813) ***(P-11299)***
**Kc Hilites Inc** ........ E ...... 928 635-2607
13637 Cimarron Ave Gardena (90249) ***(P-11574)***
**Kc Pharmaceuticals Inc (PA)** ........ D ...... 909 598-9499
3420 Pomona Blvd Pomona (91768) ***(P-5524)***
**Kca Electronics Inc** ........ C ...... 714 239-2433
223 N Crescent Way Anaheim (92801) ***(P-12148)***
**Kcb Towers Inc** ........ D ...... 909 862-0322
27260 Meines St Highland (92346) ***(P-531)***
**Kdc Inc (HQ)** ........ C ...... 714 828-7000
4462 Corporate Center Dr Los Alamitos (90720) ***(P-459)***
**Kdc Systems, Los Alamitos** *Also Called: Kdc Inc* ***(P-459)***
**Kdc/One Chatsworth Inc (DH)** ........ D ...... 818 709-1345
20245 Sunburst St Chatsworth (91311) ***(P-5997)***
**Kdc/One Chatsworth Inc** ........ C ...... 818 709-1345
20320 Prairie St Chatsworth (91311) ***(P-5998)***
**Kdf Enterprises LLC** ........ C ...... 803 928-7073
3941 Park Dr El Dorado Hills (95762) ***(P-9429)***
**KDF Inc** ........ E ...... 408 779-3731
15875 Concord Cir Morgan Hill (95037) ***(P-10923)***
**Kdr Holding Inc (PA)** ........ F ...... 510 230-2777
47448 Fremont Blvd Fremont (94538) ***(P-17755)***
**Kearneys Aluminum Foundry Inc (PA)** ........ E ...... 559 233-2591
2660 S Dearing Ave Fresno (93725) ***(P-7812)***
**Kechika, Rcho Sta Marg** *Also Called: Point Conception Inc* ***(P-2801)***
**Keco Inc** ........ E ...... 619 298-3800
3475 Kurtz St San Diego (92110) ***(P-16823)***
**Keebler, Tracy** *Also Called: Keebler Company* ***(P-1279)***
**Keebler Company** ........ C ...... 209 836-0302
1550 N Chrisman Rd Tracy (95304) ***(P-1279)***
**Keenan Farms Inc** ........ D ...... 559 945-1400
31510 Plymouth Ave Kettleman City (93239) ***(P-39)***
**Keepcool USA LLC (PA)** ........ F ...... 925 962-1832
25 Orinda Way Ste 210 Orinda (94563) ***(P-2959)***
**Keiser Corporation (PA)** ........ D ...... 559 256-8000
2470 S Cherry Ave Fresno (93706) ***(P-15834)***
**Keiser Sports Health Equipment, Fresno** *Also Called: Keiser Corporation* ***(P-15834)***
**Keith Co, Pico Rivera** *Also Called: W P Keith Co Inc* ***(P-10062)***
**Keith E Archambeau Sr Inc** ........ E ...... 818 718-6110
20615 Plummer St Chatsworth (91311) ***(P-8482)***
**Kelco, Oxnard** *Also Called: Kim Laube & Company Inc* ***(P-6000)***
**Kelco Sales & Engineering, Norwalk** *Also Called: Polley Inc* ***(P-10107)***
**Kelcourt Plastics Inc (DH)** ........ D ...... 949 361-0774
1000 Calle Recodo San Clemente (92673) ***(P-6882)***
**Kellermyer Bergensons Svcs LLC (PA)** ........ E ...... 760 631-5111
3605 Ocean Ranch Blvd Ste 200 Oceanside (92056) ***(P-10570)***
**Kelley Blue Book Co Inc (DH)** ........ D ...... 949 770-7704
195 Technology Dr Irvine (92618) ***(P-4269)***
**Kellogg Garden Product, Lockeford** *Also Called: Kellogg Supply Inc* ***(P-6177)***
**Kellogg Supply Inc** ........ C ...... 209 727-3130
12686 Locke Rd Lockeford (95237) ***(P-6177)***
**Kelly Pneumatics Inc** ........ F ...... 800 704-7552
1611 Babcock St Newport Beach (92663) ***(P-13260)***
**Kelly-Moore Paint Company Inc (HQ)** ........ C ...... 650 592-8337
1390 El Camino Real Ste 300 San Carlos (94070) ***(P-6089)***
**Kelly-Moore Paint Company Inc** ........ E ...... 650 595-1654
320 Industrial Rd San Carlos (94070) ***(P-6090)***
**Kelly-Moore Paints, San Carlos** *Also Called: Kelly-Moore Paint Company Inc* ***(P-6089)***
**Kelly-Moore Paints, San Carlos** *Also Called: Kelly-Moore Paint Company Inc* ***(P-6090)***
**Kelmscott Communications LLC** ........ B ...... 949 475-1900
2485 Da Vinci Irvine (92614) ***(P-4660)***
**Kelpac Medical, San Clemente** *Also Called: Kelcourt Plastics Inc* ***(P-6882)***
**Kelytech Corporation** ........ E ...... 408 935-0888
1482 Gladding Ct Milpitas (95035) ***(P-13017)***
**Kemac Technology Inc** ........ E ...... 626 334-1519
503 S Vincent Ave Azusa (91702) ***(P-10924)***
**Kemira Water Solutions Inc** ........ E ...... 909 350-5678
14000 San Bernardino Ave Fontana (92335) ***(P-5098)***
**Kemira Water Solutions Inc** ........ E ...... 909 350-5678
14000 San Bernardino Ave Fontana (92335) ***(P-6301)***
**Kemiron Pacific, Fontana** *Also Called: Kemira Water Solutions Inc* ***(P-6301)***
**Kemper Enterprises Inc** ........ F ...... 909 627-6191
13595 12th St Chino (91710) ***(P-7957)***
**Kempton Machine Works Inc** ........ F ...... 714 990-0596
4070 E Leaverton Ct Anaheim (92807) ***(P-9680)***
**Ken's Spray Equipment, Inc., Compton** *Also Called: Kens Spray Equipment LLC* ***(P-9086)***
**Kenco Engineering Inc** ........ E ...... 916 782-8494
2155 Pfe Rd Roseville (95747) ***(P-9430)***
**Kenco Wear Parts, Roseville** *Also Called: Kenco Engineering Inc* ***(P-9430)***
**Kendall-Jackson Wine Estates (HQ)** ........ B ...... 707 544-4000
425 Aviation Blvd Santa Rosa (95403) ***(P-1646)***
**Kendon Industries Inc** ........ F ...... 714 630-7144
3711 E La Palma Ave Anaheim (92806) ***(P-14121)***
**Kenefick Ranches LLC** ........ E ...... 707 942-6175
2200 Pickett Rd Calistoga (94515) ***(P-1647)***
**Keney Manufacturing Co (PA)** ........ F ...... 209 358-6474
586 Broadway Ave Atwater (95301) ***(P-3247)***
**Keney's Cabinets, Atwater** *Also Called: Keney Manufacturing Co* ***(P-3247)***
**Kenjitsu USA Corp** ........ F ...... 619 734-5862
9830 Siempre Viva Rd Ste 14 San Diego (92154) ***(P-13018)***
**Kennedy Athletics, Carson** *Also Called: Cali-Fame Los Angeles Inc* ***(P-2842)***
**Kennedy Name Plate Co** ........ E ...... 323 585-0121
4501 Pacific Blvd Vernon (90058) ***(P-9085)***
**Kennerley-Spratling Inc (PA)** ........ C ...... 510 351-8230
2116 Farallon Dr San Leandro (94577) ***(P-6883)***
**Kennerley-Spratling Inc** ........ C ...... 408 944-9407
2308 Zanker Rd San Jose (95131) ***(P-6884)***
**Kennfoods Usa LLC** ........ E ...... 209 932-8132
861 Performance Dr Stockton (95206) ***(P-1355)***

ALPHABETIC

Employee Codes: A=Over 500 employees, B=251-500
C=101-250, D=51-100, E=20-50, F=10-19, G=1-9
2025 Harris California
Manufacturers Directory
© Mergent Inc. 1-800-342-5647
1111

**Kenny The Printer, Orange** *Also Called: American PCF Prtrs College Inc (P-4510)*
**Kens Spray Equipment LLC** .................................................. C ...... 310 635-9995
1900 W Walnut St Compton (90220) *(P-9086)*
**Kensington Computer Pdts Group, Burlingame** *Also Called: Acco Brands Corporation (P-10301)*
**Kensington Laboratories LLC (PA)** .......................................... F ...... 510 324-0126
6200 Village Pkwy Dublin (94568) *(P-11330)*
**Kenvue Brands LLC** ................................................................ C ...... 310 642-1150
5760 W 96th St Los Angeles (90045) *(P-5999)*
**Kenwait Die Casting Company, Sun Valley** *Also Called: Kenwalt Die Casting Corp (P-7813)*
**Kenwalt Die Casting Corp** ...................................................... E ...... 818 768-5800
8719 Bradley Ave Sun Valley (91352) *(P-7813)*
**Kenwood Vineyards, Kenwood** *Also Called: Pernod Ricard Usa LLC (P-1704)*
**Kenzo Estate Inc** .................................................................... E ...... 707 254-7572
3200 Monticello Rd Napa (94558) *(P-93)*
**Kepner Plas Fabricators Inc** .................................................. E ...... 562 543-4472
3131 Lomita Blvd Torrance (90505) *(P-6885)*
**Keri Systems Inc (PA)** .............................................................. D ...... 408 435-8400
302 Enzo Dr Ste 190 San Jose (95138) *(P-13261)*
**Kerio Technologies Inc** .......................................................... E ...... 409 880-7011
111 W Saint John St Ste 1100 San Jose (95113) *(P-18465)*
**Kerleylegacy63 Inc** ................................................................ D ...... 714 630-7286
3000-3010 La Jolla St Anaheim (92806) *(P-10925)*
**Kern Delta Co LLC** .................................................................. E ...... 559 276-2855
2513 W Shaw Ave Ste 101 Fresno (93711) *(P-953)*
**Kern Energy, Bakersfield** *Also Called: Kern Oil & Refining Co (P-6340)*
**Kern Engineering, Chino** *Also Called: R Kern Engineering & Mfg Corp (P-12894)*
**Kern Oil & Refining Co (HQ)** .................................................. C ...... 661 845-0761
7724 E Panama Ln Bakersfield (93307) *(P-6340)*
**Kern Steel Fabrication Inc (PA)** .............................................. D ...... 661 327-9588
627 Williams St Bakersfield (93305) *(P-8164)*
**Kern Valley Sun, Lake Isabella** *Also Called: Wick Communications Co (P-4221)*
**Kernridge Division, Mc Kittrick** *Also Called: Aera Energy LLC (P-120)*
**Kerr Corporation (HQ)** .......................................................... C ...... 714 516-7400
1717 W Collins Ave Orange (92867) *(P-15461)*
**Kerry Inc** ................................................................................ D ...... 760 396-2116
64405 Lincoln St Mecca (92254) *(P-765)*
**Kerv Interactive, Sherman Oaks** *Also Called: Grabit Interactive Inc (P-17788)*
**Kesa Incorporated** ................................................................ E ...... 714 956-2827
960 E Discovery Ln Anaheim (92801) *(P-19057)*
**Kesmor Associates** ................................................................ E ...... 213 629-2300
610 S Broadway Ste 717 Los Angeles (90014) *(P-15695)*
**Kessil, Richmond** *Also Called: Dicon Fiberoptics Inc (P-12960)*
**Ketab Corporation** ................................................................ F ...... 310 477-7477
12701 Van Nuys Blvd Ste H Pacoima (91331) *(P-17638)*
**Ketera Technologies Inc (DH)** ................................................ E ...... 408 572-9500
3055 Olin Ave Ste 2200 San Jose (95128) *(P-18466)*
**Ketos Inc** ................................................................................ D ...... 408 550-2162
420 S Hillview Dr Milpitas (95035) *(P-18983)*
**Kettenbach LP** ........................................................................ E ...... 877 532-2123
16052 Beach Blvd Ste 221 Huntington Beach (92647) *(P-15462)*
**Keurig Green Mountain Inc** .................................................. E ...... 909 557-6513
26875 Pioneer Ave Redlands (92374) *(P-1897)*
**Kevala Inc** .............................................................................. E ...... 415 712-7829
550 California St San Francisco (94104) *(P-18467)*
**Kevin Orthopedic, Riverside** *Also Called: Foot In Motion Inc (P-15348)*
**Kevin Whaley** ........................................................................ E ...... 619 596-4000
9565 Pathway St Santee (92071) *(P-9221)*
**Kevin White** .......................................................................... F ...... 562 231-6642
9918 Ramona St Apt 1 Bellflower (90706) *(P-4142)*
**Kevin's Natural Foods, Stockton** *Also Called: Calchef Foods LLC (P-976)*
**Kevita, Oxnard** *Also Called: Kevita Inc (P-1898)*
**Kevita Inc (HQ)** ...................................................................... D ...... 805 200-2250
2220 Celsius Ave Ste A Oxnard (93030) *(P-1898)*
**Key Code Media Inc (PA)** ...................................................... E ...... 818 303-3900
270 S Flower St Burbank (91502) *(P-10172)*
**Key Container, South Gate** *Also Called: Liberty Container Company (P-3864)*
**Key Energy Services Inc** ........................................................ E ...... 831 627-2404
62391 Sargents Rd San Ardo (93450) *(P-245)*
**Key Essentials Inc** .................................................................. D
1916 S Tubeway Ave Commerce (90040) *(P-2012)*

**Key-Bak, Ontario** *Also Called: West Coast Chain Mfg Co (P-13329)*
**Keyline Sales Inc** .................................................................... E ...... 562 904-3910
9768 Firestone Blvd Downey (90241) *(P-16769)*
**Keysight Technologies Inc (PA)** ............................................ A ...... 800 829-4444
1400 Fountaingrove Pkwy Santa Rosa (95403) *(P-14427)*
**Keysight Technologies Inc** .................................................... D ...... 408 553-3290
5301 Stevens Creek Blvd Santa Clara (95051) *(P-14542)*
**Keysight Technologies Inc** .................................................... F ...... 916 788-5571
10090 Foothills Blvd Roseville (95747) *(P-14543)*
**Keyspan, Walnut Creek** *Also Called: Innosys Incorporated (P-17929)*
**Keyssa Inc (PA)** ...................................................................... E ...... 408 637-2300
3945 Freedom Cir Ste 560 Santa Clara (95054) *(P-12512)*
**Keystone Dental Inc** .............................................................. E ...... 781 328-3324
5 Holland Ste 209 Irvine (92618) *(P-15463)*
**Keystone Dental Inc** .............................................................. E ...... 781 328-3382
13645 Alton Pkwy Ste A Irvine (92618) *(P-15464)*
**Keystone Door & Bldg Sup Inc** .............................................. E ...... 916 623-8100
1037 N Market Blvd Ste 9 Sacramento (95834) *(P-495)*
**Keystone Door & Building Sup, Sacramento** *Also Called: Keystone Door & Bldg Sup Inc (P-495)*
**Keystone Textile Inc** .............................................................. F ...... 213 622-7755
1201 Mateo St Los Angeles (90021) *(P-2454)*
**Kezar Life Sciences, South San Francisco** *Also Called: Kezar Life Sciences Inc (P-5525)*
**Kezar Life Sciences Inc (PA)** .................................................. E ...... 650 822-5600
4000 Shoreline Ct Ste 300 South San Francisco (94080) *(P-5525)*
**Kf Fiberglass Inc (PA)** ............................................................ F ...... 562 869-1536
8247 Phlox St Downey (90241) *(P-13524)*
**KG Technologies Inc (PA)** ...................................................... F ...... 888 513-1874
6028 State Farm Dr Rohnert Park (94928) *(P-13019)*
**Kgs Electronics, Arcadia** *Also Called: Gar Enterprises (P-16524)*
**Khan Academy Inc** ................................................................ D ...... 650 336-5426
1200 Villa St Ste 200 Mountain View (94041) *(P-18468)*
**Kharma Clothing LLC** ............................................................ F ...... 323 494-7705
5066 W Jefferson Blvd Los Angeles (90016) *(P-2863)*
**Khuus Inc** .............................................................................. D ...... 408 522-8000
1778 Mccarthy Blvd Milpitas (95035) *(P-10926)*
**Kiara Sky Professional Nails, Bakersfield** *Also Called: Glam and Glits Nail Design Inc (P-5981)*
**Kibblwhite Prcsion McHning Inc** .......................................... E ...... 650 359-4704
580 Crespi Dr Ste H Pacifica (94044) *(P-14062)*
**Kibo Software Inc** ................................................................ F ...... 415 425-1833
617 2nd St Petaluma (94952) *(P-18469)*
**Kids Healthy Foods LLC** ........................................................ E ...... 949 260-4950
2030 Main St Ste 1300 Irvine (92614) *(P-17191)*
**Kids Line LLC** ........................................................................ C ...... 310 660-0110
10541 Humbolt St Los Alamitos (90720) *(P-2932)*
**Kie-Con Inc** .......................................................................... D ...... 925 754-9494
3551 Wilbur Ave Antioch (94509) *(P-7350)*
**Kieran Label Corp** ................................................................ E ...... 619 449-4457
2321 Siempre Viva Ct Ste 101 San Diego (92154) *(P-4904)*
**Kieu Hoang Winery LLC** ...................................................... E ...... 707 253-1615
1285 Dealy Ln Napa (94559) *(P-1648)*
**Kifuki USA Co Inc (HQ)** ........................................................ D ...... 626 334-8090
15547 1st St Irwindale (91706) *(P-696)*
**Kik, Santa Fe Springs** *Also Called: Kik-Socal Inc (P-5911)*
**Kik Custom Products, Torrance** *Also Called: Prestone Products Corporation (P-6318)*
**Kik Pool Additives Inc** .......................................................... C ...... 909 390-9912
5160 E Airport Dr Ontario (91761) *(P-6302)*
**Kik-Socal Inc** ........................................................................ A ...... 562 946-6427
9028 Dice Rd Santa Fe Springs (90670) *(P-5911)*
**Kikkoman, San Francisco** *Also Called: Kikkoman Sales Usa Inc (P-17192)*
**Kikkoman Foods Inc** ............................................................ F ...... 916 355-8078
1000 Glenn Dr Folsom (95630) *(P-980)*
**Kikkoman Sales Usa Inc (HQ)** .............................................. E ...... 415 956-7750
50 California St Ste 3600 San Francisco (94111) *(P-17192)*
**Kilam, Fremont** *Also Called: Kilam Inc (P-17076)*
**Kilam Inc** .............................................................................. C ...... 510 943-4040
47685 Lakeview Blvd Fremont (94538) *(P-17076)*
**Kilgore Enterprises LLC** ........................................................ E ...... 925 885-8999
2005 San Jose Dr Unit 258 Antioch (94509) *(P-246)*
**Kilgore Machine Company Inc** ............................................ E ...... 714 540-3659
2312 S Susan St Santa Ana (92704) *(P-10927)*

## ALPHABETIC SECTION — Kitchen Expo

Killion Industries Inc (PA) .......... D ...... 760 727-5102
1380 Poinsettia Ave Vista (92081) *(P-3661)*

Kilovac, Carpinteria *Also Called: Te Connectivity Corporation (P-11352)*

Kim & Cami Productions Inc .......... E ...... 323 584-1300
2950 Leonis Blvd Vernon (90058) *(P-2780)*

Kim Laube & Company Inc .......... E ...... 805 240-1300
2221 Statham Blvd Oxnard (93033) *(P-6000)*

Kim Lighting & Mfg, City Of Industry *Also Called: Kim Lighting Inc (P-11604)*

Kim Lighting Inc .......... A ...... 626 968-5666
16555 Gale Ave City Of Industry (91745) *(P-11604)*

Kimball Electronics Ind Inc .......... E ...... 669 234-1110
5215 Hellyer Ave Ste 130 San Jose (95138) *(P-12149)*

Kimberley Wine Vinegars, Acampo *Also Called: California Concentrate Company (P-998)*

Kimberly Machine Inc .......... E ...... 714 539-0151
12822 Joy St Garden Grove (92840) *(P-10928)*

Kimco Iron Inc .......... F ...... 714 293-6442
8235 Inverness Grn Buena Park (90621) *(P-8633)*

Kimlor Innovative HM Fashions, Santa Ana *Also Called: Kimlor Mills Inc (P-16415)*

Kimlor Mills Inc .......... D ...... 803 531-2037
18142 Blue Ridge Dr Santa Ana (92705) *(P-16415)*

Kinamad, Camarillo *Also Called: VME Acquisition Corp (P-15428)*

Kinamed Inc .......... E ...... 805 384-2748
820 Flynn Rd Camarillo (93012) *(P-15372)*

Kind Led Grow Lights, Santa Rosa *Also Called: Supercloset (P-7966)*

Kindeva Drug Delivery LP .......... B ...... 818 341-1300
19901 Nordhoff St Northridge (91324) *(P-5526)*

Kindred Litho Incorporated .......... E ...... 909 944-4015
10833 Bell Ct Rancho Cucamonga (91730) *(P-4661)*

Kindredbio Equine Inc .......... E ...... 888 608-2542
1555 Bayshore Hwy Ste 200 Burlingame (94010) *(P-5527)*

Kinematic, Sonora *Also Called: Kinematic Automation Inc (P-15144)*

Kinematic Automation Inc .......... D ...... 209 532-3200
21085 Longeway Rd Sonora (95370) *(P-15144)*

Kinemetrics Inc (DH) .......... D ...... 626 795-2220
222 Vista Ave Pasadena (91107) *(P-19400)*

King Bros Enterprises LLC .......... C ...... 661 257-3262
29101 The Old Rd Valencia (91355) *(P-6682)*

King Bros Industries .......... C
29101 The Old Rd Valencia (91355) *(P-6886)*

King Ex Chinese Fd & Donut, North Hollywood *Also Called: King Express Inc (P-17591)*

King Express Inc .......... F ...... 818 503-2772
12053 Vanowen St North Hollywood (91605) *(P-17591)*

King Graphics, San Diego *Also Called: Colmol Inc (P-4863)*

King Henrys Inc .......... E ...... 818 536-3692
29124 Hancock Pkwy 1 Valencia (91355) *(P-2096)*

King Holding Corporation .......... A ...... 586 254-3900
360 N Crescent Dr Beverly Hills (90210) *(P-8760)*

King Instrument Company Inc .......... E ...... 714 891-0008
12700 Pala Dr Garden Grove (92841) *(P-14428)*

King Nutronics LLC .......... E ...... 818 887-5460
6421 Independence Ave Woodland Hills (91367) *(P-14429)*

King Nutronics Corporation, Woodland Hills *Also Called: King Nutronics LLC (P-14429)*

King Plastics Inc .......... D ...... 714 997-7540
840 N Elm St Orange (92867) *(P-6887)*

King Shock Technology Inc .......... D ...... 719 394-3754
12472 Edison Way Garden Grove (92841) *(P-13525)*

King Taco Restaurant Inc (PA) .......... D ...... 323 266-3585
3421 E 14th St Los Angeles (90023) *(P-17592)*

King Wire Partitions Inc .......... E ...... 323 256-4848
6044 N Figueroa St Los Angeles (90042) *(P-8702)*

Kingcom(us) LLC (DH) .......... E ...... 424 744-5697
3100 Ocean Park Blvd Santa Monica (90405) *(P-18470)*

Kingdom Matress Company, Commerce *Also Called: Kingdom Mattress Co Inc (P-3530)*

Kingdom Mattress Co Inc .......... F ...... 562 630-5531
2425 S Malt Ave Commerce (90040) *(P-3530)*

Kingfa Global Inc .......... F ...... 909 212-5413
1455 S Archibald Ave Ontario (91761) *(P-8761)*

Kingman Industries, Tustin *Also Called: Johnston International Corporation (P-10097)*

Kingman Industries Inc .......... E ...... 951 698-1812
26370 Beckman Ct Ste A Murrieta (92562) *(P-5876)*

Kings & Convicts Bp LLC (HQ) .......... E ...... 858 790-6900
9045 Carroll Way San Diego (92121) *(P-1441)*

Kings & Convicts Bp LLC .......... C ...... 619 255-7213
2215 India St San Diego (92101) *(P-1442)*

Kings & Convicts Bp LLC .......... D ...... 619 295-2337
5401 Linda Vista Rd Ste 406 San Diego (92110) *(P-1443)*

Kings Asian Gourmet Inc .......... E ...... 415 222-6100
683 Brannan St Unit 304 San Francisco (94107) *(P-862)*

Kings Hawaiian Bakery, Gardena *Also Called: Kings Hawaiian Bakery W Inc (P-17593)*

Kings Hawaiian Bakery W Inc (HQ) .......... E ...... 310 533-3250
1411 W 190th St Gardena (90248) *(P-17593)*

Kings Oil Tools Inc (PA) .......... E ...... 805 238-9311
2235 Spring St Paso Robles (93446) *(P-17852)*

Kings River Casting Inc .......... F ...... 559 875-8250
1350 North Ave Sanger (93657) *(P-3633)*

Kingsburg Cultivator Inc .......... E ...... 559 897-3662
40190 Road 36 Kingsburg (93631) *(P-9365)*

Kingseal Corporation .......... F ...... 562 944-3100
12681 Corral Pl Santa Fe Springs (90670) *(P-6888)*

Kingsford, Oakland *Also Called: Kingsford Products Company LLC (P-6118)*

Kingsford Products Company LLC (HQ) .......... D ...... 510 271-7000
1221 Broadway Fl 13 Oakland (94612) *(P-6118)*

Kingsolver Inc .......... F ...... 562 945-7590
8417 Secura Way Santa Fe Springs (90670) *(P-15931)*

Kingson Mold & Machine Inc .......... E ...... 714 871-0221
1350 Titan Way Brea (92821) *(P-9631)*

Kingspan Insulated Panels Inc .......... C ...... 209 531-9091
2000 Morgan Rd Modesto (95358) *(P-8673)*

Kingston Digital Inc (DH) .......... E ...... 714 435-2600
17600 Newhope St Fountain Valley (92708) *(P-10393)*

Kingston Technology Company .......... A ...... 310 729-3394
17600 Newhope St Fountain Valley (92708) *(P-10250)*

Kingston Technology Company Inc (HQ) .......... A ...... 714 435-2600
17600 Newhope St Fountain Valley (92708) *(P-16530)*

Kingston Technology Corp (PA) .......... B ...... 714 435-2600
17600 Newhope St Fountain Valley (92708) *(P-10394)*

Kinkisharyo (usa) Inc .......... C ...... 424 276-1803
300 Continental Blvd Ste 300 El Segundo (90245) *(P-14050)*

Kinkisharyo Int LLC (HQ) .......... F ...... 424 276-1803
1960 E Grand Ave Ste 1210 El Segundo (90245) *(P-14051)*

Kino Flo Lighting Systems, Burbank *Also Called: Nomoflo Enterprises Inc (P-11548)*

Kins Capital LLC (PA) .......... F ...... 650 575-4456
4 Palo Alto Sq Ste 200 Palo Alto (94306) *(P-18471)*

Kintera Inc (HQ) .......... C ...... 858 795-3000
9605 Scranton Rd Ste 200 San Diego (92121) *(P-18472)*

Kioxia America Inc (PA) .......... C ...... 408 526-2400
2610 Orchard Pkwy San Jose (95134) *(P-12513)*

Kipe Molds Inc .......... F ...... 714 572-9576
340 E Crowther Ave Placentia (92870) *(P-9632)*

Kirby Manufacturing Inc (PA) .......... D ...... 209 723-0778
484 S Hwy 59 Merced (95341) *(P-9366)*

Kirk Containers, City Of Commerce *Also Called: Arthurmade Plastics Inc (P-6726)*

Kirkhill Inc .......... A ...... 714 529-4901
300 E Cypress St Brea (92821) *(P-6456)*

Kirkhill Inc .......... D ...... 562 803-1117
1451 S Carlos Ave Ontario (91761) *(P-6507)*

Kirkhill Inc (HQ) .......... C ...... 714 529-4901
300 E Cypress St Brea (92821) *(P-13886)*

Kirkhill Manufacturing Company, Ontario *Also Called: KMC Acquisition LLC (P-6509)*

Kirkhill Rubber Company .......... D ...... 562 803-1117
2500 E Thompson St Long Beach (90805) *(P-6508)*

Kisca, Los Angeles *Also Called: Komarov Enterprises Inc (P-2724)*

Kiss Packaging Systems, Vista *Also Called: Accutek Packaging Equipment Co (P-10009)*

Kitara Media Corp (HQ) .......... F
2010 Main St Ste 900 Irvine (92614) *(P-17779)*

Kitch Engineering Inc .......... E ...... 818 897-7133
12320 Montague St Pacoima (91331) *(P-10929)*

Kitchen and Rail, Arroyo Grande *Also Called: Corbett Vineyards LLC (P-1518)*

Kitchen Cuts LLC .......... D ...... 323 560-7415
6045 District Blvd Maywood (90270) *(P-648)*

Kitchen Expo .......... F
7458 La Jolla Blvd La Jolla (92037) *(P-566)*

**Kitchen Pro Cabinetry Inc** ............................................. E ...... 877 210-6361
11347 Vanowen St North Hollywood (91605) *(P-3248)*

**Kitchens Now Inc** ............................................................ E ...... 916 229-8224
6047 Power Inn Rd Sacramento (95824) *(P-3249)*

**Kitcor Corporation** ......................................................... E ...... 323 875-2820
9959 Glenoaks Blvd Sun Valley (91352) *(P-8857)*

**Kite Hill, Hayward** *Also Called: Lyrical Foods Inc (P-2270)*

**Kite Pharma Inc (HQ)** ................................................... D ...... 310 824-9999
2400 Broadway Ste 100 Santa Monica (90404) *(P-19459)*

**Kite, A Gilead Company, Santa Monica** *Also Called: Kite Pharma Inc (P-19459)*

**Kittrich Corporation (PA)** .............................................. C ...... 714 736-1000
1585 W Mission Blvd Pomona (91766) *(P-3723)*

**Kittyhawk Inc (PA)** .......................................................... E ...... 714 895-5024
11651 Monarch St Garden Grove (92841) *(P-7887)*

**Kittyhawk Products, Garden Grove** *Also Called: Kpi Services Inc (P-7889)*

**Kittyhawk Products CA LLC** ......................................... E ...... 714 895-5024
11651 Monarch St Garden Grove (92841) *(P-7888)*

**Kiva Brands Inc** .............................................................. F ...... 510 592-8711
2300 N Loop Rd Alameda (94502) *(P-1342)*

**Kiva Confections, Oakland** *Also Called: Kiva Manufacturing Inc (P-16162)*

**Kiva Manufacturing Inc** ................................................ E ...... 510 780-0777
445 Lesser St Oakland (94601) *(P-16162)*

**Kive Company** ................................................................ E ...... 747 212-0337
15800 Arminta St Van Nuys (91406) *(P-18473)*

**Kjos Music, San Diego** *Also Called: Neil A Kjos Music Company (P-4436)*

**Kl Decorator Sales** ......................................................... E ...... 562 920-0268
10120 Artesia Pl Bellflower (90706) *(P-3152)*

**KLA Corporation** ............................................................. F ...... 408 986-5600
5451 Patrick Henry Dr Santa Clara (95054) *(P-12514)*

**KLA Corporation (PA)** .................................................... B ...... 408 875-3000
1 Technology Dr Milpitas (95035) *(P-14793)*

**KLA-Tencor, Milpitas** *Also Called: KLA Corporation (P-14793)*

**Klatch Coffee Inc (PA)** ................................................... E ...... 909 981-4031
9325 Feron Blvd Rancho Cucamonga (91730) *(P-17594)*

**Klean Kanteen Inc** ......................................................... D ...... 530 592-4552
3960 Morrow Ln Chico (95928) *(P-7922)*

**Kleen Maid Inc** ................................................................ F ...... 323 581-3000
11450 Sheldon St Sun Valley (91352) *(P-2933)*

**Kleenrite, Madera** *Also Called: Better Cleaning Systems Inc (P-11415)*

**Klein Bros Holdings Ltd** ................................................ E ...... 209 465-5033
3101 W March Ln Ste B Stockton (95219) *(P-1356)*

**Klein Bros Snacks, Stockton** *Also Called: Klein Bros Holdings Ltd (P-1356)*

**Klein Electronics, Escondido** *Also Called: Klein Electronics Inc (P-16712)*

**Klein Electronics Inc** ..................................................... E ...... 760 781-3220
349 N Vinewood St Escondido (92029) *(P-16712)*

**Klein Foods Inc** ............................................................... D ...... 707 431-1533
11455 Old Redwood Hwy Healdsburg (95448) *(P-19)*

**Kleiner Prkins Cfeld Byers LLC (PA)** ........................... E ...... 650 233-2750
2750 Sand Hill Rd Menlo Park (94025) *(P-17756)*

**Klentysoft Inc** ................................................................. C ...... 707 518-9640
440 N Barranca Ave # 2331 Covina (91723) *(P-18474)*

**Kleverness Incorporated** .............................................. F ...... 213 559-2480
340 S Lemon Ave 2291 Walnut (91789) *(P-17554)*

**Klh Consulting Incorporated** ....................................... D ...... 707 575-9986
2324 Bethards Dr Santa Rosa (95405) *(P-19564)*

**Klippenstein Corporation** ............................................. E ...... 559 834-4258
2246 E Date Ave Fresno (93706) *(P-10022)*

**Klk Forte Industry Inc (PA)** ........................................... E ...... 323 415-9181
1535 Rio Vista Ave Los Angeles (90023) *(P-2781)*

**Klm Laboratories Inc** .................................................... D ...... 661 295-2600
28280 Alta Vista Ave Valencia (91355) *(P-16584)*

**Klm Orthotic, Valencia** *Also Called: Klm Laboratories Inc (P-16584)*

**Klooma Holdings Inc** ..................................................... E ...... 305 747-3315
113 N San Vicente Blvd Beverly Hills (90211) *(P-18475)*

**Kloudgin, Sunnyvale** *Also Called: Kloudgin Inc (P-18476)*

**Kloudgin Inc (PA)** ........................................................... E ...... 704 904-4321
440 N Wolfe Rd Sunnyvale (94085) *(P-18476)*

**Kloudspot Inc** ................................................................. D ...... 800 709-2211
1285 Oakmead Pkwy Sunnyvale (94085) *(P-18477)*

**Klune Industries Inc (DH)** ............................................. B ...... 818 503-8100
7323 Coldwater Canyon Ave North Hollywood (91605) *(P-13887)*

**Km Printing Production Inc** ......................................... F ...... 626 821-0008
218 Longden Ave Irwindale (91706) *(P-4662)*

**Kmb Foods Inc (PA)** ....................................................... E ...... 626 447-0545
1010 S Sierra Way San Bernardino (92408) *(P-649)*

**KMC Acquisition LLC (PA)** ............................................ E ...... 562 396-0121
1451 S Carlos Ave Ontario (91761) *(P-6509)*

**Kme Fire, Fontana** *Also Called: Kovatch Mobile Equipment Corp (P-13362)*

**Kmp Numatech Pacific, Pomona** *Also Called: Numatech West (kmp) LLC (P-3870)*

**Kmr Label LLC** ................................................................ E ...... 310 603-8910
1360 W Walnut Pkwy Compton (90220) *(P-4823)*

**KMW Communications, Fullerton** *Also Called: Gigatera Communications (P-12985)*

**Knauf Insulation, Shasta Lake** *Also Called: Knauf Insulation Inc (P-7579)*

**Knauf Insulation Inc** ..................................................... A ...... 530 275-9665
3100 Ashby Rd Shasta Lake (96019) *(P-7579)*

**Knife River Construction, Chico** *Also Called: Baldwin Contracting Co Inc (P-373)*

**Knight LLC (HQ)** ............................................................. D ...... 949 595-4800
15340 Barranca Pkwy Irvine (92618) *(P-10098)*

**Knightsbridge Plastics Inc** ........................................... D ...... 510 440-8444
3075 Osgood Ct Fremont (94539) *(P-6889)*

**Knightscope, Mountain View** *Also Called: Knightscope Inc (P-13262)*

**Knightscope Inc** ............................................................. D ...... 650 924-1025
1070 Terra Bella Ave Mountain View (94043) *(P-13262)*

**Knisley Aircraft Exhaust, Loomis** *Also Called: Knisley Welding Inc (P-19207)*

**Knisley Welding Inc** ...................................................... E ...... 916 652-5891
3450 Swetzer Rd Loomis (95650) *(P-19207)*

**Knit Generation Group Inc** .......................................... E ...... 213 221-5081
3818 S Broadway Los Angeles (90037) *(P-2420)*

**Kno Inc** ............................................................................. D ...... 408 844-8120
2200 Mission College Blvd Santa Clara (95054) *(P-18478)*

**Kns Industrial Supply, Santa Fe Springs** *Also Called: International Consulting Unltd (P-7664)*

**Knt Inc** .............................................................................. C ...... 510 651-7163
39760 Eureka Dr Newark (94560) *(P-10930)*

**Knt Manufacturing, Newark** *Also Called: Knt Inc (P-10930)*

**Knt Manufacturing Inc** .................................................. D ...... 510 896-1699
39760 Eureka Dr Newark (94560) *(P-16163)*

**Kobe Protection Group, Emeryville** *Also Called: Tanium Inc (P-18864)*

**Kobelco Compressors Amer Inc** ................................. D ...... 951 739-3030
301 N Smith Ave Corona (92878) *(P-9964)*

**Kobelco Compressors Amer Inc (DH)** ....................... B ...... 951 739-3030
1450 W Rincon St Corona (92880) *(P-9965)*

**Kobis Windows & Doors Mfg Inc** ................................ E ...... 818 764-6400
7326 Laurel Canyon Blvd North Hollywood (91605) *(P-3250)*

**Koda Farms Inc** .............................................................. E ...... 209 392-2191
22540 Russell Ave South Dos Palos (93665) *(P-1080)*

**KODIAK, Palo Alto** *Also Called: Kodiak Sciences Inc (P-5528)*

**Kodiak Cartoners Inc** .................................................... F ...... 559 266-4844
2550 Se Ave, Ste 101 Fresno (93706) *(P-10023)*

**Kodiak Precision Inc (PA)** ............................................. F ...... 510 234-4165
444 S 1st St Richmond (94804) *(P-10931)*

**Kodiak Sciences Inc (PA)** ............................................. D ...... 650 281-0850
1200 Page Mill Rd Palo Alto (94304) *(P-5528)*

**Kofax Limited (PA)** ........................................................ E ...... 949 783-1000
15211 Laguna Canyon Rd Irvine (92618) *(P-18479)*

**Koffler Elec Mech Apprtus Repr** ................................ D ...... 510 567-0630
527 Whitney St San Leandro (94577) *(P-16656)*

**Koffler Electrical Mechanical, San Leandro** *Also Called: Koffler Elec Mech Apprtus Repr (P-16656)*

**Kokatat Inc** ...................................................................... C ...... 707 822-7621
5350 Ericson Way Arcata (95521) *(P-2782)*

**Kollmorgen Corporation** .............................................. D ...... 805 696-1236
33 S La Patera Ln Santa Barbara (93117) *(P-11274)*

**Koltov Inc (PA)** ................................................................ E ...... 805 764-0280
300 S Lewis Rd Ste A Camarillo (93012) *(P-7148)*

**Komar Apparel Supply, Los Angeles** *Also Called: Mdc Interior Solutions LLC (P-2905)*

**Komar Distribution Services, Jurupa Valley** *Also Called: Charles Komar & Sons Inc (P-2828)*

**Komarov Enterprises Inc** ............................................. D ...... 213 244-7000
10939 Venice Blvd Los Angeles (90034) *(P-2724)*

**Komex International Inc** .............................................. F ...... 323 233-9005
736 E 29th St Los Angeles (90011) *(P-2675)*

**Konami, Hawthorne** *Also Called: Konami Digital Entrmt Inc (P-18480)*

## ALPHABETIC SECTION

Konami Digital Entrmt Inc (DH) .................................. E ...... 310 220-8100
  1 Konami Way Hawthorne (90250) *(P-18480)*
Konark Silicone Tech Inc .................................. F ...... 562 372-5415
  4725 E Bryson St Anaheim (92807) *(P-6890)*
Kone Inc .................................. E ...... 714 890-7080
  1540 Scenic Ave # 100 Costa Mesa (92626) *(P-19266)*
Kone Inc .................................. D ...... 510 351-5141
  15021 Wicks Blvd San Leandro (94577) *(P-19267)*
Konecranes Inc .................................. E ...... 909 930-0108
  1620 S Carlos Ave Ontario (91761) *(P-9501)*
Konecranes Inc .................................. E ...... 562 903-1371
  10310 Pioneer Blvd Ste 2 Santa Fe Springs (90670) *(P-9502)*
Konigsberg Instruments Inc .................................. E ...... 626 775-6500
  1017 S Mountain Ave Monrovia (91016) *(P-15145)*
Kontron America Incorporated (PA) .................................. F ...... 800 822-7522
  9477 Waples St Ste 150 San Diego (92121) *(P-10173)*
Koolfog Inc (PA) .................................. F ...... 760 321-9203
  31290 Plantation Dr Thousand Palms (92276) *(P-10504)*
Koos Manufacturing Inc .................................. A ...... 323 249-1000
  2741 Seminole Ave South Gate (90280) *(P-19101)*
Kopykake Enterprises Inc (PA) .................................. F ...... 310 373-8906
  3699 W 240th St Torrance (90505) *(P-8858)*
Koral Activewear, Santa Monica *Also Called: Koral LLC (P-2628)*
Koral Industries LLC (PA) .................................. E ...... 323 585-5343
  1334 3rd Street Promenade Ste 200 Santa Monica (90401) *(P-2783)*
Koral LLC .................................. E ...... 323 391-1060
  1334 3rd Street Promenade Ste 200 Santa Monica (90401) *(P-2628)*
Koral Los Angeles, Santa Monica *Also Called: Koral Industries LLC (P-2783)*
Korbel Champagne Cellers, Guerneville *Also Called: F Korbel & Bros (P-1559)*
Korden Inc .................................. E ...... 909 988-8979
  601 S Milliken Ave Ste H Ontario (91761) *(P-3604)*
Korea Times, Los Angeles *Also Called: The Korea Times Los Angeles Inc (P-4208)*
Koros USA Inc .................................. E ...... 805 529-0825
  610 Flinn Ave Moorpark (93021) *(P-15146)*
Kortick Manufacturer Co, Pittsburg *Also Called: Frase Enterprises (P-11479)*
Kos Inc .................................. E ...... 650 231-2044
  1205 N Miller St Palo Alto (94303) *(P-16319)*
Kosakura Associates, Irvine *Also Called: CK Manufacturing & Trading Inc (P-3651)*
Koshland Pharm Cstm Cmpnding P, San Francisco *Also Called: Koshland Pharmacy Inc (P-5529)*
Koshland Pharmacy Inc .................................. F ...... 415 344-0600
  301 Folsom St Ste B San Francisco (94105) *(P-5529)*
Kosta Browne, Sebastopol *Also Called: KB Wines LLC (P-1645)*
Kosta Browne Winery, Sebastopol *Also Called: Kosta Browne Wines LLC (P-1649)*
Kosta Browne Wines LLC .................................. E ...... 707 823-7430
  220 Morris St Sebastopol (95472) *(P-1649)*
Kovatch Mobile Equipment Corp .................................. E ...... 951 685-1224
  14562 Manzanita Dr Fontana (92335) *(P-13362)*
Kovin Corporation Inc .................................. E ...... 858 558-0100
  9240 Mira Este Ct San Diego (92126) *(P-4663)*
Kovio Inc .................................. D ...... 408 503-7300
  2865 Zanker Rd San Jose (95134) *(P-12515)*
KP Concrete & Steel Inc .................................. F ...... 909 461-4163
  3835 E 9th St Pomona (91766) *(P-523)*
Kp LLC (PA) .................................. D ...... 510 346-0729
  13951 Washington Ave San Leandro (94578) *(P-4664)*
Kp LLC .................................. E ...... 510 346-0729
  13951 Washington Ave San Leandro (94578) *(P-4665)*
Kp LLC .................................. E ...... 209 466-6761
  1134 Enterprise St Stockton (95204) *(P-4666)*
Kpcb, Menlo Park *Also Called: Kleiner Prkins Cfeld Byers LLC (P-17756)*
Kpi Services Inc .................................. E ...... 714 895-5024
  11651 Monarch St Garden Grove (92841) *(P-7889)*
Kq Integrated Solutions Inc .................................. C ...... 408 654-0428
  3380 Keller St Santa Clara (95054) *(P-10932)*
Kraco Enterprises LLC .................................. C ...... 310 639-0666
  505 E Euclid Ave Compton (90222) *(P-17454)*
Kraft Foods, Buena Park *Also Called: Mondelez Global LLC (P-654)*
Kraft Foods, Fullerton *Also Called: Kraft Heinz Foods Company (P-898)*
Kraft Foods, Fresno *Also Called: Kraft Heinz Foods Company (P-899)*
Kraft Heinz Foods Company .................................. E ...... 949 250-4080
  2450 White Rd Irvine (92614) *(P-863)*
Kraft Heinz Foods Company .................................. D ...... 714 870-8235
  1500 E Walnut Ave Fullerton (92831) *(P-898)*
Kraft Heinz Foods Company .................................. E ...... 559 441-8515
  2494 S Orange Ave Fresno (93725) *(P-899)*
Kranem, San Jose *Also Called: Kranem Corporation (P-18481)*
Kranem Corporation .................................. C ...... 650 319-6743
  560 S Winchester Blvd Ste 500 San Jose (95128) *(P-18481)*
Krasnes Inc .................................. D ...... 619 232-2066
  2222 Commercial St San Diego (92113) *(P-2881)*
KRATOS, San Diego *Also Called: Kratos Def & SEC Solutions Inc (P-14082)*
Kratos Def & SEC Solutions Inc (PA) .................................. C ...... 858 812-7300
  10680 Treena St Ste 600 San Diego (92131) *(P-14082)*
Kratos Microwave Inc .................................. D ...... 408 541-0596
  5870 Hellyer Ave Ste 70 San Jose (95138) *(P-11872)*
Kratos Unmnned Arial Systems I (HQ) .................................. C ...... 916 991-1990
  5381 Raley Blvd Sacramento (95838) *(P-19401)*
Krave Jerky, Sonoma *Also Called: Krave Pure Foods Inc (P-650)*
Krave Pure Foods Inc .................................. D ...... 707 939-9176
  117 W Napa St Ste A Sonoma (95476) *(P-650)*
Kretus Group Inc (PA) .................................. E ...... 714 738-6640
  1129 N Patt St Anaheim (92801) *(P-16474)*
Kretus Inc .................................. F ...... 714 694-2061
  1055 W Struck Ave Orange (92867) *(P-6091)*
Kreysler & Associates, American Canyon *Also Called: William Kreysler & Assoc Inc (P-7081)*
Kri Star Enterprises Inc .................................. E ...... 800 579-8819
  360 Sutton Pl Santa Rosa (95407) *(P-7351)*
Kribi Enterprises Inc .................................. F ...... 310 594-1222
  322 Culver Blvd Playa Del Rey (90293) *(P-17620)*
Krieger Speciality Pdts LLC (DH) .................................. D ...... 562 695-0645
  4880 Gregg Rd Pico Rivera (90660) *(P-8272)*
Krieger Steel Products, Pico Rivera *Also Called: Krieger Speciality Pdts LLC (P-8272)*
Kristich-Monterey Pipe Company .................................. F ...... 831 724-4186
  225 Salinas Rd Ste B Royal Oaks (95076) *(P-7352)*
Kroeger Eqp Sup Co A Cal Corp .................................. E ...... 559 485-9900
  2645 South Chestnut At Jensen Fresno (93725) *(P-13526)*
Kroeger Equipment, Fresno *Also Called: Kroeger Eqp Sup Co A Cal Corp (P-13526)*
Krohn Division, Fair Oaks *Also Called: Rice Corporation (P-1081)*
KRONOS BIO, San Mateo *Also Called: Kronos Bio Inc (P-5530)*
Kronos Bio Inc (PA) .................................. E ...... 650 781-5200
  1300 S El Camino Real Ste 400 San Mateo (94402) *(P-5530)*
Krueger International Inc .................................. E ...... 949 748-7000
  16510 Bake Pkwy Ste 100 Irvine (92618) *(P-3634)*
Kruger Foods Inc .................................. C ...... 209 941-8518
  18362 E Highway 4 Stockton (95215) *(P-981)*
Krupp Brothers LLC (PA) .................................. F ...... 707 226-2215
  1345 Hestia Way Napa (94558) *(P-1650)*
Kruse and Son Inc .................................. E ...... 626 358-4536
  235 Kruse Ave Monrovia (91016) *(P-651)*
Kruse Pet Holdings LLC (HQ) .................................. E ...... 559 302-4880
  1111 N Miller Park Ct Visalia (93291) *(P-1106)*
Kryler Corp .................................. E ...... 714 871-9611
  1217 E Ash Ave Fullerton (92831) *(P-8978)*
Krystal Enterprises, Riverside *Also Called: Krystal Infinity LLC (P-13415)*
Krystal Infinity LLC .................................. B
  6915 Arlington Ave Riverside (92504) *(P-13415)*
Krystal Ventures LLC .................................. E ...... 213 507-2215
  17 Shell Bch Newport Coast (92657) *(P-15696)*
Krytar Inc .................................. E ...... 408 734-5999
  1288 Anvilwood Ave Sunnyvale (94089) *(P-13020)*
KS Engineering Inc .................................. F ...... 562 483-7788
  14948 Shoemaker Ave Santa Fe Springs (90670) *(P-13888)*
Ksc Industries Inc .................................. E ...... 619 671-0110
  9771 Clairemont Mesa Blvd Ste E San Diego (92124) *(P-11671)*
Ksm Corp .................................. E ...... 408 514-2400
  102 Persian Dr Ste 203 Sunnyvale (94089) *(P-12516)*
KSM Garment Inc .................................. E ...... 323 585-8811
  5613 Maywood Ave Maywood (90270) *(P-2676)*
Kssm LLC .................................. F ...... 707 433-7427
  4155 Wine Creek Rd Healdsburg (95448) *(P-1651)*

# Ksu Corporation

**Ksu Corporation** .................................................... F ...... 951 409-7055
3 Emmy Ln Ladera Ranch (92694) *(P-8165)*

**KT Engineering Corporation** .................................. F ...... 310 537-3818
2016 E Vista Bella Way Rancho Dominguez (90220) *(P-10933)*

**Ktc-Tu Corporation** ............................................... E ...... 714 435-2600
17600 Newhope St Fountain Valley (92708) *(P-12517)*

**Kti Incorporated** .................................................. D ...... 909 434-1888
3011 N Laurel Ave Rialto (92377) *(P-7353)*

**Kts Kitchens Inc** ................................................... C ...... 310 764-0850
1065 E Walnut St Ste C Carson (90746) *(P-2247)*

**Kubecost, San Francisco** *Also Called: Stackwatch Inc (P-18832)*

**KUDos&co Inc** ...................................................... F ...... 650 799-9104
470 Ramona St Palo Alto (94301) *(P-4424)*

**Kugler Wines LLC** ................................................ E ...... 630 306-4634
300 N 12th St Ste 4b Lompoc (93436) *(P-1652)*

**Kui Co Inc** ........................................................... E ...... 949 369-7949
266 Calle Pintoresco San Clemente (92672) *(P-6891)*

**Kuic Inc** ............................................................... C ...... 707 446-0200
555 Mason St Ste 245 Vacaville (95688) *(P-16327)*

**Kuic-FM, Vacaville** *Also Called: Kuic Inc (P-16327)*

**Kukdong Apparel America Inc** ................................ E
17100 Pioneer Blvd Ste 230 Artesia (90701) *(P-19102)*

**Kulicke & Soffa Industries, Santa Ana** *Also Called: Kulicke Sffa Wedge Bonding Inc (P-13263)*

**Kulicke Sffa Wedge Bonding Inc** ............................ C ...... 949 660-0440
1821 E Dyer Rd Ste 200 Santa Ana (92705) *(P-13263)*

**Kulr Technology Corporation** ................................. D ...... 408 663-5247
4863 Shawline St Ste B San Diego (92111) *(P-12518)*

**Kum Kang Trading USA Inc** .................................. E ...... 562 531-6111
6433 Alondra Blvd Paramount (90723) *(P-6001)*

**Kumar Industries** .................................................. E ...... 909 591-0722
4775 Chino Ave Chino (91710) *(P-8166)*

**Kumon, Los Gatos** *Also Called: Tamana Corporation (P-19353)*

**Kunde Enterprises Inc** .......................................... D ...... 707 833-5501
9825 Sonoma Hwy Kenwood (95452) *(P-1653)*

**Kunde Estate Winery, Kenwood** *Also Called: Kunde Enterprises Inc (P-1653)*

**Kuprion Inc** .......................................................... E ...... 408 206-0122
4425 Fortran Dr San Jose (95134) *(P-12519)*

**Kura Oncology Inc (PA)** ........................................ E ...... 858 500-8800
12730 High Bluff Dr Ste 400 San Diego (92130) *(P-5531)*

**Kurz Instruments Inc** ............................................ D ...... 831 646-5911
2411 Garden Rd Monterey (93940) *(P-14363)*

**Kurz Transfer Products LP** ................................... D ...... 951 738-9521
415 N Smith Ave Corona (92878) *(P-16164)*

**Kuster Co Oil Well Services** .................................. E ...... 562 595-0661
2900 E 29th St Long Beach (90806) *(P-247)*

**Kuster Company, Long Beach** *Also Called: Kuster Co Oil Well Services (P-247)*

**Kustom Kanopies Inc** ............................................ E ...... 801 399-3400
210 Senior Cir Lompoc (93436) *(P-358)*

**Kut From The Kloth, City Of Industry** *Also Called: Swatfame Inc (P-17501)*

**Kuz & Kirb** ........................................................... E ...... 310 539-6116
23911 Garnier St Ste C Torrance (90505) *(P-7970)*

**Kuzz FM, Bakersfield** *Also Called: Buck Owens Production Co Inc (P-16326)*

**Kval Inc** ............................................................... C ...... 707 762-4363
825 Petaluma Blvd S Petaluma (94952) *(P-9754)*

**Kval Machinery Co, Petaluma** *Also Called: Kval Inc (P-9754)*

**Kvl Holdings Inc (PA)** ........................................... E ...... 831 678-2132
37700 Foothill Rd Soledad (93960) *(P-20)*

**Kvr Investment Group Inc** ..................................... D ...... 818 896-1102
12113 Branford St Sun Valley (91352) *(P-9873)*

**Kw Automotive North Amer Inc** .............................. E ...... 800 445-3767
300 W Pontiac Way Clovis (93612) *(P-13527)*

**Kwdz Manufacturing LLC (PA)** ............................. D ...... 323 526-3526
337 S Anderson St Los Angeles (90033) *(P-2855)*

**Kwik Bond Polymers LLC** ..................................... E ...... 866 434-1772
923 Teal Dr Ste A Benicia (94510) *(P-6235)*

**Kwikset Corporation** ............................................. A ...... 949 672-4000
19701 Da Vinci Foothill Ranch (92610) *(P-8009)*

**Kwj Engineering Inc (PA)** ..................................... E ...... 510 794-4296
8430 Central Ave Ste C Newark (94560) *(P-14891)*

**Kycon Inc** ............................................................ E ...... 408 494-0330
305 Digital Dr Morgan Hill (95037) *(P-16713)*

**Kyma Medical Technologies Inc** ............................. F ...... 650 386-5089
2000 Ringwood Ave San Jose (95131) *(P-15550)*

**Kyoceara, Costa Mesa** *Also Called: Kyocera Tycom Corporation (P-9559)*

**Kyocera America Inc** ............................................ E ...... 858 576-2600
8611 Balboa Ave San Diego (92123) *(P-12520)*

**Kyocera AVX Cmpnnts San Dego I (DH)** ............... E ...... 858 550-3820
5501 Oberlin Dr Ste 100 San Diego (92121) *(P-11873)*

**Kyocera International Inc (HQ)** ............................. D ...... 858 492-1456
8611 Balboa Ave San Diego (92123) *(P-12521)*

**Kyocera Medical Tech Inc** .................................... E ...... 909 557-2360
1289 Bryn Mawr Ave Ste A Redlands (92374) *(P-15373)*

**Kyocera Precision Tools, Orange** *Also Called: Kyocera SGS Precision Tls Inc (P-9681)*

**Kyocera SGS Precision Tls Inc** ............................. D ...... 888 848-9266
1814 W Collins Ave Orange (92867) *(P-9681)*

**Kyocera Sld Laser Inc (HQ)** ................................. E ...... 805 696-6999
485 Pine Ave Goleta (93117) *(P-13264)*

**Kyocera Sld Laser Inc** ......................................... E ...... 805 696-6999
6500 Kaiser Dr Fremont (94555) *(P-13265)*

**Kyocera Sld Laser Inc** ......................................... E ...... 310 808-4542
111 Castilian Dr Goleta (93117) *(P-13266)*

**Kyocera Tycom Corporation** ................................. B ...... 714 428-3600
3565 Cadillac Ave Costa Mesa (92626) *(P-9559)*

**Kyolic, Mission Viejo** *Also Called: Wakunaga of America Co Ltd (P-5715)*

**Kyowa Kirin Inc** ................................................... E ...... 858 952-7000
9420 Athena Cir La Jolla (92037) *(P-5532)*

**Kyriba Corp (PA)** ................................................. E ...... 858 210-3560
4435 Eastgate Mall Ste 200 San Diego (92121) *(P-18482)*

**Kythera Biopharmaceuticals Inc** ........................... C ...... 818 587-4500
30930 Russell Ranch Rd Fl 3 Westlake Village (91362) *(P-5533)*

**Kyverna Therapeutics Inc** .................................... D ...... 510 925-2492
5980 Horton St Ste 550 Emeryville (94608) *(P-5844)*

**L & H Mold & Engineering Inc (PA)** ...................... E ...... 909 930-1547
140 Atlantic St Pomona (91768) *(P-6892)*

**L & H Molds, Pomona** *Also Called: L & H Mold & Engineering Inc (P-6892)*

**L & L Diamond Co** ............................................... F ...... 213 622-5752
1801 Beverly Blvd Los Angeles (90057) *(P-17647)*

**L & L Distributors, Los Angeles** *Also Called: L&L Manufacturing Co Inc (P-2784)*

**L & L Printers Carlsbad LLC** ................................ E ...... 760 477-0321
6200 Yarrow Dr Carlsbad (92011) *(P-4667)*

**L & M Machining Corporation** .............................. D ...... 714 414-0923
550 S Melrose St Placentia (92870) *(P-12887)*

**L & N Fixtures Inc** .............................................. F ...... 626 442-4778
2214 Tyler Ave El Monte (91733) *(P-3662)*

**L & S Stone and Fireplace Shop, San Marcos** *Also Called: L&S Stone LLC (P-7541)*

**L & T Precision LLC** ............................................ C ...... 858 513-7874
12105 Kirkham Rd Poway (92064) *(P-8483)*

**L & T Precision Engrg Inc** ................................... E ...... 408 441-1890
2395 Qume Dr San Jose (95131) *(P-10934)*

**L A Cstm AP & Promotions Inc (PA)** .................... E ...... 562 595-1770
2680 Temple Ave Long Beach (90806) *(P-2629)*

**L A Gauge Company Inc** ..................................... D ...... 818 767-7193
7440 San Fernando Rd Sun Valley (91352) *(P-10935)*

**L A Girl, Ontario** *Also Called: Beauty 21 Cosmetics Inc (P-17029)*

**L A Glo Inc** ......................................................... E ...... 323 932-0091
1451 Hi Point St Los Angeles (90035) *(P-2708)*

**L A Hearne Company (PA)** .................................. D ...... 831 385-5441
512 Metz Rd King City (93930) *(P-17272)*

**L A Hq Inc** .......................................................... E ...... 310 880-7433
5363 Wilshire Blvd Los Angeles (90036) *(P-16165)*

**L A Lighting, El Monte** *Also Called: Los Angeles Ltg Mfg Co Inc (P-16658)*

**L A Press, Los Angeles** *Also Called: LA Printing & Graphics Inc (P-4669)*

**L A Propoint Inc** .................................................. E ...... 818 767-6800
10870 La Tuna Canyon Rd Sun Valley (91352) *(P-9290)*

**L A Steel Craft Products (PA)** .............................. E ...... 626 798-7401
1975 Lincoln Ave Pasadena (91103) *(P-15835)*

**L A Supply Co** .................................................... E ...... 949 470-9900
4241 E Brickell St Ontario (91761) *(P-4905)*

**L B Construction, Roseville** *Also Called: Lancaster Burns Cnstr Inc (P-476)*

**L C Miller Company** ............................................ E ...... 323 268-3611
717 Monterey Pass Rd Monterey Park (91754) *(P-10056)*

## ALPHABETIC SECTION — La Mousse

**L C Pringle Sales Inc (PA)** ............................................. E ...... 714 892-1524
12020 Western Ave Garden Grove (92841) *(P-3724)*

**L F P Inc (PA)** ................................................................ D ...... 323 651-3525
8484 Wilshire Blvd Ste 900 Beverly Hills (90211) *(P-4270)*

**L Foppiano Wine Co** ...................................................... E ...... 707 433-2736
12707 Old Redwood Hwy Healdsburg (95448) *(P-1654)*

**L K Lehman Trucking** .................................................... E ...... 209 532-5586
19333 Industrial Dr Sonora (95370) *(P-7460)*

**L M I, Ontario** *Also Called: Larry Mthvin Installations Inc (P-7230)*

**L M Scofield Company (DH)** ........................................... E ...... 323 720-3000
12767 Imperial Hwy Santa Fe Springs (90670) *(P-6303)*

**L P McNear Brick Co Inc** ............................................... D ...... 415 453-7702
1 Mcnear Brickyard Rd San Rafael (94901) *(P-7295)*

**L R Enterprises, Milpitas** *Also Called: Lre Silicon Services (P-12534)*

**L Space, Irvine** *Also Called: Lspace America LLC (P-2476)*

**L Spark** ......................................................................... E ...... 805 626-0511
1140 Kendall Rd Ste A San Luis Obispo (93401) *(P-15697)*

**L T Litho & Printing Co** ................................................. E ...... 949 466-8584
16811 Noyes Ave Irvine (92606) *(P-4668)*

**L T Seroge Inc** .............................................................. F ...... 951 354-7141
7400 Jurupa Ave Riverside (92504) *(P-13267)*

**L Y Z Ltd (PA)** ............................................................... F ...... 415 445-9505
210 Post St San Francisco (94108) *(P-2709)*

**L-3 Cmmnications Sonoma Eo Inc** ................................ C ...... 707 568-3000
428 Aviation Blvd Santa Rosa (95403) *(P-15647)*

**L-3 Communication, San Leandro** *Also Called: L3 Technologies Inc (P-11880)*

**L-3 Interstate Electronics, Anaheim** *Also Called: L3harris Interstate Elec Corp (P-14545)*

**L-3 Telemetry & Rf Products, San Diego** *Also Called: L3 Technologies Inc (P-11876)*

**L-Com, Irvine** *Also Called: Infinite Electronics Inc (P-12999)*

**L.A. Sleeve, Santa Fe Springs** *Also Called: Los Angeles Sleeve Co Inc (P-13531)*

**L&L Manufacturing Co Inc** ............................................ B
12400 Wilshire Blvd Ste 360 Los Angeles (90025) *(P-2784)*

**L&S Stone LLC (DH)** ..................................................... E ...... 760 736-3232
1370 Grand Ave Ste B San Marcos (92078) *(P-7541)*

**L&W Stone Corporation (PA)** ....................................... D
55 Independence Cir Ste 108 Chico (95973) *(P-16475)*

**L3 Technologies Inc** ..................................................... D ...... 818 367-0111
15825 Roxford St Sylmar (91342) *(P-11874)*

**L3 Technologies Inc** ..................................................... B ...... 858 552-9500
9020 Balboa Ave San Diego (92123) *(P-11875)*

**L3 Technologies Inc** ..................................................... B ...... 858 279-0411
9020 Balboa Ave San Diego (92123) *(P-11876)*

**L3 Technologies Inc** ..................................................... C ...... 714 758-4222
602 E Vermont Ave Anaheim (92805) *(P-11877)*

**L3 Technologies Inc** ..................................................... D ...... 805 683-3881
7414 Hollister Ave Goleta (93117) *(P-11878)*

**L3 Technologies Inc** ..................................................... D ...... 858 552-9716
10180 Barnes Canyon Rd San Diego (92121) *(P-11879)*

**L3 Technologies Inc** ..................................................... C ...... 858 499-0284
2700 Merced St San Leandro (94577) *(P-11880)*

**L3 Technologies Inc** ..................................................... E ...... 714 956-9200
901 E Ball Rd Anaheim (92805) *(P-14201)*

**L3 Technologies Inc** ..................................................... C ...... 760 431-6800
5957 Landau Ct Carlsbad (92008) *(P-14202)*

**L3 Technologies Inc** ..................................................... D ...... 805 584-1717
200 W Los Angeles Ave Simi Valley (93065) *(P-14203)*

**L3 Technologies Inc** ..................................................... C ...... 818 367-0111
28022 Industry Dr Valencia (91355) *(P-14204)*

**L3harris Interstate Elec Corp** ..................................... D ...... 714 758-3395
604 E Vermont Ave Anaheim (92805) *(P-11881)*

**L3harris Interstate Elec Corp** ..................................... E ...... 714 758-0500
600 E Vermont Ave Anaheim (92805) *(P-14544)*

**L3harris Interstate Elec Corp (DH)** ............................. B ...... 714 758-0500
602 E Vermont Ave Anaheim (92805) *(P-14545)*

**L3harris Interstate Elec Corp** ..................................... D ...... 714 758-0500
708 E Vermont Ave Anaheim (92805) *(P-14546)*

**L3harris Interstate Elec Corp** ..................................... D ...... 858 552-9500
3033 Science Park Rd San Diego (92121) *(P-14547)*

**L3harris Technologies Inc** .......................................... B ...... 818 901-2523
7821 Orion Ave Van Nuys (91406) *(P-14205)*

**L3harris Technologies Inc** .......................................... E ...... 310 481-6000
12121 Wilshire Blvd Ste 910 Los Angeles (90025) *(P-14206)*

**L3harris Technologies Inc** .......................................... C ...... 626 305-6230
1400 S Shamrock Ave Monrovia (91016) *(P-14207)*

**La Aloe LLC** ................................................................ E ...... 888 968-2563
2301 E 7th St Ste A152 Los Angeles (90023) *(P-1010)*

**La Apparel, Los Angeles** *Also Called: Los Angeles Apparel Inc (P-2904)*

**La Barca Tortilleria Inc** ............................................... E ...... 323 268-1744
3047 Whittier Blvd Los Angeles (90023) *(P-2248)*

**La Bath Vanity Inc (PA)** .............................................. F ...... 909 303-3323
1071 W 9th St Upland (91786) *(P-3251)*

**La Bonita, Norwalk** *Also Called: Dianas Mexican Food Pdts Inc (P-2185)*

**La Bottleworks Inc** ..................................................... E ...... 323 724-4076
1605 Beach St Montebello (90640) *(P-1899)*

**La Brea Bakery Cafe Inc** ............................................ A ...... 818 742-4242
14490 Catalina St San Leandro (94577) *(P-1220)*

**LA Cabinet & Millwork Inc** ......................................... E ...... 323 227-5000
3005 Humboldt St Los Angeles (90031) *(P-3663)*

**La Cascada Inc** .......................................................... F ...... 510 452-3663
1940 Union St Ste 10 Oakland (94607) *(P-864)*

**La Chapalita Inc (PA)** ................................................ E ...... 626 443-8556
1724 Chico Ave El Monte (91733) *(P-2249)*

**La Colonial, San Jose** *Also Called: Robles Bros Inc (P-2339)*

**La Colonial Mexican Foods, Monterey Park** *Also Called: La Colonial Tortilla Pdts Inc (P-2250)*

**La Colonial Tortilla Pdts Inc** ..................................... C ...... 626 289-3647
543 Monterey Pass Rd Monterey Park (91754) *(P-2250)*

**La Copa De Oro** ........................................................ E ...... 714 554-9925
3321 W 1st St Santa Ana (92703) *(P-2251)*

**La Costa Coffee Roasting Co (PA)** ........................... E ...... 760 438-8160
6965 El Camino Real Ste 208 Carlsbad (92009) *(P-17427)*

**La Dye & Print Inc** .................................................... E ...... 310 327-3200
13416 Estrella Ave Gardena (90248) *(P-17093)*

**LA Envelope Incorporated** ........................................ E ...... 323 838-9300
1053 S Vail Ave Montebello (90640) *(P-4010)*

**La Espanola Meats Inc** ............................................. E ...... 310 539-0455
25020 Doble Ave Harbor City (90710) *(P-652)*

**La Fe Tortilleria Factory, San Marcos** *Also Called: La Fe Tortilleria Inc (P-2252)*

**La Fe Tortilleria Inc (PA)** .......................................... E ...... 760 752-8350
1512 Linda Vista Dr San Marcos (92078) *(P-2252)*

**La Flora Del Sur, Los Angeles** *Also Called: Walker Foods Inc (P-940)*

**La Fortaleza Inc** ....................................................... D ...... 323 261-1211
525 N Ford Blvd Los Angeles (90022) *(P-2253)*

**LA Gem and Jewelry Design** .................................... D ...... 213 488-1290
3232 E Washington Blvd Los Angeles (90058) *(P-15698)*

**LA Gem and Jewelry Design (PA)** ............................ E ...... 213 488-1290
659 S Broadway Fl 7 Los Angeles (90014) *(P-15699)*

**La Gloria Flour Tortillas, Los Angeles** *Also Called: La Gloria Foods Corp (P-2255)*

**La Gloria Foods Corp (PA)** ....................................... D ...... 323 262-0410
3455 E 1st St Los Angeles (90063) *(P-2254)*

**La Gloria Foods Corp** .............................................. E ...... 323 263-6755
3285 E Cesar E Chavez Ave Los Angeles (90063) *(P-2255)*

**La Gloria Tortilleria, Los Angeles** *Also Called: La Gloria Foods Corp (P-2254)*

**La Habra Stucco, Riverside** *Also Called: Parex Usa Inc (P-17341)*

**LA Hardwood Flooring Inc (PA)** ............................... F ...... 818 361-0099
9880 San Fernando Rd Pacoima (91331) *(P-3096)*

**La Indiana Tamales Inc** ........................................... F ...... 323 262-4682
1142 S Indiana St Los Angeles (90023) *(P-865)*

**La Jolla Baking Co, San Diego** *Also Called: Fusion Food Factory (P-1207)*

**La Jolla Group Inc (PA)** ........................................... B ...... 949 428-2800
14350 Myford Rd Irvine (92606) *(P-19103)*

**La La Land Production & Design** ............................. E ...... 323 406-9223
1701 S Santa Fe Ave Los Angeles (90021) *(P-7088)*

**La Linen Inc** ............................................................ E ...... 213 745-4004
1760 E 15th St Los Angeles (90021) *(P-17536)*

**La Mamba LLC** ........................................................ E ...... 323 526-3526
150 N Myers St Los Angeles (90033) *(P-2677)*

**La Mejor Inc** ............................................................ E ...... 559 747-0739
684 S Farmersville Blvd Farmersville (93223) *(P-2256)*

**La Mejor Restaurant, Farmersville** *Also Called: La Mejor Inc (P-2256)*

**La Mexicana LLC** .................................................... E ...... 323 277-3660
6535 Caballero Blvd Unit A Buena Park (90620) *(P-1037)*

**La Mousse, Gardena** *Also Called: La Mousse Desserts Inc (P-1038)*

**La Mousse Desserts Inc ................................................** E ...... 310 478-6051
18211 S Broadway Gardena (90248) *(P-1038)*

**La Opinion LP (HQ) ..................................................** D ...... 213 891-9191
915 Wilshire Blvd Ste 915 Los Angeles (90017) *(P-4143)*

**La Opinion LP ........................................................** B ...... 213 896-2222
210 E Washington Blvd Los Angeles (90015) *(P-4144)*

**La Pachanga Foods Inc ............................................** E ...... 209 522-2222
708 L St Modesto (95354) *(P-604)*

**La Palm Furnitures & ACC Inc (PA) ..............................** E ...... 310 217-2700
1650 W Artesia Blvd Gardena (90248) *(P-2992)*

**La Parent Magazine (PA) ..........................................** F ...... 818 264-2222
5855 Topanga Canyon Blvd Ste 150 Woodland Hills (91367) *(P-4271)*

**La Paz Products Inc ...............................................** F ...... 714 990-0982
345 Oak Pl Brea (92821) *(P-2013)*

**LA Pillow & Fiber Inc ..............................................** D ...... 323 724-7969
7633 Bequette Ave Pico Rivera (90660) *(P-2934)*

**La Princesita Tortilleria Inc (PA) .................................** F ...... 323 267-0673
3432 E Cesar E Chavez Ave Los Angeles (90063) *(P-2257)*

**LA Printing & Graphics Inc ......................................** E ...... 310 527-4526
13951 S Main St Los Angeles (90061) *(P-4669)*

**La Quinta Brewing Company LLC ...............................** D ...... 760 200-2597
74714 Technology Dr Palm Desert (92211) *(P-1444)*

**La Quinta Cliff House, La Quinta** Also Called: TS Enterprises Inc *(P-17608)*

**La Rancherita Tortilleria Deli, Santa Ana** Also Called: MRS Foods Incorporated *(P-2288)*

**La Rocks, Los Angeles** Also Called: LA Gem and Jewelry Design *(P-15699)*

**La Rosa Tortilla Factory Inc .....................................** C ...... 831 728-5332
26 Menker St Watsonville (95076) *(P-2258)*

**La Sentinel Newspaper, Los Angeles** Also Called: Los Angeles Sentinel Inc *(P-4150)*

**LA Signal ..............................................................** F ...... 909 599-2201
155 N Eucla Ave La Puente (91744) *(P-460)*

**LA Spas Inc ...........................................................** C ...... 714 630-1150
1325 N Blue Gum St Anaheim (92806) *(P-16166)*

**La Spec Industries Inc ............................................** F ...... 323 588-8746
2315 E 52nd St Vernon (90058) *(P-11540)*

**LA Supply Company LLC .......................................** F ...... 310 980-3404
15040 Desman Rd La Mirada (90638) *(P-6150)*

**La Tapatia Tortilleria Inc .........................................** C ...... 559 441-1030
104 E Belmont Ave Fresno (93701) *(P-2259)*

**La Times ..............................................................** D ...... 213 237-2279
202 W 1st St Ste 500 Los Angeles (90012) *(P-4145)*

**La Tolteca Mexican Foods, Azusa** Also Called: Arrietta Incorporated *(P-17368)*

**La Tortilla Factory Inc ............................................** B ...... 707 586-4000
3300 Westwind Blvd Santa Rosa (95403) *(P-17193)*

**LA Triumph Inc .....................................................** E ...... 562 404-7657
13336 Alondra Blvd Cerritos (90703) *(P-2597)*

**LA Turbine (HQ) ....................................................** D ...... 661 294-8290
28557 Industry Dr Valencia (91355) *(P-9312)*

**La Xpress Air & Heating Svcs ..................................** D ...... 310 856-9678
6400 E Washington Blvd Ste 121 Commerce (90040) *(P-4425)*

**La- Rochelle, Livermore** Also Called: Steven Kent LLC *(P-1762)*

**La's Totally Awesome, Buena Park** Also Called: Awesome Products Inc *(P-5890)*

**La6721 LLC ..........................................................** F ...... 323 484-4070
1275 E 6th St Los Angeles (90021) *(P-16000)*

**Lab Clean Inc .......................................................** E ...... 714 689-0063
3627 Briggeman Dr Los Alamitos (90720) *(P-5912)*

**Lab Clear, Oakland** Also Called: Diamond Tool and Die Inc *(P-10811)*

**Lab Health Medical, Anaheim** Also Called: Teco Diagnostics *(P-5782)*

**Labarge/Stc Inc ....................................................** E ...... 281 207-1400
600 Anton Blvd Costa Mesa (92626) *(P-12522)*

**Label Art - HM Es-E Stik Lbels .................................** E ...... 510 465-1125
290 27th St Oakland (94612) *(P-4906)*

**Label Art of California, Oakland** Also Called: Label Art - HM Es-E Stik Lbels *(P-4906)*

**Label Division, Modesto** Also Called: G3 Enterprises Inc *(P-17828)*

**Label House, Ontario** Also Called: L A Supply Co *(P-4905)*

**Label ID Technologies Inc ......................................** F ...... 619 661-5566
2275 Michael Faraday Dr Ste 4 San Diego (92154) *(P-4907)*

**Label Impressions, Anaheim** Also Called: Brook & Whittle Limited *(P-4855)*

**Label Impressions Inc ............................................** E ...... 714 634-3466
1831 W Sequoia Ave Orange (92868) *(P-4908)*

**Label Innovators, Livermore** Also Called: Vintage 99 Label Mfg Inc *(P-3959)*

**Label Shoppe, The, City Of Industry** Also Called: Labels-R-Us Inc *(P-17632)*

**Label Specialties Inc .............................................** F ...... 714 961-8074
704 Dunn Way Placentia (92870) *(P-4909)*

**Label-Aire, Fullerton** Also Called: Label-Aire Inc *(P-10024)*

**Label-Aire Inc (PA) ................................................** D ...... 714 449-5155
550 Burning Tree Rd Fullerton (92833) *(P-10024)*

**Labelbox, San Francisco** Also Called: Labelbox Inc *(P-18483)*

**Labelbox Inc (PA) ..................................................** F ...... 415 294-0791
510 Treat Ave San Francisco (94110) *(P-18483)*

**Labelbox Inc .........................................................** C ...... 415 294-0791
510 Treat Ave San Francisco (94110) *(P-18484)*

**Labeling Hurst Systems LLC ...................................** F ...... 818 701-0710
20747 Dearborn St Chatsworth (91311) *(P-4910)*

**Labels-R-Us Inc ....................................................** E ...... 626 333-4001
1121 Fullerton Rd City Of Industry (91748) *(P-17632)*

**Labeltex Mills Inc (PA) ...........................................** C ...... 323 582-0228
5301 S Santa Fe Ave Vernon (90058) *(P-15912)*

**Labeltronix LLC (HQ) .............................................** D ...... 800 429-4321
2419 E Winston Rd Anaheim (92806) *(P-4911)*

**Labonita Diana's Mexican Food, Carson** Also Called: Dianas Mexican Food Pdts Inc *(P-17374)*

**Labor Law Center Inc ............................................** E ...... 800 745-9970
3501 W Garry Ave Santa Ana (92704) *(P-4670)*

**Laborer, San Francisco** Also Called: H&Gbygiselleco *(P-98)*

**Laborlawcenter.com, Santa Ana** Also Called: Labor Law Center Inc *(P-4670)*

**Labrucherie Produce LLC ......................................** E ...... 760 352-2170
1407 S La Brucherie Rd El Centro (92243) *(P-2260)*

**Labs Upwest .........................................................** F ...... 650 272-6529
550 California Ave Ste 100 Palo Alto (94306) *(P-18485)*

**Laclede Inc ...........................................................** E ...... 310 605-4280
2103 E University Dr Rancho Dominguez (90220) *(P-15465)*

**Laclede Research Center, Rancho Dominguez** Also Called: Laclede Inc *(P-15465)*

**Laco Inc ...............................................................** C ...... 775 461-2960
6767 Preston Ave Livermore (94551) *(P-12888)*

**Lactalis Heritage Dairy Inc .....................................** C ...... 559 685-0790
10800 Avenue 184 Tulare (93274) *(P-723)*

**Ladder, Palo Alto** Also Called: Ladder Financial Inc *(P-17939)*

**Ladder Financial Inc .............................................** E ...... 844 533-7206
100 Forest Ave Palo Alto (94301) *(P-17939)*

**Ladera Vineyards LLC ..........................................** F ...... 707 965-2445
150 White Cottage Rd S Angwin (94508) *(P-1655)*

**Ladera Winery LLC ...............................................** E ...... 707 965-2445
150 White Cottage Rd S Angwin (94508) *(P-1656)*

**LAdesserts Inc ......................................................** E ...... 323 588-2522
1433 E Gage Ave Los Angeles (90001) *(P-17363)*

**Lady Family Wines ...............................................** F ...... 707 944-8642
1473 Yountville Cross Rd Yountville (94599) *(P-1657)*

**Ladybug Medical Supply, Chatsworth** Also Called: Loveis Corp *(P-15153)*

**Laetitia Vineyard & Winery Inc ...............................** D ...... 805 481-1772
453 Laetitia Vineyard Dr Arroyo Grande (93420) *(P-1658)*

**Laetitia Winery, Arroyo Grande** Also Called: Laetitia Vineyard & Winery Inc *(P-1658)*

**Lagun Engineering Solutions, Harbor City** Also Called: Republic Machinery Co Inc *(P-9565)*

**Laguna Beach Magazine, Laguna Beach** Also Called: Firebrand Media LLC *(P-4609)*

**Laguna Clay Company, City Of Industry** Also Called: Jon Brooks Inc *(P-7570)*

**Laguna Cookie Company Inc .................................** D ...... 714 546-6855
4041 W Garry Ave Santa Ana (92704) *(P-1280)*

**Laguna Oaks Vnyards Winery Inc ...........................** E ...... 707 568-2455
5700 Occidental Rd Santa Rosa (95401) *(P-1659)*

**Lahlouh, Burlingame** Also Called: Lahlouh Inc *(P-4671)*

**Lahlouh Inc (PA) ...................................................** C ...... 650 692-6600
1649 Adrian Rd Burlingame (94010) *(P-4671)*

**Laird Coatings Corporation ...................................** D ...... 714 894-5252
15541 Commerce Ln Huntington Beach (92649) *(P-6092)*

**Laird Family Estate LLC (PA) ..................................** F ...... 707 257-0360
5055 Solano Ave Napa (94558) *(P-1660)*

**Laird Manufacturing, Merced** Also Called: Laird Mfg LLC *(P-9367)*

**Laird Mfg LLC (PA) ................................................** E ...... 209 722-4145
531 S State Highway 59 Merced (95341) *(P-9367)*

**Laird Plastics, Santa Fe Springs** Also Called: Plastics Family Holdings Inc *(P-17232)*

**Laird R & F Products Inc (DH) ................................** E ...... 760 916-9410
2091 Rutherford Rd Carlsbad (92008) *(P-14208)*

# ALPHABETIC SECTION

**Laird Technologies Inc** ............................................................... E ...... 408 544-9500
2040 Fortune Dr Ste 102 San Jose (95131) *(P-14430)*

**Lake County Publishing Co Inc** .................................................. D ...... 707 263-5636
415 Talmage Rd Ste A Ukiah (95482) *(P-4146)*

**Lake County Record-Bee, Ukiah** *Also Called: Lake County Publishing Co Inc (P-4146)*

**Lakeshirts LLC** ............................................................................. E ...... 805 239-1290
1400 Railroad St Ste 104 Paso Robles (93446) *(P-2993)*

**Lakim Industries Incorporated (PA)** ........................................... E ...... 310 637-8900
389 Rood Rd Calexico (92231) *(P-15932)*

**Lakos, Fresno** *Also Called: Lakos Corporation (P-16824)*

**Lakos Corporation (HQ)** ............................................................. E ...... 559 255-1601
1365 N Clovis Ave Fresno (93727) *(P-16824)*

**LAM RESEARCH, Fremont** *Also Called: Lam Research Corporation (P-12526)*

**Lam Research Corporation** ........................................................ E ...... 408 434-6109
3590 N 1st St Ste 200 San Jose (95134) *(P-12523)*

**Lam Research Corporation** ........................................................ E ...... 510 572-8400
1 Portola Ave Livermore (94551) *(P-12524)*

**Lam Research Corporation** ........................................................ F ...... 209 597-2194
1201 Voyager St Livermore (94550) *(P-12525)*

**Lam Research Corporation (PA)** ................................................ A ...... 510 572-0200
4650 Cushing Pkwy Fremont (94538) *(P-12526)*

**Lamar Tool & Die Casting Inc** ................................................... D ...... 209 545-5525
4230 Technology Dr Modesto (95356) *(P-7618)*

**Lamart California Inc** ................................................................. E ...... 973 772-6262
7560 Bristow Ct Ste C San Diego (92154) *(P-7580)*

**Lamart Corporation** ................................................................... C ...... 510 489-8100
2600 Central Ave Ste E Union City (94587) *(P-7562)*

**Lamb Fuels Inc** .......................................................................... E ...... 619 777-9135
10723 Prospect Ave Santee (92071) *(P-6151)*

**Lambda, San Jose** *Also Called: Lambda Inc (P-17940)*

**Lambda Inc** ................................................................................ E ...... 650 741-0738
2510 Zanker Rd San Jose (95131) *(P-17940)*

**Lambda Research Optics Inc** .................................................... D ...... 714 327-0600
1695 Macarthur Blvd Costa Mesa (92626) *(P-14682)*

**Lambs & Ivy Inc** ........................................................................ E ...... 310 322-3800
2042 E Maple Ave El Segundo (90245) *(P-2935)*

**Lamer Street Kreations Corp** .................................................... E ...... 909 305-4824
13815 Arrow Blvd Fontana (92335) *(P-19402)*

**Laminated Shim Company Inc** .................................................. E ...... 951 273-3900
1691 California Ave Corona (92881) *(P-9291)*

**Laminating Company of America** .............................................. E ...... 949 587-3300
20322 Windrow Dr Ste 100 Lake Forest (92630) *(P-12150)*

**Laminating Company of America, Lake Forest** *Also Called: Tri-Star Laminates Inc (P-12243)*

**Laminating Technologies, Anaheim** *Also Called: Yti Enterprises Inc (P-3432)*

**Lamkin Corporation (PA)** ........................................................... F ...... 619 661-7090
6530 Gateway Park Dr San Diego (92154) *(P-5173)*

**Lamps Plus Inc** .......................................................................... E ...... 805 642-9007
4723 Telephone Rd Ventura (93003) *(P-11541)*

**Lamsco West Inc** ...................................................................... D ...... 661 295-8620
29101 The Old Rd Santa Clarita (91355) *(P-6893)*

**Lancaster Burns Cnstr Inc** ........................................................ C ...... 916 624-8404
8655 Washington Blvd Roseville (95678) *(P-476)*

**Lancer Orthodontics Inc (PA)** .................................................... E ...... 760 744-5585
2726 Loker Ave W Carlsbad (92010) *(P-15466)*

**Land O'Lakes, Tulare** *Also Called: Land OLakes Inc (P-724)*

**Land O'Lakes, Orland** *Also Called: Land OLakes Inc (P-725)*

**Land OLakes Inc** ....................................................................... D ...... 559 687-8287
400 S M St Tulare (93274) *(P-724)*

**Land OLakes Inc** ....................................................................... E ...... 530 865-7626
3601 County Road C Orland (95963) *(P-725)*

**Landing Gear, Los Angeles** *Also Called: Judy Ann of California Inc (P-2672)*

**Landmark Electronics Inc** .......................................................... E ...... 626 967-2857
990 N Amelia Ave San Dimas (91773) *(P-13021)*

**Landmark Mfg Inc** ..................................................................... E ...... 760 941-6626
4112 Avenida De La Plata Oceanside (92056) *(P-10936)*

**Landmark Motor Cycle ACC, Oceanside** *Also Called: Landmark Mfg Inc (P-10936)*

**Landsberg Flflment Sltons Div, Fontana** *Also Called: Orora Packaging Solutions (P-17017)*

**Landsberg Los Angeles Div 1001, Montebello** *Also Called: Orora Packaging Solutions (P-17008)*

**Landsberg Orange Cnty Div 1025, Buena Park** *Also Called: Orora Packaging Solutions (P-17009)*

**Landsberg Snta Brbara Div 1046, Oxnard** *Also Called: Orora Packaging Solutions (P-17012)*

**Landscape Communications Inc** ............................................... E ...... 714 979-5276
14771 Plaza Dr Ste A Tustin (92780) *(P-4272)*

**Landscape Contract National, Tustin** *Also Called: Landscape Communications Inc (P-4272)*

**Landscape Contractor, Salinas** *Also Called: Uv Landscaping LLC (P-7302)*

**Lane International Trading Inc** .................................................. C ...... 510 489-7364
33155 Transit Ave Union City (94587) *(P-7110)*

**Lane Safety Co Inc** ................................................................... E ...... 707 746-4820
340 W Channel Rd Ste F Benicia (94510) *(P-17868)*

**Lange Precision Inc** ................................................................. F ...... 714 870-5420
1106 E Elm Ave Fullerton (92831) *(P-10937)*

**Langer Juice Company Inc (PA)** ............................................... C ...... 626 336-3100
16195 Stephens St City Of Industry (91745) *(P-17428)*

**Langer Juice Company Inc** ....................................................... B ...... 626 336-3100
16185 Stephens St City Of Industry (91744) *(P-1011)*

**Langers Juice, City Of Industry** *Also Called: Langer Juice Company Inc (P-17428)*

**Langetwins Inc** ......................................................................... E ...... 209 339-4055
1298 E Jahant Rd Acampo (95220) *(P-1661)*

**Langetwins Wine Company Inc** ............................................... E ...... 209 334-9780
1525 E Jahant Rd Acampo (95220) *(P-1662)*

**Langetwins Winery & Vineyards, Acampo** *Also Called: Langetwins Wine Company Inc (P-1662)*

**Langills General Machine Inc** ................................................... E ...... 916 452-0167
7850 14th Ave Sacramento (95826) *(P-10938)*

**Langlois Company** ................................................................... E ...... 951 360-3900
10810 San Sevaine Way Jurupa Valley (91752) *(P-1087)*

**Langlois Fancy Frozen Foods Inc** ........................................... E ...... 949 497-1741
2975 Laguna Canyon Rd Laguna Beach (92651) *(P-1039)*

**Langlois Flour Company, Jurupa Valley** *Also Called: Langlois Company (P-1087)*

**Langston Companies Inc** ......................................................... C ...... 559 688-3839
2500 S K St Tulare (93274) *(P-3991)*

**Langtry Farms LLC** .................................................................. F ...... 707 987-2772
21000 Butts Canyon Rd Middletown (95461) *(P-1663)*

**Language Los Angeles, Burbank** *Also Called: Eastwest Clothing Inc (P-2663)*

**Lanic Aerospace, Rancho Cucamonga** *Also Called: Lanic Engineering Inc (P-13889)*

**Lanic Engineering Inc (PA)** ...................................................... E ...... 877 763-0411
12144 6th St Rancho Cucamonga (91730) *(P-13889)*

**Lansair Corporation** ................................................................ F ...... 661 294-9503
25228 Anza Dr Santa Clarita (91355) *(P-10939)*

**Lansas Products, Lodi** *Also Called: Vander Lans & Sons Inc (P-10608)*

**Lansky Sharpeners, Oakland** *Also Called: Levine Arthur Lansky & Assoc (P-7959)*

**Lansmont, Monterey** *Also Called: Ppt Group Corp (P-19506)*

**Lapco West, Cerritos** *Also Called: Lapco West LLC (P-13528)*

**Lapco West LLC** ..................................................................... E ...... 562 348-4850
13140 Midway Pl Cerritos (90703) *(P-13528)*

**Laptalo Enterprises Inc (PA)** ................................................... D ...... 408 727-6633
2360 Zanker Rd San Jose (95131) *(P-8484)*

**Lara Manufacturing Inc** ........................................................... E ...... 408 778-0811
16235 Vineyard Blvd Morgan Hill (95037) *(P-8485)*

**Lares Research** ...................................................................... E ...... 530 345-1767
295 Lockheed Ave Chico (95973) *(P-15467)*

**Larin Corp** .............................................................................. E ...... 909 464-0605
5651 Schaefer Ave Chino (91710) *(P-7958)*

**Laritech Inc** ............................................................................ C ...... 805 529-5000
5898 Condor Dr Moorpark (93021) *(P-12151)*

**Lark Ellen Farm, Ojai** *Also Called: Pure Simple Foods LLC (P-360)*

**Larkin Precision Machining Inc** ............................................... E ...... 831 438-2700
175 El Pueblo Rd Ste 10 Scotts Valley (95066) *(P-10940)*

**Larry Fisher & Sons Ltd Partnr** ............................................... F ...... 559 252-2575
5242 E Home Ave Fresno (93727) *(P-16416)*

**Larry Mthvin Installations Inc (HQ)** ........................................ C ...... 909 563-1700
501 Kettering Dr Ontario (91761) *(P-7230)*

**Larry Mthvin Installations Inc** ................................................. D ...... 209 368-2105
128 N Cluff Ave Lodi (95240) *(P-7231)*

**Larry Spun Products Inc** ........................................................ E ...... 323 881-6300
1533 S Downey Rd Los Angeles (90023) *(P-8859)*

**Larsens** .................................................................................. F ...... 831 476-3009
1041 17th Ave Ste A Santa Cruz (95062) *(P-2977)*

**Larson Al Boat Shop** .............................................................. D ...... 310 514-4100
1046 S Seaside Ave San Pedro (90731) *(P-14007)*

**Larson Packaging Company LLC** ............................................. E ...... 408 946-4971
1000 Yosemite Dr Milpitas (95035) *(P-3326)*

**Larson Picture Frames, Santa Fe Springs** *Also Called: Larson-Juhl US LLC (P-3419)*

**Larson-Juhl US LLC** ............................................................... E ...... 562 946-6873
12206 Bell Ranch Dr Santa Fe Springs (90670) *(P-3419)*

**Las Animas Con & Bldg Sup Inc** ........................................... E ...... 831 425-4084
146 Encinal St Santa Cruz (95060) *(P-7461)*

**Las Animas Concrete, Santa Cruz** *Also Called: Las Animas Con & Bldg Sup Inc (P-7461)*

**Las Colinas** ............................................................................. F ...... 714 528-8100
600 S Jefferson St Ste M Placentia (92870) *(P-10571)*

**Las Glondrinas Mexican Fd Pdts (PA)** ................................. **F ...... 949 240-3440**
27124 Paseo Espada Ste 803 San Juan Capistrano (92675) *(P-17595)*

**Laselva Beach Spice Co Inc** ................................................. F ...... 831 724-4500
453 Mcquaide Dr Watsonville (95076) *(P-2261)*

**Laser Division, Milpitas** *Also Called: Spectra-Physics Inc (P-13310)*

**Laser Imaging International, Van Nuys** *Also Called: E Alko Inc (P-15894)*

**Laser Industries Inc** .............................................................. D ...... 714 532-3271
1351 Manhattan Ave Fullerton (92831) *(P-10941)*

**Laser Operations LLC** ........................................................... E ...... 818 986-0000
15632 Roxford St Rancho Cascades (91342) *(P-12527)*

**Laser Recharge Inc (PA)** ...................................................... E ...... 916 813-2717
8250 Belvedere Ave Ste C Sacramento (95826) *(P-15897)*

**Laser Reference Inc** ............................................................. F ...... 408 361-0220
786 E Mcglincy Ln Campbell (95008) *(P-14342)*

**Laser Tech, Riverside** *Also Called: L T Seroge Inc (P-13267)*

**Laser Technologies, San Fernando** *Also Called: Laser Technologies & Services LLC (P-15648)*

**Laser Technologies & Services LLC** ..................................... D
1175 Aviation Pl San Fernando (91340) *(P-15648)*

**Lasercard Corporation** ......................................................... D ...... 650 969-4428
1875 N Shoreline Blvd Mountain View (94043) *(P-13197)*

**Lasercare, Irvine** *Also Called: Lasercare Technologies Inc (P-15898)*

**Lasercare Technologies Inc (PA)** ........................................ E ...... 310 202-4200
14370 Myford Rd Ste 100 Irvine (92606) *(P-15898)*

**Lasergraphics Inc** ................................................................. E ...... 949 753-8282
20 Ada Irvine (92618) *(P-10395)*

**Lasergraphics General Business, Irvine** *Also Called: Lasergraphics Inc (P-10395)*

**Laserod Technologies LLC** .................................................. E ...... 310 328-5869
20312 Gramercy Pl Torrance (90501) *(P-10942)*

**Laspec Lighting, Vernon** *Also Called: La Spec Industries Inc (P-11540)*

**Lassen Forest Products Inc** ................................................. E ...... 530 527-7677
22829 Casale Rd Red Bluff (96080) *(P-3313)*

**Lassonde Pappas and Co Inc** ............................................... E ...... 909 923-4041
1755 E Acacia St Ontario (91761) *(P-2262)*

**Lastline LLC (DH)** ................................................................. D ...... 877 671-3239
3401 Hillview Ave Palo Alto (94304) *(P-18486)*

**Lastline, Inc., Palo Alto** *Also Called: Lastline LLC (P-18486)*

**LAT LLC** .................................................................................. E ...... 323 233-3017
2618 Fruitland Ave Vernon (90058) *(P-2785)*

**Latexco West, Santa Fe Springs** *Also Called: Sleepcomp West LLC (P-6662)*

**Lathrop Engineering, Morgan Hill** *Also Called: Paramit Corporation (P-12186)*

**Lathrop Woodworks, Lathrop** *Also Called: Rafael Sandoval (P-3076)*

**Latigo Inc** .............................................................................. E ...... 323 583-8000
4371 E 49th St Vernon (90058) *(P-2475)*

**Latina & Associates Inc (PA)** ............................................... E ...... 619 426-1491
1031 Bay Blvd Chula Vista (91911) *(P-4147)*

**Latitude 1, Stockton** *Also Called: Kennfoods Usa LLC (P-1355)*

**Lattice Data Inc** .................................................................... E ...... 650 800-7262
801 El Camino Real Menlo Park (94025) *(P-18487)*

**Lattice Engines Inc (DH)** ..................................................... **C ...... 877 460-0010**
1820 Gateway Dr Ste 200 San Mateo (94404) *(P-18984)*

**Lattice Semiconductor Corp** ................................................ B ...... 408 826-6000
2115 Onel Dr San Jose (95131) *(P-12528)*

**Laumiere Gourmet Fruits Co LLC** ........................................ F ...... 661 218-9768
3331 Pegasus Dr Ste 101 Bakersfield (93308) *(P-954)*

**Launchpint Elc Prplsion Sltons** ........................................... E ...... 805 683-9659
320 Storke Rd Ste 100 Goleta (93117) *(P-13890)*

**Launchpoint Eps, Goleta** *Also Called: Launchpint Elc Prplsion Sltons (P-13890)*

**Lauras Orgnal Bston Brwnies In** ......................................... F ...... 619 855-3258
2735 Cactus Rd Ste 101 San Diego (92154) *(P-1221)*

**Lauren Anthony & Co Inc** ..................................................... E ...... 619 590-1141
11425 Woodside Ave Ste B Santee (92071) *(P-3446)*

**Lausmann Lumber & Moulding Co** ...................................... E ...... 916 652-9201
3370 Rippey Rd Loomis (95650) *(P-3072)*

**Lava Athletica Inc** ................................................................ F ...... 909 859-1287
9661 Garvey Ave Ste 112-528 South El Monte (91733) *(P-2903)*

**Lava Cap Winery, Placerville** *Also Called: Lava Springs Inc (P-1664)*

**Lava Products, Fullerton** *Also Called: Minaloas Inc (P-4695)*

**Lava Springs Inc** .................................................................. E ...... 530 621-0175
2221 Fruitridge Rd Placerville (95667) *(P-1664)*

**Lavash Corporation of America** .......................................... E ...... 323 663-5249
2835 Newell St Los Angeles (90039) *(P-1222)*

**Lave Apparel, San Diego** *Also Called: Tequila Blues Inc (P-17103)*

**Lavender Ridge Vineyard Inc** .............................................. E ...... 209 728-2441
425a Main St Murphys (95247) *(P-1665)*

**Lavi Industries LLC (PA)** ..................................................... **D ...... 877 275-5284**
27810 Avenue Hopkins Valencia (91355) *(P-8634)*

**Lawley's Trucking, Stockton** *Also Called: Lawleys Inc (P-1133)*

**Lawleys Inc** ........................................................................... E ...... 209 337-1170
4554 Qantas Ln Stockton (95206) *(P-1133)*

**Lawrence Equipment, El Monte** *Also Called: Lawrence Equipment Leasing Inc (P-9803)*

**Lawrence Equipment Leasing Inc (PA)** ............................. **C ...... 626 442-2894**
2034 Peck Rd El Monte (91733) *(P-9803)*

**Lawrence Roll Up Doors Inc (PA)** ...................................... **E ...... 626 962-4163**
4525 Littlejohn St Baldwin Park (91706) *(P-8273)*

**Layline Automation** ............................................................. D ...... 415 758-0044
1005 Northgate Dr San Rafael (94903) *(P-17941)*

**Laymon Candy Co Inc** ........................................................... E ...... 909 825-4408
276 Commercial Rd San Bernardino (92408) *(P-17148)*

**Layne Laboratories Inc** ....................................................... F ...... 805 242-7918
4303 Huasna Rd Arroyo Grande (93420) *(P-1134)*

**Layton Printing, La Verne** *Also Called: Layton Printing & Mailing (P-4672)*

**Layton Printing & Mailing** ................................................... F ...... 909 592-4419
1538 Arrow Hwy La Verne (91750) *(P-4672)*

**Lb Beadels LLC** .................................................................... E ...... 562 726-1700
70 Atlantic Ave Long Beach (90802) *(P-1316)*

**Lbi - USA, Chatsworth** *Also Called: Lehrer Brllnprfktion Werks Inc (P-6895)*

**Lca Promotions Inc** .............................................................. E ...... 818 773-9170
3073 Cicero Ct Simi Valley (93063) *(P-4912)*

**LCD&d, Chatsworth** *Also Called: Lighting Control & Design Inc (P-11609)*

**Lcf Wine Company LLC** ........................................................ F ...... 209 334-9782
1525 E Jahant Rd Acampo (95220) *(P-1666)*

**Lcoa, Lake Forest** *Also Called: Laminating Company of America (P-12150)*

**Lcptracker Inc** ...................................................................... E ...... 714 669-0052
117 E Chapman Ave Orange (92866) *(P-18488)*

**Lcr-Dixon Corporation** ......................................................... F ...... 404 307-1695
2048 Union St Apt 4 San Francisco (94123) *(P-18489)*

**Ld Products Inc** .................................................................... C ...... 888 321-2552
2501 E 28th St Signal Hill (90755) *(P-3785)*

**Lddf Inc** ................................................................................. F ...... 707 995-7145
9781 Point Lakeview Rd Ste 3 Kelseyville (95451) *(P-14548)*

**LDI, Monterey** *Also Called: Steiner Eoptics Inc (P-13311)*

**Le Belge Chocolatier Inc** ...................................................... E ...... 707 258-9200
761 Skyway Ct Napa (94558) *(P-1317)*

**Le Elegant Bath Inc** .............................................................. C ...... 951 734-0238
13405 Estelle St Corona (92879) *(P-6683)*

**Le Petite Fleur, Santa Rosa** *Also Called: Tumelo Inc (P-6327)*

**Leach Grain & Milling Co Inc** ............................................... E ...... 562 869-4451
8131 Pivot St Downey (90241) *(P-17273)*

**Leach International Corp (DH)** .......................................... **B ...... 714 736-7537**
6900 Orangethorpe Ave Buena Park (90620) *(P-13891)*

**Leadcrunch, San Diego** *Also Called: Leadcrunch Inc (P-18490)*

**Leadcrunch Inc (PA)** ........................................................... **E ...... 888 708-6649**
750 B St Ste 1630 San Diego (92101) *(P-18490)*

**Leader Emergency Vehicles, South El Monte** *Also Called: Leader Industries Inc (P-16277)*

**Leader Industries Inc** .......................................................... C ...... 626 575-0880
10941 Weaver Ave South El Monte (91733) *(P-16277)*

**Leading Edge Aviation Svcs Inc** .......................................... A ...... 714 556-0576
5251 California Ave Ste 170 Irvine (92617) *(P-447)*

**Leading Industry Inc** ............................................................ D ...... 805 385-4100
1151 Pacific Ave Oxnard (93033) *(P-6894)*

## ALPHABETIC SECTION

**Leadingway Corporation (PA)** .................................................. F ...... 949 509-6589
4199 Campus Dr Ste 550 Irvine (92612) *(P-18985)*

**Leadingway Knowledge Systems, Irvine** *Also Called: Leadingway Corporation (P-18985)*

**Leadman Electronics USA Inc (PA)** ........................................ E ...... 408 380-4567
382 Laurelwood Rd Santa Clara (95054) *(P-10174)*

**Leads360 LLC** ........................................................................ E ...... 888 843-1777
207 Hindry Ave Inglewood (90301) *(P-18491)*

**League of California Cities (PA)** .............................................. D ...... 916 658-8200
1400 K St Fl 4 Sacramento (95814) *(P-19550)*

**Leal Vineyards Inc** ................................................................. F ...... 408 778-1978
1978 Willow Springs Rd Morgan Hill (95037) *(P-17774)*

**Lean Merch, Huntington Beach** *Also Called: HB Products LLC (P-4890)*

**Leap, San Francisco** *Also Called: Leapfrog Power Inc (P-18492)*

**Leapfrog Enterprises Inc (HQ)** ............................................... B ...... 510 420-5000
2200 Powell St Ste 500 Emeryville (94608) *(P-15757)*

**Leapfrog Power Inc (PA)** ........................................................ E ...... 415 409-9783
1700 Montgomery St Ste 200 San Francisco (94111) *(P-18492)*

**Leapyear Technologies Inc** ..................................................... E ...... 510 542-9193
612 Howard St Ste 500 San Francisco (94105) *(P-18493)*

**Learjet Inc** ............................................................................... E ...... 818 894-8241
16750 Schoenborn St North Hills (91343) *(P-13675)*

**Learning Explorer Inc** ............................................................. F ...... 888 909-9035
924 Anacapa St Ste 4i Santa Barbara (93101) *(P-18494)*

**Learning Ovations Inc** ............................................................ E ...... 734 904-1459
16 Coltrane Ct Irvine (92617) *(P-19352)*

**Learning Resources Inc** ......................................................... E ...... 800 995-4436
19700 S Vermont Ave Torrance (90502) *(P-16167)*

**Learning Squared Inc** ............................................................. C ...... 650 567-9995
935 Benecia Ave Sunnyvale (94085) *(P-15758)*

**Leather Pro Inc** ....................................................................... E ...... 818 833-8822
12900 Bradley Ave Sylmar (91342) *(P-7149)*

**Leather.com, National City** *Also Called: San Diego Leather Inc (P-17513)*

**Lebata Inc** ............................................................................... E ...... 949 253-2800
4621 Teller Ave Ste 130 Newport Beach (92660) *(P-7462)*

**Lecroy Prtocol Solutions Group, Milpitas** *Also Called: Teledyne Lecroy Inc (P-14590)*

**Leda Corporation** ................................................................... E ...... 714 841-7821
7080 Kearny Dr Huntington Beach (92648) *(P-14114)*

**Leda Multimedia, Chino** *Also Called: Shop4techcom (P-10283)*

**Ledconn, Brea** *Also Called: Ledconn Corp (P-11605)*

**Ledconn Corp** ......................................................................... E ...... 714 256-2111
301 Thor Pl Brea (92821) *(P-11605)*

**Ledengin Inc** ........................................................................... E ...... 408 922-7200
651 River Oaks Pkwy San Jose (95134) *(P-12529)*

**Ledson Winery & Vineyards, Santa Rosa** *Also Called: Steven N Ledson (P-349)*

**Ledtronics Inc (PA)** ................................................................. E ...... 310 534-1505
23105 Kashiwa Ct Torrance (90505) *(P-12530)*

**Ledvance LLC** ........................................................................ E ...... 909 923-3003
1651 S Archibald Ave Ontario (91761) *(P-11427)*

**Lee Brothers Inc** .................................................................... E ...... 650 964-9650
1011 Timothy Dr San Jose (95133) *(P-982)*

**Lee Kum Kee (usa) Foods Inc (PA)** ....................................... D ...... 626 709-1888
14455 Don Julian Rd City Of Industry (91746) *(P-983)*

**Lee Kum Kee (usa) Inc (DH)** .................................................. E ...... 626 709-1888
14841 Don Julian Rd City Of Industry (91746) *(P-17194)*

**Lee Mar Aquarium & Pet Sups, Vista** *Also Called: Lee-Mar Aquarium & Pet Sups (P-17299)*

**Lee Pharmaceuticals** ............................................................. D ...... 626 442-3141
1434 Santa Anita Ave South El Monte (91733) *(P-6002)*

**Lee Publishing Company** ....................................................... F ...... 916 284-0022
1825 Del Paso Blvd Ste 2 Sacramento (95815) *(P-4148)*

**Lee Ray Sandblasting, Santa Fe Springs** *Also Called: Cji Process Systems Inc (P-8308)*

**Lee Thomas Inc (PA)** .............................................................. E ...... 310 532-7560
13800 S Figueroa St Los Angeles (90061) *(P-2786)*

**Lee-Mar Aquarium & Pet Sups** .............................................. D ...... 760 727-1300
2459 Dogwood Way Vista (92081) *(P-17299)*

**Lee's Enterprise, Chatsworth** *Also Called: Molnar Engineering Inc (P-10990)*

**Lee's Kitchen, City Of Industry** *Also Called: Lee Kum Kee (usa) Inc (P-17194)*

**Leebe, Los Angeles** *Also Called: Leebe Apparel Inc (P-2678)*

**Leebe Apparel Inc** .................................................................. E ...... 323 897-5585
3499 S Main St Los Angeles (90007) *(P-2678)*

**Leemah Corporation (PA)** ...................................................... C ...... 415 394-1288
155 S Hill Dr Brisbane (94005) *(P-12034)*

**Leemah Electronics Inc** ......................................................... C ...... 415 394-1288
1080 Samson St San Francisco (94111) *(P-16343)*

**Leemah Electronics Inc (HQ)** ................................................ E ...... 415 394-1288
155 S Hill Dr Brisbane (94005) *(P-12152)*

**Leemarc Industries LLC** ........................................................ D ...... 760 598-0505
340 Rancheros Dr Ste 172 San Marcos (92069) *(P-2630)*

**Leeper's Stair Products, Corona** *Also Called: Leepers Wood Turning Co Inc (P-3153)*

**Leepers Wood Turning Co Inc (PA)** ....................................... E ...... 562 422-6525
341 Bonnie Cir Ste 104 Corona (92878) *(P-3153)*

**Lees Concrete Materials Inc** .................................................. F ...... 559 486-2440
200 S Pine St Madera (93637) *(P-7463)*

**Lees Imperial Welding Inc** ...................................................... C ...... 510 657-4900
3300 Edison Way Fremont (94538) *(P-8167)*

**Leet Technology Inc** ............................................................... F ...... 877 238-4492
1427 S Robertson Blvd Los Angeles (90035) *(P-13529)*

**Leewood Press Inc** ................................................................. E ...... 415 896-0513
398 Beach Rd Burlingame (94010) *(P-4673)*

**Leeyo, San Jose** *Also Called: Leeyo Software Inc (P-18495)*

**Leeyo Software Inc (HQ)** ....................................................... E ...... 408 988-5800
2841 Junction Ave Ste 201 San Jose (95134) *(P-18495)*

**Lefiell, Santa Fe Springs** *Also Called: Lefiell Manufacturing Company (P-13892)*

**Lefiell Manufacturing Company** ............................................. C ...... 562 921-3411
13700 Firestone Blvd Santa Fe Springs (90670) *(P-13892)*

**Left Coast Brewing Company** ................................................ F ...... 949 218-3961
1245 Puerta Del Sol San Clemente (92673) *(P-1445)*

**Left Coast Brewing Company, San Clemente** *Also Called: Left Coast Brewing Company (P-1445)*

**Left Coast T-Shirt Company** ................................................... E ...... 805 547-1622
755 Fiero Ln Ste A San Luis Obispo (93401) *(P-4913)*

**Leftbank Art, La Mirada** *Also Called: Outlook Resources Inc (P-2998)*

**Lefty Production Co LLC** ....................................................... E ...... 323 515-9266
318 W 9th St Ste 1010 Los Angeles (90015) *(P-2787)*

**Legacy Commercial Holdings Inc** .......................................... E ...... 818 767-6626
28939 Avenue Williams Valencia (91355) *(P-3447)*

**Legacy Epoch LLC** ................................................................. D ...... 844 673-7305
21011 Warner Center Ln Ste A Woodland Hills (91367) *(P-1135)*

**Legacy Reinforcing Steel LLC** ............................................... D ...... 619 646-0205
1057 Tierra Del Rey Ste F Chula Vista (91910) *(P-532)*

**Legacy Vulcan LLC** ................................................................. F ...... 559 434-1202
11599 Old Friant Rd Fresno (93730) *(P-7464)*

**Legal Vision Group LLC** ......................................................... E ...... 310 945-5550
2030 Paddock Ln Norco (92860) *(P-4674)*

**Legend Pump & Well Service Inc** .......................................... E ...... 909 384-1000
1324 W Rialto Ave San Bernardino (92410) *(P-162)*

**Legendary Foods LLC** ............................................................ E ...... 888 698-1708
2601 Colorado Ave Santa Monica (90404) *(P-17403)*

**Legendary Headwear, San Diego** *Also Called: Legendary Holdings Inc (P-2845)*

**Legendary Holdings Inc** ......................................................... E ...... 619 872-6100
2295 Paseo De Las Americas Ste 19 San Diego (92154) *(P-2845)*

**Legends Apparel & I C Ink, Stockton** *Also Called: IC Ink Image Co Inc (P-4894)*

**Leggett & Platt Incorporated** .................................................. F ...... 209 839-8230
2015 N Macarthur Dr Tracy (95376) *(P-3531)*

**Leggett & Platt Incorporated** .................................................. D ...... 909 937-1010
1050 S Dupont Ave Ontario (91761) *(P-3532)*

**Leggett & Platt 0768, Poway** *Also Called: Valley Metals LLC (P-7673)*

**Legion Creative Group** ........................................................... E ...... 323 498-1100
500 N Brand Blvd Ste 1800 Glendale (91203) *(P-4914)*

**Leham Millet West, Santa Ana** *Also Called: Lehman Millet Incorporated (P-5759)*

**Lehigh Southwest Cement Co** ................................................ F ...... 408 996-4271
24001 Stevens Creek Blvd Cupertino (95014) *(P-7257)*

**Lehigh Southwest Cement Co (DH)** ...................................... F ...... 972 653-5500
2300 Clayton Rd Ste 300 Concord (94520) *(P-7258)*

**Lehman Foods Inc** ................................................................. E ...... 818 837-7600
1145 Arroyo St Ste B San Fernando (91340) *(P-2263)*

**Lehman Millet Incorporated** ................................................... E ...... 714 850-7900
3 Macarthur Pl Ste 700 Santa Ana (92707) *(P-5759)*

**Lehmans Manufacturing Co Inc** ............................................. F ...... 559 486-1700
4960 E Jensen Ave Fresno (93725) *(P-8168)*

**Lehrer Brllnprfktion Werks Inc** .............................................. D ...... 818 407-1890
20801 Nordhoff St Chatsworth (91311) *(P-6895)*

**Leica Biosystems Imaging Inc (HQ)** ...................................... C ...... 760 539-1100
1360 Park Center Dr Vista (92081) *(P-14683)*

**Leica Geosystems Hds LLC** .................................................. D ...... 925 790-2300
5000 Executive Pkwy Ste 500 San Ramon (94583) *(P-14892)*

**Leidos Inc** .................................................. C ...... 858 826-9090
2985 Scott St Vista (92081) *(P-19460)*

**Leidos Inc** .................................................. D ...... 858 826-6000
Naval Air Station San Diego (92135) *(P-19461)*

**Leidos Government Services Inc** .................................................. C ...... 323 721-6979
500 N Via Val Verde Montebello (90640) *(P-19039)*

**Leigh Jerry California Inc (PA)** .................................................. C ...... 818 909-6200
7860 Nelson Rd Van Nuys (91402) *(P-2856)*

**Leiner Health Products, Carson** *Also Called: Leiner Health Products Inc (P-5534)*

**Leiner Health Products, Garden Grove** *Also Called: Leiner Health Products Inc (P-5535)*

**Leiner Health Products Inc (DH)** .................................................. C ...... 631 200-2000
901 E 233rd St Carson (90745) *(P-5534)*

**Leiner Health Products Inc** .................................................. E ...... 714 898-9936
7366 Orangewood Ave Garden Grove (92841) *(P-5535)*

**Leiter's Compounding, San Jose** *Also Called: Wedgewood Connect (P-5716)*

**Lejon Tulliani, Corona** *Also Called: Shirinian-Shaw Inc (P-2884)*

**Lekos Dye & Finishing Inc (PA)** .................................................. D ...... 310 763-0900
3131 E Harcourt St Compton (90221) *(P-2448)*

**Leland Stanford Junior Univ** .................................................. E ...... 650 723-5553
557 Escondido Mall Stanford (94305) *(P-4426)*

**Lemo USA Inc** .................................................. D ...... 707 206-3700
635 Park Ct Rohnert Park (94928) *(P-16714)*

**Lennox, Fresno** *Also Called: Lennox International Inc (P-10505)*

**Lennox International Inc** .................................................. C ...... 559 490-0078
1155 E North Ave Ste 102 Fresno (93725) *(P-10505)*

**Lenntek Corporation** .................................................. E ...... 310 534-2738
1610 Lockness Pl Torrance (90501) *(P-11882)*

**Lenovo (united States) Inc** .................................................. D ...... 510 813-3331
602 Charcot Ave San Jose (95131) *(P-10175)*

**Lens C-C Inc (PA)** .................................................. D ...... 800 772-3911
1750 N Loop Rd Ste 150 Alameda (94502) *(P-15606)*

**Lensvector Inc** .................................................. D ...... 669 247-5095
6203 San Ignacio Ave Ste 110 San Jose (95119) *(P-15607)*

**Lenthor Engineering Inc** .................................................. C ...... 408 945-8787
311 Turquoise St Milpitas (95035) *(P-12153)*

**Lenz Precision Technology Inc** .................................................. E ...... 650 966-1784
355 Pioneer Way Ste A Mountain View (94041) *(P-10943)*

**Lenz Technology, Mountain View** *Also Called: Lenz Precision Technology Inc (P-10943)*

**Leo Lam Inc** .................................................. E ...... 925 484-3690
1348 Terminal St West Sacramento (95691) *(P-4675)*

**Leoben Company** .................................................. E ...... 951 284-9653
16692 Burke Ln Huntington Beach (92647) *(P-16168)*

**Leoch Battery Corporation (DH)** .................................................. D ...... 949 588-5853
20322 Valencia Cir Lake Forest (92630) *(P-11275)*

**Leon Krous Drilling Inc** .................................................. E ...... 818 833-4654
9300 Borden Ave Sun Valley (91352) *(P-163)*

**Leonard Craft Co LLC** .................................................. D ...... 714 549-0678
1815 Ritchey St Ste B Santa Ana (92705) *(P-15700)*

**Leonard's Guide, Glendora** *Also Called: G R Leonard & Co Inc (P-4401)*

**Leonardo Logging and Cnstr Inc** .................................................. E ...... 707 725-1809
604 L St Fortuna (95540) *(P-3049)*

**Leonards Carpet Service Inc (PA)** .................................................. D ...... 714 630-1930
1121 N Red Gum St Anaheim (92806) *(P-3664)*

**Leonards Molded Products Inc** .................................................. E ...... 661 253-2227
25031 Anza Dr Valencia (91355) *(P-6510)*

**Leonesse Cellars, Temecula** *Also Called: Temecula Valley Winery MGT LLC (P-1776)*

**Leonesse Cellars LLC** .................................................. E ...... 951 302-7601
38311 De Portola Rd Temecula (92592) *(P-1667)*

**Leotek Electronics USA LLC** .................................................. E ...... 408 380-1788
1955 Lundy Ave San Jose (95131) *(P-16001)*

**Leprino Foods Company** .................................................. B ...... 209 835-8340
2401 N Macarthur Dr Tracy (95376) *(P-726)*

**Leprino Foods Company** .................................................. C ...... 559 924-7722
490 F St Lemoore (93245) *(P-727)*

**Leprino Foods Company** .................................................. C ...... 559 924-7939
351 Belle Haven Dr Lemoore (93245) *(P-728)*

**Lerexa Winery, Livingston** *Also Called: E & J Gallo Winery (P-1550)*

**Lesco, Torrance** *Also Called: American Ultraviolet West Inc (P-9480)*

**Leslie Heavy Haul, Sonora** *Also Called: Leslie Heavy Haul LLC (P-19104)*

**Leslie Heavy Haul LLC** .................................................. E ...... 209 840-1664
18971 Hess Ave Sonora (95370) *(P-19104)*

**Lester Lithograph Inc** .................................................. E ...... 714 491-3981
1128 N Gilbert St Anaheim (92801) *(P-4676)*

**Lets Do Lunch** .................................................. B ...... 310 523-3664
310 W Alondra Blvd Gardena (90248) *(P-2264)*

**Letterhead Factory Inc** .................................................. F ...... 310 538-3321
1007 E Dominguez St Ste H Carson (90746) *(P-4677)*

**Levecke LLC** .................................................. E ...... 951 681-8600
10810 Inland Ave Jurupa Valley (91752) *(P-1668)*

**Level, Los Altos** *Also Called: Markov Corporation (P-19484)*

**Level 99, Gardena** *Also Called: Phoenix Textile Inc (P-17097)*

**Levena Biopharma Us Inc** .................................................. E ...... 858 720-1439
11760 Sorrento Valley Rd Ste N San Diego (92121) *(P-5536)*

**Levi Strauss, San Francisco** *Also Called: Levi Strauss & Co (P-2586)*

**Levi Strauss & Co (PA)** .................................................. A ...... 415 501-6000
1155 Battery St San Francisco (94111) *(P-2586)*

**Levi Strauss International (HQ)** .................................................. D ...... 415 501-6000
1155 Battery St San Francisco (94111) *(P-2631)*

**Levine Arthur Lansky & Assoc (PA)** .................................................. F ...... 415 234-6020
3914 Delmont Ave Oakland (94605) *(P-7959)*

**Levita Magnetics Intl Corp** .................................................. E ...... 530 456-6627
453 Ravendale Dr Ste G Mountain View (94043) *(P-15147)*

**Leviton Manufacturing Co Inc** .................................................. F ...... 619 205-8600
6020 Progressive Ave Ste 500 San Diego (92154) *(P-11462)*

**Levmar Inc** .................................................. F ...... 925 680-8723
1666 Willow Pass Rd Pittsburg (94565) *(P-8486)*

**Lewisgoetz, Sacramento** *Also Called: Valley Rubber & Gasket Company Inc (P-16904)*

**Lexani, Corona** *Also Called: Lexani Wheel Corporation (P-7619)*

**Lexani Wheel Corporation** .................................................. E ...... 951 808-4220
1121 Olympic Dr Corona (92881) *(P-7619)*

**Lexco Imports Inc** .................................................. E ...... 800 883-1454
1455 S Campus Ave Ontario (91761) *(P-9222)*

**Lexington, North Hollywood** *Also Called: Lexington Acquisition Inc (P-8169)*

**Lexington Acquisition Inc** .................................................. C ...... 818 768-5768
11125 Vanowen St North Hollywood (91605) *(P-8169)*

**Lexor Inc** .................................................. D ...... 714 444-4144
7400 Hazard Ave Westminster (92683) *(P-16169)*

**Lexstar Inc (PA)** .................................................. F ...... 845 947-1415
4959 Kalamis Way Oceanside (92056) *(P-11542)*

**Lexus of Stevens Creek, San Jose** *Also Called: S J Automotive LLC (P-11094)*

**Ley Grand Foods Corporation** .................................................. E ...... 626 336-2244
287 S 6th Ave La Puente (91746) *(P-2265)*

**Leyden Energy Inc** .................................................. E ...... 408 776-2779
1100 La Avenida St Ste A Mountain View (94043) *(P-13022)*

**Lezat, Los Angeles** *Also Called: Kharma Clothing LLC (P-2863)*

**Lf Illumination LLC** .................................................. D ...... 818 885-1335
9200 Deering Ave Chatsworth (91311) *(P-11543)*

**Lf Sportswear Inc (PA)** .................................................. E ...... 310 437-4100
13336 Beach Ave Marina Del Rey (90292) *(P-2679)*

**Lf Visuals Inc** .................................................. F ...... 760 345-5571
39620 Entrepreneur Ln Palm Desert (92211) *(P-2548)*

**Lg Innotek Usa Inc** .................................................. D ...... 408 234-6356
2540 N 1st St Ste 400 San Jose (95131) *(P-14209)*

**Lg Nanoh2o LLC** .................................................. E ...... 424 218-4000
21250 Hawthorne Blvd Ste 330 Torrance (90503) *(P-6304)*

**Lg Nanoh2o, Inc., Torrance** *Also Called: Lg Nanoh2o LLC (P-6304)*

**Lg-Ericsson USA Inc** .................................................. E ...... 877 828-2673
20 Mason Irvine (92618) *(P-11774)*

**Lg-Led Solutions Limited** .................................................. E ...... 626 587-8506
15902 Halliburton Rd Ste A Hacienda Heights (91745) *(P-11606)*

**LGarde Inc** .................................................. E ...... 714 259-0771
15181 Woodlawn Ave Tustin (92780) *(P-10251)*

**Lgc Biosearch Technologies, Petaluma** *Also Called: Biosearch Technologies Inc (P-5811)*

**Lgc Wireless LLC** .................................................. C ...... 408 952-2400
541 E Trimble Rd San Jose (95131) *(P-11883)*

**Lgg Industrial Inc** .................................................. D ...... 562 802-7782
15500 Blackburn Ave Norwalk (90650) *(P-6457)*

**Lgg Industrial Inc** .................................................. D ...... 916 366-9340
10182 Croydon Way Sacramento (95827) *(P-16880)*

## ALPHABETIC SECTION — Linde Gas & Equipment Inc

Lhl Construction Inc .................................................................. E ...... 916 782-9001
   1370 Furneaux Rd Olivehurst (95961) *(P-533)*

Lhoist North America Ariz Inc ................................................. E ...... 831 449-9117
   11771 Old Stage Road Salinas (93908) *(P-317)*

Lhv Power Corporation (PA) ..................................................... E ...... 619 258-7700
   10221 Buena Vista Ave Ste A Santee (92071) *(P-13023)*

Libby Laboratories Inc ............................................................. E ...... 510 527-5400
   1700 6th St Berkeley (94710) *(P-6003)*

Liberty Container Company ................................................... C ...... 323 564-4211
   4224 Santa Ana St South Gate (90280) *(P-3864)*

Liberty Diversified Intl Inc ......................................................... C ...... 858 391-7302
   13100 Danielson St Poway (92064) *(P-3695)*

Liberty Film, Commerce *Also Called: Liberty Packg & Extruding Inc (P-3970)*

Liberty Industries ..................................................................... F ...... 626 575-3206
   10754 Lower Azusa Rd El Monte (91731) *(P-10944)*

Liberty Love, Commerce *Also Called: Cure Apparel Llc (P-2662)*

Liberty Packaging, Poway *Also Called: Liberty Diversified Intl Inc (P-3695)*

Liberty Packg & Extruding Inc ............................................... E ...... 323 722-5124
   3015 Supply Ave Commerce (90040) *(P-3970)*

Liberty Packing Company LLC (PA) ................................... D ...... 209 826-7100
   724 Main St Woodland (95695) *(P-17170)*

Liberty Paper, Los Angeles *Also Called: D D Office Products Inc (P-3765)*

Liberty Photo Products, San Clemente *Also Called: Liberty Synergistics Inc (P-16881)*

Liberty School, Paso Robles *Also Called: Treana Winery LLC (P-1789)*

Liberty Synergistics Inc ........................................................... D ...... 949 361-1100
   1041 Calle Trepadora San Clemente (92673) *(P-16881)*

Liberty Vegetable Oil Company ............................................ E ...... 562 921-3567
   15760 Ventura Blvd Encino (91436) *(P-1399)*

Licap Technologies Inc ........................................................... D ...... 916 329-8099
   9795 Business Park Dr Ste A Sacramento (95827) *(P-5099)*

Licher Direct Mail Inc ............................................................... E ...... 626 795-3333
   980 Seco St Pasadena (91103) *(P-4678)*

Lidestri Foods Inc ..................................................................... B ...... 559 251-1000
   568 S Temperance Ave Fresno (93727) *(P-2266)*

Lief Labs, Valencia *Also Called: Lief Organics LLC (P-766)*

Lief Organics LLC (PA) ............................................................ E ...... 661 775-2500
   28903 Avenue Paine Valencia (91355) *(P-766)*

Life Guard Gloves, City Of Industry *Also Called: Durasafe Inc (P-16581)*

Life Is Life LLC ......................................................................... E ...... 310 584-7541
   2611 Cottonwood Ave Moreno Valley (92553) *(P-729)*

Life Paint Company (PA) ......................................................... E ...... 562 944-6391
   12927 Sunshine Ave Santa Fe Springs (90670) *(P-6093)*

Life Science Outsourcing Inc ................................................ D ...... 714 672-1090
   830 Challenger St Brea (92821) *(P-15148)*

Life Specialty Coatings, Santa Fe Springs *Also Called: Life Paint Company (P-6093)*

Life Technologies, Carlsbad *Also Called: Life Technologies Corporation (P-14684)*

Life Technologies Corporation (HQ) .................................. C ...... 760 603-7200
   5781 Van Allen Way Carlsbad (92008) *(P-5760)*

Life Technologies Corporation ............................................ B ...... 760 918-0135
   5791 Van Allen Way Carlsbad (92008) *(P-14684)*

Life Technologies Corporation ............................................ E ...... 760 918-4259
   5791 Van Allen Way Carlsbad (92008) *(P-14685)*

Lifeaid Beverage Company LLC ........................................... E ...... 888 558-1113
   2833 Mission St Santa Cruz (95060) *(P-1900)*

Lifearound2angels, Sacramento *Also Called: Emilykate LLC (P-17916)*

Lifefactory Inc .......................................................................... E ...... 415 729-9820
   3 Harbor Dr Ste 200 Sausalito (94965) *(P-7183)*

Lifescience, Hercules *Also Called: Bio-RAD Laboratories Inc (P-14630)*

Lifesource Water Systems Inc (PA) ..................................... E ...... 626 792-4214
   911 E Colorado Blvd Ste 100 Pasadena (91106) *(P-10572)*

Lifestream, San Bernardino *Also Called: Lifestream Blood Bank (P-19337)*

Lifestream Blood Bank (PA) ................................................... C ...... 909 885-6503
   384 W Orange Show Rd San Bernardino (92412) *(P-19337)*

Lifetile, Lathrop *Also Called: Royal Westlake Roofing LLC (P-16290)*

Lifetime Memory Products Inc ............................................. E ...... 949 794-9000
   2505 Da Vinci Ste A Irvine (92614) *(P-12154)*

Lifeward Ca Inc ........................................................................ D ...... 510 270-5900
   48368 Milmont Dr Fremont (94538) *(P-15836)*

Lifoam Industries LLC ............................................................ E ...... 714 891-5035
   15671 Industry Ln Huntington Beach (92649) *(P-3865)*

Lift By Encore, Huntington Beach *Also Called: Encore Seats Inc (P-13836)*

Lift By Encore, Huntington Beach *Also Called: Irish Interiors Inc (P-13875)*

Lift It, Pomona *Also Called: Lift-It Manufacturing Co Inc (P-2536)*

Lift-It Manufacturing Co Inc ................................................... E ...... 909 469-2251
   1603 W 2nd St Pomona (91766) *(P-2536)*

Light, Redwood City *Also Called: Light Labs Inc (P-14794)*

Light & Motion Industries ....................................................... D ...... 831 645-1525
   711 Neeson Rd Marina (93933) *(P-11607)*

Light Composite Corporation ............................................... E ...... 949 858-8820
   22322 Gilberto Rcho Sta Marg (92688) *(P-8010)*

Light Composites Inc ............................................................. E ...... 619 339-0638
   12170 Paine Pl Poway (92064) *(P-13676)*

Light Fixture Industries, Vista *Also Called: Exit Light Co Inc (P-11530)*

Light Helmets, Carlsbad *Also Called: Safer Sports Inc (P-15850)*

Light House, Torrance *Also Called: Takuyo Corporation (P-4205)*

Light Labs Inc .......................................................................... D ...... 650 257-8100
   725 Shasta St Redwood City (94063) *(P-14794)*

Light Soda On Tap, San Francisco *Also Called: Northern California Equipment (P-17859)*

Light Vast Inc .......................................................................... E ...... 800 358-0499
   1202 Monte Vista Ave Ste 1 Upland (91786) *(P-11608)*

Lightbit Corporation ............................................................... F ...... 650 988-9500
   411 Clyde Ave Mountain View (94043) *(P-12889)*

Lightcap Industries Inc .......................................................... E ...... 909 930-3772
   1612 S Cucamonga Ave Ontario (91761) *(P-8170)*

Lightera, Sunnyvale *Also Called: Luminus Inc (P-11610)*

Lightform, Carpinteria *Also Called: Forms and Surfaces Company LLC (P-7333)*

Lighting Control & Design Inc ............................................. E ...... 323 226-0000
   9144 Deering Ave Chatsworth (91311) *(P-11609)*

Lighting Technologies Intl LLC ............................................ C ...... 626 480-0755
   13700 Live Oak Ave Baldwin Park (91706) *(P-16657)*

Lightpointe Communications Inc ....................................... E ...... 858 834-4083
   8515 Arjons Dr Ste G San Diego (92126) *(P-16715)*

Lightpointe Wireless, San Diego *Also Called: Lightpointe Communications Inc (P-16715)*

Lights of America Inc (PA) ................................................... B ...... 909 594-7883
   13602 12th St Ste B Chino (91710) *(P-11497)*

Lightspeed Software Inc ....................................................... F ...... 661 716-7600
   1800 19th St Bakersfield (93301) *(P-18496)*

Lightway Industries ................................................................ F ...... 661 257-0286
   28435 Industry Dr Valencia (91355) *(P-11544)*

Lightworks Optics Inc ............................................................ D ...... 714 247-7100
   14192 Chambers Rd Tustin (92780) *(P-14795)*

Lili Panaderia, Lodi *Also Called: Del Castillo Foods Inc (P-2181)*

Lily Bleu Inc ............................................................................ E ...... 310 225-2522
   1406 W 178th St Gardena (90248) *(P-17094)*

Lily Samii Collection, San Francisco *Also Called: L Y Z Ltd (P-2709)*

Lilypad Ev LLC ........................................................................ E ...... 866 525-9723
   4591 Pacheco Blvd Martinez (94553) *(P-13174)*

Lime Light Crm Inc ................................................................. F ...... 800 455-9645
   89 De Boom St San Francisco (94107) *(P-7523)*

Liminal Insights Inc ................................................................ E ...... 310 702-5803
   1175 Park Ave Emeryville (94608) *(P-13024)*

Limited Access Unlimited Inc ............................................. F ...... 619 294-3682
   5220 Anna Ave Ste A San Diego (92110) *(P-9368)*

Limos By Tiffany Inc .............................................................. E ...... 951 657-2680
   23129 Cajalco Rd Perris (92570) *(P-13416)*

Limsons, Woodland Hills *Also Called: Limsons It Services LLC (P-19040)*

Limsons It Services LLC ....................................................... E ...... 323 988-5546
   21255 Burbank Blvd Ste 120 Woodland Hills (91367) *(P-19040)*

Lin Engineering Inc ............................................................... C ...... 408 919-0200
   16245 Vineyard Blvd Morgan Hill (95037) *(P-11276)*

Lin Frank Distillers ................................................................ E ...... 707 437-1092
   2455 Huntington Dr Fairfield (94533) *(P-1840)*

Lincoln Composite Mtls Inc ................................................ F ...... 714 898-8350
   5451 Commercial Dr Huntington Beach (92649) *(P-5174)*

Lind Marine Incorporated (PA) ........................................... E ...... 707 762-7251
   1175 Nimitz Ave Ste 120 Vallejo (94592) *(P-1136)*

Lindblade Metal Works, La Mirada *Also Called: Lindblade Metalworks Inc (P-8171)*

Lindblade Metalworks Inc .................................................. E ...... 714 670-7172
   14355 Macaw St La Mirada (90638) *(P-8171)*

Linde Gas & Equipment Inc ................................................ D ...... 559 237-5521
   2771 S Maple Ave Fresno (93725) *(P-5045)*

## ALPHABETIC SECTION

**Linde Gas & Equipment Inc** .................................................. E ..... 800 225-8247
  203 Golden State Blvd Turlock (95380) *(P-5046)*
**Linde Inc** ............................................................................. E ..... 510 223-9593
  2995 Atlas Rd San Pablo (94806) *(P-5047)*
**Linde Inc** ............................................................................. E ..... 909 390-0283
  5705 E Airport Dr Ontario (91761) *(P-5048)*
**Linde Inc** ............................................................................. C ..... 510 451-4100
  901 Embarcadero Oakland (94606) *(P-5049)*
**Linden Nut, Linden** Also Called: *Pearl Crop Inc* *(P-2316)*
**Linden Steel & Cnstr Inc** ................................................... E ..... 209 239-2160
  17863 Ideal Pkwy Manteca (95336) *(P-248)*
**Lindsay Windows California LLC** ...................................... F ..... 760 247-1082
  13510 Central Rd Apple Valley (92308) *(P-8274)*
**Lindsey Doors Inc** ............................................................ E ..... 760 775-1959
  81101 Indio Blvd Ste D16 Indio (92201) *(P-6584)*
**Lindsey Manufacturing Co** ................................................ C ..... 626 969-3471
  760 N Georgia Ave Azusa (91702) *(P-8798)*
**Lindsey Mfg, Indio** Also Called: *Lindsey Doors Inc* *(P-6584)*
**Lindsey Systems, Azusa** Also Called: *Lindsey Manufacturing Co* *(P-8798)*
**Linea Pelle, Van Nuys** Also Called: *Linea Pelle Inc* *(P-7089)*
**Linea Pelle Inc (PA)** .......................................................... F ..... 310 231-9950
  7107 Valjean Ave Van Nuys (91406) *(P-7089)*
**Lineage, Vernon** Also Called: *American Fruits & Flavors LLC* *(P-1983)*
**LINEAGE, Carlsbad** Also Called: *Lineage Cell Therapeutics Inc* *(P-5845)*
**Lineage Cell Therapeutics Inc (PA)** .................................. E ..... 510 521-3390
  2173 Salk Ave Ste 200 Carlsbad (92008) *(P-5845)*
**Linear Industries Ltd (PA)** ................................................. E ..... 626 303-1130
  1850 Enterprise Way Monrovia (91016) *(P-16882)*
**Linear Integrated Systems Inc** ......................................... F ..... 510 490-9160
  4042 Clipper Ct Fremont (94538) *(P-12531)*
**Linear Technology LLC (HQ)** ............................................ A ..... 408 432-1900
  1630 Mccarthy Blvd Milpitas (95035) *(P-12532)*
**Linen Lovers, Ontario** Also Called: *Jomar Table Linens Inc* *(P-2931)*
**Linen Salvage Et Cie LLC** ................................................. E ..... 323 904-3100
  1073 Stearns Dr Los Angeles (90035) *(P-17537)*
**Liner Technologies Inc** ..................................................... E ..... 909 594-6610
  4821 Chino Ave Chino (91710) *(P-6896)*
**Linfinity Microelectronics, Garden Grove** Also Called: *Microsemi Corp - Anlog Mxed Sg* *(P-12571)*
**Ling's, South El Monte** Also Called: *Out of Shell LLC* *(P-2307)*
**Links Medical Products Inc (PA)** ...................................... E ..... 949 753-0001
  9249 Research Dr Irvine (92618) *(P-15149)*
**Linksoul LLC** ..................................................................... E ..... 760 231-7069
  530 S Coast Hwy Oceanside (92054) *(P-2421)*
**Linksys Usa Inc** ................................................................ D ..... 949 270-8500
  121 Theory Irvine (92617) *(P-16716)*
**Linn Energy LLC** ............................................................... E ..... 714 257-1600
  2000 Tonner Canyon Rd Brea (92821) *(P-188)*
**Linn Western Operating, Brea** Also Called: *Linn Energy LLC* *(P-188)*
**Linn's Main Bin, Cambria** Also Called: *Linns Fruit Bin Inc* *(P-17399)*
**Linnco LLC** ........................................................................ A ..... 661 616-3900
  5201 Truxtun Ave Bakersfield (93309) *(P-189)*
**Linns Fruit Bin Inc (PA)** ..................................................... E ..... 805 927-1499
  2535 Village Ln Ste A Cambria (93428) *(P-17399)*
**Linoleum Sales Co Inc (PA)** ............................................. D ..... 510 652-1032
  1000 W Grand Ave Oakland (94607) *(P-7175)*
**Linquip Corporation** .......................................................... F ..... 925 998-2480
  440 N Wolfe Rd Sunnyvale (94085) *(P-4427)*
**Linzer Products, San Fernando** Also Called: *Ahi Investment Inc* *(P-17283)*
**Lion Packing Co, Selma** Also Called: *Lion Raisins Inc* *(P-955)*
**Lion Raisins Inc (PA)** ........................................................ C ..... 559 834-6677
  9500 S De Wolf Ave Selma (93662) *(P-955)*
**Lip Service, Burbank** Also Called: *The Original Cult Inc* *(P-2815)*
**Lippert Components Inc** ................................................... F ..... 949 259-4000
  1270 Puerta Del Sol San Clemente (92673) *(P-13363)*
**Lippert Components Inc** ................................................... F ..... 574 312-6277
  1361 Calle Avanzado San Clemente (92673) *(P-13364)*
**Lippert Components Inc** ................................................... E ..... 909 873-0061
  168 S Spruce Ave Rialto (92376) *(P-13365)*
**Lippert Components Mfg Inc** ............................................ E ..... 909 628-5557
  1021 Walnut Ave Pomona (91766) *(P-7232)*

**Liqui-Box Corporation** ....................................................... E ..... 916 381-7054
  5000 Warehouse Way Sacramento (95826) *(P-6897)*
**Liquid Death Mountain Water** .......................................... E ..... 818 521-5500
  1447 2nd St Ste 200 Santa Monica (90401) *(P-1901)*
**Liquid Gold** ........................................................................ E ..... 415 660-5142
  1040 Hyde St San Francisco (94109) *(P-1446)*
**Liquid Graphics Inc** .......................................................... C ..... 949 486-3588
  2701 S Harbor Blvd Unit A Santa Ana (92704) *(P-2632)*
**Liquid Instruments Inc (PA)** ............................................. F ..... 619 332-6230
  12526 High Bluff Dr Ste 150 San Diego (92130) *(P-14549)*
**Liquidspace Inc** ................................................................ E ..... 855 254-7843
  2225 E Bayshore Rd # 200 Palo Alto (94303) *(P-18497)*
**Lisa Factory Inc** ............................................................... D ..... 213 536-5326
  144 N Swall Dr Beverly Hills (90211) *(P-2576)*
**Lisi Aerospace** .................................................................. E ..... 310 326-8110
  2600 Skypark Dr Torrance (90505) *(P-15150)*
**Lisi Aerospace, City Of Industry** Also Called: *Monadnock Company* *(P-8018)*
**Lisi Aerospace North Amer Inc** ........................................ A ..... 310 326-8110
  2602 Skypark Dr Torrance (90505) *(P-7689)*
**List Biological Labs Inc** .................................................... E ..... 408 866-6363
  540 Division St Campbell (95008) *(P-5846)*
**List Labs, Campbell** Also Called: *List Biological Labs Inc* *(P-5846)*
**Lite Extrusions, Gardena** Also Called: *Lite Extrusions Mfg Inc* *(P-6585)*
**Lite Extrusions Mfg Inc** .................................................... E ..... 323 770-4298
  15025 S Main St Gardena (90248) *(P-6585)*
**Lite On Land Inc** .............................................................. E ..... 559 203-2322
  35846 Powerhouse Rd Auberry (93602) *(P-3050)*
**Lite-On Technology Intl Inc (HQ)** ..................................... E ..... 408 945-0222
  720 S Hillview Dr Milpitas (95035) *(P-10396)*
**Litegear, Burbank** Also Called: *Litegear Inc* *(P-11428)*
**Litegear Inc** ...................................................................... E ..... 818 358-8542
  4406 W Vanowen St Burbank (91505) *(P-11428)*
**Lites On West Soho, Oceanside** Also Called: *Lexstar Inc* *(P-11542)*
**Lith-O-Roll Corporation** .................................................... E ..... 626 579-0340
  9521 Telstar Ave El Monte (91731) *(P-9770)*
**Lithocraft Co, Anaheim** Also Called: *Man-Grove Industries Inc* *(P-4688)*
**Lithographix Inc (PA)** ....................................................... B ..... 323 770-1000
  12250 Crenshaw Blvd Hawthorne (90250) *(P-4679)*
**Lithos Energy Inc** ............................................................. E ..... 415 944-5482
  28345 Industrial Blvd Hayward (94545) *(P-13145)*
**Lithotype Company Inc (PA)** ........................................... D ..... 650 871-1750
  333 Point San Bruno Blvd South San Francisco (94080) *(P-4680)*
**Litmus Automation Inc (PA)** ............................................ D ..... 765 418-7405
  2350 Mission College Blvd Ste 1020 Santa Clara (95054) *(P-16531)*
**Liton Lighting, Los Angeles** Also Called: *Eema Industries Inc* *(P-11591)*
**Little Brothers Bakery, Gardena** Also Called: *Little Brothers Bakery LLC* *(P-1223)*
**Little Brothers Bakery LLC** .............................................. D ..... 310 225-3790
  320 W Alondra Blvd Gardena (90248) *(P-1223)*
**Little Castle Furniture Co Inc** .......................................... E ..... 805 278-4646
  301 Todd Ct Oxnard (93030) *(P-3478)*
**Little Folk Visuals, Palm Desert** Also Called: *Lf Visuals Inc* *(P-2548)*
**Little Green Forks, Duarte** Also Called: *Tanner Research Inc* *(P-19478)*
**Littlejohn-Reuland Corporation** ....................................... E ..... 323 587-5255
  4575 Pacific Blvd Vernon (90058) *(P-461)*
**Live Action General Engrg Inc** ........................................ C ..... 559 292-2900
  2972 Larkin Ave Clovis (93612) *(P-424)*
**Live Fresh Corporation** .................................................... C ..... 909 478-0895
  1055 E Cooley Ave San Bernardino (92408) *(P-1012)*
**Live Journal Inc** ............................................................... E ..... 415 230-3600
  6363 Skyline Blvd Oakland (94611) *(P-4149)*
**Liveaction Inc (PA)** .......................................................... E ..... 888 881-1116
  901 Campisi Way Ste 222 Campbell (95008) *(P-18498)*
**Liveoffice LLC** .................................................................. E ..... 877 253-2793
  900 Corporate Pointe Culver City (90230) *(P-18499)*
**Livescribe Inc** ................................................................... E
  930 Roosevelt Irvine (92620) *(P-10397)*
**Living Ecology** .................................................................. E ..... 951 371-4982
  240 Crouse Dr Corona (92879) *(P-17041)*
**Living To 100 Club LLC** ................................................... F ..... 858 272-3992
  4231 Balboa Ave Ste 316 San Diego (92117) *(P-16170)*

# ALPHABETIC SECTION — Lombard Medical Tech Inc

**Living Way Industries Inc** .................................................. F ...... 661 298-3200
20734 Centre Pointe Pkwy Santa Clarita (91350) *(P-4681)*

**Living Wellness Partners LLC** ............................................. E ...... 800 642-3754
3305 Tyler St Carlsbad (92008) *(P-2267)*

**Livingston's, North Highlands** *Also Called: Livingstons Concrete Svc Inc (P-7465)*

**Livingstons Concrete Svc Inc (PA)** ..................................... E ...... 916 334-4313
5416 Roseville Rd North Highlands (95660) *(P-7465)*

**Livingstons Concrete Svc Inc** ............................................. E ...... 916 334-4313
5416 Roseville Rd North Highlands (95660) *(P-7466)*

**Livingstons Concrete Svc Inc** ............................................. E ...... 916 334-4313
2915 Lesvos Ct Lincoln (95648) *(P-7467)*

**Lixit Corporation (PA)** ......................................................... D ...... 800 358-8254
100 Coombs St Napa (94559) *(P-16171)*

**Lj Smith Stair Systems, Corona** *Also Called: Novo Manufacturing LLC (P-3168)*

**Ljg, Irvine** *Also Called: La Jolla Group Inc (P-19103)*

**Llamas Plastics Inc** ............................................................. C ...... 818 362-0371
12970 Bradley Ave Sylmar (91342) *(P-13893)*

**LLC Lyons Magnus (PA)** ..................................................... B ...... **559 268-5966**
3158 E Hamilton Ave Fresno (93702) *(P-900)*

**LLC Lyons Magnus** ............................................................. C ...... 559 268-5966
1636 S 2nd St Fresno (93702) *(P-901)*

**LLC Walker West** ................................................................ D ...... 800 767-9378
5500 Jurupa St Ontario (91761) *(P-3696)*

**LLC Walker West** ................................................................ C ...... 909 390-4300
1555 S Vintage Ave Ontario (91761) *(P-6898)*

**LLC Walker West** ................................................................ D ...... 951 685-9660
11445 Pacific Ave Fontana (92337) *(P-8487)*

**Lloyd Design Corporation** ................................................... D ...... 818 768-6001
19731 Nordhoff St Northridge (91324) *(P-13530)*

**Lloyd Mats, Northridge** *Also Called: Lloyd Design Corporation (P-13530)*

**LMC Enterprises (PA)** ........................................................ D ...... **562 602-2116**
6401 Alondra Blvd Paramount (90723) *(P-5913)*

**LMC Enterprises** ................................................................ E ...... 310 632-7124
19402 S Susana Rd Compton (90221) *(P-5914)*

**LMI, Lodi** *Also Called: Larry Mthvin Installations Inc (P-7231)*

**LMI, Windsor** *Also Called: Luthiers Mercantile Intl Inc (P-17666)*

**LMS** ...................................................................................... E ...... 909 623-8781
1462 E 9th St Pomona (91766) *(P-16172)*

**LMS Reinforcing Steel Group, Corona** *Also Called: LMS Reinforcing Steel Usa LP (P-8703)*

**LMS Reinforcing Steel Usa LP (HQ)** ................................... F ...... **951 307-0972**
26365 Earthmover Cir Corona (92883) *(P-8703)*

**Lmw Enterprises LLC** ......................................................... E ...... 562 944-1969
10558 Norwalk Blvd Santa Fe Springs (90670) *(P-10506)*

**Lni Custom Manufacturing Inc** ........................................... E ...... 310 978-2000
15542 Broadway Center St Gardena (90248) *(P-8635)*

**Loaded Boards Inc** ............................................................. F ...... 310 839-1800
10575 Virginia Ave Culver City (90232) *(P-14063)*

**Loard's Ice Cream and Candies, San Leandro** *Also Called: Loco Ventures Inc (P-806)*

**Lob.com, San Francisco** *Also Called: Lobcom Inc (P-4682)*

**Lobby Traffic Systems Inc (PA)** .......................................... F ...... **800 486-8606**
8583 Irvine Center Dr # 10 Irvine (92618) *(P-14893)*

**Lobcom Inc** ........................................................................... C ...... 415 894-9979
2261 Market St Pmb 5668 San Francisco (94114) *(P-4682)*

**Lobue Laser & Eye Medical Ctrs** ........................................ F ...... 951 696-1135
40740 California Oaks Rd Murrieta (92562) *(P-15551)*

**Local Foodz Cali Inc** ............................................................ E ...... 650 242-5651
1552 Beach St Ste C Emeryville (94608) *(P-19358)*

**Local Savers LLC** ............................................................... F ...... 916 672-1006
10535 Estckton Blvd Ste F Elk Grove (95624) *(P-4915)*

**Lock America Inc** ................................................................ F ...... 951 277-5180
9168 Stellar Ct Corona (92883) *(P-8011)*

**Lock People, The, San Diego** *Also Called: Hodge Products Inc (P-8002)*

**Lock-N-Stitch Inc** ................................................................. E ...... 209 632-2345
1015 S Soderquist Rd Turlock (95380) *(P-10945)*

**Lock-Ridge Tool Company Inc** ........................................... D ...... 909 865-8309
145 N 8th Ave Upland (91786) *(P-8860)*

**Lockheed Martin, Sunnyvale** *Also Called: Lockheed Martin Corporation (P-11884)*

**Lockheed Martin, San Jose** *Also Called: Lockheed Martin Corporation (P-11885)*

**Lockheed Martin, San Jose** *Also Called: Lockheed Martin Corporation (P-13677)*

**Lockheed Martin, Tracy** *Also Called: Lockheed Martin Corporation (P-13678)*

**Lockheed Martin, Palo Alto** *Also Called: Lockheed Martin Corporation (P-14211)*

**Lockheed Martin, Coronado** *Also Called: Lockheed Martin Corporation (P-14214)*

**Lockheed Martin Aeronautics Co, Palmdale** *Also Called: Lockheed Martin Corporation (P-14212)*

**Lockheed Martin Corporation** ............................................. E ...... 408 742-4321
1111 Lockheed Martin Way Sunnyvale (94089) *(P-11884)*

**Lockheed Martin Corporation** ............................................. D ...... 408 473-3000
3130 Zanker Rd San Jose (95134) *(P-11885)*

**Lockheed Martin Corporation** ............................................. B ...... 408 761-1276
669 Mary Evelyn Dr San Jose (95123) *(P-13677)*

**Lockheed Martin Corporation** ............................................. B ...... 408 756-3008
2655 S Macarthur Dr Tracy (95376) *(P-13678)*

**Lockheed Martin Corporation** ............................................. D ...... 408 756-5751
1111 Lockheed Martin Way Bldg 195a Sunnyvale (94089) *(P-14210)*

**Lockheed Martin Corporation** ............................................. E ...... 650 424-2000
3251 Hanover St Palo Alto (94304) *(P-14211)*

**Lockheed Martin Corporation** ............................................. A ...... 661 572-7428
1011 Lockheed Way Palmdale (93599) *(P-14212)*

**Lockheed Martin Corporation** ............................................. E ...... 805 571-2346
346 Bollay Dr Goleta (93117) *(P-14213)*

**Lockheed Martin Corporation** ............................................. C ...... 619 437-7230
Nas North Island Coronado (92118) *(P-14214)*

**Lockheed Martin Corporation** ............................................. D ...... 760 952-4200
17452 Wheeler Rd Helendale (92342) *(P-14215)*

**Lockheed Martin Orincon Corp (HQ)** ................................. C ...... **858 455-5530**
10325 Meanley Dr San Diego (92131) *(P-14216)*

**Lockheed Mrtin Unmnned Intgrte** ....................................... E ...... 805 503-4340
125 Venture Dr Ste 110 San Luis Obispo (93401) *(P-14217)*

**Lockwood Industries LLC (HQ)** ......................................... C ...... **661 702-6999**
28525 Industry Dr Valencia (91355) *(P-12533)*

**Loco Ventures Inc** ............................................................... E ...... 510 351-0405
2000 Wayne Ave San Leandro (94577) *(P-806)*

**Lodestone LLC** .................................................................... E ...... 714 970-0900
4769 E Wesley Dr Anaheim (92807) *(P-9726)*

**Lodestone Pacific, Anaheim** *Also Called: R H Barden Inc (P-12854)*

**Lodi Iron Works Inc (PA)** .................................................... E ...... **209 368-5395**
820 S Sacramento St Lodi (95240) *(P-7677)*

**Lofta** ..................................................................................... E ...... 858 299-8000
9225 Brown Deer Rd San Diego (92121) *(P-2936)*

**Lofty Coffee Inc** ................................................................... D ...... 760 230-6747
97 N Coast Highway 101 Ste 101 Encinitas (92024) *(P-17596)*

**Log(n) LLC** ........................................................................... E ...... 323 839-4538
5651 Dreyer Pl Oakland (94619) *(P-4428)*

**Logans Candies** .................................................................. F ...... 909 984-5410
125 W B St Ontario (91762) *(P-17404)*

**Logicube, Chatsworth** *Also Called: Logicube Inc (P-10398)*

**Logicube Inc (PA)** ............................................................... E ...... **888 494-8832**
19755 Nordhoff Pl Chatsworth (91311) *(P-10398)*

**Logility Inc** ........................................................................... D ...... 858 565-4238
4885 Greencraig Ln 200 San Diego (92123) *(P-17942)*

**Loginext, Fremont** *Also Called: Loginext Solutions Inc (P-18500)*

**Loginext Solutions Inc (PA)** ............................................... D ...... **510 894-6225**
5002 Spring Crest Ter Fremont (94536) *(P-18500)*

**Logistical Support LLC** ...................................................... C ...... 818 341-3344
20409 Prairie St Chatsworth (91311) *(P-13715)*

**Logistics, Fresno** *Also Called: Service Express Inc (P-4464)*

**Logitech Inc** ......................................................................... A ...... 510 795-8500
3 Jenner Ste 180 Irvine (92618) *(P-10399)*

**Logitech Inc** ......................................................................... B ...... 972 947-7100
2053 E Jay St Ontario (91764) *(P-10400)*

**Logitech Inc (HQ)** ............................................................... B ...... **510 795-8500**
3930 N 1st St San Jose (95134) *(P-10401)*

**Logo Expressions, Ontario** *Also Called: Dennis Foland Inc (P-16974)*

**Lola Belle Brands LLC** ........................................................ F ...... 855 226-3526
629 S Palm Ave Alhambra (91803) *(P-17494)*

**Loma Vista Medical Inc** ....................................................... F ...... 650 490-4747
863 Mitten Rd Ste A100a Burlingame (94010) *(P-15151)*

**Lombard Enterprises Inc** ..................................................... E ...... 562 692-7070
3619 San Gabriel River Pkwy Pico Rivera (90660) *(P-4683)*

**Lombard Graphics, Pico Rivera** *Also Called: Lombard Enterprises Inc (P-4683)*

**Lombard Medical Tech Inc (PA)** ......................................... E ...... **949 379-3750**
6440 Oak Cyn Ste 200 Irvine (92618) *(P-15152)*

---

Employee Codes: A=Over 500 employees, B=251-500
C=101-250, D=51-100, E=20-50, F=10-19, G=1-9

## Lomeli's Gardens | ALPHABETIC SECTION

**Lomeli's Gardens, Lockeford** *Also Called: Lomelis Statuary Inc (P-7593)*
**Lomelis Statuary Inc (PA)** ......................................................... E ...... 209 367-1131
   11921 E Brandt Rd Lockeford (95237) *(P-7593)*
**Lonely Planet Publications Inc** .................................................. D ...... 510 250-6400
   124 Linden St Oakland (94607) *(P-4429)*
**Long Machine Inc** ....................................................................... E ...... 951 296-0194
   27450 Colt Ct Temecula (92590) *(P-10946)*
**Long-Lok LLC** .............................................................................. E ...... 424 209-8726
   20531 Belshaw Ave Carson (90746) *(P-13894)*
**Long-Lok Fasteners Corporation** ............................................... F ...... 424 213-4570
   20531 Belshaw Ave Carson (90746) *(P-16756)*
**LONGBOARD, La Jolla** *Also Called: Longboard Pharmaceuticals Inc (P-5537)*
**Longboard Pharmaceuticals Inc** ................................................ E ...... 858 789-9283
   4275 Executive Sq Ste 950 La Jolla (92037) *(P-5537)*
**Lonix Pharmaceutical Inc** ........................................................... F ...... 626 287-4700
   5001 Earle Ave Rosemead (91770) *(P-767)*
**Lonza Biologics Inc** .................................................................... F ...... 510 265-3095
   21075 Alexander Ct Hayward (94545) *(P-5538)*
**Loop Ai Labs, San Francisco** *Also Called: Loop Ai Labs Inc (P-18501)*
**Loop Ai Labs Inc** ........................................................................ E ...... 415 980-3655
   404 Bryant St San Francisco (94107) *(P-18501)*
**Loop Inc** ...................................................................................... E ...... 888 385-6674
   115 Eucalyptus Dr El Segundo (90245) *(P-13175)*
**Lopez Pallet Inc** .......................................................................... F ...... 909 823-0865
   11080 Redwood Ave Fontana (92337) *(P-3349)*
**Lor-Van Manufacturing LLC** ...................................................... E ...... 408 980-1045
   3307 Edward Ave Santa Clara (95054) *(P-8488)*
**Lord & Sons Inc (PA)** .................................................................. **E ...... 408 293-4841**
   430 E Trimble Rd San Jose (95131) *(P-16883)*
**Lore Io Inc** ................................................................................... E ...... 408 256-1521
   100 S Murphy Ave Ste 200 Sunnyvale (94086) *(P-18502)*
**Loren Electric Sign & Lighting, Whittier** *Also Called: Exiton Inc (P-15974)*
**Lorenz Inc** ................................................................................... E ...... 760 427-1815
   1749 Stergios Rd Calexico (92231) *(P-13268)*
**Lorenzo USA, Solana Beach** *Also Called: Simon Golub & Sons Inc (P-16971)*
**Lorom West, Fremont** *Also Called: Cable Connection Inc (P-11443)*
**Los Angeles Apparel Inc (PA)** .................................................... D ...... 213 275-3120
   1020 E 59th St Los Angeles (90001) *(P-2904)*
**Los Angeles Brass Products, Huntington Park** *Also Called: Los Angles Pump Valve Pdts Inc (P-9930)*
**Los Angeles Bus Jurnl Assoc** ................................................... F ...... 323 549-5225
   11150 Santa Monica Blvd Ste 350 Los Angeles (90025) *(P-4273)*
**Los Angeles Business Journal, Los Angeles** *Also Called: Cbj LP (P-4236)*
**Los Angeles Fiber Co, Vernon** *Also Called: Marspring Corporation (P-3533)*
**Los Angeles Galvanizing Co** ...................................................... D ...... 323 583-2263
   2518 E 53rd St Huntington Park (90255) *(P-9087)*
**Los Angeles Ltg Mfg Co Inc** ...................................................... D ...... 626 454-8300
   10141 Olney St El Monte (91731) *(P-16658)*
**Los Angeles Plant, Cypress** *Also Called: Hitachi Automotive Systems (P-11272)*
**Los Angeles Poultry Co Inc** ....................................................... D ...... 323 232-1619
   4816 Long Beach Ave Los Angeles (90058) *(P-697)*
**Los Angeles Sentinel Inc** ........................................................... D ...... 323 299-3800
   3800 Crenshaw Blvd Los Angeles (90008) *(P-4150)*
**Los Angeles Sleeve Co Inc** ....................................................... E ...... 562 945-7578
   12051 Rivera Rd Santa Fe Springs (90670) *(P-13531)*
**Los Angeles Times, El Segundo** *Also Called: Los Angles Tmes Cmmnctions LLC (P-4151)*
**Los Angeles Wraps, Torrance** *Also Called: Sirena Incorporated (P-4961)*
**Los Angles Pump Valve Pdts Inc** ............................................... E ...... 323 277-7788
   2528 E 57th St Huntington Park (90255) *(P-9930)*
**Los Angles Tmes Cmmnctions LLC (PA)** ................................. **A ...... 213 237-5000**
   2300 E Imperial Hwy El Segundo (90245) *(P-4151)*
**Los Bagels Inc (PA)** .................................................................... **E ...... 707 822-3150**
   1061 I St Ste 101 Arcata (95521) *(P-17415)*
**Los Banos Abattoir Co** ............................................................... E ...... 209 826-2212
   1312 W Pacheco Blvd Los Banos (93635) *(P-605)*
**Los Banos Rock and Ready Mix, Los Banos** *Also Called: Azusa Rock LLC (P-297)*
**Los Cabos Mexican Foods, Santa Fe Springs** *Also Called: MCI Foods Inc (P-2278)*
**Los Californias Winery, Fresno** *Also Called: Full Circle Brewing Co Ltd LLC (P-1432)*
**Los Gatos Tomato Products LLC (PA)** ..................................... **F ...... 559 945-2700**
   7041 N Van Ness Blvd Fresno (93711) *(P-902)*

**Los Pericos Food Products LLC** ............................................... E ...... 909 623-5625
   2301 Valley Blvd Pomona (91768) *(P-2268)*
**Lost & Wander, Vernon** *Also Called: Vxb & Orfwid Inc (P-2821)*
**Lost Coast Brewery & Cafe, Eureka** *Also Called: Table Bluff Brewing Inc (P-1463)*
**Lost Dutchmans Minings Assn (DH)** ........................................ **E ...... 951 699-4749**
   43445 Business Park Dr Ste 113 Temecula (92590) *(P-104)*
**Lotus, Chino** *Also Called: Lotus & Windoware Inc (P-16429)*
**Lotus & Windoware Inc (PA)** ..................................................... **F ...... 909 606-8866**
   14450 Yorba Ave Chino (91710) *(P-16429)*
**Lotus Bed Solutions LLC** .......................................................... F ...... 415 756-5099
   4600 Greenholme Dr Apt 3 Sacramento (95842) *(P-3448)*
**Lotus Hygiene Systems Inc** ...................................................... E ...... 714 259-8805
   1621 E Saint Andrew Pl Santa Ana (92705) *(P-7277)*
**Lotus Labels, Brea** *Also Called: President Enterprise LLC (P-4940)*
**Lotus Orient Corp (PA)** .............................................................. **F ...... 626 285-5796**
   411 S California St San Gabriel (91776) *(P-2710)*
**Lotus Trolley Bags, Carlsbad** *Also Called: Golden Eye Media Usa Inc (P-17001)*
**Lotusflare Inc** .............................................................................. D ...... 626 695-5634
   2350 Mission College Blvd Santa Clara (95054) *(P-18503)*
**Lou Ana Foods, Brea** *Also Called: Ventura Foods LLC (P-1409)*
**Loud Mfg, Thousand Oaks** *Also Called: Midnight Manufacturing LLC (P-5248)*
**Louden Madelon, Vernon** *Also Called: National Corset Supply House (P-2833)*
**Louidar LLC** ................................................................................. E ...... 951 676-5047
   33820 Rancho California Rd Temecula (92591) *(P-1669)*
**Louis Sardo Upholstery Inc (PA)** .............................................. **D ...... 310 327-0532**
   512 W Rosecrans Ave Gardena (90248) *(P-3635)*
**Lounge Fly, Walnut** *Also Called: Loungefly LLC (P-15905)*
**Loungefly LLC** ........................................................................... E ...... 818 718-5600
   108 S Mayo Ave Walnut (91789) *(P-15905)*
**Loupe, San Francisco** *Also Called: Plangrid Inc (P-18679)*
**Louroe Electronics Inc** ............................................................... E ...... 818 994-6498
   6955 Valjean Ave Van Nuys (91406) *(P-19058)*
**Love Stitch, Los Angeles** *Also Called: Clothing Illustrated Inc (P-2746)*
**Loveis Corp** ................................................................................. F ...... 818 408-9504
   9588 Topanga Canyon Blvd Chatsworth (91311) *(P-15153)*
**Low Cost Interlock Inc** ............................................................... D ...... 844 387-0326
   2038 W Park Ave Redlands (92373) *(P-13176)*
**Lowpensky Moulding** ................................................................. F ...... 415 822-7422
   900 Palou Ave San Francisco (94124) *(P-3154)*
**Loyal, San Francisco** *Also Called: Cellular Longevity Inc (P-19501)*
**Loyalty Juggernaut Inc** .............................................................. B ...... 650 283-5081
   2100 Geng Rd Ste 210 Palo Alto (94303) *(P-18504)*
**Lozano Caseworks Inc** .............................................................. D ...... 909 783-7530
   242 W Hanna St Colton (92324) *(P-496)*
**Lozano Enterprises, Los Angeles** *Also Called: La Opinion LP (P-4143)*
**Lpa Insurance Agency Inc** ........................................................ D ...... 916 286-7850
   3800 Watt Ave Ste 147 Sacramento (95821) *(P-18505)*
**Lpcc 6008, Ontario** *Also Called: Leggett & Platt Incorporated (P-3532)*
**Lps Agency Sales & Posting Inc** .............................................. F ...... 714 247-7500
   3210 El Camino Real Ste 200 Irvine (92602) *(P-4916)*
**Lrc Coil Company, Santa Fe Springs** *Also Called: Lmw Enterprises LLC (P-10506)*
**Lre Silicon Services** ................................................................... F ...... 408 262-8725
   1235 Torres Ave Milpitas (95035) *(P-12534)*
**LSI Corporation (DH)** ................................................................. **A ...... 408 433-8000**
   1320 Ridder Park Dr San Jose (95131) *(P-12535)*
**LSI Logic, San Jose** *Also Called: LSI Corporation (P-12535)*
**Lso, San Diego** *Also Called: Cri 2000 LP (P-3416)*
**Lspace America LLC** ................................................................. D ...... 949 750-2292
   14420 Myford Rd Irvine (92606) *(P-2476)*
**Lt Foods Americas Inc (HQ)** ..................................................... **F ...... 562 340-4040**
   11130 Warland Dr Cypress (90630) *(P-1061)*
**Lta Research & Exploration LLC (PA)** ..................................... **D ...... 408 396-0577**
   642 N Pastoria Ave Sunnyvale (94085) *(P-19533)*
**LTI Boyd** ...................................................................................... A ...... 800 554-0200
   600 S Mcclure Rd Modesto (95357) *(P-9739)*
**LTI Holdings Inc (PA)** ................................................................. **F ...... 925 271-8041**
   5960 Inglewood Dr Ste 115 Pleasanton (94588) *(P-5221)*
**Ltr, South Gate** *Also Called: Lunday-Thagard Company (P-6402)*
**Lubeco Inc** .................................................................................. E ...... 562 602-1791
   6859 Downey Ave Long Beach (90805) *(P-6397)*

## ALPHABETIC SECTION — Luxer Corporation

**Lubricating Specialties Company** .............................. C ...... 562 776-4000
  8015 Paramount Blvd Pico Rivera (90660) *(P-6398)*

**Lubrication Scientifics Inc** ....................................... F ...... 714 557-0664
  17651 Armstrong Ave Irvine (92614) *(P-9158)*

**Lubrication Scientifics LLC** ..................................... E ...... 714 557-0664
  17651 Armstrong Ave Irvine (92614) *(P-10099)*

**Lubrizol Global Management Inc** ............................. E ...... 805 239-1550
  3115 Propeller Dr Paso Robles (93446) *(P-6305)*

**Lucare Corporation** .................................................. F ...... 818 583-7731
  1292 Journeys End Dr La Canada Flintridge (91011) *(P-15649)*

**Lucas & Lewellen Vineyards Inc (PA)** ....................... E ...... 805 686-9336
  1645 Copenhagen Dr Solvang (93463) *(P-17267)*

**Lucas Labs, Gilroy** *Also Called: Lucas/Signatone Corporation (P-14550)*

**Lucas Lwllen Vnyrds Tasting Rm, Solvang** *Also Called: Lucas & Lewellen Vineyards Inc (P-17267)*

**Lucas/Signatone Corporation (PA)** ........................... E ...... 408 848-2851
  393 Tomkins Ct Ste J Gilroy (95020) *(P-14550)*

**Lucent Diamonds Inc** .............................................. E ...... 424 781-7127
  6303 Owensmouth Ave Fl 10 Woodland Hills (91367) *(P-15710)*

**Lucerne Foods Inc** .................................................. A ...... 925 951-4724
  5918 Stoneridge Mall Rd Pleasanton (94588) *(P-2269)*

**Lucero Cables Inc** .................................................. C ...... 408 498-6001
  193 Stauffer Blvd San Jose (95125) *(P-13025)*

**Lucid, Newark** *Also Called: Atieva Inc (P-13340)*

**Lucid Group Inc (PA)** ............................................... A ...... 510 648-3553
  7373 Gateway Blvd Newark (94560) *(P-13366)*

**Lucid Motors, Newark** *Also Called: Lucid Usa Inc (P-13367)*

**Lucid Usa Inc (HQ)** .................................................. C ...... 510 648-3553
  7373 Gateway Blvd Newark (94560) *(P-13367)*

**Lucira Health, Emeryville** *Also Called: Lucira Health Inc (P-5761)*

**Lucira Health Inc** .................................................... D ...... 510 350-7162
  1315 63rd St Emeryville (94608) *(P-5761)*

**Lucite Intl Prtnr Holdings Inc** .................................. D ...... 760 929-0001
  5441 Avenida Encinas Ste B Carlsbad (92008) *(P-15837)*

**Lucix, Camarillo** *Also Called: Lucix Corporation (P-13026)*

**Lucix Corporation (HQ)** ........................................... D ...... 805 987-6645
  800 Avenida Acaso Ste E Camarillo (93012) *(P-13026)*

**Luckinta Corporation** .............................................. E
  7307 Alexis Manor Pl San Jose (95120) *(P-8979)*

**Lucky Line Products Inc** ........................................ E ...... 858 549-6699
  7890 Dunbrook Rd San Diego (92126) *(P-8012)*

**Lucky You, San Diego** *Also Called: Cyberbasket Inc (P-17655)*

**Lucky-13 Apparel, Los Alamitos** *Also Called: Blue Sphere Inc (P-2558)*

**Ludfords Inc** .......................................................... E ...... 909 948-0797
  3038 Pleasant St Riverside (92507) *(P-903)*

**Lugano Diamonds & Jewelry Inc (HQ)** ..................... D ...... 949 625-7722
  545 Newport Center Dr Newport Beach (92660) *(P-17648)*

**Luidia Inc** ............................................................... E ...... 650 413-7500
  591 W Hamilton Ave Ste 205 Campbell (95008) *(P-19462)*

**Luma Comfort, Cypress** *Also Called: Luma Comfort LLC (P-11408)*

**Luma Comfort LLC** ................................................. E ...... 855 963-9247
  6600 Katella Ave Cypress (90630) *(P-11408)*

**Lumaprints** ............................................................ F ...... 800 380-6038
  955 E Ball Rd Anaheim (92805) *(P-4684)*

**Lumar Metals, Rancho Cucamonga** *Also Called: Lur Inc (P-8636)*

**Lumasense Technologies Inc (HQ)** ......................... D ...... 408 727-1600
  888 Tasman Dr # 100 Milpitas (95035) *(P-15552)*

**Lumedx Corporation (PA)** ........................................ F ...... 510 419-1000
  555 12th St Ste 2060 Oakland (94607) *(P-17943)*

**Lumenis, Livermore** *Also Called: Rh USA Inc (P-15244)*

**Lumenis Be Inc** ....................................................... B ...... 877 586-3647
  2077 Gateway Pl Ste 300 San Jose (95110) *(P-15154)*

**Lumenis Inc (HQ)** .................................................... C ...... 408 764-3000
  2077 Gateway Pl Ste 300 San Jose (95110) *(P-15155)*

**Lumenova Ai Inc** ..................................................... E ...... 310 694-2461
  1419 Beaudry Blvd, 1419 Beaudry Blvd Glendale (91208) *(P-18506)*

**Lumens** .................................................................. E ...... 916 231-1952
  1906 L St Sacramento (95811) *(P-11331)*

**LUMENS, Sacramento** *Also Called: Lumens (P-11331)*

**Lumens Integration Inc** ........................................... E ...... 510 657-8367
  4116 Clipper Ct Fremont (94538) *(P-15650)*

**LUMENTUM, San Jose** *Also Called: Lumentum Holdings Inc (P-12003)*

**Lumentum Holdings Inc (PA)** ................................... C ...... 408 546-5483
  1001 Ridder Park Dr San Jose (95131) *(P-12003)*

**Lumiata Inc** ............................................................ E ...... 916 607-2442
  489 S El Camino Real San Mateo (94402) *(P-19463)*

**Lumigrow Inc** .......................................................... E ...... 800 514-0487
  6550 Vallejo St Ste 200 Emeryville (94608) *(P-11545)*

**Lumileds LLC (DH)** .................................................. E ...... 408 964-2900
  370 W Trimble Rd San Jose (95131) *(P-14551)*

**Lumin, Laguna Beach** *Also Called: Pangaea Holdings Inc (P-6017)*

**Luminit LLC** ............................................................ E ...... 310 320-1066
  1850 W 205th St Torrance (90501) *(P-14796)*

**Luminostics Inc** ...................................................... E ...... 408 858-7103
  48389 Fremont Blvd Fremont (94538) *(P-15156)*

**Luminus, Sunnyvale** *Also Called: Luminus Devices Inc (P-11611)*

**Luminus Inc (HQ)** ................................................... C ...... 408 708-7000
  1145 Sonora Ct Sunnyvale (94086) *(P-11610)*

**Luminus Devices Inc** ............................................. C ...... 978 528-8000
  1145 Sonora Ct Sunnyvale (94086) *(P-11611)*

**Luna Imaging Inc** ................................................... E ...... 323 908-1400
  2702 Media Center Dr Los Angeles (90065) *(P-18507)*

**Luna Vineyards Inc** ................................................. E ...... 707 255-2474
  2921 Silverado Trl Napa (94558) *(P-1670)*

**Lunar Energy Inc (PA)** ............................................. F ...... 408 475-4137
  755 Ravendale Dr Mountain View (94043) *(P-13269)*

**Lunas Sheet Metal Inc** ............................................ F ...... 408 492-1260
  3125 Molinaro St Ste 102 Santa Clara (95054) *(P-8489)*

**Lunch Bunch, Los Angeles** *Also Called: Lunch Bunch Co (P-17123)*

**Lunch Bunch Co** ..................................................... F ...... 310 383-5233
  4351 Melrose Ave Los Angeles (90029) *(P-17123)*

**Lund Motion Products Inc** ...................................... E ...... 888 983-2204
  3172 Nasa St Brea (92821) *(P-13532)*

**Lunday-Thagard Company** ...................................... B ...... 562 928-6990
  9301 Garfield Ave South Gate (90280) *(P-6379)*

**Lunday-Thagard Company (HQ)** .............................. C ...... 562 928-7000
  9302 Garfield Ave South Gate (90280) *(P-6402)*

**Lundberg Designs, San Francisco** *Also Called: Thomas Lundberg (P-3513)*

**Lundberg Family Farms, Richvale** *Also Called: Wehah Farm Inc (P-1085)*

**Lundberg Family Farms, Richvale** *Also Called: Wehah-Lundberg Inc (P-1086)*

**Lundberg Survey Incorporated** ............................... E ...... 805 383-2400
  911 Via Alondra Camarillo (93012) *(P-4274)*

**Lupitas Bakery Inc (PA)** .......................................... F ...... 323 752-2391
  1848 W Florence Ave Los Angeles (90047) *(P-1224)*

**Luppen Holdings Inc (PA)** ....................................... E ...... 323 581-8121
  3050 Leonis Blvd Vernon (90058) *(P-8861)*

**Lur Inc** ................................................................... F ...... 909 623-4999
  9936 Albany Ave Rancho Cucamonga (91701) *(P-8636)*

**Luran Inc** ................................................................ F ...... 661 257-6303
  24927 Avenue Tibbitts Ste K Valencia (91355) *(P-10947)*

**Lusive Decor** .......................................................... D ...... 323 227-9207
  3400 Medford St Los Angeles (90063) *(P-19565)*

**Lusk Quality Machine Products** ............................. E ...... 661 272-0630
  39457 15th St E Palmdale (93550) *(P-10948)*

**Lusso Cloud Inc** ..................................................... F ...... 714 307-4414
  2431 W Coast Hwy Ste 201 Newport Beach (92663) *(P-7119)*

**Lustre-Cal, Lodi** *Also Called: Lustre-Cal Nameplate Corp (P-4918)*

**Lustre-Cal LLC** ....................................................... D ...... 206 370-1600
  715 S Guild Ave Lodi (95240) *(P-4917)*

**Lustre-Cal Nameplate Corp** .................................... D ...... 209 370-1600
  715 S Guild Ave Lodi (95240) *(P-4918)*

**Lustros Inc** ............................................................. E ...... 619 449-4800
  9025 Carlton Hills Blvd Ste A Santee (92071) *(P-102)*

**Lutema, San Diego** *Also Called: MI Technologies Inc (P-6913)*

**Luthiers Mercantile Intl Inc** .................................... F ...... 707 433-1823
  7975 Cameron Dr Ste 1600 Windsor (95492) *(P-17666)*

**Luthman Backlund Foods USA Inc** ......................... F ...... 310 994-9444
  214 Main St Pmb 300 El Segundo (90245) *(P-807)*

**Luxe Light and Home, Los Angeles** *Also Called: Lusive Decor (P-19565)*

**Luxer Corporation** .................................................. C ...... 415 390-0123
  5040 Dudley Blvd Mcclellan (95652) *(P-3573)*

**Luxer One**     ALPHABETIC SECTION

**Luxer One, Mcclellan** *Also Called: Luxer Corporation (P-3573)*
**Luxfer Gas Cylinder, Riverside** *Also Called: Luxfer Inc (P-13895)*
**Luxfer Inc** ................................................................... E ...... 951 684-5110
  1995 3rd St Riverside (92507) *(P-7742)*
**Luxfer Inc** ................................................................... E ...... 951 351-4100
  6825 Jurupa Ave Riverside (92504) *(P-8799)*
**Luxfer Inc (DH)** ........................................................ D ...... 951 684-5110
  3016 Kansas Ave Bldg 1 Riverside (92507) *(P-13895)*
**Luxim Corp** ............................................................... F ...... 408 734-1096
  3542 Bassett St Santa Clara (95054) *(P-11429)*
**Luxshare-Ict Inc** ....................................................... D ...... 408 957-0535
  480 N Mccarthy Blvd Ste 280 Milpitas (95035) *(P-16173)*
**Luxtera LLC** ............................................................. C ...... 760 448-3520
  2320 Camino Vida Roble Ste 100 Carlsbad (92011) *(P-12536)*
**Ly Brothers Corporation (PA)** ................................ D ...... 510 782-2118
  1963 Sabre St Hayward (94545) *(P-1225)*
**Ly Brothers Corporation** ........................................ D ...... 510 782-2118
  20389 Corsair Blvd Hayward (94545) *(P-1226)*
**Lymi Inc (PA)** ............................................................ D ...... 844 701-0139
  2263 E Vernon Ave Vernon (90058) *(P-17095)*
**Lynam Industries Inc (PA)** ..................................... D ...... 951 360-1919
  11027 Jasmine St Fontana (92337) *(P-8490)*
**Lyncean Technologies Inc** ..................................... F ...... 650 320-8300
  47633 Westinghouse Dr Fremont (94539) *(P-15504)*
**Lynch Ready Mix Concrete Co** .............................. F ...... 805 647-2817
  11011 Azahar St Ste 4 Ventura (93004) *(P-7468)*
**Lyncole Grunding Solutions LLC** .......................... E ...... 310 214-4000
  369 Van Ness Way Torrance (90501) *(P-11463)*
**Lyncole Xit Grounding, Torrance** *Also Called: Lyncole Grunding Solutions LLC (P-11463)*
**Lynde-Ordway Company Inc** ................................. F ...... 714 957-1311
  5402 Commercial Dr Huntington Beach (92649) *(P-10462)*
**Lynn Products Inc** .................................................. A ...... 310 530-5966
  2645 W 237th St Torrance (90505) *(P-10402)*
**Lynx Enterprises Inc** ............................................... C ...... 209 833-3400
  724 E Grant Line Rd Ste B Tracy (95304) *(P-8491)*
**Lynx Software Technologies Inc (PA)** .................. D ...... 408 979-3900
  855 Embedded Way San Jose (95138) *(P-18508)*
**Lyrical Foods Inc** .................................................... C ...... 510 784-0955
  3180 Corporate Pl Hayward (94545) *(P-2270)*
**Lytle Screen Printing Inc** ....................................... F ...... 714 969-2424
  21572 Surveyor Cir Huntington Beach (92646) *(P-9751)*
**Lytx Inc (PA)** ............................................................. B ...... 858 430-4000
  9785 Towne Centre Dr San Diego (92121) *(P-14218)*
**M & B Window Fashions, Los Angeles** *Also Called: Hd Window Fashions Inc (P-3720)*
**M & G Jewelers Inc** ................................................. D ...... 909 989-2929
  10823 Edison Ct Rancho Cucamonga (91730) *(P-17649)*
**M & H Electric Fabricators Inc** .............................. E ...... 562 926-9552
  13537 Alondra Blvd Santa Fe Springs (90670) *(P-13177)*
**M & H Uniforms, Burlingame** *Also Called: Murphy HARtelius/M&h Uniforms (P-17078)*
**M & J Precision, Morgan Hill** *Also Called: Lara Manufacturing Inc (P-8485)*
**M & L Pharmaceutical Inc** ...................................... F ...... 909 890-0078
  629 S Allen St San Bernardino (92408) *(P-5539)*
**M & L Precision Machining Inc (PA)** ..................... E ...... 408 436-3955
  18665 Madrone Pkwy Morgan Hill (95037) *(P-10949)*
**M & M Bakery Products Inc** .................................. D ...... 510 235-0274
  1900 Garden Tract Rd Richmond (94801) *(P-17597)*
**M & O Perry Industries Inc** .................................... E ...... 951 734-9838
  412 N Smith Ave Corona (92878) *(P-10025)*
**M & R Company, Lodi** *Also Called: Reynolds Packing Co (P-85)*
**M & R Engineering Co** ............................................ F ...... 714 991-8480
  227 E Meats Ave Orange (92865) *(P-8725)*
**M & R Plating Corporation** .................................... F ...... 818 896-2700
  12375 Montague St Pacoima (91331) *(P-8980)*
**M & W Engineering Inc** .......................................... E ...... 530 676-7185
  3880 Dividend Dr Ste 100 Shingle Springs (95682) *(P-10950)*
**M A G, Santa Maria** *Also Called: Microwave Applications Group (P-19405)*
**M A G Engineering Mfg Co** .................................... E
  17305 Demler St Irvine (92614) *(P-8013)*
**M and M Stamping Corp** ........................................ F ...... 909 590-2704
  13821 Oaks Ave Chino (91710) *(P-8172)*
**M C C, Torrance** *Also Called: Medical Chemical Corporation (P-6309)*

**M C E, Torrance** *Also Called: Magnetic Component Engrg LLC (P-9292)*
**M C E, Salinas** *Also Called: Magnetic Circuit Elements Inc (P-13028)*
**M C I Manufacturing (PA)** ....................................... E ...... 408 456-2700
  1020 Rock Ave San Jose (95131) *(P-8492)*
**M Calosso & Son** ....................................................    209 466-8994
  1947 E Miner Ave Stockton (95205) *(P-17274)*
**M D H Burner & Boiler Co Inc** ............................... F ...... 562 630-2875
  12106 Center St South Gate (90280) *(P-9991)*
**M D Manufacturing Inc** .......................................... F ...... 661 283-7550
  34970 Mcmurtrey Ave Bakersfield (93308) *(P-10573)*
**M E D Inc** ................................................................... D ...... 562 921-0464
  14001 Marquardt Ave Santa Fe Springs (90670) *(P-13533)*
**M E I, Santa Barbara** *Also Called: Motion Engineering Inc (P-10412)*
**M E T, Murrieta** *Also Called: Medical Extrusion Tech Inc (P-6908)*
**M F G West, Adelanto** *Also Called: Molded Fiber GL Companies - W (P-6919)*
**M G A Investment Co Inc** ....................................... F ...... 805 543-9050
  3211 Broad St Ste 201 San Luis Obispo (93401) *(P-4430)*
**M I P, Covina** *Also Called: Moores Ideal Products LLC (P-15761)*
**M K Products Inc** .................................................... D ...... 949 798-1234
  16882 Armstrong Ave Irvine (92606) *(P-9727)*
**M Klemme Technology Corp** ................................ E ...... 760 727-0593
  1384 Poinsettia Ave Ste F Vista (92081) *(P-11672)*
**M M S, Claremont** *Also Called: Micro Matrix Systems (P-8868)*
**M Nexon Inc** ............................................................. E ...... 213 858-5930
  222 N Pacific Coast Hwy Ste 300 El Segundo (90245) *(P-18509)*
**M O S Plastics, San Jose** *Also Called: Kennerley-Spratling Inc (P-6884)*
**M P A, Ione** *Also Called: Mp Associates Inc (P-6251)*
**M P N Inc** ................................................................... F ...... 562 921-0748
  14600 Marquardt Ave Santa Fe Springs (90670) *(P-13534)*
**M R C, Fremont** *Also Called: Manufacturing Resource Corp (P-19105)*
**M S E, Burbank** *Also Called: Matthews Studio Equipment Inc (P-15651)*
**M T R, Newark** *Also Called: Membrane Technology & RES Inc (P-19466)*
**M T S, Bakersfield** *Also Called: MTS Stimulation Services Inc (P-252)*
**M Tek Corporation** .................................................. F ...... 530 888-9609
  169 Borland Ave Auburn (95603) *(P-19268)*
**M W Reid Welding Inc** ............................................ D ...... 619 401-5880
  781 Oconner St El Cajon (92020) *(P-8173)*
**M W Sausse & Co Inc (PA)** ..................................... D ...... 661 257-3311
  28744 Witherspoon Pkwy Valencia (91355) *(P-11332)*
**M Z J, Chino Hills** *Also Called: Victory Intl Group LLC (P-16953)*
**M-5 Steel Mfg Inc (PA)** ............................................ E ...... 323 263-9383
  1353 Philadelphia St Pomona (91766) *(P-8493)*
**M-H Ironworks Inc** .................................................. D
  1000 S Seaward Ave Ventura (93001) *(P-16622)*
**M-I LLC** ..................................................................... E ...... 661 321-5400
  4400 Fanucchi Way Shafter (93263) *(P-249)*
**M-I Swaco, Shafter** *Also Called: M-I LLC (P-249)*
**M-Industrial Enterprises LLC** ................................ E ...... 949 413-7513
  11 Via Onagro Rcho Sta Marg (92688) *(P-10951)*
**M-Pulse Microwave Inc** .......................................... E ...... 408 432-1480
  576 Charcot Ave San Jose (95131) *(P-12537)*
**M.A.g Engineering & Mfg, Irvine** *Also Called: M A G Engineering Mfg Co (P-8013)*
**M.C. Gill, El Monte** *Also Called: Castle Industries Inc of California (P-8407)*
**M&B Sciences Inc** ................................................... E ...... 858 812-8735
  4445 Eastgate Mall San Diego (92121) *(P-19464)*
**M&J Design Inc** ....................................................... E ...... 714 687-9918
  1303 S Claudina St Anaheim (92805) *(P-3479)*
**M&J Design Furniture, Anaheim** *Also Called: M&J Design Inc (P-3479)*
**M2 Antenna Systems Inc** ....................................... F ...... 559 221-2271
  4402 N Selland Ave Fresno (93722) *(P-13027)*
**M3 Products Inc** ..................................................... E ...... 626 371-1900
  15134 Matisse Cir La Mirada (90638) *(P-3697)*
**M724 Inc** ................................................................... F ...... 951 314-1333
  949 N Cataract Ave Ste E San Dimas (91773) *(P-3506)*
**Maas Brothers Inc** .................................................. D ...... 925 294-8200
  285 S Vasco Rd Livermore (94551) *(P-9088)*
**Maas Brothers Powder Coating, Livermore** *Also Called: Maas Brothers Inc (P-9088)*
**Maas Energy Works LLC** ....................................... C ...... 530 710-8545
  1730 South St Redding (96001) *(P-16344)*

# ALPHABETIC SECTION
## Magnaflow Performance

**Maas-Hansen Steel, Westminster** *Also Called: Neighborhood Steel LLC (P-16625)*

**Mabel Baas Inc** .................................................................. E ...... 805 520-8075
3960 Royal Ave Simi Valley (93063) *(P-9089)*

**Mac Cal Company** .............................................................. D ...... 408 441-1435
2520 Zanker Rd San Jose (95131) *(P-8494)*

**Mac Cal Manufacturing, San Jose** *Also Called: Mac Cal Company (P-8494)*

**Mac M Mc Cully Corporation** ............................................. E ...... 805 529-0661
5316 Kazuko Ct Moorpark (93021) *(P-11277)*

**Mac M McCully Co, Moorpark** *Also Called: Mac M Mc Cully Corporation (P-11277)*

**Mac Publishing LLC (DH)** .................................................. E ...... 415 243-0505
501 2nd St Ste 600 San Francisco (94107) *(P-4275)*

**Mac Thin Films Inc** ............................................................. E ...... 707 791-1656
2721 Giffen Ave Santa Rosa (95407) *(P-7233)*

**Macbee Engineering, Upland** *Also Called: Engineered Machinery Group Inc (P-9717)*

**Macchia Inc** ........................................................................ F ...... 209 333-2600
7099 E Peltier Rd Acampo (95220) *(P-1671)*

**Macdonald Carbide Co** ...................................................... E ...... 626 960-4034
525 S Prospero Dr West Covina (91791) *(P-9633)*

**Macdonald Screen Print, Modesto** *Also Called: Sign Designs Inc (P-16035)*

**Machado Backhoe Inc** ....................................................... E ...... 209 634-4836
22332 Third Ave Stevinson (95374) *(P-545)*

**Machine Building Spc Inc** .................................................. E ...... 323 666-8289
1977 Blake Ave Los Angeles (90039) *(P-9804)*

**Machine Craft of San Diego** ............................................... F ...... 858 642-0509
7204 Babilonia St Carlsbad (92009) *(P-10952)*

**Machine Precision Components** ........................................ F ...... 562 404-0500
14014 Dinard Ave Santa Fe Springs (90670) *(P-10953)*

**Machine Vision Products Inc (PA)** ..................................... E ...... 760 438-1138
3270 Corporate Vw Ste D Vista (92081) *(P-14797)*

**Machine Zone LLC** ............................................................. E ...... 650 320-1678
1900 S Norfolk St Ste 350 San Mateo (94403) *(P-18510)*

**Machined-Art, San Jose** *Also Called: Gentec Manufacturing Inc (P-10858)*

**Machinetek LLC** .................................................................. F ...... 760 438-6644
1985 Palomar Oaks Way Carlsbad (92011) *(P-13896)*

**Machining and Frame Division, San Jose** *Also Called: Mass Precision Inc (P-8499)*

**Macintyre Corp** ................................................................... E ...... 800 229-3560
5285 Diamond Heights Blvd San Francisco (94131) *(P-10507)*

**Mack & Reiss Inc** ............................................................... D ...... 510 434-9122
5601 San Leandro St Ste 3 Oakland (94621) *(P-2864)*

**Mack Packaging Inc** .......................................................... E ...... 760 752-3500
1239 Linda Vista Dr San Marcos (92078) *(P-17300)*

**Mackenzie Laboratories Inc** .............................................. F ...... 909 394-9007
1163 Nicole Ct Glendora (91740) *(P-12538)*

**Mackie International Inc (PA)** ............................................. E ...... 951 346-0530
4193 Flat Rock Dr Ste 200 Riverside (92505) *(P-808)*

**Maclac Co, San Francisco** *Also Called: R J McGlennon Company Inc (P-6109)*

**Macom, Newport Beach** *Also Called: Mindspeed Technologies LLC (P-12585)*

**Macom Technology Solutions Inc** .................................... D ...... 408 542-8872
18275 Serene Dr Morgan Hill (95037) *(P-11886)*

**Macom Technology Solutions Inc** .................................... E ...... 408 387-7741
471 El Camino Real Ste 210 Santa Clara (95050) *(P-12539)*

**Macpherson Oil Company LLC** ......................................... E ...... 661 556-6096
24118 Round Mountain Rd Bakersfield (93308) *(P-190)*

**Macpherson Wstn TI Sup Co LLC** .................................... F ...... 714 666-4100
1160 N Tustin Ave Anaheim (92807) *(P-16757)*

**Macro Air Technologies, San Bernardino** *Also Called: Macroair Technologies Inc (P-9992)*

**Macro Industries Inc** ......................................................... E ...... 909 606-2218
14178 Albers Way Chino (91710) *(P-16174)*

**Macro Plastics Inc (DH)** .................................................... E ...... 707 437-1200
2250 Huntington Dr Fairfield (94533) *(P-6899)*

**Macroair Technologies Inc (PA)** ....................................... E ...... 909 890-2270
794 S Allen St San Bernardino (92408) *(P-9992)*

**Macronix America Inc (HQ)** ............................................... D ...... 408 262-8887
680 N Mccarthy Blvd Ste 200 Milpitas (95035) *(P-16717)*

**Macs Lift Gate Inc (PA)** ..................................................... E ...... 562 529-3465
2801 E South St Long Beach (90805) *(P-16175)*

**Macworld Magazine, San Francisco** *Also Called: Mac Publishing LLC (P-4275)*

**Mad Catz, San Diego** *Also Called: Mad Catz Inc (P-10403)*

**Mad Catz Inc** ...................................................................... C ...... 858 790-5008
10680 Treena St Ste 500 San Diego (92131) *(P-10403)*

**Mad Engine, Irvine** *Also Called: Mad Engine Global LLC (P-2477)*

**Mad Engine Global LLC (HQ)** ........................................... D ...... 858 558-5270
7 Studebaker Irvine (92618) *(P-2477)*

**Mad River Brewing Company Inc** ..................................... E ...... 707 668-4151
101 Taylor Way Blue Lake (95525) *(P-17621)*

**Madaco Safety Products Inc** ............................................ F ...... 909 614-1756
1313 N Grand Ave 249 Walnut (91789) *(P-16979)*

**Made and Modern Hard Goods Inc** .................................. D ...... 707 366-9180
2260 Cordelia Rd Ste 400 Fairfield (94534) *(P-9755)*

**Made Media LLC** ................................................................ E ...... 866 263-6233
2337 Roscomare Rd Ste 2302 Los Angeles (90077) *(P-16338)*

**Made Merch, Los Angeles** *Also Called: Made Media LLC (P-16338)*

**Madera Fina, Fremont** *Also Called: Commercial Casework Inc (P-3120)*

**Madisn/Grham Clor Graphics Inc** ..................................... B ...... 323 261-7171
150 N Myers St Los Angeles (90033) *(P-4685)*

**Madison Inc of Oklahoma** ................................................. D ...... 918 224-6990
18000 Studebaker Rd Cerritos (90703) *(P-8174)*

**Madison Industries (HQ)** ................................................... E ...... 562 484-5099
17201 Darwin Ave Hesperia (92345) *(P-8674)*

**Madison Reed Inc** .............................................................. E ...... 415 225-0872
548 Market St San Francisco (94104) *(P-17711)*

**Madison Reed Color Bar III, San Francisco** *Also Called: Madison Reed Inc (P-17711)*

**Madison Street Press, Oakland** *Also Called: Inter-City Printing Co Inc (P-4653)*

**Madn Aircraft Hinge** .......................................................... E ...... 661 257-3430
26911 Ruether Ave Ste Q Santa Clarita (91351) *(P-13679)*

**Madrigal Family Winery LLC** ............................................ F ...... 415 887-9539
3718 Saint Helena Hwy Calistoga (94515) *(P-1672)*

**Madruga Iron Works Inc** ................................................... E ...... 209 832-7003
305 Gandy Dancer Dr Tracy (95377) *(P-8175)*

**Madsen Products Incorporated** ....................................... F ...... 714 894-1816
15321 Connector Ln Huntington Beach (92649) *(P-10954)*

**Maf Industries Inc (HQ)** .................................................... D ...... 559 897-2905
36470 Highway 99 Traver (93673) *(P-10026)*

**Mag Aerospace Industries LLC** ....................................... B ...... 801 400-7944
1500 Glenn Curtiss St Carson (90746) *(P-8042)*

**Mag Instrument Inc (PA)** ................................................... B ...... 909 947-1006
2001 S Hellman Ave Ontario (91761) *(P-11612)*

**Magenta Buyer LLC (HQ)** .................................................. E ...... 650 935-9500
428 University Ave Palo Alto (94301) *(P-18511)*

**Maggio Estates, Lodi** *Also Called: Oak Ridge Winery LLC (P-1694)*

**Maggiora Baking Co, Richmond** *Also Called: M & M Bakery Products Inc (P-17597)*

**Magic Apparel & Magic Headwear, Compton** *Also Called: Magic Apparel Group Inc (P-2846)*

**Magic Apparel Group Inc** ................................................. E ...... 310 223-4000
1100 W Walnut St Compton (90220) *(P-2846)*

**Magic Jump Inc** ................................................................. E ...... 818 847-1313
9165 Glenoaks Blvd Sun Valley (91352) *(P-17857)*

**Magic Plastics Inc (PA)** .................................................... E ...... 800 369-0303
25215 Avenue Stanford Santa Clarita (91355) *(P-6900)*

**Magic Ram Inc** ................................................................... F ...... 213 380-5555
3540 Wilshire Blvd Ste 716 Los Angeles (90010) *(P-10404)*

**Magic Software Enterprises Inc** ....................................... E ...... 949 250-1718
530 Technology Dr Ste 100 Irvine (92618) *(P-18512)*

**Magic Technologies Inc** .................................................... A ...... 408 263-1484
463 S Milpitas Blvd Milpitas (95035) *(P-10252)*

**Magic Touch Software Intl** ............................................... E ...... 800 714-6490
950 Boardwalk Ste 200 San Marcos (92078) *(P-18513)*

**Magicall Inc** ........................................................................ E ...... 805 484-4300
4550 Calle Alto Camarillo (93012) *(P-11278)*

**Magico LLc** ........................................................................ E ...... 510 649-9700
3170 Corporate Pl Hayward (94545) *(P-11673)*

**Magma, Escondido** *Also Called: One Stop Systems Inc (P-10418)*

**Magma Inc** .......................................................................... E ...... 858 530-2511
9918 Via Pasar San Diego (92126) *(P-10405)*

**Magma Products LLC** ....................................................... D ...... 562 627-0500
3940 Pixie Ave Lakewood (90712) *(P-11391)*

**Magna Tool Inc** .................................................................. E ...... 714 826-2500
5594 Market Pl Cypress (90630) *(P-10955)*

**Magnachip Semiconductor Corp** ..................................... F ...... 408 625-5999
60 S Market St Ste 750 San Jose (95113) *(P-12540)*

**Magnaflow Performance, Oceanside** *Also Called: Car Sound Exhaust System Inc (P-13470)*

## Magnaslow — ALPHABETIC SECTION

Magnaslow, Rcho Sta Marg *Also Called: Car Sound Exhaust System Inc (P-13471)*

Magnasync-Moviola, Burbank *Also Called: Magnasync/Moviola Corporation (P-11674)*

Magnasync/Moviola Corporation .................................................. E ...... 818 845-8066
  1400 W Burbank Blvd Burbank (91506) *(P-11674)*

Magnebit Holding Corp .................................................................. E ...... 858 573-0727
  9474 La Cuesta Dr La Mesa (91941) *(P-14552)*

Magnell Associate Inc .................................................................... B ...... 626 271-1320
  17708 Rowland St City Of Industry (91748) *(P-10176)*

Magnesium Alloy Pdts Co Inc ....................................................... E ...... 310 605-1440
  2420 N Alameda St Compton (90222) *(P-7814)*

Magnesium Alloy Products Co LP ................................................. E ...... 323 636-2276
  2420 N Alameda St Compton (90222) *(P-7815)*

Magnet Sales & Mfg Co Inc (HQ) ................................................. D ...... 310 391-7213
  11250 Playa Ct Culver City (90230) *(P-7284)*

Magnet Systems Inc ....................................................................... E ...... 650 329-5904
  2300 Geng Rd Ste 100 Palo Alto (94303) *(P-18514)*

Magnetic Circuit Elements Inc ..................................................... F ...... 831 757-8752
  1540 Moffett St Salinas (93905) *(P-13028)*

Magnetic Coils Inc ........................................................................... D ...... 707 459-5994
  150 San Hedrin Cir Willits (95490) *(P-12844)*

Magnetic Component Engrg LLC (PA) ........................................ D ...... 310 784-3100
  2830 Lomita Blvd Torrance (90505) *(P-9292)*

Magnetic Design Labs Inc ............................................................ F ...... 714 558-3355
  1636 E Edinger Ave Ste I Santa Ana (92705) *(P-13029)*

Magnetic Metals Corporation ...................................................... F ...... 714 828-4625
  2475 W La Palma Ave Anaheim (92801) *(P-9584)*

Magnetic Sensors Corporation .................................................... E ...... 714 630-8380
  1365 N Mccan St Anaheim (92806) *(P-13030)*

Magnetika Inc (PA) ......................................................................... D ...... 310 527-8100
  2041 W 139th St Gardena (90249) *(P-16659)*

Magnetron Power Inventions Inc ................................................ E ...... 310 462-6970
  2226 W 232nd St Torrance (90501) *(P-191)*

Magnit LLC (PA) ............................................................................... D ...... 516 437-3300
  2635 Iron Point Rd Ste 270 Folsom (95630) *(P-18515)*

Magnum Semiconductor Inc ........................................................ C ...... 408 934-3700
  6024 Silver Creek Valley Rd San Jose (95138) *(P-12541)*

Magnus Medical Inc ....................................................................... D ...... 415 231-7407
  1350 Bayshore Hwy Ste 600 Burlingame (94010) *(P-15157)*

Magnuson Products LLC ............................................................... E ...... 805 642-8833
  1990 Knoll Dr Ste A Ventura (93003) *(P-13535)*

Magnuson Superchargers, Ventura *Also Called: Magnuson Products LLC (P-13535)*

Magor Mold LLC ............................................................................. D ...... 909 592-3663
  420 S Lone Hill Ave San Dimas (91773) *(P-9634)*

Magparts (HQ) ................................................................................. C ...... 626 334-7897
  1545 W Roosevelt St Azusa (91702) *(P-7848)*

Magtech & Power Conversion Inc .............................................. E ...... 714 451-0106
  1146 E Ash Ave Fullerton (92831) *(P-12845)*

Magtek Inc (PA) .............................................................................. C ...... 562 546-6400
  1710 Apollo Ct Seal Beach (90740) *(P-10406)*

Mahana Therapeutics Inc (PA) .................................................... D ...... 650 483-4720
  201 Mission St Ste 1200 San Francisco (94105) *(P-15158)*

Mahar Manufacturing Corp (PA) ................................................. E ...... 323 581-9988
  2834 E 46th St Vernon (90058) *(P-15731)*

Maier Manufacturing Inc ............................................................... E ...... 530 272-9036
  416 Crown Point Cir Ste 1 Grass Valley (95945) *(P-14064)*

Mail Handling Group Inc .............................................................. C ...... 952 975-5000
  2840 Madonna Dr Fullerton (92835) *(P-4686)*

Mail Handling Services, Fullerton *Also Called: Mail Handling Group Inc (P-4686)*

Mailbird Inc ..................................................................................... F ...... 650 830-9891
  2600 El Camino Real Ste 601 Palo Alto (94306) *(P-18516)*

Main Electric Supply Co LLC ........................................................ E ...... 323 753-5131
  8146 Byron Rd Whittier (90606) *(P-16660)*

Main Electric Supply Co LLC ........................................................ E ...... 805 654-8600
  1700 Morse Ave Ventura (93003) *(P-16661)*

Main Electric Supply Co LLC ........................................................ E ...... 858 737-7000
  4674 Cardin St San Diego (92111) *(P-16662)*

Main Steel LLC ................................................................................ D ...... 951 231-4949
  3100 Jefferson St Riverside (92504) *(P-8981)*

Mainline, Torrance *Also Called: Mainline Equipment Inc (P-11887)*

Mainline Equipment Inc ............................................................... D ...... 800 444-2288
  20917 Higgins Ct Torrance (90501) *(P-11887)*

Mainspring Energy Inc .................................................................. B ...... 408 529-5651
  3601 Haven Ave Menlo Park (94025) *(P-8780)*

Mainstreet Communication Inc (PA) ......................................... F ...... 951 682-2005
  4093 Market St Riverside (92501) *(P-17814)*

Mainstreet Media Group LLC ...................................................... C ...... 408 842-6400
  6400 Monterey Rd Gilroy (95020) *(P-4152)*

Maintech Incorporated ................................................................. C ...... 714 921-8000
  2401 N Glassell St Orange (92865) *(P-17944)*

Maintech Resources Inc ............................................................... E ...... 562 804-0664
  5042 Northwestern Way Westminster (92683) *(P-550)*

Maintex Inc (PA) ............................................................................. C ...... 800 446-1888
  13300 Nelson Ave City Of Industry (91746) *(P-5915)*

Maison Goyard, San Francisco *Also Called: Goyard Miami LLC (P-7131)*

Majestic Garlic Inc ......................................................................... F ...... 951 677-0555
  2222 Foothill Blvd Ste E La Canada (91011) *(P-984)*

Majestic Print Inc ........................................................................... F ...... 951 509-2539
  4017 Trail Creek Rd Riverside (92505) *(P-4687)*

Majestic Printing Systems, Riverside *Also Called: Majestic Print Inc (P-4687)*

Majestic Steel Usa Inc ................................................................... E ...... 800 445-6374
  620 Clark Ave Pittsburg (94565) *(P-8495)*

Major Gloves & Safety Inc ........................................................... E ...... 626 330-8022
  250 Turnbull Canyon Rd City Of Industry (91745) *(P-17770)*

Makabi 26 Inc ................................................................................. F ...... 323 588-7666
  2850 E 44th St Vernon (90058) *(P-6901)*

Make Community LLC ................................................................... E ...... 707 200-3714
  150 Todd Rd Ste 100 Santa Rosa (95407) *(P-4276)*

Makesy, Irvine *Also Called: Wood Candle Wick Tech Inc (P-16272)*

Makino Inc ....................................................................................... E ...... 714 444-4334
  17800 Newhope St Ste H Fountain Valley (92708) *(P-9682)*

Makplate, Gilroy *Also Called: Makplate Inc (P-8982)*

Makplate Inc .................................................................................... E ...... 408 842-7572
  5780 Obata Way Ste F Gilroy (95020) *(P-8982)*

Mal, San Diego *Also Called: Myanimelist LLC (P-4434)*

Malakan Inc (PA) ............................................................................. F ...... 310 910-9270
  11035 Sherman Way Sun Valley (91352) *(P-3286)*

Malbon Golf LLC ............................................................................. E ...... 323 433-4028
  1740 Stanford St Santa Monica (90404) *(P-15838)*

Malcolm Demille Inc ...................................................................... F ...... 805 929-4353
  650 S Frontage Rd Nipomo (93444) *(P-15701)*

Malibu Kitchen, Malibu *Also Called: Marys Country Kitchen (P-1288)*

Malibu Leather Inc ......................................................................... C ...... 310 985-0707
  510 W 6th St Ste 1002 Los Angeles (90014) *(P-7150)*

Mallard Creek Inc ........................................................................... F ...... 916 645-1681
  4095 Duluth Ave Rocklin (95765) *(P-3073)*

Mallin Casual Furniture, Los Angeles *Also Called: Minson Corporation (P-3483)*

Malmberg Engineering Inc .......................................................... E ...... 925 606-6500
  655 Deep Valley Dr Ste 125 Rllng Hls Est (90274) *(P-10956)*

Maloof Naman Builders ................................................................ D ...... 818 775-0040
  9614 Cozycroft Ave Chatsworth (91311) *(P-16792)*

Malwarebytes, Santa Clara *Also Called: Malwarebytes Inc (P-18517)*

Malwarebytes Inc (PA) ................................................................. B ...... 408 852-4336
  3979 Freedom Cir Fl 12 Santa Clara (95054) *(P-18517)*

Mama Mellaces Old World Treats, Carlsbad *Also Called: Mfb Liquidation Inc (P-1359)*

Mammoth Media Inc .................................................................... D ...... 832 315-0833
  1447 2nd St Santa Monica (90401) *(P-4153)*

Mammoth Water, Montebello *Also Called: Unix Packaging LLC (P-1970)*

Man-Grove Industries Inc ............................................................ D ...... 714 630-3020
  1201 N Miller St Anaheim (92806) *(P-4688)*

Mananalu Inc .................................................................................. E ...... 805 222-0046
  8605 Santa Monica Blvd Pmb 82374 West Hollywood (90069) *(P-1902)*

Mandala, Vista *Also Called: Oceanside Glasstile Company (P-7270)*

Mandeville Modular Inc ............................................................... F ...... 888 662-8458
  39510 Middleton St Palmdale (93551) *(P-352)*

Mandiant Inc ................................................................................... E ...... 408 321-6300
  630 Alder Dr Milpitas (95035) *(P-18518)*

Maneri Sign Co Inc ........................................................................ E ...... 310 327-6261
  2722 S Fairview St Santa Ana (92704) *(P-16002)*

Maney Aircraft, Ontario *Also Called: Maney Aircraft Inc (P-13897)*

Maney Aircraft Inc ......................................................................... E ...... 909 390-2500
  1305 S Wanamaker Ave Ontario (91761) *(P-13897)*

## ALPHABETIC SECTION

Mango Materials Inc .................................................................. F ...... 650 440-0430
  800 Buchanan St Berkeley (94710) *(P-5175)*

Mangomint Inc ......................................................................... E ...... 310 496-8677
  10401 Venice Blvd 497 Los Angeles (90034) *(P-18519)*

Manhattan Beachwear LLC (PA) .............................................. D ...... 657 384-2110
  10855 Business Center Dr Ste C Cypress (90630) *(P-2865)*

Manhattan Confectioners Inc .................................................. F ...... 310 257-0260
  2530 W 237th St Torrance (90505) *(P-1318)*

Manhattan Stitching Co, Buena Park Also Called: Manhattan Stitching Co Inc *(P-2994)*

Manhattan Stitching Co Inc ...................................................... E ...... 714 521-9479
  8362 Artesia Blvd Ste E Buena Park (90621) *(P-2994)*

Manley Laboratories Inc .......................................................... E ...... 909 627-4256
  13880 Magnolia Ave Chino (91710) *(P-11888)*

Mann+hmmel Wtr Fluid Sltons In (DH) ..................................... D ...... 805 964-8003
  93 S La Patera Ln Goleta (93117) *(P-10574)*

Manna, La Jolla Also Called: Manna Health LLC *(P-5540)*

Manna Health LLC .................................................................. E ...... 877 576-2662
  216 Nautilus St La Jolla (92037) *(P-5540)*

Mannkind Corporation ............................................................. B ...... 818 661-5000
  30930 Russell Ranch Rd Ste 300 Westlake Village (91362) *(P-5541)*

Manson Western LLC ............................................................. C ...... 424 201-8800
  625 Alaska Ave Torrance (90503) *(P-4335)*

Manteca Bulletin, Manteca Also Called: Morris Newspaper Corp Cal *(P-4162)*

Mantels & More Corp .............................................................. E ...... 323 869-9764
  2909 Tanager Ave Commerce (90040) *(P-483)*

Mantels & More Corp .............................................................. F ...... 323 869-9764
  2909 Tanager Ave Commerce (90040) *(P-7542)*

Manticore Games Inc .............................................................. E ...... 650 799-6145
  1390 Buckingham Way Hillsborough (94010) *(P-18520)*

Mantle Inc ............................................................................... E ...... 415 655-3555
  1950 Cesar Chavez San Francisco (94124) *(P-9635)*

Manufactur ............................................................................. E ...... 213 613-1246
  411 S Main St Unit 422 Los Angeles (90013) *(P-16176)*

Manufacture, Vernon Also Called: BTS Trading Inc *(P-2405)*

MANUFACTURE, Irvine Also Called: Connectec Company Inc *(P-11446)*

Manufacture, Commerce Also Called: D I F Group Inc *(P-19513)*

Manufactured Solutions LLC ................................................... E ...... 714 548-6915
  9601 Janice Cir Villa Park (92861) *(P-16177)*

Manufacturer, Ventura Also Called: Novotech Nutraceuticals Inc *(P-777)*

Manufacturer, Hollister Also Called: Advantage Truss Company LLC *(P-3290)*

Manufacturer, Redding Also Called: Purity Pool Inc *(P-7965)*

Manufacturer, Roseville Also Called: Swiss-Tech Machining LLC *(P-8733)*

Manufacturer, Novato Also Called: Ranch Systems Inc *(P-9379)*

Manufacturer, Paramount Also Called: Z-Tronix Inc *(P-13129)*

Manufacturer, Lake Forest Also Called: Sonnet Technologies Inc *(P-13308)*

Manufacturer and Distributor, Corona Also Called: Approved Aeronautics LLC *(P-13782)*

Manufacturers Coml Fin LLC .................................................. E ...... 530 477-5011
  13185 Nevada City Ave Grass Valley (95945) *(P-8071)*

Manufacturers of Wood Products, Santa Barbara Also Called: Architctral Mllwk Snta Barbara *(P-3110)*

Manufacturing, Anaheim Also Called: Bloomfield Food Inc *(P-583)*

Manufacturing, Valencia Also Called: King Henrys Inc *(P-2096)*

Manufacturing, Vallejo Also Called: Western Dovetail Incorporated *(P-3461)*

Manufacturing, Richmond Also Called: Ats Products Inc *(P-6728)*

Manufacturing, Temecula Also Called: Marathon Finishing Systems Inc *(P-8496)*

Manufacturing, Valencia Also Called: CURRAN ENGINEERING COMPANY I *(P-8622)*

Manufacturing, Woodland Also Called: Crist Group Inc *(P-9844)*

Manufacturing, Chino Also Called: Manley Laboratories Inc *(P-11888)*

Manufacturing, San Diego Also Called: Continental Controls Corp *(P-14397)*

Manufacturing Facility, Davis Also Called: Schilling Robotics LLC *(P-19418)*

Manufacturing Logistics Inc .................................................... E ...... 916 387-9700
  8135 Elder Creek Rd Sacramento (95824) *(P-17195)*

Manufacturing Resource Corp ................................................. E ...... 510 438-9600
  44853 Fremont Blvd Fremont (94538) *(P-19105)*

Manufacturing/Distribrution, Long Beach Also Called: Jf Fixtures & Design LLC *(P-19100)*

Manufacturing/Machining, Santa Clara Also Called: Applied Manufacturing Group *(P-12313)*

Manutronics Inc ...................................................................... F ...... 408 262-6579
  736 S Hillview Dr Milpitas (95035) *(P-13031)*

Manzana Products Co Inc ....................................................... E ...... 707 823-5313
  9141 Green Valley Rd Sebastopol (95472) *(P-904)*

Map Pharmaceuticals Inc ........................................................ C ...... 650 625-8790
  2400 Bayshore Pkwy Ste 200 Mountain View (94043) *(P-5542)*

Mapcargo Global Logistics (PA) .............................................. D ...... 310 297-8300
  2501 Santa Fe Ave Redondo Beach (90278) *(P-16307)*

Mapei Corporation .................................................................. D ...... 909 475-4100
  5415 Industrial Pkwy San Bernardino (92407) *(P-5176)*

Maple Clamp, San Francisco Also Called: Lowpensky Moulding *(P-3154)*

Maple Imaging LLC (HQ) ........................................................ E ...... 805 373-4545
  1049 Camino Dos Rios Thousand Oaks (91360) *(P-13032)*

Maplebear Inc (PA) ................................................................. A ...... 888 246-7822
  50 Beale St Ste 600 San Francisco (94105) *(P-19010)*

Maplight Therapeutics Inc ....................................................... E ...... 207 653-8478
  800 Chesapeake Dr Redwood City (94063) *(P-5543)*

Mapquest Holdings LLC .......................................................... B ...... 310 256-4882
  4235 Redwood Ave Los Angeles (90066) *(P-14219)*

Mar Cor Purification Inc .......................................................... E ...... 800 633-3080
  6351 Orangethorpe Ave Buena Park (90620) *(P-10575)*

Mar Cor Purification Inc .......................................................... F ...... 510 397-0025
  2606 Barrington Ct Hayward (94545) *(P-10576)*

Mar Engineering Company ..................................................... E ...... 818 765-4805
  7350 Greenbush Ave North Hollywood (91605) *(P-10957)*

Marathon Finishing Systems Inc ............................................. E ...... 310 791-5601
  42355 Rio Nedo Temecula (92590) *(P-8496)*

Marathon Industries Inc .......................................................... C ...... 661 286-1520
  20950 Centre Pointe Pkwy Santa Clarita (91350) *(P-16372)*

Marathon Petroleum Corporation ............................................ E ...... 925 370-3290
  150 Solano Way Martinez (94553) *(P-17253)*

Marathon Products Incorporated ............................................. E ...... 510 562-6450
  14500 Doolittle Dr San Leandro (94577) *(P-14894)*

Marathon Truck Bodies, Santa Clarita Also Called: Marathon Industries Inc *(P-16372)*

Maravai Lfscences Holdings Inc (PA) ...................................... E ...... 858 546-0004
  10770 Wateridge Cir Ste 200 San Diego (92121) *(P-5544)*

MARAVAI LIFESCIENCES, San Diego Also Called: Maravai Lfscences Holdings Inc *(P-5544)*

Marble Security Inc ................................................................ F ...... 408 737-4300
  68 Willow Rd Menlo Park (94025) *(P-18521)*

Marbleworks, Huntington Beach Also Called: Tile & Marble Design Co Inc *(P-485)*

Marburg Technology Inc ......................................................... F ...... 408 262-8400
  304 Turquoise St Milpitas (95035) *(P-10407)*

Marcel Electronics Inc ............................................................ E ...... 714 974-8590
  130 W Bristol Ln Orange (92865) *(P-12155)*

March Plasma Systems, Concord Also Called: Nordson March Inc *(P-9970)*

March Products Inc ................................................................ D ...... 909 622-4800
  4645 Troy Ct Jurupa Valley (92509) *(P-16178)*

March Vision Care Inc ............................................................ E ...... 310 665-0975
  6701 Center Dr W Ste 790 Los Angeles (90045) *(P-15608)*

Marchem Solvay Group, Long Beach Also Called: Energy Solutions (us) LLC *(P-5092)*

Marchem Technologies LLC ................................................... E ...... 310 638-9352
  20851 S Santa Fe Ave Carson (90810) *(P-5100)*

Marco Fine Arts Galleries Inc .................................................. E ...... 310 615-1818
  4860 W 147th St Hawthorne (90250) *(P-4919)*

Marco Products, Los Angeles Also Called: Augerscope Inc *(P-7947)*

Marcoa Media LLC (PA) ......................................................... E ...... 858 635-9627
  9955 Black Mountain Rd San Diego (92126) *(P-4431)*

Mare Island Dry Dock LLC ...................................................... D ...... 707 652-7356
  1180 Nimitz Ave Vallejo (94592) *(P-14008)*

Mare Island Ship Yard, Vallejo Also Called: Mare Island Ship Yard LLC *(P-14009)*

Mare Island Ship Yard LLC ..................................................... D ...... 760 877-0291
  1180 Nimitz Ave Vallejo (94592) *(P-14009)*

Mareblu Naturals, Anaheim Also Called: 180 Snacks Inc *(P-1297)*

Marelich Mechanical Co Inc (HQ) ........................................... D ...... 510 785-5500
  24041 Amador St Hayward (94544) *(P-425)*

Marflex, Vernon Also Called: Marspring Corporation *(P-2516)*

Marfred Industries .................................................................. B
  12708 Branford St Sun Valley (91353) *(P-3866)*

Margaret O'Leary, San Francisco Also Called: Margaret OLeary Inc *(P-2788)*

Margaret OLeary Inc (PA) ....................................................... D ...... 415 354-6663
  50 Dorman Ave San Francisco (94124) *(P-2788)*

Marge Carson Inc (PA) ........................................................... D ...... 626 571-1111
  555 W 5th St Los Angeles (90013) *(P-3480)*

**Marian Inc**            ALPHABETIC SECTION

Marian Inc .................................................................. E ...... 408 645-5355
   19550 Vallco Pkwy Unit 214 Cupertino (95014) *(P-13270)*

Mariani Bros, Marysville *Also Called: Mariani Packing Co Inc (P-956)*

Mariani Packing Co Inc (PA) ................................... B ...... 707 452-2800
   500 Crocker Dr Vacaville (95688) *(P-83)*

Mariani Packing Co Inc .............................................. C ...... 530 749-6565
   9281 State Highway 70 Marysville (95901) *(P-956)*

Mariani Winery, Saratoga *Also Called: Savannah Chanelle Vineyards (P-1741)*

Mariannes Ice Cream LLC (PA) ............................. E ...... 831 457-1447
   1201 Fair Ave Santa Cruz (95060) *(P-809)*

Mariannes Ice Cream LLC ........................................ E ...... 831 713-4746
   218 State Park Dr Aptos (95003) *(P-810)*

Marich Confectionery Co Inc .................................... C ...... 831 634-4700
   2101 Bert Dr Hollister (95023) *(P-1319)*

Marie Callender's Pie Shops, Rancho Palos Verdes *Also Called: Pie Rise Ltd (P-17601)*

Marie Edward Vineyards Inc .................................... E ...... 661 363-5038
   6901 E Brundage Ln Bakersfield (93307) *(P-9369)*

Marietta Cellars Incorporated ................................... F ...... 707 433-2747
   22295 Chianti Rd Geyserville (95441) *(P-1673)*

Marietta Marketing, Geyserville *Also Called: Marietta Cellars Incorporated (P-1673)*

Marika LLC .................................................................. D ...... 323 888-7755
   5553 Bandini Blvd B Bell (90201) *(P-2789)*

Marin Brewing Company Inc .................................... F ...... 415 461-4677
   15 Rowland Way Novato (94945) *(P-17598)*

Marin Food Specialties Inc ....................................... E ...... 925 634-6126
   14800 Byron Hwy Byron (94514) *(P-866)*

Marin Independent Journal, Novato *Also Called: California Newspapers Inc (P-4082)*

Marin Mountain Bikes (PA) ....................................... F ...... 415 382-6000
   1450 Technology Ln Ste 100 Petaluma (94954) *(P-16938)*

Marin Sun Farms Inc (PA) ........................................ E ...... 415 663-8997
   1522 Petaluma Blvd N Petaluma (94952) *(P-606)*

Marina Graphic Center Inc ........................................ C ...... 310 970-1777
   12901 Cerise Ave Hawthorne (90250) *(P-4689)*

Marina Shipyard, Long Beach *Also Called: Indel Engineering Inc (P-14036)*

Marine & Industrial Svcs Inc .................................... F ...... 925 757-8791
   2391 W 10th St Antioch (94509) *(P-9265)*

Marine & Rest Fabricators Inc ................................. E ...... 619 232-7267
   3768 Dalbergia St San Diego (92113) *(P-8497)*

Marine Corps United States ..................................... C ...... 760 577-6716
   Usmc Barstow (92311) *(P-9431)*

Marine Fenders Intl Inc .............................................. E ...... 310 834-7037
   452 W Valley Blvd Rialto (92376) *(P-6902)*

Marine Interiors, San Diego *Also Called: US Joiner LLC (P-399)*

Marine Outfitters, Carlsbad *Also Called: Matthew Smith Crampton (P-14040)*

Marine Spill Response Corp ..................................... E ...... 707 442-6087
   990 W Waterfront Dr Eureka (95501) *(P-14686)*

Mariner Systems Inc (PA) ......................................... E ...... 305 266-7255
   114 C Ave Coronado (92118) *(P-19106)*

Marino Enterprises Inc .............................................. E ...... 909 476-0343
   10671 Civic Center Dr Rancho Cucamonga (91730) *(P-13898)*

Maripro, Goleta *Also Called: L3 Technologies Inc (P-11878)*

Maritime Solutions LLC ............................................. E ...... 619 234-2676
   1616 Newton Ave San Diego (92113) *(P-14039)*

Maritime Telecom Netwrk Inc, Los Angeles *Also Called: Eeg 3 LLC (P-11848)*

Marjan Stone Inc ........................................................ E ...... 619 825-6000
   2758 Via Orange Way Spring Valley (91978) *(P-16476)*

Mark Christopher Chevrolet Inc (PA) ...................... C ...... 909 321-5860
   2131 E Convention Center Way Ontario (91764) *(P-17440)*

Mark Christopher Hummer, Ontario *Also Called: Mark Christopher Chevrolet Inc (P-17440)*

Mark Optics Inc .......................................................... E ...... 714 545-6684
   1424 E Saint Gertrude Pl Santa Ana (92705) *(P-14798)*

Mark V Products, Corona *Also Called: 2nd Gen Productions Inc (P-5885)*

Markar & Pemko Products, Ventura *Also Called: Assa Abloy ACC Door Cntrls Gro (P-7976)*

Market Fixtures Unlimited Inc (PA) .......................... F ...... 562 803-5553
   13235 Woodruff Ave Downey (90242) *(P-16785)*

Marketo Inc (HQ) ....................................................... C ...... 650 376-2303
   901 Mariners Island Blvd Ste 200 San Mateo (94404) *(P-17945)*

Marketshare Inc (PA) ................................................ D ...... 408 262-0677
   2001 Tarob Ct Milpitas (95035) *(P-16003)*

Markit Forestry MGT LLC .......................................... F ...... 279 444-0033
   14330 Musso Rd Auburn (95603) *(P-101)*

Markland Industries Inc (PA) .................................... E ...... 714 245-2850
   21 Merano Laguna Niguel (92677) *(P-14065)*

Marko Foam Products, Huntington Beach *Also Called: Marko Foam Products Inc (P-6647)*

Marko Foam Products Inc (PA) ............................... E ...... 949 417-3307
   17592 Metzler Ln Huntington Beach (92647) *(P-6647)*

Markov Corporation ................................................... E ...... 650 207-9445
   1225 Magdalena Ct Los Altos (94024) *(P-19484)*

Marlee Manufacturing Inc ......................................... E ...... 909 390-3222
   4711 E Guasti Rd Ontario (91761) *(P-15159)*

Marlin Designs LLC .................................................... C ...... 949 637-7257
   13845 Alton Pkwy Ste C Irvine (92618) *(P-3481)*

Marlin Equity Partners LLC (PA) ............................. D ...... 310 364-0100
   1301 Manhattan Ave Hermosa Beach (90254) *(P-17733)*

Marman Industries Inc .............................................. D ...... 909 392-2136
   1701 Earhart La Verne (91750) *(P-9636)*

Marmot Mountain, Rohnert Park *Also Called: Marmot Mountain LLC (P-2633)*

Marmot Mountain LLC (HQ) ..................................... C ...... 888 357-3262
   5789 State Farm Dr Ste 100 Rohnert Park (94928) *(P-2633)*

Maroney Company ..................................................... F ...... 818 882-2722
   9016 Winnetka Ave Northridge (91324) *(P-10958)*

Marples Gears Inc ..................................................... E ...... 626 570-1744
   1310 Mountain View Cir Azusa (91702) *(P-10041)*

Marqeta, Oakland *Also Called: Marqeta Inc (P-18522)*

Marqeta Inc (PA) ........................................................ A ...... 877 962-7738
   180 Grand Ave Ste 600 Oakland (94612) *(P-18522)*

Marquez & Marquez Food PR, South Gate *Also Called: Marquez Marquez Inc (P-2097)*

Marquez Marquez Inc ............................................... E ...... 562 408-0960
   11821 Industrial Ave South Gate (90280) *(P-2097)*

Marrone Bio Innovations, Davis *Also Called: Pro Farm Group Inc (P-6205)*

Marrs Printing Inc ....................................................... D ...... 909 594-9459
   860 Tucker Ln City Of Industry (91789) *(P-4690)*

Mars Air Curtains, Gardena *Also Called: Mars Air Systems LLC (P-9993)*

Mars Air Systems LLC ............................................... D ...... 310 532-1555
   14716 S Broadway Gardena (90248) *(P-9993)*

MArs Engineering Company Inc (PA) ..................... E ...... 510 483-0541
   699 Montague St San Leandro (94577) *(P-10959)*

Mars Food North America, Rancho Dominguez *Also Called: Mars Food Us LLC (P-2271)*

Mars Food Us LLC (HQ) ........................................... B ...... 310 933-0670
   2001 E Cashdan St Ste 201 Rancho Dominguez (90220) *(P-2271)*

Mars Petcare Us Inc .................................................. D ...... 760 261-7900
   13243 Nutro Way Victorville (92395) *(P-1107)*

Mars Petcare Us Inc .................................................. E ...... 909 887-8131
   2765 Lexington Way San Bernardino (92407) *(P-1108)*

Mars Printing and Packaging, City Of Industry *Also Called: Marrs Printing Inc (P-4690)*

Marseille Networks Inc .............................................. F ...... 408 689-0303
   3211 Scott Blvd Ste 205 Santa Clara (95054) *(P-12542)*

Marshall Advertising and Design Inc ....................... E ...... 714 545-5757
   2729 Bristol St Ste 100 Costa Mesa (92626) *(P-17780)*

Marshall Electronics Inc (PA) ................................... D ...... 310 333-0606
   20608 Madrona Ave Torrance (90503) *(P-11675)*

Marspring Corporation (PA) ...................................... E ...... 323 589-5637
   4920 S Boyle Ave Vernon (90058) *(P-2516)*

Marspring Corporation .............................................. D ...... 310 484-6849
   5190 S Santa Fe Ave Vernon (90058) *(P-3533)*

Martek Power, Torrance *Also Called: Sure Power Inc (P-13096)*

Martin Archery, Los Angeles *Also Called: Martin Sports Inc (P-15839)*

Martin Bauer Inc ......................................................... F ...... 310 669-2100
   20710 S Alameda St Long Beach (90810) *(P-2014)*

Martin Bauer Inc., Long Beach *Also Called: Martin Bauer Inc (P-2014)*

Martin Chancey Corporation .................................... E ...... 510 972-6300
   525 Malloy Ct Corona (92878) *(P-6903)*

Martin E-Z Stick Labels ............................................. F ...... 562 906-1577
   12921 Sunnyside Pl Santa Fe Springs (90670) *(P-4920)*

Martin Furniture, San Diego *Also Called: Gilbert Martin Wdwkg Co Inc (P-3550)*

Martin Group Inc (PA) ............................................... E ...... 707 433-3900
   1470 Grove St Healdsburg (95448) *(P-3420)*

Martin Integrated, Orange *Also Called: Martin Integrated Systems (P-477)*

Martin Integrated Systems ........................................ E ...... 714 998-9100
   1525 W Orange Grove Ave Ste D Orange (92868) *(P-477)*

Martin Sports Inc (PA) ............................................... E ...... 509 529-2554
   1100 Glendon Ave Ste 920 Los Angeles (90024) *(P-15839)*

## ALPHABETIC SECTION — Mastiff Design

**Martin Sprocket & Gear Inc** .................................... D ...... 916 441-7172
1199 Vine St Sacramento (95811) *(P-10042)*

**Martin Sprocket & Gear Inc** .................................... F ...... 323 728-8117
5920 Triangle Dr Commerce (90040) *(P-10043)*

**Martin/Brattrud Inc** ................................................. D ...... 323 770-4171
1231 W 134th St Gardena (90247) *(P-3482)*

**Martinelli Envmtl Graphics** ................................... F ...... 415 468-4000
1829 Egbert Ave San Francisco (94124) *(P-16004)*

**Martinez & Turek, Rialto** *Also Called: Martinez and Turek Inc (P-10960)*

**Martinez and Turek Inc** ......................................... C ...... 909 820-6800
300 S Cedar Ave Rialto (92376) *(P-10960)*

**Martinez Refinery, Martinez** *Also Called: Marathon Petroleum Corporation (P-17253)*

**Martini Prati Winery, Santa Rosa** *Also Called: Conetech Custom Services LLC (P-1515)*

**Martins Metal Fabrication & Welding Inc** ............ E ...... 707 678-4117
7260 Lewis Rd Vacaville (95687) *(P-19208)*

**Martins Quality Truck Body Inc** ............................ F ...... 310 632-5978
1831 W El Segundo Blvd Compton (90222) *(P-13368)*

**Marton Precision Mfg LLC** .................................... E ...... 714 808-6523
1365 S Acacia Ave Fullerton (92831) *(P-13716)*

**Maruchan Inc** ........................................................ C ...... 949 789-2300
1902 Deere Ave Irvine (92606) *(P-2115)*

**Maruchan Inc (HQ)** ............................................... B ...... 949 789-2300
15800 Laguna Canyon Rd Irvine (92618) *(P-2272)*

**Maruhachi Ceramics America Inc** ........................ E ...... 800 736-6221
1985 Sampson Ave Corona (92879) *(P-7274)*

**Maruichi American Corporation** ............................ D ...... 562 903-8600
11529 Greenstone Ave Santa Fe Springs (90670) *(P-7666)*

**Marukan Vinegar, Paramount** *Also Called: Marukan Vinegar U S A Inc (P-2273)*

**Marukan Vinegar U S A Inc (HQ)** .......................... E ...... 562 630-6060
16203 Vermont Ave Paramount (90723) *(P-2273)*

**Marukan Vinegar U S A Inc** .................................. E ...... 562 630-6060
7755 Monroe St Paramount (90723) *(P-2274)*

**Marukome USA Inc (HQ)** ...................................... F ...... 949 863-0110
17132 Pullman St Irvine (92614) *(P-2275)*

**Marvac Scientific Mfg Co** ..................................... F ...... 925 825-4636
3231 Monument Way Ste I Concord (94518) *(P-14343)*

**Marvel Parent LLC (HQ)** ...................................... D ...... 650 321-4910
1950 University Ave Ste 350 Palo Alto (94303) *(P-17946)*

**Marvell, Santa Clara** *Also Called: Marvell Semiconductor Inc (P-12545)*

**Marvell Semiconductor Inc** .................................. E ...... 916 605-3700
890 Glenn Dr Folsom (95630) *(P-12543)*

**Marvell Semiconductor Inc** .................................. A ...... 949 614-7700
15485 Sand Canyon Ave Irvine (92618) *(P-12544)*

**Marvell Semiconductor Inc (HQ)** .......................... A ...... 408 222-2500
5488 Marvell Ln Santa Clara (95054) *(P-12545)*

**Marvell Technology Group Ltd** ............................. C ...... 408 222-2500
5488 Marvell Ln Santa Clara (95054) *(P-12546)*

**Marvin Group The, Inglewood** *Also Called: Marvin Land Systems Inc (P-13369)*

**Marvin Land Systems Inc** ..................................... E ...... 310 674-5030
261 W Beach Ave Inglewood (90302) *(P-13369)*

**Marvin Test Solutions Inc** .................................... D ...... 949 263-2222
1770 Kettering Irvine (92614) *(P-14553)*

**Marway Power Solutions, Santa Ana** *Also Called: Marway Power Systems Inc (P-10408)*

**Marway Power Systems Inc (PA)** .......................... E ...... 714 917-6200
1721 S Grand Ave Santa Ana (92705) *(P-10408)*

**Marwell Corporation** ............................................. F ...... 909 794-4192
1094 Wabash Ave Mentone (92359) *(P-11246)*

**Mary Ann's, Sacramento** *Also Called: Mary Anns Baking Co Inc (P-1227)*

**Mary Anns Baking Co Inc** .................................... C ...... 916 681-7444
8371 Carbide Ct Sacramento (95828) *(P-1227)*

**Marys Country Kitchen** ......................................... F ...... 310 456-7845
3900 Cross Creek Rd Ste 3 Malibu (90265) *(P-1288)*

**Mascorro Leather Inc** ............................................ E ...... 323 724-6759
5921 Sheila St Commerce (90040) *(P-7157)*

**Mashka Jewelry LLC** ............................................. E ...... 415 273-9330
1400 Grant Ave San Francisco (94133) *(P-15702)*

**MASIMO, Irvine** *Also Called: Masimo Corporation (P-15555)*

**Masimo Americas Inc** ............................................ E ...... 949 297-7000
52 Discovery Irvine (92618) *(P-15160)*

**Masimo Consumer, Carlsbad** *Also Called: Dei Holdings Inc (P-11991)*

**Masimo Corporation** .............................................. E ...... 949 297-7000
40 Parker Irvine (92618) *(P-15553)*

**Masimo Corporation** .............................................. E ...... 949 297-7000
9600 Jeronimo Rd Irvine (92618) *(P-15554)*

**Masimo Corporation (PA)** ..................................... **B** ...... **949 297-7000**
52 Discovery Irvine (92618) *(P-15555)*

**Masimo Corporation** .............................................. F ...... 949 297-7000
15776 Laguna Canyon Rd Irvine (92618) *(P-15556)*

**Masimo Semiconductor Inc** .................................. F ...... 603 595-8900
52 Discovery Irvine (92618) *(P-12547)*

**Mask-Off Company Inc** ......................................... F ...... 626 359-3261
345 W Maple Ave Monrovia (91016) *(P-6236)*

**Mason Electric Co** ................................................ B ...... 818 361-3366
13955 Balboa Blvd Rancho Cascades (91342) *(P-13899)*

**Masongate Inc** ...................................................... E ...... 323 415-8544
2800 Ayers Ave Vernon (90058) *(P-867)*

**Masonite International Corp** ................................ E ...... 209 463-3503
3632 Petersen Rd Stockton (95215) *(P-3155)*

**Mass Precision Inc** ............................................... C ...... 408 954-0200
46555 Landing Pkwy Fremont (94538) *(P-8498)*

**Mass Precision Inc (PA)** ....................................... **C** ...... **408 954-0200**
2110 Oakland Rd San Jose (95131) *(P-8499)*

**Mass Systems, Baldwin Park** *Also Called: Ametek Ameron LLC (P-14386)*

**Mast Biosurgery, San Diego** *Also Called: Mast Biosurgery USA Inc (P-15161)*

**Mast Biosurgery USA Inc** ..................................... E ...... 858 550-8050
6749 Top Gun St Ste 108 San Diego (92121) *(P-15161)*

**Mast Technologies LLC** ....................................... F ...... 858 452-1700
8380 Camino Santa Fe Ste 200 San Diego (92121) *(P-6094)*

**Masten Space, Mojave** *Also Called: Masten Space Systems Inc (P-14083)*

**Masten Space Systems Inc** .................................. E ...... 888 488-8455
1570 Sabovich St 25 Mojave (93501) *(P-14083)*

**Master Arts Engraving, Anaheim** *Also Called: Master Arts Inc (P-5027)*

**Master Arts Inc** ..................................................... F ...... 714 240-4550
3737 E Miraloma Ave Anaheim (92806) *(P-5027)*

**Master Builder Solutions, Newark** *Also Called: BASF Corporation (P-6130)*

**Master Builders LLC** ............................................ A ...... 909 987-1758
9060 Haven Ave Rancho Cucamonga (91730) *(P-6306)*

**Master Enterprises Inc** ......................................... E ...... 626 442-1821
2025 Lee Ave South El Monte (91733) *(P-8500)*

**Master Fab Inc** ...................................................... F ...... 951 277-4772
2279 Eagle Glen Pkwy Ste 112 Corona (92883) *(P-8862)*

**Master Machine Products, Riverside** *Also Called: Metric Machining (P-10975)*

**Master of Code Global** .......................................... E ...... 650 200-8490
541 Jefferson Ave Ste 104 Redwood City (94063) *(P-18523)*

**Master Plastics, Vacaville** *Also Called: Master Plastics California Inc (P-6904)*

**Master Plastics California Inc** .............................. E ...... 707 451-3168
820 Eubanks Dr Vacaville (95688) *(P-6904)*

**Master Powder Coating Inc** .................................. F ...... 562 863-4135
13721 Bora Dr Santa Fe Springs (90670) *(P-9090)*

**Master Precision Machining** ................................ E ...... 408 727-0185
2199 Ronald St Santa Clara (95050) *(P-10961)*

**Master Research & Mfg Inc** .................................. D ...... 562 483-8789
13528 Pumice St Norwalk (90650) *(P-13900)*

**Master-Halco Inc** .................................................. F ...... 909 350-4740
27474 5th St Highland (92346) *(P-7645)*

**Masterbilt Atmtn Solutions Inc** ............................ E ...... 858 748-6700
12568 Kirkham Ct Poway (92064) *(P-9740)*

**Masterbrand Cabinets LLC** .................................. E ...... 951 682-1535
3700 S Riverside Ave Colton (92324) *(P-3252)*

**Masterbrand Cabinets LLC** .................................. E ...... 909 989-2992
5576 Inland Empire Blvd Ontario (91764) *(P-3253)*

**Masterclass, San Francisco** *Also Called: Yanka Industries Inc (P-19307)*

**Masterite Division, Los Angeles** *Also Called: Dcx-Chol Enterprises Inc (P-12030)*

**Masterpiece Artist Canvas LLC** .......................... E ...... 619 710-2500
1401 Air Wing Rd San Diego (92154) *(P-2422)*

**Masters In Metal Inc** ............................................ F ...... 805 988-1992
131 Lombard St Oxnard (93030) *(P-7283)*

**Mastey De Paris Inc** ............................................. E ...... 661 257-4814
24841 Avenue Tibbitts Valencia (91355) *(P-6004)*

**Mastiff Design, Poway** *Also Called: Ramona Research Inc (P-11927)*

**Mat Cactus Mfg Co** ............................................. E ...... 626 969-0444
930 W 10th St Azusa (91702) *(P-2517)*

**Matchbook Wine Company** .................................. E ...... 530 662-1032
12300 Co. Road 92b Zamora (95698) *(P-21)*

**Matches Inc** .......................................................... B ...... 760 899-1919
1700 E Araby St Ste 64 Palm Springs (92264) *(P-5222)*

**Matchmaster Dyg & Finshg Inc (PA)** .................. C ...... 323 232-2061
3750 S Broadway Los Angeles (90007) *(P-2504)*

**Material Control Inc** ............................................ D ...... 661 617-6033
6901 District Blvd Ste A Bakersfield (93313) *(P-9293)*

**Material Sciences Corporation** ........................... E ...... 562 699-4550
3730 Capitol Ave City Of Industry (90601) *(P-7730)*

**Material Security Inc** ........................................... D ...... 408 649-9882
33 New Montgomery St San Francisco (94105) *(P-18524)*

**Material Technology Intl, Richmond** Also Called: MTI Corporation *(P-13040)*

**Materials Innovation, Sunnyvale** Also Called: Jsr Micro Inc *(P-6149)*

**Matheson Tri-Gas Inc** .......................................... E ...... 626 334-2905
16125 Ornelas St Irwindale (91706) *(P-5050)*

**Matheson Tri-Gas Inc** .......................................... E ...... 510 793-2559
6775 Central Ave Newark (94560) *(P-5051)*

**Matheson Tri-Gas Inc** .......................................... E ...... 925 229-4350
651 Solano Way Pacheco (94553) *(P-16825)*

**Mathews Ready Mix LLC** ..................................... E ...... 530 893-8856
1619 Skyway Chico (95928) *(P-7469)*

**Mathews Ready Mix LLC** ..................................... E ...... 530 671-2400
249 Lamon St Yuba City (95991) *(P-7470)*

**Mathews Readymix, Yuba City** Also Called: Mathews Ready Mix LLC *(P-7470)*

**Mathy Machine Inc** .............................................. E ...... 619 448-0404
9315 Wheatlands Rd Santee (92071) *(P-10962)*

**Mathy Winery LLC** ............................................... E ...... 707 431-2700
8533 Dry Creek Rd Geyserville (95441) *(P-1674)*

**Matich Corporation (PA)** ...................................... D ...... 909 382-7400
1596 E Harry Shepard Blvd San Bernardino (92408) *(P-375)*

**Matri Kart** .............................................................. E ...... 858 609-0933
448 W Market St San Diego (92101) *(P-10177)*

**Matrix, Commerce** Also Called: Matrix International Tex Inc *(P-17063)*

**Matrix, Palmdale** Also Called: Africajun LLC *(P-19293)*

**Matrix Document Imaging Inc** ............................. F ...... 626 966-9959
527 E Rowland St Ste 214 Covina (91723) *(P-4921)*

**Matrix International Tex Inc** ................................ E ...... 323 582-9100
1363 S Bonnie Beach Pl Commerce (90023) *(P-17063)*

**Matrix USA Inc** ..................................................... E ...... 714 825-0404
2730 S Main St Santa Ana (92707) *(P-12156)*

**Matsuda House Printing Inc** ................................ E ...... 310 532-1533
1825 W 169th St Ste A Gardena (90247) *(P-4691)*

**Matsui International Co Inc (HQ)** ........................ E ...... 310 767-7812
1501 W 178th St Gardena (90248) *(P-6307)*

**Matsushita International Corp (PA)** .................... D ...... 949 498-1000
1141 Via Callejon San Clemente (92673) *(P-17757)*

**Mattco Forge Inc (HQ)** ......................................... F ...... 562 634-8635
16443 Minnesota Ave Paramount (90723) *(P-8781)*

**Mattco Forge Inc** ................................................. E ...... 562 634-8635
7530 Jackson St Paramount (90723) *(P-8782)*

**Mattel, El Segundo** Also Called: Mattel Inc *(P-15732)*

**Mattel, El Segundo** Also Called: Mattel Direct Import Inc *(P-15759)*

**Mattel Inc (PA)** ..................................................... A ...... 310 252-2000
333 Continental Blvd El Segundo (90245) *(P-15732)*

**Mattel Direct Import Inc (HQ)** .............................. E ...... 310 252-2000
333 Continental Blvd El Segundo (90245) *(P-15759)*

**Matteo LLC** ........................................................... E ...... 213 617-2813
1000 E Cesar E Chavez Ave Los Angeles (90033) *(P-2937)*

**Mattermark, San Francisco** Also Called: Fullcontact Inc *(P-17925)*

**Matternet Inc (PA)** ................................................ E ...... 650 260-2727
355 Ravendale Dr Mountain View (94043) *(P-13901)*

**MATTERPORT, Sunnyvale** Also Called: Matterport Inc *(P-18525)*

**Matterport Inc (PA)** .............................................. D ...... 650 641-2241
352 E Java Dr Sunnyvale (94089) *(P-18525)*

**Matthew Smith Crampton** .................................... E ...... 760 840-8404
300 Carlsbad Village Dr Ste 108a Carlsbad (92008) *(P-14040)*

**Matthew Warren Inc** ............................................. E ...... 805 928-3851
901 W Mccoy Ln Santa Maria (93455) *(P-9177)*

**Matthew Warren Inc** ............................................. D ...... 800 237-5225
5959 Triumph St Commerce (90040) *(P-9202)*

**Matthew Warren Inc** ............................................. E ...... 714 630-7840
3850 E Miraloma Ave Anaheim (92806) *(P-15913)*

**Matthews Studio Equipment Inc** ......................... E ...... 818 843-6715
4520 W Valerio St Burbank (91505) *(P-15651)*

**Mattson Technology Inc (HQ)** ............................. E ...... 510 657-5900
47131 Bayside Pkwy Fremont (94538) *(P-12548)*

**Matz Rubber Company Inc** .................................. E ...... 323 849-5170
1209 Chestnut St Burbank (91506) *(P-6511)*

**Maul Mfg Inc (PA)** ................................................ E ...... 714 641-0727
3041 S Shannon St Santa Ana (92704) *(P-10963)*

**Maurer Marine Inc** ................................................ F ...... 949 645-7673
873 W 17th St Costa Mesa (92627) *(P-14041)*

**Maurice & Maurice Engrg Inc** ............................. E ...... 760 949-5151
17579 Mesa St Ste B4 Hesperia (92345) *(P-7709)*

**Maurice Kraiem & Company** ............................... E ...... 213 629-0038
228 S Beverly Dr Beverly Hills (90212) *(P-16969)*

**Mauser Usa LLC** .................................................. E ...... 209 205-1135
2777 N State Highway 59 Bldg C Merced (95348) *(P-3906)*

**Mave Enterprises Inc** .......................................... E ...... 818 767-4533
11555 Cantara St Ste B-E North Hollywood (91605) *(P-1320)*

**Mavens Creamery LLC** ........................................ E ...... 408 216-9270
1701 S 7th St Ste 7 San Jose (95112) *(P-811)*

**Maverick Abrasives Corporation** ........................ D ...... 714 854-9531
4340 E Miraloma Ave Anaheim (92807) *(P-7555)*

**Maverick Aerospace Inc** ..................................... F ...... 714 578-1700
3718 Capitol Ave City Of Industry (90601) *(P-13902)*

**Maverick Aerospace LLC** .................................... D ...... 714 578-1700
3718 Capitol Ave City Of Industry (90601) *(P-13903)*

**Maverick Desk, Gardena** Also Called: New Maverick Desk Inc *(P-3575)*

**Maverick Therapeutics Inc** ................................. E ...... 650 684-7140
3260 Bayshore Blvd Brisbane (94005) *(P-5545)*

**Mawi Dna Technologies Inc** ............................... E ...... 510 256-5186
1252 Quarry Ln Pleasanton (94566) *(P-19465)*

**Max Leon Inc (PA)** ............................................... D ...... 626 797-6886
3100 New York Dr Ste 100 Pasadena (91107) *(P-2790)*

**Max Machinery Inc** .............................................. E ...... 707 433-2662
33 Healdsburg Ave Ste A Healdsburg (95448) *(P-14431)*

**Max Muscle, Anaheim** Also Called: Joe Wells Enterprises Inc *(P-2626)*

**Max Process Eqp Globl LLC** ............................... E ...... 707 433-7281
1420 Healdsburg Ave Healdsburg (95448) *(P-10964)*

**Max Process Equipment, Healdsburg** Also Called: Max Process Eqp Globl LLC *(P-10964)*

**Max Q, Ontario** Also Called: Maximum Quality Metal Pdts Inc *(P-8176)*

**Max Studio.com, Pasadena** Also Called: Max Leon Inc *(P-2790)*

**Max Windsor Floors, Rancho Cucamonga** Also Called: Three Wise Men Inc *(P-16436)*

**Maxair Systems, Irvine** Also Called: Bio-Medical Devices Inc *(P-15006)*

**Maxar Space LLC** ................................................ A ...... 916 605-5448
5130 Robert J Mathews Pkwy El Dorado Hills (95762) *(P-11889)*

**Maxar Space LLC** ................................................ C ...... 650 852-4000
3825 Fabian Way Palo Alto (94303) *(P-13033)*

**Maxar Space LLC (HQ)** ....................................... D ...... 650 852-4000
3875 Fabian Way Palo Alto (94303) *(P-16339)*

**Maxco Supply Inc** ............................................... C ...... 559 638-8449
2059 E Olsen Ave Reedley (93654) *(P-3804)*

**Maxco Supply Inc** ............................................... E ...... 559 646-8449
605 S Zediker Ave Parlier (93648) *(P-17002)*

**Maxim Equipment Inc** ......................................... F ...... 209 649-7225
339 Doak Blvd Ripon (95366) *(P-6365)*

**Maxim Integrated, San Jose** Also Called: Maxim Integrated Products LLC *(P-12549)*

**Maxim Integrated Products LLC (HQ)** ................ A ...... 408 601-1000
160 Rio Robles San Jose (95134) *(P-12549)*

**Maxim International Holdg Inc (DH)** ................... E ...... 408 737-7600
160 Rio Robles San Jose (95134) *(P-12550)*

**Maxim Lighting Intl Inc** ....................................... D ...... 626 956-4200
247 Vineland Ave City Of Industry (91746) *(P-11498)*

**Maxima Racing Oils, Santee** Also Called: South West Lubricants Inc *(P-6400)*

**Maximum Quality Metal Pdts Inc** ........................ E ...... 909 902-5018
1017 E Acacia St Ontario (91761) *(P-8176)*

**Maxlinear Inc (PA)** ............................................... E ...... 760 692-0711
5966 La Place Ct Ste 100 Carlsbad (92008) *(P-12551)*

# ALPHABETIC SECTION — McLeod Racing LLC

**Maxlinear Communications LLC (HQ)** .................................... F
5966 La Place Ct Ste 100 Carlsbad (92008) *(P-12552)*

**Maxon Industries Inc** .......................................... D ...... 562 464-0099
11921 Slauson Ave Santa Fe Springs (90670) *(P-13536)*

**Maxon Lift Corp (PA)** .......................................... C ...... 562 464-0099
11921 Slauson Ave Santa Fe Springs (90670) *(P-16826)*

**Maxtrol Corporation** ........................................... E ...... 714 245-0506
1701 E Edinger Ave Ste B6 Santa Ana (92705) *(P-12157)*

**Maxus Group, Walnut** Also Called: Prophecy Technology LLC *(P-10424)*

**Maxwell, San Diego** Also Called: Maxwell Technologies Inc *(P-13178)*

**Maxwell Alarm Screen Mfg Inc** .......................... E ...... 818 773-5533
20327 Nordhoff St Chatsworth (91311) *(P-16005)*

**Maxwell Petersen Associates** ............................ F ...... 714 230-3150
412 Olive Ave Ste 208 Huntington Beach (92648) *(P-4277)*

**Maxwell Sign and Decal Div, Chatsworth** Also Called: Maxwell Alarm Screen Mfg Inc *(P-16005)*

**Maxwell Technologies Inc** ................................. D ...... 858 503-3493
3912 Calle Fortunada San Diego (92123) *(P-11376)*

**Maxwell Technologies Inc (HQ)** ......................... D ...... 858 503-3300
3888 Calle Fortunada San Diego (92123) *(P-13178)*

**Maxxess Systems Inc (PA)** ................................. F ...... 714 772-1000
135 S State College Blvd Ste 200 Brea (92821) *(P-18526)*

**Maxxon Company, City Of Industry** Also Called: Dennison Inc *(P-8624)*

**Maxzone Vehicle Lighting Corp (HQ)** ................ E ...... 909 822-3288
15889 Slover Ave Unit A Fontana (92337) *(P-16388)*

**May Holdings Inc** ............................................... F ...... 714 563-2772
4883 E La Palma Ave Ste 503 Anaheim (92807) *(P-15557)*

**Maya Steel Fabrications Inc** .............................. D ...... 310 532-8830
301 E Compton Blvd Gardena (90248) *(P-8177)*

**Mayer Baking Co, Torrance** Also Called: Kopykake Enterprises Inc *(P-8858)*

**Mayoni Enterprises** ............................................ D ...... 818 896-0026
10320 Glenoaks Blvd Pacoima (91331) *(P-8501)*

**Mazda Motor of America Inc (HQ)** .................... B ...... 949 727-1990
200 Spectrum Center Dr Ste 100 Irvine (92618) *(P-13370)*

**Mazda North Amercn Operations, Irvine** Also Called: Mazda Motor of America Inc *(P-13370)*

**Mazona Inc** ......................................................... D ...... 209 538-3667
1885 Kinser Rd Ceres (95307) *(P-8275)*

**Mazzei Injector Company LLC** .......................... E ...... 661 363-6500
500 Rooster Dr Bakersfield (93307) *(P-10577)*

**MB Sports Inc** .................................................... E ...... 209 357-4153
280 Airpark Rd Atwater (95301) *(P-14042)*

**Mbf Interiors Inc** ................................................ F ...... 858 565-2944
7831 Ostrow St San Diego (92111) *(P-2915)*

**Mbtechnology** .................................................... E ...... 559 233-2181
188 S Teilman Ave Fresno (93706) *(P-6380)*

**Mc, Windsor** Also Called: Staubli Electrical Connectors Inc *(P-12897)*

**Mc Allister Industries Inc (PA)** ........................... E ...... 858 755-0683
731 S Highway 101 Ste 2 Solana Beach (92075) *(P-4824)*

**Mc Cann's Engineering & Mfg Co, La Mirada** Also Called: MEMC Liquidating Corporation *(P-9806)*

**Mc Electronics LLC** ........................................... B ...... 831 637-1651
1891 Airway Dr Hollister (95023) *(P-12158)*

**MC Metal Inc** ...................................................... F ...... 415 822-2288
1347 Donner Ave San Francisco (94124) *(P-8637)*

**MC Truss Inc** ...................................................... D ...... 559 876-3630
1144 Academy Ave Sanger (93657) *(P-3314)*

**Mc William & Son Inc** ........................................ F ...... 626 969-1821
421 S Irwindale Ave Azusa (91702) *(P-8863)*

**McAfee LLC (DH)** ............................................... D ...... 888 847-8766
6220 America Ctr Dr San Jose (95002) *(P-18527)*

**McAfee Corp (HQ)** ............................................. D ...... 866 622-3911
6220 America Center Dr San Jose (95002) *(P-18528)*

**McAfee Enterprise, Palo Alto** Also Called: Magenta Buyer LLC *(P-18511)*

**McAfee Finance 2 LLC** ...................................... A ...... 888 847-8766
2821 Mission College Blvd Santa Clara (95054) *(P-18529)*

**McBain Systems A Cal Ltd Prtnr** ...................... E ...... 805 581-6800
810 Lawrence Dr Newbury Park (91320) *(P-16602)*

**McBride Sisters Collection, Oakland** Also Called: McBride Sisters Collections *(P-1675)*

**McBride Sisters Collections** .............................. E ...... 510 671-0739
6114 La Salle Ave Pmb 280 Oakland (94611) *(P-1675)*

**McC Control Systems, Vacaville** Also Called: McC Control Systems LP *(P-10578)*

**McC Control Systems LP** .................................. E ...... 707 449-0341
859 Cotting Ct Ste G Vacaville (95688) *(P-10578)*

**McC Controls LLC** ............................................. E ...... 218 847-1317
859 Cotting Ct Ste G Vacaville (95688) *(P-10579)*

**McCain & Mccain Inc** ........................................ F ...... 661 322-7764
3801 Gilmore Ave Bakersfield (93308) *(P-10965)*

**McCain Manufacturing Inc** ................................ D ...... 760 295-9290
2633 Progress St Vista (92081) *(P-8178)*

**McCalls Country Canning Inc** ............................ F ...... 951 461-2277
41735 Cherry St Murrieta (92562) *(P-16179)*

**McClatchy Newspapers Inc (DH)** ...................... A ...... 916 321-1855
1601 Alhambra Blvd Ste 100 Sacramento (95816) *(P-4154)*

**McConnell Cabinets Inc** .................................... A ...... 626 937-2200
13110 Louden Ln City Of Industry (91746) *(P-3254)*

**McConnells Fine Ice Creams LLC** .................... E ...... 805 963-8813
800 Del Norte Blvd Oxnard (93030) *(P-17132)*

**McCoppin Enterprises** ....................................... F ...... 818 240-4840
6641 San Fernando Rd Glendale (91201) *(P-10966)*

**McCormick & Co** ............................................... D ...... 831 775-3485
340 El Camino Real S Salinas (93901) *(P-2276)*

**McCormick & Company Inc** .............................. F ...... 831 775-3350
340 El Camino Real S Ste 20 Salinas (93901) *(P-2277)*

**McCrometer Inc (HQ)** ........................................ C ...... 951 652-6811
3255 W Stetson Ave Hemet (92545) *(P-14432)*

**McDaniel Inc** ...................................................... F ...... 909 591-8353
10807 Monte Vista Ave Montclair (91763) *(P-7690)*

**McDaniel Manufacturing Inc** ............................. F ...... 530 626-6336
6180 Enterprise Dr Ste D Diamond Springs (95619) *(P-8014)*

**McDavis and Gumbys Inc** ................................. C ...... 800 736-7363
1 Fleetwood Way Corona (92879) *(P-16448)*

**McDowell Craig Off Systems Inc** ...................... D ...... 562 921-4441
13146 Firestone Blvd Norwalk (90650) *(P-3605)*

**McDowell-Craig Office Furn, Norwalk** Also Called: McDowell Craig Off Systems Inc *(P-3605)*

**McE, Rancho Cordova** Also Called: Nidec Motor Corporation *(P-9474)*

**McElroy Metal, Adelanto** Also Called: McElroy Metal Mill Inc *(P-8675)*

**McElroy Metal Mill Inc** ....................................... E ...... 760 246-5545
17031 Koala Rd Adelanto (92301) *(P-8675)*

**McEvoy of Marin LLC** ........................................ E ...... 707 467-1999
1600 Barlow Ln Sebastopol (95472) *(P-1400)*

**McEvoy of Marin LLC (PA)** ................................ E ...... 707 778-2307
5935 Red Hill Rd Petaluma (94952) *(P-1401)*

**McEvoy Ranch, Petaluma** Also Called: McEvoy of Marin LLC *(P-1401)*

**McFiebow Inc (PA)** ............................................ E ...... 310 327-7474
17025 S Main St Gardena (90248) *(P-7354)*

**McFiebow Inc** ..................................................... E ...... 310 327-7474
13238 S Figueroa St Los Angeles (90061) *(P-7355)*

**McGrayel Company** ........................................... E ...... 559 299-7660
5361 S Villa Ave Fresno (93725) *(P-6308)*

**McGuff Otsurcing Solutions Inc** ........................ E ...... 800 603-4795
2921 W Macarthur Blvd Ste 142 Santa Ana (92704) *(P-5546)*

**McGuire Grinding Inc** ........................................ F ...... 805 238-9000
2754 Concrete Ct Paso Robles (93446) *(P-10967)*

**MCI Foods Inc** ................................................... C ...... 562 977-4000
13013 Molette St Santa Fe Springs (90670) *(P-2278)*

**McK Enterprises Inc** .......................................... D ...... 805 483-5292
910 Commercial Ave Oxnard (93030) *(P-2279)*

**McKeever Danlee Confectionary** ...................... C ...... 626 334-8964
760 N Mckeever Ave Azusa (91702) *(P-1321)*

**McKenna Boiler Works Inc** ................................ E ...... 323 221-1171
2601 Industry St Oceanside (92054) *(P-19269)*

**McKenna Labs Inc (PA)** .................................... E ...... 714 687-6888
1601 E Orangethorpe Ave Fullerton (92831) *(P-5547)*

**McLane Manufacturing Inc** ............................... D ...... 562 633-8158
6814 Foster Bridge Blvd Bell Gardens (90201) *(P-9397)*

**McLellan Equipment Inc** ................................... E ...... 559 582-8100
13221 Crown Ave Hanford (93230) *(P-13417)*

**McLellan Industries Inc** ..................................... D ...... 650 873-8100
13221 Crown Ave Hanford (93230) *(P-13418)*

**McLeod Racing, Anaheim** Also Called: McLeod Racing LLC *(P-13537)*

**McLeod Racing LLC** .......................................... E ...... 714 630-2764
1570 Lakeview Loop Anaheim (92807) *(P-13537)*

# McLoud
## ALPHABETIC SECTION

**McLoud, San Francisco** *Also Called: mCloud Tchnlgs (USA) Inc (P-18530)*

**mCloud Tchnlgs (USA) Inc** ............................................. F ...... 866 420-1781
580 California St San Francisco (94104) *(P-18530)*

**McM Fabricators Inc** ...................................................... C ...... 661 589-2774
720 Commerce Way Shafter (93263) *(P-8179)*

**McMahon Steel Company Inc** ........................................ C ...... 619 671-9700
1880 Nirvana Ave Chula Vista (91911) *(P-8015)*

**McManis Family Vineyards Inc** ...................................... E ...... 209 599-1186
18700 E River Rd Ripon (95366) *(P-1676)*

**McNab Ridge, Ukiah** *Also Called: McNab Ridge Winery LLC (P-1677)*

**McNab Ridge Winery LLC** ............................................. F ...... 707 462-2423
2350 Mcnab Ranch Rd Ukiah (95482) *(P-1677)*

**McNaughton Newspapers** ............................................. E ...... 530 756-0800
325 G St Davis (95616) *(P-4155)*

**McNaughton Newspapers Inc (PA)**............................... **D ...... 707 425-4646**
1250 Texas St Fairfield (94533) *(P-4156)*

**McNeal Enterprises Inc** ................................................. D ...... 408 922-7290
2031 Ringwood Ave San Jose (95131) *(P-6905)*

**McNear Brick & Block, San Rafael** *Also Called: L P McNear Brick Co Inc (P-7295)*

**McNeilus Truck and Mfg Inc** ......................................... E ...... 909 370-2100
401 N Pepper Ave Colton (92324) *(P-13419)*

**McNichols, Cerritos** *Also Called: McNichols Company (P-16623)*

**McNichols Company** ..................................................... F ...... 562 921-3344
14108 Arbor Pl Cerritos (90703) *(P-16623)*

**MCP Industries Inc (PA)**............................................... **F ...... 951 736-1881**
708 S Temescal St Ste 101 Corona (92879) *(P-6512)*

**McRoskey Mattress Company** ...................................... E ...... 415 861-4532
1400 Minnesota St San Francisco (94107) *(P-3534)*

**McStarlite, Harbor City** *Also Called: Basmat Inc (P-8388)*

**McWane Inc** ................................................................... F ...... 559 834-4630
2581 S Golden State Blvd Apt A Fowler (93625) *(P-7678)*

**McWhirter Steel Inc** ...................................................... D ...... 661 951-8998
42211 7th St E Lancaster (93535) *(P-8180)*

**MD COMMERCIAL, Fallbrook** *Also Called: Breakmart LLC (P-17845)*

**MD Engineering Inc** ...................................................... E ...... 951 736-5390
1550 Consumer Cir Corona (92878) *(P-10968)*

**MD Stainless Services** .................................................. E ...... 562 904-7022
8241 Phlox St Downey (90241) *(P-9266)*

**Md-Staff, Temecula** *Also Called: Applied Statistics & MGT Inc (P-18057)*

**Mdc Interior Solutions LLC** .......................................... E ...... 800 621-4006
6900 E Washington Blvd Los Angeles (90040) *(P-2905)*

**Mdc Precision LLC** ....................................................... E ...... 510 265-3500
23874b Cabot Blvd Hayward (94545) *(P-9159)*

**Mdc Precision LLC (PA)**............................................... **D ...... 510 265-3500**
30962 Santana St Hayward (94544) *(P-9966)*

**Mdc Vacuum, Hayward** *Also Called: Mdc Precision LLC (P-9966)*

**Mdh, Monrovia** *Also Called: Radcal Corporation (P-14912)*

**Mdi General Contracting, Redding** *Also Called: Metals Direct Inc (P-8507)*

**Mdm Solutions LLC** ...................................................... B ...... 800 669-6361
575 Anton Blvd Ste 300 Costa Mesa (92626) *(P-250)*

**ME & My Big Ideas LLC** ............................................... C ...... 240 348-5240
6261 Katella Ave Ste 150 Cypress (90630) *(P-16949)*

**Meadow Decor Inc** ........................................................ F ...... 909 923-2558
1477 E Cedar St Ste F Ontario (91761) *(P-2938)*

**Meadows Mechanical, Gardena** *Also Called: Meadows Sheet Metal and AC Inc (P-8502)*

**Meadows Sheet Metal and AC Inc** ................................ E ...... 310 615-1125
333 Crown Vista Dr Gardena (90248) *(P-8502)*

**Means Engineering Inc** ................................................. D ...... 760 931-9452
5927 Geiger Ct Carlsbad (92008) *(P-14687)*

**Measure Uas Inc** ........................................................... E ...... 714 916-6166
5862 Bolsa Ave Ste 104 Huntington Beach (92649) *(P-14895)*

**Measurement Specialties Inc** ....................................... D ...... 530 273-4608
424 Crown Point Cir Grass Valley (95945) *(P-14554)*

**Measurement Specialties Inc** ....................................... C ...... 818 701-2750
9131 Oakdale Ave Ste 170 Chatsworth (91311) *(P-14896)*

**Meat Packers Butchers Sup Inc** ................................... F ...... 323 268-8514
2820 E Washington Blvd Los Angeles (90023) *(P-9805)*

**Mechanical Associates, Fresno** *Also Called: Pacific Gold Marketing Inc (P-546)*

**Mechanized Science Seals Inc** ..................................... E ...... 714 898-5602
5322 Mcfadden Ave Huntington Beach (92649) *(P-14897)*

**Meclec Metal Finishing Inc** .......................................... E ...... 559 797-0101
5945 E Harvard Ave Fresno (93727) *(P-8983)*

**Mecpro Inc** .................................................................... E ...... 408 727-9757
980 George St Santa Clara (95054) *(P-10969)*

**Med Couture Inc** ........................................................... D ...... 214 231-2500
15301 Ventura Blvd Sherman Oaks (91403) *(P-2598)*

**Med-Pharmex Inc** ......................................................... C ...... 909 593-7875
2727 Thompson Creek Rd Pomona (91767) *(P-5548)*

**Medallia Inc (HQ)**......................................................... **C ...... 650 321-3000**
6220 Stoneridge Mall Rd Fl 2 Pleasanton (94588) *(P-18531)*

**Medallia Parent LP (PA)**.............................................. **D ...... 650 321-3000**
6220 Stoneridge Mall Rd Fl 2 Pleasanton (94588) *(P-19485)*

**Medallion Industries Inc** .............................................. F ...... 925 449-9040
4771 Arroyo Vis Ste F Livermore (94551) *(P-16449)*

**Medata LLC (HQ)**........................................................ **D ...... 714 918-1310**
5 Peters Canyon Rd Ste 250 Irvine (92606) *(P-18532)*

**Medeanalytics Inc** ......................................................... E ...... 925 248-8118
4160 Dublin Blvd Ste 200 Dublin (94568) *(P-18533)*

**Mededge Inc** ................................................................. F ...... 310 392-9843
319 Windward Ave Venice (90291) *(P-15162)*

**Medegen LLC (DH)**...................................................... **E ...... 909 390-9080**
4501 E Wall St Ontario (91761) *(P-6906)*

**Medegen Inc** ................................................................. C ...... 909 390-9080
930 S Wanamaker Ave Ontario (91761) *(P-6907)*

**Medennium Inc (PA)**.................................................... **E ...... 949 789-9000**
9 Parker Ste 150 Irvine (92618) *(P-15609)*

**Medeologix Inc** ............................................................. E ...... 510 431-3221
32940 Alvarado Niles Rd Ste 400 Union City (94587) *(P-15163)*

**Medeologix LLC** ........................................................... E ...... 408 432-6388
2200 Zanker Rd Ste F San Jose (95131) *(P-15164)*

**Medeonbio Inc** .............................................................. F ...... 650 397-5100
452 Oakmead Pkwy Sunnyvale (94085) *(P-15165)*

**Medgear, Cerritos** *Also Called: LA Triumph Inc (P-2597)*

**Medgle, San Mateo** *Also Called: Lumiata Inc (P-19463)*

**Media Blast & Abrasive Inc** ......................................... F ...... 714 257-0484
591 Apollo St Brea (92821) *(P-10580)*

**Media Gobbler Inc** ........................................................ F ...... 323 203-3222
6427 W Sunset Blvd Los Angeles (90028) *(P-18534)*

**Media Nation, Lake Forest** *Also Called: Media Nation Enterprises LLC (P-16006)*

**Media Nation Enterprises LLC** .................................... E ...... 714 371-9494
25361 Commercentre Dr Ste 100 Lake Forest (92630) *(P-16006)*

**Media Nation Enterprises LLC (PA)**........................... **E ...... 888 502-8222**
15271 Barranca Pkwy Irvine (92618) *(P-16007)*

**Media Nation USA, Irvine** *Also Called: Media Nation Enterprises LLC (P-16007)*

**Media News, Paradise** *Also Called: Califrnia Nwspapers Ltd Partnr (P-4088)*

**Media News Groups, Vacaville** *Also Called: Reporter (P-4184)*

**Media Print Services Inc** ............................................. F ...... 866 935-5077
10012 Del Almendra Dr Oakdale (95361) *(P-17832)*

**Medianews Group Inc** .................................................. B ...... 408 920-5713
4 N 2nd St Ste 800 San Jose (95113) *(P-4157)*

**Mediatech Inc** ............................................................... E ...... 530 666-9868
1242 Commerce Ave Woodland (95776) *(P-5549)*

**Mediatech Inc** ............................................................... E ...... 530 666-9825
1215 Commerce Ave Woodland (95776) *(P-5847)*

**Mediatech Inc** ............................................................... E ...... 530 666-9868
1242 Commerce Ave Woodland (95776) *(P-5848)*

**Mediatek, San Jose** *Also Called: Mediatek USA Inc (P-10178)*

**Mediatek USA Inc (HQ)**............................................... **E ...... 408 526-1899**
2840 Junction Ave San Jose (95134) *(P-10178)*

**Mediatek USA Inc** ........................................................ C ...... 408 526-1899
1 Ada Ste 200 Irvine (92618) *(P-10179)*

**Mediballoon, Inc., Union City** *Also Called: Medeologix Inc (P-15163)*

**Medical Analysis Systems Inc (DH)**............................ **C ...... 510 979-5000**
46360 Fremont Blvd Fremont (94538) *(P-14688)*

**Medical Brkthrugh Mssage Chirs** ................................ E ...... 408 677-7702
24971 Avenue Stanford Valencia (91355) *(P-16180)*

**Medical Chemical Corporation** .................................... E ...... 310 787-6800
19250 Van Ness Ave Torrance (90501) *(P-6309)*

**Medical Depot Inc** ........................................................ D ...... 877 224-0946
548 W Merrill Ave Rialto (92376) *(P-15166)*

**Medical Device, Pleasanton** *Also Called: Mawi Dna Technologies LLC (P-19465)*

## ALPHABETIC SECTION — Meggitt Western Design Inc

Medical Device Bus Svcs Inc .................................................. E ...... 858 560-4165
  5644 Kearny Mesa Rd Ste I San Diego (92111) *(P-15374)*

Medical Device Bus Svcs Inc .................................................. E ...... 916 285-9125
  1174 National Dr Ste 100 Sacramento (95834) *(P-15375)*

Medical Device Manufacturing, Brea Also Called: Life Science Outsourcing Inc *(P-15148)*

Medical Extrusion Tech Inc (PA) ............................................. E ...... 951 698-4346
  26608 Pierce Cir Ste A Murrieta (92562) *(P-6908)*

Medical Illumination International Inc (PA) ........................... F ...... 818 838-3025
  19749 Dearborn St Chatsworth (91311) *(P-11546)*

Medical Instr Dev Labs Inc ....................................................... E ...... 510 357-3952
  557 Mccormick St San Leandro (94577) *(P-15167)*

Medical Packaging Corporation ............................................. D ...... 805 388-2383
  941 Avenida Acaso Camarillo (93012) *(P-15376)*

Medical Tactile Inc .................................................................... E ...... 310 641-8228
  5500 W Rosecrans Ave Ste A Hawthorne (90250) *(P-15168)*

Medicool Inc .............................................................................. F ...... 310 782-2200
  20460 Gramercy Pl Torrance (90501) *(P-15169)*

Mediland Corporation .............................................................. D ...... 562 630-9696
  15 Longitude Way Corona (92881) *(P-7176)*

Medimizer, San Diego Also Called: Medimizer Software *(P-17947)*

Medimizer Software .................................................................. E ...... 760 642-2000
  9920 Pacific Heights Blvd Ste 150 San Diego (92121) *(P-17947)*

Medisense, Alameda Also Called: Abbott Diabetes Care Inc *(P-5727)*

Meditab Software Inc ................................................................ C ...... 844 463-3482
  8795 Folsom Blvd Ste 205 Sacramento (95826) *(P-18535)*

Medius, Morgan Hill Also Called: Babylon Printing Inc *(P-4525)*

Medivation Inc ........................................................................... C ...... 415 812-6345
  499 Illinois St San Francisco (94158) *(P-5550)*

Medivation Inc (HQ) ................................................................. D ...... 415 543-3470
  525 Market St Ste 2800 San Francisco (94105) *(P-5551)*

Medivision Optics, Anaheim Also Called: May Holdings Inc *(P-15557)*

Medlin & Sons, Whittier Also Called: Medlin and Son Engrg Svc Inc *(P-10970)*

Medlin and Son Engrg Svc Inc ................................................ E ...... 562 464-5889
  12484 Whittier Blvd Whittier (90602) *(P-10970)*

Medlin Ramps ............................................................................ E ...... 877 463-3546
  14903 Marquardt Ave Santa Fe Springs (90670) *(P-9585)*

Medline Industries LP .............................................................. D ...... 209 585-3260
  5701 Promontory Pkwy Ste 100 Tracy (95377) *(P-15377)*

Medline Industries LP .............................................................. E ...... 951 296-2600
  42500 Winchester Rd Temecula (92590) *(P-15378)*

Medplast Group Inc .................................................................. A ...... 510 657-5800
  45581 Northport Loop W Fremont (94538) *(P-6909)*

Medrics Corp .............................................................................. F ...... 415 704-7404
  353 Sacramento St Ste 1820 San Francisco (94111) *(P-18536)*

Medrio Inc (PA) ......................................................................... D ...... 415 963-3700
  345 California St Ste 325 San Francisco (94104) *(P-18537)*

Medsco Fabrication & Dist Inc ................................................ D ...... 323 263-0511
  938 N Eastern Ave Los Angeles (90063) *(P-8181)*

Medtronic, Carlsbad Also Called: Medtronic Inc *(P-15170)*
Medtronic, Santa Clara Also Called: Medtronic Inc *(P-15172)*
Medtronic, San Diego Also Called: Medtronic Inc *(P-15173)*
Medtronic, Irvine Also Called: Medtronic Inc *(P-15174)*
Medtronic, Santa Rosa Also Called: Medtronic Cardiovascular *(P-15177)*
Medtronic, Northridge Also Called: Medtronic Minimed Inc *(P-15178)*
Medtronic, Irvine Also Called: Medtronic PS Medical Inc *(P-15179)*
Medtronic, Santa Rosa Also Called: Medtronic Inc *(P-15379)*

Medtronic Inc ............................................................................. E ...... 760 214-3009
  2101 Faraday Ave Carlsbad (92008) *(P-15170)*

Medtronic Inc ............................................................................. A ...... 949 474-3943
  1851 E Deere Ave Santa Ana (92705) *(P-15171)*

Medtronic Inc ............................................................................. D ...... 408 548-6618
  3062 Bunker Hill Ln Santa Clara (95054) *(P-15172)*

Medtronic Inc ............................................................................. E ...... 949 798-3934
  1659 Gailes Blvd San Diego (92154) *(P-15173)*

Medtronic Inc ............................................................................. C ...... 949 837-3700
  9775 Toledo Way Irvine (92618) *(P-15174)*

Medtronic Inc ............................................................................. E ...... 707 541-3144
  5345 Skylane Blvd Santa Rosa (95403) *(P-15175)*

Medtronic Inc ............................................................................. C ...... 707 541-3281
  3576 Unocal Pl Bldg B Santa Rosa (95403) *(P-15379)*

Medtronic 3f Therapeutics Inc ................................................ F ...... 949 399-1675
  1851 E Deere Ave Santa Ana (92705) *(P-15558)*

Medtronic Ats Medical Inc ....................................................... C ...... 949 380-9333
  1851 E Deere Ave Santa Ana (92705) *(P-15176)*

Medtronic Cardiovascular ........................................................ A ...... 707 545-1156
  3576 Unocal Pl Santa Rosa (95403) *(P-15177)*

Medtronic Minimed Inc (DH) ................................................... A ...... 800 646-4633
  18000 Devonshire St Northridge (91325) *(P-15178)*

Medtronic PS Medical Inc (DH) .............................................. C ...... 805 571-3769
  5290 California Ave # 100 Irvine (92617) *(P-15179)*

Medtronic Spine LLC ............................................................... A ...... 408 548-6500
  1221 Crossman Ave Sunnyvale (94089) *(P-15180)*

Medtronic Vascular Inc ............................................................ E ...... 707 522-2250
  3576 Unocal Pl Santa Rosa (95403) *(P-15380)*

Medwand Solutions Inc ........................................................... E ...... 770 363-7053
  23162 Arroyo Vis Rancho Santa Margari (92688) *(P-15181)*

Medway Plastics Corporation ................................................. C ...... 562 630-1175
  2250 E Cherry Industrial Cir Long Beach (90805) *(P-6910)*

Medzon Health .......................................................................... E ...... 844 860-8584
  2099 S State College Blvd Ste 360 Anaheim (92806) *(P-15182)*

Mee Audio, City Of Industry Also Called: S2e Inc *(P-11694)*

Meeder Equipment Company (PA) ........................................ E ...... 559 485-0979
  3495 S Maple Ave Fresno (93725) *(P-9874)*

Meeder Equipment Company ................................................. F ...... 909 463-0600
  12323 6th St Rancho Cucamonga (91739) *(P-19403)*

Meehleis Modular Buildings Inc ............................................. D ...... 209 334-4637
  1303 E Lodi Ave Lodi (95240) *(P-19432)*

Meem Worldwide Logistics LLC ............................................. F ...... 347 666-9680
  5756 Jean Dr Union City (94587) *(P-9528)*

Meg Company Inc (PA) ........................................................... F ...... 310 372-8033
  1860 W 205th St Torrance (90501) *(P-17301)*

Mega Brands America Inc (DH) .............................................. D ...... 949 727-9009
  333 Continental Blvd El Segundo (90245) *(P-15760)*

Mega Creation Inc .................................................................... E ...... 510 741-9998
  228 Linus Pauling Dr Hercules (94547) *(P-6005)*

Mega Fluid Systems Inc .......................................................... E ...... 971 277-9000
  6161 Industrial Way Ste A Livermore (94551) *(P-12553)*

Mega Force Corporation .......................................................... E ...... 408 956-9989
  2035 Otoole Ave San Jose (95131) *(P-10409)*

Megachips LSI USA Corporation ........................................... D ...... 408 570-0555
  910 E Hamilton Ave Ste 120 Campbell (95008) *(P-12554)*

Megachips Technology America Corporation ...................... D ...... 408 570-0555
  2755 Orchard Pkwy San Jose (95134) *(P-12555)*

Megaforce, San Jose Also Called: Mega Force Corporation *(P-10409)*

Meggitt (orange County) Inc ................................................... D ...... 408 739-3533
  355 N Pastoria Ave Sunnyvale (94085) *(P-14220)*

Meggitt (orange County) Inc (DH) .......................................... C ...... 949 493-8181
  4 Marconi Irvine (92618) *(P-14898)*

Meggitt (san Diego) Inc (HQ) .................................................. C ...... 858 824-8976
  6650 Top Gun St San Diego (92121) *(P-13904)*

Meggitt Aerospace, Sunnyvale Also Called: Meggitt (orange County) Inc *(P-14220)*
Meggitt Arcft Braking Systems, Gardena Also Called: Nasco Aircraft Brake Inc *(P-13914)*
Meggitt Control Systems, North Hollywood Also Called: Meggitt North Hollywood Inc *(P-13907)*

Meggitt Defense Systems Inc ................................................. B ...... 949 465-7700
  9801 Muirlands Blvd Irvine (92618) *(P-13905)*

Meggitt North Hollywood Inc .................................................. E ...... 818 691-6258
  10092 Foxrun Rd Santa Ana (92705) *(P-13906)*

Meggitt North Hollywood Inc (DH) ......................................... C ...... 818 765-8160
  12838 Saticoy St North Hollywood (91605) *(P-13907)*

Meggitt Polymers & Composites, San Diego Also Called: Meggitt (san Diego) Inc *(P-13904)*
Meggitt Polymers & Composites, Simi Valley Also Called: Meggitt-Usa Inc *(P-13909)*

Meggitt Safety Systems Inc (DH) ........................................... C ...... 805 584-4100
  1785 Voyager Ave Simi Valley (93063) *(P-13271)*

Meggitt Safety Systems Inc .................................................... D ...... 442 792-3217
  11661 Sorrento Valley Rd San Diego (92121) *(P-13272)*

Meggitt Safety Systems Inc .................................................... D ...... 805 584-4100
  1785 Voyager Ave Simi Valley (93063) *(P-13908)*

Meggitt Sensing Systems, Irvine Also Called: Meggitt (orange County) Inc *(P-14898)*

Meggitt Western Design Inc ................................................... C ...... 949 465-7700
  9801 Muirlands Blvd Irvine (92618) *(P-14364)*

**Meggitt-Usa Inc (DH)** .................................................. B ...... 805 526-5700
1955 Surveyor Ave Simi Valley (93063) *(P-13909)*

**Megiddo Global LLC** ........................................................ E ...... 844 477-7007
17101 Central Ave Ste 1c Carson (90746) *(P-15381)*

**Meguiars Inc (HQ)** ............................................................ E ...... 949 752-8000
213 Technology Dr Irvine (92618) *(P-5916)*

**MEI PHARMA, San Diego** *Also Called: MEI Pharma Inc (P-5552)*

**MEI Pharma Inc** ................................................................. E ...... 858 369-7100
11455 El Camino Real Ste 250 San Diego (92130) *(P-5552)*

**MEI Rigging & Crating LLC** .......................................... D ...... 714 712-5888
14555 Alondra Blvd La Mirada (90638) *(P-9875)*

**Meissner Corporation** ................................................... E ...... 805 388-9911
1001 Flynn Rd Camarillo (93012) *(P-12846)*

**Meissner Filtration Pdts Inc (PA)** ................................. E ...... 805 388-9911
1001 Flynn Rd Camarillo (93012) *(P-12847)*

**Meissner Mfg Co Inc (PA)** ............................................ D ...... 818 678-0400
21701 Prairie St Chatsworth (91311) *(P-10581)*

**Meivac, San Jose** *Also Called: Ferrotec (usa) Corporation (P-12431)*

**Mekong Printing Inc** ....................................................... E ...... 714 558-9595
2421 W 1st St Santa Ana (92703) *(P-4692)*

**Melcast, Cerritos** *Also Called: Molino Company (P-4699)*

**Melco Steel Inc** ................................................................ E ...... 626 334-7875
1100 W Foothill Blvd Azusa (91702) *(P-8320)*

**Melfred Borzall Inc** .......................................................... E ...... 805 614-4344
2712 Airpark Dr Santa Maria (93455) *(P-9560)*

**Melin LLC** ......................................................................... E ...... 323 489-3274
10 Faraday Irvine (92618) *(P-15840)*

**Melissa Trinidad** .............................................................. E ...... 805 536-0954
3589 Vine St Paso Robles (93446) *(P-6006)*

**Melkonian Enterprises Inc** ............................................. E ...... 559 217-0749
2730 S De Wolf Ave Sanger (93657) *(P-957)*

**Mellace Family Brands Cal Inc** ..................................... E ...... 760 448-1940
6195 El Camino Real Carlsbad (92009) *(P-1357)*

**Mellanox Technologies Inc** ........................................... C ...... 408 970-3400
2530 Zanker Rd San Jose (95131) *(P-12556)*

**Mellanox Technologies Inc (DH)** .................................. E ...... 408 970-3400
2530 Zanker Rd San Jose (95131) *(P-12557)*

**Melles Griot Inc** ............................................................... D ...... 760 438-2254
2051 Palomar Airport Rd Carlsbad (92011) *(P-14799)*

**Mellinger Engineering Inc** ............................................. F ...... 707 935-1100
20366 8th St E Sonoma (95476) *(P-19404)*

**Melmarc Products Inc** .................................................... C ...... 714 549-2170
752 S Campus Ave Ontario (91761) *(P-2995)*

**Melrose, Hayward** *Also Called: Melrose Nameplate Label Co Inc (P-9091)*

**Melrose Nameplate Label Co Inc (PA)** ........................ E ...... 510 732-3100
26575 Corporate Ave Hayward (94545) *(P-9091)*

**Melton Intl Tackle Inc** ..................................................... E ...... 714 978-9192
1375 S State College Blvd Anaheim (92806) *(P-17667)*

**Membrane Technology & RES Inc (PA)** ...................... E ...... 650 328-2228
39630 Eureka Dr Newark (94560) *(P-19466)*

**MEMC Liquidating Corporation** ................................... C ...... 818 637-7200
4570 Colorado Blvd La Mirada (90638) *(P-9806)*

**Memora Health Inc** ......................................................... D ...... 480 335-7348
548 Market St San Francisco (94104) *(P-18538)*

**Memorex Products Inc** ................................................... C ...... 562 653-2800
17777 Center Court Dr N Ste 800 Cerritos (90703) *(P-16683)*

**Memory Experts Intl USA Inc (HQ)** ............................... E ...... 714 258-3000
2102 Business Center Dr Irvine (92612) *(P-10253)*

**Memry Corporation** ........................................................ E ...... 650 463-3400
4065 Campbell Ave Menlo Park (94025) *(P-15183)*

**Menasha, Tracy** *Also Called: Menasha Packaging Company LLC (P-3867)*

**Menasha Packaging Company LLC** ............................. E ...... 951 660-5361
1550 N Chrisman Rd Tracy (95304) *(P-3867)*

**Menches Tool & Die Inc** ................................................. E ...... 510 476-1160
30995 San Benito St Hayward (94544) *(P-10971)*

**Mendicino Wine Company, Ukiah** *Also Called: Parducci Wine Estates LLC (P-1703)*

**Mendocino, Santa Rosa** *Also Called: Mendocino Forest Pdts Co LLC (P-16451)*

**Mendocino Brewing Company Inc (HQ)** ..................... F ...... 707 744-1015
1601 Airport Rd Ukiah (95482) *(P-1447)*

**Mendocino Forest Pdts Co LLC** ................................... C ...... 707 468-1431
850 Kunzler Ranch Rd Ukiah (95482) *(P-16450)*

**Mendocino Forest Pdts Co LLC (PA)** ........................... E ...... 707 620-2961
3700 Old Redwood Hwy Ste 200 Santa Rosa (95403) *(P-16451)*

**Mendocino Forest Pdts Co LLC** ................................... D ...... 707 485-6800
6375 N State St Calpella (95418) *(P-16452)*

**Menke Marketing Devices, Santa Fe Springs** *Also Called: Menke Marking Devices Inc (P-16827)*

**Menke Marking Devices Inc** .......................................... E ...... 562 921-1380
10440 Pioneer Blvd Ste 4 Santa Fe Springs (90670) *(P-16827)*

**Mentor Worldwide LLC (DH)** ......................................... C ...... 800 636-8678
31 Technology Dr Ste 200 Irvine (92618) *(P-15382)*

**Mepco Label Systems** ................................................... D ...... 209 946-0201
1313 S Stockton St Lodi (95240) *(P-4922)*

**Mer-Kote Products Inc** ................................................... E ...... 714 778-2266
4125 E La Palma Ave Ste 250 Anaheim (92807) *(P-5177)*

**Mer-Mar Electronics, Hesperia** *Also Called: Geeriraj Inc (P-12121)*

**Mer-Mar Electronics Inc** ................................................ F ...... 760 244-6149
7042 Santa Fe Ave E Ste A1 Hesperia (92345) *(P-12159)*

**Meraqi Medical Inc** ......................................................... E ...... 669 222-7710
47225 Fremont Blvd Fremont (94538) *(P-15184)*

**Mercado Latino Inc** ........................................................ D ...... 310 537-1062
1420 W Walnut St Compton (90220) *(P-16181)*

**Merced Screw Products Inc** .......................................... E ...... 209 723-7706
1861 Grogan Ave Merced (95341) *(P-8726)*

**Mercer Foods, Modesto** *Also Called: Mercer Foods LLC (P-958)*

**Mercer Foods LLC (PA)** ................................................. B ...... 877 743-5373
1836 Lapham Dr Modesto (95354) *(P-958)*

**Mercfuel LLC (HQ)** .......................................................... F ...... 281 442-3000
2780 Skypark Dr Ste 300 Torrance (90505) *(P-6152)*

**Merchants Metals, Riverside** *Also Called: Merchants Metals LLC (P-7646)*

**Merchants Metals LLC** .................................................. C ...... 951 686-1888
6466 Mission Blvd Riverside (92509) *(P-7646)*

**Merci Life LLC** ................................................................. F ...... 317 341-4109
321 N Pass Ave Ste 144 Burbank (91505) *(P-5247)*

**Merco Manufacturing Co, Walnut** *Also Called: Aero Pacific Corporation (P-13743)*

**Mercotac Inc** .................................................................... F ...... 760 431-7723
6195 Corte Del Cedro Ste 100 Carlsbad (92011) *(P-11464)*

**Mercury Computer System Inc** ..................................... E ...... 760 494-9600
1815 Aston Ave Ste 107 Carlsbad (92008) *(P-10180)*

**Mercury Fuels, Torrance** *Also Called: Mercfuel LLC (P-6152)*

**Mercury LLC - Rf Integrated Solutions** ....................... C ...... 805 388-1345
1000 Avenida Acaso Camarillo (93012) *(P-13034)*

**Mercury Magnetics Inc** .................................................. E ...... 818 998-7791
21520 Blythe St Canoga Park (91304) *(P-12848)*

**Mercury Metal Die & Ltr Co Inc (PA)** ............................ F ...... 951 674-8717
600 3rd St Ste A Lake Elsinore (92530) *(P-9092)*

**Mercury Mission Systems LLC** .................................... E ...... 310 320-3088
20701 Manhattan Pl Torrance (90501) *(P-19467)*

**Mercury Plastics Inc (HQ)** ............................................. B ...... 626 961-0165
14825 Salt Lake Ave City Of Industry (91746) *(P-3971)*

**Mercury Plastics Inc** ...................................................... D ...... 323 264-2400
2939 E Washington Blvd Los Angeles (90023) *(P-6562)*

**Mercury Security Products LLC** .................................. F ...... 562 986-9105
4811 Airport Plaza Dr Ste 300 Long Beach (90815) *(P-13273)*

**Mercury Systems Inc** ..................................................... D ...... 510 252-0870
48025 Fremont Blvd Fremont (94538) *(P-10181)*

**Mercury Systems Inc** ..................................................... C ...... 805 388-1345
400 Del Norte Blvd Oxnard (93030) *(P-12160)*

**Mercury Systems Inc** ..................................................... C ...... 805 751-1100
300 Del Norte Blvd Oxnard (93030) *(P-12161)*

**Mercury Systems - Trsted Mssio, Fremont** *Also Called: Mercury Systems - Trusted Mission Solutions Inc (P-10182)*

**Mercury Systems - Trusted Mission Solutions Inc** ... D ...... 510 252-0870
47200 Bayside Pkwy Fremont (94538) *(P-10182)*

**Mercy Hospital, Bakersfield** *Also Called: Dean L Davis MD (P-19356)*

**Meredith Publishing, San Francisco** *Also Called: Hawkeye Acquisition Inc (P-4330)*

**Meredith Vineyard Estate Inc** ....................................... F ...... 707 823-7466
636 Gold Ridge Rd Sebastopol (95472) *(P-1678)*

**Merelex Corporation** ...................................................... E ...... 310 208-0551
10884 Weyburn Ave Los Angeles (90024) *(P-5101)*

**Mereo Biopharma 5 Inc** .................................................. D ...... 650 995-8200
800 W El Camino Real Ste 180 Mountain View (94040) *(P-5553)*

# ALPHABETIC SECTION — Metalite Manufacturing

**Merge4 Mfg Inc** ............................................................. E ...... 831 239-5566
6353 Glen Haven Rd Soquel (95073) *(P-16182)*

**Merger Sub Gotham 2 LLC** ............................................ C ...... 714 462-4603
6261 Katella Ave Ste 250 Cypress (90630) *(P-6911)*

**Merical, Anaheim** *Also Called: B & C Nutritional Products Inc (P-5231)*

**Meridian Gold Inc** ........................................................... B ...... 209 785-3222
4461 Rock Creek Rd Copperopolis (95228) *(P-105)*

**Meridian Graphics Inc** ................................................... D ...... 949 833-3500
2652 Dow Ave Tustin (92780) *(P-4693)*

**Meridian Growers Proc Inc** ............................................ F ...... 559 458-7272
13559 Firebaugh Blvd Madera (93637) *(P-1358)*

**Meridian Moulding Inc** ................................................... F ...... 951 279-5220
330 Cessna Cir Corona (92878) *(P-16980)*

**Meridian Project Systems Inc** ....................................... C ...... 916 294-2000
1720 Prairie City Rd Ste 120 Folsom (95630) *(P-18539)*

**Meridian Supply, Meridian** *Also Called: Davis Machine Shop Inc (P-9348)*

**Meridian Systems, Folsom** *Also Called: Meridian Project Systems Inc (P-18539)*

**Meridian Vineyards, Paso Robles** *Also Called: Treasury Wine Estates Americas (P-33)*

**Meridianlink, Costa Mesa** *Also Called: Meridianlink Inc (P-17948)*

**Meridianlink Inc (PA)** .................................................... D ...... 714 708-6950
3560 Hyland Ave Ste 200 Costa Mesa (92626) *(P-17948)*

**Merit Aluminum Inc (PA)** ............................................... C ...... 951 735-1770
2480 Railroad St Corona (92880) *(P-7743)*

**Merit Assembly, Fremont** *Also Called: Meritronics Materials Inc (P-12163)*

**Merit Cables Incorporated** ............................................ E ...... 714 918-1932
830 N Poinsettia St Santa Ana (92701) *(P-15185)*

**Merit Day Food Service, Pico Rivera** *Also Called: Three Sons Inc (P-17166)*

**Merit Medical Systems Inc** ............................................ E ...... 801 208-4793
6 Journey Ste 125 Aliso Viejo (92656) *(P-15186)*

**Meritek Electronics Corp (PA)** ...................................... D ...... 626 373-1728
5160 Rivergrade Rd Baldwin Park (91706) *(P-9876)*

**Merito.com, Van Nuys** *Also Called: Chef Merito LLC (P-2164)*

**Meritronics Inc (PA)** ...................................................... E ...... 408 969-0888
500 Yosemite Dr Ste 108 Milpitas (95035) *(P-12162)*

**Meritronics Materials Inc** ............................................... F ...... 408 390-5642
42660 Christy St Fremont (94538) *(P-12163)*

**Merle Norman Cosmetics, Los Angeles** *Also Called: Merle Norman Cosmetics Inc (P-6007)*

**Merle Norman Cosmetics Inc (PA)** ............................... B ...... 310 641-3000
9130 Bellanca Ave Los Angeles (90045) *(P-6007)*

**Merlin Solar Technologies Inc (HQ)** ............................. E ...... 844 637-5461
5225 Hellyer Ave Ste 200 San Jose (95138) *(P-12558)*

**Merqbiz LLC** ................................................................... E ...... 855 637-7249
300 Continental Blvd Ste 640 El Segundo (90245) *(P-17668)*

**Merrick Engineering Inc (PA)** ........................................ C ...... 951 737-6040
1275 Quarry St Corona (92879) *(P-6912)*

**Merrill Farms LLC (PA)** ................................................. E ...... 831 424-7365
18900 Portola Dr Ste 100 Salinas (93908) *(P-6)*

**Merrill's Packaging Supply, Burlingame** *Also Called: Merrills Packaging Inc (P-6563)*

**Merrills Packaging Inc** .................................................. D ...... 650 259-5959
1529 Rollins Rd Burlingame (94010) *(P-6563)*

**Merrimans Incorporated** ............................................... E ...... 909 795-5301
32195 Dunlap Blvd Yucaipa (92399) *(P-8182)*

**Merry An Cejka** ............................................................... E ...... 323 560-3949
4601 Cecilia St Cudahy (90201) *(P-10972)*

**Merry Edwards Wines, Sebastopol** *Also Called: Meredith Vineyard Estate Inc (P-1678)*

**Merryvale Vineyards LLC** ............................................. E ...... 707 963-2225
1000 Main St Saint Helena (94574) *(P-1679)*

**Meru Networks, Sunnyvale** *Also Called: Meru Networks Inc (P-12004)*

**Meru Networks Inc (HQ)** ............................................... F ...... 408 215-5300
894 Ross Dr Sunnyvale (94089) *(P-12004)*

**Mesa Industries Inc** ....................................................... E ...... 626 712-1708
1419 Palomares St La Verne (91750) *(P-9432)*

**Mesa/Boogie Limited (HQ)** ........................................... D ...... 707 765-1805
1317 Ross St Petaluma (94954) *(P-11676)*

**Mesotech International Inc** ........................................... E ...... 916 368-2020
2731 Citrus Rd Ste D Rancho Cordova (95742) *(P-14689)*

**Messer LLC** .................................................................... D ...... 310 533-8394
2535 Del Amo Blvd Torrance (90503) *(P-5052)*

**Messer LLC** .................................................................... D ...... 916 381-1606
5858 88th St Sacramento (95828) *(P-5053)*

**Messer LLC** .................................................................... E ...... 562 903-1290
13117 Meyer Rd Whittier (90605) *(P-5054)*

**Mestek Inc** ...................................................................... C ...... 310 835-7500
1220 E Watson Center Rd Carson (90745) *(P-10508)*

**Meta Platforms Tech LLC (HQ)** .................................... E ...... 650 543-4800
1 Hacker Way Menlo Park (94025) *(P-18540)*

**Metabolic Response Modifiers, Oceanside** *Also Called: Chemi-Source Inc (P-17031)*

**Metacrine, San Diego** *Also Called: Metacrine Inc (P-5554)*

**Metacrine Inc** ................................................................. E ...... 858 369-7800
3985 Sorrento Valley Blvd Ste C San Diego (92121) *(P-5554)*

**METAGENOMI, Emeryville** *Also Called: Metagenomi Inc (P-19468)*

**Metagenomi Inc (PA)** ..................................................... E ...... 510 871-4880
5959 Horton St Fl 7 Emeryville (94608) *(P-19468)*

**Metal Air Filters, Chula Vista** *Also Called: American Metal Filter Company (P-9979)*

**Metal Art of California Inc (PA)** .................................... D ...... 714 532-7100
640 N Cypress St Orange (92867) *(P-16008)*

**Metal Buildings & Components, Fowler** *Also Called: Borga Inc (P-8657)*

**Metal Chem, Chatsworth** *Also Called: Metal Chem Inc (P-8984)*

**Metal Chem Inc** .............................................................. E ...... 818 727-9951
21514 Nordhoff St Chatsworth (91311) *(P-8984)*

**Metal Coaters, Rancho Cucamonga** *Also Called: Nci Group Inc (P-8678)*

**Metal Coaters California Inc** ........................................ D ...... 909 987-4681
9123 Center Ave Rancho Cucamonga (91730) *(P-9093)*

**Metal Coaters System, Rancho Cucamonga** *Also Called: Metal Coaters California Inc (P-9093)*

**Metal Container Corporation** ....................................... C ...... 951 360-4500
10980 Inland Ave Jurupa Valley (91752) *(P-7923)*

**Metal Container Corporation** ....................................... C ...... 951 354-0444
7155 Central Ave Riverside (92504) *(P-7924)*

**Metal Cutting Service** .................................................... F ...... 626 968-4764
16233 Gale Ave City Of Industry (91745) *(P-10973)*

**Metal Engineering Inc** ................................................... E ...... 626 334-1819
1642 S Sacramento Ave Ontario (91761) *(P-8503)*

**Metal Fd Hhld Pdts Pckging Div, Oakdale** *Also Called: Ball Corporation (P-7918)*

**Metal Finishing Pntg Lab Tstg, Oxnard** *Also Called: Elite Metal Finishing LLC (P-8959)*

**Metal Improvement Company LLC** .............................. C ...... 323 585-2168
2588 Industry Way Ste A Lynwood (90262) *(P-7890)*

**Metal Improvement Company LLC** .............................. D ...... 818 983-1952
6940 Farmdale Ave North Hollywood (91605) *(P-7891)*

**Metal Improvement Company LLC** .............................. E ...... 949 855-8010
35 Argonaut Ste A1 Laguna Hills (92656) *(P-7892)*

**Metal Improvement Company LLC** .............................. D ...... 818 407-6280
20751 Superior St Chatsworth (91311) *(P-7893)*

**Metal Improvement Company LLC** .............................. E ...... 925 960-1090
7655 Longard Rd Bldg A Livermore (94551) *(P-7894)*

**Metal Improvement Company LLC** .............................. E ...... 714 546-4160
2151 S Hathaway St Santa Ana (92705) *(P-7895)*

**Metal Manufacturing Co Inc** ......................................... E ...... 916 922-3484
2240 Evergreen St Sacramento (95815) *(P-8276)*

**Metal Master Inc** ............................................................ E ...... 858 292-8880
4611 Overland Ave San Diego (92123) *(P-8504)*

**Metal Products Engineering, Vernon** *Also Called: Luppen Holdings Inc (P-8861)*

**Metal Sales, Woodland** *Also Called: Metal Sales Manufacturing Corp (P-8505)*

**Metal Sales Manufacturing Corp** ................................. E ...... 707 826-2653
1326 Paddock Pl Woodland (95776) *(P-8505)*

**Metal Supply LLC** .......................................................... D ...... 562 634-9940
11810 Center St South Gate (90280) *(P-8183)*

**Metal Surfaces Intl LLC** ................................................ C ...... 562 927-1331
6060 Shull St Bell Gardens (90201) *(P-8985)*

**Metal Tek Company** ...................................................... E ...... 661 832-6011
3801 S H St Bakersfield (93304) *(P-8184)*

**Metal Works Supply, Oroville** *Also Called: Smb Industries Inc (P-8217)*

**Metal Works Supply, Oroville** *Also Called: Smb Industries Inc (P-8218)*

**Metal-Fab Services Indust Inc** ..................................... E ...... 714 630-7771
2500 E Miraloma Way Anaheim (92806) *(P-8506)*

**Metalagraphics, Moorpark** *Also Called: Glendee Corp (P-10861)*

**Metalagraphics, Moorpark** *Also Called: Glendee Corp (P-10862)*

**Metalfx, Willits** *Also Called: Advanced Mfg & Dev Inc (P-8363)*

**Metalite Manufacturing, Pacoima** *Also Called: Hanmar LLC (P-8848)*

**Metalite Manufacturing Company** .................................................. E ...... 818 890-2802
11441 Bradley Ave Pacoima (91331) *(P-8864)*
**Metalite Mfg Companys, Pacoima** *Also Called: Metalite Manufacturing Company (P-8864)*
**Metalore Inc** .................................................................................. E ...... 310 643-0360
750 S Douglas St El Segundo (90245) *(P-10974)*
**Metals Direct Inc** .......................................................................... E ...... 530 605-1931
6771 Eastside Rd Redding (96001) *(P-8507)*
**Metals USA, Brea** *Also Called: Metals USA Building Pdts LP (P-7759)*
**Metals USA Building Pdts LP (DH)** ............................................. A ...... 713 946-9000
955 Columbia St Brea (92821) *(P-7759)*
**Metals USA Building Pdts LP** ..................................................... D ...... 800 325-1305
1951 S Parco Ave Ste C Ontario (91761) *(P-7760)*
**Metals USA Building Pdts LP** ..................................................... C ...... 714 522-7852
6450 Caballero Blvd Ste A Buena Park (90620) *(P-8185)*
**Metalset Inc** ................................................................................. E ...... 510 233-9998
1200 Hensley St Richmond (94801) *(P-8186)*
**Metarom USA Inc** ....................................................................... E ...... 619 449-0299
1725 Gillespie Way Ste 101 El Cajon (92020) *(P-2015)*
**Metcal, Cypress** *Also Called: OK International Inc (P-9728)*
**Metco Fourslide Manufacturing, Gardena** *Also Called: Metco Manufacturing Inc (P-8865)*
**Metco Manufacturing Inc** ............................................................ E ...... 310 516-6547
17540 S Denver Ave Gardena (90248) *(P-8865)*
**Metcoe Skylight Specialites, Gardena** *Also Called: Weiss Sheet Metal Company (P-518)*
**Method Home Care, San Francisco** *Also Called: Method Products Inc (P-5877)*
**Method Products Inc** .................................................................. C ...... 415 931-3947
631 Howard St Fl 5 San Francisco (94105) *(P-5877)*
**Metlsaw Systems Inc** ................................................................. E ...... 707 746-6200
2950 Bay Vista Ct Benicia (94510) *(P-9561)*
**Metra Biosystems Inc (DH)** ....................................................... E ...... 408 616-4300
2981 Copper Rd Santa Clara (95051) *(P-5762)*
**Metric Equipment Sales Inc** ....................................................... D ...... 510 264-0887
25841 Industrial Blvd Ste 200 Hayward (94545) *(P-16718)*
**Metric Machining (PA)** ............................................................... E ...... 909 947-9222
3263 Trade Center Dr Riverside (92507) *(P-10975)*
**Metric Precision, Huntington Beach** *Also Called: AMG Torrance LLC (P-13777)*
**Metric Products Inc (PA)** ........................................................... E ...... 310 815-9000
4630 Leahy St Culver City (90232) *(P-2838)*
**Metricstream Inc (PA)** ............................................................... C ...... 650 620-2955
6201 America Center Dr Ste 240 San Jose (95002) *(P-18541)*
**Metrie El & El LLC (DH)** ............................................................ F ...... 909 591-0339
9129 Remington Ave Chino (91710) *(P-3156)*
**Metro Caseworks, Fremont** *Also Called: Goldfire Corporation (P-490)*
**Metro Poly Corporation** ............................................................. E ...... 510 357-9898
1651 Aurora Dr San Leandro (94577) *(P-3972)*
**Metro Publishing Inc** .................................................................. E ...... 707 527-1200
445 Center St Healdsburg (95448) *(P-4158)*
**Metro Truck Body Inc** ................................................................. E ...... 310 532-5570
240 Citation Cir Corona (92878) *(P-19147)*
**Metromedia Technologies Inc** .................................................... E ...... 818 552-6500
311 Parkside Dr San Fernando (91340) *(P-10410)*
**Metropolitan News Company** .................................................... E ...... 951 369-5890
3540 12th St Riverside (92501) *(P-4159)*
**Metropolitan News Company, Los Angeles** *Also Called: Grace Communications Inc (P-4123)*
**Metrosa, Healdsburg** *Also Called: Metro Publishing Inc (P-4158)*
**Metrotech Corporation (PA)** ...................................................... D ...... 408 734-3880
3251 Olcott St Santa Clara (95054) *(P-14221)*
**Mettler Electronics Corp** ............................................................ E ...... 714 533-2221
1333 S Claudina St Anaheim (92805) *(P-15187)*
**Mettler-Toledo Rainin LLC (HQ)** ............................................... C ...... 510 564-1600
7500 Edgewater Dr Oakland (94621) *(P-14899)*
**Meus, Cypress** *Also Called: Mitsubishi Electric Us Inc (P-16721)*
**Mevsa, Cypress** *Also Called: Mitsubshi Elc Vsual Sltons AME (P-13039)*
**Mexapparel Inc (PA)** ................................................................. E ...... 323 364-8600
2344 E 38th St Vernon (90058) *(P-2599)*
**Mexi, Santa Cruz** *Also Called: Seltzer Revolutions Inc (P-1844)*
**Meyco Machine and Tool Inc** .................................................... E ...... 714 435-1546
11579 Martens River Cir Fountain Valley (92708) *(P-9683)*
**Meyenburg Goat Milk Products, Turlock** *Also Called: Jackson-Mitchell Inc (P-840)*
**Meyer & Reeder Inc** .................................................................. F ...... 714 388-0146
2800 S Main St Ste I Santa Ana (92707) *(P-3255)*

**Meyer Cookware Industries Inc** ................................................ E ...... 707 551-2800
1 Meyer Plz Vallejo (94590) *(P-8866)*
**Meyer Corporation US (HQ)** ..................................................... D ...... 707 551-2800
1 Meyer Plz Vallejo (94590) *(P-8867)*
**Meyer Corporation US** .............................................................. E ...... 707 399-2100
2001 Meyer Way Fairfield (94533) *(P-16430)*
**Meyer Sound Laboratories Inc (PA)** ........................................ C ...... 510 486-1166
2832 San Pablo Ave Berkeley (94702) *(P-11677)*
**Meyer Sound Labs, Berkeley** *Also Called: Meyer Sound Laboratories Inc (P-11677)*
**Meyer Wines, Vallejo** *Also Called: Meyer Corporation US (P-8867)*
**Meza Pallets Inc** ........................................................................ F ...... 909 829-0223
14619 Merrill Ave Fontana (92335) *(P-3350)*
**Meziere Enterprises Inc** ............................................................ E ...... 800 208-1755
220 S Hale Ave Ste A Escondido (92029) *(P-10976)*
**Mezzetta, American Canyon** *Also Called: G L Mezzetta Inc (P-890)*
**Mf Inc** ......................................................................................... C ...... 213 627-2498
2010 E 15th St Los Angeles (90021) *(P-2680)*
**Mfb Liquidation Inc** ................................................................... E ...... 760 448-1940
6195 El Camino Real Carlsbad (92009) *(P-1359)*
**Mfb Worldwide Inc (PA)** ........................................................... F ...... 323 562-2339
4901 Patata St Ste 201-204 Cudahy (90201) *(P-2549)*
**Mfi Construction Inc** ................................................................. E ...... 626 565-2015
417 E San Bernardino Rd Covina (91723) *(P-497)*
**Mflex, Irvine** *Also Called: Multi-Fineline Electronix Inc (P-12167)*
**Mflex Delaware Inc** ................................................................... A ...... 949 453-6800
101 Academy Ste 250 Irvine (92617) *(P-12164)*
**Mgl, Anaheim** *Also Called: Michael Gerald Ltd (P-17077)*
**MGM Brakes** .............................................................................. D ...... 707 894-3333
1184 S Cloverdale Blvd Cloverdale (95425) *(P-13538)*
**MGM Drywall Inc** ....................................................................... D ...... 408 292-4085
1050 Commercial St Ste 102 San Jose (95112) *(P-478)*
**MGM Transformer Co** ............................................................... D ...... 323 726-0888
5701 Smithway St Commerce (90040) *(P-11217)*
**Mgr Design International Inc** .................................................... C ...... 805 981-6400
1950 Williams Dr Oxnard (93036) *(P-16183)*
**MGT Industries Inc (PA)** .......................................................... D ...... 310 516-5900
13889 S Figueroa St Los Angeles (90061) *(P-2791)*
**MI Rancho Tortilla Factory, Elk Grove** *Also Called: Berber Food Manufacturing LLC (P-2137)*
**MI Technologies Inc** .................................................................. A ...... 619 710-2637
2215 Paseo De Las Americas Ste 30 San Diego (92154) *(P-6913)*
**Mi9, Pleasanton** *Also Called: Software Development Inc (P-18806)*
**Miasole** ...................................................................................... B ...... 408 919-5700
2590 Walsh Ave Santa Clara (95051) *(P-12559)*
**Miasole, Santa Clara** *Also Called: Miasole Hi-Tech Corp (P-12560)*
**Miasole Hi-Tech Corp (DH)** ...................................................... C ...... 408 919-5700
3211 Scott Blvd Ste 201 Santa Clara (95054) *(P-12560)*
**Michael and Company, Lockeford** *Also Called: Woodside Investment Inc (P-9305)*
**Michael Gerald Ltd** .................................................................... E ...... 562 921-9611
7051 E Avenida De Santiago Anaheim (92807) *(P-17077)*
**Michael Telfer (PA)** ................................................................... D ...... 925 228-1515
211 Foster St Martinez (94553) *(P-376)*
**Michel-Schlumberger, Healdsburg** *Also Called: Kssm LLC (P-1651)*
**Michelsen Packaging California, Fresno** *Also Called: Michelsen Packaging Co Cal (P-3930)*
**Michelsen Packaging Co Cal** ................................................... E ...... 559 237-3819
4165 S Cherry Ave Fresno (93706) *(P-3930)*
**Micrel Incorporated** ................................................................... A ...... 408 944-0800
2180 Fortune Dr San Jose (95131) *(P-12561)*
**Micrel LLC** ................................................................................. A ...... 408 944-0800
1849 Fortune Dr San Jose (95131) *(P-12562)*
**Micrel LLC** ................................................................................. B ...... 408 944-0800
1931 Fortune Dr San Jose (95131) *(P-12563)*
**Micrel LLC** ................................................................................. A ...... 408 944-0800
2180 Fortune Dr San Jose (95131) *(P-12564)*
**Micrel Semiconductor, San Jose** *Also Called: Micrel Incorporated (P-12561)*
**Micrel Semiconductor, San Jose** *Also Called: Micrel LLC (P-12562)*
**Micro Analog Inc** ....................................................................... C ...... 909 392-8277
1861 Puddingstone Dr La Verne (91750) *(P-12565)*
**Micro Connectors Inc** ............................................................... E ...... 510 266-0299
2700 Mccone Ave Hayward (94545) *(P-10411)*
**Micro Focus, Menlo Park** *Also Called: Micro Focus (us) Inc (P-18542)*

## ALPHABETIC SECTION

**Micro Focus, Pleasanton** *Also Called: Micro Focus LLC (P-18543)*
**Micro Focus (us) Inc (DH)** .................................................. D ...... 301 838-5000
2440 Sand Hill Rd Ste 302 Menlo Park (94025) *(P-18542)*
**Micro Focus LLC** ........................................................... D ...... 925 784-3242
6701 Koll Center Pkwy # 300 Pleasanton (94566) *(P-18543)*
**Micro Lambda Wireless Inc** ........................................ E ...... 510 770-9221
46515 Landing Pkwy Fremont (94538) *(P-13035)*
**Micro Lithography Inc** ............................................... C ...... 408 747-1769
1247 Elko Dr Sunnyvale (94089) *(P-14433)*
**Micro Matrix Systems** ............................................... E ...... 909 626-8544
1899 Salem Ct Claremont (91711) *(P-8868)*
**Micro Space Products, Hawthorne** *Also Called: K & E Inc (P-13883)*
**Micro Steel Inc** ........................................................ E ...... 818 348-8701
7850 Alabama Ave Canoga Park (91304) *(P-14115)*
**Micro Surface Engr Inc (PA)** ..................................... E ...... 323 582-7348
1550 E Slauson Ave Los Angeles (90011) *(P-7908)*
**Micro Tech Systems, Milpitas** *Also Called: Mt Systems Inc (P-9880)*
**Micro Therapeutics Inc (HQ)** .................................... E ...... 949 837-3700
9775 Toledo Way Irvine (92618) *(P-15188)*
**Micro Tool & Manufacturing Inc** ............................... E ...... 619 582-2884
6494 Federal Blvd Lemon Grove (91945) *(P-9684)*
**Micro-Mechanics Inc** ................................................ E ...... 408 779-2927
465 Woodview Ave Morgan Hill (95037) *(P-16719)*
**Micro-Mode Products Inc** ........................................ C ...... 619 449-3844
1870 John Towers Ave El Cajon (92020) *(P-11890)*
**Micro-TEC, Chatsworth** *Also Called: Wallace E Miller Inc (P-11182)*
**Micro-Vu, Windsor** *Also Called: Micro-Vu Corp California (P-14800)*
**Micro-Vu Corp California (PA)** .................................. D ...... 707 838-6272
7909 Conde Ln Windsor (95492) *(P-14800)*
**Micro/Sys Inc** .......................................................... E ...... 818 244-4600
158 W Pomona Ave Monrovia (91016) *(P-10183)*
**Microblend Inc** ........................................................ E ...... 330 998-4602
543 Country Club Dr Simi Valley (93065) *(P-6095)*
**Microblend Technologies, Simi Valley** *Also Called: Microblend Inc (P-6095)*
**Microchip Technology** .............................................. E ...... 408 474-3640
1931 Fortune Dr San Jose (95131) *(P-12566)*
**Microchip Technology Inc** ........................................ E ...... 408 735-9110
450 Holger Way San Jose (95134) *(P-12567)*
**Microcool** ................................................................. F ...... 760 322-1111
72216 Northshore St Ste 103 Thousand Palms (92276) *(P-14434)*
**Microcosm Inc** ......................................................... E ...... 310 539-2306
3111 Lomita Blvd Torrance (90505) *(P-14102)*
**Microdental Laboratories, Livermore** *Also Called: Microdental Laboratories Inc (P-15468)*
**Microdental Laboratories Inc** ................................... E ...... 800 229-0936
7475 Southfront Rd Livermore (94551) *(P-15468)*
**Microfab Manufacturing Inc** ..................................... F ...... 760 744-7240
220 Distribution St San Marcos (92078) *(P-8508)*
**Microfab Mfg Shtmtl Pdts, San Marcos** *Also Called: Microfab Manufacturing Inc (P-8508)*
**Microfabrica Inc** ...................................................... E ...... 888 964-2763
7911 Haskell Ave Van Nuys (91406) *(P-13036)*
**Microform Precision LLC** ......................................... D ...... 916 419-0580
4244 S Market Ct Ste A Sacramento (95834) *(P-8509)*
**Microgenics Corporation (HQ)** ................................. C ...... 510 979-9147
46500 Kato Rd Fremont (94538) *(P-14690)*
**Microgenics Corporation** ......................................... A ...... 510 979-5000
44660 Osgood Rd Fremont (94539) *(P-14691)*
**Microland Electronics Corp (PA)** .............................. E ...... 408 441-1688
1883 Ringwood Ave San Jose (95131) *(P-16532)*
**Microlease, Hayward** *Also Called: Metric Equipment Sales Inc (P-16718)*
**Micrometals Inc (PA)** ............................................... C ...... 714 970-9400
5615 E La Palma Ave Anaheim (92807) *(P-13037)*
**Micromold Inc** .......................................................... F ...... 951 684-7130
2100 Iowa Ave Riverside (92507) *(P-6914)*
**Micron Instruments, Simi Valley** *Also Called: Piezo-Metrics Inc (P-12632)*
**Micron Machine Company** ....................................... E ...... 858 486-5900
3337 Highway 67 Ramona (92065) *(P-10977)*
**Micron Technology Inc** ............................................ C ...... 916 458-3003
2235 Iron Point Rd Folsom (95630) *(P-12568)*
**Micronova Manufacturing Inc** .................................. E ...... 310 784-6990
3431 Lomita Blvd Torrance (90505) *(P-2939)*

**Microphor Inc** ........................................................... E ...... 707 459-5563
452 E Hill Rd Willits (95490) *(P-7278)*
**Microplate, Inglewood** *Also Called: Multichrome Company Inc (P-8987)*
**Micropoint Bioscience Inc** ....................................... E ...... 408 588-1682
3521 Leonard Ct Santa Clara (95054) *(P-5763)*
**Microsemi, Garden Grove** *Also Called: Microsemi Corporation (P-12576)*
**Microsemi Communications Inc (DH)** ...................... D ...... 805 388-3700
4721 Calle Carga Camarillo (93012) *(P-12569)*
**Microsemi Corp - Anlog Mxed Sg** ............................ A ...... 408 643-6000
3850 N 1st St San Jose (95134) *(P-12570)*
**Microsemi Corp - Anlog Mxed Sg (DH)** .................... D ...... 714 898-8121
11861 Western Ave Garden Grove (92841) *(P-12571)*
**Microsemi Corp - Santa Ana, Garden Grove** *Also Called: Microsemi Corporation (P-12573)*
**Microsemi Corp- Rf Integrated** ................................. F ...... 408 954-8314
3870 N 1st St San Jose (95134) *(P-12572)*
**Microsemi Corp-Power MGT Group** ......................... C ...... 714 994-6500
11861 Western Ave Garden Grove (92841) *(P-11333)*
**Microsemi Corporation** ............................................ C ...... 714 898-7112
11861 Western Ave Garden Grove (92841) *(P-12573)*
**Microsemi Corporation** ............................................ E ...... 408 643-6000
3850 N 1st St San Jose (95134) *(P-12574)*
**Microsemi Corporation** ............................................ C ...... 650 318-4200
3870 N 1st St San Jose (95134) *(P-12575)*
**Microsemi Corporation (HQ)** .................................... E ...... 949 380-6100
11861 Western Ave Garden Grove (92841) *(P-12576)*
**Microsemi Crp- Rf Intgrted Slt (DH)** .......................... C ...... 916 850-8640
105 Lake Forest Way Folsom (95630) *(P-12577)*
**Microsemi Frequency Time Corp (DH)** ..................... C ...... 480 792-7200
3870 N 1st St San Jose (95134) *(P-11334)*
**Microsemi Frequency Time Corp** ............................. D ...... 408 433-0910
2300 Orchard Pkwy San Jose (95131) *(P-12578)*
**Microsemi Rfis, Folsom** *Also Called: Microsemi Crp- Rf Intgrted Slt (P-12577)*
**Microsemi Soc Corp (DH)** ........................................ D ...... 408 643-6000
3850 N 1st St San Jose (95134) *(P-12579)*
**Microsemi Soc Corp** ................................................ C ...... 650 318-4200
2051 Stierlin Ct Mountain View (94043) *(P-12580)*
**Microsemi Stor Solutions Inc (DH)** .......................... D ...... 408 239-8000
1380 Bordeaux Dr Sunnyvale (94089) *(P-12581)*
**Microsemi Stor Solutions Inc** .................................. E ...... 916 788-3300
101 Creekside Ridge Ct Ste 100 Roseville (95678) *(P-12582)*
**Microsoft, Irvine** *Also Called: Microsoft Corporation (P-18544)*
**Microsoft Corporation** ............................................. E ...... 949 263-3000
3 Park Plz Ste 1800 Irvine (92614) *(P-18544)*
**Micross HI Rel Pwr Sltions Inc** ................................ C ...... 408 434-5000
2520 Junction Ave San Jose (95134) *(P-12583)*
**Micross Holdings Inc** ............................................... D ...... 215 997-3200
11150 Santa Monica Blvd Ste 750 Los Angeles (90025) *(P-12584)*
**Microtech Systems Inc** ............................................ F ...... 650 596-1900
1336 Brommer St Santa Cruz (95062) *(P-13198)*
**Microvention Inc (DH)** ............................................. C ...... 714 258-8000
35 Enterprise Aliso Viejo (92656) *(P-15189)*
**Microvention Terumo, Aliso Viejo** *Also Called: Microvention Inc (P-15189)*
**Microwave Applications Group** ............................... E ...... 805 928-5711
3030 Industrial Pkwy Santa Maria (93455) *(P-19405)*
**Microwave Dynamics LLC** ....................................... F ...... 949 679-7788
16541 Scientific Irvine (92618) *(P-11891)*
**Microwave Power Products Inc** ............................... B ...... 650 846-2900
811 Hansen Way Palo Alto (94304) *(P-12035)*
**Microwave Power Products Div, Palo Alto** *Also Called: Communications & Pwr Inds LLC (P-11833)*
**Microwave Technology Inc (HQ)** .............................. E ...... 510 651-6700
4268 Solar Way Fremont (94538) *(P-13038)*
**Micrus Endovascular LLC (HQ)** ............................... C ...... 408 433-1400
821 Fox Ln San Jose (95131) *(P-15190)*
**Mid Labs, San Leandro** *Also Called: Medical Instr Dev Labs Inc (P-15167)*
**Mid Valley Dairy, Turlock** *Also Called: Super Store Industries (P-816)*
**Mid-State Concrete Pdts Inc** ................................... E ...... 805 928-2855
1625 E Donovan Rd Ste C Santa Maria (93454) *(P-7356)*
**Mid-West Fabricating Co** ........................................ E ...... 562 698-9615
8623 Dice Rd Santa Fe Springs (90670) *(P-13539)*
**Mid-West Wholesale Hardware Co** ......................... E ...... 714 630-4751
1641 S Sunkist St Anaheim (92806) *(P-8016)*

## ALPHABETIC SECTION

**Midland Tractor Company** .................................................. D ...... 559 674-8757
1901 W Cleveland Ave Madera (93637) *(P-9370)*

**Midnight Manufacturing LLC** .............................................. E ...... 714 833-6130
2535 Conejo Spectrum St Bldg 4 Thousand Oaks (91320) *(P-5248)*

**Midnight Oil Agency LLC** ................................................... B ...... 818 295-6100
3800 W Vanowen St Ste 101 Burbank (91505) *(P-4694)*

**Midnight Oil Agency, Inc., Burbank** *Also Called: Midnight Oil Agency LLC (P-4694)*

**Midstream Energy Partners USA** ........................................ E ...... 661 765-4087
9224 Tupman Rd Tupman (93276) *(P-115)*

**Midthrust, Los Angeles** *Also Called: Midthrust Imports Inc (P-2485)*

**Midthrust Imports Inc** ........................................................ E ...... 213 749-6651
830 E 14th Pl Los Angeles (90021) *(P-2485)*

**Midway Games West Inc** ................................................... C ...... 408 434-3700
675 Sycamore Dr Milpitas (95035) *(P-16184)*

**Mighty Green, Costa Mesa** *Also Called: Inveco Inc (P-8975)*

**Mikada Cabinets, Los Angeles** *Also Called: Mikada Cabinets LLC (P-3256)*

**Mikada Cabinets LLC** ......................................................... D ...... 713 681-6116
11777 San Vicente Blvd Los Angeles (90049) *(P-3256)*

**Mikawaya, Vernon** *Also Called: Mochi Ice Cream Company LLC (P-1228)*

**Mike Dyell Machine Shop Inc (PA)** ..................................... F ...... 909 350-4101
160 S Linden Ave Rialto (92376) *(P-10978)*

**Mike Jensen Farms LLC** .................................................... C ...... 559 897-4192
13138 S Bethel Ave Kingsburg (93631) *(P-43)*

**Mike Kenney Tool Inc** ........................................................ E ...... 714 577-9262
588 Porter Way Placentia (92870) *(P-10979)*

**Mike Murach & Associates Inc** .......................................... E ...... 559 440-9071
3730 W Swift Ave Fresno (93722) *(P-4336)*

**Mike Russ School, San Diego** *Also Called: Russ Mike Financial Training (P-17738)*

**Mikelson Machine Shop Inc** .............................................. E ...... 626 448-3920
2546 Merced Ave South El Monte (91733) *(P-10980)*

**Mikes Metal Works Inc** ..................................................... F ...... 619 440-8804
3552 Fowler Canyon Rd Jamul (91935) *(P-8187)*

**Mikes Sheet Metal Pdts Inc** .............................................. E ...... 916 348-3800
3315 Elkhorn Blvd North Highlands (95660) *(P-8510)*

**Mikhail Darafeev Inc (PA)** ................................................. E ...... 909 613-1818
5075 Edison Ave Chino (91710) *(P-3449)*

**Mil-Spec Magnetics Inc** ..................................................... D ...... 909 598-8116
169 Pacific St Pomona (91768) *(P-12849)*

**Mila Usa Inc** ...................................................................... E ...... 540 206-4306
1 Belvedere Pl Ste 200 Mill Valley (94941) *(P-11409)*

**Milco Waterjet, Huntington Beach** *Also Called: Milco Wire Edm Inc (P-10981)*

**Milco Wire Edm Inc** ........................................................... F ...... 714 373-0098
15221 Connector Ln Huntington Beach (92649) *(P-10981)*

**Mileiq Inc** .......................................................................... D ...... 415 528-7722
548 Market St San Francisco (94104) *(P-18545)*

**Milestone Holdco Inc** ........................................................ A ...... 650 376-2300
901 Mariners Island Blvd San Mateo (94404) *(P-17747)*

**Milgard Manufacturing LLC** ............................................... B ...... 480 763-6000
26879 Diaz Rd Temecula (92590) *(P-6915)*

**Milgard Manufacturing LLC** ............................................... C ...... 805 581-6325
355 E Easy St Simi Valley (93065) *(P-7234)*

**Milgard Windows, Temecula** *Also Called: Milgard Manufacturing LLC (P-6915)*

**Milgard-Simi Valley, Simi Valley** *Also Called: Milgard Manufacturing LLC (P-7234)*

**Military Advantage Inc** ..................................................... E ...... 530 788-0221
17600 25th St Bldg 2434 Beale Afb (95903) *(P-2561)*

**Military Aircraft Parts (PA)** ................................................ E ...... 916 635-8010
116 Oxburough Dr Folsom (95630) *(P-13910)*

**Milk Specialties Company** ................................................. E ...... 559 732-1220
715 N Divisadero St Visalia (93291) *(P-5555)*

**Mill Industries Inc** ............................................................. D ...... 415 862-4394
950 Elm Ave Ste 200 San Bruno (94066) *(P-11410)*

**Mill Yard, Arcata** *Also Called: Bracut International Corp (P-17323)*

**Millcraft Inc** ....................................................................... D ...... 714 632-9621
2850 E White Star Ave Anaheim (92806) *(P-3157)*

**Millennial Brands LLC** ....................................................... E ...... 925 230-0617
126 W 9th St Los Angeles (90015) *(P-7117)*

**Millennium Metalcraft Inc** ................................................ E ...... 510 657-4700
3201 Osgood Cmn Fremont (94539) *(P-8511)*

**Millennium Space Systems Inc (HQ)** ................................. E ...... 310 683-5840
2265 E El Segundo Blvd El Segundo (90245) *(P-11892)*

**Millenworks** ...................................................................... D ...... 714 426-5500
1361 Valencia Ave Tustin (92780) *(P-13371)*

**Miller Brewing Co** ............................................................. F ...... 626 353-1604
15801 1st St Irwindale (91706) *(P-1448)*

**Miller Castings Inc (PA)** .................................................... B ...... 562 695-0461
2503 Pacific Park Dr Whittier (90601) *(P-7691)*

**Miller Castings Inc** ............................................................ E ...... 562 695-0461
12245 Coast Dr Whittier (90601) *(P-10982)*

**Miller Cnc, Chula Vista** *Also Called: Miller Machine Works LLC (P-10983)*

**Miller Gasket Co, San Fernando** *Also Called: J Miller Co Inc (P-6455)*

**Miller Hot Dogs, Lodi** *Also Called: Miller Packing Company (P-653)*

**Miller Machine Works LLC** ................................................ F ...... 619 501-9866
789 Anita St Chula Vista (91911) *(P-10983)*

**Miller Marine** .................................................................... E ...... 619 791-1500
2275 Manya St San Diego (92154) *(P-14010)*

**Miller Packing Company** ................................................... E ...... 209 339-2310
1122 Industrial Way Lodi (95240) *(P-653)*

**Miller Products Inc** ........................................................... D ...... 209 467-2470
2315 Station Dr Stockton (95215) *(P-3952)*

**Miller Woodworking Inc** ................................................... E ...... 310 257-6806
1429 259th St Harbor City (90710) *(P-3158)*

**Millers Fab & Weld Corp** ................................................... E ...... 951 359-3100
6100 Industrial Ave Riverside (92504) *(P-8188)*

**Millers Woodworking, Tustin** *Also Called: GL Woodworking Inc (P-3139)*

**Million Corporation** ........................................................... D ...... 626 969-1888
1300 W Optical Dr Ste 600 Irwindale (91702) *(P-4923)*

**Millipart Inc (PA)** ............................................................... F ...... 626 963-4101
412 W Carter Dr Glendora (91740) *(P-10984)*

**Mills Acquisition Corporation** ........................................... E
1035 22nd Ave Oakland (94606) *(P-8512)*

**Millwood Cabinet Co Inc** .................................................. F ...... 661 327-0371
2321 Virginia Ave Bakersfield (93307) *(P-3257)*

**Millwork Company Inc** ..................................................... F ...... 760 788-1533
607 Brazos St Ste C Ramona (92065) *(P-3159)*

**Millwork Div, Oroville** *Also Called: Setzer Forest Products Inc (P-3080)*

**Millworks Etc Inc** .............................................................. E ...... 805 499-3400
2230 Statham Blvd Ste 100 Oxnard (93033) *(P-8277)*

**Millworks By Design Inc** ................................................... D ...... 818 597-1326
4525 Runway St Simi Valley (93063) *(P-3160)*

**Millworx, Corona** *Also Called: Millworx Prcsion Machining Inc (P-10985)*

**Millworx Prcsion Machining Inc** ........................................ E ...... 951 371-2683
506 Malloy Ct Corona (92878) *(P-10985)*

**Milodon Incorporated** ...................................................... E ...... 805 577-5950
2250 Agate Ct Simi Valley (93065) *(P-13540)*

**Milpitas Materials Company** ............................................. E ...... 650 969-4401
1125 N Milpitas Blvd Milpitas (95035) *(P-16477)*

**Milwaukee Hand Truck, Los Angeles** *Also Called: Gleason Industrial Pdts Inc (P-9519)*

**Min-E-Con LLC** .................................................................. D ...... 949 250-0087
17312 Eastman Irvine (92614) *(P-12890)*

**Mina-Tree Signs Incorporated (PA)** ................................... E ...... 209 941-2921
1233 E Ronald St Stockton (95205) *(P-16009)*

**Minaloas Inc** ..................................................................... E ...... 949 951-7191
2358 E Walnut Ave Fullerton (92831) *(P-4695)*

**Minaris Medical America Inc** ............................................ C ...... 650 961-5501
630 Clyde Ct Mountain View (94043) *(P-19328)*

**Mindbody, San Luis Obispo** *Also Called: Mindbody Inc (P-19011)*

**Mindbody Inc (PA)** ............................................................ C ...... 877 755-4279
651 Tank Farm Rd San Luis Obispo (93401) *(P-19011)*

**Mindera Corp** .................................................................... E ...... 858 810-6070
1221 Liberty Way Vista (92081) *(P-5849)*

**Mindful Meats, Petaluma** *Also Called: Marin Sun Farms Inc (P-606)*

**Mindray Ds Usa Inc** .......................................................... A ...... 650 230-2800
2100 Gold St San Jose (95002) *(P-5764)*

**Mindray Innvtion Ctr Slcon Vly, San Jose** *Also Called: Mindray Ds Usa Inc (P-5764)*

**Mindrum Precision Inc** ..................................................... E ...... 909 989-1728
10000 4th St Rancho Cucamonga (91730) *(P-14482)*

**Mindrum Precision Products, Rancho Cucamonga** *Also Called: Mindrum Precision Inc (P-14482)*

**Mindshare Design Inc** ...................................................... E ...... 510 904-6900
475 14th St Ste 250 Oakland (94612) *(P-17949)*

Mindshow Inc .................................................................................. D ...... 213 531-0277
  811 W 7th St Ste 500 Los Angeles (90017) *(P-18546)*
Mindsnacks Inc .................................................................................. E ...... 415 875-9817
  1390 Market St Ste 200 San Francisco (94102) *(P-18547)*
Mindsource Inc .................................................................................. D ...... 650 314-6400
  995 Montague Expy Ste 121 Milpitas (95035) *(P-17950)*
Mindspeed Technologies LLC (HQ) .................................................. D ...... 949 579-3000
  4000 Macarthur Blvd Newport Beach (92660) *(P-12585)*
Mindtickle Inc (PA) ............................................................................. E ...... 973 400-1717
  535 Mission St Fl 14 San Francisco (94105) *(P-18548)*
Mineral Earth Sciences LLC .............................................................. D ...... 650 532-9590
  100 Mayfield Ave Mountain View (94043) *(P-9371)*
Minerva, Santa Clara *Also Called: Minerva Surgical Inc (P-15191)*
Minerva Surgical Inc .......................................................................... C ...... 855 646-7874
  4255 Burton Dr Santa Clara (95054) *(P-15191)*
Minh Phung Incorporated .................................................................. E ...... 714 379-0606
  15216 Weststate St Westminster (92683) *(P-17196)*
Minimatics Inc (PA) ............................................................................ E ...... 650 969-5630
  15500 Concord Cir Morgan Hill (95037) *(P-16720)*
Minnesota Premier Publications, Sebastopol *Also Called: Southwest Journal Inc (P-4199)*
Minorities & Success, Torrance *Also Called: Minority Success Pubg Group (P-4278)*
Minority Success Pubg Group ........................................................... E ...... 310 736-2462
  23505 Crenshaw Blvd Torrance (90505) *(P-4278)*
Minsley Inc ......................................................................................... E ...... 909 458-1100
  989 S Monterey Ave Ontario (91761) *(P-2280)*
Minson Corporation ........................................................................... B ...... 323 513-1041
  11701 Wilshire Blvd Ste 15a Los Angeles (90025) *(P-3483)*
Mint Grips, Benicia *Also Called: Gibbs Plastic & Rubber LLC (P-6496)*
Mint Software Inc .............................................................................. D ...... 650 944-6000
  280 Hope St Mountain View (94041) *(P-18549)*
Minton Door Company (PA) .............................................................. E ...... 650 961-9800
  1150 Elko Dr Sunnyvale (94089) *(P-16453)*
Minturn Nut Co Inc ............................................................................ E ...... 559 665-8500
  8800 Minturn Rd Le Grand (95333) *(P-17405)*
Minus K Technology Inc ................................................................... C ...... 310 348-9656
  460 Hindry Ave Ste C Inglewood (90301) *(P-14900)*
Mipox International Corp .................................................................. E ...... 650 638-9830
  1065 E Hillsdale Blvd Ste 401 Foster City (94404) *(P-7556)*
Mir Group Inc .................................................................................... E ...... 408 432-1000
  2200 Zanker Rd Ste B San Jose (95131) *(P-7235)*
Mir Mosaic, San Jose *Also Called: Mir Group Inc (P-7235)*
Miracle Greens Inc ........................................................................... F ...... 800 521-5867
  8477 Steller Dr Culver City (90232) *(P-768)*
Miradry, Irvine *Also Called: Mist Inc (P-15383)*
Miradry Inc ........................................................................................ D ...... 408 579-8700
  2790 Walsh Ave Santa Clara (95051) *(P-15559)*
Mirama Enterprises Inc ..................................................................... D ...... 858 587-8866
  6469 Flanders Dr San Diego (92121) *(P-11392)*
Miramar Plant 33, San Diego *Also Called: Robertsons Ready Mix Ltd (P-7492)*
Mirantis Inc (PA) ................................................................................ F ...... 650 963-9828
  900 E Hamilton Ave Ste 650 Campbell (95008) *(P-18986)*
Mirapoint Software Inc ...................................................................... D ...... 650 286-7200
  1600 Seaport Blvd Ste 400 Redwood City (94063) *(P-11893)*
Mirion Technologies (us) Inc (HQ) .................................................... C ...... 925 543-0800
  3000 Executive Pkwy Ste 518 San Ramon (94583) *(P-14901)*
MIRUM, Foster City *Also Called: Mirum Pharmaceuticals Inc (P-5556)*
Mirum Pharmaceuticals Inc (PA) ...................................................... C ...... 650 667-4085
  989 E Hillsdale Blvd Ste 300 Foster City (94404) *(P-5556)*
Mismo, Oakland *Also Called: Log(n) LLC (P-4428)*
Miss Cristina, Los Angeles *Also Called: Miss Kim Inc (P-2711)*
Miss Kim Inc ..................................................................................... F ...... 213 741-0888
  363 Patton St Apt 3 Los Angeles (90026) *(P-2711)*
Mission AG Resources LLC ............................................................. E ...... 559 591-3333
  6801 Avenue 430 Unit A Reedley (93654) *(P-769)*
Mission Bell Mfg Co Inc ................................................................... B ...... 408 778-2036
  16100 Jacqueline Ct Morgan Hill (95037) *(P-498)*
Mission Brewery Inc ........................................................................ E ...... 619 818-7451
  1441 L St San Diego (92101) *(P-17622)*
Mission Concrete Products, Gilroy *Also Called: Quinn Development Co (P-7297)*
Mission Crtical Composites LLC ...................................................... E ...... 714 831-2100
  15400 Graham St Ste 102 Huntington Beach (92649) *(P-13911)*

Mission Flavors Fragrances Inc ....................................................... F ...... 949 461-3344
  25882 Wright El Toro (92610) *(P-2016)*
Mission Foods, Commerce *Also Called: Gruma Corporation (P-2094)*
Mission Foods, Rancho Cucamonga *Also Called: Gruma Corporation (P-2095)*
Mission Foods, Fresno *Also Called: Gruma Corporation (P-2224)*
Mission Hockey Company (PA) ....................................................... F ...... 949 585-9390
  12 Goodyear Ste 100 Irvine (92618) *(P-15841)*
Mission Kleensweep Prod Inc ......................................................... D ...... 323 223-1405
  13644 Live Oak Ln Baldwin Park (91706) *(P-5878)*
Mission Laboratories, Baldwin Park *Also Called: Mission Kleensweep Prod Inc (P-5878)*
Mission Microwave Tech LLC (PA) .................................................. D ...... 951 893-4925
  6060 Phyllis Dr Cypress (90630) *(P-11894)*
Mission Park Hotel LP ..................................................................... E ...... 408 809-3838
  1950 Wyatt Dr Santa Clara (95054) *(P-5102)*
Mission Plastics Inc ........................................................................ C ...... 909 947-7287
  1930 S Parco Ave Ontario (91761) *(P-6916)*
Mission Ready Mix, Ventura *Also Called: Lynch Ready Mix Concrete Co (P-7468)*
Mission Rubber Co, Corona *Also Called: MCP Industries Inc (P-6512)*
Mission Rubber Company LLC ....................................................... D ...... 951 736-1313
  1660 Leeson Ln Corona (92879) *(P-9188)*
Mission Tool and Mfg Co Inc .......................................................... E ...... 510 782-8383
  3440 Arden Rd Hayward (94545) *(P-10986)*
Mission Vly Cab / Counter Tech, Poway *Also Called: B Young Enterprises Inc (P-3218)*
Mist Inc ............................................................................................ C ...... 408 940-8700
  3333 Michelson Dr Ste 650 Irvine (92612) *(P-15383)*
Mistic Products, Los Angeles *Also Called: Brybradan Inc (P-16101)*
Misto Lino ........................................................................................ F ...... 925 284-6565
  3585 Mt Diablo Blvd Lafayette (94549) *(P-2550)*
Misyd Corp (PA) ............................................................................... D ...... 213 742-1800
  30 Fremont Pl Los Angeles (90005) *(P-2857)*
Mitac Information Systems Corp .................................................... E ...... 510 668-3507
  44131 Nobel Dr Fremont (94538) *(P-10184)*
Mitac Information Systems Corp (DH) ........................................... C ...... 510 284-3000
  39889 Eureka Dr Newark (94560) *(P-10254)*
Mitchell Fabrication ......................................................................... E ...... 909 590-0393
  4564 Mission Blvd Montclair (91763) *(P-8189)*
Mitchell Instruments, Vista *Also Called: Mitchell Instruments Co Inc (P-14902)*
Mitchell Instruments Co Inc ........................................................... F ...... 760 744-2690
  2875 Scott St Ste 101 Vista (92081) *(P-14902)*
Mitchell Processing LLC ................................................................. E ...... 909 519-5759
  2778 Pomona Blvd Pomona (91768) *(P-6513)*
Mitchell Repair Info Co LLC (HQ) ................................................... E ...... 858 391-5000
  16067 Babcock St San Diego (92127) *(P-4432)*
Mitchell Rubber Products LLC (PA) ................................................ C ...... 951 681-5655
  1880 Iowa Ave Ste 400 Riverside (92507) *(P-6514)*
Mitchell1, San Diego *Also Called: Mitchell Repair Info Co LLC (P-4432)*
Mitchellamazing, Montclair *Also Called: Amazing Steel Company (P-8093)*
Mitco Industries Inc (PA) ................................................................ E ...... 909 877-0800
  2235 S Vista Ave Bloomington (92316) *(P-10987)*
Mitek, San Diego *Also Called: Mitek Systems Inc (P-18550)*
Mitek Systems Inc (PA) .................................................................. D ...... 619 269-6800
  770 1st Ave Ste 425 San Diego (92101) *(P-18550)*
Mitra Chem, Mountain View *Also Called: Mitra Future Technologies Inc (P-16663)*
Mitra Future Technologies Inc ....................................................... D ...... 650 695-1245
  1245 Terra Bella Ave Mountain View (94043) *(P-16663)*
Mitratech Holdings Inc ................................................................... C ...... 323 964-0000
  5900 Wilshire Blvd Ste 1500 Los Angeles (90036) *(P-18551)*
Mitsubishi Cement Corporation ..................................................... B ...... 562 495-0600
  1150 Pier F Ave Long Beach (90802) *(P-7259)*
Mitsubishi Cement Corporation ..................................................... C ...... 760 248-7373
  5808 State Highway 18 Lucerne Valley (92356) *(P-7260)*
Mitsubishi Chemical Carbon Fiber and Composites, Inc., Irvine *Also Called: Mitsubishi Chemical Crbn Fbr (P-6237)*
Mitsubishi Chemical Crbn Fbr ....................................................... C ...... 800 929-5471
  1822 Reynolds Ave Irvine (92614) *(P-6237)*
Mitsubishi Electric Us Inc (DH) ...................................................... C ...... 714 220-2500
  5900 Katella Ave Ste A Cypress (90630) *(P-16721)*
Mitsubshi Chem Advnced Mtls In .................................................. E ...... 209 464-2701
  3837 Imperial Way Stockton (95215) *(P-5178)*
Mitsubshi Chem Crbn Fibr Cmpst (DH) ......................................... C ...... 916 386-1733
  5900 88th St Sacramento (95828) *(P-11300)*

**Mitsubshi Elc Vsual Sltons AME** ............................................................ C ...... 800 553-7278
10833 Valley View St Ste 300 Cypress (90630) *(P-13039)*

**Mittera Group Inc** ............................................................................... E ...... 562 598-2446
3791 Catalina St Los Alamitos (90720) *(P-4696)*

**Mittera-CA, Los Alamitos** *Also Called: Mittera Group Inc (P-4696)*

**Mixed Nuts Inc** .................................................................................... E ...... 323 587-6887
7909 Crossway Dr Pico Rivera (90660) *(P-1360)*

**Mixel Inc** ............................................................................................... D ...... 408 436-8500
97 E Brokaw Rd Ste 250 San Jose (95112) *(P-12586)*

**Mixmode Inc** ....................................................................................... E ...... 858 225-2352
111 W Micheltorena St Ste 300-A Santa Barbara (93101) *(P-18552)*

**Mixmor Inc** .......................................................................................... F ...... 323 664-1941
3131 Casitas Ave Los Angeles (90039) *(P-9433)*

**Miyoko's Creamery, Petaluma** *Also Called: Miyokos Kitchen (P-705)*

**Miyokos Kitchen** ................................................................................ E ...... 415 521-5313
1622 Corporate Cir Petaluma (94954) *(P-705)*

**Mizari Enterprises Inc (PA)** .............................................................. E ...... 323 549-9400
5455 Wilshire Blvd Ste 1410 Los Angeles (90036) *(P-16981)*

**Mizkan America Inc** ........................................................................... D ...... 831 728-2061
46 Walker St Watsonville (95076) *(P-2281)*

**Mizkan America Inc** ........................................................................... C ...... 909 484-8743
10037 8th St Rancho Cucamonga (91730) *(P-2282)*

**Mizuho Orthopedic Systems Inc (HQ)** ............................................ E ...... 510 429-1500
30031 Ahern Ave Union City (94587) *(P-15192)*

**Mizuho Orthopedic Systems Inc** .................................................... C ...... 510 429-1500
30063 Ahern Ave Union City (94587) *(P-15193)*

**Mizuho OSI, Union City** *Also Called: Mizuho Orthopedic Systems Inc (P-15192)*

**Mj Best Videographer LLC** ............................................................... C ...... 209 208-8432
14005 S Berendo Ave Apt 3 Gardena (90247) *(P-11678)*

**Mj-Pak, Irvine** *Also Called: Plastoker Inc (P-6970)*

**Mjc America Ltd (PA)** ......................................................................... E ...... 888 876-5387
20035 E Walnut Dr N Walnut (91789) *(P-11411)*

**Mjc Engineering and Tech Inc** ......................................................... F ...... 714 890-0618
15401 Assembly Ln Huntington Beach (92649) *(P-9586)*

**Mjck Corporation** ............................................................................... F ...... 888 992-8437
3222 E Washington Blvd Vernon (90058) *(P-2478)*

**Mjw Inc** ................................................................................................. D ...... 323 778-8900
1328 W Slauson Ave Los Angeles (90044) *(P-9931)*

**Mk Davidson Inc** ................................................................................. E ...... 949 698-2963
3333 W Coast Hwy Ste 200 Newport Beach (92663) *(P-12005)*

**Mk Diamond Products Inc (PA)** ....................................................... D ...... 310 539-5221
1315 Storm Pkwy Torrance (90501) *(P-9713)*

**Mk Luxury Group, Beverly Hills** *Also Called: Maurice Kraiem & Company (P-16969)*

**Mk Magnetics Inc** ............................................................................... D ...... 760 246-6373
17030 Muskrat Ave Adelanto (92301) *(P-7647)*

**Mk Manufacturing, Irvine** *Also Called: M K Products Inc (P-9727)*

**Mk Printing, Santa Ana** *Also Called: Mekong Printing Inc (P-4692)*

**Mkm Customs, Roseville** *Also Called: Sinister Mfg Company Inc (P-13575)*

**Mks Instruments Inc** ......................................................................... E ...... 408 750-0300
3625 Peterson Way Santa Clara (95054) *(P-19270)*

**Mkt Innovations** ................................................................................. D ...... 714 524-7668
588 Porter Way Placentia (92870) *(P-10988)*

**Mkt Innovations, Placentia** *Also Called: Mike Kenney Tool Inc (P-10979)*

**ML Kishigo Mfg Co LLC** .................................................................... D ...... 949 852-1963
11250 Slater Ave Fountain Valley (92708) *(P-2906)*

**Mly Technix Corp** ............................................................................... E ...... 650 384-1456
2005 De La Cruz Blvd Ste 180 Santa Clara (95050) *(P-18553)*

**Mmb, Lodi** *Also Called: Meehleis Modular Buildings Inc (P-19432)*

**Mmi Services Inc** ............................................................................... C ...... 661 589-9366
4042 Patton Way Bakersfield (93308) *(P-251)*

**Mmi Sonora, Sonora** *Also Called: Arch Medical Solutions - Sonora LLC (P-12916)*

**Mmp Sheet Metal Inc** ......................................................................... E ...... 562 691-1055
501 Commercial Way La Habra (90631) *(P-8513)*

**MMR Technologies Inc** ..................................................................... F ...... 650 962-9620
72 Bonaventura Dr San Jose (95134) *(P-9877)*

**Mmxviii Holdings Inc** ......................................................................... E ...... 800 672-3974
20251 Sw Acacia St Ste 120 Newport Beach (92660) *(P-16010)*

**Mng Newspapers, San Jose** *Also Called: California Newspapers Partnr (P-4083)*

**Mnm Corporation (PA)** ....................................................................... E ...... 213 627-3737
110 E 9th St Ste A777 Los Angeles (90079) *(P-4279)*

**Mnm Manufacturing Inc** .................................................................... D ...... 310 898-1099
3019 E Harcourt St Compton (90221) *(P-8278)*

**Mob Scene LLC** .................................................................................. C ...... 323 648-7200
8447 Wilshire Blvd Ste 100 Beverly Hills (90211) *(P-17781)*

**Mob Scene Creative Productions, Beverly Hills** *Also Called: Mob Scene LLC (P-17781)*

**Mobile Equipment Appraisers, Bakersfield** *Also Called: Mobile Equipment Company (P-9503)*

**Mobile Equipment Company** ........................................................... E ...... 661 327-8476
3610 Gilmore Ave Bakersfield (93308) *(P-9503)*

**Mobile Modular Management Corp** ................................................ C ...... 800 819-1084
11450 Mission Blvd Jurupa Valley (91752) *(P-8676)*

**Mobility Solutions Inc (PA)** .............................................................. E ...... 858 278-0591
7895 Convoy Ct Ste 11 San Diego (92111) *(P-16585)*

**Mobilityware, Irvine** *Also Called: Upstanding LLC (P-18904)*

**Mobis, Fountain Valley** *Also Called: Mobis Parts America LLC (P-13541)*

**Mobis Parts America LLC** ................................................................ E ...... 949 450-0014
10550 Talbert Ave # 4 Fountain Valley (92708) *(P-13541)*

**Mobiveil Inc** ......................................................................................... E ...... 408 791-2977
2535 Augustine Dr Santa Clara (95054) *(P-12587)*

**Moc Products Company Inc (PA)** ................................................... D ...... 818 794-3500
12306 Montague St Pacoima (91331) *(P-6310)*

**Mocean, Newport Beach** *Also Called: Crossport Mocean (P-2559)*

**Mochi Ice Cream Company LLC (PA)** ............................................ E ...... 323 587-5504
5563 Alcoa Ave Vernon (90058) *(P-1228)*

**Mod 2, Los Angeles** *Also Called: Mod2 Inc (P-18554)*

**Mod-Electronics Inc** .......................................................................... E ...... 310 322-2136
142 Sierra St El Segundo (90245) *(P-15677)*

**Mod2 Inc** .............................................................................................. F ...... 213 747-8424
3317 S Broadway Los Angeles (90007) *(P-18554)*

**Modalai Inc** .......................................................................................... E ...... 858 247-7053
10855 Sorrento Valley Rd Ste 2 San Diego (92121) *(P-12165)*

**Modalityai Inc** ..................................................................................... F ...... 415 200-8535
149 New Montgomery St Fl 4 San Francisco (94105) *(P-18555)*

**Mode, Mountain View** *Also Called: Mode Analytics Inc (P-18556)*

**Mode Analytics Inc** ............................................................................ E ...... 415 271-7599
444 Castro St Ste 1000 Mountain View (94041) *(P-18556)*

**Model Lyfe** ........................................................................................... F ...... 224 325-5933
5405 Wilshire Blvd Los Angeles (90036) *(P-4280)*

**Model Lyfe Magazine, Los Angeles** *Also Called: Model Lyfe (P-4280)*

**Model Match Inc** ................................................................................. F ...... 949 525-9405
209 Avenida Fabricante Ste 150 San Clemente (92672) *(P-18557)*

**Modelo Group Inc** .............................................................................. E ...... 562 446-5091
16751 Millikan Ave Irvine (92606) *(P-19406)*

**Modern Aire Ventilating, North Hollywood** *Also Called: Modern-Aire Ventilating Inc (P-8514)*

**Modern Blind Factory, San Diego** *Also Called: Mbf Interiors Inc (P-2915)*

**Modern Campus USA Inc (PA)** ........................................................ D ...... 805 484-9400
1320 Flynn Rd Ste 100 Camarillo (93012) *(P-17951)*

**Modern Candle Co Inc** ....................................................................... E ...... 323 441-0104
12884 Bradley Ave Sylmar (91342) *(P-17302)*

**Modern Candles, Sylmar** *Also Called: Modern Candle Co Inc (P-17302)*

**Modern Ceramics Mfg Inc** ................................................................ E ...... 408 383-0554
2240 Lundy Ave San Jose (95131) *(P-7198)*

**Modern Concepts Inc** ........................................................................ D ...... 310 637-0013
3121 E Ana St E Rncho Dmngz (90221) *(P-6917)*

**Modern Custom Fabrication Inc** ..................................................... E ...... 559 264-4741
4922 E Jensen Ave Fresno (93725) *(P-8321)*

**Modern Embroidery Inc** .................................................................... E ...... 714 436-9960
3701 W Moore Ave Santa Ana (92704) *(P-2996)*

**Modern Engine Inc** ............................................................................. E ...... 818 409-9494
701 Sonora Ave Glendale (91201) *(P-10989)*

**Modern Gourmet Foods, Santa Ana** *Also Called: Coastal Cocktails Inc (P-17184)*

**Modern Luxury Media LLC (HQ)** ..................................................... E ...... 404 443-0004
243 Vallejo St San Francisco (94111) *(P-4281)*

**Modern Plating, Los Angeles** *Also Called: Alco Plating Corp (P-8910)*

**Modern Postcard, Carlsbad** *Also Called: Iris Group Inc (P-4901)*

**Modern Printing & Mailing Inc** ......................................................... E ...... 619 222-0535
3535 Enterprise St San Diego (92110) *(P-4697)*

**Modern Studio Equipment Inc** ........................................................ F ...... 818 764-8574
16200 Stagg St Van Nuys (91406) *(P-15652)*

**Modern Welding Company of California Inc** ................................ E ...... 559 275-9353
4141 N Brawley Ave Fresno (93722) *(P-8190)*

## ALPHABETIC SECTION — Monopole Inc

Modern Woodworks, Canoga Park *Also Called: Modern Woodworks Inc (P-11547)*
Modern Woodworks Inc .................................................. E ...... 800 575-3475
  7949 Deering Ave Canoga Park (91304) *(P-11547)*
Modern-Aire Ventilating Inc .......................................... E ...... 818 765-9870
  7319 Lankershim Blvd North Hollywood (91605) *(P-8514)*
Modern-Twist, Emeryville *Also Called: Stasher Inc (P-17023)*
Modernica, Vernon *Also Called: Modernica Inc (P-17522)*
Modernica Inc (PA) ......................................................... E ...... 323 826-1600
  2901 Saco St Vernon (90058) *(P-17522)*
Modesto Industrial Elec Co Inc .................................... D ...... 559 292-4714
  2516 N Sunnyside Ave Fresno (93727) *(P-462)*
Modesto Industrial Electrical Co Inc (PA) .................. D ...... 209 527-2800
  1417 Coldwell Ave Modesto (95350) *(P-463)*
Modesto Milling Inc ........................................................ E ...... 209 523-9167
  142 Linley Ave Empire (95319) *(P-1137)*
Modified Plastics Inc (PA) ............................................ E ...... 714 546-4667
  1240 E Glenwood Pl Santa Ana (92707) *(P-6918)*
Moducom, La Crescenta *Also Called: Modular Communications Systems (P-11895)*
Modular Communications Systems ............................ F ...... 818 764-1333
  2629 Foothill Blvd La Crescenta (91214) *(P-11895)*
Modular Medical, San Diego *Also Called: Modular Medical Inc (P-15194)*
Modular Medical Inc (PA) ............................................. E ...... 858 800-3500
  10740 Thornmint Rd San Diego (92127) *(P-15194)*
Modular Metal Fabricators Inc ..................................... C ...... 951 242-3154
  24600 Nandina Ave Moreno Valley (92551) *(P-8515)*
Modular Office Solutions Inc ........................................ E ...... 909 476-4200
  11701 6th St Rancho Cucamonga (91730) *(P-3606)*
Modular Wind Energy Inc .............................................. D ...... 562 304-6782
  1709 Apollo Ct Seal Beach (90740) *(P-9313)*
Modus Advanced Inc ..................................................... D ...... 925 960-8700
  2772 Loker Ave W Carlsbad (92010) *(P-6515)*
Modutek Corp ................................................................... E ...... 408 362-2000
  6387 San Ignacio Ave San Jose (95119) *(P-14435)*
Mody Entrepreneurs Inc ................................................. F ...... 858 292-8100
  8975 Complex Dr San Diego (92123) *(P-4698)*
Moehair Usa Inc ............................................................... F ...... 888 663-7032
  1061 S Melrose St Ste A Placentia (92870) *(P-6008)*
Moeller Mfg & Sup LLC .................................................. E ...... 714 999-5551
  630 E Lambert Rd Brea (92821) *(P-8017)*
Mogami, Torrance *Also Called: Marshall Electronics Inc (P-11675)*
Mogan David Wine, Ripon *Also Called: Wine Group Inc (P-1831)*
Mogul ................................................................................. E ...... 424 245-4331
  10106 Sunbrook Dr Beverly Hills (90210) *(P-13542)*
Mohawk Industries Inc .................................................... E ...... 909 357-1064
  9687 Transportation Way Fontana (92335) *(P-2518)*
Mohawk Land & Cattle Co Inc ....................................... D ...... 408 436-1800
  1660 Old Bayshore Hwy San Jose (95112) *(P-607)*
Mohawk Western Plastics Inc ........................................ E ...... 909 593-7547
  1496 Arrow Hwy La Verne (91750) *(P-3973)*
Mohin Inc ........................................................................... E ...... 925 798-5572
  5040 Commercial Cir Ste A Concord (94520) *(P-9294)*
Moisture Register Products, Rancho Cucamonga *Also Called: Aqua Measure Instrument Co (P-14845)*
Mojave Foods Corporation (HQ) ................................... D ...... 323 890-8900
  6200 E Slauson Ave Los Angeles (90040) *(P-2283)*
Mojave Foods Corporation ............................................. C ...... 323 890-8900
  6000 E Slauson Ave Commerce (90040) *(P-2284)*
Mojo Networks Inc (HQ) .................................................. E ...... 650 961-1111
  5453 Great America Pkwy Santa Clara (95054) *(P-18558)*
Molaniki Distributor, Sunnyvale *Also Called: Wayne (P-788)*
Molded Fiber GL Companies - W ................................. D ...... 760 246-4042
  9400 Holly Rd Adelanto (92301) *(P-6919)*
Moldex, Culver City *Also Called: Moldex-Metric Inc (P-15384)*
Moldex-Metric Inc ............................................................. B ...... 310 837-6500
  10111 Jefferson Blvd Culver City (90232) *(P-15384)*
Molding Corporation America ....................................... E ...... 818 890-7877
  10349 Norris Ave Pacoima (91331) *(P-6920)*
Molding Solutions Inc ...................................................... D ...... 707 575-1218
  3225 Regional Pkwy Santa Rosa (95403) *(P-6921)*
Moldings Plus Inc ............................................................. E ...... 909 947-3310
  1856 S Grove Ave Ontario (91761) *(P-3161)*

Mole-Richardson Co Ltd (PA) ....................................... D ...... 323 851-0111
  12154 Montague St Pacoima (91331) *(P-11613)*
Moleaer Inc ....................................................................... D ...... 424 558-3567
  3232 W El Segundo Blvd Hawthorne (90250) *(P-9932)*
Molecular Bio Products, San Diego *Also Called: Thermo Fisher Scientific Inc (P-14739)*
Molecular Bioproducts Inc (DH) ................................... C ...... 858 453-7551
  9389 Waples St San Diego (92121) *(P-14692)*
Molecular Bioproducts Svc Corp (HQ) ....................... E ...... 858 875-7696
  10636 Scripps Summit Ct Ste 130 San Diego (92131) *(P-16603)*
Molecular Databank, Burlingame *Also Called: Collabrative DRG Discovery Inc (P-18193)*
Molecular Devices LLC (HQ) ........................................ C ...... 408 747-1700
  3860 N 1st St San Jose (95134) *(P-14693)*
Molecular Probes Inc ..................................................... E ...... 760 603-7200
  5781 Van Allen Way Carlsbad (92008) *(P-5765)*
Molecule Labs Inc ........................................................... E ...... 925 473-8200
  524 Stone Rd Ste A Benicia (94510) *(P-6153)*
Moleculum ......................................................................... F ...... 714 619-5139
  3128 Red Hill Ave Costa Mesa (92626) *(P-6341)*
Molino Company .............................................................. D ...... 323 726-1000
  13712 Alondra Blvd Cerritos (90703) *(P-4699)*
Mollie Stone Market, Greenbrae *Also Called: Albeco Inc (P-17365)*
Molnar Engineering Inc ................................................. E ...... 818 993-3495
  20731 Marilla St Chatsworth (91311) *(P-10990)*
Mom Enterprises LLC .................................................... E ...... 415 694-3799
  1001 Canal Blvd Unit C-1 Richmond (94804) *(P-5557)*
Momeni Engineering LLC ............................................. E ...... 714 897-9301
  5451 Argosy Ave Huntington Beach (92649) *(P-10991)*
Momentum Management LLC ..................................... F ...... 310 329-2599
  1206 W Jon St Torrance (90502) *(P-6516)*
Momentum Textiles LLC (PA) ....................................... E ...... 949 833-8886
  17811 Fitch Irvine (92614) *(P-17064)*
Momentum Textiles Wallcovering, Irvine *Also Called: Momentum Textiles LLC (P-17064)*
Monaco Baking Company, Fullerton *Also Called: Phenix Gourmet LLC (P-1282)*
Monadnock Company ..................................................... C ...... 626 964-6581
  16728 Gale Ave City Of Industry (91745) *(P-8018)*
Monarch Corporation ....................................................... F ...... 714 744-5098
  726 W Angus Ave Ste H Orange (92868) *(P-16011)*
Monarch Litho Inc (PA) ................................................... E ...... 323 727-0300
  1501 Date St Montebello (90640) *(P-4700)*
Monarch Prcision Deburring Inc .................................. F ...... 714 258-0342
  1514 E Edinger Ave Ste C Santa Ana (92705) *(P-10992)*
Monco Products Inc ........................................................ E ...... 714 891-2788
  7562 Acacia Ave Garden Grove (92841) *(P-6922)*
Mondelez Global LLC ..................................................... F ...... 714 690-7428
  6201 Knott Ave Buena Park (90620) *(P-654)*
Mondelez Global LLC ..................................................... D ...... 909 605-0140
  5815 Clark St Ontario (91761) *(P-17197)*
Monex, Newport Beach *Also Called: Monex Deposit A Cal Ltd Partnr (P-17650)*
Monex Deposit A Cal Ltd Partnr ................................... D ...... 800 444-8317
  4910 Birch St Newport Beach (92660) *(P-17650)*
Monier Lifetile, Rialto *Also Called: Royal Westlake Roofing LLC (P-7386)*
Moniker General, San Diego *Also Called: Moniker General LLC (P-3097)*
Moniker General LLC ..................................................... F ...... 619 255-8772
  2860 Sims Rd San Diego (92106) *(P-3097)*
Mono Engineering Corp ................................................. E ...... 818 772-4998
  20977 Knapp St Chatsworth (91311) *(P-10993)*
Monobind Sales Inc (PA) ............................................... E ...... 949 951-2665
  100 N Pointe Dr Lake Forest (92630) *(P-15195)*
Monocent, Northridge *Also Called: Monocent Inc (P-5766)*
Monocent Inc .................................................................... F ...... 424 310-0777
  8920 Quartz Ave Northridge (91324) *(P-5766)*
Monogram Aerospace Fas Inc ..................................... C ...... 323 722-4760
  3423 Garfield Ave Commerce (90040) *(P-8019)*
Monogram Biosciences Inc .......................................... B ...... 650 635-1100
  345 Oyster Point Blvd South San Francisco (94080) *(P-5767)*
Monogram Systems, Carson *Also Called: Mag Aerospace Industries LLC (P-8042)*
Monogram Systems, Carson *Also Called: Zodiac Wtr Waste Aero Systems (P-13997)*
Monolith Materials Inc .................................................... E ...... 650 933-4957
  662 Laurel St San Carlos (94070) *(P-5103)*
Monopole Inc .................................................................... F ...... 818 500-8585
  4661 Alger St Los Angeles (90039) *(P-6096)*

## ALPHABETIC SECTION

**Monroe Magnus LLC (HQ)** .................................................. F ...... 714 771-2630
1110 E Elm Ave Fullerton (92831) *(P-16758)*

**Monroeone, Fullerton** *Also Called: Monroe Magnus LLC (P-16758)*

**Monrow, Los Angeles** *Also Called: Monrow LLC (P-2681)*

**Monrow LLC** .................................................. E ...... 213 741-6007
1404 S Main St Ste C Los Angeles (90015) *(P-2681)*

**Monsanto, Oxnard** *Also Called: Monsanto Company (P-6202)*

**Monsanto Company** .................................................. E ...... 805 827-2341
2700 Camino Del Sol Oxnard (93030) *(P-6202)*

**MONSTER, Corona** *Also Called: Monster Beverage Corporation (P-1905)*

**Monster Inc (PA)** .................................................. B ...... 415 840-2000
601 Gateway Blvd Ste 900 South San Francisco (94080) *(P-16982)*

**Monster Beverage 1990 Corporation** .................................................. A ...... 951 739-6200
1 Monster Way Corona (92879) *(P-1903)*

**Monster Beverage Company** .................................................. E ...... 866 322-4466
1990 Pomona Rd Corona (92878) *(P-1904)*

**Monster Beverage Corporation (PA)** .................................................. A ...... 951 739-6200
1 Monster Way Corona (92879) *(P-1905)*

**Monster City Studios** .................................................. E ...... 559 498-0540
411 S West Ave Fresno (93706) *(P-6648)*

**Monster Products, South San Francisco** *Also Called: Monster Inc (P-16982)*

**Monster Tool LLC** .................................................. C ...... 760 477-1000
2470 Ash St U 2 Vista (92081) *(P-7960)*

**Montage Technology Inc** .................................................. E ...... 408 982-2788
101 Metro Dr Ste 500 San Jose (95110) *(P-12588)*

**Montague Company** .................................................. C ...... 510 785-8822
1830 Stearman Ave Hayward (94545) *(P-10582)*

**Montavista Software LLC (DH)** .................................................. D ...... 408 572-8000
2315 N 1st St 4th Fl San Jose (95131) *(P-18559)*

**Montclair Bronze Inc** .................................................. E ...... 909 986-2664
2535 E 57th St Huntington Park (90255) *(P-7855)*

**Monte Vista Farming Co LLC** .................................................. E ...... 209 874-1866
5043 N Montpelier Rd Denair (95316) *(P-40)*

**Monte Vista Farming Company, Denair** *Also Called: California Royale LLC (P-76)*

**Montebello Container, Santa Fe Springs** *Also Called: Cflute Corp (P-3830)*

**Montebello Plastics LLC** .................................................. E ...... 323 728-6814
601 W Olympic Blvd Montebello (90640) *(P-6564)*

**Monterey Agresources, Fresno** *Also Called: Monterey Chemical Company (P-6203)*

**Monterey Canyon LLC (PA)** .................................................. D ...... 213 741-0209
1515 E 15th St Los Angeles (90021) *(P-2792)*

**Monterey Chemical Company** .................................................. D ...... 559 499-2100
3654 S Willow Ave Fresno (93725) *(P-6203)*

**Monterey County Herald Company (DH)** .................................................. E ...... 831 372-3311
2200 Garden Rd # 101 Monterey (93940) *(P-4160)*

**Monterey Fish Company Inc (PA)** .................................................. E ...... 831 775-0522
960 S Sanborn Rd Salinas (93901) *(P-2056)*

**Monterey Herald, Monterey** *Also Called: Monterey County Herald Company (P-4160)*

**Monterey Mechanical Co (PA)** .................................................. E ...... 510 632-3173
8275 San Leandro St Oakland (94621) *(P-426)*

**Monterey Mushrooms LLC** .................................................. E ...... 408 779-4191
642 Hale Ave Morgan Hill (95037) *(P-52)*

**Monterey Mushrooms-Morgan Hill, Morgan Hill** *Also Called: Monterey Mushrooms LLC (P-52)*

**Monterey Pasta Company, Salinas** *Also Called: Pulmuone Foods Usa Inc (P-2326)*

**Monterey Structural Steel Inc** .................................................. F ...... 831 768-1277
404 W Beach St Watsonville (95076) *(P-8191)*

**Monterey Wine Company LLC** .................................................. F ...... 831 386-1100
1010 Industrial Way King City (93930) *(P-1680)*

**Montesquieu Winery, San Diego** *Also Called: WG Best Weinkellerei Inc (P-1825)*

**Monticello Cellars Inc** .................................................. E ...... 707 253-2802
4242 Big Ranch Rd Napa (94558) *(P-1681)*

**Montrail, Richmond** *Also Called: Mountain Hardwear Inc (P-2978)*

**Moog Aircraft Group, Torrance** *Also Called: Moog Inc (P-14222)*

**Moog Inc** .................................................. B ...... 310 533-1178
1218 W Jon St Torrance (90502) *(P-11335)*

**Moog Inc** .................................................. B ...... 310 533-1178
20263 S Western Ave Torrance (90501) *(P-14222)*

**Moog Inc** .................................................. C ...... 818 341-5156
21339 Nordhoff St Chatsworth (91311) *(P-14223)*

**Moog Inc** .................................................. B ...... 805 618-3900
7406 Hollister Ave Goleta (93117) *(P-14224)*

**Moog Jon Street Warehouse, Torrance** *Also Called: Moog Inc (P-11335)*

**Mooney Farms** .................................................. D ...... 530 899-2661
1220 Fortress St Chico (95973) *(P-84)*

**Mooney Inds Prcsion McHning In** .................................................. F ...... 818 998-0199
8744 Remmet Ave Canoga Park (91304) *(P-10994)*

**Mooney International, Chino** *Also Called: Soaring America Corporation (P-13691)*

**Moore Business Forms, Temecula** *Also Called: R R Donnelley & Sons Company (P-16994)*

**Moore Farms Inc** .................................................. F ...... 661 854-5588
916 S Derby St Arvin (93203) *(P-2285)*

**Moore Industries, North Hills** *Also Called: Moore Industries-International Inc (P-14436)*

**Moore Industries-International Inc (PA)** .................................................. C ...... 818 894-7111
16650 Schoenborn St North Hills (91343) *(P-14436)*

**Moore Quality Galvanizing Inc** .................................................. E ...... 559 673-2822
3001 Falcon Dr Madera (93637) *(P-9094)*

**Moores Ideal Products LLC** .................................................. E ...... 626 339-9007
830 W Golden Grove Way Covina (91722) *(P-15761)*

**Moose, El Segundo** *Also Called: Moose Toys LLC (P-15733)*

**Moose Boats LLC** .................................................. F ...... 707 778-9828
1175 Nimitz Ave Ste 150 Vallejo (94592) *(P-14043)*

**Moose Toys LLC** .................................................. D ...... 310 341-4642
737 Campus Sq W El Segundo (90245) *(P-15733)*

**Mophie Inc (DH)** .................................................. D ...... 888 866-7443
15495 Sand Canyon Ave Ste 400 Irvine (92618) *(P-11896)*

**Moquin Press Inc** .................................................. D ...... 650 592-0575
555 Harbor Blvd Belmont (94002) *(P-4701)*

**Moravek, Brea** *Also Called: Moravek Biochemicals Inc (P-5104)*

**Moravek Biochemicals Inc (PA)** .................................................. E ...... 714 990-2018
577 Mercury Ln Brea (92821) *(P-5104)*

**Moreflavor Inc (PA)** .................................................. E ...... 800 600-0033
701 Willow Pass Rd Unit 1 Pittsburg (94565) *(P-1449)*

**Morehouse Foods Inc** .................................................. E ...... 626 854-1655
760 Epperson Dr City Of Industry (91748) *(P-985)*

**Morehouse-Cowles LLC** .................................................. E ...... 909 627-7222
13930 Magnolia Ave Chino (91710) *(P-9878)*

**Moreland Manufacturing Inc** .................................................. E ...... 714 426-1411
17406 Mount Cliffwood Cir Fountain Valley (92708) *(P-4924)*

**Morettis Design Collection Inc** .................................................. E ...... 310 638-5555
16926 Keegan Ave Ste C Carson (90746) *(P-3450)*

**Morgan & Slates Mfg & Sup Inc (PA)** .................................................. F ...... 559 582-4417
12918 Hanford Armona Rd Hanford (93230) *(P-17357)*

**Morgan Advanced Ceramics Inc** .................................................. E ...... 530 823-3401
13079 Earhart Ave Auburn (95602) *(P-5105)*

**Morgan Advanced Ceramics Inc (HQ)** .................................................. C ...... 510 491-1100
2425 Whipple Rd Hayward (94544) *(P-7266)*

**Morgan Advanced Materials Inc** .................................................. F ...... 530 823-3401
13079 Earhart Ave Auburn (95602) *(P-7269)*

**Morgan Fabrics, Los Angeles** *Also Called: Morgan Fabrics Corporation (P-17065)*

**Morgan Fabrics Corporation (PA)** .................................................. D ...... 323 583-9981
4265 Exchange Ave Los Angeles (90058) *(P-17065)*

**Morgan Gallacher Inc** .................................................. E ...... 562 695-1232
8707 Millergrove Dr Santa Fe Springs (90670) *(P-5917)*

**Morgan Manufacturing Inc** .................................................. F ...... 707 763-6848
521 2nd St Petaluma (94952) *(P-7961)*

**Morgan Marine, Simi Valley** *Also Called: Catalina Yachts Inc (P-14030)*

**Morgan Polymer Seals LLC** .................................................. B ...... 619 498-9221
3303 2475a Paseo De Las Americas San Diego (92154) *(P-9879)*

**Morgan Technical Ceramics Inc** .................................................. D ...... 510 491-1100
2425 Whipple Rd Hayward (94544) *(P-7594)*

**Morgan-Royce Industries, Fremont** *Also Called: Morgan-Royce Industries Inc (P-12166)*

**Morgan-Royce Industries Inc** .................................................. E ...... 510 440-8500
47730 Westinghouse Dr Fremont (94539) *(P-12166)*

**Morin Corporation** .................................................. E ...... 909 428-3747
10707 Commerce Way Fontana (92337) *(P-8677)*

**Morin West, Fontana** *Also Called: Morin Corporation (P-8677)*

**Morinaga Nutritional Foods Inc (HQ)** .................................................. F ...... 310 787-0200
3838 Del Amo Blvd Ste 201 Torrance (90503) *(P-2286)*

**Morning Star, Los Banos** *Also Called: The Morning Star Packing Company L P (P-932)*

**Morning Star Company The, Woodland** *Also Called: Liberty Packing Company LLC (P-17170)*

**Morning Star Packing, Williams** *Also Called: Morning Star Packing Co LP (P-906)*

**Morning Star Packing Co LP** .................................................. E ...... 209 826-8000
12045 Ingomar Grade Los Banos (93635) *(P-905)*

# ALPHABETIC SECTION — Mp Mine Operations LLC

**Morning Star Packing Co LP** .................................................. E ...... 530 473-3600
2211 Old Highway 99w Williams (95987) *(P-906)*

**Morpheus Space Inc (PA)** ...................................................... F ...... 562 766-8470
2101 E El Segundo Blvd El Segundo (90245) *(P-14103)*

**Morrell's Metal Finishing, Compton** *Also Called: Morrells Electro Plating Inc (P-8986)*

**Morrells Electro Plating Inc** ................................................ E ...... 310 639-1024
436 E Euclid Ave Compton (90222) *(P-8986)*

**Morrill Industries Inc** ............................................................ D ...... 209 838-2550
24754 E River Rd Escalon (95320) *(P-9189)*

**Morris Crullo World Evangelism (PA)** ................................ D ...... 858 277-2200
875 Hotel Cir S # 2 San Diego (92108) *(P-19368)*

**Morris Group International, City Of Industry** *Also Called: Acorn Engineering Company (P-6265)*

**Morris Multimedia Inc** .......................................................... E ...... 661 259-1234
26330 Diamond Pl Ste 100 Santa Clarita (91350) *(P-4161)*

**Morris Newspaper Corp Cal (HQ)** ...................................... D ...... 209 249-3500
531 E Yosemite Ave Manteca (95336) *(P-4162)*

**Morris Publications (PA)** ..................................................... E ...... 209 847-3021
122 S 3rd Ave Oakdale (95361) *(P-4163)*

**Morris, Phyllis, Los Angeles** *Also Called: Phyllis Morris Originals (P-16418)*

**Morse Micro Inc** ..................................................................... D ...... 949 501-7080
40 Waterworks Way Irvine (92618) *(P-12589)*

**Mortech Manufacturing, Azusa** *Also Called: Joseph Manufacturing Co Inc (P-3632)*

**Mortex Apparel, Burbank** *Also Called: Mortex Corporation (P-2634)*

**Mortex Corporation** ............................................................... C
40 E Verdugo Ave Burbank (91502) *(P-2634)*

**Morton Grinding Inc** .............................................................. C ...... 661 298-0895
201 E Avenue K15 Lancaster (93535) *(P-15914)*

**Morton Manufacturing, Lancaster** *Also Called: Morton Grinding Inc (P-15914)*

**Morton Salt Inc** ...................................................................... D ...... 562 437-0071
1050 Pier F Ave Long Beach (90802) *(P-6311)*

**Mosaic Brands Inc** ................................................................. E ...... 925 322-8700
3266 Buskirk Ave Pleasant Hill (94523) *(P-16185)*

**Moseys Production Machinists Inc (PA)** ........................... E ...... 714 693-4840
1550 Lakeview Loop Anaheim (92807) *(P-10995)*

**MOSplastics Inc** .................................................................... F ...... 408 944-9407
2308 Zanker Rd San Jose (95131) *(P-6923)*

**Moss Prcsion McHning Shetmetal, Hayward** *Also Called: Moss Precision Inc (P-10996)*

**Moss Precision Inc** ............................................................... D ...... 510 785-2235
3200 Arden Rd Hayward (94545) *(P-10996)*

**Mota Group Inc (PA)** ............................................................. E ...... 408 370-1248
60 S Market St Ste 1100 San Jose (95113) *(P-13199)*

**Motech Americas LLC** .......................................................... B ...... 302 451-7500
1300 Valley Vista Dr Ste 207 Diamond Bar (91765) *(P-19469)*

**Mother Jones, San Francisco** *Also Called: Foundation For Nat Progress (P-4257)*

**Mother Lode Plas Molding Inc** ............................................ D ...... 209 532-5146
1480 E Pescadero Ave Tracy (95304) *(P-6924)*

**Mother Lode Prtg & Pubg Co Inc** ....................................... E ...... 530 344-5030
2889 Ray Lawyer Dr Placerville (95667) *(P-4164)*

**Motherly Inc** ........................................................................... E ...... 917 860-9926
1725 Oakdell Dr Menlo Park (94025) *(P-4433)*

**Motion Control Engineering Inc** ......................................... B ...... 916 638-4011
11380 White Rock Rd Rancho Cordova (95742) *(P-9473)*

**Motion Engineering Inc (DH)** ............................................... D ...... 805 696-1200
33 S La Patera Ln Santa Barbara (93117) *(P-10412)*

**Motion Industries Inc** ........................................................... E ...... 858 602-1500
12550 Stowe Dr Poway (92064) *(P-16884)*

**Motionloft Inc** ......................................................................... E ...... 415 580-7671
13681 Newport Ave Ste 8 Tustin (92780) *(P-14694)*

**Motiv Design Group Inc** ....................................................... F ...... 408 441-0611
430 Perrymont Ave San Jose (95125) *(P-10997)*

**Motiv Power Systems Inc** .................................................... C ...... 650 458-4804
2745 Boeing Way Stockton (95206) *(P-13420)*

**Motivational Systems Inc (PA)** ........................................... D ...... 619 474-8246
2200 Cleveland Ave National City (91950) *(P-17833)*

**Motive Nation, Downey** *Also Called: Rockview Dairies Inc (P-17209)*

**Motivemetrics** ........................................................................ E ...... 800 216-5207
425 Sherman Ave Ste 300 Palo Alto (94306) *(P-11737)*

**Motomotion USA Corporation** ............................................. F ...... 626 538-4866
1008 S Baldwin Ave Ste G Arcadia (91007) *(P-3098)*

**Motor Warehouse, Sacramento** *Also Called: Dana Motors Inc (P-16379)*

**Motorcar Parts of America Inc (PA)** ................................... A ...... 310 212-7910
2929 California St Torrance (90503) *(P-13543)*

**Motorola, Sunnyvale** *Also Called: Motorola Mobility LLC (P-11898)*

**Motorola, San Diego** *Also Called: Motorola Mobility LLC (P-16722)*

**Motorola Mobility LLC** .......................................................... E ...... 408 919-0600
2121 Tasman Dr Santa Clara (95054) *(P-11897)*

**Motorola Mobility LLC** .......................................................... E ...... 847 576-5000
809 Eleventh Ave Bldg 4 Sunnyvale (94089) *(P-11898)*

**Motorola Mobility LLC** .......................................................... D ...... 858 455-1500
6450 Sequence Dr San Diego (92121) *(P-16722)*

**Motorola Sltons Cnnctivity Inc (HQ)** ................................. D ...... 951 719-2100
42555 Rio Nedo Temecula (92590) *(P-11899)*

**Motors & Controls Whse Inc** .............................................. E ...... 714 956-0480
1440 N Burton Pl Anaheim (92806) *(P-16723)*

**Motorvac Technologies Inc** ................................................. E ...... 714 558-4822
1431 Village Way Santa Ana (92705) *(P-10998)*

**Moulding Company** .............................................................. D ...... 925 798-7525
5117 Commercial Cir Concord (94520) *(P-3162)*

**Mount Palomar Winery, Temecula** *Also Called: Louidar LLC (P-1669)*

**Mount Veeder Winery, Napa** *Also Called: Tpwc Inc (P-1788)*

**Mountain Democrat, Placerville** *Also Called: Mother Lode Prtg & Pubg Co Inc (P-4164)*

**Mountain F Enterprises Inc** ................................................. E ...... 530 626-4127
950 Iron Point Rd Ste 210 Folsom (95630) *(P-3051)*

**Mountain Hardwear Inc** ........................................................ A ...... 510 558-3000
1414 Harbour Way S Ste 1005 Richmond (94804) *(P-2978)*

**Mountain Materials Inc** ........................................................ E ...... 619 445-4150
1117 Tavern Rd Alpine (91901) *(P-7471)*

**Mountain News & Shopper, Lake Arrowhead** *Also Called: Hi-Desert Publishing Company (P-4131)*

**Mountain Water Ice Company** ............................................ E ...... 760 722-7611
2843 Benet Rd Oceanside (92058) *(P-16284)*

**Mountain Water Ice Company Inc (PA)** ............................. D ...... 310 638-0321
17011 Central Ave Carson (90746) *(P-2111)*

**Mountain Winery, Saratoga** *Also Called: Chateau Masson LLC (P-1505)*

**Mountanos Brothers Coffee Co (PA)** ................................. E ...... 707 774-8800
1331 Commerce St Petaluma (94954) *(P-17198)*

**Mountanos Family Coffee & Tea, Petaluma** *Also Called: Mountanos Brothers Coffee Co (P-17198)*

**Mountz Inc (HQ)** .................................................................... E ...... 408 292-2214
1080 N 11th St San Jose (95112) *(P-14437)*

**Mouse Graphics, Costa Mesa** *Also Called: Orange Coast Reprographics Inc (P-4713)*

**Mousepad Designs, Cerritos** *Also Called: Mpd Holdings Inc (P-10414)*

**Movano, Pleasanton** *Also Called: Movano Inc (P-15560)*

**Movano Inc** ............................................................................. E ...... 408 393-1209
6800 Koll Center Pkwy Ste 160 Pleasanton (94566) *(P-15560)*

**Moveworks Inc (PA)** ............................................................. E ...... 408 435-5100
1400 Terra Bella Ave Mountain View (94043) *(P-18560)*

**Moving Image Technologies LLC** ....................................... E ...... 714 751-7998
17760 Newhope St Ste B Fountain Valley (92708) *(P-15653)*

**Moviola Digital, Burbank** *Also Called: Filmtools Inc (P-17653)*

**Moxa Americas Inc** ............................................................... E ...... 714 528-6777
601 Valencia Ave Ste 100 Brea (92823) *(P-10413)*

**Moximed Inc (PA)** .................................................................. F ...... 510 887-3300
46602 Landing Pkwy Fremont (94538) *(P-15196)*

**Moyes Custom Furniture Inc** .............................................. E ...... 714 729-0234
1884 Pomona Rd Corona (92878) *(P-19182)*

**Moz Designs, Oakland** *Also Called: Ngo Metals Inc (P-8638)*

**Mozaik LLC** ............................................................................ E ...... 562 207-1900
245 W Carl Karcher Way Anaheim (92801) *(P-3815)*

**Mp Aero LLC** .......................................................................... D ...... 818 901-9828
7701 Woodley Ave Van Nuys (91406) *(P-567)*

**Mp Associates Inc** ................................................................ C ...... 209 274-4715
6555 Jackson Valley Rd Ione (95640) *(P-6251)*

**Mp Biomedicals, Irvine** *Also Called: Mp Biomedicals LLC (P-14695)*

**Mp Biomedicals LLC (HQ)** ................................................... E ...... 949 833-2500
6 Thomas Irvine (92618) *(P-14695)*

**Mp Express, Salinas** *Also Called: Albert Maldonado (P-17804)*

**Mp Materials Corp** ................................................................ D ...... 702 844-6111
67750 Bailey Rd Mountain Pass (92366) *(P-110)*

**Mp Mine Operations LLC** ..................................................... C ...... 702 277-0848
67750 Bailey Rd Mountain Pass (92366) *(P-336)*

**Mp Solutions Inc** .................................................................... E
21818 S Wilmington Ave Ste 411 Carson (90810) *(P-14225)*

**MPA, Torrance** *Also Called: Motorcar Parts of America Inc (P-13543)*

**Mpbs Industries, Los Angeles** *Also Called: Meat Packers Butchers Sup Inc (P-9805)*

**Mpd Holdings Inc** .................................................................... E ...... 213 210-2591
16200 Commerce Way Cerritos (90703) *(P-10414)*

**Mpi, Camarillo** *Also Called: Multilayer Prototypes Inc (P-12168)*

**Mpi America Inc** ...................................................................... F ...... 408 770-3650
2360 Qume Dr Ste C San Jose (95131) *(P-12590)*

**Mpi Label Systems, Stockton** *Also Called: Miller Products Inc (P-3952)*

**Mpl Brands Inc (PA)** ................................................................ E ...... 888 513-3022
71 Liberty Ship Way Sausalito (94965) *(P-1682)*

**Mpm & Associates, Van Nuys** *Also Called: Mpm Building Services Inc (P-5918)*

**Mpm Building Services Inc** .................................................... E ...... 818 708-9676
7011 Hayvenhurst Ave Ste F Van Nuys (91406) *(P-5918)*

**Mpo Videotronics Inc (PA)** ..................................................... D ...... 805 499-8513
5069 Maureen Ln Moorpark (93021) *(P-15654)*

**Mpower Electronics Inc (PA)** ................................................. D ...... 408 320-1266
2910 Scott Blvd Santa Clara (95054) *(P-16664)*

**Mpp Brea Div 6079, Brea** *Also Called: Orora Packaging Solutions (P-17005)*

**Mpp Fullerton Div 6061, Fullerton** *Also Called: Orora Packaging Solutions (P-17010)*

**Mpp San Diego Div 6064, San Marcos** *Also Called: Orora Packaging Solutions (P-17006)*

**Mpressions, Anaheim** *Also Called: Dean Hesketh Company Inc (P-4871)*

**MPS Anzon LLC** ....................................................................... C ...... 626 471-3553
11911 Clark St Arcadia (91006) *(P-15385)*

**MPS International Ltd** ............................................................. E ...... 408 826-0600
79 Great Oaks Blvd San Jose (95119) *(P-12591)*

**MPS Medical Inc** ...................................................................... E ...... 714 672-1090
785 Challenger St Brea (92821) *(P-15197)*

**Mq Power, Cypress** *Also Called: Multiquip Inc (P-16665)*

**Mr Bug, Anaheim** *Also Called: Reels Inc (P-16396)*

**Mr Dj Inc** ................................................................................... E ...... 213 744-0044
1800 E Washington Blvd Los Angeles (90021) *(P-11679)*

**Mr Lock, Corona** *Also Called: Lock America Inc (P-8011)*

**MR Mold & Engineering Corp** ................................................ E ...... 714 996-5511
1150 Beacon St Brea (92821) *(P-9637)*

**Mr Plastics** ................................................................................ E ...... 510 895-0774
844 Doolittle Dr San Leandro (94577) *(P-17228)*

**Mr S Leather** ............................................................................. E ...... 415 863-7764
385 8th St San Francisco (94103) *(P-2882)*

**Mr Tortilla Inc** ........................................................................... E ...... 818 233-8932
1112 Arroyo St San Fernando (91340) *(P-2287)*

**Mro Maryruth LLC** .................................................................. C ...... 424 343-6650
1171 S Robertson Blvd Ste 148 Los Angeles (90035) *(P-5249)*

**Mrp Inc** ...................................................................................... E ...... 909 825-4800
150 S La Cadena Dr Colton (92324) *(P-1229)*

**Mrs Appletree's Bakery, Baldwin Park** *Also Called: Distinct Indulgence Inc (P-1183)*

**MRS Foods Incorporated (PA)** ................................................ E ...... 714 554-2791
4406 W 5th St Santa Ana (92703) *(P-2288)*

**Mrv, Chatsworth** *Also Called: Mrv Communications Inc (P-12592)*

**Mrv Communications Inc** ....................................................... B ...... 818 773-0900
20520 Nordhoff St Chatsworth (91311) *(P-12592)*

**Mrv Crane, Delano** *Also Called: Mrv Service Air Inc (P-19172)*

**Mrv Service Air Inc** ................................................................. F ...... 661 725-3400
937 High St Delano (93215) *(P-19172)*

**Mrv Systems LLC** .................................................................... E ...... 800 645-7114
6370 Lusk Blvd Ste F100 San Diego (92121) *(P-14555)*

**MS Aerospace Inc** ................................................................... B ...... 818 833-9095
13928 Balboa Blvd Sylmar (91342) *(P-8762)*

**Ms Bellows, Huntington Beach** *Also Called: Mechanized Science Seals Inc (P-14897)*

**Ms Carita Inc** ............................................................................ E ...... 925 243-1720
2159 Research Dr Livermore (94550) *(P-4925)*

**MS Industrial Shtmtl Inc** ........................................................ C ...... 951 272-6610
1731 Pomona Rd Corona (92878) *(P-8516)*

**MS Intertrade Inc (PA)** ............................................................ E ...... 707 837-8057
2221 Bluebell Dr Ste A Santa Rosa (95403) *(P-2057)*

**Ms-Tech Corporation** .............................................................. E ...... 562 404-9727
1911 Sampson Ave Corona (92879) *(P-10999)*

**MSC-La, City Of Industry** *Also Called: Material Sciences Corporation (P-7730)*

**Msci Barra, Berkeley** *Also Called: Barra LLC (P-18091)*

**Mscsoftware Corporation** ...................................................... A ...... 714 540-8900
5161 California Ave Ste 200 Irvine (92617) *(P-18561)*

**MSF Inc** ..................................................................................... F ...... 650 592-0239
5763 Drakes Dr Discovery Bay (94505) *(P-3698)*

**MSI Hvac, Fontana** *Also Called: AC Pro Inc (P-16773)*

**MSM Industries Inc** ................................................................. E ...... 951 735-0834
12660 Magnolia Ave Riverside (92503) *(P-19407)*

**Msquared, Fresno** *Also Called: M2 Antenna Systems Inc (P-13027)*

**Mt Poso Cgnrtion A Cal Ltd PR** .............................................. E ...... 661 663-3155
10000 Stockdale Hwy Ste 100 Bakersfield (93311) *(P-16345)*

**Mt Systems Inc** ........................................................................ F ...... 510 651-5277
580 Cottonwood Dr Milpitas (95035) *(P-9880)*

**MTA, San Diego** *Also Called: MTA Moving Tech In Amer Inc (P-10308)*

**MTA Moving Tech In Amer Inc** ............................................... E ...... 619 651-7208
10065 Via De La Amistad Ste A1 San Diego (92154) *(P-10308)*

**Mtc Worldwide Corp** ............................................................... D ...... 626 839-6800
17837 Rowland St City Of Industry (91748) *(P-16533)*

**Mtd Kitchen Inc** ....................................................................... D ...... 818 764-2254
13213 Sherman Way North Hollywood (91605) *(P-3163)*

**Mtech Inc** .................................................................................. F ...... 530 894-5091
1072 Marauder St Ste 210 Chico (95973) *(P-6925)*

**MTI Adventurewear, Arcata** *Also Called: Wing Inflatables Inc (P-7082)*

**MTI Corporation** ...................................................................... E ...... 510 525-3070
860 S 19th St Richmond (94804) *(P-13040)*

**MTI De Baja Inc** ....................................................................... E ...... 951 654-2333
915 Industrial Way San Jacinto (92582) *(P-14226)*

**MTI Laboratory Inc** ................................................................. E ...... 310 955-3700
201 Continental Blvd Ste 300 El Segundo (90245) *(P-11900)*

**Mtil, El Segundo** *Also Called: MTI Laboratory Inc (P-11900)*

**Mtroiz International** ................................................................ E ...... 661 998-8013
150 S Kenmore Ave Los Angeles (90004) *(P-16724)*

**MTS Solutions LLC** ................................................................. E ...... 661 589-5804
7131 Charity Ave Bakersfield (93308) *(P-6342)*

**MTS Stimulation Services Inc (PA)** ....................................... F ...... 661 589-5804
7131 Charity Ave Bakersfield (93308) *(P-252)*

**Muhlhauser Enterprises Inc (PA)** ........................................... F ...... 909 877-2792
25825 Adams Ave Murrieta (92562) *(P-8192)*

**Muhlhauser Steel, Murrieta** *Also Called: Muhlhauser Enterprises Inc (P-8192)*

**Muhlhauser Steel Inc** .............................................................. E ...... 909 877-2792
25825 Adams Ave Murrieta (92562) *(P-8193)*

**Mulechain Inc** .......................................................................... D ...... 888 456-8881
2901 W Coast Hwy Ste 200 Newport Beach (92663) *(P-16280)*

**Mulesoft LLC** ........................................................................... A ...... 800 596-4880
415 Mission St Fl 3 San Francisco (94105) *(P-18562)*

**Mulesoft, Inc., San Francisco** *Also Called: Mulesoft LLC (P-18562)*

**Mulgrew Arcft Components Inc** ............................................ D ...... 626 256-1375
1810 S Shamrock Ave Monrovia (91016) *(P-13912)*

**Mulholland Brand, Canoga Park** *Also Called: Mulholland Security Ctrs LLC (P-8279)*

**Mulholland Brothers (PA)** ....................................................... E ...... 415 824-5995
1710 4th St Berkeley (94710) *(P-3484)*

**Mulholland Brothers** ............................................................... E ...... 510 280-5485
11840 Dorothy St Apt 301 Los Angeles (90049) *(P-16289)*

**Mulholland Security Ctrs LLC** ................................................ D ...... 800 562-5770
21260 Deering Ct Canoga Park (91304) *(P-8279)*

**Mullen Auto Sales, Brea** *Also Called: Mullen Technologies Inc (P-13372)*

**Mullen Technologies Inc (PA)** ................................................ E ...... 714 613-1900
1405 Pioneer St Brea (92821) *(P-13372)*

**Multani Logistics, Hayward** *Also Called: Do Dine Inc (P-18246)*

**Multi Plastics, Santa Fe Springs** *Also Called: Multi-Plastics Inc (P-5179)*

**Multi-Color Corporation** ......................................................... D ...... 707 931-7400
21 Executive Way Napa (94558) *(P-4926)*

**Multi-Color Napa/Sonoma, Napa** *Also Called: Collotype Labels USA Inc (P-4862)*

**Multi-Fineline Electronix Inc (HQ)** ......................................... A ...... 949 453-6800
101 Academy Ste 250 Irvine (92617) *(P-12167)*

**Multi-Link International Corp** ................................................ E ...... 562 941-5380
933 Montecito Dr San Gabriel (91776) *(P-6649)*

**Multi-Plastics Inc** .................................................................... E ...... 562 692-1202
11625 Los Nietos Rd Santa Fe Springs (90670) *(P-5179)*

**Multibeam Corporation** .......................................................... E ...... 408 980-1800
3951 Burton Dr Santa Clara (95054) *(P-9881)*

## ALPHABETIC SECTION — N V Cast Stone LLC

**Multichip Assembly Inc** .................................................. E ...... 408 451-2345
270 E Brokaw Rd San Jose (95112) *(P-12593)*

**Multichrome Company Inc (PA)** ..................................... E ...... 310 216-1086
1013 W Hillcrest Blvd Inglewood (90301) *(P-8987)*

**Multicoat Products Inc** ................................................... F ...... 949 888-7100
23331 Antonio Pkwy Rcho Sta Marg (92688) *(P-6097)*

**Multilayer Prototypes Inc** ............................................... F ...... 805 498-9390
2320 Terra Bella Ln Camarillo (93012) *(P-12168)*

**Multimek Inc** ................................................................... E ...... 408 653-1300
357 Reed St Santa Clara (95050) *(P-12169)*

**Multiquip Inc (DH)** .......................................................... B ...... 310 537-3700
6141 Katella Ave Ste 200 Cypress (90630) *(P-16665)*

**Multitaskr** ........................................................................ F ...... 619 391-3371
2576 Catamaran Way Chula Vista (91914) *(P-3258)*

**Multitest Elctrnic Systems Inc (DH)** .............................. B ...... 408 988-6544
3021 Kenneth St Santa Clara (95054) *(P-14556)*

**Multivest, San Dimas** *Also Called: Webmetro (P-18930)*

**Multivitamin Direct Inc** .................................................. E ...... 408 573-7292
2178 Paragon Dr San Jose (95131) *(P-5250)*

**Mum Industries Inc** ........................................................ D ...... 800 729-1314
2320 Meyers Ave Escondido (92029) *(P-5180)*

**Mumm NAPA Valley, Rutherford** *Also Called: Pernod Ricard Usa LLC (P-1705)*

**Munchkin Inc** .................................................................. E ...... 818 893-5000
27334 San Bernardino Ave Redlands (92374) *(P-6609)*

**Munchkin Inc (PA)** .......................................................... C ...... 800 344-2229
7835 Gloria Ave Van Nuys (91406) *(P-6610)*

**Munekata America Inc** .................................................. B ...... 619 661-8080
2320 Paseo De Las Americas Ste 112 San Diego (92154) *(P-13041)*

**Munger Bros LLC** ........................................................... A ...... 661 721-0390
786 Road 188 Delano (93215) *(P-46)*

**Munger Farm, Delano** *Also Called: Munger Bros LLC (P-46)*

**Munn & Perkins, Modesto** *Also Called: Reed Group (P-379)*

**Munselle Vineyards LLC** ............................................... F ...... 707 857-9988
2859 Dry Creek Rd Healdsburg (95448) *(P-1683)*

**Murad, Los Angeles** *Also Called: Murad LLC (P-5559)*

**Murad LLC (HQ)** ............................................................. C ...... 310 726-0600
2121 Park Pl Fl 1 El Segundo (90245) *(P-5558)*

**Murad LLC** ...................................................................... D ...... 310 906-3100
8207 W 3rd St Los Angeles (90048) *(P-5559)*

**Murcal, Palmdale** *Also Called: Murcal Inc (P-16666)*

**Murcal Inc** ....................................................................... E ...... 661 272-4700
41343 12th St W Palmdale (93551) *(P-16666)*

**Murdoc Technology LLC** ................................................ E ...... 559 497-1580
5683 E Fountain Way Fresno (93727) *(P-13042)*

**Murphy HARtelius/M&h Uniforms (PA)** ........................ E ...... 650 344-2997
845 Stanton Rd Burlingame (94010) *(P-17078)*

**Murray Trailers, Stockton** *Also Called: Pacifico Inc (P-13618)*

**Murrays Iron Works Inc (PA)** ......................................... C ...... 323 521-1100
7355 E Slauson Ave Commerce (90040) *(P-3507)*

**Murrietta Circuits** ........................................................... C ...... 714 970-2430
5000 E Landon Dr Anaheim (92807) *(P-12170)*

**Mursion Inc** ..................................................................... C ...... 415 746-9631
2443 Fillmore St Pmb 515 San Francisco (94115) *(P-18563)*

**Musco Family Olive Co, Tracy** *Also Called: Olive Musco Products Inc (P-914)*

**Musicmatch Inc** .............................................................. C ...... 858 485-4300
16935 W Bernardo Dr Ste 270 San Diego (92127) *(P-18564)*

**Muth Machine Works (HQ)** ............................................ E ...... 714 527-2239
8042 Katella Ave Stanton (90680) *(P-11000)*

**Mutual Liquid Gas & Eqp Co Inc (PA)** .......................... E ...... 310 515-0553
17117 S Broadway Gardena (90248) *(P-16828)*

**Mutual Propane, Gardena** *Also Called: Mutual Liquid Gas & Eqp Co Inc (P-16828)*

**Mux Inc (PA)** .................................................................... F ...... 510 402-2257
50 Beale St Fl 9 San Francisco (94105) *(P-18565)*

**Mventix, Woodland Hills** *Also Called: Mventix Inc (P-19107)*

**Mventix Inc (PA)** .............................................................. D ...... 818 337-3747
21600 Oxnard St Ste 1700 Woodland Hills (91367) *(P-19107)*

**Mvinix Corporation** ........................................................ E ...... 408 321-9109
1759 Mccarthy Blvd Milpitas (95035) *(P-17543)*

**Mw Compnnts - Anheim Ideal Fas, Anaheim** *Also Called: Matthew Warren Inc (P-15913)*

**Mw Components - Corona, Corona** *Also Called: Ameriflex Inc (P-9247)*

**Mw McWong International Inc (PA)** .............................. F ...... 916 371-8080
1921 Arena Blvd Sacramento (95834) *(P-11614)*

**Mws Precision Wire Inds Inc** ........................................ D ...... 818 991-8553
3000 Camino Del Sol Oxnard (93030) *(P-16624)*

**Mws Wire Industries, Oxnard** *Also Called: Mws Precision Wire Inds Inc (P-16624)*

**Mx No Fear, Carlsbad** *Also Called: J2 Llc (P-2624)*

**MXF Designs Inc** ............................................................ D ...... 323 266-1451
5327 Valley Blvd Los Angeles (90032) *(P-2682)*

**Mxic, Milpitas** *Also Called: Macronix America Inc (P-16717)*

**My Eye Media LLC** ......................................................... D ...... 818 559-7200
2211 N Hollywood Way Burbank (91505) *(P-18566)*

**My Machine Inc** .............................................................. F ...... 626 214-9223
5140 Commerce Dr Baldwin Park (91706) *(P-11001)*

**My Michelle, La Puente** *Also Called: Mymichelle Company LLC (P-2683)*

**My Tech USA, Corona** *Also Called: Hardy Frames Inc (P-7614)*

**Myanimelist LLC** ............................................................ F ...... 714 423-8289
8445 Camino Santa Fe Ste 210 San Diego (92121) *(P-4434)*

**Mycase, San Diego** *Also Called: Appfolio Inc (P-18052)*

**Mycelium Enterprises LLC** ........................................... E ...... 657 251-0016
10632 Trask Ave Garden Grove (92843) *(P-5251)*

**Mydax Inc** ....................................................................... F ...... 530 888-6662
12260 Shale Ridge Ln Ste 4 Auburn (95602) *(P-10509)*

**Mye Technologies Inc** ................................................... E ...... 661 964-0217
25060 Avenue Stanford Valencia (91355) *(P-13274)*

**Myers & Sons Hi-Way Safety Inc (PA)** ......................... D ...... 909 591-1781
13310 5th St Chino (91710) *(P-16012)*

**Myers Mixers LLC** .......................................................... E ...... 323 560-4723
8376 Salt Lake Ave Cudahy (90201) *(P-10100)*

**Myevaluationscom Inc** .................................................. E ...... 646 422-0554
11111 W Olympic Blvd Ste 401 Los Angeles (90064) *(P-17952)*

**Mygrant Glass Company Inc** ....................................... E ...... 858 455-8022
10220 Camino Santa Fe San Diego (92121) *(P-13544)*

**Mymichelle Company LLC (HQ)** .................................. B ...... 626 934-4166
13077 Temple Ave La Puente (91746) *(P-2683)*

**Myntahl Corporation** ..................................................... E ...... 510 413-0002
48273 Lakeview Blvd Fremont (94538) *(P-13043)*

**Myojo USA Inc** ............................................................... F ...... 909 464-1411
6220 Prescott Ct Chino (91710) *(P-2116)*

**Myokardia Inc (HQ)** ....................................................... D ...... 650 741-0900
1000 Sierra Point Pkwy Brisbane (94005) *(P-5560)*

**Myotek Industries Incorporated (DH)** .......................... D ...... 949 502-3776
1278 Glenneyre St Ste 431 Laguna Beach (92651) *(P-13179)*

**Myron L Company** ......................................................... D ...... 760 438-2021
2450 Impala Dr Carlsbad (92010) *(P-14438)*

**Mysmile Oral Care Inc** .................................................. E ...... 909 908-4615
8238 Mayten Ave Rancho Cucamonga (91730) *(P-5919)*

**Mytee Products Inc** ....................................................... E ...... 858 679-1191
13655 Stowe Dr Poway (92064) *(P-10583)*

**Mytra Inc** ........................................................................ E ...... 650 539-8070
111 Pine Ave South San Francisco (94080) *(P-9741)*

**Myvr.com, Corte Madera** *Also Called: Jomu Mist Incorporated (P-18460)*

**Mywi Fabricators Inc** .................................................... F ...... 626 279-6994
2115 Edwards Ave 2119 South El Monte (91733) *(P-8194)*

**Mzla Technologies Corporation** .................................. E ...... 650 903-0800
149 New Montgomery St Fl 4 San Francisco (94105) *(P-18567)*

**N Ck's, El Segundo** *Also Called: Luthman Backlund Foods USA Inc (P-807)*

**N D C, Fremont** *Also Called: Confluent Medical Tech Inc (P-15048)*

**N D E Inc** ........................................................................ E ...... 408 727-3955
3301 Keller St Santa Clara (95054) *(P-13044)*

**N G S, Sacramento** *Also Called: New Generation Software Inc (P-18582)*

**N H Research LLC (DH)** ................................................ D ...... 949 474-3900
16601 Hale Ave Irvine (92606) *(P-14557)*

**N J M, Stockton** *Also Called: NJ Mc Cutchen Inc (P-11009)*

**N K Cabinets Inc** ........................................................... E ...... 818 897-7909
13290 Paxton St Pacoima (91331) *(P-3259)*

**N M Floor Coverings Inc** .............................................. F ...... 760 931-8274
5651 Palmer Way Ste D Carlsbad (92010) *(P-3099)*

**N Philanthropy LLC** ....................................................... F ...... 213 278-0754
1132 E 12th St Los Angeles (90021) *(P-19108)*

**N V Cast Stone LLC** ...................................................... E ...... 707 261-6615
2003 Seville Dr Napa (94559) *(P-7357)*

**N/S Corporation (PA)** .................................................. D ...... 310 412-7074
28309 Avenue Crocker Valencia (91355) *(P-10584)*

**N2 Aero, Van Nuys** *Also Called: N2 Development Inc (P-13913)*

**N2 Development Inc** ........................................................ F ...... 323 210-3251
6849 Hayvenhurst Ave Van Nuys (91406) *(P-13913)*

**N7 Creamery Inc** ............................................................. F ...... 909 922-8422
35458 Byron Trl Beaumont (92223) *(P-812)*

**Nabisco, Ontario** *Also Called: Mondelez Global LLC (P-17197)*

**Nabors Well Services Co** .................................................. D ...... 805 648-2731
2567 N Ventura Ave # C Ventura (93001) *(P-253)*

**Nabors Well Services Co** .................................................. C ...... 661 588-6140
1025 Earthmover Ct Bakersfield (93314) *(P-254)*

**Nabors Well Services Co** .................................................. D ...... 310 639-7074
19431 S Santa Fe Ave Compton (90221) *(P-255)*

**Nabors Well Services Co** .................................................. C ...... 661 392-7668
1954 James Rd Bakersfield (93308) *(P-256)*

**Nabors Well Services Co** .................................................. C ...... 661 589-3970
7515 Rosedale Hwy Bakersfield (93308) *(P-257)*

**Nada Appraisal Guide, Costa Mesa** *Also Called: National Appraisal Guides Inc (P-4435)*

**Nadalie USA, Calistoga** *Also Called: Tonnellerie Francaise French C (P-3376)*

**Nadolife Inc** ..................................................................... E ...... 619 522-0077
1025 Orange Ave Coronado (92118) *(P-7938)*

**Nady Systems Inc** ............................................................ E ...... 510 652-2411
3341 Vincent Rd Pleasant Hill (94523) *(P-11680)*

**Nafhc, Santa Maria** *Also Called: North American Fire Hose Corp (P-6426)*

**Nagles Veal Inc** ................................................................ E ...... 909 383-7075
1411 E Base Line St San Bernardino (92410) *(P-608)*

**Nagra, San Francisco** *Also Called: Opentv Inc (P-18625)*

**NAI, Carlsbad** *Also Called: Natural Alternatives Intl Inc (P-5252)*

**Naia Inc** .......................................................................... E ...... 510 724-2479
736 Alfred Nobel Dr Hercules (94547) *(P-813)*

**Nailpro, Encino** *Also Called: Creative Age Publications Inc (P-4242)*

**Nakagawa Manufacturing USA Inc** .................................... E ...... 510 782-0197
1709 Junction Ct San Jose (95112) *(P-3786)*

**Nakamura-Beeman Inc** .................................................... E ...... 562 696-1400
8520 Wellsford Pl Santa Fe Springs (90670) *(P-3574)*

**Naked Juice Co Glendora Inc (HQ)** .................................... E ...... 626 873-2600
1333 S Mayflower Ave Ste 100 Monrovia (91016) *(P-17429)*

**Nalco Champion, Bakersfield** *Also Called: Championx LLC (P-5082)*

**Nalco Water, Placentia** *Also Called: Nalco Wtr Prtrtment Sltons LLC (P-10585)*

**Nalco Wtr Prtrtment Sltons LLC** ....................................... ...... 714 792-0708
1961 Petra Ln Placentia (92870) *(P-10585)*

**Nally & Millie, Los Angeles** *Also Called: MXF Designs Inc (P-2682)*

**Namar Company, Paramount** *Also Called: Namar Foods (P-959)*

**Namar Foods** .................................................................. E ...... 562 531-2744
6830 Walthall Way Paramount (90723) *(P-959)*

**Nan McKay and Associates Inc** ......................................... D ...... 619 258-1855
1810 Gillespie Way Ste 202 El Cajon (92020) *(P-19534)*

**Nana Wall Systems, Corte Madera** *Also Called: Nana Wall Systems Inc (P-8280)*

**Nana Wall Systems Inc** .................................................... E ...... 415 383-3148
100 Meadowcreek Dr Ste 250 Corte Madera (94925) *(P-8280)*

**Nancys Specialty Foods** ................................................... B ...... 510 494-1100
2400 Olympic Blvd Ste 8 Lafayette (94595) *(P-2289)*

**Nanez Mfg Inc (PA)** .......................................................... F ...... 408 830-9903
164 Commercial St Sunnyvale (94086) *(P-11002)*

**Nano Filter Inc** ................................................................. D ...... 949 316-8866
22310 Bonita St Carson (90745) *(P-16186)*

**Nanofilm, Westlake Village** *Also Called: Interntional Photo Plates Corp (P-8974)*

**Nanofocus Inc** ................................................................. E ...... 408 435-2777
2360 Qume Dr Ste B San Jose (95131) *(P-14558)*

**Nanografix Corporation** ................................................... F ...... 858 524-3295
3820 Valley Centre Dr Ste 705 San Diego (92130) *(P-4702)*

**Nanoknee, Arroyo Grande** *Also Called: Applied Orthopedic Design (P-15323)*

**Nanoprecision Products Inc** ............................................. E ...... 310 597-4991
802 Calle Plano Camarillo (93012) *(P-8869)*

**Nanosilicon Inc** ............................................................... E ...... 408 263-7341
2461 Autumnvale Dr San Jose (95131) *(P-12594)*

**Nanoskin Car Care Products, Santa Fe Springs** *Also Called: Total Import Solutions Inc (P-16404)*

**Nanosolar Inc** .................................................................. B
2434 Rock St Apt 14 Mountain View (94043) *(P-16770)*

**Nanosys, Milpitas** *Also Called: Nanosys Inc (P-12595)*

**Nanosys Inc (HQ)** ............................................................ E ...... 408 240-6700
233 S Hillview Dr Milpitas (95035) *(P-12595)*

**Nanotronics Automation, Hollister** *Also Called: Nanotronics Imaging Inc (P-13275)*

**Nanotronics Imaging Inc** .................................................. E ...... 831 630-0700
777 Flynn Rd Hollister (95023) *(P-13275)*

**Nanovea Inc (PA)** ............................................................. E ...... 949 461-9292
6 Morgan Ste 156 Irvine (92618) *(P-14696)*

**Nantenergy LLC** .............................................................. D ...... 310 905-4866
2040 E Mariposa Ave El Segundo (90245) *(P-11279)*

**NAPA Cellars, Oakville** *Also Called: Sutter Home Winery Inc (P-1770)*

**NAPA Register, Napa** *Also Called: NAPA Valley Publishing Co (P-4165)*

**NAPA Select Vineyard Svcs Inc** ......................................... F ...... 707 294-2637
5 Financial Plz Ste 200 Napa (94558) *(P-1684)*

**NAPA Valley Cast Stone, Napa** *Also Called: N V Cast Stone LLC (P-7357)*

**NAPA Valley PSI Inc** ......................................................... D ...... 707 255-0177
651 Trabajo Ln Napa (94559) *(P-19362)*

**NAPA Valley Publishing Co** ............................................... D ...... 707 226-3711
1615 Soscol Ave Napa (94559) *(P-4165)*

**NAPA Wine Company LLC** ................................................ E ...... 707 944-8669
7830 St Helena Hwy # 40 Oakville (94562) *(P-1685)*

**Naprotek LLC (PA)** ........................................................... E ...... 408 830-5000
90 Rose Orchard Way San Jose (95134) *(P-12171)*

**Narayan Corporation** ....................................................... E ...... 310 719-7330
13432 Estrella Ave Gardena (90248) *(P-6611)*

**Narcotics Anonymous Wrld Svcs I (PA)** ............................. E ...... 818 773-9999
19737 Nordhoff Pl Chatsworth (91311) *(P-4337)*

**Narda Microwave West, Folsom** *Also Called: Stellant Systems Inc (P-11952)*

**Nasco Aircraft Brake Inc** ................................................... D ...... 310 532-4430
13300 Estrella Ave Gardena (90248) *(P-13914)*

**Nasco Gourmet Foods Inc** ................................................ D ...... 714 279-2100
22720 Savi Ranch Pkwy Yorba Linda (92887) *(P-907)*

**Nashville Wire Pdts Mfg Co LLC** ....................................... F ...... 714 736-0081
10727 Commerce Way Ste C Fontana (92337) *(P-9223)*

**Nasmyth Tmf Inc** ............................................................. D ...... 818 954-9504
29102 Hancock Pkwy Valencia (91355) *(P-8988)*

**Naso Industries Corporation** ............................................ E ...... 805 650-1231
3007 Bunsen Ave Ste Q Ventura (93003) *(P-12172)*

**Naso Technologies, Ventura** *Also Called: Naso Industries Corporation (P-12172)*

**Nassco** ........................................................................... ...... 619 929-3019
7470 Mission Valley Rd San Diego (92108) *(P-14011)*

**Nassco, San Diego** *Also Called: International Mfg Tech Inc (P-7616)*

**Nasty Gal Inc (HQ)** ........................................................... E ...... 213 542-3436
2049 Century Park E Ste 3400 Los Angeles (90067) *(P-17495)*

**Natals Inc** ........................................................................ C ...... 323 475-6033
1370 N St Andrews Pl Los Angeles (90028) *(P-5561)*

**Natel Engineering, Chatsworth** *Also Called: Epic Technologies LLC (P-11762)*

**Natel Engineering Company LLC (PA)** .............................. C ...... 818 495-8617
9340 Owensmouth Ave Chatsworth (91311) *(P-13045)*

**Natel Engineering Holdings Inc** ........................................ ...... 818 734-6500
9340 Owensmouth Ave Chatsworth (91311) *(P-12173)*

**Nates Fine Foods LLC** ...................................................... E ...... 310 897-2690
8880 Industrial Ave Ste 100 Roseville (95678) *(P-1040)*

**Nathan Anthony Furniture, Vernon** *Also Called: Yen-Nhai Inc (P-3495)*

**National Advanced Endoscopy De** .................................... E ...... 818 227-2720
22134 Sherman Way Canoga Park (91303) *(P-17712)*

**National Appraisal Guides Inc** .......................................... E ...... 714 556-8511
3186 Airway Ave Ste K Costa Mesa (92626) *(P-4435)*

**National Band Saw Company** ........................................... ...... 661 294-9552
1055 W Avenue L12 Lancaster (93534) *(P-9807)*

**National Bevpak, Hayward** *Also Called: Shasta Beverages Inc (P-1963)*

**National Business Group Inc (PA)** ..................................... D ...... 818 221-6000
15319 Chatsworth St Mission Hills (91345) *(P-17853)*

**National Cement Co Cal Inc (DH)** ...................................... E ...... 818 728-5200
15821 Ventura Blvd Ste 475 Encino (91436) *(P-7472)*

**National Cement Company Inc (HQ)** ................................. E ...... 818 728-5200
15821 Ventura Blvd Ste 475 Encino (91436) *(P-7261)*

**National Cement Company Inc** ......................................... D ...... 323 923-4466
2626 E 26th St Vernon (90058) *(P-7473)*

**National Cement Ready Mix, Encino** *Also Called: National Ready Mixed Con Co (P-7477)*

## ALPHABETIC SECTION — Nautilus Seafood

National Cnstr Rentals Inc .................... D ...... 510 563-4000
  1300 Business Center Dr San Leandro (94577) *(P-17858)*

National Coatings Corporation .................... E ...... 805 388-7112
  1201 Calle Suerte Camarillo (93012) *(P-6381)*

National Construction Rental, San Leandro *Also Called: National Cnstr Rentals Inc (P-17858)*

National Copy Cartridge, Tustin *Also Called: US Print & Toner Inc (P-15902)*

National Corset Supply House (PA) .................... D ...... 323 261-0265
  3240 E 26th St Vernon (90058) *(P-2833)*

National Diversified Sales Inc (HQ) .................... C ...... 559 562-9888
  21300 Victory Blvd Ste 215 Woodland Hills (91367) *(P-6926)*

National Emblem, Long Beach *Also Called: Enrich Enterprises Inc (P-2990)*

National Emblem (PA) .................... C ...... 310 515-5055
  3925 E Vernon St Long Beach (90815) *(P-2997)*

National Ewp Inc .................... F ...... 909 931-4014
  5566 Arrow Hwy Montclair (91763) *(P-108)*

National Explrtion Wells Pumps, Montclair *Also Called: National Ewp Inc (P-108)*

National Glass Systems Inc .................... E ...... 408 835-5124
  258 Boulay Ct Morgan Hill (95037) *(P-541)*

National Graphics LLC .................... E ...... 805 644-9212
  200 N Elevar St Oxnard (93030) *(P-4703)*

National Hot Rod Association (PA) .................... C ...... 626 914-4761
  140 Via Verde Ste 100 San Dimas (91773) *(P-19308)*

National Hrdwood Flrg Moulding, Van Nuys *Also Called: Katzirs Floor & HM Design Inc (P-16428)*

National Instruments Corp .................... E ...... 408 610-6800
  4600 Patrick Henry Dr Santa Clara (95054) *(P-14559)*

National Jurist, San Diego *Also Called: Cypress Magazines Inc (P-4245)*

National Logistics Team LLC .................... E ...... 951 369-5841
  21496 Main St Grand Terrace (92313) *(P-16281)*

National Manufacturing Co .................... A ...... 800 346-9445
  19701 Da Vinci Lake Forest (92610) *(P-8020)*

National Media Inc .................... F ...... 310 372-0388
  2615 Pacific Coast Hwy Ste 329 Hermosa Beach (90254) *(P-4166)*

National Media Inc (HQ) .................... E ...... 310 377-6877
  609 Deep Valley Dr Ste 200 Rllng Hls Est (90274) *(P-4167)*

National Metal Stampings Inc .................... D ...... 661 945-1157
  42110 8th St E Lancaster (93535) *(P-8870)*

National O Rings, Downey *Also Called: Hutchinson Seal Corporation (P-6452)*

National Packaging Products, Commerce *Also Called: Yavar Manufacturing Co Inc (P-3920)*

National Print + Promo .................... E ...... 707 576-6375
  2321 Circadian Way Santa Rosa (95407) *(P-4704)*

National Ready Mixed Con Co .................... F ...... 818 768-0050
  9010 Norris Ave Sun Valley (91352) *(P-7474)*

National Ready Mixed Con Co .................... F ...... 323 245-5539
  4549 Brazil St Los Angeles (90039) *(P-7475)*

National Ready Mixed Con Co .................... F ...... 818 884-0893
  6969 Deering Ave Canoga Park (91303) *(P-7476)*

National Ready Mixed Con Co (DH) .................... E ...... 818 728-5200
  15821 Ventura Blvd Ste 475 Encino (91436) *(P-7477)*

National Ready Mixed Con Co .................... F ...... 562 865-6211
  11725 Artesia Blvd Artesia (90701) *(P-7478)*

National Ready Mixed Con Co .................... F ...... 661 252-8181
  27050 Ruether Ave Canyon Country (91351) *(P-7479)*

National Ready Mixed Con Co .................... F ...... 949 552-5566
  16282 Construction Cir E Irvine (92606) *(P-7480)*

National Resilience Inc (PA) .................... E ...... 888 737-2460
  3115 Merryfield Row Ste 200 San Diego (92121) *(P-5562)*

National Semiconductor Corp (HQ) .................... A ...... 408 721-5000
  2900 Semiconductor Dr Santa Clara (95051) *(P-12596)*

National Sign & Marketing Corp .................... D ...... 909 591-4742
  13580 5th St Chino (91710) *(P-16013)*

National Signal LLC .................... D ...... 714 441-7707
  14489 Industry Cir La Mirada (90638) *(P-14131)*

National Stl & Shipbuilding Co (HQ) .................... B ...... 619 544-3400
  2798 Harbor Dr San Diego (92113) *(P-14012)*

National Tour Intgrted Rsrces .................... E ...... 949 215-6330
  23141 Arroyo Vis Ste 100 Rcho Sta Marg (92688) *(P-19535)*

National Tube & Steel, Mission Hills *Also Called: National Business Group Inc (P-17853)*

National Wholesale Lumber, Pixley *Also Called: Correa Pallet Inc (P-3336)*

National Wire and Cable, Los Angeles *Also Called: National Wire and Cable Corporation (P-7648)*

National Wire and Cable Corporation .................... C ...... 323 225-5611
  136 N San Fernando Rd Los Angeles (90031) *(P-7648)*

Nationwide and International, Oceanside *Also Called: Amflex Plastics Incorporated (P-6424)*

Nationwide Boiler Incorporated (PA) .................... E ...... 510 490-7100
  42400 Christy St Fremont (94538) *(P-8322)*

Nationwide Technologies .................... E ...... 909 340-2770
  3684 W Uva Ln San Bernardino (92407) *(P-18568)*

Native .................... E ...... 562 217-9338
  201 California St Ste 450 San Francisco (94111) *(P-6009)*

Native, San Francisco *Also Called: Native Data Inc (P-18569)*

Native Data Inc .................... F ...... 855 466-9494
  185 Berry St Ste 6850 San Francisco (94107) *(P-18569)*

Native Deodorants, San Francisco *Also Called: Zenlen Inc (P-6064)*

Natividad Plant Us24, Salinas *Also Called: Lhoist North America Ariz Inc (P-317)*

Natren Inc .................... D ...... 805 371-4737
  3105 Willow Ln Thousand Oaks (91361) *(P-2290)*

Natrol Inc .................... C ...... 818 739-6000
  21411 Prairie St Chatsworth (91311) *(P-5563)*

Natrol LLC (PA) .................... C ...... 800 262-8765
  15233 Ventura Blvd Fl 900 Sherman Oaks (91403) *(P-5564)*

Natrol LLC .................... E ...... 818 739-6000
  9454 Jordan Ave Chatsworth (91311) *(P-17042)*

Natron Energy Inc (PA) .................... D ...... 408 498-5828
  3542 Bassett St Santa Clara (95054) *(P-13146)*

Natural Alternatives Intl Inc .................... F ...... 800 848-2646
  5928 Farnsworth Ct Carlsbad (92008) *(P-770)*

Natural Alternatives Intl Inc (PA) .................... C ...... 760 736-7700
  1535 Faraday Ave Carlsbad (92008) *(P-5252)*

Natural Balance Pet Foods LLC .................... D ...... 800 829-4493
  1224 Montague Unit 1 Pacoima (91331) *(P-1138)*

Natural Balance Pet Foods LLC (PA) .................... D ...... 800 829-4493
  19425 Soledad Canyon Rd # 302 Canyon Country (91351) *(P-1139)*

Natural Decadence LLC .................... F ...... 707 444-2629
  5720 West End Rd Ste 2 Arcata (95521) *(P-1289)*

Natural Envmtl Protection Co .................... E ...... 909 620-8028
  750 S Reservoir St Pomona (91766) *(P-5181)*

Natural Food Mill, Corona *Also Called: Food For Life Baking Co Inc (P-1201)*

Natural Latex Company, The, Camarillo *Also Called: Sleep Technologies Inc (P-3539)*

Natural Thoughts Incorporated .................... E ...... 619 582-0027
  4757 Old Cliffs Rd San Diego (92120) *(P-6010)*

Naturalife Eco Vite Labs .................... D ...... 310 370-1563
  20433 Earl St Torrance (90503) *(P-771)*

Nature Qulty A Cal Ltd Partnr .................... F
  9351 Fairview Rd Hollister (95023) *(P-1013)*

Nature-Cide, Canoga Park *Also Called: Pacific Shore Holdings Inc (P-5592)*

Nature's Flavors, Orange *Also Called: Newport Flavors & Fragrances (P-2017)*

Naturener USA LLC (HQ) .................... E ...... 415 217-5500
  435 Pacific Ave Fl 4 San Francisco (94133) *(P-11280)*

Natures Flavors .................... E ...... 714 744-3700
  833 N Elm St Orange (92867) *(P-2291)*

Naturvet, Temecula *Also Called: Garmon Corporation (P-1096)*

Naturvet, Temecula *Also Called: Garmon Corporation (P-1097)*

Naturvet, Temecula *Also Called: Garmon Corporation (P-1098)*

Naturvet, Temecula *Also Called: Garmon Corporation (P-1099)*

Naturvet, Temecula *Also Called: Garmon Corporation (P-1127)*

Natus, Pleasanton *Also Called: Natus Medical Incorporated (P-15563)*

Natus Inc .................... D ...... 626 355-3746
  38 W Sierra Madre Blvd Los Alamitos (90720) *(P-7136)*

Natus Medical Incorporated .................... D ...... 650 802-0400
  6701 Koll Center Pkwy # 120 Pleasanton (94566) *(P-15561)*

Natus Medical Incorporated .................... D ...... 858 260-2590
  5955 Pacific Center Blvd San Diego (92121) *(P-15562)*

Natus Medical Incorporated (HQ) .................... E ...... 925 223-6700
  6701 Koll Center Pkwy Ste 120 Pleasanton (94566) *(P-15563)*

Natus Newborn Care, Pleasanton *Also Called: Natus Medical Incorporated (P-15561)*

Natvar, City Of Industry *Also Called: Tekni-Plex Inc (P-4054)*

Nautica Opco LLC .................... B ...... 909 297-7243
  950 Barrington Ave Ontario (91764) *(P-2635)*

Nautilus Seafood, Wilmington *Also Called: J Deluca Fish Company Inc (P-2055)*

Naval Coating Inc .................................................. C ...... 619 234-8366
  2080 Cambridge Ave Cardiff By The Sea (92007) *(P-568)*
Navarro Vineyard, Philo *Also Called: Navarro Vineyards LLC (P-1686)*
Navarro Vineyards LLC ............................................ E ...... 707 895-3686
  5601 Highway 128 Philo (95466) *(P-1686)*
Navco Security Systems, Fullerton *Also Called: North American Video Corp (P-16726)*
Navcom Technology Inc (HQ) ................................ D ...... 310 381-2000
  20780 Madrona Ave Torrance (90503) *(P-11901)*
Navis LP .................................................................. C ...... 408 512-2505
  2001 Gateway Pl Ste 200 San Jose (95110) *(P-18570)*
Nawgan Beverages, Dana Point *Also Called: Nawgan Products LLC (P-17199)*
Nawgan Products LLC ............................................ F ...... 949 542-4425
  34232 Pacific Coast Hwy Ste D Dana Point (92629) *(P-17199)*
Naxcor Inc ............................................................... F ...... 650 328-9398
  320 Logue Ave # 200 Mountain View (94043) *(P-5768)*
Nbcuniversal Television Dist, Universal City *Also Called: Universal Cy Stdios Prdctons L (P-19298)*
Nbp, Claremont *Also Called: New Bedford Panoramex Corp (P-11615)*
Nbs Design Inc ....................................................... B ...... 805 966-9383
  1940 Milmont Dr Milpitas (95035) *(P-12174)*
Nbs Systems Inc (PA) ............................................ E ...... 217 999-3472
  2477 E Orangethorpe Ave Fullerton (92831) *(P-4990)*
Nbty Manufacturing LLC ........................................ C ...... 714 765-8323
  5115 E La Palma Ave Anaheim (92807) *(P-5565)*
NC America LLC ..................................................... E ...... 949 447-6287
  400 Spectrum Center Dr Fl 18 Irvine (92618) *(P-17953)*
NC Dynamics, Long Beach *Also Called: NC Dynamics LLC (P-11004)*
NC Dynamics Incorporated .................................... C ...... 562 634-7392
  6925 Downey Ave Long Beach (90805) *(P-11003)*
NC Dynamics LLC ................................................... C ...... 562 634-7392
  3401 E 69th St Long Beach (90805) *(P-11004)*
Nc4 Soltra LLC ....................................................... D ...... 408 489-5579
  21515 Hawthorne Blvd Ste 520 Torrance (90503) *(P-18571)*
Nca Laboratories Inc ............................................. E ...... 916 852-7029
  11305 Sunrise Gold Cir Rancho Cordova (95742) *(P-11681)*
Ncc Group Escrow Assoc LLC ............................... F ...... 678 381-2768
  123 Mission St Ste 900 San Francisco (94105) *(P-11738)*
Ncdi, Long Beach *Also Called: NC Dynamics Incorporated (P-11003)*
Nci Group Inc ......................................................... E ...... 909 987-4681
  9123 Center Ave Rancho Cucamonga (91730) *(P-8678)*
Ncim, Rancho Cordova *Also Called: Northern California Injection Molding LLC (P-6935)*
Ncla Inc .................................................................. F ...... 562 926-6252
  1388 W Foothill Blvd Azusa (91702) *(P-4042)*
Ncoup Inc (PA) ........................................................ E ...... 510 739-4010
  825 Corporate Way Fremont (94539) *(P-18572)*
Ncstar Inc .............................................................. E ...... 866 627-8278
  18031 Cortney Ct City Of Industry (91748) *(P-14801)*
NDC Technologies Inc ........................................... D ...... 626 960-3300
  5314 Irwindale Ave Irwindale (91706) *(P-14903)*
Nds, Woodland Hills *Also Called: National Diversified Sales Inc (P-6926)*
Nds, Fresno *Also Called: Agrifim Irrigation Pdts Inc (P-9335)*
Ndsp Crp, San Jose *Also Called: Ndsp Delaware Inc (P-12597)*
Ndsp Delaware Inc ................................................. E ...... 408 626-1640
  224 Airport Pkwy Ste 400 San Jose (95110) *(P-12597)*
Ne-Mo's, Escondido *Also Called: Nemos Bakery Inc (P-1290)*
Nea Electronics Inc ............................................... E ...... 805 292-4010
  14370 White Sage Rd Moorpark (93021) *(P-12891)*
Neal Feay Company ............................................... D ...... 805 967-4521
  133 S La Patera Ln Goleta (93117) *(P-7744)*
Nearfield Systems Inc ........................................... D ...... 310 525-7000
  19730 Magellan Dr Torrance (90502) *(P-14560)*
Neato Robotics Inc (HQ) ........................................ E ...... 510 795-1351
  3590 N 1st St Ste 200 San Jose (95134) *(P-9742)*
Neb Cal Printing, San Diego *Also Called: Kovin Corporation Inc (P-4663)*
Nebia, San Francisco *Also Called: Brondell Inc (P-17030)*
Nectave Inc ............................................................ F ...... 714 736-9811
  3309 E Miraloma Ave Ste 105 Anaheim (92806) *(P-2292)*
Nefab Packaging Inc ............................................. D ...... 408 678-2500
  8477 Central Ave Newark (94560) *(P-3327)*
Neft Vodka USA Inc ................................................ F ...... 415 846-0359
  144 Penn St El Segundo (90245) *(P-4927)*

Neighborhood Church, Visalia *Also Called: Neighborhood Mennonite (P-19369)*
Neighborhood Mennonite ...................................... E ...... 559 732-9107
  5505 W Riggin Ave Visalia (93291) *(P-19369)*
Neighborhood Steel LLC (HQ) ............................... E ...... 714 236-8700
  5555 Garden Grove Blvd Ste 250 Westminster (92683) *(P-16625)*
Neighbrhood Bus Advrtsment Ltd ......................... E ...... 442 300-1803
  14752 Crenshaw Blvd Gardena (90249) *(P-16187)*
Neil A Kjos Music Company (PA) ........................... E ...... 858 270-9800
  4382 Jutland Dr San Diego (92117) *(P-4436)*
Neil Jones Food Company ..................................... E ...... 831 637-0573
  711 Sally St Hollister (95023) *(P-908)*
Neil Jones Food Company ..................................... E ...... 559 659-5100
  2502 N St Firebaugh (93622) *(P-909)*
Neill Aircraft Co ..................................................... B ...... 562 432-7981
  1260 W 15th St Long Beach (90813) *(P-13915)*
Neilmed Pharmaceuticals Inc (PA) ....................... B ...... 707 525-3784
  498 Aviation Blvd Santa Rosa (95403) *(P-5566)*
Neilsen-Kuljian Inc ................................................ E ...... 800 959-4014
  3511 Charter Park Dr San Jose (95136) *(P-14561)*
Neiman & Company, Van Nuys *Also Called: Neiman/Hoeller Inc (P-16014)*
Neiman/Hoeller Inc ............................................... D ...... 818 781-8600
  6842 Valjean Ave Van Nuys (91406) *(P-16014)*
NEKTAR, San Francisco *Also Called: Nektar Therapeutics (P-5567)*
Nektar Therapeutics (PA) ...................................... D ...... 415 482-5300
  455 Mission Bay Blvd S San Francisco (94158) *(P-5567)*
Nektar Therapeutics ............................................. D ...... 650 622-1790
  150 Industrial Rd San Carlos (94070) *(P-5568)*
Nel Hydrogen Inc ................................................... E ...... 650 543-3180
  2389 Verna Ct San Leandro (94577) *(P-5055)*
Nelco Products Inc ................................................ C ...... 714 879-4293
  1100 E Kimberly Ave Anaheim (92801) *(P-6586)*
Nelgo Industries Inc .............................................. E ...... 760 433-6434
  598 Airport Rd Oceanside (92058) *(P-11005)*
Nelgo Manufacturing, Oceanside *Also Called: Nelgo Industries Inc (P-11005)*
Nellix Inc ................................................................ E ...... 650 213-8700
  2 Musick Irvine (92618) *(P-15198)*
Nellson Nutraceutical LLC .................................... F ...... 626 812-6522
  1000 Etiwanda Ave Ontario (91761) *(P-2293)*
Nellxo LLC ............................................................. E ...... 909 320-8501
  5990 Bald Eagle Dr Fontana (92336) *(P-8871)*
Nelson & Sons Inc ................................................. F ...... 707 462-3755
  550 Nelson Ranch Rd Ukiah (95482) *(P-1687)*
Nelson Adams Naco Corporation .......................... E ...... 909 256-8938
  420 S E St San Bernardino (92401) *(P-3451)*
Nelson Case, Placentia *Also Called: Nelson Case Corporation (P-3328)*
Nelson Case Corporation ...................................... E ...... 714 528-2215
  650 S Jefferson St Ste A Placentia (92870) *(P-3328)*
Nelson Family Vineyard, Ukiah *Also Called: Nelson & Sons Inc (P-1687)*
Nelson Name Plate Company (PA) ........................ E ...... 323 663-3971
  708 Nogales St City Of Industry (91748) *(P-9095)*
Nelson Sports Inc (PA) .......................................... E ...... 562 944-8081
  12810 Florence Ave Santa Fe Springs (90670) *(P-7120)*
Nelson-Miller, City Of Industry *Also Called: Nelson Name Plate Company (P-9095)*
Nemos Bakery Inc (HQ) ......................................... D ...... 760 741-5725
  416 N Hale Ave Escondido (92029) *(P-1290)*
Neo Tech, Chatsworth *Also Called: Natel Engineering Company LLC (P-13045)*
Neo Tech, Chatsworth *Also Called: Oncore Manufacturing LLC (P-19408)*
Neo Tech Aqua Solutions Inc ................................ F ...... 858 571-6590
  3853 Calle Fortunada San Diego (92123) *(P-6312)*
Neo Tech Inc .......................................................... F ...... 510 360-2222
  48119 Warm Springs Blvd Fremont (94539) *(P-12175)*
Neo Tech Natel Epic Oncore, Chatsworth *Also Called: Oncore Manufacturing Svcs Inc (P-12182)*
Neoconix Inc .......................................................... E ...... 408 530-9393
  4020 Moorpark Ave Ste 108 San Jose (95117) *(P-12598)*
Neogov, El Segundo *Also Called: Governmentjobscom Inc (P-18360)*
Neology, Carlsbad *Also Called: Neology Inc (P-14562)*
Neology Inc (PA) .................................................... D ...... 858 391-0260
  1917 Palomar Oaks Way Ste 110 Carlsbad (92008) *(P-14562)*
Neomend Inc .......................................................... D ...... 949 783-3300
  60 Technology Dr Irvine (92618) *(P-15199)*

## ALPHABETIC SECTION

Neon Rose, San Diego *Also Called: Neon Rose Inc (P-5056)*
Neon Rose Inc ............................................................................ E ...... 619 218-6103
5158 Bristol Rd San Diego (92116) *(P-5056)*
Neonode, San Jose *Also Called: Neonode Inc (P-13046)*
Neonode Inc (PA)..................................................................... E ...... 408 496-6722
2880 Zanker Rd San Jose (95134) *(P-13046)*
Neopacific Holdings Inc ........................................................ E ...... 818 786-2900
14940 Calvert St Van Nuys (91411) *(P-6927)*
Neosem Technology Inc (HQ).............................................. E ...... 925 303-4613
4659 Las Positas Rd Ste C Livermore (94551) *(P-14563)*
Nepco, Pomona *Also Called: Natural Envmtl Protection Co (P-5181)*
Neptec Optical Solutions, Fremont *Also Called: Neptec Os Inc (P-7789)*
Neptec Os Inc ........................................................................... E ...... 510 687-1101
454 Kato Ter Fremont (94539) *(P-7789)*
Neptune Foods, Vernon *Also Called: Fishermans Pride Prcessors Inc (P-2053)*
Nerdist Channel LLC ............................................................. E ...... 818 333-2705
2900 W Alameda Ave Unit 1500 Burbank (91505) *(P-11902)*
Nerdist Industries, Burbank *Also Called: Nerdist Channel LLC (P-11902)*
Nero, Garden Grove *Also Called: Vorsteiner Inc (P-17468)*
Nes Holding GMBH, San Jose *Also Called: Networked Energy Services Corp (P-13276)*
Nesco Fabricators, Vallejo *Also Called: Xkt Engineering Inc (P-8356)*
Nestle Confections Factory, Modesto *Also Called: Nestle Usa Inc (P-776)*
Nestle Dist Ctr & Logistics, Jurupa Valley *Also Called: Nestle Usa Inc (P-1041)*
Nestle Dsd, Fresno *Also Called: Nestle Usa Inc (P-772)*
Nestle Purina Factory, Maricopa *Also Called: Nestle Purina Petcare Company (P-1109)*
Nestle Purina Petcare Company ........................................ C ...... 661 769-8261
1710 Golden Cat Rd Maricopa (93252) *(P-1109)*
Nestle Purina Petcare Company ........................................ E ...... 314 982-1000
800 N Brand Blvd Fl 5 Glendale (91203) *(P-1110)*
Nestle Usa Inc ......................................................................... D ...... 559 834-2554
4065 E Therese Ave Fresno (93725) *(P-772)*
Nestle Usa Inc ......................................................................... D ...... 877 463-7853
3285 De Forest Cir Jurupa Valley (91752) *(P-773)*
Nestle Usa Inc ......................................................................... C ...... 661 398-3536
7301 District Blvd Bakersfield (93313) *(P-774)*
Nestle Usa Inc ......................................................................... C ...... 818 549-6000
800 N Brand Blvd Glendale (91203) *(P-775)*
Nestle Usa Inc ......................................................................... B ...... 209 574-2000
736 Garner Rd Modesto (95357) *(P-776)*
Nestle Usa Inc ......................................................................... B ...... 951 360-7200
3450 Dulles Dr Jurupa Valley (91752) *(P-1041)*
Net Optics Inc ......................................................................... D ...... 408 737-7777
5301 Stevens Creek Blvd Santa Clara (95051) *(P-18573)*
Net Shapes Inc (PA) ............................................................... D ...... 909 947-3231
1336 E Francis St Ste B Ontario (91761) *(P-7692)*
Netafim Irrigation Inc (HQ) .................................................. B ...... 559 453-6800
5470 E Home Ave Fresno (93727) *(P-16800)*
Netafim USA, Fresno *Also Called: Netafim Irrigation Inc (P-16800)*
Netapp, San Jose *Also Called: Netapp Inc (P-10255)*
Netapp Inc (PA)....................................................................... A ...... 408 822-6000
3060 Olsen Dr San Jose (95128) *(P-10255)*
Netensity Corporation .......................................................... E ...... 855 222-8488
1068 Balin Ct Folsom (95630) *(P-18574)*
Netflix, Los Gatos *Also Called: Netflix Inc (P-16333)*
Netflix Inc (PA)......................................................................... C ...... 408 540-3700
121 Albright Way Los Gatos (95032) *(P-16333)*
Netgear Inc (PA)...................................................................... C ...... 408 907-8000
350 E Plumeria Dr San Jose (95134) *(P-11775)*
Nethra Imaging Inc (PA)....................................................... E ...... 408 257-5880
2855 Bowers Ave Santa Clara (95051) *(P-12599)*
Netlinx Publishing Solutions, Sacramento *Also Called: System Integrators Inc (P-18995)*
NETLIST, Irvine *Also Called: Netlist Inc (P-12600)*
Netlist Inc (PA)......................................................................... E ...... 949 435-0025
111 Academy Ste 100 Irvine (92617) *(P-12600)*
Netlogic Microsystems LLC ................................................ A ...... 408 454-3000
3975 Freedom Cir Santa Clara (95054) *(P-12601)*
Netmarble Us Inc ................................................................... D ...... 213 222-7712
600 Wilshire Blvd Ste 1100 Los Angeles (90005) *(P-4437)*
Netronix Integration Inc (HQ) ............................................. D ...... 800 600-3939
360 Turtle Creek Ct San Jose (95125) *(P-464)*

Netsarang Inc .......................................................................... F ...... 669 204-3301
4701 Patrick Henry Dr Bldg 22 Santa Clara (95054) *(P-18575)*
Netskope Inc (PA).................................................................... A ...... 800 979-6988
2445 Augustine Dr 3rd Fl Santa Clara (95054) *(P-18576)*
NETSOL, Encino *Also Called: Netsol Technologies Inc (P-18577)*
Netsol Technologies Inc (PA).............................................. D ...... 818 222-9195
16000 Ventura Blvd Ste 770 Encino (91436) *(P-18577)*
Netsource Technology Inc .................................................. F ...... 949 713-0800
951 Calle Negocio Ste B San Clemente (92673) *(P-16725)*
Netsuite Inc (DH) .................................................................... A ...... 650 627-1000
2955 Campus Dr Ste 100 San Mateo (94403) *(P-18578)*
Network Automation Inc ..................................................... E ...... 213 738-1700
3530 Wilshire Blvd Ste 1800 Los Angeles (90010) *(P-18579)*
Network Sltons Prvider USA Inc ........................................ E ...... 213 985-2173
1240 Rosecrans Ave Manhattan Beach (90266) *(P-19566)*
Network Television Time Inc .............................................. E ...... 877 468-8899
3929 Clearford Ct Westlake Village (91361) *(P-4438)*
Network Video Technologies, Fremont *Also Called: Network Video Technologies Inc (P-12892)*
Network Video Technologies Inc (PA).............................. E ...... 650 462-8100
551 Brown Rd Fremont (94539) *(P-12892)*
Networked Energy Services Corp (PA)............................ E ...... 408 622-9900
780 Montague Expy Ste 401 San Jose (95131) *(P-13276)*
Networks Electronic Co LLC ............................................... E ...... 818 341-0440
9750 De Soto Ave Chatsworth (91311) *(P-9139)*
Netwrix Corporation ............................................................. D ...... 888 638-9749
300 Spectrum Center Dr Ste 200 Irvine (92618) *(P-18580)*
Neurasignal Inc ...................................................................... E ...... 877 638-7251
1109 Westwood Blvd Los Angeles (90024) *(P-15564)*
Neurelis Inc (PA)..................................................................... E ...... 858 251-2111
3430 Carmel Mountain Rd Ste 300 San Diego (92121) *(P-5569)*
NEUROCRINE, San Diego *Also Called: Neurocrine Biosciences Inc (P-5850)*
Neurocrine Biosciences Inc (PA)....................................... B ...... 858 617-7600
12780 El Camino Real San Diego (92130) *(P-5850)*
Neurogesx Inc ........................................................................ E ...... 650 358-3300
999 Baker Way Ste 200 San Mateo (94404) *(P-5570)*
Neuron Fuel Inc ..................................................................... E ...... 408 537-3966
280 Hope St Mountain View (94041) *(P-17954)*
NEUROPACE, Mountain View *Also Called: Neuropace Inc (P-15200)*
Neuropace Inc ........................................................................ C ...... 650 237-2700
455 Bernardo Ave Mountain View (94043) *(P-15200)*
Neuroptics Inc ........................................................................ E ...... 949 250-9792
9223 Research Dr Irvine (92618) *(P-15201)*
Neurovasc Technologies Inc .............................................. E ...... 949 258-9946
3 Jenner Ste 100 Irvine (92618) *(P-15202)*
Neutraderm Inc ...................................................................... E ...... 818 534-3190
20660 Nordhoff St Chatsworth (91311) *(P-6011)*
Neutrogena, Los Angeles *Also Called: Kenvue Brands LLC (P-5999)*
Neutronic Stamping & Plating, Corona *Also Called: Ravlich Enterprises LLC (P-9004)*
Neuvector Inc ......................................................................... E ...... 408 455-4034
2880 Zanker Rd Ste 100 San Jose (95134) *(P-15655)*
Nevada Heat Treating LLC (PA)......................................... E ...... 510 790-2300
37955 Central Ct Ste D Newark (94560) *(P-19209)*
Never Boring Design Associates ...................................... E ...... 209 526-9136
1016 14th St Modesto (95354) *(P-17834)*
Nevro Corp (PA)...................................................................... A ...... 650 251-0005
1800 Bridge Pkwy Redwood City (94065) *(P-15203)*
Nevwest Inc ............................................................................ F ...... 619 420-8100
1225 Exposition Way Ste 140 San Diego (92154) *(P-14227)*
New Age Enclosures, Santa Maria *Also Called: Alltec Integrated Mfg Inc (P-6704)*
New Amsterdam Spirits, Modesto *Also Called: E & J Gallo Winery (P-1546)*
New Bedford Panoramex Corp ......................................... E ...... 909 982-9806
1480 N Claremont Blvd Claremont (91711) *(P-11615)*
New Bi US Gaming LLC ....................................................... D ...... 858 592-2472
10920 Via Frontera Ste 420 San Diego (92127) *(P-18581)*
New Brunswick Industries Inc ........................................... E ...... 619 448-4900
5656 La Jolla Blvd La Jolla (92037) *(P-12176)*
New Cal Metals Inc ............................................................... E ...... 916 652-7424
3495 Swetzer Rd Loomis (95650) *(P-8517)*
New Century Audio / Video Inc ......................................... F ...... 408 341-1950
450 El Paseo De Saratoga San Jose (95130) *(P-11682)*

# New Century Industries Inc — ALPHABETIC SECTION

New Century Industries Inc .................................................. E ...... 562 634-9551
7231 Rosecrans Ave Paramount (90723) *(P-13545)*

New Century Snacks, Commerce *Also Called: Snak Club LLC (P-1366)*

New Century Snacks LLC .................................................... E ...... 323 278-9578
5560 E Slauson Ave Commerce (90040) *(P-1361)*

New Chef Fashion Inc ........................................................... D ...... 323 581-0300
3223 E 46th St Los Angeles (90058) *(P-2562)*

New Classic Furniture, Fontana *Also Called: New Classic HM Furnishing Inc (P-3485)*

New Classic HM Furnishing Inc (PA) ................................ E ...... 909 484-7676
7351 Mcguire Ave Fontana (92336) *(P-3485)*

New Cntury Mtals Southeast Inc ........................................ C ...... 562 356-6804
15723 Shoemaker Ave Norwalk (90650) *(P-7764)*

New Desserts LLC .................................................................. D ...... 415 780-6860
5000 Fulton Dr Fairfield (94534) *(P-17200)*

New Desserts, Inc., Fairfield *Also Called: New Desserts LLC (P-17200)*

New Dimension Electronics, Santa Clara *Also Called: N D E Inc (P-13044)*

New Dimension One Spas Inc (DH) ................................. C ...... 800 345-7727
1819 Aston Ave Ste 105 Carlsbad (92008) *(P-16188)*

New Fashion Products Inc .................................................. C ...... 310 354-0090
3600 E Olympic Blvd Los Angeles (90023) *(P-2793)*

New Flyer of America Inc .................................................... C ...... 909 456-3566
2880 Jurupa St Ontario (91761) *(P-13373)*

New Frontier Foods Inc ....................................................... F ...... 713 501-0292
1424 Chapin Ave Burlingame (94010) *(P-2098)*

New Generation Athlete LLC ............................................. F ...... 661 316-2209
680 Lighthouse Ave Unit 51688 Pacific Grove (93950) *(P-2794)*

New Generation Engrg Cnstr Inc ....................................... E ...... 424 329-3950
22815 Frampton Ave Torrance (90501) *(P-16478)*

New Generation Software Inc ............................................ E ...... 916 920-2200
3835 N Freeway Blvd Ste 200 Sacramento (95834) *(P-18582)*

New Generation Wellness Inc (PA) .................................. C ...... 949 863-0340
46 Corporate Park Ste 200 Irvine (92606) *(P-5571)*

New Glaspro Inc .................................................................... E ...... 800 776-2368
9401 Ann St Santa Fe Springs (90670) *(P-7236)*

New Gordon Industries, Santa Fe Springs *Also Called: New Gordon Industries LLC (P-8872)*

New Gordon Industries LLC ............................................... E ...... 562 483-7378
13750 Rosecrans Ave Santa Fe Springs (90670) *(P-8872)*

New Green Day LLC ............................................................. E ...... 323 566-7603
1710 E 111th St Los Angeles (90059) *(P-3758)*

New Harbinger Publications Inc (PA) ............................... E ...... 510 652-0215
5674 Shattuck Ave Oakland (94609) *(P-4338)*

New Haven Companies Inc ................................................ D ...... 818 686-7020
13571 Vaughn St Unit E San Fernando (91340) *(P-2551)*

New Hong Kong Noodle Co Inc ........................................ E ...... 650 588-6425
360 Swift Ave Ste 22 South San Francisco (94080) *(P-2294)*

New Horizon Foods, Union City *Also Called: New Horizon Foods Inc (P-2295)*

New Horizon Foods Inc ....................................................... E ...... 510 489-8600
33440 Western Ave Union City (94587) *(P-2295)*

NEW HORIZONS CENTER & WORKSHOP, North Hills *Also Called: New Hrzns Srving Indvdals With (P-19348)*

New Hrzns Srving Indvdals With (PA) .............................. D ...... 818 894-9301
15725 Parthenia St North Hills (91343) *(P-19348)*

New Iem LLC .......................................................................... B ...... 510 656-1600
48205 Warm Springs Blvd Fremont (94539) *(P-11247)*

New Inspiration Brdcstg Co Inc (HQ) ............................... E ...... 805 987-0400
4880 Santa Rosa Rd Camarillo (93012) *(P-16328)*

New Leaf Biofuel LLC .......................................................... E ...... 619 236-8500
2285 Newton Ave San Diego (92113) *(P-6343)*

New Maverick Desk Inc ....................................................... C ...... 310 217-1554
15100 S Figueroa St Gardena (90248) *(P-3575)*

New Prduct Intgrtion Sltons In (HQ) ................................. E ...... 408 944-9178
685 Jarvis Dr Ste A Morgan Hill (95037) *(P-7649)*

New Pride Corporation ........................................................ D ...... 323 584-6608
5101 Pacific Blvd Vernon (90058) *(P-17096)*

New Pride Tire LLC (HQ) .................................................... E ...... 510 567-8800
2900 Main St Bldg 137 Ste 201a Alameda (94501) *(P-19152)*

New Pride Tire LLC .............................................................. E ...... 310 631-7000
1511 E Orangethorpe Ave Ste D Fullerton (92831) *(P-19153)*

New Printing, Van Nuys *Also Called: Digital Room Holdings Inc (P-4873)*

New Relic Inc (HQ) ............................................................... A ...... 650 777-7600
188 Spear St Fl 11 San Francisco (94105) *(P-18583)*

New Source Technology LLC ............................................. F ...... 925 462-6888
6678 Owens Dr Ste 105 Pleasanton (94588) *(P-15565)*

New Spirit Naturals Inc (PA) ............................................... E ...... 909 592-4445
615 W Allen Ave San Dimas (91773) *(P-19319)*

New Tech Solutions Inc ....................................................... E ...... 510 353-4070
4179 Business Center Dr Fremont (94538) *(P-17555)*

New Technology Plastics Inc ............................................. E ...... 562 941-6034
7110 Fenwick Ln Westminster (92683) *(P-5182)*

New Times Media Group, San Luis Obispo *Also Called: Slo New Times Inc (P-4197)*

New United Motor Manufacturing Inc .............................. A ...... 510 498-5500
45500 Fremont Blvd Fremont (94538) *(P-13546)*

New Vavin Inc ........................................................................ E ...... 707 963-5972
3222 Ehlers Ln Saint Helena (94574) *(P-1688)*

New Vision Display Inc (DH) .............................................. E ...... 916 786-8111
1430 Blue Oaks Blvd Ste 100 Roseville (95747) *(P-13047)*

New Wave Embroidery ........................................................ F ...... 323 727-0076
909 S Greenwood Ave Ste B Montebello (90640) *(P-19109)*

New Wave Industries Ltd (DH) .......................................... F ...... 800 882-8854
3315 Orange Grove Ave North Highlands (95660) *(P-10586)*

New West Products Inc ....................................................... E ...... 619 671-9022
7520 Airway Rd Ste 1 San Diego (92154) *(P-6928)*

New World Library, Novato *Also Called: Whatever Publishing Inc (P-4494)*

New World Medical Incorporated ..................................... F ...... 909 466-4304
10763 Edison Ct Rancho Cucamonga (91730) *(P-15204)*

New-Indy Containerboard, Ontario *Also Called: New-Indy Ontario LLC (P-3788)*

New-Indy Containerboard, Oxnard *Also Called: New-Indy Oxnard LLC (P-3789)*

New-Indy Containerboard LLC (DH) ................................ D ...... 909 296-3400
3500 Porsche Way Ste 150 Ontario (91764) *(P-3787)*

New-Indy Ontario LLC .......................................................... C ...... 909 390-1055
5100 Jurupa St Ontario (91761) *(P-3788)*

New-Indy Oxnard LLC .......................................................... C ...... 805 986-3881
5936 Perkins Rd Oxnard (93033) *(P-3789)*

Newbasis LLC ........................................................................ C ...... 951 787-0600
2626 Kansas Ave Riverside (92507) *(P-7358)*

Newbasis West LLC ............................................................. C ...... 951 787-0600
2626 Kansas Ave Riverside (92507) *(P-7359)*

Newby Rubber Inc ................................................................ E ...... 661 327-5137
320 Industrial St Bakersfield (93307) *(P-6517)*

Newcomb Spring Corp ........................................................ E ...... 714 995-5341
8380 Cerritos Ave Stanton (90680) *(P-9203)*

Newcomb Spring of California, Stanton *Also Called: Newcomb Spring Corp (P-9203)*

Newegg.com, City Of Industry *Also Called: Magnell Associate Inc (P-10176)*

Newell Brands Inc ................................................................. E ...... 760 246-2700
17182 Nevada St Victorville (92394) *(P-6929)*

Newhall Signal, Santa Clarita *Also Called: Signal (P-4194)*

Newlife2 (PA) ......................................................................... E ...... 805 549-8093
4855 Morabito Pl San Luis Obispo (93401) *(P-10101)*

Newlight Technologies Inc ................................................. E ...... 714 556-4500
14382 Astronautics Ln Huntington Beach (92647) *(P-6930)*

Newlon Rouge LLC .............................................................. E ...... 310 458-7737
1640 5th St Ste 218 Santa Monica (90401) *(P-4168)*

Newly Weds Foods Inc ........................................................ D ...... 209 491-7777
437 S Mcclure Rd Modesto (95357) *(P-2296)*

Newman and Sons Inc (PA) ............................................... E ...... 805 522-1646
2655 1st St Ste 210 Simi Valley (93065) *(P-7360)*

Newman Bros California Inc (PA) ..................................... F ...... 951 782-0102
1901 Massachusetts Ave Riverside (92507) *(P-3164)*

Newman Flange & Fitting Co, Newman *Also Called: Titan Newman Inc (P-16900)*

Newmar Power LLC ............................................................. C ...... 800 854-3906
1580 Sunflower Ave Costa Mesa (92626) *(P-12821)*

Newport, Irvine *Also Called: Newport Corporation (P-14344)*

Newport Brass, Santa Ana *Also Called: Brasstech Inc (P-8047)*

Newport Corporation ............................................................ D ...... 408 980-4300
3635 Peterson Way Santa Clara (95054) *(P-13277)*

Newport Corporation (HQ) ................................................. B ...... 949 863-3144
1791 Deere Ave Irvine (92606) *(P-14344)*

Newport Electronics Inc ...................................................... D ...... 714 540-4914
2229 S Yale St Santa Ana (92704) *(P-9882)*

Newport Energy ..................................................................... E ...... 408 230-7545
19200 Von Karman Ave Ste 400 Irvine (92612) *(P-192)*

## ALPHABETIC SECTION — Nichols Pistachio

**Newport Fab  LLC** .................................................. D ...... 949 435-8000
4321 Jamboree Rd Newport Beach (92660) *(P-12602)*

**Newport Fish, South San Francisco** *Also Called: Tardio Enterprises  Inc (P-2065)*

**Newport Flavors & Fragrances** ............................. E ...... 714 771-2200
833 N Elm St Orange (92867) *(P-2017)*

**Newport Glassworks, Stanton** *Also Called: Newport Optcal Inds Hldngs Ltd (P-14802)*

**Newport Laminates  Inc** ........................................ E ...... 714 545-8335
3121 W Central Ave Santa Ana (92704) *(P-6931)*

**Newport Medical Instrs Inc** ................................... D ...... 949 642-3910
1620 Sunflower Ave Costa Mesa (92626) *(P-15205)*

**Newport Optcal Inds Hldngs Ltd (PA)** .................. E ...... 714 484-8100
10564 Fern Ave Stanton (90680) *(P-14802)*

**Newport Plastics  LLC (PA)** ................................. F ...... 800 854-8402
3200 E Birch St Ste B Brea (92821) *(P-6932)*

**Newton Heat Treating Co Inc** ............................... D ...... 626 964-6528
19235 E Walnut Dr N City Of Industry (91748) *(P-7896)*

**Newton Vineyard, Napa** *Also Called: Newton Vineyard LLC (P-1689)*

**Newton Vineyard LLC (DH)** .................................. E ...... 707 204-7423
1040 Main St Ste 204 Napa (94559) *(P-1689)*

**Newton Vineyard LLC** ........................................... C ...... 707 204-7410
1 California Dr Yountville (94599) *(P-1690)*

**Newvac  LLC (HQ)** ................................................ F ...... 310 525-1205
9330 De Soto Ave Chatsworth (91311) *(P-11465)*

**Newvac  LLC** ........................................................ C ...... 310 990-0401
9330 De Soto Ave Chatsworth (91311) *(P-12036)*

**Newvac  LLC** ........................................................ E ...... 747 202-7333
9330 De Soto Ave Chatsworth (91311) *(P-13048)*

**Newvac Division, Chatsworth** *Also Called: Newvac LLC (P-12036)*

**Nexcoil Steel  LLC** ................................................ F ...... 209 900-1919
1265 Shaw Rd Stockton (95215) *(P-7659)*

**Nexenta By Ddn  Inc** ............................................ E ...... 408 791-3300
2025 Gateway Pl Ste 160 San Jose (95110) *(P-18584)*

**Nexgen Container  LLC** ........................................ D ...... 559 553-7500
7182 Rasmussen Ave Visalia (93291) *(P-3868)*

**Nexgen Pharma, Irvine** *Also Called: New Generation Wellness  Inc (P-5571)*

**Nexgen Power Systems  Inc** ................................ E ...... 408 230-7698
3151 Jay St Ste 201 Santa Clara (95054) *(P-12603)*

**Nexgrill Industries, Chino** *Also Called: Nexgrill Industries  Inc (P-16431)*

**Nexgrill Industries  Inc (PA)** ................................. D ...... 909 598-8799
14050 Laurelwood Pl Chino (91710) *(P-16431)*

**Nexlogic Technologies  LLC** ................................. D ...... 408 436-8150
2085 Zanker Rd San Jose (95131) *(P-12177)*

**Nexogy  Inc** ........................................................... D ...... 305 358-8952
10967 Via Frontera San Diego (92127) *(P-18585)*

**Nexon America, El Segundo** *Also Called: M Nexon Inc (P-18509)*

**Nexrange Industries, City Of Industry** *Also Called: Duro Corporation (P-11389)*

**Nexsan, Sunnyvale** *Also Called: Nexsan Technologies Inc (P-10257)*

**Nexsan Technologies (US) LL** ............................. F ...... 408 724-9809
1287 Anvilwood Ave Sunnyvale (94089) *(P-10256)*

**Nexsan Technologies Inc** ..................................... C
1289 Anvilwood Ave Sunnyvale (94089) *(P-10257)*

**Nexstar Pharmaceutical, San Dimas** *Also Called: Gilead Sciences  Inc (P-5464)*

**Next Chapter  Inc** ................................................. E ...... 559 665-7473
16000 Avenue 25 Chowchilla (93610) *(P-7361)*

**Next Day Frame  Inc** ............................................. D ...... 310 886-0851
11560 Wright Rd Lynwood (90262) *(P-3555)*

**Next Day Printed Tees** .......................................... F ...... 619 420-8618
3523 Main St Ste 601 Chula Vista (91911) *(P-3013)*

**Next Generation, Commerce** *Also Called: J & F Design Inc (P-2767)*

**Next Intent, San Luis Obispo** *Also Called: Next Intent  Inc (P-11006)*

**Next Intent  Inc** ..................................................... E ...... 805 781-6755
865 Via Esteban San Luis Obispo (93401) *(P-11006)*

**Next Level Apparel, Torrance** *Also Called: Ys Garments LLC (P-2696)*

**Next Phase Solar, Berkeley** *Also Called: Sunsystem Technology LLC (P-12746)*

**Next Point Bearing Group  LLC** ........................... E ...... 818 988-1880
28364 Avenue Crocker Valencia (91355) *(P-9952)*

**Next Semiconductor Tech Inc** .............................. E ...... 858 707-7060
4115 Sorrento Valley Blvd San Diego (92121) *(P-12604)*

**Nextclientcom  Inc** ................................................ E ...... 661 222-7755
25000 Avenue Stanford Valencia (91355) *(P-4439)*

**Nextest Systems Corporation** .............................. C ...... 408 960-2331
875 Embedded Way San Jose (95138) *(P-14564)*

**Nextest Systems Teradyne Co, San Jose** *Also Called: Nextest Systems Corporation (P-14564)*

**Nextev, San Jose** *Also Called: Nio Usa  Inc (P-13374)*

**Nextex International, South Gate** *Also Called: Nextrade  Inc (P-2552)*

**Nextgen Healthcare  Inc (HQ)** .............................. B ...... 949 255-2600
18111 Von Karman Ave Ste 600 Irvine (92612) *(P-18586)*

**Nexthealth West Hollywood Inc** ........................... F ...... 310 295-2075
24955 Pacific Coast Hwy Ste 203 Malibu (90265) *(P-19320)*

**Nextinput  Inc (PA)** ................................................ E ...... 408 770-9293
980 Linda Vista Ave Mountain View (94043) *(P-11336)*

**Nextivity  Inc (PA)** ................................................. E ...... 858 485-9442
16550 W Bernardo Dr Ste 550 San Diego (92127) *(P-11903)*

**Nextmod  Inc** ......................................................... E ...... 909 740-3120
6361 Box Springs Blvd Riverside (92507) *(P-3387)*

**Nextpatient  Inc** ..................................................... E ...... 617 504-4726
655 Victoria St San Francisco (94127) *(P-18587)*

**Nextracker Inc (PA)** .............................................. D ...... 510 270-2500
6200 Paseo Padre Pkwy Fremont (94555) *(P-18588)*

**Nextracker LLC (HQ)** ........................................... C ...... 510 270-2500
6200 Paseo Padre Pkwy Fremont (94555) *(P-18589)*

**Nextrade  Inc (PA)** ................................................ E ...... 562 944-9950
12411 Industrial Ave South Gate (90280) *(P-2552)*

**Nextroll  Inc (PA)** .................................................. A ...... 415 236-3956
201 California St Ste 500 San Francisco (94111) *(P-18590)*

**Nexus Dx  Inc** ........................................................ E ...... 858 410-4600
6759 Mesa Ridge Rd San Diego (92121) *(P-15206)*

**Nexxen Apparel  Inc (PA)** ..................................... F ...... 323 267-9900
1555 Los Palos St Los Angeles (90023) *(P-2795)*

**Nexxen Group LLC (PA)** ...................................... D ...... 425 279-1222
535 Mission St Fl 14 San Francisco (94105) *(P-16320)*

**Neyenesch Printers  Inc** ....................................... D ...... 619 297-2281
2750 Kettner Blvd San Diego (92101) *(P-4705)*

**NFC Innovation Center, San Jose** *Also Called: Ensurge Micropower Inc (P-12973)*

**Ngcodec Inc** ........................................................... E ...... 408 766-4382
440 N Wolfe Rd Ste 2187 Sunnyvale (94085) *(P-12605)*

**Ngd Systems  Inc** ................................................. E ...... 949 870-9148
3019 Wilshire Blvd Santa Monica (90403) *(P-10258)*

**NGK North America  Inc** ....................................... F ...... 925 292-5372
7100 National Dr Livermore (94550) *(P-11007)*

**Ngm Biopharmaceuticals  Inc (PA)** ...................... C ...... 650 243-5555
333 Oyster Point Blvd South San Francisco (94080) *(P-5572)*

**Ngmbio, South San Francisco** *Also Called: Ngm Biopharmaceuticals  Inc (P-5572)*

**Ngo Metals  Inc** ..................................................... E ...... 510 632-0853
711 Kevin Ct Oakland (94621) *(P-8638)*

**Ngrok  Inc** .............................................................. D ...... 415 323-4184
548 Market St Pmb 26741 San Francisco (94104) *(P-18591)*

**Nguoi Viet Newspaper, Westminster** *Also Called: Nguoi Viet Vtnamese People Inc (P-4169)*

**Nguoi Viet Vtnamese People Inc (PA)** ................. E ...... 714 892-9414
14771 Moran St Westminster (92683) *(P-4169)*

**Nhk Laboratories  Inc (PA)** ................................... E ...... 562 903-5835
12230 Florence Ave Santa Fe Springs (90670) *(P-5573)*

**Nhk Laboratories Inc** ............................................ D ...... 562 204-5002
10603 Norwalk Blvd Santa Fe Springs (90670) *(P-5574)*

**Nhr, Irvine** *Also Called: N H Research  LLC (P-14557)*

**Nhra, San Dimas** *Also Called: National Hot Rod Association (P-19308)*

**Nhs  Inc** ................................................................. D ...... 831 459-7800
104 Bronson St Ste 9 Santa Cruz (95062) *(P-15842)*

**Ni Microwave Components, Santa Clara** *Also Called: National Instruments Corp (P-14559)*

**Niacc-Avitech Technologies Inc (PA)** .................. D ...... 559 291-2500
245 W Dakota Ave Clovis (93612) *(P-19271)*

**Nice North America LLC (DH)** .............................. C ...... 760 438-7000
5919 Sea Otter Pl Ste 100 Carlsbad (92010) *(P-17713)*

**Nicholas Michael Designs LLC** ............................ C ...... 714 562-8101
2330 Raymer Ave Fullerton (92833) *(P-3556)*

**Nichols Farms, Hanford** *Also Called: Nichols Pistachio (P-1362)*

**Nichols Lumber & Hardware Co** .......................... D ...... 626 960-4802
13470 Dalewood St Baldwin Park (91706) *(P-16454)*

**Nichols Pistachio** .................................................. C ...... 559 584-6811
13762 1st Ave Hanford (93230) *(P-1362)*

**Nick Sciabica & Sons A Corp** ............................................. E ...... 209 577-5067
  2150 Yosemite Blvd Modesto (95354) *(P-1402)*

**Nick's Cabinet Doors, Azusa** *Also Called: Nicks Door Corporation (P-3165)*

**Nicks Door Corporation** ................................................. F ...... 626 812-6491
  1052 W Kirkwall Rd Azusa (91702) *(P-3165)*

**Nico Nat Mfg Corp** ........................................................... E ...... 323 721-1900
  2624 Yates Ave Commerce (90040) *(P-3665)*

**Niconat Manufacturing, Commerce** *Also Called: Nico Nat Mfg Corp (P-3665)*

**Nicro Inc** ........................................................................... E ...... 209 848-8826
  635 Delano Dr Oakdale (95361) *(P-427)*

**Nidec Genmark Automation Inc (DH)** .......................... C ...... 510 897-3400
  46723 Lakeview Blvd Fremont (94538) *(P-16829)*

**Nidec Motor Corporation** ............................................... B ...... 916 463-9200
  11380 White Rock Rd Rancho Cordova (95742) *(P-9474)*

**Nidek Incorporated** ........................................................ E ...... 800 223-9044
  2040 Corporate Ct San Jose (95131) *(P-16596)*

**Niebam-Cppola Estate Winery LP** ................................ E ...... 415 291-1700
  916 Kearny St San Francisco (94133) *(P-1691)*

**Niebam-Cppola Estate Winery LP (PA)** ....................... C ...... 707 968-1100
  1991 St Helena Hwy Rutherford (94573) *(P-1692)*

**Nieco Corporation** .......................................................... D ...... 707 838-3226
  7950 Cameron Dr Windsor (95492) *(P-10587)*

**Niedwick Corporation** .................................................... E ...... 714 771-9999
  967 N Eckhoff St Orange (92867) *(P-11008)*

**Niedwick Machine Co, Orange** *Also Called: Niedwick Corporation (P-11008)*

**Nifty Package Co Inc** ..................................................... E ...... 714 863-6058
  175 S Cambridge St Orange (92866) *(P-17303)*

**Nighthawk Flight Systems Inc** ..................................... E ...... 760 727-4900
  1370 Decision St Ste D Vista (92081) *(P-14228)*

**Niitakaya Usa Inc (PA)** .................................................. E ...... 323 720-5050
  1801 Aeros Way Montebello (90640) *(P-17201)*

**Nike Inc** ........................................................................... F ...... 949 616-4042
  20001 Ellipse Foothill Ranch (92610) *(P-2847)*

**Nikkel Iron Works Corporation** .................................... F ...... 661 746-4904
  17045 S Central Valley Hwy Shafter (93263) *(P-9372)*

**Nikkiso Acd, Santa Ana** *Also Called: Acd LLC (P-8296)*

**Nikkiso Cosmodyne, Seal Beach** *Also Called: Cosmodyne LLC (P-9842)*

**Nikkiso Cryoquip, Escondido** *Also Called: Integrted Crygnic Slutions LLC (P-9870)*

**Nikko Enterprise Corporation** ...................................... E ...... 562 941-6080
  13168 Sandoval St Santa Fe Springs (90670) *(P-2058)*

**Niknejad Inc** .................................................................... E ...... 310 477-0407
  6855 Hayvenhurst Ave Van Nuys (91406) *(P-4706)*

**Nikon, Belmont** *Also Called: Nikon Research Corp America (P-14565)*

**Nikon AM Synergy Inc** .................................................. E ...... 310 607-0188
  3550 E Carson St Long Beach (90808) *(P-7635)*

**Nikon Research Corp America** .................................... E ...... 800 446-4566
  1399 Shoreway Rd Belmont (94002) *(P-14565)*

**Nile Ai Inc** ....................................................................... E ...... 818 689-9107
  15260 Ventura Blvd Ste 1410 Sherman Oaks (91403) *(P-18592)*

**Nils Inc (PA)** .................................................................... F ...... 714 755-1600
  12572 Western Ave Garden Grove (92841) *(P-2796)*

**Nils Skiwear, Garden Grove** *Also Called: Nils Inc (P-2796)*

**Nimble Storage Inc** ....................................................... A ...... 408 432-9600
  900 N Mccarthy Blvd Milpitas (95035) *(P-10259)*

**Nimbus Water Systems** ................................................ F
  42445 Avenida Alvarado Temecula (92590) *(P-10588)*

**Nimsoft Inc (HQ)** ............................................................ E ...... 408 796-3400
  3965 Freedom Cir Fl 6 Santa Clara (95054) *(P-12606)*

**Nina Mia Inc** .................................................................... D ...... 714 773-5588
  826 Enterprise Way Fullerton (92831) *(P-2297)*

**Nina Religion, Huntington Park** *Also Called: Saydel Inc (P-6034)*

**Ninas Mexican Foods Inc** ............................................. E ...... 909 468-5888
  20631 Valley Blvd Ste A Walnut (91789) *(P-2298)*

**Nine Stars Group (usa) Inc** .......................................... F ...... 866 978-2778
  1775 S Business Pkwy Ontario (91761) *(P-17714)*

**Niner Wine Estates LLC** ............................................... E ...... 805 239-2233
  2400 W Highway 46 Paso Robles (93446) *(P-1693)*

**Ninestars, Ontario** *Also Called: Nine Stars Group (usa) Inc (P-17714)*

**Ninja Jump Inc** ................................................................ D ...... 323 255-5418
  3221 N San Fernando Rd Los Angeles (90065) *(P-15762)*

**Ninjatech Ai** ..................................................................... E ...... 408 444-5101
  4410 El Camino Real Ste 100 Los Altos (94022) *(P-16534)*

**Ninth Avenue Foods, City Of Industry** *Also Called: Heritage Distributing Company (P-761)*

**Nio Usa Inc** ..................................................................... C ...... 408 518-7000
  3151 Zanker Rd San Jose (95134) *(P-13374)*

**Nippon Industries Inc** ................................................... E ...... 707 427-3127
  2430 S Watney Way Fairfield (94533) *(P-1042)*

**Nippon Trends Food Service Inc (PA)** ........................ D ...... 408 479-0558
  631 Giguere Ct Ste A1 San Jose (95133) *(P-2299)*

**Nipro Optics Inc** ............................................................ E ...... 949 215-1151
  7 Marconi Irvine (92618) *(P-14803)*

**Niron Inc** ......................................................................... F ...... 909 598-1526
  20541 Earlgate St Walnut (91789) *(P-9638)*

**Nis America Inc** ............................................................. E ...... 714 540-1122
  4 Hutton Centre Dr Ste 650 Santa Ana (92707) *(P-18593)*

**Nissan North America Inc** ........................................... A ...... 310 768-3700
  18501 S Figueroa St Gardena (90248) *(P-19536)*

**Nissin Foods USA Company Inc (DH)** ....................... C ...... 310 327-8478
  2001 W Rosecrans Ave Gardena (90249) *(P-2117)*

**Niterder Tchncal Ltg Vdeo Syst** ................................. E ...... 858 268-9316
  12255 Crosthwaite Cir Ste A Poway (92064) *(P-11616)*

**Niterider, Poway** *Also Called: Niterder Tchncal Ltg Vdeo Syst (P-11616)*

**Nitinol Development Corp** ........................................... A ...... 510 683-2000
  47533 Westinghouse Dr Fremont (94539) *(P-15610)*

**Nitinol Devices & Components, Fremont** *Also Called: Nitinol Development Corp (P-15610)*

**Nitricity Inc** ..................................................................... E ...... 303 475-6197
  44530 S Grimmer Blvd Fremont (94538) *(P-6178)*

**Nitto, Oceanside** *Also Called: Nitto Denko Technical Corp (P-19486)*

**Nitto Avecia Pharma Svcs Inc (DH)** ........................... F ...... 949 951-4425
  10 Vanderbilt Irvine (92618) *(P-5575)*

**Nitto Denko Technical Corp** ........................................ D ...... 760 435-7011
  501 Via Del Monte Oceanside (92058) *(P-19486)*

**Nittobo America Inc (HQ)** ............................................ F ...... 951 677-5629
  41900 Brown St Murrieta (92562) *(P-5851)*

**Nium Inc** ......................................................................... E ...... 732 492-6908
  85 2nd St Fl 2 San Francisco (94105) *(P-18594)*

**Nivagen Pharmaceuticals Inc (PA)** ............................. D ...... 916 364-1662
  3050 Fite Cir Ste 100 Sacramento (95827) *(P-5576)*

**Nivek Industries Inc** ...................................................... E ...... 714 545-8855
  230 E Dyer Rd Ste K Santa Ana (92707) *(P-11466)*

**NJ Mc Cutchen Inc** ........................................................ E ...... 209 466-9704
  123 W Sonora St Stockton (95203) *(P-11009)*

**Nk Technologies, San Jose** *Also Called: Neilsen-Kuljian Inc (P-14561)*

**NKARTA, South San Francisco** *Also Called: Nkarta Inc (P-5577)*

**Nkarta Inc** ....................................................................... C ...... 925 407-1049
  1150 Veterans Blvd South San Francisco (94080) *(P-5577)*

**NL&a Collections Inc** ................................................... E ...... 323 277-6266
  6323 Maywood Ave Huntington Park (90255) *(P-11499)*

**Nlms Elite Construction Co** ........................................ F ...... 626 205-8417
  1254 S Waterman Ave San Bernardino (92408) *(P-345)*

**NM Holdco Inc** ............................................................... C ...... 323 663-3971
  2800 Casitas Ave Los Angeles (90039) *(P-9096)*

**NM Machining Inc** ......................................................... E ...... 408 972-8978
  175 Lewis Rd Ste 25 San Jose (95111) *(P-11010)*

**NMB (usa) Inc (HQ)** ...................................................... E ...... 818 709-1770
  9730 Independence Ave Chatsworth (91311) *(P-9953)*

**NMB Tech, Chatsworth** *Also Called: NMB (usa) Inc (P-9953)*

**Nmc Group Inc** .............................................................. E ...... 714 223-3525
  300 E Cypress St Brea (92821) *(P-16885)*

**Nmsp Inc (DH)** ............................................................... D ...... 310 484-2322
  2205 W 126th St Ste A Hawthorne (90250) *(P-13547)*

**Nmsp Inc** ........................................................................ E ...... 951 734-2453
  1451 E 6th St Corona (92879) *(P-13548)*

**NN Jaeschke Inc** ........................................................... E ...... 858 550-7900
  9610 Waples St San Diego (92121) *(P-97)*

**No Boundaries Inc** ........................................................ E ...... 619 266-2349
  789 Gateway Center Way San Diego (92102) *(P-4707)*

**No Frill Franchising Inc** ............................................... F ...... 858 642-4848
  7310 Miramar Rd San Diego (92126) *(P-4928)*

**No Nuts, Camarillo** *Also Called: No Nuts LLC (P-1322)*

**No Nuts LLC** .................................................................. F ...... 805 309-2420
  750 Calle Plano Camarillo (93012) *(P-1322)*

**No Pressure Landscape Services, Murrieta** *Also Called: No Prssure Prssure Wshg Svcs L (P-5920)*

**No Prssure Prssure Wshg Svcs L** .................................................. E ...... 951 477-1988
41880 Kalmia St Ste 165 Murrieta (92562) *(P-5920)*

**No Second Thoughts Inc** .......................................................... D ...... 619 428-5992
1333 30th St Ste D San Diego (92154) *(P-2563)*

**No Starch Press Inc** ................................................................ F ...... 415 863-9900
329 Primrose Rd Burlingame (94010) *(P-4440)*

**Noah Medical Corporation** ....................................................... D ...... 718 564-3717
2075 Zanker Rd San Jose (95131) *(P-14904)*

**Noah Pharmaceuticals Inc** ....................................................... E ...... 707 631-0921
1380 San Andreas Rd Watsonville (95076) *(P-5253)*

**Noah's, Los Gatos** *Also Called: Einstein Noah Rest Group Inc (P-713)*

**Noah's, San Francisco** *Also Called: Einstein Noah Rest Group Inc (P-17410)*

**Noah's Bagels, Redwood City** *Also Called: Einstein Noah Rest Group Inc (P-17411)*

**Noah's New York Bagels, Westminster** *Also Called: Einstein Noah Rest Group Inc (P-712)*

**Nobbe Orthopedics Inc** ........................................................... E ...... 805 687-7508
3010 State St Santa Barbara (93105) *(P-2839)*

**Noble Brewer Beer Company** .................................................... E ...... 510 766-2337
562 Whitney St San Leandro (94577) *(P-2075)*

**Noble Energy, Seal Beach** *Also Called: Samedan Oil Corporation (P-196)*

**Noble Metals, San Diego** *Also Called: Johnson Matthey Inc (P-7721)*

**Nobles Medical Tech Inc** ......................................................... E ...... 714 427-0398
17080 Newhope St Fountain Valley (92708) *(P-15207)*

**Noel Technologies, Campbell** *Also Called: Semi Automation & Tech Inc (P-12686)*

**Nok Nok Labs Inc** ................................................................... F ...... 650 433-1300
2890 Zanker Rd Ste 203 San Jose (95134) *(P-18595)*

**Nokia Inc** ............................................................................... A ...... 408 530-7600
200 S Mathilda Ave Sunnyvale (94086) *(P-11904)*

**Nokia of America Corporation** ................................................. E ...... 818 880-3500
2000 Corporate Center Dr Newbury Park (91320) *(P-11776)*

**Nokia of America Corporation** ................................................. F ...... 408 878-6500
520 Almanor Ave Sunnyvale (94085) *(P-12607)*

**Noll/Norwesco LLC** ................................................................ C ...... 209 234-1600
1320 Performance Dr Stockton (95206) *(P-8518)*

**Nolo** ..................................................................................... C ...... 510 549-1976
6801 Koll Center Pkwy Ste 300 Pleasanton (94566) *(P-4339)*

**Nology Engineering Inc** ........................................................... F ...... 760 591-0888
1333 Keystone Way Vista (92081) *(P-13549)*

**Nominum Inc** ........................................................................ C ...... 650 381-6000
3355 Scott Blvd Fl 3 Santa Clara (95054) *(P-18596)*

**Nomnomnow Inc** ................................................................... D ...... 415 991-0669
371 3rd St Oakland (94607) *(P-1111)*

**Nomoflo Enterprises Inc** ......................................................... D ...... 818 767-6528
2840 N Hollywood Way Burbank (91505) *(P-11548)*

**Nongshim, Rancho Cucamonga** *Also Called: Nongshim America Inc (P-17116)*

**Nongshim America Inc (HQ)** .................................................... C ...... 909 481-3698
12155 6th St Rancho Cucamonga (91730) *(P-17116)*

**Nooma Bio Inc** ...................................................................... F ...... 408 309-9375
250 Natural Bridges Dr Santa Cruz (95060) *(P-14697)*

**Noopl, Sacramento** *Also Called: Noopl Inc (P-11683)*

**Noopl Inc** ............................................................................. E ...... 916 400-3976
1210 G St Ste B Sacramento (95814) *(P-11683)*

**Noozhawk** ............................................................................ F ...... 805 456-7267
1327a State St Santa Barbara (93101) *(P-4170)*

**Nor-Cal Beverage Co Inc** ......................................................... E ...... 916 372-1700
1375 Terminal St West Sacramento (95691) *(P-1906)*

**Nor-Cal Beverage Co Inc (PA)** .................................................. B ...... 916 372-0600
2150 Stone Blvd West Sacramento (95691) *(P-17259)*

**Nor-Cal Beverage Co Inc** ......................................................... D ...... 714 526-8600
1226 N Olive St Anaheim (92801) *(P-19110)*

**Nor-Cal Overhead Inc** ............................................................. F ...... 925 240-5141
1799 Carpenter Rd Unit C Oakley (94561) *(P-17336)*

**Nor-Cal Products Inc (DH)** ...................................................... C ...... 530 842-4457
1967 S Oregon St Yreka (96097) *(P-9190)*

**Nor-Cal Vans Inc** ................................................................... F ...... 530 892-0150
1100 Marauder St Chico (95973) *(P-13421)*

**Nora Lighting Inc** .................................................................. C ...... 323 767-2600
6505 Gayhart St Commerce (90040) *(P-16667)*

**Norac Pharma, Azusa** *Also Called: S&B Pharma Inc (P-5268)*

**Noranco Corona Division, Corona** *Also Called: Noranco Manufacturing (usa) Acquisition Corp (P-9685)*

**Noranco Manufacturing (usa) Acquisition Corp** .......................... C ...... 951 721-8400
345 Cessna Cir Ste 102 Corona (92880) *(P-9685)*

**Norberts Athletic Products Inc** ................................................ F ...... 310 830-6672
354 W Gardena Blvd Gardena (90248) *(P-15843)*

**Norcal Beverage Co, Anaheim** *Also Called: Nor-Cal Beverage Co Inc (P-19110)*

**Norcal Building Materials, Santa Rosa** *Also Called: Northern Cal Bldg Mtls Inc (P-17337)*

**Norcal Materials Inc** .............................................................. E ...... 650 365-4811
941 Bransten Rd San Carlos (94070) *(P-7481)*

**Norcal Triangles Inc** .............................................................. D ...... 530 740-7750
4476 Skyway Dr Olivehurst (95961) *(P-3315)*

**Norchem Corporation (PA)** ..................................................... E ...... 323 221-0221
5649 Alhambra Ave Los Angeles (90032) *(P-9883)*

**Norco Industries Inc (PA)** ....................................................... C ...... 310 639-4000
365 W Victoria St Compton (90220) *(P-10102)*

**Norco Injection Molding Inc** ................................................... D ...... 909 393-4000
14325 Monte Vista Ave Chino (91710) *(P-6933)*

**Norco Plastics, Chino** *Also Called: Norco Injection Molding Inc (P-6933)*

**Norco Plastics Inc** ................................................................. D ...... 909 393-4000
14325 Monte Vista Ave Chino (91710) *(P-6934)*

**Norco Printing Inc** ................................................................. F ...... 510 569-2200
4588 Grenadier Pl Castro Valley (94546) *(P-5021)*

**Norden Millimeter Inc** ........................................................... E ...... 530 642-9123
5441 Merchant Cir Ste C Placerville (95667) *(P-11905)*

**Nordhavn Yachts, Dana Point** *Also Called: Pacific Asian Enterprises Inc (P-19114)*

**Nordic Naturals Inc** .............................................................. C ...... 800 662-2544
111 Jennings Way Watsonville (95076) *(P-1386)*

**Nordic Naturals Mfg Inc** ........................................................ E ...... 800 662-2544
111 Jennings Way Watsonville (95076) *(P-5254)*

**Nordon Yestech, Carlsbad** *Also Called: Nordson Corporation (P-9969)*

**Nordson, Carlsbad** *Also Called: Nordson Dage Inc (P-15505)*

**Nordson Asymtek, Carlsbad** *Also Called: Nordson Corporation (P-9968)*

**Nordson Asymtek, Carlsbad** *Also Called: Nordson California Inc (P-13200)*

**Nordson Asymtek, Carlsbad** *Also Called: Nordson Asymtek Inc (P-14439)*

**Nordson Asymtek Inc** ............................................................ C ...... 760 431-1919
2747 Loker Ave W Carlsbad (92010) *(P-14439)*

**Nordson California Inc** .......................................................... D ...... 760 918-8490
2747 Loker Ave W Carlsbad (92010) *(P-13200)*

**Nordson Corporation** ............................................................ D ...... 760 419-6551
2747 Loker Ave W Carlsbad (92010) *(P-9967)*

**Nordson Corporation** ............................................................ C ...... 760 431-1919
2747 Loker Ave W Carlsbad (92010) *(P-9968)*

**Nordson Corporation** ............................................................ E ...... 760 431-1919
2765 Loker Ave W Carlsbad (92010) *(P-9969)*

**Nordson Dage Inc** ................................................................. E ...... 440 985-4496
2747 Loker Ave W Carlsbad (92010) *(P-15505)*

**Nordson March Inc (HQ)** ....................................................... E ...... 925 827-1240
2470 Bates Ave Ste A Concord (94520) *(P-9970)*

**Nordson March Inc** .............................................................. D ...... 925 827-1240
2762 Loker Ave W Carlsbad (92010) *(P-9971)*

**Nordson Medical (ca) LLC** ...................................................... E ...... 657 215-4200
7612 Woodwind Dr Huntington Beach (92647) *(P-15208)*

**Nordson Test Insptn Amrcas Inc** ............................................. E ...... 760 918-8471
2765 Loker Ave W Carlsbad (92010) *(P-9972)*

**Norfield Acquisition LLC (HQ)** ................................................ E ...... 800 824-6242
422 Otterson Dr Chico (95928) *(P-9756)*

**Norfox, City Of Industry** *Also Called: Norman Fox & Co (P-17247)*

**Norlaine Inc** ......................................................................... C ...... 626 961-2471
1449 W Industrial Park St Covina (91722) *(P-16189)*

**Norman Fox & Co (PA)** .......................................................... E ...... 800 632-1777
14970 Don Julian Rd City Of Industry (91746) *(P-17247)*

**Norman Fox & Co** ................................................................. E ...... 323 973-4900
5511 S Boyle Ave Vernon (90058) *(P-17248)*

**Norman Industrial Mtls Inc (PA)** ............................................. C ...... 818 729-3333
8300 San Fernando Rd Sun Valley (91352) *(P-16626)*

**Norman Industrial Mtls Inc** .................................................... E ...... 949 250-3343
2481 Alton Pkwy Irvine (92606) *(P-16627)*

**Norman International, Vernon** *Also Called: Norman Paper and Foam Co Inc (P-3974)*

**Norman Paper and Foam Co Inc** ............................................. E ...... 323 582-7132
4501 S Santa Fe Ave Vernon (90058) *(P-3974)*

**Normont Hydraulic Sls Svc Inc** ........................................... F ...... 951 676-2155
43123 Business Park Dr Temecula (92590) *(P-16830)*

**Norotos Inc** ..................................................................... C ...... 714 662-3113
201 E Alton Ave Santa Ana (92707) *(P-11011)*

**Norpak, Hayward** *Also Called: Norton Packaging Inc (P-6936)*

**Norstar Office Products Inc (PA)** .................................... E ...... 323 262-1919
5353 Jillson St Commerce (90040) *(P-3576)*

**Nortech, Nevada City** *Also Called: Nortech Waste LLC (P-16360)*

**Nortech Waste LLC** ......................................................... C ...... 916 645-5230
219 Reward St Nevada City (95959) *(P-16360)*

**North American Fire Hose Corp** ..................................... D ...... 805 922-7076
910 Noble Way Santa Maria (93454) *(P-6426)*

**North American Pet Products, Corona** *Also Called: Pet Partners Inc (P-16201)*

**North American Seal & Pkg Co, Fresno** *Also Called: San Joaquin Hydraulic Inc (P-16893)*

**North American Video Corp (PA)** .................................... E ...... 714 779-7499
1335 S Acacia Ave Fullerton (92831) *(P-16726)*

**North Amrcn Foam Ppr Cnverters** ................................. E ...... 818 255-3383
11835 Wicks St Sun Valley (91352) *(P-6650)*

**North Amrcn Specialty Pdts LLC** ................................... F ...... 209 365-7500
300 S Beckman Rd Lodi (95240) *(P-5183)*

**North Area News (PA)** .................................................... E ...... 916 486-1248
2612 El Camino Ave Sacramento (95821) *(P-4171)*

**NORTH ATLANTIC BOOKS, Berkeley** *Also Called: Society For The Study Ntiv Art (P-4346)*

**NORTH BAY INDUSTRIES, Rohnert Park** *Also Called: North Bay Rhblitation Svcs Inc (P-3032)*

**North Bay Plywood Inc** ................................................... E ...... 707 224-7849
510 Northbay Dr Napa (94559) *(P-3166)*

**North Bay Rhblitation Svcs Inc (PA)** ............................... C ...... 707 585-1991
649 Martin Ave Rohnert Park (94928) *(P-3032)*

**North Beam Inc** ............................................................... E ...... 860 940-4569
338 Main St Unit 32d San Francisco (94105) *(P-18597)*

**North Cal Wood Products Inc** ........................................ E ...... 707 462-0686
700 Kunzler Ranch Rd Ukiah (95482) *(P-3074)*

**North Coast Brewing Co Inc (PA)** ................................... E ...... 707 964-2739
455 N Main St Fort Bragg (95437) *(P-1450)*

**North Coast Brewing Co Inc** .......................................... E ...... 707 964-3400
444 N Main St Fort Bragg (95437) *(P-1451)*

**North Coast Industries, Sausalito** *Also Called: Tony Marterie & Associates Inc (P-2718)*

**North County Sand and Grav Inc** ................................... F ...... 951 928-2881
26160 Jackson Ave Murrieta (92563) *(P-318)*

**North County Times (DH)** ............................................... C ...... 800 533-8830
350 Camino De La Reina San Diego (92108) *(P-4172)*

**North County Times** ........................................................ E ...... 951 676-4315
28441 Rancho California Rd Ste 103 Temecula (92590) *(P-4173)*

**North Park Beer Co., San Diego** *Also Called: K A McNair Brewing Co LLC (P-1438)*

**North Ranch Management Corp** .................................... D ...... 800 410-2153
9754 Deering Ave Chatsworth (91311) *(P-17538)*

**North Star Acquisition Inc** .............................................. D ...... 310 515-2200
14912 S Broadway Gardena (90248) *(P-8704)*

**North Star Company, Gardena** *Also Called: North Star Acquisition Inc (P-8704)*

**North State Renewables LLC** ......................................... E ...... 530 343-6076
15 Shippee Rd Oroville (95965) *(P-1387)*

**North Valley Fleet Svcs Inc (PA)** ..................................... F ...... 916 374-8850
3115 Coke St West Sacramento (95691) *(P-19161)*

**North West Pharmanaturals, Brea** *Also Called: Beacon Manufacturing Inc (P-5232)*

**North West Pharmanaturals Inc** .................................... E ...... 714 529-0980
1000 Beacon St Brea (92821) *(P-5255)*

**Northeast Newspapers Inc** ............................................ E ...... 213 727-1117
621 W Beverly Blvd Montebello (90640) *(P-4174)*

**Northern Aggregates Inc** ............................................... E ...... 707 459-3929
500 Cropley Ln Willits (95490) *(P-300)*

**Northern Cal Bldg Mtls Inc (PA)** ..................................... E ...... 707 546-9422
1534 Copperhill Pkwy Santa Rosa (95403) *(P-17337)*

**Northern California Equipment** ..................................... E ...... 415 648-6262
1920 Ingalls St San Francisco (94124) *(P-17859)*

**Northern California Injection Molding LLC** .................... F ...... 916 853-0717
2691 Mercantile Dr Rancho Cordova (95742) *(P-6935)*

**Northern Division, Pittsburg** *Also Called: Arb Inc (P-16286)*

**Northland Process Piping Inc** ........................................ E ...... 559 925-9724
400 E St Lemoore (93245) *(P-8195)*

**Northrdge Tr-Mdlity Imging Inc** ...................................... F ...... 818 709-2468
2140 Eastman Ave Ventura (93003) *(P-14345)*

**Northrop Grmman Arospc Systems, Palmdale** *Also Called: Northrop Grumman Corporation (P-14232)*

**Northrop Grmman Def Mssion Sys, San Diego** *Also Called: Northrop Grumman Systems Corp (P-14238)*

**Northrop Grmman Elctrnic Syste, Azusa** *Also Called: Northrop Grumman Systems Corp (P-14251)*

**Northrop Grmman Innvtion Syste** ................................. D ...... 818 887-8100
9401 Corbin Ave Northridge (91324) *(P-14229)*

**Northrop Grmman Innvtion Syste** ................................. B ...... 858 621-5700
9617 Distribution Ave San Diego (92121) *(P-14230)*

**Northrop Grmmn Spce & Mssn Sys** .............................. B ...... 310 812-4321
2501 Santa Fe Ave Redondo Beach (90278) *(P-13550)*

**Northrop Grumman CMS, Woodland Hills** *Also Called: Northrop Grumman Systems Corp (P-14271)*

**Northrop Grumman Corporation** ................................... C ...... 310 332-1000
1 Hornet Way El Segundo (90245) *(P-14231)*

**Northrop Grumman Corporation** ................................... E ...... 661 272-7334
3520 E Avenue M Palmdale (93550) *(P-14232)*

**Northrop Grumman Corporation** ................................... E ...... 310 332-0461
500 N Douglas St El Segundo (90245) *(P-14233)*

**Northrop Grumman Corporation** ................................... E ...... 949 260-9800
19782 Macarthur Blvd Irvine (92612) *(P-14234)*

**Northrop Grumman Corporation** ................................... E ...... 310 864-7342
198 Willow Grove Pl Escondido (92027) *(P-14235)*

**Northrop Grumman Corporation** ................................... A ...... 858 967-1221
18701 Caminito Pasadero San Diego (92128) *(P-14236)*

**Northrop Grumman Mar Systems, Sunnyvale** *Also Called: Northrop Grumman Systems Corp (P-13681)*

**Northrop Grumman Space, San Diego** *Also Called: Northrop Grumman Systems Corp (P-14257)*

**Northrop Grumman Space & Mission Systems Corp** .... A ...... 703 280-2900
6379 San Ignacio Ave San Jose (95119) *(P-18987)*

**Northrop Grumman Systems Corp** ................................ C ...... 310 812-5149
1 Space Park Blvd Redondo Beach (90278) *(P-11906)*

**Northrop Grumman Systems Corp** ................................ B ...... 661 272-7000
3520 E Avenue M Palmdale (93550) *(P-13680)*

**Northrop Grumman Systems Corp** ................................ A ...... 408 735-3011
401 E Hendy Ave Ms 33-3 Sunnyvale (94086) *(P-13681)*

**Northrop Grumman Systems Corp** ................................ B ...... 310 812-1089
1 Space Park Blvd Redondo Beach (90278) *(P-13682)*

**Northrop Grumman Systems Corp** ................................ B ...... 310 812-4321
1 Space Park Blvd # D1 1024 Redondo Beach (90278) *(P-13683)*

**Northrop Grumman Systems Corp** ................................ C ...... 858 514-9020
9326 Spectrum Center Blvd San Diego (92123) *(P-14237)*

**Northrop Grumman Systems Corp** ................................ A ...... 410 765-5589
9326 Spectrum Center Blvd San Diego (92123) *(P-14238)*

**Northrop Grumman Systems Corp** ................................ C ...... 818 715-2597
21200 Burbank Blvd Woodland Hills (91367) *(P-14239)*

**Northrop Grumman Systems Corp** ................................ E ...... 925 416-1080
5627 Stoneridge Dr Ste 310 Pleasanton (94588) *(P-14240)*

**Northrop Grumman Systems Corp** ................................ D ...... 760 380-4268
Building 806 Fort Irwin (92310) *(P-14241)*

**Northrop Grumman Systems Corp** ................................ A ...... 818 887-8110
9401 Corbin Ave Northridge (91324) *(P-14242)*

**Northrop Grumman Systems Corp** ................................ F ...... 858 592-2535
16707 Via Del Campo Ct San Diego (92127) *(P-14243)*

**Northrop Grumman Systems Corp** ................................ C ...... 703 968-1239
6379 San Ignacio Ave San Jose (95119) *(P-14244)*

**Northrop Grumman Systems Corp** ................................ D ...... 805 315-5728
1467 Fairway Dr Santa Maria (93455) *(P-14245)*

**Northrop Grumman Systems Corp** ................................ B ...... 858 592-4518
15120 Innovation Dr San Diego (92128) *(P-14246)*

**Northrop Grumman Systems Corp** ................................ D ...... 650 604-6056
Mountain View (94035) *(P-14247)*

**Northrop Grumman Systems Corp** ................................ C ...... 805 987-8831
760 Paseo Camarillo Ste 200 Camarillo (93010) *(P-14248)*

**Northrop Grumman Systems Corp** ................................ D ...... 805 987-9739
5161 Verdugo Way Camarillo (93012) *(P-14249)*

**Northrop Grumman Systems Corp** ................................ D ...... 818 249-5252
2550 Honolulu Ave Montrose (91020) *(P-14250)*

**Northrop Grumman Systems Corp** ................................ A ...... 626 812-1000
1100 W Hollyvale St Azusa (91702) *(P-14251)*

# ALPHABETIC SECTION

**Northrop Grumman Systems Corp** .................... D ...... 661 540-0446
3520 E Avenue M Palmdale (93550) *(P-14252)*

**Northrop Grumman Systems Corp** .................... B ...... 916 570-4454
5441 Luce Ave Mcclellan (95652) *(P-14253)*

**Northrop Grumman Systems Corp** .................... C ...... 855 737-8364
1 Space Park Blvd Redondo Beach (90278) *(P-14254)*

**Northrop Grumman Systems Corp** .................... D ...... 310 812-4321
2477 Manhattan Beach Blvd Redondo Beach (90278) *(P-14255)*

**Northrop Grumman Systems Corp** .................... A ...... 626 812-1464
1111 W 3rd St Azusa (91702) *(P-14256)*

**Northrop Grumman Systems Corp** .................... D ...... 858 514-9000
9326 Spectrum Center Blvd San Diego (92123) *(P-14257)*

**Northrop Grumman Systems Corp** .................... B ...... 310 332-1000
1 Hornet Way El Segundo (90245) *(P-14258)*

**Northrop Grumman Systems Corp** .................... D ...... 703 713-4096
862 E Hospitality Ln San Bernardino (92408) *(P-14259)*

**Northrop Grumman Systems Corp** .................... D ...... 805 278-2074
2700 Camino Del Sol Oxnard (93030) *(P-14260)*

**Northrop Grumman Systems Corp** .................... D ...... 858 621-7395
7130 Miramar Rd Ste 100b San Diego (92121) *(P-14261)*

**Northrop Grumman Systems Corp** .................... C ...... 714 240-6521
6033 Bandini Blvd Commerce (90040) *(P-14262)*

**Northrop Grumman Systems Corp** .................... D ...... 714 240-6521
600 Pine Ave Goleta (93117) *(P-14263)*

**Northrop Grumman Systems Corp** .................... D ...... 480 355-7716
400 Continental Blvd El Segundo (90245) *(P-14264)*

**Northrop Grumman Systems Corp** .................... D ...... 703 406-5474
20 Ryan Ranch Rd Ste 214 Monterey (93940) *(P-14265)*

**Northrop Grumman Systems Corp** .................... B ...... 858 618-4349
17066 Goldentop Rd San Diego (92127) *(P-14266)*

**Northrop Grumman Systems Corp** .................... B ...... 408 735-2241
401 E Hendy Ave Sunnyvale (94086) *(P-14267)*

**Northrop Grumman Systems Corp** .................... B ...... 310 556-4911
6411 W Imperial Hwy Los Angeles (90045) *(P-14268)*

**Northrop Grumman Systems Corp** .................... A ...... 818 715-4040
21240 Burbank Blvd Ms 29 Woodland Hills (91367) *(P-14269)*

**Northrop Grumman Systems Corp** .................... C ...... 805 684-6641
2601 Camino Del Sol Oxnard (93030) *(P-14270)*

**Northrop Grumman Systems Corp** .................... B ...... 818 715-4854
21240 Burbank Blvd Woodland Hills (91367) *(P-14271)*

**Northstar Engineering, Rancho Cucamonga** *Also Called: James Magna Ltd (P-19164)*

**Northwest Circuits Corp** .................... D ...... 619 661-1701
8660 Avenida Costa Blanca San Diego (92154) *(P-12178)*

**Northwest Exteriors Inc (PA)** .................... E ...... 916 851-1632
11200 Sun Center Dr Rancho Cordova (95670) *(P-499)*

**Northwest Pallets, Sacramento** *Also Called: Northwest Pallets LLC (P-3869)*

**Northwest Pallets LLC** .................... E ...... 916 736-2787
3264 Ramona Ave Sacramento (95826) *(P-3869)*

**Northwest Pipe Company** .................... C ...... 760 246-3191
12351 Rancho Rd Adelanto (92301) *(P-7667)*

**Northwest Signs, Santa Cruz** *Also Called: Jeff Frank (P-15993)*

**Northwestern Converting Co** .................... D ...... 800 959-3402
2395 Railroad St Corona (92878) *(P-2940)*

**Northwestern Inc** .................... E ...... 818 786-1581
10153-1/2 Riverside Dr #250 Toluca Lake (91602) *(P-3167)*

**Northwood Design Partners Inc** .................... E ...... 510 731-6505
1550 Atlantic St Union City (94587) *(P-3577)*

**Norton Packaging Inc (PA)** .................... D ...... **510 786-1922**
20670 Corsair Blvd Hayward (94545) *(P-6936)*

**Norton Packaging Inc** .................... E ...... 323 588-6167
5800 S Boyle Ave Vernon (90058) *(P-6937)*

**Norton Packaging Inc** .................... E ...... 510 786-1922
2868 W Winton Ave Hayward (94545) *(P-6938)*

**Nortra Cables Inc** .................... D ...... 408 942-1106
570 Gibraltar Dr Milpitas (95035) *(P-13049)*

**Norway Topco LP (PA)** .................... F ...... **435 655-6000**
1950 University Ave Palo Alto (94303) *(P-5256)*

**Nothing To Wear Inc** .................... F ...... 310 328-0408
630 Maple Ave Torrance (90503) *(P-2684)*

**Nothing To Wear Inc (PA)** .................... E ...... 310 328-0408
630 Maple Ave Torrance (90503) *(P-2685)*

**Nothwest Pipe Company, Tracy** *Also Called: Nwpc LLC (P-8323)*

**Noticiero Semanal Advertising** .................... F ...... 559 784-5000
115 E Oak Ave Porterville (93257) *(P-4175)*

**Notthoff Engineering L A Inc** .................... E ...... 714 894-9802
5416 Argosy Ave Huntington Beach (92649) *(P-13916)*

**Noushig Inc** .................... E ...... 805 983-2903
451 Lombard St Oxnard (93030) *(P-1230)*

**Nov Inc** .................... E ...... 714 978-1900
759 N Eckhoff St Orange (92868) *(P-9465)*

**Nova, Huntington Park** *Also Called: NL&a Collections Inc (P-11499)*

**Nova Eye, Fremont** *Also Called: Nova Eye Inc (P-15209)*

**Nova Eye Inc** .................... E ...... 510 291-1300
41316 Christy St Fremont (94538) *(P-15209)*

**Nova Lifestyle Inc (PA)** .................... E ...... **323 888-9999**
6565 E Washington Blvd Commerce (90040) *(P-3452)*

**Nova Measuring Instruments Inc** .................... E ...... 408 510-7400
3342 Gateway Blvd Fremont (94538) *(P-14566)*

**Nova Medical Products, Carson** *Also Called: Nova Ortho-Med Inc (P-16586)*

**Nova Module LP** .................... E ...... 415 323-0520
7901 Oakport St Ste 4250 Oakland (94621) *(P-18598)*

**Nova Ortho-Med Inc (PA)** .................... E ...... **310 352-3600**
1470 Beachey Pl Carson (90746) *(P-16586)*

**Nova Steel Company, Corona** *Also Called: Ckkm Inc (P-16613)*

**Novalogic Inc** .................... D ...... 818 880-1997
27489 Agoura Rd Ste 300 Agoura Hills (91301) *(P-17955)*

**Novartis Bphrmctcal Oprtons -, Vacaville** *Also Called: Novartis Pharmaceuticals Corp (P-5769)*

**Novartis Insttes For Bmdcal R** .................... C ...... 510 923-4248
5959 Horton St Emeryville (94608) *(P-5578)*

**Novartis Pharmaceuticals Corp** .................... C ...... 862 778-8300
1121 L St Ste 211 Sacramento (95814) *(P-5579)*

**Novartis Pharmaceuticals Corp** .................... B ...... 707 452-8081
2010 Cessna Dr Vacaville (95688) *(P-5769)*

**Novasignal, Los Angeles** *Also Called: Neurasignal Inc (P-15564)*

**Novastor Corporation (PA)** .................... E ...... **805 579-6700**
29209 Canwood St Ste 200 Agoura Hills (91301) *(P-18599)*

**Novate Industrial Cnstr Svcs, West Sacramento** *Also Called: Novate Solutions Inc (P-19567)*

**Novate Solutions Inc** .................... F ...... 916 641-2725
4781 Pell Dr Sacramento (95838) *(P-11337)*

**Novate Solutions Inc (PA)** .................... E ...... **866 668-2830**
2101 Stone Blvd Ste 210 West Sacramento (95691) *(P-19567)*

**Novato Advance Newspaper, Novato** *Also Called: St Louis Post-Dispatch LLC (P-4200)*

**Novellus Systems Inc** .................... A ...... 408 943-9700
4000 N 1st St San Jose (95134) *(P-9884)*

**Novo Brasil Brewing Co., Chula Vista** *Also Called: Otay Lakes Brewery LLC (P-1452)*

**Novo Manufacturing LLC** .................... D ...... 951 479-4620
341 Bonnie Cir Ste 104 Corona (92878) *(P-3168)*

**Novo Manufacturing LLC** .................... E ...... 949 609-0544
25956 Commercentre Dr Lake Forest (92630) *(P-3169)*

**Novo Nordisk Inc** .................... A ...... 510 299-9508
6300 Dumbarton Cir Fremont (94555) *(P-5580)*

**Novolex Bagcraft Inc** .................... D ...... 626 912-2481
17625 Railroad St Rowland Heights (91748) *(P-3975)*

**Novonutrients, Sunnyvale** *Also Called: Oakbio Inc (P-6154)*

**Novotech Nutraceuticals Inc** .................... E ...... 805 676-1098
2897 Palma Dr Ventura (93003) *(P-777)*

**Nowdocs, Brea** *Also Called: Nowdocs International Inc (P-4929)*

**Nowdocs International Inc** .................... E ...... 714 986-1559
3230 E Imperial Hwy Ste 302 Brea (92821) *(P-4929)*

**Npg Inc (PA)** .................... D ...... **951 940-0200**
1354 Jet Way Perris (92571) *(P-6366)*

**Npi Services Inc** .................... F ...... 714 850-0550
1580 Corporate Dr Ste 124 Costa Mesa (92626) *(P-12179)*

**Npi Solutions, Morgan Hill** *Also Called: New Prduct Intgrtion Sltons In (P-7649)*

**Npms Natural Products Mil Svcs, Gardena** *Also Called: Sabater Usa Inc (P-2346)*

**Nr2b Research Inc** .................... B ...... 650 393-6500
2121 S El Camino Real Ste 1000 San Mateo (94403) *(P-18600)*

**NRC, Milpitas** *Also Called: NRC Manufacturing Inc (P-13050)*

**NRC Manufacturing Inc** .................... F ...... 510 438-9400
500 Yosemite Dr Ste 108 Milpitas (95035) *(P-13050)*

---

Employee Codes: A=Over 500 employees, B=251-500
C=101-250, D=51-100, E=20-50, F=10-19, G=1-9

2025 Harris California Manufacturers Directory

© Mergent Inc. 1-800-342-5647

## ALPHABETIC SECTION

Nreach Online Services Inc .................................................. B ...... 425 301-9168
   303 Twin Dolphin Dr Ste 6080 Redwood City (94065) *(P-18601)*
NRG Motorsports Inc .................................................. D ...... 714 541-1173
   861 E Lambert Rd La Habra (90631) *(P-13551)*
NS Wash Systems, Valencia *Also Called: N/S Corporation (P-10584)*
Nsa Holdings Inc .................................................. E ...... 951 686-1400
   888 Marlborough Ave Riverside (92507) *(P-6939)*
Nsi - Natural Sourcing Intl, Encino *Also Called: Nsi Group LLC (P-19111)*
Nsi Group LLC (PA) .................................................. F ...... 818 639-8335
   17031 Ventura Blvd Encino (91316) *(P-19111)*
Nss Enterprises .................................................. E ...... 408 970-9200
   3380 Viso Ct Santa Clara (95054) *(P-4708)*
Nst, San Diego *Also Called: No Second Thoughts Inc (P-2563)*
NTL Precision Machining Inc .................................................. F ...... 408 298-6650
   1355 Vander Way San Jose (95112) *(P-11012)*
Ntm Consulting Services Inc .................................................. E ...... 510 744-3901
   39300 Civic Center Dr Ste 250 Fremont (94538) *(P-19041)*
Ntrust Infotech Inc .................................................. D ...... 562 207-1600
   230 Commerce Ste 180 Irvine (92602) *(P-18602)*
NTS, Fremont *Also Called: New Tech Solutions Inc (P-17555)*
Nu Health Products, Walnut *Also Called: Nu-Health Products Co (P-5257)*
Nu Venture Diving Co .................................................. E ...... 805 815-4044
   1600 Beacon Pl Oxnard (93033) *(P-9973)*
Nu-Health Products Co .................................................. E ...... 909 869-0666
   20875 Currier Rd Walnut (91789) *(P-5257)*
Nu-Hope Laboratories Inc .................................................. E ...... 818 899-7711
   12640 Branford St Pacoima (91331) *(P-15210)*
Nubs Plastics Inc .................................................. E ...... 760 598-2525
   991 Park Center Dr Vista (92081) *(P-6940)*
Nuconic Packaging LLC .................................................. E ...... 323 588-9033
   4889 Loma Vista Ave Vernon (90058) *(P-6941)*
Nucor Bldg Systems Utah LLC .................................................. D ...... 209 608-7701
   1100 Pinot Noir Dr Lodi (95240) *(P-7620)*
Nucor Warehouse Systems Inc (HQ) .................................................. C ...... 323 588-4261
   3851 S Santa Fe Ave Vernon (90058) *(P-7668)*
Nuface, Vista *Also Called: Carol Cole Company (P-15035)*
Nugeneration Technologies LLC (PA) .................................................. F ...... 415 747-2768
   1155 Park Ave Emeryville (94608) *(P-6313)*
Nugentec, Emeryville *Also Called: Nugeneration Technologies LLC (P-6313)*
Nulaid Foods Inc (PA) .................................................. D ...... 209 599-2121
   200 W 5th St Ripon (95366) *(P-17134)*
Numano Sake Company, Berkeley *Also Called: Takara Sake USA Inc (P-1846)*
Numatech West (kmp) LLC .................................................. D ...... 909 706-3627
   1201 E Lexington Ave Pomona (91766) *(P-3870)*
Numatic Engineering Inc .................................................. E ...... 818 768-1200
   7915 Ajay Dr Sun Valley (91352) *(P-14440)*
Numecent Inc .................................................. E ...... 949 833-2800
   18565 Jamboree Rd Irvine (92612) *(P-18603)*
Numerical Technologies Inc .................................................. C ...... 408 919-1910
   70 W Plumeria Dr San Jose (95134) *(P-18604)*
Nummi, Fremont *Also Called: New United Motor Manufacturing Inc (P-13546)*
Numotion, Cypress *Also Called: Atg - Designing Mobility Inc (P-16574)*
Nuphoton Technologies Inc .................................................. E ...... 951 696-8366
   41610 Corning Pl Murrieta (92562) *(P-13278)*
Nuprodx Inc .................................................. F ...... 415 472-1699
   161 S Vasco Rd Ste G Livermore (94551) *(P-15386)*
Nura, Irvine *Also Called: Nura USA LLC (P-5581)*
Nura USA LLC .................................................. E ...... 949 946-5700
   2652 White Rd Irvine (92614) *(P-5581)*
Nurlink Technology Corp .................................................. F ...... 408 205-5363
   5910 Pacific Center Blvd Ste 310 San Diego (92121) *(P-12608)*
Nuro Inc .................................................. A ...... 650 476-2687
   1300 Terra Bella Ave Ste 200 Mountain View (94043) *(P-9885)*
Nuseed Americas Inc (HQ) .................................................. E ...... 800 345-3330
   990 Riverside Pkwy Ste 140 West Sacramento (95605) *(P-6204)*
Nuset Inc .................................................. E ...... 626 246-1668
   2432 Peck Rd City Of Industry (90601) *(P-8021)*
Nusil, Carpinteria *Also Called: Nusil Technology LLC (P-6518)*
Nusil Technology LLC (DH) .................................................. B ...... 805 684-8780
   1050 Cindy Ln Carpinteria (93013) *(P-6518)*

Nuspace Inc (HQ) .................................................. E ...... 562 497-3200
   4401 E Donald Douglas Dr Long Beach (90808) *(P-11013)*
Nutanix, San Jose *Also Called: Nutanix Inc (P-18605)*
Nutanix Inc (PA) .................................................. A ...... 408 216-8360
   1740 Technology Dr Ste 150 San Jose (95110) *(P-18605)*
Nutiva .................................................. C ...... 510 255-2700
   213 W Cutting Blvd Richmond (94804) *(P-2300)*
Nutra-Blend LLC .................................................. B ...... 559 661-6161
   2140 W Industrial Ave Madera (93637) *(P-1140)*
Nutra-Figs, Fresno *Also Called: San Joaquin Figs Inc (P-963)*
Nutrasumma Inc .................................................. E ...... 866 866-3993
   1315 John Reed Ct City Of Industry (91745) *(P-778)*
Nutrawise, Irvine *Also Called: Nutrawise Health & Beauty LLC (P-5582)*
Nutrawise Health & Beauty LLC .................................................. D ...... 888 271-8976
   9600 Toledo Way Irvine (92618) *(P-5582)*
Nutri Granulations, La Mirada *Also Called: JM Huber Micropowders Inc (P-5097)*
Nutribiotic, Lakeport *Also Called: Globalridge LLC (P-5242)*
Nutrien AG Solutions Inc .................................................. F ...... 805 488-3646
   2150 Eastman Ave Oxnard (93030) *(P-6179)*
Nutrien AG Solutions Inc .................................................. F ...... 209 551-1424
   3348 Claus Rd Modesto (95355) *(P-6189)*
Nutrius, Kingsburg *Also Called: Nutrius LLC (P-1141)*
Nutrius LLC (PA) .................................................. E ...... 559 897-5862
   39494 Clarkson Dr Kingsburg (93631) *(P-1141)*
Nutstar Software LLC .................................................. F ...... 209 250-1324
   1460 W 18th St Merced (95340) *(P-18606)*
Nuvair, Oxnard *Also Called: Nu Venture Diving Co (P-9973)*
Nuvasive Inc .................................................. F ...... 858 909-1800
   4223 Ponderosa Ave Ste C San Diego (92123) *(P-15211)*
Nuvasive Inc (HQ) .................................................. D ...... 858 909-1800
   7475 Lusk Blvd San Diego (92121) *(P-15212)*
Nuvet Labs, Westlake Village *Also Called: Vitavet Labs Inc (P-16264)*
Nuvia Inc .................................................. E ...... 408 654-9696
   2811 Mission College Blvd Fl 7 Santa Clara (95054) *(P-12609)*
Nuvo, Chatsworth *Also Called: Medical Illumination International Inc (P-11546)*
Nuvosun Inc .................................................. E ...... 510 304-2351
   1565 Barber Ln Milpitas (95035) *(P-12610)*
Nuvve Holding Corp (PA) .................................................. E ...... 619 456-5161
   2488 Historic Decatur Rd Ste 200 San Diego (92106) *(P-11218)*
Nuwest Milling LLC .................................................. F ...... 209 883-1163
   4636 Geer Rd Hughson (95326) *(P-1142)*
Nux Group Inc .................................................. E ...... 323 780-4700
   5164 Alcoa Ave Vernon (90058) *(P-2423)*
Nvent Thermal LLC .................................................. B ...... 650 474-7414
   899 Broadway St Redwood City (94063) *(P-14365)*
Nvidia, Santa Clara *Also Called: Nvidia Corporation (P-12612)*
Nvidia, Menlo Park *Also Called: Swiftstack Inc (P-18854)*
Nvidia Corporation .................................................. E ...... 408 486-2715
   2530 Zanker Rd San Jose (95131) *(P-12611)*
Nvidia Corporation (PA) .................................................. A ...... 408 486-2000
   2788 San Tomas Expy Santa Clara (95051) *(P-12612)*
Nvidia US Investment Company .................................................. E ...... 408 615-2500
   2701 San Tomas Expy Santa Clara (95050) *(P-11907)*
Nwe Technology Inc .................................................. C ...... 408 919-6100
   1688 Richard Ave Santa Clara (95050) *(P-10260)*
Nwp Services Corporation (DH) .................................................. C ...... 949 253-2500
   535 Anton Blvd Ste 1100 Costa Mesa (92626) *(P-18607)*
Nwpc LLC .................................................. D ...... 209 836-5050
   10100 W Linne Rd Tracy (95377) *(P-8323)*
Nxedge Csl LLC .................................................. D ...... 408 727-0893
   529 Aldo Ave Santa Clara (95054) *(P-8989)*
Nxgn Management LLC .................................................. E ...... 949 255-2600
   18111 Von Karman Ave Ste 600 Irvine (92612) *(P-18608)*
Nxp, San Jose *Also Called: Nxp Semiconductors Usa Inc (P-12613)*
Nxp Semiconductors Usa Inc .................................................. A ...... 408 518-5500
   411 E Plumeria Dr San Jose (95134) *(P-12613)*
Nxp Usa Inc .................................................. B ...... 408 518-5500
   411 E Plumeria Dr San Jose (95134) *(P-12614)*
Nyansa Inc .................................................. E ...... 650 446-7818
   430 Cowper St Ste 250 Palo Alto (94301) *(P-18609)*

**Nylok LLC** ............................................................................. E ...... 714 635-3993
313 N Euclid Way Anaheim (92801) *(P-8763)*

**Nylok Western Fastener, Anaheim** *Also Called: Nylok LLC (P-8763)*

**Nylon Molding, Brea** *Also Called: Nmc Group Inc (P-16885)*

**Nypro Healthcare Baja, Chula Vista** *Also Called: Nypro Inc (P-6942)*

**Nypro Inc** ............................................................................. D ...... 619 498-9250
505 Main St Rm 107 Chula Vista (91911) *(P-6942)*

**Nypro San Diego Inc** ............................................................. D ...... 619 482-7033
505 Main St Chula Vista (91911) *(P-6943)*

**Nyx Cosmetics, Torrance** *Also Called: Nyx Los Angeles Inc (P-6012)*

**Nyx Los Angeles Inc** ............................................................. C ...... 323 869-9420
588 Crenshaw Blvd Torrance (90503) *(P-6012)*

**Nzxt Inc (PA)** ....................................................................... B ...... 626 385-8272
605 E Huntington Dr Ste 213 Monrovia (91016) *(P-16535)*

**O & S California Inc** ............................................................. B ...... 619 661-1800
9731 Siempre Viva Rd Ste E San Diego (92154) *(P-13279)*

**O & S Precision Inc** ............................................................. E ...... 818 718-8876
20630 Nordhoff St Chatsworth (91311) *(P-11014)*

**O & S Properties Inc (PA)** .................................................... D ...... 626 579-1084
1817 Chico Ave South El Monte (91733) *(P-19272)*

**O C M, Los Angeles** *Also Called: Old Country Millwork Inc (P-9719)*

**O C McDonald Co Inc** .......................................................... C ...... 408 295-2182
1150 W San Carlos St San Jose (95126) *(P-428)*

**O H I Company** .................................................................... E ...... 209 466-8921
820 S Pershing Ave Stockton (95206) *(P-9808)*

**O Industries Corporation** .................................................... F ...... 310 719-2289
1930 W 139th St Gardena (90249) *(P-3100)*

**O M Y A, Lucerne Valley** *Also Called: Omya California Inc (P-5106)*

**O P F, Oxnard** *Also Called: Oxnard Prcsion Fabrication Inc (P-8522)*

**O P I Products Inc (HQ)** ....................................................... B ...... 818 759-8688
13034 Saticoy St North Hollywood (91605) *(P-6013)*

**O.C. Metro Magazine, Newport Beach** *Also Called: Churm Publishing Inc (P-4092)*

**O.C.components, Costa Mesa** *Also Called: Orange County Components Inc (P-16727)*

**O'Dell Printing Company, San Rafael** *Also Called: Syriani Brothers Corp (P-4777)*

**O'Hagin Manufacturing, Rohnert Park** *Also Called: OHagin Manufacturing Company (P-16190)*

**O'Neal U S A, Camarillo** *Also Called: Jim ONeal Distributing Inc (P-17482)*

**O'Neill Vintners & Distillers, Parlier** *Also Called: ONeill Beverages Co LLC (P-22)*

**O'Neill Vintners & Distillers, Larkspur** *Also Called: ONeill Beverages Co LLC (P-23)*

**O'Neill Wetsuits, Santa Cruz** *Also Called: ONeill Wetsuits LLC (P-6519)*

**Oai, Milpitas** *Also Called: Optical Associates Inc (P-14807)*

**Oak Paper Products Co LLC (PA)** ........................................ C ...... 323 268-0507
3686 E Olympic Blvd Los Angeles (90023) *(P-17003)*

**Oak Ridge Winery LLC** ........................................................ E ...... 209 369-4768
6100 E. Hwy 12 Victor Rd Lodi (95240) *(P-1694)*

**Oakbio Inc** ........................................................................... F ...... 888 591-9413
1292 Anvilwood Ct Sunnyvale (94089) *(P-6154)*

**Oakcroft Associates Inc (PA)** .............................................. E ...... 323 261-5122
750 Monterey Pass Rd Monterey Park (91754) *(P-16793)*

**Oakdale Shell, Modesto** *Also Called: Vintners Distributors Inc (P-1820)*

**Oakhurst Industries Inc** ..................................................... C ...... 510 265-2400
3265 Investment Blvd Hayward (94545) *(P-17117)*

**Oakley Inc (DH)** .................................................................. A ...... 949 951-0991
1 Icon Foothill Ranch (92610) *(P-15611)*

**Oakmead Printing, Sunnyvale** *Also Called: Oakmead Prtg Reproduction Inc (P-4709)*

**Oakmead Prtg Reproduction Inc** ......................................... E ...... 408 734-5505
233 E Weddell Dr Ste G Sunnyvale (94089) *(P-4709)*

**Oakville Pump Service Inc** .................................................. F ...... 707 944-2471
2310 Laurel St Ste 1 Napa (94559) *(P-429)*

**Oasis Materials, Poway** *Also Called: Oasis Materials Company LLC (P-13051)*

**Oasis Materials Company LLC (DH)** ................................... E ...... 858 486-8846
12131 Community Rd Poway (92064) *(P-13051)*

**Oasis Medical Inc (PA)** ........................................................ D ...... 909 305-5400
510-528 S Vermont Ave Glendora (91741) *(P-15612)*

**Oberon Design and Mfg LLC** ............................................... E ...... 415 865-5440
1076 Illinois St San Francisco (94107) *(P-16432)*

**OBryant Electric Inc** ........................................................... E ...... 949 341-0025
3 Banting Irvine (92618) *(P-13280)*

**Obsidian Ridge Wine Company** .......................................... E ...... 707 939-7625
21684 8th St E Sonoma (95476) *(P-1695)*

**Oc Acquisition LLC (HQ)** ..................................................... C ...... 650 506-7000
500 Oracle Pkwy Redwood City (94065) *(P-17956)*

**Oc Direct Shower Door, Orange** *Also Called: Dennis DiGiorgio (P-7218)*

**Oc Metals, Santa Ana** *Also Called: Oc Metals Inc (P-8519)*

**Oc Metals Inc** ...................................................................... E ...... 714 668-0783
2720 S Main St Ste B Santa Ana (92707) *(P-8519)*

**Occidental Leather, Santa Rosa** *Also Called: Occidental Manufacturing LLC (P-7158)*

**Occidental Manufacturing LLC** .......................................... C ...... 707 824-2560
3500 N Laughlin Rd Ste 100 Santa Rosa (95403) *(P-7158)*

**Occidental Petroleum Corporation of California** ................ A
10889 Wilshire Blvd Los Angeles (90024) *(P-136)*

**Occidental Petroleum Investment Co Inc** ........................... A ...... 310 208-8800
10889 Wilshire Blvd Fl 10 Los Angeles (90024) *(P-193)*

**Occidental Systems Inc** ...................................................... F ...... 800 902-4393
131a Stony Cir Ste 500 Santa Rosa (95401) *(P-18610)*

**Ocdm, Tustin** *Also Called: Orange County Direct Mail Inc (P-17800)*

**Ocean Direct LLC (HQ)** ........................................................ C ...... 424 266-9300
13771 Gramercy Pl Gardena (90249) *(P-2059)*

**Ocean Fresh LLC (PA)** ........................................................ E ...... 707 964-1389
344 N Franklin St Fort Bragg (95437) *(P-2040)*

**Ocean Fresh Seafood Products, Fort Bragg** *Also Called: Ocean Fresh LLC (P-2040)*

**Ocean Protecta Incorporated** ............................................. E ...... 714 891-2628
14708 Biola Ave La Mirada (90638) *(P-14044)*

**Ocean Technology Systems, Santa Ana** *Also Called: Undersea Systems Intl Inc (P-13321)*

**Ocean's Halo, Burlingame** *Also Called: New Frontier Foods Inc (P-2098)*

**Oceania Inc** ......................................................................... E ...... 562 926-8886
14209 Gannet St La Mirada (90638) *(P-6565)*

**Oceania International LLC** ................................................. E ...... 949 407-8904
23661 Birtcher Dr Lake Forest (92630) *(P-7765)*

**Oceanic, San Leandro** *Also Called: American Underwater Products (P-15778)*

**Oceanscience, Poway** *Also Called: Tern Design Ltd (P-14462)*

**Oceanside Glasstile Company (PA)** .................................... B ...... 760 929-4000
2445 Grand Ave Vista (92081) *(P-7270)*

**Oceanwide Repairs, Long Beach** *Also Called: APR Engineering Inc (P-13998)*

**Ocelot Engineering Inc** ....................................................... C ...... 800 841-2960
555 S H St San Bernardino (92410) *(P-17483)*

**Oci, Santa Fe Springs** *Also Called: Office Chairs Inc (P-3578)*

**Ocinet Inc** ........................................................................... F ...... 213 280-0989
8718 Cleta St Downey (90241) *(P-986)*

**Ocip, Anaheim** *Also Called: Orange County Indus Plas Inc (P-17229)*

**Ockam Inc** .......................................................................... E ...... 415 407-3800
535 Mission St Fl 14 San Francisco (94105) *(P-18611)*

**Oclaro, Milpitas** *Also Called: Oclaro Fiber Optics Inc (P-12615)*

**Oclaro (north America) Inc (DH)** ........................................ B ...... 408 383-1400
252 Charcot Ave San Jose (95131) *(P-11777)*

**Oclaro Fiber Optics Inc (DH)** .............................................. C ...... 408 383-1400
400 N Mccarthy Blvd Milpitas (95035) *(P-12615)*

**Oclaro Subsystems Inc** ....................................................... C ...... 408 383-1400
400 N Mccarthy Blvd Milpitas (95035) *(P-11778)*

**Oclaro Technology Inc** ........................................................ A ...... 408 383-1400
400 N Mccarthy Blvd Milpitas (95035) *(P-14804)*

**Ocli, Santa Rosa** *Also Called: Optical Coating Laboratory LLC (P-9097)*

**Ocm Pe Holdings LP** ........................................................... A ...... 213 830-6213
333 S Grand Ave Fl 28 Los Angeles (90071) *(P-13052)*

**OCP Group Inc** .................................................................... C ...... 858 279-7400
7130 Engineer Rd San Diego (92111) *(P-10309)*

**Ocpc Inc** ............................................................................. D ...... 949 475-1900
2485 Da Vinci Irvine (92614) *(P-4710)*

**Ocs America Inc (DH)** ......................................................... E ...... 310 417-0650
22912 Lockness Ave Torrance (90501) *(P-19112)*

**Ocs Bookstore, Torrance** *Also Called: Ocs America Inc (P-19112)*

**Oculeve Inc** ......................................................................... F ...... 415 745-3784
4410 Rosewood Dr Pleasanton (94588) *(P-5583)*

**Oculus, Menlo Park** *Also Called: Meta Platforms Tech LLC (P-18540)*

**Ocz Enterprise, San Jose** *Also Called: Zco Liquidating Corporation (P-10300)*

**Odcombe Press (nashville)** ................................................ E ...... 615 793-5414
2801 Townsgate Rd Westlake Village (91361) *(P-4711)*

**Odenberg Inc** ...................................................................... E ...... 916 371-0700
875 Embarcadero Dr West Sacramento (95605) *(P-9809)*

**Odi Manufacturing LLC** .................................................................. C ...... 951 786-4750
708 S Temescal St Ste 101 Corona (92879) *(P-6944)*

**Odyssey Innovative Designs, San Gabriel** *Also Called: Hsiao & Montano Inc (P-7133)*

**Oea International Incorporated** .................................................... E ...... 408 778-6747
155 E Main Ave Ste 130 Morgan Hill (95037) *(P-18612)*

**OEM, Orange** *Also Called: Premier Filters Inc (P-10108)*

**Oem LLC** ........................................................................................ E ...... 714 449-7500
311 S Highland Ave Fullerton (92832) *(P-11015)*

**OEM Materials, Santa Ana** *Also Called: OEM Materials & Supplies Inc (P-3790)*

**OEM Materials & Supplies Inc** ..................................................... E ...... 714 564-9600
1500 Ritchey St Santa Ana (92705) *(P-3790)*

**Oepic Semiconductors Inc** .......................................................... E ...... 408 747-0388
1231 Bordeaux Dr Sunnyvale (94089) *(P-12616)*

**Off Broadway, La Verne** *Also Called: Fortress Inc (P-3567)*

**Office Chairs Inc** ......................................................................... D ...... 562 802-0464
14815 Radburn Ave Santa Fe Springs (90670) *(P-3578)*

**Office Libations, San Leandro** *Also Called: Noble Brewer Beer Company (P-2075)*

**Office Master Inc** ......................................................................... D ...... 909 392-5678
1110 Mildred St Ontario (91761) *(P-16417)*

**Office Star Products, Ontario** *Also Called: Blumenthal Distributing Inc (P-16411)*

**Officia Imaging Inc (PA)** ............................................................... E ...... 858 348-0831
5636 Ruffin Rd San Diego (92123) *(P-17715)*

**Offline Inc (PA)** ............................................................................ E ...... 213 742-9001
2931 S Alameda St Vernon (90058) *(P-2600)*

**Ofs Brands Holdings Inc** ............................................................. A ...... 714 903-2257
5559 Mcfadden Ave Huntington Beach (92649) *(P-3579)*

**Oggi's Sports Brewhouse Pizza, Encinitas** *Also Called: Oggis Pizza & Brewing Company (P-17599)*

**Oggis Pizza & Brewing Company** ............................................... E ...... 760 944-8170
305 Encinitas Blvd Encinitas (92024) *(P-17599)*

**Ogio, Carlsbad** *Also Called: Ogio International Inc (P-7138)*

**Ogio International Inc** ................................................................. D ...... 800 326-6325
508 Constitution Ave Camarillo (93012) *(P-7137)*

**Ogio International Inc (HQ)** ......................................................... E ...... 801 619-4100
2180 Rutherford Rd Carlsbad (92008) *(P-7138)*

**Ogio Powersports, Camarillo** *Also Called: Ogio International Inc (P-7137)*

**Ogleby Sisters Soap** .................................................................... E ...... 212 518-1172
1804 Garnet Ave San Diego (92109) *(P-17772)*

**OH Juice Inc** ................................................................................. F ...... 619 318-0207
5631 Palmer Way Ste A Carlsbad (92010) *(P-910)*

**OHagin Manufacturing Company** ............................................... D ...... 707 322-2402
210 Classic Ct Ste 100 Rohnert Park (94928) *(P-16190)*

**OHara Metal Products** ................................................................. E ...... 707 863-9090
4949 Fulton Dr Ste E Fairfield (94534) *(P-9178)*

**Ohio, San Francisco** *Also Called: Ohio Inc (P-3580)*

**Ohio Inc** ........................................................................................ F ...... 415 647-6446
630 Treat Ave San Francisco (94110) *(P-3580)*

**Ohline Corporation** ..................................................................... E ...... 310 327-4630
1930 W 139th St Gardena (90249) *(P-3170)*

**Ohmega Solenoid Co Inc** ............................................................ E ...... 562 944-7948
10912 Painter Ave Santa Fe Springs (90670) *(P-11219)*

**Ohmio Inc** .................................................................................... F ...... 818 818-8268
1900 Powell St Ste 700 Emeryville (94608) *(P-11281)*

**Ohmium International Inc (PA)** ................................................... F ...... 775 237-2077
39672 Eureka Dr Newark (94560) *(P-5057)*

**Ohmnilabs Incorporated** ............................................................ D ...... 408 675-9565
591 Yosemite Dr Milpitas (95035) *(P-9743)*

**Oil Field Services, Santa Maria** *Also Called: Pacific Petroleum California Inc (P-264)*

**Oil Well Service, Santa Paula** *Also Called: Oil Well Service Company (P-260)*

**Oil Well Service Company** .......................................................... D ...... 661 746-4809
10255 Enos Ln Shafter (93263) *(P-258)*

**Oil Well Service Company (PA)** .................................................. C ...... 562 612-0600
1241 E Burnett St Signal Hill (90755) *(P-259)*

**Oil Well Service Company** .......................................................... D ...... 805 525-2103
1015 Mission Rock Rd Santa Paula (93060) *(P-260)*

**Oil-Dri Corporation America** ....................................................... E ...... 661 765-7194
950 Petroleum Club Rd Taft (93268) *(P-5921)*

**OK International Inc (DH)** ............................................................ C ...... 714 799-9910
10800 Valley View St Cypress (90630) *(P-9728)*

**OKeeffes Inc** ................................................................................. D ...... 209 386-1645
2001 Grogan Ave Merced (95341) *(P-7199)*

**OKeeffes Inc** ................................................................................. D ...... 209 388-9072
220 S R St Merced (95341) *(P-17338)*

**OKeeffes Inc (PA)** ......................................................................... E ...... 415 822-4222
100 N Hill Dr Ste 12 Brisbane (94005) *(P-7237)*

**Okera Inc** ...................................................................................... D ...... 415 741-3282
600 California St Fl 15 San Francisco (94108) *(P-18613)*

**Okonite Company Inc** ................................................................. C ...... 805 922-6682
2900 Skyway Dr Santa Maria (93455) *(P-7790)*

**OKTA, San Francisco** *Also Called: Okta Inc (P-18614)*

**Okta Inc (PA)** ................................................................................ A ...... 888 722-7871
100 1st St Ste 600 San Francisco (94105) *(P-18614)*

**Ola Nation LLC** ............................................................................ E ...... 310 256-0638
915 W Barbara Ave West Covina (91790) *(P-2712)*

**Olam Food Ingriedients, Fresno** *Also Called: Olam LLC (P-1)*

**Olam LLC** ..................................................................................... E ...... 559 446-6420
205 E River Park Cir Ste 310 Fresno (93720) *(P-1)*

**Olam Spices and Vegetables, Woodland** *Also Called: Olam West Coast Inc (P-913)*

**Olam Tomato Processors Inc** ..................................................... B ...... 559 447-1390
1175 S 19th Ave Lemoore (93245) *(P-911)*

**Olam Tomato Processors Inc (DH)** ............................................. E ...... 559 447-1390
205 E River Park Cir Ste 310 Fresno (93720) *(P-912)*

**Olam West Coast Inc** .................................................................. C ...... 530 473-4290
1400 Churchill Downs Ave Woodland (95776) *(P-913)*

**Old Bbh Inc** .................................................................................. A ...... 858 715-4000
280 10th Ave San Diego (92101) *(P-655)*

**Old Castle Inclosure Solution, Madera** *Also Called: Oldcastle Infrastructure Inc (P-7363)*

**Old Country Millwork Inc (PA)** ..................................................... E ...... 323 234-2940
5855 Hooper Ave Los Angeles (90001) *(P-9719)*

**Old Durham Wood Inc** ................................................................. E ...... 530 342-7381
1156 Oroville Chico Hwy Durham (95938) *(P-99)*

**Old English Mil & Woodworks, Santa Clarita** *Also Called: Old English Mil Woodworks Inc (P-3171)*

**Old English Mil Woodworks Inc (PA)** ......................................... E ...... 661 294-9171
27772 Avenue Scott Santa Clarita (91355) *(P-3171)*

**Old Guys Rule, Ventura** *Also Called: Streamline Dsign Slkscreen Inc (P-2645)*

**Old New York Bagel Deli Co Inc (PA)** ......................................... F ...... 805 484-3354
4972 Verdugo Way Camarillo (93012) *(P-1231)*

**Old New York Deli & Bagel Co, Camarillo** *Also Called: Old New York Bagel Deli Co Inc (P-1231)*

**Old Spc Inc** .................................................................................. E ...... 310 533-0748
202 W 140th St Los Angeles (90061) *(P-8990)*

**Oldcast Precast (DH)** .................................................................. E ...... 951 788-9720
2434 Rubidoux Blvd Riverside (92509) *(P-7362)*

**Oldcastle Buildingenvelope Inc** ................................................. C ...... 510 651-2292
6850 Stevenson Blvd Fremont (94538) *(P-17349)*

**Oldcastle Infrastructure Inc** ....................................................... E ...... 559 675-1813
801 S Pine St Madera (93637) *(P-7363)*

**Oldcastle Infrastructure Inc** ....................................................... E ...... 909 428-3700
10650 Hemlock Ave Fontana (92337) *(P-7364)*

**Oldcastle Infrastructure Inc** ....................................................... E ...... 925 846-8183
3786 Valley Ave Pleasanton (94566) *(P-7365)*

**Oldcastle Infrastructure Inc** ....................................................... E ...... 951 683-8200
2512 Harmony Grove Rd Escondido (92029) *(P-7366)*

**Oldcastle Infrastructure Inc** ....................................................... E ...... 209 235-1173
2960 S Highway 99 Stockton (95215) *(P-7367)*

**Oldcastle Infrastructure Inc** ....................................................... E ...... 951 928-8713
19940 Hansen Ave Nuevo (92567) *(P-7368)*

**Oldcastle Infrastructure Inc** ....................................................... D ...... 559 674-8093
801 S Pine St Madera (93637) *(P-9295)*

**Oldcastle Prcast Enclsure Slto, Riverside** *Also Called: Carson Industries LLC (P-6766)*

**Olde Thompson LLC (DH)** ........................................................... E ...... 805 983-0388
3250 Camino Del Sol Oxnard (93030) *(P-6314)*

**Olde Thompson LLC** ................................................................... E ...... 805 983-0388
2300 Celsius Ave Oxnard (93030) *(P-17202)*

**Olde World Corporation** .............................................................. E ...... 209 384-1337
360 Grogan Ave Merced (95341) *(P-3666)*

**Olea Kiosks Inc** ............................................................................ D ...... 562 924-2644
13845 Artesia Blvd Cerritos (90703) *(P-10415)*

**OLEMA ONCOLOGY, San Francisco** *Also Called: Olema Pharmaceuticals Inc (P-5584)*

**Olema Pharmaceuticals Inc (PA)** ................................................ D ...... 415 651-3316
780 Brannan St San Francisco (94103) *(P-5584)*

# ALPHABETIC SECTION

Oleumtech Corporation .................................................................. D ...... 949 305-9009
   19762 Pauling Foothill Ranch (92610) *(P-14441)*

Olin Chlor Alkali Logistics ............................................................. C ...... 562 692-0510
   11600 Pike St Santa Fe Springs (90670) *(P-5034)*

Olin Chlor Alkali Logistics ............................................................. C ...... 209 835-5424
   26700 S Banta Rd Tracy (95304) *(P-5035)*

Olipop Inc ...................................................................................... D ...... 510 560-5709
   360 Grand Ave # 259 Oakland (94610) *(P-1907)*

Oliso Inc ........................................................................................ F ...... 415 864-7600
   1200 Harbour Way S # 215 Richmond (94804) *(P-11412)*

Olivarez Honey Bees Inc .............................................................. D ...... 530 865-0298
   6398 County Road 20 Orland (95963) *(P-70)*

Olive Corto L P .............................................................................. F ...... 888 832-0051
   10201 Live Oak Rd Stockton (95212) *(P-1403)*

Olive Media Products Inc .............................................................. F ...... 415 908-3870
   555 Howard St San Francisco (94105) *(P-11684)*

Olive Musco Products Inc (PA) .................................................... C ...... 866 965-4837
   17950 Via Nicolo Tracy (95377) *(P-914)*

Olive Musco Products Inc ............................................................ E ...... 530 865-4111
   Swift & 5th St Orland (95963) *(P-987)*

Olive Oil Factory LLC (PA) ........................................................... E ...... 707 426-3400
   770 Chadbourne Rd Fairfield (94534) *(P-1404)*

Olive Pit LLC ................................................................................. F ...... 530 824-4667
   2156 Solano St Corning (96021) *(P-17430)*

Olive Refinish ............................................................................... E ...... 805 273-5072
   19014 Pacific Coast Hwy Malibu (90265) *(P-6098)*

Oliver De Silva Inc (PA) ............................................................... E ...... 925 829-9220
   11555 Dublin Blvd Dublin (94568) *(P-303)*

Oliver Healthcare Packaging Co ................................................. D ...... 714 864-3500
   1145 N Ocean Cir Anaheim (92806) *(P-16831)*

Olivera Egg Ranch LLC .............................................................. D ...... 408 258-8074
   3315 Sierra Rd San Jose (95132) *(P-698)*

Olivera Foods, San Jose *Also Called: Olivera Egg Ranch LLC (P-698)*

Olivet International Inc (PA) ....................................................... D ...... 951 681-8888
   11015 Hopkins St Mira Loma (91752) *(P-16983)*

Olivia Companies LLC ................................................................ E ...... 415 962-5700
   434 Brannan St San Francisco (94107) *(P-16305)*

Olivia Cruises & Resorts, San Francisco *Also Called: Olivia Companies LLC (P-16305)*

Olli Salumeria Americana LLC ................................................... D
   1301 Rocky Point Dr Oceanside (92056) *(P-609)*

Olloclip, Huntington Beach *Also Called: Premier Systems Usa Inc (P-16540)*

Olson and Co Steel ..................................................................... C ...... 559 224-7811
   3488 W Ashlan Ave Fresno (93722) *(P-8196)*

Olson and Co Steel (PA) ............................................................. C ...... 510 567-2200
   1941 Davis St San Leandro (94577) *(P-8639)*

Olson Industrial Systems, Santee *Also Called: Olson Irrigation Systems (P-9373)*

Olson Irrigation Systems ............................................................ E ...... 619 562-3100
   10910 Wheatlands Ave Ste A Santee (92071) *(P-9373)*

Olson Meat Company ................................................................. E ...... 530 865-8111
   7301 Cutler Ave Orland (95963) *(P-610)*

Olt Solar, San Jose *Also Called: Orbotech Lt Solar LLC (P-12622)*

Olympic Cascade Publishing (DH) ............................................. E ...... 916 321-1000
   2100 Q St Sacramento (95816) *(P-4176)*

Olympus Water Holdings IV LP (PA) .......................................... E ...... 310 739-6325
   360 N Crescent Dr Bldg S Beverly Hills (90210) *(P-5922)*

Om Mushroom Superfood .......................................................... E ...... 858 779-1275
   5931 Priestly Dr Ste 101 Carlsbad (92008) *(P-915)*

Om Smart Seating, Ontario *Also Called: Office Master Inc (P-16417)*

Om Tactical, Van Nuys *Also Called: Rizzo Inc (P-15399)*

Omar Leather Co .......................................................................... F ...... 323 227-5220
   4557 Valley Blvd Los Angeles (90032) *(P-7159)*

Omc-Thc Liquidating Inc ............................................................. E ...... 858 486-8846
   12131 Community Rd Poway (92064) *(P-8072)*

Omega Diamond Inc ................................................................... F ...... 530 889-8977
   10125 Ophir Rd Newcastle (95658) *(P-9686)*

Omega Ii Inc ................................................................................ E ...... 619 920-6650
   3525 Main St Chula Vista (91911) *(P-8324)*

Omega Industrial Marine, Chula Vista *Also Called: Omega Ii Inc (P-8324)*

Omega Leads Inc ........................................................................ E ...... 310 394-6786
   1509 Colorado Ave Santa Monica (90404) *(P-13053)*

Omega Precision ......................................................................... E ...... 562 946-2491
   13040 Telegraph Rd Santa Fe Springs (90670) *(P-11016)*

Omega Products Corp (HQ) ....................................................... D ...... 951 737-7447
   1681 California Ave Corona (92881) *(P-7595)*

Omega Products Corp ................................................................ E ...... 916 635-3335
   8111 Fruitridge Rd Sacramento (95826) *(P-7596)*

Omega Products Corp ................................................................ E ...... 714 935-0900
   282 S Anita Dr 3rd Fl Orange (92868) *(P-7597)*

Omega Products International, Corona *Also Called: Omega Products Corp (P-7595)*

Omex Agrifluids Inc ..................................................................... F ...... 559 661-6138
   1675 Dockery Ave Selma (93662) *(P-6180)*

Omex USA, Selma *Also Called: Omex Agrifluids Inc (P-6180)*

Omics Group Inc .......................................................................... B ...... 650 268-9744
   5716 Corsa Ave Ste 110 Westlake Village (91362) *(P-4282)*

Omics Group Inc .......................................................................... B ...... 650 268-9744
   731 Gull Ave Foster City (94404) *(P-4283)*

Omni Connection Intl Inc ............................................................. B ...... 951 898-6232
   126 Via Trevizio Corona (92879) *(P-13054)*

Omni Duct Systems, West Sacramento *Also Called: ECB Corp (P-8438)*

Omni Enclosures Inc ................................................................... E ...... 619 579-6664
   505 Raleigh Ave El Cajon (92020) *(P-3667)*

Omni Metal Finishing Inc (PA) ................................................... D ...... 714 979-9414
   11639 Coley River Cir Fountain Valley (92708) *(P-8991)*

Omni Optical Products Inc (PA) ................................................. E ...... 714 634-5700
   17282 Eastman Irvine (92614) *(P-14905)*

Omni Optical Products Inc ......................................................... E ...... 714 692-1400
   22605 La Palma Ave Ste 505 Yorba Linda (92887) *(P-19273)*

Omni Pacific, El Cajon *Also Called: Omni Enclosures Inc (P-3667)*

Omni Resource Recovery Inc .................................................... C ...... 909 327-2900
   1495 N 8th St Ste 150 Colton (92324) *(P-6945)*

Omni Seals, Rancho Cucamonga *Also Called: Smith International Inc (P-9466)*

Omni Seals Inc ............................................................................ D ...... 909 946-0181
   11031 Jersey Blvd Ste A Rancho Cucamonga (91730) *(P-6474)*

Omni-Pak Industries, Anaheim *Also Called: Nbty Manufacturing LLC (P-5565)*

Omnia Leather Motion Inc .......................................................... C ...... 909 393-4400
   4950 Edison Ave Chino (91710) *(P-2941)*

Omniduct, Buena Park *Also Called: ECB Corp (P-416)*

Omnimax International LLC ....................................................... D ...... 951 928-1000
   28921 Us Highway 74 Sun City (92585) *(P-8281)*

Omnimax International LLC ....................................................... F ...... 951 928-1000
   28921 Us Highway 74 Sun City (92585) *(P-8520)*

Omniprint Inc ............................................................................... E ...... 949 833-0080
   1923 E Deere Ave Santa Ana (92705) *(P-10416)*

Omnisil ......................................................................................... E ...... 805 644-2514
   5401 Everglades St Ventura (93003) *(P-12617)*

Omnissa LLC ............................................................................... A ...... 650 239-7600
   590 E Middlefield Rd Mountain View (94043) *(P-18615)*

Omnitracs Midco LLC ................................................................. E ...... 858 651-5812
   9276 Scranton Rd Ste 200 San Diego (92121) *(P-18616)*

Omnivision Technologies Inc (PA) ............................................. A ...... 408 567-3000
   4275 Burton Dr Santa Clara (95054) *(P-12618)*

Omniyig Inc .................................................................................. E ...... 408 988-0843
   630 Chelsea Xing San Jose (95138) *(P-13055)*

Omron Delta Tau, Chatsworth *Also Called: Delta Tau Data Systems Inc Cal (P-10086)*

Omron Robotics Safety Tech Inc (HQ) ...................................... C ...... 925 245-3400
   4225 Hacienda Dr Pleasanton (94588) *(P-9489)*

Omya California Inc .................................................................... D ...... 760 248-7306
   7299 Crystal Creek Rd Lucerne Valley (92356) *(P-5106)*

Omya Inc ...................................................................................... D ...... 760 248-5200
   7299 Crystal Creek Rd Lucerne Valley (92356) *(P-5107)*

On Premise Products Inc ............................................................ E ...... 619 562-1486
   8021 Wing Ave El Cajon (92020) *(P-16191)*

On Semcndctor Cnnctvity Sltons ................................................ B ...... 669 209-5500
   1704 Automation Pkwy San Jose (95131) *(P-12619)*

On Semiconductor, Sunnyvale *Also Called: Fairchild Semicdtr Intl Inc (P-12430)*

On Semiconductor, Santa Clara *Also Called: Semicndctor Cmponents Inds LLC (P-12687)*

On Semiconductor, Santa Clara *Also Called: Semicndctor Cmponents Inds LLC (P-12688)*

On Target Marketing ................................................................... E ...... 209 723-1691
   429 Grogan Ave Merced (95341) *(P-17835)*

On-Line Power Incorporated (PA) ............................................. E ...... 323 721-5017
   14000 S Broadway Los Angeles (90061) *(P-11220)*

On24 Inc (PA) .............................................................................. B ...... 415 369-8000
   50 Beale St Fl 8 San Francisco (94105) *(P-18617)*

# Onanon Inc — ALPHABETIC SECTION

**Onanon Inc** .................................................................................. E ...... 408 262-8990
720 S Milpitas Blvd Milpitas (95035) *(P-12893)*

**Oncocyte Corporation (PA)** ........................................................ F ...... 949 409-7600
15 Cushing Irvine (92602) *(P-5770)*

**Oncology Care Systems Group, Concord** *Also Called: Siemens Med Solutions USA Inc* *(P-15578)*

**Oncor Corp** ................................................................................... E ...... 562 944-0230
13115 Barton Rd Ste G-H Whittier (90605) *(P-17043)*

**ONCOR CORP, Whittier** *Also Called: Oncor Corp (P-17043)*

**Oncore Manufacturing LLC** ........................................................ D ...... 510 516-5488
6600 Stevenson Blvd Fremont (94538) *(P-12180)*

**Oncore Manufacturing LLC** ........................................................ C ...... 760 737-6777
237 Via Vera Cruz San Marcos (92078) *(P-12181)*

**Oncore Manufacturing LLC (HQ)** ............................................... A ...... 818 734-6500
9340 Owensmouth Ave Chatsworth (91311) *(P-19408)*

**Oncore Manufacturing Svcs Inc** ................................................. C ...... 510 360-2222
9340 Owensmouth Ave Chatsworth (91311) *(P-12182)*

**Oncore Velocity, San Marcos** *Also Called: Oncore Manufacturing LLC (P-12181)*

**Ondax Inc** .................................................................................... F ...... 626 357-9600
850 E Duarte Rd Monrovia (91016) *(P-14805)*

**One Bella Casa Inc** ..................................................................... E ...... 707 746-8300
101 Lucas Valley Rd Ste 130 San Rafael (94903) *(P-2942)*

**One Hat One Hand LLC** ............................................................. E ...... 415 822-2020
1335 Yosemite Ave San Francisco (94124) *(P-2848)*

**One Step Gps LLC** ..................................................................... D ...... 818 659-2031
675 Glenoaks Blvd Unit C San Fernando (91340) *(P-14272)*

**One Stop Label Corporation** ...................................................... F ...... 909 230-9380
1641 S Baker Ave Ontario (91761) *(P-4930)*

**One Stop Systems Inc (PA)** ....................................................... E ...... 760 745-9883
2235 Enterprise St Ste 110 Escondido (92029) *(P-10417)*

**One Stop Systems Inc** ............................................................... E ...... 858 530-2511
2235 Enterprise St Ste 110 Escondido (92029) *(P-10418)*

**One Structural Inc** ...................................................................... E ...... 626 252-0778
19326 Ventura Blvd Ste 200 Tarzana (91356) *(P-261)*

**One Touch Office Technology, Torrance** *Also Called: One Touch Solutions Inc (P-9771)*

**One Touch Solutions Inc** ........................................................... F ...... 310 320-6868
370 Amapola Ave Ste 106 Torrance (90501) *(P-9771)*

**One Up Manufacturing LLC** ....................................................... E ...... 310 749-8347
550 E Airline Way Gardena (90248) *(P-3805)*

**One Wheel, Santa Cruz** *Also Called: Future Motion Inc (P-15815)*

**One World Meat Company LLC** ................................................. F ...... 800 782-1670
6363 Knott Ave Buena Park (90620) *(P-656)*

**One-Way Manufacturing Inc** ...................................................... E ...... 714 630-8833
1195 N Osprey Cir Anaheim (92807) *(P-9267)*

**ONeil Capital Management Inc** .................................................. C ...... 310 448-6400
12655 Beatrice St Los Angeles (90066) *(P-4825)*

**ONeil Digital Solutions LLC** ..................................................... C ...... 310 448-6407
12655 Beatrice St Los Angeles (90066) *(P-4712)*

**ONeill Beverages Co LLC** ......................................................... C ...... 559 638-3544
8418 S Lac Jac Ave Parlier (93648) *(P-22)*

**ONeill Beverages Co LLC (PA)** ................................................. D ...... 559 638-3544
101 Larkspur Landing Cir Ste 350 Larkspur (94939) *(P-23)*

**ONeill Beverages Co LLC** ......................................................... E ...... 805 239-1616
2975 Mitchell Ranch Way Paso Robles (93446) *(P-1696)*

**ONeill Wetsuits LLC (PA)** .......................................................... D ...... 831 475-7500
1071 41st Ave Santa Cruz (95062) *(P-6519)*

**Onelogin Inc (DH)** ...................................................................... C ...... 415 645-6830
848 Battery St San Francisco (94111) *(P-18618)*

**Onesignal, San Mateo** *Also Called: Onesignal Inc (P-18619)*

**Onesignal Inc (PA)** ..................................................................... C ...... 408 506-0701
201 S B St Ste 200 San Mateo (94401) *(P-18619)*

**Onesource Distributors LLC (DH)** ............................................ E ...... 760 966-4500
3951 Oceanic Dr Oceanside (92056) *(P-13281)*

**Onesource Distributors LLC** .................................................... E ...... 925 827-9988
2500 Bisso Ln Ste 100a Concord (94520) *(P-16668)*

**Oneto Metal Products Corp** ....................................................... E ...... 916 681-6555
7485 Reese Rd Sacramento (95828) *(P-7660)*

**Onex Rf Inc** ................................................................................. E ...... 626 358-6639
1824 Flower Ave Duarte (91010) *(P-9729)*

**Oni Inc** ......................................................................................... E ...... 415 301-8526
101 Jefferson Dr Menlo Park (94025) *(P-14698)*

**Onq Solutions Inc (PA)** .............................................................. E ...... 650 351-4245
25821 Industrial Blvd Hayward (94545) *(P-3699)*

**Onshore Technologies Inc** ........................................................ E ...... 310 533-4888
2771 Plaza Del Amo Ste 802-803 Torrance (90503) *(P-13056)*

**Ontario Foam Products, Ontario** *Also Called: Androp Packaging Inc (P-3819)*

**Ontic Engineering and Mfg Inc (PA)** ......................................... D ...... 818 678-6555
20400 Plummer St Chatsworth (91311) *(P-16921)*

**Onto Innovation Inc** ................................................................... C ...... 408 545-6000
1550 Buckeye Dr Milpitas (95035) *(P-14567)*

**Onto Innovation Inc** ................................................................... F ...... 408 545-6000
1550 Buckeye Dr Milpitas (95035) *(P-14568)*

**Ontraport Inc** .............................................................................. D ...... 855 668-7276
2030 Alameda Padre Serra Ste 200 Santa Barbara (93103) *(P-18620)*

**Onvantage Inc** ............................................................................. D ...... 408 562-3388
3290 Freedom Cir # 200 Santa Clara (95054) *(P-18621)*

**Onymos Inc** ................................................................................. E ...... 650 504-8037
1600 El Camino Real Menlo Park (94025) *(P-18622)*

**Onyx Industries Inc (PA)** ........................................................... D ...... 310 539-8830
1227 254th St Harbor City (90710) *(P-8727)*

**Onyx Industries Inc** ................................................................... D ...... 310 851-6161
521 W Rosecrans Ave Gardena (90248) *(P-8728)*

**Onyx Optics Inc** ......................................................................... F ...... 925 833-1969
6551 Sierra Ln Dublin (94568) *(P-14806)*

**Onyx Pharmaceuticals Inc** ........................................................ A ...... 650 266-0000
1 Amgen Center Dr Newbury Park (91320) *(P-5585)*

**Onyx Power Inc** .......................................................................... C ...... 714 513-1500
4011 W Carriage Dr Santa Ana (92704) *(P-11221)*

**Oorja Corporation** ...................................................................... E ...... 510 659-1899
45473 Warm Springs Blvd Fremont (94539) *(P-12620)*

**Ooshirts Inc (PA)** ....................................................................... D ...... 866 660-8667
39899 Balentine Dr Ste 220 Newark (94560) *(P-4931)*

**Op Games, The, Carlsbad** *Also Called: USAopoly Inc (P-15771)*

**Opal Moon Winery LLC** ............................................................. F ...... 707 996-0420
21690 8th St E Ste A Sonoma (95476) *(P-1697)*

**Opal Service Inc (PA)** ................................................................ E ...... 714 935-0900
282 S Anita Dr Orange (92868) *(P-7598)*

**Open Systems Inc** ..................................................................... E ...... 317 566-6662
5250 Lankershim Blvd Ste 620 North Hollywood (91601) *(P-18623)*

**Openai Inc (PA)** .......................................................................... E ...... 650 387-6701
1960 Bryant St San Francisco (94110) *(P-18624)*

**Openfive, San Jose** *Also Called: Alphawave Semi Inc (P-12292)*

**Opentv Inc** .................................................................................. B ...... 415 962-5000
275 Sacramento St San Francisco (94111) *(P-18625)*

**Openwave Mobility Inc (DH)** ..................................................... E ...... 650 480-7200
303 Twin Dolphin Dr Ste 600 Redwood City (94065) *(P-18626)*

**Opera Patisserie** ........................................................................ D ...... 858 536-5800
8480 Redwood Creek Ln San Diego (92126) *(P-1291)*

**Opera Patisserie, San Diego** *Also Called: Opera Patisserie (P-1291)*

**Opera Software International As** .............................................. E ...... 650 625-8470
1875 S Grant St Ste 750 San Mateo (94402) *(P-18627)*

**Ophir Rf, Los Angeles** *Also Called: Ophir Rf Inc (P-11908)*

**Ophir Rf Inc** ................................................................................ E ...... 310 306-5556
5300 Beethoven St Fl 3 Los Angeles (90066) *(P-11908)*

**Ophthonix Inc** ............................................................................. E ...... 760 842-5600
900 Glenneyre St Laguna Beach (92651) *(P-15613)*

**Oplink, Fremont** *Also Called: Oplink Communications LLC (P-16340)*

**Oplink Communications LLC (DH)** .......................................... E ...... 510 933-7200
46360 Fremont Blvd Fremont (94538) *(P-16340)*

**Opolo Vineyards Inc** .................................................................. F ...... 805 238-9593
2801 Townsgate Rd Ste 123 Westlake Village (91361) *(P-1698)*

**Opscruise Inc** ............................................................................. E ...... 916 204-4369
5255 Stevens Creek Blvd Ste 179 Santa Clara (95051) *(P-18628)*

**Opshub Inc** ................................................................................. F ...... 650 701-1800
1000 Elwell Ct Ste 217 Palo Alto (94303) *(P-17957)*

**Optec Displays Inc** .................................................................... D ...... 866 924-5239
1700 S De Soto Pl Ste A Ontario (91761) *(P-16015)*

**Optec Laser Systems LLC** ........................................................ E ...... 858 220-1070
11622 El Camino Real Ste 100 San Diego (92130) *(P-4932)*

**Optex Incorporated** .................................................................... E ...... 800 966-7839
10741 Walker St Cypress (90630) *(P-12006)*

**Opti-Forms Inc** ........................................................................... E ...... 951 296-1300
42310 Winchester Rd Temecula (92590) *(P-8992)*

## ALPHABETIC SECTION — Orange County Thermal Inds Inc

Optibase Inc (HQ) .................................................. E ...... 800 451-5101
   931 Benecia Ave Sunnyvale (94085) *(P-10419)*

Optic Arts Holdings Inc ........................................ E ...... 213 250-6069
   716 Monterey Pass Rd Monterey Park (91754) *(P-11549)*

Optical Associates Inc ......................................... E ...... 408 232-0600
   464 S Hillview Dr Milpitas (95035) *(P-14807)*

Optical Coating Laboratory LLC (HQ) ................ B ...... 707 545-6440
   2789 Northpoint Pkwy Santa Rosa (95407) *(P-9097)*

Optical Corporation (DH) ..................................... E ...... 818 725-9750
   9731 Topanga Canyon Pl Chatsworth (91311) *(P-14808)*

Optical Physics Company ..................................... F ...... 818 880-2907
   4133 Guardian St # G Simi Valley (93063) *(P-14809)*

Optical Zonu Corporation ..................................... F ...... 818 780-9701
   7510 Hazeltine Ave Van Nuys (91405) *(P-11779)*

Optim, Pleasanton *Also Called: Unchained Labs (P-19332)*

Optimedica Corporation ........................................ E ...... 408 850-8600
   510 Cottonwood Dr Milpitas (95035) *(P-15213)*

Optimiscorp ............................................................ D ...... 310 230-2780
   200 Mantua Rd Pacific Palisades (90272) *(P-18629)*

Optimum Solutions Group LLC ............................ F ...... 415 954-7100
   419 Ponderosa Ct Lafayette (94549) *(P-18630)*

Optiscan, Fremont *Also Called: Optiscan Biomedical Corp (P-15214)*

Optiscan Biomedical Corp .................................... E ...... 510 342-5800
   35452 Galen Pl Fremont (94536) *(P-15214)*

Optiva Inc .............................................................. D ...... 650 616-7600
   384 Oyster Point Blvd Ste 16 South San Francisco (94080) *(P-6315)*

Optivus Proton Therapy Inc ................................. D ...... 909 799-8300
   1475 Victoria Ct San Bernardino (92408) *(P-14906)*

Optiwise Ai Inc ..................................................... F ...... 408 480-0482
   37298 Aleppo Dr Newark (94560) *(P-18631)*

Optiwise.ai, Newark *Also Called: Optiwise Ai Inc (P-18631)*

Optiworks Inc (PA) ............................................... D ...... 510 438-4560
   47211 Bayside Pkwy Fremont (94538) *(P-7200)*

Opto 22 .................................................................. C ...... 951 695-3000
   43044 Business Park Dr Temecula (92590) *(P-13057)*

Opto Diode Corporation ........................................ E ...... 805 499-0335
   1260 Calle Suerte Camarillo (93012) *(P-12621)*

Opto-Knowledge Systems Inc .............................. E ...... 310 756-0520
   19805 Hamilton Ave Torrance (90502) *(P-19470)*

Optofidelity Inc ..................................................... E ...... 669 241-8383
   20863 Stevens Creek Blvd Ste 540 Cupertino (95014) *(P-19409)*

Optoknowledge, Torrance *Also Called: Opto-Knowledge Systems Inc (P-19470)*

Optoma Technology, Fremont *Also Called: Optoma Technology Inc (P-15656)*

Optoma Technology Inc ....................................... C ...... 510 897-8600
   47697 Westinghouse Dr Fremont (94539) *(P-15656)*

Optoplex Corporation ........................................... B ...... 510 490-9930
   48500 Kato Rd Fremont (94538) *(P-11780)*

Optosigma Corporation ........................................ E ...... 949 851-5881
   1540 Scenic Ave Costa Mesa (92626) *(P-14810)*

Optotest Corp., Camarillo *Also Called: Santec California Corporation (P-14821)*

Optronics, Goleta *Also Called: Karl Storz Imaging Inc (P-14890)*

Opus One, Oakville *Also Called: Opus One Winery LLC (P-1699)*

Opus One Winery LLC (PA) ................................. D ...... 707 944-9442
   7900 St Helena Hwy Oakville (94562) *(P-1699)*

Oracle, San Mateo *Also Called: Netsuite Inc (P-18578)*

Oracle, Pleasanton *Also Called: Oracle Corporation (P-18633)*

Oracle, Rocklin *Also Called: Oracle Corporation (P-18634)*

Oracle, Rocklin *Also Called: Oracle Corporation (P-18635)*

Oracle, Redwood City *Also Called: Oracle Corporation (P-18636)*

Oracle, Mission Viejo *Also Called: Oracle Corporation (P-18637)*

Oracle, Santa Clara *Also Called: Oracle Corporation (P-18638)*

Oracle, Redwood City *Also Called: Oracle Japan Holding Inc (P-18641)*

Oracle, Belmont *Also Called: Oracle Systems Corporation (P-18642)*

Oracle, San Mateo *Also Called: Oracle Systems Corporation (P-18643)*

Oracle, Belmont *Also Called: Oracle Systems Corporation (P-18644)*

Oracle, Pleasanton *Also Called: Oracle Systems Corporation (P-18646)*

Oracle America Inc ............................................... E ...... 408 276-4300
   4220 Network Cir Santa Clara (95054) *(P-10185)*

Oracle America Inc (HQ) ..................................... A ...... 650 506-7000
   500 Oracle Pkwy Redwood Shores (94065) *(P-10186)*

Oracle America Inc ............................................... F ...... 303 272-6473
   1001 Sunset Blvd Rocklin (95765) *(P-10187)*

Oracle America Inc ............................................... F ...... 925 694-3314
   5815 Owens Dr Pleasanton (94588) *(P-10188)*

Oracle America Inc ............................................... F ...... 858 625-5044
   9540 Towne Centre Dr San Diego (92121) *(P-10189)*

Oracle America Inc ............................................... E ...... 408 276-7534
   4230 Leonard Stocking Dr Santa Clara (95054) *(P-10190)*

Oracle America Inc ............................................... C ...... 408 276-3331
   4120 Network Cir Santa Clara (95054) *(P-18632)*

Oracle Corporation ............................................... E ...... 877 767-2253
   5805 Owens Dr Pleasanton (94588) *(P-18633)*

Oracle Corporation ............................................... B ...... 916 315-3500
   1001 Sunset Blvd Rocklin (95765) *(P-18634)*

Oracle Corporation ............................................... E ...... 916 315-3500
   6020 West Oaks Blvd Ste 200 Rocklin (95765) *(P-18635)*

Oracle Corporation ............................................... E ...... 415 834-9731
   200 Oracle Pkwy Redwood City (94065) *(P-18636)*

Oracle Corporation ............................................... B ...... 626 315-7513
   1 Bolero Mission Viejo (92692) *(P-18637)*

Oracle Corporation ............................................... D ...... 408 986-8800
   3005 Bunker Hill Ln Santa Clara (95054) *(P-18638)*

Oracle Corporation ............................................... E ...... 650 506-7000
   500 Oracle Pkwy Redwood City (94065) *(P-18639)*

Oracle International Corp (HQ) ............................ F ...... 650 506-7000
   500 Oracle Pkwy Redwood City (94065) *(P-18640)*

Oracle Japan Holding Inc (HQ) ............................ D ...... 650 506-7000
   500 Oracle Pkwy Redwood City (94065) *(P-18641)*

Oracle Systems Corporation ................................ E ...... 650 654-7606
   301 Island Pkwy Belmont (94002) *(P-18642)*

Oracle Systems Corporation ................................ F ...... 650 506-6780
   500 Oracle Pwky San Mateo (94403) *(P-18643)*

Oracle Systems Corporation ................................ F ...... 650 506-5062
   501 Island Pkwy Belmont (94002) *(P-18644)*

Oracle Systems Corporation ................................ E ...... 650 506-5887
   300 Oracle Pkwy Redwood City (94065) *(P-18645)*

Oracle Systems Corporation ................................ E ...... 925 694-3000
   5840 Owens Dr Pleasanton (94588) *(P-18646)*

Oracle Systems Corporation (HQ) ....................... A ...... 650 506-7000
   500 Oracle Pkwy Redwood City (94065) *(P-19042)*

Oracle Taleo LLC (HQ) ........................................ D ...... 925 452-3000
   4140 Dublin Blvd Ste 400 Dublin (94568) *(P-18647)*

Oracle Usa Inc ..................................................... A ...... 650 506-7000
   500 Oracle Pkwy Redwood City (94065) *(P-18648)*

Orange Bakery Inc (HQ) ...................................... F ...... 949 863-1377
   17751 Cowan Irvine (92614) *(P-1232)*

Orange Bang Inc .................................................. E ...... 818 833-1000
   13115 Telfair Ave Sylmar (91342) *(P-1908)*

Orange Circle Studio Corp (PA) ........................... D ...... 949 727-0800
   2 Technology Dr Irvine (92618) *(P-4933)*

Orange Cnty Name Plate Co Inc ......................... D ...... 714 522-7693
   13201 Arctic Cir Santa Fe Springs (90670) *(P-16016)*

Orange Coast Magazine, Los Angeles *Also Called: Orange Coast Magazine LLC (P-4284)*

Orange Coast Magazine LLC ............................... D ...... 949 862-1133
   5900 Wilshire Blvd # 10 Los Angeles (90036) *(P-4284)*

Orange Coast Reprographics Inc ......................... E ...... 949 548-5571
   659 W 19th St Costa Mesa (92627) *(P-4713)*

Orange County Business Journal, Irvine *Also Called: Cbj LP (P-4238)*

Orange County Components Inc ......................... F ...... 714 979-3597
   3184 Airway Ave Ste C Costa Mesa (92626) *(P-16727)*

Orange County Direct Mail Inc ............................. E ...... 714 444-4412
   2672 Dow Ave Tustin (92780) *(P-17800)*

Orange County Erectors Inc ................................. E ...... 714 502-8455
   517 E La Palma Ave Anaheim (92801) *(P-8679)*

Orange County Indus Plas Inc (PA) ..................... E ...... 714 632-9450
   4811 E La Palma Ave Anaheim (92807) *(P-17229)*

Orange County Printing, Irvine *Also Called: Kelmscott Communications LLC (P-4660)*

Orange County Screw Pdts Inc ............................ E ...... 714 630-7433
   2993 E La Palma Ave Anaheim (92806) *(P-11017)*

Orange County Thermal Inds Inc (PA) ................. D ...... 714 279-9416
   1940 N Glassell St Orange (92865) *(P-479)*

**Orange Woodworks Inc** ............................................................. E ...... 714 997-2600
1215 N Parker St Orange (92867) *(P-3172)*

**Oraya Therapeutics Inc** ............................................................. E ...... 510 456-3700
3 Twin Dolphin Dr Ste 175 Redwood City (94065) *(P-14811)*

**Orbis Bioaid, Santa Rosa** *Also Called: Orbis Wheels Inc (P-6946)*

**Orbis Intelligent Systems Inc** ................................................... E ...... 858 737-4469
5675 Ruffin Rd Ste 110 San Diego (92123) *(P-14442)*

**Orbis Wheels Inc** ........................................................................ F ...... 415 548-4160
789 Lombardi Ct Ste 204 Santa Rosa (95407) *(P-6946)*

**Orbita Corp (PA)** ........................................................................ F ...... 213 746-4783
1136 Crocker St Los Angeles (90021) *(P-2871)*

**Orbital Sciences LLC** ................................................................ C ...... 703 406-5000
2401 E El Segundo Blvd Ste 200 El Segundo (90245) *(P-14273)*

**Orbital Sciences LLC** ................................................................ C ...... 818 887-8345
1151 W Reeves Ave Ridgecrest (93555) *(P-14274)*

**Orbital Sciences LLC** ................................................................ B ...... 805 734-5400
Talo Rd Bldg 1555 Lompoc (93437) *(P-14275)*

**Orbital Sciences LLC** ................................................................ C ...... 858 618-1847
16707 Via Del Campo Ct San Diego (92127) *(P-14276)*

**Orbitel International LLC** .......................................................... E ...... 626 369-7050
15304 Valley Blvd City Of Industry (91746) *(P-4934)*

**Orbo Corporation (PA)** ............................................................. E ...... 562 806-6171
1000 S Euclid St La Habra (90631) *(P-3636)*

**Orbo Manufacturing Inc** ........................................................... E ...... 562 222-4535
1000 S Euclid St La Habra (90631) *(P-3014)*

**Orbotech Lt Solar LLC** .............................................................. E ...... 408 414-3777
5970 Optical Ct San Jose (95138) *(P-12622)*

**Orca Arms, Calabasas** *Also Called: Orca Arms LLC (P-15844)*

**Orca Arms LLC** .......................................................................... D ...... 858 586-0503
26500 Agoura Rd Calabasas (91302) *(P-15844)*

**Orca Systems Inc** ...................................................................... F ...... 858 679-9175
3990 Old Town Ave Ste C307 San Diego (92110) *(P-12623)*

**Orca Technologies, San Clemente** *Also Called: Orca Technologies LLC (P-11909)*

**Orca Technologies LLC** ............................................................ F ...... 949 682-3289
934 Calle Negocio Ste B San Clemente (92673) *(P-11909)*

**Orchard Equipment Mfg, Gridley** *Also Called: Bianchi Orchard Systems Inc (P-9341)*

**Orchard Harvest, Yuba City** *Also Called: Orchard Machinery Corp Disc (P-9374)*

**Orchard Machinery Corp Disc (PA)** ........................................ D ...... 530 673-2822
2700 Colusa Hwy Yuba City (95993) *(P-9374)*

**Orchid MPS** ................................................................................ D ...... 714 549-9203
3233 W Harvard St Santa Ana (92704) *(P-15215)*

**Orchid Orthopedis, Arcadia** *Also Called: MPS Anzon LLC (P-15385)*

**Orco Block & Hardscape (PA)** ................................................. D ...... 714 527-2239
11100 Beach Blvd Stanton (90680) *(P-7296)*

**Orcon Aerospace** ...................................................................... F ...... 510 489-8100
2600 Central Ave Ste E Union City (94587) *(P-13917)*

**Orcon Aerospace, Union City** *Also Called: Lamart Corporation (P-7562)*

**Oreco Duct Systems Inc** ........................................................... C ...... 626 337-8832
5119 Azusa Canyon Rd Baldwin Park (91706) *(P-8521)*

**OReilly Media Inc (PA)** .............................................................. C ...... 707 827-7000
1005 Gravenstein Hwy N Sebastopol (95472) *(P-4441)*

**Orexigen, La Jolla** *Also Called: Orexigen Therapeutics Inc (P-5586)*

**Orexigen Therapeutics Inc** ....................................................... D ...... 858 875-8600
3344 N Torrey Pines Ct Ste 200 La Jolla (92037) *(P-5586)*

**Orfila Vineyards & Winery, Escondido** *Also Called: Orfila Vineyards Inc (P-1700)*

**Orfila Vineyards Inc** ................................................................... F ...... 760 738-6500
13455 San Pasqual Rd Escondido (92025) *(P-1700)*

**Orgain LLC** ................................................................................. E ...... 888 881-4246
16631 Millikan Ave Irvine (92606) *(P-5258)*

**Organic, Rancho Dominguez** *Also Called: Organic By Nature Inc (P-5259)*

**Organic By Nature Inc (PA)** ..................................................... E ...... 562 901-0177
2610 Homestead Pl Rancho Dominguez (90220) *(P-5259)*

**Organic Milling Inc (PA)** ........................................................... D ...... 800 638-8686
505 W Allen Ave San Dimas (91773) *(P-2301)*

**Organic Milling Corporation** ..................................................... E ...... 909 599-0961
505 W Allen Ave San Dimas (91773) *(P-2302)*

**Organic Spices (PA)** ................................................................. E ...... 510 440-1044
4180 Business Center Dr Fremont (94538) *(P-2303)*

**Organicgirl LLC** .......................................................................... A ...... 831 758-7800
900 Work St Salinas (93901) *(P-2304)*

**Orgatech Omegalux, Riverside** *Also Called: Western Lighting Inds Inc (P-16680)*

**Oric Pharmaceuticals Inc** ......................................................... D ...... 650 388-5600
240 E Grand Ave Fl 2 South San Francisco (94080) *(P-5587)*

**Orientex, Pittsburg** *Also Called: Ramar International Corp (P-614)*

**Orientex Foods, Pittsburg** *Also Called: Ramar International Corp (P-814)*

**Origin, West Sacramento** *Also Called: Origin Materials Inc (P-5852)*

**Origin LLC** .................................................................................. E ...... 818 848-1648
119 E Graham Pl Burbank (91502) *(P-16192)*

**Origin Materials Inc (PA)** .......................................................... E ...... 916 231-9329
930 Riverside Pkwy Ste 10 West Sacramento (95605) *(P-5852)*

**Original Glass Design, San Jose** *Also Called: Beveled Edge Inc (P-7213)*

**Original Parts Group Inc (PA)** .................................................. D ...... 562 594-1000
1770 Saturn Way Seal Beach (90740) *(P-17455)*

**Original Pennysaver, The, Brea** *Also Called: Pennysaver USA Publishing LLC (P-4446)*

**Orion Chandelier Inc** ................................................................. F ...... 714 668-9668
2202 S Wright St Santa Ana (92705) *(P-11550)*

**Orion Group World LLC** ........................................................... C ...... 415 602-5233
143 Seminary Dr Apt Q Mill Valley (94941) *(P-19113)*

**Orion Ornamental Iron Inc** ........................................................ E ...... 818 752-0688
6918 Tujunga Ave North Hollywood (91605) *(P-8022)*

**Orion Plastics Corporation** ....................................................... D ...... 310 223-0370
700 W Carob St Compton (90220) *(P-5184)*

**Orion Tech, City Of Industry** *Also Called: Compucase Corporation (P-10233)*

**Orlandini Entps Pcf Die Cast** .................................................... C ...... 323 725-1332
6155 S Eastern Ave Commerce (90040) *(P-7867)*

**Orlando Precision, Huntington Beach** *Also Called: Orlando Spring Corp (P-9204)*

**Orlando Spring Corp** ................................................................. E ...... 562 594-8411
5341 Argosy Ave Huntington Beach (92649) *(P-9204)*

**Orly International Inc (PA)** ....................................................... D ...... 818 994-1001
7710 Haskell Ave Van Nuys (91406) *(P-6014)*

**Ormat Technologies Inc** ........................................................... E ...... 760 337-8872
855 Dogwood Rd Heber (92249) *(P-16346)*

**Ormco Corporation** .................................................................... E ...... 909 962-5705
200 S Kraemer Blvd Brea (92821) *(P-15469)*

**Ormco Corporation (HQ)** .......................................................... D ...... 714 516-7400
1717 W Collins Ave Orange (92867) *(P-15470)*

**Ormet Circuits Inc** ...................................................................... E ...... 858 831-0010
6555 Nancy Ridge Dr Ste 200 San Diego (92121) *(P-13058)*

**Oro Grande Cement Plant, Oro Grande** *Also Called: Calportland Company (P-7250)*

**Orora North America, Buena Park** *Also Called: Orora Packaging Solutions (P-17004)*

**Orora Packaging Solutions (HQ)** ............................................. D ...... 714 562-6000
6600 Valley View St Buena Park (90620) *(P-17004)*

**Orora Packaging Solutions** ...................................................... E ...... 714 984-2300
3200 Enterprise St Brea (92821) *(P-17005)*

**Orora Packaging Solutions** ...................................................... E ...... 760 510-7170
664 N Twin Oaks Valley Rd San Marcos (92069) *(P-17006)*

**Orora Packaging Solutions** ...................................................... E ...... 510 487-1211
33463 Western Ave Union City (94587) *(P-17007)*

**Orora Packaging Solutions** ...................................................... C ...... 323 832-2000
1640 S Greenwood Ave Montebello (90640) *(P-17008)*

**Orora Packaging Solutions** ...................................................... E ...... 714 525-4900
7001 Village Dr Ste 155 Buena Park (90621) *(P-17009)*

**Orora Packaging Solutions** ...................................................... D ...... 714 278-6000
1901 E Rosslynn Ave Fullerton (92831) *(P-17010)*

**Orora Packaging Solutions** ...................................................... E ...... 626 284-9524
3201 W Mission Rd Alhambra (91803) *(P-17011)*

**Orora Packaging Solutions** ...................................................... E ...... 805 278-5040
2146 Eastman Ave Oxnard (93030) *(P-17012)*

**Orora Packaging Solutions** ...................................................... D ...... 916 645-8100
1221 Tara Ct Rocklin (95765) *(P-17013)*

**Orora Packaging Solutions** ...................................................... F ...... 510 896-4750
8311 Central Ave Newark (94560) *(P-17014)*

**Orora Packaging Solutions** ...................................................... F ...... 714 773-0124
1911 E Rosslynn Ave Fullerton (92831) *(P-17015)*

**Orora Packaging Solutions** ...................................................... C ...... 714 562-6002
6200 Caballero Blvd Buena Park (90620) *(P-17016)*

**Orora Packaging Solutions** ...................................................... D ...... 909 770-5400
13397 Marlay Ave Fontana (92337) *(P-17017)*

**Orora Visual LLC** ....................................................................... D ...... 714 879-2400
1600 E Valencia Dr Fullerton (92831) *(P-4935)*

# ALPHABETIC SECTION — Owens Corning Sales LLC

Orphan Medical Inc .................................................................. D ...... 650 496-3777
  3180 Porter Dr Palo Alto (94304) *(P-5588)*
Orthaheel, San Rafael *Also Called: Vionic Group LLC (P-7112)*
Ortho Engineering Inc (PA) ...................................................... E ...... 310 559-5996
  17402 Chatsworth St Ste 200 Granada Hills (91344) *(P-15387)*
Ortho Organizers Inc ............................................................... C ...... 760 448-8600
  1822 Aston Ave Carlsbad (92008) *(P-15471)*
Ortho-Clinical Diagnostics Inc ................................................. E ...... 908 704-5910
  1401 Red Hawk Cir Apt E307 Fremont (94538) *(P-5771)*
Ortho-Clinical Diagnostics Inc ................................................. E ...... 714 639-2323
  612 W Katella Ave Ste B Orange (92867) *(P-5772)*
Orthodental International Inc .................................................. D ...... 760 357-8070
  280 Campillo St Ste J Calexico (92231) *(P-15472)*
Orthodyne Electronics Corporation (HQ) .................................. C ...... 949 660-0440
  16700 Red Hill Ave Irvine (92606) *(P-13282)*
Orthofix Medical Inc ................................................................. E ...... 214 937-2000
  501 Mercury Dr Sunnyvale (94085) *(P-15216)*
Orthogroup Inc ........................................................................ F ...... 916 859-0881
  11280 Sanders Dr Ste A Rancho Cordova (95742) *(P-15217)*
Oryx, Fremont *Also Called: Oryx Advanced Materials Inc (P-10261)*
Oryx Advanced Materials Inc (PA) ........................................... E ...... 510 249-1157
  46458 Fremont Blvd Fremont (94538) *(P-10261)*
Osca-Arcosa, San Diego *Also Called: O & S California Inc (P-13279)*
OSI Digital Inc (PA) ................................................................. E ...... 818 992-2700
  26745 Malibu Hills Rd Agoura Hills (91301) *(P-19043)*
OSI Electronics Inc (HQ) ......................................................... D ...... 310 978-0516
  12533 Chadron Ave Hawthorne (90250) *(P-12183)*
OSI Industries LLC ................................................................. B ...... 951 684-4500
  1155 Mt Vernon Ave Riverside (92507) *(P-2305)*
OSI Optoelectronics Inc .......................................................... E ...... 805 987-0146
  1240 Avenida Acaso Camarillo (93012) *(P-12624)*
OSI Optoelectronics Inc (HQ) .................................................. C ...... 310 978-0516
  12525 Chadron Ave Hawthorne (90250) *(P-12625)*
OSI Software, San Leandro *Also Called: Osisoft LLC (P-17958)*
OSI Subsidiary Inc .................................................................. F ...... 310 978-0516
  12525 Chadron Ave Hawthorne (90250) *(P-13283)*
OSI Systems Inc (PA) ............................................................. A ...... 310 978-0516
  12525 Chadron Ave Hawthorne (90250) *(P-12626)*
Osisoft LLC (DH) ..................................................................... B ...... 510 297-5800
  1600 Alvarado St San Leandro (94577) *(P-17958)*
Osmosis Technology Inc ......................................................... E ...... 714 670-9303
  6900 Hermosa Cir Buena Park (90620) *(P-10589)*
Osmotik, Buena Park *Also Called: Osmosis Technology Inc (P-10589)*
Ospreydata Inc ........................................................................ F ...... 619 971-4662
  32242 Paseo Adelanto C San Juan Capistrano (92675) *(P-14699)*
Osr Enterprises Inc ................................................................. E ...... 805 925-1831
  1910 E Stowell Rd Santa Maria (93454) *(P-18649)*
Osram Sylvania Inc ................................................................. D ...... 858 748-5077
  13350 Gregg St Ste 101 Poway (92064) *(P-11430)*
Oss, Escondido *Also Called: One Stop Systems Inc (P-10417)*
Osseon LLC ............................................................................ F ...... 707 636-5940
  2301 Circadian Way Ste 300 Santa Rosa (95407) *(P-15218)*
Osseon Therapeutics Inc ........................................................ E ...... 707 636-5940
  2305 Circadian Way Santa Rosa (95407) *(P-15219)*
Ossur Americas Inc ................................................................. C ...... 949 382-3883
  19762 Pauling Foothill Ranch (92610) *(P-15388)*
Ossur Americas Inc (HQ) ........................................................ D ...... 800 233-6263
  200 Spectrum Center Dr Ste 700 Irvine (92618) *(P-15389)*
Ostial Corporation ................................................................... E ...... 408 541-1007
  747 Camden Ave Campbell (95008) *(P-15390)*
OT Precision Machining Inc ..................................................... E ...... 408 435-8818
  1450 Seareel Ln San Jose (95131) *(P-11018)*
Otafuku Foods Inc ................................................................... E ...... 562 404-4700
  13117 Molette St Santa Fe Springs (90670) *(P-2306)*
Otay Lakes Brewery LLC ......................................................... E ...... 619 768-0172
  901 Lane Ave Ste 100 Chula Vista (91914) *(P-1452)*
Oti Engineering Cons Inc ........................................................ E ...... 209 586-1022
  24926 State Highway 108 Mi Wuk Village (95346) *(P-11910)*
Otis Elevator Company ........................................................... D ...... 408 727-1231
  470 Lakeside Dr Ste D Sunnyvale (94085) *(P-16832)*
Otis Elevator Company ........................................................... D ...... 858 560-5881
  3949 Viewridge Ave San Diego (92123) *(P-16833)*
Otonomy, San Diego *Also Called: Otonomy Inc (P-5589)*
Otonomy Inc ............................................................................ D ...... 619 323-2200
  4796 Executive Dr San Diego (92121) *(P-5589)*
Otsuka America Inc ................................................................. E ...... 408 867-3233
  80 Railroad Ave Milpitas (95035) *(P-1701)*
OTTERAI INC ......................................................................... E ...... 650 250-6322
  800 W El Camino Real Ste 170 Mountain View (94040) *(P-17959)*
Otto Instrument Service Inc (PA) ............................................. E ...... 909 930-5800
  1441 Valencia Pl Ontario (91761) *(P-13918)*
Ouster Inc (PA) ....................................................................... E ...... 415 987-6972
  350 Treat Ave Ste 1 San Francisco (94110) *(P-14907)*
Out of Shell LLC ..................................................................... C ...... 626 401-1923
  9658 Remer St South El Monte (91733) *(P-2307)*
Outback Inc (PA) ..................................................................... E ...... 559 293-3880
  4201 W Shaw Ave Ste 106 Fresno (93722) *(P-7482)*
Outback Materials, Fresno *Also Called: Outback Inc (P-7482)*
Outdoor Dimensions LLC ........................................................ C ...... 714 578-9555
  5325 E Hunter Ave Anaheim (92807) *(P-3421)*
Outdoor Products, Los Angeles *Also Called: Outdoor Rcrtion Group Hldngs L (P-2960)*
Outdoor Rcrtion Group Hldngs L (PA) ..................................... E ...... 323 226-0830
  3450 Mount Vernon Dr Los Angeles (90008) *(P-2960)*
Outer Rebel Inc ....................................................................... F ...... 949 246-2421
  3211 W Macarthur Blvd Santa Ana (92704) *(P-2907)*
Outex, La Canada Flintridge *Also Called: Lucare Corporation (P-15649)*
Outform Group Inc .................................................................. E ...... 510 431-5872
  30526 San Antonio St Hayward (94544) *(P-3999)*
Outform Group Inc .................................................................. E ...... 510 433-1586
  33195 Lewis St Union City (94587) *(P-4000)*
Outform Group Inc .................................................................. F ...... 510 487-1122
  1320 Performance Dr Stockton (95206) *(P-16017)*
Outfront Media LLC ................................................................. E ...... 323 222-7171
  1731 Workman St Los Angeles (90031) *(P-17786)*
Outlaw Beverage Inc ............................................................... F ...... 310 424-5077
  3945 Freedom Cir Ste 560 Santa Clara (95054) *(P-1453)*
Outlook Resources Inc ............................................................ D ...... 562 623-9328
  14930 Alondra Blvd La Mirada (90638) *(P-2998)*
Output Inc ............................................................................... F ...... 888 803-3175
  3014 Worthen Ave Los Angeles (90039) *(P-18650)*
Outreach Corporation .............................................................. B ...... 888 938-7356
  600 California St Fl 7 San Francisco (94108) *(P-18651)*
OUTSET, San Jose *Also Called: Outset Medical Inc (P-15566)*
Outset Medical Inc .................................................................. B ...... 669 231-8200
  3052 Orchard Dr San Jose (95134) *(P-15566)*
Outsource Manufacturing Inc .................................................. D ...... 760 795-1295
  2460 Ash St Vista (92081) *(P-12627)*
Ovation R&G LLC (PA) ........................................................... F ...... 310 430-7575
  2850 Ocean Park Blvd Ste 225 Santa Monica (90405) *(P-11911)*
Oven Fresh Bakery Incorporated ............................................. F ...... 650 366-9201
  23188 Foley St Hayward (94545) *(P-1233)*
Overair Inc .............................................................................. E ...... 949 503-7503
  3001 S Susan St Santa Ana (92704) *(P-13684)*
Overhill Farms Inc (DH) .......................................................... C ...... 323 582-9977
  2727 E Vernon Ave Vernon (90058) *(P-2308)*
Overland Storage Inc (HQ) ..................................................... D ...... 408 283-4700
  2633 Camino Ramon Ste 325 San Ramon (94583) *(P-10262)*
Overland Storage Inc .............................................................. B ...... 858 571-5555
  2633 Camino Ramon San Ramon (94583) *(P-10263)*
Overland Vehicle Systems LLC .............................................. E ...... 833 226-4863
  9830 Norwalk Blvd Ste 130 Santa Fe Springs (90670) *(P-2979)*
Overland-Tandberg, San Ramon *Also Called: Overland Storage Inc (P-10262)*
Overview Corporation .............................................................. F ...... 415 795-9020
  736 Clementina St San Francisco (94103) *(P-15657)*
Owb Packers LLC ................................................................... D ...... 760 351-2700
  57 Shank Rd Brawley (92227) *(P-611)*
Owen Oil Tools LP ................................................................... D ...... 661 637-1380
  5001 Standard St Bakersfield (93308) *(P-262)*
Owen Trailers Inc .................................................................... E ...... 951 361-4557
  9020 Jurupa Rd Riverside (92509) *(P-13617)*
Owens Corning, Compton *Also Called: Owens Corning Sales LLC (P-6382)*
Owens Corning Sales LLC ...................................................... C ...... 310 631-1062
  1501 N Tamarind Ave Compton (90222) *(P-6382)*

---

Employee Codes: A=Over 500 employees, B=251-500
C=101-250, D=51-100, E=20-50, F=10-19, G=1-9

Owens Design Incorporated (PA) .................................................. E ...... 510 659-1800
  47427 Fremont Blvd Fremont (94538) *(P-11019)*
Owens-Brockway Glass Cont Inc ................................................. E ...... 510 436-2000
  3600 Alameda Ave Oakland (94601) *(P-7184)*
OWENS-BROCKWAY GLASS CONTAINER, INC., Oakland *Also Called: Owens-Brockway Glass Cont Inc (P-7184)*
Owsla Touring LLC ............................................................. E ...... 818 385-1933
  16000 Ventura Blvd Ste 600 Encino (91436) *(P-4442)*
Oxbase Inc ................................................................... E ...... 707 824-2560
  3500 N Laughlin Rd 100 Santa Rosa (95403) *(P-7160)*
Oxerra Americas LLC .......................................................... D ...... 323 269-7311
  3700 E Olympic Blvd Los Angeles (90023) *(P-5062)*
Oxford Instrs Asylum RES Inc (HQ) ............................................ D ...... 805 696-6466
  7416 Hollister Ave Santa Barbara (93117) *(P-14700)*
Oxford Instrs X-Ray Tech Inc ................................................. D ...... 831 439-9729
  360 El Pueblo Rd Scotts Valley (95066) *(P-13059)*
Oxford Nanoimaging Inc ....................................................... D ...... 858 999-8860
  11045 Roselle St Ste 3 San Diego (92121) *(P-14701)*
Oxide Computer Company ....................................................... E ...... 510 922-1392
  1251 Park Ave Emeryville (94608) *(P-10191)*
Oxnard 2 Warehouse, Oxnard *Also Called: Sunrise Growers Inc (P-2365)*
Oxnard Lemon Company ......................................................... F ...... 805 483-1173
  2001 Sunkist Cir Oxnard (93033) *(P-1014)*
Oxnard Pallet Company, Oxnard *Also Called: E Vasquez Distributors Inc (P-3340)*
Oxnard Prcsion Fabrication Inc ............................................... E ...... 805 985-0447
  2200 Teal Club Rd Oxnard (93030) *(P-8522)*
OXY, Los Angeles *Also Called: Occidental Petroleum Corporation of California (P-136)*
Oxystrap International Inc ................................................... E ...... 800 699-6901
  8705 Complex Dr San Diego (92123) *(P-6520)*
Oyewan Inc ................................................................... E ...... 909 869-6200
  20501 Earlgate St Walnut (91789) *(P-6015)*
Ozeki Sake (usa) Inc (HQ) .................................................... E ...... 831 637-9217
  249 Hillcrest Rd Hollister (95023) *(P-1702)*
Ozeri, Ventura *Also Called: Commonpath LLC (P-7216)*
Ozig LLC ..................................................................... E ...... 510 588-7952
  490 43rd St Ste 206 Oakland (94609) *(P-8043)*
Ozotech Inc (PA) ............................................................. F ...... 530 842-4189
  1015 S Main St Yreka (96097) *(P-10590)*
P & L Concrete Products Inc .................................................. E ...... 209 838-1448
  1900 Roosevelt Ave Escalon (95320) *(P-7483)*
P & L Development LLC ........................................................ C ...... 323 567-2482
  11865 Alameda St Lynwood (90262) *(P-5590)*
P & L Specialties ............................................................ F ...... 707 573-3141
  1650 Almar Pkwy Santa Rosa (95403) *(P-9886)*
P & R Paper Supply Co Inc .................................................... C ...... 619 671-2400
  1350 Piper Ranch Rd San Diego (92154) *(P-4043)*
P A P, Anaheim *Also Called: Precision Anodizing & Pltg Inc (P-8998)*
P A S U Inc .................................................................. E ...... 619 421-1151
  1891 Nirvana Ave Chula Vista (91911) *(P-8523)*
P A X Industries, Costa Mesa *Also Called: Tk Pax Inc (P-6433)*
P B M, Chico *Also Called: PBM Supply & Mfg Inc (P-16887)*
P C A Electronics Inc ........................................................ E ...... 818 892-0761
  16799 Schoenborn St North Hills (91343) *(P-16728)*
P C S, Hollister *Also Called: Pride Conveyance Systems Inc (P-9491)*
P C S C, Torrance *Also Called: Proprietary Controls Systems (P-14910)*
P I Inc ...................................................................... D ...... 209 527-8020
  3511 Finch Rd Modesto (95357) *(P-8282)*
P K Metal, Los Angeles *Also Called: P Kay Metal Inc (P-7766)*
P K Selective Metal Pltg Inc ................................................. F ...... 408 988-1910
  415 Mathew St Santa Clara (95050) *(P-8993)*
P Kay Metal Inc (PA) ......................................................... E ...... 323 585-5058
  2448 E 25th St Los Angeles (90058) *(P-7766)*
P L C Lighting, Chatsworth *Also Called: PLC Imports Inc (P-16670)*
P L D S, Milpitas *Also Called: Philips Lt-On Dgtal Sltons USA (P-10264)*
P L M, Los Angeles *Also Called: Prudential Lighting Corp (P-11553)*
P M C, Cypress *Also Called: Plastic Molded Components Inc (P-6961)*
P M I, San Diego *Also Called: Pacific Maritime Inds Corp (P-8197)*
P M S D Inc (PA) ............................................................. D ...... 408 988-5235
  3411 Leonard Ct Santa Clara (95054) *(P-11020)*
P M S D Inc .................................................................. E ...... 408 727-5322
  3411 Leonard Ct Santa Clara (95054) *(P-11021)*

P P I, Rancho Cordova *Also Called: Paper Processors Inc (P-3792)*
P P I, Corona *Also Called: Preproduction Plastics Inc (P-6980)*
P R L, City Of Industry *Also Called: Prl Glass Systems Inc (P-7240)*
P R P Multisource Inc ........................................................ E ...... 951 681-6100
  3836 Wacker Dr Jurupa Valley (91752) *(P-10027)*
P S E Boilers, Santa Fe Springs *Also Called: Pacific Steam Equipment Inc (P-8325)*
P S I, Beaumont *Also Called: Precision Stampings Inc (P-11468)*
P T I, Riverside *Also Called: Products/Techniques Inc (P-6107)*
P T I, Torrance *Also Called: Plasma Technology Incorporated (P-9108)*
P T I, Santa Ana *Also Called: Parpro Technologies Inc (P-12187)*
P T Industries Inc ........................................................... F ...... 562 961-3431
  3220 Industry Dr Signal Hill (90755) *(P-8524)*
P T P, Carson *Also Called: Pacific Toll Processing Inc (P-16312)*
P V T Supply, Yorba Linda *Also Called: Wagner Plate Works West Inc (P-8351)*
P W S, San Luis Obispo *Also Called: Protective Wther Strctures Inc (P-359)*
P-Tabun, El Cajon *Also Called: Pf Bakeries Llc (P-17205)*
P.S. Services, Anaheim *Also Called: 3s Sign Services Inc (P-15934)*
P&P International Inc ........................................................ E ...... 559 891-9888
  2014 2nd St Selma (93662) *(P-17018)*
P5 Graphics and Displays Inc ................................................. E ...... 714 808-1645
  625 Fee Ana St Placentia (92870) *(P-17836)*
Pabco Building Products LLC .................................................. D ...... 916 645-3341
  601 7th St Lincoln (95648) *(P-7275)*
Pabco Building Products LLC .................................................. C ...... 510 792-9555
  37851 Cherry St Newark (94560) *(P-7525)*
Pabco Building Products LLC .................................................. E ...... 510 792-1577
  37849 Cherry St Newark (94560) *(P-7526)*
Pabco Building Products LLC (HQ) ............................................. E ...... 510 792-1577
  10811 International Dr Rancho Cordova (95670) *(P-7527)*
Pabco Building Products LLC .................................................. C ...... 323 581-6113
  4460 Pacific Blvd Vernon (90058) *(P-7528)*
Pabco Gypsum, Newark *Also Called: Pabco Building Products LLC (P-7525)*
Pabco Paper, Vernon *Also Called: Pabco Building Products LLC (P-7528)*
Pac Fill Inc ................................................................. E ...... 818 409-0117
  5471 W San Fernando Rd Los Angeles (90039) *(P-841)*
Pac Foundries Inc ............................................................ C ...... 805 986-1308
  705 Industrial Way Port Hueneme (93041) *(P-7856)*
Pac-Dent Inc ................................................................. E ...... 909 839-0888
  670 Endeavor Cir Brea (92821) *(P-15473)*
Pac-Rancho Inc (HQ) .......................................................... C ...... 909 987-4721
  11000 Jersey Blvd Rancho Cucamonga (91730) *(P-7693)*
Pac-Refco Inc ................................................................ E ...... 760 956-8600
  2230 Ottawa Rd Ste A Apple Valley (92307) *(P-10510)*
Pacbell, San Francisco *Also Called: Pacific Bell Telephone Company (P-16321)*
PACBIO, Menlo Park *Also Called: Pacific Biosciences Cal Inc (P-14702)*
Pace, Visalia *Also Called: Pace International LLC (P-5923)*
Pace International LLC ....................................................... F ...... 559 651-4877
  8030 W Doe Ave Visalia (93291) *(P-5923)*
Pace Lithographers Inc ....................................................... E ...... 626 913-2108
  18030 Cortney Ct City Of Industry (91748) *(P-19575)*
Pace Marketing Communications, City Of Industry *Also Called: Pace Lithographers Inc (P-19575)*
Pace Punches Inc ............................................................. D ...... 949 428-2750
  297 Goddard Irvine (92618) *(P-9639)*
Pace Transducer Co, Canoga Park *Also Called: C J Instruments Incorporated (P-14851)*
Pacer Print .................................................................. E ...... 888 305-3144
  4101 Guardian St Simi Valley (93063) *(P-4714)*
Pacer Technology (HQ) ........................................................ C ...... 909 987-0550
  3281 E Guasti Rd Ste 260 Ontario (91761) *(P-6238)*
Pacesetter Inc ............................................................... B ...... 323 773-0591
  4946 Florence Ave Bell (90201) *(P-15567)*
Pacesetter Inc ............................................................... B ...... 818 493-2715
  13150 Telfair Ave Sylmar (91342) *(P-15568)*
Pacesetter Inc ............................................................... C ...... 925 730-4171
  6035 Stoneridge Dr Pleasanton (94588) *(P-15569)*
Pacesetter Inc (DH) .......................................................... A ...... 818 362-6822
  15900 Valley View Ct Sylmar (91342) *(P-15570)*
Pacesetter Fabrics LLC (HQ) .................................................. F ...... 213 741-9999
  11450 Sheldon St Sun Valley (91352) *(P-2553)*

## ALPHABETIC SECTION — Pacific Fibre & Rope Co Inc

**Pachama Inc** .................................................. E ...... 650 338-9394
2261 Market St Ste 4303 San Francisco (94114) *(P-17960)*

**Pacific Aggregates Inc** ........................................ D ...... 951 245-2460
28251 Lake St Lake Elsinore (92530) *(P-7484)*

**Pacific Airframe & Engineering, Oxnard** *Also Called: American Airframe Inc (P-13776)*

**Pacific Alloy Casting Company Inc** ............................. C ...... 562 928-1387
5900 Firestone Blvd Fl 1 South Gate (90280) *(P-7679)*

**Pacific American Fish Co Inc (PA)** ............................. C ...... 323 319-1551
5525 S Santa Fe Ave Vernon (90058) *(P-2041)*

**Pacific Analogix Semiconductor, Santa Clara** *Also Called: Analogix Semiconductor Inc (P-12309)*

**Pacific Archtectural Mllwk Inc** ................................ E ...... 562 905-9282
1435 Pioneer St Brea (92821) *(P-3173)*

**Pacific Archtectural Mllwk Inc** ................................ D ...... 714 525-2059
101 E Commwl Ave Ste A Fullerton (92832) *(P-3174)*

**Pacific Archtectural Mllwk Inc** ................................ D ...... 562 905-3200
1031 S Leslie St La Habra (90631) *(P-3175)*

**Pacific Artglass Corporation** .................................. E ...... 310 516-7828
125 W 157th St Gardena (90248) *(P-7238)*

**Pacific Asian Enterprises Inc (PA)** ............................ E ...... 949 496-4848
25001 Dana Dr Dana Point (92629) *(P-19114)*

**Pacific Athletic Wear Inc** ..................................... D ...... 714 751-8006
7340 Lampson Ave Garden Grove (92841) *(P-2797)*

**Pacific Award Metals Inc (HQ)** ................................. D ...... 626 814-4410
1450 Virginia Ave Baldwin Park (91706) *(P-8525)*

**Pacific Award Metals Inc** ...................................... E ...... 360 694-9530
10302 Birtcher Dr Jurupa Valley (91752) *(P-8526)*

**Pacific Award Metals Inc** ...................................... D ...... 909 390-9880
10302 Birtcher Dr Jurupa Valley (91752) *(P-16492)*

**Pacific Barcode Inc** ........................................... E ...... 951 587-8717
27531 Enterprise Cir W Ste 201c Temecula (92590) *(P-9772)*

**Pacific Bell Directory** ........................................ A ...... 800 303-3000
101 Spear St Fl 5 San Francisco (94105) *(P-4443)*

**Pacific Bell Telephone Company (HQ)** ........................... A ...... 415 542-9000
430 Bush St Fl 3 San Francisco (94108) *(P-16321)*

**Pacific Biosciences Cal Inc (PA)** .............................. C ...... 650 521-8000
1305 Obrien Dr Menlo Park (94025) *(P-14702)*

**Pacific Biotech Inc** ........................................... E ...... 858 552-1100
10165 Mckellar Ct San Diego (92121) *(P-5773)*

**Pacific Boat Trailers, Corona** *Also Called: Pacific Boat Trailers Inc (P-17488)*

**Pacific Boat Trailers Inc (PA)** ................................ F ...... 909 902-0094
2855 Sampson Ave Corona (92879) *(P-17488)*

**Pacific Broach & Engrg Assoc** .................................. F ...... 714 632-5678
1513 N Kraemer Blvd Anaheim (92806) *(P-11022)*

**Pacific Cast Cnstr Wtrproofing** ................................ E ...... 760 298-3170
390 Oak Ave Ste A Carlsbad (92008) *(P-346)*

**Pacific Cast Fther Cushion LLC (HQ)** ........................... C ...... 562 801-9995
7600 Industry Ave Pico Rivera (90660) *(P-2943)*

**Pacific Cast Products, Ontario** *Also Called: Alumistar Inc (P-7835)*

**Pacific Casual LLC** ............................................ F ...... 805 445-8310
1060 Avenida Acaso Camarillo (93012) *(P-3508)*

**Pacific Catch, Corte Madera** *Also Called: Pacific Catch Inc (P-1143)*

**Pacific Catch Inc** ............................................. E ...... 415 504-6905
770 Tamalpais Dr Ste 210 Corte Madera (94925) *(P-1143)*

**Pacific Ceramics Inc** .......................................... E ...... 408 747-4600
3524 Bassett St Santa Clara (95054) *(P-7271)*

**Pacific Choice Brands Inc (PA)** ................................ C ...... 559 892-5365
4652 E Date Ave Fresno (93725) *(P-988)*

**Pacific Clay Products Inc** ..................................... C ...... 661 857-1401
14741 Lake St Lake Elsinore (92530) *(P-16479)*

**Pacific Clears, Eureka** *Also Called: Schmidbauer Lumber Inc (P-3078)*

**Pacific Coachworks Inc** ........................................ C ...... 951 686-7294
3411 N Perris Blvd Bldg 1 Perris (92571) *(P-14122)*

**Pacific Coast Bach Label Inc** .................................. E ...... 213 612-0314
3015 S Grand Ave Los Angeles (90007) *(P-2505)*

**Pacific Coast Bolt, Santa Fe Springs** *Also Called: Birmingham Fastener & Sup Inc (P-7984)*

**Pacific Coast Building Products Inc (PA)** ...................... C ...... 916 631-6500
10811 International Dr Rancho Cordova (95670) *(P-7529)*

**Pacific Coast Cabling Inc (PA)** ................................ E ...... 818 407-1911
20717 Prairie St Chatsworth (91311) *(P-465)*

**Pacific Coast Coml Interiors, Carlsbad** *Also Called: N M Floor Coverings Inc (P-3099)*

**Pacific Coast Feather Cushion, Pico Rivera** *Also Called: Pacific Cast Fther Cushion LLC (P-2943)*

**Pacific Coast Foam, San Diego** *Also Called: PCF Group LLC (P-17304)*

**Pacific Coast Home Furn Inc (PA)** .............................. F ...... 323 838-7808
2424 Saybrook Ave Commerce (90040) *(P-2944)*

**Pacific Coast Ingredients (PA)** ................................ F ...... 831 316-7137
170 Technology Cir Scotts Valley (95066) *(P-2018)*

**Pacific Coast Ingredients** ..................................... E ...... 831 316-7137
200 Technology Cir Scotts Valley (95066) *(P-2019)*

**Pacific Coast Lacquer, Los Angeles** *Also Called: Berg Lacquer Co (P-17281)*

**Pacific Coast Lighting, Ventura** *Also Called: Lamps Plus Inc (P-11541)*

**Pacific Coast Lighting Inc (HQ)** ............................... F ...... 800 709-9004
20238 Plummer St Chatsworth (91311) *(P-11617)*

**Pacific Coast Lighting Group, Chatsworth** *Also Called: Pacific Coast Lighting Inc (P-11617)*

**Pacific Coast Mfg Inc** ......................................... D ...... 909 627-7040
5270 Edison Ave Chino (91710) *(P-11393)*

**Pacific Coast Optics LLC** ...................................... F ...... 916 789-0111
10604 Industrial Ave # 100 Roseville (95678) *(P-9887)*

**Pacific Coast Producers** ....................................... C ...... 530 662-8661
1376 Lemen Ave Woodland (95776) *(P-916)*

**Pacific Coast Producers (PA)** .................................. B ...... 209 367-8800
631 N Cluff Ave Lodi (95240) *(P-917)*

**Pacific Coast Producers** ....................................... C ...... 530 533-4311
1601 Mitchell Ave Oroville (95965) *(P-918)*

**Pacific Coast Producers** ....................................... C ...... 209 334-3352
741 S Stockton St Lodi (95240) *(P-919)*

**Pacific Coast Retreaders, Alameda** *Also Called: New Pride Tire LLC (P-19152)*

**Pacific Coast Supply LLC** ...................................... F ...... 916 339-8100
5550 Roseville Rd North Highlands (95660) *(P-3316)*

**Pacific Coast Supply LLC** ...................................... E ...... 559 651-2185
30158 Road 68 Visalia (93291) *(P-7530)*

**Pacific Coast Supply LLC** ...................................... E ...... 707 546-7317
879 N Wright Rd Santa Rosa (95407) *(P-16455)*

**Pacific Communications, Irvine** *Also Called: Allergan Usa Inc (P-5309)*

**Pacific Consolidated Inds LLC** ................................. D ...... 951 479-0860
12201 Magnolia Ave Riverside (92503) *(P-10103)*

**Pacific Contntl Textiles Inc** .................................. D ...... 310 639-1500
2880 E Ana St Compton (90221) *(P-2506)*

**Pacific Contours Corporation** .................................. D ...... 714 693-1260
5340 E Hunter Ave Anaheim (92807) *(P-13919)*

**Pacific Cookie Company Inc (PA)** ............................... E ...... 831 429-9709
303 Potrero St Ste 40 Santa Cruz (95060) *(P-17416)*

**Pacific Copy and Print** ........................................ E ...... 916 928-8434
9950 Horn Rd Sacramento (95827) *(P-17815)*

**Pacific Corrugated Pipe Co LLC** ................................ E ...... 916 383-4891
5999 Power Inn Rd Sacramento (95824) *(P-7369)*

**Pacific Crest Corporation (HQ)** ................................ D ...... 408 481-8070
510 De Guigne Dr Sunnyvale (94085) *(P-11912)*

**Pacific Culinary Group Inc** .................................... E ...... 626 284-1328
566 Monterey Pass Rd Monterey Park (91754) *(P-2309)*

**Pacific Defense, El Segundo** *Also Called: Pacific Defense Strategies Inc (P-14277)*

**Pacific Defense Strategies Inc (PA)** ........................... E ...... 310 722-6050
400 Continental Blvd Ste 100 El Segundo (90245) *(P-14277)*

**Pacific Die Casting, Commerce** *Also Called: Orlandini Entps Pcf Die Cast (P-7867)*

**Pacific Die Casting Corp** ...................................... C ...... 323 725-1308
6155 S Eastern Ave Commerce (90040) *(P-7816)*

**Pacific Die Cut Industries** .................................... D ...... 510 732-8103
3399 Arden Rd Hayward (94545) *(P-6458)*

**Pacific Diversified Capital Co** ................................ D ...... 619 696-2000
101 Ash St San Diego (92101) *(P-14908)*

**Pacific Door & Cabinet Company** ................................ E ...... 559 439-3822
7050 N Harrison Ave Pinedale (93650) *(P-3176)*

**Pacific Drilling Co., San Diego** *Also Called: Limited Access Unlimited Inc (P-9368)*

**Pacific Duct Inc** .............................................. F ...... 909 635-1335
5499 Brooks St Montclair (91763) *(P-8527)*

**Pacific Earthscape, Mckinleyville** *Also Called: Ford Logging Inc (P-3045)*

**Pacific Embroidery, Anaheim** *Also Called: Pacific Embroidery LLC (P-19115)*

**Pacific Embroidery LLC** ........................................ F ...... 714 630-4757
1189 N Kraemer Blvd Anaheim (92806) *(P-19115)*

**Pacific Fibre & Rope Co Inc** ................................... F ...... 310 834-4567
2700 Rose Ave Ste R Signal Hill (90755) *(P-2537)*

# Pacific Foam — ALPHABETIC SECTION

**Pacific Foam, Ontario** Also Called: Induspac California Inc *(P-5163)*

**Pacific Forge Inc** .................................................................. D ...... 909 390-0701
10641 Etiwanda Ave Fontana (92337) *(P-8783)*

**Pacific Galvanizing Inc** ...................................................... E ...... 510 261-7331
715 46th Ave Oakland (94601) *(P-9098)*

**Pacific Gas and Electric Co** ............................................... B ...... 925 779-7745
2111 Hillcrest Ave Antioch (94509) *(P-16347)*

**Pacific Gas and Electric Co** ............................................... B ...... 415 695-3513
2180 Harrison St San Francisco (94110) *(P-16348)*

**Pacific Glass, Gardena** Also Called: Pacific Artglass Corporation *(P-7238)*

**Pacific Gold Marketing Inc** ................................................ E ...... 559 272-8168
745 Broadway St Fresno (93721) *(P-546)*

**Pacific Handy Cutter Inc (DH)** .......................................... E ...... **714 662-1033**
170 Technology Dr Irvine (92618) *(P-7962)*

**Pacific Hardware Sales, Anaheim** Also Called: A J Fasteners Inc *(P-8741)*

**Pacific Heritg HM Fashion Inc** ........................................... E ...... 909 598-5200
901 Lawson St City Of Industry (91748) *(P-16433)*

**Pacific Holdings 137 Company** .......................................... F ...... 209 527-0108
137 N Hart Rd Modesto (95358) *(P-2310)*

**Pacific Hospitality Design Inc** ........................................... E ...... 323 278-7998
2620 S Malt Ave Commerce (90040) *(P-3637)*

**Pacific Industries, Modesto** Also Called: P I Inc *(P-8282)*

**Pacific Instruments Inc** .................................................... E ...... 925 827-9010
4080 Pike Ln Concord (94520) *(P-14909)*

**Pacific Integrated Mfg Inc** ................................................ C ...... 619 921-3464
4364 Bonita Rd Ste 454 Bonita (91902) *(P-15220)*

**Pacific Intl Rice Mills, Woodland** Also Called: Farmers Rice Cooperative *(P-1078)*

**Pacific Lighting & Electrical, Sacramento** Also Called: Mw McWong International Inc *(P-11614)*

**Pacific Lock Company (PA)** .............................................. E ...... **661 294-3707**
25605 Hercules St Valencia (91355) *(P-8023)*

**Pacific Ltg & Standards Co** ............................................... E ...... 310 603-9344
2815 Los Flores Blvd Lynwood (90262) *(P-11551)*

**Pacific Magnetics, Chula Vista** Also Called: Pacmag Inc *(P-13060)*

**Pacific Manufacturing MGT Inc** ........................................ D ...... 323 263-9000
3110 E 12th St Los Angeles (90023) *(P-3700)*

**Pacific Marine Sheet Metal Corporation** ........................... C ...... 858 869-8900
2650 Jamacha Rd Ste 147 Pmb El Cajon (92019) *(P-8528)*

**Pacific Maritime Inds Corp** ............................................... C ...... 619 575-8141
1790 Dornoch Ct San Diego (92154) *(P-8197)*

**Pacific Metal Products, Los Angeles** Also Called: Basic Industries Intl Inc *(P-8301)*

**Pacific Metal Stampings Inc** ............................................. E ...... 661 257-7656
28415 Witherspoon Pkwy Valencia (91355) *(P-8873)*

**Pacific Mfg Inc San Diego** ................................................ E ...... 619 423-0316
1520 Corporate Center Dr San Diego (92154) *(P-11023)*

**Pacific Miniatures, Fullerton** Also Called: Pacmin Incorporated *(P-16194)*

**Pacific Modern Homes Inc** ............................................... E ...... 916 685-9514
9723 Railroad St Elk Grove (95624) *(P-8529)*

**Pacific Natural Spices, Commerce** Also Called: Pacific Spice Company Inc *(P-2311)*

**Pacific Neon** ...................................................................... E ...... 916 927-0527
2939 Academy Way Sacramento (95815) *(P-16018)*

**Pacific Northwest Pubg Co Inc** .......................................... B ...... 916 321-1828
2100 Q St Sacramento (95816) *(P-4177)*

**Pacific Oil Cooler Service Inc** ........................................... E ...... 909 593-8400
1677 Curtiss Ct La Verne (91750) *(P-16301)*

**Pacific Ozone Technology, Inc., Benicia** Also Called: Evoqua Water Technologies LLC *(P-11372)*

**Pacific Packaging McHy LLC** ............................................ E ...... 951 393-2200
200 River Rd Corona (92878) *(P-9810)*

**Pacific Pallet Exchange Inc** ............................................... E ...... 916 448-5589
3350 51st Ave Sacramento (95823) *(P-3351)*

**Pacific Panel Products, Irwindale** Also Called: Pacific Panel Products Corp *(P-3422)*

**Pacific Panel Products Corp** ............................................. E ...... 626 851-0444
15601 Arrow Hwy Irwindale (91706) *(P-3422)*

**Pacific Paper, Rancho Cucamonga** Also Called: Pacific Pprbd Converting LLC *(P-4044)*

**Pacific Paper Tube LLC (PA)** ............................................ E ...... 510 562-8823
4343 E Fremont St Stockton (95215) *(P-3907)*

**Pacific Perforating Inc** ..................................................... E ...... 661 768-9224
25090 Highway 33 Fellows (93224) *(P-263)*

**Pacific Petroleum California Inc** ....................................... B ...... 805 925-1947
1615 E Betteravia Rd Ste A Santa Maria (93454) *(P-264)*

**Pacific Pharma Inc** ............................................................ A ...... 714 246-4600
18600 Von Karman Ave Irvine (92612) *(P-5591)*

**Pacific Piston Ring Co Inc** ................................................. D ...... 310 836-3322
3620 Eastham Dr Culver City (90232) *(P-10622)*

**Pacific Plas Injection Molding, Vista** Also Called: Diversified Plastics Inc *(P-6807)*

**Pacific Plastics Inc** ............................................................ D ...... 714 990-9050
111 S Berry St Brea (92821) *(P-6600)*

**Pacific Plastics & Engineering, Soquel** Also Called: Harkness Enterprises Inc *(P-6849)*

**Pacific Plating, Sun Valley** Also Called: Kvr Investment Group Inc *(P-9873)*

**Pacific Play Tents Inc** ....................................................... F ...... 323 269-0431
2801 E 12th St Los Angeles (90023) *(P-2980)*

**Pacific Plaza Imports Inc (PA)** .......................................... F ...... **925 349-4000**
3018 Willow Pass Rd Ste 102 Concord (94519) *(P-2042)*

**Pacific Plstcs-Njction Molding, Vista** Also Called: J A English II Inc *(P-6869)*

**Pacific Powder Coating Inc** ............................................... E ...... 916 381-1154
8637 23rd Ave Sacramento (95826) *(P-9099)*

**Pacific Power Systems Integration Inc** ............................. E ...... 562 281-0500
14729 Spring Ave Santa Fe Springs (90670) *(P-16669)*

**Pacific Pprbd Converting LLC (PA)** ................................... E ...... **909 476-6466**
8865 Utica Ave Ste A Rancho Cucamonga (91730) *(P-4044)*

**Pacific Precision Inc** ......................................................... E ...... 909 392-5610
1318 Palomares St La Verne (91750) *(P-8729)*

**Pacific Precision Metals Inc** .............................................. C ...... 951 226-1500
1100 E Orangethorpe Ave Ste 253 Anaheim (92801) *(P-8874)*

**Pacific Precision Products, Irvine** Also Called: Pacific Precision Products Mfg Inc *(P-13920)*

**Pacific Precision Products Mfg Inc** ................................... E ...... 949 727-3844
9671 Irvine Ctr Dr Koll Ctr Ii Bldg 6 Irvine (92618) *(P-13920)*

**Pacific Press, Anaheim** Also Called: Wasser Filtration Inc *(P-10121)*

**Pacific Prime Meats LLC** .................................................. D ...... 310 523-3664
3501 E Vernon Ave Vernon (90058) *(P-612)*

**Pacific Printing, Fresno** Also Called: Pan Pacific Printing Press Inc *(P-4717)*

**Pacific Process Systems Inc (PA)** ..................................... D ...... **661 321-9681**
7401 Rosedale Hwy Bakersfield (93308) *(P-265)*

**Pacific Quality Packaging Corp** ......................................... D ...... 714 257-1234
660 Neptune Ave Brea (92821) *(P-3871)*

**Pacific Refrigerator Company, Apple Valley** Also Called: Pac-Refco Inc *(P-10510)*

**Pacific Res Inst For Pub Plicy (PA)** ................................... F ...... **415 989-0833**
1 Embarcadero Ctr San Francisco (94111) *(P-19487)*

**Pacific Rim Printers & Mailers, Culver City** Also Called: Econ-O-Plate Inc *(P-4601)*

**Pacific Roller Die Co Inc** .................................................. F ...... 510 244-7286
1321 W Winton Ave Hayward (94545) *(P-11024)*

**Pacific Rubber & Packing Inc (PA)** ................................... E ...... **650 595-5888**
1160 Industrial Rd Ste 3 San Carlos (94070) *(P-16886)*

**Pacific Scientific, Hollister** Also Called: Pacific Scientific Energetic *(P-6316)*

**Pacific Scientific Company (DH)** ....................................... E ...... **805 526-5700**
1785 Voyager Ave Simi Valley (93063) *(P-14278)*

**Pacific Scientific Energetic (HQ)** ....................................... B ...... **831 637-3731**
3601 Union Rd Hollister (95023) *(P-6316)*

**Pacific Screw Products Inc** ............................................... D ...... 650 583-9682
1331 Old County Rd Ste C Belmont (94002) *(P-11025)*

**Pacific Seismic Products Inc** ............................................. E ...... 661 942-4499
233 E Avenue H8 Lancaster (93535) *(P-9160)*

**Pacific Sewer Maintenance Corp** ...................................... F ...... 800 292-9927
4008 Via Rio Ave Oceanside (92057) *(P-7680)*

**Pacific Ship Repr Fbrction Inc (PA)** .................................. B ...... **619 232-3200**
1625 Rigel St San Diego (92113) *(P-14013)*

**Pacific Shore Holdings Inc** ................................................ E ...... 818 998-0996
8236 Remmet Ave Canoga Park (91304) *(P-5592)*

**Pacific Shoring Products LLC (PA)** ................................... F ...... **707 575-9014**
265 Roberts Ave Santa Rosa (95407) *(P-9100)*

**Pacific Sky Supply Inc** ...................................................... D ...... 818 768-3700
8230 San Fernando Rd Sun Valley (91352) *(P-13921)*

**Pacific Solartech, Fremont** Also Called: China Custom Manufacturing Ltd *(P-6774)*

**Pacific Southwest Cont LLC** ............................................. E ...... 559 651-5500
9525 W Nicholas Ct Visalia (93291) *(P-3872)*

**Pacific Southwest Cont LLC (PA)** ..................................... B ...... **209 526-0444**
4530 Leckron Rd Modesto (95357) *(P-3931)*

**Pacific Southwest Cont LLC** ............................................. E ...... 209 526-0444
671 Mariposa Rd Modesto (95354) *(P-3932)*

**Pacific Spice Company Inc** ............................................... C ...... 323 726-9190
6430 E Slauson Ave Commerce (90040) *(P-2311)*

## ALPHABETIC SECTION — Palermo Family LP

**Pacific Standard Print, Sacramento** *Also Called: American Lithographers Inc (P-4509)*

**Pacific States Felt Mfg Co Inc** ............................................. F ..... 510 783-2357
23850 Clawiter Rd Ste 20 Hayward (94545) *(P-6459)*

**Pacific Steam Equipment Inc** ............................................ E ..... 562 906-9292
11748 Slauson Ave Santa Fe Springs (90670) *(P-8325)*

**Pacific Steel, Chula Vista** *Also Called: Simec USA Corporation (P-7627)*

**Pacific Steel Inc** ................................................................... E ..... 619 477-3925
1700 Cleveland Ave National City (91950) *(P-16961)*

**Pacific Steel Group** .............................................................. E ..... 707 669-3136
2301 Napa Vallejo Hwy Napa (94558) *(P-8705)*

**Pacific Steel Group, Napa** *Also Called: Pacific Steel Group (P-8705)*

**Pacific Steel Group LLC (PA)** ............................................ C ..... 858 251-1100
4805 Murphy Canyon Rd San Diego (92123) *(P-8706)*

**Pacific Stone Design Inc** ................................................... E ..... 714 836-5757
1201 E Wakeham Ave Santa Ana (92705) *(P-7370)*

**Pacific Supply, North Highlands** *Also Called: Pacific Coast Supply LLC (P-3316)*

**Pacific Supply, Visalia** *Also Called: Pacific Coast Supply LLC (P-7530)*

**Pacific Supply, Santa Rosa** *Also Called: Pacific Coast Supply LLC (P-16455)*

**Pacific Tank & Cnstr Inc** ..................................................... E ..... 805 237-2929
17995 E Highway 46 Shandon (93461) *(P-8326)*

**Pacific Tech Products Ontario, Union City** *Also Called: California Performance Packg (P-6625)*

**Pacific Toll Processing Inc** ................................................ E ..... 310 952-4992
24724 Wilmington Ave Carson (90745) *(P-16312)*

**Pacific Transformer Corp** .................................................. D ..... 714 779-0450
5399 E Hunter Ave Anaheim (92807) *(P-11222)*

**Pacific Truck Tank Inc** ........................................................ E ..... 916 379-9280
7029 Florin Perkins Rd Ste A Sacramento (95828) *(P-13422)*

**Pacific Urethanes, Ontario** *Also Called: Pacific Urethanes LLC (P-2945)*

**Pacific Urethanes LLC** ....................................................... C ..... 909 390-8400
1671 Champagne Ave Ste A Ontario (91761) *(P-2945)*

**Pacific Utility Products Inc** ............................................... E ..... 951 493-8394
2430 Railroad St Corona (92880) *(P-13284)*

**Pacific Vial Mfg Inc** ............................................................. E ..... 323 721-7004
2738 Supply Ave Commerce (90040) *(P-7185)*

**Pacific Wave Systems Inc** ................................................. D ..... 714 893-0152
2525 W 190th St Torrance (90504) *(P-11913)*

**Pacific West, Anaheim** *Also Called: Pacific West Litho Inc (P-4715)*

**Pacific West Forest Products** ........................................... F ..... 530 899-7313
13434 Browns Valley Dr Chico (95973) *(P-8707)*

**Pacific West Litho Inc** ........................................................ D ..... 714 579-0868
3291 E Miraloma Ave Anaheim (92806) *(P-4715)*

**Pacific Western Systems Inc (PA)** .................................... E ..... 650 961-8855
505 E Evelyn Ave Mountain View (94041) *(P-14569)*

**Pacific Wire Products Inc** ................................................. E ..... 818 755-6400
10725 Vanowen St North Hollywood (91605) *(P-9224)*

**Pacific World Corporation (PA)** ....................................... D ..... 949 598-2400
757 S Alameda St Ste 280 Los Angeles (90021) *(P-6016)*

**Pacifica Beauty LLC** ............................................................ D ..... 844 332-8440
1090 Eugenia Pl Ste 200 Carpinteria (93013) *(P-16193)*

**Pacifica Foods LLC** ............................................................. C ..... 951 371-3123
1581 N Main St Orange (92867) *(P-989)*

**Pacifica International, Carpinteria** *Also Called: Pacifica Beauty LLC (P-16193)*

**Pacifico Inc** ............................................................................ E ..... 209 466-0266
1754 E Mariposa Rd Stockton (95205) *(P-13618)*

**Pacira Pharmaceuticals Inc** ............................................. D ..... 858 625-2424
10578 Science Center Dr San Diego (92121) *(P-5593)*

**Paciugo** ................................................................................. E ..... 714 536-5388
122 Main St Ste 122 Huntington Beach (92648) *(P-7939)*

**Pack West Machinery, Corona** *Also Called: Pacific Packaging McHy LLC (P-9810)*

**Packaging America - Sacramento, Mcclellan** *Also Called: PCA Central Cal Corrugated LLC (P-3877)*

**Packaging Corporation America** ..................................... D ..... 323 263-7581
4240 Bandini Blvd Vernon (90058) *(P-3873)*

**Packaging Corporation America** ..................................... E ..... 909 888-7008
879 E Rialto Ave San Bernardino (92408) *(P-3874)*

**Packaging Corporation America** ..................................... C ..... 562 927-7741
9700 E Frontage Rd Ste 20 South Gate (90280) *(P-3875)*

**Packaging Innovators LLC** ............................................... D ..... 925 371-2000
6850 Brisa St Livermore (94550) *(P-17019)*

**Packaging Manufacturing Inc** ......................................... C ..... 619 498-9199
2285 Michael Faraday Dr Ste 12 San Diego (92154) *(P-4716)*

**Packaging Spectrum, Los Angeles** *Also Called: Advance Paper Box Company (P-3818)*

**Packaging Systems Inc** ..................................................... E ..... 661 253-5700
26435 Summit Cir Santa Clarita (91350) *(P-6239)*

**Packers Bar M, Los Angeles** *Also Called: Serv-Rite Meat Company Inc (P-616)*

**Packline Technologies Inc** ............................................... E ..... 559 591-3150
5929 Avenue 408 Dinuba (93618) *(P-10028)*

**Packline USA LLC** ............................................................... E ..... 909 392-8000
9555 Hyssop Dr Rancho Cucamonga (91730) *(P-7186)*

**Paclights, Chino** *Also Called: Paclights LLC (P-11552)*

**Paclights LLC (PA)** .............................................................. F ..... 800 980-6386
15318 El Prado Rd Chino (91708) *(P-11552)*

**Pacmag Inc** ........................................................................... E ..... 619 872-0343
87 Georgina St Chula Vista (91910) *(P-13060)*

**Pacmet Aerospace, Corona** *Also Called: Pacmet Aerospace LLC (P-9329)*

**Pacmet Aerospace LLC** .................................................... D ..... 909 218-8889
224 Glider Cir Corona (92878) *(P-9329)*

**Pacmin Incorporated (PA)** ............................................... D ..... 714 447-4478
2021 Raymer Ave Fullerton (92833) *(P-16194)*

**Pacobond Inc** ...................................................................... E ..... 818 768-5002
9344 Glenoaks Blvd Sun Valley (91352) *(P-3992)*

**Pacon, Livermore** *Also Called: Pacon Mfg Inc (P-11026)*

**Pacon Inc** .............................................................................. C ..... 626 814-4654
4249 Puente Ave Baldwin Park (91706) *(P-3791)*

**Pacon Mfg Inc** ..................................................................... E ..... 925 961-0445
4777 Bennett Dr Ste H Livermore (94551) *(P-11026)*

**Pacsgear Inc** ......................................................................... D ..... 925 225-6100
4309 Hacienda Dr Ste 500 Pleasanton (94588) *(P-18652)*

**Pactech, San Jose** *Also Called: Saco Enterprises Inc (P-16631)*

**Pactiv LLC** ............................................................................. D ..... 209 983-1930
4545 Qantas Ln Stockton (95206) *(P-3876)*

**Pactiv LLC** ............................................................................. C ..... 661 392-4000
2024 Norris Rd Bakersfield (93308) *(P-6947)*

**Pactron** ................................................................................. D ..... 408 329-5500
3000 Patrick Henry Dr Santa Clara (95054) *(P-12184)*

**Pactron, Santa Clara** *Also Called: Pactron (P-12184)*

**Pactum, Mountain View** *Also Called: Pactum Ai Inc (P-17556)*

**Pactum Ai Inc (PA)** ............................................................. E ..... 669 289-9041
800 W El Camino Real Ste 180 Mountain View (94040) *(P-17556)*

**Pacwest Air Filter LLC** ....................................................... E ..... 951 698-2228
26550 Adams Ave Murrieta (92562) *(P-9994)*

**Pacwood, Cottonwood** *Also Called: Plum Valley Inc (P-3075)*

**Padoma Wind Power LLC (DH)** ....................................... F ..... 858 731-5001
7777 Fay Ave Ste 200 La Jolla (92037) *(P-19471)*

**Pafco, Vernon** *Also Called: Pacific American Fish Co Inc (P-2041)*

**Paige LLC (HQ)** .................................................................... C ..... 310 733-2100
10119 Jefferson Blvd Culver City (90232) *(P-2686)*

**Paige Floor Cvg Specialists, National City** *Also Called: Paige Sitta & Associates Inc (P-14014)*

**Paige Premium Denim, Culver City** *Also Called: Paige LLC (P-2686)*

**Paige Sitta & Associates Inc (PA)** .................................... E ..... 619 233-5912
2050 Wilson Ave Ste B National City (91950) *(P-14014)*

**Paiho North America Corp** ............................................... E ..... 661 257-6611
16051 El Prado Rd Chino (91708) *(P-15915)*

**Paint-Chem Inc** ................................................................... F ..... 213 747-7725
1680 Miller Ave Los Angeles (90063) *(P-6099)*

**Paisano Publications LLC (PA)** ....................................... D ..... 818 889-8740
28210 Dorothy Dr Agoura Hills (91301) *(P-4285)*

**Paisano Publications Inc** .................................................. D ..... 818 889-8740
28210 Dorothy Dr Agoura Hills (91301) *(P-4286)*

**Paisleyriversoapco, Paso Robles** *Also Called: Melissa Trinidad (P-6006)*

**Pak Group LLC** .................................................................... E ..... 626 316-6555
236 N Chester Ave Ste 200 Pasadena (91106) *(P-1281)*

**Pak West Paper & Packaging, Santa Ana** *Also Called: Blower-Dempsay Corporation (P-3822)*

**Paklab, Chino** *Also Called: Universal Packg Systems Inc (P-6050)*

**Paladar Mfg Inc** .................................................................. D ..... 760 775-4222
53973 Polk St Coachella (92236) *(P-15720)*

**Palamida Inc** ........................................................................ E ..... 415 777-9400
215 2nd St Lbby 2 San Francisco (94105) *(P-16536)*

**Palermo Family LP (PA)** .................................................... E ..... 213 542-3300
140 W Providencia Ave Burbank (91502) *(P-2312)*

**Palette Life Sciences Inc (PA)** ............................................. D ...... 805 869-7020
27 E Cota St Ste 402 Santa Barbara (93101) *(P-5260)*

**Palisades Beach Club, Los Angeles** *Also Called: Fortune Swimwear LLC (P-2470)*

**Pall Corporation** ............................................................. C ...... 858 455-7264
4116 Sorrento Valley Blvd San Diego (92121) *(P-10104)*

**Pallet Depot Inc** ............................................................. D ...... 916 645-0490
19049 Avenue 242 Lindsay (93247) *(P-3352)*

**Pallet Masters Inc** ......................................................... D ...... 323 758-1713
655 E Florence Ave Los Angeles (90001) *(P-3353)*

**Palletmasters, Woodland** *Also Called: Palletmasters LLC (P-3354)*

**Palletmasters LLC** ......................................................... F ...... 510 715-1242
104 Matmor Rd Woodland (95776) *(P-3354)*

**Pallets Unlimited Inc** ..................................................... F ...... 916 408-1914
2390 Athens Ave Lincoln (95648) *(P-3355)*

**Palm Inc (HQ)** ............................................................... B ...... 408 617-7000
950 W Maude Ave Sunnyvale (94085) *(P-11914)*

**Palmaz Vineyards, Napa** *Also Called: Cedar Knoll Vineyards Inc (P-1499)*

**Palmer Tank & Construction Inc** .................................. E ...... 661 834-1110
2464 S Union Ave Bakersfield (93307) *(P-266)*

**Palo Alto Networks Inc (PA)** ........................................ B ...... 408 753-4000
3000 Tannery Way Santa Clara (95054) *(P-18653)*

**Palomar Products Inc** ................................................... D ...... 949 766-5300
23042 Arroyo Vis Rcho Sta Marg (92688) *(P-12007)*

**Palomar Tech Companies (PA)** ................................... D ...... 760 931-3600
6305 El Camino Real Carlsbad (92009) *(P-13285)*

**Palomar Technologies Inc (PA)** .................................. E ...... 760 931-3600
6305 El Camino Real Carlsbad (92009) *(P-9888)*

**Palos Verdes Building Corp (PA)** ................................ C ...... 951 371-8090
1675 Sampson Ave Corona (92879) *(P-13147)*

**Palpilot International Corp (PA)** ................................... E ...... 408 855-8866
500 Yosemite Dr Milpitas (95035) *(P-12185)*

**Palyon Medical Corporation** ........................................ E
28432 Constellation Rd Valencia (91355) *(P-15571)*

**Pamco, Sun Valley** *Also Called: Precision Arcft Machining Inc (P-11045)*

**Pamco Machine Works Inc** ......................................... E ...... 909 941-7260
9359 Feron Blvd Rancho Cucamonga (91730) *(P-11027)*

**Pamela's Products, Ukiah** *Also Called: Pamelas Products Incorporated (P-1234)*

**Pamelas Products Incorporated** .................................. D ...... 707 462-6605
1 Carousel Ln Ste D Ukiah (95482) *(P-1234)*

**Pampanga Food Company Inc** .................................... E ...... 714 773-0537
1835 N Orangethorpe Park Ste A Anaheim (92801) *(P-657)*

**Pan Pacific Plastics Mfg Inc (PA)** ................................ E ...... 510 785-6888
26551 Danti Ct Hayward (94545) *(P-6948)*

**Pan Pacific Printing Press Inc** ..................................... E ...... 559 252-1624
1899 N Helm Ave Fresno (93727) *(P-4717)*

**Pan-O-Rama Baking Inc** ............................................. F ...... 415 522-5500
500 Florida St San Francisco (94110) *(P-1235)*

**Pana-Pacific Corporation (HQ)** .................................... E ...... 559 457-4700
838 N Laverne Ave Fresno (93727) *(P-13552)*

**Pana-Pacific Corporation** ............................................. C ...... 559 499-1891
541 Division St Campbell (95008) *(P-13553)*

**Panadent Corporation** ................................................. E ...... 909 783-1841
580 S Rancho Ave Colton (92324) *(P-15474)*

**Panapacific Shipping, Fresno** *Also Called: Brix Group Inc (P-13216)*

**Panasonic Avionics Corporation (DH)** ......................... B ...... 949 672-2000
3347 Michelson Dr Ste 100 Irvine (92612) *(P-19410)*

**Panasonic Disc Manufacturing Corporation of America** ...... C ...... 310 783-4800
20000 Mariner Ave Ste 200 Torrance (90503) *(P-11739)*

**Panavision Group, Woodland Hills** *Also Called: Panavision Inc (P-17860)*

**Panavision Hollywood, Los Angeles** *Also Called: Panavision Inc (P-15658)*

**Panavision Inc** .............................................................. E ...... 323 464-3800
6735 Selma Ave Los Angeles (90028) *(P-15658)*

**Panavision Inc (PA)** ..................................................... A ...... 818 316-1000
6101 Variel Ave Woodland Hills (91367) *(P-17860)*

**Panavision International LP (HQ)** ................................ B ...... 818 316-1080
6101 Variel Ave Woodland Hills (91367) *(P-15659)*

**Pandadoc Inc** ................................................................ E ...... 415 860-0176
400 Spear St Apt 217 San Francisco (94105) *(P-18654)*

**Panel Products, Long Beach** *Also Called: Simulator PDT Solutions LLC (P-14306)*

**Pangaea Holdings Inc** .................................................. E ...... 402 704-7546
1968 S Coast Hwy Pmb 3080 Laguna Beach (92651) *(P-6017)*

**Pankl Aerospace Systems** ........................................... D ...... 562 207-6300
16615 Edwards Rd Cerritos (90703) *(P-7868)*

**Pankl Engine Systems Inc** ........................................... E ...... 949 428-8788
1902 Mcgaw Ave Irvine (92614) *(P-13554)*

**Pannaway, Fremont** *Also Called: Enablence Systems Inc (P-18280)*

**Pannonia Group Inc** ..................................................... E ...... 310 846-4496
5441 W 104th St Los Angeles (90045) *(P-17791)*

**Pano Logic Inc** .............................................................. E ...... 650 743-1773
1100 La Avenida St Ste A Mountain View (94043) *(P-10420)*

**Panoramic Software Corporation** ................................ F ...... 877 558-8526
9650 Research Dr Irvine (92618) *(P-18655)*

**Panosoft, Irvine** *Also Called: Panoramic Software Corporation (P-18655)*

**Panrosa Enterprises Inc** .............................................. D ...... 951 339-5888
550 Monica Cir Corona (92878) *(P-5879)*

**Papa Cantella's Sausage Plant, Vernon** *Also Called: Papa Cantellas Incorporated (P-658)*

**Papa Cantellas Incorporated** ...................................... D ...... 323 584-7272
3341 E 50th St Vernon (90058) *(P-658)*

**Papaya** .......................................................................... E ...... 310 740-6774
14140 Ventura Blvd Ste 209 Sherman Oaks (91423) *(P-18656)*

**Pape Material Handling Inc** ......................................... D ...... 562 692-9311
2600 Peck Rd City Of Industry (90601) *(P-9529)*

**Paper Pulp & Film** ........................................................ E ...... 559 233-1151
2822 S Maple Ave Fresno (93725) *(P-4045)*

**Paper Processors Inc** ................................................... E
2583 Mercantile Dr Rancho Cordova (95742) *(P-3792)*

**Paper Surce Converting Mfg Inc** ................................. E ...... 323 583-3800
4800 S Santa Fe Ave Vernon (90058) *(P-3793)*

**Paperboard Packaging Corp** ....................................... D ...... 530 671-9000
800 N Walton Ave Yuba City (95993) *(P-3933)*

**Papercutters Inc** ........................................................... E ...... 323 888-1330
6900 Washington Blvd Montebello (90640) *(P-3934)*

**Papi, Glendale** *Also Called: Glenair Inc (P-11456)*

**Pappy's Fine Foods, Fresno** *Also Called: Pappys Meat Company Inc (P-2313)*

**Pappys Meat Company Inc** ......................................... E ...... 559 291-0218
5663 E Fountain Way Fresno (93727) *(P-2313)*

**Papyrus, Petaluma** *Also Called: Schurman Fine Papers (P-4997)*

**Para Plate, Cerritos** *Also Called: Para-Plate & Plastics Co Inc (P-9773)*

**Para Tech Coating, Laguna Hills** *Also Called: Metal Improvement Company LLC (P-7892)*

**Para-Plate & Plastics Co Inc** ....................................... E ...... 562 404-3434
15910 Shoemaker Ave Cerritos (90703) *(P-9773)*

**Parablu Inc** .................................................................... E ...... 408 775-6571
38350 Fremont Blvd # 203 Fremont (94536) *(P-18657)*

**Parachute Home Inc** .................................................... C ...... 310 903-0353
3525 Eastham Dr Culver City (90232) *(P-2946)*

**Paradigm Contract Mfg LLC** ........................................ F ...... 714 889-7074
5531 Belle Ave Cypress (90630) *(P-16195)*

**Paradigm Label Inc** ...................................................... F ...... 951 372-9212
1177 N Grove St Anaheim (92806) *(P-4936)*

**Paradigm Packaging East LLC** ................................... E ...... 909 985-2750
9595 Utica Ave Rancho Cucamonga (91730) *(P-6949)*

**Paradigm Packaging West, Rancho Cucamonga** *Also Called: Paradigm Packaging East LLC (P-6949)*

**Paradise Kitchen Doors, Pomona** *Also Called: Gonzalez Feliciano (P-3140)*

**Paradise Post Inc** ......................................................... C ...... 530 872-5581
5399 Clark Rd Paradise (95969) *(P-4178)*

**Paragon Building Products Inc (PA)** ........................... E ...... 951 549-1155
2191 5th St Ste 111 Norco (92860) *(P-7371)*

**Paragon Controls Incorporated** ................................... F ...... 707 579-1424
2371 Circadian Way Santa Rosa (95407) *(P-14366)*

**Paragon II Real Estate, Fresno** *Also Called: Paragon Industries II Inc (P-17340)*

**Paragon Industries Inc** ................................................. E ...... 818 833-0550
16450 Foothill Blvd Ste 100 Sylmar (91342) *(P-484)*

**Paragon Industries Inc (PA)** ........................................ D ...... 559 275-5000
4285 N Golden State Blvd Fresno (93722) *(P-17339)*

**Paragon Industries II Inc** .............................................. D ...... 559 275-5000
4285 N Golden State Blvd Fresno (93722) *(P-17340)*

**Paragon Label, Petaluma** *Also Called: Resource Label Group LLC (P-4950)*

**Paragon Laboratories, Torrance** *Also Called: Naturalife Eco Vite Labs (P-771)*

**Paragon Machine Works Inc** ....................................... D ...... 510 232-3223
253 S 25th St Richmond (94804) *(P-11028)*

# ALPHABETIC SECTION — Pasadena Newspapers Inc

**Paragon Plastics Co Div, Chino** *Also Called: Consolidated Plastics Corp (P-17227)*
**Paragon Precision, Valencia** *Also Called: Princeton Tool Inc (P-13719)*
**Paragon Swiss** ................................................................. E ...... 408 748-1617
  545 Aldo Ave Ste 1 Santa Clara (95054) *(P-11029)*
**Parallax Incorporated** ...................................................... E ...... 916 624-8333
  599 Menlo Dr Ste 100 Rocklin (95765) *(P-10192)*
**Parallax Research, Rocklin** *Also Called: Parallax Incorporated (P-10192)*
**Parallel 6 Inc (PA)** ........................................................... E ...... 619 452-1750
  1455 Frazee Rd Ste 900 San Diego (92108) *(P-17961)*
**Parallel Machines Inc** ...................................................... F ...... 669 467-2638
  2445 Augustine Dr Ste 150 Santa Clara (95054) *(P-18658)*
**Parallelm, Santa Clara** *Also Called: Parallel Machines Inc (P-18658)*
**Parametric Manufacturing Inc** ......................................... F ...... 408 654-9845
  3465 Edward Ave Santa Clara (95054) *(P-11030)*
**Paramit Corporation (PA)** ................................................ D ...... 408 782-5600
  18735 Madrone Pkwy Morgan Hill (95037) *(P-12186)*
**Paramont Metal & Supply Co, Paramount** *Also Called: George Jue Mfg Co Inc (P-9711)*
**Paramount Asphalt, Paramount** *Also Called: Paramount Petroleum Corp (P-6344)*
**Paramount Citrus, Delano** *Also Called: Wonderful Company LLC (P-42)*
**Paramount Citrus Packing Co, Delano** *Also Called: Wonderful Citrus Packing LLC (P-90)*
**Paramount Dairy Inc** ........................................................ C ...... 562 361-1800
  15255 Texaco Ave Paramount (90723) *(P-842)*
**Paramount Farms, Los Angeles** *Also Called: Wonderful Pstchios Almonds LLC (P-1370)*
**Paramount Forge Inc** ....................................................... E ...... 323 775-6803
  1721 E Colon St Wilmington (90744) *(P-8784)*
**Paramount Machine Co Inc** ............................................. E ...... 909 484-3600
  10824 Edison Ct Rancho Cucamonga (91730) *(P-11031)*
**Paramount Metal & Supply Inc** ....................................... E ...... 562 634-8180
  8140 Rosecrans Ave Paramount (90723) *(P-8640)*
**Paramount Panels Inc (PA)** ............................................. E ...... 909 947-8008
  1531 E Cedar St Ontario (91761) *(P-6950)*
**Paramount Petroleum Corp (DH)** .................................... C ...... 562 531-2060
  14700 Downey Ave Paramount (90723) *(P-6344)*
**Paramount Tool & Machine Co, Redwood City** *Also Called: Talos Corporation (P-11136)*
**Paramount Window & Doors, San Bernardino** *Also Called: Paramount Windows & Doors (P-3177)*
**Paramount Windows & Doors** ......................................... F ...... 909 888-4688
  723 W Mill St San Bernardino (92410) *(P-3177)*
**Parcell Steel, Corona** *Also Called: Parcell Steel Corp (P-8198)*
**Parcell Steel Corp** .......................................................... C ...... 951 471-3200
  26365 Earthmover Cir Corona (92883) *(P-8198)*
**Parco LLC (DH)** ............................................................. C ...... 909 947-2200
  1801 S Archibald Ave Ontario (91761) *(P-6460)*
**Parducci Wine Estates LLC** ............................................ E ...... 707 463-5350
  501 Parducci Rd Ukiah (95482) *(P-1703)*
**Parent Is Sitecore USA Holding, San Francisco** *Also Called: Sitecore Usa Inc (P-18792)*
**Parentsquare Inc** ............................................................ D ...... 888 496-3168
  6144 Calle Real Ste 200a Goleta (93117) *(P-18659)*
**Parex Usa Inc (DH)** ........................................................ E ...... 714 778-2266
  2150 Eastridge Ave Riverside (92507) *(P-7599)*
**Parex Usa Inc** ................................................................. F ...... 510 444-2497
  111290 S Vallejo Ct French Camp (95231) *(P-16480)*
**Parex Usa Inc** ................................................................. E ...... 951 653-3549
  2150 Eastridge Ave Riverside (92507) *(P-17341)*
**Paris Precision LLC** ....................................................... C ...... 805 239-2500
  1650 Ramada Dr Paso Robles (93446) *(P-8530)*
**Parisa Lingerie & Swim Wear, Calabasas** *Also Called: Afr Apparel International Inc (P-2827)*
**Park Avenue Cleaners Inc** .............................................. E ...... 209 832-3706
  2529 N Tracy Blvd Tracy (95376) *(P-17765)*
**Park Engineering and Mfg Co** ......................................... E ...... 714 521-4660
  6430 Roland St Buena Park (90621) *(P-11032)*
**Park Steel Co Inc** ........................................................... F ...... 310 638-6101
  515 E Pine St Compton (90222) *(P-8199)*
**Park West Enterprises Inc** .............................................. F ...... 909 383-8341
  2586 Shenandoah Way San Bernardino (92407) *(P-1388)*
**Park's Prtg & Lithographic Co, Modesto** *Also Called: Village Instant Printing Inc (P-4804)*
**Parker Aerospace, Irvine** *Also Called: Parker-Hannifin Corporation (P-13923)*
**Parker Boiler Co, Commerce** *Also Called: Sid E Parker Boiler Mfg Co Inc (P-8335)*
**Parker Meggitt, Simi Valley** *Also Called: Meggitt Safety Systems Inc (P-13271)*

**Parker Powis Inc** ............................................................. D ...... 510 848-2463
  2929 5th St Berkeley (94710) *(P-10463)*
**Parker Service Center, Buena Park** *Also Called: Parker-Hannifin Corporation (P-6427)*
**Parker-Hannifin Corporation** ........................................... D ...... 714 522-8840
  8460 Kass Dr Buena Park (90621) *(P-6427)*
**Parker-Hannifin Corporation** ........................................... D ...... 562 404-1938
  14087 Borate St Santa Fe Springs (90670) *(P-8327)*
**Parker-Hannifin Corporation** ........................................... C ...... 619 661-7000
  7664 Panasonic Way San Diego (92154) *(P-10633)*
**Parker-Hannifin Corporation** ........................................... D ...... 951 280-3800
  221 Helicopter Cir Corona (92878) *(P-10634)*
**Parker-Hannifin Corporation** ........................................... E ...... 707 584-7558
  5500 Business Park Dr Rohnert Park (94928) *(P-10635)*
**Parker-Hannifin Corporation** ........................................... C ...... 707 584-7558
  5500 Business Park Dr Rohnert Park (94928) *(P-11338)*
**Parker-Hannifin Corporation** ........................................... C ...... 310 608-5600
  19610 S Rancho Way Rancho Dominguez (90220) *(P-12850)*
**Parker-Hannifin Corporation** ........................................... C ...... 949 833-3000
  16666 Von Karman Ave Irvine (92606) *(P-13717)*
**Parker-Hannifin Corporation** ........................................... E ...... 805 484-8533
  3800 Calle Tecate Camarillo (93012) *(P-13922)*
**Parker-Hannifin Corporation** ........................................... C ...... 949 833-3000
  14300 Alton Pkwy Irvine (92618) *(P-13923)*
**Parker-Hannifin Corporation** ........................................... C ...... 510 235-9590
  250 Canal Blvd Richmond (94804) *(P-14443)*
**Parkhouse Tire, San Diego** *Also Called: Parkhouse Tire Service Inc (P-17456)*
**Parkhouse Tire, Bell Gardens** *Also Called: Parkhouse Tire Service Inc (P-17457)*
**Parkhouse Tire Service Inc** ............................................. E ...... 858 565-8473
  4660 Ruffner St San Diego (92111) *(P-17456)*
**Parkhouse Tire Service Inc (PA)** ..................................... D ...... 562 928-0421
  6006 Shull St Bell Gardens (90201) *(P-17457)*
**Parkinson Enterprises Inc** ............................................... D ...... 714 626-0275
  135 S State College Blvd Ste 625 Brea (92821) *(P-3581)*
**Parkoworld Inc** ................................................................ F ...... 818 686-6900
  10314 Norris Ave Ste B Pacoima (91331) *(P-16019)*
**Parks Group Ey** .............................................................. E ...... 209 576-2568
  1515 10th St Modesto (95354) *(P-4718)*
**Parma Floors Inc** ............................................................ F ...... 408 638-0247
  2079 Hartog Dr San Jose (95131) *(P-16075)*
**Parmatech Corporation** ................................................... D ...... 707 778-2266
  2221 Pine View Way Petaluma (94954) *(P-7909)*
**Parmela Creamery, Moreno Valley** *Also Called: Life Is Life LLC (P-729)*
**Parmeter Logging and Excav Inc** .................................... F ...... 707 632-5610
  6040 Cazadero Hwy Cazadero (95421) *(P-547)*
**Parpro Technologies Inc** ................................................. C ...... 714 545-8886
  2700 S Fairview St Santa Ana (92704) *(P-12187)*
**Parquet By Dian** ............................................................. D ...... 310 527-3779
  16601 S Main St Gardena (90248) *(P-3101)*
**Parrot Communications Intl Inc** ....................................... E ...... 818 567-4700
  25461 Rye Canyon Rd Valencia (91355) *(P-4444)*
**Parrot Media Network, Valencia** *Also Called: Parrot Communications Intl Inc (P-4444)*
**Partner Concepts Inc** ...................................................... D ...... 805 745-7199
  811 Camino Viejo Santa Barbara (93108) *(P-4287)*
**Partner Printing, Glendale** *Also Called: Colour Concepts Inc (P-4562)*
**Partners 1993 Inc** ........................................................... F ...... 818 352-7800
  3501 Ocean View Blvd Glendale (91208) *(P-11740)*
**Partnrship Prmnt Ptro Chnse En, Long Beach** *Also Called: Tidelands Oil Production Inc (P-141)*
**Partsflex Inc** ................................................................... E ...... 408 677-7121
  1775 Park St Ste 77 Selma (93662) *(P-3015)*
**Partyaid, Santa Cruz** *Also Called: Anomalies International Inc (P-1865)*
**Parvus Therapeutics Us Inc** ............................................ F ...... 415 805-8251
  750 Gateway Blvd South San Francisco (94080) *(P-5594)*
**Parylene Coating Services Inc** ........................................ E ...... 281 391-7665
  35 Argonaut Aliso Viejo (92656) *(P-9101)*
**Pasadena Newspapers Inc** ............................................. F ...... 562 698-0955
  6737 Bright Ave Ste 109 Whittier (90601) *(P-4179)*
**Pasadena Newspapers Inc (PA)** ..................................... C ...... 626 578-6300
  605 E Huntington Dr Ste 100 Monrovia (91016) *(P-4180)*
**Pasadena Newspapers Inc** ............................................. C ...... 707 442-1711
  930 6th St Eureka (95501) *(P-4181)*

**Pasadena Refining System Inc** ............................................................ B ...... 713 920-1874
6001 Bollinger Canyon Rd San Ramon (94583) *(P-6345)*

**Pasadena Star-News, Monrovia** *Also Called: Pasadena Newspapers Inc (P-4180)*

**Pascal Patisserie** .................................................................................. F ...... 818 712-9375
21040 Victory Blvd Woodland Hills (91367) *(P-1236)*

**Pascal Systems, West Sacramento** *Also Called: Heco Inc (P-10040)*

**Pasco, Buena Park** *Also Called: Yeager Enterprises Corp (P-7560)*

**Pasco Scientific (PA)** ............................................................................ C ...... 916 786-3800
10101 Foothills Blvd Roseville (95747) *(P-14703)*

**Pasco Scientific, Roseville** *Also Called: Pasco Scientific (P-14703)*

**Paso Robles Tank Inc (HQ)** ................................................................. D ...... 805 227-1641
825 26th St Paso Robles (93446) *(P-7621)*

**Pass, Orange** *Also Called: Prototype & Short-Run Svcs Inc (P-8879)*

**Pass Laboratories Inc** .......................................................................... F ...... 530 878-5350
13395 New Airport Rd Ste G Auburn (95602) *(P-11685)*

**Passport Food Group LLC** .................................................................. C ...... 909 627-7312
2539 E Philadelphia St Ontario (91761) *(P-2314)*

**Passport Foods (svc) LLC** ................................................................... C ...... 909 627-7312
2539 E Philadelphia St Ontario (91761) *(P-2315)*

**Passport Technology Usa Inc** ............................................................. E ...... 818 957-5471
400 N Brand Blvd Ste 800 Glendale (91203) *(P-19274)*

**Password Enterprise Inc** ..................................................................... E ...... 562 988-8889
3200 E 29th St Long Beach (90806) *(P-17669)*

**Passy-Muir Inc (PA)** ............................................................................. E ...... 949 833-8255
17992 Mitchell S Ste 200 Irvine (92614) *(P-15391)*

**Pasta Mia, Fullerton** *Also Called: Nina Mia Inc (P-2297)*

**Pasta Piccinini Inc** ................................................................................ E ...... 626 798-0841
950 N Fair Oaks Ave Pasadena (91103) *(P-17203)*

**Pasta Prima, Benicia** *Also Called: Valley Fine Foods Company LLC (P-1066)*

**Patagonia Inc (HQ)** .............................................................................. B ...... 805 643-8616
259 W Santa Clara St Ventura (93001) *(P-2636)*

**Patagonia Works (PA)** ........................................................................ B ...... 805 643-8616
259 W Santa Clara St Ventura (93001) *(P-17511)*

**Pathwater, Fremont** *Also Called: Pathwater Inc (P-1909)*

**Pathwater Inc** ........................................................................................ E ...... 510 518-0014
44137 Fremont Blvd Fremont (94538) *(P-1909)*

**Patient Safety Technologies Inc** ......................................................... E ...... 949 387-2277
15440 Laguna Canyon Rd Ste 150 Irvine (92618) *(P-15392)*

**Patientpop Inc** ....................................................................................... D ...... 844 487-8399
214 Wilshire Blvd Santa Monica (90401) *(P-18660)*

**Patina Products, Arroyo Grande** *Also Called: Layne Laboratories Inc (P-1134)*

**Patina V, Covina** *Also Called: Norlaine Inc (P-16189)*

**Patio Guys, Orange** *Also Called: Guys Patio Inc (P-19181)*

**Patio Industries, Ontario** *Also Called: Western States Wholesale Inc (P-7305)*

**Patric Communications Inc (PA)** ........................................................ D ...... 619 579-2898
15215 Alton Pkwy Ste 200 Irvine (92618) *(P-466)*

**Patrick Industries Inc** ........................................................................... E ...... 909 350-4440
13414 Slover Ave Fontana (92337) *(P-16481)*

**Patriot Memory, Fremont** *Also Called: Patriot Memory Inc (P-12628)*

**Patriot Memory Inc (PA)** ..................................................................... C ...... 510 979-1021
2925 Bayview Dr Fremont (94538) *(P-12628)*

**Patriot Polishing Company** ................................................................. F ...... 310 903-7409
47260 Wrangler Rd Aguanga (92536) *(P-5924)*

**Patriot Products, Irwindale** *Also Called: Pertronix Inc (P-13180)*

**Patron Solutions LLC** .......................................................................... C ...... 949 823-1700
5171 California Ave Ste 200 Irvine (92617) *(P-18661)*

**Patsons Media Group, Santa Clara** *Also Called: Patsons Press (P-4719)*

**Patsons Press** ....................................................................................... E ...... 408 567-0911
3000 Scott Blvd Ste 101 Santa Clara (95054) *(P-4719)*

**Patten Christian Schools, Oakland** *Also Called: Christian Evang Chrches Amer I (P-19343)*

**Patten Co Inc** ........................................................................................ E ...... 707 826-2887
3701 Mt Diablo Blvd Lafayette (94549) *(P-6521)*

**Patten Group, Lafayette** *Also Called: Patten Co Inc (P-6521)*

**Patterson Dental Supply Inc** ............................................................... E ...... 925 603-6350
5087 Commercial Cir Concord (94520) *(P-15475)*

**Patterson Kincaid LLC** ........................................................................ E ...... 323 584-3559
5175 S Soto St Vernon (90058) *(P-2798)*

**Paul Baker Printing Inc** ....................................................................... E ...... 916 969-8317
4251 Gateway Park Blvd Sacramento (95834) *(P-4720)*

**Paul Ferrante Inc** .................................................................................. E ...... 310 854-4412
8464 Melrose Pl West Hollywood (90069) *(P-16196)*

**Paul Graham Drilling, Rio Vista** *Also Called: Paul Graham Drilling & Svc Co (P-164)*

**Paul Graham Drilling & Svc Co** .......................................................... C ...... 707 374-5123
2500 Airport Rd Rio Vista (94571) *(P-164)*

**Paul Hubbs Construction Co Inc (PA)** .............................................. F ...... 951 360-3990
542 W C St Colton (92324) *(P-304)*

**Paul R Briles Inc** ................................................................................... A ...... 310 323-6222
1700 W 132nd St Gardena (90249) *(P-8764)*

**Paul-Munroe Entertech Division, Brea** *Also Called: Curtiss-Wright Flow Ctrl Corp (P-9184)*

**Paulco Precision Inc** ............................................................................ E ...... 310 679-4900
13916 Cordary Ave Hawthorne (90250) *(P-11033)*

**Pauley Plastic LLC** .............................................................................. F ...... 760 240-3737
17177 Navajo Rd Apple Valley (92307) *(P-6951)*

**Pauli Systems Inc** ................................................................................. E ...... 707 429-2434
1820 Walters Ct Fairfield (94533) *(P-11034)*

**Paulson Manufacturing Corp (PA)** ..................................................... D ...... 951 676-2451
46752 Rainbow Canyon Rd Temecula (92592) *(P-15393)*

**Pavement Recycling Systems Inc** ..................................................... D ...... 661 948-5599
48028 90th St W Lancaster (93536) *(P-6367)*

**Paver Decor Masonry Inc** ................................................................... E ...... 909 795-8474
987 Calimesa Blvd Calimesa (92320) *(P-377)*

**Pavestone LLC** ..................................................................................... E ...... 530 795-4400
27600 County Road 90 Winters (95694) *(P-7543)*

**Pavex Construction Co, Seaside** *Also Called: Granite Rock Co (P-7449)*

**Pavilions, Pleasanton** *Also Called: Vons Companies Inc (P-17389)*

**Paw Prints Inc** ....................................................................................... F ...... 650 365-4077
3166 Bay Rd Redwood City (94063) *(P-4937)*

**Pawloyalty Software Inc** ..................................................................... F ...... 866 594-6848
876 4th St E Sonoma (95476) *(P-18662)*

**Pax Labs Inc** ......................................................................................... C ...... 415 829-2336
660 Alabama St Ste 2 San Francisco (94110) *(P-4)*

**Pax Tag & Label Inc** ............................................................................ E ...... 626 579-2000
9528 Rush St Ste C El Monte (91733) *(P-4938)*

**Paxata Inc** .............................................................................................. D ...... 650 542-7897
1800 Seaport Blvd # 1 Redwood City (94063) *(P-18663)*

**Paydarfar Industries Inc** ...................................................................... D ...... 949 481-3267
26054 Acero Mission Viejo (92691) *(P-16537)*

**Payjoy Inc (PA)** ..................................................................................... E ...... 888 632-1922
655 4th St San Francisco (94107) *(P-18664)*

**Payless Kitchen Cabinets, Glendale** *Also Called: Carpet Wagon-Glendale Inc (P-3230)*

**Paylocity Holding Corporation** .......................................................... A ...... 847 956-4850
2107 Livingston St Oakland (94606) *(P-18665)*

**Payne Magnetics Corporation** ........................................................... D ...... 626 332-6207
854 W Front St Covina (91722) *(P-12851)*

**Paysonic, Union City** *Also Called: Spacesonics Incorporated (P-8576)*

**Pazo Inc** ................................................................................................. E ...... 786 786-1195
505 Cento Ct Pleasanton (94566) *(P-18666)*

**Pb Fasteners, Gardena** *Also Called: Paul R Briles Inc (P-8764)*

**Pb Loader Corporation** ....................................................................... E ...... 800 350-8521
5778 W Barstow Ave Fresno (93722) *(P-9434)*

**Pbb Inc** .................................................................................................. E ...... 909 923-6250
1311 E Philadelphia St Ontario (91761) *(P-16759)*

**Pbc Companies, Anaheim** *Also Called: Peterson Brothers Cnstr Inc (P-524)*

**Pbf & E LLC** .......................................................................................... E ...... 213 427-0340
3014 W Olympic Blvd Los Angeles (90006) *(P-17600)*

**Pbk International LLC** ......................................................................... E ...... 866 727-7195
717 E Compton Blvd Rancho Dominguez (90220) *(P-17523)*

**PBM Supply & Mfg Inc** ........................................................................ E ...... 530 345-1334
324 Meyers St Chico (95928) *(P-16887)*

**PC Cleaner, Pasadena** *Also Called: Realdefense LLC (P-19060)*

**PC Mechanical Inc** ............................................................................... E ...... 805 925-2888
2803 Industrial Pkwy Santa Maria (93455) *(P-267)*

**PC Specialists Inc (HQ)** ...................................................................... C ...... 858 566-1900
11860 Community Rd Ste 160 Poway (92064) *(P-16538)*

**PC Vaughan Mfg Corp** ........................................................................ D ...... 805 278-2555
1278 Mercantile St Oxnard (93030) *(P-6952)*

**PC World Magazine, San Francisco** *Also Called: Idg Consumer & Smb Inc (P-4266)*

**PCA, Santa Clara** *Also Called: Polishing Corporation America (P-12634)*

**PCA Aerospace Inc (PA)** .................................................................... D ...... 714 841-1750
17800 Gothard St Huntington Beach (92647) *(P-13924)*

# ALPHABETIC SECTION — Pelco Inc

**PCA Aerospace Inc** .................................................. E ...... 714 901-5209
15282 Newsboy Cir Huntington Beach (92649) *(P-13925)*

**PCA Central Cal Corrugated LLC** ............................ D ...... 916 614-0580
4841 Urbani Ave Mcclellan (95652) *(P-3877)*

**PCA/Los Angeles 349, Vernon** *Also Called: Packaging Corporation America (P-3873)*

**PCA/South Gate 378, South Gate** *Also Called: Packaging Corporation America (P-3875)*

**Pcb Fabrication Facility, San Marcos** *Also Called: Hughes Circuits Inc (P-12131)*

**Pcbc Holdco Inc** .......................................................... E ...... 562 944-9549
12748 Florence Ave Santa Fe Springs (90670) *(P-16888)*

**PCC Aerostructures, North Hollywood** *Also Called: Klune Industries Inc (P-13887)*

**PCC Fluid Fittings, Gardena** *Also Called: Precision Castparts Corp (P-7694)*

**PCC Network Solutions, Chatsworth** *Also Called: Pacific Coast Cabling Inc (P-465)*

**PCC Rollmet Inc** .......................................................... D ...... 949 221-5333
1822 Deere Ave Irvine (92606) *(P-7712)*

**PCC Structurals Inc** .................................................... C ...... 510 568-6400
414 Hester St San Leandro (94577) *(P-7869)*

**PCC Structurals-San Leandro, San Leandro** *Also Called: PCC Structurals Inc (P-7869)*

**PCF Group LLC** ........................................................... F ...... 858 455-1274
8585 Miramar Pl San Diego (92121) *(P-17304)*

**Pcfs 2000, San Diego** *Also Called: Pcfs Solutions (P-17557)*

**Pcfs Solutions** ............................................................. E ...... 714 674-0009
6353 El Cajon Blvd Ste 124 San Diego (92115) *(P-17557)*

**Pch Sheet Metal & AC Inc** ........................................... F ...... 949 361-9905
118 Calle De Los Molinos San Clemente (92672) *(P-8531)*

**PCI, Riverside** *Also Called: Pacific Consolidated Inds LLC (P-10103)*

**PCI, Santa Rosa** *Also Called: Paragon Controls Incorporated (P-14366)*

**PCI Industries Inc** ....................................................... E ...... 323 889-6770
700 S Vail Ave Montebello (90640) *(P-8532)*

**PCI Industries Inc** ....................................................... E ...... 323 728-0004
6501 Potello St Commerce (90040) *(P-8533)*

**PCI Industries Inc** ....................................................... E ...... 323 889-6770
700 S Vail Ave Montebello (90640) *(P-16197)*

**PCI Industries Inc** ....................................................... E ...... 323 728-0004
6490 Fleet St Commerce (90040) *(P-16198)*

**Pct, Compton** *Also Called: Pacific Contntl Textiles Inc (P-2506)*

**Pct Enterprises Inc** ..................................................... C ...... 925 412-3341
4255 Hopyard Rd Pleasanton (94588) *(P-3582)*

**Pct Enterprises Inc (PA)** .............................................. D ...... 925 634-5552
145 Middlefield Ct Brentwood (94513) *(P-3583)*

**Pct-Gw Carbide Tools Usa Inc** ................................... F ...... 562 921-7898
13701 Excelsior Dr Santa Fe Springs (90670) *(P-5108)*

**Pcx Aerosystems - Santa Ana, Santa Ana** *Also Called: Integral Aerospace LLC (P-13874)*

**Pd Group** ..................................................................... E ...... 760 674-3028
41945 Boardwalk Ste L Palm Desert (92211) *(P-16020)*

**Pdc-Identicard, Valencia** *Also Called: Precision Dynamics Corporation (P-3953)*

**Pdf Print Communications Inc (PA)** ........................... D ...... 562 426-6978
2630 E 28th St Long Beach (90755) *(P-4721)*

**PDF SOLUTIONS, Santa Clara** *Also Called: Pdf Solutions Inc (P-18667)*

**Pdf Solutions Inc (PA)** ................................................ C ...... 408 280-7900
2858 De La Cruz Blvd Santa Clara (95050) *(P-18667)*

**PDM Solutions Inc** ...................................................... E ...... 858 348-1000
8451 Miralani Dr Ste J San Diego (92126) *(P-12188)*

**PDM Steel Service Centers Inc** .................................. E ...... 408 988-3000
3500 Bassett St Santa Clara (95054) *(P-16628)*

**PDM Steel Service Centers Inc (HQ)** ......................... D ...... 209 943-0513
3535 E Myrtle St Stockton (95205) *(P-16629)*

**Pdma Ventures Inc** ..................................................... E ...... 714 777-8770
22951 La Palma Ave Yorba Linda (92887) *(P-15476)*

**Pdplay, Escondido** *Also Called: Progressive Design Playgrounds (P-569)*

**Pdu Lad Corporation (PA)** ........................................... E ...... 626 442-7711
11165 Valley Spring Ln North Hollywood (91602) *(P-9102)*

**Peabody Engineering, Corona** *Also Called: Peabody Engineering & Sup Inc (P-9889)*

**Peabody Engineering & Sup Inc** ................................ E ...... 951 734-7711
13435 Estelle St Corona (92879) *(P-9889)*

**Peaches, Sherman Oaks** *Also Called: Med Couture Inc (P-2598)*

**Peak Plastics, San Jose** *Also Called: Peak Technology Entps Inc (P-17230)*

**Peak Property Management Sftwr, Berkeley** *Also Called: I Manageproperty Inc (P-18397)*

**Peak Technology Inc** .................................................. F ...... 760 745-8297
1835 S Centre City Pkwy Escondido (92025) *(P-12629)*

**Peak Technology Entps Inc** ....................................... E ...... 408 748-1102
6951 Via Del Oro San Jose (95119) *(P-17230)*

**Peanut Shell, Union City** *Also Called: Farallon Brands Inc (P-15748)*

**Pearl Crop Inc** ............................................................. E ...... 209 982-9933
17641 French Camp Rd Ripon (95366) *(P-1372)*

**Pearl Crop Inc** ............................................................. E ...... 209 887-3731
8452 Demartini Ln Linden (95236) *(P-2316)*

**Pearl Therapeutics Inc** ............................................... D ...... 650 305-2600
200 Cardinal Way Redwood City (94063) *(P-5595)*

**Pearson Engineering Corp** ........................................ F ...... 626 442-7436
2505 Loma Ave South El Monte (91733) *(P-9103)*

**Pebble Mobility Inc** ..................................................... E ...... 650 209-0799
2800 Bayview Dr Fremont (94538) *(P-13555)*

**PEC, Torrance** *Also Called: Products Engineering Corp (P-7964)*

**PEC Tool, Torrance** *Also Called: Fun Properties Inc (P-7953)*

**Pecc, San Diego** *Also Called: Precision Engine Controls Corp (P-9314)*

**Pacific Grinding, Fullerton** *Also Called: Kryler Corp (P-8978)*

**Peck Road Gravel Pit** .................................................. F ...... 626 574-7570
128 Live Oak Ave Monrovia (91016) *(P-319)*

**Peco Inspx** ................................................................... F ...... 209 576-3345
1616 Culpepper Ave Ste A Modesto (95351) *(P-11339)*

**Pedavena Mould and Die Co Inc** ............................... E ...... 310 327-2814
12464 Mccann Dr Santa Fe Springs (90670) *(P-11035)*

**Pedego LLC (PA)** ........................................................ E ...... 800 646-8604
11230 Grace Ave Fountain Valley (92708) *(P-17635)*

**Pedego Electric Bikes, Fountain Valley** *Also Called: Pedego LLC (P-17635)*

**Pedi, San Diego** *Also Called: Providien Injction Molding Inc (P-6988)*

**Peei, Los Angeles** *Also Called: Playboy Enterprises Intl Inc (P-4450)*

**Peerles Coffee and Tea, Oakland** *Also Called: Peerless Coffee Company Inc (P-2076)*

**Peerless Coffee Company Inc** .................................. D ...... 510 763-1763
260 Oak St Oakland (94607) *(P-2076)*

**Peerless Injection Molding LLC** ............................... E ...... 714 689-1920
14321 Corp Dr Garden Grove (92843) *(P-6953)*

**Peerless Materials Company** ................................... E ...... 323 266-0313
4442 E 26th St Vernon (90058) *(P-5925)*

**Peet's Coffee, Emeryville** *Also Called: Peets Coffee Inc (P-17431)*

**Peets Coffee Inc (DH)** ................................................ D ...... 510 594-2100
1400 Park Ave Emeryville (94608) *(P-17431)*

**Peets Coffee & Tea LLC (DH)** .................................... E ...... 510 594-2100
1400 Park Ave Emeryville (94608) *(P-2077)*

**Peets Coffee & Tea LLC** ............................................. E ...... 408 558-9535
1875 S Bascom Ave Campbell (95008) *(P-2078)*

**Pega Precision Inc** ..................................................... E ...... 408 776-3700
18800 Adams Ct Morgan Hill (95037) *(P-8534)*

**Pegasus Foods, Los Angeles** *Also Called: Astrochef LLC (P-1026)*

**Pegasus Interprint Inc** ............................................... E ...... 800 926-9873
7111 Hayvenhurst Ave Van Nuys (91406) *(P-4722)*

**Pegasus One, Fullerton** *Also Called: Aspirez Inc (P-17883)*

**Pegasus Solar, Richmond** *Also Called: Pegasus Solar Inc (P-17342)*

**Pegasus Solar Inc** ...................................................... E ...... 510 210-3797
506 W Ohio Ave Richmond (94804) *(P-17342)*

**Peggs Company Inc (PA)** .......................................... C ...... 800 242-8416
4851 Felspar St Riverside (92509) *(P-19275)*

**Peggy S Lane Inc** ....................................................... D ...... 510 483-1202
2701 Merced St San Leandro (94577) *(P-6684)*

**Peju Province Winery, Rutherford** *Also Called: Peju Prvnce Wnery A Cal Ltd PR (P-17629)*

**Peju Prvnce Wnery A Cal Ltd PR** .............................. D ...... 800 446-7358
8466 Saint Helena Hwy Rutherford (94573) *(P-17629)*

**Peking Noodle Co Inc** ................................................ E ...... 323 223-0897
1514 N San Fernando Rd Los Angeles (90065) *(P-2118)*

**Pel Manufacturing and Lsg Corp** .............................. F ...... 310 530-7145
3200 Kashiwa St Torrance (90505) *(P-5013)*

**Pel Mfg & Leasing, Torrance** *Also Called: Pel Manufacturing and Lsg Corp (P-5013)*

**Pel Wholesale Inc** ...................................................... E ...... 925 373-3628
6818 Patterson Pass Rd # H Livermcre (94550) *(P-16984)*

**Pelagic Pressure Systems Corp** .............................. D ...... 510 569-3100
480 Mccormick St San Leandro (94577) *(P-9687)*

**Pelco, Fresno** *Also Called: Pelco Inc (P-19059)*

**Pelco Inc (HQ)** ............................................................ A ...... 559 292-1981
625 W Alluvial Ave Fresno (93711) *(P-19059)*

**Pelican, Torrance** *Also Called: Pelican Products Inc (P-11618)*
**Pelican Products Inc (PA)**..........................................................C ...... 310 326-4700
  23215 Early Ave Torrance (90505) *(P-11618)*
**Pelican Rope Works** ................................................................F ...... 714 545-0116
  1600 E Mcfadden Ave Santa Ana (92705) *(P-2538)*
**Pelicantunes Inc** ......................................................................F ...... 925 838-8484
  3950 Valley Ave Ste A Pleasanton (94566) *(P-19310)*
**Pellenc America Inc (DH)** ........................................................E ...... 707 568-7286
  3171 Guerneville Rd Santa Rosa (95401) *(P-9375)*
**Peltek Holdings Inc** ..................................................................E ...... 949 855-8010
  35 Argonaut Ste A1 Laguna Hills (92656) *(P-9104)*
**Peltier Winery, Acampo** *Also Called: R & G Schatz Farms Inc (P-24)*
**Pelton-Shepherd Industries Inc (PA)**......................................E ...... 209 460-0893
  812 W Luce St Ste B Stockton (95203) *(P-2112)*
**Peluso Cheese, Los Banos** *Also Called: Romalv Group LLC (P-731)*
**Pem, Buena Park** *Also Called: Park Engineering and Mfg Co (P-11032)*
**Pemko Manufacturing Co** ........................................................C ...... 800 283-9988
  4226 Transport St Ventura (93003) *(P-8283)*
**Pen Manufacturing, Anaheim** *Also Called: Pen Manufacturing LLC (P-11036)*
**Pen Manufacturing LLC** ...........................................................E ...... 714 992-0950
  1808 N American St Anaheim (92801) *(P-11036)*
**Pencil Grip Inc (PA)**.................................................................F ...... 310 315-3545
  21200 Superior St Ste A Chatsworth (91311) *(P-4021)*
**Pendulum Instruments, Redwood City** *Also Called: Pendulum Instruments Inc (P-13286)*
**Pendulum Instruments Inc** ......................................................E ...... 866 644-1230
  1123 Madison Ave Redwood City (94061) *(P-13286)*
**Penfield Products Inc** ..............................................................E ...... 916 635-0231
  11300 Trade Center Dr Ste A Rancho Cordova (95742) *(P-8535)*
**Pengcheng Aluminum Enterprise Inc USA** ............................E ...... 909 598-7933
  19605 E Walnut Dr N Walnut (91789) *(P-7745)*
**Pengo Wireline of California Inc** .............................................F ...... 661 327-9900
  3529 Standard St Bakersfield (93308) *(P-268)*
**Penguin Natural Foods Inc** ......................................................E ...... 323 488-6000
  5659 Mansfield Way Bell (90201) *(P-2317)*
**Penguin Natural Foods Inc (PA)**..............................................E ...... 323 727-7980
  4400 Alcoa Ave Vernon (90058) *(P-2318)*
**Penguin Pumps Incorporated** ..................................................E ...... 818 504-2391
  7932 Ajay Dr Sun Valley (91352) *(P-9933)*
**Penguin Solutions, Milpitas** *Also Called: Penguin Solutions Inc (P-12630)*
**Penguin Solutions Inc (PA)**......................................................C ...... 510 623-1231
  1390 Mccarthy Blvd Milpitas (95035) *(P-12630)*
**Peninsula Metal Fabrication, San Jose** *Also Called: Hardcraft Industries Inc (P-8466)*
**Peninsula Metal Fabrication, San Jose** *Also Called: I & A Inc (P-8471)*
**Peninsula Packaging LLC (DH)**................................................D ...... 559 594-6813
  1030 N Anderson Rd Exeter (93221) *(P-16199)*
**Peninsula Publishing Inc** .........................................................E ...... 949 631-1307
  1602 Monrovia Ave Newport Beach (92663) *(P-4445)*
**Peninsula Road Materials, Redwood City** *Also Called: Granite Rock Company (P-6364)*
**Peninsula Spring Corporation** .................................................F ...... 408 848-3361
  6750 Silacci Way Gilroy (95020) *(P-9205)*
**Penn Elcom Inc (HQ)** ...............................................................E ...... 714 230-6200
  7465 Lampson Ave Garden Grove (92841) *(P-16760)*
**Penn Elcom Hardware, Garden Grove** *Also Called: Penn Elcom Inc (P-16760)*
**Penn Engineering Components** ...............................................E ...... 818 503-1511
  29045 Avenue Penn Valencia (91355) *(P-16761)*
**Pennoyer-Dodge Co** .................................................................E ...... 818 547-2100
  6650 San Fernando Rd Glendale (91201) *(P-9688)*
**Penny & Giles Drive Technology, Brea** *Also Called: Curtiss-Wrght Cntrls Intgrted (P-15330)*
**Penny Ice Creamery, The, Santa Cruz** *Also Called: Glass Jar Inc (P-803)*
**Pennysaver USA Publishing LLC** ............................................A ...... 866 640-3900
  2830 Orbiter St Brea (92821) *(P-4446)*
**Penrose Studios Inc** ................................................................F ...... 703 354-1801
  223 Mississippi St Ste 3 San Francisco (94107) *(P-4447)*
**Pensieve Foods** .......................................................................E ...... 323 938-8666
  1782 Industrial Way Los Angeles (90023) *(P-2319)*
**Penta Financial Inc** ..................................................................F ...... 818 882-3872
  14399 Princeton Ave Moorpark (93021) *(P-12037)*
**Penta Laboratories, Moorpark** *Also Called: Penta Financial Inc (P-12037)*
**Penta Laboratories LLC** ..........................................................F ...... 818 882-3872
  14399 Princeton Ave Moorpark (93021) *(P-12038)*

**Pentacare Skin Systems, San Dimas** *Also Called: New Spirit Naturals Inc (P-19319)*
**Pentair, San Diego** *Also Called: EMR Final Ctrl US Holdg Corp (P-9920)*
**Pentair Equipment Protection, San Diego** *Also Called: Schroff Inc (P-19178)*
**Pentair Water Treatment, Costa Mesa** *Also Called: Shurflo LLC (P-9940)*
**Pentel of America Ltd (DH)**.....................................................C ...... 310 320-3831
  2715 Columbia St Torrance (90503) *(P-16992)*
**Pentrate Metal Processing** .....................................................E ...... 323 269-2121
  3517 E Olympic Blvd Los Angeles (90023) *(P-8994)*
**PENUMBRA, Alameda** *Also Called: Penumbra Inc (P-15221)*
**Penumbra Inc (PA)**..................................................................B ...... 510 748-3200
  1 Penumbra Alameda (94502) *(P-15221)*
**Penwal Industries Inc** .............................................................D ...... 909 466-1555
  10611 Acacia St Rancho Cucamonga (91730) *(P-369)*
**People Center Inc** ...................................................................E ...... 415 737-5780
  430 California St San Francisco (94104) *(P-18668)*
**Peopleadmin Inc (DH)**.............................................................E ...... 877 637-5800
  150 Parkshore Dr Folsom (95630) *(P-18669)*
**Peoplefinders Ngt Por Priof** ...................................................E ...... 916 341-0227
  1915 21st St Sacramento (95811) *(P-4448)*
**Peoplesense, Rancho Murieta** *Also Called: Glocol Inc (P-16275)*
**Pep West, Inc., San Diego** *Also Called: Schroff Inc (P-9939)*
**Pepper Plant, The, Gilroy** *Also Called: Blossom Valley Foods Inc (P-1989)*
**Pepsi Beverages, Fresno** *Also Called: Bottling Group LLC (P-1869)*
**Pepsi Beverages, Fresno** *Also Called: Bottling Group LLC (P-1871)*
**Pepsi Co, Oakland** *Also Called: Svc Mfg Inc A Corp (P-1967)*
**Pepsi-Cola, Mojave** *Also Called: Pepsi-Cola Metro Btlg Co Inc (P-1911)*
**Pepsi-Cola, Buena Park** *Also Called: Pepsi-Cola Metro Btlg Co Inc (P-1913)*
**Pepsi-Cola, Santa Clara** *Also Called: Pepsi-Cola Metro Btlg Co Inc (P-1914)*
**Pepsi-Cola, Carson** *Also Called: Pepsi-Cola Metro Btlg Co Inc (P-1915)*
**Pepsi-Cola, Benicia** *Also Called: Pepsi-Cola Metro Btlg Co Inc (P-1917)*
**Pepsi-Cola, San Fernando** *Also Called: Pepsi-Cola Metro Btlg Co Inc (P-1919)*
**Pepsi-Cola, Hayward** *Also Called: Pepsi-Cola Metro Btlg Co Inc (P-1920)*
**Pepsi-Cola, Sacramento** *Also Called: Pepsi-Cola Metro Btlg Co Inc (P-1922)*
**Pepsi-Cola, Fresno** *Also Called: Roger Enrico (P-1956)*
**Pepsi-Cola, Riverside** *Also Called: Pepsi-Cola Metro Btlg Co Inc (P-16786)*
**Pepsi-Cola, Santa Rosa** *Also Called: Pepsi-Cola Metro Btlg Co Inc (P-17204)*
**Pepsi-Cola Bottling Group** ......................................................D ...... 661 635-1100
  215 E 21st St Bakersfield (93305) *(P-1910)*
**Pepsi-Cola Metro Btlg Co Inc** .................................................E ...... 661 824-2051
  2471 Nadeau St Mojave (93501) *(P-1911)*
**Pepsi-Cola Metro Btlg Co Inc** .................................................E ...... 805 739-2160
  2345 Thompson Way Santa Maria (93455) *(P-1912)*
**Pepsi-Cola Metro Btlg Co Inc** .................................................C ...... 714 522-9635
  6261 Caballero Blvd Buena Park (90620) *(P-1913)*
**Pepsi-Cola Metro Btlg Co Inc** .................................................E ...... 408 617-2200
  4699 Old Ironsides Dr Ste 150 Santa Clara (95054) *(P-1914)*
**Pepsi-Cola Metro Btlg Co Inc** .................................................C ...... 310 327-4222
  19700 Figueroa St Carson (90745) *(P-1915)*
**Pepsi-Cola Metro Btlg Co Inc** .................................................D ...... 209 367-7140
  4225 Pepsi Pl Stockton (95215) *(P-1916)*
**Pepsi-Cola Metro Btlg Co Inc** .................................................D ...... 707 746-5404
  4701 Park Rd Benicia (94510) *(P-1917)*
**Pepsi-Cola Metro Btlg Co Inc** .................................................C ...... 858 560-6735
  10057 Marathon Pkwy Lakeside (92040) *(P-1918)*
**Pepsi-Cola Metro Btlg Co Inc** .................................................D ...... 818 898-3829
  1200 Arroyo St San Fernando (91340) *(P-1919)*
**Pepsi-Cola Metro Btlg Co Inc** .................................................C ...... 510 781-3600
  29000 Hesperian Blvd Hayward (94545) *(P-1920)*
**Pepsi-Cola Metro Btlg Co Inc** .................................................D ...... 949 643-5700
  27717 Aliso Creek Rd Aliso Viejo (92656) *(P-1921)*
**Pepsi-Cola Metro Btlg Co Inc** .................................................C ...... 916 423-1000
  7550 Reese Rd Sacramento (95828) *(P-1922)*
**Pepsi-Cola Metro Btlg Co Inc** .................................................E ...... 951 697-3200
  6659 Sycamore Canyon Blvd Riverside (92507) *(P-16786)*
**Pepsi-Cola Metro Btlg Co Inc** .................................................D ...... 707 535-4560
  3029 Coffey Ln Santa Rosa (95403) *(P-17204)*
**Pepsico** ....................................................................................E ...... 562 818-9429
  1650 E Central Ave San Bernardino (92408) *(P-1923)*
**Pepsico, Riverside** *Also Called: Bottling Group LLC (P-1872)*

# ALPHABETIC SECTION                                                                                   Petra

Pepsico, Redding *Also Called: John Fitzpatrick & Sons (P-1896)*
Pepsico, Bakersfield *Also Called: Pepsi-Cola Bottling Group (P-1910)*
Pepsico, Santa Maria *Also Called: Pepsi-Cola Metro Btlg Co Inc (P-1912)*
Pepsico, Stockton *Also Called: Pepsi-Cola Metro Btlg Co Inc (P-1916)*
Pepsico, Lakeside *Also Called: Pepsi-Cola Metro Btlg Co Inc (P-1918)*
Pepsico, Aliso Viejo *Also Called: Pepsi-Cola Metro Btlg Co Inc (P-1921)*
Pepsico, Beverly Hills *Also Called: Pepsico Inc (P-1924)*
Pepsico, Baldwin Park *Also Called: Pepsico Inc (P-1925)*
Pepsico, Walnut *Also Called: Pepsico Inc (P-1926)*

Pepsico Inc ............................................................................ F ...... 323 785-2820
 8530 Wilshire Blvd Ste 300 Beverly Hills (90211) *(P-1924)*

Pepsico Inc ............................................................................ E ...... 626 338-5531
 4416 Azusa Canyon Rd Baldwin Park (91706) *(P-1925)*

Pepsico Inc ............................................................................ E ...... 909 718-8229
 20445 Business Pkwy Walnut (91789) *(P-1926)*

Peraton Technology Svcs Inc .......................................... E ...... 571 313-6000
 2750 Womble Rd Ste 202 San Diego (92106) *(P-19495)*

Perceptimed Inc ................................................................. E ...... 650 941-7000
 365 San Antonio Rd Mountain View (94040) *(P-9890)*

Perera Cnstr & Design Inc .............................................. E ...... 909 484-6350
 2890 Inland Empire Blvd Ste 102 Ontario (91764) *(P-109)*

Perez Distributing Fresno Inc (PA) ................................. F ...... 800 638-3512
 103 S Academy Ave Sanger (93657) *(P-5596)*

Perfect Banner, The, Aliso Viejo *Also Called: Perfect Impression Inc (P-19116)*

Perfect Choice Mfrs Inc .................................................... E ...... 714 792-0322
 17819 Gillette Ave Irvine (92614) *(P-16200)*

Perfect Impression Inc ..................................................... E ...... 949 305-0797
 27111 Aliso Creek Rd Ste 145 Aliso Viejo (92656) *(P-19116)*

Perfect Puree of NAPA Vly LLC ..................................... F ...... 707 261-5100
 2700 Napa Valley Corporate Dr Napa (94558) *(P-1015)*

Perfection Pet Foods, LLC, Visalia *Also Called: Kruse Pet Holdings LLC (P-1106)*
Performance Aluminum, Ontario *Also Called: Performance Aluminum Products (P-7817)*

Performance Aluminum Products .................................. E ...... 909 391-4131
 520 S Palmetto Ave Ontario (91762) *(P-7817)*

Performance Coatings Inc ............................................... E ...... 707 462-3023
 360 Lake Mendocino Dr Ukiah (95482) *(P-6100)*

Performance Composites Inc ......................................... C ...... 310 328-6661
 1418 S Alameda St Compton (90221) *(P-7201)*

Performance Forge Inc .................................................... E ...... 323 722-3460
 7401 Telegraph Rd Montebello (90640) *(P-8785)*

Performance Machine, La Palma *Also Called: Performance Machine Inc (P-14066)*

Performance Machine Inc ............................................... C ...... 714 523-3000
 6892 Marlin Cir La Palma (90623) *(P-14066)*

Performance Machine Tech Inc ..................................... E ...... 661 294-8617
 25141 Avenue Stanford Valencia (91355) *(P-11037)*

Performance Materials Corp (HQ) ................................. D ...... 805 482-1722
 1150 Calle Suerte Camarillo (93012) *(P-5185)*

Performance Matters LLC (DH) ..................................... F ...... 801 453-0136
 150 Parkshore Dr Folsom (95630) *(P-18670)*

Performance Motorsports Inc ......................................... B ...... 714 898-9763
 5100 Campus Dr Ste 100 Newport Beach (92660) *(P-10623)*

Performance Pipe Div, San Ramon *Also Called: Chevron Phillips Chem Co LP (P-5145)*
Performance Plastics, San Diego *Also Called: Rock West Composites Inc (P-5196)*

Performance Plastics Inc ................................................. D ...... 714 343-3928
 7919 Saint Andrews Ave San Diego (92154) *(P-13926)*

Performance Polymer Tech LLC ................................... E ...... 916 677-1414
 8801 Washington Blvd Ste 109 Roseville (95678) *(P-6475)*

Performance Powder Inc ................................................. E ...... 714 632-0600
 2940 E La Jolla St Ste A Anaheim (92806) *(P-9105)*

Performance Trailer Inc ................................................... E ...... 559 673-6300
 2901 Falcon Dr Madera (93637) *(P-17489)*

Performance Water Products Inc .................................. F ...... 714 736-0137
 6902 Aragon Cir Buena Park (90620) *(P-17680)*

Performex Machining Inc ................................................ E ...... 650 595-2228
 963 Terminal Way San Carlos (94070) *(P-11038)*

Performnce Engineered Pdts Inc .................................. E ...... 909 594-7487
 3270 Pomona Blvd Pomona (91768) *(P-6954)*

Perfumer's Apprentice, Scotts Valley *Also Called: Pacific Coast Ingredients (P-2018)*
Perfumer's Apprentice, Scotts Valley *Also Called: Pacific Coast Ingredients (P-2019)*

Pericom Semiconductor Corp (HQ) ............................... D ...... 408 232-9100
 1545 Barber Ln Milpitas (95035) *(P-14570)*

Peridot Corporation ........................................................... D ...... 925 461-8830
 1072 Serpentine Ln Pleasanton (94566) *(P-8875)*

Perillo Industries Inc ......................................................... E ...... 805 498-9838
 2150 Anchor Ct Ste A Newbury Park (91320) *(P-16729)*

Perimeter Solutions LP .................................................... E ...... 909 983-0772
 10667 Jersey Blvd Rancho Cucamonga (91730) *(P-5109)*

Periscope LLC ................................................................... E ...... 323 327-5115
 3247 Bennett Dr Los Angeles (90068) *(P-14812)*

Perm Light, Tustin *Also Called: Permlight Products Inc (P-12631)*
Permaswage USA, Gardena *Also Called: Designed Metal Connections Inc (P-13822)*

Permlight Products Inc .................................................... E ...... 714 508-0729
 420 W 6th St Tustin (92780) *(P-12631)*

Pernod Ricard Usa LLC ................................................... D ...... 707 833-5891
 9592 Sonoma Hwy Kenwood (95452) *(P-1704)*

Pernod Ricard Usa LLC ................................................... D ...... 707 967-7770
 8445 Silverado Trl Rutherford (94573) *(P-1705)*

Perricone Juices, Beaumont *Also Called: Beaumont Juice LLC (P-877)*
Perrin Craft, San Marcos *Also Called: Dispensing Dynamics Intl Inc (P-6804)*
Perry Industries, Corona *Also Called: M & O Perry Industries Inc (P-10025)*

Perrys Custom Chopping LLC ...................................... F ...... 209 667-8777
 21365 Williams Ave Hilmar (95324) *(P-9376)*

Perseption, Vernon *Also Called: W & W Concept Inc (P-2822)*
Persian Bks Englsh-Prsian Bks, Pacoima *Also Called: Ketab Corporation (P-17638)*

Person & Covey Inc .......................................................... E ...... 818 937-5000
 616 Allen Ave Glendale (91201) *(P-6018)*

Personnel Concepts, Ontario *Also Called: Aio Acquisition Inc (P-4361)*

Pertronix Inc ........................................................................ E ...... 909 599-5955
 15601 Cypress Ave Unit B Irwindale (91706) *(P-13180)*

Pesenti Winery, Saint Helena *Also Called: Turley Wine Cellars Inc (P-1804)*

Pet Partners Inc (PA) ....................................................... C ...... 951 279-9888
 450 N Sheridan St Corona (92878) *(P-16201)*

Petadata Software LLC ................................................... E ...... 203 306-9949
 39159 Paseo Padre Pkwy Ste 116 Fremont (94538) *(P-18671)*

Petaluma Acquisitions LLC ............................................ D ...... 707 763-1904
 2700 Lakeville Hwy Petaluma (94954) *(P-699)*

Petaluma Acquistion LLC ............................................... C ...... 707 763-1904
 1500 Cader Ln Petaluma (94954) *(P-700)*

Petaluma Poultry Processors, Petaluma *Also Called: Petaluma Acquistion LLC (P-700)*

Petalumaidence Opco LLC ............................................ C ...... 707 763-4109
 101 Monroe St Petaluma (94954) *(P-1706)*

Petco, Los Angeles *Also Called: Petco Animal Sups Stores Inc (P-17716)*

Petco Animal Sups Stores Inc ....................................... F ...... 323 852-1370
 8161 Beverly Blvd Los Angeles (90048) *(P-17716)*

Petcube Inc (PA) ............................................................... E ...... 424 302-6107
 555 De Haro St Ste 280a San Francisco (94107) *(P-11686)*

Peter ..................................................................................... E ...... 916 588-9954
 2850 Gateway Oaks Dr Sacramento (95833) *(P-3993)*

Peter Brasseler Holdings LLC ....................................... D ...... 805 658-2643
 4837 Mcgrath St Ventura (93003) *(P-15222)*

Peter Brasseler Holdings LLC ....................................... D ...... 805 650-5209
 4837 Mcgrath St J Ventura (93003) *(P-16587)*

Peter Cohen Companies, Los Angeles *Also Called: Piet Retief Inc (P-2800)*

Peter Grimm Ltd ................................................................ E ...... 800 664-4287
 550 Rancheros Dr San Marcos (92069) *(P-2849)*

Peter Michael Winery, Calistoga *Also Called: Sugarloaf Farming Corporation (P-1766)*
Petersen Precision, Redwood City *Also Called: Petersen Precision Engrg LLC (P-11039)*

Petersen Precision Engrg LLC ...................................... C ...... 650 365-4373
 611 Broadway St Redwood City (94063) *(P-11039)*

Peterson Brothers Cnstr Inc ........................................... A ...... 714 278-0488
 2929 E White Star Ave Anaheim (92806) *(P-524)*

Peterson's Spices, Pico Rivera *Also Called: GPde Slva Spces Incrporation (P-2223)*

Petes Road Service Inc (PA) ......................................... D ...... 714 446-1207
 2230 E Orangethorpe Ave Fullerton (92831) *(P-16409)*

Petit Pot LLC ...................................................................... E ...... 650 488-7432
 4221 Horton St Emeryville (94608) *(P-2320)*

Petits Pains & Co LP ........................................................ E ...... 650 692-6000
 1730 Gilbreth Rd Burlingame (94010) *(P-1237)*

Petra, San Francisco *Also Called: Arcbyt Inc (P-9408)*

# ALPHABETIC SECTION

Petra-1 LP ............................................................................. F ...... 866 334-3702
  12386 Osborne Pl Pacoima (91331) *(P-6019)*
Petro-Lud Inc ....................................................................... E ...... 661 747-4779
  12625 Jomani Dr Ste 104 Bakersfield (93312) *(P-165)*
Petrochem, Long Beach *Also Called: Petrochem Insulation Inc (P-480)*
Petrochem Insulation Inc ..................................................... C ...... 310 638-6663
  3117 E South St Long Beach (90805) *(P-480)*
Petrochem Manufacturing Inc .............................................. E ...... 760 603-0961
  6168 Innovation Way Carlsbad (92009) *(P-6368)*
Petroleum Sales Inc ............................................................ F ...... 415 256-1600
  2066 Redwood Hwy Greenbrae (94904) *(P-137)*
Petwise, Novato *Also Called: Worldwise Inc (P-17318)*
Pexco Aerospace Inc ........................................................... E ...... 714 894-9922
  5451 Argosy Ave Huntington Beach (92649) *(P-5186)*
Pezeme, Los Angeles *Also Called: Choon Inc (P-2703)*
Pezzi King Vineyards, Healdsburg *Also Called: Strategic Capital Incorporated (P-19539)*
Pf Bakeries Llc ..................................................................... E ...... 858 263-4863
  1375 Fayette St El Cajon (92020) *(P-17205)*
PF Candle Co ....................................................................... E ...... 323 284-8431
  2213 W Sunset Blvd Los Angeles (90026) *(P-16202)*
Pf Candle Co, Commerce *Also Called: Pommes Frites Candle Co (P-16206)*
Pfeiffer Vacuum Valves & Engrg, Yreka *Also Called: Nor-Cal Products Inc (P-9190)*
Pfenex, San Diego *Also Called: Pfenex Inc (P-5597)*
Pfenex Inc ............................................................................ D ...... 858 352-4400
  10790 Roselle St San Diego (92121) *(P-5597)*
Pfi Acquisition, Menlo Park *Also Called: Purfresh Inc (P-9893)*
Pfizer, San Diego *Also Called: Pfizer Inc (P-5598)*
Pfizer, San Diego *Also Called: Pfizer Inc (P-5599)*
Pfizer Inc ............................................................................... D ...... 858 622-3000
  10777 Science Center Dr San Diego (92121) *(P-5598)*
Pfizer Inc ............................................................................... D ...... 858 622-3001
  10646 Science Center Dr San Diego (92121) *(P-5599)*
Pfp, Chula Vista *Also Called: Precision Fiber Products Inc (P-7792)*
Pfs, Sylmar *Also Called: Professnal Fnshg Systems Sups (P-8877)*
PG Emminger Inc ................................................................. E ...... 925 313-5830
  4036 Pacheco Blvd # A Martinez (94553) *(P-3668)*
PG&e, Antioch *Also Called: Pacific Gas and Electric Co (P-16347)*
PG&e, San Francisco *Also Called: Pacific Gas and Electric Co (P-16348)*
Pgac Corp (PA) ..................................................................... D ...... 858 560-8213
  9630 Ridgehaven Ct Ste B San Diego (92123) *(P-3935)*
Pgc Construction Inc ........................................................... E ...... 760 549-4121
  41731 Corporate Center Ct Murrieta (92562) *(P-347)*
Pgc Scientiifics, San Diego *Also Called: Molecular Bioproducts Svc Corp (P-16603)*
Pgi, San Diego *Also Called: Pgac Corp (P-3935)*
Pgi, City Of Industry *Also Called: Pgi Pacific Graphics Intl (P-4723)*
Pgi Pacific Graphics Intl ...................................................... E ...... 626 336-7707
  14938 Nelson Ave City Of Industry (91744) *(P-4723)*
Pgp International Inc (DH) ................................................... C ...... 530 662-5056
  351 Hanson Way Woodland (95776) *(P-2321)*
PH Design, Commerce *Also Called: Pacific Hospitality Design Inc (P-3637)*
PH Dip Inc ............................................................................ E ...... 909 869-8083
  18560 San Jose Ave City Of Industry (91748) *(P-15763)*
PH Labs, San Diego *Also Called: Provision Health Corp (P-5615)*
Phantom Access Systems LLC ........................................... F ...... 949 753-1280
  631 Wald Irvine (92618) *(P-13287)*
Phantom Cyber Corporation ............................................... E ...... 650 208-5151
  2479 E Bayshore Rd Ste 185 Palo Alto (94303) *(P-18672)*
Phaostron Instr Electronic Co ............................................. D ...... 626 969-6801
  717 N Coney Ave Azusa (91702) *(P-11248)*
Phaostron Instr Electronic Co, Azusa *Also Called: Phaostron Instr Electronic Co (P-11248)*
Pharma Pac, Grover Beach *Also Called: H J Harkins Company Inc (P-5474)*
Pharmaceutic Litho Label Inc ............................................. D ...... 805 285-5162
  3990 Royal Ave Simi Valley (93063) *(P-5600)*
Pharmachem Laboratories LLC ......................................... E ...... 714 630-6000
  2929 E White Star Ave Anaheim (92806) *(P-779)*
PHARMACHEM LABORATORIES, LLC, Anaheim *Also Called: Pharmachem Laboratories LLC (P-779)*
Pharmaco-Kinesis Corporation ........................................... E ...... 310 641-2700
  10604 S La Cienega Blvd Inglewood (90304) *(P-15223)*

Pharmacyclics Inc ............................................................... A ...... 408 774-0330
  995 E Arques Ave Sunnyvale (94085) *(P-5601)*
Pharmacyclics LLC (HQ) ..................................................... D ...... 408 215-3000
  1000 Gateway Blvd South San Francisco (94080) *(P-5602)*
Pharmatek, San Diego *Also Called: Catalent Pharma Solutions Inc (P-5397)*
Pharmavite LLC (DH) ........................................................... B ...... 818 221-6200
  8531 Fallbrook Ave West Hills (91304) *(P-5261)*
Pharmavite LLC .................................................................... F ...... 818 221-6200
  1150 Aviation Pl San Fernando (91340) *(P-5262)*
Pharmion Corporation ......................................................... E ...... 858 335-5744
  12481 High Bluff Dr Ste 200 San Diego (92130) *(P-5603)*
Phase 2 Cellars LLC ............................................................ F ...... 805 782-0300
  4910 Edna Rd San Luis Obispo (93401) *(P-1707)*
Phase Four Inc .................................................................... F ...... 310 648-8454
  12605 S Van Ness Ave Hawthorne (90250) *(P-14104)*
Phase II, San Diego *Also Called: Phase II Products Inc (P-3725)*
Phase II Products Inc (PA) .................................................. F ...... 619 236-9699
  16875 W Bernardo Dr San Diego (92127) *(P-3725)*
Phatboykustomz, Rancho Dominguez *Also Called: Pbk International LLC (P-17523)*
PHC, Irvine *Also Called: Pacific Handy Cutter Inc (P-7962)*
PHC, Irvine *Also Called: PHC Merger Inc (P-7963)*
PHC Merger Inc .................................................................... E ...... 714 662-1033
  17819 Gillette Ave Irvine (92614) *(P-7963)*
PHC Sharp Holdings Inc (HQ) ............................................. E ...... 714 662-1033
  17819 Gillette Ave Irvine (92614) *(P-7940)*
Phenix Enterprises Inc (PA) ................................................ E ...... 909 469-0411
  1785 Mount Vernon Ave Pomona (91768) *(P-13423)*
Phenix Gourmet LLC ........................................................... C ...... 562 404-5028
  4225 N Palm St Fullerton (92835) *(P-1282)*
Phenix Technology, Riverside *Also Called: Phenix Technology Corporation (P-10105)*
Phenix Technology Corporation (PA) ................................. F ...... 951 272-4938
  3453 Durahart St Riverside (92507) *(P-10105)*
Phenix Truck Bodies and Eqp, Pomona *Also Called: Phenix Enterprises Inc (P-13423)*
Phenomenex Inc (HQ) ......................................................... C ...... 310 212-0555
  411 Madrid Ave Torrance (90501) *(P-14704)*
PHI (PA) ................................................................................ F ...... 626 968-9680
  14955 Salt Lake Ave City Of Industry (91746) *(P-9587)*
PHI Hydraulics, City Of Industry *Also Called: PHI (P-9587)*
Phiaro Incorporated ............................................................ E ...... 949 727-1261
  9016 Research Dr Irvine (92618) *(P-16203)*
Phibro Animal Health Corp ................................................. E ...... 562 698-8036
  8851 Dice Rd Santa Fe Springs (90670) *(P-6317)*
Phibro-Tech Inc ................................................................... E ...... 562 698-8036
  8851 Dice Rd Santa Fe Springs (90670) *(P-5110)*
Phifer Incorporated ............................................................. D ...... 626 968-0438
  14408 Nelson Ave City Of Industry (91744) *(P-9225)*
Phifer Western, City Of Industry *Also Called: Phifer Incorporated (P-9225)*
Phihong USA Corp (HQ) ...................................................... D ...... 510 445-0100
  47800 Fremont Blvd Fremont (94538) *(P-16539)*
Phil Wood & Company ........................................................ F ...... 408 298-1540
  1125 N 7th St # A San Jose (95112) *(P-9296)*
Philadelphia Gear, Santa Fe Springs *Also Called: Timken Gears & Services Inc (P-8789)*
Philatron International ........................................................ E ...... 562 802-2570
  15645 Clanton Cir Santa Fe Springs (90670) *(P-7791)*
Philatron International (PA) ................................................ D ...... 562 802-0452
  15315 Cornet St Santa Fe Springs (90670) *(P-13288)*
Philip B, West Hollywood *Also Called: Philip B Inc (P-5263)*
Philip B Inc .......................................................................... E ...... 888 376-8236
  9053 Nemo St West Hollywood (90069) *(P-5263)*
Philip B Botanicals Products ............................................. F ...... 202 759-0650
  9053 Nemo St West Hollywood (90069) *(P-6020)*
Philippe Charriol USA, San Diego *Also Called: Alor International Ltd (P-15680)*
Philips ................................................................................... D ...... 916 337-8008
  3721 Valley Centre Dr Ste 500 San Diego (92130) *(P-11687)*
Philips Image Gded Thrapy Corp (DH) ............................... B ...... 800 228-4728
  3721 Valley Centre Dr Ste 500 San Diego (92130) *(P-15572)*
Philips Image Gded Thrapy Corp ....................................... B ...... 916 281-2932
  2451 Mercantile Dr Ste 200 Rancho Cordova (95742) *(P-15573)*
Philips Lt-On Dgtal Sltons USA (DH) ................................. E ...... 510 687-1800
  720 S Hillview Dr Milpitas (95035) *(P-10264)*

## ALPHABETIC SECTION — Pinnacle Manufacturing Corp

Philips North America LLC .................................................. C ...... 909 574-1800
   11201 Iberia St Ste A Jurupa Valley (91752) *(P-11500)*

Philips Semiconductors, San Jose *Also Called: Nxp Usa Inc (P-12614)*

Phillips 66 Co Carbon Group .................................................. E ...... 805 489-4050
   2555 Willow Rd Arroyo Grande (93420) *(P-9891)*

Phillips Industries, Santa Fe Springs *Also Called: R A Phillips Industries Inc (P-13562)*

Phillps-Mdisize Costa Mesa LLC .................................................. C ...... 949 477-9495
   3545 Harbor Blvd Costa Mesa (92626) *(P-15224)*

Phoenix Cars LLC .................................................. E ...... 909 987-0815
   1500 Lakeview Loop Anaheim (92807) *(P-13375)*

Phoenix Cpitl Group Hldngs LLC .................................................. E ...... 303 749-0074
   18575 Jamboree Rd Ste 830 Irvine (92612) *(P-194)*

Phoenix Custom Packaging, Santa Fe Springs *Also Called: Camper Packaging LLC (P-752)*

Phoenix Day Inc .................................................. F ...... 415 822-4414
   3431 Regatta Blvd Richmond (94804) *(P-11501)*

Phoenix Deventures Inc .................................................. E ...... 408 782-6240
   18655 Madrone Pkwy Ste 180 Morgan Hill (95037) *(P-15225)*

Phoenix Engineering, Orange *Also Called: His Industries Inc (P-10020)*

Phoenix Footwear Group Inc (PA) .................................................. F ...... 760 602-9688
   2236 Rutherford Rd Ste 113 Carlsbad (92008) *(P-7111)*

Phoenix Marketing Services Inc .................................................. D ...... 909 399-4000
   651 Wharton Dr Claremont (91711) *(P-4724)*

Phoenix Motor Inc .................................................. E ...... 909 987-0815
   140 Blue Ravine Rd Folsom (95630) *(P-11377)*

Phoenix Motor Inc (DH) .................................................. E ...... 909 987-0815
   1500 Lakeview Loop Anaheim (92807) *(P-13556)*

Phoenix Motorcars, Anaheim *Also Called: Phoenix Cars LLC (P-13375)*

Phoenix Motorcars, Anaheim *Also Called: Phoenix Motor Inc (P-13556)*

Phoenix Pharmaceuticals Inc .................................................. E ...... 650 558-8898
   330 Beach Rd Burlingame (94010) *(P-5604)*

Phoenix Technologies Ltd (HQ) .................................................. E ...... 408 570-1000
   150 S Los Robles Ave Ste 500 Pasadena (91101) *(P-18673)*

Phoenix Textile Inc (PA) .................................................. D ...... 310 715-7090
   14600 S Broadway Gardena (90248) *(P-17097)*

Phoenix Wheel Company Inc .................................................. E ...... 760 598-1960
   2611 Commerce Way Ste D Vista (92081) *(P-16389)*

Phonesuit Inc .................................................. E ...... 310 774-0282
   1431 7th St Ste 201 Santa Monica (90401) *(P-11915)*

Phorus Inc .................................................. D ...... 310 995-2521
   5220 Las Virgenes Rd Calabasas (91302) *(P-19303)*

Photo Fabricators Inc .................................................. D ...... 818 781-1010
   7648 Burnet Ave Van Nuys (91405) *(P-12189)*

Photo Printing Pros, Goleta *Also Called: Surf To Summit Inc (P-15863)*

Photo Research, Chatsworth *Also Called: Photo Research Inc (P-14813)*

Photo Research Inc .................................................. E ...... 818 341-5151
   9731 Topanga Canyon Pl Chatsworth (91311) *(P-14813)*

Photo-Sonics Inc (PA) .................................................. E ...... 818 842-2141
   9131 Independence Ave Chatsworth (91311) *(P-15660)*

Photon Dynamics Inc .................................................. C ...... 408 723-7118
   5970 Optical Ct San Jose (95138) *(P-14571)*

Photon Dynamics Inc .................................................. C ...... 408 226-9900
   17 Great Oaks Blvd San Jose (95119) *(P-14572)*

Photon Dynamics Inc (HQ) .................................................. C ...... 408 226-9900
   5970 Optical Ct San Jose (95138) *(P-14573)*

Photonics Division, Carlsbad *Also Called: L3 Technologies Inc (P-14202)*

Photronics California, Burbank *Also Called: Photronics Inc (P-15661)*

Photronics Inc (DH) .................................................. B ...... 203 740-5653
   2428 N Ontario St Burbank (91504) *(P-15661)*

Photronics Inc .................................................. C ...... 760 294-1896
   1760 Arroyo Gln Escondido (92026) *(P-15662)*

Phs / Mwa .................................................. C ...... 951 695-1008
   42374 Avenida Alvarado # A Temecula (92590) *(P-16302)*

Phs/Mwa Aviation Services, Temecula *Also Called: Phs / Mwa (P-16302)*

Phyllis Morris Originals (PA) .................................................. F ...... 310 289-6868
   8772 Beverly Blvd Los Angeles (90048) *(P-16418)*

Physicans Formula Holdings Inc (HQ) .................................................. E ...... 626 334-3395
   22067 Ferrero Walnut (91789) *(P-6021)*

Physicians Formula, Walnut *Also Called: Physicans Formula Holdings Inc (P-6021)*

Physicians Formula Inc (DH) .................................................. D ...... 626 334-3395
   22067 Ferrero City Of Industry (91789) *(P-6022)*

Physicians Formula Cosmt Inc .................................................. D ...... 626 334-3395
   22067 Ferrero City Of Industry (91789) *(P-6023)*

PI Variables, Tustin *Also Called: PI Variables Inc (P-12008)*

PI Variables Inc .................................................. E ...... 949 415-9411
   3002 Dow Ave Ste 138 Tustin (92780) *(P-12008)*

Piano Disc, Sacramento *Also Called: Burgett Incorporated (P-16973)*

Picarro Inc (PA) .................................................. C ...... 408 962-3900
   3105 Patrick Henry Dr Santa Clara (95054) *(P-14705)*

Pickering Laboratories Inc .................................................. E ...... 650 694-6700
   1280 Space Park Way Mountain View (94043) *(P-5111)*

Picnic At Ascot Inc .................................................. E ...... 310 674-3098
   3237 W 131st St Hawthorne (90250) *(P-3374)*

Picnic Basket, The, Santa Cruz *Also Called: Glass Jar Inc (P-802)*

Picnic Time Inc .................................................. D ...... 805 529-7400
   5131 Maureen Ln Moorpark (93021) *(P-16204)*

Pico Metal Products Inc .................................................. E ...... 562 944-0626
   10640 Springdale Ave Santa Fe Springs (90670) *(P-8536)*

Pico Metal Products Since 1919, Santa Fe Springs *Also Called: Pico Metal Products Inc (P-8536)*

Pico Pica Foods, Wilmington *Also Called: Juanitas Foods (P-861)*

Picosys Incorporated .................................................. D ...... 805 962-3333
   320 N Nopal St Santa Barbara (93103) *(P-9689)*

Pictsweet Company .................................................. B ...... 805 928-4414
   732 Hanson Way Santa Maria (93458) *(P-1043)*

Pie Rise Ltd .................................................. E ...... 310 832-4559
   29051 S Western Ave Rancho Palos Verdes (90275) *(P-17601)*

Piedmont Plastics, La Mirada *Also Called: Regal-Piedmont Plastics LLC (P-17234)*

Piedras Machine Corporation .................................................. E ...... 562 602-1500
   15154 Downey Ave Ste B Paramount (90723) *(P-11040)*

Piercan Usa Inc .................................................. D ...... 760 599-4543
   160 Bosstick Blvd San Marcos (92069) *(P-2486)*

Pierce Magnetics, Pomona *Also Called: Fong Engineering Enterprise (P-12980)*

Pierco Incorporated .................................................. F ...... 909 251-7100
   680 Main St Riverside (92501) *(P-16205)*

Pierre Mitri (PA) .................................................. F ...... 213 747-1838
   1138 Wall St Los Angeles (90015) *(P-2799)*

Piet Retief Inc .................................................. E ...... 323 732-8312
   1914 6th Ave Los Angeles (90018) *(P-2800)*

Piezo-Metrics Inc (PA) .................................................. E ...... 805 522-4676
   4584 Runway St Simi Valley (93063) *(P-12632)*

Pigeon and Poodle, City Of Industry *Also Called: Ardmore Home Design Inc (P-3465)*

Pilatus Unmanned, Huntington Beach *Also Called: Measure Uas Inc (P-14895)*

Pillar Data Systems Inc .................................................. B ...... 408 503-4000
   2840 Junction Ave San Jose (95134) *(P-10265)*

Pillow Pets, San Marcos *Also Called: CJ Products Inc (P-2925)*

Pillsbury, Glendale *Also Called: Pillsbury Company LLC (P-1062)*

Pillsbury Company LLC .................................................. E ...... 818 522-3952
   220 S Kenwood St Ste 202 Glendale (91205) *(P-1062)*

Pilot Software Inc .................................................. E ...... 650 230-2830
   3410 Hillview Ave Palo Alto (94304) *(P-18674)*

Pin Concepts, Sun Valley *Also Called: Pincraft Inc (P-15906)*

Pin Hsiao & Associates LLC .................................................. D ...... 209 665-4176
   1316 Dupont Ct Manteca (95336) *(P-1238)*

Pina Vineyard Management LLC .................................................. E ...... 707 944-2229
   7960 Silverado Trl Napa (94558) *(P-94)*

Pincraft Inc .................................................. E ...... 818 248-0077
   7933 Ajay Dr Sun Valley (91352) *(P-15906)*

Pine Grove Group Inc .................................................. E ...... 209 295-7733
   25500 State Highway 88 Pioneer (95666) *(P-13289)*

Pine Ridge Vineyards, Napa *Also Called: Pine Ridge Winery LLC (P-1708)*

Pine Ridge Winery LLC (HQ) .................................................. E ...... 707 253-7500
   5901 Silverado Trl Napa (94558) *(P-1708)*

Pine Ridge Winery LLC .................................................. D ...... 707 260-0330
   700 Grove St Healdsburg (95448) *(P-1709)*

Pinky Los Angeles, Burbank *Also Called: Vesture Group Incorporated (P-2869)*

Pinnacle Diversified Inc .................................................. F ...... 510 400-7929
   1248 San Luis Obispo St Hayward (94544) *(P-4725)*

Pinnacle Industrial Supply Inc (PA) .................................................. E ...... 619 710-4255
   1612 Pacific Rim Ct San Diego (92154) *(P-16889)*

Pinnacle Manufacturing Corp .................................................. E ...... 408 778-6100
   17680 Butterfield Blvd Ste 100 Morgan Hill (95037) *(P-8537)*

Pinnacle Plastic Containers, Oxnard *Also Called: Leading Industry Inc (P-6894)*
Pinnacle Precision Shtmtl Corp (HQ) ............................................. D ...... 714 777-3129
   5410 E La Palma Ave Anaheim (92807) *(P-8538)*
Pinnacle Precision Shtmtl Corp ............................................................. D ...... 714 777-3129
   5410 E La Palma Ave Anaheim (92807) *(P-8539)*
Pinnacle Press, Hayward *Also Called: Pinnacle Diversified Inc (P-4725)*
Pinnacle Solutions Inc .............................................................................. D ...... 209 523-8300
   1700 Mchenry Ave Ste 45 Modesto (95350) *(P-19117)*
Pinnacle Stair Group Inc ......................................................................... E ...... 209 832-3200
   1875 N Macarthur Dr Tracy (95376) *(P-3178)*
Pinnpack Capital Holdings LLC ............................................................. C ...... 805 385-4100
   1151 Pacific Ave Oxnard (93033) *(P-6955)*
Pinnpack Packaging, Oxnard *Also Called: Pinnpack Capital Holdings LLC (P-6955)*
Pioneer Broach Company (PA) ............................................................. E ...... 323 728-1263
   6434 Telegraph Rd Commerce (90040) *(P-9690)*
Pioneer Circuits Inc .................................................................................. B ...... 714 641-3132
   3021 S Shannon St Santa Ana (92704) *(P-12190)*
Pioneer Custom Elec Pdts Corp ............................................................. D ...... 562 944-0626
   10640 Springdale Ave Santa Fe Springs (90670) *(P-11223)*
Pioneer Diecasters Inc ............................................................................. F ...... 323 245-6561
   4209 Chevy Chase Dr Los Angeles (90039) *(P-7818)*
Pioneer Magnetics Inc ............................................................................. C ...... 310 829-6751
   1745 Berkeley St Santa Monica (90404) *(P-13061)*
Pioneer Metal Finishing, Union City *Also Called: Electrochem Solutions LLC (P-8952)*
Pioneer North America Inc (DH) ........................................................... F ...... 310 952-2000
   970 W 190th St Ste 360 Torrance (90502) *(P-16684)*
Pioneer North America Inc ..................................................................... C ...... 310 952-2000
   2050 W 190th St Ste 100 Torrance (90504) *(P-16685)*
Pioneer Packing Inc (PA) ......................................................................... E ...... 714 540-9751
   2430 S Grand Ave Santa Ana (92705) *(P-17020)*
Pioneer Photo Albums Inc (PA) ............................................................. C ...... 818 882-2161
   9801 Deering Ave Chatsworth (91311) *(P-5003)*
Pioneer Sands LLC .................................................................................... E ...... 661 746-5789
   9952 Enos Lane Bakersfield (93314) *(P-329)*
Pioneer Sands LLC .................................................................................... E ...... 949 728-0171
   31302 Ortega Hwy San Juan Capistrano (92675) *(P-330)*
Pioneer Speakers Inc ............................................................................... A ...... 310 952-2000
   2050 W 190th St Ste 100 Torrance (90504) *(P-11688)*
Pionyr Immunotherapeutics Inc ........................................................... E ...... 415 226-7503
   2 Tower Pl # 8 South San Francisco (94080) *(P-5605)*
PIP Printing, Downey *Also Called: Jeb-Phi Inc (P-4657)*
PIP Printing, Mission Viejo *Also Called: Postal Instant Press Inc (P-4728)*
PIP Printing, Riverside *Also Called: Mainstreet Communication Inc (P-17814)*
Pipeline, Rolling Hills Estate *Also Called: Graphic Prints Inc (P-3008)*
Pipeline Products Inc ............................................................................... F ...... 760 744-8907
   1650 Linda Vista Dr Ste 110 San Marcos (92078) *(P-10106)*
Pipeline Trading Systems LLC ............................................................... E ...... 415 293-8159
   1 Market St San Francisco (94105) *(P-13290)*
Pipline, Oxnard *Also Called: West Coast Wldg & Piping Inc (P-19221)*
Pipsticks, San Luis Obispo *Also Called: Pipsticks Inc (P-4022)*
Pipsticks Inc ............................................................................................... E ...... 805 439-1692
   872 Higuera St San Luis Obispo (93401) *(P-4022)*
Piranha Ems Inc ........................................................................................ E ...... 408 520-3963
   2681 Zanker Rd San Jose (95134) *(P-10193)*
Piranha Pipe & Precast, Chowchilla *Also Called: Next Chapter Inc (P-7361)*
Pitman Farms ............................................................................................. D ...... 559 585-3330
   10365 Iona Ave Hanford (93230) *(P-1144)*
Pivot3 Inc ................................................................................................... C ...... 512 807-2666
   614 Lighthouse Ave Ste C Pacific Grove (93950) *(P-18675)*
Pivotal Aero LLC ....................................................................................... D ...... 404 641-9131
   1029 Corporation Way Palo Alto (94303) *(P-13685)*
Pivotal Systems, Fremont *Also Called: Pivotal Systems Corporation (P-11340)*
Pivotal Systems Corporation ................................................................. E ...... 510 770-9125
   48389 Fremont Blvd Ste 100 Fremont (94538) *(P-11340)*
Pixar (DH) .................................................................................................. B ...... 510 922-3000
   1200 Park Ave Emeryville (94608) *(P-19295)*
Pixar Animation Studios, Emeryville *Also Called: Pixar (P-19295)*
Pj Printers Inc ............................................................................................ E ...... 714 779-8484
   1530 Lakeview Loop Anaheim (92807) *(P-4726)*
Pjk Winery LLC .......................................................................................... E ...... 707 431-8333
   4900 W Dry Creek Rd Healdsburg (95448) *(P-1710)*

Pjy LLC ........................................................................................................ E ...... 323 583-7737
   3251 Leonis Blvd Vernon (90058) *(P-2424)*
Pk1 Inc (HQ) ............................................................................................. D ...... 559 662-1910
   401 S Granada Dr Madera (93637) *(P-3878)*
Pl Development, Lynwood *Also Called: P & L Development LLC (P-5590)*
Pl Machine Corporation ......................................................................... E ...... 714 892-1100
   10716 Reagan St Los Alamitos (90720) *(P-11041)*
Placer Waterworks Inc ............................................................................ E ...... 530 742-9675
   1325 Furneaux Rd Plumas Lake (95961) *(P-8200)*
Plainfield Companies, Brea *Also Called: Plainfield Molding Inc (P-6956)*
Plainfield Molding Inc ............................................................................. D ...... 815 436-7806
   135 S State College Blvd # 200 Brea (92821) *(P-6956)*
Plainfield Stamping-Illinois, Brea *Also Called: Plainfield Tool and Engineering Inc (P-6957)*
Plainfield Tool and Engineering Inc .................................................... B ...... 815 436-5671
   135 South College Blvd Ste 200 Brea (92821) *(P-6957)*
Planar Monolithics Inds Inc ................................................................... E ...... 916 542-1401
   4921 Robert J Mathews Pkwy Ste 1 El Dorado Hills (95762) *(P-13062)*
Planet, San Francisco *Also Called: Planet Labs Pbc (P-11916)*
Planet DDS, Irvine *Also Called: Planet DDS Inc (P-18676)*
Planet DDS Inc (PA) ................................................................................ E ...... 800 861-5098
   17872 Gillette Ave Ste 250 Irvine (92614) *(P-18676)*
Planet Forward Inc ................................................................................... E ...... 800 861-3787
   2443 Fillmore St San Francisco (94115) *(P-18677)*
Planet FWD, San Francisco *Also Called: Planet Forward Inc (P-18677)*
Planet Green, Chatsworth *Also Called: Planet Green Cartridges Inc (P-15899)*
Planet Green Cartridges Inc ................................................................. D ...... 818 725-2596
   20724 Lassen St Chatsworth (91311) *(P-15899)*
Planet Innovation Inc .............................................................................. E ...... 847 943-7270
   2720 Loker Ave W Ste P Carlsbad (92010) *(P-15226)*
Planet Labs Pbc (PA) ............................................................................... D ...... 415 829-3313
   645 Harrison St Fl 4 San Francisco (94107) *(P-11916)*
Planet One Products Inc (PA) ............................................................... F ...... 707 794-8000
   1445 N Mcdowell Blvd Petaluma (94954) *(P-3669)*
Planetizen, Los Angeles *Also Called: Planetizen Inc (P-4449)*
Planetizen Inc ............................................................................................ E ...... 877 260-7526
   3530 Wilshire Blvd Ste 1285 Los Angeles (90010) *(P-4449)*
Planful Inc (HQ) ....................................................................................... C ...... 650 249-7100
   150 Spear St Ste 1850 San Francisco (94105) *(P-18678)*
Plangrid Inc (HQ) .................................................................................... D ...... 800 646-0796
   2111 Mission St Ste 400 San Francisco (94110) *(P-18679)*
Planing Mill & Lbr. Co., Sacramento *Also Called: Burnett Sons Planing Mill Lbr (P-17326)*
Plansee USA LLC ...................................................................................... D ...... 760 438-9090
   1491 Poinsettia Ave Ste 138 Vista (92081) *(P-12633)*
Plant, San Francisco *Also Called: Plant/Allison Corporation (P-3179)*
Plant 1, North Highlands *Also Called: Livingstons Concrete Svc Inc (P-7466)*
Plant 2, Harbor City *Also Called: Hansen Engineering Co (P-13857)*
Plant 3, Lincoln *Also Called: Livingstons Concrete Svc Inc (P-7467)*
Plant Ranch LLC ....................................................................................... F ...... 818 384-9727
   242 N Avenue 25 Ste 114 Los Angeles (90031) *(P-2322)*
Plant/Allison Corporation ...................................................................... E ...... 415 285-0500
   300 Newhall St San Francisco (94124) *(P-3179)*
Planted Solar Inc ...................................................................................... E ...... 650 861-1455
   1901 Poplar St Oakland (94607) *(P-8073)*
Plantel Nurseries Inc (PA) ..................................................................... E ...... 805 349-8952
   2775 E Clark Ave Santa Maria (93455) *(P-50)*
Plantel Tranplanting Services, Santa Maria *Also Called: Plantel Nurseries Inc (P-50)*
Plantronics, Scotts Valley *Also Called: Plantronics Inc (P-13063)*
Plantronics Inc .......................................................................................... D ...... 714 897-0808
   12082 Western Ave Garden Grove (92841) *(P-10194)*
Plantronics Inc (HQ) ............................................................................... A ...... 831 420-3002
   100 Enterprise Way Ste A300 Scotts Valley (95066) *(P-13063)*
Plas-Tal Manufacturing Co, Santa Fe Springs *Also Called: Brunton Enterprises Inc (P-8107)*
Plascor Inc ................................................................................................. C ...... 951 328-1010
   972 Columbia Ave Riverside (92507) *(P-6612)*
Plasidyne Engineering & Mfg ............................................................... E ...... 562 531-0510
   3230 E 59th St Long Beach (90805) *(P-6958)*
Plaskolite West LLC ................................................................................. E ...... 310 637-2103
   2225 E Del Amo Blvd Compton (90220) *(P-5187)*
Plasma Coating Corporation ................................................................ E ...... 310 532-1951
   1900 W Walnut St Compton (90220) *(P-9106)*

# ALPHABETIC SECTION — Plz Corp

**Plasma Division, Corona** *Also Called: PVA Tepla America Inc (P-11057)*

**Plasma Rggedized Solutions Inc** ............................................................. E ...... 714 893-6063
5452 Business Dr Huntington Beach (92649) *(P-8995)*

**Plasma Rggedized Solutions Inc (PA)** ................................................... D ...... 408 954-8405
2284 Ringwood Ave Ste A San Jose (95131) *(P-9107)*

**Plasma Technology Incorporated (PA)** ................................................. D ...... 310 320-3373
1754 Crenshaw Blvd Torrance (90501) *(P-9108)*

**Plastic and Metal Center Inc** ................................................................. E ...... 949 770-0610
23162 La Cadena Dr Laguna Hills (92653) *(P-6959)*

**Plastic Dress-Up, North Hollywood** *Also Called: Pdu Lad Corporation (P-9102)*

**Plastic Engineering Tech LLC** .............................................................. F ...... 909 390-1323
4502 Brickell Privado St Ontario (91761) *(P-6960)*

**Plastic Molded Components Inc** ........................................................... E ...... 714 229-0133
5920 Lakeshore Dr Cypress (90630) *(P-6961)*

**Plastic Package, Sacramento** *Also Called: Jadra Inc (P-6871)*

**Plastic Processing Co, Gardena** *Also Called: Narayan Corporation (P-6611)*

**Plastic Processing Corp** ....................................................................... F ...... 310 719-7330
13432 Estrella Ave Gardena (90248) *(P-6962)*

**Plastic Sales, Long Beach** *Also Called: Plastic Sales Southern Inc (P-17231)*

**Plastic Sales Southern Inc** ................................................................... E ...... 714 375-7900
425 Havana Ave Long Beach (90814) *(P-17231)*

**Plastic Services and Products** ............................................................. A ...... 818 896-1101
12243 Branford St Sun Valley (91352) *(P-6651)*

**Plastic Technologies Inc** ...................................................................... E ...... 951 360-6055
4720 Felspar St Riverside (92509) *(P-6963)*

**Plasticolor, Fullerton** *Also Called: Plasticolor Molded Pdts Inc (P-17458)*

**Plasticolor Molded Pdts Inc (PA)** ......................................................... C ...... 714 525-3880
801 S Acacia Ave Fullerton (92831) *(P-17458)*

**Plastics Development Corp** ................................................................. E ...... 949 492-0217
960 Calle Negocio San Clemente (92673) *(P-6964)*

**Plastics Family Holdings Inc** ............................................................... F ...... 626 333-7678
15317 Don Julian Rd City Of Industry (91745) *(P-5188)*

**Plastics Family Holdings Inc** ............................................................... D ...... 858 560-1551
5535 Ruffin Rd San Diego (92123) *(P-6566)*

**Plastics Family Holdings Inc** ............................................................... F ...... 310 928-4100
19801 S Rancho Way Unit B Rancho Dominguez (90220) *(P-6965)*

**Plastics Family Holdings Inc** ............................................................... E ...... 562 464-9929
12991 Marquardt Ave Santa Fe Springs (90670) *(P-17232)*

**Plastics Plus Technology Inc** ............................................................... E ...... 909 747-0555
1495 Research Dr Redlands (92374) *(P-6966)*

**Plastics Research Corporation** ............................................................ D ...... 909 391-9050
1400 S Campus Ave Ontario (91761) *(P-6587)*

**Plastifab Inc** ......................................................................................... E ...... 909 596-1927
1425 Palomares St La Verne (91750) *(P-6588)*

**Plastifab San Diego** ............................................................................ F ...... 858 679-6600
12145 Paine St Poway (92064) *(P-17233)*

**Plastifab/Leed Plastics, La Verne** *Also Called: Plastifab Inc (P-6588)*

**Plastikon Automotive, Hayward** *Also Called: Plastikon Industries (P-6967)*

**Plastikon Healthcare LLC** .................................................................... E ...... 785 330-7100
688 Sandoval Way Hayward (94544) *(P-5774)*

**Plastikon Industries (PA)** ..................................................................... C ...... 510 400-1010
688 Sandoval Way Hayward (94544) *(P-6967)*

**Plastikon Industries Inc** ....................................................................... C ...... 510 487-1010
30260 Santucci Ct Hayward (94544) *(P-6968)*

**PLASTIKON INDUSTRIES, INC., Hayward** *Also Called: Plastikon Industries Inc (P-6968)*

**Plastique Unique Inc** ........................................................................... F ...... 310 839-3968
3383 Livonia Ave Los Angeles (90034) *(P-6969)*

**Plastoker Inc** ....................................................................................... F ...... 714 598-5920
12 Morgan Irvine (92618) *(P-6970)*

**Plastopan, Los Angeles** *Also Called: Plastopan Industries Inc (P-3908)*

**Plastopan Industries Inc (PA)** .............................................................. E ...... 323 231-2225
812 E 59th St Los Angeles (90001) *(P-3908)*

**Plastpro 2000 Inc (PA)** ......................................................................... C ...... 310 693-8600
5200 W Century Blvd Los Angeles (90045) *(P-6971)*

**Plastpro Doors, Los Angeles** *Also Called: Plastpro 2000 Inc (P-6971)*

**Plasvacc USA Inc** ............................................................................... F ...... 805 434-0321
1535 Templeton Rd Templeton (93465) *(P-15227)*

**Plateronics Processing, Chatsworth** *Also Called: Plateronics Processing Inc (P-8996)*

**Plateronics Processing Inc** .................................................................. E ...... 818 341-2191
9164 Independence Ave Chatsworth (91311) *(P-8996)*

**Platform Science Inc (PA)** ................................................................... C ...... 844 475-8724
9560 Towne Centre Dr # 200 San Diego (92121) *(P-17962)*

**Plating, Chatsworth** *Also Called: Electro Adapter Inc (P-11451)*

**Platinum, Fullerton** *Also Called: Ultra Wheel Company (P-13597)*

**Platinum Distribution, Yorba Linda** *Also Called: Nasco Gourmet Foods Inc (P-907)*

**Platinum Performance Inc (HQ)** .......................................................... E ...... 800 553-2400
90 Thomas Rd Buellton (93427) *(P-17044)*

**Platinum Visual Systems, Corona** *Also Called: ABC School Equipment Inc (P-16598)*

**Plaxicon Co, Rancho Cucamonga** *Also Called: Plaxicon Holding Corporation (P-6613)*

**Plaxicon Holding Corporation** ............................................................. B ...... 909 944-6868
10660 Acacia St Rancho Cucamonga (91730) *(P-6613)*

**Play-I, San Mateo** *Also Called: Wonder Workshop Inc (P-17998)*

**Playboy Enterprises Inc** ....................................................................... D ...... 310 424-1800
10960 Wilshire Blvd Fl 22 Los Angeles (90024) *(P-4288)*

**Playboy Enterprises Intl Inc** ................................................................. D ...... 310 424-1800
10960 Wilshire Blvd Ste 2200 Los Angeles (90024) *(P-4450)*

**Playboy Japan Inc** ............................................................................... F ...... 310 424-1800
9346 Civic Center Dr # 200 Beverly Hills (90210) *(P-4289)*

**Players West Amusements Inc (PA)** ................................................... E ...... 805 983-1400
2360 Sturgis Rd Ste A Oxnard (93030) *(P-19311)*

**Playfirst Inc** ......................................................................................... C ...... 415 738-4600
160 Spear St Fl 13 San Francisco (94105) *(P-18680)*

**Playhut, Inc., City Of Industry** *Also Called: PH Dip Inc (P-15763)*

**Playmax Surfacing Inc** ........................................................................ F ...... 951 250-6039
1950 Compton Ave Ste 111 Corona (92881) *(P-6522)*

**Playvox, Sunnyvale** *Also Called: Arcaris Inc (P-18062)*

**Plaze De Caviar, Concord** *Also Called: Pacific Plaza Imports Inc (P-2042)*

**PLC Imports Inc** .................................................................................. E ...... 818 349-1600
9667 Owensmouth Ave Ste 201 Chatsworth (91311) *(P-16670)*

**Pleasant Grove Farms, Pleasant Grove** *Also Called: Sills Farms Inc (P-57)*

**Pleasanton Ready Mix Con Inc** .......................................................... F ...... 925 846-3226
3400 Boulder St Pleasanton (94566) *(P-7485)*

**Pleasanton Readymix Concrete, Pleasanton** *Also Called: Pleasanton Ready Mix Con Inc (P-7485)*

**Pleasanton Tool & Mfg Inc** .................................................................. E ...... 925 426-0500
1181 Quarry Ln Ste 450 Pleasanton (94566) *(P-11042)*

**Plenty Unlimited Inc (PA)** .................................................................... D ...... 650 735-3737
570 Eccles Ave South San Francisco (94080) *(P-56)*

**Plenty Unlimited Inc** ............................................................................ F ...... 415 735-3737
126 E Oris St Compton (90222) *(P-2323)*

**Plenums Plus LLC** .............................................................................. D ...... 619 422-5515
67 Brisbane St Chula Vista (91910) *(P-8540)*

**Plexus Optix Inc** .................................................................................. E ...... 800 852-7600
3333 Quality Dr Rancho Cordova (95670) *(P-7202)*

**Plh Products Inc** .................................................................................. B ...... 714 739-6622
10541 Calle Lee Ste 119 Los Alamitos (90720) *(P-3398)*

**Pls Diabetic Shoe Company Inc** ......................................................... E ...... 818 734-7080
21500 Osborne St Canoga Park (91304) *(P-6419)*

**Plt Enterprises Inc** ............................................................................... D ...... 805 389-5335
809 Calle Plano Camarillo (93012) *(P-11467)*

**Pluckys Dump Rental LLC** .................................................................. E ...... 323 540-3510
10136 Bowman Ave South Gate (90280) *(P-8328)*

**Plugg ME LNc** ..................................................................................... E ...... 949 705-4472
18100 Von Karman Ave Ste 850 Irvine (92612) *(P-18681)*

**Plum Valley Inc** ................................................................................... E ...... 530 262-6262
3308 Cyclone Ct Cottonwood (96022) *(P-3075)*

**Plunge, Lincoln** *Also Called: Reboot Labs LLC (P-6685)*

**Plural Publishing Inc** ........................................................................... E ...... 858 492-1555
9177 Aero Dr San Diego (92123) *(P-4340)*

**Plus Products, Adelanto** *Also Called: Carberry LLC (P-16108)*

**Plusai Inc** ............................................................................................ D ...... 408 508-4758
3315 Scott Blvd Santa Clara (95054) *(P-18682)*

**Plutoshift Inc** ....................................................................................... F ...... 213 400-2104
530 Lytton Ave Fl 2 Palo Alto (94301) *(P-18683)*

**Plycraft Industries Inc** ......................................................................... C ...... 323 587-8101
2100 E Slauson Ave Huntington Park (90255) *(P-3287)*

**Plz Corp** ............................................................................................... E ...... 805 498-4531
840 Tourmaline Dr Newbury Park (91320) *(P-5058)*

**Plz Corp** ............................................................................................... D ...... 951 683-2912
2321 3rd St Riverside (92507) *(P-6024)*

Plz Corp ............................................................................ D ...... 909 393-9475
  14425 Yorba Ave Chino (91710) *(P-6025)*
Plz Corp ............................................................................ C ...... 951 683-2912
  2375 3rd St Riverside (92507) *(P-6026)*
PM Corporate Group Inc (PA) ....................................... D ...... 800 343-3139
  2285 Michael Faraday Dr Ste 12 San Diego (92154) *(P-4727)*
PM Packaging, Mcclellan *Also Called: Dome Printing & Packaging LLC (P-4594)*
PM Packaging, San Diego *Also Called: PM Corporate Group Inc (P-4727)*
Pmb Group, Poway *Also Called: Pmb Group Inc (P-16588)*
Pmb Group Inc .................................................................. F ...... 619 690-7300
  12778 Brookprinter Pl Poway (92064) *(P-16588)*
Pmc Inc ............................................................................. C ...... 562 905-3101
  345 Saratoga Ave Santa Clara (95050) *(P-6652)*
Pmc Inc (HQ) .................................................................... D ...... 818 896-1101
  12243 Branford St Sun Valley (91352) *(P-13927)*
PMC Global Inc (PA) ....................................................... D ...... 818 896-1101
  12243 Branford St Sun Valley (91352) *(P-6653)*
PMC Leaders In Chemicals Inc (HQ) ............................ C ...... 818 896-1101
  12243 Branford St Sun Valley (91352) *(P-6654)*
PMI, Carlsbad *Also Called: Petrochem Manufacturing Inc (P-6368)*
Pmic, Los Angeles *Also Called: Practice Management Info Corp (P-4341)*
Pmp Forge, El Cajon *Also Called: Jmmca Inc (P-8779)*
Pmr Precision Mfg & Rbr Co Inc ................................... E ...... 909 605-7525
  1330 Etiwanda Ave Ontario (91761) *(P-6523)*
PNa Construction Tech Inc ............................................ E ...... 661 326-1700
  301 Espee St Ste E Bakersfield (93301) *(P-8541)*
PNC Proactive Nthrn Cont LLC ..................................... E ...... 909 390-5624
  602 S Rockefeller Ave Ste A Ontario (91761) *(P-3879)*
Pneudraulics Inc ............................................................. B ...... 909 980-5366
  8575 Helms Ave Rancho Cucamonga (91730) *(P-14279)*
Pneumatic Conveying Inc (PA) ..................................... F ...... 866 557-5214
  960 E Grevillea Ct Ontario (91761) *(P-9490)*
Pni Sensor, Santa Rosa *Also Called: Protonex LLC (P-12642)*
Pni Sensor Corporation ................................................. E ...... 707 566-2260
  2331 Circadian Way Santa Rosa (95407) *(P-16922)*
Pnk Enterprises Inc ........................................................ E ...... 818 765-3770
  12901 Saticoy St North Hollywood (91605) *(P-17717)*
Pnm Company .................................................................. E ...... 559 291-1986
  2547 N Business Park Ave Fresno (93727) *(P-11043)*
Pocino Foods Company ................................................. D ...... 626 968-8000
  14250 Lomitas Ave City Of Industry (91746) *(P-659)*
Pocket, San Francisco *Also Called: Read It Later Inc (P-18724)*
Pocket Gems, San Francisco *Also Called: Pocket Gems Inc (P-15764)*
Pocket Gems Inc (PA) .................................................... C ...... 415 371-1333
  126 Post St Fl 3 San Francisco (94108) *(P-15764)*
Poco Dolce, San Francisco *Also Called: Poco Dolce Chocolates (P-1343)*
Poco Dolce Chocolates ................................................... F ...... 415 255-1443
  2419 3rd St San Francisco (94107) *(P-1343)*
Point 360 ........................................................................... F ...... 415 989-6245
  1025 Sansome St San Francisco (94111) *(P-19304)*
Point Conception Inc ..................................................... E ...... 949 589-6890
  23121 Arroyo Vis Ste A Rcho Sta Marg (92688) *(P-2801)*
Pokka Beverages, American Canyon *Also Called: Amcan Beverages Inc (P-1849)*
Polar Power, Gardena *Also Called: Polar Power Inc (P-13181)*
Polar Power Inc ............................................................... D ...... 310 830-9153
  249 E Gardena Blvd Gardena (90248) *(P-13181)*
Polar Service Center ...................................................... F ...... 916 643-4689
  4432 Winters Ave Mcclellan (95652) *(P-17459)*
Polarion Software Inc .................................................... D ...... 877 572-4005
  1001 Marina Village Pkwy Ste 403 Alameda (94501) *(P-18684)*
Polaris E-Commerce Inc ................................................ E ...... 714 907-0582
  1941 E Occidental St Santa Ana (92705) *(P-9934)*
Polaris Music, Los Angeles *Also Called: Eti Systems (P-14410)*
Polaris Pharmaceuticals Inc (PA) ................................ F ...... 858 452-6688
  9990 Mesa Rim Rd San Diego (92121) *(P-5606)*
Polishing Corporation America .................................... F ...... 888 892-3377
  442 Martin Ave Santa Clara (95050) *(P-12634)*
Polishing The Professional, Culver City *Also Called: Davina Douthard Inc (P-19557)*
Polley Inc (PA) ................................................................. F ...... 562 868-9861
  11936 Front St Norwalk (90650) *(P-10107)*

Pollstar LLC ..................................................................... D ...... 559 271-7900
  1100 Glendon Ave Ste 2100 Los Angeles (90024) *(P-4451)*
Pollstar.com, Los Angeles *Also Called: Pollstar LLC (P-4451)*
Poly Pak America Inc ..................................................... D ...... 323 264-2400
  2939 E Washington Blvd Los Angeles (90023) *(P-6567)*
Poly Processing Company LLC .................................... E ...... 209 982-4904
  8055 Ash St French Camp (95231) *(P-5189)*
Poly-Fiber Inc (PA) .......................................................... F ...... 951 684-4280
  4343 Fort Dr Riverside (92509) *(P-6101)*
Poly-Seal Industries ........................................................ F ...... 510 843-9722
  725 Channing Way Berkeley (94710) *(P-6524)*
Poly-Tainer Inc (PA) ........................................................ C ...... 805 526-3424
  450 W Los Angeles Ave Simi Valley (93065) *(P-6614)*
Polyalloys Injected Metals Inc ...................................... D ...... 310 715-9800
  14000 Avalon Blvd Los Angeles (90061) *(P-9449)*
Polycell Packaging Corporation ................................... E ...... 562 483-6000
  12851 Midway Pl Cerritos (90703) *(P-17305)*
Polycom Inc ...................................................................... E ...... 925 924-6151
  4750 Willow Rd Pleasanton (94588) *(P-10195)*
Polycom Inc ...................................................................... E ...... 209 830-5083
  25212 S Schulte Rd Tracy (95377) *(P-10196)*
Polycom Inc (DH) ............................................................ D ...... 831 426-5858
  6001 America Center Dr San Jose (95002) *(P-11781)*
Polycraft Inc ..................................................................... E ...... 951 296-0860
  42075 Avenida Alvarado Temecula (92590) *(P-4939)*
Polycycle Solutions LLC ................................................ D ...... 626 856-2100
  4516 Azusa Canyon Rd Irwindale (91706) *(P-6615)*
Polyfet Rf Devices Inc .................................................... E ...... 805 484-9582
  1110 Avenida Acaso Camarillo (93012) *(P-12635)*
Polymer Coating Services, Aliso Viejo *Also Called: Parylene Coating Services Inc (P-9101)*
Polymer Concepts Tech Pby Inc .................................. F ...... 760 240-4999
  13522 Manhasset Rd Apple Valley (92308) *(P-5190)*
Polymer Logistics Inc .................................................... D ...... 951 567-2900
  1725 Sierra Ridge Dr Riverside (92507) *(P-6972)*
Polymer Technology Group, The, Berkeley *Also Called: DSM Biomedical Inc (P-19451)*
Polymeric Technology Inc ............................................. E ...... 510 895-6001
  1900 Marina Blvd San Leandro (94577) *(P-6525)*
Polymerpak LLC .............................................................. C ...... 559 651-1965
  6941 W Goshen Ave Visalia (93291) *(P-6973)*
Polypeptide Laboratories Inc (DH) .............................. E ...... 310 782-3569
  365 Maple Ave Torrance (90503) *(P-19329)*
Polypeptide Labs San Diego LLC ................................. D ...... 858 408-0808
  9395 Cabot Dr San Diego (92126) *(P-5607)*
Polytec Products Corporation ...................................... E ...... 650 322-7555
  3390 Valley Square Ln San Jose (95117) *(P-11044)*
Pometta's, Sonoma *Also Called: Sonoma Gourmet Inc (P-992)*
Pommes Frites Candle Co ............................................. E ...... 213 488-2016
  7300 E Slauson Ave Commerce (90040) *(P-16206)*
Pomona Box Co, La Habra *Also Called: Votaw Wood Products Inc (P-3365)*
Pomona Quality Foam LLC ........................................... D ...... 909 628-7844
  1279 Philadelphia St Pomona (91766) *(P-6655)*
Pomona Service Center, Pomona *Also Called: Altec Industries Inc (P-19159)*
Ponder Environmental Svcs Inc ................................... E ...... 661 589-7771
  19484 Broken Ct Shafter (93263) *(P-19552)*
Ponton Industries, Yorba Linda *Also Called: Tom Ponton Industries Inc (P-19544)*
Pontrelli & Larricchia Ltd .............................................. E ...... 323 583-6690
  6080 Malburg Way Vernon (90058) *(P-17163)*
Pontrlli-Laricchia Sausage Mfg, Vernon *Also Called: Pontrelli & Larricchia Ltd (P-17163)*
Pool Water Products Inc (PA) ....................................... F ...... 949 756-1666
  17872 Mitchell N Ste 250 Irvine (92614) *(P-16939)*
Poolmaster Inc (PA) ........................................................ E ...... 916 567-9800
  770 Del Paso Rd Sacramento (95834) *(P-15765)*
Poor Richard's Press, San Luis Obispo *Also Called: Prpco (P-4742)*
Poor Richards Press, San Luis Obispo *Also Called: Ws Packaging-Blake Printery (P-4815)*
Pop 82, Buena Park *Also Called: Pop 82 Inc (P-2440)*
Pop 82 Inc ......................................................................... F ...... 714 523-8500
  8211 Orangethorpe Ave Buena Park (90621) *(P-2440)*
Pop Chips, E Rncho Dmngz *Also Called: Sonora Mills Foods Inc (P-2356)*
Popla International Inc .................................................. E ...... 909 923-6899
  1740 S Sacramento Ave Ontario (91761) *(P-1088)*

## ALPHABETIC SECTION

**Popout Inc (PA)** .................................................................. D ..... 415 691-7447
731 Market St Ste 200 San Francisco (94103) *(P-18685)*

**Popsalot Gourmet Popcorn, Paramount** *Also Called: Popsalot LLC (P-2099)*

**Popsalot LLC** ..................................................................... E ..... 213 761-0156
7723 Somerset Blvd Paramount (90723) *(P-2099)*

**Populus, San Francisco** *Also Called: Populus Technologies Inc (P-18686)*

**Populus Technologies Inc** ............................................... E ..... 415 364-8048
177 Post St Ste 200 San Francisco (94108) *(P-18686)*

**Port Plastics, City Of Industry** *Also Called: Plastics Family Holdings Inc (P-5188)*

**Porta-Bote International, Redwood City** *Also Called: Kaye Sandy Enterprises Inc (P-14038)*

**Portable Clers Sls Rentals Inc** ........................................ F ..... 760 747-9591
1250 Pacific Oaks Pl Ste 101 Escondido (92029) *(P-17542)*

**Porter Boiler Service Inc** ................................................. E ..... 562 426-2528
1166 E 23rd St Signal Hill (90755) *(P-19276)*

**Porter Hire Ltd** ................................................................... E ..... 951 674-9999
13013 Temescal Canyon Rd Corona (92883) *(P-17861)*

**Porterville Recorder, Porterville** *Also Called: Noticiero Semanal Advertising (P-4175)*

**Porthos Ventures Inc** ....................................................... F ..... 415 339-2790
33 Filbert Ave Sausalito (94965) *(P-1711)*

**Portola Minerals Company** .............................................. D ..... 209 533-0127
24599 Marble Quarry Rd Columbia (95310) *(P-301)*

**Portos Bakery & Cafe, Burbank** *Also Called: Portos Bakery Burbank Inc (P-17417)*

**Portos Bakery Burbank Inc** ............................................. E ..... 818 846-9100
3614 W Magnolia Blvd Burbank (91505) *(P-17417)*

**Posca Brothers Dental Lab Inc** ...................................... D ..... 562 427-1811
641 W Willow St Long Beach (90806) *(P-19334)*

**POSEIDA, San Diego** *Also Called: Poseida Therapeutics Inc (P-5853)*

**Poseida Therapeutics Inc (PA)** ....................................... B ..... 858 779-3100
9390 Towne Centre Dr Ste 200 San Diego (92121) *(P-5853)*

**Posh Bakery Inc** ................................................................ C ..... 408 980-8451
20488 Stevens Creek Blvd Ste 2010 Cupertino (95014) *(P-17418)*

**Poshmark Inc (HQ)** ........................................................... F ..... 650 262-4771
203 Redwood Shores Pkwy Fl 8 Redwood City (94065) *(P-18687)*

**Positive Concepts Inc (PA)** ............................................. E ..... 714 685-5800
2021 N Glassell St Orange (92865) *(P-4046)*

**Positon Inc** ......................................................................... F ..... 650 600-1924
825 Oak Grove Ave Ste B401 Menlo Park (94025) *(P-18688)*

**Positronics Incorporated** ................................................. E ..... 925 931-0211
173 Spring St Ste 120 Pleasanton (94566) *(P-9744)*

**Postal Instant Press Inc (HQ)** ......................................... E ..... 949 348-5000
26722 Plaza Mission Viejo (92691) *(P-4728)*

**Postvision Inc** .................................................................... F ..... 818 840-0777
2605 E Foothill Blvd Ste 103 Glendora (91740) *(P-10266)*

**Potrero Medical Inc** .......................................................... D ..... 888 635-7280
26142 Eden Landing Rd Hayward (94545) *(P-15228)*

**Potter Roemer LLC (HQ)** ................................................. E ..... 626 855-4890
17451 Hurley St City Of Industry (91744) *(P-16456)*

**Powder Coating, South El Monte** *Also Called: Island Powder Coating (P-9082)*

**Powder Painting By Sundial, Sun Valley** *Also Called: Sundial Industries Inc (P-9126)*

**Powdercoat Services LLC** ............................................... E ..... 714 533-2251
1747 W Lincoln Ave Ste K Anaheim (92801) *(P-9109)*

**Power - Trim Co** ................................................................ F ..... 714 523-8560
6060 Phyllis Dr Cypress (90630) *(P-9398)*

**Power Automation Systems, Lathrop** *Also Called: California Natural Products (P-2154)*

**Power Brands Consulting LLC** ....................................... E ..... 818 989-9646
5805 Sepulveda Blvd Ste 501 Van Nuys (91411) *(P-1454)*

**Power Crunch, Irvine** *Also Called: Bio-Nutritional RES Group Inc (P-750)*

**Power Design Manufacturing LLC** ................................. E ..... 408 437-1931
1130 Ringwood Ct San Jose (95131) *(P-12191)*

**Power Design Services, San Jose** *Also Called: Power Design Manufacturing LLC (P-12191)*

**Power Fasteners Inc** ........................................................ E ..... 323 232-4362
650 E 60th St Los Angeles (90001) *(P-8765)*

**POWER INTEGRATIONS, San Jose** *Also Called: Power Integrations Inc (P-12636)*

**Power Integrations Inc (PA)** ............................................ B ..... 408 414-9200
5245 Hellyer Ave San Jose (95138) *(P-12636)*

**Power One, Santa Clara** *Also Called: Bel Power Solutions Inc (P-12831)*

**Power Pt Inc** ...................................................................... E ..... 714 826-7407
9292 Nancy St Cypress (90630) *(P-9530)*

**Power Pt Inc (PA)** ............................................................. E ..... 951 490-4149
1500 Crafton Ave Bldg 100 Mentone (92359) *(P-9531)*

**Power Services, Los Angeles** *Also Called: On-Line Power Incorporated (P-11220)*

**Power Standards Lab Inc** ................................................ E ..... 510 522-4400
980 Atlantic Ave Ste 100 Alameda (94501) *(P-14574)*

**Power-Right Industries LLC** ............................................ F ..... 909 628-4397
4722 W Mission Blvd Ontario (91762) *(P-13557)*

**Powerhouse Diesel Services Incorporated** ................. E ..... 707 747-6737
4700 E 2nd St Benicia (94510) *(P-16834)*

**Powerhouse Engineering Inc** ......................................... F ..... 650 226-3560
101 Industrial Way Ste 13 Belmont (94002) *(P-16207)*

**Powerlift Dumbwaiters Inc** .............................................. F ..... 800 409-5438
2444 Georgia Slide Rd Georgetown (95634) *(P-9475)*

**Powers Holdings Inc** ........................................................ F ..... 559 651-2222
1601 Clancy Ct Visalia (93291) *(P-13064)*

**Powerschool Group LLC (HQ)** ........................................ C ..... 916 790-1509
150 Parkshore Dr Folsom (95630) *(P-18689)*

**Powerschool Holdings Inc (PA)** ..................................... A ..... 877 873-1550
150 Parkshore Dr Folsom (95630) *(P-18690)*

**Powerside, Alameda** *Also Called: Power Standards Lab Inc (P-14574)*

**Powersphyr Inc** ................................................................. E ..... 925 736-8299
4115 Blackhawk Plaza Cir Ste 100 Danville (94506) *(P-10073)*

**Powertronix Inc** ................................................................. E ..... 650 345-6800
1120 Chess Dr Foster City (94404) *(P-11224)*

**Powwow Inc** ....................................................................... E ..... 877 800-4381
71 Stevenson St Ste 400 San Francisco (94105) *(P-18691)*

**Ppd Holding LLC (PA)** ...................................................... D ..... 310 733-2100
10119 Jefferson Blvd Culver City (90232) *(P-2601)*

**Ppf, Garden Grove** *Also Called: Pure Process Filtration Inc (P-16783)*

**PPG Aerospace, Berkeley** *Also Called: PRC - Desoto International Inc (P-6106)*

**PPG Aerospace, Valencia** *Also Called: PRC - Desoto International Inc (P-6240)*

**PPG Aerospace, Mojave** *Also Called: PRC - Desoto International Inc (P-6241)*

**PPG Aerospace, Sylmar** *Also Called: Sierracin/Sylmar Corporation (P-7027)*

**PPG Industries Inc** ............................................................ F ..... 562 692-4010
10060 Mission Mill Rd City Of Industry (90601) *(P-6102)*

**PPG Industries Inc** ............................................................ E ..... 714 894-5252
15541 Commerce Ln Huntington Beach (92649) *(P-6103)*

**PPG Industries Inc** ............................................................ E ..... 661 824-4532
11601 United St Mojave (93501) *(P-6104)*

**PPG Paints** .......................................................................... F ..... 818 362-6711
12780 San Fernando Rd Sylmar (91342) *(P-6105)*

**Ppp LLC** .............................................................................. E ..... 323 832-9627
601 W Olympic Blvd Montebello (90640) *(P-6974)*

**Ppst Inc (PA)** ...................................................................... E ..... 800 421-1921
17692 Fitch Irvine (92614) *(P-13065)*

**Ppt Group Corp (HQ)** ....................................................... E ..... 831 655-6600
17 Mandeville Ct Monterey (93940) *(P-19506)*

**PQ LLC** ................................................................................ C ..... 323 326-1100
8401 Quartz Ave South Gate (90280) *(P-5112)*

**Practice Management Info Corp (PA)** ........................... F ..... 323 954-0224
4727 Wilshire Blvd Ste 302 Los Angeles (90010) *(P-4341)*

**Pranalytica Inc** ................................................................... F ..... 310 458-3345
1101 Colorado Ave Santa Monica (90401) *(P-15229)*

**Prata Inc** ............................................................................. E ..... 512 823-1002
202 Bicknell Ave Santa Monica (90405) *(P-18692)*

**Pratt & Whitney Eng Svcs Inc** ......................................... A ..... 714 373-0110
11190 Valley View St Cypress (90630) *(P-13718)*

**Pratt Industries Inc** ........................................................... C ..... 770 922-0117
2131 E Louise Ave Lathrop (95330) *(P-3794)*

**Pratt Lathrop Corrugating LLC** ....................................... F ..... 209 670-0900
2131 E Louise Ave Lathrop (95330) *(P-3880)*

**Pratt Robert Mann Packg LLC** ....................................... E ..... 831 789-8300
340 El Camino Real S Ste 36 Salinas (93901) *(P-3881)*

**Pratt Whitney Engine Services, Cypress** *Also Called: Pratt & Whitney Eng Svcs Inc (P-13718)*

**Praxair, Fresno** *Also Called: Linde Gas & Equipment Inc (P-5045)*

**Praxair, Turlock** *Also Called: Linde Gas & Equipment Inc (P-5046)*

**Praxair, San Pablo** *Also Called: Linde Inc (P-5047)*

**Praxair, Oakland** *Also Called: Linde Inc (P-5049)*

**Praxair, Santa Ana** *Also Called: Praxair Distribution Inc (P-5059)*

**Praxair Distribution Inc** ................................................... F ..... 714 564-7311
1555 E Edinger Ave Santa Ana (92705) *(P-5059)*

**PRC, Ontario** *Also Called: Plastics Research Corporation (P-6587)*

PRC - Desoto International Inc .................................................. D ...... 510 526-1525
1608 4th St Ste C2 Berkeley (94710) *(P-6106)*

PRC - Desoto International Inc (HQ) ........................................ B ...... 661 678-4209
24811 Avenue Rockefeller Valencia (91355) *(P-6240)*

PRC - Desoto International Inc .................................................. C ...... 661 824-4532
11601 United St Mojave (93501) *(P-6241)*

PRC Composites LLC ................................................................... E ...... 909 464-1520
13477 12th St Chino (91710) *(P-6975)*

PRC Composites LLC (PA) ......................................................... D ...... 909 391-2006
1400 S Campus Ave Ontario (91761) *(P-6976)*

Prd Company, Hayward *Also Called: Pacific Roller Die Co Inc (P-11024)*

Pre-Con Products ....................................................................... D ...... 805 527-0841
240 W Los Angeles Ave Simi Valley (93065) *(P-7372)*

Pre-Insulated Metal Tech Inc (HQ) ........................................... E ...... 707 359-2280
929 Aldridge Rd Vacaville (95688) *(P-8680)*

Pre/Plastics Inc ........................................................................... E ...... 530 823-1820
12600 Locksley Ln Ste 100 Auburn (95602) *(P-6977)*

Precast Con Tech Unlimited LLC ............................................. D ...... 530 749-6501
1260 Furneaux Rd Olivehurst (95961) *(P-7373)*

Precast Innovations Inc ............................................................ E ...... 714 921-4060
1670 N Main St Orange (92867) *(P-7374)*

Precious Metals Plating Co Inc ................................................ F ...... 714 546-6271
2635 Orange Ave Santa Ana (92707) *(P-8997)*

Precise Aerospace Mfg LLC ...................................................... E ...... 951 898-0500
22951 La Palma Ave Yorba Linda (92887) *(P-6978)*

Precise Die and Finishing .......................................................... E ...... 818 773-9337
9400 Oso Ave Chatsworth (91311) *(P-9640)*

Precise Industries Inc ................................................................ C ...... 714 482-2333
610 Neptune Ave Brea (92821) *(P-8542)*

Precise Iron Doors Inc ............................................................... E ...... 818 338-6269
12331 Foothill Blvd Sylmar (91342) *(P-8284)*

Precise Media Services Inc ....................................................... E ...... 909 481-3305
888 Vintage Ave Ontario (91764) *(P-11741)*

Precise Plastic Products, Yorba Linda *Also Called: Precise Aerospace Mfg LLC (P-6978)*

Precise-Full Service Media, Ontario *Also Called: Precise Media Services Inc (P-11741)*

Precision Aerial Services Inc .................................................... F ...... 909 484-8259
2020 Lowell St Rialto (92377) *(P-19169)*

Precision Aerospace Corp ........................................................ D ...... 909 945-9604
11155 Jersey Blvd Ste A Rancho Cucamonga (91730) *(P-13928)*

Precision Anodizing & Pltg Inc ................................................. D ...... 714 996-1601
1601 N Miller St Anaheim (92806) *(P-8998)*

Precision Arcft Machining Inc ................................................. E ...... 818 768-5900
10640 Elkwood St Sun Valley (91352) *(P-11045)*

Precision Cabinets, Brentwood *Also Called: Pct Enterprises Inc (P-3583)*

Precision Castparts Corp .......................................................... F ...... 310 323-6200
14800 S Figueroa St Gardena (90248) *(P-7694)*

Precision Cnc Mil & Turning, Scotts Valley *Also Called: Larkin Precision Machining Inc (P-10940)*

Precision Coil Spring Company ................................................ C ...... 626 444-0561
10107 Rose Ave El Monte (91731) *(P-9206)*

Precision Companies Inc .......................................................... F ...... 909 548-2700
15088 La Palma Dr Chino (91710) *(P-3180)*

Precision Contacts Inc .............................................................. E ...... 916 939-4147
990 Suncast Ln El Dorado Hills (95762) *(P-11917)*

Precision Cutting Tools Inc ...................................................... E ...... 562 921-7898
5572 Fresca Dr La Palma (90623) *(P-9691)*

Precision Cutting Tools LLC ..................................................... E ...... 562 921-7898
5572 Fresca Dr La Palma (90623) *(P-9692)*

Precision Deburring Services ................................................... E ...... 562 944-4497
4440 Manning Rd Pico Rivera (90660) *(P-9562)*

Precision Design Source, Pleasanton *Also Called: Pct Enterprises Inc (P-3582)*

Precision Die Cutting, LLC, Chino *Also Called: Team Technologies Inc (P-9652)*

Precision Doors & Millwork Co, Chino *Also Called: Precision Companies Inc (P-3180)*

Precision Dynamics Corporation (HQ) .................................... C ...... 818 897-1111
25124 Springfield Ct Ste 200 Valencia (91355) *(P-3953)*

Precision Engine Controls Corp (DH) ...................................... C ...... 858 792-3217
11661 Sorrento Valley Rd San Diego (92121) *(P-9314)*

Precision Fiber Products Inc .................................................... E ...... 408 946-4040
642 Palomar St Chula Vista (91911) *(P-7792)*

Precision Fluid Controls Inc .................................................... C ...... 916 626-3029
1751 Aviation Blvd Ste 200 Lincoln (95648) *(P-13929)*

Precision Forging Dies Inc ........................................................ E ...... 562 861-1878
10710 Sessler St South Gate (90280) *(P-9641)*

Precision Frrites Ceramics Inc ................................................. D ...... 714 901-7622
5432 Production Dr Huntington Beach (92649) *(P-7285)*

Precision Glass & Optics, Santa Ana *Also Called: Buk Optics Inc (P-14764)*

Precision Graphics, Redwood City *Also Called: Tilley Manufacturing Co Inc (P-6470)*

Precision Hermetic, Redlands *Also Called: Precision Hermetic Tech Inc (P-13066)*

Precision Hermetic Tech Inc .................................................... D ...... 909 381-6011
1940 W Park Ave Redlands (92373) *(P-13066)*

Precision Label LLC ................................................................... E ...... 760 757-7533
659 Benet Rd Oceanside (92058) *(P-3936)*

Precision Litho Inc .................................................................... E ...... 760 727-9400
1185 Joshua Way Vista (92081) *(P-4729)*

Precision Machining, Pacifica *Also Called: Kibblwhite Prcsion McHning Inc (P-14062)*

Precision Machining & Fab, Anaheim *Also Called: Precision Waterjet Inc (P-11047)*

Precision Manufacturing .......................................................... F ...... 408 460-2435
301 Derek Pl Roseville (95678) *(P-11046)*

Precision Metal Crafts Inc ........................................................ E ...... 562 468-7080
11965 Rivera Rd Santa Fe Springs (90670) *(P-8201)*

Precision Millwork LLC ............................................................. F ...... 661 402-5021
14300 Davenport Rd Ste 4a Agua Dulce (91390) *(P-3181)*

Precision Offset Inc .................................................................. D ...... 949 752-1714
15201 Woodlawn Ave Tustin (92780) *(P-4730)*

Precision One Medical Inc ....................................................... D ...... 760 945-7966
3923 Oceanic Dr Ste 200 Oceanside (92056) *(P-15477)*

Precision Optical, Costa Mesa *Also Called: Sellers Optical Inc (P-14823)*

Precision Plastics, Sacramento *Also Called: Fresno Precision Plastics Inc (P-6833)*

Precision Plastics Packaging, Anaheim *Also Called: Interlink Inc (P-4654)*

Precision Printers, Grass Valley *Also Called: Igraphics (P-4896)*

Precision Pwdred Met Parts Inc ............................................... E ...... 909 595-5656
145 Atlantic St Pomona (91768) *(P-7910)*

Precision Resource Inc ............................................................. C ...... 714 891-4439
5803 Engineer Dr Huntington Beach (92649) *(P-8876)*

Precision Resource Cal Div, Huntington Beach *Also Called: Precision Resource Inc (P-8876)*

Precision Resources, Hawthorne *Also Called: Paulco Precision Inc (P-11033)*

Precision Services Group, Tustin *Also Called: Precision Offset Inc (P-4730)*

Precision Sheet Metal, Gardena *Also Called: Artistic Welding (P-8381)*

Precision Silicones, Chino *Also Called: Wacker Chemical Corporation (P-6167)*

Precision Stampings Inc (PA) ................................................... E ...... 951 845-1174
500 Egan Ave Beaumont (92223) *(P-11468)*

Precision Steel Products Inc .................................................... E ...... 310 523-2002
13124 Avalon Blvd Los Angeles (90061) *(P-8543)*

Precision Swiss Products Inc ................................................... D
1911 Tarob Ct Milpitas (95035) *(P-15394)*

Precision Tube Bending ............................................................ D ...... 562 921-6723
13626 Talc St Santa Fe Springs (90670) *(P-13930)*

Precision Waterjet, Orange *Also Called: Jbb Inc (P-13258)*

Precision Waterjet Inc .............................................................. E ...... 888 538-9287
4900 E Hunter Ave Anaheim (92807) *(P-11047)*

Precision Welding Inc ............................................................... E ...... 661 729-3436
241 Enterprise Pkwy Lancaster (93534) *(P-8202)*

Precision Wire Products Inc (PA) ............................................. C ...... 323 890-9100
6150 Sheila St Commerce (90040) *(P-9226)*

Precision Works, Indio *Also Called: Cabinets By Prcision Works Inc (P-3224)*

Preco Aircraft Motors Inc ......................................................... E ...... 626 799-3549
1133 Mission St South Pasadena (91030) *(P-13182)*

Pred, San Diego *Also Called: Pred Technologies Usa Inc (P-13067)*

Pred Technologies Usa Inc ....................................................... D ...... 858 999-2114
4901 Morena Blvd San Diego (92117) *(P-13067)*

Predator Motorsports Inc ......................................................... F ...... 760 734-1749
1250 Distribution Way Vista (92081) *(P-6979)*

Predii Inc ..................................................................................... E ...... 415 269-1146
2211 Park Blvd Palo Alto (94306) *(P-18693)*

Prefab Innovations Inc ............................................................. E ...... 559 582-3871
1801 Santa Clara St Fresno (93721) *(P-348)*

Preferred Mfg Svcs Inc (PA) ..................................................... D ...... 530 677-2675
4261 Business Dr Cameron Park (95682) *(P-11048)*

Preferred Printing & Packaging Inc ......................................... E ...... 909 923-2053
1493 E Philadelphia St Ontario (91761) *(P-3806)*

## ALPHABETIC SECTION

Preferred Testing Labs Inc .................................................. F ...... 714 999-1616
  1435 S Allec St Anaheim (92805) *(P-12192)*
Premier Coatings Inc .......................................................... D ...... 209 982-5585
  7910 Longe St Stockton (95206) *(P-9110)*
Premier Cold Storage & Pkg LLC .................................... C ...... 949 444-8859
  1071 E 233rd St Carson (90745) *(P-16285)*
Premier Filters Inc ............................................................. E ...... 657 226-0091
  952 N Elm St Orange (92867) *(P-10108)*
Premier Finishing, Stockton Also Called: Premier Coatings Inc *(P-9110)*
Premier Floor Care Inc (PA) ............................................ E ...... 925 679-4901
  5179 Lone Tree Way Antioch (94531) *(P-17847)*
Premier Fuel Delivery Service, Riverside Also Called: Premier Fuel Distributors Inc *(P-17254)*
Premier Fuel Distributors Inc .......................................... C ...... 760 423-3610
  156 E La Cadena Dr Riverside (92507) *(P-17254)*
Premier Gear & Machining Inc ....................................... E ...... 951 278-5505
  2360 Pomona Rd Corona (92880) *(P-8786)*
Premier Magnetics Inc ...................................................... E ...... 949 452-0511
  20381 Barents Sea Cir Lake Forest (92630) *(P-12852)*
Premier Mop & Broom, Corona Also Called: Northwestern Converting Co *(P-2940)*
Premier Organics ................................................................ E ...... 866 237-8688
  810 81st Ave Ste B Oakland (94621) *(P-1363)*
Premier Packaging LLC .................................................... E ...... 909 749-5123
  10700 Business Dr Ste 100 Fontana (92337) *(P-6656)*
Premier Power Renewable Energy Inc ............................ E ...... 916 939-0400
  4961 Windplay Dr Ste 100 El Dorado Hills (95762) *(P-8074)*
Premier Print & Mail Inc ................................................... F ...... 916 503-5300
  2615 Del Monte St West Sacramento (95691) *(P-17801)*
Premier Solar Energy Inc .................................................. E ...... 530 450-9450
  1359 E Lassen Ave Chico (95973) *(P-12637)*
Premier Steel Structures Inc ............................................ E ...... 951 356-6655
  13345 Estelle St Corona (92879) *(P-8203)*
Premier Systems Usa Inc (PA) ........................................ F ...... 657 204-9861
  16291 Gothard St Huntington Beach (92647) *(P-16540)*
Premier Trailer Mfg Inc ..................................................... E ...... 559 651-2212
  30517 Ivy Rd Visalia (93291) *(P-14132)*
Premier Wireless Inc ......................................................... E ...... 925 776-1070
  4010 Watson Plaza Dr Ste 245 Lakewood (90712) *(P-11918)*
Premier Woodworking LLC ............................................... E ...... 916 999-0050
  5800 Alder Ave Sacramento (95828) *(P-3182)*
Premiere Recycle, San Jose Also Called: Jonna Corporation Inc *(P-8319)*
Premio Inc (PA) .................................................................. C ...... 626 839-3100
  918 Radecki Ct City Of Industry (91748) *(P-10197)*
Premise Data Corporation (PA) ....................................... F ...... 415 419-8750
  535 Mission St San Francisco (94105) *(P-18694)*
Premisys Communications Inc (HQ) ............................... C ...... 510 777-7000
  70011 Oakport St Oakland (94621) *(P-11782)*
Premium Pet Foods, Irwindale Also Called: J&R Taylor Brothers Assoc Inc *(P-1103)*
Premium Seals LLC (PA) .................................................. C ...... 619 207-7603
  19270 Tenaja Rd Murrieta (92562) *(P-6461)*
Premium Windows, Corona Also Called: Mediland Corporation *(P-7176)*
Preplastics, Auburn Also Called: Pre/Plastics Inc *(P-6977)*
Preproduction Plastics Inc ............................................... E ...... 951 340-9680
  210 Teller St Corona (92879) *(P-6980)*
Pres-Tek Plastics Inc (PA) ................................................ E ...... 909 360-1600
  10700 7th St Rancho Cucamonga (91730) *(P-6981)*
Presbia, Aliso Viejo Also Called: Presbibio LLC *(P-15614)*
Presbibio LLC ..................................................................... E ...... 949 502-7010
  36 Plateau Aliso Viejo (92656) *(P-15614)*
Prescient Holdings Group LLC ........................................ E ...... 858 790-7004
  10181 Scripps Gateway Ct San Diego (92131) *(P-5608)*
Presentation Folder Inc .................................................... E ...... 714 289-7000
  1130 N Main St Orange (92867) *(P-4001)*
Presentertek Inc ................................................................ E ...... 916 251-7190
  3710 N Lakeshore Blvd Loomis (95650) *(P-12009)*
Preserve Inc ........................................................................ E ...... 800 995-1607
  1355 Paulson Rd Turlock (95380) *(P-5926)*
Preserve International, Turlock Also Called: Preserve Inc *(P-5926)*
Preserved Treescapes International Inc ......................... D ...... 760 631-6789
  180 Vallecitos De Oro San Marcos (92069) *(P-16208)*
Preserved Treescapes Intl, San Marcos Also Called: Preserved Treescapes International Inc *(P-16208)*

President Enterprise LLC .................................................. E ...... 714 671-9577
  655 Tamarack Ave Brea (92821) *(P-4940)*
Presidio Brands Inc (PA) ................................................... E ...... 877 875-5225
  100 Shoreline Hwy Ste A200 Mill Valley (94941) *(P-17045)*
Presidio Systems Inc ......................................................... E ...... 925 362-8400
  159 Wright Brothers Ave Livermore (94551) *(P-467)*
Presort Center of Fresno LLC .......................................... E ...... 559 498-6151
  496 S Uruapan Way Dinuba (93618) *(P-17802)*
Presort Center, The, Visalia Also Called: Central Valley Presort Inc *(P-17796)*
Press Colorcom, Santa Fe Springs Also Called: Ace Commercial Inc *(P-4500)*
Press Democrat, The, Santa Rosa Also Called: Santa Rosa Press Democrat Inc *(P-4192)*
Press Forge Company ....................................................... D ...... 562 531-4962
  7700 Jackson St Paramount (90723) *(P-8787)*
Press-Enterprise Company (PA) ...................................... A ...... 951 684-1200
  3450 14th St Riverside (92501) *(P-4182)*
Pressure Profile Systems Inc .......................................... F ...... 310 641-8100
  5757 W Century Blvd Ste 600 Los Angeles (90045) *(P-14444)*
Prestige Flag, San Diego Also Called: Prestige Flag & Banner Co Inc *(P-3033)*
Prestige Flag & Banner Co Inc ......................................... D ...... 619 497-2220
  591 Camino De La Reina Ste 917 San Diego (92108) *(P-3033)*
Prestige Graphics Inc ....................................................... E ...... 858 560-8213
  9630 Ridgehaven Ct Ste B San Diego (92123) *(P-16993)*
Prestige Mold Incorporated ............................................. D ...... 909 980-6600
  11040 Tacoma Dr Rancho Cucamonga (91730) *(P-9642)*
Presto Inc ............................................................................ F ...... 760 336-1455
  2472 Stapleton Ave Imperial (92251) *(P-17963)*
Preston Vineyards Inc ....................................................... F ...... 707 433-3372
  9282 W Dry Creek Rd Healdsburg (95448) *(P-1712)*
Preston Vineyards & Winery, Healdsburg Also Called: Preston Vineyards Inc *(P-1712)*
Prestone Products Corporation ....................................... E ...... 424 271-4836
  19500 Mariner Ave Torrance (90503) *(P-6318)*
Previously Known As Smile Inc, San Francisco Also Called: Textexpander Inc *(P-18876)*
Prevost Car (us) Inc .......................................................... F ...... 951 202-2064
  28702 Hall Rd Hayward (94545) *(P-13376)*
Prevost Car (us) Inc .......................................................... D ...... 951 360-2550
  3384 De Forest Cir Mira Loma (91752) *(P-16390)*
Prey Inc ............................................................................... F ...... 415 780-9090
  548 Market St San Francisco (94104) *(P-18695)*
Prezero US Packaging LLC .............................................. D ...... 800 767-5278
  3155 S 5th Ave Oroville (95965) *(P-6657)*
Price Industries Inc ........................................................... D ...... 858 673-4451
  10883 Thornmint Rd San Diego (92127) *(P-7622)*
Price Manufacturing Co Inc ............................................. E ...... 951 371-5660
  372 N Smith Ave Corona (92878) *(P-8730)*
Price Pfister Brass Mfg, Lake Forest Also Called: Price Pfister Inc *(P-8054)*
Price Pfister Inc ................................................................. A ...... 949 672-4000
  19701 Da Vinci Lake Forest (92610) *(P-8054)*
Price Products Incorporated ............................................ E ...... 760 745-5602
  106 State Pl Escondido (92029) *(P-11049)*
Pride Conveyance Systems Inc (PA) .............................. D ...... 831 637-1787
  1700 Shelton Dr Hollister (95023) *(P-9491)*
Pride Industries (PA) ......................................................... C ...... 916 788-2100
  10030 Foothills Blvd Roseville (95747) *(P-16294)*
Pride Industries, Roseville Also Called: Pride Industries One Inc *(P-16209)*
Pride Industries One Inc .................................................. A ...... 916 788-2100
  10030 Foothills Blvd Roseville (95747) *(P-16209)*
Pride Line Products, Stockton Also Called: Value Products Inc *(P-5884)*
Prima Fleur Botanicals Inc .............................................. F ...... 415 455-0957
  84 Galli Dr Novato (94949) *(P-6027)*
Primal Elements, Huntington Beach Also Called: Primal Elements Inc *(P-17046)*
Primal Elements Inc .......................................................... D ...... 714 899-0757
  18062 Redondo Cir Huntington Beach (92648) *(P-17046)*
Primal Pet Foods ............................................................... E ...... 415 642-7400
  5100 Fulton Dr Fairfield (94534) *(P-1112)*
Primal Pet Foods Inc ........................................................ E ...... 415 642-7400
  801 Chadbourne Rd Ste 103 Fairfield (94534) *(P-1113)*
Primal Pet Foods Inc (PA) ................................................ D ...... 415 642-7400
  535 Watt Dr Ste B Fairfield (94534) *(P-1114)*
Primapharma Inc ............................................................... E ...... 858 259-0969
  3443 Tripp Ct San Diego (92121) *(P-5609)*

**Primary Color Systems Corp**     ALPHABETIC SECTION

Primary Color Systems Corp .................................................. D ...... 818 643-5944
3500 W Burbank Blvd Burbank (91505) *(P-4731)*

Primary Color Systems Corp (PA) ........................................... B ...... 949 660-7080
11130 Holder St Ste 210 Cypress (90630) *(P-4941)*

Primary Color Systems Corp .................................................. D ...... 310 841-0250
401 Coral Cir El Segundo (90245) *(P-4942)*

Primavera Foods USA, Fresno *Also Called: Fiore Di Pasta Inc (P-2199)*

Prime Converting Corporation ................................................ E ...... 909 476-9500
9121 Pittsburgh Ave Ste 100 Rancho Cucamonga (91730) *(P-4047)*

Prime Engineering, Fresno *Also Called: Axiom Industries Inc (P-15324)*

Prime Forming & Cnstr Sups Inc .............................................. E ...... 714 547-6710
1500a E Chestnut Ave Santa Ana (92701) *(P-7375)*

Prime Heat Incorporated ....................................................... F ...... 619 449-6623
1844 Friendship Dr Ste A El Cajon (92020) *(P-10057)*

Prime Plastic Products Inc .................................................... F ...... 760 734-3900
1351 Distribution Way Ste 8 Vista (92081) *(P-6982)*

Prime Plating, Sun Valley *Also Called: Schmidt Industries Inc (P-9011)*

Prime Technologies ............................................................. F ...... 818 568-0482
19850 Pacific Coast Hwy Malibu (90265) *(P-12193)*

Prime Wheel Corporation ....................................................... B ...... 310 326-5080
23920 Vermont Ave Harbor City (90710) *(P-13558)*

Prime Wheel Corporation ....................................................... E ...... 310 819-4123
17680 S Figueroa St Gardena (90248) *(P-13559)*

Prime Wheel Corporation (PA) ................................................. A ...... 310 516-9126
17705 S Main St Gardena (90248) *(P-13560)*

Prime Wheel of Figueroa, Gardena *Also Called: Prime Wheel Corporation (P-13559)*

Prime Wire & Cable Inc (HQ) .................................................. E ...... 888 445-9955
1330 Valley Vista Dr Diamond Bar (91765) *(P-7793)*

Prime Wire & Cable Inc ........................................................ D ...... 323 266-2010
11701 6th St Rancho Cucamonga (91730) *(P-7794)*

Primenano Inc .................................................................. F ...... 650 300-5115
4701 Patrick Henry Dr Bldg 8 Santa Clara (95054) *(P-12638)*

Primex, Vacaville *Also Called: McC Controls LLC (P-10579)*

Primex Farms LLC (PA) .......................................................... E ...... 661 758-7790
16070 Wildwood Rd Wasco (93280) *(P-1364)*

Primordial Diagnostics Inc .................................................... E ...... 800 462-1926
3233 Mission Oaks Blvd Ste P Camarillo (93012) *(P-14445)*

Primus Inc ...................................................................... D ...... 714 527-2261
17901 Jamestown Ln Huntington Beach (92647) *(P-16021)*

Primus Pipe and Tube Inc (DH) ................................................ D ...... 562 808-8000
5855 Obispo Ave Long Beach (90805) *(P-7669)*

Primus Power Corporation ...................................................... E ...... 510 342-7600
3967 Trust Way Hayward (94545) *(P-13162)*

Prince Kona Food LLC .......................................................... D ...... 209 430-7814
2284 Britton Ct Valley Springs (95252) *(P-2020)*

Prince Lionheart Inc (PA) ..................................................... E ...... 805 922-2250
2421 Westgate Rd Santa Maria (93455) *(P-6983)*

Princess Paper Inc ............................................................. E ...... 323 588-4777
4455 Fruitland Ave Vernon (90058) *(P-4003)*

Princess Paradise, Walnut *Also Called: Diana Did-It Designs Inc (P-2898)*

Princeton Case-West Inc ....................................................... E ...... 805 928-8840
1444 W Mccoy Ln Santa Maria (93455) *(P-6984)*

Princeton Technology Inc ...................................................... E ...... 949 851-7776
1691 Browning Irvine (92606) *(P-10421)*

Princeton Tool Inc ............................................................. F ...... 661 257-1380
25620 Rye Canyon Rd Ste A Valencia (91355) *(P-13719)*

Principle Plastics ............................................................. E ...... 310 532-3411
1136 W 135th St Gardena (90247) *(P-6420)*

Pringle's Draperies, Garden Grove *Also Called: L C Pringle Sales Inc (P-3724)*

Print Ink LLC .................................................................. F ...... 925 829-3950
6918 Sierra Ct Dublin (94568) *(P-4943)*

Print Printing, Placentia *Also Called: Crescent Inc (P-4578)*

Print Shop, San Bernardino *Also Called: San Brnrdino Cmnty College Dst (P-4958)*

Printec Ht Electronics LLC .................................................... E ...... 714 484-7597
501 Sally Pl Fullerton (92831) *(P-12639)*

Printed Image, The, Chico *Also Called: Srl Apparel Inc (P-2495)*

Printegra Corp ................................................................. D ...... 714 692-2221
23281 La Palma Ave Yorba Linda (92887) *(P-4991)*

Printery Inc ................................................................... F ...... 949 757-1930
1762 Kaiser Ave Irvine (92614) *(P-4732)*

Printing 4him, Ontario *Also Called: Ultimate Print Source Inc (P-4796)*

Printing Connection , The, Newbury Park *Also Called: HJS Graphics (P-4632)*

Printing Management Associates ............................................... F ...... 562 407-9977
17128 Edwards Rd Cerritos (90703) *(P-4733)*

Printing Palace Inc (PA) ...................................................... F ...... 310 451-5151
2300 Lincoln Blvd Santa Monica (90405) *(P-4734)*

Printivity, San Diego *Also Called: Printivity LLC (P-4735)*

Printivity LLC ................................................................. E ...... 877 649-5463
8840 Kenamar Dr Ste 405 San Diego (92121) *(P-4735)*

Printograph Inc ............................................................... E ...... 818 252-3000
7625 N San Fernando Rd Burbank (91505) *(P-4736)*

Printpack Inc ................................................................. D ...... 925 469-0601
5870 Stoneridge Mall Rd Ste 200 Pleasanton (94588) *(P-3976)*

Printronix LLC (PA) ........................................................... E ...... 714 368-2300
7700 Irvine Center Dr Ste 700 Irvine (92618) *(P-10422)*

Printrunner LLC ............................................................... E ...... 888 296-5760
8000 Haskell Ave Van Nuys (91406) *(P-4737)*

Prints 4 Life ................................................................. E ...... 661 942-2233
43145 Business Ctr Pkwy Lancaster (93535) *(P-4738)*

Printsafe Inc ................................................................. E ...... 858 748-8600
11895 Community Rd Ste B Poway (92064) *(P-16541)*

Printworx Inc ................................................................. F ...... 831 722-7147
195 Aviation Way Ste 201 Watsonville (95076) *(P-10423)*

Priority Archtctral Grphics In ............................................... E ...... 415 850-9836
1260 Egbert Ave San Francisco (94124) *(P-16022)*

Priority Lighting Inc ......................................................... F ...... 800 709-1119
77551 El Duna Ct Ste H Palm Desert (92211) *(P-17539)*

Priority Posting and Pubg Inc ................................................ F ...... 714 338-2568
17501 Irvine Blvd Ste 1 Tustin (92780) *(P-4452)*

Prism Aerospace ............................................................... E ...... 951 582-2850
3087 12th St Riverside (92507) *(P-8544)*

Prism Inks .................................................................... E ...... 408 744-6710
824 W Ahwanee Ave Sunnyvale (94085) *(P-6260)*

Prism Software Corporation ................................................... E ...... 949 855-3100
184 Technology Dr Ste 201 Irvine (92618) *(P-18696)*

Private, Sacramento *Also Called: Eisenbeiss Inc (P-19255)*

Private Brand Mdsg Corp ...................................................... E ...... 213 749-0191
214 W Olympic Blvd Los Angeles (90015) *(P-2713)*

Prl Aluminum Inc ............................................................. D ...... 626 968-7507
14760 Don Julian Rd City Of Industry (91746) *(P-7746)*

Prl Glass Systems Inc ........................................................ D ...... 877 775-2586
14760 Don Julian Rd City Of Industry (91746) *(P-7239)*

Prl Glass Systems Inc (PA) ................................................... C ...... 626 961-5890
13644 Nelson Ave City Of Industry (91746) *(P-7240)*

Pro America Premium Tools, Baldwin Park *Also Called: American Kal Enterprises Inc (P-16745)*

Pro American Premium Tools, Baldwin Park *Also Called: Kal-Cameron Manufacturing Corp (P-7956)*

Pro Cal, South Gate *Also Called: Productivity California Inc (P-6986)*

Pro Circuit Products Inc (PA) ................................................ E ...... 951 738-8050
2771 Wardlow Rd Corona (92882) *(P-17484)*

Pro Circuit Products & Racing, Corona *Also Called: Pro Circuit Products Inc (P-17484)*

Pro Circuits Manufacturing Inc ............................................... E ...... 858 899-4747
16464 Via Esprillo San Diego (92127) *(P-19176)*

Pro Circuits Mfg Inds, San Diego *Also Called: Pro Circuits Manufacturing Inc (P-19176)*

Pro Design Group Inc ......................................................... E ...... 310 767-1032
438 E Alondra Blvd Gardena (90248) *(P-6985)*

Pro Detention Inc ............................................................ D ...... 714 881-3680
2238 N Glassell St Ste E Orange (92865) *(P-7650)*

Pro Document Solutions Inc (PA) .............................................. E ...... 805 238-6680
1760 Commerce Way Paso Robles (93446) *(P-4739)*

Pro Farm Group Inc (PA) ...................................................... C ...... 530 750-2800
1530 Drew Ave Davis (95618) *(P-6205)*

Pro Group, Irvine *Also Called: Progroup (P-4945)*

Pro Installations Inc (HQ) ................................................... E
10948 Willow Ct Ste 100 San Diego (92127) *(P-505)*

Pro Lab Orthotics Inc ........................................................ E ...... 707 257-4400
575 Airpark Rd Napa (94558) *(P-6526)*

Pro Pacific Pest Control, San Marcos *Also Called: Corkys Pest Control Inc (P-17844)*

Pro Spot International Inc ................................................... F ...... 760 407-1414
5932 Sea Otter Pl Carlsbad (92010) *(P-13291)*

# ALPHABETIC SECTION  Prolab Digital Imaging

**Pro Spray Equipment, San Bernardino** *Also Called: Wcs Distributing Inc (P-16856)*
**Pro Tech Thermal Services** .................................................. E ...... 951 272-5808
  1954 Tandem Norco (92860) *(P-7897)*
**Pro Tool Services Inc** ........................................................ F ...... 661 393-9222
  1704 Sunnyside Ct Bakersfield (93308) *(P-9693)*
**Pro Tour Memorabilia LLC** ................................................. E ...... 424 303-7200
  700 N San Vicente Blvd Ste G696 West Hollywood (90069) *(P-3423)*
**Pro Vote Solutions, Paso Robles** *Also Called: Pro Document Solutions I Inc (P-4739)*
**Pro-Action Products, Van Nuys** *Also Called: Neopacific Holdings Inc (P-6927)*
**Pro-Cast Products Inc (PA)** ................................................ E ...... 909 793-7602
  27417 3rd St Highland (92346) *(P-7376)*
**Pro-Cision Machining, Morgan Hill** *Also Called: KDF Inc (P-10923)*
**PRO-DEX, Irvine** *Also Called: Pro-Dex Inc (P-15230)*
**Pro-Dex Inc (PA)** ............................................................... C ...... 949 769-3200
  2361 Mcgaw Ave Irvine (92614) *(P-15230)*
**Pro-Lite Inc** ..................................................................... F ...... 714 668-9988
  3505 Cadillac Ave Ste D Costa Mesa (92626) *(P-16023)*
**Pro-Mart Industries Inc** ..................................................... E ...... 949 428-7700
  17421 Von Karman Ave Irvine (92614) *(P-2947)*
**Pro-Tek Manufacturing, Livermore** *Also Called: Pro-Tek Manufacturing Inc (P-8545)*
**Pro-Tek Manufacturing Inc** ................................................ E ...... 925 454-8100
  4849 Southfront Rd Livermore (94551) *(P-8545)*
**Proactive Northern Container, Ontario** *Also Called: PNC Proactive Nthrn Cont LLC (P-3879)*
**Procede Software LP** ....................................................... E ...... 858 450-4800
  6815 Flanders Dr Ste 200 San Diego (92121) *(P-18697)*
**Procelebrity, Arcadia** *Also Called: Tee Top of California Inc (P-17082)*
**PROCEPT BIOROBOTICS, San Jose** *Also Called: Procept Biorobotics Corp (P-15231)*
**Procept Biorobotics Corp (PA)** ........................................... B ...... 650 232-7200
  150 Baytech Dr San Jose (95134) *(P-15231)*
**Process Fab Inc** .............................................................. C ...... 562 921-1979
  13153 Lakeland Rd Santa Fe Springs (90670) *(P-11050)*
**Process Insghts - Gded Wave In** ........................................ E ...... 919 264-9651
  2121 Aviation Dr Upland (91786) *(P-14446)*
**Process Insghts - Gded Wave In (HQ)** ................................ E ...... 916 638-4944
  3033 Gold Canal Dr Rancho Cordova (95670) *(P-14706)*
**Process Specialties Inc** ................................................... E ...... 209 832-1344
  1660 W Linne Rd Ste A Tracy (95377) *(P-12640)*
**Process Stainless Lab Inc (PA)** ......................................... E ...... 408 980-0535
  1280 Memorex Dr Santa Clara (95050) *(P-8999)*
**Processes By Martin Inc** .................................................. E ...... 310 637-1855
  12150 Alameda St Lynwood (90262) *(P-9111)*
**Procisedx Inc** ................................................................. E ...... 858 382-4598
  9449 Carroll Park Dr San Diego (92121) *(P-14346)*
**Proco Products Inc (PA)** .................................................. E ...... 209 943-6088
  2431 Wigwam Dr Stockton (95205) *(P-6527)*
**Procore Technologies Inc (PA)** ......................................... A ...... 866 477-6267
  6309 Carpinteria Ave Carpinteria (93013) *(P-17964)*
**Procter & Gamble, Oxnard** *Also Called: Procter & Gamble Paper Pdts Co (P-4004)*
**Procter & Gamble, Sacramento** *Also Called: Procter & Gamble Mfg Co (P-5880)*
**Procter & Gamble Mfg Co** ................................................ B ...... 916 383-3800
  8201 Fruitridge Rd Sacramento (95826) *(P-5880)*
**Procter & Gamble Mfg Co** ................................................ E ...... 916 442-3135
  1415 L St Sacramento (95814) *(P-16210)*
**Procter & Gamble Paper Pdts Co** ..................................... A ...... 805 485-8871
  800 N Rice Ave Oxnard (93030) *(P-4004)*
**Prodigy Surface Tech Inc** ................................................ E ...... 408 492-9390
  807 Aldo Ave Ste 103 Santa Clara (95054) *(P-9000)*
**Produce World Inc** .......................................................... D ...... 510 441-1449
  37293 3rd St Fremont (94536) *(P-2324)*
**Producers Meat and Prov Inc** ........................................... E ...... 619 232-7593
  7651 Saint Andrews Ave San Diego (92154) *(P-17164)*
**Product Slingshot Inc (DH)** .............................................. E ...... 760 929-9380
  2221 Rutherford Rd Carlsbad (92008) *(P-9643)*
**Product Solutions Inc** ..................................................... E ...... 714 545-9757
  1182 N Knollwood Cir Anaheim (92801) *(P-10591)*
**Productboard Inc (PA)** .................................................... C ...... 844 472-6273
  333 Bush St San Francisco (94104) *(P-9532)*
**Production Data Inc** ........................................................ E ...... 661 327-4776
  1210 33rd St Bakersfield (93301) *(P-269)*
**Production Engineering & Mch** .......................................... E ...... 909 721-2455
  14955 Hilton Dr Fontana (92336) *(P-19330)*
**Production Engineering & Mch, Fontana** *Also Called: Cavallo & Cavallo Inc (P-10765)*
**Production Lapping Company** ........................................... F ...... 626 359-0611
  120 E Chestnut Ave Pmb 124 Monrovia (91016) *(P-11051)*
**Productivity California Inc** ............................................... F ...... 562 923-3100
  10533 Sessler Dr South Gate (90280) *(P-6986)*
**Productos Oropeza, Santa Ana** *Also Called: La Copa De Oro (P-2251)*
**Productplan LLC** ............................................................. E ...... 805 618-2975
  10 E Yanonali St Ste 2a Santa Barbara (93101) *(P-18698)*
**Products Engineering Corp** .............................................. E ...... 310 787-4500
  2645 Maricopa St Torrance (90503) *(P-7964)*
**Products/Techniques Inc** ................................................ F ...... 909 877-3951
  20282 Opus Dr Riverside (92507) *(P-6107)*
**Professional Cabinet Solutions** ........................................ C ...... 909 614-2900
  2111 Eastridge Ave Riverside (92507) *(P-3260)*
**Professional Finishing Inc** ............................................... D ...... 510 233-7629
  770 Market Ave Richmond (94801) *(P-9112)*
**Professional Image Inc** ................................................... F ...... 513 984-1111
  10516 Sierra Estates Dr Auburn (95602) *(P-17306)*
**Professional Lumper Svc Inc** ........................................... E ...... 209 613-5397
  1943 Alex Way Turlock (95382) *(P-9533)*
**Professional Plastics Inc (PA)** .......................................... E ...... 714 446-6500
  1810 E Valencia Dr Fullerton (92831) *(P-5191)*
**Professional Print & Mail, Fresno** *Also Called: Professional Print & Mail Inc (P-4740)*
**Professional Print & Mail Inc** ............................................ E ...... 559 237-7468
  2818 E Hamilton Ave Fresno (93721) *(P-4740)*
**Professnal Fnshg Systems Sups** ...................................... F ...... 818 365-8888
  12341 Gladstone Ave Sylmar (91342) *(P-8877)*
**Profile Planing Mill, Santa Ana** *Also Called: Strata Forest Products Inc (P-3089)*
**Proform Finishing Products LLC** ...................................... E ...... 562 435-4465
  1850 Pier B St Long Beach (90813) *(P-7531)*
**Proformance Manufacturing Inc** ....................................... E ...... 951 279-1230
  1922 Elise Cir Corona (92879) *(P-8878)*
**Prognomiq Inc** ................................................................ E ...... 774 254-1569
  1900 Alameda De Las Pulgas San Mateo (94403) *(P-14707)*
**Prographics Inc** .............................................................. E ...... 626 287-0417
  9200 Lower Azusa Rd Rosemead (91770) *(P-4741)*
**Prographics Screenprinting Inc** ........................................ E ...... 760 744-4555
  1975 Diamond St San Marcos (92078) *(P-4944)*
**Progress Software Corporation** ........................................ D ...... 650 341-7733
  800 W El Camino Real Mountain View (94040) *(P-18699)*
**Progressive Design Playgrounds** ...................................... F ...... 760 597-5990
  2235 Meyers Ave Escondido (92029) *(P-569)*
**Progressive Frame & Fabg Co** ......................................... E ...... 323 589-9933
  5050 Everett Ct Vernon (90058) *(P-8204)*
**Progressive Label Inc** ..................................................... E ...... 323 415-9770
  2545 Yates Ave Commerce (90040) *(P-4048)*
**Progressive Manufacturing, Anaheim** *Also Called: Progrssive Intgrated Solutions (P-4946)*
**Progressive Marketing, Yorba Linda** *Also Called: Progressive Marketing Pdts Inc (P-8681)*
**Progressive Marketing Pdts Inc** ........................................ D ...... 714 888-1700
  4571 Avenida Del Este Yorba Linda (92886) *(P-8681)*
**Progressive Technology** ................................................. F ...... 916 632-6715
  4130 Citrus Ave Ste 17 Rocklin (95677) *(P-7272)*
**Progrip Cargo Control, Lodi** *Also Called: USA Products Group (P-15873)*
**Progroup** ....................................................................... E ...... 949 748-5400
  17622 Armstrong Ave Irvine (92614) *(P-4945)*
**Progrssive Intgrated Solutions** ........................................ D ...... 714 237-0980
  3291 E Miraloma Ave Anaheim (92806) *(P-4946)*
**Progrssive Stl Fabricators Inc** ......................................... F ...... 619 460-7150
  9188 Harness St Spring Valley (91977) *(P-8205)*
**Project Management, Rcho Sta Marg** *Also Called: M-Industrial Enterprises LLC (P-10951)*
**Project Social T LLC** ....................................................... E ...... 323 266-4500
  615 S Clarence St Los Angeles (90023) *(P-2687)*
**Project Sutter Holdings LLC (HQ)** .................................... E ...... 916 669-7408
  11370 Sunrise Park Dr Rancho Cordova (95742) *(P-11619)*
**Projectdiscovery Inc** ....................................................... E ...... 510 681-4441
  548 Market St San Francisco (94104) *(P-18700)*
**Projectoris Inc** ............................................................... D ...... 917 972-5553
  582 Market St Ste 1005 San Francisco (94104) *(P-18701)*
**Prolab, Napa** *Also Called: Pro Lab Orthotics Inc (P-6526)*
**Prolab Digital Imaging, Los Angeles** *Also Called: Pannonia Group Inc (P-17791)*

Prolabs Factory Inc .................................................. E ...... 818 646-3677
  15001 Oxnard St Van Nuys (91411) *(P-6028)*
Prolacta Bioscience Inc .......................................... B ...... 626 599-9260
  1800 Highland Ave Duarte (91010) *(P-780)*
Prolacta Bioscience Inc (PA) .................................. C ...... 626 599-9260
  757 Baldwin Park Blvd City Of Industry (91746) *(P-5854)*
Prolacta Facility LLC .............................................. F ...... 626 599-9260
  757 Baldwin Park Blvd City Of Industry (91746) *(P-5855)*
Prolifics Testing Inc ................................................ E ...... 925 485-9535
  24025 Park Sorrento Ste 405 Calabasas (91302) *(P-17965)*
Proline Concrete Tools Inc .................................. E ...... 760 758-7240
  4645 North Ave Ste 102 Oceanside (92056) *(P-9892)*
Proline Metal Fabricators Inc ................................ E ...... 510 438-0300
  42650 Osgood Rd Fremont (94539) *(P-8206)*
Proma Inc ............................................................... E ...... 310 327-0035
  730 Kingshill Pl Carson (90746) *(P-15478)*
Promart Dazz, Irvine *Also Called: Pro-Mart Industries Inc (P-2947)*
Promax Tools LP .................................................... E ...... 916 638-0501
  11312 Sunrise Gold Cir Rancho Cordova (95742) *(P-9563)*
Promega Biosciences LLC .................................... D ...... 805 544-8524
  277 Granada Dr San Luis Obispo (93401) *(P-5264)*
Promenade Software Inc ...................................... E ...... 949 333-4634
  16 Technology Dr Ste 100 Irvine (92618) *(P-18702)*
Promesys Division, Santa Clara *Also Called: KLA Corporation (P-12514)*
Prometheus Biosciences Inc ................................ D ...... 858 422-4300
  3050 Science Park Rd San Diego (92121) *(P-5610)*
Prometheus Laboratories Inc ................................ B ...... 858 824-0895
  9410 Carroll Park Dr San Diego (92121) *(P-5611)*
Promex, Santa Clara *Also Called: Promex Industries Incorporated (P-12641)*
Promex Industries Incorporated (PA) .................... D ...... 408 496-0222
  3075 Oakmead Village Dr Santa Clara (95051) *(P-12641)*
Prominex Inc .......................................................... F ...... 858 242-1541
  6181 Cornerstone Ct E Ste 106 San Diego (92121) *(P-11052)*
Promises Promises Inc ........................................ E ...... 213 749-7725
  3121 S Grand Ave Los Angeles (90007) *(P-2714)*
Promontory LLC .................................................... F ...... 707 944-1441
  1601 Oakville Grade Rd Oakville (94562) *(P-1713)*
Promotion Xpress Prtg Graphics, San Leandro *Also Called: Akido Printing Inc (P-4506)*
Promotonal Design Concepts Inc .......................... D ...... 626 579-4454
  9872 Rush St South El Monte (91733) *(P-6528)*
Prompt Precision Metals Inc ................................ E ...... 209 531-1210
  1649 E Whitmore Ave Ceres (95307) *(P-8546)*
Pronto Products Co (PA) ...................................... E ...... 619 661-6995
  9850 Siempre Viva Rd San Diego (92154) *(P-10592)*
Pronto Products Co .............................................. E ...... 800 377-6680
  1801 W Olympic Blvd Pasadena (91199) *(P-11053)*
Proof of Concept Poc Lab, Sunnyvale *Also Called: Juniper Networks Inc (P-18981)*
Proofpoint Inc ........................................................ E ...... 408 571-6400
  2216 Otoole Ave San Jose (95131) *(P-18703)*
Propel Fuels California Inc .................................... F ...... 916 716-7605
  1815 19th St Sacramento (95811) *(P-6155)*
Property Care Building Svc LLC ............................ E ...... 626 623-6420
  126 La Porte St Ste F Arcadia (91006) *(P-17848)*
Propertyradar Inc .................................................. E ...... 530 550-8801
  12242 Business Park Dr Ste 20 Truckee (96161) *(P-18704)*
Propertyradar.com, Truckee *Also Called: Propertyradar Inc (P-18704)*
Prophecy Technology LLC .................................... F ...... 909 598-7998
  339 Cheryl Ln Walnut (91789) *(P-10424)*
Proplas Technologies, Garden Grove *Also Called: Peerless Injection Molding LLC (P-6953)*
Proponent, Brea *Also Called: Proponent Inc (P-16923)*
Proponent Inc (PA) ................................................ C ...... 714 223-5400
  3120 Enterprise St Brea (92821) *(P-16923)*
Proprietary Controls Systems ................................ E ...... 310 303-3600
  3830 Del Amo Blvd # 102 Torrance (90503) *(P-14910)*
Propstream, Lake Forest *Also Called: Equimine (P-18289)*
Prorack Gas Products, Santa Ana *Also Called: Cramer-Decker Industries (P-16579)*
Pros Incorporated ................................................ D ...... 661 589-5400
  3400 Patton Way Bakersfield (93308) *(P-270)*
Proshot Golf, Newport Beach *Also Called: Proshot Investors LLC (P-11919)*
Proshot Investors LLC .......................................... F ...... 949 586-9500
  14 Corporate Plaza Dr Ste 120 Newport Beach (92660) *(P-11919)*

Prospect Enterprises Inc (PA) .............................. C ...... 213 599-5700
  625 Kohler St Los Angeles (90021) *(P-17158)*
Prospectra Contract Flooring, San Diego *Also Called: Pro Installations Inc (P-505)*
Prost LLC .............................................................. E ...... 619 954-4189
  8179 Center St La Mesa (91942) *(P-1455)*
Prosthtic Orthtic Group Ornge .............................. F ...... 949 242-2237
  26300 La Alameda Ste 120 Mission Viejo (92691) *(P-15395)*
Prosurg Inc ............................................................ E ...... 408 945-4040
  2195 Trade Zone Blvd San Jose (95131) *(P-15232)*
Protab Laboratories .............................................. D ...... 949 713-1301
  30321 Esperanza Rcho Sta Marg (92688) *(P-5612)*
Protab Laboratories (PA) ...................................... D ...... 949 635-1930
  25892 Towne Centre Dr Foothill Ranch (92610) *(P-5613)*
Protagonist Games LLC ........................................ E ...... 512 785-4946
  10755 Scripps Poway Pkwy San Diego (92131) *(P-18705)*
PROTAGONIST THERAPEUTICS, Newark *Also Called: Protagonist Therapeutics Inc (P-5614)*
Protagonist Therapeutics Inc (PA) ........................ D ...... 510 474-0170
  7707 Gateway Blvd Ste 140 Newark (94560) *(P-5614)*
Protec, Hercules *Also Called: Mega Creation Inc (P-6005)*
Protec Arisawa America Inc .................................. E ...... 760 599-4800
  2455 Ash St Vista (92081) *(P-8329)*
Protech Design & Manufacturing, San Diego *Also Called: PDM Solutions Inc (P-12188)*
Protech Materials, Hayward *Also Called: Protech Materials Inc (P-7830)*
Protech Materials Inc ............................................ F ...... 510 887-5870
  20919 Cabot Blvd Hayward (94545) *(P-7830)*
Protech Systems, Riverside *Also Called: Alectro Inc (P-11203)*
Protective Wther Strctures Inc .............................. F ...... 805 547-8797
  5290 Orcutt Rd San Luis Obispo (93401) *(P-359)*
Protempis (usa) LLC ............................................ E ...... 408 410-3222
  2151 Otoole Ave Ste 60 San Jose (95131) *(P-10464)*
Proterra (PA) .......................................................... A ...... 864 438-0000
  1815 Rollins Rd Burlingame (94010) *(P-13183)*
Proterra Operating Company Inc .......................... B ...... 864 438-0000
  393 Cheryl Ln City Of Industry (91789) *(P-13377)*
Proterra Operating Company Inc (HQ) .................. D
  1815 Rollins Rd Burlingame (94010) *(P-13378)*
Proterra Powered LLC (DH) .................................. B ...... 864 516-0068
  1815 Rollins Rd Burlingame (94010) *(P-13184)*
Proteus Digital Health Inc (PA) .............................. D ...... 650 632-4031
  2600 Bridge Pkwy Redwood City (94065) *(P-5856)*
Proteus Industries Inc .......................................... E ...... 650 964-4163
  340 Pioneer Way Mountain View (94041) *(P-14447)*
Prothena Corp Pub Ltd Co .................................... E ...... 650 837-8550
  331 Oyster Point Blvd South San Francisco (94080) *(P-5265)*
Proto Homes LLC .................................................. E ...... 310 271-7544
  11301 W Olympic Blvd Los Angeles (90064) *(P-14123)*
Proto Services Inc ................................................ E ...... 408 719-9088
  1991 Concourse Dr San Jose (95131) *(P-12010)*
Protocast, Chatsworth *Also Called: John List Corporation (P-9718)*
Protoform, Banning *Also Called: DT Mattson Enterprises Inc (P-15746)*
Protonex LLC ........................................................ F ...... 707 566-2260
  2331 Circadian Way Santa Rosa (95407) *(P-12642)*
Protool Co, Tustin *Also Called: Bernhardt and Bernhardt Inc (P-9541)*
Prototek Dgtal Mfg Scrmnto LLC .......................... E ...... 916 851-9285
  11341 Sunrise Park Dr Rancho Cordova (95742) *(P-11054)*
Prototek Holdings LLC (PA) .................................. E ...... 800 403-9777
  215 Devcon Dr San Jose (95112) *(P-8547)*
Prototype & Short-Run Svcs Inc .......................... E ...... 714 449-9661
  1310 W Collins Ave Orange (92867) *(P-8879)*
Prototype Engineering and Manufacturing Inc ...... E ...... 310 532-6305
  140 E 162nd St Gardena (90248) *(P-19411)*
Prototype Express LLC ........................................ E ...... 714 751-3533
  3506 W Lake Center Dr Ste D Santa Ana (92704) *(P-13292)*
Prototype Industries Inc (PA) ................................ F ...... 949 680-4890
  26035 Acero Ste 100 Mission Viejo (92691) *(P-4453)*
Protype, Orange *Also Called: G P Manufacturing Inc (P-10848)*
Proulx Manufacturing Inc ...................................... E ...... 909 980-0662
  11433 6th St Rancho Cucamonga (91730) *(P-6987)*
Provac Sales Inc .................................................... E ...... 831 462-8900
  3131 Soquel Dr Ste A Soquel (95073) *(P-9935)*

# ALPHABETIC SECTION — Pura Naturals Inc

**Provena Foods Inc (HQ)** .................................................. D ...... 909 627-1082
5010 Eucalyptus Ave Chino (91710) *(P-660)*

**Provena Foods Inc** .......................................................... C ...... 209 858-5555
251 Darcy Pkwy Lathrop (95330) *(P-661)*

**Provenance Technologies Inc** ......................................... F ...... 415 796-6281
650 California St Ste 07-126 San Francisco (94108) *(P-18706)*

**Provide, San Francisco** *Also Called: Provide Inc (P-18707)*

**Provide Inc** ...................................................................... E ...... 877 341-0617
268 Bush St # 2921 San Francisco (94104) *(P-18707)*

**Providence Publications LLC** ......................................... E ...... 916 774-4000
1620 Santa Clara Dr Ste 115 Roseville (95661) *(P-4454)*

**Providien LLC (HQ)** ......................................................... C ...... 480 344-5000
6740 Nancy Ridge Dr San Diego (92121) *(P-15233)*

**Providien Injction Molding Inc** ....................................... D ...... 760 931-1844
6740 Nancy Ridge Dr San Diego (92121) *(P-6988)*

**Providien Machining & Metals LLC** ................................ D ...... 818 367-3161
12840 Bradley Ave Sylmar (91342) *(P-15234)*

**Providien Machining Mtls Corp, Sylmar** *Also Called: Providien Machining & Metals LLC (P-15234)*

**Providien Thermoforming LLC** ....................................... E ...... 858 850-1591
6740 Nancy Ridge Dr San Diego (92121) *(P-6568)*

**Providien Thermoforming, Inc., San Diego** *Also Called: Providien Thermoforming LLC (P-6568)*

**Provisio Medical Inc** ....................................................... E ...... 508 740-9940
10815 Rancho Bernardo Rd Ste 110 San Diego (92127) *(P-19338)*

**Provision Health Corp** .................................................... F ...... 619 240-3263
9760 Via De La Amistad San Diego (92154) *(P-5615)*

**Provivi Inc** ........................................................................ D ...... 310 828-2307
1701 Colorado Ave Santa Monica (90404) *(P-6156)*

**Proxim Wireless Corporation (PA)** ................................. D ...... 408 383-7600
2114 Ringwood Ave San Jose (95131) *(P-12011)*

**Prp Seats, Temecula** *Also Called: Kamm Industries Inc (P-3011)*

**Prpco** .............................................................................. E ...... 805 543-6844
2226 Beebee St San Luis Obispo (93401) *(P-4742)*

**Prs Industries, Ontario** *Also Called: Inland Powder Coating Corp (P-9079)*

**Prudential Lighting Corp (PA)** ........................................ C ...... 213 477-1694
1774 E 21st St Los Angeles (90058) *(P-11553)*

**Pryor Products** ............................................................... E ...... 760 724-8244
1819 Peacock Blvd Oceanside (92056) *(P-15235)*

**Prysm, Milpitas** *Also Called: Prysm Inc (P-16211)*

**Prysm Inc (PA)** ................................................................ D ...... 408 586-1127
513 Fairview Way Milpitas (95035) *(P-16211)*

**PS Print, LLC, Oakland** *Also Called: TYT LLC (P-4795)*

**PSC, Visalia** *Also Called: Pacific Southwest Cont LLC (P-3872)*

**PSC Industrial Outsourcing LP** ...................................... D ...... 661 833-9991
200 Old Yard Dr Bakersfield (93307) *(P-271)*

**Pscmb Repairs Inc** ........................................................ E ...... 626 448-7778
12145 Slauson Ave Santa Fe Springs (90670) *(P-11055)*

**Psemi Corporation (DH)** ................................................ D ...... 858 731-9400
9369 Carroll Park Dr San Diego (92121) *(P-12643)*

**Psg, San Diego** *Also Called: Pacific Steel Group LLC (P-8706)*

**Psg California LLC (HQ)** ................................................ B ...... 909 422-1700
22069 Van Buren St Grand Terrace (92313) *(P-9936)*

**PSI, El Cajon** *Also Called: Derosa Enterprises Inc (P-8431)*

**PSI, San Jose** *Also Called: Proto Services Inc (P-12010)*

**PSI, Milpitas** *Also Called: PSI Water Technologies Inc (P-14448)*

**PSI Pharma Support America Inc** ................................. E ...... 267 464-2500
401 California Dr Burlingame (94010) *(P-5616)*

**PSI Water Technologies Inc** .......................................... E ...... 408 819-3043
550 Sycamore Dr Milpitas (95035) *(P-14448)*

**Psiquantum Corp (PA)** ................................................... F ...... 650 427-0000
700 Hansen Way Palo Alto (94304) *(P-10198)*

**PSM, Oceanside** *Also Called: Pacific Sewer Maintenance Corp (P-7680)*

**PSM Industries Inc (PA)** ................................................ D ...... 888 663-8256
14000 Avalon Blvd Los Angeles (90061) *(P-9297)*

**Pssc Labs** ...................................................................... F ...... 949 380-7288
20432 N Sea Cir Lake Forest (92630) *(P-10267)*

**PSW Inc** .......................................................................... F ...... 951 371-7100
281 Corporate Terrace St Corona (92879) *(P-2325)*

**Psyonic Inc** .................................................................... E ...... 888 779-6642
9999 Businesspark Ave Ste B San Diego (92131) *(P-15396)*

**Pt Systems Inc** ............................................................... F ...... 925 676-0709
2350 Whitman Rd Ste B Concord (94518) *(P-19412)*

**Ptb, Azusa** *Also Called: Ptb Sales Inc (P-13068)*

**Ptb Sales Inc (PA)** ......................................................... E ...... 626 334-0500
1361 Mountain View Cir Azusa (91702) *(P-13068)*

**PTEC Solutions Inc (PA)** ............................................... C ...... 510 358-3578
48633 Warm Springs Blvd Fremont (94539) *(P-19413)*

**Pterodynamics, Moorpark** *Also Called: Pterodynamics Inc (P-13686)*

**Pterodynamics Inc** ........................................................ F ...... 719 257-3103
14165 Huron Ct Moorpark (93021) *(P-13686)*

**PTi Sand & Gravel Inc** ................................................... E ...... 951 272-0140
14925 River Rd Eastvale (92880) *(P-320)*

**Pti Technologies Inc (DH)** ............................................. C ...... 805 604-3700
501 Del Norte Blvd Oxnard (93030) *(P-13931)*

**Ptm & W Industries Inc** ................................................. E ...... 562 946-4511
10640 Painter Ave Santa Fe Springs (90670) *(P-6589)*

**Ptm Images, West Hollywood** *Also Called: Pro Tour Memorabilia LLC (P-3423)*

**Ptm Images LLC** ........................................................... F ...... 310 881-8053
555 W 5th St Los Angeles (90013) *(P-3747)*

**Ptr Manufacturing Inc** ................................................... E ...... 510 477-9654
33390 Transit Ave Union City (94587) *(P-11056)*

**Ptr Sheet Metal & Fabrication, Union City** *Also Called: Ptr Manufacturing Inc (P-11056)*

**Public Fclities Resources Dept, Santa Ana** *Also Called: County of Orange (P-19576)*

**Public Library of Science (PA)** ..................................... C ...... 415 624-1200
1265 Battery St Ste 200 San Francisco (94111) *(P-19346)*

**Public Utilites Emts, San Diego** *Also Called: City of San Diego (P-14644)*

**Public Works, Stockton** *Also Called: City of Stockton (P-3614)*

**Public Works, Dept of, Malibu** *Also Called: County of Los Angeles (P-9417)*

**Public Works, Dept of, La Puente** *Also Called: County of Los Angeles (P-9418)*

**Publish Brand Inc** .......................................................... F ...... 714 890-1908
15731 Graham St Huntington Beach (92649) *(P-4455)*

**Publishers Development Corp** ..................................... E ...... 858 605-0200
225 W Valley Pkwy Ste 100 Escondido (92025) *(P-4290)*

**Publishers Distribution Svcs, Ventura** *Also Called: Homes & Land of Ventura (P-4132)*

**Puente Ready Mix Services Inc (PA)** ............................ E ...... 626 968-0711
209 N California Ave City Of Industry (91744) *(P-7486)*

**Puglia Engineering Inc** .................................................. C ...... 415 861-7447
Foot Of 20th St Pier 70 San Francisco (94107) *(P-14015)*

**Pulitzer Community Newspapers, Hanford** *Also Called: Hanford Sentinel Inc (P-4125)*

**Pull-N-Pac, Huntington Park** *Also Called: Crown Poly Inc (P-3965)*

**Pulltarps Manufacturing, El Cajon** *Also Called: Roll-Rite LLC (P-2981)*

**Pulltarps Manufacturing, El Cajon** *Also Called: Transportation Equipment Inc (P-2985)*

**Pulmuone Foods Usa Inc** .............................................. B ...... 831 753-6262
340 El Camino Real S Ste 35 Salinas (93901) *(P-2326)*

**Pulp Studio Incorporated** .............................................. D ...... 310 815-4999
2100 W 139th St Gardena (90249) *(P-17837)*

**Pulse A Yageo Company, San Diego** *Also Called: Pulse Electronics Corporation (P-13069)*

**Pulse Electronics Inc (HQ)** ........................................... B ...... 858 674-8100
15255 Innovation Dr Ste 100 San Diego (92128) *(P-11225)*

**Pulse Electronics Corporation (HQ)** ............................. E ...... 858 674-8100
15255 Innovation Dr Ste 100 San Diego (92128) *(P-13069)*

**Pulse Instruments** ........................................................ E ...... 310 515-5330
22301 S Western Ave Ste 107 Torrance (90501) *(P-14575)*

**Pulse Instruments, Camarillo** *Also Called: Primordial Diagnostics Inc (P-14445)*

**Pulse Shower Spas Inc** ................................................. F ...... 831 724-7300
297 Anna St Watsonville (95076) *(P-7279)*

**PUMA BIOTECHNOLOGY, Los Angeles** *Also Called: Puma Biotechnology Inc (P-5617)*

**Puma Biotechnology Inc (PA)** ...................................... C ...... 424 248-6500
10880 Wilshire Blvd Ste 2150 Los Angeles (90024) *(P-5617)*

**Pump-A-Head, San Diego** *Also Called: Keco Inc (P-16823)*

**Punch Press Products Inc** ............................................ D ...... 323 581-7151
2035 E 51st St Vernon (90058) *(P-9644)*

**Punkpost, San Francisco** *Also Called: Punkpost LLC (P-4996)*

**Punkpost LLC** ............................................................... E ...... 415 818-7677
41 Federal St Unit 4 San Francisco (94107) *(P-4996)*

**Pur-Clean Pressure Car Wash, North Highlands** *Also Called: New Wave Industries Ltd (P-10586)*

**Pura Naturals Inc** .......................................................... E ...... 949 273-8100
3401 Space Center Ct Ste 811a Jurupa Valley (91752) *(P-3535)*

**Pura Naturals Inc (HQ)** ............................................................. F ...... 949 273-8100
23615 El Toro Rd Ste X300 Lake Forest (92630) *(P-6029)*

**Pure Flo Water, Escondido** *Also Called: Pure-Flo Water Co (P-1927)*

**Pure Nature Foods LLC** ........................................................... E ...... 530 723-5269
700 Santa Anita Dr Ste A Woodland (95776) *(P-2100)*

**Pure Process Filtration Inc** ...................................................... F ...... 714 891-6527
11582 Markon Dr Garden Grove (92841) *(P-16783)*

**Pure Project LLC** ..................................................................... D ...... 760 552-7873
1305 Hot Springs Way Vista (92081) *(P-1456)*

**Pure Simple Foods LLC** ........................................................... E ...... 805 272-8448
420 Bryant Cir Ste B Ojai (93023) *(P-360)*

**Pure Storage, Santa Clara** *Also Called: Pure Storage Inc (P-18708)*

**Pure Storage Inc (PA)** .............................................................. A ...... 800 379-7873
2555 Augustine Dr Santa Clara (95054) *(P-18708)*

**Pure Wafer Inc** ......................................................................... C ...... 408 945-8112
2240 Ringwood Ave San Jose (95131) *(P-12644)*

**Pure-Flo Water Co (PA)** ........................................................... D ...... 619 596-4130
2169 Orange Ave Escondido (92029) *(P-1927)*

**Pureformance Cables, Torrance** *Also Called: Lynn Products Inc (P-10402)*

**Puretek Corporation** ................................................................. C ...... 818 361-3949
7900 Nelson Rd Unit A Panorama City (91402) *(P-5618)*

**Puretek Corporation (PA)** ........................................................ E ...... 818 361-3316
1145 Arroyo St Ste D San Fernando (91340) *(P-5619)*

**Purewave Networks Inc** ........................................................... E ...... 650 528-5200
3951 Burton Dr Santa Clara (95054) *(P-11920)*

**Purfresh Inc** .............................................................................. E ...... 510 580-0700
1350 Willow Rd Ste 102 Menlo Park (94025) *(P-9893)*

**Puri Tech Inc** ............................................................................ E ...... 951 360-8380
3167 Progress Cir Jurupa Valley (91752) *(P-10593)*

**Puritan Bakery Inc** ................................................................... C ...... 310 830-5451
1624 E Carson St Carson (90745) *(P-17419)*

**Purity Pool Inc** ......................................................................... E ...... 800 527-1961
9533 Crossroads Dr Redding (96003) *(P-7965)*

**Puroflux Corporation** ............................................................... F ...... 805 579-0216
2121 Union Pl Simi Valley (93065) *(P-12853)*

**Puronics Incorporated (HQ)** .................................................... E ...... 925 456-7000
7503 Southfront Rd Livermore (94551) *(P-10594)*

**Purotecs Inc** ............................................................................. F ...... 925 215-0380
216 Lindbergh Ave Livermore (94551) *(P-9894)*

**Purple Wine Production Company** ......................................... C ...... 707 829-6100
9119 Graton Rd Graton (95444) *(P-1714)*

**Purus International Inc** ............................................................ F ...... 760 775-4500
82860 Avenue 45 Indio (92201) *(P-6529)*

**Purveyors Kitchen** .................................................................... E ...... 530 823-8527
2043 Airpark Ct Ste 30 Auburn (95602) *(P-920)*

**Putah Creek Cafe, Winters** *Also Called: Buckhorn Cafe Inc (P-17566)*

**Puyallup Herald, Sacramento** *Also Called: Olympic Cascade Publishing (P-4176)*

**PVA Tepla America Inc (HQ)** .................................................. E ...... 951 371-2500
251 Corporate Terrace St Corona (92879) *(P-11057)*

**Pvai US Opco Inc** ..................................................................... E ...... 703 929-6807
4125 Hopyard Rd Pleasanton (94588) *(P-18709)*

**Pvd Coatings, Huntington Beach** *Also Called: California Faucets Inc (P-8049)*

**Pvd Coatings LLC** .................................................................... F ...... 714 899-4892
5271 Argosy Ave Huntington Beach (92649) *(P-9113)*

**Pvd Modular LLC** ..................................................................... E ...... 510 962-5100
1684 Decoto Rd Ste 215 Union City (94587) *(P-12645)*

**Pvp Advanced Eo Systems Inc (DH)** ...................................... E ...... 714 508-2740
14312 Franklin Ave Ste 100 Tustin (92780) *(P-14814)*

**Pw Eagle Inc** ............................................................................ A ...... 800 621-4404
5200 W Century Blvd Los Angeles (90045) *(P-6601)*

**PW Gillibrand Co Inc (PA)** ...................................................... E ...... 805 526-2195
4537 Ish Dr Simi Valley (93063) *(P-331)*

**Pxise Energy Solutions LLC** ................................................... E ...... 619 696-2944
1455 Frazee Rd Ste 150 San Diego (92108) *(P-13293)*

**Pyr, San Diego** *Also Called: Pyr Preservation Services (P-14016)*

**Pyr Preservation Services** ...................................................... E ...... 619 338-8395
2393 Newton Ave Ste B San Diego (92113) *(P-14016)*

**Pyramid Graphics** .................................................................... F ...... 650 871-0290
325 Harbor Way South San Francisco (94080) *(P-4743)*

**Pyramid Mold & Tool** ............................................................... D ...... 909 476-2555
10155 Sharon Cir Rancho Cucamonga (91730) *(P-9645)*

**Pyramid Printing and Graphics, South San Francisco** *Also Called: Pyramid Graphics (P-4743)*

**Q & B Foods Inc (DH)** .............................................................. D ...... 626 334-8090
15547 1st St Irwindale (91706) *(P-990)*

**Q C A, San Jose** *Also Called: Quality Circuit Assembly Inc (P-12198)*

**Q C M Inc** .................................................................................. E ...... 714 414-1173
285 Gemini Ave Brea (92821) *(P-11378)*

**Q Com Inc** ................................................................................. E ...... 949 833-1000
17782 Cowan Irvine (92614) *(P-11341)*

**Q Microwave Inc** ...................................................................... D ...... 619 258-7322
1591 Pioneer Way El Cajon (92020) *(P-13070)*

**Q Team** ..................................................................................... E ...... 714 228-4465
6400 Dale St Buena Park (90621) *(P-4744)*

**Q Technology Inc** .................................................................... E ...... 925 373-3456
336 Lindbergh Ave Livermore (94551) *(P-11620)*

**Q-See, Anaheim** *Also Called: Digital Periph Solutions Inc (P-11648)*

**Q-Vio LLC** .................................................................................. F ...... 858 777-8299
10211 Pacific Mesa Blvd Ste 401 San Diego (92121) *(P-13071)*

**Q1 Test Inc** ............................................................................... E ...... 909 390-9718
1100 S Grove Ave Ste B2 Ontario (91761) *(P-13932)*

**Qad, Santa Barbara** *Also Called: Qad Inc (P-18711)*

**Qad Inc** ..................................................................................... F ...... 805 684-6614
6450 Via Real Carpinteria (93013) *(P-18710)*

**Qad Inc (HQ)** ............................................................................ C ...... 805 566-6000
101 Innovation Pl Santa Barbara (93108) *(P-18711)*

**Qantel Technologies Inc** ......................................................... E ...... 510 731-2080
9812 Vasquez Cir Loomis (95650) *(P-10199)*

**QApel Medical Inc** .................................................................... D ...... 510 738-6255
4245 Technology Dr Fremont (94538) *(P-15236)*

**Qc Manufacturing Inc** .............................................................. D ...... 951 325-6340
26040 Ynez Rd Temecula (92591) *(P-9995)*

**Qc Poultry, Montebello** *Also Called: Ingenue Inc (P-695)*

**Qdos Inc** ................................................................................... E ...... 949 362-8888
200 Spectrum Center Dr Ste 300 Irvine (92618) *(P-18712)*

**QED Software LLC** .................................................................. E ...... 310 214-3118
211 E Ocean Blvd Long Beach (90802) *(P-18713)*

**Qf Liquidation Inc (PA)** ........................................................... C ...... 949 930-3400
25242 Arctic Ocean Dr Lake Forest (92630) *(P-13561)*

**Qfi Prv Aerospace, Torrance** *Also Called: Quality Forming LLC (P-13933)*

**Qg LLC** ...................................................................................... A ...... 209 384-0444
2201 Cooper Ave Merced (95348) *(P-4745)*

**Qg Printing Corp** ..................................................................... E ...... 951 571-2500
6688 Box Springs Blvd Riverside (92507) *(P-4291)*

**Qg Printing IL LLC** ................................................................... C ...... 951 571-2500
6688 Box Springs Blvd Riverside (92507) *(P-4746)*

**Qlogic LLC (DH)** ...................................................................... C ...... 949 389-6000
15485 Sand Canyon Ave Irvine (92618) *(P-12646)*

**Qmp Inc** .................................................................................... E ...... 661 294-6860
25070 Avenue Tibbitts Valencia (91355) *(P-10595)*

**Qorvo California Inc** ................................................................ E ...... 805 480-5050
950 Lawrence Dr Newbury Park (91320) *(P-13072)*

**Qorvo US, Newbury Park** *Also Called: Qorvo California Inc (P-13072)*

**Qorvo Us Inc** ............................................................................ D ...... 408 493-4304
3099 Orchard Dr San Jose (95134) *(P-12647)*

**Qostronics Inc** ......................................................................... E ...... 408 719-1286
2044 Corporate Ct San Jose (95131) *(P-12194)*

**Qpc Fiber Optic LLC** ............................................................... E ...... 949 361-8855
27612 El Lazo Laguna Niguel (92677) *(P-7795)*

**Qpc Laser, Rancho Cascades** *Also Called: Laser Operations LLC (P-12527)*

**Qpe** ............................................................................................ F ...... 949 263-0381
1372 Mcgaw Ave Irvine (92614) *(P-4826)*

**Qre Operating LLC** .................................................................. D ...... 213 225-5900
707 Wilshire Blvd Ste 4600 Los Angeles (90017) *(P-195)*

**Qsc LLC (PA)** ........................................................................... C ...... 800 854-4079
1675 Macarthur Blvd Costa Mesa (92626) *(P-11689)*

**Qsc Audio, Costa Mesa** *Also Called: Qsc LLC (P-11689)*

**Qspac Industries Inc** .............................................................. D ...... 562 407-3868
15020 Marquardt Ave Santa Fe Springs (90670) *(P-6242)*

**Qst Ingredients and Packg Inc** .............................................. F ...... 909 989-4343
9734 6th St Rancho Cucamonga (91730) *(P-2327)*

**Quad Graphics, Riverside** *Also Called: Qg Printing IL LLC (P-4746)*

## ALPHABETIC SECTION

**Quality Packaging and Engrg**

Quad R Tech, Harbor City *Also Called: Onyx Industries Inc (P-8727)*
Quad/Graphics Inc .................................................................. D ..... 951 689-1122
   6688 Box Springs Blvd Riverside (92507) *(P-4747)*
Quad/Graphics Inc .................................................................. E ..... 916 371-9500
   1201 Shore St West Sacramento (95691) *(P-17782)*
QUAD/GRAPHICS INC., Riverside *Also Called: Quad/Graphics Inc (P-4747)*
Quadricio Inc ........................................................................... E ..... 408 337-2429
   330 Primrose Rd Ste 306 Burlingame (94010) *(P-12648)*
Quadriga Americas LLC ........................................................ E ..... 424 634-4900
   17800 S Main St Ste 113 Gardena (90248) *(P-4456)*
Quadrotech Solutions Inc (PA) .............................................. E ..... 949 754-8000
   20 Enterprise Aliso Viejo (92656) *(P-18714)*
Quady Winery Inc ................................................................... F ..... 559 673-8068
   13181 Road 24 Madera (93637) *(P-1715)*
Quaker, Whittier *Also Called: AC Products Inc (P-6215)*
Quaker City Plating ................................................................ C ..... 562 945-3721
   11729 Washington Blvd Whittier (90606) *(P-9001)*
Quaker City Plating & Silvrsm, Whittier *Also Called: Quaker City Plating (P-9001)*
Quaker Oats, Oakland *Also Called: Quaker Oats Company (P-2021)*
Quaker Oats Company ........................................................... C ..... 510 261-5800
   5625 International Blvd Oakland (94621) *(P-2021)*
Qual-Pro Corporation (HQ) .................................................... C ..... 310 329-7535
   18510 S Figueroa St Gardena (90248) *(P-12195)*
Qualcomm, San Diego *Also Called: Qualcomm Incorporated (P-11921)*
Qualcomm, San Diego *Also Called: Qualcomm Incorporated (P-11922)*
Qualcomm, Santa Clara *Also Called: Qualcomm Incorporated (P-11923)*
Qualcomm, San Diego *Also Called: Qualcomm Incorporated (P-11924)*
Qualcomm, Carlsbad *Also Called: Qualcomm Incorporated (P-12651)*
Qualcomm, Santa Clara *Also Called: Qualcomm Incorporated (P-12652)*
Qualcomm, San Jose *Also Called: Qualcomm Incorporated (P-12653)*
Qualcomm, San Diego *Also Called: Qualcomm Incorporated (P-12654)*
Qualcomm, San Diego *Also Called: Qualcomm Incorporated (P-12655)*
Qualcomm, San Diego *Also Called: Qualcomm Incorporated (P-12656)*
Qualcomm, San Diego *Also Called: Qualcomm Incorporated (P-12657)*
Qualcomm, San Diego *Also Called: Qualcomm Incorporated (P-12658)*
Qualcomm Atheros Inc (HQ) ................................................. A ..... 408 773-5200
   1700 Technology Dr San Jose (95110) *(P-12649)*
Qualcomm Datacenter Tech Inc (HQ) ................................... E ..... 858 567-1121
   5775 Morehouse Dr San Diego (92121) *(P-12650)*
Qualcomm Incorporated ........................................................ C ..... 858 587-1121
   4243 Campus Point Ct San Diego (92121) *(P-11921)*
Qualcomm Incorporated ........................................................ E ..... 202 263-0008
   5775 Morehouse Dr San Diego (92121) *(P-11922)*
Qualcomm Incorporated ........................................................ B ..... 858 587-1121
   3165 Kifer Rd Santa Clara (95051) *(P-11923)*
Qualcomm Incorporated (PA) ................................................ A ..... 858 587-1121
   5775 Morehouse Dr San Diego (92121) *(P-11924)*
Qualcomm Incorporated ........................................................ E ..... 858 651-8481
   2016 Palomar Airport Rd Ste 100 Carlsbad (92011) *(P-12651)*
Qualcomm Incorporated ........................................................ E ..... 408 216-6797
   3135 Kifer Rd Santa Clara (95051) *(P-12652)*
Qualcomm Incorporated ........................................................ D ..... 408 546-2000
   1700 Technology Dr San Jose (95110) *(P-12653)*
Qualcomm Incorporated ........................................................ E ..... 619 341-2920
   5828 Pacific Center Blvd Ste 100 San Diego (92121) *(P-12654)*
Qualcomm Incorporated ........................................................ E ..... 858 909-0316
   5751 Pacific Center Blvd San Diego (92121) *(P-12655)*
Qualcomm Incorporated ........................................................ C ..... 858 587-1121
   9393 Waples St Ste 150 San Diego (92121) *(P-12656)*
Qualcomm Incorporated ........................................................ D ..... 858 587-1121
   10555 Sorrento Valley Rd San Diego (92121) *(P-12657)*
Qualcomm Incorporated ........................................................ D ..... 858 587-1121
   5525 Morehouse Dr San Diego (92121) *(P-12658)*
Qualcomm Mems Technologies Inc ...................................... E ..... 858 587-1121
   5775 Morehouse Dr San Diego (92121) *(P-12012)*
Qualcomm Technologies Inc (HQ) ........................................ B ..... 858 587-1121
   5775 Morehouse Dr San Diego (92121) *(P-12659)*
Qualcomm Technologies Inc .................................................. E ..... 858 587-1121
   5745 Pacific Center Blvd San Diego (92121) *(P-12660)*
Qualcomm Technologies Inc .................................................. E ..... 858 658-3040
   10350 Sorrento Valley Rd San Diego (92121) *(P-12661)*
Qualer Inc ................................................................................. E ..... 858 224-9516
   9477 Waples St San Diego (92121) *(P-18715)*
Quali-Tech Manufacturing, Calexico *Also Called: Lakim Industries Incorporated (P-15932)*
Qualigen Inc (HQ) ................................................................... E ..... 760 918-9165
   2042 Corte Del Nogal Ste B Carlsbad (92011) *(P-14347)*
Qualio Inc (PA) ........................................................................ E ..... 415 795-7331
   268 Bush St San Francisco (94104) *(P-18716)*
Qualitask Inc ........................................................................... E ..... 714 237-0900
   2840 E Gretta Ln Anaheim (92806) *(P-11058)*
Qualitau Incorporated (PA) ................................................... D ..... 408 675-3034
   2270 Martin Ave Santa Clara (95050) *(P-14576)*
Qualitek Inc (HQ) .................................................................... D ..... 408 734-8686
   1116 Elko Dr Sunnyvale (94089) *(P-12196)*
Qualitek Inc ............................................................................. D ..... 408 752-8422
   1272 Forgewood Ave Sunnyvale (94089) *(P-12197)*
Quality Aluminum Forge LLC (HQ) ...................................... E ..... 714 639-8191
   793 N Cypress St Orange (92867) *(P-8800)*
Quality Aluminum Forge LLC ............................................... C ..... 714 639-8191
   794 N Cypress St Orange (92867) *(P-8801)*
Quality Aluminum Forge Div, Orange *Also Called: Gel Industries Inc (P-8797)*
Quality Cabinet and Fixture Co (HQ) ................................... E ..... 619 266-1011
   7955 Saint Andrews Ave San Diego (92154) *(P-3261)*
Quality Cabinet Shop Inc ...................................................... E ..... 209 948-0431
   3256 Tomahawk Dr Stockton (95205) *(P-3262)*
Quality Circuit Assembly Inc ................................................ D ..... 408 441-1001
   161 Baypointe Pkwy San Jose (95134) *(P-12198)*
Quality Control Plating Inc ................................................... E ..... 909 605-0206
   4425 E Airport Dr Ste 113 Ontario (91761) *(P-9002)*
Quality Control Solutions Inc ............................................... F ..... 951 676-1616
   43339 Business Park Dr Ste 101 Temecula (92590) *(P-14911)*
Quality Controlled Mfg Inc .................................................... D ..... 619 443-3997
   9429 Abraham Way Santee (92071) *(P-11059)*
Quality Distributor, El Cajon *Also Called: Benny Enterprises Inc (P-17258)*
Quality Door & Trim, Stockton *Also Called: J & J Quality Door Inc (P-3148)*
Quality Doors & Trim, Lakeport *Also Called: Young & Family Inc (P-3210)*
Quality Fabrication Inc (PA) ................................................. D ..... 818 407-5015
   4020 Garner Rd Riverside (92501) *(P-8548)*
Quality First Woodworks Inc ................................................ C ..... 714 632-0480
   1264 N Lakeview Ave Anaheim (92807) *(P-3424)*
Quality Foam Packaging, Lake Elsinore *Also Called: Aerofoam Industries Inc (P-3612)*
Quality Foam Packaging Inc ................................................ E ..... 951 245-4429
   31855 Corydon St Lake Elsinore (92530) *(P-6658)*
Quality Forming LLC ............................................................. D ..... 310 539-2855
   22906 Frampton Ave Torrance (90501) *(P-13933)*
Quality Grinding Co Inc ........................................................ F ..... 714 228-2100
   6800 Caballero Blvd Buena Park (90620) *(P-9694)*
Quality Heat Treating Inc ...................................................... E ..... 818 840-8212
   3305 Burton Ave Burbank (91504) *(P-7898)*
Quality Industry Repair, Santa Fe Springs *Also Called: Pscmb Repairs Inc (P-11055)*
Quality Industry Repair Inc .................................................. F ..... 626 448-7778
   1815 Potrero Ave South El Monte (91733) *(P-11060)*
Quality Machine Engrg Inc ................................................... E ..... 707 528-1900
   2559 Grosse Ave Santa Rosa (95404) *(P-11061)*
Quality Machining & Design Inc .......................................... E ..... 408 224-7976
   2857 Aiello Dr San Jose (95111) *(P-9895)*
Quality Marble & Granite, Ontario *Also Called: Regards Enterprises Inc (P-3408)*
Quality Metal Fabrication LLC ............................................. E ..... 530 887-7388
   2350 Wilbur Way Auburn (95602) *(P-8549)*
Quality Metal Spinning, Palo Alto *Also Called: Quality Mtal Spnning McHning I (P-8880)*
Quality Mtal Spnning McHning I ........................................... E ..... 650 858-2491
   4047 Transport St Palo Alto (94303) *(P-8880)*
Quality Naturally Foods Inc .................................................. E ..... 626 854-6363
   17769 Railroad St City Of Industry (91748) *(P-17206)*
Quality Naturally Foods Inc (PA) ......................................... E ..... 626 854-6363
   18830 San Jose Ave City Of Industry (91748) *(P-17207)*
QUALITY NATURALLYU FOODS, INC., City Of Industry *Also Called: Quality Naturally Foods Inc (P-17206)*
Quality Packaging and Engrg, Irvine *Also Called: Qpe Inc (P-4826)*

## Quality Powder Coating — ALPHABETIC SECTION

**Quality Powder Coating, Bakersfield** *Also Called: Elyte Inc (P-9067)*

**Quality Resources Dist LLC** .................................................... E ...... 510 378-6861
16254 Beaver Rd Adelanto (92301) *(P-16212)*

**Quality Rubber Sourcing Inc** ................................................... F ...... 805 544-7770
3988 Short St Ste 110 San Luis Obispo (93401) *(P-6530)*

**Quality Service Pac Industry, Santa Fe Springs** *Also Called: Qspac Industries Inc (P-6242)*

**Quality Shutters Inc** ............................................................... E ...... 951 683-4939
3359 Chicago Ave Ste A Riverside (92507) *(P-3183)*

**Quality Steel Fabricators Inc** .................................................. E ...... 858 748-8400
13275 Gregg St Poway (92064) *(P-8708)*

**Quality Systems, San Diego** *Also Called: Quality Systems Intgrated Corp (P-12200)*

**Quality Systems Intgrated Corp** .............................................. C ...... 858 536-3128
7098 Miratech Dr Ste 170 San Diego (92121) *(P-12199)*

**Quality Systems Intgrated Corp (PA)** ....................................... C ...... 858 587-9797
6740 Top Gun St San Diego (92121) *(P-12200)*

**Quality Tech Mfg Inc** ............................................................. E ...... 909 465-9565
170 W Mindanao St Bloomington (92316) *(P-13687)*

**Quality Technology Solutions** ................................................. F ...... 559 804-4522
788 S Peach Ave Reedley (93654) *(P-468)*

**Quality Transformer & Elec** .................................................... E ...... 408 935-0231
963 Ames Ave Milpitas (95035) *(P-11226)*

**Quality Transformer & Elec Co, Milpitas** *Also Called: Quality Transformer & Elec (P-11226)*

**Qualitylogic Inc** .................................................................... C ...... 208 424-1905
2245 1st St Ste 103 Simi Valley (93065) *(P-10425)*

**Quallion LLC** ........................................................................ C ...... 818 833-2000
12744 San Fernando Rd Ste 100 Sylmar (91342) *(P-13163)*

**Qualls Stud Welding Pdts Inc** ................................................. E ...... 562 923-7883
9459 Washburn Rd Downey (90242) *(P-16835)*

**Qualys Inc (PA)** .................................................................... A ...... 650 801-6100
919 E Hillsdale Blvd Ste 400 Foster City (94404) *(P-17966)*

**Quanergy Perception Tech Inc (HQ)** ........................................ E ...... 408 245-9500
433 Lakeside Dr Sunnyvale (94085) *(P-14280)*

**Quantal International Inc** ....................................................... E ...... 415 644-0754
455 Market St Ste 1200 San Francisco (94105) *(P-18717)*

**Quantcast Corporation (PA)** ................................................... D ...... 800 293-5706
795 Folsom St Fl 5 San Francisco (94107) *(P-17967)*

**Quanten Consortium Angola LLC** ............................................ E ...... 408 955-0768
1161-70 Ringwood Ct San Jose (95131) *(P-6346)*

**Quantic M-Wave** ................................................................... F ...... 805 499-8825
82 W Cochran St Ste B Simi Valley (93065) *(P-16730)*

**Quantic Mwd, Irvine** *Also Called: Microwave Dynamics LLC (P-11891)*

**Quanticel Pharmaceuticals Inc** ............................................... E ...... 858 956-3747
9393 Towne Centre Dr Ste 110 San Diego (92121) *(P-5620)*

**Quantimetrix** ........................................................................ D ...... 310 536-0006
2005 Manhattan Beach Blvd Redondo Beach (90278) *(P-5775)*

**Quantmshift Communications Inc** .......................................... F ...... 800 804-8266
12657 Alcosta Blvd San Ramon (94583) *(P-18718)*

**Quantum** ............................................................................. E ...... 323 709-8880
220 S Glasgow Ave Inglewood (90301) *(P-10268)*

**QUANTUM, San Jose** *Also Called: Quantum Corporation (P-10269)*

**Quantum Automation (PA)** ..................................................... E ...... 714 854-0800
4400 E La Palma Ave Anaheim (92807) *(P-16671)*

**Quantum Corporation (PA)** ..................................................... C ...... 408 944-4000
224 Airport Pkwy Ste 550 San Jose (95110) *(P-10269)*

**Quantum Corporation** ............................................................ E ...... 949 856-7800
141 Innovation Dr Ste 100 Irvine (92617) *(P-10270)*

**Quantum Corporation, Irvine** *Also Called: Certance LLC (P-10231)*

**Quantum Design Inc (PA)** ....................................................... C ...... 858 481-4400
10307 Pacific Center Ct San Diego (92121) *(P-14708)*

**Quantum Design International, San Diego** *Also Called: Quantum Design Inc (P-14708)*

**Quantum Global Tech LLC (HQ)** .............................................. C ...... 215 892-9300
26462 Corporate Ave Hayward (94545) *(P-5927)*

**Quantum Magnetics LLC** ........................................................ A ...... 714 258-4400
1251 E Dyer Rd Ste 140 Santa Ana (92705) *(P-14709)*

**Quantum Networks LLC** ......................................................... E ...... 212 993-5899
3412 Garfield Ave Commerce (90040) *(P-17670)*

**Quantum Technologies, Lake Forest** *Also Called: Qf Liquidation Inc (P-13561)*

**Quantum3d Inc (PA)** .............................................................. F ...... 408 600-2500
920 Hillview Ct Ste 145 Milpitas (95035) *(P-14281)*

**Quantumcamp Inc** ................................................................. F ...... 650 933-5467
4010 Opal St Oakland (94609) *(P-10271)*

**Quantumclean, Hayward** *Also Called: Quantum Global Tech LLC (P-5927)*

**Quantumscape Battery Inc** ..................................................... C ...... 408 452-2000
1730 Technology Dr San Jose (95110) *(P-12662)*

**Quantumscape Corporation (PA)** ............................................. A ...... 408 452-2000
1730 Technology Dr San Jose (95110) *(P-12663)*

**Quantumsphere Inc** .............................................................. F ...... 714 545-6266
28981 Modjeska Peak Ln Trabuco Canyon (92679) *(P-7911)*

**Quark Pharmaceuticals Inc (DH)** ............................................. E ...... 510 402-4020
495 N Whisman Rd Ste 100 Mountain View (94043) *(P-5621)*

**Quarterwave Corp** ................................................................. E ...... 707 793-9105
1500 Valley House Dr Ste 100 Rohnert Park (94928) *(P-19568)*

**Quartic Solutions LLC** ............................................................ E ...... 858 377-8470
1427 Chalcedony St San Diego (92109) *(P-16542)*

**Quartics Inc** ......................................................................... E ...... 949 679-2672
15241 Laguna Canyon Rd Ste 200 Irvine (92618) *(P-12664)*

**Quashnick Tool Corporation** ................................................... E ...... 209 334-5283
225 N Guild Ave Lodi (95240) *(P-6989)*

**Quatro Composites, Poway** *Also Called: Quatro Composites LLC (P-13934)*

**Quatro Composites LLC** ......................................................... C ...... 712 707-9200
13250 Gregg St Ste A1 Poway (92064) *(P-13934)*

**Queen Beach Printers Inc** ...................................................... E ...... 562 436-8201
937 Pine Ave Long Beach (90813) *(P-4748)*

**Quemetco West LLC** .............................................................. E ...... 626 330-2294
720 S 7th Ave City Of Industry (91746) *(P-7722)*

**Quest, Aliso Viejo** *Also Called: Quadrotech Solutions Inc (P-18714)*

**Quest Diagnostics, Ukiah** *Also Called: Quest Diagnostics Incorporated (P-19331)*

**Quest Diagnostics Incorporated** .............................................. F ...... 707 462-7553
1165 S Dora St Ste A1 Ukiah (95482) *(P-19331)*

**Quest Inds - Stockton Plant, Stockton** *Also Called: By Quest LLC (P-4856)*

**Quest International, Irvine** *Also Called: Quest Intl Monitor Svc Inc (P-19021)*

**Quest Intl Monitor Svc Inc (PA)** .............................................. D ...... 949 581-9900
60 Parker 65 Irvine (92618) *(P-19021)*

**Quest Software Inc** ............................................................... D ...... 949 754-8000
4 Polaris Way Aliso Viejo (92656) *(P-18719)*

**Quest Software Inc (PA)** ......................................................... A ...... 949 754-8000
20 Enterprise Ste 100 Aliso Viejo (92656) *(P-18988)*

**Quest Solution, Garden Grove** *Also Called: Bar Code Specialties Inc (P-10331)*

**Questivity Inc** ....................................................................... F ...... 408 615-1781
1680 Civic Center Dr Ste 209 Santa Clara (95050) *(P-18720)*

**Quetzal, San Francisco** *Also Called: Quetzal Group Inc (P-17602)*

**Quetzal Group Inc** ................................................................. E ...... 415 673-4181
1234 Polk St San Francisco (94109) *(P-17602)*

**Quick Crete Products Corp** ..................................................... C ...... 951 737-6240
731 Parkridge Ave Norco (92860) *(P-7377)*

**Quick Draw and Machining Inc** ............................................... F ...... 805 644-7882
4869 Mcgrath St Ste130 Ventura (93003) *(P-8881)*

**Quickbooks Capital, Mountain View** *Also Called: Intuit Financing Inc (P-18429)*

**QUICKLOGIC, San Jose** *Also Called: Quicklogic Corporation (P-12665)*

**Quicklogic Corporation (PA)** ................................................... E ...... 408 990-4000
2220 Lundy Ave San Jose (95131) *(P-12665)*

**Quickrete, Corona** *Also Called: Quikrete California LLC (P-7378)*

**Quid LLC** ............................................................................. C ...... 415 813-5300
3960 Freedom Cir Ste 200 Santa Clara (95054) *(P-17968)*

**Quidel Corporation** ............................................................... E ...... 858 552-1100
10165 Mckellar Ct San Diego (92121) *(P-5776)*

**Quidel Corporation (HQ)** ........................................................ D ...... 858 552-1100
9975 Summers Ridge Rd San Diego (92121) *(P-5777)*

**Quidelortho Corporation (PA)** ................................................. E ...... 858 552-1100
9975 Summers Ridge Rd San Diego (92121) *(P-5778)*

**Quiel Bros Elc Sign Svc Co Inc** ............................................... E ...... 909 885-4476
272 S I St San Bernardino (92410) *(P-16024)*

**Quietrock, Rancho Cordova** *Also Called: Pabco Building Products LLC (P-7527)*

**Quik-Pak, Hayward** *Also Called: Delphon Industries LLC (P-6797)*

**Quikrete California LLC (DH)** .................................................. E ...... 951 277-3155
3940 Temescal Canyon Rd Corona (92883) *(P-7378)*

**Quikrete California LLC** ......................................................... E ...... 510 490-4670
6950 Stevenson Blvd Fremont (94538) *(P-7379)*

**Quikrete California LLC** ......................................................... E ...... 916 689-8840
7705 Wilbur Way Sacramento (95828) *(P-7380)*

**Quikrete Companies LLC** ....................................................... E ...... 559 781-1949
14200 Road 284 Porterville (93257) *(P-7381)*

# ALPHABETIC SECTION

Quikrete Companies LLC .................................................. E ...... 510 490-4670
   6950 Stevenson Blvd Fremont (94538) *(P-7382)*
Quikrete Companies LLC .................................................. E ...... 323 875-1367
   11145 Tuxford St Sun Valley (91352) *(P-7383)*
Quikrete Companies LLC .................................................. E ...... 510 490-4670
   7705 Wilbur Way Sacramento (95828) *(P-7384)*
Quikrete Northern California, Porterville *Also Called: Quikrete Companies LLC (P-7381)*
Quikrete of Atlanta, Fremont *Also Called: Quikrete Companies LLC (P-7382)*
Quiksilver/Dc Shoes, Mira Loma *Also Called: DC Shoes Inc (P-17087)*
Quikstor, Encino *Also Called: Calstar Systems Group Inc (P-13217)*
Quilt In A Day Inc ............................................................ E ...... 760 591-0929
   1955 Diamond St San Marcos (92078) *(P-17671)*
Quince Therapeutics Inc (PA) ........................................ F ...... 415 910-5717
   611 Gateway Blvd Fl 2 South San Francisco (94080) *(P-5857)*
Quinn Development Co .................................................. F
   5787 Obata Way Gilroy (95020) *(P-7297)*
Quinoa Corporation ........................................................ E ...... 707 462-6605
   1 Carousel Ln Ste D Ukiah (95482) *(P-1239)*
Quinstar Technology Inc ................................................ D ...... 310 320-1111
   24085 Garnier St Torrance (90505) *(P-16731)*
QUINSTREET, Foster City *Also Called: Quinstreet Inc (P-19118)*
Quinstreet Inc (PA) .......................................................... E ...... 650 578-7700
   950 Tower Ln Ste 600 Foster City (94404) *(P-19118)*
Quintessa Vineyards, Saint Helena *Also Called: Huneeus Vintners LLC (P-1617)*
Quite Powerful Enterprises LLC .................................... F ...... 800 782-0915
   626 Wilshire Blvd Ste 410 Los Angeles (90017) *(P-4342)*
Quivira Vineyards, Healdsburg *Also Called: Pjk Winery LLC (P-1710)*
Quoc Viet Foods .............................................................. F ...... 714 519-3199
   830 Williamson Ave Fullerton (92832) *(P-2328)*
Quoc Viet Foods .............................................................. F ...... 714 283-3663
   1967 N Glassell St Orange (92865) *(P-2329)*
Quoc Viet Foods (PA) ...................................................... E ...... 714 283-3663
   12221 Monarch St Garden Grove (92841) *(P-2330)*
Quorex Pharm Inc (PA) ................................................... E ...... 760 602-1910
   2232 Rutherford Rd Carlsbad (92008) *(P-5622)*
Qwilt Inc ........................................................................... E ...... 650 249-6521
   275 Shoreline Dr Ste 510 Redwood City (94065) *(P-4457)*
Qxq Inc ............................................................................. E ...... 510 252-1522
   44113 S Grimmer Blvd Fremont (94538) *(P-14577)*
Qycell Corporation .......................................................... E ...... 909 390-6644
   600 Etiwanda Ave Ontario (91761) *(P-5192)*
Qyk Brands LLC ............................................................... C ...... 833 795-7664
   12101 Western Ave Garden Grove (92841) *(P-17047)*
R & B Wire Products Inc ................................................. E ...... 714 549-3355
   2902 W Garry Ave Santa Ana (92704) *(P-9227)*
R & D Fasteners, Rancho Cucamonga *Also Called: Doubleco Incorporated (P-8752)*
R & D Metal Fabricators Inc ............................................ E ...... 714 891-4878
   5250 Rancho Rd Huntington Beach (92647) *(P-8550)*
R & D Nova Inc ................................................................. F ...... 951 781-7332
   2934 E Garvey Ave S Ste 104 West Covina (91791) *(P-15574)*
R & D Steel Inc ................................................................. E ...... 310 631-6183
   7930 E Tarma St Long Beach (90808) *(P-8207)*
R & D Tech, Milpitas *Also Called: Hytek R&D Inc (P-12133)*
R & G Precision Machining Inc ...................................... E ...... 760 630-8602
   2585 Jason Ct Oceanside (92056) *(P-11062)*
R & G Schatz Farms Inc ................................................. F ...... 209 367-4881
   22150 N Kennefick Rd Acampo (95220) *(P-24)*
R & I, Ontario *Also Called: R & I Industries Inc (P-8208)*
R & I Industries Inc ......................................................... E ...... 909 923-7747
   1876 S Taylor Ave Ontario (91761) *(P-8208)*
R & J Fabricators Inc ...................................................... E ...... 951 817-0300
   1121 Railroad St Ste 102 Corona (92882) *(P-3748)*
R & J Material Handling Inc ........................................... F ...... 951 735-0000
   345 Adams Cir Corona (92882) *(P-16836)*
R & K Industrial Products Co ........................................ E ...... 510 234-7212
   1945 7th St Richmond (94801) *(P-9298)*
R & L Enterprises Inc ..................................................... E ...... 559 233-1608
   1955 S Mary St Fresno (93721) *(P-11063)*
R & M Painting Inc .......................................................... F ...... 209 576-2576
   2928 Yosemite Blvd Modesto (95354) *(P-448)*

R & R Ductwork, Santa Fe Springs *Also Called: R & R Ductwork LLC (P-8551)*
R & R Ductwork LLC ....................................................... F ...... 562 944-9660
   12820 Lakeland Rd Santa Fe Springs (90670) *(P-8551)*
R & R Industries, San Clemente *Also Called: Rosen & Rosen Industries Inc (P-15847)*
R & R Industries Inc ....................................................... E ...... 800 234-5611
   204 Avenida Fabricante San Clemente (92672) *(P-2908)*
R & R Rubber Molding Inc ............................................. E ...... 626 575-8105
   2444 Loma Ave South El Monte (91733) *(P-6531)*
R & R Services Corporation .......................................... F ...... 818 889-2562
   3595 Old Conejo Rd Newbury Park (91320) *(P-6532)*
R & S Automation Inc ..................................................... E ...... 800 962-3111
   283 W Bonita Ave Pomona (91767) *(P-8285)*
R & S Manufacturing Inc (HQ) ....................................... E ...... 510 429-1788
   33955 7th St Union City (94587) *(P-8286)*
R & S Manufacturing & Sup Inc .................................... F ...... 909 622-5881
   16616 Garfield Ave Paramount (90723) *(P-6108)*
R & S Ovrhd Doors So-Cal Inc ...................................... E ...... 714 680-0600
   1617 N Orangethorpe Way Anaheim (92801) *(P-19277)*
R & S Processing Co Inc ............................................... D ...... 562 531-0738
   15712 Illinois Ave Paramount (90723) *(P-6533)*
R & S Rolling Door Products, Union City *Also Called: R & S Manufacturing Inc (P-8286)*
R A Phillips Industries Inc (PA) .................................... E ...... 562 781-2121
   12012 Burke St Santa Fe Springs (90670) *(P-13562)*
R A Reed Electric Company (PA) .................................. E ...... 323 587-2284
   5503 S Boyle Ave Vernon (90058) *(P-19231)*
R B III Associates Inc .................................................... C ...... 760 471-5370
   2386 Faraday Ave Ste 125 Carlsbad (92008) *(P-2725)*
R B R Meat Company Inc .............................................. E ...... 323 973-4868
   5151 Alcoa Ave Vernon (90058) *(P-613)*
R C Furniture Inc ............................................................ D ...... 626 964-4100
   1111 Jellick Ave City Of Industry (91748) *(P-3486)*
R C I P Inc ....................................................................... F ...... 714 630-1239
   1476 N Hundley St Anaheim (92806) *(P-11064)*
R C Industries, Anaheim *Also Called: R C I P Inc (P-11064)*
R D D USA Division, Commerce *Also Called: RDD Enterprises Inc (P-17512)*
R D Mathis Company ..................................................... E ...... 562 426-7049
   2840 Gundry Ave Signal Hill (90755) *(P-7636)*
R D Rubber Technology Corp ....................................... E ...... 562 941-4800
   12870 Florence Ave Santa Fe Springs (90670) *(P-6476)*
R H Barden Inc ............................................................... F ...... 714 970-0900
   4769 E Wesley Dr Anaheim (92807) *(P-12854)*
R H Strasbaugh (PA) ...................................................... E ...... 805 541-6424
   825 Buckley Rd San Luis Obispo (93401) *(P-9564)*
R I M, Loomis *Also Called: Rimnetics Inc (P-7005)*
R J McGlennon Company Inc (PA) ............................... E ...... 415 552-0311
   198 Utah St San Francisco (94103) *(P-6109)*
R J Miles Co, Colfax *Also Called: Scott Miles (P-17343)*
R J Reynolds Tobacco Company .................................. D ...... 858 625-8453
   8380 Miramar Mall Ste 117 San Diego (92121) *(P-2396)*
R K Fabrication Inc ........................................................ F ...... 714 630-9654
   1283 N Grove St Anaheim (92806) *(P-5193)*
R K I, Union City *Also Called: Rki Instruments Inc (P-16838)*
R K Larrabee Company Inc ........................................... D ...... 925 828-9420
   7800 Las Positas Rd Livermore (94551) *(P-11282)*
R Kern Engineering & Mfg Corp ................................... D ...... 909 664-2440
   13912 Mountain Ave Chino (91710) *(P-12894)*
R Lang Company ............................................................ D ...... 559 651-0701
   8240 W Doe Ave Visalia (93291) *(P-8287)*
R M Baker Machine and TI Inc ...................................... F ...... 562 697-4007
   815 W Front St Covina (91722) *(P-11065)*
R M I, Gardena *Also Called: Rotational Molding Inc (P-7009)*
R M I, Van Nuys *Also Called: Rothlisberger Mfg A Cal Corp (P-11091)*
R O S, San Diego *Also Called: Remote Ocean Systems Inc (P-11621)*
R Planet Earth LLC ......................................................... C ...... 213 320-0601
   3200 Fruitland Ave Vernon (90058) *(P-16361)*
R R Donnelley, San Diego *Also Called: R R Donnelley & Sons Company (P-4947)*
R R Donnelley & Sons Company .................................. E ...... 619 527-4600
   955 Gateway Center Way San Diego (92102) *(P-4947)*
R R Donnelley & Sons Company .................................. D ...... 310 516-3100
   19681 Pacific Gateway Dr Torrance (90502) *(P-4948)*

**R R Donnelley & Sons Company** .................................................. D ...... 951 296-2890
40610 County Center Dr Ste 100 Temecula (92591) *(P-16994)*
**R T C Group** ........................................................................................ E ...... 949 226-2000
905 Calle Amanecer Ste 250 San Clemente (92673) *(P-4292)*
**R T I, Morgan Hill** *Also Called: Robson Technologies Inc (P-11084)*
**R Torre & Company Inc (PA)** ....................................................... D ...... 800 775-1925
2000 Marina Blvd San Leandro (94577) *(P-2022)*
**R Torre & Company Inc** ............................................................... E ...... 800 775-1925
1952 Williams St San Leandro (94577) *(P-2023)*
**R V Best Inc** ......................................................................................... E ...... 619 448-7300
9335 Stevens Rd Santee (92071) *(P-6990)*
**R W I, Campbell** *Also Called: Ron Witherspoon Inc (P-9696)*
**R W Swarens Associates Inc** ........................................................ E ...... 626 579-0943
10768 Lower Azusa Rd El Monte (91731) *(P-11554)*
**R Zamora Inc** ...................................................................................... E ...... 760 597-1130
4645 North Ave Ste 102 Oceanside (92056) *(P-8882)*
**R-Cold Inc** ........................................................................................... D ...... 951 436-5476
1221 S G St Perris (92570) *(P-10511)*
**R&D Metal, Huntington Beach** *Also Called: R & D Metal Fabricators Inc (P-8550)*
**R&K Industrial Wheels, Richmond** *Also Called: R & K Industrial Products Co (P-9298)*
**R&M Deese Inc** .................................................................................. E ...... 951 734-7342
1875 Sampson Ave Corona (92879) *(P-16025)*
**R&M Supply Inc** ................................................................................ D ...... 951 552-9860
420 Harley Knox Blvd Perris (92571) *(P-9399)*
**R1 Concepts Inc (PA)** ..................................................................... E ...... 714 777-2323
13140 Midway Pl Cerritos (90703) *(P-16391)*
**R2 Semiconductor Inc** .................................................................... F ...... 408 745-7400
3600 W Bayshore Rd Ste 205 Palo Alto (94303) *(P-12666)*
**R2 Technologies Inc** ........................................................................ E ...... 925 378-4400
6517 Sierra Ln Dublin (94568) *(P-15237)*
**R3 Performance Products Inc** ..................................................... F ...... 760 909-0846
531 Old Woman Springs Rd Yucca Valley (92284) *(P-13563)*
**RA Industries LLC** ........................................................................... E ...... 714 557-2322
900 Glenneyre St Laguna Beach (92651) *(P-11066)*
**Raceamerica Inc** .............................................................................. F ...... 408 988-6188
62 Bonaventura Dr San Jose (95134) *(P-11342)*
**Raceline Wheels, Garden Grove** *Also Called: Allied Wheel Components Inc (P-13454)*
**Racepak LLC** ...................................................................................... E ...... 949 709-5555
30402 Esperanza Rcho Sta Marg (92688) *(P-13564)*
**Racing Power Company** ................................................................. E ...... 909 468-3690
815 Tucker Ln Walnut (91789) *(P-13565)*
**Rack & Riddle, Healdsburg** *Also Called: RB Wine Associates LLC (P-1719)*
**Rack Installation Services Inc** ..................................................... E ...... 909 261-2243
1256 Brooks St Ste E Ontario (91762) *(P-3701)*
**Rack Shelves, Fresno** *Also Called: Fresno Rack & Shelving Inc (P-3688)*
**Rackmountpro.com, La Puente** *Also Called: Yang-Ming International Corp (P-19001)*
**Raco, Berkeley** *Also Called: Raco Manufacturing & Engrg Co (P-13294)*
**Raco Manufacturing & Engrg Co** ............................................... E ...... 510 658-6713
727 Allston Way Ste B Berkeley (94710) *(P-13294)*
**Radcal Corporation** ......................................................................... E ...... 626 357-7921
426 W Duarte Rd Monrovia (91016) *(P-14912)*
**Radford Cabinets Inc** ..................................................................... D ...... 661 729-8931
216 E Avenue K8 Lancaster (93535) *(P-3453)*
**Radian Audio Engineering Inc** ..................................................... E ...... 714 288-8900
2720 Kimball Ave Pomona (91767) *(P-11925)*
**Radian Heat Sinks, Santa Clara** *Also Called: Radian Thermal Products Inc (P-7870)*
**Radian Memory Systems Inc** ....................................................... E ...... 818 222-4080
5010 N Pkwy Ste 205 Calabasas (91302) *(P-10272)*
**Radian Thermal Products Inc** ..................................................... D ...... 408 988-6200
2160 Walsh Ave Santa Clara (95050) *(P-7870)*
**Radiance Beauty & Wellness Inc** ................................................ E ...... 818 812-9740
9419 Mason Ave Chatsworth (91311) *(P-6030)*
**Radiant Graph Inc** ............................................................................ E ...... 857 928-3248
3525 16th St San Francisco (94114) *(P-19119)*
**Radiant Logic Inc (HQ)** ................................................................. E ...... 415 209-6800
818 5th Ave San Rafael (94901) *(P-18721)*
**Radiation Protection & Spc Inc** .................................................. F ...... 714 771-7702
5991 Short St Yorba Linda (92886) *(P-8552)*
**Radiator Specialty Company** ....................................................... D ...... 707 252-0122
935 Enterprise Way Napa (94558) *(P-6319)*

**Radiology Support Devices Inc** ................................................... E ...... 310 518-0527
1501 W 178th St Gardena (90248) *(P-15238)*
**Raditek Inc (PA)** ............................................................................... D ...... 408 266-7404
1702l Meridian Ave Ste 127 San Jose (95125) *(P-11926)*
**Radix, Los Angeles** *Also Called: Radix Textile Inc (P-17066)*
**Radix Textile Inc** .............................................................................. D ...... 323 234-1667
600 E Washington Blvd Ste C2 Los Angeles (90015) *(P-17066)*
**Rae Systems Inc (DH)** ................................................................... E ...... 408 952-8200
1349 Moffett Park Dr Sunnyvale (94089) *(P-14913)*
**Rael Inc** ................................................................................................ E ...... 800 573-1516
6940 Beach Blvd Unit D301 Buena Park (90621) *(P-4005)*
**Raemica Inc** ........................................................................................ E ...... 909 864-1990
7759 Victoria Ave Highland (92346) *(P-662)*
**Rafael Sandoval** ................................................................................ E ...... 209 858-4173
16175 Mckinley Ave Lathrop (95330) *(P-3076)*
**Rafco Products Brickform, Rancho Cucamonga** *Also Called: Rafco-Brickform LLC (P-9695)*
**Rafco-Brickform LLC (PA)** ........................................................... D ...... 909 484-3399
11061 Jersey Blvd Rancho Cucamonga (91730) *(P-9695)*
**Rago & Son Inc** ................................................................................ D ...... 510 536-5700
1029 51st Ave Oakland (94601) *(P-8883)*
**RAH Industries Inc (PA)** ................................................................ C ...... 661 295-5190
24800 Avenue Rockefeller Valencia (91355) *(P-8553)*
**Rahn Industries, Whittier** *Also Called: Rahn Industries Incorporated (P-10512)*
**Rahn Industries Incorporated (PA)** ............................................ E ...... 562 908-0680
2630 Pacific Park Dr Whittier (90601) *(P-10512)*
**Railroad Signals, Rancho Cucamonga** *Also Called: Highball Signal Inc (P-11998)*
**Railstech Inc** ...................................................................................... E ...... 267 315-2998
730 Arizona Ave Santa Monica (90401) *(P-18722)*
**Rain Bird, Azusa** *Also Called: Rain Bird Corporation (P-9191)*
**Rain Bird Corporation** .................................................................... D ...... 626 812-3400
970 W Sierra Madre Ave Azusa (91702) *(P-8055)*
**Rain Bird Corporation (PA)** ......................................................... C ...... 626 812-3400
970 W Sierra Madre Ave Azusa (91702) *(P-9191)*
**Rain Bird Corporation** .................................................................... E ...... 619 674-4068
9491 Ridgehaven Ct San Diego (92123) *(P-9377)*
**Rain Bird Golf Division, Azusa** *Also Called: Rain Bird Corporation (P-8055)*
**Rain For Rent, Bakersfield** *Also Called: Western Oilfields Supply Co (P-17865)*
**Rain Oncology Inc (PA)** ................................................................. D ...... 510 953-5559
8000 Jarvis Ave Ste 204 Newark (94560) *(P-5623)*
**Rain Therapeutics, Newark** *Also Called: Rain Oncology Inc (P-5623)*
**Rainbeau, San Francisco** *Also Called: Jjs Mae Inc (P-2773)*
**Rainbo Record Mfg Corp (PA)** .................................................... E ...... 818 280-1100
8960 Eton Ave Canoga Park (91304) *(P-11742)*
**Rainbo Records & Cassettes, Canoga Park** *Also Called: Rainbo Record Mfg Corp (P-11742)*
**Rainbow Farms, Denair** *Also Called: Valley Fresh Foods Inc (P-66)*
**Rainbow Light** .................................................................................... E ...... 831 429-9089
125 Mcpherson St Santa Cruz (95060) *(P-5266)*
**Raindance, Pleasanton** *Also Called: Raindance Technologies Inc (P-14710)*
**Raindance Technologies Inc** ........................................................ E ...... 978 495-3300
5731 W Las Positas Blvd Pleasanton (94588) *(P-14710)*
**Rainmaker Solutions Inc** ............................................................... F ...... 855 463-5843
121 Sierra St El Segundo (90245) *(P-6428)*
**Raise 3d, Irvine** *Also Called: Raise 3d Inc (P-16543)*
**Raise 3d Inc** ....................................................................................... F ...... 888 963-9028
43 Tesla Irvine (92618) *(P-16543)*
**Raise 3d Technologies Inc** ........................................................... E ...... 949 482-2040
43 Tesla Irvine (92618) *(P-10426)*
**Raison DEtre Bakery LLC** ............................................................. D ...... 650 952-8889
179 Starlite St South San Francisco (94080) *(P-2101)*
**Raj Manufacturing LLC** .................................................................. E ...... 714 838-3110
2712 Dow Ave Tustin (92780) *(P-2802)*
**Raj Manufacturing Inc (PA)** ......................................................... F ...... 714 838-3110
2712 Dow Ave Tustin (92780) *(P-2803)*
**Rajswim, Tustin** *Also Called: Raj Manufacturing LLC (P-2802)*
**Rakar Incorporated** ......................................................................... E ...... 805 487-2721
1680 Universe Cir Oxnard (93033) *(P-6991)*
**Rakworx Inc** ....................................................................................... C ...... 949 215-1362
1 Mason Irvine (92618) *(P-19022)*
**Ralco Holdings Inc (DH)** ............................................................... C ...... 949 440-5094
13861 Rosecrans Ave Santa Fe Springs (90670) *(P-16392)*

## ALPHABETIC SECTION

Ralec USA Electronic Corp, Baldwin Park *Also Called: Meritek Electronics Corp (P-9876)*
**Rally Holdings LLC** ............................................................................ A ...... 817 919-6833
17771 Mitchell N Irvine (92614) *(P-16393)*
**Ralph E Ames Machine Works** ........................................................... E ...... 310 328-8523
2301 Dominguez Way Torrance (90501) *(P-11067)*
Ralph Wilson Plastics, Santa Fe Springs *Also Called: Wilsonart LLC (P-16293)*
**Ralphs-Pugh Co Inc** ............................................................................ D ...... 707 745-6222
3931 Oregon St Benicia (94510) *(P-9492)*
Ralphs-Pugh Co., Benicia *Also Called: Ralphs-Pugh Co Inc (P-9492)*
**Ram Board Inc** .................................................................................... E ...... 818 848-0400
27460 Avenue Scott Unit A Valencia (91355) *(P-16076)*
**Ram Mechanical Inc** ........................................................................... D ...... 209 531-9155
3506 Moore Rd Ceres (95307) *(P-430)*
**Rama Corporation** .............................................................................. E ...... 951 654-7351
600 W Esplanade Ave San Jacinto (92583) *(P-10058)*
**Rama Food Manufacture Corp (PA)** ................................................... F ...... 909 923-5305
1486 E Cedar St Ontario (91761) *(P-2331)*
**Ramador Inc** ....................................................................................... D ...... 209 245-6979
12225 Steiner Rd Plymouth (95669) *(P-1716)*
**Ramar International Corp** ................................................................... E ...... 925 432-4267
539 Garcia Ave Ste E Pittsburg (94565) *(P-614)*
**Ramar International Corp (PA)** ........................................................... E ...... 925 439-9009
1101 Railroad Ave Pittsburg (94565) *(P-814)*
RAMBUS, San Jose *Also Called: Rambus Inc (P-12669)*
**Rambus Inc** ......................................................................................... E ...... 408 462-8000
4353 N 1st St # 100 San Jose (95134) *(P-12667)*
**Rambus Inc** ......................................................................................... E ...... 919 960-6600
4453 N 1st St San Jose (95134) *(P-12668)*
**Rambus Inc (PA)** ................................................................................ C ...... 408 462-8000
4453 N 1st St Ste 100 San Jose (95134) *(P-12669)*
**RAMCAR Batteries Inc** ....................................................................... E ...... 323 726-1212
2700 Carrier Ave Commerce (90040) *(P-16394)*
**Ramcast Ornamental Sup Co Inc** ....................................................... E ...... 909 469-4767
1450 E Mission Blvd Pomona (91766) *(P-16630)*
Ramcast Steel, Pomona *Also Called: Ramcast Ornamental Sup Co Inc (P-16630)*
Ramda Metal Specialties, Gardena *Also Called: Ramda Metal Specialties Inc (P-8554)*
**Ramda Metal Specialties Inc** .............................................................. E ...... 310 538-2136
13012 Crenshaw Blvd Gardena (90249) *(P-8554)*
**Rami Designs Inc** ............................................................................... F ...... 949 588-8288
24 Hammond Ste E Irvine (92618) *(P-8641)*
**Ramirez Pallets Inc** ............................................................................. E ...... 909 822-2066
8431 Sultana Ave Fontana (92335) *(P-3356)*
**Ramisons Inc** ...................................................................................... F ...... 714 323-7134
1534 S Harbor Blvd Anaheim (92802) *(P-17603)*
**Ramko Injection Inc** ........................................................................... D ...... 951 929-0360
3551 Tanya Ave Hemet (92545) *(P-6992)*
**Ramko Mfg Inc** ................................................................................... D ...... 951 652-3510
3500 Tanya Ave Hemet (92545) *(P-11068)*
**Ramona Research Inc** ....................................................................... F ...... 858 679-0717
13741 Danielson St Ste J Poway (92064) *(P-11927)*
**Ramp Engineering Inc** ....................................................................... E ...... 562 531-8030
6850 Walthall Way Paramount (90723) *(P-11069)*
Ramp Restaurant , The, San Francisco *Also Called: St Francis Marine Center (P-17606)*
**Rampone Industries LLC** .................................................................. E ...... 714 265-0200
168 E Liberty Ave Anaheim (92801) *(P-9228)*
**Rams Gate Winery LLC** .................................................................... E ...... 707 721-8700
28700 Arnold Dr Sonoma (95476) *(P-1717)*
**Ramsay Highlander Inc** ..................................................................... E ...... 831 675-3453
45 Gonzales River Rd Gonzales (93926) *(P-9378)*
**Ramtec Associates Inc** ..................................................................... E ...... 714 996-7477
3200 E Birch St Ste B Brea (92821) *(P-6993)*
**Ranch Systems Inc** ........................................................................... F ...... 415 884-2770
865 Sweetser Ave Ste A Novato (94945) *(P-9379)*
**Rancho Foods Inc** ............................................................................. D ...... 323 585-0503
2528 E 37th St Vernon (90058) *(P-17165)*
Rancho Sisquoc Winery, Santa Maria *Also Called: Flood Ranch Company (P-1570)*
Rand Machine Works, Fresno *Also Called: R & L Enterprises Inc (P-11063)*
**Randal Optimal Nutrients LLC** .......................................................... E ...... 707 528-1800
1595 Hampton Way Santa Rosa (95407) *(P-5624)*
**Rando AAA Hvac Inc** ........................................................................ E ...... 408 293-4717
1712 Stone Ave Ste 1 San Jose (95125) *(P-431)*

Randtron Antenna Systems, Menlo Park *Also Called: Fisica Applied Tech Inc (P-11856)*
**Rangeme USA LLC** ........................................................................... E ...... 510 688-0995
821 Folsom St San Francisco (94107) *(P-4458)*
**Rangers Die Casting Co** .................................................................... E ...... 310 764-1800
10828 Alameda St Lynwood (90262) *(P-7819)*
Rani Therapeutics, San Jose *Also Called: Rani Therapeutics Holdings Inc (P-5626)*
**Rani Therapeutics LLC** .................................................................... D ...... 408 457-3700
2051 Ringwood Ave San Jose (95131) *(P-5625)*
**Rani Therapeutics Holdings Inc (PA)** ............................................... D ...... 408 457-3700
2051 Ringwood Ave San Jose (95131) *(P-5626)*
**Ranir LLC** .......................................................................................... E ...... 866 373-7374
6 Centerpointe Dr Ste 640 La Palma (90623) *(P-5627)*
Rankin and Rankin, Olivehurst *Also Called: Lhl Construction Inc (P-533)*
**Rankin-Delux Inc (PA)** ...................................................................... F ...... 951 685-0081
3245 Corridor Dr Eastvale (91752) *(P-10596)*
Ransome Manufacturing, Fresno *Also Called: Meeder Equipment Company (P-9874)*
**Rantec Microwave Systems Inc** ....................................................... E ...... 760 744-1544
2066 Wineridge Pl Escondido (92029) *(P-11928)*
**Rantec Microwave Systems Inc (PA)** ............................................... D ...... 818 223-5000
31186 La Baya Dr Westlake Village (91362) *(P-14282)*
**RAP Security Inc** .............................................................................. D ...... 323 560-3493
4630 Cecilia St Cudahy (90201) *(P-3702)*
**Raphaels Inc** ..................................................................................... F
4460 Braeburn Rd San Diego (92116) *(P-3425)*
**Rapid Accu-Form Inc** ........................................................................ F ...... 707 745-1879
3825 Sprig Dr Benicia (94510) *(P-6994)*
Rapid Displays, Hayward *Also Called: Outform Group Inc (P-3999)*
Rapid Displays, Union City *Also Called: Outform Group Inc (P-4000)*
Rapid Lasergraphics, San Francisco *Also Called: Rapid Typographers Company (P-5022)*
Rapid Manufacturing, Anaheim *Also Called: Rapid Mfg A Cal Ltd Partnr (P-9229)*
**Rapid Mfg A Cal Ltd Partnr (PA)** ...................................................... C ...... 714 974-2432
8080 E Crystal Dr Anaheim (92807) *(P-9229)*
**Rapid Precision Mfg Inc** ................................................................... E ...... 408 617-0771
1516 Montague Expy San Jose (95131) *(P-11070)*
**Rapid Product Solutions Inc** ............................................................ E ...... 805 485-7234
2240 Celsius Ave Ste D Oxnard (93030) *(P-11071)*
**Rapid Rack Holdings Inc** .................................................................. A
1370 Valley Vista Dr Ste 100 Diamond Bar (91765) *(P-3703)*
**Rapid Rack Industries Inc** ................................................................ D
1370 Valley Vista Dr Ste 100 Diamond Bar (91765) *(P-3704)*
**Rapid Typographers Company (PA)** ................................................ F ...... 415 957-5840
836 Harrison St San Francisco (94107) *(P-5022)*
Rapidbizapps, Milpitas *Also Called: Rapidbizappscom LLC (P-17969)*
**Rapidbizappscom LLC** ..................................................................... F ...... 408 647-3050
1525 Mccarthy Blvd Ste 1101 Milpitas (95035) *(P-17969)*
Rapids Warehousing, Kerman *Also Called: Helena Industries LLC (P-17361)*
**Rapiscan Laboratories Inc (HQ)** ...................................................... D ...... 408 961-9700
46718 Fremont Blvd Fremont (94538) *(P-15506)*
**Rapiscan Laboratories Inc** .............................................................. E ...... 510 399-7101
3793 Spinnaker Ct Fremont (94538) *(P-15507)*
**Rapiscan Systems Inc (HQ)** ............................................................ C ...... 310 978-1457
2805 Columbia St Torrance (90503) *(P-15508)*
RAPT THERAPEUTICS, South San Francisco *Also Called: Rapt Therapeutics Inc (P-5628)*
**Rapt Therapeutics Inc** ..................................................................... D ...... 650 489-9000
561 Eccles Ave South San Francisco (94080) *(P-5628)*
**Rare Barrel LLC** .............................................................................. E ...... 510 984-6585
216 Amherst Ave San Mateo (94402) *(P-1457)*
Rare Barrel, The, San Mateo *Also Called: Rare Barrel LLC (P-1457)*
**Rare Breed Distilling LLC (HQ)** ....................................................... E ...... 415 315-8060
55 Francisco St Ste 100 San Francisco (94133) *(P-1841)*
**Rare Parts Inc** ................................................................................. E ...... 209 948-6005
621 Wilshire Ave Stockton (95203) *(P-16395)*
**Rascal Therapeutics Inc** ................................................................. E ...... 650 770-0192
3000 El Camino Real Bldg 4 Palo Alto (94306) *(P-5629)*
**Rasilient Systems Inc (PA)** ............................................................. E ...... 408 730-2568
3281 Kifer Rd Santa Clara (95051) *(P-16544)*
**Rasmussen Iron Works Inc** ............................................................ D ...... 562 696-8718
12028 Philadelphia St Whittier (90601) *(P-8075)*
**Raspadoxpress** ................................................................................ D ...... 818 892-6969
8610 Van Nuys Blvd Panorama City (91402) *(P-4459)*

**Rastaclat LLC**                                                                                             **ALPHABETIC SECTION**

**Rastaclat LLC** ............................................................. E ...... 424 287-0902
100 W Broadway Ste 3000 Long Beach (90802) *(P-15703)*

**Rategain Adara Inc** ..................................................... E ...... 408 691-3603
2033 Gateway Pl 5th Fl San Jose (95110) *(P-18723)*

**Ratermann Manufacturing Inc (PA)**.......................... E ...... 800 264-7793
275 S K St Livermore (94550) *(P-6995)*

**Raudmans Craig Victory Circle** ................................. F ...... 661 833-4600
700 S Mount Vernon Ave Ste 100 Bakersfield (93307) *(P-17460)*

**Ravenswood Solutions Inc (HQ)**............................... D ...... 650 241-3661
48371 Fremont Blvd Ste 105 Fremont (94538) *(P-18989)*

**Raveon Technologies Corp** ....................................... E ...... 760 444-5995
2320 Cousteau Ct Vista (92081) *(P-11929)*

**Ravig Inc** ..................................................................... D ...... 925 526-1234
510 Garcia Ave Ste E Pittsburg (94565) *(P-16545)*

**Ravioli Factory, Napa** *Also Called: Dominics Orgnal Gnova Deli Inc (P-17377)*

**Ravlich Enterprises LLC** ............................................ E ...... 310 533-0748
202 W 140th St Los Angeles (90061) *(P-9003)*

**Ravlich Enterprises LLC (PA)**.................................... E ...... 714 964-8900
100 Business Center Dr Corona (92878) *(P-9004)*

**Raw Farm LLC** ........................................................... E ...... 559 846-9732
7221 S Jameson Ave Fresno (93706) *(P-59)*

**Raw Juicery Inc** ......................................................... F ...... 213 221-6081
915 Mateo St Ste 207 Los Angeles (90021) *(P-1016)*

**Rawson Custom Cabinets Inc** .................................. E ...... 408 779-9838
1115 Holly Oak Cir San Jose (95120) *(P-3263)*

**Ray Moles Farms Inc (PA)**......................................... E ...... 559 444-0324
9503 S Hughes Ave Fresno (93706) *(P-960)*

**Ray Products Company Inc** ...................................... E ...... 888 776-9014
1700 Chablis Ave Ontario (91761) *(P-6996)*

**Ray Road Vineyards, Lodi** *Also Called: Thomas Allen Vnyrds Winery LLC (P-1781)*

**Ray Therapeutics Inc** ................................................. E ...... 858 617-8610
1 Sansome St San Francisco (94104) *(P-5630)*

**Raychem Product Division, Redwood City** *Also Called: Te Connectivity Corporation (P-12900)*

**Rayco Electronic Mfg Inc** .......................................... E ...... 310 329-2660
1220 W 130th St Gardena (90247) *(P-12855)*

**Raydiance Inc** ............................................................ F ...... 408 764-4000
1100 La Avenida St Mountain View (94043) *(P-19488)*

**Rayes Inc (PA)**........................................................... F ...... 785 726-4885
252 Mariah Cir Corona (92879) *(P-15397)*

**Raykorvay Inc** ............................................................ F ...... 714 632-8680
1070 N Kraemer Pl Anaheim (92806) *(P-15734)*

**Raymond Vineyard & Cellar Inc (DH)**........................ E ...... 707 963-3141
849 Zinfandel Ln Saint Helena (94574) *(P-25)*

**Raymonds Little Print Shop Inc** ............................... B ...... 510 353-3608
41454 Christy St Fremont (94538) *(P-4749)*

**Rayotek Scientific, San Diego** *Also Called: Rayotek Scientific LLC (P-7241)*

**Rayotek Scientific LLC** ............................................. E ...... 858 558-3671
8845 Rehco Rd San Diego (92121) *(P-7241)*

**Raypak Inc (DH)**........................................................ B ...... 805 278-5300
2151 Eastman Ave Oxnard (93030) *(P-8076)*

**Raytheon, El Segundo** *Also Called: Raytheon Company (P-14283)*

**Raytheon, El Segundo** *Also Called: Raytheon Company (P-14284)*

**Raytheon, Fullerton** *Also Called: Raytheon Company (P-14285)*

**Raytheon, Goleta** *Also Called: Raytheon Company (P-14287)*

**Raytheon, San Diego** *Also Called: Raytheon Company (P-14288)*

**Raytheon, El Segundo** *Also Called: Raytheon Company (P-14289)*

**Raytheon, El Segundo** *Also Called: Raytheon Company (P-14290)*

**Raytheon Applied Sgnal Tech In** ............................... C ...... 310 436-7000
2000 E El Segundo Blvd El Segundo (90245) *(P-11930)*

**Raytheon Applied Sgnal Tech In (DH)**...................... D ...... 408 749-1888
100 Headquarters Dr San Jose (95134) *(P-11931)*

**Raytheon Applied Sgnal Tech In** .............................. D ...... 714 917-0255
160 N Riverview Dr Ste 300 Anaheim (92808) *(P-12013)*

**Raytheon Company** ................................................... C ...... 805 967-5511
6380 Hollister Ave Goleta (93117) *(P-13295)*

**Raytheon Company** ................................................... E ...... 310 647-9438
2000 E El Segundo Blvd El Segundo (90245) *(P-14283)*

**Raytheon Company** ................................................... D ...... 310 647-1000
1921 E Mariposa Ave El Segundo (90245) *(P-14284)*

**Raytheon Company** ................................................... F ...... 714 446-2584
1801 Hughes Dr Fullerton (92833) *(P-14285)*

**Raytheon Company** ................................................... C ...... 714 732-0119
1801 Hughes Dr Fullerton (92833) *(P-14286)*

**Raytheon Company** ................................................... C ...... 805 562-4611
75 Coromar Dr Goleta (93117) *(P-14287)*

**Raytheon Company** ................................................... D ...... 858 571-6598
8650 Balboa Ave San Diego (92123) *(P-14288)*

**Raytheon Company** ................................................... B ...... 310 647-1000
2000 E El Segundo Blvd El Segundo (90245) *(P-14289)*

**Raytheon Company** ................................................... A ...... 310 647-9438
2000 E El Segundo Blvd El Segundo (90245) *(P-14290)*

**Raytheon Dgital Force Tech LLC (DH)**..................... E ...... 858 546-1244
6779 Mesa Ridge Rd Ste 150 San Diego (92121) *(P-14291)*

**Rayzebio Inc (HQ)**..................................................... F ...... 619 937-2754
5505 Morehouse Dr Ste 300 San Diego (92121) *(P-5631)*

**Rayzist Photomask Inc (PA)**..................................... D ...... 760 727-8561
955 Park Center Dr Vista (92081) *(P-15900)*

**Razor, Cerritos** *Also Called: Razor USA LLC (P-14067)*

**Razor USA LLC (PA)**.................................................. D ...... 562 345-6000
12723 166th St Cerritos (90703) *(P-14067)*

**Razvi Inc** .................................................................... E ...... 925 242-1200
824 La Gonda Way Danville (94526) *(P-19012)*

**RB Wine Associates LLC** .......................................... E ...... 209 365-9463
1 Winemaster Way Ste D Lodi (95240) *(P-1718)*

**RB Wine Associates LLC (PA)**.................................. D ...... 707 433-8400
499 Moore Ln Healdsburg (95448) *(P-1719)*

**Rbc Transport Dynamics Corp** ................................. C ...... 203 267-7001
3131 W Segerstrom Ave Santa Ana (92704) *(P-16890)*

**Rbd Online Inc** .......................................................... E ...... 800 681-1757
1800 Lombardi Ln Santa Rosa (95407) *(P-7289)*

**Rbf Group International** ............................................ F ...... 626 333-5700
1441 W 2nd St Pomona (91766) *(P-3584)*

**Rbf Lifestyle Holdings, Pomona** *Also Called: Rbf Group International (P-3584)*

**Rbf Lifestyle Holdings LLC** ...................................... E ...... 626 333-5700
1441 W 2nd St Pomona (91766) *(P-3585)*

**Rbm Conveyor Systems Inc** ..................................... E ...... 909 620-1333
1570 W Mission Blvd Pomona (91766) *(P-9811)*

**Rbz Vineyards LLC** ................................................... E ...... 805 542-0133
2324 W Highway 46 Paso Robles (93446) *(P-1720)*

**RC Readymix Co Inc** ................................................. E ...... 925 449-7785
1227 Greenville Rd Livermore (94550) *(P-7487)*

**Rcbs, Sacramento** *Also Called: River City Building Supply Inc (P-16482)*

**Rcd Engineering Inc** ................................................. E ...... 530 292-3133
17100 Salmon Mine Rd Nevada City (95959) *(P-11343)*

**RCP Block & Brick Inc (PA)**...................................... D ...... 619 460-9101
8240 Broadway Lemon Grove (91945) *(P-7298)*

**RCP Block & Brick Inc** ............................................. E ...... 619 448-2240
8755 N Magnolia Ave Santee (92071) *(P-7299)*

**RCP Block & Brick Inc** ............................................. E ...... 619 474-1516
75 N 4th Ave Chula Vista (91910) *(P-7300)*

**RCP Block & Brick Inc** ............................................. E ...... 760 753-1164
577 N Vulcan Ave Encinitas (92024) *(P-7301)*

**Rcrv Inc (PA)**............................................................. E ...... 323 235-8070
4715 S Alameda St Vernon (90058) *(P-2587)*

**Rdc Machine Inc** ....................................................... E ...... 408 970-0721
2011 Stone Ave San Jose (95125) *(P-11072)*

**RDD Enterprises Inc** ................................................. F ...... 213 746-0020
4638 E Washington Blvd Commerce (90040) *(P-2564)*

**RDD Enterprises Inc** ................................................. F ...... 213 742-0666
4638 E Washington Blvd Commerce (90040) *(P-17512)*

**RDfabricators Inc** ..................................................... F ...... 714 634-2078
11880 Western Ave Stanton (90680) *(P-8555)*

**RDM Industries** ......................................................... E ...... 714 690-0380
14310 Gannet St La Mirada (90638) *(P-16837)*

**Rdmm Legacy Inc** ..................................................... E ...... 323 232-2147
724 E 60th St Los Angeles (90001) *(P-17067)*

**RDS Wire & Cable Incorporated** ............................... F ...... 310 323-7131
225 E Gardena Blvd Gardena (90248) *(P-9230)*

**RE Tranquillity 8 LLC** ................................................ D ...... 415 675-1500
300 California St Fl 7 San Francisco (94104) *(P-8077)*

**Reach Technology Inc** .............................................. E ...... 510 770-1417
4575 Cushing Pkwy Fremont (94538) *(P-13073)*

## ALPHABETIC SECTION — Reed Electric & Field Service

Reaction Technology Inc (HQ) .................................................. E ...... 408 970-9601
 1590 Buckeye Dr Milpitas (95035) *(P-12670)*
Read It Later Inc .................................................................... E ...... 415 692-6111
 233 Samsone St Ste 1200 San Francisco (94104) *(P-18724)*
Ready Industries Inc ............................................................... F ...... 213 749-2041
 1520 E 15th St Los Angeles (90021) *(P-4750)*
Ready Pac Foods, Irwindale *Also Called: Ready Pac Produce Inc (P-2333)*
Ready Pac Foods Inc (HQ) ...................................................... A ...... 626 856-8686
 4401 Foxdale St Irwindale (91706) *(P-2332)*
Ready Pac Produce Inc (DH) .................................................... E ...... 800 800-4088
 4401 Foxdale St Irwindale (91706) *(P-2333)*
Ready Reproductions, Los Angeles *Also Called: Ready Industries Inc (P-4750)*
Readymix - Cordelia R/M, Suisun City *Also Called: Cemex Cnstr Mtls PCF LLC (P-7316)*
Readymix - Union City Rm, Union City *Also Called: Cemex Cnstr Mtls PCF LLC (P-7423)*
Readymix -Redlands Rm Dual, Highland *Also Called: Cemex Cnstr Mtls PCF LLC (P-7422)*
Readymix- Lodi Rm, Lodi *Also Called: Cemex Cnstr Mtls PCF LLC (P-7424)*
Reagent Chemical & RES Inc .................................................. E ...... 909 796-4059
 1454 S Sunnyside Ave San Bernardino (92408) *(P-5113)*
Reagent World Inc .................................................................. F ...... 909 947-7779
 18401 Von Karman Ave Irvine (92612) *(P-16604)*
Real Estate Image Inc (PA) ...................................................... C ...... 714 502-3900
 1415 S Acacia Ave Fullerton (92831) *(P-17803)*
Real Estate Trainers Inc .......................................................... E ...... 800 282-2352
 212 Towne Centre Pl Ste 100 Anaheim (92806) *(P-19349)*
Real Marketing ........................................................................ E ...... 858 847-0335
 8470 Redwood Creek Ln Ste 200 San Diego (92126) *(P-4460)*
Real Mex Foods Inc ................................................................. D ...... 714 523-0031
 5660 Katella Ave Ste 200 Cypress (90630) *(P-17118)*
Real Plating Inc ....................................................................... E ...... 909 623-2304
 1245 W 2nd St Pomona (91766) *(P-9005)*
Real Seal, Escondido *Also Called: REAL Seal Co Inc (P-6462)*
REAL Seal Co Inc .................................................................... E ...... 760 743-7263
 1971 Don Lee Pl Escondido (92029) *(P-6462)*
Real Software Systems LLC (PA) ............................................. E ...... 818 313-8000
 21255 Burbank Blvd Ste 220 Woodland Hills (91367) *(P-18725)*
Real Vision Foods, Irvine *Also Called: Real Vision Foods LLC (P-1044)*
Real Vision Foods LLC ............................................................ E ...... 253 228-5050
 72 Knollglen Irvine (92614) *(P-1044)*
Realdefense LLC (PA) ............................................................. E ...... 801 895-7907
 150 S Los Robles Ave Ste 400 Pasadena (91101) *(P-19060)*
Realscout Inc .......................................................................... F ...... 650 397-6500
 480 Ellis St Ste 203 Mountain View (94043) *(P-18726)*
Realtruck, Anaheim *Also Called: Realtruck Enterprise Inc (P-13424)*
Realtruck Enterprise Inc ......................................................... E ...... 956 324-5337
 1747 W Lincoln Ave Ste K Anaheim (92801) *(P-13424)*
Reaps Company LLC ............................................................... E ...... 212 256-1186
 1950 S Santa Fe Ave Ste 109 Los Angeles (90021) *(P-16213)*
Reason Foundation ................................................................. E ...... 310 391-2245
 5737 Mesmer Ave Los Angeles (90230) *(P-19120)*
Rebbl, Emeryville *Also Called: Rebbl Inc (P-843)*
Rebbl Inc ................................................................................. E ...... 855 732-2500
 5900 Hollis St Ste L Emeryville (94608) *(P-843)*
Rebecca International Inc ....................................................... E ...... 323 973-2602
 4587 E 48th St Vernon (90058) *(P-2999)*
Rebel Jeans, Los Angeles *Also Called: Be Bop Clothing (P-2738)*
Reboot Labs LLC ..................................................................... D ...... 916 926-1716
 1721 Aviation Blvd Ste 100 Lincoln (95648) *(P-6685)*
Reborn Bath Solutions, Anaheim *Also Called: Reborn Cabinets LLC (P-3264)*
Reborn Cabinets LLC (PA) ....................................................... B ...... 714 630-2220
 5515 E La Palma Ave Ste 250 Anaheim (92807) *(P-3264)*
Rebound Therapeutics Corp .................................................... E ...... 949 305-8111
 13900 Alton Pkwy Ste 120 Irvine (92618) *(P-15239)*
Rec Inc .................................................................................... F ...... 760 727-8006
 2442 Cades Way Vista (92081) *(P-10109)*
Receptos Inc ........................................................................... E ...... 858 652-5700
 3033 Science Park Rd Ste 300 San Diego (92121) *(P-5632)*
Recoating-West Inc (PA) ......................................................... E ...... 916 652-8290
 4170 Douglas Blvd Ste 120 Granite Bay (95746) *(P-8556)*
Recognition Products Mfg, San Jose *Also Called: Stryker Enterprises Inc (P-9300)*
Recold, Brea *Also Called: SPX Cooling Tech LLC (P-8338)*

Recommind Inc (HQ) ............................................................... D ...... 415 394-7899
 550 Kearny St Ste 700 San Francisco (94108) *(P-13201)*
Reconserve Inc (HQ) ............................................................... E ...... 310 458-1574
 2811 Wilshire Blvd Ste 410 Santa Monica (90403) *(P-1145)*
Reconserve of Maryland, Santa Monica *Also Called: Dext Company of Maryland (P-1124)*
Record Technology Inc (PA) .................................................... E ...... 805 484-2747
 486 Dawson Dr Ste 4s Camarillo (93012) *(P-11743)*
Record The, Stockton *Also Called: Dow Jones Lmg Stockton Inc (P-4105)*
Recorder .................................................................................. E ...... 877 256-2472
 1035 Market St San Francisco (94103) *(P-4183)*
Recruitment Services Inc ........................................................ E ...... 213 364-1960
 3600 Wilshire Blvd Ste 1526 Los Angeles (90010) *(P-4293)*
Recycled Aggregate Mtls Co Inc, Simi Valley *Also Called: ACC Ca Inc (P-6359)*
Recycled Paper Products, Santa Fe Springs *Also Called: Gabriel Container (P-3845)*
Recycled Spaces Inc ............................................................... F ...... 530 587-3394
 10157 Donner Pass Rd Truckee (96161) *(P-3557)*
Recycler Classified, Sherman Oaks *Also Called: E Z Buy & E Z Sell Recycl Corp (P-4106)*
Red Bay Coffee Company Inc ................................................. E ...... 510 409-1076
 3098 E 10th St Oakland (94601) *(P-2079)*
Red Brick Corporation ............................................................. F ...... 323 549-9444
 5364 Venice Blvd Los Angeles (90019) *(P-4751)*
Red Bull Media Hse N Amer Inc .............................................. D ...... 310 393-4647
 1630 Stewart St Ste A Santa Monica (90404) *(P-1928)*
Red Digital Cinema Camera Co, Foothill Ranch *Also Called: Redcom LLC (P-15663)*
Red Gate Software Inc ............................................................ E ...... 626 993-3949
 144 W Colorado Blvd Ste 200 Pasadena (91105) *(P-18727)*
Red Hat Inc ............................................................................. E ...... 650 567-9039
 444 Castro St Ste 1200 Mountain View (94041) *(P-18728)*
Red Line Synthetic Oil Corporation ......................................... F ...... 707 745-6100
 6100 Egret Ct Benicia (94510) *(P-6399)*
Red Rock Pallet Company ....................................................... E ...... 530 852-7744
 81153 Red Rock Rd La Quinta (92253) *(P-16308)*
Redbarn Pet Products Inc (PA) ............................................... C ...... 562 495-7315
 3229 E Spring St Ste 310 Long Beach (90806) *(P-17307)*
Redbarn Premium Pet Products, Long Beach *Also Called: Redbarn Pet Products Inc (P-17307)*
Redcom LLC ............................................................................ B ...... 949 404-4084
 94 Icon Foothill Ranch (92610) *(P-15663)*
Redding Printing Co Inc (PA) ................................................... E ...... 530 243-0525
 1130 Continental St Redding (96001) *(P-4752)*
Redefined Industries LLC ........................................................ E ...... 909 991-9927
 9681 Business Center Dr Ste B Rancho Cucamonga (91730) *(P-16214)*
Redfern Integrated Optics Inc ................................................. E ...... 408 970-3500
 3350 Scott Blvd Bldg 1 Santa Clara (95054) *(P-14815)*
Redlands Daily Facts, Redlands *Also Called: Califrnia Nwspapers Ltd Partnr (P-4087)*
Redline Detection LLC (PA) ..................................................... E ...... 714 579-6961
 828 W Taft Ave Orange (92865) *(P-14914)*
Redline Prcision Machining Inc ............................................... F ...... 909 483-1273
 907 E Francis St Ontario (91761) *(P-11073)*
Redman Equipment & Mfg Co ................................................. E ...... 310 329-1134
 19800 Normandie Ave Torrance (90502) *(P-19278)*
Redseal Inc ............................................................................. C ...... 408 641-2200
 1300 El Camino Real Ste 300 Menlo Park (94025) *(P-18729)*
Redstone Print & Mail Inc ....................................................... C ...... 925 335-9090
 910 Riverside Pkwy Ste 40 West Sacramento (95605) *(P-4753)*
Redtrac, Bakersfield *Also Called: Water Associates LLC (P-11976)*
Redwood Coast Petroleum Inc ................................................ D ...... 707 546-0766
 444 Yolanda Ave Ste A Santa Rosa (95404) *(P-17255)*
Redwood Scientific Tech Inc ................................................... E ...... 310 693-5401
 245 E Main St Ste 115 Alhambra (91801) *(P-5633)*
Redwood Wellness LLC .......................................................... E ...... 323 843-2676
 1950 W Corporate Way Anaheim (92801) *(P-2554)*
Reed LLC ................................................................................. E ...... 909 287-2100
 13822 Oaks Ave Chino (91710) *(P-9937)*
Reed & Graham Inc (PA) ......................................................... E ...... 408 287-1400
 690 Sunol St San Jose (95126) *(P-6347)*
Reed & Graham Inc ................................................................. E ...... 888 381-0800
 26 Light Sky Ct Sacramento (95828) *(P-6369)*
Reed Brothers Security, San Leandro *Also Called: Security Central Inc (P-19281)*
Reed Electric & Field Service, Vernon *Also Called: R A Reed Electric Company (P-19231)*

## Reed Family Companies — ALPHABETIC SECTION

Reed Family Companies (PA) .................................................. E ...... 209 521-9771
  928 12th St Ste 700 Modesto (95354) *(P-378)*
Reed Group (HQ) ................................................................... E ...... 209 521-7423
  928 12th St Ste 700 Modesto (95354) *(P-379)*
Reed International ................................................................. F ...... 209 874-2719
  13024 Lake Rd Hickman (95323) *(P-9435)*
Reed International (HQ) .......................................................... E ...... 209 874-2357
  13024 Lake Rd Hickman (95323) *(P-9450)*
Reed Manufacturing, Chino Also Called: Reed LLC *(P-9937)*
Reed Manufacturing Inc ......................................................... E ...... 831 637-5641
  205 Apollo Way Ste A Hollister (95023) *(P-7695)*
Reed Mariculture Inc .............................................................. F ...... 408 377-1065
  900 E Hamilton Ave Ste 100 Campbell (95008) *(P-1146)*
Reedex Inc ............................................................................. E ...... 714 894-0311
  15526 Commerce Ln Huntington Beach (92649) *(P-13074)*
Reedley Irrigation & Supply, Reedley Also Called: Fortier & Fortier Inc *(P-16798)*
Reef, Carlsbad Also Called: South Cone Inc *(P-17111)*
Reel Efx Inc ............................................................................ E ...... 818 762-1710
  5539 Riverton Ave North Hollywood (91601) *(P-16215)*
Reel Picture Productions LLC ................................................ E ...... 858 587-0301
  5330 Eastgate Mall San Diego (92121) *(P-13202)*
Reels Inc ................................................................................ D ...... 714 446-9606
  301 E Orangethorpe Ave Anaheim (92801) *(P-16396)*
Reeve Store Equipment Company (PA) ................................... D ...... 562 949-2535
  9131 Bermudez St Pico Rivera (90660) *(P-3705)*
Reeves Extruded Products Inc .............................................. D ...... 661 854-5970
  1032 Stockton Ave Arvin (93203) *(P-6997)*
Refinitiv, San Francisco Also Called: Refinitiv US LLC *(P-4294)*
Refinitiv US LLC ..................................................................... C ...... 415 344-6000
  50 California St San Francisco (94111) *(P-4294)*
Reflex Corporation ................................................................. E ...... 760 931-9009
  2401 Mountain View Dr Carlsbad (92008) *(P-3034)*
Reflexion Medical Inc ............................................................ C ...... 650 239-9070
  25841 Industrial Blvd Ste 275 Hayward (94545) *(P-15575)*
Reformation, Vernon Also Called: Lymi Inc *(P-17095)*
Refresco Beverages US Inc ................................................... C ...... 951 685-0481
  11751 Pacific Ave Fontana (92337) *(P-921)*
Refresco Beverages US Inc ................................................... E ...... 909 915-1400
  631 S Waterman Ave San Bernardino (92408) *(P-1929)*
Refresco Beverages US Inc ................................................... E ...... 909 915-1430
  499 E Mill St San Bernardino (92408) *(P-1930)*
Refresco Beverages US Inc ................................................... F ...... 909 915-1432
  1455 Research Dr Unit A Redlands (92374) *(P-1931)*
Refriderator Manufacturers LLC ............................................ E ...... 562 229-0500
  17018 Edwards Rd Cerritos (90703) *(P-11398)*
Refrigeration Hdwr Sup Corp ................................................ D ...... 800 537-8300
  9255 Deering Ave Chatsworth (91311) *(P-16787)*
Refrigerator Manufacturers Inc (PA) ....................................... E ...... 562 926-2006
  17018 Edwards Rd Cerritos (90703) *(P-11399)*
Refrigerator Manufacturers LLC ............................................ E ...... 562 926-2006
  17018 Edwards Rd Cerritos (90703) *(P-10513)*
Refrigrated Trck Solutions LLC .............................................. E ...... 323 594-4500
  1115 E Dominguez St Carson (90746) *(P-13619)*
Regal Electronics Inc (PA) ...................................................... E ...... 408 988-2288
  820 Charcot Ave San Jose (95131) *(P-13075)*
Regal-Piedmont Plastics LLC ................................................ E ...... 562 404-4014
  17000 Valley View Ave La Mirada (90638) *(P-17234)*
Regards Enterprises Inc ........................................................ F ...... 909 983-0655
  731 S Taylor Ave Ontario (91761) *(P-3408)*
Regent, Valencia Also Called: Regent Aerospace Corporation *(P-16924)*
Regent Aerospace Corporation (PA) ...................................... C ...... 661 257-3000
  28110 Harrison Pkwy Valencia (91355) *(P-16924)*
Registrar of Voters Office, Oakland Also Called: County of Alameda *(P-14475)*
Regusci Vineyard MGT Inc .................................................... E ...... 707 254-0403
  5584 Silverado Trl Napa (94558) *(P-1721)*
Regusci Winery, Napa Also Called: Regusci Vineyard MGT Inc *(P-1721)*
Reh Company ....................................................................... D ...... 559 351-1916
  1703 W Olive Ave Fresno (93728) *(P-6348)*
Reh Company ....................................................................... C ...... 559 997-3617
  5792 N Palm Ave Fresno (93704) *(P-6349)*
Rehau Construction LLC ....................................................... D ...... 951 549-9017
  1250 Corona Pointe Ct Ste 301 Corona (92879) *(P-6998)*

Rehrig Pacific Company (HQ) ................................................. C ...... 323 262-5145
  4010 E 26th St Los Angeles (90058) *(P-6999)*
Rehrig Pacific Holdings Inc (PA) ............................................. D ...... 323 262-5145
  900 Corporate Center Dr Monterey Park (91754) *(P-7000)*
Reid Metal Finishing, Santa Ana Also Called: Electrode Technologies Inc *(P-8953)*
Reid Plastics Customer Svcs, City Of Industry Also Called: Altium Packaging LLC *(P-6708)*
Reid Products, Apple Valley Also Called: Reid Products Inc *(P-11074)*
Reid Products Inc ................................................................. E ...... 760 240-1355
  21430 Waalew Rd Apple Valley (92307) *(P-11074)*
Reinhold Industries Inc (DH) .................................................. C ...... 562 944-3281
  12827 Imperial Hwy Santa Fe Springs (90670) *(P-7001)*
Relational Center ................................................................... E ...... 323 935-1807
  2717 S Robertson Blvd Apt 1 Los Angeles (90034) *(P-18730)*
Relationalai Inc ..................................................................... D ...... 650 307-8776
  2120 University Ave Berkeley (94704) *(P-18731)*
Relativity Space Inc (PA) ....................................................... B ...... 424 393-4309
  3500 E Burnett St Long Beach (90815) *(P-14105)*
Relax Medical Systems Inc ................................................... F ...... 800 405-7677
  3260 E Willow St Signal Hill (90755) *(P-16216)*
Relay Robotics Inc ................................................................ E ...... 833 735-2976
  271 E Hacienda Ave Campbell (95008) *(P-10110)*
Reldom Corporation .............................................................. E ...... 562 498-3346
  3241 Industry Dr Signal Hill (90755) *(P-13296)*
Reliable Container Corporation ............................................. B ...... 562 861-6226
  9206 Santa Fe Springs Rd Santa Fe Springs (90670) *(P-3882)*
Reliable Fire SEC Slutions Inc .............................................. E ...... 559 277-3754
  6339 Highway 145 Madera (93637) *(P-13297)*
Reliable Lumber and Hardware, Riverside Also Called: Reliable Wholesale Lumber Inc *(P-16457)*
Reliable Packaging Systems Inc ........................................... F ...... 714 572-1094
  1300 N Jefferson St Anaheim (92807) *(P-6243)*
Reliable Sheet Metal Works, Fullerton Also Called: Gard Inc *(P-8456)*
Reliable Tape Products, Vernon Also Called: Chua & Sons Co Inc *(P-2451)*
Reliable Wholesale Lumber Inc ............................................ F ...... 951 300-2500
  1450 Citrus St Riverside (92507) *(P-16457)*
Reliable Wholesale Lumber Inc (PA) ..................................... D ...... 714 848-8222
  7600 Redondo Cir Huntington Beach (92648) *(P-16458)*
Reliance Carpet Cushion, Huntington Park Also Called: Reliance Upholstery Sup Co Inc *(P-2948)*
Reliance Machine Products Inc ............................................ E ...... 510 438-6760
  4265 Solar Way Fremont (94538) *(P-11075)*
Reliance Upholstery Sup Co Inc ........................................... D ...... 323 321-2300
  4920 S Boyle Ave Huntington Park (90255) *(P-2948)*
Reliance Worldwide Corporation ........................................... D ...... 770 863-4005
  2750 E Mission Blvd Ontario (91761) *(P-9161)*
Reliant Ems, Fremont Also Called: Reliant Engrg & Mfg Svcs Inc *(P-19414)*
Reliant Engrg & Mfg Svcs Inc ............................................... E ...... 510 252-1973
  47366 Fremont Blvd Fremont (94538) *(P-19414)*
Reliant Foodservice, Temecula Also Called: Canadas Finest Foods Inc *(P-1000)*
Relief-Mart Inc ...................................................................... E ...... 805 379-4300
  28505 Canwood St Ste C Agoura Hills (91301) *(P-17718)*
Relton Corporation ................................................................ D ...... 800 423-1505
  317 Rolyn Pl Arcadia (91007) *(P-6320)*
Remco, Stockton Also Called: Rock Engineered McHy Co Inc *(P-6350)*
Remco Mch & Fabrication Inc .............................................. F ...... 909 877-3530
  1966 S Date Ave Bloomington (92316) *(P-11076)*
Remec Brdband Wrless Ntwrks LL ........................................ C ...... 858 312-6900
  82 Coromar Dr Goleta (93117) *(P-11932)*
Remec Broadband Wireless LLC .......................................... C ...... 858 312-6900
  82 Coromar Dr Goleta (93117) *(P-11933)*
Remec Defense & Space Inc ................................................ A ...... 858 560-1301
  9404 Chesapeake Dr San Diego (92123) *(P-14292)*
Remedly Inc .......................................................................... E ...... 650 265-8449
  407 Sansome St Fl 4 San Francisco (94111) *(P-18732)*
Remel Inc ............................................................................. A ...... 916 425-2651
  46500 Kato Rd Fremont (94538) *(P-14711)*
Remo Inc (PA) ....................................................................... B ...... 661 294-5600
  28110 Industry Dr Valencia (91355) *(P-15721)*
Remote Ocean Systems Inc (PA) .......................................... E ...... 858 565-8500
  9581 Ridgehaven Ct San Diego (92123) *(P-11621)*
Rempex Pharmaceuticals Inc ............................................... E ...... 858 875-2840
  3013 Science Park Rd 1st Fl San Diego (92121) *(P-5634)*

# ALPHABETIC SECTION

Remstek Corp, Temecula *Also Called: Inners Tasks LLC (P-10166)*

Renaissance Doors & Windows, Rcho Sta Marg *Also Called: Renaissnce Frnch Dors Sash Inc (P-3184)*

Renaissnce Frnch Dors Sash Inc (PA) .................................................. C ...... 714 578-0090
38 Segada Rcho Sta Marg (92688) *(P-3184)*

Renau Corporation .................................................................................. E ...... 818 341-1994
9309 Deering Ave Chatsworth (91311) *(P-14449)*

Renau Electronic Laboratories, Chatsworth *Also Called: Renau Corporation (P-14449)*

Renee Claire Inc, Los Angeles *Also Called: Camp Smidgemore Inc (P-2742)*

Renesas Design North Amer Inc (DH) ................................................. E ...... 408 845-8500
6024 Silver Creek Valley Rd San Jose (95138) *(P-12671)*

Renesas Design North Amer Inc ........................................................... C ...... 408 327-8800
1515 Wyatt Dr Santa Clara (95054) *(P-12672)*

Renesas Electronics Amer Inc ............................................................... B ...... 408 432-8888
915 Murphy Ranch Rd Milpitas (95035) *(P-12673)*

Renesas Electronics Amer Inc ............................................................... A ...... 408 588-6750
240a Lawrence Ave South San Francisco (94080) *(P-12674)*

Renesas Electronics Amer Inc ............................................................... D ...... 408 432-8888
1001 Murphy Ranch Rd Milpitas (95035) *(P-12675)*

Renesas Electronics America Inc .......................................................... A ...... 408 432-8888
1001 Murphy Ranch Rd Milpitas (95035) *(P-13076)*

Renkus-Heinz Inc (PA) ........................................................................... D ...... 949 588-9997
19201 Cook St Foothill Ranch (92610) *(P-11690)*

Rennovia Inc ............................................................................................ F ...... 650 804-7400
3040 Oakmead Village Dr Santa Clara (95051) *(P-6157)*

Reno Jones Inc ........................................................................................ E ...... 707 422-4300
2373 N Watney Way Fairfield (94533) *(P-17308)*

Reno News & Review, Chico *Also Called: Chico Community Publishing (P-4090)*

Reno Tenco, Boron *Also Called: Rio Tinto Minerals Inc (P-117)*

Renovaro, Los Angeles *Also Called: Renovaro Inc (P-5635)*

Renovaro Inc (PA) ................................................................................... E ...... 305 918-1980
2080 Century Park E Ste 906 Los Angeles (90067) *(P-5635)*

Rent What, Compton *Also Called: Sew What Inc (P-2919)*

Rentech Inc (PA) ..................................................................................... E ...... 310 571-9800
10880 Wilshire Blvd Ste 1101 Los Angeles (90024) *(P-6403)*

Rentech Ntrgn Pasadena Spa LLC ....................................................... E ...... 310 571-9805
10877 Wilshire Blvd Ste 710 Los Angeles (90024) *(P-6181)*

Renwood Winery, Plymouth *Also Called: Ramador Inc (P-1716)*

Reny & Co Inc .......................................................................................... F ...... 626 962-3078
4505 Littlejohn St Baldwin Park (91706) *(P-7002)*

Renymed, Baldwin Park *Also Called: Reny & Co Inc (P-7002)*

Renzenberger Inc .................................................................................... B ...... 530 283-3314
2096 E Main St Quincy (95971) *(P-13425)*

Renzoni Vineyards Inc ............................................................................ E ...... 951 302-8466
37350 De Portola Rd Temecula (92592) *(P-26)*

Reotemp Instrument Corporation (PA) ................................................. D ...... 858 784-0710
10656 Roselle St San Diego (92121) *(P-14450)*

Repair Tech International, Van Nuys *Also Called: Repairtech International Inc (P-16303)*

Repairtech International Inc ................................................................... E ...... 818 989-2681
7850 Gloria Ave Van Nuys (91406) *(P-16303)*

Repet Inc ................................................................................................... C ...... 909 594-5333
14207 Monte Vista Ave Chino (91710) *(P-6590)*

Replacement Parts Inds Inc .................................................................... E ...... 818 882-8611
625 Cochran St Simi Valley (93065) *(P-15479)*

Replicant Solutions Inc ........................................................................... C ...... 415 854-3296
1 Letterman Dr # 3500 San Francisco (94129) *(P-18733)*

Replico Corporation ................................................................................ D ...... 408 842-8600
18625 Sutter Blvd Ste 300 Morgan Hill (95037) *(P-18734)*

Replicon, Palo Alto *Also Called: Replicon Software Inc (P-17970)*

Replicon Software Inc ............................................................................. E ...... 650 286-9200
1718 Waverley St Palo Alto (94301) *(P-17970)*

Reporter ..................................................................................................... F ...... 707 448-6401
916 Cotting Ln Vacaville (95688) *(P-4184)*

Repsco Inc ................................................................................................ E ...... 888 727-7261
5300 Claus Rd Ste 2 Riverbank (95367) *(P-6591)*

Republic Bag Inc (PA) ............................................................................ D ...... 951 734-9740
580 E Harrison Blvd Corona (92879) *(P-3977)*

Republic Fence Co Inc (PA) .................................................................. E ...... 818 341-5723
11309 Danube Ave Granada Hills (91344) *(P-570)*

Republic Floor, Montebello *Also Called: Reu Distribution LLC (P-16434)*

Republic Flooring, Montebello *Also Called: Hardwood Flrg Liquidators Inc (P-3094)*

Republic Machinery Co Inc (PA) ........................................................... E ...... 310 518-1100
800 Sprucelake Dr Harbor City (90710) *(P-9565)*

Reputationcom Inc (PA) ......................................................................... B ...... 800 888-0924
6111 Bollinger Canyon Rd Ste 500 San Ramon (94583) *(P-18735)*

Rerubber LLC ........................................................................................... F ...... 909 786-2811
7372 Sonoma Creek Ct Rancho Cucamonga (91739) *(P-16362)*

Rescue 42 Inc .......................................................................................... F ...... 530 891-3473
370 Ryan Ave Ste 120 Chico (95973) *(P-10111)*

Research Metal Industries Inc ............................................................... E ...... 310 352-3200
1970 W 139th St Gardena (90249) *(P-11077)*

Research Tool & Die Works LLC .......................................................... D ...... 310 639-5722
17124 Keegan Ave Carson (90746) *(P-8884)*

Resers Fine Foods Inc ........................................................................... E ...... 503 643-6431
15100 Jack Tone Rd Manteca (95336) *(P-2334)*

Resers Fine Foods Inc ........................................................................... F ...... 503 643-6431
3261 Lionshead Ave Ste 100 Carlsbad (92010) *(P-9812)*

Resers Fine Foods Inc ........................................................................... E ...... 503 643-6431
3285 Corporate Vw Vista (92081) *(P-9813)*

Resideo Buoy, Santa Cruz *Also Called: Buoy Labs Inc (P-18131)*

Resilience, San Diego *Also Called: National Resilience Inc (P-5562)*

Resilience Us Inc (HQ) ........................................................................... E ...... 984 202-0854
3115 Merryfield Row Ste 200 San Diego (92121) *(P-5636)*

Resin Designs LLC ................................................................................. E ...... 510 413-0115
39714 Eureka Dr Newark (94560) *(P-6244)*

Resinart Corporation ............................................................................... E ...... 949 642-3665
1621 Placentia Ave Costa Mesa (92627) *(P-7003)*

Resinart Plastics, Costa Mesa *Also Called: Resinart Corporation (P-7003)*

Resinate Materials Group Inc ................................................................ F ...... 800 891-2955
6451 El Camino Real Ste C Carlsbad (92009) *(P-5194)*

Resmed, Chatsworth *Also Called: Resmed Motor Technologies Inc (P-11283)*

Resmed, San Diego *Also Called: Resmed Inc (P-15241)*

Resmed Corp ........................................................................................... E ...... 858 746-2400
14040 Danielson St Poway (92064) *(P-15240)*

Resmed Corp (HQ) ................................................................................. D ...... 858 836-5000
9001 Spectrum Center Blvd San Diego (92123) *(P-15576)*

Resmed Inc (PA) ..................................................................................... A ...... 858 836-5000
9001 Spectrum Center Blvd San Diego (92123) *(P-15241)*

Resmed Motor Technologies Inc .......................................................... C ...... 818 428-6400
9540 De Soto Ave Chatsworth (91311) *(P-11283)*

Resonant, San Mateo *Also Called: Resonant Inc (P-12676)*

Resonant Inc ............................................................................................ D ...... 805 308-9803
1875 S Grant St Ste 750 San Mateo (94402) *(P-12676)*

Resonate I Inc (PA) ................................................................................. C ...... 408 545-5500
90 Great Oaks Blvd Ste 205 San Jose (95119) *(P-17971)*

Resonetics LLC ....................................................................................... F ...... 603 886-6772
4602 2nd St Ste 5 Davis (95618) *(P-13298)*

Resonetics, LLC, Davis *Also Called: Resonetics LLC (P-13298)*

Resource Collection Inc ......................................................................... E ...... 310 219-3272
3771 W 242nd St Ste 205 Torrance (90505) *(P-17849)*

Resource Label Group LLC .................................................................. E ...... 310 603-8910
1360 W Walnut Pkwy Compton (90220) *(P-4827)*

Resource Label Group LLC .................................................................. D ...... 714 619-7100
1511 E Edinger Ave Santa Ana (92705) *(P-4949)*

Resource Label Group LLC .................................................................. E ...... 707 773-4363
3810 Cypress Dr Petaluma (94954) *(P-4950)*

Resource Label Group LLC .................................................................. E ...... 510 477-0707
39611 Eureka Dr Newark (94560) *(P-4951)*

Response Envelope Inc (PA) ................................................................ C ...... 909 923-5855
1340 S Baker Ave Ontario (91761) *(P-4952)*

Response Genetics Inc .......................................................................... C ...... 323 224-3900
1640 Marengo St Ste 7 Los Angeles (90033) *(P-5779)*

Responsible Metal Fab Inc .................................................................... E ...... 408 734-0713
1256 Lawrence Station Rd Sunnyvale (94089) *(P-8557)*

Resq Manufacturing ................................................................................ E ...... 916 638-6786
11430 White Rock Rd Rancho Cordova (95742) *(P-16217)*

Result Group Inc ..................................................................................... D ...... 480 777-7130
2603 Main St Ste 710 Irvine (92614) *(P-18990)*

Retail, Los Angeles *Also Called: Bake Usa Inc (P-1164)*

Retail Content Service Inc ..................................................................... E ...... 415 890-2097
440 N Wolfe Rd Sunnyvale (94085) *(P-4461)*

Retail Print Media Inc     ALPHABETIC SECTION

Retail Print Media Inc .................................................. E ...... 424 488-6950
   2355 Crenshaw Blvd Ste 135 Torrance (90501) *(P-4953)*

Retail Pro International LLC (HQ) ................................. D ...... 916 605-7200
   400 Plaza Dr Ste 200 Folsom (95630) *(P-17972)*

Retail Pro Software, Folsom *Also Called: Retail Pro International LLC (P-17972)*

Retail Solutions, San Jose *Also Called: Retail Solutions Incorporated (P-18736)*

Retail Solutions Incorporated (HQ) ............................... E ...... 650 390-6100
   100 Century Center Ct Ste 800 San Jose (95112) *(P-18736)*

Retail Zipline Inc (PA) .................................................. D ...... 510 390-4904
   2370 Market St Ste 436 San Francisco (94114) *(P-18737)*

Retech Systems LLC .................................................... D ...... 707 462-6522
   168 Washington Ave Ste B Ukiah (95482) *(P-8078)*

Rethink Label Systems, Anaheim *Also Called: Labeltronix LLC (P-4911)*

Rettig Machine Inc ...................................................... E ...... 909 793-7811
   301 Kansas St Redlands (92373) *(P-19210)*

Retzlaff Vineyards, Livermore *Also Called: Robert Taylor (P-1728)*

Reu Distribution LLC ................................................... A ...... 323 201-4200
   7227 Telegraph Rd Montebello (90640) *(P-16434)*

Reuland Electric Co (PA) ............................................. C ...... 626 964-6411
   17969 Railroad St City Of Industry (91748) *(P-11284)*

Reuser Inc .................................................................. F ...... 707 894-4224
   370 Santana Dr Cloverdale (95425) *(P-3077)*

Reuters Television La, North Hollywood *Also Called: Thomson Reuters Corporation (P-11966)*

Rev Vac 7777 Inc ........................................................ E ...... 661 392-0355
   1907 Nute St Bakersfield (93312) *(P-272)*

Reva Medical Inc (PA) ................................................. E ...... 858 966-3000
   5751 Copley Dr Ste B San Diego (92111) *(P-15398)*

Revasum Inc ............................................................... C ...... 805 541-6424
   825 Buckley Rd San Luis Obispo (93401) *(P-12677)*

Revco Industries Inc (PA) ............................................ E ...... 562 777-1588
   10747 Norwalk Blvd Santa Fe Springs (90670) *(P-16891)*

Revco Products ........................................................... D ...... 714 891-6688
   7221 Acacia Ave Garden Grove (92841) *(P-18738)*

Reveal Biosciences Inc ............................................... E ...... 858 274-3663
   80 Empire Dr Lake Forest (92630) *(P-19472)*

Reveal Imaging, Vista *Also Called: Leidos Inc (P-19460)*

Reveal Windows & Doors, La Habra *Also Called: Pacific Archtectural Mllwk Inc (P-3175)*

Revera Incorporated .................................................... E ...... 408 510-7400
   3090 Oakmead Village Dr Santa Clara (95051) *(P-10427)*

Revere Data LLC ......................................................... E ...... 415 782-0454
   1 California St Ste 1900 San Francisco (94111) *(P-19121)*

Reverse Medical, Irvine *Also Called: Reverse Medical Corporation (P-15242)*

Reverse Medical Corporation ....................................... E ...... 949 215-0660
   13700 Alton Pkwy Ste 167 Irvine (92618) *(P-15242)*

Revir Therapeutics Inc ................................................ F ...... 415 794-7166
   150 N Hill Dr Ste 19 Brisbane (94005) *(P-5637)*

Reviver, Granite Bay *Also Called: Revivermx Inc (P-11934)*

Revivermx Inc ............................................................. E ...... 916 580-3495
   4170 Douglas Blvd Ste 200 Granite Bay (95746) *(P-11934)*

Revjet Corporation ....................................................... C ...... 650 508-2215
   981 Industrial Rd Ste D San Carlos (94070) *(P-18739)*

Revlon Inc ................................................................... D ...... 619 372-1379
   1125 Joshua Way Ste 12 Vista (92081) *(P-6031)*

Revo Powetrains, San Jose *Also Called: Wrightspeed Inc (P-13606)*

Revolan Systems, San Jose *Also Called: Tera-Lite Inc (P-506)*

Revup Software Inc ..................................................... F ...... 415 231-2315
   101 Redwood Shores Pkwy Ste 125 Redwood City (94065) *(P-18740)*

Rex Creamery, Commerce *Also Called: Heritage Distributing Company (P-838)*

Rexhall Industries Inc .................................................. E ...... 661 726-5470
   26857 Tannahill Ave Canyon Country (91387) *(P-13625)*

Rexnord Industries LLC ............................................... E ...... 805 583-5514
   2175 Union Pl Simi Valley (93065) *(P-9814)*

Reyes Coca-Cola Bottling LLC (PA) ............................. B ...... 213 744-8616
   3 Park Plz Ste 600 Irvine (92614) *(P-1932)*

Reyes Coca-Cola Bottling LLC ..................................... D ...... 661 324-6531
   4320 Ride St Bakersfield (93313) *(P-1933)*

Reyes Coca-Cola Bottling LLC ..................................... C ...... 408 436-3700
   1555 Old Bayshore Hwy San Jose (95112) *(P-1934)*

Reyes Coca-Cola Bottling LLC ..................................... D ...... 562 803-8100
   8729 Cleta St Downey (90241) *(P-1935)*

Reyes Coca-Cola Bottling LLC ..................................... C ...... 510 667-6300
   14655 Wicks Blvd San Leandro (94577) *(P-1936)*

Reyes Coca-Cola Bottling LLC ..................................... D ...... 559 264-4631
   3220 E Malaga Ave Fresno (93725) *(P-1937)*

Reyes Coca-Cola Bottling LLC ..................................... E ...... 805 644-2211
   5335 Walker St Ventura (93003) *(P-1938)*

Reyes Coca-Cola Bottling LLC ..................................... D ...... 209 466-9501
   4101 Gateway Park Blvd Sacramento (95834) *(P-1939)*

Reyes Coca-Cola Bottling LLC ..................................... D ...... 760 396-4500
   86375 Industrial Way Coachella (92236) *(P-1940)*

Reyes Coca-Cola Bottling LLC ..................................... E ...... 805 925-2629
   120 E Jones St Santa Maria (93454) *(P-1941)*

Reyes Coca-Cola Bottling LLC ..................................... D ...... 831 755-8300
   715 Vandenberg St Salinas (93905) *(P-1942)*

Reyes Coca-Cola Bottling LLC ..................................... C ...... 909 980-3121
   11900 Cabernet Dr Fontana (92337) *(P-1943)*

Reyes Coca-Cola Bottling LLC ..................................... E ...... 805 614-3702
   1000 Fairway Dr Santa Maria (93455) *(P-1944)*

Reyes Coca-Cola Bottling LLC ..................................... E ...... 559 264-4631
   971 E North Ave Fresno (93725) *(P-1945)*

Reyes Coca-Cola Bottling LLC ..................................... D ...... 530 241-4315
   1580 Beltline Rd Redding (96003) *(P-1946)*

Reyes Coca-Cola Bottling LLC ..................................... B ...... 619 266-6300
   5255 Federal Blvd San Diego (92105) *(P-1947)*

Reyes Coca-Cola Bottling LLC ..................................... C ...... 323 278-2600
   666 Union St Montebello (90640) *(P-1948)*

Reyes Coca-Cola Bottling LLC ..................................... E ...... 530 743-6533
   1430 Melody Rd Marysville (95901) *(P-1949)*

Reyes Coca-Cola Bottling LLC ..................................... D ...... 714 974-1901
   700 W Grove Ave Orange (92865) *(P-1950)*

Reyes Coca-Cola Bottling LLC ..................................... E ...... 707 747-2000
   530 Getty Ct Benicia (94510) *(P-1951)*

Reyes Coca-Cola Bottling LLC ..................................... E ...... 213 744-8659
   1338 E 14th St Los Angeles (90021) *(P-1952)*

Reyes Coca-Cola Bottling LLC ..................................... C ...... 925 830-6500
   2633 Camino Ramon Ste 300 San Ramon (94583) *(P-1953)*

Reyes Coca-Cola Bottling LLC ..................................... E ...... 760 241-2653
   17220 Nutro Way Victorville (92395) *(P-1954)*

Reyes Coca-Cola Bottling LLC ..................................... E ...... 760 352-1561
   126 S 3rd St El Centro (92243) *(P-1955)*

Reyes Coca-Cola Bottling LLC ..................................... D ...... 818 362-4307
   12925 Bradley Ave Sylmar (91342) *(P-17208)*

Reynaldos Mexican Food Co LLC (PA) ........................ C ...... 562 803-3188
   3301 E Vernon Ave Vernon (90058) *(P-2335)*

Reynard Corporation .................................................... E ...... 949 366-8866
   1020 Calle Sombra San Clemente (92673) *(P-14816)*

Reynolds Packing Co (PA) ........................................... F ...... 209 369-2725
   33 E Tokay St Lodi (95240) *(P-85)*

Reynolds Paper Mill, Commerce *Also Called: Tzeng Long USA Inc (P-16965)*

Reyrich Plastics Inc .................................................... E ...... 909 484-8444
   1704 S Vineyard Ave Ontario (91761) *(P-7004)*

Rezex Corporation ....................................................... E ...... 213 622-2015
   1930 E 51st St Vernon (90058) *(P-2507)*

Rezo Therapeutics Inc ................................................ E ...... 650 704-5577
   455 Mission Bay Blvd S Ste 525 San Francisco (94158) *(P-5638)*

Rezolute Inc (PA) ........................................................ E ...... 650 206-4507
   275 Shoreline Dr Ste 500 Redwood City (94065) *(P-5639)*

Rf America-Ids Inc ...................................................... F ...... 866 578-5533
   17609 Ventura Blvd Ste 115 Encino (91316) *(P-15480)*

Rf Digital Corporation .................................................. C ...... 949 610-0008
   1601 Pacific Coast Hwy Ste 290 Hermosa Beach (90254) *(P-12678)*

Rf Industries Ltd (PA) .................................................. D ...... 858 549-6340
   16868 Via Del Campo Ct Ste 200 San Diego (92127) *(P-12895)*

Rf Surgical Systems LLC ............................................. D ...... 855 522-7027
   5927 Landau Ct Carlsbad (92008) *(P-15243)*

Rfaxis Inc .................................................................... F ...... 949 825-6300
   7595 Irvine Center Dr Ste 200 Irvine (92618) *(P-12679)*

Rfc Wire Forms, Ontario *Also Called: Rfc Wire Forms Inc (P-9231)*

Rfc Wire Forms Inc ..................................................... D ...... 909 467-0559
   525 Brooks St Ontario (91762) *(P-9231)*

Rfid4u, Concord *Also Called: Esmart Source Inc (P-18290)*

## ALPHABETIC SECTION

RG Costumes & Accessories Inc .................................................. E ...... 626 858-9559
   726 Arrow Grand Cir Covina (91722) *(P-2909)*

Rgb Spectrum ............................................................................... D ...... 510 814-7000
   1101 Marina Village Pkwy Ste 101 Alameda (94501) *(P-10428)*

Rgb Systems Inc (PA) ................................................................. C ...... 714 491-1500
   1025 E Ball Rd Ste 100 Anaheim (92805) *(P-10429)*

RGF Enterprises Inc .................................................................... E ...... 951 734-6922
   220 Citation Cir Corona (92878) *(P-9114)*

Rggd Inc (PA) .............................................................................. E ...... 323 581-6617
   4950 S Santa Fe Ave Vernon (90058) *(P-16985)*

Rgm Products Inc ........................................................................ B ...... 559 499-2222
   3301 Navone Rd Stockton (95215) *(P-6383)*

Rgs Industries, Santa Clara *Also Called: Rockys Gasket Shop Inc (P-6463)*

RH Peterson Co (PA) ................................................................... C ...... 626 369-5085
   14724 Proctor Ave City Of Industry (91746) *(P-11394)*

Rh USA Inc .................................................................................. E ...... 925 245-7900
   455 N Canyons Pkwy Ste B Livermore (94551) *(P-15244)*

Rhapsody Clothing Inc ................................................................. D ...... 213 614-8887
   810 E Pico Blvd Ste 24 Los Angeles (90021) *(P-2804)*

Rhino Linings Corporation (PA) .................................................... D ...... 858 450-0441
   9747 Businesspark Ave San Diego (92131) *(P-6110)*

Rhys Vineyards LLC .................................................................... E ...... 650 419-2050
   11715 Skyline Blvd Los Gatos (95033) *(P-1722)*

RI, Santa Clara *Also Called: Roos Instruments Inc (P-14581)*

Rialto Concrete Products, Rialto *Also Called: Kti Incorporated (P-7353)*

Ric, Santa Ana *Also Called: Rickenbacker International Corporation (P-15722)*

Ricardo Defense Inc (DH) ............................................................ E ...... 805 882-1884
   3757 State St Santa Barbara (93105) *(P-13566)*

Ricaurte Precision Inc ................................................................. E ...... 714 667-0632
   1550 E Mcfadden Ave Santa Ana (92705) *(P-11078)*

Rice Corporation (PA) .................................................................. E ...... 916 784-7745
   11140 Fair Oaks Blvd Ste 101 Fair Oaks (95628) *(P-1081)*

Rice Field Corporation ................................................................. C ...... 626 968-6917
   14500 Valley Blvd City Of Industry (91746) *(P-663)*

Rich Chicks LLC .......................................................................... E ...... 209 879-4104
   13771 Gramercy Pl Gardena (90249) *(P-701)*

Rich Limited, Oceanside *Also Called: Britcan Inc (P-3681)*

Rich Products Corporation ........................................................... E ...... 714 338-1145
   3401 W Segerstrom Ave Santa Ana (92704) *(P-1292)*

Rich Products Corporation ........................................................... E ...... 559 486-7380
   320 O St Fresno (93721) *(P-2060)*

Rich Products Corporation ........................................................... C ...... 562 946-6750
   12805 Busch Pl Santa Fe Springs (90670) *(P-2336)*

Richard C Thurston ..................................................................... F ...... 619 440-6165
   360 N Magnolia Ave El Cajon (92020) *(P-17769)*

Richard K Gould Inc .................................................................... E ...... 916 371-5943
   788 Northport Dr West Sacramento (95691) *(P-6321)*

Richard Tyler, Alhambra *Also Called: Tyler Trafficante Inc (P-2569)*

Richards Machining Co Inc .......................................................... F ...... 408 526-9219
   382 Martin Ave Santa Clara (95050) *(P-11079)*

Richards Neon Shop Inc .............................................................. E ...... 951 279-6767
   4375 Prado Rd Ste 102 Corona (92878) *(P-16026)*

Richardson Rfpd Inc ................................................................... E ...... 669 342-3985
   1732 N 1st St Ste 300 San Jose (95110) *(P-14578)*

Richardson Steel Inc ................................................................... E ...... 619 697-5892
   9102 Harness St Ste A Spring Valley (91977) *(P-8209)*

Richwood Meat Company Inc ...................................................... D ...... 209 722-8171
   2751 N Santa Fe Ave Merced (95348) *(P-615)*

Rick's Hitches & Welding, El Cajon *Also Called: CLP Inc (P-19186)*

Rickenbacker International Corporation ....................................... D ...... 714 545-5574
   3895 S Main St Santa Ana (92707) *(P-15722)*

Rickshaw Bagworks Inc .............................................................. E ...... 415 904-8368
   904 22nd St San Francisco (94107) *(P-2961)*

Ricoh Electronics Inc .................................................................. D ...... 714 259-1220
   17482 Pullman St Irvine (92614) *(P-10465)*

Ricoh Electronics Inc .................................................................. C ...... 714 566-6079
   2310 Redhill Ave Santa Ana (92705) *(P-15664)*

Ricoh Prtg Systems Amer Inc (HQ) .............................................. B ...... 805 578-4000
   2390 Ward Ave Ste A Simi Valley (93065) *(P-10430)*

Ricon Corporation ....................................................................... C ...... 818 267-3000
   1135 Aviation Pl San Fernando (91340) *(P-16218)*

Riddle Ranches Inc ..................................................................... E ...... 209 874-9784
   12013 El Pomar Ave Waterford (95386) *(P-41)*

Ridge Wallet LLC ......................................................................... E ...... 818 636-2832
   2448 Main St Santa Monica (90405) *(P-7151)*

Ridge Wallet, The, Santa Monica *Also Called: Ridge Wallet LLC (P-7151)*

Ridgeline, Stockton *Also Called: Rgm Products Inc (P-6383)*

Ridgeline Engineering Company, Vista *Also Called: Rec Inc (P-10109)*

Riedon Inc (PA) ........................................................................... C
   300 Cypress Ave Alhambra (91801) *(P-12823)*

Rieke LLC .................................................................................... C ...... 707 238-9250
   1200 Valley House Dr Ste 100 Rohnert Park (94928) *(P-8812)*

Rigel Pharmaceuticals Inc (PA) .................................................... C ...... 650 624-1100
   611 Gateway Blvd Ste 900 South San Francisco (94080) *(P-5640)*

Right Angle Solutions Inc ............................................................ E ...... 951 934-3081
   6315 Pedley Rd Jurupa Valley (92509) *(P-432)*

Right Hand Manufacturing Inc .................................................... C ...... 619 819-5056
   180 Otay Lakes Rd Ste 205 Bonita (91902) *(P-11344)*

Right Manufacturing LLC ............................................................ E ...... 858 566-7002
   7949 Stromesa Ct Ste G San Diego (92126) *(P-9268)*

Rightway, Vernon *Also Called: R B R Meat Company Inc (P-613)*

Rigos Equipment Mfg LLC .......................................................... E ...... 626 813-6621
   14501 Joanbridge St Baldwin Park (91706) *(P-8558)*

Rigos Sheet Metal, Baldwin Park *Also Called: Rigos Equipment Mfg LLC (P-8558)*

Riki, Davis *Also Called: Riki Fashion inc (P-2688)*

Riki Fashion Inc ........................................................................... F ...... 530 756-8048
   815 Sweetbriar Rd Davis (95616) *(P-2688)*

Rima Enterprises Inc ................................................................... D ...... 714 893-4534
   16417 Ladona Cir Huntington Beach (92649) *(P-9774)*

Rima-System, Huntington Beach *Also Called: Rima Enterprises Inc (P-9774)*

Rimnetics Inc .............................................................................. F ...... 916 652-5555
   3141 Swetzer Rd Loomis (95650) *(P-7005)*

Rincon Engineering Tech ............................................................. E ...... 805 684-4144
   6325 Carpinteria Ave Carpinteria (93013) *(P-11080)*

Rincon Iron Inc ............................................................................ F ...... 805 455-2904
   531 Montgomery Ave Oxnard (93036) *(P-8642)*

Rincon Ironworks, Oxnard *Also Called: Rincon Iron Inc (P-8642)*

Ring, Hawthorne *Also Called: Ring LLC (P-11227)*

Ring Container Tech LLC ............................................................ D ...... 209 238-3426
   3643 Finch Rd Modesto (95357) *(P-6616)*

Ring Container Tech LLC ............................................................ D ...... 909 350-8416
   8275 Almeria Ave Fontana (92335) *(P-6617)*

Ring LLC (HQ) ............................................................................. B ...... 310 929-7085
   12515 Cerise Ave Hawthorne (90250) *(P-11227)*

Ring of Fire, Van Nuys *Also Called: Rof LLC (P-2602)*

Rio Pluma Company LLC (HQ) .................................................... E ...... 530 846-5200
   1900 State Highway 99 Gridley (95948) *(P-922)*

Rio Tinto Minerals Inc ................................................................. C ...... 760 762-7121
   14486 Borax Rd Boron (93516) *(P-117)*

Rios-Lovell Estate Winery ........................................................... E ...... 925 443-0434
   6500 Tesla Rd Livermore (94550) *(P-1723)*

Rios-Lovell Winery, Livermore *Also Called: Rios-Lovell Estate Winery (P-1723)*

Riot Games, Los Angeles *Also Called: Riot Games Inc (P-18741)*

Riot Games Inc (DH) ................................................................... E ...... 310 207-1444
   12333 W Olympic Blvd Los Angeles (90064) *(P-18741)*

Riot Glass Inc .............................................................................. E ...... 800 580-2303
   17941 Brookshire Ln Huntington Beach (92647) *(P-13299)*

Rip Curl Inc ................................................................................. E ...... 714 422-3617
   193 Avenida La Pata San Clemente (92673) *(P-15845)*

Rip Curl Inc (DH) ......................................................................... D ...... 714 422-3600
   3030 Airway Ave Costa Mesa (92626) *(P-15846)*

Rip Curl USA, Costa Mesa *Also Called: Rip Curl Inc (P-15846)*

Rip-Tie Inc .................................................................................. F ...... 510 577-0200
   883 San Leandro Blvd San Leandro (94577) *(P-2539)*

Ripon Mfg Co ............................................................................... E ...... 209 599-2148
   652 S Stockton Ave Ripon (95366) *(P-9815)*

Rippey Corporation ..................................................................... D ...... 916 939-4332
   5000 Hillsdale Cir El Dorado Hills (95762) *(P-16546)*

Rippling, San Francisco *Also Called: People Center Inc (P-18668)*

Risa Tech Inc ............................................................................... E ...... 949 951-5815
   27442 Portola Pkwy Ste 200 Foothill Ranch (92610) *(P-17973)*

Risco Inc ............................................................................................ E ...... 951 769-2899
390 Risco Cir Beaumont (92223) *(P-8766)*

Rise Baking Company LLC ............................................................ D ...... 909 825-7343
2111 W Valley Blvd Colton (92324) *(P-1240)*

Rising Dough Bakery, Sacramento Also Called: Manufacturing Logistics Inc *(P-17195)*

Rising Tide Bottleworks LLC ......................................................... F ...... 619 725-0844
3986 30th St San Diego (92104) *(P-2337)*

Risvolds Inc ..................................................................................... D ...... 323 770-2674
1234 W El Segundo Blvd Gardena (90247) *(P-2338)*

Rite Engineering & Manufacturing Corporation ........................ E ...... 562 862-2135
5832 Garfield Ave Commerce (90040) *(P-8330)*

Rite Screen, Rancho Cucamonga Also Called: J T Walker Industries Inc *(P-8269)*

Ritec, Simi Valley Also Called: Rugged Info Tech Eqp Corp *(P-10431)*

Ritual, Los Angeles Also Called: Natals Inc *(P-5561)*

Rival Iq Corporation ........................................................................ F ...... 206 395-8572
3945 Freedom Cir Santa Clara (95054) *(P-18742)*

River City Building Supply Inc ...................................................... F ...... 916 375-8322
801 Striker Ave Sacramento (95834) *(P-16482)*

River City Millwork Inc .................................................................. E ...... 916 364-8981
3045 Fite Cir Sacramento (95827) *(P-3185)*

River City Printers LLC .................................................................. E ...... 916 638-8400
4251 Gateway Park Blvd Sacramento (95834) *(P-4754)*

River City Waste Recyclers LLC (PA) ........................................... F ...... 916 383-5511
8940 Elder Creek Rd Sacramento (95829) *(P-16363)*

River Ranch Raisins Inc ................................................................. E ...... 559 843-2294
4087 N Howard Ave Kerman (93630) *(P-961)*

River Ready Mix, Forestville Also Called: Canyon Rock Co Inc *(P-310)*

Riverbed Technology LLC (HQ) .................................................... D ...... 415 247-8800
275 Shoreline Dr Ste 350 Redwood City (94065) *(P-16547)*

Riverbench LLC ............................................................................... E ...... 805 324-4100
137 Anacapa St Santa Barbara (93101) *(P-1724)*

Rivermeadow Software Inc ........................................................... E ...... 617 448-4990
120 W Main St Los Gatos (95030) *(P-18743)*

Riverside Biltin Jrupa This We, Riverside Also Called: Metropolitan News Company *(P-4159)*

Riverside Cement Holdings Company ........................................ B ...... 951 774-2500
1500 Rubidoux Blvd Riverside (92509) *(P-7262)*

Riverside Foundary, Riverside Also Called: Oldcast Precast *(P-7362)*

Rivian, Irvine Also Called: Rivian Automotive Inc *(P-13379)*

Rivian Automotive Inc (PA) ........................................................... B ...... 888 748-4261
14600 Myford Rd Irvine (92606) *(P-13379)*

Rivian Automotive LLC .................................................................. D ...... 309 249-8777
1648 Ashley Way Colton (92324) *(P-13380)*

Rivian Automotive LLC .................................................................. D ...... 888 748-4261
14451 Myford Rd Tustin (92780) *(P-13381)*

Riviana Foods Inc ........................................................................... D ...... 530 458-8512
2870 Niagara Rd Colusa (95932) *(P-17221)*

Rivulis Irrigation Inc (HQ) ............................................................. E ...... 858 578-1860
7545 Carroll Rd San Diego (92121) *(P-9380)*

Rix Industries (PA) .......................................................................... D ...... 707 747-5900
4900 Industrial Way Benicia (94510) *(P-9974)*

Riye Group LLC ............................................................................... E ...... 820 203-9215
2110 W 103rd St Los Angeles (90047) *(P-4462)*

Rizo-Lopez Foods Inc .................................................................... B ...... 800 626-5587
201 S Mcclure Rd Modesto (95357) *(P-730)*

Rizzo Inc .......................................................................................... E ...... 818 781-6891
7720 Airport Business Pkwy Van Nuys (91406) *(P-15399)*

RJ Acquisition Corp (PA) ............................................................... C ...... 323 318-1107
3260 E 26th St Los Angeles (90058) *(P-4954)*

Rjp Framing Holding Co ............................................................... F ...... 916 817-1427
1139 Sibley St Ste 100 Folsom (95630) *(P-3186)*

Rki Instruments Inc (PA) ............................................................... E ...... 510 441-5656
33248 Central Ave Union City (94587) *(P-16838)*

Rko General Inc .............................................................................. D ...... 916 351-8515
Highway 50 & Aerojet Road Rancho Cordova (95670) *(P-14293)*

Rks Inc (HQ) .................................................................................... F ...... 858 571-4444
1955 Cordell Ct Ste 104 El Cajon (92020) *(P-13300)*

Rlh Industries Inc ........................................................................... E ...... 714 532-1672
936 N Main St Orange (92867) *(P-11783)*

Rm Esop Inc .................................................................................... C ...... 831 789-8300
340 El Camino Real S Ste 36 Salinas (93901) *(P-3883)*

Rm Pallets, Turlock Also Called: Rm Pallets Inc *(P-3357)*

Rm Pallets Inc .................................................................................. F ...... 209 632-9887
2512 Paulson Rd Turlock (95380) *(P-3357)*

Rm Partners Inc .............................................................................. E ...... 714 765-5725
1439 S State College Blvd Anaheim (92806) *(P-17528)*

RMC, Ripon Also Called: Ripon Mfg Co *(P-9815)*

RMC Engineering Co Inc (PA) ....................................................... E ...... 408 842-2525
255 Mayock Rd Gilroy (95020) *(P-11081)*

RMC Pacific Materials LLC (PA) ................................................... C
6601 Koll Center Pkwy Ste 300 Pleasanton (94566) *(P-7263)*

Rmf Salt Holdings LLC ................................................................... F ...... 510 477-9600
2217 S Shore Ctr # 200 Alameda (94501) *(P-6032)*

Rmi, Livermore Also Called: Ratermann Manufacturing Inc *(P-6995)*

RMR Products Inc (PA) .................................................................. E ...... 818 890-0896
11011 Glenoaks Blvd Ste 1 Pacoima (91331) *(P-7385)*

RMS, Signal Hill Also Called: Relax Medical Systems Inc *(P-16216)*

Rnbs Corporation ........................................................................... E ...... 714 998-1828
725 S Paseo Prado Anaheim (92807) *(P-17672)*

Rnd Contractors Inc ....................................................................... E ...... 909 429-8500
14796 Jurupa Ave Ste A Fontana (92337) *(P-8210)*

Rnd Enterprises, Chatsworth Also Called: BDR Industries Inc *(P-10332)*

Rnj Printing Corporation ............................................................... F ...... 310 638-7768
116 23rd Pl Manhattan Beach (90266) *(P-4755)*

RNS Channel Letters, Corona Also Called: Richards Neon Shop Inc *(P-16026)*

Ro Gar Mfg, El Centro Also Called: Rogar Manufacturing Inc *(P-13078)*

Roach Bros Inc ................................................................................ D ...... 707 964-9240
23550 Shady Ln Fort Bragg (95437) *(P-3052)*

Road Champs Inc ........................................................................... C ...... 310 456-7799
22619 Pacific Coast Hwy Ste 250 Malibu (90265) *(P-15766)*

Road Runner Sports, San Diego Also Called: Road Runner Sports Inc *(P-17673)*

Road Runner Sports Inc (PA) ....................................................... D ...... 858 974-4200
5549 Copley Dr San Diego (92111) *(P-17673)*

Road Vista, San Diego Also Called: Gamma Scientific Inc *(P-14870)*

Roadmax Products, Chino Also Called: Svevia Usa Inc *(P-15892)*

Roadwire Distinctive Inds, Santa Fe Springs Also Called: Distinctive Inds Texas Inc *(P-2877)*

Roadzen Inc (PA) ............................................................................ B ...... 650 414-3530
111 Anza Blvd Ste 109 Burlingame (94010) *(P-18744)*

Rob Inc ............................................................................................. D ...... 562 806-5589
6760 Foster Bridge Blvd Bell Gardens (90201) *(P-2588)*

Robar Enterprises Inc (PA) ........................................................... C ...... 760 244-5456
17671 Bear Valley Rd Hesperia (92345) *(P-7488)*

Robb Curtco Media LLC ................................................................ E ...... 310 589-7700
22741 Pacific Coast Hwy Ste 401 Malibu (90265) *(P-4295)*

Robb-Jack Corporation (PA) ......................................................... D ...... 916 645-6045
3300 Nicolaus Rd Ste 1 Lincoln (95648) *(P-9566)*

Robecks Wldg & Fabrication Inc ................................................. E ...... 408 287-0202
1150 Mabury Rd Ste 1 San Jose (95133) *(P-8211)*

Roberson Construction ................................................................. E ...... 626 578-1936
22 Central Ct Pasadena (91105) *(P-3726)*

Robert C Worth Inc ........................................................................ D ...... 661 942-6601
15846 Liggett St North Hills (91343) *(P-3265)*

Robert F Chapman Inc ................................................................... D ...... 661 940-9482
43100 Exchange Pl Lancaster (93535) *(P-8559)*

Robert H Oliva Inc .......................................................................... E ...... 818 700-1035
19863 Nordhoff St Northridge (91324) *(P-11082)*

Robert H Peterson Company, City Of Industry Also Called: RH Peterson Co *(P-11394)*

Robert Heely Construction, Bakersfield Also Called: Robert Heely Construction LP *(P-273)*

Robert Heely Construction LP (PA) ............................................. E ...... 661 617-1400
5401 Woodmere Dr Bakersfield (93313) *(P-273)*

Robert J Alandt & Sons ................................................................. E ...... 559 275-1391
4692 N Brawley Ave Fresno (93722) *(P-8212)*

Robert Jones ................................................................................... F ...... 707 829-9864
742 S Main St Sebastopol (95472) *(P-17461)*

Robert Kaufman Co Inc (PA) ........................................................ C ...... 310 538-3482
129 W 132nd St Los Angeles (90061) *(P-17657)*

Robert Kaufman Fabrics, Los Angeles Also Called: Robert Kaufman Co Inc *(P-17657)*

Robert M Hadley Company Inc ................................................... D ...... 805 658-7286
4054 Transport St Ste B Ventura (93003) *(P-12856)*

Robert Michael Ltd ........................................................................ B ...... 562 758-6789
10035 Geary Ave Santa Fe Springs (90670) *(P-3487)*

Robert Mondavi Corporation (HQ) ............................................. D ...... 707 967-2100
166 Gateway Rd E Napa (94558) *(P-1725)*

# ALPHABETIC SECTION

**Robert Mondavi Corporation** .................................................. A ...... 209 365-2995
770 N Guild Ave Lodi (95240) *(P-1726)*

**Robert Mondavi Winery** ........................................................ D ...... 707 738-5727
7801 St. Helena Hwy Oakville (94562) *(P-1727)*

**Robert R Wix Inc (PA)** .......................................................... E ...... 209 537-4561
2140 Pine St Ceres (95307) *(P-4955)*

**Robert Rnzoni Vineyards Winery, Temecula** *Also Called: Renzoni Vineyards Inc (P-26)*

**Robert Talbott Inc (PA)** ........................................................ E ...... 831 649-6000
24560 Silver Cloud Ct Ste 201 Monterey (93940) *(P-2565)*

**Robert Taylor** ...................................................................... F ...... 925 447-8941
1356 S Livermore Ave Livermore (94550) *(P-1728)*

**Robert W Cameron & Co Inc** ................................................ E ...... 707 769-1617
149 Kentucky St Ste 7 Petaluma (94952) *(P-4343)*

**Robert's Engineering, Anaheim** *Also Called: Roberts Precision Engrg Inc (P-11083)*

**Robert's Lumber, Bloomington** *Also Called: Roberts Lumber Sales Inc (P-16459)*

**Roberta, Los Angeles** *Also Called: L A Glo Inc (P-2708)*

**Roberto Martinez Inc** ............................................................ F ...... 800 257-6462
1050 Calle Cordillera Ste 103 San Clemente (92673) *(P-15704)*

**Roberts Container Corporation** ............................................ E ...... 818 727-1700
9131 Oakdale Ave Ste 110 Chatsworth (91311) *(P-19122)*

**Roberts Cosmetics and Cntrs, Chatsworth** *Also Called: Roberts Container Corporation (P-19122)*

**Roberts Engineers, Paramount** *Also Called: Total-Western Inc (P-282)*

**Roberts Ferry Nut Company Inc** ............................................ E ...... 209 874-3247
20493 Yosemite Blvd Waterford (95386) *(P-1323)*

**Roberts Lumber Sales Inc** .................................................... D ...... 909 350-9164
2661 S Lilac Ave Bloomington (92316) *(P-16459)*

**Roberts Precision Engrg Inc** ................................................ E ...... 714 635-4485
1345 S Allec St Anaheim (92805) *(P-11083)*

**Roberts Research Laboratory** .............................................. F ...... 310 320-7310
23150 Kashiwa Ct Torrance (90505) *(P-9140)*

**Robertshaw Controls Company** ............................................ D ...... 951 893-6233
1751 3rd St Ste 102 Norco (92860) *(P-14367)*

**Robertson-Ceco II Corporation** ............................................ D ...... 209 727-5504
12101 E Brandt Rd Lockeford (95237) *(P-8682)*

**Robertson's, Corona** *Also Called: Robertsons Rdymx Ltd A Cal Ltd (P-7489)*

**Robertsons Rdymx Ltd A Cal Ltd (PA)** .................................. D ...... 951 493-6500
200 S Main St Ste 200 Corona (92882) *(P-7489)*

**Robertsons Rdymx Ltd A Cal Ltd** .......................................... C ...... 909 425-2930
27401 3rd St Highland (92346) *(P-7490)*

**Robertsons Ready Mix Ltd** .................................................. D ...... 760 244-7239
9635 C Ave Hesperia (92345) *(P-7491)*

**Robertsons Ready Mix Ltd** .................................................. D ...... 800 834-7557
5692 Eastgate Dr San Diego (92121) *(P-7492)*

**Robertsons Ready Mix Ltd** .................................................. D ...... 760 373-4815
7900 Moss Ave California City (93505) *(P-7493)*

**Robertsons Ready Mix Ltd** .................................................. D ...... 951 685-4600
1310 Simpson Way Escondido (92029) *(P-7494)*

**Robin's Jeans, Bell Gardens** *Also Called: Rob Inc (P-2588)*

**Robinson Enterprises Investment Co Inc** .............................. D ...... 530 265-5844
293 Lower Grass Valley Rd Ste 201 Nevada City (95959) *(P-3053)*

**Robinson Farms Feed Company** .......................................... D ...... 209 466-7915
7000 S Inland Dr Stockton (95206) *(P-1147)*

**Robinson Helicopter Co Inc (PA)** .......................................... A ...... 310 539-0508
2901 Airport Dr Torrance (90505) *(P-13935)*

**Robinson Pharma Inc** .......................................................... C ...... 714 241-0235
3701 W Warner Ave Santa Ana (92704) *(P-5641)*

**Robinson Pharma Inc** .......................................................... C ...... 714 241-0235
3300 W Segerstrom Ave Santa Ana (92704) *(P-5642)*

**Robinson Pharma Inc (PA)** .................................................. B ...... 714 241-0235
3330 S Harbor Blvd Santa Ana (92704) *(P-5643)*

**Robinson Printing, Temecula** *Also Called: Robinson Printing Inc (P-4956)*

**Robinson Printing Inc** .......................................................... E ...... 951 296-0300
42685 Rio Nedo Temecula (92590) *(P-4956)*

**Robinson Timber, Nevada City** *Also Called: Robinson Enterprises Investment Co Inc (P-3053)*

**Robles Bros Inc (PA)** ............................................................ E ...... 408 436-5551
1700 Rogers Ave San Jose (95112) *(P-2339)*

**ROBLOX, San Mateo** *Also Called: Roblox Corporation (P-18745)*

**Roblox Corporation (PA)** ...................................................... A ...... 888 858-2569
970 Park Pl San Mateo (94403) *(P-18745)*

**Robo 3d Inc** ........................................................................ E ...... 844 476-2233
5070 Santa Fe St Ste C San Diego (92109) *(P-4756)*

**Robo 3d Printer, San Diego** *Also Called: Robo 3d Inc (P-4756)*

**Robot-Gxg Inc** .................................................................... E ...... 660 324-0030
8960 Toronto Ave Rancho Cucamonga (91730) *(P-11691)*

**Robot27, Irvine** *Also Called: Robotic Software Solutions Inc (P-9938)*

**Robotic Software Solutions Inc** ............................................ E ...... 855 762-6827
550 Wald Irvine (92618) *(P-9938)*

**Roboto Games Inc** .............................................................. E ...... 650 380-5966
72 E 3rd Ave San Mateo (94401) *(P-15767)*

**Robson Technologies Inc** .................................................... E ...... 408 779-8008
135 E Main Ave Ste 130 Morgan Hill (95037) *(P-11084)*

**ROC-Aire Corp** .................................................................... E ...... 909 784-3385
2198 Pomona Blvd Pomona (91768) *(P-11085)*

**Roche Diagnostics Corporation** ............................................ C ...... 650 491-7251
1 Dna Way South San Francisco (94080) *(P-5644)*

**Roche Molecular Systems Inc** .............................................. E ...... 650 225-1000
1 Dna Way South San Francisco (94080) *(P-5645)*

**Roche Sequencing Solutions Inc** .......................................... F ...... 408 386-5414
5945 Optical Ct San Jose (95138) *(P-5646)*

**Roche Sequencing Solutions Inc** .......................................... F ...... 925 854-6246
2841 Scott Blvd Santa Clara (95050) *(P-15245)*

**Rock Engineered McHy Co Inc** ............................................ F ...... 925 447-0805
1627 Army Ct Ste 1 Stockton (95206) *(P-6350)*

**Rock Revival, Vernon** *Also Called: Rcrv Inc (P-2587)*

**Rock Springs Industries Inc** ................................................ E ...... 707 443-9323
300 S Bay Depot Rd Fields Landing (95537) *(P-5195)*

**Rock Structures-Rip Rap** .................................................... E ...... 951 371-1112
11126 Silverton Ct Corona (92881) *(P-7581)*

**Rock Systems, Red Bluff** *Also Called: Tedon Specialties A Cal Corp (P-11141)*

**Rock Wall Wine Company Inc** .............................................. E ...... 510 522-5700
2301 Monarch St Alameda (94501) *(P-1729)*

**Rock West Composites Inc (PA)** .......................................... D ...... 858 537-6260
7625 Panasonic Way San Diego (92154) *(P-5196)*

**Rock West Composites Inc** .................................................. E ...... 858 537-6260
7625 Panasonic Way San Diego (92154) *(P-19415)*

**Rock World Merchandise, Anaheim** *Also Called: Bring Rokk LLC (P-2591)*

**Rock-Ola Manufacturing Corp** .............................................. D ...... 310 328-1306
1445 Sepulveda Blvd Torrance (90501) *(P-11692)*

**Rocker Industries, Huntington Beach** *Also Called: Rocker Solenoid Company (P-13077)*

**Rocker Solenoid Company** .................................................. D ...... 310 534-5660
5492 Bolsa Ave Huntington Beach (92649) *(P-13077)*

**Rocket Composites Inc** ...................................................... E ...... 916 873-8840
1790 Terminal St West Sacramento (95691) *(P-11086)*

**Rocket Ems Inc** .................................................................. B ...... 408 727-3700
2950 Patrick Henry Dr Santa Clara (95054) *(P-12201)*

**Rocket Lab Usa Inc (PA)** .................................................... E ...... 714 465-5737
3881 Mcgowen St Long Beach (90808) *(P-14084)*

**Rocket Lab Usa Inc** ............................................................ E ...... 714 465-5737
4022 E Conant St Long Beach (90808) *(P-14085)*

**Rocket Shop, Folsom** *Also Called: Aerojet Rocketdyne Inc (P-13747)*

**Rockjock, Corona** *Also Called: John Currie Performance Group (P-9872)*

**Rockler Companies Inc** ...................................................... F ...... 714 282-1157
1955 N Tustin St Orange (92865) *(P-17358)*

**Rockler Woodworking and Hdwr, Orange** *Also Called: Rockler Companies Inc (P-17358)*

**Rockley Photonics Inc (HQ)** ................................................ C ...... 626 304-9960
17252 Armstrong Ave Ste E Irvine (92614) *(P-12680)*

**Rockley Photonics Inc** ........................................................ F ...... 408 579-9210
333 W San Carlos St Ste 850 San Jose (95110) *(P-12681)*

**Rockridge Press, Oakland** *Also Called: Callisto Media Inc (P-4318)*

**Rockstar San Diego Inc** ...................................................... D ...... 760 929-0700
2200 Faraday Ave Ste 200 Carlsbad (92008) *(P-19013)*

**Rockview Dairies Inc (PA)** .................................................. C ...... 562 927-5511
7011 Stewart And Gray Rd Downey (90241) *(P-17209)*

**Rockwell Collins Inc** .......................................................... B ...... 707 422-1880
3530 Branscombe Rd Fairfield (94533) *(P-13936)*

**Rockwell Collins Inc** .......................................................... E ...... 714 929-3000
1733 Alton Pkwy Irvine (92606) *(P-14294)*

**Rockwell Collins Inc** .......................................................... D ...... 714 929-3000
1733 Alton Pkwy Irvine (92606) *(P-14295)*

**Rockwell Collins Inc** .................................................. E ...... 760 768-4732
1757 Carr Rd Ste 100 Calexico (92231) *(P-13937)*

**Rockwell Enterprises Inc** ............................................ E ...... 626 796-1511
20327 Regina Ave Torrance (90503) *(P-17309)*

**Rocky Point RTD, Oceanside** Also Called: Belching Beaver Brewery *(P-17613)*

**Rockys Gasket Shop Inc** ............................................. F ...... 408 980-9190
445 Laurelwood Rd Santa Clara (95054) *(P-6463)*

**Rode Microphones LLC (DH)** ..................................... C ...... 310 328-7456
2745 Raymond Ave Signal Hill (90755) *(P-11693)*

**Rodney Strong Vineyards, Healdsburg** Also Called: Klein Foods Inc *(P-19)*

**Rodriguez Brothers Auto Parts (PA)** ............................ F ...... 714 772-7278
812 N Anaheim Blvd Anaheim (92805) *(P-17462)*

**Roederer Estate Inc** ................................................... F ...... 707 895-2288
4501 Highway 128 Philo (95466) *(P-27)*

**Roederer Estate Winery, Philo** Also Called: Roederer Estate Inc *(P-27)*

**Roettele Industries** ..................................................... F ...... 909 606-8252
15485 Dupont Ave Chino (91710) *(P-6464)*

**Rof LLC** ..................................................................... E ...... 818 933-4000
7800 Airport Business Pkwy Van Nuys (91406) *(P-2602)*

**Rof Ferrari Lending 1 LLC** .......................................... C ...... 510 351-5520
14234 Catalina St San Leandro (94577) *(P-17381)*

**Rogar Manufacturing Inc** ........................................... C ...... 760 335-3700
866 E Ross Ave El Centro (92243) *(P-13078)*

**Roger Enrico** ............................................................. E ...... 559 485-5050
1150 E North Ave Fresno (93725) *(P-1956)*

**Roger Industry** ........................................................... F ...... 714 896-0765
11552 Knott St Ste 5 Garden Grove (92841) *(P-12202)*

**Roger R Caruso Enterprises Inc** ................................. E ...... 714 778-6006
2911 Norton Ave Lynwood (90262) *(P-3358)*

**Rogers Corporation** .................................................... D ...... 562 404-8942
13937 Rosecrans Ave Santa Fe Springs (90670) *(P-6534)*

**Rogers Holding Company Inc** .................................... E ...... 714 257-4850
1130 Columbia St Brea (92821) *(P-13938)*

**Rogerson Aircraft Corporation (PA)** ............................ D ...... 949 660-0666
16940 Von Karman Ave Irvine (92606) *(P-14296)*

**Rogerson Kratos** ........................................................ C ...... 626 449-3090
403 S Raymond Ave Pasadena (91105) *(P-14297)*

**Rogue Games, Sherman Oaks** Also Called: Rogue Games Inc *(P-17974)*

**Rogue Games Inc** ...................................................... E ...... 650 483-8008
4056 Ventura Canyon Ave Sherman Oaks (91423) *(P-17974)*

**Rohde & Schwarz Usa Inc** ......................................... E ...... 818 846-3600
2255 N Ontario St Ste 150 Burbank (91504) *(P-14579)*

**Rohde & Schwarz Usa Inc** ......................................... E ...... 818 846-3600
409 Dixon Landing Rd Milpitas (95035) *(P-14580)*

**Rohr Inc (HQ)** ............................................................. A ...... 619 691-4111
850 Lagoon Dr Chula Vista (91910) *(P-13939)*

**Rohrback Cosasco Systems Inc (DH)** ......................... D ...... 562 949-0123
11841 Smith Ave Santa Fe Springs (90670) *(P-14451)*

**Rojo's, Cypress** Also Called: Simply Fresh LLC *(P-2063)*

**Roland Corporation US (HQ)** ..................................... C ...... 323 890-3700
5100 S Eastern Ave Los Angeles (90040) *(P-16986)*

**Rolenn Manufacturing Inc (PA)** .................................. E ...... 951 682-1185
2065 Roberta St Riverside (92507) *(P-7006)*

**Roll Along Vans Inc** ................................................... E ...... 714 528-9600
1350 E Yorba Linda Blvd Placentia (92870) *(P-13567)*

**Roll-A-Shade LLC (PA)** .............................................. E ...... 951 245-5077
12101 Madera Way Riverside (92503) *(P-3727)*

**Roll-Rite LLC** .............................................................. E ...... 619 449-8860
1404 N Marshall Ave El Cajon (92020) *(P-2981)*

**Roller Bones, Goleta** Also Called: Skate One Corp *(P-15856)*

**Rollin J. Lobaugh, Belmont** Also Called: Pacific Screw Products Inc *(P-11025)*

**Rolling Hills Vineyard Inc** .......................................... E ...... 310 541-5098
4213 Pascal Pl Pls Vrds Pnsl (90274) *(P-1730)*

**Rolls Royce, Oakland** Also Called: Rolls-Royce Engine Services-Oakland Inc *(P-13720)*

**Rolls-Royce Corporation** ............................................ B ...... 510 635-1500
7200 Earhart Rd Oakland (94621) *(P-17441)*

**Rolls-Royce Engine Services-Oakland Inc** ................. B ...... 510 635-1500
7200 Earhart Rd Oakland (94621) *(P-13720)*

**Rolls-Royce High Temperature Composites Inc** ........ E ...... 714 375-4085
5730 Katella Ave Cypress (90630) *(P-7600)*

**Rolls-Royce Htc, Cypress** Also Called: Rolls-Royce High Temperature Composites Inc *(P-7600)*

**Roma Moulding Inc** .................................................... E ...... 626 334-2539
6230 N Irwindale Ave Irwindale (91702) *(P-3426)*

**Romac, Yorba Linda** Also Called: Romac Supply Co Inc *(P-11249)*

**Romac Supply Co Inc** ................................................ D ...... 323 721-5810
17722 Neff Ranch Rd Yorba Linda (92886) *(P-11249)*

**Romakk Engineering, Northridge** Also Called: Robert H Oliva Inc *(P-11082)*

**Romakk Engineering, Northridge** Also Called: Vision Aerospace LLC *(P-13988)*

**Romalv Group LLC** .................................................... E ...... 213 272-1026
429 H St Los Banos (93635) *(P-731)*

**Roman Cthlic Diocese of Orange** ............................... C ...... 949 766-6000
22062 Antonio Pkwy Rcho Sta Marg (92688) *(P-19345)*

**Romar Innovations, Murrieta** Also Called: Romar Innovations Inc *(P-14348)*

**Romar Innovations Inc** .............................................. D ...... 951 296-3480
38429 Innovation Ct Murrieta (92563) *(P-14348)*

**Rombauer Vineyards LLC (HQ)** ................................. D ...... 707 963-5170
3522 Silverado Trl N Saint Helena (94574) *(P-1731)*

**Romeo Packing Company** ......................................... E ...... 650 728-3393
106 Princeton Ave Half Moon Bay (94019) *(P-3994)*

**Romeros Engineering Inc** .......................................... E ...... 909 481-1170
9175 Milliken Ave Rancho Cucamonga (91730) *(P-11087)*

**Romeros Food Products Inc (PA)** .............................. D ...... 562 802-1858
15155 Valley View Ave Santa Fe Springs (90670) *(P-2340)*

**Romex Textiles Inc (PA)** ............................................ E ...... 213 749-9090
2454 E 27th St Vernon (90058) *(P-17068)*

**Romla Co** ................................................................... E ...... 619 946-1224
9668 Heinrich Hertz Dr Ste D San Diego (92154) *(P-8560)*

**Romla Ventilator Co, San Diego** Also Called: Romla Co *(P-8560)*

**Ron Teeguarden Enterprises Inc (PA)** ........................ E ...... 323 556-8188
10940 Wilshire Blvd Los Angeles (90024) *(P-5267)*

**Ron Witherspoon Inc** ................................................. D ...... 831 633-3568
13525 Blackie Rd Castroville (95012) *(P-11088)*

**Ron Witherspoon Inc (PA)** ......................................... E ...... 408 370-6620
1551 Dell Ave Campbell (95008) *(P-9696)*

**Ron's Pharmacy Services, San Diego** Also Called: Guardian Phrm Southern Cal LLC *(P-7340)*

**Ronan Engineering Company (PA)** ............................ D ...... 661 702-1344
28209 Avenue Stanford Valencia (91355) *(P-14452)*

**Ronan Engnrng/Rnan Msrment Div, Valencia** Also Called: Ronan Engineering Company *(P-14452)*

**Roncelli Plastics Inc** .................................................. C ...... 800 250-6516
330 W Duarte Rd Monrovia (91016) *(P-11089)*

**Ronco Plastics, Tustin** Also Called: Ronco Plastics Inc *(P-7007)*

**Ronco Plastics Inc** ..................................................... E ...... 714 259-1385
15022 Parkway Loop Ste B Tustin (92780) *(P-7007)*

**Ronford Products Inc** ................................................ E ...... 909 622-7446
1116 E 2nd St Pomona (91766) *(P-7008)*

**Ronlo Engineering Ltd** .............................................. E ...... 805 388-3227
955 Flynn Rd Camarillo (93012) *(P-11090)*

**Ronman Products Inc** ................................................ F ...... 714 994-3700
8440 Kass Dr Buena Park (90621) *(P-7912)*

**Roo-Hide Saddlery LLC** ............................................. F ...... 877 766-4433
341 Crown Ct Bldg C Imperial (92251) *(P-7161)*

**Roofscreen Mfg Inc** ................................................... E ...... 831 421-9230
347 Coral St Santa Cruz (95060) *(P-8683)*

**Roos Instruments Inc** ................................................ E ...... 408 748-8589
2285 Martin Ave Santa Clara (95050) *(P-14581)*

**Roostify Inc** ............................................................... E ...... 888 908-2470
180 Howard St Ste 100 San Francisco (94105) *(P-17728)*

**Roots Community Health Center** ............................... D ...... 510 777-1177
9925 International Blvd Ste 5 Oakland (94603) *(P-5881)*

**Roplast Industries Inc** ............................................... C ...... 530 532-9500
3155 S 5th Ave Oroville (95965) *(P-3978)*

**Ros Electrical Sup Eqp Co LLC** ................................. E ...... 562 695-9000
9529 Slauson Ave Pico Rivera (90660) *(P-16672)*

**Rosa Brothers Milk Co Inc (PA)** ................................ E ...... 559 582-8825
10090 2nd Ave Hanford (93230) *(P-815)*

**Roscoe Moss Company, Los Angeles** Also Called: Roscoe Moss Manufacturing Co *(P-7670)*

**Roscoe Moss Manufacturing Co (PA)** ........................ D ...... 323 261-4185
4360 Worth St Los Angeles (90063) *(P-7670)*

**Rose Art Industries, El Segundo** Also Called: Mega Brands America Inc *(P-15760)*

**Rose Batteries, San Jose** Also Called: Rose Electronics Distrg Co LLC *(P-16732)*

# ALPHABETIC SECTION                                                                                          Rsa Conference LLC

Rose Electronics Distrg Co LLC ............................................... E ...... 408 943-0200
   2030 Ringwood Ave San Jose (95131) *(P-16732)*
Rose Joaquin Inc ....................................................................... F ...... 209 632-0616
   410 S Golden State Blvd Turlock (95380) *(P-16839)*
Rose Lilla Inc ............................................................................. E ...... 888 519-8889
   1050 S Cypress St La Habra (90631) *(P-15916)*
Rose Manufacturing Group Inc ............................................... E ...... 760 407-0232
   2525 Jason Ct Ste 102 Oceanside (92056) *(P-9006)*
Rose Tarlow-Melrose House, West Hollywood *Also Called: Rtmh Inc (P-3489)*
Rosedale Medical, Fremont *Also Called: Intuity Medical Inc (P-15130)*
Roselm Industries Inc .............................................................. E ...... 626 442-6840
   2510 Seaman Ave South El Monte (91733) *(P-11935)*
Rosemead Electrical Supply ................................................... E ...... 562 298-4190
   9150 Dice Rd Santa Fe Springs (90670) *(P-13301)*
Rosemount Analytical Inc ....................................................... A ...... 713 396-8880
   2400 Barranca Pkwy Irvine (92606) *(P-11345)*
Rosen & Rosen Industries Inc ............................................... D ...... 949 361-9238
   204 Avenida Fabricante San Clemente (92672) *(P-15847)*
Rosen Electronics, Ontario *Also Called: Rosen Electronics LLC (P-16987)*
Rosen Electronics LLC ........................................................... D ...... 951 898-9808
   2500 E Francis St Ontario (91761) *(P-16987)*
Roseville Precision Inc ............................................................ E ...... 916 645-1628
   1180 Tara Ct Rocklin (95765) *(P-8561)*
Roshan Trading Inc ................................................................. E ...... 213 622-9904
   3631 Union Pacific Ave Los Angeles (90023) *(P-2449)*
Roskam Baking Company LLC ............................................. C ...... 909 599-0961
   505 W Allen Ave San Dimas (91773) *(P-2341)*
Roskam Baking Company LLC ............................................. B ...... 909 305-0185
   305 S Acacia St Ste A San Dimas (91773) *(P-2342)*
Ross Bindery Inc ..................................................................... C ...... 562 623-4565
   15310 Spring Ave Santa Fe Springs (90670) *(P-5014)*
Ross Engineering Corporation ............................................... E ...... 408 377-4621
   540 Westchester Dr Campbell (95008) *(P-14582)*
Ross Name Plate Company .................................................... E ...... 323 725-6812
   2 Red Plum Cir Monterey Park (91755) *(P-16027)*
Ross Periodicals, Novato *Also Called: Excellence Magazine Inc (P-4254)*
Ross Racing Pistons ............................................................... D ...... 310 536-0100
   625 S Douglas St El Segundo (90245) *(P-10624)*
Rossmoor, Walnut Creek *Also Called: Golden Rain Foundation (P-17742)*
Rossmoor Pastries MGT Inc .................................................. D ...... 562 498-2253
   2325 Redondo Ave Signal Hill (90755) *(P-1241)*
Rostar Filters, Oxnard *Also Called: PC Vaughan Mfg Corp (P-6952)*
Rotating Prcsion McHanisms Inc ........................................... E ...... 818 349-9774
   8750 Shirley Ave Northridge (91324) *(P-11936)*
Rotational Molding Inc ........................................................... D ...... 310 327-5401
   17038 S Figueroa St Gardena (90248) *(P-7009)*
Rotax Incorporated .................................................................. E ...... 323 589-5999
   2940 Leonis Blvd Vernon (90058) *(P-2805)*
Rotech Engineering, Placentia *Also Called: Rotech Engineering Inc (P-13079)*
Rotech Engineering Inc ........................................................... E ...... 714 632-0532
   1020 S Melrose St Ste A Placentia (92870) *(P-13079)*
Roth Wood Products Ltd ......................................................... E ...... 408 723-8888
   2260 Canoas Garden Ave San Jose (95125) *(P-3749)*
Rothlisberger Mfg A Cal Corp ................................................. F ...... 818 786-9462
   14718 Arminta St Van Nuys (91402) *(P-11091)*
Roto Dynamics Inc ................................................................... E ...... 714 685-0183
   1925 N Lime St Orange (92865) *(P-7010)*
Roto Power Inc ........................................................................ F ...... 951 751-9850
   191 Granite St Ste A Corona (92879) *(P-7011)*
Roto-Lite Inc ............................................................................. F ...... 909 923-4353
   84701 Avenue 48 Coachella (92236) *(P-7012)*
Rotoplas, Merced *Also Called: Acuantia Inc (P-5132)*
Rotron Incorporated ................................................................ C ...... 619 593-7400
   474 Raleigh Ave El Cajon (92020) *(P-9996)*
Round Hill Cellars .................................................................... D ...... 707 968-3200
   1680 Silverado Trl S Saint Helena (94574) *(P-1732)*
Roundtool Laboratories, Huntington Beach *Also Called: Tool Alliance Corporation (P-9703)*
Router Works Inc .................................................................... F ...... 760 599-9280
   2555 Progress St Vista (92081) *(P-11092)*
Rovi Corporation ..................................................................... F ...... 408 562-8400
   2 Circle Star Way San Carlos (94070) *(P-18746)*
Rowar Corporation .................................................................. F ...... 916 626-3030
   4025 Cincinnatti Ave Sacramento (94203) *(P-571)*
Rox Medical Inc (PA) ............................................................... F ...... **949 276-8968**
   150 Calle Iglesia Ste A San Clemente (92672) *(P-15246)*
Roy E Hanson Jr Mfg (PA) ...................................................... D ...... 213 747-7514
   1600 E Washington Blvd Los Angeles (90021) *(P-8331)*
Royal Adhesives & Sealants LLC ........................................... E ...... 310 830-9904
   800 E Anaheim St Wilmington (90744) *(P-6322)*
Royal Blue Inc ......................................................................... E ...... 310 888-0156
   9025 Wilshire Blvd Ste 301 Beverly Hills (90211) *(P-2949)*
Royal Cabinets, Pomona *Also Called: Royal Cabinets Inc (P-3266)*
Royal Cabinets, Pomona *Also Called: Royal Industries Inc (P-3267)*
Royal Cabinets Inc .................................................................. A ...... 909 629-8565
   1299 E Phillips Blvd Pomona (91766) *(P-3266)*
Royal Circuit Solutions LLC (DH) .......................................... D ...... 831 636-7789
   21 Hamilton Ct Hollister (95023) *(P-12203)*
Royal Coatings, Simi Valley *Also Called: Mabel Baas Inc (P-9089)*
Royal Custom Designs LLC ................................................... C ...... 909 591-8990
   13951 Monte Vista Ave Chino (91710) *(P-3488)*
Royal Gold LLC ....................................................................... F ...... 707 822-4653
   600 F St Ste 3 Arcata (95521) *(P-6190)*
Royal Industries, Eastvale *Also Called: Royal Range California Inc (P-11395)*
Royal Industries Inc ................................................................ C ...... 909 629-8565
   1299 E Phillips Blvd Pomona (91766) *(P-3267)*
Royal Interpack North Amer Inc ............................................. E ...... 951 787-6925
   475 Palmyrita Ave Riverside (92507) *(P-7013)*
Royal Mountain King, Copperopolis *Also Called: Meridian Gold Inc (P-105)*
Royal Plasticware, Gardena *Also Called: La Palm Furnitures & ACC Inc (P-2992)*
Royal Range California Inc ..................................................... D ...... 951 360-1600
   3245 Corridor Dr Eastvale (91752) *(P-11395)*
Royal Welding & Fabricating, Fullerton *Also Called: Cook and Cook Incorporated (P-8313)*
Royal Westlake Roofing LLC .................................................. E ...... 909 822-4407
   3511 N Riverside Ave Rialto (92377) *(P-7386)*
Royal Westlake Roofing LLC .................................................. F ...... 209 982-1473
   9508 S Harlan Rd French Camp (95231) *(P-7387)*
Royal Westlake Roofing LLC .................................................. E ...... 209 983-1600
   342 Roth Rd Lathrop (95330) *(P-16290)*
Royal Wine Corporation .......................................................... E ...... 805 983-1560
   3201 Camino Del Sol Oxnard (93030) *(P-1733)*
Royal-Pedic Mattress Mfg LLC (PA) ....................................... E ...... **310 278-9594**
   341 N Robertson Blvd Beverly Hills (90211) *(P-17524)*
Royalty, Irvine *Also Called: Royalty Carpet Mills Inc (P-2519)*
Royalty Carpet Mills Inc .......................................................... A ...... 949 474-4000
   17111 Red Hill Ave Irvine (92614) *(P-2519)*
Rozge Cosmoceutical, Van Nuys *Also Called: CDM Corp (P-17692)*
Rpc Inc ...................................................................................... E ...... 619 334-6244
   1100 N Magnolia Ave Ste H El Cajon (92020) *(P-274)*
RPC Legacy Inc ....................................................................... E ...... 818 787-9000
   14600 Arminta St Van Nuys (91402) *(P-8024)*
RPI, Simi Valley *Also Called: Replacement Parts Inds Inc (P-15479)*
Rplanet Erth Los Angles Hldngs ............................................ D ...... 833 775-2638
   5300 S Boyle Ave Vernon (90058) *(P-7014)*
RPM, Northridge *Also Called: Rotating Prcsion McHanisms Inc (P-11936)*
RPM Media, Torrance *Also Called: Retail Print Media Inc (P-4953)*
RPM Plastic Molding Inc ......................................................... E ...... 714 630-9300
   2821 E Miraloma Ave Anaheim (92806) *(P-7015)*
RPM Products Inc (PA) ........................................................... E ...... **949 888-8543**
   23201 Antonio Pkwy Rancho Santa Margari (92688) *(P-6465)*
RPS, Yorba Linda *Also Called: Radiation Protection & Spc Inc (P-8552)*
RPS Inc ..................................................................................... E ...... 818 350-8088
   20331 Corisco St Chatsworth (91311) *(P-9232)*
Rpsz Construction LLC ........................................................... C ...... 314 677-5831
   1201 W 5th St Ste T340 Los Angeles (90017) *(P-15848)*
Rrd Pckaging Solutions - Vista, Vista *Also Called: Precision Litho Inc (P-4729)*
Rrds Inc (PA) ............................................................................ F ...... **949 482-6200**
   12 Goodyear Ste 100 Irvine (92618) *(P-14817)*
Rrz Enterprises Inc ................................................................. F ...... 714 683-2820
   5521 Schaefer Ave Chino (91710) *(P-17079)*
Rsa Conference LLC ............................................................... E ...... 415 707-2833
   166 Geary St Ste 1500 San Francisco (94108) *(P-18747)*

**Rsa Engineered Products LLC** .................................................. D ...... 805 584-4150
110 W Cochran St Ste A Simi Valley (93065) *(P-13940)*

**RSI, Anaheim** *Also Called: RSI Home Products LLC (P-3510)*

**RSI Home Products, Anaheim** *Also Called: American Woodmark Corporation (P-3215)*

**RSI Home Products Inc** .................................................. C ...... 949 720-1116
620 Newport Center Dr Ste 1030 Newport Beach (92660) *(P-3509)*

**RSI Home Products LLC (HQ)** .................................................. A ...... 714 449-2200
400 E Orangethorpe Ave Anaheim (92801) *(P-3510)*

**Rsk Tool Incorporated** .................................................. E ...... 310 537-3302
410 W Carob St Compton (90220) *(P-7016)*

**RSR Steel Fabrication Inc** .................................................. E ...... 760 244-2210
11040 I Ave Hesperia (92345) *(P-7623)*

**Rt Western Inc** .................................................. E ...... 415 677-9202
160 Mendell St San Francisco (94124) *(P-572)*

**Rt Western Construction Svcs, San Francisco** *Also Called: Rt Western Inc (P-572)*

**RT&d, Carson** *Also Called: Research Tool & Die Works LLC (P-8884)*

**RTC Aerospace, Chatsworth** *Also Called: Logistical Support LLC (P-13715)*

**RTC Aerospace, Chatsworth** *Also Called: Cliffdale Manufacturing LLC (P-14109)*

**RTC Arspace - Chtswrth Div Inc (PA)** .................................................. D ...... 818 341-3344
20409 Prairie St Chatsworth (91311) *(P-10629)*

**Rte Welding, Fontana** *Also Called: Tikos Tanks Inc (P-19218)*

**Rtec-Instruments Inc** .................................................. E ...... 408 456-0801
1810 Oakland Rd Ste B San Jose (95131) *(P-14712)*

**Rti Los Angeles, Norwalk** *Also Called: New Cntury Mtals Southeast Inc (P-7764)*

**Rtie Holdings LLC** .................................................. F ...... 714 765-8200
1800 E Via Burton Anaheim (92806) *(P-13080)*

**Rtm Products Inc** .................................................. E ...... 562 926-2400
13120 Arctic Cir Santa Fe Springs (90670) *(P-7624)*

**Rtmex Inc** .................................................. C ...... 619 391-9913
1202 Piper Ranch Rd San Diego (92154) *(P-3102)*

**Rtmh Inc (PA)** .................................................. F ...... 323 651-2202
425 N Robertson Blvd West Hollywood (90048) *(P-3489)*

**Rtr Industries LLC (PA)** .................................................. E ...... 714 996-0050
4430 E Miraloma Ave Ste B Anaheim (92807) *(P-10625)*

**RTS Powder Coating Inc (PA)** .................................................. E ...... 909 393-5404
15121 Sierra Bonita Ln Chino (91710) *(P-9115)*

**Rtx Corporation** .................................................. E ...... 408 779-9121
600 Metcalf Rd San Jose (95138) *(P-13721)*

**Ru Vango Winery, Napa** *Also Called: Ego One LLC (P-1552)*

**Rubber Plastic & Metal Pdts, Rancho Santa Margari** *Also Called: RPM Products Inc (P-6465)*

**Rubber Teck Division, Long Beach** *Also Called: Rubbercraft Corp Cal Ltd (P-6477)*

**Rubber-Cal Inc** .................................................. D ...... 714 772-3000
18424 Mount Langley St Fountain Valley (92708) *(P-6535)*

**Rubbercraft Corp Cal Ltd (HQ)** .................................................. C ...... 562 354-2800
3701 E Conant St Long Beach (90808) *(P-6477)*

**Ruben & Leon Inc** .................................................. E ...... 323 937-4445
5002 Venice Blvd Los Angeles (90019) *(P-19177)*

**Ruben Ortiz, Sacramento** *Also Called: Capitol Steel Products (P-8117)*

**Rubicon Gear, Corona** *Also Called: Rubicon Gear Inc (P-8788)*

**Rubicon Gear Inc** .................................................. D ...... 951 356-3800
225 Citation Cir Corona (92878) *(P-8788)*

**Rubik Built LLC** .................................................. F ...... 209 408-0626
1004 Reno Ave Modesto (95351) *(P-19537)*

**Rubrik, Palo Alto** *Also Called: Rubrik Inc (P-19014)*

**Rubrik Inc (PA)** .................................................. A ...... 844 478-2745
3495 Deer Creek Rd Palo Alto (94304) *(P-19014)*

**Ruby Ribbon Inc** .................................................. E ...... 650 449-4470
4607 Lakeview Canyon Rd Pmb 405 Westlake Village (91361) *(P-17098)*

**Ruby Rox, Los Angeles** *Also Called: Misyd Corp (P-2857)*

**Rucker & Kolls Inc (PA)** .................................................. F ...... 408 934-9875
1064 Yosemite Dr Milpitas (95035) *(P-9896)*

**Ruckus Networks, Sunnyvale** *Also Called: Ruckus Wireless LLC (P-11937)*

**Ruckus Wireless LLC (DH)** .................................................. E ...... 650 265-4200
350 W Java Dr Sunnyvale (94089) *(P-11937)*

**Rudd Winery, Oakville** *Also Called: Rudd Wines Inc (P-1734)*

**Rudd Wines Inc (PA)** .................................................. E ...... 707 944-8577
500 Oakville Crossroad Oakville (94562) *(P-1734)*

**Ruffstuff Inc** .................................................. E ...... 916 600-1945
3237 Rippey Rd Ste 200 Loomis (95650) *(P-13568)*

**Rugby Laboratories Inc (DH)** .................................................. D ...... 951 270-1400
311 Bonnie Cir Corona (92878) *(P-17048)*

**Ruggable LLC** .................................................. B ...... 310 295-0098
17809 S Broadway Gardena (90248) *(P-17674)*

**Rugged Info Tech Eqp Corp** .................................................. D ...... 805 577-9710
25 E Easy St Simi Valley (93065) *(P-10431)*

**Rugged Notebooks, Anaheim** *Also Called: Rnbs Corporation (P-17672)*

**Rugged Systems Inc** .................................................. C ...... 858 391-1006
13000 Danielson St Ste Q Poway (92064) *(P-10200)*

**Ruggeri Marble and Granite Inc** .................................................. D ...... 310 513-2155
25028 Vermont Ave Harbor City (90710) *(P-7544)*

**Ruiz Flour Tortillas, Riverside** *Also Called: Ruiz Mexican Foods Inc (P-2343)*

**Ruiz Mexican Foods Inc (PA)** .................................................. C ...... 909 947-7811
1200 Marlborough Ave Ste A Riverside (92507) *(P-2343)*

**Rukli Inc** .................................................. E ...... 818 981-9137
4150 Puente Ave Baldwin Park (91706) *(P-16219)*

**Rumiano Cheese Co (PA)** .................................................. C ...... 530 934-5438
101 Harvest Dr Willows (95988) *(P-732)*

**Rumiano Cheese Co** .................................................. E ...... 707 465-1535
511 9th St Crescent City (95531) *(P-733)*

**Runway, Los Angeles** *Also Called: Runway Beauty Inc (P-4185)*

**Runway Beauty Inc** .................................................. F ...... 844 240-2250
6075 Rodgerton Dr Los Angeles (90068) *(P-4185)*

**Runway Liquidation LLC (HQ)** .................................................. D ...... 323 589-2224
2761 Fruitland Ave Vernon (90058) *(P-17099)*

**Rupe's Hydraulics Sales & Svc, San Marcos** *Also Called: Hydralic Systems Cmponents Inc (P-19262)*

**Rupert Gibbon & Spider Inc** .................................................. E ...... 800 442-0455
1147 Healdsburg Ave Healdsburg (95448) *(P-6111)*

**Rush Business Forms Inc** .................................................. E ...... 714 630-5661
3860 E Eagle Dr Ste A Anaheim (92807) *(P-17640)*

**Rush Pcb Inc** .................................................. E ...... 408 496-6013
500 Yosemite Dr Ste 106 Milpitas (95035) *(P-19123)*

**Rush Press Inc** .................................................. E ...... 619 296-7874
955 Gateway Center Way San Diego (92102) *(P-4757)*

**Russ Bassett Corp** .................................................. C ...... 562 945-2445
8189 Byron Rd Whittier (90606) *(P-3454)*

**Russ International Inc** .................................................. E ...... 310 329-7121
1658 W 132nd St Gardena (90249) *(P-8562)*

**Russ Mike Financial Training** .................................................. F ...... 800 724-5661
8322 Clairemont Mesa Blvd San Diego (92111) *(P-17738)*

**Russell Fabrication Corp** .................................................. E ...... 661 861-8495
4940 Gilmore Ave Bakersfield (93308) *(P-9269)*

**Russell Mechanical Inc** .................................................. D ...... 916 635-2522
3251 Monier Cir Ste A Rancho Cordova (95742) *(P-433)*

**Russian River Vineyards, Forestville** *Also Called: Topolos At Rssian River Vinyrd (P-32)*

**Russian River Winery Inc** .................................................. F ...... 707 824-2005
2191 Laguna Rd Santa Rosa (95401) *(P-1735)*

**Rusty Surfboards, San Diego** *Also Called: Rusty Surfboards Inc (P-15849)*

**Rusty Surfboards Inc (PA)** .................................................. F ...... 858 578-0414
8495 Commerce Ave San Diego (92121) *(P-15849)*

**Rutherford Hill Winery** .................................................. B ...... 707 963-1871
200 Rutherford Hill Rd Rutherford (94573) *(P-1736)*

**Rutherford Wine Company, Saint Helena** *Also Called: Round Hill Cellars (P-1732)*

**Rvision Inc** .................................................. E ...... 408 437-5777
2992 Scott Blvd Santa Clara (95054) *(P-14818)*

**Rvl Packaging Inc** .................................................. C ...... 818 735-5000
31330 Oak Crest Dr Westlake Village (91361) *(P-19124)*

**Rwh Inc** .................................................. E ...... 818 782-2350
15115 Oxnard St Van Nuys (91411) *(P-7495)*

**Rwi, Granite Bay** *Also Called: Recoating-West Inc (P-8556)*

**Rwnm Inc** .................................................. E
1240 Simpson Way Escondido (92029) *(P-11228)*

**Rxsafe, Vista** *Also Called: Rxsafe LLC (P-9897)*

**Rxsafe LLC** .................................................. D ...... 760 593-7161
2453 Cades Way Bldg A Vista (92081) *(P-9897)*

**RXSIGHT, Aliso Viejo** *Also Called: Rxsight Inc (P-15615)*

**Rxsight Inc (PA)** .................................................. D ...... 949 521-7830
100 Columbia Ste 120 Aliso Viejo (92656) *(P-15615)*

**Ryan Mc Teer** .................................................. F ...... 559 217-1450
5920 E Shields Ave Ste 103 Fresno (93727) *(P-2916)*

# ALPHABETIC SECTION — Sabina Motors & Controls

Ryan Press, Buena Park *Also Called: Q Team (P-4744)*
RYL Inc .................................................................................................. E ...... 213 503-7968
   2738 Supply Ave Commerce (90040) *(P-17310)*
Ryland Custom Welding Inc ................................................................ F ...... 408 781-2509
   1815 Monterey Hwy San Jose (95112) *(P-19211)*
Rysigo Technologies Corp (PA) .......................................................... F ...... 408 621-9274
   119 Lyon St Apt A San Francisco (94117) *(P-18748)*
Rytan Inc .............................................................................................. F ...... 310 328-6553
   1648 W 134th St Gardena (90249) *(P-9567)*
Ryte Sport, Tustin *Also Called: Ryte Ventures LLC (P-2637)*
Ryte Ventures LLC (PA) ..................................................................... F ...... 925 323-7195
   15471 Red Hill Ave Tustin (92780) *(P-2637)*
Ryvec Inc ............................................................................................. E ...... 714 520-5592
   251 E Palais Rd Anaheim (92805) *(P-5063)*
Ryvid Inc (PA) ..................................................................................... F ...... 949 691-3495
   12090 Carson St Ste H504 Hawaiian Gardens (90716) *(P-13569)*
S & H Cabinets and Mfg Inc ................................................................ E ...... 909 357-0551
   10860 Mulberry Ave Fontana (92337) *(P-3586)*
S & H Machine Inc ............................................................................... E ...... 626 448-5062
   9928 Hayward Way South El Monte (91733) *(P-9170)*
S & H Rubber Co .................................................................................. E ...... 714 525-0277
   1141 E Elm Ave Fullerton (92831) *(P-6536)*
S & H Welding Inc ................................................................................ F ...... 916 386-8921
   8604 Elder Creek Rd Sacramento (95828) *(P-8332)*
S & K Theatrical Drap Inc .................................................................... F ...... 818 503-0596
   7313 Varna Ave North Hollywood (91605) *(P-2917)*
S & M Professionals Inc (PA) ............................................................. E ...... 805 988-7677
   710 Graves Ave Oxnard (93030) *(P-1148)*
S & R Architectural Metals Inc ............................................................ E ...... 714 226-0108
   2609 W Woodland Dr Anaheim (92801) *(P-8213)*
S & S Bakery, Vista *Also Called: Baked In The Sun (P-1165)*
S & S Bindery Inc ................................................................................. E ...... 909 596-2213
   2366 1st St La Verne (91750) *(P-5015)*
S & S Carbide Tool Inc ........................................................................ E ...... 619 670-5214
   2830 Via Orange Way Ste D Spring Valley (91978) *(P-9646)*
S & S Foods LLC, Azusa *Also Called: CTI Foods Azusa LLC (P-638)*
S & S Numerical Control Inc ............................................................... E ...... 818 341-4141
   19841 Nordhoff St Northridge (91324) *(P-11093)*
S & S Paving Inc ................................................................................... E ...... 818 591-0668
   23875 Ventura Blvd Ste 202 Calabasas (91302) *(P-380)*
S & W Plastic Stores Inc (PA) ............................................................. E ...... 909 390-0090
   14270 Albers Way Chino (91710) *(P-17235)*
S & W Plastics Supply, Chino *Also Called: S & W Plastic Stores Inc (P-17235)*
S 2 K, Simi Valley *Also Called: S2k Graphics Inc (P-16028)*
S A Top-U Corporation ........................................................................ E ...... 951 916-4025
   1794 Illinois Ave Perris (92571) *(P-17651)*
S Bravo Systems Inc ........................................................................... E ...... 323 888-4133
   2929 Vail Ave Los Angeles (90040) *(P-8333)*
S C Coatings Corporation ................................................................... E ...... 951 461-9777
   41775 Elm St Ste 302 Murrieta (92562) *(P-9116)*
S C Hydraulic Engineering, Brea *Also Called: Southern Cal Hydrlic Engrg Cor (P-16843)*
S C I Industries Inc .............................................................................. E
   1433 Adelia Ave El Monte (91733) *(P-13570)*
S C S, North Highlands *Also Called: Security Contractor Svcs Inc (P-16495)*
S D I, Visalia *Also Called: Spraying Devices Inc (P-9383)*
S D I, Camarillo *Also Called: Structural Diagnostics Inc (P-14926)*
S D M, Chino *Also Called: Syntech Development & Mfg Inc (P-7048)*
S D S, Ontario *Also Called: Specialized Dairy Service Inc (P-9382)*
S E - G I Products Inc ......................................................................... C ...... 949 297-8530
   20521 Teresita Way Lake Forest (92630) *(P-8288)*
S E M, Fremont *Also Called: Streamline Electronics Mfg Inc (P-12231)*
S F Technology, Cerritos *Also Called: UFO Designs (P-13596)*
S J Automotive LLC ............................................................................. F ...... 408 296-2223
   3333 Stevens Creek Blvd San Jose (95117) *(P-11094)*
S J S Products, Loomis *Also Called: Jamcor Corporation (P-16709)*
S K Laboratories Inc ........................................................................... D ...... 714 695-9800
   5420 E La Palma Ave Anaheim (92807) *(P-5647)*
S K Labs, Anaheim *Also Called: S K Laboratories Inc (P-5647)*
S K S Enterprises Inc (PA) .................................................................. E ...... 209 599-4095
   11830 French Camp Rd Manteca (95336) *(P-64)*
S L Fusco Inc (PA) ............................................................................... E ...... 310 868-1010
   1966 E Via Arado Rancho Dominguez (90220) *(P-9568)*
S M S Briners Inc ................................................................................. E ...... 209 941-8515
   17750 E Highway 4 Stockton (95215) *(P-991)*
S Martinelli & Company ...................................................................... E ...... 831 768-3958
   257 Kearney Ext Watsonville (95076) *(P-923)*
S Martinelli & Company ...................................................................... E ...... 831 768-3958
   1260 W Beach St Watsonville (95076) *(P-924)*
S Martinelli & Company (PA) .............................................................. D ...... 831 724-1126
   735 W Beach St Watsonville (95076) *(P-2344)*
S Martinelli & Company ...................................................................... D ...... 831 724-1126
   345 Harvest Dr Watsonville (95076) *(P-2345)*
S Q I, San Jose *Also Called: Silicon Quest International Inc (P-12704)*
S R C Devices Inccustomer ................................................................ B ...... 866 772-8668
   6295 Ferris Sq Ste D San Diego (92121) *(P-11346)*
S R Machining, Norco *Also Called: S R Machining-Properties LLC (P-11096)*
S R Machining Inc ................................................................................ E ...... 951 520-9486
   640 Parkridge Ave Norco (92860) *(P-11095)*
S R Machining-Properties LLC .......................................................... C ...... 951 520-9486
   640 Parkridge Ave Norco (92860) *(P-11096)*
S S, South Gate *Also Called: Shultz Steel Company LLC (P-8802)*
S S I, Long Beach *Also Called: Seal Science Inc (P-6466)*
S S Schaffer Co Inc ............................................................................ F ...... 323 560-1430
   5637 District Blvd Vernon (90058) *(P-9569)*
S Studio Inc ......................................................................................... F ...... 213 388-7400
   3030 W 6th St Los Angeles (90020) *(P-2726)*
S-Curve Technologies Inc ................................................................... E ...... 909 584-8898
   601 Valley Blvd Unit C Big Bear City (92314) *(P-7018)*
S&B Development Group LLC .......................................................... E ...... 213 446-2818
   1901 Avenue Of The Stars 235 Los Angeles (90067) *(P-2441)*
S&B Filters Inc (PA) ............................................................................ E ...... 909 947-0015
   15461 Slover Ave Ste A Fontana (92337) *(P-13571)*
S&B Industry Inc .................................................................................. E ...... 909 569-4155
   105 S Puente St Brea (92821) *(P-7017)*
S&B Pharma Inc ................................................................................... D ...... 626 334-2908
   405 S Motor Ave Azusa (91702) *(P-5268)*
S&E Gourmet Cuts Inc ....................................................................... C ...... 909 370-0155
   1055 E Cooley Ave San Bernardino (92408) *(P-17149)*
S&S Flavours, Brea *Also Called: Scisorek & Son Flavors Inc (P-2024)*
S&S Precision Mfg Inc ........................................................................ E ...... 714 754-6664
   2101 S Yale St Santa Ana (92704) *(P-11097)*
S2e Inc .................................................................................................. F ...... 626 965-1008
   817 Lawson St City Of Industry (91748) *(P-11694)*
S2k Graphics Inc ................................................................................. E ...... 818 885-3900
   4686 Industrial St Simi Valley (93063) *(P-16028)*
S3 Graphics Inc ................................................................................... E ...... 510 687-4900
   940 Mission Ct Fremont (94539) *(P-12682)*
SA Camp Pump and Drilling Co, Bakersfield *Also Called: SA Camp Pump Company (P-19279)*
SA Camp Pump Company ................................................................. D ...... 661 399-2976
   17876 Zerker Rd Bakersfield (93308) *(P-19279)*
SA Photonics, LLC, Los Gatos *Also Called: Caci Photonics LLC (P-14165)*
SA Serving Lines Inc .......................................................................... E ...... 714 848-7529
   226 W Carleton Ave Orange (92867) *(P-8563)*
Saags Products LLC .......................................................................... E ...... 510 678-3412
   1799 Factor Ave San Leandro (94577) *(P-664)*
Saba Software Inc (DH) ..................................................................... D ...... 877 722-2101
   4120 Dublin Blvd Ste 200 Dublin (94568) *(P-18749)*
Sabater Usa Inc (PA) .......................................................................... E ...... 310 518-2227
   14824 S Main St Gardena (90248) *(P-2346)*
Sabater Usa Inc .................................................................................. F ...... 310 518-2227
   1904 1/2 E Dominguez St Carson (90810) *(P-17210)*
Sabel, Vista *Also Called: Surgistar Inc (P-15271)*
Sabia, San Diego *Also Called: Sabia incorporated (P-14453)*
Sabia Incorporated (PA) ..................................................................... E ...... 858 217-2200
   10919 Technology Pl Ste A San Diego (92127) *(P-14453)*
Sabic Innovative Plas US LLC ........................................................... E ...... 559 264-4100
   3311 E Central Ave Fresno (93725) *(P-5197)*
Sabic Polymershapes, Fresno *Also Called: Sabic Innovative Plas US LLC (P-5197)*
Sabina Motors & Controls, Anaheim *Also Called: Motors & Controls Whse Inc (P-16723)*

**Sable Industries, Oceanside** Also Called: Surgistar Inc *(P-15272)*
**Sabot Publishing Inc (PA)**......................................E ...... 310 356-4100
300 Continental Blvd Ste 650 El Segundo (90245) *(P-4296)*
**Sabre Sciences Inc** ..................................................F ...... 760 448-2750
2233 Faraday Ave Ste K Carlsbad (92008) *(P-5269)*
**Sabrin Corporation** ..................................................F ...... 626 792-3813
2836 E Walnut St Pasadena (91107) *(P-13941)*
**Sabritec** ......................................................................B ...... 714 371-1100
1550 Scenic Ave Ste 150 Costa Mesa (92626) *(P-12896)*
**Sac-TEC Labs Inc (PA)**...........................................E ...... 310 375-5295
24311 Wilmington Ave Carson (90745) *(P-12683)*
**Sacahn JV** ..................................................................D ...... 858 924-1110
15916 Bernardo Center Dr San Diego (92127) *(P-6351)*
**Saco Enterprises Inc** .................................................E ...... 408 526-9363
2260 Trade Zone Blvd San Jose (95131) *(P-16631)*
**Sacramento Bee, Sacramento** Also Called: McClatchy Newspapers Inc *(P-4154)*
**Sacramento Business Journal, Sacramento** Also Called: American City Bus Journals Inc *(P-4064)*
**Sacramento Cash and Carry, Rocklin** Also Called: Soniya Valley LLC *(P-16235)*
**Sacramento Coca-Cola Btlg Inc (HQ)**......................B ...... 916 928-2300
4101 Gateway Park Blvd Sacramento (95834) *(P-1957)*
**Sacramento Coca-Cola Btlg Inc** ...............................D ...... 209 541-3200
1733 Morgan Rd Ste 200 Modesto (95358) *(P-1958)*
**Sacramento Container Corp** ....................................C ...... 916 614-0580
4841 Urbani Ave Mcclellan (95652) *(P-3884)*
**Sacramento Cooling Systems Inc** ............................F ...... 559 253-9660
5466 E Lamona Ave Ste 1022 Fresno (93727) *(P-14915)*
**Sacramento Div, West Sacramento** Also Called: Quad/Graphics Inc *(P-17782)*
**Sacramento E.D.M., Inc., Rancho Cordova** Also Called: Prototek Dgtal Mfg Scrmnto LLC *(P-11054)*
**Sacramento News & Review, Sacramento** Also Called: Chico Community Publishing *(P-4091)*
**Sacramento Observer, The, Sacramento** Also Called: Lee Publishing Company *(P-4148)*
**Sacramento Packing Inc** ..........................................B ...... 530 671-4488
833 Tudor Rd Yuba City (95991) *(P-962)*
**Sacramento Rendering Co** ......................................D ...... 916 363-4821
11350 Kiefer Blvd Sacramento (95830) *(P-1389)*
**Sacramento Rendering Co, Sacramento** Also Called: SRC Milling Co LLC *(P-1390)*
**Sacramento Stucco Co** ............................................E ...... 916 372-7442
1550 Parkway Blvd West Sacramento (95691) *(P-16483)*
**Saddleback Educational Inc** ....................................F ...... 714 640-5200
3130 Clay St Newport Beach (92663) *(P-4344)*
**Saddleback Educational Pubg, Newport Beach** Also Called: Saddleback Educational Inc *(P-4344)*
**Saddlemen, Compton** Also Called: Saddlemen Corporation *(P-16397)*
**Saddlemen Corporation** ...........................................C ...... 310 638-1222
17801 S Susana Rd Compton (90221) *(P-16397)*
**SAE Engineering Inc** ................................................E ...... 408 492-1784
15500 Concord Cir # 150 Morgan Hill (95037) *(P-8564)*
**Saehan Electronics America Inc (PA)**.....................D ...... 858 496-1500
7880 Airway Rd Ste B5g San Diego (92154) *(P-12204)*
**Saeilo Manufacturing Inds, Santa Fe Springs** Also Called: SMI Ca Inc *(P-11115)*
**Saf West, Redding** Also Called: Southern Alum Finshg Co Inc *(P-7761)*
**Saf-T-Cab Inc (PA)**...................................................E ...... 559 268-5541
3241 S Parkway Dr Fresno (93725) *(P-13426)*
**Saf-T-Co Supply** .......................................................E ...... 714 547-9975
1300 E Normandy Pl Santa Ana (92705) *(P-11481)*
**Safari Books Online LLC (PA)**................................D ...... 707 827-7000
1003 Gravenstein Hwy N Sebastopol (95472) *(P-19347)*
**Safariland LLC** .........................................................B ...... 909 923-7300
4700 E Airport Dr Ontario (91761) *(P-15400)*
**Safc Pharma, Carlsbad** Also Called: Sigma-Aldrich Corporation *(P-6323)*
**Safe Haven, San Fernando** Also Called: Valeda Company LLC *(P-15425)*
**Safe Path Products, Chico** Also Called: Van Duerr Industries Inc *(P-16497)*
**Safe Plating Inc** ........................................................D ...... 626 810-1872
18001 Railroad St City Of Industry (91748) *(P-9007)*
**Safe Publishing Company** .......................................D ...... 805 973-1300
400 Del Norte Blvd Oxnard (93030) *(P-4957)*
**Safeguard Envirogroup Inc** .....................................E ...... 626 512-7585
153 Lowell Ave Glendora (91741) *(P-14713)*
**Safer Sports Inc** .......................................................E ...... 760 444-0082
5670 El Camino Real Ste B Carlsbad (92008) *(P-15850)*

**Safesmart Access Inc** .............................................E ...... 310 410-1525
13238 Florence Ave Santa Fe Springs (90670) *(P-19061)*
**Safety Network, Fresno** Also Called: Safety Ntwrk Traffic Signs Inc *(P-12014)*
**Safety Ntwrk Traffic Signs Inc** ................................E ...... 559 291-8000
1345 N Rabe Ave Fresno (93727) *(P-12014)*
**Safety Products Holdings LLC** ...............................E ...... 714 662-1033
170 Technology Dr Irvine (92618) *(P-9570)*
**Safetychain Software Inc (PA)**................................E ...... 415 233-9474
7599 Redwood Blvd Ste 205 Novato (94945) *(P-18750)*
**Safeway, San Francisco** Also Called: Safeway Inc *(P-17382)*
**Safeway Inc** ..............................................................A ...... 415 661-3220
1200 Irving St Ste 2 San Francisco (94122) *(P-17382)*
**Safeway Sign Company** ..........................................E ...... 760 246-7070
9875 Yucca Rd Adelanto (92301) *(P-16029)*
**Saffola Quality Foods, Ontario** Also Called: Ventura Foods LLC *(P-707)*
**Saffron & Sage LLC** .................................................F ...... 619 933-2340
2555 State St Ste 101 San Diego (92101) *(P-17775)*
**Safran Aerospace, Carson** Also Called: Safran Usa Inc *(P-11469)*
**Safran Cabin - Cypress, Cypress** Also Called: Safran Cabin Inc *(P-13948)*
**Safran Cabin Galleys Us Inc (HQ)**..........................A ...... 714 861-7300
17311 Nichols Ln Huntington Beach (92647) *(P-13942)*
**Safran Cabin Inc** ......................................................C ...... 909 652-9700
8595 Milliken Ave Ste 101 Rancho Cucamonga (91730) *(P-13943)*
**Safran Cabin Inc** ......................................................C ...... 714 901-2672
12472 Industry St Garden Grove (92841) *(P-13944)*
**Safran Cabin Inc** ......................................................C ...... 805 922-3013
2850 Skyway Dr Santa Maria (93455) *(P-13945)*
**Safran Cabin Inc** ......................................................C ...... 619 671-0430
6754 Calle De Linea Ste 111 San Diego (92154) *(P-13946)*
**Safran Cabin Inc (HQ)**..............................................B ...... 714 934-0000
5701 Bolsa Ave Huntington Beach (92647) *(P-13947)*
**Safran Cabin Inc** ......................................................C ...... 562 344-4780
12240 Warland Dr Cypress (90630) *(P-13948)*
**Safran Cabin Inc** ......................................................C ...... 619 661-6292
2695 Customhouse Ct Ste 111 San Diego (92154) *(P-13949)*
**Safran Cabin Inc** ......................................................D ...... 714 934-0000
1500 Glenn Curtiss St Carson (90746) *(P-13950)*
**Safran Cabin Inc** ......................................................C ...... 714 891-1906
7330 Lincoln Way Garden Grove (92841) *(P-13951)*
**Safran Cabin Tijuana S.a De Cv, San Diego** Also Called: Safran Cabin Inc *(P-13949)*
**Safran Defense & Space Inc** ...................................D ...... 805 373-9340
2665 Park Center Dr Ste A Simi Valley (93065) *(P-14819)*
**Safran Defense & Space Inc** ...................................D ...... 603 296-0469
2960 Airway Ave Ste A103 Costa Mesa (92626) *(P-14820)*
**Safran Power Units, San Diego** Also Called: Safran Pwr Units San Diego LLC *(P-13722)*
**Safran Pwr Units San Diego LLC** ...........................D ...... 858 223-2228
4255 Ruffin Rd Ste 100 San Diego (92123) *(P-13722)*
**Safran Seats Santa Maria LLC** ...............................A ...... 805 922-5995
2641 Airpark Dr Santa Maria (93455) *(P-13952)*
**Safran Usa Inc** .........................................................A ...... 310 884-7198
1500 Glenn Curtiss St Carson (90746) *(P-11469)*
**Safti, Merced** Also Called: OKeeffes Inc *(P-17338)*
**Safti First, Merced** Also Called: OKeeffes Inc *(P-7199)*
**Safti First, Brisbane** Also Called: OKeeffes Inc *(P-7237)*
**Sage Goddess Inc** ...................................................E ...... 650 733-6639
21010 Figueroa St Carson (90745) *(P-15705)*
**Sage Instruments Inc** ..............................................D ...... 831 761-1000
135 Aviation Way Ste 19 Watsonville (95076) *(P-14583)*
**Sage Plastics Long Beach Corp** .............................D ...... 562 423-3900
2210 E Artesia Blvd Long Beach (90805) *(P-7019)*
**Sage Publications Inc (PA)**......................................C ...... 805 499-0721
2455 Teller Rd Thousand Oaks (91320) *(P-4345)*
**Sage Software Inc** ...................................................F ...... 650 579-3628
1380 Tartan Trail Rd Burlingame (94010) *(P-18751)*
**Sage Software Inc** ...................................................D ...... 949 753-1222
7595 Irvine Center Dr Ste 200 Irvine (92618) *(P-19018)*
**Sage Software Holdings Inc (HQ)**...........................B ...... 866 530-7243
6561 Irvine Center Dr Irvine (92618) *(P-18752)*
**SAI Industries** ..........................................................E ...... 818 842-6144
631 Allen Ave Glendale (91201) *(P-9136)*

# ALPHABETIC SECTION — San Diego Composites Inc

Saic, San Diego *Also Called: Leidos Inc (P-19461)*

Saigon Fabrication Ltd ............... E ...... 408 693-2340
5750 Hellyer Ave Ste 20 San Jose (95138) *(P-19416)*

Saildrone, Alameda *Also Called: Saildrone Inc (P-9745)*

Saildrone Inc ............... C ...... 415 670-9700
1050 W Tower Ave Alameda (94501) *(P-9745)*

Sailing Innovation (us) Inc ............... A ...... 626 965-6665
17870 Castleton St Ste 220 City Of Industry (91748) *(P-17652)*

Saint Germain Foundation (PA) ............... F ...... 530 235-2994
1120 Stonehedge Dr Dunsmuir (96025) *(P-19370)*

Saint Jseph Communications Inc (PA) ............... E ...... 626 331-3549
1243 E Shamwood St West Covina (91790) *(P-19296)*

Saint Nicolas Vineyard, Soledad *Also Called: Kvl Holdings Inc (P-20)*

Saint Nine America Inc ............... E ...... 562 921-5300
10700 Norwalk Blvd Santa Fe Springs (90670) *(P-15851)*

Saint-Gobain Ceramics Plas Inc ............... C ...... 714 701-3900
4905 E Hunter Ave Anaheim (92807) *(P-6158)*

Saint-Gobain Performance Plas, San Diego *Also Called: Saint-Gobain Solar Gard LLC (P-6569)*

Saint-Gobain Prfmce Plas Corp ............... C ...... 714 893-0470
7301 Orangewood Ave Garden Grove (92841) *(P-5198)*

Saint-Gobain Prfmce Plas Corp ............... D ...... 714 630-5818
7301 Orangewood Ave Garden Grove (92841) *(P-5199)*

Saint-Gobain Solar Gard LLC (DH) ............... D ...... 866 300-2674
4540 Viewridge Ave San Diego (92123) *(P-6569)*

Saintsbury LLC ............... F ...... 707 252-0592
1500 Los Carneros Ave Napa (94559) *(P-1737)*

Saitech Inc ............... F ...... 510 440-0256
42640 Christy St Fremont (94538) *(P-17558)*

Saitex (usa) LLC ............... F ...... 323 391-6116
6074 Malburg Way Vernon (90058) *(P-2425)*

Saiyr Sweets LLC ............... F ...... 916 667-1407
10292 Marlaw Way Elk Grove (95757) *(P-1324)*

Sal J Acsta Sheetmetal Mfg Inc ............... D ...... 408 275-6370
930 Remillard Ct San Jose (95122) *(P-8565)*

Salad Cosmo, Dixon *Also Called: Salad Cosmo USA Corporation (P-2347)*

Salad Cosmo USA Corporation ............... E ...... 707 678-6633
5944 Dixon Ave W Dixon (95620) *(P-2347)*

Saladinos Foodservice, Fresno *Also Called: US Foods Inc (P-17120)*

Sale 121 Corp (PA) ............... E ...... 888 233-7667
1467 68th Ave Sacramento (95822) *(P-10273)*

Saleen Automotive Inc (PA) ............... E ...... 800 888-8945
2735 Wardlow Rd Corona (92882) *(P-8808)*

Saleen Incorporated (PA) ............... C ...... 714 400-2121
2735 Wardlow Rd Corona (92882) *(P-13382)*

Salem Music Network Inc ............... F ...... 805 987-0400
4880 Santa Rosa Rd Ste 300 Camarillo (93012) *(P-11938)*

Sales & Marketing, San Francisco *Also Called: Outreach Corporation (P-18651)*

Sales & Mktg Professionals, Oxnard *Also Called: S & M Professionals Inc (P-1148)*

Salescatcher, Orange *Also Called: Salescatcher LLC (P-18753)*

Salescatcher LLC ............... E ...... 714 376-6700
1570 N Batavia St Orange (92867) *(P-18753)*

Salesforce, San Francisco *Also Called: Salesforce Inc (P-18754)*

Salesforce Inc (PA) ............... A ...... 415 901-7000
415 Mission St Fl 3 San Francisco (94105) *(P-18754)*

SALESFORCE.COM, INC., Santa Monica *Also Called: Salesforcecom Inc (P-18755)*

Salesforcecom Inc ............... E ...... 310 752-7000
1442 2nd St Santa Monica (90401) *(P-18755)*

Salesforcecom Landmark ............... F ...... 650 653-4500
1 Market St Ste 400 San Francisco (94105) *(P-18756)*

Salesforceorg LLC ............... B ...... 415 901-7000
415 Mission St Fl 3 San Francisco (94105) *(P-18757)*

Salico Farms Inc ............... C ...... 760 344-5375
4231 Us Highway 86 Ste 4 Brawley (92227) *(P-868)*

Salient Global Technologies, Pittsburg *Also Called: Ravig Inc (P-16545)*

Salinas Valley Wax Paper, Salinas *Also Called: Salinas Valley Wax Paper Co (P-4049)*

Salinas Valley Wax Paper Co ............... E ...... 831 424-2747
1111 Abbott St Salinas (93901) *(P-4049)*

Salis International Inc ............... E ...... 303 384-3588
3921 Oceanic Dr Ste 802 Oceanside (92056) *(P-15887)*

Sallingers Spclty Scrnprint Em ............... E ...... 714 532-6627
1080 N Batavia St Ste L Orange (92867) *(P-17838)*

Salman, Brea *Also Called: Parkinson Enterprises Inc (P-3581)*

Salsbury Industries, Carson *Also Called: Salsbury Industries Inc (P-3707)*

Salsbury Industries Inc ............... D ...... 323 846-6700
1010 E 62nd St Los Angeles (90001) *(P-3706)*

Salsbury Industries Inc (PA) ............... C ...... 800 624-5269
18300 Central Ave Carson (90746) *(P-3707)*

Salutron Incorporated (PA) ............... E ...... 510 795-2876
8371 Central Ave Ste A Newark (94560) *(P-15577)*

Sam Israel Viner, Marina Del Rey *Also Called: Samvco (P-11413)*

Sam Schaffer Inc ............... E ...... 323 263-7524
3015 E Echo Hill Way Orange (92867) *(P-19280)*

Sam's Super Market, Fresno *Also Called: Sams Italian Deli & Mkt Inc (P-17383)*

Samax Precision Inc ............... E ...... 408 245-9555
926 W Evelyn Ave Sunnyvale (94086) *(P-11098)*

Sambrailo Packaging ............... E ...... 831 726-3210
1750 San Juan Rd Aromas (95004) *(P-17021)*

Samedan Oil Corporation ............... B ...... 661 319-5038
1360 Landing Ave Seal Beach (90740) *(P-196)*

Sample Tile and Stone Inc ............... E ...... 951 776-8562
1410 Richardson St San Bernardino (92408) *(P-7545)*

Sams Italian Deli & Mkt Inc ............... F ...... 559 229-9333
2415 N 1st St Fresno (93703) *(P-17383)*

Samsara Winery and Tasting Rm ............... E ...... 805 845-8001
6485 Calle Real Ste E Goleta (93117) *(P-1738)*

Samson Pharmaceuticals Inc ............... E ...... 323 722-3066
5635 Smithway St Commerce (90040) *(P-5648)*

Samsung Biologics America Inc ............... F ...... 650 898-9717
600 Gateway Blvd South San Francisco (94080) *(P-5649)*

Samsung International Inc (DH) ............... E ...... 619 671-6001
333 H St Ste 6000 Chula Vista (91910) *(P-16733)*

Samtech Automotive Usa Inc ............... E ...... 310 638-9955
1130 E Dominguez St Carson (90746) *(P-9588)*

Samtech International, Carson *Also Called: Samtech Automotive Usa Inc (P-9588)*

Samuel Son & Co (usa) Inc ............... E ...... 951 781-7800
2345 Fleetwood Dr Riverside (92509) *(P-7747)*

Samuel Raoof ............... F ...... 818 534-3180
20660 Nordhoff St Chatsworth (91311) *(P-6033)*

Samvco ............... F ...... 310 980-5680
14016 Bora Bora Way Marina Del Rey (90292) *(P-11413)*

San Antonio Gift Shop, Los Angeles *Also Called: San Antonio Winery Inc (P-1739)*

San Antonio Winery Inc (PA) ............... C ...... 323 223-1401
737 Lamar St Los Angeles (90031) *(P-1739)*

San Benito Supply (PA) ............... C ...... 831 637-5526
1060 Nash Rd Hollister (95023) *(P-7388)*

San Bernabe Vineyards ............... E ...... 831 385-4897
53001 Oasis Rd King City (93930) *(P-28)*

San Bernabe Vineyards LLC ............... E ...... 209 824-3501
12001 S Highway 99 Manteca (95336) *(P-1740)*

San Bernandina Steel, Stockton *Also Called: Herrick Corporation (P-8150)*

San Bernardino Canning Co., San Bernardino *Also Called: Refresco Beverages US Inc (P-1930)*

San Bernardino County Sun, The, San Bernardino *Also Called: Sun Cmpany of San Brnrdino Cal (P-4203)*

San Bernardino Sheet Plant, San Bernardino *Also Called: Packaging Corporation America (P-3874)*

San Brnrdino Cmnty College Dst ............... D ...... 909 888-6511
701 S Mount Vernon Ave San Bernardino (92410) *(P-4958)*

San Dego Nghborhood Newspapers, Gardena *Also Called: Community Media Corporation (P-4097)*

San Dego Prcsion Machining Inc ............... E ...... 858 499-0379
9375 Ruffin Ct San Diego (92123) *(P-7625)*

San Dego Second Chance Program ............... E ...... 619 266-2506
6145 Imperial Ave San Diego (92114) *(P-19359)*

San Diego Ace Inc ............... C ...... 619 206-7339
5363 Sweetwater Trl San Diego (92130) *(P-7020)*

San Diego Arcft Interiors Inc ............... E ...... 619 474-1997
2381 Boswell Rd Chula Vista (91914) *(P-3455)*

San Diego Business Journal, San Diego *Also Called: Cbj LP (P-4239)*

San Diego Composites Inc ............... D ...... 858 751-0450
9220 Activity Rd Ste 100 San Diego (92126) *(P-19417)*

# ALPHABETIC SECTION

San Diego Crating & Pkg Inc ........................................... F ...... 858 748-0100
  12678 Brookprinter Pl Poway (92064) *(P-3885)*

San Diego Custom Cabinets ............................................ E ...... 858 256-0933
  683 Vernon Way El Cajon (92020) *(P-3268)*

San Diego Daily Transcript ............................................. D ...... 619 232-4381
  34 Emerald Gln Laguna Niguel (92677) *(P-3795)*

San Diego Die Cutting Inc ................................................ E ...... 619 297-4453
  3112 Moore St San Diego (92110) *(P-17022)*

San Diego Electric Sign Inc ............................................. F ...... 619 258-1775
  1890 Cordell Ct Ste 105 El Cajon (92020) *(P-16030)*

San Diego Leather Inc ..................................................... F ...... 619 477-2900
  340 National City Blvd National City (91950) *(P-17513)*

San Diego Magazine, San Diego *Also Called: San Diego Magazine Pubg Co (P-4297)*

San Diego Magazine Pubg Co ........................................ E ...... 619 230-9292
  1230 Columbia St Ste 800 San Diego (92101) *(P-4297)*

San Diego Marble & Tile, San Diego *Also Called: Alkal Tile Inc (P-17321)*

San Diego Pcb Design LLC ............................................. F ...... 858 271-5722
  461 Whitby Gln Escondido (92027) *(P-12205)*

San Diego Powder Coating, El Cajon *Also Called: BJS&t Enterprises Inc (P-9055)*

San Diego Precast Concrete Inc (DH) ........................... E ...... 619 240-8000
  2735 Cactus Rd San Diego (92154) *(P-7389)*

San Diego Printers, San Diego *Also Called: Three Man Corporation (P-4975)*

San Diego Ready Mix, San Diego *Also Called: Superior Ready Mix Concrete LP (P-17346)*

San Diego Sign Company Inc .......................................... E ...... 888 748-7446
  5960 Pascal Ct Carlsbad (92008) *(P-16892)*

San Diego Union Tribune, The, San Diego *Also Called: San Diego Union-Tribune LLC (P-4187)*

San Diego Union-Tribune LLC ........................................ E ...... 619 299-3131
  1920 Main St Irvine (92614) *(P-4186)*

San Diego Union-Tribune LLC (PA) ............................... A ...... 619 299-3131
  600 B St Ste 1201 San Diego (92101) *(P-4187)*

San Dieguito Printers, San Marcos *Also Called: San Dieguito Publishers Inc (P-4758)*

San Dieguito Publishers Inc ............................................. D ...... 760 593-5139
  1880 Diamond St San Marcos (92078) *(P-4758)*

San Fernando Valley Bus Jurnl, Los Angeles *Also Called: Cbj LP (P-4237)*

San Francisco Bath Salt Co, Alameda *Also Called: Rmf Salt Holdings LLC (P-6032)*

San Francisco Bay Brand Inc (PA) ................................. E ...... 510 792-7200
  8239 Enterprise Dr Newark (94560) *(P-1149)*

San Francisco Bay Coffee Co, Lincoln *Also Called: Jbr Inc (P-2243)*

San Francisco Bay Guardian, San Francisco *Also Called: Bay Guardian Company (P-4074)*

San Francisco Business Times, San Francisco *Also Called: Business Jrnl Publications Inc (P-4079)*

San Francisco Foods Inc ................................................ D ...... 510 357-7343
  14054 Catalina St San Leandro (94577) *(P-1045)*

San Francisco Herb & Natural Food Co Inc ................ D ...... 510 770-1215
  47444 Kato Rd Fremont (94538) *(P-17211)*

San Francisco Herb Tea & Spice, Fremont *Also Called: San Francisco Herb & Natural Food Co Inc (P-17211)*

San Francisco Ship Repair Inc ....................................... C ...... 415 861-7447
  Foot Of 20th St Pier 70 San Francisco (94107) *(P-14017)*

San Group Biotech Usa Inc ............................................ F ...... 760 599-8855
  1260 Avenida Chelsea Vista (92081) *(P-6206)*

San Joaquin Figs Inc ....................................................... E ...... 559 224-4492
  3564 N Hazel Ave Fresno (93722) *(P-963)*

San Joaquin Hydraulic Inc (PA) ..................................... F ...... 559 264-7325
  530 Van Ness Ave Fresno (93721) *(P-16893)*

San Joaquin Magazine .................................................... E ...... 209 625-8313
  1463 Moffat Blvd Ste 4 Manteca (95336) *(P-17277)*

San Joaquin Refining Co Inc ......................................... C ...... 661 327-4257
  3500 Shell St Bakersfield (93388) *(P-6352)*

San Joaquin Valley Dairymen, Turlock *Also Called: California Dairies Inc (P-704)*

San Joaquin Window Inc ................................................ C ...... 909 946-3697
  1455 Columbia Ave Riverside (92507) *(P-8289)*

San Jose Awning, San Jose *Also Called: San Jose Awning Company Inc (P-2982)*

San Jose Awning Company Inc .................................... E ...... 408 350-7000
  755 Chestnut St Ste E San Jose (95110) *(P-2982)*

San Jose Business Journal ............................................ C ...... 408 295-3800
  125 S Market St Fl 11 San Jose (95113) *(P-4188)*

San Jose Die Casting Corp ............................................ E ...... 408 262-6500
  600 Business Park Dr Ste 100 Lincoln (95648) *(P-7820)*

San Jose Mercury-News LLC (DH) ................................ A ...... 408 920-5000
  4 N 2nd St Fl 8 San Jose (95113) *(P-4189)*

San Jose Office, San Jose *Also Called: Lg Innotek Usa Inc (P-14209)*

San Luis Obspo Cocmmnty Clgdst ............................. F ...... 805 591-6200
  2800 Buena Vista Dr Paso Robles (93446) *(P-4190)*

San Marcos Trading Company, San Marcos *Also Called: GK Foods Inc (P-1060)*

San Mateo Times, San Mateo *Also Called: Alameda Newspapers Inc (P-4063)*

San Rafael Rock Quarry Inc (HQ) ................................ D ...... 415 459-7740
  2350 Kerner Blvd Ste 200 San Rafael (94901) *(P-305)*

San Rafael Rock Quarry Inc ......................................... E ...... 510 970-7700
  961 Western Dr Richmond (94801) *(P-6370)*

San-I-Pak Pacific Inc ....................................................... D ...... 209 836-2310
  23535 S Bird Rd Tracy (95304) *(P-8334)*

Sanchez Business Inc .................................................... E ...... 415 282-2400
  250 Napoleon St Ste M San Francisco (94124) *(P-17604)*

Sanctuary Clothing, Burbank *Also Called: Sanctuary Clothing LLC (P-17496)*

Sanctuary Clothing LLC (PA) ........................................ E ...... 818 505-0018
  3611 N San Fernando Blvd Burbank (91505) *(P-17496)*

Sandberg Furniture, Vernon *Also Called: Sandberg Furniture Mfg Co Inc (P-3456)*

Sandberg Furniture Mfg Co Inc (PA) ........................... C ...... 323 582-0711
  5705 Alcoa Ave Vernon (90058) *(P-3456)*

Sandberg Industries Inc (PA) ........................................ D ...... 949 660-9473
  2921 Daimler St Santa Ana (92705) *(P-13081)*

Sandee Plastic Extrusions ............................................. E ...... 323 979-4020
  14932 Gwenchris Ct Paramount (90723) *(P-7021)*

Sandel, Vista *Also Called: Sandel Avionics Inc (P-14299)*

Sandel Avionics, Vista *Also Called: Sandel Avionics Inc (P-14298)*

Sandel Avionics Inc ....................................................... C ...... 760 727-4900
  2405 Dogwood Way Vista (92081) *(P-14298)*

Sandel Avionics Inc (PA) .............................................. E ...... 760 727-4900
  1370 Decision St Ste D Vista (92081) *(P-14299)*

Sanders Candy Factory Inc ......................................... E ...... 626 814-2038
  5051 Calmview Ave Baldwin Park (91706) *(P-1325)*

Sanders Composites Inc (HQ) ..................................... E ...... 562 354-2800
  3701 E Conant St Long Beach (90808) *(P-13953)*

Sanders Composites Industries, Long Beach *Also Called: Sanders Composites Inc (P-13953)*

Sanders Inds Holdings Inc (PA) ................................... F ...... 562 354-2920
  3701 E Conant St Long Beach (90808) *(P-5200)*

Sanders Prcsion Tmber Flling I (PA) ............................ E ...... 530 938-4120
  9509 N Old Stage Rd Weed (96094) *(P-3054)*

Sandia Plastics Inc ......................................................... E ...... 714 901-8400
  15571 Container Ln Huntington Beach (92649) *(P-7022)*

Sandisk LLC (DH) ........................................................... C ...... 408 801-1000
  951 Sandisk Dr Milpitas (95035) *(P-10274)*

Sandman Inc (PA) .......................................................... D ...... 408 947-0669
  1404 S 7th St San Jose (95112) *(P-7390)*

Sandpiper of California Inc ........................................... D ...... 619 424-2222
  687 Anita St Ste A Chula Vista (91911) *(P-7139)*

Sandra Gruca .................................................................. E ...... 714 661-6464
  16993 Bluewater Ln Huntington Beach (92649) *(P-13572)*

Sandusky Lee LLC .......................................................... E ...... 661 854-5551
  16125 Widmere Rd Arvin (93203) *(P-3511)*

Sandys Drapery Inc (PA) ............................................... E ...... 510 445-0112
  48374 Milmont Dr Bldg A Fremont (94538) *(P-2918)*

SANGAMO, Richmond *Also Called: Sangamo Therapeutics Inc (P-5858)*

Sangamo Therapeutics Inc (PA) .................................. B ...... 510 970-6000
  501 Canal Blvd Richmond (94804) *(P-5858)*

Sangraf International Inc ............................................... E ...... 216 800-9999
  3171 Independence Dr Livermore (94551) *(P-11301)*

Sani-Tech West, Inc., Camarillo *Also Called: Sanisure Inc (P-6429)*

Sanie Manufacturing Company ................................... F ...... 714 751-7700
  320 E Alton Ave Santa Ana (92707) *(P-8643)*

Sanisure (HQ) .................................................................. D ...... 805 389-0400
  1020 Flynn Rd Camarillo (93012) *(P-6429)*

Sanitary Stainless Welding Inc .................................... E ...... 559 233-7116
  2550 S East Ave Ste 101b Fresno (93706) *(P-19212)*

Sanko Electronics America Inc (HQ) ........................... F ...... 310 618-1677
  2587 Otay Center Dr San Diego (92154) *(P-13573)*

Sanluisina, Chino Hills *Also Called: Andrew LLC (P-1052)*

**Sanmina, San Jose** *Also Called: Sanmina Corporation (P-12212)*
Sanmina Corporation ........................................................... D ...... 510 897-2000
427535 Christy St Fremont (94538) *(P-8566)*
Sanmina Corporation ........................................................... E ...... 408 964-3500
2700 N 1st St San Jose (95134) *(P-12206)*
Sanmina Corporation ........................................................... E ...... 408 964-3500
2701 Zanker Rd San Jose (95134) *(P-12207)*
Sanmina Corporation ........................................................... B ...... 408 964-6400
2050 Bering Dr San Jose (95131) *(P-12208)*
Sanmina Corporation ........................................................... E ...... 408 964-3500
2036 Bering Dr San Jose (95131) *(P-12209)*
Sanmina Corporation ........................................................... C ...... 408 557-7210
60 E Plumeria Dr Bldg 2 San Jose (95134) *(P-12210)*
Sanmina Corporation ........................................................... D ...... 714 371-2800
2945 Airway Ave Costa Mesa (92626) *(P-12211)*
Sanmina Corporation (PA) .................................................... A ...... 408 964-3500
2700 N 1st St San Jose (95134) *(P-12212)*
Sanmina Corporation ........................................................... C ...... 510 494-2421
8455 Cabot Ct Newark (94560) *(P-12213)*
Sanmina Corporation ........................................................... C ...... 714 913-2200
2950 Red Hill Ave Costa Mesa (92626) *(P-12214)*
**Sanmina-Sci, San Jose** *Also Called: Sanmina Corporation (P-12209)*
Sanovas Inc ........................................................................... E ...... 415 729-9391
2597 Kerner Blvd San Rafael (94901) *(P-15247)*
Sansani Cleaning Solutions LLC ......................................... F ...... 310 630-9033
551 E 64th St Apt 3 Long Beach (90805) *(P-10597)*
Santa Ana Plating (PA) ........................................................ D ...... 310 923-8305
1726 E Rosslynn Ave Fullerton (92831) *(P-9008)*
Santa Barbara Control Systems ......................................... F ...... 805 683-8833
5375 Overpass Rd Santa Barbara (93111) *(P-14454)*
Santa Barbara Design Studio (PA) ..................................... D ...... 805 966-3883
1600 Pacific Ave Oxnard (93033) *(P-7290)*
Santa Barbara Independent Inc ......................................... E ...... 805 965-5205
1715 State St Santa Barbara (93101) *(P-4191)*
Santa Barbara Infrared Inc (DH) ......................................... D ...... 805 965-3669
30 S Calle Cesar Chavez Ste D Santa Barbara (93103) *(P-14300)*
Santa Barbara Instrument GP Inc ...................................... E ...... 925 463-3410
150 Castilian Dr Goleta (93117) *(P-15665)*
**Santa Clara Facility, Santa Clara** *Also Called: Summit Interconnect Inc (P-12235)*
Santa Clara Plating Co Inc .................................................. D ...... 408 727-9315
1773 Grant St Santa Clara (95050) *(P-9009)*
Santa Clarita Signs ............................................................. E ...... 661 291-1188
26330 Diamond Pl Santa Clarita (91350) *(P-16031)*
Santa Croce LLC ................................................................. F ...... 707 227-7834
1097 Nimitz Ave Vallejo (94592) *(P-1842)*
Santa Cruz Bicycles LLC .................................................... D ...... 831 459-7560
2841 Mission St Santa Cruz (95060) *(P-14068)*
**Santa Cruz Bikes, Santa Cruz** *Also Called: Santa Cruz Bicycles LLC (P-14068)*
Santa Cruz Guitar Corporation ........................................... E ...... 831 425-0999
151 Harvey West Blvd Ste C Santa Cruz (95060) *(P-15723)*
**Santa Cruz Skateboards, Santa Cruz** *Also Called: Nhs Inc (P-15842)*
Santa Fe Enterprises Inc ..................................................... E ...... 562 692-7596
11654 Pike St Santa Fe Springs (90670) *(P-9647)*
Santa Fe Footwear Corporation ......................................... F ...... 562 941-9689
9988 Santa Fe Springs Rd Santa Fe Springs (90670) *(P-7121)*
Santa Fe Machine Works Inc ............................................. E ...... 909 350-6877
14578 Rancho Vista Dr Fontana (92335) *(P-11099)*
**Santa Fe Supply Company, Santa Fe Springs** *Also Called: Philatron International (P-13288)*
Santa Maria Enrgy Holdings LLC ....................................... E ...... 805 938-3320
2811 Airpark Dr Santa Maria (93455) *(P-197)*
Santa Maria Tire Inc (PA) .................................................... D ...... 805 347-4793
2170 Hutton Rd Bldg A Nipomo (93444) *(P-17463)*
**Santa Monica Daily Press, Santa Monica** *Also Called: Newlon Rouge LLC (P-4168)*
Santa Monica Millworks ..................................................... E ...... 805 643-0010
2568 Channel Dr Ventura (93003) *(P-3269)*
**Santa Monica Propeller, Santa Monica** *Also Called: Santa Monica Propeller Svc Inc (P-13954)*
Santa Monica Propeller Svc Inc ......................................... F ...... 310 390-6233
3135 Donald Douglas Loop S Santa Monica (90405) *(P-13954)*
**Santa Monica Seafood, Rancho Dominguez** *Also Called: Santa Monica Seafood Company (P-2061)*
Santa Monica Seafood Company (PA) ............................... D ...... 310 886-7900
18531 S Broadwick St Rancho Dominguez (90220) *(P-2061)*

**Santa Mrgrita Cthlc High Schl, Rcho Sta Marg** *Also Called: Roman Cthlic Diocese of Orange (P-19345)*
Santa Rosa Press Democrat Inc (HQ) ................................ B ...... 707 546-2020
427 Mendocino Ave Santa Rosa (95401) *(P-4192)*
Santa Rosa Seafood Retail Inc .......................................... E ...... 707 579-2085
946 Santa Rosa Ave Santa Rosa (95404) *(P-17397)*
Santa Rosa Stain .................................................................. E ...... 707 544-7777
1400 Airport Blvd Santa Rosa (95403) *(P-14127)*
Santana Formal Accessories Inc ....................................... F ...... 818 898-3677
707 Arroyo St Ste B San Fernando (91340) *(P-2566)*
Santarus Inc ......................................................................... F ...... 858 314-5700
3611 Valley Centre Dr Ste 400 San Diego (92130) *(P-5650)*
**Sante Specialty Foods, Santa Clara** *Also Called: Aharoni & Steele Inc (P-17423)*
Santec Inc ............................................................................ E ...... 310 542-0063
3501 Challenger St Fl 2 Torrance (90503) *(P-8056)*
Santec California Corporation ............................................ E ...... 805 987-1700
4750 Calle Quetzal Camarillo (93012) *(P-14821)*
**Santex Group, Carlsbad** *Also Called: A R Santex LLC (P-17873)*
Santier Inc ........................................................................... D ...... 858 271-1993
10103 Carroll Canyon Rd San Diego (92131) *(P-12684)*
**Santini Fine Wines, San Lorenzo** *Also Called: Santini Foods Inc (P-781)*
Santini Foods Inc ................................................................ C ...... 510 317-8888
16505 Worthley Dr San Lorenzo (94580) *(P-781)*
Santoshi Corporation .......................................................... E ...... 626 444-7118
2439 Seaman Ave El Monte (91733) *(P-9010)*
**Sanyo Fisher Company, San Diego** *Also Called: Sanyo North America Corp (P-19569)*
Sanyo Foods Corp America (DH) ....................................... E ...... 714 891-3671
11955 Monarch St Garden Grove (92841) *(P-2119)*
Sanyo Manufacturing Corporation ..................................... D ...... 619 661-1134
2055 Sanyo Ave San Diego (92154) *(P-11695)*
Sanyo North America Corp ................................................ B ...... 619 661-1134
2055 Sanyo Ave San Diego (92154) *(P-19569)*
**Sap AG, Palo Alto** *Also Called: Sap America Inc (P-18758)*
Sap America Inc .................................................................. E ...... 650 849-4000
3410 Hillview Ave Palo Alto (94304) *(P-18758)*
Sap Labs LLC (DH) ............................................................. B ...... 650 849-4000
3410 Hillview Ave Palo Alto (94304) *(P-18759)*
Sapar Usa Inc (HQ) ............................................................. E ...... 510 441-9500
1610 Delta Ct Unit 1 Hayward (94544) *(P-665)*
Sapphire Chandelier LLC .................................................. D ...... 714 879-3660
505 Porter Way Placentia (92870) *(P-11555)*
Sapphire Energy Inc ........................................................... D ...... 858 768-4700
10996 Torreyana Rd Ste 280 San Diego (92121) *(P-5270)*
Sapphire Manufacturing Inc .............................................. E ...... 714 401-3117
505 Porter Way Placentia (92870) *(P-8644)*
Sappi North America Inc .................................................... E ...... 714 456-0600
21700 Copley Dr Ste 165 Diamond Bar (91765) *(P-3796)*
**SAPS, Fremont** *Also Called: Acm Research Inc (P-10531)*
Sapu Bioscience LLC ......................................................... E ...... 650 635-7018
10840 Thornmint Rd Ste 118 San Diego (92127) *(P-5651)*
Saputo Cheese USA Inc ..................................................... B ...... 559 687-8411
800 E Paige Ave Tulare (93274) *(P-734)*
Saputo Cheese USA Inc ..................................................... D ...... 262 307-6738
691 Inyo Ave Newman (95360) *(P-735)*
Saputo Cheese USA Inc ..................................................... B ...... 559 687-9999
901 E Levin Ave Tulare (93274) *(P-736)*
Saputo Cheese USA Inc ..................................................... A ...... 562 862-7686
5611 Imperial Hwy South Gate (90280) *(P-737)*
Saputo Cheese USA Inc ..................................................... C ...... 209 854-6461
299 5th Ave Gustine (95322) *(P-844)*
**Sara, Cypress** *Also Called: Scientfic Applctons RES Assoc (P-11380)*
**Sarabian Farms, Sanger** *Also Called: Virginia Sarabian (P-34)*
Saramark Inc ........................................................................ E ...... 408 971-3881
15660 Mckinley Ave Lathrop (95330) *(P-8684)*
**Saratech, Mission Viejo** *Also Called: Paydarfar Industries Inc (P-16537)*
**Sardee, Stockton** *Also Called: Sardee Industries Inc (P-10029)*
Sardee Industries Inc ......................................................... E ...... 209 466-1526
2731 E Myrtle St Stockton (95205) *(P-10029)*
**Sardo Bus & Coach Upholstery, Gardena** *Also Called: Louis Sardo Upholstery Inc (P-3635)*
**Saroni Total Food Ingredients, Oakland** *Also Called: Sugar & Rice Saroni Inc (P-17216)*

Sas Manufacturing Inc ............................................................. E ...... 951 734-1808
   405 N Smith Ave Corona (92878) *(P-13082)*
Sas Safety, Cerritos *Also Called: Sas Safety Corporation (P-15401)*
Sas Safety Corporation ............................................................ D ...... 562 427-2775
   17785 Center Court Dr N Cerritos (90703) *(P-15401)*
Sas Textiles Inc ...................................................................... D ...... 323 277-5555
   3100 E 44th St Vernon (90058) *(P-2487)*
Sass Labs Inc ......................................................................... E ...... 404 731-7284
   121 W Washington Ave Ste 212 Sunnyvale (94086) *(P-18760)*
Sat, Sacramento *Also Called: Lpa Insurance Agency Inc (P-18505)*
Satco, El Segundo *Also Called: Satco Inc (P-3359)*
Satco Inc (PA) ........................................................................ C ...... 310 322-4719
   1601 E El Segundo Blvd El Segundo (90245) *(P-3359)*
Satellite Av LLC ...................................................................... E ...... 916 677-0720
   4021 Alvis Ct Ste 5 Rocklin (95677) *(P-17544)*
Satellite Security Corporation ................................................. E ...... 877 437-4199
   6779 Mesa Ridge Rd Ste 100 San Diego (92121) *(P-11939)*
Satellite Telework Centers Inc ................................................ F ...... 831 222-2100
   5900 Butler Ln Ste 103 Scotts Valley (95066) *(P-14584)*
Saticoy Foods Corporation ..................................................... E ...... 805 647-5266
   554 Todd Rd Santa Paula (93060) *(P-925)*
Satterfield Aerospace, Northridge *Also Called: S & S Numerical Control Inc (P-11093)*
Saturn Fasteners Inc .............................................................. C ...... 818 973-1807
   425 S Varney St Burbank (91502) *(P-8025)*
Sauer Brands Inc ................................................................... D ...... 805 597-8900
   184 Suburban Rd San Luis Obispo (93401) *(P-2348)*
Saunco Air Technologies, Hickman *Also Called: Reed International (P-9450)*
Sauvage Inc (PA) ................................................................... F ...... 858 408-0100
   7717 Formula Pl San Diego (92121) *(P-2638)*
Savage & Cooke, Vallejo *Also Called: Santa Croce LLC (P-1842)*
Savage Industries ................................................................... E ...... 415 845-6264
   48 Linda St San Francisco (94110) *(P-16220)*
Savage Machining Inc ............................................................ E ...... 805 584-8047
   2235 1st St Ste 116 Simi Valley (93065) *(P-11100)*
Savannah Chanelle Vineyards ................................................ F ...... 301 758-2338
   23600 Big Basin Way Saratoga (95070) *(P-1741)*
Save Mart Supermarkets Disc ................................................ C ...... 530 222-6740
   1330 Churn Creek Rd Redding (96003) *(P-17384)*
Save The Sound, San Francisco *Also Called: Olive Media Products Inc (P-11684)*
Savedaily Inc ......................................................................... F ...... 562 795-7500
   1503 S Coast Dr Ste 330 Costa Mesa (92626) *(P-18761)*
Savi Customs, San Diego *Also Called: Crazy Industries (P-15801)*
Savi Technology Holdings Inc ................................................ B ...... 650 316-4950
   615 Tasman Dr Sunnyvale (94089) *(P-16221)*
Savicom, Oakland *Also Called: Mindshare Design Inc (P-17949)*
Savioke, Campbell *Also Called: Working Robot Inc (P-10124)*
Savitsky Stin Bcon Bcci A Cal, Los Angeles *Also Called: Ground Control Business MGT (P-2438)*
Saviynt Inc (PA) ..................................................................... B ...... 310 641-1664
   1301 E El Segundo Blvd Ste D El Segundo (90245) *(P-18762)*
Saw Daily Service Inc ............................................................ E ...... 323 564-1791
   4481 Firestone Blvd South Gate (90280) *(P-16894)*
Sawmill, Ukiah *Also Called: Mendocino Forest Pdts Co LLC (P-16450)*
Sayari Shahrzad .................................................................... E ...... 310 903-6368
   4822 Aqueduct Ave Encino (91436) *(P-17080)*
Saydel Inc (PA) ..................................................................... F ...... 323 585-2800
   2475 E Slauson Ave Huntington Park (90255) *(P-6034)*
Sazerac Company Inc ............................................................ D ...... 310 604-8717
   2202 E Del Amo Blvd Carson (90749) *(P-1843)*
SBC, San Francisco *Also Called: Pacific Bell Directory (P-4443)*
Sbig Astronomical Instruments, Goleta *Also Called: Santa Barbara Instrument GP Inc (P-15665)*
Sbir, Santa Barbara *Also Called: Santa Barbara Infrared Inc (P-14300)*
Sbm Dairies Inc ..................................................................... B ...... 626 923-3000
   17851 Railroad St City Of Industry (91748) *(P-1959)*
Sbnw LLC (PA) ...................................................................... C ...... 213 234-5122
   5600 W Adams Blvd Los Angeles (90016) *(P-7146)*
Sbr Sports Inc ....................................................................... F ...... 800 620-4094
   2806 Willis St Santa Ana (92705) *(P-15852)*
Sbragia Family Vineyards LLC ............................................... F ...... 707 473-2992
   9990 Dry Creek Rd Geyserville (95441) *(P-1742)*

SBS, Fremont *Also Called: South Bay Solutions Inc (P-11119)*
SC Barns, Santa Rosa *Also Called: G Hartley Inc (P-368)*
SC Bloom Network Inc ........................................................... E ...... 415 650-8015
   300 Pioneer St Santa Cruz (95060) *(P-16222)*
SC Liquidation Company LLC ................................................ C ...... 714 482-1006
   566 Vanguard Way Brea (92821) *(P-3954)*
Scafco Corporation ................................................................ E ...... 559 256-9911
   2443 Foundry Park Ave Fresno (93706) *(P-7913)*
Scafco Corporation ................................................................ E ...... 415 852-7974
   2050 Farallon Dr San Leandro (94577) *(P-16223)*
Scafco Corporation ................................................................ E ...... 209 670-8053
   2525 S Airport Way Stockton (95206) *(P-16224)*
Scafco Steel Stud Mfg, San Leandro *Also Called: Scafco Corporation (P-16223)*
Scalable, Newark *Also Called: Ooshirts Inc (P-4931)*
Scalable Press ....................................................................... F ...... 877 752-9060
   41454 Christy St Fremont (94538) *(P-4193)*
Scale Computing Inc ............................................................. F ...... 650 212-0132
   2121 S El Camino Real Ste 500 San Mateo (94403) *(P-10275)*
Scaled Composites LLC ......................................................... B ...... 661 824-4541
   1624 Flight Line Mojave (93501) *(P-13688)*
Scales, Covina *Also Called: American Scale Co Inc (P-16506)*
Scality Inc ............................................................................. E ...... 650 356-8500
   149 New Montgomery St Fl 4 San Francisco (94105) *(P-10276)*
Scandic Springs Inc ............................................................... E ...... 510 352-3700
   700 Montague St San Leandro (94577) *(P-8885)*
Scarrott Metallurgical Co, Los Angeles *Also Called: Interntnal Mtllrgical Svcs LLC (P-7886)*
Scat Enterprises Inc ............................................................... D ...... 310 370-5501
   1400 Kingsdale Ave Ste B Redondo Beach (90278) *(P-16398)*
Scb Distributors, Gardena *Also Called: A B P Inc (P-17282)*
Scb Division, Bell Gardens *Also Called: Cal Southern Braiding Inc (P-12930)*
Scelzi Enterprises Inc (PA) ..................................................... E ...... 559 237-5541
   2286 E Date Ave Fresno (93706) *(P-13427)*
Scenic Express Inc ................................................................ E ...... 323 254-4351
   9380 San Fernando Rd Sun Valley (91352) *(P-573)*
Sceptre Inc ............................................................................ E ...... 626 369-3698
   16800 Gale Ave City Of Industry (91745) *(P-13083)*
Schaeffler Group USA Inc ...................................................... E ...... 949 234-9799
   34700 Pacific Coast Hwy Ste 203 Capistrano Beach (92624) *(P-9954)*
Schawk, San Francisco *Also Called: Sgk LLC (P-5028)*
Schea Holdings Inc ................................................................ E ...... 818 998-3636
   9812 Independence Ave Chatsworth (91311) *(P-16032)*
Schecter Guitar Research Inc ................................................. E ...... 818 767-1029
   10953 Pendleton St Sun Valley (91352) *(P-15724)*
Scheid Family Wines, Salinas *Also Called: Scheid Vineyards Inc (P-29)*
Scheid Vineyards Inc (PA) ..................................................... D ...... 831 455-9990
   305 Hilltown Rd Salinas (93908) *(P-29)*
Schell & Kampeter Inc ........................................................... D ...... 209 983-4900
   250 Roth Rd Lathrop (95330) *(P-1115)*
Scher Tire Inc (PA) ................................................................ E ...... 951 343-3100
   3863 Tyler St Riverside (92503) *(P-19154)*
Scheu Manufacturing Company (PA) ..................................... F ...... 909 982-8933
   297 Stowell St Upland (91786) *(P-8079)*
Schilling Robotics LLC ........................................................... E ...... 530 753-6718
   201 Cousteau Pl Davis (95618) *(P-19418)*
Schilling Robotics LLC (DH) ................................................... D ...... 530 753-6718
   260 Cousteau Pl Ste 200 Davis (95618) *(P-19419)*
Schindler, San Leandro *Also Called: Schindler Elevator Corporation (P-9476)*
Schindler Elevator Corporation .............................................. E ...... 510 382-2075
   555 Mccormick St San Leandro (94577) *(P-9476)*
Schlumberger Technology Corp ............................................. D ...... 661 864-4721
   6120 Snow Rd Bakersfield (93308) *(P-275)*
Schmeiser Farm Equipment, Fresno *Also Called: T G Schmeiser Co Inc (P-8030)*
Schmid, Watsonville *Also Called: Sierrathermal Inc (P-10059)*
Schmidbauer Lumber Inc (PA) ............................................... C ...... 707 443-7024
   1099 W Waterfront Dr Eureka (95501) *(P-3078)*
Schmidbauer Lumber Inc ....................................................... D ...... 707 822-7607
   1017 Samoa Blvd Arcata (95521) *(P-3079)*
Schmidt Industries Inc ........................................................... D ...... 818 768-9100
   11321 Goss St Sun Valley (91352) *(P-9011)*
Schmitt Superior Classics, Redding *Also Called: William R Schmitt (P-3062)*

# ALPHABETIC SECTION

Schneder Elc Bldngs Amrcas Inc .................................................. E ..... 925 463-7100
5735 W Las Positas Blvd Ste 400 Pleasanton (94588) *(P-13302)*

Schneder Elc Slar Invrters USA, Livermore *Also Called: Schneider Electric Solar Inverters Usa Inc (P-11379)*

Schneider Elc Buildings LLC .......................................................... C ..... 310 900-2385
100 W Victoria St Long Beach (90805) *(P-13303)*

Schneider Electric ........................................................................... E ..... 949 713-9200
1660 Scenic Ave Costa Mesa (92626) *(P-13304)*

Schneider Electric Solar Inverters Usa Inc ................................... B ..... 925 245-1935
250 S Vasco Rd Livermore (94551) *(P-11379)*

Schneiders Manufacturing Inc ....................................................... E ..... 818 771-0082
11122 Penrose St Sun Valley (91352) *(P-11101)*

Schnoogs ......................................................................................... D ..... 209 532-5279
19051 Standard Rd Sonora (95370) *(P-7941)*

Scholastic Sports Inc ...................................................................... D ..... 858 496-9221
4878 Ronson Ct Ste Kl San Diego (92111) *(P-4759)*

Scholle Ipn Packaging Inc ............................................................. C ..... 209 384-3100
2500 Cooper Ave Merced (95348) *(P-7023)*

SCHOLLE IPN PACKAGING, INC., Merced *Also Called: Scholle Ipn Packaging Inc (P-7023)*

Scholten Surgical Instrs Inc .......................................................... F ..... 209 365-1393
170 Commerce St Ste 101 Lodi (95240) *(P-15248)*

School Apparel Inc (PA) ................................................................. D ..... 650 777-4500
838 Mitten Rd Burlingame (94010) *(P-2727)*

School Innovations Achievement (HQ) ......................................... E ..... 800 487-9234
5200 Golden Foothill Pkwy El Dorado Hills (95762) *(P-18763)*

Schramsberg Vineyards Company ................................................ E ..... 707 942-4558
1400 Schramsberg Rd Calistoga (94515) *(P-30)*

Schrey & Sons Mold Co Inc .......................................................... E ..... 661 294-2260
24735 Avenue Rockefeller Valencia (91355) *(P-9648)*

Schroeder Iron Corporation .......................................................... E ..... 909 428-6471
8417 Beech Ave Fontana (92335) *(P-8214)*

Schroff Inc ....................................................................................... A ..... 800 525-4682
7328 Trade St San Diego (92121) *(P-9939)*

Schroff Inc ....................................................................................... C ..... 858 740-2400
7328 Trade St San Diego (92121) *(P-19178)*

Schuberth North America LLC ..................................................... F ..... 949 215-0893
12707 High Bluff Dr Ste 200 San Diego (92130) *(P-8886)*

Schuff Steel Company .................................................................... E ..... 209 938-0869
10100 Trinity Pkwy Ste 400 Stockton (95219) *(P-534)*

Schulz Engineering, Sylmar *Also Called: Dg Engineering Corp (P-14180)*

Schurman Fine Papers ................................................................... C ..... 707 765-2514
36 Petaluma Blvd N Petaluma (94952) *(P-4997)*

Schurman Fine Papers ................................................................... E ..... 714 549-0212
3333 Bristol St Costa Mesa (92626) *(P-16840)*

Schweitzers Metal Fabricators, Azusa *Also Called: Todd Street Inc (P-8348)*

Schwing America Inc ..................................................................... C ..... 909 681-6430
3351 Grapevine St Bldg A Jurupa Valley (91752) *(P-9436)*

SCI, Pomona *Also Called: Structural Composites Inds LLC (P-8341)*

SCI, El Monte *Also Called: S C I Industries Inc (P-13570)*

SCI-Pharm, Pomona *Also Called: Scientific Pharmaceuticals Inc (P-15481)*

Sciabica's, Modesto *Also Called: Nick Sciabica & Sons A Corp (P-1402)*

Scicon Technologies Corp (PA) ..................................................... E ..... 661 295-8630
27525 Newhall Ranch Rd Ste 2 Valencia (91355) *(P-19420)*

Sciencell Research Labs Inc ......................................................... E ..... 760 602-8549
1610 Faraday Ave Carlsbad (92008) *(P-19496)*

Scientfc Applctons RES Assoc (PA) ............................................. D ..... 714 224-4410
6300 Gateway Dr Cypress (90630) *(P-11380)*

Scientific Cutting Tools Inc .......................................................... E ..... 805 584-9495
220 W Los Angeles Ave Simi Valley (93065) *(P-9697)*

Scientific Drilling Intl Inc ............................................................. E ..... 661 831-0736
31101 Coberly Rd Shafter (93263) *(P-166)*

Scientific Hardware Systems, Gilroy *Also Called: Technical Reps Intl Inc (P-16252)*

Scientific Learning Corp ............................................................... E ..... 510 444-3500
300 Frank H Ogawa Plz Ste 600 Oakland (94612) *(P-18764)*

Scientific Metal Finishing Inc ....................................................... E ..... 408 970-9011
3180 Molinaro St Santa Clara (95054) *(P-9117)*

Scientific Pharmaceuticals Inc ...................................................... E ..... 909 595-9922
3221 Producer Way Pomona (91768) *(P-15481)*

Scientific Specialties Inc .............................................................. D ..... 209 333-2120
1310 Thurman St Lodi (95240) *(P-6570)*

Scientific Surface Inds Inc ............................................................ F ..... 805 499-5100
855 Rancho Conejo Blvd Newbury Park (91320) *(P-3670)*

Scientific-Atlanta LLC ................................................................... E ..... 619 679-6000
13112 Evening Creek Dr S San Diego (92128) *(P-14301)*

Sciforma Corporation .................................................................... E ..... 408 899-0398
600 B St Ste 300 San Diego (92101) *(P-17975)*

Scilex Pharmaceuticals Inc ........................................................... E ..... 650 430-3238
960 San Antonio Rd Palo Alto (94303) *(P-5652)*

Scilex Pharmaceuticals Inc (HQ) .................................................. F ..... 949 441-2270
4955 Directors Pl Ste 100 San Diego (92121) *(P-19125)*

Scintera Networks Inc ................................................................... E ..... 408 636-2600
160 Rio Robles San Jose (95134) *(P-12685)*

Scisorek & Son Flavors Inc .......................................................... E ..... 714 524-0550
2951 Enterprise St Brea (92821) *(P-2024)*

Sciton Inc (PA) ................................................................................ C ..... 650 493-9155
925 Commercial St Palo Alto (94303) *(P-15249)*

Scn Bestco, Santa Cruz *Also Called: Harmony Foods LLC (P-5476)*

Scoggan Company Inc (PA) .......................................................... E ..... 916 371-3984
704 Houston St West Sacramento (95691) *(P-16399)*

Sconza Candy Company ................................................................ D ..... 209 845-3700
1 Sconza Candy Ln Oakdale (95361) *(P-1326)*

Scope, San Diego *Also Called: Scope Orthtics Prosthetics Inc (P-17719)*

Scope AR, San Francisco *Also Called: Scope Technologies US Inc (P-18765)*

Scope City (PA) ............................................................................... E ..... 805 522-6646
2978 Topaz Ave Simi Valley (93063) *(P-14822)*

Scope Orthtics Prosthetics Inc (DH) ............................................ E ..... 858 292-7448
7720 Cardinal Ct San Diego (92123) *(P-17719)*

Scope Packaging Inc ...................................................................... E ..... 714 998-4411
13400 Nelson Ave City Of Industry (91746) *(P-3886)*

Scope Technologies US Inc (PA) .................................................. E ..... 855 207-2673
575 Market St Fl 4 San Francisco (94105) *(P-18765)*

Scopely Inc (DH) ............................................................................. C ..... 323 400-6618
3505 Hayden Ave Culver City (90232) *(P-18766)*

Score Sports, Wilmington *Also Called: American Soccer Company Inc (P-17508)*

Scorelate Inc ................................................................................... E ..... 818 602-9176
91301 Fairview Pl Ste 2 Agoura Hills (91301) *(P-18767)*

Scosche Industries Inc .................................................................. C ..... 805 486-4450
1550 Pacific Ave Oxnard (93033) *(P-11696)*

Scott A Humphreys Inc (PA) ......................................................... E ..... 805 581-2971
4600 Industrial St Simi Valley (93063) *(P-8567)*

Scott Ag LLC ................................................................................... E ..... 707 545-4519
1275 N Dutton Ave Santa Rosa (95401) *(P-16033)*

Scott Architectural, Fairfield *Also Called: Scott Lamp Company Inc (P-11556)*

Scott Craft Co, Cudahy *Also Called: Merry An Cejka (P-10972)*

Scott Lamp Company Inc .............................................................. D ..... 707 864-2066
355 Watt Dr Fairfield (94534) *(P-11556)*

Scott Manufacturing Solutions, Chino *Also Called: Scott Mfg Solutions Inc (P-11381)*

Scott Mfg Solutions Inc ................................................................. C ..... 909 594-9637
5051 Edison Ave Chino (91710) *(P-11381)*

Scott Miles ...................................................................................... E ..... 530 346-2294
Railroad & Oak St Colfax (95713) *(P-17343)*

Scott Turbon Mixer Inc., Adelanto *Also Called: Ebara Mixers Inc (P-9787)*

Scottex Inc ...................................................................................... E ..... 310 516-1411
12828 S Broadway Los Angeles (90061) *(P-3035)*

Scotts Company LLC ..................................................................... E ..... 661 387-9555
742 Industrial Way Shafter (93263) *(P-6182)*

Scotts Seafood Roundhouse ......................................................... D ..... 916 989-6711
824 Sutter St Folsom (95630) *(P-2062)*

Scotts Temecula Operations LLC (DH) ........................................ E ..... 951 719-1700
42375 Remington Ave Temecula (92590) *(P-9400)*

Scotts Valley Magnetics Inc ......................................................... E ..... 831 438-3600
300 El Pueblo Rd Ste 107 Scotts Valley (95066) *(P-12857)*

Scotts- Hyponex, Jurupa Valley *Also Called: Hyponex Corporation (P-6175)*

Scotts- Hyponex, Linden *Also Called: Hyponex Corporation (P-6176)*

Scottxscott Inc ............................................................................... E ..... 310 622-2775
3453 Union Pacific Ave Los Angeles (90023) *(P-19126)*

Scpe, Walnut *Also Called: Cal Southern Packg Eqp Inc (P-16808)*

Scq Construction, Cupertino *Also Called: Stevens Creek Quarry Inc (P-382)*

Scrap Tire Company, Ballico *Also Called: Golden By-Products Inc (P-9861)*

Screen Printers Resource Inc ....................................................... F ..... 714 441-1155
3164 E La Palma Ave Anaheim (92806) *(P-4959)*

Screen Spe Usa LLC (DH) ............................................................. E ..... 408 523-9140
3151 Jay St Ste 210 Santa Clara (95054) *(P-9898)*

Screen Tech Inc ............................................................. D ...... 408 885-9750
   4754 Bennett Dr Livermore (94551) *(P-8568)*

Screening Systems Inc (PA) ........................................ E ...... 949 855-1751
   36 Blackbird Ln Aliso Viejo (92656) *(P-14714)*

Screenmeet.com, San Francisco *Also Called: Projectoris Inc (P-18701)*

Screw Conveyor Pacific Corp .................................... C ...... 559 651-2131
   7807 W Doe Ave Visalia (93291) *(P-9493)*

Screwmatic Inc ............................................................ D ...... 626 334-7831
   925 W 1st St Azusa (91702) *(P-11102)*

Scribner Plastics ......................................................... F ...... 916 638-1515
   11455 Hydraulics Dr Rancho Cordova (95742) *(P-7024)*

Scripps Laboratories ................................................. E ...... 858 546-5800
   6838 Flanders Dr San Diego (92121) *(P-5859)*

Scripto-Tokai Corporation (HQ) ............................... D ...... 909 930-5000
   2055 S Haven Ave Ontario (91761) *(P-16225)*

Scry Ai, San Jose *Also Called: Scry Analytics Inc (P-18768)*

Scry Ai, Saratoga *Also Called: Scry Analytics Inc (P-18769)*

Scry Analytics Inc (PA) .............................................. E ...... 408 740-8017
   2635 N 1st St Ste 200 San Jose (95131) *(P-18768)*

Scry Analytics Inc .................................................... B ...... 408 740-8017
   12835 Pheasant Ridge Rd Saratoga (95070) *(P-18769)*

Scully Leather Wear, Oxnard *Also Called: Scully Sportswear Inc (P-2883)*

Scully Sportswear Inc (PA) ....................................... E ...... 805 483-6339
   1701 Pacific Ave Oxnard (93033) *(P-2883)*

Scw Contracting Corporation ................................. D ...... 760 728-1308
   2525 Old Highway 395 Fallbrook (92028) *(P-388)*

SD Electric Sign, El Cajon *Also Called: San Diego Electric Sign Inc (P-16030)*

SD Fresh Products, San Diego *Also Called: Cg Financial LLC (P-852)*

SDC Technologies Inc (HQ) ..................................... E ...... 714 939-8300
   45 Parker Ste 100 Irvine (92618) *(P-9118)*

Sdi, Simi Valley *Also Called: Special Devices Incorporated (P-13577)*

Sdi LLC ......................................................................... E ...... 949 351-1866
   21 Morgan Ste 150 Irvine (92618) *(P-11103)*

Sdi Industries Inc (DH) ............................................. C ...... 818 890-6002
   24307 Magic Mountain Pkwy # 443 Valencia (91355) *(P-9494)*

SDS Industries Inc ..................................................... C ...... 818 492-3500
   10241 Norris Ave Pacoima (91331) *(P-8290)*

SE Software Inc ......................................................... F ...... 888 504-9876
   3000 Olympic Blvd Bldg 4 Santa Monica (90404) *(P-18770)*

Sea Electric LLC .......................................................... E ...... 424 376-3660
   436 Alaska Ave Torrance (90503) *(P-11285)*

Sea Magazine, Fountain Valley *Also Called: Duncan McIntosh Company Inc (P-4249)*

Sea Shield Marine Products Inc .............................. E ...... 909 594-2507
   20832 Currier Rd Walnut (91789) *(P-7821)*

Seabiscuit Motorsports Inc ..................................... E ...... 714 898-9763
   10800 Valley View St Cypress (90630) *(P-10626)*

Seaboard Envelope Co Inc ...................................... E ...... 626 960-4559
   15601 Cypress Ave Irwindale (91706) *(P-4011)*

Seaborn Canvas, San Pedro *Also Called: Juanita F Wade (P-3031)*

Seacatch Seafoods, El Monte *Also Called: Atlantis Seafood LLC (P-2047)*

Seachrome, Long Beach *Also Called: Seachrome Corporation (P-8044)*

Seachrome Corporation ........................................... C ...... 310 427-8010
   1906 E Dominguez St Long Beach (90810) *(P-8044)*

Seacloud Software LLC ............................................. F ...... 650 318-1172
   2021 Fillmore St Pmb 9071 San Francisco (94115) *(P-18771)*

Seaco Technologies Inc ........................................... E ...... 661 326-1522
   280 El Cerrito Dr Bakersfield (93305) *(P-10598)*

Seacomp Inc (PA) ....................................................... E ...... 760 918-6722
   1525 Faraday Ave Carlsbad (92008) *(P-11382)*

Seagate Systems, Fremont *Also Called: Seagate Technology LLC (P-10280)*

Seagate Systems (us) Inc (DH) ................................ D ...... 510 687-5200
   46831 Lakeview Blvd Fremont (94538) *(P-10277)*

Seagate Technology, Fremont *Also Called: Seagate Technology LLC (P-10279)*

Seagate Technology LLC .......................................... B ...... 405 324-4799
   10200 S De Anza Blvd Cupertino (95014) *(P-10278)*

Seagate Technology LLC (DH) ................................ A ...... 800 732-4283
   47488 Kato Rd Fremont (94538) *(P-10279)*

Seagate Technology LLC .......................................... B ...... 510 624-3728
   47488 Kato Rd Fremont (94538) *(P-10280)*

Seagate US LLC .......................................................... F ...... 408 658-1000
   10200 S De Anza Blvd Cupertino (95014) *(P-10281)*

Seagra Technology Inc ............................................. E ...... 408 230-8706
   816 W Ahwanee Ave Sunnyvale (94085) *(P-10432)*

Seal & Packing Supply, Bakersfield *Also Called: Shar-Craft Inc (P-16896)*

Seal For Life Industries LLC (HQ) ........................... E ...... 619 671-0932
   2290 Enrico Fermi Dr Ste 22 San Diego (92154) *(P-6245)*

Seal Methods Inc (PA) ............................................... D ...... 562 944-0291
   11915 Shoemaker Ave Santa Fe Springs (90670) *(P-3955)*

Seal Science Inc (HQ) ............................................... D ...... 949 253-3130
   3701 E Conant St Long Beach (90808) *(P-6466)*

Seal Software Incorporated (HQ) ........................... F ...... 650 938-7325
   1990 N California Blvd Ste 500 Walnut Creek (94596) *(P-18772)*

Sealed Air Corporation ............................................. C ...... 559 675-0152
   1835 W Almond Ave Madera (93637) *(P-6659)*

Sealed Air Corporation ............................................. C ...... 909 594-1791
   19440 Arenth Ave City Of Industry (91748) *(P-6660)*

Sealed Air Corporation ............................................. E ...... 619 421-9003
   2311 Boswell Rd Ste 8 Chula Vista (91914) *(P-6661)*

Sealy Mattress, Richmond *Also Called: Sealy Mattress Mfg Co LLC (P-3536)*

Sealy Mattress Mfg Co LLC ...................................... D ...... 510 235-7171
   1130 7th St Richmond (94801) *(P-3536)*

Seam Labs Inc ............................................................ E ...... 415 815-5509
   2948 20th St Ste 308-302 San Francisco (94110) *(P-18773)*

Seaport Stainless, Richmond *Also Called: Andrus Sheet Metal Inc (P-8375)*

Seaquake Brewing, Crescent City *Also Called: Smith River Brewing Company (P-17623)*

Searing Industries, Rancho Cucamonga *Also Called: Searing Industries Inc (P-7626)*

Searing Industries Inc ............................................. C ...... 909 948-3030
   8901 Arrow Rte Rancho Cucamonga (91730) *(P-7626)*

Searles Valley Minerals Inc ...................................... C ...... 760 372-2259
   80201 Trona Rd Trona (93562) *(P-334)*

Searles Valley Minerals Inc ...................................... C ...... 760 672-2053
   13068 Main St Trona (93562) *(P-335)*

Seaspace Corporation .............................................. E ...... 858 746-1100
   9155 Brown Deer Rd San Diego (92121) *(P-11940)*

Seaspine Inc ............................................................... D ...... 760 727-8399
   5770 Armada Dr Carlsbad (92008) *(P-15402)*

Seaspine Orthopedics Corp (DH) ........................... E ...... 866 942-8698
   5770 Armada Dr Carlsbad (92008) *(P-15403)*

Seatel Inc (DH) ........................................................... C ...... 925 798-7979
   4030 Nelson Ave Concord (94520) *(P-11941)*

Seating Concepts LLC .............................................. E ...... 619 491-3159
   4229 Ponderosa Ave Ste B San Diego (92123) *(P-3638)*

Seating Resource, Azusa *Also Called: Holguin & Holguin Inc (P-3626)*

Seaurchin. Io., San Francisco *Also Called: Algolia Inc (P-18036)*

Seaward Products Corp ........................................... D ...... 562 699-7997
   3721 Capitol Ave City Of Industry (90601) *(P-10514)*

Seb, Chino *Also Called: Specilty Enzymes Btechnologies (P-6160)*

Sebastiani Vineyards Inc ......................................... D ...... 707 933-3200
   389 4th St E Sonoma (95476) *(P-1743)*

Sebastiani Vineyards & Winery, Sonoma *Also Called: Sebastiani Vineyards Inc (P-1743)*

SEC, Moorpark *Also Called: Semiconductor Equipment Corp (P-12690)*

Sechrist Industries Inc ............................................. A ...... 714 579-8400
   4225 E La Palma Ave Anaheim (92807) *(P-15250)*

Seco Industries, Commerce *Also Called: Specialty Enterprises Co (P-6663)*

Seco Manufacturing Company Inc ........................ C ...... 530 225-8155
   4155 Oasis Rd Redding (96003) *(P-14916)*

Secom, Gardena *Also Called: Secom International (P-18991)*

Secom International (PA) ......................................... D ...... 310 641-1290
   15905 S Broadway Gardena (90248) *(P-18991)*

Second Generation Inc ............................................ D
   21650 Oxnard St Ste 500 Woodland Hills (91367) *(P-2806)*

Second Source Medical LLC, San Jose *Also Called: Medeologix LLC (P-15164)*

Second Street Properties ......................................... A
   1333 2nd St Berkeley (94710) *(P-7699)*

Secpod Technologies ............................................... E ...... 405 385-9890
   303 Twin Dolphin Dr Fl 6 Redwood City (94065) *(P-18774)*

Sector9, San Diego *Also Called: Bravo Sports (P-15794)*

Secugen Corporation ............................................... E ...... 408 727-7787
   2445 Augustine Dr Ste 150 Santa Clara (95054) *(P-10433)*

Secura Key, Chatsworth *Also Called: Soundcraft Inc (P-13309)*

Secure Comm Systems Inc (HQ) ............................. C ...... 714 547-1174
   1740 E Wilshire Ave Santa Ana (92705) *(P-11942)*

# ALPHABETIC SECTION — Senariotek LLC

Secure Computing Corporation (DH) .......... E ...... 408 979-2020
3965 Freedom Cir # 4 Santa Clara (95054) *(P-18775)*

Security 20/20 Inc .......... F ...... 310 475-7780
8543 Venice Blvd Los Angeles (90034) *(P-17720)*

Security Central Inc .......... E ...... 510 652-2477
2950 Alvarado St Ste D San Leandro (94577) *(P-19281)*

Security Classification Inc .......... E ...... 707 301-6052
2339 Gold Meadow Way Gold River (95670) *(P-19127)*

Security Contractor Svcs Inc (PA) .......... D ...... 916 338-4200
5339 Jackson St North Highlands (95660) *(P-16495)*

Security Front Desk, Mc Kittrick *Also Called: Aera Energy Services Company (P-152)*

Security Pro USA, Los Angeles *Also Called: Security 20/20 Inc (P-17720)*

Security Systems Installation, Vallejo *Also Called: Done Right Security Inc (P-19053)*

Security Textile Corporation .......... E ...... 213 747-2673
1457 E Washington Blvd Los Angeles (90021) *(P-3016)*

Securus Inc .......... E
14284 Danielson St Poway (92064) *(P-8645)*

Sedas Printing Inc .......... F ...... 323 469-1034
5335 Santa Monica Blvd Los Angeles (90029) *(P-4760)*

Sedona Ventures Inc (PA) .......... C ...... 916 932-1300
100 Blue Ravine Rd Folsom (95630) *(P-19128)*

See's Candies, San Francisco *Also Called: Sees Candies Inc (P-1327)*

See's Candies, South San Francisco *Also Called: Sees Candy Shops Incorporated (P-1328)*

Seed Dynamics Inc .......... D ...... 831 424-1177
1081b Harkins Rd Salinas (93901) *(P-86)*

Seed Factory Northwest Inc (PA) .......... E ...... 209 634-8522
4319 Jessup Rd Ceres (95307) *(P-1150)*

Seedorff Acme, Anaheim *Also Called: A P Seedorff & Company Inc (P-11303)*

Seektech, San Diego *Also Called: Seescan Inc (P-9714)*

SEER, Redwood City *Also Called: Seer Inc (P-14715)*

Seer Inc (PA) .......... C ...... 650 453-0000
3800 Bridge Pkwy Ste 102 Redwood City (94065) *(P-14715)*

Sees Candies Inc (DH) .......... B ...... 800 347-7337
210 El Camino Real S San Francisco (94132) *(P-1327)*

Sees Candy Shops Incorporated (HQ) .......... E ...... 650 761-2490
210 El Camino Real South San Francisco (94080) *(P-1328)*

Seescan Inc (PA) .......... C ...... 858 244-3300
3855 Ruffin Rd San Diego (92123) *(P-9714)*

Sega Holdings USA Inc .......... A ...... 415 701-6000
9737 Lurline Ave Chatsworth (91311) *(P-16226)*

Sega of America Inc (DH) .......... E ...... 949 788-0455
140 Progress Ste 100 Irvine (92618) *(P-16950)*

Segale Bros Wood Products Inc .......... E ...... 510 300-1170
1705 Sabre St Hayward (94545) *(P-500)*

Seghesio Family Vineyards, Healdsburg *Also Called: Pine Ridge Winery LLC (P-1709)*

Seghesio Wineries Inc .......... E ...... 707 433-3579
700 Grove St Healdsburg (95448) *(P-1744)*

Segmentio Inc .......... B ...... 844 611-0621
101 Spear St Fl 1 San Francisco (94105) *(P-10434)*

Seguin Mreau NAPA Coperage Inc (PA) .......... F ...... 707 252-3408
151 Camino Dorado Napa (94558) *(P-16895)*

Segundo Metal Products, Inc., Livermore *Also Called: Advantage Metal Products Inc (P-8364)*

Segway Inc .......... C ...... 603 222-6000
405 E Santa Clara St Ste 100 Arcadia (91006) *(P-14069)*

Seiko Epson, Los Alamitos *Also Called: Epson America Inc (P-10365)*

Seirus Innovation, Poway *Also Called: Seirus Innovative ACC Inc (P-15853)*

Seirus Innovative ACC Inc .......... D ...... 858 513-1212
13975 Danielson St Poway (92064) *(P-15853)*

Seismic Software Inc (HQ) .......... D ...... 714 404-7069
12390 El Camino Real Ste 300 San Diego (92130) *(P-18776)*

Sekai Electronics Inc (PA) .......... E ...... 949 783-5740
38 Waterworks Way Irvine (92618) *(P-11943)*

Selane Products Inc (PA) .......... D ...... 818 998-7460
9129 Lurline Ave Chatsworth (91311) *(P-15482)*

Select Data, Anaheim *Also Called: Select Data Inc (P-17976)*

Select Data Inc .......... C ...... 714 577-1000
4175 E La Palma Ave Ste 205 Anaheim (92807) *(P-17976)*

Select Harvest Usa LLC .......... D ...... 530 865-7286
7418 County Road 24 Orland (95963) *(P-1365)*

Select Imaging LLC .......... F ...... 925 803-1210
6398 Dougherty Rd Ste 27 Dublin (94568) *(P-4761)*

Select Supplements, Watsonville *Also Called: Nordic Naturals Mfg Inc (P-5254)*

Selectabed, Agoura Hills *Also Called: Relief-Mart Inc (P-17718)*

Selectiva Systems Inc .......... D ...... 408 297-1336
2051 Junction Ave Ste 225 San Jose (95131) *(P-17977)*

Selectra Industries Corp .......... D ...... 323 581-8500
5166 Alcoa Ave Vernon (90058) *(P-2834)*

Self Esteem, Montebello *Also Called: All Access Apparel Inc (P-2851)*

Self Realization Fellowship, Los Angeles *Also Called: Self-Realization Fellowship Ch (P-19371)*

Self-Realization Fellowship Ch (PA) .......... E ...... 323 225-2471
3880 San Rafael Ave Los Angeles (90065) *(P-19371)*

Seller Best Publishing .......... E ...... 626 765-9750
253 N San Gabriel Blvd Pasadena (91107) *(P-4463)*

Sellers Optical Inc .......... D ...... 949 631-6800
320 Kalmus Dr Costa Mesa (92626) *(P-14823)*

Selma Pallet Inc .......... D ...... 559 896-7171
1651 Pacific St Selma (93662) *(P-3360)*

Seltzer Revolutions Inc .......... F ...... 604 765-9966
2911 Branciforte Dr Santa Cruz (95065) *(P-1844)*

Semacon Business Machines, San Diego *Also Called: Dove Business Machine Inc (P-16502)*

Semano Inc .......... E ...... 510 489-2360
31757 Knapp St Hayward (94544) *(P-9012)*

Semco .......... E ...... 909 799-9666
1495 S Gage St San Bernardino (92408) *(P-14917)*

Semco, Vista *Also Called: Systems Engineering & MGT Co (P-19423)*

Semco Enterprises Inc .......... F ...... 626 333-2237
475 Wilson Way City Of Industry (91744) *(P-7767)*

Semi Automation & Tech Inc .......... E ...... 408 374-9549
1510 Dell Ave Ste C Campbell (95008) *(P-12686)*

Semi-Kinetics Inc .......... D ...... 949 830-7364
20191 Windrow Dr Ste A Lake Forest (92630) *(P-12215)*

Semicndctor Cmponents Inds LLC .......... E ...... 408 660-2699
3001 Stender Way Santa Clara (95054) *(P-12687)*

Semicndctor Cmponents Inds LLC .......... F ...... 408 542-1000
2975 Stender Way Santa Clara (95054) *(P-12688)*

Semicoa Corporation .......... D ...... 714 979-1900
333 Mccormick Ave Costa Mesa (92626) *(P-12689)*

Semiconductor, Santa Clara *Also Called: Glf Integrated Power Inc (P-12446)*

Semiconductor Equipment Corp .......... F ...... 805 529-2293
5154 Goldman Ave Moorpark (93021) *(P-12690)*

Semiconductor Process Eqp LLC .......... E ...... 661 257-0934
27963 Franklin Pkwy Valencia (91355) *(P-12691)*

Semiconductor Technologies Inc .......... B ...... 408 240-7000
3901 N 1st St San Jose (95134) *(P-19507)*

Semiconductors, San Jose *Also Called: Mixel Inc (P-12586)*

Semifab Inc .......... D ...... 408 414-5928
2027 Otoole Ave San Jose (95131) *(P-14455)*

Seminis Inc (DH) .......... B ...... 805 485-7317
2700 Camino Del Sol Oxnard (93030) *(P-19473)*

Semiq Incorporated .......... F ...... 949 273-4373
20692 Prism Pl Lake Forest (92630) *(P-12692)*

SEMLER SCIENTIFIC, Santa Clara *Also Called: Semler Scientific Inc (P-15251)*

Semler Scientific Inc .......... D ...... 877 774-4211
2340-2348 Walsh Ave Ste 2344 Santa Clara (95051) *(P-15251)*

Semotus Inc .......... E ...... 408 667-2046
20 S Santa Cruz Ave Ste 300 Los Gatos (95030) *(P-18777)*

Sempra Global (HQ) .......... D ...... 619 696-2000
488 8th Ave San Diego (92101) *(P-11229)*

Semprius, Mountain View *Also Called: Semprius Inc (P-19474)*

Semprius Inc .......... D
1100 La Avenida St Ste A Mountain View (94043) *(P-19474)*

Semtech, Camarillo *Also Called: Semtech Corporation (P-12693)*

Semtech Corporation (PA) .......... C ...... 805 498-2111
200 Flynn Rd Camarillo (93012) *(P-12693)*

Semtek Innvtive Solutions Corp .......... F ...... 858 436-2270
12777 High Bluff Dr Ste 225 San Diego (92130) *(P-10435)*

Senariotek LLC .......... E ...... 707 237-6822
1201 Corporate Cntr Pkwy Santa Rosa (95407) *(P-14585)*

**Senba USA, Hayward** *Also Called: United Foods Intl USA Inc (P-2383)*

**Sencha Naturals Inc** ............................................................... F ...... 213 353-9908
1101 Monterey Pass Rd Ste A Monterey Park (91754) *(P-1329)*

**Sendmail Inc** ............................................................................ C ...... 510 594-5400
892 Ross Dr Sunnyvale (94089) *(P-16322)*

**Sendx Medical Inc (DH)** ......................................................... E ...... 760 930-6300
1945 Palomar Oaks Way Ste 100 Carlsbad (92011) *(P-15252)*

**Seneca** ..................................................................................... E ...... 209 815-3023
2801 Finch Rd Modesto (95354) *(P-2349)*

**Senetrics International, Berkeley** *Also Called: Sensys Networks Inc (P-12015)*

**Senfeng Laser Usa Inc** .......................................................... F ...... 562 319-8053
5989 Rickenbacker Rd Commerce (90040) *(P-13305)*

**Senga Engineering Inc** ......................................................... E ...... 714 549-8011
1525 E Warner Ave Santa Ana (92705) *(P-11104)*

**Senior Flexonics, San Diego** *Also Called: Senior Operations LLC (P-11106)*

**Senior Operations LLC** ......................................................... D ...... 818 350-8499
28510 Industry Dr Valencia (91355) *(P-9171)*

**Senior Operations LLC** ......................................................... C ...... 858 278-8400
9150 Balboa Ave San Diego (92123) *(P-11105)*

**Senior Operations LLC** ......................................................... D ...... 858 278-8400
9106 Balboa Ave San Diego (92123) *(P-11106)*

**Senior Operations LLC** ......................................................... D ...... 909 627-2723
790 Greenfield Dr El Cajon (92021) *(P-11107)*

**Senior Operations LLC** ......................................................... C ...... 858 278-8400
9106 Balboa Ave San Diego (92123) *(P-11108)*

**Senior Operations LLC** ......................................................... B ...... 818 260-2900
2980 N San Fernando Blvd Burbank (91504) *(P-13955)*

**Senju Comtek Corp** ............................................................... F ...... 408 792-3830
1171 N 4th St Ste 80 San Jose (95112) *(P-7914)*

**Senju Fire Protection Corp** .................................................. F ...... 949 333-1281
8850 Research Dr Irvine (92618) *(P-10112)*

**Senju Sprinkler, Irvine** *Also Called: Senju Fire Protection Corp (P-10112)*

**Sensarray Corporation** ......................................................... D ...... 408 875-3000
7 Technology Dr Milpitas (95035) *(P-14456)*

**Sensata Technologies Inc** .................................................... D ...... 805 716-0322
1461 Lawrence Dr Thousand Oaks (91320) *(P-19044)*

**Sensbey Inc (PA)** ................................................................... F ...... 650 697-2032
833 Mahler Rd Ste 3 Burlingame (94010) *(P-9730)*

**Sensemetrics Inc** ................................................................... E ...... 619 738-8300
750 B St Ste 1630 San Diego (92101) *(P-12694)*

**Sensient Dehydrated Flavors, Turlock** *Also Called: Sensient Ntral Ingredients LLC (P-2350)*

**Sensient Dehydrated Flavors Company** ............................. A ...... 209 667-2777
151 S Walnut Rd Turlock (95380) *(P-964)*

**Sensient Ntral Ingredients LLC (HQ)** .................................. E ...... 209 667-2777
151 S Walnut Rd Turlock (95380) *(P-2350)*

**Sensient Ntral Ingredients LLC** ........................................... E ...... 209 667-2777
1700 Kibby Rd Merced (95341) *(P-2351)*

**Sensor Concepts LLC** .......................................................... D ...... 925 443-9001
7950 National Dr Livermore (94550) *(P-14302)*

**Sensor Systems Inc** .............................................................. B ...... 818 341-5366
8929 Fullbright Ave Chatsworth (91311) *(P-14303)*

**Sensorex Corporation** .......................................................... D ...... 714 895-4344
11751 Markon Dr Garden Grove (92841) *(P-14457)*

**Sensoscientific LLC** ............................................................. E ...... 800 279-3101
685 Cochran St Ste 200 Simi Valley (93065) *(P-14458)*

**Sensys Networks Inc** ............................................................ D ...... 510 548-4620
1608 4th St Ste 110 Berkeley (94710) *(P-12015)*

**Sente Inc** ................................................................................. E ...... 760 753-5400
701 Palomar Airport Rd Ste 300 Carlsbad (92011) *(P-19321)*

**Senti, South San Francisco** *Also Called: Senti Biosciences Inc (P-5860)*

**Senti Biosciences Inc (PA)** ................................................... E ...... 650 239-2030
2 Corporate Dr Fl 1 South San Francisco (94080) *(P-5860)*

**Sentinel Peak Rsources Cal LLC** ........................................ D ...... 661 395-5214
1200 Discovery Dr Ste 100 Bakersfield (93309) *(P-198)*

**Sentinel Peak Rsources Cal LLC** ........................................ D ...... 323 298-2200
5640 S Fairfax Ave Los Angeles (90056) *(P-199)*

**Sentinelone, Mountain View** *Also Called: Sentinelone Inc (P-18778)*

**Sentinelone Inc (PA)** ............................................................. A ...... 855 868-3733
444 Castro St Ste 400 Mountain View (94041) *(P-18778)*

**Sentons Usa Inc** .................................................................... E ...... 408 732-9000
627 River Oaks Pkwy San Jose (95134) *(P-18779)*

**Sentran LLC (PA)** .................................................................. F ...... 888 545-8988
4355 E Lowell St Ste F Ontario (91761) *(P-14918)*

**Sentynl Therapeutics Inc** ..................................................... E ...... 888 227-8725
420 Stevens Ave Ste 200 Solana Beach (92075) *(P-5653)*

**Sep Group Inc** ....................................................................... E ...... 858 876-4621
11374 Turtleback Ln San Diego (92127) *(P-19421)*

**Separation Engineering Inc** ................................................. E ...... 760 489-0101
931 S Andreasen Dr Ste A Escondido (92029) *(P-10113)*

**Sepasoft Inc** .......................................................................... E ...... 916 939-1684
1262 Hawks Flight Ct Ste 190 El Dorado Hills (95762) *(P-18780)*

**Sephora Co LLC (PA)** ........................................................... E ...... 760 798-7654
6103 Obispo Ave Long Beach (90805) *(P-6035)*

**Sepragen Corporation** .......................................................... E ...... 510 475-0650
33470 Western Ave Union City (94587) *(P-14716)*

**Sequelae Inc** .......................................................................... D ...... 801 628-0256
101 W Bdwy Fl 9 San Diego (92101) *(P-18781)*

**Sequent Medical Inc** ............................................................. D ...... 949 830-9600
35 Enterprise Aliso Viejo (92656) *(P-15253)*

**Sequent Software Inc** ........................................................... F
4699 Old Ironsides Dr Ste 470 Santa Clara (95054) *(P-18782)*

**Sequoia Nut Company, Earlimart** *Also Called: Custom Almonds (P-1350)*

**Sequoia Steel and Supply Co** .............................................. F ...... 559 485-4100
1407 N Clark St Fresno (93703) *(P-17344)*

**Serampore Inds Private Ltd Inc** ........................................... F ...... 877 921-6111
8333 Almeria Ave Fontana (92335) *(P-11109)*

**Serco Mold Inc (PA)** .............................................................. E ...... 626 331-0517
2009 Wright Ave La Verne (91750) *(P-7025)*

**Sercomp LLC (PA)** ................................................................ D ...... 805 299-0020
5401 Tech Cir Ste 200 Moorpark (93021) *(P-15901)*

**Seres, Milpitas** *Also Called: SF Motors Inc (P-13383)*

**Seres Inc** ................................................................................ C ...... 214 585-3356
1504 Mccarthy Blvd Milpitas (95035) *(P-13185)*

**Series, San Francisco** *Also Called: All Blue Labs Inc (P-18039)*

**Serious Energy Inc** ............................................................... D ...... 408 541-8000
1250 Elko Dr Sunnyvale (94089) *(P-3639)*

**Serious Windows, Sunnyvale** *Also Called: Serious Energy Inc (P-3639)*

**Serpa Packaging Solutions, Visalia** *Also Called: Serpa Packaging Solutions LLC (P-10030)*

**Serpa Packaging Solutions LLC** ......................................... D ...... 559 651-2339
7020 W Sunnyview Ave Visalia (93291) *(P-10030)*

**Serpac Electronic Enclosures, La Verne** *Also Called: Serco Mold Inc (P-7025)*

**Serra Laser and Waterjet Inc** ............................................... E ...... 714 680-6211
1740 N Orangethorpe Park Anaheim (92801) *(P-13306)*

**Serra Manufacturing Corp (PA)** ........................................... D ...... 310 537-4560
3039 E Las Hermanas St Compton (90221) *(P-8887)*

**Serra Systems Inc (HQ)** ....................................................... F ...... 707 433-5104
126 Mill St Healdsburg (95448) *(P-18783)*

**Serrala Americas Inc** ............................................................ D ...... 650 655-3939
17485 Monterey St Ste 201 Morgan Hill (95037) *(P-18784)*

**Serrano Industries Inc** .......................................................... E ...... 562 777-8180
9922 Tabor Pl Santa Fe Springs (90670) *(P-11110)*

**Serta Simmons Bedding LLC** .............................................. E ...... 951 807-8467
23700 Cactus Ave Moreno Valley (92553) *(P-3537)*

**Sertec Precision Machining** ................................................ F ...... 714 842-2023
16787 Beach Blvd Huntington Beach (92647) *(P-11111)*

**Serv-Rite Meat Company Inc** ............................................... D ...... 323 227-1911
2515 N San Fernando Rd Los Angeles (90065) *(P-616)*

**Serve Robotics Inc** ............................................................... D ...... 818 860-1352
730 Broadway St Redwood City (94063) *(P-10114)*

**Servexo** .................................................................................. C ...... 323 527-9994
1411 W 190th St Ste 475 Gardena (90248) *(P-13307)*

**Servexo Protective Service, Gardena** *Also Called: Servexo (P-13307)*

**Service Express Inc** ............................................................. E ...... 559 495-4790
3619 S Fowler Ave Fresno (93725) *(P-4464)*

**Service Printing Co, San Leandro** *Also Called: Edelstein Printing Co (P-4602)*

**Service Warehouse, The, Gardena** *Also Called: The Service Warehouse Inc (P-16849)*

**Serviceaide Inc (PA)** ............................................................. D ...... 650 206-8988
2445 Augustine Dr Ste 150 Santa Clara (95054) *(P-18785)*

**SERVICENOW, Santa Clara** *Also Called: Servicenow Inc (P-19045)*

**Servicenow Inc (PA)** ............................................................. E ...... 408 501-8550
2225 Lawson Ln Santa Clara (95054) *(P-19045)*

## ALPHABETIC SECTION

Servitek Electric Inc .................................................... E ...... 626 227-1650
618 Brea Canyon Rd Ste J City Of Industry (91789) *(P-16349)*
Servitek Electric Hawaii, City Of Industry *Also Called: Servitek Electric Inc (P-16349)*
Sesa Inc (PA) ............................................................. E ...... 714 779-9700
20391 Via Guadalupe Yorba Linda (92887) *(P-17839)*
Sesame Software Inc (PA) ........................................ E ...... 408 550-7999
5201 Great America Pkwy Ste 320 Santa Clara (95054) *(P-18786)*
Setco LLC ................................................................. C ...... 812 424-2904
4875 E Hunter Ave Anaheim (92807) *(P-7026)*
Settlers Jerky Inc ...................................................... E ...... 909 444-3999
307 Paseo Sonrisa Walnut (91789) *(P-666)*
Setton International Foods, Terra Bella *Also Called: Setton Pstchio Terra Bella Inc (P-17212)*
Setton Pstchio Terra Bella Inc (HQ) ......................... F ...... 559 535-6050
9370 Road 234 Terra Bella (93270) *(P-17212)*
Setzer Forest Products Inc ...................................... C ...... 530 534-8100
1980 Kusel Rd Oroville (95966) *(P-3080)*
SETZER FOREST PRODUCTS INC (PA) ................ C ...... 916 442-2555
2555 3rd St Ste 200 Sacramento (95818) *(P-3187)*
Seven Sisters of New Orleans, Whittier *Also Called: Indio Products Inc (P-16601)*
Seven Up Btlg Co San Francisco (HQ) ................... C ...... 925 938-8777
2875 Prune Ave Fremont (94539) *(P-1960)*
Seven Up Btlg Co San Francisco ........................... C ...... 831 632-0777
11205 Commercial Pkwy Castroville (95012) *(P-1961)*
Seven Up Btlg Co San Francisco ........................... C ...... 916 929-7777
2670 Land Ave Sacramento (95815) *(P-1962)*
Seven-Up Bottling, Petaluma *Also Called: American Bottling Company (P-1851)*
Seven-Up Bottling, Ukiah *Also Called: American Bottling Company (P-1852)*
Seven-Up Bottling, Fremont *Also Called: Seven Up Btlg Co San Francisco (P-1960)*
Seven-Up Bottling, Castroville *Also Called: Seven Up Btlg Co San Francisco (P-1961)*
Seven-Up Bottling, Sacramento *Also Called: Seven Up Btlg Co San Francisco (P-1962)*
Seven-Up Btlg Co Marysville, Sacramento *Also Called: American Bottling Company (P-1860)*
Seventh Heaven Inc ................................................. E ...... 408 287-8945
1025 S 5th St San Jose (95112) *(P-3036)*
Sew What Inc ........................................................... E ...... 310 639-6000
1978 E Gladwick St Compton (90220) *(P-2919)*
Sew-Eurodrive Inc .................................................... E ...... 510 487-3560
30599 San Antonio St Hayward (94544) *(P-10044)*
Sewby LLC ................................................................ E ...... 310 494-7705
5066 W Jefferson Blvd Los Angeles (90016) *(P-2715)*
Sewer Rodding Equipment Co (PA) ........................ E ...... 310 301-9009
3217 Carter Ave Marina Del Rey (90292) *(P-10599)*
Sewing Collection Inc (PA) ...................................... D ...... 323 264-2223
3113 E 26th St Vernon (90058) *(P-6467)*
Sextant Wines, Paso Robles *Also Called: Rbz Vineyards LLC (P-1720)*
Sexy Hair Concepts LLC ......................................... E ...... 818 435-0800
21551 Prairie St Chatsworth (91311) *(P-17721)*
Seymour Duncan, Santa Barbara *Also Called: Duncan Carter Corporation (P-15713)*
SF Motors Inc (DH) .................................................. C ...... 408 617-7878
1504 Mccarthy Blvd Milpitas (95035) *(P-13383)*
SF Tube Inc .............................................................. E ...... 510 785-9148
23099 Connecticut St Hayward (94545) *(P-9270)*
Sfc, Perris *Also Called: Stretch Forming Corporation (P-8585)*
SFE, Santa Fe Springs *Also Called: Santa Fe Enterprises Inc (P-9647)*
SFJ Pharmaceuticals Inc ......................................... E ...... 925 223-6233
5000 Hopyard Rd Ste 330 Pleasanton (94588) *(P-5654)*
Sfo Apparel .............................................................. C ...... 415 468-8816
41 Park Pl # 43 Brisbane (94005) *(P-2807)*
Sfrlc Inc .................................................................... E ...... 562 693-2776
12306 Washington Blvd Whittier (90606) *(P-6537)*
Sfs, Brea *Also Called: Kirkhill Inc (P-13886)*
SGB Better Baking Co LLC ..................................... D ...... 818 787-9992
14528 Blythe St Van Nuys (91402) *(P-1242)*
SGB Bubbles Baking Co LLC ................................. D ...... 818 786-1700
15215 Keswick St Van Nuys (91405) *(P-1243)*
SGB Enterprises Inc ................................................ E ...... 661 294-8306
24844 Anza Dr Ste A Valencia (91355) *(P-10310)*
SGC International Inc .............................................. F ...... 323 318-2998
6489 Corvette St Commerce (90040) *(P-7177)*
Sgk LLC .................................................................... E ...... 415 438-6700
650 Townsend St Ste 160 San Francisco (94103) *(P-5028)*

Sgl Composites Inc (DH) ......................................... D ...... 424 329-5250
1551 W 139th St Gardena (90249) *(P-3909)*
Sgl Technic LLC (DH) .............................................. E ...... 661 257-0500
28176 Avenue Stanford Valencia (91355) *(P-7571)*
Sgps Inc ................................................................... D ...... 310 538-4175
15823 S Main St Gardena (90248) *(P-16227)*
Sgt Dresser-Rand, Chula Vista *Also Called: Curtiss-Wright Corporation (P-19250)*
Shade Structures, Orange *Also Called: Shade Structures Inc (P-8685)*
Shade Structures Inc .............................................. E ...... 714 427-6980
115 E 2nd St Ste 101 Tustin (92780) *(P-8569)*
Shade Structures Inc .............................................. E ...... 714 427-6980
1085 N Main St Ste C Orange (92867) *(P-8685)*
Shademaster Products, Santee *Also Called: R V Best Inc (P-6990)*
Shadow Security App Inc ....................................... F ...... 310 388-9371
19709 Ventura Blvd Pmb 105-1017 Woodland Hills (91364) *(P-469)*
Shafer Vineyards .................................................... F ...... 707 944-2877
6154 Silverado Trl Napa (94558) *(P-1745)*
Shaka Wear, Los Angeles *Also Called: Gino Corporation (P-2573)*
Shamir, San Diego *Also Called: Shamir Insight Inc (P-7203)*
Shamir Insight Inc ................................................... D ...... 858 514-8330
9938 Via Pasar San Diego (92126) *(P-7203)*
Shamrock Companies, The, Anaheim *Also Called: Shamrock Supply Company Inc (P-16762)*
Shamrock Fireplace, San Rafael *Also Called: Ebac Investments Inc (P-7444)*
Shamrock Materials of Cotati, Cotati *Also Called: Ebac Investments Inc (P-7443)*
Shamrock Office Solutions .................................... F ...... 408 791-6432
743 Ames Ave Milpitas (95035) *(P-16504)*
Shamrock Supply Company Inc (PA) .................... D ...... 714 575-1800
3366 E La Palma Ave Anaheim (92806) *(P-16762)*
Shanghai Anc Electronic Tech, Moorpark *Also Called: Anc Technology Inc (P-12054)*
Shani Darden Skincare Inc .................................... E ...... 310 745-3150
1800 Century Park E Ste 400 Los Angeles (90067) *(P-6036)*
Shannon Ridge Inc (PA) ......................................... E ...... 707 281-6780
2150 Argonaut Rd Lakeport (95453) *(P-1746)*
Shannon Ridge Inc ................................................. E ...... 707 281-6780
4350 Thomas Dr Lakeport (95453) *(P-1747)*
Shannon's Imperial Brand, Fresno *Also Called: Athens Baking Company Inc (P-1160)*
Shapco Inc ............................................................... D ...... 559 834-1342
5220 S Peach Ave Fresno (93725) *(P-9271)*
Shapco Inc (PA) ...................................................... F ...... 310 264-1666
1666 20th St Ste 100 Santa Monica (90404) *(P-16632)*
Shape Memory Applications, San Jose *Also Called: Johnson Matthey Inc (P-15138)*
Shape Products, Oakland *Also Called: Vulpine Inc (P-6329)*
Shapell Industries .................................................. F ...... 323 655-7330
1990 S Bundy Dr Ste 500 Los Angeles (90025) *(P-16228)*
Shar-Craft Inc (PA) .................................................. E ...... 661 324-4985
1103 33rd St Bakersfield (93301) *(P-16896)*
Shara-Tex Inc .......................................................... E ...... 323 587-7200
3338 E Slauson Ave Vernon (90058) *(P-2482)*
Sharethis Inc (PA) ................................................... E ...... 650 641-0191
3000 El Camino Real Ste 5-150 Palo Alto (94306) *(P-19489)*
Sharon Havriluk ...................................................... E ...... 714 630-1313
1164 N Kraemer Pl Anaheim (92806) *(P-5004)*
Sharp, Torrance *Also Called: Sharp Industries Inc (P-16841)*
Sharp Dimension Inc .............................................. E ...... 510 656-8938
4240 Business Center Dr Fremont (94538) *(P-11112)*
Sharp Industries Inc (PA) ....................................... E ...... 310 370-5990
3501 Challenger St Fl 2 Torrance (90503) *(P-16841)*
Sharpcast, Los Angeles *Also Called: Sugarsync Inc (P-18846)*
Sharpmart LLC ....................................................... E ...... 619 278-1473
3911 Cleveland Ave San Diego (92103) *(P-6037)*
Shasta Beverages Inc (DH) ................................... D ...... 954 581-0922
26901 Indl Blvd Hayward (94545) *(P-1963)*
Shasta Beverages Inc ............................................ D ...... 714 523-2280
14405 Artesia Blvd La Mirada (90638) *(P-1964)*
Shasta Electronic Mfg Svcs Inc ............................. F ...... 408 436-1267
525 E Brokaw Rd San Jose (95112) *(P-10201)*
Shasta Ems, San Jose *Also Called: Shasta Electronic Mfg Svcs Inc (P-10201)*
Shasta Forest Products Inc ................................... E ...... 530 842-2787
1423 Montague Rd Yreka (96097) *(P-3427)*
Shasta Green Inc .................................................... E ...... 530 335-4924
35586a State Highway 299 E Burney (96013) *(P-3055)*

**Shasta Wood Products Inc** ............................................. E ...... 530 378-6880
19751 Hirsch Ct Anderson (96007) *(P-3428)*

**Shattuck Group, The, Oxnard** *Also Called: Steelworks Etc Inc (P-8292)*

**Shaver Specialty Co Inc** ............................................. E ...... 310 370-6941
20608 Earl St Torrance (90503) *(P-9816)*

**Shaw Bakers LLC (PA)** ............................................. E ...... **650 273-1440**
320b Shaw Rd South San Francisco (94080) *(P-17213)*

**Shaw Bakers LLC** ............................................. C ...... 650 273-1440
14490 Catalina St San Leandro (94577) *(P-17214)*

**Shaw Industries Group Inc** ............................................. E ...... 562 430-4445
11411 Valley View St Cypress (90630) *(P-2520)*

**Shaxon Industries Inc** ............................................. D ...... 714 779-1140
337 W Freedom Ave Orange (92865) *(P-10282)*

**Sheathing Technologies Inc** ............................................. E ...... 408 782-2720
675 Jarvis Dr Ste A Morgan Hill (95037) *(P-15254)*

**Sheet Metal Engineering** ............................................. E ...... 805 306-0390
1780 Voyager Ave Simi Valley (93063) *(P-8570)*

**Sheet Metal Service** ............................................. F ...... 714 446-0196
2310 E Orangethorpe Ave Anaheim (92806) *(P-8571)*

**Sheffield Manufacturing Inc** ............................................. D ...... 310 320-1473
9131 Glenoaks Blvd Sun Valley (91352) *(P-11113)*

**Sheffield Platers Inc** ............................................. D ...... 858 546-8484
9850 Waples St San Diego (92121) *(P-9013)*

**Sheila Street Properties Inc (PA)** ............................................. D ...... **323 838-9208**
5900 Sheila St Commerce (90040) *(P-9014)*

**Shelby Carroll Intl Inc (PA)** ............................................. E ...... **310 327-5072**
7927 Garden Grove Blvd Garden Grove (92841) *(P-13384)*

**Shelcore Inc (PA)** ............................................. E ...... **818 883-2400**
7811 Lemona Ave Van Nuys (91405) *(P-15768)*

**Shelcore Toys, Van Nuys** *Also Called: Shelcore Inc (P-15768)*

**Shell Catalysts & Tech LP** ............................................. D ...... 925 370-9675
10 Mococo Rd Martinez (94553) *(P-5114)*

**Shell Catalysts & Tech LP** ............................................. D ...... 925 458-9045
2840 Willow Pass Rd Pittsburg (94565) *(P-5115)*

**Shell Chemical LP** ............................................. E ...... 925 313-8601
10 Mococo Rd Martinez (94553) *(P-5116)*

**Shelter & Indus Svcs Mexico, San Diego** *Also Called: Jaime Enterprise Group (P-351)*

**Shelton Inc** ............................................. E
1225 8th St Berkeley (94710) *(P-1344)*

**Sheng-Kee of California Inc** ............................................. D ...... 415 468-3800
201 S Hill Dr Brisbane (94005) *(P-17420)*

**Shepard Bros Inc (PA)** ............................................. C ...... **562 697-1366**
503 S Cypress St La Habra (90631) *(P-10600)*

**Shepard-Thomason Company** ............................................. D ...... 714 773-5539
901 S Leslie St La Habra (90631) *(P-13574)*

**Shercon LLC** ............................................. D
18704 S Ferris Pl Rancho Dominguez (90220) *(P-6538)*

**Shercon, Inc., Rancho Dominguez** *Also Called: Shercon LLC (P-6538)*

**Sherline Products, Vista** *Also Called: Sherline Products Incorporated (P-9571)*

**Sherline Products Incorporated** ............................................. E ...... 760 727-5181
3235 Executive Rdg Vista (92081) *(P-9571)*

**Sherpa Clinical Packaging LLC** ............................................. E ...... 858 282-0928
6920 Carroll Rd San Diego (92121) *(P-3937)*

**Sherrill M Campbell Corporation** ............................................. F ...... 209 392-6103
15142 Merrill Ave Dos Palos (93620) *(P-19213)*

**Sherry Kline, Commerce** *Also Called: Pacific Coast Home Furn Inc (P-2944)*

**Sheryl Lowe Designs LLC** ............................................. E ...... 805 969-1742
1187 Coast Village Rd Ste 156 Santa Barbara (93108) *(P-19129)*

**Sheward & Son & Sons (PA)** ............................................. E ...... **714 556-6055**
14352 Chambers Rd Tustin (92780) *(P-3728)*

**Shield AI Inc (PA)** ............................................. A ...... **619 719-5740**
600 W Broadway Ste 250 San Diego (92101) *(P-13689)*

**Shifamed LLC** ............................................. E ...... 408 364-1242
590 Division St Campbell (95008) *(P-17869)*

**Shift Calendars Inc** ............................................. F ...... 626 967-5862
809 N Glendora Ave Covina (91724) *(P-4762)*

**Shift Packaging LLC** ............................................. F ...... 206 412-4253
14261 Proctor Ave Ste A La Puente (91746) *(P-5882)*

**Shikai Products, Santa Rosa** *Also Called: Trans-India Products Inc (P-6046)*

**Shim-It Corporation** ............................................. F ...... 951 734-8300
1691 California Ave Corona (92881) *(P-13956)*

**Shimada Enterprises Inc** ............................................. E ...... 562 802-8811
14009 Dinard Ave Santa Fe Springs (90670) *(P-11622)*

**Shine Food Inc (PA)** ............................................. E ...... **310 329-3829**
19216 Normandie Ave Torrance (90502) *(P-869)*

**Shine Food Inc** ............................................. D ...... 310 533-6010
21100 S Western Ave Torrance (90501) *(P-1046)*

**Shinko Electric America Inc (DH)** ............................................. E ...... **408 232-0499**
2077 Gateway Pl Ste 250 San Jose (95110) *(P-16734)*

**Ship & Shore Environmental Inc** ............................................. E ...... 562 997-0233
2474 N Palm Dr Signal Hill (90755) *(P-16842)*

**Ship Smart Inc** ............................................. E ...... 831 661-4841
783 Rio Del Mar Blvd Ste 9 Aptos (95003) *(P-3938)*

**Shippo, San Francisco** *Also Called: Popout Inc (P-18685)*

**Shipscience LLC** ............................................. F ...... 800 303-6644
268 N Santa Cruz Ave Los Gatos (95030) *(P-16341)*

**Shire** ............................................. E ...... 805 372-3000
1445 Lawrence Dr Newbury Park (91320) *(P-5655)*

**Shire Rgenerative Medicine Inc** ............................................. E ...... 858 754-5396
11095 Torreyana Rd San Diego (92121) *(P-5656)*

**Shirinian-Shaw Inc** ............................................. E ...... 951 736-1229
1229 Railroad St Corona (92882) *(P-2884)*

**Shlbao Distributors, Sacramento** *Also Called: Peter (P-3993)*

**Shmaze Custom Coatings, Lake Forest** *Also Called: Shmaze Industries Inc (P-9119)*

**Shmaze Industries Inc** ............................................. E ...... 949 583-1448
20792 Canada Rd Lake Forest (92630) *(P-9119)*

**Shock Doctor Inc** ............................................. E ...... 657 383-4400
11488 Slater Ave Fountain Valley (92708) *(P-15854)*

**Shock Doctor Inc (PA)** ............................................. D ...... **800 233-6956**
11488 Slater Ave Fountain Valley (92708) *(P-15855)*

**Shock Doctor Sports, Fountain Valley** *Also Called: Shock Doctor Inc (P-15855)*

**Shockwave Medical Inc (HQ)** ............................................. B ...... **510 279-4262**
5403 Betsy Ross Dr Santa Clara (95054) *(P-15255)*

**Shop -Ncal Rmx Fixed Maint Sho, Fairfield** *Also Called: Cemex Cnstr Mtls PCF LLC (P-7421)*

**Shop Buru, Los Angeles** *Also Called: Bu Ru LLC (P-17660)*

**Shop4techcom** ............................................. E ...... 909 248-2725
13745 Seminole Dr Chino (91710) *(P-10283)*

**Shore Front LLC** ............................................. E ...... 714 612-3751
3973 Trolley Ct Brea (92823) *(P-2352)*

**Shore Western Manufacturing** ............................................. E ...... 626 357-3251
19888 Quiroz Ct Walnut (91789) *(P-14717)*

**Shorett Printing Inc (PA)** ............................................. E ...... **714 545-4689**
250 W Rialto Ave San Bernardino (92408) *(P-4960)*

**Short Load Concrete Inc** ............................................. E ...... 714 524-7013
605 E Commercial St Anaheim (92801) *(P-7496)*

**Shortcuts Software Inc** ............................................. E ...... 714 622-6600
7711 Center Ave Ste 550 Huntington Beach (92647) *(P-18787)*

**Show Group Production Services, Gardena** *Also Called: Sgps Inc (P-16227)*

**Show Off Time, Ventura** *Also Called: Fnc Medical Corporation (P-5978)*

**Showdogs Inc** ............................................. E ...... 760 603-3269
168 S Pacific St San Marcos (92078) *(P-3729)*

**Shower Glass & Mirror Co, Santa Clara** *Also Called: South Bay Showers Inc (P-542)*

**Showerdoordirect LLC** ............................................. F ...... 310 327-8060
20100 Normandie Ave Torrance (90502) *(P-8572)*

**Shred Labs LLC** ............................................. E ...... 781 285-8622
8033 W Sunset Blvd # 1112 Los Angeles (90046) *(P-18788)*

**Shrin LLC** ............................................. D ...... 714 850-0303
900 E Arlee Pl Anaheim (92805) *(P-16400)*

**Shultz Steel Company LLC** ............................................. B ...... **323 357-3200**
5321 Firestone Blvd South Gate (90280) *(P-8802)*

**Shurflo LLC** ............................................. B ...... **714 371-1550**
3545 Harbor Gtwy S Ste 103 Costa Mesa (92626) *(P-9940)*

**Shye West Inc (PA)** ............................................. E ...... **949 486-4598**
43 Corporate Park Ste 102 Irvine (92606) *(P-16034)*

**Shyft Group Inc** ............................................. D ...... 323 276-1933
1130 S Vail Ave Montebello (90640) *(P-13385)*

**Shyft Group Inc** ............................................. D ...... 916 921-2639
4242 Forcum Ave Bldg B-640 Mcclellan (95652) *(P-13386)*

**Si, Fontana** *Also Called: California Steel Inds Inc (P-7609)*

**Si Manufacturing Inc** ............................................. E ...... 714 956-7110
1440 S Allec St Anaheim (92805) *(P-12858)*

# ALPHABETIC SECTION — Sierra Resource Management

Si-Bone, Santa Clara *Also Called: Si-Bone Inc (P-15404)*
Si-Bone Inc (PA) .................................................................. B ...... 408 207-0700
   471 El Camino Real Ste 101 Santa Clara (95050) *(P-15404)*
Si-Ware Systems Inc ........................................................... D ...... 650 257-9680
   101 Jefferson Dr Fl 1 Menlo Park (94025) *(P-12695)*
Siblings Investment Inc ....................................................... E ...... 510 668-0368
   43951 Boscell Rd Fremont (94538) *(P-16548)*
Sicor Inc (HQ) ....................................................................... A ...... 949 455-4700
   19 Hughes Irvine (92618) *(P-5657)*
Sid E Parker Boiler Mfg Co Inc ........................................... D ...... 323 727-9800
   5930 Bandini Blvd Commerce (90040) *(P-8335)*
Sid-Mar Inc ........................................................................... F ...... 213 626-8121
   23303 La Palma Ave Yorba Linda (92887) *(P-17641)*
Sidco Labelling Systems, Gilroy *Also Called: Context Engineering Co (P-8831)*
Sids Carpet Barn (PA) ........................................................ E ...... 619 477-7000
   132 W 8th St National City (91950) *(P-16435)*
Sidus Solutions LLC ........................................................... F ...... 619 275-5533
   7352 Trade St San Diego (92121) *(P-11944)*
Siegfried Irvine, Irvine *Also Called: Alliance Medical Products Inc (P-14959)*
Siegfried Irvine, Irvine *Also Called: Alliance Medical Products Inc (P-14960)*
Siemens Energy Inc ............................................................ E ...... 949 448-0600
   6 Journey Ste 200 Aliso Viejo (92656) *(P-4465)*
Siemens Energy Inc ............................................................ E ...... 310 223-0660
   18502 S Dominguez Hills Dr Rancho Dominguez (90220) *(P-9975)*
Siemens Hlthcare Dgnostics Inc ........................................ D ...... 310 645-8200
   5210 Pacific Concourse Dr Los Angeles (90045) *(P-15256)*
Siemens Industry Inc .......................................................... C ...... 916 681-3000
   7464 French Rd Sacramento (95828) *(P-14368)*
Siemens Industry Inc .......................................................... E ...... 916 553-4444
   3650 Industrial Blvd Ste 100 West Sacramento (95691) *(P-14369)*
Siemens Med Solutions USA Inc ....................................... B ...... 925 293-5430
   757 Arnold Dr Martinez (94553) *(P-11784)*
Siemens Med Solutions USA Inc ....................................... B ...... 650 694-5747
   3120 Hansen Way Palo Alto (94304) *(P-15257)*
Siemens Med Solutions USA Inc ....................................... A ...... 925 246-8200
   4040 Nelson Ave Concord (94520) *(P-15578)*
Siemens Medical Solutions, Los Angeles *Also Called: Siemens Hlthcare Dgnostics Inc (P-15256)*
Siemens Mobility Inc ........................................................... E ...... 714 284-0206
   1026 E Lacy Ave Anaheim (92805) *(P-11785)*
Siemens Mobility Inc ........................................................... A ...... 916 681-3000
   7464 French Rd Sacramento (95828) *(P-13387)*
Siemens Mobility Inc ........................................................... D ...... 916 621-2700
   5301 Price Ave Mcclellan (95652) *(P-19162)*
Siemens Rail Automation Corp .......................................... D ...... 909 532-5405
   9568 Archibald Ave Rancho Cucamonga (91730) *(P-12016)*
Sienna Corporation ............................................................. C ...... 510 440-0200
   41350 Christy St Fremont (94538) *(P-8573)*
Sientra, Irvine *Also Called: Sientra Inc (P-15405)*
Sientra Inc (HQ) ................................................................... E ...... 805 562-3500
   3333 Michelson Dr Ste 650 Irvine (92612) *(P-15405)*
Sierra, Compton *Also Called: Sierra Cheese Manufacturing Company Inc (P-738)*
Sierra Alloys Company, Irwindale *Also Called: STS Metals Inc (P-8803)*
Sierra Aluminum, Riverside *Also Called: Samuel Son & Co (usa) Inc (P-7747)*
Sierra Aluminum Company ................................................ E ...... 951 781-7800
   2345 Fleetwood Dr Riverside (92509) *(P-7748)*
Sierra Assembly Technology LLC ..................................... F ...... 909 606-7700
   14764 Yorba Ct Unit T1 Chino (91710) *(P-12216)*
Sierra Automated Sys/Eng Corp ....................................... E ...... 818 840-6749
   2821 Burton Ave Burbank (91504) *(P-11945)*
Sierra Automated Systems, Burbank *Also Called: Sierra Automated Sys/Eng Corp (P-11945)*
Sierra Cheese Manufacturing Company Inc .................... E ...... 310 635-1216
   916 S Santa Fe Ave Compton (90221) *(P-738)*
Sierra Chemical Company, West Sacramento *Also Called: Richard K Gould Inc (P-6321)*
Sierra Circuits Inc (PA) ....................................................... D ...... 408 735-7137
   1108 W Evelyn Ave Sunnyvale (94086) *(P-12217)*
Sierra CP Engineering, Monterey *Also Called: Sierra Instruments Inc (P-14459)*
Sierra Design Mfg Inc (PA) ................................................ E ...... 925 443-3140
   2602 Superior Dr Livermore (94550) *(P-11575)*
Sierra Electrotek LLC .......................................................... D ...... 414 762-1390
   1108 W Evelyn Ave Sunnyvale (94086) *(P-12218)*

Sierra Feeds, Reedley *Also Called: Mission AG Resources LLC (P-769)*
Sierra Finish Carpentry, Fresno *Also Called: Ryan Mc Teer (P-2916)*
Sierra Instruments Inc (HQ) ............................................... D ...... 831 373-0200
   5 Harris Ct Bldg L Monterey (93940) *(P-14459)*
Sierra Metal Fabricators Inc .............................................. E ...... 530 265-4591
   529 Searls Ave Nevada City (95959) *(P-8215)*
Sierra Metalk Fabricators, Nevada City *Also Called: Sierra Metal Fabricators Inc (P-8215)*
Sierra Monitor, Milpitas *Also Called: Sierra Monitor Corporation (P-14919)*
Sierra Monitor Corporation (HQ) ....................................... D ...... 408 262-6611
   1991 Tarob Ct Milpitas (95035) *(P-14919)*
Sierra Monolithics Inc (HQ) ............................................... E ...... 310 698-1000
   103 W Torrance Blvd Redondo Beach (90277) *(P-19570)*
Sierra Mountain, Sonora *Also Called: Sierra Mountain Cnstr Inc (P-19360)*
Sierra Mountain Cnstr Inc .................................................. D ...... 209 928-1900
   13919 Mono Way Sonora (95370) *(P-19360)*
Sierra Nevada Brewing Co (PA) ........................................ B ...... 530 893-3520
   1075 E 20th St Chico (95928) *(P-1458)*
Sierra Nevada Cheese Co Inc (PA) ................................... D ...... 530 934-8660
   6505 County Road 39 Willows (95988) *(P-739)*
Sierra Nevada Corporation ................................................ E ...... 510 446-8400
   39465 Paseo Padre Pkwy Ste 2900 Fremont (94538) *(P-11946)*
Sierra Nevada Corporation ................................................ C ...... 408 395-2004
   985 University Ave Ste 4 Los Gatos (95032) *(P-14304)*
Sierra Nevada Corporation ................................................ D ...... 916 985-8799
   145 Parkshore Dr Folsom (95630) *(P-14305)*
SIERRA NEVADA CORPORATION, Fremont *Also Called: Sierra Nevada Corporation (P-11946)*
SIERRA NEVADA CORPORATION, Los Gatos *Also Called: Sierra Nevada Corporation (P-14304)*
SIERRA NEVADA CORPORATION, Folsom *Also Called: Sierra Nevada Corporation (P-14305)*
Sierra Office Supply & Prtg, Sacramento *Also Called: Sierra Office Systems Pdts Inc (P-4763)*
Sierra Office Systems Pdts Inc (PA) ................................. D ...... 916 369-0491
   9950 Horn Rd Ste 5 Sacramento (95827) *(P-4763)*
Sierra Oncology, San Mateo *Also Called: Sierra Oncology Inc (P-5658)*
Sierra Oncology Inc (HQ) ................................................... D ...... 650 376-8679
   1820 Gateway Dr Ste 110 San Mateo (94404) *(P-5658)*
Sierra Pacific Engrg & Pdts, Long Beach *Also Called: SPEP Acquisition Corp (P-8028)*
Sierra Pacific Industries ..................................................... C ...... 530 283-2820
   1538 Lee Rd Quincy (95971) *(P-3081)*
Sierra Pacific Industries ..................................................... C ...... 530 378-8301
   14980 Camage Ave Sonora (95370) *(P-3082)*
Sierra Pacific Industries ..................................................... E ...... 530 335-3681
   Hwy 299 E Burney (96013) *(P-3083)*
Sierra Pacific Industries ..................................................... C ...... 530 365-3721
   19758 Riverside Ave Anderson (96007) *(P-3084)*
Sierra Pacific Industries ..................................................... E ...... 530 644-2311
   3950 Carson Rd Camino (95709) *(P-3085)*
Sierra Pacific Industries ..................................................... D ...... 916 645-1631
   1440 Lincoln Blvd Lincoln (95648) *(P-3086)*
Sierra Pacific Industries ..................................................... E ...... 530 824-2474
   Alameda Rd Corning (96021) *(P-3188)*
SIERRA PACIFIC INDUSTRIES, Quincy *Also Called: Sierra Pacific Industries (P-3081)*
SIERRA PACIFIC INDUSTRIES, Sonora *Also Called: Sierra Pacific Industries (P-3082)*
SIERRA PACIFIC INDUSTRIES, Burney *Also Called: Sierra Pacific Industries (P-3083)*
SIERRA PACIFIC INDUSTRIES, Anderson *Also Called: Sierra Pacific Industries (P-3084)*
SIERRA PACIFIC INDUSTRIES, Camino *Also Called: Sierra Pacific Industries (P-3085)*
SIERRA PACIFIC INDUSTRIES, Lincoln *Also Called: Sierra Pacific Industries (P-3086)*
SIERRA PACIFIC INDUSTRIES, Corning *Also Called: Sierra Pacific Industries (P-3188)*
Sierra Pacific Industries Inc .............................................. B ...... 530 527-9620
   11605 Reading Rd Red Bluff (96080) *(P-3087)*
Sierra Pacific Industries Inc (PA) ...................................... D ...... 530 378-8000
   19794 Riverside Ave Anderson (96007) *(P-3088)*
Sierra Pacific Industries Inc .............................................. D ...... 530 529-5108
   11400 Reading Rd Red Bluff (96080) *(P-3189)*
Sierra Pacific Packaging, Oroville *Also Called: Graphic Packaging Intl LLC (P-4885)*
Sierra Precision, Anaheim *Also Called: 3d Instruments LLC (P-14380)*
Sierra Precision Optics Inc ................................................ E ...... 530 885-6979
   12830 Earhart Ave Auburn (95602) *(P-14824)*
Sierra Proto Express, Sunnyvale *Also Called: Sierra Circuits Inc (P-12217)*
Sierra Resource Management, Jamestown *Also Called: Sierra Resource Management Inc (P-3056)*

---

Employee Codes: A=Over 500 employees, B=251-500
C=101-250, D=51-100, E=20-50, F=10-19, G=1-9

Sierra Resource Management Inc ............................................. F ...... 209 984-1146
  12015 La Grange Rd Jamestown (95327) *(P-3056)*
Sierra Technical Services Inc ................................................... F ...... 661 823-1092
  101 Commercial Way Unit D Tehachapi (93561) *(P-7696)*
Sierra Trim Inc ........................................................................ E ...... 916 259-2966
  3137 Swetzer Rd Ste B Loomis (95650) *(P-501)*
Sierra-Tahoe Ready Mix Inc .................................................. E ...... 530 541-1877
  1526 Emerald Bay Rd South Lake Tahoe (96150) *(P-7497)*
Sierracin Corporation (HQ) ...................................................... A ...... 818 741-1656
  12780 San Fernando Rd Sylmar (91342) *(P-6112)*
Sierracin/Sylmar Corporation ................................................. A ...... 818 362-6711
  12780 San Fernando Rd Sylmar (91342) *(P-7027)*
Sierramotion Inc ..................................................................... F ...... 916 259-1868
  3295 Swetzer Rd Loomis (95650) *(P-11286)*
Sierrapine A California Limited Partnership .............................. B ...... 800 676-3339
  1050 Melody Ln Ste 160 Roseville (95678) *(P-3190)*
Sierrathermal Inc (DH) .......................................................... E ...... 831 763-0113
  200 Westridge Dr Watsonville (95076) *(P-10059)*
Sifive Inc (PA) ....................................................................... D ...... 415 673-2836
  2625 Augustine Dr Ste 201 Santa Clara (95054) *(P-12696)*
Sigen, San Jose *Also Called: Silicon Genesis Corporation (P-12700)*
Sight Machine Inc ................................................................. D ...... 888 461-5739
  243 Vallejo St San Francisco (94111) *(P-18789)*
SIGHT SCIENCES, Menlo Park *Also Called: Sight Sciences Inc (P-15258)*
Sight Sciences Inc (PA) ......................................................... C ...... 877 266-1144
  4040 Campbell Ave Ste 100 Menlo Park (94025) *(P-15258)*
Sigma, Fremont *Also Called: Sigma Designs Inc (P-12697)*
Sigma Designs Inc ................................................................ A ...... 510 897-0200
  47467 Fremont Blvd Fremont (94538) *(P-12697)*
Sigma Mfg & Logistics LLC .................................................... E ...... 916 781-3052
  851 Eagle Ridge Cir Folsom (95630) *(P-10202)*
Sigma Supply & Dist Inc ........................................................ F ...... 818 246-4624
  701 W Harvard St Glendale (91204) *(P-16589)*
Sigma-Aldrich Corporation ..................................................... E ...... 760 710-6213
  6211 El Camino Real Carlsbad (92009) *(P-6323)*
Sigmatronix Inc ..................................................................... F ...... 714 436-1618
  2109 S Susan St Santa Ana (92704) *(P-11697)*
Sign Designs Inc .................................................................... E ...... 209 524-4484
  204 Campus Way Modesto (95350) *(P-16035)*
Sign Industries Inc ................................................................. E ...... 909 930-0303
  2101 Carrillo Privado Ontario (91761) *(P-16036)*
Sign Mart, Orange *Also Called: Metal Art of California Inc (P-16008)*
Sign Specialists Corporation ................................................... E ...... 714 641-0064
  111 W Dyer Rd Ste F Santa Ana (92707) *(P-16037)*
Sign Technology Inc .............................................................. E ...... 916 372-1200
  1700 Enterprise Blvd Ste F West Sacramento (95691) *(P-16038)*
Sign-A-Rama, Redding *Also Called: Jar Ventures Inc (P-15992)*
Sign-A-Rama, Palm Desert *Also Called: Pd Group (P-16020)*
Signage Solutions Corporation ................................................ E ...... 714 491-0299
  2231 S Dupont Dr Anaheim (92806) *(P-16039)*
Signal ................................................................................... E ...... 661 259-1234
  26330 Diamond Pl Ste 100 Santa Clarita (91350) *(P-4194)*
Signal Hill Petroleum Inc ........................................................ E ...... 562 595-6440
  2633 Cherry Ave Signal Hill (90755) *(P-200)*
Signal Newspaper, The, Santa Clarita *Also Called: Morris Multimedia Inc (P-4161)*
Signal Pharmaceuticals LLC ................................................... C ...... 858 795-4700
  10300 Campus Point Dr Ste 100 San Diego (92121) *(P-5659)*
Signature Control Systems ..................................................... D ...... 949 580-3640
  16485 Laguna Canyon Rd Ste 130 Irvine (92618) *(P-9381)*
Signature Flexible Packg LLC (PA) ......................................... E ...... 909 598-7844
  19310 San Jose Ave City Of Industry (91748) *(P-6246)*
Signature Flexible Packg LLC ................................................ F ...... 949 475-2300
  17032 Armstrong Ave Irvine (92614) *(P-6247)*
Signature Fresh, City Of Industry *Also Called: Ssre Holdings LLC (P-617)*
Signature Tech Group Inc ...................................................... F ...... 818 890-7611
  11960 Borden Ave San Fernando (91340) *(P-13084)*
Signco, Yorba Linda *Also Called: Sesa Inc (P-17839)*
Signet Armorlite Inc (DH) ....................................................... B ...... 760 744-4000
  5803 Newton Dr Ste A Carlsbad (92008) *(P-15616)*
Signgroup/Karman, Chatsworth *Also Called: Schea Holdings Inc (P-16032)*

Signify North America Corp .................................................... C ...... 732 563-3000
  3350 Enterprise Dr Bloomington (92316) *(P-11557)*
Signifyd Inc (PA) .................................................................... B ...... 866 220-1415
  99 Almaden Blvd Ste 400 San Jose (95113) *(P-18790)*
Signode Industrial Group LLC ................................................. E ...... 209 931-0917
  3901 Navone Rd Stockton (95215) *(P-4050)*
Signresource LLC .................................................................. C ...... 323 771-2098
  6135 District Blvd Maywood (90270) *(P-16040)*
Signs and Services Company ................................................. E ...... 714 761-8200
  10980 Boatman Ave Stanton (90680) *(P-16041)*
Signsusa.com, Santa Fe Springs *Also Called: Inkovation Inc (P-4646)*
Signtech, West Sacramento *Also Called: Sign Technology Inc (P-16038)*
Signtech, San Diego *Also Called: Signtech Electrical Advg Inc (P-16042)*
Signtech Electrical Advg Inc ................................................... C ...... 619 527-6100
  4444 Federal Blvd San Diego (92102) *(P-16042)*
Signtronix Inc ........................................................................ D ...... 310 534-7500
  1445 Sepulveda Blvd Torrance (90501) *(P-16043)*
Sigona's Farmers Market, Redwood City *Also Called: Brothers Pride Produce Inc (P-17398)*
Sigtronics Corporation ............................................................ E ...... 909 305-9399
  178 E Arrow Hwy San Dimas (91773) *(P-12017)*
Sika Corporation .................................................................... F ...... 562 941-0231
  12767 Imperial Hwy Santa Fe Springs (90670) *(P-6324)*
Sila Nanotechnologies Inc (PA) .............................................. C ...... 408 475-7452
  2470 Mariner Square Loop Alameda (94501) *(P-13148)*
Silao Tortilleria, Rowland Heights *Also Called: Silao Tortilleria Inc (P-2353)*
Silao Tortilleria Inc ................................................................ E ...... 626 961-0761
  18316 Senteno St Rowland Heights (91748) *(P-2353)*
Silc Technologies Inc ............................................................. D ...... 626 375-1231
  181 W Huntington Dr Ste 200 Monrovia (91016) *(P-12698)*
Silevo, Fremont *Also Called: Silevo Inc (P-434)*
Silevo Inc .............................................................................. E ...... 510 771-1360
  1055 Page Ave Fremont (94538) *(P-434)*
Silgan, Woodland Hills *Also Called: Silgan Can Company (P-7925)*
Silgan, Woodland Hills *Also Called: Silgan Containers Corporation (P-7926)*
Silgan, Modesto *Also Called: Silgan Containers Mfg Corp (P-7928)*
Silgan, Antioch *Also Called: Silgan Containers Mfg Corp (P-7929)*
Silgan, Riverbank *Also Called: Silgan Containers Mfg Corp (P-7930)*
Silgan, Woodland Hills *Also Called: Silgan Containers Mfg Corp (P-7931)*
Silgan Can Company ............................................................. C ...... 818 348-3700
  21600 Oxnard St Ste 1600 Woodland Hills (91367) *(P-7925)*
Silgan Containers Corporation (DH) ........................................ D ...... 818 710-3700
  21600 Oxnard St Ste 1600 Woodland Hills (91367) *(P-7926)*
Silgan Containers LLC (HQ) .................................................. D ...... 818 710-3700
  21600 Oxnard St Ste 1600 Woodland Hills (91367) *(P-7927)*
Silgan Containers Mfg Corp ................................................... E ...... 209 521-6469
  4000 Yosemite Blvd Modesto (95357) *(P-7928)*
Silgan Containers Mfg Corp ................................................... E ...... 925 778-8000
  2200 Wilbur Ave Antioch (94509) *(P-7929)*
Silgan Containers Mfg Corp ................................................... E ...... 209 869-3601
  3250 Patterson Rd Riverbank (95367) *(P-7930)*
Silgan Containers Mfg Corp (DH) ........................................... C ...... 818 710-3700
  21600 Oxnard St Ste 1600 Woodland Hills (91367) *(P-7931)*
Silica Engineering Group, Milpitas *Also Called: Superior Quartz Inc (P-7713)*
Silicon Genesis Corporation .................................................... E ...... 408 228-5885
  46816 Lakeview Blvd Fremont (94538) *(P-12699)*
Silicon Genesis Corporation (PA) ............................................ E ...... 408 228-5858
  145 Baytech Dr San Jose (95134) *(P-12700)*
Silicon Graphics Intl Corp (HQ) ............................................... C ...... 669 900-8000
  940 N Mccarthy Blvd Milpitas (95035) *(P-10436)*
Silicon Graphics Intl Inc ......................................................... F ...... 669 900-8000
  900 N Mccarthy Blvd Milpitas (95035) *(P-10203)*
Silicon Image Inc (HQ) .......................................................... E ...... 408 616-4000
  2115 Onel Dr San Jose (95131) *(P-12701)*
Silicon Light Machines Corp (DH) ........................................... F ...... 408 240-4700
  6660 Via Del Oro San Jose (95119) *(P-12702)*
Silicon Microstructures Inc ..................................................... D ...... 408 473-9700
  1701 Mccarthy Blvd Milpitas (95035) *(P-11347)*
Silicon Motion Inc ................................................................. D ...... 408 501-5300
  690 N Mccarthy Blvd Ste 200 Milpitas (95035) *(P-12703)*
Silicon Quest International Inc ................................................ D ...... 408 496-1000
  4425 Fortran Dr San Jose (95134) *(P-12704)*

## ALPHABETIC SECTION

Silicon Tech Inc .................................................... A ...... 949 476-1130
  3009 Daimler St Santa Ana (92705) *(P-10284)*
Silicon Turnkey Solutions Inc (HQ) ......................... F ...... **408 904-0200**
  1804 Mccarthy Blvd Milpitas (95035) *(P-12705)*
SILICON TURNKEY SOLUTIONS INC. DBA HI RELIABILITY MICROELECTRONICS, Milpitas
  *Also Called: Silicon Turnkey Solutions Inc (P-12705)*
Silicon Valley Mfg Inc ........................................... E ...... 510 791-9450
  6520 Central Ave Newark (94560) *(P-11114)*
Silicon Valley Mfg., Newark *Also Called: Svm Machining Inc (P-11129)*
Silicon Valley X-Ray, San Jose *Also Called: Bruker Nano Inc (P-14641)*
Silicon Vly McRelectronics Inc .............................. E ...... 408 844-7100
  2985 Kifer Rd Santa Clara (95051) *(P-12706)*
Siliconcore, Milpitas *Also Called: Siliconcore Technology Inc (P-12707)*
Siliconcore Technology Inc (PA) ............................ F ...... **408 946-8185**
  890 Hillview Ct Ste 120 Milpitas (95035) *(P-12707)*
Siliconix Incorporated (HQ) ................................... A ...... **408 988-8000**
  2585 Junction Ave San Jose (95134) *(P-12708)*
Silicontech, Santa Ana *Also Called: Silicon Tech Inc (P-10284)*
Silicor Materials, Sunnyvale *Also Called: Silicor Materials Inc (P-9120)*
Silicor Materials Inc ............................................... D ...... 408 962-3100
  985 Almanor Ave Sunnyvale (94085) *(P-9120)*
Silitronics, Santa Clara *Also Called: Silitronics Inc (P-13085)*
Silitronics Inc ......................................................... E ...... 408 605-1148
  2388 Walsh Ave Santa Clara (95051) *(P-13085)*
Silitronics Solutions Inc ........................................ E ...... 408 605-1148
  2388 Walsh Ave Santa Clara (95051) *(P-9899)*
Silk Road Medical, Sunnyvale *Also Called: Silk Road Medical Inc (P-15259)*
Silk Road Medical Inc ........................................... B ...... 408 720-9002
  1213 Innsbruck Dr Sunnyvale (94089) *(P-15259)*
Silk Screen Shirts Inc ............................................ E ...... 760 233-3900
  6185 El Camino Real Carlsbad (92009) *(P-2494)*
Siller Aviation, Yuba City *Also Called: Siller Brothers Inc (P-3057)*
Siller Brothers Inc (PA) ......................................... E ...... **530 673-0734**
  1250 Smith Rd Yuba City (95991) *(P-3057)*
Sills Farms Inc ....................................................... E ...... 916 655-3391
  5072 Pacific Ave Pleasant Grove (95668) *(P-57)*
Silmar Division, Hawthorne *Also Called: Ip Corporation (P-5167)*
Silton Cases, Fresno *Also Called: International Cases & Mfg Inc (P-7134)*
Siluria Technologies Inc ........................................ E ...... 415 978-2170
  409 Illinois St San Francisco (94158) *(P-138)*
Silva Sausage Co ................................................... E ...... 408 293-5437
  5935 Rossi Ln Gilroy (95020) *(P-667)*
Silver Creek Industries LLC .................................. C ...... 951 943-5393
  2830 Barrett Ave Perris (92571) *(P-370)*
Silver Oak, Oakville *Also Called: Silver Oak Wine Cellars LLC (P-1749)*
Silver Oak Wine Cellars LLC ................................ F ...... 707 942-7082
  7300 Highway 128 Healdsburg (95448) *(P-1748)*
Silver Oak Wine Cellars LLC (PA) ........................ F ...... **707 942-7022**
  915 Oakville Cross Rd Oakville (94562) *(P-1749)*
Silver Peak Systems LLC (HQ) ............................. C ...... **408 935-1800**
  2860 De La Cruz Blvd Ste 100 Santa Clara (95050) *(P-12709)*
Silverado Vineyards ............................................... E ...... 707 257-1770
  6121 Silverado Trl Napa (94558) *(P-1750)*
Silveron Industries Inc .......................................... F ...... 909 598-4533
  182 S Brent Cir City Of Industry (91789) *(P-11348)*
Silverrest, Fullerton *Also Called: Brentwood Home LLC (P-3522)*
Silvester California, Los Angeles *Also Called: Silvestri Studio Inc (P-16229)*
Silvestri Studio Inc (PA) ........................................ D ...... **323 277-4420**
  8125 Beach St Los Angeles (90001) *(P-16229)*
Silvus Technologies Inc (PA) ................................ E ...... **310 479-3333**
  10990 Wilshire Blvd Ste 1500 Los Angeles (90024) *(P-11947)*
Sim Ideation, Irvine *Also Called: Specialty Interior Mfg Inc (P-16402)*
Simba Recycling, San Marcos *Also Called: Arna Trading Inc (P-3754)*
Simec USA Corporation ......................................... E ...... 619 474-7081
  333 H St Ste 5000 Chula Vista (91910) *(P-7627)*
Simex-Iwerks, Valencia *Also Called: Iwerks Entertainment Inc (P-13257)*
Simmons Family Corporation ................................ D ...... 951 278-4563
  350 W Rincon St Corona (92880) *(P-6592)*
Simmons Stairways Inc ......................................... E ...... 408 920-0105
  255 Apollo Way # B Hollister (95023) *(P-3191)*

Simo Holdings Inc ................................................. B ...... 760 931-9550
  611 Gateway Blvd Ste 120 South San Francisco (94080) *(P-2577)*
Simon G Jewelry Inc ............................................. E ...... 818 500-8595
  528 State St Glendale (91203) *(P-16970)*
Simon Golub & Sons Inc (DH) ............................. D
  514 Via De La Valle Ste 210 Solana Beach (92075) *(P-16971)*
Simonton Windows, Vacaville *Also Called: Fortune Brands Windows Inc (P-6830)*
Simple Green, Huntington Beach *Also Called: Sunshine Makers Inc (P-5929)*
Simple Science Inc ............................................... E ...... 949 335-1099
  1626 Ohms Way Costa Mesa (92627) *(P-19130)*
Simple Solar Industries LLC ................................ E ...... 844 907-0705
  661 Brea Canyon Rd Ste 1 Walnut (91789) *(P-12710)*
Simplex Filler Inc ................................................... F ...... 707 265-6801
  640 Airpark Rd Ste A Napa (94558) *(P-10031)*
Simplex Filler Co, Napa *Also Called: Simplex Filler Inc (P-10031)*
Simplex Supplies Inc ............................................ F ...... 618 594-6450
  1370 Valley Vista Dr Ste 200 Diamond Bar (91765) *(P-8216)*
Simplexgrinnell, San Diego *Also Called: Johnson Cntrls Fire Prtction L (P-12002)*
Simpliphi Power Inc .............................................. E ...... 805 640-6700
  3100 Camino Del Sol Oxnard (93030) *(P-13149)*
Simply Display ...................................................... E ...... 888 767-0676
  12200 Los Nietos Rd Santa Fe Springs (90670) *(P-16044)*
Simply Fresh LLC ................................................. C ...... 714 562-5000
  11215 Knott Ave Ste A Cypress (90630) *(P-2063)*
Simply Straws LLC ............................................... E ...... 855 787-2974
  515 Bay Hill Dr Newport Beach (92660) *(P-7204)*
Simpplr Inc (PA) .................................................... C ...... 650 396-2646
  3 Twin Dolphin Dr Ste 160 Redwood City (94065) *(P-18791)*
Simpson Coatings Group Inc .............................. E ...... 650 873-5990
  401 S Canal St A South San Francisco (94080) *(P-6113)*
Simpson Industries Inc ......................................... E ...... 310 605-1224
  20611 Belshaw Ave Carson (90746) *(P-5660)*
Simpson Manufacturing Co Inc ............................ E ...... 209 234-7775
  5151 S Airport Way Stockton (95206) *(P-7557)*
Simpson Manufacturing Co Inc (PA) .................... C ...... **925 560-9000**
  5956 W Las Positas Blvd Pleasanton (94588) *(P-7915)*
Simpson Strong-Tie Company Inc ....................... C ...... 714 871-8373
  12246 Holly St Riverside (92509) *(P-3317)*
Simpson Strong-Tie Company Inc (HQ) .............. C ...... **925 560-9000**
  5956 W Las Positas Blvd Pleasanton (94588) *(P-8709)*
Simpson Strong-Tie Company Inc ....................... D ...... 209 234-7775
  5151 S Airport Way Stockton (95206) *(P-8710)*
Simpson Strong-Tie Intl Inc (DH) ......................... D ...... **925 560-9000**
  5956 W Las Positas Blvd Pleasanton (94588) *(P-8711)*
Simpsonsimpson Industries, Carson *Also Called: Simpson Industries Inc (P-5660)*
Sims Group USA Corporation ............................... E ...... 408 494-4242
  1900 Monterey Hwy San Jose (95112) *(P-16962)*
Sims Software, Carlsbad *Also Called: Stratcom Systems Inc (P-17983)*
Sims/LMC Recyclers, San Jose *Also Called: Sims Group USA Corporation (P-16962)*
Simso Tex, Compton *Also Called: Simso Tex Sublimation (P-3017)*
Simso Tex Sublimation (PA) ................................. E ...... **310 885-9717**
  3028 E Las Hermanas St Compton (90221) *(P-3017)*
Simulator PDT Solutions LLC ............................... E ...... 310 830-3331
  21818 S Wilmington Ave Ste 411 Long Beach (90810) *(P-14306)*
Sincere Orient Commercial Corp ......................... D ...... 626 333-8882
  15222 Valley Blvd City Of Industry (91746) *(P-2354)*
Sincere Orient Food Company, City Of Industry *Also Called: Sincere Orient Commercial Corp (P-2354)*
Sinclair & Valentine, Watsonville *Also Called: Sv Labs Corporation (P-17053)*
Sinclair Systems, Fresno *Also Called: Atlas Pacific Engineering Co (P-9778)*
Sinecera Inc .......................................................... D ...... 626 962-1087
  5397 3rd St Irwindale (91706) *(P-19131)*
Sing Kung Corp ..................................................... E ...... 626 358-5838
  12061 Clark St Arcadia (91006) *(P-1063)*
Sing Tao Daily, Burlingame *Also Called: Sing Tao Newspapers (P-4195)*
Sing Tao Newspapers (DH) .................................. D ...... **650 808-8800**
  1818 Gilbreth Rd Ste 108 Burlingame (94010) *(P-4195)*
Sing Tao Newspapers Ltd .................................... D ...... 626 956-8200
  17059 Green Dr City Of Industry (91745) *(P-4196)*
Sing Tao Nwspapers Los Angeles, City Of Industry *Also Called: Sing Tao Newspapers Ltd (P-4196)*

**Singer Vehicle Design LLC (PA)** ............................................. C ...... 213 592-2728
19500 S Vermont Ave Torrance (90502) *(P-19170)*

**Singod Investors Vi LLC** ..................................................... D ...... 714 326-7800
1600 S Clementine St Anaheim (92802) *(P-5117)*

**Singtel Enterprise SEC US Inc** ........................................... A ...... 650 508-6800
901 Marshall St Ste 125 Redwood City (94063) *(P-18992)*

**SINGULAR GENOMICS, San Diego** *Also Called: Singular Genomics Systems Inc (P-14718)*

**Singular Genomics Systems Inc (PA)** ................................. C ...... 858 333-7830
3010 Science Park Rd San Diego (92121) *(P-14718)*

**Singular Genomics Systems Inc** ........................................ D ...... 619 703-8135
10010 Mesa Rim Rd San Diego (92121) *(P-14719)*

**Singulex, Alameda** *Also Called: Singulex Inc (P-19497)*

**Singulex Inc** ........................................................................ B ...... 510 995-9000
1701 Harbor Bay Pkwy Ste 200 Alameda (94502) *(P-19497)*

**Sinister Mfg Company Inc** ................................................. E ...... 916 772-9253
2025 Opportunity Dr Ste 7 Roseville (95678) *(P-13575)*

**Sinosource Intl Co Inc** ........................................................ F ...... 650 697-6668
282 Harbor Way South San Francisco (94080) *(P-7546)*

**Sip & Sonder LLC** .............................................................. F ...... 908 309-3739
108 S Market St Inglewood (90301) *(P-2355)*

**Siplast Inc** .......................................................................... E ...... 408 490-4268
1754 Technology Dr Ste 120-E San Jose (95110) *(P-6384)*

**Sir Speedy, Mission Viejo** *Also Called: Sir Speedy Inc (P-4764)*

**Sir Speedy, Whittier** *Also Called: Ss Whittier LLC (P-4770)*

**Sir Speedy Inc (HQ)** ........................................................... E ...... 949 348-5000
26722 Plaza Mission Viejo (92691) *(P-4764)*

**Sirena Incorporated** ........................................................... F ...... 866 548-5353
22717 S Western Ave Torrance (90501) *(P-4961)*

**Sirf Technology Holdings Inc** ............................................. A ...... 408 523-6500
1060 Rincon Cir San Jose (95131) *(P-12711)*

**Sirna Therapeutics Inc** ...................................................... E ...... 415 512-7200
1700 Owens St San Francisco (94158) *(P-5661)*

**Siskiyou Daily News, Yreka** *Also Called: Gatehouse Media LLC (P-4119)*

**Siskiyou Forest Products (PA)** ........................................... E ...... 530 378-6980
6275 State Highway 273 Anderson (96007) *(P-3192)*

**Sisneros Inc** ........................................................................ F ...... 562 777-9797
12717 Los Nietos Rd Santa Fe Springs (90670) *(P-3607)*

**Sisneros Office Furntiure, Santa Fe Springs** *Also Called: Sisneros Inc (P-3607)*

**Sissell Bros** ......................................................................... E ...... 323 261-0106
4322 E 3rd St Los Angeles (90022) *(P-7391)*

**Sistema US Inc** ................................................................... E ...... 707 773-2200
775 Southpoint Blvd Petaluma (94954) *(P-7028)*

**Sit On It, Buena Park** *Also Called: Exemplis LLC (P-3600)*

**Sitecore Usa Inc (DH)** ........................................................ C ...... 415 380-0600
44 Montgomery St Ste 3340 San Francisco (94104) *(P-18792)*

**Sitek Process Solutions** ..................................................... E ...... 916 797-9000
233 Technology Way Ste 3 Rocklin (95765) *(P-12712)*

**Siteserver Inc** ..................................................................... F ...... 805 579-7831
4514 Ish Dr Simi Valley (93063) *(P-19571)*

**Sitetraker** ............................................................................ E ...... 650 868-5164
420 Florence St Palo Alto (94301) *(P-11744)*

**SITIME, Santa Clara** *Also Called: Sitime Corporation (P-12713)*

**Sitime Corporation (PA)** ..................................................... B ...... 408 328-4400
5451 Patrick Henry Dr Santa Clara (95054) *(P-12713)*

**Sitonit, Cypress** *Also Called: Exemplis LLC (P-3602)*

**Sittin Pretty Natural Dog Bky, Ontario** *Also Called: JE Rich Company (P-1104)*

**Sius Products and Distr Inc (PA)** ....................................... F ...... 510 382-1700
1065 46th Ave Oakland (94601) *(P-3979)*

**Siwibi Wholesale** ................................................................ E ...... 650 448-1041
625 Ellis St Mountain View (94043) *(P-11230)*

**Six Sigma, Milpitas** *Also Called: Winslow Automation Inc (P-12804)*

**Sizzix, Lake Forest** *Also Called: Ellison Educational Eqp Inc (P-9759)*

**Sjm Facility, Irvine** *Also Called: St Jude Medical LLC (P-5672)*

**Sk Chemicals America Inc** ................................................. F ...... 949 336-8088
3 Park Plz Ste 430 Irvine (92614) *(P-5201)*

**Sk Drapes, North Hollywood** *Also Called: S & K Theatrical Drap Inc (P-2917)*

**Sk Foods LP** ........................................................................ C ...... 559 924-6500
1175 19th Ave Lemoore (93245) *(P-926)*

**Sk Hynix Mmory Sltons Amer Inc** ...................................... B ...... 408 514-3500
3103 N 1st St San Jose (95134) *(P-12714)*

**Sk Hynix Nand PDT Sltions Corp (HQ)** .............................. C ...... 858 863-3069
10951 White Rock Rd Rancho Cordova (95670) *(P-12715)*

**Sk Pharmteco Inc (HQ)** ...................................................... E ...... 888 330-2232
12460 Akron St Ste 100 Rancho Cordova (95742) *(P-5662)*

**Skalli Vineyards, Rutherford** *Also Called: St Supery Inc (P-1759)*

**Skanska USA Cvil W Cal Dst Inc (DH)** .............................. A ...... 951 684-5360
1995 Agua Mansa Rd Riverside (92509) *(P-381)*

**Skat-Trak** ............................................................................. F ...... 909 795-2505
654 Avenue K Calimesa (92320) *(P-6412)*

**Skate One Corp** .................................................................. D ...... 805 964-1330
6860 Cortona Dr Ste B Goleta (93117) *(P-15856)*

**Skaug Truck Body Works** .................................................. F ...... 818 365-9123
1404 1st St San Fernando (91340) *(P-13428)*

**SKB Corporation (PA)** ........................................................ B ...... 714 637-1252
434 W Levers Pl Orange (92867) *(P-7029)*

**Skdy of San Diego Inc** ........................................................ E ...... 858 552-9033
6455 Weathers Pl San Diego (92121) *(P-19132)*

**SKECHERS, Manhattan Beach** *Also Called: Skechers Collection LLC (P-6421)*

**SKECHERS, Manhattan Beach** *Also Called: Skechers USA Inc (P-7122)*

**Skechers Collection LLC** .................................................... E ...... 310 318-3100
228 Manhattan Beach Blvd Manhattan Beach (90266) *(P-6421)*

**Skechers Factory Outlet 335, Moreno Valley** *Also Called: Skechers USA Inc (P-17110)*

**Skechers USA Inc (PA)** ...................................................... D ...... 310 318-3100
228 Manhattan Beach Blvd Ste 200 Manhattan Beach (90266) *(P-7122)*

**Skechers USA Inc** .............................................................. E ...... 951 242-4307
29800 Eucalyptus Ave Moreno Valley (92555) *(P-17110)*

**Skechers USA Inc II** ........................................................... A ...... 800 746-3411
228 Manhattan Beach Blvd Ste 200 Manhattan Beach (90266) *(P-17504)*

**Skedulo Inc** ......................................................................... F ...... 415 640-1997
548 Market St Ste 80260 San Francisco (94104) *(P-18793)*

**Skell Inc** .............................................................................. F ...... 310 392-3288
2401 Lincoln Blvd Ste C Santa Monica (90405) *(P-6207)*

**SKF Aptitude Exchange, San Diego** *Also Called: SKF Condition Monitoring Inc (P-14920)*

**SKF Condition Monitoring Inc (DH)** ................................... C ...... 858 496-3400
9444 Balboa Ave Ste 150 San Diego (92123) *(P-14920)*

**Ski Air Conditioning Company** ........................................... E ...... 530 626-4010
5528 Merchant Cir Placerville (95667) *(P-435)*

**Skinmedica Inc** ................................................................... B ...... 760 929-2600
18655 Teller Ave Irvine (92612) *(P-5663)*

**Skinny Minnie, Maywood** *Also Called: Ev R Inc (P-2758)*

**Skintight** .............................................................................. E ...... 310 829-4120
11740 San Vicente Blvd Ste 208 Los Angeles (90049) *(P-15857)*

**Sks Die Cast & Machining Inc (PA)** .................................. E ...... 510 523-2541
1849 Oak St Alameda (94501) *(P-7822)*

**Skuid Inc** ............................................................................. D ...... 800 515-2535
2121 N California Blvd Ste 350 Walnut Creek (94596) *(P-18794)*

**Skurka Aerospace Inc (DH)** ............................................... E ...... 805 484-8884
4600 Calle Bolero Camarillo (93012) *(P-11287)*

**Sky One Inc** ........................................................................ F ...... 909 622-3333
1793 W 2nd St Pomona (91766) *(P-7282)*

**Sky Parent Inc (PA)** ........................................................... F ...... 650 362-0488
5470 Great America Pkwy Santa Clara (95054) *(P-18795)*

**Sky Rider Equipment Co Inc** .............................................. E ...... 714 632-6890
1180 N Blue Gum St Anaheim (92806) *(P-3538)*

**Skyco Shading Systems Inc** .............................................. E ...... 714 708-3038
3411 W Fordham Ave Santa Ana (92704) *(P-17540)*

**Skydio Inc (PA)** ................................................................... D ...... 855 463-5902
3000 Clearview Way Bldg E San Mateo (94402) *(P-13690)*

**Skylane Farms, Turlock** *Also Called: Valley Fresh Foods Inc (P-67)*

**Skyline Alterations Inc (PA)** ............................................... E ...... 530 549-4010
5626 Riverland Dr Anderson (96007) *(P-3058)*

**Skyline Displays of San Diego, San Diego** *Also Called: Skdy of San Diego Inc (P-19132)*

**Skyline Homes Inc** ............................................................. C ...... 951 654-9321
499 W Esplanade Ave San Jacinto (92583) *(P-3388)*

**Skyline Homes Inc** ............................................................. C ...... 530 666-0974
1720 E Beamer St Woodland (95776) *(P-3389)*

**Skylock Industries LLC** ...................................................... D ...... 626 334-2391
1290 W Optical Dr Azusa (91702) *(P-13957)*

**Skylon, Perris** *Also Called: Eci Water Ski Products Inc (P-17633)*

**Skyview Aviation Llc** .......................................................... E ...... 209 830-7666
5749 S Tracy Blvd Tracy (95377) *(P-17862)*

## ALPHABETIC SECTION

**Skyworks, Irvine** *Also Called: Skyworks Solutions Inc (P-12719)*
Skyworks Solutions Inc ............................................................ F ...... 301 874-6408
1767 Carr Rd Ste 105 Calexico (92231) *(P-11383)*
Skyworks Solutions Inc ............................................................ F ...... 949 231-3550
1778 Zinetta Rd Ste A Calexico (92231) *(P-12716)*
Skyworks Solutions Inc ............................................................ E ...... 805 480-4400
2427 W Hillcrest Dr Newbury Park (91320) *(P-12717)*
Skyworks Solutions Inc ............................................................ E ...... 805 480-4227
730 Lawrence Dr Newbury Park (91320) *(P-12718)*
Skyworks Solutions Inc (PA) .................................................... A ...... 949 231-3000
5260 California Ave Irvine (92617) *(P-12719)*
SI3 Technologies LLC ............................................................... F ...... 619 365-4275
416 W San Ysidro Blvd Ste L-5 San Ysidro (92173) *(P-10285)*
Slabs Inc ..................................................................................... E ...... 424 289-0275
12555 W Jefferson Blvd Los Angeles (90066) *(P-18796)*
**Slack, San Francisco** *Also Called: Slack Technologies Inc (P-18797)*
Slack Technologies Inc (HQ) .................................................... B ...... 970 299-4848
500 Howard St Ste 100 San Francisco (94105) *(P-18797)*
Slam Specialties LLC ............................................................... F ...... 559 348-9038
5837 E Brown Ave Fresno (93727) *(P-13576)*
**Slawomira Sobczyk, Milpitas** *Also Called: Yuhas Tooling & Machining Inc (P-11199)*
**SLC, Truckee** *Also Called: Software Licensing Consultants (P-18807)*
**Sld Laser, Goleta** *Also Called: Kyocera Sld Laser Inc (P-13264)*
Sleep Technologies Inc ............................................................ F ...... 866 931-1964
3233 Mission Oaks Blvd Ste C Camarillo (93012) *(P-3539)*
Sleepcomp West LLC ............................................................... E ...... 562 946-3222
10006 Santa Fe Springs Rd Santa Fe Springs (90670) *(P-6662)*
Slide Systems Inc .................................................................... F ...... 310 539-3416
1448 240th St Harbor City (90710) *(P-8888)*
**Slimsuit, Bell** *Also Called: Carol Wior Inc (P-2744)*
Slo Cider LLC ............................................................................ F ...... 805 439-0865
3419 Roberto Ct San Luis Obispo (93401) *(P-1751)*
Slo New Times Inc ................................................................... E ...... 805 546-8208
1010 Marsh St San Luis Obispo (93401) *(P-4197)*
Sloan Electric Corporation ...................................................... E ...... 619 239-5174
3520 Main St San Diego (92113) *(P-16673)*
Slouber Enterprises (PA) ......................................................... E ...... 530 273-2080
11885 Sunrise Ln Grass Valley (95945) *(P-14720)*
Sly Trunk LLC ........................................................................... E ...... 408 540-6411
481 N Santa Cruz Ave # 120 Los Gatos (95030) *(P-7140)*
**SM Tire, Nipomo** *Also Called: Santa Maria Tire Inc (P-17463)*
**Smac, Carlsbad** *Also Called: Systems Mchs Atmtn Cmpnnts Cor (P-11351)*
**Small City Cider Co., Geyserville** *Also Called: Mathy Winery LLC (P-1674)*
**Small Hand Foods, Hayward** *Also Called: Still Room LLC (P-2026)*
Small Precision Tools Inc ........................................................ D ...... 707 762-5880
1330 Clegg St Petaluma (94954) *(P-12720)*
Small Vines Viticulture Inc ..................................................... F ...... 707 823-0886
2160 Green Hill Rd Sebastopol (95472) *(P-1752)*
Small Wnders Hndcrfted Mntres ............................................ F ...... 818 703-7450
7033 Canoga Ave Ste 5 Canoga Park (91303) *(P-16230)*
Small World Trading Co .......................................................... C ...... 415 945-1900
90 Windward Way San Rafael (94901) *(P-6038)*
Smarsh Inc ................................................................................ C ...... 650 631-6300
900 Veterans Blvd Ste 500 Redwood City (94063) *(P-18798)*
Smart LLC ................................................................................. E ...... 866 822-3670
3501 Sepulveda Blvd Torrance (90505) *(P-7030)*
Smart Elec & Assembly Inc .................................................... C ...... 714 772-2651
2000 W Corporate Way Anaheim (92801) *(P-12219)*
**Smart Electronics, Anaheim** *Also Called: Smart Elec & Assembly Inc (P-12219)*
Smart Erp Solutions Inc (PA) .................................................. E ...... 925 271-0200
3875 Hopyard Rd Ste 180 Pleasanton (94588) *(P-17978)*
**Smart Foam Pads, Lake Forest** *Also Called: Advanced Innvtive Rcvery Tech (P-3517)*
Smart Fog ................................................................................. E ...... 800 921-5230
1017 L St Pmb 319 Sacramento (95814) *(P-10515)*
Smart Foods LLC ..................................................................... E ...... 800 284-2250
3398 Leonis Blvd Vernon (90058) *(P-1373)*
Smart Modular Tech De Inc (HQ) ........................................... C ...... 510 623-1231
45800 Northport Loop W Fremont (94538) *(P-12721)*
Smart Modular Technologies (wwh) Inc ............................... A ...... 510 623-1231
39870 Eureka Dr Newark (94560) *(P-12722)*
Smart Modular Technologies Inc (HQ) .................................. C ...... 510 623-1231
39870 Eureka Dr Newark (94560) *(P-12723)*
**Smart Spectrometer, Pleasanton** *Also Called: Atonarp Us Inc (P-14617)*
Smart Start Early Childhood ................................................... F ...... 916 984-3800
101 Hazelmere Dr Folsom (95630) *(P-19364)*
**Smart TV & Sound, Chico** *Also Called: Videomaker Inc (P-4304)*
Smart World LLC ..................................................................... E ...... 510 933-9700
48225 Lakeview Blvd Fremont (94538) *(P-19133)*
Smart-Tek Services Inc (HQ) .................................................. F ...... 858 798-1644
11838 Bernardo Plaza Ct Ste 250 San Diego (92128) *(P-18799)*
**Smartcover Systems, Escondido** *Also Called: Hadronex Inc (P-16354)*
**Smarthomepro, Irvine** *Also Called: Smartlabs Inc (P-17722)*
Smartlabs Inc ........................................................................... D ...... 800 762-7846
1621 Alton Pkwy Ste 100 Irvine (92606) *(P-17722)*
**Smartlogic, San Jose** *Also Called: Smartlogic Semaphore Inc (P-18800)*
Smartlogic Semaphore Inc ..................................................... C ...... 408 213-9500
111 N Market St Ste 365 San Jose (95113) *(P-18800)*
Smartthings Inc (PA) ............................................................... F ...... 757 633-2308
665 Clyde Ave Mountain View (94043) *(P-17359)*
Smb Industries Inc .................................................................. E ...... 530 538-0101
558 Georgia Pacific Way Oroville (95965) *(P-8217)*
Smb Industries Inc (PA) .......................................................... E ...... 530 534-6266
550 Georgia Pacific Way Oroville (95965) *(P-8218)*
SMC Grease Specialist Inc ..................................................... E ...... 951 788-6042
1600 W Pellisier Rd Colton (92324) *(P-16364)*
SMC Products Inc ................................................................... D ...... 949 753-1099
22651 Lambert St Ste 105 Lake Forest (92630) *(P-16951)*
**Smg, Torrance** *Also Called: Storm Manufacturing Group Inc (P-9162)*
SMI Architectural Millwork Inc .............................................. E ...... 714 567-0112
2116 W Chestnut Ave Santa Ana (92703) *(P-17345)*
SMI Ca Inc ................................................................................ E ...... 562 926-9407
14340 Iseli Rd Santa Fe Springs (90670) *(P-11115)*
SMI Holdings Inc ..................................................................... E ...... 800 232-2612
28420 Witherspoon Pkwy Valencia (91355) *(P-11288)*
**SMI Millwork, Santa Ana** *Also Called: SMI Architectural Millwork Inc (P-17345)*
**Smith Brothers, San Diego** *Also Called: Smith Brothers Mfg Corp (P-11116)*
Smith Brothers Mfg Corp ........................................................ F ...... 619 296-3171
5304 Banks St San Diego (92110) *(P-11116)*
Smith International Inc .......................................................... C ...... 909 906-7900
11031 Jersey Blvd Ste A Rancho Cucamonga (91730) *(P-9466)*
**Smith Ironworks, Hesperia** *Also Called: Endura Steel Inc (P-16619)*
Smith River Brewing Company (PA) ...................................... F ...... 707 465-4444
400 Front St Crescent City (95531) *(P-17623)*
**Smithfield Foods, Los Angeles** *Also Called: Clougherty Packing LLC (P-592)*
Smiths Action Plastics Inc (PA) ............................................. F ...... 714 836-4141
645 S Santa Fe St Santa Ana (92705) *(P-6686)*
Smiths Detection Inc .............................................................. C ...... 410 612-2625
39714 Eureka Dr Newark (94560) *(P-14307)*
Smiths Detection LLC ............................................................. A ...... 510 739-2400
7151 Gateway Blvd Newark (94560) *(P-14308)*
Smiths Interconnect Inc ......................................................... D ...... 805 267-0100
375 Conejo Ridge Ave Thousand Oaks (91361) *(P-13086)*
Smiths Intrcnnect Americas Inc ............................................ B ...... 714 371-1100
1231 E Dyer Rd Ste 235 Santa Ana (92705) *(P-13087)*
Smiths Shade & Linoleum Co Inc .......................................... E ...... 619 299-2228
6588 Federal Blvd Lemon Grove (91945) *(P-17529)*
**SMK, Chula Vista** *Also Called: SMK Manufacturing Inc (P-10311)*
SMK Manufacturing Inc .......................................................... E ...... 619 216-6400
1055 Tierra Del Rey Ste F Chula Vista (91910) *(P-10311)*
**Sml Space Maintainers Labs, Chatsworth** *Also Called: Selane Products Inc (P-15482)*
**Smooth-Bor Plastics, Laguna Hills** *Also Called: Steward Plastics Inc (P-7044)*
Smoothreads Inc ..................................................................... E ...... 800 536-5959
13750 Stowe Dr Ste A Poway (92064) *(P-3018)*
SMS Fabrications Inc ............................................................. E ...... 951 351-6828
11698 Warm Springs Rd Riverside (92505) *(P-8574)*
Smtc Manufacturing Corp Cal ................................................ A ...... 510 737-0700
431 Kato Ter Fremont (94539) *(P-12220)*
Smucker Natural Foods Inc (HQ) ........................................... C ...... 530 899-5000
37 Speedway Ave Chico (95928) *(P-1965)*
Sna Electronics Inc ................................................................. E ...... 510 656-3903
3249 Laurelview Ct Fremont (94538) *(P-12221)*

**Snack It Forward LLC** — ALPHABETIC SECTION

Snack It Forward LLC .................................................... E ...... 310 242-5517
  6080 Center Dr Ste 600 Los Angeles (90045) *(P-2102)*

Snail Inc (PA) ................................................................ E ...... 310 988-0643
  12049 Jefferson Blvd Culver City (90230) *(P-17979)*

SNAIL GAMES, Culver City *Also Called: Snail Inc (P-17979)*

Snak Club LLC ............................................................ C ...... 323 278-9578
  5560 E Slauson Ave Commerce (90040) *(P-1366)*

Snak-King LLC (PA) .................................................... B ...... 626 336-7711
  16150 Stephens St City Of Industry (91745) *(P-2103)*

Snap, Sunnyvale *Also Called: Spiracur Inc (P-15265)*

Snap Inc (PA) .............................................................. A ...... 310 399-3339
  3000 31st St Ste C Santa Monica (90405) *(P-17980)*

Snap Inc ...................................................................... D ...... 310 745-0632
  579 Toyopa Dr Pacific Palisades (90272) *(P-18801)*

Snap Pack Mail, Oakdale *Also Called: Media Print Services Inc (P-17832)*

SNAPCHAT, Santa Monica *Also Called: Snap Inc (P-17980)*

Snaplogic Inc (PA) ....................................................... C ...... 888 494-1570
  1825 S Grant St Ste 550 San Mateo (94402) *(P-18802)*

Snapnrack Inc ............................................................. E ...... 877 732-2860
  775 Fiero Ln Ste 200 San Luis Obispo (93401) *(P-8026)*

Snapshot Hair & Extensions LLC ................................. F ...... 877 783-5658
  2892 N Bellflower Blvd Long Beach (90815) *(P-16231)*

Snapware Corporation ................................................ C ...... 951 361-3100
  2325 Cottonwood Ave Riverside (92508) *(P-7031)*

Snapwiz Inc ................................................................ C ...... 510 328-3277
  39300 Civic Center Dr Ste 310 Fremont (94538) *(P-18803)*

Snickerdoodle Labs Inc .............................................. F ...... 408 807-9426
  3242 San Rivas Dr San Jose (95148) *(P-18804)*

Snowflake Designs Corporation .................................. E ...... 559 291-6234
  2893 Larkin Ave Clovis (93612) *(P-2479)*

Snowline Engineering, Cameron Park *Also Called: Preferred Mfg Svcs Inc (P-11048)*

Snowmass Apparel Inc (PA) ........................................ E ...... 949 788-0617
  15225 Alton Pkwy Irvine (92618) *(P-17100)*

Snowpure LLC ............................................................ E ...... 949 240-2188
  130 Calle Iglesia Ste A San Clemente (92672) *(P-10601)*

Snowpure Water Technologies, San Clemente *Also Called: Snowpure LLC (P-10601)*

Snowshoe Brewing, Arnold *Also Called: Snowshoe Brewing Co LLC (P-17605)*

Snowshoe Brewing Co LLC (PA) ................................. E ...... 209 795-2272
  2050 Hwy 4 Arnold (95223) *(P-17605)*

Snowsound USA, Santa Fe Springs *Also Called: Atlantic Representations Inc (P-3497)*

Snyder Industries LLC ................................................ E ...... 559 665-7611
  800 Commerce Dr Chowchilla (93610) *(P-7032)*

So Cal Graphics, San Diego *Also Called: Bretkeri Corporation (P-4853)*

SO Tech/Spcl Op Tech Inc (PA) .................................... E ...... 310 202-9007
  206 Star Of India Ln Carson (90746) *(P-17069)*

So-Cal Strl Stl Fbrication Inc ....................................... E ...... 909 877-1299
  130 S Spruce Ave Rialto (92376) *(P-8219)*

So-Cal Value Added, Camarillo *Also Called: Plt Enterprises Inc (P-11467)*

Soaptronic LLC ........................................................... E ...... 949 465-8955
  19771 Pauling Foothill Ranch (92610) *(P-5928)*

Soaring America Corporation ...................................... E ...... 909 270-2628
  8354 Kimball Ave # F360 Chino (91708) *(P-13691)*

Sobon Wine Company LLC ......................................... F ...... 209 245-4457
  12300 Steiner Rd Plymouth (95669) *(P-1753)*

Socal Auto Supply Inc ................................................ E ...... 302 360-8373
  21418 Osborne St Canoga Park (91304) *(P-17767)*

Socal Garment Works LLC ......................................... E ...... 323 300-5717
  4700 S Boyle Ave Ste C Vernon (90058) *(P-2426)*

Socal Labs LLC .......................................................... F ...... 813 857-5207
  68739 Summit Dr Cathedral City (92234) *(P-16232)*

Socal Technologies LLC ............................................. E ...... 619 635-1128
  1305 Oakdale Ave El Cajon (92021) *(P-19046)*

Socco Plastic Coating Company ................................. E ...... 909 987-4753
  11251 Jersey Blvd Rancho Cucamonga (91730) *(P-9121)*

Social Brands LLC ..................................................... E ...... 415 728-1761
  6575 Simson St Oakland (94605) *(P-16233)*

Social Gaming Network, Culver City *Also Called: Jam City Inc (P-17553)*

Social Junky Inc ......................................................... E ...... 213 999-1275
  7874 Palmetto Ave Fontana (92336) *(P-19134)*

Social Print Studio ...................................................... F ...... 805 551-5328
  548 Market St # 16617 San Francisco (94104) *(P-4765)*

Social Thinking, Santa Clara *Also Called: Think Social Publishing Inc (P-4479)*

Societal CDMO San Diego LLC ................................... D ...... 858 623-1520
  6828 Nancy Ridge Dr Ste 100 San Diego (92121) *(P-5664)*

Society For The Study Ntiv Art .................................... E ...... 510 549-4270
  2526 Martin Luther King Jr Way Berkeley (94704) *(P-4346)*

SOCKET COMMUNICATIONS, Fremont *Also Called: Socket Mobile Inc (P-18805)*

Socket Mobile Inc (PA) ................................................ D ...... 510 933-3000
  40675 Encyclopedia Cir Fremont (94538) *(P-18805)*

Socksmith Design Inc (PA) ......................................... E ...... 831 426-6416
  1515 Pacific Ave Santa Cruz (95060) *(P-2459)*

Soderberg Manufacturing Co Inc ................................. D ...... 909 595-1291
  20821 Currier Rd Walnut (91789) *(P-11576)*

Sofa U Love LLC (PA) ................................................. E ...... 323 464-3397
  1207 N Western Ave Los Angeles (90029) *(P-3490)*

Soffa Electric Inc ........................................................ E ...... 323 728-0230
  5901 Corvette St Commerce (90040) *(P-14460)*

Sofie, Gilroy *Also Called: Sofie Co (P-5665)*

Sofie Co ...................................................................... — ...... 408 842-0520
  5900b Obata Way Gilroy (95020) *(P-5665)*

Soft Gel Technologies Inc (HQ) ................................... E ...... 323 726-0700
  6982 Bandini Blvd Los Angeles (90040) *(P-5666)*

Soft-Touch Tissue, Vernon *Also Called: Paper Surce Converting Mfg Inc (P-3793)*

Softbank Robotics America Inc (DH) ........................... F ...... 844 737-7371
  2 Embarcadero Ctr Fl 8 San Francisco (94111) *(P-9495)*

Softline Home Fashions Inc ........................................ E ...... 310 630-4848
  13130 S Normandie Ave Gardena (90249) *(P-17070)*

Softub Inc (PA) ............................................................ D ...... 858 602-1920
  24700 Avenue Rockefeller Valencia (91355) *(P-16234)*

Software, Pleasanton *Also Called: Cambrian Lab Inc (P-18144)*

Software Development Inc .......................................... E ...... 925 847-8823
  4900 Hopyard Rd Pleasanton (94588) *(P-18806)*

Software Licensing Consultants .................................. E ...... 925 371-1277
  12030 Donner Pass Rd Ste 1 Truckee (96161) *(P-18807)*

Sogno Toscano Tuscan Dream .................................... A ...... 718 581-9494
  820 Aladdin Ave San Leandro (94577) *(P-1405)*

Soilmoisture Equipment Corp ..................................... E ...... 805 964-3525
  601 Pine Ave Ste A Goleta (93117) *(P-14921)*

Sol De Oro, Fresno *Also Called: La Tapatia Tortilleria Inc (P-2259)*

Sol-Pak Thermoforming Inc ........................................ E ...... 323 582-3333
  3388 Fruitland Ave Vernon (90058) *(P-7033)*

Solano Clinical Research, Petaluma *Also Called: Dow Pharmaceutical Sciences Inc (P-14654)*

Solano Diagnostics Imaging ........................................ F ...... 707 646-4646
  1101 B Gale Wilson Blvd Ste 100 Fairfield (94533) *(P-14922)*

Solar 4 America, Livermore *Also Called: Solarjuice American Inc (P-9437)*

Solar Art, Laguna Hills *Also Called: Budget Enterprises Llc (P-7164)*

Solar Atmospheres Inc ............................................... E ...... 909 217-7400
  8606 Live Oak Ave Fontana (92335) *(P-7899)*

Solar Electronics Company, North Hollywood *Also Called: A T Parker Inc (P-13207)*

Solar Shading Systems, Tustin *Also Called: Sheward & Son & Sons (P-3728)*

Solar Turbines Incorporated (HQ) ................................ A ...... 619 544-5352
  2200 Pacific Hwy San Diego (92101) *(P-9315)*

Solar Turbines Incorporated ....................................... E ...... 619 544-5321
  2660 Sarnen St San Diego (92154) *(P-9316)*

Solar Turbines Incorporated ....................................... C ...... 858 694-6110
  9330 Sky Park Ct San Diego (92123) *(P-9317)*

Solar Turbines Incorporated ....................................... D ...... 858 715-2060
  9250 Sky Park Ct A San Diego (92123) *(P-9318)*

Solar Turbines Intl Co (DH) ......................................... E ...... 619 544-5000
  2200 Pacific Hwy San Diego (92101) *(P-9319)*

Solara Health Inc ........................................................ E ...... 650 270-4500
  50 Fox Hill Rd Woodside (94062) *(P-18808)*

Solaredge, Milpitas *Also Called: Solaredge Technologies Inc (P-11384)*

Solaredge Technologies Inc (PA) ................................. D ...... 510 498-3200
  700 Tasman Dr Milpitas (95035) *(P-11384)*

Solarflare Communications Inc (DH) ........................... D ...... 949 581-6830
  7505 Irvine Center Dr Ste 100 Irvine (92618) *(P-10204)*

Solaris Paper Inc ........................................................ C ...... 714 687-6657
  505 N Euclid St Ste 630 Anaheim (92801) *(P-10466)*

Solarius Development, Inc., San Jose *Also Called: Nanofocus Inc (P-14558)*

Solarjuice American Inc (PA) ...................................... B ...... 925 474-8821
  6764 Preston Ave Ste A Livermore (94551) *(P-9437)*

# ALPHABETIC SECTION — Sonoma Media Investments LLC

**Solarreserve LLC (PA)** .................................................. F ...... 310 315-2200
520 Broadway 6th Fl Santa Monica (90401) *(P-8080)*

**Solarroofs.com, Carmichael** *Also Called: ACR Solar International Corp (P-17320)*

**Solartis, Manhattan Beach** *Also Called: Solartis LLC (P-17981)*

**Solartis LLC** .................................................................. E ...... 310 251-4861
1601 N Sepulveda Blvd Ste 606 Manhattan Beach (90266) *(P-17981)*

**Solatube, Vista** *Also Called: Solatube International Inc (P-8291)*

**Solatube International Inc (DH)** ................................. D ...... 888 765-2882
2210 Oak Ridge Way Vista (92081) *(P-8291)*

**Soldermask Inc** ............................................................ F ...... 714 842-1987
17905 Metzler Ln Huntington Beach (92647) *(P-12222)*

**SOLE Designs Inc** ........................................................ F ...... 626 452-8642
11685 Mcbean Dr El Monte (91732) *(P-3491)*

**Sole Society Group Inc** .............................................. C ...... 310 220-0808
11248 Playa Ct # B Culver City (90230) *(P-7093)*

**Sole Technology Inc (PA)** ........................................... D ...... 949 460-2020
26921 Fuerte Lake Forest (92630) *(P-7123)*

**Solecta Inc (PA)** .......................................................... E ...... 760 630-9643
4113 Avenida De La Plata Oceanside (92056) *(P-2530)*

**Solectek Corporation** ................................................. E ...... 858 450-1220
8375 Camino Santa Fe Ste A San Diego (92121) *(P-11948)*

**Soleffect** ....................................................................... F ...... 323 275-9945
10125 Freeman Ave Santa Fe Springs (90670) *(P-3730)*

**Soleno Therapeutics Inc (PA)** .................................... F ...... 650 213-8444
100 Marine Pkwy Ste 400 Redwood City (94065) *(P-5667)*

**Soleo Health, Inglewood** *Also Called: Biomed California Inc (P-5373)*

**Soleo Health Inc** .......................................................... F ...... 844 362-7360
1324 W Winton Ave Hayward (94545) *(P-5668)*

**Soleus International, Walnut** *Also Called: Mjc America Ltd (P-11411)*

**Solevy Co LLC** ............................................................. D ...... 661 622-4880
28918 Hancock Pkwy Valencia (91355) *(P-6039)*

**Soli-Bond Inc** ............................................................... F ...... 661 631-1633
4230 Foster Ave Bakersfield (93308) *(P-276)*

**Solid Oak Software Inc (PA)** ...................................... E ...... 805 568-5415
319 W Mission St Santa Barbara (93101) *(P-16549)*

**Solid State Devices Inc** .............................................. C ...... 562 404-4474
14701 Firestone Blvd La Mirada (90638) *(P-12724)*

**Solid State Optronics, San Jose** *Also Called: Synapse Semiconductor Corp (P-12752)*

**Solid-Scope, Carson** *Also Called: Solid-Scope Machining Co Inc (P-8027)*

**Solid-Scope Machining Co Inc** .................................. F ...... 310 523-2366
17925 Adria Maru Ln Carson (90746) *(P-8027)*

**Solidcore Systems Inc (DH)** ...................................... D ...... 408 387-8400
3965 Freedom Cir Santa Clara (95054) *(P-18809)*

**Solidigm, Rancho Cordova** *Also Called: Sk Hynix Nand PDT Sltions Corp (P-12715)*

**Soligen 2006, Santa Ana** *Also Called: DC Partners Inc (P-7842)*

**Solmetric Corporation** ................................................ E ...... 707 823-4600
117 Morris St Ste 100 Sebastopol (95472) *(P-14923)*

**Solo Clip Inc** ................................................................ E ...... 626 448-8118
1988 W Holt Ave Pomona (91768) *(P-15617)*

**Solo Enterprise Corp** .................................................. E ...... 626 961-3591
220 N California Ave City Of Industry (91744) *(P-11117)*

**Solo Golf, City Of Industry** *Also Called: Solo Enterprise Corp (P-11117)*

**Solomon Colors Inc** .................................................... E ...... 909 873-9444
1371 Laurel Ave Rialto (92376) *(P-5064)*

**Solon Corporation** ...................................................... F ...... 520 807-1300
44 Montgomery St Ste 2040 San Francisco (94104) *(P-8081)*

**Solow** ............................................................................ E ...... 323 664-7772
2907 Glenview Ave Los Angeles (90039) *(P-2808)*

**Solta Medical Distribution LLC** ................................. C ...... 510 782-2286
25901 Industrial Blvd Hayward (94545) *(P-15579)*

**Solut Inc** ....................................................................... E ...... 760 758-7240
4645 North Ave Ste 102 Oceanside (92056) *(P-3797)*

**Solutions Unlimited, Fullerton** *Also Called: Wilsons Art Studio Inc (P-4985)*

**Solv Energy LLC** ......................................................... C ...... 858 622-4040
16798 W Bernardo Dr San Diego (92128) *(P-18810)*

**Solvari Corp** ................................................................. E ...... 909 509-8228
2060 S Haven Ave Ontario (91761) *(P-17685)*

**Solvay America Inc** ..................................................... C ...... 714 688-4403
1440 N Kraemer Blvd Anaheim (92806) *(P-5118)*

**Solvay America Inc** ..................................................... D ...... 225 361-3376
645 N Cypress St Orange (92867) *(P-5119)*

**Solvay America Inc** ..................................................... D ...... 562 906-3300
12801 Ann St Santa Fe Springs (90670) *(P-5120)*

**Solvay America LLC** ................................................... D ...... 713 525-4000
1191 N Hawk Cir Anaheim (92807) *(P-5121)*

**SOLVAY AMERICA, INC., Anaheim** *Also Called: Solvay America Inc (P-5118)*

**SOLVAY AMERICA, INC., Orange** *Also Called: Solvay America Inc (P-5119)*

**SOLVAY AMERICA, INC., Santa Fe Springs** *Also Called: Solvay America Inc (P-5120)*

**Solvay Chemicals Inc** ................................................. E ...... 714 744-5610
645 N Cypress St Orange (92867) *(P-5122)*

**Solvay Composite Materials, Anaheim** *Also Called: Cytec Engineered Materials Inc (P-7841)*

**Solvay Draka Inc (DH)** ................................................ C ...... 323 725-7010
6900 Elm St Commerce (90040) *(P-6571)*

**Solvay USA Inc** ............................................................ E ...... 805 591-3314
7305 Morro Rd Ste 200 Atascadero (93422) *(P-6159)*

**Somacis Inc** ................................................................. C ...... 858 513-2200
13500 Danielson St Poway (92064) *(P-12223)*

**Some Crust Bakery, Claremont** *Also Called: Feemster Co Inc (P-1192)*

**Somers Orear Stphan Stl Fbrcto, Santa Clara** *Also Called: SOS Steel Company Inc (P-535)*

**Sommer, Juliana Choy, San Francisco** *Also Called: Priority Archtctral Grphics In (P-16022)*

**Son of A Barista Usa LLC** .......................................... E ...... 323 788-8718
5125 Wheeler Ridge Rd Arvin (93203) *(P-2080)*

**Sonaca North America, Vista** *Also Called: Versaform Corporation (P-8608)*

**Sonance** ........................................................................ F ...... 949 492-7777
212 Avenida Fabricante San Clemente (92672) *(P-11698)*

**Sonance, San Clemente** *Also Called: Dana Innovations (P-11647)*

**Sondors Inc** .................................................................. E ...... 323 372-3000
2710 Yates Ave Commerce (90040) *(P-14070)*

**SONENDO, Laguna Hills** *Also Called: Sonendo Inc (P-15483)*

**Sonendo Inc (PA)** ........................................................ C ...... 949 766-3636
26061 Merit Cir Ste 102 Laguna Hills (92653) *(P-15483)*

**Sonendo Acquisition Corp** ......................................... E ...... 858 558-3696
6235 Lusk Blvd San Diego (92121) *(P-18811)*

**Sonfarrel** ....................................................................... E ...... 714 630-7280
3000 E La Jolla St Anaheim (92806) *(P-7034)*

**Sonfarrel Aerospace LLC** ........................................... D ...... 714 630-7280
3010 E La Jolla St Anaheim (92806) *(P-7849)*

**Songs Music Publishing LLC** .................................... F ...... 323 939-3511
7656 W Sunset Blvd Los Angeles (90046) *(P-4466)*

**Sonic Manufacturing Tech Inc** .................................. D ...... 510 580-8551
47931 Westinghouse Dr Fremont (94539) *(P-12224)*

**Sonic Manufacturing Tech Inc** .................................. D ...... 510 573-3065
44051 Nobel Dr Fremont (94538) *(P-12225)*

**Sonic Manufacturing Tech Inc (PA)** .......................... C ...... 510 580-8500
47951 Westinghouse Dr Fremont (94539) *(P-12226)*

**Sonic Vr, San Diego** *Also Called: Sonic Vr LLC (P-18812)*

**Sonic Vr LLC** ................................................................ F ...... 206 227-8585
225 Broadway Ste 650 San Diego (92101) *(P-18812)*

**Sonim Technologies Inc (PA)** .................................... E ...... 650 378-8100
4445 Eastgate Mall Ste 200 San Diego (92121) *(P-11786)*

**Sonix, Torrance** *Also Called: Lenntek Corporation (P-11882)*

**Soniya Valley LLC** ....................................................... F ...... 916 221-4313
1160 Tara Ct Ste A Rocklin (95765) *(P-16235)*

**Sonnet Technologies Inc** ........................................... E ...... 949 587-3500
25 Empire Dr Ste 200 Lake Forest (92630) *(P-13308)*

**Sonoco Industrial Products Div, City Of Industry** *Also Called: Sonoco Products Company (P-3807)*

**Sonoco Products Company** ....................................... D ...... 626 369-6611
166 Baldwin Park Blvd City Of Industry (91746) *(P-3807)*

**Sonoco Products Company** ....................................... D ...... 562 921-0881
12851 Leyva St Norwalk (90650) *(P-3808)*

**Sonoco Prtective Solutions Inc** ................................. D ...... 510 785-0220
3466 Enterprise Ave Hayward (94545) *(P-3887)*

**Sonoma County Winegrowers** ................................... E ...... 707 522-5860
3245 Guerneville Rd Santa Rosa (95401) *(P-1754)*

**Sonoma Foods, Santa Rosa** *Also Called: MS Intertrade Inc (P-2057)*

**Sonoma Gourmet Inc** .................................................. E ...... 707 939-3700
21684 8th St E Ste 100 Sonoma (95476) *(P-992)*

**Sonoma Magazine, Santa Rosa** *Also Called: Sonoma Media Investments LLC (P-4198)*

**Sonoma Media Investments LLC (PA)** ..................... D ...... 707 526-8563
416 B St Ste C Santa Rosa (95401) *(P-4198)*

**Sonoma Photonics Inc** ............................................. E ...... 707 568-1202
1750 Northpoint Pkwy Ste C Santa Rosa (95407) *(P-12859)*

**Sonoma Stainless Inc** ............................................. F ...... 707 546-3945
170 Todd Rd Santa Rosa (95407) *(P-8336)*

**Sonoma Wine Hardware Inc** ..................................... E ...... 650 866-3020
360 Swift Ave Ste 34 South San Francisco (94080) *(P-1755)*

**Sonoma-Cutrer Vineyards LLC (DH)** ........................... E ...... 707 528-1181
4401 Slusser Rd Windsor (95492) *(P-31)*

**Sonomay Wine, Graton** *Also Called: Purple Wine Production Company (P-1714)*

**Sonora Bakery Inc** ................................................. E ...... 323 269-2253
4484 Whittier Blvd Los Angeles (90022) *(P-17421)*

**Sonora Mills Foods Inc (PA)** .................................... C ...... 310 639-5333
3064 E Maria St E Rncho Dmngz (90221) *(P-2356)*

**Sonos, Goleta** *Also Called: Sonos Inc (P-11699)*

**Sonos Inc (PA)** ..................................................... D ...... 805 965-3001
301 Coromar Dr Goleta (93117) *(P-11699)*

**Sonova USA Inc** .................................................... D ...... 510 743-3900
47257 Fremont Blvd Fremont (94538) *(P-15406)*

**Sonsray Inc** ......................................................... E ...... 323 585-1271
23935 Madison St Torrance (90505) *(P-11118)*

**Sony Biotechnology Inc** .......................................... D ...... 800 275-5963
1730 N 1st St 2nd Fl San Jose (95112) *(P-18813)*

**Sony Broadcast Products, San Jose** *Also Called: Sony Electronics Inc (P-10437)*

**Sony Electronics Inc** .............................................. E ...... 408 352-4000
1730 N 1st St San Jose (95112) *(P-10437)*

**Sony Electronics Inc (DH)** ....................................... A ...... 858 942-2400
16535 Via Esprillo 1 San Diego (92127) *(P-11700)*

**Sony Electronics Inc** .............................................. C ...... 858 942-2400
16530 Via Esprillo San Diego (92127) *(P-11701)*

**Sony Media Cloud Services LLC** ................................ E ...... 877 683-9124
10202 Washington Blvd Culver City (90232) *(P-19297)*

**Sony Pictures Entrmt Inc** ........................................ E ...... 310 244-4000
10202 Washington Blvd Culver City (90232) *(P-15666)*

**Sony Pictures Mpic Group, Culver City** *Also Called: Sony Pictures Entrmt Inc (P-15666)*

**Sony Style, San Diego** *Also Called: Sony Electronics Inc (P-11701)*

**Soojians Inc** ........................................................ E ...... 559 875-5511
89 Academy Ave Sanger (93657) *(P-1283)*

**Sopact Inc** .......................................................... E ...... 510 226-8535
280 Chantecler Dr Fremont (94539) *(P-18814)*

**Sophie Buhai LLC** ................................................. F ...... 949 302-8762
2658 Griffith Park Blvd # 417 Los Angeles (90039) *(P-2584)*

**Soraa Inc (PA)** ..................................................... D ...... 510 456-2200
6500 Kaiser Dr Ste 110 Fremont (94555) *(P-12725)*

**Sorenson Engineering Inc (PA)** ................................. C ...... 909 795-2434
32032 Dunlap Blvd Yucaipa (92399) *(P-8731)*

**Sorma USA LLC** ................................................... B ...... 559 651-1269
231 S Kelsey St Visalia (93291) *(P-3980)*

**Sorrento Networks Corporation (HQ)** ......................... F ...... 510 577-1400
7195 Oakport St Oakland (94621) *(P-11787)*

**Sorrento Networks I Inc** ......................................... D ...... 303 803-9405
55 Almaden Blvd San Jose (95113) *(P-11788)*

**Sorrento Therapeutics Inc (PA)** ................................ D ...... 858 203-4100
4955 Directors Pl San Diego (92121) *(P-5861)*

**SOS Beauty Inc** .................................................... E ...... 424 285-1405
9100 Wilshire Blvd Ste 500w Beverly Hills (90212) *(P-17049)*

**SOS Steel Company Inc** .......................................... E ...... 408 727-6363
1160 Richard Ave Santa Clara (95050) *(P-535)*

**Sota Extracts Inc** .................................................. F ...... 612 889-4049
468 Yolanda Ave Ste 203 Santa Rosa (95404) *(P-16236)*

**Sotec USA LLC** .................................................... F ...... 909 525-5861
3076 S Edenglen Ave Ontario (91761) *(P-9451)*

**Sotera Wireless Inc** ............................................... C ...... 858 427-4620
5841 Edison Pl Ste 140 Carlsbad (92008) *(P-15580)*

**Sound Agriculture Company** ..................................... E ...... 512 650-8290
6401 Hollis St Ste 100 Emeryville (94608) *(P-5862)*

**Sound Image, Escondido** *Also Called: Cal Southern Sound Image Inc (P-16693)*

**Sound Investment Group** ........................................ F ...... 714 515-4001
16402 Gothard St Ste E Huntington Beach (92647) *(P-16401)*

**Sound Seal Inc** ..................................................... E ...... 760 806-6400
4675 North Ave Oceanside (92056) *(P-7582)*

**Sound United, Carlsbad** *Also Called: Dei Headquarters Inc (P-11990)*

**Soundboks Inc** ..................................................... F ...... 310 774-0480
1968 S Coast Hwy Pmb 2510 Laguna Beach (92651) *(P-17863)*

**Soundcoat Company Inc** ......................................... D ...... 631 242-2200
16901 Armstrong Ave Irvine (92606) *(P-11349)*

**Soundcraft Inc** ..................................................... E ...... 818 882-0020
20301 Nordhoff St Chatsworth (91311) *(P-13309)*

**SOUNDHOUND, Santa Clara** *Also Called: Soundhound Ai Inc (P-18815)*

**Soundhound Ai Inc (PA)** ......................................... F ...... 408 441-3200
5400 Betsy Ross Dr Santa Clara (95054) *(P-18815)*

**SOUNDTHINKING, Fremont** *Also Called: Soundthinking Inc (P-18816)*

**Soundthinking Inc (PA)** .......................................... B ...... 510 794-3100
39300 Civic Center Dr Ste 300 Fremont (94538) *(P-18816)*

**Soup Bases Loaded Inc** .......................................... E ...... 909 230-6890
2355 E Francis St Ontario (91761) *(P-2357)*

**Source Code LLC** .................................................. E ...... 562 903-1500
9808 Alburtis Ave Santa Fe Springs (90670) *(P-10205)*

**Source It USA Inc** ................................................. E ...... 714 318-4428
1150 S Olive St Los Angeles (90015) *(P-18993)*

**Source One Cable Technology Inc** .............................. D ...... 408 376-3400
6680 Via Del Oro San Jose (95119) *(P-13088)*

**Source One Technologies, San Jose** *Also Called: Source One Cable Technology Inc (P-13088)*

**Source Photonics Usa Inc (PA)** ................................. C ...... 818 773-9044
8521 Fallbrook Ave Ste 200 West Hills (91304) *(P-12726)*

**Source Photonics Usa Inc** ....................................... F ...... 818 407-5007
8917 Fullbright Ave Chatsworth (91311) *(P-12727)*

**Source Scientific LLC** ............................................ E ...... 949 231-5096
2144 Michelson Dr Irvine (92612) *(P-15260)*

**Souriau Usa Inc (DH)** ............................................ E ...... 805 238-2840
1740 Commerce Way Paso Robles (93446) *(P-11470)*

**South Bay Diversfd Systems Inc** ................................ F ...... 510 784-3094
1841 National Ave Hayward (94545) *(P-8575)*

**South Bay Foundry Inc (HQ)** ................................... E ...... 909 383-1823
895 Inland Center Dr San Bernardino (92408) *(P-8220)*

**South Bay International Inc** ..................................... E ...... 909 718-5000
8570 Hickory Ave Rancho Cucamonga (91739) *(P-3540)*

**South Bay Marble Inc** ............................................ F ...... 650 592-7416
797 Industrial Rd San Carlos (94070) *(P-7547)*

**South Bay Salt Works, Chula Vista** *Also Called: Ggtw LLC (P-6289)*

**South Bay Showers Inc** .......................................... E ...... 408 988-3484
540 Martin Ave Santa Clara (95050) *(P-542)*

**South Bay Solutions Inc (PA)** ................................... E ...... 650 843-1800
37399 Centralmont Pl Fremont (94536) *(P-11119)*

**South Bay Welding, El Cajon** *Also Called: M W Reid Welding Inc (P-8173)*

**South Bay Wire & Cable Co LLC (PA)** ......................... D ...... 951 659-2183
54125 Maranatha Dr Idyllwild (92549) *(P-7651)*

**South Coast Baking LLC (PA)** ................................... D ...... 949 851-9654
1711 Kettering Irvine (92614) *(P-1284)*

**South Coast Baking Co., Irvine** *Also Called: South Coast Baking LLC (P-1284)*

**South Coast Circuits LLC** ........................................ D ...... 714 966-2108
3506 W Lake Center Dr Ste A Santa Ana (92704) *(P-12227)*

**South Coast Iron, Placentia** *Also Called: Ironwood Fabrication Inc (P-8778)*

**South Coast Materials Co, San Diego** *Also Called: Forterra Pipe & Precast LLC (P-7336)*

**South Coast Screen and Casing** ................................ F ...... 310 632-3200
19112 S Santa Fe Ave Compton (90221) *(P-9467)*

**South Coast Stairs Inc** ........................................... E ...... 949 858-1685
30251 Tomas Rcho Sta Marg (92688) *(P-3193)*

**South Coast Water, Santa Ana** *Also Called: Hannah Industries Inc (P-10563)*

**South Coast Winery Inc** .......................................... E ...... 951 587-9463
34843 Rancho California Rd Temecula (92591) *(P-1756)*

**South Coast Winery Resort Spa, Temecula** *Also Called: South Coast Winery Inc (P-1756)*

**South Cone Inc** .................................................... C ...... 760 431-2300
5935 Darwin Ct Carlsbad (92008) *(P-17111)*

**South Gate Brewing Company** .................................. E ...... 559 692-2739
40233 Enterprise Dr Oakhurst (93644) *(P-10602)*

**South Gate Engineering LLC** .................................... C ...... 909 628-2779
13477 Yorba Ave Chino (91710) *(P-8337)*

**South Skyline Firefighters** ....................................... F ...... 408 354-0025
12900 Skyline Blvd Los Gatos (95033) *(P-10115)*

**South Skyline Vlntr Fire Rscue, Los Gatos** *Also Called: South Skyline Firefighters (P-10115)*

## ALPHABETIC SECTION — Spansion LLC

**South Valley Materials Inc** .......................................... F ..... 559 594-4142
1132 N Belmont Rd Exeter (93221) *(P-7498)*

**South Valley Materials Inc (HQ)** .................................. D ..... 559 277-7060
114 E Shaw Ave Ste 100 Fresno (93710) *(P-7499)*

**South Valley Materials Inc** .......................................... F ..... 559 582-0532
7761 Hanford Armona Rd Hanford (93230) *(P-7500)*

**South West Lubricants Inc** .......................................... D ..... 619 449-5000
9266 Abraham Way Santee (92071) *(P-6400)*

**Southcoast Cabinet Inc (PA)** ....................................... E ..... 909 594-3089
755 Pinefalls Ave Walnut (91789) *(P-3270)*

**Southcoast Welding & Mfg LLC** ................................... B ..... 619 429-1337
2591 Faivre St Ste 1 Chula Vista (91911) *(P-19214)*

**Southeast Kern Weekender, Tehachapi** *Also Called: Tehachapi News Inc (P-4207)*

**Southern Alum Finshg Co Inc** ..................................... D ..... 530 244-7518
4356 Caterpillar Rd Redding (96003) *(P-7761)*

**Southern Cal Disc Tire Co Inc** ..................................... C ..... 760 634-2202
107 N El Camino Real Encinitas (92024) *(P-17464)*

**Southern Cal Hydrlic Engrg Cor** .................................. E ..... 714 257-4800
1130 Columbia St Brea (92821) *(P-16843)*

**Southern Cal Tchnical Arts Inc** .................................... E ..... 714 524-2626
370 E Crowther Ave Placentia (92870) *(P-11120)*

**Southern Cal Trck Bdies Sls In** .................................... F ..... 909 469-1132
1131 E 2nd St Pomona (91766) *(P-13429)*

**Southern California Plas Inc** ....................................... D ..... 714 751-7084
3122 Maple St Santa Ana (92707) *(P-7035)*

**Southern California Plating Co** ................................... E ..... 619 231-1481
3261 National Ave San Diego (92113) *(P-9015)*

**Southern California Trane, Brea** *Also Called: Trane US Inc (P-10521)*

**Southern Electronics, Pomona** *Also Called: Electrocube Inc (P-12969)*

**Southerncarlson Inc** .................................................... F ..... 916 375-8322
801 Striker Ave Sacramento (95834) *(P-16484)*

**Southland Box Company** ........................................... C ..... 323 583-2231
4201 Fruitland Ave Vernon (90058) *(P-3888)*

**Southland Container Corp** ......................................... C ..... 909 937-9781
1600 Champagne Ave Ontario (91761) *(P-3889)*

**Southland Envelope LLC** ........................................... C ..... 619 449-3553
8830 Siempre Viva Rd San Diego (92154) *(P-4012)*

**Southland Paving Inc** ................................................. D ..... 760 747-6895
361 N Hale Ave Escondido (92029) *(P-525)*

**Southland Polymers Inc** ............................................. E ..... 562 921-0444
14030 Gannet St Santa Fe Springs (90670) *(P-5202)*

**Southland Ready Mix Concrete, Escondido** *Also Called: Superior Ready Mix Concrete LP (P-7510)*

**Southland Technology Inc** ......................................... D ..... 858 694-0932
8053 Vickers St San Diego (92111) *(P-16550)*

**Southland Tool Mfg Inc** .............................................. F ..... 714 632-8198
1430 N Hundley St Anaheim (92806) *(P-9698)*

**Southwest Boulder & Stone Inc (PA)** ........................... E ..... 760 451-3333
5002 2nd St Fallbrook (92028) *(P-17723)*

**Southwest Concrete Products** ................................... E ..... 909 983-9789
519 S Benson Ave Ontario (91762) *(P-7392)*

**Southwest Contractors (PA)** ...................................... E ..... 661 588-0484
136 Allen Rd # 100 Bakersfield (93314) *(P-389)*

**Southwest Data Products, San Bernardino** *Also Called: Innovative Metal Inds Inc (P-8699)*

**Southwest Greene Intl Inc** ......................................... D ..... 760 639-4960
4055b Calle Platino Oceanside (92056) *(P-8889)*

**Southwest Hide Co** .................................................... E ..... 209 382-5633
925 Crows Landing Rd Modesto (95351) *(P-17223)*

**Southwest Hide Co, Modesto** *Also Called: Southwest Hide Co (P-17223)*

**Southwest Journal Inc** ............................................... F ..... 612 825-9205
3727 Burnside Rd Sebastopol (95472) *(P-4199)*

**Southwest Machine & Plastic Co** ............................... E ..... 626 963-6919
620 W Foothill Blvd Glendora (91741) *(P-13958)*

**Southwest Manufacturing Svcs, El Cajon** *Also Called: Pacific Marine Sheet Metal Corporation (P-8528)*

**Southwest Offset Prtg Co Inc (PA)** .............................. B ..... 310 965-9154
13650 Gramercy Pl Gardena (90249) *(P-4766)*

**Southwest Plastics Co, Glendora** *Also Called: Southwest Machine & Plastic Co (P-13958)*

**Southwest Products Corporation** ............................... F ..... 360 887-7400
2875 Cherry Ave Signal Hill (90755) *(P-9330)*

**Southwest Products Corporation** ............................... E ..... 209 745-6000
85 Enterprise Ct Ste B Galt (95632) *(P-9331)*

**Southwest Products LLC** ............................................ C ..... 619 263-8000
8411 Siempre Viva Rd San Diego (92154) *(P-2358)*

**Southwest Sign Company, Corona** *Also Called: Fovell Enterprises Inc (P-15979)*

**Southwest Sign Systems, El Centro** *Also Called: Western Electrical Advg Co (P-16066)*

**Southwestern Industries Inc (PA)** ............................... D ..... 310 608-4422
2615 Homestead Pl Rancho Dominguez (90220) *(P-9572)*

**Southwestern Wire Inc** ............................................... F ..... 916 333-5289
4318 Dudley Blvd Mcclellan (95652) *(P-7652)*

**Southwind Foods LLC (PA)** ........................................ C ..... 323 262-8222
20644 S Fordyce Ave Carson (90810) *(P-2043)*

**Southwire Company LLC** ........................................... D ..... 909 989-2888
9199 Cleveland Ave Ste 100 Rancho Cucamonga (91730) *(P-7731)*

**Southwire Inc** ............................................................ B ..... 310 886-8300
20250 S Alameda St Compton (90221) *(P-7732)*

**Southwire Inc (HQ)** .................................................... F ..... 310 884-8500
11695 Pacific Ave Fontana (92337) *(P-7733)*

**Soxnet Inc** ................................................................. F ..... 626 934-9400
235 S 6th Ave La Puente (91746) *(P-2460)*

**Soy Sauce Productions LLC** ....................................... F ..... 818 213-1092
30700 Russell Ranch Rd Ste 250 Westlake Village (91362) *(P-993)*

**Soyfoods of America** ................................................. E ..... 626 358-3836
1091 Hamilton Rd Duarte (91010) *(P-2359)*

**Sp, City Of Industry** *Also Called: Scope Packaging Inc (P-3886)*

**Sp Controls Inc** ......................................................... F ..... 650 392-7880
930 Linden Ave South San Francisco (94080) *(P-10438)*

**Sp Craftech I LLC** ...................................................... E ..... 714 630-8117
2941 E La Jolla St Anaheim (92806) *(P-7036)*

**Sp Crankshaft, Irvine** *Also Called: Pankl Engine Systems Inc (P-13554)*

**Spa De Soleil Inc** ....................................................... E ..... 818 504-3200
10443 Arminta St Sun Valley (91352) *(P-17050)*

**Space Components, Commerce** *Also Called: Atk Space Systems LLC (P-14155)*

**Space Components Division, San Diego** *Also Called: Atk Space Systems LLC (P-14156)*

**Space Exploration Tech Corp** ..................................... C ..... 310 848-4410
731 Kelp Rd Slc-4 Vandenberg Afb (93437) *(P-13692)*

**Space Exploration Tech Corp** ..................................... C ..... 310 363-6289
2980 Nimitz Rd Long Beach (90802) *(P-14086)*

**Space Exploration Tech Corp** ..................................... C ..... 714 330-8668
2700 Miner St San Pedro (90731) *(P-14087)*

**Space Exploration Tech Corp** ..................................... C ..... 323 754-1285
12520 Wilkie Ave Gardena (90249) *(P-14088)*

**Space Exploration Tech Corp** ..................................... C ..... 310 889-4968
3976 Jack Northrop Ave Hawthorne (90250) *(P-14089)*

**Space Exploration Tech Corp (PA)** .............................. B ..... 310 363-6000
1 Rocket Rd Hawthorne (90250) *(P-14090)*

**Space Micro Inc** ........................................................ C ..... 858 332-0700
15378 Avenue Of Science Ste 200 San Diego (92128) *(P-11949)*

**Space Systems Division, El Segundo** *Also Called: Orbital Sciences LLC (P-14273)*

**Space Time Insight Inc** .............................................. E ..... 650 513-8550
1850 Gateway Dr Ste 125 San Mateo (94404) *(P-18817)*

**Space Vector Corporation** ......................................... E ..... 818 734-2600
20520 Nordhoff St Chatsworth (91311) *(P-14309)*

**Space-Lok Inc** ........................................................... C ..... 310 527-6150
13306 Halldale Ave Gardena (90249) *(P-13959)*

**Spaceship Company, The, Tustin** *Also Called: Galactic Co LLC (P-14080)*

**Spacesonics Incorporated** ......................................... D ..... 650 610-0999
30300 Union City Blvd Union City (94587) *(P-8576)*

**Spacestor Inc** ............................................................ E ..... 310 410-0220
16411 Carmenita Rd Cerritos (90703) *(P-3587)*

**Spacex, Long Beach** *Also Called: Space Exploration Tech Corp (P-14086)*

**Spacex, San Pedro** *Also Called: Space Exploration Tech Corp (P-14087)*

**Spacex, Hawthorne** *Also Called: Space Exploration Tech Corp (P-14089)*

**Spacex, Hawthorne** *Also Called: Space Exploration Tech Corp (P-14090)*

**Spacex LLC** ................................................................ A ..... 310 970-5845
12533 Crenshaw Blvd Hawthorne (90250) *(P-14091)*

**Spacex Wilkie, Gardena** *Also Called: Space Exploration Tech Corp (P-14088)*

**Span-O-Matic Inc** ....................................................... E ..... 714 256-4700
825 Columbia St Brea (92821) *(P-8577)*

**Spangler Industries Inc** ............................................. C ..... 951 735-5000
1711 N Delilah St Corona (92879) *(P-6539)*

**Spansion LLC (DH)** .................................................... C ..... 512 691-8500
198 Champion Ct San Jose (95134) *(P-12728)*

---

Employee Codes: A=Over 500 employees, B=251-500
C=101-250, D=51-100, E=20-50, F=10-19, G=1-9

Spar Sausage Co ALPHABETIC SECTION

**Spar Sausage Co** ........ F ...... 510 614-8100
688 Williams St San Leandro (94577) ***(P-668)***

**Sparitual, Van Nuys** *Also Called: Orly International Inc* ***(P-6014)***

**Sparkcentral Inc (HQ)** ........ **D ...... 866 559-6229**
535 Mission St Fl 14 San Francisco (94105) ***(P-4467)***

**Sparkcognition Inc (PA)** ........ **D ...... 844 205-7173**
7901 Stoneridge Dr Ste 555 Pleasanton (94588) ***(P-18818)***

**Sparkletts Water, Los Angeles** *Also Called: Ds Services of America Inc* ***(P-1887)***

**Sparks Exhbits Envrnments Corp** ........ E ...... 562 941-0101
3143 S La Cienega Blvd Los Angeles (90016) ***(P-16237)***

**Sparks Los Angeles, Los Angeles** *Also Called: Sparks Exhbits Envrnments Corp* ***(P-16237)***

**Sparktech Software LLC** ........ E ...... 818 330-9098
1419 Beaudry Blvd Glendale (91208) ***(P-18819)***

**Sparling Instruments LLC** ........ E ...... 626 444-0571
4097 Temple City Blvd El Monte (91731) ***(P-14483)***

**Sparqtron Corporation** ........ D ...... 510 657-7198
5079 Brandin Ct Fremont (94538) ***(P-12228)***

**Spartan Inc** ........ D ...... 661 327-1205
3030 M St Bakersfield (93301) ***(P-8221)***

**Spartan Manufacturing Co** ........ E ...... 714 894-1955
7081 Patterson Dr Garden Grove (92841) ***(P-11121)***

**Spartan Truck Company Inc** ........ E ...... 818 899-1111
12266 Branford St Sun Valley (91352) ***(P-13430)***

**Spartech Plastics, La Mirada** *Also Called: Alchem Plastics Inc* ***(P-6581)***

**Spates Fabricators, Thermal** *Also Called: Spates Fabricators Inc* ***(P-3318)***

**Spates Fabricators Inc** ........ D ...... 760 397-4122
85435 Middleton St Thermal (92274) ***(P-3318)***

**Spatial Labs Inc** ........ E ...... 424 289-0275
12555 W Jefferson Blvd Ste 220 Los Angeles (90066) ***(P-18820)***

**Spatz Corporation** ........ C ...... 805 487-2122
1600 Westar Dr Oxnard (93033) ***(P-6040)***

**Spatz Laboratories, Oxnard** *Also Called: Spatz Corporation* ***(P-6040)***

**Spaulding Crusher Parts, Perris** *Also Called: Spaulding Equipment Company* ***(P-9452)***

**Spaulding Equipment Company (PA)** ........ **E ...... 951 943-4531**
75 Paseo Adelanto Perris (92570) ***(P-9452)***

**SPD Manufacturing Inc** ........ F ...... 985 302-1902
1101 E Truslow Ave Fullerton (92831) ***(P-2442)***

**Speakeasy Ales & Lagers Inc** ........ E ...... 415 642-3371
1195 Evans Ave San Francisco (94124) ***(P-1459)***

**Speakeasy Tech Inc** ........ F ...... 650 581-9701
525 Brannan St Ste 100 San Francisco (94107) ***(P-18821)***

**Speakercraft LLC** ........ D ...... 951 685-1759
12471 Riverside Dr Mira Loma (91752) ***(P-11702)***

**Spearman Aerospace Inc** ........ E ...... 714 523-4751
9215 Greenleaf Ave Santa Fe Springs (90670) ***(P-19422)***

**Spears Manufacturing Co** ........ E ...... 818 364-1611
15860 Olden St Rancho Cascades (91342) ***(P-6602)***

**Spears Manufacturing Co (PA)** ........ **C ...... 818 364-1611**
15853 Olden St Rancho Cascades (91342) ***(P-16801)***

**Spec, Valencia** *Also Called: Semiconductor Process Eqp LLC* ***(P-12691)***

**Spec Engineering Company Inc** ........ E ...... 818 780-3045
13754 Saticoy St Panorama City (91402) ***(P-11122)***

**Spec Formliners Inc** ........ E ...... 714 429-9500
1038 E 4th St Santa Ana (92701) ***(P-7393)***

**Spec Tool Company** ........ E ...... 323 723-9533
11805 Wakeman St Santa Fe Springs (90670) ***(P-13960)***

**Spec-Built Systems Inc** ........ D ...... 619 661-8100
2150 Michael Faraday Dr San Diego (92154) ***(P-8578)***

**Special Devices Incorporated** ........ A ...... 805 387-1000
2655 1st St Ste 125 Simi Valley (93065) ***(P-13577)***

**Special Event Audio Svcs Inc** ........ E ...... 800 518-9144
35889 Shetland Hls E Fallbrook (92028) ***(P-19306)***

**Special Operations Tech, Carson** *Also Called: SO Tech/Spcl Op Tech Inc* ***(P-17069)***

**Special Products Group, Chula Vista** *Also Called: Sealed Air Corporation* ***(P-6661)***

**Specialist Media Group, Carlsbad** *Also Called: L & L Printers Carlsbad LLC* ***(P-4667)***

**Specialists In Cstm Sftwr Inc** ........ E ...... 310 315-9660
2574 Wellesley Ave Los Angeles (90064) ***(P-18822)***

**Speciality Labs, Fullerton** *Also Called: Magtech & Power Conversion Inc* ***(P-12845)***

**Specialized Coating Services, Fremont** *Also Called: Specialized Coating Svcs LLC* ***(P-9122)***

**Specialized Coating Svcs LLC (HQ)** ........ **E ...... 510 226-8700**
42680 Christy St Fremont (94538) ***(P-9122)***

**Specialized Dairy Service Inc** ........ E ...... 909 923-3420
1710 E Philadelphia St Ontario (91761) ***(P-9382)***

**Specialized Milling Corp** ........ E ...... 909 357-7890
10330 Elm Ave Fontana (92337) ***(P-6114)***

**Specialty Baking Inc** ........ D ...... 408 298-6950
3134 Capelaw Ct San Jose (95135) ***(P-17215)***

**Specialty Baking Co., San Jose** *Also Called: Specialty Baking Inc* ***(P-17215)***

**Specialty Brands Incorporated** ........ A ...... 909 477-4851
4200 Concours Ste 100 Ontario (91764) ***(P-1047)***

**Specialty Coating Systems Inc** ........ D ...... 909 390-8818
4435 E Airport Dr Ste 100 Ontario (91761) ***(P-9123)***

**Specialty Division, Santa Fe Springs** *Also Called: Distinctive Industries* ***(P-3005)***

**Specialty Enterprises Co** ........ D ...... 323 726-9721
6858 E Acco St Commerce (90040) ***(P-6663)***

**Specialty Fabrications Inc** ........ E ...... 805 579-9730
2674 Westhills Ct Simi Valley (93065) ***(P-8579)***

**Specialty Finishes, Fontana** *Also Called: Specialized Milling Corp* ***(P-6114)***

**Specialty Granules LLC** ........ E ...... 209 274-5323
1900 State Hwy 104 Ione (95640) ***(P-7572)***

**Specialty Hose Xpress, Hilmar** *Also Called: Specialty Hose Xpress LLC* ***(P-6430)***

**Specialty Hose Xpress LLC** ........ E ...... 209 226-1031
7515 Lander Ave Hilmar (95324) ***(P-6430)***

**Specialty Interior Mfg Inc** ........ E ...... 714 296-8618
16751 Millikan Ave Irvine (92606) ***(P-16402)***

**Specialty Minerals Inc** ........ C ...... 760 248-5300
6565 Meridian Rd Lucerne Valley (92356) ***(P-5123)***

**Specialty Motions Inc** ........ E ...... 951 735-8722
5480 Smokey Mountain Way Yorba Linda (92887) ***(P-9955)***

**Specialty Motors, Valencia** *Also Called: SMI Holdings Inc* ***(P-11288)***

**Specialty Paper Mills Inc** ........ C ...... 562 692-8737
8844 Millergrove Dr Santa Fe Springs (90670) ***(P-3798)***

**Specialty Sales LLC** ........ D ...... 559 862-6611
4672 E Drummond Ave Fresno (93725) ***(P-17051)***

**Specialty Steel Service, Stockton** *Also Called: PDM Steel Service Centers Inc* ***(P-16629)***

**Specialty Tools Inc** ........ F ...... 818 827-8138
11912 Sheldon St Sun Valley (91352) ***(P-7037)***

**Specialty Truck Parts Inc (PA)** ........ **E ...... 408 998-7272**
7700 Arroyo Cir Gilroy (95020) ***(P-17465)***

**Specific Diagnostics Inc** ........ D ...... 650 938-6800
130 Baytech Dr San Jose (95134) ***(P-15261)***

**Specilized Packg Solutions Inc (PA)** ........ **D ...... 510 494-5670**
38505 Cherry St Ste H Newark (94560) ***(P-3375)***

**Specilty Enzymes Btechnologies** ........ F ...... 909 613-1660
13591 Yorba Ave Chino (91710) ***(P-6160)***

**Specilty Enzymes Btechnologies, Chino** *Also Called: Cal-India Foods International* ***(P-6136)***

**Specilty Mtals Fabrication Inc** ........ F ...... 619 937-6100
11222 Woodside Ave N Santee (92071) ***(P-2531)***

**Specilzed Packg Solutions-Wood, Newark** *Also Called: Specilized Packg Solutions Inc* ***(P-3375)***

**Speck Products, San Mateo** *Also Called: Speculative Product Design LLC* ***(P-7141)***

**Spectra Apparel, Chino** *Also Called: Rrz Enterprises Inc* ***(P-17079)***

**Spectra Color Inc** ........ E ...... 951 277-0200
9116 Stellar Ct Corona (92883) ***(P-5065)***

**Spectra USA, Chino** *Also Called: Isiqalo LLC* ***(P-2474)***

**Spectra Watermakers, Petaluma** *Also Called: Katadyn Desalination LLC* ***(P-11407)***

**Spectra-Physics Inc (DH)** ........ **D ...... 877 835-9620**
1565 Barber Ln Milpitas (95035) ***(P-13310)***

**Spectra-Physics Laser Div, Santa Clara** *Also Called: Newport Corporation* ***(P-13277)***

**Spectral Dynamics, San Jose** *Also Called: Spectral Dynamics Inc* ***(P-14924)***

**Spectral Dynamics Inc (PA)** ........ **E ...... 760 761-0440**
2199 Zanker Rd San Jose (95131) ***(P-14924)***

**Spectral Labs, San Diego** *Also Called: Spectral Labs Incorporated* ***(P-14925)***

**Spectral Labs Incorporated** ........ E ...... 858 451-0540
15920 Bernardo Center Dr San Diego (92127) ***(P-14925)***

**Spectrolab Inc** ........ B ...... 818 365-4611
12500 Gladstone Ave Sylmar (91342) ***(P-13089)***

**Spectron LLC (PA)** ........ **E ...... 805 642-0400**
2291 Portola Rd Ste A Ventura (93003) ***(P-14721)***

**Spectrum Assembly Inc** ........ C ...... 760 930-4000
6300 Yarrow Dr Ste 100 Carlsbad (92011) ***(P-12229)***

## ALPHABETIC SECTION — Spp Process Technology Systems

**Spectrum Bags, Cerritos** *Also Called: Ips Industries Inc (P-6866)*
**Spectrum Brands Hdwr HM Imprv, Foothill Ranch** *Also Called: Kwikset Corporation (P-8009)*
**Spectrum Electronics, Carlsbad** *Also Called: Spectrum Assembly Inc (P-12229)*
**Spectrum Inc** .................................................. C ...... 310 885-4600
  18617 S Broadwick St Rancho Dominguez (90220) *(P-15262)*
**Spectrum Intl Holdings** .................................... A ...... 626 333-7225
  14421 Bonelli St City Of Industry (91746) *(P-3708)*
**Spectrum Lab & Phrm Pdts, Gardena** *Also Called: Spectrum Laboratory Pdts Inc (P-17249)*
**Spectrum Label, Newark** *Also Called: Resource Label Group LLC (P-4951)*
**Spectrum Label Corporation** ........................... E ...... 510 477-9374
  30803 San Clemente St Hayward (94544) *(P-4962)*
**Spectrum Laboratories, Rancho Dominguez** *Also Called: Spectrum Inc (P-15262)*
**Spectrum Laboratory Pdts Inc** .......................... E ...... 520 292-3103
  14422 S San Pedro St Gardena (90248) *(P-17249)*
**Spectrum Lighting, Santa Fe Springs** *Also Called: Dab Inc (P-11493)*
**Spectrum Lithograph Inc** .................................. E ...... 510 438-9192
  4300 Business Center Dr Fremont (94538) *(P-4767)*
**Spectrum Naturals, Petaluma** *Also Called: Spectrum Organic Products LLC (P-1406)*
**Spectrum Organic Products LLC** ..................... E ...... 888 343-6637
  2201 S Mcdowell Boulevard Ext Petaluma (94954) *(P-1406)*
**Spectrum Plating Company, Los Angeles** *Also Called: Ravlich Enterprises LLC (P-9003)*
**Spectrum Prsthtcs/Rthtics Rddi** ....................... E ...... 530 243-4500
  1844 South St Redding (96001) *(P-15407)*
**Spectrum Scientific Inc** .................................... E ...... 949 260-9900
  16692 Hale Ave Ste A Irvine (92606) *(P-14825)*
**Spectrum Systems SF** ..................................... E ...... 415 361-2429
  1331 Old County Rd Belmont (94002) *(P-11502)*
**Speculative Product Design LLC (HQ)** ........... E ...... 650 462-2040
  400 S El Camino Real Ste 1200 San Mateo (94402) *(P-7141)*
**Speed Society LLC** .......................................... F ...... 760 402-6838
  4122 Sorrento Valley Blvd Ste 104 San Diego (92121) *(P-4468)*
**Speed Ventures** ................................................ E ...... 323 461-4795
  901 N Fairfax Ave # 207 West Hollywood (90046) *(P-11482)*
**Speedo USA, Cypress** *Also Called: Speedo USA Inc (P-2639)*
**Speedo USA Inc** ............................................... B ...... 657 465-3800
  6251 Katella Ave Cypress (90630) *(P-2639)*
**Speedpress Sign Supply, Carlsbad** *Also Called: Coplan & Coplan Inc (P-9669)*
**Speedpro East Bay, Alameda** *Also Called: Ericson Owens Enterprises (P-15971)*
**Speedway Copy Systems Inc** .......................... E ...... 415 495-4330
  275 E L St Benicia (94510) *(P-17816)*
**Speedway Digital Printing, Benicia** *Also Called: Speedway Copy Systems Inc (P-17816)*
**Speedy Circuits, Huntington Beach** *Also Called: Coast To Coast Circuits Inc (P-12080)*
**Speedy Circuits, Anaheim** *Also Called: Excello Circuits Inc (P-12096)*
**Spencer Forrest Inc** ......................................... E
  11777 San Vicente Blvd Ste 650 Los Angeles (90049) *(P-17675)*
**Spenuzza Inc (HQ)** .......................................... D ...... 951 281-1830
  1128 Sherborn St Corona (92879) *(P-10603)*
**SPEP Acquisition Corp (PA)** ........................... D ...... 310 608-0693
  4041 Via Oro Ave Long Beach (90810) *(P-8028)*
**Sphere Alliance Inc** ......................................... E ...... 951 352-2400
  3087 12th St Riverside (92507) *(P-5203)*
**SPI Energy Co Ltd** ........................................... B ...... 408 919-8000
  4803 Urbani Ave Mcclellan (95652) *(P-12729)*
**SPI Solar Inc (PA)** ........................................... B ...... 408 919-8000
  4803 Urbani Ave Mcclellan (95652) *(P-8082)*
**Spicy Chix Inc** .................................................. F ...... 562 293-7690
  1753 E 21st St Los Angeles (90058) *(P-2835)*
**Spidell Publishing Inc** ...................................... E ...... 714 776-7850
  1134 N Gilbert St Anaheim (92801) *(P-4469)*
**Spikes Inc (PA)** ................................................ E ...... 855 287-7453
  4000 Executive Pkwy Ste 250 San Ramon (94583) *(P-18823)*
**Spikes Security, San Ramon** *Also Called: Spikes Inc (P-18823)*
**Spill Magic Inc** ................................................. E ...... 714 557-2001
  630 Young St Santa Ana (92705) *(P-3799)*
**Spin Products Inc** ............................................ E ...... 909 590-7000
  13878 Yorba Ave Chino (91710) *(P-7038)*
**Spinal Elements, Carlsbad** *Also Called: Spinal Elements Holdings Inc (P-15263)*
**Spinal Elements Holdings Inc** .......................... C ...... 877 774-6255
  3115 Melrose Dr Ste 200 Carlsbad (92010) *(P-15263)*

**Spine View Inc** .................................................. D ...... 510 490-1753
  110 Pioneer Way Ste A Mountain View (94041) *(P-15264)*
**Spinergy Inc** ..................................................... D ...... 760 496-2121
  1709 La Costa Meadows Dr San Marcos (92078) *(P-14071)*
**Spinlaunch Inc** ................................................. C ...... 650 516-7746
  3816 Stineman Ct Long Beach (90808) *(P-14106)*
**Spintek Filtration Inc** ........................................ F ...... 714 236-9190
  10863 Portal Dr Los Alamitos (90720) *(P-10116)*
**Spira Manufacturing Corp** ................................ E ...... 818 764-8222
  650 Jessie St San Fernando (91340) *(P-6468)*
**Spiracur Inc** ...................................................... D ...... 650 364-1544
  1180 Bordeaux Dr Sunnyvale (94089) *(P-15265)*
**Spiral Ppr Tube & Core Co Inc** ........................ E ...... 562 801-9705
  5200 Industry Ave Pico Rivera (90660) *(P-3910)*
**Spiratec Solutions Inc** ...................................... F ...... 925 357-1103
  190 S Orchard Ave Ste B220 Vacaville (95688) *(P-13578)*
**Spire Manufacturing Inc** ................................... E ...... 510 226-1070
  2526 Qume Dr Ste 18 San Jose (95131) *(P-11471)*
**Spirent Calabasas, Calabasas** *Also Called: Spirent Communications Inc (P-16551)*
**Spirent Communications Inc** ............................ C ...... 408 752-7100
  2350 Mission College Blvd Santa Clara (95054) *(P-11950)*
**Spirent Communications Inc (HQ)** .................. B ...... 818 676-2300
  27349 Agoura Rd Calabasas (91301) *(P-16551)*
**Spirit Active Wear, Los Angeles** *Also Called: Spirit Clothing Company (P-2641)*
**Spirit Clothing Company** ................................. D ...... 213 784-5372
  2137 E 37th St Vernon (90058) *(P-2640)*
**Spirit Clothing Company (PA)** ......................... C ...... 213 784-0251
  2211 E 37th St Los Angeles (90058) *(P-2641)*
**Spitzlift, San Diego** *Also Called: Hirok Inc (P-9427)*
**Splits 59 LLC** ................................................... F ...... 310 827-5200
  527 Colyton St Los Angeles (90013) *(P-2809)*
**Splunk, San Francisco** *Also Called: Splunk Inc (P-18824)*
**Splunk Inc (HQ)** ............................................... C ...... 415 848-8400
  270 Brannan St San Francisco (94107) *(P-18824)*
**Spm, Anaheim** *Also Called: Bace Manufacturing Inc (P-6732)*
**Spooners Woodworks, Poway** *Also Called: Spooners Woodworks Inc (P-3671)*
**Spooners Woodworks Inc** ............................... C ...... 858 679-9086
  12460 Kirkham Ct Poway (92064) *(P-3671)*
**Sport Boat Trailers** .......................................... F ...... 209 892-5388
  430 C St Patterson (95363) *(P-14133)*
**Sport Card Co LLC** .......................................... B ...... 800 873-7332
  5830 El Camino Real Carlsbad (92008) *(P-4768)*
**Sport Kites Inc** ................................................. F ...... 714 998-6359
  500 W Blueridge Ave Orange (92865) *(P-13693)*
**Sport Tek, Commerce** *Also Called: Sportek International Inc (P-17081)*
**Sportek International Inc** ................................. F ...... 213 239-6700
  2425 S Eastern Ave Commerce (90040) *(P-17081)*
**Sportifeye Optics Inc** ....................................... E ...... 877 742-5000
  1854 Business Center Dr Duarte (91010) *(P-15618)*
**Sports Boosters Inc (PA)** ................................ F ...... 888 541-5561
  9320 Chesapeake Dr Ste 118 San Diego (92123) *(P-17783)*
**Sports Street Marketing A California Limited Partnership** ... E ...... 510 527-4664
  1609 4th St Berkeley (94710) *(P-2025)*
**Sports Venue Padding Inc** ............................... E ...... 562 404-9343
  14135 Artesia Blvd Cerritos (90703) *(P-6664)*
**Sportsman Steel Gun Safe, Long Beach** *Also Called: Sportsmen Steel Safe Fabg Co (P-9299)*
**Sportsmen Steel Safe Fabg Co (PA)** .............. E ...... 562 984-0244
  6311 N Paramount Blvd Long Beach (90805) *(P-9299)*
**Sportsmobile West** .......................................... E ...... 559 233-8267
  3631 S Bagley Ave Fresno (93725) *(P-19148)*
**Sportsrobe Inc** ................................................. E ...... 310 559-3999
  8654 Hayden Pl Culver City (90232) *(P-2642)*
**Spotlite America Corporation (PA)** .................. E ...... 310 829-0200
  9937 Jefferson Blvd Ste 110 Culver City (90232) *(P-7205)*
**Spotlite Power Corporation** ............................. E ...... 310 838-2367
  9937 Jefferson Blvd Ste 110 Culver City (90232) *(P-11558)*
**Spoton Computing Inc** ..................................... E ...... 650 293-7464
  548 Market St San Francisco (94104) *(P-18825)*
**Spotter Global Inc** ............................................ C ...... 515 817-3726
  1204 N Miller St Unit A Anaheim (92806) *(P-8890)*
**Spp Process Technology Systems, San Jose** *Also Called: ATI Liquidating Inc (P-9835)*

**Spragues Ready Mix, Irwindale** *Also Called: Spragues Rock and Sand Company (P-7501)*
**Spragues Rock and Sand Company (PA)** .................................................. E ...... 626 445-2125
230 Longden Ave Irwindale (91706) *(P-7501)*
**Spray Enclosure Tech Inc** .................................................. E ...... 909 419-7011
1427 N Linden Ave Rialto (92376) *(P-8580)*
**Spray Systems Inc** .................................................. E ...... 909 397-7511
1363 E Grand Ave Pomona (91766) *(P-11123)*
**Spray Tech, Rialto** *Also Called: Spray Enclosure Tech Inc (P-8580)*
**Spraying Devices Inc** .................................................. F ...... 559 734-5555
447 E Caldwell Ave Visalia (93277) *(P-9383)*
**Spreadco Inc** .................................................. E ...... 760 351-0747
803 Us Highway 78 Brawley (92227) *(P-2500)*
**Spreckels Sugar Company Inc** .................................................. B ...... 760 344-3110
395 W Keystone Rd Brawley (92227) *(P-1296)*
**Spring Discovery Inc** .................................................. E ...... 917 572-1552
1121 Industrial Rd # 500 San Carlos (94070) *(P-5669)*
**Spring Industries, Ventura** *Also Called: Juengermann Inc (P-9176)*
**Spring Mountain Vineyards Inc** .................................................. E ...... 707 967-4188
2805 Spring Mountain Rd Saint Helena (94574) *(P-1757)*
**Spring R&D & Stamp Inc** .................................................. F ...... 909 465-5166
5757 Chino Ave Chino (91710) *(P-8891)*
**Spring Technologies Corp** .................................................. E ...... 310 230-4000
10170 Culver Blvd Culver City (90232) *(P-18826)*
**Springcoin Inc** .................................................. E ...... 310 494-6928
4551 Glencoe Ave Marina Del Rey (90292) *(P-18827)*
**Sprintray Inc (PA)** .................................................. D ...... 800 914-8004
2710 Media Center Dr Los Angeles (90065) *(P-15484)*
**Sprite Industries Incorporated** .................................................. E ...... 951 735-1015
1791 Railroad St Corona (92880) *(P-14722)*
**Sprite Showers, Corona** *Also Called: Sprite Industries Incorporated (P-14722)*
**Sproutime, Sun Valley** *Also Called: Foodology LLC (P-2202)*
**SPRUCE, South San Francisco** *Also Called: Spruce Biosciences Inc (P-5670)*
**Spruce Biosciences Inc** .................................................. E ...... 415 655-4168
611 Gateway Blvd Ste 740 South San Francisco (94080) *(P-5670)*
**SPS Technologies LLC** .................................................. E ...... 714 892-5571
12570 Knott St Garden Grove (92841) *(P-13961)*
**SPS Technologies LLC** .................................................. B ...... 714 545-9311
1224 E Warner Ave Santa Ana (92705) *(P-15917)*
**SPS Technologies LLC** .................................................. B ...... 714 371-1925
1224 E Warner Ave Santa Ana (92705) *(P-15918)*
**Spt Microtechnologies** .................................................. E ...... 408 571-1400
1755 Junction Ave San Jose (95112) *(P-12730)*
**Spts, San Jose** *Also Called: Spts Technologies Inc (P-9900)*
**Spts Technologies Inc (HQ)** .................................................. C ...... 408 571-1400
2381 Bering Dr San Jose (95131) *(P-9900)*
**SPX Cooling Tech LLC** .................................................. F ...... 714 529-6080
550 Mercury Ln Brea (92821) *(P-8338)*
**SPX Flow Us LLC** .................................................. E ...... 949 455-8150
26561 Rancho Pkwy S Lake Forest (92630) *(P-8339)*
**Spy Inc (PA)** .................................................. D ...... 760 804-8420
1896 Rutherford Rd Carlsbad (92008) *(P-15619)*
**Spyder3d LLC** .................................................. F ...... 714 256-1122
620 Lunar Ave Brea (92821) *(P-4769)*
**Spyglass Pharma Inc** .................................................. E ...... 949 284-6904
27061 Aliso Creek Rd Ste 100 Aliso Viejo (92656) *(P-5671)*
**Spyrus Inc (PA)** .................................................. E ...... 408 392-9131
103 Bonaventura Dr San Jose (95134) *(P-10439)*
**Squab Producers Calif Inc** .................................................. D ...... 209 537-4744
409 Primo Way Modesto (95358) *(P-17135)*
**Squaglia Manufacturing Company (PA)** .................................................. E ...... 650 965-9644
275 Polaris Ave Mountain View (94043) *(P-11124)*
**Square Deal Mat Fctry & Uphl, Chico** *Also Called: Square Deal Mattress Factory (P-3541)*
**Square Deal Mattress Factory** .................................................. E ...... 530 342-2510
1354 Humboldt Ave Chico (95928) *(P-3541)*
**Square Enix Inc** .................................................. C ...... 310 846-0400
999 N Pacific Coast Hwy Fl 3 El Segundo (90245) *(P-16552)*
**Square H Brands Inc (PA)** .................................................. E ...... 323 267-4600
2731 S Soto St Vernon (90058) *(P-669)*
**Square International Svcs Inc** .................................................. D ...... 415 375-3176
1955 Broadway Ste 600 Oakland (94612) *(P-10286)*
**Squelch Inc** .................................................. E ...... 650 241-2700
3945 Freedom Cir Ste 560 Santa Clara (95054) *(P-18828)*

**Sr Plastics Company LLC** .................................................. E ...... 951 479-5394
692 Parkridge Ave Norco (92860) *(P-7039)*
**Sr Shroeder Inc** .................................................. F ...... 707 693-8166
1150 N 1st St Dixon (95620) *(P-17485)*
**Sra Oss Inc** .................................................. D ...... 408 855-8200
2114 Ringwood Ave San Jose (95131) *(P-18829)*
**Srax Inc (PA)** .................................................. D ...... 323 205-6109
1014 S Westlake Blvd # 14-299 Westlake Village (91361) *(P-18830)*
**SRC, Linden** *Also Called: Stockton Rubber Mfgcoinc (P-6540)*
**SRC Haverhill, Santa Rosa** *Also Called: Winchester SRC Cables Corp (P-13124)*
**SRC Milling Co LLC** .................................................. E ...... 916 363-4821
11350 Kiefer Blvd Sacramento (95830) *(P-1390)*
**Sream Inc** .................................................. E ...... 951 245-6999
12869 Temescal Canyon Rd Ste A Corona (92883) *(P-7242)*
**Srl Apparel Inc** .................................................. E ...... 530 898-9525
2209 Park Ave Chico (95928) *(P-2495)*
**Srm Contracting & Paving, San Diego** *Also Called: Superior Ready Mix Concrete LP (P-7505)*
**Sroodtuo, Paramount** *Also Called: Top Line Mfg Inc (P-8031)*
**SRS, Sunnyvale** *Also Called: Stanford Research Systems Inc (P-14724)*
**Ss Brewtech, Temecula** *Also Called: CM Brewing Technologies LLC (P-10552)*
**Ss Whittier LLC** .................................................. E ...... 562 698-7513
7240 Greenleaf Ave Whittier (90602) *(P-4770)*
**Ssco Manufacturing Inc** .................................................. E ...... 619 628-1022
8155 Mercury Ct Ste 100 San Diego (92111) *(P-9731)*
**Sscor Inc** .................................................. F ...... 818 504-4054
11064 Randall St Sun Valley (91352) *(P-15266)*
**Ssdi, La Mirada** *Also Called: Solid State Devices Inc (P-12724)*
**Ssi, Lodi** *Also Called: Scientific Specialties Inc (P-6570)*
**Ssi, Valley Center** *Also Called: Survival Systems Intl Inc (P-19283)*
**Ssi G Debbas Chocolatier LLC** .................................................. E ...... 559 294-2071
2794 N Larkin Ave Fresno (93727) *(P-1345)*
**Ssi Surfaces, Newbury Park** *Also Called: Scientific Surface Inds Inc (P-3670)*
**Ssl Mda Holdings Inc** .................................................. F ...... 650 852-4000
3825 Fabian Way Palo Alto (94303) *(P-11951)*
**Ssre Holdings LLC** .................................................. D ...... 800 314-2098
18901 Railroad St City Of Industry (91748) *(P-617)*
**SSS, Carlsbad** *Also Called: Silk Screen Shirts Inc (P-2494)*
**Sst Rg LLC** .................................................. B ...... 408 735-9110
1171 Sonora Ct Sunnyvale (94086) *(P-12731)*
**Sst Technologies** .................................................. E ...... 562 803-3361
6305 El Camino Real Carlsbad (92009) *(P-12732)*
**Sst Vacuum Reflow Systems, Carlsbad** *Also Called: Sst Technologies (P-12732)*
**St Clair Plastics Inc** .................................................. E ...... 562 946-3115
10031 Freeman Ave Santa Fe Springs (90670) *(P-5204)*
**St Clement Vineyards, Saint Helena** *Also Called: Treasury Wine Estates Americas (P-1800)*
**St Francis Marine Center** .................................................. E ...... 415 621-2876
835 Terry A Francois Blvd San Francisco (94158) *(P-17606)*
**St George Spirits Inc (PA)** .................................................. F ...... 510 769-1601
2601 Monarch St Alameda (94501) *(P-1758)*
**St John Knits, Anaheim** *Also Called: St John Knits Inc (P-2810)*
**St John Knits, Irvine** *Also Called: St John Knits Intl Inc (P-2811)*
**St John Knits Inc (DH)** .................................................. B ...... 877 750-1171
5515 E La Palma Ave Ste 100 Anaheim (92807) *(P-2810)*
**St John Knits Intl Inc (HQ)** .................................................. C ...... 949 863-1171
17522 Armstrong Ave Irvine (92614) *(P-2811)*
**St Jude Medical LLC** .................................................. E ...... 949 769-5000
2375 Morse Ave Irvine (92614) *(P-5672)*
**St Jude Medical LLC** .................................................. D ...... 408 738-4883
645 Almanor Ave Sunnyvale (94085) *(P-15267)*
**St Louis Post-Dispatch LLC** .................................................. C ...... 415 892-1516
1068 Machin Ave Novato (94945) *(P-4200)*
**St Louis Post-Dispatch LLC** .................................................. D ...... 707 762-4541
830 Petaluma Blvd N Petaluma (94952) *(P-4201)*
**St Paul Brands Inc** .................................................. E ...... 714 903-1000
11842 Monarch St Garden Grove (92841) *(P-5223)*
**St Supertec, Paramount** *Also Called: Supertec Machinery Inc (P-9573)*
**St Supery Inc (DH)** .................................................. E ...... 707 963-4507
8440 St Helena Hwy Rutherford (94573) *(P-1759)*
**St Worth Container LLC** .................................................. D ...... 909 390-4550
727 S Wanamaker Ave Ontario (91761) *(P-3890)*

## ALPHABETIC SECTION

STA Pharmaceutical US LLC .................................................. E ...... 609 606-6499
  6114 Nancy Ridge Dr San Diego (92121) *(P-5673)*
**STAAR, Lake Forest** *Also Called: Staar Surgical Company (P-15620)*
Staar Surgical Company (PA) ................................................. A ...... 626 303-7902
  25510 Commercentre Dr Lake Forest (92630) *(P-15620)*
Staar Surgical Company ........................................................ F ...... 626 303-7902
  15102 Red Hill Ave Tustin (92780) *(P-15621)*
Stabile Plating Company Inc ................................................. E ...... 626 339-9091
  1150 E Edna Pl Covina (91724) *(P-9016)*
Stable Auto Corporation ........................................................ E ...... 415 967-2719
  124 Jupiter St Encinitas (92024) *(P-13186)*
Stack Plastics Inc ................................................................... E ...... 650 361-8600
  3525 Haven Ave Menlo Park (94025) *(P-7040)*
Stacked Energy Inc ................................................................ E ...... 618 420-9244
  2380 Bering Dr San Jose (95131) *(P-13150)*
Stackla Inc ............................................................................. D ...... 415 789-3304
  548 Market St San Francisco (94104) *(P-18831)*
Stackwatch Inc ...................................................................... E ...... 301 202-4542
  315 Montgomery St Fl 9 San Francisco (94104) *(P-18832)*
**Staco Switch, Irvine** *Also Called: Staco Systems Inc (P-11250)*
Staco Systems Inc (HQ) ........................................................ D ...... 949 297-8700
  7 Morgan Irvine (92618) *(P-11250)*
Stadco (HQ) ........................................................................... D ...... 323 227-8888
  107 S Avenue 20 Los Angeles (90031) *(P-9699)*
Staffing Industry Analysts Inc ............................................... E ...... 650 390-6200
  1975 W El Camino Real Ste 304 Mountain View (94040) *(P-4470)*
**Staffing Industry Report, Mountain View** *Also Called: Staffing Industry Analysts Inc (P-4470)*
**Stages West, San Leandro** *Also Called: Ariat International Inc (P-7153)*
Stags Leap Wine Cellars LLC (PA) ....................................... C ...... 707 944-2020
  5766 Silverado Trl Napa (94558) *(P-1760)*
Staidson Biopharma Inc ........................................................ F ...... 800 345-1899
  2600 Hilltop Dr Bldg A San Pablo (94806) *(P-5674)*
**Stailess Polishing Co., Oakland** *Also Called: General Grinding Inc (P-10856)*
Stainless Fixtures Inc ........................................................... E ...... 909 622-1615
  1250 E Franklin Ave Pomona (91766) *(P-3750)*
Stainless Stl Fabricators Inc ................................................. D ...... 714 739-9904
  15120 Desman Rd La Mirada (90638) *(P-16844)*
**Stair Service, Hollister** *Also Called: Simmons Stairways Inc (P-3191)*
**Stake Fastener, Chino** *Also Called: Dupree Inc (P-8754)*
Stalfab Inc .............................................................................. E ...... 831 786-1600
  131 Algen Ln Watsonville (95076) *(P-9817)*
Stalker Software Inc ............................................................. E ...... 415 569-2280
  6 Tara View Rd Belvedere Tiburon (94920) *(P-18833)*
**Standard Armament, Glendale** *Also Called: SAI Industries (P-9136)*
**STANDARD BIOTOOLS, South San Francisco** *Also Called: Standard Biotools Inc (P-14723)*
Standard Biotools Inc (PA) ................................................... C ...... 650 266-6000
  2 Tower Pl Ste 2000 South San Francisco (94080) *(P-14723)*
Standard Cable Usa Inc ........................................................ F ...... 949 888-0842
  23126 Arroyo Vis Rcho Sta Marg (92688) *(P-9233)*
Standard Cognition Corp (PA) .............................................. E ...... 415 324-4156
  548 Market St # 96346 San Francisco (94104) *(P-18834)*
Standard Concrete Products Inc (HQ) .................................. E ...... 310 829-4537
  13550 Live Oak Ln Baldwin Park (91706) *(P-7502)*
Standard Fiber LLC ............................................................... E ...... 650 872-6528
  919 E Hillsdale Blvd Ste 100 Foster City (94404) *(P-2427)*
Standard Filter Corporation (PA) .......................................... E ...... 866 443-3615
  3801 Ocean Ranch Blvd Ste 107 Oceanside (92056) *(P-9997)*
**Standard Industries, Anaheim** *Also Called: Si Manufacturing Inc (P-12858)*
Standard Sales Llc (PA) ........................................................ E ...... 323 269-0510
  2801 E 12th St Los Angeles (90023) *(P-15858)*
**Standard Tool & Die Co, Los Angeles** *Also Called: Stadco (P-9699)*
Standard Wire & Cable Co (PA) ........................................... E ...... 310 609-1811
  2050 E Vista Bella Way Rancho Dominguez (90220) *(P-7796)*
Standardvision LLC ............................................................... E ...... 323 222-3630
  3370 N San Fernando Rd Ste 206 Los Angeles (90065) *(P-16045)*
Standdesk Inc ........................................................................ E ...... 213 634-0665
  5042 Wilshire Blvd # 44689 Los Angeles (90036) *(P-3558)*
**Standish Precision Products, Fallbrook** *Also Called: Fallbrook Industries Inc (P-8842)*
Standridge Granite Corporation ............................................ E ...... 562 946-6334
  9437 Santa Fe Springs Rd Santa Fe Springs (90670) *(P-7548)*

Staness Jonekos Entps Inc ................................................... E ...... 818 606-2710
  4000 W Magnolia Blvd Ste D Burbank (91505) *(P-2360)*
**Stanford Advanced Materials, Lake Forest** *Also Called: Oceania International LLC (P-7765)*
Stanford Business Magazine ................................................ E ...... 650 723-2146
  655 Knight Way Stanford (94305) *(P-4771)*
Stanford Daily Publishing Corp ............................................. E ...... 650 723-2555
  456 Panama Mall Stanford (94305) *(P-4202)*
**Stanford Daily, The, Stanford** *Also Called: Stanford Daily Publishing Corp (P-4202)*
Stanford Mu Corporation ....................................................... E ...... 310 605-2888
  20725 Annalee Ave Carson (90746) *(P-14116)*
Stanford Research Systems Inc ........................................... D ...... 408 744-9040
  1290 Reamwood Ave Ste D Sunnyvale (94089) *(P-14724)*
Stanford Sign & Awning Inc (PA) .......................................... E ...... 619 423-6200
  2556 Faivre St Chula Vista (91911) *(P-16046)*
**Stanford University Libraries, Stanford** *Also Called: Leland Stanford Junior Univ (P-4426)*
**Stang Industrial Products, Chino** *Also Called: Stang Industries Inc (P-16238)*
Stang Industries Inc .............................................................. F ...... 914 479-9810
  8778 Kimball Ave Chino (91708) *(P-16238)*
Stangenes Industries Inc (PA) .............................................. D ...... 650 855-9926
  1052 E Meadow Cir Palo Alto (94303) *(P-12860)*
Stanislaus Food Products Co (PA) ....................................... D ...... 209 548-3537
  1202 D St Modesto (95354) *(P-927)*
Stanley Electric Motor Co Inc ............................................... E ...... 209 464-7321
  222 N Wilson Way Stockton (95205) *(P-19232)*
**Stanley National Hardware, Lake Forest** *Also Called: National Manufacturing Co (P-8020)*
**Stansport, Los Angeles** *Also Called: Standard Sales Llc (P-15858)*
Stantec Consulting Svcs Inc ................................................ E ...... 916 434-5062
  1245 Fiddyment Rd Lincoln (95648) *(P-10604)*
Stanton Carpet Corp .............................................................. E ...... 562 945-8711
  2209 Pine Ave Manhattan Beach (90266) *(P-2521)*
**Stanza, San Francisco** *Also Called: Spoton Computing Inc (P-18825)*
Stanzino Inc ........................................................................... C ...... 818 602-5171
  17937 Santa Rita St Encino (91316) *(P-2428)*
Stanzino Inc (PA) ................................................................... E ...... 213 746-8822
  16325 S Avalon Blvd Gardena (90248) *(P-2429)*
**Stapleton, Gridley** *Also Called: Stapleton - Spence Packing Co (P-928)*
Stapleton - Spence Packing Co (PA) .................................... D ...... 408 297-8815
  1900 State Highway 99 Gridley (95948) *(P-928)*
**Star Building Products, Fresno** *Also Called: E-Z Haul Ready Mix Inc (P-7439)*
**Star Building Systems, Lockeford** *Also Called: Robertson-Ceco II Corporation (P-8682)*
**Star Concrete, San Jose** *Also Called: Sandman Inc (P-7390)*
Star Die Casting Inc .............................................................. D ...... 562 698-0627
  12209 Slauson Ave Santa Fe Springs (90670) *(P-8029)*
**Star Food Snacks, Colton** *Also Called: Star Food Snacks Intl Inc (P-670)*
Star Food Snacks Intl Inc ..................................................... D ...... 909 825-8882
  125 E Laurel St Colton (92324) *(P-670)*
Star Link Company Inc ......................................................... F ...... 310 787-8299
  3300 Fujita St Torrance (90505) *(P-17840)*
Star Milling Co ....................................................................... D ...... 951 657-3143
  23901 Water St Perris (92570) *(P-1151)*
**Star Nail International, Valencia** *Also Called: Star Nail Products Inc (P-17052)*
Star Nail Products Inc .......................................................... D ...... 661 257-3376
  29120 Avenue Paine Valencia (91355) *(P-17052)*
Star Pacific Inc ...................................................................... E ...... 510 471-6555
  27462 Sunrise Farm Rd Los Altos Hills (94022) *(P-5883)*
Star Plastic Design ................................................................ D ...... 310 530-7119
  25914 President Ave Harbor City (90710) *(P-7041)*
Star Sanitation Services ....................................................... E ...... 831 754-6794
  4 Harris Rd Salinas (93901) *(P-7042)*
Star Shield Solutions LLC .................................................... D ...... 866 662-4477
  4315 Santa Ana St Ontario (91761) *(P-7043)*
Star Stainless Screw Co ....................................................... E ...... 510 489-6569
  30150 Ahern Ave Union City (94587) *(P-7628)*
Star Star .................................................................................. E ...... 310 901-1079
  621 W Rosecrans Ave Ste 1 Gardena (90248) *(P-8581)*
**Star Trac, Irvine** *Also Called: Star Trac Health & Fitness Inc (P-15859)*
**Star Trac, Irvine** *Also Called: Unisen Inc (P-15871)*
**Star Trac Fitness, Irvine** *Also Called: Star Trac Strength Inc (P-15860)*
Star Trac Health & Fitness Inc ............................................. E ...... 714 669-1660
  14410 Myford Rd Irvine (92606) *(P-15859)*

## ALPHABETIC SECTION

**Star Trac Strength Inc** .................................................. B ...... 714 669-1660
14410 Myford Rd Irvine (92606) *(P-15860)*

**Star-Luck Enterprise Inc** .................................................. F ...... 661 665-9999
11807 Harrington St Bakersfield (93311) *(P-14461)*

**Starco Enterprises Inc (PA)** .................................................. D ...... 323 266-7111
3137 E 26th St Los Angeles (90058) *(P-9901)*

**Stark Awning & Canvas, Chula Vista** Also Called: Stark Mfg Co *(P-2983)*

**Stark Mfg Co** .................................................. E ...... 619 425-5880
76 Broadway Chula Vista (91910) *(P-2983)*

**Starmont Winery, Saint Helena** Also Called: Merryvale Vineyards LLC *(P-1679)*

**Starrett Kinemetric Engrg Inc** .................................................. E ...... 949 348-1213
26052 Merit Cir Ste 103 Laguna Hills (92653) *(P-9700)*

**Startech Semiconductor Inc** .................................................. D ...... 510 668-7000
48720 Kato Rd Fremont (94538) *(P-12733)*

**Startel Corporation (PA)** .................................................. D ...... 949 863-8700
16 Goodyear B-125 Irvine (92618) *(P-17982)*

**Stasher Inc** .................................................. D ...... 510 531-2100
1310 63rd St Emeryville (94608) *(P-17023)*

**Stason Pharmaceuticals Inc (PA)** .................................................. F ...... 949 380-0752
11 Morgan Irvine (92618) *(P-5675)*

**Statco Engrg & Fabricators LLC (DH)** .................................................. E ...... 714 375-6300
7595 Reynolds Cir Huntington Beach (92647) *(P-16845)*

**State Fish Co Inc** .................................................. C ...... 310 547-9530
624 W 9th St Ste 100 San Pedro (90731) *(P-2064)*

**State Pipe & Supply Inc** .................................................. E ...... 909 356-5670
2180 N Locust Ave Rialto (92377) *(P-7629)*

**State Ready Mix Inc** .................................................. F ...... 805 647-2817
3127 Los Angeles Ave Oxnard (93036) *(P-7503)*

**State Ready Mix Inc (PA)** .................................................. E ...... 805 647-2817
1011 Azahar St Ste 1 Ventura (93004) *(P-7504)*

**Statek, Orange** Also Called: Statek Corporation *(P-13090)*

**Statek Corporation (HQ)** .................................................. C ...... 714 639-7810
512 N Main St Orange (92868) *(P-13090)*

**Statek Corporation** .................................................. C ...... 714 639-7810
1449 W Orange Grove Ave Orange (92868) *(P-13091)*

**Stater Bros Markets** .................................................. E ...... 714 963-0949
10114 Adams Ave Huntington Beach (92646) *(P-17385)*

**Stater Bros Markets** .................................................. E ...... 714 991-5310
1131 N State College Blvd Anaheim (92806) *(P-17386)*

**Statewide Distributors, Ontario** Also Called: USA Sales Inc *(P-2397)*

**Statewide Trffic Sfety Sgns In (HQ)** .................................................. E ...... 949 553-8272
2722 S Fairview St Fl 2 Santa Ana (92704) *(P-12018)*

**Statewide Trffic Sfety Sgns In** .................................................. E ...... 559 291-8500
3049 S Golden State Frontage Rd Fresno (93725) *(P-16047)*

**Statewide Trffic Sfety Sgns In** .................................................. E ...... 714 468-1919
2722 S Fairview St Santa Ana (92704) *(P-16048)*

**Statewide Trffic Sfety Sgns In** .................................................. E ...... 530 222-8023
6479 Eastside Rd Redding (96001) *(P-16049)*

**Statewide Trffic Sfety Sgns In** .................................................. E ...... 707 825-6927
40 S G St Arcata (95521) *(P-16050)*

**Statewide Trffic Sfety Sgns In** .................................................. E ...... 949 553-8272
1100 Main St Ste 100 Irvine (92614) *(P-16051)*

**Stationery Exchange, Yorba Linda** Also Called: Sid-Mar Inc *(P-17641)*

**Stats Chippac Inc (DH)** .................................................. E ...... 510 979-8000
880 N Mccarthy Blvd Ste 250 Milpitas (95035) *(P-12734)*

**Stats Chippac Test Svcs Inc (DH)** .................................................. F ...... 510 979-8000
46429 Landing Pkwy Fremont (94538) *(P-12735)*

**Stauber, Fullerton** Also Called: Stauber Prfmce Ingredients Inc *(P-5272)*

**Stauber California Inc** .................................................. D ...... 714 441-3900
4120 N Palm St Fullerton (92835) *(P-5271)*

**Stauber Prfmce Ingredients Inc (HQ)** .................................................. D ...... 714 441-3900
4120 N Palm St Fullerton (92835) *(P-5272)*

**Stauber USA, Fullerton** Also Called: Stauber California Inc *(P-5271)*

**Staubli Electrical Connectors Inc (DH)** .................................................. F ...... 707 838-0530
100 Market St Windsor (95492) *(P-12897)*

**Stavatti Industries Ltd** .................................................. E ...... 651 238-5369
3670 El Camino Dr San Bernardino (92404) *(P-106)*

**Stavros Enterprises Inc** .................................................. E ...... 888 463-2293
681 Arrow Grand Cir Covina (91722) *(P-19282)*

**Stci, Rancho Cucamonga** Also Called: Superior Tank Co Inc *(P-8343)*

**Steady Clothing Inc** .................................................. F ...... 714 444-2058
2851 E White Star Ave Ste A Anaheim (92806) *(P-2643)*

**Steadymed Therapeutics Inc** .................................................. E ...... 925 361-7111
2603 Camino Ramon Ste 350 San Ramon (94583) *(P-5676)*

**Stealth Aerospace, Commerce** Also Called: Fastener Dist Holdings LLC *(P-16874)*

**Stearns Product Dev Corp (PA)** .................................................. D ...... 951 657-0379
20281 Harvill Ave Perris (92570) *(P-10117)*

**Stec Inc (HQ)** .................................................. B ...... 415 222-9996
3355 Michelson Dr Ste 100 Irvine (92612) *(P-10287)*

**Stecher Enterprises Inc** .................................................. F ...... 714 484-6900
8536 Central Ave Stanton (90680) *(P-9207)*

**Steel Products International, Los Angeles** Also Called: Precision Steel Products Inc *(P-8543)*

**Steel Services Co, Vernon** Also Called: S S Schaffer Co Inc *(P-9569)*

**Steel Structures Inc** .................................................. E ...... 559 673-8021
28777 Avenue 15 1/2 Madera (93638) *(P-8340)*

**Steel Works Etc, Oxnard** Also Called: Millworks Etc Inc *(P-8277)*

**Steel-Tech Industrial Corp** .................................................. E ...... 951 270-0144
1268 Sherborn St Corona (92879) *(P-8222)*

**Steelcase Authorized Dealer, Camarillo** Also Called: BKM Office Environments Inc *(P-17515)*

**Steelco USA, Chino** Also Called: Wcs Equipment Holdings LLC *(P-7701)*

**Steelco USA, Chino** Also Called: Wcs Equipment Holdings LLC *(P-8610)*

**Steelcraft LLC** .................................................. F ...... 888 261-4537
2120 California Ave Corona (92881) *(P-8809)*

**Steeldeck Inc** .................................................. E ...... 323 290-2100
13147 S Western Ave Gardena (90249) *(P-16239)*

**Steeldyne Industries** .................................................. E ...... 714 630-6200
2871 E La Cresta Ave Anaheim (92806) *(P-8582)*

**Steele Wines, Kelseyville** Also Called: Steele Wines Inc *(P-1761)*

**Steele Wines Inc** .................................................. E ...... 707 279-9475
4350 Thomas Dr Kelseyville (95451) *(P-1761)*

**Steelscape LLC** .................................................. F ...... 909 987-4711
11200 Arrow Rte Rancho Cucamonga (91730) *(P-9124)*

**Steelwedge Software Inc** .................................................. D ...... 925 460-1700
3875 Hopyard Rd Ste 300 Pleasanton (94588) *(P-18835)*

**Steelworks Etc Inc** .................................................. F ...... 805 487-3000
2230 Statham Blvd Ste 100 Oxnard (93033) *(P-8292)*

**Steico, Oceanside** Also Called: Steico Industries Inc *(P-8892)*

**Steico Industries Inc** .................................................. C ...... 760 438-8015
1814 Ord Way Oceanside (92056) *(P-8892)*

**Stein Industries Inc (PA)** .................................................. E ...... 714 522-4560
4005 Artesia Ave Fullerton (92833) *(P-8583)*

**Steinbeck Brewing Company** .................................................. D ...... 510 886-9823
1082 B St Hayward (94541) *(P-1460)*

**Steiner Eoptics Inc** .................................................. D ...... 831 373-0701
70 Garden Ct Ste 200 Monterey (93940) *(P-13311)*

**Steiny & Company, Corona** Also Called: Computer Service Company *(P-11988)*

**Stell Industries Inc** .................................................. E ...... 951 369-8777
1951 S Parco Ave Ste B Ontario (91761) *(P-8686)*

**Stellant Systems Inc** .................................................. C ...... 916 351-4500
107 Woodmere Rd Folsom (95630) *(P-11952)*

**Stellant Systems Inc (DH)** .................................................. A ...... 310 517-6000
3100 Lomita Blvd Torrance (90505) *(P-14310)*

**Stellar Cyber Inc** .................................................. D ...... 408 548-0860
2590 N 1st St Ste 360 San Jose (95131) *(P-18836)*

**Stellar Engineering, Anaheim** Also Called: APT Manufacturing LLC *(P-9540)*

**Stellar Exploration Inc** .................................................. E ...... 805 459-1425
835 Airport Dr San Luis Obispo (93401) *(P-14092)*

**Stellar Microelectronics Inc** .................................................. C ...... 661 775-3500
9340 Owensmouth Ave Chatsworth (91311) *(P-12736)*

**Stellartech Research Corp (PA)** .................................................. C ...... 408 331-3000
560 Cottonwood Dr Milpitas (95035) *(P-19475)*

**Stem Inc (PA)** .................................................. E ...... 877 374-7836
100 California St Ste 1400 San Francisco (94111) *(P-11289)*

**Stem US Holdings Inc (HQ)** .................................................. D
100 Rollins Rd Millbrae (94030) *(P-14586)*

**Step, Palo Alto** Also Called: Step Mobile Inc *(P-18837)*

**Step Mobile Inc** .................................................. E ...... 203 913-9229
380 Portage Ave Palo Alto (94306) *(P-18837)*

**Step Tools Unlimited Inc** .................................................. E ...... 408 988-8898
18434 Technology Dr Morgan Hill (95037) *(P-9701)*

**Stepan Company** .................................................. C ...... 714 776-9870
1208 N Patt St Anaheim (92801) *(P-5205)*

## ALPHABETIC SECTION

**Stepladder Creamery, Cambria** *Also Called: Stepladder Farmstead Crmry LLC (P-740)*
**Stepladder Farmstead Crmry LLC** .................................................. E ...... 415 606-8559
   4450 San Simeon Creek Rd Cambria (93428) *(P-740)*
**Steri-Tek, Fremont** *Also Called: Smart World LLC (P-19133)*
**Sterigenics US LLC** ....................................................................... F ...... 951 340-0700
   344 Bonnie Cir Corona (92878) *(P-19508)*
**Steril-Aire Inc** ............................................................................... E ...... 818 565-1128
   25060 Avenue Stanford Ste 160 Valencia (91355) *(P-11623)*
**Steris, San Diego** *Also Called: Steris Corporation (P-15408)*
**Steris Corporation** ........................................................................ D ...... 858 586-1166
   9020 Activity Rd Ste D San Diego (92126) *(P-15408)*
**Steris Corporation** ........................................................................ C ...... 510 439-4500
   503 Canal Blvd Richmond (94804) *(P-15409)*
**Steris Isomedix, Temecula** *Also Called: Isomedix Operations Inc (P-15367)*
**Sterisyn Inc** .................................................................................. E ...... 805 991-9694
   11969 Challenger Ct Moorpark (93021) *(P-5677)*
**Sterisyn Scientific, Moorpark** *Also Called: Sterisyn Inc (P-5677)*
**Sterling Carpets & Flooring, Anaheim** *Also Called: Rm Partners Inc (P-17528)*
**Sterling Pacific Meat Co., Commerce** *Also Called: Interstate Meat Co Inc (P-9798)*
**Sterling Sleep Systems, Westminster** *Also Called: American Pacific Plastic Fabricators Inc (P-5135)*
**Sterling Vineyards, Calistoga** *Also Called: Treasury Wine Estates Americas (P-1796)*
**Steven Handelman Studios Inc (PA)** ............................................ E ...... 805 884-9070
   716 N Milpas St Santa Barbara (93103) *(P-7682)*
**Steven Kent LLC** .......................................................................... F ...... 925 243-6442
   2245 S Vasco Rd Livermore (94550) *(P-1762)*
**Steven Label Corporation (PA)** .................................................... C ...... 562 698-9971
   11926 Burke St Santa Fe Springs (90670) *(P-17071)*
**Steven N Ledson** .......................................................................... D ...... 707 537-3810
   7335 Sonoma Hwy Santa Rosa (95409) *(P-349)*
**Stevenot Winery & Imports Inc (PA)** ............................................ E ...... 209 728-0638
   2690 San Domingo Rd Murphys (95247) *(P-1763)*
**Stevens Creek Quarry Inc (PA)** .................................................... D ...... 408 253-2512
   21771 Stevens Creek Blvd Ste 100 Cupertino (95014) *(P-382)*
**Steves Plating Corporation** .......................................................... C ...... 818 842-2184
   3111 N San Fernando Blvd Burbank (91504) *(P-3709)*
**Steward Plastics Inc** ..................................................................... D ...... 949 581-9530
   23322 Del Lago Dr Laguna Hills (92653) *(P-7044)*
**Stewart & Jasper Marketing Inc (PA)** .......................................... C ...... 209 862-9600
   3500 Shiells Rd Newman (95360) *(P-1367)*
**Stewart & Jasper Orchards, Newman** *Also Called: Stewart & Jasper Marketing Inc (P-1367)*
**Stewart Filmscreen Corp (PA)** ..................................................... C ...... 310 784-5300
   1161 Sepulveda Blvd Torrance (90502) *(P-15667)*
**Stewart Superior** .......................................................................... F ...... 510 346-9811
   14487 Griffith St San Leandro (94577) *(P-16897)*
**Stewart Tool Company** ................................................................ D ...... 916 635-8321
   3647 Omec Cir Rancho Cordova (95742) *(P-9702)*
**Stewart/Walker Company, Tracy** *Also Called: Altium Packaging LLC (P-6709)*
**Stg Machine, Santa Clara** *Also Called: James Stout (P-10903)*
**Stic-Adhesive Products Co Inc** ..................................................... C ...... 323 268-2956
   3950 Medford St Los Angeles (90063) *(P-6248)*
**Stickypos, Santa Ana** *Also Called: Documotion Research Inc (P-4593)*
**Stigtec Mfg, San Marcos** *Also Called: Ed Stiglic (P-10819)*
**Stila Cosmetics, Glendale** *Also Called: Stila Styles LLC (P-6041)*
**Stila Styles LLC (HQ)** .................................................................. E ...... 866 784-5201
   801 N Brand Blvd Ste 910 Glendale (91203) *(P-6041)*
**Still Room LLC** ............................................................................. E ...... 510 847-1930
   2624 Barrington Ct Hayward (94545) *(P-2026)*
**Stillhouse LLC** .............................................................................. E ...... 323 498-1111
   8201 Beverly Blvd Ste 300 Los Angeles (90048) *(P-1845)*
**Stines Machine Inc** ...................................................................... E ...... 760 599-9955
   2481 Coral St Vista (92081) *(P-11125)*
**Stir Foods, Orange** *Also Called: Pacifica Foods LLC (P-989)*
**Stir Foods LLC** ............................................................................. E ...... 714 871-9231
   1851 N Delilah St Corona (92879) *(P-1048)*
**Stitch Industries Inc** ..................................................................... E ...... 888 282-0842
   767 S Alameda St Ste 360 Los Angeles (90021) *(P-3492)*
**Stitch Labs Inc** ............................................................................. E ...... 415 323-0630
   1455 Market St Ste 600 San Francisco (94103) *(P-19518)*
**Stmicroelectronics Inc** ................................................................. F ...... 408 919-8400
   2755 Great America Way Santa Clara (95054) *(P-12737)*

**Stoble LLC** ................................................................................... E ...... 530 990-3607
   418 Broadway St Chico (95928) *(P-2081)*
**Stockton Rubber Mfgcoinc** .......................................................... E ...... 209 887-1172
   5023 N Flood Rd Linden (95236) *(P-6540)*
**Stockton Tri-Industries LLC** ........................................................ E ...... 209 948-9701
   2141 E Anderson St Stockton (95205) *(P-9496)*
**Stoll Metalcraft Inc** ...................................................................... C ...... 661 295-0401
   24808 Anza Dr Valencia (91355) *(P-8584)*
**Stolo Cabinets Inc (PA)** ............................................................... E ...... 714 529-7303
   860 Challenger St Brea (92821) *(P-3588)*
**Stolo Custom Cabinets, Brea** *Also Called: Stolo Cabinets Inc (P-3588)*
**Stone Brewing Co LLC** ................................................................ C ...... 619 269-2100
   2816 Historic Decatur Rd Ste 116 San Diego (92106) *(P-1461)*
**Stone Brewing Co LLC** ................................................................ C ...... 760 294-7899
   1977 Citracado Pkwy Escondido (92029) *(P-1462)*
**Stone Brewing Co LLC (DH)** ....................................................... E ...... 760 294-7866
   1999 Citracado Pkwy Escondido (92029) *(P-17624)*
**Stone Brewing Co., Escondido** *Also Called: Stone Brewing Co LLC (P-17624)*
**Stone Bridge Cellars Inc (PA)** ..................................................... E ...... 707 963-2745
   200 Taplin Rd Saint Helena (94574) *(P-1764)*
**Stone Canyon Inds Holdings LLC (PA)** ...................................... E ...... 424 316-2061
   1875 Century Park E Ste 320 Los Angeles (90067) *(P-19538)*
**Stone Canyon Industries LLC** ..................................................... A ...... 310 570-4869
   1875 Century Park E Ste 320 Los Angeles (90067) *(P-7045)*
**Stone Entertainment, Costa Mesa** *Also Called: Volcom LLC (P-19142)*
**Stone Harbor Inc** ......................................................................... F ...... 323 277-2777
   5015 District Blvd Vernon (90058) *(P-2555)*
**Stonecrop Technologies LLC** ..................................................... E ...... 781 659-0007
   103 H St Ste B Petaluma (94952) *(P-11953)*
**Stonecushion Inc (PA)** ................................................................. E ...... 707 433-1911
   1400 Lytton Springs Rd Healdsburg (95448) *(P-1765)*
**Stonegate Winery, Napa** *Also Called: California Wine Company (P-9)*
**Stony Apparel Corp (PA)** ............................................................. C ...... 323 981-9080
   1201 S Grand Ave Los Angeles (90015) *(P-2689)*
**Stop Look Plastics Inc, La Habra** *Also Called: Stop-Look Sign Co Intl Inc (P-16052)*
**Stop-Look Sign Co Intl Inc** .......................................................... F ...... 562 690-7576
   401 Commercial Way La Habra (90631) *(P-16052)*
**Stoptech** ...................................................................................... F ...... 310 933-1100
   21046 Figueroa St Carson (90745) *(P-13579)*
**Store 3, El Cajon** *Also Called: Wetzels Pretzels LLC (P-17422)*
**Store Intelligence Inc** .................................................................. E ...... 925 433-9520
   6700 Koll Center Pkwy Ste 109 Pleasanton (94566) *(P-13092)*
**Stories International Inc** ............................................................. E ...... 310 242-8409
   400 Corporate Pointe Culver City (90230) *(P-4471)*
**Storm, Torrance** *Also Called: Storm Industries Inc (P-9384)*
**Storm Industries Inc (PA)** ........................................................... D ...... 310 534-5232
   970 W 190th St Torrance (90502) *(P-9384)*
**Storm Manufacturing Group Inc** ................................................ D ...... 310 326-8287
   23201 Normandie Ave Torrance (90501) *(P-9162)*
**Storm Tee's, Huntington Park** *Also Called: Abgb Designs Inc (P-2652)*
**Storm8 Inc** ................................................................................... F ...... 650 596-8600
   2400 Bridge Pkwy Ste 2 Redwood City (94065) *(P-18838)*
**Storm8 Entertainment, Redwood City** *Also Called: Storm8 Inc (P-18838)*
**Storopack Inc** ............................................................................... E ...... 562 803-5582
   12007 Woodruff Ave Downey (90241) *(P-5206)*
**Storyland Studios, Lake Elsinore** *Also Called: Harrington & Sons Inc (P-7591)*
**Stoughton Printing Co** ................................................................. F ...... 626 961-3678
   130 N Sunset Ave City Of Industry (91744) *(P-4772)*
**Stout Industrial Tech Inc** ............................................................. F ...... 831 455-1004
   90 Monterey Salinas Hwy Salinas (93908) *(P-9385)*
**Stracon Inc** ................................................................................... F ...... 949 851-2288
   1672 Kaiser Ave Ste 1 Irvine (92614) *(P-13312)*
**Straight Down Clothing Company, San Luis Obispo** *Also Called: Straight Down Enterprises (P-2644)*
**Straight Down Enterprises (PA)** .................................................. E ...... 805 543-3086
   625 Clarion Ct San Luis Obispo (93401) *(P-2644)*
**Straight Smile LLC (HQ)** ............................................................. F ...... 424 389-4551
   3435 Ocean Park Blvd Ste 107-252 Santa Monica (90405) *(P-15485)*
**Strand Art Company Inc** ............................................................. E ...... 714 777-0444
   4700 E Hunter Ave Anaheim (92807) *(P-7046)*

**Strand Products Inc (PA)** .................................................................. E ...... 800 343-7985
  2233 Knoll Dr Ventura (93003) *(P-15581)*
**Strasbaugh, San Luis Obispo** *Also Called: R H Strasbaugh (P-9564)*
**Strat Edge, Santee** *Also Called: Stratedge Corporation (P-12738)*
**Strata Forest Products Inc (PA)** ........................................................... E ...... 714 751-0800
  2600 S Susan St Santa Ana (92704) *(P-3089)*
**Strata USA Llc** .................................................................................... E ...... 888 878-7282
  333 City Blvd W Fl 17 Orange (92868) *(P-17681)*
**Stratas Foods LLC** ............................................................................. D ...... 559 495-4506
  3390 S Chestnut Ave Fresno (93725) *(P-1407)*
**Stratcom Systems Inc** ....................................................................... E ...... 858 481-9292
  2701 Loker Ave W Ste 130 Carlsbad (92010) *(P-17983)*
**Stratedge Corporation** ...................................................................... E ...... 866 424-4962
  9424 Abraham Way Santee (92071) *(P-12738)*
**Strategic Capital Incorporated** ........................................................... E ...... 707 473-4310
  3225 W Dry Creek Rd Healdsburg (95448) *(P-19539)*
**Strategic Distribution L P** ................................................................ C
  15301 Ventura Blvd Sherman Oaks (91403) *(P-2603)*
**Strategic Industry Inc** ........................................................................ E ...... 559 419-9481
  1440 Draper St Ste C Kingsburg (93631) *(P-277)*
**Strategic Insights Inc** ........................................................................ F ...... 858 452-7500
  9191 Towne Centre Dr Ste 401 San Diego (92122) *(P-18839)*
**Strategic Materials Inc** ...................................................................... F ...... 323 415-0166
  3211 E 26th St Vernon (90058) *(P-16963)*
**Strategic Mechanical Inc** .................................................................. C ...... 559 291-1952
  4661 E Commerce Ave Fresno (93725) *(P-436)*
**Strategic Medical Ventures LLC** ........................................................ E ...... 949 355-5212
  280 Newport Center Dr Newport Beach (92660) *(P-15509)*
**Strategy Companion Corp** ................................................................ D ...... 714 460-8398
  100 Pacifica Ste 220 Irvine (92618) *(P-18840)*
**Stratoflex Product Division, Camarillo** *Also Called: Parker-Hannifin Corporation (P-13922)*
**Stratos Manufacturing LLC** ............................................................... F ...... 408 839-0054
  9885 Mesa Rim Rd Ste 112 San Diego (92121) *(P-17311)*
**Stratos Renewables Corporation** ...................................................... E ...... 310 402-5901
  9440 Santa Monica Blvd Ste 401 Beverly Hills (90210) *(P-6161)*
**Stratus Group Duo LLC** .................................................................... E ...... 323 581-3663
  4401 S Downey Rd Vernon (90058) *(P-1966)*
**Straus Family Creamery Inc (PA)** ..................................................... D ...... 707 776-2887
  1105 Industrial Ave Ste 200 Petaluma (94952) *(P-706)*
**Streamline Avionics Inc** .................................................................... E ...... 949 861-8151
  17672 Armstrong Ave Irvine (92614) *(P-11231)*
**Streamline Circuits LLC** ................................................................... B ...... 408 727-1418
  1410 Martin Ave Santa Clara (95050) *(P-12230)*
**Streamline Dsign Slkscreen Inc (PA)** ................................................ D ...... 805 884-1025
  1299 S Wells Rd Ventura (93004) *(P-2645)*
**Streamline Electronics Mfg Inc** ......................................................... E ...... 408 263-3600
  4285 Technology Dr Fremont (94538) *(P-12231)*
**Streamsets Inc** .................................................................................. D ...... 415 851-1018
  1875 S Grant St Ste 810 San Mateo (94402) *(P-17984)*
**Strech Plastics Incorporated** ............................................................. E ...... 951 922-2224
  900 John St Ste J Banning (92220) *(P-16925)*
**Street Smart 247, El Segundo** *Also Called: Street Smart LLC (P-18841)*
**Street Smart LLC** .............................................................................. E ...... 866 924-4644
  100 N Pacific Coast Hwy El Segundo (90245) *(P-18841)*
**Streeter Printing Inc** .......................................................................... F ...... 858 566-0866
  9880 Via Pasar Ste C San Diego (92126) *(P-4773)*
**Streets Ahead Inc** ............................................................................. E ...... 323 277-0860
  5510 S Soto St Unit B Vernon (90058) *(P-2885)*
**Streivor Inc** ........................................................................................ F ...... 925 960-9090
  2150 Kitty Hawk Rd Livermore (94551) *(P-15708)*
**Streivor Air Systems, Livermore** *Also Called: Streivor Inc (P-15708)*
**Stremicks Heritage Foods LLC (HQ)** ................................................ B ...... 714 775-5000
  4002 Westminster Ave Santa Ana (92703) *(P-845)*
**Stress-O-Pedic, Ontario** *Also Called: Stress-O-Pedic Mattress Co Inc (P-3542)*
**Stress-O-Pedic Mattress Co Inc** ....................................................... D ...... 909 605-2010
  2060 S Wineville Ave Ste A Ontario (91761) *(P-3542)*
**Stretch Art, Gardena** *Also Called: Ar-Ce Inc (P-15883)*
**Stretch Forming Corporation** ............................................................ D ...... 951 443-0911
  804 S Redlands Ave Perris (92570) *(P-8585)*
**Streuter Fastel Timtel, San Clemente** *Also Called: Streuter Technologies Inc (P-16633)*
**Streuter Technologies Inc** ................................................................. F ...... 949 369-7676
  208 Avenida Fabricante Ste 200 San Clemente (92672) *(P-16633)*

**Strike Technology Inc** ....................................................................... E ...... 562 437-3428
  24311 Wilmington Ave Carson (90745) *(P-13093)*
**Striker Co** .......................................................................................... F ...... 562 861-2216
  1230 N Jefferson St Anaheim (92807) *(P-9125)*
**Stringking Inc (PA)** ........................................................................... E ...... 310 503-8901
  19100 S Vermont Ave Gardena (90248) *(P-2567)*
**Strocal Inc** ......................................................................................... B ...... 209 948-4646
  4651 Quail Lakes Dr Stockton (95207) *(P-536)*
**Stromasys Inc** ................................................................................... D ...... 919 239-8450
  871 Marlborough Ave Ste 100 Riverside (92507) *(P-18842)*
**Strong Hand Tools, Santa Fe Springs** *Also Called: Valtra Inc (P-16853)*
**Strottman, Irvine** *Also Called: Strottman International Inc (P-15735)*
**Strottman International Inc (PA)** ...................................................... E ...... 949 623-7900
  28 Executive Park Ste 200 Irvine (92614) *(P-15735)*
**Structural Composites Inds LLC (DH)** ............................................. E ...... 909 594-7777
  336 Enterprise Pl Pomona (91768) *(P-8341)*
**Structural Diagnostics Inc** ................................................................ E ...... 805 987-7755
  650 Via Alondra Camarillo (93012) *(P-14926)*
**Structural Stl Fabricators Inc** ............................................................ E ...... 714 761-1695
  10641 Sycamore Ave Stanton (90680) *(P-8223)*
**Structure Therapeutics Inc** ............................................................... D ...... 628 229-9277
  611 Gateway Blvd Ste 223 South San Francisco (94080) *(P-5678)*
**Structurecast, Bakersfield** *Also Called: Golden Empire Con Pdts Inc (P-7339)*
**Stryder Corp (PA)** ............................................................................. D ...... 415 981-8400
  225 Bush St Fl 12 San Francisco (94104) *(P-18843)*
**Stryker Corporation** .......................................................................... E ...... 650 667-4460
  4085 Campbell Ave Ste 200 Menlo Park (94025) *(P-15268)*
**Stryker Dre Ai, Menlo Park** *Also Called: Stryker Corporation (P-15268)*
**Stryker Endoscopy, San Jose** *Also Called: Stryker Sales LLC (P-15410)*
**Stryker Enterprises Inc** ..................................................................... E ...... 408 295-6300
  1358 E San Fernando St San Jose (95116) *(P-9300)*
**Stryker Neurovascular, Fremont** *Also Called: Stryker Sales LLC (P-15269)*
**Stryker Sales LLC** ............................................................................ E ...... 510 413-2500
  47900 Bayside Pkwy Fremont (94538) *(P-15269)*
**Stryker Sales LLC** ............................................................................ E ...... 800 624-4422
  5900 Optical Ct San Jose (95138) *(P-15410)*
**STS, Tehachapi** *Also Called: Sierra Technical Services Inc (P-7696)*
**STS Metals Inc** .................................................................................. D ...... 626 969-6711
  5467 Ayon Ave Irwindale (91706) *(P-8803)*
**Stuart David Inc (PA)** ....................................................................... E ...... 209 537-7449
  3419 Railroad Ave Ceres (95307) *(P-3457)*
**Stuart F Cooper Co** ........................................................................... C ...... 213 747-7141
  1565 E 23rd St Los Angeles (90011) *(P-4828)*
**Stuart-Dean Co Inc** ........................................................................... E ...... 714 544-4460
  14731 Franklin Ave Ste L Tustin (92780) *(P-9017)*
**Stuart's Fine Furniture, Ceres** *Also Called: Stuart David Inc (P-3457)*
**Stud Welding Products, Downey** *Also Called: Qualls Stud Welding Pdts Inc (P-16835)*
**Student Sports LLC** .......................................................................... F ...... 310 791-1142
  23954 Madison St Torrance (90505) *(P-2522)*
**Studio Depot, Pacoima** *Also Called: Mole-Richardson Co Ltd (P-11613)*
**Studio OH, Irvine** *Also Called: Orange Circle Studio Corp (P-4933)*
**Studio Systems Inc (PA)** .................................................................. E ...... 323 634-3400
  5700 Wilshire Blvd Ste 600 Los Angeles (90036) *(P-4472)*
**Studio9d8 Inc** .................................................................................... E ...... 626 350-0832
  9743 Alesia St South El Monte (91733) *(P-2480)*
**Sturgeon Services Intl Inc** ................................................................. B ...... 661 322-4408
  3511 Gilmore Ave Bakersfield (93308) *(P-9438)*
**Style Media Group Inc** ...................................................................... E ...... 916 988-9888
  909 Mormon St Folsom (95630) *(P-4298)*
**Styrotek Inc** ....................................................................................... C ...... 661 725-4957
  345 Road 176 Delano (93215) *(P-6665)*
**Suba Tech, Fremont** *Also Called: Suba Technology Inc (P-12232)*
**Suba Technology Inc** ........................................................................ D ...... 408 434-6500
  46501 Landing Pkwy Fremont (94538) *(P-12232)*
**Subject, Beverly Hills** *Also Called: Subject Technologies Inc (P-18844)*
**Subject Technologies Inc** ................................................................. E ...... 310 243-6484
  345 N Maple Dr Beverly Hills (90210) *(P-18844)*
**Sublimation Inc** ................................................................................. E ...... 888 994-2726
  2537 Willow St Unit 6 Oakland (94607) *(P-16240)*
**Sublime, Oakland** *Also Called: Sublimation Inc (P-16240)*

# ALPHABETIC SECTION — Sun Microsystems

**Sublitex Inc** .................................................................. E ...... 323 582-9596
1515 E 15th St Los Angeles (90021) *(P-2716)*

**Sublitex Sublimation Tech**, Los Angeles *Also Called: Sublitex Inc (P-2716)*

**Submersible Systems LLC** .............................................. F ...... 714 842-6566
7413 Slater Ave Huntington Beach (92647) *(P-15861)*

**Substance Abuse Program** ............................................. E ...... 951 791-3350
1370 S State St Ste A Hemet (92543) *(P-12739)*

**Subtle Luxury**, Torrance *Also Called: Nothing To Wear Inc (P-2684)*

**Subtle Medical Inc** ........................................................ E ...... 650 397-8709
883 Santa Cruz Ave Ste 205 Menlo Park (94025) *(P-18845)*

**Suburban Steel Inc (PA)** ................................................ E ...... **559 268-6281**
706 W California Ave Fresno (93706) *(P-8224)*

**Sudwerk**, Davis *Also Called: Sudwerk Privatbrauerei Hubsch (P-17607)*

**Sudwerk Privatbrauerei Hubsch** .................................... D ...... 530 756-2739
2001 2nd St Davis (95618) *(P-17607)*

**Sue Wong**, Los Angeles *Also Called: S Studio Inc (P-2726)*

**Suess Properties Inc** ..................................................... F ...... 209 334-2081
18378 Atkins Rd Lodi (95240) *(P-16241)*

**Sugar & Rice Saroni** ...................................................... E ...... 510 261-9670
727 Kennedy St Oakland (94606) *(P-17216)*

**Sugar Bowl Bakery**, Hayward *Also Called: Ly Brothers Corporation (P-1225)*

**Sugar Bowl Bakery**, Hayward *Also Called: Ly Brothers Corporation (P-1226)*

**Sugar Foods**, Westlake Village *Also Called: Sugar Foods LLC (P-6162)*

**Sugar Foods LLC** ........................................................... D ...... 323 727-8290
6190 E Slauson Ave Commerce (90040) *(P-1244)*

**Sugar Foods LLC (HQ)** ................................................... E ...... **805 396-5000**
3059 Townsgate Rd Ste 101 Westlake Village (91361) *(P-6162)*

**Sugar Foods LLC** ........................................................... C ...... 818 768-7900
9500 El Dorado Ave Sun Valley (91352) *(P-19135)*

**Sugarfina Inc** ................................................................ E ...... 855 784-2734
377 Santana Row San Jose (95128) *(P-1330)*

**Sugarfina Inc** ................................................................ E ...... 424 290-0777
840 S Pacific Coast Hwy El Segundo (90245) *(P-1331)*

**Sugarfina Inc** ................................................................ E ...... 424 284-8518
20 Hugus Aly Pasadena (91103) *(P-1332)*

**Sugarfina Inc** ................................................................ E ...... 855 784-2734
9495 Santa Monica Blvd Beverly Hills (90210) *(P-1333)*

**Sugarfina Inc** ................................................................ E ...... 949 301-9482
4353 La Jolla Village Dr San Diego (92122) *(P-1334)*

**Sugarfina Inc** ................................................................ E ...... 818 302-0765
779 Americana Way Glendale (91210) *(P-1335)*

**Sugarloaf Farming Corporation** ..................................... E ...... 707 942-4459
12400 Ida Clayton Rd Calistoga (94515) *(P-1766)*

**Sugarsync Inc** ............................................................... E ...... 650 571-5105
6922 Hollywood Blvd Ste 500 Los Angeles (90028) *(P-18846)*

**Suitecentric Lcc** ............................................................ E ...... 760 520-1611
5857 Owens Ave Ste 300 Carlsbad (92008) *(P-11745)*

**Suja Juice**, Oceanside *Also Called: Suja Life LLC (P-17432)*

**Suja Life LLC (PA)** ........................................................ E ...... **855 879-7852**
3841 Ocean Ranch Blvd Oceanside (92056) *(P-17432)*

**Sukarne**, City Of Industry *Also Called: Viz Cattle Corporation (P-624)*

**Sullins Connector Solutions**, San Marcos *Also Called: Sullins Electronics Corp (P-11472)*

**Sullins Electronics Corp** ................................................ D ...... 760 744-0125
801 E Mission Rd # B San Marcos (92069) *(P-11472)*

**Sullivans Stone Factory Inc** .......................................... E ...... 760 347-5535
83778 Avenue 45 Indio (92201) *(P-7549)*

**Sulzer Bingham Pumps**, Santa Fe Springs *Also Called: Sulzer Pump Services (us) Inc (P-9941)*

**Sulzer Elctr-Mchncal Svcs US I** ..................................... E ...... 909 825-7971
620 S Rancho Ave Colton (92324) *(P-19233)*

**Sulzer Pump Services (us) Inc** ...................................... E ...... 562 903-1000
9856 Jordan Cir Santa Fe Springs (90670) *(P-9941)*

**Sulzer Pump Solutions US Inc** ...................................... E ...... 916 925-8508
1650 Bell Ave Ste 140 Sacramento (95838) *(P-9942)*

**Sumco USA Sales Corporation** ...................................... A ...... 408 352-3880
2099 Gateway Pl Ste 400 San Jose (95110) *(P-12740)*

**Sumiden Wire Products Corp** ........................................ E ...... 615 446-3199
1412 El Pinal Dr Stockton (95205) *(P-9234)*

**Sumitomo Pharma America Inc** .................................... C ...... 650 392-0222
2000 Sierra Point Pkwy Brisbane (94005) *(P-5679)*

**Sumitronics USA Inc** ..................................................... E ...... 619 661-0450
9335 Airway Rd Ste 212 San Diego (92154) *(P-12233)*

**Summer Fridays LLC** ..................................................... E ...... 612 804-0868
9180 Wilshire Blvd Beverly Hills (90212) *(P-6042)*

**Summer Rio Corp (PA)** .................................................. F ...... **626 854-1498**
17501 Rowland St City Of Industry (91748) *(P-6422)*

**Summerwood Winery & Inn Inc** .................................... E ...... 805 227-1365
2175 Arbor Rd Paso Robles (93446) *(P-17762)*

**Summit Electric & Data Inc** .......................................... F ...... 661 775-9901
27913 Smyth Dr Valencia (91355) *(P-13313)*

**Summit Enterprises Inc** ................................................ E ...... 858 679-2100
2471 Montecito Rd Ste A Ramona (92065) *(P-4051)*

**Summit Erosion Control**, Ramona *Also Called: Summit Enterprises Inc (P-4051)*

**Summit ESP LLC** ........................................................... F ...... 805 585-0595
27655 Avenue Hopkins Unit B Santa Clarita (91355) *(P-10516)*

**Summit Forest Products**, Cerritos *Also Called: J Summitt Inc (P-3149)*

**Summit Interconnect**, Santa Ana *Also Called: South Coast Circuits LLC (P-12227)*

**Summit Interconnect Inc (HQ)** ..................................... C ...... **714 239-2433**
223 N Crescent Way Anaheim (92801) *(P-12234)*

**Summit Interconnect Inc** ............................................. C ...... 408 727-1418
1401 Martin Ave Santa Clara (95050) *(P-12235)*

**Summit Interconnect - Anaheim**, Anaheim *Also Called: Kca Electronics Inc (P-12148)*

**Summit Interconnect Hollister**, Hollister *Also Called: Royal Circuit Solutions LLC (P-12203)*

**Summit Interconnect Orange**, Orange *Also Called: Fabricated Components Corp (P-12098)*

**Summit Intrconnect Santa Clara**, Santa Clara *Also Called: Streamline Circuits LLC (P-12230)*

**Summit Machine LLC** .................................................... C ...... 909 923-2744
2880 E Philadelphia St Ontario (91761) *(P-13962)*

**Summit Microelectronics Inc** ........................................ E ...... 408 523-1000
757 N Mary Ave Sunnyvale (94085) *(P-12741)*

**Summit Steel Works Corporation** .................................. E ...... 408 510-5880
850 Faulstich Ct San Jose (95112) *(P-8225)*

**Summit Therapeutics Sub Inc** ...................................... C ...... 617 225-4455
2882 Sand Hill Rd Ste 106 Menlo Park (94025) *(P-5680)*

**Sumopti** ........................................................................ E ...... 650 331-1126
742 Moreno Ave Palo Alto (94303) *(P-18847)*

**Sun Badge Co** ............................................................... E ...... 909 930-1444
2248 S Baker Ave Ontario (91761) *(P-16242)*

**Sun Basket Inc (PA)** ..................................................... C ...... **866 786-2758**
501 Folsom St Fl 3 San Francisco (94105) *(P-2361)*

**Sun Basket Inc** ............................................................. D ...... 408 669-4418
1 Clarence Pl Unit 14 San Francisco (94107) *(P-2362)*

**Sun Basket Inc** ............................................................. D ...... 925 240-1512
18675 Madrone Pkwy Morgan Hill (95037) *(P-2363)*

**Sun Chemical Corporation** ............................................ E ...... 562 946-2327
12963 Park St Santa Fe Springs (90670) *(P-6261)*

**Sun Chemical Corporation** ............................................ D ...... 510 618-1302
1599 Factor Ave San Leandro (94577) *(P-6262)*

**Sun Cmpany of San Brnrdino Cal (HQ)** ......................... B ...... **909 889-9666**
4030 Georgia Blvd San Bernardino (92407) *(P-4203)*

**Sun Dairy Co**, Los Angeles *Also Called: Pac Fill Inc (P-841)*

**Sun Deep Cosmetics**, Hayward *Also Called: Sun Deep Inc (P-6043)*

**Sun Deep Inc (PA)** ........................................................ D ...... **510 441-2525**
31285 San Clemente St Hayward (94544) *(P-6043)*

**Sun Diego**, San Diego *Also Called: Athleisure Inc (P-17509)*

**Sun Ice USA**, Riverside *Also Called: Mackie International Inc (P-808)*

**Sun Industries**, Torrance *Also Called: Sun Industries Corporation (P-9998)*

**Sun Industries Corporation** ........................................... E ...... 310 782-1188
370 Amapola Ave Ste 101 Torrance (90501) *(P-9998)*

**Sun Industries Filtration**, City Of Industry *Also Called: Sun Industries Filtration Corp (P-9999)*

**Sun Industries Filtration Corp** ...................................... E ...... 310 782-1188
14322 Bonelli St City Of Industry (91746) *(P-9999)*

**Sun Light & Power** ....................................................... D ...... 510 845-2997
1035 Folger Ave Berkeley (94710) *(P-19136)*

**Sun Manufacturing Solutions**, San Jose *Also Called: Sun Sheetmetal Solutions Inc (P-8586)*

**Sun Microsystems**, Santa Clara *Also Called: Oracle America Inc (P-10185)*

**Sun Microsystems**, Redwood Shores *Also Called: Oracle America Inc (P-10186)*

**Sun Microsystems**, Rocklin *Also Called: Oracle America Inc (P-10187)*

**Sun Microsystems**, Pleasanton *Also Called: Oracle America Inc (P-10188)*

**Sun Microsystems**, San Diego *Also Called: Oracle America Inc (P-10189)*

**Sun Microsystems, Santa Clara** *Also Called: Oracle America Inc (P-10190)*
**Sun Pac Storage Containers Inc** ......................................................... F ...... 949 458-2347
23222 Olive Ave Ste A Lake Forest (92630) *(P-3361)*
**Sun Plastics Inc** ......................................................................................... E ...... 323 888-6999
7140 E Slauson Ave Commerce (90040) *(P-3981)*
**Sun Power Security Gates Inc** ................................................................ F ...... 209 722-3990
438 Tyler Rd Merced (95341) *(P-7653)*
**Sun Power Source (PA)** ............................................................................ F ...... 805 644-2520
1650 Palma Dr Ventura (93003) *(P-11624)*
**Sun Precision Machining Inc** .................................................................. F ...... 951 817-0056
1651 Market St Ste A Corona (92880) *(P-11126)*
**Sun Rich Foods Intl Corp** ........................................................................ F ...... 714 632-7577
1240 N Barsten Way Anaheim (92806) *(P-2364)*
**Sun Sheetmetal Solutions Inc** ................................................................ E ...... 408 445-8047
3565 Charter Park Dr San Jose (95136) *(P-8586)*
**Sun Sports Apparels, Irvine** *Also Called: Sunsports Inc (P-4963)*
**Sun Stone Sales, Temecula** *Also Called: Sunstone Components Group Inc (P-8893)*
**Sun Ten Laboratories Inc** ........................................................................ E ...... 949 587-1238
9250 Jeronimo Rd Irvine (92618) *(P-5681)*
**Sun Ten Labs Liquidation Co** .................................................................. F ...... 949 587-0509
9250 Jeronimo Rd Irvine (92618) *(P-17217)*
**Sun Tropics Inc** ......................................................................................... F ...... 925 202-2221
4000 Executive Pkwy Ste 190 San Ramon (94583) *(P-1017)*
**Sun Valley Extrusion, Los Angeles** *Also Called: Sun Valley Products Inc (P-7749)*
**Sun Valley Floral Group LLC** ................................................................. A ...... 707 826-8700
3160 Upper Bay Rd Arcata (95521) *(P-16243)*
**Sun Valley Ltg Standards Inc** ................................................................. D ...... 661 233-2000
660 W Avenue O Palmdale (93551) *(P-11559)*
**Sun Valley Products Inc** .......................................................................... E ...... 818 247-8350
4640 Sperry St Los Angeles (90039) *(P-7749)*
**Sun Valley Products Inc (HQ)** ................................................................. E ...... 818 247-8350
4626 Sperry St Los Angeles (90039) *(P-7750)*
**Sun Valley Rice, Arbuckle** *Also Called: Sun Valley Rice Company LLC (P-1082)*
**Sun Valley Rice Company LLC** ............................................................... D ...... 530 476-3000
7050 Eddy Rd Arbuckle (95912) *(P-1082)*
**Sun Vlley Rsins Inc A Cal Corp** .............................................................. F ...... 559 233-8070
9595 S Hughes Ave Fresno (93706) *(P-965)*
**Sun-Gro Commodities Inc (PA)** .............................................................. E ...... 661 393-2612
34575 Famoso Rd Bakersfield (93308) *(P-1152)*
**Sun-Mate Corp** .......................................................................................... F ...... 818 700-0572
19730 Ventura Blvd Ste 18 Woodland Hills (91364) *(P-15769)*
**Sunbeam, Fontana** *Also Called: Sunbeam Products Inc (P-11396)*
**Sunbeam Products Inc** ............................................................................ F ...... 951 727-3901
13052 Jurupa Ave Fontana (92337) *(P-11396)*
**Sunbritetv LLC (DH)** ................................................................................. F ...... 805 214-7250
2630 Townsgate Rd Ste F Westlake Village (91361) *(P-11954)*
**Sunco Lighting Inc** ................................................................................... E ...... 844 334-9938
27811 Hancock Pkwy Ste A Valencia (91355) *(P-16674)*
**Suncoast Post, Ontario** *Also Called: Suncoast Post-Tension Ltd (P-16763)*
**Suncoast Post-Tension Ltd** .................................................................... F ...... 909 673-0490
1528 E Cedar St Ontario (91761) *(P-16763)*
**Suncore Inc** ............................................................................................... E ...... 949 450-0054
15 Hubble Ste 200 Irvine (92618) *(P-12742)*
**Sundance Custom Golf Carts, El Cajon** *Also Called: Sundance Custom Golf Carts Inc (P-16926)*
**Sundance Custom Golf Carts Inc** .......................................................... F ...... 619 449-0822
1240 Vernon Way El Cajon (92020) *(P-16926)*
**Sundance Spas, Chino** *Also Called: Jacuzzi Brands LLC (P-16154)*
**Sundance Spas, Irvine** *Also Called: Sundance Spas Inc (P-16244)*
**Sundance Spas Inc (DH)** ......................................................................... D ...... 909 606-7733
17872 Gillette Ave Ste 300 Irvine (92614) *(P-16244)*
**Sunderstorm LLC** ..................................................................................... E ...... 818 605-6682
1146 N Central Ave Glendale (91202) *(P-16245)*
**Sundial Industries Inc** ............................................................................. E ...... 818 767-4477
8421 Telfair Ave Sun Valley (91352) *(P-9126)*
**Sundial Powder Coatings Inc** ................................................................ E ...... 818 767-4477
8421 Telfair Ave Sun Valley (91352) *(P-9127)*
**Sundown Foods, Fontana** *Also Called: Sundown Foods USA Inc (P-929)*
**Sundown Foods USA Inc** ........................................................................ E ...... 909 606-6797
10891 Business Dr Fontana (92337) *(P-929)*

**Sundown Liquidating Corp (PA)** ............................................................. D ...... 714 540-8950
401 Goetz Ave Santa Ana (92707) *(P-7178)*
**Suneva Medical Inc (PA)** ......................................................................... E ...... 858 550-9999
5870 Pacific Center Blvd San Diego (92121) *(P-6044)*
**Suneye, Sebastopol** *Also Called: Solmetric Corporation (P-14923)*
**Sunfusion Energy Systems Inc** ............................................................. E ...... 800 544-0282
9020 Kenamar Dr Ste 204 San Diego (92121) *(P-13151)*
**Sungard, Calabasas** *Also Called: Sungard Treasury Systems Inc (P-18848)*
**Sungard Treasury Systems Inc** ............................................................. C ...... 818 223-2300
23975 Park Sorrento Ste 100 Calabasas (91302) *(P-18848)*
**Sungear Inc** ............................................................................................... E ...... 858 549-3166
8535 Arjons Dr Ste G San Diego (92126) *(P-13963)*
**Sunkist Growers Inc** ................................................................................ E ...... 909 983-9811
531 W Poplar Ave Tipton (93272) *(P-87)*
**Sunkist Growers Inc** ................................................................................ E ...... 844 694-5406
10730 Bell Ct Rancho Cucamonga (91730) *(P-9818)*
**Sunkist Growers Inc (PA)** ........................................................................ C ...... 661 290-8900
27770 Entertainment Dr Valencia (91355) *(P-17171)*
**Sunkist Growers Inc** ................................................................................ F ...... 559 752-4256
11407 Avenue 144 Tipton (93272) *(P-17172)*
**Sunland Aerospace Fasteners** .............................................................. D ...... 818 485-8929
12920 Pierce St Pacoima (91331) *(P-8767)*
**Sunlink Corporation** ................................................................................ F ...... 415 925-9650
2131 Williams St San Leandro (94577) *(P-12743)*
**Sunn America Inc** .................................................................................... E ...... 909 944-5756
10280 Indiana Ct Rancho Cucamonga (91730) *(P-17864)*
**Sunny Sky Products, Fullerton** *Also Called: Dr Smoothie Brands LLC (P-1999)*
**Sunny Sky Products, Fullerton** *Also Called: Dr Smoothie Enterprises LLC (P-2000)*
**Sunnygem, Wasco** *Also Called: Sunnygem LLC (P-930)*
**Sunnygem LLC (PA)** ................................................................................. C ...... 661 758-0491
500 N F St Wasco (93280) *(P-930)*
**Sunnytech Biz Inc** .................................................................................... F ...... 408 943-8100
150 River Oaks Pkwy Ste 100 San Jose (95134) *(P-12236)*
**Sunnyvale Fluid Sys Tech Inc (PA)** ....................................................... E ...... 510 933-2500
3393 W Warren Ave Fremont (94538) *(P-16898)*
**Sunnyvalley Smoked Meats Inc** ............................................................ C ...... 209 825-0288
2475 W Yosemite Ave Manteca (95337) *(P-671)*
**Sunon Inc (PA)** .......................................................................................... E ...... 714 255-0208
1760 Yeager Ave La Verne (91750) *(P-10000)*
**Sunopta Food Solutions, Scotts Valley** *Also Called: Sunopta Globl Orgnic Ingrdnts (P-994)*
**Sunopta Fruit Group Inc** ........................................................................ D ...... 323 774-6000
12128 Center St South Gate (90280) *(P-2027)*
**Sunopta Globl Orgnic Ingrdnts (HQ)** .................................................... E ...... 831 685-6506
100 Enterprise Way Ste B101 Scotts Valley (95066) *(P-994)*
**Sunopta Grains and Foods Inc** ............................................................. D ...... 323 774-6000
12128 Center St South Gate (90280) *(P-1064)*
**Sunoptics Prismatic Skylights, Sacramento** *Also Called: Washoe Equipment Inc (P-11508)*
**Sunpower, Richmond** *Also Called: Sunpower Corporation (P-12744)*
**Sunpower By Green Convergence, Valencia** *Also Called: Green Convergence (P-16767)*
**Sunpower Corporation (HQ)** .................................................................. C ...... 408 240-5500
880 Harbour Way S Ste 600 Richmond (94804) *(P-12744)*
**Sunpreme Inc** ........................................................................................... E ...... 408 419-9281
4701 Patrick Henry Dr Bldg 25 Santa Clara (95054) *(P-12745)*
**Sunridge Farms, Royal Oaks** *Also Called: Falcon Trading Company (P-2196)*
**Sunrise Bistro, Walnut Creek** *Also Called: Joroda Inc (P-17589)*
**Sunrise Farms LLC** ................................................................................. D ...... 707 778-6450
395 Liberty Rd Petaluma (94952) *(P-17136)*
**Sunrise Fresh Fruit and Nut Co, Stockton** *Also Called: Sunrise Fresh LLC (P-966)*
**Sunrise Fresh LLC** .................................................................................. D ...... 209 932-0192
237 N Golden Gate Ave Stockton (95205) *(P-966)*
**Sunrise Growers Inc** ............................................................................... A ...... 612 619-9545
2640 Sturgis Rd Oxnard (93030) *(P-2365)*
**Sunrise Med HM Hlth Care Group, Chula Vista** *Also Called: Vcp Mobility Holdings Inc (P-15426)*
**Sunrise Medical (us) LLC** ....................................................................... E ...... 559 292-2171
2842 N Business Park Ave Fresno (93727) *(P-16590)*
**Sunrise Mfg Inc (PA)** ............................................................................... E ...... 916 635-6262
2665 Mercantile Dr Rancho Cordova (95742) *(P-4052)*
**SUNRUN, San Francisco** *Also Called: Sunrun Inc (P-437)*
**Sunrun Inc (PA)** ........................................................................................ B ...... 415 580-6900
600 California St Fl 18 San Francisco (94108) *(P-437)*

# ALPHABETIC SECTION

**Sunrun Solar** ............................................................... F ...... 833 324-5886
775 Fiero Ln Ste 200 San Luis Obispo (93401) *(P-8083)*

**Sunsation Inc** ............................................................. E ...... 909 542-0280
100 S Cambridge Ave Claremont (91711) *(P-1018)*

**Sunset Magazine, Oakland** *Also Called: Sunset Publishing Corporation (P-4299)*

**Sunset Moulding Co (PA)** .......................................... E ...... 530 790-2700
2231 Paseo Rd Live Oak (95953) *(P-3090)*

**Sunset Publishing Corporation (HQ)** ....................... C ...... 800 777-0117
55 Harrison St Ste 200 Oakland (94607) *(P-4299)*

**Sunset Signs and Printing Inc** .................................. E ...... 714 255-9104
2906 E Coronado St Anaheim (92806) *(P-16053)*

**Sunsets Inc** ................................................................ E ...... 310 784-3600
24511 Frampton Ave Harbor City (90710) *(P-2481)*

**Sunsets Separates, Harbor City** *Also Called: Sunsets Inc (P-2481)*

**Sunshine, Montebello** *Also Called: Sunshine Fpc Inc (P-3982)*

**Sunshine Fpc Inc** ....................................................... D ...... 323 721-8168
1600 Gage Rd Montebello (90640) *(P-3982)*

**Sunshine Makers Inc (PA)** ........................................ D ...... 562 795-6000
15922 Pacific Coast Hwy Huntington Beach (92649) *(P-5929)*

**Sunsports Inc** ............................................................ F
7 Holland Irvine (92618) *(P-4963)*

**Sunstar Spa Covers Inc (HQ)** ................................... E ...... 858 602-1950
26074 Avenue Hall Ste 13 Valencia (91355) *(P-16246)*

**Sunstone Components Group Inc (HQ)** .................. E ...... 951 296-5010
42136 Avenida Alvarado Temecula (92590) *(P-8893)*

**Sunsweet Dryers** ....................................................... C ...... 530 824-5854
23760 Loleta Ave Corning (96021) *(P-967)*

**Sunsweet Dryers** ....................................................... C ...... 530 846-5578
26 E Evans Reimer Rd Gridley (95948) *(P-968)*

**Sunsweet Growers Inc** .............................................. D ...... 530 824-5376
23760 Loleta Ave Corning (96021) *(P-969)*

**Sunsweet Growers Inc (PA)** ..................................... A ...... 800 417-2253
901 N Walton Ave Yuba City (95993) *(P-970)*

**Sunsystem Technology LLC** ..................................... C ...... 510 984-2027
2802 10th St Berkeley (94710) *(P-12746)*

**Suntech International Usa LLC** ................................ F ...... 833 282-3731
6060 Corte Del Cedro Carlsbad (92011) *(P-11955)*

**Suntsu, Irvine** *Also Called: Suntsu Electronics Inc (P-13094)*

**Suntsu Electronics Inc (PA)** ..................................... F ...... 949 783-7300
142 Technology Dr Ste 150 Irvine (92618) *(P-13094)*

**Sunvair, Valencia** *Also Called: Sunvair Inc (P-13964)*

**Sunvair Inc (HQ)** ........................................................ E ...... 661 294-3777
29145 The Old Rd Valencia (91355) *(P-13964)*

**Sunwest Industries Inc** ............................................. E ...... 714 712-6233
648 N Eckhoff St Orange (92868) *(P-16940)*

**Sunwest Milling Inc** .................................................. D ...... 530 868-5421
507 Bannock St Biggs (95917) *(P-1083)*

**Supacolor, Hawthorne** *Also Called: Supacolor Usa Inc (P-4964)*

**Supacolor Usa Inc** ..................................................... D ...... 844 973-2862
12705 Daphne Ave Hawthorne (90250) *(P-4964)*

**Super Center Concepts Inc** ...................................... C ...... 323 241-6789
10211 Avalon Blvd Los Angeles (90003) *(P-17387)*

**Super Center Concepts Inc** ...................................... C ...... 323 562-8980
7300 Atlantic Ave Cudahy (90201) *(P-17388)*

**Super Color Digital, Irvine** *Also Called: Super Color Digital LLC (P-4965)*

**Super Color Digital LLC (PA)** ................................... E ...... 949 622-0010
16761 Hale Ave Irvine (92606) *(P-4965)*

**Super Dyeing and Finishing, Santa Fe Springs** *Also Called: Super Dyeing LLC (P-2496)*

**Super Dyeing LLC** ...................................................... D ...... 562 692-9500
8825 Millergrove Dr Santa Fe Springs (90670) *(P-2496)*

**Super Glue, Ontario** *Also Called: Pacer Technology (P-6238)*

**Super Micro Computer Inc (PA)** ............................... A ...... 408 503-8000
980 Rock Ave San Jose (95131) *(P-10206)*

**Super Store Industries** ............................................. D ...... 209 668-2100
2600 Spengler Way Turlock (95380) *(P-816)*

**Super Struct Bldg Systems Inc** ................................ E ...... 760 322-2522
1251 Montalvo Way Ste F Palm Springs (92263) *(P-3608)*

**Super Welding Southern Cal Inc** .............................. E ...... 619 239-8003
1668 Newton Ave San Diego (92113) *(P-574)*

**Super73 Inc (PA)** ....................................................... E ...... 949 258-9245
2722 Michelson Dr Ste 125 Irvine (92612) *(P-14072)*

**Superbam Inc** ............................................................. E ...... 310 845-5784
214 Main St El Segundo (90245) *(P-4473)*

**Supercloset** ................................................................ E ...... 831 588-7829
2321 Circadian Way Santa Rosa (95407) *(P-7966)*

**Supercolor, Irvine** *Also Called: Digital Supercolor Inc (P-4591)*

**Supergiant Games LLC** ............................................. E ...... 714 488-5642
521 Gough St San Francisco (94102) *(P-18849)*

**Superheat Fgh Services Inc** ..................................... F ...... 925 808-6711
1940 Olivera Rd Ste C Concord (94520) *(P-7900)*

**Superior, La Mirada** *Also Called: Superior Storage Tank Inc (P-8342)*

**Superior Awning Inc** ................................................. E ...... 818 780-7200
14555 Titus St Panorama City (91402) *(P-2984)*

**Superior Connector Plating Inc** ............................... E ...... 714 774-1174
1901 E Cerritos Ave Anaheim (92805) *(P-9018)*

**Superior Duct Fabrication Inc** .................................. C ...... 909 620-8565
1683 Mount Vernon Ave Pomona (91768) *(P-8587)*

**Superior Electric Mtr Svc Inc** .................................. F ...... 323 583-1040
4622 Alcoa Ave Vernon (90058) *(P-19234)*

**Superior Equipment Company Inc** ........................... E ...... 707 256-3600
2301 Napa Vallejo Hwy Napa (94558) *(P-16368)*

**Superior Equipment Solutions** ................................. D ...... 323 722-7900
1085 Bixby Dr City Of Industry (91745) *(P-11397)*

**Superior Essex Inc** .................................................... C ...... 909 481-4804
5250 Ontario Mills Pkwy Ste 300 Ontario (91764) *(P-7797)*

**Superior Farms, Sacramento** *Also Called: Ellensburg Lamb Company Inc (P-595)*

**Superior Farms, Sacramento** *Also Called: Transhumance Holding Co Inc (P-618)*

**Superior Farms, Dixon** *Also Called: Transhumance Holding Co Inc (P-619)*

**Superior Farms, Sacramento** *Also Called: Transhumance Inc (P-620)*

**Superior Food Machinery Inc** ................................... E ...... 562 949-0396
8311 Sorensen Ave Santa Fe Springs (90670) *(P-9819)*

**Superior Jig Inc** ......................................................... E ...... 714 525-4777
1540 N Orangethorpe Way Anaheim (92801) *(P-9649)*

**Superior Kitchen Cabinets Inc** ................................. E ...... 209 247-0097
1703 Voumard Ranch Dr Turlock (95382) *(P-3271)*

**Superior Lithographics Inc** ....................................... D ...... 323 263-8400
3055 Bandini Blvd Vernon (90058) *(P-4774)*

**Superior Metal Shapes Inc** ....................................... E ...... 909 947-3455
4730 Eucalyptus Ave Chino (91710) *(P-7751)*

**Superior Metals Inc** .................................................. F ...... 408 938-3488
838 Jury Ct Ste B San Jose (95112) *(P-8588)*

**Superior Mold Co** ...................................................... E ...... 909 947-7028
1927 E Francis St Ontario (91761) *(P-7047)*

**Superior Mold Co** ...................................................... E ...... 714 751-7084
3122 Maple St Santa Ana (92707) *(P-9650)*

**Superior Nut Co Inc** .................................................. F ...... 323 223-2431
5200 Valley Blvd Los Angeles (90032) *(P-17150)*

**Superior Packing Co, Dixon** *Also Called: Ellensburg Lamb Company Inc (P-594)*

**Superior Plating, Anaheim** *Also Called: Superior Connector Plating Inc (P-9018)*

**Superior Press, Santa Fe Springs** *Also Called: Superior Printing Inc (P-4966)*

**Superior Printing Inc** ................................................ D ...... 888 590-7998
9440 Norwalk Blvd Santa Fe Springs (90670) *(P-4966)*

**Superior Quality Foods Inc** ...................................... D ...... 909 923-4733
2355 E Francis St Ontario (91761) *(P-870)*

**Superior Quartz Inc** .................................................. F ...... 408 844-9663
1126 Yosemite Dr Milpitas (95035) *(P-7713)*

**Superior Ready Mix Concrete, Corona** *Also Called: Superior Ready Mix Concrete LP (P-7509)*

**Superior Ready Mix Concrete, Thousand Palms** *Also Called: Superior Ready Mix Concrete LP (P-7513)*

**Superior Ready Mix Concrete LP** ............................. D ...... 619 265-0955
7192 Mission Gorge Rd San Diego (92120) *(P-7505)*

**Superior Ready Mix Concrete LP** ............................. D ...... 619 265-0296
7500 Mission Gorge Rd San Diego (92120) *(P-7506)*

**Superior Ready Mix Concrete LP** ............................. D ...... 760 352-4341
802 E Main St El Centro (92243) *(P-7507)*

**Superior Ready Mix Concrete LP** ............................. D ...... 760 728-1128
1564 Mission Rd Escondido (92029) *(P-7508)*

**Superior Ready Mix Concrete LP** ............................. D ...... 951 277-3553
24635 Temescal Canyon Rd Corona (92883) *(P-7509)*

**Superior Ready Mix Concrete LP (PA)** .................... E ...... 760 745-0556
1564 Mission Rd Escondido (92029) *(P-7510)*

| Company | Code | Phone |
|---|---|---|
| **Superior Ready Mix Concrete LP** | D | 951 658-9225 |
| 1130 N State St Hemet (92543) *(P-7511)* | | |
| **Superior Ready Mix Concrete LP** | D | 619 443-7510 |
| 12494 Highway 67 Lakeside (92040) *(P-7512)* | | |
| **Superior Ready Mix Concrete LP** | D | 760 343-3418 |
| 72270 Varner Rd Thousand Palms (92276) *(P-7513)* | | |
| **Superior Ready Mix Concrete LP** | D | 858 695-0666 |
| 9245 Camino Santa Fe San Diego (92121) *(P-17346)* | | |
| **Superior Sensor Technology Inc** | E | 408 703-2950 |
| 103 Cooper Ct Los Gatos (95032) *(P-14370)* | | |
| **Superior Signs & Installation (PA)** | D | 562 495-3808 |
| 1700 W Anaheim St Long Beach (90813) *(P-16054)* | | |
| **Superior Spring Company** | E | 714 490-0881 |
| 1260 S Talt Ave Anaheim (92806) *(P-9208)* | | |
| **Superior Storage Tank Inc** | F | 714 226-1914 |
| 14700 Industry Cir La Mirada (90638) *(P-8342)* | | |
| **Superior Super Warehouse, Cudahy** *Also Called: Super Center Concepts Inc (P-17388)* | | |
| **Superior Tank Co Inc (PA)** | E | 909 912-0580 |
| 9500 Lucas Ranch Rd Rancho Cucamonga (91730) *(P-8343)* | | |
| **Superior Thread Rolling Co** | D | 818 504-3626 |
| 12801 Wentworth St Arleta (91331) *(P-11127)* | | |
| **Superior Touch, Ontario** *Also Called: Superior Quality Foods Inc (P-870)* | | |
| **Superior Trailer Works** | E | 909 350-0185 |
| 13700 Slover Ave Fontana (92337) *(P-9534)* | | |
| **Superior Warehouse, Los Angeles** *Also Called: Super Center Concepts Inc (P-17387)* | | |
| **Superior Window Coverings Inc** | E | 818 762-6685 |
| 7683 N San Fernando Rd Burbank (91505) *(P-2920)* | | |
| **Superior-Studio Spc Inc** | E | 323 278-0100 |
| 2239 Yates Ave Commerce (90040) *(P-16247)* | | |
| **Supermedia LLC** | E | 562 594-5101 |
| 3131 Katella Ave Los Alamitos (90720) *(P-4474)* | | |
| **Supermicro, San Jose** *Also Called: Super Micro Computer Inc (P-10206)* | | |
| **Supernal LLC** | C | 202 422-3275 |
| 15555 Laguna Canyon Rd Irvine (92618) *(P-7850)* | | |
| **Superpak, Tustin** *Also Called: Durabag Company Inc (P-3966)* | | |
| **Superprint Lithographics, Santa Fe Springs** *Also Called: Superprint Lithographics Inc (P-4775)* | | |
| **Superprint Lithographics Inc** | F | 562 698-8001 |
| 8332 Secura Way Santa Fe Springs (90670) *(P-4775)* | | |
| **Supersonic ADS Inc** | E | 650 825-6010 |
| 17 Bluxome St San Francisco (94107) *(P-16055)* | | |
| **Supersprings International Inc** | E | 805 745-5553 |
| 5251 6th St Carpinteria (93013) *(P-9179)* | | |
| **Supertec Machinery Inc** | F | 562 220-1675 |
| 6435 Alondra Blvd Paramount (90723) *(P-9573)* | | |
| **Supertex Inc (HQ)** | D | 408 222-8888 |
| 1235 Bordeaux Dr Sunnyvale (94089) *(P-12747)* | | |
| **Supervision of Shipbuilding, San Diego** *Also Called: United States Dept of Navy (P-14020)* | | |
| **Superwinch, San Dimas** *Also Called: Superwinch LLC (P-16403)* | | |
| **Superwinch LLC** | E | 800 323-2031 |
| 320 W Covina Blvd San Dimas (91773) *(P-16403)* | | |
| **Superwinch Holding LLC** | D | 860 412-1476 |
| 3945 Freedom Cir Ste 560 Santa Clara (95054) *(P-9439)* | | |
| **Supherb Farms** | C | 209 633-3600 |
| 300 Dianne Dr Turlock (95380) *(P-2366)* | | |
| **Supherb Farms, Turlock** *Also Called: Supherb Farms (P-2366)* | | |
| **Supira Medical Inc** | E | 408 560-2500 |
| 590 Division St Campbell (95008) *(P-15270)* | | |
| **Supplier Diversity Program, Carlsbad** *Also Called: Life Technologies Corporation (P-14685)* | | |
| **Support Equipment, Escondido** *Also Called: C & H Machine Inc (P-10758)* | | |
| **Support Sales, Redwood City** *Also Called: Oracle Systems Corporation (P-18645)* | | |
| **Support Systems Intl Corp** | D | 510 234-9090 |
| 136 S 2nd St Dept B Richmond (94804) *(P-13095)* | | |
| **Support Technologies Inc** | F | 949 442-2957 |
| 1939 Deere Ave Irvine (92606) *(P-18850)* | | |
| **Supportpay, Mountain View** *Also Called: Ittavi Inc (P-18450)* | | |
| **Supracor Inc** | E | 408 432-1616 |
| 2050 Corporate Ct San Jose (95131) *(P-3543)* | | |
| **Supreme Enterprise, Santa Fe Springs** *Also Called: Kingsolver Inc (P-15931)* | | |
| **Supreme Graphics Inc** | F | 310 531-8300 |
| 1201 N Miller St Anaheim (92806) *(P-4776)* | | |
| **Supreme Machine Products Inc** | F | 909 974-0349 |
| 302 Sequoia Ave Ontario (91761) *(P-11128)* | | |
| **Supreme Truck Bodies Cal Inc** | E | 800 827-0753 |
| 22135 Alessandro Blvd Moreno Valley (92553) *(P-13431)* | | |
| **Sure Grip International** | D | 562 923-0724 |
| 5519 Rawlings Ave South Gate (90280) *(P-15862)* | | |
| **Sure Power Inc** | F | 619 661-6292 |
| 9255 Customhouse Plz San Diego (92154) *(P-11290)* | | |
| **Sure Power Inc** | F | 310 542-8561 |
| 1111 Knox St Torrance (90502) *(P-13096)* | | |
| **Surecall, Fremont** *Also Called: Cellphone-Mate Inc (P-11824)* | | |
| **Surefire LLC** | E | 714 545-9444 |
| 18300 Mount Baldy Cir Fountain Valley (92708) *(P-15411)* | | |
| **Surefire LLC** | E | 714 545-9444 |
| 17680 Newhope St Ste B Fountain Valley (92708) *(P-15412)* | | |
| **Surefire LLC** | E | 714 545-9444 |
| 17760 Newhope St Ste A Fountain Valley (92708) *(P-15413)* | | |
| **Surefire LLC** | E | 714 641-0483 |
| 2110 S Anne St Santa Ana (92704) *(P-15414)* | | |
| **Surefire LLC** | E | 714 545-9444 |
| 2121 S Yale St Santa Ana (92704) *(P-15415)* | | |
| **Surefire LLC** | E | 714 641-0483 |
| 2300 S Yale St Santa Ana (92704) *(P-15416)* | | |
| **Surefire LLC (PA)** | C | 714 545-9444 |
| 18300 Mount Baldy Cir Fountain Valley (92708) *(P-11625)* | | |
| **Surf Loch LLC** | F | 858 454-1777 |
| 9747 Olson Dr San Diego (92121) *(P-13314)* | | |
| **Surf Ride** | F | 760 433-4020 |
| 1909 S Coast Hwy Oceanside (92054) *(P-2646)* | | |
| **Surf To Summit Inc** | F | 805 964-1896 |
| 7234 Hollister Ave Goleta (93117) *(P-15863)* | | |
| **Surface Art Ems, San Jose** *Also Called: Surface Art Engineering Inc (P-12748)* | | |
| **Surface Art Engineering Inc** | E | 408 433-4700 |
| 81 Bonaventura Dr San Jose (95134) *(P-12748)* | | |
| **Surface Engineering Spc** | E | 408 734-8810 |
| 919 Hamlin Ct Sunnyvale (94089) *(P-9752)* | | |
| **Surface Optics Corporation** | E | 858 675-7404 |
| 11555 Rancho Bernardo Rd San Diego (92127) *(P-14587)* | | |
| **Surface Pumps Inc (PA)** | D | 661 393-1545 |
| 3301 Unicorn Rd Bakersfield (93308) *(P-16846)* | | |
| **Surface Techniques Corporation (PA)** | E | 510 887-6000 |
| 25673 Nickel Pl Hayward (94545) *(P-3672)* | | |
| **Surface Technologies Corp** | E | 619 564-8320 |
| 3170 Commercial St San Diego (92113) *(P-11350)* | | |
| **Surface Technology, Hayward** *Also Called: Surface Techniques Corporation (P-3672)* | | |
| **Surface-Tech LLC** | F | 619 880-0265 |
| 888 Prospect St Ste 200 La Jolla (92037) *(P-6371)* | | |
| **Surgeon Worldwide Inc** | E | 707 501-7962 |
| 3855 S Hill St Los Angeles (90037) *(P-7118)* | | |
| **Surgical Specialties, San Diego** *Also Called: Corza Medical Inc (P-15055)* | | |
| **Surgistar Inc (PA)** | E | 760 598-2480 |
| 2310 La Mirada Dr Vista (92081) *(P-15271)* | | |
| **Surgistar Inc** | F | 760 431-7400 |
| 4751 Oceanside Blvd Ste G Oceanside (92056) *(P-15272)* | | |
| **Surplus Solutions LLC** | F | 760 696-8788 |
| 30220 Commerce Ct Murrieta (92563) *(P-14349)* | | |
| **Surrounding Elements LLC** | E | 949 582-9000 |
| 33051 Calle Aviador Ste A San Juan Capistrano (92675) *(P-3512)* | | |
| **Surrozen Inc (PA)** | E | 650 489-9000 |
| 171 Oyster Point Blvd Ste 300 South San Francisco (94080) *(P-5863)* | | |
| **Surrozen Operating Inc (HQ)** | E | 650 918-8818 |
| 171 Oyster Point Blvd South San Francisco (94080) *(P-5682)* | | |
| **Surtec Inc** | E | 209 820-3700 |
| 2350 Interlaken Ct Lodi (95242) *(P-5930)* | | |
| **Surtec System, The, Lodi** *Also Called: Surtec Inc (P-5930)* | | |
| **Surveillance Systems Group Inc** | F | 877 687-3939 |
| 4193 Flat Rock Dr Ste 200 Riverside (92505) *(P-19137)* | | |
| **Survios Inc** | E | 310 736-1503 |
| 4501 Glencoe Ave Marina Del Rey (90292) *(P-18994)* | | |
| **Survival Systems Intl Inc (PA)** | D | 760 749-6800 |
| 34140 Valley Center Rd Valley Center (92082) *(P-19283)* | | |

# ALPHABETIC SECTION

Suspender Factory Inc .................................................. E ...... 510 547-5400
1425 63rd St Emeryville (94608) *(P-2910)*

Suspender Factory of S F, Emeryville *Also Called: Suspender Factory Inc (P-2910)*

Suss McRtec Phtnic Systems Inc ................................... D ...... 951 817-3700
2520 Palisades Dr Corona (92882) *(P-13315)*

Suss McRtec Prcsion Phtmask In .................................. F ...... 415 494-3113
821 San Antonio Rd Palo Alto (94303) *(P-15668)*

Suss Microtec Inc (HQ) ................................................. C ...... 408 940-0300
2520 Palisades Dr Corona (92882) *(P-9902)*

Sustainable Care Company Inc ..................................... E ...... 310 210-7090
633 W 5th St Fl 28 Los Angeles (90071) *(P-5931)*

SUTRO BIOPHARMA, South San Francisco *Also Called: Sutro Biopharma Inc (P-5864)*

Sutro Biopharma Inc (PA) ............................................. B ...... 650 881-6500
111 Oyster Point Blvd Ste 100 South San Francisco (94080) *(P-5864)*

Sutter Buttes Mfg, Gridley *Also Called: Sutter Buttes Mfg LLC (P-575)*

Sutter Buttes Mfg LLC .................................................. F ...... 530 846-9960
1221 Independence Pl Gridley (95948) *(P-575)*

Sutter Buttes Olive Oil, Yuba City *Also Called: California Olive and Vine LLC (P-1394)*

Sutter Buttes Rubber Co LLC (PA) ................................ F ...... 530 846-9533
286 W Evans Reimer Rd Gridley (95948) *(P-6431)*

Sutter Home Winery Inc (PA) ........................................ C ...... 707 963-3104
100 St Helena Hwy (Hwy. 29) S Saint Helena (94574) *(P-1767)*

Sutter Home Winery Inc ............................................... F ...... 707 963-5928
18655 Jacob Brack Rd Lodi (95242) *(P-1768)*

Sutter Home Winery Inc ............................................... E ...... 707 963-3104
560 Gateway Dr Napa (94558) *(P-1769)*

Sutter Home Winery Inc ............................................... E ...... 707 944-2565
7481 St Helena Hwy S Oakville (94562) *(P-1770)*

Sutter Home Winery Inc ............................................... E ...... 800 967-4663
277 Saint Helena Hwy S Hwy29 Saint Helena (94574) *(P-1771)*

Sutter Home Winery Inc ............................................... E ...... 707 645-0661
303 Green Island Rd Vallejo (94503) *(P-17630)*

Sutter Instrument Corp ................................................. D ...... 415 883-0128
1 Digital Dr Novato (94949) *(P-14725)*

Suzhou South ............................................................... B ...... 626 322-0101
18351 Colima Rd Ste 82 Rowland Heights (91748) *(P-10460)*

Suzuki Motor of America Inc (HQ) ................................. C ...... 714 996-7040
3251 E Imperial Hwy Brea (92821) *(P-17442)*

Suzuki USA, Brea *Also Called: Suzuki Motor of America Inc (P-17442)*

Sv Labs Corporation (PA) ............................................. D ...... 831 722-9526
480 Airport Blvd Watsonville (95076) *(P-17053)*

Sv Probe Inc ................................................................. B ...... 480 635-4700
6680 Via Del Oro San Jose (95119) *(P-14588)*

SV PROBE, INC., San Jose *Also Called: Sv Probe Inc (P-14588)*

Svc Mfg Inc A Corp ....................................................... E ...... 510 261-5800
5625 International Blvd Oakland (94621) *(P-1967)*

Svendsen Marine Distributing, Alameda *Also Called: Svendsens Boat Works Inc (P-16927)*

Svendsens Boat Works Inc ........................................... D ...... 510 522-2886
2900 Main St Ste 1900 Alameda (94501) *(P-16927)*

Svevia Usa Inc ............................................................. F ...... 909 559-4134
13643 5th St Chino (91710) *(P-15892)*

Svf Flow Controls Inc ................................................... E ...... 562 802-2255
5595 Fresca Dr La Palma (90623) *(P-16847)*

Svm Machining Inc ....................................................... F ...... 510 791-9450
6520 Central Ave Newark (94560) *(P-11129)*

Svo Enterprise LLC ...................................................... E ...... 626 406-4770
9854 Baldwin Pl El Monte (91731) *(P-2872)*

SW Fixtures Inc ............................................................ F ...... 909 595-2506
3940 Valley Blvd Ste C Walnut (91789) *(P-3673)*

SW Sustainability Solutions Inc .................................... E ...... 510 429-8692
33278 Central Ave Ste 102 Union City (94587) *(P-2488)*

Swabplus Inc ................................................................ E ...... 909 987-7898
9669 Hermosa Ave Rancho Cucamonga (91730) *(P-6469)*

Swagelok Northern California, Fremont *Also Called: Sunnyvale Fluid Sys Tech Inc (P-16898)*

Swan Fence Incorporated ............................................. E ...... 310 669-8000
600 W Manville St Compton (90220) *(P-17347)*

Swaner Hardwood Co Inc (PA) ..................................... D ...... 818 953-5350
5 W Magnolia Blvd Burbank (91502) *(P-3288)*

Swanson Family Estate (DH) ........................................ E ...... 707 754-4018
1271 Manley Ln Rutherford (94573) *(P-1772)*

Swarco McCain Inc (DH) .............................................. C ...... 760 727-8100
2365 Oak Ridge Way Vista (92081) *(P-16848)*

Swarm Aero, Oxnard *Also Called: Autonomous Defense Tech Corp (P-19052)*

Swartz Glass Co Inc (PA) ............................................. F ...... 310 392-0001
821 Lincoln Blvd Venice (90291) *(P-17350)*

Swatfame Inc (PA) ........................................................ B ...... 626 961-7928
16425 Gale Ave City Of Industry (91745) *(P-17101)*

Swave Photonics Inc .................................................... E ...... 408 963-9958
1610 Canary Dr Sunnyvale (94087) *(P-12749)*

Sway-A-Way Inc ........................................................... E ...... 818 700-9712
8031 Remmet Ave Canoga Park (91304) *(P-13580)*

Sweco, Sutter *Also Called: Sweco Products Inc (P-19284)*

Sweco Products Inc (PA) .............................................. E ...... 530 673-8949
8949 Colusa Hwy Sutter (95982) *(P-19284)*

Sweden & Martina Inc .................................................. E ...... 844 862-7846
600 Anton Blvd Ste 1134 Costa Mesa (92626) *(P-15273)*

Sweet Factory Express, Livermore *Also Called: DSD Merchandisers LLC (P-17400)*

Sweetener Products Inc (PA) ........................................ E ...... 323 234-2200
2050 E 38th St Vernon (90058) *(P-17218)*

Sweetener Products Company, Vernon *Also Called: Sweetener Products Inc (P-17218)*

Sweetie Pies LLC ......................................................... F ...... 707 257-7280
520 Main St Napa (94559) *(P-1245)*

Sweis Inc (PA) .............................................................. D ...... 310 375-0558
20000 Mariner Ave Torrance (90503) *(P-16910)*

Swell Cafe, The, San Diego *Also Called: Swell Coffee Roasting Co LP (P-17219)*

Swell Coffee Roasting Co LP ........................................ E ...... 619 504-9244
501 W Broadway Ste 290 San Diego (92101) *(P-17219)*

Swift Autonomy Inc ...................................................... E ...... 800 547-9438
1141 A Via Callejon San Clemente (92673) *(P-13694)*

Swift Beef Company ..................................................... C ...... 951 571-2237
15555 Meridian Pkwy Riverside (92518) *(P-672)*

Swift Engineering, San Clemente *Also Called: Swift Engineering Inc (P-13965)*

Swift Engineering Inc ................................................... D ...... 949 492-6608
1141a Via Callejon San Clemente (92673) *(P-13965)*

Swift Fab, Gardena *Also Called: Carla Senter (P-8405)*

Swift Solar Inc .............................................................. E ...... 650 297-7943
981 Bing St San Carlos (94070) *(P-12750)*

Swiftcomply, Pleasanton *Also Called: Swiftcomply US Opco Inc (P-18851)*

Swiftcomply US Opco Inc ............................................. F ...... 650 430-4341
6701 Koll Center Pkwy Ste 250 Pleasanton (94566) *(P-18851)*

Swiftlane Inc ................................................................. F ...... 833 607-9438
743 Clementina St San Francisco (94103) *(P-18852)*

Swiftly Inc ..................................................................... C ...... 415 894-5223
49 Stevenson St Ste 700 San Francisco (94105) *(P-18853)*

Swiftstack Inc (HQ) ...................................................... D ...... 408 486-2000
423 Central Ave Menlo Park (94025) *(P-18854)*

Swim Cap Company , The, Chula Vista *Also Called: Next Day Printed Tees (P-3013)*

Swinerton Builders, San Diego *Also Called: Solv Energy LLC (P-18810)*

Swiss Dairy, City Of Industry *Also Called: Dean Socal LLC (P-833)*

Swiss Machine Products, Anaheim *Also Called: Farrell Brothers Holding Corp (P-10835)*

Swiss Screw Products Inc ............................................ E ...... 408 748-8400
339 Mathew St Santa Clara (95050) *(P-11130)*

Swiss Wire EDM ........................................................... F ...... 714 540-2903
3505 Cadillac Ave Ste J1 Costa Mesa (92626) *(P-11131)*

Swiss-Micron Inc .......................................................... D ...... 949 589-0430
22361 Gilberto Ste A Rcho Sta Marg (92688) *(P-8732)*

Swiss-Tech Machining LLC .......................................... E ...... 916 797-6010
10564 Industrial Ave Roseville (95678) *(P-8733)*

Switch Bulb Company Inc ............................................. D ...... 408 457-3821
225 Charcot Ave San Jose (95131) *(P-11431)*

Switch Lighting, San Jose *Also Called: Switch Bulb Company Inc (P-11431)*

Switchboard Software Inc ............................................. E ...... 415 425-3660
268 Bush St San Francisco (94104) *(P-18855)*

Switchboard Software Inc ............................................. F ...... 415 506-9095
115 Sansome St Fl 7 San Francisco (94104) *(P-18856)*

Switching Systems, Anaheim *Also Called: Xp Power Inc (P-13128)*

Swm, El Cajon *Also Called: Delstar Technologies Inc (P-6557)*

Syar Industries, Healdsburg *Also Called: Syar Industries Inc (P-7514)*

Syar Industries Inc ....................................................... E ...... 707 643-3261
885 Lake Herman Rd Vallejo (94591) *(P-302)*

Syar Industries Inc ....................................................... F ...... 707 433-3366
13666 Healdsburg Ave Healdsburg (95448) *(P-7514)*

**Syar Industries LLC (HQ)** .................................................. E ...... 707 252-8711
  2301 Napa Vallejo Hwy Napa (94558) *(P-16485)*
**SYAR INDUSTRIES, INC., Vallejo** *Also Called: Syar Industries Inc (P-302)*
**Sybase, Dublin** *Also Called: Sybase Inc (P-18857)*
**Sybase Inc (DH)** ................................................................. E ...... 925 236-5000
  One Sybase Dr Dublin (94568) *(P-18857)*
**Sybridge Technologies Ala Inc** ......................................... F ...... 909 476-2555
  10155 Sharon Cir Rancho Cucamonga (91730) *(P-9651)*
**Sybron Dental Specialties Inc** .......................................... E ...... 909 596-0276
  1332 S Lone Hill Ave Glendora (91740) *(P-15486)*
**Sybron Dental Specialties Inc (PA)** ................................... C ...... 714 516-7400
  1717 W Collins Ave Orange (92867) *(P-15487)*
**Sybron Endo, Orange** *Also Called: Ormco Corporation (P-15470)*
**Symantec, Mountain View** *Also Called: Gen Digital Inc (P-12442)*
**SymantEC SEC Holdings I Inc** .......................................... E ...... 650 527-8000
  350 Ellis St Mountain View (94043) *(P-12751)*
**Symbolic Displays Inc** ...................................................... D ...... 714 258-2811
  1917 E Saint Andrew Pl Santa Ana (92705) *(P-13966)*
**Symcoat Metal Processing Inc** ......................................... E ...... 858 451-3313
  7887 Dunbrook Rd Ste C San Diego (92126) *(P-9019)*
**Symed Corporation** ........................................................... E ...... 707 255-3300
  215 Gateway Rd W Ste 101 Napa (94558) *(P-19434)*
**Symprotek Co** ................................................................... E ...... 408 956-0700
  950 Yosemite Dr Milpitas (95035) *(P-12237)*
**Symyx Technologies Inc** ................................................... B ...... 408 764-2000
  2804 Mission College Blvd Ste 240 Santa Clara (95054) *(P-19476)*
**Synapse Semiconductor Corp** .......................................... D ...... 408 293-4600
  15 Great Oaks Blvd San Jose (95119) *(P-12752)*
**Synapsense, Folsom** *Also Called: Wmn Corp (P-10298)*
**SYNAPTICS, San Jose** *Also Called: Synaptics Incorporated (P-10441)*
**Synaptics Inc** ..................................................................... F ...... 949 483-5594
  1929 Main St Ste 105 Irvine (92614) *(P-10440)*
**Synaptics Incorporated (PA)** ............................................. B ...... 408 904-1100
  1109 Mckay Dr San Jose (95131) *(P-10441)*
**Synaptics LLC** ................................................................... B ...... 408 904-1100
  1109 Mckay Dr San Jose (95131) *(P-10442)*
**Synbiotics LLC** .................................................................. E ...... 858 451-3771
  16420 Via Esprillo San Diego (92127) *(P-5780)*
**Synchronized Technologies Inc** ........................................ F ...... 213 368-3760
  7536 Tyrone Ave Van Nuys (91405) *(P-10443)*
**Synchrotech, Van Nuys** *Also Called: Synchronized Technologies Inc (P-10443)*
**Synder Inc (PA)** ................................................................. E ...... 707 451-6060
  4941 Allison Pkwy Vacaville (95688) *(P-12861)*
**Synder California Container, Chowchilla** *Also Called: Central California Cont Mfg (P-6769)*
**Synder Filtration, Vacaville** *Also Called: Synder Inc (P-12861)*
**Synear Foods, Chatsworth** *Also Called: Synear Foods Usa LLC (P-361)*
**Synear Foods Usa LLC** ..................................................... E ...... 818 341-3588
  9601 Canoga Ave Chatsworth (91311) *(P-361)*
**Synergetic Tech Group Inc** ............................................... E ...... 909 305-4711
  1712 Earhart La Verne (91750) *(P-13967)*
**Synergeyes, Carlsbad** *Also Called: Synergeyes Inc (P-14826)*
**Synergeyes Inc (HQ)** ......................................................... D ...... 760 476-9410
  2236 Rutherford Rd Ste 115 Carlsbad (92008) *(P-14826)*
**Synergistic Research Inc** .................................................. F ...... 949 476-0000
  11208 Young River Ave Fountain Valley (92708) *(P-9235)*
**Synergy Beverages, Vernon** *Also Called: Gts Living Foods LLC (P-1892)*
**Synergy Direct Response, Santa Ana** *Also Called: Cowboy Direct Response (P-15961)*
**Synergy Health Ast LLC (DH)** ............................................ E ...... 858 586-1166
  9020 Activity Rd Ste D San Diego (92126) *(P-15274)*
**Synergy Microsystems Inc** ................................................ C ...... 858 452-0020
  28965 Avenue Penn Valencia (91355) *(P-10207)*
**Syneron Inc (DH)** ............................................................... D ...... 866 259-6661
  3 Goodyear Ste A Irvine (92618) *(P-15582)*
**Syneron Candela, Irvine** *Also Called: Syneron Inc (P-15582)*
**Synertech PM Inc** .............................................................. F ...... 714 898-9151
  11711 Monarch St Garden Grove (92841) *(P-7871)*
**Syng Inc (PA)** .................................................................... D ...... 770 354-0915
  120 Mildred Ave Venice (90291) *(P-11703)*
**Synopsys, Sunnyvale** *Also Called: Synopsys Inc (P-18858)*
**Synopsys Inc (PA)** ............................................................. B ...... 650 584-5000
  675 Almanor Ave Sunnyvale (94085) *(P-18858)*

**Synplicity Inc (HQ)** ............................................................ C ...... 650 584-5000
  690 E Middlefield Rd Mountain View (94043) *(P-18859)*
**Synsus Prvate Lbel Prtners LLC** ...................................... D ...... 713 714-0225
  980 Rancheros Dr San Marcos (92069) *(P-5932)*
**Syntech Development & Mfg Inc (PA)** .............................. E ...... 909 465-5554
  13948 Mountain Ave Chino (91710) *(P-7048)*
**Synthorx, La Jolla** *Also Called: Synthorx Inc (P-5683)*
**Synthorx Inc** ...................................................................... E ...... 858 352-5100
  11099 N Torrey Pines Rd Ste 190 La Jolla (92037) *(P-5683)*
**Syntiant Corp (PA)** ............................................................ E ...... 949 774-4887
  7555 Irvine Center Dr Ste 200 Irvine (92618) *(P-12753)*
**Syntron Bioresearch Inc** ................................................... B ...... 760 930-2200
  2774 Loker Ave W Carlsbad (92010) *(P-5781)*
**Synvasive Technology Inc** ................................................ F ...... 916 939-3913
  4925 Robert J Mathews Pkwy Ste 130 El Dorado Hills (95762) *(P-15275)*
**Synventive Engineering Inc** .............................................. E ...... 312 848-8717
  3301 Michelson Dr Apt 1534 Irvine (92612) *(P-9589)*
**Sypris Data Systems Inc (HQ)** .......................................... E ...... 909 962-9400
  160 Via Verde San Dimas (91773) *(P-10288)*
**Syriani Brothers Corp** ....................................................... E ...... 707 585-2718
  237 Picnic Ave Apt 24 San Rafael (94901) *(P-4777)*
**Syspro, Tustin** *Also Called: Syspro Impact Software Inc (P-16553)*
**Syspro Impact Software Inc** ............................................. C ...... 714 437-1000
  1735 Flight Way Tustin (92782) *(P-16553)*
**Systech, Escondido** *Also Called: Systech Corporation (P-12019)*
**Systech Corporation** ......................................................... E ...... 858 674-6500
  118 State Pl Ste 101 Escondido (92029) *(P-12019)*
**System Integrators Inc** ..................................................... C ...... 916 830-2400
  1740 N Market Blvd Sacramento (95834) *(P-18995)*
**System Studies Incorporated (PA)** ................................... E ...... 831 475-5777
  21340 E Cliff Dr Santa Cruz (95062) *(P-11789)*
**System Studies Incorporated** ........................................... E ...... 831 475-5777
  2900 Research Park Dr Soquel (95073) *(P-11790)*
**System Supply Stationery Corp** ....................................... F ...... 310 223-0880
  1251 E Walnut St Carson (90746) *(P-16995)*
**System1 Inc (PA)** .............................................................. B ...... 310 924-6037
  4235 Redwood Ave Los Angeles (90066) *(P-18860)*
**Systems Engineering & MGT Co (PA)** .............................. E ...... 760 727-7800
  1430 Vantage Ct Vista (92081) *(P-19423)*
**Systems Mchs Atmtn Cmpnnts Cor (PA)** ......................... C ...... 760 929-7575
  5807 Van Allen Way Carlsbad (92008) *(P-11351)*
**Systems Plus Lumber, Anderson** *Also Called: Haisch Construction Co Inc (P-3309)*
**Systems Technology Inc** ................................................... D ...... 909 799-9950
  1350 Riverview Dr San Bernardino (92408) *(P-10032)*
**Syston Cable Technology Corp** ........................................ E ...... 888 679-7866
  15278 El Prado Rd Chino (91710) *(P-13316)*
**Systron Donner Inertial, Concord** *Also Called: Systron Donner Inertial Inc (P-13097)*
**Systron Donner Inertial, Walnut Creek** *Also Called: Carros Sensors Systems Co LLC (P-14855)*
**Systron Donner Inertial Inc** .............................................. C ...... 925 979-4400
  2700 Systron Dr Concord (94518) *(P-13097)*
**T & F Sheet Mtls Fab McHning I** ...................................... E ...... 310 516-8548
  15607 New Century Dr Gardena (90248) *(P-8589)*
**T & H Store Fixtures, Commerce** *Also Called: Teichman Enterprises Inc (P-3710)*
**T & J Sausage Kitchen, Anaheim** *Also Called: T&J Sausage Kitchen Inc (P-673)*
**T & M Machining** ............................................................... E ...... 805 983-6716
  331 Irving Dr Oxnard (93030) *(P-11132)*
**T & T Box Company Inc** .................................................... E ...... 909 465-0848
  602 N Cypress St Orange (92867) *(P-3919)*
**T & T Enterprises, Corona** *Also Called: Thalasinos Enterprises Inc (P-16899)*
**T & T Foods Inc** ................................................................. E ...... 323 588-2158
  3080 E 50th St Vernon (90058) *(P-871)*
**T & W Converters Inc** ....................................................... F ...... 818 241-1707
  15020 Marquardt Ave Santa Fe Springs (90670) *(P-17024)*
**T B B Inc** ............................................................................ F ...... 559 222-4100
  3586 N Hazel Ave Fresno (93722) *(P-16554)*
**T C B, Sacramento** *Also Called: Thermal Conductive Bonding Inc (P-12768)*
**T E B Inc** ............................................................................ F ...... 909 941-8100
  14288 Central Ave Ste B Chino (91710) *(P-11133)*
**T E M P, Gardena** *Also Called: Thermlly Engnred Mnfctred Pdts (P-8346)*

## ALPHABETIC SECTION

T F Louderback Inc .................................................. C ...... 510 965-6120
  700 National Ct Richmond (94804) *(P-17260)*
T F X, Oxnard *Also Called: Trans Fx Inc (P-16255)*
T G H Aviation, Auburn *Also Called: The Gyro House (P-19286)*
T G Schmeiser Co Inc .............................................. E ...... 559 486-4569
  3160 E California Ave Fresno (93702) *(P-8030)*
T G T Enterprises Inc ............................................... C ...... 858 413-0300
  12650 Danielson Ct Poway (92064) *(P-19540)*
T Hasegawa USA Inc .............................................. E ...... 949 461-3344
  25882 Wright Foothill Ranch (92610) *(P-2028)*
T Hasegawa USA Inc .............................................. E ...... 714 522-1900
  8720 Rochester Ave Rancho Cucamonga (91730) *(P-2029)*
T Hasegawa USA Inc (HQ) ....................................... E ...... **714 522-1900**
  14017 183rd St Cerritos (90703) *(P-2030)*
T Hasegawa USA Inc .............................................. E ...... 951 264-1121
  2026 Cecilia Cir Corona (92881) *(P-2367)*
T I B Inc .................................................................... F ...... 619 562-3071
  9525 Pathway St Santee (92071) *(P-11134)*
T Joseph Raoof MD Inc ........................................... F ...... 818 788-5060
  16133 Ventura Blvd Ste 340 Encino (91436) *(P-19322)*
T L Fabrications LP ................................................. D ...... 562 802-3980
  2921 E Coronado St Anaheim (92806) *(P-19215)*
T L Timmerman Cnstr Inc ....................................... E ...... 760 244-2532
  9845 Santa Fe Ave E Hesperia (92345) *(P-3319)*
T M B, San Fernando *Also Called: Jme Inc (P-16655)*
T M C, Berkeley *Also Called: Terminal Manufacturing Co LLC (P-8227)*
T M Cobb Company (PA) ......................................... E ...... 951 248-2400
  500 Palmyrita Ave Riverside (92507) *(P-3194)*
T M Cobb Company ................................................ D ...... 209 948-5358
  2651 E Roosevelt St Stockton (95205) *(P-3195)*
T M I, Gardena *Also Called: Timbucktoo Manufacturing Inc (P-10606)*
T M P Services Inc (PA) .......................................... E ...... 951 213-3900
  2929 Kansas Ave Riverside (92507) *(P-8687)*
T R I, Yucaipa *Also Called: Technical Resource Industries (P-11473)*
T S I, Valencia *Also Called: Tape Specialty Inc (P-16736)*
T S M, Los Angeles *Also Called: Tubular Specialties Mfg Inc (P-7280)*
T T S Construction Corporation ............................... E ...... 209 333-7788
  1220 E Pine St Lodi (95240) *(P-398)*
T W I, Sunnyvale *Also Called: Thomas West Inc (P-2950)*
T Y R, Huntington Beach *Also Called: Tyr Sport Inc (P-17106)*
T-1 Lighting Inc ....................................................... F ...... 626 234-2328
  9929 Pioneer Blvd Santa Fe Springs (90670) *(P-11560)*
T-Rex Grilles, Corona *Also Called: T-Rex Truck Products Inc (P-8810)*
T-Rex Products Incorporated .................................. F ...... 619 482-4424
  7920 Airway Rd Ste A6 San Diego (92154) *(P-16248)*
T-Rex Truck Products Inc ....................................... D ...... 800 287-5900
  2365 Railroad St Corona (92878) *(P-8810)*
T.B.S. Irrigation, Santee *Also Called: TBs Irrigation Products Inc (P-8057)*
T/O Printing, Westlake Village *Also Called: Thousand Oaks Prtg & Spc Inc (P-19139)*
T/Q Systems Inc ..................................................... E ...... 949 455-0478
  25131 Arctic Ocean Dr Lake Forest (92630) *(P-11135)*
T&J Sausage Kitchen Inc ........................................ E ...... 714 632-8350
  2831 E Miraloma Ave Anaheim (92806) *(P-673)*
T&S Manufacturing Tech LLC ................................. F ...... 408 441-0285
  1530 Oakland Rd Ste 120 San Jose (95112) *(P-8226)*
T2c Inc ................................................................... F ...... 213 741-5232
  1348 S Flower St Los Angeles (90015) *(P-2690)*
T3 Micro Inc (PA) .................................................... F ...... 310 452-2888
  301 Arizona Ave Ste 230 Santa Monica (90401) *(P-11414)*
Ta Aerospace Co .................................................... C ...... 661 702-0448
  28065 Franklin Pkwy Valencia (91355) *(P-5207)*
Ta Aerospace Co (DH) ............................................ C ...... **661 775-1100**
  28065 Franklin Pkwy Valencia (91355) *(P-6541)*
Ta Division, Valencia *Also Called: Ta Aerospace Co (P-5207)*
TA Industries Inc (HQ) ............................................ F ...... 562 466-1000
  11130 Bloomfield Ave Santa Fe Springs (90670) *(P-16771)*
Tab32, Roseville *Also Called: Integrated Charts Inc (P-18424)*
Tabc Inc (DH) ......................................................... C ...... 562 984-3305
  6375 N Paramount Blvd Long Beach (90805) *(P-13432)*
Taber Company Inc ................................................ D ...... 714 543-7100
  121 Waterworks Way Ste 100 Irvine (92618) *(P-3196)*

Tablas Creek Vnyrd A Cal Ltd P .............................. F ...... 805 237-1231
  9339 Adelaida Rd Paso Robles (93446) *(P-1773)*
Table Bluff Brewing Inc (PA) ................................... E ...... **707 445-4480**
  617 4th St Eureka (95501) *(P-1463)*
Tabor Communications Inc ..................................... E ...... 858 625-0070
  8445 Camino Santa Fe Ste 101 San Diego (92121) *(P-4475)*
TAC Yamas, Pleasanton *Also Called: Schneder Elc Bldngs Amrcas Inc (P-13302)*
Tackett Volume Press Inc ....................................... E ...... 916 374-8991
  1348 Terminal St West Sacramento (95691) *(P-4778)*
Tacna International Corp ........................................ F ...... 619 661-1261
  9255 Customhouse Plz Ste G San Diego (92154) *(P-19541)*
Taco Works Inc ....................................................... E ...... 805 541-1556
  3424 Sacramento Dr San Luis Obispo (93401) *(P-2104)*
Tactical Command Inds Inc (DH) ............................ E ...... **925 219-1097**
  4700 E Airport Dr Ontario (91761) *(P-12020)*
Tactical Communications Corp ............................... E ...... 805 987-4100
  473 Post St Camarillo (93010) *(P-12021)*
Tactical Micro Inc (DH) ........................................... F ...... **714 547-1174**
  1740 E Wilshire Ave Santa Ana (92705) *(P-13317)*
Tacticombat Inc ...................................................... F ...... 626 315-4433
  11640 Mcbean Dr El Monte (91732) *(P-15864)*
Tacticon Armament, Rancho Cordova *Also Called: Concealed Carrier LLC (P-9138)*
Tactsquad, Corona *Also Called: Amwear USA Inc (P-2556)*
Tacupeto Chips & Salsa Inc ................................... F ...... 760 597-9400
  1330 Distribution Way Ste A Vista (92081) *(P-2105)*
Taft Production Company ....................................... D ...... 661 765-7194
  950 Petroleum Club Rd Taft (93268) *(P-118)*
Taft Street Inc ........................................................ E ...... 707 823-2049
  2030 Barlow Ln Sebastopol (95472) *(P-1774)*
Taft Street Winery, Sebastopol *Also Called: Taft Street Inc (P-1774)*
Tag Rag, Los Angeles *Also Called: Fetish Group Inc (P-2620)*
Tag Toys Inc .......................................................... D ...... 310 639-4566
  1810 S Acacia Ave Compton (90220) *(P-16249)*
Tagnos Inc ............................................................. E ...... 949 305-0806
  555 W 5th St Fl 34 Los Angeles (90013) *(P-18861)*
Tagtime Usa Inc ..................................................... B ...... 323 587-1555
  4601 District Blvd Vernon (90058) *(P-4053)*
Tahiti Cabinets Inc ................................................. D ...... 714 693-0618
  5419 E La Palma Ave Anaheim (92807) *(P-3751)*
Tahiti Trading Company, Riverside *Also Called: Tropical Functional Labs LLC (P-784)*
Tailgate Printing Inc ............................................... D ...... 714 966-3035
  2930 S Fairview St Santa Ana (92704) *(P-4779)*
Tait & Associates Inc ............................................. E ...... 714 560-8222
  2131 S Dupont Dr Anaheim (92806) *(P-8344)*
Tajen Graphics Inc ................................................. E ...... 714 527-3122
  2100 W Lincoln Ave Ste B Anaheim (92801) *(P-4780)*
Tajima Usa Inc ....................................................... E ...... 310 604-8200
  19925 S Susana Rd Compton (90221) *(P-9753)*
Takara Bio Usa Inc (DH) ........................................ E ...... **650 919-7300**
  2560 Orchard Pkwy San Jose (95131) *(P-19477)*
Takara Sake USA Inc (DH) ..................................... F ...... **510 540-8250**
  708 Addison St Berkeley (94710) *(P-1846)*
Take A Break Paper ............................................... E ...... 323 333-7773
  1048 W Gardena Blvd Gardena (90247) *(P-4204)*
Take It For Granite Inc ........................................... E ...... 408 790-2812
  345 Phelan Ave San Jose (95112) *(P-295)*
Takuyo Corporation ................................................ F ...... 310 782-6927
  970 W 190th St Ste 620 Torrance (90502) *(P-4205)*
Takyo Tyco, Los Angeles *Also Called: Ruben & Leon Inc (P-19177)*
Talbert Archtctral Panl Door I ................................. D ...... 714 671-9700
  711 S Stimson Ave City Of Industry (91745) *(P-3197)*
Talbott Ties, Monterey *Also Called: Robert Talbott Inc (P-2565)*
Talco Foam Inc (PA) .............................................. F ...... **916 492-8840**
  1631 Enterprise Blvd Ste 30 West Sacramento (95691) *(P-6542)*
Talco Foam Products, West Sacramento *Also Called: Talco Foam Inc (P-6542)*
Talco Plastics Inc ................................................... D ...... 562 630-1224
  3270 E 70th St Long Beach (90805) *(P-7049)*
Talco Plastics Inc (PA) ........................................... D ...... **951 531-2000**
  1000 W Rincon St Corona (92878) *(P-16365)*
Talena Inc ............................................................... E ...... 408 649-6338
  2860 Zanker Rd Ste 109 San Jose (95134) *(P-18862)*

**Talimar Systems Inc** | **ALPHABETIC SECTION**

**Talimar Systems Inc** ............................................................. E ...... 714 557-4884
3105 W Alpine St Santa Ana (92704) *(P-3640)*

**Talix Inc** ............................................................................. D ...... 628 220-3885
660 3rd St San Francisco (94107) *(P-18863)*

**Tall Tree Insurance Company** .............................................. D ...... 650 857-1501
1501 Page Mill Rd Palo Alto (94304) *(P-10208)*

**Talladium Inc (PA)** ............................................................. E ...... **661 295-0900**
27360 Muirfield Ln Valencia (91355) *(P-15488)*

**Talley Metal Fabrication, San Jacinto** *Also Called: J Talley Corporation (P-8629)*

**Talley Oil Inc** ..................................................................... E ...... 559 673-9011
12483 Road 29 Madera (93638) *(P-383)*

**Talley Vineyards** ................................................................ F ...... 805 489-0446
3031 Lopez Dr Arroyo Grande (93420) *(P-1775)*

**Tallgrass Pictures LLC** ........................................................ E ...... 619 227-2701
710 13th St Ste 300 San Diego (92101) *(P-1246)*

**Talmo & Chinn Inc** ............................................................. E ...... 626 443-1741
9537 Telstar Ave Ste 131 El Monte (91731) *(P-12754)*

**Talon Innovations, Fremont** *Also Called: Ichor Systems Inc (P-12471)*

**Talon International Inc (PA)** ............................................... C ...... 818 444-4100
21900 Burbank Blvd Ste 101 Woodland Hills (91367) *(P-17072)*

**Talos Corporation** .............................................................. E ...... 713 328-3071
512 2nd Ave Redwood City (94063) *(P-11136)*

**Talphera, San Mateo** *Also Called: Talphera Inc (P-5684)*

**Talphera Inc** ...................................................................... F ...... 650 216-3500
1850 Gateway Dr Ste 175 San Mateo (94404) *(P-5684)*

**Talsco, Garden Grove** *Also Called: Jvr Sheetmetal Fabrication Inc (P-13674)*

**Talsco Inc** .......................................................................... E ...... 714 841-2464
7101 Patterson Dr Garden Grove (92841) *(P-13968)*

**Tam Printing Inc** ................................................................ F ...... 714 224-4488
2961 E White Star Ave Anaheim (92806) *(P-4781)*

**Tamaki Rice Corporation** ................................................... E ...... 530 473-2862
1701 Abel Rd Williams (95987) *(P-1084)*

**Tamalpais Coml Cabinetry Inc** ........................................... E ...... 510 231-6800
200 9th St Richmond (94801) *(P-3272)*

**Tamana Corporation** ......................................................... F ...... 408 358-0747
455 Los Gatos Blvd Ste 10 Los Gatos (95032) *(P-19353)*

**Tamarack Sprng Mutl Wtr Co Inc (PA)** ................................. E ...... 209 369-2761
125 N Church St Lodi (95240) *(P-4206)*

**Tamco (HQ)** ....................................................................... E ...... **909 899-0660**
5425 Industrial Pkwy San Bernardino (92407) *(P-7630)*

**Tamco** ............................................................................... B ...... 949 552-9714
1000 Quail St Ste 260 Newport Beach (92660) *(P-8712)*

**Tammy Taylor Nails Inc** ...................................................... E ...... 949 250-9287
2001 E Deere Ave Santa Ana (92705) *(P-5208)*

**Tampico Spice Co Incorporated** ......................................... E ...... 323 235-3154
5901 S Central Ave # 5941 Los Angeles (90001) *(P-2368)*

**Tampico Spice Company, Los Angeles** *Also Called: Tampico Spice Co Incorporated (P-2368)*

**Tamshell, Corona** *Also Called: Tamshell Corp (P-7050)*

**Tamshell Corp** ................................................................... D ...... 951 272-9395
545 Monica Cir Corona (92878) *(P-7050)*

**Tamura Corporation of America (HQ)** ................................. E ...... **800 472-6624**
277 Rancheros Dr Ste 190 San Marcos (92069) *(P-16735)*

**Tanco Inc** ........................................................................... E ...... 209 523-8365
2310 N Walnut Rd Turlock (95382) *(P-438)*

**Tandem Design Inc** ............................................................ E ...... 714 978-7272
1916 W 144th St Gardena (90249) *(P-16250)*

**TANDEM DIABETES CARE, San Diego** *Also Called: Tandem Diabetes Care Inc (P-15276)*

**Tandem Diabetes Care Inc (PA)** .......................................... A ...... **858 366-6900**
12400 High Bluff Dr San Diego (92130) *(P-15276)*

**Tandem Exhibit, Gardena** *Also Called: Tandem Design Inc (P-16250)*

**Tandex Test Labs Inc** ......................................................... E ...... 626 962-7166
15849 Business Center Dr Irwindale (91706) *(P-19509)*

**Tanfield Engrg Systems US Inc** ........................................... F ...... 559 443-6602
2686 S Maple Ave Fresno (93725) *(P-9440)*

**Tangent Computer Inc (PA)** ............................................... E ...... **800 342-9388**
191 Airport Blvd Burlingame (94010) *(P-17559)*

**Tangerine Express Inc** ....................................................... E ...... 702 260-6650
4870 Adohr Ln A Camarillo (93012) *(P-17724)*

**Tangerine Office Systems, Camarillo** *Also Called: Tangerine Express Inc (P-17724)*

**Tanget Fastnet, Burlingame** *Also Called: Tangent Computer Inc (P-17559)*

**Tangible Science LLC** ......................................................... E ...... 650 241-1045
750 Broadway St Redwood City (94063) *(P-15622)*

**Tangle Inc** ......................................................................... E ...... 650 616-7900
310 Littlefield Ave South San Francisco (94080) *(P-6543)*

**Tangle Creations, South San Francisco** *Also Called: Tangle Inc (P-6543)*

**Tango Systems LLC** ........................................................... D ...... 408 526-2330
1980 Concourse Dr San Jose (95131) *(P-11432)*

**Tanimura & Antle, Salinas** *Also Called: Tanimura Antle Fresh Foods Inc (P-7)*

**Tanimura Antle Fresh Foods Inc (PA)** .................................. D ...... **831 455-2950**
1 Harris Rd Salinas (93908) *(P-7)*

**Tanium Inc** ........................................................................ A ...... 510 704-0202
2100 Powell St 3rd Fl Emeryville (94608) *(P-18864)*

**Tank Depot, Hanford** *Also Called: Acuantia Inc (P-6695)*

**Tanka Inc** .......................................................................... D ...... 650 656-9560
303 Twin Dolphin Dr Ste 600 Redwood City (94065) *(P-18865)*

**Tanko Streetlighting Inc** .................................................... E ...... 415 254-7579
220 Bay Shore Blvd San Francisco (94124) *(P-11561)*

**Tanko Streetlighting Services, San Francisco** *Also Called: Tanko Streetlighting Inc (P-11561)*

**Tanner Research Inc** .......................................................... E ...... 626 471-9700
1851 Huntington Dr Duarte (91010) *(P-19478)*

**Tanoshi Inc** ....................................................................... F ...... 949 677-5261
505 14th St Ste 900 Oakland (94612) *(P-18866)*

**Tap, San Leandro** *Also Called: Tap Plastics Inc A Cal Corp (P-5209)*

**Tap Plastics Inc A Cal Corp (PA)** ........................................ F ...... **510 357-3755**
3011 Alvarado St Ste A San Leandro (94577) *(P-5209)*

**Tapatio Foods LLC** ............................................................ F ...... 323 587-8933
4685 District Blvd Vernon (90058) *(P-931)*

**Tapatio Hot Sauce, Vernon** *Also Called: Tapatio Foods LLC (P-931)*

**Tape and Label Converters Inc** .......................................... E ...... 562 945-3486
8231 Allport Ave Santa Fe Springs (90670) *(P-3956)*

**Tape Specialty Inc** ............................................................ E ...... 661 702-9030
26017 Huntington Ln Ste C Valencia (91355) *(P-16736)*

**Tapemation Machining Inc (PA)** ........................................ E ...... **831 438-3069**
13 Janis Way Scotts Valley (95066) *(P-11137)*

**Tapingo, San Francisco** *Also Called: Tapingo Inc (P-18867)*

**Tapingo Inc (DH)** .............................................................. E ...... 415 283-5222
39 Stillman St San Francisco (94107) *(P-18867)*

**Taproom Beer Co** .............................................................. E ...... 619 539-7738
2000 El Cajon Blvd San Diego (92104) *(P-1464)*

**Taracom Corporation** ....................................................... F ...... 408 691-6655
1735 N 1st St Ste 301a San Jose (95112) *(P-10209)*

**Taral Plastics, Corona** *Also Called: Martin Chancey Corporation (P-6903)*

**Tarana Wireless Inc (PA)** ................................................... F ...... 408 351-4085
630 Alder Dr Milpitas (95035) *(P-11956)*

**Tarantino Wholesale Fd Distrs, San Diego** *Also Called: Producers Meat and Prov Inc (P-17164)*

**Tardio Enterprises Inc** ...................................................... E ...... 650 877-7200
457 S Canal St South San Francisco (94080) *(P-2065)*

**Target Mdia Prtners Intractive, North Hollywood** *Also Called: Target Mdia Prtners Intrctive (P-4967)*

**Target Mdia Prtners Intrctive (HQ)** ................................... E ...... **323 930-3123**
5200 Lankershim Blvd Ste 350 North Hollywood (91601) *(P-4967)*

**Target Technology Company LLC** ..................................... E ...... 949 788-0909
3420 Bristol St Costa Mesa (92626) *(P-13203)*

**Targeted Medical Pharma Inc** ........................................... F ...... 310 474-9809
2980 N Beverly Glen Cir Ste 100 Los Angeles (90077) *(P-19339)*

**Targus US LLC** .................................................................. E ...... 714 765-5555
1211 N Miller St Anaheim (92806) *(P-7142)*

**Taricco Corp** ..................................................................... F ...... 562 437-5433
1500 W 16th St Long Beach (90813) *(P-8345)*

**Tarrant Capital Ip LLC (PA)** ............................................... A ...... **415 743-1500**
345 California St Ste 3300 San Francisco (94104) *(P-17734)*

**Tarsus Pharmaceuticals Inc** .............................................. C ...... 949 409-9820
15440 Laguna Canyon Rd Ste 160 Irvine (92618) *(P-5865)*

**Tartan Fashion Inc** ........................................................... E ...... 626 575-2828
4357 Rowland Ave El Monte (91731) *(P-2647)*

**Tartine LP** ........................................................................ E ...... 415 487-2600
600 Guerrero St San Francisco (94110) *(P-1247)*

**Tartine Bakery & Cafe, San Francisco** *Also Called: Tartine LP (P-1247)*

**Tarulli Tire Inc (PA)** .......................................................... E ...... **714 630-4722**
376 Broadway Costa Mesa (92627) *(P-19155)*

# ALPHABETIC SECTION — Teambridge LLC

**Tascent Inc** .................................................................. F ...... 650 799-4611
475 Alberto Way Ste 200 Los Gatos (95032) *(P-13318)*

**Taseon Inc** ................................................................... F ...... 408 240-7800
515 S Flower St Fl 25 Los Angeles (90071) *(P-14589)*

**Tasker Metal Products** ............................................ F ...... 213 765-5400
1823 S Hope St Los Angeles (90015) *(P-13581)*

**Taste Nirvana International, Corona** *Also Called: PSW Inc (P-2325)*

**Tastepoint By Iff, Corona** *Also Called: Tastepoint Inc (P-6163)*

**Tastepoint Inc** ........................................................... C ...... 951 734-6620
790 E Harrison St Corona (92879) *(P-6163)*

**Tasting Room, Murphys** *Also Called: Lavender Ridge Vineyard Inc (P-1665)*

**Tastries Bakery, Bakersfield** *Also Called: Cathys Creations Inc (P-17408)*

**Tattooed Chef Inc (PA)**............................................. E ...... **562 602-0822**
6305 Alondra Blvd Paramount (90723) *(P-2369)*

**Tatung Company America Inc (HQ)**...................... D ...... **310 637-2105**
2157 Mount Shasta Dr San Pedro (90732) *(P-11957)*

**Tau Motors, Redwood City** *Also Called: Tau Motors Inc (P-13187)*

**Tau Motors Inc** .......................................................... F ...... 650 486-1033
1104 Main St Redwood City (94063) *(P-13187)*

**Taurus Fabrication Inc** ............................................ E ...... 530 268-2650
22838 Industrial Pl Grass Valley (95949) *(P-11138)*

**Tavis Corporation** ..................................................... D ...... 209 966-2027
3636 State Highway 49 S Mariposa (95338) *(P-19479)*

**Tavistock Restaurants LLC** .................................... C ...... 714 939-8686
20 City Blvd W Ste R1 Orange (92868) *(P-17625)*

**Tawa Supermarket Inc (PA)**.................................... C ...... **714 521-8899**
6281 Regio Ave Buena Park (90620) *(P-1049)*

**Tay Ho, Santa Ana** *Also Called: West Lake Food Corporation (P-625)*

**Tayco Engineering Inc** ............................................ C ...... 714 952-2240
10874 Hope St Cypress (90630) *(P-14093)*

**Taylor Communications Inc** .................................. E ...... 916 340-0200
3885 Seaport Blvd Ste 40 West Sacramento (95691) *(P-4992)*

**Taylor Digital** ............................................................. E ...... 949 391-3333
101 W Avenida Vista Hermosa Ste 122 San Clemente (92672) *(P-4968)*

**Taylor Farms, San Juan Bautista** *Also Called: Earthbound Farm LLC (P-80)*

**Taylor Graphics Inc** ................................................. E ...... 949 752-5200
1582 Browning Irvine (92606) *(P-4969)*

**Taylor Guitars, El Cajon** *Also Called: Taylor-Listug Inc (P-16988)*

**Taylor Investments LLC** ......................................... E ...... 530 273-4135
13355 Nevada City Ave Grass Valley (95945) *(P-9976)*

**Taylor Maid Farms LLC** ......................................... E ...... 707 824-9110
6790 Mckinley Ave Sebastopol (95472) *(P-2082)*

**Taylor Wings Inc** ....................................................... E ...... 916 851-9464
11496 Refinement Rd Ste A Rancho Cordova (95742) *(P-8590)*

**Taylor-Dunn Manufacturing LLC (HQ)**................. D ...... **714 956-4040**
2114 W Ball Rd Anaheim (92804) *(P-9535)*

**Taylor-Listug Inc (PA)**.............................................. C ...... **619 258-1207**
1980 Gillespie Way El Cajon (92020) *(P-16988)*

**Taylord Products Intl Inc (PA)**................................ C ...... **619 247-6544**
4505 Lister St San Diego (92110) *(P-3809)*

**Tbc Shared Services LLC** ...................................... A ...... 707 829-9864
742 S Main St Sebastopol (95472) *(P-17466)*

**Tbdx Inc** ...................................................................... E ...... 415 225-1391
1212 Broadway Plz Ste 2100 Walnut Creek (94596) *(P-9820)*

**TBs Irrigation Products Inc** ................................... E ...... 619 579-0520
8787 Olive Ln Bldg 3 Santee (92071) *(P-8057)*

**Tbyci LLC** ................................................................... F ...... 805 985-6800
3615 Victoria Ave Oxnard (93035) *(P-14045)*

**TC Steel** ...................................................................... E ...... 707 773-2150
3700 Lakeville Hwy Ste 215 Petaluma (94954) *(P-19216)*

**Tcho, Emeryville** *Also Called: Tcho Ventures Inc (P-1346)*

**Tcho Ventures Inc** .................................................... E ...... 415 981-0189
1900 Powell St Ste 600 Emeryville (94608) *(P-1346)*

**TCI Engineering Inc** ................................................. D ...... 909 984-1773
1416 Brooks St Ontario (91762) *(P-13388)*

**TCI International Inc (DH)**...................................... C ...... **510 687-6100**
3541 Gateway Blvd Fremont (94538) *(P-11958)*

**TCI Texarkana Inc** .................................................... D ...... 562 808-8000
3855 Obispo Ave Long Beach (90805) *(P-7734)*

**Manufacturing LLC** ............................................... E ...... 213 488-8400
744 E 11th St Los Angeles (90023) *(P-2812)*

**TCS, Chatsworth** *Also Called: Telemtry Cmmnctons Systems Inc (P-11963)*

**TCS Space & Component Tech, Torrance** *Also Called: Trident Space & Defense LLC (P-12773)*

**Tcw Trends Inc** ......................................................... E ...... 310 533-5177
2886 Columbia St Torrance (90503) *(P-2813)*

**Td Synnex Corporation** .......................................... F ...... 510 656-3333
6551 W Schulte Rd Ste 100 Tracy (95377) *(P-10210)*

**Tdg Aerospace Inc** .................................................. F ...... 760 466-1040
2180 Chablis Ct Ste 106 Escondido (92029) *(P-13969)*

**Tdg Operations LLC** ............................................... D ...... 559 781-4116
600 Se St Porterville (93257) *(P-2523)*

**Tdi Signs** .................................................................... E ...... 562 436-5188
13158 Arctic Cir Santa Fe Springs (90670) *(P-16056)*

**Tdi2 Custom Packaging Inc** .................................. F ...... 714 751-6782
17391 Mount Cliffwood Cir Fountain Valley (92708) *(P-3983)*

**Tdk Electronics Inc** ................................................. C ...... 858 715-4200
8787 Complex Dr Ste 200 San Diego (92123) *(P-13098)*

**Tdmi, Gardena** *Also Called: Twin Dragon Marketing Inc (P-2431)*

**Tdo Software, Inc., San Diego** *Also Called: Sonendo Acquisition Corp (P-18811)*

**Te Circuit Protection, Fremont** *Also Called: Te Connectivity Ltd (P-13099)*

**Te Connectivity, Grass Valley** *Also Called: Measurement Specialties Inc (P-14554)*

**Te Connectivity Corporation** ................................ E ...... 805 684-4560
550 Linden Ave Carpinteria (93013) *(P-11352)*

**Te Connectivity Corporation** ................................ C ...... 650 361-3333
300 Constitution Dr Menlo Park (94025) *(P-12898)*

**Te Connectivity Corporation** ................................ D ...... 760 757-7500
3390 Alex Rd Oceanside (92058) *(P-12899)*

**Te Connectivity Corporation** ................................ D ...... 650 361-2495
501 Oakside Ave Side Redwood City (94063) *(P-12900)*

**Te Connectivity Ltd** ................................................. E ...... 650 361-4923
6900 Paseo Padre Pkwy Fremont (94555) *(P-13099)*

**Te Connectivity MOG, El Cajon** *Also Called: Brantner and Associates Inc (P-12866)*

**Te Connectivity MOG Inc (PA)**.............................. F ...... **650 361-5292**
501 Oakside Ave Redwood City (94063) *(P-7206)*

**Tea Financial Services** ........................................... E ...... 951 301-8884
32100 Menifee Rd Menifee (92584) *(P-16941)*

**Tea Tree Essentials, Rancho Santa Margari** *Also Called: Forespar Products Corp (P-7995)*

**Teaaroma Inc** ............................................................. F ...... 310 525-3400
841 E Artesia Blvd Carson (90746) *(P-1368)*

**Teac, Santa Fe Springs** *Also Called: Teac America Inc (P-16555)*

**Teac America Inc (HQ)**............................................ F ...... **323 726-0303**
10410 Pioneer Blvd Santa Fe Springs (90670) *(P-16555)*

**Teacher Created Materials Inc** ............................. C ...... 714 891-2273
5301 Oceanus Dr Huntington Beach (92649) *(P-4476)*

**Teacher Created Resources Inc** .......................... C ...... 714 230-7060
12621 Western Ave Garden Grove (92841) *(P-4347)*

**Teachers Curriculum Inst LLC (PA)**..................... E ...... **800 497-6138**
2440 W El Camino Real Ste 400 Mountain View (94040) *(P-4348)*

**Teague Custom Marine Inc** ................................... F ...... 661 295-7000
28115 Avenue Stanford Valencia (91355) *(P-19285)*

**Teal Electronics Corporation (PA)**....................... D ...... **858 558-9000**
10350 Sorrento Valley Rd San Diego (92121) *(P-11353)*

**Tealove Inc** ................................................................. E ...... 714 408-8245
9810 Sierra Ave Ste A Fontana (92335) *(P-17433)*

**Team, San Jose** *Also Called: Team Research Inc (P-16556)*

**Team Inc** ..................................................................... E ...... 310 514-2312
1515 240th St Harbor City (90710) *(P-7901)*

**Team Air Inc (PA)**...................................................... E ...... **909 823-1957**
12771 Brown Ave Riverside (92509) *(P-10517)*

**Team Air Conditioning Eqp, Riverside** *Also Called: Team Air Inc (P-10517)*

**Team Industrial Services, Harbor City** *Also Called: Team Inc (P-7901)*

**Team Manufacturing Inc** ........................................ E ...... 310 639-0251
2625 Homestead Pl Rancho Dominguez (90220) *(P-8894)*

**Team Research Inc** ................................................. E ...... 408 452-8788
1911 Hartog Dr San Jose (95131) *(P-16556)*

**Team Technologies Inc** .......................................... D ...... 626 334-5000
4675 Vinita Ct Chino (91710) *(P-9652)*

**Team USA (PA)**.......................................................... F ...... **323 826-9888**
2154 E 51st St Vernon (90058) *(P-13389)*

**Teambridge LLC** ....................................................... E ...... 415 323-5571
604 Mission St Fl 10 San Francisco (94105) *(P-18868)*

## ALPHABETIC SECTION

**Teamohana Inc** ............................................................. E ...... 415 650-9767
2067 Golden Gate Ave San Francisco (94115) *(P-18869)*

**Teamraderie Inc** ............................................................ E ...... 650 402-0030
171 Main St # 510 Los Altos (94022) *(P-18870)*

**Teamsable Inc** ................................................................ E ...... 408 452-8788
1911 Hartog Dr San Jose (95131) *(P-16557)*

**Teamwork Athletic Apparel, Carlsbad** *Also Called: R B III Associates Inc (P-2725)*

**Tearlab Corporation** ....................................................... E ...... 858 455-6006
42309 Winchester Rd Ste I Temecula (92590) *(P-15277)*

**Teasdale Foods, Atwater** *Also Called: Teasdale Foods Inc (P-2370)*

**Teasdale Foods Inc** ....................................................... D ...... 209 358-5616
901 Packers St Atwater (95301) *(P-2370)*

**TEC, Rancho Dominguez** *Also Called: Thermal Equipment Corporation (P-14351)*

**TEC Color Craft (PA)** ..................................................... E ...... 909 392-9000
1860 Wright Ave La Verne (91750) *(P-4970)*

**TEC Color Craft Products, La Verne** *Also Called: TEC Color Craft (P-4970)*

**TEC Lighting Inc** ............................................................ F ...... 714 529-5068
115 Arovista Cir Brea (92821) *(P-11626)*

**TEC-Pro, Torrance** *Also Called: Medicool Inc (P-15169)*

**Tecan, Morgan Hill** *Also Called: Tecan Systems Inc (P-14350)*

**Tecan Systems Inc** ....................................................... D ...... 408 953-3100
18635 Sutter Blvd Morgan Hill (95037) *(P-14350)*

**Tecfar Manufacturing Inc** ............................................. F ...... 818 767-0677
8525 Telfair Ave Sun Valley (91352) *(P-11139)*

**Tech Circuits, Santa Clara** *Also Called: Apct-Wallingford Inc (P-12057)*

**Tech West, Fresno** *Also Called: Tech West Vacuum Inc (P-15489)*

**Tech West Vacuum Inc** ................................................. E ...... 559 291-1650
2625 N Argyle Ave Fresno (93727) *(P-15489)*

**Techmer Pm Inc** ............................................................ B ...... 310 632-9211
18420 S Laurel Park Rd Compton (90220) *(P-5210)*

**Techni Cast Corp, South Gate** *Also Called: Techni-Cast Corp (P-7872)*

**Techni-Cast Corp** ........................................................... D ...... 562 923-4585
11220 Garfield Ave South Gate (90280) *(P-7872)*

**Techni-Tools, Moorpark** *Also Called: Testequity LLC (P-19180)*

**Technic Inc** .................................................................... E ...... 714 632-0200
1170 N Hawk Cir Anaheim (92807) *(P-9020)*

**Technical Arts, Placentia** *Also Called: Southern Cal Tchnical Arts Inc (P-11120)*

**Technical Cable Concepts Inc** ..................................... E ...... 714 835-1081
350 Lear Ave Costa Mesa (92626) *(P-13100)*

**Technical Devices, Torrance** *Also Called: Winther Technologies Inc (P-9732)*

**Technical Devices Company, Torrance** *Also Called: Belhome Inc (P-9722)*

**Technical Heaters Inc** ................................................... F ...... 818 361-7185
10959 Tuxford St Sun Valley (91352) *(P-6432)*

**Technical Instr San Francisco (PA)** ............................ E ...... 650 651-3000
1826 Rollins Rd Ste 100 Burlingame (94010) *(P-16605)*

**Technical Instrument SF, Burlingame** *Also Called: Technical Instr San Francisco (P-16605)*

**Technical Manufacturing W LLC** ................................ E ...... 661 295-7226
24820 Avenue Tibbitts Valencia (91355) *(P-16251)*

**Technical Micro Cons Inc (PA)** .................................... E ...... 310 559-3982
807 N Park View Dr Ste 150 El Segundo (90245) *(P-19542)*

**Technical Reps Intl Inc** ................................................. F ...... 408 848-8868
8525 Forest St Ste C Gilroy (95020) *(P-16252)*

**Technical Resource Industries (PA)** .......................... E ...... 909 446-1109
12854 Daisy Ct Yucaipa (92399) *(P-11473)*

**Technical Services, Mountain View** *Also Called: Northrop Grumman Systems Corp (P-14247)*

**Technical Services, San Bernardino** *Also Called: Northrop Grumman Systems Corp (P-14259)*

**Technicolor, Hollywood** *Also Called: Technicolor Usa Inc (P-11705)*

**Technicolor Connected USA, Lebec** *Also Called: Technicolor Usa Inc (P-11704)*

**Technicolor Disc Services Corp (HQ)** ........................ C ...... 805 445-1122
3601 Calle Tecate Ste 120 Camarillo (93012) *(P-13204)*

**Technicolor Usa Inc** ...................................................... A ...... 661 496-1309
4049 Industrial Parkway Dr Lebec (93243) *(P-11704)*

**Technicolor Usa Inc** ...................................................... C ...... 530 478-3000
400 Providence Mine Rd Nevada City (95959) *(P-11959)*

**Technicolor Usa Inc (HQ)** ............................................. A ...... 317 587-4287
6040 W Sunset Blvd Hollywood (90028) *(P-11705)*

**Technicote Inc** ............................................................... E ...... 951 372-0627
1587 E Bentley Dr Ste 101 Corona (92879) *(P-6249)*

**Technifex Products LLC** .............................................. E ...... 661 294-3800
25261 Rye Canyon Rd Valencia (91355) *(P-7558)*

**Techniform International Corp** .................................... C ...... 909 877-6886
375 S Cactus Ave Rialto (92376) *(P-11140)*

**Technipfmc Usa Inc** ...................................................... F ...... 949 238-4150
6400 Oak Cyn Ste 100 Irvine (92618) *(P-9468)*

**Technoconcepts Inc** ..................................................... E ...... 818 988-3364
6060 Sepulveda Blvd Ste 202 Van Nuys (91411) *(P-11960)*

**Technology Integration Group, Poway** *Also Called: PC Specialists Inc (P-16538)*

**Technology Management Concepts, El Segundo** *Also Called: Technical Micro Cons Inc (P-19542)*

**Technology Training Corp** ........................................... D ...... 310 644-7777
3238 W 131st St Hawthorne (90250) *(P-4782)*

**Technology Training Corp (PA)** .................................. F ...... 310 320-8110
369 Van Ness Way Ste 735 Torrance (90501) *(P-19138)*

**Technoprobe America Inc** ............................................ E ...... 408 573-9911
2526 Qume Dr Ste 27 San Jose (95131) *(P-12755)*

**Technosylva Inc (PA)** ................................................... F ...... 619 292-1935
7590 Fay Ave Ste 300 La Jolla (92037) *(P-16558)*

**Technotronix Inc** ........................................................... E ...... 714 630-9200
1381 N Hundley St Anaheim (92806) *(P-12238)*

**Technovative Applications** .......................................... D ...... 714 996-0104
3160 Enterprise St Ste A Brea (92821) *(P-14311)*

**Techtron Products Inc** ................................................. E ...... 510 293-3500
2694 W Winton Ave Hayward (94545) *(P-11503)*

**Techture Inc** ................................................................... E ...... 323 347-6209
1010 Wilshire Blvd Apt 1206 Los Angeles (90017) *(P-4477)*

**Tecnadyne, San Diego** *Also Called: Tecnova Advanced Systems Inc (P-14312)*

**Tecnico Corporation** ..................................................... F ...... 619 426-7385
3636 Gateway Center Ave San Diego (92102) *(P-14018)*

**Tecnova Advanced Systems Inc** ................................. E ...... 858 586-9660
9770 Carroll Centre Rd Ste A San Diego (92126) *(P-14312)*

**Teco Diagnostics** .......................................................... D ...... 714 693-7788
1268 N Lakeview Ave Anaheim (92807) *(P-5782)*

**Tecomet, Azusa** *Also Called: Tecomet Inc (P-15278)*

**Tecomet Inc** ................................................................... A ...... 626 334-1519
503 S Vincent Ave Azusa (91702) *(P-15278)*

**Tecon Pacific, Ontario** *Also Called: Clark - Pacific Corporation (P-7320)*

**Tect Aerospace, San Francisco** *Also Called: Turbine Eng Cmpnents Tech Corp (P-13725)*

**Tecxel, Oceanside** *Also Called: R Zamora Inc (P-8882)*

**Ted Pella Inc (PA)** ......................................................... E ...... 530 243-2200
4595 Mountain Lakes Blvd Redding (96003) *(P-14726)*

**Tedon Specialties A Cal Corp** ..................................... F ...... 530 527-6600
1255 Vista Way Red Bluff (96080) *(P-11141)*

**Tee -N -Jay Manufacturing Inc** .................................... E ...... 818 504-2961
9145 Glenoaks Blvd Sun Valley (91352) *(P-8591)*

**Tee Styled Inc** ................................................................ E ...... 323 983-9988
4640 E La Palma Ave Anaheim (92807) *(P-4971)*

**Tee Top of California Inc (PA)** .................................... E ...... 626 303-1868
11801 Goldring Rd Arcadia (91006) *(P-17082)*

**Teeco Products Inc** ...................................................... E ...... 916 688-3535
7471 Reese Rd Sacramento (95828) *(P-13582)*

**Teeki** ............................................................................... F ...... 323 835-6397
1105 N Topanga Canyon Blvd Topanga (90290) *(P-17102)*

**Tegile Systems Inc** ....................................................... C ...... 510 791-7900
7999 Gateway Blvd Ste 120 Newark (94560) *(P-19480)*

**Tehachapi News Inc (PA)** ............................................ F ...... 661 822-6828
411 N Mill St Tehachapi (93561) *(P-4207)*

**Tei Struthers Wells, Santa Fe Springs** *Also Called: Wells Struthers Corporation (P-8353)*

**Teichert Inc** .................................................................... C ...... 530 587-3811
13879 Butterfield Dr Truckee (96161) *(P-321)*

**Teichert Inc** .................................................................... D ...... 209 832-4150
36314 S Bird Rd Tracy (95304) *(P-322)*

**Teichert Inc** .................................................................... E ...... 530 787-3468
27944 County Road 19a Esparto (95627) *(P-323)*

**Teichert Inc** .................................................................... C ...... 530 885-4244
2601 State Highway 49 Cool (95614) *(P-324)*

**Teichert Inc** .................................................................... D ...... 530 749-12??
3331 Walnut Ave Marysville (95901) *(P-325)*

**Teichert Inc** .................................................................... C ...... 530 743-????
4249 Hammonton Smartville Rd Marysville (95901) *(P-326)*

**Teichert Inc** .................................................................... C ...... 916 351-????
3417 Grant Line Rd Rancho Cordova (95742) *(P-327)*

## ALPHABETIC SECTION — Telesis Bio Inc

Teichert Inc .................................................................................................. D ...... 916 386-6900
8760 Kiefer Blvd Sacramento (95826) *(P-328)*

Teichert Inc (PA) ......................................................................................... C ...... **916 484-3011**
5200 Franklin Dr Ste 115 Pleasanton (94588) *(P-7515)*

Teichert Inc .................................................................................................. D ...... 916 386-6974
8609 Jackson Rd Sacramento (95826) *(P-7516)*

Teichert Inc .................................................................................................. E ...... 916 783-7132
721 Berry St Roseville (95678) *(P-7517)*

Teichert Aggregates, Truckee *Also Called: Teichert Inc (P-321)*
Teichert Aggregates, Tracy *Also Called: Teichert Inc (P-322)*
Teichert Aggregates, Esparto *Also Called: Teichert Inc (P-323)*
Teichert Aggregates, Cool *Also Called: Teichert Inc (P-324)*
Teichert Aggregates, Marysville *Also Called: Teichert Inc (P-325)*
Teichert Aggregates, Marysville *Also Called: Teichert Inc (P-326)*
Teichert Aggregates, Rancho Cordova *Also Called: Teichert Inc (P-327)*
Teichert Aggregates, Sacramento *Also Called: Teichert Inc (P-328)*
Teichert Construction, Sacramento *Also Called: A Teichert & Son Inc (P-16462)*
Teichert Readymix, Sacramento *Also Called: Teichert Inc (P-7516)*
Teichert Readymix, Roseville *Also Called: Teichert Inc (P-7517)*

Teichman Enterprises Inc ....................................................................... E ...... 323 278-9000
6100 Bandini Blvd Commerce (90040) *(P-3710)*

Teikoku Pharma USA, San Jose *Also Called: Teikoku Pharma Usa Inc (P-5685)*

Teikoku Pharma Usa Inc (HQ) ................................................................ D ...... **408 501-1800**
1718 Ringwood Ave San Jose (95131) *(P-5685)*

Teikuro Corporation ................................................................................. E ...... 510 487-4797
31499 Hayman St Hayward (94544) *(P-9021)*

Tekia Inc ..................................................................................................... E ...... 949 699-1300
17 Hammond Ste 414 Irvine (92618) *(P-15623)*

Teklam, Corona *Also Called: Simmons Family Corporation (P-6592)*

Tekni-Plex Inc ............................................................................................ D ...... 909 589-4366
19555 Arenth Ave City Of Industry (91748) *(P-4054)*

Teknor Apex, City Of Industry *Also Called: Teknor Color Company (P-5212)*

Teknor Apex Company ............................................................................ C ...... 626 968-4656
420 S 6th Ave City Of Industry (91746) *(P-5211)*

Teknor Color Company ........................................................................... E ...... 626 336-7709
420 S 6th Ave City Of Industry (91746) *(P-5212)*

Tektest Inc ................................................................................................. E ...... 626 446-6175
5108 Azusa Canyon Rd Baldwin Park (91706) *(P-12901)*

Telair International, Anaheim *Also Called: AAR Manufacturing Inc (P-8295)*

Telatemp Corp .......................................................................................... F ...... 714 414-0343
2910 E La Palma Ave Ste C Anaheim (92806) *(P-14927)*

Telecommunications Engrg Assoc ........................................................ F ...... 650 590-1801
1160 Industrial Rd Ste 15 San Carlos (94070) *(P-11961)*

Teledyne, San Diego *Also Called: Teledyne Instruments Inc (P-12758)*
Teledyne, Los Angeles *Also Called: Teledyne Technologies Inc (P-13106)*
Teledyne Analytical Instrs, City Of Industry *Also Called: Teledyne Instruments Inc (P-14930)*
Teledyne API, San Diego *Also Called: Teledyne Instruments Inc (P-14929)*
Teledyne Battery Products, Redlands *Also Called: Teledyne Technologies Inc (P-13152)*
Teledyne Controls, El Segundo *Also Called: Teledyne Technologies Inc (P-13104)*

Teledyne Controls LLC ............................................................................ A ...... 310 765-3600
501 Continental Blvd El Segundo (90245) *(P-14313)*

Teledyne Cougar Inc ................................................................................ C ...... 408 522-3838
1274 Terra Bella Ave Mountain View (94043) *(P-13101)*

Teledyne Defense Elec LLC .................................................................... C ...... 408 737-0992
765 Sycamore Dr Milpitas (95035) *(P-12756)*

Teledyne Defense Elec LLC .................................................................... C ...... 916 638-3344
11361 Sunrise Park Dr Rancho Cordova (95742) *(P-13102)*

Teledyne Defense Elec LLC (HQ) ........................................................... E ...... **650 691-9800**
1274 Terra Bella Ave Mountain View (94043) *(P-13103)*

Teledyne Dgital Imaging US Inc ............................................................. F ...... 408 736-6000
765 Sycamore Dr Milpitas (95035) *(P-14928)*

Teledyne E2v Hirel Electronics, Milpitas *Also Called: Teledyne Defense Elec LLC (P-12756)*

Teledyne E2v Inc ...................................................................................... C ...... 408 737-0992
765 Sycamore Dr Milpitas (95035) *(P-12757)*

Teledyne Etm (HQ) ................................................................................... D ...... **510 797-1100**
35451 Dumbarton Ct Newark (94560) *(P-11962)*

Teledyne Flir LLC ..................................................................................... C ...... 805 964-9797
6769 Hollister Ave Goleta (93117) *(P-14314)*

Teledyne Flir Cml Systems Inc (DH) ...................................................... B ...... **805 964-9797**
6769 Hollister Ave Goleta (93117) *(P-14727)*

Teledyne Hanson Research Inc ............................................................. E ...... 818 882-7266
9810 Variel Ave Chatsworth (91311) *(P-14728)*

Teledyne Hirel Electronics, Milpitas *Also Called: Teledyne E2v Inc (P-12757)*
Teledyne Impulse, San Diego *Also Called: Impulse Enterprise (P-11459)*
Teledyne Impulse, San Diego *Also Called: Teledyne Instruments Inc (P-11474)*

Teledyne Instruments Inc ....................................................................... D ...... 858 842-3100
9855 Carroll Canyon Rd San Diego (92131) *(P-11474)*

Teledyne Instruments Inc ....................................................................... E ...... 858 842-3127
9855 Carroll Canyon Rd San Diego (92131) *(P-12758)*

Teledyne Instruments Inc ....................................................................... C ...... 858 842-2600
14020 Stowe Dr Poway (92064) *(P-14315)*

Teledyne Instruments Inc ....................................................................... E ...... 818 882-7266
9810 Variel Ave Chatsworth (91311) *(P-14729)*

Teledyne Instruments Inc ....................................................................... D ...... 619 239-5959
9970 Carroll Canyon Rd Ste A San Diego (92131) *(P-14929)*

Teledyne Instruments Inc ....................................................................... C ...... 626 934-1500
16830 Chestnut St City Of Industry (91748) *(P-14930)*

Teledyne Instruments Inc ....................................................................... E ...... 858 657-9800
9970 Carroll Canyon Rd San Diego (92131) *(P-14931)*

Teledyne Lecroy Inc ................................................................................. C ...... 408 727-6600
765 Sycamore Dr Milpitas (95035) *(P-14590)*

Teledyne Lecroy Inc ................................................................................. E ...... 434 984-4500
1049 Camino Dos Rios Thousand Oaks (91360) *(P-14591)*

Teledyne Microwave Solutions, Rancho Cordova *Also Called: Teledyne Defense Elec LLC (P-13102)*
Teledyne Microwave Solutions, Mountain View *Also Called: Teledyne Defense Elec LLC (P-13103)*
Teledyne Optmum Optcal Systems, Camarillo *Also Called: Teledyne Scentific Imaging LLC (P-14827)*
Teledyne RAD-Icon Imaging, Milpitas *Also Called: Teledyne Dgital Imaging US Inc (P-14928)*

Teledyne RAD-Icon Imaging Corp ......................................................... F ...... 408 736-6000
765 Sycamore Dr Milpitas (95035) *(P-14932)*

Teledyne Rd Instruments, Poway *Also Called: Teledyne Instruments Inc (P-14315)*

Teledyne Rd Instruments Inc ................................................................. C ...... 858 842-2600
14020 Stowe Dr Poway (92064) *(P-14316)*

Teledyne Redlake Masd LLC (DH) ......................................................... E ...... **805 373-4545**
1049 Camino Dos Rios Thousand Oaks (91360) *(P-14730)*

Teledyne Reson Inc ................................................................................. E ...... 805 964-6260
5212 Verdugo Way Camarillo (93012) *(P-16928)*

Teledyne Reynolds Inc ............................................................................ C ...... 310 823-5491
1001 Knox St Torrance (90502) *(P-6252)*

Teledyne Scentific Imaging LLC ............................................................. D
4153 Calle Tesoro Camarillo (93012) *(P-14827)*

Teledyne Seabotix Inc ............................................................................. D ...... 619 239-5959
2877 Historic Decatur Rd Ste 100 San Diego (92106) *(P-9746)*

TELEDYNE TECHNOLOGIES, Thousand Oaks *Also Called: Teledyne Technologies Inc (P-13105)*

Teledyne Technologies Inc ..................................................................... B ...... 310 765-3600
501 Continental Blvd El Segundo (90245) *(P-13104)*

Teledyne Technologies Inc (PA) ............................................................. C ...... **805 373-4545**
1049 Camino Dos Rios Thousand Oaks (91360) *(P-13105)*

Teledyne Technologies Inc ..................................................................... B ...... 310 822-8229
12964 Panama St Los Angeles (90066) *(P-13106)*

Teledyne Technologies Inc ..................................................................... D ...... 909 793-3131
840 W Brockton Ave Redlands (92374) *(P-13152)*

Teleflora, Los Angeles *Also Called: The Wonderful Company LLC (P-1780)*
Telemetry Systems, Goleta *Also Called: Acroamatics Inc (P-11797)*

Telemtry Cmmnctons Systems Inc ....................................................... E ...... 818 718-6248
10020 Remmet Ave Chatsworth (91311) *(P-11963)*

Telenav, Santa Clara *Also Called: Telenav Inc (P-14317)*

Telenav Inc (PA) ....................................................................................... A ...... **408 245-3800**
2540 Mission College Blvd Ste 100 Santa Clara (95054) *(P-14317)*

Telenet, El Segundo *Also Called: Telenet Voip Inc (P-19179)*

Telenet Voip Inc ....................................................................................... D ...... 310 253-9000
850 N Park View Dr El Segundo (90245) *(P-19179)*

Telesign Holdings Inc (HQ) ..................................................................... E ...... **310 740-9700**
13274 Fiji Way Ste 600 Marina Del Rey (90292) *(P-18871)*

TELESIS BIO, San Diego *Also Called: Telesis Bio Inc (P-14731)*

Telesis Bio Inc (PA) ................................................................................. E ...... **858 228-4115**
10431 Wateridge Cir Ste 150 San Diego (92121) *(P-14731)*

Telestar International Corp .............................................. E ...... 818 582-3018
  5536 Balboa Blvd Encino (91316) *(P-19543)*
Telestar Material, Encino Also Called: Telestar International Corp *(P-19543)*
Teletronics Technology Corp .............................................. E ...... 661 273-7033
  190 Sierra Ct Ste A3 Palmdale (93550) *(P-14318)*
Telewave Inc .............................................. E ...... 408 929-4400
  48421 Milmont Dr Fremont (94538) *(P-11964)*
Telirite Technical Svcs Inc .............................................. E ...... 510 440-3888
  2857 Lakeview Ct Fremont (94538) *(P-12239)*
Tellabs Access LLC (HQ) .............................................. E ...... 630 798-8671
  338 Pier Ave Hermosa Beach (90254) *(P-12022)*
Tellkamp Systems Inc (PA) .............................................. E ...... 562 802-1621
  15523 Carmenita Rd Santa Fe Springs (90670) *(P-14371)*
Tellme Networks Inc .............................................. B ...... 650 693-1009
  1065 La Avenida St Mountain View (94043) *(P-4478)*
Tellus Solutions Inc .............................................. E ...... 408 850-2942
  3080 Olcott St Ste D103 Santa Clara (95054) *(P-18872)*
Temblor Brewing LLC .............................................. E ...... 661 489-4855
  3200 Buck Owens Blvd Bakersfield (93308) *(P-1465)*
Temecula Quality Plating Inc .............................................. E ...... 951 296-9875
  42147 Roick Dr Temecula (92590) *(P-9022)*
Temecula T-Shirt Printers Inc .............................................. E ...... 951 296-0184
  41607 Enterprise Cir N Ste A Temecula (92590) *(P-4972)*
Temecula Valley Winery MGT LLC .............................................. D ...... 951 699-8896
  27495 Diaz Rd Temecula (92590) *(P-1776)*
Temeka Advertising Inc .............................................. D ...... 951 277-2525
  9073 Pulsar Ct Corona (92883) *(P-3674)*
Temeka Group, Corona Also Called: Temeka Advertising Inc *(P-3674)*
Tempest Technology Corporation .............................................. E ...... 800 346-2143
  4708 N Blythe Ave Fresno (93722) *(P-10001)*
Temple Custom Jewelers LLC .............................................. E ...... 800 988-3844
  1640 Camino Del Rio N Ste 220 San Diego (92108) *(P-15706)*
Tempo Communications Inc (PA) .............................................. D ...... 800 642-2155
  1390 Aspen Way Vista (92081) *(P-16323)*
Tempo Industries, Irvine Also Called: Wpmg Inc *(P-11569)*
Tempo Industries Inc .............................................. C ...... 415 552-8074
  2137 E 55th St Vernon (90058) *(P-3544)*
Tempo Plastic Co .............................................. F ...... 559 651-7711
  1227 N Miller Park Ct Visalia (93291) *(P-6666)*
Tempted Apparel Corp .............................................. E ...... 323 859-2480
  4516 Loma Vista Ave Vernon (90058) *(P-2814)*
Temptron Engineering Inc .............................................. E ...... 818 346-4900
  7823 Deering Ave Canoga Park (91304) *(P-14933)*
Ten Publishing Media LLC .............................................. F ...... 760 722-7777
  2052 Corte Del Nogal Ste 100 Carlsbad (92011) *(P-4300)*
Tenaya Therapeutics Inc .............................................. C ...... 760 310-9976
  171 Oyster Point Blvd Ste 500 South San Francisco (94080) *(P-5866)*
Tencate Performance Composite, Camarillo Also Called: Performance Materials Corp *(P-5185)*
Tend Insights Inc .............................................. E ...... 510 619-9289
  46567 Fremont Blvd Fremont (94538) *(P-17545)*
Tenenblatt Corporation .............................................. C ...... 323 232-2061
  3750 Broadway Pl Los Angeles (90007) *(P-2483)*
Tenergy Corporation .............................................. D ...... 510 687-0388
  436 Kato Ter Fremont (94539) *(P-13153)*
Tenex Health Inc .............................................. D ...... 949 454-7500
  26902 Vista Ter Lake Forest (92630) *(P-15279)*
Tenma America Corporation .............................................. C ...... 619 754-2250
  333 H St Ste 5000 Chula Vista (91910) *(P-7051)*
Tenney A Norquist, Turlock Also Called: Tanco Inc *(P-438)*
Tenon Medical, Los Gatos Also Called: Tenon Medical Inc *(P-15280)*
Tenon Medical Inc .............................................. E ...... 408 649-5760
  104 Cooper Ct Los Gatos (95032) *(P-15280)*
Tensorcom Inc .............................................. E ...... 760 496-3264
  3530 John Hopkins Ct San Diego (92121) *(P-12759)*
Tenstorrent Usa Inc .............................................. E ...... 737 262-8464
  2600 Great America Way Ste 501 Santa Clara (95054) *(P-10211)*
Tensys Medical Inc .............................................. E ...... 858 552-1941
  12625 High Bluff Dr Ste 213 San Diego (92130) *(P-15583)*
Teon Therapeutics Inc .............................................. F ...... 650 832-1421
  555 Twin Dolphin Dr Ste 120 Redwood City (94065) *(P-5686)*

Tequila Blues Inc .............................................. F ...... 310 526-8002
  2475 Paseo De Las Americas # 1053 San Diego (92154) *(P-17103)*
Tequila Clase Azul, San Francisco Also Called: Tequilas Premium Inc *(P-1847)*
Tequilas Premium Inc .............................................. F ...... 415 399-0496
  470 Columbus Ave Ste 210 San Francisco (94133) *(P-1847)*
Tera-Lite Inc .............................................. E ...... 408 288-8655
  1631 S 10th St San Jose (95112) *(P-506)*
TERADATA, San Diego Also Called: Teradata Corporation *(P-18873)*
Teradata Corporation (PA) .............................................. A ...... 866 548-8348
  17095 Via Del Campo San Diego (92127) *(P-18873)*
Teradata Operations Inc (HQ) .............................................. D ...... 937 242-4030
  17095 Via Del Campo San Diego (92127) *(P-10212)*
Teradek LLC .............................................. F ...... 949 743-5780
  8 Mason Irvine (92618) *(P-17725)*
Teradyne Inc .............................................. D ...... 818 991-2900
  30701 Agoura Rd Agoura Hills (91301) *(P-13107)*
Teradyne Inc .............................................. F ...... 408 960-2400
  875 Embedded Way San Jose (95138) *(P-14592)*
Terarecon Inc .............................................. E ...... 650 372-1100
  93141 Civic Ct Dr Fremont (94538) *(P-10444)*
Terawatt Infrastructure Inc .............................................. F ...... 785 251-0751
  85 2nd St San Francisco (94105) *(P-13188)*
Terawatt Infrastructure Inc .............................................. E ...... 415 837-1946
  49 Stevenson St Ste 600 San Francisco (94105) *(P-13189)*
Teridian Semiconductor Corp (DH) .............................................. D ...... 714 508-8800
  6440 Oak Cyn Ste 100 Irvine (92618) *(P-12760)*
Teridian Smicdtr Holdings Corp (DH) .............................................. F ...... 714 508-8800
  6440 Oak Cyn Ste 100 Irvine (92618) *(P-12761)*
Terminal Manufacturing Co LLC .............................................. E ...... 510 526-3071
  707 Gilman St Berkeley (94710) *(P-8227)*
Termo Company .............................................. E ...... 562 595-7401
  3275 Cherry Ave Long Beach (90807) *(P-201)*
Tern Design Ltd .............................................. E ...... 760 754-2400
  14020 Stowe Dr Poway (92064) *(P-14462)*
Terns Pharmaceuticals Inc (PA) .............................................. E ...... 650 525-5535
  1065 E Hillsdale Blvd Ste 100 Foster City (94404) *(P-5687)*
Terra Furniture Inc .............................................. E
  549 E Edna Pl Hacienda Heights (91745) *(P-3493)*
Terra Nova Technologies Inc .............................................. D ...... 619 596-7400
  10770 Rockville St Ste A Santee (92071) *(P-9497)*
Terra Universal Inc (PA) .............................................. D ...... 714 526-0100
  800 S Raymond Ave Fullerton (92831) *(P-10002)*
Terrasat Communications Inc .............................................. E ...... 408 782-5911
  315 Digital Dr Morgan Hill (95037) *(P-11965)*
Terravant Wine, Buellton Also Called: Terravant Wine Company LLC *(P-1777)*
Terravant Wine Company LLC .............................................. C ...... 805 688-4245
  35 Industrial Way Buellton (93427) *(P-1777)*
Terravia Holdings Inc .............................................. E
  1 Tower Pl Ste 600 South San Francisco (94080) *(P-2371)*
Terravino, Pasadena Also Called: Eurobizusa Inc *(P-1557)*
Terry Grimes Graphic Center of Sacramento Inc .............................................. E ...... 916 453-1332
  3925 Power Inn Rd Sacramento (95826) *(P-4783)*
Terry Hinge & Hardware, Van Nuys Also Called: RPC Legacy Inc *(P-8024)*
Terry Town Corporation .............................................. D ...... 619 421-5354
  8851 Kerns St Ste 100 San Diego (92154) *(P-2873)*
Terumo Americas Holding Inc .............................................. E ...... 714 258-8001
  1311 Valencia Ave Tustin (92780) *(P-14732)*
Terviva Inc .............................................. D ...... 510 501-3707
  980 Atlantic Ave Ste 105 Alameda (94501) *(P-1374)*
Tesca, Los Angeles Also Called: Tesca Usa Inc *(P-3019)*
Tesca Usa Inc .............................................. E ...... 586 991-0744
  333 S Grand Ave Ste 4100 Los Angeles (90071) *(P-3019)*
Tesco Controls Inc .............................................. D ...... 916 395-8800
  42015 Remington Ave Ste 102 Temecula (92590) *(P-14593)*
TESCO CONTROLS, INC., Temecula Also Called: Tesco Controls Inc *(P-14593)*
Tesla Inc .............................................. B ...... 209 647-7037
  18260 S Harlan Rd Lathrop (95330) *(P-13390)*
Tesla Inc .............................................. C ...... 510 249-3500
  45500 Fremont Blvd Fremont (94538) *(P-13391)*
Tesla Inc .............................................. B ...... 650 681-5000
  47700 Kato Rd Fremont (94538) *(P-13392)*

Tesla Inc .................................................................................. B ...... 650 681-5800
4180 El Camino Real Palo Alto (94306) *(P-13393)*

Tesla Inc .................................................................................. F ...... 510 690-5451
39800 Fremont Blvd Fremont (94538) *(P-13394)*

Tesla Inc .................................................................................. A ...... 510 249-3650
45500 Fremont Blvd Fremont (94538) *(P-13395)*

Tesla Inc .................................................................................. D ...... 510 766-6688
901 Page Ave Fremont (94538) *(P-13396)*

Tesla Factory, Fremont *Also Called: Tesla Inc (P-13391)*

Tesla Factory, Fremont *Also Called: Tesla Inc (P-13395)*

Tesla Motors, Fremont *Also Called: Tesla Inc (P-13392)*

Tesla Store Menlo Park, Palo Alto *Also Called: Tesla Inc (P-13393)*

Tesla Vineyards Lp .................................................................. E ...... 925 456-2500
4590 Tesla Rd Livermore (94550) *(P-1778)*

Teslarati LLC ........................................................................... F ...... 323 405-7657
11040 Bollinger Canyon Rd Ste E879 San Ramon (94582) *(P-17985)*

Tesoro Refining & Mktg Co LLC ............................................. D ...... 562 728-2215
5905 N Paramount Blvd Long Beach (90805) *(P-6353)*

Tessa Mia Corp ........................................................................ E ...... 877 740-5757
9565 Vassar Ave Chatsworth (91311) *(P-3273)*

Tessenderlo Kerley Inc ........................................................... E ...... 559 485-0114
5247 E Central Ave Fresno (93725) *(P-5124)*

Tessera, San Jose *Also Called: Tessera Inc (P-12762)*

Tessera Inc (DH) ..................................................................... E ...... 408 321-6000
3025 Orchard Pkwy San Jose (95134) *(P-12762)*

Tessera Global Services Inc .................................................. F ...... 408 321-6000
140 Scott Dr Menlo Park (94025) *(P-12763)*

Tessera Intellectual Prpts Inc ................................................. E ...... 408 321-6000
3025 Orchard Pkwy San Jose (95134) *(P-12764)*

Tessera Intllctual Prprty Corp ................................................ F ...... 408 321-6000
3025 Orchard Pkwy San Jose (95134) *(P-12765)*

Tessera Technologies Inc (DH) ............................................. C ...... 408 321-6000
3025 Orchard Pkwy San Jose (95134) *(P-12766)*

Tessitura Network Inc ............................................................. C ...... 888 643-5778
2295 Fletcher Pkwy Ste 101 El Cajon (92020) *(P-18874)*

Test Enterprises Inc (PA) ....................................................... E ...... 408 542-5900
1288 Reamwood Ave Sunnyvale (94089) *(P-14463)*

Testament Apparel, Vernon *Also Called: Clue Clothing Corp (P-2747)*

Testarossa Vineyards LLC ..................................................... E ...... 408 354-6150
300 College Ave Ste A Los Gatos (95030) *(P-1779)*

Testarossa Winery, Los Gatos *Also Called: Testarossa Vineyards LLC (P-1779)*

Testequity LLC (HQ) ............................................................... D ...... 805 498-9733
6100 Condor Dr Moorpark (93021) *(P-19180)*

Tethys Bioscience Inc ............................................................ C ...... 888 483-8497
5858 Horton St Ste 280 Emeryville (94608) *(P-5783)*

Tetra Tech Ec Inc .................................................................... E ...... 949 809-5000
17885 Von Karman Ave Ste 500 Irvine (92614) *(P-14733)*

Teva Parenteral Medicines Inc .............................................. A ...... 949 455-4700
19 Hughes Irvine (92618) *(P-5688)*

Texaco, San Ramon *Also Called: Texaco Inc (P-17476)*

Texaco, San Ramon *Also Called: Texaco Overseas Holdings Inc (P-17477)*

Texaco Inc (HQ) ...................................................................... A ...... 925 842-1000
6001 Bollinger Canyon Rd San Ramon (94583) *(P-17476)*

Texaco Overseas Holdings Inc (DH) ..................................... F ...... 510 242-5357
6001 Bollinger Canyon Rd San Ramon (94583) *(P-17477)*

Texarkana Aluminum, Long Beach *Also Called: TCI Texarkana Inc (P-7734)*

Texas Instruments, Santa Clara *Also Called: Texas Instruments Incorporated (P-12767)*

Texas Instruments Incorporated ........................................... E ...... 669 721-5000
2900 Semiconductor Dr Santa Clara (95051) *(P-12767)*

Texas Tst Inc ........................................................................... E ...... 951 685-2155
13428 Benson Ave Chino (91710) *(P-7723)*

Texican Inc .............................................................................. E ...... 310 384-7000
21031 Ventura Blvd Ste 1000 Woodland Hills (91364) *(P-18875)*

Texollini Inc ............................................................................. C ...... 310 537-3400
2575 E El Presidio St Long Beach (90810) *(P-2533)*

Textexpander Inc .................................................................... E ...... 510 289-4000
548 Market St # 37453 San Francisco (94104) *(P-18876)*

Textile Unlimited Corporation (PA) ....................................... D ...... 310 263-7400
20917 Higgins Ct Torrance (90501) *(P-2578)*

Textron Aviation Inc ............................................................... C ...... 916 929-5656
5850 Citation Way Sacramento (95837) *(P-13695)*

Tfb Games Inc ......................................................................... E ...... 707 582-0005
5401 Old Redwood Hwy Ste 109 Petaluma (94954) *(P-18877)*

TFC Manufacturing Inc ........................................................... D ...... 562 426-9559
4001 Watson Plaza Dr Lakewood (90712) *(P-8592)*

Tfd Incorporated ..................................................................... E ...... 714 630-7127
39 Heritage Irvine (92604) *(P-14828)*

Tfi of California Inc (DH) ........................................................ E ...... 844 362-3222
10646 Fulton Ct Rancho Cucamonga (91730) *(P-674)*

Tfn Architectural Signage Inc (PA) ........................................ E ...... 714 556-0990
527 Fee Ana St Placentia (92870) *(P-16057)*

Tgs, Chatsworth *Also Called: Truly Green Solutions LLC (P-11629)*

Thai Union North America Inc (HQ) ...................................... F ...... 424 397-8556
2150 E Grand Ave El Segundo (90245) *(P-2044)*

Thalasinos Enterprises Inc .................................................... E ...... 951 340-0911
1220 Railroad St Corona (92882) *(P-16899)*

Thales Avionics Inc ................................................................ E ...... 949 381-3033
48 Discovery Irvine (92618) *(P-13970)*

Thales Avionics Inc ................................................................ E ...... 949 790-2500
51 Discovery Ste 100 Irvine (92618) *(P-13971)*

Thales Avionics Inc ................................................................ E ...... 949 829-5808
9975 Toledo Way Irvine (92618) *(P-13972)*

Tharco, San Lorenzo *Also Called: Tharco Holdings Inc (P-3892)*

Tharco Container Inc .............................................................. A ...... 510 276-8600
2222 Grant Ave San Lorenzo (94580) *(P-3891)*

Tharco Holdings Inc ............................................................... A ...... 303 373-1860
2222 Grant Ave San Lorenzo (94580) *(P-3892)*

Thatcher's Gourmet Popcorn, Pittsburg *Also Called: Gourmet Plus Inc (P-17402)*

The Adhesive Products Inc (PA) ............................................ E ...... 510 526-7616
520 Cleveland Ave Albany (94710) *(P-6250)*

The Alternative Copy Shop Inc .............................................. D ...... 805 569-2116
3887 State St Ste 12 Santa Barbara (93105) *(P-17817)*

The Bobrick Corporation (PA) ............................................... D ...... 818 764-1000
6901 Tujunga Ave North Hollywood (91605) *(P-3711)*

The China Press, San Gabriel *Also Called: Asia-Pacific California Inc (P-4068)*

The Clearwater Company, Rancho Cordova *Also Called: Nca Laboratories Inc (P-11681)*

The Copley Press Inc ............................................................. A ...... 858 454-0411
7776 Ivanhoe Ave La Jolla (92037) *(P-19064)*

The Enkeboll Co ...................................................................... E ...... 310 532-1400
16506 Avalon Blvd Carson (90746) *(P-3198)*

The Full Void 2 Inc .................................................................. B ...... 818 891-5999
16320 Roscoe Blvd Ste 100 Van Nuys (91406) *(P-4349)*

The Godfor Plbg Wtr Filtration, Carlsbad *Also Called: Goodfor LLC (P-12842)*

The Goodwin Company, Garden Grove *Also Called: Goodwin Ammonia Company LLC (P-5875)*

The Gyro House (PA) .............................................................. F ...... 530 823-6204
2389 Rickenbacker Way Auburn (95602) *(P-19286)*

The Heat Factory Inc .............................................................. E ...... 760 893-8300
2793 Loker Ave W Carlsbad (92010) *(P-3984)*

The Hunter Spice Inc .............................................................. D ...... 805 597-8900
184 Suburban Rd San Luis Obispo (93401) *(P-2372)*

The Korea Times Los Angeles Inc (PA) ................................ C ...... 323 692-2000
3731 Wilshire Blvd Ste 1000 Los Angeles (90010) *(P-4208)*

The Ligature Inc (HQ) ............................................................. E ...... 323 585-6000
4909 Alcoa Ave Vernon (90058) *(P-4784)*

The Lubrizol Corporation ....................................................... F ...... 949 212-1863
30211 Avenida De Las Bandera Rancho Santa Margari (92688) *(P-6325)*

The Lunada Bay Corporation (PA) ......................................... E ...... 714 490-1313
2000 E Winston Rd Anaheim (92806) *(P-2866)*

The Morning Star Company (PA) ........................................... D ...... 530 666-6600
724 Main St Ste 202 Woodland (95695) *(P-17870)*

The Morning Star Packing Company L P (PA) ..................... E ...... 209 826-8000
13448 Volta Rd Los Banos (93635) *(P-932)*

The Orange County Printing Co, Irvine *Also Called: Ocpc Inc (P-4710)*

The Original Cult Inc .............................................................. D ...... 323 260-7308
40 E Verdugo Ave Burbank (91502) *(P-2815)*

The Rutter Group, North Hollywood *Also Called: West Publishing Corporation (P-4354)*

The Service Warehouse Inc ................................................... F ...... 310 329-9110
17819 S Figueroa St Gardena (90248) *(P-16849)*

The Sign Man, Orange *Also Called: Monarch Corporation (P-16011)*

The Strand Energy Company ................................................. B ...... 213 225-5900
515 S Flower St Ste 4800 Los Angeles (90071) *(P-139)*

The Sun .................................................................................................... F ...... 619 405-7702
852 Hollister St Unit B San Diego (92154) *(P-4209)*

The Sweet Life Enterprises Inc .............................................................. C ...... 949 261-7400
2350 Pullman St Santa Ana (92705) *(P-1065)*

The Timing Inc ......................................................................................... E ...... 323 589-5577
2807 S Santa Fe Ave Vernon (90058) *(P-17104)*

The Wave, Manhattan Beach *Also Called: Wave Community Newspapers Inc (P-4219)*

The White Sheet, Palm Desert *Also Called: Associated Desert Shoppers Inc (P-4367)*

The Wine Appreciation Guild Ltd ............................................................ F ...... 650 866-3020
360 Swift Ave Unit 3040 South San Francisco (94080) *(P-4350)*

The Wonderful Company LLC (PA) ........................................................ C ...... 310 966-5700
11444 W Olympic Blvd Fl 10 Los Angeles (90064) *(P-1780)*

The/Studio ................................................................................................ E ...... 213 233-1633
360 E 2nd St Ste 800 Los Angeles (90012) *(P-4973)*

Thebrain Technologies LP ...................................................................... F ...... 310 751-5000
11522 W Washington Blvd Los Angeles (90066) *(P-18878)*

Theodore, Los Angeles *Also Called: Country Club Fashions Inc (P-17492)*

Theorem LLC, Woodland Hills *Also Called: Citrusbyte LLC (P-17897)*

Theory LLC ............................................................................................... F ...... 415 376-9065
412 Jackson St San Francisco (94111) *(P-2728)*

Therabreath, Los Angeles *Also Called: Dr Harold Katz LLC (P-17663)*

Therapeutic Industries Inc ..................................................................... F ...... 760 343-2502
72096 Dunham Way Ste E Thousand Palms (92276) *(P-15281)*

Therapeutic RES Faculty LLC ................................................................ C ...... 209 472-2240
3120 W March Ln Stockton (95219) *(P-4974)*

Therasense Inc ........................................................................................ E ...... 510 749-5400
1360 S Loop Rd Alameda (94502) *(P-15282)*

Theravance Biopharma Us Inc .............................................................. C ...... 650 808-6000
901 Gateway Blvd South San Francisco (94080) *(P-5689)*

Therm Core Products, San Bernardino *Also Called: Caldesso LLC (P-17691)*

Therm Pacific, Commerce *Also Called: Hkf Inc (P-16781)*

Therm-X of California Inc (HQ) .............................................................. D ...... 510 441-7566
3200 Investment Blvd Hayward (94545) *(P-14934)*

Therma LLC .............................................................................................. A ...... 408 347-3400
1601 Las Plumas Ave San Jose (95133) *(P-8593)*

Thermal Conductive Bonding Inc (PA) ................................................. E ...... 408 920-0255
6210 88th St Sacramento (95828) *(P-12768)*

Thermal Dynamics, Ontario *Also Called: Thmx Holdings LLC (P-13584)*

Thermal Electronics Inc ......................................................................... F
403 W Minthorn St Lake Elsinore (92530) *(P-13108)*

Thermal Energy Solutions Inc .............................................................. E ...... 661 489-4100
100 Quantico Ave Bakersfield (93307) *(P-390)*

Thermal Engineering, Cerritos *Also Called: Thermal Engrg Intl USA Inc (P-19424)*

Thermal Engrg Intl USA Inc (HQ) .......................................................... D ...... 323 726-0641
18000 Studebaker Rd Ste 400 Cerritos (90703) *(P-19424)*

Thermal Equipment Corporation .......................................................... E ...... 310 328-6600
2146 E Gladwick St Rancho Dominguez (90220) *(P-14351)*

Thermal Idntification Tech Inc (PA) ...................................................... F ...... 408 656-6809
2707 Saturn St Brea (92821) *(P-14734)*

Thermal Rite, Commerce *Also Called: Crowntonka California Inc (P-10493)*

Thermal Solutions Mfg Inc .................................................................... E ...... 909 796-0754
1390 S Tippecanoe Ave Ste B San Bernardino (92408) *(P-13583)*

Thermal Structures Inc (DH) ................................................................. B ...... 951 736-9911
2362 Railroad St Corona (92878) *(P-13723)*

Thermal Structures Inc ........................................................................... E ...... 951 256-8051
2380 Railroad St Corona (92878) *(P-13724)*

Thermal-Vac Technology Inc ................................................................ E ...... 714 997-2601
1221 W Struck Ave Orange (92867) *(P-7902)*

Thermalflex, San Diego *Also Called: Tacna International Corp (P-19541)*

Thermalrite, Rancho Cucamonga *Also Called: Everidge Inc (P-10500)*

Thermaprint Corporation ........................................................................ E ...... 949 583-0800
11 Autry Ste B Irvine (92618) *(P-15669)*

Thermasol Steam Bath, Simi Valley *Also Called: DMA Enterprises Inc (P-16126)*

Thermcraft Inc ......................................................................................... F ...... 916 363-9411
3762 Bradview Dr Sacramento (95827) *(P-4785)*

Thermech Corporation ........................................................................... E ...... 714 533-3183
1773 W Lincoln Ave Ste I Anaheim (92801) *(P-3939)*

Thermech Engineering, Anaheim *Also Called: Thermech Corporation (P-3939)*

Thermionics Laboratory Inc .................................................................. D ...... 510 786-0680
3118 Depot Rd Hayward (94545) *(P-9023)*

Thermionics Laboratory Inc .................................................................. E ...... 530 272-3436
10230 Twin Pines Pl Grass Valley (95949) *(P-10605)*

Thermionics Laboratory Inc (HQ) ......................................................... E ...... 510 538-3304
3118 Depot Rd Hayward (94545) *(P-14352)*

Thermlly Engnred Mnfctred Pdts .......................................................... E ...... 310 523-9934
543 W 135th St Gardena (90248) *(P-8346)*

Thermo Finnigan LLC (HQ) .................................................................... B ...... 408 965-6000
355 River Oaks Pkwy San Jose (95134) *(P-14735)*

Thermo Fisher, Sunnyvale *Also Called: Dionex Corporation (P-14650)*

Thermo Fisher Scientific ........................................................................ E ...... 603 430-2203
750 Laurelwood Rd Santa Clara (95054) *(P-14736)*

Thermo Fisher Scientific ........................................................................ B ...... 408 894-9835
355 River Oaks Pkwy San Jose (95134) *(P-14737)*

Thermo Fisher Scientific, Carlsbad *Also Called: Life Technologies Corporation (P-5760)*

Thermo Fisher Scientific, Santa Clara *Also Called: Fiberlite Centrifuge LLC (P-14666)*

Thermo Fisher Scientific, Carlsbad *Also Called: Thermo Fisher Scientific Inc (P-14742)*

Thermo Fisher Scientific Inc ................................................................. E ...... 781 622-1000
5823 Newton Dr Carlsbad (92008) *(P-14738)*

Thermo Fisher Scientific Inc ................................................................. D ...... 858 453-7551
9389 Waples St San Diego (92121) *(P-14739)*

Thermo Fisher Scientific Inc ................................................................. E ...... 408 731-5056
3380 Central Expy Santa Clara (95051) *(P-14740)*

Thermo Fisher Scientific Inc ................................................................. D ...... 760 603-7200
5791 Van Allen Way Carlsbad (92008) *(P-14741)*

Thermo Fisher Scientific Inc ................................................................. F ...... 760 268-8641
5781 Van Allen Way Carlsbad (92008) *(P-14742)*

Thermo Fisher Scientific Inc ................................................................. E ...... 925 600-2522
6055 Sunol Blvd Bldg D Pleasanton (94566) *(P-14743)*

Thermo Fisher Scientific Inc ................................................................. E ...... 408 965-6200
355 River Oaks Pkwy San Jose (95134) *(P-14744)*

Thermo Fisher Scientific Inc ................................................................. E ...... 650 246-5265
180 Oyster Point Blvd South San Francisco (94080) *(P-14745)*

Thermo Fsher Scntific Psg Corp (HQ) .................................................. C ...... 760 603-7200
5791 Van Allen Way Carlsbad (92008) *(P-14746)*

Thermo Fsher Scntific Psg Corp ........................................................... E ...... 609 865-5869
777 Mariposa St San Francisco (94107) *(P-14747)*

Thermo Power Industries ....................................................................... E ...... 562 799-0087
10570 Humbolt St Los Alamitos (90720) *(P-481)*

Thermo Power Industries, Los Alamitos *Also Called: Thermo Power Industries (P-481)*

Thermo Trilogy, Wasco *Also Called: Certis USA LLC (P-6195)*

Thermo-Fusion Inc .................................................................................. E ...... 510 782-7755
2342 American Ave Hayward (94545) *(P-7903)*

Thermobile, Santa Ana *Also Called: Hood Manufacturing Inc (P-6856)*

Thermocraft ............................................................................................. D ...... 619 813-2985
2554 Commercial St San Diego (92113) *(P-10518)*

Thermodyne International Ltd ............................................................... C ...... 909 923-9945
1841 S Business Pkwy Ontario (91761) *(P-7052)*

Thermofinnegan, San Jose *Also Called: Thermo Fisher Scientific (P-14737)*

Thermogenesis Holdings Inc (PA) ........................................................ E ...... 916 858-5100
2711 Citrus Rd Rancho Cordova (95742) *(P-15283)*

Thermolab, Sun Valley *Also Called: Technical Heaters Inc (P-6432)*

Thermometrics Corporation (PA) .......................................................... F ...... 818 886-3755
18714 Parthenia St Northridge (91324) *(P-14464)*

Thermonics, Sunnyvale *Also Called: Test Enterprises Inc (P-14463)*

Thermtronix Corporation (PA) ............................................................... E ...... 760 246-4500
17129 Muskrat Ave Adelanto (92301) *(P-10060)*

Theta Oilfield Services Inc .................................................................... E ...... 661 633-2792
5201 California Ave Ste 370 Bakersfield (93309) *(P-278)*

THETRADEDESK, Ventura *Also Called: Trade Desk Inc (P-17989)*

Thewrap .................................................................................................... E ...... 424 273-4787
2260 S Centinela Ave Ste 150 Los Angeles (90064) *(P-4210)*

Thg Brands Inc ........................................................................................ E ...... 844 694-8327
1810 Abalone Ave Torrance (90501) *(P-2373)*

Thi Inc ...................................................................................................... D ...... 714 444-4643
1525 E Edinger Ave Santa Ana (92705) *(P-15284)*

Thiele Technologies Inc ......................................................................... D ...... 559 638-8484
1949 E Manning Ave Reedley (93654) *(P-10033)*

Thiessen Products Inc ............................................................................ C ...... 805 482-6913
555 Dawson Dr Ste A Camarillo (93012) *(P-11142)*

Thin Film Devices, Irvine *Also Called: Tfd Incorporated (P-14828)*

# ALPHABETIC SECTION — Tiancheng Intl Inc USA

**Thin-Lite Corporation** .................................................. E ...... 805 987-5021
530 Constitution Ave Camarillo (93012) *(P-11627)*

**Thingap, Camarillo** *Also Called: Thingap Inc (P-11291)*

**Thingap Inc** ...................................................................... E ...... 805 477-9741
4035 Via Pescador Camarillo (93012) *(P-11291)*

**Think Social Publishing Inc** ....................................... E ...... 408 557-8595
404 Saratoga Ave Ste 200 Santa Clara (95050) *(P-4479)*

**Think Surgical, Fremont** *Also Called: Think Surgical Inc (P-15417)*

**Think Surgical Inc** ........................................................ C ...... 510 249-2300
47201 Lakeview Blvd Fremont (94538) *(P-15417)*

**Thinkcp Technologies, Irvine** *Also Called: H Co Computer Products (P-10240)*

**Third Culture Food Group Inc** .................................... E ...... 650 479-4585
2701 8th St Berkeley (94710) *(P-1248)*

**Third Floor North Company, Placentia** *Also Called: Tfn Architectural Signage Inc (P-16057)*

**Thirdlove, San Francisco** *Also Called: Thirdlove Inc (P-17105)*

**Thirdlove Inc** ................................................................... C ...... 415 692-0089
555 Market St Fl 13 San Francisco (94105) *(P-17105)*

**Thirty Three Threads Inc (PA)** ................................... E ...... 877 486-3769
1330 Park Center Dr Vista (92081) *(P-2648)*

**Thistle Health Inc** ........................................................ B ...... 917 587-2341
1000 Van Ness Ave Ste 10004 San Francisco (94109) *(P-2374)*

**Thistle Roller Co Inc** .................................................... E ...... 323 685-5322
209 Van Norman Rd Montebello (90640) *(P-9775)*

**Thmx Holdings LLC** ..................................................... C ...... 909 390-3944
4850 E Airport Dr Ontario (91761) *(P-13584)*

**Thomas Allen Vnyrds Winery LLC** ............................. E ...... 209 288-7880
5573 W Woodbridge Rd Lodi (95242) *(P-1781)*

**Thomas Burt** .................................................................. F ...... 626 301-9065
5095 Brooks St Montclair (91763) *(P-4786)*

**Thomas Container & Packaging, Orange** *Also Called: T & T Box Company Inc (P-3919)*

**Thomas Fogarty Winery LLC** .................................... E ...... 650 851-6777
19501 Skyline Blvd Woodside (94062) *(P-1782)*

**Thomas Leonardini** ...................................................... F ...... 707 963-9454
1563 Saint Helena Hwy S Saint Helena (94574) *(P-1783)*

**Thomas Lundberg** ......................................................... E ...... 415 695-0110
2620 3rd St San Francisco (94107) *(P-3513)*

**Thomas Products, Madera** *Also Called: Nutra-Blend LLC (P-1140)*

**Thomas Products LLC** ................................................. D ...... 559 661-6161
2140 W Industrial Ave Madera (93637) *(P-1153)*

**Thomas Welding & Machine Inc** ................................ E ...... 530 893-8940
1308 W 8th Ave Chico (95926) *(P-19217)*

**Thomas West Inc (PA)** ................................................. E ...... 408 481-3850
470 Mercury Dr Sunnyvale (94085) *(P-2950)*

**Thomas-Swan Sign Company Inc** ............................. E ...... 415 621-1511
2717 Goodrick Ave Richmond (94801) *(P-16058)*

**Thompco Inc** .................................................................. E ...... 805 933-8048
899 Mission Rock Rd Santa Paula (93060) *(P-16794)*

**Thompson ADB Industries, Westminster** *Also Called: Thompson Industries Ltd (P-13973)*

**Thompson Gundrilling Inc** ........................................... E ...... 323 873-4045
13840 Saticoy St Van Nuys (91402) *(P-7681)*

**Thompson Industries Ltd** ............................................ C ...... 310 679-9193
7155 Fenwick Ln Westminster (92683) *(P-13973)*

**Thompson Magnetics Inc** ............................................ E ...... 951 676-0243
42255 Baldaray Cir Ste C Temecula (92590) *(P-13109)*

**Thompson Pipe Group Inc (PA)** ................................ E ...... 909 822-0200
3011 N Laurel Ave Rialto (92377) *(P-4055)*

**Thompson Tank Inc** ...................................................... F ...... 562 869-7711
8029 Phlox St Downey (90241) *(P-8347)*

**Thomson Industries Inc** .............................................. E ...... 619 661-6292
2695 Customhouse Ct San Diego (92154) *(P-11143)*

**Thomson International Inc** .......................................... F ...... 661 845-1111
11220 S Vineland Rd Bakersfield (93307) *(P-58)*

**Thomson Lnear Motion Optimized, San Diego** *Also Called: Thomson Industries Inc (P-11143)*

**Thomson Reuters Corporation** .................................. E ...... 310 287-2360
3280 Motor Ave Ste 200 Los Angeles (90034) *(P-4480)*

**Thomson Reuters Corporation** .................................. E ...... 949 400-7782
163 Albert Pl Costa Mesa (92627) *(P-4481)*

**Thomson Reuters Corporation** .................................. E ...... 877 518-2761
5161 Lankershim Blvd North Hollywood (91601) *(P-11966)*

**Thor Electronics of California, Salinas** *Also Called: Abrams Electronics Inc (P-11437)*

**Thoratec LLC (HQ)** ....................................................... C ...... 925 847-8600
6035 Stoneridge Dr Pleasanton (94588) *(P-15584)*

**Thorne Research Inc** ................................................... F ...... 707 297-3458
533 Stone Rd Benicia (94510) *(P-782)*

**Thornton Technologies, Oceanside** *Also Called: Thornton Technology Corp (P-16929)*

**Thornton Technology Corp** ......................................... E ...... 760 471-9969
2608 Temple Heights Dr Oceanside (92056) *(P-16929)*

**Thornton Winery** ........................................................... D ...... 951 699-0099
32575 Rancho California Rd Temecula (92591) *(P-1784)*

**Thorpe Technologies Inc (DH)** .................................. E ...... 562 903-8230
449 W Allen Ave Ste 119 San Dimas (91773) *(P-19425)*

**Thorsens Plumbing & AC, Turlock** *Also Called: Thorsens-Norquist Inc (P-516)*

**Thorsens-Norquist Inc** ................................................. D ...... 209 524-5296
2310 N Walnut Rd Turlock (95382) *(P-516)*

**Thoughtspot Inc (PA)** .................................................. C ...... 800 508-7008
444 Castro St Ste 1000 Mountain View (94041) *(P-18879)*

**Thousand LLC** ............................................................... E ...... 310 745-0110
915 Mateo St Ste 302 Los Angeles (90021) *(P-15865)*

**Thousand Oaks Prtg & Spc Inc** .................................. C ...... 818 706-8330
5334 Sterling Center Dr Westlake Village (91361) *(P-19139)*

**Thousandeyes LLC (HQ)** ............................................. D ...... 415 513-4526
500 Terry A Francois Blvd San Francisco (94158) *(P-18880)*

**Thq Inc** ........................................................................... A ...... 818 591-1310
21900 Burbank Blvd Woodland Hills (91367) *(P-18881)*

**Thq San Diego, Woodland Hills** *Also Called: Thq Inc (P-18881)*

**Three Man Corporation** ............................................... E ...... 858 684-5200
10025 Huennekens St San Diego (92121) *(P-4975)*

**Three Sons Inc** .............................................................. D ...... 562 801-4100
5201 Industry Ave Pico Rivera (90660) *(P-17166)*

**Three Sticks Wines LLC** .............................................. E ...... 707 996-3328
143 W Spain St Sonoma (95476) *(P-1785)*

**Three Stone Hearth, Berkeley** *Also Called: Three Stone Hearth LLC (P-2375)*

**Three Stone Hearth LLC** ............................................. E ...... 510 981-1334
1581 University Ave Berkeley (94703) *(P-2375)*

**Three Wise Men Inc** ..................................................... E ...... 909 477-6698
11818 San Marino St Ste B Rancho Cucamonga (91730) *(P-16436)*

**Three-D Plastics Inc (PA)** ........................................... E ...... 323 849-1316
430 N Varney St Burbank (91502) *(P-7053)*

**Three-D Traffics Works, Burbank** *Also Called: Three-D Plastics Inc (P-7053)*

**Threshold Enterprises Ltd** .......................................... E ...... 831 425-3955
165 Technology Dr Watsonville (95076) *(P-5273)*

**Threshold Enterprises Ltd (PA)** ................................. C ...... 831 438-6851
23 Janis Way Scotts Valley (95066) *(P-5274)*

**Threshold Enterprises Ltd** .......................................... E ...... 831 461-6413
11 Janis Way Scotts Valley (95066) *(P-5275)*

**Threshold Enterprises Ltd** .......................................... E ...... 831 461-6343
19 Janis Way Scotts Valley (95066) *(P-5276)*

**Threshold Enterprises Ltd** .......................................... E ...... 831 466-4014
2280 Delaware Ave Santa Cruz (95060) *(P-5277)*

**Thrifty Oil Co (PA)** ........................................................ F ...... 562 921-3581
13116 Imperial Hwy Santa Fe Springs (90670) *(P-17739)*

**Thrio Inc** ......................................................................... E ...... 858 299-7191
5230 Las Virgenes Rd Ste 210 Calabasas (91302) *(P-18882)*

**Throughput Inc** ............................................................. F ...... 215 606-8552
2100 Geng Rd Palo Alto (94303) *(P-11746)*

**Thums Long Beach Company** .................................... C ...... 562 624-3400
111 W Ocean Blvd Ste 800 Long Beach (90802) *(P-140)*

**Thunderbird, San Francisco** *Also Called: Mzla Technologies Corporation (P-18567)*

**Thunderbolt Manufacturing Inc** .................................. E ...... 714 632-0397
641 S State College Blvd Fullerton (92831) *(P-11144)*

**Thunderbolt Sales Inc** .................................................. F ...... 209 869-4561
3400 Patterson Rd Riverbank (95367) *(P-3404)*

**Thunderworks Division, Santee** *Also Called: Decatur Electronics Inc (P-14179)*

**Thursby Software Systems LLC** ............................... E ...... 817 478-5070
1900 Carnegie Ave Santa Ana (92705) *(P-18883)*

**Thyssenkrupp Bilstein Amer Inc** ................................ E ...... 858 386-5900
13225 Danielson St # 100 Poway (92064) *(P-13585)*

**TI Limited LLC (PA)** ..................................................... D ...... 323 877-5991
20335 Ventura Blvd Ste 231-239 Woodland Hills (91364) *(P-18884)*

**TI Wire, Walnut** *Also Called: Tree Island Wire (USA) Inc (P-7656)*

**Tiancheng Intl Inc USA** ................................................ F ...... 909 947-5577
2851 E Philadelphia St Ontario (91761) *(P-5690)*

**Tianello Inc** ............................................................. C ...... 323 231-0599
138 W 38th St Los Angeles (90037) *(P-2691)*

**Tianello By Steve Barraza, Los Angeles** *Also Called: Tianello Inc (P-2691)*

**Tibco Software Federal, Inc., Santa Clara** *Also Called: Cloud Software Group Federal (P-18179)*

**Ticketscom LLC (DH)** ............................................. E ...... 714 327-5400
2100 E Grand Ave Ste 600 El Segundo (90245) *(P-19305)*

**Tide Rock Holdings LLC (PA)** ................................ E ...... 858 204-7438
343 S Highway 101 Ste 200 Solana Beach (92075) *(P-8594)*

**Tidelands Oil Production Inc** .................................. E ...... 562 436-9918
301 E Ocean Blvd St 300 Long Beach (90802) *(P-141)*

**Tidings** ..................................................................... E ...... 213 637-7360
3424 Wilshire Blvd Los Angeles (90010) *(P-4211)*

**Tiffany Coach Builders, Perris** *Also Called: Warlock Industries (P-13397)*

**Tiffany Coachworks, Perris** *Also Called: Limos By Tiffany Inc (P-13416)*

**Tifg, San Jose** *Also Called: Take It For Granite Inc (P-295)*

**Tig/M LLC** ................................................................ E ...... 818 709-8500
9160 Jordan Ave Chatsworth (91311) *(P-9498)*

**Tiger Business Holdings Inc** .................................. F ...... 714 763-4180
32052 Sea Island Dr Dana Point (92629) *(P-12240)*

**Tiger Case Hole Services, Signal Hill** *Also Called: Tiger Cased Hole Services Inc (P-279)*

**Tiger Cased Hole Services Inc** ............................... E ...... 562 426-4044
2828 Junipero Ave Signal Hill (90755) *(P-279)*

**Tiger Tanks Inc** ....................................................... E ...... 661 363-8335
3397 Edison Hwy Bakersfield (93307) *(P-14128)*

**Tigerconnect Inc (PA)** ............................................. D ...... 310 401-1820
2054 Broadway Santa Monica (90404) *(P-19047)*

**Tikos Tanks Inc** ...................................................... F ...... 951 757-8014
14561 Hawthorne Ave Fontana (92335) *(P-19218)*

**Tikun Olam Adelanto LLC** ...................................... E ...... 833 468-4586
541 S Spring St Unit 213 Los Angeles (90013) *(P-5278)*

**Tile & Marble Design Co Inc** .................................. E ...... 714 847-6472
7421 Vincent Cir Huntington Beach (92648) *(P-485)*

**Tilera, San Jose** *Also Called: Ezchip Semiconductor Inc (P-10152)*

**Tiling and Stone Counter Tops, Ontario** *Also Called: Calvillo Construction Corp (P-343)*

**Tilley Manufacturing Co Inc (PA)** ........................... D ...... 650 365-3598
2734 Spring St Redwood City (94063) *(P-6470)*

**Tilton Engineering Inc** ............................................ E ...... 805 688-2353
25 Easy St Buellton (93427) *(P-13586)*

**Timber Products Co Ltd Partnr** .............................. D ...... 530 842-2310
130 N Phillipe Ln Yreka (96097) *(P-3289)*

**Timberlake Cabinet, Rancho Cordova** *Also Called: American Woodmark Corporation (P-3214)*

**Timbucktoo Manufacturing Inc** .............................. E ...... 310 323-1134
1633 W 134th St Gardena (90249) *(P-10606)*

**Timbuk2, San Francisco** *Also Called: Timbuk2 Designs Inc (P-2962)*

**Timbuk2 Designs Inc (HQ)** ..................................... F ...... 415 252-4300
400 Alabama St Ste 201 San Francisco (94110) *(P-2962)*

**Timbuk2 Designs Inc** .............................................. E ...... 800 865-2513
2031 Cessna Dr Vacaville (95688) *(P-2963)*

**Timco, Hesperia** *Also Called: T L Timmerman Cnstr Inc (P-3319)*

**Timco/Cal Rf Inc** ..................................................... E ...... 805 582-1777
3910 Royal Ave Ste A Simi Valley (93063) *(P-12902)*

**Time Masters, Glendale** *Also Called: AMG Employee Management Inc (P-15674)*

**Timec Companies Inc** ............................................. E ...... 661 322-8177
6861 Charity Ave Bakersfield (93308) *(P-9903)*

**Timec Southern California, Bakersfield** *Also Called: Timec Companies Inc (P-9903)*

**Timely Prefinished Steel, Pacoima** *Also Called: SDS Industries Inc (P-8290)*

**Timemed Labeling Systems Inc (DH)** .................... D ...... 818 897-1111
27770 Entertainment Dr Ste 200 Valencia (91355) *(P-6544)*

**Times Herald, Hayward** *Also Called: Alameda Newspapers Inc (P-4062)*

**Times Media Incorporated** .................................... E ...... 408 494-7000
1900 Camden Ave San Jose (95124) *(P-4212)*

**Timevalue Software** ............................................... E ...... 949 727-1800
22 Mauchly Irvine (92618) *(P-18885)*

**Timing Fashion, Vernon** *Also Called: The Timing Inc (P-17104)*

**Timken Gears & Services Inc** ................................. E ...... 310 605-2600
12935 Imperial Hwy Santa Fe Springs (90670) *(P-8789)*

**Tini Aerospace Inc** ................................................. E ...... 415 524-2124
2505 Kerner Blvd San Rafael (94901) *(P-14319)*

**Tink Inc** ................................................................... E ...... 530 895-0897
2361 Durham Dayton Hwy Durham (95938) *(P-9441)*

**Tinker & Rasor** ........................................................ E ...... 909 890-0700
791 S Waterman Ave San Bernardino (92408) *(P-14320)*

**Tinyco Inc** ............................................................... C ...... 415 644-8101
225 Bush St Ste 1900 San Francisco (94104) *(P-17560)*

**Tiodize, Huntington Beach** *Also Called: Tiodize Co Inc (P-9128)*

**Tiodize Co Inc (PA)** ................................................ F ...... 714 898-4377
5858 Engineer Dr Huntington Beach (92649) *(P-9128)*

**Tiodize Co Inc** ......................................................... E ...... 714 898-4377
15701 Industry Ln Huntington Beach (92649) *(P-17256)*

**Tire Centers West LLC** .......................................... F ...... 619 596-8473
12208 Industry Rd Lakeside (92040) *(P-17467)*

**Titan, Camarillo** *Also Called: Titan Metal Fabricators Inc (P-8228)*

**Titan Medical Enterprises Inc** ............................... F ...... 562 903-7236
11100 Greenstone Ave Santa Fe Springs (90670) *(P-5691)*

**Titan Metal Fabricators Inc (PA)** ........................... D ...... 805 487-5050
352 Balboa Cir Camarillo (93012) *(P-8228)*

**Titan Newman Inc (PA)** .......................................... E ...... 209 862-2977
1649 L St Newman (95360) *(P-16900)*

**Titan Oilfield Services, Bakersfield** *Also Called: Titan Oilfield Services Inc (P-280)*

**Titan Oilfield Services Inc** ..................................... D ...... 661 861-1630
21535 Kratzmeyer Rd Bakersfield (93314) *(P-280)*

**Titans of Cnc Inc** .................................................... E ...... 916 203-2430
4041 Alvis Ct Rocklin (95677) *(P-9904)*

**Titleist, Carlsbad** *Also Called: Acushnet Company (P-15773)*

**Tivoli LLC** ................................................................ E ...... 714 957-6101
17110 Armstrong Ave Irvine (92614) *(P-11433)*

**Tj Aerospace, Garden Grove** *Also Called: Tj Aerospace Inc (P-13974)*

**Tj Aerospace Inc** .................................................... E ...... 714 891-3564
12601 Monarch St Garden Grove (92841) *(P-13974)*

**Tjs Metal Manufacturing Inc** .................................. E ...... 310 604-1545
10847 Drury Ln Lynwood (90262) *(P-8646)*

**Tk Classics LLC** ..................................................... E ...... 916 209-5500
3771 Channel Dr Ste 100 West Sacramento (95691) *(P-3514)*

**Tk Elevator Corporation** ........................................ C ...... 510 476-1900
14400 Catalina St San Leandro (94577) *(P-16850)*

**Tk Pax Inc** ............................................................... E ...... 714 850-1330
1545 Macarthur Blvd Costa Mesa (92626) *(P-6433)*

**TI Enterprises LLC** ................................................ C ...... 805 981-8393
2750 Park View Ct Ste 240 Oxnard (93036) *(P-4301)*

**Tl Machine Inc** ........................................................ D ...... 714 554-4154
14272 Commerce Dr Garden Grove (92843) *(P-8734)*

**TL Shield & Associates Inc** ................................... E ...... 818 509-8228
1030 Arroyo St San Fernando (91340) *(P-9477)*

**Tli Enterprises Inc (PA)** .......................................... E ...... 510 538-3304
3118 Depot Rd Hayward (94545) *(P-14353)*

**Tli-Grass Valley, Hayward** *Also Called: Thermionics Laboratory Inc (P-14352)*

**Tlm International Inc** ............................................. F ...... 650 952-2257
860 Mahler Rd Burlingame (94010) *(P-11420)*

**Tlmf Inc** ................................................................... D ...... 212 764-2334
1515 E 15th St Los Angeles (90021) *(P-2717)*

**Tls Productions Inc** ............................................... E ...... 810 220-8577
6 Venture Irvine (92618) *(P-576)*

**TMC Aero, Murrieta** *Also Called: TMC Ice Protection Systems LLC (P-14321)*

**TMC Aero, Los Angeles** *Also Called: TMC Ice Protection Systems LLC (P-14322)*

**TMC Ice Protection Systems LLC** ........................ E ...... 951 677-6934
25775 Jefferson Ave Murrieta (92562) *(P-14321)*

**TMC Ice Protection Systems LLC (PA)** ............... E ...... 951 677-6934
10850 Wilshire Blvd Ste 1250 Los Angeles (90024) *(P-14322)*

**TMI Products Inc** ................................................... C ...... 951 272-1996
1493 E Bentley Dr Ste 102 Corona (92879) *(P-13587)*

**TMI Visualogic, Corona** *Also Called: TMI Products Inc (P-13587)*

**TMJ Concepts, Ventura** *Also Called: TMJ Solutions LLC (P-15285)*

**TMJ Solutions LLC** ................................................ D ...... 805 650-3391
6059 King Dr Ventura (93003) *(P-15285)*

**TMW Corporation (PA)** .......................................... C ...... 818 362-5665
15148 Bledsoe St Sylmar (91342) *(P-13975)*

**Tmx Engineering and Mfg Corp** ............................ D ...... 714 641-5884
2141 S Standard Ave Santa Ana (92707) *(P-11145)*

**TN Sheet Metal Inc** ................................................ F ...... 714 593-0100
18385 Bandilier Cir Fountain Valley (92708) *(P-8595)*

## ALPHABETIC SECTION — Toray Prfmce Mtls Corp USA

Tnh Development LLC ............................................... F ...... 847 525-3960
1990 Olivera Rd Ste B Concord (94520) *(P-391)*

TNT Industrial Contractors Inc (PA)........................... E ...... 916 395-8400
3800 Happy Ln Sacramento (95827) *(P-9442)*

TNT Plastic Molding Inc (PA)....................................... D ...... 951 808-9700
725 E Harrison St Corona (92879) *(P-7054)*

Toad & Co, Santa Barbara *Also Called: Toad & Co International Inc (P-2816)*

Toad & Co International Inc (PA)................................. E ...... 800 865-8623
2020 Alameda Padre Serra Ste 125 Santa Barbara (93103) *(P-2816)*

Tobar Industries Inc ................................................... E ...... 408 778-3901
875 Jarvis Dr Ste 120 Morgan Hill (95037) *(P-8596)*

Tobar Industries Inc ................................................... D ...... 408 494-3530
912 Olinder Ct San Jose (95122) *(P-11475)*

Tobin Steel Company Inc ........................................... D ...... 714 541-2268
817 E Santa Ana Blvd Santa Ana (92701) *(P-8229)*

Toca Boca Inc ............................................................. F ...... 415 352-9028
848 Folsom St Ste 201 San Francisco (94107) *(P-18886)*

Today Pvc Bending Inc .............................................. E ...... 714 953-5707
995 E Discovery Ln Anaheim (92801) *(P-11483)*

Todd Street Inc ........................................................... E ...... 626 815-1175
770 N Todd Ave Azusa (91702) *(P-8348)*

Toesox, Vista *Also Called: Thirty Three Threads Inc (P-2648)*

Togetherbuycom .......................................................... F ...... 714 379-4600
11621 Markon Dr Garden Grove (92841) *(P-13588)*

Tognazzini Beverage Service .................................... F ...... 805 928-1144
241 Roemer Way Santa Maria (93454) *(P-1968)*

Tok America, Milpitas *Also Called: Tokyo Ohka Kogyo America Inc (P-5125)*

Tokalabs, San Jose *Also Called: Allied Telesis Inc (P-10319)*

Tokyo Ohka Kogyo America Inc ................................. E ...... 408 956-9901
190 Topaz St Milpitas (95035) *(P-5125)*

Tokyopop Inc (PA)....................................................... D ...... 323 920-5967
4136 Del Rey Ave Marina Del Rey (90292) *(P-4351)*

Tolar Manufacturing Co Inc ....................................... E ...... 951 808-0081
258 Mariah Cir Corona (92879) *(P-8230)*

Toleeto Fastener International ................................... E ...... 619 662-1355
1580 Jayken Way Chula Vista (91911) *(P-15919)*

Tolemar LLC ................................................................ E ...... 657 200-3840
6412 Maple Ave Westminster (92683) *(P-11434)*

Toller Enterprises Inc (PA)......................................... E ...... 805 374-9455
2251 Townsgate Rd Westlake Village (91361) *(P-17480)*

Tollhouse Window Company ...................................... C ...... 800 287-7996
1665 Tollhouse Rd Clovis (93611) *(P-3199)*

Tolosa Winery, San Luis Obispo *Also Called: Courtside Cellars LLC (P-1520)*

Tom Anderson Guitarworks ....................................... F ...... 805 498-1747
845 Rancho Conejo Blvd Newbury Park (91320) *(P-15725)*

Tom Ponton Industries Inc ......................................... F ...... 714 998-9073
22901 Savi Ranch Pkwy Ste B Yorba Linda (92887) *(P-19544)*

Tom Sawyer Software Corp (PA)................................ E ...... 510 682-6313
1997 El Dorado Ave Berkeley (94707) *(P-19048)*

Tom York Enterprises Inc .......................................... E ...... 323 581-6194
2050 E 48th St Vernon (90058) *(P-7055)*

Toma Tek, Firebaugh *Also Called: Neil Jones Food Company (P-909)*

Tomato Press, Westley *Also Called: Just Tomatoes Inc (P-82)*

Tomi Engineering Inc ................................................. D ...... 714 556-1474
414 E Alton Ave Santa Ana (92707) *(P-11146)*

Tomitribe Corporation ................................................ E ...... 310 526-7676
1519 6th St Apt 503 Santa Monica (90401) *(P-17986)*

Tomorrows Look Inc .................................................. D ...... 949 596-8400
17462 Von Karman Ave Irvine (92614) *(P-2497)*

Tomra, West Sacramento *Also Called: Odenberg Inc (P-9809)*

Tomra Food, Visalia *Also Called: Tomra Sorting Inc (P-10118)*

Tomra Sorting Inc ...................................................... E ...... 877 402-1755
728 N American St Visalia (93291) *(P-10118)*

Toms Metal Specialists Inc ........................................ E ...... 415 822-7971
1416 Wallace Ave San Francisco (94124) *(P-8231)*

Toms Welding & Fabrication, San Francisco *Also Called: Toms Metal Specialists Inc (P-8231)*

Tonbo Biosciences, San Diego *Also Called: Tonbo Biotechnologies Corp (P-5126)*

Tonbo Biotechnologies Corp ..................................... E ...... 858 888-7300
10840 Thornmint Rd San Diego (92127) *(P-5126)*

Tone It Up LLC ........................................................... E ...... 310 376-7645
1110 Manhattan Ave Manhattan Beach (90266) *(P-17434)*

Toneonel Lavash, Los Angeles *Also Called: Lavash Corporation of America (P-1222)*

Tonkean Inc ................................................................ D ...... 646 215-0493
44 Montgomery St San Francisco (94104) *(P-18887)*

Tonnage Industrial LLC ............................................. F ...... 800 893-9681
2130 W Cowles St Long Beach (90813) *(P-16901)*

Tonnellerie Francaise French C ................................ F ...... 707 942-9301
1401 Tubbs Ln Calistoga (94515) *(P-3376)*

Tonnellerie Radoux Usa Inc ...................................... F ...... 707 284-2888
480 Aviation Blvd Santa Rosa (95403) *(P-3377)*

Tonusa LLC ................................................................. F ...... 626 961-8700
16770 E Johnson Dr City Of Industry (91745) *(P-3274)*

Tony Marterie & Associates Inc ................................ E ...... 415 331-7150
28 Liberty Ship Way Fl 2 Sausalito (94965) *(P-2718)*

Too Good Gourmet, San Lorenzo *Also Called: Too Good Gourmet Inc (P-17220)*

Too Good Gourmet Inc (PA)....................................... E ...... 510 317-8150
2380 Grant Ave San Lorenzo (94580) *(P-17220)*

Tool Alliance Corporation .......................................... E ...... 714 373-5864
5372 Mcfadden Ave Huntington Beach (92649) *(P-9703)*

Tool Components Inc (PA)......................................... E ...... 310 323-5613
240 E Rosecrans Ave Gardena (90248) *(P-16634)*

Tool Specialty Co, Los Angeles *Also Called: Tosco - Tool Specialty Company (P-11147)*

Toolbox Medical Innovations, Carlsbad *Also Called: Foundry Med Innovations Inc (P-15090)*

Toor Knives Inc .......................................................... F ...... 619 328-6118
1488 Pioneer Way Ste 8 El Cajon (92020) *(P-16902)*

Tooth and Nail Winery ............................................... E ...... 805 369-6100
3090 Anderson Rd Paso Robles (93446) *(P-1786)*

Top Brands Distribution Inc ...................................... F ...... 858 578-0319
9675 Distribution Ave San Diego (92121) *(P-741)*

Top Heavy Clothing Company Inc (PA)..................... D ...... 951 442-8839
28381 Vincent Moraga Dr Temecula (92590) *(P-2579)*

Top Line Mfg Inc ........................................................ E ...... 562 633-0605
7032 Alondra Blvd Paramount (90723) *(P-8031)*

Top Shelf Manufacturing LLC ................................... F ...... 209 834-8185
1851 Paradise Rd Ste A Tracy (95304) *(P-15286)*

Top Shelf Orthopedics, Tracy *Also Called: Top Shelf Manufacturing LLC (P-15286)*

Top Source, The, Anaheim *Also Called: Block Tops Inc (P-3646)*

Top-Shelf Fixtures LLC .............................................. D ...... 909 627-7423
5263 Schaefer Ave Chino (91710) *(P-9236)*

Topaz Lighting Company LLC ................................... E ...... 818 838-3123
225 Parkside Dr San Fernando (91340) *(P-11562)*

Topaz Systems Inc (PA)............................................. E ...... 805 520-8282
875 Patriot Dr Ste A Moorpark (93021) *(P-10445)*

Topcon, Livermore *Also Called: Topcon Positioning Systems Inc (P-14935)*

Topcon Positioning Systems Inc (DH)....................... C ...... 925 245-8300
7400 National Dr Livermore (94550) *(P-14935)*

Topgolf Callaway Brands Corp (PA).......................... B ...... 760 931-1771
2180 Rutherford Rd Carlsbad (92008) *(P-15866)*

Topline Manufacturing Inc ........................................ F ...... 562 633-0605
7032 Alondra Blvd Paramount (90723) *(P-16253)*

Topolos At Rssian River Vinyrd ................................ E ...... 707 887-1575
5700 Hwy 116 Forestville (95436) *(P-32)*

Topper Manufacturing Corp ...................................... F ...... 310 375-5000
23880 Madison St Torrance (90505) *(P-10607)*

Toppik, Los Angeles *Also Called: Spencer Forrest Inc (P-17675)*

Topson Downs, Culver City *Also Called: Topson Downs California LLC (P-17497)*

Topson Downs California Inc .................................... C ...... 310 558-0300
3545 Motor Ave Los Angeles (90034) *(P-2729)*

Topson Downs California LLC (PA)........................... C ...... 310 558-0300
3840 Watseka Ave Culver City (90232) *(P-17497)*

**TOPSON DOWNS OF CALIFORNIA, INC., Los Angeles** *Also Called: Topson Downs California Inc (P-2729)*

Torani Syrups & Flavors, San Leandro *Also Called: R Torre & Company Inc (P-2022)*

Toray Advanced Composites USA Inc (DH).............. C ...... 408 465-8500
18255 Sutter Blvd Morgan Hill (95037) *(P-5213)*

Toray Advnced Cmpsites ADS LLC .......................... D ...... 707 359-3400
2450 Cordelia Rd Fairfield (94534) *(P-5214)*

Toray Membrane Usa Inc (DH)................................... D ...... 858 218-2360
13435 Danielson St Poway (92064) *(P-6326)*

Toray PMC, Camarillo *Also Called: Toray Prfmce Mtls Corp USA (P-11302)*

Toray Prfmce Mtls Corp USA ..................................... F ...... 805 402-6664
1150 Calle Suerte Camarillo (93012) *(P-11302)*

---

Employee Codes: A=Over 500 employees, B=251-500
C=101-250, D=51-100, E=20-50, F=10-19, G=1-9

**Torn & Glasser Inc**                                                                                              **ALPHABETIC SECTION**

Torn & Glasser Inc ............................................................ E ...... 909 706-4100
   1845 W Mt Vernon Ave Pomona (91768) *(P-1369)*

Torn Ranch Inc (PA) .......................................................... D ...... 415 506-3000
   2198 S Mcdowell Boulevard Ext Petaluma (94954) *(P-1336)*

Toro Company .................................................................... C ...... 619 562-2950
   1588 N Marshall Ave El Cajon (92020) *(P-9386)*

Toro Company .................................................................... C ...... 951 688-9221
   5825 Jasmine St Riverside (92504) *(P-9387)*

Torr Industries Inc ............................................................. E ...... 530 247-6909
   4564 Caterpillar Rd Redding (96003) *(P-17987)*

Torrance Refining Company LLC ................................... A ...... 310 212-2800
   3700 W 190th St Torrance (90504) *(P-6354)*

Torrance Steel Window Co Inc ...................................... E ...... 310 328-9181
   1819 Abalone Ave Torrance (90501) *(P-8293)*

Torrence Aluminum Window, Redlands *Also Called: Window Enterprises Inc (P-8294)*

Torres Fence Co Inc ........................................................ E ...... 559 237-4141
   2357 S Orange Ave Fresno (93725) *(P-577)*

Tortoise Industries Inc ..................................................... E ...... 323 258-7776
   3052 Treadwell St Los Angeles (90065) *(P-9129)*

Tortoise Tube, Los Angeles *Also Called: Tortoise Industries Inc (P-9129)*

Tosco - Tool Specialty Company ................................... E ...... 323 232-3561
   1011 E Slauson Ave Los Angeles (90011) *(P-11147)*

Toshiba, Irvine *Also Called: Toshiba Amer Elctrnic Cmpnnts (P-11706)*

Toshiba, South San Francisco *Also Called: Toshiba America Mri Inc (P-15586)*

Toshiba Amer Elctrnic Cmpnnts ..................................... B ...... 408 526-2400
   2610 Orchard Pkwy San Jose (95134) *(P-10289)*

Toshiba Amer Elctrnic Cmpnnts (DH) ............................ B ...... 949 462-7700
   5231 California Ave Irvine (92617) *(P-11706)*

Toshiba Amer Info Systems Inc ..................................... C ...... 949 583-3000
   9740 Irvine Blvd Fl 1 Irvine (92618) *(P-10213)*

Toshiba America Inc ........................................................ A ...... 212 596-0600
   5241 California Ave Ste 200 Irvine (92617) *(P-11707)*

Toshiba America Inc ........................................................ C ...... 212 596-0600
   280 Utah Ave South San Francisco (94080) *(P-15585)*

Toshiba America Mri Inc ................................................. C ...... 650 737-6686
   280 Utah Ave Ste 200 South San Francisco (94080) *(P-15586)*

Toska Inc ........................................................................... F ...... 213 746-0088
   1100 S San Pedro St Ste I6 Los Angeles (90015) *(P-2817)*

Total Accnting Bkkping Sltions ....................................... F ...... 818 981-0600
   6345 Balboa Blvd Ste 160 Encino (91316) *(P-5005)*

Total Beauty Media Inc ................................................... F ...... 310 295-9593
   1158 26th St Ste 535 Santa Monica (90403) *(P-4302)*

Total Concept Enterprises Inc ........................................ F ...... 559 485-8413
   3745 E Jensen Ave Fresno (93725) *(P-15920)*

Total Cost Involved, Ontario *Also Called: TCI Engineering Inc (P-13388)*

Total Gym Commercial LLC ........................................... F ...... 858 586-6080
   100 Chesterfield Dr # G Cardiff By The Sea (92007) *(P-15867)*

Total Health Environment LLC ....................................... E ...... 714 637-1010
   743 W Taft Ave Orange (92865) *(P-16591)*

Total Import Solutions Inc .............................................. F ...... 562 691-6818
   14700 Radburn Ave Santa Fe Springs (90670) *(P-16404)*

Total Intermodal Services Inc (PA) ................................ E ...... 562 427-6300
   7101 Jackson St Paramount (90723) *(P-16296)*

Total Mont LLC ................................................................. E ...... 562 983-1374
   790 W 12th St Long Beach (90813) *(P-7243)*

Total Process Solutions LLC ......................................... E ...... 661 829-7910
   1400 Norris Rd Bakersfield (93308) *(P-9943)*

Total Resources Intl Inc (PA) ......................................... E ...... 909 594-1220
   420 S Lemon Ave Walnut (91789) *(P-15418)*

Total Structures, Ventura *Also Called: Total Structures Inc (P-11628)*

Total Structures Inc ......................................................... E ...... 805 676-3322
   1696 Walter St Ventura (93003) *(P-11628)*

Total Tire Recycling, Sacramento *Also Called: AAA Signs Inc (P-19150)*

Total Warehouse, Anaheim *Also Called: Total Warehouse Inc (P-16291)*

Total Warehouse Inc ....................................................... C ...... 714 332-3082
   2895 E Miraloma Ave Anaheim (92806) *(P-16291)*

Total-Western Inc ............................................................. E ...... 707 747-5506
   3985 Teal Ct Benicia (94510) *(P-281)*

Total-Western Inc (HQ) .................................................... E ...... 562 220-1450
   8049 Somerset Blvd Paramount (90723) *(P-282)*

Totally Bamboo, Escondido *Also Called: Hollywood Chairs (P-3444)*

Totalrewards Software Inc ............................................. E ...... 916 632-1000
   2208 Plaza Dr Ste 100 Rocklin (95765) *(P-18888)*

Totex Manufacturing Inc ................................................. D ...... 310 326-2028
   3050 Lomita Blvd Torrance (90505) *(P-7056)*

Totten Tubes Inc (PA) ...................................................... D ...... 626 812-0220
   500 W Danlee St Azusa (91702) *(P-16635)*

Totus Medicines Inc ........................................................ E ...... 510 501-4832
   1480 64th St Emeryville (94608) *(P-5692)*

Touch International Display Enhancements Corp ...... E ...... 512 646-0310
   11231 Jola Ln Garden Grove (92843) *(P-14829)*

Touch Litho Company ..................................................... F ...... 562 927-8899
   7215 E Gage Ave Commerce (90040) *(P-4787)*

Touchstone Pistachio Co LLC ....................................... C ...... 559 535-0110
   19570 Avenue 88 Terra Bella (93270) *(P-9821)*

Touchtone Corporation ................................................... E ...... 714 755-2810
   3151 Airway Ave Ste I3 Costa Mesa (92626) *(P-17988)*

Toughbuilt, Irvine *Also Called: Toughbuilt Industries Inc (P-7967)*

Toughbuilt Industries Inc (PA) ........................................ B ...... 949 528-3100
   8669 Research Dr Irvine (92618) *(P-7967)*

Tour Master, Calabasas Hills *Also Called: Helmet House LLC (P-17075)*

Tournesol Siteworks LLC (PA) ........................................ D ...... 800 542-2282
   2930 Faber St Union City (94587) *(P-578)*

Tow Industries, West Covina *Also Called: Baatz Enterprises Inc (P-13342)*

Tower 26 Inc ..................................................................... E ...... 347 366-2706
   8826 Bradley Ave Ste B Sun Valley (91352) *(P-16254)*

Tower Industries Inc ........................................................ C ...... 909 947-2723
   1720 S Bon View Ave Ontario (91761) *(P-11148)*

Tower Mechanical Products Inc ..................................... C ...... 714 947-2723
   1720 S Bon View Ave Ontario (91761) *(P-14323)*

Tower Semicdtr Newport Bch Inc (DH) .......................... A ...... 949 435-8000
   4321 Jamboree Rd Newport Beach (92660) *(P-12769)*

Tower Semiconductor Usa Inc ....................................... F ...... 408 770-1320
   2570 N 1st St Ste 480 San Jose (95131) *(P-12770)*

Towerjazz, Newport Beach *Also Called: Tower Semicdtr Newport Bch Inc (P-12769)*

Towmaster Tire & Wheel, Anaheim *Also Called: Greenball Corp (P-16408)*

Townsend Design, Bakersfield *Also Called: Townsend Industries Inc (P-15421)*

Townsend Industries Inc ................................................ D ...... 661 837-1795
   4401 Stine Rd Bakersfield (93313) *(P-15419)*

Townsend Industries Inc ................................................ D ...... 661 837-1795
   4833 N Hills Dr Bakersfield (93308) *(P-15420)*

Townsend Industries Inc (DH) ........................................ C ...... 661 837-1795
   4615 Shepard St Bakersfield (93313) *(P-15421)*

Townsteel Inc ................................................................... D ...... 626 965-8917
   17901 Railroad St City Of Industry (91748) *(P-8032)*

Toy Barn, Oxnard *Also Called: Players West Amusements Inc (P-19311)*

Toymax International Inc (HQ) ....................................... D ...... 310 456-7799
   22619 Pacific Coast Hwy Malibu (90265) *(P-15770)*

Toyo Tire Hldings Americas Inc (HQ) ........................... E ...... 714 229-6100
   3565 Harbor Blvd Costa Mesa (92626) *(P-6413)*

Toyota Logistics Services Inc (DH) .............................. C ...... 310 468-4000
   19001 S Western Ave Torrance (90501) *(P-17443)*

TP Products, San Fernando *Also Called: Triumph Precision Products (P-8735)*

TP Solar Inc ...................................................................... F ...... 562 808-2171
   16310 Downey Ave Paramount (90723) *(P-10061)*

Tpg Growth, San Francisco *Also Called: Tpg Partners III LP (P-142)*

Tpg Growth, San Francisco *Also Called: Tarrant Capital Ip LLC (P-17734)*

Tpg Partners III LP (DH) .................................................. E ...... 415 743-1500
   345 California St Ste 3300 San Francisco (94104) *(P-142)*

Tpi, Madera *Also Called: Thomas Products LLC (P-1153)*

Tpl Communications, Panorama City *Also Called: D X Communications Inc (P-11839)*

Tps Aviation Inc (PA) ...................................................... D ...... 510 475-1010
   1515 Crocker Ave Hayward (94544) *(P-16737)*

Tpsi, Paramount *Also Called: TP Solar Inc (P-10061)*

Tpwc Inc (HQ) ................................................................... D ...... 877 283-5934
   1178 Galleron Rd Saint Helena (94574) *(P-1787)*

Tpwc Inc ........................................................................... D ...... 707 224-4039
   1999 Mount Veeder Rd Napa (94558) *(P-1788)*

Tr Manufacturing LLC (HQ) ............................................ C ...... 408 235-2900
   840 N Mccarthy Blvd Milpitas (95035) *(P-13110)*

Trackonomy Systems Inc (PA) ....................................... B ...... 833 872-2566
   214 Devcon Dr San Jose (95112) *(P-18889)*

# ALPHABETIC SECTION — Treasury Chateau & Estates

Tractor Beverage Co ............................................. E ...... 909 855-4106
512 Briarwood Ter Ventura (93001) *(P-1969)*

Tracy Industries Inc ............................................. C ...... 562 692-9034
3200 E Guasti Rd Ste 100 Ontario (91761) *(P-9332)*

Tracy Press Inc ................................................... E ...... 209 835-3030
145 W 10th St Tracy (95376) *(P-4213)*

Tracy Renewable Energy ..................................... E ...... 831 224-2513
4750 Holly Dr Tracy (95304) *(P-371)*

Trade Desk Inc (PA) ............................................. B ...... 805 585-3434
42 N Chestnut St Ventura (93001) *(P-17989)*

Trade Litho Inc .................................................... F ...... 510 965-6501
110 L St Ste 1 Antioch (94509) *(P-4788)*

Trade Lithography, Antioch *Also Called: Trade Litho Inc (P-4788)*

Trademark Construction Co Inc (PA) .................. D ...... 760 489-5647
15916 Bernardo Center Dr San Diego (92127) *(P-13190)*

Trademark Cosmetics LLC ................................. E ...... 951 683-2631
545 Columbia Ave Riverside (92507) *(P-6045)*

Trademark Plastics, Inc., Riverside *Also Called: Dek Industry Inc (P-9849)*

Tradenet Enterprise Inc ...................................... D ...... 888 595-3956
1580 Magnolia Ave Corona (92879) *(P-16059)*

Tradin Organics USA LLC ................................... E ...... 831 685-6565
15 Parade St Ste A Aptos (95003) *(P-2376)*

Traditional Medicinals Inc (PA) .......................... C ...... 707 823-8911
4515 Ross Rd Sebastopol (95472) *(P-2377)*

Traditions Prepared Meals LLC ......................... E ...... 916 534-4937
849 F St West Sacramento (95605) *(P-2378)*

Traffic Control & Safety Corp ............................. E ...... 858 679-7292
13755 Blaisdell Pl Poway (92064) *(P-16060)*

Traffic Management Pdts Inc .............................. A ...... 800 763-3999
4900 Airport Plaza Dr Ste 300 Long Beach (90815) *(P-18890)*

Traffic Signal Maintenance, Fremont *Also Called: Econolite (P-19090)*

Traffic Works Inc ................................................. E ...... 323 582-0616
5720 Soto St Huntington Park (90255) *(P-6572)*

Traffix Devices Inc (PA) ..................................... F ...... 949 361-5663
160 Avenida La Pata San Clemente (92673) *(P-12023)*

Train Reaction, Huntington Beach *Also Called: West Coast Trends Inc (P-15876)*

Trak Machine Tools, Rancho Dominguez *Also Called: Southwestern Industries Inc (P-9572)*

Trane, Walnut *Also Called: Trane US Inc (P-10519)*

Trane, San Diego *Also Called: Trane US Inc (P-10520)*

Trane Technologies Company LLC ..................... F ...... 323 583-4771
2845 Pellissier Pl City Of Industry (90601) *(P-9944)*

Trane US Inc ....................................................... E ...... 626 913-7913
20450 E Walnut Dr N Walnut (91789) *(P-10519)*

Trane US Inc ....................................................... C ...... 858 292-0833
3565 Corporate Ct Fl 1 San Diego (92123) *(P-10520)*

Trane US Inc ....................................................... D ...... 626 913-7123
3253 E Imperial Hwy Brea (92821) *(P-10521)*

Tranpak Inc ......................................................... E ...... 800 827-2474
1209 Victory Ln Madera (93637) *(P-3362)*

Trans Bay Steel Corporation (PA) ...................... E ...... 510 277-3756
536 Cleveland Ave Berkeley (94710) *(P-8232)*

Trans Fx Inc ........................................................ F ...... 805 485-6110
2361 Eastman Ave Oxnard (93030) *(P-16255)*

Trans Western Polymers Inc .............................. B ...... 925 449-7800
7539 Las Positas Rd Livermore (94551) *(P-3985)*

Trans-Dapt California Inc .................................... E ...... 562 921-0404
12438 Putnam St Whittier (90602) *(P-13589)*

Trans-India Products Inc .................................... E ...... 707 544-0298
3330 Coffey Ln Ste A Santa Rosa (95403) *(P-6046)*

Transcendia Inc .................................................. E ...... 909 944-9981
9000 9th St Ste 140 Rancho Cucamonga (91730) *(P-17236)*

Transchem Coatings, Los Angeles *Also Called: Paint-Chem Inc (P-6099)*

Transco, El Monte *Also Called: Transgo LLC (P-13591)*

Transcom Telecommunication Inc ..................... E ...... 562 424-9616
1390 E Burnett St Ste C Signal Hill (90755) *(P-11967)*

Transcontinental Nrthern CA 20 ......................... C ...... 510 580-7700
47540 Kato Rd Fremont (94538) *(P-4976)*

Transcontinental US LLC .................................... E ...... 909 390-8866
5601 Santa Ana St Ontario (91761) *(P-3986)*

Transdigm Inc ..................................................... D ...... 323 269-9181
5000 Triggs St Commerce (90022) *(P-13976)*

Transducer Techniques LLC .............................. E ...... 951 719-3965
42480 Rio Nedo Temecula (92590) *(P-14936)*

Transfer Flow Inc ................................................ D ...... 530 893-5209
1444 Fortress St Chico (95973) *(P-13590)*

Transfirst Corporation ........................................ E ...... 831 424-2911
900 E Blanco Rd Salinas (93901) *(P-14372)*

Transgo LLC ....................................................... F ...... 626 443-7456
2621 Merced Ave El Monte (91733) *(P-13591)*

Transhumance Holding Co Inc (PA) ................... E ...... 530 758-3091
2530 River Plaza Dr Ste 200 Sacramento (95833) *(P-618)*

Transhumance Holding Co Inc ........................... C ...... 707 693-2303
7390 Rio Dixon Rd Dixon (95620) *(P-619)*

Transhumance Inc .............................................. B ...... 530 758-3091
2530 River Plaza Dr Ste 200 Sacramento (95833) *(P-620)*

Transico Inc ........................................................ E ...... 714 835-6000
1240 Pioneer St Ste A Brea (92821) *(P-13111)*

Transilwrap Company, Rancho Cucamonga *Also Called: Transcendia Inc (P-17236)*

Translarity Inc (PA) ............................................. F ...... 510 371-7900
46575 Fremont Blvd Fremont (94538) *(P-14594)*

Translattice Inc (PA) ........................................... F ...... 408 749-8478
3398 Londonderry Dr Santa Clara (95050) *(P-10214)*

Transline Technology Inc ................................... E ...... 714 533-8300
1106 S Technology Cir Anaheim (92805) *(P-12241)*

Translogic Incorporated ...................................... E ...... 714 890-0058
5641 Engineer Dr Huntington Beach (92649) *(P-14465)*

Transom Capital Group LLC (PA) ....................... E ...... 424 293-2818
10990 Wilshire Blvd Ste 440 Los Angeles (90024) *(P-17758)*

Transonic Combustion Inc .................................. E ...... 805 465-5145
461 Calle San Pablo Camarillo (93012) *(P-9333)*

Transparent Products Inc ................................... E ...... 661 294-9787
28064 Avenue Stanford Unit E Valencia (91355) *(P-10312)*

Transphorm Inc (DH) .......................................... C ...... 805 456-1300
75 Castilian Dr Ste 200 Goleta (93117) *(P-12771)*

Transportation Equipment Inc ............................ E ...... 619 449-8860
1404 N Marshall Ave El Cajon (92020) *(P-2985)*

Transportation Power LLC .................................. E ...... 858 248-4255
2057 Aldergrove Ave Escondido (92029) *(P-13592)*

Transpower, Escondido *Also Called: Transportation Power LLC (P-13592)*

Transsight LLC .................................................... E ...... 510 415-6301
6200 Stoneridge Mall Rd Ste 300 Pleasanton (94588) *(P-19572)*

Transwestern Publishing, San Diego *Also Called: Transwestern Publishing Company LLC (P-4482)*

Transwestern Publishing Company LLC ............ A ...... 858 467-2800
8344 Clairemont Mesa Blvd San Diego (92111) *(P-4482)*

Trantronics Inc .................................................... E ...... 949 553-1234
1822 Langley Ave Irvine (92614) *(P-12242)*

Trashy Lingerie, West Hollywood *Also Called: 402 Shoes Inc (P-2826)*

Travelers Choice Travelware ............................. D ...... 909 529-7688
2805 S Reservoir St Pomona (91766) *(P-7143)*

Travelling Pic Show Company ........................... F ...... 323 769-1115
1000 Kenfield Ave Los Angeles (90049) *(P-15670)*

TRAVERE, San Diego *Also Called: Travere Therapeutics Inc (P-5693)*

Travere Therapeutics Inc (PA) ........................... B ...... 888 969-7879
3611 Valley Centre Dr Ste 300 San Diego (92130) *(P-5693)*

Travis Snyder ...................................................... F ...... 909 338-6302
27248 Hwy 189 Ste Ab-06 Blue Jay (92317) *(P-9443)*

TravisMathew LLC (HQ) ..................................... E ...... 562 799-6900
15202 Graham St Huntington Beach (92649) *(P-2649)*

Traxero North America LLC ................................ D ...... 423 497-1164
1730 E Holly Ave Ste 740 El Segundo (90245) *(P-18891)*

Traxx Corporation ............................................... D ...... 909 623-8032
1201 E Lexington Ave Pomona (91766) *(P-16256)*

Trayer Engineering Corporation ......................... D ...... 415 285-7770
1569 Alvarado St San Leandro (94577) *(P-11251)*

Tre Milano LLC ................................................... E ...... 310 260-8888
2730 Monterey St Ste 101 Torrance (90503) *(P-16257)*

Treana Winery LLC ............................................. E ...... 805 237-2932
4280 Second Wind Way Paso Robles (93447) *(P-1789)*

Treasure Garden Inc (PA) .................................. E ...... 626 814-0168
13401 Brooks Dr Baldwin Park (91706) *(P-17362)*

Treasury Chateau & Estates ............................... C ...... 707 299-2600
10300 Chalk Hill Rd Healdsburg (95448) *(P-1790)*

## Treasury Wine Estates Americas — ALPHABETIC SECTION

Treasury Wine Estates Americas ..... E ...... 805 237-6000
7000 E Highway 46 Paso Robles (93446) *(P-33)*

Treasury Wine Estates Americas ..... D ...... 707 880-9967
630 Airpark Rd Napa (94558) *(P-1791)*

Treasury Wine Estates Americas ..... F ...... 707 312-0081
6480 Finnell Rd Yountville (94599) *(P-1792)*

Treasury Wine Estates Americas (HQ) ..... B ...... 707 259-4500
555 Gateway Dr Napa (94558) *(P-1793)*

Treasury Wine Estates Americas ..... E ...... 707 935-1357
21468 8th St E Ste A Sonoma (95476) *(P-1794)*

Treasury Wine Estates Americas ..... F ...... 707 942-4945
2010 Diamond Mountain Rd Calistoga (94515) *(P-1795)*

Treasury Wine Estates Americas ..... F ...... 707 564-8477
1111 Dunaweal Ln Calistoga (94515) *(P-1796)*

Treasury Wine Estates Americas ..... F ...... 707 299-3112
300 Lakeside Dr 25th Fl Oakland (94612) *(P-1797)*

Treasury Wine Estates Americas ..... E ...... 707 257-5300
1250 Cuttings Wharf Rd Napa (94559) *(P-1798)*

Treasury Wine Estates Americas ..... E ...... 707 963-4812
1000 Pratt Ave Saint Helena (94574) *(P-1799)*

Treasury Wine Estates Americas ..... E ...... 707 963-7221
2867 Saint Helena Hwy N Saint Helena (94574) *(P-1800)*

Treasury Wine Estates Americas ..... D ...... 707 963-7115
2000 Saint Helena Hwy N Saint Helena (94574) *(P-1801)*

Treasury Wine Estates Americas ..... E ...... 707 967-5200
1960 Saint Helena Hwy Rutherford (94573) *(P-1848)*

Treau Inc ..... E ...... 866 945-3514
375 Alabama St Ste 220 San Francisco (94110) *(P-10522)*

Tree House Pad & Paper Inc ..... D ...... 800 213-4184
2341 Pomona Rd Ste 108 Corona (92878) *(P-4023)*

Tree Island Wire (usa) Inc ..... C ...... 909 594-7511
13470 Philadelphia Ave Fontana (92337) *(P-7654)*

Tree Island Wire (usa) Inc ..... C ...... 909 595-6617
3880 W Valley Blvd Pomona (91769) *(P-7655)*

Tree Island Wire (usa) Inc ..... C ...... 909 899-1673
5080 Hallmark Pkwy San Bernardino (92407) *(P-9237)*

Tree Island Wire (USA) Inc (DH) ..... C ...... 909 594-7511
3880 Valley Blvd Walnut (91789) *(P-7656)*

Tree Island Wire USA, San Bernardino *Also Called: Tree Island Wire (usa) Inc (P-9237)*

Tree Nuts LLC ..... E ...... 209 669-6400
451 W F St Turlock (95380) *(P-17151)*

Tree Service, Folsom *Also Called: Mountain F Enterprises Inc (P-3051)*

Tree Service Unlimited, Cameron Park *Also Called: Tsu/Tree Service Unlimited Inc (P-100)*

Treescapes and Plant Works ..... E ...... 760 631-6789
1248 Los Vallecitos Blvd San Marcos (92069) *(P-16258)*

Trefethen Family Vineyards, Napa *Also Called: Trefethen Vineyards Winery Inc (P-1802)*

Trefethen Vineyards Winery Inc ..... E ...... 707 255-7700
1160 Oak Knoll Ave Napa (94558) *(P-1802)*

Treivush Industries Inc ..... D ...... 213 745-7774
940 W Washington Blvd Los Angeles (90015) *(P-2818)*

Trelborg Sling Sltions US Inc ..... E ...... 805 239-4284
3077 Rollie Gates Dr Paso Robles (93446) *(P-7057)*

Trellborg Sling Sltions US Inc (DH) ..... C ...... 714 415-0280
2761 Walnut Ave Tustin (92780) *(P-15287)*

Trelleborg Sealing Solutions ..... D ...... 805 239-4284
3034 Propeller Dr Paso Robles (93446) *(P-15288)*

TRELLEBORG SEALING SOLUTIONS TUSTIN, INC., Paso Robles *Also Called: Trelleborg Sealing Solutions (P-15288)*

Trellisware Technologies Inc (HQ) ..... C ...... 858 753-1600
10641 Scripps Summit Ct Ste 100 San Diego (92131) *(P-16314)*

Tremont Group Incorporated ..... E ...... 530 662-5442
201 East St Woodland (95776) *(P-17275)*

Trenchless Pipe Company Inc ..... E ...... 530 275-9400
3410 Bronze Ct Shasta Lake (96019) *(P-6603)*

Trend Design Inc ..... F ...... 805 498-0457
1200 Lawrence Dr Ste 465 Newbury Park (91320) *(P-17841)*

Trend Graphics Screenprinting, Newbury Park *Also Called: Trend Design Inc (P-17841)*

Trend Manor Furn Mfg Co Inc ..... E ...... 626 964-6493
17047 Gale Ave City Of Industry (91745) *(P-3458)*

Trend Micro Incorporated ..... D ...... 408 257-1500
3031 Tisch Way San Jose (95128) *(P-16559)*

Trend Micro Incorporated ..... B ...... 408 257-1500
10101 N De Anza Blvd Cupertino (95014) *(P-16560)*

Trend Offset Printing, Los Alamitos *Also Called: Trend Offset Printing Services Inc (P-4789)*

Trend Offset Printing Services Inc (HQ) ..... E ...... 562 598-2446
3701 Catalina St Los Alamitos (90720) *(P-4789)*

TREND OFFSET PRINTING SERVICES INCORPORATED, Los Alamitos *Also Called: Trend Offset Printing Svcs Inc (P-4790)*

Trend Offset Printing Svcs Inc ..... B ...... 562 598-2446
3791 Catalina St Los Alamitos (90720) *(P-4790)*

Trend Technologies, Chino *Also Called: Trend Technologies LLC (P-8597)*

Trend Technologies LLC (DH) ..... C ...... 909 597-7861
4626 Eucalyptus Ave Chino (91710) *(P-8597)*

Trendsetter Solar Products Inc ..... F ...... 707 443-5652
818 Broadway Eureka (95501) *(P-439)*

Trensor, Foothill Ranch *Also Called: Trensor LLC (P-19426)*

Trensor LLC ..... F ...... 949 379-6730
27051 Towne Centre Dr Foothill Ranch (92610) *(P-19426)*

Trepanning Specialities Inc ..... E ...... 562 633-8110
16201 Illinois Ave Paramount (90723) *(P-11149)*

Trepanning Specialties, Paramount *Also Called: Trepanning Specialities Inc (P-11149)*

Treston IAC LLC ..... E ...... 714 990-8997
8175 E Brookdale Ln Anaheim (92807) *(P-3752)*

Tri Counties Trucking ..... E ...... 530 692-5388
1263 Reed Rd Yuba City (95991) *(P-13433)*

Tri Fab Associates Inc ..... D ...... 510 651-7628
48351 Lakeview Blvd Fremont (94538) *(P-8598)*

Tri Models Inc ..... D ...... 714 896-0823
5191 Oceanus Dr Huntington Beach (92649) *(P-13696)*

Tri Precision Sheetmetal Inc ..... E ...... 714 632-8838
1104 N Armando St Anaheim (92806) *(P-8599)*

Tri Tool Inc (HQ) ..... D ...... 916 288-6100
3041 Sunrise Blvd Rancho Cordova (95742) *(P-16851)*

Tri-C Manufacturing Inc ..... E ...... 916 371-1700
517 Houston St West Sacramento (95691) *(P-9905)*

Tri-City Print & Mail, West Sacramento *Also Called: Premier Print & Mail Inc (P-17801)*

Tri-Continent Scientific Inc ..... D ...... 530 273-8888
12740 Earhart Ave Auburn (95602) *(P-14484)*

Tri-Dim Filter Corporation ..... E ...... 626 826-5893
26550 Adams Ave Murrieta (92562) *(P-10003)*

Tri-Fitting Mfg, South El Monte *Also Called: Tri-Fitting Mfg Company (P-13977)*

Tri-Fitting Mfg Company ..... F ...... 626 442-2000
10414 Rush St South El Monte (91733) *(P-13977)*

Tri-J Metal Heat Treating Co (PA) ..... F ...... 909 622-9999
327 E Commercial St Pomona (91767) *(P-7904)*

Tri-Net Inc ..... E ...... 909 483-3555
14721 Hilton Dr Fontana (92336) *(P-14595)*

Tri-Net Technology Inc ..... D ...... 909 598-8818
21709 Ferrero Walnut (91789) *(P-10446)*

Tri-Star Dyeing & Finshg Inc ..... D ...... 562 483-0123
15125 Marquardt Ave Santa Fe Springs (90670) *(P-2450)*

Tri-Star Laminates Inc ..... E ...... 949 587-3200
20322 Windrow Dr Ste 100 Lake Forest (92630) *(P-12243)*

Tri-State Stairway Corp ..... F ...... 559 268-0875
706 W California Ave Fresno (93706) *(P-8647)*

Tri-Tech Metals Inc ..... F ...... 909 948-1401
9039 Charles Smith Ave Rancho Cucamonga (91730) *(P-16636)*

Tri-Tech Precision Inc ..... F ...... 714 970-1363
1863 N Case St Orange (92865) *(P-13978)*

Tri-Tek Electronics, Valencia *Also Called: Interconnect Solutions Co LLC (P-13002)*

Tri-Union Seafoods LLC (DH) ..... D ...... 424 397-8556
2150 E Grand Ave El Segundo (90245) *(P-17159)*

Tri-Valley Corporation ..... E ...... 661 864-0500
4927 Calloway Dr Ste 101 Bakersfield (93312) *(P-143)*

Triad Global Group, Acampo *Also Called: Global Wine Group (P-1589)*

Triamid Cnstr Centl Cal Inc ..... E ...... 916 858-0397
3130 Fite Cir Ste 1 Sacramento (95827) *(P-353)*

Triangle Coatings Inc (PA) ..... E ...... 510 895-8000
4763 Bennett Dr Livermore (94551) *(P-6115)*

Triangle Paint, Livermore *Also Called: Triangle Coatings Inc (P-6115)*

Triangle Rock Product Inc ..... C ...... 209 826-5066
22101 W Sunset Ave Los Banos (93635) *(P-16486)*

# ALPHABETIC SECTION

Triangle Rock Products, Los Banos *Also Called: Triangle Rock Product Inc (P-16486)*
Triangle Rock Products  LLC .................................................. C ...... 818 553-8820
500 N Brand Blvd Ste 500 Glendale (91203) *(P-306)*

Triangle Tool & Die Corp .......................................................... F ...... 562 944-2117
13189 Flores St Santa Fe Springs (90670) *(P-11150)*

Trianglehardalloys, Santa Fe Springs *Also Called: Triangle Tool & Die Corp (P-11150)*

Tribe Mdia Corp A Cal Nnprfit ................................................... E ...... 213 368-1661
3250 Wilshire Blvd Los Angeles (90010) *(P-4214)*

Trical  Inc ................................................................................ E ...... 559 651-0736
28679 Rd 68 Visalia (93277) *(P-6208)*

Trical  Inc (PA)........................................................................ **E ...... 831 637-0195**
8100 Arroyo Cir Gilroy (95020) *(P-6209)*

Trical  Inc ................................................................................ E ...... 831 637-0195
8770 Hwy 25 Hollister (95023) *(P-6210)*

Trical  Inc ................................................................................ E ...... 951 737-6960
1029 Railroad St Corona (92882) *(P-6211)*

Trical  Inc ................................................................................ E ...... 661 824-2494
1667 Purdy Rd Mojave (93501) *(P-6212)*

Trick or Treat Stdios Hldngs L .................................................. E ...... 831 713-9665
1005 17th Ave Santa Cruz (95062) *(P-16259)*

Trico Leasing Company  LLC ................................................... D ...... 877 259-9997
30154 Rhone Dr Rancho Palos Verdes (90275) *(P-16903)*

Tricom Research  Inc ............................................................... D ...... 949 250-6024
17791 Sky Park Cir Ste J Irvine (92614) *(P-11968)*

Tricom Research  Inc ............................................................... D ...... 949 250-6024
17791 Sky Park Cir Ste J Irvine (92614) *(P-11969)*

Tricopp  Inc (PA)..................................................................... **E ...... 925 520-5807**
39899 Balentine Dr Ste 265 Newark (94560) *(P-19573)*

Tricor Refining  LLC ................................................................ E ...... 661 393-7110
1134 Manor St Bakersfield (93308) *(P-6355)*

Tridecs Corporation ................................................................. E ...... 510 785-2620
3513 Arden Rd Hayward (94545) *(P-11151)*

Trident Maritime Systems  Inc .................................................. D ...... 619 346-3800
651 Drucker Ln San Diego (92154) *(P-14019)*

Trident Microsystems Inc ......................................................... A ...... 408 962-5000
1170 Kifer Rd Sunnyvale (94086) *(P-12772)*

Trident Plating  Inc ................................................................... E ...... 562 906-2556
10046 Romandel Ave Santa Fe Springs (90670) *(P-9024)*

Trident Space & Defense LLC .................................................. E ...... 310 214-5500
19951 Mariner Ave Torrance (90503) *(P-12773)*

Trident Technologies, San Diego *Also Called: Chemtreat  Inc (P-6274)*

Trifo, Santa Clara *Also Called: Trifo  Inc (P-10119)*
Trifo  Inc ................................................................................. E ...... 408 326-2242
4633 Old Ironsides Dr Ste 300 Santa Clara (95054) *(P-10119)*

Trifoil Imaging, Ventura *Also Called: Northrdge Tr-Mdlity Imging Inc (P-14345)*

Triformix  Inc .......................................................................... F ...... 707 545-7645
487 Aviation Blvd Ste 100 Santa Rosa (95403) *(P-7058)*

Trijicon Electro Optics, Auburn *Also Called: IRD Acquisitions  LLC (P-15604)*

Trillium Pump USA, Fresno *Also Called: Trillium Pumps Usa  Inc (P-9945)*
Trillium Pumps Usa  Inc (HQ).................................................. C ...... 559 442-4000
2495 S Golden State Blvd Fresno (93706) *(P-9945)*

Trilore Technologies Inc .......................................................... E ...... 925 295-0734
3000 Danville Blvd Ste F # 525 Alamo (94507) *(P-7851)*

Trim Quick, Corona *Also Called: Vinylvisions Company  LLC (P-6116)*

Trim-Lok Inc (PA).................................................................... **C ...... 714 562-0500**
6855 Hermosa Cir Buena Park (90620) *(P-7059)*

Trimas Aerospace, Simi Valley *Also Called: Rsa Engineered Products  LLC (P-13940)*

Trimble Inc ............................................................................. E ...... 916 294-2000
1720 Prairie City Rd Ste 100 Folsom (95630) *(P-14324)*

Trimble Military & Advnced Sys ................................................ D ...... 408 481-8000
510 De Guigne Dr Sunnyvale (94085) *(P-14325)*

Trinchero Family Estates, Saint Helena *Also Called: Sutter Home Winery  Inc (P-1767)*

Trinchero Family Estates, Lodi *Also Called: Sutter Home Winery  Inc (P-1768)*

Trinet Communications  Inc (PA).............................................. **F ...... 925 294-1720**
6567 Brisa St Livermore (94550) *(P-16738)*

Trinet Zenefits, San Francisco *Also Called: Yourpeople  Inc (P-18950)*

Trinity Engineering ................................................................. F ...... 707 585-2959
583 Martin Ave Rohnert Park (94928) *(P-19427)*

Trinity International Inds LLC ................................................... E ...... 800 985-5506
1041 E 230th St Carson (90745) *(P-7060)*

Trinity Lighweight, Frazier Park *Also Called: Trnlwb  LLC (P-16260)*
Trinity Process Solutions Inc ................................................... E ...... 714 701-1112
4740 E Bryson St Anaheim (92807) *(P-9272)*

Trinity Robotics Automtn LLC .................................................. F ...... 562 690-4525
4582 Brickell Privado St Ontario (91761) *(P-9747)*

Trinity Sports Inc .................................................................... B ...... 323 277-9288
2067 E 55th St Vernon (90058) *(P-2719)*

Trinity Woodworks  Inc ............................................................ E ...... 760 639-5351
2620 Temple Heights Dr Oceanside (92056) *(P-3200)*

Trinium Technologies, Long Beach *Also Called: QED Software LLC (P-18713)*

Trio, Azusa *Also Called: Trio Engineered Products  Inc (P-9444)*
Trio Engineered Products  Inc (HQ).......................................... E ...... 626 851-3966
505 W Foothill Blvd Azusa (91702) *(P-9444)*

Trio Manufacturing, El Segundo *Also Called: Trio Manufacturing  Inc (P-13979)*
Trio Manufacturing  Inc ........................................................... C ...... 310 640-6123
601 Lairport St El Segundo (90245) *(P-13979)*

Trio Metal Stamping, City Of Industry *Also Called: Trio Metal Stamping  Inc (P-8600)*
Trio Metal Stamping  Inc ......................................................... D ...... 626 336-1228
15318 Proctor Ave City Of Industry (91745) *(P-8600)*

Trion Worlds Inc ..................................................................... B ...... 650 631-9800
2400 Bridge Pkwy 100 Redwood City (94065) *(P-18892)*

Triple A Containers Inc ........................................................... D ...... 562 404-7433
16069 Shoemaker Ave Cerritos (90703) *(P-3893)*

Triple Aught Design  LLC ........................................................ E ...... 415 318-8252
660 22nd St San Francisco (94107) *(P-17514)*

Triple D and DS ..................................................................... E
4040 Calle Platino Ste 105 Oceanside (92056) *(P-4056)*

Triple Five Nutrition  LLC ......................................................... E ...... 310 502-2277
17120 S Figueroa St Ste B Gardena (90248) *(P-783)*

Triple H Food Processors  LLC ................................................ D ...... 951 352-5700
5821 Wilderness Ave Riverside (92504) *(P-2379)*

Triquint Semiconductor  Inc ..................................................... F ...... 408 577-6344
3099 Orchard Dr San Jose (95134) *(P-12774)*

Triquint Wj  Inc ....................................................................... D ...... 408 577-6200
3099 Orchard Dr San Jose (95134) *(P-11970)*

Trireme Medical  LLC ............................................................. E ...... 925 931-1300
7060 Koll Center Pkwy Ste 300 Pleasanton (94566) *(P-15289)*

Tritex Trading Inc ................................................................... F ...... 949 413-8454
7171 Warner Ave Ste B348 Huntington Beach (92647) *(P-2430)*

Triton, Newport Beach *Also Called: Triton Chandelier  Inc (P-11563)*
Triton Chandelier  Inc ............................................................. F ...... 714 957-9600
1301 Dove St Ste 900 Newport Beach (92660) *(P-11563)*

Triton Enterprises  LLC ........................................................... E ...... 925 230-8395
5638 Wells Ln San Ramon (94582) *(P-19574)*

Triumph Acttion Systems - VInc ............................................... C ...... 661 702-7537
28150 Harrison Pkwy Valencia (91355) *(P-13980)*

Triumph Equipment  Inc .......................................................... F ...... 909 947-5983
13434 S Ontario Ave Ontario (91761) *(P-13981)*

Triumph Group, Valencia *Also Called: Triumph Acttion Systems - VInc (P-13980)*

Triumph Group, Calexico *Also Called: Triumph Insulation Systems LLC (P-13982)*

Triumph Insulation Systems LLC ............................................. A ...... 760 618-7543
1754 Carr Rd Ste 103 Calexico (92231) *(P-13982)*

Triumph Precision Products .................................................... F ...... 818 897-4700
13636 Vaughn St Ste A San Fernando (91340) *(P-8735)*

Triumph Proc - Embee Div Inc ................................................ B ...... 714 546-9842
2158 S Hathaway St Santa Ana (92705) *(P-9025)*

Triumph Processing  Inc ......................................................... C ...... 323 563-1338
2605 Industry Way Lynwood (90262) *(P-9026)*

Triumph Structures, City Of Industry *Also Called: Triumph Structures - Everett Inc (P-13983)*

Triumph Structures - Brea, Chatsworth *Also Called: Alatus Aerosystems (P-13767)*

Triumph Structures - Everett Inc ............................................. C ...... 425 348-4100
17055 Gale Ave City Of Industry (91745) *(P-13983)*

Triune Enterprises  Inc ........................................................... E ...... 310 719-1600
13711 S Normandie Ave Gardena (90249) *(P-3940)*

Triune Enterprises Mfg, Gardena *Also Called: Triune Enterprises  Inc (P-3940)*

Trius Therapeutics LLC .......................................................... C ...... 858 452-0370
4747 Executive Dr Ste 1100 San Diego (92121) *(P-5694)*

Trivad  Inc ............................................................................. C ...... 650 286-1086
880 Mitten Rd Ste 107 Burlingame (94010) *(P-16561)*

Trivascular  Inc (DH)............................................................... E ...... 707 543-8800
2 Musick Irvine (92618) *(P-15290)*

Trivascular Technologies Inc (HQ) .................................................. C ...... 707 543-8800
  2 Musick Irvine (92618) *(P-15291)*
Triview, La Habra *Also Called: Triview Glass Industries LLC (P-7244)*
Triview Glass Industries LLC .................................................. D ...... 626 363-7980
  279 Shawnan Ln La Habra (90631) *(P-7244)*
Triw1969 Inc .................................................. E ...... 619 593-3636
  877 Vernon Way El Cajon (92020) *(P-7905)*
Trixxi Clothing Company Inc (PA) .................................................. E ...... 323 585-4200
  6817 E Acco St Commerce (90040) *(P-2720)*
Trlg Corporate Holdings LLC (PA) .................................................. C ...... 323 266-3072
  1888 Rosecrans Ave Manhattan Beach (90266) *(P-2867)*
TRM Manufacturing Inc .................................................. C ...... 951 256-8550
  375 Trm Cir Corona (92879) *(P-6573)*
Trnlwb LLC .................................................. A ...... 661 245-3736
  17410 Lockwood Valley Rd Frazier Park (93225) *(P-16260)*
Trojan Battery Company LLC (DH) .................................................. C ...... 562 236-3000
  12380 Clark St Santa Fe Springs (90670) *(P-13164)*
Trojan Battery Holdings LLC .................................................. E ...... 800 423-6569
  12380 Clark St Santa Fe Springs (90670) *(P-13154)*
Tronex Technology Incorporated .................................................. E ...... 707 426-2550
  2860 Cordelia Rd Ste 230 Fairfield (94534) *(P-7968)*
Tronson Manufacturing Inc .................................................. E ...... 408 533-0369
  3421 Yale Way Fremont (94538) *(P-11152)*
Tropical Asphalt LLC (PA) .................................................. F ...... 714 739-1408
  14435 Macaw St La Mirada (90638) *(P-6385)*
Tropical Functional Labs LLC .................................................. E ...... 951 688-2619
  7111 Arlington Ave Ste F Riverside (92503) *(P-784)*
Tropical Preserving Co Inc .................................................. E ...... 213 748-5108
  5 Lewiston Ct Ladera Ranch (92694) *(P-933)*
Tropical Roofing Products CA, La Mirada *Also Called: Tropical Asphalt LLC (P-6385)*
Tropicale Foods LLC (PA) .................................................. E ...... 909 635-1000
  1237 W State St Ontario (91762) *(P-817)*
Tropicana, City Of Industry *Also Called: Tropicana Products Inc (P-934)*
Tropicana Products Inc .................................................. E ...... 626 968-1299
  240 N Orange Ave City Of Industry (91744) *(P-934)*
Tropitone Furniture Co Inc (DH) .................................................. B ...... 949 595-2010
  5 Marconi Irvine (92618) *(P-3515)*
Tropos Technologies Inc .................................................. F ...... 408 571-6104
  16890 Church St Bldg 1a Morgan Hill (95037) *(P-13593)*
Trov Inc .................................................. E ...... 925 478-5500
  1423 Broadway Oakland (94612) *(P-18893)*
Troy Metal Products, Goleta *Also Called: Neal Feay Company (P-7744)*
Troy Products, Montebello *Also Called: Troy Sheet Metal Works Inc (P-8811)*
Troy Sheet Metal Works Inc (PA) .................................................. D ...... 323 720-4100
  1024 S Vail Ave Montebello (90640) *(P-8811)*
Troy-Csl Lighting Inc .................................................. C ...... 626 336-4511
  14508 Nelson Ave City Of Industry (91744) *(P-11504)*
Trs Rentelco, Jurupa Valley *Also Called: Mobile Modular Management Corp (P-8676)*
Tru Form Industries, Santa Fe Springs *Also Called: Tru-Form Industries Inc (P-8895)*
Tru Machining .................................................. F ...... 510 573-3408
  45979 Warm Springs Blvd Ste 8 Fremont (94539) *(P-11153)*
Tru-Cut Inc .................................................. E ...... 310 630-0422
  141 E 157th St Gardena (90248) *(P-9401)*
Tru-Duct Inc .................................................. E ...... 619 660-3858
  2515 Industry St Oceanside (92054) *(P-8601)*
Tru-Fit Manufacturing, Lathrop *Also Called: Accurate Heating & Cooling Inc (P-8360)*
Tru-Form Industries Inc (PA) .................................................. D ...... 562 802-2041
  14511 Anson Ave Santa Fe Springs (90670) *(P-8895)*
Tru-Form Plastics Inc .................................................. E ...... 310 327-9444
  14600 Hoover St Westminster (92683) *(P-7061)*
Truabutment Inc (PA) .................................................. F ...... 714 956-1488
  17666 Fitch Irvine (92614) *(P-15490)*
Truaire, Santa Fe Springs *Also Called: TA Industries Inc (P-16771)*
True Botanicals Inc .................................................. D ...... 415 420-0403
  1 Lovell Ave Mill Valley (94941) *(P-6047)*
True Cast Concrete Products, Sun Valley *Also Called: Quikrete Companies LLC (P-7383)*
True Classic Tees LLC .................................................. E ...... 323 419-1092
  26635 Agoura Rd Ste 105 Calabasas (91302) *(P-2580)*
True Design Inc .................................................. F ...... 562 699-2001
  9427 Norwalk Blvd Santa Fe Springs (90670) *(P-3275)*

True Digital Surgery, Goleta *Also Called: Digital Surgery Systems Inc (P-15070)*
True Fresh Hpp LLC .................................................. E ...... 949 922-8801
  6535 Caballero Blvd Unit B Buena Park (90620) *(P-14373)*
True Investments LLC .................................................. E ...... 949 258-9720
  2260 University Dr Newport Beach (92660) *(P-17759)*
True Investments LLC .................................................. E ...... 949 258-9720
  6535 Caballero Blvd Unit B Buena Park (90620) *(P-17760)*
True Leaf Farms LLC (PA) .................................................. C ...... 831 623-4667
  1275 San Justo Rd San Juan Bautista (95045) *(P-971)*
True Leaf Technologies, Cotati *Also Called: Biotherm Hydronic Inc (P-8061)*
True Position Technologies LLC .................................................. D ...... 661 294-0030
  24900 Avenue Stanford Valencia (91355) *(P-11154)*
True Precision Machining Inc .................................................. E ...... 805 964-4545
  175 Industrial Way Buellton (93427) *(P-11155)*
True Religion Apparel Inc (HQ) .................................................. B ...... 323 266-3072
  500 W 190th St Ste 300 Gardena (90248) *(P-2589)*
True Religion Brand Jeans, Gardena *Also Called: True Religion Apparel Inc (P-2589)*
True Warrior LLC .................................................. E ...... 661 237-6588
  21226 Lone Star Way Santa Clarita (91390) *(P-2911)*
Trueclass, Foothill Ranch *Also Called: Twila True Collaborations LLC (P-6049)*
Truepill Inc (PA) .................................................. F ...... 855 910-8606
  3121 Diablo Ave Hayward (94545) *(P-5695)*
Truepoint Solutions LLC (PA) .................................................. E ...... 916 259-1293
  3262 Penryn Rd Ste 100b Loomis (95650) *(P-18996)*
Truevision 3d Surgical, Goleta *Also Called: Truevision Systems Inc (P-15292)*
Truevision Systems Inc .................................................. E ...... 805 963-9700
  315 Bollay Dr Ste 101 Goleta (93117) *(P-15292)*
Trufocus, Watsonville *Also Called: Trufocus Corporation (P-15510)*
Trufocus Corporation .................................................. F ...... 831 761-9981
  468 Westridge Dr Watsonville (95076) *(P-15510)*
Truframe, Visalia *Also Called: R Lang Company (P-8287)*
Truitt Oilfield Maint Corp .................................................. B ...... 661 871-4099
  1051 James Rd Bakersfield (93308) *(P-283)*
Trulite GL Alum Solutions LLC .................................................. D ...... 800 877-8439
  19430 San Jose Ave City Of Industry (91748) *(P-7752)*
Truly Green Solutions LLC .................................................. E ...... 818 206-4404
  9601 Variel Ave Chatsworth (91311) *(P-11629)*
Trumaker & Co., San Francisco *Also Called: Trumaker Inc (P-2568)*
Trumaker Inc .................................................. E ...... 415 662-3836
  228 Grant Ave Fl 2 San Francisco (94108) *(P-2568)*
Trumed Systems Incorporated .................................................. E ...... 844 878-6331
  4370 La Jolla Village Dr Ste 200 San Diego (92122) *(P-10523)*
Truroots LLC .................................................. E ...... 530 899-5000
  37 Speedway Ave Chico (95928) *(P-2380)*
Truss Engineering Inc .................................................. E ...... 209 527-6387
  477 Zeff Rd Modesto (95351) *(P-3320)*
Trussworks International Inc .................................................. D ...... 714 630-2772
  1275 E Franklin Ave Pomona (91766) *(P-8233)*
Trust Automation Inc .................................................. D ...... 805 544-0761
  125 Venture Dr Ste 110 San Luis Obispo (93401) *(P-19428)*
Trusteel LLC .................................................. F ...... 530 802-0420
  416 Crown Point Cir Ste 1 Grass Valley (95945) *(P-7631)*
Tryad Service Corporation .................................................. D ...... 661 391-1524
  5900 E Lerdo Hwy Shafter (93263) *(P-284)*
TS Enterprises Inc .................................................. E ...... 760 360-5991
  78250 Highway 111 La Quinta (92253) *(P-17608)*
TSC Precision Machining Inc .................................................. F ...... 714 542-3182
  1311 E Saint Gertrude Pl Ste A Santa Ana (92705) *(P-11156)*
Tscg Ventures Inc .................................................. E ...... 408 409-3274
  550 Santa Rosa Dr Los Gatos (95032) *(P-4791)*
Tsdi America Inc .................................................. F ...... 650 430-3776
  1065 E Hillsdale Blvd Ste 416 Foster City (94404) *(P-11292)*
Tshirtguyscom (PA) .................................................. F ...... 619 500-5271
  11264 Chula Vista Ave San Jose (95127) *(P-4977)*
Tsmc North America (HQ) .................................................. B ...... 408 382-8000
  2851 Junction Ave San Jose (95134) *(P-19545)*
Tsmc Technology Inc .................................................. F ...... 408 382-8052
  2851 Junction Ave San Jose (95134) *(P-12775)*
Tst Inc (PA) .................................................. B ...... 951 685-2155
  13428 Benson Ave Chino (91710) *(P-7724)*
Tst Inc .................................................. E ...... 310 835-0115
  2132 E Dominguez St Long Beach (90810) *(P-16964)*

## ALPHABETIC SECTION

**TST Molding LLC** .................................................. E ...... 951 296-6200
   42322 Avenida Alvarado Temecula (92590) *(P-7062)*

**Tst/Impreso Inc** ................................................... E ...... 909 357-7190
   10589 Business Dr Fontana (92337) *(P-4993)*

**Tsu/Tree Service Unlimited Inc** ........................... E ...... 530 626-8733
   4080 Plaza Goldorado Cir Cameron Park (95682) *(P-100)*

**TT Elctrnics Pwr Sltons US Inc** ............................ C ...... 626 967-6021
   1330 E Cypress St Covina (91724) *(P-13112)*

**TT Electronics, Brea** *Also Called: Bi Technologies Corporation (P-12923)*

**TTI Floor Care North Amer Inc** ............................ D ...... 440 996-2802
   13055 Valley Blvd Fontana (92335) *(P-6434)*

**TTI Performance Exhaust, Corona** *Also Called: Tube Technologies Inc (P-13594)*

**TTM, Santa Ana** *Also Called: Ttm Technologies Inc (P-12248)*

**Ttm Printed Circuit Group Inc** ............................. C ...... 408 486-3100
   407 Mathew St Santa Clara (95050) *(P-12244)*

**Ttm Printed Circuit Group Inc (HQ)** ..................... C ...... **714 327-3000**
   2630 S Harbor Blvd Santa Ana (92704) *(P-12245)*

**Ttm Technologies Inc** ......................................... B ...... 408 486-3100
   407 Mathew St Santa Clara (95050) *(P-12246)*

**Ttm Technologies Inc** ......................................... B ...... 714 241-0303
   2630 S Harbor Blvd Santa Ana (92704) *(P-12247)*

**Ttm Technologies Inc (PA)** .................................. B ...... **714 327-3000**
   200 Sandpointe Ave Ste 400 Santa Ana (92707) *(P-12248)*

**Ttm Technologies Inc** ......................................... B ...... 714 688-7200
   3140 E Coronado St Anaheim (92806) *(P-12249)*

**Ttm Technologies Inc** ......................................... C ...... 858 874-2701
   5037 Ruffner St San Diego (92111) *(P-12250)*

**Ttm Technologies Inc** ......................................... C ...... 408 280-0422
   355 Turtle Creek Ct San Jose (95125) *(P-12251)*

**Ttn Machining Inc** .............................................. F ...... 619 303-4573
   9105 Olive Dr Spring Valley (91977) *(P-11157)*

**TTT Concrete, Lakeside** *Also Called: Superior Ready Mix Concrete LP (P-7512)*

**TTT Innovations, Chatsworth** *Also Called: TTT Innovations LLC (P-16261)*

**TTT Innovations LLC** .......................................... E ...... 818 201-8828
   20850 Plummer St Chatsworth (91311) *(P-16261)*

**TTT-Cubed Inc** ................................................... D ...... 510 656-2325
   1120 Auburn St Fremont (94538) *(P-14596)*

**Tu Madre Romana Inc** ........................................ C ...... 323 321-6041
   13633 S Western Ave Gardena (90249) *(P-2381)*

**Tu-K Industries LLC** .......................................... E ...... 562 927-3365
   5702 Firestone Pl South Gate (90280) *(P-6048)*

**Tube Lighting Products, El Cajon** *Also Called: Tujayar Enterprises Inc (P-11564)*

**Tube One, Riverside** *Also Called: Tube One Industries Inc (P-7671)*

**Tube One Industries Inc** ..................................... F ...... 951 300-2998
   4055 Garner Rd Riverside (92501) *(P-7671)*

**Tube Technologies Inc** ....................................... E ...... 951 371-4878
   1555 Consumer Cir Corona (92878) *(P-13594)*

**Tube-Tainer Inc** ................................................. E ...... 562 945-3711
   8174 Byron Rd Whittier (90606) *(P-3911)*

**Tubemogul Inc** ................................................... A ...... 510 653-0126
   1250 53rd St Ste 1 Emeryville (94608) *(P-18894)*

**Tubing Seal Cap Co, Anaheim** *Also Called: Pacific Precision Metals Inc (P-8874)*

**Tubit Enterprises Inc** ......................................... E ...... 530 335-5085
   21640 S Vallejo St Burney (96013) *(P-3059)*

**Tuboscope, Bakersfield** *Also Called: Tuboscope Pipeline Svcs Inc (P-285)*

**Tuboscope Nat Oilwell Varco, Bakersfield** *Also Called: Tuboscope Pipeline Svcs Inc (P-286)*

**Tuboscope Pipeline Svcs Inc** .............................. F ...... 661 328-5500
   3003 Fairhaven Dr Ste B Bakersfield (93308) *(P-285)*

**Tuboscope Pipeline Svcs Inc** .............................. F ...... 661 321-3400
   4621 Burr St Bakersfield (93308) *(P-286)*

**Tubular Specialties Mfg Inc** ................................ D ...... 310 515-4801
   13011 S Spring St Los Angeles (90061) *(P-7280)*

**Tuff Stuff Products** ............................................. B ...... 559 535-5778
   9600 Road 256 Terra Bella (93270) *(P-5215)*

**Tuff Stuff Products, Terra Bella** *Also Called: Tuff Stuff Products (P-5215)*

**Tuffer Manufacturing Co Inc** .............................. E ...... 714 526-3077
   163 E Liberty Ave Anaheim (92801) *(P-14326)*

**Tuffstuff Fitness Intl Inc** .................................... D ...... 909 629-1600
   155 N Riverview Dr Anaheim (92808) *(P-15868)*

**Tujayar Enterprises Inc** ...................................... E ...... 619 442-0577
   1346 Pioneer Way El Cajon (92020) *(P-11564)*

**Tulavi Therapeutics Inc** ...................................... E ...... 877 885-2841
   160 Knowles Dr Los Gatos (95032) *(P-15293)*

**Tulip Pubg & Graphics Inc** .................................. E ...... 510 898-0000
   1003 Canal Blvd Richmond (94804) *(P-4792)*

**Tully-Wihr Company** .......................................... C ...... 530 346-2649
   148 Whitcomb Ave Colfax (95713) *(P-4793)*

**Tumelo Inc** ......................................................... E ...... 707 523-4411
   420 Tesconi Cir Ste B Santa Rosa (95401) *(P-6327)*

**Tungsten Automation Corp (PA)** ........................ B ...... **949 783-1000**
   15211 Laguna Canyon Rd Irvine (92618) *(P-17990)*

**Tur-Bo Jet Products Co Inc** ................................ D ...... 626 285-1294
   5025 Earle Ave Rosemead (91770) *(P-12862)*

**Turbine Eng Cmpnents Tech Corp** ...................... C ...... 415 626-2000
   1211 Old Albany Road San Francisco (94103) *(P-13725)*

**Turbine Repair Services LLC (PA)** ....................... E ...... **909 947-2256**
   1838 E Cedar St Ontario (91761) *(P-9320)*

**Turbo Debt Relief** .............................................. F ...... 949 244-1907
   23181 Verdugo Dr Ste 100a Laguna Hills (92653) *(P-4483)*

**Turbo Intl Partners LLC** ..................................... E ...... 760 476-1444
   2151 Las Palmas Dr Ste E Carlsbad (92011) *(P-8790)*

**Turbosand, Anderson** *Also Called: Voorwood Company (P-9757)*

**Turbotax, San Diego** *Also Called: Intuit Inc (P-18436)*

**Turkhan Nuts, Ripon** *Also Called: Pearl Crop Inc (P-1372)*

**Turley Wine Cellars** ........................................... E ...... 209 245-3938
   11076 Bell Rd Plymouth (95669) *(P-1803)*

**Turley Wine Cellars Inc** ..................................... E ...... 707 968-2700
   3358 Saint Helena Hwy N Saint Helena (94574) *(P-1804)*

**Turlock Journal** ................................................. F ...... 209 634-9141
   121 S Center St # 2 Turlock (95380) *(P-4215)*

**Turlock Poker Room, Turlock** *Also Called: Central Valley Gaming LLC (P-19313)*

**Turlock Rendering, Crows Landing** *Also Called: Darling Ingredients Inc (P-1384)*

**Turnbull Wine Cellars** ........................................ E ...... 707 963-5839
   8210 St Helena Hwy Oakville (94562) *(P-1805)*

**Turner Designs Inc** ............................................ E ...... 408 749-0994
   1995 N 1st St San Jose (95112) *(P-14748)*

**Turner Dsgns Hydrcrbon Instrs** .......................... E ...... 559 253-1414
   2023 N Gateway Blvd Ste 101 Fresno (93727) *(P-13319)*

**Turner Fiberfill Inc** ............................................ E ...... 323 724-7957
   1600 Date St Montebello (90640) *(P-5224)*

**Turnkey Industries, Madera** *Also Called: Performance Trailer Inc (P-17489)*

**Turnongreen Inc** ................................................ E ...... 510 657-2635
   1421 Mccarthy Blvd Milpitas (95035) *(P-11293)*

**Turntide Technologies Inc (PA)** .......................... E ...... **877 776-8470**
   1295 Forgewood Ave Sunnyvale (94089) *(P-11294)*

**Turnupseed Electric Service** .............................. D ...... 559 686-1541
   1580 S K St Tulare (93274) *(P-470)*

**Turret Lathe Specialists Inc** ............................... F ...... 714 520-0058
   875 S Rose Pl Anaheim (92805) *(P-11158)*

**Turtle Storage Ltd** ............................................. E ...... 805 933-3688
   401 S Beckwith Rd Santa Paula (93060) *(P-3712)*

**Turtleback Case, Sylmar** *Also Called: Leather Pro Inc (P-7149)*

**Tusker Medical Inc** ............................................ E ...... 650 223-6900
   155 Jefferson Dr Menlo Park (94025) *(P-15587)*

**TV Ears Inc** ........................................................ E ...... 619 797-1600
   2701 Via Orange Way Ste 1 Spring Valley (91978) *(P-16739)*

**TW Graphics, Commerce** *Also Called: TW Graphics Group Company (P-6263)*

**TW Graphics Group Company (PA)** .................... F ...... **323 721-1400**
   3323 S Malt Ave Commerce (90040) *(P-6263)*

**Twdc Enterprises 18 Corp (HQ)** ......................... A ...... **818 560-1000**
   500 S Buena Vista St Burbank (91521) *(P-16330)*

**Twed-Dells Inc** .................................................. E ...... 714 754-6900
   1900 S Susan St Santa Ana (92704) *(P-7245)*

**Twila True Collaborations LLC** ........................... E ...... 949 258-9720
   27156 Burbank Foothill Ranch (92610) *(P-6049)*

**TWILIO, San Francisco** *Also Called: Twilio Inc (P-18895)*

**Twilio Inc (PA)** ................................................... A ...... **415 390-2337**
   101 Spear St Fl 5 San Francisco (94105) *(P-18895)*

**Twin Bridges Technologies LLC** ......................... F ...... 707 591-4500
   30286 Oakbrook Rd Hayward (94544) *(P-16562)*

**Twin Coast Metrology Inc (PA)** .......................... F ...... **310 709-2308**
   333 Washington Blvd Ste 362 Marina Del Rey (90292) *(P-14830)*

---

Employee Codes: A=Over 500 employees, B=251-500
C=101-250, D=51-100, E=20-50, F=10-19, G=1-9

## Twin Dragon Marketing Inc — ALPHABETIC SECTION

Twin Dragon Marketing Inc (PA) .......................................... E ...... 310 715-7070
  14600 S Broadway Gardena (90248) *(P-2431)*

Twin Eagles, Inc., Cerritos *Also Called: Dcec Holdings Inc (P-11387)*

Twin Oaks Growers Intl, San Marcos *Also Called: Twin Oaks Growers Intl Inc (P-51)*

Twin Oaks Growers Intl Inc ................................................ E ...... 760 744-5581
  1969 Marilyn Ln San Marcos (92069) *(P-51)*

Twin Peak Industries Inc ..................................................... E ...... 800 259-5906
  12420 Montague St Ste E Pacoima (91331) *(P-15869)*

Twin Peaks Winery Inc ........................................................ D ...... 707 944-8642
  1473 Yountville Cross Rd Yountville (94599) *(P-1806)*

Twin Power Indus Solutions, Murrieta *Also Called: Twin Power Usa LLC (P-471)*

Twin Power Usa LLC ............................................................ E ...... 714 609-6014
  40424 Jacob Way Murrieta (92563) *(P-471)*

Twist Tite Mfg Inc ................................................................ E ...... 562 229-0990
  13344 Cambridge St Santa Fe Springs (90670) *(P-8768)*

Twisted Oak Winery LLC (PA) ............................................ F ...... 209 728-3000
  4280 Red Hill Rd Vallecito (95251) *(P-1807)*

Twitch Interactive Inc .......................................................... A
  350 Bush St Fl 2 San Francisco (94104) *(P-4484)*

Two Brothers Racing Inc .................................................... F ...... 714 550-6070
  3474 Niki Way Riverside (92507) *(P-14073)*

Two Lads Inc (PA) ................................................................ E ...... 323 584-0064
  5001 Hampton St Vernon (90058) *(P-15921)*

Two Pitchers Brewing Company, Oakland *Also Called: W G Barr Beverage Company LP (P-1467)*

Txd International Usa Inc ................................................... F ...... 909 947-6568
  2336 S Vineyard Ave # A Ontario (91761) *(P-4216)*

Txi Riverside Cement, Riverside *Also Called: Riverside Cement Holdings Company (P-7262)*

Tyler Trafficante Inc (PA) .................................................... E ...... 323 869-9299
  700 S Palm Ave Alhambra (91803) *(P-2569)*

Tynker, Mountain View *Also Called: Neuron Fuel Inc (P-17954)*

Typecraft Inc ........................................................................ E ...... 626 795-8093
  2040 E Walnut St Pasadena (91107) *(P-4794)*

Typecraft Wood & Jones, Pasadena *Also Called: Typecraft Inc (P-4794)*

Tyr Sport Inc (HQ) ............................................................... F ...... 714 897-0799
  5559 Mcfadden Ave Huntington Beach (92649) *(P-17106)*

TYRA, Carlsbad *Also Called: Tyra Biosciences Inc (P-5696)*

Tyra Biosciences Inc .......................................................... E ...... 619 728-4760
  2656 State St Carlsbad (92008) *(P-5696)*

TYT LLC (HQ) ....................................................................... C ...... 510 444-3933
  2861 Mandela Pkwy Oakland (94608) *(P-4795)*

Tyte Jeans, Commerce *Also Called: 4 What Its Worth Inc (P-2605)*

Tyvak Nn-Satellite Systems Inc ......................................... E ...... 805 264-4319
  1288 W Mccoy Ln Santa Maria (93455) *(P-14094)*

Tyvak Nn-Satellite Systems Inc ......................................... E ...... 949 753-1020
  400 Spectrum Center Dr Irvine (92618) *(P-14095)*

Tyvak Nn-Satellite Systems Inc (DH) ................................ E ...... 949 753-1020
  15330 Barranca Pkwy Irvine (92618) *(P-14096)*

Tz, Los Angeles *Also Called: Toska Inc (P-2817)*

Tzeng Long USA Inc (PA) .................................................. E ...... 323 722-5353
  2301 Vail Ave Commerce (90040) *(P-16965)*

U F P, San Marcos *Also Called: Unique Functional Products (P-13620)*

U I G, Lake Forest *Also Called: United Industries Group Inc (P-19429)*

U M C, Costa Mesa *Also Called: Universal Motion Components Co Inc (P-10045)*

U S Architectural Lighting, Palmdale *Also Called: US Pole Company Inc (P-11566)*

U S C, Burbank *Also Called: Universal Switching Corp (P-11476)*

U S Circuit Inc ..................................................................... D ...... 760 489-1413
  2071 Wineridge Pl Escondido (92029) *(P-13113)*

U S Enterprise Corporation ................................................ F ...... 510 487-8877
  30560 San Antonio St Hayward (94544) *(P-995)*

U S Fabrications, Hayward *Also Called: South Bay Diversfd Systems Inc (P-8575)*

U S L, San Luis Obispo *Also Called: Ultra-Stereo Labs Inc (P-13320)*

U S Medical Instruments Inc (PA) ..................................... E ...... 619 661-5500
  888 Prospect St Ste 100 La Jolla (92037) *(P-15294)*

U S Precision Manufacturing, Riverside *Also Called: US Precision Sheet Metal Inc (P-8604)*

U S Saw & Blades, Santa Ana *Also Called: US Saws Inc (P-9445)*

U S Technical Institute, Placentia *Also Called: US Computers Inc (P-10447)*

U S Weatherford L P ........................................................... C ...... 661 589-9483
  2815 Fruitvale Ave Bakersfield (93308) *(P-287)*

U S Wheel Corporation ....................................................... E ...... 714 892-0021
  15702 Producer Ln Huntington Beach (92649) *(P-13595)*

U W G Southern California Div, Los Angeles *Also Called: Unified Grocers Inc (P-16292)*

U-Blox San Diego Inc ......................................................... E ...... 858 847-9611
  12626 High Bluff Dr Ste 200 San Diego (92130) *(P-11791)*

U-C Components Inc (PA) .................................................. E ...... 408 782-1929
  18700 Adams Ct Morgan Hill (95037) *(P-8769)*

U-Nited Printing and Copy Ctr, Van Nuys *Also Called: Printrunner LLC (P-4737)*

U-Tech Media Usa LLC ....................................................... C ...... 408 597-1600
  1105 Montague Expy Milpitas (95035) *(P-13205)*

U.S. Battery Mfg Co, Corona *Also Called: Palos Verdes Building Corp (P-13147)*

U.S. Continental, Corona *Also Called: US Continental Marketing Inc (P-5934)*

U.S. Horizon Mfg, Valencia *Also Called: US Horizon Manufacturing Inc (P-7179)*

U.S. Specialty Vehicles, Yorba Linda *Also Called: American HX Auto Trade Inc (P-13338)*

Ubiq, San Diego *Also Called: Ubiq Security Inc (P-16563)*

Ubiq Security Inc ................................................................ E ...... 888 434-6674
  4660 La Jolla Village Dr Ste 100 San Diego (92122) *(P-16563)*

Ubiquiti Networks Inc ......................................................... D ...... 408 942-3085
  91 E Tasman Dr San Jose (95134) *(P-18997)*

Ubm Canon LLC (DH) ......................................................... E ...... 310 445-4200
  2901 28th St Ste 100 Santa Monica (90405) *(P-4303)*

Ubtech Robotics Corp ........................................................ E ...... 213 261-7153
  767 S Alameda St Ste 250 Los Angeles (90021) *(P-9748)*

Ucan Zippers, Los Angeles *Also Called: Catame Inc (P-15909)*

Ucc Guide Inc ..................................................................... F ...... 800 345-3822
  225 Cabrillo Hwy S Ste 200c Half Moon Bay (94019) *(P-4485)*

Uce Holdings Inc ................................................................ D ...... 213 217-4235
  411 Center St Los Angeles (90012) *(P-2382)*

Uct, Hayward *Also Called: Ultra Clean Tech Systems Svc I (P-12776)*

Udelv Inc .............................................................................. E ...... 650 376-3785
  30516 Union City Blvd Union City (94587) *(P-17991)*

UFO Designs (PA) ............................................................... F ...... 714 892-4420
  5812 Machine Dr Huntington Beach (92649) *(P-7063)*

UFO Designs ....................................................................... E ...... 562 924-5763
  16730 Gridley Rd Cerritos (90703) *(P-13596)*

UFO Inc ................................................................................ E ...... 323 588-5450
  2110 Belgrave Ave Huntington Park (90255) *(P-7064)*

Ufp Technologies Inc ......................................................... E ...... 714 662-0277
  20211 S Susana Rd Compton (90221) *(P-6667)*

Ug Storage, Vernon *Also Called: Urgent Gear Inc (P-17083)*

Ui Medical LLC .................................................................... E ...... 562 453-1515
  1670 W Park Ave Redlands (92373) *(P-4006)*

Ujet Inc (PA) ........................................................................ F ...... 855 242-8538
  535 Mission St Fl 14 San Francisco (94105) *(P-18896)*

Uke Corporation .................................................................. D ...... 858 513-9100
  13400 Danielson St Poway (92064) *(P-15870)*

Ullman Sails Inc (PA) ......................................................... F ...... 714 432-1860
  2710 S Croddy Way Santa Ana (92704) *(P-2986)*

Ultimate Ears Consumer LLC ............................................ B ...... 949 502-8340
  3 Jenner Ste 180 Irvine (92618) *(P-15422)*

Ultimate Metal Finishing Corp .......................................... E ...... 323 890-9100
  6150 Sheila St Commerce (90040) *(P-9130)*

Ultimate Paper Box Company, City Of Industry *Also Called: Boxes R Us Inc (P-3824)*

Ultimate Print Source Inc .................................................. E ...... 909 947-5292
  2070 S Hellman Ave Ontario (91761) *(P-4796)*

Ultimate Solutions, Huntington Beach *Also Called: Sandia Plastics Inc (P-7022)*

Ultimate Sound Inc ............................................................. B ...... 909 861-6200
  1200 S Diamond Bar Blvd Ste 200 Diamond Bar (91765) *(P-11708)*

Ultimatum Records LLC ..................................................... F ...... 925 353-5202
  4695 Chabot Dr Ste 200 Pleasanton (94588) *(P-11709)*

Ultra Built Kitchens Inc ..................................................... E ...... 323 232-3362
  1814 E 43rd St Los Angeles (90058) *(P-3276)*

Ultra Chem Labs Corp ....................................................... F ...... 909 605-1640
  1370 Valley Vista Dr Diamond Bar (91765) *(P-5933)*

Ultra Clean Tech Systems Svc I (HQ) .............................. C ...... 510 576-4400
  26462 Corporate Ave Hayward (94545) *(P-12776)*

Ultra Communications Inc ................................................ E ...... 760 652-0011
  990 Park Center Dr Ste H Vista (92081) *(P-16324)*

Ultra Glass .......................................................................... F ...... 916 338-3911
  4001 Vista Park Ct Ste 1 Sacramento (95834) *(P-7246)*

## ALPHABETIC SECTION

**Ultra Pro Acquisition LLC** .......................................... E ...... 323 725-1975
  6049 E Slauson Ave Commerce (90040) *(P-5006)*

**Ultra Pro International LLC** ........................................ C ...... 323 890-2100
  6049 E Slauson Ave Commerce (90040) *(P-16952)*

**Ultra TEC Manufacturing Inc** ...................................... F ...... 714 542-0608
  1025 E Chestnut Ave Santa Ana (92701) *(P-9906)*

**Ultra Wheel Company** ................................................ E ...... 714 449-7100
  586 N Gilbert St Fullerton (92833) *(P-13597)*

**Ultra-Stereo Labs Inc** ................................................ E ...... 805 549-0161
  181 Bonetti Dr San Luis Obispo (93401) *(P-13320)*

**ULTRAGENYX, Novato** *Also Called: Ultragenyx Pharmaceutical Inc (P-5697)*

**Ultragenyx Pharmaceutical Inc (PA)** ............................. A ...... 415 483-8800
  60 Leveroni Ct Novato (94949) *(P-5697)*

**Ultraglas Inc** ........................................................... E ...... 818 772-7744
  3392 Hampton Ct Thousand Oaks (91362) *(P-16496)*

**Ultragraphics Inc** .................................................... E ...... 818 295-3994
  2800 N Naomi St Burbank (91504) *(P-17819)*

**Ultramar Inc** ........................................................... D ...... 661 944-2496
  9508 E Palmdale Blvd Palmdale (93591) *(P-6356)*

**Ultramet** ................................................................ D ...... 818 899-0236
  12173 Montague St Pacoima (91331) *(P-9027)*

**Ultrasigns Electrical Advg, San Diego** *Also Called: Jones Sign Co Inc (P-15996)*

**Ultrasil LLC** ............................................................ E ...... 510 266-3700
  3527 Breakwater Ave Hayward (94545) *(P-12777)*

**Ultratech, San Jose** *Also Called: Ultratech Inc (P-9907)*

**Ultratech Inc** .......................................................... B ...... 408 321-8835
  3050 Zanker Rd San Jose (95134) *(P-9907)*

**Ultron Systems Inc** ................................................. F ...... 805 529-1485
  5105 Maureen Ln Moorpark (93021) *(P-12778)*

**Ultura, Long Beach** *Also Called: Ultura Inc (P-19553)*

**Ultura Inc** .............................................................. C ...... 562 661-4999
  3605 Long Beach Blvd Ste 201 Long Beach (90807) *(P-19553)*

**Umc, Sunnyvale** *Also Called: Umc Group (usa) (P-12779)*

**Umc Acquisition Corp (PA)** ....................................... E ...... 562 940-0300
  9151 Imperial Hwy Downey (90242) *(P-7768)*

**Umc Group (usa)** .................................................... D ...... 408 523-7800
  488 De Guigne Dr Sunnyvale (94085) *(P-12779)*

**Umec, Union City** *Also Called: United Mech Met Fbricators Inc (P-8603)*

**Umgd, Santa Monica** *Also Called: Universal Mus Group Dist Corp (P-4486)*

**Umgee, Los Angeles** *Also Called: Umgee USA Inc (P-2692)*

**Umgee USA Inc** ..................................................... F ...... 323 526-9138
  1565 E 23rd St Los Angeles (90011) *(P-2692)*

**Umo Steel, Union City** *Also Called: United Misc & Orna Stl Inc (P-8235)*

**Umpco Inc** ............................................................. D ...... 714 897-3531
  7100 Lampson Ave Garden Grove (92841) *(P-8033)*

**Un Deux Trois Inc (PA)** ........................................... E ...... 323 588-1067
  2301 E 7th St Los Angeles (90023) *(P-2868)*

**Unbrako LLC** ......................................................... F ...... 310 817-2400
  11939 Woodruff Ave Downey (90241) *(P-16764)*

**Unbroken Studios LLC** ............................................ D ...... 310 741-2670
  2120 Park Pl Ste 110 El Segundo (90245) *(P-18897)*

**Unchained Labs (PA)** .............................................. C ...... 925 587-9800
  4747 Willow Rd Pleasanton (94588) *(P-19332)*

**Uncountable Inc (PA)** ............................................. F ...... 650 208-5949
  415 Brannan St San Francisco (94107) *(P-18898)*

**Undersea Systems Intl Inc** ...................................... D ...... 714 754-7848
  3133 W Harvard St Santa Ana (92704) *(P-13321)*

**Underwater Kinetics, Poway** *Also Called: Uke Corporation (P-15870)*

**Underwraps Costume Corporation** ............................ F ...... 818 349-5300
  9600 Irondale Ave Chatsworth (91311) *(P-2912)*

**Underwraps Costumes, Chatsworth** *Also Called: Underwraps Costume Corporation (P-2912)*

**Uneekor Inc** .......................................................... D ...... 888 262-6498
  15770 Laguna Canyon Rd Ste 100 Irvine (92618) *(P-18899)*

**Unger Fabrik LLC (PA)** ............................................ C ...... 626 469-8080
  18525 Railroad St City Of Industry (91748) *(P-2693)*

**UNI Filter Inc** ........................................................ F ...... 714 535-6933
  1468 Manhattan Ave Fullerton (92831) *(P-13598)*

**UNI Poly Inc** ......................................................... F ...... 510 357-9898
  2040 Williams San Leandro (94577) *(P-3987)*

**UNI-Caps LLC** ....................................................... E ...... 714 529-8400
  540 Lambert Rd Brea (92821) *(P-5279)*

**UNI-Fab Industries Inc** ............................................ D ...... 408 945-9733
  5020 Brandin Ct Fremont (94538) *(P-9238)*

**UNI-Pixel, Santa Clara** *Also Called: UNI-Pixel Inc (P-6574)*

**UNI-Pixel Inc** ......................................................... D ...... 281 825-4500
  4699 Old Ironsides Dr Ste 300 Santa Clara (95054) *(P-6574)*

**UNI-Sport Inc** ........................................................ E ...... 310 217-4587
  16933 Gramercy Pl Gardena (90247) *(P-4797)*

**Unicel, Chatsworth** *Also Called: Meissner Mfg Co Inc (P-10581)*

**Unico Mechanical, Benicia** *Also Called: Unico Mechanical Corp (P-11159)*

**Unico Mechanical Corp (PA)** .................................... E ...... 707 745-9970
  1209 Polk St Benicia (94510) *(P-11159)*

**Unicor, Lompoc** *Also Called: Federal Prison Industries (P-15978)*

**Unicorn Group, Novato** *Also Called: Forest Investment Group Inc (P-4614)*

**Unifi Software Inc** .................................................. E ...... 732 614-9522
  1810 Gateway Dr Ste 380 San Mateo (94404) *(P-18900)*

**Unified Field Services Corp** ..................................... E ...... 661 325-8962
  6906 Downing Ave Bakersfield (93308) *(P-144)*

**Unified Grocers Inc** ................................................ C ...... 323 232-6124
  457 E Martin Luther King Jr Blvd Los Angeles (90011) *(P-16292)*

**Unified Nutrimeals** ................................................. D ...... 323 923-9335
  5469 Ferguson Dr Commerce (90022) *(P-17609)*

**Unigen Corporation (PA)** ......................................... C ...... 510 896-1818
  39730 Eureka Dr Newark (94560) *(P-12780)*

**Unimark, Gardena** *Also Called: Matsui International Co Inc (P-6307)*

**Uninet Imaging Inc (PA)** ......................................... F ...... 424 675-3300
  3308 W El Segundo Blvd Hawthorne (90250) *(P-16500)*

**Union Carbide Corporation** ...................................... E ...... 310 214-5300
  19206 Hawthorne Blvd Torrance (90503) *(P-3810)*

**Union Chemicar America Inc** ................................... F ...... 949 770-7072
  3151 Airway Ave Costa Mesa (92626) *(P-6575)*

**Union Mine Iron** .................................................... E ...... 916 985-0332
  12525 Quicksilver Dr Rancho Cordova (95742) *(P-8234)*

**Union Sup Comsy Solutions Inc** ............................... B ...... 785 357-5005
  2301 E Pacifica Pl Rancho Dominguez (90220) *(P-17119)*

**Union Technology Corp** .......................................... E ...... 323 266-6871
  718 Monterey Pass Rd Monterey Park (91754) *(P-16740)*

**Uniproducts, North Highlands** *Also Called: Mikes Sheet Metal Pdts Inc (P-8510)*

**Unique Carpets Ltd** ................................................ D ...... 951 352-8125
  7360 Jurupa Ave Riverside (92504) *(P-16437)*

**Unique Functional Products** .................................... C ...... 760 744-1610
  135 Sunshine Ln San Marcos (92069) *(P-13620)*

**Unique Functional Products, San Marcos** *Also Called: Dexter Axle Company (P-13616)*

**Unique Lighting Systems Inc** ................................... E ...... 800 955-4831
  5825 Jasmine St Riverside (92504) *(P-11630)*

**Unique Sales, Vernon** *Also Called: Zk Enterprises Inc (P-2651)*

**Uniquify Inc (PA)** ................................................... E ...... 408 235-8810
  2323 Owen St # 101 Santa Clara (95054) *(P-13114)*

**Unirex Corp** .......................................................... E ...... 323 589-4000
  2288 E 27th St Vernon (90058) *(P-12781)*

**Unirex Technologies, Vernon** *Also Called: Unirex Corp (P-12781)*

**Unisen Inc** ............................................................ E ...... 714 669-1660
  14410 Myford Rd Irvine (92606) *(P-15871)*

**Unisun Multinational, Azusa** *Also Called: Ht Multinational Inc (P-13515)*

**United Aeronautical Corp** ........................................ E ...... 818 764-2102
  7360 Laurel Canyon Blvd North Hollywood (91605) *(P-16930)*

**United Bakery Equipment Co Inc (PA)** ...................... D ...... 310 635-8121
  15315 Marquardt Ave Santa Fe Springs (90670) *(P-10034)*

**United Biologics Inc** ............................................... E ...... 949 345-7490
  1642 Kaiser Ave Irvine (92614) *(P-15423)*

**United Brands Company Inc** .................................... E ...... 619 461-5220
  5930 Cornerstone Ct W Ste 170 San Diego (92121) *(P-2031)*

**United Cabinet Company Inc** ................................... E ...... 909 796-3015
  1510 S Mountain View Ave San Bernardino (92408) *(P-3277)*

**United California, Downey** *Also Called: United Drill Bushing Corp (P-9704)*

**United California Corporation** .................................. E ...... 562 803-1521
  12200 Woodruff Ave Downey (90241) *(P-9653)*

**United Carports LLC** .............................................. E ...... 800 757-6742
  7280 Sycamore Canyon Blvd Ste 1 Riverside (92508) *(P-8688)*

**United Compost & Organics Inc** ............................... E ...... 707 443-4369
  1900 Bendixsen St Samoa (95564) *(P-6183)*

# United Compost And Organics, Inc.

**ALPHABETIC SECTION**

**United Compost And Organics, Inc., Samoa** *Also Called: United Compost & Organics Inc* *(P-6183)*

**United Detector Technology, Hawthorne** *Also Called: OSI Optoelectronics Inc* *(P-12625)*

**United Distlrs Vintners N Amer, San Francisco** *Also Called: Diageo North America Inc* *(P-1538)*

United Drill Bushing Corp ............................................................ C ...... 562 803-1521
  12200 Woodruff Ave Downey (90241) *(P-9704)*

United Duralume Products Inc .................................................... F ...... 714 773-4011
  350 S Raymond Ave Fullerton (92831) *(P-8602)*

United Fiber Inc ............................................................................ E ...... 510 783-6904
  1680 W Winton Ave Ste 7 Hayward (94545) *(P-5225)*

United Foods Intl USA Inc (DH) .................................................. E ...... 510 264-5850
  23447 Cabot Blvd Hayward (94545) *(P-2383)*

**United Garment, Oakland** *Also Called: Imperial Garment Inds Inc* *(P-2862)*

United Industries Group Inc ........................................................ E ...... 949 759-3200
  11 Rancho Cir Lake Forest (92630) *(P-19429)*

United International Tech Inc ...................................................... E ...... 818 772-9400
  9207 Deering Ave Ste B Chatsworth (91311) *(P-12252)*

United Launch Alliance LLC ....................................................... B ...... 303 269-5876
  1579 Utah Ave, Bldg. 7525 Vandenberg Afb (93437) *(P-14097)*

United Mech Met Fbricators Inc .................................................. E ...... 510 537-4744
  33353 Lewis St Union City (94587) *(P-8603)*

United Medical Devices LLC ...................................................... E ...... 310 551-4100
  16250 Ventura Blvd Encino (91436) *(P-15295)*

United Mfg Assembly Inc ............................................................ D ...... 510 490-4680
  44169 Fremont Blvd Fremont (94538) *(P-19510)*

United Misc & Orna Stl Inc .......................................................... E ...... 510 429-8755
  4700 Horner St Union City (94587) *(P-8235)*

**United Orthopedic Corp USA, Irvine** *Also Called: Uoc USA Inc* *(P-15296)*

**United Pacific Designs, Vernon** *Also Called: UPD INC* *(P-15736)*

United Pallet Services Inc ........................................................... C ...... 209 538-5844
  4043 Crows Landing Rd Modesto (95358) *(P-3363)*

United Pharma LLC ..................................................................... C ...... 714 738-8999
  2317 Moore Ave Fullerton (92833) *(P-5698)*

United Pipe & Stl Fabrication ...................................................... E ...... 661 489-4100
  100 Quantico Ave Bakersfield (93307) *(P-8236)*

United Precision Corp ................................................................. E ...... 818 576-9540
  20810 Plummer St Chatsworth (91311) *(P-11160)*

United Scope LLC (HQ) .............................................................. E ...... 714 942-3202
  3210 El Camino Real Irvine (92602) *(P-14831)*

United Security Products Inc ...................................................... E ...... 800 227-1592
  12675 Danielson Ct Ste 405 Poway (92064) *(P-13322)*

**United Sign Systems, Modesto** *Also Called: Johnson United Inc* *(P-15995)*

**United Spiral Pipe, Pittsburg** *Also Called: United Spiral Pipe LLC* *(P-7672)*

United Spiral Pipe LLC ............................................................... C ...... 925 526-3100
  900 E 3rd St Pittsburg (94565) *(P-7672)*

**United Sports Brands, Fountain Valley** *Also Called: Shock Doctor Inc* *(P-15854)*

United States Bakery .................................................................. E ...... 323 232-6124
  457 E Martin Luther King Jr Blvd Los Angeles (90011) *(P-1249)*

United States Dept of Navy ........................................................ A ...... 619 556-6033
  32nd St Naval Sta San Diego (92136) *(P-14020)*

United States Gypsum Company ............................................... D ...... 908 232-8900
  401 Van Ness Ave Torrance (90501) *(P-7532)*

United States Gypsum Company ............................................... C ...... 760 358-3200
  3810 Evan Hewes Hwy Imperial (92251) *(P-7533)*

United States Logistics Group .................................................... E ...... 562 989-9555
  2700 Rose Ave Ste A Signal Hill (90755) *(P-13621)*

United States Tile Co .................................................................. C ...... 951 739-4613
  909 Railroad St Corona (92882) *(P-7276)*

United Sttes Thrmlctric Cnsrti ..................................................... E ...... 530 345-8000
  13267 Contractors Dr Ste D Chico (95973) *(P-14466)*

United Sunshine American Industries Corporation ..................... E
  2808 E Marywood Ln Orange (92867) *(P-9239)*

United Surface Solutions LLC .................................................... E ...... 562 693-0202
  11901 Burke St Santa Fe Springs (90670) *(P-9908)*

United Western Enterprises Inc .................................................. E ...... 805 389-1077
  850 Flynn Rd Ste 200 Camarillo (93012) *(P-9131)*

United Western Industries Inc .................................................... E ...... 559 226-7236
  3515 N Hazel Ave Fresno (93722) *(P-11161)*

**Unitek Miyachi International, San Jose** *Also Called: Directed Light Inc* *(P-16812)*

Unitek Technology Inc ................................................................ F ...... 909 930-5700
  10211 Bellegrave Ave Jurupa Valley (91752) *(P-10215)*

**UNITY, San Francisco** *Also Called: Unity Software Inc* *(P-17992)*

Unity Biotechnology Inc .............................................................. F ...... 650 416-1192
  285 E Grand Ave South San Francisco (94080) *(P-19481)*

Unity Forest Products Inc ........................................................... E ...... 530 671-7152
  1162 Putman Ave Yuba City (95991) *(P-3201)*

Unity Software Inc (PA) ............................................................... B ...... 415 638-9950
  30 3rd St San Francisco (94103) *(P-17992)*

**Universal Christian Music Pubg, Santa Monica** *Also Called: Universal Music Publishing Inc* *(P-4487)*

Universal Ctrl Solutions Corp ..................................................... F ...... 818 898-3380
  19770 Bahama St Northridge (91324) *(P-11354)*

Universal Cushion Company Inc (PA) ........................................ E ...... 323 887-8000
  1610 Mandeville Canyon Rd Los Angeles (90049) *(P-2951)*

**Universal Custom Cabinets, Pacoima** *Also Called: N K Cabinets Inc* *(P-3259)*

**Universal Custom Design, Elk Grove** *Also Called: Universal Custom Display* *(P-16061)*

Universal Custom Display .......................................................... C ...... 916 714-2505
  9104 Elkmont Dr Ste 100 Elk Grove (95624) *(P-16061)*

Universal Cy Stdios Prdctons L (DH) ......................................... E ...... 818 777-1000
  100 Universal City Plz Universal City (91608) *(P-19298)*

Universal Defense ...................................................................... E ...... 909 626-4178
  412 Cucamonga Ave Claremont (91711) *(P-8349)*

Universal Elastic & Garment Supply Inc .................................... E ...... 213 748-2995
  2200 S Alameda St Vernon (90058) *(P-2455)*

**Universal Framing Products, Santa Clarita** *Also Called: Universal Wood Moulding Inc* *(P-16438)*

Universal Hosiery Inc ................................................................. D ...... 661 702-8444
  28337 Constellation Rd Valencia (91355) *(P-2461)*

**Universal Meat Company, Rancho Cucamonga** *Also Called: Formosa Meat Company Inc* *(P-640)*

Universal Meditech Inc ............................................................... E ...... 559 366-7798
  1320 E Fortune Ave Ste 102 Fresno (93725) *(P-16073)*

Universal Metal Plating ............................................................... F ...... 626 969-7932
  704 S Taylor Ave Montebello (90640) *(P-9028)*

Universal Metal Plating (PA) ....................................................... F ...... 626 969-7931
  626 1/2 S Gerhart Ave Los Angeles (90022) *(P-19149)*

Universal Molding Company (HQ) .............................................. C ...... 310 886-1750
  9151 Imperial Hwy Downey (90242) *(P-7769)*

**Universal Molding Company, Downey** *Also Called: Umc Acquisition Corp* *(P-7768)*

Universal Motion Components Co Inc ....................................... E ...... 714 437-9600
  2920 Airway Ave Costa Mesa (92626) *(P-10045)*

Universal Mus Group Dist Corp (DH) ......................................... D ...... 310 235-4700
  2220 Colorado Ave Santa Monica (90404) *(P-4486)*

Universal Music Group Inc (HQ) ................................................ D ...... 310 865-0770
  2220 Colorado Ave Santa Monica (90404) *(P-19140)*

Universal Music Publishing Inc .................................................. D ...... 310 235-4700
  1601 Cloverfield Blvd Santa Monica (90404) *(P-4487)*

Universal Orthodontic Lab Inc ................................................... F ...... 562 484-0500
  11917 Front St Norwalk (90650) *(P-15491)*

Universal Packg Systems Inc (PA) ............................................ A ...... 909 517-2442
  14570 Monte Vista Ave Chino (91710) *(P-6050)*

Universal Plant Svcs Cal Inc ..................................................... D ...... 310 618-1600
  20545 Belshaw Ave # A Carson (90746) *(P-11162)*

**Universal Plastic Mold, Baldwin Park** *Also Called: Upm Inc* *(P-9654)*

Universal Printing Svcs Inc ........................................................ F ...... 951 788-1500
  26012 Atlantic Ocean Dr Lake Forest (92630) *(P-4798)*

**Universal Products, Rancho Cucamonga** *Also Called: Proulx Manufacturing Inc* *(P-6987)*

Universal Propulsion Co Inc ...................................................... B ...... 707 399-1867
  3530 Branscombe Rd Fairfield (94533) *(P-13984)*

Universal Prtein Spplmnts Corp ................................................ F ...... 732 545-3130
  3441 Gato Ct Riverside (92507) *(P-5699)*

Universal Punch Corp ................................................................ D ...... 714 556-4488
  4001 W Macarthur Blvd Santa Ana (92704) *(P-9590)*

Universal Screw Products ......................................................... F ...... 310 371-1170
  20421 Earl St Torrance (90503) *(P-8736)*

Universal Steel Services Inc ..................................................... E ...... 626 960-1455
  5034 Heintz St Baldwin Park (91706) *(P-8237)*

Universal Studios Company LLC (DH) ..................................... A ...... 818 777-1000
  100 Universal City Plz North Hollywood (91608) *(P-19299)*

**Universal Surveillance Systems, Rancho Cucamonga** *Also Called: Universal Surveillance Systems LLC* *(P-13323)*

Universal Surveillance Systems LLC ........................................ D ...... 909 484-7870
  11172 Elm Ave Rancho Cucamonga (91730) *(P-13323)*

## ALPHABETIC SECTION

Universal Switching Corp .................................................. E ...... 818 785-0200
7671 N San Fernando Rd Burbank (91505) *(P-11476)*

Universal Wood Moulding Inc (PA) ....................................... E ...... 661 362-6262
21139 Centre Pointe Pkwy Santa Clarita (91350) *(P-16438)*

University Cal Press Fundation (PA) .................................... D ...... 510 642-4247
155 Grand Ave Ste 400 Oakland (94612) *(P-4352)*

University Frames Inc ...................................................... E ...... 714 575-5100
3060 E Miraloma Ave Anaheim (92806) *(P-3429)*

University Plating Co, San Jose *Also Called: Hane and Hane Inc (P-8969)*

University Readers, Solana Beach *Also Called: Cognella Inc (P-4380)*

Uniweb, Corona *Also Called: Uniweb Inc (P-3713)*

Uniweb Inc (PA) ............................................................. D ...... 951 279-7999
222 S Promenade Ave Corona (92879) *(P-3713)*

Unix Packaging LLC (PA) ................................................. D ...... 213 627-5050
9 Minson Way Montebello (90640) *(P-1970)*

Unlimited Innovations Inc ................................................... E ...... 714 998-0866
180 N Rverview Dr Ste 320 Anaheim (92808) *(P-18901)*

Unorth, San Jose *Also Called: Mota Group Inc (P-13199)*

Uns Electric Inc ............................................................... E ...... 714 690-3660
6565 Valley View St La Palma (90623) *(P-16675)*

Unspun Inc ..................................................................... E ...... 207 577-8745
6655 Hollis St Emeryville (94608) *(P-2590)*

Untangle, San Jose *Also Called: Untangle Holdings Inc (P-18902)*

Untangle Holdings Inc (PA) ............................................... E ...... 408 598-4299
25 Metro Dr Ste 210 San Jose (95110) *(P-18902)*

Uoc USA Inc .................................................................. F ...... 949 328-3366
15251 Alton Pkwy Ste 100 Irvine (92618) *(P-15296)*

UPD INC ....................................................................... D ...... 323 588-8811
4507 S Maywood Ave Vernon (90058) *(P-15736)*

Upguard Inc (PA) ............................................................ E ...... 888 882-3223
723 N Shoreline Blvd Mountain View (94043) *(P-18903)*

Upland Fab Inc ............................................................... E ...... 909 986-6565
1445 Brooks St Ste L Ontario (91762) *(P-11163)*

Upm Inc ........................................................................ B ...... 626 962-4001
13245 Los Angeles St Baldwin Park (91706) *(P-9654)*

Upm Raflatac Inc ............................................................ F ...... 909 390-4657
1105 Auto Center Dr Ontario (91761) *(P-3957)*

Upper Deck Company (PA) ............................................... E ...... 800 873-7332
5830 El Camino Real Carlsbad (92008) *(P-4488)*

Upright, Fresno *Also Called: Tanfield Engrg Systems US Inc (P-9440)*

Upside Fods Engrg Prod Innvtio, Emeryville *Also Called: Upside Foods Inc (P-2384)*

Upside Foods Inc ............................................................ D ...... 510 588-1224
6001 Shellmound St Ste 115 # 125 Emeryville (94608) *(P-2384)*

Upstanding LLC .............................................................. C ...... 949 788-9900
440 Exchange Ste 100 Irvine (92602) *(P-18904)*

Uptimeai Inc .................................................................. E ...... 415 935-1195
611 Gateway Blvd South San Francisco (94080) *(P-18905)*

Upwing Energy Inc ......................................................... F ...... 562 293-1660
16323 Shoemaker Ave Cerritos (90703) *(P-288)*

Uqora Inc ...................................................................... E ...... 888 313-1372
4250 Executive Sq La Jolla (92037) *(P-785)*

Urban Armor Gear LLC (HQ) ........................................... E ...... 949 329-0500
1601 Alton Pkwy Irvine (92606) *(P-7065)*

Urban Concepts, Vernon *Also Called: Anns Trading Company Inc (P-17284)*

Urban Expressions Inc ..................................................... E ...... 310 593-4574
5500 Union Pacific Ave Commerce (90022) *(P-7147)*

Urban Farmer Store Inc (DH) ............................................ E ...... 415 661-2204
2833 Vicente St San Francisco (94116) *(P-16802)*

Urban Insight Inc ............................................................ D ...... 213 792-2000
3530 Wilshire Blvd Ste 1285 Los Angeles (90010) *(P-18998)*

Uremet Corporation ......................................................... E ...... 657 257-4027
7012 Belgrave Ave Garden Grove (92841) *(P-5216)*

Urethane Masters Inc ...................................................... F ...... 651 829-1032
455 54th St Ste 102 San Diego (92114) *(P-6668)*

Urgent Gear Inc ............................................................. F ...... 213 741-9926
1955 E 48th St Vernon (90058) *(P-17083)*

Urgent Upfits, Rancho Cordova *Also Called: Form & Fusion Mfg Inc (P-8843)*

Urocare Products Inc ...................................................... F ...... 909 621-6013
2735 Melbourne Ave Pomona (91767) *(P-6545)*

US Apothecary Crown Labs, Santa Fe Springs *Also Called: Titan Medical Enterprises Inc (P-5691)*

US Architectural Lighting, Palmdale *Also Called: Sun Valley Ltg Standards Inc (P-11559)*

US Armor Corporation ..................................................... E ...... 562 207-4240
10715 Bloomfield Ave Santa Fe Springs (90670) *(P-15424)*

US Blanks LLC (PA) ........................................................ E ...... 310 225-6774
14700 S San Pedro St Gardena (90248) *(P-5217)*

US Borax Inc ................................................................. A ...... 760 762-7000
14486 Borax Rd Boron (93516) *(P-5127)*

US Bowling Corporation ................................................... F ...... 909 548-0644
5480 Schaefer Ave Chino (91710) *(P-15872)*

US Computers Inc .......................................................... F ...... 714 528-0514
181 W Orangethorpe Ave Ste C Placentia (92870) *(P-10447)*

US Concrete Precast, San Diego *Also Called: San Diego Precast Concrete Inc (P-7389)*

US Continental Marketing Inc (PA) ..................................... D ...... 951 808-8888
310 Reed Cir Corona (92879) *(P-5934)*

US Cotton LLC .............................................................. D ...... 559 651-3015
7100 W Sunnyview Ave Visalia (93291) *(P-6051)*

US Critical, Lake Forest *Also Called: US Critical LLC (P-10290)*

US Critical LLC (PA) ....................................................... E ...... 949 916-9326
6 Orchard Ste 150 Lake Forest (92630) *(P-10290)*

US Critical LLC .............................................................. E ...... 800 884-8945
25422 Trabuco Rd # 320 Lake Forest (92630) *(P-10291)*

US Dental Inc ................................................................ E ...... 562 404-3500
13043 166th St Cerritos (90703) *(P-15492)*

US Dies Inc (PA) ............................................................ E ...... 209 664-1402
1992 Rockefeller Dr Ste 300 Ceres (95307) *(P-9655)*

US Donuts & Yogurt ........................................................ F ...... 562 695-8867
11719 Whittier Blvd Whittier (90601) *(P-17610)*

US Duty Gear Inc ........................................................... F ...... 909 391-8800
1946 S Grove Ave Ontario (91761) *(P-7162)*

US Electrical Services Inc ................................................. E ...... 714 982-1534
1501 E Orangethorpe Ave Ste 140 Fullerton (92831) *(P-16676)*

US Energy Technologies Inc .............................................. E ...... 714 617-8800
14370 Myford Road Ste 100 Walnut (91789) *(P-11565)*

US Foods Inc ................................................................. A ...... 559 271-3700
3325 W Figarden Dr Fresno (93711) *(P-17120)*

US Foods Inc ................................................................. C ...... 714 670-3500
15155 Northam St La Mirada (90638) *(P-17121)*

US Hanger Company LLC ................................................ E ...... 310 323-8030
17501 S Denver Ave Gardena (90248) *(P-7657)*

US Horizon Manufacturing Inc ........................................... E ...... 661 775-1675
28539 Industry Dr Valencia (91355) *(P-7179)*

US Hybrid Corporation (HQ) ............................................. E ...... 310 212-1200
2660 Columbia St Torrance (90503) *(P-13599)*

US Industrial Tool & Sup Co ............................................. E ...... 310 464-8400
14083 S Normandie Ave Gardena (90249) *(P-9591)*

US Joiner LLC ............................................................... E ...... 619 233-3993
2800 Harbor Dr San Diego (92113) *(P-399)*

US Lighting Tech, Walnut *Also Called: US Energy Technologies Inc (P-11565)*

US Logistics, Signal Hill *Also Called: United States Logistics Group (P-13621)*

US Megano Wine, Healdsburg *Also Called: Chateau Diana LLC (P-1504)*

US Motor Works LLC (PA) ................................................ E ...... 562 404-0488
14722 Anson Ave Santa Fe Springs (90670) *(P-13600)*

US Pipe Fabrication LLC ................................................. E ...... 530 742-5171
3387 Plumas Arboga Rd Marysville (95901) *(P-6604)*

US Pole Company Inc (PA) .............................................. D ...... 800 877-6537
660 W Avenue O Palmdale (93551) *(P-11566)*

US Polymers Inc (PA) ..................................................... D ...... 323 728-3023
1057 S Vail Ave Montebello (90640) *(P-7066)*

US Polymers Inc ............................................................ D ...... 323 727-6888
5910 Bandini Blvd Commerce (90040) *(P-7753)*

US Precision Sheet Metal Inc ............................................ D ...... 951 276-2611
4020 Garner Rd Riverside (92501) *(P-8604)*

US Print & Toner Inc ....................................................... E ...... 619 562-6995
14751 Franklin Ave Ste B Tustin (92780) *(P-15902)*

US Radiator Corporation (PA) ........................................... E ...... 323 826-0965
4423 District Blvd Vernon (90058) *(P-13601)*

US Rigging Supply Corp .................................................. E ...... 714 545-7444
1600 E Mcfadden Ave Santa Ana (92705) *(P-9240)*

US Rubber Recycling Inc ................................................. E ...... 909 825-1200
1231 Lincoln St Colton (92324) *(P-6546)*

US Saws Inc (PA) ........................................................... F ...... 860 668-2402
3702 W Central Ave Santa Ana (92704) *(P-9445)*

**US Sensor Corp** .................................................................... D ...... 714 639-1000
1832 W Collins Ave Orange (92867) *(P-12782)*

**US Technical Ceramics Inc** ................................................. E ...... 408 779-0303
15400 Concord Cir Morgan Hill (95037) *(P-16487)*

**US Tower, Woodlake** *Also Called: US Tower Corp (P-8238)*

**US Tower Corp (PA)** ............................................................ E ...... 785 524-9966
1099 W Ropes Ave Woodlake (93286) *(P-8238)*

**US Union Tool Inc (HQ)** ...................................................... E ...... 714 521-6242
1260 N Fee Ana St Anaheim (92807) *(P-9574)*

**US Weldments, Fremont** *Also Called: Ichor Systems Inc (P-12469)*

**US Wheel, Huntington Beach** *Also Called: U S Wheel Corporation (P-13595)*

**USA Extruded Plastics Inc** .................................................. F ...... 714 991-6061
965 E Discovery Ln Anaheim (92801) *(P-7067)*

**USA Industries, Orange** *Also Called: United Sunshine American Industries Corporation (P-9239)*

**USA Products Group (PA)** ................................................... E ...... 209 334-1460
1300 E Vine St Lodi (95240) *(P-15873)*

**USA Sales Inc** ....................................................................... E ...... 909 390-9606
1560 S Archibald Ave Ontario (91761) *(P-2397)*

**USA Tolerance Rings** .......................................................... E ...... 415 457-6711
831 Sir Francis Drake Blvd San Anselmo (94960) *(P-7916)*

**USA Vision Systems Inc (HQ)** ............................................. E ...... 949 583-1519
9301 Irvine Blvd Irvine (92618) *(P-13324)*

**USAopoly Inc** ....................................................................... D ...... 760 431-5910
5999 Avenida Encinas Ste 150 Carlsbad (92008) *(P-15771)*

**Used Tank Sales of California, Fresno** *Also Called: Central Valley Tank of Cal (P-8304)*

**Usertesting, Los Gatos** *Also Called: Usertesting Inc (P-18906)*

**Usertesting Inc (PA)** ............................................................ D ...... 888 877-1882
1484 Pollard Rd Los Gatos (95032) *(P-18906)*

**USG Ceilings Plus LLC** ..................................................... E ...... 323 724-8166
6711 E Washington Blvd Commerce (90040) *(P-8896)*

**Usit Co, Gardena** *Also Called: US Industrial Tool & Sup Co (P-9591)*

**Usk Manufacturing Inc** ....................................................... E ...... 510 471-7555
720 Zwissig Way Union City (94587) *(P-8605)*

**Usl Parallel Products Cal** ................................................... E ...... 909 980-1200
12281 Arrow Rte Rancho Cucamonga (91739) *(P-6164)*

**Usmpc Buyer Inc** ................................................................. E ...... 909 473-3027
4062 Georgia Blvd San Bernardino (92407) *(P-7583)*

**USP Inc** ................................................................................. D ...... 760 842-7700
1818 Ord Way Oceanside (92056) *(P-6052)*

**Ustc, Chico** *Also Called: United Sttes Thrmlctric Cnsrti (P-14466)*

**Utak Laboratories Inc** ........................................................ E ...... 661 294-3935
25020 Avenue Tibbitts Valencia (91355) *(P-6165)*

**Utap Printing Co Inc** .......................................................... F ...... 650 588-2818
1423 San Mateo Ave South San Francisco (94080) *(P-4799)*

**Utc, Mas, Costa Mesa** *Also Called: Honeywell SEC Americas LLC (P-11999)*

**Utility Refrigerator** .............................................................. E ...... 818 764-6200
12160 Sherman Way North Hollywood (91605) *(P-10524)*

**Utility Trailer Manufacturing (PA)** ...................................... B ...... 626 965-1514
17295 Railroad St Ste A City Of Industry (91748) *(P-13622)*

**Utility Trailer Mfg Co** .......................................................... C ...... 909 594-6026
17295 Railroad St Ste A City Of Industry (91748) *(P-13623)*

**Utility Trailer Mfg Co** .......................................................... C ...... 909 428-8300
15567 Valley Blvd Fontana (92335) *(P-13624)*

**Utility Trlr Sls Southern Cal, Fontana** *Also Called: Utility Trailer Mfg Co (P-13624)*

**Utility Vault, Fontana** *Also Called: Oldcastle Infrastructure Inc (P-7364)*

**Utility Vault, Pleasanton** *Also Called: Oldcastle Infrastructure Inc (P-7365)*

**Utility Vault, Escondido** *Also Called: Oldcastle Infrastructure Inc (P-7366)*

**Utility Vault, Madera** *Also Called: Oldcastle Infrastructure Inc (P-9295)*

**Uttam Composites LLC** ..................................................... F ...... 714 894-5300
11700 Monarch St Garden Grove (92841) *(P-8350)*

**Uv Landscaping LLC** .......................................................... F ...... 831 275-5296
477 Old Natividad Rd Salinas (93906) *(P-7302)*

**Uwe, Camarillo** *Also Called: United Western Enterprises Inc (P-9131)*

**V & F Fabrication Company Inc** ......................................... E ...... 714 265-0630
13902 Seaboard Cir Garden Grove (92843) *(P-8239)*

**V & M Company** ................................................................... F ...... 310 532-5633
14024 Avalon Blvd Los Angeles (90061) *(P-9029)*

**V & M Precision Grinding Co., Brea** *Also Called: Rogers Holding Company Inc (P-13938)*

**V & P Scientific Inc** ............................................................. F ...... 858 455-0643
9823 Pacific Heights Blvd Ste T San Diego (92121) *(P-14749)*

**V & S Engineering Company Ltd** ....................................... E ...... 714 898-7869
5766 Research Dr Huntington Beach (92649) *(P-11164)*

**V 3, Oxnard** *Also Called: V3 Printing Corporation (P-4800)*

**V B I, Simi Valley** *Also Called: Vanderhorst Brothers Industries Inc (P-11170)*

**V G S, Salinas** *Also Called: Vegetable Growers Supply Co (P-17312)*

**V M I, Visalia** *Also Called: Voltage Multipliers Inc (P-12796)*

**V M P Inc** .............................................................................. F ...... 661 294-9934
24830 Avenue Tibbitts Valencia (91355) *(P-8737)*

**V Q Orthocare, Vista** *Also Called: Vision Quest Industries Inc (P-15427)*

**V R Gifts, Brea** *Also Called: Vesuki Inc (P-17656)*

**V S S, West Sacramento** *Also Called: Vss International Inc (P-384)*

**V Sattui Winery** .................................................................... D ...... 707 963-7774
1111 White Ln Saint Helena (94574) *(P-17631)*

**V Tech, Patterson** *Also Called: V-Tech Manufacturing Inc (P-11165)*

**V Twest Inc** ........................................................................... F ...... 714 521-2167
16222 Phoebe Ave La Mirada (90638) *(P-3675)*

**V Twin Magazine, Agoura Hills** *Also Called: Paisano Publications LLC (P-4285)*

**V-T Industries Inc** ................................................................ D ...... 714 521-2008
9818 Firestone Blvd Downey (90241) *(P-7068)*

**V-Tech Manufacturing Inc** .................................................. E ...... 408 730-9200
505 Baldwin Rd Patterson (95363) *(P-11165)*

**V-Wave Inc** ........................................................................... E ...... 818 629-2164
29219 Canwood St Ste 100 Agoura Hills (91301) *(P-15297)*

**V/ Twins, Agoura Hills** *Also Called: Paisano Publications Inc (P-4286)*

**V&H Performance LLC** ...................................................... D ...... 562 921-7461
13861 Rosecrans Ave Santa Fe Springs (90670) *(P-14074)*

**V3, Oxnard** *Also Called: Ventura Printing Inc (P-4803)*

**V3 Printing Corporation** ..................................................... D ...... 805 981-2600
200 N Elevar St Oxnard (93030) *(P-4800)*

**V3 Systems, El Dorado Hills** *Also Called: V3 Systems Scrtyautomation Inc (P-19141)*

**V3 Systems Scrtyautomation Inc** ...................................... E ...... 916 543-1543
4925 Robert J Mathews Pkwy Ste 100 El Dorado Hills (95762) *(P-19141)*

**Vacaville Fruit Co Inc (PA)** ................................................. E ...... 707 448-5292
2055 Cessna Dr Ste 200 Vacaville (95688) *(P-972)*

**Vacco Industries (DH)** ........................................................ C ...... 626 443-7121
10350 Vacco St South El Monte (91733) *(P-9192)*

**Vacuum Engrg & Mtls Co Inc** ............................................. E ...... 408 871-9900
390 Reed St Santa Clara (95050) *(P-5128)*

**Vae Industries Corporation** ............................................... E ...... 714 842-7500
5402 Research Dr Huntington Beach (92649) *(P-2987)*

**Vaga Industries, South El Monte** *Also Called: Pearson Engineering Corp (P-9103)*

**Vahe Enterprises Inc** .......................................................... D ...... 323 235-6657
750 E Slauson Ave Los Angeles (90011) *(P-13434)*

**Val Plastic USA L L C** ......................................................... F ...... 909 390-9600
4570 Eucalyptus Ave Ste C Chino (91710) *(P-9388)*

**Val USA Manufacturer Inc** ................................................. E ...... 626 839-8069
1050 W Central Ave Ste A Brea (92821) *(P-16262)*

**Valco Planer Works Inc** ...................................................... E ...... 323 582-6355
6131 Maywood Ave Huntington Park (90255) *(P-9656)*

**Valco Precision Works, Huntington Park** *Also Called: Valco Planer Works Inc (P-9656)*

**Valdera Inc** ........................................................................... E ...... 415 323-6646
548 Market St Ste 85314 San Francisco (94104) *(P-18907)*

**Valdor Fiber Optics Inc (PA)** ............................................. F ...... 510 293-1212
1838 D St Hayward (94541) *(P-14597)*

**Valeant Biomedicals Inc (DH)** ............................................ D ...... 949 461-6000
1 Enterprise Aliso Viejo (92656) *(P-17250)*

**Valeda Company LLC** ........................................................ E ...... 800 421-8700
13571 Vaughn St Unit E San Fernando (91340) *(P-15425)*

**Valence Los Angeles, Gardena** *Also Called: Coast Plating Inc (P-8942)*

**Valence Lynwood, Lynwood** *Also Called: Triumph Processing Inc (P-9026)*

**Valence Surface Tech LLC** ................................................ F ...... 562 531-7666
7718 Adams St Paramount (90723) *(P-8240)*

**Valencia Mold, Valencia** *Also Called: Valencia Plastics Inc (P-7069)*

**Valencia Pipe Company** ..................................................... E ...... 661 257-3923
28305 Livingston Ave Valencia (91355) *(P-6605)*

**Valencia Plastics Inc** .......................................................... F ...... 661 257-0066
25611 Hercules St Valencia (91355) *(P-7069)*

**Valent, San Ramon** *Also Called: Valent USA LLC (P-6213)*

**Valent USA LLC (DH)** ......................................................... D ...... 925 256-2700
4600 Norris Canyon Rd San Ramon (94583) *(P-6213)*

# ALPHABETIC SECTION — Valutics Inc

**Valero, Wilmington** *Also Called: Valero Ref Company-California (P-6357)*
**Valero Energy Corporation** .............................................. B ...... 707 745-7011
3400 E 2nd St Benicia (94510) *(P-17478)*
**Valero Ref Company-California** ...................................... A ...... 562 491-6754
2401 E Anaheim St Wilmington (90744) *(P-6357)*
**Valet Cstm Cabiners & Closets, Campbell** *Also Called: Valet Organizers Inc (P-3278)*
**Valet Organizers Inc** ......................................................... E ...... 408 370-1041
1190 Dell Ave Ste J Campbell (95008) *(P-3278)*
**Valew Welding & Fabrication, Adelanto** *Also Called: Hayes Welding Inc (P-19197)*
**Valex Corp (HQ)** ................................................................ D ...... 805 658-0944
6080 Leland St Ventura (93003) *(P-9030)*
**Valiant Technical Services Inc** ......................................... D ...... 757 628-9500
1785 Utah Ave Lompoc (93437) *(P-14021)*
**Valiantica Inc (PA)** ............................................................ E ...... 408 694-3803
9170 Irvine Center Dr Irvine (92618) *(P-18908)*
**Validyne Engineering Corp** .............................................. E ...... 818 886-8488
8626 Wilbur Ave Northridge (91324) *(P-14937)*
**Valimet Inc (PA)** ................................................................ D ...... 209 444-1600
431 Sperry Rd Stockton (95206) *(P-7917)*
**Valitor Inc** .......................................................................... F ...... 510 813-8611
2956 San Pablo Ave Berkeley (94702) *(P-5700)*
**Vallejo Building Materials, Napa** *Also Called: Syar Industries LLC (P-16485)*
**Valley Box Co Inc** ............................................................. E ...... 619 449-2882
10611 Prospect Ave Santee (92071) *(P-17025)*
**Valley Business Printers Inc** ............................................ D ...... 818 362-7771
6355 Topanga Canyon Blvd Ste 225 Woodland Hills (91367) *(P-4801)*
**Valley Cabinet, El Cajon** *Also Called: Vcsd Inc (P-3279)*
**Valley Chrome Plating Inc (PA)** ........................................ D ...... 559 298-8094
1028 Hoblitt Ave Clovis (93612) *(P-9031)*
**Valley Communications Inc (PA)** ..................................... D ...... 916 349-7300
6921 Roseville Rd Sacramento (95842) *(P-472)*
**Valley Enerprises Inc** ........................................................ E ...... 951 789-0843
18600 Van Buren Blvd Riverside (92508) *(P-16062)*
**Valley Fabrication Inc** ....................................................... E ...... 831 757-5151
1056 Pellet Ave Salinas (93901) *(P-9389)*
**Valley Fig Growers** ........................................................... E ...... 559 349-1686
2028 S 3rd St Fresno (93702) *(P-88)*
**Valley Fine Foods Company LLC (PA)** ............................ D ...... 707 746-6888
3909 Park Rd Ste H Benicia (94510) *(P-1066)*
**Valley Fine Foods Company Inc** ...................................... C ...... 530 671-7200
300 Epley Dr Yuba City (95991) *(P-2385)*
**VALLEY FINE FOODS COMPANY, INC., Yuba City** *Also Called: Valley Fine Foods Company Inc (P-2385)*
**Valley Forge, Azusa** *Also Called: Valley Forge Acquisition Corp (P-8791)*
**Valley Forge Acquisition Corp** ......................................... F ...... 626 969-8701
444 S Motor Ave Azusa (91702) *(P-8791)*
**Valley Fresh Inc (HQ)** ....................................................... E ...... 209 943-5411
1404 S Fresno Ave Stockton (95206) *(P-621)*
**Valley Fresh Foods Inc** .................................................... E ...... 209 669-5600
3600 E Linwood Ave Turlock (95380) *(P-65)*
**Valley Fresh Foods Inc** .................................................... E ...... 209 669-5510
1220 Hall Rd Denair (95316) *(P-66)*
**Valley Fresh Foods Inc (PA)** ............................................ F ...... 209 669-5600
3600 E Linwood Ave Turlock (95380) *(P-67)*
**Valley Garlic LLC** .............................................................. E ...... 559 934-1763
500 Enterprise Pkwy Coalinga (93210) *(P-996)*
**Valley Images, San Jose** *Also Called: Valley Images LLC (P-4978)*
**Valley Images LLC** ........................................................... F ...... 408 279-6777
1925 Kyle Park Ct San Jose (95125) *(P-4978)*
**Valley Iron Works Inc** ....................................................... E ...... 209 368-7037
127 E Harney Ln Lodi (95240) *(P-537)*
**Valley Lahvosh Baking Co Inc** ......................................... E ...... 559 485-2700
502 M St Fresno (93721) *(P-1250)*
**Valley Metal Supply Inc** ................................................... F ...... 818 837-6566
12950 Bradley Ave Sylmar (91342) *(P-16493)*
**Valley Metal Treating Inc** ................................................. E ...... 909 623-6316
355 Se End Ave Pomona (91766) *(P-7906)*
**Valley Metals LLC** ............................................................ E ...... 858 513-1300
13125 Gregg St Poway (92064) *(P-7673)*
**Valley Milk LLC** ................................................................. D ...... 209 410-6701
400 N Washington Rd Turlock (95380) *(P-60)*

**Valley News Gardens, Gardena** *Also Called: Gardena Valley News Inc (P-4117)*
**Valley Oak Cabinets, Santa Ynez** *Also Called: Valley Oaks Industries (P-3589)*
**Valley Oaks Industries** ..................................................... F ...... 805 688-2754
3550 E Highway 246 Ste Ae Santa Ynez (93460) *(P-3589)*
**Valley of Moon Winery** ..................................................... E ...... 707 939-4500
134 Church St Sonoma (95476) *(P-1808)*
**Valley Packline Solutions** ................................................ E ...... 559 638-7821
5259 Avenue 408 Reedley (93654) *(P-9822)*
**Valley Pallet Inc** ................................................................ F ...... 916 381-7954
6060 Midway St Sacramento (95828) *(P-3364)*
**Valley Perforating LLC** ..................................................... E ...... 661 324-4964
3201 Gulf St Bakersfield (93308) *(P-11166)*
**Valley Power Services Inc** ............................................... D ...... 909 969-9345
425 S Hacienda Blvd City Of Industry (91745) *(P-11295)*
**Valley Power Systems Inc** ............................................... E ...... 510 635-8991
2070 Farallon Dr San Leandro (94577) *(P-16852)*
**Valley Precision Met Pdts Inc** .......................................... E ...... 661 607-0100
27771 Avenue Hopkins Valencia (91355) *(P-8606)*
**Valley Precision Metal Pdts, Valencia** *Also Called: Valley Precision Met Pdts Inc (P-8606)*
**Valley Printers, Woodland Hills** *Also Called: Valley Business Printers Inc (P-4801)*
**Valley Printing, Ceres** *Also Called: Robert R Wix Inc (P-4955)*
**Valley Processing, Long Beach** *Also Called: Hexpol Compounding CA Inc (P-6499)*
**Valley Protein, Fresno** *Also Called: Cencal Foods LLC (P-678)*
**Valley Protein LLC** ............................................................ D ...... 559 498-7115
1828 E Hedges Ave Fresno (93703) *(P-675)*
**Valley Resource Center, Hemet** *Also Called: Valley Resource Center Inc (P-19363)*
**Valley Resource Center Inc (PA)** ..................................... E ...... 951 766-8659
1285 N Santa Fe St Hemet (92543) *(P-19363)*
**Valley Rock Lndscpe Material** ......................................... E ...... 916 652-7209
4018 Taylor Rd Loomis (95650) *(P-7303)*
**Valley Rubber & Gasket, Sacramento** *Also Called: Lgg Industrial Inc (P-16880)*
**Valley Rubber & Gasket Company Inc** ........................... D ...... 916 369-8885
10182 Croydon Way Sacramento (95827) *(P-16904)*
**Valley Services Electronics** ............................................. C ...... 408 284-7700
6190 San Ignacio Ave San Jose (95119) *(P-12253)*
**Valley Sheet Metal, South San Francisco** *Also Called: Frank M Booth Inc (P-418)*
**Valley Spuds, Oxnard** *Also Called: McK Enterprises Inc (P-2279)*
**Valley Stairway Inc** .......................................................... F ...... 559 299-0151
5684 E Shields Ave Fresno (93727) *(P-8648)*
**Valley Sun Products Inc** ................................................... D ...... 209 862-1200
3324 Orestimba Rd Newman (95360) *(P-2386)*
**Valley Tool & Mfg Co Inc** ................................................. E ...... 209 883-4093
2507 Tully Rd Hughson (95326) *(P-11167)*
**Valley Tool and Machine Co Inc** ..................................... D ...... 909 595-2205
111 Explorer St Pomona (91768) *(P-11168)*
**Valley View Foods Inc** ..................................................... D ...... 530 673-7356
7547 Sawtelle Ave Yuba City (95991) *(P-935)*
**Valley Welding & Machine Works, Fresno** *Also Called: Garabedian Bros Inc (P-10851)*
**Valley-Todeco Inc** ............................................................. C ...... 800 992-4444
135 N Unruh Ave City Of Industry (91744) *(P-8770)*
**Valmark Industries Inc** ..................................................... C ...... 925 960-9900
7900 National Dr Livermore (94550) *(P-3958)*
**Valmark Interface Solutions, Livermore** *Also Called: Valmark Industries Inc (P-3958)*
**Valmetal Tulare Inc** .......................................................... D ...... 559 685-0340
2955 S K St Tulare (93274) *(P-9390)*
**Valmont Ctngs Clwest Glvnizing, Long Beach** *Also Called: Valmont Industries Inc (P-9132)*
**Valmont Industries Inc** ..................................................... E ...... 310 549-2200
2226 E Dominguez St Long Beach (90810) *(P-9132)*
**Valor Compounding Pharmacy, Berkeley** *Also Called: Valor Compounding Pharmacy Inc (P-5701)*
**Valor Compounding Pharmacy Inc** ................................. D ...... 855 554-2889
2461 Shattuck Ave Berkeley (94704) *(P-5701)*
**Valterra Products LLC (HQ)** ............................................. E ...... 818 898-1671
15235 Brand Blvd Ste A101 Mission Hills (91345) *(P-9193)*
**Valtra Inc (PA)** .................................................................. E ...... 562 949-8625
8750 Pioneer Blvd Santa Fe Springs (90670) *(P-16853)*
**Value Products Inc** ........................................................... E ...... 209 345-3817
2128 Industrial Dr Stockton (95206) *(P-5884)*
**Valutics Inc** ....................................................................... E ...... 408 823-3597
34332 Eucalyptus Ter Fremont (94555) *(P-18909)*

## Van Can Company — ALPHABETIC SECTION

Van Can Company .................................................................. C ...... 858 391-8084
13230 Evening Creek Dr S Ste 212 San Diego (92128) *(P-7932)*

Van Duerr Industries Inc ...................................................... E ...... 530 893-1596
21 Valley Ct Chico (95973) *(P-16497)*

Van Sark Inc (PA) .................................................................. D ...... 510 635-1111
410 Harriet St San Francisco (94103) *(P-3494)*

Van-Mulder Sheet Metal Inc ................................................ E ...... 510 569-9123
2437 Radley Ct Hayward (94545) *(P-517)*

Van's Gifts, Long Beach *Also Called: Farm Street Designs Inc (P-17265)*

Vance & Hines, Santa Fe Springs *Also Called: V&H Performance LLC (P-14074)*

Vander Lans & Sons Inc (PA) ............................................... E ...... 209 334-4115
1320 S Sacramento St Lodi (95240) *(P-10608)*

Vander-Bend Manufacturing Inc .......................................... C ...... 916 631-6375
3510 Luyung Dr Rancho Cordova (95742) *(P-11169)*

Vander-Bend Manufacturing Inc .......................................... C ...... 408 245-5150
2701 Orchard Pkwy San Jose (95131) *(P-13115)*

Vanderhorst Brothers Industries Inc ................................... D ...... 805 583-3333
1715 Surveyor Ave Simi Valley (93063) *(P-11170)*

Vanderhulst Associates Inc ................................................. E ...... 408 727-1313
3300 Victor Ct Santa Clara (95054) *(P-11171)*

Vanderra Resources LLC ..................................................... B ...... 817 439-2220
1801 Century Park E Ste 2400 Los Angeles (90067) *(P-289)*

Vandersteen Audio .............................................................. E ...... 559 582-0324
116 W 4th St Hanford (93230) *(P-11710)*

Vanderveer Industrial Plas LLC ........................................... E ...... 714 579-7700
515 S Melrose St Placentia (92870) *(P-6593)*

Vanderveer Industrial Plastics, Placentia *Also Called: Vanderveer Industrial Plas LLC (P-6593)*

Vanguard Electronics Company (PA) .................................. E ...... 714 842-3330
18292 Enterprise Ln Huntington Beach (92648) *(P-12863)*

Vanguard Industries East Inc ............................................... E ...... 800 433-1334
2440 Impala Dr Carlsbad (92010) *(P-3037)*

Vanguard Industries West Inc (PA) ..................................... C ...... 760 438-4437
2440 Impala Dr Carlsbad (92010) *(P-3038)*

Vanguard Marketing, Scotts Valley *Also Called: Threshold Enterprises Ltd (P-5274)*

Vanguard Space Tech Inc .................................................... C ...... 858 587-4210
4398 Corporate Center Dr Los Alamitos (90720) *(P-13985)*

Vanguard Tool & Manufacturing, Rancho Cucamonga *Also Called: Vanguard Tool & Mfg Co Inc (P-8897)*

Vanguard Tool & Mfg Co Inc ............................................... E ...... 909 980-9392
8388 Utica Ave Rancho Cucamonga (91730) *(P-8897)*

Variman Manufacturing, Murrieta *Also Called: Vmc International LLC (P-15493)*

Vanlaw Food Products Inc (HQ) .......................................... D ...... 714 870-9091
2325 Moore Ave Fullerton (92833) *(P-997)*

Vanomation Inc .................................................................... F ...... 877 228-2992
9241 Research Dr Irvine (92618) *(P-10035)*

Vans Inc (DH) ....................................................................... B ...... 714 755-4000
1588 S Coast Dr Costa Mesa (92626) *(P-6423)*

Vans Manufacturing Inc ....................................................... F ...... 805 522-6267
330 E Easy St Ste C Simi Valley (93065) *(P-11172)*

Vans Shoes, Costa Mesa *Also Called: Vans Inc (P-6423)*

Vantage Apparel, Santa Ana *Also Called: Vantage Custom Classics Inc (P-17084)*

Vantage Associates Inc ....................................................... E ...... 800 995-8322
1565 Macarthur Blvd Costa Mesa (92626) *(P-6687)*

Vantage Associates Inc ....................................................... D ...... 562 968-1400
12333 Los Nietos Rd Santa Fe Springs (90670) *(P-7070)*

Vantage Associates Inc ....................................................... E ...... 562 968-1400
1565 Macarthur Blvd Costa Mesa (92626) *(P-13986)*

Vantage Associates Inc (PA) ............................................... E ...... 619 477-6940
1565 Macarthur Blvd Costa Mesa (92626) *(P-14117)*

Vantage Custom Classics Inc .............................................. C ...... 714 755-1133
1815 Ritchey St Santa Ana (92705) *(P-17084)*

Vantage Led, Corona *Also Called: Tradenet Enterprise Inc (P-16059)*

Vantage Master Machine Company, Costa Mesa *Also Called: Vantage Associates Inc (P-13986)*

Vantage Point Products Corp (PA) ...................................... E ...... 562 946-1718
9234 Hall Rd Downey (90241) *(P-11711)*

Vantage Vehicle Group, Corona *Also Called: Vantage Vehicle Intl Inc (P-13191)*

Vantage Vehicle Intl Inc ....................................................... E ...... 951 735-1200
1740 N Delilah St Corona (92879) *(P-13191)*

Vantec Thermal Technologies, Fremont *Also Called: Siblings Investment Inc (P-16548)*

Vantiq Inc (PA) ..................................................................... E ...... 650 346-1114
1990 N California Blvd Ste 640 Walnut Creek (94596) *(P-18910)*

Vape Craft LLC .................................................................... E ...... 760 295-7484
2100 Palomar Airport Rd Ste 210 Carlsbad (92011) *(P-17682)*

Vapex-Genex-Precision, Los Angeles *Also Called: Electrical Rebuilders Sls Inc (P-13169)*

Vapor Delux Inc ................................................................... E ...... 818 370-8308
2148 Glendale Galleria Glendale (91210) *(P-5007)*

Vaquero Energy Inc ............................................................. E ...... 661 616-0600
4700 Stockdale Hwy Ste 120 Bakersfield (93309) *(P-290)*

Vaquero Energy Incorporated ............................................. E ...... 661 363-7240
15545 Hermosa Rd Bakersfield (93307) *(P-145)*

Vaquero Hunter Inc., Bakersfield *Also Called: Vaquero Energy Inc (P-290)*

Varda Space Industries Inc ................................................. D ...... 833 707-0020
225 S Aviation Blvd El Segundo (90245) *(P-14098)*

Varex Imaging West LLC (HQ) ............................................ E ...... 408 565-0850
2175 Mission College Blvd Santa Clara (95054) *(P-15511)*

Varian, Palo Alto *Also Called: Varian Medical Systems Inc (P-15588)*

Varian Inc ............................................................................. A ...... 650 213-8000
3100 Hansen Way Palo Alto (94304) *(P-14750)*

Varian Medical Systems Inc ................................................ E ...... 650 213-8000
3120 Hansen Way Palo Alto (94304) *(P-15298)*

Varian Medical Systems Inc ................................................ D ...... 650 493-4000
3045 Hanover St Palo Alto (94304) *(P-15299)*

Varian Medical Systems Inc (DH) ....................................... A ...... 650 493-4000
3100 Hansen Way Palo Alto (94304) *(P-15588)*

Varmour Networks Inc (HQ) ................................................ E ...... 650 564-5100
1825 S Grant St San Mateo (94402) *(P-18911)*

Varni Brothers Corporation ................................................. D ...... 209 464-7778
1109 W Anderson St Stockton (95206) *(P-1971)*

Varni Brothers Corporation (DH) ........................................ D ...... 209 521-1777
400 Hosmer Ave Modesto (95351) *(P-17261)*

Vas Engineering Inc ............................................................ E ...... 858 569-1601
4750 Viewridge Ave San Diego (92123) *(P-13116)*

Vascular Therapies, Irvine *Also Called: Covidien LP (P-15061)*

Vat Incorporated (DH) ......................................................... E ...... 800 935-1446
655 River Oaks Pkwy San Jose (95134) *(P-16905)*

Vaughans Industrial Repair Inc .......................................... E ...... 562 633-2660
16224 Garfield Ave Paramount (90723) *(P-16854)*

Vault Prep Inc ...................................................................... E ...... 310 971-9091
2500 Broadway Ste F125 Santa Monica (90404) *(P-7394)*

Vault Pro ............................................................................... F ...... 800 299-6929
13607 Pumice St Santa Fe Springs (90670) *(P-9301)*

Vave Health Inc .................................................................... F ...... 650 387-7059
3031 Tisch Way San Jose (95128) *(P-15589)*

VAXART, South San Francisco *Also Called: Vaxart Inc (P-5702)*

Vaxart Inc (PA) ..................................................................... E ...... 650 550-3500
170 Harbor Way Ste 300 South San Francisco (94080) *(P-5702)*

VAXCYTE, San Carlos *Also Called: Vaxcyte Inc (P-5867)*

Vaxcyte Inc (PA) .................................................................. D ...... 650 837-0111
825 Industrial Rd Ste 300 San Carlos (94070) *(P-5867)*

Vbc Bottling Co., Modesto *Also Called: Varni Brothers Corporation (P-17261)*

Vbc Holdings Inc .................................................................. E ...... 310 322-7357
134 Main St El Segundo (90245) *(P-1251)*

Vbc Tracy LLC (PA) ............................................................. E ...... 215 259-7509
2302 Paradise Rd Tracy (95304) *(P-3399)*

Vcc, Carlsbad *Also Called: Visual Communications Company LLC (P-13118)*

Vclad Laminates Inc ............................................................ E ...... 626 442-2100
2103 Seaman Ave South El Monte (91733) *(P-6594)*

Vcom Solutions, San Ramon *Also Called: Quantmshift Communications Inc (P-18718)*

Vcp Mobility Holdings Inc ................................................... E ...... 619 213-6500
745 Design Ct Ste 602 Chula Vista (91911) *(P-15426)*

Vcsd Inc ................................................................................ E ...... 619 579-6886
585 Vernon Way El Cajon (92020) *(P-3279)*

Vdp Direct LLC (PA) ............................................................. E ...... 858 300-4510
5520 Ruffin Rd Ste 111 San Diego (92123) *(P-4802)*

Veal Connection Corporation ............................................. E ...... 707 992-0932
1987 Grosse Ave Santa Rosa (95404) *(P-622)*

Vectice Inc ............................................................................ E ...... 650 399-0114
785 Market St Ste 700 San Francisco (94103) *(P-18912)*

Vector, Huntington Beach *Also Called: Vector Launch LLC (P-9141)*

# ALPHABETIC SECTION — Vericool Inc

Vector Data LLC .................................................................. D ...... 408 933-3266
801 Addison St Berkeley (94710) *(P-10216)*

Vector Electronics & Tech Inc ............................................ E ...... 818 985-8208
11115 Vanowen St North Hollywood (91605) *(P-12254)*

Vector Laboratories, Newark *Also Called: Vector Laboratories Inc (P-5868)*

Vector Laboratories Inc (PA) ............................................ D ...... 800 227-6666
6737 Mowry Ave Newark (94560) *(P-5868)*

Vector Launch LLC (PA) ..................................................... E ...... 202 888-3063
15261 Connector Ln Huntington Beach (92649) *(P-9141)*

Vector Resources Inc (PA) ................................................. C ...... 310 436-1000
20917 Higgins Ct Torrance (90501) *(P-473)*

Vectorusa, Torrance *Also Called: Vector Resources Inc (P-473)*

Vectron Inc ......................................................................... F ...... 858 621-2400
345 6th Ave San Diego (92101) *(P-9909)*

Vedabio Inc ........................................................................ F ...... 858 310-1330
11125 Flintkote Ave Ste A San Diego (92121) *(P-5784)*

Veeco Electro Fab Inc ....................................................... E ...... 714 630-8020
1176 N Osprey Cir Anaheim (92807) *(P-12255)*

Veeco Process Equipment Inc ......................................... D ...... 805 967-2700
112 Robin Hill Rd Goleta (93117) *(P-11173)*

Veeco Process Equipment Inc ......................................... D ...... 408 321-8835
355 E Trimble Rd San Jose (95131) *(P-13325)*

Veeco Process Equipment Inc ......................................... C ...... 805 967-1400
112 Robin Hill Rd Goleta (93117) *(P-14751)*

Veeva, Pleasanton *Also Called: Veeva Systems Inc (P-18913)*

Veeva Systems Inc (PA) .................................................... C ...... 925 452-6500
4280 Hacienda Dr Pleasanton (94588) *(P-18913)*

Veex, Fremont *Also Called: Veex Inc (P-14467)*

Veex Inc .............................................................................. F ...... 510 651-0500
2827 Lakeview Ct Fremont (94538) *(P-14467)*

Veezee Inc .......................................................................... E ...... 949 265-0800
121 Waterworks Way Irvine (92618) *(P-2694)*

Vefo Inc ............................................................................... E ...... 909 598-3856
3202 Factory Dr Pomona (91768) *(P-6669)*

Vege - Kurl Inc ................................................................... D ...... 818 956-5582
412 W Cypress St Glendale (91204) *(P-6053)*

Vege-Mist Inc ..................................................................... D ...... 310 353-2300
407 E Redondo Beach Blvd Gardena (90248) *(P-10525)*

Vege-Tech Company, Glendale *Also Called: Vege - Kurl Inc (P-6053)*

Vegetable Growers Supply Co (PA) ................................. E ...... 831 759-4600
1360 Merrill St Salinas (93901) *(P-17312)*

Veinviewer, Cypress *Also Called: Christie Medical Holdings Inc (P-15525)*

VELDONA, San Diego *Also Called: Ainos Inc (P-19437)*

Velher LLC ......................................................................... E ...... 619 494-6310
350 10th Ave Ste 1000 San Diego (92101) *(P-14598)*

Vello Systems Inc ............................................................. F ...... 650 324-7688
1530 Obrien Dr Menlo Park (94025) *(P-11792)*

Velo3d Inc (PA) .................................................................. E ...... 408 610-3915
511 Division St Campbell (95008) *(P-9776)*

Velodyne LLC (HQ) ........................................................... E ...... 669 275-2251
5521 Hellyer Ave San Jose (95138) *(P-18914)*

Velodyne Acoustics Inc ................................................... D ...... 408 465-2800
850 Tanglewood Dr Lafayette (94549) *(P-11712)*

Velodyne Lidar, San Jose *Also Called: Velodyne LLC (P-18914)*

Velodyne Lidar Usa Inc (DH) ........................................... E ...... 669 275-2251
5521 Hellyer Ave San Jose (95138) *(P-13602)*

Velsam, Santa Rosa *Also Called: Veal Connection Corporation (P-622)*

Velti Inc .............................................................................. D
150 California St 10th Fl San Francisco (94111) *(P-18915)*

Velti USA, San Francisco *Also Called: Velti Inc (P-18915)*

Velvet Heart, Los Angeles *Also Called: Tcj Manufacturing LLC (P-2812)*

Ventana Micro Systems Inc ............................................. F ...... 408 816-8852
20813 Stevens Creek Blvd Ste 250 Cupertino (95014) *(P-12783)*

Ventek International, Petaluma *Also Called: Caracal Enterprises LLC (P-10470)*

Ventek International Inc .................................................. E ...... 707 773-3373
1260 Holm Rd Ste A Petaluma (94954) *(P-10472)*

Ventex Corp ....................................................................... E ...... 408 436-2929
2153 Otoole Ave Ste 10 San Jose (95131) *(P-19287)*

Ventritex, Sylmar *Also Called: Pacesetter Inc (P-15570)*

Ventura Aerospace Inc .................................................... F ...... 818 540-3130
31355 Agoura Rd Westlake Village (91361) *(P-13987)*

Ventura Coastal LLC (PA) ................................................ E ...... 805 653-7000
2325 Vista Del Mar Dr Ventura (93001) *(P-1019)*

Ventura County Lemon Coop .......................................... D ...... 805 385-3345
2620 Sakioka Dr Oxnard (93030) *(P-17173)*

Ventura Feed and Pet Sups Inc ....................................... E ...... 805 648-5035
980 E Front St Ventura (93001) *(P-17505)*

Ventura Foods LLC ........................................................... E ...... 323 262-9157
2900 Jurupa St Ontario (91761) *(P-707)*

Ventura Foods LLC ........................................................... D ...... 714 257-3700
2900 Jurupa St Ontario (91761) *(P-1408)*

Ventura Foods LLC (PA) ................................................... C ...... 714 257-3700
40 Pointe Dr Brea (92821) *(P-1409)*

Ventura Harbor Boatyard Inc .......................................... E ...... 805 654-1433
1415 Spinnaker Dr Ventura (93001) *(P-14046)*

Ventura Hydrulic Mch Works Inc .................................... E ...... 805 656-1760
1555 Callens Rd Ventura (93003) *(P-11174)*

Ventura Pacific Co, Oxnard *Also Called: Ventura County Lemon Coop (P-17173)*

Ventura Printing Inc (PA) ................................................. D ...... 805 981-2600
200 N Elevar St Oxnard (93030) *(P-4803)*

Ventura Technology Group .............................................. F ...... 805 581-0800
855 E Easy St Ste 104 Simi Valley (93065) *(P-12784)*

Venturedyne Ltd ............................................................... D ...... 909 793-2788
1320 W Colton Ave Redlands (92374) *(P-10004)*

Ventus Medical Inc ........................................................... E ...... 408 200-5299
1100 La Avenida St Ste A Mountain View (94043) *(P-15300)*

Venus Alloys Inc (PA) ....................................................... E ...... 714 635-8800
1415 S Allec St Anaheim (92805) *(P-7823)*

Venus Bridal Gowns, San Gabriel *Also Called: Lotus Orient Corp (P-2710)*

Venus Concept Inc ........................................................... D ...... 408 489-4925
1800 Bering Dr San Jose (95112) *(P-15301)*

Venus Foods Inc ............................................................... E ...... 626 369-5188
770 S Stimson Ave City Of Industry (91745) *(P-623)*

Venus Group Inc (PA) ....................................................... D ...... 949 609-1299
25861 Wright Foothill Ranch (92610) *(P-16439)*

Venus Laboratories Inc .................................................... D ...... 714 891-3100
11150 Hope St Cypress (90630) *(P-5129)*

Venus Textiles, Foothill Ranch *Also Called: Venus Group Inc (P-16439)*

Veolia Wts Services Usa Inc ........................................... D ...... 562 942-2200
7777 Industry Ave Pico Rivera (90660) *(P-10609)*

Veolia Wts Usa Inc ........................................................... D ...... 805 545-3743
8.5 Miles Nw Avila Beach Avila Beach (93424) *(P-6328)*

Ver Sales Inc (PA) ............................................................. E ...... 818 567-3000
2509 N Naomi St Burbank (91504) *(P-16637)*

Vera Bradley Inc ................................................................ E ...... 858 320-9020
4525 La Jolla Village Dr San Diego (92122) *(P-17501)*

Vera Therapeutics Inc (PA) ............................................. E ...... 650 770-0077
8000 Marina Blvd Ste 120 Brisbane (94005) *(P-5703)*

Veracyte, South San Francisco *Also Called: Veracyte Inc (P-19333)*

Veracyte Inc (PA) .............................................................. D ...... 650 243-6300
6000 Shoreline Ct Ste 300 South San Francisco (94080) *(P-19333)*

Verana Health Inc ............................................................. C ...... 888 774-0077
360 3rd St Ste 425 San Francisco (94107) *(P-18916)*

Veratex, Chatsworth *Also Called: Avitex Inc (P-2401)*

Verb Surgical Inc .............................................................. D ...... 408 438-3363
5490 Great America Pkwy Santa Clara (95054) *(P-15302)*

Vercity Protect Inc ............................................................ F ...... 917 689-0989
1625 El Paseo St San Luis Obispo (93401) *(P-16592)*

Verdagy Inc ....................................................................... F ...... 831 800-0250
11500 Dolan Rd Bldg 17 Moss Landing (95039) *(P-5060)*

Verdant Robotics Inc ....................................................... E ...... 202 510-5040
3167 Corporate Pl Hayward (94545) *(P-9391)*

Verdeco Recycling Inc ..................................................... E ...... 323 537-4617
8685 Bowers Ave South Gate (90280) *(P-16366)*

Verdugo Tool & Engrg Co Inc ......................................... F ...... 818 998-1101
20600 Superior St Chatsworth (91311) *(P-8898)*

Verenium Corporation ..................................................... C ...... 858 431-8500
3550 John Hopkins Ct San Diego (92121) *(P-6166)*

Verge Genomics ................................................................ E ...... 312 489-7455
131 Oyster Point Blvd South San Francisco (94080) *(P-5785)*

Vericool Inc ....................................................................... E ...... 925 337-0808
7066 Las Positas Rd Ste C Livermore (94551) *(P-10036)*

**Veridiam Inc (DH)** .................................................. D ...... 619 448-1000
1717 N Cuyamaca St El Cajon (92020) *(P-9705)*
**Verifone Inc** ........................................................... F ...... 858 436-2270
440 Stevens Ave Ste 200 Solana Beach (92075) *(P-10448)*
**Verifone Intrmdate Hldings Inc** ............................. C ...... 408 232-7800
2099 Gateway Pl San Jose (95110) *(P-10461)*
**Verinata Health Inc** ............................................... D ...... 650 632-1680
200 Lincoln Centre Dr Foster City (94404) *(P-19482)*
**Verint Americas Inc** .............................................. E ...... 408 830-5400
2250 Walsh Ave Ste 120 Santa Clara (95050) *(P-17993)*
**Veris Manufacturing, Brea** Also Called: Q C M Inc *(P-11378)*
**Verisilicon Inc (HQ)** .............................................. F ...... 408 844-8560
2150 Gold St Ste 200 San Jose (95002) *(P-12785)*
**Veristone Products, Jurupa Valley** Also Called: Architectural Veneer Systems *(P-7310)*
**Veritas Software Global LLC** ................................ F ...... 650 335-8000
1600 Plymouth St Mountain View (94043) *(P-18917)*
**Verizon, Los Alamitos** Also Called: Supermedia LLC *(P-4474)*
**Veronica Foods, Oakland** Also Called: Veronica Foods Company *(P-1410)*
**Veronica Foods Company** ................................... E ...... 510 535-6833
1991 Dennison St Oakland (94606) *(P-1410)*
**Versa Products (PA)** ............................................. C ...... 310 353-7100
14105 Avalon Blvd Los Angeles (90061) *(P-3609)*
**Versaclimber, Santa Ana** Also Called: Heart Rate Inc *(P-15820)*
**Versafab Corp (PA)** ............................................... E ...... 800 421-1822
15919 S Broadway Gardena (90248) *(P-8607)*
**Versaform Corporation** ........................................ D ...... 760 599-4477
1377 Specialty Dr Vista (92081) *(P-8608)*
**Versatables.com, Los Angeles** Also Called: Versa Products *(P-3609)*
**Versatile Power Inc** .............................................. E ...... 408 341-4600
743 Camden Ave Ste B Campbell (95008) *(P-15303)*
**Verseon Corporation (PA)** .................................... E ...... 510 225-9000
47000 Warm Springs Blvd Ste 3 Fremont (94539) *(P-5704)*
**Verseon International Corp (PA)** .......................... E ...... 510 225-9000
47000 Warm Springs Blvd Ste 3 Fremont (94539) *(P-5705)*
**Vertechs Enterprises Inc (PA)** .............................. E ...... 858 578-3900
1071 Industrial Pl El Cajon (92020) *(P-7831)*
**Vertechs Enterprises Inc** ..................................... F ...... 858 578-3900
400 Raleigh Ave El Cajon (92020) *(P-13726)*
**Vertex China, Pomona** Also Called: Sky One Inc *(P-7282)*
**Vertex Lcd Inc** ....................................................... E ...... 714 223-7111
600 S Jefferson St Ste K Placentia (92870) *(P-13117)*
**Vertex Phrmctcals San Dego LLC (HQ)** ............... C ...... 858 404-6600
3215 Merryfield Row San Diego (92121) *(P-5706)*
**Vertical Circuits Inc** ............................................. E ...... 831 438-3887
10 Victor Sq Ste 100 Scotts Valley (95066) *(P-12786)*
**Vertical Fiber Technologies, Montebello** Also Called: Vft Inc *(P-2952)*
**Vertiflex Inc** .......................................................... E ...... 442 325-5900
25155 Rye Canyon Loop Valencia (91355) *(P-15304)*
**Vertiv, Irvine** Also Called: Vertiv Corporation *(P-14468)*
**Vertiv Corporation** ............................................... D ...... 949 457-3600
35 Parker Irvine (92618) *(P-14468)*
**Vertos Medical Inc LLC** ........................................ D ...... 949 349-0008
95 Enterprise Ste 325 Aliso Viejo (92656) *(P-15305)*
**Vertosa Inc** ............................................................ E ...... 510 550-5850
1630 N Main St Ste 363 Walnut Creek (94596) *(P-5280)*
**Very Special Chocolats Inc** .................................. C ...... 626 334-7838
760 N Mckeever Ave Azusa (91702) *(P-1347)*
**Verys, Santa Ana** Also Called: Verys LLC *(P-19049)*
**Verys LLC** ............................................................. C ...... 949 423-3295
1251 E Dyer Rd Ste 210 Santa Ana (92705) *(P-19049)*
**Vescio Manufacturing Intl, Santa Fe Springs** Also Called: Vescio Threading Co *(P-11175)*
**Vescio Threading Co** ............................................ D ...... 562 802-1868
14002 Anson Ave Santa Fe Springs (90670) *(P-11175)*
**Vest Tube LLC** ...................................................... D ...... 800 421-6370
6023 Alcoa Ave Los Angeles (90058) *(P-9720)*
**Vesta, Corona** Also Called: Extrumed Inc *(P-6824)*
**Vesture Group Incorporated** ................................ D ...... 818 842-0200
3405 W Pacific Ave Burbank (91505) *(P-2869)*
**Vesuki Inc** ............................................................. F ...... 562 245-4000
1350 W Lambert Rd Ste A Brea (92821) *(P-17656)*

**Vet National Inc** ..................................................... E ...... 805 692-8487
3621 State St Santa Barbara (93105) *(P-16677)*
**Vet National Mail, Santa Barbara** Also Called: Vet National Inc *(P-16677)*
**Vetpowered, San Diego** Also Called: Vetpowered LLC *(P-11176)*
**Vetpowered LLC** .................................................. F ...... 619 269-7116
2717 Boston Ave San Diego (92113) *(P-11176)*
**Vetronix Corporation** ........................................... C ...... 805 966-2000
2030 Alameda Padre Serra Santa Barbara (93103) *(P-13603)*
**Veza Technologies Inc** ......................................... C ...... 510 870-8692
122 Lansberry Ct Los Gatos (95032) *(P-18918)*
**Vft Inc** ................................................................... E ...... 323 728-2280
1040 S Vail Ave Montebello (90640) *(P-2952)*
**VI Degrees Collective, Valencia** Also Called: Solevy Co LLC *(P-6039)*
**Vi-Star Gear Co Inc** .............................................. E ...... 323 774-3750
7312 Jefferson St Paramount (90723) *(P-8792)*
**Via Embedded Store, Fremont** Also Called: Via Technologies Inc *(P-12787)*
**Via Technologies Inc** ........................................... C ...... 510 683-3300
940 Mission Ct Fremont (94539) *(P-12787)*
**Viacyte Inc** ............................................................ D ...... 858 455-3708
5580 Morehouse Dr Ste 100 San Diego (92121) *(P-19498)*
**Vian Enterprises Inc** ............................................. D ...... 530 885-1997
2120 Precision Pl Auburn (95603) *(P-11177)*
**Vianh Company Inc** ............................................. F ...... 714 590-9808
13841 A Better Way Ste 10c Garden Grove (92843) *(P-11178)*
**Viant Medical LLC** ............................................... C ...... 510 657-5800
45581 Northport Loop W Fremont (94538) *(P-7071)*
**VIASAT, Carlsbad** Also Called: Viasat Inc *(P-11971)*
**Viasat Inc (PA)** ...................................................... A ...... 760 476-2200
6155 El Camino Real Carlsbad (92009) *(P-11971)*
**Viavi Solutions Inc** ............................................... F ...... 408 546-5000
1750 Automation Pkwy San Jose (95131) *(P-12788)*
**Viavi Solutions Inc** ............................................... D ...... 408 577-1478
80 Rose Orchard Way San Jose (95134) *(P-12789)*
**Viavi Solutions Inc** ............................................... C ...... 707 545-6440
2789 Northpoint Pkwy Santa Rosa (95407) *(P-13326)*
**Viavi Solutions Inc** ............................................... C ...... 408 546-5000
430 N Mccarthy Blvd Milpitas (95035) *(P-14752)*
**Vibra Finish Co (PA)** ............................................. E ...... 805 578-0033
2220 Shasta Way Simi Valley (93065) *(P-7559)*
**Vibrahone, Simi Valley** Also Called: Vibra Finish Co *(P-7559)*
**Vibrant Sciences LLC** .......................................... C ...... 408 203-9383
3521 Leonard Ct Santa Clara (95054) *(P-14753)*
**Vibrex, Valencia** Also Called: M W Sausse & Co Inc *(P-11332)*
**Vicarious, Union City** Also Called: Vicarious Fpc Inc *(P-16564)*
**Vicarious Fpc Inc** ................................................. E ...... 415 604-3278
1320 Decoto Rd Ste 200 Union City (94587) *(P-16564)*
**Vicolo Pizza, Hayward** Also Called: Vicolo Wholesale LLC *(P-1067)*
**Vicolo Wholesale LLC (PA)** .................................. E ...... 510 475-6019
31112 San Clemente St Hayward (94544) *(P-1067)*
**Victor Packing Inc** ................................................ E ...... 559 673-5908
11687 Rd 27 1/2 Madera (93637) *(P-973)*
**Victor Wire & Cable Inc** ....................................... F ...... 310 842-9933
12915 S Spring St Los Angeles (90061) *(P-7798)*
**Victorville Daily Press, Victorville** Also Called: Gatehouse Media LLC *(P-4121)*
**Victory Archery** .................................................... F ...... 866 934-6565
1945 Kellogg Ave Carlsbad (92008) *(P-17636)*
**Victory Circle Chassis & Parts, Bakersfield** Also Called: Raudmans Craig Victory Circle *(P-17460)*
**Victory Custom Athletics** .................................... E ...... 818 349-8476
2001 Anchor Ct Ste A Newbury Park (91320) *(P-2819)*
**Victory Display & Store Fixs, Compton** Also Called: Gemco Display and Str Fixs LLC *(P-16567)*
**Victory Foam Inc (PA)** .......................................... D ...... 949 474-0690
3 Holland Irvine (92618) *(P-17313)*
**Victory Intl Group LLC** ......................................... C ...... 949 407-5888
14748 Pipeline Ave Ste B Chino Hills (91709) *(P-16953)*
**Victory Koredrry, Huntington Beach** Also Called: Victory Professional Pdts Inc *(P-2820)*
**Victory Professional Pdts Inc** ............................. E ...... 714 887-0621
5601 Engineer Dr Huntington Beach (92649) *(P-2820)*
**Victory Sportswear, Duarte** Also Called: Victory Sportswear Inc *(P-17314)*

# ALPHABETIC SECTION — Virco Mfg Corporation

Victory Sportswear Inc .................................................. E ...... 866 308-0798
2381 Buena Vista St Duarte (91010) *(P-17314)*

Vida & Co .................................................................... E ...... 415 379-4325
353 Kearny St San Francisco (94108) *(P-17503)*

VIDA NUEVA, Los Angeles Also Called: Tidings *(P-4211)*

Videoamp Inc (PA) ........................................................ D ...... 424 272-7774
12121 Bluff Creek Dr Playa Vista (90094) *(P-18919)*

Videomaker Inc ............................................................. E ...... 530 891-8410
645 Mangrove Ave Chico (95926) *(P-4304)*

Videssence LLC (PA) ..................................................... E ...... 626 579-0943
10768 Lower Azusa Rd El Monte (91731) *(P-11505)*

Vidovation Corporation ................................................ F ...... 949 777-5435
1035 N Armando St Ste V Anaheim (92806) *(P-11972)*

Vie De France 108, Vernon Also Called: Vie De France Yamazaki Inc *(P-17611)*

Vie De France Yamazaki Inc ......................................... A ...... 323 582-1241
3046 E 50th St Vernon (90058) *(P-17611)*

Vie-Del Company (PA) ................................................. D ...... 559 834-2525
11903 S Chestnut Ave Fresno (93725) *(P-936)*

Vie-Del Company ......................................................... E ...... 559 896-3065
13363 S Indianola Ave Kingsburg (93631) *(P-1809)*

View Rite Manufacturing ............................................. E ...... 415 468-3856
455 Allan St Daly City (94014) *(P-3676)*

Viewsonic, Brea Also Called: Viewsonic Corporation *(P-10449)*

Viewsonic Corporation (PA) ......................................... C ...... 909 444-8888
10 Pointe Dr Ste 200 Brea (92821) *(P-10449)*

Vigilant Drone Defense Inc .......................................... E ...... 424 275-8282
1055 W 7th St 33rd Fl Los Angeles (90017) *(P-9302)*

Vigilent Corporation (PA) ............................................ E ...... 888 305-4451
1111 Broadway Fl 3 Oakland (94607) *(P-14374)*

Vigobyte Tape Corporation .......................................... A ...... 866 803-8446
2498 Roll Dr Ste 916 San Diego (92154) *(P-10292)*

Vigor Marine LLC ......................................................... D ...... 619 474-4352
1636 Wilson Ave National City (91950) *(P-14022)*

Vigor Systems Inc ........................................................ E ...... 866 748-4467
4660 La Jolla Village Dr Ste 500 San Diego (92122) *(P-11973)*

Vijall Inc ...................................................................... E ...... 818 700-0071
21900 Marilla St Chatsworth (91311) *(P-17251)*

Viking Products, Orange Also Called: Pro Detention Inc *(P-7650)*

Viking Products Inc ..................................................... E ...... 949 379-5100
20 Doppler Irvine (92618) *(P-9706)*

Viking Rubber Products Inc ......................................... F ...... 310 868-5200
2600 Homestead Pl Compton (90220) *(P-6547)*

Viking Therapeutics Inc (PA) ....................................... E ...... 858 704-4660
9920 Pacific Heights Blvd Ste 350 San Diego (92121) *(P-5707)*

Villa Amorosa .............................................................. D ...... 707 967-6272
4045 Saint Helena Hwy Calistoga (94515) *(P-1810)*

Villa Del Lago LLC (PA) ................................................ E ...... 707 963-2134
540 Technology Way Napa (94558) *(P-1811)*

Villa Dolce Gelato, Van Nuys Also Called: Dolce Dolci LLC *(P-798)*

Villa Furniture Mfg Co ................................................. C ...... 714 535-7272
16440 Manning Way Cerritos (90703) *(P-3641)*

Villa International, Cerritos Also Called: Villa Furniture Mfg Co *(P-3641)*

Villa Roma Sausage Co, Ontario Also Called: Heatherfield Foods Inc *(P-601)*

Villa Toscano Winery ................................................... F ...... 209 245-3800
10600 Shenandoah Rd Plymouth (95669) *(P-1812)*

Village Center Ultramar, Palmdale Also Called: Ultramar Inc *(P-6356)*

Village Green Foods Inc .............................................. E ...... 949 261-0111
1732 Kaiser Ave Irvine (92614) *(P-2387)*

Village Instant Printing Inc ......................................... E ...... 209 576-2568
1515 10th St Modesto (95354) *(P-4804)*

Village Marine Technology, Gardena Also Called: Aqua Pro Properties Vii LP *(P-9831)*

Village News Inc ......................................................... E ...... 760 451-3488
41740 Enterprise Cir S Temecula (92590) *(P-4217)*

Vim Tools, La Verne Also Called: Durston Manufacturing Company *(P-7951)*

Vimco, Santa Rosa Also Called: Randal Optimal Nutrients LLC *(P-5624)*

Vin-Max, San Leandro Also Called: MArs Engineering Company Inc *(P-10959)*

Vina Concha Y Tora USA, Hopland Also Called: Fetzer Vineyards *(P-1565)*

Vinatronic Inc ............................................................. F ...... 714 845-3480
15571 Industry Ln Huntington Beach (92649) *(P-12256)*

Vincent Electric Motor Company, Oakland Also Called: Vincent Electric Company *(P-19235)*

Vincent Electric Company (PA) .................................. E ...... 510 639-4500
8383 Baldwin St Oakland (94621) *(P-19235)*

Vincerx Pharma Inc (PA) ............................................ F ...... 650 800-6676
260 Sheridan Ave Ste 400 Palo Alto (94306) *(P-5708)*

Vindicia Inc ................................................................ C ...... 650 264-4700
1000 Sansome St Ste 200 San Francisco (94111) *(P-18920)*

Vine Village Incorporated .......................................... E ...... 707 255-4006
4059 Old Sonoma Rd Napa (94559) *(P-19365)*

Vineburg Wine Company Inc (PA) .............................. E ...... 707 938-5277
2000 Denmark St Sonoma (95476) *(P-1813)*

Vineyard Post Acute, Petaluma Also Called: Petalumaidence Opco LLC *(P-1706)*

Vineyards and Winery, Sebastopol Also Called: Iron Horse Vineyards *(P-1620)*

Vineyards of Monterey, Santa Rosa Also Called: Jackson Family Wines Inc *(P-1628)*

Vino Farms Inc (PA) ................................................... E ...... 209 334-6975
1377 E Lodi Ave Lodi (95240) *(P-95)*

Vino Vault Inc (PA) .................................................... F ...... 323 937-9463
5800 W 3rd St Los Angeles (90036) *(P-1814)*

Vinotheque Wine Cellars ........................................... F ...... 209 466-9463
1738 E Alpine Ave Stockton (95205) *(P-10526)*

Vintage 99 Label Mfg Inc (PA) ................................... E ...... 925 294-5270
611 Enterprise Ct Livermore (94550) *(P-3959)*

Vintage Image, South San Francisco Also Called: The Wine Appreciation Guild Ltd *(P-4350)*

Vintage Production California, Santa Clarita Also Called: California Resources Prod Corp *(P-131)*

Vintage Wine Estates, Santa Rosa Also Called: Vintage Wine Estates Inc CA *(P-1819)*

Vintage Wine Estates Inc CA ..................................... D ...... 800 330-4064
15000 Hwy 12 Glen Ellen (95442) *(P-1815)*

Vintage Wine Estates Inc CA ..................................... D ...... 707 921-2600
1091 Saint Helena Hwy S Saint Helena (94574) *(P-1816)*

Vintage Wine Estates Inc CA ..................................... E ...... 415 495-1350
251 Rhode Island St Ste 203 San Francisco (94103) *(P-1817)*

Vintage Wine Estates Inc CA ..................................... E ...... 805 503-9660
3070 Limestone Way Unit C Paso Robles (93446) *(P-1818)*

Vintage Wine Estates Inc CA (HQ) ............................. E ...... 877 289-9463
205 Concourse Blvd Santa Rosa (95403) *(P-1819)*

Vintellus Inc .............................................................. F ...... 510 972-4710
19918 Wellington Ct Saratoga (95070) *(P-18921)*

Vintners Daughter LLC ............................................. F ...... 415 906-6735
38 Keyes Ave San Francisco (94129) *(P-6054)*

Vintners Distributors Inc ......................................... D ...... 209 551-6422
1728 Oakdale Rd Modesto (95355) *(P-1820)*

Vinventions Usa LLC (PA) ........................................ C ...... 919 460-2200
888 Prospect St La Jolla (92037) *(P-7072)*

Vinyl Technology LLC (PA) ....................................... C ...... 626 443-5257
200 Railroad Ave Monrovia (91016) *(P-3941)*

Vinylvisions Company LLC ...................................... E ...... 800 321-8746
1233 Enterprise Ct Corona (92882) *(P-6116)*

Violin Memory Inc (PA) ........................................... C ...... 650 396-1500
4555 Great America Pkwy Ste 150 Santa Clara (95054) *(P-10293)*

Vionic Group LLC .................................................... D ...... 415 526-6932
4040 Civic Center Dr Ste 430 San Rafael (94903) *(P-7112)*

Vioptix Inc ............................................................... F ...... 510 226-5860
39655 Eureka Dr Newark (94560) *(P-19499)*

VIP Manufacturing & Engrg Corp ............................ D ...... 408 727-6545
1084 Martin Ave Santa Clara (95050) *(P-13727)*

VIP Mfg & Engr, Santa Clara Also Called: VIP Manufacturing & Engrg Corp *(P-13727)*

VIP Rubber Company Inc (PA) ................................ C ...... 562 905-3456
540 S Cypress St La Habra (90631) *(P-6548)*

Viptela Inc .............................................................. E ...... 408 663-6759
510 Mccarthy Blvd Milpitas (95035) *(P-10450)*

Vir Biotechnology Inc (PA) ..................................... B ...... 415 906-4324
1800 Owens St Fl 11 San Francisco (94158) *(P-5869)*

VIRACTA, Cardiff Also Called: Viracta Therapeutics Inc *(P-5709)*

Viracta Therapeutics Inc (PA) ................................ E ...... 858 400-8470
2533 S Coast Highway 101 Ste 210 Cardiff (92007) *(P-5709)*

Virage Logic Corporation (HQ) ............................... B ...... 650 584-5000
700 E Middlefield Rd Bldg C Mountain View (94043) *(P-12790)*

Virco Inc (HQ) ......................................................... E ...... 310 533-0474
2027 Harpers Way Torrance (90501) *(P-16419)*

Virco Mfg Corporation (PA) .................................... D ...... 310 533-0474
2027 Harpers Way Torrance (90501) *(P-3642)*

**Virgil Walker Inc** ............................................................ F ...... 661 797-4101
24856 Avenue Rockefeller Valencia (91355) *(P-8241)*

**VIRGIN GALACTIC, Tustin** *Also Called: Virgin Galactic Holdings Inc (P-14099)*

**Virgin Galactic Holdings Inc (PA)**................................... E ...... 949 774-7640
1700 Flight Way Ste 400 Tustin (92782) *(P-14099)*

**Virgin Orbit Holdings Inc (HQ)**..................................... F ...... 562 388-4400
4022 E Conant St Long Beach (90808) *(P-14327)*

**Virginia Park LLC** ........................................................... F ...... 816 592-0776
2225 Via Cerro Ste A Riverside (92509) *(P-2388)*

**Virginia Park Foods, Riverside** *Also Called: Virginia Park LLC (P-2388)*

**Virginia Sarabian** ........................................................... E ...... 559 493-2900
2816 S Leonard Ave Sanger (93657) *(P-34)*

**Virtis, Los Angeles** *Also Called: Virtis-Us LLC (P-19062)*

**Virtis-Us LLC (PA)**.......................................................... F ...... 855 796-1457
11601 Wilshire Blvd 5th Fl Los Angeles (90025) *(P-19062)*

**Virtium, Rcho Sta Marg** *Also Called: Virtium Technology Inc (P-12791)*

**Virtium Technology Inc** ................................................. E ...... 949 888-2444
30052 Tomas Rcho Sta Marg (92688) *(P-12791)*

**Virtual Technologies Inc** ............................................... E ...... 408 597-3400
1380 Piper Dr Milpitas (95035) *(P-16263)*

**Visalia Electric Motor Service, Visalia** *Also Called: Visalia Electric Motor Sp Inc (P-19236)*

**Visalia Electric Motor Sp Inc** ........................................ E ...... 559 651-0606
7515 W Sunnyview Ave Visalia (93291) *(P-19236)*

**Visby Medical Inc** .......................................................... C ...... 408 650-8878
3010 N 1st St San Jose (95134) *(P-14938)*

**Vishay Siliconix LLC** ..................................................... A ...... 408 988-8000
2585 Junction Ave San Jose (95134) *(P-12792)*

**Vishay Spectoral Electronics, Ontario** *Also Called: Vishay Thin Film LLC (P-12793)*

**Vishay Thin Film LLC** ................................................... E ...... 909 923-3313
4051 Greystone Dr Ontario (91761) *(P-12793)*

**Visible Graphics Inc** ..................................................... F ...... 818 787-0477
9736 Eton Ave Chatsworth (91311) *(P-16063)*

**Vision Aerospace LLC** .................................................. E ...... 818 700-1035
19863 Nordhoff St Northridge (91324) *(P-13988)*

**Vision Collective Inc** .................................................... E ...... 562 597-4000
109 Wappo Ave Calistoga (94515) *(P-4489)*

**Vision Design Studio, Calistoga** *Also Called: Vision Collective Inc (P-4489)*

**Vision Engineering, Palmdale** *Also Called: Vision Engrg Met Stamping Inc (P-11567)*

**Vision Engrg Met Stamping Inc** ................................... D ...... 661 575-0933
114 Grand Cypress Ave Palmdale (93551) *(P-11567)*

**Vision Envelope & Prtg Co Inc (PA)**............................. E ...... 310 324-7062
13707 S Figueroa St Los Angeles (90061) *(P-4013)*

**Vision Imaging Supplies Inc** ....................................... E ...... 818 885-4515
9540 Cozycroft Ave Chatsworth (91311) *(P-15903)*

**Vision Quest Industries Inc** ........................................ C ...... 949 261-6382
1390 Decision St Ste A Vista (92081) *(P-15427)*

**Vision Systems Inc** ...................................................... D ...... 619 258-7300
11322 Woodside Ave N Santee (92071) *(P-7754)*

**Visionaire Lighting, Long Beach** *Also Called: Visionaire Lighting LLC (P-11568)*

**Visionaire Lighting LLC** .............................................. D ...... 310 512-6480
3780 Kilroy Airport Way Long Beach (90806) *(P-11568)*

**Visionary Contact Lens Inc** ........................................ E ...... 714 237-1900
2940 E Miraloma Ave Anaheim (92806) *(P-15624)*

**Visionary Electronics Inc** ........................................... F ...... 415 751-8811
141 Parker Ave San Francisco (94118) *(P-12794)*

**Visionary Sleep LLC** ................................................... D ...... 909 605-2010
2060 S Wineville Ave Ste A Ontario (91761) *(P-3545)*

**Visionary Vr Inc** ........................................................... E ...... 323 868-7443
409 N Plymouth Blvd Los Angeles (90004) *(P-18922)*

**Visioncare Devices Inc** .............................................. E ...... 530 364-2271
6100 Bellevue Ln Anderson (96007) *(P-16593)*

**Visioneer Inc (PA)**........................................................ E ...... 925 251-6300
5696 Stewart Ave Fremont (94538) *(P-10451)*

**Visions Paint Recycling, Sacramento** *Also Called: Visions Recycling Inc (P-16367)*

**Visions Recycling Inc** ................................................ E ...... 916 564-9121
4105 S Market Ct Ste A Sacramento (95834) *(P-16367)*

**Vista Industrial Products Inc** .................................... C ...... 760 599-5050
3210 Executive Rdg Vista (92081) *(P-11179)*

**Vista Metals Corp (PA)**................................................ C ...... 909 823-4278
13425 Whittram Ave Fontana (92335) *(P-7755)*

**Vista Outdoor Inc** ....................................................... E ...... 831 461-7500
5550 Scotts Valley Dr Scotts Valley (95066) *(P-15874)*

**Vista Paint Corporation (PA)**...................................... C ...... 714 680-3800
2020 E Orangethorpe Ave Fullerton (92831) *(P-17351)*

**Vista Point Technologies Inc** .................................... E ...... 408 576-7000
847 Gibraltar Dr Milpitas (95035) *(P-11974)*

**Vista Steel Co Inc** ....................................................... E ...... 805 653-1189
331 W Lewis St Ventura (93001) *(P-400)*

**VISTA STEEL CO INC, Ventura** *Also Called: Vista Steel Co Inc (P-400)*

**Vista Steel Company (PA)**........................................... E ...... 805 964-4732
6100 Francis Botello Rd Ste C Goleta (93117) *(P-8242)*

**Vista Way Corporation** ............................................... E ...... 408 586-8107
472 Vista Way Milpitas (95035) *(P-4805)*

**VISTAGEN, South San Francisco** *Also Called: Vistagen Therapeutics Inc (P-5710)*

**Vistagen Therapeutics Inc**.......................................... E ...... 650 577-3600
343 Allerton Ave South San Francisco (94080) *(P-5710)*

**Visual Communications Company LLC** ................... C ...... 800 522-5546
2173 Salk Ave Ste 175 Carlsbad (92008) *(P-13118)*

**Visual Information Systems Co, Chino** *Also Called: National Sign & Marketing Corp (P-16013)*

**Visualize Led, San Diego** *Also Called: Visualizeled Inc (P-11435)*

**Visualizeled Inc** ........................................................... F ...... 703 919-5559
1531 Rigel St San Diego (92113) *(P-11435)*

**Visualon Inc (PA)**.......................................................... E ...... 408 645-6618
19925 Stevens Creek Blvd Cupertino (95014) *(P-18923)*

**Vit Best, Tustin** *Also Called: Vitabest Nutrition Inc (P-5711)*

**VIT Products Inc** .......................................................... E ...... 760 480-6702
2063 Wineridge Pl Escondido (92029) *(P-8034)*

**Vita Forte Inc (PA)**........................................................ F ...... 831 626-0555
19350 Cachagua Rd Carmel Valley (93924) *(P-362)*

**Vita Juice Corporation** .............................................. D ...... 818 899-1195
10725 Sutter Ave Pacoima (91331) *(P-937)*

**Vita-Herb Nutriceuticals Inc** ..................................... E ...... 714 632-3726
172 E La Jolla St Placentia (92870) *(P-17435)*

**Vita-Pakt Citrus Products Co (PA)**............................ E ...... 626 332-1101
10000 Stockdale Hwy Ste 390 Bakersfield (93311) *(P-938)*

**Vitabest Nutrition Inc (HQ)**........................................ F ...... 714 832-9700
2802 Dow Ave Tustin (92780) *(P-5711)*

**Vitabri Canopies, Huntington Beach** *Also Called: Vae Industries Corporation (P-2987)*

**Vitachrome Graphics, Montrose** *Also Called: Vitachrome Graphics Group Inc (P-4979)*

**Vitachrome Graphics Group Inc** .............................. E ...... 818 957-0900
3710 Park Pl Montrose (91020) *(P-4979)*

**Vitajoy USA Inc** ........................................................... E ...... 626 965-8830
14165 Ramona Ave Chino (91710) *(P-5281)*

**Vital Connect Inc** ....................................................... C ...... 408 963-4600
2870 Zanker Rd Ste 100 San Jose (95134) *(P-15590)*

**Vitalbulk Inc** ............................................................... F ...... 855 885-2855
440 Kings Village Rd Scotts Valley (95066) *(P-786)*

**Vitamins Unlimited, Brea** *Also Called: North West Pharmanaturals Inc (P-5255)*

**Vitatech Nutritional Sciences Inc** ............................. B ...... 714 832-9700
2802 Dow Ave Tustin (92780) *(P-5712)*

**Vitavet Labs Inc** .......................................................... E ...... 818 865-2600
5717 Corsa Ave Westlake Village (91362) *(P-16264)*

**Vitawest Nutraceuticals Inc** ..................................... E ...... 888 557-8012
1502 Arrow Hwy La Verne (91750) *(P-787)*

**Vitek Indus Video Pdts Inc** ....................................... E ...... 661 294-8043
28492 Constellation Rd Valencia (91355) *(P-15671)*

**Vitesse Manufacturing & Dev** .................................. C ...... 805 388-3700
11861 Western Ave Garden Grove (92841) *(P-12795)*

**Vitesse Semiconductor, Garden Grove** *Also Called: Vitesse Manufacturing & Dev (P-12795)*

**Vitrek LLC (PA)**............................................................ E ...... 858 689-2755
12169 Kirkham Rd Ste C Poway (92064) *(P-14599)*

**Vitro Flat Glass LLC** ................................................... C ...... 559 485-4660
3333 S Peach Ave Fresno (93725) *(P-7180)*

**Vitron Electronic Services Inc** .................................. D ...... 408 251-1600
5400 Hellyer Ave San Jose (95138) *(P-12257)*

**Vitron Electronics Mfg & Svcs, San Jose** *Also Called: Vitron Electronic Services Inc (P-12257)*

**Viv Labs Inc** ................................................................ E ...... 650 268-9837
665 Clyde Ave Mountain View (94043) *(P-18924)*

**Viva Concepts, Vernon** *Also Called: Viva Holdings LLC (P-4024)*

**Viva Holdings LLC (PA)**.............................................. F ...... 818 243-1363
4210 Charter St Vernon (90058) *(P-4024)*

## ALPHABETIC SECTION — Vossloh Signaling LLC

Viva Life Science Inc .................................................. C ...... 949 645-6100
350 Paularino Ave Costa Mesa (92626) *(P-17054)*

Viva Print LLC (HQ) .................................................... F ...... 818 243-1363
1025 N Brand Blvd Ste 300 Glendale (91202) *(P-4025)*

VIVANI, Alameda *Also Called: Vivani Medical Inc (P-15306)*

Vivani Medical Inc (PA) ............................................... F ...... 415 506-8462
1350 S Loop Rd Ste 100 Alameda (94502) *(P-15306)*

Vivax-Metrotech, Santa Clara *Also Called: Metrotech Corporation (P-14221)*

Vive Organic Inc ........................................................ E ...... 877 774-9291
2554 Lincoln Blvd Ste 772 Venice (90291) *(P-939)*

Vivid Inc ................................................................... E ...... 408 982-9101
180 E Sunnyoaks Ave Bldg 1 Campbell (95008) *(P-9133)*

Vivint Inc .................................................................. B ...... 805 790-7209
651 N Armstrong Ave Ste 101 Fresno (93727) *(P-14375)*

Vivometrics Inc .......................................................... E ...... 805 667-2225
16030 Ventura Blvd Ste 470 Encino (91436) *(P-15591)*

Vivotein LLC .............................................................. F ...... 918 344-8742
231 S Pleasant Ave Ontario (91761) *(P-1154)*

Vivus, Campbell *Also Called: Vivus LLC (P-5713)*

Vivus LLC (PA) ........................................................... E ...... 650 934-5200
900 E Hamilton Ave Ste 550 Campbell (95008) *(P-5713)*

Viz Cattle Corporation ................................................ E ...... 310 884-5260
17800 Castleton St Ste 435 City Of Industry (91748) *(P-624)*

Viz Media LLC ........................................................... C ...... 415 546-7073
1355 Market St Ste 200 San Francisco (94103) *(P-4305)*

Viz Media Music, San Francisco *Also Called: Viz Media LLC (P-4305)*

Vizcon, San Clemente *Also Called: Traffix Devices Inc (P-12023)*

VIZIO, Irvine *Also Called: Vizio Holding Corp (P-11715)*

Vizio Inc ................................................................... C ...... 213 746-7730
2601 S Bdwy Unit B Los Angeles (90007) *(P-11713)*

Vizio Inc (HQ) ........................................................... C ...... 855 833-3221
39 Tesla Irvine (92618) *(P-11714)*

Vizio Holding Corp (PA) .............................................. E ...... 949 428-2525
39 Tesla Irvine (92618) *(P-11715)*

Vizualogic LLC .......................................................... C ...... 407 509-3421
1493 E Bentley Dr Corona (92879) *(P-9910)*

Vline Industries, Simi Valley *Also Called: Computer Metal Products Corp (P-8414)*

Vmc International LLC ................................................ F ...... 760 723-1498
25799 Jefferson Ave Murrieta (92562) *(P-15493)*

VME Acquisition Corp (PA) .......................................... F ...... 805 384-2748
820 Flynn Rd Camarillo (93012) *(P-15428)*

Vmware, Palo Alto *Also Called: Vmware LLC (P-18925)*

Vmware LLC (HQ) ...................................................... A ...... 650 427-6000
3421 Hillview Ave Palo Alto (94304) *(P-18925)*

Vnomic, Cupertino *Also Called: Vnomic Inc (P-18926)*

Vnomic Inc ................................................................ E ...... 408 641-3810
19925 Stevens Creek Blvd Ste 100 Cupertino (95014) *(P-18926)*

Vnu Business, San Juan Capistrano *Also Called: Emerald X LLC (P-4252)*

Vnus Medical Technologies Inc .................................... E ...... 408 360-7200
5799 Fontanoso Way San Jose (95138) *(P-15307)*

Vocera, San Jose *Also Called: Vocera Communications Inc (P-12024)*

Vocera Communications Inc (HQ) ................................ E ...... 408 882-5100
3030 Orchard Pkwy San Jose (95134) *(P-12024)*

Vode, Sonoma *Also Called: Vode Lighting LLC (P-11506)*

Vode Lighting LLC ..................................................... F ...... 707 996-9898
21684 8th St E Ste 700 Sonoma (95476) *(P-11506)*

Voestalpine High Prfmce Mtls, Walnut *Also Called: Edro Engineering LLC (P-9619)*

Vogue Developement, Irvine *Also Called: Vogue Enterprise Inc (P-16440)*

Vogue Enterprise Inc .................................................. F ...... 949 833-9787
1801 Kettering Irvine (92614) *(P-16440)*

Voice Assist Inc ......................................................... F ...... 949 655-6400
100 Spectrum Center Dr Ste 900 Irvine (92618) *(P-13119)*

Voice of San Diego ..................................................... D ...... 619 325-0525
110 W A St Ste 650 San Diego (92101) *(P-4218)*

Voiceboard Corporation ............................................... F ...... 805 389-3100
473 Post St Camarillo (93010) *(P-10217)*

Volcano, San Diego *Also Called: Philips Image Gded Thrapy Corp (P-15572)*

Volcano Therapeutics, Rancho Cordova *Also Called: Philips Image Gded Thrapy Corp (P-15573)*

Volcom LLC (HQ) ....................................................... C ...... 949 646-2175
1740 Monrovia Ave Costa Mesa (92627) *(P-19142)*

Volex De Mexico, San Ysidro *Also Called: Volex Inc (P-7073)*

Volex Inc .................................................................. E ...... 619 205-4900
511 E San Ysidro Blvd 509 San Ysidro (92173) *(P-7073)*

Volk Enterprises Inc ................................................... D ...... 209 632-3826
618 S Kilroy Rd Turlock (95380) *(P-9241)*

Volta Charging LLC .................................................... D ...... 415 735-5169
155 De Haro St San Francisco (94103) *(P-17787)*

Volta Industries Inc (DH) ............................................. E ...... 415 583-3805
155 De Haro St San Francisco (94103) *(P-16265)*

Voltage Multipliers Inc (PA) ......................................... C ...... 559 651-1402
8711 W Roosevelt Ave Visalia (93291) *(P-12796)*

Volterra Semiconductor LLC (DH) ................................. E ...... 408 601-1000
160 Rio Robles San Jose (95134) *(P-12797)*

Volterra Semiconductor LLC ........................................ C ...... 510 743-1200
3839 Spinnaker Ct Fremont (94538) *(P-12798)*

Voltpost Inc .............................................................. E ...... 908 868-1527
1345 Howard St San Francisco (94103) *(P-13327)*

Voltus Inc ................................................................. E ...... 646 248-4342
2443 Fillmore St Pmb 380-3427 San Francisco (94115) *(P-14376)*

Volume Press, West Sacramento *Also Called: Tackett Volume Press Inc (P-4778)*

Volumetric Bldg Companies LLC ................................... E ...... 623 236-5322
2302 Paradise Rd Tracy (95304) *(P-3321)*

Voluspa, Irvine *Also Called: Flame and Wax Inc (P-16129)*

Vomar, Canoga Park *Also Called: Vomar Products Inc (P-4980)*

Vomar Products Inc ................................................... E ...... 818 610-5115
7800 Deering Ave Canoga Park (91304) *(P-4980)*

Vomela, Santa Fe Springs *Also Called: Vomela Specialty Company (P-4806)*

Vomela Specialty Company ......................................... C ...... 562 944-3853
9810 Bell Ranch Dr Santa Fe Springs (90670) *(P-4806)*

Vomela Specialty Company ......................................... D ...... 650 877-8000
1342 San Mateo Ave South San Francisco (94080) *(P-16064)*

Von Hoppen Ice Cream ............................................... F ...... 858 695-9111
8221 Arjons Dr Ste A San Diego (92126) *(P-818)*

Vonnic Inc ................................................................. E ...... 626 964-2345
16610 Gale Ave City Of Industry (91745) *(P-19063)*

Vons 2030, Stevenson Ranch *Also Called: Vons Companies Inc (P-17390)*

Vons 2111, Newhall *Also Called: Vons Companies Inc (P-17395)*

Vons 2124, Tujunga *Also Called: Vons Companies Inc (P-17393)*

Vons 2381, Corona *Also Called: Vons Companies Inc (P-17394)*

Vons 2407, Brawley *Also Called: Vons Companies Inc (P-17392)*

Vons 2560, Grover Beach *Also Called: Vons Companies Inc (P-17391)*

Vons Companies Inc (DH) ........................................... A ...... 925 467-3000
5918 Stoneridge Mall Rd Pleasanton (94588) *(P-17389)*

Vons Companies Inc ................................................... C ...... 661 254-3570
25850 The Old Rd Stevenson Ranch (91381) *(P-17390)*

Vons Companies Inc ................................................... C ...... 805 481-2492
1758 W Grand Ave Grover Beach (93433) *(P-17391)*

Vons Companies Inc ................................................... C ...... 760 351-3002
475 W Main St Brawley (92227) *(P-17392)*

Vons Companies Inc ................................................... C ...... 818 353-4917
7789 Foothill Blvd Tujunga (91042) *(P-17393)*

Vons Companies Inc ................................................... C ...... 951 278-8284
535 N Mckinley St Corona (92879) *(P-17394)*

Vons Companies Inc ................................................... C ...... 661 259-9214
24160 Lyons Ave Newhall (91321) *(P-17395)*

Voorwood Company .................................................... E ...... 530 365-3311
2350 Barney Rd Anderson (96007) *(P-9757)*

Vorsteiner, Garden Grove *Also Called: Togetherbuycom (P-13588)*

Vorsteiner Inc ........................................................... E ...... 714 379-4600
11621 Markon Dr Garden Grove (92841) *(P-17468)*

Vortech, Oxnard *Also Called: Vortech Engineering Inc (P-10005)*

Vortech Engineering Inc ............................................. E ...... 805 247-0226
1650 Pacific Ave Oxnard (93033) *(P-10005)*

Vortex Doors, Irvine *Also Called: Vortex Industries LLC (P-502)*

Vortex Industries LLC (PA) ......................................... E ...... 714 434-8000
20 Odyssey Irvine (92618) *(P-502)*

Vortox Air Technology Inc .......................................... E ...... 909 621-3843
121 S Indian Hill Blvd Claremont (91711) *(P-10006)*

Vossloh Signaling LLC ................................................ E ...... 530 272-8194
12799 Loma Rica Dr Grass Valley (95945) *(P-17994)*

**Vossloh Signaling Usa Inc** .................................................... E ...... 530 272-8194
12799 Loma Rica Dr Grass Valley (95945) *(P-8793)*

**Votaw, Santa Fe Springs** *Also Called: Votaw Precision Technologies (P-14328)*

**Votaw Precision Technologies** ............................................... C ...... 562 944-0661
13153 Lakeland Rd Santa Fe Springs (90670) *(P-14328)*

**Votaw Wood Products Inc** ...................................................... E ...... 714 871-0932
301 W Imperial Hwy La Habra (90631) *(P-3365)*

**Vox Network Solutions Inc** ..................................................... C ...... 650 989-1000
130 Produce Ave Ste C South San Francisco (94080) *(P-11793)*

**Voyant Beauty, Chatsworth** *Also Called: Aware Products LLC (P-5945)*

**Vpet Usa LLC** ............................................................................ D ...... 909 605-1668
12925b Marlay Ave Fontana (92337) *(P-7074)*

**Vpt Direct, Downey** *Also Called: Vantage Point Products Corp (P-11711)*

**Vsmpo-Tirus US Inc** ................................................................ D ...... 909 230-9020
2850 E Cedar St Ontario (91761) *(P-7770)*

**Vss International Inc (HQ)** ..................................................... D ...... 916 373-1500
3785 Channel Dr West Sacramento (95691) *(P-384)*

**Vti Instruments Corporation (HQ)** ........................................ E ...... 949 955-1894
2031 Main St Irvine (92614) *(P-13328)*

**Vtl Amplifiers Inc** .................................................................... E ...... 909 627-5944
4774 Murietta St Ste 10 Chino (91710) *(P-11716)*

**Vts Medical Systems, Richmond** *Also Called: Steris Corporation (P-15409)*

**Vts Sheetmetal Specialist Co** ................................................ E ...... 714 237-1420
13831 Seaboard Cir Garden Grove (92843) *(P-8609)*

**Vudu Inc** ................................................................................... D ...... 408 492-1010
2901 Tasman Dr Ste 101 Santa Clara (95054) *(P-17546)*

**Vulcan Construction Mtls LLC** ............................................... E ...... 408 213-4270
346 Mathew St Santa Clara (95050) *(P-7518)*

**Vulcan Construction Mtls LLC** ............................................... E ...... 661 810-2285
35800 146th St E Pearblossom (93553) *(P-7519)*

**Vulcan Materials Co** ................................................................ C ...... 760 737-3486
849 W Washington Ave Escondido (92025) *(P-7520)*

**Vulpine Inc** .............................................................................. E ...... 510 534-1186
1127 57th Ave Oakland (94621) *(P-6329)*

**Vurger Co (usa) Corp** .............................................................. E ...... 929 318-9546
1800 Century Park E Ste 600 Los Angeles (90067) *(P-1252)*

**Vxb & Orfwid Inc** ..................................................................... E ...... 213 222-0030
5041 S Santa Fe Ave Unit B Vernon (90058) *(P-2821)*

**Vybion Inc** ............................................................................... F ...... 607 227-2502
584 Oak St Monterey (93940) *(P-5226)*

**Vyshnavi Info Tech India Prvat** .............................................. F ...... 408 454-6218
2603 Camino Ramon Ste 200 San Ramon (94583) *(P-17995)*

**Vytalogy Wellness LLC** .......................................................... C ...... 818 867-4440
15233 Ventura Blvd Sherman Oaks (91403) *(P-5282)*

**W & F Mfg Inc** .......................................................................... E ...... 818 394-6060
10635 Keswick St Sun Valley (91352) *(P-8035)*

**W & W Concept Inc** ................................................................. D ...... 323 803-3090
4890 S Alameda St Vernon (90058) *(P-2822)*

**W A Benjamin Electric Co** ...................................................... E ...... 213 749-7731
1615 Staunton Ave Los Angeles (90021) *(P-11252)*

**W B Mason Co Inc** .................................................................. E ...... 888 926-2766
5911 E Washington Blvd Commerce (90040) *(P-17642)*

**W B Mason Co Inc** .................................................................. E ...... 888 926-2766
4100 Whipple Rd Union City (94587) *(P-17643)*

**W B Powell Inc** ........................................................................ D ...... 951 270-0095
630 Parkridge Ave Norco (92860) *(P-3202)*

**W B Walton Enterprises Inc** .................................................. E ...... 951 683-0930
4185 Hallmark Pkwy San Bernardino (92407) *(P-11975)*

**W C Q, Fremont** *Also Called: West Coast Quartz Corporation (P-7207)*

**W Cellars Inc** ........................................................................... F ...... 714 655-2025
333 S Grand Ave Ste 3400 Los Angeles (90071) *(P-1466)*

**W D Schock Corp** .................................................................... E ...... 951 277-3377
1232 E Pomona St Santa Ana (92707) *(P-14047)*

**W E Plemons McHy Svcs Inc** ................................................. E ...... 559 646-6630
13479 E Industrial Dr Parlier (93648) *(P-10037)*

**W F F H Inc** .............................................................................. F ...... 805 735-9255
216 E Laurel Ave Lompoc (93436) *(P-16266)*

**W G Barr Beverage Company LP** .......................................... E ...... 510 999-4939
2344 Webster St Oakland (94612) *(P-1467)*

**W G Holt Inc** ............................................................................ D ...... 949 859-8800
101 Columbia Aliso Viejo (92656) *(P-12799)*

**W L Gore & Associates Inc** ................................................... C ...... 928 864-2705
2890 De La Cruz Blvd Santa Clara (95050) *(P-15308)*

**W L Rubottom Co** ................................................................... D ...... 805 648-6943
320 W Lewis St Ventura (93001) *(P-3280)*

**W Machine Works Inc** ............................................................ E ...... 818 890-8049
13814 Del Sur St San Fernando (91340) *(P-11180)*

**W O K, Corona** *Also Called: Rayes Inc (P-15397)*

**W P Keith Co Inc** .................................................................... E ...... 562 948-3636
8323 Loch Lomond Dr Pico Rivera (90660) *(P-10062)*

**W Plastics Inc** ......................................................................... 800 442-9727
41573 Dendy Pkwy Ste 2543 Temecula (92590) *(P-6576)*

**W R E Colortech, Berkeley** *Also Called: Western Roto Engravers Inc (P-4983)*

**W R Grace & Co** ...................................................................... F ...... 562 927-8513
7237 E Gage Ave Commerce (90040) *(P-5130)*

**W R Grace & Co-Conn** ............................................................ F ...... 760 244-6107
17434 Mojave St Hesperia (92345) *(P-14754)*

**W R Grace Construction Pdts, Commerce** *Also Called: W R Grace & Co (P-5130)*

**W R Meadows Inc** ................................................................... E ...... 909 469-2606
2300 Valley Blvd Pomona (91768) *(P-7395)*

**W S West, Fresno** *Also Called: Gea Farm Technologies Inc (P-5905)*

**W T E, Ontario** *Also Called: Wallner Expac Inc (P-9749)*

**W T F, Hayward** *Also Called: Western Truck Fabrication Inc (P-13435)*

**W. R. Meadows Southern Cal, Pomona** *Also Called: W R Meadows Inc (P-7395)*

**W/S Packaging Group Inc** ..................................................... E ...... 714 992-2574
531 Airpark Dr Fullerton (92833) *(P-4057)*

**W3II People Inc** ....................................................................... F ...... 800 790-1563
570 10th St # 3 Oakland (94607) *(P-6055)*

**W5 Concepts Inc** ..................................................................... E ...... 323 231-2415
2049 E 38th St Vernon (90058) *(P-2695)*

**Waag, Van Nuys** *Also Called: Wsw Corp (P-13607)*

**Wabash, Moreno Valley** *Also Called: Supreme Truck Bodies Cal Inc (P-13431)*

**Wabash National Trlr Ctrs Inc** .............................................. E ...... 765 771-5300
16025 Slover Ave Fontana (92337) *(P-16405)*

**Wac Lighting, Ontario** *Also Called: Wangs Alliance Corporation (P-11507)*

**Wacker Biotech US Inc** .......................................................... E ...... 858 875-4700
10390 Pacific Center Ct San Diego (92121) *(P-5714)*

**Wacker Chemical Corporation** ............................................. D ...... 909 590-8822
13910 Oaks Ave Chino (91710) *(P-6167)*

**Wadco Industries Inc** ............................................................ E ...... 909 874-7800
2625 S Willow Ave Bloomington (92316) *(P-8243)*

**Wadco Steel Sales, Bloomington** *Also Called: Wadco Industries Inc (P-8243)*

**Waddington North America Inc** ........................................... C ...... 626 913-4022
1135 Samuelson St City Of Industry (91748) *(P-7075)*

**Waev Inc (PA)** .......................................................................... E ...... 714 956-4040
2114 W Ball Rd Anaheim (92804) *(P-9536)*

**Wafer Process Systems Inc** ................................................. F ...... 408 445-3010
3641 Charter Park Dr San Jose (95136) *(P-12800)*

**Wafer Reclaim Services LLC** ................................................ C ...... 408 945-8112
2240 Ringwood Ave San Jose (95131) *(P-12801)*

**Wafergen Bio-Systems Inc** .................................................... D ...... 877 923-3746
34700 Campus Dr Fremont (94555) *(P-14755)*

**Wafergen Biosystems, Fremont** *Also Called: Wafergen Bio-Systems Inc (P-14755)*

**Wafernet Inc** ............................................................................ F ...... 408 437-9747
2142 Paragon Dr San Jose (95131) *(P-12802)*

**Waggl Inc (PA)** ........................................................................ D ...... 415 399-9949
1750 Bridgeway Ste B103 Sausalito (94965) *(P-18927)*

**Wagner Die Supply Inc (PA)** .................................................. E ...... 909 947-3044
2041 Elm Ct Ontario (91761) *(P-9657)*

**Wagner Plate Works West Inc (PA)** ..................................... E ...... 562 531-6050
28100 Shady Meadow Ln Yorba Linda (92887) *(P-8351)*

**Wagner Wine Company, Rutherford** *Also Called: Caymus Vineyards (P-1498)*

**Wahlco, Chino** *Also Called: Wahlco Inc (P-11181)*

**Wahlco Inc** ............................................................................... C ...... 714 979-7300
4774 Murietta St Ste 3 Chino (91710) *(P-11181)*

**Waitwhile Inc** ........................................................................... E ...... 888 983-0869
548 Market St San Francisco (94104) *(P-17996)*

**Wakool Transport** ................................................................... D ...... 626 723-3100
19130 San Jose Ave Rowland Heights (91748) *(P-9537)*

**Wakunaga of America Co Ltd (HQ)** ..................................... D ...... 949 855-2776
23501 Madero Mission Viejo (92691) *(P-5715)*

## ALPHABETIC SECTION — Waterman Valve LLC

**Walashek Industrial & Mar Inc** .......... D ...... 206 624-2880
3890 Industrial Way Benicia (94510) *(P-14023)*

**Walashek Industrial & Mar Inc** .......... E ...... 619 498-1711
1428 Mckinley Ave National City (91950) *(P-14024)*

**Walden Structures Inc** .......... B ...... 909 389-9100
1000 Bristol St N # 126 Newport Beach (92660) *(P-3400)*

**Walin Group Inc** .......... E ...... 714 444-5980
1117 Baker St Ste A Costa Mesa (92626) *(P-10120)*

**Walk Vascular LLC** .......... E ...... 949 752-9642
3200 Lakeside Dr Santa Clara (95054) *(P-16594)*

**Walker, Ontario** Also Called: Walker Spring & Stamping Corp *(P-8899)*

**Walker Design Inc** .......... E ...... 818 252-7788
9255 San Fernando Rd Sun Valley (91352) *(P-14025)*

**Walker Engineering Enterprises, Sun Valley** Also Called: Walker Design Inc *(P-14025)*

**Walker Foods Inc** .......... D ...... 323 268-5191
237 N Mission Rd Los Angeles (90033) *(P-940)*

**Walker Products** .......... E ...... 714 554-5151
14291 Commerce Dr Garden Grove (92843) *(P-13604)*

**WALKER PRODUCTS, Garden Grove** Also Called: Walker Products *(P-13604)*

**Walker Spring & Stamping Corp** .......... C ...... 909 390-4300
1555 S Vintage Ave Ontario (91761) *(P-8899)*

**Wallaby Organic, American Canyon** Also Called: Wallaby Yogurt Company LLC *(P-819)*

**Wallaby Yogurt Company LLC** .......... E ...... 855 925-4636
110 Mezzetta Ct Ste B American Canyon (94503) *(P-819)*

**Wallace E Miller Inc** .......... F ...... 818 998-0444
9155 Alabama Ave Ste B Chatsworth (91311) *(P-11182)*

**Wallace Wood Products** .......... F ...... 951 654-9311
1247 S Buena Vista St Ste C San Jacinto (92583) *(P-3677)*

**Wallner Expac Inc (PA)** .......... D ...... 909 481-8800
1274 S Slater Cir Ontario (91761) *(P-9749)*

**Wally & Pat Enterprises** .......... E ...... 310 532-2031
13530 S Budlong Ave Gardena (90247) *(P-16267)*

**Wally's Natural Products, Auburn** Also Called: Wallys Natural *(P-17315)*

**Wallys Natural** .......... E ...... 530 887-0396
11837 Kemper Rd Ste 5 Auburn (95603) *(P-17315)*

**Walmart, Lodi** Also Called: Walmart Inc *(P-17364)*

**Walmart Inc** .......... E ...... 209 368-6658
1601 S Lower Sacramento Rd Ste A Lodi (95242) *(P-17364)*

**Walt, Saint Helena** Also Called: Hall Wines LLC *(P-1608)*

**Walt Dsney Imgnring RES Dev In** .......... E ...... 714 781-3152
1200 N Miller St Unit D Anaheim (92806) *(P-2913)*

**Walt Pinot Noir** .......... F ...... 707 933-4440
380 1st St W Sonoma (95476) *(P-1821)*

**Walter Foster Publishing Inc** .......... E ...... 949 380-7510
6 Orchard Ste 100 Lake Forest (92630) *(P-4353)*

**Walter N Coffman Inc** .......... D ...... 619 266-2642
5180 Naranja St San Diego (92114) *(P-6670)*

**Walters & Wolf Glass Company** .......... D ...... 510 226-9800
41450 Cowbell Rd Fremont (94538) *(P-7396)*

**Walters & Wolf Precast** .......... C ...... 510 226-9800
41450 Boscell Rd Fremont (94538) *(P-7397)*

**Walters Wholesale Electric Co (HQ)** .......... E ...... 714 784-1900
200 N Berry St Brea (92821) *(P-16678)*

**Walton Company Inc** .......... E ...... 714 847-8800
17900 Sampson Ln Huntington Beach (92647) *(P-3430)*

**Walton Electric Corporation** .......... C ...... 909 981-5051
755 N Central Ave Ste A Upland (91786) *(P-12025)*

**Walton Industries Inc** .......... E ...... 559 495-4004
1220 E North Ave Fresno (93725) *(P-6117)*

**Wamco Inc (PA)** .......... F ...... 714 545-5560
17752 Fitch Irvine (92614) *(P-16679)*

**Waneshear Technologies LLC** .......... E ...... 707 462-4761
3471 N State St Ukiah (95482) *(P-9758)*

**Wangs Alliance Corporation** .......... E ...... 909 230-9401
1750 S Archibald Ave Ontario (91761) *(P-11507)*

**Warco, Orange** Also Called: West American Rubber Co LLC *(P-6549)*

**Warco, Orange** Also Called: West American Rubber Co LLC *(P-6550)*

**Wardley Industrial Inc** .......... E ...... 209 932-1088
907 Stokes Ave Stockton (95210) *(P-6671)*

**Ware Jared Construction, Olivehurst** Also Called: Builtware Fabrication Inc *(P-19246)*

**Warlock Industries** .......... E ...... 951 657-2680
23129 Cajalco Rd Ste A Perris (92570) *(P-13397)*

**Warmboard Inc** .......... E ...... 831 685-9276
100 Enterprise Way Ste G300 Scotts Valley (95066) *(P-10063)*

**Warmelin Precision Products, Hawthorne** Also Called: DL Horton Enterprises Inc *(P-10814)*

**Warner Chappell Music Inc (DH)** .......... C ...... 310 441-8600
777 S Santa Fe Ave Los Angeles (90021) *(P-4490)*

**Warner Enterprises Inc** .......... E ...... 530 241-4000
1577 Beltline Rd Redding (96003) *(P-3060)*

**Warner Geometric Music, Los Angeles** Also Called: Warner Chappell Music Inc *(P-4490)*

**Warren & Baerg Mfg Inc** .......... E ...... 559 591-6790
39950 Road 108 Dinuba (93618) *(P-9392)*

**Warren Collins and Assoc Inc (PA)** .......... E ...... 909 548-6708
300 E Eucalyptus Ave Ontario (91762) *(P-401)*

**Warren E & P, Long Beach** Also Called: Warren E&P Inc *(P-202)*

**Warren E&P Inc** .......... D ...... 214 393-9688
400 Oceangate Ste 200 Long Beach (90802) *(P-202)*

**Wasco Hardfacing Co** .......... D ...... 559 485-5860
4585 E Citron Ave Fresno (93725) *(P-9393)*

**Wasco Sales and Marketing Inc** .......... E ...... 805 739-2747
2245 A St Santa Maria (93455) *(P-11477)*

**Wasco Switches & Sensors, Santa Maria** Also Called: Wasco Sales and Marketing Inc *(P-11477)*

**Washington Garment Dyeing (PA)** .......... E ...... 213 747-1111
1341 E Washington Blvd Los Angeles (90021) *(P-2501)*

**Washington Grment Dyg Fnshg In** .......... E ...... 213 747-1111
1332 E 18th St Los Angeles (90021) *(P-2498)*

**Washington Iron Works, Gardena** Also Called: Washington Orna Ir Works Inc *(P-579)*

**Washington Orna Ir Works Inc (PA)** .......... D ...... 310 327-8660
17926 S Broadway Gardena (90248) *(P-579)*

**Washington Orna Ir Works Inc** .......... E ...... 310 327-8660
17913 S Main St Gardena (90248) *(P-8649)*

**Washoe Equipment Inc** .......... F ...... 916 395-4700
6201 27th St Sacramento (95822) *(P-11508)*

**Wasser Filtration Inc (PA)** .......... D ...... 714 696-6450
1215 N Fee Ana St Anaheim (92807) *(P-10121)*

**Wastech Controls & Engrg LLC** .......... D ...... 818 998-3500
20600 Nordhoff St Chatsworth (91311) *(P-16855)*

**Watch L.A., Los Angeles** Also Called: Pierre Mitri *(P-2799)*

**Water Associates LLC** .......... E ...... 661 281-6077
5060 California Ave Bakersfield (93309) *(P-11976)*

**Water Filter Exchange Inc** .......... F ...... 818 808-2541
875 N Todd Ave Azusa (91702) *(P-10122)*

**Water One, Benicia** Also Called: Water One Industries Inc *(P-10610)*

**Water One Industries Inc (PA)** .......... E ...... 707 747-4300
5410 Gateway Plaza Dr Benicia (94510) *(P-10610)*

**Water Purification, Rancho Dominguez** Also Called: Parker-Hannifin Corporation *(P-12850)*

**Water Restoration Inc** .......... F ...... 760 673-7374
31855 Date Palm Dr Ste 3 Cathedral City (92234) *(P-580)*

**Water Treatment Plant, Riverside** Also Called: City of Riverside *(P-10548)*

**Water Treatment Services, Chico** Also Called: B and F Solutions Inc *(P-10542)*

**Water Well Solutions, Exeter** Also Called: Willitts Eqp & Engrg Co Inc *(P-17360)*

**Water Works Inc** .......... E ...... 858 499-0119
5490 Complex St Ste 601 San Diego (92123) *(P-10611)*

**Water Works Manufacturing, Marysville** Also Called: US Pipe Fabrication LLC *(P-6604)*

**Wateranywhere, Vista** Also Called: Applied Membranes Inc *(P-10536)*

**Waterco of Central States Inc** .......... E ...... 916 290-4591
1908 D St Sacramento (95811) *(P-1972)*

**Watercrest Inc** .......... E ...... 909 390-3944
4850 E Airport Dr Ontario (91761) *(P-8352)*

**Waterfi LLC** .......... F ...... 619 438-0058
4379 30th St Ste 2 San Diego (92104) *(P-16741)*

**Waterford Almond Hller Sheller, Waterford** Also Called: Riddle Ranches Inc *(P-41)*

**Waterfront Design Group LLC** .......... E ...... 213 746-5800
122 E Washington Blvd Los Angeles (90015) *(P-2650)*

**Waterman Industries, Exeter** Also Called: Waterman Industries Inc *(P-9194)*

**Waterman Industries, Exeter** Also Called: Waterman Valve LLC *(P-10612)*

**Waterman Industries Inc** .......... D ...... 559 562-8661
25500 Road 204 Exeter (93221) *(P-9194)*

**Waterman Valve LLC (HQ)** .......... C ...... 559 562-4000
25500 Road 204 Exeter (93221) *(P-10612)*

# Watermark — ALPHABETIC SECTION

**Watermark, Riverside** *Also Called: Irrometer Company Inc (P-14886)*

**Waters Edge Wineries Inc** ............................................. E ...... 909 468-9463
8560 Vineyard Ave Ste 408 Rancho Cucamonga (91730) *(P-1822)*

**Waters Edge Winery, Rancho Cucamonga** *Also Called: Waters Edge Wineries Inc (P-1822)*

**Watersentinel, Temecula** *Also Called: Aquamor LLC (P-10539)*

**Watershed Technology Inc (PA)** ................................... D ...... 650 561-5438
360 9th St San Francisco (94103) *(P-18928)*

**Waterstone Faucets, Murrieta** *Also Called: Waterstone Faucets LLC (P-16772)*

**Waterstone Faucets LLC** ................................................ C ...... 951 304-0520
41180 Raintree Ct Murrieta (92562) *(P-16772)*

**Waterway Plastics, Oxnard** *Also Called: B & S Plastics Inc (P-6730)*

**Watkins Manufacturing Corp** ........................................ B ...... 760 598-6464
1325 Hot Springs Way Vista (92081) *(P-6688)*

**Watkins Manufacturing Corp (HQ)** ............................... C ...... 760 598-6464
1280 Park Center Dr Vista (92081) *(P-16268)*

**Watkins Wellness, Vista** *Also Called: Watkins Manufacturing Corp (P-16268)*

**Watson Marlow Fluid Tech Group, San Jose** *Also Called: Asepco (P-9144)*

**Watts Machining Inc** ...................................................... E ...... 408 654-9300
3370 Victor Ct Santa Clara (95054) *(P-11183)*

**Watts Regulator Co** ........................................................ C ...... 530 666-2493
1485 Tanforan Ave Woodland (95776) *(P-9163)*

**Watts Water Technology, Woodland** *Also Called: Watts Regulator Co (P-9163)*

**Wattzon, Mountain View** *Also Called: Glyntai Inc (P-18354)*

**Wave Community Newspapers Inc (PA)** ....................... E ...... 323 290-3000
1007 N Sepulveda Blvd Manhattan Beach (90266) *(P-4219)*

**Wavenet Inc (PA)** ........................................................... F ...... 310 885-4200
707 E Sepulveda Blvd Carson (90745) *(P-7799)*

**Wavestream Corporation (HQ)** ..................................... C ...... 909 599-9080
545 W Terrace Dr San Dimas (91773) *(P-13120)*

**Wawona Frozen Foods (PA)** .......................................... C ...... 559 299-2901
100 W Alluvial Ave Clovis (93611) *(P-2389)*

**Wax Jean By Ambiance, Los Angeles** *Also Called: Ambiance USA Inc (P-2734)*

**Way Out West Inc** .......................................................... F ...... 310 769-6937
1440 W 135th St Gardena (90249) *(P-2604)*

**Way To Be Designs LLC** ................................................ E ...... 510 476-6200
30987 San Clemente St Hayward (94544) *(P-17316)*

**Wayfarers, Alamo** *Also Called: Edner Corporation (P-1189)*

**Wayne** ............................................................................ E ...... 669 206-2179
640 W California Ave Sunnyvale (94086) *(P-788)*

**Wayne Tool & Die Co** .................................................... E ...... 818 364-1611
15853 Olden St Sylmar (91342) *(P-7632)*

**Waynes Tire Inc (PA)** .................................................... F ...... 805 928-2661
895 Via Las Aguilas Arroyo Grande (93420) *(P-19156)*

**Waytobe Prmtonal Pdts Uniforms, Hayward** *Also Called: Way To Be Designs LLC (P-17316)*

**Wb Machining & Mech Design** ..................................... E ...... 408 453-5005
1670 Zanker Rd San Jose (95112) *(P-11184)*

**Wb Music Corp (DH)** ..................................................... C ...... 310 441-8600
10585 Santa Monica Blvd Ste 200 Los Angeles (90025) *(P-4491)*

**Wbi Inc** .......................................................................... A ...... 800 673-4968
8201 Woodley Ave Van Nuys (91406) *(P-15672)*

**Wbt Group LLC** ............................................................. E ...... 323 735-1201
1401 S Shamrock Ave Monrovia (91016) *(P-16269)*

**Wbt Industries, Monrovia** *Also Called: Wbt Group LLC (P-16269)*

**Wc, Fairfield** *Also Called: West-Com Nrse Call Systems Inc (P-11977)*

**Wc Music Corp., Los Angeles** *Also Called: Wb Music Corp (P-4491)*

**Wcbm Company (PA)** .................................................... E ...... 323 262-3274
1812 W 135th St Gardena (90249) *(P-15922)*

**Wcp Solutions, Sacramento** *Also Called: West Coast Paper Company (P-16907)*

**Wcp West Coast Glass LLC** ........................................... D ...... 562 653-9797
17730 Crusader Ave Cerritos (90703) *(P-7076)*

**Wcr Incorporated** .......................................................... F ...... 559 266-8374
4636 E Drummond Ave Fresno (93725) *(P-19288)*

**Wcs Distributing Inc** ..................................................... E ...... 909 888-2015
268 W Orange Show Ln San Bernardino (92408) *(P-16856)*

**Wcs Equipment Holdings LLC** ..................................... D ...... 909 993-5700
1350 E Lexington Ave Pomona (91766) *(P-7700)*

**Wcs Equipment Holdings LLC (HQ)** ........................... E ...... 909 393-8405
13568 Vintage Pl Chino (91710) *(P-7701)*

**Wcs Equipment Holdings LLC** ..................................... D ...... 909 393-8405
13066 14th St Chino (91710) *(P-8610)*

**WD, San Jose** *Also Called: Western Digital Tech Inc (P-10297)*

**WD Media LLC** .............................................................. B ...... 408 576-2000
1710 Automation Pkwy San Jose (95131) *(P-10294)*

**Wd-40 Company** ........................................................... C ...... 619 275-1400
9715 Businesspark Ave San Diego (92131) *(P-6358)*

**WD-40 Company (PA)** .................................................. C ...... 619 275-1400
9715 Businesspark Ave San Diego (92131) *(P-6401)*

**We Do Graphics Inc** ...................................................... E ...... 714 997-7390
1150 N Main St Orange (92867) *(P-4807)*

**We Imagine Inc** ............................................................. D ...... 818 709-0064
9371 Canoga Ave Chatsworth (91311) *(P-12258)*

**We Own Everything Records LLC** ............................... F ...... 323 208-9454
620 W Huntington Dr Unit 103 Arcadia (91007) *(P-5008)*

**We The Pie People LLC** ................................................ E ...... 818 349-1880
9909 Topanga Canyon Blvd # 159 Chatsworth (91311) *(P-820)*

**We're Organized Northern Cal, Rancho Cordova** *Also Called: Garage Cabinet Warehouse Inc (P-489)*

**Wealthfront Corporation** ............................................. E ...... 650 249-4258
261 Hamilton Ave Ste 10 Palo Alto (94301) *(P-17735)*

**Weapons System Division, Northridge** *Also Called: Northrop Grumman Systems Corp (P-14242)*

**Wearlinq Inc** .................................................................. E ...... 650 785-8742
1819 Polk St Pmb 148 San Francisco (94109) *(P-16595)*

**Weartech International Inc** .......................................... E ...... 714 683-2430
1177 N Grove St Anaheim (92806) *(P-9956)*

**Weatherford International LLC** ................................... F ...... 805 933-0242
201 Hallock Dr Santa Paula (93060) *(P-291)*

**Web Traffic School, Oakland** *Also Called: Interactive Solutions Inc (P-18426)*

**Webedoctor Inc** ............................................................. F ...... 714 990-3999
335 N Puente St Ste B Brea (92821) *(P-18929)*

**Weber, Rancho Cucamonga** *Also Called: American Fruits & Flavors LLC (P-1984)*

**Weber Drilling Co Inc** .................................................. E ...... 310 670-7708
4028 W 184th St Torrance (90504) *(P-11185)*

**Weber Metals Inc (HQ)** ................................................ E ...... 562 602-0260
16706 Garfield Ave Paramount (90723) *(P-8804)*

**Weber Metals Inc** .......................................................... B ...... 562 543-3316
233 E Manville St Compton (90220) *(P-8805)*

**Weber Orthopedic LP (PA)** .......................................... D ...... 800 221-5465
1185 E Main St Santa Paula (93060) *(P-15429)*

**Weber Precision Graphics, Santa Ana** *Also Called: Artisan Nameplate Awards Corp (P-4843)*

**Weber Printing Company Inc** ...................................... E ...... 310 639-5064
1124 E Del Amo Blvd Long Beach (90807) *(P-4808)*

**Webmetro** ...................................................................... D ...... 909 599-8885
160 Via Verde Ste 1 San Dimas (91773) *(P-18930)*

**Webroot Inc** .................................................................. E ...... 650 292-6600
1855 S Grant St Ste 100 San Mateo (94402) *(P-18931)*

**Webtoon Entertainment Inc (PA)** ............................... A ...... 323 297-3410
5700 Wilshire Blvd Ste 220 Los Angeles (90036) *(P-4492)*

**Weckerle Cosmetic, Torrance** *Also Called: Weckerle Cosmetics Usa Inc (P-17055)*

**Weckerle Cosmetics Usa Inc** ........................................ E ...... 310 328-7000
525 Maple Ave Torrance (90503) *(P-17055)*

**Weco, Woodland** *Also Called: Woodside Electronics Corp (P-19291)*

**Weddingolala, City Of Industry** *Also Called: Orbitel International LLC (P-4934)*

**Wedemeyer Bakery, South San Francisco** *Also Called: Windmill Corporation (P-1255)*

**Wedgewood Connect** .................................................... E ...... 855 321-3477
17 Great Oaks Blvd San Jose (95119) *(P-5716)*

**Weekend Balita, La Crescenta** *Also Called: Balita Media Inc (P-4072)*

**Weeks Drilling and Pump Co (PA)** .............................. E ...... 707 823-3184
6100 Sebastopol Ave Sebastopol (95472) *(P-440)*

**Wehah Farm Inc** ............................................................ B ...... 530 538-3500
5311 Midway Richvale (95974) *(P-1085)*

**Wehah-Lundberg Inc** .................................................... C ...... 530 882-4551
5311 Midway Richvale (95974) *(P-1086)*

**WEI Laboratories Inc** ................................................... E ...... 408 970-8700
3002 Scott Blvd Santa Clara (95054) *(P-872)*

**WEI-Chuan USA Inc (PA)** ............................................. C ...... 626 225-7168
6655 Garfield Ave Bell Gardens (90201) *(P-17124)*

**Weider Health and Fitness** .......................................... B ...... 818 884-6800
21100 Erwin St Woodland Hills (91367) *(P-2032)*

**Weidner Archtctral Sgng/Huse S** ................................ D ...... 800 561-7446
5001 24th St Sacramento (95822) *(P-16065)*

# ALPHABETIC SECTION — West Coast Metal Stamping

**Weidnerca, Sacramento** *Also Called: Weidner Archtctral Sgng/Huse S (P-16065)*

**Weiser Lock Corporation** ................................................. F ...... 949 672-4000
19701 Da Vinci Foothill Ranch (92610) *(P-8036)*

**Weiss Sheet Metal Company** ........................................... E ...... 310 354-2700
1715 W 135th St Gardena (90249) *(P-518)*

**Weiss-Mcnair LLC (DH)** ................................................... D ...... 530 891-6214
100 Loren Ave Chico (95928) *(P-9394)*

**Welaco, Bakersfield** *Also Called: Well Analysis Corporation Inc (P-3061)*

**Welbilt Fdsrvice Companies LLC** .................................... B ...... 323 245-3761
1210 N Red Gum St Anaheim (92806) *(P-10527)*

**Welbilt Inc** ............................................................................ E ...... 310 339-1555
3835 E Thousand Oaks Blvd Unit 315 Westlake Village (91362) *(P-292)*

**Welcome Skateboards Inc** ................................................ E ...... 949 305-9200
26792 Vista Ter Lake Forest (92630) *(P-15875)*

**Weld-It Co, Orange** *Also Called: Sam Schaffer Inc (P-19280)*

**Weld-On Adhesives, Compton** *Also Called: Ips Corporation (P-6234)*

**Weldcraft Industries Inc** ................................................... F ...... 559 784-4322
18794 Avenue 96 Terra Bella (93270) *(P-9395)*

**Weldex Corporation** .......................................................... B ...... 714 761-2100
6751 Katella Ave Cypress (90630) *(P-12803)*

**Weldlogic Inc** ..................................................................... D ...... 805 375-1670
2651 Lavery Ct Newbury Park (91320) *(P-19219)*

**Weldlogic Gas & Supply, Newbury Park** *Also Called: Weldlogic Inc (P-19219)*

**Weldmac Manufacturing Company** ................................ C ...... 619 440-2300
1451 N Johnson Ave El Cajon (92020) *(P-11186)*

**Weldmac Manufacturing Company** ................................ E ...... 619 440-2300
1533 N Johnson Ave El Cajon (92020) *(P-11187)*

**Weldstone Portable Welders, Anaheim** *Also Called: Lodestone LLC (P-9726)*

**Weldway Inc** ........................................................................ E ...... 209 847-8083
521 Hi Tech Pkwy Oakdale (95361) *(P-8244)*

**Well Above Bottling & Canning** ....................................... E ...... 916 918-1946
8250 Industrial Ave Roseville (95678) *(P-7187)*

**Well Analysis Corporation Inc (PA)** ................................ E ...... 661 283-9510
5500 Woodmere Dr Bakersfield (93313) *(P-3061)*

**Wella Corporation (HQ)** ................................................... C ...... 800 422-2336
4500 Park Granada # 100 Calabasas (91302) *(P-6056)*

**Wellex Corporation (PA)** ................................................... C ...... 510 743-1818
551 Brown Rd Fremont (94539) *(P-13121)*

**Wellington Foods Inc (PA)** .............................................. C ...... 951 547-7000
1930 California Ave Corona (92881) *(P-789)*

**Wells Dental Inc** ................................................................ F ...... 707 937-0521
5860 Flynn Creek Rd Comptche (95427) *(P-15494)*

**Wells Media Group Inc (PA)** ............................................ F ...... 619 584-1100
3570 Camino Del Rio N Ste 100 San Diego (92108) *(P-19341)*

**Wells Precision Machining, Comptche** *Also Called: Wells Dental Inc (P-15494)*

**Wells Struthers Corporation** ........................................... E ...... 814 726-1000
10375 Slusher Dr Santa Fe Springs (90670) *(P-8353)*

**Welovefine, Los Angeles** *Also Called: Mf Inc (P-2680)*

**Wems Inc (PA)** ................................................................... D ...... 310 644-0251
4650 W Rosecrans Ave Hawthorne (90250) *(P-10007)*

**Wems Electronics, Hawthorne** *Also Called: Wems Inc (P-10007)*

**Wen U Luv Liquidation LLC** ............................................. E ...... 323 456-8821
8383 Wilshire Blvd Ste 800 Beverly Hills (90211) *(P-17502)*

**Wente Bros** ......................................................................... E ...... 925 456-2286
7701 Las Positas Rd Livermore (94551) *(P-1823)*

**Wente Bros** ......................................................................... E ...... 831 674-5642
37995 Elm Ave Greenfield (93927) *(P-1824)*

**Wente Bros (PA)** ................................................................ D ...... 925 456-2300
5050 Arroyo Rd Livermore (94550) *(P-19546)*

**Wente Brothers Winery, Greenfield** *Also Called: Wente Bros (P-1824)*

**Wente Family Estates, Livermore** *Also Called: Wente Bros (P-1823)*

**Wente Vineyards, Livermore** *Also Called: Wente Bros (P-19546)*

**Wepower LLC** ..................................................................... E ...... 866 385-9463
32 Journey Ste 250 Aliso Viejo (92656) *(P-9321)*

**Werfen, San Diego** *Also Called: Inova Diagnostics Inc (P-19456)*

**Werner Co** ........................................................................... E ...... 209 383-3989
1810 Grogan Ave Merced (95341) *(P-9303)*

**Werner Corporation** .......................................................... E ...... 951 277-4586
25050 Maitri Rd Corona (92883) *(P-7521)*

**Wes Go Inc** ......................................................................... E ...... 818 504-1200
8211 Lankershim Blvd North Hollywood (91605) *(P-4981)*

**Wes Manufacturing Inc** .................................................... E ...... 408 727-0750
431 Greenwood Dr Santa Clara (95054) *(P-11188)*

**Wesanco Inc** ...................................................................... E ...... 714 739-4989
14870 Desman Rd La Mirada (90638) *(P-13989)*

**Wescam Sonoma Operations, Santa Rosa** *Also Called: L-3 Cmmnications Sonoma Eo Inc (P-15647)*

**Wesfac Inc (HQ)** ................................................................ F ...... 562 861-2160
9300 Hall Rd Downey (90241) *(P-10613)*

**Wesley Allen Inc** ................................................................ C ...... 323 231-4275
1001 E 60th St Los Angeles (90001) *(P-3516)*

**Wespac, Downey** *Also Called: Wesfac Inc (P-10613)*

**Wessco International, Los Angeles** *Also Called: Wessco Intl Ltd A Cal Ltd Prtn (P-3039)*

**Wessco Intl Ltd A Cal Ltd Prtn (PA)** ............................... D ...... 310 477-4272
11400 W Olympic Blvd Ste 450 Los Angeles (90064) *(P-3039)*

**Wessex Industries Inc** ...................................................... E ...... 562 944-5760
8619 Red Oak St Rancho Cucamonga (91730) *(P-9273)*

**West American Rubber Co LLC (PA)** .............................. C ...... 714 532-3355
1337 W Braden Ct Orange (92868) *(P-6549)*

**West American Rubber Co LLC** ...................................... C ...... 714 532-3355
750 N Main St Orange (92868) *(P-6550)*

**West Area Opportunity Center, Santa Monica** *Also Called: Casa De Hermandad (P-15798)*

**West Bay Imports Inc** ....................................................... E ...... 323 720-5777
7245 Oxford Way Commerce (90040) *(P-17317)*

**West Bent Bolt Division, Santa Fe Springs** *Also Called: Mid-West Fabricating Co (P-13539)*

**West Bond Inc (PA)** .......................................................... E ...... 714 978-1551
1551 S Harris Ct Anaheim (92806) *(P-11189)*

**West Cast Stl Proc Hldings LLC (PA)** ............................. E ...... 909 393-8405
13568 Vintage Pl Chino (91710) *(P-7633)*

**West Coast Aerospace Inc (PA)** ...................................... D ...... 310 518-3167
220 W E St Wilmington (90744) *(P-15923)*

**West Coast Aerospace Inc** .............................................. F ...... 310 518-0633
24224 Broad St Carson (90745) *(P-16906)*

**West Coast Beauty Supply Co** ........................................ A ...... 707 748-4800
5001 Industrial Way Benicia (94510) *(P-16911)*

**West Coast Button Mfg Co, Gardena** *Also Called: Wcbm Company (P-15922)*

**West Coast Catrg Trcks Mfg Inc** ..................................... F ...... 323 278-1279
1217 Goodrich Blvd Commerce (90022) *(P-3459)*

**West Coast Chain Mfg Co** ............................................... E ...... 909 923-7800
4245 Pacific Privado Ontario (91761) *(P-13329)*

**West Coast Corporation** .................................................. E ...... 909 923-7800
4245 Pacific Privado Ontario (91761) *(P-13330)*

**West Coast Coupon Inc** ................................................... E ...... 818 341-2400
9400 Oso Ave Chatsworth (91311) *(P-17792)*

**West Coast Cryogenics Inc** ............................................. E ...... 800 657-0545
503 W Larch Rd Ste K Tracy (95304) *(P-9911)*

**West Coast Cryogenics Services, Tracy** *Also Called: West Coast Cryogenics Inc (P-9911)*

**West Coast Energy Systems LLC (HQ)** .......................... D ...... 209 870-1900
7100 Longe St Ste 300 Stockton (95206) *(P-19430)*

**West Coast Fab Inc** .......................................................... F ...... 510 529-0177
700 S 32nd St Richmond (94804) *(P-8611)*

**West Coast Foundry LLC (HQ)** ....................................... E ...... 323 583-1421
2450 E 53rd St Huntington Park (90255) *(P-7702)*

**West Coast Furn Framers Inc** ......................................... E ...... 760 669-5275
24006 Tahquitz Rd Apple Valley (92307) *(P-3103)*

**West Coast Gasket Co** ..................................................... D ...... 714 869-0123
300 Ranger Ave Brea (92821) *(P-6471)*

**West Coast Iron Inc** .......................................................... D ...... 619 464-8456
9302 Jamacha Rd Spring Valley (91977) *(P-551)*

**West Coast Labels, Placentia** *Also Called: Cinton LLC (P-3947)*

**West Coast Laboratories Inc** .......................................... E ...... 310 527-6163
156 E 162nd St Gardena (90248) *(P-5717)*

**West Coast Laboratories Inc (PA)** .................................. F ...... 323 321-4774
116 E Alondra Blvd Gardena (90248) *(P-5718)*

**West Coast Machining Inc** .............................................. F ...... 562 229-1087
14560 Marquardt Ave Santa Fe Springs (90670) *(P-11190)*

**West Coast Magnetics, Stockton** *Also Called: Wjlp Company Inc (P-12864)*

**West Coast Manufacturing, Stanton** *Also Called: West Coast Manufacturing Inc (P-8900)*

**West Coast Manufacturing Inc** ....................................... E ...... 714 897-4221
11822 Western Ave Stanton (90680) *(P-8900)*

**West Coast Metal Stamping, Irvine** *Also Called: Perfect Choice Mfrs Inc (P-16200)*

## ALPHABETIC SECTION

West Coast Metal Stamping Incorporated .................... E ...... 714 792-0322
  550 W Crowther Ave Placentia (92870) *(P-8901)*

West Coast Mfg & Whsng, Ontario *Also Called: Idx Los Angeles LLC (P-3691)*

West Coast Milling, Lancaster *Also Called: Pavement Recycling Systems Inc (P-6367)*

West Coast Motor Sports, Perris *Also Called: West Coast Yamaha Inc (P-10074)*

West Coast Naturals LLC .................... E ...... 310 467-3007
  4585 Firestone Blvd South Gate (90280) *(P-2033)*

West Coast Operations, Chula Vista *Also Called: East Cast Repr Fabrication LLC (P-8133)*

West Coast Paper Company .................... E ...... 916 599-1113
  600 Sequoia Pacific Blvd Sacramento (95811) *(P-16907)*

West Coast Pvd Inc .................... E ...... 714 822-6362
  3280 Corporate Vw Vista (92081) *(P-9032)*

West Coast Quartz Corporation (HQ) .................... D ...... 510 249-2160
  1000 Corporate Way Fremont (94539) *(P-7207)*

West Coast Sales Office & Whse, Oxnard *Also Called: Amiad USA Inc (P-10533)*

West Coast Service Center, Ontario *Also Called: Vsmpo-Tirus US Inc (P-7770)*

West Coast Surfaces Inc .................... E ...... 951 699-0600
  27620 Commerce Center Dr Ste 107 Temecula (92590) *(P-507)*

West Coast Switchgear (DH) .................... D ...... 562 802-3441
  13837 Bettencourt St Cerritos (90703) *(P-11253)*

West Coast Trends Inc .................... E ...... 714 843-9288
  17811 Jamestown Ln Huntington Beach (92647) *(P-15876)*

West Coast Trimming Corp .................... E ...... 323 587-0701
  7100 Wilson Ave Los Angeles (90001) *(P-2456)*

West Coast Venture Capital LLC (PA) .................... D ...... 408 725-0700
  10050 Bandley Dr Cupertino (95014) *(P-11794)*

West Coast Vinyl Windows, Cerritos *Also Called: Wcp West Coast Glass LLC (P-7076)*

West Coast Welding & Cnstr .................... F ...... 805 604-1222
  390 S Del Norte Blvd Oxnard (93030) *(P-19220)*

West Coast Wldg & Piping Inc .................... D ...... 805 246-5841
  760 W Hueneme Rd Oxnard (93033) *(P-19221)*

West Coast Wood Preserving LLC .................... C ...... 661 833-0429
  5601 District Blvd Bakersfield (93313) *(P-3405)*

West Coast Yamaha Inc .................... E ...... 951 943-2061
  1622 Illinois Ave Perris (92571) *(P-10074)*

West Coast-Accudyne Inc .................... E ...... 562 927-2546
  7180 Scout Ave Bell (90201) *(P-9592)*

West Grant Vineyards, Geyserville *Also Called: Sbragia Family Vineyards LLC (P-1742)*

West Lake Food Corporation (PA) .................... E ...... 714 973-2286
  301 N Sullivan St Santa Ana (92703) *(P-625)*

West Newport Oil Company .................... E ...... 949 631-1100
  5300 W Coast Hwy Newport Beach (92663) *(P-146)*

West Point Spc Contg Inc .................... F ...... 619 784-2524
  2704 Transportation Ave Ste C National City (91950) *(P-9446)*

West Publishing Corporation .................... A ...... 800 747-3161
  5161 Lankershim Blvd North Hollywood (91601) *(P-4354)*

West Publishing Corporation .................... A ...... 619 296-7862
  2801 Camino Del Rio S San Diego (92108) *(P-4493)*

West Star Industries, Stockton *Also Called: Hackett Industries Inc (P-9795)*

West Valley Aviation Inc .................... F ...... 559 659-7378
  1011 12th St Firebaugh (93622) *(P-13990)*

West Valley Plating Inc .................... F ...... 818 709-1684
  21061 Superior St Ste A Chatsworth (91311) *(P-9033)*

West Valley Precision Inc .................... E ...... 408 519-5959
  2055 Otoole Ave San Jose (95131) *(P-8902)*

West Wood Products Inc (PA) .................... F ...... 310 631-8978
  2943 E Las Hermanas St Compton (90221) *(P-16460)*

West-Bag Inc .................... E ...... 323 264-0750
  1161 Monterey Pass Rd Monterey Park (91754) *(P-7077)*

West-Com Nrse Call Systems Inc (PA) .................... E ...... 707 428-5900
  2200 Cordelia Rd Fairfield (94534) *(P-11977)*

West-Mark, Ceres *Also Called: Certified Stainless Svc Inc (P-8306)*

West-Mark, Atwater *Also Called: Certified Stainless Svc Inc (P-8307)*

West-Tech Mechanical Inc .................... F ...... 909 635-1170
  5589 Brooks St Ste A Montclair (91763) *(P-441)*

Westaire Engineering Inc .................... F ...... 323 587-3347
  5820 S Alameda St Vernon (90058) *(P-10528)*

Westak, Sunnyvale *Also Called: Qualitek Inc (P-12196)*

Westak, Sunnyvale *Also Called: Qualitek Inc (P-12197)*

Westak Inc (PA) .................... D ...... 408 734-8686
  1116 Elko Dr Sunnyvale (94089) *(P-12259)*

Westak International Sales Inc (HQ) .................... C ...... 408 734-8686
  1116 Elko Dr Sunnyvale (94089) *(P-12260)*

Westar Nutrition Corp (PA) .................... E ...... 949 645-6100
  350 Paularino Ave Costa Mesa (92626) *(P-5283)*

Westates Inc .................... E ...... 714 523-7600
  6800 Orangethorpe Ave Ste H Buena Park (90620) *(P-17676)*

Westates Automotive Promotions, Buena Park *Also Called: Westates Inc (P-17676)*

Westbridge, Vista *Also Called: San Group Biotech Usa Inc (P-6206)*

Westco, Livermore *Also Called: Westco Iron Works Inc (P-8246)*

Westco Industries Inc .................... E ...... 909 874-8700
  2625 S Willow Ave Bloomington (92316) *(P-8245)*

Westco Iron Works Inc (PA) .................... D ...... 925 961-9152
  1080 Concannon Blvd Ste 110 Livermore (94550) *(P-8246)*

Westcoast Brush Mfg Inc .................... E ...... 909 627-7170
  1330 Philadelphia St Pomona (91766) *(P-15933)*

Westcoast Iron, Spring Valley *Also Called: West Coast Iron Inc (P-551)*

Westcoast Precision Inc .................... D ...... 408 943-9998
  2091 Fortune Dr San Jose (95131) *(P-9912)*

Westcoast Rotor Inc .................... E ...... 310 327-5050
  119 W 154th St Gardena (90248) *(P-16857)*

Westcott Designs Inc .................... E ...... 510 367-7229
  4455 Park Rd Benicia (94510) *(P-3460)*

Westec Plastics Corporation .................... D ...... 925 454-3400
  6757 Las Positas Rd Ste A Livermore (94551) *(P-7078)*

Westech Inv Advisors LLC (HQ) .................... E ...... 650 234-4300
  104 La Mesa Dr Ste 102 Portola Valley (94028) *(P-1050)*

Westech Products Inc (PA) .................... E ...... 951 279-4496
  1242 Enterprise Ct Corona (92882) *(P-15888)*

Westech Wax Products, Corona *Also Called: Westech Products Inc (P-15888)*

Westeel Builders .................... F ...... 858 524-4353
  287 Vernon Way El Cajon (92020) *(P-8247)*

Western Allied Corporation .................... E ...... 562 944-6341
  12046 Florence Ave Santa Fe Springs (90670) *(P-442)*

Western Bagel Baking Corp (PA) .................... C ...... 818 786-5847
  7814 Sepulveda Blvd Van Nuys (91405) *(P-1253)*

Western Bagel Baking Corp .................... E ...... 818 887-5451
  21749 Ventura Blvd Woodland Hills (91364) *(P-1254)*

Western Bay Sheet Metal Inc .................... E ...... 619 233-1753
  1410 Hill St El Cajon (92020) *(P-8248)*

Western Blended Products, West Sacramento *Also Called: Sacramento Stucco Co (P-16483)*

Western Cactus Growers Inc .................... E ...... 760 726-1710
  1860 Monte Vista Dr Vista (92084) *(P-9402)*

Western Case Incorporated .................... D ...... 951 214-6380
  231 E Alessandro Blvd Riverside (92508) *(P-7079)*

WESTERN CITY MAGAZINE, Sacramento *Also Called: League of California Cities (P-19550)*

Western Cnc Inc .................... D ...... 760 597-7000
  1001 Park Center Dr Vista (92081) *(P-11191)*

Western Concrete Products, Pleasanton *Also Called: Central Precast Concrete Inc (P-7317)*

Western Converting Spc Inc .................... E ...... 909 392-4578
  15601 Cypress Ave Baldwin Park (91706) *(P-4982)*

Western Corrugated Design Inc .................... E ...... 562 695-9295
  8741 Pioneer Blvd Santa Fe Springs (90670) *(P-3894)*

Western Costume Co (HQ) .................... E ...... 818 760-0900
  11041 Vanowen St North Hollywood (91605) *(P-17776)*

Western Design, Irvine *Also Called: Meggitt Western Design Inc (P-14364)*

Western Digital .................... D ...... 510 557-7553
  19600 S Western Ave Torrance (90501) *(P-13122)*

Western Digital, Milpitas *Also Called: Sandisk LLC (P-10274)*

WESTERN DIGITAL, San Jose *Also Called: Western Digital Corporation (P-10295)*

Western Digital, Irvine *Also Called: Western Digital Corporation (P-13123)*

Western Digital Corporation (PA) .................... A ...... 408 717-6000
  5601 Great Oaks Pkwy San Jose (95119) *(P-10295)*

Western Digital Corporation .................... E ...... 949 672-7000
  3337 Michelson Dr Irvine (92612) *(P-10296)*

Western Digital Corporation .................... E ...... 949 672-7000
  3355 Michelson Dr Ste 100 Irvine (92612) *(P-13123)*

Western Digital Tech Inc (HQ) .................... A ...... 408 801-1000
  5601 Great Oaks Pkwy San Jose (95119) *(P-10297)*

Western Dning - Schneider Cafe .................... F ...... 559 292-1981
  3500 Never Forget Ln Clovis (93612) *(P-13331)*

**Western Dovetail Incorporated** .......................................... E ...... 707 556-3683
1101 Nimitz Ave Ste 209 Vallejo (94592) *(P-3461)*

**Western Electrical Advg Co** .......................................... E ...... 760 352-0471
853 S Dogwood Rd El Centro (92243) *(P-16066)*

**Western Environmental Inc** .......................................... E ...... 760 396-0222
62150 Gene Welmas Dr Mecca (92254) *(P-14377)*

**Western Equipment Mfg, Corona** *Also Called: Western Equipment Mfg Inc (P-9447)*

**Western Equipment Mfg Inc** .......................................... E ...... 951 284-2000
1160 Olympic Dr Corona (92881) *(P-9447)*

**Western Fab Inc** .......................................... F ...... 760 949-1441
9823 E Ave Hesperia (92345) *(P-9304)*

**Western Fabricators, Hesperia** *Also Called: Western Fab Inc (P-9304)*

**Western Fiberglass Inc (PA)** .......................................... E ...... 707 523-2050
1555 Copperhill Pkwy Santa Rosa (95403) *(P-7208)*

**Western Filter A Division of Donaldson Company Inc** .......................................... D ...... 661 295-0800
26235 Technology Dr Valencia (91355) *(P-10123)*

**Western Foam, Newark** *Also Called: Induspac California Inc (P-5164)*

**Western Foods LLC** .......................................... C ...... 530 601-5991
440 N Pioneer Ave Ste 200 Woodland (95776) *(P-1068)*

**Western Gage Corporation** .......................................... E ...... 805 445-1410
3316 Maya Linda Ste A Camarillo (93012) *(P-9707)*

**Western Golf Car Mfg Inc** .......................................... D ...... 760 671-6691
69391 Dillon Rd Desert Hot Springs (92241) *(P-15877)*

**Western Golf Car Sales Co, Desert Hot Springs** *Also Called: Western Golf Car Mfg Inc (P-15877)*

**Western Grinding Service Inc** .......................................... E ...... 650 591-2635
2375 De La Cruz Blvd Santa Clara (95050) *(P-11192)*

**Western Hardware Company** .......................................... F ...... 909 595-6201
161 Commerce Way Walnut (91789) *(P-8037)*

**Western Highway Products, Huntington Beach** *Also Called: Primus Inc (P-16021)*

**Western Hose & Gasket, National City** *Also Called: Westflex Inc (P-6435)*

**Western Hydrostatics Inc (PA)** .......................................... E ...... 951 784-2133
1956 Keats Dr Riverside (92501) *(P-10636)*

**Western Insulfoam, Chino** *Also Called: Carlisle Construction Mtls LLC (P-16489)*

**Western Integrated Mtls Inc (PA)** .......................................... E ...... 562 634-2823
3310 E 59th St Long Beach (90805) *(P-3203)*

**Western Lighting Inds Inc** .......................................... E ...... 626 969-6820
12203 Magnolia Ave Ste 1 Riverside (92503) *(P-16680)*

**Western Meat Processing Inc** .......................................... E ...... 209 521-1843
725 Zeff Rd Modesto (95351) *(P-626)*

**Western Mesquite Mines Inc** .......................................... E ...... 928 341-4653
6502 E Us Highway 78 Brawley (92227) *(P-7714)*

**Western Metal Supply Co Inc** .......................................... F ...... 760 233-7800
530 State Pl Escondido (92029) *(P-8689)*

**Western Methods, Santa Ana** *Also Called: Western Methods Machinery Corporation (P-13991)*

**Western Methods Machinery Corporation** .......................................... C ...... 949 252-6600
2344 Pullman St Santa Ana (92705) *(P-13991)*

**Western Mfg & Distrg LLC** .......................................... E ...... 805 988-1010
835 Flynn Rd Camarillo (93012) *(P-14075)*

**Western Mill Fabricators Inc** .......................................... E ...... 714 993-3667
670 S Jefferson St Ste B Placentia (92870) *(P-3753)*

**Western Mountaineering, San Jose** *Also Called: Seventh Heaven Inc (P-3036)*

**Western Oil & Spreading, Martinez** *Also Called: Michael Telfer (P-376)*

**Western Oilfields Supply Co (PA)** .......................................... C ...... 661 399-9124
3404 State Rd Bakersfield (93308) *(P-17865)*

**Western Operations, Rancho Cucamonga** *Also Called: Gentex Corporation (P-19454)*

**Western Outdoor News, San Clemente** *Also Called: Western Outdoors Publications (P-4220)*

**Western Outdoors Publications (PA)** .......................................... E ...... 949 366-0030
901 Calle Amanecer Ste 115 San Clemente (92673) *(P-4220)*

**Western Pacific Signal LLC** .......................................... F ...... 510 276-6400
15890 Foothill Blvd San Leandro (94577) *(P-12026)*

**Western Pavement Preservation, Modesto** *Also Called: George Reed Inc (P-522)*

**Western PCF Stor Solutions Inc (PA)** .......................................... D ...... 909 451-0303
300 E Arrow Hwy San Dimas (91773) *(P-3714)*

**Western Plastics Temecula, Temecula** *Also Called: W Plastics Inc (P-6576)*

**Western Precision Aero LLC** .......................................... E ...... 714 893-7999
11600 Monarch St Garden Grove (92841) *(P-11193)*

**Western Printing and Label, Orange** *Also Called: Westlabel LLC (P-4810)*

**Western Psychological Services, Torrance** *Also Called: Manson Western LLC (P-4335)*

**Western Pump Inc (PA)** .......................................... D ...... 619 239-9988
3235 F St San Diego (92102) *(P-19289)*

**Western Quartz Products Inc** .......................................... F ...... 805 238-3524
2432 Spring St Paso Robles (93446) *(P-11436)*

**Western Real Estate News, South San Francisco** *Also Called: Business Extension Bureau Ltd (P-4233)*

**Western Refining Inc** .......................................... D ...... 510 538-1679
25225 Mission Blvd Hayward (94544) *(P-16858)*

**Western Refining Inc** .......................................... D ...... 310 834-1297
22232 Wilmington Ave Carson (90745) *(P-16859)*

**Western Refining Inc** .......................................... D ...... 323 264-8500
4357 E Cesar E Chavez Ave Los Angeles (90022) *(P-16860)*

**Western Refining Inc** .......................................... D ...... 714 708-2200
1201 Baker St Costa Mesa (92626) *(P-16861)*

**Western Roto Engravers Inc** .......................................... E ...... 510 525-2950
1225 6th St Berkeley (94710) *(P-4983)*

**Western Saw, Oxnard** *Also Called: Western Saw Manufacturers Inc (P-7971)*

**Western Saw Manufacturers Inc** .......................................... E ...... 805 981-0999
3200 Camino Del Sol Oxnard (93030) *(P-7971)*

**Western Sheld Acquisitions LLC (PA)** .......................................... F ...... 310 527-6212
3760 Kilroy Airport Way Ste 500 Long Beach (90806) *(P-4829)*

**Western Sign Company Inc** .......................................... E ...... 916 933-3765
6221a Enterprise Dr Ste A Diamond Springs (95619) *(P-16067)*

**Western Sign Systems, San Marcos** *Also Called: Western Sign Systems Inc (P-16068)*

**Western Sign Systems Inc** .......................................... E ...... 760 736-6070
261 S Pacific St San Marcos (92078) *(P-16068)*

**Western Square Industries Inc** .......................................... E ...... 209 944-0921
1621 N Brdwy Stockton (95205) *(P-8650)*

**Western Stabilization, Dixon** *Also Called: J & A Jeffery Inc (P-16153)*

**Western State Design Inc** .......................................... D ...... 510 786-9271
2331 Tripaldi Way Hayward (94545) *(P-10475)*

**Western States Envelope Corp** .......................................... D ...... 714 449-0909
2301 Raymer Ave Fullerton (92833) *(P-4984)*

**Western States Glass, Long Beach** *Also Called: Total Mont LLC (P-7243)*

**Western States Glass, Sacramento** *Also Called: Wsglass Holdings Inc (P-14833)*

**Western States Packaging Inc** .......................................... E ...... 818 686-6045
13276 Paxton St Pacoima (91331) *(P-3988)*

**Western States Wholesale Inc (PA)** .......................................... D ...... 909 947-0028
1420 S Bon View Ave Ontario (91761) *(P-7304)*

**Western States Wholesale Inc** .......................................... C ...... 909 947-0028
1600 E Francis St Ontario (91761) *(P-7305)*

**Western Supreme Inc** .......................................... C ...... 213 627-3861
846 Produce Ct Los Angeles (90021) *(P-702)*

**Western Telematic Inc** .......................................... E ...... 949 586-9950
5 Sterling Irvine (92618) *(P-10452)*

**Western Truck Fabrication Inc** .......................................... E ...... 510 785-9994
1923 W Winton Ave Hayward (94545) *(P-13435)*

**Western Tube & Conduit Corp (HQ)** .......................................... D ...... 310 537-6300
2001 E Dominguez St Long Beach (90810) *(P-11484)*

**Western Valve, Bakersfield** *Also Called: Western Valve Inc (P-9164)*

**Western Valve Inc** .......................................... E ...... 661 327-7660
201 Industrial St Bakersfield (93307) *(P-9164)*

**Western Web, Samoa** *Also Called: Western Web Inc (P-4809)*

**Western Web Inc** .......................................... E ...... 707 444-6236
1900 Bendixsen St Ste 2 Samoa (95564) *(P-4809)*

**Westfab Manufacturing Inc** .......................................... E ...... 408 727-0550
3370 Keller St Santa Clara (95054) *(P-8612)*

**Westfall Technik, Walnut** *Also Called: 10 Day Parts Inc (P-6689)*

**Westfall Technik, Walnut** *Also Called: AMS Plastics Inc (P-6716)*

**Westfall Technik, Riverside** *Also Called: AMS Plastics Inc (P-6717)*

**Westfall Technik, Walnut** *Also Called: Fairway Injection Molds Inc (P-9622)*

**Westflex Inc (PA)** .......................................... E ...... 619 474-7400
325 W 30th St National City (91950) *(P-6435)*

**Westgate Hardwoods Inc (PA)** .......................................... E ...... 530 892-0300
9296 Midway Durham (95938) *(P-3204)*

**Westgate Manufacturing, Vernon** *Also Called: Westgate Mfg Inc (P-13332)*

**Westgate Mfg Inc** .......................................... D ...... 323 826-9490
2462 E 28th St Vernon (90058) *(P-13332)*

**Westin, San Dimas** *Also Called: Westin Automotive Products Inc (P-3020)*

**Westin Automotive Products Inc (PA)** .......................................... E ...... 626 960-6762
320 W Covina Blvd San Dimas (91773) *(P-3020)*

**Westinghouse A Brake Tech Corp** .......................................... E ...... 707 459-5563
452 E Hill Rd Willits (95490) *(P-7281)*

**Westlabel LLC (PA)** ............................................................ E ...... 714 532-3946
675 N Main St Orange (92868) *(P-4810)*

**Westlake Audio Inc (PA)** ...................................................... F ...... 805 499-3686
2696 Lavery Ct Ste 18 Newbury Park (91320) *(P-11717)*

**Westlake Royal Stone LLC** ................................................... D ...... 800 255-1727
3817 Ocean Ranch Blvd Oceanside (92056) *(P-7550)*

**Westland Technologies Inc** .................................................. D ...... 800 877-7734
107 S Riverside Dr Modesto (95354) *(P-6478)*

**Westmark, Atwater** *Also Called: Certified Stainless Svc Inc (P-8305)*

**Westmont Industries LLC (PA)** ............................................. F ...... 562 944-6137
10805 Painter Ave Uppr Santa Fe Springs (90670) *(P-9504)*

**Westport Scandinavia, Watsonville** *Also Called: Nordic Naturals Inc (P-1386)*

**Westridge Laboratories Inc** .................................................. E ...... 714 259-9400
1671 E Saint Andrew Pl Santa Ana (92705) *(P-6057)*

**Westrock Cp LLC** ................................................................... D ...... 951 273-7900
2577 Research Dr Corona (92882) *(P-4811)*

**Westrock Rkt LLC** ................................................................. C ...... 559 441-1181
1854 E Home Ave Fresno (93703) *(P-3816)*

**Westrock Rkt LLC** ................................................................. E ...... 714 978-2895
749 N Poplar St Orange (92868) *(P-3895)*

**Westrock Rkt LLC** ................................................................. E ...... 559 497-1662
3366 E Muscat Ave Fresno (93725) *(P-3896)*

**Westrock Rkt LLC** ................................................................. D ...... 818 729-0610
100 E Tujunga Ave Ste 102 Burbank (91502) *(P-3897)*

**Westrock Rkt LLC** ................................................................. D ...... 559 567-3501
1401 S Madera Ave Kerman (93630) *(P-3898)*

**Westside Accessories Inc (PA)** ............................................. F ...... 626 858-5452
8920 Vernon Ave Ste 128 Montclair (91763) *(P-2886)*

**Westside Bldg San Diego LLC** .............................................. E ...... 858 566-4343
11620 Sorrento Valley Rd San Diego (92121) *(P-16461)*

**Westside Building Materials, San Jose** *Also Called: Central Concrete Supply Co Inc (P-7433)*

**Westside Building Materials, San Diego** *Also Called: Westside Bldg San Diego LLC (P-16461)*

**Westside Equipment Co (DH)** ............................................... F ...... 209 856-4700
2500 W Industrial Ave Madera (93637) *(P-16803)*

**Westside Pallet Inc** ............................................................... E ...... 209 862-3941
2138 L St Newman (95360) *(P-3366)*

**Westside Resources Inc** ....................................................... E ...... 800 944-3939
8350 Research Dr Irvine (92618) *(P-15495)*

**Westwood Building Materials Co** ........................................ E ...... 310 643-9158
15708 Inglewood Ave Lawndale (90260) *(P-7522)*

**Westwood Laboratories LLC** ................................................ E ...... 626 969-3305
766 S Ayon Ave Azusa (91702) *(P-6058)*

**Westwood Laboratories LLC (PA)** ........................................ E ...... 626 969-3305
710 S Ayon Ave Azusa (91702) *(P-6059)*

**Wet (PA)** ................................................................................ C ...... 818 769-6200
10847 Sherman Way Sun Valley (91352) *(P-19143)*

**Wet Design, Sun Valley** *Also Called: Wet (P-19143)*

**Wetmore Cutting Tools, Chino** *Also Called: Wetmore Tool and Engrg Co (P-9708)*

**Wetmore Tool and Engrg Co** ................................................ D ...... 909 364-1000
5091 G St Chino (91710) *(P-9708)*

**Wetzels Pretzels LLC** ............................................................ E ...... 619 588-1074
525 Parkway Plz Unit 525 El Cajon (92020) *(P-17422)*

**Wfb Archives Inc** .................................................................. D
13500 Danielson St Poway (92064) *(P-12261)*

**Wg, Campbell** *Also Called: Wg Security Products Inc (P-13333)*

**WG Best Weinkellerei Inc** ..................................................... F ...... 858 627-1747
868 W E St San Diego (92101) *(P-1825)*

**Wg Security Products Inc (PA)** ............................................ E ...... 408 241-8000
591 W Hamilton Ave Ste 260 Campbell (95008) *(P-13333)*

**Whalen Furniture Manufacturing, San Diego** *Also Called: Whalen LLC (P-3462)*

**Whalen LLC (DH)** ................................................................. E ...... 619 423-9948
1578 Air Wing Rd San Diego (92154) *(P-3462)*

**Whaley, Kevin Enterprises, Santee** *Also Called: Kevin Whaley (P-9221)*

**Whaling Packaging Co** ......................................................... E ...... 310 518-6021
21020 S Wilmington Ave Carson (90810) *(P-16311)*

**Wham-O Inc** .......................................................................... D ...... 818 963-4200
6301 Owensmouth Ave Ste 700 Woodland Hills (91367) *(P-16954)*

**Wharf, The, Ventura** *Also Called: Ventura Feed and Pet Sups Inc (P-17505)*

**Whatever Publishing Inc** ...................................................... F ...... 415 884-2100
14 Pamaron Way Ste 1 Novato (94949) *(P-4494)*

**Wheel and Tire Club Inc** ....................................................... E ...... 800 901-6003
1909 S Susan St Ste D Santa Ana (92704) *(P-7634)*

**Whipple Industries Inc** ......................................................... F ...... 559 442-1261
3292 N Weber Ave Fresno (93722) *(P-10008)*

**Whipple Superchargers, Fresno** *Also Called: Whipple Industries Inc (P-10008)*

**Whistlestop MTA, Fresno** *Also Called: Dantel Inc (P-11759)*

**White Bottle Inc** ................................................................... E ...... 949 788-1998
10579 Dale Ave Stanton (90680) *(P-7080)*

**White Fire Tagets, San Bernardino** *Also Called: Reagent Chemical & RES Inc (P-5113)*

**White Oak Frozen Foods, Merced** *Also Called: Jain Farm Fresh Foods Inc (P-952)*

**Whitefox Defense Tech Inc** ................................................... D ...... 805 225-4506
854 Monterey St San Luis Obispo (93401) *(P-7832)*

**Whitehall Lane Winery, Saint Helena** *Also Called: Thomas Leonardini (P-1783)*

**Whites Steel Inc (PA)** ........................................................... F ...... 760 347-3401
45524 Towne St Indio (92201) *(P-538)*

**Whitestone Industries Inc** .................................................... E ...... 888 567-2234
4632 District Blvd Bakersfield (93313) *(P-16270)*

**Whitewater Rock & Sup Co Inc** ............................................ E ...... 760 325-2747
58645 Old Highway 60 Whitewater (92282) *(P-16488)*

**Whiting Door Mfg Corp** ........................................................ D ...... 909 877-0120
301 S Milliken Ave Ontario (91761) *(P-19290)*

**Whitlock Industries Inc** ........................................................ F ...... 760 231-9262
609 Mission Ave Oceanside (92054) *(P-16271)*

**Whitlock Surfboards, Oceanside** *Also Called: Whitlock Industries Inc (P-16271)*

**Whitmor Plstic Wire Cable Corp (PA)** ................................. E ...... 661 257-2400
27737 Avenue Hopkins Santa Clarita (91355) *(P-9242)*

**Whitmor Plstic Wire Cable Corp** ......................................... E ...... 661 257-2400
28420 Avenue Stanford Valencia (91355) *(P-9243)*

**Whitmor Wire and Cable, Santa Clarita** *Also Called: Whitmor Plstic Wire Cable Corp (P-9242)*

**Whitmor Wirenetics, Valencia** *Also Called: Whitmor Plstic Wire Cable Corp (P-9243)*

**Whittaker Corporation** ......................................................... E ...... 805 526-5700
1955 Surveyor Ave Fl 2 Simi Valley (93063) *(P-13992)*

**Whittier Fertilizer Company** ................................................ D ...... 562 699-3461
9441 Kruse Rd Pico Rivera (90660) *(P-6184)*

**Whittier Filtration Inc (DH)** ................................................. E ...... 714 986-5300
120 S State College Blvd Ste 175 Brea (92821) *(P-10614)*

**Whittier Mailing Products Inc (PA)** .................................... F ...... 562 464-3000
13019 Park St Santa Fe Springs (90670) *(P-10467)*

**Whizz Systems, Santa Clara** *Also Called: Whizz Systems Inc (P-12262)*

**Whizz Systems Inc (PA)** ....................................................... E ...... 408 207-0400
3240 Scott Blvd Santa Clara (95054) *(P-12262)*

**Who What Wear, West Hollywood** *Also Called: Clique Brands Inc (P-4240)*

**Wholesale, Sacramento** *Also Called: Coral Port LLC (P-17291)*

**Wholesale and Retail, South El Monte** *Also Called: Lava Athletica Inc (P-2903)*

**Wholesale Art and Framing Inc** .......................................... F ...... 916 851-0770
3068 Sunrise Blvd Ste E Rancho Cordova (95742) *(P-3431)*

**Wholesale Displays, Carlsbad** *Also Called: San Diego Sign Company Inc (P-16892)*

**Wholesale Shade, San Marcos** *Also Called: Showdogs Inc (P-3729)*

**Wi2wi, San Jose** *Also Called: Wi2wi Inc (P-11978)*

**Wi2wi Inc (PA)** ..................................................................... E ...... 408 416-4200
1879 Lundy Ave Ste 218 San Jose (95131) *(P-11978)*

**Wick Communications Co** .................................................... E ...... 760 379-3667
6404 Lake Isabella Blvd Lake Isabella (93240) *(P-4221)*

**Wick Communications Co** .................................................... E ...... 650 726-4424
714 Kelly St Half Moon Bay (94019) *(P-4222)*

**Widly Inc** ............................................................................... C ...... 951 279-0900
785 E Harrison St Ste 100 Corona (92879) *(P-3546)*

**Wiedenbach-Brown, Fullerton** *Also Called: US Electrical Services Inc (P-16676)*

**Wiegmann & Rose, Benicia** *Also Called: Xchanger Manufacturing Corp (P-8355)*

**Wiens Cellars LLC** ................................................................ E ...... 951 694-9892
35550 Via Del Ponte Temecula (92592) *(P-1826)*

**Wilbur Curtis Co Inc** ............................................................. B ...... 800 421-6150
6913 Acco St Montebello (90640) *(P-17748)*

**Wilbur Packing Company Inc** .............................................. D ...... 530 671-4911
1500 Eager Rd Live Oak (95953) *(P-89)*

**Wilcox AG Products, Walnut Grove** *Also Called: Wilcox Brothers Inc (P-9396)*

**Wilcox Brothers Inc** .............................................................. D ...... 916 776-1784
14180 State Highway 160 Walnut Grove (95690) *(P-9396)*

**Wilcox Machine Co** ............................................................... D ...... 562 927-5353
7180 Scout Ave Bell Gardens (90201) *(P-11194)*

# ALPHABETIC SECTION

Wild Earth Inc ..................................................................... E ...... 510 206-6559
  2865 7th St Berkeley (94710) *(P-1116)*
Wild Lizard, Los Angeles *Also Called: Bb Co Inc (P-2737)*
Wild Turkey Distillery, San Francisco *Also Called: Rare Breed Distilling LLC (P-1841)*
Wildbrine, Santa Rosa *Also Called: Wildbrine LLC (P-941)*
Wildbrine LLC (PA) ................................................................ E ...... 707 657-7607
  322 Bellevue Ave Santa Rosa (95407) *(P-941)*
Wildcat Discovery Tech Inc ................................................. D ...... 858 550-1980
  6255 Ferris Sq Ste A San Diego (92121) *(P-19483)*
Wilden Pump, Grand Terrace *Also Called: Psg California LLC (P-9936)*
Wildfire Interactive Inc ........................................................ C ...... 650 253-0000
  1600 Amphitheatre Pkwy Mountain View (94043) *(P-18932)*
Wildflower Health Inc ......................................................... E ...... 415 430-7543
  2443 Fillmore St # 380 Pmb 6499 San Francisco (94115) *(P-18933)*
Will-Mann Inc ....................................................................... E ...... 714 870-0350
  225 E Santa Fe Ave Fullerton (92832) *(P-8613)*
Will's Fresh Foods, San Leandro *Also Called: Woolery Enterprises Inc (P-2391)*
Willard Marine Inc ............................................................... D ...... 714 666-2150
  4602 North Ave Oceanside (92056) *(P-14048)*
Willey Printing Company (PA) ............................................. E ...... 209 524-4811
  1405 10th St Modesto (95354) *(P-4812)*
William Kreysler & Assoc Inc ............................................. E ...... 707 552-3500
  501 Green Island Rd American Canyon (94503) *(P-7081)*
William R Schmitt ................................................................ E ...... 530 243-3069
  18135 Clear Creek Rd Redding (96001) *(P-3062)*
William Stucky & Assoc LLC ............................................. E ...... 415 788-2441
  6059 Sycamore Ter Pleasanton (94566) *(P-17997)*
Williams & Selyem LLC ..................................................... F ...... 707 536-9685
  981 Airway Ct Ste E-F Santa Rosa (95403) *(P-1827)*
Williams Aerospace & Mfg Inc (DH) .................................. E ...... 805 586-8699
  999 Avenida Acaso Camarillo (93012) *(P-16931)*
Williams Aerospace and Mfg, Chula Vista *Also Called: Allclear Aerospace & Def Inc (P-13773)*
Williams Comfort Products, Colton *Also Called: Williams Furnace Co (P-10529)*
Williams Furnace Co (DH) .................................................. C ...... 562 450-3602
  250 W Laurel St Colton (92324) *(P-10529)*
Willis Construction Co Inc ................................................. C ...... 831 623-2900
  2261 San Juan Hwy San Juan Bautista (95045) *(P-7398)*
Willis Machine Inc ............................................................... E ...... 805 604-4500
  11000 Alto Dr Oak View (93022) *(P-11195)*
Willits Redwood Company Inc .......................................... E ...... 707 459-4549
  220 Franklin Ave Willits (95490) *(P-3091)*
Willitts Eqp & Engrg Co Inc ............................................... E ...... 559 594-5020
  30548 Road 196 Exeter (93221) *(P-17360)*
Willow, Vernon *Also Called: Complete Clothing Company (P-2704)*
Willow, Mountain View *Also Called: Exploramed Nc7 LLC (P-15537)*
Willow Technology Inc ....................................................... E ...... 360 393-4962
  215 Cummins Ln Mckinleyville (95519) *(P-18934)*
Wills Wing, Orange *Also Called: Sport Kites Inc (P-13693)*
Wilmar, Vernon *Also Called: Jobbers Meat Packing Co LLC (P-603)*
Wilmar Oils Fats Stockton LLC .......................................... E ...... 925 627-1600
  2008 Port Road B Stockton (95203) *(P-1375)*
Wilmington Instrument Co Inc (PA) .................................. F ...... 310 834-1133
  332 N Fries Ave Wilmington (90744) *(P-14600)*
Wilorco, Carson *Also Called: Strike Technology Inc (P-13093)*
Wilsey Foods Inc ................................................................. A ...... 714 257-3700
  40 Pointe Dr Brea (92821) *(P-1411)*
Wilshire Precision Pdts Inc ................................................ E ...... 818 765-4571
  7353 Hinds Ave North Hollywood (91605) *(P-11196)*
Wilson Artisan Wineries, Healdsburg *Also Called: Stonecushion Inc (P-1765)*
Wilson Creek Winery, Temecula *Also Called: Wilson Creek Wnery Vnyards Inc (P-1828)*
Wilson Creek Wnery Vnyards Inc ..................................... C ...... 951 699-9463
  35960 Rancho California Rd Temecula (92591) *(P-1828)*
Wilson Cycles Sports Corp ................................................ E ...... 951 894-5545
  26145 Jefferson Ave Ste 205 Murrieta (92562) *(P-17444)*
Wilson Trophy Co California .............................................. F ...... 916 927-9733
  1724 Frienza Ave Sacramento (95815) *(P-17726)*
Wilsonart LLC ...................................................................... E ...... 562 921-7426
  13911 Gannet St Santa Fe Springs (90670) *(P-16293)*
Wilsons Art Studio Inc ........................................................ D ...... 714 870-7030
  501 S Acacia Ave Fullerton (92831) *(P-4985)*

Wilwood Engineering (PA) .................................................. C ...... 805 388-1188
  4700 Calle Bolero Camarillo (93012) *(P-13605)*
Win Foods Corporation ...................................................... D ...... 510 487-8877
  30560 San Antonio St Hayward (94544) *(P-2390)*
Win Soon Inc ....................................................................... D ...... 323 564-5070
  4569 Firestone Blvd South Gate (90280) *(P-846)*
Win-Dor Inc (PA) ................................................................. C ...... 714 576-2030
  450 Delta Ave Brea (92821) *(P-503)*
Winbond Electronics Corp Amer ....................................... D ...... 408 943-6666
  2727 N 1st St San Jose (95134) *(P-16742)*
Winc Inc ............................................................................... C ...... 855 282-5829
  927 S Santa Fe Ave Los Angeles (90021) *(P-1829)*
Winchester Interconnect EC LLC ...................................... D ...... 714 230-6122
  12691 Monarch St Garden Grove (92841) *(P-16743)*
Winchester SRC Cables Corp ............................................ F ...... 707 573-1900
  5590 Skylane Blvd Santa Rosa (95403) *(P-13124)*
Winchster Interconnect Rf Corp ........................................ A ...... 707 573-1900
  5590 Skylane Blvd Santa Rosa (95403) *(P-13125)*
Winchster Intrcnnect CM CA Inc ....................................... C ...... 800 848-4257
  1810 Diamond St San Marcos (92078) *(P-7800)*
Winchster Intrcnnect Micro LLC ....................................... C ...... 714 637-7099
  1872 N Case St Orange (92865) *(P-12903)*
Wind River, Alameda *Also Called: Wind River Systems Inc (P-18935)*
Wind River Systems Inc (DH) ............................................ A ...... 510 748-4100
  500 Wind River Way Alameda (94501) *(P-18935)*
Wind River Systems Inc ..................................................... F ...... 858 824-3100
  12770 High Bluff Dr Ste 300 San Diego (92130) *(P-18936)*
Windjmmer Capitl Investors III, Santa Ana *Also Called: Jwc Environmental Inc (P-16821)*
Windmill Corporation .......................................................... F ...... 650 873-1000
  314 Harbor Way South San Francisco (94080) *(P-1255)*
Window Enterprises Inc ...................................................... E ...... 951 943-4894
  430 Nevada St Redlands (92373) *(P-8294)*
Windows Hawaii, Rancho Cordova *Also Called: Northwest Exteriors Inc (P-499)*
Windsor Foods, Hayward *Also Called: Ajinomoto Foods North Amer Inc (P-1021)*
Windsor Foods, Ontario *Also Called: Ajinomoto Foods North Amer Inc (P-1022)*
Windsor Foods, Ontario *Also Called: Windsor Quality Food Company Ltd (P-1051)*
Windsor Mill, Willits *Also Called: Windsor Willits Company (P-3206)*
Windsor Oaks Vineyards, Windsor *Also Called: Windsor Oaks Vineyards LLP (P-1830)*
Windsor Oaks Vineyards LLP ............................................ E ...... 707 433-4050
  10810 Hillview Rd Windsor (95492) *(P-1830)*
Windsor One, Petaluma *Also Called: Windsor Willits Company (P-3205)*
Windsor Quality Food Company Ltd ................................. A ...... 713 843-5200
  4200 Concours Ste 100 Ontario (91764) *(P-1051)*
Windsor Willits Company (PA) .......................................... E ...... 707 665-9663
  737 Southpoint Blvd Ste H Petaluma (94954) *(P-3205)*
Windsor Willits Company ................................................... D ...... 707 459-8568
  661 Railroad Ave Willits (95490) *(P-3206)*
Windy City Express, Oakland *Also Called: Edys Grand Ice Cream (P-799)*
Wine Chemicals, San Leandro *Also Called: Copper Harbor Company Inc (P-6277)*
Wine Country Cases Inc .................................................... D ...... 707 967-4805
  621 Airpark Rd Napa (94558) *(P-3378)*
Wine Group Inc (HQ) .......................................................... C ...... 209 599-4111
  17000 E State Highway 120 Ripon (95366) *(P-1831)*
Winfield Locks Inc .............................................................. A ...... 949 722-5400
  1721 Whittier Ave Costa Mesa (92627) *(P-8038)*
Wing Hing, Los Angeles *Also Called: Wing Hing Foods LLC (P-873)*
Wing Hing Foods LLC ........................................................ D ...... 323 232-8899
  1659 E 23rd St Los Angeles (90011) *(P-873)*
Wing Hing Noodle Company, Ontario *Also Called: Passport Food Group LLC (P-2314)*
Wing Inflatables (HQ) ......................................................... E ...... 707 826-2887
  1220 5th St Arcata (95521) *(P-7082)*
Wing Master, Clovis *Also Called: Valley Chrome Plating Inc (P-9031)*
Wing Nien Company, Hayward *Also Called: U S Enterprise Corporation (P-995)*
Wing Nien Foods, Hayward *Also Called: Win Foods Corporation (P-2390)*
Winnov Inc ........................................................................... E ...... 888 315-9460
  3945 Freedom Cir Ste 560 Santa Clara (95054) *(P-11718)*
Winonics Inc ........................................................................ C ...... 714 626-3755
  1257 S State College Blvd Fullerton (92831) *(P-12263)*
Winslow Automation Inc .................................................... D ...... 408 262-9004
  905 Montague Expy Milpitas (95035) *(P-12804)*

---

Employee Codes: A=Over 500 employees, B=251-500
C=101-250, D=51-100, E=20-50, F=10-19, G=1-9

## ALPHABETIC SECTION

**Winstronices International Inc** ........................................... E ...... 510 226-7588
3817 Spinnaker Ct Fremont (94538) *(P-7801)*

**Winstronics, Fremont** *Also Called: Winstronices International Inc (P-7801)*

**Wintec, Newark** *Also Called: Wintec Industries Inc (P-12805)*

**Wintec Industries Inc (HQ)** ................................................. E ...... 510 953-7421
8674 Thornton Ave Newark (94560) *(P-12805)*

**Winter & Bain Mfg Inc (PA)** ................................................. F ...... 213 749-3568
1417 Elwood St Los Angeles (90021) *(P-9478)*

**Winther Technologies Inc (PA)** ........................................... E ...... 310 618-8437
560 Alaska Ave Torrance (90503) *(P-9732)*

**Wintriss Engineering Corp** ................................................... E ...... 858 550-7300
9010 Kenamar Dr Ste 101 San Diego (92121) *(P-14832)*

**Wipro LLC** ........................................................................... E ...... 650 316-3555
425 National Ave Ste 200 Mountain View (94043) *(P-18999)*

**Wipro Technologies, Mountain View** *Also Called: Wipro LLC (P-18999)*

**Wira Co, El Monte** *Also Called: Jans Enterprises Corporation (P-17190)*

**Wire Bonding Tools, Petaluma** *Also Called: Small Precision Tools Inc (P-12720)*

**Wire Cut Company Inc** ........................................................ E ...... 714 994-1170
6750 Caballero Blvd Buena Park (90620) *(P-11197)*

**Wire Harness & Cable Assembly, Santa Monica** *Also Called: Omega Leads Inc (P-13053)*

**Wire Technology Corporation** ............................................. E ...... 310 635-6935
9527 Laurel St Los Angeles (90002) *(P-7802)*

**Wired, San Francisco** *Also Called: Wired Ventures Inc (P-4306)*

**Wired Ventures Inc** .............................................................. C ...... 415 276-8400
520 3rd St Ste 305 San Francisco (94107) *(P-4306)*

**Wireless Technology Inc** ..................................................... E ...... 805 339-9696
2064 Eastman Ave Ste 113 Ventura (93003) *(P-11719)*

**Wirenetics Co, Valencia** *Also Called: Circle W Enterprises Inc (P-9214)*

**Wiretech Inc (PA)** ................................................................ D ...... 323 722-4933
6440 Canning St Commerce (90040) *(P-7658)*

**Wirex Systems** .................................................................... E ...... 408 799-4498
100 S Murphy Ave Ste 200 Sunnyvale (94086) *(P-18937)*

**Wirz & Co** ............................................................................ F ...... 909 825-6970
444 Colton Ave Colton (92324) *(P-4813)*

**Wiser Foods Inc** .................................................................. D ...... 310 895-0888
5405 E Village Rd Unit 8219 Long Beach (90808) *(P-1973)*

**Wisk Aero LLC (PA)** ............................................................ B ...... 650 641-0920
2700 Broderick Way Mountain View (94043) *(P-13697)*

**Wit Group** ........................................................................... E ...... 530 243-4447
1822 Buenaventura Blvd Ste 101 Redding (96001) *(P-1974)*

**Wixen Music Publishing Inc** ................................................ F ...... 818 591-7355
27200 Agoura Rd Ste 201 Agoura Hills (91301) *(P-4355)*

**Wizard Graphics Inc** ........................................................... F ...... 530 893-3636
411 Otterson Dr Ste 20 Chico (95973) *(P-4986)*

**WJB Bearings Inc** ................................................................ E ...... 909 598-6238
535 Brea Canyon Rd City Of Industry (91789) *(P-8806)*

**Wjlp Company Inc** .............................................................. D ...... 800 628-1123
4848 Frontier Way Ste 100 Stockton (95215) *(P-12864)*

**Wkf (friedman Enterprises Inc (PA)** .................................... F ...... 925 673-9100
2334 Stagecoach Rd Ste B Stockton (95215) *(P-13728)*

**Wm Bolthouse Farms Inc (HQ)** .......................................... A ...... 800 467-4683
7200 E Brundage Ln Bakersfield (93307) *(P-1020)*

**WM TECHNOLOGY, Irvine** *Also Called: Wm Technology Inc (P-18938)*

**Wm Technology Inc (PA)** ................................................... E ...... 646 699-3750
41 Discovery Irvine (92618) *(P-18938)*

**Wme Bi LLC** ........................................................................ D ...... 877 592-2472
17075 Camino San Diego (92127) *(P-18939)*

**Wmn Corp** ........................................................................... E ...... 916 294-0110
340 Palladio Pkwy Ste 530 Folsom (95630) *(P-10298)*

**Wna City of Industry, City Of Industry** *Also Called: Waddington North America Inc (P-7075)*

**Wohler Technologies Inc** .................................................... E ...... 510 870-0810
1280 San Luis Obispo St Hayward (94544) *(P-11979)*

**Wolfe Industries, Santa Fe Springs** *Also Called: C Wolfe Industries Inc (P-8825)*

**Wolfgang Enterprise Inc** ..................................................... F ...... 951 848-7680
13977 The Merge St Unit B Eastvale (92880) *(P-19144)*

**Wolfpack Inc** ....................................................................... E ...... 760 736-4500
2440 Grand Ave Ste B Vista (92081) *(P-16069)*

**Wolfpack Sign Group, Vista** *Also Called: Wolfpack Inc (P-16069)*

**Wonder Ice Cream Inc (PA)** ............................................... E ...... 510 818-9102
2338 Walsh Ave Santa Clara (95051) *(P-821)*

**Wonder Workshop Inc (PA)** ............................................... E ...... 408 785-7981
116c E 25th Ave San Mateo (94403) *(P-17998)*

**Wonderful Citrus Packing LLC (HQ)** .................................. B ...... 661 720-2400
1901 S Lexington St Delano (93215) *(P-90)*

**Wonderful Citrus Packing LLC** .......................................... F ...... 661 720-2400
1701 S Lexington St Delano (93215) *(P-942)*

**Wonderful Company LLC** ................................................... B ...... 661 720-2400
1901 S Lexington St Delano (93215) *(P-42)*

**Wonderful Pstchios Almonds LLC (HQ)** ............................ E ...... 310 966-5700
11444 W Olympic Blvd Fl 10 Los Angeles (90064) *(P-1370)*

**Wonderware Corporation (DH)** .......................................... B ...... 949 727-3200
26561 Rancho Pkwy S Lake Forest (92630) *(P-18940)*

**Wood Candle Wick Tech Inc** .............................................. D ...... 310 488-5885
9750 Irvine Blvd Ste 106 Irvine (92618) *(P-16272)*

**Wood Connection Inc** ......................................................... E ...... 209 577-1044
4701 N Star Way Modesto (95356) *(P-3207)*

**Wood Space Industries Inc** ................................................ F ...... 714 996-4552
429 W Levers Pl Orange (92867) *(P-16295)*

**Wood Tech Inc** .................................................................... D ...... 510 534-4930
4611 Malat St Oakland (94601) *(P-3463)*

**Wood-N-Wood Products Cal Inc (PA)** ............................... E ...... 559 896-3636
2247 W Birch Ave Fresno (93711) *(P-3379)*

**Wood-N-Wood Products Cal Inc** ....................................... F ...... 559 896-3636
13598 S Golden State Blvd Selma (93662) *(P-3380)*

**Woodbridge Winery** ............................................................ F ...... 209 369-5861
5950 E Woodbridge Rd Acampo (95220) *(P-1832)*

**Wooden Window Inc** .......................................................... E ...... 510 893-1157
849 29th St Oakland (94608) *(P-3208)*

**Woodland Fire Department, Woodland** *Also Called: City of Woodland (P-19577)*

**Woodline Cabinets, Fairfield** *Also Called: Woodline Partners Inc (P-3281)*

**Woodline Partners Inc** ........................................................ E ...... 707 864-5445
5165 Fulton Dr Fairfield (94534) *(P-3281)*

**Woodpecker Cabinets Inc** .................................................. E ...... 310 404-4805
21512 Nordhoff St Chatsworth (91311) *(P-3282)*

**Woodridge Press Inc** .......................................................... E ...... 949 475-1900
2485 Da Vinci Irvine (92614) *(P-4814)*

**Woodside Electronics Corp** ............................................... D ...... 530 666-9190
1311 Blue Grass Pl Woodland (95776) *(P-19291)*

**Woodside Investment Inc** .................................................. D ...... 209 787-8040
12405 E Brandt Rd Lockeford (95237) *(P-9305)*

**Woodward Drilling Company Inc** ....................................... E ...... 707 374-4300
550 River Rd Rio Vista (94571) *(P-167)*

**Woodward Duarte, Duarte** *Also Called: Woodward Hrt Inc (P-13993)*

**Woodward Hrt Inc (HQ)** ..................................................... A ...... 661 294-6000
25200 Rye Canyon Rd Santa Clarita (91355) *(P-11355)*

**Woodward Hrt Inc** .............................................................. C ...... 626 359-9211
1700 Business Center Dr Duarte (91010) *(P-13993)*

**Woodwork Pioneers Corp** .................................................. E ...... 714 991-1017
1757 S Claudina Way Anaheim (92805) *(P-3209)*

**Woody's, Denair** *Also Called: Woodys Poultry Supply (P-372)*

**Woodys Poultry Supply** ..................................................... F ...... 209 634-2948
2900 E Monte Vista Ave Denair (95316) *(P-372)*

**Woolery Enterprises Inc** ..................................................... E ...... 510 357-5700
1991 Republic Ave San Leandro (94577) *(P-2391)*

**Woongjin Coway USA Inc., Los Angeles** *Also Called: Coway Usa Inc (P-17699)*

**Word For Today** .................................................................. E ...... 714 825-9673
3232 W Macarthur Blvd # A Santa Ana (92704) *(P-17677)*

**Wordsmart Corporation** ..................................................... E
10025 Mesa Rim Rd San Diego (92121) *(P-18941)*

**Workboard Inc (PA)** ............................................................ C ...... 650 294-4480
487 Seaport Ct Ste 100 Redwood City (94063) *(P-18942)*

**Workbook Inc** ..................................................................... E ...... 323 856-0008
110 N Doheny Dr Beverly Hills (90211) *(P-4495)*

**Working Computer, Oceanside** *Also Called: Clients & Profits Inc (P-16514)*

**Working Nurse, Los Angeles** *Also Called: Recruitment Services Inc (P-4293)*

**Working Robot Inc** .............................................................. E ...... 408 809-5600
583c Division St Campbell (95008) *(P-10124)*

**Workrite Ergonomics, Petaluma** *Also Called: Workrite Ergonomics LLC (P-3590)*

**Workrite Ergonomics LLC** .................................................. C ...... 707 780-6400
2277 Pine View Way Ste 100 Petaluma (94954) *(P-3590)*

**Workspot Inc (PA)** .............................................................. E ...... 888 426-8113
1999 S Bascom Ave Ste 1000 Campbell (95008) *(P-18943)*

## ALPHABETIC SECTION — Xdr Radiology

**World Centric** .................................................. D ...... 707 241-9190
1500 Valley House Dr Ste 210 Rohnert Park (94928) *(P-4058)*

**World Centric, Rohnert Park** *Also Called: World Centric (P-4058)*

**World Class Cheerleading Inc** ...................... E ...... 877 923-2645
20212 Hart St Winnetka (91306) *(P-15878)*

**World History Group LLC** ............................. E ...... 703 779-8322
9720 Wilshire Blvd Beverly Hills (90212) *(P-4307)*

**World Journal Inc (PA)** ................................. D ...... 650 692-9936
1633 Bayshore Hwy Ste 231 Burlingame (94010) *(P-4223)*

**World Journal La LLC (HQ)** .......................... C ...... 323 268-4982
1588 Corporate Center Dr Monterey Park (91754) *(P-4224)*

**World Oil Corp** ............................................. C ...... 562 928-0100
9302 Garfield Ave South Gate (90280) *(P-147)*

**World Oil Marketing Company (PA)** ............. E ...... 562 928-0100
9302 Garfield Ave South Gate (90280) *(P-17396)*

**World Peas Brand, Los Angeles** *Also Called: Snack It Forward LLC (P-2102)*

**WORLD SERVICE OFFICE, Chatsworth** *Also Called: Narcotics Annymous Wrld Svcs I (P-4337)*

**World Trade Printing Company, Garden Grove** *Also Called: Wtpc Inc (P-4816)*

**World Water Inc** ........................................... E ...... 562 940-1964
9848 Everest St Downey (90242) *(P-14469)*

**World Wind & Solar, Tehachapi** *Also Called: World Wind Electrical Svcs Inc (P-474)*

**World Wind & Solar, Paso Robles** *Also Called: Worldwind Services LLC (P-475)*

**World Wind Electrical Svcs Inc** .................... A ...... 661 822-4877
228 W Tehachapi Blvd Tehachapi (93561) *(P-474)*

**Worldwide, Monrovia** *Also Called: Worldwide Energy and Mfg USA (P-12806)*

**Worldwide Aeros Corp** ................................. D ...... 818 344-3999
3971 Fredonia Dr Los Angeles (90068) *(P-13698)*

**Worldwide Energy and Mfg USA (PA)** .......... D ...... 650 692-7788
1800 S Myrtle Ave Monrovia (91016) *(P-12806)*

**Worldwide Envmtl Pdts Inc (PA)** .................. D ...... 714 990-2700
1100 Beacon St Brea (92821) *(P-14470)*

**Worldwide Specialties Inc** ........................... C ...... 323 587-2200
2420 Modoc St Los Angeles (90021) *(P-2392)*

**Worldwind Services LLC** ............................. A ...... 661 822-4877
1222 Vine St Ste 301 Paso Robles (93446) *(P-475)*

**Worldwise Inc (DH)** ..................................... D ...... 415 721-7400
6 Hamilton Landing Ste 150 Novato (94949) *(P-17318)*

**Worth Data Inc** ............................................ F ...... 831 458-9938
623 Swift St Santa Cruz (95060) *(P-10453)*

**Worthington Cylinder Corp** .......................... C ...... 909 594-7777
336 Enterprise Pl Pomona (91768) *(P-8354)*

**Wowyow Inc** ................................................ F ...... 844 496-9969
3919 30th St San Diego (92104) *(P-18944)*

**Wpmg Inc** .................................................... E ...... 949 442-1601
1961 Mcgaw Ave Irvine (92614) *(P-11569)*

**Wrex Products, Chico** *Also Called: Wrex Products Inc Chico (P-7083)*

**Wrex Products Inc Chico** ............................. D ...... 530 895-3838
25 Wrex Ct Chico (95928) *(P-7083)*

**Wright Business Graphics Calif, Chino** *Also Called: Wright Business Graphics LLC (P-4994)*

**Wright Business Graphics LLC** .................... E ...... 909 614-6700
13602 12th St Ste A Chino (91710) *(P-4994)*

**Wright Engineered Plastics Inc, Santa Rosa** *Also Called: Wright Engineered Plastics LLC (P-9658)*

**Wright Engineered Plastics LLC** .................. E ...... 707 575-1218
3681 N Laughlin Rd Santa Rosa (95403) *(P-9658)*

**Wright Pharma Inc** ...................................... E ...... 209 549-9771
700 Kiernan Ave Ste A Modesto (95356) *(P-5719)*

**Wrights Supply Inc** ..................................... E ...... 661 254-8400
25838 Springbrook Ave Santa Clarita (91350) *(P-19237)*

**Wrightspeed Inc** .......................................... E ...... 866 960-9482
150 Almaden Blvd San Jose (95113) *(P-13606)*

**Wrkco Inc** .................................................... E ...... 310 532-8988
1025 W 190th St Ste 450 Gardena (90248) *(P-3811)*

**Wrkco Inc** .................................................... E ...... 770 448-2193
14103 Borate St Santa Fe Springs (90670) *(P-3812)*

**Wrs Materials, San Jose** *Also Called: Pure Wafer Inc (P-12644)*

**Wrs Materials, San Jose** *Also Called: Wafer Reclaim Services LLC (P-12801)*

**Ws Packaging-Blake Printery** ...................... E ...... 805 543-6844
2224 Beebee St San Luis Obispo (93401) *(P-4815)*

**Wsglass Holdings Inc** .................................. F ...... 916 388-5885
180 Main Ave Sacramento (95838) *(P-14833)*

**Wsw Corp (PA)** ............................................ E ...... 818 989-5008
16000 Strathern St Van Nuys (91406) *(P-13607)*

**Wti, Ventura** *Also Called: Wireless Technology Inc (P-11719)*

**Wtpc Inc** ...................................................... E ...... 714 903-2500
12082 Western Ave Garden Grove (92841) *(P-4816)*

**Wun, Goleta** *Also Called: Yardi Kube Inc (P-18949)*

**Wunder-Bar, Vacaville** *Also Called: Automatic Bar Controls Inc (P-10483)*

**Wunder-Mold Inc** ......................................... E ...... 707 448-2349
790 Eubanks Dr Vacaville (95688) *(P-7084)*

**WV Communications Inc** ............................. E ...... 805 376-1820
1125 Business Center Cir Ste A Newbury Park (91320) *(P-11980)*

**Wyatt Precision Machine Inc** ....................... E ...... 562 634-0524
3301 E 59th St Long Beach (90805) *(P-8738)*

**Wyatt Technology, Goleta** *Also Called: Wyatt Technology LLC (P-14756)*

**Wyatt Technology LLC (HQ)** ........................ C ...... 805 681-9009
6330 Hollister Ave Goleta (93117) *(P-14756)*

**Wycen Foods Inc (PA)** ................................. F ...... 510 351-1987
560 Estabrook St San Leandro (94577) *(P-676)*

**Wylatti Resource MGT Inc** ........................... E ...... 707 983-8135
23601 Cemetery Ln Covelo (95428) *(P-3063)*

**Wymore Inc** ................................................. E ...... 760 352-2045
697 S Dogwood Rd El Centro (92243) *(P-19222)*

**Wynd Technologies Inc** ............................... E ...... 617 438-3694
1037 S Claremont St San Mateo (94402) *(P-19292)*

**Wyndcrest Dd Florida, Los Angeles** *Also Called: Digital Domain Media Group Inc (P-17826)*

**Wyndham Collection LLC** ............................ E ...... 888 522-8476
1175 Aviation Pl San Fernando (91340) *(P-3283)*

**Wyrefab Inc** ................................................. E ...... 310 523-2147
15711 S Broadway Gardena (90248) *(P-9244)*

**Wytcote Inc** ................................................. F ...... 877 472-5587
3 Park Plz Ste 480 Irvine (92614) *(P-19000)*

**Wyvern Technologies** .................................. E ...... 714 966-0710
1205 E Warner Ave Santa Ana (92705) *(P-13126)*

**X Hyper** ....................................................... E ...... 530 673-7099
17600 Newhope St Fountain Valley (92708) *(P-11720)*

**X Therm** ...................................................... E ...... 510 441-7566
3325 Investment Blvd Hayward (94545) *(P-14378)*

**X-1 Audio Inc** .............................................. F ...... 858 623-0339
5771 Copley Dr San Diego (92111) *(P-11721)*

**X-Chair LLC** ................................................ E ...... 844 492-4247
6415 Katella Ave Ste 200 Cypress (90630) *(P-3610)*

**X-Igent Printing Inc** ..................................... F ...... 323 837-9779
1001 Goodrich Blvd Commerce (90022) *(P-4817)*

**X-Ray Technology Group, Scotts Valley** *Also Called: Oxford Instrs X-Ray Tech Inc (P-13059)*

**X-Scan Imaging Corporation** ....................... E ...... 408 432-9888
107 Bonaventura Dr San Jose (95134) *(P-19511)*

**X1 Discovery Inc** ......................................... E ...... 877 999-1347
251 S Lake Ave Ste 800 Pasadena (91101) *(P-17999)*

**Xactly Corporation (HQ)** ............................. D ...... 408 977-3132
221 Los Gatos Saratoga Rd Los Gatos (95030) *(P-18000)*

**Xandex Inc** .................................................. E ...... 707 763-7799
1360 Redwood Way Ste A Petaluma (94954) *(P-14601)*

**Xantech LLC** ............................................... E ...... 818 362-0353
1690 Corporate Cir Petaluma (94954) *(P-11722)*

**Xavier Group** ............................................... F ...... 844 928-4378
707 Wilshire Blvd Ste 4375 Los Angeles (90017) *(P-6060)*

**Xbloom, Walnut Creek** *Also Called: Tbdx Inc (P-9820)*

**XCEL, Palo Alto** *Also Called: Xcelmobility Inc (P-18945)*

**Xcelmobility Inc** .......................................... D ...... 650 320-1728
2225 E Bayshore Rd Ste 200 Palo Alto (94303) *(P-18945)*

**Xchanger Manufacturing Corp** .................... E ...... 510 632-8828
849 Jackson St Benicia (94510) *(P-8355)*

**Xcor, Mojave** *Also Called: Xcor Aerospace Inc (P-14100)*

**Xcor Aerospace Inc** ..................................... D ...... 661 824-4714
1314 Flight Line Mojave (93501) *(P-14100)*

**Xcvi LLC (PA)** .............................................. D ...... 213 749-2661
15236 Burbank Blvd Sherman Oaks (91411) *(P-2432)*

**Xdr Radiology, Los Angeles** *Also Called: Cyber Medical Imaging Inc (P-15444)*

# XEL Group

## ALPHABETIC SECTION

**XEL Group, Laguna Hills** *Also Called: XEL USA Inc (P-12807)*
**XEL USA Inc** ............................................................................... E ...... 949 425-8686
   25231 Paseo De Alicia Laguna Hills (92653) *(P-12807)*

**Xencor, Pasadena** *Also Called: Xencor Inc (P-5720)*
**Xencor Inc** .................................................................................. B ...... 626 305-5900
   465 N Halstead St Ste 200 Pasadena (91107) *(P-5720)*

**Xenowulf, Valencia** *Also Called: C 232 Inc (P-18965)*
**Xerox** ......................................................................................... E ...... 714 895-7500
   12833 Monarch St Garden Grove (92841) *(P-10468)*

**Xerox International Partners (DH)** .......................................... E
   2100 Geng Rd Ste 210 Palo Alto (94303) *(P-9777)*

**Xerxes Corporation** .................................................................. C ...... 714 630-0012
   1210 N Tustin Ave Anaheim (92807) *(P-5218)*

**Xgrass Turf Direct, Anaheim** *Also Called: Leonards Carpet Service Inc (P-3664)*
**Xiamen Hongfa Electroacoustic, Lake Forest** *Also Called: Hongfa America Inc (P-11325)*
**Xicato Inc** .................................................................................. E ...... 866 223-8395
   102 Cooper Ct Los Gatos (95032) *(P-11509)*

**Xidas Inc** ................................................................................... F ...... 949 930-0147
   46 Waterworks Way Irvine (92618) *(P-13127)*

**Xilinx, San Jose** *Also Called: Xilinx Inc (P-17761)*
**Xilinx Inc (HQ)** .......................................................................... A ...... 408 559-7778
   2100 Logic Dr San Jose (95124) *(P-17761)*

**Xilinx Development Corporation (DH)** ................................... F ...... 408 559-7778
   2100 All Programable San Jose (95124) *(P-12808)*

**Ximed Medical Systems, San Jose** *Also Called: Prosurg Inc (P-15232)*
**Xintec Corporation (PA)** ........................................................... E ...... 510 832-2130
   1660 S Loop Rd Alameda (94502) *(P-15309)*

**Xirgo Technologies LLC** .......................................................... D ...... 805 319-4079
   188 Camino Ruiz Fl 2 Camarillo (93012) *(P-13334)*

**Xirrus Inc** .................................................................................. E ...... 805 262-1600
   2545 W Hillcrest Dr Ste 220 Newbury Park (91320) *(P-14471)*

**Xitron Technologies, Poway** *Also Called: Vitrek LLC (P-14599)*
**Xkt Engineering Inc** ................................................................. D ...... 707 562-2500
   390 Railroad Ave Vallejo (94592) *(P-8356)*

**Xlsoft Corporation** .................................................................... F ...... 949 453-2781
   12 Mauchly Ste K Irvine (92618) *(P-18946)*

**Xmultiple Technologies (PA)** ................................................... E ...... 805 579-1100
   1919 Williams St Ste 325 Simi Valley (93065) *(P-10218)*

**Xmultiple/Xrjax, Simi Valley** *Also Called: Xmultiple Technologies (P-10218)*
**XO BABYPLUTO FADED PARADISE XO** ................................ E ...... 650 750-5025
   3442 E 8th St Los Angeles (90023) *(P-19145)*

**Xoft Inc** ...................................................................................... E ...... 408 493-1500
   101 Nicholson Ln San Jose (95134) *(P-15310)*

**XOS, Los Angeles** *Also Called: Xos Inc (P-13608)*
**Xos Inc (PA)** .............................................................................. E ...... 818 316-1890
   3550 Tyburn St Ste 100 Los Angeles (90065) *(P-13608)*

**Xos Fleet Inc (HQ)** ................................................................... E ...... 818 316-1890
   3550 Tyburn St Ste 100 Los Angeles (90065) *(P-13398)*

**Xos Trucks, Los Angeles** *Also Called: Xos Fleet Inc (P-13398)*
**Xp Power Inc** ............................................................................. D ...... 714 712-2642
   1590 S Sinclair St Anaheim (92806) *(P-13128)*

**Xperi Inc (PA)** ............................................................................ D ...... 408 519-9100
   2190 Gold St San Jose (95002) *(P-18947)*

**Xpower Manufacture Inc** ........................................................ E ...... 626 285-3301
   668 S 6th Ave City Of Industry (91746) *(P-14379)*

**Xr LLC** ....................................................................................... E ...... 714 847-9292
   15251 Pipeline Ln Huntington Beach (92649) *(P-15430)*

**Xrp Inc (PA)** .............................................................................. F ...... 562 861-4765
   5630 Imperial Hwy South Gate (90280) *(P-17469)*

**Xs Scuba Inc (PA)** ..................................................................... E ...... 714 424-0434
   4040 W Chandler Ave Santa Ana (92704) *(P-15879)*

**Xtandi, San Francisco** *Also Called: Medivation Inc (P-5551)*
**Xtime Inc** ................................................................................... E ...... 650 508-4300
   1400 Bridge Pkwy Ste 200 Redwood City (94065) *(P-18948)*

**Xtraction Inc** ............................................................................. F ...... 800 273-4137
   3688 E Central Ave Ste 103 Fresno (93725) *(P-3547)*

**Xy Corp Inc** ............................................................................... F ...... 760 323-0333
   1258 Montalvo Way Ste A Palm Springs (92262) *(P-9593)*

**Xylem Water Solutions USA Inc** ............................................. D ...... 949 474-1679
   17342 Cowan Irvine (92614) *(P-9946)*

**Xylem Water Systems (california) Inc** .................................... E ...... 619 575-7466
   830 Bay Blvd Ste 101 Chula Vista (91911) *(P-9947)*

**Xyratex, Fremont** *Also Called: Seagate Systems (us) Inc (P-10277)*
**Xzavier, Vernon** *Also Called: Mjck Corporation (P-2478)*
**Y B S Enterprises Inc** .............................................................. F ...... 818 848-7790
   3114 W Vanowen St Burbank (91505) *(P-11795)*

**Y I C, Carson** *Also Called: Yun Industrial Co Ltd (P-12264)*
**Y K K U S A, Anaheim** *Also Called: YKK (usa) Inc (P-15924)*
**Yaesu Usa Inc** .......................................................................... E ...... 714 827-7600
   6125 Phyllis Dr Cypress (90630) *(P-11981)*

**Yageo America, San Jose** *Also Called: Yageo America Corporation (P-12824)*
**Yageo America Corporation** .................................................. E ...... 408 240-6200
   2550 N 1st St Ste 480 San Jose (95131) *(P-12824)*

**Yagi Brothers Produce LLC, Livingston** *Also Called: Ybp Holdings LLC (P-2393)*
**Yamagata America Inc** ............................................................ C ...... 858 751-1010
   3760 Convoy St Ste 219 San Diego (92111) *(P-4496)*

**Yamaha Corporation of America (HQ)** .................................. B ...... 714 522-9011
   6600 Orangethorpe Ave Buena Park (90620) *(P-16989)*

**Yamaha Guitar Group Inc (HQ)** .............................................. C ...... 818 575-3600
   26580 Agoura Rd Calabasas (91302) *(P-15726)*

**Yamaha Guitar Group Inc** ....................................................... E ...... 818 575-3900
   26664 Agoura Rd Calabasas (91302) *(P-15727)*

**Yamaha Music Corporation U S A, Buena Park** *Also Called: Yamaha Corporation of America (P-16989)*
**Yamasa Enterprises** ................................................................ E ...... 213 626-2211
   515 Stanford Ave Los Angeles (90013) *(P-2045)*

**Yamasa Fish Cake, Los Angeles** *Also Called: Yamasa Enterprises (P-2045)*
**Yamazaki Baking Co Ltd** ........................................................ E ...... 323 581-5218
   335 E 2nd St Ste 223 Los Angeles (90012) *(P-1256)*

**Yanchewski & Wardell Entps Inc** ........................................... D ...... 760 754-1960
   2241 La Mirada Dr Vista (92081) *(P-10615)*

**Yanfeng, Hayward** *Also Called: Yanfeng Intl Auto Tech US I LL (P-13609)*
**Yanfeng Intl Auto Tech US I LL** ............................................. E ...... 616 886-3622
   30559 San Antonio St Hayward (94544) *(P-13609)*

**Yang-Ming International Corp** ................................................ E ...... 626 956-0100
   595 Yorbita Rd La Puente (91744) *(P-19001)*

**Yanka Industries Inc** ............................................................... C ...... 855 981-8208
   660 4th St Ste 443 San Francisco (94107) *(P-19307)*

**Yankon Industries Inc (PA)** ..................................................... E ...... 909 591-2345
   13445 12th St Chino (91710) *(P-11570)*

**Yardi Kube Inc** ......................................................................... D ...... 805 699-2040
   430 S Fairview Ave Goleta (93117) *(P-18949)*

**Yardney Water MGT Systems, Riverside** *Also Called: Yardney Water MGT Systems Inc (P-10616)*
**Yardney Water MGT Systems Inc** ......................................... E ...... 951 656-6716
   6666 Box Springs Blvd Riverside (92507) *(P-10616)*

**Yasheng Group** ........................................................................ A ...... 650 363-8345
   251 Ginko Ter Sunnyvale (94086) *(P-6214)*

**Yates Gear Inc** ......................................................................... D ...... 530 222-4606
   330 N Brand Blvd Ste 700 Glendale (91203) *(P-7163)*

**Yavar Manufacturing Co Inc** .................................................. E ...... 323 722-2040
   1900 S Tubeway Ave Commerce (90040) *(P-3920)*

**Yawitz Inc** ................................................................................. E ...... 909 865-5599
   1379 Ridgeway St Pomona (91768) *(P-11510)*

**Yb Media LLC** .......................................................................... E ...... 310 467-5804
   1534 Plaza Ln # 146 Burlingame (94010) *(P-4497)*

**Ybcc Inc** ................................................................................... E ...... 626 213-3945
   17800 Castleton St Ste 386 City Of Industry (91748) *(P-790)*

**Ybp Holdings LLC** ................................................................... E ...... 209 394-7311
   5614 Lincoln Blvd Livingston (95334) *(P-2393)*

**YC Cable Usa Inc (HQ)** ........................................................... D ...... 510 824-2788
   48010 Fremont Blvd Fremont (94538) *(P-11478)*

**Yeager Enterprises Corp** ........................................................ D ...... 714 994-2040
   7100 Village Dr Buena Park (90621) *(P-7560)*

**Yebo Group LLC** ..................................................................... C ...... 949 502-3317
   2652 Dow Ave Tustin (92780) *(P-17644)*

**Yebo Printing, Tustin** *Also Called: Yebo Group LLC (P-17644)*
**Yen-Nhai Inc** ............................................................................ E ...... 323 584-1315
   4940 District Blvd Vernon (90058) *(P-3495)*

**Yes To Carrots, Santa Clara** *Also Called: Yes To Inc (P-6061)*

# ALPHABETIC SECTION

**Yes To Inc** .................................................................................. E ...... 626 365-1976
3945 Freedom Cir Ste 560 Santa Clara (95054) *(P-6061)*

**Yesco, Fremont** *Also Called: Young Electric Sign Company (P-16070)*

**Yesco, Sacramento** *Also Called: Young Electric Sign Company (P-16071)*

**Yesco, Jurupa Valley** *Also Called: Young Electric Sign Company (P-16072)*

**Yesterdays Sportswear, Paso Robles** *Also Called: Lakeshirts LLC (P-2993)*

**Yg Laboratories Inc** .................................................................. E ...... 714 474-2800
11520 Warner Ave Fountain Valley (92708) *(P-6062)*

**Yield Engineering Systems Inc (PA)** ....................................... C ...... 510 954-6889
3178 Laurelview Ct Fremont (94538) *(P-12809)*

**Yinlun Tdi LLC (HQ)** ................................................................. E ...... 909 390-3944
10668 N Trademark Pkwy Rancho Cucamonga (91730) *(P-13610)*

**YKK (usa) Inc** ............................................................................ E ...... 714 701-1200
5001 E La Palma Ave Anaheim (92807) *(P-15924)*

**Yla Inc** ........................................................................................ D ...... 707 359-3400
2450 Cordelia Rd Fairfield (94534) *(P-7601)*

**Ymi Jeanswear, Los Angeles** *Also Called: YMi Jeanswear Inc (P-17498)*

**YMi Jeanswear Inc** ................................................................... D ...... 213 746-6681
1015 Wall St Ste 115 Los Angeles (90015) *(P-2823)*

**YMi Jeanswear Inc (PA)** ........................................................... F ...... 323 581-7700
1155 S Boyle Ave Los Angeles (90023) *(P-17498)*

**Yobs, Los Angeles** *Also Called: Yobs Technologies Inc (P-19300)*

**Yobs Technologies Inc** ............................................................. E ...... 213 713-3825
615 Childs Way Tro 370 Los Angeles (90089) *(P-19300)*

**Yokohama Corp North America (HQ)** ..................................... C ...... 540 389-5426
1 Macarthur Pl Santa Ana (92707) *(P-6414)*

**Yokohama Tire, Santa Ana** *Also Called: Yokohama Corp North America (P-6414)*

**Yokohama Tire Corporation (DH)** ........................................... C ...... 714 870-3800
1 Macarthur Pl Ste 900 Santa Ana (92707) *(P-16410)*

**Yokohama Tire USA, Santa Ana** *Also Called: Yokohama Tire Corporation (P-16410)*

**Yolo Ice & Creamery Inc** .......................................................... F ...... 530 662-7337
1462 Churchill Downs Ave Woodland (95776) *(P-17133)*

**Yonekyu USA Inc** ...................................................................... D ...... 323 581-4194
611 N 20th St Montebello (90640) *(P-677)*

**Yorba Linda Country Club, Garden Grove** *Also Called: Sanyo Foods Corp America (P-2119)*

**York International Corporation** .............................................. F ...... 916 283-7650
1307 Striker Ave Ste 100 Sacramento (95834) *(P-10530)*

**Yosemite Farms** ........................................................................ E ...... 209 383-3411
2341 N St Merced (95340) *(P-17406)*

**Yosemite Meat Company Inc** .................................................. D ...... 209 524-5117
601 Zeff Rd Modesto (95351) *(P-17167)*

**Yosemite Vly Beef Pkg Co Inc** ................................................. E ...... 626 435-0170
970 E Sandy Mush Rd Merced (95341) *(P-627)*

**Yoshimasa, South El Monte** *Also Called: Yoshimasa Display Case Inc (P-3678)*

**Yoshimasa Display Case Inc** .................................................. E ...... 213 637-9999
10808 Weaver Ave South El Monte (91733) *(P-3678)*

**Youbar Inc (PA)** ......................................................................... D ...... 626 537-1851
445 Wilson Way City Of Industry (91744) *(P-17152)*

**Youcare Pharma (usa) Inc** ....................................................... D ...... 951 258-3114
132 Business Center Dr Corona (92878) *(P-5721)*

**Young & Family Inc** ................................................................... E ...... 707 263-8877
64 Soda Bay Rd Lakeport (95453) *(P-3210)*

**Young Dental, Cerritos** *Also Called: US Dental Inc (P-15492)*

**Young Electric Sign Company** ................................................. E ...... 510 877-7815
46750 Fremont Blvd Ste 101 Fremont (94538) *(P-16070)*

**Young Electric Sign Company** ................................................. E ...... 916 419-8101
875 National Dr Ste 107 Sacramento (95834) *(P-16071)*

**Young Electric Sign Company** ................................................. C ...... 909 923-7668
10235 Bellegrave Ave Jurupa Valley (91752) *(P-16072)*

**Young Engineering & Mfg Inc (PA)** ......................................... E ...... 909 394-3225
560 W Terrace Dr San Dimas (91773) *(P-14472)*

**Young Engineers Inc** ................................................................ D ...... 949 581-9411
25841 Commercentre Dr Lake Forest (92630) *(P-8039)*

**Young Machine Inc** ................................................................... F ...... 909 464-0405
12282 Colony Ave Chino (91710) *(P-11198)*

**Young Sung (usa) Inc** ............................................................... F ...... 213 427-2580
1122 S Alvarado St Los Angeles (90006) *(P-3040)*

**Younger Mfg Co (PA)** ................................................................ B ...... 310 783-1533
2925 California St Torrance (90503) *(P-15625)*

**Younger Optics, Torrance** *Also Called: Younger Mfg Co (P-15625)*

**Youngvity Essntial Lf Sciences, Chula Vista** *Also Called: Al Global Corporation (P-17659)*

**Yourpeople Inc (HQ)** ................................................................ E ...... 888 249-3263
50 Beale St Ste 1000 San Francisco (94105) *(P-18950)*

**Youth To People Inc** ................................................................. D ...... 309 648-5500
888 N Douglas St El Segundo (90245) *(P-6063)*

**Youthglow, Fountain Valley** *Also Called: Yg Laboratories Inc (P-6062)*

**Yreka Division, Yreka** *Also Called: Timber Products Co Ltd Partnr (P-3289)*

**Ys Garments LLC (HQ)** ............................................................ F ...... 310 631-4955
588 Crenshaw Blvd Torrance (90503) *(P-2696)*

**Yti Enterprises Inc** .................................................................... F ...... 714 632-8696
1260 S State College Pkwy Anaheim (92806) *(P-3432)*

**Yuba Cy Wste Wtr Trtmnt Fcilty** .............................................. E ...... 530 822-7698
302 Burns Dr Yuba City (95991) *(P-10617)*

**Yuba Rver Mlding Mill Work Inc (PA)** ..................................... E ...... 530 742-2168
3757 Feather River Blvd Olivehurst (95961) *(P-3211)*

**Yuciapa & Calimesa News Mirror, Yucaipa** *Also Called: Hi-Desert Publishing Company (P-4129)*

**Yuhas Tooling & Machining Inc** .............................................. F ...... 408 934-9196
1031 Pecten Ct Milpitas (95035) *(P-11199)*

**Yuja Inc (PA)** ............................................................................. C ...... 888 257-2278
84 W Santa Clara St Ste 400 San Jose (95113) *(P-18951)*

**Yukeep LLC** ............................................................................... F ...... 888 855-2568
4540 Kearny Villa Rd Ste 203 San Diego (92123) *(P-16325)*

**Yum Yum Donut Shop, City Of Industry** *Also Called: Quality Naturally Foods Inc (P-17207)*

**Yumi, Los Angeles** *Also Called: Caer Inc (P-851)*

**Yun Industrial Co Ltd** ............................................................... E ...... 310 715-1898
161 Selandia Ln Carson (90746) *(P-12264)*

**Ywd Cartoners, Fresno** *Also Called: Kodiak Cartoners Inc (P-10023)*

**Yyk Enterprises Operations LLC (PA)** .................................... C ...... 619 474-6229
3475 E St San Diego (92102) *(P-581)*

**Z C & R Coating For Optics Inc** ............................................... E ...... 310 381-3060
1401 Abalone Ave Torrance (90501) *(P-14834)*

**Z Industries, Los Angeles** *Also Called: Active Window Products (P-8251)*

**Z Microsystems, San Diego** *Also Called: Zmicro Inc (P-19002)*

**Z P M Inc** .................................................................................... E ...... 805 681-3511
5770 Thornwood Dr Ste C Goleta (93117) *(P-10618)*

**Z-Line Designs Inc** ................................................................... D ...... 925 743-4000
181 Pullman St Livermore (94551) *(P-3611)*

**Z-Tronix Inc** ............................................................................... E ...... 562 808-0800
6327 Alondra Blvd Paramount (90723) *(P-13129)*

**Zaca Mesa Winery, Los Olivos** *Also Called: Cushman Winery Corporation (P-17263)*

**Zacky Farms, Fresno** *Also Called: ZF In Liquidation LLC (P-703)*

**Zadara Storage Inc** .................................................................. D ...... 949 251-0360
6 Venture Ste 140 Irvine (92618) *(P-10299)*

**Zadro Inc** ................................................................................... E ...... 714 892-9200
14462 Astronautics Ln Ste 101 Huntington Beach (92647) *(P-7247)*

**Zadro Products Inc** .................................................................. E ...... 714 892-9200
14462 Astronautics Ln Ste 101 Huntington Beach (92647) *(P-7248)*

**Zaitun Printing & Graphics Inc** ............................................... F ...... 402 305-0109
16260 Church St Ste 100 Morgan Hill (95037) *(P-4818)*

**Zamboni, Paramount** *Also Called: Zamboni Company Usa Inc (P-9913)*

**Zamboni Company Usa Inc** ..................................................... E ...... 562 633-0751
15714 Colorado Ave Paramount (90723) *(P-9913)*

**Zander, Baldwin Park** *Also Called: Sanders Candy Factory Inc (P-1325)*

**Zapp Packaging Inc** ................................................................. D ...... 909 930-1500
1921 S Business Pkwy Ontario (91761) *(P-3813)*

**Zapworldcom** ............................................................................ B ...... 707 525-8658
300 Stony Point Rd Spc 249 Petaluma (94952) *(P-11296)*

**Zbe Inc** ....................................................................................... E ...... 805 576-1600
1035 Cindy Ln Carpinteria (93013) *(P-11356)*

**Zco Liquidating Corporation** .................................................. A ...... 408 733-8400
6373 San Ignacio Ave San Jose (95119) *(P-10300)*

**Zebra Technologies Corporation** ............................................ D ...... 805 579-1800
30601 Agoura Rd Agoura Hills (91301) *(P-10454)*

**Zeda Inc** ..................................................................................... F ...... 510 225-8412
47929 Fremont Blvd Fremont (94538) *(P-15311)*

**Zeek Management Group LLC** ................................................ F ...... 424 570-0531
21720 Avalon Blvd Ste 102-B Carson (90745) *(P-17612)*

**Zeghani, Glendale** *Also Called: Simon G Jewelry Inc (P-16970)*

**Zeltiq Aesthetics Inc** ................................................................ C ...... 925 474-2519
6723 Sierra Ct Dublin (94568) *(P-15312)*

**Zeltiq Aesthetics Inc** — C ...... 925 474-2519
7085 Las Positas Rd Ste G Livermore (94551) *(P-15313)*

**Zeltiq Aesthetics Inc** — C ...... 925 474-2500
7041 Las Positas Rd Livermore (94551) *(P-15314)*

**Zeltiq Aesthetics Inc (DH)** — D ...... 925 474-2500
4410 Rosewood Dr Pleasanton (94588) *(P-15315)*

**Zenbooth Inc** — E ...... 510 646-8368
650 University Ave Unit 10 Berkeley (94710) *(P-3591)*

**Zendesk, San Francisco** Also Called: Zendesk Inc *(P-18952)*

**Zendesk Inc (HQ)** — A ...... 415 418-7506
181 Fremont St Fl 17 San Francisco (94105) *(P-18952)*

**Zenith Manufacturing Inc** — E ...... 818 767-2106
3087 12th St Riverside (92507) *(P-13994)*

**Zenith Screw Products Inc** — E ...... 562 941-0281
10910 Painter Ave Santa Fe Springs (90670) *(P-8739)*

**Zenith Specialty Bag, Rowland Heights** Also Called: Novolex Bagcraft Inc *(P-3975)*

**Zenlen Inc** — E ...... 415 834-8238
201 California St San Francisco (94111) *(P-6064)*

**Zenni Optical Inc (PA)** — D ...... 800 211-2105
448 Ignacio Blvd Ste 332 Novato (94949) *(P-15626)*

**Zentera Systems Inc** — E ...... 408 436-4811
1525 Mccarthy Blvd Ste 1104 Milpitas (95035) *(P-18953)*

**Zenverge Inc** — D ...... 408 350-5052
2680 Zanker Rd Ste 200 San Jose (95134) *(P-12810)*

**Zeons Inc** — B ...... 323 302-8299
291 S La Cienega Blvd Ste 102 Beverly Hills (90211) *(P-7209)*

**Zep Solar Llc (DH)** — E ...... 415 479-6900
151 Mitchell Blvd Ste 104 San Rafael (94903) *(P-12811)*

**Zephyr, San Jose** Also Called: D Software Inc *(P-18221)*

**Zephyr Manufacturing Co Inc** — D ...... 310 410-4907
201 Hindry Ave Inglewood (90301) *(P-9715)*

**Zephyr Tool Group, Inglewood** Also Called: Zephyr Manufacturing Co Inc *(P-9715)*

**Zero Base, Fremont** Also Called: Zerobase Energy LLC *(P-13155)*

**Zero Gravity Labs Inc** — E ...... 707 653-6287
548 Market St Pmb 33721 San Francisco (94104) *(P-18954)*

**Zero Motorcycles, Scotts Valley** Also Called: Zero Motorcycles Inc *(P-17486)*

**Zero Motorcycles Inc** — C ...... 831 438-3500
380 El Pueblo Rd Scotts Valley (95066) *(P-17486)*

**Zerobase Energy LLC** — E ...... 888 530-9376
46609 Fremont Blvd Fremont (94538) *(P-13155)*

**Zet-Tek Machining, Yorba Linda** Also Called: Zet-Tek Precision Machining *(P-11200)*

**Zet-Tek Precision Machining (PA)** — F ...... 714 777-8770
22951 La Palma Ave Yorba Linda (92887) *(P-11200)*

**Zet-Tek Precision Machining, Yorba Linda** Also Called: Pdma Ventures Inc *(P-15476)*

**Zettler Components Inc (PA)** — C ...... 949 831-5000
75 Columbia Orange (92868) *(P-12027)*

**Zettler Magnetics Inc** — C ...... 949 831-5000
2410 Birch St Vista (92081) *(P-11232)*

**Zevia, Encino** Also Called: Zevia Pbc *(P-1976)*

**Zevia LLC** — D ...... 310 202-7000
15821 Ventura Blvd Ste 145 Encino (91436) *(P-1975)*

**Zevia Pbc (PA)** — E ...... 424 343-2654
15821 Ventura Blvd Ste 135 Encino (91436) *(P-1976)*

**ZF Array Technology Inc** — E ...... 408 433-9920
2302 Trade Zone Blvd San Jose (95131) *(P-12265)*

**ZF In Liquidation LLC** — A ...... 559 486-2310
2020 S East Ave Fresno (93721) *(P-703)*

**Zhong W Ang Group, Walnut** Also Called: Pengcheng Aluminum Enterprise Inc USA *(P-7745)*

**Zi Machine Manufacturing, El Dorado Hills** Also Called: 478826 Limited *(P-10642)*

**Zia Aamir** — E ...... 714 337-7861
2043 Imperial St Los Angeles (90021) *(P-8249)*

**Zico, El Segundo** Also Called: Zico Beverages LLC *(P-1977)*

**Zico Beverages LLC (HQ)** — E ...... 866 729-9426
2101 E El Segundo Blvd Ste 403 El Segundo (90245) *(P-1977)*

**Ziegenfelder Company** — D ...... 909 590-0493
12290 Colony Ave Chino (91710) *(P-822)*

**Ziegenfelder Company** — D ...... 909 509-0493
12262 Colony Ave Chino (91710) *(P-823)*

**Zilog Inc** — E ...... 408 513-1500
6800 Santa Teresa Blvd San Jose (95119) *(P-12812)*

**Zilog Inc (DH)** — E ...... 408 513-1500
1590 Buckeye Dr Milpitas (95035) *(P-12813)*

**Zimmer Biomet Fegan Inc** — F ...... 707 863-0291
1640 Jeni Ln Fairfield (94534) *(P-15431)*

**Zimmer Dental Inc** — B ...... 800 854-7019
1900 Aston Ave Carlsbad (92008) *(P-15432)*

**Zimmer Melia & Associates Inc (PA)** — E ...... 615 377-0118
6832 Presidio Dr Huntington Beach (92648) *(P-15433)*

**Zinio Systems Inc** — D ...... 415 494-2700
114 Sansome St 4th Fl San Francisco (94104) *(P-18955)*

**Zinus Inc (HQ)** — E ...... 925 417-2100
5731 Promontory Pkwy Tracy (95377) *(P-3548)*

**Zion Automotive Group, Cerritos** Also Called: R1 Concepts Inc *(P-16391)*

**Zipco, Riverside** Also Called: Zenith Manufacturing Inc *(P-13994)*

**Zircon, Campbell** Also Called: Zircon Corporation *(P-9716)*

**Zircon Corporation (HQ)** — E ...... 408 866-8600
1580 Dell Ave Campbell (95008) *(P-9716)*

**Zk Enterprises Inc** — E ...... 213 622-7012
4368 District Blvd Vernon (90058) *(P-2651)*

**Zm Trucks, Torrance** Also Called: Zo Motors North America LLC *(P-11577)*

**Zmicro Inc (PA)** — D ...... 858 831-7000
9820 Summers Ridge Rd San Diego (92121) *(P-19002)*

**Zmp Aquisition Corporation** — F ...... 714 278-6500
4141 N Palm St Fullerton (92835) *(P-11357)*

**Znyx, Fremont** Also Called: Znyx Networks Inc *(P-10455)*

**Znyx Networks Inc** — D
48421 Milmont Dr Fremont (94538) *(P-10455)*

**Zo Motors North America LLC** — E ...... 310 792-7077
21250 Hawthorne Blvd Ste 500 Torrance (90503) *(P-11577)*

**Zo Skin Health Inc (DH)** — D ...... 949 988-7524
9685 Research Dr Irvine (92618) *(P-6065)*

**Zodiac Aerospace** — E ...... 909 652-9700
11340 Jersey Blvd Rancho Cucamonga (91730) *(P-13995)*

**Zodiac Interconnect US** — F ...... 707 535-2700
3780 Flightline Dr Santa Rosa (95403) *(P-13996)*

**Zodiac Pool Solutions, Carlsbad** Also Called: Fluidra North America LLC *(P-10559)*

**Zodiac Pool Systems LLC (DH)** — C ...... 760 599-9600
2882 Whiptail Loop Ste 100 Carlsbad (92010) *(P-10619)*

**Zodiac Wtr Waste Aero Systems** — D ...... 310 884-7000
1500 Glenn Curtiss St Carson (90746) *(P-13997)*

**Zoetis Inc** — C ...... 510 474-9259
30411 Whipple Rd Union City (94587) *(P-5722)*

**Zogenix, Emeryville** Also Called: Zogenix Inc *(P-5723)*

**Zogenix Inc (HQ)** — E ...... 510 550-8300
5959 Horton St Ste 500 Emeryville (94608) *(P-5723)*

**Zola Acai, San Jose** Also Called: Amazon Prsrvation Partners Inc *(P-875)*

**Zola Electric Labs Inc** — E ...... 650 542-6939
3130 20th St Ste 225 San Francisco (94110) *(P-12814)*

**Zoll Circulation Inc** — C ...... 408 541-2140
2000 Ringwood Ave San Jose (95131) *(P-15592)*

**Zollner Electronics Inc** — E ...... 408 434-5400
575 Cottonwood Dr Milpitas (95035) *(P-12266)*

**Zonda Media, Newport Beach** Also Called: Hanley Wood Media Inc *(P-4412)*

**Zonson Company Inc** — E ...... 760 597-0338
3197 Lionshead Ave Carlsbad (92010) *(P-15880)*

**Zonu, Van Nuys** Also Called: Optical Zonu Corporation *(P-11779)*

**Zoo Med Laboratories Inc** — C ...... 805 542-9988
3650 Sacramento Dr San Luis Obispo (93401) *(P-16273)*

**Zoo Printing Inc (PA)** — E ...... 310 253-7751
1225 Los Angeles St Glendale (91204) *(P-4819)*

**Zoo Printing Trade Printer, Glendale** Also Called: Zoo Printing Inc *(P-4819)*

**Zooey Apparel Inc** — E ...... 310 315-2880
1526 Cloverfield Blvd Ste C Santa Monica (90404) *(P-2824)*

**Zoomifier Corporation (PA)** — B ...... 800 255-5303
8048 Golden Eagle Way Pleasanton (94588) *(P-18956)*

**Zoot Sports Inc** — E ...... 760 681-3587
2719 Loker Ave W Ste B Carlsbad (92010) *(P-2825)*

**Zoove Corp., Campbell** Also Called: Zoove LLC *(P-18001)*

**Zoove LLC** — E ...... 954 448-5442
1901 S Bascom Ave Ste 400 Campbell (95008) *(P-18001)*

**Zoox Inc (HQ)** .................................................................... E ...... 650 539-9669
 1149 Chess Dr Foster City (94404) *(P-13399)*
**Zoox Labs, Foster City** *Also Called: Zoox Inc (P-13399)*
**Zoria Farms Inc (PA)** ........................................................ B ...... 559 673-6368
 3487 Mckee Rd Ste 54 San Jose (95127) *(P-974)*
**Zosano, Los Angeles** *Also Called: Zp Opco Inc (P-5725)*
**Zosano Pharma, Fremont** *Also Called: Zosano Pharma Corporation (P-5724)*
**Zosano Pharma Corporation (PA)** ................................... E ...... 510 745-1200
 34790 Ardentech Ct Fremont (94555) *(P-5724)*
**Zp Opco Inc** ...................................................................... E ...... 510 745-1200
 34790 Ardentech Ct Los Angeles (90071) *(P-5725)*
**Zpower LLC** ..................................................................... C ...... 805 445-7789
 5171 Clareton Dr Agoura Hills (91301) *(P-11385)*
**Zs Pharma Inc** ................................................................. E ...... 650 753-1823
 1100 Park Pl Fl 3 San Mateo (94403) *(P-5726)*
**Zscaler, San Jose** *Also Called: Zscaler Inc (P-18002)*
**Zscaler Inc (PA)** .............................................................. A ...... 408 533-0288
 120 Holger Way San Jose (95134) *(P-18002)*
**Zuca Inc** ........................................................................... E ...... 408 377-9822
 320 S Milpitas Blvd Milpitas (95035) *(P-7144)*
**Zumen Inc** ........................................................................ F ...... 564 444-6964
 340 S Lemon Ave Ste 3677 Walnut (91789) *(P-18957)*
**Zuo, Oakland** *Also Called: Zuo Modern Contemporary Inc (P-11511)*
**Zuo Modern Contemporary Inc (PA)** ............................... E ...... 510 877-4087
 80 Swan Way Ste 150 Oakland (94621) *(P-11511)*
**Zuora, Redwood City** *Also Called: Zuora Inc (P-18958)*
**Zuora Inc (PA)** B
 101 Redwood Shores Pkwy Ste 100 Redwood City (94065) *(P-18958)*
**Zuza LLC** ......................................................................... D ...... 760 494-9000
 2304 Faraday Ave Carlsbad (92008) *(P-4820)*
**Zwift Inc (PA)** ................................................................... B ...... 855 469-9438
 111 W Ocean Blvd Ste 1800 Long Beach (90802) *(P-18959)*
**Zygo Corporation** ............................................................. E ...... 408 434-1000
 3350 Scott Blvd Ste 4901 Santa Clara (95054) *(P-14757)*
**Zygo Corporation** ............................................................. E ...... 714 918-7433
 2031 Main St Irvine (92614) *(P-14835)*
**Zygo Epo** .......................................................................... F ...... 510 243-7592
 3900 Lakeside Dr Richmond (94806) *(P-14836)*
**Zygo Optical Systems, Irvine** *Also Called: Zygo Corporation (P-14835)*
**Zynga, San Mateo** *Also Called: Zynga Inc (P-19015)*
**Zynga Inc (HQ)** ................................................................ C ...... 855 449-9642
 1200 Park Pl Ste 100 San Mateo (94403) *(P-19015)*
**Zyris Inc** ........................................................................... E ...... 805 560-9888
 6868 Cortona Dr Ste A Santa Barbara (93117) *(P-15496)*
**Zytek Corp (PA)** ............................................................... E ...... 408 520-4287
 1755 Mccarthy Blvd Milpitas (95035) *(P-12267)*
**Zytek Ems, Milpitas** *Also Called: Zytek Corp (P-12267)*

# COUNTY/CITY CROSS-REFERENCE INDEX

**Alameda**
Alameda
Albany
Berkeley
Castro Valley
Dublin
Emeryville
Fremont
Hayward
Kensington
Livermore
Newark
Oakland
Pleasanton
San Leandro
San Lorenzo
Sunol
Union City

**Amador**
Ione
Pioneer
Plymouth
Sutter Creek

**Butte**
Biggs
Chico
Durham
Gridley
Nelson
Oroville
Paradise
Richvale

**Calaveras**
Arnold
Copperopolis
Murphys
Vallecito
Valley Springs

**Colusa**
Arbuckle
Colusa
Maxwell
Princeton
Williams

**Contra Costa**
Alamo
Antioch
Brentwood
Byron
Clayton
Concord
Crockett
Danville
Discovery Bay
Hercules
Lafayette
Martinez
Moraga
Oakley
Orinda
Pacheco
Pinole
Pittsburg
Pleasant Hill

Richmond
San Pablo
San Ramon
Walnut Creek

**Del Norte**
Crescent City

**El Dorado**
Cameron Park
Camino
Cool
Diamond Springs
El Dorado Hills
Georgetown
Placerville
Shingle Springs
Somerset
South Lake Tahoe

**Fresno**
Auberry
Caruthers
Clovis
Coalinga
Del Rey
Firebaugh
Fowler
Fresno
Kerman
Kingsburg
Parlier
Pinedale
Reedley
Sanger
Selma

**Glenn**
Glenn
Orland
Willows

**Humboldt**
Arcata
Blue Lake
Eureka
Fields Landing
Fortuna
Hoopa
Mckinleyville
Samoa
Scotia

**Imperial**
Brawley
Calexico
Calipatria
El Centro
Heber
Imperial

**Inyo**
Bishop
Darwin

**Kern**
Arvin
Bakersfield
Boron

Buttonwillow
California City
Delano
Edison
Fellows
Frazier Park
Inyokern
Lake Isabella
Lebec
Maricopa
Mc Farland
Mc Kittrick
Mojave
Ridgecrest
Shafter
Taft
Tehachapi
Tupman
Wasco

**Kings**
Corcoran
Hanford
Kettleman City
Lemoore

**Lake**
Kelseyville
Lakeport
Lower Lake
Middletown

**Los Angeles**
Agoura Hills
Agua Dulce
Alhambra
Altadena
Arcadia
Arleta
Artesia
Azusa
Baldwin Park
Bell
Bell Gardens
Bellflower
Beverly Hills
Burbank
Calabasas
Calabasas Hills
Canoga Park
Canyon Country
Carson
Castaic
Cerritos
Chatsworth
City Of Commerce
City Of Industry
Claremont
Commerce
Compton
Covina
Cudahy
Culver City
Diamond Bar
Downey
Duarte
E Rncho Dmngz
East Rancho Domingue
El Monte

El Segundo
Encino
Gardena
Glendale
Glendora
Granada Hills
Hacienda Heights
Harbor City
Hawaiian Gardens
Hawthorne
Hermosa Beach
Hollywood
Huntington Park
Inglewood
Irwindale
La Canada
La Canada Flintridge
La Crescenta
La Mirada
La Puente
La Verne
Lakewood
Lancaster
Lawndale
Littlerock
Long Beach
Los Angeles
Lynwood
Malibu
Manhattan Beach
Marina Del Rey
Maywood
Mission Hills
Monrovia
Montebello
Monterey Park
Montrose
Newhall
North Hills
North Hollywood
Northridge
Norwalk
Pacific Palisades
Pacoima
Palmdale
Palos Verdes Estates
Panorama City
Paramount
Pasadena
Pearblossom
Pico Rivera
Playa Del Rey
Playa Vista
Pls Vrds Pnsl
Pomona
Porter Ranch
Rancho Cascades
Rancho Dominguez
Rancho Palos Verdes
Redondo Beach
Rlng Hls Est
Rolling Hills
Rolling Hills Estate
Rosemead
Rowland Heights
San Dimas
San Fernando
San Gabriel
San Marino

San Pedro
Santa Clarita
Santa Fe Springs
Santa Monica
Saugus
Sherman Oaks
Sierra Madre
Signal Hill
South El Monte
South Gate
South Pasadena
Stevenson Ranch
Studio City
Sun Valley
Sylmar
Tarzana
Temple City
Toluca Lake
Topanga
Torrance
Tujunga
Universal City
Valencia
Valley Village
Van Nuys
Venice
Vernon
Walnut
West Covina
West Hills
West Hollywood
Whittier
Wilmington
Winnetka
Woodland Hills

**Madera**
Chowchilla
Coarsegold
Madera
Oakhurst

**Marin**
Belvedere Tiburon
Corte Madera
Greenbrae
Larkspur
Mill Valley
Novato
San Anselmo
San Rafael
Sausalito

**Mariposa**
Mariposa

**Mendocino**
Boonville
Branscomb
Calpella
Comptche
Covelo
Fort Bragg
Hopland
Philo
Redwood Valley
Ukiah
Willits

2025 Harris California Manufacturers Directory

# COUNTY/CITY CROSS-REFERENCE

### Merced
Atwater
Ballico
Dos Palos
Gustine
Hilmar
Le Grand
Livingston
Los Banos
Merced
South Dos Palos
Stevinson

### Mono
Mammoth Lakes

### Monterey
Aromas
Carmel Valley
Castroville
Gonzales
Greenfield
King City
Marina
Monterey
Moss Landing
Pacific Grove
Salinas
San Ardo
Seaside
Soledad

### Napa
American Canyon
Angwin
Calistoga
Napa
Oakville
Rutherford
Saint Helena
Vallejo
Yountville

### Nevada
Grass Valley
Nevada City
Penn Valley
Truckee

### Orange
Aliso Viejo
Anaheim
Brea
Buena Park
Capistrano Beach
Corona Del Mar
Costa Mesa
Cypress
Dana Point
El Toro
Foothill Ranch
Fountain Valley
Fullerton
Garden Grove
Huntington Beach
Irvine
La Habra
La Palma
Ladera Ranch
Laguna Beach
Laguna Hills
Laguna Niguel
Lake Forest
Los Alamitos
Mission Viejo
Newport Beach
Newport Coast
Orange
Placentia
Rancho Santa Margari
Rcho Sta Marg
San Clemente
San Juan Capistrano
Santa Ana
Seal Beach
Stanton
Trabuco Canyon
Tustin
Villa Park
Westminster
Yorba Linda

### Placer
Auburn
Colfax
Granite Bay
Lincoln
Loomis
Newcastle
Rocklin
Roseville

### Plumas
Chester
Quincy

### Riverside
Aguanga
Banning
Beaumont
Blythe
Cabazon
Calimesa
Canyon Lake
Cathedral City
Coachella
Corona
Desert Hot Springs
Eastvale
Hemet
Idyllwild
Indio
Jurupa Valley
La Quinta
Lake Elsinore
Mecca
Menifee
Mira Loma
Moreno Valley
Murrieta
Norco
Nuevo
Palm Desert
Palm Springs
Perris
Riverside
Romoland
San Jacinto
Sun City
Temecula
Thermal
Thousand Palms
Whitewater
Wildomar

### Sacramento
Antelope
Carmichael
Citrus Heights
Elk Grove
Fair Oaks
Folsom
Galt
Gold River
Mather
Mcclellan
North Highlands
Rancho Cordova
Rancho Murieta
Sacramento
Walnut Grove
Wilton

### San Benito
Hollister
San Juan Bautista

### San Bernardino
Adelanto
Apple Valley
Barstow
Big Bear City
Big Bear Lake
Bloomington
Blue Jay
Chino
Chino Hills
Colton
Fontana
Fort Irwin
Grand Terrace
Helendale
Hesperia
Highland
Lake Arrowhead
Loma Linda
Lucerne Valley
Lytle Creek
Mentone
Montclair
Mountain Pass
Newberry Springs
Ontario
Oro Grande
Rancho Cucamonga
Redlands
Rialto
San Bernardino
Trona
Upland
Victorville
Yucaipa
Yucca Valley

### San Diego
Alpine
Bonita
Bonsall
Cardiff
Cardiff By The Sea
Carlsbad
Chula Vista
Coronado
Del Mar
El Cajon
Encinitas
Escondido
Fallbrook
Jamul
La Jolla
La Mesa
Lakeside
Lemon Grove
National City
Oceanside
Pala
Poway
Ramona
San Diego
San Marcos
San Ysidro
Santa Ysabel
Santee
Solana Beach
Spring Valley
Tecate
Valley Center
Vista

### San Francisco
San Francisco

### San Joaquin
Acampo
Escalon
French Camp
Lathrop
Linden
Lockeford
Lodi
Manteca
Ripon
Stockton
Tracy

### San Luis Obispo
Arroyo Grande
Atascadero
Avila Beach
Cambria
Grover Beach
Morro Bay
Nipomo
Paso Robles
Pismo Beach
San Luis Obispo
San Miguel
Shandon
Templeton

### San Mateo
Belmont
Brisbane
Burlingame
Colma
Daly City
El Granada
Foster City
Half Moon Bay
Hillsborough
La Honda
Menlo Park
Millbrae
Moss Beach
Pacifica
Portola Valley
Redwood City
Redwood Shores
San Bruno
San Carlos
San Mateo
South San Francisco
Woodside

### Santa Barbara
Buellton
Carpinteria
Goleta
Lompoc
Los Olivos
New Cuyama
Orcutt
Santa Barbara
Santa Maria
Santa Ynez
Solvang
Vandenberg Afb

### Santa Clara
Alviso
Campbell
Cupertino
East Palo Alto
Gilroy
Los Altos
Los Altos Hills
Los Gatos
Milpitas
Monte Sereno
Morgan Hill
Mountain View
Palo Alto
San Jose
San Martin
Santa Clara
Saratoga
Stanford
Sunnyvale

### Santa Cruz
Aptos
Capitola
Davenport
Los Gatos
Royal Oaks
Santa Cruz
Scotts Valley
Soquel
Watsonville

### Shasta
Anderson
Burney
Cottonwood
Redding
Shasta Lake

### Siskiyou
Dunsmuir
Etna
Weed
Yreka

### Solano
Benicia
Dixon
Fairfield
Rio Vista
Suisun City
Vacaville
Vallejo

### Sonoma
Cazadero
Cloverdale

## COUNTY/CITY CROSS-REFERENCE

Cotati
Forestville
Geyserville
Glen Ellen
Graton
Guerneville
Healdsburg
Kenwood
Petaluma
Rohnert Park
Santa Rosa
Sebastopol
Sonoma
Windsor

### Stanislaus

Ceres
Crows Landing
Denair
Empire
Hickman
Hughson
Modesto
Newman
Oakdale
Patterson
Riverbank
Salida
Turlock
Waterford
Westley

### Sutter

Live Oak
Meridian
Pleasant Grove
Sutter
Yuba City

### Tehama

Corning
Red Bluff

### Trinity

Junction City
Lewiston

### Tulare

Dinuba
Earlimart
Exeter
Farmersville
Lindsay
Pixley
Porterville
Strathmore
Terra Bella
Tipton
Traver
Tulare
Visalia
Woodlake

### Tuolumne

Columbia
Jamestown
Mi Wuk Village
Sonora

### Ventura

Camarillo
Fillmore
Moorpark
Newbury Park
Oak Park
Oak View
Ojai
Oxnard
Port Hueneme
Santa Paula
Santa Rosa Valley
Simi Valley
Somis
Thousand Oaks
Ventura
Westlake Village

### Yolo

Davis
Esparto
West Sacramento
Winters
Woodland
Zamora

### Yuba

Beale Afb
Marysville
Olivehurst
Plumas Lake

# GEOGRAPHIC SECTION

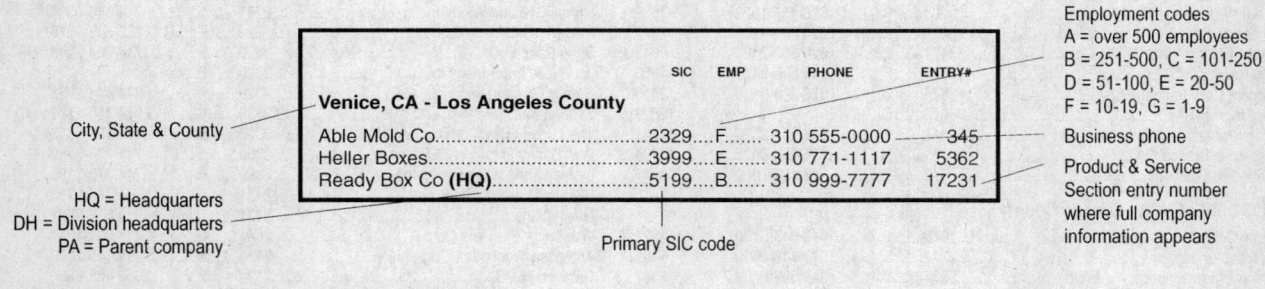

- Listings in this section are sorted alphabetically by city.
- Listings within each city are sorted alphabetically by company name.

|  | SIC | EMP | PHONE | ENTRY# |
|---|---|---|---|---|
| **ACAMPO, CA - San Joaquin County** | | | | |
| R & G Schatz Farms Inc | 0172 | F | 209 367-4881 | 24 |
| California Concentrate Company | 2037 | E | 209 334-9112 | 998 |
| Calva Products LLC (PA) | 2048 | E | 800 328-9680 | 1121 |
| Calva Products Co Inc | 2048 | E | 209 339-1516 | 1122 |
| Global Wine Group | 2084 | E | 209 340-8500 | 1589 |
| Langetwins Inc | 2084 | E | 209 339-4055 | 1661 |
| Langetwins Wine Company Inc | 2084 | E | 209 334-9780 | 1662 |
| Lcf Wine Company LLC | 2084 | E | 209 334-9782 | 1666 |
| Macchia Inc | 2084 | E | 209 333-2600 | 1671 |
| Woodbridge Winery | 2084 | F | 209 369-5861 | 1832 |
| **ADELANTO, CA - San Bernardino County** | | | | |
| Flavor House Inc | 2087 | E | 760 246-9131 | 2004 |
| Furniture Technologies Inc | 2426 | E | 760 246-9180 | 3092 |
| California Silica Products LLC | 2819 | D | 909 947-0028 | 5075 |
| Dar-Ken Inc | 3053 | E | 760 246-4010 | 6445 |
| Fiber Care Baths Inc | 3088 | E | 760 246-0019 | 6678 |
| Hee Environmental Engineering LLC | 3089 | E | 760 530-1409 | 6850 |
| Molded Fiber GL Companies - W | 3089 | D | 760 246-4042 | 6919 |
| Clark - Pacific Corporation | 3272 | E | 626 962-8755 | 7319 |
| Mk Magnetics Inc | 3315 | D | 760 246-6373 | 7647 |
| Northwest Pipe Company | 3317 | C | 760 246-3191 | 7667 |
| McElroy Metal Mill Inc | 3448 | E | 760 246-5545 | 8675 |
| Cageco Inc | 3523 | E | 800 605-4859 | 9344 |
| Ebara Mixers Inc | 3556 | E | 760 246-3430 | 9787 |
| Thermtronix Corporation (PA) | 3567 | E | 760 246-4500 | 10060 |
| Andersen Industries Inc | 3715 | E | 760 246-8766 | 13611 |
| General Atomic Aeron | 3721 | C | 760 388-8208 | 13663 |
| Ducommun Aerostructures Inc | 3728 | E | 760 246-4191 | 13828 |
| Safeway Sign Company | 3993 | E | 760 246-7070 | 16029 |
| Carberry LLC (HQ) | 3999 | E | 800 564-0842 | 16108 |
| Quality Resources Dist LLC | 3999 | E | 510 378-6861 | 16212 |
| Hayes Welding Inc (PA) | 7692 | D | 760 246-4878 | 19197 |
| **AGOURA HILLS, CA - Los Angeles County** | | | | |
| 1st Century Builders Inc | 1521 | F | 818 254-7183 | 342 |
| Acorn Newspaper Inc | 2711 | F | 818 706-0266 | 4061 |
| Paisano Publications LLC (PA) | 2721 | D | 818 889-8740 | 4285 |
| Paisano Publications Inc | 2721 | D | 818 889-8740 | 4286 |
| Wixen Music Publishing Inc | 2731 | F | 818 591-7355 | 4355 |
| Evergreen Licensing LLC | 2833 | F | 844 270-2700 | 5239 |
| Bendpak Inc (PA) | 3559 | C | 805 933-9970 | 9838 |
| Edge Solutions Consulting Inc (PA) | 3571 | E | 818 591-3500 | 10149 |
| Internet Machines Corporation (PA) | 3577 | D | 818 575-2100 | 10390 |
| Zebra Technologies Corporation | 3577 | D | 805 579-1800 | 10454 |
| Zpower LLC | 3629 | C | 805 445-7789 | 11385 |
| Teradyne Inc | 3679 | D | 818 991-2900 | 13107 |
| Aptiv Services Us LLC | 3714 | B | 818 661-6667 | 13459 |
| V-Wave Inc | 3841 | E | 818 629-2164 | 15297 |
| Relief-Mart Inc | 5999 | E | 805 379-4300 | 17718 |
| Novalogic Inc | 7371 | D | 818 880-1997 | 17955 |
| Novastor Corporation (PA) | 7372 | E | 805 579-6700 | 18599 |
| Scorelate Inc | 7372 | E | 818 602-9176 | 18767 |
| OSI Digital Inc (PA) | 7379 | E | 818 992-2700 | 19043 |
| **AGUA DULCE, CA - Los Angeles County** | | | | |
| Agua Dulce Vineyards LLC | 2084 | E | 661 268-7402 | 1473 |
| Precision Millwork LLC | 2431 | F | 661 402-5021 | 3181 |

|  | SIC | EMP | PHONE | ENTRY# |
|---|---|---|---|---|
| **AGUANGA, CA - Riverside County** | | | | |
| Patriot Polishing Company | 2842 | F | 310 903-7409 | 5924 |
| **ALAMEDA, CA - Alameda County** | | | | |
| Eat Just Inc (PA) | 2035 | D | 844 423-6637 | 977 |
| Donsuemor Inc | 2051 | D | 888 420-4441 | 1185 |
| Firebrand Pbc | 2051 | D | 510 594-9213 | 1194 |
| Kiva Brands Inc | 2066 | F | 510 592-8711 | 1342 |
| Terviva Inc | 2076 | D | 510 501-3707 | 1374 |
| Rock Wall Wine Company Inc | 2084 | E | 510 522-5700 | 1729 |
| St George Spirits Inc (PA) | 2084 | F | 510 769-1601 | 1758 |
| Golden West Envelope Corp | 2677 | E | 510 452-5419 | 4008 |
| Fleenor Company Inc | 2679 | E | 800 433-2531 | 4039 |
| Center For Cllbrtive Classroom | 2731 | D | 510 533-0213 | 4319 |
| Abbott Diabetes Care Sls Corp | 2834 | D | 510 749-5400 | 5287 |
| Abbott Diabetes Care Inc (HQ) | 2835 | D | 855 632-8658 | 5727 |
| Exelixis Inc (PA) | 2836 | D | 650 837-7000 | 5828 |
| Rmf Salt Holdings LLC | 2844 | F | 510 477-9600 | 6032 |
| Heliotrope Technologies Inc | 3211 | F | 510 871-3980 | 7172 |
| Sks Die Cast & Machining Inc (PA) | 3363 | E | 510 523-2541 | 7822 |
| Saildrone Inc | 3549 | C | 415 670-9700 | 9745 |
| Rgb Spectrum | 3577 | D | 510 814-7000 | 10428 |
| Allied Engineering and Production Corporation | 3599 | E | 510 522-1500 | 10700 |
| ABB Inc | 3612 | E | 510 987-7111 | 11201 |
| Black Point Products Inc | 3661 | E | 510 232-7723 | 11754 |
| Clear-Com LLC (HQ) | 3663 | A | 510 337-6600 | 11826 |
| Sila Nanotechnologies Inc (PA) | 3691 | C | 408 475-7452 | 13148 |
| Imprint Energy Inc | 3692 | E | 510 847-7027 | 13161 |
| Bay Ship & Yacht Co (PA) | 3731 | C | 510 337-9122 | 14000 |
| Astra Space Inc (PA) | 3761 | E | 866 278-7217 | 14077 |
| Exelixis Inc | 3824 | B | 650 837-7000 | 14479 |
| Power Standards Lab Inc | 3825 | E | 510 522-4400 | 14574 |
| Penumbra Inc (PA) | 3841 | B | 510 748-3200 | 15221 |
| Therasense Inc | 3841 | E | 510 749-5400 | 15282 |
| Vivani Medical Inc (PA) | 3841 | F | 415 506-8462 | 15306 |
| Xintec Corporation (PA) | 3841 | E | 510 832-2130 | 15309 |
| Lens C-C Inc (PA) | 3851 | D | 800 772-3911 | 15606 |
| Ericson Owens Enterprises | 3993 | F | 510 500-5491 | 15971 |
| Svendsens Boat Works Inc | 5088 | D | 510 522-2886 | 16927 |
| Golden State Imports Intl Inc (PA) | 5094 | F | 510 995-1320 | 16967 |
| Polarion Software Inc | 7372 | D | 877 572-4005 | 18684 |
| Wind River Systems Inc (DH) | 7372 | A | 510 748-4100 | 18935 |
| New Pride Tire LLC (HQ) | 7534 | E | 510 567-8800 | 19152 |
| Asterias Biotherapeutics Inc | 8731 | D | 510 456-3800 | 19443 |
| Singulex Inc | 8733 | B | 510 995-9000 | 19497 |
| Doer Marine Operations | 8748 | E | 510 530-9388 | 19558 |
| **ALAMO, CA - Contra Costa County** | | | | |
| Edner Corporation | 2051 | F | 925 831-1248 | 1189 |
| Trilore Technologies Inc | 3365 | E | 925 295-0734 | 7851 |
| Heirloom Computing Inc (PA) | 7372 | E | 510 709-7245 | 18381 |
| Gridbright Inc | 7373 | F | 925 899-9025 | 18979 |
| **ALBANY, CA - Alameda County** | | | | |
| The Adhesive Products Inc (PA) | 2891 | E | 510 526-7616 | 6250 |
| **ALHAMBRA, CA - Los Angeles County** | | | | |
| Tyler Trafficante Inc (PA) | 2311 | E | 323 869-9299 | 2569 |
| Gracing Brand Management Inc | 2369 | B | 626 297-2472 | 2861 |
| Asia-Pacific California Inc (PA) | 2711 | F | 323 318-2254 | 4067 |

# ALHAMBRA, CA

| | SIC | EMP | PHONE | ENTRY# |
|---|---|---|---|---|
| Copy Solutions Inc. | 2752 | E | 323 307-0900 | 4572 |
| Redwood Scientific Tech Inc. | 2834 | E | 310 693-5401 | 5633 |
| Great Wall International Corp. | 3281 | F | 626 457-1022 | 7538 |
| Alhambra Foundry Company Ltd. | 3321 | E | 626 289-4294 | 7674 |
| Coast To Coast Met Finshg Corp. | 3471 | E | 626 282-2122 | 8943 |
| Dsp Winner Inc. | 3631 | F | 858 336-9471 | 11388 |
| Emcore Corporation (PA) | 3674 | C | 626 293-3400 | 12419 |
| Riedon Inc (PA) | 3676 | C | | 12823 |
| Orora Packaging Solutions | 5113 | E | 626 284-9524 | 17011 |
| Lola Belle Brands LLC | 5621 | F | 855 226-3526 | 17494 |
| Embodied Labs Inc. | 7372 | E | 323 421-7600 | 18277 |

## ALISO VIEJO, CA - Orange County

| | SIC | EMP | PHONE | ENTRY# |
|---|---|---|---|---|
| Pepsi-Cola Metro Btlg Co Inc. | 2086 | D | 949 643-5700 | 1921 |
| Siemens Energy Inc. | 2741 | E | 949 448-0600 | 4465 |
| Avanir Pharmaceuticals Inc (DH) | 2834 | D | 949 389-6700 | 5347 |
| Biovail Technologies Ltd. | 2834 | D | 703 995-2400 | 5378 |
| Spyglass Pharma Inc. | 2834 | E | 949 284-6904 | 5671 |
| Epicuren Discovery. | 2835 | D | 949 588-5807 | 5750 |
| Custom Iron Corporation. | 3441 | F | 949 939-4379 | 8127 |
| Parylene Coating Services Inc. | 3479 | E | 281 391-7665 | 9101 |
| Wepower LLC. | 3511 | E | 866 385-9463 | 9321 |
| Centon Electronics Inc (PA) | 3572 | D | 949 855-9111 | 10230 |
| Ace Tube Bending. | 3599 | E | 949 362-2220 | 10667 |
| Astronic. | 3672 | C | 949 454-1180 | 12062 |
| Indie Semiconductor Inc (PA) | 3674 | E | 949 608-0854 | 12475 |
| Ixys Intgrted Crcits Div AV In. | 3674 | A | 949 831-4622 | 12508 |
| W G Holt Inc. | 3674 | D | 949 859-8800 | 12799 |
| Screening Systems Inc (PA) | 3826 | E | 949 855-1751 | 14714 |
| Glaukos Corporation (PA) | 3841 | C | 949 367-9600 | 15101 |
| Merit Medical Systems Inc. | 3841 | E | 801 208-4793 | 15186 |
| Microvention Inc (DH) | 3841 | C | 714 258-8000 | 15189 |
| Sequent Medical Inc. | 3841 | D | 949 830-9600 | 15253 |
| Vertos Medical Inc LLC. | 3841 | E | 949 349-0008 | 15305 |
| Presbibio LLC. | 3851 | E | 949 502-7010 | 15614 |
| Rxsight Inc (PA) | 3851 | D | 949 521-7830 | 15615 |
| Valeant Biomedicals Inc (DH) | 5169 | D | 949 461-6000 | 17250 |
| Gaikai Inc. | 7372 | D | | 18339 |
| Global Wave Group. | 7372 | E | 949 916-9800 | 18353 |
| Quadrotech Solutions Inc (PA) | 7372 | E | 949 754-8000 | 18714 |
| Quest Software Inc. | 7372 | D | 949 754-8000 | 18719 |
| Quest Software Inc (PA) | 7373 | A | 949 754-8000 | 18988 |
| Perfect Impression Inc. | 7389 | E | 949 305-0797 | 19116 |

## ALPINE, CA - San Diego County

| | SIC | EMP | PHONE | ENTRY# |
|---|---|---|---|---|
| Mountain Materials Inc. | 3273 | E | 619 445-4150 | 7471 |

## ALTADENA, CA - Los Angeles County

| | SIC | EMP | PHONE | ENTRY# |
|---|---|---|---|---|
| Honeybee Robotics LLC. | 3569 | D | 303 774-7613 | 10094 |
| 3becom Inc (PA) | 7372 | F | 818 726-0007 | 18004 |
| Blue Marble Rehab Inc. | 7372 | F | 626 296-6400 | 18118 |

## ALVISO, CA - Santa Clara County

| | SIC | EMP | PHONE | ENTRY# |
|---|---|---|---|---|
| Flextronics America LLC. | 3672 | C | 512 425-4129 | 12103 |
| Flextronics Ap LLC (DH) | 3679 | C | 408 576-7000 | 12979 |

## AMERICAN CANYON, CA - Napa County

| | SIC | EMP | PHONE | ENTRY# |
|---|---|---|---|---|
| Wallaby Yogurt Company LLC. | 2024 | E | 855 925-4636 | 819 |
| G L Mezzetta Inc (PA) | 2033 | C | 707 648-1050 | 890 |
| Barry Callebaut USA LLC. | 2066 | D | 707 642-8200 | 1337 |
| Hess Collection Winery. | 2084 | D | 707 255-1144 | 1612 |
| Amcan Beverages Inc. | 2086 | D | 707 557-0500 | 1849 |
| Coca-Cola Company American Cyn. | 2086 | E | 707 556-1220 | 1881 |
| Amcor Flexibles LLC. | 2671 | E | 707 257-6481 | 3921 |
| William Kreysler & Assoc Inc. | 3089 | E | 707 552-3500 | 7081 |
| Envirocare International Inc. | 3564 | E | 707 638-6800 | 9985 |
| Alcan Packg Capsules Cal LLC. | 5085 | E | 707 257-6481 | 16862 |

## ANAHEIM, CA - Orange County

| | SIC | EMP | PHONE | ENTRY# |
|---|---|---|---|---|
| Capsule Manufacturing Inc. | 1389 | D | 949 245-4151 | 212 |
| Control Air Conditioning Corporation. | 1711 | B | 714 777-8600 | 414 |
| C G Systems LLC. | 1731 | E | 714 632-8882 | 452 |
| Donco & Sons Inc. | 1731 | E | 714 779-0099 | 455 |
| Peterson Brothers Cnstr Inc. | 1771 | A | 714 278-0488 | 524 |
| A-1 Enterprises Inc. | 1799 | E | 714 630-3390 | 552 |
| Bravo Sign & Design Inc. | 1799 | F | 714 284-0500 | 556 |
| Bloomfield Food Inc. | 2011 | E | 714 779-7273 | 583 |
| Pampanga Food Company Inc. | 2013 | E | 714 773-0537 | 657 |
| T&J Sausage Kitchen Inc. | 2013 | E | 714 632-8350 | 673 |
| Pharmachem Laboratories LLC. | 2023 | E | 714 630-6000 | 779 |
| 180 Snacks Inc. | 2064 | E | 714 238-1192 | 1297 |
| Nectave Inc. | 2099 | E | 714 736-9811 | 2292 |
| Sun Rich Foods Intl Corp. | 2099 | F | 714 632-7577 | 2364 |
| Fantasia Distribution Inc. | 2131 | F | 714 817-8300 | 2398 |
| Alstyle Apparel LLC. | 2211 | A | 714 765-0400 | 2400 |
| Harrys Dye and Wash Inc. | 2261 | E | 714 446-0300 | 2492 |
| Redwood Wellness LLC. | 2299 | E | 323 843-2676 | 2554 |
| Bring Rokk LLC. | 2326 | F | 714 904-2243 | 2591 |
| Joe Wells Enterprises Inc. | 2329 | E | | 2626 |
| Steady Clothing Inc. | 2329 | F | 714 444-2058 | 2643 |
| St John Knits Inc (DH) | 2339 | B | 877 750-1171 | 2810 |
| The Lunada Bay Corporation (PA) | 2369 | E | 714 490-1313 | 2866 |
| Walt Dsney Imgnring RES Dev In. | 2389 | E | 714 781-3152 | 2913 |
| Display Fabrication Group Inc. | 2399 | E | 714 373-2100 | 3026 |
| Highland Lumber Sales Inc. | 2431 | E | 714 778-2293 | 3145 |
| Millcraft Inc. | 2431 | D | 714 632-9621 | 3157 |
| Woodwork Pioneers Corp. | 2431 | E | 714 991-1017 | 3209 |
| American Woodmark Corporation. | 2434 | B | 714 449-2200 | 3215 |
| Cabinets R US. | 2434 | E | 562 483-6886 | 3225 |
| Reborn Cabinets LLC (PA) | 2434 | B | 714 630-2220 | 3264 |
| D-Mac Inc. | 2451 | E | 714 808-3918 | 3383 |
| Outdoor Dimensions LLC. | 2499 | C | 714 578-9555 | 3421 |
| Quality First Woodworks Inc. | 2499 | C | 714 632-4040 | 3424 |
| University Frames Inc. | 2499 | E | 714 575-5100 | 3429 |
| Yti Enterprises Inc. | 2499 | F | 714 632-8696 | 3432 |
| M&J Design Inc. | 2512 | E | 714 687-9918 | 3479 |
| RSI Home Products LLC (HQ) | 2514 | A | 714 449-2200 | 3510 |
| Sky Rider Equipment Co Inc. | 2515 | E | 714 632-6890 | 3538 |
| Furniture Solutions Inc. | 2521 | E | 714 666-0424 | 3568 |
| Block Tops Inc (PA) | 2541 | E | 714 978-5080 | 3646 |
| Leonards Carpet Service Inc (PA) | 2541 | D | 714 630-1930 | 3664 |
| Tahiti Cabinets Inc. | 2599 | E | 714 693-0618 | 3751 |
| Treston IAC LLC. | 2599 | E | 714 990-8997 | 3752 |
| International Paper Company. | 2621 | E | 714 776-6060 | 3773 |
| Mozaik LLC. | 2652 | E | 562 207-1900 | 3815 |
| Jellco Container Inc. | 2653 | D | 714 666-2728 | 3861 |
| Absolute Packaging Inc. | 2657 | E | 714 630-3020 | 3916 |
| Thermech Corporation. | 2671 | E | 714 333-7155 | 3939 |
| Felix Schoeller North Amer Inc. | 2672 | E | 315 298-8425 | 3950 |
| Apple Paper Converting Inc. | 2679 | E | 714 632-3195 | 4029 |
| Digital Label Solutions LLC. | 2679 | E | 714 982-5000 | 4036 |
| Affluent Target Marketing Inc. | 2721 | E | 714 446-6280 | 4229 |
| Spidell Publishing Inc. | 2741 | E | 714 776-7850 | 4469 |
| Anchored Prints. | 2752 | E | 714 929-9317 | 4513 |
| Creative Press LLC. | 2752 | E | 714 774-5060 | 4576 |
| Creative Press LLC (PA) | 2752 | E | 714 774-5060 | 4577 |
| Inland Litho LLC. | 2752 | D | 714 993-6000 | 4648 |
| Interlink Inc. | 2752 | D | 714 905-7700 | 4654 |
| Lester Lithograph Inc. | 2752 | E | 714 491-3981 | 4676 |
| Lumaprints. | 2752 | F | 800 380-6038 | 4684 |
| Man-Grove Industries Inc. | 2752 | D | 714 630-3020 | 4688 |
| Pacific West Litho Inc. | 2752 | D | 714 579-0868 | 4715 |
| Pj Printers Inc. | 2752 | E | 714 779-8484 | 4726 |
| Supreme Graphics Inc. | 2752 | F | 310 531-8300 | 4776 |
| Tajen Graphics Inc. | 2752 | E | 714 527-3122 | 4780 |
| Tam Printing Inc. | 2752 | F | 714 224-4488 | 4781 |
| Adcraft Products Co Inc. | 2759 | E | 714 776-1230 | 4836 |
| Brook & Whittle Limited. | 2759 | E | 714 634-3466 | 4855 |
| C T L Printing Inds Inc. | 2759 | E | 714 635-2980 | 4857 |
| Dean Hesketh Company Inc. | 2759 | E | 714 236-2138 | 4871 |
| Labeltronix LLC (HQ) | 2759 | D | 800 429-4321 | 4911 |
| Paradigm Label Inc. | 2759 | F | 951 372-9212 | 4936 |
| Progrssive Intgrated Solutions. | 2759 | D | 714 237-0980 | 4946 |
| Screen Printers Resource Inc. | 2759 | E | 714 441-1155 | 4959 |
| Tee Styled Inc. | 2759 | E | 323 983-9988 | 4971 |
| Sharon Havriluk. | 2782 | E | 714 630-1313 | 5004 |
| Castle Press. | 2791 | E | 800 794-0858 | 5017 |
| Master Arts Inc. | 2796 | F | 714 240-4550 | 5027 |
| Ryvec Inc. | 2816 | E | 714 520-5592 | 5063 |
| Cytec Solvay Group. | 2819 | F | 714 630-9400 | 5085 |
| Singod Investors Vi LLC. | 2819 | E | 714 326-7800 | 5117 |
| Solvay America Inc. | 2819 | C | 714 688-4403 | 5118 |
| Solvay America LLC. | 2819 | D | 713 525-4000 | 5121 |
| Cytec Engineered Materials Inc. | 2821 | E | 714 632-8444 | 5150 |
| Mer-Kote Products Inc. | 2821 | E | 714 778-2266 | 5177 |
| R K Fabrication Inc. | 2821 | F | 714 630-9654 | 5193 |
| Stepan Company. | 2821 | C | 714 776-9870 | 5205 |
| Xerxes Corporation. | 2821 | C | 714 630-0012 | 5218 |
| B & C Nutritional Products Inc. | 2833 | D | 714 238-7225 | 5231 |
| Excelsior Nutrition Inc. | 2833 | D | 657 999-5188 | 5241 |
| Gmp Laboratories America Inc (PA) | 2834 | D | 714 630-2467 | 5466 |
| Nbty Manufacturing LLC. | 2834 | C | 714 765-8323 | 5565 |
| S K Laboratories Inc. | 2834 | E | 714 695-9800 | 5647 |
| Teco Diagnostics. | 2835 | D | 714 693-7788 | 5782 |
| Botanx LLC. | 2844 | E | 714 854-1601 | 5950 |
| Firmenich. | 2869 | D | 714 535-2871 | 6146 |

# GEOGRAPHIC SECTION — ANAHEIM, CA

| Company | SIC | EMP | PHONE | ENTRY# |
|---|---|---|---|---|
| Saint-Gobain Ceramics Plas Inc | 2869 | C | 714 701-3900 | 6158 |
| Reliable Packaging Systems Inc | 2891 | F | 714 572-1094 | 6243 |
| Firmenich Incorporated | 2899 | C | 714 535-2871 | 6285 |
| Graffiti Shield Inc | 3081 | E | 714 575-1100 | 6561 |
| Nelco Products Inc | 3083 | C | 714 879-4293 | 6586 |
| Clean Cut Technologies LLC | 3086 | D | 714 864-3500 | 6628 |
| Foam Concepts Inc | 3086 | E | 714 693-1037 | 6634 |
| Foam Plastics & Rbr Pdts Corp | 3086 | E | 714 779-0990 | 6638 |
| Aquatic Co | 3088 | E | 714 993-1220 | 6674 |
| Anaheim Custom Extruders Inc | 3089 | E | 714 693-8508 | 6718 |
| Bace Manufacturing Inc (HQ) | 3089 | A | 714 630-6002 | 6732 |
| Beemak Plastics LLC | 3089 | D | 800 421-4393 | 6738 |
| Berry Global Inc | 3089 | D | 714 777-5200 | 6741 |
| Charmaine Plastics Inc | 3089 | D | 714 630-8117 | 6771 |
| Edco Plastics Inc | 3089 | E | 714 772-1986 | 6815 |
| GT Styling Corp | 3089 | E | 714 644-9214 | 6848 |
| Konark Silicone Tech Inc | 3089 | F | 562 372-5415 | 6890 |
| RPM Plastic Molding Inc | 3089 | E | 714 630-9300 | 7015 |
| Setco LLC | 3089 | C | 812 424-2904 | 7026 |
| Sonfarrel | 3089 | E | 714 630-7280 | 7034 |
| Sp Craftech I LLC | 3089 | E | 714 630-8117 | 7036 |
| Strand Art Company Inc | 3089 | E | 714 777-0444 | 7046 |
| USA Extruded Plastics Inc | 3089 | F | 714 991-6061 | 7067 |
| Targus US LLC | 3161 | E | 714 765-5555 | 7142 |
| Custom Industries Inc | 3231 | E | 714 779-9101 | 7217 |
| Elysium Tiles Inc | 3253 | F | 714 991-7885 | 7267 |
| Short Load Concrete Inc | 3273 | E | 714 524-7013 | 7496 |
| Maverick Abrasives Corporation | 3291 | E | 714 854-9531 | 7555 |
| Anaheim Extrusion Co Inc | 3354 | D | 714 630-3111 | 7735 |
| Cablesys LLC | 3357 | E | 562 356-3222 | 7776 |
| Venus Alloys Inc (PA) | 3363 | E | 714 635-8800 | 7823 |
| Cytec Engineered Materials Inc | 3365 | C | 714 632-1174 | 7841 |
| Sonfarrel Aerospace LLC | 3365 | D | 714 630-7280 | 7849 |
| Craftsman Unity LLC | 3423 | E | 714 776-8995 | 7950 |
| B & B Specialties Inc (PA) | 3429 | E | 714 985-3000 | 7981 |
| Mid-West Wholesale Hardware Co | 3429 | E | 714 630-4751 | 8016 |
| Aerofab Corporation | 3441 | F | 714 635-0902 | 8090 |
| Hitech Metal Fabrication Corp | 3441 | D | 714 635-3505 | 8151 |
| S & R Architectural Metals Inc | 3441 | E | 714 226-0108 | 8213 |
| Janus International Group LLC | 3442 | F | 714 503-6120 | 8270 |
| AAR Manufacturing Inc | 3443 | C | 714 634-8807 | 8295 |
| Tait & Associates Inc | 3443 | E | 714 560-8222 | 8344 |
| AMF Anaheim LLC | 3444 | C | 714 363-9206 | 8374 |
| California Chassis Inc | 3444 | C | 714 666-8511 | 8401 |
| Fabrication Network Inc | 3444 | F | 714 393-5282 | 8451 |
| International West Inc | 3444 | E | 714 632-9190 | 8476 |
| Metal-Fab Services Indust Inc | 3444 | E | 714 630-7771 | 8506 |
| Pinnacle Precision Shtmtl Corp (HQ) | 3444 | D | 714 777-3129 | 8538 |
| Pinnacle Precision Shtmtl Corp | 3444 | D | 714 777-3129 | 8539 |
| Sheet Metal Service | 3444 | F | 714 446-0196 | 8571 |
| Steeldyne Industries | 3444 | E | 714 630-6200 | 8582 |
| Tri Precision Sheetmetal Inc | 3444 | E | 714 632-8838 | 8599 |
| K & J Wire Products Corp | 3446 | E | 714 816-0360 | 8631 |
| Orange County Erectors Inc | 3448 | E | 714 502-8455 | 8679 |
| A J Fasteners Inc | 3452 | E | 714 630-1556 | 8741 |
| Butler Inc | 3452 | F | 310 323-3114 | 8748 |
| CBS Fasteners LLC | 3452 | E | 714 779-6368 | 8749 |
| Dgl Holdings Inc | 3452 | E | 714 630-7840 | 8751 |
| Nylok LLC | 3452 | E | 714 635-3993 | 8763 |
| Ascent Manufacturing LLC | 3469 | E | 714 540-6414 | 8819 |
| Brice Tool & Stamping Inc | 3469 | F | 714 630-6400 | 8824 |
| Pacific Precision Metals Inc | 3469 | C | 951 226-1500 | 8874 |
| Spotter Global Inc | 3469 | C | 515 817-3726 | 8890 |
| Advance-Tech Plating Inc | 3471 | F | 714 630-7093 | 8907 |
| Artistic Pltg & Met Finshg Inc | 3471 | E | 619 661-1691 | 8925 |
| Black Oxide Industries Inc | 3471 | E | 714 870-9610 | 8931 |
| Precision Anodizing & Pltg Inc | 3471 | D | 714 996-1601 | 8998 |
| Superior Connector Plating Inc | 3471 | E | 714 774-1174 | 9018 |
| Technic Inc | 3471 | E | 714 632-0200 | 9020 |
| Crest Coating Inc | 3479 | D | 714 635-7090 | 9060 |
| Performance Powder Inc | 3479 | E | 714 632-0600 | 9105 |
| Powdercoat Services LLC | 3479 | E | 714 533-2251 | 9109 |
| Striker Co | 3479 | F | 562 861-2216 | 9125 |
| Superior Spring Company | 3495 | E | 714 490-0881 | 9208 |
| Anaheim Wire Products Inc | 3496 | E | 714 563-8300 | 9210 |
| Rampone Industries LLC | 3496 | E | 714 265-0200 | 9228 |
| Rapid Mfg A Cal Ltd Partnr (PA) | 3496 | C | 714 974-2432 | 9229 |
| Bassani Manufacturing | 3498 | E | 714 630-1821 | 9250 |
| One-Way Manufacturing Inc | 3498 | E | 714 630-8833 | 9267 |
| Trinity Process Solutions Inc | 3498 | E | 714 701-1112 | 9272 |
| J&S Goodwin Inc (HQ) | 3537 | D | 714 956-4040 | 9525 |
| Taylor-Dunn Manufacturing LLC (HQ) | 3537 | D | 714 956-4040 | 9535 |
| Waev Inc (PA) | 3537 | E | 714 956-4040 | 9536 |
| APT Manufacturing LLC | 3541 | F | 714 632-0040 | 9540 |
| US Union Tool Inc (HQ) | 3541 | E | 714 521-6242 | 9574 |
| Magnetic Metals Corporation | 3542 | F | 714 828-4625 | 9584 |
| Gemini Mfg & Engrg Inc | 3544 | E | 714 999-0010 | 9625 |
| Superior Jig Inc | 3544 | E | 714 525-4777 | 9649 |
| Kempton Machine Works Inc | 3545 | F | 714 990-0596 | 9680 |
| Southland Tool Mfg Inc | 3545 | F | 714 632-8198 | 9698 |
| Lodestone LLC | 3548 | E | 714 970-0900 | 9726 |
| Weartech International Inc | 3562 | F | 714 683-2430 | 9956 |
| Adwest Technologies Inc (HQ) | 3564 | E | 714 632-8595 | 9977 |
| Hepa Corporation | 3564 | D | 714 630-5700 | 9989 |
| Wasser Filtration Inc (PA) | 3569 | D | 714 696-6450 | 10121 |
| Cemtrol Inc | 3571 | F | 714 666-6606 | 10141 |
| Foreseeson Custom Displays Inc (PA) | 3577 | E | 714 300-0540 | 10369 |
| Rgb Systems Inc (PA) | 3577 | C | 714 491-1500 | 10429 |
| Solaris Paper Inc | 3579 | C | 714 687-6657 | 10466 |
| Welbilt Fdsrvice Companies LLC | 3585 | B | 323 245-3761 | 10527 |
| Product Solutions Inc | 3589 | E | 714 545-9757 | 10591 |
| Rtr Industries LLC (PA) | 3592 | E | 714 996-0050 | 10625 |
| 3d Machine Co Inc | 3599 | E | 714 777-8985 | 10640 |
| A & D Precision Mfg Inc | 3599 | E | 714 779-2714 | 10647 |
| Bechler Cams Inc | 3599 | F | 714 774-5150 | 10741 |
| Cheek Machine Corp | 3599 | E | 714 279-9486 | 10774 |
| Cresco Manufacturing Inc | 3599 | E | 714 525-2326 | 10792 |
| Farrell Brothers Holding Corp | 3599 | F | 714 630-3417 | 10835 |
| Jaco Engineering | 3599 | E | 714 991-1680 | 10901 |
| Kerleylegacy63 Inc | 3599 | D | 714 630-7286 | 10925 |
| Moseys Production Machinists Inc (PA) | 3599 | E | 714 693-4840 | 10995 |
| Orange County Screw Pdts Inc | 3599 | E | 714 630-7433 | 11017 |
| Pacific Broach & Engrg Assoc | 3599 | F | 714 632-5678 | 11022 |
| Pen Manufacturing LLC | 3599 | E | 714 992-0950 | 11036 |
| Precision Waterjet Inc | 3599 | E | 888 538-9287 | 11047 |
| Qualitask Inc | 3599 | E | 714 237-0900 | 11058 |
| R C I P Inc | 3599 | F | 714 630-1239 | 11064 |
| Roberts Precision Engrg Inc | 3599 | E | 714 635-4485 | 11083 |
| Turret Lathe Specialists Inc | 3599 | F | 714 520-0058 | 11158 |
| West Bond Inc (PA) | 3599 | E | 714 978-1551 | 11189 |
| Pacific Transformer Corp | 3612 | D | 714 779-0450 | 11222 |
| A P Seedorff & Company Inc | 3625 | E | 714 252-5330 | 11303 |
| Anaheim Automation Inc | 3625 | E | 714 992-6990 | 11307 |
| Hestan Commercial Corporation | 3639 | C | 714 869-2380 | 11419 |
| Today Pvc Bending Inc | 3644 | E | 714 953-5707 | 11483 |
| Intense Lighting LLC | 3646 | D | 714 630-9877 | 11539 |
| Birchwood Lighting Inc | 3648 | E | 714 550-7118 | 11583 |
| Emazing Lights LLC | 3648 | F | 626 628-6482 | 11594 |
| Anacom General Corporation | 3651 | E | 714 774-8484 | 11635 |
| Digital Periph Solutions Inc | 3651 | E | 714 998-3440 | 11648 |
| Interntnl Cnnctors Cable Corp | 3661 | C | 888 275-4422 | 11772 |
| Siemens Mobility Inc | 3661 | E | 714 284-0206 | 11785 |
| L3 Technologies Inc | 3663 | C | 714 758-4222 | 11877 |
| L3harris Interstate Elec Corp | 3663 | D | 714 758-3395 | 11881 |
| Vidovation Corporation | 3663 | F | 949 777-5435 | 11972 |
| Econolite Control Products Inc (PA) | 3669 | C | 714 630-3700 | 11992 |
| Raytheon Applied Sgnal Tech In | 3669 | D | 714 917-0255 | 12013 |
| American Circuit Tech Inc (PA) | 3672 | E | 714 777-2480 | 12051 |
| APT Electronics Inc | 3672 | C | 714 687-6760 | 12058 |
| Chad Industries Incorporated | 3672 | E | 714 938-0080 | 12076 |
| Copper Clad Mltilayer Pdts Inc | 3672 | E | 714 237-1388 | 12082 |
| Excello Circuits Inc | 3672 | D | 714 993-0560 | 12096 |
| Jabil Inc | 3672 | E | 714 938-0080 | 12143 |
| Kca Electronics Inc | 3672 | C | 714 239-2433 | 12148 |
| Murrietta Circuits | 3672 | C | 714 970-2430 | 12170 |
| Preferred Testing Labs Inc | 3672 | F | 714 999-1616 | 12192 |
| Smart Elec & Assembly Inc | 3672 | C | 714 772-2651 | 12219 |
| Summit Interconnect Inc (HQ) | 3672 | C | 714 239-2433 | 12234 |
| Technotronix Inc | 3672 | E | 714 630-9200 | 12238 |
| Transline Technology Inc | 3672 | E | 714 533-8300 | 12241 |
| Ttm Technologies Inc | 3672 | B | 714 688-7200 | 12249 |
| Veeco Electro Fab Inc | 3672 | E | 714 630-8020 | 12255 |
| R H Barden Inc | 3677 | F | 714 970-0900 | 12854 |
| Si Manufacturing Inc | 3677 | E | 714 956-7110 | 12858 |
| Cristek Interconnects LLC (DH) | 3678 | C | 714 696-5200 | 12875 |
| C & S Assembly Inc | 3679 | F | 866 779-8939 | 12928 |
| General Power Systems Inc | 3679 | E | 714 956-9321 | 12984 |
| Interlog Corporation | 3679 | E | 714 529-7808 | 13005 |
| Jasper Electronics | 3679 | E | 714 917-0749 | 13011 |
| Magnetic Sensors Corporation | 3679 | E | 714 630-8380 | 13030 |
| Micrometals Inc (PA) | 3679 | C | 714 970-9400 | 13037 |
| Rtie Holdings LLC | 3679 | F | 714 765-8200 | 13080 |
| Xp Power Inc | 3679 | D | 714 712-2642 | 13128 |
| Asco Power Services Inc | 3699 | F | 714 283-4000 | 13213 |
| Serra Laser and Waterjet Inc | 3699 | E | 714 680-6211 | 13306 |
| Phoenix Cars LLC | 3711 | E | 909 987-0815 | 13375 |

Employee Codes: A=Over 500 employees, B=251-500, C=101-250, D=51-100, E=20-50, F=10-19, G=1-9

## ANAHEIM, CA

| Company | SIC | EMP | PHONE | ENTRY# |
|---|---|---|---|---|
| Realtruck Enterprise Inc. | 3713 | E | 956 324-5337 | 13424 |
| American Fabrication Corp (PA) | 3714 | D | 714 632-1709 | 13456 |
| McLeod Racing LLC | 3714 | E | 714 630-2764 | 13537 |
| Phoenix Motor Inc (DH) | 3714 | E | 909 987-0815 | 13556 |
| Aerospace Parts Holdings Inc | 3728 | A | 949 877-3630 | 13757 |
| Arden Engineering Inc (DH) | 3728 | E | 949 877-3642 | 13783 |
| Astro Spar Inc | 3728 | E | 626 839-7858 | 13789 |
| B/E Aerospace Macrolink | 3728 | E | 714 777-8800 | 13796 |
| Cadence Aerospace LLC (HQ) | 3728 | D | 949 877-8600 | 13800 |
| Cadence Aerospace LLC | 3728 | F | 425 353-0405 | 13801 |
| Cal Tech Precision Inc | 3728 | D | 714 992-4130 | 13802 |
| Canyon Composites Incorporated | 3728 | E | 714 991-8181 | 13804 |
| D & D Gear Incorporated | 3728 | C | 714 692-6570 | 13819 |
| Dretloh Aircraft Supply Inc | 3728 | F | 714 632-6982 | 13826 |
| Ferra Aerospace Inc | 3728 | E | 918 787-2220 | 13839 |
| Gear Manufacturing Inc | 3728 | E | 714 792-2895 | 13847 |
| Giddens Industries Inc (DH) | 3728 | C | | 13850 |
| Gledhill/Lyons Inc | 3728 | E | 714 502-0274 | 13851 |
| Goodrich Corporation | 3728 | C | 714 984-1461 | 13854 |
| Pacific Contours Corporation | 3728 | D | 714 693-1260 | 13919 |
| Kendon Industries Inc | 3792 | F | 714 630-7144 | 14121 |
| DG Performance Spc Inc | 3799 | D | 714 961-8850 | 14129 |
| Apex Technology Holdings Inc | 3812 | A | 321 270-3630 | 14145 |
| Cummins Aerospace LLC (PA) | 3812 | E | 714 879-2800 | 14175 |
| Employer Defense Group | 3812 | E | 949 200-0137 | 14184 |
| L3 Technologies Inc | 3812 | E | 714 956-9200 | 14201 |
| Tuffer Manufacturing Co Inc | 3812 | E | 714 526-3077 | 14326 |
| 3d Instruments LLC | 3823 | D | 714 399-9200 | 14380 |
| L3harris Interstate Elec Corp | 3825 | E | 714 758-0500 | 14544 |
| L3harris Interstate Elec Corp (DH) | 3825 | B | 714 758-0500 | 14545 |
| L3harris Interstate Elec Corp | 3825 | D | 714 758-0500 | 14546 |
| Endress & Hauser Conducta Inc | 3826 | E | 800 835-5474 | 14661 |
| Fire & Gas Detection Tech Inc | 3829 | F | 714 671-8500 | 14866 |
| Telatemp Corp | 3829 | F | 714 414-0343 | 14927 |
| Medzon Health | 3841 | E | 844 860-8584 | 15182 |
| Mettler Electronics Corp | 3841 | E | 714 533-2221 | 15187 |
| Sechrist Industries Inc | 3841 | A | 714 579-8400 | 15250 |
| Hanger Prsthtics Orthtics W In (HQ) | 3842 | E | 714 961-2112 | 15356 |
| Danville Materials LLC | 3843 | E | 714 399-0334 | 15447 |
| May Holdings Inc | 3845 | F | 714 563-2772 | 15557 |
| Visionary Contact Lens Inc | 3851 | E | 714 237-1900 | 15624 |
| Raykorvay Inc | 3942 | F | 714 632-8680 | 15734 |
| Golf Supply House Usa Inc | 3949 | D | 714 983-0050 | 15818 |
| Greenfields Outdoor Fitnes Inc | 3949 | F | 888 315-9037 | 15819 |
| Tuffstuff Fitness Intl Inc | 3949 | D | 909 629-1600 | 15868 |
| Matthew Warren Inc | 3965 | E | 714 630-7840 | 15913 |
| YKK (usa) Inc | 3965 | E | 714 701-1200 | 15924 |
| 3s Sign Services Inc | 3993 | E | 714 683-1120 | 15934 |
| Coast Sign Incorporated | 3993 | C | 714 520-9144 | 15957 |
| Signage Solutions Corporation | 3993 | E | 714 491-0299 | 16039 |
| Sunset Signs and Printing Inc | 3993 | E | 714 255-9104 | 16053 |
| Jorge Ulloa | 3999 | F | 714 630-0499 | 16156 |
| LA Spas Inc | 3999 | C | 714 630-1150 | 16166 |
| Total Warehouse Inc | 4225 | C | 714 332-3082 | 16291 |
| Aircraft Repair & Overhaul Svc (PA) | 4581 | E | 714 630-9494 | 16299 |
| Competition Clutch Inc | 5013 | E | 800 809-6598 | 16378 |
| Empi Inc | 5013 | D | 714 446-9606 | 16383 |
| Reels Inc | 5013 | D | 714 446-9606 | 16396 |
| Shrin LLC | 5013 | E | 714 850-0303 | 16400 |
| Greenball Corp (PA) | 5014 | E | 714 782-3060 | 16408 |
| Best Cheer Stone Inc (PA) | 5032 | E | 714 399-1588 | 16465 |
| Kretus Group Inc (PA) | 5032 | E | 714 738-6640 | 16474 |
| Genesis Computer Systems Inc | 5045 | E | 714 632-3648 | 16525 |
| Quantum Automation (PA) | 5063 | E | 714 854-0800 | 16671 |
| Motors & Controls Whse Inc | 5065 | E | 714 956-0480 | 16723 |
| B & B Specialties Inc | 5072 | D | 714 985-3075 | 16746 |
| Chuaolson Enterprises Inc | 5072 | E | 714 630-4751 | 16748 |
| Macpherson Wstn Tl Sup Co LLC | 5072 | E | 714 666-4100 | 16757 |
| Shamrock Supply Company Inc (PA) | 5072 | D | 714 575-1800 | 16762 |
| Dust Collector Services Inc | 5075 | E | 714 237-1690 | 16777 |
| George T Hall Co Inc (PA) | 5075 | E | 909 825-9751 | 16780 |
| Aggressive Engineering Corp | 5084 | F | 714 995-8313 | 16805 |
| Oliver Healthcare Packaging Co | 5084 | D | 714 864-3500 | 16831 |
| Ft 2 Inc | 5099 | C | 714 765-5555 | 16976 |
| Michael Gerald Ltd | 5136 | E | 562 921-9611 | 17077 |
| Harris Freeman & Co Inc (PA) | 5149 | B | 714 765-7525 | 17189 |
| Orange County Indus Plas Inc (PA) | 5162 | E | 714 632-9450 | 17229 |
| Stater Bros Markets | 5411 | E | 714 991-5310 | 17386 |
| Emergency Vehicle Group Inc | 5511 | E | 714 238-0110 | 17438 |
| Rodriguez Brothers Auto Parts (PA) | 5531 | F | 714 772-7278 | 17462 |
| Iheartraves LLC | 5632 | F | 626 628-6482 | 17500 |
| Rm Partners Inc | 5713 | E | 714 765-5725 | 17528 |
| Ramisons Inc | 5812 | F | 714 323-7134 | 17603 |
| Rush Business Forms Inc | 5943 | E | 714 630-5661 | 17640 |
| Melton Intl Tackle Inc | 5961 | E | 714 978-9192 | 17667 |
| Rnbs Corporation | 5961 | E | 714 998-1828 | 17672 |
| Caballero & Sons Inc | 6221 | E | 562 368-1644 | 17731 |
| GBS Linens Inc (PA) | 7213 | D | 714 778-6448 | 17766 |
| Consolidated Design West Inc | 7336 | E | 714 999-1476 | 17824 |
| Infosend Inc (PA) | 7338 | E | 714 993-2690 | 17842 |
| Anamex Corporation (PA) | 7371 | E | 714 779-7055 | 17880 |
| Select Data Inc | 7371 | E | 714 577-1000 | 17976 |
| Bpoms/Hro Inc (HQ) | 7372 | D | 714 974-2670 | 18123 |
| Unlimited Innovations Inc | 7372 | E | 714 998-0866 | 18901 |
| Bcp Systems Inc | 7378 | D | 714 202-3900 | 19020 |
| Etherwan Systems Inc | 7379 | D | 714 779-3800 | 19035 |
| G4s Justice Services LLC | 7382 | E | 800 589-6003 | 19056 |
| Kesa Incorporated | 7382 | E | 714 956-2827 | 19057 |
| Nor-Cal Beverage Co Inc | 7389 | D | 714 526-8600 | 19110 |
| Pacific Embroidery LLC | 7389 | F | 714 630-4757 | 19115 |
| T L Fabrications LP | 7692 | D | 562 802-3980 | 19215 |
| R & S Ovrhd Doors So-Cal Inc | 7699 | E | 714 680-0600 | 19277 |
| Real Estate Trainers Inc | 8249 | E | 800 282-2352 | 19349 |
| Fortel Traffic Inc | 8711 | F | 714 701-9800 | 19395 |
| Concrete West Construction Inc | 8742 | F | 949 448-9940 | 19524 |

## ANDERSON, CA - Shasta County

| Company | SIC | EMP | PHONE | ENTRY# |
|---|---|---|---|---|
| Cascade Comfort Service Inc | 1711 | E | 530 365-5350 | 408 |
| Elizabeth Headrick | 2411 | F | 530 247-8000 | 3044 |
| Skyline Alterations Inc (PA) | 2411 | E | 530 549-4010 | 3058 |
| Sierra Pacific Industries | 2421 | C | 530 365-3721 | 3084 |
| Sierra Pacific Industries Inc (PA) | 2421 | D | 530 378-8000 | 3088 |
| Siskiyou Forest Products (PA) | 2431 | E | 530 378-6980 | 3192 |
| Haisch Construction Co Inc | 2439 | F | 530 378-6800 | 3309 |
| Shasta Wood Products Inc | 2499 | E | 530 378-6880 | 3428 |
| Checchi Enterprises Inc | 2752 | E | 530 378-1207 | 4548 |
| Voorwood Company | 3553 | E | 530 365-3311 | 9757 |
| Visioncare Devices Inc | 5047 | E | 530 364-2271 | 16593 |

## ANGWIN, CA - Napa County

| Company | SIC | EMP | PHONE | ENTRY# |
|---|---|---|---|---|
| Ladera Vineyards LLC | 2084 | F | 707 965-2445 | 1655 |
| Ladera Winery LLC | 2084 | E | 707 965-2445 | 1656 |

## ANTELOPE, CA - Sacramento County

| Company | SIC | EMP | PHONE | ENTRY# |
|---|---|---|---|---|
| Babyfits LLC | 3161 | E | 916 544-7018 | 7127 |

## ANTIOCH, CA - Contra Costa County

| Company | SIC | EMP | PHONE | ENTRY# |
|---|---|---|---|---|
| Kilgore Enterprises LLC | 1389 | E | 925 885-8999 | 246 |
| Freschi Air Systems Inc | 1711 | D | 925 827-9761 | 419 |
| Chep (usa) Inc | 2448 | F | 925 234-4970 | 3334 |
| Trade Litho Inc | 2752 | F | 510 965-6501 | 4788 |
| General Graphic Chem Co Inc | 2899 | F | 510 879-7010 | 6288 |
| Bond Manufacturing Co Inc (PA) | 3272 | D | 866 771-2663 | 7314 |
| Kie-Con Inc | 3272 | D | 925 754-9494 | 7350 |
| Georgia-Pacific LLC | 3275 | D | 925 757-2870 | 7524 |
| Silgan Containers Mfg Corp | 3411 | E | 925 778-8000 | 7929 |
| Allied Container Systems Inc | 3448 | C | 925 944-7600 | 8652 |
| Marine & Industrial Svcs Inc | 3498 | F | 925 757-8791 | 9265 |
| Pacific Gas and Electric Co | 4911 | B | 925 779-7745 | 16347 |
| Premier Floor Care Inc (PA) | 7349 | E | 925 679-4901 | 17847 |

## APPLE VALLEY, CA - San Bernardino County

| Company | SIC | EMP | PHONE | ENTRY# |
|---|---|---|---|---|
| West Coast Furn Framers Inc | 2426 | E | 760 669-5275 | 3103 |
| Polymer Concepts Tech Pby Inc | 2821 | F | 760 240-4999 | 5190 |
| American Integrity Corp | 3089 | E | 760 247-1082 | 6713 |
| Pauley Plastic LLC | 3089 | F | 760 240-3737 | 6951 |
| Cemex Cement Inc | 3273 | C | 760 381-7616 | 7419 |
| Lindsay Windows California LLC | 3442 | F | 760 247-1082 | 8274 |
| Consolidated Frt Systems LLC | 3537 | E | 310 424-9924 | 9509 |
| Dicken Enterprises Inc | 3567 | E | 760 246-7333 | 10049 |
| Induction Technology Corp | 3567 | E | 760 246-7333 | 10053 |
| Pac-Refco Inc | 3585 | E | 760 956-8600 | 10510 |
| Reid Products Inc | 3599 | E | 760 240-1355 | 11074 |
| Biodefensor Corporation | 5075 | E | 888 899-2956 | 16774 |

## APTOS, CA - Santa Cruz County

| Company | SIC | EMP | PHONE | ENTRY# |
|---|---|---|---|---|
| Mariannes Ice Cream LLC | 2024 | E | 831 713-4746 | 810 |
| Tradin Organics USA LLC | 2099 | E | 831 685-6565 | 2376 |
| Ship Smart Inc | 2671 | E | 831 661-4841 | 3938 |

## ARBUCKLE, CA - Colusa County

| Company | SIC | EMP | PHONE | ENTRY# |
|---|---|---|---|---|
| California Family Foods LLC | 2044 | D | 530 476-3326 | 1072 |
| Sun Valley Rice Company LLC | 2044 | D | 530 476-3000 | 1082 |
| Grindstone Wines LLC | 2084 | E | 530 393-2162 | 1603 |
| Cal Vsta Erosion Ctrl Pdts LLC | 3531 | E | 530 476-0706 | 9412 |

# GEOGRAPHIC SECTION

AZUSA, CA

| | SIC | EMP | PHONE | ENTRY# |
|---|---|---|---|---|

### ARCADIA, CA - Los Angeles County

| Company | SIC | EMP | PHONE | ENTRY# |
|---|---|---|---|---|
| Sing Kung Corp | 2041 | E | 626 358-5838 | 1063 |
| Motomotion USA Corporation | 2426 | F | 626 538-4866 | 3098 |
| Harvest Pack Inc | 2656 | F | 888 727-7225 | 3915 |
| We Own Everything Records LLC | 2782 | F | 323 208-9454 | 5008 |
| Relton Corporation | 2899 | D | 800 423-1505 | 6320 |
| Danco Anodizing Inc (PA) | 3471 | E | 626 445-3303 | 8949 |
| Bendick Precision Inc | 3599 | F | 626 445-0217 | 10746 |
| Ev Charging Solutions Inc | 3694 | D | 866 300-3827 | 13170 |
| Segway Inc | 3751 | C | 603 222-6000 | 14069 |
| MPS Anzon LLC | 3842 | E | 626 471-3553 | 15385 |
| Gar Enterprises (PA) | 5045 | D | 626 574-1175 | 16524 |
| Big Tree Sales Inc | 5092 | F | 626 672-0048 | 16944 |
| Tee Top of California Inc (PA) | 5136 | E | 626 303-1868 | 17082 |
| Property Care Building Svc LLC | 7349 | E | 626 623-6420 | 17848 |

### ARCATA, CA - Humboldt County

| Company | SIC | EMP | PHONE | ENTRY# |
|---|---|---|---|---|
| Cypress Grove Chevre Inc | 2022 | D | 707 825-1100 | 710 |
| Desserts On Us Inc | 2051 | F | 707 822-0160 | 1182 |
| Natural Decadence LLC | 2053 | F | 707 444-2629 | 1289 |
| Kokatat Inc | 2339 | C | 707 822-7621 | 2782 |
| Schmidbauer Lumber Inc | 2421 | D | 707 822-7607 | 3079 |
| Crestmark Millwork Inc | 2431 | E | 707 822-4034 | 3123 |
| JR Stephens Company | 2434 | E | 707 825-0100 | 3245 |
| Royal Gold LLC | 2875 | F | 707 822-4653 | 6190 |
| Wing Inflatables Inc (HQ) | 3089 | E | 707 826-2887 | 7082 |
| C & K Johnson Industries Inc | 3444 | E | 707 822-7687 | 8397 |
| Cummins Pacific LLC | 3714 | E | 707 822-7392 | 13480 |
| Holly Yashi Inc | 3911 | D | 707 822-0389 | 15694 |
| Statewide Trffic Sfety Sgns In | 3993 | E | 707 825-6927 | 16050 |
| Sun Valley Floral Group LLC | 3999 | A | 707 826-8700 | 16243 |
| Bracut International Corp | 5211 | E | 707 826-9850 | 17323 |
| Los Bagels Inc (PA) | 5461 | E | 707 822-3150 | 17415 |

### ARLETA, CA - Los Angeles County

| Company | SIC | EMP | PHONE | ENTRY# |
|---|---|---|---|---|
| Superior Thread Rolling Co | 3599 | D | 818 504-3626 | 11127 |

### ARNOLD, CA - Calaveras County

| Company | SIC | EMP | PHONE | ENTRY# |
|---|---|---|---|---|
| Snowshoe Brewing Co LLC (PA) | 5812 | E | 209 795-2272 | 17605 |

### AROMAS, CA - Monterey County

| Company | SIC | EMP | PHONE | ENTRY# |
|---|---|---|---|---|
| Granite Rock Co | 1442 | E | 831 768-2300 | 313 |
| Gregory Patterson | 3446 | E | 831 636-1015 | 8627 |
| Sambrailo Packaging | 5113 | E | 831 726-3210 | 17021 |

### ARROYO GRANDE, CA - San Luis Obispo County

| Company | SIC | EMP | PHONE | ENTRY# |
|---|---|---|---|---|
| Layne Laboratories Inc | 2048 | E | 805 242-7918 | 1134 |
| Coastal Vineyard Services LLC | 2084 | E | 805 441-4465 | 1513 |
| Corbett Vineyards LLC | 2084 | E | 805 782-9463 | 1518 |
| Laetitia Vineyard & Winery Inc | 2084 | D | 805 481-1772 | 1658 |
| Talley Vineyards | 2084 | E | 805 489-0446 | 1775 |
| Crosno Construction Inc | 3441 | E | 805 343-7437 | 8126 |
| Phillips 66 Co Carbon Group | 3559 | E | 805 489-4050 | 9891 |
| Applied Orthopedic Design | 3842 | E | 805 481-3685 | 15323 |
| Waynes Tire Inc (PA) | 7534 | F | 805 928-2661 | 19156 |

### ARTESIA, CA - Los Angeles County

| Company | SIC | EMP | PHONE | ENTRY# |
|---|---|---|---|---|
| California Dairies Inc | 2026 | D | 562 809-2595 | 830 |
| National Ready Mixed Con Co | 3273 | F | 562 865-6211 | 7478 |
| Cal Plate (PA) | 3555 | D | 562 403-3000 | 9763 |
| Kukdong Apparel America Inc | 7389 | E | | 19102 |

### ARVIN, CA - Kern County

| Company | SIC | EMP | PHONE | ENTRY# |
|---|---|---|---|---|
| Son of A Barista Usa LLC | 2095 | E | 323 788-8718 | 2080 |
| Moore Farms Inc | 2099 | F | 661 854-5588 | 2285 |
| Sandusky Lee LLC | 2514 | E | 661 854-5551 | 3511 |
| Reeves Extruded Products Inc | 3089 | D | 661 854-5970 | 6997 |
| Grimmway Enterprises Inc | 8741 | C | 661 854-6200 | 19517 |

### ATASCADERO, CA - San Luis Obispo County

| Company | SIC | EMP | PHONE | ENTRY# |
|---|---|---|---|---|
| 13 Stars | 2711 | F | 805 466-4086 | 4059 |
| Chemlogics Group LLC | 2869 | E | 805 591-3314 | 6139 |
| Solvay USA Inc | 2869 | E | 805 591-3314 | 6159 |

### ATWATER, CA - Merced County

| Company | SIC | EMP | PHONE | ENTRY# |
|---|---|---|---|---|
| Joseph Gallo Cheese Company LP | 2022 | C | 209 394-7984 | 721 |
| Teasdale Foods Inc | 2099 | D | 209 358-5616 | 2370 |
| Keney Manufacturing Co (PA) | 2434 | F | 209 358-6474 | 3247 |
| Global Diversified Inds Inc (PA) | 2452 | F | 559 665-5800 | 3396 |
| Certified Stainless Svc Inc | 3443 | D | 209 356-3300 | 8305 |
| Certified Stainless Svc Inc | 3443 | D | 209 537-4747 | 8307 |
| Global Modular Inc (HQ) | 3448 | E | 209 676-8029 | 8669 |
| MB Sports Inc | 3732 | E | 209 357-4153 | 14042 |

### AUBERRY, CA - Fresno County

| Company | SIC | EMP | PHONE | ENTRY# |
|---|---|---|---|---|
| Lite On Land Inc | 2411 | E | 559 203-2322 | 3050 |

### AUBURN, CA - Placer County

| Company | SIC | EMP | PHONE | ENTRY# |
|---|---|---|---|---|
| Markit Forestry MGT LLC | 0851 | F | 279 444-0033 | 101 |
| Absinthe Group Inc | 2033 | E | 530 823-8527 | 874 |
| Purveyors Kitchen | 2033 | E | 530 823-8527 | 920 |
| Auburn Trader Inc (DH) | 2711 | E | 530 888-7653 | 4071 |
| API Marketing | 2752 | F | 916 632-1946 | 4515 |
| Morgan Advanced Ceramics Inc | 2819 | E | 530 823-3401 | 5105 |
| Pre/Plastics Inc | 3089 | E | 530 823-1820 | 6977 |
| Morgan Advanced Materials Inc | 3253 | E | 530 823-3401 | 7269 |
| Quality Metal Fabrication LLC | 3444 | E | 530 887-7388 | 8549 |
| Broach Masters Inc | 3545 | E | 530 885-1939 | 9663 |
| Mydax Inc | 3585 | F | 530 888-6662 | 10509 |
| Armstrong Technology Sv Inc | 3599 | F | 530 888-6262 | 10717 |
| Vian Enterprises Inc | 3599 | D | 530 885-1997 | 11177 |
| Pass Laboratories Inc | 3651 | F | 530 878-5350 | 11685 |
| Tri-Continent Scientific Inc | 3824 | D | 530 273-8888 | 14484 |
| Dimaxx Technologies LLC | 3827 | F | 530 888-1942 | 14772 |
| Sierra Precision Optics Inc | 3827 | E | 530 885-6979 | 14824 |
| Aqua Sierra Controls Inc | 3829 | F | 530 823-3241 | 14846 |
| IRD Acquisitions LLC | 3851 | D | 530 210-2966 | 15604 |
| C Ceronix Incorporated | 3861 | E | 530 886-6400 | 15631 |
| Auburn Alehouse LP | 5181 | E | 530 885-2537 | 17257 |
| Professional Image Inc | 5199 | F | 513 984-1111 | 17306 |
| Wallys Natural | 5199 | E | 530 887-0396 | 17315 |
| Hyland LLC | 7371 | F | 440 788-5045 | 17927 |
| M Tek Corporation | 7699 | F | 530 888-9609 | 19268 |
| The Gyro House (PA) | 7699 | F | 530 823-6204 | 19286 |
| Intermotive Inc | 8742 | E | 530 823-1048 | 19531 |

### AVILA BEACH, CA - San Luis Obispo County

| Company | SIC | EMP | PHONE | ENTRY# |
|---|---|---|---|---|
| Veolia Wts Usa Inc | 2899 | D | 805 545-3743 | 6328 |

### AZUSA, CA - Los Angeles County

| Company | SIC | EMP | PHONE | ENTRY# |
|---|---|---|---|---|
| CTI Foods Azusa LLC | 2013 | C | 626 633-1609 | 638 |
| McKeever Danlee Confectionary | 2064 | C | 626 334-8964 | 1321 |
| Very Special Chocolats Inc | 2066 | C | 626 334-7838 | 1347 |
| Mat Cactus Mfg Co | 2273 | E | 626 969-0444 | 2517 |
| Bojer Inc | 2392 | E | 626 334-1711 | 2923 |
| Nicks Door Corporation | 2431 | F | 626 812-6491 | 3165 |
| Carters Metal Fabricators Inc | 2522 | E | 626 815-4225 | 3595 |
| Holguin & Holguin Inc | 2531 | E | 626 815-0168 | 3626 |
| Joseph Manufacturing Co Inc | 2531 | D | 626 334-1471 | 3632 |
| I2k LLC | 2599 | E | 626 788-0247 | 3745 |
| Ncla Inc | 2679 | F | 562 926-6252 | 4042 |
| Artisan Screen Printing Inc | 2759 | E | 626 815-2700 | 4844 |
| S&B Pharma Inc | 2833 | D | 626 334-2908 | 5268 |
| Bbeautiful LLC | 2844 | E | 626 610-2332 | 5947 |
| Westwood Laboratories LLC | 2844 | E | 626 969-3305 | 6058 |
| Westwood Laboratories LLC (PA) | 2844 | E | 626 969-3305 | 6059 |
| D W Mack Co Inc | 3053 | E | 626 969-1817 | 6443 |
| Calportland Company | 3273 | E | 626 334-3226 | 7414 |
| California Amforge Corporation | 3312 | C | 626 334-4931 | 7608 |
| Inwesco Incorporated (HQ) | 3315 | D | 626 334-7115 | 7644 |
| Inovativ Inc | 3334 | E | 626 969-5300 | 7707 |
| Magparts (HQ) | 3365 | E | 626 334-7897 | 7848 |
| Rain Bird Corporation | 3432 | D | 626 812-3400 | 8055 |
| Melco Steel Inc | 3443 | E | 626 334-7875 | 8320 |
| Todd Street Inc | 3443 | E | 626 815-1175 | 8348 |
| Valley Forge Acquisition Corp | 3462 | E | 626 969-8701 | 8791 |
| Lindsey Manufacturing Co | 3463 | C | 626 969-3471 | 8798 |
| Mc William & Son Inc | 3469 | F | 626 969-1821 | 8863 |
| AMCS | 3479 | E | 626 334-9160 | 9045 |
| Rain Bird Corporation (PA) | 3494 | C | 626 812-3400 | 9191 |
| Gale Banks Engineering | 3519 | C | 626 969-9600 | 9328 |
| Trio Engineered Products Inc (HQ) | 3531 | E | 626 851-3966 | 9444 |
| Ancra International LLC | 3537 | C | 626 765-4818 | 9505 |
| Ancra International LLC (HQ) | 3537 | C | 626 765-4800 | 9506 |
| Marples Gears Inc | 3566 | E | 626 570-1744 | 10041 |
| Water Filter Exchange Inc | 3569 | F | 818 808-2541 | 10122 |
| Acme Portable Machines Inc | 3571 | E | 626 610-1888 | 10127 |
| A & B Aerospace Inc | 3599 | E | 626 334-2976 | 10645 |
| Chipmasters Manufacturing Inc (PA) | 3599 | F | 626 804-8178 | 10775 |
| Kemac Technology Inc | 3599 | E | 626 334-1519 | 10924 |
| Screwmatic Inc | 3599 | D | 626 334-7831 | 11102 |
| Phaostron Instr Electronic Co | 3613 | D | 626 969-6801 | 11248 |
| Ptb Sales Inc (PA) | 3679 | E | 626 334-0500 | 13068 |
| Ht Multinational Inc | 3714 | E | 909 325-8582 | 13515 |
| Skylock Industries LLC | 3728 | D | 626 334-2391 | 13957 |
| Northrop Grumman Systems Corp | 3812 | A | 626 812-1000 | 14251 |
| Northrop Grumman Systems Corp | 3812 | A | 626 812-1464 | 14256 |

# AZUSA, CA

## GEOGRAPHIC SECTION

| Company | SIC | EMP | PHONE | ENTRY# |
|---|---|---|---|---|
| Tecomet Inc. | 3841 | A | 626 334-1519 | 15278 |
| BK Signs Inc. | 3993 | F | 626 334-5600 | 15948 |
| Cemex Cement Inc. | 5032 | C | 626 969-1747 | 16466 |
| Totten Tubes Inc (PA) | 5051 | D | 626 812-0220 | 16635 |
| Arrietta Incorporated | 5411 | E | 626 334-0302 | 17368 |

## BAKERSFIELD, CA - Kern County

| Company | SIC | EMP | PHONE | ENTRY# |
|---|---|---|---|---|
| Generis Holdings LP (PA) | 0161 | C | 661 366-7209 | 5 |
| Thomson International Inc. | 0191 | F | 661 845-1111 | 58 |
| Illume Agriculture LLC | 0762 | C | 661 587-5198 | 92 |
| Aera Energy LLC | 1311 | A | 661 665-5000 | 119 |
| Berry Petroleum Company LLC (HQ) | 1311 | E | 661 616-3900 | 123 |
| Hathaway LLC | 1311 | E | 661 393-2004 | 134 |
| Tri-Valley Corporation | 1311 | E | 661 864-0500 | 143 |
| Unified Field Services Corp. | 1311 | E | 661 325-8962 | 144 |
| Vaquero Energy Incorporated | 1311 | E | 661 363-7240 | 145 |
| Aera Energy Services Company (HQ) | 1381 | A | 661 665-5000 | 151 |
| Elysium Jennings LLC | 1381 | C | 661 679-1700 | 157 |
| Excalibur Well Services Corp. | 1381 | C | 661 589-5338 | 158 |
| Geo Guidance Drilling Svcs Inc (PA) | 1381 | E | 661 833-9999 | 159 |
| Golden State Drilling Inc. | 1381 | D | 661 589-0730 | 160 |
| Gunnar Lllp | 1381 | F | 281 690-0322 | 161 |
| Petro-Lud Inc. | 1381 | E | 661 747-4779 | 165 |
| California Resources Corp. | 1382 | D | 661 395-8000 | 172 |
| E & B Ntral Resources Mgt Corp (PA) | 1382 | D | 661 387-8500 | 180 |
| Freeport-Mcmoran Oil & Gas LLC | 1382 | C | 661 322-7600 | 184 |
| Linnco LLC | 1382 | A | 661 616-3900 | 189 |
| Macpherson Oil Company LLC | 1382 | E | 661 556-6096 | 190 |
| Sentinel Peak Rsources Cal LLC | 1382 | D | 661 395-5214 | 198 |
| Ally Enterprises | 1389 | E | 661 412-9933 | 204 |
| Anatesco Inc. | 1389 | F | 661 399-6990 | 205 |
| Basic Energy Services Inc. | 1389 | E | 661 588-3800 | 207 |
| C & H Testing Service Inc (PA) | 1389 | E | 661 589-4030 | 209 |
| C&J Well Services LLC | 1389 | A | 661 589-5220 | 210 |
| Casing Specialties Inc. | 1389 | E | 661 399-5522 | 213 |
| Central California Cnstr Inc. | 1389 | E | 661 978-8230 | 215 |
| CJ Berry Well Services MGT LLC | 1389 | A | 661 589-5220 | 217 |
| CL Knox Inc. | 1389 | D | 661 837-0477 | 219 |
| Cummings Vacuum Service Inc. | 1389 | D | 661 746-1786 | 221 |
| Engineered Well Svc Intl Inc | 1389 | F | 866 913-6283 | 228 |
| First Energy Services Inc. | 1389 | E | 661 387-1972 | 230 |
| Grayson Service Inc. | 1389 | F | 661 589-5444 | 231 |
| Halliburton Company | 1389 | D | 661 393-8111 | 234 |
| Hills Wldg & Engrg Contr Inc. | 1389 | D | 661 746-5400 | 237 |
| John M Phillips LLC | 1389 | E | 661 327-3118 | 243 |
| Mmi Services Inc. | 1389 | C | 661 589-9366 | 251 |
| MTS Stimulation Services Inc (PA) | 1389 | F | 661 589-5804 | 252 |
| Nabors Well Services Co. | 1389 | C | 661 588-6140 | 254 |
| Nabors Well Services Co. | 1389 | C | 661 392-7668 | 256 |
| Nabors Well Services Co. | 1389 | C | 661 589-3970 | 257 |
| Owen Oil Tools LP | 1389 | D | 661 637-1380 | 262 |
| Pacific Process Systems Inc (PA) | 1389 | D | 661 321-9681 | 265 |
| Palmer Tank & Construction Inc. | 1389 | E | 661 834-1110 | 266 |
| Pengo Wireline of California Inc. | 1389 | F | 661 327-9900 | 268 |
| Production Data Inc. | 1389 | E | 661 327-4776 | 269 |
| Pros Incorporated | 1389 | E | 661 589-5400 | 270 |
| PSC Industrial Outsourcing LP | 1389 | E | 661 833-9991 | 271 |
| Rev Vac 7777 Inc. | 1389 | E | 661 392-0355 | 272 |
| Robert Heely Construction LP (PA) | 1389 | E | 661 617-1400 | 273 |
| Schlumberger Technology Corp. | 1389 | D | 661 864-4721 | 275 |
| Soli-Bond Inc. | 1389 | F | 661 631-1633 | 276 |
| Theta Oilfield Services Inc. | 1389 | E | 661 633-2792 | 278 |
| Titan Oilfield Services Inc. | 1389 | D | 661 861-1630 | 280 |
| Truitt Oilfield Maint Corp | 1389 | B | 661 871-4099 | 283 |
| Tuboscope Pipeline Svcs Inc. | 1389 | F | 661 328-5500 | 285 |
| Tuboscope Pipeline Svcs Inc. | 1389 | F | 661 321-3400 | 286 |
| U S Weatherford L P | 1389 | C | 661 589-9483 | 287 |
| Vaquero Energy Inc. | 1389 | E | 661 616-0600 | 290 |
| Pioneer Sands LLC | 1446 | E | 661 746-5789 | 329 |
| Construction Specialty Svc Inc. | 1623 | D | 661 864-7573 | 387 |
| Southwest Contractors (PA) | 1623 | E | 661 588-0484 | 389 |
| Thermal Energy Solutions Inc. | 1623 | E | 661 489-4100 | 390 |
| Davidson Enterprises Inc. | 1799 | E | 661 325-2145 | 560 |
| Nestle Usa Inc | 2023 | C | 661 398-3536 | 774 |
| Vita-Pakt Citrus Products Co (PA) | 2033 | E | 626 332-1101 | 938 |
| Laumiere Gourmet Fruits Co LLC | 2034 | F | 661 218-9768 | 954 |
| Wm Bolthouse Farms Inc (HQ) | 2037 | A | 800 467-4683 | 1020 |
| Sun-Gro Commodities Inc (PA) | 2048 | E | 661 393-2612 | 1152 |
| Temblor Brewing LLC | 2082 | E | 661 489-4855 | 1465 |
| Giumarra Vineyards Corporation | 2084 | C | 661 395-7000 | 1588 |
| American Bottling Company | 2086 | D | 661 323-7921 | 1853 |
| Crystal Geyser Water Company | 2086 | E | 661 323-6296 | 1883 |
| Crystal Geyser Water Company | 2086 | E | 661 321-0896 | 1884 |
| Pepsi-Cola Bottling Group | 2086 | D | 661 635-1100 | 1910 |
| Reyes Coca-Cola Bottling LLC | 2086 | D | 661 324-6531 | 1933 |
| Alfred Louie Incorporated | 2099 | E | 661 831-2520 | 2125 |
| American Yeast Corporation | 2099 | E | 661 834-1050 | 2126 |
| Well Analysis Corporation Inc (PA) | 2411 | E | 661 283-9510 | 3061 |
| Millwood Cabinet Co Inc. | 2434 | F | 661 327-0371 | 3257 |
| Hoover Treated Wood Pdts Inc. | 2491 | C | 661 833-0429 | 3403 |
| West Coast Wood Preserving LLC | 2491 | C | 661 833-0429 | 3405 |
| Johnson Controls Inc. | 2531 | F | 661 862-5706 | 3631 |
| Harrell Holdings (PA) | 2711 | E | 661 322-5627 | 4126 |
| Amber Chemical Inc. | 2819 | E | 661 325-2072 | 5068 |
| Championx LLC | 2819 | E | 661 834-0454 | 5082 |
| Glam and Glits Nail Design Inc. | 2844 | D | 661 393-4800 | 5981 |
| Kern Oil & Refining Co (HQ) | 2911 | C | 661 845-0761 | 6340 |
| MTS Solutions LLC | 2911 | E | 661 589-5804 | 6342 |
| San Joaquin Refining Co Inc. | 2911 | C | 661 327-4257 | 6352 |
| Tricor Refining LLC | 2911 | E | 661 393-7110 | 6355 |
| Delta Trading LP | 2951 | E | 661 834-5560 | 6361 |
| Asphalt Dr Inc. | 2952 | E | 661 437-5995 | 6372 |
| Newby Rubber Inc. | 3069 | E | 661 327-5137 | 6517 |
| Hancor Inc. | 3084 | D | 661 366-1520 | 6597 |
| Domino Plastics Mfg Inc. | 3089 | E | 661 396-3744 | 6808 |
| Pactiv LLC | 3089 | C | 661 392-4000 | 6947 |
| Golden Empire Con Pdts Inc. | 3272 | D | 661 833-4490 | 7339 |
| Consolidated Fibrgls Pdts Co | 3296 | E | 661 323-6026 | 7575 |
| Kern Steel Fabrication Inc (PA) | 3441 | D | 661 327-9588 | 8164 |
| Metal Tek Company | 3441 | E | 661 832-6011 | 8184 |
| Spartan Inc. | 3441 | D | 661 327-1205 | 8221 |
| United Pipe & Stl Fabrication | 3441 | E | 661 489-4100 | 8236 |
| PNa Construction Tech Inc. | 3444 | E | 661 326-1700 | 8541 |
| Jts Modular Inc. | 3448 | E | 661 835-9270 | 8672 |
| 3g Rebar Inc. | 3449 | F | 661 588-0294 | 8690 |
| Elyte Inc. | 3479 | F | 661 832-1000 | 9067 |
| Bvi International Inc. | 3491 | E | 661 834-1775 | 9147 |
| Western Valve Inc. | 3491 | E | 661 327-7660 | 9164 |
| Russell Fabrication Corp. | 3498 | E | 661 861-8495 | 9269 |
| Material Control Inc. | 3499 | D | 661 617-6033 | 9293 |
| Marie Edward Vineyards Inc. | 3523 | E | 661 363-5038 | 9369 |
| Altec Inc. | 3531 | E | 661 679-4177 | 9404 |
| Sturgeon Services Intl Inc. | 3531 | B | 661 322-4408 | 9438 |
| Chancellor Oil Tools Inc. | 3533 | E | 661 324-2213 | 9458 |
| Downhole Stabilization Inc. | 3533 | E | 661 631-1044 | 9461 |
| Global Elastomeric Pdts Inc. | 3533 | D | 661 831-5380 | 9463 |
| Kba Engineering LLC | 3533 | D | 661 323-0487 | 9464 |
| Mobile Equipment Company | 3536 | E | 661 327-8476 | 9503 |
| Ensign US Drlg Cal Inc (HQ) | 3541 | E | 661 589-0111 | 9554 |
| Pro Tool Services Inc. | 3545 | F | 661 393-9222 | 9693 |
| Timec Companies Inc. | 3559 | E | 661 322-8177 | 9903 |
| Total Process Solutions LLC | 3561 | E | 661 829-7910 | 9943 |
| Acco Engineered Systems Inc. | 3585 | E | 661 631-1975 | 10476 |
| M D Manufacturing Inc. | 3589 | F | 661 283-7550 | 10573 |
| Mazzei Injector Company LLC | 3589 | E | 661 363-6500 | 10577 |
| Seaco Technologies Inc. | 3589 | E | 661 326-1522 | 10598 |
| B & B Pipe and Tool Co. | 3599 | E | 661 323-8208 | 10730 |
| Bakersfield Machine Co Inc. | 3599 | D | 661 709-1992 | 10736 |
| Energy Link Indus Svcs Inc. | 3599 | E | 661 765-4444 | 10827 |
| McCain & Mccain Inc. | 3599 | F | 661 322-7764 | 10965 |
| Valley Perforating LLC | 3599 | D | 661 324-4964 | 11166 |
| Water Associates LLC | 3663 | E | 661 281-6077 | 11976 |
| Custom Truck One Source LP | 3713 | E | 316 627-2608 | 13406 |
| Douglass Truck Bodies Inc | 3713 | E | 661 327-0258 | 13408 |
| Tiger Tanks Inc. | 3795 | E | 661 363-8335 | 14128 |
| Computational Systems Inc. | 3823 | D | 661 832-5306 | 14396 |
| Star-Luck Enterprise Inc. | 3823 | E | 661 665-9999 | 14461 |
| Townsend Industries Inc. | 3842 | D | 661 837-1795 | 15419 |
| Townsend Industries Inc. | 3842 | D | 661 837-1795 | 15420 |
| Townsend Industries Inc (DH) | 3842 | E | 661 837-1795 | 15421 |
| Whitestone Industries Inc. | 3999 | E | 888 567-2234 | 16270 |
| Buck Owens Production Co Inc (PA) | 4832 | E | 661 326-1011 | 16326 |
| Mt Poso Cgnrtion A Cal Ltd PR | 4911 | E | 661 663-3155 | 16345 |
| Cameron West Coast Inc. | 5082 | D | | 16788 |
| Ace Hydraulic Sales & Svc Inc. | 5084 | E | 661 327-0571 | 16804 |
| Drill Cool Systems Inc (PA) | 5084 | F | 661 633-2665 | 16813 |
| Industrial Data Communications | 5084 | E | 661 589-4477 | 16818 |
| Surface Pumps Inc (PA) | 5084 | D | 661 393-1545 | 16846 |
| Custom Building Products LLC | 5085 | D | 661 393-0422 | 16869 |
| Dhv Industries Inc. | 5085 | D | 661 392-8948 | 16872 |
| Shar-Craft Inc. | 5085 | E | 661 324-4985 | 16896 |
| Geo Drilling Fluids Inc (PA) | 5169 | E | 661 325-5919 | 17245 |
| Emser Tile LLC | 5211 | E | 661 837-4400 | 17330 |
| Cathys Creations Inc. | 5461 | F | 661 322-1110 | 17408 |
| Raudmans Craig Victory Circle | 5531 | F | 661 833-4600 | 17460 |
| Jipcob Inc. | 5812 | C | 661 859-1111 | 17587 |

| Company | SIC | EMP | PHONE | ENTRY# |
|---|---|---|---|---|
| Western Oilfields Supply Co (PA) | 7359 | C | 661 399-9124 | 17865 |
| Lightspeed Software Inc | 7372 | F | 661 716-7600 | 18496 |
| Bakersfield Elc Mtr Repr Inc | 7694 | F | 661 327-3583 | 19225 |
| Electric Motor Works Inc | 7694 | E | 661 327-4271 | 19228 |
| SA Camp Pump Company | 7699 | D | 661 399-2976 | 19279 |
| Covenant Community Svcs Inc | 8322 | E | 661 829-6999 | 19355 |
| Dean L Davis MD | 8322 | E | 661 632-5000 | 19356 |

### BALDWIN PARK, CA - Los Angeles County

| Company | SIC | EMP | PHONE | ENTRY# |
|---|---|---|---|---|
| Distinct Indulgence Inc | 2051 | E | 818 546-1700 | 1183 |
| Sanders Candy Factory Inc | 2064 | E | 626 814-2038 | 1325 |
| Pepsico Inc | 2086 | E | 626 338-5531 | 1925 |
| Pacon Inc | 2621 | C | 626 814-4654 | 3791 |
| Western Converting Spc Inc | 2759 | E | 909 392-4578 | 4982 |
| Checkworks Inc | 2782 | D | 626 333-1444 | 4999 |
| Mission Kleensweep Prod Inc | 2841 | D | 323 223-1405 | 5878 |
| Hemosure Inc | 2899 | E | 888 436-6787 | 6291 |
| Hillcor Distribution Inc | 3089 | F | 626 960-8789 | 6854 |
| Reny & Co Inc | 3089 | F | 626 962-3078 | 7002 |
| Standard Concrete Products Inc (HQ) | 3273 | E | 310 829-4537 | 7502 |
| Kal-Cameron Manufacturing Corp (HQ) | 3423 | D | 626 338-7308 | 7956 |
| Universal Steel Services Inc | 3441 | E | 626 960-1455 | 8237 |
| Lawrence Roll Up Doors Inc (PA) | 3442 | E | 626 962-4163 | 8273 |
| Fabtronics Inc | 3444 | E | 626 962-3293 | 8452 |
| Oreco Duct Systems Inc | 3444 | C | 626 337-8832 | 8521 |
| Pacific Award Metals Inc (HQ) | 3444 | D | 626 814-4410 | 8525 |
| Rigos Equipment Mfg LLC | 3444 | E | 626 813-6621 | 8558 |
| Upm Inc | 3544 | B | 626 962-4001 | 9654 |
| G & I Islas Industries Inc (PA) | 3556 | E | 626 960-5020 | 9793 |
| Meritek Electronics Corp (PA) | 3559 | D | 626 373-1728 | 9876 |
| Global Silicon Electronics Inc | 3572 | E | 626 336-1888 | 10239 |
| George Fischer Inc (HQ) | 3599 | C | 626 571-2770 | 10859 |
| My Machine Inc | 3599 | F | 626 214-9223 | 11001 |
| Tektest Inc | 3678 | E | 626 446-6175 | 12901 |
| Inovit Inc | 3714 | F | 626 444-4775 | 13520 |
| Cera Inc | 3821 | E | 626 814-2688 | 14331 |
| Ametek Ameron LLC (HQ) | 3823 | D | 626 856-0101 | 14386 |
| Georg Fischer Signet LLC | 3823 | E | 626 571-2770 | 14418 |
| Freudenberg Medical LLC | 3841 | C | 626 814-9684 | 15092 |
| Denovo Dental Inc | 3843 | E | 626 480-0182 | 15449 |
| Condor Outdoor Products Inc (PA) | 3949 | E | 626 358-3270 | 15800 |
| Rukli Inc | 3999 | F | 818 981-9137 | 16219 |
| Classic Concepts Inc (PA) | 5023 | F | 323 266-8993 | 16422 |
| Nichols Lumber & Hardware Co | 5031 | D | 626 960-4802 | 16454 |
| Lighting Technologies Intl LLC | 5063 | C | 626 480-0755 | 16657 |
| American Kal Enterprises Inc (PA) | 5072 | E | 626 338-7308 | 16745 |
| Cedarwood-Young Company | 5093 | E | 626 962-4047 | 16958 |
| Cremi Mex Inc | 5143 | E | 323 235-0004 | 17127 |
| Treasure Garden Inc (PA) | 5261 | E | 626 814-0168 | 17362 |
| Alphatech General Inc | 7699 | D | 626 337-4640 | 19241 |

### BALLICO, CA - Merced County

| Company | SIC | EMP | PHONE | ENTRY# |
|---|---|---|---|---|
| Golden By-Products Inc | 3559 | D | 209 668-4855 | 9861 |

### BANNING, CA - Riverside County

| Company | SIC | EMP | PHONE | ENTRY# |
|---|---|---|---|---|
| IMS Products Inc | 3751 | F | 951 653-7720 | 14060 |
| DT Mattson Enterprises Inc | 3944 | E | 951 849-9781 | 15746 |
| Strech Plastics Incorporated | 5088 | E | 951 922-2224 | 16925 |

### BARSTOW, CA - San Bernardino County

| Company | SIC | EMP | PHONE | ENTRY# |
|---|---|---|---|---|
| Green Valley Foods Product | 2022 | F | 760 964-1105 | 717 |
| Kar Ice Service Inc (PA) | 2097 | F | 760 256-2648 | 2110 |
| Five Star Food Containers Inc | 3086 | D | 626 437-6219 | 6633 |
| Marine Corps United States | 3531 | C | 760 577-6716 | 9431 |

### BEALE AFB, CA - Yuba County

| Company | SIC | EMP | PHONE | ENTRY# |
|---|---|---|---|---|
| Military Advantage Inc | 2311 | E | 530 788-0221 | 2561 |
| Goodrich Corporation | 3728 | F | 530 788-9214 | 13856 |

### BEAUMONT, CA - Riverside County

| Company | SIC | EMP | PHONE | ENTRY# |
|---|---|---|---|---|
| N7 Creamery Inc | 2024 | F | 909 922-8422 | 812 |
| Beaumont Juice LLC | 2033 | E | 951 769-7171 | 877 |
| Dpp 2020 Inc (DH) | 3089 | E | 951 845-3161 | 6811 |
| Anderson Chrnesky Strl Stl Inc | 3441 | D | 951 769-5700 | 8096 |
| Risco Inc | 3452 | E | 951 769-2899 | 8766 |
| Precision Stampings Inc (PA) | 3643 | E | 951 845-1174 | 11468 |
| CJ Foods Mfg Beaumont LLC | 3999 | D | 951 916-9300 | 16117 |

### BELL, CA - Los Angeles County

| Company | SIC | EMP | PHONE | ENTRY# |
|---|---|---|---|---|
| Penguin Natural Foods Inc | 2099 | E | 323 488-6000 | 2317 |
| Fam LLC (PA) | 2231 | D | 323 888-7755 | 2446 |
| Carol Wior Inc | 2339 | E | 562 927-0052 | 2744 |
| Marika LLC | 2339 | D | 323 888-7755 | 2789 |
| Hain Celestial Group Inc | 2844 | C | 323 859-0553 | 5985 |
| Custom Building Products LLC | 2891 | C | 323 582-0846 | 6225 |
| West Coast-Accudyne Inc | 3542 | E | 562 927-2546 | 9592 |
| Pacesetter Inc | 3845 | B | 323 773-0591 | 15567 |
| Dg Brands Inc | 5137 | D | 323 268-0220 | 17088 |
| H & T Seafood Inc | 5146 | E | 323 526-0888 | 17157 |
| El Aviso Magazine | 5192 | E | 323 586-9199 | 17276 |

### BELL GARDENS, CA - Los Angeles County

| Company | SIC | EMP | PHONE | ENTRY# |
|---|---|---|---|---|
| Rob Inc | 2325 | D | 562 806-5589 | 2588 |
| Carnevale & Lohr Inc | 3281 | E | 562 927-8311 | 7535 |
| Infinity Kitchen Products Inc | 3444 | F | 562 806-5771 | 8472 |
| Eurocraft Archtectural Met Inc | 3446 | E | 323 771-1323 | 8625 |
| Metal Surfaces Intl LLC | 3471 | C | 562 927-1331 | 8985 |
| McLane Manufacturing Inc | 3524 | D | 562 633-8158 | 9397 |
| Barber Welding and Mfg Co | 3599 | E | 562 928-2570 | 10737 |
| Wilcox Machine Co | 3599 | D | 562 927-5353 | 11194 |
| Cal Southern Braiding Inc | 3679 | E | 562 927-5531 | 12930 |
| Flexco Inc | 3728 | E | 562 927-2525 | 13841 |
| WEI-Chuan USA Inc (PA) | 5142 | C | 626 225-7168 | 17124 |
| Parkhouse Tire Service Inc (PA) | 5531 | D | 562 928-0421 | 17457 |

### BELLFLOWER, CA - Los Angeles County

| Company | SIC | EMP | PHONE | ENTRY# |
|---|---|---|---|---|
| Arctic Glacier USA Inc | 2097 | E | 800 562-1990 | 2107 |
| KI Decorator Sales | 2431 | E | 562 920-0268 | 3152 |
| Cutting Edge Creative LLC | 2542 | D | 562 907-7007 | 3683 |
| Kevin White | 2711 | F | 562 231-6642 | 4142 |
| Bryant Rubber Corp | 3053 | C | 310 530-2530 | 6439 |
| Danco Valve Company | 3491 | E | 562 925-2588 | 9155 |

### BELMONT, CA - San Mateo County

| Company | SIC | EMP | PHONE | ENTRY# |
|---|---|---|---|---|
| Fineline Carpentry Inc | 2434 | E | 650 592-2442 | 3240 |
| Moquin Press Inc | 2752 | D | 650 592-0575 | 4701 |
| Cutting Edge Machining Inc (PA) | 3599 | E | 408 738-8677 | 10795 |
| Pacific Screw Products Inc | 3599 | D | 650 583-9682 | 11025 |
| Spectrum Systems SF | 3645 | E | 415 361-2429 | 11502 |
| General Radar Corp (PA) | 3812 | F | 650 304-9033 | 14193 |
| Nikon Research Corp America | 3825 | E | 800 446-4566 | 14565 |
| Powerhouse Engineering Inc | 3999 | F | 650 226-3560 | 16207 |
| Folio3 Software Inc | 7372 | E | 650 802-8668 | 18318 |
| Oracle Systems Corporation | 7372 | F | 650 654-7606 | 18642 |
| Oracle Systems Corporation | 7372 | F | 650 506-5062 | 18644 |

### BELVEDERE TIBURON, CA - Marin County

| Company | SIC | EMP | PHONE | ENTRY# |
|---|---|---|---|---|
| Stalker Software Inc | 7372 | E | 415 569-2280 | 18833 |

### BENICIA, CA - Solano County

| Company | SIC | EMP | PHONE | ENTRY# |
|---|---|---|---|---|
| Total-Western Inc | 1389 | E | 707 747-5506 | 281 |
| Thorne Research Inc | 2023 | F | 707 297-3458 | 782 |
| Valley Fine Foods Company LLC (PA) | 2041 | D | 707 746-6888 | 1066 |
| Pepsi-Cola Metro Btlg Co Inc | 2086 | E | 707 746-5404 | 1917 |
| Reyes Coca-Cola Bottling LLC | 2086 | E | 707 747-2000 | 1951 |
| Cork Supply USA Inc | 2499 | D | 707 746-0353 | 3415 |
| Westcott Designs Inc | 2511 | E | 510 367-7229 | 3460 |
| Gibson Printing & Pubg Inc | 2711 | E | 707 745-0733 | 4122 |
| Molecule Labs Inc | 2869 | E | 925 473-8200 | 6153 |
| Kwik Bond Polymers LLC | 2891 | E | 866 434-1772 | 6235 |
| Red Line Synthetic Oil Corporation | 2992 | F | 707 745-6100 | 6399 |
| East Bay Tire Co | 3011 | E | 707 747-5613 | 6409 |
| Gibbs Plastic & Rubber LLC | 3069 | F | 707 746-7300 | 6496 |
| Rapid Accu-Form Inc | 3089 | F | 707 745-1879 | 6994 |
| Benicia Fabrication & Mch Inc | 3443 | C | 707 745-8111 | 8302 |
| Xchanger Manufacturing Corp | 3443 | E | 510 632-8828 | 8355 |
| Cameron International Corp | 3533 | E | 707 752-8800 | 9457 |
| Ralphs-Pugh Co Inc | 3535 | D | 707 745-6222 | 9492 |
| Metlsaw Systems Inc | 3541 | E | 707 746-6200 | 9561 |
| Flowserve Corporation | 3561 | F | 707 748-4900 | 9923 |
| Rix Industries (PA) | 3563 | D | 707 745-5900 | 9974 |
| Water One Industries Inc (PA) | 3589 | E | 707 747-4300 | 10610 |
| Unico Mechanical Corp (PA) | 3599 | E | 707 745-9970 | 11159 |
| Evoqua Water Technologies LLC | 3629 | E | 707 747-9600 | 11372 |
| Custom Coils Inc | 3677 | F | 707 752-8633 | 12836 |
| Crane Co | 3679 | E | 707 748-7166 | 12948 |
| Walashek Industrial & Mar Inc | 3731 | D | 206 624-2880 | 14023 |
| Dusouth Industries | 3823 | E | 707 745-5117 | 14405 |
| Dunlop Manufacturing Inc (PA) | 3931 | D | 707 745-2722 | 15714 |
| Powerhouse Diesel Services Incorporated | 5084 | E | 707 747-6737 | 16834 |
| West Coast Beauty Supply Co | 5087 | A | 707 748-4800 | 16911 |
| Harv 81 Usa Inc | 5199 | E | 707 746-0353 | 17297 |
| Valero Energy Corporation | 5541 | B | 707 745-7011 | 17478 |
| Speedway Copy Systems Inc | 7334 | E | 415 495-4330 | 17816 |
| Lane Safety Co Inc | 7363 | E | 707 746-4820 | 17868 |

# BERKELEY, CA

**GEOGRAPHIC SECTION**

| | SIC | EMP | PHONE | ENTRY# |
|---|---|---|---|---|

## BERKELEY, CA - Alameda County

| Company | SIC | EMP | PHONE | ENTRY# |
|---|---|---|---|---|
| Wild Earth Inc | 2047 | E | 510 206-6559 | 1116 |
| Doughtronics Inc **(PA)** | 2051 | E | 510 524-1327 | 1187 |
| Doughtronics Inc | 2051 | E | 510 843-2978 | 1188 |
| Third Culture Food Group Inc | 2051 | E | 650 479-4585 | 1248 |
| Shelton Inc | 2066 | E | | 1344 |
| Takara Sake USA Inc **(DH)** | 2085 | F | 510 540-8250 | 1846 |
| Sports Street Marketing A Californi | 2087 | E | 510 527-4664 | 2025 |
| Annies Inc **(HQ)** | 2099 | D | 510 558-7500 | 2127 |
| Three Stone Hearth LLC | 2099 | E | 510 981-1334 | 2375 |
| Bebop Sensors Inc | 2296 | E | 503 875-4990 | 2532 |
| Berkeley Mllwk & Furn Co Inc | 2511 | E | 510 549-2854 | 3435 |
| Mulholland Brothers **(PA)** | 2512 | E | 415 824-5995 | 3484 |
| Zenbooth Inc | 2521 | E | 510 646-8368 | 3591 |
| Evolv Surfaces Inc | 2542 | C | 415 767-4600 | 3685 |
| Berkeleyside LLC | 2711 | E | 510 671-0380 | 4075 |
| Indepndent Brkley Stdnt Pubg I | 2711 | E | 510 548-8300 | 4133 |
| Society For The Study Ntiv Art | 2731 | E | 510 549-4270 | 4346 |
| Associted Stdnts of The Univ CA | 2741 | D | 510 590-7874 | 4368 |
| Autumn Press Inc | 2752 | E | 510 654-4545 | 4519 |
| Western Roto Engravers Inc | 2759 | E | 510 525-2950 | 4983 |
| Bayer Corporation | 2821 | E | 412 777-2000 | 5140 |
| Mango Materials Inc | 2821 | F | 650 440-0430 | 5175 |
| Aduro Gvax Inc | 2834 | E | 510 848-4400 | 5300 |
| Bayer Healthcare LLC | 2834 | C | 510 705-7545 | 5359 |
| Bayer Healthcare LLC | 2834 | D | 510 705-4421 | 5360 |
| Carmot Therapeutics Inc | 2834 | F | 888 402-4674 | 5396 |
| Gu | 2834 | E | 510 527-4664 | 5471 |
| Valitor Inc | 2834 | F | 510 813-8611 | 5700 |
| Valor Compounding Pharmacy Inc | 2834 | D | 855 554-2889 | 5701 |
| Caribou Biosciences Inc | 2836 | C | 510 982-6030 | 5815 |
| Libby Laboratories Inc | 2844 | E | 510 527-5400 | 6003 |
| Janco Chemical Corporation | 2851 | E | 510 527-9770 | 6088 |
| PRC - Desoto International Inc | 2851 | D | 510 526-1525 | 6106 |
| Poly-Seal Industries | 3069 | F | 510 843-9722 | 6524 |
| Hanson Aggrgtes Md-Pacific Inc | 3273 | F | 510 526-1611 | 7452 |
| Second Street Properties | 3325 | A | | 7699 |
| Cellmobility Inc | 3399 | E | 510 549-3300 | 7907 |
| Terminal Manufacturing Co LLC | 3441 | E | 510 526-3071 | 8227 |
| Trans Bay Steel Corporation **(PA)** | 3441 | E | 510 277-3756 | 8232 |
| Graysix Company | 3444 | E | 510 845-5936 | 8460 |
| Bierwith Forge & Tool Inc | 3462 | D | 510 526-5034 | 8773 |
| Cal Electro-Coatings Inc | 3471 | E | 510 849-4075 | 8936 |
| Vector Data LLC | 3571 | D | 408 933-3266 | 10216 |
| Parker Powis Inc | 3579 | D | 510 848-2463 | 10463 |
| Holophane Corporation | 3646 | A | 510 540-0156 | 11538 |
| Meyer Sound Laboratories Inc **(PA)** | 3651 | C | 510 486-1166 | 11677 |
| Iteris Inc | 3669 | F | 510 540-7647 | 12001 |
| Sensys Networks Inc | 3669 | D | 510 548-4620 | 12015 |
| Sunsystem Technology LLC | 3674 | C | 510 984-2027 | 12746 |
| Coreshell Technologies Inc | 3692 | E | 415 265-4887 | 13158 |
| 3d Robotics Inc **(PA)** | 3699 | D | 415 599-1404 | 13206 |
| Raco Manufacturing & Engrg Co | 3699 | E | 510 658-6713 | 13294 |
| Ivu Traffic Technologies Inc | 3714 | F | 415 655-2200 | 13521 |
| Heliospace Corporation | 3769 | E | 415 385-6803 | 14112 |
| Bayer Corporation | 3841 | D | 510 705-5000 | 14996 |
| Channel Medsystems Inc | 3841 | E | 603 318-5084 | 15039 |
| Avid Technology Inc | 3861 | E | 510 486-8302 | 15629 |
| Cemex Corp | 5032 | C | 800 992-3639 | 16470 |
| 4d Sight Inc | 7372 | E | 415 425-1321 | 18007 |
| Barra LLC **(HQ)** | 7372 | B | 510 548-5442 | 18091 |
| Blu Banyan Inc | 7372 | E | 510 929-1070 | 18116 |
| Curacubby Inc | 7372 | D | 415 200-3373 | 18215 |
| Disruptive Games Inc | 7372 | E | 310 922-6658 | 18244 |
| Geopogo | 7372 | E | 510 918-7083 | 18346 |
| I Manageproperty Inc | 7372 | E | 510 665-0665 | 18397 |
| Relationalai Inc | 7372 | D | 650 307-8776 | 18731 |
| Tom Sawyer Software Corp **(PA)** | 7379 | E | 510 682-6313 | 19048 |
| Sun Light & Power | 7389 | D | 510 845-2997 | 19136 |
| DSM Biomedical Inc | 8731 | C | 510 841-8800 | 19451 |

## BEVERLY HILLS, CA - Los Angeles County

| Company | SIC | EMP | PHONE | ENTRY# |
|---|---|---|---|---|
| Atlas Lithium Corporation | 1499 | D | 833 661-7900 | 337 |
| Alexander International Inc | 2051 | E | 424 285-8080 | 1155 |
| Sugarfina Inc | 2064 | E | 855 784-2734 | 1333 |
| Fast Track Energy Drink LLc | 2086 | E | 310 281-2045 | 1888 |
| Pepsico Inc | 2086 | F | 323 785-2820 | 1924 |
| Alanic International Corp | 2299 | E | 855 525-2642 | 2540 |
| Lisa Factory Inc | 2321 | D | 213 536-5326 | 2576 |
| Etro USA Incorporated | 2331 | E | 310 248-2855 | 2664 |
| Instant Tuck Inc | 2392 | E | 310 955-8824 | 2929 |
| Royal Blue Inc | 2392 | E | 310 888-0156 | 2949 |
| ERA Products Inc | 2531 | F | 310 324-4908 | 3624 |
| L F P Inc **(PA)** | 2721 | D | 323 651-3525 | 4270 |
| Playboy Japan Inc | 2721 | F | 310 424-1800 | 4289 |
| World History Group LLC | 2721 | E | 703 779-8322 | 4307 |
| Workbook Inc | 2741 | E | 323 856-0008 | 4495 |
| Olympus Water Holdings IV LP **(PA)** | 2842 | E | 310 739-6325 | 5922 |
| Hunniface LLC | 2844 | F | 424 966-0281 | 5989 |
| Summer Fridays LLC | 2844 | E | 612 804-0868 | 6042 |
| Stratos Renewables Corporation | 2869 | E | 310 402-5901 | 6161 |
| Zeons Inc | 3229 | B | 323 302-8299 | 7209 |
| American Solar LLC | 3433 | E | 323 250-1307 | 8059 |
| King Holding Corporation | 3452 | A | 586 254-3900 | 8760 |
| B-Reel Films Inc | 3571 | E | 917 388-3836 | 10138 |
| Ateliere Crtive Tech Hldg Corp | 3577 | E | 855 466-9696 | 10330 |
| Dasol Inc | 3641 | C | 310 327-6700 | 11423 |
| Mogul | 3714 | E | 424 245-4331 | 13542 |
| Greene & Company | 3911 | E | 212 203-1107 | 15693 |
| Maurice Kraiem & Company | 5094 | E | 213 629-0038 | 16969 |
| SOS Beauty Inc | 5122 | E | 424 285-1405 | 17049 |
| Wen U Luv Liquidation LLC | 5632 | E | 323 456-8821 | 17502 |
| Royal-Pedic Mattress Mfg LLC **(PA)** | 5712 | E | 310 278-9594 | 17524 |
| Gores Group LLC **(PA)** | 6211 | D | 310 209-3010 | 17730 |
| Mob Scene LLC | 7311 | C | 323 648-7200 | 17781 |
| 1on1 LLC | 7372 | E | 310 998-7473 | 18003 |
| Ateliere Creative Tech Inc | 7372 | E | 800 921-4252 | 18071 |
| Klooma Holdings Inc | 7372 | E | 305 747-3315 | 18475 |
| Subject Technologies Inc | 7372 | E | 310 243-6484 | 18844 |

## BIG BEAR CITY, CA - San Bernardino County

| Company | SIC | EMP | PHONE | ENTRY# |
|---|---|---|---|---|
| S-Curve Technologies Inc | 3089 | E | 909 584-8898 | 7018 |

## BIG BEAR LAKE, CA - San Bernardino County

| Company | SIC | EMP | PHONE | ENTRY# |
|---|---|---|---|---|
| Big Bear Bowling Barn Inc | 1799 | E | 909 878-2695 | 555 |
| Hi-Desert Publishing Company | 5994 | E | 909 866-3456 | 17683 |

## BIGGS, CA - Butte County

| Company | SIC | EMP | PHONE | ENTRY# |
|---|---|---|---|---|
| Sunwest Milling Inc | 2044 | D | 530 868-5421 | 1083 |

## BISHOP, CA - Inyo County

| Company | SIC | EMP | PHONE | ENTRY# |
|---|---|---|---|---|
| Cal-Tron Corporation | 3089 | E | 760 873-8491 | 6757 |

## BLOOMINGTON, CA - San Bernardino County

| Company | SIC | EMP | PHONE | ENTRY# |
|---|---|---|---|---|
| Aspire Bakeries LLC | 2052 | C | 714 478-4656 | 1262 |
| Frito-Lay North America Inc | 2096 | F | 909 877-0902 | 2092 |
| Dura Technologies Inc | 2851 | C | 909 877-8477 | 6082 |
| Hogan Co Inc | 3315 | E | 909 421-0245 | 7643 |
| Wadco Industries Inc | 3441 | E | 909 874-7800 | 8243 |
| Westco Industries Inc | 3441 | E | 909 874-8700 | 8245 |
| Cummins Pacific LLC | 3519 | F | 909 877-0433 | 9322 |
| Hydraulic Shop Inc | 3537 | E | 909 875-9336 | 9523 |
| Heater Designs Inc | 3567 | E | 909 421-0971 | 10052 |
| Mitco Industries Inc **(PA)** | 3599 | E | 909 877-0800 | 10987 |
| Remco Mch & Fabrication Inc | 3599 | F | 909 877-3530 | 11076 |
| Signify North America Corp | 3646 | E | 732 563-3000 | 11557 |
| Cooper Lighting LLC | 3648 | B | 909 605-6615 | 11588 |
| Cooper Crouse-Hinds LLC | 3699 | E | 951 241-8766 | 13226 |
| Quality Tech Mfg Inc | 3721 | E | 909 465-9565 | 13687 |
| Roberts Lumber Sales Inc | 5031 | D | 909 350-9164 | 16459 |
| Atlas Pacific Corporation **(PA)** | 5093 | E | 909 421-1200 | 16956 |

## BLUE JAY, CA - San Bernardino County

| Company | SIC | EMP | PHONE | ENTRY# |
|---|---|---|---|---|
| Travis Snyder | 3531 | F | 909 338-6302 | 9443 |

## BLUE LAKE, CA - Humboldt County

| Company | SIC | EMP | PHONE | ENTRY# |
|---|---|---|---|---|
| Mad River Brewing Company Inc | 5813 | E | 707 668-4151 | 17621 |

## BLYTHE, CA - Riverside County

| Company | SIC | EMP | PHONE | ENTRY# |
|---|---|---|---|---|
| Blythe Energy Inc | 1321 | F | 760 922-9950 | 148 |
| Crawford Associates | 1771 | E | 760 922-6804 | 520 |

## BONITA, CA - San Diego County

| Company | SIC | EMP | PHONE | ENTRY# |
|---|---|---|---|---|
| International Plating Svc LLC **(PA)** | 3471 | E | 619 454-2135 | 8973 |
| Right Hand Manufacturing Inc | 3625 | C | 619 819-5056 | 11344 |
| Pacific Integrated Mfg Inc | 3841 | C | 619 921-3464 | 15220 |
| Crockett & Coinc **(PA)** | 7992 | E | 619 267-6410 | 19309 |

## BONSALL, CA - San Diego County

| Company | SIC | EMP | PHONE | ENTRY# |
|---|---|---|---|---|
| Finishline Certified Welding L | 7692 | F | 760 271-6364 | 19193 |

## BOONVILLE, CA - Mendocino County

| Company | SIC | EMP | PHONE | ENTRY# |
|---|---|---|---|---|
| Anderson Valley Brewing Inc | 2082 | E | 707 895-2337 | 1412 |

## BORON, CA - Kern County

| Company | SIC | EMP | PHONE | ENTRY# |
|---|---|---|---|---|
| Rio Tinto Minerals Inc | 1241 | C | 760 762-7121 | 117 |

| Company | SIC | EMP | PHONE | ENTRY# |
|---|---|---|---|---|
| US Borax Inc | 2819 | A | 760 762-7000 | 5127 |

## BRANSCOMB, CA - Mendocino County

| Company | SIC | EMP | PHONE | ENTRY# |
|---|---|---|---|---|
| Harwood Products | 2431 | C | 707 984-1601 | 3144 |

## BRAWLEY, CA - Imperial County

| Company | SIC | EMP | PHONE | ENTRY# |
|---|---|---|---|---|
| Owb Packers LLC | 2011 | D | 760 351-2700 | 611 |
| Salico Farms Inc | 2032 | C | 760 344-5375 | 868 |
| Fiesta Mexican Foods Inc | 2051 | E | 760 344-3580 | 1193 |
| Spreckels Sugar Company Inc | 2063 | B | 760 344-3110 | 1296 |
| Spreadco Inc | 2262 | E | 760 351-0747 | 2500 |
| Western Mesquite Mines Inc | 3339 | E | 928 341-4653 | 7714 |
| Broma Applicators LLC | 5191 | E | 760 351-0101 | 17269 |
| Vons Companies Inc | 5411 | C | 760 351-3002 | 17392 |

## BREA, CA - Orange County

| Company | SIC | EMP | PHONE | ENTRY# |
|---|---|---|---|---|
| Linn Energy LLC | 1382 | E | 714 257-1600 | 188 |
| Win-Dor Inc (PA) | 1751 | C | 714 576-2030 | 503 |
| Fresh Start Bakeries Inc | 2051 | A | 714 256-8900 | 1203 |
| Ventura Foods LLC (PA) | 2079 | C | 714 257-3700 | 1409 |
| Wilsey Foods Inc | 2079 | A | 714 257-3700 | 1411 |
| La Paz Products Inc | 2087 | F | 714 990-0982 | 2013 |
| Scisorek & Son Flavors Inc | 2087 | E | 714 524-0550 | 2024 |
| Benevolence Food Products LLC | 2099 | E | 888 832-3738 | 2136 |
| Shore Front LLC | 2099 | E | 714 612-3751 | 2352 |
| BOa Inc | 2329 | E | 714 256-8960 | 2614 |
| AST Sportswear Inc (PA) | 2361 | D | 714 223-2030 | 2852 |
| Absolute Screenprint Inc | 2396 | E | 714 529-2120 | 3000 |
| Pacific Archtectural Mllwk Inc | 2431 | E | 562 905-9282 | 3173 |
| Parkinson Enterprises Inc | 2521 | D | 714 626-0275 | 3581 |
| Stolo Cabinets Inc (PA) | 2521 | E | 714 529-7303 | 3588 |
| Pacific Quality Packaging Corp | 2653 | E | 714 257-1234 | 3871 |
| Avery Dennison Corporation | 2672 | B | 714 674-8500 | 3942 |
| SC Liquidation Company LLC | 2672 | C | 714 482-1006 | 3954 |
| Avery Dennison Office Products Co Inc | 2678 | A | | 4014 |
| Avery Products Corporation (DH) | 2678 | E | 714 674-8500 | 4017 |
| Educational Ideas Incorporated | 2731 | E | 714 990-4332 | 4328 |
| Pennysaver USA Publishing LLC | 2741 | A | 866 640-3900 | 4446 |
| Coyle Reproductions Inc (PA) | 2752 | C | 866 269-5373 | 4575 |
| Spyder3d LLC | 2752 | F | 714 256-1122 | 4769 |
| Nowdocs International Inc | 2759 | E | 714 986-1559 | 4929 |
| President Enterprise LLC | 2759 | E | 714 671-9577 | 4940 |
| Moravek Biochemicals Inc (PA) | 2819 | E | 714 990-2018 | 5104 |
| Beacon Manufacturing Inc | 2833 | E | 714 529-0980 | 5232 |
| North West Pharmanaturals Inc | 2833 | E | 714 529-0980 | 5255 |
| UNI-Caps LLC | 2833 | E | 714 529-8400 | 5279 |
| Kirkhill Inc | 3053 | A | 714 529-4901 | 6456 |
| West Coast Gasket Co | 3053 | D | 714 869-0123 | 6471 |
| Pacific Plastics Inc | 3084 | D | 714 990-9050 | 6600 |
| Foxconn Electronics Inc | 3089 | E | 714 988-9230 | 6831 |
| Newport Plastics LLC (PA) | 3089 | F | 800 854-8402 | 6932 |
| Plainfield Molding Inc | 3089 | D | 815 436-7806 | 6956 |
| Plainfield Tool and Engineering Inc | 3089 | B | 815 436-5671 | 6957 |
| Ramtec Associates Inc | 3089 | E | 714 996-7477 | 6993 |
| S&B Industry Inc | 3089 | E | 909 569-4155 | 7017 |
| Metals USA Building Pdts LP (DH) | 3355 | A | 713 946-9000 | 7759 |
| Consolidated Aerospace Mfg LLC | 3429 | D | 714 989-2802 | 7989 |
| Moeller Mfg & Sup LLC | 3429 | E | 714 999-5551 | 8017 |
| SPX Cooling Tech LLC | 3443 | F | 714 529-6080 | 8338 |
| Precise Industries Inc | 3444 | C | 714 482-2333 | 8542 |
| Span-O-Matic Inc | 3444 | E | 714 256-4700 | 8577 |
| 3-V Fastener Co Inc | 3452 | D | 949 888-7700 | 8740 |
| Bristol Industries LLC | 3452 | C | 714 990-4121 | 8747 |
| Caran Precision Engineering & Manuf (PA) | 3469 | D | 714 447-5400 | 8829 |
| Imperial Cal Products Inc | 3469 | E | 714 990-9100 | 8851 |
| Electronic Precision Spc Inc | 3471 | E | 714 256-8950 | 8958 |
| Amada America Inc | 3479 | D | 714 739-2111 | 9044 |
| Curtiss-Wright Flow Ctrl Corp | 3491 | E | 949 271-7500 | 9153 |
| Curtiss-Wright Flow Ctrl Corp | 3491 | D | 714 528-2301 | 9154 |
| Curtiss-Wright Flow Ctrl Corp (DH) | 3494 | D | 714 528-1365 | 9184 |
| Kingson Mold & Machine Inc | 3544 | E | 714 871-0221 | 9631 |
| MR Mold & Engineering Corp | 3544 | E | 714 996-5511 | 9637 |
| Baker Furnace Inc | 3567 | F | 714 223-7262 | 10046 |
| Moxa Americas Inc | 3577 | E | 714 528-6777 | 10413 |
| Viewsonic Corporation (PA) | 3577 | C | 909 444-8888 | 10449 |
| Trane US Inc | 3585 | D | 626 913-7123 | 10521 |
| Media Blast & Abrasive Inc | 3589 | F | 714 257-0484 | 10580 |
| Whittier Filtration Inc (DH) | 3589 | E | 714 986-5300 | 10614 |
| Able Wire Edm Inc | 3599 | E | 714 255-1967 | 10657 |
| Energy Cnvrsion Appictions Inc | 3612 | F | 714 256-2166 | 11212 |
| Q C M Inc | 3629 | E | 714 414-1173 | 11378 |
| Jade Range LLC | 3631 | C | 714 961-2400 | 11390 |
| Foxlink International Inc (HQ) | 3643 | E | 714 256-1777 | 11454 |
| Ledconn Corp | 3648 | E | 714 256-2111 | 11605 |
| TEC Lighting Inc | 3648 | F | 714 529-5068 | 11626 |
| Fine Line Circuits & Tech Inc | 3672 | E | 714 529-2942 | 12100 |
| Aeroflite Enterprises Inc | 3678 | D | 714 773-4251 | 12865 |
| Bi Technologies Corporation (HQ) | 3679 | B | 714 447-2300 | 12923 |
| Cks Solution Incorporated | 3679 | E | 714 292-6307 | 12940 |
| Transico Inc | 3679 | E | 714 835-6000 | 13111 |
| HI Uriman Inc (HQ) | 3694 | F | 714 257-2080 | 13172 |
| Clean America Inc | 3699 | F | 800 336-2946 | 13221 |
| Mullen Technologies Inc (PA) | 3711 | E | 714 613-1900 | 13372 |
| Harbor Truck Bodies Inc | 3713 | D | 714 996-0411 | 13414 |
| Lund Motion Products Inc | 3714 | E | 888 983-2204 | 13532 |
| Aerospace Engineering LLC (PA) | 3728 | D | 714 996-8178 | 13755 |
| Applied Cmpsite Structures Inc (HQ) | 3728 | E | 714 990-6300 | 13781 |
| Dynamic Fabrication Inc | 3728 | E | 714 662-2440 | 13834 |
| Kirkhill Inc (HQ) | 3728 | C | 714 529-4901 | 13886 |
| Rogers Holding Company Inc | 3728 | E | 714 257-4850 | 13938 |
| Garmin International Inc | 3812 | B | 909 444-5000 | 14189 |
| Technovative Applications | 3812 | D | 714 996-0104 | 14311 |
| Worldwide Envmtl Pdts Inc (PA) | 3823 | D | 714 990-2700 | 14470 |
| Beckman Coulter Inc | 3826 | A | 714 993-5321 | 14623 |
| Thermal Idntification Tech Inc (PA) | 3826 | F | 408 656-6809 | 14734 |
| Beckman Coulter Inc | 3841 | C | 818 970-2161 | 14998 |
| Carolina Lqiud Chmistries Corp | 3841 | E | 336 722-8910 | 15036 |
| Life Science Outsourcing Inc | 3841 | D | 714 672-1090 | 15148 |
| MPS Medical Inc | 3841 | E | 714 672-1090 | 15197 |
| Curtiss-Wrght Cntrls Intgrted | 3842 | E | 714 982-1860 | 15330 |
| Dcii North America LLC (HQ) | 3843 | E | 714 817-7000 | 15448 |
| Envista Holdings Corporation (PA) | 3843 | D | 714 817-7000 | 15455 |
| Ormco Corporation | 3843 | E | 909 962-5705 | 15469 |
| Pac-Dent Inc | 3843 | E | 909 839-0888 | 15473 |
| Val USA Manufacturer Inc | 3999 | E | 626 839-8069 | 16262 |
| Walters Wholesale Electric Co (HQ) | 5063 | C | 714 784-1900 | 16678 |
| Southern Cal Hydrlic Engrg Cor | 5084 | E | 714 257-4800 | 16843 |
| Nmc Group Inc | 5085 | E | 714 223-3525 | 16885 |
| Proponent Inc (PA) | 5088 | C | 714 223-5400 | 16923 |
| Orora Packaging Solutions | 5113 | E | 714 984-2300 | 17005 |
| Hill Brothers Chemical Company (PA) | 5169 | E | 714 998-8800 | 17246 |
| Suzuki Motor of America Inc (HQ) | 5511 | C | 714 996-7040 | 17442 |
| Jewelers Touch | 5944 | E | 714 579-1616 | 17646 |
| Vesuki Inc | 5947 | F | 562 245-4000 | 17656 |
| Maxxess Systems Inc (PA) | 7372 | F | 714 772-1000 | 18526 |
| Webedoctor Inc | 7372 | E | 714 990-3999 | 18929 |
| American Regent Inc | 8733 | E | 714 989-5058 | 19491 |

## BRENTWOOD, CA - Contra Costa County

| Company | SIC | EMP | PHONE | ENTRY# |
|---|---|---|---|---|
| Pct Enterprises Inc (PA) | 2521 | D | 925 634-5552 | 3583 |
| Brentwood Press & Pubg Co LLC | 2711 | E | 925 516-4757 | 4077 |
| Bay Standard Manufacturing Inc (PA) | 3452 | E | 925 634-1181 | 8744 |
| Bay Standard Inc | 5085 | D | 925 634-1181 | 16863 |

## BRISBANE, CA - San Mateo County

| Company | SIC | EMP | PHONE | ENTRY# |
|---|---|---|---|---|
| Sfo Apparel | 2339 | C | 415 468-8816 | 2807 |
| Fong Brothers Printing Inc (PA) | 2752 | C | 415 467-1050 | 4612 |
| Infoimage of California Inc (PA) | 2759 | D | 650 473-6388 | 4897 |
| Annexon Inc (PA) | 2834 | D | 650 822-5500 | 5325 |
| Janssen Biopharma Inc | 2834 | E | 650 452-0210 | 5510 |
| Maverick Therapeutics Inc | 2834 | E | 650 684-7140 | 5545 |
| Myokardia Inc (HQ) | 2834 | D | 650 741-0900 | 5560 |
| Revir Therapeutics Inc | 2834 | F | 415 794-7166 | 5637 |
| Sumitomo Pharma America Inc | 2834 | C | 650 392-0222 | 5679 |
| Vera Therapeutics Inc (PA) | 2834 | E | 650 770-0077 | 5703 |
| Gate Bioscience Inc | 2835 | E | 650 241-8057 | 5752 |
| OKeeffes Inc (PA) | 3231 | E | 415 822-4222 | 7237 |
| Florian Industries Inc | 3441 | F | 415 330-9000 | 8141 |
| Dolby Laboratories Inc | 3663 | E | 415 715-2500 | 11843 |
| Leemah Corporation (PA) | 3671 | C | 415 394-1288 | 12034 |
| Leemah Electronics Inc (HQ) | 3672 | E | 415 394-1288 | 12152 |
| Faster Faster Inc | 3714 | E | 323 839-0654 | 13499 |
| Cutera Inc (PA) | 3845 | C | 415 657-5500 | 15528 |
| Sheng-Kee of California Inc | 5461 | D | 415 468-3800 | 17420 |
| Day One Biopharmaceuticals Inc (PA) | 8731 | E | 650 484-0899 | 19449 |

## BUELLTON, CA - Santa Barbara County

| Company | SIC | EMP | PHONE | ENTRY# |
|---|---|---|---|---|
| Central Coast Agriculture Inc (PA) | 0191 | E | 805 694-8594 | 54 |
| Firestone Walker Inc | 2082 | D | 805 254-4205 | 1429 |
| Foley Fmly Wines Holdings Inc | 2084 | E | 805 450-7225 | 1574 |
| Terravant Wine Company LLC | 2084 | C | 805 688-4245 | 1777 |
| Aero Industries LLC | 3599 | B | 805 688-6734 | 10683 |
| True Precision Machining Inc | 3599 | E | 805 964-4545 | 11155 |
| Tilton Engineering Inc | 3714 | E | 805 688-2353 | 13586 |
| Platinum Performance Inc (HQ) | 5122 | E | 800 553-2400 | 17044 |

# BUENA PARK, CA — GEOGRAPHIC SECTION

| | SIC | EMP | PHONE | ENTRY# |
|---|---|---|---|---|

## BUENA PARK, CA - Orange County

| Company | SIC | EMP | PHONE | ENTRY# |
|---|---|---|---|---|
| ECB Corp (PA) | 1711 | D | 714 385-8900 | 416 |
| Gresean Industries Inc. | 1751 | E | | 491 |
| Mondelez Global LLC | 2013 | F | 714 690-7428 | 654 |
| One World Meat Company LLC | 2013 | F | 800 782-1670 | 656 |
| Cleughs Frozen Foods Inc | 2037 | E | | 1001 |
| La Mexicana LLC | 2038 | E | 323 277-3660 | 1037 |
| Tawa Supermarket Inc (PA) | 2038 | C | 714 521-8899 | 1049 |
| Island Snacks Inc | 2064 | E | 714 994-1228 | 1314 |
| Ameripec Inc | 2086 | C | 714 690-9191 | 1864 |
| Pepsi-Cola Metro Btlg Co Inc | 2086 | C | 714 522-9635 | 1913 |
| Pop 82 Inc | 2221 | F | 714 523-8500 | 2440 |
| Expo Dyeing & Finishing Inc | 2269 | C | 714 220-9583 | 2502 |
| Manhattan Stitching Co Inc | 2395 | E | 714 521-9479 | 2994 |
| Haley Bros Inc (HQ) | 2431 | D | 714 670-2112 | 3142 |
| Exemplis LLC | 2522 | C | 714 995-4800 | 3600 |
| Exemplis LLC | 2522 | E | 714 898-5500 | 3601 |
| Elwin Inc | 2591 | E | 714 752-6962 | 3719 |
| Blue Ribbon Cont & Display Inc | 2653 | E | 562 944-1217 | 3823 |
| Express Container Inc | 2653 | E | 909 798-3857 | 3841 |
| Rael Inc | 2676 | E | 800 573-1516 | 4005 |
| 365 Printing Inc | 2752 | F | 714 752-6990 | 4498 |
| Cyu Lithographics Inc | 2752 | E | 888 878-9898 | 4580 |
| Q Team | 2752 | E | 714 228-4465 | 4744 |
| Interntional Color Posters Inc | 2759 | E | 949 768-1005 | 4899 |
| Awesome Products Inc (PA) | 2842 | C | 714 562-8873 | 5890 |
| BASF Corporation | 2869 | E | 714 521-6085 | 6131 |
| Parker-Hannifin Corporation | 3052 | D | 714 522-8840 | 6427 |
| Creative Impressions Inc | 3081 | F | 714 521-4441 | 6555 |
| Abad Foam Inc | 3086 | E | 714 994-2223 | 6618 |
| Trim-Lok Inc (PA) | 3089 | C | 714 562-0500 | 7059 |
| Yeager Enterprises Corp | 3291 | D | 714 994-2040 | 7560 |
| Alloy Die Casting Co (PA) | 3363 | C | 714 521-9800 | 7805 |
| Ronman Products Inc | 3399 | F | 714 994-3700 | 7912 |
| Metals USA Building Pdts LP | 3441 | F | 714 522-7852 | 8185 |
| Kimco Iron Inc | 3446 | F | 714 293-6442 | 8633 |
| AW Die Engraving Inc | 3544 | E | 714 521-7910 | 9603 |
| Quality Grinding Co Inc | 3545 | F | 714 228-2100 | 9694 |
| Mar Cor Purification Inc | 3589 | E | 800 633-3080 | 10575 |
| Osmosis Technology Inc | 3589 | E | 714 670-9303 | 10589 |
| CJ Advisors Inc | 3599 | E | 714 956-3388 | 10777 |
| Hi-Tech Labels Incorporated | 3599 | E | 714 670-2150 | 10871 |
| Park Engineering and Mfg Co | 3599 | E | 714 521-4660 | 11032 |
| Wire Cut Company Inc | 3599 | E | 714 994-1170 | 11197 |
| Erika Records Inc | 3652 | E | 714 228-5420 | 11731 |
| Amcor Industries Inc | 3714 | E | 323 585-2852 | 13455 |
| Leach International Corp (DH) | 3728 | B | 714 736-7537 | 13891 |
| True Fresh Hpp LLC | 3822 | E | 949 922-8801 | 14373 |
| Communications Supply Corp | 4899 | D | 714 670-7711 | 16335 |
| Cambium Business Group Inc (PA) | 5021 | C | 714 670-1171 | 16412 |
| Atlas Construction Supply Inc | 5032 | E | 714 441-9500 | 16464 |
| Hochiki America Corporation (HQ) | 5063 | D | 714 522-2246 | 16654 |
| AM Machining Inc | 5088 | F | 714 367-0830 | 16914 |
| Yamaha Corporation of America (HQ) | 5099 | B | 714 522-9011 | 16989 |
| Orora Packaging Solutions (HQ) | 5113 | E | 714 562-6000 | 17004 |
| Orora Packaging Solutions | 5113 | E | 714 525-4900 | 17009 |
| Orora Packaging Solutions | 5113 | E | 714 562-6002 | 17016 |
| Derm Cosmetic Labs Inc (PA) | 5122 | E | 714 562-8873 | 17036 |
| G & G Door Products Inc | 5211 | E | 714 228-2008 | 17331 |
| Westates Inc | 5961 | E | 714 523-7600 | 17676 |
| Performance Water Products Inc | 5963 | F | 714 736-0137 | 17680 |
| True Investments LLC | 6799 | E | 949 258-9720 | 17760 |
| A J Parent Company Inc (PA) | 7389 | D | 714 521-1100 | 19066 |
| Bridport Erie Aviation Inc | 7699 | E | 714 634-8801 | 19245 |

## BURBANK, CA - Los Angeles County

| Company | SIC | EMP | PHONE | ENTRY# |
|---|---|---|---|---|
| Honey Isabells Inc | 0279 | E | 800 708-8485 | 69 |
| Eagle Dominion Energy Corp | 1382 | E | 270 366-4817 | 181 |
| Aries Beef LLC | 2013 | E | 818 526-4855 | 631 |
| Excelline Food Products LLC | 2038 | E | 818 701-7710 | 1034 |
| Divine Pasta Company | 2099 | E | 818 559-7440 | 2187 |
| Palermo Family LP (PA) | 2099 | E | 213 542-3300 | 2312 |
| Staness Jonekos Entps Inc | 2099 | E | 818 606-2710 | 2360 |
| Mortex Corporation | 2329 | C | | 2634 |
| Eastwest Clothing Inc (PA) | 2331 | F | 323 980-1177 | 2663 |
| The Original Cult Inc | 2339 | D | 323 260-7308 | 2815 |
| Vesture Group Incorporated | 2369 | D | 818 842-0200 | 2869 |
| Superior Window Coverings Inc | 2391 | E | 818 762-6685 | 2920 |
| Swaner Hardwood Co Inc (PA) | 2435 | D | 818 953-5350 | 3288 |
| Arte De Mexico Inc (PA) | 2522 | D | 818 753-4559 | 3593 |
| Steves Plating Corporation | 2542 | C | 818 842-2184 | 3709 |
| Westrock Rkt LLC | 2653 | E | 818 729-0610 | 3897 |
| Disney Publishing Worldwide (DH) | 2721 | D | 212 633-4400 | 4248 |
| Disney Book Group LLC (DH) | 2731 | E | 818 560-1000 | 4327 |
| Advanced Publishing Tech Inc | 2741 | F | 818 557-3035 | 4360 |
| Extreme Reach Inc | 2741 | E | 818 588-3635 | 4397 |
| Color West Inc | 2752 | C | 818 840-8881 | 4559 |
| Imagic | 2752 | D | 818 333-1670 | 4639 |
| Midnight Oil Agency LLC | 2752 | B | 818 295-6100 | 4694 |
| Primary Color Systems Corp | 2752 | E | 818 643-5944 | 4731 |
| Printograph Inc | 2752 | E | 818 252-3000 | 4736 |
| Merci Life LLC | 2833 | F | 317 341-4109 | 5247 |
| Hutchinson Arospc & Indust Inc | 3069 | E | 818 843-1000 | 6502 |
| Matz Rubber Company Inc | 3069 | E | 323 849-5170 | 6511 |
| Three-D Plastics Inc (PA) | 3089 | E | 323 849-1316 | 7053 |
| Cydwoq Inc | 3131 | E | 818 848-8307 | 7092 |
| California Insulated Wire & | 3357 | D | 818 569-4930 | 7778 |
| Burbank Steel Treating Inc | 3398 | E | 818 842-0975 | 7882 |
| Quality Heat Treating Inc | 3398 | E | 818 840-8212 | 7898 |
| Saturn Fasteners Inc | 3429 | C | 818 973-1807 | 8025 |
| ESM Aerospace Inc | 3444 | E | 818 841-3653 | 8446 |
| Connell Processing Inc (PA) | 3471 | E | 818 845-7661 | 8946 |
| Haskel International LLC (HQ) | 3561 | C | 818 843-4000 | 9928 |
| Key Code Media Inc (PA) | 3571 | E | 818 303-3900 | 10172 |
| Comco Inc | 3589 | E | 818 333-8500 | 10553 |
| Centerpoint Mfg Co Inc | 3599 | E | 818 842-2147 | 10769 |
| Fortner Eng & Mfg Inc | 3599 | E | 818 240-7740 | 10840 |
| Hydra-Electric Company (PA) | 3613 | C | 818 843-6211 | 11243 |
| Litegear Inc | 3641 | E | 818 358-8542 | 11428 |
| Universal Switching Corp | 3643 | E | 818 785-0200 | 11476 |
| Flo Kino Inc | 3646 | C | 818 767-6528 | 11533 |
| Nomoflo Enterprises Inc | 3646 | D | 818 767-6528 | 11548 |
| Dolby Laboratories Inc | 3651 | E | 818 562-1101 | 11651 |
| Doremi Labs Inc | 3651 | E | 818 562-1101 | 11654 |
| Magnasync/Moviola Corporation | 3651 | E | 818 845-8066 | 11674 |
| Hollywood Records Inc | 3652 | E | 818 560-5670 | 11735 |
| Y B S Enterprises Inc | 3661 | F | 818 848-7790 | 11795 |
| 24/7 Studio Equipment Inc | 3663 | F | 818 840-8247 | 11796 |
| Nerdist Channel LLC | 3663 | E | 818 333-2705 | 11902 |
| Sierra Automated Sys/Eng Corp | 3663 | E | 818 840-6749 | 11945 |
| Graphic Research Inc | 3672 | E | 818 886-7340 | 12125 |
| Accratronics Seals LLC | 3679 | D | 818 843-1500 | 12907 |
| Acsco Products Inc | 3714 | E | 818 953-2240 | 13439 |
| Gerhardt Gear Co Inc | 3714 | E | 818 842-6700 | 13506 |
| Bandy Manufacturing LLC | 3728 | D | 818 846-9000 | 13797 |
| Cardona Manufacturing Corp | 3728 | E | 818 841-8358 | 13807 |
| Crane Aerospace Inc | 3728 | D | 818 526-2600 | 13817 |
| Hutchinson Arospc & Indust Inc | 3728 | C | 818 843-1000 | 13859 |
| Hydro-Aire Inc (HQ) | 3728 | E | 818 526-2600 | 13864 |
| Hydro-Aire Aerospace Corp | 3728 | E | 818 526-2600 | 13865 |
| Senior Operations LLC | 3728 | B | 818 260-2900 | 13955 |
| Rohde & Schwarz Usa Inc | 3825 | E | 818 846-3600 | 14579 |
| Eckert Zegler Isotope Pdts Inc | 3829 | E | 661 309-1010 | 14862 |
| Avid Technology Inc | 3861 | D | 818 557-2520 | 15630 |
| Matthews Studio Equipment Inc | 3861 | E | 818 843-6715 | 15651 |
| Photronics Inc (DH) | 3861 | B | 203 740-5653 | 15661 |
| Hasbro Inc | 3942 | F | 818 478-4320 | 15730 |
| Insomniac Games Inc (PA) | 3944 | D | 818 729-2400 | 15752 |
| Origin LLC | 3999 | E | 818 848-1648 | 16192 |
| Twdc Enterprises 18 Corp (HQ) | 4833 | A | 818 560-1000 | 16330 |
| Ver Sales Inc (PA) | 5051 | E | 818 567-3000 | 16637 |
| Portos Bakery Burbank Inc | 5461 | E | 818 846-9100 | 17417 |
| Sanctuary Clothing LLC (PA) | 5621 | E | 818 505-0018 | 17496 |
| Filmtools Inc (PA) | 5946 | E | 323 467-1116 | 17653 |
| Dvs Media Services (PA) | 7334 | E | 818 841-6750 | 17810 |
| Ultragraphics Inc | 7335 | E | 818 295-3994 | 17819 |
| J L Fisher Inc | 7359 | D | 818 846-8366 | 17856 |
| Cheque Guard Inc | 7371 | E | 818 563-9335 | 17895 |
| Annex Pro Inc | 7372 | E | 800 682-6639 | 18046 |
| Cloudsoda Inc | 7372 | E | 303 947-8661 | 18188 |
| Jam City Inc | 7372 | D | 804 920-8760 | 18453 |
| My Eye Media LLC | 7372 | D | 818 559-7200 | 18566 |

## BURLINGAME, CA - San Mateo County

| Company | SIC | EMP | PHONE | ENTRY# |
|---|---|---|---|---|
| Crown Shtmtl & Skylights Inc | 1761 | E | 415 467-5008 | 512 |
| Petits Pains & Co LP | 2051 | E | 650 692-6000 | 1237 |
| Ed & Dons of Hawaii Inc | 2064 | D | 808 423-8200 | 1304 |
| Guittard Chocolate Holdings Co | 2066 | C | 650 697-4427 | 1340 |
| New Frontier Foods Inc | 2096 | F | 713 501-0292 | 2098 |
| School Apparel Inc (PA) | 2337 | D | 650 777-4500 | 2727 |
| Sing Tao Newspapers (DH) | 2711 | D | 650 808-8800 | 4195 |
| World Journal Inc (PA) | 2711 | D | 650 692-9936 | 4223 |
| No Starch Press Inc | 2741 | F | 415 863-9900 | 4440 |
| Yb Media LLC | 2741 | E | 310 467-5804 | 4497 |
| Asia America Enterprise Inc | 2752 | E | 650 348-2333 | 4517 |
| Clic LLC | 2752 | E | 415 421-2900 | 4554 |

# GEOGRAPHIC SECTION — CAMARILLO, CA

| Company | SIC | EMP | PHONE | ENTRY# |
|---|---|---|---|---|
| Lahlouh Inc (PA) | 2752 | C | 650 692-6600 | 4671 |
| Leewood Press Inc | 2752 | E | 415 896-0513 | 4673 |
| Attralus Inc | 2834 | E | 415 410-3268 | 5344 |
| Corvus Pharmaceuticals Inc | 2834 | E | 650 900-4520 | 5411 |
| Igencia Biotherapeutics Inc | 2834 | E | 650 231-4320 | 5485 |
| Innoviva Inc (PA) | 2834 | E | 650 238-9600 | 5495 |
| Kindredbio Equine Inc | 2834 | E | 888 608-2542 | 5527 |
| Phoenix Pharmaceuticals Inc | 2834 | E | 650 558-8898 | 5604 |
| PSI Pharma Support America Inc | 2834 | E | 267 464-2500 | 5616 |
| Garratt-Callahan Company (PA) | 2899 | D | 650 697-5811 | 6287 |
| Merrills Packaging Inc | 3081 | E | 650 259-5959 | 6563 |
| Devincenzi Metal Products Inc | 3444 | D | 650 692-5800 | 8432 |
| Sensbey Inc (PA) | 3548 | F | 650 697-2032 | 9730 |
| Acco Brands Corporation | 3575 | F | 650 572-2700 | 10301 |
| Acco Brands USA LLC | 3575 | D | 650 572-2700 | 10302 |
| Tlm International Inc | 3639 | F | 650 952-2257 | 11420 |
| Hanergy Holding (america) LLC (HQ) | 3674 | D | 650 288-3722 | 12459 |
| Quadricio Inc | 3674 | E | 408 337-2429 | 12648 |
| Caban Systems Inc | 3691 | E | 831 245-1608 | 13132 |
| Proterra Inc (PA) | 3694 | A | 864 438-0000 | 13183 |
| Proterra Powered LLC (DH) | 3694 | B | 864 516-0068 | 13184 |
| Proterra Operating Company Inc (HQ) | 3711 | D | | 13378 |
| Loma Vista Medical Inc | 3841 | F | 650 490-4747 | 15151 |
| Magnus Medical Inc | 3841 | D | 415 231-7407 | 15157 |
| Trivad Inc | 5045 | C | 650 286-1086 | 16561 |
| B & N Industries Inc (PA) | 5046 | D | 650 593-4127 | 16566 |
| Technical Instr San Francisco (PA) | 5049 | E | 650 651-3000 | 16605 |
| Abx Engineering Inc | 5065 | D | 650 552-2300 | 16686 |
| Murphy HARtelius/M&h Uniforms (PA) | 5136 | E | 650 344-2997 | 17078 |
| Tangent Computer Inc (PA) | 5734 | D | 800 342-9388 | 17559 |
| Collabrative DRG Discovery Inc | 7372 | D | 650 204-3084 | 18193 |
| Imply Data Inc (PA) | 7372 | C | 415 685-8187 | 18406 |
| Roadzen Inc (PA) | 7372 | B | 650 414-3530 | 18744 |
| Sage Software Inc | 7372 | F | 650 579-3628 | 18751 |

## BURNEY, CA - Shasta County

| Company | SIC | EMP | PHONE | ENTRY# |
|---|---|---|---|---|
| Shasta Green Inc | 2411 | E | 530 335-4924 | 3055 |
| Tubit Enterprises Inc | 2411 | E | 530 335-5085 | 3059 |
| Sierra Pacific Industries | 2421 | E | 530 335-3681 | 3083 |
| Dicalite Minerals LLC (HQ) | 3295 | E | 530 335-5451 | 7565 |

## BUTTONWILLOW, CA - Kern County

| Company | SIC | EMP | PHONE | ENTRY# |
|---|---|---|---|---|
| B W Implement Co | 3523 | E | 661 764-5254 | 9340 |

## BYRON, CA - Contra Costa County

| Company | SIC | EMP | PHONE | ENTRY# |
|---|---|---|---|---|
| Marin Food Specialties Inc | 2032 | E | 925 634-6126 | 866 |
| Campos Vineyards LLC | 2084 | E | 925 308-7963 | 1497 |

## CABAZON, CA - Riverside County

| Company | SIC | EMP | PHONE | ENTRY# |
|---|---|---|---|---|
| Centric Brands Inc | 2211 | E | 951 797-5077 | 2407 |
| Chicos Fas Inc | 5621 | F | 951 849-4069 | 17491 |
| Hadley Fruit Orchards Inc (PA) | 5961 | E | 951 849-5255 | 17665 |

## CALABASAS, CA - Los Angeles County

| Company | SIC | EMP | PHONE | ENTRY# |
|---|---|---|---|---|
| S & S Paving Inc | 1611 | E | 818 591-0668 | 380 |
| True Classic Tees LLC | 2321 | E | 323 419-1092 | 2580 |
| Afr Apparel International Inc | 2341 | E | 818 773-5000 | 2827 |
| Electric Solidus LLC | 2741 | E | 917 692-7764 | 4393 |
| Wella Corporation (HQ) | 2844 | C | 800 422-2336 | 6056 |
| Radian Memory Systems Inc | 3572 | E | 818 222-4080 | 10272 |
| Fulcrum Microsystems Inc | 3674 | D | 818 871-8100 | 12440 |
| Apex Precision Technologies Inc | 3714 | E | 317 821-1000 | 13458 |
| Ixia (HQ) | 3825 | C | 818 871-1800 | 14539 |
| Ixia | 3825 | E | 818 871-1800 | 14540 |
| Yamaha Guitar Group Inc (HQ) | 3931 | C | 818 575-3600 | 15726 |
| Yamaha Guitar Group Inc | 3931 | E | 818 575-3900 | 15727 |
| Orca Arms LLC | 3949 | D | 858 586-0503 | 15844 |
| Spirent Communications Inc (HQ) | 5045 | B | 818 676-2300 | 16551 |
| Fattail Inc (HQ) | 7371 | E | 818 615-0380 | 17919 |
| Prolifics Testing Inc | 7371 | E | 925 485-9535 | 17965 |
| Catapult Communications Corp (DH) | 7372 | E | 818 871-1800 | 18152 |
| Sungard Treasury Systems Inc | 7372 | E | 818 223-2300 | 18848 |
| Thrio Inc | 7372 | E | 858 299-7191 | 18882 |
| Dts Inc (DH) | 7819 | C | 818 436-1000 | 19302 |
| Phorus Inc | 7819 | D | 310 995-2521 | 19303 |

## CALABASAS HILLS, CA - Los Angeles County

| Company | SIC | EMP | PHONE | ENTRY# |
|---|---|---|---|---|
| Helmet House LLC (PA) | 5136 | D | 800 421-7247 | 17075 |
| Cheesecake Factory Bakery Inc | 5812 | B | 818 871-3000 | 17571 |
| Cheesecake Factory Inc (PA) | 5812 | B | 818 871-3000 | 17572 |

## CALEXICO, CA - Imperial County

| Company | SIC | EMP | PHONE | ENTRY# |
|---|---|---|---|---|
| Imperial Valley Foods Inc | 2037 | B | 760 203-1896 | 1007 |
| Bradford Soap Mexico Inc | 2841 | B | 760 768-4539 | 5872 |
| 4l Technologies Inc | 3555 | A | 817 538-0974 | 9761 |
| Skyworks Solutions Inc | 3629 | F | 301 874-6408 | 11383 |
| Celestica LLC | 3643 | D | 760 357-4880 | 11445 |
| Creation Tech Calexico Inc (HQ) | 3672 | E | | 12083 |
| Skyworks Solutions Inc | 3674 | F | 949 231-3550 | 12716 |
| Lorenz Inc | 3699 | E | 760 427-1815 | 13268 |
| Chromalloy Gas Turbine LLC | 3724 | D | 760 768-3723 | 13705 |
| Honeywell International Inc | 3724 | F | 760 312-5300 | 13711 |
| Rockwell Collins Inc | 3728 | E | 760 768-4732 | 13937 |
| Triumph Insulation Systems LLC | 3728 | A | 760 618-7543 | 13982 |
| Orthodental International Inc | 3843 | D | 760 357-8070 | 15472 |
| Clover Envmtl Solutions LLC | 3861 | E | 760 357-9277 | 15635 |
| Lakim Industries Incorporated (PA) | 3991 | E | 310 637-8900 | 15932 |
| ARC - Imperial Valley | 8093 | E | 760 768-1944 | 19335 |

## CALIFORNIA CITY, CA - Kern County

| Company | SIC | EMP | PHONE | ENTRY# |
|---|---|---|---|---|
| Creative Accents | 2273 | E | 760 373-1222 | 2512 |
| Robertsons Ready Mix Ltd | 3273 | D | 760 373-4815 | 7493 |

## CALIMESA, CA - Riverside County

| Company | SIC | EMP | PHONE | ENTRY# |
|---|---|---|---|---|
| Paver Decor Masonry Inc | 1611 | E | 909 795-8474 | 377 |
| Skat-Trak | 3011 | F | 909 795-2505 | 6412 |

## CALIPATRIA, CA - Imperial County

| Company | SIC | EMP | PHONE | ENTRY# |
|---|---|---|---|---|
| Crown Citrus Company Inc | 2037 | F | 760 348-9755 | 1002 |
| Earthrise Nutritionals LLC | 2099 | E | 760 348-5027 | 2190 |

## CALISTOGA, CA - Napa County

| Company | SIC | EMP | PHONE | ENTRY# |
|---|---|---|---|---|
| Schramsberg Vineyards Company | 0172 | E | 707 942-4558 | 30 |
| Chateau Montelena LLC | 2084 | E | 707 942-5105 | 1506 |
| Diamond Creek Vineyard | 2084 | F | 707 942-6926 | 1539 |
| Fairwinds Estate Winery LLC | 2084 | E | 707 341-5300 | 1560 |
| Kenefick Ranches LLC | 2084 | E | 707 942-6175 | 1647 |
| Madrigal Family Winery LLC | 2084 | F | 415 887-9539 | 1672 |
| Sugarloaf Farming Corporation | 2084 | E | 707 942-4459 | 1766 |
| Treasury Wine Estates Americas | 2084 | E | 707 942-4945 | 1795 |
| Treasury Wine Estates Americas | 2084 | F | 707 564-8477 | 1796 |
| Villa Amorosa | 2084 | D | 707 967-6272 | 1810 |
| Crystal Geyser Water Company (DH) | 2086 | E | 888 424-1977 | 1882 |
| Tonnellerie Francaise French C | 2449 | F | 707 942-9301 | 3376 |
| Vision Collective Inc | 2741 | E | 562 597-4000 | 4489 |

## CALPELLA, CA - Mendocino County

| Company | SIC | EMP | PHONE | ENTRY# |
|---|---|---|---|---|
| Mendocino Forest Pdts Co LLC | 5031 | D | 707 485-6800 | 16452 |

## CAMARILLO, CA - Ventura County

| Company | SIC | EMP | PHONE | ENTRY# |
|---|---|---|---|---|
| Old New York Bagel Deli Co Inc (PA) | 2051 | F | 805 484-3354 | 1231 |
| No Nuts LLC | 2064 | F | 805 309-2420 | 1322 |
| Adidas North America Inc | 2329 | E | 805 482-3475 | 2608 |
| Califrnia Dsgners Chice Cstm C | 2434 | E | 805 987-5820 | 3229 |
| Pacific Casual LLC | 2514 | F | 805 445-8310 | 3508 |
| Sleep Technologies Inc | 2515 | F | 866 931-1964 | 3539 |
| Galtech Computer Corporation | 2521 | E | 805 376-1060 | 3569 |
| International Paper Company | 2621 | E | 805 933-4347 | 3776 |
| Crockett Graphics Inc (PA) | 2653 | D | 805 987-8577 | 3836 |
| Lundberg Survey Incorporated | 2721 | E | 805 383-2400 | 4274 |
| Bestforms Inc | 2761 | E | 805 388-0503 | 4988 |
| Performance Materials Corp (HQ) | 2821 | D | 805 482-1722 | 5185 |
| Gsms Inc (PA) | 2834 | E | 805 477-9866 | 5470 |
| National Coatings Corporation | 2952 | E | 805 388-7112 | 6381 |
| Sanisure Inc (HQ) | 3052 | D | 805 389-0400 | 6429 |
| Ogio International Inc | 3161 | D | 800 326-6325 | 7137 |
| Koltov Inc (PA) | 3172 | E | 805 764-0280 | 7148 |
| Engense Inc | 3312 | E | 805 484-8317 | 7612 |
| Gc International Inc (PA) | 3365 | E | 805 389-4631 | 7845 |
| Titan Metal Fabricators Inc (PA) | 3441 | D | 805 487-5050 | 8228 |
| Abel Automatics LLC | 3451 | E | 805 388-3721 | 8713 |
| Cudoquanta Photonics Inc | 3469 | F | 805 617-0818 | 8832 |
| Nanoprecision Products Inc | 3469 | E | 310 597-4991 | 8869 |
| United Western Enterprises Inc | 3479 | E | 805 389-1077 | 9131 |
| Transonic Combustion Inc | 3519 | E | 805 465-5145 | 9333 |
| Western Gage Corporation | 3545 | E | 805 445-1410 | 9707 |
| Voiceboard Corporation | 3571 | F | 805 389-3100 | 10217 |
| Hales Engineering Coinc | 3599 | E | | 10865 |
| Hte Acquisition Inc | 3599 | E | 805 987-0520 | 10877 |
| Ronlo Engineering Ltd | 3599 | E | 805 388-3227 | 11090 |
| Thiessen Products Inc | 3599 | C | 805 482-6913 | 11142 |
| Arnold Magnetics Corporation | 3612 | D | 805 484-4221 | 11205 |
| Barta - Schoenewald Inc (PA) | 3621 | C | 805 389-1935 | 11256 |
| Magicall Inc | 3621 | E | 805 484-4300 | 11278 |
| Skurka Aerospace Inc (DH) | 3621 | E | 805 484-8884 | 11287 |
| Thingap Inc | 3621 | E | 805 477-9741 | 11291 |

# CAMARILLO, CA

## GEOGRAPHIC SECTION

| | SIC | EMP | PHONE | ENTRY# |
|---|---|---|---|---|
| Toray Prfmce Mtls Corp USA | 3624 | F | 805 402-6664 | 11302 |
| Plt Enterprises Inc | 3643 | D | 805 389-5335 | 11467 |
| Thin-Lite Corporation | 3648 | F | 805 987-5021 | 11627 |
| Gc International Inc | 3652 | E | 805 389-4631 | 11734 |
| Record Technology Inc (PA) | 3652 | E | 805 484-2747 | 11743 |
| Salem Music Network Inc | 3663 | F | 805 987-0400 | 11938 |
| Tactical Communications Corp | 3669 | E | 805 987-4100 | 12021 |
| Multilayer Prototypes Inc | 3672 | F | 805 498-9390 | 12168 |
| Attollo Engineering LLC | 3674 | D | 805 384-8046 | 12341 |
| Former Luna Subsidiary Inc (HQ) | 3674 | E | 805 987-0146 | 12435 |
| Interconnect Systems Intl LLC (DH) | 3674 | D | 805 482-2870 | 12496 |
| Microsemi Communications Inc (DH) | 3674 | E | 805 388-3700 | 12569 |
| Opto Diode Corporation | 3674 | E | 805 499-0335 | 12621 |
| OSI Optoelectronics Inc | 3674 | E | 805 987-0146 | 12624 |
| Polyfet Rf Devices Inc | 3674 | E | 805 484-9582 | 12635 |
| Semtech Corporation (PA) | 3674 | E | 805 498-2111 | 12693 |
| Johanson Technology Inc | 3675 | C | 805 575-0124 | 12820 |
| Meissner Corporation | 3677 | E | 805 388-9911 | 12846 |
| Meissner Filtration Pdts Inc (PA) | 3677 | E | 805 388-9911 | 12847 |
| Cooper Interconnect Inc (DH) | 3678 | F | 805 484-0543 | 12873 |
| Ciao Wireless Inc | 3679 | D | 805 389-3224 | 12937 |
| Gtran Inc (PA) | 3679 | E | 805 445-4500 | 12990 |
| Lucix Corporation (HQ) | 3679 | E | 805 987-6645 | 13026 |
| Mercury LLC - Rf Integrated Solutions | 3679 | E | 805 388-1345 | 13034 |
| Battery-Biz Inc | 3694 | D | 800 848-6782 | 13167 |
| Technicolor Disc Services Corp (HQ) | 3695 | E | 805 445-1122 | 13204 |
| Xirgo Technologies LLC | 3699 | D | 805 319-4079 | 13334 |
| Artisan Vehicle Systems Inc | 3711 | E | 805 402-6856 | 13339 |
| Wilwood Engineering (PA) | 3714 | C | 805 388-1188 | 13605 |
| Airborne Technologies Inc | 3728 | E | 805 389-3700 | 13763 |
| Allclear Aerospace & Def Inc | 3728 | E | 805 446-2700 | 13772 |
| Camar Aircraft Parts Co | 3728 | E | 805 389-8944 | 13803 |
| Parker-Hannifin Corporation | 3728 | E | 805 484-8533 | 13922 |
| Western Mfg & Distrg LLC | 3751 | E | 805 988-1010 | 14075 |
| Northrop Grumman Systems Corp | 3812 | C | 805 987-8831 | 14248 |
| Northrop Grumman Systems Corp | 3812 | D | 805 987-9739 | 14249 |
| Hanson Lab Solutions LLC | 3821 | E | 805 498-3121 | 14339 |
| CK Technologies Inc (PA) | 3823 | F | 805 987-4801 | 14394 |
| Innovative Integration Inc | 3823 | E | 805 520-3300 | 14423 |
| Primordial Diagnostics Inc | 3823 | E | 800 462-1926 | 14445 |
| Bruker Corporation | 3826 | F | 805 388-3326 | 14640 |
| Interglobal Waste MGT Inc | 3826 | D | 805 388-1885 | 14678 |
| Santec California Corporation | 3827 | E | 805 987-1700 | 14821 |
| Teledyne Scentific Imaging LLC | 3827 | D | | 14827 |
| Structural Diagnostics Inc | 3829 | E | 805 987-7755 | 14926 |
| Infab LLC | 3842 | D | 805 987-5255 | 15362 |
| Kinamed Inc | 3842 | E | 805 384-2748 | 15372 |
| Medical Packaging Corporation | 3842 | D | 805 388-2383 | 15376 |
| VME Acquisition Corp (PA) | 3842 | F | 805 384-2748 | 15428 |
| Belport Company Inc (PA) | 3843 | F | 805 484-1051 | 15439 |
| Cal Simba Inc (PA) | 3914 | E | 805 240-1177 | 15707 |
| K9 Ballistics Inc | 3999 | E | 844 772-3125 | 16160 |
| New Inspiration Brdcstg Co Inc (HQ) | 4832 | E | 805 987-0400 | 16328 |
| Teledyne Reson Inc | 5088 | E | 805 964-6260 | 16928 |
| Williams Aerospace & Mfg Inc (DH) | 5088 | E | 805 586-8699 | 16931 |
| Jim ONeal Distributing Inc | 5571 | E | 805 426-3300 | 17482 |
| BKM Office Environments Inc (PA) | 5712 | F | 805 339-6388 | 17515 |
| Tangerine Express Inc | 5999 | E | 702 260-6650 | 17724 |
| Modern Campus USA Inc (PA) | 7371 | D | 805 484-9400 | 17951 |
| Electronic Clearing House Inc (HQ) | 7372 | E | 805 419-8700 | 18273 |
| Gbl Systems Corporation | 7373 | E | 805 987-4345 | 18977 |
| Amt Datasouth Corp (PA) | 8731 | E | 805 388-5799 | 19440 |

## CAMBRIA, CA - San Luis Obispo County

| | SIC | EMP | PHONE | ENTRY# |
|---|---|---|---|---|
| Stepladder Farmstead Crmry LLC | 2022 | E | 415 606-8559 | 740 |
| Linns Fruit Bin Inc (PA) | 5431 | E | 805 927-1499 | 17399 |

## CAMERON PARK, CA - El Dorado County

| | SIC | EMP | PHONE | ENTRY# |
|---|---|---|---|---|
| Tsu/Tree Service Unlimited Inc | 0783 | E | 530 626-8733 | 100 |
| Entex Corporation | 2869 | F | 888 960-3689 | 6143 |
| Preferred Mfg Svcs Inc (PA) | 3599 | D | 530 677-2675 | 11048 |
| JEI | 5065 | F | 530 677-3210 | 16710 |

## CAMINO, CA - El Dorado County

| | SIC | EMP | PHONE | ENTRY# |
|---|---|---|---|---|
| Sierra Pacific Industries | 2421 | E | 530 644-2311 | 3085 |

## CAMPBELL, CA - Santa Clara County

| | SIC | EMP | PHONE | ENTRY# |
|---|---|---|---|---|
| Reed Mariculture Inc | 2048 | F | 408 377-1065 | 1146 |
| Peets Coffee & Tea LLC | 2095 | E | 408 558-9535 | 2078 |
| Valet Organizers Inc | 2434 | E | 408 370-1041 | 3278 |
| Vivus LLC (PA) | 2834 | E | 650 934-5200 | 5713 |
| List Biological Labs Inc | 2836 | E | 408 866-6363 | 5846 |
| Implus LLC | 3021 | E | 408 796-7739 | 6415 |
| Vivid Inc | 3479 | E | 408 982-9101 | 9133 |
| Ron Witherspoon Inc (PA) | 3545 | E | 408 370-6620 | 9696 |
| Zircon Corporation (HQ) | 3546 | E | 408 866-8600 | 9716 |
| Velo3d Inc (PA) | 3555 | E | 408 610-3915 | 9776 |
| Relay Robotics Inc | 3569 | E | 833 735-2976 | 10110 |
| Working Robot Inc | 3569 | E | 408 809-5600 | 10124 |
| Applied Systems Engrg Inc | 3577 | F | 408 364-0500 | 10322 |
| Firetide Inc (DH) | 3577 | E | 408 399-7771 | 10368 |
| Consoldted Hnge Mnfctured Pdts | 3599 | F | 408 379-6550 | 10789 |
| Jessee Brothers Machine Sp Inc | 3599 | E | 408 866-1755 | 10907 |
| Chargepoint Inc (HQ) | 3629 | C | 408 841-4500 | 11363 |
| Exalt Communications Inc | 3663 | D | 408 688-0200 | 11855 |
| G2 Microsystems Inc | 3672 | E | 408 879-2614 | 12119 |
| Arteris Inc (PA) | 3674 | E | 408 470-7300 | 12332 |
| Arteris Holdings Inc | 3674 | E | 408 470-7300 | 12333 |
| Jinkosolar (us) Inc | 3674 | E | 415 402-0502 | 12510 |
| Megachips LSI USA Corporation | 3674 | D | 408 570-0555 | 12554 |
| Semi Automation & Tech Inc | 3674 | E | 408 374-9549 | 12686 |
| Wg Security Products Inc (PA) | 3699 | E | 408 241-8000 | 13333 |
| Pana-Pacific Corporation | 3714 | C | 559 499-1891 | 13553 |
| Laser Reference Inc | 3821 | F | 408 361-0220 | 14342 |
| Ross Engineering Corporation | 3825 | E | 408 377-4621 | 14582 |
| Kalila Medical Inc | 3829 | E | 408 819-5175 | 14888 |
| Atia Vision Inc | 3841 | E | 408 805-0520 | 14981 |
| Supira Medical Inc | 3841 | E | 408 560-2500 | 15270 |
| Versatile Power Inc | 3841 | E | 408 341-4600 | 15303 |
| Imperative Care Inc (PA) | 3842 | B | 669 228-3814 | 15360 |
| Ostial Corporation | 3842 | E | 408 541-1007 | 15390 |
| 8x8 Inc (PA) | 4813 | B | 408 727-1885 | 16315 |
| Infinite Networks Inc | 5064 | E | 408 796-7735 | 16682 |
| Shifamed LLC | 7363 | E | 408 364-1242 | 17869 |
| Dicom Systems Inc | 7371 | E | 415 684-8790 | 17911 |
| Zoove LLC | 7371 | E | 954 448-5442 | 18001 |
| Barracuda Networks Inc (PA) | 7372 | C | 408 342-5400 | 18092 |
| Condeco Software Inc (DH) | 7372 | F | 917 677-7600 | 18198 |
| Freeagent Network Inc | 7372 | E | 650 880-3240 | 18331 |
| Liveaction Inc (PA) | 7372 | E | 888 881-1116 | 18498 |
| Workspot Inc (PA) | 7372 | E | 888 426-8113 | 18943 |
| Mirantis Inc (PA) | 7373 | F | 650 963-9828 | 18986 |
| Luidia Inc | 8731 | E | 650 413-7500 | 19462 |
| Centric Software Inc (PA) | 8742 | E | 408 574-7802 | 19523 |

## CANOGA PARK, CA - Los Angeles County

| | SIC | EMP | PHONE | ENTRY# |
|---|---|---|---|---|
| Flowers Bkg Co Henderson LLC | 2051 | D | 818 884-8970 | 1198 |
| Barrys Printing Inc | 2752 | E | 818 998-8600 | 4528 |
| Vomar Products Inc | 2759 | E | 818 610-5115 | 4980 |
| Pacific Shore Holdings Inc | 2834 | E | 818 998-0996 | 5592 |
| Den-Mat Corporation | 2844 | C | 800 445-0345 | 5970 |
| Aerojet Rocketdyne De Inc (DH) | 2869 | B | 818 586-1000 | 6122 |
| Pls Diabetic Shoe Company Inc | 3021 | E | 818 734-7080 | 6419 |
| National Ready Mixed Con Co | 3273 | F | 818 884-0893 | 7476 |
| Mulholland Security Ctrs LLC | 3442 | D | 800 562-5770 | 8279 |
| Glastar Corporation | 3559 | E | 818 341-0301 | 9860 |
| Best Data Products Inc | 3577 | D | 818 534-1414 | 10334 |
| All Swiss Turning | 3599 | E | 818 466-3076 | 10697 |
| Mooney Inds Prcsion McHning In | 3599 | F | 818 998-0199 | 10994 |
| Modern Woodworks Inc | 3646 | E | 800 575-3475 | 11547 |
| Rainbo Record Mfg Corp (PA) | 3652 | E | 818 280-1100 | 11742 |
| Mercury Magnetics Inc | 3677 | E | 818 998-7791 | 12848 |
| Sway-A-Way Inc | 3714 | E | 818 700-9712 | 13580 |
| Aerojet Rocketdyne De Inc | 3724 | B | 818 586-1000 | 13702 |
| Micro Steel Inc | 3769 | E | 818 348-8701 | 14115 |
| C J Instruments Incorporated | 3829 | E | 818 996-4131 | 14851 |
| Temptron Engineering Inc | 3829 | E | 818 346-4900 | 14933 |
| Small Wnders Hndcrfted Mntres | 3999 | F | 818 703-7450 | 16230 |
| H2w | 5099 | E | 800 578-3088 | 16978 |
| National Advanced Endoscopy De | 5999 | E | 818 227-2720 | 17712 |
| Socal Auto Supply Inc | 7213 | E | 302 360-8373 | 17767 |
| Computrition Inc (HQ) | 7371 | D | 818 961-3999 | 17900 |
| Hvantage Technologies Inc (PA) | 7371 | D | 818 661-6301 | 17926 |
| Decor Interior Design Inc | 7389 | E | 818 962-4800 | 19085 |

## CANYON COUNTRY, CA - Los Angeles County

| | SIC | EMP | PHONE | ENTRY# |
|---|---|---|---|---|
| Natural Balance Pet Foods LLC (PA) | 2048 | D | 800 829-4493 | 1139 |
| National Ready Mixed Con Co | 3273 | F | 661 252-8181 | 7479 |
| Commercial Display Systems LLC | 3585 | E | 818 361-8160 | 10490 |
| Rexhall Industries Inc | 3716 | E | 661 726-5470 | 13625 |

## CANYON LAKE, CA - Riverside County

| | SIC | EMP | PHONE | ENTRY# |
|---|---|---|---|---|
| Golding Publications | 2791 | F | 951 244-1966 | 5020 |

## CAPISTRANO BEACH, CA - Orange County

| | SIC | EMP | PHONE | ENTRY# |
|---|---|---|---|---|
| Schaeffler Group USA Inc | 3562 | E | 949 234-9799 | 9954 |

# GEOGRAPHIC SECTION
## CARLSBAD, CA

| Company | SIC | EMP | PHONE | ENTRY# |
|---|---|---|---|---|
| **CAPITOLA, CA - Santa Cruz County** | | | | |
| Alpha Machine Company Inc | 3599 | F | 831 462-7400 | 10703 |
| **CARDIFF, CA - San Diego County** | | | | |
| Viracta Therapeutics Inc (PA) | 2834 | E | 858 400-8470 | 5709 |
| **CARDIFF BY THE SEA, CA - San Diego County** | | | | |
| Naval Coating Inc | 1799 | C | 619 234-8366 | 568 |
| Total Gym Commercial LLC | 3949 | F | 858 586-6080 | 15867 |
| Igrad LLC | 7372 | E | 858 705-2917 | 18402 |
| **CARLSBAD, CA - San Diego County** | | | | |
| Pacific Cast Cnstr Wtrproofing | 1521 | E | 760 298-3170 | 346 |
| Anaergia Services LLC | 1629 | E | 760 436-8870 | 392 |
| Natural Alternatives Intl Inc | 2023 | F | 800 848-2646 | 770 |
| OH Juice Inc | 2033 | F | 619 318-0207 | 910 |
| Om Mushroom Superfood | 2033 | E | 858 779-1275 | 915 |
| Mellace Family Brands Cal Inc | 2068 | E | 760 448-1940 | 1357 |
| Mfb Liquidation Inc | 2068 | E | 760 448-1940 | 1359 |
| Bitchin Inc (PA) | 2099 | E | 760 224-7447 | 2141 |
| Bitchin Sauce LLC | 2099 | D | 737 248-2446 | 2142 |
| Living Wellness Partners LLC | 2099 | E | 800 642-3754 | 2267 |
| Centric Brands Inc | 2211 | E | 760 603-8520 | 2408 |
| Silk Screen Shirts Inc | 2261 | E | 760 233-3900 | 2494 |
| Ashworth Inc | 2329 | A | 760 438-6610 | 2612 |
| J2 Llc | 2329 | F | 760 930-1738 | 2624 |
| R B III Associates Inc | 2337 | C | 760 471-5370 | 2725 |
| Zoot Sports Inc | 2339 | E | 760 681-3587 | 2825 |
| Hemlock Hat Company | 2353 | E | 888 490-6440 | 2844 |
| Eevelle LLC | 2399 | E | 760 434-2231 | 3027 |
| Reflex Corporation | 2399 | E | 760 931-9009 | 3034 |
| Vanguard Industries East Inc | 2399 | E | 800 433-1334 | 3037 |
| Vanguard Industries West Inc (PA) | 2399 | C | 760 434-4437 | 3038 |
| N M Floor Coverings Inc | 2426 | F | 760 931-8274 | 3099 |
| Finishing Touch Moulding Inc | 2434 | D | 760 444-1019 | 3241 |
| The Heat Factory Inc | 2673 | E | 760 893-8300 | 3984 |
| Ten Publishing Media LLC | 2721 | F | 760 722-7777 | 4300 |
| Upper Deck Company (PA) | 2741 | E | 800 873-7332 | 4488 |
| Gsg Printing Inc (PA) | 2752 | E | 760 752-9500 | 4625 |
| L & L Printers Carlsbad LLC | 2752 | E | 760 477-0321 | 4667 |
| Sport Card Co LLC | 2752 | B | 800 873-7332 | 4768 |
| Zuza LLC | 2752 | D | 760 494-9000 | 4820 |
| Hudson Printing Inc | 2759 | E | 760 602-1260 | 4893 |
| Iris Group Inc | 2759 | C | 760 431-1103 | 4901 |
| Air Products and Chemicals Inc | 2813 | D | 760 931-9555 | 5039 |
| American Lithium Energy Corp | 2819 | F | 760 599-7388 | 5070 |
| Resinate Materials Group Inc | 2821 | E | 800 891-2955 | 5194 |
| Natural Alternatives Intl Inc (PA) | 2833 | C | 760 736-7700 | 5252 |
| Sabre Sciences Inc | 2833 | F | 760 448-2750 | 5269 |
| Akcea Therapeutics Inc (HQ) | 2834 | D | 617 207-0202 | 5303 |
| Carlsbad Technology Inc (DH) | 2834 | D | 760 431-8284 | 5394 |
| Carlsbad Technology Inc | 2834 | D | 760 431-8284 | 5395 |
| Design Therapeutics Inc | 2834 | C | 858 293-4900 | 5426 |
| Greenwich Biosciences LLC (DH) | 2834 | E | 760 795-2200 | 5469 |
| Hikma Pharmaceuticals USA Inc | 2834 | E | 760 683-0901 | 5480 |
| Imprimisrx LLC | 2834 | D | 844 446-6979 | 5492 |
| Ionis Pharmaceuticals Inc | 2834 | D | 760 931-9200 | 5502 |
| Ionis Pharmaceuticals Inc (PA) | 2834 | A | 760 931-9200 | 5503 |
| Ionis Pharmaceuticals Inc | 2834 | E | 760 603-3567 | 5504 |
| Quorex Pharm Inc (PA) | 2834 | E | 760 602-1910 | 5622 |
| Tyra Biosciences Inc | 2834 | E | 619 728-4760 | 5696 |
| Biosource International Inc | 2835 | E | 805 659-5759 | 5743 |
| Life Technologies Corporation (HQ) | 2835 | C | 760 603-7200 | 5760 |
| Molecular Probes Inc | 2835 | E | 760 603-7200 | 5765 |
| Syntron Bioresearch Inc | 2835 | B | 760 930-2200 | 5781 |
| Dnatrix Inc | 2836 | E | 832 930-2401 | 5824 |
| Lineage Cell Therapeutics Inc (PA) | 2836 | E | 510 521-3390 | 5845 |
| Alastin Skincare Inc | 2844 | C | 844 858-7546 | 5940 |
| Coola LLC | 2844 | E | 760 940-2125 | 5957 |
| Eden Beauty Concepts Inc | 2844 | E | 760 330-9941 | 5976 |
| Sigma-Aldrich Corporation | 2899 | E | 760 710-6213 | 6323 |
| Petrochem Manufacturing Inc | 2951 | E | 760 603-0961 | 6368 |
| Modus Advanced Inc | 3069 | D | 925 960-8700 | 6515 |
| Edge Theory Labs Inc | 3088 | F | 858 358-5386 | 6675 |
| Allbirds Inc | 3143 | F | 442 273-5519 | 7095 |
| Phoenix Footwear Group Inc (PA) | 3143 | F | 760 602-9688 | 7111 |
| Ogio International Inc (HQ) | 3161 | E | 801 619-4100 | 7138 |
| Turbo Intl Partners LLC | 3462 | E | 760 476-1444 | 8790 |
| Product Slingshot Inc (DH) | 3544 | E | 760 929-9380 | 9643 |
| Coplan & Coplan | 3545 | E | 760 268-0583 | 9669 |
| Resers Fine Foods Inc | 3556 | F | 503 643-6431 | 9812 |
| Palomar Technologies Inc (PA) | 3559 | E | 760 931-9300 | 9888 |
| Nordson Corporation | 3563 | D | 760 419-6551 | 9967 |
| Nordson Corporation | 3563 | C | 760 431-1919 | 9968 |
| Nordson Corporation | 3563 | E | 760 431-1919 | 9969 |
| Nordson March Inc | 3563 | D | 925 827-1240 | 9971 |
| Nordson Test Insptn Amrcas Inc | 3563 | E | 760 918-8471 | 9972 |
| Mercury Computer System Inc | 3571 | E | 760 494-9600 | 10180 |
| Aqua Products Inc (DH) | 3589 | E | 973 857-2700 | 10537 |
| Fluidra North America LLC (HQ) | 3589 | D | 760 599-9600 | 10559 |
| Fluidra Usa LLC (PA) | 3589 | E | 904 378-0999 | 10560 |
| Zodiac Pool Systems LLC (DH) | 3589 | C | 760 599-9600 | 10619 |
| Diligent Solutions Inc | 3599 | E | 760 814-8960 | 10812 |
| Machine Craft of San Diego | 3599 | F | 858 642-0509 | 10952 |
| Systems Mchs Atmtn Cmpnnts Cor (PA) | 3625 | C | 760 929-7575 | 11351 |
| Seacomp Inc (PA) | 3629 | E | 760 476-6722 | 11382 |
| Mercotac Inc | 3643 | E | 760 431-7723 | 11464 |
| Anchor Audio Inc | 3651 | D | 760 827-7100 | 11636 |
| Arlo Technologies Inc (PA) | 3651 | D | 408 890-3900 | 11638 |
| Ecolink Intelligent Tech Inc | 3651 | F | 855 432-6546 | 11657 |
| Suitecentric Lcc | 3652 | E | 760 520-1611 | 11745 |
| Allegiance Supply Incorporated | 3661 | E | 760 230-8018 | 11750 |
| Aethercomm Inc | 3663 | C | 760 208-6002 | 11799 |
| Atx Networks (san Diego) Corp (DH) | 3663 | E | 858 546-5050 | 11816 |
| Denso Wireless Systems America Inc | 3663 | C | 760 734-4600 | 11840 |
| Global Microwave Systems Inc | 3663 | E | 760 496-0046 | 11858 |
| Suntech International Usa LLC | 3663 | E | 833 282-3731 | 11955 |
| Viasat Inc (PA) | 3663 | A | 760 476-2200 | 11971 |
| Dei Headquarters Inc | 3669 | B | 760 598-6200 | 11990 |
| Dei Holdings Inc (HQ) | 3669 | E | 760 598-6200 | 11991 |
| H M Electronics Inc | 3669 | E | 858 535-6139 | 11997 |
| Cal-Comp USA (san Diego) Inc | 3672 | C | 858 587-6900 | 12072 |
| Electro Surface Tech Inc | 3672 | E | 760 431-8306 | 12089 |
| Spectrum Assembly Inc | 3672 | C | 760 930-4000 | 12229 |
| Luxtera LLC | 3674 | E | 760 448-3520 | 12536 |
| Maxlinear Inc (PA) | 3674 | E | 760 692-0711 | 12551 |
| Maxlinear Communications LLC (HQ) | 3674 | F | | 12552 |
| Qualcomm Incorporated | 3674 | E | 858 651-8481 | 12651 |
| Sst Technologies | 3674 | E | 562 803-3361 | 12732 |
| Goodfor LLC | 3677 | F | 833 488-3489 | 12842 |
| Visual Communications Company LLC | 3679 | C | 800 522-5546 | 13118 |
| Nordson California Inc | 3695 | D | 760 918-8490 | 13200 |
| Palomar Tech Companies (PA) | 3699 | E | 760 931-3600 | 13285 |
| Pro Spot International Inc | 3699 | F | 760 407-1414 | 13291 |
| American Rim Supply Inc | 3714 | E | 760 431-3666 | 13457 |
| Machinetek LLC | 3728 | E | 760 438-6644 | 13896 |
| Matthew Smith Crampton | 3732 | E | 760 840-8404 | 14040 |
| L3 Technologies Inc | 3812 | C | 760 431-6800 | 14202 |
| Laird R & F Products Inc (DH) | 3812 | E | 760 916-9410 | 14208 |
| Qualigen Inc (HQ) | 3821 | E | 760 918-9165 | 14347 |
| Myron L Company | 3823 | D | 760 438-2021 | 14438 |
| Nordson Asymtek Inc | 3823 | C | 760 431-1919 | 14439 |
| Neology Inc (PA) | 3825 | D | 858 391-0260 | 14562 |
| Beckman Coulter Inc | 3826 | E | 760 438-9151 | 14622 |
| Invitrogen Corp | 3826 | F | 760 476-7055 | 14679 |
| Invitrogen Ip Holdings Inc | 3826 | E | 760 603-7200 | 14680 |
| Life Technologies Corporation | 3826 | B | 760 918-0135 | 14684 |
| Life Technologies Corporation | 3826 | E | 760 918-4259 | 14685 |
| Means Engineering Inc | 3826 | D | 760 931-9452 | 14687 |
| Thermo Fisher Scientific Inc | 3826 | E | 781 622-1000 | 14738 |
| Thermo Fisher Scientific Inc | 3826 | D | 760 603-7200 | 14741 |
| Thermo Fisher Scientific Inc | 3826 | F | 760 268-8641 | 14742 |
| Thermo Fsher Scntfic Psg Corp (HQ) | 3826 | E | 760 603-7200 | 14746 |
| Idex Health & Science LLC | 3827 | E | 760 438-2131 | 14783 |
| Intevac Photonics Inc | 3827 | E | 760 476-0339 | 14788 |
| Melles Griot Inc | 3827 | D | 760 438-2254 | 14799 |
| Synergeyes Inc (HQ) | 3827 | D | 760 476-9410 | 14826 |
| California Sensor Corporation | 3829 | E | 760 438-0525 | 14854 |
| Aalto Scientific Ltd | 3841 | E | 800 748-6674 | 14939 |
| Acutus Medical Inc | 3841 | C | 442 232-6080 | 14950 |
| Alphatec Holdings Inc (PA) | 3841 | B | 760 431-9286 | 14961 |
| Bolt Medical Inc | 3841 | E | 949 287-3207 | 15017 |
| Breg Inc (HQ) | 3841 | C | 760 599-3000 | 15020 |
| Canary Medical USA LLC | 3841 | D | 760 448-5066 | 15025 |
| Carlsmed Inc | 3841 | F | 760 766-1923 | 15034 |
| Covidien Holding Inc | 3841 | E | 760 603-5020 | 15058 |
| Foundry Med Innovations Inc | 3841 | F | 888 445-2333 | 15090 |
| Genmark Diagnostics Inc (DH) | 3841 | A | 760 448-4300 | 15100 |
| Impedimed Inc (HQ) | 3841 | E | 760 585-2100 | 15114 |
| Medtronic Inc | 3841 | E | 760 214-3009 | 15170 |
| Planet Innovation Inc | 3841 | E | 847 943-7270 | 15226 |
| Rf Surgical Systems LLC | 3841 | D | 855 522-7027 | 15243 |
| Sendx Medical Inc (DH) | 3841 | E | 760 930-6300 | 15252 |
| Spinal Elements Holdings Inc | 3841 | C | 877 774-6255 | 15263 |
| Alphatec Spine Inc (HQ) | 3842 | C | 760 431-9286 | 15319 |
| Djo LLC (HQ) | 3842 | D | 800 321-9549 | 15333 |

Employee Codes: A=Over 500 employees, B=251-500
C=101-250, D=51-100, E=20-50, F=10-19, G=1-9

# CARLSBAD, CA

| Company | SIC | EMP | PHONE | ENTRY# |
|---|---|---|---|---|
| Drs Own Inc (PA) | 3842 | E | 760 804-0751 | 15335 |
| Seaspine Inc | 3842 | D | 760 727-8399 | 15402 |
| Seaspine Orthopedics Corp (DH) | 3842 | E | 866 942-8698 | 15403 |
| Zimmer Dental Inc | 3842 | B | 800 854-7019 | 15432 |
| Danville Materials LLC (HQ) | 3843 | F | 760 743-7744 | 15446 |
| Lancer Orthodontics Inc (PA) | 3843 | E | 760 744-5585 | 15466 |
| Ortho Organizers Inc | 3843 | C | 760 448-8600 | 15471 |
| Nordson Dage Inc | 3844 | E | 440 985-4496 | 15505 |
| Hygeia II Medical Group Inc | 3845 | E | 714 515-7571 | 15545 |
| Sotera Wireless Inc | 3845 | C | 858 427-4620 | 15580 |
| Signet Armorlite Inc (DH) | 3851 | B | 760 744-4000 | 15616 |
| Spy Inc (PA) | 3851 | E | 760 804-8420 | 15619 |
| USAopoly Inc | 3944 | D | 760 431-5910 | 15771 |
| Acushnet Company | 3949 | B | 760 804-6500 | 15773 |
| Aldila Inc (HQ) | 3949 | F | 858 513-1801 | 15775 |
| Aldila Golf Corp (DH) | 3949 | D | 858 513-1801 | 15777 |
| Evnroll Putters LLC | 3949 | F | 321 277-1397 | 15808 |
| Fujikura Composite America Inc | 3949 | E | 760 598-6060 | 15814 |
| Lucite Intl Prtnr Holdings Inc | 3949 | D | 760 929-0001 | 15837 |
| Safer Sports Inc | 3949 | E | 760 444-0082 | 15850 |
| Topgolf Callaway Brands Corp (PA) | 3949 | B | 760 931-1771 | 15866 |
| Zonson Company Inc | 3949 | E | 760 597-0338 | 15880 |
| New Dimension One Spas Inc (DH) | 3999 | C | 800 345-7727 | 16188 |
| Carlsbad International Export Inc | 5047 | E | 760 438-5323 | 16578 |
| San Diego Sign Company Inc | 5085 | E | 888 748-7446 | 16892 |
| Full-Swing Golf Inc | 5091 | E | 858 675-1100 | 16935 |
| Industrial Strength Corp | 5094 | F | 760 795-1068 | 16968 |
| Golden Eye Media Usa Inc | 5113 | F | 760 688-9962 | 17001 |
| Colorescience Inc | 5122 | C | 866 426-5673 | 17032 |
| South Cone Inc | 5139 | C | 760 431-2300 | 17111 |
| La Costa Coffee Roasting Co (PA) | 5499 | E | 760 438-8160 | 17427 |
| Victory Archery | 5941 | F | 866 934-6565 | 17636 |
| Vape Craft LLC | 5993 | E | 760 295-7484 | 17682 |
| Gunnar Optiks LLC | 5995 | E | 858 769-2500 | 17684 |
| Nice North America LLC (DH) | 5999 | C | 760 438-7000 | 17713 |
| A R Santex LLC (PA) | 7371 | E | 888 622-7098 | 17873 |
| Applied Spectral Imaging Inc | 7371 | F | 760 929-2840 | 17881 |
| Chromacode Inc | 7371 | E | 442 244-4369 | 17896 |
| Stratcom Systems Inc | 7371 | E | 858 481-9292 | 17983 |
| Aira Tech Corp | 7372 | C | 800 835-1934 | 18031 |
| Applied Biosystems LLC (DH) | 7372 | C | | 18054 |
| Brendan Technologies Inc | 7372 | F | 760 929-7500 | 18126 |
| Caleb Enterprises Inc | 7372 | F | 760 683-8787 | 18141 |
| Electronic Online Systems International | 7373 | D | 760 431-8400 | 18972 |
| Rockstar San Diego Inc | 7374 | D | 760 929-0700 | 19013 |
| Boughts Inc | 7379 | E | 619 895-7246 | 19032 |
| Sente Inc | 8011 | E | 760 753-5400 | 19321 |
| Sciencell Research Labs Inc | 8733 | E | 760 602-8549 | 19496 |
| Camston Wrather LLC | 8744 | C | 858 525-9999 | 19551 |

## CARMEL VALLEY, CA - Monterey County

| Company | SIC | EMP | PHONE | ENTRY# |
|---|---|---|---|---|
| Vita Forte Inc (PA) | 1541 | F | 831 626-0555 | 362 |
| Joullian Vineyards Ltd | 2084 | E | 831 659-8100 | 1640 |

## CARMICHAEL, CA - Sacramento County

| Company | SIC | EMP | PHONE | ENTRY# |
|---|---|---|---|---|
| ACR Solar International Corp | 5211 | E | 916 481-7200 | 17320 |

## CARPINTERIA, CA - Santa Barbara County

| Company | SIC | EMP | PHONE | ENTRY# |
|---|---|---|---|---|
| Nusil Technology LLC (DH) | 3069 | B | 805 684-8780 | 6518 |
| Forms and Surfaces Company LLC | 3272 | C | 805 684-8626 | 7333 |
| Forms and Surfaces Inc | 3446 | D | 805 684-8626 | 8626 |
| Supersprings International Inc | 3493 | E | 805 745-5553 | 9179 |
| Clipper Windpower PLC | 3511 | A | 805 690-3275 | 9310 |
| Dac International Inc | 3541 | E | 805 684-8307 | 9547 |
| Development Associates Contrls | 3541 | E | 805 684-8307 | 9548 |
| Hugo Venture Solutions Corp | 3599 | E | 805 684-0935 | 10878 |
| Rincon Engineering Tech | 3599 | E | 805 684-4144 | 11080 |
| Te Connectivity Corporation | 3625 | E | 805 684-4560 | 11352 |
| Zbe Inc | 3625 | E | 805 576-1600 | 11356 |
| Bega North America Inc | 3648 | D | 805 684-0533 | 11582 |
| Essex Electronics Inc | 3674 | E | 805 684-7601 | 12427 |
| Agilent Technologies Inc | 3825 | E | 805 566-6655 | 14490 |
| Agilent Technologies Inc | 3825 | E | 805 566-1405 | 14493 |
| Freudenberg Medical LLC | 3842 | D | 805 576-5308 | 15350 |
| Freudenberg Medical LLC | 3842 | E | 805 684-3304 | 15351 |
| Freudenberg Medical LLC (DH) | 3842 | C | 805 684-3304 | 15352 |
| Inhealth Technologies | 3842 | E | 800 477-5969 | 15363 |
| Pacifica Beauty Inc | 3999 | D | 844 332-8440 | 16193 |
| Dako North America Inc | 5122 | B | 805 566-6655 | 17034 |
| Procore Technologies Inc (PA) | 7371 | A | 866 477-6267 | 17964 |
| Qad Inc | 7372 | F | 805 684-6614 | 18710 |

## CARSON, CA - Los Angeles County

| Company | SIC | EMP | PHONE | ENTRY# |
|---|---|---|---|---|
| General Mills Inc | 2026 | D | 310 605-6108 | 835 |
| Giuliano-Pagano Corporation | 2051 | D | 310 537-7700 | 1210 |
| Teaaroma Inc | 2068 | F | 310 525-3400 | 1368 |
| Anheuser-Busch LLC | 2082 | E | 310 761-4600 | 1417 |
| Sazerac Company Inc | 2085 | D | 310 604-8717 | 1843 |
| Pepsi-Cola Metro Btlg Co Inc | 2086 | C | 310 327-4222 | 1915 |
| American Fruits & Flavors LLC | 2087 | E | 310 522-1844 | 1982 |
| Southwind Foods LLC (PA) | 2091 | C | 323 262-8222 | 2043 |
| Arctic Glacier USA Inc | 2097 | C | 310 638-0321 | 2106 |
| Mountain Water Ice Company Inc (PA) | 2097 | D | 310 638-0321 | 2111 |
| Bristol Farms (HQ) | 2099 | D | 310 233-4700 | 2149 |
| Cedarlane Natural Foods Inc (PA) | 2099 | D | 310 886-7720 | 2160 |
| Kts Kitchens Inc | 2099 | C | 310 764-0850 | 2247 |
| Dynamex Corporation | 2298 | E | 310 329-0399 | 2535 |
| Js Apparel Inc | 2329 | D | 310 631-6333 | 2627 |
| Cali-Fame Los Angeles Inc | 2353 | D | 310 747-5263 | 2842 |
| The Enkeboll Co | 2431 | E | 310 532-1400 | 3198 |
| Cal-Coast Pkg & Crating Inc | 2441 | E | 310 518-7215 | 3325 |
| Morettis Design Collection Inc | 2511 | E | 310 638-5555 | 3450 |
| Arktura LLC (HQ) | 2519 | E | 310 532-1050 | 3552 |
| Salsbury Industries Inc (PA) | 2542 | C | 800 624-5269 | 3707 |
| International Paper Company | 2621 | D | 310 549-5525 | 3783 |
| Empire Container Corporation | 2653 | D | 310 537-8190 | 3840 |
| Elite 4 Print Inc | 2752 | E | 310 366-1344 | 4603 |
| Letterhead Factory Inc | 2752 | F | 310 538-3321 | 4677 |
| Marchem Technologies LLC | 2819 | E | 310 638-9352 | 5100 |
| Avient Corporation | 2821 | F | 310 513-7100 | 5138 |
| Ineos Polypropylene LLC | 2821 | C | 310 847-8523 | 5166 |
| AOE International Inc | 2834 | E | | 5327 |
| Leiner Health Products Inc (DH) | 2834 | C | 631 200-2000 | 5534 |
| Simpson Industries Inc | 2834 | E | 310 605-1224 | 5660 |
| Cosway Company Inc (PA) | 2844 | D | 310 900-4100 | 5966 |
| Cosway Company Inc | 2844 | F | 310 609-3352 | 5967 |
| Dermalogica LLC (HQ) | 2844 | C | 310 900-4000 | 5971 |
| Dan-Loc Group LLC | 3053 | D | 310 538-2822 | 6444 |
| Johnson Laminating Coating Inc | 3083 | D | 310 635-4929 | 6583 |
| Altium Packaging LLC | 3089 | D | 310 952-8736 | 6606 |
| CCL Tube Inc (HQ) | 3089 | D | 310 635-4444 | 6768 |
| Trinity International Inds LLC | 3089 | E | 800 985-5506 | 7060 |
| Avalon Glass & Mirror Company | 3231 | F | 323 321-8806 | 7212 |
| Howmet Corporation | 3324 | A | 310 847-8152 | 7686 |
| Belden Inc | 3357 | A | 310 639-9473 | 7773 |
| Wavenet Inc (PA) | 3357 | E | 310 885-4200 | 7799 |
| Solid-Scope Machining Co Inc | 3429 | F | 310 523-2366 | 8027 |
| Mag Aerospace Industries LLC | 3431 | B | 801 400-7944 | 8042 |
| Capital Cooking Equipment Inc | 3433 | E | 562 903-1168 | 8063 |
| Crate Modular Inc | 3448 | D | 310 405-0829 | 8662 |
| Designed Metal Connections Inc | 3451 | E | 310 323-6200 | 8721 |
| Huck International Inc | 3452 | C | 310 830-8200 | 8758 |
| Research Tool & Die Works LLC | 3469 | D | 310 639-5722 | 8884 |
| Calwest Galvanizing Corp | 3479 | F | 310 549-2200 | 9056 |
| Samtech Automotive Usa Inc | 3542 | E | 310 638-9955 | 9588 |
| Mestek Inc | 3585 | C | 310 835-7500 | 10508 |
| A & R Engineering Co Inc | 3599 | E | 310 603-9060 | 10649 |
| Cardic Machine Products Inc | 3599 | F | 310 884-3400 | 10764 |
| Universal Plant Svcs Cal Inc | 3599 | D | 310 618-1600 | 11162 |
| DMC Power Inc (PA) | 3643 | D | 310 323-1616 | 11450 |
| Safran Usa Inc | 3643 | A | 310 884-7198 | 11469 |
| Dmf Inc | 3645 | D | 323 934-7779 | 11494 |
| Yun Industrial Co Ltd | 3672 | E | 310 715-1898 | 12264 |
| Sac-TEC Labs Inc (PA) | 3674 | E | 310 375-5295 | 12683 |
| Daico Industries Inc | 3679 | D | 310 507-3242 | 12953 |
| Strike Technology Inc | 3679 | E | 562 437-3428 | 13093 |
| Coast Wire & Plastic Tech LLC | 3699 | A | 310 639-9473 | 13222 |
| Stoptech | 3714 | E | 310 933-1100 | 13579 |
| Refrigerated Trck Solutions LLC | 3715 | E | 323 594-4500 | 13619 |
| Boeing Company | 3721 | C | 310 522-2809 | 13641 |
| Ducommun Aerostructures Inc | 3728 | C | 310 513-7200 | 13829 |
| Ducommun Labarge Tech Inc (HQ) | 3728 | C | 310 513-7200 | 13832 |
| Hydroform USA Incorporated | 3728 | C | 310 632-6353 | 13866 |
| Long-Lok LLC | 3728 | E | 424 209-8726 | 13894 |
| Safran Cabin Inc | 3728 | D | 714 934-0000 | 13950 |
| Zodiac Wtr Waste Aero Systems | 3728 | D | 310 884-7000 | 13997 |
| Stanford Mu Corporation | 3769 | E | 310 605-2888 | 14116 |
| Mp Solutions Inc | 3812 | E | | 14225 |
| Duro-Sense Corporation | 3823 | F | 310 533-6877 | 14404 |
| Megiddo Global LLC | 3842 | E | 844 477-7007 | 15381 |
| Proma Inc | 3843 | E | 310 327-0035 | 15478 |
| Sage Goddess Inc | 3911 | E | 650 733-6639 | 15705 |
| C Preme Limited LLC | 3949 | E | 310 355-0498 | 15795 |
| Chris Putrimas | 3999 | E | 877 434-1666 | 16116 |
| Nano Filter Inc | 3999 | D | 949 316-8866 | 16186 |

# GEOGRAPHIC SECTION

## CHATSWORTH, CA

| | SIC | EMP | PHONE | ENTRY# |
|---|---|---|---|---|
| Premier Cold Storage & Pkg LLC | 4222 | C | 949 444-8859 | 16285 |
| Whaling Packaging Co | 4783 | E | 310 518-6021 | 16311 |
| Pacific Toll Processing Inc | 4785 | E | 310 952-4992 | 16312 |
| Nova Ortho-Med Inc (PA) | 5047 | E | 310 352-3600 | 16586 |
| Long-Lok Fasteners Corporation | 5072 | F | 424 213-4570 | 16756 |
| Industrial Parts Depot LLC (HQ) | 5084 | E | 310 530-1900 | 16819 |
| Western Refining Inc | 5084 | D | 310 834-1297 | 16859 |
| West Coast Aerospace Inc | 5085 | F | 310 518-0633 | 16906 |
| System Supply Stationery Corp | 5112 | E | 310 223-0880 | 16995 |
| SO Tech/Spcl Op Tech Inc (PA) | 5131 | E | 310 202-9007 | 17069 |
| Sabater Usa Inc | 5149 | F | 310 518-2227 | 17210 |
| Cirrus Enterprises LLC | 5162 | D | 310 204-6159 | 17224 |
| Dianas Mexican Food Pdts Inc | 5411 | E | 310 834-4886 | 17374 |
| Puritan Bakery Inc | 5461 | C | 310 830-5451 | 17419 |
| Zeek Management Group LLC | 5812 | F | 424 570-0531 | 17612 |
| Interface Welding | 7699 | E | 310 323-4944 | 19265 |

### CARUTHERS, CA - Fresno County

| | SIC | EMP | PHONE | ENTRY# |
|---|---|---|---|---|
| Batth Farms Inc | 0173 | D | 559 864-9421 | 36 |
| Caruthers Raisin Pkg Co Inc (PA) | 2034 | D | 559 864-9448 | 948 |

### CASTAIC, CA - Los Angeles County

| | SIC | EMP | PHONE | ENTRY# |
|---|---|---|---|---|
| Castaic Truck Stop Inc | 2911 | E | 661 295-1374 | 6332 |

### CASTRO VALLEY, CA - Alameda County

| | SIC | EMP | PHONE | ENTRY# |
|---|---|---|---|---|
| Community Media Corporation | 2711 | E | 657 337-0200 | 4096 |
| Norco Printing Inc | 2791 | F | 510 569-2200 | 5021 |

### CASTROVILLE, CA - Monterey County

| | SIC | EMP | PHONE | ENTRY# |
|---|---|---|---|---|
| American Bottling Company | 2086 | E | 831 632-0777 | 1862 |
| Seven Up Btlg Co San Francisco | 2086 | C | 831 632-0777 | 1961 |
| Biopharmaceutical RES Co LLC | 2834 | E | 704 905-8703 | 5375 |
| Fujifilm Ultra Pure Sltons Inc (DH) | 2899 | E | 831 632-2120 | 6286 |
| Ron Witherspoon Inc | 3599 | D | 831 633-3568 | 11088 |

### CATHEDRAL CITY, CA - Riverside County

| | SIC | EMP | PHONE | ENTRY# |
|---|---|---|---|---|
| Water Restoration Inc | 1799 | F | 760 673-7374 | 580 |
| Socal Labs LLC | 3999 | F | 813 857-5207 | 16232 |

### CAZADERO, CA - Sonoma County

| | SIC | EMP | PHONE | ENTRY# |
|---|---|---|---|---|
| Parmeter Logging and Excav Inc | 1794 | F | 707 632-5610 | 547 |
| Dharma Mudranalaya (PA) | 2731 | E | 707 847-3380 | 4326 |

### CERES, CA - Stanislaus County

| | SIC | EMP | PHONE | ENTRY# |
|---|---|---|---|---|
| Ram Mechanical Inc | 1711 | D | 209 531-9155 | 430 |
| Seed Factory Northwest Inc (PA) | 2048 | E | 209 634-8522 | 1150 |
| Stuart David Inc (PA) | 2511 | E | 209 537-7449 | 3457 |
| Robert R Wix Inc (PA) | 2759 | E | 209 537-4561 | 4955 |
| Aemetis Advnced Fels Keyes Inc | 2869 | E | 209 632-4511 | 6121 |
| Craftsman Cutting Dies Inc (PA) | 3423 | E | 714 776-8995 | 7949 |
| Mazona Inc | 3442 | D | 209 538-3667 | 8275 |
| Certified Stainless Svc Inc (PA) | 3443 | E | 209 537-4747 | 8306 |
| Prompt Precision Metals Inc | 3444 | E | 209 531-1210 | 8546 |
| US Dies Inc (PA) | 3544 | E | 209 664-1402 | 9655 |
| B & H Manufacturing Co Inc (PA) | 3565 | C | 209 537-5785 | 10013 |
| Bronco Wine Company (PA) | 5182 | C | 209 538-3131 | 17262 |

### CERRITOS, CA - Los Angeles County

| | SIC | EMP | PHONE | ENTRY# |
|---|---|---|---|---|
| Brea Canon Oil Co Inc | 1311 | F | 310 326-4002 | 126 |
| Upwing Energy Inc | 1389 | F | 562 293-1660 | 288 |
| Better Beverages Inc (PA) | 2087 | E | 562 924-8321 | 1987 |
| T Hasegawa USA Inc (HQ) | 2087 | E | 714 522-1900 | 2030 |
| Fleischmanns Vinegar Company Inc (DH) | 2099 | E | 562 483-4619 | 2201 |
| Dool Fna Inc | 2221 | E | 562 483-4100 | 2435 |
| Insta-Lettering Machine Co (PA) | 2253 | E | 562 404-3000 | 2473 |
| LA Triumph Inc | 2326 | E | 562 404-7657 | 2597 |
| Caravan Canopy Intl Inc | 2394 | D | 714 367-3000 | 2971 |
| Eide Industries Inc | 2394 | E | 562 402-8335 | 2973 |
| J Summitt Inc | 2431 | F | 562 236-5744 | 3149 |
| Spacestor Inc | 2521 | E | 310 410-0220 | 3587 |
| Villa Furniture Mfg Co | 2531 | C | 714 535-7272 | 3641 |
| Triple A Containers Inc | 2653 | D | 562 404-7433 | 3893 |
| Molino Company | 2752 | E | 323 726-1000 | 4699 |
| Printing Management Associates | 2752 | F | 562 407-9977 | 4733 |
| Blc Wc Inc (PA) | 2759 | C | 562 926-1452 | 4850 |
| Apperson Inc (PA) | 2761 | E | 562 356-3333 | 4987 |
| Captek Softgel Intl Inc (DH) | 2834 | B | 562 921-9511 | 5390 |
| International Coatings Co Inc (PA) | 2891 | E | 562 926-1010 | 6233 |
| Foam Molders and Specialties (PA) | 3086 | E | 562 924-7757 | 6636 |
| Foam Molders and Specialties | 3086 | E | 562 924-7757 | 6637 |
| Sports Venue Padding Inc | 3086 | E | 562 404-9343 | 6664 |
| Ips Industries Inc | 3089 | D | 562 623-2555 | 6866 |
| Wcp West Coast Glass LLC | 3089 | D | 562 653-9797 | 7076 |

| | SIC | EMP | PHONE | ENTRY# |
|---|---|---|---|---|
| Pankl Aerospace Systems | 3369 | D | 562 207-6300 | 7868 |
| Madison Inc of Oklahoma | 3441 | D | 918 224-6990 | 8174 |
| California Metal & Supply Inc | 3443 | F | 800 707-6061 | 8303 |
| Bermingham Cntrls Inc A Cal Co (PA) | 3491 | E | 562 860-0463 | 9146 |
| Para-Plate & Plastics Co Inc | 3555 | E | 562 404-3434 | 9773 |
| Hny Ramen Inc | 3556 | F | 626 586-7209 | 9797 |
| Atlas Copco Compressors LLC | 3563 | E | 562 484-6370 | 9957 |
| Aline Systems Corporation | 3565 | E | 562 229-9727 | 10011 |
| All American Print Supply Co | 3577 | E | 714 616-5834 | 10317 |
| Mpd Holdings Inc | 3577 | E | 213 210-2591 | 10414 |
| Olea Kiosks Inc | 3577 | D | 562 924-2644 | 10415 |
| ARI Industries Inc | 3585 | D | 714 993-3700 | 10482 |
| Refrigerator Manufacturers LLC | 3585 | E | 562 926-2006 | 10513 |
| Advanced Uv Inc (PA) | 3589 | E | 562 407-0299 | 10532 |
| Chemical Methods Assoc LLC (DH) | 3589 | E | 714 898-8781 | 10545 |
| West Coast Switchgear (DH) | 3613 | D | 562 802-3441 | 11253 |
| Calnetix Technologies LLC (HQ) | 3621 | D | 562 293-1660 | 11258 |
| Dcec Holdings Inc | 3631 | C | 562 802-3488 | 11387 |
| Refrigerator Manufacturers LLC | 3632 | E | 562 229-0500 | 11398 |
| Refrigerator Manufacturers Inc (PA) | 3632 | E | 562 926-2006 | 11399 |
| Big 5 Electronics Inc | 3651 | E | 562 941-4669 | 11645 |
| IPC Cal Flex Inc | 3672 | E | 714 952-0373 | 12137 |
| Corelis Inc | 3679 | E | 562 926-6727 | 12946 |
| Lapco West LLC | 3714 | E | 562 348-4850 | 13528 |
| UFO Designs | 3714 | E | 562 924-5763 | 13596 |
| Dji Service LLC | 3728 | F | 818 235-0788 | 13824 |
| Hyundai Rotem USA Corporation | 3743 | F | 215 227-6836 | 14049 |
| Razor USA LLC (PA) | 3751 | D | 562 345-6000 | 14067 |
| Sas Safety Corporation | 3842 | E | 562 427-2775 | 15401 |
| Alpha Dental of Utah Inc | 3843 | E | 562 467-7759 | 15437 |
| US Dental Inc | 3843 | E | 562 404-3500 | 15492 |
| Dji Technology Inc | 3861 | E | 818 235-0789 | 15536 |
| R1 Concepts Inc (PA) | 5013 | E | 714 777-2323 | 16391 |
| McNichols Company | 5051 | F | 562 921-3344 | 16623 |
| Memorex Products Inc | 5064 | C | 562 653-2800 | 16683 |
| Capitol Distribution Co LLC (PA) | 5149 | E | 562 404-4321 | 17180 |
| Polycell Packaging Corporation | 5199 | E | 562 483-6000 | 17305 |
| Thermal Engrg Intl USA Inc (HQ) | 8711 | D | 323 726-0641 | 19424 |
| Biospace Inc | 8731 | D | 323 932-6503 | 19447 |

### CHATSWORTH, CA - Los Angeles County

| | SIC | EMP | PHONE | ENTRY# |
|---|---|---|---|---|
| Featherock Inc (PA) | 1499 | F | 818 882-3888 | 339 |
| Synear Foods Usa LLC | 1541 | E | 818 341-3588 | 361 |
| Pacific Coast Cabling Inc (PA) | 1731 | E | 818 407-1911 | 465 |
| We The Pie People LLC | 2024 | E | 818 349-1880 | 820 |
| Earth Island LLC (HQ) | 2099 | E | 818 725-2820 | 2189 |
| Avitex (PA) | 2211 | C | 818 994-6487 | 2401 |
| Apparel Prod Svcs Globl LLC | 2339 | E | 818 700-3700 | 2735 |
| Honeydew Apparel Group Inc | 2341 | F | 818 717-9717 | 2832 |
| Academic Ch Choir Gwns Mfg Inc | 2389 | E | 818 886-8697 | 2887 |
| Underwraps Costume Corporation | 2389 | F | 818 349-5300 | 2912 |
| Califrnia Dluxe Wndows Inds In (PA) | 2431 | E | 818 349-5566 | 3116 |
| Tessa Mia Corp | 2434 | E | 877 740-5757 | 3273 |
| Woodpecker Cabinets Inc | 2434 | E | 310 404-4805 | 3282 |
| Califrnia Trade Converters Inc | 2631 | E | 818 899-1455 | 3800 |
| Pencil Grip Inc (PA) | 2678 | F | 310 315-3545 | 4021 |
| Avn Media Network Inc | 2731 | E | 818 718-5788 | 4312 |
| Narcotics Annymous Wrld Svcs I (PA) | 2731 | E | 818 773-9999 | 4337 |
| Breakaway Press Inc | 2752 | E | 818 727-7388 | 4536 |
| Cal Southern Graphics Corp (HQ) | 2752 | D | 310 559-3600 | 4541 |
| GPA Printing CA LLC (PA) | 2752 | E | 818 237-9771 | 4621 |
| Impress Communications LLC | 2752 | D | 818 701-8800 | 4643 |
| Labeling Hurst Systems LLC | 2759 | F | 818 701-0710 | 4910 |
| Pioneer Photo Albums Inc (PA) | 2782 | C | 818 882-2161 | 5003 |
| H2u Technologies Inc | 2813 | E | 626 344-0505 | 5044 |
| Erbaviva Inc | 2833 | E | 818 998-7112 | 5237 |
| Bio-Nutraceuticals Inc (PA) | 2834 | F | 818 727-0246 | 5369 |
| Natrol Inc | 2834 | E | 818 739-6000 | 5563 |
| Henkel US Operations Corp | 2843 | E | 818 435-0889 | 5936 |
| Aware Products LLC | 2844 | C | 818 206-6700 | 5945 |
| Ida Classic Inc (PA) | 2844 | C | 818 773-9042 | 5992 |
| Kdc/One Chatsworth Inc (DH) | 2844 | D | 818 709-1345 | 5997 |
| Kdc/One Chatsworth | 2844 | E | 818 709-1345 | 5998 |
| Neutraderm Inc | 2844 | E | 818 534-3190 | 6011 |
| Radiance Beauty & Wellness Inc | 2844 | E | 818 812-9740 | 6030 |
| Samuel Raoof | 2844 | E | 818 534-3180 | 6033 |
| Aerojet Rocketdyne De Inc | 2869 | E | 818 586-1000 | 6124 |
| ABC Plastics Inc | 3083 | F | 818 775-0065 | 6580 |
| 3d Cam Inc | 3089 | E | 818 773-8777 | 6690 |
| A & S Mold and Die Corp | 3089 | D | 818 341-5393 | 6691 |
| Lehrer Brllnprfktion Werks Inc | 3089 | D | 818 407-1890 | 6895 |
| Dwa Composite Specialties Inc | 3354 | F | 818 885-8654 | 7737 |
| Ftg Aerospace Inc (DH) | 3364 | E | 818 407-4024 | 7829 |

Employee Codes: A=Over 500 employees, B=251-500
C=101-250, D=51-100, E=20-50, F=10-19, G=1-9

## CHATSWORTH, CA

| Company | SIC | EMP | PHONE | ENTRY# |
|---|---|---|---|---|
| Dwa Aluminum Composites USA Inc | 3365 | E | 818 998-1504 | 7843 |
| Metal Improvement Company LLC | 3398 | D | 818 407-6280 | 7893 |
| Alliance Metal Products Inc | 3444 | C | 818 709-1204 | 8370 |
| Armorcast Products Company Inc (DH) | 3444 | C | 818 982-3600 | 8378 |
| Dynamo Aviation Inc | 3444 | D | 818 785-9561 | 8436 |
| Keith E Archambeau Sr Inc | 3444 | E | 818 718-6110 | 8482 |
| Federal Manufacturing Corp | 3452 | E | 818 341-9825 | 8755 |
| Golden Bolt LLC | 3452 | E | 818 626-8261 | 8756 |
| Verdugo Tool & Engrg Co Inc | 3469 | F | 818 998-1101 | 8898 |
| Metal Chem Inc | 3471 | E | 818 727-9951 | 8984 |
| Plateronics Processing Inc | 3471 | E | 818 341-2191 | 8996 |
| West Valley Plating Inc | 3471 | F | 818 709-1684 | 9033 |
| Networks Electronic Co LLC | 3489 | E | 818 341-0440 | 9139 |
| Aquasyn LLC | 3491 | F | 818 350-0423 | 9143 |
| RPS Inc | 3496 | E | 818 350-8088 | 9232 |
| Bey-Berk International (PA) | 3499 | E | 818 773-7534 | 9276 |
| Invelop Inc | 3523 | E | 818 772-2887 | 9360 |
| Tig/M LLC | 3535 | E | 818 709-8500 | 9498 |
| Colbrit Manufacturing Co Inc | 3544 | E | 818 709-3608 | 9613 |
| Precise Die and Finishing | 3544 | E | 818 773-9337 | 9640 |
| John List Corporation | 3547 | E | 818 882-7848 | 9718 |
| Capna Fabrication | 3556 | E | 888 416-6777 | 9782 |
| NMB (usa) Inc (HQ) | 3562 | E | 818 709-1770 | 9953 |
| Delta Tau Data Systems Inc Cal (HQ) | 3569 | C | 818 998-2095 | 10086 |
| Aleratec Inc | 3571 | E | | 10131 |
| BDR Industries Inc | 3577 | E | 818 341-2112 | 10332 |
| Ciphertex LLC | 3577 | F | 818 773-8989 | 10342 |
| Logicube Inc (PA) | 3577 | E | 888 494-8832 | 10398 |
| Meissner Mfg Co Inc (PA) | 3589 | D | 818 678-0400 | 10581 |
| RTC Arspace - Chtswrth Div Inc (PA) | 3593 | E | 818 341-3344 | 10629 |
| 3dcam International Corp | 3599 | A | 818 773-8777 | 10641 |
| Aben Machine Products Inc | 3599 | F | 818 960-4502 | 10656 |
| Aero Mechanism Precision Inc | 3599 | E | 818 886-1855 | 10684 |
| Delta Fabrication Inc | 3599 | D | 818 407-4000 | 10805 |
| Delta Hi-Tech | 3599 | C | 818 407-4000 | 10806 |
| Excel Manufacturing Inc | 3599 | E | 661 257-1900 | 10830 |
| Expand Machinery LLC | 3599 | F | 818 349-9166 | 10831 |
| Houston Ontic Inc | 3599 | F | 818 678-6555 | 10876 |
| International Precision Inc | 3599 | E | 818 882-3933 | 10889 |
| Molnar Engineering Inc | 3599 | E | 818 993-3495 | 10990 |
| Mono Engineering Corp | 3599 | E | 818 772-4998 | 10993 |
| O & S Precision Inc | 3599 | E | 818 718-8876 | 11014 |
| United Precision Corp | 3599 | E | 818 576-9540 | 11160 |
| Wallace E Miller Inc | 3599 | F | 818 998-0444 | 11182 |
| Jackson Engineering Co Inc | 3612 | E | 818 886-9567 | 11215 |
| Custom Control Sensors LLC (PA) | 3613 | C | 818 341-4610 | 11239 |
| Resmed Motor Technologies Inc | 3621 | C | 818 428-6400 | 11283 |
| Custom Control Sensors Inc | 3625 | F | 818 341-4610 | 11317 |
| Electro Adapter Inc | 3643 | D | 818 998-1198 | 11451 |
| Newvac LLC (HQ) | 3643 | F | 310 525-1205 | 11465 |
| Lf Illumination LLC | 3646 | D | 818 885-1335 | 11543 |
| Medical Illumination International Inc (PA) | 3646 | F | 818 838-3025 | 11546 |
| Lighting Control & Design Inc | 3648 | E | 323 226-0000 | 11609 |
| Pacific Coast Lighting Inc (HQ) | 3648 | F | 800 709-9004 | 11617 |
| Truly Green Solutions LLC | 3648 | E | 818 206-4404 | 11629 |
| Epic Technologies LLC | 3661 | A | 908 707-4085 | 11762 |
| Dynamic Sciences Intl Inc | 3663 | E | 818 226-6262 | 11845 |
| Telemtry Cmmnctons Systems Inc | 3663 | E | 818 718-6248 | 11963 |
| Canoga Perkins Corporation (HQ) | 3669 | D | 818 718-6300 | 11986 |
| Newvac LLC | 3671 | C | 310 990-0401 | 12036 |
| Circuit Services Llc | 3672 | E | 818 701-5391 | 12078 |
| Ftg Circuits Inc (DH) | 3672 | D | 818 407-4024 | 12118 |
| Natel Engineering Holdings Inc | 3672 | D | 818 734-6500 | 12173 |
| Oncore Manufacturing Svcs Inc | 3672 | C | 510 360-2222 | 12182 |
| United International Tech Inc | 3672 | E | 818 772-9400 | 12252 |
| We Imagine Inc | 3672 | D | 818 709-0064 | 12258 |
| Iog Products LLC | 3674 | F | 818 350-5070 | 12503 |
| Mrv Communications Inc | 3674 | B | 818 773-0900 | 12592 |
| Source Photonics Usa Inc | 3674 | F | 818 407-5007 | 12727 |
| Stellar Microelectronics Inc | 3674 | C | 661 775-3500 | 12736 |
| Dytran Instruments Inc | 3679 | C | 818 700-7818 | 12965 |
| Natel Engineering Company LLC (PA) | 3679 | C | 818 495-8617 | 13045 |
| Newvac LLC | 3679 | E | 747 202-7333 | 13048 |
| Aitech Defense Systems Inc | 3699 | D | 818 700-2000 | 13210 |
| Aitech Rugged Group Inc (PA) | 3699 | E | 818 700-2000 | 13211 |
| Soundcraft Inc | 3699 | E | 818 882-0020 | 13309 |
| Logistical Support LLC | 3724 | C | 818 341-3344 | 13715 |
| Alatus Aerosystems (PA) | 3728 | E | 610 965-1630 | 13766 |
| Alatus Aerosystems | 3728 | D | 714 732-0559 | 13767 |
| Alatus Aerosystems | 3728 | D | 626 498-7376 | 13768 |
| Align Aerospace LLC (PA) | 3728 | B | 818 727-7800 | 13769 |
| Hydraulics International Inc (PA) | 3728 | B | 818 998-1231 | 13861 |
| Hydraulics International Inc | 3728 | E | 818 998-1236 | 13862 |
| Hydraulics International Inc | 3728 | E | 818 998-1231 | 13863 |
| Cliffdale Manufacturing LLC | 3769 | C | 818 341-3344 | 14109 |
| Hydromach Inc | 3769 | E | 818 341-0915 | 14113 |
| Aeroantenna Technology Inc | 3812 | C | 818 993-3842 | 14135 |
| Firan Tech Group USA Corp (HQ) | 3812 | D | 818 407-4024 | 14186 |
| Moog Inc | 3812 | E | 818 341-5156 | 14223 |
| Sensor Systems Inc | 3812 | B | 818 341-5366 | 14303 |
| Space Vector Corporation | 3812 | E | 818 734-2600 | 14309 |
| Flowmetrics Inc | 3823 | F | 818 407-3420 | 14411 |
| Renau Corporation | 3823 | E | 818 341-1994 | 14449 |
| Intelligent Cmpt Solutions Inc (PA) | 3825 | E | 818 998-5805 | 14537 |
| Teledyne Hanson Research Inc | 3826 | E | 818 882-7266 | 14728 |
| Teledyne Instruments Inc | 3826 | E | 818 882-7266 | 14729 |
| Optical Corporation (DH) | 3827 | E | 818 725-9750 | 14808 |
| Photo Research Inc | 3827 | E | 818 341-5151 | 14813 |
| California Dynamics Corp (PA) | 3829 | E | 323 223-3882 | 14853 |
| Measurement Specialties Inc | 3829 | C | 818 701-2750 | 14896 |
| Loveis Corp | 3841 | F | 818 408-9504 | 15153 |
| Ansell Sndel Med Solutions LLC | 3842 | E | 818 534-2500 | 15322 |
| Boyd Chatsworth Inc | 3842 | D | 818 998-1477 | 15327 |
| Selane Products Inc (PA) | 3843 | E | 818 998-7460 | 15482 |
| Photo-Sonics Inc (PA) | 3861 | E | 818 842-2141 | 15660 |
| Avet Industries Inc | 3949 | F | 818 576-9895 | 15782 |
| General Ribbon Corp | 3955 | B | 818 709-1224 | 15896 |
| Planet Green Cartridges Inc | 3955 | D | 818 725-2596 | 15899 |
| Vision Imaging Supplies Inc | 3955 | E | 818 885-4515 | 15903 |
| Maxwell Alarm Screen Mfg Inc | 3993 | E | 818 773-5533 | 16005 |
| Schea Holdings Inc | 3993 | E | 818 998-3636 | 16032 |
| Visible Graphics Inc | 3993 | F | 818 787-0477 | 16063 |
| Advanced Cosmetic RES Labs Inc | 3999 | E | 818 709-9945 | 16082 |
| Sega Holdings USA Inc | 3999 | A | 415 701-4000 | 16226 |
| TTT Innovations LLC | 3999 | E | 818 201-8828 | 16261 |
| Cooner Sales Company LLC (PA) | 5051 | F | 818 882-8311 | 16616 |
| PLC Imports Inc | 5063 | E | 818 349-1600 | 16670 |
| Air Electro Inc (PA) | 5065 | C | 818 407-5400 | 16689 |
| Refrigeration Hdwr Sup Corp | 5078 | D | 800 537-8300 | 16787 |
| Maloof Naman Builders | 5082 | D | 818 775-0040 | 16792 |
| Wastech Controls & Engrg LLC | 5084 | E | 818 998-3500 | 16855 |
| Ontic Engineering and Mfg Inc (PA) | 5088 | C | 818 678-6555 | 16921 |
| Natrol LLC | 5122 | E | 818 739-6000 | 17042 |
| Chemsil Silicones Inc | 5169 | E | 818 700-0302 | 17240 |
| Vijall Inc | 5169 | E | 818 700-0071 | 17251 |
| North Ranch Management Corp | 5719 | D | 800 410-2153 | 17538 |
| Cosmetic Laboratories of America LLC | 5999 | B | 818 717-6140 | 17696 |
| Sexy Hair Concepts LLC | 5999 | E | 818 435-0800 | 17721 |
| West Coast Coupon Inc | 7319 | E | 818 341-2400 | 17792 |
| Roberts Container Corporation | 7389 | E | 818 727-1700 | 19122 |
| Ironman Inc | 7692 | E | 818 341-0980 | 19200 |
| Cali Framing Supplies LLC | 7699 | E | 818 899-7777 | 19247 |
| Duclos Lenses Inc | 7699 | F | 818 773-0600 | 19253 |
| Accunex Inc | 8711 | E | 818 882-5858 | 19373 |
| Armada Engineering LLC | 8711 | F | 818 280-5138 | 19380 |
| Oncore Manufacturing LLC (HQ) | 8711 | A | 818 734-6500 | 19408 |

## CHESTER, CA - Plumas County

| Company | SIC | EMP | PHONE | ENTRY# |
|---|---|---|---|---|
| Collins Pine Company | 2421 | E | 530 258-2111 | 3067 |
| Collins Pine Company | 2421 | D | 530 258-2131 | 3068 |

## CHICO, CA - Butte County

| Company | SIC | EMP | PHONE | ENTRY# |
|---|---|---|---|---|
| Agreserves Inc | 0173 | E | 530 343-5365 | 35 |
| Mooney Farms | 0723 | D | 530 899-2661 | 84 |
| Baldwin Contracting Co Inc (DH) | 1611 | E | 530 891-6555 | 373 |
| Beber Inc | 2026 | E | 530 487-8676 | 826 |
| Amy Lacey Project | 2032 | E | 866 422-3568 | 848 |
| California Olive Ranch Inc (PA) | 2079 | D | 530 846-8000 | 1395 |
| Sierra Nevada Brewing Co (PA) | 2082 | B | 530 893-3520 | 1458 |
| Smucker Natural Foods Inc (HQ) | 2086 | C | 530 899-5000 | 1965 |
| Stoble LLC | 2095 | E | 530 990-3607 | 2081 |
| Truroots LLC | 2099 | E | 530 899-5000 | 2380 |
| Srl Apparel Inc | 2261 | E | 530 898-9525 | 2495 |
| Chicoeco Inc | 2393 | E | 530 342-4426 | 2954 |
| Square Deal Mattress Factory | 2515 | E | 530 342-2510 | 3541 |
| Chico Community Publishing (PA) | 2711 | E | 530 894-2300 | 4090 |
| Gatehouse Media LLC | 2711 | C | 530 891-1234 | 4120 |
| Videomaker Inc | 2721 | E | 530 891-8410 | 4304 |
| Wizard Graphics Inc | 2759 | F | 530 893-3636 | 4986 |
| Chemcraft Coatings Technology Inc | 2851 | D | 530 894-3585 | 6075 |
| Duckback Acquisition Corp | 2851 | E | 530 343-3261 | 6079 |
| IL Helth Buty Natural Oils Inc | 2899 | E | 530 399-3782 | 6294 |
| Mtech Inc | 3089 | F | 530 894-5091 | 6925 |
| Wrex Products Inc Chico | 3089 | D | 530 895-3838 | 7083 |
| Mathews Ready Mix LLC | 3273 | E | 530 893-8856 | 7469 |
| Klean Kanteen Inc | 3411 | D | 530 592-4552 | 7922 |

# GEOGRAPHIC SECTION
## CHOWCHILLA, CA

| | SIC | EMP | PHONE | ENTRY# |
|---|---|---|---|---|
| Fafco Inc **(PA)** | 3433 | E | 530 332-2100 | 8066 |
| Butte Steel & Fabrication Inc. | 3441 | E | | 8108 |
| Pacific West Forest Products | 3449 | F | 530 899-7313 | 8707 |
| Weiss-Mcnair LLC **(DH)** | 3523 | D | 530 891-6214 | 9394 |
| Norfield Acquisition LLC **(HQ)** | 3553 | E | 800 824-6242 | 9756 |
| Rescue 42 Inc | 3569 | F | 530 891-3473 | 10111 |
| B and F Solutions Inc | 3589 | E | 530 343-5100 | 10542 |
| Joy Signal Technology LLC | 3643 | E | 530 891-3551 | 11460 |
| Premier Solar Energy Inc | 3674 | F | 530 450-9450 | 12637 |
| Nor-Cal Vans Inc | 3713 | F | 530 892-0150 | 13421 |
| Transfer Flow Inc | 3714 | D | 530 893-5209 | 13590 |
| United Sttes Thrmlctric Cnsrti | 3823 | E | 530 345-8000 | 14466 |
| Lares Research | 3843 | E | 530 345-1767 | 15467 |
| L&W Stone Corporation **(PA)** | 5032 | D | | 16475 |
| Van Duerr Industries Inc | 5039 | E | 530 893-1596 | 16497 |
| PBM Supply & Mfg Inc | 5085 | E | 530 345-1334 | 16887 |
| Gonzales Park LLC | 5136 | C | 530 343-8725 | 17074 |
| Davids Bridal LLC | 5621 | F | 530 342-5914 | 17493 |
| Thomas Welding & Machine Inc | 7692 | E | 530 893-8940 | 19217 |

### CHINO, CA - San Bernardino County

| | SIC | EMP | PHONE | ENTRY# |
|---|---|---|---|---|
| American Beef Packers Inc | 0751 | C | 909 628-4888 | 91 |
| Provena Foods Inc **(HQ)** | 2013 | D | 909 627-1082 | 660 |
| Fenchem **(HQ)** | 2023 | E | 909 597-8880 | 757 |
| Ziegenfelder Company | 2024 | D | 909 590-0493 | 822 |
| Ziegenfelder Company | 2024 | D | 909 509-0493 | 823 |
| Hira Paris Inc | 2064 | C | 909 634-3900 | 1310 |
| Myojo USA Inc | 2098 | F | 909 464-1411 | 2116 |
| Gluten Free Foods Mfg LLC **(PA)** | 2099 | F | 909 823-8230 | 2215 |
| Isiqalo LLC | 2253 | B | 714 683-2820 | 2474 |
| Omnia Leather Motion Inc | 2392 | C | 909 393-4400 | 2941 |
| California Wood Cstm Solutions **(PA)** | 2431 | F | 909 364-2440 | 3115 |
| Metrie EI & EI LLC **(DH)** | 2431 | F | 909 591-0339 | 3156 |
| Precision Companies Inc | 2431 | F | 909 548-2700 | 3180 |
| Corona Millworks Company **(PA)** | 2434 | D | 909 606-3288 | 3233 |
| Hanson Truss Inc | 2439 | B | 909 591-9256 | 3310 |
| Alaco Ladder Company | 2499 | E | 909 591-7561 | 3409 |
| B E & P Enterprises LLC **(PA)** | 2499 | E | 909 591-7561 | 3411 |
| Mikhail Darafeev Inc **(PA)** | 2511 | E | 909 613-1818 | 3449 |
| Royal Custom Designs LLC | 2512 | C | 909 591-8990 | 3488 |
| Eastwest Container Group Inc | 2631 | E | 626 523-1523 | 3802 |
| Contixo Inc | 2678 | E | 909 465-5668 | 4020 |
| GLS US Freight Inc | 2741 | E | 909 627-2538 | 4405 |
| Epac Los Angeles LLC | 2752 | F | 844 623-8603 | 4605 |
| Impact Printing & Graphics | 2752 | E | 909 614-1678 | 4641 |
| Wright Business Graphics LLC | 2761 | E | 909 614-6700 | 4994 |
| Ferco Color Inc **(PA)** | 2821 | E | 909 930-0773 | 5157 |
| Vitajoy USA Inc | 2833 | E | 626 965-8830 | 5281 |
| Gen Labs Inc **(PA)** | 2842 | C | 909 591-8451 | 5906 |
| Diamond Wipes Intl Inc | 2844 | D | 909 230-9888 | 5973 |
| Diamond Wipes Intl Inc **(PA)** | 2844 | D | 909 230-9888 | 5974 |
| Plz Corp | 2844 | D | 909 393-9475 | 6025 |
| Universal Packg Systems Inc **(PA)** | 2844 | A | 909 517-2442 | 6050 |
| AST Enzymes | 2869 | F | 800 608-1688 | 6127 |
| Avient Colorants USA LLC | 2869 | E | 909 606-1325 | 6128 |
| Cal-India Foods International | 2869 | E | 909 613-1660 | 6136 |
| Specilty Enzymes Btechnologies | 2869 | F | 909 613-1660 | 6160 |
| Wacker Chemical Corporation | 2869 | D | 909 590-8822 | 6167 |
| Gro-Power Inc | 2873 | E | 909 393-3744 | 6172 |
| Roettele Industries | 3053 | E | 909 606-8252 | 6464 |
| Berry Global Films LLC | 3081 | C | 909 517-2872 | 6553 |
| Flexcon Company Inc | 3081 | E | 909 465-0408 | 6559 |
| Repet Inc | 3083 | E | 909 594-5333 | 6590 |
| Jacuzzi Products Co | 3088 | B | 909 548-7732 | 6681 |
| Acorn-Gencon Plastics LLC | 3089 | E | 909 591-8461 | 6694 |
| Altium Packaging LP | 3089 | E | 909 590-7334 | 6710 |
| Berry Global Inc | 3089 | C | 909 465-9055 | 6742 |
| Dacha Enterprises Inc **(HQ)** | 3089 | E | 951 273-7777 | 6791 |
| Envision Plastics Industries LLC | 3089 | E | 909 590-7334 | 6822 |
| Karat Packaging Inc **(PA)** | 3089 | E | 626 965-8882 | 6880 |
| Liner Technologies Inc | 3089 | E | 909 594-6610 | 6896 |
| Norco Injection Molding Inc | 3089 | D | 909 393-4000 | 6933 |
| Norco Plastics Inc | 3089 | D | 909 393-4000 | 6934 |
| PRC Composites LLC | 3089 | E | 909 464-1520 | 6975 |
| Spin Products Inc | 3089 | E | 909 590-7000 | 7038 |
| Syntech Development & Mfg Inc **(PA)** | 3089 | E | 909 465-5554 | 7048 |
| West Cast Stl Proc Hldngs LLC **(PA)** | 3312 | E | 909 393-8405 | 7633 |
| Wcs Equipment Holdings LLC **(HQ)** | 3325 | E | 909 393-8405 | 7701 |
| Texas Tst Inc | 3341 | E | 951 685-2155 | 7723 |
| Tst Inc **(PA)** | 3341 | B | 951 685-2155 | 7724 |
| Superior Metal Shapes Inc | 3354 | E | 909 947-3455 | 7751 |
| Kemper Enterprises Inc | 3423 | F | 909 627-6191 | 7957 |
| Larin Corp | 3423 | E | 909 464-0605 | 7958 |
| Acornvac Inc | 3432 | E | 909 902-1141 | 8045 |
| Kumar Industries | 3441 | E | 909 591-0722 | 8166 |
| M and M Stamping Corp | 3441 | E | 909 590-2704 | 8172 |
| South Gate Engineering LLC | 3443 | C | 909 628-2779 | 8337 |
| Great Pacific Elbow LLC | 3444 | E | 909 606-5551 | 8461 |
| Trend Technologies LLC **(DH)** | 3444 | C | 909 597-7861 | 8597 |
| Wcs Equipment Holdings LLC | 3444 | D | 909 393-8405 | 8610 |
| Dupree Inc | 3452 | E | 909 597-4889 | 8754 |
| Spring R&D & Stamp Inc | 3469 | F | 909 465-5166 | 8891 |
| RTS Powder Coating Inc **(PA)** | 3479 | E | 909 393-5404 | 9115 |
| Top-Shelf Fixtures LLC | 3496 | D | 909 627-7423 | 9236 |
| Albers Mfg Co Inc **(PA)** | 3523 | E | 909 597-5537 | 9336 |
| Val Plastic USA L L C | 3523 | F | 909 390-9600 | 9388 |
| Team Technologies Inc | 3544 | D | 626 334-5000 | 9652 |
| Wetmore Tool and Engrg Co | 3545 | E | 909 364-1000 | 9708 |
| Imperial Rubber Products Inc | 3555 | E | 909 393-0528 | 9769 |
| Morehouse-Cowles LLC | 3559 | E | 909 627-7222 | 9878 |
| Reed LLC | 3561 | E | 909 287-2100 | 9937 |
| Dick Farrell Industries Inc | 3567 | F | 909 613-9424 | 10048 |
| Shop4techcom | 3572 | E | 909 248-2725 | 10283 |
| Hussmann Corporation | 3585 | B | 909 590-4910 | 10502 |
| Advanced Precision Inc | 3599 | E | 909 591-4244 | 10678 |
| Aranda Tooling LLC | 3599 | D | 714 379-6565 | 10714 |
| Arnold-Gonsalves Engrg Inc | 3599 | E | 909 465-1579 | 10719 |
| Fortune Manufacturing Inc | 3599 | F | 909 591-1547 | 10841 |
| T E B Inc | 3599 | F | 909 941-8100 | 11133 |
| Wahlco Inc | 3599 | C | 714 979-7300 | 11181 |
| Young Machine Inc | 3599 | F | 909 940-0405 | 11198 |
| Custom Magnetics Cal Inc | 3612 | E | 909 620-3877 | 11208 |
| Desco Industries Inc **(PA)** | 3629 | D | 909 627-8178 | 11369 |
| Scott Mfg Solutions Inc | 3629 | C | 909 594-9637 | 11381 |
| Pacific Coast Mfg Inc | 3631 | D | 909 627-7040 | 11393 |
| Anthony California Inc **(PA)** | 3645 | E | 909 627-0351 | 11488 |
| Artiva USA Inc **(PA)** | 3645 | E | 909 628-1388 | 11490 |
| Base Lite Corporation | 3645 | E | 909 444-2776 | 11492 |
| Lights of America Inc **(PA)** | 3645 | B | 909 594-7883 | 11497 |
| Hi-Lite Manufacturing Co Inc | 3646 | D | 909 465-1999 | 11537 |
| Paclights LLC **(PA)** | 3646 | F | 800 980-6386 | 11552 |
| Yankon Industries Inc **(PA)** | 3646 | E | 909 591-2345 | 11570 |
| Vtl Amplifiers Inc | 3651 | E | 909 627-5944 | 11716 |
| Balaji Trading Inc | 3661 | D | 909 444-7999 | 11753 |
| Fonegear LLC | 3661 | F | 909 627-7999 | 11764 |
| General Photonics Corp | 3661 | D | 909 590-5473 | 11766 |
| Manley Laboratories Inc | 3663 | E | 909 627-4256 | 11888 |
| Sierra Assembly Technology LLC | 3672 | E | 909 606-7700 | 12216 |
| American Solar Advantage Inc | 3674 | E | 877 765-2388 | 12301 |
| R Kern Engineering & Mfg Corp | 3678 | D | 909 664-2440 | 12894 |
| Enersys | 3691 | E | 909 464-8251 | 13137 |
| Syston Cable Technology Corp | 3699 | E | 888 679-7866 | 13316 |
| Esslinger Engineering Inc | 3714 | E | 909 539-0544 | 13496 |
| Soaring America Corporation | 3721 | E | 909 270-2628 | 13691 |
| Alvarado Manufacturing Co Inc | 3829 | C | 909 591-8431 | 14842 |
| US Bowling Corporation | 3949 | E | 909 548-0644 | 15872 |
| Svevia Usa Inc | 3953 | F | 909 559-4134 | 15892 |
| Paiho North America Corp | 3965 | E | 661 257-6611 | 15915 |
| Myers & Sons Hi-Way Safety Inc **(PA)** | 3993 | D | 909 591-1781 | 16012 |
| National Sign & Marketing Corp | 3993 | D | 909 591-4742 | 16013 |
| Jacuzzi Brands LLC | 3999 | D | 909 606-1416 | 16154 |
| Macro Industries Inc | 3999 | E | 909 606-2218 | 16174 |
| Stang Industries Inc | 3999 | F | 914 479-9810 | 16238 |
| Lotus & Windoware Inc **(PA)** | 5023 | D | 909 606-8866 | 16429 |
| Nexgrill Industries Inc **(PA)** | 5023 | D | 909 598-8799 | 16431 |
| Carlisle Construction Mtls LLC | 5033 | C | 909 591-7425 | 16489 |
| Aamp of Florida Inc | 5046 | E | 805 338-6800 | 16565 |
| A Plus International Inc **(PA)** | 5047 | D | 909 591-5168 | 16570 |
| Rrz Enterprises Inc | 5136 | F | 714 683-2820 | 17079 |
| Consolidated Plastics Corp **(PA)** | 5162 | E | 909 393-8222 | 17227 |
| S & W Plastic Stores Inc **(PA)** | 5162 | E | 909 390-0090 | 17235 |
| Contract Labeling Service Inc | 7389 | E | 909 937-0344 | 19084 |

### CHINO HILLS, CA - San Bernardino County

| | SIC | EMP | PHONE | ENTRY# |
|---|---|---|---|---|
| Andrew LLC | 2041 | F | 909 270-9356 | 1052 |
| Jacuzzi Products Co **(DH)** | 3088 | C | 909 606-1416 | 6680 |
| Dur-Red Products | 3444 | E | 323 771-9000 | 8435 |
| Advanced Mold Technology Inc | 3544 | F | | 9596 |
| Dynamic Enterprises Inc | 3599 | E | 562 944-0271 | 10817 |
| Victory Intl Group LLC | 5092 | C | 949 407-5888 | 16953 |

### CHOWCHILLA, CA - Madera County

| | SIC | EMP | PHONE | ENTRY# |
|---|---|---|---|---|
| Artistry In Wood | 2599 | F | 559 665-7171 | 3734 |
| Central California Cont Mfg | 3089 | E | 559 665-7611 | 6769 |
| Snyder Industries LLC | 3089 | E | 559 665-7611 | 7032 |
| Next Chapter Inc | 3272 | E | 559 665-7473 | 7361 |

Employee Codes: A=Over 500 employees, B=251-500
C=101-250, D=51-100, E=20-50, F=10-19, G=1-9

# CHOWCHILLA, CA

| | SIC | EMP | PHONE | ENTRY# |
|---|---|---|---|---|
| Certainteed LLC | 3296 | D | 559 665-4831 | 7574 |

## CHULA VISTA, CA - San Diego County

| | SIC | EMP | PHONE | ENTRY# |
|---|---|---|---|---|
| Legacy Reinforcing Steel LLC | 1791 | D | 619 646-0205 | 532 |
| Otay Lakes Brewery LLC | 2082 | E | 619 768-0172 | 1452 |
| Boochery Inc | 2085 | D | 619 207-0530 | 1834 |
| Canvas Concepts Inc | 2394 | E | 619 424-3428 | 2969 |
| Stark Mfg Co | 2394 | E | 619 425-5880 | 2983 |
| Next Day Printed Tees | 2396 | E | 619 420-8618 | 3013 |
| Multitaskr | 2434 | F | 619 391-3371 | 3258 |
| San Diego Arcft Interiors Inc | 2511 | E | 619 474-1997 | 3455 |
| Califrnia Furn Collections Inc | 2519 | C | 619 621-2455 | 3553 |
| Latina & Associates Inc (PA) | 2711 | E | 619 426-1491 | 4147 |
| Ggtw LLC | 2899 | E | 619 423-3388 | 6289 |
| Sealed Air Corporation | 3086 | E | 619 421-9003 | 6661 |
| American Design Inc | 3089 | E | 619 429-1995 | 6712 |
| Nypro Inc | 3089 | D | 619 498-9250 | 6942 |
| Nypro San Diego Inc | 3089 | D | 619 482-7033 | 6943 |
| Tenma America Corporation | 3089 | C | 619 754-2250 | 7051 |
| Sandpiper of California Inc | 3161 | D | 619 424-2222 | 7139 |
| Aker International Inc | 3199 | E | 619 423-5182 | 7152 |
| RCP Block & Brick Inc | 3271 | E | 619 474-1516 | 7300 |
| Heidelberg Mtls Sthwest Agg LL | 3273 | F | 619 425-0290 | 7453 |
| Simec USA Corporation | 3312 | E | 619 474-7081 | 7627 |
| Precision Fiber Products Inc | 3357 | E | 408 946-4040 | 7792 |
| McMahon Steel Company Inc | 3429 | C | 619 671-9700 | 8015 |
| East Cast Repr Fabrication LLC | 3441 | E | 619 591-9577 | 8133 |
| Omega Ii Inc | 3443 | E | 619 920-6650 | 8324 |
| P A S U Inc | 3444 | E | 619 421-1151 | 8523 |
| Plenums Plus LLC | 3444 | D | 619 422-5515 | 8540 |
| Curtiss-Wright Corporation | 3491 | D | 619 482-3405 | 9151 |
| Flexible Metal Inc | 3498 | C | 734 516-3017 | 9259 |
| Harcon Precision Metals Inc | 3531 | E | 619 423-5544 | 9426 |
| Xylem Water Systems (california) Inc | 3561 | E | 619 575-7466 | 9947 |
| Integrated Energy Technologies Inc | 3562 | C | 619 421-1151 | 9951 |
| American Metal Filter Company | 3564 | F | 619 628-1917 | 9979 |
| Hyspan Precision Products Inc (PA) | 3568 | D | 619 421-1355 | 10070 |
| SMK Manufacturing Inc | 3575 | E | 619 216-6400 | 10311 |
| Ace Industries Inc | 3599 | E | 619 482-2700 | 10665 |
| Advanced McHning Solutions Inc | 3599 | E | 619 671-3055 | 10676 |
| Bender Ccp Inc | 3599 | E | 619 232-5719 | 10745 |
| Miller Machine Works LLC | 3599 | F | 619 501-9866 | 10983 |
| Ichia USA Inc | 3674 | D | 619 482-2222 | 12467 |
| Pacmag Inc | 3679 | E | 619 872-0343 | 13060 |
| Allclear Aerospace & Def Inc | 3728 | E | 619 660-6220 | 13773 |
| Astor Manufacturing | 3728 | E | 661 645-5585 | 13788 |
| Rohr Inc (HQ) | 3728 | A | 619 691-4111 | 13939 |
| Colonnas Shipyard West LLC | 3731 | E | 757 545-2414 | 14001 |
| Integrated Marine Services Inc | 3731 | D | 619 429-0300 | 14005 |
| Adept Process Services Inc | 3732 | E | 619 434-3194 | 14026 |
| Bae Systems Land Armaments LP | 3812 | E | 619 455-0213 | 14161 |
| Kama-Tech Corporation | 3827 | F | 619 421-7858 | 14792 |
| Corneagen LLC | 3841 | F | 786 992-2688 | 15053 |
| Vcp Mobility Holdings Inc | 3842 | E | 619 213-6500 | 15426 |
| Toleeto Fastener International | 3965 | E | 619 662-1355 | 15919 |
| Stanford Sign & Awning Inc (PA) | 3993 | E | 619 423-6200 | 16046 |
| Samsung International Inc (DH) | 5065 | E | 619 671-6001 | 16733 |
| Heartland Meat Company Inc | 5147 | D | 619 407-3668 | 17162 |
| California Baking Company | 5149 | B | 619 591-8289 | 17179 |
| Al Global Corporation (HQ) | 5961 | E | 619 934-3980 | 17659 |
| Southcoast Welding & Mfg LLC | 7692 | B | 619 429-1337 | 19214 |
| Curtiss-Wright Corporation | 7699 | E | 619 656-4740 | 19250 |

## CITRUS HEIGHTS, CA - Sacramento County

| | SIC | EMP | PHONE | ENTRY# |
|---|---|---|---|---|
| A & A Stepping Stone Mfg Inc | 3999 | F | 916 723-1717 | 16078 |

## CITY OF COMMERCE, CA - Los Angeles County

| | SIC | EMP | PHONE | ENTRY# |
|---|---|---|---|---|
| Arthurmade Plastics Inc | 3089 | D | 323 721-7325 | 6726 |

## CITY OF INDUSTRY, CA - Los Angeles County

| | SIC | EMP | PHONE | ENTRY# |
|---|---|---|---|---|
| Home Organizers Inc | 1751 | A | 562 699-9945 | 494 |
| Ssre Holdings LLC | 2011 | D | 800 314-2098 | 617 |
| Venus Foods Inc | 2011 | E | 626 369-5188 | 623 |
| Viz Cattle Corporation | 2011 | E | 310 884-5260 | 624 |
| Derek and Constance Lee Corp (PA) | 2013 | D | 909 595-8831 | 639 |
| Gaytan Foods LLC | 2013 | E | 626 330-4553 | 645 |
| Pocino Foods Company | 2013 | D | 626 968-8000 | 659 |
| Rice Field Corporation | 2013 | E | 626 968-6917 | 663 |
| Heritage Distributing Company | 2023 | E | 626 333-9526 | 761 |
| Nutrasumma Inc | 2023 | E | 866 866-3993 | 778 |
| Ybcc Inc | 2023 | E | 626 213-3945 | 790 |
| Berkeley Farms LLC | 2026 | B | 510 265-8600 | 827 |
| Dean Socal LLC | 2026 | C | 951 734-3950 | 833 |
| Tropicana Products Inc | 2033 | E | 626 968-1299 | 934 |
| Gff Inc | 2035 | D | 323 232-6255 | 979 |
| Lee Kum Kee (usa) Foods Inc (PA) | 2035 | D | 626 709-1888 | 983 |
| Morehouse Foods Inc | 2035 | E | 626 854-1655 | 985 |
| Langer Juice Company Inc | 2037 | B | 626 336-3100 | 1011 |
| Golden State Foods Corp | 2038 | B | 626 465-7500 | 1035 |
| Harbor Green Grain LP | 2048 | E | 310 991-8089 | 1129 |
| Sbm Dairies Inc | 2086 | B | 626 923-3000 | 1959 |
| Blue Pacific Flavors Inc | 2087 | E | 626 934-0099 | 1990 |
| Snak-King LLC (PA) | 2096 | B | 626 336-7711 | 2103 |
| Best Formulations LLC | 2099 | C | 626 912-9998 | 2138 |
| Best Formulations LLC (HQ) | 2099 | E | 626 912-9998 | 2139 |
| Delori-Nutifood Products Inc | 2099 | E | 626 965-3006 | 2182 |
| Sincere Orient Commercial Corp | 2099 | D | 626 333-8882 | 2354 |
| Bentley Mills Inc (PA) | 2273 | C | 626 333-4585 | 2510 |
| American Foam Fiber & Sups Inc (PA) | 2299 | E | 626 969-7268 | 2542 |
| Antaeus Fashions Group Inc | 2329 | F | 626 452-0797 | 2610 |
| Unger Fabrik LLC (PA) | 2331 | E | 626 469-8080 | 2693 |
| Continental Marketing Svc Inc | 2393 | F | 626 626-8888 | 2955 |
| Exxel Outdoors Inc | 2399 | C | 626 369-7278 | 3028 |
| Hitex Dyeing & Finishing Inc | 2399 | E | 626 363-0160 | 3030 |
| Talbert Archtctral Panl Door I | 2431 | D | 714 671-9700 | 3197 |
| McConnell Cabinets Inc | 2434 | A | 626 937-2200 | 3254 |
| Tonusa LLC | 2434 | F | 626 961-8700 | 3274 |
| Commercial Lbr & Pallet Co Inc (PA) | 2448 | C | 626 968-0631 | 3335 |
| Fremarc Industries Inc (PA) | 2511 | D | 626 965-0802 | 3441 |
| Trend Manor Furn Mfg Co Inc | 2511 | E | 626 964-6493 | 3458 |
| Ardmore Home Design Inc (PA) | 2512 | E | 626 803-7769 | 3465 |
| BJ Liquidation Inc | 2512 | D | 626 961-7221 | 3466 |
| E J Lauren LLC | 2512 | E | 562 803-1113 | 3471 |
| R C Furniture Inc | 2512 | E | 626 964-4100 | 3486 |
| Spectrum Intl Holdings | 2542 | A | 626 333-7225 | 3708 |
| Harvard Label LLC | 2621 | C | 626 333-8881 | 3771 |
| Sonoco Products Company | 2631 | D | 626 369-6611 | 3807 |
| Boxes R Us Inc | 2653 | D | 626 820-5410 | 3824 |
| Fleetwood Fibre LLC | 2653 | C | 626 968-8503 | 3842 |
| Golden West Packg Group LLC (PA) | 2653 | B | 888 501-5893 | 3851 |
| Goldencorr Sheets LLC | 2653 | C | 626 369-6446 | 3852 |
| Hoover Containers Inc | 2653 | C | 909 444-9454 | 3858 |
| Scope Packaging Inc | 2653 | E | 714 998-4411 | 3886 |
| Bagcraftpapercon III LLC | 2673 | C | 626 961-6766 | 3962 |
| Mercury Plastics Inc (HQ) | 2673 | B | 626 961-0165 | 3971 |
| Tekni-Plex Inc | 2679 | C | 909 589-4366 | 4054 |
| Sing Tao Newspapers Ltd | 2711 | D | 626 956-8200 | 4196 |
| Ideal Printing Company | 2752 | E | 626 964-2019 | 4635 |
| K-1 Packaging Group LLC (PA) | 2752 | D | 626 964-9384 | 4659 |
| Marrs Printing Inc | 2752 | D | 909 594-9459 | 4690 |
| Pgi Pacific Graphics Intl | 2752 | E | 626 336-7707 | 4723 |
| Stoughton Printing Co | 2752 | F | 626 961-3678 | 4772 |
| Orbitel International LLC | 2759 | E | 626 369-7050 | 4934 |
| Hill Brothers Chemical Company | 2812 | F | 626 333-2251 | 5032 |
| Plastics Family Holdings Inc | 2821 | F | 626 333-7678 | 5188 |
| Teknor Apex Company | 2821 | C | 626 968-4656 | 5211 |
| Teknor Color Company | 2821 | E | 626 336-7709 | 5212 |
| Accolade Pharma USA | 2834 | E | 626 279-9699 | 5295 |
| Best Formulations LLC | 2834 | E | 626 912-9998 | 5364 |
| Health One Pharmaceutical Inc | 2834 | F | 626 279-9699 | 5478 |
| Prolacta Bioscience Inc (PA) | 2836 | C | 626 599-9260 | 5854 |
| Prolacta Facility LLC | 2836 | F | 626 599-9260 | 5855 |
| Maintex Inc (PA) | 2842 | E | 800 446-1888 | 5915 |
| Physicians Formula Inc (DH) | 2844 | D | 626 334-3395 | 6022 |
| Physicians Formula Cosmt Inc | 2844 | D | 626 334-3395 | 6023 |
| Cardinal Paint and Powder Inc | 2851 | C | 626 937-6767 | 6072 |
| PPG Industries Inc | 2851 | F | 562 692-4010 | 6102 |
| General Sealants Inc | 2891 | C | 626 961-0211 | 6229 |
| Henkel US Operations Corp | 2891 | D | 626 968-6511 | 6232 |
| Signature Flexible Packg LLC (PA) | 2891 | E | 909 598-7844 | 6246 |
| Acorn Engineering Company (PA) | 2899 | A | 800 488-8999 | 6265 |
| Summer Rio Corp (PA) | 3021 | F | 626 854-1498 | 6422 |
| Coi Rubber Products Inc | 3069 | B | 626 965-9966 | 6487 |
| Sealed Air Corporation | 3086 | C | 909 594-1791 | 6660 |
| Altium Packaging LLC | 3089 | D | 888 425-7343 | 6708 |
| Engineering Model Assoc Inc (PA) | 3089 | E | 626 912-7011 | 6820 |
| J & L Cstm Plstic Extrsons Inc | 3089 | E | 626 442-0711 | 6868 |
| Waddington North America Inc | 3089 | D | 626 913-4022 | 7075 |
| Prl Glass Systems Inc | 3231 | D | 877 775-2586 | 7239 |
| Prl Glass Systems Inc (PA) | 3231 | C | 626 961-5890 | 7240 |
| Puente Ready Mix Services Inc (PA) | 3273 | E | 626 968-0711 | 7486 |
| Jon Brooks Inc (PA) | 3295 | D | 626 330-0631 | 7570 |
| Cast Parts Inc | 3324 | C | 626 937-3444 | 7684 |
| Custom Alloy Sales Inc (PA) | 3341 | F | 626 369-3641 | 7717 |
| Quemetco West LLC | 3341 | E | 626 330-2294 | 7722 |
| Alum-A-Fold Pacific Inc | 3353 | E | 562 699-4550 | 7726 |

# GEOGRAPHIC SECTION

## COLMA, CA

| | SIC | EMP | PHONE | ENTRY# |
|---|---|---|---|---|
| Material Sciences Corporation | 3353 | E | 562 699-4550 | 7730 |
| Hydro Extrusion Usa LLC | 3354 | B | 626 964-3411 | 7740 |
| Prl Aluminum Inc | 3354 | D | 626 968-7507 | 7746 |
| Trulite GL Alum Solutions LLC | 3354 | D | 800 877-8439 | 7752 |
| Semco Enterprises Inc | 3356 | F | 626 333-2237 | 7767 |
| Aremac Heat Treating Inc | 3398 | E | 626 333-3898 | 7875 |
| Newton Heat Treating Co Inc | 3398 | D | 626 964-6528 | 7896 |
| Monadnock Company | 3429 | C | 626 964-6581 | 8018 |
| Nuset Inc | 3429 | E | 626 246-1668 | 8021 |
| Townsteel Inc | 3429 | D | 626 965-8917 | 8032 |
| Katch Inc | 3441 | E | 626 369-0958 | 8163 |
| Fanboys Window Factory Inc **(PA)** | 3442 | E | 626 280-8787 | 8266 |
| Adams-Campbell Company Ltd **(PA)** | 3444 | D | 626 330-3425 | 8361 |
| California Hydroforming Co Inc | 3444 | F | 626 912-0036 | 8402 |
| Cemco LLC **(DH)** | 3444 | D | 800 775-2362 | 8409 |
| Trio Metal Stamping Inc | 3444 | F | 626 336-1228 | 8600 |
| Dennison Inc | 3446 | E | 626 965-8917 | 8624 |
| Valley-Todeco Inc | 3452 | C | 800 992-4444 | 8770 |
| WJB Bearings Inc | 3463 | E | 909 598-6238 | 8806 |
| Safe Plating Inc | 3471 | D | 626 810-1872 | 9007 |
| Nelson Name Plate Company **(PA)** | 3479 | E | 323 663-3971 | 9095 |
| Phifer Incorporated | 3496 | D | 626 968-0438 | 9225 |
| Evans Industries Inc | 3499 | D | 626 912-1688 | 9285 |
| Pape Material Handling Inc | 3537 | E | 562 692-9311 | 9529 |
| PHI **(PA)** | 3542 | F | 626 968-9680 | 9587 |
| Trane Technologies Company LLC | 3561 | F | 323 583-4771 | 9944 |
| Sun Industries Filtration Corp | 3564 | E | 310 782-1188 | 9999 |
| Clayton Manufacturing Company **(PA)** | 3569 | C | 626 443-9381 | 10082 |
| Clayton Manufacturing Inc **(HQ)** | 3569 | D | 626 443-9381 | 10083 |
| Magnell Associate Inc | 3571 | B | 626 271-1320 | 10176 |
| Premio Inc **(PA)** | 3571 | C | 626 839-3100 | 10197 |
| Compucase Corporation | 3572 | A | 626 336-6588 | 10233 |
| Seaward Products Corp | 3585 | D | 562 699-7997 | 10514 |
| Metal Cutting Service | 3599 | F | 626 968-4764 | 10973 |
| Solo Enterprise Corp | 3599 | E | 626 961-1915 | 11117 |
| Reuland Electric Co **(PA)** | 3621 | C | 626 964-6411 | 11284 |
| Valley Power Services Inc | 3621 | D | 909 969-9345 | 11295 |
| ITT LLC | 3625 | D | 562 908-4144 | 11327 |
| Silveron Industries Inc | 3625 | F | 909 598-4533 | 11348 |
| Duro Corporation | 3631 | F | | 11389 |
| RH Peterson Co **(PA)** | 3631 | C | 626 369-5085 | 11394 |
| Superior Equipment Solutions | 3631 | D | 323 722-7900 | 11397 |
| Maxim Lighting Intl Inc | 3645 | D | 626 956-4200 | 11498 |
| Troy-Csl Lighting Inc | 3645 | C | 626 336-4511 | 11504 |
| Acuity Brands Lighting Inc | 3646 | E | 626 965-0711 | 11516 |
| Kim Lighting Inc | 3648 | A | 626 968-5666 | 11604 |
| S2e Inc | 3651 | F | 626 965-1008 | 11694 |
| D-Tech Optoelectronics Inc | 3669 | E | 626 956-1100 | 11989 |
| Adtech Photonics Inc | 3674 | E | 626 956-1000 | 12275 |
| Invenlux Corporation | 3674 | E | 626 277-4163 | 12500 |
| Cooper Interconnect Inc | 3679 | D | 617 389-7080 | 12945 |
| Sceptre Inc | 3679 | E | 626 369-3698 | 13083 |
| Battery Technology Inc **(PA)** | 3691 | D | 626 336-6878 | 13131 |
| Proterra Operating Company Inc | 3711 | B | 864 438-0000 | 13377 |
| Blackseries Campers Inc | 3715 | E | 833 822-6737 | 13613 |
| Utility Trailer Manufacturing **(PA)** | 3715 | B | 626 965-1514 | 13622 |
| Utility Trailer Mfg Co | 3715 | C | 909 594-6026 | 13623 |
| Acromil LLC **(HQ)** | 3728 | C | 626 964-2522 | 13732 |
| Acromil Corporation **(PA)** | 3728 | C | 626 964-2522 | 13734 |
| Maverick Aerospace Inc | 3728 | F | 714 578-1700 | 13902 |
| Maverick Aerospace Inc | 3728 | E | 714 578-1700 | 13903 |
| Triumph Structures - Everett Inc | 3728 | C | 425 348-4100 | 13983 |
| Chronomite Laboratories Inc | 3822 | E | 310 534-2300 | 14358 |
| Xpower Manufacture Inc | 3822 | E | 626 285-3301 | 14379 |
| Ncstar Inc | 3827 | E | 866 627-8278 | 14801 |
| Teledyne Instruments Inc | 3829 | C | 626 934-1500 | 14930 |
| Johnson Wilshire Inc | 3842 | E | 562 777-0088 | 15370 |
| Astrophysics Inc **(PA)** | 3844 | C | 909 598-5488 | 15499 |
| Jada Group Inc | 3944 | D | 626 810-8382 | 15754 |
| PH Dip Inc | 3944 | E | 909 869-8083 | 15763 |
| Easy Reach Supply LLC | 3991 | E | 601 582-7866 | 15928 |
| Gordon Brush Mfg Co Inc **(PA)** | 3991 | E | 323 724-7777 | 15930 |
| Cambro Manufacturing Company | 3999 | C | 909 354-8962 | 16106 |
| H & H Specialties Inc | 3999 | E | 626 575-0776 | 16141 |
| Cryomax USA Inc **(HQ)** | 4225 | F | 626 330-3388 | 16287 |
| Servitek Electric Inc | 4911 | E | 626 227-1650 | 16349 |
| Furniture America Cal Inc **(PA)** | 5021 | E | 866 923-8500 | 16414 |
| Pacific Heritg HM Fashion Inc | 5023 | E | 909 598-5200 | 16433 |
| Potter Roemer LLC **(HQ)** | 5031 | E | 626 855-4890 | 16456 |
| Avatar Technology Inc | 5045 | E | 909 598-7696 | 16511 |
| Mtc Worldwide Corp | 5045 | D | 626 839-6800 | 16533 |
| Alpha Imaging Technology | 5047 | F | 626 330-0808 | 16571 |
| Durasafe Inc | 5047 | F | 626 965-1588 | 16581 |
| Airgas Safety Inc | 5084 | E | 562 699-5239 | 16806 |
| Bridgestone Hosepower LLC | 5085 | E | 562 699-9500 | 16864 |
| Design International Group Inc | 5092 | E | 626 369-2289 | 16948 |
| Swatfame Inc **(PA)** | 5137 | B | 626 961-7928 | 17101 |
| Clemson Distribution Inc **(PA)** | 5143 | E | 909 595-2770 | 17126 |
| Youbar Inc **(PA)** | 5145 | D | 626 537-1851 | 17152 |
| Lee Kum Kee (usa) Inc **(DH)** | 5149 | E | 626 709-1888 | 17194 |
| Quality Naturally Foods Inc | 5149 | E | 626 854-6363 | 17206 |
| Quality Naturally Foods Inc **(PA)** | 5149 | E | 626 854-6363 | 17207 |
| Norman Fox & Co **(PA)** | 5169 | E | 800 632-1777 | 17247 |
| Dazpak Flexible Packaging LLC | 5199 | F | 909 598-7844 | 17292 |
| Consolidated Devices Inc **(HQ)** | 5251 | E | 626 965-0668 | 17352 |
| Langer Juice Company Inc **(PA)** | 5499 | C | 626 336-3100 | 17428 |
| Dna Motor Inc | 5531 | E | 626 965-8898 | 17450 |
| Dacor **(DH)** | 5719 | D | 626 799-1000 | 17533 |
| Labels-R-Us Inc | 5932 | E | 626 333-4001 | 17632 |
| Sailing Innovation (us) Inc | 5945 | A | 626 965-6665 | 17652 |
| Major Gloves & Safety Inc | 7218 | E | 626 330-8022 | 17770 |
| Asi Networks Inc | 7379 | F | 800 251-1336 | 19027 |
| Vonnic Inc | 7382 | E | 626 964-2345 | 19063 |
| Pace Lithographers Inc | 8999 | E | 626 913-2108 | 19575 |

## CLAREMONT, CA - Los Angeles County

| | SIC | EMP | PHONE | ENTRY# |
|---|---|---|---|---|
| Sunsation Inc | 2037 | E | 909 542-0280 | 1018 |
| Feemster Co Inc | 2051 | E | 909 621-9772 | 1192 |
| Green Spot Packaging Inc | 2086 | E | 909 625-8771 | 1890 |
| Claremont Courier Inc | 2711 | F | 909 621-4761 | 4094 |
| Phoenix Marketing Services Inc | 2752 | D | 909 399-4000 | 4724 |
| Universal Defense | 3443 | D | 909 626-4178 | 8349 |
| Micro Matrix Systems | 3469 | E | 909 626-8544 | 8868 |
| Conveyor Mfg & Svc Inc | 3535 | F | 909 621-0406 | 9483 |
| Vortox Air Technology Inc | 3564 | E | 909 621-3843 | 10006 |
| Baumann Engineering | 3599 | D | 909 621-4181 | 10738 |
| HI Rel Connectors Inc | 3643 | B | 909 626-1820 | 11458 |
| New Bedford Panoramex Corp | 3648 | E | 909 982-9806 | 11615 |
| Isn Global Enterprises Inc | 7375 | F | 909 670-0601 | 19017 |

## CLAYTON, CA - Contra Costa County

| | SIC | EMP | PHONE | ENTRY# |
|---|---|---|---|---|
| Cemex Cnstr Mtls PCF LLC | 5032 | E | 925 672-4900 | 16467 |

## CLOVERDALE, CA - Sonoma County

| | SIC | EMP | PHONE | ENTRY# |
|---|---|---|---|---|
| Reuser Inc | 2421 | F | 707 894-4224 | 3077 |
| Classic Mill & Cabinet LLC | 2434 | E | 707 894-9800 | 3232 |
| Ebac Investments Inc | 3273 | F | 707 894-4425 | 7442 |
| MGM Brakes | 3714 | D | 707 894-3333 | 13538 |
| All-Coast Forest Products Inc **(PA)** | 5031 | D | 707 894-4281 | 16441 |

## CLOVIS, CA - Fresno County

| | SIC | EMP | PHONE | ENTRY# |
|---|---|---|---|---|
| Live Action General Engrg Inc | 1711 | C | 559 292-2900 | 424 |
| Wawona Frozen Foods **(PA)** | 2099 | A | 559 299-2901 | 2389 |
| Snowflake Designs Corporation | 2253 | E | 559 291-6234 | 2479 |
| Tollhouse Window Company | 2431 | C | 800 287-7996 | 3199 |
| Agri Technovation Inc | 2873 | C | 559 931-3332 | 6168 |
| Karcher Design | 3429 | D | 253 220-8244 | 8008 |
| Anlin Windows & Doors | 3442 | B | 800 287-7996 | 8253 |
| Atmf Inc | 3471 | E | 559 299-6836 | 8927 |
| Valley Chrome Plating Inc **(PA)** | 3471 | D | 559 298-8094 | 9031 |
| Western Dning - Schneider Cafe | 3699 | F | 559 292-1981 | 13331 |
| Kw Automotive North Amer Inc | 3714 | E | 800 445-3767 | 13527 |
| Calpine Containers Inc **(PA)** | 5113 | F | 559 519-7199 | 16998 |
| Hydratech LLC **(HQ)** | 7699 | D | 559 233-0876 | 19263 |
| Niacc-Avitech Technologies Inc **(PA)** | 7699 | E | 559 291-2500 | 19271 |

## COACHELLA, CA - Riverside County

| | SIC | EMP | PHONE | ENTRY# |
|---|---|---|---|---|
| Reyes Coca-Cola Bottling LLC | 2086 | D | 760 396-4500 | 1940 |
| Roto-Lite Inc | 3089 | F | 909 923-4353 | 7012 |
| Armtec Defense Products Co **(DH)** | 3489 | B | 760 398-0143 | 9137 |
| Armtec Countermeasures Co **(DH)** | 3812 | E | 760 398-0143 | 14149 |
| Paladar Mfg Inc | 3931 | D | 760 775-4222 | 15720 |
| Imperial Western Products Inc A Cal **(HQ)** | 5159 | E | 760 398-0815 | 17222 |

## COALINGA, CA - Fresno County

| | SIC | EMP | PHONE | ENTRY# |
|---|---|---|---|---|
| Harris Farms Inc **(PA)** | 0191 | C | 559 884-2435 | 55 |
| Valley Garlic LLC | 2035 | E | 559 934-1763 | 996 |
| Aera Energy Services Company | 3533 | C | 559 935-7418 | 9453 |

## COARSEGOLD, CA - Madera County

| | SIC | EMP | PHONE | ENTRY# |
|---|---|---|---|---|
| Charging Tree Corporation | 1389 | F | 559 760-5473 | 216 |

## COLFAX, CA - Placer County

| | SIC | EMP | PHONE | ENTRY# |
|---|---|---|---|---|
| Fox Barrel Cider Company Inc | 2084 | E | 530 346-9699 | 1575 |
| Tully-Wihr Company | 2752 | C | 530 346-2649 | 4793 |
| Scott Miles | 5211 | E | 530 346-2294 | 17343 |

Employee Codes: A=Over 500 employees, B=251-500
C=101-250, D=51-100, E=20-50, F=10-19, G=1-9

# COLMA, CA
GEOGRAPHIC SECTION

| | SIC | EMP | PHONE | ENTRY# |
|---|---|---|---|---|

## COLMA, CA - San Mateo County

| | | | | |
|---|---|---|---|---|
| Christy Vault Company **(PA)** | 3272 | E | 650 994-1378 | 7318 |

## COLTON, CA - San Bernardino County

| | | | | |
|---|---|---|---|---|
| Paul Hubbs Construction Co Inc **(PA)** | 1429 | F | 951 360-3990 | 304 |
| Lozano Caseworks Inc | 1751 | D | 909 783-7530 | 496 |
| Boyd Specialties LLC | 2013 | D | 909 219-5120 | 634 |
| Hawa Corporation **(PA)** | 2013 | F | 909 825-8882 | 646 |
| Star Food Snacks Intl Inc | 2013 | D | 909 825-8882 | 670 |
| Ardent Mills LLC | 2041 | E | 951 201-1170 | 1054 |
| California Churros Corporation | 2051 | B | 909 370-4777 | 1175 |
| Mrp Inc | 2051 | E | 909 825-4800 | 1229 |
| Rise Baking Company LLC | 2051 | E | 909 825-7343 | 1240 |
| Avalon Apparel LLC | 2335 | D | 323 440-4344 | 2699 |
| Masterbrand Cabinets LLC | 2434 | E | 951 682-1535 | 3252 |
| Banner Mattress Inc | 2515 | D | 909 835-4200 | 3521 |
| Clariant Corporation | 2672 | E | 909 825-1793 | 3948 |
| Wirz & Co | 2752 | F | 909 825-6970 | 4813 |
| US Rubber Recycling Inc | 3069 | E | 909 825-1200 | 6546 |
| Omni Resource Recovery Inc | 3089 | C | 909 327-2900 | 6945 |
| Cemex Materials LLC | 3273 | E | 909 825-1500 | 7431 |
| Als Garden Art Inc **(PA)** | 3299 | B | 909 424-0221 | 7586 |
| Darnell-Rose Inc | 3429 | E | 626 912-1688 | 7992 |
| Elizabeth Shutters Inc | 3442 | E | 909 825-1531 | 8264 |
| C&K Form Fabrication Inc | 3449 | E | 909 825-1882 | 8693 |
| Black Diamond Blade Company **(PA)** | 3531 | E | 800 949-9014 | 9409 |
| Williams Furnace Co **(DH)** | 3585 | C | 562 450-3602 | 10529 |
| Rivian Automotive LLC | 3711 | D | 309 249-8777 | 13380 |
| Erf Enterprises Inc | 3713 | E | 909 825-4080 | 13411 |
| McNeilus Truck and Mfg Inc | 3713 | E | 909 370-2100 | 13419 |
| Panadent Corporation | 3843 | E | 909 783-1841 | 15474 |
| Cummings Resources LLC | 3993 | E | 951 248-1130 | 15963 |
| SMC Grease Specialist Inc | 4953 | E | 951 788-6042 | 16364 |
| Brithinee Electric | 5063 | D | 909 825-7971 | 16646 |
| Greenpath Recovery West Inc | 5093 | D | 909 954-0686 | 16960 |
| Sulzer Elctr-Mchncal Svcs US I | 7694 | E | 909 825-7971 | 19233 |

## COLUMBIA, CA - Tuolumne County

| | | | | |
|---|---|---|---|---|
| Portola Minerals Company | 1422 | D | 209 533-0127 | 301 |

## COLUSA, CA - Colusa County

| | | | | |
|---|---|---|---|---|
| Farmers Rice Cooperative | 0723 | E | 530 439-2244 | 81 |
| Riviana Foods Inc | 5153 | D | 530 458-8512 | 17221 |

## COMMERCE, CA - Los Angeles County

| | | | | |
|---|---|---|---|---|
| Mantels & More Corp | 1743 | E | 323 869-9764 | 483 |
| Heritage Distributing Company **(PA)** | 2026 | E | 323 838-1225 | 838 |
| Sugar Foods LLC | 2051 | D | 323 727-8290 | 1244 |
| New Century Snacks LLC | 2068 | D | 323 278-9578 | 1361 |
| Snak Club LLC | 2068 | C | 323 278-9578 | 1366 |
| Jr Grease Services Inc | 2077 | E | 323 318-2096 | 1385 |
| Chameleon Beverage Company Inc **(PA)** | 2086 | D | 323 724-8223 | 1878 |
| Carmi Flvr & Fragrance Co Inc **(PA)** | 2087 | E | 323 888-9240 | 1993 |
| Key Essentials Inc | 2087 | D | | 2012 |
| Caffe DAmore Inc | 2095 | C | | 2068 |
| Gruma Corporation | 2096 | B | 323 803-1400 | 2094 |
| Fungs Village Inc | 2098 | E | 323 881-1600 | 2113 |
| Arevalo Tortilleria Inc | 2099 | E | 323 888-1711 | 2131 |
| Gold Coast Ingredients Inc | 2099 | D | 323 724-8935 | 2217 |
| Interntional Tea Importers Inc **(PA)** | 2099 | E | 562 801-9600 | 2240 |
| Mojave Foods Corporation | 2099 | C | 323 890-8900 | 2284 |
| Pacific Spice Company Inc | 2099 | C | 323 726-9190 | 2311 |
| Bonded Fiberloft Inc | 2211 | B | 323 726-7820 | 2404 |
| Hidden Jeans Inc | 2211 | E | 213 746-4223 | 2418 |
| American & Efird LLC | 2284 | F | 323 724-6884 | 2524 |
| RDD Enterprises Inc | 2311 | F | 213 746-0020 | 2564 |
| 4 What Its Worth Inc **(PA)** | 2329 | E | 323 728-4503 | 2605 |
| Alliance Apparel Inc | 2331 | E | 323 888-8900 | 2653 |
| Au Merrow Corporation | 2331 | F | | 2655 |
| Cure Apparel Llc | 2331 | F | 562 927-7460 | 2662 |
| Trixxi Clothing Company Inc **(PA)** | 2335 | E | 323 585-4200 | 2720 |
| DNam Apparel Industries LLC | 2339 | E | 323 859-0114 | 2756 |
| J & F Design Inc | 2339 | D | 323 526-4444 | 2767 |
| Evy of California Inc | 2361 | C | 213 746-4647 | 2853 |
| Ajg Inc | 2386 | E | 323 346-0171 | 2874 |
| Pacific Coast Home Furn Inc **(PA)** | 2392 | F | 323 838-7808 | 2944 |
| Canvas Specialty Inc | 2394 | E | | 2970 |
| Hospitality Wood Products Inc | 2431 | F | 562 806-5564 | 3146 |
| Apex Drum Company Inc | 2449 | E | 323 721-8994 | 3368 |
| Greif Inc | 2449 | E | 323 724-7500 | 3371 |
| Furniture Technics Inc | 2511 | E | 562 802-0261 | 3443 |
| JP Products LLC | 2511 | E | 310 237-6237 | 3445 |
| Nova Lifestyle Inc **(PA)** | 2511 | E | 323 888-9999 | 3452 |
| West Coast Catrg Trcks Mfg Inc | 2511 | F | 323 278-1279 | 3459 |
| Commercial Intr Resources Inc | 2512 | D | 562 926-5885 | 3469 |
| Murrays Iron Works Inc **(PA)** | 2514 | C | 323 521-1100 | 3507 |
| Kingdom Mattress Co Inc | 2515 | F | 562 630-5531 | 3530 |
| Deskmakers Inc | 2521 | E | 323 264-2260 | 3566 |
| Norstar Office Products Inc **(PA)** | 2521 | E | 323 262-1919 | 3576 |
| Ergocraft Contract Solutions | 2522 | E | | 3598 |
| Pacific Hospitality Design Inc | 2531 | E | 323 278-7998 | 3637 |
| Nico Nat Mfg Corp | 2541 | E | 323 721-1900 | 3665 |
| Teichman Enterprises Inc | 2542 | E | 323 278-9000 | 3710 |
| Yavar Manufacturing Co Inc | 2657 | E | 323 722-2040 | 3920 |
| Amcor Flexibles LLC | 2671 | A | 323 721-6777 | 3922 |
| Liberty Packg & Extruding Inc | 2673 | E | 323 722-5124 | 3970 |
| Sun Plastics Inc | 2673 | E | 323 888-6999 | 3981 |
| Progressive Label Inc | 2679 | E | 323 415-9770 | 4048 |
| Bridge Publications Inc **(PA)** | 2731 | E | 323 888-6200 | 4317 |
| La Xpress Air & Heating Svcs | 2741 | D | 310 856-9678 | 4425 |
| Colorcom Inc | 2752 | F | 323 246-4640 | 4560 |
| Touch Litho Company | 2752 | F | 562 927-8899 | 4787 |
| X-Igent Printing Inc | 2752 | F | 323 837-9779 | 4817 |
| Hanover Accessories Corp | 2782 | C | | 5002 |
| Ultra Pro Acquisition LLC | 2782 | E | 323 725-1975 | 5006 |
| W R Grace & Co | 2819 | F | 562 927-8513 | 5130 |
| Biorx Pharmaceuticals Inc | 2834 | E | 323 725-3100 | 5377 |
| Samson Pharmaceuticals Inc | 2834 | E | 323 722-3066 | 5648 |
| American Intl Inds Inc | 2844 | A | 323 728-2999 | 5943 |
| Ink Solutions LLC | 2893 | F | 323 726-8100 | 6255 |
| Ink Systems Inc **(PA)** | 2893 | D | 323 720-4000 | 6256 |
| TW Graphics Group Company **(PA)** | 2893 | F | 323 721-1400 | 6263 |
| Indio Products Inc | 2899 | E | 323 720-9117 | 6296 |
| Solvay Draka Inc **(DH)** | 3081 | C | 323 725-7010 | 6571 |
| Huhtamaki Inc | 3086 | D | 323 269-0151 | 6646 |
| Specialty Enterprises Co | 3086 | D | 323 726-9721 | 6663 |
| Bottlemate Inc **(PA)** | 3089 | E | 323 887-9009 | 6750 |
| Urban Expressions Inc | 3171 | E | 310 593-4574 | 7147 |
| Custom Leathercraft Mfg LLC | 3199 | D | | 7154 |
| Mascorro Leather Inc | 3199 | E | 323 724-6759 | 7157 |
| SGC International Inc | 3211 | F | 323 318-2998 | 7177 |
| Pacific Vial Mfg Inc | 3221 | E | 323 721-7004 | 7185 |
| Mantels & More Corp | 3281 | F | 323 869-9764 | 7542 |
| Wiretech Inc **(PA)** | 3315 | D | 323 722-4933 | 7658 |
| Globe Iron Foundry Inc | 3321 | D | 323 723-8983 | 7675 |
| Kaiser Aluminum Corporation | 3354 | D | 323 726-8011 | 7741 |
| US Polymers Inc | 3354 | D | 323 727-6888 | 7753 |
| Century Wire & Cable Inc | 3357 | D | 800 999-5566 | 7781 |
| Gehr Industries Inc **(HQ)** | 3357 | C | 323 728-5558 | 7786 |
| Pacific Die Casting Corp | 3363 | E | 323 725-1308 | 7816 |
| Alcast Mfg Inc **(PA)** | 3365 | E | 310 542-3581 | 7834 |
| Orlandini Entps Pcf Die Cast | 3369 | C | 323 725-1332 | 7867 |
| Alarin Aircraft Hinge Inc | 3429 | E | 323 725-1666 | 7974 |
| Asco Sintering Co | 3429 | E | 323 725-3550 | 7975 |
| Hollywood Bed Spring Mfg Inc **(PA)** | 3429 | D | 323 887-9500 | 8003 |
| Monogram Aerospace Fas Inc | 3429 | C | 323 722-4760 | 8019 |
| Capitol Steel Fabricators Inc | 3441 | E | 323 721-5460 | 8116 |
| Air Louvers Inc | 3442 | E | 800 554-6077 | 8252 |
| Rite Engineering & Manufacturing Corporation | 3443 | E | 562 862-2135 | 8330 |
| Sid E Parker Boiler Mfg Co Inc | 3443 | D | 323 727-9800 | 8335 |
| A-1 Metal Products Inc | 3444 | E | 323 721-3334 | 8358 |
| PCI Industries Inc | 3444 | E | 323 728-0004 | 8533 |
| Architectural Enterprises Inc | 3449 | E | 323 268-4000 | 8692 |
| USG Ceilings Plus LLC | 3469 | E | 323 724-8166 | 8896 |
| Sheila Street Properties Inc **(PA)** | 3471 | D | 323 838-9208 | 9014 |
| Haley Indus Ctings Linings Inc | 3479 | E | 323 588-8086 | 9077 |
| Ultimate Metal Finishing Corp | 3479 | E | 323 890-9100 | 9130 |
| Matthew Warren Inc | 3495 | D | 800 237-5225 | 9202 |
| Precision Wire Products Inc **(PA)** | 3496 | C | 323 890-9100 | 9226 |
| ASC Engineered Solutions LLC | 3498 | D | 800 766-0076 | 9249 |
| Ctd Machines Inc | 3541 | F | 213 689-4455 | 9546 |
| Pioneer Broach Company **(PA)** | 3545 | E | 323 728-1263 | 9690 |
| Interstate Meat Co Inc | 3556 | E | 323 838-9400 | 9798 |
| Martin Sprocket & Gear Inc | 3566 | F | 323 728-8117 | 10043 |
| Crowntonka California Inc | 3585 | E | 909 230-6720 | 10493 |
| Alloy Machining and Honing Inc | 3599 | F | 323 726-8248 | 10701 |
| MGM Transformer Co | 3612 | D | 323 726-0888 | 11217 |
| Iworks Us Inc | 3641 | D | 323 278-8363 | 11426 |
| Acclaim Lighting LLC | 3646 | E | 323 213-4626 | 11514 |
| Deco Enterprises Inc | 3646 | D | 323 726-2575 | 11524 |
| Edison Price Lighting Inc **(PA)** | 3646 | C | 718 685-0700 | 11526 |
| Element Controls Corp | 3646 | E | 323 727-2737 | 11527 |
| Hallmark Lighting LLC | 3646 | D | 818 885-5010 | 11536 |
| Elation Lighting Inc | 3648 | D | 323 582-3322 | 11592 |
| Elite Lighting | 3648 | C | 323 888-1973 | 11593 |
| Eti Sound Systems Inc | 3651 | E | 323 835-6660 | 11659 |

# GEOGRAPHIC SECTION — CONCORD, CA

| Company | SIC | EMP | PHONE | ENTRY# |
|---|---|---|---|---|
| 71yrs Inc (PA) | 3669 | D | 310 639-0390 | 11982 |
| B & B Battery (usa) Inc (PA) | 3692 | F | 323 278-1900 | 13157 |
| Senfeng Laser Usa Inc | 3699 | E | 562 319-8053 | 13305 |
| Dynaflex Products (PA) | 3713 | D | 323 724-1555 | 13409 |
| Fastener Dist Holdings LLC | 3721 | E | 213 620-9950 | 13651 |
| Transdigm Inc | 3728 | E | 323 269-9181 | 13976 |
| Sondors Inc | 3751 | E | 323 372-3000 | 14070 |
| Atk Space Systems LLC (DH) | 3812 | E | 323 722-0222 | 14155 |
| Northrop Grumman Systems Corp | 3812 | C | 714 240-6521 | 14262 |
| Soffa Electric Inc | 3823 | E | 323 728-0230 | 14460 |
| Aahs Enterprises Inc | 3993 | F | 323 838-9130 | 15936 |
| PCI Industries Inc | 3999 | E | 323 728-0004 | 16198 |
| Pommes Frites Candle Co | 3999 | E | 213 488-2016 | 16206 |
| Superior-Studio Spc Inc | 3999 | E | 323 278-0100 | 16247 |
| RAMCAR Batteries Inc | 5013 | E | 323 726-1212 | 16394 |
| Gibson Overseas Inc (PA) | 5023 | B | 323 832-8900 | 16426 |
| Insul-Therm International Inc (PA) | 5033 | E | 323 728-0558 | 16491 |
| Justman Packaging & Display (PA) | 5046 | D | 323 728-8888 | 16569 |
| Nora Lighting Inc | 5063 | C | 323 767-2600 | 16667 |
| Hkf Inc (PA) | 5075 | E | 323 225-1318 | 16781 |
| Fastener Dist Holdings LLC (HQ) | 5085 | E | 213 620-9950 | 16874 |
| Cbb Group Inc | 5092 | F | 323 888-2800 | 16946 |
| Ultra Pro International LLC | 5092 | C | 323 890-2100 | 16952 |
| Tzeng Long USA Inc (PA) | 5093 | E | 323 722-5353 | 16965 |
| Charming Trim & Packaging | 5131 | A | 415 302-7021 | 17060 |
| Matrix International Tex Inc | 5131 | E | 323 582-9100 | 17063 |
| Sportek International Inc | 5136 | F | 213 239-6700 | 17081 |
| Balance Foods Inc | 5145 | E | 323 838-5555 | 17140 |
| Century Snacks LLC | 5145 | B | 323 278-9578 | 17142 |
| Bio Hazard Inc | 5199 | E | 213 625-2116 | 17287 |
| Blisterpak Inc | 5199 | E | 323 728-5555 | 17288 |
| RYL Inc | 5199 | E | 213 503-7968 | 17310 |
| West Bay Imports Inc | 5199 | E | 323 720-5777 | 17317 |
| Dunn-Edwards Corporation (DH) | 5231 | C | 888 337-2468 | 17348 |
| RDD Enterprises Inc | 5699 | E | 213 742-0666 | 17512 |
| Unified Nutrimeals Inc | 5812 | D | 323 923-9335 | 17609 |
| W B Mason Co Inc | 5943 | E | 888 926-2766 | 17642 |
| Quantum Networks LLC | 5961 | E | 212 993-5899 | 17670 |
| Ceramic Decorating Company Inc | 7389 | E | 323 268-5135 | 19081 |
| D I F Group Inc | 8741 | E | 323 231-8800 | 19513 |

## COMPTCHE, CA - Mendocino County

| Company | SIC | EMP | PHONE | ENTRY# |
|---|---|---|---|---|
| Wells Dental Inc | 3843 | F | 707 937-0521 | 15494 |

## COMPTON, CA - Los Angeles County

| Company | SIC | EMP | PHONE | ENTRY# |
|---|---|---|---|---|
| Demenno Kerdoon | 1382 | F | 310 537-7100 | 177 |
| Nabors Well Services Co | 1389 | D | 310 639-7074 | 255 |
| Alameda Construction Svcs Inc | 1442 | E | 310 635-3277 | 307 |
| Foster Poultry Farms | 2015 | B | 310 223-1499 | 687 |
| Sierra Cheese Manufacturing Company Inc | 2022 | E | 310 635-1216 | 738 |
| Bcd Food Inc | 2099 | E | 310 323-1200 | 2135 |
| Plenty Unlimited Inc | 2099 | F | 415 735-3737 | 2323 |
| Lekos Dye & Finishing Inc (PA) | 2231 | D | 310 763-0900 | 2448 |
| Pacific Contntl Textiles Inc | 2269 | E | 310 639-1500 | 2506 |
| American Dawn Inc (PA) | 2299 | D | 800 821-2221 | 2541 |
| Edmund Kim International Inc (PA) | 2329 | E | 310 604-1100 | 2618 |
| Magic Apparel Group Inc | 2353 | E | 310 223-4000 | 2846 |
| Sew What Inc | 2391 | E | 310 639-6000 | 2919 |
| Simso Tex Sublimation (PA) | 2396 | E | 310 885-9717 | 3017 |
| Elliotts Designs Inc | 2514 | E | 310 631-4931 | 3503 |
| Jbi LLC | 2514 | E | 310 537-2910 | 3505 |
| Cri Sub 1 (DH) | 2521 | E | 310 537-1657 | 3565 |
| International Paper Company | 2621 | E | 310 639-2310 | 3777 |
| Great Eastern Entertainment Co | 2741 | E | 310 638-5058 | 4409 |
| Kmr Label LLC | 2754 | E | 310 603-8910 | 4823 |
| Resource Label Group LLC | 2754 | E | 310 603-8910 | 4827 |
| Carbon Activated Corporation (PA) | 2819 | E | 310 885-4555 | 5079 |
| Crossfield Products Corp (PA) | 2821 | E | 310 886-9100 | 5149 |
| Orion Plastics Corporation | 2821 | D | 310 223-0370 | 5184 |
| Plaskolite West LLC | 2821 | E | 310 637-2103 | 5187 |
| Techmer Pm Inc | 2821 | B | 310 632-9211 | 5210 |
| Flo-Kem Inc | 2842 | E | 310 632-7124 | 5904 |
| LMC Enterprises | 2842 | E | 310 632-7124 | 5914 |
| Henkel US Operations Corp | 2843 | C | 562 297-6840 | 5937 |
| Ips Corporation (HQ) | 2891 | C | 310 898-3300 | 6234 |
| De Menno-Kerdoon Trading Co (HQ) | 2911 | E | 310 537-7100 | 6336 |
| Owens Corning Sales LLC | 2952 | E | 310 631-1062 | 6382 |
| Viking Rubber Products Inc | 3069 | F | 310 868-5200 | 6547 |
| Foam Factory Inc | 3086 | D | 310 603-9808 | 6635 |
| Ufp Technologies Inc | 3086 | E | 714 662-0277 | 6667 |
| Advanced Materials Inc (HQ) | 3089 | E | 310 537-5444 | 6698 |
| County Plastics Corp | 3089 | E | 310 635-5400 | 6783 |
| Idemia America Corp | 3089 | C | 310 884-7900 | 6862 |
| Rsk Tool Incorporated | 3089 | E | 310 537-3302 | 7016 |
| Andrew Alexander Inc | 3111 | D | 323 752-0066 | 7085 |
| Performance Composites Inc | 3229 | C | 310 328-6661 | 7201 |
| Southwire Inc | 3353 | B | 310 886-8300 | 7732 |
| Magnesium Alloy Pdts Co Inc | 3363 | E | 310 605-1440 | 7814 |
| Magnesium Alloy Products Co LP | 3363 | E | 323 636-2276 | 7815 |
| Fleetwood Continental Inc | 3366 | D | 310 609-1477 | 7852 |
| Fs - Precision Tech Co LLC | 3369 | D | 310 638-0595 | 7864 |
| Golden Gate Steel Inc | 3441 | F | 310 638-0855 | 8147 |
| Park Steel Co Inc | 3441 | D | 310 638-6101 | 8199 |
| Mnm Manufacturing Inc | 3442 | F | 310 898-1099 | 8278 |
| Anoroc Precision Shtmtl Inc | 3444 | E | 310 515-6015 | 8376 |
| Fastener Innovation Tech Inc | 3451 | D | 310 538-1111 | 8722 |
| Continental Forge Company LLC | 3463 | D | 310 603-1014 | 8796 |
| Weber Metals Inc | 3463 | B | 562 543-3316 | 8805 |
| Innovative Stamping Inc | 3469 | E | 310 537-6996 | 8852 |
| Serra Manufacturing Corp (PA) | 3469 | E | 310 537-4560 | 8887 |
| AAA Plating & Inspection Inc | 3471 | D | 323 979-8930 | 8905 |
| BHC Industries Inc | 3471 | E | 310 632-2000 | 8930 |
| Bowman Plating Co Inc | 3471 | C | 310 639-4343 | 8933 |
| E M E Inc | 3471 | E | 310 639-1621 | 8950 |
| Morrells Electro Plating Inc | 3471 | E | 310 639-1024 | 8986 |
| Kens Spray Equipment LLC | 3479 | C | 310 635-9995 | 9086 |
| Plasma Coating Corporation | 3479 | E | 310 532-1951 | 9106 |
| Ilco Industries Inc | 3498 | E | 310 631-8655 | 9261 |
| South Coast Screen and Casing | 3533 | F | 310 632-3200 | 9467 |
| Ace Clearwater Enterprises Inc | 3544 | E | 310 538-5380 | 9594 |
| Tajima Usa Inc | 3552 | E | 310 604-8200 | 9753 |
| Barkens Hardchrome Inc | 3559 | E | 310 632-2000 | 9837 |
| Flowserve Corporation | 3561 | D | 310 667-4220 | 9922 |
| Circle Industrial Mfg Corp (PA) | 3567 | E | 310 638-5101 | 10047 |
| Norco Industries Inc (PA) | 3569 | E | 310 639-4000 | 10102 |
| Classic Tents | 3585 | E | 310 328-5060 | 10488 |
| Allan Kidd | 3643 | E | 310 762-1600 | 11439 |
| Jimway Inc | 3648 | D | 310 886-3718 | 11603 |
| Martins Quality Truck Body Inc | 3711 | F | 310 632-5978 | 13368 |
| Complete Truck Body Repair Inc | 3713 | E | 323 445-2675 | 13404 |
| AITA Clutch Inc | 3714 | E | 323 585-4140 | 13453 |
| Fmf Racing | 3751 | C | 310 631-4563 | 14058 |
| Hf Group Inc (PA) | 3861 | E | 310 605-0755 | 15643 |
| Artboxx Framing Inc | 3999 | E | 310 604-6933 | 16089 |
| Mercado Latino Inc | 3999 | D | 310 537-1062 | 16181 |
| Tag Toys Inc | 3999 | D | 310 639-4566 | 16249 |
| Dna Specialty Inc | 5013 | E | 310 767-4070 | 16381 |
| Saddlemen Corporation | 5013 | C | 310 638-1222 | 16397 |
| West Wood Products Inc (PA) | 5031 | F | 310 631-8978 | 16460 |
| Concrete Tie Industries Inc (PA) | 5032 | E | 310 628-2328 | 16473 |
| Gemco Display and Str Fixs LLC (PA) | 5046 | E | 800 262-1126 | 16567 |
| Jack Rubin & Sons Inc (PA) | 5051 | E | 310 635-5407 | 16621 |
| Florence Filter Corporation | 5075 | D | 310 637-1137 | 16779 |
| JOHN TILLMAN COMPANY (DH) | 5084 | E | 310 764-0110 | 16820 |
| Industrial Valco Inc (PA) | 5085 | E | 310 635-0711 | 16879 |
| Gourmet Foods Inc (PA) | 5141 | E | 310 632-3300 | 17114 |
| Swan Fence Incorporated | 5211 | E | 310 669-8000 | 17347 |
| Kraco Enterprises LLC | 5531 | C | 310 639-0666 | 17454 |
| Diamond Mattress Company Inc (PA) | 5712 | E | 310 638-0363 | 17518 |
| Color Ad Inc | 7311 | E | 310 632-5500 | 17777 |
| Evans Hydro Inc | 7699 | E | 310 608-5801 | 19256 |
| Dxterity Diagnostics Inc (PA) | 8733 | E | 310 537-7857 | 19493 |

## CONCORD, CA - Contra Costa County

| Company | SIC | EMP | PHONE | ENTRY# |
|---|---|---|---|---|
| Tnh Development LLC | 1623 | F | 847 525-3960 | 391 |
| Cal Ranch Inc (PA) | 2034 | E | 925 429-2900 | 946 |
| Eldorado Usa LLC | 2079 | F | 925 285-4572 | 1397 |
| Pacific Plaza Imports Inc (PA) | 2091 | F | 925 349-4000 | 2042 |
| Moulding Company | 2431 | D | 925 798-7525 | 3162 |
| C&T Publishing Inc | 2741 | E | 925 677-0377 | 4375 |
| Acme Press Inc | 2752 | F | 925 682-1111 | 4501 |
| Hnc Printing Services LLC | 2752 | E | 925 771-2080 | 4633 |
| Cerus Corporation (PA) | 2836 | C | 925 288-6000 | 5816 |
| Lehigh Southwest Cement Co (DH) | 3241 | F | 972 653-5500 | 7258 |
| Indepndent Flr Tstg Insptn Inc | 3272 | F | 925 676-7682 | 7345 |
| GGF Marble & Supply Inc | 3281 | F | 925 676-8385 | 7537 |
| Superheat Fgh Services Inc | 3398 | F | 925 808-6711 | 7900 |
| Acro Associates Inc | 3491 | E | 925 676-8828 | 9142 |
| Heraeus Medical Components LLC | 3493 | D | 925 798-4080 | 9175 |
| Mohin Inc | 3499 | E | 925 798-5572 | 9294 |
| Nordson March Inc (HQ) | 3563 | E | 925 827-1240 | 9970 |
| Alvellan Inc | 3599 | E | 925 689-2421 | 10707 |
| Seatel Inc (DH) | 3663 | C | 925 798-7979 | 11941 |
| Benchmark Electronics Inc | 3672 | E | 925 363-1151 | 12071 |
| Emcore Corporation | 3674 | C | 925 979-4500 | 12418 |
| Systron Donner Inertial Inc | 3679 | C | 925 979-4400 | 13097 |

# CONCORD, CA — GEOGRAPHIC SECTION

| | SIC | EMP | PHONE | ENTRY# |
|---|---|---|---|---|
| Marvac Scientific Mfg Co | 3821 | F | 925 825-4636 | 14343 |
| Cubic Trnsp Systems Inc | 3829 | E | 925 348-9163 | 14858 |
| Pacific Instruments Inc | 3829 | E | 925 827-9010 | 14909 |
| Fresenius Med Care Hldings Inc | 3841 | F | 888 373-1470 | 15091 |
| Kainos Dental Technologies LLC (PA) | 3841 | E | 800 331-4834 | 15140 |
| Patterson Dental Supply Inc | 3843 | E | 925 603-6350 | 15475 |
| Siemens Med Solutions USA Inc | 3845 | A | 925 246-8200 | 15578 |
| Goodie Closett LLC | 3999 | F | 980 895-0496 | 16138 |
| Onesource Distributors LLC | 5063 | E | 925 827-9988 | 16668 |
| Creation Networks Inc | 5999 | E | 925 446-4332 | 17700 |
| Carlton Senior Living Inc (PA) | 6531 | E | 925 338-2434 | 17741 |
| Concord Graphic Arts Inc | 7336 | E | 925 682-9670 | 17823 |
| Esmart Source Inc | 7372 | E | 408 739-3500 | 18290 |
| Pt Systems Inc | 8711 | F | 925 676-0709 | 19412 |

## COOL, CA - El Dorado County

| | SIC | EMP | PHONE | ENTRY# |
|---|---|---|---|---|
| Teichert Inc | 1442 | C | 530 885-4244 | 324 |

## COPPEROPOLIS, CA - Calaveras County

| | SIC | EMP | PHONE | ENTRY# |
|---|---|---|---|---|
| Meridian Gold Inc | 1041 | B | 209 785-3222 | 105 |

## CORCORAN, CA - Kings County

| | SIC | EMP | PHONE | ENTRY# |
|---|---|---|---|---|
| Camfil Usa Inc | 3564 | E | 559 992-5118 | 9982 |

## CORNING, CA - Tehama County

| | SIC | EMP | PHONE | ENTRY# |
|---|---|---|---|---|
| Sunsweet Dryers | 2034 | C | 530 824-5854 | 967 |
| Sunsweet Growers Inc | 2034 | D | 530 824-5376 | 969 |
| Bell-Carter Foods LLC | 2035 | B | 530 528-4820 | 975 |
| Sierra Pacific Industries | 2431 | E | 530 824-2474 | 3188 |
| Eco-Shell Inc | 3999 | E | 530 824-8794 | 16127 |
| Olive Pit LLC | 5499 | F | 530 824-4667 | 17430 |

## CORONA, CA - Riverside County

| | SIC | EMP | PHONE | ENTRY# |
|---|---|---|---|---|
| Chandler Aggregates Inc (PA) | 1411 | E | 951 277-1341 | 294 |
| Gail Materials Inc | 1442 | E | 951 667-6106 | 312 |
| Champion Home Builders Inc | 1521 | C | 951 256-4617 | 344 |
| Clay Corona Company (PA) | 1542 | E | 951 277-2667 | 365 |
| A Class Precision Inc | 1761 | E | 951 549-9706 | 508 |
| Wellington Foods Inc (PA) | 2023 | C | 951 547-7000 | 789 |
| Stir Foods LLC | 2038 | E | 714 871-9231 | 1048 |
| Food For Life Baking Co Inc (PA) | 2051 | D | 951 279-5090 | 1201 |
| Inw Living Ecology Opco LLC (DH) | 2064 | E | 951 371-4982 | 1313 |
| Bu LLC | 2082 | F | 951 277-7470 | 1425 |
| Monster Beverage 1990 Corporation | 2086 | A | 951 739-6200 | 1903 |
| Monster Beverage Company | 2086 | A | 866 322-4466 | 1904 |
| Monster Beverage Corporation (PA) | 2086 | A | 951 739-6200 | 1905 |
| Cadence Gourmet LLC (PA) | 2099 | F | 951 444-9269 | 2152 |
| PSW Inc | 2099 | F | 951 371-7100 | 2325 |
| T Hasegawa USA Inc | 2099 | E | 951 264-1121 | 2367 |
| Amrapur Overseas Incorporated (PA) | 2299 | E | 714 893-8808 | 2544 |
| Amwear USA Inc | 2311 | E | 800 858-6755 | 2556 |
| Shirinian-Shaw Inc | 2387 | E | 951 736-1229 | 2884 |
| Anatomic Global Inc | 2392 | C | 800 874-7237 | 2921 |
| Northwestern Converting Co | 2392 | D | 800 959-3402 | 2940 |
| CTA Manufacturing Inc | 2393 | E | 951 280-2400 | 2956 |
| Best- In- West | 2395 | E | 909 947-6507 | 2989 |
| Leepers Wood Turning Co Inc (PA) | 2431 | E | 562 422-6525 | 3153 |
| Novo Manufacturing LLC | 2431 | D | 951 479-4620 | 3168 |
| Excel Cabinets Inc | 2434 | E | 951 279-4545 | 3239 |
| American National Mfg Inc | 2515 | D | 951 273-7888 | 3519 |
| AMF Support Surfaces Inc (DH) | 2515 | E | 951 549-6800 | 3520 |
| Della Robbia Inc | 2515 | E | 951 372-9199 | 3524 |
| Widly Inc | 2515 | C | 951 279-0900 | 3546 |
| Ergononmic Comfort Design Inc | 2522 | F | 951 277-1558 | 3599 |
| Temeka Advertising Inc | 2541 | D | 951 277-2525 | 3674 |
| Uniweb Inc (PA) | 2542 | D | 951 279-7999 | 3713 |
| Century Blinds Inc | 2591 | D | 951 734-3762 | 3717 |
| Diamante Worldwide Inc | 2591 | F | 714 822-7458 | 3718 |
| R & J Fabricators Inc | 2599 | E | 951 817-0300 | 3748 |
| General Container | 2653 | D | 714 562-8700 | 3846 |
| Republic Bag Inc (PA) | 2673 | F | 951 734-9740 | 3977 |
| Tree House Pad & Paper Inc | 2678 | E | 800 213-4184 | 4023 |
| Azalea Systems Corp Inc | 2752 | E | 951 547-5910 | 4522 |
| Big Horn Wealth Management Inc | 2752 | E | 951 273-7900 | 4532 |
| Handbill Printers LP | 2752 | E | 951 547-5910 | 4628 |
| Westrock Cp LLC | 2752 | E | 951 273-7900 | 4811 |
| Spectra Color Inc | 2816 | E | 951 277-0200 | 5065 |
| Cgpc America Corporation | 2821 | E | 951 332-4100 | 5143 |
| Actavis LLC | 2834 | D | 909 270-1400 | 5296 |
| Youcare Pharma (usa) Inc | 2834 | D | 951 258-3114 | 5721 |
| Panrosa Enterprises Inc | 2841 | D | 951 339-5888 | 5879 |
| 2nd Gen Productions Inc | 2842 | F | 800 877-6282 | 5885 |
| US Continental Marketing Inc (PA) | 2842 | D | 951 808-8888 | 5934 |
| Adonis Inc | 2844 | E | 951 432-3960 | 5939 |
| Vinylvisions Company LLC | 2851 | E | 800 321-8746 | 6116 |
| Tastepoint Inc | 2869 | C | 951 734-6620 | 6163 |
| Trical Inc | 2879 | E | 951 737-6960 | 6211 |
| Technicote Inc | 2891 | E | 951 372-0627 | 6249 |
| MCP Industries Inc (PA) | 3069 | D | 951 736-1881 | 6512 |
| Playmax Surfacing Inc | 3069 | F | 951 250-6039 | 6522 |
| Spangler Industries Inc | 3069 | C | 951 735-5000 | 6539 |
| Arvinyl Laminates LP | 3081 | D | 951 371-7800 | 6552 |
| TRM Manufacturing Inc | 3081 | D | 951 256-8550 | 6573 |
| Simmons Family Corporation | 3083 | D | 951 278-4563 | 6592 |
| Dart Container Corp California (PA) | 3086 | B | 951 735-8115 | 6629 |
| Aquatic Co | 3088 | C | 714 993-1220 | 6673 |
| Le Elegant Bath Inc | 3088 | D | 951 734-0238 | 6683 |
| Carr Management Inc | 3089 | D | 951 277-4800 | 6765 |
| Dacha Enterprises Inc | 3089 | D | 951 273-7777 | 6792 |
| Extrumed Inc (DH) | 3089 | E | 951 547-7400 | 6824 |
| Fischer Mold Incorporated | 3089 | D | 951 279-1140 | 6826 |
| Hoosier Inc | 3089 | E | 951 272-3070 | 6857 |
| Martin Chancey Corporation | 3089 | E | 510 972-6300 | 6903 |
| Merrick Engineering Inc (PA) | 3089 | E | 951 737-6040 | 6912 |
| Odi Manufacturing LLC | 3089 | C | 951 786-4750 | 6944 |
| Preproduction Plastics Inc | 3089 | E | 951 340-9680 | 6980 |
| Rehau Construction LLC | 3089 | D | 951 549-9017 | 6998 |
| Roto Power Inc | 3089 | F | 951 751-9850 | 7011 |
| Tamshell Corp | 3089 | D | 951 272-9395 | 7050 |
| TNT Plastic Molding Inc (PA) | 3089 | D | 951 808-9700 | 7054 |
| Mediland Corporation | 3211 | D | 562 630-9696 | 7176 |
| Sream Inc | 3231 | E | 951 245-6999 | 7242 |
| Maruhachi Ceramics America Inc | 3259 | E | 800 736-6221 | 7274 |
| United States Tile Co | 3259 | C | 951 739-4613 | 7276 |
| Acker Stone Industries Inc (DH) | 3272 | E | 951 674-0047 | 7306 |
| Quikrete California LLC (DH) | 3272 | E | 951 277-3155 | 7378 |
| Robertsons Rdymx Ltd A Cal Ltd (PA) | 3273 | D | 951 493-6500 | 7489 |
| Superior Ready Mix Concrete LP | 3273 | E | 951 277-3553 | 7509 |
| Werner Corporation | 3273 | E | 951 277-4586 | 7521 |
| 3M Company | 3295 | E | 951 737-3441 | 7563 |
| Rock Structures-Rip Rap | 3296 | E | 951 371-1112 | 7581 |
| Omega Products Corp (HQ) | 3299 | D | 951 737-7447 | 7595 |
| Hardy Frames Inc | 3312 | D | 951 245-9525 | 7614 |
| Lexani Wheel Corporation | 3312 | E | 951 808-4220 | 7619 |
| Merit Aluminum Inc (PA) | 3354 | C | 951 735-1770 | 7743 |
| Actron Manufacturing Inc | 3429 | E | 951 371-0885 | 7973 |
| Lock America Inc | 3429 | F | 951 277-5180 | 8011 |
| Columbia Aluminum Products LLC | 3441 | D | 323 728-7361 | 8120 |
| Johasee Rebar Inc | 3441 | E | 661 589-0972 | 8159 |
| Parcell Steel Corp | 3441 | C | 951 471-3200 | 8198 |
| Premier Steel Structures Inc | 3441 | E | 951 356-6655 | 8203 |
| Steel-Tech Industrial Corp | 3441 | E | 951 270-0144 | 8222 |
| Tolar Manufacturing Co Inc | 3441 | E | 951 808-0081 | 8230 |
| Decra Roofing Systems Inc (DH) | 3444 | D | 951 272-8180 | 8428 |
| Fletcher Bldg Holdings USA Inc (DH) | 3444 | D | 951 272-8180 | 8454 |
| MS Industrial Shtmtl Inc | 3444 | C | 951 272-6610 | 8516 |
| LMS Reinforcing Steel Usa LP (HQ) | 3449 | F | 951 307-0972 | 8703 |
| Price Manufacturing Co Inc | 3451 | E | 951 371-5660 | 8730 |
| Premier Gear & Machining Inc | 3462 | E | 951 278-5505 | 8786 |
| Rubicon Gear Inc | 3462 | D | 951 356-3800 | 8788 |
| Saleen Automotive Inc (PA) | 3465 | E | 800 888-8945 | 8808 |
| Steelcraft LLC | 3465 | F | 888 261-4537 | 8809 |
| T-Rex Truck Products Inc | 3465 | D | 800 287-5900 | 8810 |
| David Engineering & Mfg Inc | 3469 | E | 951 735-5200 | 8834 |
| Master Fab Inc | 3469 | F | 951 277-4772 | 8862 |
| Proformance Manufacturing Inc | 3469 | E | 951 279-1230 | 8878 |
| Ravlich Enterprises LLC (PA) | 3471 | E | 714 964-8900 | 9004 |
| RGF Enterprises Inc | 3479 | E | 951 734-6922 | 9114 |
| Circor Aerospace Inc (DH) | 3491 | C | 951 270-6200 | 9148 |
| Crane Instrmnttion Smpling Inc | 3491 | D | 951 270-6200 | 9149 |
| Eibach Inc | 3493 | D | 951 256-8300 | 9174 |
| Mission Rubber Company LLC | 3494 | D | 951 736-1313 | 9188 |
| California Wire Products Corp | 3496 | E | 951 371-7730 | 9213 |
| Ameriflex Inc | 3498 | D | 951 737-5557 | 9247 |
| Do It American Mfg Company LLC | 3499 | F | 951 254-9204 | 9281 |
| Laminated Shim Company Inc | 3499 | E | 951 273-3900 | 9291 |
| Pacmet Aerospace LLC | 3519 | D | 909 218-8889 | 9329 |
| Western Equipment Mfg Inc | 3531 | E | 951 284-2000 | 9447 |
| Cremach Tech Inc (DH) | 3541 | E | 951 735-3194 | 9544 |
| Cremach Tech Inc | 3541 | C | 951 735-3194 | 9545 |
| David Engineering & Manufacturing Inc | 3544 | E | 951 735-5200 | 9617 |
| Noranco Manufacturing (usa) Acquisition Corp | 3545 | C | 951 721-8400 | 9685 |
| Pacific Packaging McHy LLC | 3556 | E | 951 393-2200 | 9810 |
| John Currie Performance Group | 3559 | E | 714 367-1580 | 9872 |
| Peabody Engineering & Sup Inc | 3559 | E | 951 734-7711 | 9889 |
| Suss Microtec Inc (HQ) | 3559 | C | 408 940-0300 | 9902 |

# GEOGRAPHIC SECTION — COSTA MESA, CA

| Company | SIC | EMP | PHONE | ENTRY# |
|---|---|---|---|---|
| Vizualogic LLC | 3559 | C | 407 509-3421 | 9910 |
| Kobelco Compressors Amer Inc | 3563 | D | 951 739-3030 | 9964 |
| Kobelco Compressors Amer Inc (DH) | 3563 | B | 951 739-3030 | 9965 |
| Hannan Products Corp (PA) | 3565 | F | 951 735-1587 | 10019 |
| M & O Perry Industries Inc | 3565 | E | 951 734-9838 | 10025 |
| Jhawar Industries LLC | 3567 | E | 951 340-4646 | 10055 |
| Anaco Inc | 3568 | C | 951 372-2732 | 10064 |
| Avt Inc | 3581 | E | 951 737-1057 | 10469 |
| Ace Heaters LLC | 3585 | E | 951 738-2230 | 10477 |
| Aqueous Technologies Corp | 3589 | E | 909 944-7771 | 10540 |
| Blue Desert International Inc | 3589 | D | 951 273-7575 | 10544 |
| Engineered Food Systems | 3589 | E | 714 921-9913 | 10558 |
| Spenuzza Inc (HQ) | 3589 | D | 951 281-1830 | 10603 |
| Parker-Hannifin Corporation | 3594 | D | 951 280-3800 | 10634 |
| Btl Machine | 3599 | D | 951 808-9929 | 10755 |
| F & L Tools Corporation | 3599 | F | 951 279-1555 | 10834 |
| MD Engineering Inc | 3599 | E | 951 736-5390 | 10968 |
| Millworx Prcsion Machining Inc | 3599 | E | 951 371-2683 | 10985 |
| Ms-Tech Corporation | 3599 | E | 562 404-9727 | 10999 |
| PVA Tepla America Inc (HQ) | 3599 | E | 951 371-2500 | 11057 |
| Sun Precision Machining Inc | 3599 | F | 951 817-0056 | 11126 |
| Absolute Graphic Tech USA Inc | 3625 | E | 909 597-1133 | 11304 |
| Esl Power Systems Inc | 3643 | D | 800 922-4188 | 11453 |
| Computer Service Company | 3669 | E | 951 738-1444 | 11988 |
| Corona Magnetics Inc | 3677 | C | 951 735-7558 | 12835 |
| Jayco/Mmi Inc | 3679 | E | 951 738-2000 | 13014 |
| Omni Connection Intl Inc | 3679 | B | 951 898-6232 | 13054 |
| Sas Manufacturing Inc | 3679 | E | 951 734-1808 | 13082 |
| Palos Verdes Building Corp (PA) | 3691 | C | 951 371-8090 | 13147 |
| Vantage Vehicle Intl Inc | 3694 | E | 951 735-1200 | 13191 |
| Pacific Utility Products Inc | 3699 | E | 951 493-8394 | 13284 |
| Suss McRtec Phtnic Systems Inc | 3699 | D | 951 817-3700 | 13315 |
| Saleen Incorporated (PA) | 3711 | C | 714 400-2121 | 13382 |
| Advanced Flow Engineering Inc (PA) | 3714 | E | 951 493-7155 | 13444 |
| Advanced Flow Engineering Inc | 3714 | E | 951 493-7100 | 13445 |
| Currie Enterprises | 3714 | D | 714 528-6957 | 13481 |
| Gibson Performance Corporation | 3714 | D | 951 372-1220 | 13507 |
| Hitachi Astemo Americas Inc | 3714 | B | 951 340-0702 | 13514 |
| Nmsp Inc | 3714 | E | 951 734-2453 | 13548 |
| TMI Products Inc | 3714 | C | 951 272-1996 | 13587 |
| Tube Technologies Inc | 3714 | E | 951 371-4878 | 13594 |
| Accurate Grinding and Mfg Corp | 3724 | E | 951 479-0909 | 13700 |
| International Wind Inc (PA) | 3724 | E | 562 240-3963 | 13713 |
| Thermal Structures Inc (DH) | 3724 | B | 951 736-9911 | 13723 |
| Thermal Structures Inc | 3724 | E | 951 256-8051 | 13724 |
| Acromil LLC | 3728 | D | 951 808-9929 | 13733 |
| Aero-Craft Hydraulics Inc | 3728 | E | 951 736-4690 | 13745 |
| Approved Aeronautics LLC | 3728 | E | 951 200-3730 | 13782 |
| Asturies Manufacturing Co Inc | 3728 | E | 951 270-1766 | 13790 |
| Irwin Aviation Inc | 3728 | E | 951 372-9555 | 13878 |
| Johnson Caldraul Inc | 3728 | E | 951 340-1067 | 13882 |
| Shim-It Corporation | 3728 | F | 951 734-8300 | 13956 |
| Electrasem Corp | 3822 | D | 951 371-6140 | 14360 |
| Eclypse International Corp (PA) | 3825 | E | 951 371-8008 | 14514 |
| Sprite Industries Incorporated | 3826 | E | 951 735-1015 | 14722 |
| Kap Medical | 3829 | E | 951 340-4360 | 14889 |
| All Manufacturers Inc | 3841 | C | 951 280-4200 | 14958 |
| Rayes Inc (PA) | 3842 | F | 785 726-4885 | 15397 |
| Biolase Inc | 3843 | D | 949 361-1200 | 15441 |
| Dansereau Health Products | 3843 | E | 951 549-1400 | 15445 |
| Fender Musical Instrs Corp | 3931 | A | 480 596-9690 | 15717 |
| Westech Products Inc (PA) | 3952 | E | 951 279-4496 | 15888 |
| Architectural Design Signs Inc (PA) | 3993 | D | 951 278-0680 | 15942 |
| Fovell Enterprises Inc | 3993 | E | 951 734-6275 | 15979 |
| R&M Deese Inc | 3993 | E | 951 734-7342 | 16025 |
| Richards Neon Shop Inc | 3993 | E | 951 279-6767 | 16026 |
| Tradenet Enterprise Inc | 3993 | D | 888 595-3956 | 16059 |
| Arminak Solutions LLC | 3999 | E | 626 802-7332 | 16088 |
| Cbd Living Water | 3999 | E | 800 940-3660 | 16110 |
| Developlus Inc | 3999 | C | 951 738-8595 | 16124 |
| Kurz Transfer Products LP | 3999 | D | 951 738-9521 | 16164 |
| Pet Partners Inc (PA) | 3999 | E | 951 279-9888 | 16201 |
| Combustion Associates Inc | 4911 | E | 951 272-6999 | 16342 |
| Talco Plastics Inc (PA) | 4953 | D | 951 531-2000 | 16365 |
| McDavis and Gumbys Inc | 5031 | C | 800 736-7363 | 16448 |
| ABC School Equipment Inc | 5049 | E | 951 817-2200 | 16598 |
| Ckkm Inc (PA) | 5051 | E | 951 371-8484 | 16613 |
| Corona Clipper Inc | 5072 | E | 800 847-7863 | 16750 |
| R & J Material Handling Inc | 5084 | F | 951 735-0000 | 16836 |
| Thalasinos Enterprises Inc | 5085 | E | 951 340-0911 | 16899 |
| Aqua Performance Inc | 5091 | E | 951 340-2056 | 16932 |
| Meridian Moulding Inc | 5099 | F | 951 279-5220 | 16980 |
| Living Ecology | 5122 | E | 951 371-4982 | 17041 |
| Rugby Laboratories Inc (DH) | 5122 | D | 951 270-1400 | 17048 |
| Index Fresh Inc (PA) | 5148 | D | 909 877-0999 | 17169 |
| Ganahl Lumber Company | 5211 | D | 951 278-4000 | 17332 |
| Vons Companies Inc | 5411 | C | 951 278-8284 | 17394 |
| Freedom Prfmce Exhaust Inc | 5531 | E | 951 898-4733 | 17451 |
| Pro Circuit Products Inc (PA) | 5571 | E | 951 738-8050 | 17484 |
| Pacific Boat Trailers Inc (PA) | 5599 | F | 909 902-0094 | 17488 |
| Porter Hire Ltd | 7359 | E | 951 674-9999 | 17861 |
| Eknowledge Group Inc | 7372 | E | 951 256-4076 | 18271 |
| General Water Systems | 7389 | F | 951 278-8992 | 19093 |
| Metro Truck Body Inc | 7532 | E | 310 532-5570 | 19147 |
| Moyes Custom Furniture Inc | 7641 | E | 714 729-0234 | 19182 |
| General Conveyor Inc | 7699 | E | 951 734-3460 | 19259 |
| Sterigenics US LLC | 8734 | F | 951 340-0700 | 19508 |

## CORONA DEL MAR, CA - Orange County

| Company | SIC | EMP | PHONE | ENTRY# |
|---|---|---|---|---|
| Cpaperless LLC | 3652 | E | 949 510-3365 | 11726 |

## CORONADO, CA - San Diego County

| Company | SIC | EMP | PHONE | ENTRY# |
|---|---|---|---|---|
| Nadolife Inc | 3421 | E | 619 522-0077 | 7938 |
| Lockheed Martin Corporation | 3812 | C | 619 437-7188 | 14214 |
| Coronado Brewing Company (PA) | 5813 | E | 619 437-4452 | 17615 |
| Mariner Systems Inc (PA) | 7389 | E | 305 266-7255 | 19106 |

## CORTE MADERA, CA - Marin County

| Company | SIC | EMP | PHONE | ENTRY# |
|---|---|---|---|---|
| Pacific Catch Inc | 2048 | E | 415 504-6905 | 1143 |
| Allbirds Inc | 3143 | F | 628 266-0533 | 7096 |
| Nana Wall Systems Inc | 3442 | E | 415 383-3148 | 8280 |
| Automted Mdia Proc Sltions Inc | 4813 | E | 415 332-4343 | 16316 |
| IL Fornaio (america) LLC (HQ) | 5812 | E | 415 945-0500 | 17585 |
| Jomu Mist Incorporated | 7372 | E | 415 448-7273 | 18460 |

## COSTA MESA, CA - Orange County

| Company | SIC | EMP | PHONE | ENTRY# |
|---|---|---|---|---|
| Hexagon Agility Inc | 1321 | E | 949 236-5520 | 149 |
| Mdm Solutions LLC | 1389 | B | 800 669-6361 | 250 |
| El Metate Inc | 2051 | C | 949 646-9362 | 1190 |
| Associated Microbreweries Inc | 2082 | D | 714 546-2739 | 1420 |
| Cotton Links LLC | 2321 | E | 714 444-4700 | 2570 |
| Hurley International LLC (PA) | 2329 | C | 855 655-2515 | 2623 |
| I D Brand LLC | 2396 | E | 949 422-7057 | 3009 |
| Fxc Corporation | 2399 | D | 714 557-8032 | 3029 |
| Fineline Woodworking Inc | 2431 | D | 714 540-5468 | 3137 |
| National Appraisal Guides Inc | 2741 | E | 714 556-8511 | 4435 |
| Thomson Reuters Corporation | 2741 | E | 949 400-7782 | 4481 |
| Chup Corporation | 2752 | F | 949 455-0676 | 4550 |
| Orange Coast Reprographics Inc | 2752 | E | 949 548-5571 | 4713 |
| ID Supply | 2759 | E | 949 287-9200 | 4895 |
| Westar Nutrition Corp (PA) | 2833 | E | 949 645-6100 | 5283 |
| Atp Clinical Research Inc | 2834 | F | 714 393-0787 | 5343 |
| Bio Creative Enterprises (PA) | 2844 | E | 714 352-3600 | 5948 |
| Moleculum | 2911 | F | 714 619-5139 | 6341 |
| Toyo Tire Hldings Americas Inc (HQ) | 3011 | E | 714 229-6100 | 6413 |
| Vans Inc (DH) | 3021 | B | 714 755-4000 | 6423 |
| Tk Pax Inc | 3052 | E | 714 850-1330 | 6433 |
| Union Chemicar America Inc | 3081 | F | 949 770-7072 | 6575 |
| Vantage Associates Inc | 3088 | E | 800 995-8322 | 6687 |
| CCI Industries Inc (PA) | 3089 | E | 714 662-3879 | 6767 |
| Husky Injction Mlding Systems | 3089 | D | 714 545-8200 | 6861 |
| JG Plastics Group LLC | 3089 | E | 714 751-4266 | 6877 |
| Resinart Corporation | 3089 | E | 949 642-3665 | 7003 |
| Cevians LLC (PA) | 3211 | D | 714 619-5135 | 7167 |
| Ceradyne Esk LLC | 3299 | E | 714 549-0421 | 7589 |
| Griswold Industries (PA) | 3365 | B | 949 722-4800 | 7847 |
| Baier Marine Company Inc | 3429 | E | 800 455-3917 | 7982 |
| Fxc Corporation (PA) | 3429 | E | 714 556-7400 | 7997 |
| Winfield Locks Inc | 3429 | A | 949 722-5400 | 8038 |
| Advanced Cnsrvtion Tech Dist I | 3433 | F | 714 668-1200 | 8058 |
| Coast Sheet Metal Inc | 3444 | E | 949 645-2224 | 8411 |
| Flare Group | 3471 | E | 714 549-0202 | 8961 |
| Inveco Inc | 3471 | E | 949 378-3850 | 8975 |
| Kyocera Tycom Corporation | 3541 | B | 714 428-3600 | 9559 |
| Criterion Machine Works | 3545 | E | | 9671 |
| Shurflo LLC | 3561 | B | 714 371-1550 | 9940 |
| Universal Motion Components Co Inc | 3566 | E | 714 437-9600 | 10045 |
| Walin Group Inc | 3569 | E | 714 444-5980 | 10120 |
| International Bus Mchs Corp | 3571 | E | 714 472-2237 | 10168 |
| Delphi Display Systems Inc | 3577 | D | 714 825-3400 | 10357 |
| Dynamic Cooking Systems Inc | 3589 | A | 714 372-7000 | 10556 |
| Darcy AK Corporation | 3599 | F | 949 650-5566 | 10799 |
| Swiss Wire EDM | 3599 | E | 714 540-2903 | 11131 |
| Balboa Water Group LLC (HQ) | 3625 | D | 714 384-0384 | 11311 |
| Fisher & Paykel Appliances Inc (DH) | 3639 | E | 949 790-8900 | 11418 |
| Candle Lamp Holdings LLC | 3641 | B | 951 682-9600 | 11422 |

Employee Codes: A=Over 500 employees, B=251-500, C=101-250, D=51-100, E=20-50, F=10-19, G=1-9

## COSTA MESA, CA

| | SIC | EMP | PHONE | ENTRY# |
|---|---|---|---|---|
| Flexfire Leds Inc | 3646 | E | 925 273-9080 | 11532 |
| Qsc LLC (PA) | 3651 | C | 800 854-4079 | 11689 |
| Bdfco Inc | 3669 | D | 714 228-2900 | 11983 |
| Honeywell SEC Americas LLC | 3669 | D | 949 737-7800 | 11999 |
| Npi Services Inc | 3672 | F | 714 850-0550 | 12179 |
| Sanmina Corporation | 3672 | D | 714 371-2800 | 12211 |
| Sanmina Corporation | 3672 | E | 714 913-2200 | 12214 |
| Irvine Sensors Corporation | 3674 | E | 714 444-8700 | 12505 |
| Labarge/Stc Inc | 3674 | E | 281 207-1400 | 12522 |
| Semicoa Corporation | 3674 | E | 714 979-1900 | 12689 |
| Newmar Power LLC | 3675 | C | 800 854-3906 | 12821 |
| Sabritec | 3678 | B | 714 371-1100 | 12896 |
| Technical Cable Concepts Inc | 3679 | E | 714 835-1081 | 13100 |
| Target Technology Company LLC | 3695 | E | 949 788-0909 | 13203 |
| Isc8 Inc | 3699 | E | 714 549-8211 | 13256 |
| Schneider Electric | 3699 | E | 949 713-9200 | 13304 |
| Fisker Automotive Inc | 3711 | D | | 13350 |
| Ducommun Aerostructures Inc (HQ) | 3724 | B | 310 380-5390 | 13706 |
| Ducommun Incorporated (PA) | 3728 | C | 657 335-3665 | 13831 |
| Flare Group | 3728 | E | 714 850-2080 | 13840 |
| Vantage Associates Inc | 3728 | E | 562 968-1400 | 13986 |
| Maurer Marine Inc | 3732 | F | 949 645-7673 | 14041 |
| Vantage Associates Inc (PA) | 3769 | E | 619 477-6940 | 14117 |
| Anduril Industries Inc (PA) | 3812 | A | 949 891-1607 | 14142 |
| Lambda Research Optics Inc | 3826 | E | 714 327-0600 | 14682 |
| Optosigma Corporation | 3827 | E | 949 851-5881 | 14810 |
| Safran Defense & Space Inc | 3827 | D | 603 296-0469 | 14820 |
| Sellers Optical Inc | 3827 | E | 949 631-6800 | 14823 |
| Advanced Micro Instruments Inc | 3829 | E | 714 848-5533 | 14840 |
| Newport Medical Instrs Inc | 3841 | D | 949 642-3910 | 15205 |
| Phillps-Mdisize Costa Mesa LLC | 3841 | C | 949 477-9495 | 15224 |
| Sweden & Martina Inc | 3841 | E | 844 862-7846 | 15273 |
| Caperon Designs Inc | 3944 | F | 714 552-3201 | 15743 |
| Rip Curl Inc (DH) | 3949 | D | 714 422-3600 | 15846 |
| Hartley Company | 3951 | E | 949 646-9643 | 15881 |
| Pro-Lite Inc | 3993 | F | 714 668-9988 | 16023 |
| Flora Gold Corporation (PA) | 3999 | A | 949 252-1908 | 16130 |
| Orange County Components Inc | 5065 | F | 714 979-3597 | 16727 |
| Schurman Fine Papers | 5084 | E | 714 549-0212 | 16840 |
| Western Refining Inc | 5084 | D | 714 708-2200 | 16861 |
| Viva Life Science Inc | 5122 | C | 949 645-6100 | 17054 |
| Grand Prix Road Trends Inc (PA) | 5531 | F | 949 645-7022 | 17452 |
| 511 Inc (DH) | 5699 | E | 866 451-1726 | 17506 |
| Fgr 1 LLC | 5812 | E | 800 653-3517 | 17579 |
| Marshall Advertising and Design Inc | 7311 | E | 714 545-5757 | 17780 |
| Meridianlink Inc (PA) | 7371 | D | 714 708-6950 | 17948 |
| Touchtone Corporation | 7371 | E | 714 755-2810 | 17988 |
| Nwp Services Corporation (DH) | 7372 | C | 949 253-2500 | 18607 |
| Savedaily Inc | 7372 | F | 562 795-7500 | 18761 |
| Filenet Corporation | 7373 | A | 800 345-3638 | 18974 |
| Benrich Service Company Inc (PA) | 7389 | E | 714 241-0284 | 19076 |
| Simple Science Inc | 7389 | E | 949 335-1099 | 19130 |
| Volcom LLC (HQ) | 7389 | C | 949 646-2175 | 19142 |
| Tarulli Tire Inc (PA) | 7534 | E | 714 630-4722 | 19155 |
| Kone Inc | 7699 | E | 714 890-7080 | 19266 |

## COTATI, CA - Sonoma County

| | SIC | EMP | PHONE | ENTRY# |
|---|---|---|---|---|
| Barlow and Sons Printing Inc | 2752 | F | 707 664-9773 | 4527 |
| Ebac Investments Inc | 3273 | E | 707 792-4695 | 7443 |
| Biotherm Hydronic Inc | 3433 | F | 707 794-9660 | 8061 |
| J&M Manufacturing Inc | 3679 | E | 707 795-8223 | 13009 |
| Goode Printing and Mailing LLC | 7331 | E | 707 588-8028 | 17799 |

## COTTONWOOD, CA - Shasta County

| | SIC | EMP | PHONE | ENTRY# |
|---|---|---|---|---|
| Plum Valley Inc | 2421 | E | 530 262-6262 | 3075 |
| Borden Manufacturing | 3542 | E | 530 347-6642 | 9580 |

## COVELO, CA - Mendocino County

| | SIC | EMP | PHONE | ENTRY# |
|---|---|---|---|---|
| Wylatti Resource MGT Inc | 2411 | E | 707 983-8135 | 3063 |

## COVINA, CA - Los Angeles County

| | SIC | EMP | PHONE | ENTRY# |
|---|---|---|---|---|
| Mfi Construction Inc | 1751 | E | 626 565-2015 | 497 |
| RG Costumes & Accessories Inc | 2389 | E | 626 858-9559 | 2909 |
| Shift Calendars Inc | 2752 | F | 626 967-5862 | 4762 |
| Ink Fx Corporation | 2759 | F | 909 673-1950 | 4898 |
| Matrix Document Imaging Inc | 2759 | F | 626 966-9959 | 4921 |
| Composites Horizons LLC (DH) | 2821 | C | 626 331-0861 | 5147 |
| Chemeor Inc | 2843 | F | 626 966-3808 | 5935 |
| Anvil Cases Inc | 3161 | C | 626 968-4100 | 7126 |
| Stabile Plating Company Inc | 3471 | E | 626 339-9091 | 9016 |
| Caco-Pacific Corporation (PA) | 3544 | C | 626 331-3361 | 9608 |
| Dauntless Industries Inc | 3544 | F | 626 966-4494 | 9616 |
| R M Baker Machine and Tl Inc | 3599 | F | 562 697-4007 | 11065 |
| Cobel Technologies Inc | 3613 | F | 626 332-2100 | 11237 |
| Payne Magnetics Corporation | 3677 | D | 626 332-6207 | 12851 |
| TT Elctrnics Pwr Sltons US Inc | 3679 | E | 626 967-6021 | 13112 |
| Cozzia USA LLC (HQ) | 3699 | F | 626 667-2272 | 13227 |
| Azusa Engineering Inc | 3714 | F | 626 966-4071 | 13463 |
| Composites Horizons LLC | 3728 | E | 626 331-0861 | 13813 |
| Moores Ideal Products LLC | 3944 | E | 626 339-9007 | 15761 |
| AR Industries | 3999 | F | 626 332-8918 | 16087 |
| Bright Glow Candle Company Inc (PA) | 3999 | E | 909 469-4733 | 16098 |
| Norlaine Inc | 3999 | C | 626 961-2471 | 16189 |
| American Scale Co Inc | 5045 | E | 800 773-7225 | 16506 |
| Instrumentl Inc | 7372 | E | 909 258-9291 | 18422 |
| Klentysoft Inc | 7372 | C | 707 518-9640 | 18474 |
| Stavros Enterprises Inc | 7699 | E | 888 463-2293 | 19282 |

## CRESCENT CITY, CA - Del Norte County

| | SIC | EMP | PHONE | ENTRY# |
|---|---|---|---|---|
| Rumiano Cheese Co | 2022 | E | 707 465-1535 | 733 |
| Smith River Brewing Company (PA) | 5813 | E | 707 465-4444 | 17623 |

## CROCKETT, CA - Contra Costa County

| | SIC | EMP | PHONE | ENTRY# |
|---|---|---|---|---|
| C&H Sugar Company Inc | 2063 | A | 510 787-2121 | 1295 |

## CROWS LANDING, CA - Stanislaus County

| | SIC | EMP | PHONE | ENTRY# |
|---|---|---|---|---|
| Darling Ingredients Inc | 2077 | E | 209 667-9153 | 1384 |

## CUDAHY, CA - Los Angeles County

| | SIC | EMP | PHONE | ENTRY# |
|---|---|---|---|---|
| Mfb Worldwide Inc (PA) | 2299 | F | 323 562-2339 | 2549 |
| RAP Security Inc | 2542 | D | 323 560-3493 | 3702 |
| Day-Glo Color Corp | 2816 | E | 323 560-2000 | 5061 |
| Consolidated Foundries Inc | 3365 | C | 323 773-2363 | 7840 |
| Myers Mixers LLC | 3569 | E | 323 560-4723 | 10100 |
| Merry An Cejka | 3599 | E | 323 560-3949 | 10972 |
| Super Center Concepts Inc | 5411 | C | 323 562-8980 | 17388 |

## CULVER CITY, CA - Los Angeles County

| | SIC | EMP | PHONE | ENTRY# |
|---|---|---|---|---|
| Miracle Greens Inc | 2023 | F | 800 521-5867 | 768 |
| Farchitecture Bb LLC | 2024 | E | 917 701-2777 | 800 |
| Ppd Holding LLC (PA) | 2326 | D | 310 733-2100 | 2601 |
| Sportsrobe Inc | 2329 | E | 310 559-3999 | 2642 |
| Fortune Casuals LLC (PA) | 2331 | D | 310 733-2100 | 2665 |
| Paige LLC (HQ) | 2331 | C | 310 733-2100 | 2686 |
| Metric Products Inc (PA) | 2342 | E | 310 815-9000 | 2838 |
| Parachute Home Inc | 2392 | C | 310 903-0353 | 2946 |
| Fringe Studio LLC | 2621 | E | 310 390-9900 | 3769 |
| Express Press | 2741 | E | 424 228-2261 | 4396 |
| Stories International Inc | 2741 | E | 310 242-8409 | 4471 |
| Econ-O-Plate Inc | 2752 | F | 310 342-5900 | 4601 |
| Cambridge Equities LP | 2836 | E | 858 350-2300 | 5812 |
| Henkel US Operations Corp | 2844 | E | 626 321-4100 | 5987 |
| Joico Laboratories Inc | 2844 | E | 626 321-4100 | 5995 |
| Sole Society Group Inc | 3131 | C | 310 220-0808 | 7093 |
| Spotlite America Corporation (PA) | 3229 | E | 310 829-0200 | 7205 |
| Magnet Sales & Mfg Co Inc (HQ) | 3264 | D | 310 391-7213 | 7284 |
| Integrated Tech Group Inc (PA) | 3499 | E | 310 391-7213 | 9288 |
| Borin Manufacturing Inc | 3561 | E | 310 822-1000 | 9916 |
| Pacific Piston Ring Co Inc | 3592 | D | 310 836-3322 | 10622 |
| Chargie LLC | 3621 | E | 310 621-0024 | 11259 |
| CMI Integrated Tech Inc | 3621 | E | | 11260 |
| Integrated Magnetics Inc | 3621 | E | 310 391-7213 | 11273 |
| Spotlite Power Corporation | 3646 | E | 310 838-2367 | 11558 |
| Beats Electronics LLC | 3651 | B | 424 326-4679 | 11643 |
| Apic Corporation | 3674 | D | 310 642-7975 | 12311 |
| Loaded Boards Inc | 3751 | F | 310 839-1800 | 14063 |
| Moldex-Metric Inc | 3842 | B | 310 837-6500 | 15384 |
| Given Imaging Los Angeles LLC | 3845 | C | 310 641-8492 | 15540 |
| Sony Pictures Entrmt Inc | 3861 | E | 310 244-4000 | 15666 |
| Topson Downs California LLC (PA) | 5621 | C | 310 558-0300 | 17497 |
| Jam City Inc (PA) | 5734 | E | 310 205-4800 | 17553 |
| Snail Inc (PA) | 7371 | E | 310 988-0643 | 17979 |
| Chownow Inc (PA) | 7372 | D | 888 707-2469 | 18167 |
| Liveoffice LLC | 7372 | E | 877 253-2793 | 18499 |
| Scopely Inc (DH) | 7372 | C | 323 400-6618 | 18766 |
| Spring Technologies Corp | 7372 | E | 310 230-4000 | 18826 |
| Sony Media Cloud Services LLC | 7812 | E | 877 683-9124 | 19297 |
| Davina Douthard Inc | 8748 | F | 310 540-5120 | 19557 |

## CUPERTINO, CA - Santa Clara County

| | SIC | EMP | PHONE | ENTRY# |
|---|---|---|---|---|
| Stevens Creek Quarry Inc (PA) | 1611 | D | 408 253-2512 | 382 |
| Es Operating Co | 2869 | F | | 6145 |
| Lehigh Southwest Cement Co | 3241 | E | 408 996-4271 | 7257 |
| Greenvolts Inc | 3433 | D | 415 963-4030 | 8068 |
| Hantronix Inc | 3559 | E | 408 252-1100 | 9862 |
| Seagate Technology LLC | 3572 | B | 405 324-4799 | 10278 |

# GEOGRAPHIC SECTION

## DIAMOND BAR, CA

| Company | SIC | EMP | PHONE | ENTRY# |
|---|---|---|---|---|
| Seagate US LLC | 3572 | F | 408 658-1000 | 10281 |
| West Coast Venture Capital LLC **(PA)** | 3661 | D | 408 725-0700 | 11794 |
| Amino Technologies (us) LLC **(HQ)** | 3663 | E | 408 861-1400 | 11805 |
| Anacom Inc | 3663 | E | 408 519-2062 | 11808 |
| Apple Inc **(PA)** | 3663 | A | 408 996-1010 | 11812 |
| Ventana Micro Systems Inc | 3674 | F | 408 816-8852 | 12783 |
| Marian Inc | 3699 | E | 408 645-5355 | 13270 |
| Cardeon Corporation | 3841 | E | 408 253-3319 | 15026 |
| General Surgical Innovations | 3841 | E | 408 863-2500 | 15099 |
| Bil-Jax Inc | 3999 | D | 408 446-2308 | 16096 |
| Trend Micro Incorporated | 5045 | B | 408 257-1500 | 16560 |
| Posh Bakery Inc | 5461 | C | 408 980-8451 | 17418 |
| Falkonry Inc | 7371 | D | 408 761-7108 | 17917 |
| Integem | 7371 | E | 408 459-0657 | 17932 |
| Ecrio Inc | 7372 | D | 408 973-7290 | 18260 |
| Efinix Inc **(PA)** | 7372 | E | 408 789-6917 | 18266 |
| Eos Software Inc | 7372 | E | 408 439-2903 | 18284 |
| Foxpass Inc | 7372 | F | 415 805-6350 | 18328 |
| Indium Software Inc | 7372 | E | 408 501-8844 | 18408 |
| Visualon Inc **(PA)** | 7372 | E | 408 645-6618 | 18923 |
| Vnomic Inc | 7372 | E | 408 641-3810 | 18926 |
| Optofidelity Inc | 8711 | E | 669 241-8383 | 19409 |

### CYPRESS, CA - Orange County

| Company | SIC | EMP | PHONE | ENTRY# |
|---|---|---|---|---|
| Lt Foods Americas Inc **(HQ)** | 2041 | F | 562 340-4040 | 1061 |
| Simply Fresh LLC | 2092 | C | 714 562-5000 | 2063 |
| Shaw Industries Group Inc | 2273 | E | 562 430-4445 | 2520 |
| Speedo USA Inc | 2329 | E | 657 465-3800 | 2639 |
| Manhattan Beachwear LLC **(PA)** | 2369 | D | 657 384-2110 | 2865 |
| Exemplis LLC **(PA)** | 2522 | E | 714 995-4800 | 3602 |
| X-Chair LLC | 2522 | E | 844 492-4247 | 3610 |
| Johnson Controls Inc | 2531 | E | 562 594-3200 | 3628 |
| Creative Teaching Press Inc **(PA)** | 2731 | D | 714 799-2100 | 4324 |
| Primary Color Systems Corp **(PA)** | 2759 | B | 949 660-7080 | 4941 |
| Venus Laboratories Inc | 2819 | E | 714 891-3100 | 5129 |
| Diasorin Molecular LLC | 2835 | C | 562 240-6500 | 5749 |
| Merger Sub Gotham 2 LLC | 3089 | C | 714 462-4603 | 6911 |
| Plastic Molded Components Inc | 3089 | E | 714 229-0133 | 6961 |
| Rolls-Royce High Temperature Composites Inc | 3299 | E | 714 375-4085 | 7600 |
| Dameron Alloy Foundries **(PA)** | 3325 | D | 310 631-5165 | 7698 |
| Hyatt Die Cast and Engineering Corp **(PA)** | 3363 | D | 714 826-7550 | 7809 |
| Hilti US Manufacturing Inc | 3425 | E | 714 230-7410 | 7969 |
| Power - Trim Co | 3524 | F | 714 523-8560 | 9398 |
| Cavotec Inet US Inc | 3531 | D | 714 947-0005 | 9415 |
| Cavotec US Holdings Inc **(HQ)** | 3532 | F | 714 545-7900 | 9448 |
| Power Pt Inc | 3537 | E | 714 826-7407 | 9530 |
| OK International Inc **(DH)** | 3548 | C | 714 799-9910 | 9728 |
| Seabiscuit Motorsports Inc | 3592 | E | 714 898-9763 | 10626 |
| J & F Machine Inc | 3599 | E | 714 527-3499 | 10894 |
| Magna Tool Inc | 3599 | E | 714 826-2500 | 10955 |
| Hitachi Automotive Systems | 3621 | D | 310 212-0200 | 11272 |
| Scientfic Applctons RES Assoc **(PA)** | 3629 | D | 714 224-4410 | 11380 |
| Luma Comfort LLC | 3634 | E | 855 963-9247 | 11408 |
| Mission Microwave Tech LLC **(PA)** | 3663 | D | 951 893-4925 | 11894 |
| Yaesu Usa Inc | 3663 | E | 714 827-7600 | 11981 |
| Optex Incorporated | 3669 | E | 800 966-7839 | 12006 |
| Drs Ntwork Imaging Systems LLC | 3674 | D | 714 220-3800 | 12408 |
| Weldex Corporation | 3674 | B | 714 761-2100 | 12803 |
| Mitsubshi Elc Vsual Sltons AME | 3679 | C | 800 553-7278 | 13039 |
| Pratt & Whitney Eng Svcs Inc | 3724 | A | 714 373-0110 | 13718 |
| Cavotec Dabico US Inc | 3728 | E | 714 947-0005 | 13808 |
| Inet Airport Systems Inc | 3728 | E | 714 888-2700 | 13871 |
| Safran Cabin Inc | 3728 | E | 562 344-4780 | 13948 |
| Tayco Engineering Inc | 3761 | E | 714 952-2240 | 14093 |
| Dentis USA Corporation | 3843 | E | 323 677-4363 | 15450 |
| Christie Medical Holdings Inc | 3845 | E | 714 236-8610 | 15525 |
| Christie Digital Systems Inc **(HQ)** | 3861 | D | 714 236-8610 | 15634 |
| Fujifilm Rcrding Media USA Inc | 3861 | D | 310 536-0800 | 15641 |
| Paradigm Contract Mfg LLC | 3999 | F | 714 889-7074 | 16195 |
| Atg - Designing Mobility Inc **(DH)** | 5047 | E | 562 921-0258 | 16574 |
| Multiquip Inc **(DH)** | 5063 | B | 310 537-3700 | 16665 |
| Interntionl Tech Systems Corp | 5065 | E | 714 761-8886 | 16706 |
| Mitsubishi Electric Us Inc **(DH)** | 5065 | C | 714 220-2500 | 16721 |
| ME & My Big Ideas LLC | 5092 | E | 240 348-5240 | 16949 |
| Real Mex Foods Inc | 5141 | D | 714 523-0031 | 17118 |
| Eno Brands Inc | 5944 | E | 714 220-1318 | 17645 |
| DAndrea Vsual Cmmncations LLC | 7336 | D | 714 947-8444 | 17825 |

### DALY CITY, CA - San Mateo County

| Company | SIC | EMP | PHONE | ENTRY# |
|---|---|---|---|---|
| View Rite Manufacturing | 2541 | E | 415 468-3856 | 3676 |
| Dna Script Inc | 3826 | E | 650 457-0844 | 14652 |

### DANA POINT, CA - Orange County

| Company | SIC | EMP | PHONE | ENTRY# |
|---|---|---|---|---|
| Tiger Business Holdings Inc | 3672 | F | 714 763-4180 | 12240 |
| Kanstul Musical Instrs Inc | 3931 | E | 714 563-1000 | 15719 |
| Nawgan Products LLC | 5149 | F | 949 542-4425 | 17199 |
| Pacific Asian Enterprises Inc **(PA)** | 7389 | E | 949 496-4848 | 19114 |

### DANVILLE, CA - Contra Costa County

| Company | SIC | EMP | PHONE | ENTRY# |
|---|---|---|---|---|
| Heathorn & Assoc Contrs Inc | 1711 | E | 510 351-7578 | 423 |
| Powersphyr Inc | 3568 | E | 925 736-8299 | 10073 |
| Amber Semiconductor Inc | 3674 | E | 510 364-4680 | 12298 |
| Bradley Tanks Inc | 3795 | E | 925 831-3562 | 14124 |
| Razvi Inc | 7374 | E | 925 242-1200 | 19012 |

### DARWIN, CA - Inyo County

| Company | SIC | EMP | PHONE | ENTRY# |
|---|---|---|---|---|
| Inyoag LLC | 1081 | E | 775 427-8345 | 107 |

### DAVENPORT, CA - Santa Cruz County

| Company | SIC | EMP | PHONE | ENTRY# |
|---|---|---|---|---|
| Big Creek Lumber Company **(PA)** | 5211 | D | 831 457-5015 | 17322 |

### DAVIS, CA - Yolo County

| Company | SIC | EMP | PHONE | ENTRY# |
|---|---|---|---|---|
| Hmclause Inc **(DH)** | 0181 | C | 800 320-4672 | 49 |
| Riki Fashion Inc | 2331 | F | 530 756-8048 | 2688 |
| McNaughton Newspapers | 2711 | E | 530 756-0800 | 4155 |
| Antibodies Incorporated | 2835 | F | 800 824-8540 | 5738 |
| Expression Systems LLC **(PA)** | 2836 | E | 877 877-7421 | 5829 |
| Pro Farm Group Inc **(PA)** | 2879 | C | 530 750-2800 | 6205 |
| FMC Technologies Inc | 3533 | E | 530 753-6718 | 9462 |
| Dmg Mori Manufacturing USA Inc **(HQ)** | 3541 | D | 530 746-7400 | 9549 |
| Dmg Mori Manufacturing USA Inc | 3541 | D | 530 746-3140 | 9550 |
| Dmg Mori Digital Tech Lab Corp | 3545 | D | 530 746-7400 | 9675 |
| Elve Inc | 3663 | F | 734 846-2705 | 11849 |
| Resonetics LLC | 3699 | F | 603 886-6772 | 13298 |
| Sudwerk Privatbrauerei Hubsch | 5812 | F | 530 756-2739 | 17607 |
| Clarifi Technologies Inc | 7372 | F | 866 997-2643 | 18170 |
| Schilling Robotics LLC | 8711 | E | 530 753-6718 | 19418 |
| Schilling Robotics LLC **(DH)** | 8711 | E | 530 753-6718 | 19419 |

### DEL MAR, CA - San Diego County

| Company | SIC | EMP | PHONE | ENTRY# |
|---|---|---|---|---|
| Fine Magazine | 2721 | F | 858 261-0963 | 4255 |
| Evome Medical Technologies Inc **(PA)** | 3841 | F | 800 760-6826 | 15085 |
| Del Mar Blue Print Co Inc | 7334 | E | 858 755-5134 | 17809 |

### DEL REY, CA - Fresno County

| Company | SIC | EMP | PHONE | ENTRY# |
|---|---|---|---|---|
| Chooljian & Sons Inc **(PA)** | 0723 | E | 559 888-2031 | 79 |
| Cy Truss | 2439 | E | 559 888-2160 | 3305 |
| Chooljian & Sons Inc | 3556 | E | 559 888-2031 | 9784 |

### DELANO, CA - Kern County

| Company | SIC | EMP | PHONE | ENTRY# |
|---|---|---|---|---|
| Wonderful Company LLC | 0174 | B | 661 720-2400 | 42 |
| Munger Bros LLC | 0179 | A | 661 721-0390 | 46 |
| Wonderful Citrus Packing LLC **(HQ)** | 0723 | B | 661 720-2400 | 90 |
| Ayo Foods LLC | 2026 | E | 661 345-5457 | 825 |
| Wonderful Citrus Packing LLC | 2033 | F | 661 720-2400 | 942 |
| Asv Wines Inc **(PA)** | 2084 | F | 661 792-3159 | 1480 |
| Delano Growers Grape Products | 2087 | D | 661 725-3255 | 1997 |
| Styrotek Inc | 3086 | E | 661 725-4957 | 6665 |
| Anthony Welded Products Inc **(PA)** | 3537 | E | 661 721-7211 | 9507 |
| City of Delano | 3589 | E | 661 721-3352 | 10547 |
| Mrv Service Air Inc | 7623 | E | 661 725-3400 | 19172 |
| Crowne Cold Storage LLC | 8742 | E | 661 725-6458 | 19525 |

### DENAIR, CA - Stanislaus County

| Company | SIC | EMP | PHONE | ENTRY# |
|---|---|---|---|---|
| Monte Vista Farming Co LLC | 0173 | E | 209 874-1866 | 40 |
| Valley Fresh Foods Inc | 0252 | E | 209 669-5510 | 66 |
| California Royale LLC | 0723 | E | 209 874-1866 | 76 |
| Woodys Poultry Supply | 1542 | E | 209 634-2948 | 372 |
| Central Valley Concrete Inc | 1711 | E | 209 667-0161 | 410 |

### DESERT HOT SPRINGS, CA - Riverside County

| Company | SIC | EMP | PHONE | ENTRY# |
|---|---|---|---|---|
| Dreamfields California LLC | 2671 | E | 310 691-9739 | 3926 |
| Western Golf Car Mfg Inc | 3949 | D | 760 671-6691 | 15877 |

### DIAMOND BAR, CA - Los Angeles County

| Company | SIC | EMP | PHONE | ENTRY# |
|---|---|---|---|---|
| Genius Products Nt Inc | 2086 | C | 510 671-0219 | 1889 |
| Dynamic Woodworks Inc | 2431 | F | 562 483-8400 | 3132 |
| Rapid Rack Holdings Inc | 2542 | A | | 3703 |
| Rapid Rack Industries Inc | 2542 | D | | 3704 |
| Sappi North America Inc | 2621 | E | 714 456-0600 | 3796 |
| Ultra Chem Labs Corp | 2842 | F | 909 605-1640 | 5933 |
| Prime Wire & Cable Inc **(HQ)** | 3357 | E | 888 445-9955 | 7793 |
| Simplex Supplies Inc | 3441 | E | 618 594-6450 | 8216 |
| Gohz Inc | 3621 | E | 800 603-1219 | 11271 |
| Ultimate Sound Inc | 3651 | B | 909 861-6200 | 11708 |

Employee Codes: A=Over 500 employees, B=251-500, C=101-250, D=51-100, E=20-50, F=10-19, G=1-9

# DIAMOND BAR, CA

| | SIC | EMP | PHONE | ENTRY# |
|---|---|---|---|---|
| Ecmm Services Inc. | 3955 | C | 714 988-9388 | 15895 |
| Motech Americas LLC | 8731 | B | 302 451-7500 | 19469 |

## DIAMOND SPRINGS, CA - El Dorado County

| | SIC | EMP | PHONE | ENTRY# |
|---|---|---|---|---|
| Demtech Services Inc. | 3089 | E | 530 621-3200 | 6799 |
| McDaniel Manufacturing Inc. | 3429 | F | 530 626-6336 | 8014 |
| Western Sign Company Inc. | 3993 | E | 916 933-3765 | 16067 |

## DINUBA, CA - Tulare County

| | SIC | EMP | PHONE | ENTRY# |
|---|---|---|---|---|
| Warren & Baerg Mfg Inc | 3523 | E | 559 591-6790 | 9392 |
| Packline Technologies Inc. | 3565 | E | 559 591-3150 | 10028 |
| Presort Center of Fresno LLC | 7331 | E | 559 498-6151 | 17802 |
| Integrated Voting Systems Inc. | 7389 | E | 559 498-0281 | 19097 |

## DISCOVERY BAY, CA - Contra Costa County

| | SIC | EMP | PHONE | ENTRY# |
|---|---|---|---|---|
| MSF Inc. | 2542 | F | 650 592-0239 | 3698 |

## DIXON, CA - Solano County

| | SIC | EMP | PHONE | ENTRY# |
|---|---|---|---|---|
| Bellingham Marine Inds Inc. | 1629 | E | 707 678-2385 | 393 |
| Greiner Heating Air & Elc Inc. | 1711 | E | 707 678-1784 | 422 |
| Ellensburg Lamb Company Inc. | 2011 | D | 707 678-3091 | 594 |
| Transhumance Holding Co Inc. | 2011 | E | 707 693-2303 | 619 |
| Gold Star Foods Inc. | 2099 | E | 909 843-9600 | 2218 |
| Salad Cosmo USA Corporation | 2099 | E | 707 678-6633 | 2347 |
| Hemostat Laboratories Inc (PA) | 2836 | E | 707 678-9594 | 5837 |
| Grow West LLC | 2873 | E | 707 678-5542 | 6173 |
| INX International Ink Co. | 2893 | E | 707 693-2990 | 6259 |
| Cardinal Glass Industries Inc. | 3231 | C | 323 319-0070 | 7214 |
| Castlelite Block LLC (PA) | 3271 | E | 707 678-3465 | 7294 |
| Cemex Materials LLC | 3273 | D | 707 678-4311 | 7426 |
| Altec Industries Inc. | 3531 | E | 707 678-0800 | 9405 |
| Altec Industries Inc. | 3531 | E | 707 678-0800 | 9406 |
| Global Rental Co Inc. | 3531 | C | 707 693-2520 | 9423 |
| J & A Jeffery Inc. | 3999 | E | 707 678-0369 | 16153 |
| Carlisle Construction Mtls LLC | 5033 | D | 707 678-6900 | 16490 |
| Sr Shroeder Inc. | 5571 | E | 707 693-8166 | 17485 |

## DOS PALOS, CA - Merced County

| | SIC | EMP | PHONE | ENTRY# |
|---|---|---|---|---|
| Sherrill M Campbell Corporation | 7692 | F | 209 392-6103 | 19213 |

## DOWNEY, CA - Los Angeles County

| | SIC | EMP | PHONE | ENTRY# |
|---|---|---|---|---|
| Ocinet Inc. | 2035 | F | 213 280-0989 | 986 |
| Reyes Coca-Cola Bottling LLC | 2086 | D | 562 803-8100 | 1935 |
| Instant Web LLC | 2752 | C | 562 658-2020 | 4649 |
| Jeb-Phi Inc. | 2752 | F | 562 861-0863 | 4657 |
| Storopack Inc. | 2821 | F | 562 803-5582 | 5206 |
| Hutchinson Seal Corporation (DH) | 3053 | C | 248 375-4190 | 6452 |
| Bradley Manufacturing Co Inc. | 3089 | E | 562 923-5556 | 6751 |
| V-T Industries Inc. | 3089 | D | 714 521-2008 | 7068 |
| Umc Acquisition Corp (PA) | 3356 | E | 562 940-0300 | 7768 |
| Universal Molding Company (HQ) | 3356 | C | 310 886-1750 | 7769 |
| Thompson Tank Inc. | 3443 | F | 562 869-7711 | 8347 |
| Cal Pipe Manufacturing Inc (PA) | 3498 | E | 562 803-4388 | 9252 |
| MD Stainless Services | 3498 | E | 562 904-7022 | 9266 |
| Detroit Diesel Corporation | 3519 | D | 562 929-7016 | 9327 |
| Downey Grinding Co. | 3541 | E | 562 803-5556 | 9553 |
| United California Corporation | 3544 | E | 562 803-1521 | 9653 |
| United Drill Bushing Corp. | 3545 | C | 562 803-1521 | 9704 |
| Can Lines Engineering Inc (PA) | 3565 | D | 562 861-2996 | 10016 |
| Wesfac Inc (HQ) | 3589 | F | 562 861-2160 | 10613 |
| Vantage Point Products Corp (PA) | 3651 | E | 562 946-1718 | 11711 |
| Commercial Truck Eqp Co LLC | 3713 | D | 562 803-4466 | 13403 |
| Ebus Inc. | 3713 | F | 562 904-3474 | 13410 |
| Kf Fiberglass Inc (PA) | 3714 | F | 562 869-1536 | 13524 |
| World Water Inc. | 3823 | E | 562 940-1964 | 14469 |
| California Ribbon Carbn Co Inc. | 3955 | D | 323 724-9100 | 15893 |
| Advanced Building Systems Inc. | 3999 | E | 818 652-4252 | 16081 |
| Unbrako LLC. | 5072 | E | 310 817-2400 | 16764 |
| Keyline Sales Inc. | 5074 | E | 562 904-3910 | 16769 |
| Market Fixtures Unlimited Inc (PA) | 5078 | F | 562 803-5553 | 16785 |
| Qualls Stud Welding Pdts Inc. | 5084 | E | 562 923-7883 | 16835 |
| Rockview Dairies Inc (PA) | 5149 | C | 562 927-5511 | 17209 |
| Leach Grain & Milling Co Inc. | 5191 | E | 562 869-4451 | 17273 |
| Florence Meat Packing Co Inc. | 5812 | E | 562 401-0760 | 17580 |
| Jobsite Stud Welding | 7692 | E | 855 885-7883 | 19205 |

## DUARTE, CA - Los Angeles County

| | SIC | EMP | PHONE | ENTRY# |
|---|---|---|---|---|
| Prolacta Bioscience Inc. | 2023 | B | 626 599-9260 | 780 |
| Soyfoods of America | 2099 | E | 626 358-3836 | 2359 |
| Cosmo Fiber Corporation (PA) | 2759 | E | 626 256-6098 | 4867 |
| Justice Bros Dist Co Inc. | 2843 | E | 626 359-9174 | 5938 |
| Onex Rf Inc. | 3548 | E | 626 358-6639 | 9729 |
| Assembly Automation Industries | 3599 | E | 626 303-2777 | 10723 |
| Delafield Corporation (PA) | 3599 | C | 626 303-0740 | 10803 |
| Accu-Sembly Inc. | 3672 | D | 626 357-3447 | 12040 |
| Woodward Hrt Inc. | 3728 | E | 626 359-9211 | 13993 |
| Sportifeye Optics Inc. | 3851 | E | 877 742-5000 | 15618 |
| Victory Sportswear Inc. | 5199 | E | 866 308-0798 | 17314 |
| Tanner Research Inc. | 8731 | E | 626 471-9700 | 19478 |

## DUBLIN, CA - Alameda County

| | SIC | EMP | PHONE | ENTRY# |
|---|---|---|---|---|
| Oliver De Silva Inc (PA) | 1429 | E | 925 829-9220 | 303 |
| A A Label Inc (PA) | 2679 | E | 925 803-5709 | 4027 |
| AMP Printing Inc. | 2752 | D | 925 556-9000 | 4512 |
| JAMES ALLYN INC. | 2752 | F | | 4656 |
| Select Imaging LLC | 2752 | F | 925 803-1210 | 4761 |
| Print Ink LLC. | 2759 | F | 925 829-3950 | 4943 |
| Immunoscience LLC | 2835 | D | 925 400-6055 | 5756 |
| Interntnal Ptro Pdts Addtves I. | 2992 | F | 925 556-5530 | 6395 |
| Ipac Inc. | 2992 | F | 925 556-5530 | 6396 |
| Kensington Laboratories LLC (PA) | 3625 | F | 510 324-0126 | 11330 |
| Carl Zeiss Meditec Inc (DH) | 3827 | F | 925 557-4100 | 14766 |
| Carl Zeiss Ophthalmic Systems | 3827 | F | 925 557-4100 | 14768 |
| Onyx Optics Inc. | 3827 | E | 925 833-1969 | 14806 |
| R2 Technologies Inc. | 3841 | E | 925 378-4400 | 15237 |
| Zeltiq Aesthetics Inc. | 3841 | C | 925 474-2519 | 15312 |
| Carl Ziss X-Ray Microscopy Inc. | 3844 | C | 925 701-3600 | 15500 |
| Edcast LLC (DH) | 7372 | E | 844 833-2278 | 18261 |
| Epicor Software Corporation | 7372 | E | 949 585-4000 | 18285 |
| Medeanalytics Inc. | 7372 | E | 925 248-8118 | 18533 |
| Oracle Taleo LLC (HQ) | 7372 | D | 925 452-3000 | 18647 |
| Saba Software Inc (DH) | 7372 | D | 877 722-2101 | 18749 |
| Sybase Inc (DH) | 7372 | E | 925 236-5000 | 18857 |

## DUNSMUIR, CA - Siskiyou County

| | SIC | EMP | PHONE | ENTRY# |
|---|---|---|---|---|
| Castle Rock Spring Water Co. | 2086 | E | 530 678-4444 | 1875 |
| Saint Germain Foundation (PA) | 8661 | F | 530 235-2994 | 19370 |

## DURHAM, CA - Butte County

| | SIC | EMP | PHONE | ENTRY# |
|---|---|---|---|---|
| Old Durham Wood Inc. | 0783 | E | 530 342-7381 | 99 |
| Westgate Hardwoods Inc (PA) | 2431 | E | 530 892-0300 | 3204 |
| Tink Inc. | 3531 | E | 530 895-0897 | 9441 |

## E RNCHO DMNGZ, CA - Los Angeles County

| | SIC | EMP | PHONE | ENTRY# |
|---|---|---|---|---|
| Sonora Mills Foods Inc (PA) | 2099 | C | 310 639-5333 | 2356 |
| Audio Video Color Corporation (PA) | 2671 | C | 424 213-7500 | 3923 |
| Modern Concepts Inc. | 3089 | D | 310 637-0013 | 6917 |
| Coy Industries Inc. | 3444 | D | 310 603-2970 | 8419 |
| Industrial Tctnics Brings Corp (DH) | 3562 | C | 310 537-3750 | 9950 |

## EARLIMART, CA - Tulare County

| | SIC | EMP | PHONE | ENTRY# |
|---|---|---|---|---|
| Cal Treehouse Almonds LLC (PA) | 2068 | E | 559 757-5020 | 1348 |
| Custom Almonds | 2068 | E | 559 346-8212 | 1350 |

## EAST PALO ALTO, CA - Santa Clara County

| | SIC | EMP | PHONE | ENTRY# |
|---|---|---|---|---|
| Global Steel Fabricators Inc. | 7692 | F | 650 321-9533 | 19195 |

## EAST RANCHO DOMINGUE, CA - Los Angeles County

| | SIC | EMP | PHONE | ENTRY# |
|---|---|---|---|---|
| International Tex Group Inc. | 2211 | F | 310 667-9030 | 2419 |

## EASTVALE, CA - Riverside County

| | SIC | EMP | PHONE | ENTRY# |
|---|---|---|---|---|
| PTi Sand & Gravel Inc. | 1442 | E | 951 272-0140 | 320 |
| K-Swiss Inc. | 3021 | E | 951 361-7501 | 6417 |
| Califrnia Indus Rfrgn Mchs Inc. | 3585 | E | 951 361-0040 | 10487 |
| Rankin-Delux Inc (PA) | 3589 | F | 951 685-0081 | 10596 |
| Jns Industries Inc. | 3599 | F | 909 923-8334 | 10912 |
| Royal Range California Inc. | 3631 | D | 951 360-1600 | 11395 |
| Wolfgang Enterprise Inc. | 7389 | F | 951 848-7680 | 19144 |

## EDISON, CA - Kern County

| | SIC | EMP | PHONE | ENTRY# |
|---|---|---|---|---|
| Giumarra Vineyards Corporation (PA) | 0172 | B | 661 395-7000 | 13 |

## EL CAJON, CA - San Diego County

| | SIC | EMP | PHONE | ENTRY# |
|---|---|---|---|---|
| Rpc Inc. | 1389 | E | 619 334-6244 | 274 |
| Azusa Rock LLC. | 1422 | E | 619 440-2363 | 296 |
| California Shtmtl Works Inc. | 1541 | E | 619 562-7010 | 357 |
| Cascade Thermal Solutions LLC (PA) | 1711 | E | 619 562-8852 | 409 |
| Metarom USA Inc. | 2087 | E | 619 449-0299 | 2015 |
| Heartland Harvest | 2099 | F | 619 729-1604 | 2230 |
| Flight Suits | 2386 | D | 619 440-2700 | 2879 |
| Roll-Rite LLC. | 2394 | E | 619 449-8860 | 2981 |
| Transportation Equipment Inc. | 2394 | E | 619 449-8860 | 2985 |
| Brassington Caseworks | 2434 | F | 619 442-7277 | 3221 |
| San Diego Custom Cabinets | 2434 | E | 858 256-0933 | 3268 |
| Vcsd Inc. | 2434 | E | 619 579-6886 | 3279 |
| First Class Packaging Inc. | 2449 | E | 619 579-7166 | 3370 |

# GEOGRAPHIC SECTION

## EL SEGUNDO, CA

| Company | SIC | EMP | PHONE | ENTRY# |
|---|---|---|---|---|
| Omni Enclosures Inc | 2541 | E | 619 579-6664 | 3667 |
| Graphic Lab Inc | 2759 | E | 858 437-9100 | 4884 |
| Delstar Technologies Inc | 3081 | E | 619 258-1503 | 6557 |
| Damar Plastics Manufacturing Inc | 3089 | E | 619 283-2300 | 6793 |
| JP Gunite Inc | 3273 | E | 619 938-0228 | 7459 |
| Vertechs Enterprises Inc (PA) | 3364 | E | 858 578-3900 | 7831 |
| Decco Castings Inc (PA) | 3369 | F | 619 444-9437 | 7860 |
| Decco Castings Inc | 3369 | E | 818 416-0068 | 7861 |
| Triw1969 Inc | 3398 | E | 619 593-3636 | 7905 |
| M W Reid Welding Inc | 3441 | D | 619 401-5880 | 8173 |
| Westeel Builders | 3441 | F | 858 524-4353 | 8247 |
| Western Bay Sheet Metal Inc | 3441 | E | 619 233-1753 | 8248 |
| Asm Construction Inc | 3444 | E | 619 449-1966 | 8383 |
| Bay Sheet Metal Inc | 3444 | E | 619 401-9270 | 8390 |
| Dave Whipple Sheet Metal Inc | 3444 | E | 619 562-6962 | 8425 |
| Derosa Enterprises Inc | 3444 | F | 760 743-5500 | 8431 |
| Pacific Marine Sheet Metal Corporation | 3444 | C | 858 869-8900 | 8528 |
| Jmmca Inc (PA) | 3462 | D | 619 448-2711 | 8779 |
| BJS&t Enterprises Inc | 3479 | E | 619 448-7795 | 9055 |
| Alturdyne Power Systems Inc | 3511 | E | 619 343-3204 | 9307 |
| Cummins Pacific LLC | 3519 | E | 619 593-3093 | 9325 |
| Greenbroz Inc | 3523 | F | 844 379-8746 | 9355 |
| Toro Company | 3523 | C | 619 562-2950 | 9386 |
| Veridiam Inc (DH) | 3545 | D | 619 448-1000 | 9705 |
| Rotron Incorporated | 3564 | E | 619 593-7400 | 9996 |
| Prime Heat Incorporated | 3567 | F | 619 449-6623 | 10057 |
| Campbell Membrane Tech Inc | 3569 | E | 619 938-2481 | 10079 |
| High Prcsion Grnding McHning I | 3599 | F | 619 440-0303 | 10872 |
| Senior Operations LLC | 3599 | D | 909 627-2723 | 11107 |
| Weldmac Manufacturing Company | 3599 | E | 619 440-2300 | 11186 |
| Weldmac Manufacturing Company | 3599 | E | 619 440-2300 | 11187 |
| Tujayar Enterprises Inc | 3646 | E | 619 442-0577 | 11564 |
| Micro-Mode Products Inc | 3663 | C | 619 449-3844 | 11890 |
| Brantner and Associates Inc (DH) | 3678 | E | 619 456-6827 | 12866 |
| Q Microwave Inc | 3679 | D | 619 258-7322 | 13070 |
| Rks Inc (PA) | 3699 | F | 858 571-4444 | 13300 |
| Gear Vendors Inc | 3714 | E | 619 562-0060 | 13505 |
| GKN Aerospace Chem-Tronics Inc (DH) | 3724 | A | 619 258-5000 | 13709 |
| Vertechs Enterprises Inc | 3724 | E | 858 578-3900 | 13726 |
| Jet Air Fbo LLC | 3728 | E | 619 448-5991 | 13881 |
| Aerowind Corporation | 3769 | F | 619 569-1960 | 14107 |
| Dn Tanks Inc | 3795 | C | 619 440-8181 | 14125 |
| Dyk Incorporated (HQ) | 3795 | E | 619 440-8181 | 14126 |
| Get Engineering Corp | 3823 | F | 619 443-8295 | 14419 |
| Calbiotech Export Inc | 3841 | E | 619 660-6162 | 15023 |
| Johnson Outdoors Inc | 3949 | D | 619 402-1023 | 15833 |
| California Neon Products | 3993 | E | 619 283-2191 | 15952 |
| Coastal Creative | 3993 | F | 858 866-6560 | 15958 |
| Inflatable Design Group Inc | 3993 | F | 619 596-6100 | 15988 |
| Integrted Sign Assoc A Cal Cor | 3993 | E | 619 579-2229 | 15990 |
| San Diego Electric Sign Inc | 3993 | F | 619 258-1775 | 16030 |
| Cal AM Manufacturing Co Inc | 3999 | F | 800 992-0499 | 16102 |
| On Premise Products Inc | 3999 | E | 619 562-1486 | 16191 |
| Toor Knives Inc | 5085 | E | 619 328-6118 | 16902 |
| Sundance Custom Golf Carts Inc | 5088 | E | 619 449-0822 | 16926 |
| Taylor-Listug Inc (PA) | 5099 | C | 619 258-1207 | 16988 |
| Graphic Business Solutions Inc | 5112 | E | 619 258-4081 | 16991 |
| Pf Bakeries LLC | 5149 | E | 858 263-4863 | 17205 |
| Benny Enterprises Inc | 5181 | E | 619 592-4455 | 17258 |
| Wetzels Pretzels LLC | 5461 | E | 619 588-1074 | 17422 |
| Richard C Thurston | 7216 | F | 619 440-6165 | 17769 |
| Cartwright Trmt Pest Ctrl Inc | 7342 | E | 619 442-9613 | 17843 |
| Tessitura Network Inc | 7372 | C | 888 643-5778 | 18874 |
| Socal Technologies LLC | 7379 | E | 619 635-1128 | 19046 |
| CLP Inc (PA) | 7692 | E | 619 444-3105 | 19186 |
| Nan McKay and Associates Inc | 8742 | D | 619 258-1855 | 19534 |

## EL CENTRO, CA - Imperial County

| Company | SIC | EMP | PHONE | ENTRY# |
|---|---|---|---|---|
| Reyes Coca-Cola Bottling LLC | 2086 | E | 760 352-1561 | 1955 |
| Labrucherie Produce LLC | 2099 | E | 760 352-2170 | 2260 |
| Associated Desert Newspaper (DH) | 2711 | E | 760 337-3400 | 4069 |
| Imperial Printers (PA) | 2752 | F | 760 352-4374 | 4642 |
| Superior Ready Mix Concrete LP | 3273 | E | 760 352-4341 | 7507 |
| Ew Corprtion Indus Fabricators (PA) | 3441 | D | 760 337-0020 | 8135 |
| Rogar Manufacturing Inc | 3679 | E | 760 335-3700 | 13078 |
| Western Electrical Advg Co | 3993 | E | 760 352-0471 | 16066 |
| Wymore Inc | 7692 | E | 760 352-2045 | 19222 |

## EL DORADO HILLS, CA - El Dorado County

| Company | SIC | EMP | PHONE | ENTRY# |
|---|---|---|---|---|
| Ampac Fine Chemicals LLC | 2834 | B | 916 245-6500 | 5319 |
| Cemex | 3273 | D | 916 941-2800 | 7417 |
| Premier Power Renewable Energy Inc | 3433 | E | 916 939-0400 | 8074 |
| Kdf Enterprises LLC | 3531 | C | 803 928-7073 | 9429 |
| Alpha Research & Tech Inc | 3571 | D | 916 431-9340 | 10133 |
| 478826 Limited | 3599 | E | 916 933-5280 | 10642 |
| Maxar Space LLC | 3663 | A | 916 605-5448 | 11889 |
| Precision Contacts Inc | 3663 | E | 916 939-4147 | 11917 |
| Bar Manufacturing Inc | 3674 | D | 916 939-0551 | 12355 |
| Blaize Inc | 3674 | B | 916 347-0050 | 12360 |
| Illinois Tool Works Inc | 3674 | D | 916 939-4332 | 12473 |
| Planar Monolithics Inds Inc | 3679 | E | 916 542-1401 | 13062 |
| Aerometals Inc | 3728 | C | 916 939-6888 | 13748 |
| Access Systems Inc | 3826 | E | 916 941-8099 | 14602 |
| Emed Technologies Corporation (PA) | 3841 | F | 916 932-0071 | 15078 |
| Synvasive Technology Inc | 3841 | F | 916 939-3913 | 15275 |
| Rippey Corporation | 5045 | D | 916 939-4332 | 16546 |
| Digital Doc LLC | 5047 | E | 916 941-8010 | 16580 |
| Axiom Advisors & Cons Inc (PA) | 7372 | E | 800 818-3010 | 18086 |
| Cree8 Inc | 7372 | F | 805 328-4204 | 18209 |
| School Innovations Achievement (HQ) | 7372 | E | 800 487-9234 | 18763 |
| Sepasoft Inc | 7372 | E | 916 939-1684 | 18780 |
| V3 Systems Scrtyautomation Inc | 7389 | E | 916 543-1543 | 19141 |

## EL GRANADA, CA - San Mateo County

| Company | SIC | EMP | PHONE | ENTRY# |
|---|---|---|---|---|
| Exclusive Fresh Inc | 5146 | E | 650 728-7321 | 17156 |

## EL MONTE, CA - Los Angeles County

| Company | SIC | EMP | PHONE | ENTRY# |
|---|---|---|---|---|
| Atlantis Seafood LLC | 2092 | D | 626 626-4900 | 2047 |
| Dianas Mexican Food Pdts Inc | 2099 | D | 626 444-0555 | 2186 |
| El Gallito Market Inc | 2099 | E | 626 442-1190 | 2191 |
| La Chapalita Inc (PA) | 2099 | E | 626 443-8556 | 2249 |
| Flexfirm Holdings LLC | 2295 | E | 323 283-1173 | 2527 |
| Andari Fashion Inc | 2329 | C | 626 575-2759 | 2609 |
| Tartan Fashion Inc | 2329 | E | 626 575-2828 | 2647 |
| Svo Enterprise LLC | 2381 | E | 626 406-4770 | 2872 |
| SOLE Designs Inc | 2512 | E | 626 452-8642 | 3491 |
| L & N Fixtures Inc | 2541 | F | 626 442-4778 | 3662 |
| Hunter Douglas Inc | 2591 | B | 858 679-7500 | 3721 |
| 88 Special Sweet Inc | 2679 | D | 909 525-7055 | 4026 |
| Epoch Times Los Angeles | 2711 | E | 626 401-1828 | 4112 |
| Pax Tag & Label Inc | 2759 | E | 626 579-2000 | 4938 |
| Gill Corporation (PA) | 3089 | E | 626 443-6094 | 6843 |
| Castle Industries Inc of California | 3444 | E | 909 390-0899 | 8407 |
| Jansen Ornamental Supply Co | 3446 | E | 626 442-0271 | 8630 |
| BIG Enterprises | 3448 | E | 626 448-1449 | 8655 |
| All New Stamping Co | 3469 | C | 626 443-8813 | 8817 |
| Santoshi Corporation | 3471 | E | 626 444-7118 | 9010 |
| Applied Coatings & Linings | 3479 | E | 626 280-6354 | 9047 |
| Precision Coil Spring Company | 3495 | C | 626 444-0561 | 9206 |
| Craneveyor Corp (PA) | 3536 | D | 626 442-1524 | 9500 |
| Lith-O-Roll Corporation | 3555 | E | 626 579-0340 | 9770 |
| Lawrence Equipment Leasing Inc (PA) | 3556 | C | 626 442-2894 | 9803 |
| Liberty Industries | 3599 | F | 626 575-3206 | 10944 |
| Justin Inc | 3612 | E | 626 444-4516 | 11216 |
| Videssence LLC (PA) | 3645 | E | 626 579-0943 | 11505 |
| R W Swarens Associates Inc | 3646 | E | 626 579-0943 | 11554 |
| Talmo & Chinn Inc | 3674 | E | 626 443-1741 | 12754 |
| S C I Industries Inc | 3714 | E | | 13570 |
| Transgo LLC | 3714 | F | 626 443-7456 | 13591 |
| Sparling Instruments LLC | 3824 | E | 626 444-0571 | 14483 |
| Tacticombat Inc | 3949 | F | 626 315-4433 | 15864 |
| Los Angeles Ltg Mfg Co Inc | 5063 | D | 626 454-8300 | 16658 |
| Jans Enterprises Corporation | 5149 | E | 626 575-2000 | 17190 |

## EL SEGUNDO, CA - Los Angeles County

| Company | SIC | EMP | PHONE | ENTRY# |
|---|---|---|---|---|
| Luthman Backlund Foods USA Inc | 2024 | F | 310 994-9444 | 807 |
| Beyond Meat Inc (PA) | 2038 | E | 866 756-4112 | 1028 |
| El Segundo Bread Bar LLC | 2051 | E | 310 615-9898 | 1191 |
| Vbc Holdings Inc | 2051 | E | 310 322-7357 | 1251 |
| Sugarfina Inc | 2064 | E | 424 290-0777 | 1331 |
| Hemilane Inc | 2085 | F | 424 277-1134 | 1839 |
| Zico Beverages LLC (HQ) | 2086 | E | 866 729-9426 | 1977 |
| Berri Pro Inc | 2087 | F | 781 929-8288 | 1986 |
| Thai Union North America Inc (HQ) | 2091 | F | 424 397-8556 | 2044 |
| Lambs & Ivy Inc | 2392 | E | 310 322-3800 | 2935 |
| Satco Inc (PA) | 2448 | C | 310 322-4719 | 3359 |
| Artissimo Designs LLC (HQ) | 2679 | E | 310 906-3700 | 4030 |
| Los Angles Tmes Cmmnctions LLC (PA) | 2711 | A | 213 237-5000 | 4151 |
| Sabot Publishing Inc (PA) | 2721 | E | 310 356-4100 | 4296 |
| Browntrout Publishers Inc (PA) | 2741 | E | 424 290-6122 | 4372 |
| Superbam Inc | 2741 | E | 310 845-5784 | 4473 |
| Continental Graphics Corp | 2752 | D | 310 662-2307 | 4571 |
| Neft Vodka USA Inc | 2759 | F | 415 846-0359 | 4927 |
| Primary Color Systems Corp | 2759 | E | 310 841-0250 | 4942 |
| Kate Somerville Skincare LLC (HQ) | 2834 | D | 323 655-7546 | 5523 |
| Murad LLC (HQ) | 2834 | C | 310 726-0600 | 5558 |

# EL SEGUNDO, CA

## GEOGRAPHIC SECTION

| Company | SIC | EMP | PHONE | ENTRY# |
|---|---|---|---|---|
| Youth To People Inc | 2844 | D | 309 648-5500 | 6063 |
| Hco Holding II Corporation | 2952 | A | 310 955-9200 | 6375 |
| Henry Company LLC (HQ) | 2952 | D | 310 955-9200 | 6376 |
| Hnc Parent Inc (PA) | 2952 | D | 310 955-9200 | 6377 |
| Rainmaker Solutions Inc | 3052 | F | 855 463-5843 | 6428 |
| Alpha Group US LLC | 3069 | E | 844 303-8936 | 6483 |
| Allbirds Inc | 3143 | F | 424 502-2383 | 7097 |
| Federal Industries Inc | 3494 | E | 310 297-4040 | 9185 |
| Craig Tools Inc | 3545 | E | 310 322-0614 | 9670 |
| Flight Microwave Corporation | 3559 | E | 310 607-9819 | 9858 |
| Belkin International Inc (DH) | 3577 | B | 310 751-5100 | 10333 |
| Ross Racing Pistons | 3592 | D | 310 536-0100 | 10624 |
| Metalore Inc | 3599 | E | 310 643-0360 | 10974 |
| Glentek Inc | 3621 | D | 310 322-3026 | 11270 |
| Nantenergy LLC | 3621 | D | 310 905-4866 | 11279 |
| Belkin Inc | 3651 | A | 800 223-5546 | 11644 |
| Boeing Satellite Systems Inc (HQ) | 3663 | E | 310 791-7450 | 11820 |
| Millennium Space Systems Inc (HQ) | 3663 | E | 310 683-5840 | 11892 |
| MTI Laboratory Inc | 3663 | E | 310 955-3700 | 11900 |
| Raytheon Applied Sgnal Tech In | 3663 | C | 310 436-7000 | 11930 |
| Display Products Inc | 3674 | E | 310 640-0442 | 12404 |
| Infineon Tech Americas Corp | 3674 | E | 310 726-8000 | 12476 |
| Infineon Tech Americas Corp | 3674 | C | 310 252-7116 | 12478 |
| Infineon Tech Americas Corp (HQ) | 3674 | A | 310 726-8200 | 12479 |
| Integra Technologies Inc | 3674 | E | 310 606-0855 | 12492 |
| J L Cooper Electronics Inc | 3679 | E | 310 322-9990 | 13008 |
| Teledyne Technologies Inc | 3679 | B | 310 765-3600 | 13104 |
| Loop Inc | 3694 | E | 888 385-6674 | 13175 |
| Allclear Inc | 3721 | E | 424 316-1596 | 13632 |
| Boeing Satellite Systems Inc | 3721 | A | 310 568-2735 | 13646 |
| Aerospace Engrg Support Corp | 3728 | E | 310 297-4050 | 13756 |
| Trio Manufacturing Inc | 3728 | C | 310 640-6123 | 13979 |
| Kinkisharyo (usa) Inc | 3743 | C | 424 276-1803 | 14050 |
| Kinkisharyo Int LLC (HQ) | 3743 | F | 424 276-1803 | 14051 |
| Abl Space Systems Company | 3761 | D | 424 321-6060 | 14076 |
| Varda Space Industries Inc | 3761 | D | 833 707-0020 | 14098 |
| Morpheus Space Inc (PA) | 3764 | F | 562 766-8470 | 14103 |
| Aerojet Rcketdyne Holdings Inc (HQ) | 3812 | D | 310 252-8100 | 14136 |
| Aerojet Rocketdyne De Inc | 3812 | A | 310 414-0110 | 14137 |
| Atk Space Systems LLC | 3812 | D | 310 343-3799 | 14158 |
| Northrop Grumman Corporation | 3812 | C | 310 332-1000 | 14231 |
| Northrop Grumman Corporation | 3812 | E | 310 332-0461 | 14233 |
| Northrop Grumman Systems Corp | 3812 | B | 310 332-1000 | 14258 |
| Northrop Grumman Systems Corp | 3812 | D | 480 355-7716 | 14264 |
| Orbital Sciences LLC | 3812 | C | 703 406-5000 | 14273 |
| Pacific Defense Strategies Inc (PA) | 3812 | E | 310 722-6050 | 14277 |
| Raytheon Company | 3812 | E | 310 647-9438 | 14283 |
| Raytheon Company | 3812 | D | 310 647-1000 | 14284 |
| Raytheon Company | 3812 | E | 310 647-1000 | 14289 |
| Raytheon Company | 3812 | A | 310 647-9438 | 14290 |
| Teledyne Controls LLC | 3812 | A | 310 765-3600 | 14313 |
| Karl Storz Endscpy-America Inc (HQ) | 3841 | C | 424 218-8100 | 15141 |
| Mod-Electronics Inc | 3873 | E | 310 322-2136 | 15677 |
| Far Out Toys Inc | 3942 | E | 310 480-7554 | 15729 |
| Mattel Inc (PA) | 3942 | A | 310 252-2000 | 15732 |
| Moose Toys LLC | 3942 | D | 310 341-4642 | 15733 |
| Fun-Gl Games LLC | 3944 | F | 213 254-5489 | 15749 |
| Mattel Direct Import Inc (HQ) | 3944 | E | 310 252-2000 | 15759 |
| Mega Brands America Inc (DH) | 3944 | D | 949 727-9009 | 15760 |
| Beach House Group LLC | 3999 | B | 310 356-6180 | 16094 |
| Dkp Designs Inc | 3999 | F | 310 322-6000 | 16125 |
| Jal Avionet USA (HQ) | 5045 | E | 310 606-1000 | 16529 |
| Square Enix Inc | 5045 | C | 310 846-0400 | 16552 |
| Boeing Stllite Systems Intl In (HQ) | 5088 | E | 310 364-4000 | 16916 |
| Com Dev Usa LLC | 5088 | D | 424 456-8000 | 16917 |
| Itochu Aviation Inc (DH) | 5088 | E | 310 640-2770 | 16920 |
| Tri-Union Seafoods LLC (DH) | 5146 | D | 424 397-8556 | 17159 |
| Chevron Corporation | 5541 | A | 310 615-5000 | 17471 |
| Gurucul Solutions LLC | 5734 | D | 213 291-6888 | 17552 |
| Merqbiz LLC | 5961 | E | 855 637-7249 | 17668 |
| Cosmetix West (PA) | 5999 | E | 310 726-3080 | 17697 |
| Intelligent Beauty LLC | 5999 | A | 310 683-0940 | 17708 |
| Asp Henry Holdings Inc | 6719 | A | 310 955-9200 | 17743 |
| Century Pk Capitl Partners LLC (PA) | 6726 | C | 310 867-2210 | 17750 |
| Crescentone Inc (HQ) | 7371 | E | 310 563-7000 | 17903 |
| BMC | 7372 | E | 310 321-5555 | 18120 |
| Governmentjobscom Inc | 7372 | C | 877 204-4442 | 18360 |
| Hr Cloud Inc | 7372 | E | 510 909-1993 | 18393 |
| Impex Technologies Inc | 7372 | F | 310 320-0280 | 18405 |
| M Nexon Inc | 7372 | E | 213 858-5930 | 18509 |
| Saviynt Inc (PA) | 7372 | B | 310 641-1664 | 18762 |
| Street Smart LLC | 7372 | E | 866 924-4644 | 18841 |
| Traxero North America LLC | 7372 | D | 423 497-1164 | 18891 |
| Unbroken Studios LLC | 7372 | D | 310 741-2670 | 18897 |
| Telenet Voip Inc | 7629 | D | 310 253-9000 | 19179 |
| Ticketscom LLC (DH) | 7922 | E | 714 327-5400 | 19305 |
| Infineon Tech Americas Corp | 8721 | A | 310 726-8000 | 19433 |
| Anthos Group Inc | 8742 | E | 888 778-2986 | 19520 |
| Technical Micro Cons Inc (PA) | 8742 | E | 310 559-3982 | 19542 |

## EL TORO, CA - Orange County

| Company | SIC | EMP | PHONE | ENTRY# |
|---|---|---|---|---|
| Beverly Hillcrest Oil Corp | 1311 | F | 949 598-7300 | 125 |
| Mission Flavors Fragrances Inc | 2087 | F | 949 461-3344 | 2016 |
| Black & Decker Corporation | 3546 | E | 949 672-4000 | 9709 |

## ELK GROVE, CA - Sacramento County

| Company | SIC | EMP | PHONE | ENTRY# |
|---|---|---|---|---|
| Elk Grove Milling Inc | 2048 | E | 916 684-2056 | 1125 |
| Saiyr Sweets LLC | 2064 | F | 916 667-1407 | 1324 |
| Glacier Valley Ice Company LP (PA) | 2097 | E | 916 394-2939 | 2108 |
| Berber Food Manufacturing LLC | 2099 | C | 510 553-0444 | 2137 |
| Decore-Ative Spc NC LLC | 2431 | C | 916 686-4700 | 3128 |
| Eew Holdings Inc | 2431 | E | 916 685-1855 | 3135 |
| Cal-Asia Truss Inc | 2439 | E | 916 685-5648 | 3296 |
| International Paper Company | 2621 | D | 916 685-9000 | 3775 |
| Local Savers LLC | 2759 | E | 916 672-1006 | 4915 |
| Hanford Ready-Mix Inc | 3273 | E | 916 405-1918 | 7450 |
| Pacific Modern Homes Inc | 3444 | E | 916 685-9514 | 8529 |
| GNB Corporation | 3541 | D | 916 395-3003 | 9555 |
| Universal Custom Display | 3993 | C | 916 714-2505 | 16061 |
| Feist Cabinets & Woodworks Inc | 5712 | E | 916 686-8230 | 17519 |
| Alldata LLC | 7372 | B | 916 684-5200 | 18040 |

## EMERYVILLE, CA - Alameda County

| Company | SIC | EMP | PHONE | ENTRY# |
|---|---|---|---|---|
| FReal Foods LLC | 2023 | D | 800 483-3218 | 759 |
| Rebbl Inc | 2026 | E | 855 732-2500 | 843 |
| Clif Bar & Company LLC (HQ) | 2064 | C | 510 596-6300 | 1303 |
| Tcho Ventures Inc | 2066 | E | 415 981-0189 | 1346 |
| Peets Coffee & Tea LLC (DH) | 2095 | E | 510 594-2100 | 2077 |
| Petit Pot LLC | 2099 | E | 650 488-7432 | 2320 |
| Upside Foods Inc | 2099 | D | 510 588-1224 | 2384 |
| Unspun Inc | 2325 | E | 207 577-8745 | 2590 |
| Suspender Factory Inc | 2389 | E | 510 547-5400 | 2910 |
| Kay Chesterfield Inc | 2512 | F | 510 533-5565 | 3477 |
| Bacchus Press Inc (PA) | 2752 | E | 510 420-5800 | 4526 |
| Beigene Usa Inc | 2833 | B | 619 733-1842 | 5233 |
| Bayer Healthcare LLC | 2834 | C | 510 597-6150 | 5358 |
| Cell Design Labs Inc | 2834 | E | 510 398-0501 | 5400 |
| Daniel Loria Novartis | 2834 | E | 510 655-8729 | 5423 |
| Novartis Insttes For Bmdcal R | 2834 | C | 510 923-4248 | 5578 |
| Totus Medicines Inc | 2834 | E | 510 501-4832 | 5692 |
| Zogenix Inc (HQ) | 2834 | E | 510 550-8300 | 5723 |
| Lucira Health Inc | 2835 | D | 510 350-7162 | 5761 |
| Tethys Bioscience Inc | 2835 | C | 888 483-8497 | 5783 |
| Dynavax Technologies Corp (PA) | 2836 | D | 510 848-5100 | 5825 |
| Gritstone Bio Inc (PA) | 2836 | C | 510 871-6100 | 5835 |
| Kyverna Therapeutics Inc | 2836 | E | 510 925-2492 | 5844 |
| Sound Agriculture Company | 2836 | E | 512 650-8290 | 5862 |
| Amyris Inc (PA) | 2869 | B | 510 450-0761 | 6126 |
| Nugeneration Technologies LLC (PA) | 2899 | F | 415 747-2768 | 6313 |
| Coulter Forge Technology Inc | 3462 | E | 510 420-3500 | 8774 |
| Geo M Martin Company (PA) | 3554 | D | 510 652-2200 | 9760 |
| Oxide Computer Company | 3571 | E | 510 922-1392 | 10191 |
| Ohmio Inc | 3621 | F | 818 818-8268 | 11281 |
| Lumigrow Inc | 3646 | E | 800 514-0487 | 11545 |
| Liminal Insights Inc | 3679 | E | 310 702-5803 | 13024 |
| Engine World LLC | 3714 | E | 510 653-4444 | 13495 |
| Bruker Cellular Analysis Inc (HQ) | 3826 | C | 510 858-2855 | 14638 |
| Eko Health Inc | 3845 | D | 844 356-3384 | 15534 |
| Leapfrog Enterprises Inc (HQ) | 3944 | B | 510 420-5000 | 15757 |
| Folkmanis Inc | 3999 | E | 510 658-7677 | 16131 |
| Stasher Inc | 5113 | D | 510 531-2100 | 17023 |
| Peets Coffee Inc (DH) | 5499 | E | 510 594-2100 | 17431 |
| Bigfix Inc | 7372 | C | 510 652-6700 | 18102 |
| Clear Skye Inc | 7372 | E | 415 619-5001 | 18172 |
| Tanium Inc | 7372 | A | 510 704-0202 | 18864 |
| Tubemogul Inc | 7372 | E | 510 653-0126 | 18894 |
| Pixar (DH) | 7812 | B | 510 922-3000 | 19295 |
| Local Foodz Cali Inc | 8322 | E | 650 242-5651 | 19358 |
| Metagenomi Inc (PA) | 8731 | E | 510 871-4880 | 19468 |

## EMPIRE, CA - Stanislaus County

| Company | SIC | EMP | PHONE | ENTRY# |
|---|---|---|---|---|
| Modesto Milling Inc | 2048 | E | 209 523-9167 | 1137 |

## ENCINITAS, CA - San Diego County

| Company | SIC | EMP | PHONE | ENTRY# |
|---|---|---|---|---|
| Coast News Inc | 2711 | D | 760 436-9737 | 4095 |
| RCP Block & Brick Inc | 3271 | E | 760 753-1164 | 7301 |

# GEOGRAPHIC SECTION — FAIRFIELD, CA

| Company | SIC | EMP | PHONE | ENTRY# |
|---|---|---|---|---|
| Cratex Manufacturing Co Inc | 3291 | D | 760 942-2877 | 7552 |
| Stable Auto Corporation | 3694 | E | 415 967-2719 | 13186 |
| Black Box Distribution LLC | 3949 | D | 760 268-1174 | 15788 |
| El Nopalito Inc (PA) | 5411 | E | 760 436-5775 | 17378 |
| Southern Cal Disc Tire Co Inc | 5531 | C | 760 634-2202 | 17464 |
| Lofty Coffee Inc | 5812 | D | 760 230-6747 | 17596 |
| Oggis Pizza & Brewing Company | 5812 | E | 760 944-8170 | 17599 |

## ENCINO, CA - Los Angeles County

| Company | SIC | EMP | PHONE | ENTRY# |
|---|---|---|---|---|
| Liberty Vegetable Oil Company | 2079 | E | 562 921-3567 | 1399 |
| Zevia LLC | 2086 | D | 310 202-7000 | 1975 |
| Zevia Pbc (PA) | 2086 | E | 424 343-2654 | 1976 |
| Stanzino Inc | 2211 | C | 818 602-5171 | 2428 |
| Etrade 24 Inc | 2299 | E | 818 712-0574 | 2546 |
| Aquarius Rags LLC (PA) | 2335 | D | 213 895-4400 | 2698 |
| ABS By Allen Schwartz LLC (HQ) | 2339 | E | 213 895-4400 | 2731 |
| Creative Age Publications Inc | 2721 | E | 818 782-7328 | 4242 |
| Ect News Network Inc | 2741 | F | 818 461-9700 | 4392 |
| Owsla Touring LLC | 2741 | E | 818 385-1933 | 4442 |
| Total Accnting Bkkping Sltions | 2782 | F | 818 981-0600 | 5005 |
| California Respiratory Care | 2899 | D | 818 379-9999 | 6272 |
| National Cement Company Inc (HQ) | 3241 | E | 818 728-5200 | 7261 |
| Concrete Holding Co Cal Inc | 3273 | A | 818 788-4228 | 7435 |
| National Cement Co Cal Inc (DH) | 3273 | E | 818 728-5200 | 7472 |
| National Ready Mixed Con Co (DH) | 3273 | E | 818 728-5200 | 7477 |
| Garage Equipment Supply Inc | 3559 | F | 805 530-0027 | 9859 |
| Calstar Systems Group Inc | 3699 | E | 818 922-2000 | 13217 |
| United Medical Devices LLC | 3841 | E | 310 551-4100 | 15295 |
| Rf America-Ids Inc | 3843 | F | 866 578-5533 | 15480 |
| Vivometrics Inc | 3845 | E | 805 667-2225 | 15591 |
| Sayari Shahrzad | 5136 | E | 310 903-6368 | 17080 |
| Artkive | 7372 | E | 310 975-9809 | 18066 |
| Culture AMP Inc (HQ) | 7372 | F | 415 326-8453 | 18213 |
| D3publisher of America Inc | 7372 | D | 310 268-0820 | 18223 |
| Ipr Software Inc | 7372 | E | 310 499-0544 | 18443 |
| Netsol Technologies Inc (PA) | 7372 | D | 818 222-9195 | 18577 |
| Nsi Group LLC (PA) | 7389 | F | 818 639-8335 | 19111 |
| Alex A Khadavi Md Inc | 8011 | E | 818 528-2500 | 19314 |
| T Joseph Raoof MD Inc | 8011 | F | 818 788-5060 | 19322 |
| Telestar International Corp | 8742 | E | 818 582-3018 | 19543 |

## ESCALON, CA - San Joaquin County

| Company | SIC | EMP | PHONE | ENTRY# |
|---|---|---|---|---|
| Escalon Premier Brands Inc | 2033 | D | 209 838-7341 | 887 |
| Eckert Cold Storage Company (PA) | 2037 | B | 209 838-4040 | 1005 |
| P & L Concrete Products Inc | 3273 | E | 209 838-1448 | 7483 |
| Morrill Industries Inc | 3494 | D | 209 838-2550 | 9189 |
| Caron Compactor Co | 3531 | E | 800 448-8236 | 9414 |
| Central Valley Industries LLC | 3999 | D | 209 838-8150 | 16115 |
| Hogan Mfg Inc (PA) | 3999 | C | 209 838-7323 | 16145 |
| Hogan Mfg Inc | 3999 | F | 209 838-2400 | 16146 |
| Hogan Mfg Inc | 3999 | C | 209 838-2400 | 16147 |

## ESCONDIDO, CA - San Diego County

| Company | SIC | EMP | PHONE | ENTRY# |
|---|---|---|---|---|
| Southland Paving Inc | 1771 | D | 760 747-6895 | 525 |
| Progressive Design Playgrounds | 1799 | F | 760 597-5990 | 569 |
| Nemos Bakery Inc (HQ) | 2053 | D | 760 741-5725 | 1290 |
| Stone Brewing Co LLC | 2082 | C | 760 294-7899 | 1462 |
| Orfila Vineyards Inc (PA) | 2084 | F | 760 738-6500 | 1700 |
| Pure-Flo Water Co (PA) | 2086 | D | 619 596-4130 | 1927 |
| Esperanzas Tortilleria | 2099 | E | 760 743-5908 | 2192 |
| Hollywood Chairs (PA) | 2511 | E | 760 471-6600 | 3444 |
| Publishers Development Corp | 2721 | E | 858 605-0200 | 4290 |
| Mum Industries Inc | 2821 | E | 800 729-1314 | 5180 |
| REAL Seal Co Inc | 3053 | E | 760 743-7263 | 6462 |
| Dcc General Engrg Contrs Inc | 3272 | D | 760 480-7400 | 7326 |
| Oldcastle Infrastructure Inc | 3272 | E | 951 683-8200 | 7366 |
| Robertsons Ready Mix Ltd | 3273 | D | 951 685-4600 | 7494 |
| Superior Ready Mix Concrete LP | 3273 | E | 760 728-1128 | 7508 |
| Superior Ready Mix Concrete LP (PA) | 3273 | E | 760 745-0556 | 7510 |
| Vulcan Materials Co | 3273 | C | 760 737-3486 | 7520 |
| Aztec Perlite Company Inc | 3295 | F | 760 741-1733 | 7564 |
| VIT Products Inc | 3429 | E | 760 480-6702 | 8034 |
| Freeberg Indus Fbrication Corp | 3441 | E | 760 737-7614 | 8143 |
| Western Metal Supply Co Inc | 3448 | F | 760 233-7800 | 8689 |
| Count Numbering Machine Inc | 3555 | E | 760 739-9357 | 9765 |
| Integrted Crygnic Slutions LLC | 3559 | E | 951 234-0899 | 9870 |
| Capstone Fire Management Inc (PA) | 3569 | E | 760 839-2290 | 10080 |
| Separation Engineering Inc | 3569 | E | 760 489-0101 | 10113 |
| One Stop Systems Inc (PA) | 3577 | E | 760 745-9883 | 10417 |
| One Stop Systems Inc | 3577 | E | 858 530-2511 | 10418 |
| C & H Machine Inc | 3599 | D | 760 746-6459 | 10758 |
| Meziere Enterprises Inc | 3599 | E | 800 208-1755 | 10976 |
| Price Products Incorporated | 3599 | E | 760 745-5602 | 11049 |
| Rwnm Inc | 3612 | E |  | 11228 |
| Bliss Holdings LLC | 3648 | E | 626 506-8696 | 11585 |
| Rantec Microwave Systems Inc | 3663 | E | 760 744-1544 | 11928 |
| Systech Corporation | 3669 | E | 858 674-6500 | 12019 |
| Hybond Inc | 3672 | F | 760 746-7105 | 12132 |
| San Diego Pcb Design LLC | 3672 | F | 858 271-5722 | 12205 |
| Peak Technology Inc | 3674 | F | 760 745-8297 | 12629 |
| Avr Global Technologies Inc (PA) | 3679 | C | 949 391-1180 | 12918 |
| U S Circuit Inc | 3679 | D | 760 489-1413 | 13113 |
| Heatshield Products Inc | 3714 | E | 760 751-0441 | 13511 |
| Transportation Power LLC | 3714 | E | 858 248-4255 | 13592 |
| Tdg Aerospace Inc | 3728 | F | 760 466-1040 | 13969 |
| Northrop Grumman Corporation | 3812 | E | 310 864-7342 | 14235 |
| Arch Med Sltons - Escndido LLC | 3841 | E | 760 432-9785 | 14976 |
| Photronics Inc | 3861 | C | 760 294-1896 | 15662 |
| Brainstormproducts LLC | 3944 | E | 760 871-1135 | 15742 |
| Adti Media LLC | 3993 | E | 951 795-4446 | 15939 |
| Hadronex Inc (PA) | 4952 | E | 760 291-1980 | 16354 |
| Cal Southern Sound Image Inc (PA) | 5065 | D | 760 737-3900 | 16693 |
| Klein Electronics Inc | 5065 | E | 760 781-3220 | 16712 |
| Portable Clers Sls Rentals Inc | 5722 | E | 760 747-9591 | 17542 |
| Stone Brewing Co LLC (DH) | 5813 | E | 760 294-7866 | 17624 |
| Dish For All Inc | 7622 | E | 760 690-3869 | 19171 |

## ESPARTO, CA - Yolo County

| Company | SIC | EMP | PHONE | ENTRY# |
|---|---|---|---|---|
| Teichert Inc | 1442 | E | 530 787-3468 | 323 |

## ETNA, CA - Siskiyou County

| Company | SIC | EMP | PHONE | ENTRY# |
|---|---|---|---|---|
| Denny Bar Company LLC | 2085 | E | 530 467-5115 | 1835 |

## EUREKA, CA - Humboldt County

| Company | SIC | EMP | PHONE | ENTRY# |
|---|---|---|---|---|
| Trendsetter Solar Products Inc | 1711 | F | 707 443-5652 | 439 |
| Table Bluff Brewing Inc (PA) | 2082 | E | 707 445-4480 | 1463 |
| Coast Seafoods Company | 2091 | D | 707 442-2947 | 2039 |
| Schmidbauer Lumber Inc (PA) | 2421 | C | 707 443-7024 | 3078 |
| Pasadena Newspapers Inc | 2711 | E | 707 442-1711 | 4181 |
| Hagadone Directories Inc | 2741 | C | 707 444-0255 | 4411 |
| Hilfiker Pipe Co | 3272 | E | 707 443-5091 | 7343 |
| Carlson Wireless Tech Inc | 3663 | E | 707 443-0100 | 11823 |
| Marine Spill Response Corp | 3826 | E | 760 442-6087 | 14686 |
| Gold Rush Coffee | 5149 | E | 707 442-2848 | 17187 |

## EXETER, CA - Tulare County

| Company | SIC | EMP | PHONE | ENTRY# |
|---|---|---|---|---|
| Central California Baking Co | 2051 | C | 559 592-2270 | 1176 |
| International Paper Company | 2621 | D | 559 592-7279 | 3774 |
| Fruit Growers Supply Company | 2653 | F | 559 592-6550 | 3844 |
| Foothills Sun-Gazette | 2711 | E | 559 592-3171 | 4114 |
| South Valley Materials Inc | 3273 | F | 559 594-4142 | 7498 |
| Waterman Industries Inc | 3494 | E | 559 562-8661 | 9194 |
| Amarillo Wind Machine LLC | 3523 | E | 559 592-4256 | 9337 |
| Exeter Mercantile Company | 3523 | F | 559 592-2121 | 9353 |
| Waterman Valve LLC (HQ) | 3589 | C | 559 562-4000 | 10612 |
| Peninsula Packaging LLC (DH) | 3999 | D | 559 594-6813 | 16199 |
| Willitts Eqp & Engrg Co Inc | 5251 | E | 559 594-5020 | 17360 |

## FAIR OAKS, CA - Sacramento County

| Company | SIC | EMP | PHONE | ENTRY# |
|---|---|---|---|---|
| Rice Corporation (PA) | 2044 | E | 916 784-7745 | 1081 |

## FAIRFIELD, CA - Solano County

| Company | SIC | EMP | PHONE | ENTRY# |
|---|---|---|---|---|
| Courage Production LLC | 2013 | D | 707 422-6300 | 637 |
| Nippon Industries Inc | 2038 | E | 707 427-3127 | 1042 |
| Primal Pet Foods | 2047 | E | 415 642-7400 | 1112 |
| Primal Pet Foods Inc | 2047 | E | 415 642-7400 | 1113 |
| Primal Pet Foods Inc (PA) | 2047 | E | 415 642-7400 | 1114 |
| Freds Foods Inc | 2052 | F | 707 639-9438 | 1275 |
| Olive Oil Factory LLC (PA) | 2079 | E | 707 426-3400 | 1404 |
| Anheuser-Busch LLC | 2082 | B | 707 429-7595 | 1415 |
| Lin Frank Distillers | 2085 | E | 707 437-1092 | 1840 |
| Woodline Partners LLC | 2434 | E | 707 864-5445 | 3281 |
| Compu-Tech Lumber Products Inc | 2439 | E | 707 437-6683 | 3304 |
| McNaughton Newspapers Inc (PA) | 2711 | D | 707 425-4646 | 4156 |
| Toray Advnced Cmpsites ADS LLC | 2821 | D | 707 359-3400 | 5214 |
| Abbott Nutrition | 2834 | E | 707 399-1100 | 5289 |
| Abbott Nutrition Mfg Inc (HQ) | 2834 | E | 707 399-1100 | 5290 |
| Abco Laboratories Inc (PA) | 2834 | E | 707 432-2200 | 5292 |
| Clorox Manufacturing Company | 2842 | E | 707 437-1051 | 5901 |
| Aurora Innovations LLC | 2873 | C | 541 359-1580 | 6169 |
| Biomerics Imp Indus Hldngs LLC | 3089 | D | 707 863-4900 | 6744 |
| Macro Plastics Inc (DH) | 3089 | E | 707 437-1200 | 6899 |
| Fabricated Glass Spc Inc | 3231 | E | 707 429-6160 | 7220 |
| Cemex Cnstr Mtls PCF LLC | 3273 | E | 707 422-2520 | 7421 |
| Halabi Inc (PA) | 3281 | C | 707 402-1600 | 7539 |
| Yla Inc | 3299 | D | 707 359-3400 | 7601 |

---

Employee Codes: A=Over 500 employees, B=251-500, C=101-250, D=51-100, E=20-50, F=10-19, G=1-9

# FAIRFIELD, CA — GEOGRAPHIC SECTION

| Company | SIC | EMP | PHONE | ENTRY# |
|---|---|---|---|---|
| Ball Metal Beverage Cont Corp | 3411 | C | 707 437-7516 | 7919 |
| Tronex Technology Incorporated | 3423 | E | 707 426-2550 | 7968 |
| OHara Metal Products | 3493 | E | 707 863-9090 | 9178 |
| Made and Modern Hard Goods Inc | 3553 | D | 707 366-9180 | 9755 |
| Pauli Systems Inc | 3599 | E | 707 429-2434 | 11034 |
| Scott Lamp Company Inc | 3646 | D | 707 864-2066 | 11556 |
| Hydrofarm LLC | 3648 | E | 707 765-9990 | 11601 |
| West-Com Nrse Call Systems Inc (PA) | 3663 | E | 707 428-5900 | 11977 |
| Boeing Arospc Operations Inc | 3721 | E | 707 437-3175 | 13640 |
| Rockwell Collins Inc | 3728 | B | 707 422-1880 | 13936 |
| Universal Propulsion Co Inc | 3728 | B | 707 399-1867 | 13984 |
| Solano Diagnostics Imaging | 3829 | F | 707 646-4646 | 14922 |
| Zimmer Biomet Fegan Inc | 3842 | F | 707 863-0291 | 15431 |
| Aalba Dent Inc | 3843 | F | 707 864-3334 | 15436 |
| Jsj Electrical Display Corp | 3993 | F | 707 747-5595 | 15997 |
| Cortech Industries LLC | 3999 | E | 818 267-8324 | 16121 |
| Meyer Corporation US | 5023 | E | 707 399-2100 | 16430 |
| New Desserts LLC | 5149 | D | 415 780-6860 | 17200 |
| Frank-Lin Distillers Pdts Ltd (PA) | 5182 | C | 408 259-8900 | 17266 |
| Reno Jones Inc | 5199 | E | 707 422-4300 | 17308 |
| Fairfield Rental Service Inc | 7353 | F | 707 422-2270 | 17851 |
| Bay-TEC Engineering | 8711 | D | 714 257-1680 | 19382 |

## FALLBROOK, CA - San Diego County

| Company | SIC | EMP | PHONE | ENTRY# |
|---|---|---|---|---|
| Grubb & Nadler Inc | 1231 | E | 760 728-0040 | 113 |
| Scw Contracting Corporation | 1623 | D | 760 728-1308 | 388 |
| Fallbrook Industries Inc | 3469 | E | 760 728-7229 | 8842 |
| Antrin Miniature Spc Inc | 3599 | F | 760 723-7605 | 10711 |
| Axelgaard Manufacturing Co | 3845 | E | 760 723-7554 | 15515 |
| Axelgaard Manufacturing Co (PA) | 3845 | D | 760 723-7554 | 15516 |
| Southwest Boulder & Stone Inc (PA) | 5999 | E | 760 451-3333 | 17723 |
| Breakmat LLC | 7349 | F | 760 310-2421 | 17845 |
| Special Event Audio Svcs Inc | 7929 | E | 800 518-9144 | 19306 |

## FARMERSVILLE, CA - Tulare County

| Company | SIC | EMP | PHONE | ENTRY# |
|---|---|---|---|---|
| La Mejor Inc | 2099 | E | 559 747-0739 | 2256 |
| Claudes Buggies Inc | 5013 | E | 559 733-8222 | 16377 |

## FELLOWS, CA - Kern County

| Company | SIC | EMP | PHONE | ENTRY# |
|---|---|---|---|---|
| Freeport-Mcmoran Oil & Gas LLC | 1382 | E | 661 768-4831 | 183 |
| Dwaynes Engineering & Cnstr | 1389 | E | 661 762-7261 | 225 |
| Pacific Perforating Inc | 1389 | E | 661 768-9224 | 263 |

## FIELDS LANDING, CA - Humboldt County

| Company | SIC | EMP | PHONE | ENTRY# |
|---|---|---|---|---|
| Rock Springs Industries Inc | 2821 | E | 707 443-9323 | 5195 |

## FILLMORE, CA - Ventura County

| Company | SIC | EMP | PHONE | ENTRY# |
|---|---|---|---|---|
| Honey Bennetts Farm | 2099 | E | 805 521-1375 | 2232 |
| Ameron International Corp | 3272 | D | 805 524-0223 | 7307 |
| Ameron International Corp | 3272 | C | 425 258-2616 | 7308 |

## FIREBAUGH, CA - Fresno County

| Company | SIC | EMP | PHONE | ENTRY# |
|---|---|---|---|---|
| Neil Jones Food Company | 2033 | E | 559 659-5100 | 909 |
| West Valley Aviation Inc | 3728 | F | 559 659-7378 | 13990 |

## FOLSOM, CA - Sacramento County

| Company | SIC | EMP | PHONE | ENTRY# |
|---|---|---|---|---|
| Kikkoman Foods Inc | 2035 | F | 916 355-8078 | 980 |
| Gekkeikan Sake (usa) Inc | 2084 | E | 916 985-3111 | 1585 |
| Scotts Seafood Roundhouse | 2092 | D | 916 989-6711 | 2062 |
| Mountain F Enterprises Inc | 2411 | E | 530 626-4127 | 3051 |
| Rjp Framing Holding Co | 2431 | F | 916 817-1427 | 3186 |
| Clarios LLC | 2531 | D | 916 294-8866 | 3619 |
| Style Media Group Inc | 2721 | E | 916 988-9888 | 4298 |
| Cemex Inc | 3273 | D | 916 941-2999 | 7418 |
| Sigma Mfg & Logistics LLC | 3571 | E | 916 781-3052 | 10202 |
| Wmn Corp | 3572 | E | 916 294-0110 | 10298 |
| Phoenix Motor Inc | 3629 | E | 909 987-0815 | 11377 |
| Stellant Systems Inc | 3663 | C | 916 351-4500 | 11952 |
| Marvell Semiconductor Inc | 3674 | E | 916 605-3700 | 12543 |
| Micron Technology Inc | 3674 | C | 916 458-3003 | 12568 |
| Microsemi Crp- Rf Intgrted Slt (DH) | 3674 | E | 916 850-8640 | 12577 |
| Aerojet Rocketdyne Inc | 3728 | C | 916 355-4000 | 13747 |
| Military Aircraft Parts (PA) | 3728 | E | 916 635-8010 | 13910 |
| General Dynmics Ots Ncvlle Inc | 3812 | D | 916 355-7700 | 14191 |
| Sierra Nevada Corporation | 3812 | D | 916 985-8799 | 14305 |
| Trimble Inc | 3812 | E | 916 294-2000 | 14324 |
| Agilent Technologies Inc | 3825 | D | 916 985-7888 | 14489 |
| Care Innovations LLC | 3845 | E | 800 450-0970 | 15523 |
| Computer Power Sftwr Group Inc (PA) | 7371 | F | 916 985-4445 | 17899 |
| Retail Pro International LLC (HQ) | 7371 | D | 916 605-7200 | 17972 |
| Hoonuit LLC (DH) | 7372 | E | 320 631-5900 | 18388 |
| Magnit LLC (PA) | 7372 | D | 516 437-3300 | 18515 |
| Meridian Project Systems Inc | 7372 | C | 916 294-2000 | 18539 |
| Netensity Corporation | 7372 | E | 855 222-8488 | 18574 |
| Peopleadmin Inc (DH) | 7372 | E | 877 637-5800 | 18669 |
| Performance Matters LLC (DH) | 7372 | F | 801 453-0136 | 18670 |
| Powerschool Group LLC (HQ) | 7372 | E | 916 790-1509 | 18689 |
| Powerschool Holdings Inc (PA) | 7372 | A | 877 873-1550 | 18690 |
| Sedona Ventures Inc (PA) | 7389 | C | 916 932-1300 | 19128 |
| Smart Start Early Childhood | 8351 | F | 916 984-3800 | 19364 |

## FONTANA, CA - San Bernardino County

| Company | SIC | EMP | PHONE | ENTRY# |
|---|---|---|---|---|
| Refresco Beverages US Inc | 2033 | C | 951 685-0481 | 921 |
| Sundown Foods USA Inc | 2033 | E | 909 606-6797 | 929 |
| Flowers Bakeries Sls Socal LLC | 2051 | E | 702 281-4797 | 1195 |
| Reyes Coca-Cola Bottling LLC | 2086 | C | 909 980-3121 | 1943 |
| Mohawk Industries Inc | 2273 | E | 909 357-1064 | 2518 |
| A&R Tarpaulins Inc | 2394 | E | 909 829-4444 | 2964 |
| GO Pallets Inc | 2448 | F | 909 823-4663 | 3344 |
| Lopez Pallet Inc | 2448 | F | 909 823-0865 | 3349 |
| Meza Pallets Inc | 2448 | F | 909 829-0223 | 3350 |
| Ramirez Pallets Inc | 2448 | F | 909 822-2066 | 3356 |
| New Classic HM Furnishing Inc (PA) | 2512 | E | 909 484-7676 | 3485 |
| S & H Cabinets and Mfg Inc | 2521 | E | 909 357-0551 | 3586 |
| Allied West Paper Corp | 2621 | D | 909 349-0710 | 3760 |
| Tst/Impreso Inc | 2761 | E | 909 357-7190 | 4993 |
| Kemira Water Solutions Inc | 2819 | E | 909 350-5678 | 5098 |
| Indorama Vntres Sstnble Sltion | 2821 | E | 951 727-8318 | 5162 |
| J-M Manufacturing Company Inc | 2821 | D | 909 822-3009 | 5170 |
| Continental Coatings Inc | 2851 | F | 909 355-1200 | 6078 |
| Specialized Milling Corp | 2851 | E | 909 357-7890 | 6114 |
| Kemira Water Solutions Inc | 2899 | E | 909 350-5678 | 6301 |
| Fontana Paper Mills Inc | 2952 | D | 909 823-4100 | 6374 |
| TTI Floor Care North Amer Inc | 3052 | D | 440 996-2802 | 6434 |
| Cannon Gasket Inc | 3053 | E | 909 355-1547 | 6440 |
| Ring Container Tech LLC | 3085 | D | 909 350-8416 | 6617 |
| Premier Packaging LLC | 3086 | E | 909 749-5123 | 6656 |
| Dorel Juvenile Group Inc | 3089 | C | 909 428-0295 | 6809 |
| Vpet Usa LLC | 3089 | D | 909 605-1668 | 7074 |
| Avilas Garden Art (PA) | 3272 | E | 909 350-4546 | 7312 |
| Hanson Roof Tile Inc | 3272 | B | 888 509-4787 | 7341 |
| Jensen Enterprises Inc | 3272 | B | 909 357-7345 | 7347 |
| Oldcastle Infrastructure Inc | 3272 | E | 909 428-3700 | 7364 |
| California Steel Inds Inc (HQ) | 3312 | C | 909 350-6300 | 7609 |
| Tree Island Wire (usa) Inc | 3315 | C | 909 594-7511 | 7654 |
| California Steel Inds Inc | 3317 | B | 909 350-6300 | 7661 |
| Southwire Inc (HQ) | 3353 | F | 310 884-8500 | 7733 |
| Vista Metals Corp (PA) | 3354 | C | 909 823-4278 | 7755 |
| American Die Casting Inc | 3364 | E | 909 356-7768 | 7825 |
| Solar Atmospheres Inc | 3398 | E | 909 217-7400 | 7899 |
| Greif Inc | 3412 | D | 909 350-2112 | 7934 |
| Allegion Access Tech LLC | 3423 | E | 909 628-9272 | 7944 |
| Fabco Steel Fabrication Inc | 3441 | E | 909 350-1535 | 8137 |
| Rnd Contractors Inc | 3441 | E | 909 429-8500 | 8210 |
| Schroeder Iron Corporation | 3441 | E | 909 428-6471 | 8214 |
| Door Components Inc | 3442 | C | 909 770-5700 | 8262 |
| LLC Walker West | 3444 | D | 951 685-9660 | 8487 |
| Lynam Industries Inc (PA) | 3444 | D | 951 360-1919 | 8490 |
| Alabama Metal Industries Corp | 3446 | E | 909 350-9280 | 8616 |
| Morin Corporation | 3448 | E | 909 428-3747 | 8677 |
| Fab Services West Inc | 3449 | D | 909 350-7500 | 8697 |
| Forged Metals Inc | 3462 | C | 909 350-9260 | 8776 |
| Pacific Forge Inc | 3462 | D | 909 390-0701 | 8783 |
| Nellxo LLC | 3469 | E | 909 320-8501 | 8871 |
| Betts Company | 3495 | E | 909 427-9988 | 9199 |
| Nashville Wire Pdts Mfg Co LLC | 3496 | F | 714 736-0081 | 9223 |
| American Security Products Co | 3499 | C | 951 685-9680 | 9274 |
| JE Thomson & Company LLC | 3537 | F | 626 334-7190 | 9526 |
| Superior Trailer Works | 3537 | E | 909 350-0185 | 9534 |
| Cvc Technologies Inc | 3565 | E | 909 355-0311 | 10017 |
| Cavallo & Cavallo Inc | 3599 | F | 909 428-6994 | 10765 |
| Santa Fe Machine Works Inc | 3599 | E | 909 350-6877 | 11099 |
| Serampore Inds Private Ltd Inc | 3599 | F | 877 921-6111 | 11109 |
| Crown Technical Systems (PA) | 3613 | C | 951 332-4170 | 11238 |
| Eaton Electrical Inc | 3625 | C | 951 685-5788 | 11320 |
| Sunbeam Products Inc | 3631 | F | 951 727-3901 | 11396 |
| Harman Professional Inc | 3651 | C | 844 776-4899 | 11666 |
| Becker Specialty Corporation | 3677 | D | 909 356-1095 | 12830 |
| DSM&t Co Inc | 3694 | C | 909 357-7960 | 13168 |
| Kovatch Mobile Equipment Corp | 3711 | E | 951 685-1224 | 13362 |
| Bab Steering Hydraulics (PA) | 3714 | E | 208 573-4502 | 13464 |
| Carlstar Group LLC | 3714 | C | 909 829-1703 | 13473 |
| S&B Filters Inc (PA) | 3714 | E | 909 947-0015 | 13571 |
| Utility Trailer Mfg Co | 3715 | C | 909 428-8300 | 13624 |
| Tri-Net Inc | 3825 | E | 909 483-3555 | 14595 |
| Maxzone Vehicle Lighting Corp (HQ) | 5013 | E | 909 822-3288 | 16388 |

# GEOGRAPHIC SECTION — FREMONT, CA

| Company | SIC | EMP | PHONE | ENTRY# |
|---|---|---|---|---|
| Wabash National Trlr Ctrs Inc | 5013 | E | 765 771-5300 | 16405 |
| James Hardie Building Pdts Inc | 5031 | D | 909 355-6500 | 16447 |
| Patrick Industries Inc | 5032 | E | 909 350-4440 | 16481 |
| Daniel Gerard Worldwide Inc | 5051 | D | 951 361-1111 | 16618 |
| AC Pro Inc (PA) | 5075 | C | 951 360-7849 | 16773 |
| Orora Packaging Solutions | 5113 | D | 909 770-5400 | 17017 |
| Tealove Inc | 5499 | E | 714 408-8245 | 17433 |
| Boyd Flotation Inc | 5712 | E | 314 997-5222 | 17516 |
| Castle Importing Inc | 5812 | E | 909 428-9200 | 17570 |
| Social Junky Inc | 7389 | E | 213 999-1275 | 19134 |
| Bridgestone Americas | 7534 | E | 909 770-8523 | 19151 |
| Jeti Inc | 7692 | F | 909 357-2966 | 19204 |
| Tikos Tanks Inc | 7692 | F | 951 757-8014 | 19218 |
| Production Engineering & Mch | 8071 | E | 909 721-2455 | 19330 |
| Fontana Resources At Work | 8331 | E | 909 428-3833 | 19361 |
| Lamer Street Kreations Corp | 8711 | E | 909 305-4824 | 19402 |

## FOOTHILL RANCH, CA - Orange County

| Company | SIC | EMP | PHONE | ENTRY# |
|---|---|---|---|---|
| T Hasegawa USA Inc | 2087 | E | 949 461-3344 | 2028 |
| Nike Inc | 2353 | F | 949 616-4042 | 2847 |
| Avion Graphics Inc | 2752 | E | 949 472-0438 | 4520 |
| Protab Laboratories (PA) | 2834 | D | 949 635-1930 | 5613 |
| Soaptronic LLC | 2842 | E | 949 465-8955 | 5928 |
| Twila True Collaborations LLC | 2844 | E | 949 258-9720 | 6049 |
| Hampton Products Intl Corp (PA) | 3429 | C | 800 562-5625 | 8000 |
| Kwikset Corporation | 3429 | A | 949 672-4000 | 8009 |
| Weiser Lock Corporation | 3429 | F | 949 672-4000 | 8036 |
| A & J Manufacturing Company | 3469 | E | 714 544-9570 | 8813 |
| Bal Seal Engineering LLC (DH) | 3495 | C | 949 460-2100 | 9197 |
| Azure Microdynamics Inc | 3599 | D | 949 699-3344 | 10729 |
| Captivate Brands Usa Inc | 3631 | F | 949 229-8927 | 11386 |
| Renkus-Heinz Inc (PA) | 3651 | D | 949 588-9997 | 11690 |
| Allied Components Intl | 3677 | E | 949 356-1780 | 12827 |
| Carttronics LLC (HQ) | 3699 | D | 888 696-2278 | 13218 |
| Gatekeeper Systems Inc (PA) | 3699 | D | 888 808-9433 | 13242 |
| Oleumtech Corporation | 3823 | E | 949 305-9009 | 14441 |
| Chroma Systems Solutions Inc (HQ) | 3825 | E | 949 297-4848 | 14505 |
| Ossur Americas Inc | 3842 | C | 949 382-3883 | 15388 |
| Oakley Inc (DH) | 3851 | A | 949 951-0991 | 15611 |
| Redcom LLC | 3861 | B | 949 404-4084 | 15663 |
| Venus Group Inc (PA) | 5023 | D | 949 609-1299 | 16439 |
| Image Options (PA) | 7319 | D | 949 586-7665 | 17790 |
| Risa Tech Inc | 7371 | E | 949 951-5815 | 17973 |
| Trensor LLC | 8711 | F | 949 379-6730 | 19426 |

## FORESTVILLE, CA - Sonoma County

| Company | SIC | EMP | PHONE | ENTRY# |
|---|---|---|---|---|
| Topolos At Rssian River Vinyrd | 0172 | E | 707 887-1575 | 32 |
| Canyon Rock Co Inc | 1442 | E | 707 887-2207 | 310 |

## FORT BRAGG, CA - Mendocino County

| Company | SIC | EMP | PHONE | ENTRY# |
|---|---|---|---|---|
| North Coast Brewing Co Inc (PA) | 2082 | E | 707 964-2739 | 1450 |
| North Coast Brewing Co Inc | 2082 | E | 707 964-3400 | 1451 |
| Ocean Fresh LLC (PA) | 2091 | E | 707 964-1389 | 2040 |
| Anderson Logging Inc | 2411 | D | 707 964-2770 | 3041 |
| Roach Bros Inc | 2411 | E | 707 964-9240 | 3052 |

## FORT IRWIN, CA - San Bernardino County

| Company | SIC | EMP | PHONE | ENTRY# |
|---|---|---|---|---|
| Northrop Grumman Systems Corp | 3812 | D | 760 380-4268 | 14241 |

## FORTUNA, CA - Humboldt County

| Company | SIC | EMP | PHONE | ENTRY# |
|---|---|---|---|---|
| Humboldt Creamery LLC | 2023 | C | 209 576-3400 | 764 |
| Leonardo Logging and Cnstr Inc | 2411 | E | 707 725-1809 | 3049 |
| Eel River Brewing Co Inc (PA) | 5813 | E | 707 725-2739 | 17616 |

## FOSTER CITY, CA - San Mateo County

| Company | SIC | EMP | PHONE | ENTRY# |
|---|---|---|---|---|
| Standard Fiber LLC | 2211 | E | 650 872-6528 | 2427 |
| Omics Group Inc | 2721 | B | 650 268-9744 | 4283 |
| Central Business Forms Inc | 2752 | E | 650 548-0918 | 4546 |
| Capnia Inc | 2834 | E | 650 213-8444 | 5386 |
| Cymabay Therapeutics Inc (PA) | 2834 | D | 650 574-3000 | 5418 |
| Forty Seven Inc (HQ) | 2834 | E | 650 352-4150 | 5445 |
| Geron Corporation | 2834 | C | 650 473-7700 | 5459 |
| Gilead Sciences Inc (PA) | 2834 | B | 650 574-3000 | 5463 |
| Mirum Pharmaceuticals Inc (PA) | 2834 | E | 650 667-4085 | 5556 |
| Terns Pharmaceuticals Inc (PA) | 2834 | E | 650 525-5535 | 5687 |
| Mipox International Corp | 3291 | E | 650 638-9830 | 7556 |
| Bertram Capital Management LLC (PA) | 3541 | C | 650 358-5000 | 9542 |
| American Precision Gear Co | 3566 | E | 650 627-8060 | 10038 |
| Powertronix Inc | 3612 | E | 650 345-6800 | 11224 |
| Tsdi America Inc | 3621 | E | 650 430-3776 | 11292 |
| Discera Inc | 3674 | F | | 12403 |
| Zoox Inc (HQ) | 3711 | E | 650 539-9669 | 13399 |
| Applied Biosystems Inc | 3826 | D | 800 327-3002 | 14613 |
| Insomniac Games Inc | 3944 | D | 650 655-1633 | 15753 |
| Qualys Inc (PA) | 7371 | A | 650 801-6100 | 17966 |
| Coupa Software Incorporated (HQ) | 7372 | C | 650 931-3200 | 18207 |
| Gridgain Systems Inc (PA) | 7372 | D | 650 241-2281 | 18365 |
| Quinstreet Inc (PA) | 7389 | E | 650 578-7700 | 19118 |
| Gilead Palo Alto Inc (HQ) | 8731 | E | 650 384-8500 | 19455 |
| Verinata Health Inc | 8731 | D | 650 632-1680 | 19482 |

## FOUNTAIN VALLEY, CA - Orange County

| Company | SIC | EMP | PHONE | ENTRY# |
|---|---|---|---|---|
| ML Kishigo Mfg Co Inc | 2389 | D | 949 852-1963 | 2906 |
| Action Bag & Cover Inc | 2393 | D | 714 965-7777 | 2953 |
| Home Plus Group Inc | 2434 | F | 714 500-3855 | 3242 |
| Tdi2 Custom Packaging Inc | 2673 | F | 714 751-6782 | 3983 |
| Duncan McIntosh Company Inc (PA) | 2721 | E | 949 660-6150 | 4249 |
| Moreland Manufacturing Inc | 2759 | E | 714 426-1411 | 4924 |
| Yg Laboratories Inc | 2844 | E | 714 474-2800 | 6062 |
| Rubber-Cal Inc | 3069 | E | 714 772-3000 | 6535 |
| Epe Industries Usa Inc (HQ) | 3086 | F | 800 315-0336 | 6632 |
| Gaffoglio Fmly Mtlcrafters Inc (PA) | 3231 | C | 714 444-2000 | 7222 |
| Atlas Sheet Metal Inc | 3444 | F | 949 600-8787 | 8386 |
| KB Sheetmetal Fabrication Inc | 3444 | E | 714 979-1780 | 8481 |
| TN Sheet Metal Inc | 3444 | F | 714 593-0100 | 8595 |
| Omni Metal Finishing Inc (PA) | 3471 | D | 714 979-9414 | 8991 |
| Synergistic Research Inc | 3496 | F | 949 476-0000 | 9235 |
| Makino Inc | 3545 | E | 714 444-4334 | 9682 |
| Meyco Machine and Tool Inc | 3545 | E | 714 435-1546 | 9683 |
| Compuvac Industries Inc | 3563 | F | 949 574-5085 | 9959 |
| Kingston Technology Company | 3572 | A | 310 729-3394 | 10250 |
| Kingston Digital Inc (DH) | 3577 | E | 714 435-2600 | 10393 |
| Kingston Technology Corp (PA) | 3577 | B | 714 435-2600 | 10394 |
| Avatar Machine LLC | 3599 | E | 714 434-2737 | 10727 |
| Infocus Cnc Machining Inc | 3599 | E | 714 979-1253 | 10885 |
| Advanced Charging Tech LLC | 3629 | E | 877 228-5922 | 11358 |
| Interconnect Solutions Co LLC (PA) | 3629 | D | 714 556-7007 | 11375 |
| Surefire LLC (PA) | 3648 | C | 714 545-9444 | 11625 |
| X Hyper | 3651 | E | 530 673-7099 | 11720 |
| Ktc-Tu Corporation | 3674 | E | 714 435-2600 | 12517 |
| Mobis Parts America LLC | 3714 | E | 949 450-0014 | 13541 |
| Nobles Medical Tech Inc | 3841 | E | 714 427-0398 | 15207 |
| Surefire LLC | 3842 | E | 714 545-9444 | 15411 |
| Surefire LLC | 3842 | E | 714 545-9444 | 15412 |
| Surefire LLC | 3842 | E | 714 545-9444 | 15413 |
| Moving Image Technologies LLC | 3861 | E | 714 751-7998 | 15653 |
| Shock Doctor Inc | 3949 | E | 657 383-4400 | 15854 |
| Shock Doctor Inc (PA) | 3949 | D | 800 233-6956 | 15855 |
| Joy Products California Inc | 3953 | E | 714 437-7250 | 15891 |
| Kingston Technology Company Inc (HQ) | 5045 | A | 714 435-2600 | 16530 |
| Pedego LLC (PA) | 5941 | E | 800 646-8604 | 17635 |
| Freightgate Inc | 7372 | E | 714 799-2833 | 18332 |

## FOWLER, CA - Fresno County

| Company | SIC | EMP | PHONE | ENTRY# |
|---|---|---|---|---|
| Boghosian Raisin Pkg Co Inc | 0723 | E | 559 834-5348 | 75 |
| Bobby Slzars Mxcan Fd Pdts Inc (PA) | 2032 | E | 559 834-4787 | 850 |
| McWane Inc | 3321 | F | 559 834-4630 | 7678 |
| Dale Brisco Inc | 3444 | E | 559 834-5926 | 8423 |
| Borga Inc | 3448 | E | 559 834-5375 | 8657 |
| Borga Stl Bldngs Cmponents Inc | 3448 | D | 559 834-5375 | 8658 |
| Gee Manufacturing Incorporated | 3999 | E | 559 834-2929 | 16134 |

## FRAZIER PARK, CA - Kern County

| Company | SIC | EMP | PHONE | ENTRY# |
|---|---|---|---|---|
| Trnlwb LLC | 3999 | A | 661 245-3736 | 16260 |

## FREMONT, CA - Alameda County

| Company | SIC | EMP | PHONE | ENTRY# |
|---|---|---|---|---|
| Silevo Inc | 1711 | E | 510 771-1360 | 434 |
| Goldfire Corporation | 1751 | F | 510 354-3666 | 490 |
| Pathwater Inc | 2086 | E | 510 518-0014 | 1909 |
| Seven Up Btlg Co San Francisco (HQ) | 2086 | C | 925 938-8777 | 1960 |
| Organic Spices (PA) | 2099 | E | 510 440-1044 | 2303 |
| Produce World Inc | 2099 | D | 510 441-1449 | 2324 |
| Bay Associates Wire Tech Corp (DH) | 2298 | E | 510 988-3800 | 2534 |
| Sandys Drapery Inc (PA) | 2391 | E | 510 445-0112 | 2918 |
| Jia Home Inc | 2392 | E | 510 490-9788 | 2930 |
| Commercial Casework Inc (PA) | 2431 | D | 510 657-7933 | 3120 |
| International Paper Company | 2621 | D | 510 490-5887 | 3772 |
| Johnson & Johnson | 2676 | D | 650 237-4878 | 4002 |
| Scalable Press | 2711 | F | 877 752-9060 | 4193 |
| Book Buddy Digital Media Inc | 2731 | E | 510 226-9074 | 4316 |
| Chinese Overseas Mktg Svc Corp | 2741 | E | 626 280-8588 | 4378 |
| Global Publishing Inc | 2741 | E | | 4404 |
| Raymonds Little Print Shop Inc | 2752 | B | 510 353-3608 | 4749 |
| Spectrum Lithograph | 2752 | E | 510 438-9192 | 4767 |
| East Private Holdings II LLC (PA) | 2759 | E | 650 357-3500 | 4875 |
| Transcontinental Nrthern CA 20 | 2759 | C | 510 580-7700 | 4976 |

Employee Codes: A=Over 500 employees, B=251-500
C=101-250, D=51-100, E=20-50, F=10-19, G=1-9

# FREMONT, CA — GEOGRAPHIC SECTION

| Company | SIC | EMP | PHONE | ENTRY# |
|---|---|---|---|---|
| American Air Liquide Inc (DH) | 2813 | D | 510 624-4000 | 5043 |
| Air Liquide Electronics US LP | 2819 | A | 510 624-4338 | 5067 |
| BASF Catalysts LLC | 2819 | E | 510 490-2150 | 5073 |
| Alexza Pharmaceuticals Inc (HQ) | 2834 | E | 650 944-7000 | 5305 |
| Boehrnger Inglheim Fremont Inc (DH) | 2834 | C | 510 608-6500 | 5381 |
| Confluent Medical Tech Inc | 2834 | E | 510 683-2000 | 5407 |
| Novo Nordisk Inc | 2834 | A | 510 299-9508 | 5580 |
| Verseon Corporation (PA) | 2834 | E | 510 225-9000 | 5704 |
| Verseon International Corp (PA) | 2834 | E | 510 225-9000 | 5705 |
| Zosano Pharma Corporation (PA) | 2834 | E | 510 745-1200 | 5724 |
| Acrometrix Corporation | 2835 | E | 707 746-8888 | 5729 |
| Ortho-Clinical Diagnostics Inc | 2835 | E | 908 704-5910 | 5771 |
| Chemetall US Inc | 2842 | E | 408 387-5340 | 5895 |
| BASF Venture Capital Amer Inc | 2869 | E | 510 445-6140 | 6133 |
| Nitricity Inc | 2873 | E | 303 475-6197 | 6178 |
| Cyantek Corporation | 2899 | E | | 6280 |
| Certainteed LLC | 2952 | D | 510 490-0890 | 6373 |
| Alphagem Bio Inc | 3089 | E | 510 999-1153 | 6705 |
| Bace Manufacturing Inc | 3089 | D | 510 657-5800 | 6733 |
| Bayview Plastic Solutions Inc | 3089 | E | 510 360-0001 | 6737 |
| China Custom Manufacturing Ltd | 3089 | A | 510 979-1920 | 6774 |
| Freetech Plastics Inc | 3089 | E | 510 651-9996 | 6832 |
| Knightsbridge Plastics Inc | 3089 | D | 510 440-8444 | 6889 |
| Medplast Group Inc | 3089 | A | 510 657-5800 | 6909 |
| Viant Medical LLC | 3089 | C | 510 657-5800 | 7071 |
| Optiworks Inc (PA) | 3229 | D | 510 438-4560 | 7200 |
| West Coast Quartz Corporation (HQ) | 3229 | D | 510 249-2160 | 7207 |
| Quikrete California LLC | 3272 | E | 510 490-4670 | 7379 |
| Quikrete Companies LLC | 3272 | E | 510 490-4670 | 7382 |
| Walters & Wolf Glass Company | 3272 | D | 510 226-9800 | 7396 |
| Walters & Wolf Precast | 3272 | C | 510 226-9800 | 7397 |
| Golden State Assembly Inc (PA) | 3353 | E | 510 226-8155 | 7728 |
| Neptec Os Inc | 3357 | E | 510 687-1101 | 7789 |
| Winstronices International Inc | 3357 | E | 510 226-7588 | 7801 |
| Bodycote Thermal Proc Inc | 3398 | E | 510 492-4200 | 7879 |
| Lees Imperial Welding Inc | 3441 | C | 510 657-4900 | 8167 |
| Proline Metal Fabricators Inc | 3441 | E | 510 438-0300 | 8206 |
| Nationwide Boiler Incorporated (PA) | 3443 | E | 510 490-7100 | 8322 |
| Celestica Inc | 3444 | D | 408 727-0880 | 8408 |
| Mass Precision Inc | 3444 | C | 408 954-0200 | 8498 |
| Millennium Metalcraft Inc | 3444 | E | 510 657-4700 | 8511 |
| Sanmina Corporation | 3444 | D | 510 897-2000 | 8566 |
| Sienna Corporation | 3444 | C | 510 440-0200 | 8573 |
| Tri Fab Associates Inc | 3444 | D | 510 651-7628 | 8598 |
| Galgon Industries Inc | 3451 | E | 510 792-8211 | 8723 |
| E2e Mfg LLC | 3469 | E | 925 862-2057 | 8838 |
| Global Plating Inc | 3471 | E | 510 659-8764 | 8966 |
| Specialized Coating Svcs LLC (HQ) | 3479 | E | 510 226-8700 | 9122 |
| UNI-Fab Industries Inc | 3496 | D | 408 945-9733 | 9238 |
| Cal-Weld Inc | 3499 | E | 510 226-0100 | 9278 |
| Altair Technologies Inc | 3559 | E | 650 508-8700 | 9825 |
| Brooks Automation Us LLC | 3559 | E | 510 661-5132 | 9840 |
| IMG Altair LLC | 3559 | D | 650 508-8700 | 9865 |
| Imtec Acculine LLC | 3559 | E | 510 770-1800 | 9866 |
| Avp Technology LLC | 3565 | E | 510 683-0157 | 10012 |
| Ball Screws & Actuators Co Inc (DH) | 3568 | D | 510 770-5932 | 10066 |
| 3par Inc (HQ) | 3571 | E | 510 445-1046 | 10125 |
| Aivres Systems Inc | 3571 | C | 510 400-7599 | 10129 |
| Bold Data Technology Inc | 3571 | E | 510 490-8296 | 10139 |
| Elma Electronic Inc (HQ) | 3571 | D | 510 656-3400 | 10150 |
| Mercury Systems Inc | 3571 | D | 510 252-0870 | 10181 |
| Mercury Systems - Trusted Mission S | 3571 | D | 510 252-0870 | 10182 |
| Mitac Information Systems Corp | 3571 | E | 510 668-3507 | 10184 |
| Highpoint Technologies Inc | 3572 | E | 408 942-5800 | 10243 |
| Oryx Advanced Materials Inc (PA) | 3572 | E | 510 249-1157 | 10261 |
| Seagate Systems (us) Inc (DH) | 3572 | D | 510 687-5200 | 10277 |
| Seagate Technology LLC (DH) | 3572 | A | 800 732-4283 | 10279 |
| Seagate Technology LLC | 3572 | B | 510 624-3728 | 10280 |
| AG Neovo Technology Corp | 3575 | F | 408 321-8210 | 10303 |
| 3dconnexion Inc | 3577 | D | 510 713-6000 | 10313 |
| Aries Research Inc | 3577 | E | 925 818-1078 | 10324 |
| Corsair Components Inc | 3577 | A | 510 657-8747 | 10351 |
| Document Capture Technologies Inc | 3577 | E | 408 436-9888 | 10358 |
| Identiv Inc (PA) | 3577 | D | 949 250-8888 | 10377 |
| Incal Technology Inc | 3577 | E | 510 657-8405 | 10378 |
| Ituner Networks Corporation | 3577 | F | 510 573-0783 | 10391 |
| Terarecon Inc | 3577 | E | 650 372-1100 | 10444 |
| Visioneer Inc (PA) | 3577 | E | 925 251-6300 | 10451 |
| Znyx Networks Inc | 3577 | D | | 10455 |
| Acm Research Inc (PA) | 3589 | C | 510 445-3700 | 10531 |
| A & D Precision Machining Inc | 3599 | E | 510 657-6781 | 10646 |
| All-Tech Machine & Engrg Inc | 3599 | E | 510 353-2000 | 10699 |
| B & G Precision Inc | 3599 | F | 510 438-9785 | 10731 |
| CDS Engineering Inc | 3599 | C | 510 252-2100 | 10767 |
| Ceramic Tech Inc | 3599 | E | 510 252-8500 | 10772 |
| Colleen & Herb Enterprises Inc | 3599 | C | 510 226-6083 | 10784 |
| D & H Mfg Co | 3599 | C | 510 770-5100 | 10796 |
| FM Industries Inc (DH) | 3599 | C | 510 668-1900 | 10838 |
| Owens Design Incorporated (PA) | 3599 | E | 510 659-1800 | 11019 |
| Reliance Machine Products Inc | 3599 | E | 510 438-6760 | 11075 |
| Sharp Dimension Inc | 3599 | E | 510 656-8938 | 11112 |
| South Bay Solutions Inc (PA) | 3599 | E | 650 843-1800 | 11119 |
| Tronson Manufacturing Inc | 3599 | E | 408 533-0369 | 11152 |
| Tru Machining | 3599 | F | 510 573-3408 | 11153 |
| Industrial Electric Mfg Inc | 3613 | C | 510 656-1600 | 11245 |
| New Iem LLC | 3613 | B | 510 656-1600 | 11247 |
| Pivotal Systems Corporation | 3625 | E | 510 770-9125 | 11340 |
| Brava Home Inc | 3634 | E | 855 276-6767 | 11401 |
| Bizlink Technology Inc (HQ) | 3643 | D | 510 252-0786 | 11442 |
| Cable Connection Inc | 3643 | D | 510 249-9000 | 11443 |
| YC Cable Usa Inc (HQ) | 3643 | D | 510 824-2788 | 11478 |
| Enlighted Inc | 3646 | D | 650 964-1094 | 11529 |
| Isomedia LLC | 3652 | E | 510 668-1656 | 11736 |
| Accordion Networks Inc | 3661 | E | 510 623-2876 | 11747 |
| Actelis Networks Inc (PA) | 3661 | E | 510 545-1045 | 11748 |
| Ayantra Inc | 3661 | F | 510 623-7526 | 11752 |
| Enablence USA Components Inc | 3661 | D | 510 226-8900 | 11761 |
| Optoplex Corporation | 3661 | B | 510 490-9930 | 11780 |
| Cellphone-Mate Inc | 3663 | E | 510 770-0469 | 11824 |
| Commscope | 3663 | E | 408 952-2454 | 11828 |
| Sierra Nevada Corporation | 3663 | D | 510 446-6400 | 11946 |
| TCI International Inc (DH) | 3663 | C | 510 687-6100 | 11958 |
| Telewave Inc | 3663 | E | 408 929-4400 | 11964 |
| All Quality & Services Inc (PA) | 3672 | D | 510 249-5800 | 12047 |
| Alpha Ems Corporation | 3672 | C | 510 498-8788 | 12048 |
| Alta Manufacturing Inc | 3672 | E | 510 668-1870 | 12049 |
| Asteelflash California Inc | 3672 | A | 510 440-2840 | 12060 |
| Bay Area Circuits Inc | 3672 | E | 510 933-9000 | 12064 |
| Bema Electronic Mfg Inc | 3672 | D | 510 490-7770 | 12066 |
| Benchmark Electronics Inc | 3672 | E | 510 360-2800 | 12070 |
| Elma Bustronic Corp | 3672 | E | 510 490-7388 | 12093 |
| Jabil Inc | 3672 | C | 510 353-1000 | 12140 |
| Jaton Corporation | 3672 | E | 510 933-8888 | 12146 |
| Meritronics Materials Inc | 3672 | F | 408 390-5642 | 12163 |
| Morgan-Royce Industries Inc | 3672 | E | 440 440-8500 | 12166 |
| Neo Tech Inc | 3672 | F | 510 360-2222 | 12175 |
| Oncore Manufacturing LLC | 3672 | E | 510 516-5488 | 12180 |
| Smtc Manufacturing Corp Cal | 3672 | A | 510 737-0700 | 12220 |
| Sna Electronics Inc | 3672 | E | 510 656-3903 | 12221 |
| Sonic Manufacturing Tech Inc | 3672 | D | 510 580-8551 | 12224 |
| Sonic Manufacturing Tech Inc | 3672 | D | 510 573-3065 | 12225 |
| Sonic Manufacturing Tech Inc (PA) | 3672 | C | 510 580-8500 | 12226 |
| Sparqtron Corporation | 3672 | D | 510 657-7198 | 12228 |
| Streamline Electronics Mfg Inc | 3672 | E | 408 263-3600 | 12231 |
| Suba Technology Inc | 3672 | D | 408 434-6500 | 12232 |
| Telirite Technical Svcs Inc | 3672 | E | 510 440-3888 | 12239 |
| Applied Ceramics Inc (PA) | 3674 | E | 510 249-9700 | 12312 |
| Applied Thin-Film Products (PA) | 3674 | C | 510 661-4287 | 12324 |
| Asyst Technologies Inc | 3674 | A | 408 329-6661 | 12337 |
| Avalanche Technology Inc | 3674 | E | 510 438-0148 | 12346 |
| Axt Inc (PA) | 3674 | E | 510 438-4700 | 12350 |
| Axt Inc | 3674 | B | 510 683-5900 | 12351 |
| Axt-Tongmei Inc | 3674 | E | 510 438-4700 | 12352 |
| Enervenue Inc | 3674 | E | 408 664-0355 | 12420 |
| Enphase Energy Inc (PA) | 3674 | A | 707 774-7000 | 12422 |
| Finisar Corporation | 3674 | F | 408 548-1000 | 12432 |
| Gigamat Technologies Inc | 3674 | F | 510 770-8008 | 12444 |
| Hayward Quartz Technology Inc | 3674 | C | 510 657-9605 | 12462 |
| Helitek Company Ltd | 3674 | E | 510 933-7688 | 12463 |
| I2a Technologies Inc | 3674 | E | 510 770-0322 | 12465 |
| Ic Sensors Inc | 3674 | E | 510 498-1570 | 12466 |
| Ichor Holdings Ltd (PA) | 3674 | D | 510 897-5200 | 12468 |
| Ichor Systems Inc | 3674 | D | 510 226-0100 | 12469 |
| Ichor Systems Inc | 3674 | E | 510 226-0100 | 12470 |
| Ichor Systems Inc (HQ) | 3674 | E | 510 897-5200 | 12471 |
| Inapac Technology Inc | 3674 | E | 408 746-0614 | 12474 |
| Innodisk Usa Corporation | 3674 | E | 510 770-9421 | 12484 |
| Lam Research Corporation (PA) | 3674 | A | 510 572-0200 | 12526 |
| Linear Integrated Systems Inc | 3674 | F | 510 490-9160 | 12531 |
| Mattson Technology Inc (HQ) | 3674 | E | 510 657-5900 | 12548 |
| Oorja Corporation | 3674 | E | 510 659-1899 | 12620 |
| Patriot Memory Inc (PA) | 3674 | C | 510 979-1021 | 12628 |
| S3 Graphics Inc | 3674 | C | 510 687-4900 | 12682 |
| Sigma Designs Inc | 3674 | A | 510 897-0200 | 12697 |
| Silicon Genesis Corporation | 3674 | E | 408 228-5885 | 12699 |
| Smart Modular Tech De Inc (HQ) | 3674 | C | 510 623-1231 | 12721 |

# GEOGRAPHIC SECTION — FRESNO, CA

| Company | SIC | EMP | PHONE | ENTRY# |
|---|---|---|---|---|
| Soraa Inc (PA) | 3674 | D | 510 456-2200 | 12725 |
| Startech Semiconductor Inc | 3674 | D | 510 668-7000 | 12733 |
| Stats Chippac Test Svcs Inc (DH) | 3674 | F | 510 979-8000 | 12735 |
| Via Technologies Inc | 3674 | C | 510 683-3300 | 12787 |
| Volterra Semiconductor LLC | 3674 | C | 510 743-1200 | 12798 |
| Yield Engineering Systems Inc (PA) | 3674 | C | 510 954-6889 | 12809 |
| Dale Vishay Electronics LLC | 3676 | E | 510 661-4287 | 12822 |
| Network Video Technologies Inc (PA) | 3678 | E | 650 462-8100 | 12892 |
| Applied Thin-Film Products | 3679 | F | 510 661-4287 | 12915 |
| Celestica LLC | 3679 | C | 510 770-5100 | 12934 |
| Compass Components Inc (PA) | 3679 | C | 510 656-4700 | 12944 |
| Gooch & Housego Palo Alto LLC (HQ) | 3679 | C | 650 856-7911 | 12988 |
| Interface Masters Tech Inc | 3679 | E | 408 676-1086 | 13004 |
| Micro Lambda Wireless Inc | 3679 | E | 510 770-9221 | 13035 |
| Microwave Technology Inc (HQ) | 3679 | E | 510 651-6700 | 13038 |
| Myntahl Corporation | 3679 | E | 510 413-0002 | 13043 |
| Reach Technology Inc | 3679 | E | 510 770-1417 | 13073 |
| Te Connectivity Ltd | 3679 | E | 650 361-4923 | 13099 |
| Wellex Corporation (PA) | 3679 | C | 510 743-1818 | 13121 |
| Tenergy Corporation | 3691 | D | 510 687-0388 | 13153 |
| Zerobase Energy LLC | 3691 | E | 888 530-9376 | 13155 |
| Enovix Corporation (PA) | 3692 | D | 510 695-2350 | 13159 |
| Enovix Operations Inc | 3692 | C | 510 695-2399 | 13160 |
| Kyocera Sld Laser Inc | 3699 | E | 805 696-6999 | 13265 |
| Tesla Inc | 3711 | C | 510 249-3500 | 13391 |
| Tesla Inc | 3711 | B | 650 681-5000 | 13392 |
| Tesla Inc | 3711 | F | 510 690-5451 | 13394 |
| Tesla Inc | 3711 | A | 510 249-3650 | 13395 |
| Tesla Inc | 3711 | D | 510 766-6688 | 13396 |
| New United Motor Manufacturing Inc | 3714 | A | 510 498-5500 | 13546 |
| Pebble Mobility Inc | 3714 | E | 650 209-0799 | 13555 |
| Cv Ingenuity Corp | 3821 | E | 508 261-8000 | 14334 |
| Intematix Corporation (PA) | 3822 | D | 510 933-3300 | 14362 |
| Veex Inc | 3823 | F | 510 651-0500 | 14467 |
| Aehr Test Systems (PA) | 3825 | D | 510 623-9400 | 14486 |
| Calogic | 3825 | E | 510 656-2900 | 14503 |
| Db Control Corp (HQ) | 3825 | D | 510 656-2325 | 14510 |
| Essai Inc (DH) | 3825 | E | 510 580-1700 | 14520 |
| Golden Altos Corporation | 3825 | E | 408 956-1010 | 14529 |
| Nova Measuring Instruments Inc | 3825 | E | 408 510-7400 | 14566 |
| Qxq Inc | 3825 | E | 510 252-1522 | 14577 |
| Translarity Inc (PA) | 3825 | F | 510 371-7900 | 14594 |
| TTT-Cubed Inc | 3825 | D | 510 656-2325 | 14596 |
| Cytek Biosciences Inc (PA) | 3826 | B | 510 657-0102 | 14649 |
| Duke Scientific Corporation | 3826 | D | 650 424-1177 | 14657 |
| Fei Efa Inc (DH) | 3826 | E | 510 897-6800 | 14665 |
| Kashiyama-Usa Inc | 3826 | F | 510 979-0070 | 14681 |
| Medical Analysis Systems Inc (DH) | 3826 | C | 510 979-5000 | 14688 |
| Microgenics Corporation (HQ) | 3826 | E | 510 979-9147 | 14690 |
| Microgenics Corporation | 3826 | A | 510 979-5000 | 14691 |
| Remel Inc | 3826 | A | 916 425-2651 | 14711 |
| Wafergen Bio-Systems Inc | 3826 | D | 877 923-3746 | 14755 |
| Jenoptik Optical Systems LLC | 3827 | E | 510 676-0019 | 14791 |
| Angioscore Inc | 3841 | C | 510 933-7900 | 14968 |
| Biogenex Laboratories (PA) | 3841 | E | 510 824-1400 | 15011 |
| Ceterix Orthopaedics Inc | 3841 | E | 650 241-1748 | 15038 |
| Confluent Medical Tech Inc | 3841 | E | 510 683-2000 | 15048 |
| Covidien Holding Inc | 3841 | C | 510 456-1500 | 15059 |
| Evolve Manufacturing Tech Inc | 3841 | D | 510 690-8959 | 15084 |
| Insound Medical Inc | 3841 | E | 510 792-4000 | 15119 |
| Intuity Medical Inc | 3841 | D | 408 530-1700 | 15130 |
| Luminostics Inc | 3841 | E | 408 858-7103 | 15156 |
| Meraqi Medical Inc | 3841 | E | 669 222-7710 | 15184 |
| Moximed Inc (PA) | 3841 | F | 510 887-3300 | 15196 |
| Nova Eye Inc | 3841 | E | 510 291-1300 | 15209 |
| Optiscan Biomedical Corp | 3841 | E | 510 342-5800 | 15214 |
| QApel Medical Inc | 3841 | D | 510 738-6255 | 15236 |
| Stryker Sales LLC | 3841 | E | 510 413-2500 | 15269 |
| Zeda Inc | 3841 | F | 510 225-8412 | 15311 |
| Sonova USA Inc | 3842 | D | 510 743-3900 | 15406 |
| Think Surgical Inc | 3842 | C | 510 249-2300 | 15417 |
| Alara Inc | 3844 | E | 510 315-5200 | 15497 |
| Lyncean Technologies Inc | 3844 | F | 650 320-8300 | 15504 |
| Rapiscan Laboratories Inc (HQ) | 3844 | D | 408 961-9700 | 15506 |
| Rapiscan Laboratories Inc | 3844 | E | 510 399-7101 | 15507 |
| Nitinol Development Corp | 3851 | A | 510 683-2000 | 15610 |
| Lumens Integration Inc | 3861 | E | 510 657-8367 | 15650 |
| Optoma Technology Inc | 3861 | C | 510 897-8600 | 15656 |
| Lifeward Ca Inc | 3949 | D | 510 270-5900 | 15836 |
| Blazer Exhibits & Graphics Inc | 3993 | E | 408 263-7000 | 15949 |
| Garnett Signs LLC | 3993 | F | 650 871-9518 | 15982 |
| Young Electric Sign Company | 3993 | E | 510 877-7815 | 16070 |
| Oplink Communications LLC (DH) | 4899 | E | 510 933-7200 | 16340 |
| Asi Computer Technologies Inc (PA) | 5045 | E | 510 226-8000 | 16508 |
| Asus Computer International | 5045 | C | 510 739-3777 | 16509 |
| Exclusive Networks Usa Inc | 5045 | E | 408 943-9193 | 16523 |
| Hyper Products Inc (DH) | 5045 | F | 714 765-5555 | 16528 |
| Phihong USA Corp (HQ) | 5045 | D | 510 445-0100 | 16539 |
| Siblings Investment Inc | 5045 | E | 510 668-0368 | 16548 |
| Delta America Ltd (HQ) | 5065 | C | 510 668-5100 | 16698 |
| Nidec Genmark Automation Inc (DH) | 5084 | C | 510 897-3400 | 16829 |
| Cofan Thermal Inc | 5085 | E | 510 490-7533 | 16867 |
| Sunnyvale Fluid Sys Tech Inc (PA) | 5085 | E | 510 933-2500 | 16898 |
| Kal-Kustom Enterprises (PA) | 5091 | F | 510 651-8400 | 16937 |
| Kilam Inc | 5136 | C | 510 943-4040 | 17076 |
| San Francisco Herb & Natural Food Co Inc | 5149 | D | 510 770-1215 | 17211 |
| Oldcastle Buildingenvelope Inc | 5231 | C | 510 651-2292 | 17349 |
| Tend Insights Inc | 5731 | D | 510 619-9289 | 17545 |
| New Tech Solutions Inc | 5734 | E | 510 353-4070 | 17555 |
| Saitech Inc | 5734 | F | 510 440-0256 | 17558 |
| Kdr Holding Inc (PA) | 6799 | F | 510 230-2777 | 17755 |
| Fictiv Inc (PA) | 7371 | C | 415 580-2509 | 17920 |
| Instant Systems Inc | 7371 | D | 510 657-8100 | 17930 |
| Alertenterprise Inc (PA) | 7372 | C | 510 440-0840 | 18035 |
| Cliosoft Inc | 7372 | F | 510 790-4732 | 18175 |
| Cloudfiles Technologies Inc | 7372 | F | 336 298-6575 | 18183 |
| Enablence Systems Inc (HQ) | 7372 | D | 510 226-8900 | 18280 |
| Loginext Solutions Inc (PA) | 7372 | D | 510 894-6225 | 18500 |
| Ncoup Inc (PA) | 7372 | D | 510 739-4010 | 18572 |
| Nextracker Inc (PA) | 7372 | D | 510 270-2500 | 18588 |
| Nextracker LLC (HQ) | 7372 | D | 510 270-2500 | 18589 |
| Parablu Inc | 7372 | E | 408 775-6571 | 18657 |
| Petadata Software LLC | 7372 | E | 203 306-9949 | 18671 |
| Snapwiz Inc | 7372 | C | 510 328-3277 | 18803 |
| Socket Mobile Inc (PA) | 7372 | D | 510 933-3000 | 18805 |
| Sopact Inc | 7372 | E | 510 226-8535 | 18814 |
| Soundthinking Inc (PA) | 7372 | B | 510 794-3100 | 18816 |
| Valutics Inc | 7372 | E | 408 823-3597 | 18909 |
| Ravensworld Solutions Inc (HQ) | 7373 | D | 650 241-3661 | 18989 |
| Ntm Consulting Services Inc | 7379 | E | 510 744-3901 | 19041 |
| Econolite | 7389 | F | 408 577-1733 | 19090 |
| Manufacturing Resource Corp | 7389 | E | 510 438-9600 | 19105 |
| Smart World LLC | 7389 | E | 510 933-9700 | 19133 |
| Jabil Silver Creek Inc (HQ) | 7692 | D | 669 255-2900 | 19203 |
| B2 Machining LLC | 7699 | F | 510 668-1360 | 19244 |
| Db Design Group Inc | 8711 | E | 408 834-1400 | 19388 |
| Hikino Associates LLC | 8711 | F | 408 781-1900 | 19397 |
| PTEC Solutions Inc (PA) | 8711 | C | 510 358-3578 | 19413 |
| Reliant Engrg & Mfg Svcs Inc | 8711 | E | 510 252-1973 | 19414 |
| ISE Labs Inc (DH) | 8734 | C | 510 687-2500 | 19505 |
| United Mfg Assembly Inc | 8734 | D | 510 490-4680 | 19510 |
| Delta Electronics Americas Ltd (DH) | 8741 | D | 510 668-5111 | 19514 |

## FRENCH CAMP, CA - San Joaquin County

| Company | SIC | EMP | PHONE | ENTRY# |
|---|---|---|---|---|
| Poly Processing Company LLC | 2821 | E | 209 982-4904 | 5189 |
| Royal Westlake Roofing LLC | 3272 | F | 209 982-1473 | 7387 |
| Parex Usa Inc | 5032 | F | 510 444-2497 | 16480 |

## FRESNO, CA - Fresno County

| Company | SIC | EMP | PHONE | ENTRY# |
|---|---|---|---|---|
| Olam LLC | 0131 | E | 559 446-6420 | 1 |
| Dave J Mendrin Inc | 0172 | F | 559 352-1700 | 10 |
| Golden State Vintners | 0172 | E | 559 266-6548 | 14 |
| Raw Farm LLC | 0241 | E | 559 846-9732 | 59 |
| Valley Fig Growers | 0723 | E | 559 349-1686 | 88 |
| Dri Clean & Restoration | 1389 | E | 559 292-1100 | 223 |
| Prefab Innovations Inc | 1521 | E | 559 582-3871 | 348 |
| Clark Bros Inc | 1629 | D | 209 392-6144 | 394 |
| Strategic Mechanical Inc | 1711 | C | 559 291-1952 | 436 |
| Modesto Industrial Elec Co Inc | 1731 | E | 559 292-4714 | 462 |
| Pacific Gold Marketing Inc | 1794 | E | 559 272-8168 | 546 |
| B-F Glass Inc | 1799 | E | 559 221-4100 | 554 |
| Torres Fence Co Inc | 1799 | E | 559 237-4141 | 577 |
| Beef Packers Inc | 2011 | B | 559 268-5586 | 582 |
| Cargill Meat Solutions Corp | 2011 | A | 559 268-5586 | 587 |
| Certified Meat Products Inc | 2011 | D | 559 256-1433 | 590 |
| Fratelli Beretta Usa Inc | 2013 | E | 559 237-9591 | 641 |
| Fratelli Beretta Usa Inc | 2013 | E | 201 438-0723 | 642 |
| Valley Protein LLC | 2013 | D | 559 498-7115 | 675 |
| Cencal Foods LLC | 2015 | F | 559 341-5742 | 678 |
| Foster Farms LLC | 2015 | E | 559 443-2750 | 682 |
| Foster Poultry Farms | 2015 | A | 559 442-3771 | 688 |
| Foster Poultry Farms | 2015 | B | 559 265-2000 | 689 |
| Gfi Poultry LLC (PA) | 2015 | E | | 692 |
| ZF In Liquidation LLC | 2015 | A | 559 486-2310 | 703 |
| Nestle Usa Inc | 2023 | D | 559 834-2554 | 772 |
| Ampersand Ice Cream LLC | 2024 | F | 559 264-8000 | 791 |

Employee Codes: A=Over 500 employees, B=251-500
C=101-250, D=51-100, E=20-50, F=10-19, G=1-9

2025 Harris California Manufacturers Directory

© Mergent Inc. 1-800-342-5647

# FRESNO, CA

GEOGRAPHIC SECTION

| | SIC | EMP | PHONE | ENTRY# |
|---|---|---|---|---|
| Helados La Tapatia Inc | 2024 | E | 559 441-1105 | 804 |
| California Dairies Inc | 2026 | D | 559 233-5154 | 829 |
| Kraft Heinz Foods Company | 2033 | E | 559 441-8515 | 899 |
| LLC Lyons Magnus (PA) | 2033 | B | 559 268-5966 | 900 |
| LLC Lyons Magnus | 2033 | C | 559 268-5966 | 901 |
| Los Gatos Tomato Products LLC (PA) | 2033 | F | 559 945-2700 | 902 |
| Olam Tomato Processors Inc (DH) | 2033 | E | 559 447-1390 | 912 |
| Vie-Del Company (PA) | 2033 | D | 559 834-2525 | 936 |
| Caro Nut Company | 2034 | C | 559 475-5471 | 947 |
| Kern Delta Co LLC | 2034 | E | 559 276-2855 | 953 |
| Ray Moles Farms Inc (PA) | 2034 | E | 559 444-0324 | 960 |
| San Joaquin Figs Inc | 2034 | E | 559 224-4492 | 963 |
| Sun Vlley Rsns Inc A Cal Corp | 2034 | F | 559 233-8070 | 965 |
| Pacific Choice Brands Inc (PA) | 2035 | E | 559 892-5365 | 988 |
| Integrated Grain & Milling Inc | 2048 | E | 559 443-6500 | 1131 |
| Athens Baking Company Inc (PA) | 2051 | E | 559 324-8535 | 1160 |
| Fresno French Bread Bakery Inc | 2051 | E | 559 268-7088 | 1204 |
| Valley Lahvosh Baking Co Inc | 2051 | E | 559 485-2700 | 1250 |
| Brownie Baker Inc | 2052 | D | 559 277-7070 | 1267 |
| International Glace Inc (PA) | 2064 | E | 559 385-7675 | 1312 |
| G Debbas Chocolatier Inc | 2066 | E | 559 294-2071 | 1339 |
| Ssi G Debbas Chocolatier LLC | 2066 | E | 559 294-2071 | 1345 |
| Caro Nut Company (HQ) | 2068 | E | 559 475-5400 | 1349 |
| Hormel Foods Corporation | 2068 | E | 559 237-9206 | 1352 |
| Darling Ingredients Inc | 2077 | E | 559 268-5325 | 1381 |
| Stratas Foods LLC | 2079 | D | 559 495-4506 | 1407 |
| Full Circle Brewing Co Ltd LLC | 2082 | F | 559 264-6323 | 1432 |
| E & J Gallo Winery | 2084 | C | 559 458-0807 | 1547 |
| American Bottling Company | 2086 | D | 559 442-1553 | 1854 |
| Bottling Group LLC | 2086 | A | 914 767-6000 | 1869 |
| Bottling Group LLC | 2086 | A | 559 485-5050 | 1871 |
| Reyes Coca-Cola Bottling LLC | 2086 | D | 559 264-4631 | 1937 |
| Reyes Coca-Cola Bottling LLC | 2086 | E | 559 264-4631 | 1945 |
| Roger Enrico | 2086 | E | 559 485-5050 | 1956 |
| Rich Products Corporation | 2092 | E | 559 486-7380 | 2060 |
| Barney & Co California LLC | 2099 | F | 559 442-1752 | 2134 |
| Fiore Di Pasta Inc | 2099 | D | 559 457-0431 | 2199 |
| Gruma Corporation | 2099 | E | 559 498-7820 | 2224 |
| La Tapatia Tortilleria Inc | 2099 | C | 559 441-1030 | 2259 |
| Lidestri Foods Inc | 2099 | B | 559 251-1000 | 2266 |
| Pappys Meat Company Inc | 2099 | E | 559 291-0218 | 2313 |
| Ryan Mc Teer | 2391 | F | 559 217-1450 | 2916 |
| DV Kap Inc | 2392 | E | 559 435-5575 | 2928 |
| Architectural Wood Design Inc | 2434 | E | 559 292-9104 | 3216 |
| Emerzian Woodworking Inc | 2434 | E | 559 292-2448 | 3238 |
| Automated Bldg Components Inc | 2439 | F | 559 485-8232 | 3293 |
| Garcias Pallets Inc | 2448 | E | 559 485-8182 | 3343 |
| Wood-N-Wood Products Cal Inc (PA) | 2449 | E | 559 896-3636 | 3379 |
| California Tiny House Inc | 2451 | F | 559 316-4500 | 3381 |
| Xtraction Inc | 2515 | F | 800 273-4137 | 3547 |
| Fresno Rack & Shelving Inc | 2542 | E | 559 275-7225 | 3688 |
| Fury Hot Chicken LLC | 2599 | F | 559 944-8061 | 3742 |
| Westrock Rkt LLC | 2652 | C | 559 441-1181 | 3816 |
| Westrock Rkt LLC | 2653 | E | 559 497-1662 | 3896 |
| Michelsen Packaging Co Cal | 2671 | E | 559 237-3819 | 3930 |
| Paper Pulp & Film | 2679 | E | 559 233-1151 | 4045 |
| Business Journal | 2721 | E | 559 490-3400 | 4234 |
| Mike Murach & Associates Inc | 2731 | E | 559 440-9071 | 4336 |
| Service Express Inc | 2741 | E | 559 495-4790 | 4464 |
| Certified Ad Services | 2752 | C | 559 233-1891 | 4547 |
| Dumont Printing Inc | 2752 | E | 559 485-6311 | 4597 |
| Pan Pacific Printing Press Inc | 2752 | E | 559 252-1624 | 4717 |
| Professional Print & Mail Inc | 2752 | E | 559 237-7468 | 4740 |
| Linde Gas & Equipment Inc | 2813 | D | 559 237-5521 | 5045 |
| Tessenderlo Kerley Inc | 2819 | E | 559 485-0114 | 5124 |
| Eezer Products Inc | 2821 | E | 559 255-4140 | 5154 |
| Sabic Innovative Plas US LLC | 2821 | E | 559 264-4100 | 5197 |
| Haleon US LP | 2834 | D | 559 650-1550 | 5475 |
| Gea Farm Technologies Inc | 2842 | E | 559 497-5074 | 5905 |
| Duncan Enterprises (PA) | 2851 | C | 559 291-4444 | 6080 |
| Walton Industries Inc | 2851 | E | 559 495-4004 | 6117 |
| Brandt Consolidated Inc | 2875 | C | 559 499-2100 | 6185 |
| CMr Marketing and RES Inc | 2879 | B | 559 499-2100 | 6198 |
| Monterey Chemical Company | 2879 | D | 559 499-2100 | 6203 |
| McGrayel Company | 2899 | E | 559 299-7660 | 6308 |
| Reh Company | 2911 | D | 559 351-1916 | 6348 |
| Reh Company | 2911 | C | 559 997-3617 | 6349 |
| Mbtechnology | 2952 | E | 559 233-2181 | 6380 |
| Monster City Studios | 3086 | E | 559 498-0540 | 6648 |
| International Cases & Mfg Inc (PA) | 3161 | E | 559 253-4111 | 7134 |
| Vitro Flat Glass LLC | 3211 | C | 559 485-4660 | 7180 |
| Forterra Inc | 3272 | E | 559 221-2070 | 7334 |
| Builders Concrete Inc (DH) | 3273 | E | 559 225-3667 | 7408 |
| Cemex Materials LLC | 3273 | D | 559 275-2241 | 7430 |
| E-Z Haul Ready Mix Inc | 3273 | E | 559 233-6603 | 7439 |
| Legacy Vulcan LLC | 3273 | E | 559 434-1202 | 7464 |
| Outback Inc (PA) | 3273 | E | 559 293-3880 | 7482 |
| South Valley Materials Inc (HQ) | 3273 | D | 559 277-7060 | 7499 |
| Kearneys Aluminum Foundry Inc (PA) | 3363 | E | 559 233-2591 | 7812 |
| Scafco Corporation | 3399 | E | 559 256-9911 | 7913 |
| T G Schmeiser Co Inc | 3429 | E | 559 486-4569 | 8030 |
| Central Vly Assembly Packg Inc | 3432 | E | 559 486-4260 | 8050 |
| Kasco Fab Inc | 3441 | D | 559 442-1018 | 8162 |
| Lehmans Manufacturing Co Inc | 3441 | E | 559 486-1700 | 8168 |
| Modern Welding Company of California Inc | 3441 | E | 559 275-9353 | 8190 |
| Olson and Co Steel | 3441 | C | 559 224-7811 | 8196 |
| Robert J Alandt & Sons | 3441 | E | 559 275-1391 | 8212 |
| Suburban Steel Inc (PA) | 3441 | E | 559 268-6281 | 8224 |
| Central Valley Tank of Cal | 3443 | F | 559 456-3500 | 8304 |
| Modern Custom Fabrication Inc | 3443 | E | 559 264-4741 | 8321 |
| Tri-State Stairway Corp | 3446 | F | 559 268-0875 | 8647 |
| Valley Stairway Inc | 3446 | F | 559 299-0151 | 8648 |
| Meclec Metal Finishing Inc | 3471 | E | 559 797-0101 | 8983 |
| Bailey Valve Inc | 3491 | E | 559 434-2838 | 9145 |
| Bermad Inc (PA) | 3494 | E | 877 577-4283 | 9183 |
| Betts Company (PA) | 3495 | D | 559 498-3304 | 9198 |
| Shapco Inc | 3498 | D | 559 834-1342 | 9271 |
| Cummins Pacific LLC | 3519 | E | 559 277-6760 | 9323 |
| Agrifim Irrigation Pdts Inc | 3523 | F | 559 443-6680 | 9335 |
| Aweta-Autoline Inc (DH) | 3523 | E | 559 244-8340 | 9339 |
| D&M Manufacturing Co LLC | 3523 | E | 559 834-4668 | 9346 |
| D-K-P Inc | 3523 | F | 559 266-2695 | 9347 |
| Hunter Industries Incorporated | 3523 | E | 559 347-0816 | 9357 |
| Irritec Usa Inc | 3523 | E | 559 275-8825 | 9361 |
| Wasco Hardfacing Co | 3523 | D | 559 485-5860 | 9393 |
| Pb Loader Corporation | 3531 | E | 800 350-8521 | 9434 |
| Tanfield Engrg Systems US Inc | 3531 | F | 559 443-6602 | 9440 |
| Crown Equipment Corporation | 3537 | E | 559 585-8000 | 9511 |
| Golden Gate Freightliner Inc | 3537 | B | 559 486-4310 | 9520 |
| Atlas Pacific Engineering Co | 3556 | E | 559 233-4500 | 9778 |
| Commercial Manufacturing | 3556 | E | 559 237-1855 | 9785 |
| Meeder Equipment Company (PA) | 3556 | E | 559 485-0979 | 9874 |
| Grundfos Pumps Manufacturing Corpor (DH) | 3561 | C | 559 292-8000 | 9927 |
| HP Water Systems Inc | 3561 | E | 559 268-4751 | 9929 |
| Trillium Pumps Usa Inc (HQ) | 3561 | C | 559 442-4000 | 9945 |
| Tempest Technology Corporation | 3564 | E | 800 346-2143 | 10001 |
| Whipple Industries Inc | 3564 | F | 559 442-1261 | 10008 |
| Klippenstein Corporation | 3565 | E | 559 834-4258 | 10022 |
| Kodiak Cartoners Inc | 3565 | F | 559 266-4844 | 10023 |
| Gusmer Enterprises Inc | 3569 | E | 908 301-1811 | 10092 |
| J P Lamborn Co (PA) | 3585 | E | 559 650-2120 | 10503 |
| Lennox International Inc | 3585 | C | 559 490-0078 | 10505 |
| Garabedian Bros Inc (PA) | 3599 | E | 559 268-5014 | 10851 |
| Pnm Company | 3599 | E | 559 291-1986 | 11043 |
| R & L Enterprises Inc | 3599 | E | 559 233-1608 | 11063 |
| United Western Industries Inc | 3599 | E | 559 226-7236 | 11161 |
| Fresno Distributing Co | 3651 | E | 559 442-8800 | 11660 |
| Dantel Inc | 3661 | E | 559 292-1111 | 11759 |
| Digital Prototype Systems Inc | 3663 | E | 559 454-1600 | 11841 |
| Safety Ntwrk Traffic Signs Inc | 3669 | E | 559 291-8000 | 12014 |
| M2 Antenna Systems Inc | 3679 | F | 559 221-2271 | 13027 |
| Murdoc Technology LLC | 3679 | E | 559 497-1580 | 13042 |
| Brix Group Inc | 3699 | E | 559 457-4750 | 13216 |
| Turner Dsgns Hydrcrbon Instrs | 3699 | E | 559 253-1414 | 13319 |
| American Carrier Systems | 3711 | F | 559 442-1500 | 13337 |
| Saf-T-Cab Inc (PA) | 3713 | E | 559 268-5541 | 13426 |
| Scelzi Enterprises Inc (PA) | 3713 | E | 559 237-5541 | 13427 |
| Kroeger Eqp Sup Co A Cal Corp | 3714 | E | 559 485-9900 | 13526 |
| Pana-Pacific Corporation (HQ) | 3714 | E | 559 457-4700 | 13552 |
| Slam Specialties LLC | 3714 | F | 559 348-9038 | 13576 |
| Vivint Inc | 3822 | B | 805 790-7209 | 14375 |
| Sacramento Cooling Systems Inc | 3829 | E | 559 253-9660 | 14915 |
| Axiom Industries Inc | 3842 | E | 559 276-1310 | 15324 |
| Tech West Vacuum Inc | 3843 | E | 559 291-1650 | 15489 |
| California Track & Engineering | 3949 | E | 559 237-2590 | 15796 |
| Keiser Corporation (PA) | 3949 | D | 559 256-8000 | 15834 |
| Total Concept Enterprises Inc | 3965 | F | 559 485-8413 | 15920 |
| A Plus Signs LLC | 3993 | E | 559 275-0700 | 15935 |
| Craigo Investments Inc | 3993 | F | 559 222-9293 | 15962 |
| Statewide Trffic Sfety Sgns In | 3993 | E | 559 291-8500 | 16047 |
| Universal Meditech Inc | 3995 | E | 559 366-7798 | 16073 |
| Brunos Iron & Metal LP | 4953 | E | 559 233-6543 | 16356 |
| Ipt Inc | 5013 | F | 559 266-6100 | 16387 |
| Larry Fisher & Sons Ltd Partnr | 5021 | F | 559 252-2575 | 16416 |
| T B B Inc | 5045 | F | 559 222-4100 | 16554 |
| Sunrise Medical (us) LLC | 5047 | E | 559 292-2171 | 16590 |

# GEOGRAPHIC SECTION

## GARDEN GROVE, CA

| Company | SIC | EMP | PHONE | ENTRY# |
|---|---|---|---|---|
| Consoldted Metal Fbrctng Coinc | 5051 | E | 559 268-7887 | 16615 |
| Allied Electric Motor Svc Inc (PA) | 5063 | D | 559 486-4222 | 16641 |
| Electric Motor Shop (PA) | 5063 | E | 559 233-1153 | 16651 |
| American Grape Harvesters Inc | 5083 | E | 559 277-7380 | 16795 |
| Jensen & Pilegard (PA) | 5083 | E | 559 268-9221 | 16799 |
| Netafim Irrigation Inc (HQ) | 5083 | B | 559 453-6800 | 16800 |
| Fresno Oxgn Wldg Suppliers Inc (PA) | 5084 | E | 559 233-6684 | 16815 |
| Lakos Corporation (HQ) | 5084 | E | 559 255-1601 | 16824 |
| California Industrial Rbr Co (PA) | 5085 | E | 559 268-7321 | 16865 |
| San Joaquin Hydraulic Inc (PA) | 5085 | F | 559 264-7325 | 16893 |
| Specialty Sales LLC | 5122 | D | 559 862-6611 | 17051 |
| US Foods Inc | 5141 | A | 559 271-3700 | 17120 |
| Holt Lumber Inc (PA) | 5211 | E | 559 233-3291 | 17333 |
| Paragon Industries Inc (PA) | 5211 | D | 559 275-5000 | 17339 |
| Paragon Industries II Inc | 5211 | D | 559 275-5000 | 17340 |
| Sequoia Steel and Supply Co | 5211 | F | 559 485-4100 | 17344 |
| Sams Italian Deli & Mkt Inc | 5411 | E | 559 229-9333 | 17383 |
| Counter Hospitality Group LLC | 5812 | D | 559 228-9735 | 17574 |
| Cooks Communications Corp | 5999 | E | 559 233-8818 | 17695 |
| Abelisk Inc (PA) | 7371 | F | 559 227-1000 | 17874 |
| Caylym Technologies Intl LLC | 7373 | E | 209 322-9596 | 18967 |
| Pelco Inc (HQ) | 7382 | A | 559 292-1981 | 19059 |
| Sportsmobile West | 7532 | E | 559 233-8267 | 19148 |
| A-1 Alternative Fuel Systems (PA) | 7549 | E | 559 485-4427 | 19166 |
| American Crier Eqp Trlr Sls LL | 7549 | F | 559 442-1500 | 19167 |
| Sanitary Stainless Welding Inc | 7692 | E | 559 233-7116 | 19212 |
| Arrow Electric Motor Service | 7694 | F | 559 266-0104 | 19223 |
| Wcr Incorporated | 7699 | F | 559 266-8374 | 19288 |
| Cwes Inc | 8748 | E | 559 346-1251 | 19556 |

## FULLERTON, CA - Orange County

| Company | SIC | EMP | PHONE | ENTRY# |
|---|---|---|---|---|
| Gaylords HRI Meats | 2011 | F | 714 526-2278 | 597 |
| Kraft Heinz Foods Company | 2033 | D | 714 870-8235 | 898 |
| Vanlaw Food Products Inc (HQ) | 2035 | D | 714 870-9091 | 997 |
| Charlies Specialties Inc | 2052 | D | 724 346-2350 | 1268 |
| Phenix Gourmet LLC | 2052 | C | 562 404-5028 | 1282 |
| Byrnes & Kiefer Co | 2087 | E | 714 554-4000 | 1991 |
| Common Collabs LLC (PA) | 2087 | F | 714 519-3245 | 1994 |
| Dr Smoothie Brands LLC | 2087 | E | 714 449-9787 | 1999 |
| Dr Smoothie Enterprises LLC | 2087 | E | 714 449-9787 | 2000 |
| Chefmaster | 2099 | E | 714 554-4000 | 2165 |
| Nina Mia Inc | 2099 | D | 714 773-5588 | 2297 |
| Quoc Viet Foods | 2099 | F | 714 519-3199 | 2328 |
| Dae Shin Usa Inc | 2221 | D | 714 578-8900 | 2434 |
| Fabtex Inc | 2221 | C | 714 538-0877 | 2437 |
| SPD Manufacturing Inc | 2221 | F | 985 302-1902 | 2442 |
| Delta Pacific Activewear Inc | 2253 | E | 714 871-9281 | 2466 |
| Anderco Inc | 2431 | E | 714 446-9508 | 3108 |
| Pacific Archtectural Mllwk Inc | 2431 | D | 714 525-2059 | 3174 |
| Accurate Laminated Pdts Inc | 2434 | E | 714 632-2773 | 3212 |
| Brentwood Home LLC (PA) | 2515 | C | 562 949-3759 | 3522 |
| Nicholas Michael Designs LLC | 2519 | C | 714 562-8101 | 3556 |
| Amtrend Corporation | 2541 | E | 714 630-2070 | 3644 |
| Advanced Equipment Corporation (PA) | 2542 | E | 714 635-5350 | 3679 |
| Corru-Kraft IV | 2653 | F | 714 773-0124 | 3833 |
| W/S Packaging Group Inc | 2679 | E | 714 992-2574 | 4057 |
| Heat Press Nation | 2741 | E | 800 215-0894 | 4413 |
| Mail Handling Group Inc | 2752 | C | 952 975-5000 | 4686 |
| Minaloas Inc | 2752 | E | 949 951-7191 | 4695 |
| Graphics 2000 LLC | 2759 | D | 714 879-1188 | 4888 |
| Orora Visual LLC | 2759 | D | 714 879-2400 | 4935 |
| Western States Envelope Corp | 2759 | D | 714 449-0909 | 4984 |
| Wilsons Art Studio Inc | 2759 | D | 714 870-7030 | 4985 |
| Nbs Systems Inc (PA) | 2761 | E | 217 999-3472 | 4990 |
| Professional Plastics Inc (PA) | 2821 | E | 714 446-6500 | 5191 |
| Cargill Incorporated | 2833 | E | 714 449-6708 | 5235 |
| Stauber California Inc | 2833 | E | 714 441-3900 | 5271 |
| Stauber Prfmce Ingredients Inc (HQ) | 2833 | E | 714 441-3900 | 5272 |
| McKenna Labs (PA) | 2834 | E | 714 687-6888 | 5547 |
| United Pharma LLC | 2834 | C | 714 738-8999 | 5698 |
| S & H Rubber Co | 3069 | E | 714 525-0277 | 6536 |
| Foam-Craft Inc | 3086 | E | 714 459-9971 | 6639 |
| Future Foam Inc | 3086 | E | 714 459-9971 | 6641 |
| Future Foam Inc | 3086 | E | 714 871-2344 | 6643 |
| Chubby Gorilla Inc (PA) | 3089 | E | 844 365-5218 | 6775 |
| Jdh Pacific Inc (PA) | 3321 | E | 562 926-8088 | 7676 |
| Howmet Globl Fstning Systems I | 3324 | D | 714 871-1550 | 7687 |
| Cook and Cook Incorporated | 3443 | E | 714 680-6669 | 8313 |
| Gard Inc | 3444 | E | 714 738-5891 | 8456 |
| Stein Industries Inc (PA) | 3444 | E | 714 522-4560 | 8583 |
| United Duralume Products Inc | 3444 | F | 714 773-4011 | 8602 |
| Will-Mann Inc | 3444 | E | 714 870-0350 | 8613 |
| Kryler Corp | 3471 | E | 714 871-9611 | 8978 |
| Santa Ana Plating (PA) | 3471 | D | 310 923-8305 | 9008 |
| Aerofit LLC | 3498 | C | 714 521-5060 | 9246 |
| Golden Pacific Seafoods Inc | 3556 | E | 714 589-8888 | 9794 |
| Terra Universal Inc (PA) | 3564 | D | 714 526-0100 | 10002 |
| Label-Aire Inc (PA) | 3565 | D | 714 449-5155 | 10024 |
| HP It Services Incorporated | 3577 | E | 714 844-7737 | 10376 |
| Jonel Engineering | 3596 | E | 714 879-2360 | 10638 |
| Ejays Machine Co Inc | 3599 | E | 714 879-0558 | 10822 |
| Lange Precision Inc | 3599 | F | 714 870-5420 | 10937 |
| Laser Industries Inc | 3599 | E | 714 532-3271 | 10941 |
| Oem LLC | 3599 | E | 714 449-7500 | 11015 |
| Thunderbolt Manufacturing Inc | 3599 | E | 714 632-0397 | 11144 |
| Direct Drive Systems Inc | 3621 | D | 714 872-5500 | 11263 |
| Zmp Aquisition Corporation | 3625 | F | 714 278-6500 | 11357 |
| Golden West Technology | 3672 | E | 714 738-3775 | 12123 |
| Winonics Inc | 3672 | C | 714 626-3755 | 12263 |
| Printec Ht Electronics LLC | 3674 | E | 714 484-7597 | 12639 |
| General Linear Systems Inc | 3677 | F | 714 994-4822 | 12841 |
| Magtech & Power Conversion Inc | 3677 | E | 714 451-0106 | 12845 |
| Gigatera Communications | 3679 | D | 714 515-1100 | 12985 |
| Ultra Wheel Company | 3714 | E | 714 449-7100 | 13597 |
| UNI Filter Inc | 3714 | F | 714 535-6933 | 13598 |
| Marton Precision Mfg LLC | 3724 | E | 714 808-6523 | 13716 |
| Adams Rite Aerospace Inc (DH) | 3728 | E | 714 278-6500 | 13736 |
| Hydraflow | 3728 | B | 714 773-2600 | 13860 |
| Consolidated Aerospace Mfg LLC (HQ) | 3812 | E | 714 989-2797 | 14172 |
| Frontgrade Technologies LLC | 3812 | D | 714 870-2420 | 14188 |
| Raytheon Company | 3812 | F | 714 446-2584 | 14285 |
| Raytheon Company | 3812 | C | 714 732-0119 | 14286 |
| Aurident Incorporated | 3843 | E | 714 870-1851 | 15438 |
| Bbe Sound Inc (PA) | 3931 | E | 714 897-6766 | 15712 |
| Hero Industries Inc | 3999 | E | 714 879-3900 | 16143 |
| Pacmin Incorporated (PA) | 3999 | D | 714 447-4478 | 16194 |
| Petes Road Service Inc (PA) | 5014 | D | 714 446-1207 | 16409 |
| US Electrical Services Inc | 5063 | E | 714 982-1534 | 16676 |
| North American Video Corp (PA) | 5065 | E | 714 779-7499 | 16726 |
| Monroe Magnus LLC (HQ) | 5072 | F | 714 771-2630 | 16758 |
| Orora Packaging Solutions | 5113 | D | 714 278-6000 | 17010 |
| Orora Packaging Solutions | 5113 | F | 714 773-0124 | 17015 |
| Vista Paint Corporation (PA) | 5231 | C | 714 680-3800 | 17351 |
| Kaylas Cake Corporation | 5461 | E | 714 869-1522 | 17414 |
| Plasticolor Molded Pdts Inc (PA) | 5531 | C | 714 525-3880 | 17458 |
| American Window Covering Inc | 7216 | F | 714 879-3880 | 17768 |
| Advanced Image Direct LLC | 7331 | E | 714 502-3900 | 17794 |
| Real Estate Image Inc (PA) | 7331 | C | 714 502-3900 | 17803 |
| Aspirez Inc | 7371 | D | 714 485-8104 | 17883 |
| New Pride Tire LLC | 7534 | E | 310 631-7000 | 19153 |
| Bon Suisse Inc | 8748 | E | 714 578-0001 | 19555 |

## GALT, CA - Sacramento County

| Company | SIC | EMP | PHONE | ENTRY# |
|---|---|---|---|---|
| Home Factories (HQ) | 2452 | F | 209 745-3001 | 3397 |
| Herburger Publications Inc (PA) | 2711 | D | 916 685-5533 | 4128 |
| Cardinal Glass Industries Inc | 3211 | C | 209 744-8940 | 7166 |
| Carsons Coatings Inc | 3469 | E | 209 745-2387 | 8830 |
| Southwest Products Corporation | 3519 | E | 209 745-6000 | 9331 |
| 4 D Industries Inc | 3999 | F | 209 745-0500 | 16077 |

## GARDEN GROVE, CA - Orange County

| Company | SIC | EMP | PHONE | ENTRY# |
|---|---|---|---|---|
| Flowers Bkg Co Henderson LLC | 2051 | D | 702 281-4797 | 1200 |
| Sanyo Foods Corp America (DH) | 2098 | E | 714 891-3671 | 2119 |
| House Foods America Corp (HQ) | 2099 | E | 714 901-4350 | 2233 |
| Quoc Viet Foods | 2099 | E | 714 283-3663 | 2330 |
| Nils Inc (PA) | 2339 | F | 714 755-1600 | 2796 |
| Pacific Athletic Wear Inc | 2339 | D | 714 751-8006 | 2797 |
| Bodywaves Inc (PA) | 2369 | E | 714 898-9900 | 2859 |
| L C Pringle Sales Inc (PA) | 2591 | E | 714 892-1524 | 3724 |
| Commercial Cstm Sting Uphl Inc | 2599 | D | 714 850-0520 | 3735 |
| Teacher Created Resources Inc | 2731 | C | 714 230-7060 | 4347 |
| Wtpc Inc | 2752 | E | 714 903-2500 | 4816 |
| Elasco Inc | 2821 | D | 714 373-4767 | 5155 |
| Elasco Urethane Inc | 2821 | E | 714 895-7031 | 5156 |
| Holcim Solutions & Pdts US LLC | 2821 | E | 714 898-0025 | 5159 |
| Saint-Gobain Prfmce Plas Corp | 2821 | C | 714 893-0470 | 5198 |
| Saint-Gobain Prfmce Plas Corp | 2821 | D | 714 630-5818 | 5199 |
| Uremet Corporation | 2821 | E | 657 257-4027 | 5216 |
| St Paul Brands Inc | 2824 | E | 714 903-1000 | 5223 |
| Mycelium Enterprises LLC | 2833 | E | 657 251-0016 | 5251 |
| A Q Pharmaceuticals Inc | 2834 | E | 714 903-1000 | 5285 |
| Beauty & Health International | 2834 | E | 714 903-9791 | 5362 |
| Leiner Health Products Inc | 2834 | E | 714 898-9936 | 5535 |
| Goodwin Ammonia Company LLC (PA) | 2841 | F | 714 894-0531 | 5874 |
| Goodwin Ammonia Company LLC | 2841 | D | 714 894-0531 | 5875 |
| Cali Chem Inc | 2844 | E | 714 265-3740 | 5952 |

Employee Codes: A=Over 500 employees, B=251-500
C=101-250, D=51-100, E=20-50, F=10-19, G=1-9

## GARDEN GROVE, CA

| | SIC | EMP | PHONE | ENTRY# |
|---|---|---|---|---|
| Everbrands Inc. | 2844 | E | 855 595-2999 | 5977 |
| Advanced Chemistry & Technology Inc. | 2891 | E | 714 373-8118 | 6216 |
| GKN Arspace Trnsprncy Systems. | 3089 | B | 714 893-7531 | 6844 |
| Jason Tool and Engineering Inc. | 3089 | E | 714 895-5067 | 6872 |
| Monco Products Inc. | 3089 | E | 714 891-2788 | 6922 |
| Peerless Injection Molding LLC. | 3089 | E | 714 689-1920 | 6953 |
| Customfab Inc. | 3111 | C | 714 891-9119 | 7086 |
| Cham-Cal Engineering Co. | 3231 | D | 714 898-9721 | 7215 |
| CTS Cement Manufacturing Corp (PA). | 3241 | E | 714 379-8260 | 7255 |
| Hyatt Die Cast Engrg Corp - S. | 3363 | E | 714 622-2131 | 7810 |
| Synertech PM Inc. | 3369 | F | 714 898-9151 | 7871 |
| Kittyhawk Inc (PA). | 3398 | E | 714 895-5024 | 7887 |
| Kittyhawk Products CA LLC. | 3398 | E | 714 895-5024 | 7888 |
| Kpi Services Inc. | 3398 | E | 714 895-5024 | 7889 |
| Container Supply Company Incorporated. | 3411 | C | 714 892-8321 | 7920 |
| Umpco Inc. | 3429 | D | 714 897-3531 | 8033 |
| V & F Fabrication Company Inc. | 3441 | E | 714 265-0630 | 8239 |
| Uttam Composites LLC | 3443 | F | 714 894-5300 | 8350 |
| F T B & Son Inc. | 3444 | E | 714 891-8003 | 8449 |
| Vts Sheetmetal Specialist Co. | 3444 | E | 714 237-1420 | 8609 |
| Tl Machine Inc. | 3451 | E | 714 554-4154 | 8734 |
| Houston Bazz Co. | 3469 | D | 714 898-2666 | 8850 |
| Coastline Metal Finishing Corp. | 3471 | D | 714 895-9099 | 8944 |
| Intra Storage Systems Inc. | 3499 | E | 714 373-2346 | 9289 |
| Innovated Solutions Inc. | 3559 | F | 949 222-1088 | 9869 |
| American Metal Bearing Company. | 3562 | E | 714 892-5527 | 9948 |
| Plantronics Inc. | 3571 | E | 714 897-0808 | 10194 |
| Bar Code Specialties Inc. | 3577 | E | 877 411-2633 | 10331 |
| Xerox | 3579 | E | 714 895-7500 | 10468 |
| Aero Dynamic Machining Inc. | 3599 | D | 714 379-1073 | 10682 |
| I Copy Inc. | 3599 | E | 562 921-0202 | 10880 |
| Kimberly Machine Inc. | 3599 | E | 714 539-0151 | 10928 |
| Spartan Manufacturing Co. | 3599 | E | 714 894-1955 | 11121 |
| Vianh Company Inc. | 3599 | F | 714 590-9808 | 11178 |
| Western Precision Aero LLC. | 3599 | E | 714 893-7999 | 11193 |
| Microsemi Corp-Power MGT Group. | 3625 | C | 714 994-6500 | 11333 |
| Coastline High Prfmce Ctngs Lt. | 3663 | F | 714 372-3263 | 11827 |
| Exigent Sensors LLC. | 3669 | E | 949 439-1321 | 11994 |
| Roger Industry. | 3672 | E | 714 896-0765 | 12202 |
| Microsemi Corp - Anlog Mxed Sg (DH). | 3674 | D | 714 898-8121 | 12571 |
| Microsemi Corporation. | 3674 | C | 714 898-7112 | 12573 |
| Microsemi Corporation (HQ). | 3674 | E | 949 380-6100 | 12576 |
| Vitesse Manufacturing & Dev. | 3674 | C | 805 388-3700 | 12795 |
| Basic Electronics Inc. | 3679 | E | 714 530-2400 | 12921 |
| Harbinger Motors Inc. | 3711 | C | 714 684-1067 | 13359 |
| Shelby Carroll Intl Inc (PA). | 3711 | E | 310 327-5072 | 13384 |
| Allied Wheel Components Inc. | 3714 | E | 800 529-4335 | 13454 |
| Driveshaftpro. | 3714 | E | 714 893-4585 | 13489 |
| King Shock Technology Inc. | 3714 | D | 719 394-3754 | 13525 |
| Togetherbuycom. | 3714 | F | 714 379-4600 | 13588 |
| Walker Products. | 3714 | E | 714 554-5151 | 13604 |
| GKN Aerospace. | 3721 | D | 714 653-7531 | 13666 |
| Jvr Sheetmetal Fabrication Inc. | 3721 | E | 714 841-2464 | 13674 |
| Align Precision - Anaheim Inc (DH). | 3728 | D | 714 961-9200 | 13770 |
| B & E Manufacturing Co Inc. | 3728 | E | 714 898-2269 | 13794 |
| C&D Zodiac Aerospace. | 3728 | E | 714 891-0683 | 13799 |
| Safran Cabin Inc. | 3728 | C | 714 901-2672 | 13944 |
| Safran Cabin Inc. | 3728 | C | 714 891-1906 | 13951 |
| SPS Technologies LLC. | 3728 | E | 714 892-5571 | 13961 |
| Talsco Inc. | 3728 | E | 714 841-2464 | 13968 |
| Tj Aerospace Inc. | 3728 | E | 714 891-3564 | 13974 |
| King Instrument Company Inc. | 3823 | E | 714 891-0008 | 14428 |
| Sensorex Corporation. | 3823 | D | 714 895-4344 | 14457 |
| Touch International Display Enhance. | 3827 | E | 512 646-0310 | 14829 |
| Hycor Biomedical LLC. | 3841 | C | 714 933-3000 | 15107 |
| Elite Screens Inc. | 3861 | E | 877 511-1211 | 15637 |
| Iron Grip Barbell Company Inc. | 3949 | D | 714 850-6900 | 15831 |
| Evans Manufacturing LLC (HQ). | 3993 | C | 714 379-6100 | 15972 |
| Expo-3 International Inc. | 3993 | E | 714 379-8383 | 15975 |
| Innovative Casework Mfg Inc. | 3999 | E | 714 890-9100 | 16151 |
| Innovative Metal Designs Inc. | 5013 | E | 714 799-6700 | 16386 |
| Caster Technology Corp (PA). | 5051 | E | 714 893-6886 | 16611 |
| Winchester Interconnect EC LLC. | 5065 | D | 714 230-6122 | 16743 |
| Penn Elcom Inc (HQ). | 5072 | E | 714 230-6200 | 16760 |
| Pure Process Filtration Inc. | 5075 | F | 714 891-6527 | 16783 |
| Bodykore Inc. | 5091 | E | 949 325-3088 | 16933 |
| Advanced Phrm Svcs Inc. | 5122 | E | 714 903-1006 | 17026 |
| Qyk Brands LLC. | 5122 | C | 833 795-7664 | 17047 |
| Vorsteiner Inc. | 5531 | E | 714 379-4600 | 17468 |
| Revco Products. | 7372 | D | 714 891-6688 | 18738 |
| Garden Grove Unified Schl Dst. | 8211 | D | 714 663-6101 | 19344 |

## GARDENA, CA - Los Angeles County

| | SIC | EMP | PHONE | ENTRY# |
|---|---|---|---|---|
| K C Restoration Co Inc. | 1389 | E | 310 280-0597 | 244 |
| Aleksandar Inc. | 1751 | F | 310 516-7700 | 486 |
| Weiss Sheet Metal Company. | 1761 | E | 310 354-2700 | 518 |
| Washington Orna Ir Works Inc (PA). | 1799 | D | 310 327-8660 | 579 |
| Rich Chicks LLC. | 2015 | E | 209 879-4104 | 701 |
| Better Nutritionals LLC. | 2023 | E | 310 356-9019 | 747 |
| Triple Five Nutrition LLC. | 2023 | E | 310 502-2277 | 783 |
| La Mousse Desserts Inc. | 2038 | E | 310 478-6051 | 1038 |
| Hannahmax Baking Inc. | 2051 | C | 310 380-6778 | 1216 |
| Little Brothers Bakery LLC. | 2051 | E | 310 225-3790 | 1223 |
| Ocean Direct LLC (HQ). | 2092 | C | 424 266-9300 | 2059 |
| Nissin Foods USA Company Inc (DH). | 2098 | C | 310 327-8478 | 2117 |
| Lets Do Lunch. | 2099 | B | 310 523-3664 | 2264 |
| Risvolds Inc. | 2099 | D | 323 770-2674 | 2338 |
| Sabater Usa Inc (PA). | 2099 | E | 310 518-2227 | 2346 |
| Tu Madre Romana Inc. | 2099 | C | 323 321-6041 | 2381 |
| Stanzino Inc (PA). | 2211 | E | 213 746-8822 | 2429 |
| Twin Dragon Marketing Inc (PA). | 2211 | E | 310 715-7070 | 2431 |
| Caitac Garment Processing Inc. | 2261 | B | 310 217-9888 | 2489 |
| Barco Uniforms Inc. | 2311 | B | 310 323-7315 | 2557 |
| Stringking Inc (PA). | 2311 | E | 310 503-8901 | 2567 |
| True Religion Apparel Inc (HQ). | 2325 | B | 323 266-3072 | 2589 |
| Way Out West Inc. | 2326 | F | 310 769-6937 | 2604 |
| Global Casuals Inc. | 2329 | E | 310 817-2828 | 2621 |
| Gloria Lance Inc (PA). | 2331 | D | 310 767-4400 | 2666 |
| La Palm Furnitures & ACC Inc (PA). | 2395 | E | 310 217-2700 | 2992 |
| D and J Marketing Inc. | 2396 | E | 310 538-1583 | 3004 |
| O Industries Corporation. | 2426 | F | 310 719-2289 | 3100 |
| Parquet By Dian. | 2426 | D | 310 527-3779 | 3101 |
| American Cabinet Works Inc. | 2431 | E | 310 715-6815 | 3107 |
| Ohline Corporation. | 2431 | E | 310 327-4630 | 3170 |
| Alan Pre-Fab Building Corp. | 2452 | E | 310 538-0333 | 3390 |
| Martin/Brattrud Inc. | 2512 | D | 323 770-4171 | 3482 |
| A M Cabinets Inc (PA). | 2521 | D | 310 532-1919 | 3559 |
| New Maverick Desk Inc. | 2521 | C | 310 217-1554 | 3575 |
| Louis Sardo Upholstery Inc (PA). | 2531 | D | 310 327-0532 | 3635 |
| Alco Designs. | 2541 | F | 310 353-2300 | 3643 |
| One Up Manufacturing LLC. | 2631 | E | 310 749-8347 | 3805 |
| Wrkco Inc. | 2631 | E | 310 532-8988 | 3811 |
| Sgl Composites Inc (DH). | 2655 | D | 424 329-5250 | 3909 |
| Triune Enterprises Inc. | 2671 | E | 310 719-1600 | 3940 |
| Community Media Corporation (PA). | 2711 | E | 714 220-0292 | 4097 |
| Gardena Valley News Inc. | 2711 | E | 310 329-6351 | 4117 |
| Take A Break Paper. | 2711 | E | 323 333-7773 | 4204 |
| Quadriga Americas LLC. | 2741 | E | 424 634-4900 | 4456 |
| Americhip Inc (PA). | 2752 | E | 310 323-3697 | 4511 |
| Matsuda House Printing Inc. | 2752 | E | 310 532-1533 | 4691 |
| Southwest Offset Prtg Co Inc (PA). | 2752 | B | 310 965-9154 | 4766 |
| UNI-Sport Inc. | 2752 | E | 310 217-4587 | 4797 |
| Continental Bdr Specialty Corp (PA). | 2782 | C | 310 324-8227 | 5000 |
| US Blanks LLC (PA). | 2821 | E | 310 225-6774 | 5217 |
| CH Laboratories Inc (PA). | 2834 | E | 310 516-8273 | 5403 |
| West Coast Laboratories Inc. | 2834 | E | 310 527-6163 | 5717 |
| West Coast Laboratories Inc (PA). | 2834 | F | 323 321-4774 | 5718 |
| Cilajet LLC. | 2842 | E | 310 320-8000 | 5896 |
| Cosway Company Inc. | 2844 | F | 310 527-9135 | 5965 |
| Grow More Inc. | 2879 | D | 310 515-1700 | 6201 |
| Independent Ink Inc (PA). | 2899 | E | 310 523-4657 | 6295 |
| Matsui International Co Inc (HQ). | 2899 | E | 310 767-7812 | 6307 |
| Evergreen Oil Inc (HQ). | 2992 | E | 949 757-7770 | 6393 |
| Principle Plastics. | 3021 | E | 310 532-3411 | 6420 |
| Lite Extrusions Mfg Inc. | 3083 | E | 323 770-4298 | 6585 |
| Narayan Corporation. | 3085 | E | 310 719-7330 | 6611 |
| Amfoam Inc (PA). | 3086 | E | 310 847-4003 | 6621 |
| Barnes Plastics Inc. | 3089 | E | 310 329-6301 | 6736 |
| Geiger Plastics Inc. | 3089 | E | 310 327-9926 | 6837 |
| Getpart La Inc. | 3089 | E | 424 331-9599 | 6841 |
| Plastic Processing Corp. | 3089 | F | 310 719-7330 | 6962 |
| Pro Design Group Inc. | 3089 | E | 310 767-1032 | 6985 |
| Rotational Molding Inc. | 3089 | D | 310 327-5401 | 7009 |
| Pacific Artglass Corporation. | 3231 | E | 310 516-7828 | 7238 |
| Arto Brick / California Pavers. | 3251 | E | 310 768-8500 | 7264 |
| McFiebow Inc (PA). | 3272 | E | 310 327-7474 | 7354 |
| US Hanger Company LLC. | 3315 | E | 310 323-8030 | 7657 |
| Precision Castparts Corp. | 3324 | F | 310 323-6200 | 7694 |
| Del Mar Industries (PA). | 3364 | D | 323 321-0600 | 7827 |
| Cast-Rite International Inc (PA). | 3369 | E | 310 532-2080 | 7859 |
| International Die Casting Inc. | 3369 | E | 310 324-2278 | 7865 |
| A and M Welding Inc. | 3441 | F | 310 329-2700 | 8085 |
| Junior Steel Co. | 3441 | E | 310 856-6868 | 8160 |
| Maya Steel Fabrications Inc. | 3441 | D | 310 532-8830 | 8177 |
| Thermlly Engnred Mnfctred Pdts. | 3443 | E | 310 523-9934 | 8346 |

# GLENDALE, CA

| Company | SIC | EMP | PHONE | ENTRY# |
|---|---|---|---|---|
| Aero ARC | 3444 | E | 310 324-3400 | 8365 |
| All-Ways Metal Inc | 3444 | E | 310 217-1177 | 8369 |
| American Aircraft Products Inc | 3444 | D | 310 532-7434 | 8372 |
| Artistic Welding | 3444 | D | 310 515-4922 | 8381 |
| Bay Cities Tin Shop Inc | 3444 | C | 310 660-0351 | 8389 |
| Carla Senter | 3444 | F | 310 366-7295 | 8405 |
| Hi-Craft Metal Products | 3444 | E | 310 323-6949 | 8468 |
| Meadows Sheet Metal and AC Inc | 3444 | E | 310 615-1125 | 8502 |
| Ramda Metal Specialties Inc | 3444 | E | 310 538-2136 | 8554 |
| Russ International Inc | 3444 | E | 310 329-7121 | 8562 |
| Star Star | 3444 | E | 310 901-1079 | 8581 |
| T & F Sheet Mtls Fab McHning I | 3444 | E | 310 516-8548 | 8589 |
| Versafab Corp (PA) | 3444 | E | 800 421-1822 | 8607 |
| Lni Custom Manufacturing Inc | 3446 | E | 310 978-2000 | 8635 |
| Washington Orna Ir Works Inc | 3446 | E | 310 327-8660 | 8649 |
| North Star Acquisition Inc | 3449 | D | 310 515-2200 | 8704 |
| GT Precision Inc | 3451 | C | 310 323-4374 | 8724 |
| Onyx Industries Inc | 3451 | D | 310 851-6161 | 8728 |
| Briles Aerospace LLC | 3452 | D | 424 320-3817 | 8746 |
| Paul R Briles Inc | 3452 | A | 310 323-6222 | 8764 |
| Binder Metal Products Inc | 3469 | E | 800 233-0896 | 8821 |
| Metco Manufacturing Inc | 3469 | E | 310 516-6547 | 8865 |
| Coast Plating Inc (PA) | 3471 | E | 323 770-0240 | 8942 |
| Gsp Metal Finishing Inc | 3471 | E | 818 744-1328 | 8967 |
| Faber Enterprises Inc | 3492 | C | 310 323-6200 | 9168 |
| RDS Wire & Cable Incorporated | 3496 | F | 310 323-7131 | 9230 |
| Wyrefab Inc | 3496 | E | 310 523-2147 | 9244 |
| Tru-Cut Inc | 3524 | E | 310 630-0422 | 9401 |
| Doringer Manufacturing Co Inc | 3541 | F | 310 366-7766 | 9552 |
| Rytan Inc | 3541 | E | 310 328-6553 | 9567 |
| US Industrial Tool & Sup Co | 3542 | E | 310 464-8400 | 9591 |
| Cast-Rite Corporation | 3559 | D | 310 532-2080 | 9609 |
| Aqua Pro Properties Vii LP | 3559 | B | 310 516-9911 | 9831 |
| Mars Air Systems LLC | 3564 | E | 310 532-1555 | 9993 |
| American Condenser & Coil LLC | 3585 | D | 310 327-8600 | 10480 |
| Vege-Mist Inc | 3585 | D | 310 353-2300 | 10525 |
| Clean Water Technology Inc (HQ) | 3589 | E | 310 380-4648 | 10550 |
| Timbucktoo Manufacturing Inc | 3589 | E | 310 323-1134 | 10606 |
| A & A Machine & Dev Co Inc | 3599 | F | 310 532-7706 | 10644 |
| A&W Precision Machining Inc | 3599 | F | 310 527-7242 | 10652 |
| Ace Air Manufacturing | 3599 | F | 310 323-7246 | 10664 |
| Brek Manufacturing Co | 3599 | C | 310 329-7638 | 10753 |
| Century Precision Engrg Inc | 3599 | E | 310 538-0015 | 10771 |
| German Machined Products Inc | 3599 | E | 310 532-4480 | 10860 |
| J & S Inc | 3599 | E | 310 719-7144 | 10896 |
| Research Metal Industries Inc | 3599 | E | 310 352-3200 | 11077 |
| California Pak Intl Inc | 3612 | E | 310 223-2500 | 11206 |
| Delta Ultraviolet Corporation | 3641 | F | 310 323-6400 | 11424 |
| Kc Hilites Inc | 3647 | E | 928 635-2607 | 11574 |
| Mj Best Videographer LLC | 3651 | C | 209 208-8432 | 11678 |
| Centron Industries Inc | 3663 | E | 310 324-6443 | 11825 |
| Qual-Pro Corporation (HQ) | 3672 | C | 310 329-7535 | 12195 |
| Inca One Corporation | 3675 | E | 310 808-0001 | 12818 |
| Rayco Electronic Mfg Inc | 3677 | E | 310 329-2660 | 12855 |
| Polar Power Inc | 3694 | D | 310 830-9153 | 13181 |
| Servexo | 3699 | C | 323 527-9994 | 13307 |
| Prime Wheel Corporation | 3714 | E | 310 819-4123 | 13559 |
| Prime Wheel Corporation (PA) | 3714 | A | 310 516-9126 | 13560 |
| Ahf-Ducommun Incorporated (HQ) | 3728 | C | 310 380-5390 | 13760 |
| Designed Metal Connections Inc (DH) | 3728 | B | 310 323-6200 | 13822 |
| Impresa Aerospace LLC | 3728 | C | 310 354-1200 | 13870 |
| Nasco Aircraft Brake Inc | 3728 | D | 310 532-4430 | 13914 |
| Space-Lok Inc | 3728 | C | 310 527-6150 | 13959 |
| Space Exploration Tech Corp | 3761 | C | 323 754-1285 | 14088 |
| Radiology Support Devices Inc | 3841 | E | 310 518-0527 | 15238 |
| Cloud B Inc | 3942 | E | 310 781-3833 | 15728 |
| I & I Sports Supply Company (PA) | 3949 | E | 310 715-6800 | 15827 |
| Norberts Athletic Products Inc | 3949 | F | 310 830-6672 | 15843 |
| Ar-Ce Inc | 3952 | F | 310 771-1960 | 15883 |
| Wcbm Company (PA) | 3965 | E | 323 262-3274 | 15922 |
| Clegg Industries Inc | 3993 | C | 310 225-3800 | 15956 |
| Neighbrhood Bus Advrtsment Ltd | 3999 | E | 442 300-1803 | 16187 |
| Sgps Inc | 3999 | D | 310 538-4175 | 16227 |
| Steeldeck Inc | 3999 | E | 323 290-2100 | 16239 |
| Tandem Design Inc | 3999 | E | 714 978-7272 | 16250 |
| Wally & Pat Enterprises | 3999 | E | 310 532-2031 | 16267 |
| Tool Components Inc (PA) | 5051 | E | 310 323-5613 | 16634 |
| Magnetika Inc (PA) | 5063 | D | 310 527-8100 | 16659 |
| Mutual Liquid Gas & Eqp Co Inc (PA) | 5084 | E | 310 515-0553 | 16828 |
| The Service Warehouse Inc | 5084 | F | 310 329-9110 | 16849 |
| Westcoast Rotor Inc | 5084 | E | 310 327-5050 | 16857 |
| Softline Home Fashions Inc | 5131 | E | 310 630-4848 | 17070 |
| La Dye & Print Inc | 5137 | E | 310 327-3200 | 17093 |
| Lily Bleu Inc | 5137 | E | 310 225-2522 | 17094 |
| Phoenix Textile Inc (PA) | 5137 | D | 310 715-7090 | 17097 |
| Spectrum Laboratory Pdts Inc | 5169 | E | 520 292-3103 | 17249 |
| A B P Inc | 5199 | F | 310 532-9400 | 17282 |
| Carson Trailer Inc (PA) | 5599 | D | 310 835-0876 | 17487 |
| B & W Tile Co Inc (PA) | 5713 | E | 310 538-9579 | 17525 |
| Air Fayre USA Inc | 5812 | C | 310 808-1061 | 17563 |
| Kings Hawaiian Bakery W Inc (HQ) | 5812 | E | 310 533-3250 | 17593 |
| Ruggable LLC | 5961 | B | 310 295-0098 | 17674 |
| Pulp Studio Incorporated | 7336 | D | 310 815-4999 | 17837 |
| Secom International (PA) | 7373 | E | 310 641-1290 | 18991 |
| Hansens Welding Inc | 7692 | E | 310 329-6888 | 19196 |
| Elite Engineering Contrs Inc | 8711 | E | 310 465-8333 | 19390 |
| Prototype Engineering and Manufacturing Inc | 8711 | E | 310 532-6305 | 19411 |
| Nissan North America Inc | 8742 | A | 310 768-3700 | 19536 |

# GEORGETOWN, CA - El Dorado County

| Company | SIC | EMP | PHONE | ENTRY# |
|---|---|---|---|---|
| Powerlift Dumbwaiters Inc | 3534 | F | 800 409-5438 | 9475 |

# GEYSERVILLE, CA - Sonoma County

| Company | SIC | EMP | PHONE | ENTRY# |
|---|---|---|---|---|
| Clos Du Bois Wines Inc | 2084 | F | 707 857-1651 | 1509 |
| Edmeades LLC | 2084 | E | 707 895-3232 | 1551 |
| Francis Coppola Winery LLC | 2084 | E | 707 857-1400 | 1577 |
| Francis Ford Cppola Prsnts LLC | 2084 | E | 707 251-3200 | 1578 |
| J Pedroncelli Winery Inc | 2084 | F | 707 857-3531 | 1625 |
| Marietta Cellars Incorporated | 2084 | E | 707 433-2747 | 1673 |
| Mathy Winery LLC | 2084 | F | 707 431-2700 | 1674 |
| Sbragia Family Vineyards LLC | 2084 | E | 707 473-2992 | 1742 |

# GILROY, CA - Santa Clara County

| Company | SIC | EMP | PHONE | ENTRY# |
|---|---|---|---|---|
| Silva Sausage Co | 2013 | E | 408 293-5437 | 667 |
| Atorias Baking Company | 2051 | E | 408 846-0876 | 1161 |
| Blossom Valley Foods Inc | 2087 | E | 408 848-5520 | 1989 |
| International Paper Company | 2621 | C | 408 847-6400 | 3780 |
| International Paper Company | 2621 | E | 408 846-2060 | 3784 |
| Mainstreet Media Group LLC | 2711 | C | 408 842-6400 | 4152 |
| Chameleon Like Inc | 2782 | D | 408 847-3661 | 4998 |
| Bayer Corporation | 2834 | E | 408 406-8491 | 5357 |
| Sofie Co | 2834 | E | 408 842-0520 | 5665 |
| Trical Inc (PA) | 2879 | E | 831 637-0195 | 6209 |
| Advance Fabrication Inc | 3069 | E | 408 779-5424 | 6482 |
| Quinn Development Company | 3271 | F | | 7297 |
| Containment Consultants Inc | 3443 | E | 408 848-6998 | 8312 |
| American Steel & Stairways Inc | 3446 | E | 408 848-2992 | 8617 |
| Context Engineering Co | 3469 | E | 408 748-9112 | 8831 |
| Makplate Inc | 3471 | E | 408 842-7572 | 8982 |
| Peninsula Spring Corporation | 3495 | F | 408 848-3361 | 9205 |
| Heinzen Manufacturing Inc | 3556 | D | 408 842-7233 | 9796 |
| Hanaps Enterprises | 3577 | D | 669 235-3810 | 10375 |
| C L Hann Industries Inc | 3599 | F | 408 293-4800 | 10759 |
| RMC Engineering Co Inc (PA) | 3599 | E | 408 842-2525 | 11081 |
| Lucas/Signatone Corporation (PA) | 3825 | E | 408 848-2851 | 14550 |
| Technical Reps Intl Inc | 3999 | F | 408 848-8868 | 16252 |
| Amcs Inc | 5014 | E | 408 846-9274 | 16406 |
| Specialty Truck Parts Inc (PA) | 5531 | E | 408 998-7272 | 17465 |

# GLEN ELLEN, CA - Sonoma County

| Company | SIC | EMP | PHONE | ENTRY# |
|---|---|---|---|---|
| Bfw Associates LLC (HQ) | 2084 | E | 707 935-3000 | 1485 |
| Vintage Wine Estates Inc CA | 2084 | D | 800 330-4064 | 1815 |

# GLENDALE, CA - Los Angeles County

| Company | SIC | EMP | PHONE | ENTRY# |
|---|---|---|---|---|
| Triangle Rock Products LLC | 1429 | C | 818 553-8820 | 306 |
| Nestle Usa Inc | 2023 | C | 818 549-6000 | 775 |
| Pillsbury Company LLC | 2041 | E | 818 522-3952 | 1062 |
| Nestle Purina Petcare Company | 2047 | E | 314 982-1000 | 1110 |
| Sugarfina Inc | 2064 | E | 818 302-0765 | 1335 |
| Custom Characters Inc | 2389 | F | 818 507-5940 | 2895 |
| Carpet Wagon-Glendale Inc (PA) | 2434 | E | 818 937-9545 | 3230 |
| Avery Dennison Foundation | 2672 | E | 626 304-2000 | 3945 |
| Earthwise Bag Company Inc | 2673 | F | 818 396-5025 | 3967 |
| Avery Dnnson Ret Info Svcs LLC (HQ) | 2678 | D | 626 304-2000 | 4015 |
| Viva Print LLC (HQ) | 2678 | E | 818 243-1363 | 4025 |
| California Community News LLC | 2711 | D | 818 843-8700 | 4081 |
| Axiomprint Inc | 2752 | F | 747 888-7777 | 4521 |
| Chromatic Inc Lithographers | 2752 | E | 818 242-5785 | 4549 |
| Color Inc | 2752 | E | 818 240-1350 | 4557 |
| Colour Concepts Inc | 2752 | C | | 4562 |
| Zoo Printing Inc (PA) | 2752 | E | 310 253-7751 | 4819 |
| 4 Over LLC (HQ) | 2759 | | 818 246-1170 | 4830 |
| Legion Creative Group | 2759 | E | 323 498-1100 | 4914 |
| Vapor Delux Inc | 2782 | E | 818 370-8308 | 5007 |
| First Person Inc | 2834 | F | 609 760-0040 | 5441 |
| Person & Covey Inc | 2844 | E | 818 937-5000 | 6018 |

Employee Codes: A=Over 500 employees, B=251-500
C=101-250, D=51-100, E=20-50, F=10-19, G=1-9

# GLENDALE, CA

| Company | SIC | EMP | PHONE | ENTRY# |
|---|---|---|---|---|
| Stila Styles LLC (HQ) | 2844 | E | 866 784-5201 | 6041 |
| Vege - Kurl Inc | 2844 | D | 818 956-5582 | 6053 |
| K-Swiss Inc (DH) | 3021 | E | 323 675-2700 | 6416 |
| K-Swiss Sales Corp | 3021 | C | 323 675-2700 | 6418 |
| Yates Gear Inc | 3199 | D | 530 222-4606 | 7163 |
| Hintex | 3272 | F | 320 400-0009 | 7344 |
| Cygnet Stampng & Fabrictng Inc (PA) | 3469 | E | 818 240-7574 | 8833 |
| Automation Plating Corporation | 3471 | E | 323 245-4951 | 8928 |
| SAI Industries | 3484 | E | 818 842-6144 | 9136 |
| Ambrit Industries Inc | 3542 | E | 818 243-1224 | 9576 |
| Pennoyer-Dodge Co | 3545 | E | 818 547-2100 | 9688 |
| Cryst Mark Inc A Swan Techno C | 3559 | E | 818 240-7520 | 9848 |
| International Bus Mchs Corp | 3571 | A | 818 553-8100 | 10169 |
| All 4-Pcb North America Inc | 3599 | F | 866 734-9403 | 10694 |
| McCoppin Enterprises | 3599 | E | 818 240-4840 | 10966 |
| Modern Engine Inc | 3599 | E | 818 409-9494 | 10989 |
| Arecont Vision LLC | 3629 | C | 818 937-0700 | 11360 |
| Glenair Inc (PA) | 3643 | B | 818 247-6000 | 11456 |
| Partners 1993 Inc | 3652 | E | 818 352-7800 | 11740 |
| Bittree Incorporated | 3663 | E | 818 500-8142 | 11819 |
| Coda Energy Holdings LLC | 3699 | F | 626 775-3900 | 13223 |
| Denttio Inc | 3843 | F | 323 254-1000 | 15452 |
| Kalap Inc | 3861 | E | 818 332-6916 | 15646 |
| AMG Employee Management Inc | 3873 | E | 323 254-7448 | 15674 |
| Sunderstorm LLC | 3999 | F | 818 605-6682 | 16245 |
| Sigma Supply & Dist Inc | 5047 | E | 818 246-4624 | 16589 |
| Simon G Jewelry Inc | 5094 | E | 818 500-8595 | 16970 |
| Alexander Henry Fabrics Inc | 5131 | E | 818 562-8200 | 17057 |
| Informtion Intgrtion Group Inc | 7372 | F | 818 956-3744 | 18418 |
| Lumenova Ai Inc | 7372 | E | 310 694-2461 | 18506 |
| Sparktech Software LLC | 7372 | E | 818 330-9098 | 18819 |
| General Networks Corporation | 7379 | D | 818 249-1962 | 19036 |
| Grandall Distributing LLC | 7389 | E | 818 242-6640 | 19094 |
| Isovac Engineering Inc | 7389 | E | 818 552-6200 | 19098 |
| Passport Technology Usa Inc | 7699 | E | 818 957-5471 | 19274 |

## GLENDORA, CA - Los Angeles County

| Company | SIC | EMP | PHONE | ENTRY# |
|---|---|---|---|---|
| CJd Construction Svcs Inc | 1389 | E | 626 335-1116 | 218 |
| Building Elctronic Contrls Inc (PA) | 1731 | E | 909 305-1600 | 451 |
| Deccofelt Corporation | 2299 | E | 626 963-8511 | 2545 |
| G R Leonard & Co Inc | 2741 | E | 847 797-8101 | 4401 |
| Calportland Company (DH) | 3241 | D | 626 852-6200 | 7252 |
| Calportland | 3273 | D | 760 343-3403 | 7412 |
| Hallmark Metals Inc | 3444 | E | 626 335-1263 | 8464 |
| Postvision Inc | 3572 | F | 818 840-0777 | 10266 |
| Millipart Inc (PA) | 3599 | F | 626 963-4101 | 10984 |
| Mackenzie Laboratories Inc | 3674 | F | 909 394-9007 | 12538 |
| Electro-Tech Products Inc | 3679 | E | 909 592-1434 | 12968 |
| Southwest Machine & Plastic Co | 3728 | E | 626 963-6919 | 13958 |
| Safeguard Envirogroup Inc | 3826 | E | 626 512-7585 | 14713 |
| Sybron Dental Specialties Inc | 3843 | E | 909 596-0276 | 15486 |
| Oasis Medical Inc (PA) | 3851 | D | 909 305-5400 | 15612 |

## GLENN, CA - Glenn County

| Company | SIC | EMP | PHONE | ENTRY# |
|---|---|---|---|---|
| Carriere Family Farms LLC | 5145 | E | 530 934-8200 | 17141 |

## GOLD RIVER, CA - Sacramento County

| Company | SIC | EMP | PHONE | ENTRY# |
|---|---|---|---|---|
| Early Morning Inc | 2599 | E | 916 871-9005 | 3737 |
| Conquip Inc | 3599 | D | 916 379-8200 | 10788 |
| Security Classification Inc | 7389 | E | 707 301-6052 | 19127 |

## GOLETA, CA - Santa Barbara County

| Company | SIC | EMP | PHONE | ENTRY# |
|---|---|---|---|---|
| Apeel Technology Inc (PA) | 0723 | B | 805 203-0146 | 73 |
| Arguello Inc | 1382 | E | 805 567-1632 | 168 |
| Freeport-Mcmoran Oil & Gas LLC | 1382 | F | 805 567-1667 | 185 |
| Alexs Tile Works Inc | 1743 | E | 805 967-5308 | 482 |
| Baba Small Batch LLC | 2038 | F | 805 439-2250 | 1027 |
| Samsara Winery and Tasting Rm | 2084 | E | 805 845-8001 | 1738 |
| Deckers Outdoor Corporation (PA) | 2389 | A | 805 967-7611 | 2896 |
| ABC - Clio Inc (HQ) | 2731 | C | 805 968-1911 | 4309 |
| Boone Printing & Graphics Inc | 2752 | D | 805 683-2349 | 4533 |
| Island View Print Works Inc | 2759 | E | 805 845-1333 | 4902 |
| Neal Feay Company | 3354 | D | 805 967-4521 | 7744 |
| AEC - Able Engineering Company Inc | 3441 | C | 805 685-2262 | 8089 |
| Vista Steel Company (PA) | 3441 | E | 805 964-4732 | 8242 |
| Ipt Holding Inc (PA) | 3469 | F | 805 683-3414 | 8853 |
| Inovati | 3479 | E | 805 571-8384 | 9081 |
| Integris Composites Inc (DH) | 3484 | E | 740 928-0326 | 9135 |
| Bardex Corporation (PA) | 3533 | D | 805 964-7747 | 9456 |
| Mann+hmmel Wtr Fluid Sltons In (DH) | 3589 | D | 805 964-8003 | 10574 |
| Z P M Inc | 3589 | E | 805 681-3511 | 10618 |
| Cnc Machining Inc | 3599 | E | 805 681-8855 | 10780 |
| Intri-Plex Technologies Inc (HQ) | 3599 | C | 805 683-3414 | 10891 |
| Veeco Process Equipment Inc | 3599 | D | 805 967-2700 | 11173 |
| Sonos Inc (PA) | 3651 | D | 805 965-3001 | 11699 |
| Calient Technologies Inc (PA) | 3661 | E | 805 695-4800 | 11755 |
| Acroamatics Inc | 3663 | F | 805 967-9909 | 11797 |
| E-Band Communications LLC | 3663 | E | 858 408-0660 | 11846 |
| L3 Technologies Inc | 3663 | D | 805 683-3881 | 11878 |
| Remec Brdband Wrless Ntwrks LL | 3663 | C | 858 312-6900 | 11932 |
| Remec Broadband Wireless LLC | 3663 | C | 858 312-6900 | 11933 |
| Atomica Corp | 3674 | C | 805 681-2807 | 12339 |
| Transphorm Inc (DH) | 3674 | C | 805 456-1300 | 12771 |
| Kyocera Sld Laser Inc (HQ) | 3699 | E | 805 696-6999 | 13264 |
| Kyocera Sld Laser Inc | 3699 | E | 310 808-4542 | 13266 |
| Raytheon Company | 3699 | C | 805 967-5511 | 13295 |
| Launchpint Elc Prplsion Sltons | 3728 | E | 805 683-9659 | 13890 |
| Atk Space Systems LLC | 3812 | D | 805 685-2262 | 14157 |
| Lockheed Martin Corporation | 3812 | E | 805 571-2346 | 14213 |
| Moog Inc | 3812 | B | 805 618-3900 | 14224 |
| Northrop Grumman Systems Corp | 3812 | D | 714 240-6521 | 14263 |
| Raytheon Company | 3812 | C | 805 562-4611 | 14287 |
| Teledyne Flir LLC | 3812 | C | 805 964-9797 | 14314 |
| Biopac Systems Inc | 3826 | C | 805 685-0066 | 14636 |
| Teledyne Flir Coml Systems Inc (DH) | 3826 | B | 805 964-9797 | 14727 |
| Veeco Process Equipment Inc | 3826 | C | 805 967-1400 | 14751 |
| Wyatt Technology LLC (HQ) | 3826 | C | 805 681-9009 | 14756 |
| Far West Technology Inc | 3829 | F | 805 964-3615 | 14865 |
| Karl Storz Imaging Inc (HQ) | 3829 | B | 805 968-5563 | 14890 |
| Soilmoisture Equipment Corp | 3829 | E | 805 964-3525 | 14921 |
| Digital Surgery Systems Inc | 3841 | E | 805 978-5400 | 15070 |
| Inogen Inc (PA) | 3841 | C | 805 562-0500 | 15117 |
| Karl Storz Endscpy-America Inc | 3841 | D | 800 964-5563 | 15142 |
| Karl Storz Imaging Inc | 3841 | E | 805 968-5563 | 15143 |
| Truevision Systems Inc | 3841 | E | 805 963-9700 | 15292 |
| Advanced Vision Science Inc | 3851 | E | 805 683-3851 | 15593 |
| Santa Barbara Instrument GP Inc | 3861 | E | 925 463-3410 | 15665 |
| Skate One Corp | 3949 | D | 805 964-1330 | 15856 |
| Surf To Summit Inc | 3949 | F | 805 964-1896 | 15863 |
| Hanson Aggrgtes Md-Pacific Inc | 4212 | F | 805 967-2371 | 16279 |
| Enerpro Inc | 5065 | E | 805 683-2114 | 16701 |
| Exxon Mobil Corporation | 5541 | E | 805 961-4093 | 17475 |
| CMC Rescue Inc | 5999 | D | 805 562-9120 | 17694 |
| Image-X Enterprises Inc | 7371 | E | 805 964-3535 | 17928 |
| Parentsquare Inc | 7372 | D | 888 496-3168 | 18659 |
| Yardi Kube Inc | 7372 | E | 805 699-2040 | 18949 |
| Intri-Plex Technologies Inc | 8731 | E | 805 845-9600 | 19457 |

## GONZALES, CA - Monterey County

| Company | SIC | EMP | PHONE | ENTRY# |
|---|---|---|---|---|
| Braga Fresh Foods LLC | 2099 | A | 831 751-5573 | 2147 |
| Ramsay Highlander Inc | 3523 | E | 831 675-3453 | 9378 |

## GRANADA HILLS, CA - Los Angeles County

| Company | SIC | EMP | PHONE | ENTRY# |
|---|---|---|---|---|
| Republic Fence Co Inc (PA) | 1799 | E | 818 341-5323 | 570 |
| Ortho Engineering Inc (PA) | 3842 | E | 310 559-5996 | 15387 |
| Financial Info Netwrk Inc | 7371 | E | 818 782-0331 | 17922 |

## GRAND TERRACE, CA - San Bernardino County

| Company | SIC | EMP | PHONE | ENTRY# |
|---|---|---|---|---|
| City News Group Inc | 2711 | E | 909 370-1200 | 4093 |
| Griswold Pump Company | 3561 | E | 909 422-1700 | 9925 |
| Psg California LLC (HQ) | 3561 | B | 909 422-1700 | 9936 |
| National Logistics Team LLC | 4215 | E | 951 369-5841 | 16281 |

## GRANITE BAY, CA - Placer County

| Company | SIC | EMP | PHONE | ENTRY# |
|---|---|---|---|---|
| Recoating-West Inc (PA) | 3444 | E | 916 652-8290 | 8556 |
| Revivermx Inc | 3663 | E | 916 580-3495 | 11934 |
| Badass Brand Inc | 5122 | E | 916 990-3873 | 17027 |

## GRASS VALLEY, CA - Nevada County

| Company | SIC | EMP | PHONE | ENTRY# |
|---|---|---|---|---|
| Hansen Bros Enterprises (PA) | 1442 | D | 530 273-3100 | 315 |
| Igraphics (PA) | 2759 | E | 530 273-2200 | 4896 |
| Trusteel LLC | 3312 | F | 530 802-0420 | 7631 |
| Benchmark Thermal Corporation | 3433 | D | 530 477-5011 | 8060 |
| Manufacturers Coml Fin LLC | 3433 | E | 530 477-5011 | 8071 |
| Vossloh Signaling Usa Inc | 3462 | E | 530 272-8194 | 8793 |
| Huntington Mechanical Labs Inc | 3563 | E | 530 273-9533 | 9963 |
| Taylor Investments LLC | 3563 | E | 530 273-4135 | 9976 |
| Thermionics Laboratory Inc | 3589 | E | 530 272-3436 | 10605 |
| Taurus Fabrication Inc | 3599 | E | 530 268-2650 | 11138 |
| Controlomatic Inc | 3621 | E | 530 205-4520 | 11262 |
| Ei Corp | 3651 | E | 530 274-1240 | 11658 |
| Maier Manufacturing Inc | 3751 | E | 530 272-9036 | 14064 |
| Measurement Specialties Inc | 3825 | D | 530 273-4608 | 14554 |
| Slouber Enterprises Inc (PA) | 3826 | E | 530 273-2080 | 14720 |
| Ih Parts America Inc | 5531 | E | 530 274-1795 | 17453 |
| Vossloh Signaling LLC | 7371 | E | 530 272-8194 | 17994 |

# GEOGRAPHIC SECTION                                                                                           HAYWARD, CA

|  | SIC | EMP | PHONE | ENTRY# |
|---|---|---|---|---|

### GRATON, CA - Sonoma County
| | | | | |
|---|---|---|---|---|
| Purple Wine Production Company | 2084 | C | 707 829-6100 | 1714 |
| Empire West Inc | 3089 | E | 707 823-1190 | 6818 |

### GREENBRAE, CA - Marin County
| | | | | |
|---|---|---|---|---|
| Petroleum Sales Inc | 1311 | F | 415 256-1600 | 137 |
| Giorgios Restaurant Italiano | 2032 | E | 415 925-0808 | 857 |
| Albeco Inc | 5411 | D | 415 461-1164 | 17365 |
| Einstein Noah Rest Group Inc | 5812 | C | 415 925-9971 | 17578 |

### GREENFIELD, CA - Monterey County
| | | | | |
|---|---|---|---|---|
| Wente Bros | 2084 | E | 831 674-5642 | 1824 |

### GRIDLEY, CA - Butte County
| | | | | |
|---|---|---|---|---|
| Sutter Buttes Mfg LLC | 1799 | F | 530 846-9960 | 575 |
| Rio Pluma Company LLC (HQ) | 2033 | E | 530 846-5200 | 922 |
| Stapleton - Spence Packing Co (PA) | 2033 | D | 408 297-8815 | 928 |
| Sunsweet Dryers | 2034 | C | 530 846-5578 | 968 |
| Sutter Buttes Rubber Co LLC (PA) | 3052 | F | 530 846-9533 | 6431 |
| Bianchi Orchard Systems Inc | 3523 | C | 530 846-5625 | 9341 |
| Casa Lupe Inc (PA) | 5812 | D | 530 846-3218 | 17569 |

### GROVER BEACH, CA - San Luis Obispo County
| | | | | |
|---|---|---|---|---|
| Hotlix (PA) | 2064 | E | 805 473-0596 | 1311 |
| H J Harkins Company Inc | 2834 | E | 805 929-1333 | 5474 |
| C F W Research & Dev Co | 3351 | F | 805 489-8750 | 7725 |
| California Fine Wire Co (PA) | 3357 | E | 805 489-5144 | 7777 |
| Vons Companies Inc | 5411 | C | 805 481-2492 | 17391 |

### GUERNEVILLE, CA - Sonoma County
| | | | | |
|---|---|---|---|---|
| F Korbel & Bros (PA) | 2084 | C | 707 824-7000 | 1559 |

### GUSTINE, CA - Merced County
| | | | | |
|---|---|---|---|---|
| Saputo Cheese USA Inc | 2026 | C | 209 854-6461 | 844 |
| John B Sanfilippo & Son Inc | 2068 | B | 209 854-2455 | 1354 |

### HACIENDA HEIGHTS, CA - Los Angeles County
| | | | | |
|---|---|---|---|---|
| Terra Furniture Inc | 2512 | E | | 3493 |
| Lg-Led Solutions Limited | 3648 | E | 626 587-8506 | 11606 |
| Brio Water Technology Inc | 5078 | E | 800 781-1680 | 16784 |

### HALF MOON BAY, CA - San Mateo County
| | | | | |
|---|---|---|---|---|
| Romeo Packing Company | 2674 | E | 650 728-3393 | 3994 |
| Wick Communications Co | 2711 | E | 650 726-4424 | 4222 |
| Ucc Guide Inc | 2741 | F | 800 345-3822 | 4485 |
| Accurate Always Inc | 3571 | E | 650 728-9428 | 10126 |
| Allvia Inc | 3674 | E | 408 234-8778 | 12290 |
| Brewery On Half Moon Bay Inc | 5812 | E | 650 728-2739 | 17565 |

### HANFORD, CA - Kings County
| | | | | |
|---|---|---|---|---|
| Central Valley Meat Co Inc (PA) | 2011 | C | 559 583-9624 | 589 |
| Rosa Brothers Milk Co Inc (PA) | 2024 | E | 559 582-8825 | 815 |
| Del Monte Foods Inc | 2033 | D | 559 639-6160 | 883 |
| George Verhoeven Grain Inc (PA) | 2048 | F | 909 605-1531 | 1128 |
| Pitman Farms | 2048 | C | 559 585-3330 | 1144 |
| Nichols Pistachio | 2068 | C | 559 584-6811 | 1362 |
| Baker Commodities Inc | 2077 | E | 559 686-4797 | 1379 |
| Hanford Sentinel Inc | 2711 | B | 559 582-0471 | 4125 |
| Acuantia Inc | 3089 | E | 559 648-8235 | 6695 |
| South Valley Materials Inc | 3273 | F | 559 582-0532 | 7500 |
| Britz Fertilizers Inc | 3523 | E | 559 582-0942 | 9343 |
| Vandersteen Audio | 3651 | E | 559 582-0324 | 11710 |
| McLellan Equipment Inc | 3713 | E | 559 582-8100 | 13417 |
| McLellan Industries Inc | 3713 | D | 650 873-8100 | 13418 |
| Morgan & Slates Mfg & Sup Inc (PA) | 5251 | F | 559 582-4417 | 17357 |

### HARBOR CITY, CA - Los Angeles County
| | | | | |
|---|---|---|---|---|
| La Espanola Meats Inc | 2013 | E | 310 539-0455 | 652 |
| Corn Maiden Foods Inc | 2032 | D | 310 784-0400 | 853 |
| Sunsets Inc | 2253 | E | 310 784-3600 | 2481 |
| Miller Woodworking Inc | 2431 | E | 310 257-6806 | 3158 |
| A & J Industries Inc | 2441 | F | 310 216-2170 | 3322 |
| Star Plastic Design | 3089 | D | 310 530-7119 | 7041 |
| Ruggeri Marble and Granite Inc | 3281 | E | 310 513-2155 | 7544 |
| Team Inc | 3398 | E | 310 514-2312 | 7901 |
| Basmat Inc (PA) | 3444 | D | 310 325-2063 | 8388 |
| Onyx Industries Inc (PA) | 3451 | D | 310 539-8830 | 8727 |
| Slide Systems Inc | 3469 | F | 310 539-3416 | 8888 |
| Republic Machinery Co Inc (PA) | 3541 | E | 310 518-1100 | 9565 |
| Hansen Engineering Co | 3599 | D | 310 534-3870 | 10867 |
| Judco Manufacturing Inc (PA) | 3643 | E | 310 534-0959 | 11461 |
| Prime Wheel Corporation | 3714 | B | 310 326-5080 | 13558 |
| Hansen Engineering Co | 3728 | E | 310 534-3870 | 13857 |

### HAWAIIAN GARDENS, CA - Los Angeles County
| | | | | |
|---|---|---|---|---|
| Consolidated Color Corporation | 2851 | E | 562 420-7714 | 6077 |
| Ryvid Inc (PA) | 3714 | F | 949 691-3495 | 13569 |

### HAWTHORNE, CA - Los Angeles County
| | | | | |
|---|---|---|---|---|
| Firstclass Foods - Trojan Inc | 2011 | C | 310 676-2500 | 596 |
| Picnic At Ascot Inc | 2449 | E | 310 674-3098 | 3374 |
| Huntington Industries Inc | 2512 | E | 323 772-5575 | 3476 |
| Lithographix Inc (PA) | 2752 | B | 323 770-1000 | 4679 |
| Marina Graphic Center Inc | 2752 | E | 310 970-1777 | 4689 |
| Technology Training Corp | 2752 | D | 310 644-7777 | 4782 |
| Marco Fine Arts Galleries Inc | 2759 | E | 310 615-1818 | 4919 |
| Supacolor Usa Inc | 2759 | D | 844 973-2862 | 4964 |
| Ip Corporation | 2821 | E | 323 757-1801 | 5167 |
| Moleaer Inc | 3561 | D | 424 558-3567 | 9932 |
| Wems Inc (PA) | 3564 | D | 310 644-0251 | 10007 |
| Amag Technology Inc (DH) | 3577 | E | 310 518-2380 | 10320 |
| Acuna Dionisio Able | 3599 | E | 310 974-4741 | 10670 |
| DL Horton Enterprises Inc | 3599 | D | 323 777-1700 | 10814 |
| Paulco Precision Inc | 3599 | F | 310 679-4900 | 11033 |
| Fulham Co Inc | 3612 | E | 323 779-2980 | 11213 |
| Ring LLC (HQ) | 3612 | B | 310 929-7085 | 11227 |
| Calpak Usa Inc | 3672 | E | 310 937-7335 | 12073 |
| OSI Electronics Inc (HQ) | 3672 | D | 310 978-0516 | 12183 |
| OSI Optoelectronics Inc (HQ) | 3674 | C | 310 978-0516 | 12625 |
| OSI Systems Inc (PA) | 3674 | A | 310 978-0516 | 12626 |
| Glen - Mac Swiss Co | 3678 | E | 310 978-4555 | 12880 |
| OSI Subsidiary Inc | 3699 | F | 310 978-0516 | 13283 |
| Nmsp Inc (DH) | 3714 | D | 310 484-2322 | 13547 |
| K & E Inc | 3728 | E | 310 675-3309 | 13883 |
| Space Exploration Tech Corp | 3761 | C | 310 889-4968 | 14089 |
| Space Exploration Tech Corp (PA) | 3761 | B | 310 363-6000 | 14090 |
| Spacex LLC | 3761 | A | 310 970-5845 | 14091 |
| Phase Four Inc | 3764 | E | 310 648-8454 | 14104 |
| Medical Tactile Inc | 3841 | E | 310 641-8228 | 15168 |
| Dolphin Medical Inc (HQ) | 3845 | E | 800 448-6506 | 15531 |
| Uninet Imaging Inc (PA) | 5043 | F | 424 675-3300 | 16500 |
| Arch Motorcycle Company Inc | 5571 | D | 970 443-1380 | 17481 |
| EC Design LLC | 5943 | E | 310 220-2362 | 17639 |
| Konami Digital Entrmt Inc (DH) | 7372 | E | 310 220-8100 | 18480 |

### HAYWARD, CA - Alameda County
| | | | | |
|---|---|---|---|---|
| Marelich Mechanical Co Inc (HQ) | 1711 | D | 510 785-5500 | 425 |
| Segale Bros Wood Products Inc | 1751 | E | 510 300-1170 | 500 |
| Van-Mulder Sheet Metal Inc | 1761 | E | 510 569-9123 | 517 |
| Columbus Foods LLC | 2011 | B | 510 921-3400 | 593 |
| Columbus Manufacturing Inc (HQ) | 2013 | D | 510 921-3423 | 636 |
| Sapar Usa Inc (HQ) | 2013 | E | 510 441-9500 | 665 |
| U S Enterprise Corporation | 2035 | F | 510 487-8877 | 995 |
| Ajinomoto Foods North Amer Inc | 2038 | B | 510 293-1838 | 1021 |
| Vicolo Wholesale LLC | 2041 | E | 510 475-6019 | 1067 |
| Goldilocks Corporation Calif (PA) | 2051 | E | 510 476-0700 | 1215 |
| Ly Brothers Corporation (PA) | 2051 | D | 510 782-2118 | 1225 |
| Ly Brothers Corporation | 2051 | D | 510 782-2118 | 1226 |
| Oven Fresh Bakery Incorporated | 2051 | F | 650 366-9201 | 1233 |
| Steinbeck Brewing Company | 2082 | D | 510 886-9823 | 1460 |
| Gallo Sales Company Inc (DH) | 2084 | C | 510 476-5000 | 1582 |
| Bottling Group LLC | 2086 | A | 510 781-3723 | 1870 |
| Pepsi-Cola Metro Btlg Co Inc | 2086 | C | 510 781-3600 | 1920 |
| Shasta Beverages Inc (DH) | 2086 | D | 954 581-0922 | 1963 |
| Still Room LLC | 2087 | E | 510 847-1930 | 2026 |
| Azuma Foods Intl Inc USA (HQ) | 2092 | D | 510 782-1112 | 2048 |
| Fante Inc (PA) | 2096 | E | 650 697-7525 | 2090 |
| Carmel Food Group Inc | 2099 | E | 510 471-4889 | 2159 |
| Clarmill Manufacturing Corp (PA) | 2099 | E | 510 476-0700 | 2168 |
| Cnc Noodle Corporation | 2099 | F | 510 732-1318 | 2171 |
| Haigs Delicacies LLC | 2099 | E | 510 782-6285 | 2225 |
| J W Floor Covering Inc | 2099 | C | 858 444-1214 | 2241 |
| Lyrical Foods Inc | 2099 | E | 510 784-0955 | 2270 |
| United Foods Intl USA Inc (DH) | 2099 | E | 510 264-5850 | 2383 |
| Win Foods Corporation | 2099 | D | 510 487-8877 | 2390 |
| Cinder Block LLC | 2261 | F | 510 957-1333 | 2490 |
| All Bay Pallet Company Inc (PA) | 2448 | E | 510 636-4131 | 3330 |
| Applied Silver Inc | 2499 | E | 888 939-4747 | 3410 |
| Clarios LLC | 2531 | E | 510 783-4000 | 3616 |
| Surface Techniques Corporation (PA) | 2541 | E | 510 887-6000 | 3672 |
| Onq Solutions Inc (PA) | 2542 | E | 650 351-4245 | 3699 |
| Corrugated Packaging Pdts Inc | 2653 | F | 650 615-9180 | 3835 |
| Sonoco Prtective Solutions Inc | 2653 | D | 510 785-0220 | 3887 |
| Outform Group Inc | 2675 | E | 510 431-5872 | 3999 |
| Alameda Newspapers Inc (DH) | 2711 | C | 510 783-6111 | 4062 |
| Joong-Ang Daily News Cal Inc | 2711 | D | 510 487-3333 | 4139 |
| Consolidated Printers Inc | 2732 | E | 510 843-8524 | 4356 |

Employee Codes: A=Over 500 employees, B=251-500
C=101-250, D=51-100, E=20-50, F=10-19, G=1-9

# HAYWARD, CA

| Company | SIC | EMP | PHONE | ENTRY# |
|---|---|---|---|---|
| Admail-Express Inc. | 2752 | E | 510 471-6200 | 4503 |
| First Impressions Printing Inc. | 2752 | E | 510 784-0811 | 4610 |
| Pinnacle Diversified Inc. | 2752 | F | 510 400-7929 | 4725 |
| Custom Label & Decal LLC | 2759 | E | 510 876-0000 | 4870 |
| Spectrum Label Corporation | 2759 | F | 510 477-9374 | 4962 |
| Folgergraphics Inc. | 2791 | E | 510 293-2294 | 5019 |
| Ekc Technology Inc (HQ) | 2819 | C | 510 784-9105 | 5089 |
| Dow Chemical Company | 2821 | D | 510 786-0100 | 5151 |
| United Fiber Inc. | 2824 | E | 510 783-6904 | 5225 |
| Frontage Laboratories Inc. | 2834 | F | 510 626-9993 | 5447 |
| Impax Laboratories LLC | 2834 | E | 510 240-6000 | 5488 |
| Impax Laboratories LLC (DH) | 2834 | A | | 5489 |
| Impax Laboratories LLC | 2834 | D | 510 240-6000 | 5490 |
| Impax Laboratories Usa LLC | 2834 | E | 510 240-6000 | 5491 |
| Lonza Biologics Inc. | 2834 | F | 510 265-3095 | 5538 |
| Soleo Health Inc. | 2834 | F | 844 362-7360 | 5668 |
| Truepill Inc (PA) | 2834 | F | 855 910-8606 | 5695 |
| Plastikon Healthcare LLC | 2835 | E | 785 330-7100 | 5774 |
| Baxter Healthcare Corporation | 2836 | D | 510 723-2000 | 5809 |
| Quantum Global Tech LLC (HQ) | 2842 | C | 215 892-9300 | 5927 |
| Allure Labs LLC | 2844 | D | 510 489-8896 | 5942 |
| Sun Deep Inc (PA) | 2844 | D | 510 441-2525 | 6043 |
| Pacific Die Cut Industries | 3053 | D | 510 732-8103 | 6458 |
| Pacific States Felt Mfg Co Inc. | 3053 | F | 510 783-2357 | 6459 |
| American Poly-Foam Company Inc. | 3086 | E | 510 786-3626 | 6620 |
| Allstate Plastics LLC | 3089 | F | 510 783-9600 | 6703 |
| Chawk Technology Intl Inc (PA) | 3089 | C | 510 330-5299 | 6772 |
| Delphon Industries LLC (PA) | 3089 | C | 510 576-2220 | 6797 |
| General Window Corporation | 3089 | C | 510 487-1122 | 6839 |
| Norton Packaging Inc (PA) | 3089 | D | 510 786-1922 | 6936 |
| Norton Packaging Inc. | 3089 | E | 510 786-1922 | 6938 |
| Pan Pacific Plastics Mfg Inc (PA) | 3089 | E | 510 785-6888 | 6948 |
| Plastikon Industries (PA) | 3089 | C | 510 400-1010 | 6967 |
| Plastikon Industries Inc. | 3089 | C | 510 487-1010 | 6968 |
| Morgan Advanced Ceramics Inc (HQ) | 3251 | C | 510 491-1100 | 7266 |
| Florence & New Itln Art Co Inc. | 3272 | E | 510 785-9674 | 7332 |
| Morgan Technical Ceramics Inc. | 3299 | D | 510 491-1100 | 7594 |
| Protech Materials Inc. | 3364 | F | 510 887-5870 | 7830 |
| Thermo-Fusion Inc. | 3398 | E | 510 782-7755 | 7903 |
| Arch Foods Inc (PA) | 3421 | F | 510 331-8352 | 7936 |
| Glazier Steel Inc. | 3441 | D | 510 471-5300 | 8146 |
| Inland Marine Industries Inc (PA) | 3444 | E | 510 785-8555 | 8473 |
| South Bay Diversfd Systems Inc. | 3444 | F | 510 784-3094 | 8575 |
| Associated Screw Machine Pdts. | 3451 | E | 510 783-3831 | 8717 |
| Die and Tool Products Inc. | 3469 | F | 415 822-2888 | 8836 |
| Electro-Plating Spc Inc. | 3471 | E | 510 786-1881 | 8951 |
| Semano Inc. | 3471 | E | 510 489-2360 | 9012 |
| Teikuro Corporation | 3471 | E | 510 487-4797 | 9021 |
| Thermionics Laboratory Inc. | 3471 | D | 510 786-0680 | 9023 |
| Advanced Fabrication Technology LLC | 3479 | D | 510 489-6218 | 9038 |
| Melrose Nameplate Label Co Inc (PA) | 3479 | E | 510 732-3100 | 9091 |
| Mdc Precision LLC | 3491 | E | 510 265-3500 | 9159 |
| SF Tube Inc. | 3498 | E | 510 785-9148 | 9270 |
| Verdant Robotics Inc. | 3523 | E | 202 510-5040 | 9391 |
| Flo Stor Engineering Inc (PA) | 3535 | E | 510 887-7179 | 9485 |
| Carpenter Group (PA) | 3536 | E | 415 285-1954 | 9499 |
| Crown Equipment Corporation | 3537 | E | 510 471-7272 | 9514 |
| Computer Plastics | 3544 | E | 510 785-3600 | 9614 |
| Aperia Technologies Inc (PA) | 3559 | D | 650 741-3231 | 9829 |
| Mdc Precision LLC (PA) | 3563 | D | 510 265-3500 | 9966 |
| Sew-Eurodrive Inc. | 3566 | E | 510 487-3560 | 10044 |
| Ampex Data Systems Corporation (HQ) | 3572 | D | 650 367-2011 | 10223 |
| Jupiter Systems Inc. | 3575 | E | 510 675-1000 | 10307 |
| Micro Connectors Inc. | 3577 | E | 510 266-0299 | 10411 |
| Western State Design Inc. | 3582 | D | 510 786-9271 | 10475 |
| Mar Cor Purification Inc. | 3589 | F | 510 397-0025 | 10576 |
| Montague Company | 3589 | C | 510 785-8822 | 10582 |
| Autocam Acquisition Inc. | 3599 | E | | 10726 |
| Detention Device Systems | 3599 | E | 510 783-0771 | 10809 |
| I M T Precision Inc. | 3599 | E | 510 324-8926 | 10881 |
| Menches Tool & Die Inc. | 3599 | E | 510 476-1160 | 10971 |
| Mission Tool and Mfg Co Inc. | 3599 | E | 510 782-8383 | 10986 |
| Moss Precision Inc. | 3599 | D | 510 785-2235 | 10996 |
| Pacific Roller Die Co Inc. | 3599 | E | 510 244-7286 | 11024 |
| Tridecs Corporation | 3599 | E | 510 785-2620 | 11151 |
| Farasis Energy Usa Inc. | 3621 | D | 510 732-6600 | 11267 |
| Advance Carbon Products Inc. | 3624 | E | 510 293-5930 | 11297 |
| Applied Photon Technology Inc. | 3641 | E | 510 780-9500 | 11421 |
| Techtron Products Inc. | 3645 | E | 510 293-3500 | 11503 |
| Earthquake Sound Corporation | 3651 | F | 510 732-1000 | 11656 |
| Magico LLc | 3651 | E | 510 649-9700 | 11673 |
| Wohler Technologies Inc. | 3663 | E | 510 870-0810 | 11979 |
| Infineon Tech N Amer Corp. | 3674 | C | 919 768-0315 | 12481 |
| Ultra Clean Tech Systems Svc I (HQ) | 3674 | C | 510 576-4400 | 12776 |
| Ultrasil LLC | 3674 | E | 510 266-3700 | 12777 |
| Lithos Energy Inc. | 3691 | E | 415 944-5482 | 13145 |
| Primus Power Corporation | 3692 | E | 510 342-7600 | 13162 |
| Prevost Car (us) Inc. | 3711 | F | 951 202-2064 | 13376 |
| Western Truck Fabrication Inc. | 3713 | E | 510 785-9994 | 13435 |
| Advanced Transit Dynamics Inc. | 3714 | D | 510 619-8245 | 13446 |
| Yanfeng Intl Auto Tech US I LL | 3714 | E | 616 886-3622 | 13609 |
| Ao Sky Corporation | 3812 | E | 510 264-0402 | 14144 |
| Davis Instruments Corporation | 3812 | D | 510 732-9229 | 14176 |
| Thermionics Laboratory Inc (HQ) | 3821 | E | 510 538-3304 | 14352 |
| Tli Enterprises Inc (PA) | 3821 | E | 510 538-3304 | 14353 |
| X Therm | 3822 | E | 510 441-7566 | 14378 |
| Integrated Flow Systems LLC (HQ) | 3823 | D | 510 659-4900 | 14424 |
| Valdor Fiber Optics Inc (PA) | 3825 | F | 510 293-1212 | 14597 |
| Biolog Inc (PA) | 3826 | E | 800 284-4949 | 14634 |
| EMD Millipore Corporation | 3826 | E | 510 576-1367 | 14658 |
| Illumina Inc. | 3826 | E | 510 670-9300 | 14675 |
| C&C Building Automation Co Inc. | 3829 | E | 650 292-7450 | 14852 |
| Therm-X of California Inc (HQ) | 3829 | E | 510 441-7566 | 14934 |
| Potrero Medical Inc. | 3841 | D | 888 635-7280 | 15228 |
| Reflexion Medical Inc. | 3845 | C | 650 239-9070 | 15575 |
| Solta Medical Distribution LLC | 3845 | E | 510 782-2286 | 15579 |
| Beeline Group LLC | 3993 | E | 510 477-5400 | 15947 |
| J S Hckley Archtctral Sgnage | 3993 | E | 510 940-2608 | 15991 |
| Justipher Inc. | 3993 | F | 510 918-6800 | 15998 |
| Ametek Inc. | 5045 | E | 510 431-6718 | 16507 |
| Twin Bridges Technologies LLC | 5045 | F | 707 591-4500 | 16562 |
| Cnet Technology Corporation | 5065 | C | 408 392-9966 | 16695 |
| Dynamic Security Tech Inc. | 5065 | E | 510 786-1121 | 16699 |
| Metric Equipment Sales Inc. | 5065 | D | 510 264-0805 | 16718 |
| Tps Aviation Inc (PA) | 5065 | E | 510 475-1010 | 16737 |
| Ironridge Inc (DH) | 5074 | E | 800 227-9523 | 16768 |
| California Hydronics Corp (PA) | 5075 | E | 510 293-1993 | 16775 |
| Western Refining Inc. | 5084 | E | 510 538-1679 | 16858 |
| Oakhurst Industries Inc. | 5141 | C | 510 265-2400 | 17117 |
| Blue River Seafood Inc. | 5146 | D | 510 300-6800 | 17153 |
| Way To Be Designs LLC | 5199 | E | 510 476-6200 | 17316 |
| Dapper Tire Co Inc. | 5531 | F | 510 780-1616 | 17449 |
| Harvest Food Products Co Inc. | 5812 | D | 510 675-0383 | 17583 |
| Do Dine Inc. | 7372 | F | 510 583-7546 | 18246 |
| Hester Fabrication Inc. | 7692 | F | 530 227-6867 | 19198 |
| Gymdoc Inc. | 7699 | F | 510 886-4321 | 19260 |
| Corrpro Companies Inc. | 8711 | E | 510 614-8800 | 19385 |

# HEALDSBURG, CA - Sonoma County

| Company | SIC | EMP | PHONE | ENTRY# |
|---|---|---|---|---|
| E & J Gallo Winery | 0172 | F | 707 431-5400 | 12 |
| J Vineyards & Winery LP | 0172 | D | 707 431-5400 | 18 |
| Klein Foods Inc. | 0172 | D | 707 431-1533 | 19 |
| Adams Winery LLC | 2084 | F | 707 395-6126 | 1470 |
| AVV Winery Co LLC | 2084 | E | 707 433-7209 | 1481 |
| Chateau Diana LLC (PA) | 2084 | F | 707 433-6992 | 1504 |
| Constlltion Brnds US Oprtons I | 2084 | E | 707 433-8268 | 1517 |
| Davero Farms & Winery LLC | 2084 | F | 707 431-8000 | 1529 |
| Dry Creek Vineyard Inc. | 2084 | E | 707 433-1000 | 1543 |
| E & J Gallo Winery | 2084 | E | 707 431-1946 | 1548 |
| Ferrar-Crano Vnyrds Winery LLC (PA) | 2084 | D | 707 433-6700 | 1564 |
| Haus Beverage Inc. | 2084 | E | 503 939-5298 | 1611 |
| Hirsch Winery LLC | 2084 | F | 707 847-3001 | 1615 |
| Jean-Clude Bsset Wines USA Inc. | 2084 | F | 707 963-6903 | 1633 |
| Jordan Vineyard & Winery LP | 2084 | D | 707 431-5250 | 1637 |
| Justin Vineyards & Winery LLC | 2084 | F | 805 591-3260 | 1642 |
| Jvw Corporation | 2084 | D | 707 431-5250 | 1643 |
| Kssm LLC | 2084 | F | 707 433-7427 | 1651 |
| L Foppiano Wine Co. | 2084 | F | 707 433-2736 | 1654 |
| Munselle Vineyards LLC | 2084 | F | 707 857-9988 | 1683 |
| Pine Ridge Winery LLC | 2084 | D | 707 260-0330 | 1709 |
| Pjk Winery LLC | 2084 | F | 707 431-8333 | 1710 |
| Preston Vineyards Inc. | 2084 | F | 707 433-3372 | 1712 |
| RB Wine Associates LLC (PA) | 2084 | D | 707 433-8400 | 1719 |
| Seghesio Wineries Inc. | 2084 | E | 707 433-3579 | 1744 |
| Silver Oak Wine Cellars LLC | 2084 | F | 707 942-7082 | 1748 |
| Stonecushion Inc (PA) | 2084 | E | 707 433-1911 | 1765 |
| Treasury Chateau & Estates. | 2084 | C | 707 299-2600 | 1790 |
| Martin Group Inc (PA) | 2499 | E | 707 433-3900 | 3420 |
| Metro Publishing Inc. | 2711 | E | 707 527-1200 | 4158 |
| Rupert Gibbon & Spider Inc. | 2851 | E | 800 442-0455 | 6111 |
| Syar Industries Inc. | 3273 | E | 707 433-3366 | 7514 |
| Criveller California Corp. | 3556 | F | 707 431-2211 | 9786 |
| Max Process Eqp Globl LLC | 3599 | E | 707 433-7281 | 10964 |
| DJ Grey Company Inc. | 3679 | F | 707 431-2779 | 12962 |
| General Dynmics Ots Ncvlle Inc (DH) | 3728 | D | 707 473-9200 | 13849 |
| Max Machinery Inc. | 3823 | E | 707 433-2662 | 14431 |

# GEOGRAPHIC SECTION

HUNTINGTON BEACH, CA

| | SIC | EMP | PHONE | ENTRY# |
|---|---|---|---|---|
| Capital Lumber Company | 5031 | E | 707 433-7070 | 16444 |
| E & M Electric and McHy Inc (PA) | 5084 | E | 707 433-5578 | 16814 |
| Healdsburg Lumber Company Inc | 5251 | D | 707 431-9663 | 17355 |
| Costeaux French Bakery Inc | 5812 | D | 707 433-1913 | 17573 |
| Serra Systems Inc (HQ) | 7372 | F | 707 433-5104 | 18783 |
| Eandm | 7694 | E | 707 473-3137 | 19227 |
| Strategic Capital Incorporated | 8742 | E | 707 473-4310 | 19539 |

## HEBER, CA - Imperial County

| | SIC | EMP | PHONE | ENTRY# |
|---|---|---|---|---|
| Gibson & Schaefer Inc (PA) | 3273 | E | 619 352-3535 | 7448 |
| Ormat Technologies Inc | 4911 | E | 760 337-8872 | 16346 |

## HELENDALE, CA - San Bernardino County

| | SIC | EMP | PHONE | ENTRY# |
|---|---|---|---|---|
| Lockheed Martin Corporation | 3812 | D | 760 952-4200 | 14215 |

## HEMET, CA - Riverside County

| | SIC | EMP | PHONE | ENTRY# |
|---|---|---|---|---|
| EZ Lube LLC | 2992 | D | 951 766-1996 | 6394 |
| Ramko Injection Inc | 3089 | D | 951 929-0360 | 6992 |
| Califrnia Prcast Stone Mfg Inc | 3272 | F | 951 657-7913 | 7315 |
| Superior Ready Mix Concrete LP | 3273 | D | 951 658-9225 | 7511 |
| Ramko Mfg Inc | 3599 | D | 951 652-3510 | 11068 |
| Substance Abuse Program | 3674 | E | 951 791-3350 | 12739 |
| McCrometer Inc (HQ) | 3823 | C | 951 652-6811 | 14432 |
| Valley Resource Center Inc (PA) | 8331 | E | 951 766-8659 | 19363 |

## HERCULES, CA - Contra Costa County

| | SIC | EMP | PHONE | ENTRY# |
|---|---|---|---|---|
| Naia Inc | 2024 | E | 510 724-2479 | 813 |
| Mega Creation Inc | 2844 | E | 510 741-9998 | 6005 |
| A & B Die Casting Company Inc | 3363 | F | 877 708-0009 | 7803 |
| Benda Tool & Model Works Inc | 3544 | E | 510 741-3170 | 9607 |
| Bio-RAD Laboratories Inc | 3826 | C | 510 741-1000 | 14628 |
| Bio-RAD Laboratories Inc | 3826 | E | 510 232-7000 | 14629 |
| Bio-RAD Laboratories Inc | 3826 | E | 510 741-6999 | 14630 |
| Bio-RAD Laboratories Inc | 3826 | E | 510 741-6709 | 14631 |
| Bio-RAD Laboratories Inc (PA) | 3826 | A | 510 724-7000 | 14632 |
| Bio-RAD Laboratories Inc | 3826 | E | 510 741-6916 | 14633 |
| Bio-RAD Export LLC (HQ) | 3845 | F | 510 724-7000 | 15518 |

## HERMOSA BEACH, CA - Los Angeles County

| | SIC | EMP | PHONE | ENTRY# |
|---|---|---|---|---|
| National Media Inc | 2711 | F | 310 372-0388 | 4166 |
| Hammitt Inc | 3161 | D | 310 292-5200 | 7132 |
| Tellabs Access LLC (HQ) | 3669 | E | 630 798-8671 | 12022 |
| Rf Digital Corporation | 3674 | C | 949 610-0008 | 12678 |
| Marlin Equity Partners LLC (PA) | 6282 | D | 310 364-0100 | 17733 |
| Advanced Corporate Svcs Inc | 8748 | E | 310 937-6848 | 19554 |

## HESPERIA, CA - San Bernardino County

| | SIC | EMP | PHONE | ENTRY# |
|---|---|---|---|---|
| Hesperia Unified School Dst | 2099 | D | 760 948-1051 | 2231 |
| Brown Hnycutt Truss Systems In | 2439 | F | 760 244-8887 | 3295 |
| Hesperia Holding Inc | 2439 | E | 760 244-8787 | 3311 |
| T L Timmerman Cnstr Inc | 2439 | E | 760 244-2532 | 3319 |
| Brent-Wood Products Inc | 2499 | E | 800 400-7335 | 3412 |
| Robar Enterprises Inc (PA) | 3273 | C | 760 244-5456 | 7488 |
| Robertsons Ready Mix Ltd | 3273 | E | 760 244-7239 | 7491 |
| RSR Steel Fabrication Inc | 3312 | E | 760 244-2210 | 7623 |
| Maurice & Maurice Engrg Inc | 3334 | E | 760 949-5151 | 7709 |
| Madison Industries (HQ) | 3448 | E | 562 484-5099 | 8674 |
| Western Fab Inc | 3499 | F | 760 949-1441 | 9304 |
| CAr Enterprises Inc | 3578 | E | 760 947-6411 | 10457 |
| Dial Precision Inc | 3599 | F | 760 947-3557 | 10810 |
| Geeriraj Inc | 3672 | F | 760 244-6149 | 12121 |
| Mer-Mar Electronics Inc | 3672 | F | 760 244-6149 | 12159 |
| W R Grace & Co-Conn | 3826 | F | 760 244-6107 | 14754 |
| Endura Steel Inc (HQ) | 5051 | F | 760 244-9325 | 16619 |

## HICKMAN, CA - Stanislaus County

| | SIC | EMP | PHONE | ENTRY# |
|---|---|---|---|---|
| Frantz Wholesale Nursery LLC | 0181 | E | 209 874-1459 | 48 |
| Reed International | 3531 | F | 209 874-2719 | 9435 |
| Reed International (HQ) | 3532 | F | 209 874-2357 | 9450 |

## HIGHLAND, CA - San Bernardino County

| | SIC | EMP | PHONE | ENTRY# |
|---|---|---|---|---|
| Kcb Towers Inc | 1791 | D | 909 862-0322 | 531 |
| Raemica Inc | 2013 | E | 909 864-1990 | 662 |
| Pro-Cast Products Inc (PA) | 3272 | E | 909 793-7602 | 7376 |
| Cemex Cnstr Mtls PCF LLC | 3273 | E | 909 335-3105 | 7422 |
| Robertsons Rdymx Ltd A Cal Ltd | 3273 | C | 909 425-2930 | 7490 |
| Master-Halco Inc | 3315 | F | 909 350-4740 | 7645 |
| Cco Holdings LLC | 4841 | C | 909 742-8273 | 16332 |

## HILLSBOROUGH, CA - San Mateo County

| | SIC | EMP | PHONE | ENTRY# |
|---|---|---|---|---|
| Manticore Games Inc | 7372 | E | 650 799-6145 | 18520 |

## HILMAR, CA - Merced County

| | SIC | EMP | PHONE | ENTRY# |
|---|---|---|---|---|
| Americore Inc | 1796 | D | 209 632-5679 | 548 |
| Hilmar Cheese Company Inc | 2022 | B | 209 667-6076 | 719 |
| Hilmar Whey Protein Inc (PA) | 2023 | E | 209 667-6076 | 762 |
| Hilmar Whey Protein Inc | 2023 | B | 209 667-6076 | 763 |
| Specialty Hose Xpress LLC | 3052 | E | 209 226-1031 | 6430 |
| Perrys Custom Chopping LLC | 3523 | F | 209 667-8777 | 9376 |

## HOLLISTER, CA - San Benito County

| | SIC | EMP | PHONE | ENTRY# |
|---|---|---|---|---|
| Neil Jones Food Company | 2033 | E | 831 637-0573 | 908 |
| B & R Farms LLC | 2034 | E | 831 637-9168 | 944 |
| Nature Qulty A Cal Ltd Partnr | 2037 | F | | 1013 |
| Marich Confectionery Co Inc | 2064 | C | 831 634-4700 | 1319 |
| Ozeki Sake (usa) Inc (HQ) | 2084 | E | 831 637-9217 | 1702 |
| Cedar Valley Manufacturing Inc | 2429 | E | 831 636-8110 | 3104 |
| Simmons Stairways Inc | 2431 | E | 408 920-0105 | 3191 |
| Advantage Truss Company LLC | 2439 | E | 831 635-0377 | 3290 |
| Alpha Teknova Inc (PA) | 2836 | D | 831 637-1100 | 5789 |
| Trical Inc | 2879 | E | 831 637-0195 | 6210 |
| Pacific Scientific Energetic (HQ) | 2899 | B | 831 637-3731 | 6316 |
| San Benito Supply (PA) | 3272 | C | 831 637-5526 | 7388 |
| Hollister Landscape Supply Inc | 3273 | D | 831 636-8750 | 7458 |
| Reed Manufacturing Inc | 3324 | E | 831 637-5641 | 7695 |
| International Hort Tech LLC | 3523 | E | 831 637-1800 | 9359 |
| Pride Conveyance Systems Inc (PA) | 3535 | E | 831 637-1787 | 9491 |
| Mc Electronics LLC | 3672 | E | 831 637-1651 | 12158 |
| Royal Circuit Solutions LLC (DH) | 3672 | E | 831 636-7789 | 12203 |
| Nanotronics Imaging Inc | 3699 | E | 831 630-0700 | 13275 |
| Bae Systems Land Armaments LP | 3812 | E | 831 637-0356 | 14162 |
| Associated R V Ent Inc | 5013 | E | 831 636-9566 | 16373 |
| Grillin & Chillin Inc | 5812 | E | 831 637-2337 | 17582 |

## HOLLYWOOD, CA - Los Angeles County

| | SIC | EMP | PHONE | ENTRY# |
|---|---|---|---|---|
| Body Glove International LLC | 2329 | E | 310 374-3441 | 2615 |
| Technicolor Usa Inc (HQ) | 3651 | A | 317 587-4287 | 11705 |

## HOOPA, CA - Humboldt County

| | SIC | EMP | PHONE | ENTRY# |
|---|---|---|---|---|
| Hoopa Forest Industries | 2411 | E | 530 625-4281 | 3046 |

## HOPLAND, CA - Mendocino County

| | SIC | EMP | PHONE | ENTRY# |
|---|---|---|---|---|
| Fetzer Vineyards (HQ) | 2084 | C | 707 744-1250 | 1565 |

## HUGHSON, CA - Stanislaus County

| | SIC | EMP | PHONE | ENTRY# |
|---|---|---|---|---|
| Bella Viva Orchards Inc | 0191 | E | 209 883-9015 | 53 |
| Alpine Pacific Nut Co Inc | 0722 | E | 209 667-8688 | 71 |
| Nuwest Milling LLC | 2048 | F | 209 883-1163 | 1142 |
| Hughson Nut Inc (DH) | 2068 | D | 209 883-0403 | 1353 |
| California Trusframe LLC | 2439 | E | 209 883-8000 | 3299 |
| California Truss Company | 2439 | C | 209 883-8000 | 3302 |
| Calaveras Materials Inc (HQ) | 3273 | E | 209 883-0448 | 7410 |
| Grossi Fabrication Inc | 3496 | F | 209 883-2817 | 9219 |
| Valley Tool & Mfg Co Inc | 3599 | E | 209 883-4093 | 11167 |
| Cal Cat Industries LLC | 3999 | E | 209 883-4890 | 16103 |

## HUNTINGTON BEACH, CA - Orange County

| | SIC | EMP | PHONE | ENTRY# |
|---|---|---|---|---|
| Tile & Marble Design Co Inc | 1743 | E | 714 847-6472 | 485 |
| Armor Dermalogics LLC | 2023 | E | 714 202-6424 | 743 |
| Creative Costuming Designs Inc | 2211 | E | 714 895-0982 | 2411 |
| Tritex Trading Inc | 2211 | F | 949 413-8454 | 2430 |
| Gearment Inc (PA) | 2269 | C | 866 236-5476 | 2503 |
| DC Shoes LLC (PA) | 2329 | D | 714 889-4206 | 2616 |
| TravisMathew LLC (HQ) | 2329 | E | 562 799-6900 | 2649 |
| Bare Nothings Inc (PA) | 2339 | E | 714 848-8532 | 2736 |
| Jolyn Clothing Company LLC | 2339 | E | 714 794-2149 | 2775 |
| Victory Professional Pdts Inc | 2339 | E | 714 887-0621 | 2820 |
| Vae Industries Corporation | 2394 | E | 714 842-7500 | 2987 |
| Walton Company Inc | 2499 | E | 714 847-8800 | 3430 |
| Ofs Brands Holdings Inc | 2521 | A | 714 903-2257 | 3579 |
| Highmark Smart Reliable Seating Inc | 2522 | C | 714 903-2257 | 3603 |
| JCM Industries Inc (PA) | 2542 | E | 714 902-9000 | 3692 |
| K-Jack Engineering Co Inc | 2542 | D | 310 327-8389 | 3694 |
| Lifoam Industries LLC | 2653 | E | 714 891-5035 | 3865 |
| Harris Industries Inc (PA) | 2672 | E | 714 898-8048 | 3951 |
| Maxwell Petersen Associates | 2721 | F | 714 230-3150 | 4277 |
| Publish Brand Inc | 2741 | F | 714 890-1908 | 4455 |
| Teacher Created Materials Inc | 2741 | C | 714 891-2273 | 4476 |
| Inkwright LLC | 2752 | E | 714 892-3300 | 4647 |
| HB Products LLC | 2759 | E | 714 799-6967 | 4890 |
| Lincoln Composite Mtls Inc | 2821 | F | 714 898-8350 | 5174 |
| Pexco Aerospace Inc | 2821 | E | 714 894-9922 | 5186 |
| Sunshine Makers Inc (PA) | 2842 | D | 562 795-6000 | 5929 |
| Laird Coatings Corporation | 2851 | D | 714 894-5252 | 6092 |
| PPG Industries Inc | 2851 | E | 714 894-5252 | 6103 |

Employee Codes: A=Over 500 employees, B=251-500
C=101-250, D=51-100, E=20-50, F=10-19, G=1-9

# HUNTINGTON BEACH, CA

| Company | SIC | EMP | PHONE | ENTRY# |
|---|---|---|---|---|
| Custom Building Products LLC (DH) | 2891 | D | 800 272-8786 | 6224 |
| Home & Body Company (PA) | 2899 | B | 714 842-8000 | 6292 |
| Marko Foam Products Inc (PA) | 3086 | E | 949 417-3307 | 6647 |
| Advanced Cmpsite Pdts Tech Inc | 3089 | E | 714 895-5544 | 6696 |
| Bent Manufacturing Co Inc | 3089 | D | 714 842-0600 | 6739 |
| Cambro Manufacturing Company | 3089 | B | 714 848-1555 | 6759 |
| Cambro Manufacturing Company (PA) | 3089 | B | 714 848-1555 | 6760 |
| Cambro Manufacturing Company | 3089 | D | 714 848-1555 | 6761 |
| Delfin Design & Mfg Inc | 3089 | E | 949 888-4644 | 6796 |
| Newlight Technologies Inc | 3089 | E | 714 556-4500 | 6930 |
| Sandia Plastics Inc | 3089 | E | 714 901-8400 | 7022 |
| UFO Designs (PA) | 3089 | F | 714 892-4420 | 7063 |
| Donoco Industries Inc | 3229 | D | 714 893-7889 | 7194 |
| Zadro Inc | 3231 | E | 714 892-9200 | 7247 |
| Zadro Products Inc | 3231 | E | 714 892-9200 | 7248 |
| Precision Frrites Ceramics Inc | 3264 | D | 714 901-7622 | 7285 |
| Dynamet Incorporated | 3356 | E | 714 375-3150 | 7762 |
| Paciugo | 3421 | E | 714 536-5388 | 7939 |
| Advanced Cutting Tools Inc | 3423 | E | 714 842-9376 | 7942 |
| California Faucets Inc | 3432 | E | 657 400-1639 | 8048 |
| California Faucets Inc (PA) | 3432 | E | 800 822-8855 | 8049 |
| R & D Metal Fabricators Inc | 3444 | E | 714 891-4878 | 8550 |
| Precision Resource Inc | 3469 | C | 714 891-4439 | 8876 |
| Cal-Aurum Industries | 3471 | E | 714 898-0996 | 8937 |
| Plasma Rggedized Solutions Inc | 3471 | E | 714 893-6063 | 8995 |
| Pvd Coatings LLC | 3479 | F | 714 899-4892 | 9113 |
| Tiodize Co Inc (PA) | 3479 | F | 714 898-4377 | 9128 |
| Vector Launch LLC (PA) | 3489 | E | 202 888-3063 | 9141 |
| Iconn Engineering LLC | 3495 | E | 714 696-8826 | 9201 |
| Orlando Spring Corp | 3495 | E | 562 594-8411 | 9204 |
| American Precision Hydraulics | 3542 | E | 714 903-8610 | 9578 |
| Mjc Engineering and Tech Inc | 3542 | F | 714 890-0618 | 9586 |
| Crenshaw Die and Mfg Corp | 3544 | D | 949 475-5505 | 9615 |
| Guhring Inc | 3545 | E | 714 841-3582 | 9678 |
| Tool Alliance Corporation | 3545 | E | 714 373-5864 | 9703 |
| Lytle Screen Printing Inc | 3552 | F | 714 969-2424 | 9751 |
| Rima Enterprises Inc | 3555 | D | 714 893-4534 | 9774 |
| Fotis and Son Imports Inc (PA) | 3556 | F | 714 894-9022 | 9790 |
| Lynde-Ordway Company Inc | 3579 | F | 714 957-1311 | 10462 |
| Aero-Mechanical Engrg Inc | 3599 | F | 323 682-0961 | 10686 |
| Aerodynamic Engineering Inc | 3599 | E | 714 891-2651 | 10687 |
| Aerodyne Prcsion Machining Inc | 3599 | E | 714 891-1311 | 10688 |
| Buena Park Tool & Engrg Inc | 3599 | F | 714 843-6215 | 10756 |
| Fibreform Electronics Inc | 3599 | E | 714 898-9641 | 10837 |
| Hytron Mfg Co Inc | 3599 | D | 714 903-6701 | 10879 |
| Johnson Manufacturing Inc | 3599 | E | 714 903-0393 | 10913 |
| Kadan Consultants Incorporated | 3599 | F | 562 988-1165 | 10919 |
| Madsen Products Incorporated | 3599 | F | 714 894-1816 | 10954 |
| Milco Wire Edm Inc | 3599 | F | 714 373-0098 | 10981 |
| Momeni Engineering LLC | 3599 | E | 714 897-9301 | 10991 |
| Sertec Precision Machining | 3599 | F | 714 842-2023 | 11111 |
| V & S Engineering Company Ltd | 3599 | E | 714 898-7869 | 11164 |
| Coast To Coast Circuits Inc (PA) | 3672 | E | 714 891-9441 | 12080 |
| Soldermask Inc | 3672 | F | 714 842-1987 | 12222 |
| Vinatronic Inc | 3672 | E | 714 845-3480 | 12256 |
| Vanguard Electronics Company (PA) | 3677 | E | 714 842-3330 | 12863 |
| Reedex Inc | 3679 | E | 714 894-0311 | 13074 |
| Rocker Solenoid Company | 3679 | D | 310 534-5660 | 13077 |
| Riot Glass Inc | 3699 | E | 800 580-2303 | 13299 |
| Dynatrac Products LLC | 3714 | E | 714 596-4461 | 13490 |
| Dynatrac Products Co Inc | 3714 | F | 714 596-4461 | 13491 |
| Sandra Gruca | 3714 | E | 714 661-6464 | 13572 |
| U S Wheel Corporation | 3714 | E | 714 892-0021 | 13595 |
| Boeing Intllctual Prprty Lcnsi | 3721 | C | 562 797-2020 | 13645 |
| Tri Models Inc | 3721 | D | 714 896-0823 | 13696 |
| Irish International | 3724 | C | 949 559-0930 | 13714 |
| Airtech International Inc (PA) | 3728 | C | 714 899-8100 | 13765 |
| AMG Torrance LLC (DH) | 3728 | F | 310 515-2584 | 13777 |
| Encore Seats Inc | 3728 | E | 949 559-0930 | 13836 |
| Irish Interiors Inc (HQ) | 3728 | C | 949 559-0930 | 13875 |
| Irish Interiors Inc | 3728 | C | 562 344-1700 | 13876 |
| Mission Crtical Composites LLC | 3728 | E | 714 831-2100 | 13911 |
| Notthoff Engineering L A Inc | 3728 | E | 714 894-9802 | 13916 |
| PCA Aerospace Inc (PA) | 3728 | E | 714 841-1750 | 13924 |
| PCA Aerospace Inc | 3728 | E | 714 901-5209 | 13925 |
| Safran Cabin Galleys Us Inc (HQ) | 3728 | A | 714 861-7300 | 13942 |
| Safran Cabin Inc (HQ) | 3728 | B | 714 934-0000 | 13947 |
| Boeing Company | 3761 | B | 714 896-3311 | 14079 |
| American Automated Engrg Inc | 3769 | C | 714 898-9951 | 14108 |
| Leda Corporation | 3769 | E | 714 841-7821 | 14114 |
| Gardner Systems Inc | 3821 | F | 714 668-9018 | 14337 |
| Translogic Incorporated | 3823 | E | 714 890-0058 | 14465 |
| Blue-White Industries Ltd (PA) | 3824 | D | 714 893-8529 | 14473 |
| Enhanced Vision Systems Inc (HQ) | 3827 | D | 800 440-9476 | 14774 |
| Measure Uas Inc | 3829 | E | 714 916-6166 | 14895 |
| Mechanized Science Seals Inc | 3829 | E | 714 898-5602 | 14897 |
| Electronic Waveform Lab Inc | 3841 | E | 714 843-0463 | 15076 |
| Nordson Medical (ca) LLC | 3841 | D | 657 215-4200 | 15208 |
| Xr LLC | 3842 | E | 714 847-9292 | 15430 |
| Zimmer Melia & Associates Inc (PA) | 3842 | E | 615 377-0118 | 15433 |
| Kettenbach LP | 3843 | E | 877 532-2123 | 15462 |
| Submersible Systems LLC | 3949 | F | 714 842-6566 | 15861 |
| West Coast Trends Inc | 3949 | E | 714 843-9288 | 15876 |
| Primus Inc | 3993 | D | 714 527-2261 | 16021 |
| Leoben Company | 3999 | E | 951 284-9653 | 16168 |
| Sound Investment Group | 5013 | F | 714 515-4001 | 16401 |
| Reliable Wholesale Lumber Inc (PA) | 5031 | E | 714 848-8222 | 16458 |
| Premier Systems Usa Inc (PA) | 5045 | F | 657 204-9861 | 16540 |
| Bartco Lighting Inc | 5063 | E | 714 230-3200 | 16645 |
| Statco Engrg & Fabricators LLC (DH) | 5084 | E | 714 375-6300 | 16845 |
| Primal Elements Inc | 5122 | D | 714 899-0757 | 17046 |
| Tyr Sport Inc (HQ) | 5137 | F | 714 897-0799 | 17106 |
| Tiodize Co Inc | 5172 | E | 714 898-4377 | 17256 |
| Stater Bros Markets | 5411 | E | 714 963-0949 | 17385 |
| Graphic Ink Corp | 7336 | E | 714 901-2805 | 17829 |
| Applied Business Software Inc | 7372 | E | 562 426-2188 | 18055 |
| Benchmarkone | 7372 | F | 314 288-0399 | 18099 |
| Shortcuts Software Inc | 7372 | F | 714 622-6600 | 18787 |
| Great Western Grinding Inc | 7389 | F | 714 890-6592 | 19095 |
| Acceliot Inc | 8731 | F | 657 845-4250 | 19435 |

## HUNTINGTON PARK, CA - Los Angeles County

| Company | SIC | EMP | PHONE | ENTRY# |
|---|---|---|---|---|
| Abgb Designs Inc | 2331 | F |  | 2652 |
| Citizens of Humanity LLC (PA) | 2339 | C | 323 923-1240 | 2745 |
| Reliance Upholstery Sup Co Inc | 2392 | E | 323 321-2300 | 2948 |
| G - L Veneer Co Inc (PA) | 2435 | D | 323 582-5203 | 3284 |
| Plycraft Industries Inc | 2435 | C | 323 587-8101 | 3287 |
| Crown Poly Inc | 2673 | E | 323 585-5522 | 3965 |
| Cal-Pac Chemical Co Inc | 2819 | E | 323 585-2178 | 5074 |
| Saydel Inc (PA) | 2844 | F | 323 585-2800 | 6034 |
| Traffic Works Inc | 3081 | E | 323 582-0616 | 6572 |
| UFO Inc | 3089 | E | 323 588-5450 | 7064 |
| West Coast Foundry LLC (HQ) | 3325 | E | 323 583-1421 | 7702 |
| Montclair Bronze Inc | 3366 | E | 909 986-2664 | 7855 |
| Canterbury Designs Inc | 3446 | E | 323 936-7111 | 8620 |
| Bodycote Thermal Proc Inc | 3471 | D | 323 583-1231 | 8932 |
| Los Angeles Galvanizing Co | 3479 | D | 323 583-2263 | 9087 |
| Valco Planer Works Inc | 3544 | E | 323 582-6355 | 9656 |
| Los Angles Pump Valve Pdts Inc | 3561 | E | 323 277-7788 | 9930 |
| NL&a Collections Inc | 3645 | E | 323 277-6266 | 11499 |
| Aircraft Xray Laboratories Inc | 8734 | D | 323 587-4141 | 19500 |

## IDYLLWILD, CA - Riverside County

| Company | SIC | EMP | PHONE | ENTRY# |
|---|---|---|---|---|
| South Bay Wire & Cable Co LLC (PA) | 3315 | D | 951 659-2183 | 7651 |

## IMPERIAL, CA - Imperial County

| Company | SIC | EMP | PHONE | ENTRY# |
|---|---|---|---|---|
| Roo-Hide Saddlery LLC | 3199 | F | 877 766-4433 | 7161 |
| United States Gypsum Company | 3275 | C | 760 358-3200 | 7533 |
| Empire Southwest LLC | 3531 | E | 760 545-6200 | 9421 |
| Presto Inc | 7371 | F | 760 336-1455 | 17963 |

## INDIO, CA - Riverside County

| Company | SIC | EMP | PHONE | ENTRY# |
|---|---|---|---|---|
| Whites Steel Inc (PA) | 1791 | F | 760 347-3401 | 538 |
| Cabinets By Prcision Works Inc | 2434 | F | 760 342-1133 | 3224 |
| Purus International Inc | 3069 | F | 760 775-4500 | 6529 |
| Lindsey Doors Inc | 3083 | E | 760 775-1959 | 6584 |
| Coronet Concrete Products Inc (PA) | 3273 | E | 760 398-2441 | 7437 |
| Sullivans Stone Factory Inc | 3281 | E | 760 347-5535 | 7549 |

## INGLEWOOD, CA - Los Angeles County

| Company | SIC | EMP | PHONE | ENTRY# |
|---|---|---|---|---|
| Flowers Bkg Co Henderson LLC | 2051 | D | 310 695-9846 | 1199 |
| Goodman Food Products Inc (PA) | 2099 | C | 310 674-3180 | 2222 |
| Sip & Sonder LLC | 2099 | F | 908 309-3739 | 2355 |
| K B Socks Inc (DH) | 2252 | D | 310 670-3235 | 2458 |
| Biomed California Inc | 2834 | D | 310 665-1121 | 5373 |
| Hunter Vaughan LLC | 2844 | C | 626 534-7050 | 5990 |
| Multichrome Company Inc (PA) | 3471 | E | 310 216-1086 | 8987 |
| Zephyr Manufacturing Co Inc | 3546 | D | 310 410-4907 | 9715 |
| Quantum | 3572 | E | 323 709-8880 | 10268 |
| Engineered Magnetics Inc | 3629 | E | 310 649-9000 | 11370 |
| Empower Rf Systems Inc (PA) | 3663 | D | 310 412-8100 | 11850 |
| Doorking Inc (PA) | 3699 | C | 310 645-0023 | 13234 |
| Marvin Land Systems Inc | 3711 | E | 310 674-5030 | 13369 |
| Autonomous Medical Devices Inc | 3826 | E | 310 641-2700 | 14619 |
| Minus K Technology Inc | 3829 | C | 310 348-9656 | 14900 |
| Pharmaco-Kinesis Corporation | 3841 | E | 310 641-2700 | 15223 |

# GEOGRAPHIC SECTION — IRVINE, CA

| Company | SIC | EMP | PHONE | ENTRY# |
|---|---|---|---|---|
| Leads360 LLC | 7372 | E | 888 843-1777 | 18491 |

## INYOKERN, CA - Kern County

| Company | SIC | EMP | PHONE | ENTRY# |
|---|---|---|---|---|
| Firequick Products Inc | 3569 | F | 760 371-4279 | 10090 |
| Herbert Rizzardini | 5251 | F | 760 377-4571 | 17356 |

## IONE, CA - Amador County

| Company | SIC | EMP | PHONE | ENTRY# |
|---|---|---|---|---|
| Mp Associates Inc | 2892 | C | 209 274-4715 | 6251 |
| Isp Granule Products Inc | 3295 | C | 209 274-2930 | 7568 |
| Specialty Granules Inc | 3295 | E | 209 274-5323 | 7572 |

## IRVINE, CA - Orange County

| Company | SIC | EMP | PHONE | ENTRY# |
|---|---|---|---|---|
| Newport Energy | 1382 | E | 408 230-7545 | 192 |
| Phoenix Cpitl Group Hldngs LLC | 1382 | E | 303 749-0074 | 194 |
| De Vries International Inc (PA) | 1389 | E | 949 252-1212 | 222 |
| Baywa RE Operation Svcs LLC | 1711 | E | 949 398-3915 | 405 |
| Leading Edge Aviation Svcs Inc | 1721 | A | 714 556-0576 | 447 |
| Patric Communications Inc (PA) | 1731 | D | 619 579-2898 | 466 |
| Vortex Industries LLC (PA) | 1751 | E | 714 434-8000 | 502 |
| Developers General Contracting | 1799 | F | 949 351-7872 | 562 |
| Tls Productions Inc | 1799 | E | 810 220-8577 | 576 |
| Hormel Foods Corp Svcs LLC | 2013 | E | 949 753-5350 | 647 |
| Bio-Nutritional RES Group Inc | 2023 | C | 714 427-6990 | 750 |
| Bioray Inc | 2023 | F | 949 305-7454 | 751 |
| Danone Us LLC | 2024 | E | 949 474-9670 | 797 |
| Good Culture LLC | 2026 | E | 949 545-9945 | 837 |
| Kraft Heinz Foods Company | 2032 | E | 949 250-4080 | 863 |
| Real Vision Foods LLC | 2038 | E | 253 228-5050 | 1044 |
| Hillside Farms Corporation | 2047 | F | 888 846-9653 | 1100 |
| Orange Bakery Inc (HQ) | 2051 | F | 949 863-1377 | 1232 |
| South Coast Baking LLC (PA) | 2052 | D | 949 851-9654 | 1284 |
| Ezaki Glico USA Corporation | 2064 | F | 949 251-0144 | 1306 |
| Reyes Coca-Cola Bottling LLC (PA) | 2086 | B | 213 744-8616 | 1932 |
| Golden State Foods Corp (PA) | 2087 | E | 949 247-8000 | 2008 |
| Maruchan | 2098 | C | 949 789-2300 | 2115 |
| Maruchan Inc (HQ) | 2099 | B | 949 789-2300 | 2272 |
| Marukome USA Inc (HQ) | 2099 | F | 949 863-0110 | 2275 |
| Village Green Foods Inc | 2099 | E | 949 261-0111 | 2387 |
| Babylon International LLC | 2211 | E | 323 433-4104 | 2402 |
| Lspace America LLC | 2253 | D | 949 750-2292 | 2476 |
| Mad Engine Global LLC (HQ) | 2253 | E | 858 558-5270 | 2477 |
| Tomorrows Look Inc | 2261 | D | 949 596-8400 | 2497 |
| INX Prints Inc | 2262 | E | 949 660-9190 | 2499 |
| Royalty Carpet Mills Inc | 2273 | A | 949 474-4000 | 2519 |
| Birdwell Enterprises Inc | 2329 | E | 714 557-7040 | 2613 |
| Veezee Inc | 2331 | E | 949 265-0800 | 2694 |
| Boardriders Wholesale LLC | 2339 | E | 949 916-3060 | 2739 |
| St John Knits Intl Inc (HQ) | 2339 | C | 949 863-1171 | 2811 |
| Coop Home Goods LLC | 2392 | E | 888 316-1886 | 2926 |
| Pro-Mart Industries Inc | 2392 | E | 949 428-7700 | 2947 |
| Taber Company Inc | 2431 | D | 714 543-7100 | 3196 |
| Dellarobbia Inc (PA) | 2512 | E | 949 251-9532 | 3470 |
| Marlin Designs LLC | 2512 | C | 949 637-7257 | 3481 |
| Tropitone Furniture Co Inc (DH) | 2514 | B | 949 595-2010 | 3515 |
| Craftwood Industries Inc | 2522 | E | 616 796-1209 | 3596 |
| Krueger International Inc | 2531 | E | 949 748-7000 | 3634 |
| CK Manufacturing & Trading Inc | 2541 | E | 949 529-3400 | 3651 |
| Cycle News Inc (PA) | 2711 | E | 949 863-7082 | 4100 |
| San Diego Union-Tribune LLC | 2711 | B | 619 299-3131 | 4186 |
| Advanstar Communications Inc | 2721 | D | 714 513-8400 | 4227 |
| Cbj LP | 2721 | E | 949 833-8373 | 4238 |
| Haymarket Worldwide Inc | 2721 | E | 949 417-6700 | 4263 |
| HIC Corporation (PA) | 2721 | F | 949 261-1636 | 4264 |
| Kelley Blue Book Co Inc (DH) | 2721 | D | 949 770-7704 | 4269 |
| Acorn Publishing LLC | 2741 | E | 714 471-6973 | 4359 |
| Informa Business Media Inc | 2741 | E | 949 252-1146 | 4415 |
| Advanced Vsual Image Dsign LLC | 2752 | E | 951 279-2138 | 4505 |
| Digital Supercolor Inc | 2752 | D | 949 622-0010 | 4591 |
| DOT Printer Inc (PA) | 2752 | D | 949 474-1100 | 4596 |
| Kelmscott Communications LLC | 2752 | B | 949 475-1900 | 4660 |
| L T Litho & Printing Co | 2752 | E | 949 466-8584 | 4668 |
| Ocpc Inc | 2752 | D | 949 475-1900 | 4710 |
| Printery Inc | 2752 | F | 949 757-1930 | 4732 |
| Woodridge Press Inc | 2752 | E | 949 475-1900 | 4814 |
| Qpe Inc | 2754 | F | 949 263-0381 | 4826 |
| ABC Imaging of Washington | 2759 | E | 949 419-3728 | 4832 |
| Cnm Marketing Inc | 2759 | E | 866 792-5265 | 4860 |
| Lps Agency Sales & Posting Inc | 2759 | F | 714 247-7500 | 4916 |
| Orange Circle Studio Corp (PA) | 2759 | D | 949 727-0800 | 4933 |
| Progroup Inc | 2759 | E | 949 748-5400 | 4945 |
| Sunsports Inc | 2759 | F | | 4963 |
| Super Color Digital LLC (PA) | 2759 | E | 949 622-0010 | 4965 |
| Taylor Graphics Inc | 2759 | E | 949 752-5200 | 4969 |
| Sk Chemicals America Inc | 2821 | F | 949 336-8088 | 5201 |
| Bio-RAD Laboratories Inc | 2833 | C | 949 598-1200 | 5234 |
| Orgain LLC | 2833 | E | 888 881-4246 | 5258 |
| Allergan Sales LLC (DH) | 2834 | A | 862 261-7000 | 5307 |
| Allergan Spclty Thrpeutics Inc | 2834 | A | 714 246-4500 | 5308 |
| Allergan Usa Inc (DH) | 2834 | D | 714 427-1900 | 5309 |
| Amare Global LP | 2834 | E | 888 898-8551 | 5312 |
| Anchen Pharmaceuticals Inc | 2834 | C | 949 639-8100 | 5324 |
| Earthrise Nutritionals LLC (HQ) | 2834 | E | 949 623-0980 | 5429 |
| Edwards Lifesciences LLC (HQ) | 2834 | A | 949 250-2500 | 5430 |
| Formex LLC | 2834 | E | 858 529-6600 | 5443 |
| International Vitamin Corp | 2834 | C | 949 664-5500 | 5499 |
| Ista Pharmaceuticals Inc | 2834 | B | 949 788-6000 | 5507 |
| New Generation Wellness Inc (PA) | 2834 | E | 949 863-0340 | 5571 |
| Nitto Avecia Pharma Svcs Inc (DH) | 2834 | F | 949 951-4425 | 5575 |
| Nura USA LLC | 2834 | E | 949 946-5700 | 5581 |
| Nutrawise Health & Beauty LLC | 2834 | D | 888 271-8976 | 5582 |
| Pacific Pharma Inc | 2834 | A | 714 246-4600 | 5591 |
| Sicor Inc (HQ) | 2834 | A | 949 455-4700 | 5657 |
| Skinmedica Inc | 2834 | B | 760 929-2600 | 5663 |
| St Jude Medical LLC | 2834 | E | 949 769-5000 | 5672 |
| Stason Pharmaceuticals Inc (PA) | 2834 | F | 949 380-0752 | 5675 |
| Sun Ten Laboratories Inc | 2834 | E | 949 587-1238 | 5681 |
| Teva Parenteral Medicines Inc | 2834 | A | 949 455-4700 | 5688 |
| Biomerica Inc (PA) | 2835 | F | 949 645-2111 | 5741 |
| Oncocyte Corporation (PA) | 2835 | F | 949 409-7600 | 5770 |
| Cg Oncology Inc | 2836 | D | 949 409-3700 | 5817 |
| Tarsus Pharmaceuticals Inc | 2836 | E | 949 409-9820 | 5865 |
| California Scents LLC | 2842 | F | | 5894 |
| Meguiars Inc (HQ) | 2842 | E | 949 752-8000 | 5916 |
| Zo Skin Health Inc (DH) | 2844 | D | 949 988-7524 | 6065 |
| FSI Coating Technologies Inc | 2851 | E | 949 540-1140 | 6086 |
| Desmond Ventures Inc | 2891 | C | 949 474-0400 | 6226 |
| Henkel Chemical Management LLC | 2891 | C | 888 943-6535 | 6231 |
| Mitsubishi Chemical Crbn Fbr | 2891 | C | 800 929-5471 | 6237 |
| Signature Flexible Packg LLC | 2891 | F | 949 475-2300 | 6247 |
| Apoliotek International Inc | 2899 | F | 800 787-1244 | 6268 |
| Diamon Fusion Intl Inc | 2899 | F | 949 388-8000 | 6282 |
| Evergreen Holdings Inc | 2992 | C | 949 757-7770 | 6392 |
| Dinsmore & Associates LLC | 3081 | F | 714 641-7111 | 6558 |
| Jsn Packaging Products Inc | 3082 | D | 949 458-0050 | 6579 |
| Daz Inc | 3083 | F | 949 724-8800 | 6582 |
| Ctr America | 3089 | F | 323 332-1417 | 6788 |
| Jsn Industries Inc | 3089 | D | 949 458-0050 | 6878 |
| Plastoker Inc | 3089 | F | 714 598-5920 | 6970 |
| Urban Armor Gear LLC (HQ) | 3089 | E | 949 329-0500 | 7065 |
| Bloom Designs Corp | 3161 | F | 949 250-4929 | 7128 |
| Gary Bale Redi-Mix Con Inc | 3273 | D | 949 786-9441 | 7447 |
| National Ready Mixed Con Co | 3273 | F | 949 552-5566 | 7480 |
| 3M Technical Ceramics Inc (HQ) | 3299 | D | 949 862-9600 | 7584 |
| 3M Technical Ceramics Inc | 3299 | E | 949 756-0642 | 7585 |
| Cwi Steel Technologies Corporation | 3325 | E | 949 476-7600 | 7697 |
| PCC Rollmet Inc | 3339 | D | 949 221-5333 | 7712 |
| Supernal LLC | 3365 | C | 202 422-3275 | 7850 |
| Joseph Company Intl Inc | 3411 | E | | 7921 |
| PHC Sharp Holdings Inc (HQ) | 3421 | E | 714 662-1033 | 7940 |
| Pacific Handy Cutter Inc (DH) | 3423 | E | 714 662-1033 | 7962 |
| PHC Merger Inc | 3423 | E | 714 662-1033 | 7963 |
| Toughbuilt Industries Inc (PA) | 3423 | B | 949 528-3100 | 7967 |
| Jonathan Engnred Slutions Corp (HQ) | 3429 | E | 714 665-4400 | 8007 |
| M A G Engineering Mfg Co | 3429 | E | | 8013 |
| Columbia Sanitary Products Inc | 3432 | E | 949 474-0777 | 8052 |
| Cartel Industries LLC | 3444 | E | 949 474-3200 | 8406 |
| Delafoil Holdings Inc (PA) | 3444 | E | 949 752-4580 | 8429 |
| Rami Designs Inc | 3446 | F | 949 588-8288 | 8641 |
| Global Pcci (gpc) (PA) | 3469 | C | 757 637-9000 | 8847 |
| Electrolurgy Inc | 3471 | D | 949 250-4494 | 8955 |
| Global Metal Solutions Inc | 3471 | E | 949 872-2995 | 8965 |
| SDC Technologies Inc (HQ) | 3479 | E | 714 939-8300 | 9118 |
| Lubrication Scientifics Inc | 3491 | F | 714 557-0664 | 9158 |
| Griswold Controls LLC (PA) | 3494 | D | 949 559-6000 | 9187 |
| Cummins Pacific LLC (HQ) | 3519 | D | 949 253-6000 | 9324 |
| Signature Control Systems | 3523 | D | 949 580-3640 | 9381 |
| Control Systems Intl Inc | 3533 | D | 949 238-4150 | 9459 |
| Technipfmc Usa Inc | 3533 | F | 949 238-4150 | 9468 |
| Safety Products Holdings LLC | 3541 | E | 714 662-1033 | 9570 |
| Synventive Engineering Inc | 3542 | E | 312 848-8717 | 9589 |
| Barrot Corporation | 3544 | E | 949 852-1640 | 9606 |
| Pace Punches Inc | 3544 | D | 949 428-2750 | 9639 |
| Viking Products Inc | 3545 | E | 949 379-5100 | 9706 |
| M K Products Inc | 3548 | D | 949 798-1234 | 9727 |
| Cryoport Systems LLC (HQ) | 3559 | F | 949 470-2300 | 9847 |
| Aquatec International Inc | 3561 | D | 949 225-2200 | 9915 |

Employee Codes: A=Over 500 employees, B=251-500, C=101-250, D=51-100, E=20-50, F=10-19, G=1-9

# IRVINE, CA — GEOGRAPHIC SECTION

| Company | SIC | EMP | PHONE | ENTRY# |
|---|---|---|---|---|
| Robotic Software Solutions Inc. | 3561 | E | 855 762-6827 | 9938 |
| Xylem Water Solutions USA Inc. | 3561 | D | 949 474-1679 | 9946 |
| Vanomation Inc. | 3565 | F | 877 228-2992 | 10035 |
| Knight LLC (HQ) | 3569 | D | 949 595-4800 | 10098 |
| Lubrication Scientific LLC | 3569 | E | 714 557-0664 | 10099 |
| Senju Fire Protection Corp. | 3569 | F | 949 333-1281 | 10112 |
| Cybernet Manufacturing Inc. | 3571 | A | 949 600-8000 | 10146 |
| Dynabook Americas Inc (HQ) | 3571 | B | 949 583-3000 | 10147 |
| Gateway Inc (DH) | 3571 | C | 949 471-7000 | 10155 |
| Gateway US Retail Inc. | 3571 | C | 949 471-7000 | 10156 |
| I/O Magic Corporation | 3571 | E | 949 707-4800 | 10164 |
| Mediatek USA Inc. | 3571 | C | 408 526-1899 | 10179 |
| Solarflare Communications Inc (DH) | 3571 | D | 949 581-6830 | 10204 |
| Toshiba Amer Info Systems Inc. | 3571 | C | 949 583-3000 | 10213 |
| Certance LLC (HQ) | 3572 | B | 949 856-7800 | 10231 |
| H Co Computer Products (PA) | 3572 | E | 949 833-3222 | 10240 |
| Memory Experts Intl USA Inc (HQ) | 3572 | E | 714 258-3000 | 10253 |
| Quantum Corporation | 3572 | E | 949 856-7800 | 10270 |
| Stec Inc (HQ) | 3572 | B | 415 222-9996 | 10287 |
| Western Digital Corporation | 3572 | E | 949 672-7000 | 10296 |
| Zadara Storage Inc. | 3572 | D | 949 251-0360 | 10299 |
| Gateway Manufacturing LLC | 3575 | E | 949 471-7000 | 10305 |
| Cs Systems Inc. | 3577 | E | 949 475-9100 | 10354 |
| Emulex Corporation (DH) | 3577 | C | | 10363 |
| Encrypted Access Corporation | 3577 | C | 714 371-4125 | 10364 |
| Finis LLC | 3577 | E | 949 250-4929 | 10367 |
| Incipio Technologies Inc (PA) | 3577 | E | 888 893-1638 | 10379 |
| Innovative Tech & Engrg Inc. | 3577 | E | 949 955-2501 | 10383 |
| Lasergraphics Inc. | 3577 | E | 949 753-8282 | 10395 |
| Livescribe Inc. | 3577 | E | | 10397 |
| Logitech Inc. | 3577 | A | 510 795-8500 | 10399 |
| Princeton Technology Inc. | 3577 | E | 949 851-7776 | 10421 |
| Printronix LLC (PA) | 3577 | E | 714 368-2300 | 10422 |
| Raise 3d Technologies Inc. | 3577 | E | 949 482-2040 | 10426 |
| Synaptics Inc. | 3577 | F | 949 483-5594 | 10440 |
| Western Telematic Inc. | 3577 | E | 949 586-9950 | 10452 |
| Ricoh Electronics Inc. | 3579 | D | 714 259-1220 | 10465 |
| Jacuzzi Inc (DH) | 3589 | C | 909 606-7733 | 10568 |
| Cp-Carrillo Inc. | 3592 | C | 949 567-9000 | 10620 |
| Cp-Carrillo Inc (DH) | 3592 | C | 949 567-9000 | 10621 |
| Coast Composites Inc. | 3599 | E | 949 455-0665 | 10782 |
| Computer Assisted Mfg Tech LLC | 3599 | E | 949 263-8911 | 10785 |
| Sdi LLC | 3599 | E | 949 351-1866 | 11103 |
| Streamline Avionics Inc. | 3612 | E | 949 861-8151 | 11231 |
| Iconn Inc. | 3613 | D | 800 286-6742 | 11244 |
| Staco Systems Inc (HQ) | 3613 | E | 949 297-8700 | 11250 |
| ITT Cannon LLC | 3625 | C | 714 557-4700 | 11326 |
| Q Com Inc. | 3625 | E | 949 833-1000 | 11341 |
| Rosemount Analytical Inc. | 3625 | A | 713 396-8880 | 11345 |
| Soundcoat Company Inc. | 3625 | D | 631 242-2200 | 11349 |
| Composite Technology Corp. | 3629 | C | 949 428-8500 | 11365 |
| Tivoli LLC | 3641 | E | 714 957-6101 | 11433 |
| Connectec Company Inc (PA) | 3643 | D | 949 252-1077 | 11446 |
| Ctc Global Corporation (PA) | 3643 | C | 949 428-8500 | 11447 |
| Wpmg Inc. | 3646 | E | 949 442-1601 | 11569 |
| Acti Corporation Inc. | 3651 | E | 949 753-0352 | 11632 |
| Henrys Adio Vsual Slutions Inc. | 3651 | E | 714 258-7238 | 11668 |
| Toshiba Amer Elctrnic Cmpnnts (DH) | 3651 | B | 949 462-7700 | 11706 |
| Toshiba America Inc. | 3651 | A | 212 596-0600 | 11707 |
| Vizio Inc (HQ) | 3651 | C | 855 833-3221 | 11714 |
| Vizio Holding Corp (PA) | 3651 | E | 949 428-2525 | 11715 |
| Lg-Ericsson USA Inc. | 3661 | E | 877 828-2673 | 11774 |
| Anydata Corporation | 3663 | C | 949 900-6040 | 11811 |
| Fleet Management Solutions Inc. | 3663 | E | 800 500-6009 | 11857 |
| Microwave Dynamics LLC | 3663 | F | 949 679-7788 | 11891 |
| Mophie Inc (DH) | 3663 | D | 888 866-7443 | 11896 |
| Sekai Electronics Inc (PA) | 3663 | E | 949 783-5740 | 11943 |
| Tricom Research Inc. | 3663 | D | 949 250-6024 | 11968 |
| Tricom Research Inc. | 3663 | D | 949 250-6024 | 11969 |
| General Monitors Inc (DH) | 3669 | C | 949 581-4464 | 11996 |
| Choose Manufacturing Co LLC | 3672 | E | 714 327-1698 | 12077 |
| Concept Development Llc | 3672 | E | 949 623-8000 | 12081 |
| Irvine Electronics LLC | 3672 | D | 949 250-0315 | 12138 |
| Lifetime Memory Products Inc. | 3672 | E | 949 794-9000 | 12154 |
| Mflex Delaware Inc. | 3672 | A | 949 453-6800 | 12164 |
| Multi-Fineline Electronix Inc (HQ) | 3672 | A | 949 453-6800 | 12167 |
| Trantronics Inc. | 3672 | E | 949 553-1234 | 12242 |
| Adex Electronics Inc. | 3674 | F | 949 597-1772 | 12274 |
| Aeroflex Incorporated | 3674 | E | 800 843-1553 | 12281 |
| American Arium | 3674 | E | 949 623-7090 | 12300 |
| Baywa RE Epc LLC | 3674 | F | 949 398-3915 | 12356 |
| Baywa RE Solar Projects LLC (DH) | 3674 | F | 949 398-3915 | 12357 |
| Broadcom Corporation | 3674 | C | 949 926-5000 | 12363 |
| Broadcom Corporation | 3674 | E | 714 376-5029 | 12364 |
| Clariphy Communications Inc (DH) | 3674 | D | 949 861-3074 | 12382 |
| Conexant Systems LLC (HQ) | 3674 | E | 949 483-4600 | 12389 |
| Cooper Microelectronics Inc. | 3674 | E | 949 553-8352 | 12391 |
| Hanwha Energy USA Holdings Corp (HQ) | 3674 | E | 949 748-5996 | 12460 |
| Hanwha Q Cells Usa Inc. | 3674 | E | 706 671-3077 | 12461 |
| Marvell Semiconductor Inc. | 3674 | A | 949 614-7700 | 12544 |
| Masimo Semiconductor Inc. | 3674 | F | 603 595-8900 | 12547 |
| Morse Micro Inc. | 3674 | D | 949 501-7080 | 12589 |
| Netlist Inc (PA) | 3674 | E | 949 435-0025 | 12600 |
| Qlogic LLC (DH) | 3674 | C | 949 389-6000 | 12646 |
| Quartics Inc. | 3674 | E | 949 679-2672 | 12664 |
| Rfaxis Inc. | 3674 | F | 949 825-6300 | 12679 |
| Rockley Photonics Inc (HQ) | 3674 | C | 626 304-9960 | 12680 |
| Skyworks Solutions Inc (PA) | 3674 | A | 949 231-3000 | 12719 |
| Suncore Inc. | 3674 | E | 949 450-0054 | 12742 |
| Syntiant Corp (PA) | 3674 | E | 949 774-4887 | 12753 |
| Teridian Semiconductor Corp (DH) | 3674 | D | 714 508-8800 | 12760 |
| Teridian Smicdtr Holdings Corp (DH) | 3674 | F | 714 508-8800 | 12761 |
| Astron Corporation | 3677 | E | 949 458-7277 | 12829 |
| Circuit Assembly Corp (PA) | 3678 | F | 949 855-7887 | 12869 |
| Corsair Elec Connectors Inc. | 3678 | C | 949 833-0273 | 12874 |
| Infinite Electronics Intl Inc (DH) | 3678 | E | 949 261-1920 | 12883 |
| Infinite Electronics Intl Inc. | 3678 | F | 949 261-1920 | 12884 |
| Min-E-Con LLC | 3678 | D | 949 250-0087 | 12890 |
| 3y Power Technology Inc. | 3679 | F | 949 450-0152 | 12904 |
| Advanced Waveguide Tech. | 3679 | E | 949 297-3564 | 12908 |
| American Audio Component Inc. | 3679 | E | 909 596-3788 | 12912 |
| Bi-Search International Inc. | 3679 | E | 714 258-4500 | 12924 |
| Bivar Inc. | 3679 | E | 949 951-8808 | 12925 |
| Dynalloy Inc. | 3679 | E | 714 436-1206 | 12964 |
| Emerging Display Technologies Corpo (HQ) | 3679 | F | 949 296-8300 | 12971 |
| EMI Solutions LLC | 3679 | E | 949 206-9960 | 12972 |
| Fema Electronics Corporation | 3679 | E | 714 825-0140 | 12978 |
| Infinite Electronics Inc (HQ) | 3679 | E | 949 261-1920 | 12999 |
| Interctive Dsplay Slutions Inc. | 3679 | E | 949 727-1959 | 13003 |
| Ppst Inc (PA) | 3679 | E | 800 421-1921 | 13065 |
| Suntsu Electronics Inc (PA) | 3679 | F | 949 783-7300 | 13094 |
| Voice Assist Inc. | 3679 | E | 949 655-6400 | 13119 |
| Western Digital Corporation | 3679 | E | 949 672-7000 | 13123 |
| Xidas Inc. | 3679 | E | 949 930-0147 | 13127 |
| Enevate Corporation | 3691 | D | 949 243-0399 | 13138 |
| Farstone Technology Inc. | 3695 | C | 949 336-4321 | 13196 |
| Agents West Inc. | 3699 | E | 949 614-0293 | 13209 |
| OBryant Electric Inc. | 3699 | E | 949 341-0025 | 13280 |
| Orthodyne Electronics Corporation (HQ) | 3699 | C | 949 660-0440 | 13282 |
| Phantom Access Systems LLC | 3699 | F | 949 753-1280 | 13287 |
| Stracon Inc. | 3699 | F | 949 851-2288 | 13312 |
| USA Vision Systems Inc (HQ) | 3699 | E | 949 583-1519 | 13324 |
| Vti Instruments Corporation (HQ) | 3699 | E | 949 955-1894 | 13328 |
| Karma Automotive LLC | 3711 | A | 855 565-2762 | 13361 |
| Mazda Motor of America Inc (HQ) | 3711 | A | 949 727-1990 | 13370 |
| Rivian Automotive Inc (PA) | 3711 | B | 888 748-4261 | 13379 |
| Gredes Corporation | 3714 | E | 714 262-9150 | 13509 |
| Innova Electronics Corporation | 3714 | E | 714 241-6800 | 13519 |
| Pankl Engine Systems Inc. | 3714 | E | 949 428-8788 | 13554 |
| American Scence Tech As T Corp. | 3721 | D | 310 773-1978 | 13634 |
| Boeing | 3721 | E | 949 623-2222 | 13639 |
| Parker-Hannifin Corporation | 3724 | C | 949 833-3000 | 13717 |
| A-Info Inc. | 3728 | E | 949 346-7326 | 13730 |
| Coast Composites LLC (PA) | 3728 | D | 949 455-0665 | 13809 |
| Eaton Corporation | 3728 | F | 714 272-4700 | 13835 |
| Fmh Aerospace Corp. | 3728 | D | 714 751-1000 | 13844 |
| Meggitt Defense Systems Inc. | 3728 | B | 949 465-7700 | 13905 |
| Pacific Precision Products Mfg Inc. | 3728 | E | 949 727-3844 | 13920 |
| Parker-Hannifin Corporation | 3728 | C | 949 833-3000 | 13923 |
| Thales Avionics Inc. | 3728 | E | 949 381-3033 | 13970 |
| Thales Avionics Inc. | 3728 | E | 949 790-2500 | 13971 |
| Thales Avionics Inc. | 3728 | E | 949 829-5808 | 13972 |
| Super73 Inc (PA) | 3751 | E | 949 258-9245 | 14072 |
| Tyvak Nn-Satellite Systems Inc. | 3761 | E | 949 753-1020 | 14095 |
| Tyvak Nn-Satellite Systems Inc (DH) | 3761 | E | 949 753-1020 | 14096 |
| Eaton Aerospace LLC | 3812 | E | 949 452-9500 | 14181 |
| Northrop Grumman Corporation | 3812 | E | 949 260-9800 | 14234 |
| Rockwell Collins Inc. | 3812 | E | 714 929-3000 | 14294 |
| Rockwell Collins Inc. | 3812 | D | 714 929-3000 | 14295 |
| Rogerson Aircraft Corporation (PA) | 3812 | D | 949 660-0666 | 14296 |
| Newport Corporation (HQ) | 3821 | B | 949 863-3144 | 14344 |
| Meggitt Western Design Inc. | 3822 | E | 949 465-7700 | 14364 |
| Biodot Inc (HQ) | 3823 | D | 949 440-3685 | 14389 |
| Futek Advanced Sensor Tech Inc. | 3823 | C | 949 465-0900 | 14416 |
| Graphtec America Inc (DH) | 3823 | E | 949 770-6010 | 14420 |
| Vertiv Corporation | 3823 | D | 949 457-3600 | 14468 |

# GEOGRAPHIC SECTION

IRVINE, CA

| Company | SIC | EMP | PHONE | ENTRY# |
|---|---|---|---|---|
| Emcor Facilities Services Inc | 3824 | C | 949 475-6020 | 14478 |
| Astronics Test Systems Inc (HQ) | 3825 | C | 800 722-2528 | 14499 |
| Equus Products Inc | 3825 | E | 714 424-6779 | 14517 |
| Hid Global Corporation | 3825 | D | 949 732-2000 | 14533 |
| Hid Global Corporation | 3825 | F | 949 466-9508 | 14534 |
| Marvin Test Solutions Inc | 3825 | D | 949 263-2222 | 14553 |
| N H Research LLC (DH) | 3825 | E | 949 474-3900 | 14557 |
| Broadley-James Corporation (PA) | 3826 | D | 949 829-5555 | 14637 |
| Capillary Biomedical Inc | 3826 | E | 949 317-1701 | 14642 |
| Combimatrix Corporation (PA) | 3826 | E | 949 753-0624 | 14647 |
| Horiba Americas Holding Inc (HQ) | 3826 | A | 949 250-4811 | 14671 |
| Horiba Instruments Inc (DH) | 3826 | C | 949 250-4811 | 14672 |
| Mp Biomedicals LLC (HQ) | 3826 | E | 949 833-2500 | 14695 |
| Nanovea Inc (PA) | 3826 | E | 949 461-9292 | 14696 |
| Tetra Tech Ec Inc | 3826 | E | 949 809-5000 | 14733 |
| Nipro Optics Inc | 3827 | E | 949 215-1151 | 14803 |
| Rrds Inc (PA) | 3827 | F | 949 482-6200 | 14817 |
| Spectrum Scientific Inc | 3827 | E | 949 260-9900 | 14825 |
| Tfd Incorporated | 3827 | E | 714 630-7127 | 14828 |
| United Scope LLC (HQ) | 3827 | E | 714 942-3202 | 14831 |
| Zygo Corporation | 3827 | E | 714 918-7433 | 14835 |
| Horiba International Corp | 3829 | A | 949 250-4811 | 14880 |
| International Sensor Tech | 3829 | E | 949 452-9000 | 14885 |
| Lobby Traffic Systems Inc (PA) | 3829 | F | 800 486-8606 | 14893 |
| Meggitt (orange County) Inc (DH) | 3829 | C | 949 493-8181 | 14898 |
| Omni Optical Products Inc (PA) | 3829 | E | 714 634-5700 | 14905 |
| Acclarent Inc | 3841 | B | 650 687-5888 | 14947 |
| Advanced Sterlization (HQ) | 3841 | C | 800 595-0200 | 14951 |
| Alcon Lensx Inc (DH) | 3841 | D | 949 753-1393 | 14954 |
| Alcon Research Ltd | 3841 | D | 949 387-2142 | 14955 |
| Alcon Vision LLC | 3841 | A | 949 753-6488 | 14957 |
| Alliance Medical Products Inc (DH) | 3841 | E | 949 768-4690 | 14959 |
| Alliance Medical Products Inc | 3841 | E | 949 664-9616 | 14960 |
| Applied Cardiac Systems Inc | 3841 | D | 949 855-9366 | 14970 |
| Aspen Medical Products LLC | 3841 | D | 949 681-0200 | 14979 |
| B Braun Medical Inc | 3841 | E | 949 660-3151 | 14989 |
| B Braun Medical Inc | 3841 | F | 949 660-2581 | 14990 |
| B Braun Medical Inc | 3841 | A | 610 691-5400 | 14991 |
| Baxter Healthcare Corporation | 3841 | F | 949 250-2500 | 14994 |
| Baxter Healthcare Corporation | 3841 | C | 949 474-6301 | 14995 |
| Bio-Medical Devices Inc | 3841 | E | 949 752-9642 | 15006 |
| Bio-Medical Devices Intl Inc | 3841 | E | 949 752-9642 | 15007 |
| Cas Medical Systems Inc (HQ) | 3841 | D | 203 488-6056 | 15037 |
| Chen-Tech Industries Inc (DH) | 3841 | E | 949 855-6716 | 15041 |
| Clearflow Inc (PA) | 3841 | E | 714 916-5010 | 15044 |
| Covidien LP | 3841 | C | 949 837-3700 | 15061 |
| Devax Inc | 3841 | E | 949 461-0450 | 15064 |
| Diality Inc | 3841 | D | 949 916-5851 | 15069 |
| Endologix Inc (PA) | 3841 | E | 949 595-7200 | 15080 |
| Endologix Canada LLC | 3841 | D | 949 595-7200 | 15081 |
| Envveno Medical Corporation | 3841 | E | 949 261-2900 | 15082 |
| Fluxergy Inc | 3841 | F | 949 305-4201 | 15087 |
| Fluxergy Inc | 3841 | F | 949 305-4201 | 15088 |
| Hoya Surgical Optics Inc | 3841 | F | 909 680-3900 | 15106 |
| I-Flow LLC | 3841 | A | 800 448-3569 | 15110 |
| Inari Medical Inc (PA) | 3841 | A | 877 927-4747 | 15116 |
| Interventional Spine Inc | 3841 | F | 949 472-0006 | 15125 |
| Irvine Biomedical Inc | 3841 | C | 949 851-3053 | 15133 |
| Ivantis Inc (PA) | 3841 | F | 949 600-9650 | 15135 |
| Joimax Inc | 3841 | E | 949 859-3472 | 15139 |
| Links Medical Products Inc (PA) | 3841 | E | 949 753-0001 | 15149 |
| Lombard Medical Tech Inc (PA) | 3841 | E | 949 379-3750 | 15152 |
| Masimo Americas Inc | 3841 | E | 949 297-7000 | 15160 |
| Medtronic Inc | 3841 | C | 949 837-3700 | 15174 |
| Medtronic PS Medical Inc (DH) | 3841 | C | 805 571-3769 | 15179 |
| Micro Therapeutics Inc (HQ) | 3841 | E | 949 837-3700 | 15188 |
| Nellix Inc | 3841 | E | 650 213-8700 | 15198 |
| Neomend Inc | 3841 | D | 949 783-3300 | 15199 |
| Neuroptics Inc | 3841 | E | 949 250-9792 | 15201 |
| Neurovasc Technologies Inc | 3841 | E | 949 258-9946 | 15202 |
| Pro-Dex Inc (PA) | 3841 | C | 949 769-3200 | 15230 |
| Rebound Therapeutics Inc | 3841 | E | 949 305-8111 | 15239 |
| Reverse Medical Corporation | 3841 | E | 949 215-0660 | 15242 |
| Source Scientific LLC | 3841 | E | 949 231-5096 | 15260 |
| Trivascular Inc (DH) | 3841 | E | 707 543-8800 | 15290 |
| Trivascular Technologies Inc (HQ) | 3841 | C | 707 543-8800 | 15291 |
| Uoc USA Inc | 3841 | F | 949 328-3366 | 15296 |
| Biomet Inc | 3842 | E | 949 453-3200 | 15325 |
| Breathe Technologies Inc | 3842 | E | 949 988-7700 | 15328 |
| Edwards Lifesciences Corp | 3842 | C | 949 250-2500 | 15338 |
| Edwards Lifesciences Corp | 3842 | F | 949 250-3522 | 15339 |
| Edwards Lifesciences Corp (PA) | 3842 | A | 949 250-2500 | 15340 |
| Edwards Lifesciences Corp | 3842 | E | 949 553-0611 | 15341 |
| Ethicon Inc | 3842 | B | 949 581-5799 | 15345 |
| Interpore Cross Intl Inc (DH) | 3842 | D | 949 453-3200 | 15364 |
| Mentor Worldwide LLC (DH) | 3842 | C | 800 636-8678 | 15382 |
| Mist Inc | 3842 | C | 408 940-8700 | 15383 |
| Ossur Americas Inc (HQ) | 3842 | D | 800 233-6263 | 15389 |
| Passy-Muir Inc (PA) | 3842 | E | 949 833-8255 | 15391 |
| Patient Safety Technologies Inc | 3842 | E | 949 387-2277 | 15392 |
| Sientra Inc (HQ) | 3842 | E | 805 562-3500 | 15405 |
| Ultimate Ears Consumer LLC | 3842 | B | 949 502-8340 | 15422 |
| United Biologics Inc | 3842 | E | 949 345-7490 | 15423 |
| 3M Company | 3843 | B | 949 863-1360 | 15434 |
| Bien Air Usa Inc | 3843 | D | 949 477-6050 | 15440 |
| Evolve Dental Technologies Inc | 3843 | F | 949 713-0909 | 15456 |
| Keystone Dental Inc | 3843 | E | 781 328-3324 | 15463 |
| Keystone Dental Inc | 3843 | E | 781 328-3382 | 15464 |
| Truabutment Inc (PA) | 3843 | F | 714 956-1488 | 15490 |
| Westside Resources Inc | 3843 | E | 800 944-3939 | 15495 |
| Immport Therapeutics Inc | 3844 | F | 949 679-4068 | 15503 |
| Ampronix LLC | 3845 | D | 949 273-8000 | 15513 |
| Beta Bionics Inc | 3845 | E | 949 297-6635 | 15517 |
| Biosense Webster Inc (HQ) | 3845 | C | 909 839-8500 | 15521 |
| Edwards Lifesciences US Inc (HQ) | 3845 | E | 949 250-2500 | 15533 |
| Flexicare Incorporated | 3845 | E | 949 450-9999 | 15538 |
| Johnson Jhnson Srgcal Vsion In (HQ) | 3845 | B | 949 581-5799 | 15549 |
| Masimo Corporation | 3845 | E | 949 297-7000 | 15553 |
| Masimo Corporation | 3845 | E | 949 297-7000 | 15554 |
| Masimo Corporation (PA) | 3845 | E | 949 297-7000 | 15555 |
| Masimo Corporation | 3845 | E | 949 297-7000 | 15556 |
| Syneron Inc (DH) | 3845 | D | 866 259-6661 | 15582 |
| Barton Perreira LLC | 3851 | E | 949 305-5360 | 15594 |
| Eyeonics Inc | 3851 | E | 949 788-6000 | 15601 |
| Medennium Inc (PA) | 3851 | E | 949 789-9000 | 15609 |
| Tekia Inc | 3851 | E | 949 699-1300 | 15623 |
| Advexure LLC | 3861 | E | 920 917-9566 | 15627 |
| Thermaprint Corporation | 3861 | E | 949 583-0800 | 15669 |
| Strottman International Inc (PA) | 3942 | E | 949 623-7900 | 15735 |
| Bandai Nmco Toys Clictbles AME (DH) | 3944 | D | 949 271-6000 | 15740 |
| Bell Sports Inc (HQ) | 3949 | D | 469 417-6600 | 15787 |
| Diamond Baseball Company Inc | 3949 | E | 949 409-9300 | 15803 |
| Hyper Ice Inc (PA) | 3949 | E | 949 565-4994 | 15825 |
| Melin LLC | 3949 | E | 323 489-3274 | 15840 |
| Mission Hockey Company (PA) | 3949 | F | 949 585-9390 | 15841 |
| Star Trac Health & Fitness Inc | 3949 | E | 714 669-1660 | 15859 |
| Star Trac Strength Inc | 3949 | B | 714 669-1660 | 15860 |
| Unisen Inc | 3949 | E | 714 669-1660 | 15871 |
| Lasercare Technologies Inc (PA) | 3955 | E | 310 202-4200 | 15898 |
| Foampro Mfg Inc | 3991 | D | 949 252-0112 | 15929 |
| Media Nation Enterprises LLC (PA) | 3993 | E | 888 502-8222 | 16007 |
| Shye West Inc (PA) | 3993 | E | 949 486-4598 | 16034 |
| Statewide Trffic Sfety Sgns In | 3993 | E | 949 553-8272 | 16051 |
| Above & Beyond Balloons Inc | 3999 | E | 949 586-8470 | 16079 |
| Flame and Wax Inc | 3999 | C | 949 752-4000 | 16129 |
| House of Lashes | 3999 | E | 714 515-4162 | 16149 |
| Perfect Choice Mfrs Inc | 3999 | E | 714 792-0322 | 16200 |
| Phiaro Incorporated | 3999 | E | 949 727-1261 | 16203 |
| Sundance Spas Inc (DH) | 3999 | D | 909 606-7733 | 16244 |
| Wood Candle Wick Tech Inc | 3999 | D | 310 488-5885 | 16272 |
| Agility Logistics Corp (DH) | 4731 | E | 714 617-6300 | 16306 |
| 3h Communication Systems Inc | 4812 | E | 949 529-1583 | 16313 |
| Jynormus LLC | 4813 | F | 949 436-2112 | 16318 |
| Rally Holdings LLC | 5013 | A | 817 919-6833 | 16393 |
| Specialty Interior Mfg Inc | 5013 | E | 714 296-8618 | 16402 |
| Vogue Enterprise Inc | 5023 | F | 949 833-9787 | 16440 |
| Aluratek Inc | 5045 | E | 866 580-1978 | 16505 |
| D-Link Systems Incorporated | 5045 | C | 714 885-6000 | 16516 |
| Dane Elec Corp USA (HQ) | 5045 | E | 949 450-2900 | 16517 |
| Hitachi Solutions America Ltd (DH) | 5045 | E | 949 242-1300 | 16526 |
| Raise 3d Inc | 5045 | F | 888 963-9028 | 16543 |
| Balt Usa LLC | 5047 | D | 949 788-1443 | 16576 |
| Reagent World Inc | 5049 | F | 909 947-7779 | 16604 |
| Norman Industrial Mtls Inc | 5051 | E | 949 250-3343 | 16627 |
| Wamco Inc (PA) | 5063 | F | 714 545-5560 | 16679 |
| Jae Electronics Inc (HQ) | 5065 | E | 949 753-2600 | 16707 |
| Linksys Usa Inc | 5065 | D | 949 270-8500 | 16716 |
| Pool Water Products Inc (PA) | 5091 | F | 949 756-1666 | 16939 |
| Sega of America Inc (DH) | 5092 | E | 949 788-0455 | 16950 |
| Momentum Textiles LLC (PA) | 5131 | E | 949 833-8886 | 17064 |
| Snowmass Apparel Inc (PA) | 5137 | E | 949 788-0617 | 17100 |
| Asics America Corporation (HQ) | 5139 | C | 949 453-8888 | 17108 |
| Bizpack LLC | 5149 | F | 562 786-5159 | 17176 |
| Kids Healthy Foods LLC | 5149 | E | 949 260-4950 | 17191 |
| Sun Ten Labs Liquidation Co | 5149 | F | 949 587-0509 | 17217 |
| Victory Foam Inc (PA) | 5199 | D | 949 474-0690 | 17313 |

Employee Codes: A=Over 500 employees, B=251-500
C=101-250, D=51-100, E=20-50, F=10-19, G=1-9

## IRVINE, CA

| Company | SIC | EMP | PHONE | ENTRY# |
|---|---|---|---|---|
| Impressions Vanity Company (PA) | 5719 | E | 844 881-0790 | 17535 |
| Alignmed Inc. | 5999 | F | 866 987-5433 | 17687 |
| Arbonne International LLC (DH) | 5999 | E | 949 770-2610 | 17688 |
| Arbonne International Dist Inc. | 5999 | C | 800 272-6663 | 17689 |
| Smartlabs Inc. | 5999 | D | 800 762-7846 | 17722 |
| Teradek LLC | 5999 | E | 949 743-5780 | 17725 |
| Decision Ready Solutions Inc | 6162 | E | 949 400-1126 | 17727 |
| Kitara Media Corp (HQ) | 7311 | F | | 17779 |
| Certified Wtr Dmage Rstrtion E | 7349 | E | 800 417-1776 | 17846 |
| Big Cart Corporation | 7371 | E | 949 250-7064 | 17887 |
| NC America LLC | 7371 | E | 949 447-6287 | 17953 |
| Startel Corporation (PA) | 7371 | D | 949 863-8700 | 17982 |
| Tungsten Automation Corp (PA) | 7371 | B | 949 783-1000 | 17990 |
| Activision Blizzard Inc | 7372 | D | 949 955-1380 | 18015 |
| Advisys Inc. | 7372 | E | 949 250-0794 | 18025 |
| Alphastar Tech Solutions LLC | 7372 | F | 562 961-7827 | 18041 |
| Astea International Inc. | 7372 | E | 949 784-5000 | 18070 |
| Blind Squirrel Games Inc | 7372 | E | 714 460-0860 | 18111 |
| Blizzard Entertainment Inc (DH) | 7372 | D | 949 955-1380 | 18113 |
| Calamp Corp (PA) | 7372 | C | 949 600-5600 | 18140 |
| Cloudcover Iot Inc (PA) | 7372 | E | 888 511-2022 | 18182 |
| Cloudvirga Inc. | 7372 | D | 949 799-2643 | 18189 |
| Club Speed LLC (PA) | 7372 | E | 951 817-7073 | 18190 |
| Compugroup Medical Inc. | 7372 | E | 949 789-0500 | 18196 |
| Dacenso Inc. | 7372 | E | 888 513-9367 | 18224 |
| Dorado Network Systems Corp. | 7372 | C | 650 227-7300 | 18249 |
| Eagle Topco LP | 7372 | A | 949 585-4329 | 18259 |
| Egl Holdco Inc | 7372 | A | 800 678-7423 | 18268 |
| Eturns Inc. | 7372 | E | 949 265-2626 | 18292 |
| Foundation Inc. | 7372 | E | 310 294-8955 | 18326 |
| Global Cash Card Inc. | 7372 | C | 949 751-0360 | 18352 |
| Illumnate Educatn Holdings Inc (PA) | 7372 | E | 949 656-3133 | 18403 |
| Joycity Annex Inc. | 7372 | F | 949 892-0956 | 18461 |
| Justenough Software Corp Inc (HQ) | 7372 | E | 949 706-5400 | 18463 |
| Kofax Limited (PA) | 7372 | B | 949 783-1000 | 18479 |
| Magic Software Enterprises Inc. | 7372 | E | 949 250-1718 | 18512 |
| Medata LLC (HQ) | 7372 | D | 714 918-1310 | 18532 |
| Microsoft Corporation | 7372 | E | 949 263-3000 | 18544 |
| Mscsoftware Corporation | 7372 | A | 714 540-8900 | 18561 |
| Netwrix Corporation | 7372 | D | 888 638-9749 | 18580 |
| Nextgen Healthcare Inc (HQ) | 7372 | B | 949 255-2600 | 18586 |
| Ntrust Infotech Inc. | 7372 | D | 562 207-1600 | 18602 |
| Numecent Inc. | 7372 | E | 949 833-2800 | 18603 |
| Nxgn Management LLC | 7372 | E | 949 255-2600 | 18608 |
| Panoramic Software Corporation | 7372 | F | 877 558-8526 | 18655 |
| Patron Solutions LLC | 7372 | C | 949 823-1700 | 18661 |
| Planet DDS Inc (PA) | 7372 | E | 800 861-5098 | 18676 |
| Plugg ME LNc | 7372 | E | 949 705-4472 | 18681 |
| Prism Software Corporation | 7372 | E | 949 855-3100 | 18696 |
| Promenade Software Inc. | 7372 | E | 949 333-4634 | 18702 |
| Qdos Inc. | 7372 | E | 949 362-8888 | 18712 |
| Sage Software Holdings Inc (HQ) | 7372 | B | 866 530-7243 | 18752 |
| Strategy Companion Corp. | 7372 | D | 714 460-8398 | 18840 |
| Support Technologies Inc. | 7372 | F | 949 442-2957 | 18850 |
| Timevalue Software | 7372 | E | 949 727-1800 | 18885 |
| Uneekor Inc. | 7372 | D | 888 262-6498 | 18899 |
| Upstanding LLC | 7372 | C | 949 788-9900 | 18904 |
| Valiantica Inc (PA) | 7372 | E | 408 694-3803 | 18908 |
| Wm Technology Inc (PA) | 7372 | E | 646 699-3750 | 18938 |
| Xlsoft Corporation | 7372 | F | 949 453-2781 | 18946 |
| Alteryx Inc (PA) | 7373 | E | 888 836-4274 | 18962 |
| Greenwave Reality Inc. | 7373 | E | 714 805-9283 | 18978 |
| Leadingway Corporation (PA) | 7373 | F | 949 509-6589 | 18985 |
| Result Group Inc. | 7373 | E | 480 777-7130 | 18990 |
| Wytcote Inc. | 7373 | F | 877 472-5587 | 19000 |
| Sage Software Inc. | 7375 | D | 949 753-1222 | 19018 |
| Quest Intl Monitor Svc Inc (PA) | 7378 | E | 949 581-9900 | 19021 |
| Rakworx Inc. | 7378 | C | 949 215-1362 | 19022 |
| Blytheco Inc (PA) | 7379 | E | 949 583-9500 | 19031 |
| La Jolla Group Inc (PA) | 7389 | B | 949 428-2800 | 19103 |
| Cor Medica Technology | 8011 | E | 949 353-4554 | 19315 |
| Learning Ovations Inc. | 8299 | E | 734 904-1459 | 19352 |
| ACS Engineering Inc. | 8711 | E | 949 297-3777 | 19374 |
| Modelo Group Inc. | 8711 | E | 562 446-5091 | 19406 |
| Panasonic Avionics Corporation (DH) | 8711 | B | 949 672-2000 | 19410 |
| Fluxergy Inc (PA) | 8731 | E | 949 305-4201 | 19452 |

## IRWINDALE, CA - Los Angeles County

| Company | SIC | EMP | PHONE | ENTRY# |
|---|---|---|---|---|
| Kifuki USA Co Inc (HQ) | 2015 | D | 626 334-8090 | 696 |
| Huy Fong Foods Inc. | 2033 | E | 626 286-8328 | 893 |
| Q & B Foods Inc (DH) | 2035 | D | 626 334-8090 | 990 |
| J&R Taylor Brothers Assoc Inc | 2047 | D | 626 334-9301 | 1103 |
| Miller Brewing Co. | 2082 | F | 626 353-1604 | 1448 |
| Califrnia Cstm Frits Flvors LL (PA) | 2087 | E | 626 736-4130 | 1992 |
| Ready Pac Foods Inc (HQ) | 2099 | A | 626 856-8686 | 2332 |
| Ready Pac Produce Inc (DH) | 2099 | A | 800 800-4088 | 2333 |
| Decore-Ative Spc NC LLC | 2431 | C | 626 960-7731 | 3127 |
| Pacific Panel Products Corp. | 2499 | E | 626 851-0444 | 3422 |
| Roma Moulding Inc. | 2499 | E | 626 334-2539 | 3426 |
| Go2zero Strategies LLC | 2611 | F | 626 840-1850 | 3757 |
| Seaboard Envelope Co Inc. | 2677 | E | 626 960-4559 | 4011 |
| Alpha Printing & Graphics Inc. | 2752 | E | 626 851-9800 | 4508 |
| Km Printing Production Inc. | 2752 | F | 626 821-0008 | 4662 |
| Million Corporation | 2759 | D | 626 969-1888 | 4923 |
| Matheson Tri-Gas Inc. | 2813 | E | 626 334-2905 | 5050 |
| Esmond Natural Inc. | 2833 | E | 626 337-1588 | 5238 |
| Baxco Pharmaceutical Inc (PA) | 2834 | F | 626 610-7088 | 5356 |
| Bimeda Inc. | 2834 | C | 626 815-1680 | 5368 |
| Chem Arrow Corp. | 2992 | E | 626 358-2255 | 6388 |
| Polycycle Solutions LLC | 3085 | D | 626 856-2100 | 6615 |
| Altium Packaging | 3089 | E | 626 856-2100 | 6707 |
| Spragues Rock and Sand Company (PA) | 3273 | E | 626 445-2125 | 7501 |
| Davis Wire Corporation (HQ) | 3315 | E | 626 969-7651 | 7639 |
| STS Metals Inc. | 3463 | D | 626 969-6711 | 8803 |
| A & M Engineering Inc. | 3599 | D | 626 813-2020 | 10648 |
| Arrow Engineering | 3599 | E | 626 960-2816 | 10720 |
| Cni Mfg Inc. | 3599 | F | 626 962-6646 | 10781 |
| Fine Pctch Elctrnic Assmbly LLC | 3672 | E | 626 337-2800 | 12101 |
| Pertronix Inc. | 3694 | E | 909 599-5955 | 13180 |
| NDC Technologies Inc. | 3829 | D | 626 960-3300 | 14903 |
| Johnson & Johnson | 3842 | B | 909 839-8650 | 15369 |
| Blue Ridge Home Fashions Inc. | 5131 | E | 626 960-6069 | 17059 |
| Sinecera Inc. | 7389 | D | 626 962-1087 | 19131 |
| Tandex Test Labs Inc. | 8734 | E | 626 962-7166 | 19509 |
| Calibre International LLC | 8743 | C | 626 969-4660 | 19548 |

## JAMESTOWN, CA - Tuolumne County

| Company | SIC | EMP | PHONE | ENTRY# |
|---|---|---|---|---|
| Sierra Resource Management Inc. | 2411 | F | 209 984-1146 | 3056 |
| Chicken Rnch Economic Dev Corp. | 2711 | E | 209 984-9066 | 4089 |

## JAMUL, CA - San Diego County

| Company | SIC | EMP | PHONE | ENTRY# |
|---|---|---|---|---|
| Mikes Metal Works Inc. | 3441 | F | 619 440-8804 | 8187 |

## JUNCTION CITY, CA - Trinity County

| Company | SIC | EMP | PHONE | ENTRY# |
|---|---|---|---|---|
| Eagle Rock Incorporated | 3531 | F | 530 623-4444 | 9420 |

## JURUPA VALLEY, CA - Riverside County

| Company | SIC | EMP | PHONE | ENTRY# |
|---|---|---|---|---|
| Right Angle Solutions Inc. | 1711 | E | 951 934-3081 | 432 |
| Hartmark Cab Design & Mfg Inc. | 1799 | E | 909 591-9153 | 563 |
| Nestle Usa Inc. | 2023 | D | 877 463-7853 | 773 |
| Del Real LLC (PA) | 2038 | D | 951 681-0395 | 1032 |
| Nestle Usa Inc. | 2038 | B | 951 360-7200 | 1041 |
| Langlois Company | 2045 | E | 951 360-3900 | 1087 |
| Levecke LLC | 2084 | E | 951 681-8600 | 1668 |
| A and G Inc (HQ) | 2329 | A | 714 765-0400 | 2606 |
| Activeapparel Inc (PA) | 2329 | F | 951 361-0060 | 2607 |
| Charles Komar & Sons Inc. | 2341 | B | 951 934-1377 | 2828 |
| Advanced Innvtive Rcvery Tech. | 2515 | E | 949 273-8100 | 3518 |
| Pura Naturals Inc. | 2515 | E | 949 273-8100 | 3535 |
| Calpaco Papers Inc (PA) | 2679 | C | 323 767-2800 | 4033 |
| Adam Nutrition Inc. | 2834 | C | 951 361-1120 | 5298 |
| Hyponex Corporation | 2873 | C | 909 597-2811 | 6175 |
| Architectural Veneer Systems | 3272 | E | 951 824-1079 | 7310 |
| Aluminum Die Casting Co Inc. | 3363 | D | 951 681-3900 | 7806 |
| Metal Container Corporation | 3411 | E | 951 360-4500 | 7923 |
| Pacific Award Metals Inc. | 3444 | E | 360 694-9530 | 8526 |
| Hart & Cooley Inc. | 3446 | E | 951 332-5132 | 8628 |
| Mobile Modular Management Corp. | 3448 | C | 800 819-1084 | 8676 |
| Schwing America Inc. | 3531 | C | 909 681-6430 | 9436 |
| Brothers Machine & Tool Inc. | 3542 | E | 951 361-9454 | 9581 |
| Cte California Tl & Engrg Inc. | 3545 | E | | 9672 |
| P R P Multisource Inc. | 3565 | E | 951 681-6100 | 10027 |
| Unitek Technology Inc. | 3571 | F | 909 930-5700 | 10215 |
| Puri Tech Inc. | 3589 | E | 951 360-6830 | 10593 |
| Brothers Machine & Tool Inc (PA) | 3599 | F | 951 361-2909 | 10754 |
| Philips North America LLC | 3645 | C | 909 574-1800 | 11500 |
| Genbody America LLC | 3841 | E | 949 561-0664 | 15098 |
| Enhance America Inc. | 3993 | E | 951 361-3000 | 15970 |
| Young Electric Sign Company | 3993 | C | 909 923-7668 | 16072 |
| March Products Inc. | 3999 | D | 909 622-4800 | 16178 |
| Highline Aftermarket LLC | 5013 | D | 951 361-0331 | 16385 |
| Pacific Award Metals Inc. | 5033 | D | 909 390-9880 | 16492 |

## KELSEYVILLE, CA - Lake County

| Company | SIC | EMP | PHONE | ENTRY# |
|---|---|---|---|---|
| Steele Wines Inc. | 2084 | E | 707 279-9475 | 1761 |
| Lddf Inc. | 3825 | F | 707 995-7145 | 14548 |

# GEOGRAPHIC SECTION

## KENSINGTON, CA - Alameda County

| Company | SIC | EMP | PHONE | ENTRY# |
|---|---|---|---|---|
| Harvest Thermal Inc | 3585 | F | 408 597-7152 | 10501 |

## KENWOOD, CA - Sonoma County

| Company | SIC | EMP | PHONE | ENTRY# |
|---|---|---|---|---|
| Kunde Enterprises Inc | 2084 | D | 707 833-5501 | 1653 |
| Pernod Ricard Usa LLC | 2084 | D | 707 833-5891 | 1704 |

## KERMAN, CA - Fresno County

| Company | SIC | EMP | PHONE | ENTRY# |
|---|---|---|---|---|
| Central Cal Almond Grwers Assn (PA) | 0723 | E | 559 846-5377 | 77 |
| River Ranch Raisins Inc | 2034 | E | 559 843-2294 | 961 |
| Baker Commodities Inc | 2077 | E | 559 237-4320 | 1378 |
| Westrock Rkt LLC | 2653 | D | 559 567-3501 | 3898 |
| California Mfg & Engrg Co LLC | 3531 | C | 559 842-1500 | 9413 |
| Helena Industries LLC | 5261 | D | 559 846-5303 | 17361 |

## KETTLEMAN CITY, CA - Kings County

| Company | SIC | EMP | PHONE | ENTRY# |
|---|---|---|---|---|
| Keenan Farms Inc | 0173 | D | 559 945-1400 | 39 |

## KING CITY, CA - Monterey County

| Company | SIC | EMP | PHONE | ENTRY# |
|---|---|---|---|---|
| San Bernabe Vineyards | 0172 | E | 831 385-4897 | 28 |
| Monterey Wine Company LLC | 2084 | F | 831 386-1100 | 1680 |
| Casey Printing Inc | 2752 | E | 831 385-3221 | 4543 |
| L A Hearne Company (PA) | 5191 | D | 831 385-5441 | 17272 |

## KINGSBURG, CA - Fresno County

| Company | SIC | EMP | PHONE | ENTRY# |
|---|---|---|---|---|
| Mike Jensen Farms LLC | 0175 | C | 559 897-4192 | 43 |
| Strategic Industry Inc | 1389 | E | 559 419-9481 | 277 |
| Foster Farms LLC | 2015 | E | 559 897-1081 | 680 |
| Del Monte Foods Inc | 2033 | F | 559 419-9214 | 885 |
| Nutrius LLC (PA) | 2048 | E | 559 897-5862 | 1141 |
| Vie-Del Company | 2084 | E | 559 896-3065 | 1809 |
| Guardian Industries LLC | 3211 | B | 559 891-8867 | 7170 |
| Guss Automation LLC | 3523 | F | 559 897-0245 | 9356 |
| Kingsburg Cultivator Inc | 3523 | E | 559 897-3662 | 9365 |
| Cencal Cnc Inc | 3599 | E | 559 897-8706 | 10768 |
| F R O Inc | 8748 | E | 559 891-0237 | 19559 |

## LA CANADA, CA - Los Angeles County

| Company | SIC | EMP | PHONE | ENTRY# |
|---|---|---|---|---|
| Majestic Garlic Inc | 2035 | F | 951 677-0555 | 984 |

## LA CANADA FLINTRIDGE, CA - Los Angeles County

| Company | SIC | EMP | PHONE | ENTRY# |
|---|---|---|---|---|
| Lucare Corporation | 3861 | F | 818 583-7731 | 15649 |
| Bis Computer Solutions Inc (PA) | 7371 | E | 818 248-4282 | 17889 |

## LA CRESCENTA, CA - Los Angeles County

| Company | SIC | EMP | PHONE | ENTRY# |
|---|---|---|---|---|
| Hamo Construction | 1389 | E | 818 415-3334 | 236 |
| Balita Media Inc | 2711 | F | 818 552-4503 | 4072 |
| Modular Communications Systems | 3663 | F | 818 764-1333 | 11895 |

## LA HABRA, CA - Orange County

| Company | SIC | EMP | PHONE | ENTRY# |
|---|---|---|---|---|
| Albd Electric and Cable | 1731 | D | 949 440-1216 | 449 |
| Orbo Manufacturing Inc | 2396 | E | 562 222-4535 | 3014 |
| Pacific Archtectural Mllwk Inc | 2431 | D | 562 905-3200 | 3175 |
| Votaw Wood Products Inc | 2448 | E | 714 871-0932 | 3365 |
| Eurotec Seating Incorporated | 2531 | E | 562 806-6171 | 3625 |
| Orbo Corporation (PA) | 2531 | E | 562 806-6171 | 3636 |
| VIP Rubber Company Inc (PA) | 3069 | C | 562 905-3456 | 6548 |
| Triview Glass Industries LLC | 3231 | D | 626 363-7980 | 7244 |
| Mmp Sheet Metal Inc | 3444 | E | 562 691-1055 | 8513 |
| Jcr Aircraft Deburring LLC | 3471 | D | 714 870-4427 | 8976 |
| J C Ford Company (HQ) | 3556 | E | 714 871-7361 | 9799 |
| B&W Custom Restaurant Eqp Inc | 3589 | E | 714 578-0332 | 10543 |
| Shepard Bros Inc (PA) | 3589 | C | 562 697-1366 | 10600 |
| NRG Motorsports Inc | 3714 | D | 714 541-1173 | 13551 |
| Shepard-Thomason Company | 3714 | E | 714 773-5539 | 13574 |
| Rose Lilla Inc | 3965 | E | 888 519-8889 | 15916 |
| K S Designs Inc | 3993 | E | 562 929-3973 | 15999 |
| Stop-Look Sign Co Intl Inc | 3993 | F | 562 690-7576 | 16052 |

## LA HONDA, CA - San Mateo County

| Company | SIC | EMP | PHONE | ENTRY# |
|---|---|---|---|---|
| Clos De La Tech LLC | 2084 | E | 650 722-3038 | 1508 |

## LA JOLLA, CA - San Diego County

| Company | SIC | EMP | PHONE | ENTRY# |
|---|---|---|---|---|
| Groundmetrics Inc | 1389 | F | 619 786-8023 | 232 |
| Kitchen Expo | 1799 | F | | 566 |
| Uqora Inc | 2023 | E | 888 313-1372 | 785 |
| Berenice 2 AM Corp | 2024 | F | 858 255-8693 | 793 |
| Dvele Inc (PA) | 2452 | F | 805 323-3711 | 3393 |
| Display Supply Chain Cons LLC | 2541 | F | 512 577-3672 | 3654 |
| Jumper Media LLC | 2741 | D | 831 333-6202 | 4422 |
| Dm Luxury LLC | 2759 | E | 858 366-9721 | 4874 |
| Ambrx Inc (PA) | 2834 | D | 858 875-2400 | 5314 |
| Auspex Pharmaceuticals Inc | 2834 | E | 858 558-2400 | 5346 |
| Equillium Inc (PA) | 2834 | E | 858 412-5302 | 5435 |
| Kyowa Kirin Inc | 2834 | E | 858 952-7000 | 5532 |
| Longboard Pharmaceuticals Inc | 2834 | E | 858 789-9283 | 5537 |
| Manna Health LLC | 2834 | E | 877 576-2662 | 5540 |
| Orexigen Therapeutics Inc | 2834 | D | 858 875-8600 | 5586 |
| Synthorx Inc | 2834 | E | 858 352-5100 | 5683 |
| Ambrx Biopharma Inc | 2836 | D | 858 875-2400 | 5791 |
| Inhibrx Inc (HQ) | 2836 | C | 858 795-4220 | 5842 |
| Surface-Tech LLC | 2951 | F | 619 880-0265 | 6371 |
| Vinventions Usa LLC (PA) | 3089 | E | 919 460-2200 | 7072 |
| Ensemble Communications Inc | 3663 | C | 858 458-1400 | 11852 |
| New Brunswick Industries Inc | 3672 | E | 619 448-4900 | 12176 |
| International RES Dev Corp Nev (PA) | 3694 | F | 858 488-9900 | 13173 |
| Agilent Technologies Inc | 3825 | D | 858 373-6300 | 14492 |
| U S Medical Instruments Inc (PA) | 3841 | E | 619 661-5500 | 15294 |
| Technosylva Inc (PA) | 5045 | F | 619 292-1935 | 16558 |
| Edgewave Inc | 7372 | D | 800 782-3762 | 18263 |
| Eventscom Inc | 7372 | E | 858 257-2300 | 18293 |
| The Copley Press Inc | 7383 | A | 858 454-0411 | 19064 |
| Coi Pharmaceuticals Inc | 8731 | E | 858 750-4700 | 19448 |
| Padoma Wind Power LLC (DH) | 8731 | F | 858 731-5001 | 19471 |
| Ech Real Estate Developers LLC | 8741 | E | 619 996-9269 | 19515 |

## LA MESA, CA - San Diego County

| Company | SIC | EMP | PHONE | ENTRY# |
|---|---|---|---|---|
| California Countertop Inc (PA) | 1799 | F | 619 460-0205 | 557 |
| Prost LLC | 2082 | E | 619 954-4189 | 1455 |
| Magnebit Holding Corp | 3825 | E | 858 573-0727 | 14552 |

## LA MIRADA, CA - Los Angeles County

| Company | SIC | EMP | PHONE | ENTRY# |
|---|---|---|---|---|
| Bop Renewables Inc | 1382 | F | 714 418-4420 | 170 |
| Gemsa Enterprises LLC | 2079 | E | 714 521-1736 | 1398 |
| Shasta Beverages Inc | 2086 | B | 714 523-2280 | 1964 |
| Outlook Resources Inc | 2395 | D | 562 623-9328 | 2998 |
| Harbor Furniture Mfg Inc (PA) | 2512 | E | 323 636-1201 | 3475 |
| V Twest Inc | 2541 | F | 714 521-2167 | 3675 |
| M3 Products Inc | 2542 | E | 626 371-1900 | 3697 |
| Badger Paperboard Cal LLC | 2671 | F | 657 529-0456 | 3924 |
| Golden Kraft Inc | 2679 | B | 562 926-8888 | 4041 |
| JM Huber Micropowders Inc | 2819 | E | 714 994-7855 | 5097 |
| Captek Softgel Intl Inc | 2834 | E | 657 325-0412 | 5391 |
| LA Supply Company LLC | 2869 | F | 310 980-3404 | 6150 |
| INX International Ink Co | 2893 | F | 630 382-1800 | 6257 |
| Tropical Asphalt LLC (PA) | 2952 | F | 714 739-1408 | 6385 |
| Oceania Inc | 3081 | E | 562 926-8886 | 6565 |
| Alchem Plastics Inc | 3083 | C | 714 523-2260 | 6581 |
| Lindblade Metalworks Inc | 3441 | E | 714 670-7172 | 8171 |
| Superior Storage Tank Inc | 3443 | F | 714 226-1914 | 8342 |
| Fooma America Inc | 3549 | E | 310 921-0717 | 9737 |
| MEMC Liquidating Corporation | 3556 | C | 818 637-7200 | 9806 |
| MEI Rigging & Crating LLC | 3559 | D | 714 712-5888 | 9875 |
| Iqair North America Inc | 3564 | E | 877 715-4247 | 9990 |
| General Grinding & Mfg Co LLC | 3593 | F | 562 921-7033 | 10627 |
| Jmg Machine Inc | 3599 | E | 714 522-6221 | 10911 |
| American Power Solutions Inc | 3648 | E | 714 626-0300 | 11580 |
| Gallagher Rental Inc | 3648 | E | 714 690-1559 | 11598 |
| Solid State Devices Inc | 3674 | C | 562 404-4474 | 12724 |
| Wesanco Inc | 3728 | E | 714 739-4989 | 13989 |
| Ocean Protecta Incorporated | 3732 | E | 714 891-2628 | 14044 |
| National Signal LLC | 3799 | D | 714 441-7707 | 14131 |
| RDM Industries | 5084 | E | 714 690-0380 | 16837 |
| Stainless Stl Fabricators Inc | 5084 | D | 714 739-9904 | 16844 |
| US Foods Inc | 5141 | E | 714 670-3500 | 17121 |
| Regal-Piedmont Plastics LLC | 5162 | E | 562 404-4014 | 17234 |
| Calwax LLC (DH) | 5169 | E | 626 969-4334 | 17239 |
| IL Fornaio (america) LLC | 5812 | C | 714 752-7052 | 17586 |
| Georgia-Pacific LLC | 5999 | E | 562 926-8888 | 17704 |

## LA PALMA, CA - Orange County

| Company | SIC | EMP | PHONE | ENTRY# |
|---|---|---|---|---|
| CJ Foods Inc (HQ) | 2099 | D | 714 367-7200 | 2167 |
| Ranir LLC | 2834 | E | 866 373-7374 | 5627 |
| Precision Cutting Tools Inc | 3545 | E | 562 921-7898 | 9691 |
| Precision Cutting Tools LLC | 3545 | E | 562 921-7898 | 9692 |
| Fisker Group Inc (HQ) | 3711 | A | 833 434-7537 | 13351 |
| Fisker Inc (PA) | 3711 | E | 833 434-7537 | 13352 |
| Performance Machine Inc | 3751 | C | 714 523-3000 | 14066 |
| Uns Electric Inc | 5063 | E | 714 690-3660 | 16675 |
| Svf Flow Controls Inc | 5084 | E | 562 802-2255 | 16847 |
| Atlantic Richfield Company (DH) | 5541 | A | 800 333-3991 | 17470 |
| Evocative Inc | 7372 | D | 888 365-2656 | 18296 |

## LA PUENTE, CA - Los Angeles County

| Company | SIC | EMP | PHONE | ENTRY# |
|---|---|---|---|---|
| LA Signal | 1731 | F | 909 599-2201 | 460 |
| Ley Grand Foods Corporation | 2099 | E | 626 336-2244 | 2265 |

Employee Codes: A=Over 500 employees, B=251-500 C=101-250, D=51-100, E=20-50, F=10-19, G=1-9

## LA PUENTE, CA

| Company | SIC | EMP | PHONE | ENTRY# |
|---|---|---|---|---|
| Soxnet Inc. | 2252 | F | 626 934-9400 | 2460 |
| Mymichelle Company LLC (HQ) | 2331 | B | 626 934-4166 | 2683 |
| Cortez Pallets Service Inc (PA) | 2448 | F | 626 961-9891 | 3337 |
| Genesis Tc Inc. | 2512 | E | 626 968-4455 | 3473 |
| Shift Packaging LLC | 2841 | F | 206 412-4253 | 5882 |
| Cad Works Inc. | 3441 | E | 626 336-5491 | 8110 |
| County of Los Angeles | 3531 | E | 626 968-3312 | 9418 |
| Yang-Ming International Corp | 7373 | E | 626 956-0100 | 19001 |

### LA QUINTA, CA - Riverside County

| Company | SIC | EMP | PHONE | ENTRY# |
|---|---|---|---|---|
| Red Rock Pallet Company | 4731 | E | 530 852-7744 | 16308 |
| TS Enterprises Inc. | 5812 | E | 760 360-5991 | 17608 |

### LA VERNE, CA - Los Angeles County

| Company | SIC | EMP | PHONE | ENTRY# |
|---|---|---|---|---|
| Vitawest Nutraceuticals Inc. | 2023 | E | 888 557-8012 | 787 |
| G & M Mattress and Foam Corporation | 2515 | D | 909 593-1000 | 3526 |
| Fortress Inc. | 2521 | E | 909 593-8600 | 3567 |
| Mohawk Western Plastics Inc. | 2673 | E | 909 593-7547 | 3973 |
| Layton Printing & Mailing | 2752 | F | 909 592-4419 | 4672 |
| TEC Color Craft (PA) | 2759 | E | 909 392-9000 | 4970 |
| S & S Bindery Inc. | 2789 | E | 909 596-2213 | 5015 |
| Gilead Sciences Inc. | 2834 | D | 650 522-2771 | 5462 |
| Plastifab Inc. | 3083 | E | 909 596-1927 | 6588 |
| Serco Mold Inc (PA) | 3089 | E | 626 331-0517 | 7025 |
| Durston Manufacturing Company | 3423 | F | 909 593-1506 | 7951 |
| Aero-Clssics Heat Trnsf Pdts I | 3443 | E | 909 596-1630 | 8297 |
| Pacific Precision Inc. | 3451 | E | 909 392-5610 | 8729 |
| Mesa Industries Inc. | 3531 | E | 626 712-1708 | 9432 |
| Crown Equipment Corporation | 3537 | E | 626 968-0556 | 9512 |
| Marman Industries Inc. | 3544 | D | 909 392-2136 | 9636 |
| Juicy Whip Inc. | 3556 | E | 909 392-7500 | 9802 |
| Boom Industrial Inc. | 3559 | D | 909 495-3555 | 9839 |
| Sunon Inc (PA) | 3564 | E | 714 255-0208 | 10000 |
| Beonca Machine Inc. | 3599 | F | 909 392-9991 | 10747 |
| Inseat Solutions LLC. | 3634 | E | 562 447-1780 | 11406 |
| Micro Analog Inc. | 3674 | C | 909 392-8277 | 12565 |
| DPI Labs Inc. | 3728 | E | 909 392-5777 | 13825 |
| Synergetic Tech Group Inc. | 3728 | E | 909 305-4711 | 13967 |
| Pacific Oil Cooler Service Inc. | 4581 | E | 909 593-8400 | 16301 |

### LADERA RANCH, CA - Orange County

| Company | SIC | EMP | PHONE | ENTRY# |
|---|---|---|---|---|
| Tropical Preserving Co Inc. | 2033 | E | 213 748-5108 | 933 |
| Bau Furniture Mfg Inc. | 2511 | D | 949 643-2729 | 3433 |
| Ksu Corporation | 3441 | F | 951 409-7055 | 8165 |
| Enchannel Medical Ltd | 3841 | E | 949 694-6802 | 15079 |

### LAFAYETTE, CA - Contra Costa County

| Company | SIC | EMP | PHONE | ENTRY# |
|---|---|---|---|---|
| Nancys Specialty Foods | 2099 | B | 510 494-1100 | 2289 |
| Misto Lino | 2299 | E | 925 284-6565 | 2550 |
| Econoday Inc. | 2741 | F | 925 299-5350 | 4391 |
| Acp Ventures | 2752 | F | 925 297-0100 | 4502 |
| Patten Co Inc. | 3069 | E | 707 826-2887 | 6521 |
| Velodyne Acoustics Inc. | 3651 | D | 408 465-2800 | 11712 |
| Dynamic Graphics Inc (PA) | 7371 | E | 510 522-0700 | 17915 |
| Franz Inc. | 7372 | E | 510 452-2000 | 18330 |
| Optimum Solutions Group LLC | 7372 | F | 415 954-7100 | 18630 |

### LAGUNA BEACH, CA - Orange County

| Company | SIC | EMP | PHONE | ENTRY# |
|---|---|---|---|---|
| Langlois Fancy Frozen Foods Inc. | 2038 | E | 949 497-1741 | 1039 |
| Flavor Infusion LLC. | 2087 | E | 949 715-4369 | 2005 |
| Cantare Foods Inc. | 2099 | E | | 2157 |
| Firebrand Media LLC | 2752 | E | 949 715-4100 | 4609 |
| Pangaea Holdings Inc. | 2844 | E | 402 704-7546 | 6017 |
| RA Industries LLC | 3599 | E | 714 557-2322 | 11066 |
| Myotek Industries Incorporated (DH) | 3694 | D | 949 502-3776 | 13179 |
| Ophthonix Inc. | 3851 | E | 760 842-5600 | 15613 |
| K31 Road Engineering LLC | 3999 | E | 305 928-1968 | 16159 |
| Cabo Foods Inc (PA) | 5149 | E | 949 463-2373 | 17178 |
| Soundboks Inc. | 7359 | F | 310 774-0480 | 17863 |
| Data Processing Design Inc. | 7371 | E | 714 695-1000 | 17906 |
| Atlantis Computing Inc. | 7372 | E | 650 917-9471 | 18072 |

### LAGUNA HILLS, CA - Orange County

| Company | SIC | EMP | PHONE | ENTRY# |
|---|---|---|---|---|
| Bingo Publishers Incorporated | 2741 | E | 949 581-5410 | 4370 |
| Turbo Debt Relief | 2741 | F | 949 244-1907 | 4483 |
| Chavers Gasket Corporation | 3053 | E | 949 472-8118 | 6441 |
| Eurotech Showers Inc. | 3088 | E | 949 716-4099 | 6677 |
| Plastic and Metal Center Inc | 3089 | E | 949 770-0610 | 6959 |
| Steward Plastics Inc. | 3089 | D | 949 581-9530 | 7044 |
| Budget Enterprises Llc | 3211 | E | 949 697-9544 | 7164 |
| Associated Cnstr & Engrg Inc (PA) | 3272 | E | 949 455-2682 | 7311 |
| Metal Improvement Company LLC | 3398 | E | 949 855-8010 | 7892 |
| Cmt Sheet Metal | 3443 | F | 949 679-9868 | 8309 |
| Peltek Holdings Inc. | 3479 | E | 949 855-8010 | 9104 |
| Starrett Kinemetric Engrg Inc. | 3545 | E | 949 348-1213 | 9700 |
| Garrett Precision Inc. | 3599 | F | 949 855-9710 | 10852 |
| Djh Enterprises | 3663 | E | 714 424-6500 | 11842 |
| XEL USA Inc. | 3674 | E | 949 425-8686 | 12807 |
| Ecliptek Inc. | 3679 | F | 714 433-1200 | 12966 |
| Fox Enterprises LLC (HQ) | 3679 | E | 239 693-0099 | 12981 |
| Sonendo Inc (PA) | 3843 | C | 949 766-3636 | 15483 |
| Cynergy Prof Systems LLC | 5065 | E | 800 776-7978 | 16697 |
| Brainchip Inc (HQ) | 7372 | F | 949 784-0040 | 18125 |

### LAGUNA NIGUEL, CA - Orange County

| Company | SIC | EMP | PHONE | ENTRY# |
|---|---|---|---|---|
| Beverages & More Inc. | 2086 | C | 949 643-3020 | 1867 |
| San Diego Daily Transcript | 2621 | D | 619 232-4381 | 3795 |
| Qpc Fiber Optic LLC. | 3357 | E | 949 361-8855 | 7795 |
| Markland Industries Inc (PA) | 3751 | E | 714 245-2850 | 14065 |
| Alcon Vision LLC. | 3841 | B | 949 753-6218 | 14956 |
| Confluent Medical Tech Inc. | 3841 | E | 949 448-7056 | 15049 |
| Confluent Medical Tech Inc. | 3841 | D | 949 448-7056 | 15050 |
| Interface Associates Inc. | 3841 | E | 949 448-7056 | 15122 |
| Diversified Waterscapes Inc. | 8742 | F | 949 582-5414 | 19527 |

### LAKE ARROWHEAD, CA - San Bernardino County

| Company | SIC | EMP | PHONE | ENTRY# |
|---|---|---|---|---|
| Gildan USA Inc. | 2252 | E | 909 485-1475 | 2457 |
| Hi-Desert Publishing Company | 2711 | E | 909 336-3555 | 4131 |

### LAKE ELSINORE, CA - Riverside County

| Company | SIC | EMP | PHONE | ENTRY# |
|---|---|---|---|---|
| Hakes Sash & Door Inc. | 1751 | C | 951 674-2414 | 492 |
| Aerofoam Industries Inc. | 2531 | D | 951 245-4429 | 3612 |
| Quality Foam Packaging Inc. | 3086 | E | 951 245-4429 | 6658 |
| Pacific Aggregates Inc. | 3273 | E | 951 245-2460 | 7484 |
| Harrington & Sons Inc. | 3299 | E | 951 674-0998 | 7591 |
| Boozak Inc. | 3444 | E | 951 245-6045 | 8393 |
| Mercury Metal Die & Ltr Co Inc (PA) | 3479 | F | 951 674-8717 | 9092 |
| American Compaction Eqp Inc. | 3531 | E | 949 661-2921 | 9407 |
| Jose Perez | 3535 | E | 920 318-6527 | 9488 |
| Thermal Electronics Inc. | 3679 | F | | 13108 |
| Hilz Cable Assemblies Inc. | 3829 | F | 951 245-0499 | 14877 |
| Pacific Clay Products Inc. | 5032 | C | 661 857-1401 | 16479 |
| Albertsons LLC. | 5411 | E | 951 245-4461 | 17367 |
| Champion Motosports Inc (PA) | 5531 | E | 951 245-9464 | 17448 |

### LAKE FOREST, CA - Orange County

| Company | SIC | EMP | PHONE | ENTRY# |
|---|---|---|---|---|
| Hardy & Harper Inc. | 1611 | C | 714 444-1851 | 374 |
| Big Train Inc. | 2024 | C | 949 340-8800 | 794 |
| Crumbl Cookies. | 2052 | D | 949 519-0791 | 1269 |
| ABC Custom Wood Shutters Inc. | 2431 | E | 949 595-0300 | 3105 |
| Novo Manufacturing LLC. | 2431 | E | 949 609-0544 | 3169 |
| Sun Pac Storage Containers Inc. | 2448 | F | 949 458-2347 | 3361 |
| Advanced Innvtive Rcvery Tech (PA) | 2515 | F | 949 273-8100 | 3517 |
| Cod USA Inc. | 2531 | E | 949 381-7367 | 3621 |
| Walter Foster Publishing Inc. | 2731 | E | 949 380-7510 | 4353 |
| Universal Printing Svcs Inc. | 2752 | F | 951 788-1500 | 4798 |
| Pura Naturals Inc (HQ) | 2844 | E | 949 273-8100 | 6029 |
| JB Brananne Inc. | 3089 | E | 949 215-7704 | 6873 |
| Sole Technology Inc (PA) | 3149 | D | 949 460-2020 | 7123 |
| Oceania International LLC. | 3356 | E | 949 407-8904 | 7765 |
| Dynacast LLC. | 3364 | C | 949 707-1211 | 7828 |
| Baldwin Hardware Corporation (DH) | 3429 | A | 949 672-4000 | 7983 |
| National Manufacturing Co. | 3429 | A | 800 346-9445 | 8020 |
| Young Engineers Inc. | 3429 | D | 949 581-9411 | 8039 |
| Price Pfister Inc. | 3432 | E | 949 672-4000 | 8054 |
| S E - G I Products Inc. | 3442 | C | 949 297-8530 | 8288 |
| SPX Flow Us LLC. | 3443 | E | 949 455-8150 | 8339 |
| Camisasca Automotive Mfg Inc. | 3469 | E | 949 452-0195 | 8827 |
| Camisasca Automotive Mfg Inc (PA) | 3469 | E | 949 452-0195 | 8828 |
| Shmaze Industries Inc. | 3479 | E | 949 583-1448 | 9119 |
| Campbell Engineering Inc. | 3545 | E | 949 859-3306 | 9665 |
| Ellison Educational Eqp Inc (PA) | 3554 | E | 949 598-8822 | 9759 |
| Fanuc America Corporation. | 3559 | D | 949 595-2700 | 9856 |
| Cameo Technologies Inc. | 3572 | E | 949 672-7000 | 10229 |
| Gigamem LLC. | 3572 | E | 949 461-9999 | 10238 |
| I/Omagic Corporation (PA) | 3572 | E | 949 707-4800 | 10245 |
| Pssc Labs. | 3572 | F | 949 380-7288 | 10267 |
| US Critical LLC (PA) | 3572 | E | 949 916-9326 | 10290 |
| US Critical LLC. | 3572 | E | 800 884-8945 | 10291 |
| IMC Networks Corp (PA) | 3575 | E | 949 465-3000 | 10306 |
| American Deburring Inc. | 3599 | E | 949 457-9790 | 10709 |
| T/Q Systems Inc. | 3599 | E | 949 455-0478 | 11135 |
| Leoch Battery Corporation (DH) | 3621 | D | 949 588-5853 | 11275 |
| Hongfa America Inc. | 3625 | E | 714 669-2888 | 11325 |
| Focus Industries Inc. | 3646 | E | 949 830-1350 | 11535 |
| Greenshine New Energy LLC. | 3648 | D | 949 609-9636 | 11599 |

| Company | SIC | EMP | PHONE | ENTRY# |
|---|---|---|---|---|
| Laminating Company of America | 3672 | E | 949 587-3300 | 12150 |
| Semi-Kinetics Inc | 3672 | D | 949 830-7364 | 12215 |
| Tri-Star Laminates Inc | 3672 | E | 949 587-3200 | 12243 |
| Advantest Test Solutions Inc | 3674 | D | 949 523-6900 | 12280 |
| Semiq Incorporated | 3674 | F | 949 273-4373 | 12692 |
| Premier Magnetics Inc | 3677 | E | 949 452-0511 | 12852 |
| Assa Abloy AB | 3692 | A | 949 672-4003 | 13156 |
| Sonnet Technologies Inc | 3699 | E | 949 587-3500 | 13308 |
| Qf Liquidation Inc (PA) | 3714 | C | 949 930-3400 | 13561 |
| AC&a Enterprises LLC (HQ) | 3724 | E | 949 716-3511 | 13699 |
| Karem Aircraft Inc | 3728 | E | 949 859-4444 | 13885 |
| Chroma Systems Solutions Inc | 3825 | E | 949 600-6400 | 14506 |
| Monobind Sales Inc (PA) | 3841 | E | 949 951-2665 | 15195 |
| Tenex Health Inc | 3841 | D | 949 454-7500 | 15279 |
| Biolase Inc (PA) | 3843 | D | | 15442 |
| Staar Surgical Company (PA) | 3851 | A | 626 303-7902 | 15620 |
| Aminco International USA Inc | 3911 | D | 949 457-3261 | 15683 |
| Associated Electrics Inc (HQ) | 3944 | F | 949 544-7500 | 15739 |
| Welcome Skateboards Inc | 3949 | E | 949 305-9200 | 15875 |
| Media Nation Enterprises LLC | 3993 | E | 714 371-9494 | 16006 |
| SMC Products Inc | 5092 | D | 949 753-1099 | 16951 |
| Equimine | 7372 | E | 877 204-9040 | 18289 |
| Wonderware Corporation (DH) | 7372 | B | 949 727-3200 | 18940 |
| United Industries Group Inc | 8711 | E | 949 759-3200 | 19429 |
| Reveal Biosciences Inc | 8731 | E | 858 274-3663 | 19472 |
| Caelus Corporation | 8741 | E | 949 877-7170 | 19512 |
| Ibaset Inc (PA) | 8748 | E | 949 598-5200 | 19562 |

### LAKE ISABELLA, CA - Kern County

| Company | SIC | EMP | PHONE | ENTRY# |
|---|---|---|---|---|
| Wick Communications Co | 2711 | E | 760 379-3667 | 4221 |

### LAKEPORT, CA - Lake County

| Company | SIC | EMP | PHONE | ENTRY# |
|---|---|---|---|---|
| Shannon Ridge Inc (PA) | 2084 | E | 707 281-6780 | 1746 |
| Shannon Ridge Inc | 2084 | E | 707 281-6780 | 1747 |
| Young & Family Inc | 2431 | E | 707 263-8877 | 3210 |
| Globalridge LLC | 2833 | F | 800 225-4345 | 5242 |

### LAKESIDE, CA - San Diego County

| Company | SIC | EMP | PHONE | ENTRY# |
|---|---|---|---|---|
| Enniss Inc | 1442 | E | 619 561-1101 | 311 |
| Pepsi-Cola Metro Btlg Co Inc | 2086 | C | 858 560-6735 | 1918 |
| Superior Ready Mix Concrete LP | 3273 | D | 619 443-7510 | 7512 |
| Blue Star Steel Inc | 3441 | E | 619 448-5520 | 8104 |
| Clark Steel Fabricators Inc | 3446 | E | 619 390-1502 | 8621 |
| Tire Centers West LLC | 5531 | F | 619 596-8473 | 17467 |

### LAKEWOOD, CA - Los Angeles County

| Company | SIC | EMP | PHONE | ENTRY# |
|---|---|---|---|---|
| Industrial Gasket and Sup Co | 3053 | E | 310 530-1771 | 6453 |
| TFC Manufacturing Inc | 3444 | D | 562 426-9559 | 8592 |
| Magma Products LLC | 3631 | D | 562 627-0500 | 11391 |
| Premier Wireless Inc | 3663 | E | 925 776-1070 | 11918 |
| Eve Hair Inc (PA) | 5199 | E | 562 377-1020 | 17295 |

### LANCASTER, CA - Los Angeles County

| Company | SIC | EMP | PHONE | ENTRY# |
|---|---|---|---|---|
| Harvest Farms Inc | 2038 | D | 661 945-3636 | 1036 |
| Radford Cabinets Inc | 2511 | E | 661 729-8931 | 3453 |
| Antelope Valley Newspapers Inc | 2711 | E | 661 940-1000 | 4065 |
| Aerotech News and Review Inc (PA) | 2721 | E | 661 945-5634 | 4228 |
| Prints 4 Life | 2752 | E | 661 942-2233 | 4738 |
| Pavement Recycling Systems Inc | 2951 | D | 661 948-5599 | 6367 |
| Griff Industries Inc | 3089 | F | 661 728-0111 | 6847 |
| Arrow Transit Mix | 3273 | E | 661 945-7600 | 7404 |
| McWhirter Steel Inc | 3441 | D | 661 951-8998 | 8180 |
| Precision Welding Inc | 3441 | E | 661 729-3436 | 8202 |
| Robert F Chapman Inc | 3444 | D | 661 940-9482 | 8559 |
| National Metal Stampings Inc | 3469 | E | 661 945-1157 | 8870 |
| Pacific Seismic Products Inc | 3491 | E | 661 942-4499 | 9160 |
| National Band Saw Company | 3556 | F | 661 294-9552 | 9807 |
| Aerotech Precision Machining | 3599 | F | 661 802-7185 | 10691 |
| J & R Machine Works | 3599 | E | 661 945-8826 | 10895 |
| A V Poles and Lighting Inc | 3646 | E | 661 945-2731 | 11513 |
| Advanced Clutch Technology Inc | 3714 | E | 661 940-7555 | 13443 |
| Morton Grinding Inc | 3965 | C | 661 298-0895 | 15914 |

### LARKSPUR, CA - Marin County

| Company | SIC | EMP | PHONE | ENTRY# |
|---|---|---|---|---|
| ONeill Beverages Co LLC (PA) | 0172 | D | 559 638-3544 | 23 |
| G L Mezzetta Inc | 2033 | D | 707 648-1050 | 889 |

### LATHROP, CA - San Joaquin County

| Company | SIC | EMP | PHONE | ENTRY# |
|---|---|---|---|---|
| Provena Foods Inc | 2013 | C | 209 858-5555 | 661 |
| Schell & Kampeter Inc | 2047 | D | 209 983-4900 | 1115 |
| Horizon Snack Foods Inc | 2053 | D | 925 373-7700 | 1287 |
| California Natural Products | 2099 | B | 209 858-2525 | 2154 |
| Rafael Sandoval | 2421 | E | 209 858-4173 | 3076 |
| Boise Cascade Company | 2621 | C | 209 983-4114 | 3762 |
| Pratt Industries Inc | 2621 | C | 770 922-0117 | 3794 |
| Pratt Lathrop Corrugating LLC | 2653 | F | 209 670-0900 | 3880 |
| Fuel Total Systems California Corporation | 3069 | E | | 6495 |
| Carpenter Co | 3086 | D | 209 982-4800 | 6627 |
| Captive Plastics Inc | 3089 | D | 209 858-9188 | 6764 |
| Con-Fab California Corporation (PA) | 3272 | D | 209 249-4700 | 7321 |
| Accurate Heating & Cooling Inc | 3444 | E | 209 858-4125 | 8360 |
| Eclipse Metal Fabrication Inc | 3444 | E | 650 298-8731 | 8439 |
| Cbc Steel Buildings LLC | 3448 | E | 209 858-2425 | 8659 |
| Saramark Inc | 3448 | E | 408 971-3881 | 8684 |
| Tesla Inc | 3711 | B | 209 647-7037 | 13390 |
| Royal Westlake Roofing LLC | 4225 | E | 209 983-1600 | 16290 |

### LAWNDALE, CA - Los Angeles County

| Company | SIC | EMP | PHONE | ENTRY# |
|---|---|---|---|---|
| Westwood Building Materials Co | 3273 | E | 310 643-9158 | 7522 |
| Curry Company LLC | 3545 | E | 310 643-8400 | 9673 |

### LE GRAND, CA - Merced County

| Company | SIC | EMP | PHONE | ENTRY# |
|---|---|---|---|---|
| Minturn Nut Co Inc | 5441 | E | 559 665-8500 | 17405 |

### LEBEC, CA - Kern County

| Company | SIC | EMP | PHONE | ENTRY# |
|---|---|---|---|---|
| Technicolor Usa Inc | 3651 | A | 661 496-1309 | 11704 |

### LEMON GROVE, CA - San Diego County

| Company | SIC | EMP | PHONE | ENTRY# |
|---|---|---|---|---|
| RCP Block & Brick Inc (PA) | 3271 | D | 619 460-9101 | 7298 |
| Jci Metal Products (PA) | 3441 | D | 619 229-8206 | 8158 |
| Micro Tool & Manufacturing Inc | 3545 | E | 619 582-2884 | 9684 |
| Smiths Shade & Linoleum Co Inc | 5714 | E | 619 299-2228 | 17529 |

### LEMOORE, CA - Kings County

| Company | SIC | EMP | PHONE | ENTRY# |
|---|---|---|---|---|
| Bennett & Bennett Inc | 1711 | E | 559 582-9336 | 406 |
| Gar Bennett LLC | 1711 | E | 559 582-9336 | 420 |
| Leprino Foods Company | 2022 | C | 559 924-7722 | 727 |
| Leprino Foods Company | 2022 | C | 559 924-7939 | 728 |
| Olam Tomato Processors Inc | 2033 | B | 559 447-1390 | 911 |
| Sk Foods LP | 2033 | C | 559 924-6500 | 926 |
| Agusa | 2099 | E | 559 924-4785 | 2120 |
| Northland Process Piping Inc | 3441 | E | 559 925-9724 | 8195 |

### LEWISTON, CA - Trinity County

| Company | SIC | EMP | PHONE | ENTRY# |
|---|---|---|---|---|
| EH Suda Inc | 3599 | E | 530 778-9830 | 10821 |

### LINCOLN, CA - Placer County

| Company | SIC | EMP | PHONE | ENTRY# |
|---|---|---|---|---|
| Jbr Inc (PA) | 2099 | C | 916 258-8000 | 2243 |
| Sierra Pacific Industries | 2421 | C | 916 645-1631 | 3086 |
| Pallets Unlimited Inc | 2448 | F | 916 408-1914 | 3355 |
| Reboot Labs LLC | 3088 | D | 916 926-1716 | 6685 |
| Basalite Building Products LLC | 3251 | C | 916 645-3341 | 7265 |
| Pabco Building Products LLC | 3259 | D | 916 645-3341 | 7275 |
| Jhc Materials Inc | 3272 | E | 916 645-3870 | 7349 |
| Livingstons Concrete Svc Inc | 3273 | E | 916 334-4313 | 7467 |
| San Jose Die Casting Corp | 3363 | E | 408 262-6500 | 7820 |
| Robb-Jack Corporation (PA) | 3541 | D | 916 645-6045 | 9566 |
| Stantec Consulting Svcs Inc | 3589 | E | 916 434-5062 | 10604 |
| Precision Fluid Controls Inc | 3728 | C | 916 626-3029 | 13929 |
| Alpha Dyno Nobel (PA) | 5169 | E | 916 645-3377 | 17238 |

### LINDEN, CA - San Joaquin County

| Company | SIC | EMP | PHONE | ENTRY# |
|---|---|---|---|---|
| Pearl Crop Inc | 2099 | E | 209 887-3731 | 2316 |
| Hyponex Corporation | 2873 | E | 209 887-3845 | 6176 |
| Stockton Rubber Mfgcoinc | 3069 | E | 209 887-1172 | 6540 |

### LINDSAY, CA - Tulare County

| Company | SIC | EMP | PHONE | ENTRY# |
|---|---|---|---|---|
| Califrnia Citrus Producers Inc | 2037 | D | 559 562-5169 | 999 |
| Pallet Depot Inc | 2448 | D | 916 645-0490 | 3352 |
| Harvest Container Company | 2653 | E | 559 562-1394 | 3853 |

### LITTLEROCK, CA - Los Angeles County

| Company | SIC | EMP | PHONE | ENTRY# |
|---|---|---|---|---|
| Hi-Grade Materials Co | 3273 | D | 661 533-3100 | 7455 |

### LIVE OAK, CA - Sutter County

| Company | SIC | EMP | PHONE | ENTRY# |
|---|---|---|---|---|
| Wilbur Packing Company Inc | 0723 | D | 530 671-4911 | 89 |
| Sunset Moulding Co (PA) | 2421 | E | 530 790-2700 | 3090 |
| Coe Orchard Equipment Inc | 3523 | A | 530 695-5121 | 9345 |

### LIVERMORE, CA - Alameda County

| Company | SIC | EMP | PHONE | ENTRY# |
|---|---|---|---|---|
| Cosco Fire Protection Inc | 1731 | D | 925 455-2751 | 454 |
| Presidio Systems Inc (PA) | 1731 | E | 925 362-8400 | 467 |
| Darcie Kent Vineyards LLC | 2084 | E | 925 243-9040 | 1527 |
| Garre Vineyard and Winery Inc | 2084 | E | 925 371-8200 | 1584 |
| Rios-Lovell Estate Winery | 2084 | E | 925 443-0434 | 1723 |
| Robert Taylor | 2084 | F | 925 447-8941 | 1728 |

Employee Codes: A=Over 500 employees, B=251-500, C=101-250, D=51-100, E=20-50, F=10-19, G=1-9

# LIVERMORE, CA

| Company | SIC | EMP | PHONE | ENTRY# |
|---|---|---|---|---|
| Steven Kent LLC | 2084 | F | 925 243-6442 | 1762 |
| Tesla Vineyards Lp | 2084 | E | 925 456-2500 | 1778 |
| Wente Bros | 2084 | E | 925 456-2286 | 1823 |
| Z-Line Designs Inc | 2522 | D | 925 743-4000 | 3611 |
| Golden Bear Packaging Inc | 2653 | E | 925 455-4283 | 3850 |
| Heritage Paper LLC **(PA)** | 2653 | C | 925 449-1148 | 3856 |
| Valmark Industries Inc | 2672 | C | 925 960-9900 | 3958 |
| Vintage 99 Label Mfg Inc **(PA)** | 2672 | E | 925 294-5270 | 3959 |
| Trans Western Polymers Inc | 2673 | B | 925 449-7800 | 3985 |
| Ms Carita Inc | 2759 | E | 925 243-1720 | 4925 |
| GS Cosmeceutical Usa Inc | 2844 | D | 925 371-5000 | 5983 |
| Triangle Coatings Inc **(PA)** | 2851 | E | 510 895-8000 | 6115 |
| Amerimade Technology Inc | 3089 | E | 925 243-9090 | 6715 |
| Ratermann Manufacturing Inc **(PA)** | 3089 | E | 800 264-7793 | 6995 |
| Westec Plastics Corporation | 3089 | D | 925 454-3400 | 7078 |
| Allbirds Inc | 3143 | F | 925 800-3331 | 7102 |
| RC Readymix Co Inc | 3273 | C | 925 449-7785 | 7487 |
| Aria Technologies Inc | 3357 | C | 925 447-7500 | 7771 |
| Cooling Source Inc | 3363 | C | 925 292-1293 | 7807 |
| Metal Improvement Company LLC | 3398 | E | 925 960-1090 | 7894 |
| Westco Iron Works Inc **(PA)** | 3441 | D | 925 961-9152 | 8246 |
| Advantage Metal Products Inc | 3444 | D | 925 667-2009 | 8364 |
| Pro-Tek Manufacturing Inc | 3444 | E | 925 454-8100 | 8545 |
| Screen Tech Inc | 3444 | D | 408 885-9750 | 8568 |
| Fusion Coatings Inc | 3479 | F | 925 443-8083 | 9071 |
| Maas Brothers Inc | 3479 | D | 925 294-8200 | 9088 |
| Jifco Inc | 3498 | E | 925 449-4665 | 9262 |
| Solarjuice American Inc **(PA)** | 3531 | B | 925 474-8821 | 9437 |
| Cha Industries Inc | 3559 | E | 510 683-8554 | 9841 |
| Purotecs Inc | 3559 | F | 925 215-0380 | 9894 |
| Vericool Inc | 3565 | E | 925 337-0808 | 10036 |
| Ferrotec (usa) Corporation **(HQ)** | 3568 | D | 408 964-7700 | 10067 |
| Gdca Inc | 3577 | E | 925 456-9900 | 10373 |
| Puronics Incorporated **(HQ)** | 3589 | E | 925 456-7000 | 10594 |
| Altamont Manufacturing Inc | 3599 | F | 925 371-5401 | 10704 |
| Fred Matter Inc | 3599 | E | 925 371-1234 | 10844 |
| IMG Companies LLC **(HQ)** | 3599 | D | 925 273-1100 | 10882 |
| NGK North America Inc | 3599 | E | 925 292-5372 | 11007 |
| Pacon Mfg Inc | 3599 | E | 925 961-0445 | 11026 |
| R K Larrabee Company Inc | 3621 | D | 925 828-9420 | 11282 |
| Sangraf International Inc | 3624 | E | 216 800-9999 | 11301 |
| Schneider Electric Solar Inverters Usa Inc | 3629 | B | 925 245-1935 | 11379 |
| Sierra Design Mfg Inc **(PA)** | 3647 | E | 925 443-3140 | 11575 |
| Q Technology Inc | 3648 | E | 925 373-3456 | 11620 |
| Jabil Inc | 3672 | E | 925 447-2000 | 12144 |
| Formfactor Inc **(PA)** | 3674 | C | 925 290-4000 | 12436 |
| Inphenix Inc | 3674 | E | 925 606-8809 | 12488 |
| Lam Research Corporation | 3674 | E | 510 572-8400 | 12524 |
| Lam Research Corporation | 3674 | F | 209 597-2194 | 12525 |
| Mega Fluid Systems Inc | 3674 | E | 971 277-9000 | 12553 |
| Laco Inc | 3678 | C | 775 461-2960 | 12888 |
| Gillig LLC **(HQ)** | 3713 | E | 510 264-5000 | 13413 |
| Fabco Holdings Inc | 3714 | A | 925 454-9500 | 13498 |
| Aerospace Composite Products **(PA)** | 3728 | F | 925 443-5900 | 13750 |
| Allclear Aerospace & Def Inc | 3728 | E | 954 239-7844 | 13774 |
| Sensor Concepts LLC | 3812 | D | 925 443-9001 | 14302 |
| Neosem Technology Inc **(HQ)** | 3825 | E | 925 303-4613 | 14563 |
| Topcon Positioning Systems Inc **(DH)** | 3829 | C | 925 245-8300 | 14935 |
| Rh USA Inc | 3841 | E | 925 245-7900 | 15244 |
| Zeltiq Aesthetics Inc | 3841 | C | 925 474-2519 | 15313 |
| Zeltiq Aesthetics Inc | 3841 | C | 925 474-2500 | 15314 |
| Nuprodx Inc | 3842 | F | 415 472-1699 | 15386 |
| Microdental Laboratories Inc | 3843 | E | 800 229-0936 | 15468 |
| Streivor Inc | 3914 | E | 925 960-9090 | 15708 |
| Gpodisplay | 3993 | F | 510 659-9855 | 15985 |
| Medallion Industries Inc | 5031 | F | 925 449-9040 | 16449 |
| Cable Wholesalecom Inc | 5045 | E | 925 455-0800 | 16512 |
| Architectural GL & Alum Co Inc **(HQ)** | 5051 | C | 510 444-6100 | 16607 |
| Trinet Communications Inc **(PA)** | 5065 | F | 925 294-1720 | 16738 |
| Pel Wholesale Inc | 5099 | E | 925 373-3628 | 16984 |
| Packaging Innovators LLC | 5113 | D | 925 371-2000 | 17019 |
| Darcie Kent Winery LLC | 5182 | C | 925 443-5368 | 17264 |
| DSD Merchandisers LLC **(DH)** | 5441 | F | 925 449-2044 | 17400 |
| Elb US Inc | 5999 | E | 925 400-6175 | 17701 |
| Individual Software Inc | 7372 | E | 925 734-6767 | 18409 |
| Assay Technology Inc | 7389 | E | 925 461-8880 | 19072 |
| Wente Bros **(PA)** | 8742 | D | 925 456-2300 | 19546 |

## LIVINGSTON, CA - Merced County

| Company | SIC | EMP | PHONE | ENTRY# |
|---|---|---|---|---|
| Foster Farms LLC **(HQ)** | 0252 | D | 209 394-7901 | 62 |
| Foster Poultry Farms LLC | 0254 | B | 209 394-7901 | 68 |
| Foster Poultry Farms | 2015 | A | 209 394-7901 | 684 |
| Foster Poultry Farms | 2015 | C | 209 394-7901 | 685 |
| Foster Poultry Farms LLC **(PA)** | 2015 | C | 209 394-7901 | 691 |
| Foster Poultry Farms | 2048 | C | 209 394-7950 | 1126 |
| E & J Gallo Winery | 2084 | D | 209 394-6200 | 1550 |
| Hughson Nut Inc | 2099 | C | 209 394-6005 | 2234 |
| Ybp Holdings LLC | 2099 | E | 209 394-7311 | 2393 |

## LOCKEFORD, CA - San Joaquin County

| Company | SIC | EMP | PHONE | ENTRY# |
|---|---|---|---|---|
| Kellogg Supply Inc | 2873 | C | 209 727-3130 | 6177 |
| Lomelis Statuary Inc **(PA)** | 3299 | E | 209 367-1131 | 7593 |
| Robertson-Ceco II Corporation | 3448 | C | 209 727-5504 | 8682 |
| Woodside Investment Inc | 3499 | D | 209 787-8040 | 9305 |

## LODI, CA - San Joaquin County

| Company | SIC | EMP | PHONE | ENTRY# |
|---|---|---|---|---|
| Reynolds Packing Co **(PA)** | 0723 | F | 209 369-2725 | 85 |
| Vino Farms Inc **(PA)** | 0762 | E | 209 334-6975 | 95 |
| T T S Construction Corporation | 1629 | E | 209 333-7788 | 398 |
| Valley Iron Works Inc | 1791 | E | 209 368-7037 | 537 |
| Delta Specialties Inc | 1793 | F | 209 937-9650 | 540 |
| Miller Packing Company | 2013 | E | 209 339-2310 | 653 |
| Pacific Coast Producers **(PA)** | 2033 | B | 209 367-8800 | 917 |
| Pacific Coast Producers | 2033 | C | 209 334-3352 | 919 |
| Archer-Daniels-Midland Company | 2041 | F | 209 339-1252 | 1053 |
| Cottage Bakery Inc | 2051 | B | 209 334-3616 | 1178 |
| Baywood Cellars Inc | 2084 | E | 415 606-4640 | 1483 |
| Bwsc LLC | 2084 | E | 424 353-1767 | 1491 |
| Goldstone Land Company LLC | 2084 | E | 209 368-3113 | 1599 |
| Kautz Vineyards Inc | 2084 | E | 209 369-1911 | 1644 |
| Oak Ridge Winery LLC | 2084 | E | 209 369-4768 | 1694 |
| RB Wine Associates LLC | 2084 | E | 209 365-9463 | 1718 |
| Robert Mondavi Corporation | 2084 | A | 209 365-2995 | 1726 |
| Sutter Home Winery Inc | 2084 | F | 707 963-5928 | 1768 |
| Thomas Allen Vnyrds Winery LLC | 2084 | E | 209 288-7880 | 1781 |
| Del Castillo Foods Inc | 2099 | E | 209 369-2877 | 2181 |
| Design Woodworking Inc **(PA)** | 2431 | E | 209 334-6674 | 3130 |
| Tamarack Sprng Mutl Wtr Co Inc **(PA)** | 2711 | E | 209 369-2751 | 4206 |
| Lustre-Cal LLC | 2759 | D | 206 370-1600 | 4917 |
| Lustre-Cal Nameplate Corp | 2759 | D | 209 370-1600 | 4918 |
| Mepco Industries Inc | 2759 | D | 209 946-0201 | 4922 |
| North Amrcn Specialty Pdts LLC | 2821 | F | 209 365-7500 | 5183 |
| Surtec Inc | 2842 | D | 209 820-3700 | 5930 |
| Holz Rubber Company Inc | 3069 | C | 209 368-7171 | 6501 |
| Scientific Specialties Inc | 3081 | D | 209 333-2120 | 6570 |
| Dart Container Corp California | 3086 | D | 209 333-8088 | 6630 |
| Quashnick Tool Corporation | 3089 | E | 209 334-5283 | 6989 |
| Larry Mthvin Installations Inc | 3231 | D | 209 368-2105 | 7231 |
| Cemex Cnstr Mtls PCF LLC | 3273 | C | 855 292-8453 | 7424 |
| Nucor Bldg Systems Utah LLC | 3312 | D | 209 608-7701 | 7620 |
| Lodi Iron Works Inc **(PA)** | 3321 | E | 209 368-5395 | 7677 |
| Belco Cabinets Inc | 3442 | F | 209 334-5437 | 8256 |
| Dependable Precision Mfg Inc | 3444 | E | 209 369-1055 | 8430 |
| AG Industrial Mfg Inc | 3523 | E | 209 369-1994 | 9334 |
| Vander Lans & Sons Inc **(PA)** | 3589 | E | 209 334-4115 | 10608 |
| Campbell Grinding Inc | 3599 | F | 209 339-8838 | 10763 |
| Armorstruxx LLC | 3728 | E | 209 365-9400 | 13786 |
| American Mstr Tech Scntfic Inc | 3841 | C | 209 368-4031 | 14965 |
| Scholten Surgical Instrs Inc | 3841 | F | 209 365-1393 | 15248 |
| USA Products Group **(PA)** | 3949 | E | 209 334-1460 | 15873 |
| Suess Properties Inc | 3999 | F | 209 334-2081 | 16241 |
| Walmart Inc | 5311 | E | 209 368-6658 | 17364 |
| Bull Outdoor Products Inc | 5712 | E | 909 770-8626 | 17517 |
| Meehleis Modular Buildings Inc | 8712 | D | 209 334-4637 | 19432 |

## LOMA LINDA, CA - San Bernardino County

| Company | SIC | EMP | PHONE | ENTRY# |
|---|---|---|---|---|
| Dvele Inc | 2451 | E | 909 796-2561 | 3384 |
| Dvele Omega Corporation | 2451 | D | 909 796-2561 | 3385 |

## LOMPOC, CA - Santa Barbara County

| Company | SIC | EMP | PHONE | ENTRY# |
|---|---|---|---|---|
| Babcock Enterprises Inc | 0172 | E | 805 736-1455 | 8 |
| Horizon Well Logging Inc | 1389 | E | 805 733-0972 | 239 |
| Imerys Minerals California Inc **(HQ)** | 1499 | D | 805 736-1221 | 341 |
| Kustom Kanopies Inc | 1541 | E | 801 399-3400 | 358 |
| Hilliard Bruce Vineyards LLC **(PA)** | 2084 | E | 805 736-5366 | 1614 |
| Kugler Wines LLC | 2084 | E | 630 306-4634 | 1652 |
| Celite Corporation | 2819 | F | 805 736-1221 | 5081 |
| Valiant Technical Services Inc | 3731 | D | 757 628-9500 | 14021 |
| Orbital Sciences LLC | 3812 | B | 805 734-5400 | 14275 |
| Federal Prison Industries | 3993 | F | 805 735-2771 | 15978 |
| W F F H Inc | 3999 | F | 805 735-9255 | 16266 |

## LONG BEACH, CA - Los Angeles County

| Company | SIC | EMP | PHONE | ENTRY# |
|---|---|---|---|---|
| Beta Operating Company LLC | 1311 | D | 562 628-1526 | 124 |
| California Resources Corp **(PA)** | 1311 | D | 888 848-4754 | 129 |
| Thums Long Beach Company | 1311 | C | 562 624-3400 | 140 |

# GEOGRAPHIC SECTION — LOS ALAMITOS, CA

| Company | SIC | EMP | PHONE | ENTRY# |
|---|---|---|---|---|
| Tidelands Oil Production Inc. | 1311 | E | 562 436-9918 | 141 |
| Dick Howells Hole Drlg Svc Inc | 1381 | F | 562 633-9898 | 156 |
| Termo Company | 1382 | E | 562 595-7401 | 201 |
| Warren E&P Inc | 1382 | D | 214 393-9688 | 202 |
| B & B Pipe and Tool Co (PA) | 1389 | E | 562 424-0704 | 206 |
| Kuster Co Oil Well Services | 1389 | E | 562 595-0661 | 247 |
| Petrochem Insulation Inc | 1742 | C | 310 638-6663 | 480 |
| Lb Beadels LLC | 2064 | E | 562 726-1700 | 1316 |
| Wiser Foods Inc | 2086 | D | 310 895-0888 | 1973 |
| Martin Bauer Inc | 2087 | F | 310 669-2100 | 2014 |
| Everson Spice Company Inc | 2099 | E | 562 595-4785 | 2193 |
| Texollini Inc | 2297 | C | 310 537-3400 | 2533 |
| L A Cstm AP & Promotions Inc (PA) | 2329 | E | 562 595-1770 | 2629 |
| Brentwood Originals Inc (PA) | 2392 | E | 310 637-6804 | 2924 |
| Enrich Enterprises Inc | 2395 | E | 310 515-5055 | 2990 |
| National Emblem Inc (PA) | 2395 | C | 310 515-5055 | 2997 |
| Western Integrated Mtls Inc (PA) | 2431 | E | 562 634-2823 | 3203 |
| Harding Containers Intl Inc | 2448 | F | 310 549-7272 | 3346 |
| F-J-E Inc | 2541 | E | 562 437-7466 | 3656 |
| Jbi LLC (PA) | 2599 | C | 310 886-8034 | 3746 |
| Continental Graphics Corp | 2752 | D | 714 827-1752 | 4568 |
| Continental Graphics Corp | 2752 | D | 714 503-4200 | 4570 |
| Crestec Usa Inc | 2752 | C | 310 327-9000 | 4579 |
| Pdf Print Communications Inc (PA) | 2752 | C | 562 426-6978 | 4721 |
| Queen Beach Printers Inc | 2752 | E | 562 436-8201 | 4748 |
| Weber Printing Company Inc | 2752 | C | 310 639-5064 | 4808 |
| Western Sheld Acquisitions LLC (PA) | 2754 | E | 310 527-6212 | 4829 |
| Airgas Inc | 2813 | D | 510 429-4216 | 5040 |
| Eco Services Operations Corp | 2819 | D | 310 885-6719 | 5088 |
| Energy Solutions (us) LLC | 2819 | B | 310 669-5300 | 5092 |
| Sanders Inds Holdings Inc (PA) | 2821 | F | 562 354-2920 | 5200 |
| Evolife Scientific Llc | 2833 | E | 888 750-0310 | 5240 |
| Sephora Co LLC (PA) | 2844 | E | 760 798-7654 | 6035 |
| Morton Salt Inc | 2899 | D | 562 437-0071 | 6311 |
| Tesoro Refining & Mktg Co LLC | 2911 | D | 562 728-2215 | 6353 |
| Lubeco Inc | 2992 | E | 562 602-1791 | 6397 |
| Bryant Rubber Corp (PA) | 3053 | E | 310 530-2530 | 6438 |
| Seal Science Inc (HQ) | 3053 | D | 949 253-3130 | 6466 |
| Rubbercraft Corp Cal Ltd (HQ) | 3061 | C | 562 354-2800 | 6477 |
| Hexpol Compounding CA Inc (DH) | 3069 | D | 626 961-0311 | 6499 |
| Kirkhill Rubber Company | 3069 | D | 562 803-1117 | 6508 |
| G B Remanufacturing Inc | 3089 | D | 562 272-7333 | 6835 |
| Jacobson Plastics Inc | 3089 | D | 562 433-4911 | 6870 |
| Medway Plastics Corporation | 3089 | C | 562 630-1175 | 6910 |
| Plasidyne Engineering & Mfg | 3089 | E | 562 531-0510 | 6958 |
| Sage Plastics Long Beach Corp | 3089 | D | 562 423-3900 | 7019 |
| Talco Plastics Inc | 3089 | D | 562 630-1224 | 7049 |
| Total Mont LLC | 3231 | E | 562 983-1374 | 7243 |
| Mitsubishi Cement Corporation | 3241 | B | 562 495-0600 | 7259 |
| Proform Finishing Products LLC | 3275 | E | 562 435-4465 | 7531 |
| American Plant Services Inc (PA) | 3312 | E | 562 630-1773 | 7603 |
| Nikon AM Synergy Inc | 3313 | E | 310 607-0188 | 7635 |
| Primus Pipe and Tube Inc (DH) | 3317 | D | 562 808-8000 | 7669 |
| Certified Alloy Products Inc | 3341 | C | 562 595-6621 | 7716 |
| TCI Texarkana Inc | 3353 | E | 562 808-8000 | 7734 |
| SPEP Acquisition Corp (PA) | 3429 | D | 310 608-0693 | 8028 |
| Seachrome Corporation | 3431 | C | 310 427-8010 | 8044 |
| Foss Maritime Company | 3441 | F | 562 437-6098 | 8142 |
| R & D Steel Inc | 3441 | E | 310 631-6183 | 8207 |
| Taricco Corp | 3443 | F | 562 437-5433 | 8345 |
| Cowelco | 3444 | E | 562 432-5766 | 8418 |
| H Roberts Construction | 3448 | D | 562 590-4825 | 8670 |
| Wyatt Precision Machine Inc | 3451 | E | 562 634-0524 | 8738 |
| Dae-IL Usa Inc | 3471 | E | 562 422-4046 | 8947 |
| Fine Quality Metal Finshg Inc | 3471 | F | 562 983-7425 | 8960 |
| Fusion Finish LLC | 3479 | F | 562 619-1189 | 9072 |
| Valmont Industries Inc | 3479 | E | 310 549-2200 | 9132 |
| Crane Co | 3492 | C | 562 426-2531 | 9166 |
| Cunico Corporation | 3498 | E | 562 733-4600 | 9255 |
| Sportsmen Steel Safe Fabg Co (PA) | 3499 | E | 562 984-0244 | 9299 |
| Crown Equipment Corporation | 3537 | D | 310 952-6600 | 9516 |
| Sansani Cleaning Solutions LLC | 3589 | F | 310 630-9033 | 10597 |
| Berns Bros Inc | 3599 | F | 562 437-0471 | 10749 |
| Cavanaugh Machine Works Inc | 3599 | E | 562 437-1126 | 10766 |
| Frontier Engrg & Mfg Tech Inc (PA) | 3599 | E | 310 767-1227 | 10845 |
| NC Dynamics Incorporated | 3599 | E | 562 634-7392 | 11003 |
| NC Dynamics LLC | 3599 | C | 562 634-7392 | 11004 |
| Nuspace Inc (HQ) | 3599 | E | 562 497-3200 | 11013 |
| Kbr Inc | 3624 | E | 562 436-9281 | 11299 |
| Control Switches Intl Inc | 3625 | E | 562 498-7331 | 11313 |
| Western Tube & Conduit Corp (HQ) | 3644 | D | 310 537-6300 | 11484 |
| Visionaire Lighting LLC | 3646 | D | 310 512-6480 | 11568 |
| Ixys Long Beach Inc (DH) | 3674 | E | 562 296-6584 | 12509 |
| Mercury Security Products LLC | 3699 | F | 562 986-9105 | 13273 |
| Schneider Elc Buildings LLC | 3699 | C | 310 900-2385 | 13303 |
| Tabc Inc (DH) | 3713 | A | 562 984-3305 | 13432 |
| Acme Headlining Co | 3714 | D | 562 432-0281 | 13438 |
| Aibot US Operation Inc | 3721 | E | 562 283-3286 | 13631 |
| Boeing Company | 3721 | A | 562 496-1000 | 13643 |
| Boeing Company | 3721 | A | 562 593-5511 | 13644 |
| Gulfstream Aerospace Corp GA | 3721 | A | 562 420-1818 | 13668 |
| Jetzero Inc (PA) | 3721 | E | 949 474-8222 | 13671 |
| A & A Aerospace Inc | 3728 | E | 562 901-6803 | 13729 |
| Neill Aircraft Co | 3728 | B | 562 432-7981 | 13915 |
| Sanders Composites Inc (HQ) | 3728 | E | 562 354-2800 | 13953 |
| APR Engineering Inc | 3731 | E | 562 983-3800 | 13998 |
| Indel Engineering Inc | 3732 | E | 562 594-0995 | 14036 |
| Rocket Lab Usa Inc (PA) | 3761 | E | 714 465-5737 | 14084 |
| Rocket Lab Usa Inc | 3761 | E | 714 465-5737 | 14085 |
| Space Exploration Tech Corp | 3761 | C | 310 363-6289 | 14086 |
| Relativity Space Inc (PA) | 3764 | B | 424 393-4309 | 14105 |
| Spinlaunch Inc | 3764 | C | 650 516-7746 | 14106 |
| Custom Fibreglass Mfg Co | 3792 | E | 562 432-5454 | 14119 |
| Simulator PDT Solutions LLC | 3812 | E | 310 830-3331 | 14306 |
| Virgin Orbit Holdings Inc (HQ) | 3812 | F | 562 388-4400 | 14327 |
| Fundamental Tech Intl Inc | 3823 | E | 562 595-0661 | 14415 |
| Beauty Health Company (PA) | 3841 | B | 800 603-4996 | 14997 |
| Hydrafacial LLC | 3841 | E | 562 391-2052 | 15108 |
| Hydrafacial LLC (HQ) | 3841 | C | 800 603-4996 | 15109 |
| Ferraco Inc (HQ) | 3842 | E | 562 988-2414 | 15346 |
| Rastaclat LLC | 3911 | E | 424 287-0902 | 15703 |
| Superior Signs & Installation (PA) | 3993 | D | 562 495-3808 | 16054 |
| Carberry LLC | 3999 | E | 562 264-5078 | 16109 |
| Guzzler Manufacturing Inc | 3999 | F | 562 436-0250 | 16140 |
| Macs Lift Gate Inc (PA) | 3999 | E | 562 529-3465 | 16175 |
| Snapshot Hair & Extensions LLC | 3999 | F | 877 783-5658 | 16231 |
| Aviation Repair Solutions Inc | 4581 | F | 562 437-2825 | 16300 |
| Denso Pdts & Svcs Americas Inc (DH) | 5013 | B | 310 834-6352 | 16380 |
| Clarendon Specialty Fas Inc | 5072 | D | 714 842-2603 | 16749 |
| Tonnage Industrial LLC | 5085 | E | 800 893-9681 | 16901 |
| Aircraft Hardware West | 5088 | E | 562 961-9324 | 16913 |
| Intex Properties S Bay Corp (HQ) | 5091 | D | 310 549-5400 | 16936 |
| Tst Inc | 5093 | E | 310 835-0115 | 16964 |
| A W Chang Corporation (PA) | 5131 | E | 310 764-2000 | 17056 |
| Plastic Sales Southern Inc | 5162 | E | 714 375-7900 | 17231 |
| Farm Street Designs Inc | 5182 | E | 562 985-0026 | 17265 |
| Redbarn Pet Products Inc (PA) | 5199 | C | 562 495-7315 | 17307 |
| Belmont Brewing Company Inc | 5812 | E | 562 433-3891 | 17564 |
| Password Enterprise Inc | 5961 | E | 562 988-8889 | 17669 |
| Design Science Inc | 7371 | E | 562 442-4779 | 17909 |
| QED Software LLC | 7372 | E | 310 214-3118 | 18713 |
| Traffic Management Pdts Inc | 7372 | A | 800 763-3999 | 18890 |
| Zwift Inc (PA) | 7372 | B | 855 469-9438 | 18959 |
| Jf Fixtures & Design LLC | 7389 | E | 562 437-7466 | 19100 |
| Cw Industries Inc (PA) | 7692 | E | 562 432-5421 | 19188 |
| DK Valve & Supply Inc | 7699 | E | 562 529-8400 | 19251 |
| Posca Brothers Dental Lab Inc | 8072 | D | 562 427-1811 | 19334 |
| Aunt Rubys LLC | 8742 | E | 562 326-6783 | 19521 |
| Ultura Inc | 8744 | C | 562 661-4999 | 19553 |

## LOOMIS, CA - Placer County

| Company | SIC | EMP | PHONE | ENTRY# |
|---|---|---|---|---|
| Sierra Trim Inc | 1751 | E | 916 259-2966 | 501 |
| Lausmann Lumber & Moulding Co | 2421 | E | 916 652-9201 | 3072 |
| Gary Doupnik Manufacturing Inc | 2452 | E | 916 652-9291 | 3395 |
| Rimnetics Inc | 3089 | F | 916 652-5555 | 7005 |
| Valley Rock Lndscpe Material | 3271 | E | 916 652-7209 | 7303 |
| New Cal Metals Inc | 3444 | E | 916 652-7424 | 8517 |
| Qantel Technologies Inc | 3571 | E | 510 731-2080 | 10199 |
| Sierramotion Inc | 3621 | F | 916 259-1868 | 11286 |
| Presentertek Inc | 3669 | E | 916 251-7190 | 12009 |
| Ruffstuff Inc | 3714 | E | 916 660-1945 | 13568 |
| Applimotion Inc | 5063 | D | 916 652-3118 | 16642 |
| Jamcor Corporation (PA) | 5065 | E | 916 652-7713 | 16709 |
| Truepoint Solutions LLC (PA) | 7373 | E | 916 259-1293 | 18996 |
| Knisley Welding Inc | 7692 | E | 916 652-5891 | 19207 |

## LOS ALAMITOS, CA - Orange County

| Company | SIC | EMP | PHONE | ENTRY# |
|---|---|---|---|---|
| Kdc Inc (HQ) | 1731 | C | 714 828-7000 | 459 |
| Thermo Power Industries | 1742 | E | 562 799-0087 | 481 |
| Bloomfield Bakers | 2052 | A | 626 610-2253 | 1266 |
| Blue Sphere Inc | 2311 | E | 714 953-7555 | 2558 |
| Kids Line LLC | 2392 | C | 310 660-0110 | 2932 |
| Plh Products Inc | 2452 | B | 714 739-6622 | 3398 |
| Supermedia LLC | 2741 | E | 562 594-5101 | 4474 |
| Mittera Group Inc | 2752 | E | 562 598-2446 | 4696 |
| Trend Offset Printing Services Inc (HQ) | 2752 | E | 562 598-2446 | 4789 |

Employee Codes: A=Over 500 employees, B=251-500
C=101-250, D=51-100, E=20-50, F=10-19, G=1-9

# LOS ALAMITOS, CA

## GEOGRAPHIC SECTION

| | SIC | EMP | PHONE | ENTRY# |
|---|---|---|---|---|
| Trend Offset Printing Svcs Inc | 2752 | B | 562 598-2446 | 4790 |
| Lab Clean Inc | 2842 | E | 714 689-0063 | 5912 |
| Natus Inc | 3161 | D | 626 355-3746 | 7136 |
| Grating Pacific Inc (PA) | 3441 | E | 562 598-4314 | 8148 |
| Spintek Filtration Inc | 3569 | F | 714 236-9190 | 10116 |
| Epson America Inc (DH) | 3577 | A | 800 463-7766 | 10365 |
| Pl Machine Corporation | 3599 | E | 714 892-1100 | 11041 |
| Alliance Spacesystems LLC | 3624 | C | 714 226-1400 | 11298 |
| Dwi Enterprises | 3651 | E | 714 842-2236 | 11655 |
| Epson Electronics America Inc (DH) | 3674 | E | 408 922-0200 | 12423 |
| Arrowhead Products Corporation | 3728 | A | 714 822-2513 | 13787 |
| Vanguard Space Tech Inc | 3728 | C | 858 587-4210 | 13985 |
| Flowline Inc | 3829 | E | 562 598-3015 | 14869 |
| Absolute Sign Inc | 3993 | F | 562 592-5838 | 15938 |

## LOS ALTOS, CA - Santa Clara County

| | SIC | EMP | PHONE | ENTRY# |
|---|---|---|---|---|
| Cothera Biopharma Inc | 2834 | E | 510 364-1930 | 5413 |
| Ninjatech Ai | 5045 | E | 408 444-5101 | 16534 |
| Jemstep Inc | 7372 | E | 650 966-6500 | 18455 |
| Teamraderie Inc | 7372 | E | 650 402-0030 | 18870 |
| Aae Systems Inc | 7373 | F | 408 732-1710 | 18960 |
| Ahntech Inc (PA) | 8711 | D | 650 861-3987 | 19375 |
| Markov Corporation | 8732 | E | 650 207-9445 | 19484 |

## LOS ALTOS HILLS, CA - Santa Clara County

| | SIC | EMP | PHONE | ENTRY# |
|---|---|---|---|---|
| Star Pacific Inc | 2841 | E | 510 471-6555 | 5883 |

## LOS ANGELES, CA - Los Angeles County

| | SIC | EMP | PHONE | ENTRY# |
|---|---|---|---|---|
| Greenscreen | 0781 | E | 310 837-0526 | 96 |
| Breitburn Energy Partners LP | 1311 | A | 213 225-5900 | 127 |
| Breitburn GP LLC | 1311 | E | 213 225-5900 | 128 |
| Occidental Petroleum Corporation of California | 1311 | A | | 136 |
| The Strand Energy Company | 1311 | B | 213 225-5900 | 139 |
| Breitburn Energy Holdings LLC | 1382 | E | 213 225-5900 | 171 |
| Freeport-Mcmoran Oil & Gas LLC | 1382 | C | 323 298-2200 | 186 |
| Occidental Petroleum Investment Co Inc | 1382 | A | 310 208-8800 | 193 |
| Qre Operating LLC | 1382 | D | 213 225-5900 | 195 |
| Sentinel Peak Rsources Cal LLC | 1382 | E | 323 298-2200 | 199 |
| Cal-Quake Construction Inc | 1389 | E | 323 931-2969 | 211 |
| Hirsh Inc | 1389 | E | 213 622-9441 | 238 |
| Vanderra Resources LLC | 1389 | B | 817 439-2220 | 289 |
| China Pacific Inc | 1542 | F | 323 222-9580 | 364 |
| Himco National Inc | 1731 | F | 323 231-9104 | 457 |
| Clougherty Packing LLC (DH) | 2011 | B | 323 583-4621 | 592 |
| Serv-Rite Meat Company Inc | 2011 | E | 323 227-1911 | 616 |
| Commodity Sales Co | 2015 | C | 323 980-5463 | 679 |
| Los Angeles Poultry Co Inc | 2015 | D | 323 232-1619 | 697 |
| Western Supreme Inc | 2015 | C | 213 627-3861 | 702 |
| Pac Fill Inc | 2026 | E | 818 409-0117 | 841 |
| Caer Inc | 2032 | E | 415 879-9864 | 851 |
| Dolores Canning Co Inc | 2032 | E | 323 263-9155 | 854 |
| La Indiana Tamales Inc | 2032 | F | 323 262-4682 | 865 |
| Wing Hing Foods LLC | 2032 | D | 323 232-8899 | 873 |
| Jackson Manufacturing LLC | 2033 | F | 213 399-9300 | 896 |
| Walker Foods Inc | 2033 | E | 323 268-5191 | 940 |
| J Hellman Frozen Foods Inc (PA) | 2037 | E | 213 243-9105 | 1008 |
| La Aloe LLC | 2037 | E | 888 968-2563 | 1010 |
| Raw Juicery Inc | 2037 | F | 213 221-6081 | 1016 |
| Astrochef LLC | 2038 | D | 213 627-9860 | 1026 |
| Crave Foods Inc | 2038 | E | 562 900-7272 | 1030 |
| East West Tea Company LLC | 2043 | C | 310 275-9891 | 1070 |
| Arthur Dogswell LLC (PA) | 2047 | E | 888 559-8833 | 1093 |
| Bake Usa Inc | 2051 | E | 415 629-8274 | 1164 |
| Bakers Kneaded LLC | 2051 | E | 310 819-8700 | 1166 |
| Frisco Baking Company Inc | 2051 | C | 323 225-6111 | 1205 |
| Global Impact Inv Partners LLC | 2051 | E | 310 592-2000 | 1211 |
| Lavash Corporation of America | 2051 | E | 323 663-5249 | 1222 |
| Lupitas Bakery Inc (PA) | 2051 | F | 323 752-2391 | 1224 |
| United States Bakery | 2051 | E | 323 232-6124 | 1249 |
| Vurger Co (usa) Corp | 2051 | E | 929 318-9546 | 1252 |
| Yamazaki Baking Co Ltd | 2051 | E | 323 581-5218 | 1256 |
| Amays Bakery & Noodle Co Inc (PA) | 2052 | D | 213 626-2713 | 1258 |
| Aspire Bakeries Holdco LLC (HQ) | 2052 | C | 844 992-7747 | 1259 |
| Aspire Bakeries LLC (DH) | 2052 | E | 844 992-7747 | 1260 |
| Aspire Bakeries Midco LLC (DH) | 2052 | F | 844 992-7747 | 1263 |
| Grandville Llc | 2052 | F | 213 382-3878 | 1276 |
| J & J Snack Foods Corp Cal (HQ) | 2052 | D | 323 581-0171 | 1278 |
| Wonderful Pstchios Almonds LLC (HQ) | 2068 | E | 310 966-5700 | 1370 |
| Darling Ingredients Inc | 2077 | E | 323 583-6311 | 1382 |
| Karl Strauss Brewing Company | 2082 | F | 213 228-2739 | 1439 |
| W Cellars Inc | 2082 | F | 714 655-2025 | 1466 |
| San Antonio Winery Inc (PA) | 2084 | C | 323 223-1401 | 1739 |
| The Wonderful Company LLC (PA) | 2084 | C | 310 966-5700 | 1780 |
| Vino Vault Inc (PA) | 2084 | F | 323 937-9463 | 1814 |
| Winc Inc | 2084 | C | 855 282-5829 | 1829 |
| Stillhouse LLC | 2085 | E | 323 498-1111 | 1845 |
| Aquahydrate Inc | 2086 | E | 310 559-5058 | 1866 |
| Cce | 2086 | F | 213 744-8909 | 1876 |
| Ds Services of America Inc | 2086 | E | 323 551-5724 | 1887 |
| Reyes Coca-Cola Bottling LLC | 2086 | E | 213 744-8659 | 1952 |
| American Fruits & Flavors LLC | 2087 | E | 818 899-9574 | 1979 |
| American Fruits & Flavors LLC | 2087 | E | 818 899-9574 | 1980 |
| American Fruits & Flavors LLC | 2087 | D | 213 624-1831 | 1981 |
| De La Calle Co (PA) | 2087 | F | 650 465-0093 | 1996 |
| Felbro Food Products Inc | 2087 | E | 323 936-5266 | 2002 |
| Herbalife Manufacturing LLC (DH) | 2087 | E | 866 866-4744 | 2009 |
| Yamasa Enterprises | 2091 | E | 213 626-2211 | 2045 |
| Eberine Enterprises Inc | 2095 | E | 323 587-1111 | 2069 |
| Gourmet Coffee Warehouse Inc (PA) | 2095 | E | 323 871-8930 | 2072 |
| Snack It Forward LLC | 2096 | E | 310 242-5517 | 2102 |
| Peking Noodle Co Inc | 2098 | E | 323 223-0897 | 2118 |
| Albany Farms Inc (PA) | 2099 | E | 877 832-8269 | 2123 |
| C & F Foods Inc | 2099 | B | 626 723-1000 | 2150 |
| Camino Real Foods Inc (PA) | 2099 | E | 323 585-6599 | 2156 |
| Countertop | 2099 | E | 323 788-3591 | 2174 |
| Everytable Pbc | 2099 | E | 323 296-0311 | 2194 |
| Jsl Foods Inc (PA) | 2099 | D | 323 223-2484 | 2245 |
| La Barca Tortilleria Inc | 2099 | E | 323 268-1744 | 2248 |
| La Fortaleza Inc | 2099 | D | 323 261-1211 | 2253 |
| La Gloria Foods Corp (PA) | 2099 | D | 323 262-0410 | 2254 |
| La Gloria Foods Corp | 2099 | E | 323 263-6755 | 2255 |
| La Princesita Tortilleria Inc (PA) | 2099 | F | 323 267-0673 | 2257 |
| Mojave Foods Corporation (HQ) | 2099 | D | 323 890-8900 | 2283 |
| Pensieve Foods | 2099 | E | 323 938-8666 | 2319 |
| Plant Ranch LLC | 2099 | F | 818 384-9727 | 2322 |
| Tampico Spice Co Incorporated | 2099 | E | 323 235-3154 | 2368 |
| Uce Holdings Inc | 2099 | D | 213 217-4235 | 2382 |
| Worldwide Specialties Inc | 2099 | E | 323 587-2200 | 2392 |
| Centric Brands Inc | 2211 | F | 323 837-3700 | 2409 |
| Colormax Industries Inc (PA) | 2211 | E | 213 748-6600 | 2410 |
| East Shore Garment Company LLC | 2211 | E | 323 923-4454 | 2412 |
| Factory One Studio Inc | 2211 | D | 323 752-1670 | 2414 |
| G Kagan and Sons Inc (PA) | 2211 | E | 323 583-1400 | 2416 |
| Grey Studio Inc | 2211 | F | 323 780-8111 | 2417 |
| Knit Generation Group Inc | 2211 | E | 213 221-5001 | 2420 |
| Ground Control Business MGT (DH) | 2221 | E | 310 315-6200 | 2438 |
| Juicy Couture Inc | 2221 | C | 888 824-8826 | 2439 |
| S&B Development Group LLC | 2221 | E | 213 446-2818 | 2441 |
| Cmk Manufacturing LLC | 2231 | E | | 2444 |
| Roshan Trading Inc | 2231 | E | 213 622-9904 | 2449 |
| Keystone Textile Inc | 2241 | F | 213 622-7755 | 2454 |
| West Coast Trimming Corp | 2241 | E | 323 587-0701 | 2456 |
| Byer California | 2253 | C | 323 780-7615 | 2463 |
| Crew Knitwear LLC | 2253 | D | 323 526-3888 | 2464 |
| Design Knit Inc | 2253 | E | 213 742-1234 | 2467 |
| Fortune Swimwear LLC (HQ) | 2253 | E | 310 733-2130 | 2470 |
| Grand West Inc (PA) | 2253 | E | 323 235-2700 | 2472 |
| Tenenblatt Corporation | 2257 | C | 323 232-2061 | 2483 |
| Azitex Trading Corp | 2259 | D | 213 745-7072 | 2484 |
| Midthrust Imports Inc | 2259 | E | 213 749-6651 | 2485 |
| Washington Grment Dyg Fnshg In | 2261 | E | 213 747-1111 | 2498 |
| Washington Garment Dyeing (PA) | 2262 | E | 213 747-1111 | 2501 |
| Matchmaster Dyg & Finshg Inc (PA) | 2269 | E | 323 232-2061 | 2504 |
| Pacific Coast Bach Label Inc | 2269 | E | 213 612-0314 | 2505 |
| Durkan Patterned Carpets Inc | 2273 | C | 310 838-2898 | 2513 |
| Interfaceflor LLC | 2273 | D | 213 741-2139 | 2515 |
| AMpm Maintenance Corporation | 2299 | E | 424 230-1300 | 2543 |
| New Chef Fashion Inc | 2311 | D | 323 581-0300 | 2562 |
| Distro Worldwide LLC | 2321 | E | 818 849-0953 | 2572 |
| Gino Corporation | 2321 | E | 323 234-7979 | 2573 |
| Fashiongo | 2323 | E | 213 745-2667 | 2583 |
| Sophie Buhai LLC | 2323 | F | 949 302-8762 | 2584 |
| Aries 33 LLC | 2329 | E | 310 355-8330 | 2611 |
| Doh Quest LLC | 2329 | E | 213 651-3441 | 2617 |
| Fear of God LLC | 2329 | D | 213 235-7985 | 2619 |
| Fetish Group Inc (PA) | 2329 | E | 323 587-7873 | 2620 |
| Jh Design Group | 2329 | D | 213 747-5700 | 2625 |
| Spirit Clothing Company (PA) | 2329 | C | 213 784-0251 | 2641 |
| Waterfront Design Group LLC | 2329 | E | 213 746-5800 | 2650 |
| C-Quest Inc | 2331 | E | 323 980-1400 | 2659 |
| Colon Manufacturing Inc (PA) | 2331 | F | 213 749-6149 | 2660 |
| Guru Knits Inc | 2331 | D | 323 235-9424 | 2667 |
| GUSB Inc | 2331 | E | 323 233-0044 | 2668 |
| Harari Inc (PA) | 2331 | E | 323 734-5302 | 2669 |
| Harkham Industries Inc (PA) | 2331 | E | 323 586-4600 | 2670 |
| J Heyri Inc | 2331 | E | 323 588-1234 | 2671 |

# GEOGRAPHIC SECTION — LOS ANGELES, CA

| Company | SIC | EMP | PHONE | ENTRY# |
|---|---|---|---|---|
| Judy Ann of California Inc | 2331 | C | 213 623-9233 | 2672 |
| K Too | 2331 | E | 213 747-7766 | 2673 |
| Komex International Inc | 2331 | F | 323 233-9005 | 2675 |
| La Mamba LLC | 2331 | E | 323 526-3526 | 2677 |
| Leebe Apparel Inc | 2331 | E | 323 897-5585 | 2678 |
| Mf Inc | 2331 | C | 213 627-2498 | 2680 |
| Monrow LLC | 2331 | E | 213 741-6007 | 2681 |
| MXF Designs Inc | 2331 | D | 323 266-1451 | 2682 |
| Project Social T LLC | 2331 | E | 323 266-4500 | 2687 |
| Stony Apparel Corp (PA) | 2331 | C | 323 981-9080 | 2689 |
| T2c Inc | 2331 | F | 213 741-5232 | 2690 |
| Tianello Inc | 2331 | C | 323 231-0599 | 2691 |
| Umgee USA Inc | 2331 | F | 323 526-9138 | 2692 |
| Avalon Apparel LLC (PA) | 2335 | C | 323 581-3511 | 2700 |
| California Blue Apparel Inc | 2335 | E | 213 745-5400 | 2701 |
| Choon Inc (PA) | 2335 | E | 213 225-2500 | 2703 |
| J C Trimming Company Inc | 2335 | D | 323 235-4458 | 2705 |
| Jodi Kristopher LLC (PA) | 2335 | D | 323 890-8000 | 2706 |
| Jwc Studio Inc (PA) | 2335 | E | 323 231-8222 | 2707 |
| L A Glo Inc | 2335 | E | 323 932-0091 | 2708 |
| Miss Kim Inc | 2335 | F | 213 741-0888 | 2711 |
| Private Brand Mdsg Corp | 2335 | E | 213 749-0191 | 2713 |
| Promises Promises Inc | 2335 | E | 213 749-7725 | 2714 |
| Sewby LLC | 2335 | E | 310 494-7705 | 2715 |
| Sublitex Inc | 2335 | E | 323 582-9596 | 2716 |
| Tlmf Inc | 2335 | D | 212 764-2334 | 2717 |
| Komarov Enterprises Inc | 2337 | D | 213 244-7000 | 2724 |
| S Studio Inc | 2337 | F | 213 388-7400 | 2726 |
| Topson Downs California Inc | 2337 | C | 310 558-0300 | 2729 |
| Ambiance USA Inc | 2339 | F | 323 587-0007 | 2732 |
| Ambiance USA Inc (PA) | 2339 | E | 323 587-0007 | 2733 |
| Ambiance USA Inc | 2339 | F | 213 765-9600 | 2734 |
| Bb Co Inc | 2339 | E | 213 550-1158 | 2737 |
| Be Bop Clothing | 2339 | B | 323 846-0121 | 2738 |
| Burning Torch Inc | 2339 | E | 323 733-7700 | 2740 |
| Camp Smidgemore Inc (DH) | 2339 | E | 323 634-0333 | 2742 |
| Carbon 38 Inc | 2339 | D | 888 723-5838 | 2743 |
| Clothing Illustrated Inc (PA) | 2339 | E | 213 403-9950 | 2746 |
| Crew Knitwear LLC (PA) | 2339 | E | 323 526-3888 | 2748 |
| Dda Holdings Inc | 2339 | E | 213 624-5200 | 2752 |
| Dmbm LLC | 2339 | E | 714 321-6032 | 2755 |
| Eska Inc | 2339 | E | 323 846-3700 | 2757 |
| Good American LLC (PA) | 2339 | E | 213 357-5100 | 2761 |
| Gypsy 05 Inc | 2339 | E | 323 265-2700 | 2762 |
| Jaya Apparel Group LLC (PA) | 2339 | D | 323 584-3500 | 2771 |
| Jd/Cmc Inc | 2339 | E | 818 767-2260 | 2772 |
| JT Design Studio Inc (PA) | 2339 | E | 213 891-1500 | 2777 |
| Klk Forte Industry Inc (PA) | 2339 | E | 323 415-9181 | 2781 |
| L&L Manufacturing Co Inc | 2339 | B | | 2784 |
| Lee Thomas Inc (PA) | 2339 | E | 310 532-7560 | 2786 |
| Lefty Production Co LLC | 2339 | E | 323 515-9266 | 2787 |
| MGT Industries Inc (PA) | 2339 | D | 310 516-5900 | 2791 |
| Monterey Canyon LLC (PA) | 2339 | D | 213 741-0209 | 2792 |
| New Fashion Products Inc | 2339 | C | 310 354-0090 | 2793 |
| Nexxen Apparel Inc (PA) | 2339 | F | 323 267-9900 | 2795 |
| Pierre Mitri (PA) | 2339 | F | 213 747-1838 | 2799 |
| Piet Retief Inc | 2339 | E | 323 732-8312 | 2800 |
| Rhapsody Clothing Inc | 2339 | D | 213 614-8887 | 2804 |
| Solow | 2339 | E | 323 664-7772 | 2808 |
| Splits 59 LLC | 2339 | F | 310 827-5200 | 2809 |
| Tcj Manufacturing LLC | 2339 | E | 213 488-8400 | 2812 |
| Toska Inc | 2339 | F | 213 746-0088 | 2817 |
| Treivush Industries Inc | 2339 | D | 213 745-7774 | 2818 |
| YMi Jeanswear Inc | 2339 | D | 213 746-6681 | 2823 |
| Delta Galil USA Inc | 2341 | B | 213 488-4859 | 2829 |
| Guess Inc (PA) | 2341 | A | 213 765-3100 | 2830 |
| Honest Company Inc (PA) | 2341 | C | 310 917-9199 | 2831 |
| Spicy Chix Inc | 2341 | F | 562 293-7690 | 2835 |
| Foh Group Inc (PA) | 2342 | E | | 2837 |
| Agron Inc (PA) | 2353 | D | 310 473-7223 | 2840 |
| Kwdz Manufacturing LLC (PA) | 2361 | D | 323 526-3526 | 2855 |
| Misyd Corp (PA) | 2361 | D | 213 742-1800 | 2857 |
| Baby Guess Inc | 2369 | E | 213 765-3100 | 2858 |
| Kharma Clothing LLC | 2369 | F | 323 494-7705 | 2863 |
| Un Deux Trois Inc (PA) | 2369 | E | 323 588-1067 | 2868 |
| Orbita Corp (PA) | 2381 | E | 213 746-4783 | 2871 |
| Chrome Hearts LLC (PA) | 2386 | E | 323 957-7544 | 2875 |
| App Winddown LLC (HQ) | 2389 | C | | 2890 |
| B2 Apparel Inc | 2389 | F | 323 233-0044 | 2891 |
| Califrnia Cstume Cllctions Inc (PA) | 2389 | B | 323 262-8383 | 2892 |
| Conquer Nation Inc | 2389 | C | 310 651-5555 | 2894 |
| Gilli Inc | 2389 | F | 213 744-9808 | 2900 |
| Havuni LLC | 2389 | E | 917 428-1183 | 2901 |
| Los Angeles Apparel Inc (PA) | 2389 | D | 213 275-3120 | 2904 |
| Mdc Interior Solutions LLC | 2389 | E | 800 621-4006 | 2905 |
| Amtex California Inc | 2391 | E | 323 859-2200 | 2914 |
| Matteo LLC | 2392 | E | 213 617-2813 | 2937 |
| Universal Cushion Company Inc (PA) | 2392 | E | 323 887-8000 | 2951 |
| Outdoor Rcrtion Group Hldngs L (PA) | 2393 | E | 323 226-0830 | 2960 |
| Gma Cover Corp | 2394 | C | | 2975 |
| Pacific Play Tents Inc | 2394 | F | 323 269-0431 | 2980 |
| American Quilting Company Inc | 2395 | F | 323 233-2500 | 2988 |
| Atelier Luxury Group LLC | 2396 | E | 310 751-2444 | 3001 |
| Security Textile Corporation | 2396 | E | 213 747-2673 | 3016 |
| Tesca Usa Inc | 2396 | E | 586 991-0744 | 3019 |
| Scottex Inc | 2399 | E | 310 516-1411 | 3035 |
| Wessco Intl Ltd A Cal Ltd Prtn (PA) | 2399 | D | 310 477-4272 | 3039 |
| Young Sung (usa) Inc | 2399 | F | 213 427-2580 | 3040 |
| Fulghum Fibres Inc (HQ) | 2421 | F | 706 651-1000 | 3069 |
| Charles Gemeiner Cabinets | 2431 | F | 323 299-8696 | 3119 |
| Bromack Company | 2434 | E | 323 227-5000 | 3222 |
| Mikada Cabinets LLC | 2434 | D | 713 681-6116 | 3256 |
| Ultra Built Kitchens Inc | 2434 | E | 323 232-3362 | 3276 |
| Arnies Supply Service Ltd (PA) | 2448 | E | 323 263-1696 | 3333 |
| Pallet Masters Inc | 2448 | D | 323 758-1713 | 3353 |
| Marge Carson Inc (PA) | 2512 | D | 626 571-1111 | 3480 |
| Minson Corporation | 2512 | E | 323 513-1041 | 3483 |
| Sofa U Love LLC (PA) | 2512 | E | 323 464-3397 | 3490 |
| Stitch Industries Inc | 2512 | E | 888 282-0842 | 3492 |
| A A Cater Truck Mfg Co Inc | 2514 | E | 323 233-2343 | 3496 |
| Wesley Allen Inc | 2514 | E | 323 231-4275 | 3516 |
| Cristal Materials Inc | 2515 | F | 323 855-1688 | 3523 |
| Don Alderson Associates Inc | 2519 | E | 310 837-5141 | 3554 |
| Standdesk Inc | 2519 | E | 213 634-0665 | 3558 |
| Angell & Giroux Inc | 2522 | E | 323 269-8596 | 3592 |
| Versa Products (PA) | 2522 | C | 310 353-7100 | 3609 |
| Borodian Inc (PA) | 2541 | F | 323 225-0500 | 3647 |
| LA Cabinet & Millwork Inc | 2541 | E | 323 227-5000 | 3663 |
| Felbro Inc | 2542 | C | 323 263-8686 | 3686 |
| Pacific Manufacturing MGT Inc | 2542 | E | 323 263-9000 | 3700 |
| Salsbury Industries Inc | 2542 | D | 323 846-6700 | 3706 |
| Hd Window Fashions Inc (DH) | 2591 | B | 213 749-6333 | 3720 |
| 6th Street Partners LLC | 2599 | E | 213 377-5277 | 3732 |
| David Haid | 2599 | E | 323 752-8096 | 3736 |
| Ptm Images LLC | 2599 | E | 310 881-8053 | 3747 |
| New Green Day LLC | 2611 | E | 323 566-7603 | 3758 |
| Boise Cascade Company | 2621 | F | 310 815-2200 | 3761 |
| D D Office Products Inc | 2621 | F | 323 582-3400 | 3765 |
| Advance Paper Box Company | 2653 | C | 323 750-2550 | 3818 |
| City Paper Box Co | 2653 | E | 323 231-5990 | 3831 |
| Plastopan Industries Inc (PA) | 2655 | E | 323 231-2225 | 3908 |
| Vision Envelope & Prtg Co Inc (PA) | 2677 | E | 310 324-7062 | 4013 |
| Argonaut | 2711 | E | 310 822-1629 | 4066 |
| Associated Students UCLA | 2711 | C | 310 825-2787 | 4070 |
| California Community News LLC (DH) | 2711 | B | 626 388-1017 | 4080 |
| California Newsppr Svc Bur Inc | 2711 | E | 213 229-5500 | 4084 |
| Daily Journal Corporation | 2711 | D | 213 229-5300 | 4101 |
| Gannett Stllite Info Ntwrk LLC | 2711 | F | 310 846-5870 | 4116 |
| Grace Communications Inc (PA) | 2711 | E | 213 628-4384 | 4123 |
| Investors Business Daily Inc (HQ) | 2711 | C | 800 831-2525 | 4136 |
| Joongangilbo Usa Inc (DH) | 2711 | C | 213 368-2512 | 4140 |
| La Opinion LP (HQ) | 2711 | D | 213 891-9191 | 4143 |
| La Opinion LP | 2711 | B | 213 896-2222 | 4144 |
| La Times | 2711 | D | 213 237-2279 | 4145 |
| Los Angeles Sentinel Inc | 2711 | D | 323 299-3800 | 4150 |
| Runway Beauty Inc | 2711 | F | 844 240-2250 | 4185 |
| The Korea Times Los Angeles Inc (PA) | 2711 | C | 323 692-2000 | 4208 |
| Thewrap | 2711 | E | 424 273-4787 | 4210 |
| Tidings | 2711 | E | 213 637-7360 | 4211 |
| Tribe Mdia Corp A Cal Nnprfit | 2711 | E | 213 368-1661 | 4214 |
| Arsenic Inc | 2721 | E | 310 701-7559 | 4230 |
| Cbj LP | 2721 | E | 323 549-5225 | 4236 |
| Cbj LP | 2721 | D | 818 676-1750 | 4237 |
| Flaunt Magazine | 2721 | F | 323 836-1044 | 4256 |
| Graphic Film Group LLC (PA) | 2721 | E | 310 887-6330 | 4261 |
| ID Matters LLC | 2721 | E | 323 822-4800 | 4265 |
| Los Angeles Bus Jurnl Assoc | 2721 | E | 323 549-5225 | 4273 |
| Mnm Corporation (PA) | 2721 | E | 213 627-3737 | 4279 |
| Model Lyfe | 2721 | E | 224 325-5933 | 4280 |
| Orange Coast Magazine LLC | 2721 | D | 949 862-1133 | 4284 |
| Playboy Enterprises Inc | 2721 | D | 310 424-1800 | 4288 |
| Recruitment Services Inc | 2721 | E | 213 364-1960 | 4293 |
| Access Books | 2731 | C | 310 920-1694 | 4310 |
| Judy O Productions Inc | 2731 | E | 323 938-8513 | 4334 |
| Practice Management Info Corp (PA) | 2731 | F | 323 954-0224 | 4341 |
| Quite Powerful Enterprises LLC | 2731 | F | 800 782-0915 | 4342 |

Employee Codes: A=Over 500 employees, B=251-500, C=101-250, D=51-100, E=20-50, F=10-19, G=1-9

# LOS ANGELES, CA — GEOGRAPHIC SECTION

| Company | SIC | EMP | PHONE | ENTRY# |
|---|---|---|---|---|
| 418 Media LLC | 2741 | E | 614 350-3960 | 4357 |
| Acceptedcom LLC | 2741 | E | 310 815-9553 | 4358 |
| American Soc Cmpsers Athors Pb | 2741 | C | 323 883-1000 | 4364 |
| Brud Inc | 2741 | F | 310 806-2283 | 4373 |
| Good Worldwide LLC | 2741 | E | 323 206-6495 | 4407 |
| Jungotv LLC | 2741 | D | 650 207-6227 | 4423 |
| Netmarble Us Inc | 2741 | D | 213 222-7712 | 4437 |
| Planetizen Inc | 2741 | E | 877 260-7526 | 4449 |
| Playboy Enterprises Intl Inc | 2741 | D | 310 424-1800 | 4450 |
| Pollstar LLC | 2741 | E | 559 271-7900 | 4451 |
| Riye Group LLC | 2741 | E | 820 203-9215 | 4462 |
| Songs Music Publishing LLC | 2741 | F | 323 939-3511 | 4466 |
| Studio Systems Inc (PA) | 2741 | E | 323 634-3400 | 4472 |
| Techture Inc | 2741 | E | 323 347-6209 | 4477 |
| Thomson Reuters Corporation | 2741 | E | 310 287-2360 | 4480 |
| Warner Chappell Music Inc (DH) | 2741 | C | 310 441-8600 | 4490 |
| Wb Music Corp (DH) | 2741 | C | 310 441-8600 | 4491 |
| Webtoon Entertainment Inc (PA) | 2741 | A | 323 297-3410 | 4492 |
| Anderson La Inc | 2752 | D | 323 460-4115 | 4514 |
| Apple Graphics Inc | 2752 | E | 626 301-4287 | 4516 |
| Boss Litho Inc | 2752 | E | 626 912-7088 | 4534 |
| Cdr Graphics Inc (PA) | 2752 | E | 310 474-7600 | 4544 |
| Digital Printing Systems Inc (PA) | 2752 | D | 626 815-1888 | 4590 |
| Ikonick LLC | 2752 | E | 516 680-7765 | 4636 |
| Ink & Color Inc | 2752 | E | 310 280-6060 | 4644 |
| LA Printing & Graphics Inc | 2752 | E | 310 527-4526 | 4669 |
| Madisn/Grham Clor Graphics Inc | 2752 | B | 323 261-7171 | 4685 |
| ONeil Digital Solutions LLC | 2752 | C | 310 448-6407 | 4712 |
| Ready Industries Inc | 2752 | F | 213 749-2041 | 4750 |
| Red Brick Corporation | 2752 | F | 323 549-9444 | 4751 |
| Sedas Printing Inc | 2752 | F | 323 469-1034 | 4760 |
| ONeil Capital Management Inc | 2754 | C | 310 448-6400 | 4825 |
| Stuart F Cooper Co | 2754 | C | 213 747-7141 | 4828 |
| American Zabin Intl Inc | 2759 | E | 213 746-3770 | 4841 |
| Consolidated Graphics Inc | 2759 | C | 323 460-4115 | 4865 |
| CR & A Custom Apparel Inc | 2759 | E | 213 749-4440 | 4868 |
| Fabfad LLC | 2759 | F | 213 488-0456 | 4879 |
| RJ Acquisition Corp (PA) | 2759 | C | 323 318-1107 | 4954 |
| The/Studio | 2759 | E | 213 233-1633 | 4973 |
| Kater-Crafts Incorporated | 2789 | E | 562 692-0665 | 5012 |
| Gemini GEL Llc | 2796 | E | 323 651-0513 | 5025 |
| Oxerra Americas LLC | 2816 | D | 323 269-7311 | 5062 |
| Merelex Corporation | 2819 | E | 310 208-0551 | 5101 |
| Huntsman Advanced Materials AM | 2821 | C | 818 265-7221 | 5160 |
| Huntsman Advnced Mtls Amrcas L | 2821 | E | 818 265-7302 | 5161 |
| Ineos Composites Us LLC | 2821 | D | 323 767-1300 | 5165 |
| Chromadex Corporation (PA) | 2833 | E | 310 388-6706 | 5236 |
| Mro Maryruth LLC | 2833 | C | 424 343-6650 | 5249 |
| Ron Teeguarden Enterprises Inc (PA) | 2833 | E | 323 556-8188 | 5267 |
| Tikun Olam Adelanto LLC | 2833 | E | 833 468-4586 | 5278 |
| Abraxis Bioscience LLC (DH) | 2834 | C | 800 564-0216 | 5293 |
| Baxalta US Inc | 2834 | A | 818 240-5600 | 5355 |
| Cougar Biotechnology Inc | 2834 | D | 310 943-8040 | 5414 |
| Dnib Unwind Inc | 2834 | C | 213 617-2717 | 5428 |
| Hylands Consumer Health Inc (PA) | 2834 | B | 310 768-0700 | 5482 |
| Murad LLC | 2834 | D | 310 906-3100 | 5559 |
| Natals Inc | 2834 | C | 323 475-6033 | 5561 |
| Puma Biotechnology Inc (PA) | 2834 | C | 424 248-6500 | 5617 |
| Renovaro Inc (PA) | 2834 | E | 305 918-1980 | 5635 |
| Soft Gel Technologies Inc (HQ) | 2834 | E | 323 726-0700 | 5666 |
| Zp Opco Inc | 2834 | E | 510 745-1200 | 5725 |
| Response Genetics Inc | 2835 | C | 323 224-3900 | 5779 |
| Armata Pharmaceuticals Inc (PA) | 2836 | E | 310 665-2928 | 5796 |
| Clarus Therapeutics Inc | 2836 | F | 847 562-4300 | 5819 |
| Grifols Biologicals LLC (DH) | 2836 | D | 323 225-2221 | 5833 |
| Sustainable Care Company Inc | 2842 | E | 310 210-7090 | 5931 |
| Kenvue Brands LLC | 2844 | C | 310 642-1150 | 5999 |
| Merle Norman Cosmetics Inc (PA) | 2844 | B | 310 641-3000 | 6007 |
| Pacific World Corporation (PA) | 2844 | D | 949 598-2400 | 6016 |
| Shani Darden Skincare Inc | 2844 | E | 310 745-3150 | 6036 |
| Xavier Group | 2844 | F | 844 928-4378 | 6060 |
| Ennis Traffic Safety Solutions | 2851 | E | 323 758-1147 | 6083 |
| Monopole Inc | 2851 | F | 818 500-8585 | 6096 |
| Paint-Chem Inc | 2851 | F | 213 747-7725 | 6099 |
| Rentech Ntrgn Pasadena Spa LLC | 2873 | E | 310 571-9805 | 6181 |
| CTS Cement Manufacturing Corp | 2891 | E | 310 472-4004 | 6223 |
| Stic-Adhesive Products Co Inc | 2891 | C | 323 268-2956 | 6248 |
| Gans Ink and Supply Co Inc (PA) | 2893 | E | 323 264-2200 | 6254 |
| American Consumer Products LLC | 2899 | D | 323 289-6610 | 6267 |
| Rentech Inc (PA) | 2999 | E | 310 571-9800 | 6403 |
| Ames Rubber Mfg Co Inc | 3069 | E | 818 240-9313 | 6484 |
| Exrox Inc | 3069 | E | 213 536-5290 | 6492 |
| Falcon Waterfree Tech LLC (HQ) | 3069 | E | 310 209-7250 | 6493 |
| Mercury Plastics Inc | 3081 | D | 323 264-2400 | 6562 |
| Poly Pak America Inc | 3081 | D | 323 264-2400 | 6567 |
| J-M Manufacturing Company Inc (PA) | 3084 | E | 310 693-8200 | 6598 |
| Pw Eagle Inc | 3084 | A | 800 621-4404 | 6601 |
| Dial Industries Inc | 3089 | D | 323 263-6878 | 6802 |
| Dial Industries Inc (PA) | 3089 | D | 323 263-6878 | 6803 |
| Housewares International Inc | 3089 | E | 323 581-3000 | 6859 |
| Jet Plastics (PA) | 3089 | E | 323 268-6706 | 6876 |
| Plastique Unique Inc | 3089 | F | 310 839-3968 | 6969 |
| Plastpro 2000 Inc (PA) | 3089 | C | 310 693-8600 | 6971 |
| Rehrig Pacific Company (HQ) | 3089 | C | 323 262-5145 | 6999 |
| Stone Canyon Industries LLC | 3089 | A | 310 570-4869 | 7045 |
| La La Land Production & Design | 3111 | E | 323 406-9223 | 7088 |
| Allbirds Inc | 3143 | F | 213 374-2354 | 7104 |
| Millennial Brands LLC | 3144 | E | 925 230-0617 | 7117 |
| Surgeon Worldwide Inc | 3144 | E | 707 501-7962 | 7118 |
| Jan-Al Innerprizes Inc | 3161 | E | 323 260-7212 | 7135 |
| Sbnw LLC (PA) | 3171 | C | 213 234-5122 | 7146 |
| Malibu Leather Inc | 3172 | C | 310 985-0707 | 7150 |
| Omar Leather Co | 3199 | F | 323 227-5220 | 7159 |
| Aputure Imaging Industries | 3229 | E | 626 295-6133 | 7190 |
| Alan Lem & Co Inc | 3231 | F | 310 538-4282 | 7210 |
| Industrial Glass Products Inc | 3231 | F | 323 526-7125 | 7227 |
| Judson Studios Inc | 3231 | E | 323 255-0131 | 7229 |
| Tubular Specialties Mfg Inc | 3261 | D | 310 515-4801 | 7280 |
| McFiebow Inc | 3272 | E | 310 327-7474 | 7355 |
| Sissell Bros | 3272 | E | 323 261-0106 | 7391 |
| National Ready Mixed Con Co | 3273 | F | 323 245-5539 | 7475 |
| Best-Way Marble & Tile Co Inc | 3281 | E | 323 266-6794 | 7534 |
| Interstate Steel Center Co Inc | 3312 | E | 323 583-0855 | 7617 |
| National Wire and Cable Corporation | 3315 | E | 323 225-5611 | 7648 |
| Roscoe Moss Manufacturing Co (PA) | 3317 | D | 323 261-4185 | 7670 |
| David H Fell & Co Inc (PA) | 3341 | E | 323 722-9992 | 7718 |
| Darfield Industries Inc (PA) | 3354 | F | 818 247-8350 | 7736 |
| Sun Valley Products Inc | 3354 | E | 818 247-8350 | 7749 |
| Sun Valley Products Inc (HQ) | 3354 | E | 818 247-8350 | 7750 |
| Arcadia Products LLC (HQ) | 3355 | C | 323 771-9819 | 7757 |
| P Kay Metal Inc (PA) | 3356 | E | 323 585-5058 | 7766 |
| Victor Wire & Cable Inc | 3357 | F | 310 842-9933 | 7798 |
| Wire Technology Corporation | 3357 | E | 310 635-6935 | 7802 |
| Pioneer Diecasters Inc | 3363 | F | 323 245-6561 | 7818 |
| Cast Partner Inc | 3369 | E | 323 876-9000 | 7858 |
| Interntnal Mtllrgical Svcs LLC | 3398 | E | 310 645-7300 | 7886 |
| Micro Surface Engr Inc (PA) | 3399 | E | 323 582-7348 | 7908 |
| Augerscope Inc | 3423 | E |  | 7947 |
| Doval Industries Inc | 3429 | D | 323 226-0335 | 7994 |
| Commercial Shtmtl Works Inc | 3441 | E | 213 748-7321 | 8122 |
| Medsco Fabrication & Dist Inc | 3441 | D | 323 263-0511 | 8181 |
| Zia Aamir | 3441 | E | 714 337-7861 | 8249 |
| Active Window Products | 3442 | D | 323 245-5185 | 8251 |
| Hehr International Inc | 3442 | C | 323 663-1261 | 8268 |
| Basic Industries Intl Inc (PA) | 3443 | E | 951 226-1500 | 8301 |
| Roy E Hanson Jr Mfg (PA) | 3443 | D | 213 747-7514 | 8331 |
| S Bravo Systems Inc | 3443 | E | 323 888-4133 | 8333 |
| Able Sheet Metal Inc (PA) | 3444 | E | 323 269-2181 | 8359 |
| Aero Precision Engineering | 3444 | E | 310 642-9747 | 8367 |
| Precision Steel Products Inc | 3444 | E | 310 523-2002 | 8543 |
| King Wire Partitions Inc | 3449 | E | 323 256-4848 | 8702 |
| Power Fasteners Inc | 3452 | E | 323 232-4362 | 8765 |
| Bandel Mfg Inc | 3469 | E | 818 246-7493 | 8820 |
| Larry Spun Products Inc | 3469 | E | 323 881-6300 | 8859 |
| Accurate Plating Company | 3471 | E | 323 268-8567 | 8906 |
| Alco Plating Corp (PA) | 3471 | E | 213 749-7561 | 8910 |
| Alpha Polishing Corporation (PA) | 3471 | D | 323 263-7593 | 8916 |
| Anodizing Industries Inc | 3471 | E | 323 227-4916 | 8920 |
| Barry Avenue Plating Co Inc | 3471 | D | 310 478-0078 | 8929 |
| Bronze-Way Plating Corporation (PA) | 3471 | E | 323 266-6933 | 8935 |
| Chromal Plating Company | 3471 | E | 323 222-0119 | 8940 |
| Electrolizing Inc | 3471 | E | 213 749-7876 | 8954 |
| Genes Plating Works Inc (PA) | 3471 | E | 323 269-8748 | 8963 |
| George Industries (HQ) | 3471 | E | 323 264-6660 | 8964 |
| Old Spc Inc | 3471 | E | 310 533-0748 | 8990 |
| Pentrate Metal Processing | 3471 | E | 323 269-2121 | 8994 |
| Ravlich Enterprises LLC | 3471 | E | 310 533-0748 | 9003 |
| V & M Company | 3471 | E | 310 532-5633 | 9029 |
| Adfa Incorporated | 3479 | E | 213 627-8004 | 9037 |
| Aircoat Inc | 3479 | F | 310 527-2258 | 9041 |
| Certified Enameling Inc (PA) | 3479 | D | 323 264-4403 | 9057 |
| NM Holdco Inc | 3479 | C | 323 663-3971 | 9096 |
| Tortoise Industries Inc | 3479 | E | 323 258-7776 | 9129 |
| American Spring Inc | 3493 | F | 310 324-2181 | 9172 |
| Bcc Dissolution Inc | 3498 | E | 323 583-3444 | 9251 |
| Edmund A Gray Co (PA) | 3498 | D | 213 625-0376 | 9257 |

Mergent email: customerrelations@mergent.com
2025 Harris California Manufacturers Directory
(P-0000) Products & Services Section entry number
(PA)=Parent Co (HQ)=Headquarters (DH)=Div Headquarters

# GEOGRAPHIC SECTION
## LOS ANGELES, CA

| | SIC | EMP | PHONE | ENTRY# |
|---|---|---|---|---|
| Flo-Mac Inc. | 3498 | F | 323 583-8751 | 9260 |
| PSM Industries Inc (PA) | 3499 | D | 888 663-8256 | 9297 |
| Vigilant Drone Defense Inc | 3499 | E | 424 275-8282 | 9302 |
| Mixmor Inc. | 3531 | F | 323 664-1941 | 9433 |
| Polyalloys Injected Metals Inc | 3532 | D | 310 715-9800 | 9449 |
| Elevator Research & Mfg Co | 3534 | F | 213 746-1914 | 9471 |
| Winter & Bain Mfg Inc (PA) | 3534 | F | 213 749-3568 | 9478 |
| Gleason Industrial Pdts Inc | 3537 | C | 574 533-1141 | 9519 |
| Avis Roto Die Co | 3544 | E | 323 255-7070 | 9602 |
| Idea Tooling and Engrg Inc | 3544 | D | 310 608-7488 | 9629 |
| Stadco (HQ) | 3545 | D | 323 227-8888 | 9699 |
| Old Country Millwork Inc (PA) | 3547 | E | 323 234-2940 | 9719 |
| Vest Tube LLC | 3547 | D | 800 421-6370 | 9720 |
| Ubtech Robotics Corp | 3556 | E | 213 261-7153 | 9748 |
| Food & Bev Innovations LLC | 3556 | F | 888 491-3772 | 9788 |
| Machine Building Spc Inc | 3556 | E | 323 666-8289 | 9804 |
| Meat Packers Butchers Sup Inc | 3556 | F | 323 268-8514 | 9805 |
| Avanzato Technology Corp | 3559 | E | 312 509-0506 | 9836 |
| Industrial Tools Inc | 3559 | E | 805 483-1111 | 9868 |
| Norchem Corporation (PA) | 3559 | E | 323 221-0221 | 9883 |
| Starco Enterprises Inc (PA) | 3559 | D | 323 266-7111 | 9901 |
| Mjw Inc | 3561 | D | 323 778-8900 | 9931 |
| Forward | 3568 | E | 310 962-2522 | 10068 |
| Allhealth | 3571 | E | 213 538-0762 | 10132 |
| Comexposium US LLC | 3577 | F | 310 598-1376 | 10349 |
| Efaxcom (DH) | 3577 | D | 323 817-3207 | 10359 |
| Magic Ram Inc | 3577 | F | 213 380-5555 | 10404 |
| Denim-Tech LLC | 3582 | D | 323 277-8998 | 10474 |
| City of Santa Monica | 3589 | C | 310 826-6712 | 10549 |
| Immotion Vr Ltd | 3599 | E | 818 813-3923 | 10883 |
| Tosco - Tool Specialty Company | 3599 | E | 323 232-3561 | 11147 |
| On-Line Power Incorporated (PA) | 3612 | E | 323 721-5017 | 11220 |
| W A Benjamin Electric Co | 3613 | E | 213 749-7731 | 11252 |
| Concurrent Holdings LLC | 3629 | A | 310 473-3065 | 11366 |
| IaMplus LLC | 3629 | D | 323 210-3852 | 11373 |
| Capital Brands Distribution L (PA) | 3634 | B | 800 523-5993 | 11402 |
| Alger-Triton Inc | 3645 | E | 310 229-9500 | 11486 |
| Alcon Lighting Inc | 3646 | E | 310 733-1248 | 11518 |
| Prudential Lighting Corp (PA) | 3646 | C | 213 477-1694 | 11553 |
| AMP Plus Inc | 3647 | D | 323 231-2600 | 11571 |
| Eema Industries Inc | 3648 | E | 323 904-0200 | 11591 |
| Absolute Usa Inc | 3651 | E | 213 744-0044 | 11631 |
| Mr Dj Inc | 3651 | E | 213 744-0044 | 11679 |
| Vizio Inc | 3651 | C | 213 746-7730 | 11713 |
| Capitol-Emi Music Inc | 3652 | A | 323 462-6252 | 11723 |
| CMH Records Inc | 3652 | E | 323 663-8098 | 11725 |
| Eeg 3 LLC (DH) | 3663 | C | | 11848 |
| Katz Millennium Sls & Mktg Inc | 3663 | C | 323 966-5066 | 11871 |
| Ophir Rf Inc | 3663 | E | 310 306-5556 | 11908 |
| Silvus Technologies Inc (PA) | 3663 | E | 310 479-3333 | 11947 |
| Bitmax LLC (PA) | 3669 | E | 323 978-7878 | 11984 |
| Dcx-Chol Enterprises Inc | 3671 | F | 310 516-1692 | 12030 |
| ABB Enterprise Software Inc | 3674 | D | 213 743-4819 | 12268 |
| Micross Holdings Inc | 3674 | D | 215 997-3200 | 12584 |
| A M I/Coast Magnetics Inc | 3677 | E | 323 936-6188 | 12825 |
| Crucial Power Products | 3679 | F | 323 721-5017 | 12949 |
| Dcx-Chol Enterprises Inc (PA) | 3679 | D | 310 516-1692 | 12955 |
| Ocm Pe Holdings LP | 3679 | A | 213 830-6213 | 13052 |
| Teledyne Technologies Inc | 3679 | B | 310 822-8229 | 13106 |
| Electrical Rebuilders Sls Inc | 3694 | D | 323 249-7545 | 13169 |
| Gores Radio Holdings LLC | 3699 | D | 310 209-3010 | 13245 |
| Flyer Defense LLC | 3711 | D | 310 324-5650 | 13353 |
| Xos Fleet Inc (HQ) | 3711 | E | 818 316-1890 | 13398 |
| Ctbla Inc | 3713 | D | 323 276-1933 | 13405 |
| Vahe Enterprises Inc | 3713 | E | 323 235-6657 | 13434 |
| C R Laurence Co Inc (HQ) | 3714 | B | 323 588-1281 | 13468 |
| Grover Products Co | 3714 | D | 323 263-9981 | 13510 |
| Leet Technology Inc | 3714 | E | 877 238-4492 | 13529 |
| Tasker Metal Products | 3714 | F | 213 765-5400 | 13581 |
| Xos Inc (PA) | 3714 | E | 818 316-1890 | 13608 |
| Worldwide Aeros Corp | 3721 | D | 818 344-3999 | 13698 |
| Coating Specialties Inc | 3728 | F | 310 639-6900 | 13810 |
| Dynamation Research Inc | 3728 | F | 909 864-2310 | 13833 |
| Helicopter Tech Co Ltd Partnr | 3728 | E | 310 523-2750 | 13858 |
| Gambol Industries Inc | 3732 | E | 562 901-2470 | 14034 |
| Proto Homes LLC | 3792 | E | 310 271-7544 | 14123 |
| L3harris Technologies Inc | 3812 | E | 310 481-6000 | 14206 |
| Mapquest Holdings LLC | 3812 | B | 310 256-4882 | 14219 |
| Northrop Grumman Systems Corp | 3812 | B | 310 556-4911 | 14268 |
| TMC Ice Protection Systems LLC (PA) | 3812 | E | 951 677-6934 | 14322 |
| Eti Systems | 3823 | D | 310 684-3664 | 14410 |
| ITI Electro-Optic Corporation (PA) | 3823 | E | 310 445-8900 | 14425 |
| ITI Electro-Optic Corporation | 3823 | E | 310 312-4526 | 14426 |
| Pressure Profile Systems Inc | 3823 | F | 310 641-8100 | 14444 |
| Ashland Group LLC | 3825 | F | 213 749-3709 | 14498 |
| First Legal Network | 3825 | C | 213 250-1111 | 14527 |
| Taseon Inc | 3825 | F | 408 240-7800 | 14589 |
| Periscope LLC | 3827 | E | 323 327-5115 | 14812 |
| Barksdale Inc (DH) | 3829 | D | 323 583-6243 | 14848 |
| Bruin Biometrics LLC | 3841 | F | 310 268-9494 | 15022 |
| Siemens Hlthcare Dgnostics Inc | 3841 | D | 310 645-8200 | 15256 |
| Dynamics Orthtics Prsthtics In | 3842 | E | 213 383-9212 | 15336 |
| Hanger Prsthtics Orthtics W In | 3842 | D | 213 250-7850 | 15357 |
| Cyber Medical Imaging Inc | 3843 | E | 888 937-9729 | 15444 |
| Sprintray Inc (PA) | 3843 | D | 800 914-8004 | 15484 |
| Neurasignal Inc | 3845 | E | 877 638-7251 | 15564 |
| March Vision Care Inc | 3851 | E | 310 665-0975 | 15608 |
| Anschutz Film Group LLC (HQ) | 3861 | E | 310 887-1000 | 15628 |
| Carolense Entrmt Group LLC | 3861 | D | 405 493-1120 | 15632 |
| Cds California LLC | 3861 | E | 818 766-5000 | 15633 |
| Fpc Inc | 3861 | E | 323 468-5778 | 15639 |
| Freestyle Filmworks LLC | 3861 | F | 818 660-2888 | 15640 |
| Panavision Inc | 3861 | E | 323 464-3800 | 15658 |
| Travelling Pic Show Company | 3861 | F | 323 769-1115 | 15670 |
| Americas Gold Inc | 3911 | E | 213 688-4904 | 15682 |
| Gem Tech Jewelry Corporation | 3911 | E | 213 623-2222 | 15691 |
| Giving Keys Inc | 3911 | E | 213 935-8791 | 15692 |
| Kesmor Associates | 3911 | E | 213 629-2300 | 15695 |
| LA Gem and Jewelry Design | 3911 | D | 213 488-1290 | 15698 |
| LA Gem and Jewelry Design (PA) | 3911 | E | 213 488-1290 | 15699 |
| Exploding Kittens LLC | 3944 | E | 310 788-8699 | 15747 |
| Gamefam Inc | 3944 | F | 310 200-6623 | 15750 |
| Ninja Jump Inc | 3944 | D | 323 255-5418 | 15762 |
| Addaday Inc | 3949 | E | 424 465-9106 | 15774 |
| Martin Sports Inc (PA) | 3949 | E | 509 529-2554 | 15839 |
| Rpsz Construction LLC | 3949 | C | 314 677-5831 | 15848 |
| Skintight | 3949 | E | 310 829-4120 | 15857 |
| Standard Sales Llc (PA) | 3949 | E | 323 269-0510 | 15858 |
| Thousand LLC | 3949 | E | 310 745-0110 | 15865 |
| Catame Inc (PA) | 3965 | F | 213 749-2610 | 15909 |
| Brush Research Mfg Co Inc | 3991 | C | 323 261-2193 | 15926 |
| La6721 LLC | 3993 | E | 323 484-4070 | 16000 |
| Standardvision LLC | 3993 | E | 323 222-3630 | 16045 |
| Accurate Staging Mfg Inc (PA) | 3999 | F | 310 324-1040 | 16080 |
| Ata-Boy Inc | 3999 | F | 323 644-0117 | 16091 |
| Beauty Tent Inc | 3999 | E | 323 717-7131 | 16095 |
| Brybradan Inc | 3999 | E | 323 230-8604 | 16101 |
| Family Industries LLC | 3999 | F | 619 306-1035 | 16128 |
| Greneker LLC | 3999 | E | 323 263-9000 | 16139 |
| L A Hq Inc | 3999 | E | 310 880-7433 | 16165 |
| Manufactur | 3999 | E | 213 613-1246 | 16176 |
| PF Candle Co | 3999 | E | 323 284-8431 | 16202 |
| Reaps Company LLC | 3999 | E | 212 256-1186 | 16213 |
| Shapell Industries | 3999 | F | 323 655-7330 | 16228 |
| Silvestri Studio Inc (PA) | 3999 | D | 323 277-4420 | 16229 |
| Sparks Exhbits Envrnments Corp | 3999 | E | 562 941-0101 | 16237 |
| Forrest Group LLC (PA) | 4111 | D | 619 808-9798 | 16274 |
| Edmund A Gray Co | 4225 | E | 213 625-2725 | 16288 |
| Mulholland Brothers | 4225 | E | 510 280-5485 | 16289 |
| Unified Grocers Inc | 4225 | C | 323 232-6124 | 16292 |
| Made Media LLC | 4899 | E | 866 263-6233 | 16338 |
| Phyllis Morris Originals (PA) | 5021 | F | 310 289-6868 | 16418 |
| AAA Electric Motor Sales & Svc | 5063 | F | 213 749-2367 | 16638 |
| Eaton Aerospace LLC | 5063 | B | 818 409-0200 | 16650 |
| Calrad Electronics Inc | 5065 | F | 323 465-2131 | 16694 |
| Mtroiz International | 5065 | E | 661 998-8013 | 16724 |
| Western Refining Inc | 5084 | D | 323 264-8500 | 16860 |
| Duhig and Co Inc | 5085 | E | | 16873 |
| Banzai | 5092 | F | 310 231-7292 | 16943 |
| 75s Corp | 5093 | E | 323 234-7708 | 16955 |
| C&C Jewelry Mfg Inc | 5094 | D | 213 623-6800 | 16966 |
| Mizari Enterprises Inc (PA) | 5099 | E | 323 549-9400 | 16981 |
| Roland Corporation US (HQ) | 5099 | C | 323 890-3700 | 16986 |
| E & S Paper Co | 5113 | E | 310 538-8700 | 16999 |
| Oak Paper Products Co LLC (PA) | 5113 | C | 323 268-0507 | 17003 |
| Dhouse Brands Inc | 5122 | E | 213 291-7576 | 17037 |
| Glamour Industries Co (PA) | 5122 | C | 323 728-2999 | 17038 |
| Morgan Fabrics Corporation (PA) | 5131 | D | 323 583-9981 | 17065 |
| Radix Textile Inc | 5131 | D | 323 234-1667 | 17066 |
| Rdmm Legacy Inc | 5131 | E | 323 232-2147 | 17067 |
| Damo Textile Inc | 5137 | E | 213 741-1323 | 17086 |
| Final Touch Apparel Inc | 5137 | E | 323 484-9621 | 17090 |
| Flirt Inc | 5137 | E | 213 748-4442 | 17091 |
| Aci International (PA) | 5139 | D | 310 889-3400 | 17107 |
| Afc Trading & Wholesale Inc | 5141 | E | 323 223-7738 | 17112 |
| Lunch Bunch Co | 5142 | F | 310 383-5233 | 17123 |

Employee Codes: A=Over 500 employees, B=251-500
C=101-250, D=51-100, E=20-50, F=10-19, G=1-9

## LOS ANGELES, CA

| | SIC | EMP | PHONE | ENTRY# |
|---|---|---|---|---|
| I Love Bracelets Inc. | 5145 | F | 310 839-5683 | 17146 |
| Superior Nut Co Inc. | 5145 | F | 323 223-2431 | 17150 |
| Prospect Enterprises Inc (PA) | 5146 | C | 213 599-5700 | 17158 |
| Al Foods Corporation (PA) | 5147 | E | 323 222-0827 | 17160 |
| App Wholesale LLC | 5149 | B | 323 980-8315 | 17174 |
| CJ America Inc (HQ) | 5149 | D | 213 338-2700 | 17182 |
| ESE INC. | 5169 | E | 213 614-0102 | 17244 |
| Berg Lacquer Co (PA) | 5198 | D | 323 261-8114 | 17281 |
| Bernet International Trdg LLC (PA) | 5199 | F | 310 873-0300 | 17286 |
| LAdesserts Inc. | 5311 | E | 323 588-2522 | 17363 |
| Super Center Concepts Inc. | 5411 | C | 323 241-6789 | 17387 |
| Sonora Bakery Inc. | 5461 | E | 323 269-2253 | 17421 |
| City Bean Inc. | 5499 | E | 323 734-0828 | 17424 |
| Al Asher & Sons Inc. | 5511 | E | 800 896-2480 | 17436 |
| Evgo Services LLC. | 5541 | B | 310 954-2900 | 17474 |
| 26 International Inc. | 5621 | F | 213 745-4224 | 17490 |
| Country Club Fashions Inc. | 5621 | E | 323 965-2707 | 17492 |
| Nasty Gal Inc (HQ) | 5621 | E | 213 542-3436 | 17495 |
| YMi Jeanswear Inc (PA) | 5621 | E | 323 581-7700 | 17498 |
| Aero Shade Co Inc (PA) | 5719 | E | 323 938-2314 | 17530 |
| Bebe Studio Inc. | 5719 | C | 213 362-2323 | 17531 |
| La Linen Inc. | 5719 | E | 213 745-4004 | 17536 |
| Linen Salvage Et Cie LLC. | 5719 | E | 323 904-3100 | 17537 |
| Calimex Deli. | 5812 | E | 323 261-7271 | 17568 |
| King Taco Restaurant Inc (PA) | 5812 | D | 323 266-3585 | 17592 |
| Pbf & E LLC. | 5812 | E | 213 427-0340 | 17600 |
| L & L Diamond Co. | 5944 | F | 213 622-5752 | 17647 |
| Robert Kaufman Co Inc (PA) | 5949 | C | 310 538-3482 | 17657 |
| Bu Ru LLC. | 5961 | F | 424 316-2878 | 17660 |
| Dr Harold Katz LLC. | 5961 | F | 323 993-8320 | 17663 |
| Spencer Forrest Inc. | 5961 | E | | 17675 |
| AAA Flag & Banner Mfg Co Inc (PA) | 5999 | C | 310 836-3200 | 17686 |
| Coway Usa Inc. | 5999 | E | 213 486-1600 | 17699 |
| Evoqua Water Technologies LLC. | 5999 | E | 213 748-8511 | 17702 |
| Petco Animal Sups Stores Inc. | 5999 | F | 323 852-1370 | 17716 |
| Security 20/20 Inc. | 5999 | F | 310 475-7780 | 17720 |
| Transom Capital Group LLC (PA) | 6799 | E | 424 293-2818 | 17758 |
| Corbis Images LLC (PA) | 7221 | E | 323 602-5700 | 17771 |
| Jet Fleet International Corp. | 7299 | E | 310 440-3820 | 17773 |
| Dg2 Worldwide Group LLC. | 7311 | E | 310 809-0899 | 17778 |
| Outfront Media LLC. | 7312 | E | 323 222-7171 | 17786 |
| Pannonia Group Inc. | 7319 | E | 310 846-4496 | 17791 |
| Concord Document Services Inc (PA) | 7334 | E | 213 745-3175 | 17806 |
| CP Document Technologies LLC. | 7334 | E | 310 575-6640 | 17807 |
| Cybercopy Inc (PA) | 7334 | F | 310 736-1001 | 17808 |
| Cinnabar. | 7336 | C | 818 842-8190 | 17822 |
| Digital Domain Media Group Inc. | 7336 | A | | 17826 |
| Bellrock Media Inc (PA) | 7371 | E | 310 315-2727 | 17886 |
| Boulevard Labs Inc. | 7371 | C | 323 310-2093 | 17890 |
| Cyberdefender Corporation. | 7371 | F | 323 449-0774 | 17905 |
| Daz Systems LLC. | 7371 | B | 310 640-1300 | 17908 |
| Myevaluationscom Inc. | 7371 | E | 646 422-0554 | 17952 |
| Adexa Inc (PA) | 7372 | E | 310 642-2100 | 18018 |
| Agencycom LLC. | 7372 | B | 415 817-3800 | 18027 |
| Cloud Sftwr Group Holdings Inc. | 7372 | F | 800 424-8749 | 18177 |
| Consensus Cloud Solutions Inc (PA) | 7372 | D | 323 860-9200 | 18200 |
| Data Appointment. | 7372 | E | 310 979-3282 | 18227 |
| Dave Inc (PA) | 7372 | B | 844 857-3283 | 18231 |
| Exactuals LLC. | 7372 | F | 310 689-7491 | 18302 |
| Flash Code Solutions LLC. | 7372 | F | 800 633-7467 | 18314 |
| Hoylu Inc. | 7372 | E | 213 440-2499 | 18391 |
| IaMplus Electronics Inc (PA) | 7372 | E | 323 210-3852 | 18398 |
| Invisble Prtection Systems Inc. | 7372 | E | 213 254-0463 | 18439 |
| Jurny Inc. | 7372 | E | 888 875-8769 | 18462 |
| Luna Imaging Inc. | 7372 | E | 323 908-1400 | 18507 |
| Mangomint Inc. | 7372 | E | 310 496-8677 | 18519 |
| Media Gobbler Inc. | 7372 | E | 323 203-3222 | 18534 |
| Mindshow Inc. | 7372 | D | 213 531-0277 | 18546 |
| Mitratech Holdings Inc. | 7372 | C | 323 964-0000 | 18551 |
| Mod2 Inc. | 7372 | F | 213 747-8424 | 18554 |
| Network Automation Inc. | 7372 | E | 213 738-1700 | 18579 |
| Output Inc. | 7372 | F | 888 803-3175 | 18650 |
| Relational Center. | 7372 | E | 323 935-1807 | 18730 |
| Riot Games Inc (DH) | 7372 | E | 310 207-1444 | 18741 |
| Shred Labs LLC. | 7372 | E | 781 285-8622 | 18788 |
| Slabs Inc. | 7372 | E | 424 289-0275 | 18796 |
| Spatial Labs Inc. | 7372 | E | 424 289-0275 | 18820 |
| Specialists In Cstm Sftwr Inc. | 7372 | E | 310 315-9660 | 18822 |
| Sugarsync Inc. | 7372 | E | 650 571-5105 | 18846 |
| System1 Inc (PA) | 7372 | B | 310 924-6037 | 18860 |
| Tagnos Inc. | 7372 | E | 949 305-0806 | 18861 |
| Thebrain Technologies LP. | 7372 | F | 310 751-5000 | 18878 |
| Visionary Vr Inc. | 7372 | E | 323 868-7443 | 18922 |
| Source It USA Inc. | 7373 | E | 714 318-4428 | 18993 |
| Urban Insight Inc. | 7373 | D | 213 792-2000 | 18998 |
| Honk Technologies Inc. | 7374 | E | 800 979-3162 | 19008 |
| Aimsight Solutions Inc. | 7379 | F | 310 313-0047 | 19025 |
| Bitscopic Inc. | 7379 | E | 650 503-3120 | 19030 |
| Elite Intractive Solutions Inc. | 7382 | E | 310 740-5426 | 19054 |
| Virtis-Us LLC (PA) | 7382 | F | 855 796-1457 | 19062 |
| Diba Fashions Inc. | 7389 | D | 323 232-3775 | 19087 |
| N Philanthropy LLC. | 7389 | F | 213 278-0754 | 19108 |
| Reason Foundation. | 7389 | E | 310 391-2245 | 19120 |
| Scottxscott Inc. | 7389 | E | 310 622-2775 | 19126 |
| XO BABYPLUTO FADED PARADISE XO. | 7389 | E | 650 750-5025 | 19145 |
| Universal Metal Plating (PA) | 7532 | F | 626 969-7931 | 19149 |
| Ruben & Leon Inc. | 7629 | E | 323 937-4445 | 19177 |
| Excel Picture Frames Inc. | 7699 | E | 323 231-0244 | 19257 |
| Fonco Creative Services. | 7812 | E | 415 254-5460 | 19294 |
| Yobs Technologies Inc. | 7812 | E | 213 713-3825 | 19300 |
| Alan Gordon Enterprises Inc. | 7819 | E | 323 466-3561 | 19301 |
| Targeted Medical Pharma Inc. | 8099 | F | 310 474-9809 | 19339 |
| Defense Specialists LLC. | 8111 | D | 818 270-7162 | 19340 |
| Greenwood Hall Inc. | 8299 | E | 310 905-8300 | 19351 |
| Braille Institute America Inc (PA) | 8322 | C | 323 663-1111 | 19354 |
| Self-Realization Fellowship Ch (PA) | 8661 | E | 323 225-2471 | 19371 |
| Fire Protection Group Amer Inc. | 8711 | E | 323 732-4200 | 19394 |
| Hatchbeauty Agency LLC (PA) | 8742 | E | 310 396-7070 | 19529 |
| Stone Canyon Inds Holdings LLC (PA) | 8742 | E | 424 316-2061 | 19538 |
| Coalition Technologies LLC. | 8743 | C | 310 827-3890 | 19549 |
| Lusive Decor. | 8748 | D | 323 227-9207 | 19565 |

### LOS BANOS, CA - Merced County

| | SIC | EMP | PHONE | ENTRY# |
|---|---|---|---|---|
| Azusa Rock LLC. | 1422 | E | 209 826-5066 | 297 |
| Los Banos Abattoir Co. | 2011 | E | 209 826-2212 | 605 |
| Romalv Group LLC. | 2022 | E | 213 272-1026 | 731 |
| Ingomar Packing Company LLC (PA) | 2033 | D | 209 826-9494 | 894 |
| Kagome Inc (HQ) | 2033 | E | 209 826-8850 | 897 |
| Morning Star Packing Co LP. | 2033 | E | 209 826-8000 | 905 |
| The Morning Star Packing Company L P (PA) | 2033 | E | 209 826-8000 | 932 |
| Cemex Corp. | 5032 | C | 800 992-3639 | 16469 |
| Triangle Rock Product Inc. | 5032 | C | 209 826-5066 | 16486 |

### LOS GATOS, CA - Santa Clara County

| | SIC | EMP | PHONE | ENTRY# |
|---|---|---|---|---|
| Einstein Noah Rest Group Inc. | 2022 | C | 408 358-5895 | 713 |

### LOS GATOS, CA - Santa Cruz County

| | SIC | EMP | PHONE | ENTRY# |
|---|---|---|---|---|
| David Bruce Winery Inc. | 2084 | F | 408 354-4214 | 1530 |
| Rhys Vineyards LLC. | 2084 | E | 650 419-2050 | 1722 |

### LOS GATOS, CA - Santa Clara County

| | SIC | EMP | PHONE | ENTRY# |
|---|---|---|---|---|
| Testarossa Vineyards LLC. | 2084 | E | 408 354-6150 | 1779 |
| Adaptive Insights LLC. | 2323 | E | 408 656-4229 | 2581 |
| Tscg Ventures Inc. | 2752 | E | 408 409-3274 | 4791 |
| Aridis Pharmaceuticals Inc (PA) | 2834 | E | 408 385-1742 | 5334 |
| Sly Trunk LLC. | 3161 | E | 408 540-6411 | 7140 |
| Assembly Systems (PA) | 3423 | E | 408 395-5313 | 7946 |

### LOS GATOS, CA - Santa Cruz County

| | SIC | EMP | PHONE | ENTRY# |
|---|---|---|---|---|
| South Skyline Firefighters. | 3569 | F | 408 354-0025 | 10115 |

### LOS GATOS, CA - Santa Clara County

| | SIC | EMP | PHONE | ENTRY# |
|---|---|---|---|---|
| Xicato Inc. | 3645 | E | 866 223-8395 | 11509 |
| Tascent Inc. | 3699 | F | 650 799-4611 | 13318 |
| Caci Photonics LLC. | 3812 | C | 408 560-3500 | 14165 |
| Sierra Nevada Corporation. | 3812 | C | 408 395-2004 | 14304 |
| Superior Sensor Technology Inc. | 3822 | E | 408 703-2950 | 14370 |
| Akura Medical Inc. | 3841 | E | 408 560-2500 | 14953 |
| Cirtec Medical Corp. | 3841 | D | 408 395-0443 | 15043 |
| Tenon Medical Inc. | 3841 | E | 408 649-5760 | 15280 |
| Tulavi Therapeutics Inc. | 3841 | E | 877 885-2841 | 15293 |
| Cryptic Studios Inc. | 3944 | D | 408 399-1969 | 15744 |
| Brightsign LLC (PA) | 3993 | D | 408 852-9263 | 15950 |
| Netflix Inc (PA) | 4841 | E | 408 540-3700 | 16333 |
| Shipscience LLC. | 4899 | F | 800 303-6644 | 16341 |
| Xactly Corporation (HQ) | 7371 | D | 408 977-3132 | 18000 |
| Facilitron Inc (PA) | 7372 | E | 800 272-2962 | 18306 |
| Rivermeadow Software Inc. | 7372 | E | 617 448-4990 | 18743 |
| Semotus Inc. | 7372 | E | 408 667-2046 | 18777 |
| Usertesting Inc (PA) | 7372 | D | 888 877-1882 | 18906 |
| Veza Technologies Inc. | 7372 | E | 510 870-8692 | 18918 |
| Ciphertrace Inc. | 7379 | D | 650 996-2142 | 19034 |
| Tamana Corporation. | 8299 | E | 408 358-0747 | 19353 |

### LOS OLIVOS, CA - Santa Barbara County

| | SIC | EMP | PHONE | ENTRY# |
|---|---|---|---|---|
| Artiste Management Company LLC. | 2084 | F | 805 686-2626 | 1479 |

# GEOGRAPHIC SECTION — MARTINEZ, CA

| Company | SIC | EMP | PHONE | ENTRY# |
|---|---|---|---|---|
| Firestone Vineyard LP | 2084 | D | 805 688-3940 | 1569 |
| Cushman Winery Corporation | 5182 | E | 805 688-9339 | 17263 |

### LOWER LAKE, CA - Lake County

| Company | SIC | EMP | PHONE | ENTRY# |
|---|---|---|---|---|
| Aloha Bay | 3999 | E | 707 994-3267 | 16084 |

### LUCERNE VALLEY, CA - San Bernardino County

| Company | SIC | EMP | PHONE | ENTRY# |
|---|---|---|---|---|
| Omya California Inc | 2819 | D | 760 248-7306 | 5106 |
| Omya Inc | 2819 | D | 760 248-5200 | 5107 |
| Specialty Minerals Inc | 2819 | C | 760 248-5300 | 5123 |
| Mitsubishi Cement Corporation | 3241 | C | 760 248-7373 | 7260 |

### LYNWOOD, CA - Los Angeles County

| Company | SIC | EMP | PHONE | ENTRY# |
|---|---|---|---|---|
| Hgc Holdings Inc | 2064 | E | 323 567-2226 | 1309 |
| First Finish Inc | 2211 | E | 310 631-6717 | 2415 |
| Aaron Corporation | 2339 | C | 323 235-5959 | 2730 |
| Kayo of California (PA) | 2339 | E | 323 233-6107 | 2779 |
| Roger R Caruso Enterprises Inc | 2448 | E | 714 778-6006 | 3358 |
| Gomen Furniture Mfg Inc | 2512 | E | 310 635-4894 | 3474 |
| Golden Mattress Co Inc | 2515 | D | 323 887-1888 | 3528 |
| Next Day Frame Inc | 2519 | D | 310 886-0851 | 3555 |
| P & L Development LLC | 2834 | C | 323 567-2482 | 5590 |
| Rangers Die Casting Co | 3363 | E | 310 764-1800 | 7819 |
| Metal Improvement Company LLC | 3398 | C | 323 585-2168 | 7890 |
| Tjs Metal Manufacturing Inc | 3446 | E | 310 604-1545 | 8646 |
| Bowman-Field Inc | 3471 | D | 310 638-8519 | 8934 |
| Triumph Processing Inc | 3471 | C | 323 563-1338 | 9026 |
| Processes By Martin Inc | 3479 | E | 310 637-1855 | 9111 |
| Ace Machine Shop Inc | 3599 | D | 310 608-2277 | 10666 |
| Pacific Ltg & Standards Co | 3646 | E | 310 603-9344 | 11551 |

### LYTLE CREEK, CA - San Bernardino County

| Company | SIC | EMP | PHONE | ENTRY# |
|---|---|---|---|---|
| Inland Pacific Coatings Inc | 3479 | E | 909 822-0594 | 9078 |

### MADERA, CA - Madera County

| Company | SIC | EMP | PHONE | ENTRY# |
|---|---|---|---|---|
| Benton Enterprises LLC | 0173 | E | 559 664-0800 | 38 |
| California Custom Proc LLC | 1541 | E | 559 416-5122 | 356 |
| Talley Oil Inc | 1611 | E | 559 673-9011 | 383 |
| Victor Packing Inc | 2034 | E | 559 673-5908 | 973 |
| Nutra-Blend LLC | 2048 | B | 559 661-6161 | 1140 |
| Thomas Products LLC | 2048 | D | 559 661-6161 | 1153 |
| Meridian Growers Proc Inc | 2068 | F | 559 458-7272 | 1358 |
| Golden Vly Grape Jice Wine LLC (PA) | 2084 | E | 559 661-4657 | 1595 |
| Golden Vly Grape Jice Wine LLC | 2084 | E | 559 661-4657 | 1596 |
| Quady Winery Inc | 2084 | F | 559 673-8068 | 1715 |
| Calbee America Incorporated | 2096 | D | 559 661-4845 | 2087 |
| Tranpak Inc | 2448 | E | 800 827-2474 | 3362 |
| Carris Reels California Inc (HQ) | 2499 | E | 802 733-9111 | 3414 |
| Georgia-Pacific LLC | 2653 | D | 559 674-4685 | 3848 |
| Pk1 Inc (HQ) | 2653 | D | 559 662-1910 | 3878 |
| Church & Dwight Co Inc | 2812 | E | 559 661-2790 | 5030 |
| Advanced Drainage Systems Inc | 3084 | D | 559 674-4989 | 6595 |
| Sealed Air Corporation | 3086 | C | 559 675-0152 | 6659 |
| Flores Family Development (HQ) | 3088 | E | 559 661-4171 | 6679 |
| Innovtive Rttional Molding Inc | 3089 | E | 559 673-4764 | 6864 |
| Oldcastle Infrastructure Inc | 3272 | E | 559 675-1813 | 7363 |
| Lees Concrete Materials Inc | 3273 | F | 559 486-2440 | 7463 |
| Gardner Family Ltd Partnership | 3429 | E | 559 675-8149 | 7998 |
| AG Machining Inc | 3441 | D | 805 531-9555 | 8091 |
| Steel Structures Inc | 3443 | E | 559 673-8021 | 8340 |
| Moore Quality Galvanizing Inc | 3479 | E | 559 673-2822 | 9094 |
| Oldcastle Infrastructure Inc | 3499 | D | 559 674-8093 | 9295 |
| Domries Enterprises Inc | 3523 | E | 559 485-4306 | 9350 |
| Midland Tractor Company | 3523 | E | 559 674-8757 | 9370 |
| Horn Machine Tools Inc (PA) | 3542 | E | 559 431-4131 | 9583 |
| John Bean Technologies Corp | 3556 | C | 559 661-3200 | 9801 |
| Baltimore Aircoil Company Inc | 3585 | C | 559 673-9231 | 10485 |
| Evapco Inc | 3585 | D | 559 673-2207 | 10499 |
| Better Cleaning Systems Inc | 3635 | E | 559 673-5700 | 11415 |
| B-K Lighting Inc | 3645 | D | 559 438-5800 | 11491 |
| Reliable Fire SEC Slutions Inc | 3699 | E | 559 277-3754 | 13297 |
| Westside Equipment Co (DH) | 5083 | F | 209 856-4700 | 16803 |
| Performance Trailer Inc | 5599 | E | 559 673-6300 | 17489 |

### MALIBU, CA - Los Angeles County

| Company | SIC | EMP | PHONE | ENTRY# |
|---|---|---|---|---|
| Marys Country Kitchen | 2053 | F | 310 456-7845 | 1288 |
| Curtco Media Group | 2721 | F | 310 589-9700 | 4243 |
| Curtco Robb Media LLC (PA) | 2721 | E | 310 589-9700 | 4244 |
| Robb Curtco Media LLC | 2721 | E | 310 589-9700 | 4295 |
| Olive Refinish | 2851 | E | 805 273-5072 | 6098 |
| Gifts International Inc | 3499 | F | 909 854-3977 | 9287 |
| County of Los Angeles | 3531 | E | 310 456-8014 | 9417 |
| Prime Technologies | 3672 | F | 818 568-0482 | 12193 |
| Horizon Surgical Systems Inc | 3842 | F | 310 876-2460 | 15358 |
| Road Champs Inc | 3944 | C | 310 456-7799 | 15766 |
| Toymax International Inc (HQ) | 3944 | D | 310 456-7799 | 15770 |
| Nexthealth West Hollywood Inc | 8011 | F | 310 295-2075 | 19320 |

### MAMMOTH LAKES, CA - Mono County

| Company | SIC | EMP | PHONE | ENTRY# |
|---|---|---|---|---|
| Footloose Incorporated | 5941 | E | 760 934-2400 | 17634 |

### MANHATTAN BEACH, CA - Los Angeles County

| Company | SIC | EMP | PHONE | ENTRY# |
|---|---|---|---|---|
| Stanton Carpet Corp | 2273 | E | 562 945-8711 | 2521 |
| Trlg Corporate Holdings LLC (PA) | 2369 | C | 323 266-3072 | 2867 |
| Wave Community Newspapers Inc (PA) | 2711 | E | 323 290-3000 | 4219 |
| Rnj Printing Corporation | 2752 | F | 310 638-7768 | 4755 |
| Skechers Collection LLC | 3021 | E | 310 318-3100 | 6421 |
| Skechers USA Inc (PA) | 3149 | D | 310 318-3100 | 7122 |
| De Nora Water Technologies LLC | 3589 | F | 310 618-9700 | 10555 |
| Enersponse Inc | 3825 | E | 949 829-3901 | 14516 |
| Tone It Up LLC | 5499 | E | 310 376-7645 | 17434 |
| Skechers USA Inc II | 5661 | A | 800 746-3411 | 17504 |
| Distillery Tech Inc | 7371 | C | 310 776-6234 | 17913 |
| Solartis LLC | 7371 | E | 310 251-4861 | 17981 |
| Network Sltons Prvider USA Inc | 8748 | E | 213 985-2173 | 19566 |

### MANTECA, CA - San Joaquin County

| Company | SIC | EMP | PHONE | ENTRY# |
|---|---|---|---|---|
| S K S Enterprises Inc (PA) | 0252 | E | 209 599-4095 | 64 |
| Linden Steel & Cnstr Inc | 1389 | E | 209 239-2160 | 248 |
| H Lima Company Inc | 1499 | E | 209 239-6787 | 340 |
| Sunnyvalley Smoked Meats Inc | 2013 | C | 209 825-0288 | 671 |
| Bimbo Bakeries Usa Inc | 2051 | E | 209 825-8647 | 1171 |
| Pin Hsiao & Associates LLC | 2051 | D | 209 665-4176 | 1238 |
| Delicato Vineyards LLC (PA) | 2084 | E | 209 824-3600 | 1535 |
| San Bernabe Vineyards LLC | 2084 | E | 209 824-3501 | 1740 |
| Frito-Lay North America Inc | 2096 | F | 209 824-3700 | 2091 |
| Resers Fine Foods Inc | 2099 | E | 503 643-6431 | 2334 |
| American Modular Systems Inc | 2452 | D | 209 825-1921 | 3391 |
| Morris Newspaper Corp Cal (HQ) | 2711 | D | 209 249-3500 | 4162 |
| Allegion Access Tech LLC | 3423 | E | 209 221-4066 | 7945 |
| Elite Shutters & Shadings Inc | 3442 | F | 209 825-1400 | 8263 |
| E-M Manufacturing Inc | 3444 | E | 209 825-1800 | 8437 |
| Dkw Precision Machining Inc | 3599 | E | 209 824-7899 | 10813 |
| Eckert Cold Storage Company | 4222 | E | 209 823-3181 | 16283 |
| San Joaquin Magazine | 5192 | E | 209 625-8313 | 17277 |

### MARICOPA, CA - Kern County

| Company | SIC | EMP | PHONE | ENTRY# |
|---|---|---|---|---|
| Aera Energy Services Company | 1381 | D | 661 665-3200 | 153 |
| Calmat Co | 1422 | B | 661 858-2673 | 298 |
| Nestle Purina Petcare Company | 2047 | C | 661 769-8261 | 1109 |

### MARINA, CA - Monterey County

| Company | SIC | EMP | PHONE | ENTRY# |
|---|---|---|---|---|
| Cemex Cnstr Mtls PCF LLC | 3241 | E | 831 883-3701 | 7254 |
| Cemex Materials LLC | 3273 | C | 831 883-3700 | 7425 |
| Light & Motion Industries | 3648 | D | 831 645-1525 | 11607 |
| Indtec Corporation | 3672 | E | 831 582-9388 | 12135 |
| Fort Ord Works Inc | 3812 | E | 831 275-1294 | 14187 |
| Eldridge Products Inc | 3823 | E | 831 648-7777 | 14408 |
| Fox Thermal Instruments Inc | 3823 | E | 831 384-4300 | 14414 |

### MARINA DEL REY, CA - Los Angeles County

| Company | SIC | EMP | PHONE | ENTRY# |
|---|---|---|---|---|
| Lf Sportswear Inc (PA) | 2331 | E | 310 437-4100 | 2679 |
| Tokyopop Inc (PA) | 2731 | D | 323 920-5967 | 4351 |
| Dr Squatch LLC | 2844 | C | 631 229-7068 | 5975 |
| Dollar Shave Club Inc (HQ) | 3541 | E | 310 975-8528 | 9551 |
| Sewer Rodding Equipment Co (PA) | 3589 | E | 310 301-9009 | 10599 |
| Samvco | 3634 | F | 310 980-5680 | 11413 |
| Eti Partners IV LLC | 3672 | E | 949 273-4990 | 12095 |
| Twin Coast Metrology Inc (PA) | 3827 | F | 310 709-2308 | 14830 |
| Gelsons Markets | 5411 | D | 310 306-3192 | 17380 |
| Apotheka Systems Inc | 7372 | E | 844 777-4455 | 18050 |
| Springcoin Inc | 7372 | E | 310 494-6928 | 18827 |
| Telesign Holdings Inc (HQ) | 7372 | D | 310 740-9700 | 18871 |
| Survios Inc | 7373 | E | 310 736-1503 | 18994 |

### MARIPOSA, CA - Mariposa County

| Company | SIC | EMP | PHONE | ENTRY# |
|---|---|---|---|---|
| Haztech Systems Inc | 2865 | E | 209 966-8088 | 6120 |
| Tavis Corporation | 8731 | D | 209 966-2027 | 19479 |

### MARTINEZ, CA - Contra Costa County

| Company | SIC | EMP | PHONE | ENTRY# |
|---|---|---|---|---|
| Michael Telfer (PA) | 1611 | D | 925 228-1515 | 376 |
| PG Emminger Inc | 2541 | E | 925 313-5830 | 3668 |
| Document Proc Solutions Inc | 2621 | E | 925 839-1182 | 3766 |
| Eco Services Operations Corp | 2819 | E | 925 313-8224 | 5087 |
| Shell Catalysts & Tech LP | 2819 | D | 925 370-9675 | 5114 |
| Shell Chemical LP | 2819 | E | 925 313-8601 | 5116 |

Employee Codes: A=Over 500 employees, B=251-500, C=101-250, D=51-100, E=20-50, F=10-19, G=1-9

# MARTINEZ, CA

GEOGRAPHIC SECTION

| | SIC | EMP | PHONE | ENTRY# |
|---|---|---|---|---|
| Siemens Med Solutions USA Inc | 3661 | B | 925 293-5430 | 11784 |
| Lilypad Ev LLC | 3694 | E | 866 525-9723 | 13174 |
| Euv Tech Inc | 3826 | D | 925 229-4388 | 14664 |
| County Quarry Products | 4953 | E | 925 682-0707 | 16357 |
| Marathon Petroleum Corporation | 5172 | E | 925 370-3290 | 17253 |

## MARYSVILLE, CA - Yuba County

| | SIC | EMP | PHONE | ENTRY# |
|---|---|---|---|---|
| Teichert Inc | 1442 | D | 530 749-1230 | 325 |
| Teichert Inc | 1442 | C | 530 743-6111 | 326 |
| Mariani Packing Co Inc | 2034 | E | 530 749-6565 | 956 |
| Reyes Coca-Cola Bottling LLC | 2086 | E | 530 743-6533 | 1949 |
| Ecmd Inc | 2431 | E | 530 741-0769 | 3133 |
| US Pipe Fabrication LLC | 3084 | E | 530 742-5171 | 6604 |
| Hf Group Inc | 3569 | F | 530 788-0288 | 10093 |

## MATHER, CA - Sacramento County

| | SIC | EMP | PHONE | ENTRY# |
|---|---|---|---|---|
| Construction Innovations LLC | 3699 | C | 855 725-9555 | 13225 |

## MAXWELL, CA - Colusa County

| | SIC | EMP | PHONE | ENTRY# |
|---|---|---|---|---|
| California Heritage Mills Inc | 2044 | E | 530 438-2100 | 1073 |

## MAYWOOD, CA - Los Angeles County

| | SIC | EMP | PHONE | ENTRY# |
|---|---|---|---|---|
| Kitchen Cuts LLC | 2013 | D | 323 560-7415 | 648 |
| KSM Garment Inc | 2331 | E | 323 585-8811 | 2676 |
| Ev R Inc | 2339 | E | 323 312-5400 | 2758 |
| Gemini Film & Bag Inc (PA) | 3089 | E | 323 582-0901 | 6838 |
| Heritage Leather Company Inc | 3111 | E | 323 983-0420 | 7087 |
| Cook Induction Heating Co Inc | 3398 | E | 323 560-1327 | 7884 |
| Signresource LLC | 3993 | C | 323 771-2098 | 16040 |

## MC FARLAND, CA - Kern County

| | SIC | EMP | PHONE | ENTRY# |
|---|---|---|---|---|
| Aptco LLC (PA) | 2821 | D | 661 792-2107 | 5137 |
| Amaretto Orchards LLC | 3999 | E | 661 399-9697 | 16085 |

## MC KITTRICK, CA - Kern County

| | SIC | EMP | PHONE | ENTRY# |
|---|---|---|---|---|
| Aera Energy LLC | 1311 | C | 661 334-3100 | 120 |
| California Resources Prod Corp | 1311 | E | 661 869-8000 | 130 |
| Aera Energy Services Company | 1381 | C | 661 665-4400 | 152 |

## MCCLELLAN, CA - Sacramento County

| | SIC | EMP | PHONE | ENTRY# |
|---|---|---|---|---|
| Luxer Corporation | 2521 | C | 415 390-0123 | 3573 |
| PCA Central Cal Corrugated LLC | 2653 | D | 916 614-0580 | 3877 |
| Sacramento Container Corp | 2653 | C | 916 614-0580 | 3884 |
| Dome Printing & Packaging LLC (HQ) | 2752 | E | 800 343-3139 | 4594 |
| Southwestern Wire Inc | 3315 | F | 916 333-5289 | 7652 |
| SPI Solar Inc (PA) | 3433 | B | 408 919-8000 | 8082 |
| Berger Steel Corporation | 3441 | E | 916 640-8778 | 8103 |
| Greenheck Fan Corporation | 3564 | D | 916 643-4616 | 9987 |
| Aviate Enterprises Inc | 3585 | E | 916 993-4000 | 10484 |
| SPI Energy Co Ltd | 3674 | B | 408 919-8000 | 12729 |
| Shyft Group Inc | 3711 | D | 916 921-2639 | 13386 |
| Northrop Grumman Systems Corp | 3812 | B | 916 570-4454 | 14253 |
| Polar Service Center | 5531 | F | 916 643-4689 | 17459 |
| Siemens Mobility Inc | 7538 | D | 916 621-2700 | 19162 |

## MCKINLEYVILLE, CA - Humboldt County

| | SIC | EMP | PHONE | ENTRY# |
|---|---|---|---|---|
| American Bottling Company | 2086 | D | 707 840-9727 | 1855 |
| Ford Logging Inc | 2411 | F | 707 840-9442 | 3045 |
| Willow Technology Inc | 7372 | E | 360 393-4962 | 18934 |

## MECCA, CA - Riverside County

| | SIC | EMP | PHONE | ENTRY# |
|---|---|---|---|---|
| Kerry Inc | 2023 | D | 760 396-2116 | 765 |
| Califrnia Nutritional Pdts Inc | 2043 | E | 760 625-3884 | 1069 |
| Western Environmental Inc | 3822 | E | 760 396-0222 | 14377 |

## MENIFEE, CA - Riverside County

| | SIC | EMP | PHONE | ENTRY# |
|---|---|---|---|---|
| Davids Natural Toothpaste Inc | 2844 | E | 949 933-1185 | 5968 |
| Big Brand Tire & Service | 3011 | D | 951 679-6266 | 6405 |
| Datatronics Romoland Inc | 3612 | D | 951 928-7700 | 11210 |
| Tea Financial Services | 5091 | E | 951 301-8884 | 16941 |

## MENLO PARK, CA - San Mateo County

| | SIC | EMP | PHONE | ENTRY# |
|---|---|---|---|---|
| Diageo North America Inc | 2085 | E | 650 329-3220 | 1837 |
| Embarcadero Media | 2711 | E | 650 854-2626 | 4110 |
| Motherly Inc | 2741 | E | 917 860-9926 | 4433 |
| Applied Molecular Trnspt Inc | 2834 | D | 650 392-0420 | 5329 |
| Dermira Inc | 2834 | B | 650 421-7200 | 5425 |
| Grail Inc (PA) | 2834 | C | 833 694-2553 | 5468 |
| Summit Therapeutics Sub Inc | 2834 | E | 617 225-4455 | 5680 |
| C S Bio Co | 2835 | D | 650 322-1111 | 5744 |
| Stack Plastics Inc | 3089 | E | 650 361-8600 | 7040 |
| Cfkba Inc (PA) | 3357 | E | 650 847-3900 | 7783 |
| Mainspring Energy Inc | 3462 | B | 408 529-5651 | 8780 |
| Blissera Corp | 3534 | F | 844 960-4141 | 9469 |
| Purfresh Inc | 3559 | E | 510 580-0700 | 9893 |
| Countryman Associates Inc | 3651 | E | 650 364-9988 | 11646 |
| Vello Systems Inc | 3661 | F | 650 324-7688 | 11792 |
| Fisica Applied Tech Inc | 3663 | C | 650 326-9500 | 11856 |
| Si-Ware Systems Inc | 3674 | D | 650 257-9680 | 12695 |
| Tessera Global Services Inc | 3674 | E | 408 321-6000 | 12763 |
| Te Connectivity Corporation | 3678 | C | 650 361-3333 | 12898 |
| Cyngn Inc (PA) | 3711 | D | 650 924-5905 | 13346 |
| Aerwins Inc | 3728 | E | 808 892-6611 | 13759 |
| Oni Inc | 3826 | E | 415 301-8526 | 14698 |
| Pacific Biosciences Cal Inc (PA) | 3826 | C | 650 521-8000 | 14702 |
| Avails Medical Inc | 3841 | E | 650 427-0460 | 14984 |
| Credence Medsystems Inc | 3841 | E | 844 263-3797 | 15062 |
| Intersect Ent Inc | 3841 | B | 650 641-2100 | 15124 |
| Memry Corporation | 3841 | E | 650 463-3400 | 15183 |
| Sight Sciences Inc (PA) | 3841 | C | 877 266-1144 | 15258 |
| Stryker Corporation | 3841 | E | 650 667-4460 | 15268 |
| Gauss Surgical Inc | 3842 | E | 650 919-4683 | 15354 |
| Conor Medsystems LLC | 3845 | E | | 15527 |
| Tusker Medical Inc | 3845 | E | 650 223-6900 | 15587 |
| Kleiner Prkins Cfeld Byers LLC (PA) | 6799 | E | 650 233-2750 | 17756 |
| Aha Labs Inc | 7372 | D | 650 575-1425 | 18030 |
| Appcoll Inc | 7372 | E | 650 223-5460 | 18051 |
| Drivescale Inc | 7372 | F | 408 849-4651 | 18254 |
| Genesys Cloud Services Inc (HQ) | 7372 | B | 650 466-1100 | 18345 |
| Gladiator Corporation | 7372 | B | 650 233-2900 | 18350 |
| Intuit Inc | 7372 | F | 650 944-6000 | 18434 |
| Lattice Data Inc | 7372 | E | 650 800-7262 | 18487 |
| Marble Security Inc | 7372 | F | 408 737-4300 | 18521 |
| Meta Platforms Tech LLC (HQ) | 7372 | E | 650 543-4800 | 18540 |
| Micro Focus (us) Inc (DH) | 7372 | D | 301 838-5000 | 18542 |
| Onymos Inc | 7372 | E | 650 504-8037 | 18622 |
| Positon Inc | 7372 | F | 650 600-1924 | 18688 |
| Redseal Inc | 7372 | C | 408 641-2200 | 18729 |
| Subtle Medical Inc | 7372 | E | 650 397-8709 | 18845 |
| Swiftstack Inc (HQ) | 7372 | D | 408 486-2000 | 18854 |
| Finsix Corporation | 7373 | E | 650 285-6400 | 18975 |
| Ideal Aerosmith Inc | 8734 | F | 650 353-3641 | 19504 |

## MENTONE, CA - San Bernardino County

| | SIC | EMP | PHONE | ENTRY# |
|---|---|---|---|---|
| Bristol Omega Inc | 2541 | E | 909 794-6862 | 3648 |
| Power Pt Inc (PA) | 3537 | E | 951 490-4149 | 9531 |
| Marwell Corporation | 3613 | F | 909 794-4192 | 11246 |

## MERCED, CA - Merced County

| | SIC | EMP | PHONE | ENTRY# |
|---|---|---|---|---|
| Richwood Meat Company Inc | 2011 | D | 209 722-8171 | 615 |
| Yosemite Vly Beef Pkg Co Inc | 2011 | E | 626 435-0170 | 627 |
| Jain Farm Fresh Foods Inc (DH) | 2034 | E | 541 481-2522 | 952 |
| Sensient Ntral Ingredients LLC | 2099 | E | 209 667-2777 | 2351 |
| Olde World Corporation | 2541 | E | 209 384-1337 | 3666 |
| Greif Inc | 2655 | D | 209 383-4396 | 3904 |
| Mauser Usa LLC | 2655 | E | 209 205-1135 | 3906 |
| Qg LLC | 2752 | A | 209 384-0444 | 4745 |
| Fortis Solutions Group LLC | 2759 | D | 800 388-1990 | 4880 |
| J&D 2050 Wardrobe Inc A California | 2759 | C | 209 384-1000 | 4903 |
| Acuantia Inc | 2821 | D | 209 723-5000 | 5132 |
| Scholle Ipn Packaging Inc | 3089 | C | 209 384-3100 | 7023 |
| OKeeffes Inc | 3229 | D | 209 386-1645 | 7199 |
| Sun Power Security Gates Inc | 3315 | F | 209 722-3990 | 7653 |
| Merced Screw Products Inc | 3451 | E | 209 723-7706 | 8726 |
| Werner Co | 3499 | E | 209 383-3989 | 9303 |
| Kirby Manufacturing Inc (PA) | 3523 | D | 209 723-0778 | 9366 |
| Laird Mfg LLC (PA) | 3523 | E | 209 722-4145 | 9367 |
| Fineline Industries Inc (PA) | 3732 | D | 209 384-0255 | 14033 |
| Central Valley Concrete Inc (PA) | 4212 | C | 209 723-8846 | 16278 |
| OKeeffes Inc | 5211 | D | 209 388-9072 | 17338 |
| Yosemite Farms | 5441 | E | 209 383-3411 | 17406 |
| On Target Marketing | 7336 | E | 209 723-1691 | 17835 |
| Nutstar Software LLC | 7372 | F | 209 250-1324 | 18606 |

## MERIDIAN, CA - Sutter County

| | SIC | EMP | PHONE | ENTRY# |
|---|---|---|---|---|
| Davis Machine Shop Inc | 3523 | E | 530 696-2577 | 9348 |

## MI WUK VILLAGE, CA - Tuolumne County

| | SIC | EMP | PHONE | ENTRY# |
|---|---|---|---|---|
| Oti Engineering Cons Inc | 3663 | E | 209 586-1022 | 11910 |

## MIDDLETOWN, CA - Lake County

| | SIC | EMP | PHONE | ENTRY# |
|---|---|---|---|---|
| Langtry Farms LLC | 2084 | F | 707 987-2772 | 1663 |

## MILL VALLEY, CA - Marin County

| | SIC | EMP | PHONE | ENTRY# |
|---|---|---|---|---|
| True Botanicals Inc | 2844 | D | 415 420-0403 | 6047 |
| Mila Usa Inc | 3634 | E | 540 206-4306 | 11409 |

# GEOGRAPHIC SECTION — MILPITAS, CA

| | SIC | EMP | PHONE | ENTRY# |
|---|---|---|---|---|
| Presidio Brands Inc (PA) | 5122 | E | 877 875-5225 | 17045 |
| Avochato Inc | 7372 | E | 415 214-8977 | 18083 |
| Chouinard & Myhre Inc | 7373 | E | 415 480-3636 | 18968 |
| Orion Group World LLC | 7389 | C | 415 602-5233 | 19113 |

## MILLBRAE, CA - San Mateo County

| | SIC | EMP | PHONE | ENTRY# |
|---|---|---|---|---|
| Stem US Holdings Inc (HQ) | 3825 | D | | 14586 |
| Jiseki Health Inc | 7372 | E | 408 763-7264 | 18457 |

## MILPITAS, CA - Santa Clara County

| | SIC | EMP | PHONE | ENTRY# |
|---|---|---|---|---|
| Dumbarton Quarry Associates (PA) | 1422 | F | 510 793-8861 | 299 |
| Bar-S Foods Co | 2013 | E | 408 941-9958 | 632 |
| Otsuka America Inc | 2084 | E | 408 867-3233 | 1701 |
| Larson Packaging Company LLC | 2441 | E | 408 946-4971 | 3326 |
| ABC Printing Inc | 2752 | F | 408 263-1118 | 4499 |
| Vista Way Corporation | 2752 | E | 408 586-8107 | 4805 |
| Tokyo Ohka Kogyo America Inc | 2819 | E | 408 956-9901 | 5125 |
| Henlius USA Inc | 2833 | C | 510 445-0305 | 5245 |
| Alector LLC | 2834 | E | 415 231-5660 | 5304 |
| Zuca Inc | 3161 | E | 408 377-9822 | 7144 |
| Alliance Fiber Optic Pdts Inc | 3229 | A | 408 736-6900 | 7188 |
| Superior Quartz Inc | 3339 | F | 408 844-9663 | 7713 |
| Crain Cutter Company Inc | 3429 | D | 408 946-6100 | 7990 |
| Ohmnilabs Incorporated | 3549 | D | 408 675-9565 | 9743 |
| Mt Systems Inc | 3559 | F | 510 651-5277 | 9880 |
| Rucker & Kolls Inc (PA) | 3559 | F | 408 934-9875 | 9896 |
| Airgard Inc (PA) | 3564 | E | 408 573-0701 | 9978 |
| Aivres Systems Inc | 3571 | C | 866 687-1430 | 10130 |
| Silicon Graphics Intl Inc | 3571 | F | 669 900-8000 | 10203 |
| Headway Technologies Inc | 3572 | A | 408 934-5300 | 10241 |
| Magic Technologies Inc | 3572 | E | 408 263-1484 | 10252 |
| Nimble Storage Inc | 3572 | A | 408 432-9600 | 10259 |
| Philips Lt-On Dgtal Sltons USA (DH) | 3572 | C | 510 687-1800 | 10264 |
| Sandisk LLC (DH) | 3572 | C | 408 801-1000 | 10274 |
| Allied Telesis Inc | 3577 | D | 408 519-6700 | 10318 |
| Bestek Manufacturing Inc | 3577 | E | 408 321-8834 | 10335 |
| Cisco Systems Inc | 3577 | D | 408 526-6200 | 10343 |
| Corsair Gaming Inc (HQ) | 3577 | E | 510 657-8747 | 10352 |
| Cpacket Networks Inc | 3577 | E | 650 969-9500 | 10353 |
| Lite-On Technology Intl Inc (HQ) | 3577 | E | 408 945-0222 | 10396 |
| Marburg Technology Inc | 3577 | F | 408 262-8400 | 10407 |
| Silicon Graphics Intl Corp (HQ) | 3577 | C | 669 900-8000 | 10436 |
| Viptela Inc | 3577 | E | 408 663-6759 | 10450 |
| Gateway Precision Inc | 3599 | E | 408 942-8849 | 10853 |
| Hammond Enterprises Inc | 3599 | E | 925 432-3537 | 10866 |
| Innovative Machining Inc | 3599 | E | 408 262-2270 | 10887 |
| Khuus Inc | 3599 | D | 408 522-8000 | 10926 |
| Yuhas Tooling & Machining Inc | 3599 | F | 408 934-9196 | 11199 |
| Quality Transformer & Elec | 3612 | E | 408 935-0231 | 11226 |
| Turnongreen Inc | 3621 | E | 510 657-2635 | 11293 |
| Silicon Microstructures Inc | 3625 | D | 408 473-9700 | 11347 |
| Solaredge Technologies Inc (PA) | 3629 | D | 510 498-3200 | 11384 |
| G D M Electronic Assembly Inc | 3643 | D | 408 945-4100 | 11455 |
| Altigen Communications Inc | 3661 | C | 408 597-9000 | 11751 |
| Oclaro Subsystems Inc | 3661 | C | 408 383-1400 | 11778 |
| Tarana Wireless Inc (PA) | 3663 | F | 408 351-4085 | 11956 |
| Vista Point Technologies Inc | 3663 | E | 408 576-7000 | 11974 |
| Asteelflash USA Corp (DH) | 3672 | E | 510 440-2840 | 12061 |
| Flex Interconnect Tech Inc | 3672 | E | 408 956-8204 | 12102 |
| Flextronics America LLC | 3672 | C | 408 576-7156 | 12104 |
| Flextronics Intl PA Inc | 3672 | F | 408 577-2489 | 12105 |
| Flextronics Intl USA Inc | 3672 | D | 408 576-7492 | 12106 |
| Flextronics Intl USA Inc | 3672 | B | 408 576-7000 | 12107 |
| Flextronics Intl USA Inc | 3672 | C | 510 814-7000 | 12108 |
| Flextronics Intl USA Inc | 3672 | E | 408 678-3268 | 12109 |
| Flextronics Intl USA Inc | 3672 | C | 408 577-4874 | 12110 |
| Flextronics Intl USA Inc | 3672 | C | 408 576-7044 | 12111 |
| Flextronics Intl USA Inc | 3672 | C | 408 576-7076 | 12112 |
| Flextronics Intl USA Inc | 3672 | E | 408 576-6769 | 12116 |
| Hytek R&D Inc (PA) | 3672 | E | 408 761-5266 | 12133 |
| Lenthor Engineering Inc | 3672 | C | 408 945-8787 | 12153 |
| Meritronics Inc (PA) | 3672 | E | 408 969-0888 | 12162 |
| Nbs Design Inc | 3672 | B | 805 966-9383 | 12174 |
| Palpilot International Corp (PA) | 3672 | E | 408 855-8866 | 12185 |
| Symprotek Co | 3672 | E | 408 956-0700 | 12237 |
| Zollner Electronics Inc | 3672 | E | 408 434-5400 | 12266 |
| Zytek Corp (PA) | 3672 | E | 408 520-4287 | 12267 |
| Beamreach Solar Inc | 3674 | E | 408 240-3800 | 12359 |
| Corsair Memory Inc (DH) | 3674 | C | 510 657-8747 | 12393 |
| Daystar Technologies Inc | 3674 | D | 408 582-7100 | 12402 |
| Frontier Semiconductor (PA) | 3674 | E | 408 432-8338 | 12439 |
| Gyrfalcon Technology Inc (PA) | 3674 | E | 408 944-9219 | 12457 |
| HI Relblity McRelectronics Inc | 3674 | D | 408 764-5500 | 12464 |
| Integra Tech Silicon Vly LLC (DH) | 3674 | C | 408 618-8700 | 12491 |
| Integrted Silicon Solution Inc (PA) | 3674 | B | 408 969-6600 | 12493 |
| Intersil Communications LLC | 3674 | A | 408 432-8888 | 12498 |
| Ixys LLC (HQ) | 3674 | D | 408 457-9000 | 12507 |
| Linear Technology LLC (HQ) | 3674 | A | 408 432-1900 | 12532 |
| Lre Silicon Services | 3674 | F | 408 262-8725 | 12534 |
| Nanosys Inc (HQ) | 3674 | E | 408 240-6700 | 12595 |
| Nuvosun Inc | 3674 | E | 510 304-2351 | 12610 |
| Oclaro Fiber Optics Inc (DH) | 3674 | C | 408 383-1400 | 12615 |
| Penguin Solutions Inc (PA) | 3674 | C | 510 623-1231 | 12630 |
| Reaction Technology Inc (HQ) | 3674 | E | 408 970-9601 | 12670 |
| Renesas Electronics Amer Inc | 3674 | B | 408 432-8888 | 12673 |
| Renesas Electronics Amer Inc | 3674 | D | 408 432-8888 | 12675 |
| Silicon Motion Inc | 3674 | E | 408 501-5300 | 12703 |
| Silicon Turnkey Solutions Inc (HQ) | 3674 | F | 408 904-0200 | 12705 |
| Siliconcore Technology Inc (PA) | 3674 | F | 408 946-8185 | 12707 |
| Stats Chippac Inc (DH) | 3674 | E | 510 979-8000 | 12734 |
| Teledyne Defense Elec LLC | 3674 | E | 408 737-0992 | 12756 |
| Teledyne E2v Inc | 3674 | C | 408 737-0992 | 12757 |
| Winslow Automation Inc | 3674 | D | 408 262-9004 | 12804 |
| Zilog Inc (DH) | 3674 | E | 408 513-1500 | 12813 |
| Aras Power Technologies (PA) | 3677 | F | 408 935-8877 | 12828 |
| High Connection Density Inc | 3678 | E | 408 743-9700 | 12881 |
| Onanon Inc | 3678 | E | 408 262-8990 | 12893 |
| Brandt Electronics Inc | 3679 | E | 408 240-0004 | 12926 |
| Digital Power Corporation (HQ) | 3679 | E | 510 657-2635 | 12961 |
| Fabri-Tech Components Inc | 3679 | F | 510 249-2000 | 12975 |
| Isolink Inc | 3679 | E | 408 946-1968 | 13007 |
| JIC Industrial Co Inc | 3679 | E | 408 935-9880 | 13015 |
| Kelytech Corporation | 3679 | E | 408 935-0888 | 13017 |
| Manutronics Inc | 3679 | F | 408 262-6579 | 13031 |
| Nortra Cables Inc | 3679 | E | 408 942-1106 | 13049 |
| NRC Manufacturing Inc | 3679 | F | 510 438-9400 | 13050 |
| Renesas Electronics America Inc | 3679 | A | 408 432-8888 | 13076 |
| Tr Manufacturing LLC (HQ) | 3679 | C | 408 235-2900 | 13110 |
| Seres Inc | 3694 | C | 214 585-3356 | 13185 |
| U-Tech Media Usa LLC | 3695 | C | 408 597-1600 | 13205 |
| Spectra-Physics Inc (DH) | 3699 | D | 877 835-9620 | 13310 |
| SF Motors Inc (DH) | 3711 | C | 408 617-7878 | 13383 |
| Quantum3d Inc (PA) | 3812 | F | 408 600-2500 | 14281 |
| PSI Water Technologies Inc | 3823 | E | 408 819-3043 | 14448 |
| Sensarray Corporation | 3823 | D | 408 875-3000 | 14456 |
| Onto Innovation Inc | 3825 | C | 408 545-6000 | 14567 |
| Onto Innovation Inc | 3825 | F | 408 545-6000 | 14568 |
| Pericom Semiconductor Corp (HQ) | 3825 | D | 408 232-9100 | 14570 |
| Rohde & Schwarz Usa Inc | 3825 | C | 818 846-3600 | 14580 |
| Teledyne Lecroy Inc | 3825 | C | 408 727-6600 | 14590 |
| Amplitude Laser Inc (PA) | 3826 | E | 408 727-3240 | 14609 |
| Viavi Solutions Inc | 3826 | C | 408 546-5000 | 14752 |
| Blue Sky Research Incorporated (PA) | 3827 | E | 408 941-6068 | 14763 |
| Carl Zeiss Meditec Inc | 3827 | B | 650 871-4747 | 14765 |
| KLA Corporation (PA) | 3827 | B | 408 875-3000 | 14793 |
| Oclaro Technology Inc | 3827 | A | 408 383-1400 | 14804 |
| Optical Associates Inc | 3827 | E | 408 232-0600 | 14807 |
| Sierra Monitor Corporation (HQ) | 3829 | D | 408 262-6611 | 14919 |
| Teledyne Dgital Imaging US Inc | 3829 | F | 408 736-6000 | 14928 |
| Teledyne RAD-Icon Imaging Corp | 3829 | F | 408 736-6000 | 14932 |
| Becton Dickinson and Company | 3841 | A | 734 812-5271 | 15000 |
| Elixir Medical Corporation | 3841 | F | 408 636-2000 | 15077 |
| Johnson Jhnson Srgcal Vsion In | 3841 | B | 408 273-4100 | 15137 |
| Optimedica Corporation | 3841 | E | 408 850-8600 | 15213 |
| Precision Swiss Products Inc | 3842 | D | | 15394 |
| Lumasense Technologies Inc (HQ) | 3845 | D | 408 727-1600 | 15552 |
| Hoya Holdings Inc (HQ) | 3861 | C | 408 654-2300 | 15644 |
| Marketshare Inc (PA) | 3993 | D | 408 262-0677 | 16003 |
| Luxshare-Ict Inc | 3999 | E | 408 957-0535 | 16173 |
| Midway Games West Inc | 3999 | C | 408 434-3700 | 16184 |
| Prysm Inc (PA) | 3999 | B | 408 586-1127 | 16211 |
| Virtual Technologies Inc | 3999 | E | 408 597-3400 | 16263 |
| Milpitas Materials Company | 5032 | E | 650 969-4401 | 16477 |
| Shamrock Office Solutions | 5044 | F | 408 791-6432 | 16504 |
| Envision Peripherals Inc (PA) | 5045 | E | 510 770-9988 | 16521 |
| Comba Telecom Inc | 5065 | F | 408 526-0180 | 16696 |
| Macronix America Inc (HQ) | 5065 | D | 408 262-8887 | 16717 |
| Mvinix Corporation | 5731 | E | 408 321-9109 | 17543 |
| Mindsource Inc | 7371 | D | 650 314-6400 | 17950 |
| Rapidbizappscom LLC | 7371 | E | 408 647-3050 | 17969 |
| Composite Software LLC (DH) | 7372 | D | 800 553-6387 | 18195 |
| Heat Software USA Inc | 7372 | B | 408 601-2800 | 18379 |
| Mandiant Inc | 7372 | A | 408 321-6300 | 18518 |
| Zentera Systems Inc | 7372 | E | 408 436-4811 | 18953 |
| At Road Inc | 7373 | A | 510 668-1638 | 18963 |
| Ketos Inc | 7373 | D | 408 550-2162 | 18983 |

Employee Codes: A=Over 500 employees, B=251-500, C=101-250, D=51-100, E=20-50, F=10-19, G=1-9

# MILPITAS, CA

| | SIC | EMP | PHONE | ENTRY# |
|---|---|---|---|---|
| Rush Pcb Inc | 7389 | E | 408 496-6013 | 19123 |
| Integrated Mfg Tech Inc | 7692 | E | 510 659-9770 | 19199 |
| Stellartech Research Corp (PA) | 8731 | C | 408 331-3000 | 19475 |

## MIRA LOMA, CA - Riverside County

| | SIC | EMP | PHONE | ENTRY# |
|---|---|---|---|---|
| Galassos Bakery (PA) | 2051 | C | 951 360-1211 | 1208 |
| Highland Plastics Inc | 3089 | C | 951 360-9587 | 6853 |
| Cryoworks Inc | 3498 | D | 951 360-0920 | 9254 |
| Speakercraft LLC | 3651 | D | 951 685-1759 | 11702 |
| Prevost Car (us) Inc | 5013 | D | 951 360-2550 | 16390 |
| Olivet International Inc (PA) | 5099 | D | 951 681-8888 | 16983 |
| DC Shoes Inc | 5137 | F | 951 361-7712 | 17087 |

## MISSION HILLS, CA - Los Angeles County

| | SIC | EMP | PHONE | ENTRY# |
|---|---|---|---|---|
| Valterra Products LLC (HQ) | 3494 | E | 818 898-1671 | 9193 |
| Electric Gate Store Inc | 3699 | C | 818 504-2300 | 13238 |
| National Business Group Inc (PA) | 7353 | D | 818 221-6000 | 17853 |

## MISSION VIEJO, CA - Orange County

| | SIC | EMP | PHONE | ENTRY# |
|---|---|---|---|---|
| Prototype Industries Inc | 2741 | F | 949 680-4890 | 4453 |
| Franchise Services Inc (PA) | 2752 | E | 949 348-5400 | 4616 |
| Postal Instant Press Inc (HQ) | 2752 | E | 949 348-5000 | 4728 |
| Sir Speedy Inc (HQ) | 2752 | E | 949 348-5000 | 4764 |
| Wakunaga of America Co Ltd (HQ) | 2834 | D | 949 855-2776 | 5715 |
| James Hardie Trading Co Inc | 2952 | E | 949 582-2378 | 6378 |
| James Hardie Building Pdts Inc | 3241 | D | 949 348-1800 | 7256 |
| Elixir Industries | 3469 | E | 949 860-5000 | 8840 |
| Ironwood Electric Inc | 3699 | E | 714 630-2350 | 13255 |
| Prosthtic Orthtic Group Ornge | 3842 | F | 949 242-2237 | 15395 |
| Paydarfar Industries Inc | 5045 | D | 949 481-3267 | 16537 |
| Foundstone Inc | 7372 | E | 949 297-5600 | 18327 |
| Oracle Corporation | 7372 | B | 626 315-7513 | 18637 |

## MODESTO, CA - Stanislaus County

| | SIC | EMP | PHONE | ENTRY# |
|---|---|---|---|---|
| Blue Diamond Growers | 0723 | C | 209 545-6221 | 74 |
| Reed Family Companies (PA) | 1611 | E | 209 521-9771 | 378 |
| Reed Group (HQ) | 1611 | E | 209 521-7423 | 379 |
| Champion Industrial Contrs Inc | 1711 | E | 209 524-6601 | 411 |
| Champion Industrial Contrs Inc (PA) | 1711 | E | 209 579-5478 | 412 |
| R & M Painting Inc | 1721 | F | 209 576-2576 | 448 |
| Modesto Industrial Electrical Co Inc (PA) | 1731 | D | 209 527-2800 | 463 |
| George Reed Inc (HQ) | 1771 | E | 877 823-2305 | 522 |
| Golden Valley Industries Inc | 2011 | E | 209 939-3370 | 598 |
| La Pachanga Foods Inc | 2011 | E | 209 522-2222 | 604 |
| Western Meat Processing Inc | 2011 | E | 209 521-1843 | 626 |
| Rizo-Lopez Foods Inc | 2022 | B | 800 626-5587 | 730 |
| Nestle Usa Inc | 2023 | B | 209 574-2000 | 776 |
| Bell-Carter Foods Inc | 2033 | E | 209 549-5939 | 879 |
| Del Monte Foods Inc | 2033 | D | 209 548-5509 | 884 |
| Stanislaus Food Products Co (PA) | 2033 | E | 209 548-3537 | 927 |
| Mercer Foods LLC (PA) | 2034 | B | 877 743-5373 | 958 |
| Flowers Baking Co Modesto LLC | 2051 | F | 209 526-5512 | 1196 |
| Flowers Baking Co Modesto LLC (HQ) | 2051 | B | 209 857-4600 | 1197 |
| Dawn Food Products Inc | 2052 | E | 517 789-4400 | 1271 |
| Bunge Oils Inc | 2079 | C | 209 574-9981 | 1393 |
| Nick Sciabica & Sons A Corp | 2079 | E | 209 577-5067 | 1402 |
| E & J Gallo Winery (PA) | 2084 | A | 209 341-3111 | 1546 |
| E & J Gallo Winery | 2084 | E | 209 341-3111 | 1549 |
| Vintners Distributors Inc | 2084 | D | 209 551-6422 | 1820 |
| Sacramento Coca-Cola Btlg Inc | 2086 | D | 209 541-3200 | 1958 |
| Frito-Lay North America Inc | 2096 | B | 209 544-5400 | 2093 |
| Newly Weds Foods Inc | 2099 | D | 209 491-7777 | 2296 |
| Pacific Holdings 137 Company | 2099 | F | 209 527-0108 | 2310 |
| Seneca | 2099 | E | 209 815-3023 | 2349 |
| First Tactical LLC | 2311 | A | 209 482-7255 | 2560 |
| Wood Connection Inc | 2431 | E | 209 577-1044 | 3207 |
| Truss Engineering Inc | 2439 | E | 209 527-6387 | 3320 |
| United Pallet Services Inc | 2448 | C | 209 538-5844 | 3363 |
| Entekra LLC | 2452 | D | 209 624-1630 | 3394 |
| International Paper Company | 2631 | C | 209 526-4700 | 3803 |
| Georgia-Pacific LLC | 2653 | E | 209 522-5201 | 3847 |
| Pacific Southwest Cont LLC (PA) | 2671 | B | 209 526-0444 | 3931 |
| Pacific Southwest Cont LLC | 2671 | E | 209 526-0444 | 3932 |
| Parks Group Ey | 2752 | E | 209 576-2568 | 4718 |
| Village Instant Printing Inc | 2752 | E | 209 576-2568 | 4804 |
| Willey Printing Company (PA) | 2752 | E | 209 524-4811 | 4812 |
| Amcor Manufacturing Inc | 2819 | F | 209 581-9687 | 5069 |
| JM Huber Corporation | 2819 | D | 209 549-9771 | 5096 |
| Wright Pharma Inc | 2834 | E | 209 549-9771 | 5719 |
| Nutrien AG Solutions Inc | 2875 | F | 209 551-1424 | 6189 |
| Westland Technologies Inc | 3061 | D | 800 877-7734 | 6478 |
| Altium Packaging LLC | 3085 | E | 209 531-9180 | 6607 |
| Ring Container Tech LLC | 3085 | D | 209 238-3426 | 6616 |
| Fabricated Extrusion Co LLC (PA) | 3089 | E | 209 529-9200 | 6825 |
| Gallo Glass Company (HQ) | 3221 | A | 209 341-3710 | 7182 |
| Allied Concrete and Supply Co | 3273 | E | 209 524-3177 | 7401 |
| Bambacigno Steel Company | 3312 | E | 209 524-9681 | 7605 |
| Lamar Tool & Die Casting Inc | 3312 | D | 209 545-5525 | 7618 |
| Silgan Containers Mfg Corp | 3411 | E | 209 521-6469 | 7928 |
| California Stl Fabricators Inc | 3441 | F | 209 566-0629 | 8112 |
| Gilwin Company | 3442 | E | 209 522-9775 | 8267 |
| P I Inc | 3442 | D | 209 527-8020 | 8282 |
| Hsi Mechanical Inc | 3444 | E | 209 408-0183 | 8470 |
| Kingspan Insulated Panels Inc | 3448 | C | 209 531-9091 | 8673 |
| JR Daniels Commercial Bldrs | 3449 | F | 209 545-6040 | 8701 |
| Jackrabbit | 3523 | F | 209 521-9325 | 9362 |
| Dayton Superior Corporation | 3537 | E | 209 869-1201 | 9517 |
| Golden Valley & Associates Inc | 3537 | E | 209 549-1549 | 9522 |
| LTI Boyd | 3549 | A | 800 554-0200 | 9739 |
| Container Graphics Corp | 3555 | D | 209 577-0181 | 9764 |
| Billington Welding & Mfg Inc | 3556 | E | 209 526-0846 | 9779 |
| E & S Precision Machine Inc | 3599 | F | 209 545-6161 | 10818 |
| Factory Technologies Inc | 3613 | E | 209 248-8420 | 11241 |
| Peco Inspx | 3625 | F | 209 576-3345 | 11339 |
| 1le California Inc | 3646 | E | 209 846-7541 | 11512 |
| Deltatrak Inc | 3829 | E | 209 579-5343 | 14860 |
| Hoya Corporation | 3851 | E | 209 579-7739 | 15602 |
| Hoya Optical Inc (PA) | 3851 | D | 209 579-7739 | 15603 |
| Johnson United Inc (PA) | 3993 | E | 209 543-1320 | 15995 |
| Sign Designs Inc | 3993 | E | 209 524-4484 | 16035 |
| Exact Corp | 5083 | E | 209 544-8600 | 16797 |
| Foster Dairy Farms (PA) | 5143 | A | 209 576-3400 | 17129 |
| Foster Dairy Products Distrg (PA) | 5143 | E | 209 576-3400 | 17130 |
| Squab Producers Calif Inc | 5144 | D | 209 537-4744 | 17135 |
| Yosemite Meat Company Inc | 5147 | E | 209 524-5117 | 17167 |
| Southwest Hide Co | 5159 | E | 209 382-5633 | 17223 |
| Enviro Tech Chemical Svcs Inc (DH) | 5169 | C | 209 581-9576 | 17243 |
| Varni Brothers Corporation (DH) | 5181 | D | 209 521-1777 | 17261 |
| Builders Firstsource Inc | 5211 | E | 209 545-0736 | 17324 |
| Howk Well & Equipment Co Inc | 5999 | E | 209 529-4110 | 17707 |
| G3 Enterprises Inc | 7336 | E | 209 341-5265 | 17828 |
| Never Boring Design Associates | 7336 | E | 209 526-9136 | 17834 |
| A & A Portables Inc | 7359 | E | 209 524-0401 | 17854 |
| Pinnacle Solutions Inc | 7389 | D | 209 523-8300 | 19117 |
| Rubik Built LLC | 8742 | F | 209 408-0626 | 19537 |

## MOJAVE, CA - Kern County

| | SIC | EMP | PHONE | ENTRY# |
|---|---|---|---|---|
| Golden Queen Mining Co LLC | 1041 | C | 661 824-4300 | 103 |
| Pepsi-Cola Metro Btlg Co Inc | 2086 | E | 661 824-2051 | 1911 |
| PPG Industries Inc | 2851 | E | 661 824-4532 | 6104 |
| Trical Inc | 2879 | E | 661 824-2494 | 6212 |
| PRC - Desoto International Inc | 2891 | C | 661 824-4532 | 6241 |
| Calportland Company | 3241 | E | 661 824-2401 | 7249 |
| Commodity Resource Envmtl Inc | 3339 | E | 661 824-2416 | 7711 |
| Innovative Coatings Technology Corporation | 3479 | C | 661 824-8101 | 9080 |
| Scaled Composites LLC | 3721 | B | 661 824-4541 | 13688 |
| Astrobotic Technology Inc | 3761 | E | 888 488-8455 | 14078 |
| Masten Space Systems Inc | 3761 | E | 888 488-8455 | 14083 |
| Xcor Aerospace Inc | 3761 | D | 661 824-4714 | 14100 |

## MONROVIA, CA - Los Angeles County

| | SIC | EMP | PHONE | ENTRY# |
|---|---|---|---|---|
| Peck Road Gravel Pit | 1442 | F | 626 574-7570 | 319 |
| Burnett & Son Meat Co Inc | 2011 | D | 626 357-2165 | 584 |
| Kruse and Son Inc | 2013 | E | 626 358-4536 | 651 |
| Gsl Tech Inc | 2023 | F | 877 572-9617 | 760 |
| Decore-Ative Spc NC LLC (PA) | 2431 | A | 626 254-9191 | 3126 |
| Vinyl Technology LLC (PA) | 2671 | C | 626 443-5257 | 3941 |
| Califrna Nwspapers Ltd Partnr (DH) | 2711 | B | 626 962-8811 | 4085 |
| Pasadena Newspapers Inc (PA) | 2711 | C | 626 578-6300 | 4180 |
| Global Compliance Inc | 2741 | E | 626 303-6855 | 4403 |
| Genzyme Corporation | 2834 | E | 626 471-9922 | 5458 |
| Decco US Post-Harvest Inc (HQ) | 2879 | F | 800 221-0925 | 6199 |
| Mask-Off Company Inc | 2891 | F | 626 359-3261 | 6236 |
| 3M Company | 3069 | E | 626 358-0136 | 6479 |
| Duracold Refrigeration Mfg LLC | 3448 | E | 626 358-1710 | 8663 |
| Jan-Kens Enameling Company Inc | 3479 | E | 626 358-1849 | 9084 |
| Amada Weld Tech Inc (HQ) | 3548 | E | 626 303-5676 | 9721 |
| Belco Packaging Systems Inc | 3565 | E | 626 357-9566 | 10014 |
| Micro/Sys Inc | 3571 | E | 818 244-4600 | 10183 |
| Aremac Associates Inc | 3599 | E | 626 303-8795 | 10715 |
| Production Lapping Company | 3599 | F | 626 359-0611 | 11051 |
| Roncelli Plastics Inc | 3599 | C | 800 250-6516 | 11089 |
| Silc Technologies Inc | 3674 | D | 626 375-1231 | 12698 |
| Worldwide Energy and Mfg USA (PA) | 3674 | D | 650 692-7788 | 12806 |
| Clary Corporation | 3679 | E | 626 359-4486 | 12941 |
| Foote Axle & Forge LLC | 3714 | E | 323 268-4151 | 13501 |

| | SIC | EMP | PHONE | ENTRY# |
|---|---|---|---|---|
| Aerovironment Inc. | 3721 | E | 626 357-9983 | 13626 |
| Aerovironment Inc. | 3721 | E | 626 357-9983 | 13627 |
| Aerovironment Inc. | 3721 | E | 626 357-9983 | 13629 |
| Ducommun Aerostructures Inc. | 3728 | E | 626 358-3211 | 13827 |
| Ducommun Incorporated | 3728 | E | 626 358-3211 | 13830 |
| Mulgrew Arcft Components Inc. | 3728 | D | 626 256-1375 | 13912 |
| L3harris Technologies Inc. | 3812 | C | 626 305-6230 | 14207 |
| Hoya Holdings Inc. | 3827 | C | 626 739-5200 | 14781 |
| Ondax Inc. | 3827 | F | 626 357-9600 | 14805 |
| Radcal Corporation | 3829 | E | 626 357-7921 | 14912 |
| Amada Weld Tech Inc. | 3841 | E | 626 303-5676 | 14963 |
| Chromologic LLC | 3841 | E | 626 381-9974 | 15042 |
| Konigsberg Instruments Inc. | 3841 | E | 626 775-6500 | 15145 |
| 3M Unitek Corporation | 3843 | B | 626 445-7960 | 15435 |
| Wbt Group LLC | 3999 | E | 323 735-1201 | 16269 |
| Nzxt Inc **(PA)** | 5045 | B | 626 385-8272 | 16535 |
| Linear Industries Ltd **(PA)** | 5085 | E | 626 303-1130 | 16882 |
| Naked Juice Co Glendora Inc **(HQ)** | 5499 | E | 626 873-2600 | 17429 |
| Executive Auto Reconditioning | 7542 | E | 626 416-3322 | 19165 |

## MONTCLAIR, CA - San Bernardino County

| | SIC | EMP | PHONE | ENTRY# |
|---|---|---|---|---|
| National Ewp Inc. | 1081 | F | 909 931-4014 | 108 |
| West-Tech Mechanical Inc. | 1711 | F | 909 635-1170 | 441 |
| Elements Food Group Inc. | 2052 | D | 909 983-2011 | 1273 |
| Ingredients By Nature LLC | 2099 | F | 909 230-6200 | 2239 |
| Westside Accessories Inc **(PA)** | 2387 | F | 626 858-5452 | 2886 |
| California Offset Printers Inc **(PA)** | 2752 | D | 818 291-1100 | 4542 |
| Thomas Burt | 2752 | F | 626 301-9065 | 4786 |
| Bluefield Associates Inc. | 2844 | E | 909 476-6027 | 5949 |
| Cpd Industries | 3089 | E | 909 465-5596 | 6784 |
| McDaniel Inc. | 3324 | F | 909 591-8353 | 7690 |
| Empire Products Inc. | 3433 | D | 909 399-3355 | 8065 |
| Amazing Steel Company | 3441 | E | 909 590-0393 | 8093 |
| Mitchell Fabrication | 3441 | E | 909 590-0393 | 8189 |
| Pacific Duct Inc. | 3444 | F | 909 635-1335 | 8527 |
| John L Conley Inc. | 3448 | D | 909 627-0981 | 8671 |
| Fittings That Fit Inc. | 3496 | F | 909 248-2808 | 9218 |
| Ampac Usa Inc. | 3589 | E | 435 291-0961 | 10535 |
| American Nail Plate Ltg Inc. | 3645 | D | 909 982-1807 | 11487 |
| Copp Industrial Mfg Inc. | 3728 | E | 909 593-7448 | 13815 |
| Expo Power Systems Inc. | 5063 | E | 800 506-9884 | 16652 |
| Industrial Wood Products Inc. | 5211 | F | 909 625-1247 | 17335 |
| Hampton Tdder Tchncal Svcs Inc. | 8734 | F | 909 628-1256 | 19503 |

## MONTE SERENO, CA - Santa Clara County

| | SIC | EMP | PHONE | ENTRY# |
|---|---|---|---|---|
| Coast Engraving Companies Inc. | 2796 | E | 408 297-2555 | 5023 |

## MONTEBELLO, CA - Los Angeles County

| | SIC | EMP | PHONE | ENTRY# |
|---|---|---|---|---|
| Yonekyu USA Inc. | 2013 | D | 323 581-4194 | 677 |
| Ingenue Inc. | 2015 | D | 323 726-8084 | 695 |
| Bimbo Bakeries Usa Inc. | 2051 | F | 323 720-6099 | 1172 |
| J & R Bottling and Distributing Inc. | 2086 | E | 323 724-4076 | 1895 |
| La Bottleworks Inc. | 2086 | E | 323 724-4076 | 1899 |
| Reyes Coca-Cola Bottling LLC | 2086 | C | 323 278-2600 | 1948 |
| Unix Packaging LLC **(PA)** | 2086 | D | 213 627-5050 | 1970 |
| Arevalo Tortilleria Inc **(PA)** | 2099 | D | 323 888-1711 | 2130 |
| Bltee LLC | 2331 | E | 213 802-1736 | 2656 |
| All Access Apparel Inc **(PA)** | 2361 | C | 323 889-4300 | 2851 |
| Vft Inc. | 2392 | E | 323 728-2280 | 2952 |
| J & M Richman Corporation | 2395 | E | 800 422-9646 | 2991 |
| Hardwood Flrg Liquidators Inc **(PA)** | 2426 | D | 323 201-4200 | 3094 |
| Big Tree Furniture & Inds Inc **(PA)** | 2511 | E | 310 894-7500 | 3436 |
| Atlas Survival Shelters LLC | 2514 | E | 323 727-7084 | 3498 |
| Gateway Mattress Co Inc. | 2515 | D | 323 725-1923 | 3527 |
| Papercutters Inc. | 2671 | E | 323 888-1330 | 3934 |
| Sunshine Fpc Inc. | 2673 | D | 323 721-8168 | 3982 |
| LA Envelope Incorporated | 2677 | E | 323 838-9300 | 4010 |
| Northeast Newspapers Inc. | 2711 | E | 213 727-1117 | 4174 |
| Monarch Litho Inc **(PA)** | 2752 | E | 323 727-0300 | 4700 |
| Turner Fiberfill Inc. | 2824 | E | 323 724-7957 | 5224 |
| Desser Tire & Rubber Co LLC **(DH)** | 3011 | E | 323 721-4900 | 6408 |
| Montebello Plastics LLC | 3081 | E | 323 728-6814 | 6564 |
| Delamo Manufacturing Inc. | 3089 | D | 323 936-3566 | 6795 |
| Ppp LLC | 3089 | F | 323 832-9627 | 6974 |
| US Polymers Inc **(PA)** | 3089 | D | 323 728-3023 | 7066 |
| Howmet Aerospace Inc. | 3353 | C | 323 728-3901 | 7729 |
| A & A Fabrication & Polsg Corp | 3441 | F | 562 696-0441 | 8084 |
| PCI Industries Inc. | 3444 | E | 323 889-6770 | 8532 |
| Performance Forge Inc. | 3462 | E | 323 722-3460 | 8785 |
| Troy Sheet Metal Works Inc **(PA)** | 3465 | D | 323 720-4100 | 8811 |
| Universal Metal Plating | 3471 | F | 626 969-7932 | 9028 |
| H & L Tooth Company **(PA)** | 3531 | D | 323 721-5146 | 9425 |
| Ingalls Conveyors Inc. | 3535 | E | 323 837-9900 | 9487 |
| Thistle Roller Co Inc. | 3555 | E | 323 685-5322 | 9775 |
| General Industrial Repair | 3599 | E | 323 278-0873 | 10857 |
| Dow-Elco Inc. | 3612 | E | 323 723-1288 | 11211 |
| Amplifier Technologies Inc **(HQ)** | 3663 | E | 323 278-0001 | 11807 |
| Shyft Group Inc. | 3711 | D | 323 276-1933 | 13385 |
| Craig Manufacturing Company **(PA)** | 3714 | D | 323 726-7355 | 13478 |
| Commerce On Demand LLC | 3999 | D | 562 360-4819 | 16120 |
| PCI Industries Inc. | 3999 | E | 323 889-6770 | 16197 |
| Reu Distribution LLC | 5023 | A | 323 201-4200 | 16434 |
| Desser Tire & Rubber Co LLC | 5088 | E | 323 837-1497 | 16919 |
| Orora Packaging Solutions | 5113 | C | 323 832-2000 | 17008 |
| 2253 Apparel LLC **(PA)** | 5137 | D | 323 837-9800 | 17085 |
| Niitakaya Usa Inc **(PA)** | 5149 | E | 323 720-5050 | 17201 |
| Katzkin Leather Inc **(PA)** | 5199 | C | 323 725-1243 | 17298 |
| Johnstone Supply Inc. | 5722 | D | 323 722-2859 | 17541 |
| Btg Textiles Inc. | 5963 | E | 323 586-9488 | 17678 |
| Desser Holding Company LLC **(HQ)** | 6719 | E | 323 721-4900 | 17745 |
| Wilbur Curtis Co Inc. | 6719 | B | 800 421-6150 | 17748 |
| Leidos Government Services Inc. | 7379 | C | 323 721-6979 | 19039 |
| New Wave Embroidery | 7389 | F | 323 727-0076 | 19109 |

## MONTEREY, CA - Monterey County

| | SIC | EMP | PHONE | ENTRY# |
|---|---|---|---|---|
| Great American Wineries Inc. | 2084 | E | 831 920-4736 | 1601 |
| California New Foods LLC | 2099 | E | 831 444-1872 | 2155 |
| Dole Fresh Vegetables Inc **(HQ)** | 2099 | C | 831 422-8871 | 2188 |
| Robert Talbott Inc **(PA)** | 2311 | E | 831 649-6000 | 2565 |
| Monterey County Herald Company **(DH)** | 2711 | E | 831 372-3311 | 4160 |
| Evan-Moor Corporation **(HQ)** | 2731 | E | 831 649-5901 | 4329 |
| Art Brand Studios LLC **(PA)** | 2741 | E | 408 201-5000 | 4365 |
| Vybion Inc. | 2824 | F | 607 227-2502 | 5226 |
| Cyberdata Corporation | 3577 | E | 831 373-2601 | 10355 |
| Steiner Eoptics Inc. | 3699 | D | 831 373-0701 | 13311 |
| Northrop Grumman Systems Corp | 3812 | D | 703 406-5474 | 14265 |
| Kurz Instruments Inc. | 3822 | D | 831 646-5911 | 14363 |
| Sierra Instruments Inc **(HQ)** | 3823 | D | 831 373-0200 | 14459 |
| Excelligence Learning Corp **(PA)** | 5999 | E | 831 333-2000 | 17703 |
| Ppt Group Corp **(HQ)** | 8734 | E | 831 655-6600 | 19506 |

## MONTEREY PARK, CA - Los Angeles County

| | SIC | EMP | PHONE | ENTRY# |
|---|---|---|---|---|
| Alltech Industries Inc. | 1731 | E | 323 450-2168 | 450 |
| Architectural Woodworking Co. | 1751 | D | 626 570-4125 | 487 |
| Sencha Naturals Inc. | 2064 | F | 213 353-9908 | 1329 |
| La Colonial Tortilla Pdts Inc. | 2099 | C | 626 289-3647 | 2250 |
| Pacific Culinary Group Inc. | 2099 | E | 626 284-1328 | 2309 |
| International Daily News Inc **(PA)** | 2711 | E | 323 265-1317 | 4135 |
| World Journal La LLC **(HQ)** | 2711 | C | 323 268-4982 | 4224 |
| Graphic Color Systems Inc. | 2752 | D | 323 283-3000 | 4622 |
| Inertech Supply Inc. | 3053 | D | 626 282-2000 | 6454 |
| Rehrig Pacific Holdings Inc **(PA)** | 3089 | D | 323 262-5145 | 7000 |
| West-Bag Inc. | 3089 | E | 323 264-0750 | 7077 |
| L C Miller Company | 3567 | E | 323 268-3611 | 10056 |
| Optic Arts Holdings Inc. | 3646 | E | 213 250-6069 | 11549 |
| Ross Name Plate Company | 3993 | E | 323 725-6812 | 16027 |
| Union Technology Corp. | 5065 | E | 323 266-6871 | 16740 |
| Oakcroft Associates Inc **(PA)** | 5082 | E | 323 261-5122 | 16793 |

## MONTROSE, CA - Los Angeles County

| | SIC | EMP | PHONE | ENTRY# |
|---|---|---|---|---|
| Vitachrome Graphics Group Inc. | 2759 | E | 818 957-0900 | 4979 |
| Northrop Grumman Systems Corp. | 3812 | D | 818 249-5252 | 14250 |
| Gloves In A Bottle Inc. | 5122 | E | 818 248-9980 | 17039 |

## MOORPARK, CA - Ventura County

| | SIC | EMP | PHONE | ENTRY# |
|---|---|---|---|---|
| Corporate Graphics & Printing | 2752 | F | 805 529-5333 | 4573 |
| Sterisyn Inc. | 2834 | E | 805 991-9694 | 5677 |
| Insparation Inc. | 2844 | E | 805 553-0820 | 5994 |
| Kamsut Incorporated | 2844 | E | 805 495-7479 | 5996 |
| Husky Injction Mlding Systems | 3089 | E | 805 523-9593 | 6860 |
| G T Water Products Inc. | 3432 | F | 805 529-2900 | 8053 |
| Topaz Systems Inc **(PA)** | 3577 | E | 805 520-8282 | 10445 |
| Glendee Corp **(PA)** | 3599 | E | 805 523-2422 | 10861 |
| Glendee Corp | 3599 | E | 805 523-2422 | 10862 |
| Mac M Mc Cully Corporation | 3621 | E | 805 529-0661 | 11277 |
| Penta Financial Inc. | 3671 | F | 818 882-3872 | 12037 |
| Penta Laboratories LLC | 3671 | F | 818 882-3872 | 12038 |
| Anc Technology Inc. | 3672 | D | 805 530-3958 | 12054 |
| Benchmark Elec Mfg Sltons Mrpa | 3672 | A | 805 532-2800 | 12068 |
| Laritech Inc. | 3672 | C | 805 529-5000 | 12151 |
| Semiconductor Equipment Corp | 3674 | F | 805 529-2293 | 12690 |
| Ultron Systems Inc. | 3674 | F | 805 529-1485 | 12778 |
| Nea Electronics Inc. | 3678 | E | 805 292-4010 | 12891 |
| Pterodynamics Inc. | 3721 | F | 719 257-3103 | 13686 |
| Ensign-Bickford Arospc Def Co. | 3812 | C | 805 292-4000 | 14185 |
| Gooch and Housego Cal LLC | 3827 | D | 805 529-3324 | 14779 |

GEOGRAPHIC

# MOORPARK, CA

| | SIC | EMP | PHONE | ENTRY# |
|---|---|---|---|---|
| Koros USA Inc | 3841 | E | 805 529-0825 | 15146 |
| Mpo Videotronics Inc (PA) | 3861 | D | 805 499-8513 | 15654 |
| Conversion Technology Co Inc (PA) | 3952 | E | 805 378-0033 | 15884 |
| Sercomp LLC (PA) | 3955 | D | 805 299-0020 | 15901 |
| Globaluxe Inc | 3999 | E | 805 583-4600 | 16136 |
| Picnic Time Inc | 3999 | D | 805 529-7400 | 16204 |
| Testequity LLC (HQ) | 7629 | E | 805 498-9933 | 19180 |

## MORAGA, CA - Contra Costa County

| | SIC | EMP | PHONE | ENTRY# |
|---|---|---|---|---|
| Intematix Corporation | 3661 | F | 925 631-9005 | 11771 |

## MORENO VALLEY, CA - Riverside County

| | SIC | EMP | PHONE | ENTRY# |
|---|---|---|---|---|
| Life Is Life LLC | 2022 | E | 310 584-7541 | 729 |
| Fine Mexican Food Products Inc | 2099 | F | 714 476-7104 | 2198 |
| Serta Simmons Bedding LLC | 2515 | E | 951 807-8467 | 3537 |
| Hsb Holdings Inc | 3011 | E | 951 214-6590 | 6411 |
| Envirnmntal Mlding Cncepts LLC | 3069 | E | 951 214-6596 | 6491 |
| Cardinal Glass Industries Inc | 3211 | C | 951 485-9007 | 7165 |
| Modular Metal Fabricators Inc | 3444 | C | 951 242-3154 | 8515 |
| CAr Enterprises Inc | 3578 | F | 951 413-6262 | 10458 |
| Harman Professional Inc | 3651 | E | 951 242-2927 | 11665 |
| California Supertrucks Inc | 3713 | F | 951 656-2903 | 13402 |
| Supreme Truck Bodies Cal Inc | 3713 | E | 800 827-0753 | 13431 |
| Accuturn Corporation | 3812 | E | 951 656-6621 | 14134 |
| Bcd Industries Corp | 3999 | F | 760 927-8988 | 16093 |
| Skechers USA Inc | 5139 | E | 951 242-4307 | 17110 |
| Certified Tire & Svc Ctrs Inc | 5531 | E | 951 656-6466 | 17447 |

## MORGAN HILL, CA - Santa Clara County

| | SIC | EMP | PHONE | ENTRY# |
|---|---|---|---|---|
| Guglielmo Emilo Winery Inc | 0172 | F | 408 779-2145 | 16 |
| Monterey Mushrooms LLC | 0182 | E | 408 779-4191 | 52 |
| Mission Bell Mfg Co Inc | 1751 | B | 408 778-2036 | 498 |
| National Glass Systems Inc | 1793 | E | 408 835-5124 | 541 |
| Emilio Guglielmo Winery Inc | 2084 | F | 408 779-2145 | 1554 |
| Don Vito Ozuna Food Corp | 2096 | E | 408 465-2010 | 2089 |
| Gobble Inc | 2099 | C | 650 847-1258 | 2216 |
| Sun Basket Inc | 2099 | D | 925 240-1512 | 2363 |
| Aircraft Covers Inc | 2394 | E | 408 738-3959 | 2967 |
| Aircraft Covers Inc (PA) | 2394 | E | 408 738-3959 | 2968 |
| California Kit Cab Door Corp (PA) | 2434 | D | 408 782-5700 | 3227 |
| Greif Inc | 2655 | D | 408 779-2161 | 3905 |
| Babylon Printing Inc | 2752 | E | 408 519-5000 | 4525 |
| Zaitun Printing & Graphics Inc | 2752 | F | 402 305-0109 | 4818 |
| Toray Advanced Composites USA Inc (DH) | 2821 | C | 408 465-8500 | 5213 |
| Anaerobe Systems | 2835 | E | 408 782-7557 | 5737 |
| New Prduct Intgrtion Sltons In (HQ) | 3315 | E | 408 944-9178 | 7649 |
| Golden State Assembly Inc | 3353 | C | 510 226-8155 | 7727 |
| Airtronics Metal Products Inc (PA) | 3444 | C | 408 977-7800 | 8368 |
| Arts Sheet Metal Mfg Inc | 3444 | E | 408 778-0606 | 8382 |
| Creative Mfg Solutions Inc | 3444 | E | 408 327-0600 | 8421 |
| Emtec Engineering | 3444 | F | 408 779-5800 | 8442 |
| Lara Manufacturing Inc | 3444 | E | 408 778-0811 | 8485 |
| Pega Precision Inc | 3444 | E | 408 778-3700 | 8534 |
| Pinnacle Manufacturing Corp | 3444 | E | 408 778-6100 | 8537 |
| SAE Engineering Inc | 3444 | E | 408 492-1784 | 8564 |
| Tobar Industries Inc | 3444 | E | 408 778-3901 | 8596 |
| U-C Components Inc (PA) | 3452 | E | 408 782-1929 | 8769 |
| Italix Company Inc | 3479 | F | 408 988-2487 | 9083 |
| Step Tools Unlimited Inc | 3545 | E | 408 988-8898 | 9701 |
| Advanced McHning Tchniques Inc | 3599 | E | 408 778-4500 | 10677 |
| Dcpm Inc | 3599 | E | 408 928-2510 | 10802 |
| Kalman Manufacturing Inc | 3599 | E | 408 776-7664 | 10920 |
| KDF Inc | 3599 | E | 408 779-3731 | 10923 |
| M & L Precision Machining Inc (PA) | 3599 | E | 408 436-3955 | 10949 |
| Robson Technologies Inc | 3599 | E | 408 779-8008 | 11084 |
| Lin Engineering Inc | 3621 | C | 408 919-0200 | 11276 |
| Anritsu Company (DH) | 3663 | B | 800 267-4878 | 11809 |
| Macom Technology Solutions Inc | 3663 | D | 408 542-8872 | 11886 |
| Terrasat Communications Inc | 3663 | E | 408 782-5911 | 11965 |
| Amtech Microelectronics Inc | 3672 | E | 408 612-8888 | 12053 |
| Flextronics Intl USA Inc | 3672 | B | 408 577-2262 | 12113 |
| Paramit Corporation (PA) | 3672 | E | 408 782-5600 | 12186 |
| All Sensors Corporation | 3674 | E | 408 776-9434 | 12289 |
| Infineon Technologies | 3674 | F | 408 779-2367 | 12483 |
| Dinan Engineering Inc | 3714 | E | 408 779-8584 | 13486 |
| Tropos Technologies Inc | 3714 | F | 408 571-6104 | 13593 |
| Global Motorsport Parts Inc | 3751 | D | 408 778-0500 | 14059 |
| Tecan Systems Inc | 3821 | D | 408 953-3100 | 14350 |
| Anritsu US Holding Inc (HQ) | 3825 | B | 408 778-2000 | 14496 |
| Duke Empirical Inc | 3841 | D | 831 420-1104 | 15072 |
| Phoenix Deventures Inc | 3841 | E | 408 782-6240 | 15225 |
| Sheathing Technologies Inc | 3841 | E | 408 782-2720 | 15254 |
| US Technical Ceramics Inc | 5032 | E | 408 779-0303 | 16487 |
| Applied Wrless Idntfctons Grou (PA) | 5065 | E | 408 779-1929 | 16690 |
| Kycon Inc | 5065 | E | 408 494-0330 | 16713 |
| Micro-Mechanics Inc | 5065 | E | 408 779-2927 | 16719 |
| Minimatics Inc (PA) | 5065 | E | 650 969-5630 | 16720 |
| Leal Vineyards Inc | 7299 | F | 408 778-1978 | 17774 |
| Oea International Incorporated | 7372 | E | 408 778-6747 | 18612 |
| Replico Corporation | 7372 | D | 408 842-8600 | 18734 |
| Serrala Americas Inc | 7372 | D | 650 655-3939 | 18784 |

## MORRO BAY, CA - San Luis Obispo County

| | SIC | EMP | PHONE | ENTRY# |
|---|---|---|---|---|
| All Good | 2844 | E | 877 239-4667 | 5941 |

## MOSS BEACH, CA - San Mateo County

| | SIC | EMP | PHONE | ENTRY# |
|---|---|---|---|---|
| Biz Performance Solutions Inc | 7372 | F | 408 844-4284 | 18107 |

## MOSS LANDING, CA - Monterey County

| | SIC | EMP | PHONE | ENTRY# |
|---|---|---|---|---|
| Verdagy Inc | 2813 | F | 831 800-0250 | 5060 |
| Calera Corporation | 2869 | E | | 6137 |

## MOUNTAIN PASS, CA - San Bernardino County

| | SIC | EMP | PHONE | ENTRY# |
|---|---|---|---|---|
| Mp Materials Corp | 1099 | D | 702 844-6111 | 110 |
| Chevron Mining Inc | 1221 | C | 760 856-7625 | 111 |
| Mp Mine Operations LLC | 1481 | C | 702 277-0848 | 336 |

## MOUNTAIN VIEW, CA - Santa Clara County

| | SIC | EMP | PHONE | ENTRY# |
|---|---|---|---|---|
| Chay & Harris Pntg Contrs Inc | 1721 | E | 650 966-1472 | 443 |
| Teachers Curriculum Inst LLC (PA) | 2731 | E | 800 497-6138 | 4348 |
| Staffing Industry Analysts Inc | 2741 | E | 650 390-6200 | 4470 |
| Tellme Networks Inc | 2741 | B | 650 693-1009 | 4478 |
| Fernqvist Retail Systems Inc (DH) | 2754 | F | 650 428-0330 | 4822 |
| Pickering Laboratories Inc | 2819 | E | 650 694-6700 | 5111 |
| Map Pharmaceuticals Inc | 2834 | E | 650 625-8790 | 5542 |
| Mereo Biopharma 5 Inc | 2834 | D | 650 995-8200 | 5553 |
| Quark Pharmaceuticals Inc (DH) | 2834 | E | 510 402-4020 | 5621 |
| Naxcor Inc | 2835 | F | 650 328-9398 | 5768 |
| Igm Biosciences Inc | 2836 | E | 650 965-7873 | 5839 |
| Mineral Earth Sciences LLC | 3523 | D | 650 532-9590 | 9371 |
| Nuro Inc | 3559 | A | 650 476-2687 | 9885 |
| Perceptimed Inc | 3559 | E | 650 941-7000 | 9890 |
| General Dynmics Mssion Systems | 3571 | D | 650 966-2000 | 10157 |
| Eye-Fi Inc | 3572 | E | 650 969-3162 | 10237 |
| Infineta Systems Inc | 3577 | E | 408 514-6650 | 10382 |
| Pano Logic Inc | 3577 | E | 650 743-1773 | 10420 |
| Auto-Chlor System of Mid S LLC | 3599 | D | 650 967-3085 | 10725 |
| Lenz Precision Technology Inc | 3599 | E | 650 966-1784 | 10943 |
| Squaglia Manufacturing Company (PA) | 3599 | E | 650 965-9644 | 11124 |
| Siwibi Wholesale | 3612 | E | 650 448-1041 | 11230 |
| Nextinput Inc (HQ) | 3625 | E | 408 770-9293 | 11336 |
| Alcatel-Lucent USA Inc | 3661 | D | 650 623-3300 | 11749 |
| Avid Systems Inc (DH) | 3663 | C | 650 526-1600 | 11817 |
| Euphonix Inc (DH) | 3663 | E | 650 526-1600 | 11854 |
| Huawei Device USA Inc | 3663 | C | 408 306-7171 | 11866 |
| Audience Inc | 3674 | B | 650 254-2800 | 12342 |
| Ceva Development Inc (HQ) | 3674 | E | 650 417-7900 | 12380 |
| Clearwell Systems Inc | 3674 | C | 877 253-2793 | 12383 |
| Enfabrica Corporation | 3674 | E | 650 206-8533 | 12421 |
| Esperanto Technologies Inc (PA) | 3674 | D | 650 319-7357 | 12425 |
| Flex Logix Technologies Inc | 3674 | D | 650 867-2904 | 12433 |
| Gen Digital Inc | 3674 | E | 781 530-2200 | 12442 |
| Global Testing Corporation | 3674 | D | 408 745-0718 | 12448 |
| Microsemi Soc Corp | 3674 | E | 650 318-4200 | 12580 |
| Symantec SEC Holdings I Inc | 3674 | E | 650 527-8000 | 12751 |
| Virage Logic Corporation (HQ) | 3674 | B | 650 584-5000 | 12790 |
| Lightbit Corporation | 3678 | F | 650 988-9500 | 12889 |
| Leyden Energy Inc | 3679 | E | 408 776-2779 | 13022 |
| Teledyne Cougar Inc | 3679 | C | 408 522-3838 | 13101 |
| Teledyne Defense Elec LLC (HQ) | 3679 | E | 650 691-9800 | 13103 |
| Capella Photonics Inc | 3695 | E | 408 360-4240 | 13192 |
| Lasercard Corporation | 3695 | D | 650 969-4428 | 13197 |
| Guzik Technical Enterprises (PA) | 3699 | E | 650 625-8000 | 13246 |
| Knightscope Inc | 3699 | E | 650 924-1025 | 13262 |
| Lunar Energy Inc (PA) | 3699 | E | 408 475-4137 | 13269 |
| Aeva Technologies Inc (PA) | 3714 | B | 650 481-7070 | 13448 |
| Wisk Aero LLC (PA) | 3721 | B | 650 641-0920 | 13697 |
| Matternet Inc | 3728 | E | 650 260-2727 | 13901 |
| Argon St Inc | 3812 | E | 650 988-4700 | 14147 |
| Asrc Aerospace Corp | 3812 | B | 650 604-5946 | 14151 |
| Northrop Grumman Systems Corp | 3812 | D | 650 604-6056 | 14247 |
| Proteus Industries Inc | 3823 | E | 650 964-4163 | 14447 |
| Pacific Western Systems Inc (PA) | 3825 | E | 650 961-8855 | 14569 |
| Alza Corporation | 3826 | A | 650 564-5000 | 14607 |
| Inscopix Inc | 3827 | C | 650 600-3886 | 14786 |
| Applied Physics Systems Inc (PA) | 3829 | C | 650 965-0500 | 14843 |

# GEOGRAPHIC SECTION

## NAPA, CA

| | SIC | EMP | PHONE | ENTRY# |
|---|---|---|---|---|
| Athelas Inc. | 3841 | E | 833 524-1318 | 14980 |
| Guidant Sales LLC | 3841 | A | 650 965-2634 | 15103 |
| Hansen Medical Inc. | 3841 | C | 650 404-5800 | 15104 |
| Levita Magnetics Intl Corp. | 3841 | E | 530 456-6627 | 15147 |
| Neuropace Inc. | 3841 | C | 650 237-2700 | 15200 |
| Spine View Inc. | 3841 | D | 510 490-1753 | 15264 |
| Ventus Medical Inc. | 3841 | E | 408 200-5299 | 15300 |
| Johnson & Johnson. | 3842 | E | 650 903-4800 | 15368 |
| Exploramed Nc7 LLC. | 3845 | C | 650 559-5805 | 15537 |
| Iridex Corporation (PA) | 3845 | C | 650 940-4700 | 15548 |
| Attivo Networks Inc. | 5045 | D | 510 623-1000 | 16510 |
| Mitra Future Technologies Inc. | 5063 | D | 650 695-1245 | 16663 |
| Nanosolar Inc. | 5074 | B | | 16770 |
| Smartthings Inc (PA) | 5251 | F | 757 633-2308 | 17359 |
| Dome9 Security Inc. | 5734 | E | 831 212-2353 | 17550 |
| Pactum Ai Inc (PA) | 5734 | E | 669 289-9041 | 17556 |
| Intellisync Corporation. | 7371 | B | 650 625-2185 | 17933 |
| Neuron Fuel Inc. | 7371 | E | 408 537-3966 | 17954 |
| OTTERAI INC | 7371 | E | 650 250-6322 | 17959 |
| Agilepoint Inc (PA) | 7372 | D | 650 968-6789 | 18028 |
| Alivecor Inc (PA) | 7372 | E | 650 396-8650 | 18038 |
| Avast Software Inc (PA) | 7372 | D | 844 340-9251 | 18080 |
| Blackberry Corporation. | 7372 | A | 650 564-0016 | 18108 |
| Blue Coat LLC. | 7372 | A | 408 220-2200 | 18117 |
| Centrl Inc. | 7372 | E | 650 641-7092 | 18157 |
| Cloudjee Inc. | 7372 | E | 866 660-6099 | 18185 |
| Cloudsimple Inc. | 7372 | D | 412 568-3487 | 18187 |
| Codefast Inc. | 7372 | E | 408 687-4700 | 18191 |
| Confluent Inc (PA) | 7372 | A | 800 439-3207 | 18199 |
| Coursera Inc (PA) | 7372 | A | 650 963-9884 | 18208 |
| Cumulus Networks Inc (HQ) | 7372 | C | 650 383-6700 | 18214 |
| Datavisor Inc. | 7372 | D | 408 331-9886 | 18229 |
| Driveai Inc. | 7372 | C | 408 693-0765 | 18252 |
| Frontegg Inc. | 7372 | F | 408 734-6573 | 18335 |
| Glyntai Inc. | 7372 | F | 650 386-6932 | 18354 |
| Guardian Analytics Inc. | 7372 | E | 650 383-9200 | 18368 |
| Habeas Inc. | 7372 | E | 650 694-3300 | 18376 |
| Inmage Systems Inc. | 7372 | D | 408 200-3840 | 18420 |
| Intuit Financing Inc. | 7372 | E | 605 944-6000 | 18429 |
| Intuit Inc. | 7372 | E | 650 944-6000 | 18431 |
| Intuit Inc. | 7372 | C | 650 944-6000 | 18432 |
| Intuit Inc (PA) | 7372 | D | 650 944-6000 | 18437 |
| Ittavi Inc. | 7372 | E | 866 246-4408 | 18450 |
| Khan Academy Inc. | 7372 | D | 650 336-5426 | 18468 |
| Mint Software Inc. | 7372 | D | 650 944-6000 | 18549 |
| Mode Analytics Inc. | 7372 | E | 415 271-7599 | 18556 |
| Moveworks Inc (PA) | 7372 | E | 408 435-5100 | 18560 |
| Omnissa LLC. | 7372 | A | 650 239-7600 | 18615 |
| Progress Software Corporation. | 7372 | D | 650 341-7733 | 18699 |
| Realscout Inc. | 7372 | F | 650 397-6500 | 18726 |
| Red Hat Inc. | 7372 | E | 650 567-9039 | 18728 |
| Sentinelone Inc (PA) | 7372 | A | 855 868-3733 | 18778 |
| Synplicity Inc (HQ) | 7372 | C | 650 584-5000 | 18859 |
| Thoughtspot Inc (PA) | 7372 | C | 800 508-7008 | 18879 |
| Upguard Inc (PA) | 7372 | F | 888 882-3223 | 18903 |
| Veritas Software Global LLC. | 7372 | F | 650 335-8000 | 18917 |
| Viv Labs Inc. | 7372 | E | 650 268-9837 | 18924 |
| Wildfire Interactive Inc. | 7372 | C | 650 253-0000 | 18932 |
| Wipro LLC. | 7373 | E | 650 316-3555 | 18999 |
| Global Automation Inc (PA) | 7379 | E | 650 316-5900 | 19037 |
| Minaris Medical America Inc. | 8071 | C | 650 961-5501 | 19328 |
| Alto Neuroscience Inc. | 8731 | D | 650 200-0412 | 19438 |
| Semprius Inc. | 8731 | D | | 19474 |
| Raydiance Inc. | 8732 | F | 408 764-4000 | 19488 |

### MURPHYS, CA - Calaveras County

| | SIC | EMP | PHONE | ENTRY# |
|---|---|---|---|---|
| Lavender Ridge Vineyard Inc. | 2084 | E | 209 728-2441 | 1665 |
| Stevenot Winery & Imports Inc (PA) | 2084 | E | 209 728-0638 | 1763 |
| Kaiser Enterprises Inc (PA) | 3498 | E | 209 728-2091 | 9264 |
| Alchemy Cafe Inc (PA) | 7378 | F | 925 825-8400 | 19019 |

### MURRIETA, CA - Riverside County

| | SIC | EMP | PHONE | ENTRY# |
|---|---|---|---|---|
| North County Sand and Grav Inc. | 1442 | F | 951 928-2881 | 318 |
| Pgc Construction Inc. | 1521 | E | 760 549-4121 | 347 |
| Twin Power Usa LLC. | 1731 | E | 714 609-6014 | 471 |
| JI Design Enterprises Inc. | 2321 | D | 714 479-0240 | 2574 |
| Global Link Sourcing Inc. | 2671 | D | 951 698-1977 | 3928 |
| Gold Prospectors Assn Amer LLC. | 2721 | E | 951 699-4749 | 4260 |
| ASPE Inc. | 2759 | F | 951 296-2595 | 4845 |
| Nittobo America Inc (HQ) | 2836 | F | 951 677-5629 | 5851 |
| Kingman Industries Inc. | 2841 | E | 951 698-1812 | 5876 |
| No Prssure Prssure Wshg Svcs L. | 2842 | E | 951 477-1988 | 5920 |
| Premium Seals LLC (PA) | 3053 | C | 619 207-7603 | 6461 |

| | SIC | EMP | PHONE | ENTRY# |
|---|---|---|---|---|
| Medical Extrusion Tech Inc (PA) | 3089 | E | 951 698-4346 | 6908 |
| Glassplax. | 3231 | F | 951 677-4800 | 7223 |
| Muhlhauser Enterprises Inc (PA) | 3441 | F | 909 877-2792 | 8192 |
| Muhlhauser Steel Inc. | 3441 | E | 909 877-2792 | 8193 |
| S C Coatings Corporation. | 3479 | E | 951 461-9777 | 9116 |
| Apex Conveyor Corp. | 3535 | F | 951 304-7808 | 9481 |
| Chip-Makers Tooling Supply Inc. | 3544 | F | 562 698-5840 | 9611 |
| Hexco International. | 3559 | C | 951 677-2081 | 9864 |
| Pacwest Air Filter LLC. | 3564 | E | 951 698-2228 | 9994 |
| Tri-Dim Filter Corporation. | 3564 | E | 626 826-5893 | 10003 |
| Fireblast Global Inc. | 3569 | E | 951 277-8319 | 10089 |
| Bigfogg Inc (PA) | 3585 | F | 951 587-2460 | 10486 |
| Cryogenic Industries Inc. | 3634 | C | 951 677-2060 | 11403 |
| Air Adhart Inc. | 3672 | E | 951 698-4452 | 12046 |
| American Industrial Manufacturing Services Inc. | 3694 | C | 951 698-3379 | 13165 |
| Nuphoton Technologies Inc. | 3699 | E | 951 696-8366 | 13278 |
| Denso Pdts & Svcs Americas Inc. | 3714 | E | 951 698-3379 | 13485 |
| Ikhana Group LLC. | 3728 | E | 951 600-0009 | 13869 |
| Coherent Aerospace & Defense Inc (HQ) | 3812 | C | 951 926-2994 | 14170 |
| TMC Ice Protection Systems LLC. | 3812 | E | 951 677-6934 | 14321 |
| Romar Innovations Inc. | 3821 | D | 951 296-3480 | 14348 |
| Surplus Solutions LLC. | 3821 | F | 760 696-8788 | 14349 |
| Abbott Vascular Inc. | 3841 | A | 408 845-3186 | 14942 |
| Vmc International LLC. | 3843 | F | 760 723-1498 | 15493 |
| Lobue Laser & Eye Medical Ctrs. | 3845 | E | 951 696-1135 | 15551 |
| Art Signworks Inc. | 3993 | E | 951 698-8484 | 15945 |
| McCalls Country Canning Inc. | 3999 | F | 951 461-2277 | 16179 |
| Avenue Medical Equipment Inc. | 5047 | E | 949 680-7444 | 16575 |
| Waterstone Faucets LLC. | 5074 | F | 951 304-0520 | 16772 |
| Copan Diagnostics Inc (DH) | 5122 | E | 951 696-6957 | 17033 |
| Wilson Cycles Sports Corp. | 5511 | E | 951 894-5545 | 17444 |

### NAPA, CA - Napa County

| | SIC | EMP | PHONE | ENTRY# |
|---|---|---|---|---|
| California Wine Company. | 0172 | E | 707 603-2203 | 9 |
| Domaine Carneros Ltd. | 0172 | D | 707 257-0101 | 11 |
| Kenzo Estate Inc. | 0762 | E | 707 254-7572 | 93 |
| Pina Vineyard Management LLC. | 0762 | E | 707 944-2229 | 94 |
| Kaufman Building & MGT Inc. | 1442 | F | 707 732-3770 | 316 |
| Oakville Pump Service Inc. | 1711 | F | 707 944-2471 | 429 |
| Perfect Puree of NAPA Vly LLC. | 2037 | E | 707 261-5100 | 1015 |
| Sweetie Pies LLC. | 2051 | F | 707 257-7280 | 1245 |
| Anettes Chocolate Factory Inc. | 2064 | F | 707 252-4228 | 1300 |
| Le Belge Chocolatier Inc. | 2064 | E | 707 258-9200 | 1317 |
| Agnes Cove LLC (PA) | 2084 | E | 707 266-6899 | 1472 |
| Antinori California. | 2084 | E | 707 265-8866 | 1476 |
| Archery Summit Winery. | 2084 | F | 707 252-9777 | 1478 |
| Barrel Ten Qarter Cir Land Inc. | 2084 | E | 209 538-3131 | 1482 |
| Bouchaine Vineyards Inc. | 2084 | E | 707 252-9065 | 1489 |
| Caldwell Vineyard LLC. | 2084 | F | 707 255-1294 | 1495 |
| Cedar Knoll Vineyards Inc. | 2084 | E | 707 226-5587 | 1499 |
| Clos Du Val Wine Company Ltd. | 2084 | E | 707 259-2200 | 1510 |
| Codorniu Napa Inc. | 2084 | E | 707 254-2148 | 1514 |
| Crimson Wine Group Ltd (PA) | 2084 | C | 800 486-0503 | 1522 |
| Darioush Khaledi Winery LLC. | 2084 | E | 707 257-2345 | 1528 |
| Del Dotto Vineyards. | 2084 | E | 707 963-2134 | 1533 |
| Del Dotto Vineyards. | 2084 | D | 707 963-2134 | 1534 |
| Delicato Vineyards LLC. | 2084 | E | 707 265-1700 | 1536 |
| Don Sbstani Sons Intl Wine Ngc. | 2084 | E | 707 337-1961 | 1542 |
| Dry Farm Wines LLC (PA) | 2084 | F | 707 944-1500 | 1544 |
| Ego One LLC. | 2084 | F | 707 253-1615 | 1552 |
| Fior Di Sole LLC (PA) | 2084 | E | 707 259-1477 | 1566 |
| Fior Di Sole LLC. | 2084 | E | 707 492-3506 | 1567 |
| Fior Di Sole LLC. | 2084 | E | 707 204-8268 | 1568 |
| Geyser Peak Winery. | 2084 | E | 707 857-9463 | 1586 |
| Golden State Vintners. | 2084 | E | 707 254-1985 | 1594 |
| H De V LLC. | 2084 | E | 541 386-9119 | 1606 |
| Hagafen Cellars Inc. | 2084 | E | 707 252-0781 | 1607 |
| Hess Collection Winery (DH) | 2084 | E | 707 255-1144 | 1613 |
| Hudson Wines LLC. | 2084 | E | 707 255-1345 | 1616 |
| Ives Bay LLC (PA) | 2084 | E | 707 266-6899 | 1621 |
| Jarvis. | 2084 | E | 707 255-5280 | 1632 |
| Kieu Hoang Winery LLC. | 2084 | E | 707 253-1615 | 1648 |
| Krupp Brothers LLC (PA) | 2084 | E | 707 226-2215 | 1650 |
| Laird Family Estate LLC (PA) | 2084 | E | 707 257-0360 | 1660 |
| Luna Vineyards Inc. | 2084 | E | 707 255-2474 | 1670 |
| Monticello Cellars Inc. | 2084 | E | 707 253-2802 | 1681 |
| NAPA Select Vineyard Svcs Inc. | 2084 | F | 707 294-2637 | 1684 |
| Newton Vineyard LLC (DH) | 2084 | E | 707 204-7423 | 1689 |
| Pine Ridge Winery LLC (HQ) | 2084 | E | 707 253-7500 | 1708 |
| Regusci Vineyard MGT Inc. | 2084 | E | 707 254-0403 | 1721 |
| Robert Mondavi Corporation (HQ) | 2084 | D | 707 967-2100 | 1725 |
| Saintsbury LLC. | 2084 | F | 707 252-0592 | 1737 |
| Shafer Vineyards. | 2084 | F | 707 944-2877 | 1745 |

Employee Codes: A=Over 500 employees, B=251-500
C=101-250, D=51-100, E=20-50, F=10-19, G=1-9

# NAPA, CA

| | SIC | EMP | PHONE | ENTRY# |
|---|---|---|---|---|
| Silverado Vineyards | 2084 | E | 707 257-1770 | 1750 |
| Stags Leap Wine Cellars LLC (PA) | 2084 | C | 707 944-2020 | 1760 |
| Sutter Home Winery Inc | 2084 | E | 707 963-3104 | 1769 |
| Tpwc Inc | 2084 | D | 707 224-4039 | 1788 |
| Treasury Wine Estates Americas | 2084 | E | 707 880-9967 | 1791 |
| Treasury Wine Estates Americas (HQ) | 2084 | B | 707 259-4500 | 1793 |
| Treasury Wine Estates Americas | 2084 | E | 707 257-5300 | 1798 |
| Trefethen Vineyards Winery Inc | 2084 | E | 707 255-7700 | 1802 |
| Villa Del Lago LLC (PA) | 2084 | E | 707 963-2134 | 1811 |
| North Bay Plywood Inc | 2431 | E | 707 224-7849 | 3166 |
| Central Valley Truss | 2439 | F | 707 963-3622 | 3303 |
| Wine Country Cases Inc | 2449 | D | 707 967-4805 | 3378 |
| NAPA Valley Publishing Co | 2711 | D | 707 226-3711 | 4165 |
| Asl Print Fx Ltd | 2752 | F | 707 927-3096 | 4518 |
| Ben Franklin Press & Label Co | 2752 | E | 707 253-8250 | 4529 |
| Bergin Screen Prtg & Etching | 2752 | E | 707 224-0111 | 4530 |
| Eurostampa California LLC | 2754 | E | 707 927-4848 | 4821 |
| Collotype Labels USA Inc (DH) | 2759 | C | 707 603-2500 | 4862 |
| Multi-Color Corporation | 2759 | D | 707 931-7400 | 4926 |
| Radiator Specialty Company | 2899 | D | 707 252-0122 | 6319 |
| Pro Lab Orthotics Inc | 3069 | E | 707 257-4400 | 6526 |
| Cultured Stone Corporation (PA) | 3272 | A | 707 255-1727 | 7325 |
| N V Cast Stone LLC | 3272 | E | 707 261-6615 | 7357 |
| Cemex Materials LLC | 3273 | C | 707 255-3035 | 7429 |
| Pacific Steel Group | 3449 | E | 707 669-3136 | 8705 |
| Babcock & Wilcox Company | 3511 | E | 707 259-1122 | 9308 |
| Simplex Filler Inc | 3565 | F | 707 265-6801 | 10031 |
| Audio Visual MGT Solutions LLC | 3651 | D | 707 254-3395 | 11639 |
| Advanced Pressure Technology | 3823 | E | 707 259-0102 | 14383 |
| County of NAPA | 3823 | E | 707 259-8620 | 14399 |
| Dexta Corporation | 3843 | E | 707 255-2454 | 15453 |
| Lixit Corporation (PA) | 3999 | D | 800 358-8254 | 16171 |
| Superior Equipment Company Inc | 4959 | E | 707 256-3600 | 16368 |
| Syar Industries LLC (HQ) | 5032 | E | 707 252-8711 | 16485 |
| Seguin Mreau NAPA Coperage Inc (PA) | 5085 | F | 707 252-3408 | 16895 |
| Dominics Orgnal Gnova Deli Inc | 5411 | D | 707 253-8686 | 17377 |
| Bert Williams and Sons Inc | 5531 | E | 707 255-7003 | 17445 |
| Joes Dwntwn Brewry & Rest Inc | 5812 | E | 707 258-2337 | 17588 |
| Fryes Printing Inc | 7334 | E | 707 253-1114 | 17812 |
| AUL Corp (DH) | 7694 | C | 707 257-9700 | 19224 |
| NAPA Valley PSI Inc | 8331 | D | 707 255-0177 | 19362 |
| Vine Village Incorporated | 8361 | E | 707 255-4006 | 19365 |
| Symed Corporation | 8721 | E | 707 255-3300 | 19434 |

## NATIONAL CITY, CA - San Diego County

| | SIC | EMP | PHONE | ENTRY# |
|---|---|---|---|---|
| Ehmcke Sheet Metal Corp | 1761 | D | 619 477-6484 | 513 |
| Family Loompya Corporation | 2099 | E | 619 477-2125 | 2197 |
| Gmi Inc | 2393 | E | 619 429-4479 | 2957 |
| Westflex Inc (PA) | 3052 | E | 619 474-7400 | 6435 |
| B and P Plastics Inc | 3089 | E | 619 477-1893 | 6731 |
| Gary Manufacturing Inc | 3089 | E | 619 429-4479 | 6836 |
| Bay City Marine Inc (PA) | 3441 | E | 619 477-3991 | 8100 |
| Carroll Metal Works Inc | 3441 | E | 619 477-9125 | 8118 |
| Fabrication Tech Inds Inc | 3441 | D | 619 477-4141 | 8138 |
| West Point Spc Contg Inc | 3531 | F | 619 784-2524 | 9446 |
| G V Industries Inc | 3599 | E | 619 474-3013 | 10849 |
| Craft Labor & Support Svcs LLC | 3731 | C | 619 336-9977 | 14003 |
| Paige Sitta & Associates Inc (PA) | 3731 | E | 619 233-5912 | 14014 |
| Vigor Marine LLC | 3731 | D | 619 474-4352 | 14022 |
| Walashek Industrial & Mar Inc | 3731 | E | 619 498-1711 | 14024 |
| Hyperbaric Technologies Inc | 3845 | D | 619 336-2022 | 15546 |
| Sids Carpet Barn (PA) | 5023 | E | 619 477-7000 | 16435 |
| Centerline Industrial Inc | 5084 | E | 858 505-0838 | 16810 |
| Pacific Steel Inc | 5093 | E | 619 477-3925 | 16961 |
| San Diego Leather Inc | 5699 | F | 619 477-2900 | 17513 |
| Motivational Systems Inc (PA) | 7336 | D | 619 474-8246 | 17833 |

## NELSON, CA - Butte County

| | SIC | EMP | PHONE | ENTRY# |
|---|---|---|---|---|
| Far West Rice Inc | 2044 | E | 530 891-1339 | 1074 |

## NEVADA CITY, CA - Nevada County

| | SIC | EMP | PHONE | ENTRY# |
|---|---|---|---|---|
| Robinson Enterprises Investment Co Inc | 2411 | D | 530 265-5844 | 3053 |
| Best Sanitizers Inc | 2842 | D | 530 265-1800 | 5892 |
| Sierra Metal Fabricators Inc | 3441 | E | 530 265-4591 | 8215 |
| Rcd Engineering Inc | 3625 | E | 530 292-3133 | 11343 |
| Grass Valley Usa LLC (PA) | 3661 | B | 800 547-8949 | 11767 |
| Grass Valley Inc (HQ) | 3663 | D | 530 265-1000 | 11859 |
| Technicolor Usa Inc | 3663 | C | 530 478-3000 | 11959 |
| Ineoquest Technologies Inc (HQ) | 3825 | F | 508 339-2497 | 14535 |
| Nortech Waste LLC | 4953 | C | 916 645-5230 | 16360 |
| Ananda Church of Self-Realztn (PA) | 8661 | D | 530 478-7560 | 19367 |

## NEW CUYAMA, CA - Santa Barbara County

| | SIC | EMP | PHONE | ENTRY# |
|---|---|---|---|---|
| E & B Ntral Resources MGT Corp | 1382 | E | 661 766-2501 | 179 |

## NEWARK, CA - Alameda County

| | SIC | EMP | PHONE | ENTRY# |
|---|---|---|---|---|
| San Francisco Bay Brand Inc (PA) | 2048 | E | 510 792-7200 | 1149 |
| Fullbloom Baking Company Inc | 2051 | D | 510 456-3638 | 1206 |
| B-K Mill and Fixtures Inc | 2434 | F | 510 713-8657 | 3219 |
| Nefab Packaging Inc | 2441 | D | 408 678-2500 | 3327 |
| Five Star Lumber Company LLC (PA) | 2448 | E | 510 795-7204 | 3341 |
| Specilized Packg Solutions Inc (PA) | 2449 | D | 510 494-5670 | 3375 |
| Ooshirts Inc (PA) | 2759 | D | 866 660-8667 | 4931 |
| Resource Label Group LLC | 2759 | E | 510 477-0707 | 4951 |
| Matheson Tri-Gas Inc | 2813 | E | 510 793-2559 | 5051 |
| Ohmium International Inc (PA) | 2813 | F | 775 237-2077 | 5057 |
| Induspac California Inc (HQ) | 2821 | E | 510 324-3626 | 5164 |
| Incarda Therapeutics Inc | 2834 | E | 510 422-5522 | 5493 |
| Protagonist Therapeutics Inc (PA) | 2834 | D | 510 474-0170 | 5614 |
| Rain Oncology Inc (PA) | 2834 | D | 510 953-5559 | 5623 |
| Vector Laboratories Inc (PA) | 2836 | E | 800 227-6666 | 5868 |
| BASF Corporation | 2869 | D | 510 796-9911 | 6130 |
| Resin Designs LLC | 2891 | E | 510 413-0115 | 6244 |
| Crown Mfg Co Inc | 3089 | E | 510 742-8800 | 6787 |
| Pabco Building Products LLC | 3275 | C | 510 792-9555 | 7525 |
| Pabco Building Products LLC | 3275 | E | 510 792-1577 | 7526 |
| Accurate Tube Bending Inc | 3498 | E | 510 790-6500 | 9245 |
| Mitac Information Systems Corp (DH) | 3572 | C | 510 284-3000 | 10254 |
| Elitegroup Cmpt Systems Inc | 3577 | C | 510 226-7333 | 10362 |
| Knt Inc | 3599 | C | 510 651-7163 | 10930 |
| Silicon Valley Mfg Inc | 3599 | E | 510 791-9450 | 11114 |
| Svm Machining Inc | 3599 | F | 510 791-9450 | 11129 |
| Freewire Technologies Inc (PA) | 3621 | E | 415 779-5515 | 11268 |
| Kateeva Inc (PA) | 3663 | C | 800 385-7802 | 11870 |
| Teledyne Etm Inc (HQ) | 3663 | D | 510 797-1100 | 11962 |
| Sanmina Corporation | 3672 | C | 510 494-2421 | 12213 |
| Smart Modular Technologies (wwh) Inc | 3674 | A | 510 623-1231 | 12722 |
| Smart Modular Technologies Inc (HQ) | 3674 | C | 510 623-1231 | 12723 |
| Unigen Corporation (PA) | 3674 | E | 510 896-1818 | 12780 |
| Wintec Industries Inc (HQ) | 3674 | E | 510 953-7421 | 12805 |
| Envia Systems Inc | 3699 | E | 510 509-1367 | 13239 |
| Atieva Inc (HQ) | 3711 | E | 510 648-3553 | 13340 |
| Lucid Group Inc (PA) | 3711 | A | 510 648-3553 | 13366 |
| Lucid Usa Inc (HQ) | 3711 | C | 510 648-3553 | 13367 |
| Adient US LLC | 3714 | E | 510 771-2300 | 13440 |
| Smiths Detection Inc | 3812 | C | 410 612-2625 | 14307 |
| Smiths Detection LLC | 3812 | A | 510 739-2400 | 14308 |
| Kwj Engineering Inc (PA) | 3829 | E | 510 794-4296 | 14891 |
| Salutron Incorporated (PA) | 3845 | E | 510 795-2876 | 15577 |
| Cellotape Inc (HQ) | 3993 | C | 510 651-5551 | 15955 |
| Knt Manufacturing Inc | 3999 | D | 510 896-1699 | 16163 |
| Elitegroup Computer Systems Ho | 5045 | C | 510 794-2952 | 16519 |
| Orora Packaging Solutions | 5113 | F | 510 896-4750 | 17014 |
| Optiwise Ai Inc | 7372 | F | 408 480-0482 | 18631 |
| Nevada Heat Treating LLC (PA) | 7692 | E | 510 790-2300 | 19209 |
| Advanced Cell Diagnostics Inc | 8731 | D | 510 576-8800 | 19436 |
| Membrane Technology & RES Inc (PA) | 8731 | E | 650 328-2228 | 19466 |
| Tegile Systems Inc | 8731 | C | 510 791-7900 | 19480 |
| Vioptix Inc | 8733 | F | 510 226-5860 | 19499 |
| Tricopp Inc (PA) | 8748 | E | 925 520-5807 | 19573 |

## NEWBERRY SPRINGS, CA - San Bernardino County

| | SIC | EMP | PHONE | ENTRY# |
|---|---|---|---|---|
| 5e Boron Americas LLC | 1474 | E | 442 292-2120 | 333 |
| Elementis Specialties Inc | 2819 | D | 760 257-9112 | 5091 |

## NEWBURY PARK, CA - Ventura County

| | SIC | EMP | PHONE | ENTRY# |
|---|---|---|---|---|
| Bnk Petroleum (us) Inc | 1382 | E | 805 484-3613 | 169 |
| Conejo Valley Heating & AC Inc | 1711 | F | 833 538-9810 | 413 |
| Victory Custom Athletics | 2339 | E | 818 349-8476 | 2819 |
| Scientific Surface Inds Inc | 2541 | F | 805 499-5100 | 3670 |
| Coast Index Co Inc | 2678 | D | 805 499-6844 | 4019 |
| Corwin Press Inc | 2741 | E | 805 499-9734 | 4383 |
| HJS Graphics | 2752 | F | 818 782-5490 | 4632 |
| Plz Corp | 2813 | E | 805 498-4531 | 5058 |
| Amgen Inc | 2834 | E | 805 447-1000 | 5317 |
| Onyx Pharmaceuticals Inc | 2834 | A | 650 266-0000 | 5585 |
| Shire | 2834 | E | 805 372-3000 | 5655 |
| Cosmetic Technologies LLC | 2844 | D | 805 376-9960 | 5961 |
| R & R Services Corporation | 3069 | F | 818 889-2562 | 6532 |
| JBW Precision Inc | 3444 | E | 805 499-1973 | 8477 |
| JW Molding Inc | 3544 | F | 805 499-2682 | 9630 |
| Diamond Ground Products Inc | 3548 | E | 805 498-8837 | 9725 |
| CHE Precision Inc | 3599 | E | 805 499-8885 | 10773 |
| Westlake Audio Inc (PA) | 3651 | F | 805 499-3686 | 11717 |
| Nokia of America Corporation | 3661 | E | 818 880-3500 | 11776 |

# GEOGRAPHIC SECTION — NORTH HOLLYWOOD, CA

| Company | SIC | EMP | PHONE | ENTRY# |
|---|---|---|---|---|
| CPI Malibu Division | 3663 | D | 805 383-1829 | 11835 |
| WV Communications Inc | 3663 | E | 805 376-1820 | 11980 |
| Skyworks Solutions Inc | 3674 | E | 805 480-4400 | 12717 |
| Skyworks Solutions Inc | 3674 | E | 805 480-4227 | 12718 |
| Qorvo California Inc | 3679 | E | 805 480-5050 | 13072 |
| Condor Pacific Industries Inc (PA) | 3812 | E | 818 889-2150 | 14171 |
| Xirrus Inc | 3823 | E | 805 262-1600 | 14471 |
| Eca Medical Instruments (DH) | 3841 | E | 805 376-2509 | 15075 |
| Tom Anderson Guitarworks | 3931 | F | 805 498-1747 | 15725 |
| Amgen Manufacturing Limited | 3999 | E | 787 656-2000 | 16086 |
| McBain Systems A Cal Ltd Prtnr | 5049 | E | 805 581-6800 | 16602 |
| Perillo Industries Inc | 5065 | E | 805 498-9838 | 16729 |
| Trend Design Inc | 7336 | F | 805 498-0457 | 17841 |
| Compulink Business Systems Inc (PA) | 7372 | C | 805 446-2050 | 18197 |
| Isolutecom Inc (PA) | 7372 | E | 805 498-6259 | 18447 |
| Weldlogic Inc | 7692 | D | 805 375-1670 | 19219 |

## NEWCASTLE, CA - Placer County

| Company | SIC | EMP | PHONE | ENTRY# |
|---|---|---|---|---|
| Omega Diamond Inc | 3545 | F | 530 889-8977 | 9686 |
| A & A Stepping Stone Mfg Inc (PA) | 5211 | E | 530 885-7481 | 17319 |

## NEWHALL, CA - Los Angeles County

| Company | SIC | EMP | PHONE | ENTRY# |
|---|---|---|---|---|
| Berry Petroleum Company LLC | 1311 | D | 661 255-6066 | 121 |
| Vons Companies Inc | 5411 | C | 661 259-9214 | 17395 |

## NEWMAN, CA - Stanislaus County

| Company | SIC | EMP | PHONE | ENTRY# |
|---|---|---|---|---|
| Saputo Cheese USA Inc | 2022 | D | 262 307-6738 | 735 |
| Stewart & Jasper Marketing Inc (PA) | 2068 | C | 209 862-9600 | 1367 |
| Valley Sun Products Inc | 2099 | D | 209 862-1200 | 2386 |
| Westside Pallet Inc | 2448 | E | 209 862-3941 | 3366 |
| Titan Newman Inc (PA) | 5085 | E | 209 862-2977 | 16900 |

## NEWPORT BEACH, CA - Orange County

| Company | SIC | EMP | PHONE | ENTRY# |
|---|---|---|---|---|
| West Newport Oil Company | 1311 | E | 949 631-1100 | 146 |
| Jaguar Energy LLC (PA) | 1389 | E | 949 706-7060 | 241 |
| A Shoc Beverage LLC | 2048 | E | 949 490-1612 | 1117 |
| Drywater Inc | 2087 | E | 844 434-0829 | 2001 |
| Cannery Seafood of Pacific LLC | 2091 | F | 949 566-0060 | 2038 |
| Crossport Mocean | 2311 | F | 949 646-1701 | 2559 |
| Hmr Building Systems LLC | 2421 | D | 951 749-4700 | 3070 |
| Walden Structures Inc | 2452 | B | 909 389-9100 | 3400 |
| RSI Home Products Inc | 2514 | C | 949 720-1116 | 3509 |
| Bristol Management Svcs Inc | 2621 | F | 714 267-7346 | 3763 |
| Churm Publishing Inc (PA) | 2711 | E | 714 796-7000 | 4092 |
| Saddleback Educational Inc | 2731 | F | 714 640-5200 | 4344 |
| Hanley Wood Media Inc (HQ) | 2741 | E | 202 736-3300 | 4412 |
| Peninsula Publishing Inc | 2741 | E | 949 631-1307 | 4445 |
| Evolus Inc (PA) | 2834 | C | 949 284-4555 | 5438 |
| International Vitamin Corporat (PA) | 2834 | D | 949 664-5500 | 5500 |
| Ivc Inc | 2834 | F | 215 671-1400 | 5508 |
| American Vanguard Corporation (PA) | 2879 | D | 949 260-1200 | 6191 |
| Amvac Chemical Corporation (HQ) | 2879 | E | 323 264-3910 | 6192 |
| Crm of America LLC (PA) | 3011 | F | 949 263-9100 | 6407 |
| Crm Co LLC (PA) | 3061 | E | 949 263-9100 | 6472 |
| Allbirds Inc | 3143 | E | 949 942-1233 | 7099 |
| Lusso Cloud Inc | 3149 | F | 714 307-4414 | 7119 |
| Simply Straws LLC | 3229 | E | 855 787-2974 | 7204 |
| A & A Ready Mixed Concrete Inc (PA) | 3273 | E | 949 253-2800 | 7399 |
| Associated Ready Mixed Con Inc (PA) | 3273 | E | 949 253-2800 | 7406 |
| Lebata Inc | 3273 | E | 949 253-2800 | 7462 |
| Tamco | 3449 | B | 949 552-9714 | 8712 |
| Hixson Metal Finishing | 3471 | D | 800 900-9798 | 8971 |
| Jacksam Corporation | 3565 | E | 800 605-3580 | 10021 |
| Performance Motorsports Inc | 3592 | B | 714 898-9763 | 10623 |
| Triton Chandelier Inc | 3646 | F | 714 507-9760 | 11563 |
| Adaptive Digital Systems Inc | 3663 | E | 949 955-3116 | 11798 |
| Proshot Investors LLC | 3663 | F | 949 586-9500 | 11919 |
| Mk Davidson Inc | 3669 | E | 949 698-2963 | 12005 |
| Conexant Holdings Inc | 3674 | A | 415 983-2706 | 12388 |
| Mindspeed Technologies LLC (HQ) | 3674 | D | 949 579-3000 | 12585 |
| Newport Fab LLC | 3674 | D | 949 435-8000 | 12602 |
| Tower Semicdtr Newport Bch Inc (DH) | 3674 | A | 949 435-8000 | 12769 |
| Kelly Pneumatics Inc | 3699 | F | 800 704-7552 | 13260 |
| Center Line Wheel Corporation | 3714 | F | 562 921-9637 | 13474 |
| Comac America Corporation | 3721 | E | 760 616-9614 | 13648 |
| Basin Marine Inc | 3732 | E | 949 673-0360 | 14029 |
| Imagegrid Inc | 3829 | E | 949 852-1000 | 14882 |
| Strategic Medical Ventures LLC | 3844 | E | 949 355-5212 | 15509 |
| Mmxviii Holdings Inc | 3993 | E | 800 672-3974 | 16010 |
| CDM Company Inc | 3999 | E | 949 644-2820 | 16113 |
| Mulechain Inc | 4212 | D | 888 456-8881 | 16280 |
| Lugano Diamonds & Jewelry Inc (HQ) | 5944 | D | 949 625-7722 | 17648 |
| Monex Deposit A Cal Ltd Partnr | 5944 | D | 800 444-8317 | 17650 |
| True Investments LLC (PA) | 6799 | E | 949 258-9720 | 17759 |
| Conversionpoint Holdings Inc | 7372 | D | 888 706-6764 | 18202 |
| Harbor Health Systems LLC | 8099 | A | 949 273-7020 | 19336 |
| Concept Technology Inc (PA) | 8711 | D | 949 854-7047 | 19384 |

## NEWPORT COAST, CA - Orange County

| Company | SIC | EMP | PHONE | ENTRY# |
|---|---|---|---|---|
| Krystal Ventures LLC | 3911 | E | 213 507-2215 | 15696 |

## NIPOMO, CA - San Luis Obispo County

| Company | SIC | EMP | PHONE | ENTRY# |
|---|---|---|---|---|
| Condition Monitoring Svcs LLC | 3826 | E | 888 359-3277 | 14648 |
| Malcolm Demille Inc | 3911 | F | 805 929-4353 | 15701 |
| Santa Maria Tire Inc (PA) | 5531 | D | 805 347-4793 | 17463 |

## NORCO, CA - Riverside County

| Company | SIC | EMP | PHONE | ENTRY# |
|---|---|---|---|---|
| A Plus Custom Metal Supply Inc | 1761 | F | 951 736-7900 | 509 |
| Better Nutritionals LLC (PA) | 2023 | D | 310 356-9019 | 746 |
| Better Nutritionals LLC | 2023 | D | 310 356-9019 | 748 |
| Better Nutritionals LLC | 2023 | D | 310 356-9019 | 749 |
| Flavor Factory Inc | 2087 | F | 951 273-9877 | 2003 |
| International E-Z Up Inc (PA) | 2394 | E | 800 742-3363 | 2976 |
| W B Powell Inc | 2431 | E | 951 270-0095 | 3202 |
| AAA Pallet Recycling & Mfg Inc | 2448 | E | 951 681-7748 | 3329 |
| Legal Vision Group LLC | 2752 | E | 310 945-5550 | 4674 |
| Sr Plastics Company LLC | 3089 | E | 951 479-5394 | 7039 |
| Paragon Building Products Inc (PA) | 3272 | E | 951 549-1155 | 7371 |
| Quick Crete Products Corp | 3272 | C | 951 737-6240 | 7377 |
| Pro Tech Thermal Services | 3398 | E | 951 272-5808 | 7897 |
| Epic Sheet Metal Inc | 3444 | F | 714 679-5917 | 8444 |
| Industrial Process Eqp Inc | 3567 | F | 714 447-0171 | 10054 |
| S R Machining Inc | 3599 | E | 951 520-9486 | 11095 |
| S R Machining-Properties LLC | 3599 | E | 951 520-9486 | 11096 |
| Avid Idntification Systems Inc (PA) | 3674 | D | 951 371-7505 | 12347 |
| Robertshaw Controls Company | 3822 | E | 951 893-6233 | 14367 |

## NORTH HIGHLANDS, CA - Sacramento County

| Company | SIC | EMP | PHONE | ENTRY# |
|---|---|---|---|---|
| Heritage Interests LLC (PA) | 1751 | D | 916 481-5030 | 493 |
| Pacific Coast Supply LLC | 2439 | F | 916 339-8100 | 3316 |
| Livingstons Concrete Svc Inc (PA) | 3273 | E | 916 334-4313 | 7465 |
| Livingstons Concrete Svc Inc | 3273 | E | 916 334-4313 | 7466 |
| Hallsten Corporation | 3441 | E | 916 331-7211 | 8149 |
| Mikes Sheet Metal Pdts Inc | 3444 | E | 916 348-3800 | 8510 |
| New Wave Industries Ltd (DH) | 3589 | F | 800 882-8854 | 10586 |
| AAA Underground Inc | 4939 | E | 916 515-9348 | 16352 |
| Builders Firstsource Inc | 5031 | B | 916 481-5030 | 16443 |
| Heritage One Door Crpentry LLC | 5031 | D | 916 481-5030 | 16446 |
| Security Contractor Svcs Inc (PA) | 5039 | D | 916 338-4200 | 16495 |

## NORTH HILLS, CA - Los Angeles County

| Company | SIC | EMP | PHONE | ENTRY# |
|---|---|---|---|---|
| Robert C Worth Inc | 2434 | D | 661 942-6601 | 3265 |
| Alpha Aviation Components Inc (PA) | 3599 | E | 818 894-8801 | 10702 |
| Learjet Inc | 3721 | E | 818 894-8241 | 13675 |
| Moore Industries-International Inc (PA) | 3823 | C | 818 894-7111 | 14436 |
| Imperial Toy LLC (PA) | 3944 | E | 818 536-6500 | 15751 |
| P C A Electronics Inc | 5065 | E | 818 892-0761 | 16728 |
| New Hrzns Srving Indvdals With (PA) | 8243 | D | 818 894-9301 | 19348 |

## NORTH HOLLYWOOD, CA - Los Angeles County

| Company | SIC | EMP | PHONE | ENTRY# |
|---|---|---|---|---|
| Mave Enterprises Inc | 2064 | E | 818 767-4533 | 1320 |
| Groundwork Coffee Roasters LLC | 2095 | C | 818 506-6020 | 2073 |
| Ahs Trinity Group Inc (PA) | 2389 | E | 818 508-2105 | 2888 |
| S & K Theatrical Drap Inc | 2391 | F | 818 503-0596 | 2917 |
| ABC Sun Control LLC | 2394 | E | 818 982-6989 | 2966 |
| Mtd Kitchen Inc | 2431 | D | 818 764-2254 | 3163 |
| Artcrafters Cabinets | 2434 | E | 818 752-8960 | 3217 |
| Kitchen Pro Cabinetry Inc | 2434 | E | 877 210-6361 | 3248 |
| Kobis Windows & Doors Mfg Inc | 2434 | E | 818 764-6400 | 3250 |
| Basaw Manufacturing Inc (PA) | 2441 | E | 818 765-6650 | 3323 |
| Basaw Manufacturing Inc | 2441 | E | 818 765-6650 | 3324 |
| A & S Case Company Inc | 2449 | E | 800 394-6181 | 3367 |
| Bobrick Washroom Equipment Inc (HQ) | 2542 | D | 818 764-1000 | 3680 |
| The Bobrick Corporation (PA) | 2542 | D | 818 764-1000 | 3711 |
| West Publishing Corporation | 2731 | A | 800 747-3161 | 4354 |
| Dolex Dollar Express Inc | 2741 | E | 818 982-2852 | 4389 |
| Dennis Bolton Enterprises Inc | 2752 | E | 818 982-1800 | 4587 |
| Graphic Visions Inc | 2752 | E | 818 845-8393 | 4624 |
| Harman Press Inc | 2752 | E | 818 432-0570 | 4629 |
| Corporate Impressions La Inc | 2759 | E | 818 761-9295 | 4866 |
| G-2 Graphic Service Inc | 2759 | D | 818 623-3100 | 4881 |
| Target Mdia Prtnrs Intrctive (HQ) | 2759 | E | 323 930-3123 | 4967 |
| Wes Go Inc | 2759 | E | 818 504-1200 | 4981 |
| Green Dragon Caregivers Inc | 2833 | F | 818 997-1368 | 5243 |
| O P I Products Inc (HQ) | 2844 | B | 818 759-8688 | 6013 |
| Johnson doc Enterprises | 3069 | E | 818 764-1543 | 6506 |

## NORTH HOLLYWOOD, CA

| | SIC | EMP | PHONE | ENTRY# |
|---|---|---|---|---|
| Hope Plastics Co Inc | 3089 | E | 818 769-5560 | 6858 |
| Metal Improvement Company LLC | 3398 | D | 818 983-1952 | 7891 |
| Cal-June Inc (PA) | 3429 | E | 323 877-4164 | 7986 |
| Orion Ornamental Iron Inc | 3429 | E | 818 752-0688 | 8022 |
| Lexington Acquisition Inc | 3441 | C | 818 768-5768 | 8169 |
| Davis California Industries Ltd | 3444 | E | 818 980-6178 | 8426 |
| Modern-Aire Ventilating Inc | 3444 | E | 818 765-9870 | 8514 |
| Astro Chrome and Polsg Corp | 3479 | E | 818 781-1463 | 9050 |
| Pdu Lad Corporation (PA) | 3479 | E | 626 442-7711 | 9102 |
| Allan Aircraft Supply Co LLC | 3494 | E | 818 765-4992 | 9180 |
| Pacific Wire Products Inc | 3496 | E | 818 755-6400 | 9224 |
| Artisan House Inc | 3499 | E | 818 767-7476 | 9275 |
| Utility Refrigerator | 3585 | E | 818 764-6200 | 10524 |
| Mar Engineering Company | 3599 | E | 818 765-4805 | 10957 |
| Wilshire Precision Pdts Inc | 3599 | E | 818 765-4571 | 11196 |
| Arte De Mexico Inc | 3646 | D | 818 753-4510 | 11519 |
| Thomson Reuters Corporation | 3663 | E | 877 518-2761 | 11966 |
| Vector Electronics & Tech Inc | 3672 | E | 818 985-8208 | 12254 |
| A T Parker Inc (PA) | 3699 | E | 818 755-1700 | 13207 |
| Avibank Mfg Inc (DH) | 3728 | C | 818 392-2100 | 13793 |
| Curtiss-Wright Controls Inc | 3728 | E | 818 503-0998 | 13818 |
| Klune Industries Inc (DH) | 3728 | B | 818 503-8100 | 13887 |
| Meggitt North Hollywood Inc (DH) | 3728 | C | 818 765-8160 | 13907 |
| Americh Corporation (PA) | 3842 | C | 818 982-1711 | 15321 |
| General Wax Co Inc (PA) | 3999 | D | 818 765-5800 | 16135 |
| Reel Efx Inc | 3999 | E | 818 762-1710 | 16215 |
| Buster and Punch Inc | 5023 | E | 818 392-3827 | 16421 |
| Electronic Hardware Limited (PA) | 5065 | E | 818 982-6100 | 16700 |
| E B Bradley Co | 5072 | F | 800 533-3030 | 16753 |
| Fastener Technology Corp | 5085 | C | 818 764-6467 | 16875 |
| United Aeronautical Corp | 5088 | C | 818 764-2102 | 16930 |
| King Express Inc | 5812 | F | 818 503-2772 | 17591 |
| Pnk Enterprises Inc | 5999 | E | 818 765-3770 | 17717 |
| Western Costume Co (HQ) | 7299 | E | 818 760-0900 | 17776 |
| Open Systems Inc | 7372 | E | 317 566-6662 | 18623 |
| Airdraulics Inc | 7539 | E | 818 982-1400 | 19163 |
| Universal Studios Company LLC (DH) | 7812 | A | 818 777-1000 | 19299 |

## NORTHRIDGE, CA - Los Angeles County

| | SIC | EMP | PHONE | ENTRY# |
|---|---|---|---|---|
| Artistry In Motion Inc | 2679 | E | 818 994-7388 | 4031 |
| Kindeva Drug Delivery LP | 2834 | B | 818 341-1300 | 5526 |
| Monocent Inc | 2835 | F | 424 310-0777 | 5766 |
| Burns Environmental Svcs Inc | 2842 | E | 800 577-4009 | 5893 |
| Instrument Bearing Factory USA | 3452 | E | 818 989-5052 | 8759 |
| Maroney Company | 3599 | F | 818 882-2722 | 10958 |
| Robert H Oliva Inc | 3599 | E | 818 700-1035 | 11082 |
| S & S Numerical Control Inc | 3599 | E | 818 341-4141 | 11093 |
| Universal Ctrl Solutions Corp | 3625 | F | 818 898-3380 | 11354 |
| Harman Professional Inc (DH) | 3651 | B | 818 893-8411 | 11667 |
| Rotating Prcsion McHanisms Inc | 3663 | E | 818 349-9774 | 11936 |
| Lloyd Design Corporation | 3714 | D | 818 768-6001 | 13530 |
| Aviation Design Group Inc | 3728 | E | 818 350-1900 | 13792 |
| Infinity Aerospace Inc (PA) | 3728 | E | 818 998-9811 | 13872 |
| Vision Aerospace LLC | 3728 | E | 818 700-1035 | 13988 |
| Alliant Tchsystems Oprtons LLC | 3812 | B | 818 887-8195 | 14139 |
| Alliant Tchsystems Oprtons LLC | 3812 | E | 818 887-8195 | 14141 |
| Arete Associates (PA) | 3812 | C | 818 885-2200 | 14146 |
| Northrop Grmman Innvtion Syste | 3812 | D | 818 887-8100 | 14229 |
| Northrop Grumman Systems Corp | 3812 | A | 818 887-8110 | 14242 |
| Chemat Technology Inc | 3821 | E | 818 727-9786 | 14332 |
| Thermometrics Corporation (PA) | 3823 | F | 818 886-3755 | 14464 |
| Validyne Engineering Corp | 3829 | E | 818 886-8488 | 14937 |
| Medtronic Minimed Inc (DH) | 3841 | A | 800 646-4633 | 15178 |
| Harman-Kardon Incorporated | 5064 | B | 818 841-4600 | 16681 |

## NORWALK, CA - Los Angeles County

| | SIC | EMP | PHONE | ENTRY# |
|---|---|---|---|---|
| Cargill Meat Solutions Corp | 2011 | E | 562 345-5240 | 585 |
| Dianas Mexican Food Pdts Inc (PA) | 2099 | E | 562 926-5802 | 2185 |
| Golden Specialty Foods LLC | 2099 | E | 562 802-2537 | 2220 |
| Cabinets 2000 LLC | 2434 | C | 562 868-0909 | 3223 |
| McDowell Craig Off Systems Inc | 2522 | D | 562 921-4441 | 3605 |
| Sonoco Products Company | 2631 | E | 562 921-0881 | 3808 |
| El Clasificado (PA) | 2711 | E | 323 837-4095 | 4108 |
| Jason Markk Inc (PA) | 2842 | E | 213 687-7060 | 5910 |
| Lgg Industrial Inc | 3053 | D | 562 802-7782 | 6457 |
| ARC Plastics Inc | 3089 | E | 562 802-3299 | 6721 |
| New Cntury Mtals Southeast Inc | 3356 | C | 562 356-6804 | 7764 |
| Aerotec Alloys Inc | 3363 | E | 562 809-1378 | 7804 |
| Argo Spring Mfg Co Inc | 3493 | D | 800 252-2740 | 9173 |
| Polley Inc (PA) | 3569 | F | 562 868-9861 | 10107 |
| Icarcover Inc | 3714 | E | 714 469-7759 | 13516 |
| Master Research & Mfg Inc | 3728 | D | 562 483-8789 | 13900 |
| Universal Orthodontic Lab Inc | 3843 | F | 562 484-0500 | 15491 |

## NOVATO, CA - Marin County

| | SIC | EMP | PHONE | ENTRY# |
|---|---|---|---|---|
| California Newspapers Inc | 2711 | A | 415 883-8600 | 4082 |
| St Louis Post-Dispatch LLC | 2711 | C | 415 892-1516 | 4200 |
| Excellence Magazine Inc | 2721 | F | 415 382-0582 | 4254 |
| Whatever Publishing Inc | 2741 | F | 415 884-2100 | 4494 |
| Forest Investment Group Inc | 2752 | F | 415 459-2330 | 4614 |
| Ultragenyx Pharmaceutical Inc (PA) | 2834 | A | 415 483-8800 | 5697 |
| Prima Fleur Botanicals Inc | 2844 | F | 415 455-0957 | 6027 |
| Cricket Company LLC | 3069 | E | 415 475-4150 | 6488 |
| Ranch Systems Inc | 3523 | F | 415 884-2770 | 9379 |
| Sutter Instrument Corp | 3826 | D | 415 883-0128 | 14725 |
| Et Water Systems LLC | 3829 | E | 415 945-9383 | 14864 |
| Zenni Optical Inc (PA) | 3851 | D | 800 211-2105 | 15626 |
| Fibres International Inc | 4953 | D | 425 455-9811 | 16359 |
| Worldwise Inc (DH) | 5199 | E | 415 721-7400 | 17318 |
| Marin Brewing Company Inc | 5812 | F | 415 461-4677 | 17598 |
| Safetychain Software Inc (PA) | 7372 | E | 415 233-9474 | 18750 |

## NUEVO, CA - Riverside County

| | SIC | EMP | PHONE | ENTRY# |
|---|---|---|---|---|
| Oldcastle Infrastructure Inc | 3272 | E | 951 928-8713 | 7368 |

## OAK PARK, CA - Ventura County

| | SIC | EMP | PHONE | ENTRY# |
|---|---|---|---|---|
| Foldimate Inc | 3634 | E | 805 876-4418 | 11405 |
| Ipraxa Software & Services | 7372 | F | 800 459-7668 | 18444 |

## OAK VIEW, CA - Ventura County

| | SIC | EMP | PHONE | ENTRY# |
|---|---|---|---|---|
| Willis Machine Inc | 3599 | E | 805 604-4500 | 11195 |

## OAKDALE, CA - Stanislaus County

| | SIC | EMP | PHONE | ENTRY# |
|---|---|---|---|---|
| Central Valley AG Grinding LLC (PA) | 0723 | C | 209 869-1721 | 78 |
| Nicro Inc | 1711 | E | 209 848-8826 | 427 |
| Sconza Candy Company | 2064 | D | 209 845-3700 | 1326 |
| American Pallet & Lumber Inc | 2448 | E | 209 847-6122 | 3332 |
| Morris Publications (PA) | 2711 | E | 209 847-3021 | 4163 |
| Formulation Technology Inc | 2834 | E | 209 847-0331 | 5444 |
| Ball Corporation | 3411 | B | 209 848-6500 | 7918 |
| Weldway Inc | 3441 | E | 209 847-8083 | 8244 |
| Accu-Swiss Inc (PA) | 3451 | F | 209 847-1016 | 8714 |
| Heighten America Inc | 3599 | E | 209 845-0455 | 10868 |
| Hi-Tech Emergency Vehicle Service Inc | 3711 | E | 209 847-3042 | 13360 |
| Custom Carbon Composite Creations Inc | 3842 | E | 209 845-2930 | 15331 |
| Media Print Services Inc | 7336 | F | 866 935-5077 | 17832 |

## OAKHURST, CA - Madera County

| | SIC | EMP | PHONE | ENTRY# |
|---|---|---|---|---|
| South Gate Brewing Company | 3589 | E | 559 692-2739 | 10602 |

## OAKLAND, CA - Alameda County

| | SIC | EMP | PHONE | ENTRY# |
|---|---|---|---|---|
| Monterey Mechanical Co (PA) | 1711 | E | 510 632-3173 | 426 |
| Dz-Fdt LLC | 1721 | E | 510 215-5253 | 444 |
| Gallagher Properties Inc (PA) | 1794 | E | 510 261-0466 | 544 |
| Edys Grand Ice Cream | 2024 | A | 510 652-8187 | 799 |
| La Cascada Inc | 2032 | F | 510 452-3663 | 864 |
| Nomnomnow Inc | 2047 | D | 415 991-0669 | 1111 |
| Athens Baking Company Inc | 2051 | F | 510 533-5705 | 1159 |
| Bread Srsly LLC | 2051 | E | 646 244-9553 | 1173 |
| Dobake Bakeries Inc | 2051 | D | 510 834-3134 | 1184 |
| Premier Organics | 2068 | E | 866 237-8688 | 1363 |
| Veronica Foods Company | 2079 | E | 510 535-6833 | 1410 |
| W G Barr Beverage Company LP | 2082 | E | 510 999-4939 | 1467 |
| McBride Sisters Collections | 2084 | E | 510 671-0739 | 1675 |
| Treasury Wine Estates Americas | 2084 | F | 707 299-3112 | 1797 |
| Olipop Inc | 2086 | D | 510 560-5709 | 1907 |
| Svc Mfg Inc A Corp | 2086 | E | 510 261-5800 | 1967 |
| Quaker Oats Company | 2087 | C | 510 261-5800 | 2021 |
| Americas Best Beverage Inc | 2095 | E | 800 723-8808 | 2066 |
| Peerless Coffee Company Inc | 2095 | D | 510 763-1763 | 2076 |
| Red Bay Coffee Company Inc | 2095 | E | 510 409-1076 | 2079 |
| Harmless Harvest Inc | 2099 | E | 347 688-6286 | 2228 |
| Agriculture Bag Mfg USA Inc (PA) | 2221 | E | 510 632-5637 | 2433 |
| Imperial Garment Inds Inc | 2369 | F | 510 834-7771 | 2862 |
| Mack & Reiss Inc | 2369 | D | 510 434-9122 | 2864 |
| Wooden Window Inc | 2431 | E | 510 893-1157 | 3208 |
| East Bay Fixture Company | 2491 | E | 510 652-4421 | 3402 |
| Wood Tech Inc | 2511 | D | 510 534-4930 | 3463 |
| Creative Wood Products Inc | 2521 | C | 510 635-5399 | 3564 |
| CJ United Food Corporation (PA) | 2656 | F | 510 895-6868 | 3913 |
| Everett Graphics Inc | 2657 | D | 510 577-6777 | 3917 |
| Agribag Inc | 2673 | E | 510 533-2388 | 3960 |
| Sius Products and Distr Inc (PA) | 2673 | F | 510 382-1700 | 3979 |
| East Bay Publishing LLC | 2711 | E | 510 879-3708 | 4107 |
| Live Journal Inc | 2711 | E | 415 230-3600 | 4149 |
| Sunset Publishing Corporation (HQ) | 2721 | C | 800 777-0117 | 4299 |
| Berrett-Koehler Publishers Inc (PA) | 2731 | F | 510 817-2277 | 4313 |

# GEOGRAPHIC SECTION

## OCEANSIDE, CA

| | SIC | EMP | PHONE | ENTRY# |
|---|---|---|---|---|
| Callisto Media Inc. | 2731 | C | 510 253-0500 | 4318 |
| Hesperian Health Guides (PA) | 2731 | E | 510 845-1447 | 4331 |
| New Harbinger Publications Inc (PA) | 2731 | E | 510 652-0215 | 4338 |
| University Cal Press Fundation (PA) | 2731 | D | 510 642-4247 | 4352 |
| Art19 LLC (DH) | 2741 | E | 866 882-7819 | 4366 |
| Center of Media Justice | 2741 | E | 510 698-3800 | 4376 |
| Log(n) LLC | 2741 | E | 323 839-4538 | 4428 |
| Lonely Planet Publications Inc. | 2741 | D | 510 250-6400 | 4429 |
| Connected Trnsp Prtners Sthern | 2752 | E | 510 542-5446 | 4566 |
| Inter-City Printing Co Inc | 2752 | F | 510 451-4775 | 4653 |
| TYT LLC (HQ) | 2752 | C | 510 444-3933 | 4795 |
| ABC Imaging of Washington | 2759 | E | 202 429-8870 | 4833 |
| Label Art - HM Es-E Stik Lbels | 2759 | E | 510 465-1125 | 4906 |
| Linde Inc. | 2813 | C | 510 451-4100 | 5049 |
| Cerexa | 2834 | F | 510 285-9200 | 5402 |
| Jane Nextgen Inc | 2835 | F | 415 722-2226 | 5758 |
| Roots Community Health Center | 2841 | D | 510 777-1177 | 5881 |
| Clorox Company (PA) | 2842 | A | 510 271-7000 | 5898 |
| Clorox Manufacturing Company (HQ) | 2842 | C | 510 271-7000 | 5900 |
| Clorox Services Company (HQ) | 2842 | D | 510 271-7000 | 5902 |
| W3ll People Inc. | 2844 | F | 800 790-1563 | 6055 |
| Dura Chemicals Inc (PA) | 2851 | E | 510 658-1987 | 6081 |
| Kingsford Products Company LLC (HQ) | 2861 | D | 510 271-7000 | 6118 |
| Clorox International Company (HQ) | 2879 | E | 510 271-7000 | 6197 |
| Vulpine Inc. | 2899 | E | 510 534-1186 | 6329 |
| AJW Construction | 2951 | E | 510 568-2300 | 6360 |
| Glad Products Company (HQ) | 3081 | C | 510 271-7000 | 6560 |
| Golden Plastics Corporation | 3089 | F | 510 569-6465 | 6845 |
| Linoleum Sales Co Inc (PA) | 3211 | D | 510 652-1032 | 7175 |
| Owens-Brockway Glass Cont Inc | 3221 | E | 510 436-2000 | 7184 |
| Arch Foods Inc. | 3421 | E | 510 868-6000 | 7935 |
| Levine Arthur Lansky & Assoc (PA) | 3423 | F | 415 234-6020 | 7959 |
| Ozig LLC | 3431 | E | 510 588-7952 | 8043 |
| Planted Solar Inc. | 3433 | E | 650 861-1455 | 8073 |
| Mills Acquisition Corporation | 3444 | E | | 8512 |
| Ngo Metals Inc. | 3446 | E | 510 632-0853 | 8638 |
| Rago & Son Inc. | 3469 | D | 510 536-5700 | 8883 |
| Advanced Grinding Incorporated | 3479 | E | 510 536-3465 | 9039 |
| Pacific Galvanizing Inc. | 3479 | E | 510 261-7331 | 9098 |
| Cable Moore Inc (PA) | 3496 | E | 510 436-8000 | 9212 |
| Feeney Inc. | 3496 | E | 510 893-9473 | 9217 |
| Bay Area Indus Filtration Inc. | 3569 | E | 510 562-6373 | 10076 |
| Quantumcamp Inc. | 3572 | F | 650 933-5467 | 10271 |
| Square International Svcs Inc | 3572 | D | 415 375-3176 | 10286 |
| Diamond Tool and Die Inc. | 3599 | E | 510 534-7050 | 10811 |
| General Grinding Inc. | 3599 | E | 510 261-5557 | 10856 |
| Zuo Modern Contemporary Inc (PA) | 3645 | E | 510 877-4087 | 11511 |
| Acuity Brands Lighting Inc. | 3646 | E | 510 845-2760 | 11515 |
| Premisys Communications Inc (HQ) | 3661 | C | 510 777-7000 | 11782 |
| Sorrento Networks Corporation (HQ) | 3661 | F | 510 577-1400 | 11787 |
| Credence Id LLC | 3663 | E | 888 243-5452 | 11838 |
| Digicom Electronics Inc | 3672 | E | 510 639-7003 | 12087 |
| GM Associates Inc. | 3679 | D | 510 430-0806 | 12987 |
| Rolls-Royce Engine Services-Oakland Inc. | 3724 | B | 510 635-1500 | 13720 |
| Vigilent Corporation (PA) | 3822 | E | 888 305-4451 | 14374 |
| County of Alameda | 3824 | E | 510 272-6964 | 14475 |
| Mettler-Toledo Rainin LLC (HQ) | 3829 | C | 510 564-1600 | 14899 |
| Fluxion Biosciences Inc. | 3841 | E | 650 241-4577 | 15089 |
| Hydrapak Inc. | 3949 | E | 510 632-8318 | 15824 |
| Arrow Sign Co (PA) | 3993 | E | 209 931-5522 | 15943 |
| Brite Industries Inc. | 3999 | D | 510 250-9330 | 16099 |
| Clamp Swing Pricing Co Inc. | 3999 | E | 510 567-1600 | 16118 |
| Kiva Manufacturing Inc. | 3999 | E | 510 780-0777 | 16162 |
| Social Brands LLC | 3999 | E | 415 728-1761 | 16233 |
| Sublimation Inc. | 3999 | E | 888 994-2726 | 16240 |
| Bay Bolt Inc. | 5072 | F | 510 532-1188 | 16747 |
| Darcoid Company of California | 5085 | E | 510 836-2449 | 16870 |
| Creative Energy Foods Inc. | 5149 | D | 510 638-8668 | 17185 |
| Sugar & Rice Saroni Inc. | 5149 | E | 510 261-9670 | 17216 |
| Rolls-Royce Corporation | 5511 | B | 510 635-1500 | 17441 |
| Clear Channel Outdoor LLC | 7312 | E | 510 835-5900 | 17785 |
| Graphic Reproduction | 7334 | F | 510 268-9980 | 17813 |
| Lumedx Corporation (PA) | 7371 | E | 510 419-1000 | 17943 |
| Mindshare Design Inc. | 7371 | E | 510 904-6900 | 17949 |
| Beautiful Slides Inc. | 7372 | E | 415 236-0955 | 18095 |
| Binti Inc. | 7372 | E | 844 424-6844 | 18105 |
| Block Inc (PA) | 7372 | E | 415 375-3176 | 18114 |
| Cloud9 Charts Inc. | 7372 | F | 510 507-3661 | 18180 |
| Dado Inc. | 7372 | E | 866 704-7210 | 18225 |
| Deem Inc (DH) | 7372 | D | 415 590-8300 | 18235 |
| Distru Corp | 7372 | E | 603 630-0282 | 18245 |
| Fivetran Inc (PA) | 7372 | A | 415 805-2799 | 18313 |
| Flipcause Inc. | 7372 | F | 800 523-1950 | 18315 |
| Higher One Payments Inc. | 7372 | E | 510 769-9888 | 18383 |
| Interactive Solutions Inc (DH) | 7372 | D | 510 214-9002 | 18426 |
| Investopedia LLC | 7372 | E | 510 985-7400 | 18438 |
| Marqeta Inc (PA) | 7372 | A | 877 962-7738 | 18522 |
| Nova Module LP | 7372 | E | 415 323-0520 | 18598 |
| Paylocity Holding Corporation | 7372 | A | 847 956-4850 | 18665 |
| Scientific Learning Corp | 7372 | E | 510 444-3500 | 18764 |
| Tanoshi Inc | 7372 | F | 949 677-5261 | 18866 |
| Trov Inc. | 7372 | E | 925 478-5500 | 18893 |
| Atc Colors Inc. | 7532 | F | 510 639-7337 | 19146 |
| Vincent Electric Company (PA) | 7694 | E | 510 639-4500 | 19235 |
| Christian Evang Chrches Amer I | 8211 | E | 510 533-8300 | 19343 |

## OAKLEY, CA - Contra Costa County

| | SIC | EMP | PHONE | ENTRY# |
|---|---|---|---|---|
| Nor-Cal Overhead Inc. | 5211 | F | 925 240-5141 | 17336 |

## OAKVILLE, CA - Napa County

| | SIC | EMP | PHONE | ENTRY# |
|---|---|---|---|---|
| Groth Vineyards and Winery | 0172 | E | 707 944-0290 | 15 |
| Far Niente Winery Inc. | 2084 | D | 707 944-2861 | 1562 |
| FN Cellars LLC | 2084 | F | 707 944-2861 | 1572 |
| NAPA Wine Company LLC | 2084 | E | 707 944-8669 | 1685 |
| Opus One Winery LLC (PA) | 2084 | D | 707 944-9442 | 1699 |
| Promontory LLC | 2084 | E | 707 944-1441 | 1713 |
| Robert Mondavi Winery | 2084 | D | 707 738-5727 | 1727 |
| Rudd Wines Inc (PA) | 2084 | E | 707 944-8577 | 1734 |
| Silver Oak Wine Cellars LLC (PA) | 2084 | F | 707 942-7022 | 1749 |
| Sutter Home Winery Inc. | 2084 | D | 707 944-2565 | 1770 |
| Turnbull Wine Cellars | 2084 | E | 707 963-5839 | 1805 |

## OCEANSIDE, CA - San Diego County

| | SIC | EMP | PHONE | ENTRY# |
|---|---|---|---|---|
| Olli Salumeria Americana LLC | 2011 | D | | 609 |
| American Food Ingredients Inc. | 2034 | E | 760 967-6287 | 943 |
| Julians Foods LLC | 2051 | E | 760 583-9358 | 1219 |
| Dibella Baking Company Inc. | 2052 | D | 951 797-4144 | 1272 |
| Hammond Inc Which Will Do Bus | 2085 | E | 925 381-5392 | 1838 |
| Linksoul LLC | 2211 | E | 760 231-7069 | 2421 |
| Solecta Inc (PA) | 2295 | E | 760 630-9643 | 2530 |
| Surf Ride | 2329 | F | 760 433-4020 | 2646 |
| Kapan - Kent Company Inc. | 2396 | E | 760 631-1716 | 3012 |
| Trinity Woodworks Inc. | 2431 | E | 760 639-5351 | 3200 |
| Britcan Inc. | 2542 | E | 760 722-2300 | 3681 |
| Solut Inc. | 2621 | E | 760 758-7240 | 3797 |
| Precision Label LLC | 2671 | E | 760 757-7533 | 3936 |
| Triple D and DS | 2679 | E | | 4056 |
| Car Sound Exhaust System Inc. | 2819 | C | 949 888-1625 | 5077 |
| Envirnmental Catalyst Tech LLC | 2819 | E | 949 459-3870 | 5093 |
| Genentech Inc. | 2834 | A | 760 231-2440 | 5450 |
| Gilead Palo Alto Inc. | 2834 | C | 760 945-7701 | 5460 |
| Guckenheimer Enterprises Inc. | 2834 | D | 760 414-3659 | 5472 |
| Ionis Pharmaceuticals Inc. | 2834 | E | 760 603-2631 | 5505 |
| Coola Sunblock | 2844 | F | 760 940-2125 | 5958 |
| USP Inc. | 2844 | D | 760 842-7700 | 6052 |
| Hydranautics (DH) | 2899 | B | 760 901-2500 | 6293 |
| Amflex Plastics Incorporated | 3052 | E | 760 643-1756 | 6424 |
| Cal-Mil Plastic Products Inc (PA) | 3089 | E | 800 321-9069 | 6756 |
| Eldorado Stone LLC (DH) | 3272 | E | 800 925-1491 | 7328 |
| Westlake Royal Stone LLC | 3281 | D | 800 255-1727 | 7550 |
| Kainalu Blue Inc. | 3296 | E | 760 806-6400 | 7578 |
| Sound Seal Inc. | 3296 | E | 760 806-6400 | 7582 |
| Pacific Sewer Maintenance Corp | 3321 | F | 800 292-9927 | 7680 |
| Campbell Certified Inc. | 3441 | E | 760 722-9353 | 8113 |
| Tru-Duct Inc. | 3444 | E | 619 660-3858 | 8601 |
| Balda HK Plastics Inc. | 3451 | E | 760 757-1100 | 8719 |
| Balda Precision Inc (DH) | 3451 | D | 760 757-1100 | 8720 |
| R Zamora Inc. | 3469 | E | 760 597-1130 | 8882 |
| Southwest Greene Intl Inc. | 3469 | D | 760 639-4960 | 8889 |
| Steico Industries Inc. | 3469 | C | 760 438-8015 | 8892 |
| Rose Manufacturing Group Inc. | 3471 | E | 760 407-0232 | 9006 |
| Buggy Whip Inc. | 3531 | F | 760 789-3230 | 9411 |
| Proline Concrete Tools Inc. | 3559 | E | 760 758-7240 | 9892 |
| Standard Filter Corporation (PA) | 3564 | E | 866 443-3615 | 9997 |
| Kellermyer Bergensons Svcs LLC (PA) | 3589 | E | 760 631-5111 | 10570 |
| Asigma Corporation | 3599 | E | 760 966-3103 | 10722 |
| BMw Precision Machining Inc. | 3599 | E | 760 439-6813 | 10750 |
| Landmark Mfg Inc. | 3599 | E | 760 941-6626 | 10936 |
| Nelgo Industries Inc. | 3599 | E | 760 433-6434 | 11005 |
| R & G Precision Machining Inc. | 3599 | E | 760 630-8602 | 11062 |
| Lexstar Inc (PA) | 3646 | F | 845 947-1415 | 11542 |
| Amerillum LLC | 3648 | D | 760 727-7675 | 11581 |
| Foxfury LLC | 3648 | E | 760 945-4231 | 11597 |
| Dynamic Vision Inc. | 3652 | E | 858 877-6200 | 11730 |
| HI Tech Electronic Mfg Corp | 3672 | D | 858 657-0908 | 12129 |
| Te Connectivity Corporation | 3678 | D | 760 757-7500 | 12899 |

Employee Codes: A=Over 500 employees, B=251-500
C=101-250, D=51-100, E=20-50, F=10-19, G=1-9

# OCEANSIDE, CA

| | SIC | EMP | PHONE | ENTRY# |
|---|---|---|---|---|
| Onesource Distributors LLC (DH) | 3699 | E | 760 966-4500 | 13281 |
| Car Sound Exhaust System Inc (PA) | 3714 | E | 949 858-5900 | 13470 |
| Hobie Cat Company (PA) | 3732 | C | 760 758-9100 | 14035 |
| Willard Marine Inc | 3732 | D | 714 666-2150 | 14048 |
| Adaptech Corporation | 3825 | F | 571 261-9823 | 14485 |
| Hexagon Mfg Intelligence Inc | 3825 | D | 760 994-1401 | 14532 |
| Dupaco Inc | 3841 | E | 760 758-4550 | 15073 |
| Pryor Products | 3841 | E | 760 724-8244 | 15235 |
| Surgistar Inc | 3841 | F | 760 431-7400 | 15272 |
| Precision One Medical Inc | 3843 | D | 760 945-7966 | 15477 |
| Absolute Board Co Inc | 3949 | E | 760 295-2201 | 15772 |
| Hobie Cat Company II LLC | 3949 | C | 760 758-9100 | 15821 |
| Salis International Inc | 3952 | E | 303 384-3588 | 15887 |
| Federal Heath Sign Company LLC | 3993 | C | 760 941-0715 | 15977 |
| Whitlock Industries Inc | 3999 | F | 760 231-9262 | 16271 |
| Mountain Water Ice Company | 4222 | E | 760 722-7611 | 16284 |
| Agri Service Inc | 4953 | E | 760 295-6255 | 16355 |
| Diakont Advanced Tech Inc | 5043 | E | 858 551-5551 | 16499 |
| Clients & Profits Inc | 5045 | F | 760 945-4334 | 16514 |
| Thornton Technology Corp | 5088 | E | 760 471-9969 | 16929 |
| Chemi-Source Inc | 5122 | E | 760 477-8177 | 17031 |
| Evkii Inc | 5461 | E | 760 721-5200 | 17412 |
| Suja Life LLC (PA) | 5499 | E | 855 879-7852 | 17432 |
| Belching Beaver Brewery | 5813 | C | 760 599-5832 | 17613 |
| McKenna Boiler Works Inc | 7699 | E | 323 221-1171 | 19269 |
| Nitto Denko Technical Corp | 8732 | D | 760 435-7011 | 19486 |

## OJAI, CA - Ventura County

| | SIC | EMP | PHONE | ENTRY# |
|---|---|---|---|---|
| Pure Simple Foods LLC | 1541 | E | 805 272-8448 | 360 |
| Canzone and Company | 3993 | F | 714 537-8175 | 15954 |

## OLIVEHURST, CA - Yuba County

| | SIC | EMP | PHONE | ENTRY# |
|---|---|---|---|---|
| Lhl Construction Inc | 1791 | E | 916 782-9001 | 533 |
| Yuba Rver Mlding Mill Work Inc (PA) | 2431 | E | 530 742-2168 | 3211 |
| D & D Cbnets - Svage Dsgns Inc | 2434 | E | 530 634-9713 | 3234 |
| Norcal Triangles Inc | 2439 | D | 530 740-7750 | 3315 |
| Ace Composites Inc | 3089 | E | 530 743-1885 | 6693 |
| Precast Con Tech Unlimited LLC | 3272 | D | 530 749-6501 | 7373 |
| Builtware Fabrication Inc | 7699 | E | 530 634-0162 | 19246 |

## ONTARIO, CA - San Bernardino County

| | SIC | EMP | PHONE | ENTRY# |
|---|---|---|---|---|
| Perera Cnstr & Design Inc | 1081 | E | 909 484-6350 | 109 |
| Calvillo Construction Corp | 1521 | E | 310 985-3911 | 343 |
| Warren Collins and Assoc Inc (PA) | 1629 | E | 909 548-6708 | 401 |
| Heatherfield Foods Inc | 2011 | E | 877 460-3060 | 601 |
| Ventura Foods LLC | 2021 | E | 323 262-9157 | 707 |
| IDB Holdings Inc (DH) | 2022 | F | 909 390-5624 | 720 |
| Tropicale Foods LLC (PA) | 2024 | E | 909 635-1000 | 817 |
| Superior Quality Foods Inc | 2032 | D | 909 923-4733 | 870 |
| Ajinomoto Foods North Amer Inc | 2038 | C | 909 477-4700 | 1022 |
| Ajinomoto Foods North Amer Inc (DH) | 2038 | D | 909 477-4700 | 1023 |
| Cardenas Markets LLC | 2038 | C | 909 923-7426 | 1029 |
| Specialty Brands Incorporated | 2038 | A | 909 477-4851 | 1047 |
| Windsor Quality Food Company Ltd | 2038 | A | 713 843-5200 | 1051 |
| Popla International Inc | 2045 | E | 909 923-6899 | 1088 |
| JE Rich Company | 2047 | E | 909 464-1872 | 1104 |
| Vivotein LLC | 2048 | F | 918 344-8742 | 1154 |
| Ventura Foods LLC | 2079 | D | 714 257-3700 | 1408 |
| Coca-Cola Company | 2086 | D | 909 975-5200 | 1880 |
| Five Star Gourmet Foods Inc (PA) | 2099 | C | 909 390-0032 | 2200 |
| Fuji Natural Foods Inc (HQ) | 2099 | E | 909 947-1008 | 2212 |
| Gold Star Foods Inc (HQ) | 2099 | E | 909 843-9600 | 2219 |
| Haliburton International Foods Inc | 2099 | B | 909 428-8520 | 2226 |
| Lassonde Pappas and Co Inc | 2099 | E | 909 923-4041 | 2262 |
| Minsley Inc | 2099 | E | 909 458-1100 | 2280 |
| Nellson Nutraceutical LLC | 2099 | F | 626 812-6522 | 2293 |
| Passport Food Group LLC | 2099 | C | 909 627-7312 | 2314 |
| Passport Foods (svc) LLC | 2099 | C | 909 627-7312 | 2315 |
| Rama Food Manufacture Corp (PA) | 2099 | F | 909 923-5305 | 2331 |
| Soup Bases Loaded Inc | 2099 | E | 909 230-6890 | 2357 |
| USA Sales Inc | 2111 | E | 909 390-9606 | 2397 |
| Nautica Opco LLC | 2329 | B | 909 297-7243 | 2635 |
| Jomar Table Linens Inc | 2392 | D | 909 390-1444 | 2931 |
| Meadow Decor Inc | 2392 | F | 909 923-2558 | 2938 |
| Pacific Urethanes LLC | 2392 | C | 909 390-8400 | 2945 |
| Gold Crest Industries Inc | 2393 | E | 909 930-9069 | 2958 |
| Castillo Maritess | 2394 | F | 949 216-0468 | 2972 |
| Melmarc Products Inc | 2395 | C | 714 549-2170 | 2995 |
| A Lot To Say Inc | 2399 | E | 877 366-8448 | 3021 |
| Action Embroidery Corp (PA) | 2399 | E | 909 983-1359 | 3022 |
| Artesia Sawdust Products Inc | 2421 | E | 909 947-5983 | 3064 |
| Hallmark Home Interiors Inc (PA) | 2426 | F | 909 947-7736 | 3093 |
| Moldings Plus Inc | 2431 | E | 909 947-3310 | 3161 |
| Elite Stone Group Inc | 2434 | E | 909 629-6988 | 3237 |
| K & Z Cabinet Co Inc | 2434 | D | 909 947-3567 | 3246 |
| Masterbrand Cabinets LLC | 2434 | E | 909 989-2992 | 3253 |
| Regards Enterprises Inc | 2493 | F | 909 983-0655 | 3408 |
| Dorel Home Furnishings Inc | 2511 | D | 909 390-5705 | 3439 |
| Chromcraft Rvngton Douglas Ind (PA) | 2512 | F | 909 930-9891 | 3467 |
| Leggett & Platt Incorporated | 2515 | D | 909 937-1010 | 3532 |
| Stress-O-Pedic Mattress Co Inc | 2515 | D | 909 605-2010 | 3542 |
| Visionary Sleep LLC | 2515 | D | 909 605-2010 | 3545 |
| Korden Inc | 2522 | E | 909 988-8979 | 3604 |
| California Mfg Cabinetry Inc | 2541 | E | 909 930-3632 | 3649 |
| Compatico Inc | 2541 | E | 616 940-1772 | 3653 |
| Ivars Display (PA) | 2541 | D | 909 923-2761 | 3658 |
| CTA Fixtures Inc | 2542 | D | 909 390-6744 | 3682 |
| Idx Los Angeles LLC | 2542 | C | 909 212-8333 | 3691 |
| LLC Walker West | 2542 | D | 800 767-9378 | 3696 |
| Rack Installation Services Inc | 2542 | E | 909 261-2243 | 3701 |
| Elegance Upholstery Inc | 2599 | F | 562 698-2584 | 3738 |
| Forbes Industries Div | 2599 | C | 909 923-4559 | 3741 |
| Crown Paper Converting Inc | 2621 | E | 909 923-5226 | 3764 |
| New-Indy Containerboard LLC (DH) | 2621 | D | 909 296-3400 | 3787 |
| New-Indy Ontario LLC | 2621 | E | 909 390-1055 | 3788 |
| Caraustar Industries Inc | 2631 | E | 951 685-5544 | 3801 |
| Preferred Printing & Packaging Inc | 2631 | E | 909 923-2053 | 3806 |
| Zapp Packaging Inc | 2631 | D | 909 930-1500 | 3813 |
| Androp Packaging Inc | 2653 | E | 909 605-8842 | 3819 |
| Commander Packaging West Inc | 2653 | E | 714 921-9350 | 3832 |
| Ecko Products Group LLC | 2653 | E | 909 628-5678 | 3839 |
| PNC Proactive Nthrn Cont LLC | 2653 | E | 909 390-5624 | 3879 |
| Southland Container Corp | 2653 | C | 909 937-9781 | 3889 |
| St Worth Container LLC | 2653 | D | 909 390-4550 | 3890 |
| Fineline Settings LLC | 2656 | E | 845 369-6100 | 3914 |
| Upm Raflatac Inc | 2672 | F | 909 390-4657 | 3957 |
| Transcontinental US LLC | 2673 | E | 909 390-8866 | 3986 |
| Encorr Sheets LLC | 2679 | E | 626 523-4661 | 4037 |
| Califrnia Nwspapers Ltd Partnr | 2711 | B | 909 987-6397 | 4086 |
| Txd International Usa Inc | 2711 | E | 909 947-6568 | 4216 |
| Aio Acquisition Inc (HQ) | 2741 | D | 800 333-3795 | 4361 |
| Advanced Color Graphics | 2752 | D | 909 930-1500 | 4504 |
| Bert-Co Industries Inc | 2752 | C | 323 669-5700 | 4531 |
| Fgs-Wi LLC | 2752 | E | 909 467-8300 | 4608 |
| GW Reed Printing Inc | 2752 | E | 909 947-0599 | 4627 |
| Ultimate Print Source Inc | 2752 | E | 909 947-5292 | 4796 |
| L A Supply Co | 2759 | E | 949 470-9900 | 4905 |
| One Stop Label Corporation | 2759 | F | 909 230-9380 | 4930 |
| Response Envelope Inc (PA) | 2759 | C | 909 923-5855 | 4952 |
| Linde Inc | 2813 | E | 909 390-0283 | 5048 |
| Induspac California Inc | 2821 | E | 909 390-4422 | 5163 |
| Qycell Corporation | 2821 | E | 909 390-6644 | 5192 |
| AMF Pharma LLC | 2834 | E | 909 930-9599 | 5316 |
| Genvivo Inc | 2834 | E | 626 441-6695 | 5457 |
| Tiancheng Intl Inc USA | 2834 | F | 909 947-5577 | 5690 |
| Amrep Inc | 2842 | B | 770 422-2071 | 5888 |
| Diamond Wipes Intl Inc | 2844 | C | 909 230-9888 | 5972 |
| Circle Green Inc | 2869 | F | 909 930-0200 | 6140 |
| Advantage Adhesives Inc | 2891 | E | 909 204-4990 | 6217 |
| Pacer Technology (HQ) | 2891 | C | 909 987-0550 | 6238 |
| Kik Pool Additives Inc | 2899 | D | 909 390-9912 | 6302 |
| Able Industrial Products Inc (PA) | 3053 | E | 909 930-1585 | 6437 |
| Parco (DH) | 3053 | C | 909 947-2200 | 6460 |
| Abba Roller LLC (DH) | 3069 | F | 909 947-1244 | 6481 |
| Kirkhill Inc | 3069 | D | 562 803-1117 | 6507 |
| KMC Acquisition LLC (PA) | 3069 | E | 562 396-0121 | 6509 |
| Pmr Precision Mfg & Rbr Co Inc | 3069 | E | 909 605-7525 | 6523 |
| Plastics Research Corporation | 3083 | D | 909 391-9050 | 6587 |
| Classic Containers Inc | 3085 | B | 909 930-3610 | 6608 |
| Akra Plastic Products Inc | 3089 | E | 909 930-1999 | 6701 |
| Armorcast Products Company Inc | 3089 | E | 909 390-1365 | 6725 |
| Axium Packaging LLC | 3089 | A | 909 969-0766 | 6729 |
| Bandlock Corporation | 3089 | D | 909 947-7500 | 6734 |
| Bericap LLC | 3089 | D | 909 390-5518 | 6740 |
| Bomatic Inc | 3089 | D | 909 947-3900 | 6749 |
| California Quality Plas Inc | 3089 | E | 909 930-5667 | 6758 |
| Dorel Juvenile Group Inc | 3089 | C | 909 390-5705 | 6810 |
| Herman Engineering & Mfg Inc | 3089 | F | 909 483-1631 | 6851 |
| Inline Plastics Inc | 3089 | E | 909 923-1033 | 6863 |
| LLC Walker West | 3089 | C | 909 390-4300 | 6898 |
| Medegen LLC (DH) | 3089 | E | 909 390-9080 | 6906 |
| Medegen Inc | 3089 | E | 909 390-9080 | 6907 |
| Mission Plastics Inc | 3089 | C | 909 947-7287 | 6916 |
| Paramount Panels Inc (PA) | 3089 | E | 909 947-8008 | 6950 |
| Plastic Engineering Tech LLC | 3089 | F | 909 390-1323 | 6960 |
| PRC Composites LLC (PA) | 3089 | D | 909 391-2006 | 6976 |

# GEOGRAPHIC SECTION — ORANGE, CA

| Company | SIC | EMP | PHONE | ENTRY# |
|---|---|---|---|---|
| Ray Products Company Inc | 3089 | E | 888 776-9014 | 6996 |
| Reyrich Plastics Inc | 3089 | E | 909 484-8444 | 7004 |
| Star Shield Solutions LLC | 3089 | D | 866 662-4477 | 7043 |
| Superior Mold Co | 3089 | E | 909 947-7028 | 7047 |
| Thermodyne International Ltd | 3089 | C | 909 923-9945 | 7052 |
| US Duty Gear Inc | 3199 | F | 909 391-8800 | 7162 |
| Larry Mthvin Installations Inc (HQ) | 3231 | C | 909 563-1700 | 7230 |
| Western States Wholesale Inc (PA) | 3271 | D | 909 947-0028 | 7304 |
| Western States Wholesale Inc | 3271 | D | 909 947-0028 | 7305 |
| Clark - Pacific Corporation | 3272 | E | 909 823-1433 | 7320 |
| Southwest Concrete Products | 3272 | E | 909 983-9789 | 7392 |
| Cemex USA Inc | 3273 | F | 909 974-5500 | 7432 |
| Foundry Service & Supplies Inc | 3299 | E | 909 284-5000 | 7590 |
| Flow Dynamics Inc | 3312 | F | 909 930-5522 | 7613 |
| Halsteel Inc (DH) | 3315 | E | 909 937-1001 | 7641 |
| Net Shapes Inc (PA) | 3324 | D | 909 947-3231 | 7692 |
| Advanced Pattern & Mold Inc | 3334 | F | 909 930-3444 | 7704 |
| Duralum Products Inc | 3355 | F | 951 736-4500 | 7758 |
| Metals USA Building Pdts LP | 3355 | D | 800 325-1305 | 7760 |
| Vsmpo-Tirus US Inc | 3356 | D | 909 230-9020 | 7770 |
| Bee Wire & Cable Inc | 3357 | E | 909 923-5800 | 7772 |
| Superior Essex Inc | 3357 | C | 909 481-4804 | 7797 |
| Performance Aluminum Products | 3363 | E | 909 391-4131 | 7817 |
| California Die Casting Inc | 3364 | E | 909 947-9947 | 7826 |
| Alumistar Inc | 3365 | E | 562 633-6673 | 7835 |
| Calidad Inc | 3365 | E | 909 947-3937 | 7837 |
| Employee Owned PCF Cast Pdts I | 3365 | E | 562 633-6673 | 7844 |
| B Stephen Cooperage Inc | 3412 | F | 909 591-2929 | 7933 |
| Everest Group USA Inc | 3423 | E | 909 923-1818 | 7952 |
| Garden Pals Inc | 3423 | E | 909 605-0200 | 7954 |
| Halex Corporation (DH) | 3423 | E | 909 629-6219 | 7955 |
| J L M C Inc | 3441 | E | 909 947-2980 | 8155 |
| Lightcap Industries Inc | 3441 | E | 909 930-3772 | 8170 |
| Maximum Quality Metal Pdts Inc | 3441 | E | 909 902-5018 | 8176 |
| R & I Industries Inc | 3441 | E | 909 923-7747 | 8208 |
| Watercrest Inc | 3443 | E | 909 390-3944 | 8352 |
| AMD International Tech LLC | 3444 | E | 909 985-8300 | 8371 |
| Compumeric Engineering Inc | 3444 | E | 909 605-7666 | 8413 |
| Empire Sheet Metal Inc | 3444 | F | 909 923-2927 | 8441 |
| Metal Engineering Inc | 3444 | E | 626 334-1819 | 8503 |
| Stell Industries Inc | 3448 | E | 951 369-8777 | 8686 |
| Db Building Fasteners Inc (PA) | 3449 | E | 909 581-6740 | 8696 |
| Alger Precision Machining LLC | 3451 | C | 909 986-4591 | 8715 |
| Athanor Group Inc | 3451 | E | 909 467-1205 | 8718 |
| Duncan Bolt Co | 3452 | F | 909 581-6740 | 8753 |
| Kingfa Global Inc | 3452 | F | 909 212-5413 | 8761 |
| Alum-Alloy Co Inc | 3463 | E | 909 986-0410 | 8794 |
| Walker Spring & Stamping Corp | 3469 | C | 909 390-4300 | 8899 |
| Danco Anodizing Inc | 3471 | C | 909 923-0562 | 8948 |
| Quality Control Plating Inc | 3471 | E | 909 605-0206 | 9002 |
| Inland Powder Coating Corp | 3479 | C | 909 947-1122 | 9079 |
| Specialty Coating Systems Inc | 3479 | D | 909 390-8818 | 9123 |
| James Jones Company | 3491 | A | 909 418-2558 | 9157 |
| Reliance Worldwide Corporation | 3491 | D | 770 863-4005 | 9161 |
| C M C Steel Fabricators Inc | 3496 | E | 909 899-9993 | 9211 |
| Lexco Imports Inc | 3496 | E | 800 883-1454 | 9222 |
| Rfc Wire Forms Inc | 3496 | D | 909 467-0559 | 9231 |
| ASC Engineered Solutions LLC | 3498 | E | 909 418-3233 | 9248 |
| Turbine Repair Services LLC (PA) | 3511 | E | 909 947-2256 | 9320 |
| Tracy Industries Inc | 3519 | C | 562 692-9034 | 9332 |
| Specialized Dairy Service Inc | 3523 | E | 909 923-3420 | 9382 |
| Sotec USA LLC | 3532 | F | 909 525-5861 | 9451 |
| Pneumatic Conveying Inc (PA) | 3535 | F | 866 557-5214 | 9490 |
| Konecranes Inc | 3536 | E | 909 930-0108 | 9501 |
| Crown Equipment Corporation | 3537 | D | 909 923-8357 | 9513 |
| Balda C Brewer Inc (DH) | 3544 | D | 909 212-0290 | 9605 |
| Wagner Die Supply Inc (PA) | 3544 | E | 909 947-3044 | 9657 |
| Broco Inc | 3548 | E | 909 483-3222 | 9723 |
| Bmci Inc | 3549 | E | 951 361-8000 | 9734 |
| Eubanks Engineering Co (PA) | 3549 | E | 909 483-2456 | 9736 |
| Trinity Robotics Automtn LLC | 3549 | F | 562 690-4525 | 9747 |
| Wallner Expac Inc (PA) | 3549 | D | 909 481-8800 | 9749 |
| Amrep Manufacturing Co LLC | 3559 | B | 877 468-9278 | 9828 |
| Envirokinetics Inc (PA) | 3559 | F | 909 621-7599 | 9853 |
| C M Automotive Systems Inc (PA) | 3563 | E | 909 869-7912 | 9958 |
| Future Commodities Intl Inc | 3565 | E | 888 588-2378 | 10018 |
| Chenbro Micom (usa) Inc | 3572 | E | 909 937-0100 | 10232 |
| Logitech Inc | 3577 | B | 972 947-7100 | 10400 |
| Aerospace and Coml Tooling Inc | 3599 | E | 909 480-5780 | 10690 |
| Am-Tek Engineering Inc | 3599 | F | 909 673-1633 | 10708 |
| Gamma Aerospace LLC | 3599 | E | 310 532-4480 | 10850 |
| Hera Technologies LLC | 3599 | E | 951 751-6191 | 10870 |
| Redline Prcision Machining Inc | 3599 | F | 909 483-1273 | 11073 |
| Supreme Machine Products Inc | 3599 | F | 909 974-0349 | 11128 |
| Tower Industries Inc | 3599 | C | 909 947-2723 | 11148 |
| Upland Fab Inc | 3599 | E | 909 986-6565 | 11163 |
| Ledvance LLC | 3641 | E | 909 923-3003 | 11427 |
| Gund Company Inc | 3644 | F | 909 890-9300 | 11480 |
| Globalux Lighting LLC | 3645 | F | 909 591-7506 | 11496 |
| Wangs Alliance Corporation | 3645 | E | 909 230-9401 | 11507 |
| Mag Instrument Inc (PA) | 3648 | B | 909 947-1006 | 11612 |
| Discopylabs | 3652 | E | 909 390-3800 | 11729 |
| Precise Media Services Inc | 3652 | E | 909 481-3305 | 11741 |
| Tactical Command Inds Inc (DH) | 3669 | E | 925 219-1097 | 12020 |
| Celestica Aerospace Tech Corp | 3672 | C | 512 310-7540 | 12075 |
| Edison Opto USA Corporation | 3674 | E | 909 284-9710 | 12415 |
| Vishay Thin Film LLC | 3674 | E | 909 923-3313 | 12793 |
| West Coast Chain Mfg Co | 3699 | E | 909 923-7800 | 13329 |
| West Coast Corporation | 3699 | E | 909 923-7800 | 13330 |
| New Flyer of America Inc | 3711 | C | 909 456-3566 | 13373 |
| TCI Engineering Inc | 3711 | D | 909 984-1773 | 13388 |
| Arrow Truck Bodies & Eqp Inc | 3713 | E | 909 947-3991 | 13401 |
| Egr Incorporated (DH) | 3714 | E | 800 757-7075 | 13493 |
| Inland Empire Drv Line Svc Inc (PA) | 3714 | F | 909 390-3030 | 13518 |
| Power-Right Industries LLC | 3714 | F | 909 628-4397 | 13557 |
| Thmx Holdings LLC | 3714 | C | 909 390-3944 | 13584 |
| Diagnostic Solutions Intl LLC | 3728 | F | 909 930-3600 | 13823 |
| Maney Aircraft Inc | 3728 | E | 909 390-2500 | 13897 |
| Otto Instrument Service Inc (PA) | 3728 | E | 909 930-5800 | 13918 |
| Q1 Test Inc | 3728 | E | 909 390-9718 | 13932 |
| Summit Machine LLC | 3728 | C | 909 923-2744 | 13962 |
| Triumph Equipment Inc | 3728 | F | 909 947-5983 | 13981 |
| Tower Mechanical Products Inc | 3812 | C | 714 947-2723 | 14323 |
| Carl Zeiss Meditec Prod LLC | 3827 | D | 877 644-4657 | 14767 |
| Sentran LLC (PA) | 3829 | F | 888 545-8988 | 14918 |
| B Braun Medical Inc | 3841 | C | 909 906-7575 | 14988 |
| Covidien | 3841 | F | 909 605-6572 | 15056 |
| Marlee Manufacturing Inc | 3841 | E | 909 923-3222 | 15159 |
| Isomedix Operations Inc | 3842 | E | 909 390-9942 | 15366 |
| Safariland LLC | 3842 | B | 909 923-7300 | 15400 |
| Ashtel Studios Inc | 3844 | E | 909 434-0911 | 15498 |
| Aliquantum International Inc | 3944 | E | 909 773-0880 | 15737 |
| American Fleet & Ret Graphics | 3993 | E | 909 937-7570 | 15941 |
| Edelmann Usa Inc (DH) | 3993 | F | 323 669-5700 | 15966 |
| Encore Image Inc | 3993 | E | 909 986-4632 | 15968 |
| Inland Signs Inc | 3993 | F | 909 923-0006 | 15989 |
| Optec Displays Inc | 3993 | D | 866 924-5239 | 16015 |
| Sign Industries Inc | 3993 | E | 909 930-0303 | 16036 |
| California Exotic Novlt LLC | 3999 | D | 909 606-1950 | 16105 |
| Cecilia Tech Inc | 3999 | F | 818 533-9888 | 16114 |
| Scripto-Tokai Corporation (HQ) | 3999 | D | 909 930-5000 | 16225 |
| Sun Badge Co | 3999 | E | 909 930-1444 | 16242 |
| Blumenthal Distributing Inc (PA) | 5021 | C | 909 930-2000 | 16411 |
| Office Master Inc | 5021 | D | 909 392-5678 | 16417 |
| Cemex Construction Mtls Inc (DH) | 5032 | E | 909 974-5500 | 16468 |
| Bionime USA Corporation | 5047 | E | 909 781-6969 | 16577 |
| DH Caster International Inc | 5072 | F | 909 930-6400 | 16751 |
| Pbb Inc | 5072 | E | 909 923-6250 | 16759 |
| Suncoast Post-Tension Ltd | 5072 | F | 909 673-0490 | 16763 |
| Index Fasteners Inc (PA) | 5085 | E | 909 923-5002 | 16877 |
| Dennis Foland Inc (PA) | 5099 | E | 909 930-9900 | 16974 |
| Rosen Electronics LLC | 5099 | D | 951 898-9808 | 16987 |
| Beauty 21 Cosmetics Inc | 5122 | C | 909 945-2220 | 17029 |
| Clover Needlecraft Inc | 5131 | E | 800 233-1703 | 17061 |
| Mondelez Global LLC | 5149 | D | 909 605-0140 | 17197 |
| Coast Plastics Inc | 5162 | E | 626 812-9174 | 17225 |
| Logans Candies | 5441 | E | 909 984-5410 | 17404 |
| Mark Christopher Chevrolet Inc (PA) | 5511 | C | 909 321-5860 | 17440 |
| Solvari Corp | 5995 | E | 909 509-8228 | 17685 |
| Nine Stars Group (usa) Inc | 5999 | F | 866 978-2778 | 17714 |
| Invapharm Inc (PA) | 6221 | E | 909 757-1818 | 17732 |
| 10-8 Retrofit Inc | 7538 | F | 909 986-5551 | 19158 |
| Whiting Door Mfg Corp | 7699 | D | 909 877-0120 | 19290 |
| Four Seasons Surgery Centers | 8011 | F | 909 933-6576 | 19316 |

## ORANGE, CA - Orange County

| Company | SIC | EMP | PHONE | ENTRY# |
|---|---|---|---|---|
| Martin Integrated Systems | 1742 | E | 714 998-9100 | 477 |
| Orange County Thermal Inds Inc (PA) | 1742 | D | 714 279-9416 | 479 |
| Beach Paving Inc | 1771 | E | 714 978-2414 | 519 |
| Bapko Metal Inc | 1791 | D | 714 639-9380 | 528 |
| Pacifica Foods LLC | 2035 | C | 951 371-3123 | 989 |
| Don Miguel Mexican Foods Inc (HQ) | 2038 | B | 714 385-4500 | 1033 |
| Chapman Cbc LLC | 2082 | E | 844 855-2337 | 1426 |
| American Bottling Company | 2086 | C | 714 974-8560 | 1857 |
| Reyes Coca-Cola Bottling LLC | 2086 | D | 714 974-1901 | 1950 |
| Newport Flavors & Fragrances | 2087 | E | 714 771-2200 | 2017 |

Employee Codes: A=Over 500 employees, B=251-500
C=101-250, D=51-100, E=20-50, F=10-19, G=1-9

## ORANGE, CA

| Company | SIC | EMP | PHONE | ENTRY# |
|---|---|---|---|---|
| Natures Flavors | 2099 | E | 714 744-3700 | 2291 |
| Quoc Viet Foods | 2099 | F | 714 283-3663 | 2329 |
| Fur Accents LLC | 2371 | F | 714 403-5286 | 2870 |
| Orange Woodworks Inc | 2431 | E | 714 997-2600 | 3172 |
| Westrock Rkt LLC | 2653 | E | 714 978-2895 | 3895 |
| Amscan Inc | 2656 | D | 714 972-2626 | 3912 |
| T & T Box Company Inc | 2657 | E | 909 465-0848 | 3919 |
| J J Foil Company Inc | 2675 | E | 714 998-9920 | 3997 |
| K & D Graphics | 2675 | E | 714 638-8900 | 3998 |
| Presentation Folder Inc | 2675 | E | 714 289-7000 | 4001 |
| Positive Concepts Inc (PA) | 2679 | E | 714 685-5800 | 4046 |
| American PCF Prtrs College Inc | 2752 | E | 949 250-3212 | 4510 |
| Eagle Graphics Inc (PA) | 2752 | F | 714 978-2200 | 4598 |
| Fisher Printing Inc (PA) | 2752 | C | 714 998-9200 | 4611 |
| We Do Graphics Inc | 2752 | E | 714 997-7390 | 4807 |
| Westlabel LLC (PA) | 2752 | E | 714 532-3946 | 4810 |
| Label Impressions Inc | 2759 | E | 714 634-3466 | 4908 |
| Solvay America Inc | 2819 | D | 225 361-3376 | 5119 |
| Solvay Chemicals Inc | 2819 | E | 714 744-5610 | 5122 |
| Coastal Enterprises | 2821 | E | 714 771-4969 | 5146 |
| Ameripharma Specialty Phrm Div | 2834 | E | 877 778-3773 | 5315 |
| Harpers Pharmacy Inc | 2834 | C | 877 778-3773 | 5477 |
| Ortho-Clinical Diagnostics Inc | 2835 | E | 714 639-2323 | 5772 |
| AM Wax Inc | 2842 | F | 714 228-1999 | 5887 |
| Kretus Inc | 2851 | F | 714 694-2061 | 6091 |
| Alliance Hose & Extrusions Inc | 2869 | F | 714 202-8500 | 6125 |
| BASF Corporation | 2869 | E | 714 921-1430 | 6129 |
| Cytec Engineered Materials Inc | 2899 | C | 714 630-9400 | 6281 |
| California Gasket and Rbr Corp (PA) | 3069 | E | 714 202-8500 | 6486 |
| West American Rubber Co LLC (PA) | 3069 | C | 714 532-3355 | 6549 |
| West American Rubber Co LLC | 3069 | C | 714 532-3355 | 6550 |
| Allen Mold Inc | 3089 | F | 714 538-6517 | 6702 |
| Duraplex Inc | 3089 | F | 714 538-1335 | 6812 |
| King Plastics Inc | 3089 | D | 714 997-7540 | 6887 |
| Roto Dynamics Inc | 3089 | E | 714 685-0183 | 7010 |
| SKB Corporation (PA) | 3089 | B | 714 637-1252 | 7029 |
| Dennis DiGiorgio | 3231 | E | 714 408-7527 | 7218 |
| Precast Innovations Inc | 3272 | E | 714 921-4060 | 7374 |
| Omega Products Corp | 3299 | E | 714 935-0900 | 7597 |
| Opal Service Inc (PA) | 3299 | E | 714 935-0900 | 7598 |
| Pro Detention Inc | 3315 | D | 714 881-3680 | 7650 |
| Thermal-Vac Technology Inc | 3398 | E | 714 997-2601 | 7902 |
| Commercial Metal Forming Inc | 3443 | E | 714 532-6321 | 8310 |
| Facility Makers Inc | 3444 | E | 714 544-1702 | 8453 |
| SA Serving Lines Inc | 3444 | E | 714 848-7529 | 8563 |
| Allied Mdular Bldg Systems Inc (PA) | 3448 | E | 714 516-1188 | 8653 |
| Shade Structures Inc | 3448 | E | 714 427-6980 | 8685 |
| M & R Engineering Co | 3451 | F | 714 991-8480 | 8725 |
| Anillo Industries LLC | 3452 | E | 714 637-7000 | 8742 |
| Independent Forge Company | 3462 | E | 714 997-7337 | 8777 |
| Gel Industries Inc | 3463 | C | 714 639-8191 | 8797 |
| Quality Aluminum Forge LLC (HQ) | 3463 | E | 714 639-8191 | 8800 |
| Quality Aluminum Forge LLC | 3463 | C | 714 639-8191 | 8801 |
| Prototype & Short-Run Svcs Inc | 3469 | E | 714 449-9661 | 8879 |
| Aquarian Coatings Corp | 3471 | F | 714 632-0230 | 8923 |
| Hightower Plating & Mfg Co LLC | 3471 | E | 714 637-9110 | 8970 |
| Fletcher Coating Co | 3479 | E | 714 637-4763 | 9070 |
| United Sunshine American Industries | 3496 | E | | 9239 |
| Nov Inc | 3533 | E | 714 978-1900 | 9465 |
| Air Tube Transfer Systems Inc | 3535 | F | 714 363-0700 | 9479 |
| Hightower Metal Products LLC | 3544 | D | 714 637-7000 | 9627 |
| Kyocera SGS Precision Tls Inc | 3545 | D | 888 848-9266 | 9681 |
| Dilco Industrial Inc | 3552 | F | 714 998-5266 | 9750 |
| His Industries Inc | 3565 | E | 949 383-4308 | 10020 |
| Premier Filters Inc | 3569 | E | 657 226-0091 | 10108 |
| Shaxon Industries Inc | 3572 | D | 714 779-1140 | 10282 |
| Data Aire Inc (HQ) | 3585 | D | 800 347-2473 | 10496 |
| G A Systems Inc | 3589 | E | 714 848-7529 | 10561 |
| Hyperion Motors LLC | 3594 | E | 714 363-5858 | 10632 |
| Advanced Ceramic Technology | 3599 | F | 714 538-2524 | 10672 |
| All Diameter Grinding Inc | 3599 | E | 714 744-1200 | 10695 |
| D Mills Grnding Machining Inc | 3599 | C | 951 697-6847 | 10798 |
| G P Manufacturing Inc | 3599 | F | 714 974-0288 | 10848 |
| Niedwick Corporation | 3599 | E | 714 771-9999 | 11008 |
| Rlh Industries Inc | 3661 | E | 714 532-1672 | 11783 |
| Zettler Components Inc (PA) | 3669 | C | 949 831-5000 | 12027 |
| Avantec Manufacturing Inc | 3672 | E | 714 532-6197 | 12063 |
| Fabricated Components Corp | 3672 | E | 714 974-8590 | 12098 |
| Marcel Electronics Inc | 3672 | E | 714 974-8590 | 12155 |
| US Sensor Corp | 3674 | D | 714 639-1000 | 12782 |
| Coil Winding Specialist Inc | 3677 | E | 714 279-9010 | 12834 |
| Winchster Intrcnnect Micro LLC | 3678 | C | 714 637-7099 | 12903 |
| Coastal Component Inds Inc | 3679 | E | 714 685-6677 | 12942 |
| Statek Corporation (HQ) | 3679 | C | 714 639-7810 | 13090 |
| Statek Corporation | 3679 | C | 714 639-7810 | 13091 |
| Jbb Inc | 3699 | E | 888 538-9287 | 13258 |
| APM Manufacturing | 3721 | C | 714 453-0100 | 13635 |
| Sport Kites Inc | 3721 | F | 714 998-6359 | 13693 |
| Ducommun Aerostructures Inc | 3724 | C | 714 637-4401 | 13707 |
| Air Cabin Engineering Inc | 3728 | E | 714 637-4111 | 13761 |
| APM Manufacturing (HQ) | 3728 | E | 714 453-0100 | 13779 |
| Arden Engineering Inc | 3728 | E | 714 998-6410 | 13784 |
| Arden Engineering Holdings Inc (DH) | 3728 | E | 714 998-6410 | 13785 |
| Tri-Tech Precision Inc | 3728 | F | 714 970-1363 | 13978 |
| Belt Drives Ltd | 3751 | E | 714 693-1313 | 14054 |
| Cleatech LLC | 3821 | E | 714 754-6668 | 14333 |
| Califrnia Anlytical Instrs Inc | 3823 | D | 714 974-5560 | 14392 |
| Fieldpiece Instruments Inc (PA) | 3825 | E | 714 634-1844 | 14526 |
| Redline Detection LLC (PA) | 3829 | E | 714 579-6961 | 14914 |
| Fusion Biotec LLC | 3841 | E | 949 264-3437 | 15093 |
| Dux Industries Inc | 3843 | D | 805 488-1122 | 15454 |
| Handpiece Parts & Products Inc | 3843 | E | 714 997-4331 | 15457 |
| Jeneric/Pentron Incorporated (HQ) | 3843 | C | 203 265-7397 | 15460 |
| Kerr Corporation (HQ) | 3843 | C | 714 516-7400 | 15461 |
| Ormco Corporation (HQ) | 3843 | D | 714 516-7400 | 15470 |
| Sybron Dental Specialties Inc (PA) | 3843 | C | 714 516-7400 | 15487 |
| John Bishop Design Inc | 3993 | E | 714 744-2300 | 15994 |
| Metal Art of California Inc (PA) | 3993 | D | 714 532-7100 | 16008 |
| Monarch Corporation | 3993 | F | 714 744-5098 | 16011 |
| Wood Space Industries Inc | 4226 | F | 714 996-4552 | 16295 |
| Cco Holdings LLC | 4841 | C | 714 509-5861 | 16331 |
| Total Health Environment LLC | 5047 | E | 714 637-1010 | 16591 |
| Everfocus Electronics Corp (HQ) | 5065 | E | 626 844-8888 | 16702 |
| Sunwest Industries Inc | 5091 | E | 714 712-6233 | 16940 |
| Nifty Package Co Inc | 5199 | E | 714 863-6058 | 17303 |
| Rockler Companies Inc | 5251 | F | 714 282-1157 | 17358 |
| Tavistock Restaurants LLC | 5813 | C | 714 939-8686 | 17625 |
| Strata USA Llc | 5963 | E | 888 878-7282 | 17681 |
| Alignment Healthcare Inc (PA) | 6324 | D | 844 310-2247 | 17736 |
| Sallingers Spclty Scrnprint Em | 7336 | E | 714 532-6627 | 17838 |
| Ashunya Inc | 7371 | D | 714 385-1900 | 17882 |
| Maintech Incorporated | 7371 | C | 714 921-8000 | 17944 |
| Lcptracker Inc | 7372 | E | 714 669-0052 | 18488 |
| Salescatcher LLC | 7372 | E | 714 376-6700 | 18753 |
| Cirtech Inc | 7389 | E | 714 921-0860 | 19082 |
| Guys Patio Inc | 7641 | E | 844 968-7485 | 19181 |
| Sam Schaffer Inc | 7699 | E | 323 263-7524 | 19280 |

## ORCUTT, CA - Santa Barbara County

| Company | SIC | EMP | PHONE | ENTRY# |
|---|---|---|---|---|
| Den-Mat Corporation (DH) | 2844 | B | 805 922-8491 | 5969 |

## ORINDA, CA - Contra Costa County

| Company | SIC | EMP | PHONE | ENTRY# |
|---|---|---|---|---|
| Keepcool USA LLC (PA) | 2393 | F | 925 962-1832 | 2959 |
| Hopscotch Press Inc | 2741 | E | 510 548-0400 | 4414 |

## ORLAND, CA - Glenn County

| Company | SIC | EMP | PHONE | ENTRY# |
|---|---|---|---|---|
| Baugher Ranch Organics Inc | 0173 | E | 530 865-4015 | 37 |
| Olivarez Honey Bees Inc | 0279 | D | 530 865-0298 | 70 |
| Olson Meat Company | 2011 | E | 530 865-8111 | 610 |
| Land OLakes Inc | 2022 | E | 530 865-7626 | 725 |
| Olive Musco Products Inc | 2035 | E | 530 865-4111 | 987 |
| Select Harvest Usa LLC | 2068 | D | 530 865-7286 | 1365 |
| Jensen Enterprises Inc | 3272 | E | 530 865-4277 | 7348 |

## ORO GRANDE, CA - San Bernardino County

| Company | SIC | EMP | PHONE | ENTRY# |
|---|---|---|---|---|
| Calportland Company | 3241 | D | 760 245-5321 | 7250 |

## OROVILLE, CA - Butte County

| Company | SIC | EMP | PHONE | ENTRY# |
|---|---|---|---|---|
| George Delallo Company Inc | 2033 | F | 530 533-3303 | 891 |
| Pacific Coast Producers | 2033 | C | 530 533-4311 | 918 |
| North State Renewables LLC | 2077 | E | 530 343-6076 | 1387 |
| Apex Enterprises Inc | 2411 | E | 530 871-0723 | 3042 |
| J W Bamford Inc | 2411 | F | 530 533-0732 | 3047 |
| Setzer Forest Products Inc | 2421 | C | 530 534-8100 | 3080 |
| Roplast Industries Inc | 2673 | C | 530 532-9500 | 3978 |
| Graphic Packaging Intl LLC | 2759 | C | 530 533-1058 | 4885 |
| Prezero US Packaging LLC | 3086 | D | 800 767-5278 | 6657 |
| Smb Industries Inc | 3441 | E | 530 538-0101 | 8217 |
| Smb Industries Inc (PA) | 3441 | E | 530 534-6266 | 8218 |
| Endeavor Homes Inc | 3531 | E | 530 534-0300 | 9422 |
| Compass Equipment Inc (PA) | 3535 | E | 530 533-7284 | 9482 |
| Conners Oro-Cal Mfg Co | 3911 | E | 530 533-5065 | 15688 |
| Country Connection Inc (PA) | 5999 | F | 530 589-5176 | 17698 |
| Baxter Wldg & Fabrication LLC | 7692 | F | 530 321-9216 | 19184 |

# GEOGRAPHIC SECTION

## PALM DESERT, CA

| | SIC | EMP | PHONE | ENTRY# |
|---|---|---|---|---|

### OXNARD, CA - Ventura County

| Company | SIC | EMP | PHONE | ENTRY# |
|---|---|---|---|---|
| Dcor LLC (PA) | 1382 | D | 805 535-2000 | 176 |
| Freeport-Mcmoran Oil & Gas LLC | 1382 | E | 805 567-1601 | 182 |
| Kaiser Air Conditioning and Sheet Metal Inc | 1761 | E | 805 988-1800 | 515 |
| J M Smucker Company | 2033 | E | 805 487-5483 | 895 |
| Oxnard Lemon Company | 2037 | F | 805 483-1173 | 1014 |
| S & M Professionals Inc (PA) | 2048 | E | 805 988-7677 | 1148 |
| Noushig Inc | 2051 | E | 805 983-2903 | 1230 |
| Royal Wine Corporation | 2084 | E | 805 983-1560 | 1733 |
| Kevita Inc (HQ) | 2086 | D | 805 200-2250 | 1898 |
| McK Enterprises Inc | 2099 | D | 805 483-5292 | 2279 |
| Sunrise Growers Inc | 2099 | A | 612 619-9545 | 2365 |
| Scully Sportswear Inc (PA) | 2386 | E | 805 483-6339 | 2883 |
| California Woodworking Inc | 2434 | E | 805 982-9090 | 3228 |
| E Vasquez Distributors Inc | 2448 | E | 805 487-8458 | 3340 |
| Little Castle Furniture Co Inc | 2512 | E | 805 278-4646 | 3478 |
| Casualway Usa LLC | 2514 | D | 805 660-7408 | 3499 |
| Ergonom Corporation (PA) | 2599 | D | 805 981-9978 | 3739 |
| Ergonom Corporation | 2599 | D | 805 981-9978 | 3740 |
| New-Indy Oxnard LLC | 2621 | C | 805 986-3881 | 3789 |
| Procter & Gamble Paper Pdts Co | 2676 | A | 805 485-8871 | 4004 |
| TI Enterprises LLC | 2721 | C | 805 981-8393 | 4301 |
| National Graphics LLC | 2752 | D | 805 644-9212 | 4703 |
| V3 Printing Corporation | 2752 | D | 805 981-2600 | 4800 |
| Ventura Printing Inc (PA) | 2752 | D | 805 981-2600 | 4803 |
| Safe Publishing Company | 2759 | D | 805 973-1300 | 4957 |
| Complyright Dist Svcs Inc | 2761 | E | 805 981-0992 | 4989 |
| Cdti Advanced Materials Inc (PA) | 2819 | C | 805 639-9458 | 5080 |
| Infratab | 2836 | E | 805 986-8880 | 5841 |
| Kim Laube & Company Inc | 2844 | E | 805 240-1300 | 6000 |
| Spatz Corporation | 2844 | C | 805 487-2122 | 6040 |
| Nutrien AG Solutions Inc | 2873 | F | 805 488-3646 | 6179 |
| Monsanto Company | 2879 | E | 805 827-2341 | 6202 |
| Olde Thompson LLC (DH) | 2899 | E | 805 983-0388 | 6314 |
| B & S Plastics Inc | 3089 | C | 805 981-0262 | 6730 |
| Cool-Pak LLC | 3089 | D | 805 981-2434 | 6780 |
| Leading Industry Inc | 3089 | E | 805 385-4100 | 6894 |
| PC Vaughan Mfg Corp | 3089 | D | 805 278-2555 | 6952 |
| Pinnpack Capital Holdings LLC | 3089 | E | 805 385-4100 | 6955 |
| Rakar Incorporated | 3089 | E | 805 487-2721 | 6991 |
| Masters In Metal Inc | 3263 | F | 805 988-1992 | 7283 |
| Santa Barbara Design Studio (PA) | 3269 | E | 805 966-3883 | 7290 |
| Diversified Minerals Inc | 3273 | E | 805 247-1069 | 7438 |
| State Ready Mix Inc | 3273 | F | 805 647-2817 | 7503 |
| Western Saw Manufacturers Inc | 3425 | E | 805 981-0999 | 7971 |
| Raypak Inc (DH) | 3433 | B | 805 278-5300 | 8076 |
| Millworks Etc Inc | 3442 | E | 805 499-3400 | 8277 |
| Steelworks Etc Inc | 3442 | F | 805 487-3000 | 8292 |
| Oxnard Prcsion Fabrication Inc | 3444 | E | 805 985-0447 | 8522 |
| Rincon Iron Inc | 3446 | F | 805 455-2904 | 8642 |
| Clamshell Structures Inc | 3448 | F | 805 988-1340 | 8661 |
| Advanced Structural Tech Inc | 3462 | C | 805 204-9133 | 8771 |
| Alliance Chemical & Envmtl | 3471 | F | 805 385-3330 | 8915 |
| Elite Metal Finishing LLC (PA) | 3471 | C | 805 983-4320 | 8959 |
| Applied Powdercoat Inc | 3479 | E | 805 981-1991 | 9048 |
| Ets Express LLC (DH) | 3479 | E | 805 278-7771 | 9068 |
| Haas Automation Inc (PA) | 3541 | A | 805 278-1800 | 9556 |
| Acme Cryogenics Inc | 3559 | E | 805 981-4500 | 9823 |
| Cryogenic Experts Inc | 3559 | E | 805 981-4500 | 9845 |
| Nu Venture Diving Co | 3563 | E | 805 815-4044 | 9973 |
| Vortech Engineering Inc | 3564 | E | 805 247-0226 | 10005 |
| Amiad USA Inc | 3589 | E | 805 988-3323 | 10533 |
| Amiad USA Inc | 3589 | E | 805 988-3323 | 10534 |
| ACC Precision Inc | 3599 | F | 805 278-9801 | 10659 |
| Aerotek Inc | 3599 | A | 805 604-3000 | 10692 |
| Rapid Product Solutions Inc | 3599 | E | 805 485-7234 | 11071 |
| T & M Machining | 3599 | E | 805 983-6716 | 11132 |
| Birns Oceanographics Inc | 3648 | F | 805 487-5393 | 11584 |
| Scosche Industries Inc | 3651 | C | 805 486-4450 | 11696 |
| Esco Technologies Inc | 3669 | E | 805 604-3875 | 11993 |
| Mercury Systems Inc | 3672 | C | 805 388-1345 | 12160 |
| Mercury Systems Inc | 3672 | C | 805 751-1100 | 12161 |
| Component Equipment Coinc | 3678 | E | 805 988-8004 | 12871 |
| Delta Microwave LLC | 3679 | D | 805 751-1100 | 12958 |
| Harwil Precision Products | 3679 | E | 805 988-6800 | 12994 |
| Simpliphi Power Inc | 3691 | E | 805 640-6700 | 13149 |
| Becker Automotive Designs Inc | 3711 | E | 805 487-5227 | 13343 |
| Borla Performance Inds Inc (PA) | 3714 | E | 805 986-8600 | 13465 |
| Granatelli Motor Sports Inc | 3714 | E | 805 486-6644 | 13508 |
| American Airframe Inc | 3728 | D | 805 240-1608 | 13776 |
| Pti Technologies Inc (DH) | 3728 | C | 805 604-3700 | 13931 |
| Tbyci LLC | 3732 | F | 805 985-6800 | 14045 |
| Northrop Grumman Systems Corp | 3812 | D | 805 278-2074 | 14260 |
| Northrop Grumman Systems Corp | 3812 | C | 805 684-6641 | 14270 |
| Catalytic Solutions Inc (HQ) | 3822 | E | 805 486-4649 | 14356 |
| Golf Sales West Inc | 3949 | E | 805 988-3363 | 15817 |
| Illah Sports Inc | 3949 | E | 805 240-7790 | 15829 |
| Beckman Industries | 3965 | F | 805 375-3003 | 15908 |
| Mgr Design International Inc | 3999 | E | 805 981-6400 | 16183 |
| Trans Fx Inc | 3999 | F | 805 485-6110 | 16255 |
| Mws Precision Wire Inds Inc | 5051 | D | 818 991-8553 | 16624 |
| Orora Packaging Solutions | 5113 | E | 805 278-5040 | 17012 |
| McConnells Fine Ice Creams LLC | 5143 | E | 805 963-8813 | 17132 |
| Ventura County Lemon Coop | 5148 | D | 805 385-3345 | 17173 |
| Olde Thompson LLC | 5149 | E | 805 983-0388 | 17202 |
| Autonomous Defense Tech Corp | 7382 | E | 805 616-2030 | 19052 |
| West Coast Welding & Cnstr | 7692 | F | 805 604-1222 | 19220 |
| West Coast Wldg & Piping Inc | 7692 | D | 805 246-5841 | 19221 |
| Players West Amusements Inc (PA) | 7993 | E | 805 983-1400 | 19311 |
| Seminis Inc (DH) | 8731 | B | 805 485-7317 | 19473 |

### PACHECO, CA - Contra Costa County

| Company | SIC | EMP | PHONE | ENTRY# |
|---|---|---|---|---|
| Biocare Medical LLC (PA) | 2835 | C | 925 603-8000 | 5739 |
| Matheson Tri-Gas Inc | 5084 | E | 925 229-4350 | 16825 |

### PACIFIC GROVE, CA - Monterey County

| Company | SIC | EMP | PHONE | ENTRY# |
|---|---|---|---|---|
| New Generation Athlete LLC | 2339 | F | 661 316-2209 | 2794 |
| Pivot3 Inc | 7372 | C | 512 807-2666 | 18675 |

### PACIFIC PALISADES, CA - Los Angeles County

| Company | SIC | EMP | PHONE | ENTRY# |
|---|---|---|---|---|
| Aadi Bioscience Inc (PA) | 2834 | E | 424 744-8055 | 5286 |
| Chilicon Power LLC (PA) | 3825 | E | 310 800-1396 | 14504 |
| Optimiscorp | 7372 | D | 310 230-2780 | 18629 |
| Snap Inc | 7372 | D | 310 745-0632 | 18801 |

### PACIFICA, CA - San Mateo County

| Company | SIC | EMP | PHONE | ENTRY# |
|---|---|---|---|---|
| Kibblwhite Prcsion McHning Inc | 3751 | E | 650 359-4704 | 14062 |

### PACOIMA, CA - Los Angeles County

| Company | SIC | EMP | PHONE | ENTRY# |
|---|---|---|---|---|
| Vita Juice Corporation | 2033 | D | 818 899-1195 | 937 |
| Hrk Pet Food Products Inc | 2048 | F | 818 897-2521 | 1130 |
| Natural Balance Pet Foods | 2048 | E | 800 829-4493 | 1138 |
| American Fruits & Flavors LLC (HQ) | 2087 | C | 818 899-9574 | 1978 |
| LA Hardwood Flooring Inc (PA) | 2426 | F | 818 361-0099 | 3096 |
| N K Cabinets Inc | 2434 | E | 818 897-7909 | 3259 |
| Western States Packaging Inc | 2673 | E | 818 686-6045 | 3988 |
| Cosmetic Enterprises Ltd | 2844 | F | 818 896-5355 | 5959 |
| Cosmetic Group Usa Inc | 2844 | C | 818 767-2889 | 5960 |
| Petra-1 LP | 2844 | E | 866 334-3702 | 6019 |
| Flamemaster Corporation | 2891 | E | 818 890-1401 | 6228 |
| Moc Products Company Inc (PA) | 2899 | D | 818 794-3500 | 6310 |
| Molding Corporation America | 3089 | E | 818 890-7877 | 6920 |
| RMR Products Inc (PA) | 3272 | F | 818 890-0896 | 7385 |
| D & M Steel Inc | 3441 | E | 818 896-2070 | 8129 |
| SDS Industries Inc | 3442 | C | 818 492-3500 | 8290 |
| American Range Corporation | 3444 | C | 818 897-0808 | 8373 |
| Mayoni Enterprises | 3444 | E | 818 896-0026 | 8501 |
| Sunland Aerospace Fasteners | 3452 | D | 818 485-8929 | 8767 |
| APT Metal Fabricators Inc | 3469 | E | 818 896-7478 | 8818 |
| Cabrac Inc | 3469 | E | 818 834-0177 | 8826 |
| Hanmar LLC (PA) | 3469 | E | 818 890-2802 | 8848 |
| Metalite Manufacturing Company | 3469 | E | 818 890-2802 | 8864 |
| M & R Plating Corporation | 3471 | F | 818 896-2700 | 8980 |
| Ultramet | 3471 | E | 818 899-0236 | 9027 |
| American Etching & Mfg | 3479 | E | 323 875-3910 | 9046 |
| Kitch Engineering Inc | 3599 | E | 818 897-7133 | 10929 |
| JKL Components Corporation | 3647 | E | 818 896-0019 | 11573 |
| Mole-Richardson Co Ltd (PA) | 3648 | D | 323 851-0111 | 11613 |
| Dw and Bb Consulting Inc | 3769 | D | 818 896-9899 | 14111 |
| Nu-Hope Laboratories Inc | 3841 | E | 818 899-7711 | 15210 |
| Twin Peak Industries Inc | 3949 | E | 800 259-5906 | 15869 |
| California Signs Inc | 3993 | E | 818 899-1888 | 15953 |
| Parkoworld Inc | 3993 | F | 818 686-6900 | 16019 |
| Energy Club Inc | 5145 | D | | 17143 |
| Ketab Corporation | 5942 | F | 310 477-7477 | 17638 |

### PALA, CA - San Diego County

| Company | SIC | EMP | PHONE | ENTRY# |
|---|---|---|---|---|
| Heidelberg Mtls Sthwest Agg LL | 3273 | F | 877 642-6766 | 7454 |

### PALM DESERT, CA - Riverside County

| Company | SIC | EMP | PHONE | ENTRY# |
|---|---|---|---|---|
| Breeze Air Conditioning LLC | 1711 | D | 760 346-0855 | 407 |
| La Quinta Brewing Company LLC | 2082 | D | 760 200-2597 | 1444 |
| Lf Visuals Inc | 2299 | E | 760 345-5571 | 2548 |
| Clarios LLC | 2531 | E | 760 200-5225 | 3618 |
| Associated Desert Shoppers Inc (DH) | 2741 | D | 760 346-1729 | 4367 |
| Daniels Inc (PA) | 2741 | E | 801 621-3355 | 4387 |

Employee Codes: A=Over 500 employees, B=251-500
C=101-250, D=51-100, E=20-50, F=10-19, G=1-9

# PALM DESERT, CA

| Company | SIC | EMP | PHONE | ENTRY# |
|---|---|---|---|---|
| Farley Paving Stone Co Inc | 3272 | D | 760 773-3960 | 7330 |
| Jordahl USA Inc | 3444 | E | 866 332-6687 | 8479 |
| Pd Group | 3993 | E | 760 674-3028 | 16020 |
| Priority Lighting Inc | 5719 | F | 800 709-1119 | 17539 |
| Advanced Realtime Systems Inc | 7371 | F | 760 636-0444 | 17876 |

## PALM SPRINGS, CA - Riverside County

| Company | SIC | EMP | PHONE | ENTRY# |
|---|---|---|---|---|
| Super Struct Bldg Systems Inc | 2522 | E | 760 322-2522 | 3608 |
| Desert Sun Publishing Co (DH) | 2711 | C | 760 322-8889 | 4103 |
| Adams Trade Press LP (PA) | 2721 | E | 760 318-7000 | 4225 |
| Desert Publications Inc (PA) | 2721 | E | 760 325-2333 | 4246 |
| Matches Inc | 2824 | B | 760 899-1919 | 5222 |
| Xy Corp Inc | 3542 | E | 760 323-0333 | 9593 |
| BMW of Palm Springs | 3545 | D | 760 324-7071 | 9662 |
| Iqd Frequency Products Inc | 3679 | E | 408 250-1435 | 13006 |
| Carefusion 207 Inc | 3841 | B | 760 778-7200 | 15028 |
| Carefusion Corporation | 3841 | E | 760 778-7200 | 15031 |
| Joe Blasco Enterprises Inc | 3999 | E | 323 467-4949 | 16155 |
| Best Signs Inc (PA) | 7389 | E | 760 320-3042 | 19077 |

## PALMDALE, CA - Los Angeles County

| Company | SIC | EMP | PHONE | ENTRY# |
|---|---|---|---|---|
| Mandeville Modular Inc | 1531 | F | 888 662-8458 | 352 |
| Dac Heating and AC | 1711 | F | 661 441-2787 | 415 |
| D & J Printing Inc | 2752 | D | 661 265-1995 | 4581 |
| Ultramar Inc | 2911 | D | 661 944-2496 | 6356 |
| Aero Bending Company | 3444 | D | 661 948-2363 | 8366 |
| Lusk Quality Machine Products | 3599 | E | 661 272-0630 | 10948 |
| Sun Valley Ltg Standards Inc | 3646 | D | 661 233-2000 | 11559 |
| US Pole Company Inc (PA) | 3646 | D | 800 877-6537 | 11566 |
| Vision Engrg Met Stamping Inc | 3646 | D | 661 575-0933 | 11567 |
| Northrop Grumman Systems Corp | 3721 | B | 661 272-7000 | 13680 |
| Lockheed Martin Corporation | 3812 | A | 661 572-7428 | 14212 |
| Northrop Grumman Corporation | 3812 | E | 661 272-7334 | 14232 |
| Northrop Grumman Systems Corp | 3812 | E | 661 540-0446 | 14252 |
| Teletronics Technology Corp | 3812 | E | 661 273-7033 | 14318 |
| Murcal Inc | 5063 | E | 661 272-4700 | 16666 |
| Africajun LLC | 7812 | E | 310 403-1673 | 19293 |

## PALO ALTO, CA - Santa Clara County

| Company | SIC | EMP | PHONE | ENTRY# |
|---|---|---|---|---|
| Fono Unlimited (PA) | 2024 | E | 650 322-4664 | 801 |
| Embarcadero Media (PA) | 2711 | D | 650 964-6300 | 4111 |
| Caviar Affair LLC | 2721 | E | 415 235-4169 | 4235 |
| Birdeye Inc (PA) | 2741 | E | 800 561-3357 | 4371 |
| Issuu Inc (PA) | 2741 | E | 844 477-8800 | 4419 |
| KUDos&co Inc | 2741 | E | 650 799-9104 | 4424 |
| Norway Topco LP (PA) | 2833 | F | 435 655-6000 | 5256 |
| Anacor Pharmaceuticals Inc | 2834 | E | 650 543-7500 | 5322 |
| Aria Pharmaceuticals Inc | 2834 | F | 650 382-2605 | 5333 |
| Bridgebio Pharma Inc (PA) | 2834 | C | 650 391-9740 | 5383 |
| Forty Seven Inc | 2834 | E | 650 352-4150 | 5446 |
| Jazz Pharmaceuticals Inc | 2834 | C | 650 496-3777 | 5518 |
| Jazz Pharmaceuticals Inc (HQ) | 2834 | E | 650 496-3777 | 5519 |
| Kodiak Sciences Inc (PA) | 2834 | D | 650 281-0850 | 5528 |
| Orphan Medical Inc | 2834 | D | 650 496-3777 | 5588 |
| Rascal Therapeutics Inc | 2834 | E | 650 770-0192 | 5629 |
| Scilex Pharmaceuticals Inc | 2834 | E | 650 430-3238 | 5652 |
| Vincerx Pharma Inc (PA) | 2834 | F | 650 800-6676 | 5708 |
| Danisco US Inc (HQ) | 2835 | C | 650 846-7500 | 5746 |
| Allbirds Inc | 3143 | F | 650 460-8040 | 7101 |
| Quality Mtal Spnning McHning I | 3469 | E | 650 858-2491 | 8880 |
| Hammon Plating Corporation | 3471 | E | 650 494-2691 | 8968 |
| Xerox International Partners (DH) | 3555 | E | | 9777 |
| Echo Labs | 3571 | E | 650 561-3446 | 10148 |
| Enterprise Svcs Asia PCF Corp | 3571 | E | 650 857-1501 | 10151 |
| Hewlett-Packard Entps LLC (PA) | 3571 | F | 650 687-5817 | 10158 |
| HP Hewlett Packard Group LLC | 3571 | F | 650 857-1501 | 10160 |
| HP Inc (PA) | 3571 | A | 650 857-1501 | 10161 |
| HP Inc | 3571 | E | 650 857-1501 | 10163 |
| Indigo America Inc | 3571 | D | 650 857-1501 | 10165 |
| Psiquantum Corp (PA) | 3571 | F | 650 427-0000 | 10198 |
| Tall Tree Insurance Company | 3571 | D | 650 857-1501 | 10208 |
| Brocade Cmmnctions Systems LLC (DH) | 3577 | A | 408 333-8000 | 10339 |
| Motivemetrics | 3652 | E | 800 216-5207 | 11737 |
| Sitetraker | 3652 | E | 650 868-5164 | 11744 |
| Throughput Inc | 3652 | F | 215 606-8552 | 11746 |
| Calmar Optcom Inc | 3661 | E | 408 733-7800 | 11756 |
| Communications & Pwr Inds LLC | 3663 | C | 650 846-3494 | 11830 |
| Communications & Pwr Inds LLC | 3663 | A | 650 846-3729 | 11831 |
| Communications & Pwr Inds LLC | 3663 | D | 650 846-2900 | 11833 |
| Higher Ground LLC (PA) | 3663 | F | 650 322-3958 | 11864 |
| Ssl Mda Holdings Inc | 3663 | F | 650 852-4000 | 11951 |
| Communications & Pwr Inds LLC (HQ) | 3671 | A | 650 846-2900 | 12029 |
| Microwave Power Products Inc | 3671 | B | 650 846-2900 | 12035 |
| Broadcom Inc (PA) | 3674 | A | 650 427-6000 | 12368 |
| R2 Semiconductor Inc | 3674 | F | 408 745-7400 | 12666 |
| Stangenes Industries Inc (PA) | 3677 | D | 650 855-9926 | 12860 |
| CPI International Holding Corp | 3679 | F | 650 846-2900 | 12947 |
| Insulation Sources Inc (PA) | 3679 | E | 650 856-8378 | 13000 |
| Maxar Space LLC | 3679 | C | 650 852-4000 | 13033 |
| Eton Corporation | 3699 | E | 650 903-3866 | 13240 |
| Tesla Inc | 3711 | B | 650 681-5800 | 13393 |
| Pivotal Aero LLC | 3721 | D | 404 641-9131 | 13685 |
| Lockheed Martin Corporation | 3812 | E | 650 424-2000 | 14211 |
| Varian Inc | 3826 | A | 650 213-8000 | 14750 |
| Sciton Inc (PA) | 3841 | C | 650 493-9155 | 15249 |
| Siemens Med Solutions USA Inc | 3841 | B | 650 694-5747 | 15257 |
| Varian Medical Systems Inc | 3841 | E | 650 213-8000 | 15298 |
| Varian Medical Systems Inc | 3841 | D | 650 493-4000 | 15299 |
| Varian Medical Systems Inc (DH) | 3845 | A | 650 493-4000 | 15588 |
| Suss McRtec Prcsion Phtmask In | 3861 | F | 415 494-3113 | 15668 |
| Boost Treadmills LLC | 3949 | F | 650 424-1827 | 15789 |
| Kos Inc | 4813 | E | 650 231-2044 | 16319 |
| Maxar Space LLC (HQ) | 4899 | D | 650 852-4000 | 16339 |
| Wealthfront Corporation | 6282 | E | 650 249-4258 | 17735 |
| Intapp Us Inc (HQ) | 7371 | C | 650 852-0400 | 17931 |
| Ladder Financial Inc | 7371 | E | 844 533-7206 | 17939 |
| Marvel Parent LLC (HQ) | 7371 | D | 650 321-4910 | 17946 |
| Opshub Inc | 7371 | F | 650 701-1800 | 17957 |
| Replicon Software Inc | 7371 | E | 650 286-9200 | 17970 |
| Abaqus Inc | 7372 | E | 415 496-9436 | 18008 |
| Adaptive Insights LLC (HQ) | 7372 | C | 650 528-7500 | 18016 |
| Adara Inc (PA) | 7372 | D | 408 876-6360 | 18017 |
| Applied Expert Systems Inc | 7372 | E | 650 617-2400 | 18056 |
| Applovin Corporation (PA) | 7372 | C | 800 839-9646 | 18058 |
| Ariba Inc (DH) | 7372 | E | 650 849-4000 | 18065 |
| AVI Networks Inc (DH) | 7372 | E | 408 628-1300 | 18082 |
| Barcelona Merger Sub 3 LLC | 7372 | A | 650 427-5000 | 18090 |
| Boomerang Commerce Inc (PA) | 7372 | E | 602 459-2578 | 18121 |
| Buzz Solutions Inc | 7372 | F | 949 637-7946 | 18133 |
| Ca Inc (HQ) | 7372 | A | 800 225-5224 | 18137 |
| Cacheflow Inc | 7372 | E | 818 659-1400 | 18138 |
| Calmcom Inc (PA) | 7372 | E | 415 236-3012 | 18142 |
| Cetas Inc | 7372 | F | 847 530-5785 | 18161 |
| Cxapp Inc | 7372 | D | 650 575-4456 | 18217 |
| D-Wave Quantum Inc | 7372 | C | 604 630-1428 | 18222 |
| Discerndx Inc | 7372 | F | 909 319-9779 | 18243 |
| Duda Mobile Inc | 7372 | C | 855 790-0003 | 18258 |
| Edvin Inc | 7372 | E | 415 800-4067 | 18265 |
| Hazelcast Inc (PA) | 7372 | E | 650 521-5453 | 18377 |
| Integral Development Corp (PA) | 7372 | E | 650 424-4500 | 18423 |
| Jacada Inc | 7372 | D | 770 352-1300 | 18452 |
| Jive Software Inc | 7372 | F | 503 295-3700 | 18458 |
| Kins Capital LLC (PA) | 7372 | F | 650 575-4456 | 18471 |
| Labs Upwest | 7372 | F | 650 272-6529 | 18485 |
| Lastline Inc (DH) | 7372 | D | 877 671-3239 | 18486 |
| Liquidspace Inc | 7372 | E | 855 254-7843 | 18497 |
| Loyalty Juggernaut Inc | 7372 | B | 650 283-5081 | 18504 |
| Magenta Buyer LLC (HQ) | 7372 | E | 650 935-9500 | 18511 |
| Magnet Systems Inc | 7372 | E | 650 329-5904 | 18514 |
| Mailbird Inc | 7372 | E | 650 830-9891 | 18516 |
| Nyansa Inc | 7372 | E | 650 446-7818 | 18609 |
| Phantom Cyber Corporation | 7372 | E | 650 208-5151 | 18672 |
| Pilot Software Inc | 7372 | E | 650 230-2830 | 18674 |
| Plutoshift Inc | 7372 | F | 213 400-2104 | 18683 |
| Predii Inc | 7372 | E | 415 269-1146 | 18693 |
| Sap America Inc | 7372 | E | 650 849-4000 | 18758 |
| Sap Labs LLC (DH) | 7372 | B | 650 849-4000 | 18759 |
| Step Mobile Inc | 7372 | E | 203 913-9229 | 18837 |
| Sumopti | 7372 | E | 650 331-1126 | 18847 |
| Vmware LLC (HQ) | 7372 | E | 650 427-6000 | 18925 |
| Xcelmobility Inc | 7372 | D | 650 320-1728 | 18945 |
| Rubrik Inc (PA) | 7374 | A | 844 478-2745 | 19014 |
| Bloomboard Inc | 8211 | E | 650 567-5656 | 19342 |
| Sharethis Inc (PA) | 8732 | E | 650 641-0191 | 19489 |

## PALOS VERDES ESTATES, CA - Los Angeles County

| Company | SIC | EMP | PHONE | ENTRY# |
|---|---|---|---|---|
| Douglas Furniture of California LLC | 2514 | A | 310 749-0003 | 3501 |

## PANORAMA CITY, CA - Los Angeles County

| Company | SIC | EMP | PHONE | ENTRY# |
|---|---|---|---|---|
| Superior Awning Inc | 2394 | E | 818 780-7200 | 2984 |
| Raspadoxpress | 2741 | D | 818 892-6969 | 4459 |
| Puretek Corporation | 2834 | C | 818 361-3949 | 5618 |
| Spec Engineering Company Inc | 3599 | E | 818 780-3045 | 11122 |
| D X Communications Inc | 3663 | E | 323 256-3000 | 11839 |

# GEOGRAPHIC SECTION — PASO ROBLES, CA

| | SIC | EMP | PHONE | ENTRY# |
|---|---|---|---|---|

### PARADISE, CA - Butte County
| Company | SIC | EMP | PHONE | ENTRY# |
|---|---|---|---|---|
| Califrnia Nwspapers Ltd Partnr | 2711 | B | 530 877-4413 | 4088 |
| Paradise Post Inc | 2711 | C | 530 872-5581 | 4178 |

### PARAMOUNT, CA - Los Angeles County
| Company | SIC | EMP | PHONE | ENTRY# |
|---|---|---|---|---|
| Drillmec Inc | 1382 | D | 281 885-0777 | 178 |
| Total-Western Inc (HQ) | 1389 | E | 562 220-1450 | 282 |
| California Air Conveying Corp | 1796 | F | 562 531-4570 | 549 |
| Ariza Cheese Co Inc | 2022 | E | 562 630-4144 | 708 |
| Ariza Global Foods Inc | 2022 | E | 562 630-4144 | 709 |
| Bindi North America Inc | 2024 | F | 562 531-4301 | 795 |
| Paramount Dairy Inc | 2026 | C | 562 361-1800 | 842 |
| Namar Foods | 2034 | E | 562 531-2744 | 959 |
| Popsalot LLC | 2096 | E | 213 761-0156 | 2099 |
| Jayone Foods Inc | 2099 | E | 562 633-7400 | 2242 |
| Jimenes Food Inc | 2099 | E | 562 602-2505 | 2244 |
| Marukan Vinegar U S A Inc (HQ) | 2099 | E | 562 630-6060 | 2273 |
| Marukan Vinegar U S A Inc | 2099 | E | 562 630-6060 | 2274 |
| Tattooed Chef Inc (PA) | 2099 | E | 562 602-0822 | 2369 |
| C S Dash Cover Inc | 2396 | F | 562 790-8300 | 3003 |
| ICI Architectural Millwork Inc | 2431 | F | 323 759-4993 | 3147 |
| Drees Wood Products Inc | 2434 | D | 562 633-7337 | 3235 |
| Graphic Trends Incorporated | 2759 | E | 562 531-2339 | 4887 |
| Hoffman Plastic Compounds Inc | 2821 | D | 323 636-3346 | 5158 |
| LMC Enterprises (PA) | 2842 | E | 562 602-2116 | 5913 |
| Kum Kang Trading USA Inc | 2844 | E | 562 531-6111 | 6001 |
| R & S Manufacturing & Sup Inc | 2851 | F | 909 622-5881 | 6108 |
| Paramount Petroleum Corp (DH) | 2911 | C | 562 531-2060 | 6344 |
| R & S Processing Co Inc | 3069 | D | 562 531-0738 | 6533 |
| Sandee Plastic Extrusions | 3089 | E | 323 979-4020 | 7021 |
| Fenico Precision Castings Inc | 3369 | E | 562 634-5000 | 7863 |
| Aerocraft Heat Treating Co Inc | 3398 | D | 562 674-2400 | 7874 |
| Avantus Aerospace Inc | 3429 | E | 562 633-6626 | 7979 |
| California Screw Products Corp | 3429 | D | 562 633-6626 | 7987 |
| Top Line Mfg Inc | 3429 | E | 562 633-0605 | 8031 |
| Valence Surface Tech LLC | 3441 | E | 562 531-7666 | 8240 |
| Jeffrey Fabrication LLC | 3444 | E | 562 634-3101 | 8478 |
| Paramount Metal & Supply Inc | 3446 | E | 562 634-8180 | 8640 |
| Blue Circle Corp | 3452 | F | 562 531-2711 | 8745 |
| Mattco Forge Inc (HQ) | 3462 | E | 562 634-8635 | 8781 |
| Mattco Forge Inc | 3462 | E | 562 634-8635 | 8782 |
| Press Forge Company | 3462 | D | 562 531-4962 | 8787 |
| Vi-Star Gear Co Inc | 3462 | E | 323 774-3750 | 8792 |
| Carlton Forge Works LLC | 3463 | B | 562 633-1131 | 8795 |
| Weber Metals Inc (HQ) | 3463 | E | 562 602-0260 | 8804 |
| Apollo Metal Spinning Co Inc | 3465 | F | 562 634-5141 | 8807 |
| Anaplex Corporation | 3471 | E | 714 522-4481 | 8919 |
| Denmac Industries Inc | 3479 | E | 562 634-2714 | 9061 |
| Supertec Machinery Inc | 3541 | F | 562 220-1675 | 9573 |
| Die Shop | 3544 | F | 562 630-4400 | 9618 |
| George Jue Mfg Co Inc | 3546 | D | 562 634-8181 | 9711 |
| Golden State Engineering Inc | 3549 | C | 562 634-3125 | 9738 |
| Excellon Acquisition LLC (HQ) | 3559 | E | 310 668-7700 | 9855 |
| Zamboni Company Usa Inc | 3559 | E | 562 633-0751 | 9913 |
| TP Solar Inc | 3567 | F | 562 808-2171 | 10061 |
| J and K Manufacturing Inc | 3599 | E | 562 630-8417 | 10898 |
| Piedras Machine Corporation | 3599 | E | 562 602-1500 | 11040 |
| Ramp Engineering Inc | 3599 | E | 562 531-8030 | 11069 |
| Trepanning Specialities Inc | 3599 | E | 562 633-8110 | 11149 |
| Amsco US Inc | 3679 | C | 562 630-0333 | 12913 |
| Z-Tronix Inc | 3679 | E | 562 808-0800 | 13129 |
| New Century Industries Inc | 3714 | E | 562 634-9551 | 13545 |
| Topline Manufacturing Inc | 3999 | F | 562 633-0605 | 16253 |
| Total Intermodal Services Inc (PA) | 4491 | E | 562 427-6300 | 16296 |
| Vaughans Industrial Repair Inc | 5084 | E | 562 633-2660 | 16854 |
| Blue Ribbon Draperies Inc | 5713 | E | 562 425-4637 | 17526 |

### PARLIER, CA - Fresno County
| Company | SIC | EMP | PHONE | ENTRY# |
|---|---|---|---|---|
| ONeill Beverages Co LLC | 0172 | C | 559 638-3544 | 22 |
| John Daniel Gonzalez | 2449 | E | 559 646-6621 | 3372 |
| W E Plemons McHy Svcs Inc | 3565 | E | 559 646-6630 | 10037 |
| Maxco Supply Inc (PA) | 5113 | E | 559 646-8449 | 17002 |

### PASADENA, CA - Los Angeles County
| Company | SIC | EMP | PHONE | ENTRY# |
|---|---|---|---|---|
| Acco Engineered Systems Inc (PA) | 1711 | A | 818 244-6571 | 402 |
| Pak Group LLC | 2052 | E | 626 316-6555 | 1281 |
| Sugarfina Inc | 2064 | E | 424 284-8518 | 1332 |
| Eurobizusa Inc | 2084 | F | 626 793-0032 | 1557 |
| AGS Usa LLC | 2335 | C | 323 588-2200 | 2697 |
| Max Leon Inc (PA) | 2339 | D | 626 797-6886 | 2790 |
| Cisco Bros Corp (PA) | 2512 | C | 323 778-8612 | 3468 |
| Roberson Construction | 2591 | E | 626 578-1936 | 3726 |
| Avery Dennison Corporation | 2672 | C | 626 304-2000 | 3943 |
| Seller Best Publishing | 2741 | E | 626 765-9750 | 4463 |
| House of Printing | 2752 | E | 626 793-7034 | 4634 |
| Licher Direct Mail Inc | 2752 | E | 626 795-3333 | 4678 |
| Typecraft Inc | 2752 | E | 626 795-8093 | 4794 |
| Arrowhead Pharmaceuticals Inc (PA) | 2834 | C | 626 304-3400 | 5337 |
| Xencor Inc | 2834 | B | 626 305-5900 | 5720 |
| Allbirds Inc | 3143 | F | 626 344-2622 | 7098 |
| Evolution Design Lab Inc | 3144 | E | 626 960-8388 | 7115 |
| Arroyo Holdings Inc (PA) | 3444 | F | 626 765-9340 | 8380 |
| Hamilton Metalcraft Inc | 3444 | E | 626 795-4811 | 8465 |
| Fvo Solutions Inc | 3479 | D | 626 449-0218 | 9073 |
| Honeybee Robotics LLC | 3569 | D | 510 207-4555 | 10095 |
| American Reliance Inc | 3571 | E | 626 443-6818 | 10134 |
| Lifesource Water Systems Inc (PA) | 3589 | E | 626 792-4214 | 10572 |
| Pronto Products Co | 3599 | E | 800 377-6680 | 11053 |
| Caelux Corporation | 3674 | E | 626 502-7033 | 12375 |
| Byd Motors LLC (DH) | 3714 | E | 213 748-3980 | 13467 |
| Coast Autonomous Inc (PA) | 3714 | E | 626 838-2469 | 13477 |
| Advanced Mtls Joining Corp (PA) | 3728 | E | 626 449-2696 | 13740 |
| Sabrin Corporation | 3728 | E | 626 792-3813 | 13941 |
| Atk Space Systems LLC | 3812 | D | 626 351-0205 | 14159 |
| Rogerson Kratos | 3812 | C | 626 449-3090 | 14297 |
| Gmto Corporation | 3827 | D | 626 204-0500 | 14778 |
| Arts Elegance Inc | 3911 | E | 626 793-4794 | 15685 |
| Black Box Project LLC | 3944 | E | 626 356-1302 | 15741 |
| L A Steel Craft Products (PA) | 3949 | E | 626 798-7401 | 15835 |
| American Multimedia TV USA | 4833 | D | 626 466-1038 | 16329 |
| Pasta Piccinini Inc | 5149 | E | 626 798-0841 | 17203 |
| George L Throop Co | 5251 | E | 626 796-0285 | 17354 |
| Foremay Inc (PA) | 7371 | E | 408 228-3468 | 17924 |
| X1 Discovery Inc | 7371 | E | 877 999-1347 | 17999 |
| De Novo Software LLC | 7372 | F | 213 814-1240 | 18233 |
| Everbridge Inc (PA) | 7372 | C | 818 230-9700 | 18294 |
| Evolution Robotics Inc | 7372 | F | 626 993-3300 | 18298 |
| Floor Covering Soft | 7372 | E | 626 683-9188 | 18316 |
| Guidance Software Inc (HQ) | 7372 | C | 626 229-9191 | 18370 |
| Phoenix Technologies Ltd (HQ) | 7372 | E | 408 570-1000 | 18673 |
| Red Gate Software Inc | 7372 | E | 626 993-3949 | 18727 |
| Realdefense LLC (PA) | 7382 | E | 801 895-7907 | 19060 |
| Kinemetrics Inc (DH) | 8711 | D | 626 795-2220 | 19400 |

### PASO ROBLES, CA - San Luis Obispo County
| Company | SIC | EMP | PHONE | ENTRY# |
|---|---|---|---|---|
| Treasury Wine Estates Americas | 0172 | E | 805 237-6000 | 33 |
| All Risk Shield Inc | 1389 | E | 866 991-7190 | 203 |
| Worldwind Services LLC | 1731 | A | 661 822-4877 | 475 |
| Firestone Walker Inc | 2082 | D | 805 226-8514 | 1428 |
| Firestone Walker Inc (PA) | 2082 | E | 805 225-5911 | 1430 |
| Calcareous Vineyard LLC | 2084 | F | 805 239-0289 | 1494 |
| Daou Vineyards LLC | 2084 | E | 805 226-5460 | 1526 |
| Eos Estate Winery | 2084 | E | 805 239-2562 | 1556 |
| Gallo Vineyards Inc | 2084 | C | 209 394-6281 | 1583 |
| Halter Properties LLC | 2084 | F | 805 226-9455 | 1609 |
| Halter Winery LLC (PA) | 2084 | E | 805 226-9455 | 1610 |
| J Lohr Winery Corporation | 2084 | E | 805 239-8900 | 1622 |
| Jada Vineyards & Winery | 2084 | E | 805 226-4200 | 1630 |
| James Tobin Cellars Inc | 2084 | E | 805 239-2204 | 1631 |
| Justin Vineyards & Winery LLC | 2084 | F | 805 238-6932 | 1641 |
| Niner Wine Estates LLC | 2084 | E | 805 239-2233 | 1693 |
| ONeill Beverages Co LLC | 2084 | E | 805 239-1616 | 1696 |
| Rbz Vineyards LLC | 2084 | E | 805 542-0133 | 1720 |
| Tablas Creek Vnyrd A Cal Ltd P | 2084 | E | 805 237-1231 | 1773 |
| Tooth and Nail Winery | 2084 | E | 805 369-6100 | 1786 |
| Treana Winery LLC | 2084 | E | 805 237-2932 | 1789 |
| Vintage Wine Estates Inc CA | 2084 | E | 805 503-9660 | 1818 |
| Lakeshirts LLC | 2395 | E | 805 239-1290 | 2993 |
| Hogue Bros Inc | 2426 | E | 805 239-1440 | 3095 |
| San Luis Obspo Cocmmnty Clgdst | 2711 | F | 805 591-6200 | 4190 |
| Pro Document Solutions Inc (PA) | 2752 | E | 805 238-6680 | 4739 |
| Melissa Trinidad | 2844 | E | 805 536-0954 | 6006 |
| Lubrizol Global Management Inc | 2899 | E | 805 239-1550 | 6305 |
| Cornucopia Tool & Plastics Inc | 3089 | E | 805 238-7660 | 6781 |
| Trellborg Sling Sltions US Inc | 3089 | E | 805 239-4284 | 7057 |
| Acme Vial & Glass Co | 3221 | E | 805 239-2666 | 7181 |
| Paso Robles Tank Inc (HQ) | 3312 | D | 805 227-1641 | 7621 |
| Paris Precision LLC | 3444 | C | 805 239-2500 | 8530 |
| AMC Machining Inc | 3449 | E | 805 238-5452 | 8691 |
| McGuire Grinding Inc | 3599 | F | 805 238-9000 | 10967 |
| Western Quartz Products Inc | 3641 | F | 805 238-3524 | 11436 |
| Souriau Usa Inc (DH) | 3643 | F | 805 238-2840 | 11470 |
| Joslyn Sunbank Company LLC | 3678 | B | 805 238-2840 | 12886 |
| Advance Adapters Inc | 3714 | E | 805 238-7000 | 13441 |
| Advance Adapters LLC | 3714 | E | 805 238-7000 | 13442 |
| Esterline Technologies Corp | 3728 | F | 805 238-2840 | 13838 |

Employee Codes: A=Over 500 employees, B=251-500
C=101-250, D=51-100, E=20-50, F=10-19, G=1-9

# PASO ROBLES, CA

| | SIC | EMP | PHONE | ENTRY# |
|---|---|---|---|---|
| Flight Environments Inc. | 3728 | E | | 13842 |
| Arbiter Systems Incorporated (PA) | 3825 | E | 805 237-3831 | 14497 |
| Applied Technologies Assoc Inc (HQ) | 3829 | C | 805 239-9100 | 14844 |
| JIT Manufacturing Inc. | 3841 | E | 805 238-5000 | 15136 |
| Trelleborg Sealing Solutions. | 3841 | D | 805 239-4284 | 15288 |
| Ctek Inc. | 4899 | E | 310 241-2973 | 16336 |
| Summerwood Winery & Inn Inc. | 7011 | E | 805 227-1365 | 17762 |
| Kings Oil Tools Inc (PA) | 7353 | E | 805 238-9311 | 17852 |
| Iqms LLC (HQ) | 7372 | C | 805 227-1122 | 18445 |
| Eagle Med Pckg Strlization Inc. | 7389 | E | 805 238-7401 | 19089 |

## PATTERSON, CA - Stanislaus County

| Designed MBL Systems Inds Inc | 1542 | F | 209 892-6298 | 367 |
| Alpine Truss LLC | 2439 | E | 209 345-0831 | 3292 |
| Hpl Contract Inc | 2521 | F | 209 892-1717 | 3570 |
| V-Tech Manufacturing Inc. | 3599 | E | 408 730-9200 | 11165 |
| Sport Boat Trailers | 3799 | E | 209 892-5388 | 14133 |

## PEARBLOSSOM, CA - Los Angeles County

| Vulcan Construction Mtls LLC | 3273 | E | 661 810-2285 | 7519 |

## PENN VALLEY, CA - Nevada County

| Firestone Walker LLC | 2082 | D | 805 225-5911 | 1431 |

## PERRIS, CA - Riverside County

| Silver Creek Industries LLC | 1542 | C | 951 943-5393 | 370 |
| Jimenez Mexican Foods Inc | 2032 | E | 951 351-0102 | 860 |
| Star Milling Co. | 2048 | D | 951 657-3143 | 1151 |
| Aoc LLC | 2295 | D | 951 657-5161 | 2525 |
| Avalon Shutters Inc | 2431 | D | 909 937-4900 | 3112 |
| California Trusframe LLC | 2439 | C | 951 657-7491 | 3298 |
| California Trusframe LLC (HQ) | 2439 | D | 951 350-4880 | 3300 |
| California Truss Company (PA) | 2439 | E | 951 657-7491 | 3301 |
| Inland Truss Inc (PA) | 2439 | D | 951 300-1758 | 3312 |
| Alpha Corporation of Tennessee | 2821 | C | 951 657-5161 | 5133 |
| J-M Manufacturing Company Inc. | 2821 | E | 951 657-7400 | 5169 |
| Accu-Blend Corporation. | 2911 | F | 626 334-7744 | 6330 |
| Goldstar Asphalt Products Inc. | 2951 | E | 951 940-1610 | 6363 |
| Npg Inc (PA) | 2951 | D | 951 940-0200 | 6366 |
| Coreslab Structures La Inc. | 3272 | C | 951 943-9119 | 7323 |
| Creative Stone Mfg Inc (PA) | 3272 | E | 800 847-8663 | 7324 |
| J & R Concrete Products Inc. | 3272 | E | 951 943-5855 | 7346 |
| Canyon Steel Fabricators Inc. | 3441 | E | 951 683-2352 | 8114 |
| Craftech Metal Forming Inc. | 3441 | E | 951 940-6444 | 8125 |
| Stretch Forming Corporation | 3444 | D | 951 443-0911 | 8585 |
| R&M Supply Inc. | 3524 | D | 951 552-9860 | 9399 |
| Spaulding Equipment Company (PA) | 3532 | E | 951 943-4531 | 9452 |
| West Coast Yamaha Inc. | 3568 | E | 951 943-2061 | 10074 |
| Stearns Product Dev Corp (PA) | 3569 | D | 951 657-0379 | 10117 |
| R-Cold Inc. | 3585 | D | 951 436-5476 | 10511 |
| Axxis Corporation. | 3599 | E | 951 436-9921 | 10728 |
| Warlock Industries. | 3711 | E | 951 657-2680 | 13397 |
| Limos By Tiffany Inc. | 3713 | E | 951 657-2680 | 13416 |
| Pacific Coachworks Inc. | 3792 | C | 951 686-7294 | 14122 |
| Claybourne Industries Inc. | 3999 | F | 951 675-4508 | 16119 |
| Herca Telecomm Services Inc. | 5082 | D | 951 940-5941 | 16789 |
| Jpl Global LLC. | 5082 | E | 888 274-7744 | 16791 |
| Griswold Industries. | 5085 | E | 951 657-1718 | 16876 |
| Global Plastics Inc. | 5093 | C | 951 657-5466 | 16959 |
| Eci Water Ski Products Inc. | 5941 | E | 951 940-9999 | 17633 |
| S A Top-U Corporation. | 5944 | E | 951 916-4025 | 17651 |

## PETALUMA, CA - Sonoma County

| Cmblu Energy Inc. | 1382 | E | 650 272-8804 | 174 |
| Marin Sun Farms Inc (PA) | 2011 | E | 415 663-8997 | 606 |
| Petaluma Acquisitions LLC | 2015 | D | 707 763-1904 | 699 |
| Petaluma Acquistion LLC. | 2015 | C | 707 763-1904 | 700 |
| Miyokos Kitchen. | 2021 | E | 415 521-5313 | 705 |
| Straus Family Creamery Inc (PA) | 2021 | D | 707 776-2887 | 706 |
| Amys Kitchen Inc (PA) | 2038 | A | 707 578-7188 | 1024 |
| Torn Ranch Inc (PA) | 2064 | D | 415 506-3000 | 1336 |
| McEvoy of Marin LLC (PA) | 2079 | E | 707 778-2307 | 1401 |
| Spectrum Organic Products LLC | 2079 | E | 888 343-6637 | 1406 |
| Adobe Road Winery. | 2084 | F | 707 939-9099 | 1471 |
| Petalumaidence Opco LLC. | 2084 | E | 707 763-4109 | 1706 |
| American Bottling Company. | 2086 | D | 707 766-9750 | 1851 |
| Windsor Willits Company (PA) | 2431 | E | 707 665-9663 | 3205 |
| Workrite Ergonomics LLC. | 2521 | E | 707 780-6400 | 3590 |
| Planet One Products Inc (PA) | 2541 | F | 707 794-8000 | 3669 |
| St Louis Post-Dispatch LLC. | 2711 | D | 707 762-4541 | 4201 |
| Robert W Cameron & Co Inc | 2731 | E | 707 769-1617 | 4343 |
| Resource Label Group LLC. | 2759 | E | 707 773-4363 | 4950 |
| Schurman Fine Papers. | 2771 | C | 707 765-2514 | 4997 |

| | SIC | EMP | PHONE | ENTRY# |
|---|---|---|---|---|
| Bausch Health Americas Inc. | 2834 | C | 707 793-2600 | 5354 |
| Biosearch Technologies Inc (HQ) | 2836 | E | 415 883-8400 | 5811 |
| Architectural Plastics Inc. | 3089 | E | 707 765-9898 | 6722 |
| Colvin-Friedman LLC | 3089 | E | 707 769-4488 | 6778 |
| Sistema US Inc. | 3089 | E | 707 773-2200 | 7028 |
| Ace Products Enterprises Inc. | 3161 | E | 707 765-1500 | 7124 |
| Empire Shower Doors Inc. | 3231 | E | 707 773-2898 | 7219 |
| Ebac Investments Inc (PA) | 3273 | E | 707 781-9000 | 7441 |
| Parmatech Corporation. | 3399 | D | 707 778-2266 | 7909 |
| Morgan Manufacturing Inc. | 3423 | F | 707 763-6848 | 7961 |
| Gcx Corporation (DH) | 3429 | E | 707 773-1100 | 7999 |
| Hydropoint Data Systems Inc. | 3523 | E | 707 769-9696 | 9358 |
| Deweyl Tool Co Inc. | 3545 | E | 707 765-5779 | 9674 |
| Kval Inc. | 3553 | C | 707 762-4363 | 9754 |
| Elliott Company. | 3563 | F | 707 665-5307 | 9962 |
| Caracal Enterprises Inc. | 3581 | E | 707 773-3373 | 10470 |
| Ventek International Inc. | 3581 | E | 707 773-3373 | 10472 |
| Donal Machine Inc. | 3599 | E | 707 763-6625 | 10815 |
| Core Brands LLC. | 3612 | D | 707 283-5900 | 11207 |
| Zapworldcom. | 3621 | B | 707 525-8658 | 11296 |
| Katadyn Desalination LLC. | 3634 | E | 415 526-2780 | 11407 |
| Hydrofarm LLC (HQ) | 3648 | E | 707 765-9990 | 11600 |
| Mesa/Boogie Limited (HQ) | 3651 | D | 707 765-1805 | 11676 |
| Xantech LLC. | 3651 | E | 818 362-0353 | 11722 |
| Stonecrop Technologies LLC. | 3663 | E | 781 659-0007 | 11953 |
| Broadcom Corporation. | 3674 | E | 707 792-9000 | 12362 |
| Small Precision Tools Inc. | 3674 | D | 707 762-5880 | 12720 |
| Gefen LLC. | 3699 | E | 818 772-9100 | 13243 |
| Aerovironment Inc. | 3721 | E | 707 206-9372 | 13628 |
| Colter & Peterson Microsystems. | 3823 | E | 707 776-4500 | 14395 |
| Xandex Inc. | 3825 | E | 707 763-7799 | 14601 |
| Dow Pharmaceutical Sciences Inc. | 3826 | C | 707 793-2600 | 14654 |
| Camelbak Products LLC (HQ) | 3949 | D | 707 792-9700 | 15797 |
| Gmpc LLC. | 3993 | E | 707 766-1702 | 15984 |
| Marin Mountain Bikes (PA) | 5091 | F | 415 382-6000 | 16938 |
| Sunrise Farms LLC. | 5144 | D | 707 778-6450 | 17136 |
| Clover-Stornetta Farms LLC (PA) | 5149 | C | 707 769-3282 | 17183 |
| Mountanos Brothers Coffee Co (PA) | 5149 | E | 707 774-8800 | 17198 |
| All-American Prtg Svcs Corp (PA) | 7334 | E | 707 762-2500 | 17805 |
| Accountmate Software Corp (PA) | 7372 | E | 707 774-7500 | 18011 |
| Kibo Software Inc. | 7372 | F | 415 425-1833 | 18469 |
| Tfb Games Inc. | 7372 | E | 707 582-0005 | 18877 |
| TC Steel. | 7692 | E | 707 773-2150 | 19216 |

## PHILO, CA - Mendocino County

| Roederer Estate Inc. | 0172 | F | 707 895-2288 | 27 |
| Husch Vineyards Inc (PA) | 2084 | E | 707 895-3216 | 1618 |
| Navarro Vineyards LLC. | 2084 | E | 707 895-3686 | 1686 |

## PICO RIVERA, CA - Los Angeles County

| Genesis Foods Corporation. | 2064 | D | 323 890-5890 | 1308 |
| Mixed Nuts Inc. | 2068 | E | 323 587-6887 | 1360 |
| GPde Slva Spces Incrporation (PA) | 2099 | D | 562 407-2643 | 2223 |
| LA Pillow & Fiber Inc. | 2392 | E | 323 724-7969 | 2934 |
| Pacific Cast Fther Cushion LLC (HQ) | 2392 | C | 562 801-9995 | 2943 |
| Reeve Store Equipment Company (PA) | 2542 | D | 562 949-2535 | 3705 |
| Bay Cities Container Corp (PA) | 2653 | D | 562 948-3751 | 3820 |
| CD Container Inc. | 2653 | D | 562 948-1910 | 3829 |
| Jkv Inc. | 2653 | E | 562 948-3000 | 3862 |
| Spiral Ppr Tube & Core Co Inc. | 2655 | E | 562 801-9705 | 3910 |
| Endpak Packaging Inc. | 2674 | D | 562 801-0281 | 3990 |
| Lombard Enterprises Inc. | 2752 | E | 562 692-7070 | 4683 |
| Whittier Fertilizer Company. | 2873 | E | 562 699-3461 | 6184 |
| Aoclsc Inc. | 2992 | C | 813 248-1988 | 6387 |
| Lubricating Specialties Company. | 2992 | E | 562 776-4000 | 6398 |
| Krieger Speciality Pdts LLC (DH) | 3442 | D | 562 695-0645 | 8272 |
| C&O Manufacturing Company Inc. | 3444 | D | 562 692-7525 | 8398 |
| Arnaco Industrial Coatings. | 3479 | E | 562 222-1022 | 9049 |
| Precision Deburring Services. | 3541 | E | 562 944-4497 | 9562 |
| W P Keith Co Inc. | 3567 | E | 562 948-3636 | 10062 |
| Veolia Wts Services Usa Inc. | 3589 | D | 562 942-2200 | 10609 |
| Feit Electric Company Inc (PA) | 3645 | E | 562 463-2852 | 11495 |
| Ros Electrical Sup Eqp Co LLC | 5063 | E | 562 695-9000 | 16672 |
| Three Sons Inc. | 5147 | D | 562 801-4100 | 17166 |
| Bakemark USA LLC (PA) | 5149 | C | 562 949-1054 | 17175 |

## PINEDALE, CA - Fresno County

| Pacific Door & Cabinet Company. | 2431 | E | 559 439-3822 | 3176 |

## PINOLE, CA - Contra Costa County

| Azk Inc. | 2844 | E | 510 724-9999 | 5946 |

# GEOGRAPHIC SECTION

## PIONEER, CA - Amador County

| Company | SIC | EMP | PHONE | ENTRY# |
|---|---|---|---|---|
| Pine Grove Group Inc | 3699 | E | 209 295-7733 | 13289 |

## PISMO BEACH, CA - San Luis Obispo County

| Company | SIC | EMP | PHONE | ENTRY# |
|---|---|---|---|---|
| Alliance Ready Mix Inc | 3273 | E | 805 556-3015 | 7400 |
| Brooks Restaurant Group Inc (PA) | 5141 | E | 559 485-8520 | 17113 |

## PITTSBURG, CA - Contra Costa County

| Company | SIC | EMP | PHONE | ENTRY# |
|---|---|---|---|---|
| Ramar International Corp | 2011 | E | 925 432-4267 | 614 |
| Ramar International Corp (PA) | 2024 | E | 925 439-9009 | 814 |
| Moreflavor Inc (PA) | 2082 | E | 800 600-0033 | 1449 |
| Authors Press | 2741 | F | 925 698-2619 | 4369 |
| Shell Catalysts & Tech LP | 2819 | D | 925 458-9045 | 5115 |
| K2 Pure Solutions Nocal LP | 2899 | E | 713 249-8057 | 6300 |
| United Spiral Pipe LLC | 3317 | C | 925 526-3100 | 7672 |
| Concord Iron Works Inc | 3441 | E | 925 432-0136 | 8123 |
| Levmar Inc | 3444 | F | 925 680-8723 | 8486 |
| Majestic Steel Usa Inc | 3444 | E | 800 445-6374 | 8495 |
| Agra Tech Inc | 3448 | F | 925 432-3399 | 8651 |
| Cemco LLC | 3448 | D | 925 473-9340 | 8660 |
| Bishop-Wisecarver Corporation (PA) | 3499 | D | 925 439-8272 | 9277 |
| Granberg Pump and Meter Ltd | 3546 | F | 707 562-2099 | 9712 |
| Alliance Laundry Systems LLC | 3582 | E | 800 464-6866 | 10473 |
| Frase Enterprises | 3644 | E | 510 856-3600 | 11479 |
| Hospital Systems Inc | 3845 | D | 925 427-7800 | 15544 |
| Arb Inc | 4225 | B | 925 432-3649 | 16286 |
| Antioch Building Materials Co (PA) | 5032 | E | 925 432-0171 | 16463 |
| Ravig Inc | 5045 | D | 925 526-1234 | 16545 |
| Bonami Baking Company Inc | 5149 | E | 925 473-9736 | 17177 |
| Corteva Agriscience LLC | 5191 | C | 925 432-5482 | 17270 |
| Gourmet Plus Inc | 5441 | E | 415 643-9945 | 17402 |
| Allied Crane Inc | 7699 | E | 925 427-9200 | 19240 |

## PIXLEY, CA - Tulare County

| Company | SIC | EMP | PHONE | ENTRY# |
|---|---|---|---|---|
| Correa Pallet Inc (PA) | 2448 | E | 559 757-1790 | 3336 |
| Air Liquide Electronics US LP | 2813 | A | 559 685-2402 | 5038 |
| Gfp Ethanol LLC | 2869 | E | 559 757-3850 | 6147 |

## PLACENTIA, CA - Orange County

| Company | SIC | EMP | PHONE | ENTRY# |
|---|---|---|---|---|
| Nelson Case Corporation | 2441 | E | 714 528-2215 | 3328 |
| Western Mill Fabricators Inc | 2599 | E | 714 993-3667 | 3753 |
| Cinton LLC | 2672 | E | 714 961-8808 | 3947 |
| CF&b Manufacturing Inc | 2673 | E | 714 744-8361 | 3964 |
| Crescent Inc | 2752 | F | 714 992-6030 | 4578 |
| Eclectic Printing & Design LLC | 2759 | F | 714 528-8040 | 4876 |
| Label Specialties Inc | 2759 | F | 714 961-8074 | 4909 |
| General Rewinding Inc | 2789 | E | 714 776-5561 | 5010 |
| Cardinal Health 414 LLC | 2834 | E | 714 572-9900 | 5393 |
| Moehair Usa Inc | 2844 | F | 888 663-7032 | 6008 |
| Arlon Graphics LLC | 3081 | C | 714 985-6300 | 6551 |
| Vanderveer Industrial Plas LLC | 3083 | E | 714 579-7700 | 6593 |
| Excalibur Extrusion Inc | 3084 | E | 714 528-8834 | 6596 |
| Fruth Custom Plastics Inc | 3089 | D | 714 993-9955 | 6834 |
| Eisel Enterprises Inc | 3272 | E | 714 993-1706 | 7327 |
| Crd Mfg Inc | 3429 | E | 714 871-3300 | 7991 |
| Diversified Trading Corp | 3429 | F | 714 237-9995 | 7993 |
| Hartwell Corporation (DH) | 3429 | C | 714 993-4200 | 8001 |
| Sapphire Manufacturing Inc | 3446 | E | 714 401-3117 | 8644 |
| Ironwood Fabrication Inc | 3462 | F | 714 576-7320 | 8778 |
| West Coast Metal Stamping Incorporated | 3469 | E | 714 792-0322 | 8901 |
| Industrial Metal Finishing Inc | 3471 | F | 714 628-8808 | 8972 |
| Hai Advnced Mtl Specialists Inc | 3479 | F | 714 414-0575 | 9076 |
| Coast Aerospace Mfg Inc | 3544 | E | 714 893-8066 | 9612 |
| Kipe Molds Inc | 3544 | F | 714 572-9576 | 9632 |
| Furnace Super Heros Inc | 3567 | E | 714 238-9009 | 10051 |
| Caldigit Inc | 3572 | F | 714 572-6668 | 10228 |
| US Computers Inc | 3577 | F | 714 528-0514 | 10447 |
| Las Colinas | 3589 | F | 714 528-8100 | 10571 |
| Nalco Wtr Prtrtment Sltons LLC | 3589 | F | 714 792-0708 | 10585 |
| Auger Industries Inc | 3599 | F | 714 577-9350 | 10724 |
| J B Tool Inc | 3599 | F | 714 993-7173 | 10899 |
| Mike Kenney Tool Inc | 3599 | F | 714 577-9262 | 10979 |
| Mkt Innovations | 3599 | D | 714 524-7668 | 10988 |
| Southern Cal Tchnical Arts Inc | 3599 | E | 714 524-2626 | 11120 |
| Sapphire Chandelier LLC | 3646 | D | 714 879-3660 | 11555 |
| Altinex | 3663 | E | 714 990-0877 | 11804 |
| Cartel Electronics LLC | 3672 | E | 714 993-0270 | 12074 |
| L & M Machining Corporation | 3678 | D | 714 414-0923 | 12887 |
| Rotech Engineering Inc | 3679 | E | 714 632-0532 | 13079 |
| Vertex Lcd Inc | 3679 | E | 714 223-7111 | 13117 |
| Roll Along Vans Inc | 3714 | E | 714 528-9600 | 13567 |
| Alva Manufacturing Inc | 3728 | E | 714 237-0925 | 13775 |
| Bioplate Inc | 3841 | E | 310 815-2100 | 15013 |
| Bioseal | 3841 | E | 714 528-4695 | 15014 |
| Tfn Architectural Signage Inc (PA) | 3993 | E | 714 556-0990 | 16057 |
| Vita-Herb Nutriceuticals Inc | 5499 | E | 714 632-3726 | 17435 |
| P5 Graphics and Displays Inc | 7336 | E | 714 808-1645 | 17836 |
| Entek Adaptive Mtl Hdlg LLC | 8711 | F | 714 854-1300 | 19393 |

## PLACERVILLE, CA - El Dorado County

| Company | SIC | EMP | PHONE | ENTRY# |
|---|---|---|---|---|
| Ski Air Conditioning Company | 1711 | E | 530 626-4010 | 435 |
| Boeger Winery Inc | 2084 | E | 530 622-8094 | 1486 |
| Lava Springs Inc | 2084 | E | 530 621-0175 | 1664 |
| El Dorado Truss Co Inc | 2439 | E | 530 622-1264 | 3306 |
| Mother Lode Prtg & Pubg Co Inc | 2711 | E | 530 344-5030 | 4164 |
| Applied Control Electronics | 3625 | E | 530 626-5181 | 11310 |
| Norden Millimeter Inc | 3663 | D | 530 642-9123 | 11905 |
| Gist Inc | 3965 | D | 530 644-8000 | 15910 |

## PLAYA DEL REY, CA - Los Angeles County

| Company | SIC | EMP | PHONE | ENTRY# |
|---|---|---|---|---|
| Chipton-Ross Inc | 3721 | D | 310 414-7800 | 13647 |
| Kribi Enterprises Inc | 5813 | F | 310 594-1222 | 17620 |

## PLAYA VISTA, CA - Los Angeles County

| Company | SIC | EMP | PHONE | ENTRY# |
|---|---|---|---|---|
| Videoamp Inc (PA) | 7372 | D | 424 272-7774 | 18919 |

## PLEASANT GROVE, CA - Sutter County

| Company | SIC | EMP | PHONE | ENTRY# |
|---|---|---|---|---|
| Sills Farms Inc | 0191 | E | 916 655-3391 | 57 |

## PLEASANT HILL, CA - Contra Costa County

| Company | SIC | EMP | PHONE | ENTRY# |
|---|---|---|---|---|
| Nady Systems Inc | 3651 | E | 510 652-2411 | 11680 |
| Mosaic Brands Inc | 3999 | E | 925 322-8700 | 16185 |
| Chemsw Inc | 7372 | F | 707 864-0845 | 18166 |

## PLEASANTON, CA - Alameda County

| Company | SIC | EMP | PHONE | ENTRY# |
|---|---|---|---|---|
| Armanino Foods Distinction Inc | 2038 | E | 510 441-9300 | 1025 |
| Archeyy & Friends LLC | 2047 | E | 703 579-7649 | 1091 |
| Diageo North America Inc | 2085 | E | 925 520-3116 | 1836 |
| American Bottling Company | 2086 | E | 925 251-3001 | 1863 |
| Lucerne Foods Inc | 2099 | A | 925 951-4724 | 2269 |
| Pct Enterprises Inc | 2521 | C | 925 412-3341 | 3582 |
| Printpack Inc | 2673 | D | 925 469-0601 | 3976 |
| Nolo | 2731 | E | 510 549-1976 | 4339 |
| Imagex Inc | 2752 | F | 925 474-8100 | 4638 |
| LTI Holdings Inc (PA) | 2822 | E | 925 271-8041 | 5221 |
| Astex Pharmaceuticals Inc (DH) | 2834 | C | 925 560-0100 | 5340 |
| Oculeve Inc | 2834 | F | 415 745-3784 | 5583 |
| SFJ Pharmaceuticals Inc | 2834 | E | 925 223-6233 | 5654 |
| Clorox Company | 2842 | F | 925 368-6000 | 5897 |
| Boyd Corporation (HQ) | 2891 | D | 209 236-1111 | 6222 |
| A B Boyd Co (PA) | 3069 | E | 888 244-6931 | 6480 |
| RMC Pacific Materials LLC (PA) | 3241 | C | | 7263 |
| Central Precast Concrete Inc | 3272 | E | 925 417-6854 | 7317 |
| Oldcastle Infrastructure Inc | 3272 | E | 925 846-8183 | 7365 |
| Cemex Cnstr Mtls PCF LLC | 3273 | E | 925 846-2824 | 7420 |
| Cemex Materials LLC | 3273 | E | 855 292-8453 | 7427 |
| Pleasanton Ready Mix Con Inc | 3273 | F | 925 846-3226 | 7485 |
| Teichert Inc (PA) | 3273 | C | 916 484-3011 | 7515 |
| Kaiser Aluminum Intl Corp | 3334 | D | 949 614-1740 | 7708 |
| Simpson Manufacturing Co Inc (PA) | 3399 | C | 925 560-9000 | 7915 |
| Conxtech Inc | 3441 | C | 510 264-9111 | 8124 |
| Simpson Strong-Tie Company Inc (HQ) | 3449 | C | 925 560-9000 | 8709 |
| Simpson Strong-Tie Intl Inc (DH) | 3449 | D | 925 560-9000 | 8711 |
| Peridot Corporation | 3469 | E | 925 461-8830 | 8875 |
| Omron Robotics Safety Tech Inc (HQ) | 3535 | C | 925 245-3400 | 9489 |
| Positronics Incorporated | 3549 | E | 925 931-0211 | 9744 |
| Oracle America Inc | 3571 | F | 925 694-3314 | 10188 |
| Polycom Inc | 3571 | E | 925 924-6151 | 10195 |
| EMC Corporation | 3572 | C | 925 600-6800 | 10235 |
| Cisco Systems Inc | 3577 | E | 925 225-2111 | 10346 |
| Inverse Solutions Inc | 3599 | E | 925 560-9100 | 10892 |
| Pleasanton Tool & Mfg Inc | 3599 | E | 925 426-0500 | 11042 |
| Amtec Industries Inc | 3613 | E | 510 887-2289 | 11235 |
| Kapsch Trafficcom Usa Inc | 3625 | E | 925 225-1600 | 11329 |
| Cooper Bussmann LLC | 3629 | E | 925 924-8500 | 11367 |
| Excelitas Technologies Corp | 3648 | C | 510 979-6500 | 11595 |
| Excelitas Technologies Corp | 3648 | E | 510 979-6500 | 11596 |
| Ultimatum Records LLC | 3651 | F | 925 353-5202 | 11709 |
| Store Intelligence Inc | 3679 | E | 925 433-9520 | 13092 |
| Accsys Technology Inc | 3699 | E | 925 462-6949 | 13208 |
| Schneder Elc Bldngs Amrcas Inc | 3699 | E | 925 463-7100 | 13302 |
| Aeye Inc (PA) | 3714 | F | 925 400-4366 | 13449 |
| Northrop Grumman Systems Corp | 3812 | E | 925 416-1080 | 14240 |
| Atonarp Us Inc | 3826 | E | 650 714-6290 | 14617 |
| Gatan Inc (HQ) | 3826 | E | 925 463-0200 | 14668 |
| Gatan International Inc | 3826 | E | 925 463-0200 | 14669 |

Employee Codes: A=Over 500 employees, B=251-500, C=101-250, D=51-100, E=20-50, F=10-19, G=1-9

# PLEASANTON, CA

## GEOGRAPHIC SECTION

| | SIC | EMP | PHONE | ENTRY# |
|---|---|---|---|---|
| Integenx Inc (HQ) | 3826 | D | 925 701-3400 | 14677 |
| Raindance Technologies Inc | 3826 | E | 978 495-3300 | 14710 |
| Thermo Fisher Scientific Inc | 3826 | E | 925 600-2522 | 14743 |
| Inneos LLC | 3827 | E | 925 226-0138 | 14785 |
| It Concepts LLC | 3827 | F | 925 401-0010 | 14790 |
| Automatic Control Engrg Corp | 3829 | E | 510 293-6040 | 14847 |
| Deltatrak Inc (PA) | 3829 | E | 925 249-2250 | 14861 |
| Hitachi Prticle Engrg Svcs Inc (DH) | 3829 | E | 215 619-4920 | 14878 |
| Cooper Medical Inc (HQ) | 3841 | E | 925 460-3600 | 15051 |
| Trireme Medical LLC | 3841 | E | 925 931-1300 | 15289 |
| Zeltiq Aesthetics Inc (DH) | 3841 | D | 925 474-2500 | 15315 |
| Inkspace Imaging Inc | 3845 | F | 925 425-7410 | 15547 |
| Movano Inc | 3845 | E | 408 393-1209 | 15560 |
| Natus Medical Incorporated | 3845 | D | 650 802-0400 | 15561 |
| Natus Medical Incorporated (HQ) | 3845 | E | 925 223-6700 | 15563 |
| New Source Technology LLC | 3845 | F | 925 462-6888 | 15565 |
| Pacesetter Inc | 3845 | C | 925 730-4171 | 15569 |
| Thoratec LLC (HQ) | 3845 | C | 925 847-8600 | 15584 |
| Coopervision Inc | 3851 | D | 925 251-2032 | 15598 |
| Accusplit (PA) | 3873 | F | 925 290-1900 | 15673 |
| AOC Technologies Inc | 5051 | B | 925 875-0808 | 16606 |
| Vons Companies Inc (DH) | 5411 | A | 925 467-3000 | 17389 |
| Smart Erp Solutions Inc (PA) | 7371 | E | 925 271-0200 | 17978 |
| William Stucky & Assoc LLC | 7371 | E | 415 788-2441 | 17997 |
| Avatier Corporation (PA) | 7372 | E | 925 217-5170 | 18081 |
| Cambrian Lab Inc | 7372 | F | 408 569-3744 | 18144 |
| Enact Systems Inc | 7372 | F | 510 828-2701 | 18281 |
| Epodium Inc | 7372 | E | 925 621-0602 | 18288 |
| Ice Mortgage Technology Inc (HQ) | 7372 | B | 855 224-8572 | 18399 |
| Medallia Inc (HQ) | 7372 | C | 650 321-3000 | 18531 |
| Micro Focus LLC | 7372 | D | 925 784-3242 | 18543 |
| Oracle Corporation | 7372 | E | 877 767-2253 | 18633 |
| Oracle Systems Corporation | 7372 | E | 925 694-3000 | 18646 |
| Pacsgear Inc | 7372 | D | 925 225-6100 | 18652 |
| Pazo Inc | 7372 | E | 786 786-1195 | 18666 |
| Pvai US Opco Inc | 7372 | E | 703 929-6807 | 18709 |
| Software Development Inc | 7372 | E | 925 847-8823 | 18806 |
| Sparkcognition Inc (PA) | 7372 | D | 844 205-7173 | 18818 |
| Steelwedge Software Inc | 7372 | D | 925 460-1700 | 18835 |
| Swiftcomply US Opco Inc | 7372 | F | 650 430-4341 | 18851 |
| Veeva Systems Inc (PA) | 7372 | E | 925 452-6500 | 18913 |
| Zoomifier Corporation (PA) | 7372 | B | 800 255-5303 | 18956 |
| Brillius Technologies Inc | 7373 | C | 510 379-9027 | 18964 |
| Future Innovations Inc | 7389 | E | 925 485-2000 | 19092 |
| Pelicantunes Inc | 7993 | E | 925 838-8484 | 19310 |
| Unchained Labs (PA) | 8071 | C | 925 587-9800 | 19332 |
| Mawi Dna Technologies LLC | 8731 | E | 510 256-5186 | 19465 |
| Medallia Parent LP (PA) | 8732 | D | 650 321-3000 | 19485 |
| Transsight LLC | 8748 | E | 510 415-6301 | 19572 |

## PLS VRDS PNSL, CA - Los Angeles County

| | SIC | EMP | PHONE | ENTRY# |
|---|---|---|---|---|
| Rolling Hills Vineyard Inc | 2084 | E | 310 541-5098 | 1730 |

## PLUMAS LAKE, CA - Yuba County

| | SIC | EMP | PHONE | ENTRY# |
|---|---|---|---|---|
| Placer Waterworks Inc | 3441 | E | 530 742-9675 | 8200 |

## PLYMOUTH, CA - Amador County

| | SIC | EMP | PHONE | ENTRY# |
|---|---|---|---|---|
| Ramador Inc | 2084 | D | 209 245-6979 | 1716 |
| Sobon Wine Company LLC | 2084 | F | 209 245-4457 | 1753 |
| Turley Wine Cellars | 2084 | E | 209 245-3938 | 1803 |
| Villa Toscano Winery | 2084 | F | 209 245-3800 | 1812 |
| Acm Machining Inc | 3599 | E | 916 804-9489 | 10669 |

## POMONA, CA - Los Angeles County

| | SIC | EMP | PHONE | ENTRY# |
|---|---|---|---|---|
| KP Concrete & Steel Inc | 1771 | F | 909 461-4163 | 523 |
| Torn & Glasser Inc | 2068 | E | 909 706-4100 | 1369 |
| Anheuser-Busch LLC | 2082 | C | 951 782-3935 | 1416 |
| Innovation Brewworks | 2082 | F | 909 979-6197 | 1435 |
| Los Pericos Food Products LLC | 2099 | E | 909 623-5625 | 2268 |
| Lift-It Manufacturing Co Inc | 2298 | E | 909 469-2251 | 2536 |
| Bragel International Inc | 2342 | E | 909 598-8808 | 2836 |
| Gonzalez Feliciano | 2431 | F | 909 236-1372 | 3140 |
| Royal Cabinets Inc | 2434 | A | 909 629-8565 | 3266 |
| Royal Industries Inc | 2434 | C | 909 629-8565 | 3267 |
| Rbf Group International | 2521 | F | 626 333-5700 | 3584 |
| Rbf Lifestyle Holdings LLC | 2521 | E | 626 333-5700 | 3585 |
| Kittrich Corporation (PA) | 2591 | C | 714 736-1000 | 3723 |
| Stainless Fixtures Inc | 2599 | E | 909 622-1615 | 3750 |
| Numatech West (kmp) LLC | 2653 | D | 909 706-3627 | 3870 |
| Federated Diversified Sls Inc | 2671 | D | 909 591-1733 | 3927 |
| California Plastix Inc | 2673 | E | 909 629-8288 | 3963 |
| Inland Envelope Company | 2677 | D | 909 622-2016 | 4009 |
| FDS Manufacturing Company (PA) | 2679 | D | 909 591-1733 | 4038 |
| K-1 Packaging Group | 2752 | C | 626 964-9384 | 4658 |
| Golden Grove Trading Inc | 2759 | F | 909 718-8000 | 4883 |
| Natural Envmtl Protection Co | 2821 | E | 909 620-8028 | 5181 |
| Essential Pharmaceutical Corp | 2834 | E | 909 623-4565 | 5437 |
| K-Max Health Products Corp | 2834 | D | 909 455-0158 | 5520 |
| Kc Pharmaceuticals Inc (PA) | 2834 | D | 909 598-9499 | 5524 |
| Med-Pharmex Inc | 2834 | C | 909 593-7875 | 5548 |
| Alere San Diego Inc | 2835 | B | 909 482-0840 | 5733 |
| Alere San Diego Inc | 2835 | B | 858 805-2000 | 5735 |
| Ecosmart Technologies Inc | 2879 | E | 770 667-0006 | 6200 |
| Mitchell Processing LLC | 3069 | E | 909 519-5759 | 6513 |
| Urocare Products Inc | 3069 | F | 909 621-6013 | 6545 |
| Pomona Quality Foam LLC | 3086 | D | 909 628-7844 | 6655 |
| Vefo Inc | 3086 | E | 909 598-3856 | 6669 |
| L & H Mold & Engineering Inc (PA) | 3089 | E | 909 930-1547 | 6892 |
| Performnce Engineered Pdts Inc | 3089 | E | 909 594-7487 | 6954 |
| Ronford Products Inc | 3089 | E | 909 622-7446 | 7008 |
| Travelers Choice Travelware | 3161 | D | 909 529-7688 | 7143 |
| Lippert Components Mfg Inc | 3231 | E | 909 628-5557 | 7232 |
| Sky One Inc | 3262 | F | 909 622-3333 | 7282 |
| Headwaters Incorporated | 3272 | E | 909 627-9066 | 7342 |
| W R Meadows Inc | 3272 | E | 909 469-2606 | 7395 |
| Tree Island Wire (usa) Inc | 3315 | C | 909 595-6617 | 7655 |
| CFI Holdings Corp | 3324 | F | 909 595-2252 | 7685 |
| Wcs Equipment Holdings LLC | 3325 | D | 909 993-5700 | 7700 |
| Consoldted Precision Pdts Corp | 3365 | D | 909 595-2252 | 7839 |
| Tri-J Metal Heat Treating Co (PA) | 3398 | F | 909 622-9999 | 7904 |
| Valley Metal Treating Inc | 3398 | E | 909 623-6316 | 7906 |
| Precision Pwdred Met Parts Inc | 3399 | E | 909 595-5656 | 7910 |
| Able Iron Works | 3441 | E | 909 397-5300 | 8086 |
| Trussworks International Inc | 3441 | D | 714 630-2772 | 8233 |
| R & S Automation Inc | 3442 | E | 800 962-3111 | 8285 |
| Structural Composites Inds LLC (DH) | 3443 | E | 909 594-7777 | 8341 |
| Worthington Cylinder Corp | 3443 | C | 909 594-7777 | 8354 |
| Equipment Design & Mfg Inc | 3444 | D | 909 594-2229 | 8445 |
| M-5 Steel Mfg Inc (PA) | 3444 | E | 323 263-9383 | 8493 |
| Superior Duct Fabrication Inc | 3444 | C | 909 620-8565 | 8587 |
| Atr Technologies Incorporated | 3446 | F | 909 399-9724 | 8619 |
| Action Stamping Inc | 3469 | E | 626 914-7466 | 8816 |
| Real Plating Inc | 3471 | E | 909 623-2304 | 9005 |
| DOT Blue Safes Corporation | 3499 | E | 909 445-8888 | 9282 |
| Industrial Design Products Inc | 3537 | E | 909 468-0693 | 9524 |
| Casa Herrera Inc (PA) | 3556 | D | 909 392-3930 | 9783 |
| Rbm Conveyor Systems Inc | 3556 | E | 909 620-1333 | 9811 |
| Central Blower Co | 3564 | E | 626 330-3182 | 9983 |
| Cooltec Refrigeration Corp | 3585 | E | 909 865-2229 | 10492 |
| Dow Hydraulic Systems Inc | 3599 | D | 909 596-6602 | 10816 |
| Holland & Herring Mfg Inc | 3599 | E | 909 469-4700 | 10875 |
| ROC-Aire Corp | 3599 | E | 909 784-3385 | 11085 |
| Spray Systems Inc | 3599 | E | 909 397-7511 | 11123 |
| Valley Tool and Machine Co Inc | 3599 | D | 909 595-2205 | 11168 |
| Yawitz Inc | 3645 | E | 909 865-5599 | 11510 |
| Radian Audio Engineering Inc | 3663 | E | 714 288-8900 | 11925 |
| Mil-Spec Magnetics Inc | 3677 | D | 909 598-8116 | 12849 |
| Electrocube Inc (PA) | 3679 | E | 909 595-1821 | 12969 |
| Fong Engineering Enterprise | 3679 | E | 909 598-8835 | 12980 |
| Phenix Enterprises Inc (PA) | 3713 | E | 909 469-0411 | 13423 |
| Southern Cal Trck Bdies Sls In | 3713 | F | 909 469-1132 | 13429 |
| American Mtal Mfg Resource Inc | 3724 | E | 909 620-4500 | 13703 |
| Analytical Industries Inc | 3823 | E | 909 392-6900 | 14387 |
| Delphi Control Systems Inc | 3823 | F | 909 593-8099 | 14401 |
| Gould & Bass Company Inc | 3825 | E | 909 623-6793 | 14530 |
| Diagnostixx of California Corp | 3841 | E | 909 482-0840 | 15068 |
| Scientific Pharmaceuticals Inc | 3843 | E | 909 595-9922 | 15481 |
| Solo Clip Inc | 3851 | E | 626 448-8118 | 15617 |
| American Rotary Broom Co Inc | 3991 | E | 909 629-9117 | 15925 |
| Westcoast Brush Mfg Inc | 3991 | E | 909 627-7170 | 15933 |
| California Acrylic Inds Inc (HQ) | 3999 | F | 909 623-8781 | 16104 |
| LMS | 3999 | E | 909 623-8781 | 16172 |
| Traxx Corporation | 3999 | D | 909 623-8032 | 16256 |
| Ramcast Ornamental Sup Co Inc | 5051 | E | 909 469-4767 | 16630 |
| Especial T Hvac Shtmtl Fttngs | 5075 | E | 909 869-9150 | 16778 |
| Injen Technology Company Ltd | 5075 | E | 909 839-0706 | 16782 |
| Als Group Inc | 5084 | E | 909 622-7555 | 16807 |
| Eastman Music Company (PA) | 5099 | E | 909 868-1777 | 16975 |
| Cape Robbin Inc | 5139 | E | 626 810-8080 | 17109 |
| Altec Industries Inc | 7538 | E | 909 444-0444 | 19159 |

## PORT HUENEME, CA - Ventura County

| | SIC | EMP | PHONE | ENTRY# |
|---|---|---|---|---|
| Consoldted Precision Pdts Corp | 3365 | D | 805 488-6451 | 7838 |
| Pac Foundries Inc | 3366 | C | 805 986-1308 | 7856 |

# GEOGRAPHIC SECTION

## RANCHO CORDOVA, CA

|  | SIC | EMP | PHONE | ENTRY# |
|---|---|---|---|---|

### PORTER RANCH, CA - Los Angeles County

| Design Todays Inc (PA) | 2339 | E | 213 745-3091 | 2754 |
| JNJ Apparel Inc | 2339 | E | 323 584-9700 | 2774 |
| C & S Plastics | 3089 | F | 818 896-2489 | 6754 |

### PORTERVILLE, CA - Tulare County

| Foster Farms LLC | 0252 | D | 559 793-5501 | 61 |
| Foster Poultry Farms | 2015 | C | 559 793-5501 | 690 |
| Distributors Processing Inc | 2087 | F | 559 781-0297 | 1998 |
| Tdg Operations LLC | 2281 | D | 559 781-4116 | 2523 |
| Noticiero Semanal Advertising | 2711 | F | 559 784-5000 | 4175 |
| Endurequest Corporation | 3089 | E | 559 783-9220 | 6819 |
| Quikrete Companies LLC | 3272 | E | 559 781-1949 | 7381 |
| Carrolls Tire Warehouse Inc (PA) | 5531 | E | 559 781-5040 | 17446 |

### PORTOLA VALLEY, CA - San Mateo County

| Westech Inv Advisors LLC (HQ) | 2038 | E | 650 234-4300 | 1050 |

### POWAY, CA - San Diego County

| Creative Foods LLC | 2099 | E | 858 748-0070 | 2175 |
| Disguise Inc (HQ) | 2389 | D | 858 391-3600 | 2899 |
| Smoothreads Inc | 2396 | E | 800 536-5959 | 3018 |
| B Young Enterprises Inc | 2434 | D | 858 748-0935 | 3218 |
| Spooners Woodworks Inc | 2541 | C | 858 679-9086 | 3671 |
| Liberty Diversified Intl Inc | 2542 | E | 858 391-7302 | 3695 |
| Hpi Liquidations Inc | 2653 | E | 858 391-7302 | 3859 |
| San Diego Crating & Pkg Inc | 2653 | F | 858 748-0100 | 3885 |
| Digitalpro Inc | 2752 | D | 858 874-7750 | 4592 |
| Alfa Scientific Designs Inc | 2835 | D | 858 513-3888 | 5736 |
| Granite Gold Inc | 2842 | D | 858 499-8933 | 5908 |
| Henkel US Operations Corp | 2844 | E | 203 655-8911 | 5986 |
| Diversfied Nano Solutions Corp | 2893 | E | 858 924-1013 | 6253 |
| Aldila Materials Tech Corp (DH) | 2895 | E | 858 486-6970 | 6264 |
| Toray Membrane Usa Inc (DH) | 2899 | D | 858 218-2360 | 6326 |
| Eagle Mold Technologies Inc | 3089 | E | 858 530-0888 | 6814 |
| K-Tube Corporation | 3317 | D | 858 513-9229 | 7665 |
| Valley Metals LLC | 3317 | E | 858 513-1300 | 7673 |
| Omc-Thc Liquidating Inc | 3433 | E | 858 486-8846 | 8072 |
| Gaines Manufacturing Inc | 3444 | E | 858 486-7100 | 8455 |
| L & T Precision LLC | 3444 | C | 858 513-7874 | 8483 |
| Securus Inc | 3446 | E |  | 8645 |
| Quality Steel Fabricators Inc | 3449 | E | 858 748-8400 | 8708 |
| Aztec Manufacturing Inc (PA) | 3452 | E | 858 513-4350 | 8743 |
| Component Surfaces Inc | 3471 | F | 858 513-3656 | 8945 |
| Advanced Machining Tooling Inc | 3544 | E | 858 486-9050 | 9595 |
| Masterbilt Atmtn Solutions Inc | 3549 | E | 858 748-6700 | 9740 |
| Delta Design Inc (HQ) | 3569 | B | 858 848-8000 | 10085 |
| Gateway Inc | 3571 | E | 858 451-9933 | 10154 |
| Rugged Systems Inc | 3571 | C | 858 391-1006 | 10200 |
| Apricorn LLC | 3577 | E | 858 513-2000 | 10323 |
| Delkin Devices Inc (PA) | 3577 | D | 858 391-1234 | 10356 |
| Integrity Municpl Systems LLC | 3589 | F | 858 486-1620 | 10566 |
| Mytee Products Inc | 3589 | E | 858 679-1191 | 10583 |
| Advanced Engineering & EDM Inc | 3599 | F | 858 679-6800 | 10673 |
| Advanced Enginering and EDM | 3599 | E | 858 679-6800 | 10674 |
| Darmark Corporation | 3599 | D | 858 679-3970 | 10801 |
| Franklins Inds San Diego Inc | 3599 | E | 858 486-9399 | 10843 |
| EPC Power Corp (PA) | 3629 | C | 858 748-5590 | 11371 |
| Osram Sylvania Inc | 3641 | D | 858 748-5077 | 11430 |
| Niterder Tchncal Ltg Vdeo Syst | 3648 | E | 858 268-9316 | 11616 |
| Broadcast Microwave Svcs LLC (PA) | 3663 | C | 858 391-3050 | 11821 |
| Ramona Research Inc | 3663 | E | 858 679-0717 | 11927 |
| Somacis Inc | 3672 | C | 858 513-2200 | 12223 |
| Wfb Archives Inc | 3672 | D |  | 12261 |
| Data Device Corporation | 3674 | E | 858 503-3300 | 12400 |
| Oasis Materials Company LLC (DH) | 3679 | E | 858 486-8846 | 13051 |
| United Security Products Inc | 3699 | E | 800 227-1592 | 13322 |
| Thyssenkrupp Bilstein Amer Inc | 3714 | E | 858 386-5900 | 13585 |
| General Atmics Arntcal Systems | 3721 | C | 858 455-3358 | 13652 |
| General Atmics Arntcal Systems | 3721 | B | 858 312-4247 | 13654 |
| General Atmics Arntcal Systems | 3721 | C | 858 455-3000 | 13655 |
| General Atmics Arntcal Systems | 3721 | C | 858 312-2810 | 13657 |
| General Atmics Arntcal Systems | 3721 | B | 858 762-6700 | 13659 |
| General Atmics Arntcal Systems (DH) | 3721 | B | 858 312-2810 | 13660 |
| General Atomic Aeron | 3721 | C | 858 455-4560 | 13661 |
| General Atomic Aeron | 3721 | C | 858 312-3428 | 13662 |
| General Atomic Aeron | 3721 | B | 858 312-2543 | 13664 |
| Light Composites Inc | 3721 | E | 619 339-0638 | 13676 |
| Quatro Composites LLC | 3728 | C | 712 707-9200 | 13934 |
| Teledyne Instruments Inc | 3812 | C | 858 842-2600 | 14315 |
| Teledyne Rd Instruments Inc | 3812 | C | 858 842-2600 | 14316 |
| Tern Design Ltd | 3823 | E | 760 754-2400 | 14462 |
| Cohu Inc (PA) | 3825 | C | 858 848-8100 | 14507 |
| Cohu Interface Solutions LLC (HQ) | 3825 | D | 858 848-8000 | 14508 |
| Delta Design (littleton) Inc | 3825 | A | 858 848-8100 | 14511 |
| J2m Test Solutions Inc | 3825 | D | 571 333-0291 | 14541 |
| Vitrek LLC (PA) | 3825 | E | 858 689-2755 | 14599 |
| Resmed Corp | 3841 | E | 858 746-2400 | 15240 |
| Decision Sciences Med Co LLC | 3845 | E | 858 602-1600 | 15530 |
| Aldila Golf Corp | 3949 | C | 858 513-1801 | 15776 |
| Hoist Fitness Systems Inc | 3949 | D | 858 578-7676 | 15822 |
| Seirus Innovative ACC Inc | 3949 | D | 858 513-1212 | 15853 |
| Uke Corporation | 3949 | D | 858 513-9100 | 15870 |
| Traffic Control & Safety Corp | 3993 | E | 858 679-7292 | 16060 |
| PC Specialists Inc (HQ) | 5045 | C | 858 566-1900 | 16538 |
| Printsafe Inc | 5045 | E | 858 748-8600 | 16541 |
| Pmb Group Inc | 5047 | F | 619 690-7300 | 16588 |
| Motion Industries Inc | 5085 | E | 858 602-1500 | 16884 |
| Plastifab San Diego | 5162 | F | 858 679-6600 | 17233 |
| Gold Mine Natural Food Company | 5961 | E | 858 537-9830 | 17664 |
| Clarity Design Inc | 7373 | F | 858 746-3500 | 18969 |
| Dynovas Inc | 7389 | F | 508 717-7494 | 19088 |
| Innovative Lab Solutions Inc | 8711 | F | 858 842-4127 | 19399 |
| ISE Corporation | 8731 | E | 858 413-1720 | 19458 |
| T G T Enterprises Inc | 8742 | C | 858 413-0300 | 19540 |

### PRINCETON, CA - Colusa County

| AA Production Services Inc | 1381 | E | 530 982-0123 | 150 |

### QUINCY, CA - Plumas County

| Sierra Pacific Industries | 2421 | C | 530 283-2820 | 3081 |
| Feather Publishing Company Inc (PA) | 2711 | E | 530 283-0800 | 4113 |
| Renzenberger Inc | 3713 | B | 530 283-3314 | 13425 |

### RAMONA, CA - San Diego County

| In-Line Fence & Railing Co Inc | 1799 | E | 760 789-0282 | 564 |
| Millwork Company Inc | 2431 | F | 760 788-1533 | 3159 |
| Summit Enterprises Inc | 2679 | E | 858 679-2100 | 4051 |
| Micron Machine Company | 3599 | E | 858 486-5900 | 10977 |
| EMD Millipore Corporation | 3826 | E | 760 788-9692 | 14659 |

### RANCHO CASCADES, CA - Los Angeles County

| Spears Manufacturing Co | 3084 | E | 818 364-1611 | 6602 |
| Laser Operations LLC | 3674 | E | 818 986-0000 | 12527 |
| Janco Corporation | 3679 | C | 818 361-3366 | 13010 |
| Mason Electric Co | 3728 | B | 818 361-3366 | 13899 |
| Spears Manufacturing Co (PA) | 5083 | C | 818 364-1611 | 16801 |

### RANCHO CORDOVA, CA - Sacramento County

| Teichert Inc | 1442 | C | 916 351-0123 | 327 |
| Russell Mechanical Inc | 1711 | D | 916 635-2522 | 433 |
| Industrial Elctrnic Systems In (PA) | 1731 | E | 916 638-1000 | 458 |
| Garage Cabinet Warehouse Inc (PA) | 1751 | E | 916 638-0123 | 489 |
| Northwest Exteriors Inc (PA) | 1751 | E | 916 851-1632 | 499 |
| Califrnia Cstm Snroms Ptio Cve | 1799 | F | 800 834-3211 | 558 |
| American Woodmark Corporation | 2434 | C | 916 851-7400 | 3214 |
| Wholesale Art and Framing Inc | 2499 | F | 916 851-0770 | 3431 |
| J & C Custom Cabinets Inc | 2521 | F | 916 638-3400 | 3572 |
| Paper Processors Inc | 2621 | E |  | 3792 |
| High Tek Usa Inc | 2673 | F | 800 504-7120 | 3969 |
| Sunrise Mfg Inc (PA) | 2679 | E | 916 635-6262 | 4052 |
| Ampac Fine Chemicals LLC (DH) | 2819 | D | 916 357-6880 | 5071 |
| Ampac Fine Chemicals LLC | 2819 | B | 916 357-6221 | 5072 |
| Fine Chemicals Holdings Corp | 2834 | A | 916 357-6880 | 5440 |
| Sk Pharmteco Inc (HQ) | 2834 | B | 888 330-2232 | 5662 |
| Elmco & Assoc (HQ) | 3088 | F | 916 383-0110 | 6676 |
| El Dorado Molds LLC | 3089 | F | 916 635-4558 | 6817 |
| Northern California Injection Molding LLC | 3089 | F | 916 853-0717 | 6935 |
| Scribner Plastics | 3089 | F | 916 638-1515 | 7024 |
| Plexus Optix Inc | 3229 | E | 800 852-7600 | 7202 |
| Folsom Ready Mix Inc (HQ) | 3273 | F | 916 851-8300 | 7446 |
| Pabco Building Products LLC (HQ) | 3275 | B | 510 792-1577 | 7527 |
| Pacific Coast Building Products Inc (PA) | 3275 | C | 916 631-6500 | 7529 |
| Union Mine Iron | 3441 | E | 916 985-0332 | 8234 |
| Bmb Metal Products Corporation | 3444 | E | 916 631-9120 | 8392 |
| Group Manufacturing Svcs Inc | 3444 | F | 916 858-3270 | 8463 |
| Kargo Master Inc | 3444 | E | 916 638-8703 | 8480 |
| Penfield Products Inc | 3444 | E | 916 635-0231 | 8535 |
| Taylor Wings Inc | 3444 | E | 916 851-9464 | 8590 |
| Form & Fusion Mfg Inc (PA) | 3469 | E | 916 638-8576 | 8843 |
| Concealed Carrier LLC | 3489 | E | 916 530-6205 | 9138 |
| Kaiser Enterprises Inc | 3498 | E | 916 203-9797 | 9263 |
| Motion Control Engineering Inc | 3534 | B | 916 638-4011 | 9473 |
| Nidec Motor Corporation | 3534 | B | 916 463-9200 | 9474 |
| Ceratizit Los Angeles LLC | 3541 | D | 310 464-8050 | 9543 |
| Promax Tools LP | 3541 | E | 916 638-0501 | 9563 |

Employee Codes: A=Over 500 employees, B=251-500
C=101-250, D=51-100, E=20-50, F=10-19, G=1-9

# RANCHO CORDOVA, CA

| | SIC | EMP | PHONE | ENTRY# |
|---|---|---|---|---|
| Stewart Tool Company | 3545 | D | 916 635-8321 | 9702 |
| Chemical Technologies Intl Inc | 3589 | F | 916 638-1315 | 10546 |
| Acm Machining Inc **(PA)** | 3599 | E | 916 852-8600 | 10668 |
| JL Haley Enterprises Inc | 3599 | C | 916 631-6375 | 10909 |
| Prototek Dgtal Mfg Scrmnto LLC | 3599 | E | 916 851-9285 | 11054 |
| Vander-Bend Manufacturing Inc | 3599 | C | 916 631-6375 | 11169 |
| Project Sutter Holdings LLC **(HQ)** | 3648 | E | 916 669-7408 | 11619 |
| Nca Laboratories Inc | 3651 | E | 916 852-7029 | 11681 |
| Sk Hynix Nand PDT Sltions Corp **(HQ)** | 3674 | C | 858 863-3069 | 12715 |
| Teledyne Defense Elec LLC | 3679 | E | 916 638-3344 | 13102 |
| Aerojet Rocketdyne Inc **(DH)** | 3764 | A | 916 355-4000 | 14101 |
| Rko General Inc | 3812 | D | 916 351-8515 | 14293 |
| Mesotech International Inc | 3826 | E | 916 368-2020 | 14689 |
| Process Insghts - Gded Wave In **(HQ)** | 3826 | E | 916 638-4944 | 14706 |
| Orthogroup Inc | 3841 | F | 916 859-0881 | 15217 |
| Thermogenesis Holdings Inc **(PA)** | 3841 | E | 916 858-5100 | 15283 |
| Philips Image Gded Thrapy Corp | 3845 | B | 916 281-2932 | 15573 |
| Athletic Sports LLC | 3993 | E | 310 709-3944 | 15946 |
| Resq Manufacturing | 3999 | E | 916 638-6786 | 16217 |
| Automotive Importing Manufacturing Inc **(PA)** | 5013 | B | 916 985-8505 | 16374 |
| Tri Tool Inc **(HQ)** | 5084 | E | 916 288-6100 | 16851 |
| Chris Alston Chassisworks Inc | 5961 | E | 916 388-0288 | 17661 |
| Ca Inc | 7371 | E | 916 463-8500 | 17893 |
| Infor (us) LLC | 7372 | E | 916 921-0883 | 18411 |
| Infor Public Sector Inc **(DH)** | 7372 | C | 916 921-0883 | 18412 |

## RANCHO CUCAMONGA, CA - San Bernardino County

| | SIC | EMP | PHONE | ENTRY# |
|---|---|---|---|---|
| Penwal Industries Inc | 1542 | D | 909 466-1555 | 369 |
| Cargill Meat Solutions Corp | 2011 | D | 909 476-3120 | 588 |
| Formosa Meat Company Inc | 2013 | E | 909 987-0470 | 640 |
| Tfi of California Inc **(DH)** | 2013 | E | 844 362-3222 | 674 |
| Waters Edge Wineries Inc | 2084 | E | 909 468-9463 | 1822 |
| American Fruits & Flavors LLC | 2087 | E | 909 291-2620 | 1984 |
| Frozen Bean Inc | 2087 | E | 855 837-6936 | 2007 |
| T Hasegawa USA Inc | 2087 | E | 714 522-1900 | 2029 |
| Aquamar Inc | 2091 | C | 909 481-4700 | 2034 |
| Gruma Corporation | 2096 | D | 909 980-3566 | 2095 |
| Mizkan America Inc | 2099 | C | 909 484-8743 | 2282 |
| Qst Ingredients and Packg Inc | 2099 | F | 909 989-4343 | 2327 |
| Hollywood Ribbon Industries Inc | 2241 | B | 323 266-0670 | 2452 |
| Ecmd Inc | 2431 | E | 909 980-1775 | 3134 |
| Ifco Systems Us LLC | 2448 | D | 909 484-4332 | 3347 |
| Brownwood Furniture Inc | 2511 | C | 909 945-5613 | 3437 |
| ES Kluft & Company Inc **(DH)** | 2515 | C | 909 373-4211 | 3525 |
| South Bay International Inc | 2515 | E | 909 718-5000 | 3540 |
| Modular Office Solutions Inc | 2522 | E | 909 476-4200 | 3606 |
| Ironwood Packaging LLC | 2671 | E | 909 581-0077 | 3929 |
| Avery Dennison Corporation | 2672 | D | 909 987-4631 | 3944 |
| Pacific Pprbd Converting LLC **(PA)** | 2679 | E | 909 476-6466 | 4044 |
| Prime Converting Corporation | 2679 | E | 909 476-9500 | 4047 |
| Chick Publications Inc | 2731 | E | 909 987-0771 | 4320 |
| Continental Graphics Corp | 2752 | D | 909 758-9800 | 4569 |
| Eclipse Prtg & Graphics LLC | 2752 | E | 909 390-2452 | 4600 |
| Kindred Litho Incorporated | 2752 | E | 909 944-4015 | 4661 |
| Heartland Label Printers LLC | 2759 | A | 909 243-7151 | 4891 |
| Air Liquid Healthcare | 2813 | E | 909 899-4633 | 5036 |
| Perimeter Solutions LP | 2819 | E | 909 983-0772 | 5109 |
| Dow Company Foundation | 2821 | C | 909 476-4127 | 5152 |
| Criticalpoint Capital LLC | 2822 | D | 909 987-9533 | 5220 |
| Amphastar Pharmaceuticals Inc **(PA)** | 2834 | C | 909 980-9484 | 5320 |
| Mysmile Oral Care Inc | 2842 | E | 909 908-4615 | 5919 |
| Usl Parallel Products Cal | 2869 | E | 909 980-1200 | 6164 |
| Master Builders LLC | 2899 | A | 909 987-1758 | 6306 |
| Swabplus Inc | 3053 | E | 909 987-7898 | 6469 |
| Omni Seals Inc | 3061 | D | 909 946-0181 | 6474 |
| Good-West Rubber Corp **(PA)** | 3069 | C | 909 987-1774 | 6497 |
| Goodwest Rubber Linings Inc | 3069 | E | 888 499-0085 | 6498 |
| Plaxicon Holding Corporation | 3085 | B | 909 944-6868 | 6613 |
| Creu LLC | 3089 | C | 909 483-4888 | 6786 |
| Diverse Optics Inc | 3089 | E | 909 593-9330 | 6806 |
| Paradigm Packaging East LLC | 3089 | E | 909 985-2750 | 6949 |
| Pres-Tek Plastics Inc **(PA)** | 3089 | E | 909 360-1600 | 6981 |
| Proulx Manufacturing Inc | 3089 | E | 909 980-0662 | 6987 |
| American Traveler Inc | 3161 | E | 909 466-4000 | 7125 |
| Packline USA LLC | 3221 | E | 909 392-8000 | 7186 |
| Searing Industries Inc | 3312 | C | 909 948-3030 | 7626 |
| Pac-Rancho Inc **(HQ)** | 3324 | C | 909 987-4721 | 7693 |
| Southwire Company LLC | 3353 | D | 909 989-2888 | 7731 |
| Prime Wire & Cable Inc | 3357 | D | 323 266-2010 | 7794 |
| American Mechanical & Mfg Inc | 3441 | F | 909 466-4713 | 8094 |
| J T Walker Industries Inc | 3442 | A | 909 481-1909 | 8269 |
| Superior Tank Co Inc **(PA)** | 3443 | E | 909 912-0580 | 8343 |
| Lur Inc | 3446 | F | 909 623-4999 | 8636 |
| Gcn Supply LLC | 3448 | E | 909 643-4603 | 8668 |
| Nci Group Inc | 3448 | E | 909 987-4681 | 8678 |
| Doubleco Incorporated | 3452 | D | 909 481-0799 | 8752 |
| Vanguard Tool & Mfg Co Inc | 3469 | E | 909 980-9392 | 8897 |
| Metal Coaters California Inc | 3479 | D | 909 987-4681 | 9093 |
| Socco Plastic Coating Company | 3479 | E | 909 987-4753 | 9121 |
| Steelscape LLC | 3479 | F | 909 987-4711 | 9124 |
| Wessex Industries Inc | 3498 | E | 562 944-5760 | 9273 |
| Executive Safe and SEC Corp | 3499 | E | 909 947-7020 | 9286 |
| Smith International Inc | 3533 | C | 909 906-7900 | 9466 |
| Prestige Mold Incorporated | 3544 | D | 909 980-6600 | 9642 |
| Pyramid Mold & Tool | 3544 | D | 909 476-2555 | 9645 |
| Sybridge Technologies Ala Inc | 3544 | F | 909 476-2555 | 9651 |
| Rafco-Brickform LLC **(PA)** | 3545 | D | 909 484-3399 | 9695 |
| Sunkist Growers Inc | 3556 | E | 844 694-5406 | 9818 |
| Everidge Inc | 3585 | E | 909 605-6419 | 10500 |
| Bernell Hydraulics Inc **(PA)** | 3594 | E | 909 899-1751 | 10630 |
| All Star Precision | 3599 | E | 909 944-8373 | 10696 |
| Intra Aerospace LLC | 3599 | E | 909 476-0343 | 10890 |
| JCPM Inc | 3599 | E | 909 484-9040 | 10905 |
| Jet Cutting Solutions Inc | 3599 | E | 909 948-2424 | 10908 |
| Pamco Machine Works Inc | 3599 | E | 909 941-7260 | 11027 |
| Paramount Machine Co Inc | 3599 | E | 909 484-3600 | 11031 |
| Romeros Engineering Inc | 3599 | E | 909 481-1170 | 11087 |
| Electro Switch Corp | 3613 | D | 909 581-0855 | 11240 |
| Fluorescent Supply Co Inc | 3646 | E | 909 948-8878 | 11534 |
| Robot-Gxg Inc | 3651 | E | 660 324-0030 | 11691 |
| Digital Flex Media Inc | 3652 | D | 909 484-8440 | 11727 |
| Highball Signal Inc | 3669 | E | 310 961-1122 | 11998 |
| Siemens Rail Automation Corp | 3669 | D | 909 532-5405 | 12016 |
| B & G Electronic Assembly Inc | 3679 | F | 909 608-2077 | 12920 |
| Electro Switch Corp | 3679 | D | 909 581-0855 | 12967 |
| Hunt Electronic Usa Inc | 3699 | F | 909 987-6999 | 13248 |
| Kanex | 3699 | E | 714 332-1681 | 13259 |
| Universal Surveillance Systems LLC | 3699 | D | 909 484-7870 | 13323 |
| Greenpower Motor Company Inc | 3711 | E | 909 308-0960 | 13357 |
| Yinlun Tdi LLC **(HQ)** | 3714 | E | 909 390-3944 | 13610 |
| Air Components Inc | 3728 | E | 909 980-8224 | 13762 |
| Global Aerostructures | 3728 | F | 909 987-4888 | 13853 |
| Lanic Engineering Inc **(PA)** | 3728 | E | 877 763-0411 | 13889 |
| Marino Enterprises Inc | 3728 | E | 909 476-0343 | 13898 |
| Precision Aerospace Corp | 3728 | D | 909 945-9604 | 13928 |
| Safran Cabin Inc | 3728 | E | 909 652-9700 | 13943 |
| Zodiac Aerospace | 3728 | E | 909 652-9700 | 13995 |
| Pneudraulics Inc | 3812 | B | 909 980-5366 | 14279 |
| Mindrum Precision Inc | 3824 | E | 909 989-1728 | 14482 |
| Endress+hser Optcal Analis Inc | 3826 | E | 909 477-2329 | 14662 |
| Aaren Scientific Inc **(DH)** | 3827 | E | 909 937-1033 | 14758 |
| Aqua Measure Instrument Co | 3829 | F | 909 941-7776 | 14845 |
| Davidson Optronics Inc | 3829 | E | 626 962-5181 | 14859 |
| Eagle Labs LLC | 3841 | D | 909 481-0011 | 15074 |
| New World Medical Incorporated | 3841 | F | 909 466-4304 | 15204 |
| Alcoa Fastening Systems | 3965 | E | 909 483-2333 | 15907 |
| Butler Home Products LLC | 3991 | C | 909 476-3884 | 15927 |
| Fan Fave Inc | 3993 | E | 909 975-4999 | 15976 |
| Redefined Industries LLC | 3999 | E | 909 991-9927 | 16214 |
| Honeyville Inc | 4221 | D | 909 980-9500 | 16282 |
| Rerubber LLC | 4953 | F | 909 786-2811 | 16362 |
| Three Wise Men Inc | 5023 | E | 909 477-6698 | 16436 |
| Innovative Displayworks LLC **(HQ)** | 5046 | F | 909 447-8254 | 16568 |
| Tri-Tech Metals Inc | 5051 | F | 909 948-1401 | 16636 |
| California Box II | 5113 | D | 909 944-9202 | 16997 |
| Nongshim America Inc **(HQ)** | 5141 | C | 909 481-3698 | 17116 |
| Frito-Lay North America Inc | 5145 | E | 909 941-6218 | 17145 |
| Evolution Fresh Inc | 5148 | C | 800 794-9986 | 17168 |
| Transcendia Inc | 5162 | E | 909 944-9981 | 17236 |
| Klatch Coffee Inc **(PA)** | 5812 | E | 909 981-4031 | 17594 |
| J Filippi Vintage Co **(PA)** | 5921 | F | 909 899-5755 | 17628 |
| M & G Jewelers Inc | 5944 | D | 909 989-2929 | 17649 |
| Aqm Acquisition Corp | 6799 | F | 909 941-7776 | 17752 |
| Sunn America Inc | 7359 | E | 909 944-5766 | 17864 |
| Grisly Manor LLC | 7372 | F | 714 482-8194 | 18366 |
| H & A Transmissions Inc | 7537 | E | 909 941-9020 | 19157 |
| James Magna Ltd | 7539 | F | 909 391-2025 | 19164 |
| J&K Welding Co Inc | 7692 | E | 909 226-1372 | 19202 |
| AMP Display Inc **(PA)** | 8711 | E | 909 980-1310 | 19376 |
| Bas Engineering Inc | 8711 | F | 909 484-2575 | 19381 |
| Meeder Equipment Company | 8711 | F | 909 463-0600 | 19403 |
| Gentex Corporation | 8731 | D | 909 481-7667 | 19454 |

## RANCHO DOMINGUEZ, CA - Los Angeles County

| | SIC | EMP | PHONE | ENTRY# |
|---|---|---|---|---|
| Global Agri-Trade **(PA)** | 2076 | E | 562 320-8550 | 1371 |
| Bi Nutraceuticals Inc | 2087 | C | 310 669-2100 | 1988 |

# GEOGRAPHIC SECTION

REDWOOD CITY, CA

| | SIC | EMP | PHONE | ENTRY# |
|---|---|---|---|---|
| Ethos Seafood Group LLC | 2092 | D | 312 858-3474 | 2051 |
| Santa Monica Seafood Company (PA) | 2092 | D | 310 886-7900 | 2061 |
| Mars Food Us LLC (HQ) | 2099 | B | 310 933-0670 | 2271 |
| Carol Anderson Inc (PA) | 2335 | E | 310 638-3333 | 2702 |
| Organic By Nature Inc (PA) | 2833 | E | 562 901-0177 | 5259 |
| Biocell Laboratories Inc | 2835 | E | 310 537-3300 | 5740 |
| Giovanni Cosmetics Inc | 2844 | D | 310 952-9960 | 5980 |
| Shercon LLC | 3069 | D | | 6538 |
| Caplugs Inc | 3089 | E | 310 537-2300 | 6763 |
| Expanded Rubber & Plastics Corp | 3089 | E | 310 324-6692 | 6823 |
| Plastics Family Holdings Inc | 3089 | F | 310 928-4100 | 6965 |
| Buff and Shine Mfg Inc | 3291 | E | 310 886-5111 | 7551 |
| Standard Wire & Cable Co (PA) | 3357 | E | 310 609-1811 | 7796 |
| Aerol Co Inc | 3365 | E | 310 762-2660 | 7833 |
| Bodycote Thermal Proc Inc | 3398 | E | 310 604-8000 | 7877 |
| Adf Incorporated | 3446 | E | 310 669-9700 | 8615 |
| Team Manufacturing Inc | 3469 | E | 310 639-0251 | 8894 |
| S L Fusco Inc (PA) | 3541 | E | 310 868-1010 | 9568 |
| Southwestern Industries Inc (PA) | 3541 | D | 310 608-4422 | 9572 |
| Dresser-Rand Company | 3563 | E | 310 223-0600 | 9960 |
| Siemens Energy Inc | 3563 | E | 310 223-0660 | 9975 |
| Enlink Geoenergy Services Inc | 3585 | E | 424 242-1200 | 10498 |
| KT Engineering Corporation | 3599 | E | 310 537-3818 | 10933 |
| Grand General Accessories LLC | 3612 | E | 310 631-2589 | 11214 |
| DSA Phototech LLC | 3646 | E | 866 868-1602 | 11525 |
| Parker-Hannifin Corporation | 3677 | C | 310 608-5600 | 12850 |
| Thermal Equipment Corporation | 3821 | E | 310 328-6600 | 14351 |
| Spectrum Inc | 3841 | C | 310 885-4600 | 15262 |
| Laclede Inc | 3843 | E | 310 605-4280 | 15465 |
| Union Sup Comsy Solutions Inc | 5141 | B | 785 357-5005 | 17119 |
| Pbk International LLC | 5712 | E | 866 727-7195 | 17523 |
| Advanced Fresh Concepts Corp (PA) | 6794 | E | 310 604-3630 | 17751 |
| Bioquip Products Inc | 8731 | E | 310 667-8800 | 19446 |

## RANCHO MURIETA, CA - Sacramento County

| | SIC | EMP | PHONE | ENTRY# |
|---|---|---|---|---|
| Glocol Inc | 4111 | E | 650 224-2108 | 16275 |

## RANCHO PALOS VERDES, CA - Los Angeles County

| | SIC | EMP | PHONE | ENTRY# |
|---|---|---|---|---|
| Trico Leasing Company LLC | 5085 | D | 877 259-9997 | 16903 |
| Pie Rise Ltd | 5812 | E | 310 832-4559 | 17601 |
| CAW Cowie Inc (PA) | 7389 | E | 212 396-9007 | 19080 |

## RANCHO SANTA MARGARI, CA - Orange County

| | SIC | EMP | PHONE | ENTRY# |
|---|---|---|---|---|
| The Lubrizol Corporation | 2899 | F | 949 212-1863 | 6325 |
| RPM Products Inc (PA) | 3053 | E | 949 888-8543 | 6465 |
| Glas Werk Inc | 3229 | E | 949 766-1296 | 7195 |
| Forespar Products Corp | 3429 | D | 949 858-8820 | 7995 |
| Ats Workholding Llc (PA) | 3545 | E | 800 321-1833 | 9660 |
| Allstar Microelectronics Inc | 3572 | E | 949 546-0888 | 10222 |
| Applied Manufacturing LLC | 3841 | A | 949 713-8000 | 14971 |
| Applied Medical Corporation (PA) | 3841 | C | 949 713-8000 | 14972 |
| Applied Medical Resources Corp (HQ) | 3841 | E | 949 713-8000 | 14975 |
| Medwand Solutions Inc | 3841 | E | 770 363-7053 | 15181 |
| Foundation 9 Entertainment Inc (PA) | 7372 | C | 949 698-1500 | 18325 |

## RCHO STA MARG, CA - Orange County

| | SIC | EMP | PHONE | ENTRY# |
|---|---|---|---|---|
| Point Conception Inc | 2339 | E | 949 589-6890 | 2801 |
| Renaissnce Frnch Dors Sash Inc (PA) | 2431 | C | 714 578-0090 | 3184 |
| South Coast Stairs Inc | 2431 | E | 949 858-1685 | 3193 |
| Protab Laboratories | 2834 | D | 949 713-1301 | 5612 |
| Multicoat Products Inc | 2851 | F | 949 888-7100 | 6097 |
| At Apollo Technologies LLC | 2899 | E | 949 888-0573 | 6269 |
| Light Composite Corporation | 3429 | E | 949 858-8820 | 8010 |
| Swiss-Micron Inc | 3451 | E | 949 589-0430 | 8732 |
| IMI Critical Engineering LLC (DH) | 3491 | B | 949 858-1877 | 9156 |
| Standard Cable Usa Inc | 3496 | F | 949 888-0842 | 9233 |
| Alcast Mfg Inc | 3544 | E | 949 888-1744 | 9601 |
| Ats Tool Inc | 3572 | E | 949 713-4600 | 10236 |
| Ep Holdings Inc | 3589 | E | 877 876-2740 | 10551 |
| Clearly Filtered Inc | 3599 | F | 949 858-7400 | 10808 |
| Desco Manufacturing Company (PA) | 3599 | E | 949 858-7000 | 10839 |
| Form Grind Corporation | 3599 | E | 949 413-7513 | 10951 |
| M-Industrial Enterprises LLC | 3669 | D | 949 766-5300 | 12007 |
| Palomar Products Inc | 3674 | E | 949 888-2444 | 12791 |
| Virtium Technology Inc | 3679 | F | 949 546-8000 | 12906 |
| Abracon LLC | 3714 | E | 949 858-5900 | 13471 |
| Car Sound Exhaust System Inc | 3714 | E | 949 858-5900 | 13472 |
| Car Sound Exhaust System Inc | 3714 | E | 949 709-5555 | 13564 |
| Racepak LLC | 3841 | A | 949 713-8000 | 14973 |
| Applied Medical Dist Corp | 3841 | D | 949 459-1042 | 14974 |
| Applied Medical Resources | 3949 | F | 949 448-9940 | 15799 |
| Chapmn-Wlters Intrcoastal Corp | 5999 | E | 949 206-8547 | 17705 |
| Grandma Lucys LLC | 8211 | C | 949 766-6000 | 19345 |
| Roman Cthlic Diocese of Orange | | | | |

| | SIC | EMP | PHONE | ENTRY# |
|---|---|---|---|---|
| National Tour Intgrted Rsrces | 8742 | E | 949 215-6330 | 19535 |

## RED BLUFF, CA - Tehama County

| | SIC | EMP | PHONE | ENTRY# |
|---|---|---|---|---|
| John Wheeler Logging Inc | 2411 | C | 530 527-2993 | 3048 |
| Sierra Pacific Industries Inc | 2421 | B | 530 527-9620 | 3087 |
| Sierra Pacific Industries Inc | 2431 | D | 530 529-5108 | 3189 |
| Lassen Forest Products Inc | 2439 | E | 530 527-7677 | 3313 |
| Desotec US LLC | 3443 | E | 530 527-2664 | 8315 |
| Electro Star Indus Coating Inc | 3479 | F | 530 527-5400 | 9065 |
| Tedon Specialties A Cal Corp | 3599 | F | 530 527-6600 | 11141 |

## REDDING, CA - Shasta County

| | SIC | EMP | PHONE | ENTRY# |
|---|---|---|---|---|
| Electric Innovations Inc | 1731 | D | 530 222-3366 | 456 |
| John Fitzpatrick & Sons | 2086 | E | 530 241-3216 | 1896 |
| Reyes Coca-Cola Bottling LLC | 2086 | D | 530 241-4315 | 1946 |
| Wit Group | 2086 | E | 530 243-4447 | 1974 |
| Warner Enterprises Inc | 2411 | E | 530 241-4000 | 3060 |
| William R Schmitt | 2411 | E | 530 243-3069 | 3062 |
| Redding Printing Co Inc (PA) | 2752 | E | 530 243-0525 | 4752 |
| Cook Concrete Products Inc | 3272 | E | 530 243-2562 | 7322 |
| Southern Alum Finshg Co Inc | 3355 | D | 530 244-7518 | 7761 |
| Purity Pool Inc | 3423 | E | 800 527-1961 | 7965 |
| Ferrosaur Inc | 3441 | E | 530 246-7843 | 8139 |
| Fife Metal Fabricating Inc | 3441 | E | 530 243-4696 | 8140 |
| Gerlinger Fndry Mch Works Inc (PA) | 3441 | E | 530 243-1053 | 8145 |
| Captive-Aire Systems Inc | 3444 | C | 530 351-7150 | 8404 |
| Metals Direct Inc | 3444 | E | 530 605-1931 | 8507 |
| Emerald Kingdom Greenhouse LLC | 3448 | E | 530 241-5670 | 8664 |
| Absolute Machine Inc | 3599 | F | 530 242-6840 | 10658 |
| Ecoatm LLC | 3671 | E | 858 255-4111 | 12031 |
| Ted Pella Inc (PA) | 3826 | E | 530 243-2200 | 14726 |
| Seco Manufacturing Company Inc | 3829 | C | 530 225-8155 | 14916 |
| Spectrum Prsthtcs/Rthtics Rddi | 3842 | E | 530 243-4500 | 15407 |
| Ambr Inc (PA) | 3944 | E | 530 221-4759 | 15738 |
| Jar Ventures Inc | 3993 | E | 530 224-9655 | 15992 |
| Statewide Trffic Sfety Sgns In | 3993 | E | 530 222-8023 | 16049 |
| Maas Energy Works LLC | 4911 | C | 530 710-8545 | 16344 |
| Save Mart Supermarkets Disc | 5411 | C | 530 222-6740 | 17384 |
| Torr Industries Inc | 7371 | E | 530 247-6909 | 17987 |

## REDLANDS, CA - San Bernardino County

| | SIC | EMP | PHONE | ENTRY# |
|---|---|---|---|---|
| Bakell LLC | 1541 | D | 800 292-2137 | 354 |
| Keurig Green Mountain Inc | 2086 | D | 909 557-6513 | 1897 |
| Refresco Beverages US Inc | 2086 | F | 909 915-1432 | 1931 |
| Caseworx Inc (PA) | 2521 | E | 909 799-8550 | 3563 |
| Ui Medical LLC | 2676 | E | 562 453-1515 | 4006 |
| Continental Datalabel Inc | 2679 | F | 909 307-3600 | 4035 |
| Califrnia Nwspapers Ltd Partnr | 2711 | B | 909 793-3221 | 4087 |
| Clorox Manufacturing Company | 2842 | E | 909 307-2756 | 5899 |
| Munchkin Inc | 3085 | E | 818 893-5000 | 6609 |
| Plastics Plus Technology Inc | 3089 | E | 909 747-0555 | 6966 |
| Window Enterprises Inc | 3442 | E | 951 943-4894 | 8294 |
| Venturedyne Ltd | 3564 | D | 909 793-2788 | 10004 |
| Garner Holt Productions Inc | 3571 | E | 909 799-3030 | 10153 |
| Precision Hermetic Tech Inc | 3679 | D | 909 381-6011 | 13066 |
| Teledyne Technologies Inc | 3691 | D | 909 793-3131 | 13152 |
| Low Cost Interlock Inc | 3694 | E | 844 387-0326 | 13176 |
| Becton Dickinson and Company | 3826 | D | 909 748-7300 | 14625 |
| Kyocera Medical Tech Inc | 3842 | E | 909 557-2360 | 15373 |
| Ifit Inc | 3949 | A | 909 335-2888 | 15828 |
| Daryls Pet Shop | 3999 | E | 909 793-1788 | 16122 |
| Rettig Machine Inc | 7692 | E | 909 793-7811 | 19210 |

## REDONDO BEACH, CA - Los Angeles County

| | SIC | EMP | PHONE | ENTRY# |
|---|---|---|---|---|
| Coast Specialty Printing Co | 2752 | E | 626 359-2451 | 4556 |
| Quantimetrix | 2835 | D | 310 536-0006 | 5775 |
| Alcast Mfg Inc | 3364 | E | 310 542-3581 | 7824 |
| Northrop Grumman Systems Corp | 3663 | C | 310 812-5149 | 11906 |
| Northrop Grmmn Spce & Mssn Sys | 3714 | B | 310 812-4321 | 13550 |
| Northrop Grumman Systems Corp | 3721 | B | 310 812-1089 | 13682 |
| Northrop Grumman Systems Corp | 3721 | B | 310 812-4321 | 13683 |
| Impulse Space Inc | 3761 | E | 949 315-5540 | 14081 |
| Jariet Technologies Inc | 3812 | E | 310 698-1000 | 14200 |
| Northrop Grumman Systems Corp | 3812 | E | 855 737-8364 | 14254 |
| Northrop Grumman Systems Corp | 3812 | D | 310 812-4321 | 14255 |
| Advanced Arm Dynamics (PA) | 3842 | E | 310 372-3050 | 15316 |
| Mapcargo Global Logistics (PA) | 4731 | D | 310 297-8300 | 16307 |
| Scat Enterprises Inc | 5013 | E | 310 370-5501 | 16398 |
| Sierra Monolithics Inc (HQ) | 8748 | E | 310 698-1000 | 19570 |

## REDWOOD CITY, CA - San Mateo County

| | SIC | EMP | PHONE | ENTRY# |
|---|---|---|---|---|
| Aire Sheet Metal Inc | 1711 | E | 650 364-8081 | 403 |
| Douce De France | 2051 | F | 650 369-9644 | 1186 |

# REDWOOD CITY, CA

| Company | SIC | EMP | PHONE | ENTRY# |
|---|---|---|---|---|
| Impossible Foods Inc (PA) | 2099 | C | 650 461-4385 | 2238 |
| Biocentury Inc (PA) | 2711 | F | 650 595-5333 | 4076 |
| Qwilt Inc | 2741 | E | 650 249-6521 | 4457 |
| Paw Prints Inc | 2759 | F | 650 365-4077 | 4937 |
| Codexis Inc | 2819 | C | 650 421-8100 | 5084 |
| Antriabio Delaware Inc | 2834 | E | 303 222-2128 | 5326 |
| Armo Biosciences Inc | 2834 | E | 650 779-5075 | 5335 |
| Astrazeneca Pharmaceuticals LP | 2834 | E | 650 305-2600 | 5342 |
| Biomea Fusion Inc (PA) | 2834 | E | 650 980-9099 | 5372 |
| Bolt Biotherapeutics Inc | 2834 | D | 650 665-9295 | 5382 |
| Bristol-Myers Squibb Company | 2834 | D | 800 332-2056 | 5385 |
| Corcept Therapeutics Inc (PA) | 2834 | C | 650 327-3270 | 5410 |
| Eqrx Inc (HQ) | 2834 | D | 617 315-2255 | 5434 |
| Kartos Therapeutics Inc | 2834 | E | 650 542-0130 | 5522 |
| Maplight Therapeutics Inc | 2834 | E | 207 653-8478 | 5543 |
| Pearl Therapeutics Inc | 2834 | E | 650 305-2600 | 5595 |
| Rezolute Inc (PA) | 2834 | E | 650 206-4507 | 5639 |
| Soleno Therapeutics Inc (PA) | 2834 | F | 650 213-8444 | 5667 |
| Teon Therapeutics Inc | 2834 | F | 650 832-1421 | 5686 |
| Adverum Biotechnologies Inc (PA) | 2836 | C | 650 656-9323 | 5786 |
| Arcellx Inc | 2836 | C | 240 327-0630 | 5794 |
| Coherus Biosciences Inc (PA) | 2836 | C | 650 649-3530 | 5822 |
| Jasper Therapeutics Inc (PA) | 2836 | F | 650 549-1400 | 5843 |
| Proteus Digital Health Inc (PA) | 2836 | D | 650 632-4031 | 5856 |
| Granite Rock Company | 2951 | D | 650 482-3800 | 6364 |
| Tilley Manufacturing Co Inc (PA) | 3053 | D | 650 365-3598 | 6470 |
| David Schnur Assoc | 3089 | D | 650 363-8797 | 6794 |
| Te Connectivity MOG Inc (PA) | 3229 | F | 650 361-5292 | 7206 |
| Holt Tool & Machine Inc | 3312 | E | 650 364-2547 | 7615 |
| Cfkba Inc | 3357 | E | 650 302-6331 | 7782 |
| Ai Industries Inc (PA) | 3471 | D | 650 366-4099 | 8909 |
| Serve Robotics Inc | 3569 | D | 818 860-1352 | 10114 |
| Carbon Inc (PA) | 3577 | C | 650 285-6307 | 10341 |
| Bay Precision Machining Inc | 3599 | F | 650 365-3010 | 10739 |
| EH Suda Inc (PA) | 3599 | F | 650 622-9700 | 10820 |
| Petersen Precision Engrg LLC | 3599 | C | 650 365-4373 | 11039 |
| Talos Corporation | 3599 | E | 713 328-3071 | 11136 |
| Ampex Corporation | 3663 | C | 650 367-2011 | 11806 |
| Bigband Networks Inc | 3663 | B | 650 995-5000 | 11818 |
| Mirapoint Software Inc | 3663 | D | 650 286-7200 | 11893 |
| Advanced Circuits Inc | 3672 | C | 415 602-6834 | 12045 |
| Brantner Holding LLC (HQ) | 3678 | F | 650 361-5292 | 12867 |
| Te Connectivity Corporation | 3678 | D | 650 361-2495 | 12900 |
| Inevit Inc | 3691 | C | 650 298-6001 | 13144 |
| Tau Motors Inc | 3694 | F | 650 486-1033 | 13187 |
| Electronic Arts Redwood LLC | 3695 | A | 650 628-1500 | 13194 |
| Pendulum Instruments Inc | 3699 | E | 866 644-1230 | 13286 |
| Kaye Sandy Enterprises Inc | 3732 | E | 650 961-5334 | 14038 |
| Nvent Thermal LLC | 3822 | B | 650 474-7414 | 14365 |
| Seer Inc (PA) | 3826 | C | 650 453-0000 | 14715 |
| Light Labs Inc | 3827 | D | 650 257-8100 | 14794 |
| Oraya Therapeutics Inc | 3827 | E | 510 456-3700 | 14811 |
| Auris Health Inc (DH) | 3841 | C | 650 610-0750 | 14982 |
| Avinger Inc | 3841 | E | 650 241-7900 | 14986 |
| Biotricity Inc | 3841 | E | 650 832-1626 | 15015 |
| Dex Liquidating Co | 3841 | E | 650 364-9975 | 15065 |
| Galaxy Medical Inc | 3841 | E | 510 847-5189 | 15095 |
| Galvanize Therapeutics Inc (PA) | 3841 | F | 628 800-1154 | 15096 |
| Nevro Corp (PA) | 3841 | A | 650 251-0005 | 15203 |
| Ethicon Inc | 3842 | C | 650 306-7900 | 15344 |
| Biointellisense Inc | 3845 | E | 650 481-8140 | 15519 |
| Tangible Science LLC | 3851 | E | 650 241-1045 | 15622 |
| Balsam Brands Inc | 3999 | D | 877 442-2572 | 16092 |
| Riverbed Technology LLC (HQ) | 5045 | D | 415 247-8800 | 16547 |
| Brothers Pride Produce Inc (PA) | 5431 | E | 650 368-6993 | 17398 |
| Einstein Noah Rest Group Inc | 5461 | D | 650 299-9050 | 17411 |
| Clustrix Inc | 7371 | E | 415 501-9560 | 17898 |
| Oc Acquisition LLC (HQ) | 7371 | C | 650 506-7000 | 17956 |
| Accelerance Inc | 7372 | D | 650 472-3785 | 18010 |
| Actiance Inc | 7372 | C | 650 631-6300 | 18013 |
| Agiloft Inc (PA) | 7372 | D | 650 459-5637 | 18029 |
| Alation Inc (PA) | 7372 | B | 650 779-4440 | 18034 |
| Autogrid Systems Inc (PA) | 7372 | F | 650 461-9038 | 18079 |
| Badgeville Inc | 7372 | C | 650 323-6668 | 18089 |
| Box Inc (PA) | 7372 | B | 877 729-4269 | 18122 |
| C3 Delaware Inc | 7372 | E | 650 503-2200 | 18134 |
| C3AI INC (PA) | 7372 | A | 650 503-2200 | 18135 |
| Celigo Inc (PA) | 7372 | E | 650 579-0210 | 18155 |
| Check Point Software Tech Inc (DH) | 7372 | C | 800 429-4391 | 18165 |
| Electronic Arts Inc (PA) | 7372 | B | 650 628-1500 | 18272 |
| Flywheel Software Inc | 7372 | E | 650 260-1700 | 18317 |
| Gearbox Pubg San Francisco Inc | 7372 | E | 650 590-7700 | 18343 |
| Glasslab Inc | 7372 | E | 415 244-5584 | 18351 |
| Informatica Holdco 2 Inc | 7372 | A | 650 385-5000 | 18414 |
| Informatica Inc | 7372 | A | 650 385-5000 | 18415 |
| Informatica International Inc (DH) | 7372 | E | 650 385-5000 | 18416 |
| Informatica LLC (DH) | 7372 | B | 650 385-5000 | 18417 |
| Invoice2go LLC | 7372 | D | 650 300-5180 | 18440 |
| Master of Code Global | 7372 | E | 650 200-8490 | 18523 |
| Nreach Online Services Inc | 7372 | B | 425 301-9168 | 18601 |
| Openwave Mobility Inc (DH) | 7372 | E | 650 480-7200 | 18626 |
| Oracle Corporation | 7372 | E | 415 834-9731 | 18636 |
| Oracle Corporation | 7372 | E | 650 506-7000 | 18639 |
| Oracle International Corp (HQ) | 7372 | F | 650 506-7000 | 18640 |
| Oracle Japan Holding Inc (HQ) | 7372 | D | 650 506-7000 | 18641 |
| Oracle Systems Corporation | 7372 | E | 650 506-5887 | 18645 |
| Oracle Usa Inc | 7372 | A | 650 506-7000 | 18648 |
| Paxata Inc | 7372 | D | 650 542-7897 | 18663 |
| Poshmark Inc (HQ) | 7372 | F | 650 262-4771 | 18687 |
| Revup Software Inc | 7372 | F | 415 231-2315 | 18740 |
| Secpod Technologies | 7372 | E | 405 385-9890 | 18774 |
| Simpplr Inc (PA) | 7372 | C | 650 396-2646 | 18791 |
| Smarsh Inc | 7372 | C | 650 631-6300 | 18798 |
| Storm8 Inc | 7372 | F | 650 596-8600 | 18838 |
| Tanka Inc | 7372 | D | 650 656-9560 | 18865 |
| Trion Worlds Inc | 7372 | B | 650 631-9800 | 18892 |
| Workboard Inc (PA) | 7372 | C | 650 294-4480 | 18942 |
| Xtime Inc | 7372 | E | 650 508-4300 | 18948 |
| Zuora Inc (PA) | 7372 | B |  | 18958 |
| Singtel Enterprise SEC US Inc | 7373 | A | 650 508-6800 | 18992 |
| Digital Insight Corporation (HQ) | 7375 | C | 818 879-1010 | 19016 |
| Oracle Systems Corporation (HQ) | 7379 | A | 650 506-7000 | 19042 |

## REDWOOD SHORES, CA - San Mateo County

| Company | SIC | EMP | PHONE | ENTRY# |
|---|---|---|---|---|
| Oracle America Inc (HQ) | 3571 | A | 650 506-7000 | 10186 |

## REDWOOD VALLEY, CA - Mendocino County

| Company | SIC | EMP | PHONE | ENTRY# |
|---|---|---|---|---|
| Burgess Lumber | 2421 | E | 707 485-8072 | 3065 |

## REEDLEY, CA - Fresno County

| Company | SIC | EMP | PHONE | ENTRY# |
|---|---|---|---|---|
| Quality Technology Solutions | 1731 | F | 559 804-4522 | 468 |
| Mission AG Resources LLC | 2023 | E | 559 591-3333 | 769 |
| Maxco Supply Inc | 2631 | E | 559 638-8449 | 3804 |
| Valley Packline Solutions | 3556 | E | 559 638-7821 | 9822 |
| Thiele Technologies Inc | 3565 | D | 559 638-8484 | 10033 |
| Fortier & Fortier Inc | 5083 | E | 559 638-5774 | 16798 |

## RIALTO, CA - San Bernardino County

| Company | SIC | EMP | PHONE | ENTRY# |
|---|---|---|---|---|
| Arnett Construction Inc | 1794 | E | 909 421-7960 | 543 |
| Biscomerica Corp | 2052 | B | 909 877-5997 | 1265 |
| Thompson Pipe Group Inc (PA) | 2679 | E | 909 822-0200 | 4055 |
| Solomon Colors Inc | 2816 | E | 909 873-9444 | 5064 |
| B & B Plastics Inc | 2821 | E | 909 829-3606 | 5139 |
| Marine Fenders Intl Inc | 3089 | E | 310 834-7037 | 6902 |
| Eagle Roofing Products Fla LLC | 3259 | F | 909 822-6000 | 7273 |
| Kti Incorporated | 3272 | D | 909 434-1888 | 7353 |
| Royal Westlake Roofing LLC | 3272 | E | 909 822-4407 | 7386 |
| Burlingame Industries Inc | 3299 | C | 909 355-7000 | 7588 |
| State Pipe & Supply Inc | 3312 | E | 909 356-5670 | 7629 |
| Calcraft Corporation | 3441 | F | 909 879-2900 | 8111 |
| Columbia Steel Inc | 3441 | D | 909 874-8840 | 8121 |
| So-Cal Strl Stl Fbrication Inc | 3441 | E | 909 877-1299 | 8219 |
| Spray Enclosure Tech Inc | 3444 | E | 909 419-7011 | 8580 |
| H Wayne Lewis Inc | 3449 | E | 909 874-2213 | 8698 |
| Martinez and Turek Inc | 3599 | C | 909 820-6800 | 10960 |
| Mike Dyell Machine Shop Inc (PA) | 3599 | F | 909 350-4101 | 10978 |
| Technifirm International Corp | 3599 | C | 909 877-6886 | 11140 |
| Lippert Components Inc | 3711 | E | 909 873-0061 | 13365 |
| Medical Depot Inc | 3841 | D | 877 224-0946 | 15166 |
| B & B Plastics Recyclers Inc (PA) | 5093 | E | 909 829-3606 | 16957 |
| Burlingame Industries Inc (PA) | 7033 | D | 909 355-7000 | 17763 |
| Grisby Gaming & Tech LLC | 7379 | E | 415 463-8200 | 19038 |
| Precision Aerial Services Inc | 7549 | F | 909 484-8259 | 19169 |

## RICHMOND, CA - Contra Costa County

| Company | SIC | EMP | PHONE | ENTRY# |
|---|---|---|---|---|
| Galaxy Desserts | 2051 | C | 510 439-3160 | 1209 |
| Aak USA Richmond Corp (DH) | 2079 | D | 510 233-7660 | 1391 |
| Freshrealm Inc | 2099 | B | 888 278-4349 | 2208 |
| Nutiva | 2099 | C | 510 255-2700 | 2300 |
| Mountain Hardwear Inc | 2394 | A | 510 558-3000 | 2978 |
| Tamalpais Coml Cabinetry Inc | 2434 | E | 510 231-6800 | 3272 |
| Sealy Mattress Mfg Co LLC | 2515 | D | 510 235-7171 | 3536 |
| Ironies | 2521 | E | 510 644-2100 | 3571 |
| Tulip Pubg & Graphics Inc | 2752 | E | 510 898-0000 | 4792 |
| Bel Aire Displays | 2759 | D | 510 232-5100 | 4847 |
| Chemtrade Chemicals US LLC | 2819 | D | 510 232-7193 | 5083 |

# GEOGRAPHIC SECTION

## RIVERSIDE, CA

| | SIC | EMP | PHONE | ENTRY# |
|---|---|---|---|---|
| Chevron Oronite Company LLC | 2821 | B | 925 842-1000 | 5144 |
| Bioage Labs Inc | 2834 | D | 510 806-1445 | 5370 |
| Mom Enterprises LLC | 2834 | E | 415 694-3799 | 5557 |
| Sangamo Therapeutics Inc (PA) | 2836 | B | 510 970-6000 | 5858 |
| Chevron USA Inc | 2911 | D | 510 242-3000 | 6335 |
| International Group Inc | 2911 | D | 510 232-8704 | 6339 |
| San Rafael Rock Quarry Inc | 2951 | E | 510 970-7700 | 6370 |
| Gasket Specialties Inc (PA) | 3053 | E | 510 547-7955 | 6450 |
| Ats Products Inc (PA) | 3089 | E | 510 234-3173 | 6728 |
| Cemex Materials LLC | 3273 | C | 510 234-3616 | 7428 |
| Amt Metal Fabricators Inc | 3441 | E | 510 236-1414 | 8095 |
| Metalset Inc | 3441 | E | 510 233-9998 | 8186 |
| Andrus Sheet Metal Inc | 3444 | E | 510 232-8687 | 8375 |
| West Coast Fab Inc | 3444 | F | 510 529-0177 | 8611 |
| Professional Finishing Inc | 3479 | D | 510 233-7629 | 9112 |
| R & K Industrial Products Co | 3499 | E | 510 234-7212 | 9298 |
| Adel Park LLC | 3531 | F | 510 620-9670 | 9403 |
| Black Diamond Video Inc | 3577 | D | 510 439-4500 | 10337 |
| Kodiak Precision Inc (PA) | 3599 | F | 510 234-4165 | 10931 |
| Paragon Machine Works Inc | 3599 | D | 510 232-3223 | 11028 |
| Oliso Inc | 3634 | F | 415 864-7600 | 11412 |
| Phoenix Day Inc | 3645 | E | 415 822-4414 | 11501 |
| Alion Energy Inc | 3674 | D | 510 965-0868 | 12288 |
| Sunpower Corporation (HQ) | 3674 | C | 408 240-5500 | 12744 |
| Dicon Fiberoptics Inc | 3679 | B | 510 620-5000 | 12960 |
| MTI Corporation | 3679 | E | 510 525-3070 | 13040 |
| Support Systems Intl Corp | 3679 | D | 510 234-9090 | 13095 |
| AA Portable Power Corporation | 3691 | E | 510 525-2328 | 13130 |
| ACS Instrumentation Valves Inc | 3823 | D | 510 262-1880 | 14381 |
| Parker-Hannifin Corporation | 3823 | C | 510 235-9590 | 14443 |
| Bio-RAD Laboratories Inc | 3826 | E | 510 232-7000 | 14627 |
| Coherent Tios Inc | 3826 | E | 510 964-5600 | 14646 |
| Zygo Epo | 3827 | F | 510 243-7592 | 14836 |
| Steris Corporation | 3842 | E | 510 439-4500 | 15409 |
| Hero Arts Rubber Stamps Inc | 3953 | E | 510 232-4200 | 15890 |
| Thomas-Swan Sign Company Inc | 3993 | E | 415 621-1511 | 16058 |
| T F Louderback Inc | 5181 | C | 510 965-6120 | 17260 |
| Pegasus Solar Inc | 5211 | E | 510 210-3797 | 17342 |
| Foamordercom Inc | 5712 | F | 415 503-1188 | 17520 |
| M & M Bakery Products Inc | 5812 | D | 510 235-0274 | 17597 |

### RICHVALE, CA - Butte County

| | SIC | EMP | PHONE | ENTRY# |
|---|---|---|---|---|
| Wehah Farm Inc | 2044 | B | 530 538-3500 | 1085 |
| Wehah-Lundberg Inc | 2044 | C | 530 882-4551 | 1086 |

### RIDGECREST, CA - Kern County

| | SIC | EMP | PHONE | ENTRY# |
|---|---|---|---|---|
| American Ready Mix Inc | 3273 | F | 760 446-4556 | 7403 |
| Orbital Sciences LLC | 3812 | C | 818 887-8345 | 14274 |

### RIO VISTA, CA - Solano County

| | SIC | EMP | PHONE | ENTRY# |
|---|---|---|---|---|
| Asta Construction Co Inc (PA) | 1381 | E | 707 374-6472 | 154 |
| Dick Browns Technical Service | 1381 | F | 707 374-2133 | 155 |
| Paul Graham Drilling & Svc Co | 1381 | C | 707 374-5123 | 164 |
| Woodward Drilling Company Inc | 1381 | E | 707 374-4300 | 167 |
| Dry Vac Environmental Inc (PA) | 3826 | E | 707 374-7500 | 14656 |

### RIPON, CA - San Joaquin County

| | SIC | EMP | PHONE | ENTRY# |
|---|---|---|---|---|
| Pearl Crop Inc | 2076 | E | 209 982-9933 | 1372 |
| McManis Family Vineyards Inc | 2084 | E | 209 599-1186 | 1676 |
| Wine Group Inc (HQ) | 2084 | C | 209 599-4111 | 1831 |
| California Nuggets Inc | 2096 | E | 209 599-7131 | 2088 |
| Better Built Truss Inc | 2439 | E | 209 869-4545 | 3294 |
| Maxim Equipment Inc | 2951 | F | 209 649-7225 | 6365 |
| Jackrabbit (PA) | 3523 | D | 209 599-6118 | 9363 |
| Kamper Fabrication Inc | 3523 | E | 209 599-7137 | 9364 |
| Ripon Mfg Co | 3556 | E | 209 599-2148 | 9815 |
| Nulaid Foods Inc (PA) | 5144 | D | 209 599-2121 | 17134 |

### RIVERBANK, CA - Stanislaus County

| | SIC | EMP | PHONE | ENTRY# |
|---|---|---|---|---|
| Thunderbolt Sales Inc | 2491 | F | 209 869-4561 | 3404 |
| Repsco Inc | 3083 | E | 888 727-7261 | 6591 |
| American Laminates Inc | 3089 | E | 209 869-2536 | 6714 |
| Silgan Containers Mfg Corp | 3411 | E | 209 869-3601 | 7930 |

### RIVERSIDE, CA - Riverside County

| | SIC | EMP | PHONE | ENTRY# |
|---|---|---|---|---|
| Skanska USA Cvil W Cal Dst Inc (DH) | 1611 | A | 951 684-5360 | 381 |
| Allied Steel Co Inc | 1791 | D | 951 241-7000 | 527 |
| Swift Beef Company | 2013 | C | 951 571-2237 | 672 |
| Better Bar Manufacturing LLC | 2023 | E | 951 525-3111 | 745 |
| Tropical Functional Labs LLC | 2023 | E | 951 688-2619 | 784 |
| Mackie International Inc (PA) | 2024 | E | 951 346-0530 | 808 |
| Ludfords Inc | 2033 | E | 909 948-0797 | 903 |
| Inland Empire Foods Inc (PA) | 2034 | E | 951 682-8222 | 951 |
| Canine Caviar Pet Foods De Inc | 2047 | F | 714 223-1800 | 1095 |
| Canine Caviar Pet Foods Inc | 2048 | E | 714 223-1800 | 1123 |
| Growest Inc (PA) | 2084 | F | 951 638-1000 | 1605 |
| American Bottling Company | 2086 | D | 951 341-7500 | 1850 |
| Bottling Group LLC | 2086 | D | 951 697-3200 | 1872 |
| Inland Cold Storage | 2092 | E | 951 369-0230 | 2054 |
| OSI Industries LLC | 2099 | B | 951 684-4500 | 2305 |
| Ruiz Mexican Foods Inc (PA) | 2099 | C | 909 947-7811 | 2343 |
| Triple H Food Processors LLC | 2099 | D | 951 352-5700 | 2379 |
| Virginia Park LLC | 2099 | F | 816 592-0776 | 2388 |
| Newman Bros California Inc (PA) | 2431 | F | 951 782-0102 | 3164 |
| Quality Shutters Inc | 2431 | E | 951 683-4939 | 3183 |
| T M Cobb Company (PA) | 2431 | E | 951 248-2400 | 3194 |
| Professional Cabinet Solutions | 2434 | E | 909 614-2900 | 3260 |
| Simpson Strong-Tie Company Inc | 2439 | C | 714 871-8373 | 3317 |
| D L B Pallets (PA) | 2448 | F | 951 360-9896 | 3339 |
| G C Pallets Inc | 2448 | E | 909 357-8515 | 3342 |
| Cavco Industries Inc | 2451 | E | 951 688-5353 | 3382 |
| Fleetwood Homes California Inc (DH) | 2451 | C | 951 351-2494 | 3386 |
| Nextmod Inc | 2451 | E | 909 740-3120 | 3387 |
| Autonomous Inc | 2522 | E | 844 949-3879 | 3594 |
| Clarios LLC | 2531 | E | 951 222-0284 | 3615 |
| Ideal Products Inc | 2541 | E | 951 727-8600 | 3657 |
| Roll-A-Shade LLC (PA) | 2591 | E | 951 245-5077 | 3727 |
| Heritage Container Inc | 2653 | D | 951 360-1900 | 3854 |
| Metropolitan News Company | 2711 | E | 951 369-5890 | 4159 |
| Press-Enterprise Company (PA) | 2711 | A | 951 684-1200 | 4182 |
| Elisid Magazine | 2721 | E | 619 990-9999 | 4251 |
| Qg Printing Corp | 2721 | E | 951 571-2500 | 4291 |
| Majestic Print Inc | 2752 | F | 951 509-2539 | 4687 |
| Qg Printing IL LLC | 2752 | C | 951 571-2500 | 4746 |
| Quad/Graphics Inc | 2752 | D | 951 689-1122 | 4747 |
| Sphere Alliance Inc | 2821 | E | 951 352-2400 | 5203 |
| Cosmedx Science Inc | 2834 | E | 951 371-0509 | 5412 |
| Universal Prtein Spplmnts Corp | 2834 | F | 732 545-3130 | 5699 |
| California Interfill Inc | 2844 | E | 951 351-2619 | 5953 |
| Gar Laboratories Inc | 2844 | C | 951 788-0700 | 5979 |
| Plz Corp | 2844 | D | 951 683-2912 | 6024 |
| Plz Corp | 2844 | C | 951 683-2912 | 6026 |
| Trademark Cosmetics LLC | 2844 | E | 951 683-2631 | 6045 |
| Poly-Fiber Inc (PA) | 2851 | F | 951 684-4280 | 6101 |
| Products/Techniques Inc | 2851 | F | 909 877-3951 | 6107 |
| Mitchell Rubber Products LLC (PA) | 3069 | E | 951 681-5655 | 6514 |
| Plascor Inc | 3085 | C | 951 328-1010 | 6612 |
| Carpenter Co | 3086 | E | 951 354-7550 | 6626 |
| Advanced Engrg Mlding Tech Inc | 3089 | E | 888 264-0392 | 6697 |
| Altium Holdings LLC | 3089 | A | 951 340-9390 | 6706 |
| AMA Plastics | 3089 | B | 951 734-5600 | 6711 |
| AMS Plastics Inc | 3089 | B | 951 734-5600 | 6717 |
| Blow Molded Products Inc | 3089 | E | 951 360-6055 | 6745 |
| Bm Extrusion Inc | 3089 | E | 951 782-9020 | 6746 |
| Carson Industries LLC | 3089 | A | 951 788-9720 | 6766 |
| Hi-Rel Plastics & Molding Corp | 3089 | E | 951 354-0258 | 6852 |
| Micromold Inc | 3089 | F | 951 684-7130 | 6914 |
| Nsa Holdings Inc | 3089 | E | 951 686-1400 | 6939 |
| Plastic Technologies Inc | 3089 | E | 951 360-6055 | 6963 |
| Polymer Logistics Inc | 3089 | D | 951 567-2900 | 6972 |
| Rolenn Manufacturing Inc (PA) | 3089 | E | 951 682-1185 | 7006 |
| Royal Interpack North Amer Inc | 3089 | E | 951 787-6925 | 7013 |
| Snapware Corporation | 3089 | C | 951 361-3100 | 7031 |
| Western Case Incorporated | 3089 | E | 951 214-6380 | 7079 |
| Riverside Cement Holdings Company | 3241 | B | 951 774-2500 | 7262 |
| Newbasis LLC | 3272 | C | 951 787-0600 | 7358 |
| Newbasis West LLC | 3272 | C | 951 787-0600 | 7359 |
| Oldcast Precast (DH) | 3272 | E | 951 788-9720 | 7362 |
| Alpha Materials Inc | 3273 | E | 951 788-5150 | 7402 |
| Parex Usa Inc (DH) | 3299 | E | 714 778-2266 | 7599 |
| Borrmann Metal Center | 3312 | E | 951 367-1510 | 7606 |
| Barrette Outdoor Living Inc | 3315 | E | 800 336-2383 | 7637 |
| Dayton Superior Corporation | 3315 | E | 951 782-9517 | 7640 |
| Merchants Metals LLC | 3315 | C | 951 686-1888 | 7646 |
| Tube One Industries Inc | 3317 | F | 951 300-2998 | 7671 |
| Luxfer Inc | 3354 | E | 951 684-5110 | 7742 |
| Samuel Son & Co (usa) Inc | 3354 | E | 951 781-7800 | 7747 |
| Sierra Aluminum Company | 3354 | E | 951 781-7800 | 7748 |
| Metal Container Corporation | 3411 | C | 951 354-0444 | 7924 |
| Accurate Metal Products Inc | 3441 | C | 951 360-3594 | 8087 |
| Bell Bros Steel Inc | 3441 | F | 951 784-0903 | 8101 |
| Millers Fab & Weld Corp | 3441 | E | 951 359-1453 | 8188 |
| Crystal PCF Win & Door Sys LLC | 3442 | C | 951 779-9300 | 8261 |
| Kawneer Company Inc | 3442 | D | 951 410-4779 | 8271 |
| San Joaquin Window Inc | 3442 | C | 909 946-3697 | 8289 |
| Atco Rubber Products Inc | 3443 | F | 951 788-4345 | 8299 |

Employee Codes: A=Over 500 employees, B=251-500
C=101-250, D=51-100, E=20-50, F=10-19, G=1-9

# RIVERSIDE, CA

## GEOGRAPHIC SECTION

| | SIC | EMP | PHONE | ENTRY# |
|---|---|---|---|---|
| Ba Holdings Inc (DH) | 3443 | E | 951 684-5110 | 8300 |
| Clarkwestern Dietrich Building | 3444 | E | 951 360-3500 | 8410 |
| Doka USA Ltd | 3444 | E | 951 509-0023 | 8434 |
| Innovtive Dsign Shtmtl Pdts In | 3444 | F | 951 222-2270 | 8475 |
| Prism Aerospace | 3444 | E | 951 582-2850 | 8544 |
| Quality Fabrication Inc (PA) | 3444 | D | 818 407-5015 | 8548 |
| SMS Fabrications Inc | 3444 | E | 951 351-6828 | 8574 |
| US Precision Sheet Metal Inc | 3444 | D | 951 276-2611 | 8604 |
| T M P Services Inc (PA) | 3448 | E | 951 213-3900 | 8687 |
| United Carports LLC | 3448 | E | 800 757-6742 | 8688 |
| Esco Industries Inc | 3462 | F | 951 782-2130 | 8775 |
| Luxfer Inc | 3463 | E | 951 351-4100 | 8799 |
| Main Steel LLC | 3471 | D | 951 231-4949 | 8981 |
| Dura Coat Products Inc (PA) | 3479 | E | 951 341-6500 | 9062 |
| Ejay Filtration Inc | 3496 | E | 951 683-0805 | 9216 |
| Toro Company | 3523 | C | 951 688-9221 | 9387 |
| Jlg Industries Inc | 3531 | E | 951 358-1915 | 9428 |
| American Quality Tools Inc | 3545 | E | 951 280-4700 | 9659 |
| Karbide Inc | 3545 | E | 951 354-0900 | 9679 |
| John Bean Technologies Corp | 3556 | D | 951 222-2300 | 9800 |
| Dek Industry Inc | 3559 | C | 909 941-8810 | 9849 |
| Pacific Consolidated Inds LLC | 3569 | D | 951 479-0860 | 10103 |
| Phenix Technology Corporation (PA) | 3569 | F | 951 272-4938 | 10105 |
| Team Air Inc (PA) | 3585 | E | 909 823-1957 | 10517 |
| City of Riverside | 3589 | C | 951 351-6140 | 10548 |
| Yardney Water MGT Systems Inc | 3589 | E | 951 656-6716 | 10616 |
| Western Hydrostatics Inc (PA) | 3594 | E | 951 784-2133 | 10636 |
| Cody Cylinder Service LLC | 3599 | E | 951 786-3650 | 10783 |
| D G A Machine Shop Inc | 3599 | F | 951 354-2113 | 10797 |
| Future Tech Metals Inc | 3599 | E | 951 781-4801 | 10846 |
| Jaffa Precision Engrg Inc | 3599 | F | 951 278-8797 | 10902 |
| Jmc Closing Co LLC | 3599 | E | 951 278-9900 | 10910 |
| Metric Machining (PA) | 3599 | E | 909 947-9222 | 10975 |
| Alectro Inc | 3612 | F | 909 590-9521 | 11203 |
| Unique Lighting Systems Inc | 3648 | E | 800 955-4831 | 11630 |
| Bourns Inc (PA) | 3677 | C | 951 781-5500 | 12832 |
| Astro Seal Inc | 3679 | E | 951 787-6670 | 12917 |
| Impact LLC | 3679 | E | 714 546-6000 | 12998 |
| L T Seroge Inc | 3699 | F | 951 354-7141 | 13267 |
| Coachworks Holdings Inc | 3711 | F | 951 684-9585 | 13345 |
| Krystal Infinity LLC | 3713 | B | | 13415 |
| Automax Styling Inc | 3714 | E | 951 530-1876 | 13462 |
| Dee Engineering Inc | 3714 | E | 909 947-5616 | 13483 |
| Evans Walker Inc | 3714 | E | 951 784-7223 | 13497 |
| Owen Trailers Inc | 3715 | E | 951 361-4557 | 13617 |
| Collins Aerospace | 3728 | E | 951 351-5659 | 13812 |
| Luxfer Inc (DH) | 3728 | D | 951 684-5110 | 13895 |
| Zenith Manufacturing Inc | 3728 | E | 818 767-2106 | 13994 |
| K & N Engineering Inc (PA) | 3751 | A | 951 826-4000 | 14061 |
| Two Brothers Racing Inc | 3751 | E | 714 550-6070 | 14073 |
| Fleetwood Travel Trlrs Ind Inc (DH) | 3792 | C | 951 354-3000 | 14120 |
| Bourns Inc | 3825 | E | 951 781-5690 | 14502 |
| DOE & Ingalls Cal Oper LLC | 3826 | E | 951 801-7175 | 14653 |
| Brenner-Fiedler & Assoc Inc (PA) | 3829 | E | 562 404-2721 | 14850 |
| Irrometer Company Inc | 3829 | E | 951 682-9505 | 14886 |
| Foot In Motion Inc | 3842 | E | 312 752-0990 | 15348 |
| Cummings Resources LLC | 3993 | E | 951 248-1130 | 15964 |
| Fusion Sign & Design Inc (PA) | 3993 | F | 877 477-8777 | 15981 |
| Valley Enerprises Inc | 3993 | E | 951 789-0843 | 16062 |
| Pierco Incorporated | 3999 | F | 909 251-7100 | 16205 |
| Gtt International Inc | 5023 | E | 951 788-8729 | 16427 |
| Unique Carpets Ltd | 5023 | D | 951 352-8125 | 16437 |
| Reliable Wholesale Lumber Inc | 5031 | E | 951 300-2500 | 16457 |
| Data Physics Corporation (PA) | 5045 | F | 408 437-0100 | 16518 |
| Western Lighting Inds Inc | 5063 | E | 626 969-6820 | 16680 |
| Pepsi-Cola Metro Btlg Co Inc | 5078 | E | 951 697-3200 | 16786 |
| Hulsey Contracting Inc | 5082 | E | 951 549-3665 | 16790 |
| Cibaria International Inc | 5149 | E | 951 823-8490 | 17181 |
| Premier Fuel Distributors Inc | 5172 | C | 760 423-3610 | 17254 |
| Dixieline Lumber Company LLC | 5211 | B | 951 224-8491 | 17328 |
| Parex Usa Inc | 5211 | E | 951 653-3549 | 17341 |
| Albertsons LLC | 5411 | D | 951 656-6603 | 17366 |
| Dillon Companies Inc | 5411 | C | 951 352-8353 | 17375 |
| Commander Boats | 5551 | E | 951 273-0100 | 17479 |
| Fairprice Enterprises Inc | 5713 | D | 951 684-8578 | 17527 |
| Alin Party Supply Co | 5947 | E | 951 682-7441 | 17654 |
| Brimad Enterprises Inc | 7312 | F | 951 354-8187 | 17784 |
| Mainstreet Communication Inc (PA) | 7334 | F | 951 682-2005 | 17814 |
| CCS Inc | 7372 | E | 888 256-8901 | 18154 |
| Stromasys Inc | 7372 | D | 919 239-8450 | 18842 |
| Contract IT Experts LLC | 7389 | F | 702 466-5022 | 19083 |
| Surveillance Systems Group Inc | 7389 | F | 877 687-3939 | 19137 |
| Scher Tire Inc (PA) | 7534 | E | 951 343-3100 | 19154 |
| Grech Motors LLC (PA) | 7694 | E | 951 688-8347 | 19230 |
| Innovative Emergency Equipment | 7699 | E | 951 222-2270 | 19264 |
| Peggs Company Inc (PA) | 7699 | C | 800 242-8416 | 19275 |
| Current Renewables Engrg Inc | 8711 | F | 951 405-1733 | 19386 |
| MSM Industries Inc | 8711 | E | 951 735-0834 | 19407 |

### RLLNG HLS EST, CA - Los Angeles County

| | SIC | EMP | PHONE | ENTRY# |
|---|---|---|---|---|
| National Media Inc (HQ) | 2711 | E | 310 377-6877 | 4167 |
| Malmberg Engineering Inc | 3599 | E | 925 606-6500 | 10956 |
| Dincloud Inc | 7372 | D | 310 929-1101 | 18242 |
| Apex Energy LLC (HQ) | 8711 | F | 310 377-5579 | 19378 |

### ROCKLIN, CA - Placer County

| | SIC | EMP | PHONE | ENTRY# |
|---|---|---|---|---|
| Mallard Creek Inc | 2421 | E | 916 645-1681 | 3073 |
| Jeld-Wen Inc | 2431 | C | 916 782-4900 | 3151 |
| Amazing Facts Inc | 2731 | D | 916 434-3880 | 4311 |
| Cell Marque Corporation | 2835 | E | 916 746-8900 | 5745 |
| Progressive Technology | 3253 | F | 916 632-6715 | 7272 |
| Justified Performance LLC | 3441 | F | 916 771-8994 | 8161 |
| Roseville Precision Inc | 3444 | E | 916 645-1628 | 8561 |
| Energy Absorption Systems Inc | 3499 | C | 916 645-8181 | 9284 |
| Titans of Cnc Inc | 3559 | F | 916 203-2430 | 9904 |
| Greenheck Fan Corporation | 3564 | D | 916 626-3400 | 9988 |
| Oracle America Inc | 3571 | F | 303 272-6473 | 10187 |
| Parallax Incorporated | 3571 | E | 916 624-8333 | 10192 |
| Sitek Process Solutions | 3674 | F | 916 797-9000 | 12712 |
| Galil Motion Control Inc | 3823 | E | 800 377-6329 | 14417 |
| Asa Corporation | 3826 | F | 530 305-3720 | 14616 |
| Soniya Valley LLC | 3999 | F | 916 221-4313 | 16235 |
| Capitol Air Systems Inc | 4923 | E | 916 259-1200 | 16350 |
| Orora Packaging Solutions | 5113 | D | 916 645-8100 | 17013 |
| Satellite Av LLC | 5731 | E | 916 677-0720 | 17544 |
| Oracle Corporation | 7372 | B | 916 315-3500 | 18634 |
| Oracle Corporation | 7372 | E | 916 315-3500 | 18635 |
| Totalrewards Software Inc | 7372 | E | 916 632-1000 | 18888 |

### ROHNERT PARK, CA - Sonoma County

| | SIC | EMP | PHONE | ENTRY# |
|---|---|---|---|---|
| Marmot Mountain LLC (HQ) | 2329 | C | 888 357-3262 | 2633 |
| North Bay Rhblitation Svcs Inc (PA) | 2399 | C | 707 585-1991 | 3032 |
| World Centric | 2679 | D | 707 241-9190 | 4058 |
| Asm Precision Inc | 3444 | F | 707 584-7950 | 8384 |
| Rieke LLC | 3466 | C | 707 238-9250 | 8812 |
| Parker-Hannifin Corporation | 3594 | F | 707 584-7558 | 10635 |
| Parker-Hannifin Corporation | 3625 | C | 707 584-7558 | 11338 |
| KG Technologies Inc (PA) | 3679 | F | 888 513-1874 | 13019 |
| Idex Health & Science LLC (HQ) | 3821 | D | 707 588-2000 | 14340 |
| Alembic Inc | 3931 | F | 707 523-2611 | 15711 |
| OHagin Manufacturing Company | 3999 | D | 707 322-2402 | 16190 |
| Lemo USA Inc | 5065 | D | 707 206-3700 | 16714 |
| Designit Global LLC | 8711 | E | 707 584-4000 | 19389 |
| Trinity Engineering | 8711 | F | 707 585-2959 | 19427 |
| Quarterwave Corp | 8748 | E | 707 793-9105 | 19568 |

### ROLLING HILLS, CA - Los Angeles County

| | SIC | EMP | PHONE | ENTRY# |
|---|---|---|---|---|
| California Digital Inc (PA) | 3577 | D | 310 217-0500 | 10340 |

### ROLLING HILLS ESTATE, CA - Los Angeles County

| | SIC | EMP | PHONE | ENTRY# |
|---|---|---|---|---|
| Graphic Prints Inc | 2396 | E | 310 870-1239 | 3008 |

### ROMOLAND, CA - Riverside County

| | SIC | EMP | PHONE | ENTRY# |
|---|---|---|---|---|
| Datatronic Distribution Inc | 3612 | F | | 11209 |

### ROSEMEAD, CA - Los Angeles County

| | SIC | EMP | PHONE | ENTRY# |
|---|---|---|---|---|
| Lonix Pharmaceutical Inc | 2023 | F | 626 287-4700 | 767 |
| Chinese Overseas Mktg Svc Corp (PA) | 2741 | D | 626 280-8588 | 4379 |
| Prographics Inc | 2752 | E | 626 287-0417 | 4741 |
| BF Suma Pharmaceuticals Inc | 2834 | D | 626 285-8366 | 5367 |
| Tur-Bo Jet Products Co Inc | 3677 | D | 626 285-1294 | 12862 |
| Hermetic Seal Corporation (DH) | 3679 | E | 626 443-8931 | 12995 |
| HCC Industries Leasing Inc (HQ) | 3823 | F | 626 443-8933 | 14422 |
| Beckman Instruments Inc | 3826 | D | 626 309-0110 | 14624 |
| J F McCaughin Co | 3952 | F | 626 573-3000 | 15886 |

### ROSEVILLE, CA - Placer County

| | SIC | EMP | PHONE | ENTRY# |
|---|---|---|---|---|
| Heron Innovators Inc | 1629 | F | 916 408-6601 | 397 |
| Lancaster Burns Cnstr Inc | 1742 | C | 916 624-8404 | 476 |
| Nates Fine Foods LLC | 2038 | E | 310 897-2690 | 1040 |
| California Bottling Company | 2086 | E | 916 772-1000 | 1873 |
| Sierrapine A California Limited Partnership | 2431 | B | 800 676-3339 | 3190 |
| Providence Publications LLC | 2741 | E | 916 774-4000 | 4454 |
| HB Fuller Company | 2891 | E | 916 787-6000 | 6230 |
| Performance Polymer Tech LLC | 3061 | E | 916 677-1414 | 6475 |
| Well Above Bottling & Canning | 3221 | E | 916 918-1946 | 7187 |

# GEOGRAPHIC SECTION

**SACRAMENTO, CA**

| | SIC | EMP | PHONE | ENTRY# |
|---|---|---|---|---|
| Basalite Building Products LLC (HQ) | 3272 | E | 707 678-1901 | 7313 |
| Teichert Inc | 3273 | E | 916 783-7132 | 7517 |
| Camblin Steel Service Inc | 3449 | D | 916 644-1300 | 8694 |
| Swiss-Tech Machining LLC | 3451 | E | 916 797-6010 | 8733 |
| Advanced Metal Finishing LLC | 3471 | E | 530 888-7772 | 8908 |
| Kenco Engineering Inc | 3531 | E | 916 782-8494 | 9430 |
| Harris & Bruno Machine Co Inc (PA) | 3555 | D | 916 781-7676 | 9768 |
| Pacific Coast Optics LLC | 3559 | F | 916 789-0111 | 9887 |
| Iosafe Inc | 3572 | F | 888 984-6723 | 10248 |
| Precision Manufacturing | 3599 | F | 408 460-2435 | 11046 |
| Arrive Technologies Inc | 3674 | F | 916 715-9775 | 12331 |
| Ca Inc | 3674 | E | 800 405-5540 | 12374 |
| Microsemi Stor Solutions Inc | 3674 | E | 916 788-3300 | 12582 |
| New Vision Display Inc (DH) | 3679 | E | 916 786-8111 | 13047 |
| Sinister Mfg Company Inc | 3714 | E | 916 772-9253 | 13575 |
| Garner Products Inc | 3812 | F | 916 784-0200 | 14190 |
| Keysight Technologies Inc | 3825 | E | 916 788-5571 | 14543 |
| Pasco Scientific (PA) | 3826 | C | 916 786-3800 | 14703 |
| Pride Industries One Inc | 3999 | A | 916 788-2100 | 16209 |
| Pride Industries (PA) | 4226 | E | 916 788-2100 | 16294 |
| Industrial Cont Svcs - CA N LL | 5085 | D | 916 781-2775 | 16878 |
| Empire Paper Corporation | 5112 | F | 510 534-2700 | 16990 |
| Bel Air Mart | 5411 | D | 916 786-6101 | 17369 |
| Integrated Charts Inc | 7372 | E | 855 698-2232 | 18424 |
| Act-On Software Inc | 7379 | E | 503 530-1555 | 19024 |

## ROWLAND HEIGHTS, CA - Los Angeles County

| | SIC | EMP | PHONE | ENTRY# |
|---|---|---|---|---|
| Cosmos Food Co Inc | 2099 | E | 323 221-9142 | 2173 |
| Silao Tortilleria Inc | 2099 | E | 626 961-0761 | 2353 |
| Novolex Bagcraft Inc | 2673 | D | 626 912-2481 | 3975 |
| Wakool Transport | 3537 | D | 626 723-3100 | 9537 |
| Istarusa Group | 3571 | E | 888 989-1189 | 10170 |
| Suzhou South | 3578 | B | 626 322-0101 | 10460 |

## ROYAL OAKS, CA - Santa Cruz County

| | SIC | EMP | PHONE | ENTRY# |
|---|---|---|---|---|
| Falcon Trading Company (PA) | 2099 | C | 831 786-7000 | 2196 |
| Kristich-Monterey Pipe Company | 3272 | F | 831 724-4186 | 7352 |
| Cal Southern Seafood Inc (PA) | 5146 | E | 805 698-8262 | 17155 |

## RUTHERFORD, CA - Napa County

| | SIC | EMP | PHONE | ENTRY# |
|---|---|---|---|---|
| Honig Vineyard and Winery LLC | 0172 | E | 707 963-5618 | 17 |
| Cakebread Cellars | 2084 | D | 707 963-5221 | 1493 |
| Caymus Vineyards | 2084 | E | 707 963-4204 | 1498 |
| Frogs Leap Winery | 2084 | E | 707 963-4704 | 1580 |
| Grgich Hills Cellar | 2084 | E | 707 963-2784 | 1602 |
| Inglenook | 2084 | E | 707 968-1100 | 1619 |
| Niebam-Cppola Estate Winery LP (PA) | 2084 | C | 707 968-1100 | 1692 |
| Pernod Ricard Usa LLC | 2084 | D | 707 967-7770 | 1705 |
| Rutherford Hill Winery | 2084 | B | 707 963-1871 | 1736 |
| St Supery Inc (DH) | 2084 | E | 707 963-4507 | 1759 |
| Swanson Family Estate (DH) | 2084 | E | 707 754-4018 | 1772 |
| Treasury Wine Estates Americas | 2085 | E | 707 967-5200 | 1848 |
| Peju Prvnce Wnery A Cal Ltd PR | 5921 | D | 800 446-7358 | 17629 |

## SACRAMENTO, CA - Sacramento County

| | SIC | EMP | PHONE | ENTRY# |
|---|---|---|---|---|
| Teichert Inc | 1442 | D | 916 386-6900 | 328 |
| Triamid Cnstr Centl Cal Inc | 1531 | E | 916 858-0397 | 353 |
| Valley Communications Inc (PA) | 1731 | E | 916 349-7300 | 472 |
| Keystone Door & Bldg Sup Inc | 1751 | E | 916 623-8100 | 495 |
| Bagatelos Glass Systems Inc (PA) | 1793 | E | 916 364-3600 | 539 |
| Rowar Corporation | 1799 | F | 916 626-3030 | 571 |
| Ellensburg Lamb Company Inc (HQ) | 2011 | F | 530 758-3091 | 595 |
| Transhumance Holding Co Inc (PA) | 2011 | E | 530 758-3091 | 618 |
| Transhumance Inc | 2011 | B | 530 758-3091 | 620 |
| Crystal Cream & Butter Co (HQ) | 2026 | E | 916 444-7200 | 831 |
| HP Hood LLC | 2026 | B | 916 379-9266 | 839 |
| Farmers Rice Cooperative (PA) | 2044 | E | 916 923-5100 | 1075 |
| Freeport Bakery Inc | 2051 | E | 916 442-4256 | 1202 |
| Mary Anns Baking Co Inc | 2051 | C | 916 681-7444 | 1227 |
| Bennetts Baking Company | 2053 | F | 916 481-3349 | 1285 |
| Sacramento Rendering Co | 2077 | D | 916 363-4821 | 1389 |
| SRC Milling Co LLC | 2077 | E | 916 363-4821 | 1390 |
| American Bottling Company | 2086 | E | 916 929-3575 | 1860 |
| American Bottling Company | 2086 | D | 916 929-7777 | 1861 |
| Pepsi-Cola Metro Btlg Co Inc | 2086 | E | 916 423-1000 | 1922 |
| Reyes Coca-Cola Bottling LLC | 2086 | B | 209 466-9501 | 1939 |
| Sacramento Coca-Cola Btlg Inc (HQ) | 2086 | B | 916 928-2300 | 1957 |
| Seven Up Btlg Co San Francisco | 2086 | C | 916 929-7777 | 1962 |
| Watercor of Central States Inc | 2086 | E | 916 290-4591 | 1972 |
| Blue Diamond Growers | 2099 | C | 916 446-8464 | 2143 |
| Chefsattraction LLC | 2099 | E | 310 800-3778 | 2166 |
| Diamond Blue Growers (PA) | 2099 | A | 800 987-2329 | 2183 |
| Gh Foods Ca LLC (DH) | 2099 | B | 916 844-1140 | 2213 |
| Danoc Manufacturing Corp | 2337 | F | 916 455-2876 | 2722 |
| California Cab & Store Fix | 2431 | E | 916 386-1340 | 3113 |
| Califrnia Mantel Fireplace Co (PA) | 2431 | E | 916 925-5775 | 3117 |
| Composite Technology Intl Inc | 2431 | D | 916 551-1850 | 3121 |
| Dorris Lumber and Moulding Co (PA) | 2431 | D | 916 452-7531 | 3131 |
| Premier Woodworking LLC | 2431 | E | 916 999-0050 | 3182 |
| River City Millwork Inc | 2431 | E | 916 364-8981 | 3185 |
| SETZER FOREST PRODUCTS INC (PA) | 2431 | C | 916 442-2555 | 3187 |
| California Cabinet & Str Fixs | 2434 | E | 916 681-0901 | 3226 |
| John C Destefano | 2434 | E | 916 276-4056 | 3244 |
| Kitchens Now Inc | 2434 | E | 916 229-8224 | 3249 |
| General Truss Company Inc | 2439 | F | 916 388-9300 | 3307 |
| Pacific Pallet Exchange Inc | 2448 | E | 916 448-5589 | 3351 |
| Valley Pallet Inc | 2448 | F | 916 381-7954 | 3364 |
| California Cascade Industries | 2491 | C | 916 736-3353 | 3401 |
| Beauty Craft Furniture Corp | 2511 | E | 916 428-2238 | 3434 |
| Lotus Bed Solutions LLC | 2511 | F | 415 756-5099 | 3448 |
| Capitol Store Fixtures | 2521 | E | 916 646-9096 | 3562 |
| Clerprem USA Corp | 2531 | E | 415 856-9001 | 3620 |
| Evergreen Paper and Energy LLC (PA) | 2611 | D | 802 357-1003 | 3756 |
| Capital Corrugated LLC | 2653 | D | 916 388-7848 | 3828 |
| Northwest Pallets LLC | 2653 | E | 916 736-2787 | 3869 |
| Admail West Inc | 2655 | D | 916 554-5755 | 3899 |
| Peter | 2674 | E | 916 588-9954 | 3993 |
| Imperial Trade Bindery Inc | 2675 | E | 916 443-6142 | 3996 |
| American City Bus Journals Inc | 2711 | C | 916 447-7661 | 4064 |
| Chico Community Publishing | 2711 | C | 916 498-1234 | 4091 |
| El Dorado Newspapers (DH) | 2711 | E | 916 321-1826 | 4109 |
| Jck Legacy Company (HQ) | 2711 | D | 916 321-1844 | 4137 |
| Lee Publishing Company | 2711 | F | 916 284-0022 | 4148 |
| McClatchy Newspapers Inc (DH) | 2711 | A | 916 321-1855 | 4154 |
| North Area News (PA) | 2711 | E | 916 486-1248 | 4171 |
| Olympic Cascade Publishing (DH) | 2711 | E | 916 321-1000 | 4176 |
| Pacific Northwest Pubg Co Inc | 2711 | B | 916 321-1828 | 4177 |
| Comstock Publishing Inc | 2721 | F | 916 364-1000 | 4241 |
| Inside East Sacramento | 2741 | E | 916 443-5087 | 4417 |
| Peoplefinders Ngt Por Priof | 2741 | E | 916 341-0227 | 4448 |
| American Lithographers Inc | 2752 | D | 916 441-5392 | 4509 |
| Commerce Printing Services | 2752 | D | 916 442-8100 | 4563 |
| Delta Print Group LLC | 2752 | E | 916 928-0801 | 4585 |
| Fong Fong Prtrs Lthgrphers Inc | 2752 | E | 916 739-1313 | 4613 |
| Fruitridge Prtg Lithograph Inc (PA) | 2752 | E | 916 452-9213 | 4618 |
| Gsl Fine Lithographers | 2752 | E | 916 231-1410 | 4626 |
| Paul Baker Printing Inc | 2752 | E | 916 969-8317 | 4720 |
| River City Printers LLC | 2752 | E | 916 638-8400 | 4754 |
| Sierra Office Systems Pdts Inc (PA) | 2752 | D | 916 369-0491 | 4763 |
| Terry Grimes Graphic Center of Sacramento Inc | 2752 | E | 916 453-1332 | 4783 |
| Thermcraft Inc | 2752 | F | 916 363-9411 | 4785 |
| Consolidated Eagle Press Inc | 2759 | E | 916 383-7850 | 4864 |
| Delta Web Printing Inc | 2759 | E | 916 375-0044 | 4872 |
| Hironaka Promotions LLC | 2759 | E | 916 631-8470 | 4892 |
| Messer LLC | 2813 | D | 916 381-1606 | 5053 |
| Licap Technologies Inc | 2819 | D | 916 329-8099 | 5099 |
| Nivagen Pharmaceuticals Inc (PA) | 2834 | D | 916 364-1662 | 5576 |
| Novartis Pharmaceuticals Corp | 2834 | C | 862 778-8300 | 5579 |
| Procter & Gamble Mfg Co | 2841 | B | 916 383-3800 | 5880 |
| Envirnmntal Cmpliance Pros Inc | 2842 | E | 916 953-9006 | 5903 |
| Propel Fuels California Inc | 2869 | F | 916 716-7605 | 6155 |
| Innovative Healthcare Svcs LLC | 2899 | E | 909 280-0559 | 6297 |
| Reed & Graham Inc | 2951 | E | 888 381-0800 | 6369 |
| D & T Fiberglass Inc | 3089 | E | 916 383-9012 | 6790 |
| Fresno Precision Plastics Inc | 3089 | D | 916 689-5284 | 6833 |
| Jadra Inc | 3089 | D | 916 921-3399 | 6871 |
| Liqui-Box Corporation | 3089 | E | 916 381-7054 | 6897 |
| Atlas Specialties Corporation (PA) | 3231 | E | 503 636-8182 | 7211 |
| Ultra Glass | 3231 | F | 916 338-3911 | 7246 |
| Cemex California Cement LLC | 3241 | B | 760 381-7616 | 7253 |
| Forterra Pipe & Precast LLC | 3272 | D | 916 379-9695 | 7337 |
| Pacific Corrugated Pipe Co LLC | 3272 | E | 916 383-4891 | 7369 |
| Quikrete California LLC | 3272 | E | 916 689-8840 | 7380 |
| Quikrete Companies LLC | 3272 | E | 510 490-4670 | 7384 |
| Elite Ready-Mix LLC | 3273 | E | 916 366-4627 | 7445 |
| Teichert Inc | 3273 | D | 916 386-6974 | 7516 |
| Intexforms Inc | 3299 | D | 916 388-9933 | 7592 |
| Omega Products Corp | 3299 | E | 916 635-3335 | 7596 |
| Oneto Metal Products Corp | 3316 | E | 916 681-6555 | 7660 |
| Capitol Iron Works Inc | 3441 | E | 916 381-1554 | 8115 |
| Capitol Steel Products | 3441 | E | 916 383-3368 | 8117 |
| Davison Iron Works Inc | 3441 | E | 916 381-2121 | 8132 |
| Intake Screens Inc | 3441 | F | 916 665-2727 | 8153 |
| Architectural Blomberg LLC | 3442 | E | 916 428-8060 | 8254 |
| Blomberg Building Materials (PA) | 3442 | D | 916 428-8060 | 8258 |
| Metal Manufacturing Co Inc | 3442 | E | 916 922-3484 | 8276 |

Employee Codes: A=Over 500 employees, B=251-500
C=101-250, D=51-100, E=20-50, F=10-19, G=1-9

# SACRAMENTO, CA

## GEOGRAPHIC SECTION

| | SIC | EMP | PHONE | ENTRY# |
|---|---|---|---|---|
| ITW Blding Cmponents Group Inc | 3443 | E | 916 387-0116 | 8318 |
| S & H Welding Inc | 3443 | F | 916 386-8921 | 8332 |
| Atco Rubber Products Inc | 3444 | D | 916 649-8690 | 8385 |
| Microform Precision LLC | 3444 | D | 916 419-0580 | 8509 |
| A&A Metal Finishing Entps LLC | 3471 | E | 916 442-1063 | 8904 |
| Aluminum Coating Tech Inc | 3471 | E | 916 442-1063 | 8917 |
| Class a Powdercoat Inc | 3479 | E | 916 681-7474 | 9058 |
| Pacific Powder Coating Inc | 3479 | E | 916 381-1154 | 9099 |
| TNT Industrial Contractors Inc (PA) | 3531 | E | 916 395-8400 | 9442 |
| Elevator Industries Inc | 3534 | F | 916 921-1495 | 9470 |
| Fremont Package Express | 3537 | F | 916 541-1812 | 9518 |
| Elite Service Experts Inc (PA) | 3559 | E | 916 568-1400 | 9851 |
| Elliott Company | 3561 | E | 916 920-5451 | 9919 |
| Sulzer Pump Solutions US Inc | 3561 | E | 916 925-8508 | 9942 |
| Ebara Technologies Inc (DH) | 3563 | D | 916 920-5451 | 9961 |
| Martin Sprocket & Gear Inc | 3566 | E | 916 441-7172 | 10042 |
| Sale 121 Corp (PA) | 3572 | E | 888 233-7667 | 10273 |
| Smart Fog | 3585 | E | 800 921-5230 | 10515 |
| York International Corporation | 3585 | F | 916 283-7650 | 10530 |
| Langills General Machine Inc | 3599 | E | 916 452-0167 | 10938 |
| Mitsubshi Chem Crbn Fibr Cmpst (DH) | 3624 | C | 916 386-1733 | 11300 |
| Elevator Controls Company LLC | 3625 | D | 916 428-1708 | 11321 |
| Lumens | 3625 | E | 916 231-1952 | 11331 |
| Novate Solutions Inc | 3625 | F | 916 641-2725 | 11337 |
| Washoe Equipment Inc | 3645 | F | 916 395-4700 | 11508 |
| Mw McWong International Inc (PA) | 3648 | F | 916 371-8080 | 11614 |
| Noopl Inc | 3651 | E | 916 400-3976 | 11683 |
| Aldetec Inc | 3663 | E | 916 453-3382 | 11801 |
| Jampro Antennas Inc (PA) | 3663 | E | 916 383-1177 | 11869 |
| Thermal Conductive Bonding Inc (PA) | 3674 | E | 408 920-0255 | 12768 |
| Golden State Fire Appratus Inc | 3711 | E | 916 330-1638 | 13355 |
| Siemens Mobility Inc | 3711 | A | 916 681-3000 | 13387 |
| Pacific Truck Tank Inc | 3713 | E | 916 379-9280 | 13422 |
| John Boyd Enterprises Inc (PA) | 3714 | C | 916 381-4790 | 13522 |
| Teeco Products Inc | 3714 | E | 916 688-3535 | 13582 |
| Textron Aviation Inc | 3721 | C | 916 929-5656 | 13695 |
| Siemens Industry Inc | 3822 | C | 916 681-3000 | 14368 |
| California Dept Wtr Resources | 3823 | E | 916 651-9203 | 14391 |
| Wsglass Holdings Inc | 3827 | E | 916 388-5885 | 14833 |
| All Weather Inc | 3829 | D | 916 928-1000 | 14841 |
| Canyon Products Corporation | 3842 | E | 916 361-1687 | 15329 |
| Hand Biomechanics Lab Inc | 3842 | F | 916 923-5073 | 15355 |
| Medical Device Bus Svcs Inc | 3842 | E | 916 285-9125 | 15375 |
| Dentists Supply Company | 3843 | F | 888 253-1223 | 15451 |
| Poolmaster Inc (PA) | 3944 | E | 916 567-9800 | 15765 |
| Balanced Body Inc (PA) | 3949 | E | 916 388-2838 | 15784 |
| Laser Recharge Inc (PA) | 3955 | E | 916 813-2717 | 15897 |
| Ainor Signs Inc | 3993 | E | 916 348-4370 | 15940 |
| Illuminated Creations Inc | 3993 | E | 916 924-1936 | 15986 |
| Pacific Neon | 3993 | E | 916 927-0527 | 16018 |
| Weidner Archtctral Sgng/Huse S | 3993 | D | 800 561-7446 | 16065 |
| Young Electric Sign Company | 3993 | E | 916 419-8101 | 16071 |
| Destination Aesthetics Inc | 3999 | E | 916 844-4913 | 16123 |
| Procter & Gamble Mfg Co | 3999 | E | 916 442-3135 | 16210 |
| River City Waste Recyclers LLC (PA) | 4953 | E | 916 383-5511 | 16363 |
| Visions Recycling Inc | 4953 | E | 916 564-9121 | 16367 |
| Dana Motors Inc (PA) | 5013 | F | 916 920-0150 | 16379 |
| A Teichert & Son Inc (HQ) | 5032 | E | 916 484-3011 | 16462 |
| River City Building Supply Inc | 5032 | F | 916 375-8322 | 16482 |
| Southerncarlson Inc | 5032 | F | 916 375-8322 | 16484 |
| Capitol Steel Company | 5051 | F | 916 924-3195 | 16610 |
| Flight Light Inc | 5063 | F | 916 394-2800 | 16653 |
| CFM Equipment Distributors Inc (PA) | 5075 | E | 916 447-7022 | 16776 |
| Caliextractions LLC | 5084 | F | 916 519-7649 | 16809 |
| Lgg Industrial Inc | 5085 | D | 916 366-9340 | 16880 |
| Valley Rubber & Gasket Company Inc | 5085 | D | 916 369-8885 | 16904 |
| West Coast Paper Company | 5085 | E | 916 599-1113 | 16907 |
| Burgett Incorporated (PA) | 5099 | D | 916 567-9999 | 16973 |
| Manufacturing Logistics Inc | 5149 | E | 916 387-9700 | 17195 |
| Coral Port LLC | 5199 | E | 530 761-6400 | 17291 |
| Burnett Sons Planing Mill Lbr | 5211 | E | 916 442-0493 | 17326 |
| Bel Air Mart | 5411 | C | 916 739-8647 | 17370 |
| Bel Air Mart | 5411 | D | 916 920-2493 | 17371 |
| Bel Air Mart | 5411 | F | 916 972-0555 | 17372 |
| Wilson Trophy Co California | 5999 | F | 916 927-9733 | 17726 |
| Pacific Copy and Print | 7334 | E | 916 928-8434 | 17815 |
| Califrnia Srvying Drftg Sup In (PA) | 7353 | E | 916 344-0232 | 17850 |
| Goodwin-Cole Company Inc | 7359 | E | 916 381-8888 | 17855 |
| Emilykate LLC | 7371 | F | 916 761-6261 | 17916 |
| Lpa Insurance Agency Inc | 7372 | D | 916 286-7850 | 18505 |
| Meditab Software Inc | 7372 | C | 844 463-3482 | 18535 |
| New Generation Software Inc | 7372 | E | 916 920-2200 | 18582 |
| System Integrators Inc | 7373 | C | 916 830-2400 | 18995 |
| AAA Signs Inc | 7534 | D | 916 568-3456 | 19150 |
| Eisenbeiss Inc | 7699 | E | 916 262-7656 | 19255 |
| Fluid Tech Hydraulics Inc | 7699 | E | 916 681-0888 | 19258 |
| Bdg Innovations LLC (PA) | 8711 | E | 855 725-9555 | 19383 |
| Kratos Unmnned Arial Systems I (HQ) | 8711 | C | 916 991-1990 | 19401 |
| League of California Cities (PA) | 8743 | D | 916 658-8200 | 19550 |

## SAINT HELENA, CA - Napa County

| | SIC | EMP | PHONE | ENTRY# |
|---|---|---|---|---|
| Raymond Vineyard & Cellar Inc (DH) | 0172 | E | 707 963-3141 | 25 |
| Harold Smith & Son Inc | 1629 | E | 707 963-7977 | 396 |
| Burgess Cellars Inc | 2084 | E | 707 963-4766 | 1490 |
| C Mondavi & Family (PA) | 2084 | D | 707 967-2200 | 1492 |
| Chappellet Vineyard | 2084 | D | 707 286-4219 | 1502 |
| Chappellet Winery Inc (PA) | 2084 | D | 707 286-4219 | 1503 |
| Dana Estates Inc (PA) | 2084 | E | 707 963-4365 | 1524 |
| Del Dotto Vineyards | 2084 | E | 707 603-1084 | 1532 |
| Demeine Estates LLC | 2084 | E | 707 531-7838 | 1537 |
| Duckhorn Wine Company (DH) | 2084 | E | 707 963-7108 | 1545 |
| Flora Springs Wine Company | 2084 | F | 707 963-5711 | 1571 |
| FN Cellars LLC | 2084 | F | 707 967-9600 | 1573 |
| Hall Wines LLC | 2084 | E | 707 967-2626 | 1608 |
| Huneeus Vintners LLC (PA) | 2084 | F | 707 286-2724 | 1617 |
| Joseph Phelps Vineyards LLC (DH) | 2084 | E | 707 963-2745 | 1639 |
| Merryvale Vineyards LLC | 2084 | E | 707 963-2225 | 1679 |
| New Vavin Inc | 2084 | E | 707 963-5972 | 1688 |
| Rombauer Vineyards LLC (HQ) | 2084 | D | 707 963-5170 | 1731 |
| Round Hill Cellars | 2084 | E | 707 968-3200 | 1732 |
| Spring Mountain Vineyards Inc | 2084 | E | 707 967-4188 | 1757 |
| Stone Bridge Cellars Inc (PA) | 2084 | E | 707 963-2745 | 1764 |
| Sutter Home Winery Inc (PA) | 2084 | C | 707 963-3104 | 1767 |
| Sutter Home Winery Inc | 2084 | E | 800 967-4663 | 1771 |
| Thomas Leonardini | 2084 | E | 707 963-9454 | 1783 |
| Tpwc Inc (HQ) | 2084 | D | 877 283-5934 | 1787 |
| Treasury Wine Estates Americas | 2084 | E | 707 963-4812 | 1799 |
| Treasury Wine Estates Americas | 2084 | E | 707 963-7221 | 1800 |
| Treasury Wine Estates Americas | 2084 | E | 707 963-7115 | 1801 |
| Turley Wine Cellars Inc | 2084 | E | 707 968-2700 | 1804 |
| Vintage Wine Estates Inc CA | 2084 | E | 707 921-2600 | 1816 |
| Herdell Prtg & Lithography Inc | 2752 | F | 707 963-3634 | 4631 |
| Gotts Partners LP | 5812 | E | 415 213-2992 | 17581 |
| V Sattui Winery | 5921 | D | 707 963-7774 | 17631 |

## SALIDA, CA - Stanislaus County

| | SIC | EMP | PHONE | ENTRY# |
|---|---|---|---|---|
| Flory Industries (PA) | 3523 | D | 209 545-1167 | 9354 |

## SALINAS, CA - Monterey County

| | SIC | EMP | PHONE | ENTRY# |
|---|---|---|---|---|
| Grupo Flor Corporation | 0139 | D | 559 940-1070 | 3 |
| Merrill Farms LLC (PA) | 0161 | E | 831 424-7365 | 6 |
| Tanimura Antle Fresh Foods Inc (PA) | 0161 | D | 831 455-2950 | 7 |
| Scheid Vineyards Inc (PA) | 0172 | E | 831 455-9990 | 29 |
| Dole Food Company Inc | 0179 | F | 831 422-8871 | 44 |
| Seed Dynamics Inc | 0723 | D | 831 424-1177 | 86 |
| Lhoist North America Ariz Inc | 1442 | E | 831 449-9117 | 317 |
| Reyes Coca-Cola Bottling LLC | 2086 | D | 831 755-8300 | 1942 |
| Monterey Fish Company Inc (PA) | 2092 | E | 831 775-0522 | 2056 |
| Growers Ice Co | 2097 | E | 831 424-5781 | 2109 |
| Braga Fresh Foods LLC (PA) | 2099 | E | 831 756-7614 | 2146 |
| Classic Salads LLC | 2099 | E | 831 763-4520 | 2169 |
| Fresh Express Inc | 2099 | D | 831 770-7600 | 2206 |
| McCormick & Co | 2099 | E | 831 775-3485 | 2276 |
| McCormick & Company Inc | 2099 | F | 831 775-3350 | 2277 |
| Organicgirl LLC | 2099 | A | 831 758-7800 | 2304 |
| Pulmuone Foods Usa Inc | 2099 | B | 831 753-6262 | 2326 |
| International Paper Company | 2621 | E | 831 755-2100 | 3779 |
| Pratt Robert Mann Packg LLC | 2653 | E | 831 789-8300 | 3881 |
| Rm Esop Inc | 2653 | C | 831 789-8300 | 3883 |
| Salinas Valley Wax Paper Co | 2679 | E | 831 424-2747 | 4049 |
| Green Rubber-Kennedy Ag LP (PA) | 3086 | E | 831 753-6100 | 6645 |
| Star Sanitation Services | 3089 | E | 831 754-6794 | 7042 |
| Uv Landscaping LLC | 3271 | F | 831 275-5296 | 7302 |
| Associated Rebar Inc | 3441 | E | 831 758-1820 | 8097 |
| Delta Ironworks Inc | 3446 | F | 831 663-1190 | 8623 |
| Stout Industrial Tech Inc | 3523 | F | 831 455-1004 | 9385 |
| Valley Fabrication Inc | 3523 | D | 831 757-5151 | 9389 |
| Golden State Trck Trlr Repr In | 3537 | E | 888 881-8825 | 9521 |
| A&G Machine Shop Inc | 3599 | E | 831 759-2261 | 10650 |
| El Camino Machine & Wldg LLC (PA) | 3599 | E | 831 758-8309 | 10823 |
| Abrams Electronics Inc | 3643 | F | 831 758-6400 | 11437 |
| Magnetic Circuit Elements Inc | 3679 | F | 831 757-8752 | 13028 |
| Transfirst Corporation | 3822 | E | 831 424-2911 | 14372 |
| Vegetable Growers Supply Co (PA) | 5199 | E | 831 759-4600 | 17312 |
| Albert Maldonado | 7334 | F | 831 758-9040 | 17804 |
| Angkor Engineering Inc | 8711 | F | 831 256-1015 | 19377 |

# GEOGRAPHIC SECTION

## SAN DIEGO, CA

| | SIC | EMP | PHONE | ENTRY# |
|---|---|---|---|---|

### SAMOA, CA - Humboldt County

| | SIC | EMP | PHONE | ENTRY# |
|---|---|---|---|---|
| Western Web Inc | 2752 | E | 707 444-6236 | 4809 |
| United Compost & Organics Inc | 2873 | E | 707 443-4369 | 6183 |

### SAN ANSELMO, CA - Marin County

| USA Tolerance Rings | 3399 | E | 415 457-6711 | 7916 |
|---|---|---|---|---|

### SAN ARDO, CA - Monterey County

| Key Energy Services Inc | 1389 | E | 831 627-2404 | 245 |
|---|---|---|---|---|

### SAN BERNARDINO, CA - San Bernardino County

| | SIC | EMP | PHONE | ENTRY# |
|---|---|---|---|---|
| Stavatti Industries Ltd | 1041 | E | 651 238-5369 | 106 |
| Legend Pump & Well Service Inc | 1381 | E | 909 384-1000 | 162 |
| Nlms Elite Construction Co | 1521 | F | 626 205-8417 | 345 |
| Matich Corporation (PA) | 1611 | D | 909 382-7400 | 375 |
| Nagles Veal Inc | 2011 | E | 909 383-7075 | 608 |
| Kmb Foods Inc (PA) | 2013 | E | 626 447-0545 | 649 |
| Farmdale Creamery LLC | 2026 | D | 909 888-4938 | 834 |
| Live Fresh Corporation | 2037 | C | 909 478-0895 | 1012 |
| Ardent Mills LLC | 2041 | E | 909 887-3407 | 1055 |
| Mars Petcare Us Inc | 2047 | E | 909 887-8131 | 1108 |
| Adams and Brooks Inc | 2064 | C | 909 880-2305 | 1298 |
| Park West Enterprises Inc | 2077 | F | 909 383-8341 | 1388 |
| Pepsico | 2086 | E | 562 818-9429 | 1923 |
| Refresco Beverages US Inc | 2086 | E | 909 915-1400 | 1929 |
| Refresco Beverages US Inc | 2086 | E | 909 915-1430 | 1930 |
| Anitas Mexican Foods Corp (PA) | 2096 | D | 909 884-8706 | 2084 |
| Anitas Mexican Foods Corp | 2096 | D | 909 884-8706 | 2085 |
| Dean Distributors Inc | 2099 | E | 323 587-8147 | 2180 |
| Haley Bros Inc | 2431 | C | 800 854-5951 | 3141 |
| Paramount Windows & Doors | 2431 | F | 909 888-4688 | 3177 |
| United Cabinet Company Inc | 2434 | E | 909 796-3015 | 3277 |
| Nelson Adams Naco Corporation | 2511 | E | 909 256-8938 | 3451 |
| Defoe Furniture For Kids Inc | 2531 | F | 909 947-4459 | 3622 |
| Packaging Corporation America | 2653 | E | 909 888-7008 | 3874 |
| Sun Cmpany of San Brnrdino Cal (HQ) | 2711 | B | 909 889-9666 | 4203 |
| San Brnrdino Cmnty College Dst | 2759 | D | 909 888-6511 | 4958 |
| Shorett Printing Inc (PA) | 2759 | E | 714 545-4689 | 4960 |
| Reagent Chemical & RES Inc | 2819 | E | 909 796-4059 | 5113 |
| Mapei Corporation | 2821 | D | 909 475-4100 | 5176 |
| M & L Pharmaceutical Inc | 2834 | F | 909 890-0078 | 5539 |
| Innocor West LLC | 3069 | A | 909 307-3737 | 6503 |
| Back Support Systems Inc | 3086 | F | 760 329-1472 | 6624 |
| Foamex LP | 3086 | E | 909 824-8981 | 6640 |
| C-Pak Industries Inc | 3089 | E | 909 880-6017 | 6755 |
| Container Options | 3089 | E | 909 478-0045 | 6779 |
| Fiore Stone Inc | 3272 | E | 909 424-0221 | 7331 |
| Holliday Trucking Inc | 3273 | D | 888 273-2200 | 7457 |
| Sample Tile and Stone Inc | 3281 | E | 951 776-8562 | 7545 |
| Usmpc Buyer Inc | 3296 | E | 909 473-3027 | 7583 |
| Tamco (HQ) | 3312 | E | 909 899-0660 | 7630 |
| Caesar Hardware Intl Ltd | 3429 | E | 800 306-3829 | 7985 |
| South Bay Foundry Inc (HQ) | 3441 | E | 909 383-1823 | 8220 |
| Brydenscot Metal Products Inc | 3444 | F | 909 799-0088 | 8395 |
| CMC Steel Us LLC | 3449 | E | 909 646-7827 | 8695 |
| Innovative Metal Inds Inc | 3449 | D | 909 796-6200 | 8699 |
| JLJ Rebar Extreme Inc | 3449 | E | 909 381-9177 | 8700 |
| Anco International Inc | 3494 | E | 909 887-2521 | 9182 |
| American Wire Inc | 3496 | F | 909 884-9990 | 9209 |
| Tree Island Wire (usa) Inc | 3496 | C | 909 899-1673 | 9237 |
| Ground Hog Inc | 3531 | E | 909 478-5700 | 9424 |
| California PCF Trdg Co II Inc | 3537 | E | 951 218-8253 | 9508 |
| Cal-Craft Design Intl Inc | 3545 | F | | 9664 |
| Macroair Technologies Inc (PA) | 3564 | E | 909 890-2270 | 9992 |
| Systems Technology Inc | 3565 | D | 909 799-9950 | 10032 |
| W B Walton Enterprises Inc | 3663 | E | 951 683-0930 | 11975 |
| DSPM Inc | 3677 | E | 714 970-2304 | 12838 |
| Allianz Sweeper Company | 3711 | C | | 13336 |
| Global Environmental Pdts Inc | 3711 | D | 909 713-1600 | 13354 |
| Thermal Solutions Mfg Inc | 3714 | E | 909 796-0754 | 13583 |
| Northrop Grumman Systems Corp | 3812 | D | 703 713-4096 | 14259 |
| Tinker & Rasor | 3812 | E | 909 890-0700 | 14320 |
| Optivus Proton Therapy Inc | 3829 | D | 909 799-8300 | 14906 |
| Semco | 3829 | E | 909 799-9666 | 14917 |
| Quiel Bros Elc Sign Svc Co Inc | 3993 | E | 909 885-4476 | 16024 |
| California Steel Services Inc | 5051 | E | 909 796-2222 | 16609 |
| Wcs Distributing Inc | 5084 | E | 909 888-2015 | 16856 |
| Laymon Candy Co Inc | 5145 | E | 909 825-4408 | 17148 |
| S&E Gourmet Cuts Inc | 5145 | E | 909 370-0155 | 17149 |
| Bfg Supply Co LLC | 5191 | C | 909 591-0461 | 17268 |
| Ocelot Engineering Inc | 5571 | C | 800 841-2960 | 17483 |
| Caldesso LLC | 5999 | D | 909 888-2882 | 17691 |
| Nationwide Technologies Inc | 7372 | E | 909 340-2770 | 18568 |
| Jenco Productions LLC (PA) | 7389 | C | 909 381-9453 | 19099 |
| Jon Steel Erectors Inc | 7692 | E | 909 799-0005 | 19206 |
| Carbide Saw and Tool Inc | 7699 | F | 909 884-9956 | 19248 |
| Lifestream Blood Bank (PA) | 8099 | C | 909 885-6503 | 19337 |

### SAN BRUNO, CA - San Mateo County

| Mill Industries Inc | 3634 | D | 415 862-4394 | 11410 |
|---|---|---|---|---|

### SAN CARLOS, CA - San Mateo County

| | SIC | EMP | PHONE | ENTRY# |
|---|---|---|---|---|
| House of Bagels Inc (PA) | 2051 | F | 650 595-4700 | 1217 |
| Apex Die Corporation | 2675 | D | 650 592-6350 | 3995 |
| Monolith Materials Inc | 2819 | E | 650 933-4957 | 5103 |
| Allakos Inc | 2834 | C | 650 597-5002 | 5306 |
| Iovance Biotherapeutics Inc (PA) | 2834 | B | 650 260-7120 | 5506 |
| Nektar Therapeutics | 2834 | D | 650 622-1790 | 5568 |
| Spring Discovery Inc | 2834 | E | 917 572-1552 | 5669 |
| Atreca Inc | 2836 | C | 650 595-2595 | 5802 |
| Cargo Therapeutics Inc | 2836 | C | 650 499-8950 | 5814 |
| Vaxcyte Inc (PA) | 2836 | D | 650 837-0111 | 5867 |
| Kelly-Moore Paint Company Inc (HQ) | 2851 | C | 650 592-8337 | 6089 |
| Kelly-Moore Paint Company Inc | 2851 | E | 650 595-1654 | 6090 |
| Norcal Materials Inc | 3273 | E | 650 365-4811 | 7481 |
| South Bay Marble Inc | 3281 | F | 650 592-7416 | 7547 |
| Begovic Industries Inc | 3599 | E | 650 594-2861 | 10742 |
| Performex Machining Inc | 3599 | E | 650 595-2228 | 11038 |
| Telecommunications Engrg Assoc | 3663 | F | 650 590-1801 | 11961 |
| Swift Solar Inc | 3674 | E | 650 297-7943 | 12750 |
| Cellink Corporation (PA) | 3679 | D | 650 799-3018 | 12935 |
| Gmw Associates | 3829 | E | 650 802-8292 | 14873 |
| Alpine Biomed Corp | 3841 | D | 650 802-0400 | 14962 |
| Gmw Associates | 5084 | E | 650 802-8292 | 16816 |
| Pacific Rubber & Packing Inc (PA) | 5085 | E | 650 595-5888 | 16886 |
| Colabo Inc | 7372 | E | 650 288-6649 | 18192 |
| Revjet Corporation | 7372 | C | 650 508-2215 | 18739 |
| Rovi Corporation | 7372 | F | 408 562-8400 | 18746 |

### SAN CLEMENTE, CA - Orange County

| | SIC | EMP | PHONE | ENTRY# |
|---|---|---|---|---|
| Left Coast Brewing Company | 2082 | F | 949 218-3961 | 1445 |
| Custom Ingredients Inc (PA) | 2087 | E | 949 276-7995 | 1995 |
| Freshrealm Inc (PA) | 2099 | C | 800 264-1297 | 2207 |
| Futurestitch Inc | 2253 | F | 760 707-2003 | 2471 |
| Hot Shoppe Designs Inc | 2329 | E | 949 487-2828 | 2622 |
| R & R Industries Inc | 2389 | E | 800 234-5611 | 2908 |
| Western Outdoors Publications (PA) | 2711 | E | 949 366-0030 | 4220 |
| R T C Group | 2721 | E | 949 226-2000 | 4292 |
| Taylor Digital | 2759 | E | 949 391-3333 | 4968 |
| International Rubber Pdts Inc (HQ) | 3069 | D | 909 947-1244 | 6504 |
| Kelcourt Plastics Inc (DH) | 3089 | D | 949 361-0774 | 6882 |
| Kui Co Inc | 3089 | E | 949 369-7949 | 6891 |
| Plastics Development Corp | 3089 | E | 949 492-0217 | 6964 |
| Pch Sheet Metal & AC Inc | 3444 | F | 949 361-9905 | 8531 |
| Clean Wave Management Inc | 3562 | E | 949 370-0740 | 9949 |
| Code-In-Motion LLC | 3569 | F | 949 361-2633 | 10084 |
| Snowpure LLC | 3589 | E | 949 240-2188 | 10601 |
| Dana Innovations (PA) | 3651 | C | 949 492-7777 | 11647 |
| Sonance | 3651 | E | 949 492-7777 | 11698 |
| Orca Technologies LLC | 3663 | F | 949 682-3289 | 11909 |
| Traffix Devices Inc (PA) | 3669 | F | 949 361-5663 | 12023 |
| Lippert Components Inc | 3711 | F | 949 259-4000 | 13363 |
| Lippert Components Inc | 3711 | F | 574 312-6277 | 13364 |
| Fleming Metal Fabricators | 3713 | E | 323 723-8203 | 13412 |
| Bunker Corp (PA) | 3714 | D | 949 361-3935 | 13466 |
| Swift Autonomy Inc | 3721 | E | 800 547-9438 | 13694 |
| Swift Engineering Inc | 3728 | D | 949 492-6608 | 13965 |
| Reynard Corporation | 3827 | E | 949 366-8866 | 14816 |
| Composite Manufacturing Inc | 3841 | E | 949 361-7580 | 15047 |
| Dose Medical Corporation | 3841 | F | 949 367-9001 | 15071 |
| Epica Medical Innovations LLC | 3841 | E | 949 238-6323 | 15083 |
| Icu Medical Inc (PA) | 3841 | A | 949 366-2183 | 15111 |
| Rox Medical Inc (PA) | 3841 | E | 949 276-8968 | 15246 |
| Dragon Alliance Inc | 3851 | E | 760 931-4900 | 15599 |
| Electric Visual Evolution LLC (PA) | 3851 | E | 949 940-9125 | 15600 |
| Roberto Martinez Inc | 3911 | F | 800 257-6462 | 15704 |
| Rip Curl Inc | 3949 | E | 714 422-3617 | 15845 |
| Rosen & Rosen Industries Inc | 3949 | D | 949 361-9238 | 15847 |
| Elotek Systems Inc (PA) | 5045 | E | 949 366-4404 | 16520 |
| Streuter Technologies Inc | 5051 | F | 949 369-7676 | 16633 |
| Netsource Technology Inc | 5065 | E | 949 713-0800 | 16725 |
| Liberty Synergistics Inc | 5085 | D | 949 361-1100 | 16881 |
| Matsushita International Corp (PA) | 6799 | D | 949 498-1000 | 17757 |
| Ambit Software LLC | 7372 | F | 949 361-4070 | 18043 |
| Model Match Inc | 7372 | F | 949 525-9405 | 18557 |

Employee Codes: A=Over 500 employees, B=251-500
C=101-250, D=51-100, E=20-50, F=10-19, G=1-9

# SAN DIEGO, CA — GEOGRAPHIC SECTION

## SAN DIEGO, CA - San Diego County

| Company | SIC | EMP | PHONE | ENTRY# |
|---|---|---|---|---|
| NN Jaeschke Inc. | 0781 | E | 858 550-7900 | 97 |
| CP Kelco US Inc. | 1455 | E | 619 595-5000 | 332 |
| Jaime Enterprise Group | 1531 | F | 619 454-7681 | 351 |
| Biotix | 1541 | E | 858 875-5479 | 355 |
| US Joiner LLC | 1629 | E | 619 233-3993 | 399 |
| Atlas Mechanical Inc (PA) | 1711 | D | 858 554-0700 | 404 |
| Pro Installations Inc (HQ) | 1752 | E | | 505 |
| Heavy Metal Steel Company Inc | 1791 | E | 858 433-4800 | 530 |
| Demor Enterprises Inc | 1799 | E | 858 625-0003 | 561 |
| Super Welding Southern Cal Inc | 1799 | E | 619 239-8003 | 574 |
| Yyk Enterprises Operations LLC (PA) | 1799 | C | 619 474-6229 | 581 |
| Old Bbh Inc | 2013 | A | 858 715-4000 | 655 |
| Top Brands Distribution Inc | 2022 | E | 858 578-0319 | 741 |
| El Indio Shops Incorporated | 2023 | D | 619 299-0333 | 754 |
| Von Hoppen Ice Cream | 2024 | F | 858 695-9111 | 818 |
| Cg Financial LLC | 2032 | F | 619 656-2919 | 852 |
| Intelligent Blends LLC | 2043 | E | 858 888-7937 | 1071 |
| Honest Kitchen Inc | 2047 | D | 619 544-0018 | 1101 |
| Fusion Food Factory | 2051 | E | 858 578-8001 | 1207 |
| Lauras Orgnal Bston Brwnies In | 2051 | F | 619 855-3258 | 1221 |
| Tallgrass Pictures LLC | 2051 | E | 619 227-2701 | 1246 |
| Opera Patisserie | 2053 | D | 858 536-5800 | 1291 |
| Azumex Corp | 2061 | E | 858 710-8855 | 1293 |
| El Super Leon Pnchin Sncks Inc | 2064 | E | 619 426-2968 | 1305 |
| Sugarfina Inc | 2064 | E | 949 301-9482 | 1334 |
| Anheuser-Busch LLC | 2082 | D | 858 581-7000 | 1414 |
| Associated Microbreweries Inc | 2082 | D | 858 587-2739 | 1419 |
| Associated Microbreweries Inc (PA) | 2082 | E | 858 273-2739 | 1421 |
| Associated Microbreweries Inc | 2082 | D | 619 234-2739 | 1422 |
| Assocted McRbrwries Ltd A Cal | 2082 | E | 858 273-2739 | 1423 |
| Home Brew Mart Inc | 2082 | B | 858 790-6900 | 1434 |
| Jdz Inc | 2082 | D | 858 549-9888 | 1437 |
| K A McNair Brewing Co LLC | 2082 | E | 858 254-3238 | 1438 |
| Karl Strauss Brewing Company (PA) | 2082 | E | 858 273-2739 | 1440 |
| Kings & Convicts Bp LLC (HQ) | 2082 | E | 858 790-6900 | 1441 |
| Kings & Convicts Bp LLC | 2082 | C | 619 255-7213 | 1442 |
| Kings & Convicts Bp LLC | 2082 | E | 619 295-2337 | 1443 |
| Stone Brewing Co LLC | 2082 | C | 619 269-2100 | 1461 |
| Taproom Beer Co | 2082 | E | 619 539-7738 | 1464 |
| Bernardo Winery Inc (PA) | 2084 | F | 858 487-1866 | 1484 |
| Cydea Inc | 2084 | E | 800 710-9939 | 1523 |
| WG Best Weinkellerei Inc | 2084 | F | 858 627-1747 | 1825 |
| Reyes Coca-Cola Bottling LLC | 2086 | B | 619 266-6300 | 1947 |
| United Brands Company Inc | 2087 | E | 619 461-5220 | 2031 |
| Bumble Bee Foods LLC (HQ) | 2091 | F | 800 800-8572 | 2036 |
| Bumble Bee Seafoods LP | 2091 | C | 858 715-4000 | 2037 |
| Blue Nalu Inc | 2092 | E | 858 703-8703 | 2049 |
| Foods On Fly LLC | 2099 | E | 858 404-0642 | 2203 |
| Fuji Food Products Inc | 2099 | C | 619 268-3118 | 2211 |
| Healthy Times Inc | 2099 | F | 858 513-1550 | 2229 |
| Husks Unlimited (PA) | 2099 | E | 619 476-8301 | 2235 |
| Rising Tide Bottleworks LLC | 2099 | F | 619 725-0844 | 2337 |
| Southwest Products LLC | 2099 | C | 619 263-8000 | 2358 |
| Hempacco Co Inc (HQ) | 2111 | E | 619 779-0715 | 2394 |
| R J Reynolds Tobacco Company | 2111 | D | 858 625-8453 | 2396 |
| Masterpiece Artist Canvas LLC | 2211 | E | 619 710-2500 | 2422 |
| California Industrial Fabrics | 2231 | E | 619 661-7166 | 2443 |
| Balboa Manufacturing Co LLC (PA) | 2253 | E | 858 715-0060 | 2462 |
| Custom Logos Inc | 2261 | E | 858 277-1886 | 2491 |
| Industry Threadworks | 2261 | E | 858 265-6177 | 2493 |
| No Second Thoughts Inc | 2311 | D | 619 428-5992 | 2563 |
| Creative Design Industries | 2321 | C | 619 710-2525 | 2571 |
| Army of Happy LLC | 2323 | E | 704 517-9890 | 2582 |
| Sauvage Inc (PA) | 2329 | F | 858 408-0100 | 2638 |
| De Soto Clothing Inc | 2339 | F | 858 578-6672 | 2753 |
| Hylete Inc | 2339 | E | 858 225-8998 | 2765 |
| Legendary Holdings Inc | 2353 | E | 619 872-6100 | 2845 |
| A Thanks Million Inc | 2361 | F | 858 432-7744 | 2850 |
| Terry Town Corporation | 2384 | D | 619 421-5354 | 2873 |
| Coronado Leather Co Inc | 2386 | F | 619 238-0265 | 2876 |
| Krasnes Inc | 2386 | D | 619 232-2066 | 2881 |
| Mbf Interiors Inc | 2391 | F | 858 565-2944 | 2915 |
| Beme International LLC | 2392 | E | 858 751-0580 | 2922 |
| Lofta | 2392 | E | 858 299-8000 | 2936 |
| Duds By Dudes LLC | 2396 | F | 858 442-5613 | 3006 |
| Four Seasons Design Inc (PA) | 2396 | E | 619 761-5151 | 3007 |
| Autoliv Asp Inc | 2399 | E | 619 662-8018 | 3024 |
| Autoliv Safety Technology Inc | 2399 | A | 619 662-8000 | 3025 |
| Prestige Flag & Banner Co Inc | 2399 | D | 619 497-2220 | 3033 |
| Cabinets Glore Orange Cnty Inc | 2421 | E | 858 586-0555 | 3066 |
| Moniker General LLC | 2426 | F | 619 255-8772 | 3097 |
| Rtmex Inc | 2426 | C | 619 391-9913 | 3102 |
| Canyon Graphics Inc | 2431 | D | 858 646-0444 | 3118 |
| Design Synthesis Inc | 2431 | E | 858 271-8480 | 3129 |
| Jeld-Wen Inc | 2431 | C | 800 468-3667 | 3150 |
| Quality Cabinet and Fixture Co (HQ) | 2434 | E | 619 266-1011 | 3261 |
| Cri 2000 LP (PA) | 2499 | E | 619 542-1975 | 3416 |
| Raphaels Inc | 2499 | F | | 3425 |
| Whalen LLC (DH) | 2511 | E | 619 423-9948 | 3462 |
| Elite Leather LLC | 2512 | D | 909 548-8600 | 3472 |
| Ideal Mattress Company Inc | 2515 | E | 619 595-0003 | 3529 |
| Ana Global LLC (PA) | 2517 | D | 619 482-9990 | 3549 |
| Gilbert Martin Wdwkg Co Inc (PA) | 2517 | E | 800 268-5669 | 3550 |
| Bleau Consulting Inc (PA) | 2521 | D | 619 263-5550 | 3561 |
| Ecr4kids LP | 2531 | E | 619 323-2005 | 3623 |
| J L Furnishings LLC | 2531 | B | 310 605-6600 | 3627 |
| Seating Concepts LLC | 2531 | E | 619 491-3159 | 3638 |
| Bonded Window Coverings Inc | 2591 | E | 858 576-8400 | 3716 |
| Phase II Products Inc (PA) | 2591 | F | 619 236-9699 | 3725 |
| Hire Elegance | 2599 | F | 858 740-7862 | 3744 |
| Dynamic Resources Inc | 2621 | D | 619 268-3070 | 3767 |
| Taylord Products Intl Inc (PA) | 2631 | C | 619 247-6544 | 3809 |
| Corrugados De Baja California | 2653 | A | 619 662-8672 | 3834 |
| Global Packaging Solutions Inc | 2653 | B | 619 710-2661 | 3849 |
| Pgac Corp (PA) | 2671 | D | 858 560-8213 | 3935 |
| Sherpa Clinical Packaging LLC | 2671 | E | 858 282-0928 | 3937 |
| Southland Envelope LLC | 2677 | C | 619 449-3553 | 4012 |
| Avery Products Corporation | 2678 | C | 619 671-1022 | 4016 |
| Bavarian Nordic Inc | 2678 | E | 919 600-1260 | 4018 |
| P & R Paper Supply Co Inc | 2679 | E | 619 671-2400 | 4043 |
| Joong-Ang Daily News Cal Inc | 2711 | D | 858 573-1111 | 4138 |
| Kaar Drect Mail Flfillment LLC | 2711 | E | 619 382-3670 | 4141 |
| North County Times (DH) | 2711 | C | 800 533-8830 | 4172 |
| San Diego Union-Tribune LLC (PA) | 2711 | A | 619 299-3131 | 4187 |
| The Sun | 2711 | F | 619 405-7702 | 4209 |
| Voice of San Diego | 2711 | D | 619 325-0525 | 4218 |
| Cbj LP | 2721 | E | 858 277-6359 | 4239 |
| Cypress Magazines Inc | 2721 | F | 858 503-7572 | 4245 |
| San Diego Magazine Pubg Co | 2721 | E | 619 230-9292 | 4297 |
| Dawn Sign Press Inc | 2731 | E | 858 625-0600 | 4325 |
| Houghton Mifflin Harcourt Pubg | 2731 | E | 617 351-5000 | 4332 |
| Plural Publishing Inc | 2731 | E | 858 492-1555 | 4340 |
| Elsevier Inc | 2741 | E | 619 231-6616 | 4394 |
| Elsevier Inc | 2741 | D | 619 231-6616 | 4395 |
| Marcoa Media LLC (PA) | 2741 | E | 858 635-9627 | 4431 |
| Mitchell Repair Info Co LLC (HQ) | 2741 | E | 858 391-5000 | 4432 |
| Myanimelist LLC | 2741 | F | 714 423-8289 | 4434 |
| Neil A Kjos Music Company (PA) | 2741 | E | 858 270-9800 | 4436 |
| Real Marketing | 2741 | E | 858 847-0335 | 4460 |
| Speed Society LLC | 2741 | F | 760 402-6838 | 4468 |
| Tabor Communications Inc | 2741 | E | 858 625-0070 | 4475 |
| Transwestern Publishing Company LLC | 2741 | A | 858 467-2800 | 4482 |
| West Publishing Corporation | 2741 | A | 619 296-7862 | 4493 |
| Yamagata America Inc | 2741 | C | 858 751-1010 | 4496 |
| Box Co Inc | 2752 | E | 619 661-8090 | 4535 |
| Brehm Communications Inc (PA) | 2752 | E | 858 451-6200 | 4537 |
| Continental Graphics Corp | 2752 | D | 858 552-6520 | 4567 |
| Diego & Son Printing Inc | 2752 | E | 619 233-5373 | 4588 |
| Elum Designs Inc | 2752 | E | 858 650-3586 | 4604 |
| Kovin Corporation Inc | 2752 | E | 858 558-0100 | 4663 |
| Modern Printing & Mailing Inc | 2752 | E | 619 222-0535 | 4697 |
| Mody Entrepreneurs Inc | 2752 | E | 858 292-8100 | 4698 |
| Nanografix Corporation | 2752 | F | 858 524-3295 | 4702 |
| Neyenesch Printers Inc | 2752 | D | 619 297-2281 | 4705 |
| No Boundaries Inc | 2752 | E | 858 266-2349 | 4707 |
| Packaging Manufacturing Inc | 2752 | C | 619 498-9199 | 4716 |
| PM Corporate Group Inc (PA) | 2752 | D | 800 343-3139 | 4727 |
| Printivity LLC | 2752 | E | 877 649-5463 | 4735 |
| Robo 3d Inc | 2752 | E | 844 476-2233 | 4756 |
| Rush Press Inc | 2752 | E | 619 296-7874 | 4757 |
| Scholastic Sports Inc | 2752 | D | 858 496-9221 | 4759 |
| Streeter Printing Inc | 2752 | F | 858 566-0866 | 4773 |
| Vdp Direct LLC (PA) | 2752 | E | 858 300-4510 | 4802 |
| Bretkeri Corporation | 2759 | E | 858 292-4919 | 4853 |
| Colmol Inc | 2759 | E | 858 693-7575 | 4863 |
| Electronic Prtg Solutions LLC | 2759 | E | 858 576-3000 | 4877 |
| Express Business Systems Inc | 2759 | E | 858 549-9828 | 4878 |
| Kieran Label Corp | 2759 | E | 619 449-4457 | 4904 |
| Label ID Technologies Inc | 2759 | F | 619 661-5566 | 4907 |
| No Frill Franchising Inc | 2759 | E | 858 642-4848 | 4928 |
| Optec Laser Systems LLC | 2759 | E | 858 220-1070 | 4932 |
| R R Donnelley & Sons Company | 2759 | E | 619 527-4600 | 4947 |
| Three Man Corporation | 2759 | E | 858 684-5200 | 4975 |
| Found Image Press Inc | 2771 | F | 619 282-3452 | 4995 |
| Neon Rose Inc | 2813 | E | 619 218-6103 | 5056 |

## GEOGRAPHIC SECTION — SAN DIEGO, CA

| Company | SIC | EMP | PHONE | ENTRY# |
|---|---|---|---|---|
| Carbomer Inc. | 2819 | D | 858 552-0992 | 5078 |
| Tonbo Biotechnologies Corp. | 2819 | E | 858 888-7300 | 5126 |
| Lamkin Corporation (PA) | 2821 | F | 619 661-7090 | 5173 |
| Rock West Composites Inc (PA) | 2821 | D | 858 537-6260 | 5196 |
| Allermed Laboratories Inc. | 2833 | E | 858 292-1060 | 5229 |
| Green Star Labs Inc. | 2833 | E | 619 489-9020 | 5244 |
| Sapphire Energy Inc. | 2833 | D | 858 768-4700 | 5270 |
| Acadia Pharmaceuticals Inc (PA) | 2834 | A | 858 558-2871 | 5294 |
| Aegis Life Inc. | 2834 | E | 650 666-5287 | 5301 |
| Agouron Pharmaceuticals Inc (HQ) | 2834 | E | 858 622-3000 | 5302 |
| Ambit Biosciences Corporation | 2834 | D | 858 334-2100 | 5313 |
| Amylin Ohio LLC | 2834 | A | 858 552-2200 | 5321 |
| Anaptysbio Inc (PA) | 2834 | C | 858 362-6295 | 5323 |
| Applied Mlecular Evolution Inc (HQ) | 2834 | E | 858 597-4990 | 5328 |
| Arcturus Thrptics Holdings Inc (PA) | 2834 | E | 858 900-2660 | 5331 |
| Ardea Biosciences Inc. | 2834 | E | 858 625-0787 | 5332 |
| Arrowhead Pharmaceuticals Inc. | 2834 | D | 626 304-3400 | 5336 |
| ARS Pharmaceuticals Inc (PA) | 2834 | E | 858 771-9307 | 5338 |
| Atxco Inc. | 2834 | E | 650 334-2079 | 5345 |
| Avidity Biosciences Inc (PA) | 2834 | E | 858 401-7900 | 5351 |
| Capricor Therapeutics Inc (PA) | 2834 | F | 858 727-1755 | 5388 |
| Cardiff Oncology Inc. | 2834 | E | 858 952-7570 | 5392 |
| Catalent Pharma Solutions Inc. | 2834 | C | 858 805-6383 | 5397 |
| Catalent Pharma Solutions Inc. | 2834 | D | 877 587-1835 | 5398 |
| Celgene Corporation | 2834 | E | 858 795-4961 | 5399 |
| Crinetics Pharmaceuticals Inc (PA) | 2834 | D | 858 450-6464 | 5415 |
| Cv Sciences Inc (PA) | 2834 | C | 866 290-2157 | 5417 |
| Cymbiotika LLC (PA) | 2834 | E | 770 910-4945 | 5419 |
| Cymbiotika LLC | 2834 | D | 949 652-8177 | 5420 |
| Elitra Pharmaceuticals. | 2834 | D | 858 410-3030 | 5431 |
| Entos Pharmaceuticals Inc. | 2834 | F | 800 727-0884 | 5432 |
| Erasca Inc. | 2834 | C | 858 465-6511 | 5436 |
| Genetronics Inc. | 2834 | E | 858 410-3112 | 5455 |
| Genomics Inst of Nvrtis RES FN | 2834 | E | 858 812-1805 | 5456 |
| Gossamer Bio Inc (PA) | 2834 | C | 858 684-1300 | 5467 |
| Gyre Therapeutics Inc (PA) | 2834 | B | 650 266-8674 | 5473 |
| Heron Therapeutics Inc (PA) | 2834 | C | 858 251-4400 | 5479 |
| Inova Diagnostics Inc. | 2834 | C | 858 586-9900 | 5496 |
| Janssen Research & Dev LLC | 2834 | C | 858 450-2000 | 5512 |
| Janux Therapeutics Inc. | 2834 | D | 858 751-4493 | 5513 |
| Kura Oncology Inc (PA) | 2834 | E | 858 500-8800 | 5531 |
| Levena Biopharma Us Inc. | 2834 | E | 858 720-1439 | 5536 |
| Maravai Lfscences Holdings Inc (PA) | 2834 | E | 858 546-0004 | 5544 |
| MEI Pharma Inc. | 2834 | E | 858 369-7100 | 5552 |
| Metacrine Inc. | 2834 | E | 858 369-7800 | 5554 |
| National Resilience Inc (PA) | 2834 | E | 888 737-2460 | 5562 |
| Neurelis Inc (PA) | 2834 | E | 858 251-2111 | 5569 |
| Otonomy Inc. | 2834 | D | 619 323-2200 | 5589 |
| Pacira Pharmaceuticals Inc. | 2834 | D | 858 625-2424 | 5593 |
| Pfenex Inc. | 2834 | D | 858 352-4400 | 5597 |
| Pfizer Inc. | 2834 | D | 858 622-3000 | 5598 |
| Pfizer Inc. | 2834 | D | 858 622-3001 | 5599 |
| Pharmion Corporation. | 2834 | E | 858 335-5744 | 5603 |
| Polaris Pharmaceuticals Inc (PA) | 2834 | F | 858 452-6688 | 5606 |
| Polypeptide Labs San Diego LLC | 2834 | D | 858 408-0808 | 5607 |
| Prescient Holdings Group LLC | 2834 | E | 858 790-7004 | 5608 |
| Primapharma Inc. | 2834 | E | 858 259-0969 | 5609 |
| Prometheus Biosciences Inc. | 2834 | D | 858 422-4300 | 5610 |
| Prometheus Laboratories Inc. | 2834 | B | 858 824-0895 | 5611 |
| Provision Health Corp. | 2834 | F | 619 240-3263 | 5615 |
| Quanticel Pharmacueticals Inc. | 2834 | E | 858 956-3747 | 5620 |
| Rayzebio Inc (HQ) | 2834 | F | 619 937-2754 | 5631 |
| Receptos Inc. | 2834 | E | 858 652-5700 | 5632 |
| Rempex Pharmaceuticals Inc. | 2834 | E | 858 875-2840 | 5634 |
| Resilience Us Inc (HQ) | 2834 | E | 984 202-0854 | 5636 |
| Santarus Inc. | 2834 | F | 858 314-5700 | 5650 |
| Sapu Bioscience LLC | 2834 | E | 650 635-7018 | 5651 |
| Shire Rgenerative Medicine Inc. | 2834 | E | 858 754-5396 | 5656 |
| Signal Pharmaceuticals LLC | 2834 | C | 858 795-4700 | 5659 |
| Societal CDMO San Diego LLC | 2834 | D | 858 623-1520 | 5664 |
| STA Pharmaceutical US LLC | 2834 | E | 609 606-6499 | 5673 |
| Travere Therapeutics Inc (PA) | 2834 | B | 888 969-7879 | 5693 |
| Trius Therapeutics LLC | 2834 | C | 858 452-0370 | 5694 |
| Vertex Phrmctcals San Dego LLC (HQ) | 2834 | C | 858 404-6600 | 5706 |
| Viking Therapeutics Inc (PA) | 2834 | E | 858 704-4660 | 5707 |
| Wacker Biotech US Inc. | 2834 | E | 858 875-4700 | 5714 |
| Acon Laboratories Inc (PA) | 2835 | E | 858 875-8000 | 5728 |
| Alere Inc. | 2835 | D | 858 805-2000 | 5731 |
| Alere Inc. | 2835 | F | 858 805-3810 | 5732 |
| Alere San Diego Inc (DH) | 2835 | D | 858 805-2000 | 5734 |
| Bioserv Corporation | 2835 | E | 917 817-1326 | 5742 |
| Dermtech Inc (PA) | 2835 | C | 866 450-4223 | 5747 |
| Gateway Genomics LLC | 2835 | D | 858 886-7250 | 5753 |
| Gen-Probe Incorporated | 2835 | D | 858 410-8000 | 5754 |
| Inova Diagnostics Inc. | 2835 | C | 858 586-9900 | 5757 |
| Pacific Biotech Inc. | 2835 | E | 858 552-1100 | 5773 |
| Quidel Corporation | 2835 | E | 858 552-1100 | 5776 |
| Quidel Corporation (HQ) | 2835 | D | 858 552-1100 | 5777 |
| Quidelortho Corporation (PA) | 2835 | E | 858 552-1100 | 5778 |
| Synbiotics LLC | 2835 | E | 858 451-3771 | 5780 |
| Vedabio Inc. | 2835 | F | 858 310-1330 | 5784 |
| Ark Animal Health Inc. | 2836 | E | 858 203-4100 | 5795 |
| Artiva Biotherapeutics Inc. | 2836 | D | 858 267-4467 | 5797 |
| Atyr Pharma Inc (PA) | 2836 | D | 858 731-8389 | 5803 |
| Bioatla Inc. | 2836 | D | 858 558-0708 | 5810 |
| Cidara Therapeutics Inc (PA) | 2836 | D | 858 752-6170 | 5818 |
| Excellos Incorporated. | 2836 | E | 619 400-8235 | 5827 |
| Halozyme Therapeutics Inc (PA) | 2836 | D | 858 794-8889 | 5836 |
| Immunitybio Inc (PA) | 2836 | D | 844 696-5235 | 5840 |
| Neurocrine Biosciences Inc (PA) | 2836 | B | 858 617-7600 | 5850 |
| Poseida Therapeutics Inc (PA) | 2836 | B | 858 779-3100 | 5853 |
| Scripps Laboratories | 2836 | E | 858 546-5800 | 5859 |
| Sorrento Therapeutics Inc (PA) | 2836 | D | 858 203-4100 | 5861 |
| Natural Thoughts Incorporated | 2844 | E | 619 582-0027 | 6010 |
| Sharpmart LLC. | 2844 | E | 619 278-1473 | 6037 |
| Suneva Medical Inc (PA) | 2844 | E | 858 550-9999 | 6044 |
| Frazee Industries Inc. | 2851 | F | 858 626-3600 | 6085 |
| Mast Technologies LLC | 2851 | E | 858 452-1700 | 6094 |
| Rhino Linings Corporation (PA) | 2851 | D | 858 450-0441 | 6110 |
| BASF Enzymes LLC (DH) | 2869 | D | 858 431-8520 | 6132 |
| Biotix Inc. | 2869 | F | 858 875-7696 | 6135 |
| Verenium Corporation | 2869 | C | 858 431-8500 | 6166 |
| Cibus Inc. | 2879 | C | 858 450-0008 | 6196 |
| Seal For Life Industries LLC (HQ) | 2891 | E | 619 671-0932 | 6245 |
| Chemdiv Inc. | 2899 | E | 858 794-4860 | 6273 |
| Chemtreat Inc. | 2899 | D | 804 935-2000 | 6274 |
| Coatinc United States Inc. | 2899 | E | 619 638-7261 | 6276 |
| CP Kelco US Inc. | 2899 | E | 619 652-5326 | 6278 |
| Cutwater Spirits LLC (HQ) | 2899 | D | 858 672-3848 | 6279 |
| Firmenich Incorporated | 2899 | D | 858 646-8323 | 6284 |
| Neo Tech Aqua Solutions Inc. | 2899 | F | 858 571-6590 | 6312 |
| New Leaf Biofuel LLC | 2911 | E | 619 236-8500 | 6343 |
| Sacahn JV | 2911 | D | 858 924-1110 | 6351 |
| Wd-40 Company | 2911 | C | 619 275-1400 | 6358 |
| WD-40 Company (PA) | 2992 | C | 619 275-1400 | 6401 |
| Bridgestone Americas Inc. | 3011 | E | 858 874-3109 | 6406 |
| Jain Irrigation Inc. | 3052 | F | 315 782-1170 | 6425 |
| Oxystrap International Inc. | 3069 | D | 800 699-6901 | 6520 |
| Plastics Family Holdings Inc. | 3081 | D | 858 560-1551 | 6566 |
| Providien Thermoforming LLC | 3081 | E | 858 850-1591 | 6568 |
| Saint-Gobain Solar Gard LLC (DH) | 3081 | D | 866 300-2674 | 6569 |
| Atlas Roofing Corporation | 3086 | E | 626 334-5358 | 6623 |
| Urethane Masters Inc. | 3086 | F | 651 829-1032 | 6668 |
| Walter N Coffman Inc. | 3086 | D | 619 266-2642 | 6670 |
| Apon Industries Corp. | 3089 | C |  | 6720 |
| Bh-Tech Inc. | 3089 | A | 858 694-0900 | 6743 |
| Custom Engineering Plastics LP | 3089 | E | 858 452-0961 | 6789 |
| Jem-Hd Co Inc. | 3089 | E | 619 710-1443 | 6875 |
| MI Technologies Inc. | 3089 | A | 619 710-2637 | 6913 |
| New West Products Inc. | 3089 | E | 619 671-9022 | 6928 |
| Providien Injction Molding Inc. | 3089 | D | 760 931-1844 | 6988 |
| San Diego Ace Inc. | 3089 | C | 619 206-7339 | 7020 |
| Allbirds Inc. | 3143 | F | 858 987-9533 | 7103 |
| Eleanor Rigby Leather Co. | 3199 | D | 619 356-5590 | 7155 |
| Shamir Insight Inc. | 3229 | D | 858 514-8330 | 7203 |
| Rayotek Scientific LLC | 3231 | E | 858 558-3671 | 7241 |
| Forterra Pipe & Precast LLC. | 3272 | E | 858 715-5600 | 7336 |
| Guardian Phrm Southern Cal LLC | 3272 | F | 858 652-6900 | 7340 |
| San Diego Precast Concrete Inc (DH) | 3272 | E | 619 240-8000 | 7389 |
| California Commercial Asp LLC | 3273 | E | 858 513-0611 | 7411 |
| Robertsons Ready Mix Ltd. | 3273 | D | 800 834-7557 | 7492 |
| Superior Ready Mix Concrete LP | 3273 | D | 619 265-0955 | 7505 |
| Superior Ready Mix Concrete LP | 3273 | D | 619 265-0296 | 7506 |
| Hone Maxwell LLP | 3291 | F | 415 765-1754 | 7553 |
| Lamart California Inc. | 3296 | E | 973 772-6262 | 7580 |
| International Mfg Tech Inc (DH) | 3312 | D | 619 544-7741 | 7616 |
| Price Industries Inc. | 3312 | D | 858 673-4451 | 7622 |
| San Dego Prcsion Machining Inc. | 3312 | E | 858 499-0379 | 7625 |
| Initium Aerospace LLC. | 3324 | F | 818 324-3684 | 7688 |
| Argen Corporation (PA) | 3339 | C | 858 455-7900 | 7710 |
| Johnson Matthey Inc. | 3341 | C | 858 716-2400 | 7721 |
| Bridgewave Communications Inc. | 3357 | E | 408 567-6900 | 7774 |
| Centurum Information Tech Inc. | 3357 | D | 619 224-1100 | 7780 |
| Hiller Companies LLC | 3366 | E | 858 899-5008 | 7854 |
| Van Can Company. | 3411 | C | 858 391-8084 | 7932 |
| Allegion Access Tech LLC. | 3423 | E | 858 431-5940 | 7943 |

Employee Codes: A=Over 500 employees, B=251-500, C=101-250, D=51-100, E=20-50, F=10-19, G=1-9

2025 Harris California Manufacturers Directory

© Mergent Inc. 1-800-342-5647

# SAN DIEGO, CA — GEOGRAPHIC SECTION

| Company | SIC | EMP | PHONE | ENTRY# |
|---|---|---|---|---|
| Hodge Products Inc | 3429 | E | 800 778-2217 | 8002 |
| Lucky Line Products Inc | 3429 | E | 858 549-6699 | 8012 |
| Pacific Maritime Inds Corp | 3441 | C | 619 575-8141 | 8197 |
| Hyundai Translead (HQ) | 3443 | D | 619 574-1500 | 8317 |
| Arrk North America Inc | 3444 | E | 858 552-1587 | 8379 |
| Concise Fabricators Inc | 3444 | E | 520 746-3226 | 8415 |
| Marine & Rest Fabricators Inc | 3444 | E | 619 232-7267 | 8497 |
| Metal Master Inc | 3444 | E | 858 292-8880 | 8504 |
| Romla Co | 3444 | E | 619 946-1224 | 8560 |
| Spec-Built Systems Inc | 3444 | D | 619 661-8100 | 8578 |
| Pacific Steel Group LLC (PA) | 3449 | C | 858 251-1100 | 8706 |
| HI Tech Honeycomb Inc | 3469 | E | 858 974-1600 | 8849 |
| Schuberth North America LLC | 3469 | F | 949 215-0893 | 8886 |
| Sheffield Platers Inc | 3471 | D | 858 546-8484 | 9013 |
| Southern California Plating Co | 3471 | E | 619 231-1481 | 9015 |
| Symcoat Metal Processing Inc | 3471 | E | 858 451-3313 | 9019 |
| Action Powder Coating LLC | 3479 | F | 858 566-2288 | 9036 |
| All Source Company Bldg Group | 3479 | E | 858 586-0903 | 9042 |
| Alphacoat Finishing LLC | 3479 | E | 949 748-7796 | 9043 |
| Flame-Spray Inc | 3479 | E | 619 283-2007 | 9069 |
| Dha America Inc | 3496 | D | 858 925-3246 | 9215 |
| Innovive LLC (PA) | 3496 | C | 858 309-6620 | 9220 |
| Right Manufacturing LLC | 3498 | E | 858 566-7002 | 9268 |
| Precision Engine Controls Corp (DH) | 3511 | C | 858 792-3217 | 9314 |
| Solar Turbines Incorporated (HQ) | 3511 | A | 619 544-5352 | 9315 |
| Solar Turbines Incorporated | 3511 | E | 619 544-5321 | 9316 |
| Solar Turbines Incorporated | 3511 | C | 858 694-6110 | 9317 |
| Solar Turbines Incorporated | 3511 | D | 858 715-2060 | 9318 |
| Solar Turbines Intl Co (DH) | 3511 | E | 619 544-5000 | 9319 |
| DRTS Enterprises Ltd | 3523 | E | 858 270-7244 | 9352 |
| Limited Access Unlimited Inc | 3523 | F | 619 294-3682 | 9368 |
| Rain Bird Corporation | 3523 | E | 619 674-4068 | 9377 |
| Rivulis Irrigation Inc (HQ) | 3523 | E | 858 578-1860 | 9380 |
| Hirok Inc (PA) | 3531 | E | 619 713-5066 | 9427 |
| Century Design Inc | 3545 | F | 858 292-1212 | 9666 |
| California Air Tools Inc | 3546 | E | 619 407-7905 | 9710 |
| Seescan Inc (PA) | 3546 | C | 858 244-3300 | 9714 |
| Ssco Manufacturing Inc | 3548 | E | 619 628-1022 | 9731 |
| Teledyne Seabotix Inc | 3549 | D | 619 239-5959 | 9746 |
| Fabric8labs Inc | 3555 | D | 858 215-1142 | 9766 |
| Asml Us LLC | 3559 | B | 858 385-6500 | 9834 |
| CP Manufacturing Inc (HQ) | 3559 | C | 619 477-3175 | 9843 |
| Morgan Polymer Seals LLC | 3559 | B | 619 498-9221 | 9879 |
| Vectron Inc | 3559 | F | 858 621-2400 | 9909 |
| EMR Final Ctrl US Holdg Corp | 3561 | F | 858 740-2471 | 9920 |
| Schroff Inc | 3561 | A | 800 525-4682 | 9939 |
| Industrial Fire Sprnklr Co Inc | 3569 | E | 619 266-6030 | 10096 |
| Pall Corporation | 3569 | C | 858 455-7264 | 10104 |
| Continuous Computing Corp | 3571 | C | 858 882-8800 | 10144 |
| HP Inc | 3571 | B | 858 924-5117 | 10162 |
| Kontron America Incorporated (PA) | 3571 | F | 800 822-7522 | 10173 |
| Matri Kart | 3571 | E | 858 609-0933 | 10177 |
| Oracle America Inc | 3571 | F | 858 625-5044 | 10189 |
| Teradata Operations Inc (HQ) | 3571 | D | 937 242-4030 | 10212 |
| Advanced Hpc Inc | 3572 | F | 858 716-8262 | 10220 |
| Vigobyte Tape Corporation | 3575 | A | 866 803-8446 | 10292 |
| MTA Moving Tech In Amer Inc | 3575 | E | 619 651-7208 | 10308 |
| OCP Group Inc | 3575 | E | 858 279-7400 | 10309 |
| Acces I/O Products Inc | 3577 | F | 858 550-9559 | 10314 |
| Congatec Inc | 3577 | E | 858 457-2600 | 10350 |
| Exce LP | 3577 | D | 858 549-6340 | 10366 |
| Mad Catz Inc | 3577 | C | 858 790-5008 | 10403 |
| Magma Inc | 3577 | E | 858 530-2511 | 10405 |
| Semtek Innvtive Solutions Corp | 3577 | F | 858 436-2270 | 10435 |
| Asteres Inc (PA) | 3578 | E | 858 777-8600 | 10456 |
| Alliance Air Products Llc | 3585 | A | 619 664-0027 | 10478 |
| Alliance Air Products Llc (DH) | 3585 | E | 619 428-9688 | 10479 |
| Elco Rfrgn Solutions LLC | 3585 | A | 858 888-9447 | 10497 |
| Thermocraft | 3585 | D | 619 813-2985 | 10518 |
| Trane US Inc | 3585 | C | 858 292-0833 | 10520 |
| Trumed Systems Incorporated | 3585 | E | 844 878-6331 | 10523 |
| Pronto Products Co (PA) | 3589 | E | 619 661-6995 | 10592 |
| Water Works Inc | 3589 | E | 858 499-0119 | 10611 |
| Parker-Hannifin Corporation | 3594 | C | 619 661-7000 | 10633 |
| 5th Axis Inc (PA) | 3599 | C | 858 505-0432 | 10643 |
| Coredux USA LLC | 3599 | D | 858 642-0713 | 10790 |
| Futuristics Machine Inc | 3599 | E | 858 450-0644 | 10847 |
| Inno Tech Manufacturing Inc | 3599 | F | 858 565-4556 | 10886 |
| J I Machine Company Inc | 3599 | E | 858 695-1787 | 10900 |
| Pacific Mfg Inc San Diego | 3599 | E | 619 423-0316 | 11023 |
| Prominex Inc | 3599 | F | 858 242-1541 | 11052 |
| Senior Operations LLC | 3599 | C | 858 278-8400 | 11105 |
| Senior Operations LLC | 3599 | D | 858 278-8400 | 11106 |
| Senior Operations LLC | 3599 | C | 858 278-8400 | 11108 |
| Smith Brothers Mfg Corp | 3599 | E | 619 296-3171 | 11116 |
| Thomson Industries Inc | 3599 | E | 619 661-6292 | 11143 |
| Vetpowered LLC | 3599 | F | 619 269-7116 | 11176 |
| Nuvve Holding Corp (PA) | 3612 | E | 619 456-5161 | 11218 |
| Pulse Electronics Inc (HQ) | 3612 | B | 858 674-8100 | 11225 |
| Sempra Global (HQ) | 3612 | D | 619 696-2000 | 11229 |
| Aemi Holdings LLC | 3613 | D | 858 481-0210 | 11233 |
| Cal LLC Powerflex Systems | 3621 | E | 650 469-3392 | 11257 |
| Eroad Inc | 3621 | D | 503 305-2255 | 11264 |
| Eurus Energy America Corp (DH) | 3621 | F | 858 638-7115 | 11266 |
| Sure Power Inc | 3621 | F | 619 661-6292 | 11290 |
| Cal-Comp Electronics (usa) Co Ltd | 3625 | B | 858 587-6900 | 11312 |
| Crydom Inc (DH) | 3625 | E | 619 210-1590 | 11314 |
| General Dynamics Mission | 3625 | C | 619 671-5400 | 11323 |
| S R C Devices Inccustomer | 3625 | B | 866 772-8668 | 11346 |
| Surface Technologies Corp | 3625 | E | 619 564-8320 | 11350 |
| Teal Electronics Corporation (PA) | 3625 | D | 858 558-9000 | 11353 |
| Apollo Manufacturing Services | 3629 | F | 858 271-8009 | 11359 |
| Intelligent Technologies LLC | 3629 | E | 858 458-1500 | 11374 |
| Maxwell Technologies Inc | 3629 | D | 858 503-3493 | 11376 |
| Mirama Enterprises Inc | 3631 | D | 858 587-8866 | 11392 |
| Visualizeled Inc | 3641 | F | 703 919-5559 | 11435 |
| Autosplice Parent Inc (PA) | 3643 | C | 858 535-0077 | 11441 |
| Impulse Enterprise | 3643 | F | 858 565-7050 | 11459 |
| Leviton Manufacturing Co Inc | 3643 | F | 619 205-8600 | 11462 |
| Teledyne Instruments Inc | 3643 | D | 858 842-3100 | 11474 |
| Agnetix Inc | 3646 | F | 833 246-3849 | 11517 |
| Blue Planet Energy Solutions | 3646 | F | 858 947-0100 | 11520 |
| Enertron Technologies Inc | 3646 | E | 800 537-7649 | 11528 |
| Clear Blue Energy Corp | 3648 | D | 858 451-1549 | 11587 |
| Deepsea Power & Light Inc | 3648 | E | 858 576-1261 | 11590 |
| Remote Ocean Systems Inc (PA) | 3648 | E | 858 565-8500 | 11621 |
| Activeon Inc | 3651 | E | 858 798-3300 | 11633 |
| Al Shellco LLC (HQ) | 3651 | C | 570 296-6444 | 11634 |
| Goto California Inc (HQ) | 3651 | F | 619 691-8722 | 11664 |
| Ksc Industries Inc | 3651 | E | 619 671-0110 | 11671 |
| Philips | 3651 | D | 916 337-8008 | 11687 |
| Sanyo Manufacturing Corporation | 3651 | E | 619 661-1134 | 11695 |
| Sony Electronics Inc (DH) | 3651 | A | 858 942-2400 | 11700 |
| Sony Electronics Inc | 3651 | C | 858 942-2400 | 11701 |
| X-1 Audio Inc | 3651 | F | 858 623-0339 | 11721 |
| Franklin Wireless Corp | 3661 | D | 858 623-0000 | 11765 |
| Sonim Technologies Inc (PA) | 3661 | E | 650 378-8100 | 11786 |
| U-Blox San Diego Inc | 3661 | E | 858 847-9611 | 11791 |
| Airgain Inc (PA) | 3663 | E | 760 579-0200 | 11800 |
| Ectron Corporation | 3663 | E | 858 278-0600 | 11847 |
| Ingenu Inc (PA) | 3663 | E | 858 201-6000 | 11867 |
| Interdigital Inc | 3663 | D | 858 210-4800 | 11868 |
| Kyocera AVX Cmpnnts San Dego I (DH) | 3663 | E | 858 550-3820 | 11873 |
| L3 Technologies Inc | 3663 | B | 858 552-9500 | 11875 |
| L3 Technologies Inc | 3663 | E | 858 279-0411 | 11876 |
| L3 Technologies Inc | 3663 | D | 858 552-9716 | 11879 |
| Nextivity Inc (PA) | 3663 | E | 858 485-9442 | 11903 |
| Qualcomm Incorporated | 3663 | C | 858 587-1121 | 11921 |
| Qualcomm Incorporated | 3663 | E | 202 263-0008 | 11922 |
| Qualcomm Incorporated (PA) | 3663 | A | 858 587-1121 | 11924 |
| Satellite Security Corporation | 3663 | E | 877 437-4199 | 11939 |
| Seaspace Corporation | 3663 | E | 858 746-1100 | 11940 |
| Sidus Solutions LLC | 3663 | F | 619 275-5533 | 11944 |
| Solectek Corporation | 3663 | E | 858 450-1220 | 11948 |
| Space Micro Inc | 3663 | C | 858 332-0700 | 11949 |
| Vigor Systems Inc | 3663 | E | 866 748-4467 | 11973 |
| Blue Squirrel Inc | 3669 | D | 858 268-0717 | 11985 |
| Indyme Solutions LLC | 3669 | E | 858 268-0717 | 12000 |
| Johnson Cntrls Fire Prtction L | 3669 | C | 858 633-9100 | 12002 |
| Qualcomm Mems Technologies Inc | 3669 | E | 858 587-1155 | 12012 |
| Ecoatm LLC (DH) | 3671 | C | 858 999-3200 | 12032 |
| Benchmark Elec Phoenix Inc | 3672 | B | 619 397-2402 | 12069 |
| Electronic Surfc Mounted Inds | 3672 | E | 858 455-1710 | 12091 |
| Modalai Inc | 3672 | B | 858 247-7053 | 12165 |
| Northwest Circuits Corp | 3672 | D | 619 661-1701 | 12178 |
| PDM Solutions Inc | 3672 | E | 858 348-1000 | 12188 |
| Quality Systems Intgrated Corp | 3672 | C | 858 536-3128 | 12199 |
| Quality Systems Intgrated Corp (PA) | 3672 | C | 858 587-9797 | 12200 |
| Saehan Electronics America Inc (PA) | 3672 | D | 858 496-1500 | 12204 |
| Sumitronics USA Inc | 3672 | E | 619 661-0450 | 12233 |
| Ttm Technologies Inc | 3672 | E | 858 874-2701 | 12250 |
| Apta Group Inc | 3674 | E | 619 710-8170 | 12325 |
| Arm Inc | 3674 | A | 858 453-1900 | 12329 |
| Beam Global (PA) | 3674 | C | 858 799-4583 | 12358 |
| Broadcom Corporation | 3674 | C | 858 385-8800 | 12367 |
| Daylight Solutions Inc (DH) | 3674 | C | 858 432-7500 | 12401 |

## GEOGRAPHIC SECTION — SAN DIEGO, CA

| Company | SIC | EMP | PHONE | ENTRY# |
|---|---|---|---|---|
| Ikanos Communications Inc (DH) | 3674 | F | 858 587-1121 | 12472 |
| Innophase Inc | 3674 | D | 619 541-8280 | 12486 |
| Io Semiconductor Incorporated | 3674 | E | 858 362-4074 | 12502 |
| Iq-Analog Corporation | 3674 | E | 858 200-0388 | 12504 |
| Kulr Technology Corporation | 3674 | D | 408 663-5247 | 12518 |
| Kyocera America Inc | 3674 | E | 858 576-2600 | 12520 |
| Kyocera International Inc (HQ) | 3674 | D | 858 492-1456 | 12521 |
| Next Semiconductor Tech Inc | 3674 | E | 858 707-7060 | 12604 |
| Nurlink Technology Corp | 3674 | F | 408 205-5363 | 12608 |
| Orca Systems Inc | 3674 | F | 858 679-9175 | 12623 |
| Psemi Corporation (DH) | 3674 | D | 858 731-9400 | 12643 |
| Qualcomm Datacenter Tech Inc (HQ) | 3674 | F | 858 567-1121 | 12650 |
| Qualcomm Incorporated | 3674 | E | 619 341-2920 | 12654 |
| Qualcomm Incorporated | 3674 | E | 858 909-0316 | 12655 |
| Qualcomm Incorporated | 3674 | C | 858 587-1121 | 12656 |
| Qualcomm Incorporated | 3674 | E | 858 587-1121 | 12657 |
| Qualcomm Incorporated | 3674 | E | 858 587-1121 | 12658 |
| Qualcomm Technologies Inc (HQ) | 3674 | B | 858 587-1121 | 12659 |
| Qualcomm Technologies Inc | 3674 | E | 858 587-1121 | 12660 |
| Qualcomm Technologies Inc | 3674 | E | 858 658-3040 | 12661 |
| Santier | 3674 | D | 858 271-1993 | 12684 |
| Sensemetrics Inc | 3674 | E | 619 738-8300 | 12694 |
| Teledyne Instruments Inc | 3674 | E | 858 842-3127 | 12758 |
| Tensorcom Inc | 3674 | E | 760 496-3264 | 12759 |
| General Atomics Electronic Systems Inc | 3675 | E | 858 522-8495 | 12817 |
| Aem Electronics (usa) Inc (PA) | 3677 | F | 858 481-0210 | 12826 |
| Rf Industries Ltd (PA) | 3678 | D | 858 549-6340 | 12895 |
| Caes Mission Systems LLC | 3679 | E | 858 812-7300 | 12929 |
| Cali Resources Inc | 3679 | E | 619 661-5741 | 12931 |
| CCM Assembly & Mfg Inc (PA) | 3679 | E | 760 560-1310 | 12933 |
| Custom Sensors & Tech Inc | 3679 | B | 805 716-0322 | 12951 |
| Delta Group Electronics | 3679 | D | 858 569-1681 | 12957 |
| Hannspree North America Inc | 3679 | D | 909 992-5025 | 12992 |
| Integrated Microwave Corp | 3679 | E | 858 259-2600 | 13001 |
| Kenjitsu USA Corp | 3679 | F | 619 734-5862 | 13018 |
| Munekata America Inc | 3679 | B | 619 661-8080 | 13041 |
| Ormet Circuits Inc | 3679 | E | 858 831-0010 | 13058 |
| Pred Technologies Usa Inc | 3679 | D | 858 999-2114 | 13067 |
| Pulse Electronics Corporation (HQ) | 3679 | E | 858 674-8100 | 13069 |
| Q-Vio LLC | 3679 | F | 858 777-8299 | 13071 |
| Tdk Electronics Inc | 3679 | C | 858 715-4200 | 13098 |
| Vas Engineering Inc | 3679 | E | 858 569-1601 | 13116 |
| Ereplacements LLC | 3691 | E | 714 361-2652 | 13140 |
| Gold Peak Industries (north America) Inc | 3691 | E | 858 674-6099 | 13143 |
| Sunfusion Energy Systems Inc | 3691 | E | 800 544-0282 | 13151 |
| Arriver Holdco Inc | 3694 | A | 858 587-1121 | 13166 |
| Maxwell Technologies Inc (HQ) | 3694 | D | 858 503-3300 | 13178 |
| Trademark Construction Co Inc (PA) | 3694 | D | 760 489-5647 | 13190 |
| Elm System Inc | 3695 | F | 408 694-2750 | 13195 |
| Reel Picture Productions LLC | 3695 | E | 858 587-0301 | 13202 |
| Cubic Defense Applications Inc | 3699 | A | 858 277-6780 | 13228 |
| Cubic Defense Applications Inc (DH) | 3699 | A | 858 776-5664 | 13229 |
| Cubic Defense Applications Inc | 3699 | C | 858 505-2870 | 13230 |
| Cymer LLC (HQ) | 3699 | A | 858 385-7300 | 13231 |
| Hc West LLC | 3699 | B | 858 277-3473 | 13247 |
| Instruments Incorporated | 3699 | E | 858 571-1111 | 13252 |
| Meggitt Safety Systems Inc | 3699 | D | 442 792-3217 | 13272 |
| O & S California Inc | 3699 | B | 619 661-1800 | 13279 |
| Pxise Energy Solutions LLC | 3699 | E | 619 696-2944 | 13293 |
| Surf Loch LLC | 3699 | F | 858 454-1777 | 13314 |
| Azaa Investments Inc (PA) | 3711 | E | 858 569-8111 | 13341 |
| Achates Power Inc | 3714 | D | 858 535-9920 | 13437 |
| Autoliv Inc | 3714 | E | 619 661-0438 | 13461 |
| Crower Engrg & Sls Co Inc | 3714 | D | 619 661-6477 | 13479 |
| Mygrant Glass Company Inc | 3714 | E | 858 455-8022 | 13544 |
| Sanko Electronics America Inc (HQ) | 3714 | F | 310 618-1677 | 13573 |
| Boeing Company | 3721 | A | 619 545-8382 | 13642 |
| General Atomics Arntcal Systems | 3721 | B | 858 964-6700 | 13653 |
| General Atomics Arntcal Systems | 3721 | A | 858 762-6700 | 13656 |
| General Atomics Arntcal Systems | 3721 | B | 858 455-2810 | 13658 |
| Shield AI Inc (PA) | 3721 | A | 619 719-5740 | 13689 |
| Chromalloy Component Svcs Inc | 3724 | E | 858 877-2800 | 13704 |
| Honeywell Safety Pdts USA Inc | 3724 | C | 619 661-8383 | 13712 |
| Safran Pwr Units San Diego LLC | 3724 | D | 858 223-2228 | 13722 |
| Coi Ceramics Inc | 3728 | E | 858 621-5700 | 13811 |
| General Dynamics Ots Cal Inc | 3728 | C | 619 671-5411 | 13848 |
| Meggitt (san Diego) Inc (HQ) | 3728 | C | 858 824-8976 | 13904 |
| Performance Plastics Inc | 3728 | D | 714 343-3928 | 13926 |
| Safran Cabin Inc | 3728 | C | 619 671-0430 | 13946 |
| Safran Cabin Inc | 3728 | C | 619 661-6292 | 13949 |
| Sungear Inc | 3728 | E | 858 549-3166 | 13963 |
| Bae Systems San Dego Ship Repr | 3731 | A | 619 238-1000 | 13999 |
| Continental Maritime Inds Inc | 3731 | B | 619 234-8851 | 14002 |
| Hii San Diego Shipyard Inc | 3731 | B | 619 234-8851 | 14004 |
| Miller Marine | 3731 | E | 619 791-1500 | 14010 |
| Nassco | 3731 | E | 619 929-3019 | 14011 |
| National Stl & Shipbuilding Co (HQ) | 3731 | B | 619 544-3400 | 14012 |
| Pacific Ship Repr Fbrction Inc (PA) | 3731 | E | 619 232-3200 | 14013 |
| Pyr Preservation Services | 3731 | E | 619 338-8395 | 14016 |
| Tecnico Corporation | 3731 | F | 619 426-7385 | 14018 |
| Trident Maritime Systems Inc | 3731 | D | 619 346-3800 | 14019 |
| United States Dept of Navy | 3731 | A | 619 556-6033 | 14020 |
| Driscoll Inc | 3732 | E | 619 226-2500 | 14032 |
| Infinity Yachts Inc | 3732 | F | 619 431-1194 | 14037 |
| Maritime Solutions LLC | 3732 | E | 619 234-2676 | 14039 |
| Kratos Def & SEC Solutions Inc (PA) | 3761 | C | 858 812-7300 | 14082 |
| Composite Optics Incorporated | 3769 | A | 937 490-4145 | 14110 |
| Argon St Inc | 3812 | D | 703 270-6927 | 14148 |
| Atk Launch Systems LLC | 3812 | B | 858 592-2509 | 14153 |
| Atk Space Systems LLC | 3812 | C | 858 530-3047 | 14154 |
| Atk Space Systems LLC | 3812 | D | 858 621-5700 | 14156 |
| Atk Space Systems LLC | 3812 | C | 858 487-0970 | 14160 |
| Bae Systems Tech Sltons Svcs I | 3812 | D | 858 278-3042 | 14164 |
| Caes Systems LLC | 3812 | C | 858 560-1301 | 14167 |
| Coretex USA Inc | 3812 | F | 877 247-8725 | 14173 |
| Cubic Corporation (HQ) | 3812 | A | 858 277-6780 | 14174 |
| Decatur Electronics Inc (DH) | 3812 | D | 888 428-4315 | 14178 |
| Global A Lgistics Training Inc | 3812 | E | 760 688-0365 | 14194 |
| Lockheed Martin Orincon Corp (HQ) | 3812 | C | 858 455-5530 | 14216 |
| Lytx Inc (PA) | 3812 | B | 858 430-4000 | 14218 |
| Nevwest Inc | 3812 | E | 619 420-8100 | 14227 |
| Northrop Grmman Inntion Syste | 3812 | B | 858 621-5700 | 14230 |
| Northrop Grumman Corporation | 3812 | A | 858 967-1221 | 14236 |
| Northrop Grumman Systems Corp | 3812 | C | 858 514-9020 | 14237 |
| Northrop Grumman Systems Corp | 3812 | C | 410 765-5589 | 14238 |
| Northrop Grumman Systems Corp | 3812 | F | 858 592-2535 | 14243 |
| Northrop Grumman Systems Corp | 3812 | E | 858 592-4518 | 14246 |
| Northrop Grumman Systems Corp | 3812 | E | 858 514-9000 | 14257 |
| Northrop Grumman Systems Corp | 3812 | D | 858 621-7395 | 14261 |
| Northrop Grumman Systems Corp | 3812 | B | 858 618-4349 | 14266 |
| Orbital Sciences LLC | 3812 | C | 858 618-1847 | 14276 |
| Raytheon Company | 3812 | D | 858 571-6598 | 14288 |
| Raytheon Dgital Force Tech LLC (DH) | 3812 | E | 858 546-1244 | 14291 |
| Remec Defense & Space Inc | 3812 | A | 858 560-1301 | 14292 |
| Scientific-Atlanta LLC | 3812 | E | 619 679-6000 | 14301 |
| Tecnova Advanced Systems Inc | 3812 | E | 858 586-9660 | 14312 |
| Genetronics Inc | 3821 | E | 858 597-6006 | 14338 |
| Isec Incorporated | 3821 | C | 858 279-9085 | 14341 |
| Procisedx Inc | 3821 | C | 858 382-4598 | 14346 |
| Honeywell International Inc | 3822 | E | 619 671-5612 | 14361 |
| Advanced Electromagnetics Inc | 3823 | E | 619 449-9492 | 14382 |
| Continental Controls Corp | 3823 | E | 858 453-9880 | 14397 |
| Digivision Inc | 3823 | E | 858 530-0100 | 14403 |
| Embedded Designs Inc | 3823 | E | 858 673-6050 | 14409 |
| Hardy Process Solutions | 3823 | E | 858 278-2900 | 14421 |
| Orbis Intelligent Systems Inc | 3823 | E | 858 737-4469 | 14442 |
| Reotemp Instrument Corporation (PA) | 3823 | D | 858 784-0710 | 14450 |
| Sabia Incorporated (PA) | 3823 | E | 858 217-2200 | 14453 |
| D & K Engineering (HQ) | 3824 | C | 760 840-2214 | 14476 |
| Ips Group Inc (PA) | 3824 | E | 858 404-0607 | 14481 |
| Ametek Programmable Power Inc (HQ) | 3825 | B | 858 450-0085 | 14495 |
| Bae Systems Info Elctrnic Syst | 3825 | A | 858 592-5000 | 14500 |
| Bae Systems National Security Solutions Inc | 3825 | A | 858 592-5000 | 14501 |
| CONCISYS | 3825 | E | 858 292-5888 | 14509 |
| L3harris Interstate Elec Corp | 3825 | D | 858 552-9500 | 14547 |
| Liquid Instruments Inc (PA) | 3825 | F | 619 332-6230 | 14549 |
| Mrv Systems LLC | 3825 | E | 800 645-7114 | 14555 |
| Surface Optics Corporation | 3825 | E | 858 675-7404 | 14587 |
| Velher LLC | 3825 | E | 619 494-6310 | 14598 |
| Affymetrix Inc | 3826 | D | 858 642-2058 | 14603 |
| Bionano Genomics Inc (PA) | 3826 | D | 858 888-7600 | 14635 |
| City of San Diego | 3826 | C | 619 758-2310 | 14644 |
| Filmetrics Inc (HQ) | 3826 | E | 858 573-9300 | 14667 |
| Illumina Inc | 3826 | F | 800 809-4566 | 14673 |
| Illumina Inc (PA) | 3826 | B | 858 202-4500 | 14674 |
| Molecular Bioproducts Inc (DH) | 3826 | E | 858 453-7551 | 14692 |
| Oxford Nanoimaging Inc | 3826 | D | 858 999-8860 | 14701 |
| Quantum Design Inc (PA) | 3826 | C | 858 481-4400 | 14708 |
| Singular Genomics Systems Inc (PA) | 3826 | C | 858 333-7830 | 14718 |
| Singular Genomics Systems Inc | 3826 | D | 619 703-8135 | 14719 |
| Telesis Bio Inc (PA) | 3826 | E | 858 228-4115 | 14731 |
| Thermo Fisher Scientific Inc | 3826 | E | 858 453-7551 | 14739 |
| V & P Scientific Inc | 3826 | F | 858 455-0643 | 14749 |
| Hoya Corporation | 3827 | E | 858 309-6050 | 14780 |
| Wintriss Engineering Corp | 3827 | E | 858 550-7300 | 14832 |
| Fitbit LLC | 3829 | C | 415 513-1000 | 14867 |

Employee Codes: A=Over 500 employees, B=251-500, C=101-250, D=51-100, E=20-50, F=10-19, G=1-9

# SAN DIEGO, CA  GEOGRAPHIC SECTION

| Company | SIC | EMP | PHONE | ENTRY# |
|---|---|---|---|---|
| Gamma Scientific Inc. | 3829 | E | 858 635-9008 | 14870 |
| Gantner Instruments Inc. | 3829 | E | 888 512-5788 | 14871 |
| Intelliguard Group LLC | 3829 | E | 760 448-9500 | 14884 |
| Pacific Diversified Capital Co. | 3829 | E | 619 696-2000 | 14908 |
| SKF Condition Monitoring Inc (DH) | 3829 | C | 858 496-3400 | 14920 |
| Spectral Labs Incorporated. | 3829 | E | 858 451-0540 | 14925 |
| Teledyne Instruments Inc. | 3829 | D | 619 239-5959 | 14929 |
| Teledyne Instruments Inc. | 3829 | E | 858 657-9800 | 14931 |
| Accriva Dgnostics Holdings Inc (DH) | 3841 | B | 858 404-8203 | 14948 |
| Ajinomoto Althea Inc (HQ) | 3841 | E | 858 882-0123 | 14952 |
| Ameditech Inc. | 3841 | C | 858 535-1968 | 14964 |
| Apex Medical Technologies Inc. | 3841 | E | 858 535-0012 | 14969 |
| Becton Dickinson and Company | 3841 | D | 888 876-4287 | 15001 |
| Becton Dickinson and Company | 3841 | E | 858 617-2000 | 15003 |
| Biogeneral Inc. | 3841 | E | 858 453-4451 | 15010 |
| Bioject Inc. | 3841 | E | 503 692-8001 | 15012 |
| Branan Medical Corporation (PA) | 3841 | E | 949 598-7166 | 15019 |
| Carefusion 213 LLC (DH) | 3841 | B | 800 523-0502 | 15029 |
| Carefusion Corporation. | 3841 | D | 858 617-4271 | 15030 |
| Carefusion Solutions LLC (DH) | 3841 | A | 858 617-2100 | 15033 |
| Chart Sequal Technologies Inc. | 3841 | E | 858 202-3100 | 15040 |
| Companion Medical Inc. | 3841 | D | 858 522-0252 | 15046 |
| Corza Medical Inc. | 3841 | F | 619 671-0276 | 15055 |
| Covidien Holding Inc. | 3841 | C | 619 690-8500 | 15060 |
| Dexcom Inc (PA) | 3841 | A | 858 200-0200 | 15066 |
| Genalyte Inc (PA) | 3841 | F | 858 956-1200 | 15097 |
| Glysens Incorporated. | 3841 | E | 858 638-7708 | 15102 |
| Imtec Biomedical Inc. | 3841 | F | 619 316-1207 | 15115 |
| Inova Labs Inc. | 3841 | D | 866 647-0691 | 15118 |
| Integer Holdings Corporation. | 3841 | E | 619 498-9448 | 15120 |
| Integra Lfscnces Holdings Corp. | 3841 | E | 609 529-9748 | 15121 |
| International Technidyne Corp (DH) | 3841 | C | 858 263-2300 | 15123 |
| Mast Biosurgery USA Inc. | 3841 | E | 858 550-8050 | 15161 |
| Medtronic Inc. | 3841 | E | 949 798-3934 | 15173 |
| Modular Medical Inc (PA) | 3841 | E | 858 800-3500 | 15194 |
| Nexus Dx Inc. | 3841 | E | 858 410-4600 | 15206 |
| Nuvasive Inc. | 3841 | F | 858 909-1800 | 15211 |
| Nuvasive Inc (HQ) | 3841 | D | 858 909-1800 | 15212 |
| Providien LLC (HQ) | 3841 | C | 480 344-5000 | 15233 |
| Resmed Inc (PA) | 3841 | A | 858 836-5000 | 15241 |
| Synergy Health Ast LLC (DH) | 3841 | E | 858 586-1166 | 15274 |
| Tandem Diabetes Care Inc (PA) | 3841 | A | 858 366-6900 | 15276 |
| Howmedica Osteonics Corp. | 3842 | C | 800 621-6104 | 15359 |
| Medical Device Bus Svcs Inc. | 3842 | E | 858 560-4165 | 15374 |
| Psyonic Inc. | 3842 | E | 888 779-6642 | 15396 |
| Reva Medical Inc (PA) | 3842 | E | 858 966-3000 | 15398 |
| Steris Corporation. | 3842 | D | 858 586-1166 | 15408 |
| Carefusion Corporation (HQ) | 3845 | B | 858 617-2000 | 15524 |
| Coastline International. | 3845 | C | 888 748-7177 | 15526 |
| Daylight Defense LLC. | 3845 | C | 858 432-7500 | 15529 |
| Gen-Probe Sales & Service Inc. | 3845 | E | 858 410-8000 | 15539 |
| Hologic Inc. | 3845 | C | 858 410-8000 | 15542 |
| Hologic Inc. | 3845 | E | 858 410-8792 | 15543 |
| Natus Medical Incorporated. | 3845 | D | 858 260-2590 | 15562 |
| Philips Image Gded Thrapy Corp (DH) | 3845 | B | 800 228-4728 | 15572 |
| Resmed Corp (HQ) | 3845 | D | 858 836-5000 | 15576 |
| Tensys Medical Inc. | 3845 | E | 858 552-1941 | 15583 |
| Blenders Eyewear LLC. | 3851 | D | 858 490-2178 | 15595 |
| Fastec Imaging Corporation. | 3861 | E | 858 592-2342 | 15638 |
| Alor International Ltd. | 3911 | E | 858 454-0011 | 15680 |
| Temple Custom Jewelers LLC. | 3911 | E | 800 988-3844 | 15706 |
| Bravo Sports. | 3949 | E | 562 457-8916 | 15792 |
| Bravo Sports. | 3949 | E | 858 408-0083 | 15794 |
| Crazy Industries. | 3949 | E | 619 270-9090 | 15801 |
| Deuce Brand. | 3949 | F | 877 443-3823 | 15802 |
| Diving Unlimited Intl Inc. | 3949 | D | 619 236-1203 | 15804 |
| Fitness Warehouse LLC (PA) | 3949 | E | 858 578-7676 | 15813 |
| Hyperfly Inc. | 3949 | E | 760 300-0909 | 15826 |
| Indian Industries Inc. | 3949 | E | 800 467-1421 | 15830 |
| John Robert Ard. | 3949 | F | 619 326-0577 | 15832 |
| Rusty Surfboards Inc (PA) | 3949 | F | 858 578-0414 | 15849 |
| Aarrow Sign Spinners. | 3993 | F | 510 200-7326 | 15937 |
| Jones Sign Co Inc. | 3993 | C | 858 569-1400 | 15996 |
| Signtech Electrical Advg Inc. | 3993 | C | 619 527-6100 | 16042 |
| Hemp Industries. | 3999 | E | 619 458-9090 | 16142 |
| Holiday Foliage Inc. | 3999 | E | 619 661-9094 | 16148 |
| Huntington Ingalls Industries. | 3999 | E | 858 522-6000 | 16150 |
| Living To 100 Club LLC. | 3999 | E | 858 272-3992 | 16170 |
| T-Rex Products Incorporated. | 3999 | F | 619 482-4424 | 16248 |
| Air 88 Inc. | 4581 | E | 858 277-1453 | 16298 |
| Chandler Packaging A Transpak Company. | 4783 | D | 858 292-5674 | 16309 |
| Trellisware Technologies Inc (HQ) | 4812 | C | 858 753-1600 | 16314 |
| Yukeep LLC. | 4813 | F | 888 855-2568 | 16325 |
| American Green Lights LLC. | 4931 | E | 858 547-8837 | 16351 |
| Expo Industries Inc. | 5031 | D | 858 566-3110 | 16445 |
| Westside Bldg San Diego LLC. | 5031 | E | 858 566-4343 | 16461 |
| Dove Business Machine Inc. | 5044 | F | 858 638-0100 | 16502 |
| Quartic Solutions LLC. | 5045 | E | 858 377-8470 | 16542 |
| Southland Technology Inc. | 5045 | D | 858 694-0932 | 16550 |
| Ubiq Security Inc. | 5045 | E | 888 434-6674 | 16563 |
| Mobility Solutions Inc (PA) | 5047 | E | 858 278-0591 | 16585 |
| Molecular Bioproducts Svc Corp (HQ) | 5049 | E | 858 875-7696 | 16603 |
| Century Tubes Inc. | 5051 | E | 858 586-0550 | 16612 |
| Cableconn Industries Inc. | 5063 | D | 858 571-7111 | 16647 |
| Main Electric Supply Co LLC. | 5063 | E | 858 737-7000 | 16662 |
| Sloan Electric Corporation. | 5063 | E | 619 239-5174 | 16673 |
| Impact Components A California Limi. | 5065 | E | 858 634-4800 | 16705 |
| Lightpointe Communications Inc. | 5065 | E | 858 834-4083 | 16715 |
| Motorola Mobility LLC. | 5065 | D | 858 455-1500 | 16722 |
| Waterfi LLC. | 5065 | F | 619 438-0058 | 16741 |
| Eurodrip USA Inc. | 5083 | D | 559 674-2670 | 16796 |
| Keco Inc. | 5084 | E | 619 298-3800 | 16823 |
| Otis Elevator Company. | 5084 | D | 858 560-5881 | 16833 |
| Carpenter Group. | 5085 | E | 619 233-5625 | 16866 |
| Pinnacle Industrial Supply Inc (PA) | 5085 | E | 619 710-4255 | 16889 |
| Prestige Graphics Inc. | 5112 | E | 858 560-8213 | 16993 |
| San Diego Die Cutting Inc. | 5113 | E | 619 297-4453 | 17022 |
| Tequila Blues Inc. | 5137 | F | 310 526-8002 | 17103 |
| Producers Meat and Prov Inc. | 5147 | E | 619 232-7593 | 17164 |
| Swell Coffee Roasting Co LP. | 5149 | E | 619 504-9244 | 17219 |
| Clipper Oil Inc. | 5172 | E | 619 692-9701 | 17252 |
| PCF Group LLC. | 5199 | F | 858 455-1274 | 17304 |
| Stratos Manufacturing LLC. | 5199 | F | 408 839-0054 | 17311 |
| Alkal Tile Inc (PA) | 5211 | E | 858 278-7828 | 17321 |
| Dixieline Lumber Company LLC (DH) | 5211 | D | 619 224-4120 | 17327 |
| Superior Ready Mix Concrete LP. | 5211 | D | 858 695-0666 | 17346 |
| El Tigre Inc. | 5411 | C | 619 429-8212 | 17379 |
| Parkhouse Tire Service Inc. | 5531 | E | 858 565-8473 | 17456 |
| Vera Bradley Inc. | 5632 | E | 858 320-9020 | 17501 |
| Adrenaline Lacrosse Inc. | 5699 | E | 888 768-8479 | 17507 |
| Athleisure Inc. | 5699 | E | 858 866-0108 | 17509 |
| Gosecure Inc (PA) | 5734 | C | 301 442-3432 | 17551 |
| Pcfs Solutions. | 5734 | C | 714 674-0009 | 17557 |
| Carvin Corp. | 5736 | C | 858 487-1600 | 17561 |
| Cafe 21 Gaslamp Inc. | 5812 | E | 619 239-0721 | 17567 |
| Border X Brewing LLC. | 5813 | E | 619 501-0503 | 17614 |
| Harland Brewing Co LLC. | 5813 | E | 858 800-4566 | 17618 |
| Mission Brewery Inc. | 5813 | E | 619 818-7147 | 17622 |
| Cyberbasket Inc. | 5947 | F | 619 450-6700 | 17655 |
| Road Runner Sports Inc (PA) | 5961 | D | 858 974-4200 | 17673 |
| Officia Imaging Inc (PA) | 5999 | E | 858 348-0831 | 17715 |
| Scope Orthtics Prosthetics Inc (DH) | 5999 | E | 858 292-7448 | 17719 |
| Russ Mike Financial Training. | 6411 | F | 800 724-5661 | 17738 |
| Ogleby Sisters Soap. | 7231 | E | 212 518-1172 | 17772 |
| Saffron & Sage LLC. | 7299 | F | 619 933-2340 | 17775 |
| Sports Boosters Inc (PA) | 7311 | F | 888 541-5561 | 17783 |
| Full/Tech Systems Inc. | 7331 | E | 619 297-0454 | 17798 |
| Dimensional Silk Screen Inc. | 7336 | F | 619 232-9100 | 17827 |
| Cardinal Point Captains Inc. | 7363 | D | 760 438-7361 | 17867 |
| Algorithmic Objective Corp. | 7371 | E | 858 249-9580 | 17878 |
| Biosero (PA) | 7371 | E | 858 880-7376 | 17888 |
| Cubic Trnsp Systems Inc (DH) | 7371 | A | 858 268-3100 | 17904 |
| Logility Inc. | 7371 | D | 858 565-4238 | 17942 |
| Medimizer Software. | 7371 | E | 760 642-2000 | 17947 |
| Parallel 6 Inc (PA) | 7371 | E | 619 452-1750 | 17961 |
| Platform Science Inc (PA) | 7371 | C | 844 475-8724 | 17962 |
| Sciforma Corporation. | 7371 | E | 408 899-0398 | 17975 |
| Altumind Inc. | 7372 | E | 858 382-3956 | 18042 |
| Ancora Software Inc (PA) | 7372 | E | 888 476-4839 | 18044 |
| Appfolio Inc. | 7372 | C | 866 648-1536 | 18052 |
| Ascender Software Inc. | 7372 | E | 877 561-7501 | 18068 |
| Blitz Rocks Inc. | 7372 | E | 310 883-5183 | 18112 |
| Chatmeter Inc. | 7372 | D | 619 300-1050 | 18164 |
| Classy Inc. | 7372 | E | 619 961-1892 | 18171 |
| Curemetrix Inc. | 7372 | E | 858 333-5830 | 18216 |
| Dassault Systemes Biovia Corp (DH) | 7372 | E | 858 799-5000 | 18226 |
| Dcatalog Inc. | 7372 | E | 408 824-5648 | 18232 |
| Decisionlogic LLC. | 7372 | E | 858 586-0202 | 18234 |
| Digital Arbitrage Dist Inc (PA) | 7372 | E | 888 392-9474 | 18240 |
| Dreamstart Labs Inc. | 7372 | E | 408 914-1234 | 18251 |
| Edgate Holdings Inc. | 7372 | E | 858 712-9341 | 18262 |
| Galley Solutions Inc. | 7372 | E | 818 636-1538 | 18340 |
| Genasys Inc (PA) | 7372 | D | 858 676-1112 | 18344 |
| Humbl Inc. | 7372 | F | 786 738-9012 | 18395 |
| Imageware Systems Inc (PA) | 7372 | F | 858 673-8600 | 18404 |
| Intuit Inc. | 7372 | B | 858 780-2846 | 18433 |

# GEOGRAPHIC SECTION — SAN FRANCISCO, CA

| Company | SIC | EMP | PHONE | ENTRY# |
|---|---|---|---|---|
| Intuit Inc. | 7372 | E | 858 215-8000 | 18435 |
| Intuit Inc. | 7372 | B | 858 215-8000 | 18436 |
| Kazuhm Inc. | 7372 | E | 858 771-3861 | 18464 |
| Kintera Inc (HQ) | 7372 | C | 858 795-3000 | 18472 |
| Kyriba Corp (PA) | 7372 | E | 858 210-3560 | 18482 |
| Leadcrunch Inc (PA) | 7372 | E | 888 708-6649 | 18490 |
| Mitek Systems Inc (PA) | 7372 | D | 619 269-6800 | 18550 |
| Musicmatch Inc. | 7372 | C | 858 485-4300 | 18564 |
| New Bi US Gaming LLC | 7372 | E | 858 592-2472 | 18581 |
| Nexogy Inc. | 7372 | D | 305 358-8952 | 18585 |
| Omnitracs Midco LLC | 7372 | E | 858 651-5812 | 18616 |
| Procede Software LP | 7372 | E | 858 450-4800 | 18697 |
| Protagonist Games LLC | 7372 | E | 512 785-4946 | 18705 |
| Qualer Inc. | 7372 | E | 858 224-9516 | 18715 |
| Seismic Software Inc (HQ) | 7372 | D | 714 404-7069 | 18776 |
| Sequelae Inc. | 7372 | D | 801 628-0256 | 18781 |
| Smart-Tek Services Inc (HQ) | 7372 | F | 858 798-1644 | 18799 |
| Solv Energy LLC | 7372 | C | 858 622-4040 | 18810 |
| Sonendo Acquisition Corp. | 7372 | E | 858 558-3696 | 18811 |
| Sonic Vr LLC | 7372 | E | 206 227-8585 | 18812 |
| Strategic Insights Inc | 7372 | E | 858 452-7500 | 18839 |
| Teradata Corporation (PA) | 7372 | A | 866 548-8348 | 18873 |
| Wind River Systems Inc. | 7372 | F | 858 824-3100 | 18936 |
| Wme Bi LLC | 7372 | D | 877 592-2472 | 18939 |
| Wordsmart Corporation | 7372 | E | | 18941 |
| Wowyow Inc. | 7372 | F | 844 496-9969 | 18944 |
| Captiva Software Corporation (DH) | 7373 | D | 858 320-1000 | 18966 |
| Clinicomp International Inc (PA) | 7373 | D | 858 546-8202 | 18970 |
| Zmicro Inc (HQ) | 7373 | E | 858 831-7000 | 19002 |
| Bernardo Technical Services | 7379 | F | 858 779-9276 | 19029 |
| Accurate Security Pros Inc. | 7382 | E | 858 271-1155 | 19051 |
| Beaumont Nielsen Marine Inc. | 7389 | E | 619 223-2628 | 19075 |
| Scilex Pharmaceuticals Inc (HQ) | 7389 | F | 949 441-2270 | 19125 |
| Skdy of San Diego Inc. | 7389 | E | 858 552-9033 | 19132 |
| Pro Circuits Manufacturing Inc. | 7629 | E | 858 899-4747 | 19176 |
| Schroff Inc. | 7629 | C | 858 740-2400 | 19178 |
| Action Cleaning Corporation. | 7699 | E | 619 233-1881 | 19238 |
| Chromalloy San Diego Corp. | 7699 | E | 858 877-2800 | 19249 |
| Western Pump Inc (PA) | 7699 | D | 619 239-9988 | 19289 |
| James G Meyers & Associates. | 8042 | E | 858 622-2165 | 19323 |
| Biora Therapeutics Inc (PA) | 8071 | E | 833 727-2841 | 19325 |
| Biotheranostics Inc (HQ) | 8071 | F | 877 886-6739 | 19326 |
| Provisio Medical Inc. | 8099 | E | 508 740-9940 | 19338 |
| Wells Media Group Inc (PA) | 8111 | F | 619 584-1100 | 19341 |
| Essence of America. | 8322 | E | 312 805-9365 | 19357 |
| San Dego Second Chance Program. | 8322 | E | 619 266-2506 | 19359 |
| Morris Crullo World Evangelism (PA) | 8661 | D | 858 277-2200 | 19368 |
| Encore Semi Inc. | 8711 | D | 858 225-4993 | 19392 |
| Rock West Composites Inc. | 8711 | E | 858 537-6260 | 19415 |
| San Diego Composites Inc. | 8711 | E | 858 751-0450 | 19417 |
| Sep Group Inc. | 8711 | E | 858 876-4621 | 19421 |
| Architectural Mtls USA Inc. | 8712 | D | 888 219-2126 | 19431 |
| Ainos Inc (PA) | 8731 | E | 858 869-2986 | 19437 |
| Ansun Biopharma Inc. | 8731 | E | 858 452-2631 | 19441 |
| Bioduro LLC (PA) | 8731 | E | 858 529-6600 | 19445 |
| General Atomics. | 8731 | C | 858 455-4000 | 19453 |
| Inova Diagnostics Inc (HQ) | 8731 | B | 858 586-9900 | 19456 |
| Leidos Inc. | 8731 | E | 858 826-6000 | 19461 |
| M&B Sciences Inc. | 8731 | E | 858 812-8735 | 19464 |
| Wildcat Discovery Tech Inc. | 8731 | D | 858 550-1980 | 19483 |
| Peraton Technology Svcs Inc. | 8733 | E | 571 313-6000 | 19495 |
| Viacyte Inc. | 8733 | E | 858 455-3708 | 19498 |
| Blue Sky Elearn LLC | 8742 | E | 877 925-8375 | 19522 |
| Tacna International Corp. | 8742 | F | 619 661-1261 | 19541 |
| Sanyo North America Corp. | 8748 | B | 619 661-1134 | 19569 |

## SAN DIMAS, CA - Los Angeles County

| Company | SIC | EMP | PHONE | ENTRY# |
|---|---|---|---|---|
| Organic Milling Inc (PA) | 2099 | D | 800 638-8686 | 2301 |
| Organic Milling Corporation | 2099 | E | 909 599-0961 | 2302 |
| Roskam Baking Company LLC | 2099 | C | 909 599-0961 | 2341 |
| Roskam Baking Company LLC | 2099 | B | 909 305-0185 | 2342 |
| Immortal Masks Inc. | 2389 | E | 909 599-5391 | 2902 |
| Westin Automotive Products Inc (PA) | 2396 | E | 626 960-6762 | 3020 |
| M724 Inc. | 2514 | F | 951 314-1333 | 3506 |
| Western PCF Stor Solutions Inc (PA) | 2542 | D | 909 451-0303 | 3714 |
| Gilead Palo Alto Inc. | 2834 | C | 909 394-4000 | 5461 |
| Gilead Sciences Inc. | 2834 | A | 909 394-4000 | 5464 |
| Cosmobeauti Labs & Mfg Inc. | 2844 | F | 909 971-9832 | 5963 |
| Hagen-Renaker Inc (PA) | 3269 | E | 909 599-2341 | 7287 |
| Danrich Welding Co Inc. | 3444 | E | 562 634-4811 | 8424 |
| Gms Elevator Services Inc. | 3534 | E | 909 599-3904 | 9472 |
| Magor Mold LLC | 3544 | D | 909 592-3663 | 9634 |
| Bluelab Corporation Usa Inc. | 3569 | E | 909 599-1940 | 10078 |
| Sypris Data Systems Inc (HQ) | 3572 | E | 909 962-9400 | 10288 |
| Kap Manufacturing Inc. | 3599 | E | 909 599-2525 | 10921 |
| AC Propulsion Inc. | 3621 | E | 909 592-5399 | 11254 |
| Sigtronics Corporation. | 3669 | E | 909 305-9399 | 12017 |
| Landmark Electronics Inc. | 3679 | E | 626 967-2857 | 13021 |
| Wavestream Corporation (HQ) | 3679 | C | 909 599-9080 | 13120 |
| Young Engineering & Mfg Inc (PA) | 3823 | E | 909 394-3225 | 14472 |
| Hamilton Sundstrand Corp. | 3826 | C | 909 593-5300 | 14670 |
| Hamilton Sundstrand Spc Systms | 3829 | D | 909 288-5300 | 14875 |
| Elba Jewelry Inc. | 3911 | F | 909 394-5803 | 15690 |
| Superwinch LLC | 5013 | E | 800 323-2031 | 16403 |
| Webmetro | 7372 | D | 909 599-8885 | 18930 |
| National Hot Rod Association (PA) | 7948 | C | 626 914-4761 | 19308 |
| New Spirit Naturals Inc (PA) | 8011 | E | 909 592-4445 | 19319 |
| Thorpe Technologies Inc (DH) | 8711 | E | 562 903-8230 | 19425 |

## SAN FERNANDO, CA - Los Angeles County

| Company | SIC | EMP | PHONE | ENTRY# |
|---|---|---|---|---|
| Karoun Dairies Inc (PA) | 2022 | E | 818 767-7000 | 722 |
| American Bottling Company. | 2086 | D | 818 898-1471 | 1856 |
| Pepsi-Cola Metro Btlg Co Inc. | 2086 | D | 818 898-3829 | 1919 |
| Fresh & Ready Foods LLC (PA) | 2099 | D | 818 837-7600 | 2205 |
| Lehman Foods Inc. | 2099 | D | 818 837-7600 | 2263 |
| Mr Tortilla Inc. | 2099 | E | 818 233-8932 | 2287 |
| New Haven Companies Inc. | 2299 | D | 818 686-7020 | 2551 |
| Santana Formal Accessories Inc. | 2311 | F | 818 898-3677 | 2566 |
| Wyndham Collection LLC | 2434 | E | 888 522-8476 | 3283 |
| Airo Industries Company. | 2531 | E | 818 838-1008 | 3613 |
| Abex Display Systems Inc (PA) | 2653 | C | 800 537-0231 | 3817 |
| Araca Merchandise LP | 2759 | D | 818 743-5400 | 4842 |
| Pharmavite LLC | 2833 | F | 818 221-6200 | 5262 |
| Puretek Corporation (PA) | 2834 | E | 818 361-3316 | 5619 |
| J Miller Co Inc. | 3053 | E | 818 837-0181 | 6455 |
| Spira Manufacturing Corp. | 3053 | E | 818 764-8222 | 6468 |
| C A Schroeder Inc (PA) | 3296 | E | 818 365-9561 | 7573 |
| J & M Products Inc. | 3429 | D | 818 837-0205 | 8006 |
| Bellows Mfg & RES Inc. | 3441 | E | 818 838-1333 | 8102 |
| Triumph Precision Products. | 3451 | F | 818 897-4700 | 8735 |
| TL Shield & Associates Inc. | 3534 | E | 818 509-8228 | 9477 |
| Metromedia Technologies Inc. | 3577 | E | 818 552-6500 | 10410 |
| W Machine Works Inc. | 3599 | E | 818 890-8049 | 11180 |
| Topaz Lighting Company LLC | 3646 | E | 818 838-3123 | 11562 |
| Signature Tech Group Inc. | 3679 | E | 818 890-7611 | 13084 |
| Skaug Truck Body Works | 3713 | F | 818 365-9123 | 13428 |
| Frazier Aviation Inc. | 3728 | E | 818 898-1998 | 13846 |
| One Step Gps LLC | 3812 | D | 818 659-2031 | 14272 |
| J L Shepherd and Assoc Inc. | 3829 | E | 818 898-2361 | 14887 |
| Valeda Company LLC | 3842 | E | 800 421-8700 | 15425 |
| Laser Technologies & Services LLC | 3861 | D | | 15648 |
| Dg-Displays LLC. | 3993 | E | 877 358-5976 | 15965 |
| Ricon Corporation. | 3999 | C | 818 267-3000 | 16218 |
| Jme Inc (PA) | 5063 | D | 201 896-8600 | 16655 |
| Ahi Investment Inc (DH) | 5199 | E | 818 979-0030 | 17283 |
| Cousins Foods LLC. | 5411 | E | 818 767-3842 | 17373 |
| A Thread Ahead Inc. | 7389 | E | 818 837-1984 | 19067 |

## SAN FRANCISCO, CA - San Francisco County

| Company | SIC | EMP | PHONE | ENTRY# |
|---|---|---|---|---|
| Pax Labs Inc. | 0139 | C | 415 829-2336 | 4 |
| H&Gbygiselleco. | 0782 | F | 415 829-3867 | 98 |
| Grubb & Nadler Inc (PA) | 1231 | E | 415 694-6441 | 114 |
| Colombia Energy Resources Inc. | 1241 | C | | 116 |
| Siluria Technologies Inc. | 1311 | E | 415 978-2170 | 138 |
| Tpg Partners III LP (DH) | 1311 | E | 415 743-1500 | 142 |
| Halliburton Legal. | 1389 | E | 415 955-1155 | 235 |
| Sunrun Inc (PA) | 1711 | B | 415 580-6900 | 437 |
| Rt Western Inc. | 1799 | E | 415 677-9202 | 572 |
| Aphro-D LLC. | 2023 | E | 201 574-1875 | 742 |
| Aussie Bubs Inc. | 2023 | E | 888 685-1508 | 744 |
| Kings Asian Gourmet Inc. | 2032 | E | 415 222-6100 | 862 |
| Forager Project LLC (PA) | 2037 | D | 855 729-5253 | 1006 |
| Big Heart Pet Brands Inc (HQ) | 2047 | B | 415 247-3000 | 1094 |
| Andre-Boudin Bakeries Inc (HQ) | 2051 | E | 415 882-1849 | 1157 |
| Pan-O-Rama Baking Inc. | 2051 | E | 415 522-5500 | 1235 |
| Tartine LP. | 2051 | E | 415 487-2600 | 1247 |
| Sees Candies Inc (DH) | 2064 | B | 800 347-7337 | 1327 |
| Poco Dolce Chocolates. | 2066 | F | 415 255-1443 | 1343 |
| Darling Ingredients Inc. | 2077 | E | 415 647-4890 | 1383 |
| Barebottle Brewing Company Inc. | 2082 | D | 415 926-8617 | 1424 |
| Liquid Gold. | 2082 | E | 415 660-5142 | 1446 |
| Speakeasy Ales & Lagers Inc. | 2082 | E | 415 642-3371 | 1459 |
| Diageo North America Inc. | 2084 | D | 415 835-7300 | 1538 |
| Niebam-Cppola Estate Winery LP | 2084 | E | 415 291-1700 | 1691 |
| Vintage Wine Estates Inc CA | 2084 | E | 415 495-1350 | 1817 |
| Rare Breed Distilling LLC (HQ) | 2085 | E | 415 315-8060 | 1841 |

**Employee Codes:** A=Over 500 employees, B=251-500, C=101-250, D=51-100, E=20-50, F=10-19, G=1-9

# SAN FRANCISCO, CA                                               GEOGRAPHIC SECTION

| Company | SIC | EMP | PHONE | ENTRY# |
|---|---|---|---|---|
| Tequilas Premium Inc | 2085 | F | 415 399-0496 | 1847 |
| Hint Inc | 2086 | C | 415 513-4051 | 1894 |
| Jeremiahs Pick Coffee Company | 2095 | F | 415 206-9900 | 2074 |
| 4505 Meats Inc | 2096 | E | 415 255-3094 | 2083 |
| Hana Group Ops LLC | 2099 | E | 628 280-9401 | 2227 |
| Sun Basket Inc (PA) | 2099 | C | 866 786-2758 | 2361 |
| Sun Basket Inc | 2099 | D | 408 669-4418 | 2362 |
| Thistle Health Inc | 2099 | B | 917 587-2341 | 2374 |
| Allbirds Inc (PA) | 2211 | C | 628 225-4848 | 2399 |
| Trumaker Inc | 2311 | E | 415 662-3836 | 2568 |
| Levi Strauss & Co (PA) | 2325 | A | 415 501-6000 | 2586 |
| Levi Strauss International (HQ) | 2329 | D | 415 501-6000 | 2631 |
| Byer California (PA) | 2331 | A | 415 626-7844 | 2658 |
| L Y Z Ltd (PA) | 2335 | F | 415 445-9505 | 2709 |
| Theory LLC | 2337 | F | 415 376-9065 | 2728 |
| Cut Loose (PA) | 2339 | D | 415 822-2031 | 2749 |
| Jjs Mae Inc (PA) | 2339 | D | 415 255-7047 | 2773 |
| Margaret OLeary Inc (PA) | 2339 | D | 415 354-6663 | 2788 |
| One Hat One Hand LLC | 2353 | E | 415 822-2020 | 2848 |
| Jessica McClintock Inc (PA) | 2361 | C | 415 553-8200 | 2854 |
| Gb Sport Sf LLC | 2386 | E | 415 863-6171 | 2880 |
| Mr S Leather | 2386 | E | 415 863-7764 | 2882 |
| Rickshaw Bagworks Inc | 2393 | E | 415 904-8368 | 2961 |
| Timbuk2 Designs Inc (HQ) | 2393 | F | 415 252-4300 | 2962 |
| Lowpensky Moulding | 2431 | F | 415 822-7422 | 3154 |
| Plant/Allison Corporation | 2431 | E | 415 285-0500 | 3179 |
| Handle Inc | 2499 | E | 650 863-6113 | 3418 |
| Van Sark Inc (PA) | 2512 | D | 510 635-1111 | 3494 |
| Thomas Lundberg | 2514 | E | 415 695-0110 | 3513 |
| McRoskey Mattress Company | 2515 | E | 415 861-4532 | 3534 |
| Ohio Inc | 2521 | F | 415 647-6446 | 3580 |
| Arnold and Egan Mfg Co | 2541 | E | 415 822-2700 | 3645 |
| Galindo Instlltion Mvg Svcs In | 2542 | F | 415 861-4230 | 3689 |
| Bar Media Inc | 2711 | F | 415 861-5019 | 4073 |
| Bay Guardian Company | 2711 | E | 415 255-3100 | 4074 |
| Business Jrnl Publications Inc | 2711 | E | 415 989-2522 | 4079 |
| Dow Jones & Company Inc | 2711 | E | 415 765-6131 | 4104 |
| Gum Sun Times Inc (PA) | 2711 | E | 415 379-6788 | 4124 |
| Hearst Communications Inc | 2711 | E | 415 537-4200 | 4127 |
| Recorder | 2711 | E | 877 256-2472 | 4183 |
| Dwell Life Inc (PA) | 2721 | E | 415 373-5100 | 4250 |
| Foundation For Nat Progress | 2721 | E | 415 321-1700 | 4257 |
| Freedom of Press Foundation | 2721 | F | 510 995-0780 | 4259 |
| Hartle Media Ventures LLC | 2721 | F | 415 362-7797 | 4262 |
| Idg Consumer & Smb Inc (DH) | 2721 | C | 415 243-0500 | 4266 |
| Infoworld Media Group Inc (DH) | 2721 | D | 415 243-4344 | 4267 |
| Mac Publishing LLC (DH) | 2721 | E | 415 243-0505 | 4275 |
| Modern Luxury Media LLC (HQ) | 2721 | E | 404 443-0004 | 4281 |
| Refinitiv US LLC | 2721 | C | 415 344-6000 | 4294 |
| Viz Media LLC | 2721 | E | 415 546-7073 | 4305 |
| Wired Ventures Inc | 2721 | C | 415 276-8400 | 4306 |
| Blurb Inc | 2731 | E | 415 364-6300 | 4315 |
| Chronicle Books LLC (HQ) | 2731 | D | 415 537-4200 | 4321 |
| Hawkeye Acquisition Inc | 2731 | E | 415 249-2362 | 4330 |
| Comparenetworks Inc (PA) | 2741 | D | 518 238-6617 | 4382 |
| Dwell Life Inc | 2741 | F | 212 382-2010 | 4390 |
| Federated Media Publishing LLC | 2741 | C | 415 332-6955 | 4398 |
| Fundx Investment Group LLC | 2741 | F | 415 986-7979 | 4400 |
| Game Insight Publishing | 2741 | E | 415 412-5064 | 4402 |
| Guadalupe Associates Inc (PA) | 2741 | F | 415 387-2324 | 4410 |
| Inkitt Inc | 2741 | E | 978 844-1074 | 4416 |
| Pacific Bell Directory | 2741 | A | 800 303-3000 | 4443 |
| Penrose Studios Inc | 2741 | F | 703 354-1801 | 4447 |
| Rangeme USA LLC | 2741 | E | 510 688-0995 | 4458 |
| Sparkcentral Inc (HQ) | 2741 | D | 866 559-6229 | 4467 |
| Twitch Interactive Inc | 2741 | A |  | 4484 |
| Communication Services Ctr Inc | 2752 | E | 415 252-1600 | 4564 |
| Digital Mania Inc | 2752 | E | 415 896-0500 | 4589 |
| Gorman Catalog Printing Inc | 2752 | E |  | 4619 |
| Gorman Manufacturing Company Inc (PA) | 2752 | C | 650 555-0000 | 4620 |
| Integrated Digital Media | 2752 | F | 415 627-8310 | 4652 |
| Lobcom Inc | 2752 | C | 415 894-9979 | 4682 |
| Social Print Studio | 2752 | F | 805 551-5328 | 4765 |
| ABC Imaging of Washington | 2759 | E | 415 525-3874 | 4834 |
| Punkpost LLC | 2771 | E | 415 818-7677 | 4996 |
| Rapid Typographers Company (PA) | 2791 | F | 415 957-5840 | 5022 |
| Sgk LLC | 2796 | E | 415 438-6700 | 5028 |
| Ace Creations LLC | 2833 | F | 248 762-9679 | 5227 |
| 89bio Inc | 2834 | D | 415 432-9270 | 5284 |
| Aradigm Corporation | 2834 | E | 510 265-9000 | 5330 |
| Better Therapeutics (PA) | 2834 | F | 415 887-2311 | 5365 |
| Better Therapeutics Opco Inc | 2834 | F | 415 887-2311 | 5366 |
| Bioq Pharma Incorporated (PA) | 2834 | F | 415 336-6496 | 5376 |
| Blackthorn Therapeutics Inc | 2834 | E | 510 828-4062 | 5379 |
| Blade Therapeutics Inc | 2834 | E | 650 334-2079 | 5380 |
| Concentric Analgesics Inc | 2834 | E | 415 771-5129 | 5406 |
| Curae Pharma360 Inc | 2834 | E | 415 951-8700 | 5416 |
| Fibrogen Inc (PA) | 2834 | C | 415 978-1200 | 5439 |
| Hims & Hers Health Inc (PA) | 2834 | E | 415 851-0195 | 5481 |
| Jaguar Health Inc (PA) | 2834 | E | 415 371-8300 | 5509 |
| Koshland Pharmacy Inc | 2834 | F | 415 344-0600 | 5529 |
| Medivation Inc | 2834 | C | 415 812-6345 | 5550 |
| Medivation Inc (HQ) | 2834 | D | 415 543-3470 | 5551 |
| Nektar Therapeutics (PA) | 2834 | D | 415 482-5300 | 5567 |
| Olema Pharmaceuticals Inc (PA) | 2834 | E | 415 651-3316 | 5584 |
| Ray Therapeutics Inc | 2834 | E | 858 617-8610 | 5630 |
| Rezo Therapeutics Inc | 2834 | E | 650 704-5577 | 5638 |
| Sirna Therapeutics Inc | 2834 | E | 415 512-7200 | 5661 |
| Vir Biotechnology Inc (PA) | 2836 | B | 415 906-4324 | 5869 |
| Method Products Inc | 2841 | E | 415 931-3947 | 5877 |
| Caroline Chu Inc | 2844 | E | 415 279-2358 | 5954 |
| H2o Plus LLC (PA) | 2844 | D | 800 242-2284 | 5984 |
| Hims Inc (HQ) | 2844 | E | 415 851-0195 | 5988 |
| Native | 2844 | E | 562 217-9338 | 6009 |
| Vintners Daughter LLC | 2844 | F | 415 906-6735 | 6054 |
| Zenlen Inc | 2844 | E | 415 834-8238 | 6064 |
| R J McGlennon Company Inc (PA) | 2851 | E | 415 552-0311 | 6109 |
| Associated Materials Inc | 3089 | A | 415 788-5111 | 6727 |
| 1919 Investment Counsel LLC | 3131 | F | 415 500-6707 | 7090 |
| Allbirds Inc | 3143 | F | 415 469-1455 | 7094 |
| Allbirds Inc | 3143 | F | 415 802-2800 | 7100 |
| Bryr LLC | 3144 | F | 415 374-7323 | 7114 |
| Goyard Miami LLC | 3161 | C | 415 398-1110 | 7131 |
| Foggy Dog LLC | 3199 | F | 415 993-1130 | 7156 |
| Heath Ceramics Ltd | 3269 | E | 415 361-5552 | 7288 |
| Lime Light Crm Inc | 3274 | F | 800 455-9645 | 7523 |
| Candela Renewables LLC | 3433 | E | 415 515-9627 | 8062 |
| RE Tranquillity 8 LLC | 3433 | D | 415 675-1500 | 8077 |
| Solon Corporation | 3433 | E | 520 807-1300 | 8081 |
| JC Metal Specialists Inc | 3441 | E | 415 822-3878 | 8156 |
| Toms Metal Specialists Inc | 3441 | E | 415 822-7971 | 8231 |
| MC Metal Inc | 3446 | F | 415 822-2288 | 8637 |
| Arcbyt Inc (PA) | 3531 | F | 415 449-4852 | 9408 |
| Cleasby Manufacturing Co Inc (PA) | 3531 | E | 415 822-6565 | 9416 |
| Softbank Robotics America Inc (DH) | 3535 | F | 844 737-7371 | 9495 |
| Productboard Inc (PA) | 3537 | C | 844 472-6273 | 9532 |
| Mantle Inc | 3544 | E | 415 655-3555 | 9635 |
| Bright Machines Inc (PA) | 3549 | B | 415 867-4402 | 9735 |
| American Industrial Partners LP | 3559 | A | 415 788-7354 | 9827 |
| Cobalt Robotics Inc | 3571 | D | 650 781-3623 | 10142 |
| Hp Inc | 3571 | D | 415 979-3700 | 10159 |
| Scality Inc | 3572 | E | 650 356-8500 | 10276 |
| Blue Cedar Networks Inc | 3577 | E | 415 329-0401 | 10338 |
| Cisco Systems Inc | 3577 | E | 415 845-8008 | 10347 |
| Segmentio Inc | 3577 | B | 844 611-0621 | 10434 |
| Macintyre Corp | 3585 | E | 800 229-3560 | 10507 |
| Treau Inc | 3585 | E | 866 945-3514 | 10522 |
| Naturener USA LLC (HQ) | 3621 | E | 415 217-5500 | 11280 |
| Stem Inc (PA) | 3621 | E | 877 374-7836 | 11289 |
| Tanko Streetlighting Inc | 3646 | E | 415 254-7579 | 11561 |
| Dolby Laboratories Inc | 3651 | C | 415 645-5000 | 11649 |
| Dolby Laboratories Inc (PA) | 3651 | B | 415 558-0200 | 11652 |
| Dolby Labs Licensing Corp | 3651 | C | 415 558-0200 | 11653 |
| Isolation Network Inc (PA) | 3651 | D | 818 212-2600 | 11669 |
| Olive Media Products Inc | 3651 | F | 415 908-3870 | 11684 |
| Petcube Inc (PA) | 3651 | E | 424 302-6107 | 11686 |
| Clincapture | 3652 | E | 408 412-7256 | 11724 |
| Ncc Group Escrow Assoc LLC | 3652 | E | 678 381-2768 | 11738 |
| Astranis Space Tech Corp (PA) | 3663 | D | 408 829-1101 | 11815 |
| Ground Control Inc | 3663 | E | 415 508-8589 | 11860 |
| Planet Labs Pbc (PA) | 3663 | D | 415 829-3313 | 11916 |
| Carlos A Garcia | 3669 | D | 888 410-1648 | 11987 |
| Visionary Electronics Inc | 3674 | F | 415 751-8811 | 12794 |
| Zola Electric Labs Inc | 3674 | E | 650 542-6939 | 12814 |
| Terawatt Infrastructure Inc | 3694 | F | 785 251-0751 | 13188 |
| Terawatt Infrastructure Inc | 3694 | E | 415 837-1946 | 13189 |
| Recommind Inc (HQ) | 3695 | D | 415 394-7899 | 13201 |
| Aptible Inc | 3699 | D | 866 296-5003 | 13212 |
| Diy Co | 3699 | F | 844 564-6349 | 13233 |
| Ecotality Inc | 3699 | C | 415 992-3000 | 13237 |
| Ijk & Co Inc | 3699 | E | 415 826-8899 | 13249 |
| Pipeline Trading Systems LLC | 3699 | E | 415 293-8159 | 13290 |
| Voltpost Inc | 3699 | E | 908 868-1527 | 13327 |
| American Scence Tech As T Corp (PA) | 3721 | C | 415 251-2800 | 13633 |
| Turbine Eng Cmpnents Tech Corp | 3724 | C | 415 626-2000 | 13725 |
| Kargo Technologies Corp | 3731 | E | 312 925-1565 | 14006 |

# GEOGRAPHIC SECTION                                                                                    SAN FRANCISCO, CA

| Company | SIC | EMP | PHONE | ENTRY# |
|---|---|---|---|---|
| Puglia Engineering Inc | 3731 | C | 415 861-7447 | 14015 |
| San Francisco Ship Repair Inc | 3731 | C | 415 861-7447 | 14017 |
| ARC Boat Company | 3732 | D | 877 272-2443 | 14028 |
| Capella Space Corp | 3812 | D | 650 334-7734 | 14168 |
| Chevron Energy Solutions LP | 3822 | B | 415 894-4188 | 14357 |
| Voltus Inc | 3822 | E | 646 248-4342 | 14376 |
| Thermo Fsher Scntific Psg Corp | 3826 | E | 609 865-5869 | 14747 |
| Fitbit LLC (DH) | 3829 | C | 415 513-1000 | 14868 |
| Highland Technology | 3829 | E | 415 551-1700 | 14876 |
| Ouster Inc (PA) | 3829 | E | 415 987-6972 | 14907 |
| Bloomlife Inc | 3841 | E | 415 215-4251 | 15016 |
| Invuity Inc | 3841 | C | 415 665-2100 | 15131 |
| Irhythm Technologies Inc (PA) | 3841 | E | 415 632-5700 | 15132 |
| Mahana Therapeutics Inc (PA) | 3841 | D | 650 483-4720 | 15158 |
| Kaise Perma San Franc Medic Ce | 3842 | E | 415 833-2000 | 15371 |
| Halo Neuro Inc | 3845 | F | 415 851-3338 | 15541 |
| Overview Corporation | 3861 | F | 415 795-9020 | 15657 |
| Brilliant Earth Group Inc (PA) | 3911 | A | 800 691-0952 | 15687 |
| Mashka Jewelry LLC | 3911 | E | 415 273-9330 | 15702 |
| Pocket Gems Inc (PA) | 3944 | C | 415 371-1333 | 15764 |
| Ermico Enterprises Inc | 3949 | D | 415 822-6776 | 15807 |
| Eveo Inc | 3993 | D | 415 749-6777 | 15973 |
| Martinelli Envmtl Graphics | 3993 | F | 415 468-4000 | 16004 |
| Priority Archtctral Grphics In | 3993 | E | 415 850-9836 | 16022 |
| Supersonic ADS Inc | 3993 | E | 650 825-6010 | 16055 |
| Juul Labs Inc (PA) | 3999 | C | 415 829-2336 | 16157 |
| Juul Labs International Inc (HQ) | 3999 | B | 415 829-2336 | 16158 |
| Savage Industries | 3999 | E | 415 845-6264 | 16220 |
| Volta Industries Inc (DH) | 3999 | E | 415 583-3805 | 16265 |
| American Medical Response Inc | 4119 | C | 415 794-9204 | 16276 |
| Olivia Companies LLC | 4725 | E | 415 962-5700 | 16305 |
| Formagrid Inc (PA) | 4813 | B | 415 200-2040 | 16317 |
| Nexxen Group LLC (PA) | 4813 | D | 425 279-1222 | 16320 |
| Pacific Bell Telephone Company (HQ) | 4813 | A | 415 542-9000 | 16321 |
| Leemah Electronics Inc | 4911 | C | 415 394-1288 | 16343 |
| Pacific Gas and Electric Co | 4911 | B | 415 695-3513 | 16348 |
| Azulworks Inc | 4941 | C | 415 558-1507 | 16353 |
| Fellow Industries Inc (PA) | 5023 | F | 415 649-0361 | 16424 |
| Oberon Design and Mfg LLC | 5023 | E | 415 865-5440 | 16432 |
| International Bus Mchs Corp | 5044 | C | 415 545-4747 | 16503 |
| Chronicled Inc | 5045 | E | 415 355-4681 | 16513 |
| Palamida Inc | 5045 | E | 415 777-9400 | 16536 |
| Wearlinq Inc | 5047 | E | 650 785-8742 | 16595 |
| Aee Solar Inc (DH) | 5063 | E | 800 777-6609 | 16640 |
| Urban Farmer Store Inc (DH) | 5083 | E | 415 661-2204 | 16802 |
| Capcom U S A Inc (HQ) | 5092 | C | 650 350-6500 | 16945 |
| Brondell Inc | 5122 | E | 415 315-9000 | 17030 |
| Thirdlove Inc | 5137 | C | 415 692-0089 | 17105 |
| Kikkoman Sales Usa Inc (HQ) | 5149 | E | 415 956-7750 | 17192 |
| Safeway Inc | 5411 | A | 415 661-3220 | 17382 |
| Andre-Boudin Bakeries Inc | 5461 | E | 415 283-1230 | 17407 |
| Einstein Noah Rest Group Inc | 5461 | D | 415 731-1700 | 17410 |
| Dark Grdn Unique Corsetry Inc | 5632 | F | 415 431-7684 | 17499 |
| Vida & Co | 5651 | E | 415 379-4325 | 17503 |
| Triple Aught Design LLC | 5699 | E | 415 318-8252 | 17514 |
| Tinyco Inc | 5734 | C | 415 644-8101 | 17560 |
| Quetzal Group Inc | 5812 | E | 415 673-4181 | 17602 |
| Sanchez Business Inc | 5812 | E | 415 282-2400 | 17604 |
| St Francis Marine Center | 5812 | E | 415 621-2876 | 17606 |
| Harmonic Brewing LLC | 5813 | F | 415 872-6817 | 17619 |
| Delegat Usa Inc | 5921 | E | 415 538-7988 | 17626 |
| Madison Reed Inc | 5999 | E | 415 225-0872 | 17711 |
| Roostify Inc | 6163 | E | 888 908-2470 | 17728 |
| Genstar Capital LLC (PA) | 6211 | E | 415 834-2350 | 17729 |
| Tarrant Capital Ip LLC (PA) | 6282 | A | 415 743-1500 | 17734 |
| Collectivehealth Inc (PA) | 6411 | C | 844 265-3288 | 17737 |
| Francisco Partners MGT LP (PA) | 6799 | C | 415 418-2900 | 17753 |
| Golden Gate Private Equity Inc (PA) | 6799 | E | 415 983-2706 | 17754 |
| Volta Charging LLC | 7312 | D | 415 735-5169 | 17787 |
| Ace Mailing Corporation | 7331 | E | 415 863-4223 | 17793 |
| Business Services Network Corp | 7331 | D | 415 282-8161 | 17795 |
| ABC Imaging of Washington | 7336 | E | 415 869-1669 | 17820 |
| Northern California Equipment | 7359 | E | 415 648-6262 | 17859 |
| Buffer Inc (PA) | 7371 | D | 415 215-5571 | 17892 |
| Devonway Inc (DH) | 7371 | E | 415 904-4000 | 17910 |
| Fastly Inc (PA) | 7371 | B | 844 432-7859 | 17918 |
| Fleet Device Management Inc | 7371 | F | 415 651-2575 | 17923 |
| Fullcontact Inc | 7371 | E | 415 366-6587 | 17925 |
| Kaizen Technology Partners LLC | 7371 | E | 415 515-1909 | 17938 |
| Pachama Inc | 7371 | E | 650 338-9394 | 17960 |
| Quantcast Corporation (PA) | 7371 | D | 800 293-5706 | 17967 |
| Unity Software Inc (PA) | 7371 | B | 415 638-9950 | 17992 |
| Waitwhile Inc | 7371 | E | 888 983-0869 | 17996 |
| 42crunch Inc | 7372 | F | 949 316-1173 | 18005 |
| Adobe Inc | 7372 | E | 415 832-2000 | 18020 |
| Adobe Macromedia Software LLC (HQ) | 7372 | E | 415 832-2000 | 18023 |
| Afresh Technologies Inc | 7372 | D | 415 651-5068 | 18026 |
| Airbase Inc (PA) | 7372 | E | 415 625-6222 | 18032 |
| Aktana Inc (PA) | 7372 | C | 888 616-2477 | 18033 |
| Algolia Inc (PA) | 7372 | E | 415 366-9672 | 18036 |
| All Blue Labs Inc | 7372 | E | 707 492-5949 | 18039 |
| Annotation Unlimited Pbc | 7372 | E | 415 295-5689 | 18047 |
| Arable Labs Inc | 7372 | E | 510 992-4095 | 18061 |
| Area 1 Security Inc | 7372 | D | 650 924-1637 | 18064 |
| Ashby Inc | 7372 | E | 408 391-3578 | 18069 |
| Atlassian Us Inc (DH) | 7372 | E | 415 701-1110 | 18073 |
| Atob Asset Vehicle I LLC | 7372 | D | 703 663-0658 | 18074 |
| Augmedix Inc (PA) | 7372 | C | 888 669-4885 | 18075 |
| Aurora Innovation Inc | 7372 | B | 646 725-4999 | 18076 |
| Autodesk Inc (PA) | 7372 | B | 415 507-5000 | 18078 |
| Badger Maps Inc | 7372 | E | 415 592-5909 | 18088 |
| Base Crm | 7372 | F | 773 796-6266 | 18093 |
| Beats Music LLC | 7372 | D | 415 590-5104 | 18094 |
| Bee Content Design Inc (PA) | 7372 | E | 888 962-4587 | 18096 |
| Benchling Inc (PA) | 7372 | E | 415 590-2798 | 18098 |
| Bento Technologies Inc | 7372 | E | 415 887-2028 | 18100 |
| Blameless Inc | 7372 | E | 650 563-7300 | 18110 |
| Blockfreight Inc | 7372 | E | 415 815-3924 | 18115 |
| Blueshift Labs Inc | 7372 | C | 844 258-3735 | 18119 |
| Brightidea Incorporated | 7372 | E | 415 814-1387 | 18127 |
| Brilliant Worldwide Inc | 7372 | C | 650 468-2966 | 18128 |
| Broadly Inc | 7372 | E | 510 400-6039 | 18129 |
| Bugsnag Inc | 7372 | E | 415 484-8664 | 18130 |
| Canary Technologies Corp | 7372 | E | 415 578-1414 | 18145 |
| Canto Inc (PA) | 7372 | D | 415 495-6545 | 18146 |
| Care Zone Inc | 7372 | E | 206 707-9127 | 18147 |
| Certain Inc (PA) | 7372 | E | 415 353-5330 | 18158 |
| Certain Software Inc | 7372 | E | 415 353-5330 | 18159 |
| Climate Corporation (DH) | 7372 | D | 415 363-0500 | 18174 |
| Cloud Software Group Inc | 7372 | F | 415 344-0339 | 18178 |
| Cloudflare Inc (PA) | 7372 | A | 888 993-5273 | 18184 |
| Copper Crm Inc (PA) | 7372 | E | 415 989-1477 | 18203 |
| Corelight Inc | 7372 | D | 888 547-9497 | 18204 |
| Crertih Inc | 7372 | E | 415 290-6603 | 18210 |
| Datafox Intelligence Inc | 7372 | E | 415 969-2144 | 18228 |
| Deep Labs Inc (PA) | 7372 | E | 877 504-4544 | 18236 |
| Demandbase Inc (PA) | 7372 | E | 415 683-2660 | 18237 |
| Digits Financial Inc | 7372 | E | 814 634-4487 | 18241 |
| Docusign Inc (PA) | 7372 | B | 415 489-4940 | 18247 |
| Doubledutch Inc (DH) | 7372 | D | 800 748-9024 | 18250 |
| Driver Inc | 7372 | D | 415 999-4960 | 18253 |
| Drizly Inc (HQ) | 7372 | F | 774 234-1033 | 18255 |
| Dropbox Inc (PA) | 7372 | A | 415 930-7766 | 18256 |
| Eis Group Inc | 7372 | C | 415 402-2622 | 18270 |
| Elevate Labs LLC | 7372 | E | 415 875-9817 | 18275 |
| Ellipsis Health Inc | 7372 | E | 650 906-6117 | 18276 |
| Enable International Inc | 7372 | E | 628 251-1057 | 18279 |
| Epignosis LLC | 7372 | E | 646 797-2799 | 18286 |
| Etech-360 Inc (PA) | 7372 | A | 714 900-3486 | 18291 |
| Everlance Inc | 7372 | D | 872 814-6308 | 18295 |
| Evolv Technology Solutions Inc (PA) | 7372 | E | 415 444-9040 | 18299 |
| Exacttarget LLC (HQ) | 7372 | D | 415 901-7000 | 18301 |
| First Advntage Tlent MGT Svcs | 7372 | F | 415 446-3930 | 18308 |
| Firstup Inc (PA) | 7372 | B | 844 975-2533 | 18309 |
| Fitbud Inc | 7372 | E | 415 727-6264 | 18310 |
| Fitstar Inc | 7372 | A | 415 409-8348 | 18311 |
| Forge Global Inc (HQ) | 7372 | C | 415 881-1612 | 18320 |
| Forge Global Holdings Inc (PA) | 7372 | E | 415 881-1612 | 18321 |
| Fortezza Iridium Holdings Inc | 7372 | A | 415 765-6500 | 18323 |
| Framehawk Inc | 7372 | C | 415 371-9110 | 18329 |
| Frontapp Inc (PA) | 7372 | D | 415 680-3048 | 18334 |
| Fuzebox Software Corporation (DH) | 7372 | E | 415 692-4800 | 18338 |
| Get Satisfaction Inc | 7372 | E | 877 339-3997 | 18347 |
| Gitlab Inc (PA) | 7372 | F | 650 474-5175 | 18349 |
| Groove Labs Inc | 7372 | D | 650 999-0200 | 18367 |
| Gusto Inc (PA) | 7372 | C | 800 936-0383 | 18375 |
| Hearsay Systems Inc (PA) | 7372 | C | 888 399-2280 | 18378 |
| Heavyai Inc | 7372 | D | 415 997-2814 | 18380 |
| Heroku Inc | 7372 | E | 650 704-6107 | 18382 |
| Highnote Solutions Inc | 7372 | F | 415 779-6275 | 18384 |
| Hint Health Inc (PA) | 7372 | E | 415 854-6366 | 18385 |
| Hitachi Energy USA Inc | 7372 | F | 415 527-2850 | 18386 |
| Hvr Software Usa Inc | 7372 | D | 415 489-3427 | 18396 |
| Ifwe Inc (DH) | 7372 | E | 415 946-1850 | 18401 |
| Infogram Software Inc | 7372 | E | 650 319-7291 | 18410 |
| Instagis Inc (PA) | 7372 | F | 415 527-6636 | 18421 |

Employee Codes: A=Over 500 employees, B=251-500
C=101-250, D=51-100, E=20-50, F=10-19, G=1-9

# SAN FRANCISCO, CA

| | SIC | EMP | PHONE | ENTRY# |
|---|---|---|---|---|
| Integrateio Inc | 7372 | E | 888 884-6405 | 18425 |
| Intershop Communications Inc | 7372 | E | 415 844-1500 | 18428 |
| Kevala Inc | 7372 | E | 415 712-7829 | 18467 |
| Labelbox Inc (PA) | 7372 | F | 415 294-0791 | 18483 |
| Labelbox Inc | 7372 | C | 415 294-0791 | 18484 |
| Lcr-Dixon Corporation | 7372 | F | 404 307-1695 | 18489 |
| Leapfrog Power Inc (PA) | 7372 | E | 415 409-9783 | 18492 |
| Leapyear Technologies Inc | 7372 | E | 510 542-9193 | 18493 |
| Loop Ai Labs Inc | 7372 | E | 415 980-3655 | 18501 |
| Material Security Inc | 7372 | D | 408 649-9882 | 18524 |
| mCloud Tchnlgs (USA) Inc | 7372 | F | 866 420-1781 | 18530 |
| Medrics Corp | 7372 | F | 415 704-7404 | 18536 |
| Medrio Inc (PA) | 7372 | D | 415 963-3700 | 18537 |
| Memora Health Inc | 7372 | D | 480 335-7348 | 18538 |
| Mileiq Inc | 7372 | D | 415 528-7722 | 18545 |
| Mindsnacks Inc | 7372 | E | 415 875-9817 | 18547 |
| Mindtickle Inc (PA) | 7372 | E | 973 400-1717 | 18548 |
| Modalityai Inc | 7372 | F | 415 200-8535 | 18555 |
| Mulesoft LLC | 7372 | A | 800 596-4880 | 18562 |
| Mursion Inc | 7372 | C | 415 746-9631 | 18563 |
| Mux Inc (PA) | 7372 | F | 510 402-2257 | 18565 |
| Mzla Technologies Corporation | 7372 | E | 650 903-0800 | 18567 |
| Native Data Inc | 7372 | E | 855 466-9494 | 18569 |
| New Relic Inc (HQ) | 7372 | A | 650 777-7600 | 18583 |
| Nextpatient Inc | 7372 | E | 617 504-4726 | 18587 |
| Nextroll Inc (PA) | 7372 | A | 415 236-3956 | 18590 |
| Ngrok Inc | 7372 | D | 415 323-4184 | 18591 |
| Nium Inc | 7372 | E | 732 492-6908 | 18594 |
| North Beam Inc | 7372 | E | 860 940-4569 | 18597 |
| Ockam Inc | 7372 | E | 415 407-3800 | 18611 |
| Okera Inc | 7372 | D | 415 741-3282 | 18613 |
| Okta Inc (PA) | 7372 | A | 888 722-7871 | 18614 |
| On24 Inc (PA) | 7372 | B | 415 369-8000 | 18617 |
| Onelogin Inc (DH) | 7372 | C | 415 645-6830 | 18618 |
| Openai Inc (PA) | 7372 | E | 650 387-6701 | 18624 |
| Opentv Inc | 7372 | B | 415 962-5000 | 18625 |
| Outreach Corporation | 7372 | B | 888 938-7356 | 18651 |
| Pandadoc Inc | 7372 | E | 415 860-0176 | 18654 |
| Payjoy Inc (PA) | 7372 | E | 888 632-1922 | 18664 |
| People Center Inc | 7372 | E | 415 737-5780 | 18668 |
| Planet Forward Inc | 7372 | E | 800 861-3787 | 18677 |
| Planful Inc | 7372 | C | 650 249-7100 | 18678 |
| Plangrid Inc (HQ) | 7372 | D | 800 646-0796 | 18679 |
| Playfirst Inc | 7372 | C | 415 738-4600 | 18680 |
| Popout Inc (PA) | 7372 | E | 415 691-7447 | 18685 |
| Populus Technologies Inc | 7372 | E | 415 364-8048 | 18686 |
| Powwow Inc | 7372 | E | 877 800-4381 | 18691 |
| Premise Data Corporation (PA) | 7372 | F | 415 419-8750 | 18694 |
| Prey Inc | 7372 | F | 415 780-9090 | 18695 |
| Projectdiscovery Inc | 7372 | E | 510 681-4441 | 18700 |
| Projectoris Inc | 7372 | D | 917 972-5553 | 18701 |
| Provenance Technologies Inc | 7372 | E | 415 796-6281 | 18706 |
| Provide Inc | 7372 | E | 877 341-0617 | 18707 |
| Qualio Inc (PA) | 7372 | E | 415 795-7331 | 18716 |
| Quantal International Inc | 7372 | E | 415 644-0754 | 18717 |
| Read It Later Inc | 7372 | E | 415 692-6111 | 18724 |
| Remedly Inc | 7372 | E | 650 265-8449 | 18732 |
| Replicant Solutions Inc | 7372 | C | 415 854-3296 | 18733 |
| Retail Zipline Inc (PA) | 7372 | E | 510 390-4904 | 18737 |
| Rsa Conference LLC | 7372 | E | 415 707-2833 | 18747 |
| Rysigo Technologies Corp (PA) | 7372 | F | 408 621-9274 | 18748 |
| Salesforce Inc (PA) | 7372 | A | 415 901-7000 | 18754 |
| Salesforcecom Landmark | 7372 | F | 650 653-4500 | 18756 |
| Salesforceorg LLC | 7372 | B | 415 901-7000 | 18757 |
| Scope Technologies US Inc (PA) | 7372 | E | 855 207-2673 | 18765 |
| Seacloud Software LLC | 7372 | F | 650 318-1172 | 18771 |
| Seam Labs Inc | 7372 | E | 415 815-5509 | 18773 |
| Sight Machine Inc | 7372 | D | 888 461-5739 | 18789 |
| Sitecore Usa Inc (DH) | 7372 | C | 415 380-0600 | 18792 |
| Skedulo Inc | 7372 | E | 415 640-1997 | 18793 |
| Slack Technologies Inc (HQ) | 7372 | B | 970 299-4848 | 18797 |
| Speakeasy Tech Inc | 7372 | F | 650 581-9701 | 18821 |
| Splunk Inc (HQ) | 7372 | C | 415 848-8400 | 18824 |
| Spoton Computing Inc | 7372 | E | 650 293-7464 | 18825 |
| Stackla Inc | 7372 | D | 415 789-3304 | 18831 |
| Stackwatch Inc | 7372 | E | 301 202-4542 | 18832 |
| Standard Cognition Corp (PA) | 7372 | E | 415 324-4156 | 18834 |
| Stryder Corp (PA) | 7372 | D | 415 981-8400 | 18843 |
| Supergiant Games LLC | 7372 | E | 714 488-5642 | 18849 |
| Swiftlane Inc | 7372 | F | 833 607-9438 | 18852 |
| Swiftly Inc | 7372 | C | 415 894-5223 | 18853 |
| Switchboard Software Inc | 7372 | E | 415 425-3660 | 18855 |
| Switchboard Software Inc | 7372 | F | 415 506-9095 | 18856 |
| Talix Inc | 7372 | D | 628 220-3885 | 18863 |
| Tapingo Inc (DH) | 7372 | E | 415 283-5222 | 18867 |
| Teambridge LLC | 7372 | E | 415 323-5571 | 18868 |
| Teamohana Inc | 7372 | E | 415 650-9767 | 18869 |
| Textexpander Inc | 7372 | E | 510 289-4000 | 18876 |
| Thousandeyes LLC (HQ) | 7372 | D | 415 513-4526 | 18880 |
| Toca Boca Inc | 7372 | F | 415 352-9028 | 18886 |
| Tonkean Inc | 7372 | D | 646 215-0493 | 18887 |
| Twilio Inc (PA) | 7372 | A | 415 390-2337 | 18895 |
| Ujet Inc (PA) | 7372 | E | 855 242-8538 | 18896 |
| Uncountable Inc (PA) | 7372 | F | 650 208-5949 | 18898 |
| Valdera Inc | 7372 | E | 415 323-6646 | 18907 |
| Vectice Inc | 7372 | E | 650 399-0114 | 18912 |
| Velti Inc | 7372 | D | | 18915 |
| Verana Health Inc | 7372 | C | 888 774-0077 | 18916 |
| Vindicia Inc | 7372 | E | 650 264-4700 | 18920 |
| Watershed Technology Inc (PA) | 7372 | D | 650 561-5438 | 18928 |
| Wildflower Health Inc | 7372 | E | 415 430-7543 | 18933 |
| Yourpeople Inc (HQ) | 7372 | E | 888 249-3263 | 18950 |
| Zendesk Inc (HQ) | 7372 | A | 415 418-7506 | 18952 |
| Zero Gravity Labs Inc | 7372 | E | 707 653-6287 | 18954 |
| Zinio Systems Inc | 7372 | D | 415 494-2700 | 18955 |
| Aarki Inc (PA) | 7373 | D | 408 382-1180 | 18961 |
| Eero LLC | 7373 | E | 415 738-7972 | 18971 |
| Francisco Partners GP III LP (HQ) | 7373 | E | 415 418-2900 | 18976 |
| Insignia | 7373 | F | 415 777-0320 | 18980 |
| Castlight Health Inc (HQ) | 7374 | D | 415 829-1400 | 19004 |
| Jaspersoft Corporation | 7374 | C | 415 348-2300 | 19009 |
| Maplebear Inc (PA) | 7374 | A | 888 246-7822 | 19010 |
| Asana Inc (PA) | 7379 | A | 415 525-3888 | 19026 |
| Brandcast Inc | 7379 | E | 415 517-4772 | 19033 |
| Ad Art Inc (PA) | 7389 | D | 415 869-6460 | 19068 |
| Candles By Hgbyg Corp | 7389 | F | 415 655-9865 | 19079 |
| Radiant Graph Inc | 7389 | E | 857 928-3248 | 19119 |
| Revere Data LLC | 7389 | E | 415 782-0454 | 19121 |
| Auto Ex Towing & Recovery LLC | 7549 | E | 415 846-2262 | 19168 |
| Point 360 | 7819 | F | 415 989-6245 | 19304 |
| Yanka Industries Inc | 7929 | C | 855 981-8208 | 19307 |
| Public Library of Science (PA) | 8231 | E | 415 624-1200 | 19346 |
| California Academy Sciences (PA) | 8422 | A | 415 379-8000 | 19366 |
| Astronomical Soc of The PCF | 8699 | E | 415 337-1100 | 19372 |
| Pacific Res Inst For Pub Plicy (PA) | 8732 | F | 415 989-0833 | 19487 |
| Cellular Longevity Inc | 8734 | F | 707 563-9236 | 19501 |
| Stitch Labs Inc | 8741 | E | 415 323-0630 | 19518 |
| Equilibrium Management LLC | 8742 | E | 415 516-2930 | 19528 |

## SAN GABRIEL, CA - Los Angeles County

| | SIC | EMP | PHONE | ENTRY# |
|---|---|---|---|---|
| Comfort Industries Inc | 2231 | E | 562 692-8288 | 2445 |
| Lotus Orient Corp (PA) | 2335 | F | 626 285-5796 | 2710 |
| Asia-Pacific California Inc | 2711 | E | 626 281-8500 | 4068 |
| Multi-Link International Corp | 3086 | E | 562 941-5380 | 6649 |
| Hsiao & Montano Inc | 3161 | E | 626 588-2528 | 7133 |

## SAN JACINTO, CA - Riverside County

| | SIC | EMP | PHONE | ENTRY# |
|---|---|---|---|---|
| Skyline Homes Inc | 2451 | C | 951 654-9321 | 3388 |
| Wallace Wood Products | 2541 | F | 951 654-9311 | 3677 |
| Edelbrock Foundry Corp | 3363 | E | 951 654-6677 | 7808 |
| J Talley Corporation (PA) | 3446 | D | 951 654-2123 | 8629 |
| Rama Corporation | 3567 | E | 951 654-7351 | 10058 |
| CM Machine Inc | 3599 | F | 951 654-6019 | 10779 |
| MTI De Baja Inc | 3812 | E | 951 654-2333 | 14226 |

## SAN JOSE, CA - Santa Clara County

| | SIC | EMP | PHONE | ENTRY# |
|---|---|---|---|---|
| Eli Kiselman | 1389 | E | 832 886-3743 | 226 |
| Take It For Granite Inc | 1411 | E | 408 790-2812 | 295 |
| George M Robinson & Co (PA) | 1711 | E | 510 632-7017 | 421 |
| O C McDonald Co Inc | 1711 | C | 408 295-2182 | 428 |
| Rando AAA Hvac Inc | 1711 | E | 408 293-4717 | 431 |
| European Paving Designs Inc | 1721 | D | 408 283-5230 | 445 |
| Netronix Integration Inc (HQ) | 1731 | D | 800 600-3939 | 464 |
| MGM Drywall Inc | 1742 | E | 408 292-4085 | 478 |
| Floor Seal Technology Inc (PA) | 1752 | E | 408 436-8181 | 504 |
| Tera-Lite Inc | 1752 | E | 408 288-8655 | 506 |
| All Fab Prcsion Sheetmetal Inc | 1761 | D | 408 279-1099 | 511 |
| Mohawk Land & Cattle Co Inc | 2011 | D | 408 436-1800 | 607 |
| Olivera Egg Ranch LLC | 2015 | E | 408 258-8074 | 698 |
| Mavens Creamery LLC | 2024 | E | 408 216-9270 | 811 |
| Amazon Prsrvation Partners Inc | 2033 | E | 415 775-6355 | 875 |
| Zoria Farms Inc (PA) | 2034 | B | 559 673-6368 | 974 |
| Lee Brothers Inc | 2035 | E | 650 964-9650 | 982 |
| Sugarfina Inc | 2064 | E | 855 784-2734 | 1330 |
| Gordon Biersch Brewing Company (PA) | 2082 | F | 408 278-1008 | 1433 |
| J Lohr Winery Corporation (PA) | 2084 | E | 408 288-5057 | 1623 |

# GEOGRAPHIC SECTION

**SAN JOSE, CA**

| Company | SIC | EMP | PHONE | ENTRY# |
|---|---|---|---|---|
| J Lohr Winery Corporation | 2084 | E | 408 293-1345 | 1624 |
| Reyes Coca-Cola Bottling LLC | 2086 | C | 408 436-3700 | 1934 |
| Nippon Trends Food Service Inc (PA) | 2099 | D | 408 479-0558 | 2299 |
| Robles Bros Inc (PA) | 2099 | E | 408 436-5551 | 2339 |
| San Jose Awning Company Inc | 2394 | E | 408 350-7000 | 2982 |
| Seventh Heaven Inc | 2399 | E | 408 287-8945 | 3036 |
| Garage Doors Incorporated | 2431 | F | 408 293-7443 | 3138 |
| Amberwood Products Inc | 2434 | C | 408 938-1600 | 3213 |
| Rawson Custom Cabinets Inc | 2434 | E | 408 779-9838 | 3263 |
| Gonzalez Pallets Inc (PA) | 2448 | E | 408 999-0280 | 3345 |
| Supracor Inc | 2515 | E | 408 432-1616 | 3543 |
| Roth Wood Products Ltd | 2599 | E | 408 723-8888 | 3749 |
| Nakagawa Manufacturing USA Inc | 2621 | E | 510 782-0197 | 3786 |
| Boyd Gmn Inc | 2679 | C | 408 435-1666 | 4032 |
| Business Jrnl Publications Inc | 2711 | A | 408 295-3800 | 4078 |
| California Newspapers Partnr (PA) | 2711 | E | 408 920-5333 | 4083 |
| Medianews Group Inc | 2711 | B | 408 920-5713 | 4157 |
| San Jose Business Journal | 2711 | C | 408 295-3800 | 4188 |
| San Jose Mercury-News LLC (DH) | 2711 | A | 408 920-5000 | 4189 |
| Times Media Incorporated | 2711 | E | 408 494-7000 | 4212 |
| Franchise Update Inc | 2721 | F | 408 402-5681 | 4258 |
| B R Printers Inc (PA) | 2752 | D | 408 278-7711 | 4524 |
| Citation Press | 2752 | D | 408 957-9900 | 4551 |
| B A L | 2759 | E | 408 432-1980 | 4846 |
| Cupix America Inc | 2759 | D | 650 785-2122 | 4869 |
| Tshirtguyscom (PA) | 2759 | F | 619 500-5271 | 4977 |
| Valley Images LLC | 2759 | F | 408 279-6777 | 4978 |
| Multivitamin Direct Inc | 2833 | E | 408 573-7292 | 5250 |
| Biomed Industries Inc (PA) | 2834 | F | 800 824-5135 | 5374 |
| Bridgene Biosciences Inc | 2834 | E | 626 632-3188 | 5384 |
| Rani Therapeutics LLC | 2834 | D | 408 457-3700 | 5625 |
| Rani Therapeutics Holdings Inc (PA) | 2834 | D | 408 457-3700 | 5626 |
| Roche Sequencing Solutions Inc | 2834 | F | 408 386-5414 | 5646 |
| Teikoku Pharma Usa Inc (HQ) | 2834 | D | 408 501-1800 | 5685 |
| Wedgewood Connect | 2834 | E | 855 321-3477 | 5716 |
| Mindray Ds Usa Inc | 2835 | A | 650 230-2800 | 5764 |
| Cardinal Paint and Powder Inc | 2851 | E | 408 452-8522 | 6073 |
| Arelac Inc | 2891 | D | 669 267-6400 | 6218 |
| Cade Corporation | 2899 | E | 310 539-2508 | 6271 |
| Quanten Consortium Angola LLC | 2911 | E | 408 955-0768 | 6346 |
| Reed & Graham Inc (PA) | 2911 | E | 408 287-1400 | 6347 |
| Siplast Inc | 2952 | E | 408 490-4268 | 6384 |
| Burke Industries Delaware Inc (HQ) | 3069 | C | 408 297-3500 | 6485 |
| Chemical Safety Technology Inc | 3089 | E | 408 263-0984 | 6773 |
| E & F Plastics Inc | 3089 | E | 408 226-6672 | 6813 |
| Greenwaste Recovery LLC | 3089 | A | 408 283-4800 | 6846 |
| Kennerley-Spratling Inc | 3089 | C | 408 944-9407 | 6884 |
| McNeal Enterprises Inc | 3089 | D | 408 922-7290 | 6905 |
| MOSplastics Inc | 3089 | F | 408 944-9407 | 6923 |
| Counter Santana Row LP | 3131 | E | 408 610-1362 | 7091 |
| Clearedge Solutions Inc | 3229 | E | 408 434-5984 | 7193 |
| Modern Ceramics Mfg Inc | 3229 | E | 408 383-0554 | 7198 |
| Beveled Edge Inc | 3231 | F | 408 467-9900 | 7213 |
| Mir Group Inc | 3231 | E | 408 432-1000 | 7235 |
| Architctral Fcdes Unlmited Inc | 3272 | D | 408 846-5350 | 7309 |
| Sandman Inc (PA) | 3272 | D | 408 947-0669 | 7390 |
| Central Concrete Supply Co Inc (DH) | 3273 | D | 408 293-6272 | 7433 |
| Concrete Ready Mix Inc | 3273 | E | 408 224-2452 | 7436 |
| Imerys Filtration Minerals Inc (DH) | 3295 | E | 805 562-0200 | 7566 |
| Imerys Talc America Inc (DH) | 3295 | B | | 7567 |
| Dicar Inc | 3357 | E | 408 295-1106 | 7784 |
| Senju Comtek Corp | 3399 | F | 408 792-3830 | 7914 |
| Intelligent Energy Inc | 3429 | E | 562 997-3600 | 8005 |
| Gemtech Sales Corp | 3433 | E | 408 432-9900 | 8067 |
| Eligius Manufacturing Inc | 3441 | E | 408 437-0337 | 8134 |
| Robecks Wldg & Fabrication Inc | 3441 | E | 408 287-0202 | 8211 |
| Summit Steel Works Corporation | 3441 | E | 408 510-5880 | 8225 |
| T&S Manufacturing Tech LLC | 3441 | E | 408 441-0285 | 8226 |
| Blum Construction Co Inc | 3442 | F | 408 629-3740 | 8259 |
| Clear View LLC | 3442 | F | 408 271-2734 | 8260 |
| Jonna Corporation Inc | 3443 | E | 408 297-7910 | 8319 |
| A & J Precision Sheetmetal Inc | 3444 | D | 408 885-9134 | 8357 |
| Cortec Precision Shtmtl Inc (PA) | 3444 | C | 408 278-8540 | 8417 |
| Encore Industries | 3444 | E | 408 416-0501 | 8443 |
| Group Manufacturing Svcs Inc (PA) | 3444 | E | 408 436-1040 | 8462 |
| Hardcraft Industries Inc | 3444 | E | 408 432-8340 | 8466 |
| I & A Inc | 3444 | E | 408 432-8340 | 8471 |
| Laptalo Enterprises Inc (PA) | 3444 | D | 408 727-6633 | 8484 |
| M C I Manufacturing Inc (PA) | 3444 | E | 408 456-2700 | 8492 |
| Mac Cal Company | 3444 | D | 408 441-1435 | 8494 |
| Mass Precision Inc (PA) | 3444 | C | 408 954-0200 | 8499 |
| Prototek Holdings LLC (PA) | 3444 | E | 800 403-9777 | 8547 |
| Sal J Acsta Sheetmetal Mfg Inc | 3444 | D | 408 275-6370 | 8565 |
| Sun Sheetmetal Solutions Inc | 3444 | E | 408 445-8047 | 8586 |
| Superior Metals Inc | 3444 | F | 408 938-3488 | 8588 |
| Therma LLC | 3444 | A | 408 347-3400 | 8593 |
| Alumawall Inc | 3448 | D | 408 275-7165 | 8654 |
| West Valley Precision Inc | 3469 | E | 408 519-5959 | 8902 |
| A & E Anodizing | 3471 | F | 408 297-5910 | 8903 |
| Applied Anodize Inc | 3471 | E | 408 435-9191 | 8922 |
| Hane and Hane Inc | 3471 | E | 408 292-2140 | 8969 |
| Luckinta Corporation | 3471 | E | | 8979 |
| Aci Alloys Inc | 3479 | F | 408 259-7337 | 9035 |
| Plasma Rggedized Solutions Inc (PA) | 3479 | D | 408 954-8405 | 9107 |
| Asepco | 3491 | F | | 9144 |
| Cryotech International Inc | 3498 | E | 408 371-3303 | 9253 |
| Phil Wood & Company | 3499 | F | 408 298-1540 | 9296 |
| Stryker Enterprises Inc | 3499 | E | 408 295-6300 | 9300 |
| AM AND S MFG INC | 3541 | E | 408 396-3027 | 9539 |
| J&N Engineering Inc | 3541 | E | 408 680-1810 | 9557 |
| Concept Part Solutions Inc | 3545 | E | 408 748-1244 | 9668 |
| Elcon Precision LLC | 3545 | D | 408 292-7800 | 9677 |
| Neato Robotics Inc (HQ) | 3549 | E | 510 795-1351 | 9742 |
| Advanced Indus Ceramics LLC | 3559 | E | 408 955-9990 | 9824 |
| ATI Liquidating Inc | 3559 | B | 831 438-2100 | 9835 |
| Epoch International Entps Inc (PA) | 3559 | E | 510 556-1225 | 9854 |
| MMR Technologies Inc | 3559 | F | 650 962-9620 | 9877 |
| Novellus Systems Inc | 3559 | A | 408 943-9700 | 9884 |
| Quality Machining & Design Inc | 3559 | E | 408 224-7976 | 9895 |
| Spts Technologies Inc (HQ) | 3559 | C | 408 571-1400 | 9900 |
| Ultratech Inc | 3559 | B | 408 321-8835 | 9907 |
| Westcoast Precision Inc | 3559 | D | 408 943-9998 | 9912 |
| Harmonic Drive LLC | 3566 | E | 800 921-3332 | 10039 |
| Aivres Systems Inc (PA) | 3571 | E | 866 687-1430 | 10128 |
| Ampro Adlink Technology Inc | 3571 | D | 408 360-0200 | 10136 |
| Ayar Labs Inc | 3571 | E | 650 963-7200 | 10137 |
| CTS Electronics Manufacturing Solut | 3571 | B | 408 754-9800 | 10145 |
| Ezchip Semiconductor Inc | 3571 | E | 408 520-3700 | 10152 |
| Lenovo (united States) Inc | 3571 | D | 510 813-3331 | 10175 |
| Mediatek USA Inc (HQ) | 3571 | E | 408 526-1899 | 10178 |
| Piranha Ems Inc | 3571 | E | 408 520-3963 | 10193 |
| Shasta Electronic Mfg Svcs Inc | 3571 | F | 408 436-1267 | 10201 |
| Super Micro Computer Inc (PA) | 3571 | A | 408 503-8000 | 10206 |
| Taracom Corporation | 3571 | F | 408 691-6655 | 10209 |
| Appro International Inc (DH) | 3572 | D | 408 941-8100 | 10225 |
| Bluearc Corporation | 3572 | F | 408 576-6600 | 10226 |
| Hgst Inc (DH) | 3572 | C | 408 717-6000 | 10242 |
| Intelligent Storage Solution | 3572 | F | 408 428-0105 | 10247 |
| Jts Corporation | 3572 | A | 408 468-1800 | 10249 |
| Netapp Inc (PA) | 3572 | A | 408 822-6000 | 10255 |
| Pillar Data Systems Inc | 3572 | B | 408 503-4000 | 10265 |
| Quantum Corporation (PA) | 3572 | C | 408 944-4000 | 10269 |
| Toshiba Amer Elctrnic Cmpnnts | 3572 | B | 408 526-2400 | 10289 |
| WD Media LLC | 3572 | E | 408 576-2000 | 10294 |
| Western Digital Corporation (PA) | 3572 | A | 408 717-6000 | 10295 |
| Western Digital Tech Inc (HQ) | 3572 | A | 408 801-1000 | 10297 |
| Zco Liquidating Corporation | 3572 | A | 408 733-8400 | 10300 |
| Diamanti Inc (PA) | 3575 | E | 408 645-5111 | 10304 |
| Acer American Holdings Corp (DH) | 3577 | F | 408 533-7700 | 10315 |
| Allied Telesis Inc | 3577 | E | 408 519-8700 | 10319 |
| Aruba Networks Inc (HQ) | 3577 | B | 408 941-4300 | 10327 |
| Asante Technologies Inc (PA) | 3577 | E | 408 435-8388 | 10329 |
| Cisco Systems Inc | 3577 | E | 408 216-3440 | 10344 |
| Cisco Systems Inc (PA) | 3577 | A | 408 526-4000 | 10345 |
| Elisity Inc | 3577 | F | 408 839-3971 | 10361 |
| Foundry Networks Inc | 3577 | A | 408 207-1700 | 10370 |
| Intel Corporation | 3577 | A | 408 544-7000 | 10387 |
| Logitech Inc (HQ) | 3577 | B | 510 795-8500 | 10401 |
| Mega Force Corporation | 3577 | E | 408 956-9989 | 10409 |
| Sony Electronics Inc | 3577 | E | 408 352-4000 | 10437 |
| Spyrus Inc | 3577 | E | 408 392-9131 | 10439 |
| Synaptics Incorporated (PA) | 3577 | B | 408 904-1100 | 10441 |
| Synaptics LLC | 3577 | B | 408 904-1100 | 10442 |
| Verifone Intrmdate Hldings Inc | 3578 | C | 408 232-7800 | 10461 |
| Protempis (usa) LLC | 3579 | E | 408 410-3222 | 10464 |
| A&T Precision Machining Inc | 3599 | F | 408 363-1198 | 10651 |
| A-1 Jays Machining Inc (PA) | 3599 | D | 408 262-1845 | 10653 |
| Advoque Group LLC | 3599 | E | 408 560-2990 | 10680 |
| Altest Corporation | 3599 | E | 408 436-9900 | 10705 |
| Angular Machining Inc | 3599 | E | 408 954-8326 | 10710 |
| Apex Machining Inc | 3599 | E | 408 441-1335 | 10712 |
| B&Z Manufacturing Company Inc | 3599 | E | 408 943-1117 | 10734 |
| Babbitt Bearing Co Inc | 3599 | E | 408 298-1101 | 10735 |
| Citrogene Inc | 3599 | F | 408 930-5070 | 10776 |
| Cpk Manufacturing Inc | 3599 | F | 408 971-4019 | 10791 |
| Delta Matrix Inc | 3599 | E | 408 955-9140 | 10807 |

Employee Codes: A=Over 500 employees, B=251-500
C=101-250, D=51-100, E=20-50, F=10-19, G=1-9

# SAN JOSE, CA — GEOGRAPHIC SECTION

| Company | SIC | EMP | PHONE | ENTRY# |
|---|---|---|---|---|
| Elcon Inc | 3599 | E | 408 292-7800 | 10824 |
| Expedite Precision Works Inc | 3599 | E | 408 573-9600 | 10832 |
| Extreme Precision Inc | 3599 | F | 408 275-8365 | 10833 |
| Gentec Manufacturing Inc | 3599 | F | 408 432-6220 | 10858 |
| Haig Precision Mfg Corp | 3599 | D | 408 378-4920 | 10864 |
| Itsj Group Inc | 3599 | E | 408 609-6392 | 10893 |
| Jarvis Manufacturing Inc | 3599 | F | 408 226-2600 | 10904 |
| L & T Precision Engrg Inc | 3599 | E | 408 441-1890 | 10934 |
| Motiv Design Group Inc | 3599 | F | 408 441-0611 | 10997 |
| NM Machining Inc | 3599 | E | 408 972-8978 | 11010 |
| NTL Precision Machining Inc | 3599 | F | 408 298-6650 | 11012 |
| OT Precision Machining Inc | 3599 | E | 408 435-8818 | 11018 |
| Polytec Products Corporation | 3599 | E | 650 322-7555 | 11044 |
| Rapid Precision Mfg Inc | 3599 | E | 408 617-0771 | 11070 |
| Rdc Machine Inc | 3599 | E | 408 970-0721 | 11072 |
| S J Automotive LLC | 3599 | F | 408 296-2223 | 11094 |
| Wb Machining & Mech Design | 3599 | E | 408 453-5005 | 11184 |
| Asi Holdco Inc | 3621 | E | 408 913-1300 | 11255 |
| Microsemi Frequency Time Corp (DH) | 3625 | C | 480 792-7200 | 11334 |
| Raceamerica Inc | 3625 | F | 408 988-6188 | 11342 |
| Switch Bulb Company Inc | 3641 | D | 408 457-3821 | 11431 |
| Tango Systems LLC | 3641 | D | 408 526-2330 | 11432 |
| Amphenol DC Electronics Inc | 3643 | B | 408 947-4500 | 11440 |
| DC Electronics Inc | 3643 | E | 408 947-4500 | 11448 |
| Gold Technologies Inc | 3643 | E | 408 321-9568 | 11457 |
| Spire Manufacturing Inc | 3643 | E | 510 226-1070 | 11471 |
| Tobar Industries Inc | 3643 | D | 408 494-3530 | 11475 |
| New Century Audio / Video Inc | 3651 | F | 408 341-1950 | 11682 |
| Ditech Networks Inc (DH) | 3661 | E | 408 883-3636 | 11760 |
| Finisar Corporation (HQ) | 3661 | E | 408 548-1000 | 11763 |
| Infinera Corporation (HQ) | 3661 | B | 408 572-5200 | 11768 |
| Infinera International Corp (HQ) | 3661 | F | 408 572-5200 | 11769 |
| Infinera Optical Networks Inc (HQ) | 3661 | E | 630 798-8800 | 11770 |
| Jetstream Communications Inc | 3661 | E | 408 361-7000 | 11773 |
| Netgear Inc (PA) | 3661 | C | 408 907-8000 | 11775 |
| Oclaro (north America) Inc (DH) | 3661 | B | 408 383-1400 | 11777 |
| Polycom Inc (DH) | 3661 | D | 831 426-5858 | 11781 |
| Sorrento Networks I Inc | 3661 | D | 303 803-9405 | 11788 |
| Alien Technology LLC (PA) | 3663 | E | 408 782-3900 | 11803 |
| Arctic Semiconductor | 3663 | E | 408 712-3350 | 11813 |
| Canary Communications Inc | 3663 | F | 408 365-0609 | 11822 |
| Communications & Pwr Inds LLC | 3663 | F | 650 846-2900 | 11832 |
| CPI Satcom & Antenna Tech Inc | 3663 | D | 408 955-1900 | 11836 |
| Energous Corporation | 3663 | E | 408 963-0200 | 11851 |
| Harmonic Inc (PA) | 3663 | D | 408 542-2500 | 11862 |
| Herotek Inc (PA) | 3663 | E | 408 941-8399 | 11863 |
| Kratos Microwave Inc | 3663 | D | 408 541-0596 | 11872 |
| Lgc Wireless LLC | 3663 | C | 408 952-2400 | 11883 |
| Lockheed Martin Corporation | 3663 | D | 408 473-3000 | 11885 |
| Raditek Inc | 3663 | D | 408 266-7404 | 11926 |
| Raytheon Applied Sgnal Tech In (DH) | 3663 | D | 408 749-1888 | 11931 |
| Triquint Wj Inc | 3663 | D | 408 577-6200 | 11970 |
| Wi2wi Inc (PA) | 3663 | E | 408 416-4200 | 11978 |
| General Dynamics Mission | 3669 | B | 408 908-7300 | 11995 |
| Lumentum Holdings Inc (PA) | 3669 | C | 408 546-5483 | 12003 |
| Proto Services Inc | 3669 | E | 408 719-9088 | 12010 |
| Proxim Wireless Corporation (PA) | 3669 | D | 408 383-7600 | 12011 |
| Vocera Communications Inc (HQ) | 3669 | C | 408 882-5100 | 12024 |
| Ardent Systems Inc | 3672 | E | 408 526-0100 | 12059 |
| Bay Elctrnic Spport Trnics Inc | 3672 | C | 408 432-3222 | 12065 |
| Benchmark Elec Mfg Sltions Inc (HQ) | 3672 | D | 805 222-1303 | 12067 |
| CTS Corporation | 3672 | F | 408 955-9001 | 12084 |
| Electromax Inc | 3672 | E | 408 428-9474 | 12090 |
| Emsolutions Inc | 3672 | E | 510 668-1118 | 12094 |
| Flextronics Intl USA Inc | 3672 | A | 408 576-7000 | 12114 |
| Flextronics Intl USA Inc (HQ) | 3672 | A | 408 576-7000 | 12115 |
| Flextronics Logistics USA Inc (DH) | 3672 | D | 408 576-7000 | 12117 |
| General Elec Assembly Inc | 3672 | E | 408 980-8819 | 12122 |
| Gorilla Circuits (PA) | 3672 | C | 408 294-9897 | 12124 |
| Green Circuits Inc | 3672 | C | 408 526-1700 | 12126 |
| Jabil Inc | 3672 | D | 408 361-3200 | 12141 |
| Jabil Inc | 3672 | C | 408 360-3475 | 12142 |
| Jabil Inc | 3672 | B | 408 361-3200 | 12145 |
| Kimball Electronics Ind Inc | 3672 | E | 669 234-1110 | 12149 |
| Naprotek LLC (PA) | 3672 | E | 408 830-5000 | 12171 |
| Nexlogic Technologies LLC | 3672 | D | 408 436-8150 | 12177 |
| Power Design Manufacturing LLC | 3672 | E | 408 437-1931 | 12191 |
| Qostronics Inc | 3672 | E | 408 719-1286 | 12194 |
| Quality Circuit Assembly Inc | 3672 | D | 408 441-1001 | 12198 |
| Sanmina Corporation | 3672 | E | 408 964-3500 | 12206 |
| Sanmina Corporation | 3672 | E | 408 964-3500 | 12207 |
| Sanmina Corporation | 3672 | B | 408 964-6400 | 12208 |
| Sanmina Corporation | 3672 | E | 408 964-3500 | 12209 |
| Sanmina Corporation | 3672 | C | 408 557-7210 | 12210 |
| Sanmina Corporation (PA) | 3672 | A | 408 964-3500 | 12212 |
| Sunnytech Biz Inc | 3672 | F | 408 943-8100 | 12236 |
| Ttm Technologies Inc | 3672 | C | 408 280-0422 | 12251 |
| Valley Services Electronics | 3672 | C | 408 284-7700 | 12253 |
| Vitron Electronic Services Inc | 3672 | D | 408 251-1600 | 12257 |
| ZF Array Technology Inc | 3672 | E | 408 433-9920 | 12265 |
| Acacia Communications Inc | 3674 | D | 212 331-8417 | 12269 |
| Adesto Technologies Corp (DH) | 3674 | E | 408 400-0578 | 12273 |
| Advanced Analogic Tech Inc | 3674 | E | 408 330-1400 | 12276 |
| Advantest America Inc (HQ) | 3674 | D | 408 456-3600 | 12279 |
| Akm Semiconductor Inc | 3674 | E | 408 436-8580 | 12284 |
| Alacritech Inc | 3674 | E | 408 867-3809 | 12287 |
| Alphawave Semi Inc (HQ) | 3674 | E | 408 240-5700 | 12292 |
| Altera Corporation (HQ) | 3674 | C | 408 544-7000 | 12294 |
| Altierre Corporation | 3674 | E | 408 435-7343 | 12295 |
| Analog Devices Inc | 3674 | D | 408 428-2050 | 12305 |
| Analog Devices Inc | 3674 | C | 408 432-1900 | 12306 |
| Analog Devices Inc | 3674 | D | 408 727-9222 | 12307 |
| Aptina LLC | 3674 | A | 408 660-2699 | 12326 |
| Arm Inc (DH) | 3674 | B | 408 576-1500 | 12330 |
| Atmel Corporation | 3674 | E | 408 735-9110 | 12338 |
| Atp Electronics Inc | 3674 | E | 408 732-5000 | 12340 |
| Auxin Solar Inc | 3674 | E | 408 225-4380 | 12343 |
| Avago Technologies US Inc | 3674 | A | 408 433-4068 | 12344 |
| Avago Technologies US Inc | 3674 | A | 408 433-8000 | 12345 |
| Avogy Inc | 3674 | E | 408 684-5200 | 12348 |
| Bae Systems Imging Sltions Inc | 3674 | D | 408 433-2500 | 12354 |
| Bloom Energy Corporation (PA) | 3674 | B | 408 543-1500 | 12361 |
| Broadcom Corporation | 3674 | E | 408 922-7000 | 12365 |
| Broadcom Corporation (HQ) | 3674 | B | 408 433-8000 | 12366 |
| Broadcom Inc | 3674 | F | 650 427-6000 | 12369 |
| Broadcom Technologies Inc (HQ) | 3674 | D | 408 433-8000 | 12370 |
| C & D Semiconductor Svcs Inc (PA) | 3674 | D | 408 383-1888 | 12372 |
| Cavium Networks Intl Inc | 3674 | D | 650 625-7000 | 12377 |
| Cavli Inc | 3674 | E | 650 605-8166 | 12378 |
| Celestica LLC | 3674 | C | 408 574-6000 | 12379 |
| Chrontel Inc (PA) | 3674 | D | 408 383-9328 | 12381 |
| CM Manufacturing Inc | 3674 | C | 408 284-7200 | 12384 |
| Cnex Labs Inc (PA) | 3674 | E | 408 695-1045 | 12385 |
| Concept Systems Mfg Inc | 3674 | E | 408 855-8595 | 12386 |
| Core Systems LLC | 3674 | E | 510 933-2300 | 12392 |
| Credo Semiconductor Inc | 3674 | D | 408 906-8557 | 12395 |
| Cypress Semiconductor Corp (HQ) | 3674 | A | 408 943-2600 | 12397 |
| Cypress Semiconductor Intl Inc (DH) | 3674 | E | 408 943-2600 | 12398 |
| Dolphin Technology Inc | 3674 | E | 408 392-0012 | 12405 |
| Dreambig Semiconductor Inc | 3674 | D | 408 839-1232 | 12407 |
| Dsp Group Inc (HQ) | 3674 | D | 408 986-4300 | 12409 |
| Dynamic Intgrted Solutions LLC | 3674 | E | 408 727-3400 | 12411 |
| Ecomicron Inc | 3674 | E | 408 526-1020 | 12413 |
| Esilicon Corporation (DH) | 3674 | C | | 12424 |
| Ess Technology Holdings Inc (HQ) | 3674 | E | 408 643-8818 | 12426 |
| Exar Corporation (HQ) | 3674 | E | 669 265-6100 | 12428 |
| Ferrotec (usa) Corporation | 3674 | E | 408 362-1000 | 12431 |
| Flextronics Semiconductor (DH) | 3674 | E | 408 576-7000 | 12434 |
| Fortemedia Inc (PA) | 3674 | E | 408 716-8028 | 12437 |
| Foveon Inc | 3674 | E | 408 855-6800 | 12438 |
| Gainspan Corp | 3674 | E | 408 627-6500 | 12441 |
| Geo Semiconductor Inc (PA) | 3674 | F | 408 638-0400 | 12443 |
| Gigpeak Inc | 3674 | C | 408 546-3316 | 12445 |
| Grinding & Dicing Services Inc | 3674 | E | 408 451-2000 | 12455 |
| Infineon Tech Americas Corp | 3674 | A | 866 951-9519 | 12477 |
| Infineon Tech N Amer Corp (DH) | 3674 | B | 866 951-9519 | 12480 |
| Infineon Tech US Holdco Inc (HQ) | 3674 | D | 866 951-9519 | 12482 |
| Innogrit Corporation | 3674 | E | 408 785-3678 | 12485 |
| Innovion LLC (HQ) | 3674 | D | 408 501-9140 | 12487 |
| Inphi Corporation (HQ) | 3674 | C | | 12489 |
| Intermolecular Inc (HQ) | 3674 | E | 408 582-5700 | 12497 |
| Invecas Inc (HQ) | 3674 | E | 408 758-5636 | 12499 |
| Invensas Corporation | 3674 | F | 408 324-5100 | 12501 |
| Iwatt Inc (DH) | 3674 | E | 408 374-4200 | 12506 |
| Kioxia America Inc (PA) | 3674 | E | 408 526-2400 | 12513 |
| Kovio Inc | 3674 | D | 408 503-7300 | 12515 |
| Kuprion Inc | 3674 | E | 408 206-0122 | 12519 |
| Lam Research Corporation | 3674 | E | 408 434-6109 | 12523 |
| Lattice Semiconductor Corp | 3674 | B | 408 826-6000 | 12528 |
| Ledengin Inc | 3674 | E | 408 922-7200 | 12529 |
| LSI Corporation (DH) | 3674 | A | 408 433-8000 | 12535 |
| M-Pulse Microwave Inc | 3674 | E | 408 432-1480 | 12537 |
| Magnachip Semiconductor Corp | 3674 | F | 408 625-5999 | 12540 |
| Magnum Semiconductor Inc | 3674 | C | 408 934-3700 | 12541 |
| Maxim Integrated Products LLC (HQ) | 3674 | A | 408 601-1000 | 12549 |
| Maxim International Holdg Inc (DH) | 3674 | E | 408 737-7600 | 12550 |

GEOGRAPHIC SECTION SAN JOSE, CA

| | SIC | EMP | PHONE | ENTRY# |
|---|---|---|---|---|
| Megachips Technology America Corporation | 3674 | D | 408 570-0555 | 12555 |
| Mellanox Technologies Inc | 3674 | C | 408 970-3400 | 12556 |
| Mellanox Technologies Inc **(DH)** | 3674 | E | 408 970-3400 | 12557 |
| Merlin Solar Technologies Inc **(HQ)** | 3674 | E | 844 637-5461 | 12558 |
| Micrel Incorporated | 3674 | A | 408 944-0800 | 12561 |
| Micrel LLC | 3674 | A | 408 944-0800 | 12562 |
| Micrel LLC | 3674 | B | 408 944-0800 | 12563 |
| Micrel LLC | 3674 | A | 408 944-0800 | 12564 |
| Microchip Technology | 3674 | E | 408 474-3640 | 12566 |
| Microchip Technology Inc | 3674 | E | 408 735-9110 | 12567 |
| Microsemi Corp - Anlog Mxed Sg | 3674 | A | 408 643-6000 | 12570 |
| Microsemi Corp- Rf Integrated | 3674 | F | 408 954-8314 | 12572 |
| Microsemi Corporation | 3674 | E | 408 643-6000 | 12574 |
| Microsemi Corporation | 3674 | C | 650 318-4200 | 12575 |
| Microsemi Frequency Time Corp | 3674 | D | 408 433-0910 | 12578 |
| Microsemi Soc Corp **(DH)** | 3674 | D | 408 643-6000 | 12579 |
| Micross Hl Rel Pwr Sltions Inc | 3674 | C | 408 434-5000 | 12583 |
| Mixel Inc | 3674 | D | 408 436-8500 | 12586 |
| Montage Technology Inc | 3674 | E | 408 982-2788 | 12588 |
| Mpi America Inc | 3674 | F | 408 770-3650 | 12590 |
| MPS International Ltd | 3674 | E | 408 826-0600 | 12591 |
| Multichip Assembly Inc | 3674 | E | 408 451-2345 | 12593 |
| Nanosilicon Inc | 3674 | E | 408 263-7341 | 12594 |
| Ndsp Delaware Inc | 3674 | E | 408 626-1640 | 12597 |
| Neoconix Inc | 3674 | E | 408 530-9393 | 12598 |
| Nvidia Corporation | 3674 | E | 408 486-2715 | 12611 |
| Nxp Semiconductors Usa Inc | 3674 | A | 408 518-5500 | 12613 |
| Nxp Usa Inc | 3674 | B | 408 518-5500 | 12614 |
| On Semcndctor Cnnctvity Sltons | 3674 | B | 669 209-5500 | 12619 |
| Orbotech Lt Solar LLC | 3674 | E | 408 414-3777 | 12622 |
| Power Integrations Inc **(PA)** | 3674 | B | 408 414-9200 | 12636 |
| Pure Wafer Inc | 3674 | C | 408 945-8112 | 12644 |
| Qorvo Us Inc | 3674 | D | 408 493-4304 | 12647 |
| Qualcomm Atheros Inc **(HQ)** | 3674 | A | 408 773-5200 | 12649 |
| Qualcomm Incorporated | 3674 | D | 408 546-2000 | 12653 |
| Quantumscape Battery Inc | 3674 | C | 408 452-2000 | 12662 |
| Quantumscape Corporation **(PA)** | 3674 | A | 408 452-2000 | 12663 |
| Quicklogic Corporation **(PA)** | 3674 | E | 408 990-4000 | 12665 |
| Rambus Inc | 3674 | E | 408 462-8000 | 12667 |
| Rambus Inc | 3674 | E | 919 960-6600 | 12668 |
| Rambus Inc **(PA)** | 3674 | C | 408 462-8000 | 12669 |
| Renesas Design North Amer Inc **(DH)** | 3674 | E | 408 845-8500 | 12671 |
| Rockley Photonics Inc | 3674 | F | 408 579-9210 | 12681 |
| Scintera Networks Inc | 3674 | E | 408 636-2600 | 12685 |
| Silicon Genesis Corporation **(PA)** | 3674 | E | 408 228-5858 | 12700 |
| Silicon Image Inc **(HQ)** | 3674 | E | 408 616-4000 | 12701 |
| Silicon Light Machines Corp **(DH)** | 3674 | F | 408 240-4700 | 12702 |
| Silicon Quest International Inc | 3674 | D | 408 496-1000 | 12704 |
| Siliconix Incorporated **(HQ)** | 3674 | A | 408 988-8000 | 12708 |
| Sirf Technology Holdings Inc | 3674 | A | 408 523-6500 | 12711 |
| Sk Hynix Mmory Sltons Amer Inc | 3674 | B | 408 514-3500 | 12714 |
| Spansion LLC **(DH)** | 3674 | C | 512 691-8500 | 12728 |
| Spt Microtechnologies | 3674 | E | 408 571-1400 | 12730 |
| Sumco USA Sales Corporation | 3674 | A | 408 352-3880 | 12740 |
| Surface Art Engineering Inc | 3674 | E | 408 433-4700 | 12748 |
| Synapse Semiconductor Corp | 3674 | D | 408 293-4600 | 12752 |
| Technoprobe America Inc | 3674 | E | 408 573-9911 | 12755 |
| Tessera Inc **(DH)** | 3674 | E | 408 321-6000 | 12762 |
| Tessera Intellectual Prpts Inc | 3674 | E | 408 321-6000 | 12764 |
| Tessera Intllctual Prprty Corp | 3674 | F | 408 321-6000 | 12765 |
| Tessera Technologies Inc **(DH)** | 3674 | C | 408 321-6000 | 12766 |
| Tower Semiconductor Usa Inc | 3674 | F | 408 770-1320 | 12770 |
| Triquint Semiconductor Inc | 3674 | F | 408 577-6344 | 12774 |
| Tsmc Technology Inc | 3674 | F | 408 382-8052 | 12775 |
| Verisilicon Inc **(HQ)** | 3674 | F | 408 844-8560 | 12785 |
| Viavi Solutions Inc | 3674 | F | 408 546-5000 | 12788 |
| Viavi Solutions Inc | 3674 | D | 408 577-1478 | 12789 |
| Vishay Siliconix LLC | 3674 | A | 408 988-8000 | 12792 |
| Volterra Semiconductor LLC **(DH)** | 3674 | E | 408 601-1000 | 12797 |
| Wafer Process Systems Inc | 3674 | F | 408 445-3010 | 12800 |
| Wafer Reclaim Services LLC | 3674 | C | 408 945-8112 | 12801 |
| Wafernet Inc | 3674 | F | 408 437-9747 | 12802 |
| Xilinx Development Corporation **(DH)** | 3674 | F | 408 559-7778 | 12808 |
| Zenverge Inc | 3674 | D | 408 350-5052 | 12810 |
| Zilog Inc | 3674 | E | 408 513-1500 | 12812 |
| Bestronics Holdings Inc **(PA)** | 3675 | E | 408 385-7777 | 12815 |
| Jennings Technology Co LLC **(DH)** | 3675 | D | 408 292-4025 | 12819 |
| Yageo America Corporation | 3676 | E | 408 240-6200 | 12824 |
| Duel Systems Inc | 3678 | F | 408 453-9500 | 12877 |
| Aavid Thermalloy LLC | 3679 | E | 408 522-8730 | 12905 |
| Ahead Magnetics Inc | 3679 | D | 408 226-9800 | 12910 |
| Bentek Corporation | 3679 | D | 408 954-9600 | 12922 |
| Cernex Inc | 3679 | F | 408 541-9226 | 12936 |
| Csr Technology Inc **(DH)** | 3679 | E | 408 523-6500 | 12950 |
| Davberta Inc | 3679 | D | 408 453-3272 | 12954 |
| Denron Inc | 3679 | B | 408 435-8588 | 12959 |
| Ensurge Micropower Inc | 3679 | D | 408 503-7300 | 12973 |
| Fastrak Manufacturing Svcs Inc | 3679 | E | 408 298-6414 | 12977 |
| Gourmet Electronics Ltd | 3679 | E | 408 467-1100 | 12989 |
| Hti Turnkey Manufacturing Svcs | 3679 | E | 408 955-0807 | 12996 |
| Javad Ems Inc | 3679 | D | 408 770-1700 | 13012 |
| Lucero Cables Inc | 3679 | C | 408 498-6001 | 13025 |
| Neonode Inc **(PA)** | 3679 | E | 408 496-6722 | 13046 |
| Omniyig Inc | 3679 | E | 408 988-0843 | 13055 |
| Regal Electronics Inc **(PA)** | 3679 | E | 408 988-2288 | 13075 |
| Source One Cable Technology Inc | 3679 | D | 408 376-3400 | 13088 |
| Vander-Bend Manufacturing Inc **(PA)** | 3679 | C | 408 245-5150 | 13115 |
| Enpower Greentech Inc | 3691 | E | 916 220-6060 | 13139 |
| Franklinwh Energy Storage Inc | 3691 | F | 888 837-2655 | 13142 |
| Stacked Energy Inc | 3691 | E | 618 420-9244 | 13150 |
| Mota Group Inc **(PA)** | 3695 | E | 408 370-1248 | 13199 |
| Celestica Inc | 3699 | E | 416 448-5800 | 13219 |
| Central Tech Inc | 3699 | E | 408 955-0919 | 13220 |
| Ghangor Cloud Inc | 3699 | D | 408 713-3303 | 13244 |
| Ino-Tech Laser Processing Inc | 3699 | E | 408 262-1845 | 13251 |
| Intermolecular Inc | 3699 | D | 408 416-2300 | 13254 |
| Keri Systems Inc **(PA)** | 3699 | D | 408 435-8400 | 13261 |
| Networked Energy Services Corp **(PA)** | 3699 | E | 408 622-9900 | 13276 |
| Veeco Process Equipment Inc | 3699 | D | 408 321-8835 | 13325 |
| Nio Usa Inc | 3711 | C | 408 518-7000 | 13374 |
| Cepton Inc **(PA)** | 3714 | F | 408 459-7579 | 13475 |
| Cepton Technologies Inc | 3714 | C | 408 493-6246 | 13476 |
| Velodyne Lidar Usa Inc **(DH)** | 3714 | E | 669 275-2251 | 13602 |
| Wrightspeed Inc | 3714 | E | 866 960-9482 | 13606 |
| Archer Aviation Inc **(PA)** | 3721 | C | 650 272-3233 | 13636 |
| Archer Aviation Inc | 3721 | B | 650 272-3233 | 13637 |
| Archer Aviation Operating Corp | 3721 | C | 650 272-3233 | 13638 |
| Impossible Aerospace Corp | 3721 | F | 707 293-9367 | 13670 |
| Lockheed Martin Corporation | 3721 | B | 408 761-1276 | 13677 |
| Rtx Corporation | 3724 | E | 408 779-9121 | 13721 |
| Kaiser Aerospace & Electronics Corporation | 3728 | A | 949 250-1015 | 13884 |
| Deep Ocean Engineering Inc | 3732 | F | 408 436-1102 | 14031 |
| Alliant Tchsystems Oprtons LLC | 3812 | F | 408 513-3271 | 14140 |
| Astro Digital US Inc | 3812 | D | 650 804-3210 | 14152 |
| Bae Systems Land Armaments LP | 3812 | B | 408 289-0111 | 14163 |
| Caes Systems LLC | 3812 | B | 408 624-3000 | 14166 |
| Invensense Inc **(HQ)** | 3812 | C | 408 501-2200 | 14199 |
| Lg Innotek Usa Inc | 3812 | D | 408 234-6356 | 14209 |
| Northrop Grumman Systems Corp | 3812 | C | 703 968-1239 | 14244 |
| Automated Solutions Group Inc | 3822 | E | 408 432-0300 | 14354 |
| Cypress Envirosystems Inc | 3822 | E | 800 544-5411 | 14359 |
| Bruker-Michrom Inc | 3823 | E | 530 888-6498 | 14390 |
| Fortrend Engineering Corp **(PA)** | 3823 | E | 408 734-9311 | 14413 |
| Laird Technologies Inc | 3823 | E | 408 544-9500 | 14430 |
| Modutek Corp | 3823 | E | 408 362-2000 | 14435 |
| Mountz Inc **(HQ)** | 3823 | E | 408 292-2214 | 14437 |
| Semifab Inc | 3823 | D | 408 414-5928 | 14455 |
| Britelab Inc | 3824 | D | 650 961-0691 | 14474 |
| Echelon Corporation **(DH)** | 3825 | D | 408 938-5200 | 14513 |
| Eugenus Inc **(HQ)** | 3825 | D | 669 235-8244 | 14522 |
| Everactive Inc | 3825 | D | 517 256-0679 | 14523 |
| Exatron Inc | 3825 | E | 408 629-7600 | 14524 |
| Guidetech Inc | 3825 | E | 408 733-6555 | 14531 |
| Ingrasys Technology USA Inc | 3825 | D | 970 301-5069 | 14536 |
| Lumileds LLC **(DH)** | 3825 | E | 408 964-2900 | 14551 |
| Nanofocus Inc | 3825 | E | 408 435-2777 | 14558 |
| Neilsen-Kuljian Inc | 3825 | E | 800 959-4014 | 14561 |
| Nextest Systems Corporation | 3825 | C | 408 960-2331 | 14564 |
| Photon Dynamics Inc | 3825 | C | 408 723-7118 | 14571 |
| Photon Dynamics Inc | 3825 | C | 408 226-9900 | 14572 |
| Photon Dynamics Inc **(HQ)** | 3825 | C | 408 226-9900 | 14573 |
| Richardson Rfpd Inc | 3825 | E | 669 342-3985 | 14578 |
| Sv Probe Inc | 3825 | B | 480 635-4700 | 14588 |
| Teradyne Inc | 3825 | F | 408 960-2400 | 14592 |
| Bayspec Inc | 3826 | E | 408 512-5928 | 14621 |
| Bruker Corporation | 3826 | F | 510 683-4300 | 14639 |
| Bruker Nano Inc | 3826 | E | 408 230-7164 | 14641 |
| Drsd Inc | 3826 | E | 408 230-7164 | 14655 |
| Molecular Devices LLC **(HQ)** | 3826 | C | 408 747-1700 | 14693 |
| Rtec-Instruments Inc | 3826 | E | 408 456-0801 | 14712 |
| Thermo Finnigan LLC **(HQ)** | 3826 | B | 408 965-6000 | 14735 |
| Thermo Fisher Scientific | 3826 | B | 408 894-9835 | 14737 |
| Thermo Fisher Scientific Inc | 3826 | E | 408 965-6200 | 14744 |
| Turner Designs Inc | 3826 | E | 408 749-0994 | 14748 |
| Foreal Spectrum Inc | 3827 | E | 408 923-1675 | 14776 |
| Gamdan Optics Inc | 3827 | F | 669 214-2100 | 14777 |

GEOGRAPHIC

Employee Codes: A=Over 500 employees, B=251-500
C=101-250, D=51-100, E=20-50, F=10-19, G=1-9

2025 Harris California
Manufacturers Directory

© Mergent Inc. 1-800-342-5647

1385

## SAN JOSE, CA

| | SIC | EMP | PHONE | ENTRY# |
|---|---|---|---|---|
| A D A C Laboratories (inc) | 3829 | A | 408 321-9100 | 14837 |
| Comet Technologies USA Inc | 3829 | C | 408 325-8770 | 14857 |
| Geometrics Inc | 3829 | D | 408 428-4244 | 14872 |
| Noah Medical Corporation | 3829 | D | 718 564-3717 | 14904 |
| Spectral Dynamics Inc (PA) | 3829 | E | 760 761-0440 | 14924 |
| Visby Medical Inc | 3829 | C | 408 650-8878 | 14938 |
| Baxano Inc | 3841 | E | 408 514-2200 | 14993 |
| Becton Dickinson and Company | 3841 | D | 734 812-5271 | 14999 |
| Becton Dickinson and Company | 3841 | B | 408 432-9475 | 15002 |
| Dfine Inc (HQ) | 3841 | E | 408 321-9999 | 15067 |
| Icu Medical Inc | 3841 | D | 408 284-7064 | 15112 |
| Johnson Matthey Inc | 3841 | D | 408 727-2221 | 15138 |
| Lumenis Be Inc | 3841 | B | 877 586-3647 | 15154 |
| Lumenis Inc (HQ) | 3841 | C | 408 764-3000 | 15155 |
| Medeologix LLC | 3841 | E | 408 432-6388 | 15164 |
| Micrus Endovascular LLC (HQ) | 3841 | C | 408 433-1400 | 15190 |
| Procept Biorobotics Corp (PA) | 3841 | B | 650 232-7200 | 15231 |
| Prosurg Inc | 3841 | E | 408 945-4040 | 15232 |
| Specific Diagnostics Inc | 3841 | D | 650 938-6800 | 15261 |
| Venus Concept Inc | 3841 | E | 408 489-4925 | 15301 |
| Vnus Medical Technologies Inc | 3841 | E | 408 360-7200 | 15307 |
| Xoft Inc | 3841 | E | 408 493-1500 | 15310 |
| Eargo Inc (PA) | 3842 | D | 650 351-7700 | 15337 |
| Stryker Sales LLC | 3842 | E | 800 624-4422 | 15410 |
| Avantis Medical Systems Inc | 3845 | E | 408 733-1901 | 15514 |
| Kyma Medical Technologies Inc | 3845 | F | 650 386-5089 | 15550 |
| Outset Medical Inc | 3845 | B | 669 231-8200 | 15566 |
| Vave Health Inc | 3845 | F | 650 387-7059 | 15589 |
| Vital Connect Inc | 3845 | C | 408 963-4600 | 15590 |
| Zoll Circulation Inc | 3845 | C | 408 541-2140 | 15592 |
| Lensvector Inc | 3851 | D | 669 247-5095 | 15607 |
| Neuvector Inc | 3861 | E | 408 455-4034 | 15655 |
| Leotek Electronics USA LLC | 3993 | E | 408 380-1788 | 16001 |
| Parma Floors Inc | 3996 | F | 408 638-0247 | 16075 |
| Akon Incorporated | 3999 | D | 408 432-8039 | 16083 |
| Calix Inc (PA) | 4899 | A | 408 514-3000 | 16334 |
| Itron Networked Solutions Inc (HQ) | 4899 | B | 669 770-4000 | 16337 |
| B & A Friction Materials Inc | 5013 | E | 408 286-9200 | 16375 |
| Fleetpride Inc | 5013 | E | 408 286-9200 | 16384 |
| Creative Labs Inc (DH) | 5045 | C | 408 428-6600 | 16515 |
| Epmware Inc | 5045 | E | 408 614-0442 | 16522 |
| Hula Networks Inc | 5045 | F | 866 485-2638 | 16527 |
| Microland Electronics Corp (PA) | 5045 | E | 408 441-1688 | 16532 |
| Team Research Inc | 5045 | E | 408 452-8788 | 16556 |
| Teamsable Inc | 5045 | E | 408 452-8788 | 16557 |
| Trend Micro Incorporated | 5045 | D | 408 257-1500 | 16559 |
| Nidek Incorporated | 5048 | E | 800 223-9044 | 16596 |
| ABB Inc | 5049 | C | 408 770-8968 | 16597 |
| Saco Enterprises Inc | 5051 | E | 408 526-9363 | 16631 |
| Avago Technologies US Inc (HQ) | 5065 | B | 800 433-8778 | 16691 |
| Jai Inc | 5065 | E | 408 383-0300 | 16708 |
| Rose Electronics Distrg Co LLC | 5065 | E | 408 943-0200 | 16732 |
| Shinko Electric America Inc (DH) | 5065 | E | 408 232-0499 | 16734 |
| Winbond Electronics Corp Amer | 5065 | D | 408 943-6666 | 16742 |
| Directed Light Inc | 5084 | E | 408 321-8500 | 16812 |
| Lord & Sons Inc (PA) | 5085 | E | 408 293-4841 | 16883 |
| Vat Incorporated (DH) | 5085 | E | 800 935-1446 | 16905 |
| Sims Group USA Corporation | 5093 | E | 408 494-4242 | 16962 |
| Specialty Baking Inc | 5149 | D | 408 298-6950 | 17215 |
| Peak Technology Entps Inc | 5162 | E | 408 748-1102 | 17230 |
| Creative Plant Design Inc | 5193 | F | 408 452-1444 | 17279 |
| Coraltree Inc | 5734 | E | 408 215-1441 | 17549 |
| Xilinx Inc (HQ) | 6799 | A | 408 559-7778 | 17761 |
| Far Western Graphics Inc | 7334 | D | 408 481-9777 | 17811 |
| 4d Inc | 7371 | C | 408 557-4600 | 17872 |
| Bea Systems Inc (HQ) | 7371 | A | 650 506-7000 | 17885 |
| Displaylink Corp (HQ) | 7371 | F | 650 838-0481 | 17912 |
| International Bus Mchs Corp | 7371 | A | 408 463-2000 | 17934 |
| Lambda Inc | 7371 | C | 650 741-0738 | 17940 |
| Resonate I Inc (PA) | 7371 | C | 408 545-5500 | 17971 |
| Selectiva Systems Inc | 7371 | D | 408 297-1336 | 17977 |
| Zscaler Inc (PA) | 7371 | A | 408 533-0288 | 18002 |
| 42q | 7372 | E | 408 964-3222 | 18006 |
| Adobe Inc | 7372 | E | 408 536-6000 | 18021 |
| Adobe Inc (PA) | 7372 | A | 408 536-6000 | 18022 |
| Andapt Inc | 7372 | F | 408 931-4898 | 18045 |
| Aporeto Inc | 7372 | D | 408 472-7648 | 18049 |
| Aptiv Digital LLC | 7372 | D | 818 295-6789 | 18060 |
| Bill Holdings Inc (PA) | 7372 | C | 650 621-7700 | 18103 |
| Billcom LLC (HQ) | 7372 | C | 650 353-3301 | 18104 |
| Cadence Design Systems Inc (PA) | 7372 | B | 408 943-1234 | 18139 |
| Calypto Design Systems Inc | 7372 | E | 408 850-2300 | 18143 |
| Cato Networks Inc | 7372 | D | 646 975-9243 | 18153 |
| Ciphercloud Inc (HQ) | 7372 | D | 408 687-4350 | 18168 |
| Cisco Systems LLC (HQ) | 7372 | B | 650 989-6500 | 18169 |
| Cloudcar Inc | 7372 | E | 650 946-1236 | 18181 |
| Colortokens Inc (PA) | 7372 | E | 408 341-6030 | 18194 |
| D Software Inc | 7372 | E | 415 795-7466 | 18221 |
| Demandwhiz LLC | 7372 | D | 408 600-2720 | 18238 |
| Denali Software Inc (HQ) | 7372 | E | 408 943-1234 | 18239 |
| Elekta Inc | 7372 | E | 408 830-8000 | 18274 |
| Expandable Software Inc (PA) | 7372 | E | 408 261-7880 | 18304 |
| Former Nt Corp | 7372 | D | 330 702-3070 | 18322 |
| Goalsr Inc | 7372 | E | 650 453-5844 | 18355 |
| Golinks Enterprises Inc | 7372 | D | 562 715-4848 | 18356 |
| Guavus Inc | 7372 | E | 650 243-3400 | 18369 |
| Hoopla Software Inc | 7372 | E | 408 498-9600 | 18389 |
| Hpe Enterprises LLC (HQ) | 7372 | C | 650 857-5817 | 18392 |
| Kerio Technologies Inc | 7372 | E | 409 880-7011 | 18465 |
| Ketera Technologies Inc (DH) | 7372 | E | 408 572-9500 | 18466 |
| Kranem Corporation | 7372 | C | 650 319-6743 | 18481 |
| Leeyo Software Inc (HQ) | 7372 | E | 408 988-5800 | 18495 |
| Lynx Software Technologies Inc (PA) | 7372 | E | 408 979-3900 | 18508 |
| McAfee LLC (DH) | 7372 | D | 888 847-8766 | 18527 |
| McAfee Corp (HQ) | 7372 | E | 866 622-3911 | 18528 |
| Metricstream Inc (PA) | 7372 | C | 650 620-2955 | 18541 |
| Montavista Software LLC (DH) | 7372 | D | 408 572-8000 | 18559 |
| Navis LP | 7372 | E | 408 512-2505 | 18570 |
| Nexenta By Ddn Inc | 7372 | E | 408 791-3300 | 18584 |
| Nok Nok Labs Inc | 7372 | F | 650 433-1300 | 18595 |
| Numerical Technologies Inc | 7372 | C | 408 919-1910 | 18604 |
| Nutanix Inc (PA) | 7372 | A | 408 216-8360 | 18605 |
| Proofpoint Inc | 7372 | E | 408 571-6400 | 18703 |
| Rategain Adara Inc | 7372 | E | 408 691-3603 | 18723 |
| Retail Solutions Incorporated (HQ) | 7372 | E | 650 390-6100 | 18736 |
| Scry Analytics Inc (PA) | 7372 | E | 408 740-8017 | 18768 |
| Sentons Usa Inc | 7372 | E | 408 732-9000 | 18779 |
| Signifyd Inc | 7372 | B | 866 220-1415 | 18790 |
| Smartlogic Semaphore Inc | 7372 | C | 408 213-9500 | 18800 |
| Snickerdoodle Labs Inc | 7372 | F | 408 807-9426 | 18804 |
| Sony Biotechnology Inc | 7372 | D | 800 275-5963 | 18813 |
| Sra Oss Inc | 7372 | D | 408 855-8200 | 18829 |
| Stellar Cyber Inc | 7372 | E | 408 548-0860 | 18836 |
| Talena Inc | 7372 | E | 408 649-6338 | 18862 |
| Trackonomy Systems Inc (PA) | 7372 | B | 833 872-2566 | 18889 |
| Untangle Holdings Inc (PA) | 7372 | E | 408 598-4299 | 18902 |
| Velodyne LLC (HQ) | 7372 | E | 669 275-2251 | 18914 |
| Xperi Inc (PA) | 7372 | D | 408 519-9100 | 18947 |
| Yuja Inc | 7372 | C | 888 257-2278 | 18951 |
| Extreme Networks Inc | 7373 | E | 408 579-2800 | 18973 |
| Northrop Grumman Space & Mission Sy | 7373 | A | 703 280-2900 | 18987 |
| Ubiquiti Networks Inc | 7373 | D | 408 942-3085 | 18997 |
| Baytech Digital Inc | 7374 | E | 408 533-8519 | 19003 |
| A10 Networks Inc (PA) | 7379 | B | 408 325-8668 | 19023 |
| B W Padilla Inc | 7692 | E | 408 275-9834 | 19183 |
| Ryland Custom Welding Inc | 7692 | F | 408 781-2509 | 19211 |
| Ventex Corp | 7699 | E | 408 436-2929 | 19287 |
| Gener8 LLC (PA) | 8711 | D | 650 940-9898 | 19396 |
| Saigon Fabrication Ltd | 8711 | E | 408 693-2340 | 19416 |
| Alzeta Corporation | 8731 | F | 408 727-8282 | 19439 |
| Bio-Ved Pharmaceuticals Inc | 8731 | E | 408 432-4020 | 19444 |
| Takara Bio Usa Inc (DH) | 8731 | E | 650 919-7300 | 19477 |
| Semiconductor Technologies Inc | 8734 | B | 408 240-7000 | 19507 |
| X-Scan Imaging Corporation | 8734 | E | 408 432-9888 | 19511 |
| Tsmc North America (HQ) | 8742 | B | 408 382-8000 | 19545 |

## SAN JUAN BAUTISTA, CA - San Benito County

| | SIC | EMP | PHONE | ENTRY# |
|---|---|---|---|---|
| Earthbound Farm LLC (PA) | 0723 | A | 831 623-7880 | 80 |
| True Leaf Farms LLC (PA) | 2034 | C | 831 623-4667 | 971 |
| Willis Construction Co Inc | 3272 | C | 831 623-2900 | 7398 |

## SAN JUAN CAPISTRANO, CA - Orange County

| | SIC | EMP | PHONE | ENTRY# |
|---|---|---|---|---|
| Pioneer Sands LLC | 1446 | E | 949 728-0171 | 330 |
| Surrounding Elements LLC | 2514 | E | 949 582-9000 | 3512 |
| Emerald X LLC | 2721 | E | 949 226-5754 | 4252 |
| Fluidmaster Inc (PA) | 3089 | D | 949 728-2000 | 6828 |
| Ospreydata Inc | 3826 | F | 619 971-4662 | 14699 |
| Las Glondrinas Mexican Fd Pdts (PA) | 5812 | F | 949 240-3440 | 17595 |

## SAN LEANDRO, CA - Alameda County

| | SIC | EMP | PHONE | ENTRY# |
|---|---|---|---|---|
| Saags Products LLC | 2013 | E | 510 678-3412 | 664 |
| Spar Sausage Co | 2013 | E | 510 614-8100 | 668 |
| Wycen Foods Inc (PA) | 2013 | F | 510 351-1987 | 676 |
| Loco Ventures Inc | 2024 | E | 510 351-0405 | 806 |
| San Francisco Foods Inc | 2038 | D | 510 357-7343 | 1045 |
| La Brea Bakery Cafe Inc | 2051 | A | 818 742-4242 | 1220 |

# GEOGRAPHIC SECTION

## SAN MARCOS, CA

| | SIC | EMP | PHONE | ENTRY# |
|---|---|---|---|---|
| Sogno Toscano Tuscan Dream | 2079 | A | 718 581-9494 | 1405 |
| Artisan Brewers LLC | 2082 | E | 510 567-4926 | 1418 |
| Reyes Coca-Cola Bottling LLC | 2086 | C | 510 667-6300 | 1936 |
| R Torre & Company Inc (PA) | 2087 | D | 800 775-1925 | 2022 |
| R Torre & Company Inc | 2087 | E | 800 775-1925 | 2023 |
| Noble Brewer Beer Company | 2095 | E | 510 766-2337 | 2075 |
| Air Protein Inc | 2099 | E | 510 285-9097 | 2121 |
| Woolery Enterprises Inc | 2099 | E | 510 357-5700 | 2391 |
| Rip-Tie Inc | 2298 | F | 510 577-0200 | 2539 |
| Georgia-Pacific LLC | 2621 | E | 510 483-7580 | 3770 |
| Custom Paper Products LP | 2652 | D | 510 352-6880 | 3814 |
| Metro Poly Corporation | 2673 | E | 510 357-9898 | 3972 |
| UNI Poly Inc | 2673 | F | 510 357-9898 | 3987 |
| India-West Publications Inc (PA) | 2711 | E | 510 383-1140 | 4134 |
| Akido Printing Inc | 2752 | F | 510 357-0238 | 4506 |
| Dakota Press Inc | 2752 | F | 510 895-1300 | 4583 |
| Edelstein Printing Co | 2752 | E | 510 352-7890 | 4602 |
| Epac Technologies Inc (PA) | 2752 | C | 510 317-7979 | 4606 |
| Kp LLC (PA) | 2752 | D | 510 346-0729 | 4664 |
| Kp LLC | 2752 | E | 510 346-0729 | 4665 |
| Brand Marinade Holdings LLC | 2759 | F | 510 435-2002 | 4852 |
| Nel Hydrogen Inc | 2813 | E | 650 543-3180 | 5055 |
| Tap Plastics Inc A Cal Corp (PA) | 2821 | E | 510 357-3755 | 5209 |
| Columbia Cosmetics Mfrs Inc (PA) | 2844 | D | 510 562-5900 | 5956 |
| Akzo Nobel Coatings Inc | 2851 | E | 510 562-8812 | 6066 |
| INX International Ink Co | 2893 | E | 510 895-8001 | 6258 |
| Sun Chemical Corporation | 2893 | D | 510 618-1302 | 6262 |
| Copper Harbor Company Inc | 2899 | F | 510 639-4670 | 6277 |
| Polymeric Technology Inc | 3069 | E | 510 895-6001 | 6525 |
| Peggy S Lane Inc | 3088 | D | 510 483-1202 | 6684 |
| Environmental Sampling Sup Inc | 3089 | D | 510 465-4988 | 6821 |
| Kennerley-Spratling Inc (PA) | 3089 | C | 510 351-8230 | 6883 |
| Ariat International Inc (HQ) | 3199 | A | 510 477-7000 | 7153 |
| General Foundry Service Corp | 3365 | E | 510 297-5040 | 7846 |
| PCC Structurals Inc | 3369 | E | 510 568-6410 | 7869 |
| Bayfab Metals Inc | 3442 | E | 510 568-8950 | 8255 |
| Olson and Co Steel (PA) | 3446 | E | 510 567-2200 | 8639 |
| Scandic Springs Inc | 3469 | E | 510 352-3700 | 8885 |
| Schindler Elevator Corporation | 3534 | E | 510 382-2075 | 9476 |
| Pelagic Pressure Systems Corp | 3545 | D | 510 569-3100 | 9687 |
| Energy Recovery Inc (PA) | 3559 | B | 510 483-7370 | 9852 |
| Daikin Comfort Tech Mfg LP | 3585 | B | 510 265-1212 | 10494 |
| Buran and Reed Inc (PA) | 3596 | E | 888 638-5040 | 10637 |
| MArs Engineering Company Inc (PA) | 3599 | E | 510 483-0541 | 10959 |
| Trayer Engineering Corporation | 3613 | D | 415 285-7770 | 11251 |
| Airspace Systems Inc | 3625 | E | 415 226-7779 | 11305 |
| Borden Lighting | 3646 | E | 510 357-0171 | 11521 |
| L3 Technologies Inc | 3663 | C | 858 499-0284 | 11880 |
| Western Pacific Signal LLC | 3669 | F | 510 276-6400 | 12026 |
| Ampro Systems Inc | 3672 | E | 510 624-9000 | 12052 |
| Contech Solutions Incorporated | 3674 | E | 510 357-7900 | 12390 |
| Sunlink Corporation | 3674 | F | 415 925-9650 | 12743 |
| Marathon Products Incorporated | 3829 | E | 510 562-6450 | 14894 |
| Medical Instr Dev Labs Inc | 3841 | E | 510 357-3952 | 15167 |
| American Underwater Products (HQ) | 3949 | D | 800 435-3483 | 15778 |
| Scafco Corporation | 3999 | E | 415 852-7974 | 16223 |
| Koffler Elec Mech Apprtus Repr | 5063 | D | 510 567-0630 | 16656 |
| Cummins West Inc | 5084 | B | 510 351-6101 | 16811 |
| Tk Elevator Corporation | 5084 | C | 510 476-1900 | 16850 |
| Valley Power Systems Inc | 5084 | E | 510 635-8991 | 16852 |
| Continental Western Corp (PA) | 5085 | C | 510 352-3133 | 16868 |
| Stewart Superior | 5085 | F | 510 346-9811 | 16897 |
| Challenge Dairy Products Inc | 5143 | F | 510 351-3600 | 17125 |
| Shaw Bakers LLC | 5149 | C | 650 273-1440 | 17214 |
| Mr Plastics | 5162 | E | 510 895-0774 | 17228 |
| Rof Ferrari Lending 1 LLC | 5411 | C | 510 351-5520 | 17381 |
| Ghirardelli Chocolate Company (DH) | 5441 | B | 510 483-6970 | 17401 |
| Dr Hops Inc | 5921 | F | 510 863-4522 | 17627 |
| National Cnstr Rentals Inc | 7359 | D | 510 563-4000 | 17858 |
| Osisoft LLC (DH) | 7371 | B | 510 297-5800 | 17958 |
| Applied Fusion LLC | 7699 | D | 510 351-8314 | 19243 |
| Kone Inc | 7699 | E | 510 351-5141 | 19267 |
| Security Central Inc | 7699 | E | 510 652-2477 | 19281 |
| Inlyte Energy Inc | 8711 | E | 415 483-0608 | 19398 |

## SAN LORENZO, CA - Alameda County

| | SIC | EMP | PHONE | ENTRY# |
|---|---|---|---|---|
| Aidells Sausage Company Inc | 2013 | A | 510 614-5450 | 628 |
| Santini Foods Inc | 2023 | C | 510 317-8888 | 781 |
| Tharco Container Inc | 2653 | A | 510 276-8600 | 3891 |
| Tharco Holdings Inc | 2653 | A | 303 373-1860 | 3892 |
| Golden W Ppr Converting Corp | 2657 | E | 510 317-0646 | 3918 |
| Too Good Gourmet Inc (PA) | 5149 | E | 510 317-8150 | 17220 |

## SAN LUIS OBISPO, CA - San Luis Obispo County

| | SIC | EMP | PHONE | ENTRY# |
|---|---|---|---|---|
| Protective Wther Strctures Inc | 1541 | F | 805 547-8797 | 359 |
| Cattaneo Bros Inc | 2013 | E | 805 543-7188 | 635 |
| Chamisal Vineyards LLC | 2084 | F | 866 808-9463 | 1501 |
| Courtside Cellars LLC (PA) | 2084 | F | 805 782-0500 | 1520 |
| Phase 2 Cellars LLC | 2084 | F | 805 782-0300 | 1707 |
| Slo Cider LLC | 2084 | E | 805 439-0865 | 1751 |
| Taco Works Inc | 2096 | E | 805 541-1556 | 2104 |
| Sauer Brands Inc | 2099 | D | 805 597-8900 | 2348 |
| The Hunter Spice Inc | 2099 | D | 805 597-8900 | 2372 |
| Straight Down Enterprises (PA) | 2329 | E | 805 543-3086 | 2644 |
| Pipsticks Inc | 2678 | E | 805 439-1692 | 4022 |
| Slo New Times Inc | 2711 | E | 805 546-8208 | 4197 |
| M G A Investment Co Inc | 2741 | F | 805 543-9050 | 4430 |
| David B Anderson | 2752 | E | 805 489-0661 | 4584 |
| Prpco | 2752 | E | 805 543-6844 | 4742 |
| Ws Packaging-Blake Printery | 2752 | E | 805 543-6844 | 4815 |
| Left Coast T-Shirt Company | 2759 | E | 805 547-1622 | 4913 |
| Promega Biosciences LLC | 2833 | D | 805 544-8524 | 5264 |
| Quality Rubber Sourcing Inc | 3069 | F | 805 544-7770 | 6530 |
| Air-Vol Block Inc | 3271 | E | 805 543-1314 | 7291 |
| Whitefox Defense Tech Inc | 3364 | D | 805 225-4506 | 7832 |
| Inspired Flight Tech Inc | 3429 | E | 805 776-3640 | 8004 |
| Snapnrack Inc | 3429 | E | 877 732-2860 | 8026 |
| Sunrun Solar | 3433 | F | 833 324-5886 | 8083 |
| R H Strasbaugh (PA) | 3541 | E | 805 541-6424 | 9564 |
| Entegris Gp Inc | 3569 | C | 805 541-9299 | 10087 |
| Newlife2 (PA) | 3569 | E | 805 549-8093 | 10101 |
| Next Intent Inc | 3599 | E | 805 781-6755 | 11006 |
| Revasum Inc | 3674 | C | 805 541-6424 | 12677 |
| Ultra-Stereo Labs Inc | 3699 | E | 805 549-0161 | 13320 |
| Empirical Systems Arospc Inc (PA) | 3721 | E | 805 474-5900 | 13650 |
| Stellar Exploration Inc | 3761 | E | 805 459-1425 | 14092 |
| Edge Autonomy Slo LLC | 3812 | E | 805 544-0932 | 14182 |
| Lockheed Mrtin Unmnned Intgrte | 3812 | E | 805 503-4340 | 14217 |
| Crystal Engineering Corp | 3823 | E | 805 595-5477 | 14400 |
| Imdex Technology Usa LLC | 3829 | E | 805 540-2017 | 14883 |
| Fziomed Inc (PA) | 3841 | E | 805 546-0610 | 15094 |
| L Spark | 3911 | E | 805 626-0511 | 15697 |
| Ernie Ball Inc (PA) | 3931 | E | 805 544-7726 | 15716 |
| Kairos Manufacturing Inc | 3999 | F | 805 544-2216 | 16161 |
| Zoo Med Laboratories Inc | 3999 | C | 805 542-9988 | 16273 |
| Vercity Protect Inc | 5047 | F | 917 689-0989 | 16592 |
| 3i Infotech Inc | 7371 | E | 805 544-8327 | 17871 |
| Mindbody Inc (PA) | 7374 | C | 877 755-4279 | 19011 |
| Trust Automation Inc | 8711 | D | 805 544-0761 | 19428 |
| Entegris Inc | 8741 | D | 805 541-9299 | 19516 |

## SAN MARCOS, CA - San Diego County

| | SIC | EMP | PHONE | ENTRY# |
|---|---|---|---|---|
| Twin Oaks Growers Intl Inc | 0181 | E | 760 744-5581 | 51 |
| Airx Utility Surveyors Inc (PA) | 1623 | D | 760 480-2347 | 386 |
| Clear Sign & Design Inc | 1799 | E | 760 736-8111 | 559 |
| GK Foods Inc | 2041 | E | 760 752-5230 | 1060 |
| California Spirits Company LLC | 2086 | E | 619 677-7066 | 1874 |
| Fish House Foods Inc | 2092 | C | 760 597-1270 | 2052 |
| Equal Exchange Inc | 2095 | D | 619 335-6259 | 2070 |
| Culinary Specialties Inc | 2099 | E | 760 744-8220 | 2177 |
| La Fe Tortilleria Inc (PA) | 2099 | E | 760 752-8350 | 2252 |
| Piercan Usa Inc | 2259 | D | 760 599-4543 | 2486 |
| Leemarc Industries LLC | 2329 | D | 760 598-0505 | 2630 |
| Peter Grimm Ltd | 2353 | E | 800 664-4287 | 2849 |
| CJ Products Inc | 2392 | E | 760 444-4217 | 2925 |
| Showdogs Inc | 2591 | E | 760 603-3269 | 3729 |
| Arna Trading Inc (PA) | 2611 | F | 760 940-2775 | 3754 |
| Business Cards Tomorrow | 2752 | F | 760 471-2012 | 4538 |
| San Dieguito Publishers Inc | 2752 | D | 760 593-5139 | 4758 |
| Prographics Screenprinting Inc | 2759 | E | 760 744-4555 | 4944 |
| Cliniqa Corporation (HQ) | 2836 | E | 760 744-1900 | 5820 |
| Cliniqa Corporation | 2836 | E | 760 744-1900 | 5821 |
| Synsus Prvate Lbel Prtners LLC | 2842 | D | 713 714-0225 | 5932 |
| Innovative Biosciences Corp | 2844 | E | 760 603-0772 | 5993 |
| Avista Technologies Inc | 2899 | F | 760 744-0536 | 6270 |
| Dispensing Dynamics Intl Inc (PA) | 3089 | D | 626 961-3691 | 6804 |
| L&S Stone LLC (DH) | 3281 | E | 760 736-3232 | 7541 |
| Winchster Intrcnnect CM CA Inc | 3357 | C | 800 848-4257 | 7800 |
| Independent Energy Solutions Inc | 3433 | E | 760 732-9706 | 8069 |
| Crown Products Inc | 3444 | E | 760 471-1188 | 8422 |
| Microfab Manufacturing Inc | 3444 | F | 760 744-7240 | 8508 |
| Electro Tech Coatings Inc | 3479 | E | 760 746-0292 | 9066 |
| Craneworks Southwest Inc | 3537 | E | 760 735-9793 | 9510 |
| Enstrom Mold & Engineering Inc | 3544 | F | 760 744-1880 | 9620 |
| Pipeline Products Inc | 3569 | F | 760 744-8907 | 10106 |
| Accu-Tech Laser Processing Inc | 3599 | E | 760 744-6692 | 10661 |

Employee Codes: A=Over 500 employees, B=251-500
C=101-250, D=51-100, E=20-50, F=10-19, G=1-9

## SAN MARCOS, CA

| | SIC | EMP | PHONE | ENTRY# |
|---|---|---|---|---|
| Ed Stiglic | 3599 | F | 760 744-7239 | 10819 |
| K-Tech Machine Inc | 3599 | C | 800 274-9424 | 10918 |
| Sullins Electronics Corp | 3643 | D | 760 744-0125 | 11472 |
| Hughes Circuits Inc (PA) | 3672 | D | 760 744-0300 | 12130 |
| Hughes Circuits Inc | 3672 | C | 760 744-0300 | 12131 |
| Impact Project Management Inc | 3672 | E | 760 747-6616 | 12134 |
| Oncore Manufacturing LLC | 3672 | C | 760 737-6777 | 12181 |
| Bree Engineering Corp | 3679 | E | 760 510-4950 | 12927 |
| Dexter Axle Company | 3715 | D | 760 744-1610 | 13616 |
| Unique Functional Products | 3715 | E | 760 744-1610 | 13620 |
| Spinergy Inc | 3751 | D | 760 496-2121 | 14071 |
| Fluid Components Intl LLC (DH) | 3823 | F | 760 744-6950 | 14412 |
| Aci Medical LLC | 3841 | E | 760 744-4400 | 14949 |
| Bbs Manufacturing Inc | 3949 | F | 760 798-8011 | 15785 |
| Western Sign Systems Inc | 3993 | E | 760 736-6070 | 16068 |
| Hexoden Holdings Inc (PA) | 3999 | D | 858 201-3412 | 16144 |
| Preserved Treescapes International Inc | 3999 | E | 760 631-6789 | 16208 |
| Treescapes and Plant Works | 3999 | E | 760 631-6789 | 16258 |
| Hunter Industries Incorporated (PA) | 4971 | C | 760 744-5240 | 16370 |
| Bestop Baja LLC | 5013 | E | 760 560-2252 | 16376 |
| BIP Corporation | 5065 | F | 760 591-9822 | 16692 |
| Tamura Corporation of America (HQ) | 5065 | E | 800 472-6624 | 16735 |
| Orora Packaging Solutions | 5113 | E | 760 510-7170 | 17006 |
| Mack Packaging Inc | 5199 | E | 760 752-3500 | 17300 |
| Quilt In A Day Inc | 5961 | E | 760 591-0929 | 17671 |
| Corkys Pest Control Inc | 7342 | D | 760 432-8801 | 17844 |
| Magic Touch Software Intl | 7372 | E | 800 714-6490 | 18513 |
| Hydralic Systems Cmponents Inc | 7699 | E | 760 744-9350 | 19262 |
| Aquaneering LLC | 8731 | E | 858 578-2028 | 19442 |

### SAN MARINO, CA - Los Angeles County

| | SIC | EMP | PHONE | ENTRY# |
|---|---|---|---|---|
| Feihe International Inc (PA) | 2023 | A | 626 757-8885 | 756 |

### SAN MARTIN, CA - Santa Clara County

| | SIC | EMP | PHONE | ENTRY# |
|---|---|---|---|---|
| Clos La Chance Wines Inc | 2084 | E | 408 686-1050 | 1511 |
| Clos Lachance Wines LLC | 2084 | F | 408 686-1050 | 1512 |
| Admi Inc | 7372 | D | 408 776-0060 | 18019 |

### SAN MATEO, CA - San Mateo County

| | SIC | EMP | PHONE | ENTRY# |
|---|---|---|---|---|
| Rare Barrel LLC | 2082 | E | 510 984-6585 | 1457 |
| Good View Future Group Inc | 2099 | F | 408 834-5698 | 2221 |
| Alameda Newspapers Inc | 2711 | C | 650 348-4321 | 4063 |
| Jigsaw Data Corporation | 2741 | E | 650 235-8400 | 4420 |
| All Out Inc | 2759 | E | | 4838 |
| Barkerblue Inc | 2791 | E | 650 696-2100 | 5016 |
| Beigene Usa Inc | 2834 | B | 877 828-5568 | 5363 |
| Kronos Bio Inc (PA) | 2834 | E | 650 781-5200 | 5530 |
| Neurogesx Inc | 2834 | E | 650 358-3300 | 5570 |
| Sierra Oncology Inc (HQ) | 2834 | D | 650 376-8679 | 5658 |
| Talphera Inc | 2834 | F | 650 216-3500 | 5684 |
| Zs Pharma Inc | 2834 | E | 650 753-1823 | 5726 |
| Bears For Humanity Inc | 2869 | E | 866 325-1668 | 6134 |
| Calysta Inc (PA) | 2869 | F | 650 492-6880 | 6138 |
| Itouchless Housewares Pdts Inc | 3089 | E | 650 578-0578 | 6867 |
| Speculative Product Design LLC (HQ) | 3161 | E | 650 462-2040 | 7141 |
| Coen Company Inc (DH) | 3433 | E | 650 522-2100 | 8064 |
| Brelyon Inc | 3571 | E | 650 246-9426 | 10140 |
| Scale Computing Inc | 3572 | F | 650 212-0132 | 10275 |
| Brilliant Home Technology Inc | 3613 | D | 855 650-0940 | 11236 |
| Resonant Inc | 3674 | D | 805 308-9803 | 12676 |
| Skydio Inc (PA) | 3721 | D | 855 463-5902 | 13690 |
| Prognomiq Inc | 3826 | E | 774 254-1569 | 14707 |
| Gary Berke Mscp Prosthetics | 3842 | F | 650 570-5861 | 15353 |
| Cala Health Inc | 3845 | D | 415 890-3961 | 15522 |
| Gopro Inc (PA) | 3861 | B | 650 332-7600 | 15642 |
| Roboto Games Inc | 3944 | E | 650 380-5966 | 15767 |
| Conversica Inc (PA) | 5734 | C | 650 290-7674 | 17548 |
| Milestone Holdco Inc | 6719 | A | 650 376-2300 | 17747 |
| Marketo Inc (HQ) | 7371 | C | 650 376-2303 | 17945 |
| Streamsets Inc | 7371 | D | 415 851-1018 | 17984 |
| Wonder Workshop Inc (PA) | 7371 | E | 408 785-7981 | 17998 |
| Accrualify Inc | 7372 | E | 650 437-7225 | 18012 |
| Alienvault LLC (DH) | 7372 | E | 650 713-3333 | 18037 |
| Centra Software Inc | 7372 | E | 650 378-1363 | 18156 |
| Contract Wrangler Inc | 7372 | E | 408 472-6898 | 18201 |
| Coupa Holdings LLC (PA) | 7372 | E | 650 931-3200 | 18206 |
| Crowdcircle Inc | 7372 | E | 206 853-7560 | 18211 |
| Crystal Dynamics Inc (HQ) | 7372 | E | 650 421-7600 | 18212 |
| Engagio Inc | 7372 | E | 650 265-2264 | 18282 |
| Freshworks Inc (PA) | 7372 | E | 650 513-0514 | 18333 |
| Fujisoft America Inc | 7372 | E | 650 235-9422 | 18336 |
| Guidewire Software Inc (PA) | 7372 | B | 650 357-9100 | 18371 |
| Guilded LLC | 7372 | F | 415 568-8186 | 18372 |
| Jaunt Inc | 7372 | D | 650 618-6579 | 18454 |
| Jivox Corporation (HQ) | 7372 | E | 650 412-1125 | 18459 |
| Machine Zone LLC | 7372 | E | 650 320-1678 | 18510 |
| Netsuite Inc (DH) | 7372 | A | 650 627-1000 | 18578 |
| Nr2b Research Inc | 7372 | B | 650 393-6500 | 18600 |
| Onesignal Inc (PA) | 7372 | C | 408 506-0701 | 18619 |
| Opera Software International As | 7372 | E | 650 625-8470 | 18627 |
| Oracle Systems Corporation | 7372 | F | 650 506-6780 | 18643 |
| Roblox Corporation (PA) | 7372 | A | 888 858-2569 | 18745 |
| Snaplogic Inc (PA) | 7372 | C | 888 494-1570 | 18802 |
| Space Time Insight Inc | 7372 | E | 650 513-8550 | 18817 |
| Unifi Software Inc | 7372 | E | 732 614-9522 | 18900 |
| Varmour Networks Inc (HQ) | 7372 | E | 650 564-5100 | 18911 |
| Webroot Inc | 7372 | E | 650 292-6600 | 18931 |
| Lattice Engines Inc (DH) | 7373 | C | 877 460-0010 | 18984 |
| Zynga Inc (HQ) | 7374 | C | 855 449-9642 | 19015 |
| 5 Palms LLC | 7389 | C | 650 457-0539 | 19065 |
| Wynd Technologies Inc | 7699 | E | 617 438-3694 | 19292 |
| Lumiata Inc | 8731 | E | 916 607-2442 | 19463 |
| Dompe US Inc | 8733 | F | 833 366-7387 | 19492 |

### SAN MIGUEL, CA - San Luis Obispo County

| | SIC | EMP | PHONE | ENTRY# |
|---|---|---|---|---|
| Courtside Cellars LLC | 2084 | F | 805 467-2882 | 1521 |

### SAN PABLO, CA - Contra Costa County

| | SIC | EMP | PHONE | ENTRY# |
|---|---|---|---|---|
| Contra Costa Newspapers Inc | 2711 | D | 510 758-8400 | 4099 |
| Linde Inc | 2813 | E | 510 223-9593 | 5047 |
| Staidson Biopharma Inc | 2834 | F | 800 345-1899 | 5674 |
| Analytcal Scientific Instrs Inc | 3826 | E | 510 669-2250 | 14610 |

### SAN PEDRO, CA - Los Angeles County

| | SIC | EMP | PHONE | ENTRY# |
|---|---|---|---|---|
| Cleantek Electric Inc | 1731 | E | 424 400-3315 | 453 |
| State Fish Co Inc | 2092 | C | 310 547-9530 | 2064 |
| Juanita F Wade | 2399 | E | 310 519-1208 | 3031 |
| Composite Support and Sltns In | 2655 | F | 310 514-3162 | 3902 |
| Flexline Incorporated | 2796 | E | 562 921-4141 | 5024 |
| Tatung Company America Inc (HQ) | 3663 | D | 310 637-2105 | 11957 |
| Larson Al Boat Shop | 3731 | D | 310 514-4100 | 14007 |
| Space Exploration Tech Corp | 3761 | C | 714 330-8668 | 14087 |

### SAN RAFAEL, CA - Marin County

| | SIC | EMP | PHONE | ENTRY# |
|---|---|---|---|---|
| San Rafael Rock Quarry Inc (HQ) | 1429 | D | 415 459-7740 | 305 |
| Dutra Group (PA) | 1629 | D | 415 258-6876 | 395 |
| Installtion Dgtal Trnsmssons I | 1799 | F | 415 226-0020 | 565 |
| Ann Lilli Corp (PA) | 2337 | D | 415 482-9444 | 2721 |
| One Bella Casa Inc | 2392 | E | 707 746-8300 | 2942 |
| Insight Editions LP | 2731 | E | 415 526-1370 | 4333 |
| Goff Investment Group LLC | 2741 | E | 415 456-2934 | 4406 |
| Syriani Brothers Corp | 2752 | E | 707 585-2718 | 4777 |
| Biomarin Pharmaceutical Inc (PA) | 2834 | B | 415 506-6700 | 5371 |
| Imidomics Inc | 2834 | F | 415 652-4963 | 5487 |
| Small World Trading Co | 2844 | C | 415 945-1900 | 6038 |
| Aledon Inc | 2899 | E | 415 898-0044 | 6266 |
| Vionic Group LLC | 3143 | D | 415 526-6932 | 7112 |
| L P McNear Brick Co Inc | 3271 | D | 415 453-7702 | 7295 |
| Ebac Investments Inc | 3273 | E | 415 455-1575 | 7444 |
| Bok Modern LLC | 3441 | E | 415 749-6500 | 8105 |
| Ekso Bionics Inc (PA) | 3559 | E | 510 984-1761 | 9850 |
| Jeff Burgess & Associates Inc (DH) | 3651 | E | 415 256-2800 | 11670 |
| Zep Solar Llc (DH) | 3674 | E | 415 479-6900 | 12811 |
| Tini Aerospace Inc | 3812 | E | 415 524-2124 | 14319 |
| Infrastructureworld LLC | 3826 | E | 415 699-1543 | 14676 |
| Sanovas Inc | 3841 | E | 415 729-9391 | 15247 |
| Ekso Bionics Holdings Inc | 3842 | D | 510 984-1761 | 15342 |
| Dostal Studio | 3952 | E | 415 721-7080 | 15885 |
| Glass & Sash Inc (PA) | 5039 | E | 415 456-2240 | 16494 |
| Fcsi Inc | 7212 | E | 415 457-8000 | 17764 |
| Layline Automation | 7371 | D | 415 758-0044 | 17941 |
| Fair Isaac International Corp (HQ) | 7372 | A | 415 446-6000 | 18307 |
| Radiant Logic Inc (HQ) | 7372 | E | 415 209-6800 | 18721 |

### SAN RAMON, CA - Contra Costa County

| | SIC | EMP | PHONE | ENTRY# |
|---|---|---|---|---|
| Sun Tropics Inc | 2037 | F | 925 202-2221 | 1017 |
| Reyes Coca-Cola Bottling LLC | 2086 | C | 925 830-6500 | 1953 |
| Chevron Phillips Chem Co LP | 2821 | E | 909 420-5500 | 5145 |
| Steadymed Therapeutics Inc | 2834 | E | 925 361-7111 | 5676 |
| Valent USA LLC (DH) | 2879 | D | 925 256-2700 | 6213 |
| Chevron Oronite Company LLC (DH) | 2899 | E | 713 954-6060 | 6275 |
| Chevron Corporation (PA) | 2911 | A | 925 842-1000 | 6333 |
| Chevron Global Energy Inc (HQ) | 2911 | D | 925 842-1000 | 6334 |
| Pasadena Refining System Inc | 2911 | B | 713 920-1874 | 6345 |
| Flyleaf Windows Inc | 3231 | E | 925 344-1181 | 7221 |
| Overland Storage Inc (HQ) | 3572 | D | 408 283-4700 | 10262 |

# GEOGRAPHIC SECTION — SANTA ANA, CA

| Company | SIC | EMP | PHONE | ENTRY# |
|---|---|---|---|---|
| Overland Storage Inc | 3572 | B | 858 571-5555 | 10263 |
| Cti-Controltech Inc | 3625 | F | 925 208-4250 | 11315 |
| Leica Geosystems Hds LLC | 3829 | D | 925 790-2300 | 14892 |
| Mirion Technologies (us) Inc (HQ) | 3829 | C | 925 543-0800 | 14901 |
| Cooper Companies Inc (PA) | 3851 | C | 925 460-3600 | 15596 |
| Coopervision Inc | 3851 | C | 925 251-6600 | 15597 |
| Japonesque LLC | 5122 | D | 925 866-6670 | 17040 |
| Chevron USA Inc (HQ) | 5541 | B | 925 842-1000 | 17472 |
| Chevron USA Inc | 5541 | D | 925 842-0855 | 17473 |
| Texaco Inc (HQ) | 5541 | A | 925 842-1000 | 17476 |
| Texaco Overseas Holdings Inc (DH) | 5541 | F | 510 242-5357 | 17477 |
| ARC Document Solutions Inc (PA) | 7335 | C | 925 949-5100 | 17818 |
| Allianceit Inc (PA) | 7371 | F | 925 462-9787 | 17879 |
| Callidus Software Inc (HQ) | 7371 | C | 925 251-2200 | 17894 |
| Teslarati LLC | 7371 | F | 323 405-7657 | 17985 |
| Vyshnavi Info Tech India Prvat | 7371 | F | 408 454-6218 | 17995 |
| Accela Inc (PA) | 7372 | C | 925 659-3200 | 18009 |
| Autocene Inc | 7372 | F | 925 264-0045 | 18077 |
| Buyersroad Inc | 7372 | E | 937 313-4466 | 18132 |
| Cyberinc Corporation (HQ) | 7372 | E | 925 242-0777 | 18218 |
| Cylance Inc (DH) | 7372 | D | 949 375-3380 | 18220 |
| Evolphin Software Inc | 7372 | E | 888 386-4114 | 18297 |
| Five9 Inc (PA) | 7372 | A | 925 201-2000 | 18312 |
| GE Digital LLC | 7372 | B | 925 242-6200 | 18342 |
| Grid Dynamics Holdings Inc (PA) | 7372 | C | 650 523-5000 | 18364 |
| Quantmshift Communications Inc | 7372 | F | 800 804-8266 | 18718 |
| Reputationcom Inc (PA) | 7372 | B | 800 888-0924 | 18735 |
| Spikes Inc (PA) | 7372 | E | 855 287-7453 | 18823 |
| Beewise US Inc | 7379 | E | 888 706-3907 | 19028 |
| Iron Horse Ventures LLC | 8742 | E | 925 415-6141 | 19532 |
| Integrated Bldg Solutions Inc | 8748 | F | 925 244-1900 | 19563 |
| Triton Enterprises LLC | 8748 | F | 925 230-8395 | 19574 |

## SAN YSIDRO, CA – San Diego County

| Company | SIC | EMP | PHONE | ENTRY# |
|---|---|---|---|---|
| Volex Inc | 3089 | E | 619 205-4900 | 7073 |
| SI3 Technologies LLC | 3572 | F | 619 365-4275 | 10285 |

## SANGER, CA – Fresno County

| Company | SIC | EMP | PHONE | ENTRY# |
|---|---|---|---|---|
| Virginia Sarabian | 0172 | E | 559 493-2900 | 34 |
| Cargill Meat Solutions Corp | 2011 | D | 559 875-2232 | 586 |
| If Copack LLC | 2032 | E | 559 875-3354 | 858 |
| Initiative Foods LLC | 2032 | C | 559 875-3354 | 859 |
| Cobblestone Fruit | 2033 | C | 559 524-1005 | 881 |
| Melkonian Enterprises Inc | 2034 | E | 559 217-0749 | 957 |
| Dole Packaged Foods LLC | 2037 | C | 559 875-3354 | 1004 |
| Soojians Inc | 2052 | E | 559 875-5511 | 1283 |
| Gibson Wine Company | 2084 | D | 559 875-2505 | 1587 |
| If Holding Inc (PA) | 2099 | D | 559 875-3354 | 2236 |
| California Trusframe LLC | 2439 | C | 559 876-3630 | 3297 |
| MC Truss Inc | 2439 | D | 559 876-3630 | 3314 |
| Kings River Casting Inc | 2531 | F | 559 875-8250 | 3633 |
| International Paper Company | 2621 | D | 559 875-3311 | 3778 |
| Perez Distributing Fresno Inc (PA) | 2834 | F | 800 638-3512 | 5596 |
| Fresno Fab-Tech Inc | 3441 | E | 559 875-9800 | 8144 |
| Adco Manufacturing | 3565 | C | 559 875-5563 | 10010 |
| Algonquin Power Sanger LLC | 3612 | E | 559 875-0800 | 11204 |

## SANTA ANA, CA – Orange County

| Company | SIC | EMP | PHONE | ENTRY# |
|---|---|---|---|---|
| West Lake Food Corporation (PA) | 2011 | E | 714 973-2286 | 625 |
| Brothers Intl Desserts (PA) | 2024 | C | 949 655-0080 | 796 |
| Stremicks Heritage Foods LLC (HQ) | 2026 | B | 714 775-5000 | 845 |
| The Sweet Life Enterprises Inc | 2041 | E | 949 261-7400 | 1065 |
| Gold Coast Baking Company LLC | 2051 | E | 714 545-2253 | 1212 |
| D F Stauffer Biscuit Co Inc | 2052 | E | 714 546-6855 | 1270 |
| Laguna Cookie Company Inc | 2052 | D | 714 546-6855 | 1280 |
| Bonerts Incorporated | 2053 | E | 714 540-3535 | 1286 |
| Rich Products Corporation | 2053 | E | 714 338-1145 | 1292 |
| DAd Investments | 2099 | E | 714 751-8500 | 2179 |
| La Copa De Oro | 2099 | E | 714 554-9925 | 2251 |
| MRS Foods Incorporated (PA) | 2099 | E | 714 554-2791 | 2288 |
| Hook It Up | 2111 | E | 714 600-0100 | 2395 |
| Cut and Sew Co Inc | 2253 | E | 714 981-7244 | 2465 |
| Atlas Carpet Mills Inc | 2273 | C | 323 724-7930 | 2509 |
| Fabrica International Inc | 2273 | C | 949 261-7181 | 2514 |
| J Miller Canvas LLC | 2295 | E | 714 641-0052 | 2528 |
| Pelican Rope Works | 2298 | F | 714 545-0116 | 2538 |
| Fantasy Activewear Inc | 2326 | F | 714 751-0137 | 2592 |
| Image Apparel For Business Inc | 2326 | E | 714 541-5247 | 2594 |
| Liquid Graphics Inc | 2329 | C | 949 486-3588 | 2632 |
| Headmaster Inc (PA) | 2353 | E | 714 556-5244 | 2843 |
| Outer Rebel Inc | 2389 | F | 949 246-2421 | 2907 |
| Ullman Sails Inc (PA) | 2394 | F | 714 432-1860 | 2986 |
| Modern Embroidery Inc | 2395 | E | 714 436-9960 | 2996 |
| Airborne Systems N Amer CA Inc | 2399 | C | 714 662-1400 | 3023 |
| Strata Forest Products Inc (PA) | 2421 | E | 714 751-0800 | 3089 |
| Meyer & Reeder Inc | 2434 | F | 714 388-0146 | 3255 |
| Talimar Systems Inc | 2531 | E | 714 557-4884 | 3640 |
| Acme United Corporation | 2621 | E | 714 557-2001 | 3759 |
| Envelopments Inc | 2621 | E | 714 569-3300 | 3768 |
| OEM Materials & Supplies Inc | 2621 | E | 714 564-9600 | 3790 |
| Spill Magic Inc | 2621 | E | 714 557-2001 | 3799 |
| Blower-Dempsay Corporation (PA) | 2653 | E | 714 481-3800 | 3822 |
| Heritage Paper Co (HQ) | 2653 | D | 714 540-9737 | 3855 |
| A Plus Label Inc | 2679 | E | 714 229-9811 | 4028 |
| 2100 Freedom Inc (HQ) | 2711 | D | 714 796-7000 | 4060 |
| Freedom Communications Inc | 2711 | A | 714 796-7000 | 4115 |
| Entrepreneur Media LLC (PA) | 2721 | E | 949 261-2325 | 4253 |
| Foodbeast Inc | 2741 | F | 949 344-2634 | 4399 |
| B and Z Printing Inc | 2752 | E | 714 892-2000 | 4523 |
| Documocion Research Inc | 2752 | F | 714 662-3800 | 4593 |
| DOT Corp | 2752 | F | 714 708-5960 | 4595 |
| Foster Printing Company Inc | 2752 | E | 714 731-2000 | 4615 |
| Integrated Communications Inc | 2752 | E | 310 851-8066 | 4651 |
| Labor Law Center Inc | 2752 | E | 800 745-9970 | 4670 |
| Mekong Printing Inc | 2752 | E | 714 558-9595 | 4692 |
| Tailgate Printing Inc | 2752 | D | 714 966-3035 | 4779 |
| Artisan Nameplate Awards Corp | 2759 | E | 714 556-6222 | 4843 |
| Beyondgreen Biotech Inc | 2759 | F | 800 983-7221 | 4848 |
| Blackburn Alton Invstments LLC | 2759 | E | 714 731-2000 | 4849 |
| Brixen & Sons Inc | 2759 | E | 714 566-1444 | 4854 |
| Resource Label Group LLC | 2759 | D | 714 619-7100 | 4949 |
| B J Bindery Inc | 2789 | D | 714 835-7342 | 5009 |
| Praxair Distribution Inc | 2813 | F | 714 564-7311 | 5059 |
| Acp Noxtat Inc | 2821 | E | 714 547-5477 | 5131 |
| Tammy Taylor Nails Inc | 2821 | E | 949 250-9287 | 5208 |
| McGuff Otsurcing Solutions Inc | 2834 | E | 800 603-4795 | 5546 |
| Robinson Pharma Inc | 2834 | C | 714 241-0235 | 5641 |
| Robinson Pharma Inc | 2834 | C | 714 241-0235 | 5642 |
| Robinson Pharma Inc (PA) | 2834 | B | 714 241-0235 | 5643 |
| Helica Biosystems Inc | 2835 | F | 714 578-7830 | 5755 |
| Lehman Millet Incorporated | 2835 | E | 714 850-7900 | 5759 |
| Fujifilm Irvine Scientific Inc (DH) | 2836 | E | 949 261-7800 | 5832 |
| Gps Associates Inc | 2842 | E | 949 408-3162 | 5907 |
| Westridge Laboratories Inc | 2844 | E | 714 259-9400 | 6057 |
| Behr Holdings Corporation (HQ) | 2851 | E | 714 545-7101 | 6068 |
| Behr Process LLC (DH) | 2851 | A | 714 545-7101 | 6069 |
| Behr Sales Inc (HQ) | 2851 | C | 714 545-7101 | 6070 |
| Color Science Inc | 2865 | E | 714 434-1033 | 6119 |
| Axiom Materials Inc | 2891 | E | 949 623-4400 | 6219 |
| Insultech LLC (PA) | 2899 | E | 714 384-0506 | 6298 |
| Yokohama Corp North America (HQ) | 3011 | C | 540 389-5426 | 6414 |
| Ciasons Industrial Inc | 3053 | E | 714 259-0838 | 6442 |
| Freudenberg-Nok General Partnr | 3053 | C | 714 834-0602 | 6446 |
| Hdz Brothers Inc | 3053 | E | 714 953-4010 | 6451 |
| Hitt Companies | 3069 | E | 714 979-1405 | 6500 |
| Bird B Gone LLC | 3082 | D | 949 472-3122 | 6577 |
| Altium Packaging LP | 3086 | E | 714 241-6640 | 6619 |
| Smiths Action Plastics Inc (PA) | 3088 | F | 714 836-4141 | 6686 |
| Arlon LLC | 3089 | C | 714 540-2811 | 6724 |
| Clear-Ad Inc | 3089 | E | 866 627-9718 | 6776 |
| Codan US Corporation | 3089 | D | 714 545-2111 | 6777 |
| Fit-Line Inc | 3089 | E | 714 549-9091 | 6827 |
| Hood Manufacturing Inc | 3089 | D | 714 979-7681 | 6856 |
| JB Plastics Inc | 3089 | E | 714 541-8500 | 6874 |
| Modified Plastics Inc (PA) | 3089 | E | 714 546-4667 | 6918 |
| Newport Laminates Inc | 3089 | E | 714 545-8335 | 6931 |
| Southern California Plas Inc | 3089 | E | 714 751-7084 | 7035 |
| CL Solutions LLC | 3211 | D | 714 597-6499 | 7168 |
| International Skylights | 3211 | C | 800 325-4355 | 7174 |
| Sundown Liquidating Corp (PA) | 3211 | D | 714 540-8950 | 7178 |
| Twed-Dells Inc | 3231 | E | 714 754-6900 | 7245 |
| Lotus Hygiene Systems Inc | 3261 | E | 714 259-8805 | 7277 |
| Pacific Stone Design Inc | 3272 | E | 714 836-5757 | 7370 |
| Prime Forming & Cnstr Sups Inc | 3272 | E | 714 547-6710 | 7375 |
| Spec Formliners Inc | 3272 | E | 714 429-9500 | 7393 |
| Bender Ready Mix Inc | 3273 | E | 714 560-0744 | 7407 |
| Easyflex Inc | 3312 | E | 888 577-8999 | 7611 |
| Wheel and Tire Club Inc | 3312 | E | 800 901-6003 | 7634 |
| Aluminum Precision Pdts Inc (PA) | 3334 | A | 714 546-8125 | 7705 |
| Gemini Industries Inc | 3341 | D | 949 250-4011 | 7719 |
| Calmont Engrg & Elec Corp (PA) | 3357 | E | 714 549-0336 | 7779 |
| DC Partners (PA) | 3365 | E | 714 558-9444 | 7842 |
| Curtiss-Wright Surfc Tech LLC | 3398 | F | 714 546-4160 | 7885 |
| Metal Improvement Company LLC | 3398 | E | 714 546-4160 | 7895 |
| Brasstech Inc | 3432 | C | 714 796-9278 | 8046 |
| Brasstech Inc (HQ) | 3432 | C | 949 417-5207 | 8047 |

Employee Codes: A=Over 500 employees, B=251-500
C=101-250, D=51-100, E=20-50, F=10-19, G=1-9

## SANTA ANA, CA — GEOGRAPHIC SECTION

| Company | SIC | EMP | PHONE | ENTRY# |
|---|---|---|---|---|
| Tobin Steel Company Inc | 3441 | D | 714 541-2268 | 8229 |
| Accent Industries Inc (PA) | 3442 | F | 714 708-1389 | 8250 |
| Acd LLC (DH) | 3443 | E | 949 261-7533 | 8296 |
| Ajax Boiler Inc | 3443 | D | 714 437-9050 | 8298 |
| Bend-Tek Inc (PA) | 3444 | E | 714 210-8966 | 8391 |
| Cal Pac Sheet Metal Inc | 3444 | E | 714 979-2733 | 8399 |
| CPC Fabrication Inc | 3444 | F | 714 549-2426 | 8420 |
| Fabrication Concepts Corporation | 3444 | C | 714 881-2000 | 8450 |
| GKN Aerospace Camarillo Inc | 3444 | F | 805 383-6684 | 8458 |
| Oc Metals Inc | 3444 | C | 714 668-0783 | 8519 |
| Sanie Manufacturing Company | 3446 | F | 714 751-7700 | 8643 |
| Acrontos Manufacturing Inc | 3469 | E | 714 850-9133 | 8815 |
| Kaga (usa) Inc | 3469 | E | 714 540-2697 | 8855 |
| Anodyne Inc | 3471 | E | 714 549-3321 | 8921 |
| Chrome Tech Inc | 3471 | C | 714 543-4092 | 8941 |
| Electrode Technologies Inc | 3471 | E | 714 549-3771 | 8953 |
| JD Processing Inc | 3471 | E | 714 972-8161 | 8977 |
| Precious Metals Plating Co Inc | 3471 | F | 714 546-6271 | 8997 |
| Triumph Proc - Embee Div Inc | 3471 | B | 714 546-9842 | 9025 |
| Gemtech Inds Good Earth Mfg | 3479 | E | 714 848-2517 | 9074 |
| R & B Wire Products Inc | 3496 | E | 714 549-3355 | 9227 |
| US Rigging Supply Corp | 3496 | E | 714 545-7444 | 9240 |
| Ecoolthing Corp | 3499 | E | 714 368-4791 | 9283 |
| US Saws Inc (PA) | 3531 | E | 860 668-2402 | 9445 |
| K-V Engineering Inc | 3541 | D | 714 229-9977 | 9558 |
| American Pneumatic Tools Inc | 3542 | F | 562 204-1555 | 9577 |
| Universal Punch Corp | 3542 | E | 714 556-4488 | 9590 |
| Alco Manufacturing Inc | 3544 | E | 714 549-5007 | 9597 |
| Ambrit Engineering Corporation | 3544 | D | 714 557-1074 | 9598 |
| Superior Mold Co | 3544 | E | 714 751-7084 | 9650 |
| Adapt Automation Inc | 3549 | E | 714 662-4454 | 9733 |
| Cryogenic Industries Inc | 3559 | E | 714 568-0201 | 9846 |
| Newport Electronics Inc | 3559 | D | 714 540-4914 | 9882 |
| Ultra TEC Manufacturing Inc | 3559 | F | 714 542-0608 | 9906 |
| Polaris E-Commerce Inc | 3561 | F | 714 907-0582 | 9934 |
| Atr Sales Inc | 3568 | E | 714 432-8411 | 10065 |
| Silicon Tech Inc | 3572 | A | 949 476-1130 | 10284 |
| Marway Power Systems Inc (PA) | 3577 | E | 714 917-6200 | 10408 |
| Omniprint Inc | 3577 | E | 949 833-0080 | 10416 |
| Hannah Industries Inc | 3589 | F | 714 939-7873 | 10563 |
| Jwc Environmental Inc | 3589 | D | 714 662-5829 | 10569 |
| A-Z Mfg Inc | 3599 | E | 714 444-4446 | 10655 |
| Accurate Prfmce Machining Inc | 3599 | E | 714 434-7811 | 10662 |
| Advanced Joining Technologies Inc | 3599 | E | 949 756-8091 | 10675 |
| Aero-k | 3599 | E | 626 350-5125 | 10685 |
| Alco Engrg & Tooling Corp | 3599 | E | 714 556-6060 | 10693 |
| Bel-Air Machining Co | 3599 | F | 714 953-6616 | 10743 |
| Connelly Machine Wks | 3599 | E | 714 558-6855 | 10787 |
| GBF Enterprises Inc | 3599 | E | 714 979-7131 | 10854 |
| Johnson Precision Products LLC | 3599 | F | 714 824-6971 | 10914 |
| K-P Engineering Corp | 3599 | E | 714 545-7045 | 10917 |
| Kilgore Machine Company Inc | 3599 | E | 714 540-3659 | 10927 |
| Maul Mfg Inc (PA) | 3599 | E | 714 641-0727 | 10963 |
| Monarch Prcision Deburring Inc | 3599 | E | 714 258-0342 | 10992 |
| Motorvac Technologies Inc | 3599 | E | 714 558-4822 | 10998 |
| Norotos Inc | 3599 | C | 714 662-3113 | 11011 |
| Ricaurte Precision Inc | 3599 | E | 714 667-0632 | 11078 |
| S&S Precision Mfg Inc | 3599 | E | 714 754-6664 | 11097 |
| Senga Engineering Inc | 3599 | E | 714 549-8011 | 11104 |
| Tmx Engineering and Mfg Corp | 3599 | D | 714 641-5884 | 11145 |
| Tomi Engineering Inc | 3599 | D | 714 556-1474 | 11146 |
| TSC Precision Machining Inc | 3599 | F | 714 542-3182 | 11156 |
| Onyx Power Inc | 3612 | C | 714 513-1500 | 11221 |
| Cole Instrument Corp | 3621 | D | 714 556-3100 | 11261 |
| AP Parpro Inc | 3625 | E | 619 498-9004 | 11309 |
| Nivek Industries Inc | 3643 | E | 714 545-8855 | 11466 |
| Saf-T-Co Supply | 3644 | E | 714 547-9975 | 11481 |
| Orion Chandelier Inc | 3646 | F | 714 668-9668 | 11550 |
| Dana Creath Designs Ltd | 3648 | E | 714 662-0111 | 11589 |
| Aurasound Inc | 3651 | D | 949 829-4000 | 11640 |
| Sigmatronix Inc | 3651 | F | 714 436-1618 | 11697 |
| Secure Comm Systems Inc (HQ) | 3663 | C | 714 547-1174 | 11942 |
| Statewide Trffic Sfety Sgns In (HQ) | 3669 | E | 949 553-8272 | 12018 |
| Accurate Circuit Engrg Inc | 3672 | D | 714 546-2162 | 12041 |
| Dynasty Electronic Company LLC | 3672 | D | 714 550-1197 | 12088 |
| K L Electronic Inc | 3672 | E | 714 751-5611 | 12147 |
| Matrix USA Inc | 3672 | E | 714 825-0404 | 12156 |
| Maxtrol Corporation | 3672 | E | 714 245-0506 | 12157 |
| Parpro Technologies Inc | 3672 | C | 714 545-8886 | 12187 |
| Pioneer Circuits Inc | 3672 | B | 714 641-3132 | 12190 |
| South Coast Circuits LLC | 3672 | D | 714 966-2108 | 12227 |
| Ttm Printed Circuit Group Inc (HQ) | 3672 | C | 714 327-3000 | 12245 |
| Ttm Technologies Inc | 3672 | B | 714 241-0303 | 12247 |
| Ttm Technologies Inc (PA) | 3672 | B | 714 327-3000 | 12248 |
| Accelerated Memory Prod Inc | 3674 | E | 714 460-9800 | 12270 |
| Flexible Manufacturing LLC | 3678 | D | 714 259-7996 | 12879 |
| Express Manufacturing Inc (PA) | 3679 | D | 714 979-2228 | 12974 |
| IJ Research Inc | 3679 | E | 714 546-8522 | 12997 |
| Magnetic Design Labs Inc | 3679 | F | 714 558-3355 | 13029 |
| Sandberg Industries Inc (PA) | 3679 | D | 949 660-9473 | 13081 |
| Smiths Intrcnnect Americas Inc | 3679 | B | 714 371-1100 | 13087 |
| Wyvern Technologies | 3679 | E | 714 966-0710 | 13126 |
| CD Video Manufacturing Inc | 3695 | D | 714 265-0770 | 13193 |
| Kulicke Sffa Wedge Bonding Inc | 3699 | C | 949 660-0440 | 13263 |
| Prototype Express LLC | 3699 | E | 714 751-3533 | 13292 |
| Tactical Micro Inc (DH) | 3699 | F | 714 547-1174 | 13317 |
| Undersea Systems Intl Inc | 3699 | D | 714 754-7848 | 13321 |
| Greenkraft Inc | 3711 | E | 714 545-7777 | 13356 |
| AEC Group Inc | 3714 | F | 714 444-1395 | 13447 |
| Agility Fuel Systems LLC (DH) | 3714 | F | 949 236-5520 | 13450 |
| Danchuk Manufacturing Inc | 3714 | D | 714 540-4363 | 13482 |
| Garrison Manufacturing Inc | 3714 | E | 714 549-4880 | 13504 |
| Impco Technologies Inc (HQ) | 3714 | C | 714 656-1200 | 13517 |
| Overair Inc | 3721 | E | 949 503-7503 | 13684 |
| Advanced Digital Mfg LLC | 3728 | E | 714 245-0536 | 13739 |
| Aerospace Driven Tech Inc | 3728 | F | 949 553-1606 | 13751 |
| Aerospace Engineering LLC | 3728 | E | 714 641-5884 | 13754 |
| Integral Aerospace LLC | 3728 | C | 949 250-3123 | 13874 |
| Meggitt North Hollywood Inc | 3728 | E | 818 691-6258 | 13906 |
| Symbolic Displays Inc | 3728 | D | 714 258-2811 | 13966 |
| Western Methods Machinery Corporation | 3728 | C | 949 252-6600 | 13991 |
| W D Schock Corp | 3732 | E | 951 277-3377 | 14047 |
| All American Racers Inc | 3751 | C | 714 540-1771 | 14052 |
| Cult/Cvlt LLC | 3751 | E | 714 435-2858 | 14055 |
| Anduril Industries Inc | 3812 | E | 949 891-1607 | 14143 |
| Ascent Aerospace | 3812 | D | 586 726-0500 | 14150 |
| Bambeck Systems Inc (PA) | 3823 | F | 949 250-3100 | 14388 |
| E D Q Inc | 3823 | E | 714 546-6010 | 14406 |
| Autonomous Medical Devices Inc (PA) | 3826 | E | 657 660-6800 | 14618 |
| Quantum Magnetics LLC | 3826 | A | 714 258-4400 | 14709 |
| Buk Optics Inc | 3827 | E | 714 384-9620 | 14764 |
| Deltronic Corporation | 3827 | D | 714 545-5800 | 14770 |
| Infinite Optics Inc | 3827 | F | 714 557-2299 | 14784 |
| Mark Optics Inc | 3827 | E | 714 545-6684 | 14798 |
| AMO Usa Inc | 3841 | C | 714 247-8200 | 14966 |
| Medtronic Inc | 3841 | A | 949 474-3943 | 15171 |
| Medtronic Ats Medical Inc | 3841 | C | 949 380-9333 | 15176 |
| Merit Cables Incorporated | 3841 | E | 714 918-1932 | 15185 |
| Orchid MPS | 3841 | D | 714 549-9203 | 15215 |
| Thi Inc | 3841 | E | 714 444-4643 | 15284 |
| Diamond Gloves | 3842 | E | 714 667-0506 | 15332 |
| Surefire LLC | 3842 | E | 714 641-0483 | 15414 |
| Surefire LLC | 3842 | E | 714 545-9444 | 15415 |
| Surefire LLC | 3842 | E | 714 641-0483 | 15416 |
| Medtronic 3f Therapeutics Inc | 3845 | F | 949 399-1675 | 15558 |
| Ricoh Electronics Inc | 3861 | C | 714 566-6079 | 15664 |
| Leonard Craft Co LLC | 3911 | E | 714 549-0678 | 15700 |
| Rickenbacker International Corporation | 3931 | D | 714 545-5574 | 15722 |
| Heart Rate Inc | 3949 | E | 714 850-9716 | 15820 |
| Sbr Sports Inc | 3949 | F | 800 620-4094 | 15852 |
| Xs Scuba Inc (PA) | 3949 | E | 714 424-0434 | 15879 |
| Aardvark Clay & Supplies Inc (PA) | 3952 | E | 714 541-4157 | 15882 |
| Bob Siemon Designs Inc | 3961 | D | 714 549-0678 | 15904 |
| SPS Technologies LLC | 3965 | E | 714 545-9311 | 15917 |
| SPS Technologies LLC | 3965 | B | 714 371-1925 | 15918 |
| Cal-Sign Wholesale Inc | 3993 | F | 209 523-7446 | 15951 |
| Cowboy Direct Response | 3993 | E | 714 824-3780 | 15961 |
| Maneri Sign Co Inc | 3993 | E | 310 327-6261 | 16002 |
| Sign Specialists Corporation | 3993 | E | 714 641-0064 | 16037 |
| Statewide Trffic Sfety Sgns In | 3993 | E | 714 468-1919 | 16048 |
| Yokohama Tire Corporation (DH) | 5014 | C | 714 870-3800 | 16410 |
| Kimlor Mills Inc | 5021 | D | 803 531-2037 | 16415 |
| AAA Imaging & Supplies Inc | 5043 | E | 714 431-0570 | 16498 |
| Cramer-Decker Industries (PA) | 5047 | E | 714 566-3800 | 16579 |
| Advantage Manufacturing Inc | 5063 | E | 714 505-1166 | 16639 |
| Jwc Environmental Inc (DH) | 5084 | E | 949 833-3888 | 16821 |
| Rbc Transport Dynamics Corp | 5085 | C | 203 267-7001 | 16890 |
| Pioneer Packing Inc (PA) | 5113 | E | 714 540-9751 | 17020 |
| Vantage Custom Classics Inc | 5136 | C | 714 755-1133 | 17084 |
| Coastal Cocktails Inc (PA) | 5149 | E | 949 250-8951 | 17184 |
| Embee Performance LLC | 5169 | E | 714 540-1354 | 17242 |
| Jenny Silks Inc | 5193 | F | 714 597-7272 | 17280 |
| SMI Architectural Millwork Inc | 5211 | E | 714 567-0112 | 17345 |
| Blacktag Corporation | 5719 | F | 949 981-9063 | 17532 |
| Skyco Shading Systems Inc | 5719 | E | 714 708-3038 | 17540 |
| DAd Investments | 5812 | E | 714 751-8500 | 17575 |

# GEOGRAPHIC SECTION

## SANTA CLARA, CA

| | SIC | EMP | PHONE | ENTRY# |
|---|---|---|---|---|
| Word For Today | 5961 | E | 714 825-9673 | 17677 |
| Financial Statement Svcs Inc (PA) | 7331 | C | 714 436-3326 | 17797 |
| Identiv Inc | 7372 | D | 888 809-8880 | 18400 |
| Itc Sftware Slutions Group LLC (PA) | 7372 | B | 877 248-2774 | 18449 |
| Nis America Inc | 7372 | E | 714 540-1122 | 18593 |
| Thursby Software Systems LLC | 7372 | E | 817 478-5070 | 18883 |
| Verys LLC | 7379 | C | 949 423-3295 | 19049 |
| Guardsmark LLC (DH) | 7381 | C | 714 619-9700 | 19050 |
| Dekra-Lite Industries Inc | 7389 | D | 714 436-0705 | 19086 |
| American Cooling Tower Inc (PA) | 7699 | F | 714 898-2436 | 19242 |
| Custom Built Machinery Inc | 8711 | E | 714 424-9250 | 19387 |
| Embee Processing LLC | 8711 | B | 714 546-9842 | 19391 |
| Alan B Whitson Company Inc | 8742 | A | 949 955-1200 | 19519 |
| Behr Process Sales Company | 8743 | E | 714 545-7101 | 19547 |
| Iaccess Technologies Inc (PA) | 8748 | E | 714 922-9158 | 19561 |
| County of Orange | 9199 | E | 714 567-7444 | 19576 |

## SANTA BARBARA, CA - Santa Barbara County

| | SIC | EMP | PHONE | ENTRY# |
|---|---|---|---|---|
| Esperer Webstores LLC | 2023 | F | 805 880-1900 | 755 |
| Jeannines Bkg Co Santa Barbara (PA) | 2051 | F | 805 687-8701 | 1218 |
| Adriennes Gourmet Foods | 2052 | D | 805 964-6848 | 1257 |
| Riverbench LLC | 2084 | E | 805 324-4100 | 1724 |
| Kate Farms Inc | 2099 | C | 805 845-2446 | 2246 |
| Toad & Co International Inc (PA) | 2339 | E | 800 865-8623 | 2816 |
| Nobbe Orthopedics Inc | 2342 | E | 805 687-7508 | 2839 |
| Architctral Mllwk Snta Barbara | 2431 | E | 805 965-7011 | 3110 |
| Dailymedia Inc (PA) | 2711 | F | 541 821-5207 | 4102 |
| Noozhawk | 2711 | E | 805 456-7267 | 4170 |
| Santa Barbara Independent Inc | 2711 | E | 805 965-5205 | 4191 |
| Partner Concepts Inc | 2721 | D | 805 745-7199 | 4287 |
| Graphiq LLC | 2741 | C | 805 335-2433 | 4408 |
| Palette Life Sciences Inc (PA) | 2833 | E | 805 869-7020 | 5260 |
| Invenios LLC | 3231 | D | 805 962-3333 | 7228 |
| Steven Handelman Studios Inc (PA) | 3322 | E | 805 884-9070 | 7682 |
| Helistrand Inc | 3357 | E | 805 963-4518 | 7787 |
| Aqueos Corporation (PA) | 3533 | E | 805 364-0570 | 9455 |
| Picosys Incorporated | 3545 | D | 805 962-3333 | 9689 |
| Foodtools Consolidated Inc (PA) | 3556 | E | 805 962-8383 | 9789 |
| Efaxcom | 3577 | E | 805 692-0064 | 10360 |
| Motion Engineering Inc (DH) | 3577 | E | 805 696-1200 | 10412 |
| Kollmorgen Corporation | 3621 | D | 805 696-1236 | 11274 |
| Clearpathgps LLC | 3678 | E | 805 979-3442 | 12870 |
| Agile Rf Inc | 3679 | E | 805 968-5159 | 12909 |
| Freedom Photonics LLC | 3699 | E | 805 967-4900 | 13241 |
| Ricardo Defense Inc (DH) | 3714 | E | 805 882-1884 | 13566 |
| Vetronix Corporation | 3714 | C | 805 966-2000 | 13603 |
| Channel Technologies Group LLC | 3812 | A | | 14169 |
| Santa Barbara Infrared Inc (DH) | 3812 | D | 805 965-3669 | 14300 |
| Santa Barbara Control Systems | 3823 | F | 805 683-8833 | 14454 |
| International Tranducer Corp | 3825 | C | 805 683-2575 | 14538 |
| Anasys Instruments Corp | 3826 | F | 805 730-3310 | 14612 |
| Oxford Instrs Asylum RES Inc (HQ) | 3826 | D | 805 696-6466 | 14700 |
| Electro-Optical Industries LLC | 3827 | E | 805 964-6701 | 14773 |
| Ircamera LLC | 3827 | E | 805 965-9650 | 14789 |
| Arthrex Inc | 3841 | E | 805 964-8104 | 14977 |
| Hollister Incorporated | 3841 | F | 805 845-4785 | 15105 |
| Zyris Inc | 3843 | E | 805 560-9888 | 15496 |
| Duncan Carter Corporation (PA) | 3931 | D | 805 964-9749 | 15713 |
| Brandnew Industries Inc | 3953 | F | 805 964-8251 | 15889 |
| Bloomios Inc | 3999 | E | 805 222-6330 | 16097 |
| Solid Oak Software Inc (PA) | 5045 | E | 805 568-5415 | 16549 |
| Vet National Inc | 5063 | E | 805 692-8487 | 16677 |
| The Alternative Copy Shop Inc | 7334 | D | 805 569-2116 | 17817 |
| Butler Service Group Inc (HQ) | 7363 | D | 201 891-5312 | 17866 |
| Appfolio Inc (PA) | 7372 | B | 805 364-6093 | 18053 |
| Axia Technologies Inc | 7372 | E | 855 376-2942 | 18085 |
| Green Hills Software LLC (HQ) | 7372 | C | 805 965-6044 | 18362 |
| Inform Solution Incorporated | 7372 | E | 805 879-6000 | 18413 |
| Learning Explorer Inc | 7372 | F | 888 909-9035 | 18494 |
| Mixmode Inc | 7372 | E | 858 225-2352 | 18552 |
| Ontraport Inc | 7372 | D | 855 668-7276 | 18620 |
| Productplan LLC | 7372 | E | 805 618-2975 | 18698 |
| Qad Inc (HQ) | 7372 | C | 805 566-6000 | 18711 |
| Sheryl Lowe Designs LLC | 7389 | E | 805 969-1742 | 19129 |

## SANTA CLARA, CA - Santa Clara County

| | SIC | EMP | PHONE | ENTRY# |
|---|---|---|---|---|
| Envirnmntal Systems Inc Nthrn (PA) | 1711 | D | 408 980-1711 | 417 |
| SOS Steel Company Inc | 1791 | E | 408 727-6363 | 535 |
| South Bay Showers Inc | 1793 | E | 408 988-3484 | 542 |
| Wonder Ice Cream Inc (PA) | 2024 | E | 510 818-9102 | 821 |
| WEI Laboratories Inc | 2032 | E | 408 970-8700 | 872 |
| Diana Fruit Co Inc | 2033 | D | 408 727-9631 | 886 |
| Outlaw Beverage Inc | 2082 | F | 310 424-5077 | 1453 |
| Pepsi-Cola Metro Btlg Co Inc | 2086 | E | 408 617-2200 | 1914 |
| Bandmerch LLC | 2396 | E | 818 736-4800 | 3002 |
| Custom Pad and Partition Inc | 2653 | D | 408 970-9711 | 3838 |
| Carustar Industries Inc | 2655 | D | 408 845-7600 | 3901 |
| Almaden Press and Pubg LLC (PA) | 2741 | C | 408 450-7910 | 4363 |
| Cyp Online Inc | 2741 | F | 510 516-6589 | 4385 |
| Think Social Publishing Inc | 2741 | E | 408 557-8595 | 4479 |
| J P Graphics Inc | 2752 | E | 408 235-8821 | 4655 |
| Nss Enterprises | 2752 | E | 408 970-9200 | 4708 |
| Patsons Press | 2752 | E | 408 567-0911 | 4719 |
| Element Six Tech US Corp | 2819 | F | 408 986-8184 | 5090 |
| Honeywell International Inc | 2819 | D | 408 962-2000 | 5095 |
| Mission Park Hotel LP | 2819 | E | 408 809-3838 | 5102 |
| Vacuum Engrg & Mtls Co Inc | 2819 | E | 408 871-9900 | 5128 |
| Metra Biosystems Inc (DH) | 2835 | E | 408 616-4300 | 5762 |
| Micropoint Bioscience Inc | 2835 | E | 408 588-1682 | 5763 |
| B-Bridge International Inc | 2836 | E | 408 252-6200 | 5804 |
| Yes To Inc | 2844 | E | 626 365-1976 | 6061 |
| Integrated Optical Svcs Corp | 2851 | E | 408 982-9510 | 6087 |
| Rennovia Inc | 2869 | F | 650 804-7400 | 6157 |
| Rockys Gasket Shop Inc | 3053 | E | 408 980-9190 | 6463 |
| Compass Innovations Inc | 3081 | C | 408 418-3985 | 6554 |
| UNI-Pixel Inc | 3081 | D | 281 825-4500 | 6574 |
| Pmc Inc | 3086 | C | 562 905-3101 | 6652 |
| Aurora Networks Inc | 3229 | E | 408 428-9500 | 7191 |
| Halio Inc (PA) | 3231 | D | 650 416-5200 | 7226 |
| Pacific Ceramics Inc | 3253 | E | 408 747-4600 | 7271 |
| Vulcan Construction Mtls LLC | 3273 | E | 408 213-4270 | 7518 |
| All Metals Inc (PA) | 3341 | E | 408 200-7000 | 7715 |
| Intricast Company Incorporated | 3369 | E | 408 988-6200 | 7866 |
| Radian Thermal Products Inc | 3369 | D | 408 988-6200 | 7870 |
| Elite Engineering and Mfg LLC | 3443 | E | 408 988-3505 | 8316 |
| Elite E/M Inc | 3444 | E | 408 988-3505 | 8440 |
| Hill Manufacturing Company LLC | 3444 | E | 408 988-4744 | 8469 |
| Lor-Van Manufacturing LLC | 3444 | E | 408 980-1045 | 8488 |
| Lunas Sheet Metal Inc | 3444 | F | 408 492-1260 | 8489 |
| Westfab Manufacturing Inc | 3444 | E | 408 727-0550 | 8612 |
| Amex Plating Incorporated | 3471 | E | 408 986-8222 | 8918 |
| Arnolds Metal Finishing Inc | 3471 | D | 408 588-0079 | 8924 |
| Four D Metal Finishing | 3471 | E | 408 730-5722 | 8962 |
| Nxedge Csl LLC | 3471 | D | 408 727-0893 | 8989 |
| P K Selective Metal Pltg Inc | 3471 | F | 408 988-1910 | 8993 |
| Process Stainless Lab Inc (PA) | 3471 | E | 408 980-0535 | 8999 |
| Prodigy Surface Tech Inc | 3471 | E | 408 492-9390 | 9000 |
| Santa Clara Plating Co Inc | 3471 | D | 408 727-9315 | 9009 |
| B R & F Spray Inc | 3479 | E | 408 988-7582 | 9053 |
| E-Fab Inc | 3479 | E | 408 727-5218 | 9064 |
| Gilbert Spray Coat Inc | 3479 | F | 408 988-0747 | 9075 |
| Scientific Metal Finishing Inc | 3479 | E | 408 970-9011 | 9117 |
| American Precision Spring Corp | 3495 | E | 408 986-1020 | 9196 |
| Blue River Technology Inc | 3523 | D | 408 733-2583 | 9342 |
| Superwinch Holding LLC | 3531 | D | 860 412-1476 | 9439 |
| Accel Manufacturing Inc | 3541 | E | 408 727-5883 | 9538 |
| Applied Materials Inc (PA) | 3559 | A | 408 727-5555 | 9830 |
| Intevac Inc | 3559 | F | 408 986-9888 | 9871 |
| Multibeam Corporation | 3559 | E | 408 980-1800 | 9881 |
| Screen Spe Usa LLC (DH) | 3559 | E | 408 523-9140 | 9898 |
| Silitronics Solutions Inc | 3559 | E | 408 605-1148 | 9899 |
| Beam On Technology Corporation | 3569 | E | 408 982-0161 | 10077 |
| Trifo Inc | 3569 | E | 408 326-2242 | 10119 |
| Ampere Computing LLC | 3571 | E | 669 770-3700 | 10135 |
| Colfax International | 3571 | E | 408 730-2275 | 10143 |
| Innowi Inc | 3571 | E | 408 609-9404 | 10167 |
| Leadman Electronics USA Inc (PA) | 3571 | E | 408 380-4567 | 10174 |
| Oracle America Inc | 3571 | E | 408 276-4300 | 10185 |
| Oracle America Inc | 3571 | E | 408 276-7534 | 10190 |
| Tenstorrent Usa Inc | 3571 | E | 737 262-8464 | 10211 |
| Translattice Inc (PA) | 3571 | F | 408 749-8478 | 10214 |
| EMC Corporation | 3572 | E | 408 646-4406 | 10234 |
| Hitachi Vantara Corporation (DH) | 3572 | B | 858 225-2095 | 10244 |
| Nwe Technology Inc | 3572 | C | 408 919-6100 | 10260 |
| Violin Memory Inc (PA) | 3572 | E | 650 396-1500 | 10293 |
| Arista Networks Inc (PA) | 3577 | D | 408 547-5500 | 10325 |
| Fujifilm Dimatix Inc (DH) | 3577 | D | 408 565-9150 | 10371 |
| Gigamon Inc (HQ) | 3577 | D | 408 831-4000 | 10374 |
| Intel Corp Prfit Shring Rtrmen | 3577 | E | 408 765-8080 | 10385 |
| Intel Corporation | 3577 | C | 408 425-8398 | 10386 |
| Intel Services LLC (HQ) | 3577 | F | 408 765-8080 | 10388 |
| Intel Technologies Inc (HQ) | 3577 | E | 408 765-8080 | 10389 |
| Revera Incorporated | 3577 | E | 408 510-7400 | 10427 |
| Secugen Corporation | 3577 | E | 408 727-7787 | 10433 |
| A-1 Machine Manufacturing Inc (PA) | 3599 | E | 408 727-0880 | 10654 |
| Accu Machine Inc | 3599 | E | | 10660 |

Employee Codes: A=Over 500 employees, B=251-500
C=101-250, D=51-100, E=20-50, F=10-19, G=1-9

## SANTA CLARA, CA — GEOGRAPHIC SECTION

| Company | SIC | EMP | PHONE | ENTRY# |
|---|---|---|---|---|
| Adem LLC | 3599 | E | 408 727-8955 | 10671 |
| B P I Corp. | 3599 | F | 408 988-7888 | 10732 |
| Bnle Berg Holdings LLC | 3599 | D | 408 727-2374 | 10751 |
| Calmax Technology Inc. | 3599 | F | 408 506-2035 | 10760 |
| Calmax Technology Inc. | 3599 | E | 408 513-2139 | 10761 |
| Calmax Technology Inc (PA) | 3599 | E | 408 748-8660 | 10762 |
| Custom Micro Machining Inc. | 3599 | E | 510 651-9434 | 10794 |
| Darko Precision Inc. | 3599 | D | 408 988-6133 | 10800 |
| Delong Manufacturing Co Inc. | 3599 | F | 408 727-3348 | 10804 |
| Eme Technologies Inc. | 3599 | E | 408 720-8817 | 10826 |
| Excel Cnc Machining Inc. | 3599 | E | 408 970-9460 | 10829 |
| James Stout. | 3599 | E | 408 988-8582 | 10903 |
| JWP Manufacturing LLC | 3599 | E | 408 970-0641 | 10916 |
| Kq Integrated Solutions Inc. | 3599 | C | 408 654-0428 | 10932 |
| Master Precision Machining. | 3599 | E | 408 727-0185 | 10961 |
| Mecpro Inc. | 3599 | E | 408 727-9757 | 10969 |
| P M S D Inc (PA) | 3599 | D | 408 988-5235 | 11020 |
| P M S D Inc. | 3599 | E | 408 727-5322 | 11021 |
| Paragon Swiss. | 3599 | E | 408 748-1617 | 11029 |
| Parametric Manufacturing Inc. | 3599 | F | 408 654-9845 | 11030 |
| Richards Machining Co Inc. | 3599 | F | 408 526-9219 | 11079 |
| Swiss Screw Products Inc. | 3599 | E | 408 748-8400 | 11130 |
| Vanderhulst Associates Inc. | 3599 | E | 408 727-1313 | 11171 |
| Watts Machining Inc. | 3599 | E | 408 654-9300 | 11183 |
| Wes Manufacturing Inc. | 3599 | E | 408 727-0750 | 11188 |
| Western Grinding Service Inc. | 3599 | E | 650 591-2635 | 11192 |
| Animatics Corporation. | 3625 | E | 408 748-8721 | 11308 |
| Luxim Corp. | 3641 | F | 408 734-1096 | 11429 |
| Winnov Inc. | 3651 | E | 888 315-9460 | 11718 |
| Comtech Stllite Ntwrk Tech Inc. | 3663 | C | 408 213-3000 | 11834 |
| Motorola Mobility LLC. | 3663 | E | 408 919-0600 | 11897 |
| Nvidia US Investment Company. | 3663 | E | 408 615-2500 | 11907 |
| Purewave Networks Inc. | 3663 | E | 650 528-5200 | 11920 |
| Qualcom Incorporated. | 3663 | B | 858 587-1121 | 11923 |
| Spirent Communications Inc. | 3663 | C | 408 752-7100 | 11950 |
| Addison Technology Inc. | 3672 | E | 408 749-1000 | 12043 |
| Altaflex. | 3672 | D | 408 727-6614 | 12050 |
| Apct Inc (HQ) | 3672 | C | 408 727-6442 | 12055 |
| Apct Holdings LLC (PA) | 3672 | C | 408 727-6442 | 12056 |
| Apct-Wallingford Inc. | 3672 | E | 203 269-3311 | 12057 |
| Cirexx International Inc (PA) | 3672 | C | 408 988-3980 | 12079 |
| Fabrinet West Inc. | 3672 | D | 408 748-0900 | 12099 |
| Harbor Electronics Inc (PA) | 3672 | C | 408 988-6544 | 12128 |
| Multimek Inc. | 3672 | E | 408 653-1300 | 12169 |
| Pactron. | 3672 | D | 408 329-5500 | 12184 |
| Rocket Ems Inc. | 3672 | B | 408 727-3700 | 12201 |
| Streamline Circuits LLC. | 3672 | B | 408 727-1418 | 12230 |
| Summit Interconnect Inc. | 3672 | C | 408 727-1418 | 12235 |
| Ttm Printed Circuit Group Inc. | 3672 | C | 408 486-3100 | 12244 |
| Ttm Technologies Inc. | 3672 | B | 408 486-3100 | 12246 |
| Whizz Systems Inc (PA) | 3672 | E | 408 207-0400 | 12262 |
| Achronix Semiconductor Corp (PA) | 3674 | E | 408 889-4100 | 12271 |
| Actsolar Inc. | 3674 | D | 408 721-5000 | 12272 |
| Advanced Component Labs Inc. | 3674 | E | 408 327-0200 | 12277 |
| Aixtron Inc. | 3674 | C | 669 228-3759 | 12282 |
| Akeana Usa Inc. | 3674 | E | 408 332-3005 | 12283 |
| Akt America Inc (HQ) | 3674 | B | 408 563-5455 | 12285 |
| Akt America Inc. | 3674 | B | 408 563-5455 | 12286 |
| Amat. | 3674 | E | 408 563-5385 | 12296 |
| Ambarella Inc (PA) | 3674 | A | 408 734-8888 | 12297 |
| Amlogic Inc. | 3674 | E | 408 850-9688 | 12302 |
| Analog Inference Inc. | 3674 | E | 408 771-6413 | 12308 |
| Analogix Semiconductor Inc (PA) | 3674 | E | 408 988-8848 | 12309 |
| Applied Manufacturing Group. | 3674 | E | 408 855-8857 | 12313 |
| Applied Materials Inc. | 3674 | E | 408 727-5555 | 12314 |
| Applied Materials Inc. | 3674 | E | 406 752-2107 | 12315 |
| Applied Materials Inc. | 3674 | D | 408 727-5555 | 12316 |
| Applied Materials Inc. | 3674 | E | 512 272-3692 | 12317 |
| Applied Materials Inc. | 3674 | E | 408 727-5555 | 12319 |
| Applied Materials (holdings) (HQ) | 3674 | E | 408 727-5555 | 12320 |
| Applied Micro Circuits Corp (HQ) | 3674 | C | 408 542-8600 | 12321 |
| Applied Micro Circuits Corp. | 3674 | C | 408 542-8600 | 12322 |
| Applied Mtls Asia-Pacific LLC (HQ) | 3674 | E | 408 727-5555 | 12323 |
| Aquantia Corp (DH) | 3674 | E | 408 228-8300 | 12328 |
| Astera Labs Inc (PA) | 3674 | B | 408 337-9056 | 12336 |
| Broadlight Inc. | 3674 | E | 408 982-4210 | 12371 |
| Cavium LLC (DH) | 3674 | E | 408 222-2500 | 12376 |
| Condor Reliability Svcs Inc. | 3674 | E | 408 486-9600 | 12387 |
| Cortina Systems Inc (DH) | 3674 | E | 408 481-2300 | 12394 |
| Crossbar Inc. | 3674 | E | 408 884-0281 | 12396 |
| D-Tek Manufacturing. | 3674 | E | 408 588-1574 | 12399 |
| Dynamic Intgrted Solutions LLC (PA) | 3674 | F | 408 727-3400 | 12412 |
| EdgeQ Inc. | 3674 | E | 408 209-0368 | 12414 |
| Emagin Corporation. | 3674 | E | 408 327-8500 | 12416 |
| Emagin Corporation. | 3674 | E | 845 838-7989 | 12417 |
| Glf Integrated Power Inc. | 3674 | F | 408 239-4326 | 12446 |
| Globalfoundries US 2 LLC. | 3674 | E | 408 462-3900 | 12450 |
| Globalfoundries US Inc. | 3674 | A | 971 285-7461 | 12451 |
| Greenliant Systems Inc. | 3674 | C | 408 217-7400 | 12454 |
| H-Square Corporation. | 3674 | E | 408 982-9108 | 12458 |
| Intel Corporation (PA) | 3674 | A | 408 765-8080 | 12494 |
| Intel Semiconductor (us) LLC (HQ) | 3674 | E | 408 765-8080 | 12495 |
| Keyssa Inc (PA) | 3674 | E | 408 637-2300 | 12512 |
| KLA Corporation. | 3674 | F | 408 986-5600 | 12514 |
| Macom Technology Solutions Inc. | 3674 | E | 408 387-7741 | 12539 |
| Marseille Networks Inc. | 3674 | F | 408 689-0303 | 12542 |
| Marvell Semiconductor Inc (HQ) | 3674 | A | 408 222-2500 | 12545 |
| Marvell Technology Group Ltd. | 3674 | C | 408 222-2500 | 12546 |
| Miasole. | 3674 | B | 408 919-5700 | 12559 |
| Miasole Hi-Tech Corp (DH) | 3674 | E | 408 919-5700 | 12560 |
| Mobiveil Inc. | 3674 | E | 408 791-2977 | 12587 |
| National Semiconductor Corp (HQ) | 3674 | A | 408 721-5000 | 12596 |
| Nethra Imaging Inc (PA) | 3674 | E | 408 257-5881 | 12599 |
| Netlogic Microsystems LLC. | 3674 | A | 408 454-3000 | 12601 |
| Nexgen Power Systems Inc. | 3674 | E | 408 230-7698 | 12603 |
| Nimsoft Inc (HQ) | 3674 | E | 408 796-3400 | 12606 |
| Nuvia Inc. | 3674 | E | 408 654-9696 | 12609 |
| Nvidia Corporation (PA) | 3674 | A | 408 486-2000 | 12612 |
| Omnivision Technologies Inc (PA) | 3674 | A | 408 567-3000 | 12618 |
| Polishing Corporation America. | 3674 | F | 888 892-3377 | 12634 |
| Primenano Inc. | 3674 | E | 650 300-5115 | 12638 |
| Promex Industries Incorporated (PA) | 3674 | D | 408 496-0222 | 12641 |
| Qualcomm Incorporated. | 3674 | E | 408 216-6797 | 12652 |
| Renesas Design North Amer Inc. | 3674 | C | 408 327-8800 | 12672 |
| Semicndctor Cmponents Inds LLC. | 3674 | E | 408 660-2699 | 12687 |
| Semicndctor Cmponents Inds LLC. | 3674 | F | 408 542-1000 | 12688 |
| Sifive Inc (PA) | 3674 | D | 415 673-2836 | 12696 |
| Silicon Vly McRelectronics Inc. | 3674 | E | 408 844-7100 | 12706 |
| Silver Peak Systems LLC (HQ) | 3674 | C | 408 935-1800 | 12709 |
| Sitime Corporation (PA) | 3674 | B | 408 328-4400 | 12713 |
| Stmicroelectronics Inc. | 3674 | F | 408 919-8400 | 12737 |
| Sunpreme Inc. | 3674 | E | 408 419-9281 | 12745 |
| Texas Instruments Incorporated. | 3674 | E | 669 721-5000 | 12767 |
| Bel Power Solutions Inc (HQ) | 3677 | D | 866 513-2839 | 12831 |
| Coherent Asia Inc (HQ) | 3679 | C | 408 764-4000 | 12943 |
| Glimmerglass Networks Inc. | 3679 | E | 510 780-1800 | 12986 |
| N D E Inc. | 3679 | E | 408 727-3955 | 13044 |
| Silitronics Inc. | 3679 | E | 408 605-1148 | 13085 |
| Uniquify Inc (PA) | 3679 | E | 408 235-8810 | 13114 |
| Clarios LLC. | 3691 | E | 408 346-9984 | 13133 |
| Natron Energy Inc (PA) | 3691 | D | 408 498-5828 | 13146 |
| Coherent Corp. | 3699 | E | 408 764-4000 | 13224 |
| Dpss Lasers Inc. | 3699 | E | 408 988-4300 | 13235 |
| Newport Corporation. | 3699 | D | 408 980-4300 | 13277 |
| Byton North America Corp. | 3711 | C | 408 966-5078 | 13344 |
| Edisonfuture Inc (HQ) | 3711 | F | 408 919-8000 | 13348 |
| VIP Manufacturing & Engrg Corp. | 3724 | D | 408 727-6545 | 13727 |
| Metrotech Corporation (PA) | 3812 | D | 408 734-3880 | 14221 |
| Telenav Inc (PA) | 3812 | E | 408 245-3800 | 14317 |
| Applied Cells Inc. | 3821 | E | 800 960-3004 | 14329 |
| Dexerials America Corporation (HQ) | 3824 | E | 770 945-3845 | 14477 |
| Agilent Tech World Trade Inc (HQ) | 3825 | D | 408 345-8886 | 14488 |
| Agilent Technologies Inc. | 3825 | E | 408 345-8886 | 14491 |
| Agilent Technologies Inc. | 3825 | F | 408 553-7777 | 14494 |
| Excel Precision Corp USA. | 3825 | E | 408 727-4260 | 14525 |
| Keysight Technologies Inc. | 3825 | E | 408 553-3290 | 14542 |
| Multitest Elctrnic Systems Inc (DH) | 3825 | B | 408 988-6544 | 14556 |
| National Instruments Corp. | 3825 | E | 408 610-6800 | 14559 |
| Qualitau Incorporated (PA) | 3825 | D | 408 675-3034 | 14576 |
| Roos Instruments Inc. | 3825 | E | 408 748-8589 | 14581 |
| Affymetrix Inc. | 3826 | E | 408 731-5000 | 14604 |
| Agilent Technologies Inc (PA) | 3826 | A | 800 227-9770 | 14606 |
| Coherent Inc (HQ) | 3826 | A | 408 764-4000 | 14645 |
| Fiberlite Centrifuge LLC. | 3826 | D | 408 492-1109 | 14666 |
| Picarro Inc (PA) | 3826 | D | 408 962-3900 | 14705 |
| Thermo Fisher Scientific. | 3826 | E | 603 430-2203 | 14736 |
| Thermo Fisher Scientific Inc. | 3826 | E | 408 731-5056 | 14740 |
| Vibrant Sciences LLC. | 3826 | C | 408 203-9383 | 14753 |
| Zygo Corporation. | 3826 | E | 408 434-1000 | 14757 |
| Intevac Photonics Inc (PA) | 3827 | D | 408 986-9888 | 14787 |
| Redfern Integrated Optics Inc. | 3827 | F | 408 970-3500 | 14815 |
| Rvision Inc. | 3827 | E | 408 437-5777 | 14818 |
| Abbott Laboratories. | 3841 | A | 408 845-3000 | 14940 |
| Abbott Laboratories. | 3841 | B | 408 330-0057 | 14941 |
| Abbott Vascular Inc (HQ) | 3841 | C | 408 845-3000 | 14944 |
| Ablacon Inc. | 3841 | F | 303 955-5620 | 14945 |

# GEOGRAPHIC SECTION

**SANTA CRUZ, CA**

| | SIC | EMP | PHONE | ENTRY# |
|---|---|---|---|---|
| Access Closure Inc. | 3841 | B | 408 610-6500 | 14946 |
| Ancora Heart Inc. | 3841 | E | 408 727-1105 | 14967 |
| Avail Medsystems Inc. | 3841 | E | 650 772-1529 | 14983 |
| Cardiva Medical Inc. | 3841 | C | 408 470-7100 | 15027 |
| Cordis Corporation | 3841 | C | 408 273-3700 | 15052 |
| Cortex Inc. | 3841 | E | 916 501-7214 | 15054 |
| Covidien Holding Inc. | 3841 | C | 408 585-7700 | 15057 |
| Intuitive Surgical Inc. | 3841 | F | 408 523-7579 | 15129 |
| Medtronic Inc. | 3841 | D | 408 548-6618 | 15172 |
| Minerva Surgical Inc. | 3841 | C | 855 646-7874 | 15191 |
| Roche Sequencing Solutions Inc. | 3841 | F | 925 854-6246 | 15245 |
| Semler Scientific Inc. | 3841 | D | 877 774-4211 | 15251 |
| Shockwave Medical Inc (HQ) | 3841 | B | 510 279-4262 | 15255 |
| Verb Surgical Inc. | 3841 | D | 408 438-3363 | 15302 |
| W L Gore & Associates Inc. | 3841 | C | 928 864-2705 | 15308 |
| Si-Bone Inc (PA) | 3842 | B | 408 207-0700 | 15404 |
| Varex Imaging West LLC (HQ) | 3844 | E | 408 565-0850 | 15511 |
| Exo Imaging Inc. | 3845 | C | 833 633-8396 | 15536 |
| Miradry Inc. | 3845 | D | 408 579-8700 | 15559 |
| Corporate Sign Systems Inc. | 3993 | E | 408 292-1600 | 15960 |
| Litmus Automation Inc (PA) | 5045 | D | 765 418-7405 | 16531 |
| Rasilient Systems Inc (PA) | 5045 | E | 408 730-2568 | 16544 |
| Alpha Innotech Corp | 5047 | D | 408 510-5500 | 16572 |
| Walk Vascular LLC | 5047 | E | 949 752-9642 | 16594 |
| PDM Steel Service Centers Inc. | 5051 | E | 408 988-3000 | 16628 |
| Mpower Electronics Inc (PA) | 5063 | D | 408 320-1266 | 16664 |
| Advantest America Inc. | 5065 | B | 408 988-7700 | 16688 |
| Hitachi America Ltd (HQ) | 5084 | C | 914 332-5800 | 16817 |
| Gamus LLC | 5199 | E | 408 441-0170 | 17296 |
| Aharoni & Steele Inc. | 5499 | F | 408 451-9585 | 17423 |
| Vudu Inc. | 5731 | D | 408 492-1010 | 17546 |
| Computer Performance Inc. | 5734 | E | 408 330-5599 | 17547 |
| Access Systems Americas Inc. | 7371 | E | 408 400-3000 | 17875 |
| Brillio LLC | 7371 | E | 800 317-0575 | 17891 |
| Couchbase Inc (PA) | 7371 | C | 650 417-7500 | 17901 |
| Dataself Corp | 7371 | E | 888 910-9802 | 17907 |
| Dremio Corporation (PA) | 7371 | E | 408 882-3569 | 17914 |
| Quid LLC | 7371 | E | 415 813-5300 | 17968 |
| Verint Americas Inc. | 7371 | E | 408 830-5400 | 17993 |
| Awake Security LLC | 7372 | E | 833 292-5348 | 18084 |
| Big Switch Networks LLC | 7372 | E | 650 322-6510 | 18101 |
| Bitzer Mobile Inc. | 7372 | E | 866 603-8392 | 18106 |
| Ca Inc. | 7372 | C | 800 225-5224 | 18136 |
| Casemaker Inc. | 7372 | F | 408 261-8265 | 18149 |
| Cloud Software Group Federal | 7372 | E | 703 208-3900 | 18179 |
| Datera Inc. | 7372 | E | 844 432-8372 | 18230 |
| Druva Inc. | 7372 | D | 650 241-3501 | 18257 |
| Eightfold Ai Inc (PA) | 7372 | C | 650 265-7380 | 18269 |
| Forward Networks Inc. | 7372 | D | 844 393-6389 | 18324 |
| Ginsberg Holdco Inc. | 7372 | B | 408 831-4000 | 18348 |
| Graid Technology Inc (PA) | 7372 | F | 669 258-8102 | 18361 |
| Hortonworks Inc (DH) | 7372 | A | 408 916-4121 | 18390 |
| Irislogic Inc. | 7372 | E | 408 855-8741 | 18446 |
| Kno Inc. | 7372 | D | 408 844-8120 | 18478 |
| Lotusflare Inc. | 7372 | E | 626 695-5634 | 18503 |
| Malwarebytes Inc (PA) | 7372 | B | 408 852-4336 | 18517 |
| McAfee Finance 2 LLC | 7372 | A | 888 847-8766 | 18529 |
| Mly Technix Corp. | 7372 | E | 650 384-1456 | 18553 |
| Mojo Networks Inc (HQ) | 7372 | E | 650 961-1111 | 18558 |
| Net Optics Inc. | 7372 | D | 408 737-7777 | 18573 |
| Netsarang Inc. | 7372 | F | 669 204-3301 | 18575 |
| Netskope Inc (PA) | 7372 | A | 800 979-6988 | 18576 |
| Nominum Inc. | 7372 | E | 650 381-6000 | 18596 |
| Onvantage Inc. | 7372 | D | 408 562-3388 | 18621 |
| Opscruise Inc. | 7372 | E | 916 204-4369 | 18628 |
| Oracle America Inc. | 7372 | C | 408 276-3331 | 18632 |
| Oracle Corporation | 7372 | D | 408 986-8800 | 18638 |
| Palo Alto Networks Inc (PA) | 7372 | B | 408 753-4000 | 18653 |
| Parallel Machines Inc. | 7372 | F | 669 467-2638 | 18658 |
| Pdf Solutions Inc (PA) | 7372 | C | 408 280-7900 | 18667 |
| Plusai Inc. | 7372 | F | 408 508-4758 | 18682 |
| Pure Storage Inc (PA) | 7372 | A | 800 379-7873 | 18708 |
| Questivity Inc. | 7372 | F | 408 615-1781 | 18720 |
| Rival Iq Corporation | 7372 | F | 206 395-8572 | 18742 |
| Secure Computing Corporation (DH) | 7372 | E | 408 979-2020 | 18775 |
| Sequent Software Inc. | 7372 | F | | 18782 |
| Serviceaide Inc (PA) | 7372 | D | 650 206-8988 | 18785 |
| Sesame Software Inc (PA) | 7372 | E | 408 550-7999 | 18786 |
| Sky Parent Inc (PA) | 7372 | F | 650 362-0488 | 18795 |
| Solidcore Systems Inc (DH) | 7372 | D | 408 387-8400 | 18809 |
| Soundhound Ai Inc (PA) | 7372 | F | 408 441-3200 | 18815 |
| Squelch Inc. | 7372 | E | 650 241-2700 | 18828 |
| Tellus Solutions Inc. | 7372 | E | 408 850-2942 | 18872 |

| | SIC | EMP | PHONE | ENTRY# |
|---|---|---|---|---|
| Servicenow Inc (PA) | 7379 | E | 408 501-8550 | 19045 |
| Mks Instruments Inc. | 7699 | E | 408 750-0300 | 19270 |
| Cardiodx Inc. | 8071 | C | 650 475-2788 | 19327 |
| Symyx Technologies Inc. | 8731 | B | 408 764-2000 | 19476 |

## SANTA CLARITA, CA - Los Angeles County

| | SIC | EMP | PHONE | ENTRY# |
|---|---|---|---|---|
| California Resources Prod Corp (HQ) | 1311 | C | 661 869-8000 | 131 |
| Califrnia Rsrces Elk Hills LLC | 1382 | B | 661 412-0000 | 173 |
| CRC Services LLC | 1382 | F | 888 848-4754 | 175 |
| Drinkpak LLC | 2086 | A | 833 376-5725 | 1886 |
| True Warrior LLC | 2389 | E | 661 237-6588 | 2911 |
| Frametent Inc. | 2394 | E | 661 290-3375 | 2974 |
| California Millworks Corp. | 2431 | E | 661 294-2345 | 3114 |
| Old English Mil Woodworks Inc (PA) | 2431 | E | 661 294-9171 | 3171 |
| Applied Polytech Systems Inc. | 2452 | E | 818 504-9261 | 3392 |
| Hood Container Corporation | 2653 | F | 818 848-1648 | 3857 |
| Morris Multimedia Inc. | 2711 | E | 661 259-1234 | 4161 |
| Signal | 2711 | E | 661 259-1234 | 4194 |
| Daisy Publishing Company Inc. | 2741 | D | 661 295-1910 | 4386 |
| Living Way Industries Inc. | 2752 | F | 661 298-3200 | 4681 |
| 3d/International Inc. | 2842 | C | 661 250-2020 | 5886 |
| B&D Investment Partners Inc (PA) | 2842 | E | | 5891 |
| Bright Innovation Labs | 2844 | E | 661 252-3807 | 5951 |
| Packaging Innovations Inc. | 2891 | E | 661 253-5700 | 6239 |
| Certified Thermoplastics Inc. | 3089 | E | 661 222-3006 | 6770 |
| Lamsco West Inc. | 3089 | D | 661 295-8620 | 6893 |
| Magic Plastics Inc (PA) | 3089 | E | 800 369-0303 | 6900 |
| Durable Coating Inc. | 3479 | F | 805 299-8850 | 9063 |
| Curtiss-Wright Corporation | 3491 | D | 661 257-4430 | 9150 |
| Whitmor Plstic Wire Cable Corp (PA) | 3496 | F | 661 257-2400 | 9242 |
| Summit ESP LLC | 3585 | E | 805 585-0595 | 10516 |
| B&B Manufacturing Co (PA) | 3599 | C | 661 257-2161 | 10733 |
| Lansair Corporation | 3599 | F | 661 294-9503 | 10939 |
| Curtiss-Wrght Cntrls Elctrnic (DH) | 3625 | E | 661 257-4430 | 11316 |
| H2w Technologies Inc. | 3625 | F | 661 291-1620 | 11324 |
| Woodward Hrt Inc (HQ) | 3625 | A | 661 294-6000 | 11355 |
| Custom Suppression Inc. | 3677 | F | 818 718-1040 | 12837 |
| Madn Aircraft Hinge | 3721 | E | 661 257-3430 | 13679 |
| Aerospace Dynamics Intl Inc. | 3728 | B | 661 310-6986 | 13752 |
| Santa Clarita Signs | 3993 | E | 661 291-1188 | 16031 |
| Marathon Industries Inc. | 5012 | C | 661 286-1520 | 16372 |
| Universal Wood Moulding Inc (PA) | 5023 | E | 661 362-6262 | 16438 |
| Aq Lighting Group Texas Inc. | 5063 | E | 818 534-5300 | 16643 |
| Jeckys Best Inc. | 5142 | E | 661 259-1313 | 17122 |
| C Sanders Emblems LP | 5199 | E | 800 336-7467 | 17289 |
| Execuprint Inc. | 7374 | F | 818 993-8184 | 19006 |
| 5 Star Service Inc. | 7629 | E | 323 647-7777 | 19173 |
| Wrights Supply Inc. | 7694 | E | 661 254-8400 | 19237 |
| Applied Companies | 8711 | E | 661 257-0090 | 19379 |

## SANTA CRUZ, CA - Santa Cruz County

| | SIC | EMP | PHONE | ENTRY# |
|---|---|---|---|---|
| Glass Jar Inc. | 2024 | D | 831 427-9946 | 802 |
| Glass Jar Inc (PA) | 2024 | E | 831 227-2247 | 803 |
| Mariannes Ice Cream LLC (PA) | 2024 | E | 831 457-1447 | 809 |
| Bagelry Inc (PA) | 2051 | E | 831 429-8049 | 1162 |
| Beckmanns Old World Bakery Ltd | 2051 | D | 831 423-9242 | 1168 |
| Bonny Doon Winery Inc. | 2084 | E | 831 425-3625 | 1487 |
| Seltzer Revolutions Inc. | 2085 | F | 604 765-9966 | 1844 |
| Anomalies International Inc. | 2086 | D | 800 855-1113 | 1865 |
| Clean Water Stores Inc. | 2086 | F | 888 600-5426 | 1879 |
| Lifeaid Beverage Company LLC (PA) | 2086 | E | 888 558-1113 | 1900 |
| Gooder Foods Inc. | 2098 | E | 773 541-4108 | 2114 |
| Socksmith Design Inc (PA) | 2252 | E | 831 426-6416 | 2459 |
| Larsens Inc. | 2394 | E | 831 476-3009 | 2977 |
| Elements Manufacturing Inc. | 2434 | E | 831 421-9440 | 3236 |
| Garrett Moulding Company Inc. | 2499 | E | 831 426-2020 | 3417 |
| Journeyworks Publishing | 2741 | F | 831 423-1400 | 4421 |
| Community Printers Inc. | 2752 | E | 831 426-4682 | 4565 |
| Impact Creative LLC | 2752 | F | 831 824-9660 | 4640 |
| Rainbow Light | 2833 | E | 831 429-9089 | 5266 |
| Threshold Enterprises Ltd | 2833 | E | 831 466-4014 | 5277 |
| Harmony Foods LLC (PA) | 2834 | B | 831 457-3200 | 5476 |
| ONeill Wetsuits LLC (PA) | 3069 | D | 831 475-7500 | 6519 |
| K&R Products Inc. | 3089 | E | 208 935-8824 | 6879 |
| Las Animas Con & Bldg Sup Inc. | 3273 | E | 831 425-4084 | 7461 |
| Roofscreen Mfg Inc. | 3448 | E | 831 421-9230 | 8683 |
| Worth Data Inc. | 3577 | F | 831 458-9938 | 10453 |
| System Studies Incorporated (PA) | 3661 | E | 831 475-5777 | 11789 |
| Dallas Electronics Inc. | 3672 | E | 831 457-3610 | 12085 |
| Microtech Systems Inc. | 3695 | F | 650 596-1900 | 13198 |
| Joby Aero Inc (HQ) | 3721 | A | 831 426-3733 | 13672 |
| Joby Aviation Inc (PA) | 3721 | B | 831 201-6006 | 13673 |
| Santa Cruz Bicycles LLC | 3751 | D | 831 459-7560 | 14068 |

Employee Codes: A=Over 500 employees, B=251-500
C=101-250, D=51-100, E=20-50, F=10-19, G=1-9

# SANTA CRUZ, CA

| | SIC | EMP | PHONE | ENTRY# |
|---|---|---|---|---|
| Nooma Bio Inc | 3826 | F | 408 309-9375 | 14697 |
| Anatometal LLC | 3911 | E | 831 454-9880 | 15684 |
| Santa Cruz Guitar Corporation | 3931 | E | 831 425-0999 | 15723 |
| Arrow Surf Products (PA) | 3949 | F | 831 462-2791 | 15780 |
| Future Motion Inc | 3949 | D | 650 814-8643 | 15815 |
| Nhs Inc | 3949 | D | 831 459-7800 | 15842 |
| Jeff Frank | 3993 | F | 831 469-8208 | 15993 |
| SC Bloom Network Inc | 3999 | E | 415 650-8015 | 16222 |
| Trick or Treat Stdios Hldngs L | 3999 | E | 831 713-9665 | 16259 |
| Pacific Cookie Company Inc (PA) | 5461 | E | 831 429-9709 | 17416 |
| Herb KAn Company Inc | 5499 | F | 831 438-9450 | 17426 |
| Buoy Labs Inc | 7372 | F | 855 481-7112 | 18131 |
| Cycling 74 Corp | 7372 | E | 415 689-5777 | 18219 |

## SANTA FE SPRINGS, CA - Los Angeles County

| | SIC | EMP | PHONE | ENTRY# |
|---|---|---|---|---|
| Ethosenergy Field Services LLC (DH) | 1389 | E | 310 639-3523 | 229 |
| Western Allied Corporation | 1711 | E | 562 944-6341 | 442 |
| Coast Iron & Steel Co | 1791 | E | 562 946-4421 | 529 |
| Camper Packaging LLC | 2023 | F | 562 239-6167 | 752 |
| Food Technology and Design LLC (PA) | 2064 | E | 562 944-7821 | 1307 |
| Anheuser-Busch LLC | 2082 | E | 562 699-3424 | 1413 |
| Blk International LLC | 2086 | E | 424 282-3443 | 1868 |
| American Fruits & Flavors LLC | 2087 | E | 562 320-2802 | 1985 |
| J & J Processing Inc | 2087 | E | 562 926-2333 | 2010 |
| Bumble Bee Foods LLC | 2091 | E | 562 483-7474 | 2035 |
| Nikko Enterprise Corporation | 2092 | E | 562 941-6080 | 2058 |
| Apffels Coffee Inc | 2095 | E | 562 309-0400 | 2067 |
| Fuji Food Products Inc (PA) | 2099 | D | 562 404-2590 | 2210 |
| MCI Foods Inc | 2099 | C | 562 977-4000 | 2278 |
| Otafuku Foods Inc | 2099 | E | 562 404-4700 | 2306 |
| Rich Products Corporation | 2099 | C | 562 946-6396 | 2336 |
| Romeros Food Products Inc (PA) | 2099 | D | 562 802-1858 | 2340 |
| Tri-Star Dyeing & Finshg Inc | 2231 | D | 562 483-0123 | 2450 |
| Super Dyeing LLC | 2261 | D | 562 692-9500 | 2496 |
| Catalina Carpet Mills Inc (PA) | 2273 | E | 562 926-5811 | 2511 |
| Distinctive Inds Texas Inc | 2386 | E | 512 491-3500 | 2877 |
| Distinctive Inds Texas Inc | 2386 | E | 323 889-5766 | 2878 |
| Overland Vehicle Systems LLC | 2394 | E | 833 226-4863 | 2979 |
| Distinctive Industries | 2396 | B | 800 421-9777 | 3005 |
| Day Star Industries | 2431 | F | 562 926-8800 | 3125 |
| True Design Inc | 2434 | F | 562 699-2001 | 3275 |
| Larson-Juhl US LLC | 2499 | E | 562 946-6873 | 3419 |
| Robert Michael Ltd | 2512 | B | 562 758-6789 | 3487 |
| Atlantic Representations Inc (PA) | 2514 | E | 562 903-9550 | 3497 |
| Nakamura-Beeman Inc | 2521 | E | 562 696-1400 | 3574 |
| Office Chairs Inc | 2521 | D | 562 802-0464 | 3578 |
| Elite Mfg Corp | 2522 | C | 888 354-8356 | 3597 |
| Sisneros Inc | 2522 | F | 562 777-9797 | 3607 |
| Soleffect | 2591 | F | 323 275-9945 | 3730 |
| Alegacy Fdsrvice Pdts Group In | 2599 | D | 562 320-3100 | 3733 |
| International Paper Company | 2621 | D | 562 692-9465 | 3782 |
| Specialty Paper Mills Inc | 2621 | C | 562 692-8737 | 3798 |
| Wrkco Inc | 2631 | E | 770 448-2193 | 3812 |
| Bay Cities Container Corp | 2653 | F | 562 302-2552 | 3821 |
| C B Sheets Inc | 2653 | E | 562 921-1223 | 3825 |
| California Box Company (PA) | 2653 | D | 562 921-1223 | 3827 |
| Cflute Corp | 2653 | C | 562 404-6221 | 3830 |
| Gabriel Container (PA) | 2653 | C | 562 699-1051 | 3845 |
| International Paper Company | 2653 | E | 323 946-6100 | 3860 |
| Reliable Container Corporation | 2653 | B | 562 861-6226 | 3882 |
| Western Corrugated Design Inc | 2653 | E | 562 695-9295 | 3894 |
| Dorco Electronics Inc | 2655 | F | 562 623-1133 | 3903 |
| Bay Cities Container Corp | 2671 | E | 562 551-2946 | 3925 |
| Seal Methods Inc (PA) | 2672 | D | 562 944-0291 | 3955 |
| Tape and Label Converters Inc | 2672 | E | 562 945-3486 | 3956 |
| Ace Commercial Inc | 2752 | E | 562 946-6664 | 4500 |
| Alliance Printing Assoc I | 2752 | F | 562 594-7975 | 4507 |
| Ink Spot Inc | 2752 | E | 626 338-4500 | 4645 |
| Inkovation Inc | 2752 | E | 800 465-4174 | 4646 |
| Superprint Lithographics Inc | 2752 | E | 562 698-8001 | 4775 |
| Vomela Specialty Company | 2752 | C | 562 944-3853 | 4806 |
| ABC Imaging of Washington | 2759 | E | 562 375-7280 | 4835 |
| Martin E-Z Stick Labels | 2759 | F | 562 906-1577 | 4920 |
| Superior Printing Inc | 2759 | D | 888 590-7998 | 4966 |
| Ross Bindery Inc | 2789 | C | 562 623-4565 | 5014 |
| Grafico Inc | 2796 | F | 562 832-7601 | 5026 |
| Olin Chlor Alkali Logistics | 2812 | C | 562 692-0510 | 5034 |
| Airgas Usa LLC | 2813 | E | 562 945-1383 | 5041 |
| Airgas Usa LLC | 2813 | E | 562 906-8700 | 5042 |
| Pct-Gw Carbide Tools Usa Inc | 2819 | F | 562 921-7898 | 5108 |
| Phibro-Tech Inc | 2819 | E | 562 698-8036 | 5110 |
| Solvay America Inc | 2819 | D | 562 906-3300 | 5120 |
| Bdc Epoxy Systems Inc | 2821 | E | 562 944-6177 | 5141 |
| Ecowise Inc | 2821 | E | 626 759-3997 | 5153 |
| Multi-Plastics Inc | 2821 | E | 562 692-1202 | 5179 |
| Southland Polymers Inc | 2821 | E | 562 921-0444 | 5202 |
| St Clair Plastics Inc | 2821 | E | 562 946-3115 | 5204 |
| Jarrow Industries LLC (PA) | 2834 | D | 562 906-1919 | 5514 |
| Jarrow Industries LLC | 2834 | E | 562 631-9330 | 5515 |
| Jarrow Industries LLC | 2834 | E | 562 631-9330 | 5516 |
| Jarrow Industries LLC | 2834 | E | 562 631-9330 | 5517 |
| Nhk Laboratories Inc (PA) | 2834 | E | 562 903-5835 | 5573 |
| Nhk Laboratories Inc | 2834 | D | 562 204-5002 | 5574 |
| Titan Medical Enterprises Inc | 2834 | F | 562 903-7236 | 5691 |
| Kik-Socal Inc | 2842 | A | 562 946-6427 | 5911 |
| Morgan Gallacher Inc | 2842 | E | 562 695-1232 | 5917 |
| Life Paint Company (PA) | 2851 | E | 562 944-6391 | 6093 |
| Qspac Industries Inc (PA) | 2891 | D | 562 407-3868 | 6242 |
| Sun Chemical Corporation | 2893 | E | 562 946-2327 | 6261 |
| INX International Ink Co | 2899 | E | 562 404-5664 | 6299 |
| L M Scofield Company (DH) | 2899 | E | 323 720-3000 | 6303 |
| Phibro Animal Health Corp | 2899 | E | 562 698-8036 | 6317 |
| Sika Corporation | 2899 | E | 562 941-0231 | 6324 |
| Golden West Refining Company | 2911 | F | 562 921-3581 | 6338 |
| Gasket Manufacturing Co | 3053 | E | 310 217-5600 | 6449 |
| R D Rubber Technology Corp | 3061 | E | 562 941-4800 | 6476 |
| Duro Roller Company Inc | 3069 | F | 562 944-8856 | 6489 |
| Duro-Flex Rubber Products Inc | 3069 | E | 562 946-5533 | 6490 |
| Rogers Corporation | 3069 | D | 562 404-8942 | 6534 |
| Ptm & W Industries Inc | 3083 | E | 562 946-4511 | 6589 |
| Sleepcomp West LLC | 3086 | E | 562 946-3222 | 6662 |
| Barber-Webb Company Inc (PA) | 3089 | E | 541 488-4821 | 6735 |
| Bolero Inds Inc A Cal Corp | 3089 | E | 562 693-3000 | 6747 |
| Kingseal Corporation | 3089 | E | 562 944-3100 | 6888 |
| Reinhold Industries Inc (DH) | 3089 | C | 562 944-3281 | 7001 |
| Vantage Associates Inc | 3089 | D | 562 968-1400 | 7070 |
| Nelson Sports Inc (PA) | 3149 | E | 562 944-8081 | 7120 |
| Santa Fe Footwear Corporation | 3149 | F | 562 941-9689 | 7121 |
| GP Merger Sub Inc | 3231 | D | 562 946-7722 | 7225 |
| New Glaspro Inc | 3231 | E | 800 776-2368 | 7236 |
| Standridge Granite Corporation | 3281 | E | 562 946-6339 | 7548 |
| John Crane Inc | 3295 | F | 562 802-2555 | 7569 |
| Brown-Pacific Inc | 3312 | E | 562 921-3471 | 7607 |
| Rtm Products Inc | 3312 | E | 562 926-2400 | 7624 |
| International Consulting Unltd | 3317 | E | 714 449-3318 | 7664 |
| Maruichi American Corporation | 3317 | D | 562 903-8600 | 7666 |
| Heraeus Prcous Mtls N Amer LLC (DH) | 3341 | C | 562 921-7464 | 7720 |
| Fry Reglet Corporation (PA) | 3354 | D | 800 237-9773 | 7738 |
| Philatron International | 3357 | E | 562 802-2570 | 7791 |
| Bodycote Thermal Proc Inc | 3398 | E | 562 946-1717 | 7880 |
| Continental Heat Treating Inc | 3398 | E | 562 944-8808 | 7883 |
| Accuride International Inc (PA) | 3429 | E | 562 903-0200 | 7972 |
| Birmingham Fastener & Sup Inc | 3429 | E | 562 944-9549 | 7984 |
| Calmex Fireplace Eqp Mfg Inc | 3429 | E | 716 645-2901 | 7988 |
| Star Die Casting Inc | 3429 | D | 562 698-0627 | 8029 |
| Collicutt Energy Services Inc | 3432 | E | 562 944-4413 | 8051 |
| Brunton Enterprises Inc | 3441 | C | 562 945-0013 | 8107 |
| Custom Steel Fabrication Inc | 3441 | F | 562 907-2777 | 8128 |
| Precision Metal Crafts Inc | 3441 | E | 562 468-7080 | 8201 |
| Best Roll-Up Door Inc | 3442 | E | 562 802-2233 | 8257 |
| Cji Process Systems Inc | 3443 | D | 562 777-0614 | 8308 |
| Pacific Steam Equipment Inc | 3443 | E | 562 906-9292 | 8325 |
| Parker-Hannifin Corporation | 3443 | D | 562 404-1938 | 8327 |
| Wells Struthers Corporation | 3443 | E | 814 726-1000 | 8353 |
| Excel Sheet Metal Inc (PA) | 3444 | D | 562 944-0701 | 8447 |
| Grayd-A Prcsion Met Fbricators | 3444 | E | 562 944-8951 | 8459 |
| Pico Metal Products Inc | 3444 | E | 562 944-0626 | 8536 |
| R & R Ductwork LLC | 3444 | F | 562 944-9660 | 8551 |
| Zenith Screw Products Inc | 3451 | E | 562 941-0281 | 8739 |
| Twist Tite Mfg Inc | 3452 | E | 562 229-0990 | 8768 |
| Timken Gears & Services Inc | 3462 | E | 310 605-2600 | 8789 |
| A-W Engineering Company Inc | 3469 | E | 562 945-1041 | 8814 |
| C Wolfe Industries Inc | 3469 | E | 626 443-7185 | 8825 |
| Eagleware Manufacturing Co Inc | 3469 | E | 562 320-3100 | 8839 |
| Ftr Associates Inc | 3469 | E | 562 945-7504 | 8845 |
| Gasket Manufacturing Engrg Inc | 3469 | F | 310 217-5600 | 8846 |
| New Gordon Industries LLC | 3469 | E | 562 483-7378 | 8872 |
| Tru-Form Industries Inc (PA) | 3469 | D | 562 802-2041 | 8895 |
| Associated Plating Company | 3471 | E | 562 946-5525 | 8926 |
| Cal-Tron Plating Inc | 3471 | E | 562 945-1181 | 8938 |
| Electromatic | 3471 | E | 562 623-9993 | 8956 |
| Electronic Chrome Grinding Inc | 3471 | E | 562 946-6671 | 8957 |
| Trident Plating Inc | 3471 | E | 562 906-2556 | 9024 |
| Master Powder Coating Inc | 3479 | F | 562 863-4135 | 9090 |
| Foremost Spring Company Inc | 3495 | F | 562 923-0791 | 9200 |
| Vault Pro | 3499 | F | 800 299-6929 | 9301 |

# GEOGRAPHIC SECTION — SANTA MONICA, CA

| | SIC | EMP | PHONE | ENTRY# |
|---|---|---|---|---|
| Conveyor Service & Electric | 3535 | E | 562 777-1221 | 9484 |
| Konecranes Inc | 3536 | E | 562 903-1371 | 9502 |
| Westmont Industries LLC **(PA)** | 3536 | F | 562 944-6137 | 9504 |
| Medlin Ramps | 3542 | E | 877 463-3546 | 9585 |
| Express Die Supply Inc | 3544 | E | 562 903-1700 | 9621 |
| Santa Fe Enterprises Inc | 3544 | E | 562 692-7596 | 9647 |
| FPec Corporation A Cal Corp **(PA)** | 3556 | F | 562 802-3727 | 9791 |
| Superior Food Machinery Inc | 3556 | E | 562 949-0396 | 9819 |
| United Surface Solutions LLC | 3559 | E | 562 693-0202 | 9908 |
| Cascade Pump Company | 3561 | D | 562 946-1414 | 9917 |
| Sulzer Pump Services (us) Inc | 3561 | E | 562 903-1000 | 9941 |
| United Bakery Equipment Co Inc **(PA)** | 3565 | D | 310 635-8121 | 10034 |
| Industrial Sprockets Gears Inc | 3568 | E | 323 233-7221 | 10072 |
| Source Code LLC | 3571 | E | 562 903-1500 | 10205 |
| Aferin LLC | 3572 | E | 562 903-1500 | 10221 |
| Whittier Mailing Products Inc **(PA)** | 3579 | F | 562 464-3000 | 10467 |
| Lmw Enterprises LLC | 3585 | E | 562 944-1969 | 10506 |
| Gorlitz Sewer & Drain Inc | 3589 | E | 562 944-3060 | 10562 |
| Hydraulic Pneumatic Inc | 3593 | F | 562 926-1122 | 10628 |
| Aero Chip Inc | 3599 | E | 562 404-6300 | 10681 |
| Golden West Machine Inc | 3599 | E | 562 903-1111 | 10863 |
| JR Machine Company Inc | 3599 | E | 562 903-9477 | 10915 |
| Machine Precision Components | 3599 | F | 562 404-0500 | 10953 |
| Omega Precision | 3599 | E | 562 946-2491 | 11016 |
| Pedavena Mould and Die Co Inc | 3599 | E | 310 327-2814 | 11035 |
| Process Fab Inc | 3599 | C | 562 921-1979 | 11050 |
| Pscmb Repairs Inc | 3599 | E | 626 448-7778 | 11055 |
| Serrano Industries Inc | 3599 | E | 562 777-8180 | 11110 |
| SMI Ca Inc | 3599 | E | 562 926-9407 | 11115 |
| Triangle Tool & Die Corp | 3599 | F | 562 944-2117 | 11150 |
| Vescio Threading Co | 3599 | D | 562 802-1868 | 11175 |
| West Coast Machining Inc | 3599 | E | 562 229-1087 | 11190 |
| Ohmega Solenoid Co Inc | 3612 | E | 562 944-7948 | 11219 |
| Pioneer Custom Elec Pdts Corp | 3612 | D | 562 944-0626 | 11223 |
| Age Incorporated | 3613 | E | 562 483-7300 | 11234 |
| General Switchgear Inc | 3613 | E | | 11242 |
| G3 Virtus Solutions Inc | 3621 | E | 323 724-6771 | 11269 |
| Aleo Lighting Inc | 3645 | F | 877 358-8825 | 11485 |
| Artiva USA Inc | 3645 | E | 562 298-8968 | 11489 |
| Dab Inc | 3645 | D | 562 623-4773 | 11493 |
| T-1 Lighting Inc | 3646 | F | 626 234-2328 | 11560 |
| Shimada Enterprises Inc | 3648 | E | 562 802-8811 | 11622 |
| Funai Corporation Inc **(DH)** | 3651 | E | 310 787-3000 | 11661 |
| Detoronics Corp | 3678 | E | 626 579-7130 | 12876 |
| Trojan Battery Holdings LLC | 3691 | E | 800 423-6569 | 13154 |
| Trojan Battery Company LLC **(DH)** | 3692 | C | 562 236-3000 | 13164 |
| M & H Electric Fabricators Inc | 3694 | E | 562 926-9552 | 13177 |
| Philatron International **(PA)** | 3699 | D | 562 802-0452 | 13288 |
| Rosemead Electrical Supply | 3699 | E | 562 298-4190 | 13301 |
| Auto Motive Power Inc | 3714 | C | 800 894-7104 | 13460 |
| Los Angeles Sleeve Co Inc | 3714 | E | 562 945-7578 | 13531 |
| M E D Inc | 3714 | D | 562 921-0464 | 13533 |
| M P N Inc | 3714 | F | 562 921-0748 | 13534 |
| Maxon Industries Inc | 3714 | D | 562 464-0099 | 13536 |
| Mid-West Fabricating Co | 3714 | E | 562 698-9615 | 13539 |
| R A Phillips Industries Inc **(PA)** | 3714 | E | 562 781-2121 | 13562 |
| US Motor Works LLC **(PA)** | 3714 | E | 562 404-0488 | 13600 |
| Advanced Grund Systems Engrg L **(HQ)** | 3724 | E | 562 906-9300 | 13701 |
| All Power Manufacturing Co | 3728 | C | 562 802-2640 | 13771 |
| Goodrich Corporation | 3728 | D | 562 944-4441 | 13855 |
| KS Engineering Inc | 3728 | F | 562 483-7788 | 13888 |
| Lefiell Manufacturing Company | 3728 | C | 562 921-3411 | 13892 |
| Precision Tube Bending | 3728 | D | 562 921-6723 | 13930 |
| Spec Tool Company | 3728 | E | 323 723-9533 | 13960 |
| V&H Performance LLC | 3751 | D | 562 921-7461 | 14074 |
| Deca International Corp | 3812 | E | 714 367-5900 | 14177 |
| Votaw Precision Technologies | 3812 | C | 562 944-0661 | 14328 |
| Tellkamp Systems Inc **(PA)** | 3822 | E | 562 802-1621 | 14371 |
| Cosasco Inc | 3823 | D | 562 949-0123 | 14398 |
| Rohrback Cosasco Systems Inc **(DH)** | 3823 | E | 562 949-0123 | 14451 |
| I-Coat Company LLC | 3827 | E | 562 941-9989 | 14782 |
| US Armor Corporation | 3842 | E | 562 207-4240 | 15424 |
| Bravo Sports **(HQ)** | 3949 | D | 562 484-5100 | 15793 |
| Saint Nine America Inc | 3949 | E | 562 921-5300 | 15851 |
| Kingsolver Inc | 3991 | F | 562 945-7590 | 15931 |
| Orange Cnty Name Plate Co Inc | 3993 | D | 714 522-7693 | 16016 |
| Simply Display | 3993 | E | 888 767-0676 | 16044 |
| Tdi Signs | 3993 | E | 562 436-5188 | 16056 |
| Altro USA Inc | 3996 | D | 562 944-8292 | 16074 |
| Golden Supreme Inc | 3999 | E | 562 903-1063 | 16137 |
| Wilsonart LLC | 4225 | E | 562 921-7426 | 16293 |
| Diversified Logistic Svcs Inc | 4783 | E | 562 941-3600 | 16310 |
| Egge Machine Company Inc **(PA)** | 5013 | E | 562 945-3419 | 16382 |
| Ralco Holdings Inc **(DH)** | 5013 | C | 949 440-5094 | 16392 |
| Total Import Solutions Inc | 5013 | F | 562 691-6818 | 16404 |
| Galleher LLC **(PA)** | 5023 | C | 562 944-8885 | 16425 |
| Teac America Inc **(HQ)** | 5045 | F | 323 726-0303 | 16555 |
| Bergsen Inc | 5051 | E | 562 236-9787 | 16608 |
| Conquest Industries Inc | 5051 | E | 562 906-1111 | 16614 |
| Pacific Power Systems Integration Inc | 5063 | E | 562 281-0500 | 16669 |
| TA Industries Inc **(HQ)** | 5074 | E | 562 466-1000 | 16771 |
| Maxon Lift Corp **(PA)** | 5084 | C | 562 464-0099 | 16826 |
| Menke Marking Devices Inc | 5084 | E | 562 921-1380 | 16827 |
| Valtra Inc **(PA)** | 5084 | E | 562 949-8625 | 16853 |
| Pcbc Holdco Inc | 5085 | E | 562 944-9549 | 16888 |
| Revco Industries Inc **(PA)** | 5085 | E | 562 777-1588 | 16891 |
| Kaplan Indus Car Wash Sups Inc | 5087 | E | 562 921-5544 | 16909 |
| Georgia-Pacific LLC | 5113 | B | 562 861-6226 | 17000 |
| T & W Converters Inc | 5113 | E | 818 241-1707 | 17024 |
| Danne Montague King Co **(PA)** | 5122 | E | 562 944-0230 | 17035 |
| Steven Label Corporation **(PA)** | 5131 | C | 562 698-9971 | 17071 |
| Coated Fabrics Company **(HQ)** | 5162 | E | 562 298-1300 | 17226 |
| Plastics Family Holdings Inc | 5162 | E | 562 464-9929 | 17232 |
| Chus Packaging Supplies Inc | 5199 | E | 562 944-6411 | 17290 |
| Thrifty Oil Co **(PA)** | 6512 | F | 562 921-3581 | 17739 |
| Safesmart Access Inc | 7382 | E | 310 410-1525 | 19061 |
| Galaxy Brazing Co Inc | 7692 | E | 562 946-9039 | 19194 |
| E & L Electric | 7694 | F | 562 903-9272 | 19226 |
| Spearman Aerospace Inc | 8711 | E | 714 523-4751 | 19422 |

## SANTA MARIA, CA - Santa Barbara County

| | SIC | EMP | PHONE | ENTRY# |
|---|---|---|---|---|
| Plantel Nurseries Inc **(PA)** | 0181 | E | 805 349-8952 | 50 |
| Greka Integrated Inc | 1382 | C | 805 347-8700 | 187 |
| Santa Maria Enrgy Holdings LLC | 1382 | E | 805 938-3320 | 197 |
| Engel & Gray Inc | 1389 | E | 805 925-2771 | 227 |
| Pacific Petroleum California Inc | 1389 | B | 805 925-1947 | 264 |
| PC Mechanical Inc | 1389 | E | 805 925-2888 | 267 |
| Pictsweet Company | 2038 | B | 805 928-4414 | 1043 |
| ARC Vineyards LLC | 2084 | E | 805 937-3901 | 1477 |
| Central Coast Wine Warehouse **(PA)** | 2084 | F | 805 928-9210 | 1500 |
| Flood Ranch Company | 2084 | E | 805 937-3616 | 1570 |
| Foxen Vineyard Inc | 2084 | E | 805 937-4251 | 1576 |
| American Bottling Company | 2086 | D | 805 928-1001 | 1858 |
| Pepsi-Cola Metro Btlg Co Inc | 2086 | E | 805 739-2160 | 1912 |
| Reyes Coca-Cola Bottling LLC | 2086 | E | 805 925-2629 | 1941 |
| Reyes Coca-Cola Bottling LLC | 2086 | E | 805 614-3702 | 1944 |
| Tognazzini Beverage Service | 2086 | F | 805 928-1144 | 1968 |
| Curation Foods Inc **(HQ)** | 2099 | E | 800 454-1355 | 2178 |
| Amass Brands Inc | 2833 | D | 619 204-2560 | 5230 |
| North American Fire Hose Corp | 3052 | D | 805 922-7076 | 6426 |
| Alltec Integrated Mfg Inc | 3089 | E | 805 595-3500 | 6704 |
| Prince Lionheart Inc **(PA)** | 3089 | E | 805 922-2250 | 6983 |
| Princeton Case-West Inc | 3089 | E | 805 928-8840 | 6984 |
| Impo International LLC | 3144 | E | 805 922-7753 | 7116 |
| Mid-State Concrete Pdts Inc | 3272 | E | 805 928-2855 | 7356 |
| Okonite Company Inc | 3357 | C | 805 922-6682 | 7790 |
| Matthew Warren Inc | 3493 | E | 805 928-3851 | 9177 |
| Melfred Borzall Inc | 3541 | E | 805 614-4344 | 9560 |
| Fresh Venture Foods LLC | 3556 | E | 805 928-3374 | 9792 |
| Atlas Copco Mafi-Trench Co LLC **(DH)** | 3564 | C | 805 928-5757 | 9980 |
| Helical Products Company Inc | 3568 | C | 805 928-3851 | 10069 |
| Arrow Screw Products Inc | 3599 | E | 805 928-2269 | 10721 |
| Wasco Sales and Marketing Inc | 3643 | E | 805 739-2747 | 11477 |
| Gavial Engineering & Mfg Inc | 3672 | E | 805 614-0060 | 12120 |
| Gavial Holdings Inc **(PA)** | 3679 | F | 805 614-0060 | 12983 |
| Alan Johnson Prfmce Engrg Inc | 3711 | E | 805 922-1202 | 13335 |
| Safran Cabin Inc | 3728 | C | 805 922-3013 | 13945 |
| Safran Seats Santa Maria LLC | 3728 | A | 805 922-5995 | 13952 |
| Tyvak Nn-Satellite Systems Inc | 3761 | E | 805 264-4319 | 14094 |
| Northrop Grumman Systems Corp | 3812 | D | 805 315-5728 | 14245 |
| Coast Rock Products Inc | 5032 | E | 805 925-2505 | 16472 |
| Hardy Diagnostics **(PA)** | 5047 | B | 805 346-2766 | 16583 |
| Homer T Hayward Lumber Co | 5211 | E | 805 928-8557 | 17334 |
| Boot Barn Inc | 5699 | F | 805 614-9222 | 17510 |
| Osr Enterprises Inc | 7372 | E | 805 925-1831 | 18649 |
| J and D Stl Fbrication Repr LP | 7692 | F | 805 928-9674 | 19201 |
| Microwave Applications Group | 8711 | E | 805 928-5711 | 19405 |

## SANTA MONICA, CA - Los Angeles County

| | SIC | EMP | PHONE | ENTRY# |
|---|---|---|---|---|
| Dext Company of Maryland **(DH)** | 2048 | E | 310 458-1574 | 1124 |
| International Processing Corp **(DH)** | 2048 | E | 310 458-1574 | 1132 |
| Reconserve Inc **(HQ)** | 2048 | E | 310 458-1574 | 1145 |
| Bake R Us Inc | 2051 | F | 310 630-5873 | 1163 |
| Liquid Death Mountain Water | 2086 | E | 818 521-5500 | 1901 |
| Red Bull Media Hse N Amer Inc | 2086 | D | 310 393-4647 | 1928 |
| Figs Inc | 2326 | B | 424 300-8330 | 2593 |

Employee Codes: A=Over 500 employees, B=251-500
C=101-250, D=51-100, E=20-50, F=10-19, G=1-9

# SANTA MONICA, CA

| Company | SIC | EMP | PHONE | ENTRY# |
|---|---|---|---|---|
| Koral LLC | 2329 | E | 323 391-1060 | 2628 |
| Koral Industries LLC (PA) | 2339 | E | 323 585-5343 | 2783 |
| Zooey Apparel Inc | 2339 | E | 310 315-2880 | 2824 |
| Mammoth Media Inc | 2711 | D | 832 315-0833 | 4153 |
| Newlon Rouge LLC | 2711 | E | 310 458-7737 | 4168 |
| Total Beauty Media Inc | 2721 | F | 310 295-9593 | 4302 |
| Ubm Canon LLC (DH) | 2721 | E | 310 445-4200 | 4303 |
| Alg Inc | 2741 | D | 424 258-8026 | 4362 |
| C Publishing LLC | 2741 | E | 310 393-3800 | 4374 |
| Universal Mus Group Dist Corp (DH) | 2741 | E | 310 235-4700 | 4486 |
| Universal Music Publishing Inc | 2741 | E | 310 235-4700 | 4487 |
| Printing Palace Inc (PA) | 2752 | F | 310 451-5151 | 4734 |
| Archipelago Inc | 2844 | C | 213 743-9200 | 5944 |
| Provivi Inc | 2869 | D | 310 828-2307 | 6156 |
| Skell Inc | 2879 | F | 310 392-3288 | 6207 |
| Kas Engineering Inc (PA) | 3089 | E | 310 450-8925 | 6881 |
| Careismatic Group II Inc (HQ) | 3143 | F | 818 671-2100 | 7108 |
| Ridge Wallet LLC | 3172 | E | 818 636-2832 | 7151 |
| Vault Prep Inc | 3272 | E | 310 971-9091 | 7394 |
| Coast Flagstone Co | 3281 | D | 310 829-4010 | 7536 |
| Hamrock Inc | 3315 | C | 562 944-0255 | 7642 |
| Imperial Pipe Services LLC | 3317 | E | 951 682-3307 | 7663 |
| Solarreserve LLC (PA) | 3433 | F | 310 315-2200 | 8080 |
| Captive-Aire Systems Inc | 3444 | E | 310 876-8505 | 8403 |
| Eps Corporate Holdings Inc (DH) | 3498 | E | 310 204-7238 | 9258 |
| Ngd Systems Inc | 3572 | E | 949 870-9148 | 10258 |
| T3 Micro Inc | 3634 | E | 310 452-2888 | 11414 |
| Apogee Electronics Corporation | 3651 | E | 310 584-9394 | 11637 |
| Extreme Group Holdings LLC | 3652 | E | 310 899-3200 | 11732 |
| Ovation R&G LLC (PA) | 3663 | E | 310 430-7575 | 11911 |
| Phonesuit Inc | 3663 | E | 310 774-0282 | 11915 |
| Omega Leads Inc | 3679 | E | 310 394-6786 | 13053 |
| Pioneer Magnetics Inc | 3679 | C | 310 829-6751 | 13061 |
| Greenlane Infrastructure LLC | 3694 | E | 503 839-8116 | 13171 |
| Santa Monica Propeller Svc Inc | 3728 | F | 310 390-6233 | 13954 |
| Pranalytica Inc | 3841 | E | 310 458-3345 | 15229 |
| Straight Smile LLC (HQ) | 3843 | F | 424 389-4551 | 15485 |
| Carr Corporation (PA) | 3844 | E | 310 587-1113 | 15501 |
| Jakks Pacific Inc (PA) | 3944 | D | 424 268-9444 | 15756 |
| Bravo Highline LLC | 3949 | E | 562 484-5100 | 15791 |
| Casa De Hermandad (PA) | 3949 | E | 310 477-8272 | 15798 |
| Malbon Golf LLC | 3949 | E | 323 433-4028 | 15838 |
| Shapco Inc (PA) | 5051 | E | 310 264-1666 | 16532 |
| Genius Products Inc | 5099 | C | 310 453-1222 | 16977 |
| Johnny Was LLC | 5137 | D | 310 656-0600 | 17092 |
| Hokey Pokey LLC | 5143 | E | 213 361-2503 | 17131 |
| Legendary Foods LLC | 5441 | E | 888 698-1708 | 17403 |
| Clearlake Capital Group LP (PA) | 6722 | B | 310 400-8800 | 17749 |
| Kargo Global Inc | 7313 | C | 212 979-9000 | 17789 |
| Snap Inc (PA) | 7371 | A | 310 399-3339 | 17980 |
| Tomitribe Corporation | 7371 | E | 310 526-7676 | 17986 |
| Activision Blizzard Inc (HQ) | 7372 | B | 310 255-2000 | 18014 |
| Clearlake Capital Partners | 7372 | E | 310 400-8800 | 18173 |
| Cornerstone Ondemand Inc (HQ) | 7372 | C | 310 752-0200 | 18205 |
| Futur LLC | 7372 | E | 310 314-1618 | 18337 |
| Goodrx Inc (HQ) | 7372 | F | 855 268-2822 | 18358 |
| Gumgum Inc (PA) | 7372 | E | 310 260-9666 | 18373 |
| Gumgum Sports Inc | 7372 | E | 310 400-0396 | 18374 |
| Kingcom(us) LLC (DH) | 7372 | E | 424 744-5697 | 18470 |
| Patientpop Inc | 7372 | D | 844 487-8399 | 18660 |
| Prata Inc | 7372 | E | 512 823-1002 | 18692 |
| Railstech Inc | 7372 | E | 267 315-2998 | 18722 |
| Salesforcecom Inc | 7372 | D | 310 752-7000 | 18755 |
| SE Software Inc | 7372 | F | 888 504-9876 | 18770 |
| Tigerconnect Inc (PA) | 7379 | D | 310 401-1820 | 19047 |
| Advanstar Communications Inc | 7389 | E | 310 857-7500 | 19069 |
| Advanstar Communications Inc (DH) | 7389 | C | 310 857-7500 | 19070 |
| Universal Music Group Inc | 7389 | D | 310 865-0770 | 19140 |
| Kite Pharma (HQ) | 8731 | D | 310 824-9999 | 19459 |

## SANTA PAULA, CA - Ventura County

| Company | SIC | EMP | PHONE | ENTRY# |
|---|---|---|---|---|
| Carbon California Company LLC | 1311 | E | 805 933-1901 | 133 |
| Oil Well Service Company | 1389 | D | 805 525-2103 | 260 |
| Weatherford International LLC | 1389 | F | 805 933-0242 | 291 |
| Saticoy Foods Corporation | 2033 | E | 805 647-5266 | 925 |
| Calavo Growers Inc (PA) | 2099 | D | 805 525-1245 | 2153 |
| Turtle Storage Ltd | 2542 | E | 805 933-3688 | 3712 |
| Herald Printing Ltd | 2752 | E | 805 647-1870 | 4630 |
| Calpipe Industries LLC | 3312 | E | 562 803-4388 | 7610 |
| Automotive Racing Products Inc | 3429 | E | 805 525-1497 | 7978 |
| Coastal Cnting Indus Scale Inc | 3545 | E | 805 487-0403 | 9667 |
| Abrisa Industrial Glass Inc (HQ) | 3827 | E | 805 525-4902 | 14759 |
| Abrisa Technologies | 3827 | D | 805 525-4902 | 14760 |
| Weber Orthopedic LP (PA) | 3842 | D | 800 221-5465 | 15429 |
| Thompco Inc | 5082 | E | 805 933-8048 | 16794 |

## SANTA ROSA, CA - Sonoma County

| Company | SIC | EMP | PHONE | ENTRY# |
|---|---|---|---|---|
| Bo Dean Co Inc (DH) | 1411 | E | 707 576-8205 | 293 |
| Steven N Ledson | 1521 | D | 707 537-3810 | 349 |
| G Hartley Inc | 1542 | E | 707 523-3513 | 368 |
| Ahlborn Fence & Steel Inc (PA) | 1799 | E | 707 573-0742 | 553 |
| Veal Connection Corporation | 2011 | E | 707 992-0932 | 622 |
| G&G Specialty Foods Inc | 2022 | C |  | 715 |
| Wildbrine LLC (PA) | 2033 | E | 707 657-7607 | 941 |
| Conetech Custom Services LLC | 2084 | E | 707 823-2404 | 1515 |
| Grape Links Inc | 2084 | E | 707 524-8000 | 1600 |
| Jackson Family Farms LLC | 2084 | F | 707 836-2047 | 1626 |
| Jackson Family Wines Inc | 2084 | E | 707 836-2035 | 1627 |
| Jackson Family Wines Inc (PA) | 2084 | E | 707 544-4000 | 1628 |
| Kendall-Jackson Wine Estates (HQ) | 2084 | B | 707 544-4000 | 1646 |
| Laguna Oaks Vnyards Winery Inc | 2084 | E | 707 568-2455 | 1659 |
| Russian River Winery Inc | 2084 | E | 707 824-2005 | 1735 |
| Sonoma County Winegrowers | 2084 | E | 707 522-5860 | 1754 |
| Vintage Wine Estates Inc CA (HQ) | 2084 | E | 877 289-9463 | 1819 |
| Williams & Selyem LLC | 2084 | E | 707 536-9685 | 1827 |
| Dr Pepper/Seven Up Inc | 2086 | E | 707 545-7797 | 1885 |
| MS Intertrade Inc | 2092 | E | 707 837-8057 | 2057 |
| Alexander Valley Gourmet LLC | 2099 | E | 707 473-0116 | 2124 |
| Cfarms Inc (PA) | 2099 | E | 916 375-3000 | 2162 |
| Tonnellerie Radoux Usa Inc | 2449 | E | 707 284-2888 | 3377 |
| Johnson Controls Inc | 2531 | E | 707 546-3042 | 3630 |
| Johns Formica Inc | 2542 | E | 707 544-8585 | 3693 |
| Santa Rosa Press Democrat Inc (HQ) | 2711 | B | 707 546-2020 | 4192 |
| Sonoma Media Investments LLC (PA) | 2711 | E | 707 526-8563 | 4198 |
| Make Community LLC | 2721 | E | 707 200-3714 | 4276 |
| Graphic Enterprises Inc | 2752 | E | 707 528-2644 | 4623 |
| National Print + Promo | 2752 | E | 707 576-6375 | 4704 |
| Neilmed Pharmaceuticals Inc (PA) | 2834 | E | 707 525-3784 | 5566 |
| Randal Optimal Nutrients LLC | 2834 | E | 707 528-1800 | 5624 |
| Trans-India Products Inc | 2844 | E | 707 544-0298 | 6046 |
| Hawthorne Hydroponics LLC | 2873 | E | 800 221-1760 | 6174 |
| Gusmer Enterprises Inc | 2899 | E | 866 213-1131 | 6290 |
| Tumelo Inc | 2899 | E | 707 523-4411 | 6327 |
| Molding Solutions Inc | 3089 | D | 707 575-1218 | 6921 |
| Orbis Wheels Inc | 3089 | E | 415 548-4160 | 6946 |
| Triformix Inc | 3089 | F | 707 545-7645 | 7058 |
| Occidental Manufacturing Inc | 3199 | C | 707 824-2560 | 7158 |
| Oxbase Inc | 3199 | C | 707 824-2560 | 7160 |
| Western Fiberglass Inc (PA) | 3229 | E | 707 523-2050 | 7208 |
| Mac Thin Films Inc | 3231 | E | 707 791-1656 | 7233 |
| Rbd Online Inc | 3269 | E | 800 681-1757 | 7289 |
| Kri Star Enterprises Inc | 3272 | E | 800 579-8819 | 7351 |
| Supercloset | 3423 | E | 831 588-7829 | 7966 |
| Ahlborn Structural Steel Inc | 3441 | E | 707 573-0742 | 8092 |
| Iron Dog Fabrication Inc | 3441 | F | 707 579-7831 | 8154 |
| Sonoma Stainless Inc | 3443 | E | 707 546-3945 | 8336 |
| Optical Coating Laboratory LLC (HQ) | 3479 | B | 707 545-6440 | 9097 |
| Pacific Shoring Products LLC (PA) | 3479 | F | 707 575-9014 | 9100 |
| Pellenc America Inc (DH) | 3523 | E | 707 568-7286 | 9375 |
| Wright Engineered Plastics LLC | 3544 | E | 707 575-1218 | 9658 |
| Blentech Corporation | 3556 | D | 707 523-5949 | 9780 |
| P & L Specialties | 3559 | F | 707 573-3141 | 9886 |
| Filtration Group LLC | 3564 | C | 707 525-8633 | 9986 |
| Grinnell LLC | 3569 | E | 707 578-3212 | 10091 |
| Quality Machine Engrg Inc | 3599 | E | 707 528-1900 | 11061 |
| ITT LLC | 3625 | C | 707 523-2300 | 11328 |
| Protonex LLC | 3674 | E | 707 566-2260 | 12642 |
| James L Hall Co Incorporated | 3677 | D | 707 544-2436 | 12843 |
| Sonoma Photonics Inc | 3677 | E | 707 568-1202 | 12859 |
| Calculex | 3678 | E | 707 578-2307 | 12868 |
| Winchester SRC Cables Corp | 3679 | E | 707 573-1900 | 13124 |
| Winchster Interconnect Rf Corp | 3679 | A | 707 573-1900 | 13125 |
| Viavi Solutions Inc | 3699 | E | 707 545-6440 | 13326 |
| Flowmaster Inc | 3714 | D | 707 544-4761 | 13500 |
| AEG Industries Inc | 3728 | F | 707 575-0697 | 13741 |
| Zodiac Interconnect US | 3728 | F | 707 535-2700 | 13996 |
| Santa Rosa Stain | 3795 | E | 707 544-7777 | 14127 |
| Endrun Technologies LLC | 3821 | E | 707 573-8633 | 14335 |
| Paragon Controls Incorporated | 3822 | F | 707 579-1424 | 14366 |
| Air Monitor Corporation (PA) | 3823 | D | 707 544-2706 | 14384 |
| Keysight Technologies Inc (PA) | 3823 | A | 800 829-4444 | 14427 |
| Senariotek LLC | 3825 | E | 707 237-6822 | 14585 |
| Flex Products Inc | 3827 | C | 707 525-9200 | 14775 |
| Medtronic Inc | 3841 | D | 707 541-3144 | 15175 |
| Medtronic Cardiovascular | 3841 | A | 707 545-1156 | 15177 |
| Osseon LLC | 3841 | F | 707 636-5940 | 15218 |

# GEOGRAPHIC SECTION

## SELMA, CA

| | SIC | EMP | PHONE | ENTRY# |
|---|---|---|---|---|
| Osseon Therapeutics Inc. | 3841 | E | 707 636-5940 | 15219 |
| Medtronic Inc. | 3842 | C | 707 541-3281 | 15379 |
| Medtronic Vascular Inc. | 3842 | E | 707 522-2250 | 15380 |
| L-3 Cmmnications Sonoma Eo Inc. | 3861 | C | 707 568-3000 | 15647 |
| Aluma USA Inc. | 3911 | E | 707 545-9344 | 15681 |
| Emg Inc. | 3931 | D | 707 525-9941 | 15715 |
| Scott Ag LLC. | 3993 | E | 707 545-4519 | 16033 |
| Sota Extracts Inc. | 3999 | F | 612 889-4049 | 16236 |
| Mendocino Forest Pdts Co LLC (PA) | 5031 | E | 707 620-2961 | 16451 |
| Pacific Coast Supply LLC | 5031 | E | 707 546-7317 | 16455 |
| CPI International | 5049 | D | 707 521-6327 | 16599 |
| City Electric Supply | 5063 | E | 707 523-4600 | 16649 |
| Pni Sensor Corporation | 5088 | E | 707 566-2260 | 16922 |
| La Tortilla Factory Inc. | 5149 | B | 707 586-4000 | 17193 |
| Pepsi-Cola Metro Btlg Co Inc | 5149 | D | 707 535-4560 | 17204 |
| Redwood Coast Petroleum Inc. | 5172 | D | 707 546-0766 | 17255 |
| Burgess Lumber (PA) | 5211 | F | 707 542-5091 | 17325 |
| Northern Cal Bldg Mtls Inc (PA) | 5211 | E | 707 546-9422 | 17337 |
| Santa Rosa Seafood Retail Inc. | 5421 | E | 707 579-2085 | 17397 |
| Apporto Corporation | 7372 | E | 877 751-4081 | 18059 |
| Occidental Systems Inc. | 7372 | F | 800 902-4393 | 18610 |
| Deposition Sciences Inc. | 8731 | D | 707 573-6700 | 19450 |
| Klh Consulting Incorporated | 8748 | D | 707 575-9986 | 19564 |

### SANTA ROSA VALLEY, CA - Ventura County

| | SIC | EMP | PHONE | ENTRY# |
|---|---|---|---|---|
| Hyper-Tech LLC | 7389 | F | 805 988-2000 | 19096 |

### SANTA YNEZ, CA - Santa Barbara County

| | SIC | EMP | PHONE | ENTRY# |
|---|---|---|---|---|
| Gainey Vineyard | 2084 | E | 805 688-0558 | 1581 |
| Valley Oaks Industries | 2521 | F | 805 688-2754 | 3589 |

### SANTA YSABEL, CA - San Diego County

| | SIC | EMP | PHONE | ENTRY# |
|---|---|---|---|---|
| Dudleys Bakery Inc. | 5461 | E | 760 765-0488 | 17409 |

### SANTEE, CA - San Diego County

| | SIC | EMP | PHONE | ENTRY# |
|---|---|---|---|---|
| Lustros Inc. | 1021 | E | 619 449-4800 | 102 |
| Specilty Mtals Fabrication Inc. | 2295 | F | 619 937-6100 | 2531 |
| Lauren Anthony & Co Inc | 2511 | E | 619 590-1141 | 3446 |
| CCM Enterprises (PA) | 2541 | D | 619 562-2605 | 3650 |
| European Wholesale Counter | 2541 | C | 619 562-0565 | 3655 |
| Lamb Fuels Inc. | 2869 | E | 619 777-9135 | 6151 |
| South West Lubricants Inc. | 2992 | D | 619 449-5000 | 6400 |
| Delstar Holding Corp. | 3081 | E | 619 258-1503 | 6556 |
| C&M Manufacturing Company Inc (PA) | 3082 | E | 619 449-7200 | 6578 |
| Argee Mfg Co San Diego Inc. | 3089 | E | 619 449-5050 | 6723 |
| R V Best Inc. | 3089 | E | 619 448-7300 | 6990 |
| Integrity Bottles LLC | 3229 | F | 847 922-0920 | 7197 |
| RCP Block & Brick Inc. | 3271 | E | 619 448-2240 | 7299 |
| Vision Systems Inc. | 3354 | D | 619 258-7300 | 7754 |
| TBs Irrigation Products Inc. | 3432 | E | 619 579-0520 | 8057 |
| Buxcon Sheetmetal Inc. | 3444 | F | 619 937-0001 | 8396 |
| Access Professional Inc. | 3446 | F | 858 571-4444 | 8614 |
| Kevin Whaley | 3496 | E | 619 596-4000 | 9221 |
| Olson Irrigation Systems | 3523 | E | 619 562-3100 | 9373 |
| Terra Nova Technologies Inc. | 3535 | D | 619 596-7400 | 9497 |
| Ds Fibertech Corp | 3567 | E | 619 562-7001 | 10050 |
| Alts Tool & Machine Inc. | 3599 | D | 619 562-6653 | 10706 |
| Computer Intgrted McHining Inc. | 3599 | E | 619 596-9246 | 10786 |
| Mathy Machine Inc. | 3599 | E | 619 448-0404 | 10962 |
| Quality Controlled Mfg Inc. | 3599 | D | 619 443-3997 | 11059 |
| T I B Inc. | 3599 | E | 619 562-3071 | 11134 |
| Current Ways Inc. | 3629 | F | 619 596-3984 | 11368 |
| Stratedge Corporation | 3674 | E | 866 424-4962 | 12738 |
| Lhv Power Corporation (PA) | 3679 | E | 619 258-7700 | 13023 |
| Compucraft Industries Inc. | 3728 | E | 619 448-0787 | 13814 |
| Air & Gas Tech Inc. | 3732 | E | 619 955-5980 | 14027 |
| Decatur Electronics Inc. | 3812 | F | 619 596-1925 | 14179 |
| Interocean Industries Inc. | 3812 | E | 858 292-0808 | 14197 |
| Interocean Systems LLC. | 3812 | F | 858 565-8400 | 14198 |
| Acme Safety & Supply Corp (PA) | 5099 | F | 619 299-5100 | 16972 |
| Valley Box Co Inc. | 5113 | E | 619 449-2882 | 17025 |
| Business Printing Company Inc. | 7389 | F | 858 453-2111 | 19078 |

### SARATOGA, CA - Santa Clara County

| | SIC | EMP | PHONE | ENTRY# |
|---|---|---|---|---|
| Chateau Masson LLC. | 2084 | E | 408 741-7002 | 1505 |
| Savannah Chanelle Vineyards | 2084 | F | 301 758-2338 | 1741 |
| Scry Analytics Inc. | 7372 | B | 408 740-8017 | 18769 |
| Vintellus Inc. | 7372 | F | 510 972-4710 | 18921 |

### SAUGUS, CA - Los Angeles County

| | SIC | EMP | PHONE | ENTRY# |
|---|---|---|---|---|
| Hasa Inc (PA) | 2812 | D | 661 259-5848 | 5031 |

### SAUSALITO, CA - Marin County

| | SIC | EMP | PHONE | ENTRY# |
|---|---|---|---|---|
| Mpl Brands Inc (PA) | 2084 | E | 888 513-3022 | 1682 |
| Porthos Ventures Inc. | 2084 | F | 415 339-2790 | 1711 |
| Tony Marterie & Associates Inc. | 2335 | F | 415 331-7150 | 2718 |
| C P Shades Inc (PA) | 2339 | F | 415 331-4581 | 2741 |
| Lifefactory Inc. | 3221 | E | 415 729-9820 | 7183 |
| Heath Ceramics Ltd (PA) | 3253 | D | 415 332-3732 | 7268 |
| Boyd Lighting Fixture Company (PA) | 3646 | E | 415 778-4300 | 11522 |
| Humanconcepts LLC | 7372 | E | 650 581-2500 | 18394 |
| Waggl Inc (PA) | 7372 | D | 415 399-9949 | 18927 |

### SCOTIA, CA - Humboldt County

| | SIC | EMP | PHONE | ENTRY# |
|---|---|---|---|---|
| Eel River Brewing Co Inc. | 5813 | F | 707 764-1772 | 17617 |

### SCOTTS VALLEY, CA - Santa Cruz County

| | SIC | EMP | PHONE | ENTRY# |
|---|---|---|---|---|
| Vitalbulk Inc. | 2023 | F | 855 885-2855 | 786 |
| Sunopta Globl Orgnic Ingrdnts (HQ) | 2035 | E | 831 685-6506 | 994 |
| Pacific Coast Ingredients (PA) | 2087 | F | 831 316-7137 | 2018 |
| Pacific Coast Ingredients | 2087 | F | 831 316-7137 | 2019 |
| Threshold Enterprises Ltd (PA) | 2833 | C | 831 438-6851 | 5274 |
| Threshold Enterprises Ltd. | 2833 | E | 831 461-6413 | 5275 |
| Threshold Enterprises Ltd. | 2833 | E | 831 461-6343 | 5276 |
| Warmboard Inc. | 3567 | E | 831 685-9276 | 10063 |
| J A-Co Machine Works LLC. | 3599 | E | 877 429-8175 | 10897 |
| Larkin Precision Machining Inc. | 3599 | E | 831 438-2700 | 10940 |
| Tapemation Machining Inc (PA) | 3599 | E | 831 438-3069 | 11137 |
| AV Now Inc. | 3651 | E | 831 425-2500 | 11641 |
| Innerstep BSE | 3672 | D | 831 461-5600 | 12136 |
| Expert Semiconductor Tech Inc. | 3674 | E | 831 439-9300 | 12429 |
| Vertical Circuits Inc. | 3674 | E | 831 438-3887 | 12786 |
| Scotts Valley Magnetics Inc. | 3677 | E | 831 438-3600 | 12857 |
| Oxford Instrs X-Ray Tech Inc. | 3679 | E | 831 439-9729 | 13059 |
| Plantronics Inc (HQ) | 3679 | A | 831 420-3002 | 13063 |
| Fox Factory Inc. | 3714 | E | 831 274-6545 | 13503 |
| Digital Dynamics Inc. | 3823 | E | 831 438-4444 | 14402 |
| Satellite Telework Centers Inc. | 3825 | F | 831 222-2100 | 14584 |
| Vista Outdoor Inc. | 3949 | E | 831 461-7500 | 15874 |
| Zero Motorcycles Inc. | 5571 | C | 831 438-3500 | 17486 |
| Education Training & RES Assoc (PA) | 8299 | D | 831 438-4060 | 19350 |

### SEAL BEACH, CA - Orange County

| | SIC | EMP | PHONE | ENTRY# |
|---|---|---|---|---|
| Hellman Properties LLC | 1311 | F | 562 431-6022 | 135 |
| Samedan Oil Corporation | 1382 | B | 661 319-5038 | 196 |
| Dendreon Pharmaceuticals LLC (HQ) | 2834 | E | 562 252-7500 | 5424 |
| Modular Wind Energy Inc. | 3511 | D | 562 304-6782 | 9313 |
| Cosmodyne LLC. | 3559 | E | 562 795-5990 | 9842 |
| Magtek (PA) | 3577 | C | 562 546-6400 | 10406 |
| Amonix Inc. | 3674 | C | 562 344-4750 | 12303 |
| Irish Interiors Holdings Inc. | 3728 | E | 949 559-0930 | 13877 |
| Diversfied Tchncal Systems Inc (HQ) | 3825 | E | 562 493-0158 | 14512 |
| Original Parts Group Inc (PA) | 5531 | D | 562 594-1000 | 17455 |

### SEASIDE, CA - Monterey County

| | SIC | EMP | PHONE | ENTRY# |
|---|---|---|---|---|
| Granite Rock Co. | 3273 | D | 831 392-3700 | 7449 |
| Inter-City Manufacturing Inc. | 3599 | E | 831 899-3636 | 10888 |

### SEBASTOPOL, CA - Sonoma County

| | SIC | EMP | PHONE | ENTRY# |
|---|---|---|---|---|
| Weeks Drilling and Pump Co (PA) | 1711 | E | 707 823-3184 | 440 |
| Manzana Products Co Inc. | 2033 | E | 707 823-5313 | 904 |
| McEvoy of Marin LLC. | 2079 | E | 707 467-1999 | 1400 |
| Goldridgepinotcom LLC. | 2084 | D | 707 823-4464 | 1598 |
| Iron Horse Vineyards | 2084 | E | 707 887-1909 | 1620 |
| Joseph Phelps Vineyards LLC. | 2084 | E | 707 967-3717 | 1638 |
| KB Wines LLC. | 2084 | F | 707 823-7430 | 1645 |
| Kosta Browne Wines LLC. | 2084 | E | 707 823-7430 | 1649 |
| Meredith Vineyard Estate Inc. | 2084 | F | 707 823-7466 | 1678 |
| Small Vines Viticulture Inc. | 2084 | F | 707 823-0886 | 1752 |
| Taft Street Inc. | 2084 | E | 707 823-2049 | 1774 |
| Taylor Maid Farms LLC. | 2095 | E | 707 824-9110 | 2082 |
| Traditional Medicinals Inc (PA) | 2099 | C | 707 823-8911 | 2377 |
| Southwest Journal Inc. | 2711 | F | 612 825-9205 | 4199 |
| OReilly Media Inc (PA) | 2741 | C | 707 827-7000 | 4441 |
| General Hydroponics Inc. | 2875 | D | 707 824-9376 | 6187 |
| Solmetric Corporation | 3829 | E | 707 823-4600 | 14923 |
| Robert Jones | 5531 | F | 707 829-9864 | 17461 |
| Tbc Shared Services LLC. | 5531 | A | 707 829-9864 | 17466 |
| Safari Books Online LLC (PA) | 8231 | D | 707 827-7000 | 19347 |

### SELMA, CA - Fresno County

| | SIC | EMP | PHONE | ENTRY# |
|---|---|---|---|---|
| Harris Ranch Beef Company | 2011 | A | 559 896-3081 | 600 |
| Lion Raisins Inc (PA) | 2034 | C | 559 834-6677 | 955 |
| Partsflex Inc. | 2396 | E | 408 677-7121 | 3015 |
| Selma Pallet Inc. | 2448 | D | 559 896-7171 | 3360 |

Employee Codes: A=Over 500 employees, B=251-500
C=101-250, D=51-100, E=20-50, F=10-19, G=1-9

# SELMA, CA

|  | SIC | EMP | PHONE | ENTRY# |
|---|---|---|---|---|
| Wood-N-Wood Products Cal Inc | 2449 | F | 559 896-3636 | 3380 |
| Omex Agrifluids Inc | 2873 | F | 559 661-6138 | 6180 |
| Fresno Valves & Castings Inc **(PA)** | 4971 | C | 559 834-2511 | 16369 |
| P&P International Inc | 5113 | E | 559 891-9888 | 17018 |

## SHAFTER, CA - Kern County

|  | SIC | EMP | PHONE | ENTRY# |
|---|---|---|---|---|
| Garlic Company **(PA)** | 0139 | D | 661 393-4212 | 2 |
| Scientific Drilling Intl Inc | 1381 | E | 661 831-0636 | 166 |
| M-I LLC | 1389 | E | 661 321-5400 | 249 |
| Oil Well Service Company | 1389 | D | 661 746-4809 | 258 |
| Tryad Service Corporation | 1389 | E | 661 391-1524 | 284 |
| Scotts Company LLC | 2873 | E | 661 387-9555 | 6182 |
| Elk Corporation of Texas | 3272 | C | 661 391-3900 | 7329 |
| McM Fabricators Inc | 3441 | C | 661 589-2774 | 8179 |
| Nikkel Iron Works Corporation | 3523 | F | 661 746-4904 | 9372 |
| Frank Russell Inc | 3599 | E | 661 324-5575 | 10842 |
| Central California Power | 7538 | E | 661 589-2870 | 19160 |
| Ponder Environmental Svcs Inc | 8744 | E | 661 589-7771 | 19552 |

## SHANDON, CA - San Luis Obispo County

|  | SIC | EMP | PHONE | ENTRY# |
|---|---|---|---|---|
| Pacific Tank & Cnstr Inc | 3443 | E | 805 237-2929 | 8326 |

## SHASTA LAKE, CA - Shasta County

|  | SIC | EMP | PHONE | ENTRY# |
|---|---|---|---|---|
| Trenchless Pipe Company Inc | 3084 | E | 530 275-9400 | 6603 |
| Knauf Insulation Inc | 3296 | A | 530 275-9665 | 7579 |

## SHERMAN OAKS, CA - Los Angeles County

|  | SIC | EMP | PHONE | ENTRY# |
|---|---|---|---|---|
| Forever Rich International LLC | 2023 | E | 310 867-4723 | 758 |
| Xcvi LLC **(PA)** | 2211 | D | 213 749-2661 | 2432 |
| Med Couture Inc | 2326 | E | 214 231-2500 | 2598 |
| Strategic Distribution L P | 2326 | C |  | 2603 |
| E Z Buy & E Z Sell Recycl Corp **(DH)** | 2711 | C | 310 886-7808 | 4106 |
| 80lv LLC | 2731 | E | 818 435-6613 | 4308 |
| Dt123 **(PA)** | 2791 | E | 213 488-1230 | 5018 |
| Vytalogy Wellness LLC | 2833 | C | 818 867-4440 | 5282 |
| Natrol LLC **(PA)** | 2834 | C | 800 262-8765 | 5564 |
| Careismatic Brands LLC **(DH)** | 3143 | E | 818 671-2128 | 7107 |
| Careismatic Group Inc **(PA)** | 3143 | F | 818 671-2100 | 7109 |
| Envion LLC | 3564 | D | 818 217-2500 | 9984 |
| American Med O & P Clinic Inc | 3842 | E | 818 281-5747 | 15320 |
| Grabit Interactive Inc | 7313 | E | 844 472-2488 | 17788 |
| Rogue Games Inc | 7371 | E | 650 483-8008 | 17974 |
| Nile Ai Inc | 7372 | E | 818 689-9107 | 18592 |
| Papaya | 7372 | E | 310 740-6774 | 18656 |

## SHINGLE SPRINGS, CA - El Dorado County

|  | SIC | EMP | PHONE | ENTRY# |
|---|---|---|---|---|
| M & W Engineering Inc | 3599 | E | 530 676-7185 | 10950 |

## SIERRA MADRE, CA - Los Angeles County

|  | SIC | EMP | PHONE | ENTRY# |
|---|---|---|---|---|
| Group H Engineering | 1389 | E | 818 999-0999 | 233 |

## SIGNAL HILL, CA - Los Angeles County

|  | SIC | EMP | PHONE | ENTRY# |
|---|---|---|---|---|
| Signal Hill Petroleum Inc | 1382 | E | 562 595-6440 | 200 |
| Black Gold Pump & Supply Inc | 1389 | F | 323 298-0077 | 208 |
| Oil Well Service Company **(PA)** | 1389 | C | 562 612-0600 | 259 |
| Tiger Cased Hole Services Inc | 1389 | E | 562 426-4044 | 279 |
| Rossmoor Pastries MGT Inc | 2051 | D | 562 498-2253 | 1241 |
| Jnr Confection Specialty Corp | 2064 | F |  | 1315 |
| Pacific Fibre & Rope Co Inc | 2298 | F | 310 834-4567 | 2537 |
| Ld Products Inc | 2621 | C | 888 321-2552 | 3785 |
| Clariant Corporation | 2869 | F | 562 322-6647 | 6141 |
| R D Mathis Company | 3313 | E | 562 426-7049 | 7636 |
| P T Industries Inc | 3444 | F | 562 961-3431 | 8524 |
| Southwest Products Corporation | 3519 | F | 360 887-7400 | 9330 |
| Dawson Enterprises **(PA)** | 3533 | E | 562 424-8564 | 9460 |
| Rode Microphones LLC **(DH)** | 3651 | C | 310 328-7456 | 11693 |
| Transcom Telecommunication Inc | 3663 | E | 562 424-9616 | 11967 |
| Harper & Two Inc **(PA)** | 3679 | E | 562 424-3030 | 12993 |
| Reldom Corporation | 3699 | E | 562 498-3346 | 13296 |
| United States Logistics Group | 3715 | E | 562 989-9555 | 13621 |
| Asphalt Fabric and Engrg Inc | 3949 | D | 562 997-4129 | 15781 |
| Relax Medical Systems Inc | 3999 | E | 800 405-7677 | 16216 |
| Ship & Shore Environmental Inc | 5084 | E | 562 997-0233 | 16842 |
| Adaptive Tech Group Inc | 5961 | E | 562 424-1100 | 17658 |
| Porter Boiler Service Inc | 7699 | E | 562 426-2528 | 19276 |

## SIMI VALLEY, CA - Ventura County

|  | SIC | EMP | PHONE | ENTRY# |
|---|---|---|---|---|
| PW Gillibrand Co Inc **(PA)** | 1446 | E | 805 526-2195 | 331 |
| Millworks By Design Inc | 2431 | D | 818 597-1326 | 3160 |
| Clarios LLC | 2531 | E | 805 522-5555 | 3617 |
| Pacer Print | 2752 | E | 888 305-3144 | 4714 |
| Lca Promotions Inc | 2759 | E | 818 773-9170 | 4912 |
| Pharmaceutic Litho Label Inc | 2834 | D | 805 285-5162 | 5600 |
| Microblend Inc | 2851 | E | 330 998-4602 | 6095 |
| ACC Ca Inc **(HQ)** | 2951 | F | 805 522-1646 | 6359 |
| Poly-Tainer Inc **(PA)** | 3085 | C | 805 526-3424 | 6614 |
| Milgard Manufacturing LLC | 3231 | C | 805 581-6325 | 7234 |
| Newman and Sons Inc **(PA)** | 3272 | E | 805 522-1646 | 7360 |
| Pre-Con Products | 3272 | D | 805 527-0841 | 7372 |
| Vibra Finish Co **(PA)** | 3291 | E | 805 578-0033 | 7559 |
| Cal State Site Services | 3315 | E | 800 499-5757 | 7638 |
| Fiberoptic Systems Inc | 3357 | E | 805 579-6600 | 7785 |
| Delt Industries Inc | 3369 | F | 805 579-0213 | 7862 |
| Advanced Metal Mfg Inc | 3444 | E | 805 322-4161 | 8362 |
| Computer Metal Products Corp | 3444 | D | 805 520-6966 | 8414 |
| Scott A Humphreys Inc **(PA)** | 3444 | E | 805 581-2971 | 8567 |
| Sheet Metal Engineering | 3444 | E | 805 306-0390 | 8570 |
| Specialty Fabrications Inc | 3444 | E | 805 579-9730 | 8579 |
| Mabel Baas Inc | 3479 | E | 805 520-8075 | 9089 |
| Chatsworth Products Inc **(PA)** | 3499 | E | 818 735-6100 | 9279 |
| B&R Mold Inc | 3544 | F | 805 526-8665 | 9604 |
| Scientific Cutting Tools Inc | 3545 | E | 805 584-9495 | 9697 |
| Rexnord Industries LLC | 3556 | E | 805 583-5514 | 9814 |
| Xmultiple Technologies **(PA)** | 3571 | E | 805 579-1100 | 10218 |
| Qualitylogic Inc | 3577 | C | 208 424-1905 | 10425 |
| Ricoh Prtg Systems Amer Inc **(HQ)** | 3577 | B | 805 578-4000 | 10430 |
| Rugged Info Tech Eqp Corp | 3577 | E | 805 577-9710 | 10431 |
| Infinity Precision Inc | 3599 | E | 818 727-0504 | 10884 |
| Savage Machining Inc | 3599 | E | 805 584-8047 | 11100 |
| Vanderhorst Brothers Industries Inc | 3599 | D | 805 583-3333 | 11170 |
| Vans Manufacturing Inc | 3599 | F | 805 522-6267 | 11172 |
| Embedded Systems Inc | 3625 | E | 805 624-6030 | 11322 |
| Aveox Inc | 3629 | E | 805 915-0200 | 11361 |
| Dpa Labs Inc | 3674 | E | 805 581-9200 | 12406 |
| Piezo-Metrics Inc **(PA)** | 3674 | E | 805 522-4676 | 12632 |
| Ventura Technology Group | 3674 | F | 805 581-0800 | 12784 |
| Frontier Electronics Corp | 3677 | E | 805 522-9998 | 12840 |
| Puroflux Corporation | 3677 | F | 805 579-0216 | 12853 |
| Timco/Cal Rf Inc | 3678 | E | 805 582-1777 | 12902 |
| Jaxx Manufacturing Inc | 3679 | E | 805 526-4979 | 13013 |
| Meggitt Safety Systems Inc **(DH)** | 3699 | C | 805 584-4100 | 13271 |
| Enderle Fuel Injection | 3714 | E | 805 526-3838 | 13494 |
| Milodon Incorporated | 3714 | E | 805 577-5950 | 13540 |
| Special Devices Incorporated | 3714 | A | 805 387-1000 | 13577 |
| Aerovironment Inc | 3721 | E | 805 520-8350 | 13630 |
| Datron Advanced Tech Inc | 3728 | C | 805 579-2966 | 13821 |
| Meggitt Safety Systems Inc | 3728 | E | 805 584-4100 | 13908 |
| Meggitt-Usa Inc **(DH)** | 3728 | B | 805 526-5700 | 13909 |
| Rsa Engineered Products LLC | 3728 | D | 805 584-4150 | 13940 |
| Whittaker Corporation | 3728 | E | 805 526-5700 | 13992 |
| Catalina Yachts Inc **(PA)** | 3732 | E | 818 884-7700 | 14030 |
| Currie Acquisitions LLC | 3751 | E | 805 915-4900 | 14056 |
| L3 Technologies Inc | 3812 | D | 805 584-1717 | 14203 |
| Pacific Scientific Company **(DH)** | 3812 | E | 805 526-5700 | 14278 |
| Sensoscientific LLC | 3823 | E | 800 279-3101 | 14458 |
| Interscan Corporation | 3824 | E | 805 823-8301 | 14480 |
| Bemco Inc **(PA)** | 3826 | E | 805 583-4970 | 14626 |
| Entech Instruments Inc | 3826 | D | 805 527-5939 | 14663 |
| Advanced Spectral Tech Inc | 3827 | E | 805 527-7657 | 14761 |
| Optical Physics Company | 3827 | F | 818 880-2907 | 14809 |
| Safran Defense & Space Inc | 3827 | D | 805 373-9340 | 14819 |
| Scope City **(PA)** | 3827 | E | 805 522-6646 | 14822 |
| Fluid Line Technology Corp | 3841 | E | 818 998-8848 | 15086 |
| Freedom Designs Inc | 3842 | C | 805 582-0077 | 15349 |
| Replacement Parts Inds Inc | 3843 | E | 818 882-8611 | 15479 |
| S2k Graphics Inc | 3993 | E | 818 885-3900 | 16028 |
| DMA Enterprises Inc **(PA)** | 3999 | E | 805 520-2468 | 16126 |
| Quantic M-Wave | 5065 | F | 805 499-8825 | 16730 |
| Andwin Corporation **(PA)** | 5113 | E | 818 999-2828 | 16996 |
| Eurow and OReilly Corp | 5199 | E | 800 747-7452 | 17294 |
| Creative Dgtal Systems Intgrti | 7371 | F | 805 364-0555 | 17902 |
| Arxis Technology Inc | 7372 | E | 805 306-7890 | 18067 |
| CFS Tax Software Inc | 7372 | E | 805 522-1157 | 18163 |
| Siteserver Inc | 8748 | F | 805 579-7831 | 19571 |

## SOLANA BEACH, CA - San Diego County

|  | SIC | EMP | PHONE | ENTRY# |
|---|---|---|---|---|
| Cognella Inc | 2741 | D | 858 552-1120 | 4380 |
| Mc Allister Industries Inc **(PA)** | 2754 | E | 858 755-0683 | 4824 |
| Sentynl Therapeutics Inc | 2834 | E | 888 227-8725 | 5653 |
| Tide Rock Holdings LLC **(PA)** | 3444 | E | 858 204-7438 | 8594 |
| Verifone Inc | 3577 | F | 858 436-2270 | 10448 |
| Clearpoint Neuro Inc **(PA)** | 3841 | D | 949 900-6833 | 15045 |
| Simon Golub & Sons Inc **(DH)** | 5094 | D |  | 16971 |

## SOLEDAD, CA - Monterey County

|  | SIC | EMP | PHONE | ENTRY# |
|---|---|---|---|---|
| Kvl Holdings Inc **(PA)** | 0172 | E | 831 678-2132 | 20 |

# GEOGRAPHIC SECTION

## SOUTH SAN FRANCISCO, CA

| Company | SIC | EMP | PHONE | ENTRY# |
|---|---|---|---|---|
| Golden State Vintners | 2084 | E | 831 678-3991 | 1592 |

### SOLVANG, CA - Santa Barbara County

| Company | SIC | EMP | PHONE | ENTRY# |
|---|---|---|---|---|
| Alma Rosa Winery Vineyards LLC | 2084 | E | 805 688-9090 | 1475 |
| Lucas & Lewellen Vineyards Inc (PA) | 5182 | E | 805 686-9336 | 17267 |

### SOMERSET, CA - El Dorado County

| Company | SIC | EMP | PHONE | ENTRY# |
|---|---|---|---|---|
| Goldline Brands Inc | 2084 | E | 818 319-7038 | 1597 |

### SOMIS, CA - Ventura County

| Company | SIC | EMP | PHONE | ENTRY# |
|---|---|---|---|---|
| Dudes Brewing Company | 2082 | E | 424 271-2915 | 1427 |

### SONOMA, CA - Sonoma County

| Company | SIC | EMP | PHONE | ENTRY# |
|---|---|---|---|---|
| Carneros Vintners Inc | 0722 | F | 707 933-9349 | 72 |
| Krave Pure Foods Inc | 2013 | D | 707 939-9176 | 650 |
| Sonoma Gourmet Inc | 2035 | E | 707 939-3700 | 992 |
| 3 Badge Beverage Corporation | 2084 | F | 707 343-1167 | 1469 |
| Cline Cellars Inc (PA) | 2084 | E | 707 940-4000 | 1507 |
| David James LLC | 2084 | E | 925 817-9215 | 1531 |
| Enterprise Vineyards Inc | 2084 | E | 707 996-6513 | 1555 |
| Freixenet Sonoma Caves Inc | 2084 | E | 707 996-4981 | 1579 |
| Gmic Vineyards LLC | 2084 | E | 707 996-3860 | 1590 |
| Groskopf Warehouse & Logistics | 2084 | E | 707 939-3100 | 1604 |
| Jacuzzi Family Vineyards LLC | 2084 | F | 707 931-7500 | 1629 |
| Jean-Clude Bsset Wines USA Inc | 2084 | E | 800 926-1266 | 1634 |
| Obsidian Ridge Wine Company | 2084 | E | 707 939-7625 | 1695 |
| Opal Moon Winery LLC | 2084 | F | 707 996-0420 | 1697 |
| Rams Gate Winery LLC | 2084 | E | 707 721-8700 | 1717 |
| Sebastiani Vineyards Inc | 2084 | D | 707 933-3200 | 1743 |
| Three Sticks Wines LLC | 2084 | E | 707 996-3328 | 1785 |
| Treasury Wine Estates Americas | 2084 | E | 707 935-1357 | 1794 |
| Valley of Moon Winery | 2084 | E | 707 939-4500 | 1808 |
| Vineburg Wine Company Inc (PA) | 2084 | E | 707 938-5277 | 1813 |
| Walt Pinot Noir | 2084 | F | 707 933-4440 | 1821 |
| CA Creamery Holdings LLC | 2096 | E | 270 861-5956 | 2086 |
| All-Truss Inc | 2439 | E | 707 938-5595 | 3291 |
| Cameo Sonoma Limited | 2679 | D | 707 935-0202 | 4034 |
| Arbor Fence Inc | 3446 | E | 707 938-3133 | 8618 |
| Broderick General Engineering | 3531 | D | 707 996-7809 | 9410 |
| Vode Lighting LLC | 3645 | E | 707 996-9898 | 11506 |
| CCL Label Inc | 3999 | D | 707 938-7800 | 16111 |
| Fastening Systems Intl | 5072 | E | 707 935-1170 | 16754 |
| Pawloyalty Software Inc | 7372 | F | 866 594-6848 | 18662 |
| Mellinger Engineering Inc | 8711 | F | 707 935-1100 | 19404 |

### SONORA, CA - Tuolumne County

| Company | SIC | EMP | PHONE | ENTRY# |
|---|---|---|---|---|
| Sierra Pacific Industries | 2421 | C | 530 378-8301 | 3082 |
| L K Lehman Trucking | 3273 | E | 209 532-5586 | 7460 |
| Brandelli Arts Inc | 3299 | E | 714 537-0969 | 7587 |
| Schnoogs | 3421 | D | 209 532-5279 | 7941 |
| Arch Medical Solutions - Sonora LLC | 3679 | D | 209 533-1033 | 12916 |
| Kinematic Automation Inc | 3841 | E | 209 532-3200 | 15144 |
| Leslie Heavy Haul LLC | 7389 | E | 209 840-1664 | 19104 |
| Sierra Mountain Cnstr Inc | 8322 | D | 209 928-1900 | 19360 |

### SOQUEL, CA - Santa Cruz County

| Company | SIC | EMP | PHONE | ENTRY# |
|---|---|---|---|---|
| Cretex Med Cmpnent DVC Tech In | 3089 | C | 831 462-1141 | 6785 |
| Design Octaves | 3089 | E | 831 464-8500 | 6800 |
| Harkness Enterprises Inc | 3089 | D | 831 462-1141 | 6849 |
| Provac Sales Inc | 3561 | E | 831 462-8900 | 9935 |
| System Studies Incorporated | 3661 | E | 831 475-5777 | 11790 |
| Merge4 Mfg Inc | 3999 | E | 831 239-5566 | 16182 |

### SOUTH DOS PALOS, CA - Merced County

| Company | SIC | EMP | PHONE | ENTRY# |
|---|---|---|---|---|
| Koda Farms Inc | 2044 | E | 209 392-2191 | 1080 |

### SOUTH EL MONTE, CA - Los Angeles County

| Company | SIC | EMP | PHONE | ENTRY# |
|---|---|---|---|---|
| California Snack Foods Inc | 2064 | E | 626 444-4508 | 1301 |
| Botanas Mexico Inc | 2099 | F | 626 279-1512 | 2145 |
| Out of Shell LLC | 2099 | C | 626 401-1923 | 2307 |
| Cala Action Inc | 2211 | E | 213 272-9759 | 2406 |
| Studio9d8 Inc | 2253 | E | 626 350-0832 | 2480 |
| Jowett Garments Factory Inc | 2339 | E | 626 350-0515 | 2776 |
| Lava Athletica Inc | 2389 | F | 909 859-1287 | 2903 |
| Yoshimasa Display Case Inc | 2541 | E | 213 637-9999 | 3678 |
| Asia Plastics Inc | 2673 | E | 626 448-8100 | 3961 |
| Interntnal Mdction Systems Ltd | 2834 | A | 626 442-6757 | 5501 |
| Lee Pharmaceuticals | 2844 | D | 626 442-3141 | 6002 |
| Cardinal Industrial Finishes (PA) | 2851 | E | 626 444-9274 | 6071 |
| Cardinal Paint and Powder Inc | 2851 | E | 626 444-9274 | 6074 |
| Euhomy LLC | 3011 | E | 213 265-5081 | 6410 |
| Promotonal Design Concepts Inc | 3069 | D | 626 579-4454 | 6528 |
| R & R Rubber Molding Inc | 3069 | E | 626 575-8105 | 6531 |
| Vclad Laminates Inc | 3083 | E | 626 442-2100 | 6594 |
| Mywi Fabricators Inc | 3441 | F | 626 279-6994 | 8194 |
| Master Enterprises Inc | 3444 | F | 626 442-1821 | 8500 |
| Abacus Powder Coating | 3479 | E | 626 443-7556 | 9034 |
| Island Powder Coating | 3479 | E | 626 279-2460 | 9082 |
| Pearson Engineering Corp | 3479 | F | 626 442-7436 | 9103 |
| S & H Machine Inc | 3492 | E | 626 448-5062 | 9170 |
| Vacco Industries (DH) | 3494 | D | 626 443-7121 | 9192 |
| Grover Smith Mfg Corp | 3561 | E | 323 724-3444 | 9926 |
| Hoefner Corporation | 3599 | E | 626 443-3258 | 10874 |
| Mikelson Machine Shop Inc | 3599 | E | 626 448-3920 | 10980 |
| Quality Industry Repair Inc | 3599 | E | 626 448-7778 | 11060 |
| Brands Republic Inc | 3634 | E | 302 401-1195 | 11400 |
| C W Cole & Company Inc | 3646 | E | 626 443-2473 | 11523 |
| Roselm Industries Inc | 3663 | E | 626 442-6840 | 11935 |
| Fabricast Inc (PA) | 3679 | E | 626 443-3247 | 12976 |
| Halcore Group Inc | 3711 | E | 626 575-0880 | 13358 |
| Amro Fabricating Corporation (PA) | 3728 | C | 626 579-2200 | 13778 |
| Tri-Fitting Mfg Company | 3728 | F | 626 442-2000 | 13977 |
| Betensh LLC | 3873 | E | 626 841-8543 | 15675 |
| Bestsio LLC | 3911 | F | 626 841-8543 | 15686 |
| Leader Industries Inc | 4119 | C | 626 575-0880 | 16277 |
| Creative Baby Inc | 5092 | E | 626 330-2289 | 16947 |
| Hog Inc | 7336 | F | 626 279-5275 | 17830 |
| O & S Properties Inc (PA) | 7699 | D | 626 579-1084 | 19272 |

### SOUTH GATE, CA - Los Angeles County

| Company | SIC | EMP | PHONE | ENTRY# |
|---|---|---|---|---|
| World Oil Corp | 1311 | C | 562 928-0100 | 147 |
| Saputo Cheese USA Inc | 2022 | A | 562 862-7686 | 737 |
| Win Soon Inc | 2026 | D | 323 564-5070 | 846 |
| Sunopta Grains and Foods Inc | 2041 | D | 323 774-6000 | 1064 |
| Sunopta Fruit Group Inc | 2087 | D | 323 774-6000 | 2027 |
| West Coast Naturals LLC | 2087 | E | 310 467-3007 | 2033 |
| Marquez Marquez Inc | 2096 | E | 562 408-0960 | 2097 |
| Nextrade Inc (PA) | 2299 | E | 562 944-9950 | 2552 |
| AG Adriano Goldschmied Inc (PA) | 2325 | E | 323 357-1111 | 2585 |
| Janin | 2339 | E | 323 564-0995 | 2768 |
| General Veneer Mfg Co | 2435 | E | 323 564-2661 | 3285 |
| Liberty Container Company | 2653 | C | 323 564-4211 | 3864 |
| Packaging Corporation America | 2653 | C | 562 927-7741 | 3875 |
| PQ LLC | 2819 | C | 323 326-1100 | 5112 |
| Arnco | 2822 | E | 323 249-7500 | 5219 |
| Granitize Products Inc | 2842 | D | 562 923-5438 | 5909 |
| Tu-K Industries LLC | 2844 | E | 562 927-3365 | 6048 |
| Lunday-Thagard Company | 2952 | B | 562 928-6990 | 6379 |
| Demenno/Kerdoon Holdings (DH) | 2992 | D | 562 231-1550 | 6391 |
| Lunday-Thagard Company (HQ) | 2999 | C | 562 928-7000 | 6402 |
| Productivity California Inc | 3089 | F | 562 923-3100 | 6986 |
| Gwla Acquisition Corp (PA) | 3211 | E | 323 789-7800 | 7171 |
| Glasswerks La Inc (HQ) | 3231 | B | 888 789-7810 | 7224 |
| Johns Manville Corporation | 3296 | D | 323 568-2220 | 7576 |
| Artsons Manufacturing Inc | 3312 | E | 323 773-3469 | 7604 |
| Pacific Alloy Casting Company Inc | 3321 | C | 562 928-1387 | 7679 |
| Buddy Bar Casting LLC | 3365 | C | 562 861-9664 | 7836 |
| Techni-Cast Corp | 3369 | D | 562 923-4585 | 7872 |
| Accurate Steel Treating Inc | 3398 | E | 562 927-6528 | 7873 |
| Astro Aluminum Treating Co | 3398 | D | 562 923-4344 | 7876 |
| Frameless Hardware Company LLC | 3429 | E | 888 295-4531 | 7996 |
| Metal Supply LLC | 3441 | D | 562 634-9940 | 8183 |
| Pluckys Dump Rental LLC | 3443 | E | 323 540-3510 | 8328 |
| Shultz Steel Company LLC | 3463 | B | 323 357-3200 | 8802 |
| Hughes Bros Aircrafters Inc | 3544 | E | 323 773-4541 | 9628 |
| Precision Forging Dies Inc | 3544 | E | 562 861-1878 | 9641 |
| M D H Burner & Boiler Co Inc | 3564 | F | 562 630-2875 | 9991 |
| Cimc Intermodal Equipment LLC (HQ) | 3715 | D | 562 904-8600 | 13614 |
| Bell Foundry Co (PA) | 3949 | E | 323 564-5701 | 15786 |
| Sure Grip International | 3949 | D | 562 923-0724 | 15862 |
| Verdeco Recycling Inc | 4953 | E | 323 537-4617 | 16366 |
| Saw Daily Service Inc | 5085 | E | 323 564-1791 | 16894 |
| World Oil Marketing Company (PA) | 5411 | C | 562 928-0100 | 17396 |
| Xrp Inc (PA) | 5531 | F | 562 861-4765 | 17469 |
| Koos Manufacturing Inc | 7389 | A | 323 249-1000 | 19101 |

### SOUTH LAKE TAHOE, CA - El Dorado County

| Company | SIC | EMP | PHONE | ENTRY# |
|---|---|---|---|---|
| Sierra-Tahoe Ready Mix Inc | 3273 | E | 530 541-1877 | 7497 |

### SOUTH PASADENA, CA - Los Angeles County

| Company | SIC | EMP | PHONE | ENTRY# |
|---|---|---|---|---|
| Albany Farms Inc | 2099 | E | 213 330-6573 | 2122 |
| Eva Franco Inc | 2337 | F | 213 746-4776 | 2723 |
| Finesse Apparel Inc | 2339 | E | 213 747-7077 | 2759 |
| Preco Aircraft Motors Inc | 3694 | E | 626 799-3549 | 13182 |

# SOUTH SAN FRANCISCO, CA

## GEOGRAPHIC SECTION

| | SIC | EMP | PHONE | ENTRY# |
|---|---|---|---|---|

### SOUTH SAN FRANCISCO, CA - San Mateo County

| | SIC | EMP | PHONE | ENTRY# |
|---|---|---|---|---|
| Plenty Unlimited Inc (PA) | 0191 | D | 650 735-3737 | 56 |
| Compound Focus Inc | 1389 | E | 650 228-1400 | 220 |
| Frank M Booth Inc | 1711 | D | 650 871-8292 | 418 |
| Fonco Inc | 1761 | E | 650 873-4585 | 514 |
| Clara Foods Co | 2034 | F | 650 733-4015 | 949 |
| Giustos Specialty Foods LLC (PA) | 2041 | E | 650 873-6566 | 1059 |
| City Baking Company | 2051 | D | 650 332-8730 | 1177 |
| Windmill Corporation | 2051 | F | 650 873-1000 | 1255 |
| Sees Candy Shops Incorporated (HQ) | 2064 | E | 650 761-2490 | 1328 |
| Sonoma Wine Hardware Inc | 2084 | E | 650 866-3020 | 1755 |
| Tardio Enterprises Inc | 2092 | E | 650 877-7200 | 2065 |
| Raison DEtre Bakery LLC | 2096 | D | 650 952-8889 | 2101 |
| Corbion Biotech Inc (HQ) | 2099 | E | 650 780-4777 | 2172 |
| New Hong Kong Noodle Co Inc | 2099 | E | 650 588-6425 | 2294 |
| Terravia Holdings Inc | 2099 | E | | 2371 |
| Simo Holdings Inc | 2321 | B | 760 931-9550 | 2577 |
| Japanese Weekend Inc (PA) | 2339 | E | 415 621-0555 | 2769 |
| Business Extension Bureau Ltd | 2721 | F | 650 737-5700 | 4233 |
| The Wine Appreciation Guild Ltd | 2731 | F | 650 866-3020 | 4350 |
| Essence Printing Inc (PA) | 2752 | E | 650 952-5072 | 4607 |
| Lithotype Company Inc (PA) | 2752 | D | 650 871-1750 | 4680 |
| Pyramid Graphics | 2752 | E | 650 871-0290 | 4743 |
| Utap Printing Co Inc | 2752 | F | 650 588-2818 | 4799 |
| Graphic Sportswear LLC | 2759 | D | 415 206-7200 | 4886 |
| Prothena Corp Pub Ltd Co | 2833 | F | 650 837-8550 | 5265 |
| Actelion US Holding Company (HQ) | 2834 | E | 650 624-6900 | 5297 |
| Alx Oncology Holdings Inc (PA) | 2834 | D | 650 466-7125 | 5310 |
| Assembly Biosciences Inc | 2834 | D | 833 509-4583 | 5339 |
| Astrazeneca LP | 2834 | E | 650 634-0103 | 5341 |
| Chemocentryx Inc (HQ) | 2834 | E | 650 210-2900 | 5404 |
| Chempartner Inc | 2834 | E | 215 720-6650 | 5405 |
| Cor Therapeutics Inc | 2834 | B | 650 244-6800 | 5409 |
| Cytokinetics Incorporated (PA) | 2834 | B | 650 624-3000 | 5421 |
| Cytomx Therapeutics Inc | 2834 | C | 650 515-3185 | 5422 |
| Five Prime Therapeutics Inc | 2834 | D | 415 365-5600 | 5442 |
| Frontier Medicines Corporation (PA) | 2834 | E | 650 457-1005 | 5448 |
| Genentech Inc | 2834 | A | 650 467-0810 | 5449 |
| Genentech Inc | 2834 | A | 650 225-1000 | 5451 |
| Genentech Inc | 2834 | A | 650 438-2626 | 5453 |
| Genentech Usa Inc | 2834 | A | 650 225-1000 | 5454 |
| Global Blood Therapeutics Inc (HQ) | 2834 | B | 650 741-7700 | 5465 |
| Ideaya Biosciences Inc (PA) | 2834 | D | 650 443-6209 | 5483 |
| Ideaya Biosciences Inc | 2834 | D | 650 534-3568 | 5484 |
| Ignyta Inc (DH) | 2834 | E | 858 255-5959 | 5486 |
| Intermune Inc (DH) | 2834 | C | 415 466-4383 | 5498 |
| Janssen Biopharma Inc | 2834 | E | 650 635-5500 | 5511 |
| Kai Pharmaceuticals Inc | 2834 | E | 650 328-9164 | 5521 |
| Kezar Life Sciences Inc (PA) | 2834 | E | 650 822-5600 | 5525 |
| Ngm Biopharmaceuticals Inc (PA) | 2834 | E | 650 243-5555 | 5572 |
| Nkarta Inc | 2834 | C | 925 407-1049 | 5577 |
| Oric Pharmaceuticals Inc | 2834 | D | 650 388-5600 | 5587 |
| Parvus Therapeutics Us Inc | 2834 | F | 415 805-8251 | 5594 |
| Pharmacyclics LLC (HQ) | 2834 | D | 408 215-3000 | 5602 |
| Pionyr Immunotherapeutics Inc | 2834 | E | 415 226-7503 | 5605 |
| Rapt Therapeutics Inc | 2834 | D | 650 489-9000 | 5628 |
| Rigel Pharmaceuticals Inc (PA) | 2834 | C | 650 624-1100 | 5640 |
| Roche Diagnostics Corporation | 2834 | C | 650 491-7251 | 5644 |
| Roche Molecular Systems Inc | 2834 | E | 650 225-1000 | 5645 |
| Samsung Biologics America Inc | 2834 | F | 650 898-9717 | 5649 |
| Spruce Biosciences Inc | 2834 | E | 415 655-4168 | 5670 |
| Structure Therapeutics Inc | 2834 | D | 628 229-9277 | 5678 |
| Surrozen Operating Inc (HQ) | 2834 | E | 650 918-8818 | 5682 |
| Theravance Biopharma Us Inc | 2834 | C | 650 808-6000 | 5689 |
| Vaxart Inc (PA) | 2834 | E | 650 550-3500 | 5702 |
| Vistagen Therapeutics Inc (PA) | 2834 | E | 650 577-3600 | 5710 |
| Diadexus Inc | 2835 | E | 650 246-6400 | 5748 |
| Freenome Inc | 2835 | A | 650 446-6630 | 5751 |
| Monogram Biosciences Inc | 2835 | B | 650 635-1100 | 5767 |
| Verge Genomics | 2835 | D | 312 489-7455 | 5785 |
| Aligos Therapeutics Inc (PA) | 2836 | E | 800 466-6059 | 5787 |
| Allogene Therapeutics Inc (PA) | 2836 | C | 650 457-2700 | 5788 |
| Alumis Inc | 2836 | C | 650 231-6625 | 5790 |
| Astellas Gene Therapies Inc (DH) | 2836 | E | 415 818-1001 | 5798 |
| Astellas Gene Therapies Inc | 2836 | D | 415 818-1001 | 5799 |
| Astellas Gene Therapies Inc | 2836 | D | 910 578-9806 | 5800 |
| Denali Therapeutics Inc (PA) | 2836 | B | 650 866-8548 | 5823 |
| Quince Therapeutics Inc (PA) | 2836 | F | 415 910-5717 | 5857 |
| Senti Biosciences Inc (PA) | 2836 | E | 650 239-2030 | 5860 |
| Surrozen Inc (PA) | 2836 | E | 650 489-9000 | 5863 |
| Sutro Biopharma Inc (PA) | 2836 | B | 650 881-6500 | 5864 |
| Tenaya Therapeutics Inc | 2836 | C | 760 310-9976 | 5866 |
| Simpson Coatings Group Inc | 2851 | E | 650 873-5990 | 6113 |
| Optiva Inc | 2899 | D | 650 616-7600 | 6315 |
| Tangle Inc | 3069 | E | 650 616-7900 | 6543 |
| Giannini Garden Ornaments Inc | 3272 | E | 650 873-4493 | 7338 |
| Sinosource Intl Co Inc | 3281 | F | 650 697-6668 | 7546 |
| B Metal Fabrication Inc | 3441 | E | 650 615-7705 | 8099 |
| JC Metal Specialists Inc (PA) | 3441 | E | 650 827-1618 | 8157 |
| Hauslane Inc | 3444 | F | 800 929-0168 | 8467 |
| Mytra Inc | 3549 | E | 650 539-8070 | 9741 |
| Sp Controls Inc | 3577 | F | 650 392-7880 | 10438 |
| Calpico Inc | 3643 | E | 650 588-2241 | 11444 |
| Vox Network Solutions Inc | 3661 | C | 650 989-1000 | 11793 |
| Ca Inc | 3674 | E | 650 534-9000 | 12373 |
| Renesas Electronics Amer Inc | 3674 | A | 408 588-6750 | 12674 |
| Berlin Food & Lab Equipment Co | 3821 | E | 650 589-4231 | 14330 |
| Standard Biotools Inc (PA) | 3826 | C | 650 266-6000 | 14723 |
| Thermo Fisher Scientific Inc | 3826 | E | 650 246-5265 | 14745 |
| Biocheck Inc (HQ) | 3841 | F | 650 573-1968 | 15008 |
| Toshiba America Inc | 3845 | C | 212 596-0600 | 15585 |
| Toshiba America Mri Inc | 3845 | C | 650 737-6686 | 15586 |
| Boosted Inc | 3949 | E | 650 933-5151 | 15790 |
| Vomela Specialty Company | 3993 | D | 650 877-8000 | 16064 |
| D P Nicoli Inc | 5051 | F | 650 873-2999 | 16617 |
| Monster Inc (PA) | 5099 | B | 415 840-2000 | 16982 |
| Shaw Bakers LLC (PA) | 5149 | E | 650 273-1440 | 17213 |
| Aechelon Technology Inc (PA) | 7371 | C | 415 255-0120 | 17877 |
| Education Elements Inc | 7372 | D | 650 440-7860 | 18264 |
| Uptimeai Inc | 7372 | E | 415 935-1195 | 18905 |
| Veracyte Inc (PA) | 8071 | D | 650 243-6300 | 19333 |
| Unity Biotechnology Inc | 8731 | F | 650 416-1192 | 19481 |
| Abbvie Stemcentrx LLC | 8733 | D | 415 298-9242 | 19490 |
| Genentech Inc (DH) | 8733 | A | 650 225-1000 | 19494 |

### SPRING VALLEY, CA - San Diego County

| | SIC | EMP | PHONE | ENTRY# |
|---|---|---|---|---|
| West Coast Iron Inc | 1796 | D | 619 464-8456 | 551 |
| Homestead Sheet Metal | 3441 | E | 619 469-4373 | 8152 |
| Progrssive Stl Fabricators Inc | 3441 | F | 619 460-7150 | 8205 |
| Richardson Steel Inc | 3441 | E | 619 697-5892 | 8209 |
| S & S Carbide Tool Inc | 3544 | C | 619 670-5214 | 9646 |
| Ttn Machining Inc | 3599 | F | 619 303-4573 | 11157 |
| East Penn Manufacturing | 3691 | F | 619 660-0016 | 13134 |
| Bish Inc | 3728 | E | 619 660-6220 | 13798 |
| Marjan Stone Inc | 5032 | E | 619 825-6000 | 16476 |
| TV Ears Inc | 5065 | E | 619 797-1600 | 16739 |
| Deering Banjo Company Inc | 5736 | E | 619 464-8252 | 17562 |

### STANFORD, CA - Santa Clara County

| | SIC | EMP | PHONE | ENTRY# |
|---|---|---|---|---|
| Stanford Daily Publishing Corp | 2711 | E | 650 723-2555 | 4202 |
| Leland Stanford Junior Univ | 2741 | E | 650 723-5553 | 4426 |
| Stanford Business Magazine | 2752 | E | 650 723-2146 | 4771 |

### STANTON, CA - Orange County

| | SIC | EMP | PHONE | ENTRY# |
|---|---|---|---|---|
| White Bottle Inc | 3089 | E | 949 788-1998 | 7080 |
| Orco Block & Hardscape (PA) | 3271 | D | 714 527-2239 | 7296 |
| Structural Stl Fabricators Inc | 3441 | E | 714 761-1695 | 8223 |
| RDfabricators Inc | 3444 | F | 714 634-2078 | 8555 |
| West Coast Manufacturing Inc | 3469 | E | 714 897-4221 | 8900 |
| All Metals Processing of San Diego Inc | 3471 | C | 714 828-8238 | 8912 |
| All Mtals Proc Orange Cnty LLC | 3471 | C | 714 828-8238 | 8913 |
| Field Time Target Training LLC | 3483 | E | 714 677-2841 | 9134 |
| Newcomb Spring Corp | 3495 | E | 714 995-5341 | 9203 |
| Stecher Enterprises Inc | 3495 | F | 714 484-6900 | 9207 |
| Custom Pipe & Fabrication Inc (HQ) | 3498 | D | 800 553-3058 | 9256 |
| Boudraux Prcsion McHining Corp | 3599 | E | 714 894-4523 | 10752 |
| Muth Machine Works (HQ) | 3599 | E | 714 527-2239 | 11000 |
| Newport Optcal Inds Hldngs Ltd (PA) | 3827 | E | 714 484-8100 | 14802 |
| Signs and Services Company | 3993 | E | 714 761-8200 | 16041 |
| Cameron Welding Supply (PA) | 7692 | E | 714 530-9353 | 19185 |

### STEVENSON RANCH, CA - Los Angeles County

| | SIC | EMP | PHONE | ENTRY# |
|---|---|---|---|---|
| Vons Companies Inc | 5411 | C | 661 254-3570 | 17390 |

### STEVINSON, CA - Merced County

| | SIC | EMP | PHONE | ENTRY# |
|---|---|---|---|---|
| Machado Backhoe Inc | 1794 | E | 209 634-4836 | 545 |

### STOCKTON, CA - San Joaquin County

| | SIC | EMP | PHONE | ENTRY# |
|---|---|---|---|---|
| DTE Stockton LLC | 1389 | E | 209 467-3838 | 224 |
| Baldwin Contracting Co Inc | 1442 | F | 209 460-3785 | 308 |
| De La Cruz Lath and Plaster Co | 1771 | F | 209 368-8658 | 521 |
| Schuff Steel Company | 1791 | E | 209 938-0869 | 534 |
| Strocal Inc | 1791 | B | 209 948-4646 | 536 |
| Hormel Foods Corporation | 2011 | D | 800 523-4635 | 602 |
| Valley Fresh Inc (HQ) | 2011 | E | 209 943-5411 | 621 |
| Alpine Meats Inc | 2013 | E | 209 477-2691 | 629 |

# GEOGRAPHIC SECTION

**SUN VALLEY, CA**

| Company | SIC | EMP | PHONE | ENTRY# |
|---|---|---|---|---|
| Foster Farms LLC | 2015 | E | 209 948-0129 | 681 |
| Grimaud Farms California Inc (DH) | 2015 | E | 209 466-3200 | 694 |
| Sunrise Fresh LLC | 2034 | D | 209 932-0192 | 966 |
| Calchef Foods LLC (HQ) | 2035 | E | 888 638-7083 | 976 |
| Kruger Foods Inc | 2035 | C | 209 941-8518 | 981 |
| S M S Briners Inc | 2035 | E | 209 941-8515 | 991 |
| JR Simplot Company | 2037 | E | 209 941-4456 | 1009 |
| Ardent Mills LLC | 2041 | F | 209 983-6551 | 1056 |
| Corn Products Development Inc (HQ) | 2046 | E | 209 982-1920 | 1089 |
| Ingredion Incorporated | 2046 | D | 209 982-1920 | 1090 |
| Lawleys Inc | 2048 | E | 209 337-1170 | 1133 |
| Robinson Farms Feed Company | 2048 | D | 209 466-7915 | 1147 |
| Aspire Bakeries LLC | 2051 | C | 209 469-4920 | 1158 |
| Best Express Foods Inc | 2051 | B | 209 465-5540 | 1169 |
| Diamond Foods LLC (PA) | 2068 | A | 209 467-6000 | 1351 |
| Kennfoods Usa LLC | 2068 | E | 209 932-8132 | 1355 |
| Klein Bros Holdings Ltd | 2068 | E | 209 465-5033 | 1356 |
| Wilmar Oils Fats Stockton LLC | 2076 | E | 925 627-1600 | 1375 |
| Olive Corto L P | 2079 | F | 888 832-0051 | 1403 |
| Pepsi-Cola Metro Btlg Co Inc | 2086 | D | 209 367-7140 | 1916 |
| Varni Brothers Corporation | 2086 | D | 209 464-7778 | 1971 |
| Pelton-Shepherd Industries Inc (PA) | 2097 | E | 209 460-0893 | 2112 |
| Arandas Tortilla Company Inc | 2099 | E | 209 464-8675 | 2128 |
| Arandas Tortilla Company Inc (PA) | 2099 | E | 209 464-8675 | 2129 |
| J & J Quality Door Inc | 2431 | E | 209 948-5013 | 3148 |
| Masonite International Corp | 2431 | E | 209 463-3503 | 3155 |
| T M Cobb Company | 2431 | D | 209 948-5358 | 3195 |
| Quality Cabinet Shop Inc | 2434 | E | 209 948-0431 | 3262 |
| All Good Pallets Inc | 2448 | E | 209 467-7000 | 3331 |
| Cutter Lumber Products | 2448 | E | 209 982-4477 | 3338 |
| California Cedar Products Co (PA) | 2499 | E | 209 932-5002 | 3413 |
| City of Stockton | 2531 | C | 209 937-8339 | 3614 |
| Cencal Recycling LLC | 2611 | F | 209 546-8000 | 3755 |
| Cal Sheets LLC | 2653 | D | 209 234-3300 | 3826 |
| Pactiv LLC | 2653 | E | 209 983-1930 | 3876 |
| Caraustar Industries Inc | 2655 | E | 209 464-6590 | 3900 |
| Pacific Paper Tube LLC (PA) | 2655 | E | 510 562-8823 | 3907 |
| Miller Products Inc | 2672 | D | 209 467-2470 | 3952 |
| Signode Industrial Group LLC | 2679 | E | 209 931-0917 | 4050 |
| Dow Jones Lmg Stockton Inc | 2711 | C | 209 943-6397 | 4105 |
| Kp LLC | 2752 | E | 209 466-6761 | 4666 |
| By Quest LLC | 2759 | F | 209 234-0202 | 4856 |
| IC Ink Image Co Inc | 2759 | E | 209 931-3040 | 4894 |
| Therapeutic RES Faculty LLC | 2759 | C | 209 472-2240 | 4974 |
| J-M Manufacturing Company Inc | 2821 | D | 209 982-1500 | 5171 |
| Mitsubshi Chem Advnced Mtls In | 2821 | E | 209 464-2701 | 5178 |
| Value Products Inc | 2841 | E | 209 345-3817 | 5884 |
| Rock Engineered McHy Co Inc | 2911 | F | 925 447-0805 | 6350 |
| Rgm Products Inc | 2952 | B | 559 499-2222 | 6383 |
| A & D Rubber Products Co Inc (PA) | 3053 | F | 209 941-0100 | 6436 |
| Proco Products Inc (PA) | 3069 | E | 209 943-6088 | 6527 |
| Wardley Industrial Inc | 3086 | E | 209 932-1088 | 6671 |
| Advanced Polymer Technologies LLC | 3089 | E | 209 464-2701 | 6699 |
| Anderson Moulds Incorporated | 3089 | F | 209 943-1145 | 6719 |
| Calportland Company | 3241 | E | 209 469-0109 | 7251 |
| Oldcastle Infrastructure Inc | 3272 | E | 209 235-1173 | 7367 |
| Concrete Inc (DH) | 3273 | D | 209 933-6999 | 7434 |
| Simpson Manufacturing Co Inc | 3291 | E | 209 234-7775 | 7557 |
| Nexcoil Steel LLC | 3316 | F | 209 900-1919 | 7659 |
| Valimet Inc (PA) | 3399 | D | 209 444-1600 | 7917 |
| EMC Water LLC | 3431 | E | 209 616-6963 | 8040 |
| Herrick Corporation (PA) | 3441 | E | 209 956-4751 | 8150 |
| Deck West Inc | 3444 | E | 209 939-9700 | 8427 |
| Noll/Norwesco LLC | 3444 | C | 209 234-1600 | 8518 |
| Western Square Industries Inc | 3446 | E | 209 944-0921 | 8650 |
| Enviroplex Inc | 3448 | D | 209 466-8000 | 8665 |
| Simpson Strong-Tie Company Inc | 3449 | E | 209 234-7775 | 8710 |
| Ahc Enterprises Inc | 3479 | E | 209 234-2700 | 9040 |
| B & C Painting Solutions Inc | 3479 | E | 209 982-0422 | 9052 |
| Premier Coatings Inc | 3479 | D | 209 982-5585 | 9110 |
| Sumiden Wire Products Corp | 3496 | E | 615 446-3199 | 9234 |
| Aero Turbine Inc | 3511 | D | 209 983-1112 | 9306 |
| Custom Building Products Inc | 3531 | E | 209 983-8322 | 9419 |
| Stockton Tri-Industries LLC | 3535 | E | 209 948-9701 | 9496 |
| Carando Technologies Inc | 3542 | E | 209 948-6500 | 9582 |
| Hackett Industries Inc | 3556 | E | 209 955-8220 | 9795 |
| O H I Company | 3556 | E | 209 466-8921 | 9808 |
| Sardee Industries Inc | 3565 | E | 209 466-1526 | 10029 |
| Centrifuge-Systems LLC | 3569 | E | 209 583-3753 | 10081 |
| Vinotheque Wine Cellars | 3585 | F | 209 466-9463 | 10526 |
| Geiger Manufacturing Inc | 3599 | F | 209 464-7746 | 10855 |
| NJ Mc Cutchen Inc | 3599 | E | 209 466-9704 | 11009 |
| ES West Coast LLC | 3621 | E | 209 870-1900 | 11265 |
| Gallien Technology Inc (PA) | 3651 | D | 209 234-7300 | 11663 |
| Wjlp Company Inc | 3677 | D | 800 628-1123 | 12864 |
| Asco Power Technologies LP | 3699 | E | 209 931-7700 | 13214 |
| Electric Vehicles International LLC | 3711 | E | 209 939-0405 | 13349 |
| Motiv Power Systems Inc | 3713 | C | 650 458-4804 | 13420 |
| Aisin Electronics Inc | 3714 | C | 209 983-4988 | 13452 |
| Cozad Trailer Sales LLC | 3715 | E | 209 931-3000 | 13615 |
| Pacifico Inc | 3715 | E | 209 466-0266 | 13618 |
| Wkf (friedman Enterprises Inc (PA) | 3724 | F | 925 673-9100 | 13728 |
| Applied Arospc Structures Corp (PA) | 3728 | C | 209 982-0160 | 13780 |
| Exactacator Inc (PA) | 3949 | E | 209 464-8979 | 15809 |
| Arrow Sign Co | 3993 | E | 209 931-7852 | 15944 |
| Mina-Tree Signs Incorporated (PA) | 3993 | E | 209 941-2921 | 16009 |
| Outform Group Inc | 3993 | F | 510 487-1122 | 16017 |
| Scafco Corporation | 3999 | E | 209 670-8053 | 16224 |
| Rare Parts Inc | 5013 | E | 209 948-6005 | 16395 |
| Fleet Tire Inc (PA) | 5014 | E | 209 467-0154 | 16407 |
| PDM Steel Service Centers Inc (HQ) | 5051 | D | 209 943-0513 | 16629 |
| J Milano Co Inc | 5072 | E | 209 944-0902 | 16755 |
| Center State Pipe and Sup Co | 5074 | F | 209 466-0871 | 16765 |
| Delta Rubber Co Inc | 5085 | E | 209 948-0511 | 16871 |
| Cal Ranch Inc | 5146 | E | 209 465-8999 | 17154 |
| M Calosso & Son | 5191 | E | 209 466-8994 | 17274 |
| Baer Enterprises Inc | 7389 | E | 209 390-0460 | 19074 |
| Complete Welders Supply | 7692 | F | 209 462-3086 | 19187 |
| Dentonis Welding Works Inc (PA) | 7692 | E | 209 464-4930 | 19190 |
| Stanley Electric Motor Co Inc | 7694 | E | 209 464-7321 | 19232 |
| West Coast Energy Systems LLC (HQ) | 8711 | D | 209 870-1900 | 19430 |
| Daikin Comfort Tech Dist Inc | 8742 | B | 209 946-9244 | 19526 |

### STRATHMORE, CA - Tulare County

| Company | SIC | EMP | PHONE | ENTRY# |
|---|---|---|---|---|
| Bell-Carter Foods Inc | 2033 | C | 559 568-1650 | 878 |
| Cellu-Con Inc | 2879 | E | 559 568-0190 | 6194 |

### STUDIO CITY, CA - Los Angeles County

| Company | SIC | EMP | PHONE | ENTRY# |
|---|---|---|---|---|
| Harmony Infinite Inc | 2599 | F | | 3743 |
| Allbirds Inc | 3143 | F | 213 374-3533 | 7105 |
| Empire Enterprises Inc (PA) | 5021 | F | 818 784-8918 | 16413 |

### SUISUN CITY, CA - Solano County

| Company | SIC | EMP | PHONE | ENTRY# |
|---|---|---|---|---|
| Cemex Cnstr Mtls PCF LLC | 3272 | E | 800 992-3639 | 7316 |
| E B Stone & Son Inc | 5191 | E | 707 426-2500 | 17271 |

### SUN CITY, CA - Riverside County

| Company | SIC | EMP | PHONE | ENTRY# |
|---|---|---|---|---|
| Forterra Pipe & Precast LLC | 3272 | E | 951 523-7039 | 7335 |
| Omnimax International LLC | 3442 | D | 951 928-1000 | 8281 |
| Omnimax International LLC | 3444 | E | 951 928-1000 | 8520 |

### SUN VALLEY, CA - Los Angeles County

| Company | SIC | EMP | PHONE | ENTRY# |
|---|---|---|---|---|
| Leon Krous Drilling Inc | 1381 | E | 818 833-4654 | 163 |
| Scenic Express Inc | 1799 | E | 323 254-4351 | 573 |
| Glenoaks Food Inc | 2015 | E | 818 768-9091 | 693 |
| High Road Craft Ice Cream Inc (PA) | 2024 | E | 678 701-7623 | 805 |
| Gedney Foods Company | 2035 | C | 952 448-2612 | 978 |
| Aries Prepared Beef Company | 2047 | F | 818 771-0181 | 1092 |
| Foodology LLC | 2099 | D | 818 252-1888 | 2202 |
| Four Seasons Hummus Inc | 2099 | F | 305 409-0449 | 2204 |
| Pacesetter Fabrics LLC (HQ) | 2299 | E | 213 741-9999 | 2553 |
| Kleen Maid Inc | 2392 | F | 323 581-3000 | 2933 |
| Malakan Inc (PA) | 2435 | F | 310 910-9270 | 3286 |
| Acrylic Distribution Corp | 2519 | E | 818 767-8448 | 3551 |
| Columbia Showcase & Cab Co Inc | 2541 | C | 818 765-9710 | 3652 |
| Marfred Industries | 2653 | B | | 3866 |
| Pacobond Inc | 2674 | E | 818 768-5002 | 3992 |
| Colorfx Inc | 2752 | E | 818 767-7671 | 4561 |
| Insua Graphics Incorporated | 2752 | E | 818 767-7007 | 4650 |
| Cosrich Group Inc | 2844 | E | 818 686-2500 | 5964 |
| Desert Block Co Inc | 2951 | E | 661 824-2624 | 6362 |
| Technical Heaters Inc | 3052 | F | 818 361-7185 | 6432 |
| North Amrcn Foam Ppr Cnverters | 3086 | E | 818 255-3383 | 6650 |
| Plastic Services and Products | 3086 | A | 818 896-1101 | 6651 |
| PMC Global Inc (PA) | 3086 | D | 818 896-1101 | 6653 |
| PMC Leaders In Chemicals Inc (HQ) | 3086 | E | 818 896-1101 | 6654 |
| Specialty Tools Inc | 3089 | F | 818 827-8138 | 7037 |
| Encore Cases Inc | 3161 | E | 818 768-8803 | 7129 |
| Angelus Block Co Inc (PA) | 3271 | E | 714 637-8594 | 7292 |
| Quikrete Companies LLC | 3272 | E | 323 875-1367 | 7383 |
| Associated Ready Mix Con Inc | 3273 | D | 818 504-3100 | 7405 |
| Capital Ready Mix Inc | 3273 | E | 818 771-1122 | 7415 |
| E-Z Mix Inc (PA) | 3273 | E | 818 768-0568 | 7440 |
| National Ready Mixed Con Co | 3273 | F | 818 768-0050 | 7474 |
| Kenwalt Die Casting Corp | 3363 | E | 818 768-5800 | 7813 |
| W & F Mfg Inc | 3429 | E | 818 394-6060 | 8035 |

Employee Codes: A=Over 500 employees, B=251-500
C=101-250, D=51-100, E=20-50, F=10-19, G=1-9

2025 Harris California Manufacturers Directory

© Mergent Inc. 1-800-342-5647

# SUN VALLEY, CA

| Company | SIC | EMP | PHONE | ENTRY# |
|---|---|---|---|---|
| C A Buchen Corp | 3441 | E | 818 767-5408 | 8109 |
| Tee -N -Jay Manufacturing Inc | 3444 | E | 818 504-2961 | 8591 |
| Kitcor Corporation | 3469 | E | 323 875-2820 | 8857 |
| Alert Plating Company | 3471 | E | 818 771-9304 | 8911 |
| Schmidt Industries Inc | 3471 | D | 818 768-9100 | 9011 |
| Sundial Industries Inc | 3479 | E | 818 767-4477 | 9126 |
| Sundial Powder Coatings Inc | 3479 | E | 818 767-4477 | 9127 |
| L A Propoint Inc | 3499 | E | 818 767-6800 | 9290 |
| American Plastic Products Inc | 3544 | D | 818 504-1073 | 9599 |
| Art Mold Die Casting Inc | 3544 | E | 818 767-6464 | 9600 |
| Kvr Investment Group Inc | 3559 | D | 818 896-1102 | 9873 |
| Penguin Pumps Incorporated | 3561 | E | 818 504-2391 | 9933 |
| AVX Filters Corporation | 3569 | D | 818 767-6770 | 10075 |
| Impulse Industries Inc | 3581 | E | 818 767-4258 | 10471 |
| L A Gauge Company Inc | 3599 | D | 818 767-7193 | 10935 |
| Precision Arcft Machining Inc | 3599 | E | 818 768-5900 | 11045 |
| Schneiders Manufacturing Inc | 3599 | E | 818 771-0082 | 11101 |
| Sheffield Manufacturing Inc | 3599 | D | 310 320-1473 | 11113 |
| Tecfar Manufacturing Inc | 3599 | F | 818 767-0677 | 11139 |
| Abbott Technologies Inc | 3612 | E | 818 504-0644 | 11202 |
| American Grip Inc | 3648 | E | 818 768-8922 | 11579 |
| Dx Radio Systems Inc | 3663 | F | 818 252-6700 | 11844 |
| Accurate Engineering Inc | 3672 | E | 818 768-3919 | 12042 |
| De Leon Entps Elec Spclist Inc | 3672 | E | 818 252-6690 | 12086 |
| ASC Group Inc | 3674 | B | 818 896-1101 | 12334 |
| E & E TOA Corporation | 3678 | F | | 12878 |
| Spartan Truck Company Inc | 3713 | E | 818 899-1111 | 13430 |
| Forgiato Inc | 3714 | D | 818 771-9779 | 13502 |
| K & G Latirovian Inc | 3714 | D | 818 319-2862 | 13523 |
| Coronado Manufacturing LLC | 3728 | E | 818 768-5010 | 13816 |
| Pacific Sky Supply Inc | 3728 | D | 818 768-3700 | 13921 |
| Pmc Inc (HQ) | 3728 | D | 818 896-1101 | 13927 |
| Walker Design Inc | 3731 | E | 818 252-7788 | 14025 |
| Numatic Engineering Inc | 3823 | E | 818 768-1200 | 14440 |
| Sscor Inc | 3841 | F | 818 504-4054 | 15266 |
| Emergent Group Inc (DH) | 3842 | D | 818 394-2800 | 15343 |
| Schecter Guitar Research Inc | 3931 | E | 818 767-1029 | 15724 |
| Pincraft Inc | 3961 | E | 818 248-0077 | 15906 |
| Tower 26 Inc | 3999 | E | 347 366-2706 | 16254 |
| Builders Fence Company Inc (PA) | 5031 | E | 818 768-5500 | 16442 |
| Norman Industrial Mtls Inc (PA) | 5051 | C | 818 729-3333 | 16626 |
| Spa De Soleil Inc | 5122 | E | 818 504-3200 | 17050 |
| Magic Jump Inc | 7359 | E | 818 847-1313 | 17857 |
| Sugar Foods LLC | 7389 | C | 818 768-7900 | 19135 |
| Wet (PA) | 7389 | E | 818 769-6200 | 19143 |
| Dip Braze Inc | 7692 | F | 818 768-1555 | 19191 |
| Hawker Pacific Aerospace | 7699 | B | 818 765-6201 | 19261 |

## SUNNYVALE, CA - Santa Clara County

| Company | SIC | EMP | PHONE | ENTRY# |
|---|---|---|---|---|
| Fullfillment Systems Inc | 2013 | E | 408 745-7675 | 643 |
| Fullfillment Systems Inc (PA) | 2013 | D | 408 745-7675 | 644 |
| Wayne | 2023 | E | 669 206-2179 | 788 |
| Thomas West Inc (PA) | 2392 | E | 408 481-3850 | 2950 |
| Serious Energy Inc | 2531 | D | 408 541-8000 | 3639 |
| Cpp Inc | 2731 | F | 650 969-8901 | 4322 |
| Crazy Maple Studio Inc (PA) | 2741 | E | 972 757-1283 | 4384 |
| Linquip Corporation | 2741 | E | 925 998-2480 | 4427 |
| Retail Content Service Inc | 2741 | E | 415 890-2097 | 4461 |
| Oakmead Prtg Reproduction Inc | 2752 | E | 408 734-5505 | 4709 |
| Dupont De Nemours Inc | 2819 | E | 408 419-4491 | 5086 |
| American Liquid Packaging Systems Inc (PA) | 2821 | D | 408 524-7474 | 5134 |
| Adiana Inc | 2834 | B | 650 421-2900 | 5299 |
| Bayer Healthcare LLC | 2834 | E | 408 499-0606 | 5361 |
| Pharmacyclics Inc | 2834 | A | 408 774-0330 | 5601 |
| Adeza Biomedical Corporation | 2835 | A | 408 745-6491 | 5730 |
| Jsr Micro Inc (DH) | 2869 | C | 408 543-8800 | 6149 |
| Oakbio Inc | 2869 | F | 888 591-9413 | 6154 |
| Yasheng Group | 2879 | A | 650 363-8345 | 6214 |
| Bondline Elctrnic Adhsive Corp | 2891 | E | 408 830-9200 | 6220 |
| Prism Inks | 2893 | E | 408 744-6710 | 6260 |
| Diab Holdings Inc | 3086 | E | 408 598-2241 | 6631 |
| I G S Inc | 3211 | F | 408 733-4621 | 7173 |
| Hyatt Die Cast Engrg Corp - S | 3363 | E | 408 523-7000 | 7811 |
| Responsible Metal Fab Inc | 3444 | E | 408 734-0713 | 8557 |
| Silicor Materials Inc | 3479 | D | 408 962-3100 | 9120 |
| Surface Engineering Spc | 3552 | E | 408 734-8810 | 9752 |
| Graphics Microsystems LLC (DH) | 3555 | D | | 9767 |
| Figure Ai Inc | 3569 | E | 716 830-0904 | 10088 |
| Applied Micro Circuits Corp | 3572 | E | 408 523-1000 | 10224 |
| Nexsan Technologies (US) LL | 3572 | F | 408 724-9809 | 10256 |
| Nexsan Technologies Inc | 3572 | C | | 10257 |
| Aruba Networks Inc | 3577 | A | 408 227-4500 | 10326 |
| Aruba Networks Inc | 3577 | A | 408 227-4500 | 10328 |
| Fujitsu Management Services of America Inc | 3577 | C | 408 746-6000 | 10372 |
| Juniper Networks Inc (PA) | 3577 | A | 408 745-2000 | 10392 |
| Optibase Inc (HQ) | 3577 | E | 800 451-5101 | 10419 |
| Seagra Technology Inc | 3577 | E | 408 230-8706 | 10432 |
| Clover Network Inc | 3578 | D | 650 210-7888 | 10459 |
| Accurate Technology Mfg Inc | 3599 | D | 408 733-4344 | 10663 |
| Armstrong Technology Sv Inc | 3599 | D | 408 734-4434 | 10716 |
| Armstrong Technology SV Inc (PA) | 3599 | D | 408 734-4434 | 10718 |
| ERC Concepts Co Inc | 3599 | F | 408 734-5345 | 10828 |
| Nanez Mfg Inc (PA) | 3599 | F | 408 830-9903 | 11002 |
| Samax Precision Inc | 3599 | E | 408 245-9555 | 11098 |
| Turntide Technologies Inc (PA) | 3621 | E | 877 776-8470 | 11294 |
| Clearedge Power Inc | 3629 | C | 877 257-3343 | 11364 |
| Innovalight Inc | 3648 | E | 408 419-4400 | 11602 |
| Luminus Inc (HQ) | 3648 | C | 408 708-7000 | 11610 |
| Luminus Devices Inc | 3648 | C | 978 528-8000 | 11611 |
| Dolby Laboratories Inc | 3651 | E | 408 730-5543 | 11650 |
| Coadna Photonics Inc (HQ) | 3661 | D | 408 736-1100 | 11757 |
| Aruba Networks Inc | 3663 | A | 408 227-4500 | 11814 |
| Commscope | 3663 | F | 650 265-4200 | 11829 |
| Lockheed Martin Corporation | 3663 | E | 408 742-4321 | 11884 |
| Motorola Mobility LLC | 3663 | E | 847 576-5000 | 11898 |
| Nokia Inc | 3663 | A | 408 530-7600 | 11904 |
| Pacific Crest Corporation (HQ) | 3663 | D | 408 481-8070 | 11912 |
| Palm Inc (HQ) | 3663 | B | 408 617-7000 | 11914 |
| Ruckus Wireless LLC (DH) | 3663 | E | 650 265-4200 | 11937 |
| Meru Networks Inc (HQ) | 3669 | F | 408 215-5300 | 12004 |
| Electrotek Corporation | 3672 | C | 414 762-1390 | 12092 |
| Qualitek Inc (HQ) | 3672 | D | 408 734-8686 | 12196 |
| Qualitek Inc | 3672 | D | 408 752-8422 | 12197 |
| Sierra Circuits Inc (PA) | 3672 | D | 408 735-7137 | 12217 |
| Sierra Electrotek LLC | 3672 | D | 414 762-1390 | 12218 |
| Westak Inc (PA) | 3672 | D | 408 734-8686 | 12259 |
| Westak International Sales Inc (HQ) | 3672 | C | 408 734-8686 | 12260 |
| Alpha and Omega Semicdtr Inc (HQ) | 3674 | E | 408 789-0008 | 12291 |
| Alta Devices Inc | 3674 | C | 408 988-8600 | 12293 |
| AMD Far East Ltd (HQ) | 3674 | F | 408 749-4000 | 12299 |
| Analog Bits Inc (HQ) | 3674 | F | 650 279-9323 | 12304 |
| Anchor Bay Technologies Inc | 3674 | E | 888 651-1765 | 12310 |
| Applied Materials Inc | 3674 | E | 408 727-5555 | 12318 |
| Aqt Solar Inc | 3674 | E | | 12327 |
| Awbscqemgk Inc | 3674 | C | 408 988-8600 | 12349 |
| Fairchild Semicdtr Intl Inc (HQ) | 3674 | B | 408 822-2000 | 12430 |
| Globalfoundries Dresden | 3674 | A | 408 462-3900 | 12449 |
| Globalfoundries US Inc | 3674 | B | 408 462-3900 | 12452 |
| Gsi Technology Inc (PA) | 3674 | D | 408 331-8800 | 12456 |
| Jireh Semiconductor Inc | 3674 | E | | 12511 |
| Ksm Corp | 3674 | E | 408 514-2400 | 12516 |
| Microsemi Stor Solutions Inc (DH) | 3674 | D | 408 239-8000 | 12581 |
| Ngcodec Inc | 3674 | E | 408 766-4382 | 12605 |
| Nokia of America Corporation | 3674 | F | 408 878-6500 | 12607 |
| Oepic Semiconductors Inc | 3674 | C | 408 747-0388 | 12616 |
| Sst Rg LLC | 3674 | B | 408 735-9110 | 12731 |
| Summit Microelectronics Inc | 3674 | E | 408 523-1000 | 12741 |
| Supertex Inc (HQ) | 3674 | D | 408 222-8888 | 12747 |
| Swave Photonics Inc | 3674 | E | 408 963-9958 | 12749 |
| Trident Microsystems Inc | 3674 | A | 408 962-5000 | 12772 |
| Umc Group (usa) | 3674 | D | 408 523-7800 | 12779 |
| Citala US Inc | 3679 | E | 408 745-8500 | 12939 |
| De Anza Manufacturing Svcs Inc | 3679 | D | 408 734-2020 | 12956 |
| Krytar Inc | 3679 | E | 408 734-5999 | 13020 |
| Intergen Inc | 3699 | F | 408 245-2737 | 13253 |
| Northrop Grumman Systems Corp | 3721 | A | 408 735-3011 | 13681 |
| Lockheed Martin Corporation | 3812 | D | 408 756-5751 | 14210 |
| Meggitt (orange County) Inc | 3812 | D | 408 739-3533 | 14220 |
| Northrop Grumman Systems Corp | 3812 | B | 408 735-2241 | 14267 |
| Quanergy Perception Tech Inc (HQ) | 3812 | E | 408 245-9500 | 14280 |
| Trimble Military & Advnced Sys | 3812 | D | 408 481-8000 | 14325 |
| Micro Lithography Inc | 3823 | C | 408 747-1769 | 14433 |
| Test Enterprises Inc (PA) | 3823 | E | 408 542-5900 | 14463 |
| Aeroflex High Speed Test Solutions Inc | 3825 | E | 516 694-6700 | 14487 |
| Eridan Communications Inc (PA) | 3825 | E | 650 492-0657 | 14518 |
| Eta Compute Inc | 3825 | E | 650 255-1293 | 14521 |
| Affymetrix Inc (HQ) | 3826 | C | 408 731-5000 | 14605 |
| Art Robbins Instruments LLC | 3826 | E | 408 734-8400 | 14615 |
| Cepheid (HQ) | 3826 | A | 408 541-4191 | 14643 |
| Dionex Corporation | 3826 | F | 408 737-0700 | 14650 |
| Dionex Corporation (HQ) | 3826 | B | 408 737-0700 | 14651 |
| Stanford Research Systems Inc | 3826 | E | 408 744-9040 | 14724 |
| Avantier Inc | 3827 | D | 732 570-8800 | 14762 |
| Digilens Inc | 3827 | E | 408 734-0219 | 14771 |
| Horiba Instruments Inc | 3829 | D | 408 730-4772 | 14879 |
| Horiba/Stec Incorporated | 3829 | D | 408 730-4772 | 14881 |

## GEOGRAPHIC SECTION — TEMECULA, CA

| Company | SIC | EMP | PHONE | ENTRY# |
|---|---|---|---|---|
| Rae Systems Inc (DH) | 3829 | E | 408 952-8200 | 14913 |
| Arthrocare Corporation | 3841 | E | 408 736-0224 | 14978 |
| Avantec Vascular Corporation | 3841 | E | 408 329-5400 | 14985 |
| Intuitive Srgcal Oprations Inc (HQ) | 3841 | E | 408 523-2100 | 15126 |
| Intuitive Surgical Inc | 3841 | E | 408 523-4000 | 15127 |
| Intuitive Surgical Inc | 3841 | E | 408 523-7314 | 15128 |
| Medeonbio Inc | 3841 | F | 650 397-5100 | 15165 |
| Medtronic Spine LLC | 3841 | A | 408 548-6500 | 15180 |
| Orthofix Medical Inc | 3841 | E | 214 937-2000 | 15216 |
| Silk Road Medical Inc | 3841 | B | 408 720-9002 | 15259 |
| Spiracur Inc | 3841 | D | 650 364-1544 | 15265 |
| St Jude Medical LLC | 3841 | D | 408 738-4883 | 15267 |
| Intuitive Surgical Inc (PA) | 3842 | C | 408 523-2100 | 15365 |
| Hologic Inc | 3844 | E | 408 745-0975 | 15502 |
| Ebr Systems Inc (PA) | 3845 | F | 408 720-1906 | 15532 |
| Learning Squared Inc | 3944 | C | 650 567-9995 | 15758 |
| Savi Technology Holdings Inc | 3999 | B | 650 316-4950 | 16221 |
| Sendmail Inc | 4813 | C | 510 594-5400 | 16322 |
| Minton Door Company (PA) | 5031 | E | 650 961-9800 | 16453 |
| Actiontec Electronics Inc | 5065 | D | 408 752-7700 | 16687 |
| Otis Elevator Company | 5084 | D | 408 727-1231 | 16832 |
| Coadna Holdings Inc | 6719 | D | 408 736-1100 | 17744 |
| Arcaris Inc (PA) | 7372 | C | 415 854-3801 | 18062 |
| Arctic Wolf Networks Inc | 7372 | C | 888 272-8429 | 18063 |
| Azul Systems Inc (PA) | 7372 | D | 866 890-8951 | 18087 |
| Belkasoft LLC | 7372 | E | 650 272-0384 | 18097 |
| Cariden Technologies LLC | 7372 | E | 650 564-9200 | 18148 |
| Caspio Inc (PA) | 7372 | F | 650 691-0900 | 18150 |
| Cloudshield Technologies LLC | 7372 | C | 408 331-6640 | 18186 |
| Egain Corporation (PA) | 7372 | E | 408 636-4500 | 18267 |
| Entco LLC | 7372 | A | 312 580-9100 | 18283 |
| Exablox Corporation | 7372 | E | 408 773-8477 | 18300 |
| Good Technology Software Inc | 7372 | A | 408 212-7500 | 18357 |
| Goover Inc | 7372 | F | 408 748-4333 | 18359 |
| Inbenta Technologies Inc (PA) | 7372 | E | 408 213-8771 | 18407 |
| Inktomi Corporation (HQ) | 7372 | E | 650 653-2800 | 18419 |
| Intermdia Cloud Cmmnctions Inc | 7372 | A | 650 641-4000 | 18427 |
| Ipolipo Inc | 7372 | D | 408 916-5290 | 18442 |
| Ivanti Inc | 7372 | D | 408 343-8181 | 18451 |
| Jfrog Ltd (PA) | 7372 | A | 408 329-1540 | 18456 |
| Kloudgin Inc (PA) | 7372 | E | 704 904-4321 | 18476 |
| Kloudspot Inc | 7372 | D | 800 709-2211 | 18477 |
| Lore Io Inc | 7372 | E | 408 256-1521 | 18502 |
| Matterport Inc (PA) | 7372 | D | 650 641-2241 | 18525 |
| Sass Labs Inc | 7372 | E | 404 731-7284 | 18760 |
| Synopsys Inc (PA) | 7372 | B | 650 584-5000 | 18858 |
| Wirex Systems | 7372 | E | 408 799-4498 | 18937 |
| Juniper Networks Inc | 7373 | A | 408 745-2000 | 18981 |
| Juniper Networks Intl LLC | 7373 | E | 408 745-2000 | 18982 |
| Fortinet Inc (PA) | 7374 | A | 408 235-7700 | 19007 |
| Healthtap Inc | 8011 | D | 650 268-9806 | 19317 |
| Lta Research & Exploration LLC (PA) | 8742 | D | 408 396-0577 | 19533 |

### SUNOL, CA - Alameda County

| Company | SIC | EMP | PHONE | ENTRY# |
|---|---|---|---|---|
| Elliston Vineyards Inc | 2084 | D | 925 862-2377 | 1553 |
| Ge-Hitachi Nuclear Energy | 2819 | D | 925 862-4382 | 5094 |
| Hanson Aggrgtes Md-Pacific Inc | 3273 | F | 925 862-2236 | 7451 |

### SUTTER, CA - Sutter County

| Company | SIC | EMP | PHONE | ENTRY# |
|---|---|---|---|---|
| Butte Sand and Gravel | 1442 | E | 530 755-0225 | 309 |
| Sweco Products Inc (PA) | 7699 | E | 530 673-8949 | 19284 |

### SUTTER CREEK, CA - Amador County

| Company | SIC | EMP | PHONE | ENTRY# |
|---|---|---|---|---|
| Emco High Voltage Corporation | 3679 | D | 209 267-1630 | 12970 |

### SYLMAR, CA - Los Angeles County

| Company | SIC | EMP | PHONE | ENTRY# |
|---|---|---|---|---|
| Paragon Industries Inc | 1743 | E | 818 833-0550 | 484 |
| Fantasy Cookie Corporation (PA) | 2052 | E | 818 361-6901 | 1274 |
| Orange Bang Inc | 2086 | E | 818 833-1000 | 1908 |
| Clear Image Printing Inc | 2752 | E | 818 547-4684 | 4553 |
| Imagemover Inc | 2752 | F | 818 485-8840 | 4637 |
| Abbott Laboratories | 2834 | E | 818 493-2388 | 5288 |
| PPG Paints | 2851 | F | 818 362-6711 | 6105 |
| Sierracin Corporation (HQ) | 2851 | A | 818 741-1656 | 6112 |
| International Academy of Fin (PA) | 2869 | E | 818 361-7724 | 6148 |
| Gasket Associates LP (PA) | 3053 | F | 310 217-5630 | 6448 |
| Atlas Foam Products | 3086 | E | 818 837-3626 | 6622 |
| C & G Plastics | 3089 | E | 818 837-3773 | 6752 |
| Gibraltar Plastic Pdts Corp | 3089 | E | 818 365-9318 | 6842 |
| Sierracin/Sylmar Corporation | 3089 | A | 818 362-6711 | 7027 |
| Leather Pro Inc | 3172 | E | 818 833-8822 | 7149 |
| Wayne Tool & Die Co | 3312 | E | 818 364-1611 | 7632 |
| Precise Iron Doors Inc | 3442 | E | 818 338-6269 | 8284 |
| MS Aerospace Inc | 3452 | B | 818 833-9095 | 8762 |
| Professnal Fnshg Systems Sups | 3469 | F | 818 365-8888 | 8877 |
| Industrial Elctrnic Engners In | 3577 | D | 818 787-0311 | 10380 |
| Anthony Inc (DH) | 3585 | A | 818 365-9451 | 10481 |
| Kay & James Inc | 3599 | D | 818 998-0357 | 10922 |
| Eagle Access Ctrl Systems Inc | 3625 | E | 818 837-7900 | 11319 |
| L3 Technologies Inc | 3663 | D | 818 367-0111 | 11874 |
| ISU Petasys Corp | 3672 | D | 818 833-5800 | 12139 |
| Spectrolab Inc | 3679 | E | 818 365-4611 | 13089 |
| Quallion LLC | 3692 | C | 818 833-2000 | 13163 |
| Acufast Aircraft Products Inc | 3728 | E | 818 365-7077 | 13735 |
| Llamas Plastics Inc | 3728 | C | 818 362-0371 | 13893 |
| TMW Corporation (PA) | 3728 | C | 818 362-5665 | 13975 |
| Dg Engineering Corp (PA) | 3812 | E | 818 364-9024 | 14180 |
| Goldak Inc | 3812 | E | 818 240-2666 | 14195 |
| Providien Machining & Metals LLC | 3841 | D | 818 367-3161 | 15234 |
| Advanced Bionics LLC (HQ) | 3842 | B | 661 362-1400 | 15317 |
| Pacesetter Inc | 3845 | B | 818 493-2715 | 15568 |
| Pacesetter Inc (DH) | 3845 | A | 818 362-6822 | 15570 |
| Valley Metal Supply Inc | 5033 | F | 818 837-6566 | 16493 |
| All Nuts and Snacks Inc | 5145 | E | 818 367-5902 | 17137 |
| American Nuts LLC (HQ) | 5145 | F | 818 364-8855 | 17138 |
| Reyes Coca-Cola Bottling LLC | 5149 | D | 818 362-4307 | 17208 |
| Modern Candle Co Inc | 5199 | E | 323 441-0104 | 17302 |

### TAFT, CA - Kern County

| Company | SIC | EMP | PHONE | ENTRY# |
|---|---|---|---|---|
| Taft Production Company | 1241 | D | 661 765-7194 | 118 |
| Berry Petroleum Company LLC | 1311 | D | 661 769-8820 | 122 |
| Jerry Melton & Sons Cnstr Inc | 1389 | E | 661 765-5546 | 242 |
| Oil-Dri Corporation America | 2842 | E | 661 765-7194 | 5921 |

### TARZANA, CA - Los Angeles County

| Company | SIC | EMP | PHONE | ENTRY# |
|---|---|---|---|---|
| Castro Construction LLC | 1389 | E | 689 220-9145 | 214 |
| One Structural Inc | 1389 | E | 626 252-0778 | 261 |
| Anita Gelato California Inc | 2024 | E | 818 987-4055 | 792 |
| Cgm Inc | 3915 | E | 818 609-7088 | 15709 |
| Extensions Plus Inc | 5087 | E | 818 881-5611 | 16908 |

### TECATE, CA - San Diego County

| Company | SIC | EMP | PHONE | ENTRY# |
|---|---|---|---|---|
| Formula Plastics Inc | 3089 | B | 866 307-1362 | 6829 |
| Fusion Product Mfg Inc | 3544 | D | 619 819-5521 | 9624 |
| Alpha Technics Inc | 3823 | C | 949 250-6578 | 14385 |

### TEHACHAPI, CA - Kern County

| Company | SIC | EMP | PHONE | ENTRY# |
|---|---|---|---|---|
| World Wind Electrical Svcs Inc | 1731 | A | 661 822-4877 | 474 |
| Tehachapi News Inc (PA) | 2711 | E | 661 822-6828 | 4207 |
| Chemtool Incorporated | 2992 | C | 661 823-7190 | 6389 |
| Sierra Technical Services Inc | 3324 | F | 661 823-1092 | 7696 |
| GE Renewables North Amer LLC | 3511 | C | 661 823-6423 | 9311 |
| CMS Products Inc | 3577 | E | 714 424-5520 | 10348 |
| Adaptive Aerospace Corporation | 3728 | E | 661 300-0616 | 13737 |
| Henway Inc | 3965 | F | 661 822-6873 | 15911 |

### TEMECULA, CA - Riverside County

| Company | SIC | EMP | PHONE | ENTRY# |
|---|---|---|---|---|
| Renzoni Vineyards Inc | 0172 | E | 951 302-8466 | 26 |
| Lost Dutchmans Minings Assn (DH) | 1041 | E | 951 699-4749 | 104 |
| West Coast Surfaces Inc | 1752 | E | 951 699-0600 | 507 |
| Canadas Finest Foods Inc | 2037 | D | 951 296-1040 | 1000 |
| Garmon Corporation | 2047 | F | 951 296-6308 | 1096 |
| Garmon Corporation | 2047 | F | 951 296-6308 | 1097 |
| Garmon Corporation | 2047 | F | 951 296-6308 | 1098 |
| Garmon Corporation | 2047 | F | 951 296-6308 | 1099 |
| Garmon Corporation (PA) | 2048 | D | 888 628-8783 | 1127 |
| Akash Winery & Vineyards LLC | 2084 | F | 714 306-9966 | 1474 |
| Bottaia Wines LP | 2084 | E | 951 252-1799 | 1488 |
| Callaway Vineyard & Winery | 2084 | D | 951 676-4001 | 1496 |
| Danza Del Sol Winery Inc | 2084 | E | 951 302-6363 | 1525 |
| Europa Village LLC | 2084 | E | 951 506-1518 | 1558 |
| Falkner Winery Inc | 2084 | D | 951 676-6741 | 1561 |
| Fazeli Vineyards LLC | 2084 | F | 951 303-3366 | 1563 |
| Leonesse Cellars LLC | 2084 | E | 951 302-7601 | 1667 |
| Louidar Inc | 2084 | E | 951 676-5047 | 1669 |
| South Coast Winery Inc | 2084 | E | 951 587-9463 | 1756 |
| Temecula Valley Winery MGT LLC | 2084 | D | 951 699-8896 | 1776 |
| Thornton Winery | 2084 | D | 951 699-0099 | 1784 |
| Wiens Cellars LLC | 2084 | E | 951 694-9892 | 1826 |
| Wilson Creek Wnery Vnyards Inc | 2084 | C | 951 699-9463 | 1828 |
| Top Heavy Clothing Company Inc (PA) | 2321 | D | 951 442-8839 | 2579 |
| Kamm Industries Inc | 2396 | E | 800 317-6253 | 3011 |
| North County Times | 2711 | E | 951 676-4315 | 4173 |
| Village News Inc | 2711 | E | 760 451-3488 | 4217 |
| Inland Empire Media Group Inc | 2721 | E | 951 682-3026 | 4268 |
| Polycraft Inc | 2759 | E | 951 296-0860 | 4939 |

Employee Codes: A=Over 500 employees, B=251-500
C=101-250, D=51-100, E=20-50, F=10-19, G=1-9

## TEMECULA, CA

| Company | SIC | EMP | PHONE | ENTRY# |
|---|---|---|---|---|
| Robinson Printing Inc. | 2759 | E | 951 296-0300 | 4956 |
| Temecula T-Shirt Printers Inc. | 2759 | F | 951 296-0184 | 4972 |
| Abbott Vascular Inc. | 2834 | B | 951 941-2400 | 5291 |
| EMD Millipore Corporation | 2836 | D | 951 676-8080 | 5826 |
| Bostik Inc. | 2891 | E | 951 296-6425 | 6221 |
| W Plastics Inc. | 3081 | E | 800 442-9727 | 6576 |
| Bomatic Inc (DH) | 3089 | E | 909 947-3900 | 6748 |
| Milgard Manufacturing LLC | 3089 | B | 480 763-6000 | 6915 |
| TST Molding LLC | 3089 | E | 951 296-6200 | 7062 |
| Jeb Holdings Corp | 3357 | E | 951 296-9900 | 7788 |
| Marathon Finishing Systems Inc. | 3444 | E | 310 791-5601 | 8496 |
| Sunstone Components Group Inc (HQ) | 3469 | E | 951 296-5010 | 8893 |
| Opti-Forms Inc | 3471 | E | 951 296-1300 | 8992 |
| Temecula Quality Plating Inc. | 3471 | E | 951 296-9875 | 9022 |
| Aard Industries Inc. | 3495 | E | 951 296-0844 | 9195 |
| Scotts Temecula Operations LLC (DH) | 3524 | E | 951 719-1700 | 9400 |
| Pacific Barcode Inc | 3555 | E | 951 587-8717 | 9772 |
| Flowserve Corporation | 3561 | D | 951 296-2464 | 9924 |
| Qc Manufacturing Inc. | 3564 | E | 951 325-6340 | 9995 |
| Inners Tasks LLC | 3571 | E | 951 225-9696 | 10166 |
| Infineon Tech Americas Corp | 3577 | A | 951 375-6008 | 10381 |
| Aquamor LLC (PA) | 3589 | D | 951 541-9517 | 10539 |
| Axeon Water Technologies | 3589 | D | 760 723-5417 | 10541 |
| CM Brewing Technologies LLC | 3589 | F | 888 391-9990 | 10552 |
| Nimbus Water Systems | 3589 | F | | 10588 |
| 3-D Precision Machine Inc | 3599 | E | 951 296-5449 | 10639 |
| Long Machine Inc | 3599 | E | 951 296-0194 | 10946 |
| Motorola Sltons Cnnctivity Inc (HQ) | 3663 | D | 951 719-2100 | 11899 |
| Opto 22 | 3679 | C | 951 695-3000 | 13057 |
| Thompson Magnetics Inc. | 3679 | E | 951 676-0243 | 13109 |
| Douglas Technologies Group Inc | 3714 | E | 760 758-5560 | 13488 |
| Ice Management Systems Inc. | 3728 | E | 951 676-2751 | 13867 |
| Bear State Water Heating LLC | 3822 | F | 951 269-3753 | 14355 |
| Tesco Controls Inc. | 3825 | D | 916 395-8800 | 14593 |
| EMD Millipore Corporation | 3826 | D | 951 676-8080 | 14660 |
| Quality Control Solutions Inc. | 3829 | F | 951 676-1616 | 14911 |
| Transducer Techniques LLC | 3829 | E | 951 719-3965 | 14936 |
| Abbott Vascular Inc. | 3841 | A | 951 914-2400 | 14943 |
| Brightwater Medical Inc | 3841 | E | 951 290-3410 | 15021 |
| Tearlab Corporation | 3841 | E | 858 455-6006 | 15277 |
| Isomedix Operations Inc. | 3842 | D | 951 694-9340 | 15367 |
| Medline Industries LP | 3842 | E | 951 296-2600 | 15378 |
| Paulson Manufacturing Corp (PA) | 3842 | D | 951 676-2451 | 15393 |
| Artificial Grass Liquidators | 3999 | E | 951 677-3377 | 16090 |
| Phs / Mwa | 4581 | C | 951 695-1008 | 16302 |
| Normont Hydraulic Sls Svc Inc. | 5084 | E | 951 676-2155 | 16830 |
| R R Donnelley & Sons Company | 5112 | D | 951 296-2890 | 16994 |
| Advantage Chemical LLC | 5169 | E | 951 225-4631 | 17237 |
| Emser Tile LLC | 5211 | E | 951 296-3671 | 17329 |
| Karl Strauss Brewing Company | 5812 | F | 951 225-7960 | 17590 |
| Applied Statistics & MGT Inc. | 7372 | D | 951 699-4600 | 18057 |
| Empower Software Tech LLC | 7372 | F | 951 672-6257 | 18278 |
| Deans Certified Welding Inc. | 7692 | F | 760 728-0292 | 19189 |
| Hqe Systems Inc. | 8748 | D | 800 967-3036 | 19560 |

## TEMPLE CITY, CA - Los Angeles County

| Company | SIC | EMP | PHONE | ENTRY# |
|---|---|---|---|---|
| California Flexrake Corp | 3423 | E | 626 443-4026 | 7948 |
| D D Wire Co Inc (PA) | 3441 | E | 626 442-0459 | 8130 |
| Jon Davler Inc. | 5999 | E | 626 941-6558 | 17710 |

## TEMPLETON, CA - San Luis Obispo County

| Company | SIC | EMP | PHONE | ENTRY# |
|---|---|---|---|---|
| Plasvacc USA Inc. | 3841 | F | 805 434-0321 | 15227 |

## TERRA BELLA, CA - Tulare County

| Company | SIC | EMP | PHONE | ENTRY# |
|---|---|---|---|---|
| Tuff Stuff Products | 2821 | B | 559 535-5778 | 5215 |
| Weldcraft Industries Inc. | 3523 | F | 559 784-4322 | 9395 |
| Touchstone Pistachio Co LLC | 3556 | C | 559 535-0110 | 9821 |
| Setton Pstchio Terra Bella Inc (HQ) | 5149 | F | 559 535-6050 | 17212 |

## THERMAL, CA - Riverside County

| Company | SIC | EMP | PHONE | ENTRY# |
|---|---|---|---|---|
| Spates Fabricators Inc. | 2439 | D | 760 397-4122 | 3318 |

## THOUSAND OAKS, CA - Ventura County

| Company | SIC | EMP | PHONE | ENTRY# |
|---|---|---|---|---|
| Natren Inc. | 2099 | D | 805 371-4737 | 2290 |
| August Hat Company Inc (PA) | 2353 | E | 805 983-4651 | 2841 |
| Sage Publications Inc (PA) | 2731 | C | 805 499-0721 | 4345 |
| Midnight Manufacturing LLC | 2833 | E | 714 833-6130 | 5248 |
| Amgen USA Inc (HQ) | 2834 | D | 805 447-1000 | 5318 |
| Instacure Healing Products | 2834 | E | 818 222-9600 | 5497 |
| Amgen Inc (PA) | 2836 | A | 805 447-1000 | 5793 |
| Atara Biotherapeutics Inc (PA) | 2836 | E | 805 623-4211 | 5801 |
| Fujifilm Dsynth Btchnlgies Cal | 2836 | E | 914 789-8100 | 5830 |
| Fujifilm Dsynth Btchnlgies USA | 2836 | C | 805 699-5579 | 5831 |
| Ale USA Inc. | 3663 | A | 818 880-3500 | 11802 |
| Custom Sensors & Tech Inc (HQ) | 3679 | A | 805 716-0322 | 12952 |
| Kavlico Corporation (DH) | 3679 | A | 805 523-2000 | 13016 |
| Maple Imaging LLC (HQ) | 3679 | E | 805 373-4545 | 13032 |
| Smiths Interconnect Inc. | 3679 | D | 805 267-0100 | 13086 |
| Teledyne Technologies Inc (PA) | 3679 | C | 805 373-4545 | 13105 |
| Teledyne Lecroy Inc. | 3825 | E | 434 984-4500 | 14591 |
| Teledyne Redlake Masd LLC (DH) | 3826 | E | 805 373-4545 | 14730 |
| BEI North America LLC (DH) | 3829 | C | 805 716-0642 | 14849 |
| Carros Sensors Systems Co LLC (DH) | 3829 | E | 805 968-0782 | 14856 |
| Baxalta US Inc. | 3841 | A | 805 498-8664 | 14992 |
| Implant Direct Sybron Mfg LLC | 3843 | C | 818 444-3300 | 15459 |
| Easton Hockey Inc. | 3949 | A | 818 782-6445 | 15805 |
| Ultraglas Inc. | 5039 | E | 818 772-7744 | 16496 |
| Easton Baseball / Softball Inc. | 5091 | F | 800 632-7866 | 16934 |
| Sensata Technologies Inc. | 7379 | D | 805 716-0322 | 19044 |

## THOUSAND PALMS, CA - Riverside County

| Company | SIC | EMP | PHONE | ENTRY# |
|---|---|---|---|---|
| Superior Ready Mix Concrete LP | 3273 | D | 760 343-3418 | 7513 |
| Koolfog Inc (PA) | 3585 | F | 760 321-9203 | 10504 |
| Microcool | 3823 | F | 760 322-1111 | 14434 |
| Therapeutic Industries Inc. | 3841 | F | 760 343-2502 | 15281 |

## TIPTON, CA - Tulare County

| Company | SIC | EMP | PHONE | ENTRY# |
|---|---|---|---|---|
| Sunkist Growers Inc. | 0723 | E | 909 983-9811 | 87 |
| Sunkist Growers Inc. | 5148 | F | 559 752-4256 | 17172 |

## TOLUCA LAKE, CA - Los Angeles County

| Company | SIC | EMP | PHONE | ENTRY# |
|---|---|---|---|---|
| Northwestern Inc. | 2431 | E | 818 786-1581 | 3167 |

## TOPANGA, CA - Los Angeles County

| Company | SIC | EMP | PHONE | ENTRY# |
|---|---|---|---|---|
| Teeki | 5137 | F | 323 835-6397 | 17102 |

## TORRANCE, CA - Los Angeles County

| Company | SIC | EMP | PHONE | ENTRY# |
|---|---|---|---|---|
| Magnetron Power Inventions Inc. | 1382 | E | 310 462-6970 | 191 |
| Dicaperl Corporation (DH) | 1499 | D | 610 667-6640 | 338 |
| Vector Resources Inc (PA) | 1731 | C | 310 436-1000 | 473 |
| Excelpro Inc | 2022 | F | 323 415-8544 | 714 |
| Naturalife Eco Vite Labs | 2023 | D | 310 370-1563 | 771 |
| Shine Food Inc (PA) | 2032 | E | 310 329-3829 | 869 |
| Shine Food Inc. | 2038 | D | 310 533-6010 | 1046 |
| Inaba Foods (usa) Inc. | 2047 | E | 310 818-2270 | 1102 |
| Manhattan Confectioners Inc. | 2064 | F | 310 257-0260 | 1318 |
| Advanced Fresh Cncpts Frnchise | 2092 | D | 310 604-3200 | 2046 |
| Asiana Cuisine Enterprises Inc. | 2099 | A | 310 327-2223 | 2132 |
| Morinaga Nutritional Foods Inc (HQ) | 2099 | F | 310 787-0200 | 2286 |
| Thg Brands Inc. | 2099 | E | 844 694-8327 | 2373 |
| Student Sports LLC | 2273 | F | 310 791-1142 | 2522 |
| Just For Fun Inc. | 2321 | E | 310 320-1327 | 2575 |
| Textile Unlimited Corporation (PA) | 2321 | D | 310 263-7400 | 2578 |
| Image Solutions Apparel Inc. | 2326 | C | 310 464-8991 | 2595 |
| Alpinestars Usa | 2331 | D | 310 891-0222 | 2654 |
| Nothing To Wear Inc. | 2331 | F | 310 328-0408 | 2684 |
| Nothing To Wear Inc (PA) | 2331 | F | 310 328-0408 | 2685 |
| Ys Garments LLC (HQ) | 2331 | F | 310 631-4955 | 2696 |
| Dakine Equipment LLC | 2339 | E | 424 276-3618 | 2750 |
| Tcw Trends Inc. | 2339 | F | 310 533-5177 | 2813 |
| Micronova Manufacturing Inc. | 2392 | E | 310 784-6990 | 2939 |
| A-Aztec Rents & Sells Inc (PA) | 2394 | C | 310 347-3010 | 2965 |
| Doug Mockett & Company Inc. | 2511 | D | 310 318-2491 | 3440 |
| French Tradition Inc (PA) | 2511 | F | 310 719-9977 | 3442 |
| Virco Mfg Corporation (PA) | 2531 | D | 310 533-0474 | 3642 |
| Field Manufacturing Corp (PA) | 2542 | E | 310 781-9292 | 3687 |
| Union Carbide Corporation | 2631 | E | 310 214-5300 | 3810 |
| Takuyo Corporation | 2711 | F | 310 782-6927 | 4205 |
| Bbm Fairway Inc (PA) | 2721 | C | | 4231 |
| Bobit Business Media Inc. | 2721 | C | 310 533-2400 | 4232 |
| Minority Success Pubg Group | 2721 | E | 310 736-2462 | 4278 |
| Manson Western LLC | 2731 | C | 424 201-8800 | 4335 |
| Classic Litho & Design Inc. | 2752 | E | 310 224-5200 | 4552 |
| R R Donnelley & Sons Company | 2759 | E | 310 516-3100 | 4948 |
| Retail Print Media Inc. | 2759 | E | 424 488-6950 | 4953 |
| Sirena Incorporated | 2759 | F | 866 548-5353 | 4961 |
| Pel Manufacturing and Lsg Corp | 2789 | F | 310 530-7145 | 5013 |
| Arkema Inc. | 2812 | E | 310 214-5327 | 5029 |
| Jci Jones Chemicals Inc. | 2812 | E | 310 523-1629 | 5033 |
| Messer LLC | 2813 | D | 310 533-8394 | 5052 |
| Americas Styrenics LLC | 2821 | D | 424 488-3757 | 5136 |
| Bachem Americas Inc. | 2834 | E | 424 347-5600 | 5352 |
| Bachem Americas Inc (DH) | 2836 | E | 310 784-4440 | 5805 |
| Bachem Americas Inc. | 2836 | E | 310 784-4440 | 5806 |
| Bachem Americas Inc. | 2836 | E | 310 539-4171 | 5807 |
| Bachem Bioscience Inc. | 2836 | E | 310 784-7322 | 5808 |

# GEOGRAPHIC SECTION — TORRANCE, CA

| Company | SIC | EMP | PHONE | ENTRY# |
|---|---|---|---|---|
| Colonial Enterprises Inc | 2844 | E | 909 822-8700 | 5955 |
| Nyx Los Angeles Inc | 2844 | C | 323 869-9420 | 6012 |
| Commerce Coating Services Inc | 2851 | D | 310 345-1979 | 6076 |
| Mercfuel LLC (HQ) | 2869 | F | 281 442-3000 | 6152 |
| Teledyne Reynolds Inc | 2892 | C | 310 823-5491 | 6252 |
| Lg Nanoh2o LLC | 2899 | E | 424 218-4000 | 6304 |
| Medical Chemical Corporation | 2899 | E | 310 787-6800 | 6309 |
| Prestone Products Corporation | 2899 | E | 424 271-4836 | 6318 |
| Air Products and Chemicals Inc | 2911 | F | 310 212-2800 | 6331 |
| Torrance Refining Company LLC | 2911 | A | 310 212-2800 | 6354 |
| G F Cole Corporation (PA) | 3053 | F | 310 320-0601 | 6447 |
| Momentum Management LLC | 3069 | F | 310 329-2599 | 6516 |
| Kakuichi America Inc | 3084 | D | 310 539-1590 | 6599 |
| Kepner Plas Fabricators Inc | 3089 | E | 562 543-4472 | 6885 |
| Smart LLC | 3089 | E | 866 822-3670 | 7030 |
| Totex Manufacturing Inc | 3089 | D | 310 326-2028 | 7056 |
| Carley (PA) | 3229 | C | 310 325-8474 | 7192 |
| Catalina Pacific Concrete | 3273 | E | 310 532-4600 | 7416 |
| United States Gypsum Company | 3275 | D | 908 232-8900 | 7532 |
| Lisi Aerospace North Amer Inc | 3324 | A | 310 326-8110 | 7689 |
| Howmet Aerospace Inc | 3334 | B | 212 836-2674 | 7706 |
| Broadata Communications Inc | 3357 | E | 310 530-1416 | 7775 |
| Alliedsignal Arospc Svc Corp (HQ) | 3369 | E | 310 323-9500 | 7857 |
| Fun Properties Inc | 3423 | E | 310 787-4500 | 7953 |
| Products Engineering Corp | 3423 | E | 310 787-4500 | 7964 |
| Kuz & Kirb | 3425 | E | 310 539-6116 | 7970 |
| Santec Inc | 3432 | E | 310 542-0063 | 8056 |
| Torrance Steel Window Co Inc | 3442 | E | 310 328-9181 | 8293 |
| Showerdoordirect LLC | 3444 | F | 310 327-8060 | 8572 |
| Universal Screw Products | 3451 | F | 310 371-1170 | 8736 |
| Hi-Shear Corporation (DH) | 3452 | A | 310 326-8110 | 8757 |
| KB Delta Inc | 3469 | E | 310 530-1539 | 8856 |
| Kopykake Enterprises Inc (PA) | 3469 | F | 310 373-8906 | 8858 |
| Plasma Technology Incorporated (PA) | 3479 | D | 310 320-3373 | 9108 |
| Roberts Research Laboratory | 3489 | F | 310 303-7310 | 9140 |
| Storm Manufacturing Group Inc | 3491 | D | 310 326-8287 | 9162 |
| Magnetic Component Engrg LLC (PA) | 3499 | D | 310 784-3100 | 9292 |
| Storm Industries Inc (PA) | 3523 | E | 310 534-5232 | 9384 |
| American Ultraviolet West Inc | 3535 | E | 310 784-2930 | 9480 |
| Barranca Holdings Ltd | 3545 | C | 310 523-5867 | 9661 |
| Mk Diamond Products Inc (PA) | 3546 | D | 310 539-5221 | 9713 |
| Belhome Inc | 3548 | E | 310 618-8437 | 9722 |
| Creative Pathways Inc | 3548 | E | 310 530-1965 | 9724 |
| Winther Technologies Inc (PA) | 3548 | E | 310 618-8437 | 9732 |
| One Touch Solutions Inc | 3555 | F | 310 320-6868 | 9771 |
| Calpack Foods LLC | 3556 | E | 310 320-0141 | 9781 |
| Shaver Specialty Co Inc | 3556 | E | 310 370-6941 | 9816 |
| Industrial Dynamics Co Ltd (PA) | 3559 | C | 310 325-5633 | 9867 |
| Camfil Farr Inc | 3564 | E | 973 616-7300 | 9981 |
| Sun Industries Corporation | 3564 | E | 310 782-1188 | 9998 |
| Bnl Technologies Inc | 3572 | E | 310 320-7272 | 10227 |
| Bixolon America Inc | 3577 | E | 858 764-4580 | 10336 |
| Lynn Products Inc | 3577 | A | 310 530-5966 | 10402 |
| Topper Manufacturing Corp | 3589 | F | 310 375-5000 | 10607 |
| Aeroliant Manufacturing Inc | 3599 | E | 310 257-1903 | 10689 |
| Beranek LLC | 3599 | E | 310 328-9094 | 10748 |
| Century Parts Inc | 3599 | F | 310 328-0281 | 10770 |
| Ely Co Inc | 3599 | E | 310 539-5831 | 10825 |
| Laserod Technologies LLC | 3599 | E | 310 328-5869 | 10942 |
| Ralph E Ames Machine Works | 3599 | E | 310 328-8523 | 11067 |
| Sonsray Inc | 3599 | E | 323 585-1271 | 11118 |
| Weber Drilling Co Inc | 3599 | E | 310 670-7708 | 11185 |
| Sea Electric LLC | 3621 | E | 424 376-3660 | 11285 |
| Moog Inc | 3625 | B | 310 533-1178 | 11335 |
| Breville Usa Inc | 3639 | E | 310 755-3000 | 11417 |
| Irtronix Inc | 3641 | E | 310 787-1100 | 11425 |
| Aero-Electric Connector Inc (PA) | 3643 | B | 310 618-3737 | 11438 |
| Emp Connectors Inc | 3643 | E | 310 533-6799 | 11452 |
| Lyncole Grunding Solutions LLC | 3643 | E | 310 214-4000 | 11463 |
| Zo Motors North America LLC | 3647 | E | 310 792-7077 | 11577 |
| All Access Stging Prdctons Inc (PA) | 3648 | E | 310 784-2464 | 11578 |
| Pelican Products Inc (PA) | 3648 | C | 310 326-4700 | 11618 |
| Funai Corporation Inc | 3651 | D | 201 727-4560 | 11662 |
| Marshall Electronics Inc (PA) | 3651 | E | 310 333-0606 | 11675 |
| Pioneer Speakers Inc | 3651 | A | 310 952-2000 | 11688 |
| Rock-Ola Manufacturing Corp | 3651 | E | 310 328-1306 | 11692 |
| Panasonic Disc Manufacturing Corpor | 3652 | C | 310 783-4800 | 11739 |
| Antcom Corporation | 3663 | E | 310 782-1076 | 11810 |
| CPI Satcom & Antenna Tech Inc | 3663 | C | 310 539-6704 | 11837 |
| Escape Communications Inc | 3663 | F | 310 997-1300 | 11853 |
| Hadrian Automation Inc | 3663 | D | 503 807-4490 | 11861 |
| Lenntek Corporation | 3663 | E | 310 534-2738 | 11882 |
| Mainline Equipment Inc | 3663 | D | 800 444-2288 | 11887 |
| Navcom Technology Inc (HQ) | 3663 | D | 310 381-2000 | 11901 |
| Pacific Wave Systems Inc | 3663 | E | 714 893-0152 | 11913 |
| Global Comm Semiconductors LLC | 3674 | E | 310 530-7274 | 12447 |
| Ledtronics Inc (PA) | 3674 | E | 310 534-1505 | 12530 |
| Trident Space & Defense LLC | 3674 | E | 310 214-5500 | 12773 |
| Coast/Dvnced Chip Mgnetics Inc | 3677 | E | 310 370-8188 | 12833 |
| Conesys Inc | 3678 | D | 310 212-0065 | 12872 |
| J - T E C H | 3678 | C | 310 533-6700 | 12885 |
| Onshore Technologies Inc | 3679 | E | 310 533-4888 | 13056 |
| Sure Power Inc | 3679 | F | 310 542-8561 | 13096 |
| Western Digital | 3679 | D | 510 557-7553 | 13122 |
| Czv Inc | 3711 | D | 424 603-1450 | 13347 |
| Canoo Inc (PA) | 3714 | E | 424 271-2144 | 13469 |
| Edelbrock LLC | 3714 | E | 310 781-2290 | 13492 |
| Motorcar Parts of America Inc (PA) | 3714 | A | 310 212-7910 | 13543 |
| US Hybrid Corporation (HQ) | 3714 | E | 310 212-1200 | 13599 |
| Garrett Transportation I Inc (HQ) | 3724 | E | 973 455-2000 | 13708 |
| Honeywell International Inc | 3724 | A | 310 323-9500 | 13710 |
| Ace Clearwater Enterprises Inc (PA) | 3728 | D | 310 323-2140 | 13731 |
| Dasco Engineering Corp | 3728 | C | 310 326-2277 | 13820 |
| Quality Forming LLC | 3728 | E | 310 539-2855 | 13933 |
| Robinson Helicopter Co Inc (PA) | 3728 | A | 310 539-0508 | 13935 |
| Microcosm Inc | 3764 | E | 310 539-2306 | 14102 |
| Hall Associates Racg Pdts Inc | 3799 | F | 310 326-4111 | 14130 |
| General Forming Corporation | 3812 | E | 310 326-0624 | 14192 |
| Intellisense Systems Inc | 3812 | C | 310 320-1827 | 14196 |
| Moog Inc | 3812 | B | 310 533-1178 | 14222 |
| Stellant Systems Inc (DH) | 3812 | A | 310 517-6000 | 14310 |
| Fischer Cstm Cmmunications Inc (PA) | 3825 | E | 310 303-3300 | 14528 |
| Nearfield Systems Inc | 3825 | D | 310 525-7000 | 14560 |
| Pulse Instruments | 3825 | E | 310 515-5330 | 14575 |
| Phenomenex Inc (HQ) | 3826 | C | 310 212-0555 | 14704 |
| Luminit LLC | 3827 | E | 310 320-1066 | 14796 |
| Z C & R Coating For Optics Inc | 3827 | E | 310 381-3060 | 14834 |
| Proprietary Controls Systems | 3829 | E | 310 303-3600 | 14910 |
| Axiom Medical Incorporated | 3841 | E | 310 533-9020 | 14987 |
| Igenomix Usa Inc | 3841 | E | 818 919-1657 | 15113 |
| Lisi Aerospace | 3841 | E | 310 326-8110 | 15150 |
| Medicool Inc | 3841 | F | 310 782-2200 | 15169 |
| Finest Hour Holdings Inc | 3842 | E | 310 533-9966 | 15347 |
| Rapiscan Systems Inc (HQ) | 3844 | C | 310 978-1457 | 15508 |
| Younger Mfg Co (PA) | 3851 | B | 310 783-1533 | 15625 |
| Stewart Filmscreen Corp (PA) | 3861 | E | 310 784-5300 | 15667 |
| Alex and Ani LLC | 3911 | F | 310 214-3587 | 15678 |
| Crislu Corp | 3911 | E | 310 322-3444 | 15689 |
| Dreamgear LLC | 3944 | E | 310 222-5522 | 15745 |
| Elro Manufacturing Company (PA) | 3993 | E | 310 380-7444 | 15967 |
| Encore Image Group Inc (PA) | 3993 | D | 310 534-7500 | 15969 |
| George P Johnson Company | 3993 | E | 310 965-4300 | 15983 |
| Signtronix Inc | 3993 | D | 310 534-7500 | 16043 |
| Learning Resources Inc | 3999 | E | 800 995-4436 | 16167 |
| Tre Milano LLC | 3999 | E | 310 260-8888 | 16257 |
| American Honda Motor Co Inc (HQ) | 5012 | A | 310 783-2000 | 16371 |
| Virco Inc (HQ) | 5021 | E | 310 533-0474 | 16419 |
| New Generation Engrg Cnstr Inc | 5032 | E | 424 329-3950 | 16478 |
| Elers Medical Usa Inc | 5047 | E | 858 336-4900 | 16582 |
| Pioneer North America Inc (DH) | 5064 | F | 310 952-2000 | 16684 |
| Pioneer North America Inc | 5064 | C | 310 952-2000 | 16685 |
| Quinstar Technology Inc | 5065 | D | 310 320-1111 | 16731 |
| Sharp Industries Inc (PA) | 5084 | E | 310 370-5990 | 16841 |
| Sweis Inc (PA) | 5087 | D | 310 375-0558 | 16910 |
| Pentel of America Ltd (DH) | 5112 | C | 310 320-3831 | 16992 |
| Weckerle Cosmetics Usa Inc | 5122 | E | 310 328-7000 | 17055 |
| Frito-Lay North America Inc | 5145 | E | 310 224-5600 | 17144 |
| Jos Candies LLC | 5145 | F | 800 770-1946 | 17147 |
| Meg Company Inc (PA) | 5199 | F | 310 372-8033 | 17301 |
| Rockwell Enterprises Inc | 5199 | E | 626 796-1511 | 17309 |
| Jessie Lord Bakery LLC | 5461 | E | 310 533-6010 | 17413 |
| General Motors LLC | 5511 | E | 313 556-5000 | 17439 |
| Toyota Logistics Services Inc (DH) | 5511 | C | 310 468-4000 | 17443 |
| Enagic Usa Inc (PA) | 5963 | D | 310 542-7700 | 17679 |
| Star Link Company Inc | 7336 | E | 310 787-8299 | 17840 |
| Resource Collection Inc | 7349 | E | 310 219-3272 | 17849 |
| BQE Software Inc | 7372 | D | 310 602-4020 | 18124 |
| Epirus Inc | 7372 | E | 310 620-8678 | 18287 |
| Nc4 Soltra LLC | 7372 | D | 408 489-5579 | 18571 |
| CCH Incorporated | 7374 | A | 310 800-9800 | 19005 |
| Ocs America Inc (DH) | 7389 | E | 310 417-0650 | 19112 |
| Technology Training Corp (PA) | 7389 | E | 310 320-8110 | 19138 |
| Singer Vehicle Design LLC (PA) | 7549 | C | 213 592-2728 | 19170 |
| Aeroworx Inc | 7699 | E | 310 891-0300 | 19239 |
| Redman Equipment & Mfg Co | 7699 | E | 310 329-1134 | 19278 |
| Insite Digestive Health Care | 8011 | E | 626 817-2900 | 19318 |

Employee Codes: A=Over 500 employees, B=251-500
C=101-250, D=51-100, E=20-50, F=10-19, G=1-9

## TORRANCE, CA

| | SIC | EMP | PHONE | ENTRY# |
|---|---|---|---|---|
| Polypeptide Laboratories Inc (DH) | 8071 | E | 310 782-3569 | 19329 |
| Mercury Mission Systems LLC | 8731 | E | 310 320-3088 | 19467 |
| Opto-Knowledge Systems Inc | 8731 | E | 310 756-0520 | 19470 |

### TRABUCO CANYON, CA - Orange County

| | SIC | EMP | PHONE | ENTRY# |
|---|---|---|---|---|
| Quantumsphere Inc | 3399 | F | 714 545-6266 | 7911 |

### TRACY, CA - San Joaquin County

| | SIC | EMP | PHONE | ENTRY# |
|---|---|---|---|---|
| Teichert Inc | 1442 | D | 209 832-4150 | 322 |
| Tracy Renewable Energy | 1542 | E | 831 224-2513 | 371 |
| American Custom Meats LLC | 2013 | D | 209 839-8800 | 630 |
| Leprino Foods Company | 2022 | B | 209 835-8340 | 726 |
| Olive Musco Products Inc (PA) | 2033 | C | 866 965-4837 | 914 |
| Keebler Company | 2052 | E | 209 836-0302 | 1279 |
| Golden State Vintners (PA) | 2084 | F | 707 254-4900 | 1591 |
| Freshrealm Inc | 2099 | B | 800 264-1297 | 2209 |
| Hand Crfted Dutchman Doors Inc | 2431 | E | 209 833-7378 | 3143 |
| Pinnacle Stair Group Inc | 2431 | E | 209 832-3200 | 3178 |
| Barbosa Cabinets Inc | 2434 | B | 209 836-2501 | 3220 |
| Volumetric Bldg Companies LLC | 2439 | E | 623 236-5322 | 3321 |
| Jose Garcia Astorga | 2448 | E | 559 500-9338 | 3348 |
| Vbc Tracy LLC (PA) | 2452 | E | 215 259-7509 | 3399 |
| Leggett & Platt Incorporated | 2515 | F | 209 839-8230 | 3531 |
| Zinus Inc (HQ) | 2515 | E | 925 417-2100 | 3548 |
| Menasha Packaging Company LLC | 2653 | E | 951 660-5361 | 3867 |
| Tracy Press Inc | 2711 | E | 209 835-3030 | 4213 |
| Olin Chlor Alkali Logistics | 2812 | C | 209 835-5424 | 5035 |
| Dynatect Ro-Lab Inc | 3061 | E | 262 786-1500 | 6473 |
| Future Foam Inc | 3086 | F | 209 832-1886 | 6642 |
| Gloriann Farms Inc | 3086 | E | 209 221-7121 | 6644 |
| Aubin Industries Inc | 3087 | F | 800 324-0051 | 6672 |
| Altium Packaging LLC | 3089 | D | 209 820-1700 | 6709 |
| Mother Lode Plas Molding Inc | 3089 | D | 209 532-5146 | 6924 |
| Glassfab Tempering Svcs Inc (PA) | 3211 | D | 209 229-1061 | 7169 |
| Basalite Building Products LLC | 3271 | E | 209 833-3670 | 7293 |
| Madruga Iron Works Inc | 3441 | E | 209 832-7003 | 8175 |
| Nwpc LLC | 3443 | D | 209 836-5050 | 8323 |
| San-I-Pak Pacific Inc | 3443 | D | 209 836-2310 | 8334 |
| Contract Metal Products Inc | 3444 | E | 510 979-0000 | 8416 |
| Lynx Enterprises Inc | 3444 | C | 209 833-3400 | 8491 |
| Ameron International Corp | 3494 | D | 209 836-5050 | 9181 |
| Crystal Blue Inc | 3499 | E | 510 783-5888 | 9280 |
| Drilling & Trenching Sup Inc (PA) | 3545 | F | 510 895-1650 | 9676 |
| West Coast Cryogenics Inc | 3559 | E | 800 657-0545 | 9911 |
| Polycom Inc | 3571 | D | 209 830-5083 | 10196 |
| Td Synnex Corporation | 3571 | F | 510 656-3333 | 10210 |
| All-In Machining LLC | 3599 | F | 209 839-8672 | 10698 |
| Feral Productions Inc | 3599 | E | 510 791-5392 | 10836 |
| Process Specialties Inc | 3674 | E | 209 832-1344 | 12640 |
| American Trck Trlr Bdy Co Inc (PA) | 3713 | E | 209 836-8985 | 13400 |
| Lockheed Martin Corporation | 3721 | B | 408 756-3008 | 13678 |
| Action Fire Fab & Supply Inc | 3829 | E | 209 834-3460 | 14839 |
| Top Shelf Manufacturing LLC | 3841 | F | 209 834-8185 | 15286 |
| Medline Industries LP | 3842 | D | 209 585-3260 | 15377 |
| Finis Inc (PA) | 3949 | E | 925 454-0111 | 15812 |
| AP Unlimited Corporation | 5131 | F | 209 834-0287 | 17058 |
| Park Avenue Cleaners Inc | 7212 | E | 209 832-3706 | 17765 |
| Skyview Aviation Llc | 7359 | E | 209 830-7666 | 17862 |
| Clonetab Inc | 7372 | E | 209 292-5663 | 18176 |

### TRAVER, CA - Tulare County

| | SIC | EMP | PHONE | ENTRY# |
|---|---|---|---|---|
| Associated Feed & Supply Co | 2048 | C | 209 664-3323 | 1119 |
| Maf Industries Inc (HQ) | 3565 | D | 559 897-2905 | 10026 |

### TRONA, CA - San Bernardino County

| | SIC | EMP | PHONE | ENTRY# |
|---|---|---|---|---|
| Searles Valley Minerals Inc | 1479 | C | 760 372-2259 | 334 |
| Searles Valley Minerals Inc | 1479 | C | 760 672-2053 | 335 |

### TRUCKEE, CA - Nevada County

| | SIC | EMP | PHONE | ENTRY# |
|---|---|---|---|---|
| Teichert Inc | 1442 | C | 530 587-3811 | 321 |
| Horvath Holdings Inc | 2241 | F | 530 587-4700 | 2453 |
| Recycled Spaces Inc | 2519 | F | 530 587-3394 | 3557 |
| Propertyradar Inc | 7372 | E | 530 550-8801 | 18704 |
| Software Licensing Consultants | 7372 | E | 925 371-1277 | 18807 |

### TUJUNGA, CA - Los Angeles County

| | SIC | EMP | PHONE | ENTRY# |
|---|---|---|---|---|
| American Foothill Pubg Co Inc | 2759 | E | 818 352-7878 | 4840 |
| David Kopf Instruments | 3841 | E | 818 352-3274 | 15063 |
| Vons Companies Inc | 5411 | C | 818 353-4917 | 17393 |

### TULARE, CA - Tulare County

| | SIC | EMP | PHONE | ENTRY# |
|---|---|---|---|---|
| Turnupseed Electric Service | 1731 | D | 559 686-1541 | 470 |
| Golden Valley Dairy Products | 2022 | E | 559 687-1188 | 716 |
| Lactalis Heritage Dairy Inc | 2022 | C | 559 685-0790 | 723 |
| Land OLakes Inc | 2022 | D | 559 687-8287 | 724 |
| Saputo Cheese USA Inc | 2022 | B | 559 687-8411 | 734 |
| Saputo Cheese USA Inc | 2022 | B | 559 687-9999 | 736 |
| Langston Companies Inc | 2674 | C | 559 688-3839 | 3991 |
| Excelsior Metals LLC | 3441 | E | 559 346-0932 | 8136 |
| Dowdys Sales and Services Inc | 3523 | F | 559 688-6973 | 9351 |
| Valmetal Tulare Inc | 3523 | D | 559 685-0340 | 9390 |

### TUPMAN, CA - Kern County

| | SIC | EMP | PHONE | ENTRY# |
|---|---|---|---|---|
| Midstream Energy Partners USA | 1231 | E | 661 765-4087 | 115 |

### TURLOCK, CA - Stanislaus County

| | SIC | EMP | PHONE | ENTRY# |
|---|---|---|---|---|
| Valley Milk LLC | 0241 | D | 209 410-6701 | 60 |
| Gemperle Enterprises | 0252 | D | 209 667-2651 | 63 |
| Valley Fresh Foods Inc | 0252 | E | 209 669-5600 | 65 |
| Valley Fresh Foods Inc (PA) | 0252 | F | 209 669-5600 | 67 |
| Tanco Inc | 1711 | E | 209 523-8365 | 438 |
| Thorsens-Norquist Inc | 1761 | D | 209 524-5296 | 516 |
| Clausen Meat Company Inc | 2011 | E | 209 667-8690 | 591 |
| Foster Poultry Farms | 2015 | D | 209 668-5922 | 686 |
| California Dairies Inc | 2021 | C | 209 656-1942 | 704 |
| Dairy Farmers America Inc | 2022 | E | 209 667-9627 | 711 |
| Hilmar Cheese Company Inc | 2022 | B | 209 667-6076 | 718 |
| Super Store Industries | 2024 | D | 209 668-2100 | 816 |
| Golden State Mixing Inc | 2026 | E | 209 632-3656 | 836 |
| Jackson-Mitchell Inc (PA) | 2026 | E | 209 667-0786 | 840 |
| Sensient Dehydrated Flavors Company | 2034 | A | 209 667-2777 | 964 |
| Associated Feed & Supply Co (PA) | 2048 | E | 209 667-2708 | 1118 |
| Blue Diamond Growers | 2099 | C | 209 604-1501 | 2144 |
| Sensient Ntral Ingredients LLC (HQ) | 2099 | E | 209 667-2777 | 2350 |
| Superb Farms | 2099 | C | 209 633-3600 | 2366 |
| International Wood Industries Inc | 2421 | E | 209 632-3300 | 3071 |
| Superior Kitchen Cabinets Inc | 2434 | E | 209 247-0097 | 3271 |
| Rm Pallets Inc | 2448 | E | 209 632-9887 | 3357 |
| Turlock Journal | 2711 | F | 209 634-9141 | 4215 |
| Linde Gas & Equipment Inc | 2813 | E | 800 225-8247 | 5046 |
| Preserve Inc | 2842 | E | 800 995-1607 | 5926 |
| Calaveras Materials Inc | 3273 | C | 209 634-4931 | 7409 |
| Adtek Inc | 3441 | E | 209 634-0300 | 8088 |
| Cal-Coast Manufacturing Inc | 3444 | F | 209 634-9026 | 8400 |
| Volk Enterprises Inc | 3496 | D | 209 632-3826 | 9241 |
| Js Trucking Inc | 3537 | E | 209 252-0007 | 9527 |
| Professional Lumper Svc Inc | 3537 | E | 209 613-5397 | 9533 |
| Lock-N-Stitch Inc | 3599 | E | 209 632-2345 | 10945 |
| Beall Trailers of California Inc | 3715 | E | 209 669-7151 | 13612 |
| Rose Joaquin Inc | 5084 | F | 209 632-0616 | 16839 |
| Tree Nuts LLC | 5145 | E | 209 669-6400 | 17151 |
| Don Pedro Pump LLC | 7699 | E | 209 632-3161 | 19252 |
| Central Valley Gaming LLC | 7999 | E | 209 668-1010 | 19313 |

### TUSTIN, CA - Orange County

| | SIC | EMP | PHONE | ENTRY# |
|---|---|---|---|---|
| Justfoodfordogs LLC (PA) | 2047 | F | 949 722-3647 | 1105 |
| Dawn Food Products Inc | 2051 | C | 714 258-1223 | 1181 |
| Bar None Inc | 2085 | F | 714 259-8450 | 1833 |
| Ryte Ventures LLC (PA) | 2329 | F | 925 323-7195 | 2637 |
| Raj Manufacturing LLC | 2339 | F | 714 838-3110 | 2802 |
| Raj Manufacturing Inc (PA) | 2339 | F | 714 838-3110 | 2803 |
| Custom Quilting Inc | 2392 | E | 714 731-7271 | 2927 |
| GL Woodworking Inc | 2431 | D | 949 515-2192 | 3139 |
| Sheward & Son & Sons (PA) | 2591 | E | 714 556-6055 | 3728 |
| Durabag Company Inc | 2673 | D | 714 259-8811 | 3966 |
| Landscape Communications Inc | 2721 | E | 714 979-5276 | 4272 |
| Colbi Technologies Inc | 2741 | E | 714 505-9544 | 4381 |
| Diversified Printers Inc | 2741 | D | 714 994-3400 | 4388 |
| Priority Posting and Pubg Inc | 2741 | F | 714 338-2568 | 4452 |
| Meridian Graphics Inc | 2752 | D | 949 833-3500 | 4693 |
| Precision Offset Inc | 2752 | D | 949 752-1714 | 4730 |
| Docupak Inc | 2782 | F | 714 670-7944 | 5001 |
| Bjb Enterprises Inc | 2821 | E | 714 734-8450 | 5142 |
| Avid Bioservices Inc | 2834 | D | 714 508-6000 | 5348 |
| Avid Bioservices Inc | 2834 | D | 714 508-6166 | 5349 |
| Avid Bioservices Inc (PA) | 2834 | C | 714 508-6100 | 5350 |
| Vitabest Nutrition Inc (HQ) | 2834 | F | 714 832-9700 | 5711 |
| Vitatech International Sciences Inc | 2834 | B | 714 832-9700 | 5712 |
| Design West Technologies Inc | 3089 | E | 714 731-0201 | 6801 |
| Ronco Plastics Inc | 3089 | E | 714 259-1385 | 7007 |
| Ifiber Optix Inc | 3229 | E | 714 665-9796 | 7196 |
| Shade Structures Inc | 3444 | E | 714 427-6980 | 8569 |
| Braxton Caribbean Mfg Co Inc | 3469 | D | 714 508-3570 | 8823 |
| Stuart-Dean Co Inc | 3471 | E | 714 544-4460 | 9017 |
| Bernhardt and Bernhardt Inc | 3541 | E | 714 544-0708 | 9541 |
| Anajet LLC | 3555 | E | 714 662-3200 | 9762 |

# GEOGRAPHIC SECTION — VALENCIA, CA

| Company | SIC | EMP | PHONE | ENTRY# |
|---|---|---|---|---|
| Hesse Mechatronics Inc | 3559 | E | 657 720-1233 | 9863 |
| Johnston International Corporation | 3569 | E | 714 542-4487 | 10097 |
| Add-On Cmpt Peripherals LLC | 3572 | D | 949 546-8200 | 10219 |
| LGarde Inc | 3572 | E | 714 259-0771 | 10251 |
| Add-On Cmpt Peripherals Inc | 3577 | C | 949 546-8200 | 10316 |
| Compass Water Solutions Inc (HQ) | 3589 | E | 949 222-5777 | 10554 |
| PI Variables Inc | 3669 | E | 949 415-9411 | 12008 |
| Expert Assembly Services Inc | 3672 | E | 714 258-8880 | 12097 |
| Permlight Products Inc | 3674 | E | 714 508-0729 | 12631 |
| Distribution Electrnics Vlued | 3699 | E | 714 368-1717 | 13232 |
| Millenworks | 3711 | D | 714 426-5500 | 13371 |
| Rivian Automotive LLC | 3711 | D | 888 748-4261 | 13381 |
| 89908 Inc | 3714 | E | 949 221-0023 | 13436 |
| Galactic Co LLC (DH) | 3761 | E | 661 824-6600 | 14080 |
| Virgin Galactic Holdings Inc (PA) | 3761 | E | 949 774-7640 | 14099 |
| Motionloft Inc | 3826 | E | 415 580-7671 | 14694 |
| Terumo Americas Holding Inc | 3826 | E | 714 258-8001 | 14732 |
| Coherent Aerospace & Def Inc | 3827 | D | 714 247-7100 | 14769 |
| Lightworks Optics Inc | 3827 | E | 714 247-7100 | 14795 |
| Pvp Advanced Eo Systems Inc (DH) | 3827 | E | 714 508-2740 | 14814 |
| Issac Medical Inc | 3841 | B | 805 239-4284 | 15134 |
| Trellborg Sling Sltions US Inc (DH) | 3841 | C | 714 415-0280 | 15287 |
| Staar Surgical Company | 3851 | F | 626 303-7902 | 15621 |
| US Print & Toner Inc | 3955 | E | 619 562-6995 | 15902 |
| Syspro Impact Software Inc | 5045 | C | 714 437-1000 | 16553 |
| Dickeys Barbecue Rest Inc | 5812 | E | 714 602-3874 | 17576 |
| Yebo Group LLC | 5943 | C | 949 502-3317 | 17644 |
| Orange County Direct Mail Inc | 7331 | E | 714 444-4412 | 17800 |
| Autocrib Inc | 7389 | C | 714 274-0400 | 19073 |

## UKIAH, CA - Mendocino County

| Company | SIC | EMP | PHONE | ENTRY# |
|---|---|---|---|---|
| Pamelas Products Incorporated | 2051 | D | 707 462-6605 | 1234 |
| Quinoa Corporation | 2051 | E | 707 462-6605 | 1239 |
| Mendocino Brewing Company Inc (HQ) | 2082 | F | 707 744-1015 | 1447 |
| Constltion Brnds US Oprtons I | 2084 | E | 707 467-4840 | 1516 |
| Jepson Vineyard Ltd | 2084 | F | 707 468-8936 | 1635 |
| McNab Ridge Winery LLC | 2084 | F | 707 462-2423 | 1677 |
| Nelson & Sons Inc | 2084 | F | 707 462-3755 | 1687 |
| Parducci Wine Estates LLC | 2084 | F | 707 463-5350 | 1703 |
| American Bottling Company | 2086 | D | 707 462-8871 | 1852 |
| North Cal Wood Products Inc | 2421 | E | 707 462-0686 | 3074 |
| Gatehouse Media LLC | 2711 | E | 707 964-5642 | 4118 |
| Lake County Publishing Co Inc | 2711 | D | 707 263-5636 | 4146 |
| Performance Coatings Inc | 2851 | E | 707 462-3023 | 6100 |
| Cold Creek Compost Inc | 2875 | E | 707 485-5966 | 6186 |
| Retech Systems LLC | 3433 | D | 707 462-6522 | 8078 |
| Waneshear Technologies LLC | 3553 | E | 707 462-4761 | 9758 |
| Factory Pipe LLC | 3751 | E | 707 463-1322 | 14057 |
| Mendocino Forest Pdts Co LLC | 5031 | C | 707 468-1431 | 16450 |
| Quest Diagnostics Incorporated | 8071 | F | 707 462-7553 | 19331 |

## UNION CITY, CA - Alameda County

| Company | SIC | EMP | PHONE | ENTRY# |
|---|---|---|---|---|
| Tournesol Siteworks LLC (PA) | 1799 | D | 800 542-2282 | 578 |
| Dawn Food Products Inc | 2051 | E | 510 487-9007 | 1180 |
| American Licorice Company | 2064 | B | 510 487-5500 | 1299 |
| Blommer Chocolate Company Cal | 2066 | C | 510 471-4300 | 1338 |
| Irca Group USA LLC | 2066 | D | 678 679-3292 | 1341 |
| Bakemark USA LLC | 2099 | E | 510 487-8188 | 2133 |
| New Horizon Foods Inc | 2099 | E | 510 489-8600 | 2295 |
| SW Sustinability Solutions Inc | 2259 | E | 510 429-8692 | 2488 |
| Equinox Millworks Inc | 2431 | E | 510 946-9729 | 3136 |
| Northwood Design Partners Inc | 2521 | E | 510 731-6505 | 3577 |
| Outform Group Inc | 2675 | E | 510 433-1586 | 4000 |
| Chinese Overseas Mktg Svc Corp | 2741 | E | 510 476-0880 | 4377 |
| Cmy Image Corporation | 2752 | F | 510 516-6668 | 4555 |
| Fricke-Parks Press Inc | 2752 | E | 510 489-6543 | 4617 |
| Celltheon Corporation | 2834 | F | 650 743-3672 | 5401 |
| Zoetis Inc | 2834 | C | 510 474-9259 | 5722 |
| California Performance Packg | 3086 | D | 909 390-4422 | 6625 |
| Ajax - Untd Pttrns & Molds Inc | 3089 | C | 510 476-8000 | 6700 |
| Delta Yimin Technologies Inc | 3089 | E | 510 487-4411 | 6798 |
| Lane International Trading Inc | 3143 | C | 510 489-7364 | 7110 |
| Cemex Cnstr Mtls PCF LLC | 3273 | E | 855 292-8453 | 7423 |
| Hhb Holdings Inc | 3292 | C | 510 489-8100 | 7561 |
| Lamart Corporation | 3292 | E | 510 489-8100 | 7562 |
| Star Stainless Screw Co | 3312 | E | 510 489-6569 | 7628 |
| United Misc & Orna Stl Inc | 3441 | E | 510 429-8755 | 8235 |
| R & S Manufacturing Inc (HQ) | 3442 | E | 510 429-1788 | 8286 |
| Compactor Management Co LLC | 3444 | E | 510 623-2323 | 8412 |
| Gcm Medical & Oem Inc (PA) | 3444 | D | 510 475-0404 | 8457 |
| Spacesonics Incorporated | 3444 | D | 650 610-0999 | 8576 |
| United Mech Met Fbricators Inc | 3444 | E | 510 537-4744 | 8603 |
| Usk Manufacturing Inc | 3444 | E | 510 471-7555 | 8605 |
| Conklin & Conklin Incorporated | 3452 | E | 510 489-5500 | 8750 |
| Electrochem Solutions LLC | 3471 | E | 510 476-1840 | 8952 |
| Heco-Pacific Manufacturing Inc | 3535 | E | 510 487-1155 | 9486 |
| Meem Worldwide Logistics LLC | 3537 | F | 347 666-9680 | 9528 |
| Blc Wc Inc | 3565 | E | 510 489-5400 | 10015 |
| Cold Storage Manufacturing Inc | 3585 | E | 510 476-1700 | 10489 |
| Jenson Mechanical Inc | 3599 | E | 510 429-8078 | 10906 |
| Ptr Manufacturing Inc | 3599 | E | 510 477-9654 | 11056 |
| Finelite Inc (PA) | 3646 | C | 510 441-1100 | 11531 |
| Azimuth Industrial Co Inc | 3674 | E | 510 441-6000 | 12353 |
| Dust Networks Inc | 3674 | E | 510 400-2900 | 12410 |
| Pvd Modular LLC | 3674 | E | 510 962-5100 | 12645 |
| Enersys | 3691 | E | 510 887-8080 | 13136 |
| Orcon Aerospace | 3728 | F | 510 489-8100 | 13917 |
| Axygen Inc (HQ) | 3826 | D | 510 494-8900 | 14620 |
| Sepragen Corporation | 3826 | E | 510 475-0650 | 14716 |
| Abaxis Inc (HQ) | 3829 | C | 510 675-6500 | 14838 |
| Medeologix Inc | 3841 | E | 510 431-3221 | 15163 |
| Mizuho Orthopedic Systems Inc (HQ) | 3841 | E | 510 429-1500 | 15192 |
| Mizuho Orthopedic Systems Inc | 3841 | C | 510 429-1500 | 15193 |
| Aereotech LLC | 3845 | F | 626 319-5394 | 15512 |
| Farallon Brands Inc (PA) | 3944 | F | 510 550-4299 | 15748 |
| Vicarious Fpc Inc | 5045 | E | 415 604-3278 | 16564 |
| Rki Instruments Inc (PA) | 5084 | E | 510 441-5656 | 16838 |
| Orora Packaging Solutions | 5113 | C | 510 487-1211 | 17007 |
| Emerald Packaging Inc | 5199 | C | 510 429-5700 | 17293 |
| W B Mason Co Inc | 5943 | E | 888 926-2766 | 17643 |
| Gcm Holding Corporation | 6719 | B | 510 475-0404 | 17746 |
| Udelv Inc | 7371 | E | 650 376-3785 | 17991 |
| Ferguson Welding Service | 7692 | F | 510 487-5906 | 19192 |

## UNIVERSAL CITY, CA - Los Angeles County

| Company | SIC | EMP | PHONE | ENTRY# |
|---|---|---|---|---|
| Universal Cy Stdios Prdctons L (DH) | 7812 | E | 818 777-1000 | 19298 |

## UPLAND, CA - San Bernardino County

| Company | SIC | EMP | PHONE | ENTRY# |
|---|---|---|---|---|
| La Bath Vanity Inc (PA) | 2434 | F | 909 303-3323 | 3251 |
| Judith Von Hopf Inc | 2541 | E | 909 481-1884 | 3660 |
| CCL Label Inc | 2759 | D | 909 608-2655 | 4858 |
| CCL Label (delaware) Inc | 2759 | D | 909 608-2260 | 4859 |
| Holliday Trucking Inc (PA) | 3273 | D | 909 982-1553 | 7456 |
| Scheu Manufacturing Company (PA) | 3433 | F | 909 982-8933 | 8079 |
| Barzillai Manufacturing Co Inc | 3444 | F | 909 947-4200 | 8387 |
| Dimic Steel Tech Inc | 3444 | D | 909 946-6767 | 8433 |
| Exhaust Center Inc | 3444 | F | 951 685-8602 | 8448 |
| Lock-Ridge Tool Company Inc | 3469 | D | 909 865-8309 | 8860 |
| Charles Meisner Inc | 3544 | E | 909 946-8216 | 9610 |
| Engineered Machinery Group Inc | 3547 | F | 909 579-0088 | 9717 |
| Light Vast Inc | 3648 | E | 800 358-0499 | 11608 |
| Feathersoft Inc | 3652 | E | 925 230-0740 | 11733 |
| Walton Electric Corporation | 3669 | C | 909 981-5051 | 12025 |
| Gar Enterprises | 3679 | E | 909 985-4575 | 12982 |
| Innovativetek Inc | 3699 | F | 909 981-3401 | 13250 |
| Process Insghts - Gded Wave In | 3823 | E | 919 264-9651 | 14446 |
| Analytik Jena US LLC | 3826 | F | 781 376-9899 | 14611 |
| Applied Instrument Tech Inc | 3826 | E | 909 204-3700 | 14614 |

## VACAVILLE, CA - Solano County

| Company | SIC | EMP | PHONE | ENTRY# |
|---|---|---|---|---|
| Mariani Packing Co Inc (PA) | 0723 | B | 707 452-2800 | 83 |
| Vacaville Fruit Co Inc (PA) | 2034 | E | 707 448-5292 | 972 |
| Timbuk2 Designs Inc | 2393 | E | 800 865-2513 | 2963 |
| All-Weather Architectural Aluminum Inc | 2431 | D | 707 452-1600 | 3106 |
| Reporter | 2711 | F | 707 448-6401 | 4184 |
| Alza Corporation (HQ) | 2834 | A | 707 453-6400 | 5311 |
| Genentech Inc | 2834 | E | 707 454-1000 | 5452 |
| Novartis Pharmaceuticals Corp | 2835 | B | 707 452-8081 | 5769 |
| Dr Earth Inc | 2873 | F | 707 448-4676 | 6171 |
| Fortune Brands Windows Inc | 3089 | C | 707 446-7600 | 6830 |
| Master Plastics California Inc | 3089 | E | 707 451-3168 | 6904 |
| Wunder-Mold Inc | 3089 | E | 707 448-2349 | 7084 |
| Pre-Insulated Metal Tech Inc (HQ) | 3448 | E | 707 359-2280 | 8680 |
| Court Galvanizing Inc | 3479 | F | 707 448-4840 | 9059 |
| Automatic Bar Controls Inc (HQ) | 3585 | E | 707 448-5151 | 10483 |
| McC Control Systems LP | 3589 | E | 707 449-0341 | 10578 |
| McC Controls LLC | 3589 | E | 218 847-1317 | 10579 |
| Synder Inc (PA) | 3677 | E | 707 451-6060 | 12861 |
| Spiratec Solutions Inc | 3714 | F | 925 357-1103 | 13578 |
| Icon Aircraft Inc (PA) | 3728 | D | 707 564-4000 | 13868 |
| Alza Corporation | 3826 | A | 707 453-6400 | 14608 |
| Kuic Inc | 4832 | C | 707 446-0200 | 16327 |
| Martins Metal Fabrication & Welding Inc | 7692 | E | 707 678-4117 | 19208 |

## VALENCIA, CA - Los Angeles County

| Company | SIC | EMP | PHONE | ENTRY# |
|---|---|---|---|---|
| Lief Organics LLC (PA) | 2023 | E | 661 775-2500 | 766 |

Employee Codes: A=Over 500 employees, B=251-500
C=101-250, D=51-100, E=20-50, F=10-19, G=1-9

# VALENCIA, CA

| Company | SIC | EMP | PHONE | ENTRY# |
|---|---|---|---|---|
| Bestway Sandwiches Inc (PA) | 2051 | E | 818 361-1800 | 1170 |
| Chocolates A La Carte Inc | 2064 | C | 661 257-3700 | 1302 |
| King Henrys Inc | 2096 | E | 818 536-3692 | 2096 |
| Universal Hosiery Inc | 2252 | D | 661 702-8444 | 2461 |
| Contractors Wardrobe Inc (PA) | 2431 | C | 661 257-1177 | 3122 |
| Legacy Commercial Holdings Inc | 2511 | E | 818 767-6626 | 3447 |
| Fruit Growers Supply Company (PA) | 2653 | E | 888 997-4855 | 3843 |
| Precision Dynamics Corporation (HQ) | 2672 | C | 818 897-1111 | 3953 |
| Bertelsmann Inc | 2731 | A | 661 702-2700 | 4314 |
| Nextclientcom Inc | 2741 | E | 661 222-7755 | 4439 |
| Parrot Communications Intl Inc | 2741 | E | 818 567-4700 | 4444 |
| Delta Printing Solutions Inc | 2752 | E | 661 257-0584 | 4586 |
| Cosmic Plastics Inc (PA) | 2821 | F | 661 257-3274 | 5148 |
| Ta Aerospace Co | 2821 | C | 661 702-0448 | 5207 |
| Ibg Holdings Inc | 2844 | E | 661 702-8680 | 5991 |
| Mastey De Paris Inc | 2844 | E | 661 257-4814 | 6004 |
| Solevy Co LLC | 2844 | D | 661 622-4880 | 6039 |
| Utak Laboratories Inc | 2869 | E | 661 294-3935 | 6165 |
| PRC - Desoto International Inc (HQ) | 2891 | B | 661 678-4209 | 6240 |
| Leonards Molded Products Inc | 3069 | E | 661 253-2227 | 6510 |
| Ta Aerospace Co (DH) | 3069 | C | 661 775-1100 | 6541 |
| Timemed Labeling Systems Inc (DH) | 3069 | D | 818 897-1111 | 6544 |
| Valencia Pipe Company | 3084 | E | 661 257-3923 | 6605 |
| King Bros Enterprises LLC | 3088 | C | 661 257-3262 | 6682 |
| Canyon Plastics LLC | 3089 | D | 800 350-6325 | 6762 |
| King Bros Industries | 3089 | E | | 6886 |
| Valencia Plastics Inc | 3089 | F | 661 257-0066 | 7069 |
| US Horizon Manufacturing Inc | 3211 | E | 661 775-1675 | 7179 |
| Technifex Products LLC | 3291 | E | 661 294-3800 | 7558 |
| Sgl Technic LLC (DH) | 3295 | E | 661 257-0500 | 7571 |
| Galaxy Die and Engineering Inc | 3366 | E | 661 775-9301 | 7853 |
| Avibank Mfg Inc | 3429 | D | 661 257-2329 | 7980 |
| Pacific Lock Company (PA) | 3429 | E | 661 294-3707 | 8023 |
| Hydro Systems Inc (PA) | 3431 | D | 661 775-0686 | 8041 |
| Virgil Walker Inc | 3441 | F | 661 797-4101 | 8241 |
| RAH Industries Inc (PA) | 3444 | C | 661 295-5190 | 8553 |
| Stoll Metalcraft Inc | 3444 | E | 661 295-0401 | 8584 |
| Valley Precision Met Pdts Inc | 3444 | E | 661 607-0100 | 8606 |
| CURRAN ENGINEERING COMPANY I | 3446 | E | 800 643-6353 | 8622 |
| Lavi Industries LLC (PA) | 3446 | D | 877 275-5284 | 8634 |
| V M P Inc | 3451 | F | 661 294-9934 | 8737 |
| Bloomers Metal Stampings Inc | 3469 | E | 661 257-2955 | 8822 |
| Pacific Metal Stampings Inc | 3469 | E | 661 257-7656 | 8873 |
| Nasmyth Tmf Inc | 3471 | D | 818 954-9504 | 8988 |
| Curtiss-Wright Flow Control | 3491 | C | 626 851-3100 | 9152 |
| Acousticfab LLC (DH) | 3492 | E | 661 257-2242 | 9165 |
| Electrofilm Mfg Co LLC | 3492 | E | 661 257-2242 | 9167 |
| Industrial Tube Company LLC | 3492 | D | 661 295-4000 | 9169 |
| Senior Operations LLC | 3492 | D | 818 350-8499 | 9171 |
| G-G Distribution & Dev Co Inc | 3494 | E | 661 257-5700 | 9186 |
| Circle W Enterprises Inc | 3496 | E | 661 257-2400 | 9214 |
| Whitmor Plstic Wire Cable Corp | 3496 | E | 661 257-2400 | 9243 |
| LA Turbine (HQ) | 3511 | D | 661 294-8290 | 9312 |
| Sdi Industries Inc (DH) | 3535 | C | 818 890-6002 | 9494 |
| Gruber Systems Inc | 3544 | E | 661 257-0464 | 9626 |
| Schrey & Sons Mold Co Inc | 3544 | E | 661 294-2260 | 9648 |
| ASC Process Systems Inc (PA) | 3559 | C | 818 833-0088 | 9832 |
| Next Point Bearing Group LLC | 3562 | E | 818 988-1880 | 9952 |
| Indu-Electric North Amer Inc (PA) | 3568 | E | 310 578-2144 | 10071 |
| Western Filter A Division of Donald | 3569 | D | 661 295-0800 | 10123 |
| Synergy Microsystems Inc | 3571 | C | 858 452-0020 | 10207 |
| SGB Enterprises Inc | 3575 | E | 661 294-8306 | 10310 |
| Transparent Products Inc | 3575 | E | 661 294-9787 | 10312 |
| Input/Output Technology Inc | 3577 | E | 661 257-1000 | 10384 |
| Aquafine Corporation (HQ) | 3589 | D | 661 257-4770 | 10538 |
| N/S Corporation (PA) | 3589 | D | 310 412-7074 | 10584 |
| Qmp Inc | 3589 | E | 661 294-6860 | 10595 |
| Crissair Inc | 3594 | C | 661 367-3300 | 10631 |
| Advanced Tech Machining Inc | 3599 | E | 661 257-2313 | 10679 |
| Apogee Manufacturing | 3599 | F | 661 467-0440 | 10713 |
| Bayless Manufacturing LLC | 3599 | C | 661 253-3373 | 10740 |
| Classic Wire Cut Company Inc | 3599 | C | 661 257-0558 | 10778 |
| Luran Inc | 3599 | F | 661 257-6303 | 10947 |
| Performance Machine Tech Inc | 3599 | E | 661 294-8617 | 11037 |
| True Position Technologies LLC | 3599 | D | 661 294-0030 | 11154 |
| SMI Holdings Inc | 3621 | E | 800 232-2612 | 11288 |
| M W Sausse & Co Inc (PA) | 3625 | D | 661 257-3311 | 11332 |
| Capax Technologies Inc | 3629 | F | 661 257-7666 | 11362 |
| Lightway Industries | 3646 | F | 661 257-0286 | 11544 |
| Steril-Aire Inc | 3648 | E | 818 565-1128 | 11623 |
| A & M Electronics Inc | 3672 | E | 661 257-3680 | 12039 |
| Hamby Corporation | 3672 | E | 661 257-1924 | 12127 |
| Advanced Semiconductor Inc | 3674 | D | 818 982-1200 | 12278 |
| Asi Semiconductor Inc | 3674 | E | 818 982-1200 | 12335 |
| Lockwood Industries LLC (HQ) | 3674 | E | 661 702-6999 | 12533 |
| Semiconductor Process Eqp LLC | 3674 | E | 661 257-0934 | 12691 |
| Interconnect Solutions Co LLC | 3679 | D | 661 295-0020 | 13002 |
| Iwerks Entertainment Inc | 3699 | D | 661 678-1800 | 13257 |
| Mye Technologies Inc | 3699 | E | 661 964-0217 | 13274 |
| Summit Electric & Data Inc | 3699 | F | 661 775-9901 | 13313 |
| Air Flow Research Heads Inc | 3714 | E | 661 257-8124 | 13451 |
| Del West Engineering Inc (PA) | 3714 | C | 661 295-5700 | 13484 |
| Donaldson Company Inc | 3714 | E | 661 295-0800 | 13487 |
| Princeton Tool Inc | 3724 | F | 661 257-1380 | 13719 |
| Adept Fasteners Inc (PA) | 3728 | E | 661 257-6600 | 13738 |
| Aero Engineering & Mfg Co LLC | 3728 | D | 661 295-0875 | 13742 |
| Aero Sense Inc | 3728 | F | 661 257-1608 | 13744 |
| Aerospace Dynamics Intl Inc (DH) | 3728 | C | 661 257-3535 | 13753 |
| Aerospace Service & Controls | 3728 | F | 818 833-0088 | 13758 |
| Aircraft Hinge Inc | 3728 | E | 661 257-3434 | 13764 |
| Avantus Aerospace Inc (DH) | 3728 | C | 661 295-8620 | 13791 |
| Canyon Engineering Pdts Inc | 3728 | D | 661 294-0084 | 13805 |
| Flight Line Products Inc | 3728 | E | 661 775-8366 | 13843 |
| Forrest Machining LLC | 3728 | C | 661 257-0231 | 13845 |
| Global Aerospace Tech Corp | 3728 | E | 818 407-5600 | 13852 |
| ITT Aerospace Controls LLC (HQ) | 3728 | C | 315 568-7258 | 13879 |
| ITT Aerospace Controls LLC | 3728 | B | 661 295-4000 | 13880 |
| Sunvair Inc (HQ) | 3728 | E | 661 294-3777 | 13964 |
| Triumph Acttion Systems - Vlnc | 3728 | C | 661 702-7537 | 13980 |
| L3 Technologies Inc | 3812 | E | 818 367-0111 | 14204 |
| Ronan Engineering Company (PA) | 3823 | D | 661 702-1344 | 14452 |
| Eckert Zegler Isotope Pdts Inc (HQ) | 3829 | E | 661 309-1010 | 14863 |
| H2scan Corporation (PA) | 3829 | E | 661 775-9575 | 14874 |
| Boston Scientific Corporation | 3841 | E | 800 678-2575 | 15018 |
| Vertiflex Inc | 3841 | E | 442 325-5900 | 15304 |
| Advanced Bionics Corporation (HQ) | 3842 | C | 661 362-1400 | 15318 |
| Boston Scntfic Nrmdlation Corp (HQ) | 3842 | B | 661 949-4310 | 15326 |
| Talladium Inc (PA) | 3843 | E | 661 295-0900 | 15488 |
| Bioness Inc | 3845 | C | 661 362-4850 | 15520 |
| Palyon Medical Corporation | 3845 | E | | 15571 |
| Vitek Indus Video Pdts Inc | 3861 | E | 661 294-8043 | 15671 |
| Remo Inc (PA) | 3931 | B | 661 294-5600 | 15721 |
| Fasthouse Inc | 3949 | F | 661 775-5963 | 15810 |
| Fasthouse Inc (PA) | 3949 | F | 661 775-5963 | 15811 |
| Cornerstone Display Group Inc | 3993 | E | 661 705-1700 | 15959 |
| Ram Board Inc | 3996 | E | 818 848-0400 | 16076 |
| Medical Brkthrugh Mssage Chirs | 3999 | E | 408 677-7702 | 16180 |
| Softub Inc (PA) | 3999 | D | 858 602-1920 | 16234 |
| Sunstar Spa Covers Inc (HQ) | 3999 | E | 858 602-1950 | 16246 |
| Technical Manufacturing W LLC | 3999 | E | 661 295-7226 | 16251 |
| American Med & Hosp Sup Co Inc | 5047 | E | 661 294-1213 | 16573 |
| Klm Laboratories Inc | 5047 | D | 661 295-2600 | 16584 |
| Sunco Lighting Inc | 5063 | E | 844 334-9938 | 16674 |
| Tape Specialty Inc | 5065 | E | 661 702-9030 | 16736 |
| Allied International LLC | 5072 | E | 818 364-2333 | 16744 |
| Penn Engineering Components | 5072 | E | 818 503-1511 | 16761 |
| Green Convergence (PA) | 5074 | D | 661 294-9495 | 16767 |
| Air Frame Mfg & Supply Co Inc | 5088 | E | 661 257-7728 | 16912 |
| Regent Aerospace Corporation (PA) | 5088 | C | 661 257-3000 | 16924 |
| Star Nail Products Inc | 5122 | D | 661 257-3376 | 17052 |
| Sunkist Growers Inc (PA) | 5148 | C | 661 290-8900 | 17171 |
| At Battery Company Inc | 5999 | E | 661 775-2020 | 17690 |
| Black Anchor Supply Co LLC | 7336 | F | 661 309-1193 | 17821 |
| C 232 Inc | 7373 | F | 818 731-1196 | 18965 |
| Teague Custom Marine Inc | 7699 | F | 661 295-7000 | 19285 |
| Scicon Technologies Corp (PA) | 8711 | E | 661 295-8630 | 19420 |

## VALLECITO, CA - Calaveras County

| Company | SIC | EMP | PHONE | ENTRY# |
|---|---|---|---|---|
| Twisted Oak Winery LLC (PA) | 2084 | F | 209 728-3000 | 1807 |

## VALLEJO, CA - Solano County

| Company | SIC | EMP | PHONE | ENTRY# |
|---|---|---|---|---|
| Syar Industries Inc | 1422 | E | 707 643-3261 | 302 |
| Jeffco Painting & Coating Inc | 1721 | D | 707 562-1900 | 446 |
| Lind Marine Incorporated (PA) | 2048 | E | 707 762-7251 | 1136 |

## VALLEJO, CA - Napa County

| Company | SIC | EMP | PHONE | ENTRY# |
|---|---|---|---|---|
| Golden State Vintners | 2084 | E | 707 553-6480 | 1593 |

## VALLEJO, CA - Solano County

| Company | SIC | EMP | PHONE | ENTRY# |
|---|---|---|---|---|
| Santa Croce LLC | 2085 | F | 707 227-7834 | 1842 |
| Ghiringhlli Spcialty Foods Inc | 2099 | C | 707 561-7670 | 2214 |
| Western Dovetail Incorporated | 2511 | E | 707 556-3683 | 3461 |
| Jbe Inc | 2541 | F | 707 552-6800 | 3659 |
| Xkt Engineering Inc | 3443 | D | 707 562-2500 | 8356 |
| Meyer Cookware Industries Inc | 3469 | E | 707 551-2800 | 8866 |
| Meyer Corporation US (HQ) | 3469 | D | 707 551-2800 | 8867 |

# GEOGRAPHIC SECTION — VENTURA, CA

| Company | SIC | EMP | PHONE | ENTRY# |
|---|---|---|---|---|
| Dreamctchers Empwerment Netwrk | 3679 | E | 707 558-1775 | 12963 |
| Mare Island Dry Dock LLC | 3731 | D | 707 652-7356 | 14008 |
| Mare Island Ship Yard LLC | 3731 | D | 760 877-0291 | 14009 |
| Moose Boats LLC | 3732 | F | 707 778-9828 | 14043 |

## VALLEJO, CA - Napa County

| Company | SIC | EMP | PHONE | ENTRY# |
|---|---|---|---|---|
| Sutter Home Winery Inc | 5921 | E | 707 645-0661 | 17630 |

## VALLEJO, CA - Solano County

| Company | SIC | EMP | PHONE | ENTRY# |
|---|---|---|---|---|
| Done Right Security Inc | 7382 | E | 510 621-7686 | 19053 |

## VALLEY CENTER, CA - San Diego County

| Company | SIC | EMP | PHONE | ENTRY# |
|---|---|---|---|---|
| Brax Company Inc | 1781 | E | 760 749-2209 | 526 |
| Survival Systems Intl Inc (PA) | 7699 | D | 760 749-6800 | 19283 |

## VALLEY SPRINGS, CA - Calaveras County

| Company | SIC | EMP | PHONE | ENTRY# |
|---|---|---|---|---|
| Prince Kona Food LLC | 2087 | D | 209 430-7814 | 2020 |

## VALLEY VILLAGE, CA - Los Angeles County

| Company | SIC | EMP | PHONE | ENTRY# |
|---|---|---|---|---|
| Cannalogic | 3999 | F | 619 458-0775 | 16107 |

## VAN NUYS, CA - Los Angeles County

| Company | SIC | EMP | PHONE | ENTRY# |
|---|---|---|---|---|
| Mp Aero LLC | 1799 | D | 818 901-9828 | 567 |
| Dolce Dolci LLC | 2024 | F | 818 343-8400 | 798 |
| Bubbles Baking Company | 2051 | E | 818 786-1700 | 1174 |
| Danish Baking Co Inc | 2051 | D | 818 786-1700 | 1179 |
| SGB Better Baking Co LLC | 2051 | E | 818 787-9992 | 1242 |
| SGB Bubbles Baking Co LLC | 2051 | E | 818 786-1700 | 1243 |
| Western Bagel Baking Corp (PA) | 2051 | C | 818 786-5847 | 1253 |
| Aspire Bakeries LLC | 2052 | B | 818 904-8230 | 1261 |
| Power Brands Consulting LLC | 2082 | E | 818 989-9646 | 1454 |
| Chef Merito Inc | 2099 | F | 818 781-0470 | 2163 |
| Chef Merito LLC (PA) | 2099 | E | 818 787-0100 | 2164 |
| Rof LLC | 2326 | E | 818 933-4000 | 2602 |
| Kandy Kiss of California Inc | 2331 | D | | 2674 |
| Leigh Jerry California Inc (PA) | 2361 | C | 818 909-6200 | 2856 |
| Danmer Inc | 2431 | C | 516 670-5125 | 3124 |
| I and E Cabinets Inc | 2434 | E | 818 933-6480 | 3243 |
| Cpp/Belwin Inc | 2731 | D | 818 891-5999 | 4323 |
| The Full Void 2 Inc | 2731 | B | 818 891-5999 | 4349 |
| C & L Graphics Inc | 2752 | E | 818 785-8310 | 4539 |
| Color Fx Inc | 2752 | E | 877 763-7671 | 4558 |
| Niknejad Inc | 2752 | E | 310 477-0407 | 4706 |
| Pegasus Interprint Inc | 2752 | E | 800 926-9873 | 4722 |
| Printrunner LLC | 2752 | E | 888 296-5760 | 4737 |
| Digital Room Holdings Inc (HQ) | 2759 | D | 310 575-4440 | 4873 |
| Great Western Packaging LLC | 2759 | D | 818 464-3800 | 4889 |
| Investment Enterprises Inc (PA) | 2759 | D | 818 464-3800 | 4900 |
| Auto-Chlor System Wash Inc | 2842 | F | 818 376-0940 | 5889 |
| Mpm Building Services Inc | 2842 | E | 818 708-9676 | 5918 |
| Orly International Inc (PA) | 2844 | D | 818 994-1001 | 6014 |
| Prolabs Factory Inc | 2844 | E | 818 646-3677 | 6028 |
| Munchkin Inc | 3085 | C | 800 344-2229 | 6610 |
| Neopacific Holdings Inc | 3089 | E | 818 786-2900 | 6927 |
| Linea Pelle Inc (PA) | 3111 | F | 310 231-9950 | 7089 |
| Rwh Inc | 3273 | E | 818 782-2350 | 7495 |
| Thompson Gundrilling Inc | 3321 | E | 323 873-4045 | 7681 |
| RPC Legacy Inc | 3429 | E | 818 787-9000 | 8024 |
| D&A Metal Fabrication Inc | 3441 | F | 818 780-8231 | 8131 |
| Consolidated Fabricators Corp (PA) | 3443 | C | 800 635-8335 | 8311 |
| Broadway AC Htg & Shtmtl | 3444 | E | 818 781-1477 | 8394 |
| Dayton Rogers of California Inc | 3469 | C | 763 784-7714 | 8835 |
| Enterprises Industries Inc | 3469 | C | 818 989-6103 | 8841 |
| Capstone Dstr Spport Svcs Corp (PA) | 3511 | C | 818 734-5300 | 9309 |
| Synchronized Technologies Inc | 3577 | F | 213 368-3760 | 10443 |
| Rothlisberger Mfg A Cal Corp | 3599 | E | 818 786-9462 | 11091 |
| Optical Zonu Corporation | 3661 | F | 818 780-9701 | 11779 |
| Technoconcepts Inc | 3663 | E | 818 988-3364 | 11960 |
| Advanced Circuits Inc | 3672 | E | 818 345-1993 | 12044 |
| Photo Fabricators Inc | 3672 | D | 818 781-1010 | 12189 |
| Glp German Light Products Inc | 3674 | F | 818 767-8899 | 12453 |
| Alyn Industries Inc | 3679 | E | 818 988-7696 | 12911 |
| Cicon Engineering Inc (PA) | 3679 | C | 818 909-6060 | 12938 |
| Microfabrica Inc | 3679 | E | 888 964-2763 | 13036 |
| Wsw Corp (PA) | 3714 | E | 818 989-5008 | 13607 |
| Gulfstream Aerospace Corp GA | 3721 | B | 805 236-5755 | 13667 |
| Aero-Nasch Aviation Inc | 3728 | F | 818 786-5480 | 13746 |
| Aeroshear Aviation Svcs Inc (PA) | 3728 | E | 818 779-1650 | 13749 |
| N2 Development Inc | 3728 | F | 323 210-3251 | 13913 |
| Edo Communications and Countermeasu | 3812 | D | 818 464-2475 | 14183 |
| L3harris Technologies Inc | 3812 | B | 818 901-2523 | 14205 |
| Rizzo Inc | 3842 | E | 818 781-6891 | 15399 |
| Kazak-Mars Inc | 3851 | E | 818 375-1033 | 15605 |
| Modern Studio Equipment Inc | 3861 | F | 818 764-8574 | 15652 |
| Wbi Inc | 3861 | A | 800 673-4968 | 15672 |
| Allison-Kaufman Co | 3911 | F | 818 373-5100 | 15679 |
| Shelcore Inc (PA) | 3944 | E | 818 883-2400 | 15768 |
| E Alko Inc | 3955 | E | 818 587-9700 | 15894 |
| Neiman/Hoeller Inc | 3993 | D | 818 781-8600 | 16014 |
| Repairtech International Inc | 4581 | E | 818 989-2681 | 16303 |
| Katzirs Floor & HM Design Inc (PA) | 5023 | E | 818 988-9663 | 16428 |
| Anatex Enterprises Inc | 5092 | E | 818 908-1888 | 16942 |
| CDM Corp | 5999 | F | 818 787-4002 | 17692 |
| Cinema Secrets Inc | 5999 | D | 818 846-0579 | 17693 |
| 1370 Realty Corp | 6531 | F | 818 817-0092 | 17740 |
| Certemy Inc | 7372 | F | 866 907-4088 | 18160 |
| Hollywood Software Inc | 7372 | E | 818 205-2121 | 18387 |
| Kive Company | 7372 | E | 747 212-0337 | 18473 |
| Louroe Electronics Inc | 7382 | E | 818 994-6498 | 19058 |
| EDN Aviation Inc | 7699 | E | 818 988-8826 | 19254 |

## VANDENBERG AFB, CA - Santa Barbara County

| Company | SIC | EMP | PHONE | ENTRY# |
|---|---|---|---|---|
| Space Exploration Tech Corp | 3721 | C | 310 848-4410 | 13692 |
| United Launch Alliance LLC | 3761 | B | 303 269-5876 | 14097 |

## VENICE, CA - Los Angeles County

| Company | SIC | EMP | PHONE | ENTRY# |
|---|---|---|---|---|
| Vive Organic Inc | 2033 | E | 877 774-9291 | 939 |
| Indie Source | 2326 | E | 424 200-2027 | 2596 |
| Frankies Bikinis LLC | 2369 | E | 323 354-4133 | 2860 |
| Flex Company | 3069 | E | 424 209-2711 | 6494 |
| Allbirds Inc | 3143 | F | 424 295-9968 | 7106 |
| Alpargatas Usa Inc | 3144 | E | 646 277-7171 | 7113 |
| Flat Planet Inc | 3559 | E | 888 656-6872 | 9857 |
| Fellow Industries Inc | 3634 | E | 415 649-0361 | 11404 |
| Syng Inc (PA) | 3651 | D | 770 354-0915 | 11703 |
| Mededge Inc | 3841 | F | 310 392-9843 | 15162 |
| Guayaki Sstnble Rnfrest Pdts I (PA) | 5149 | C | 888 482-9254 | 17188 |
| Swartz Glass Co Inc (PA) | 5231 | F | 310 392-0001 | 17350 |
| Gamemine LLC | 7372 | E | 310 310-3105 | 18341 |

## VENTURA, CA - Ventura County

| Company | SIC | EMP | PHONE | ENTRY# |
|---|---|---|---|---|
| Floral Gift HM Decor Intl Inc | 0181 | E | 818 849-8832 | 47 |
| Calnrg Operating LLC (PA) | 1311 | E | 805 477-9805 | 132 |
| Instrument Control Services | 1389 | E | 805 642-1999 | 240 |
| Nabors Well Services Co | 1389 | D | 805 648-2731 | 253 |
| Vista Steel Co Inc | 1629 | E | 805 653-1189 | 400 |
| Novotech Nutraceuticals Inc | 2023 | E | 805 676-1098 | 777 |
| Dairy Farmers America Inc | 2026 | E | 805 653-0042 | 832 |
| HK Canning Inc (PA) | 2033 | E | 805 652-1392 | 892 |
| Ventura Coastal LLC (PA) | 2037 | E | 805 653-7000 | 1019 |
| Better Bakery LLC | 2052 | C | 661 294-9882 | 1264 |
| Reyes Coca-Cola Bottling LLC | 2086 | E | 805 644-2211 | 1938 |
| Tractor Beverage Co | 2086 | E | 909 855-4106 | 1969 |
| Fabricmate Systems Inc | 2221 | E | 805 642-7470 | 2436 |
| Patagonia Inc (HQ) | 2329 | B | 805 643-8616 | 2636 |
| Streamline Dsgn Slkscreen Inc (PA) | 2329 | D | 805 884-1025 | 2645 |
| Hearts Delight | 2339 | E | 805 648-7123 | 2763 |
| Art Glass Etc Inc | 2431 | E | 805 644-4494 | 3111 |
| Santa Monica Millworks | 2434 | E | 805 643-0010 | 3269 |
| W L Rubottom Co | 2434 | D | 805 648-6943 | 3280 |
| Goldenwood Truss Corporation | 2439 | D | 805 659-2520 | 3308 |
| Edwards Assoc Cmmnications Inc (PA) | 2672 | C | 805 658-2626 | 3949 |
| Homes & Land of Ventura | 2711 | E | 805 644-9816 | 4132 |
| Fnc Medical Corporation | 2844 | E | 805 644-7576 | 5978 |
| Jh Biotech Inc (PA) | 2875 | E | 805 650-8933 | 6188 |
| C & R Molds Inc | 3089 | E | 805 658-7098 | 6753 |
| Commonpath LLC | 3231 | C | 858 922-8116 | 7216 |
| Lynch Ready Mix Concrete Co | 3273 | F | 805 647-2817 | 7468 |
| State Ready Mix Inc (PA) | 3273 | E | 805 647-2817 | 7504 |
| Assa Abloy ACC Door Cntrls Gro | 3429 | E | 805 642-2600 | 7976 |
| Automotive Racing Products Inc (PA) | 3429 | D | 805 339-2200 | 7977 |
| Pemko Manufacturing Co | 3442 | C | 800 283-9988 | 8283 |
| Fcp Inc | 3448 | F | 805 684-1117 | 8667 |
| Quick Draw and Machining Inc | 3469 | F | 805 664-7882 | 8881 |
| Valex Corp (HQ) | 3471 | D | 805 658-0944 | 9030 |
| Bell Powder Coating Inc | 3479 | F | 805 658-2233 | 9054 |
| Juengermann Inc | 3493 | E | 805 644-7165 | 9176 |
| Cummins Pacific LLC | 3519 | C | 805 644-7281 | 9326 |
| Aqueos Corporation | 3533 | C | 805 676-4330 | 9454 |
| Aquastar Pool Products Inc | 3561 | E | 877 768-2717 | 9914 |
| HMcompany | 3599 | E | 805 650-2651 | 10873 |
| Ventura Hydrulic Mch Works Inc | 3599 | E | 805 656-1760 | 11174 |
| Dow-Key Microwave Corporation | 3625 | C | 805 650-0260 | 11318 |
| Lamps Plus Inc | 3646 | E | 805 642-9007 | 11541 |
| Sun Power Source (PA) | 3648 | F | 805 644-2520 | 11624 |
| Total Structures Inc | 3648 | E | 805 676-3322 | 11628 |

Employee Codes: A=Over 500 employees, B=251-500, C=101-250, D=51-100, E=20-50, F=10-19, G=1-9

## VENTURA, CA

| | SIC | EMP | PHONE | ENTRY# |
|---|---|---|---|---|
| Wireless Technology Inc. | 3651 | E | 805 339-9696 | 11719 |
| Coastal Connections. | 3661 | E | 805 644-5051 | 11758 |
| Naso Industries Corporation. | 3672 | E | 805 650-1231 | 12172 |
| Omnisil. | 3674 | E | 805 644-2514 | 12617 |
| Robert M Hadley Company Inc. | 3677 | D | 805 658-7286 | 12856 |
| Holland Electronics LLC. | 3678 | E | 888 628-5411 | 12882 |
| Magnuson Products LLC. | 3714 | E | 805 642-8833 | 13535 |
| Ventura Harbor Boatyard Inc. | 3732 | E | 805 654-1433 | 14046 |
| Barnett Tool & Engineering. | 3751 | D | 805 642-9435 | 14053 |
| Northrdge Tr-Mdlity Imging Inc. | 3821 | F | 818 709-2468 | 14345 |
| Spectron LLC (PA). | 3826 | E | 805 642-0400 | 14721 |
| Peter Brasseler Holdings LLC. | 3841 | D | 805 658-2643 | 15222 |
| TMJ Solutions LLC. | 3841 | E | 805 650-3391 | 15285 |
| Implantech Associates Inc. | 3842 | E | 805 289-1665 | 15361 |
| Exam Room Supply LLC. | 3845 | F | 805 298-3631 | 15535 |
| Strand Products Inc (PA). | 3845 | E | 800 343-7985 | 15581 |
| Brothers of Industry Inc. | 3999 | F | 805 628-3545 | 16100 |
| Blue Ocean Marine LLC. | 4499 | E | 805 658-2628 | 16297 |
| E J Harrison & Sons Inc. | 4953 | C | 805 647-1414 | 16358 |
| Canon Solutions America Inc. | 5044 | E | 844 443-4636 | 16501 |
| Peter Brasseler Holdings LLC. | 5047 | D | 805 650-5209 | 16587 |
| M-H Ironworks Inc. | 5051 | D | | 16622 |
| Main Electric Supply Co LLC. | 5063 | E | 805 654-8600 | 16661 |
| High Tech Pet Products. | 5065 | D | 805 644-1797 | 16704 |
| Ventura Feed and Pet Sups Inc. | 5661 | E | 805 648-5035 | 17505 |
| Patagonia Works (PA). | 5699 | B | 805 643-8616 | 17511 |
| Cold Steel Inc (PA). | 5961 | E | 805 650-8481 | 17662 |
| Trade Desk Inc (PA). | 7371 | B | 805 585-3434 | 17989 |
| Agi Holding Corp (PA). | 7997 | D | 805 667-4100 | 19312 |

## VERNON, CA - Los Angeles County

| | SIC | EMP | PHONE | ENTRY# |
|---|---|---|---|---|
| Littlejohn-Reuland Corporation. | 1731 | E | 323 587-5255 | 461 |
| Golden West Food Group Inc (PA). | 2011 | E | 888 807-3663 | 599 |
| Jobbers Meat Packing Co LLC. | 2011 | C | 323 585-6328 | 603 |
| Pacific Prime Meats LLC. | 2011 | D | 310 523-3664 | 612 |
| R B R Meat Company Inc. | 2011 | E | 323 973-4868 | 613 |
| Bar-S Foods Co. | 2013 | E | 323 589-3600 | 633 |
| Papa Cantellas Incorporated. | 2013 | D | 323 584-7272 | 658 |
| Square H Brands Inc (PA). | 2013 | E | 323 267-4600 | 669 |
| Expro Manufacturing Corporation. | 2032 | E | 323 415-8544 | 855 |
| Fresh Packing Corporation. | 2032 | E | 213 612-0136 | 856 |
| Masongate Inc. | 2032 | E | 323 415-8544 | 867 |
| T & T Foods Inc. | 2032 | E | 323 588-2158 | 871 |
| Tapatio Foods LLC. | 2033 | F | 323 587-8933 | 931 |
| Culinary Brands Inc (PA). | 2038 | E | 626 289-3000 | 1031 |
| General Mills Inc. | 2041 | E | 323 584-3433 | 1058 |
| Bakery Depot Inc. | 2051 | F | 323 261-8388 | 1167 |
| Mochi Ice Cream Company LLC (PA). | 2051 | E | 323 587-5504 | 1228 |
| Interntnal Desserts Delicacies (PA). | 2052 | F | 818 549-0056 | 1277 |
| Smart Foods LLC. | 2076 | E | 800 284-2250 | 1373 |
| Baker Commodities Inc. | 2077 | E | 323 318-8260 | 1376 |
| Baker Commodities Inc (PA). | 2077 | C | 323 268-2801 | 1377 |
| D & D Services Inc. | 2077 | E | 323 261-4176 | 1380 |
| Coast Packing Company. | 2079 | D | 323 277-7700 | 1396 |
| American Bottling Company. | 2086 | C | 323 268-7779 | 1859 |
| Gts Living Foods LLC. | 2086 | E | 323 581-7787 | 1891 |
| Gts Living Foods LLC (PA). | 2086 | A | 323 581-7787 | 1892 |
| Stratus Group Duo LLC. | 2086 | E | 323 581-3663 | 1966 |
| American Fruits & Flavors LLC. | 2087 | E | 323 881-8321 | 1983 |
| Pacific American Fish Co Inc (PA). | 2091 | C | 323 319-1551 | 2041 |
| Fishermans Pride Prcessors Inc. | 2092 | B | 323 232-1980 | 2053 |
| F Gavina & Sons Inc. | 2095 | B | 323 582-0671 | 2071 |
| Cargill Meat Solutions Corp. | 2099 | C | 515 735-9800 | 2158 |
| Clw Foods LLC. | 2099 | F | 323 432-4600 | 2170 |
| Culinary International LLC (PA). | 2099 | C | 626 289-3000 | 2176 |
| F I O Imports Inc. | 2099 | C | 323 263-5100 | 2195 |
| Overhill Farms Inc (DH). | 2099 | C | 323 582-9977 | 2308 |
| Penguin Natural Foods Inc (PA). | 2099 | E | 323 727-7980 | 2318 |
| Reynaldos Mexican Food Co LLC (PA). | 2099 | C | 562 803-3188 | 2335 |
| Belagio Enterprises Inc. | 2211 | E | 323 731-6934 | 2403 |
| BTS Trading Inc. | 2211 | E | 213 800-6755 | 2405 |
| Everybody World LLC. | 2211 | F | 213 305-9450 | 2413 |
| Nux Group Inc. | 2211 | E | 323 780-4700 | 2423 |
| Pjy LLC. | 2211 | E | 323 583-7737 | 2424 |
| Saitex (usa) LLC. | 2211 | E | 323 391-6116 | 2425 |
| Socal Garment Works LLC. | 2211 | E | 323 300-5717 | 2426 |
| Chua & Sons Co Inc. | 2241 | E | 323 588-8044 | 2451 |
| Universal Elastic & Garment Supply Inc. | 2241 | E | 213 748-2995 | 2455 |
| Fantasy Activewear Inc (PA). | 2253 | E | 213 705-4111 | 2468 |
| Fantasy Dyeing & Finishing Inc. | 2253 | E | 323 983-9988 | 2469 |
| Latigo LLC. | 2253 | E | 323 583-8000 | 2475 |
| Mjck Corporation. | 2253 | F | 888 992-8437 | 2478 |
| Shara-Tex Inc. | 2257 | E | 323 587-7200 | 2482 |
| Sas Textiles Inc. | 2259 | D | 323 277-5555 | 2487 |
| Rezex Corporation. | 2269 | E | 213 622-2015 | 2507 |
| American Cover Design 26 Inc. | 2273 | E | 323 582-8666 | 2508 |
| Marspring Corporation (PA). | 2273 | E | 323 589-5637 | 2516 |
| California Combining Corp. | 2295 | E | 323 589-5727 | 2526 |
| Kaslen Textiles LLC. | 2295 | F | 323 588-7700 | 2529 |
| J H Textiles Inc. | 2299 | E | 323 585-4124 | 2547 |
| Stone Harbor Inc. | 2299 | F | 323 277-2777 | 2555 |
| Rcrv Inc (PA). | 2325 | E | 323 235-8070 | 2587 |
| Mexapparel Inc (PA). | 2326 | E | 323 364-8600 | 2599 |
| Offline Inc (PA). | 2326 | E | 213 742-9001 | 2600 |
| Spirit Clothing Company. | 2329 | D | 213 784-5372 | 2640 |
| Zk Enterprises Inc. | 2329 | E | 213 622-7012 | 2651 |
| Bluprint Clothing Corp. | 2331 | D | 323 780-4347 | 2657 |
| Crestone LLC. | 2331 | E | 323 588-8857 | 2661 |
| W5 Concepts Inc. | 2331 | E | 323 231-2415 | 2695 |
| Complete Clothing Company (PA). | 2335 | E | 213 892-1188 | 2704 |
| Trinity Sports Inc. | 2335 | B | 323 277-9288 | 2719 |
| Clue Clothing Corp. | 2339 | F | 323 277-4500 | 2747 |
| David Grment Ctng Fsing Svc In. | 2339 | E | 323 216-1574 | 2751 |
| Gaze USA Inc. | 2339 | E | 213 622-0022 | 2760 |
| Heather By Bordeaux Inc. | 2339 | E | 213 622-0555 | 2764 |
| It Jeans Inc. | 2339 | E | 323 588-2156 | 2766 |
| Jaya Apparel Group LLC. | 2339 | F | 323 584-3500 | 2770 |
| Just For Wraps Inc (PA). | 2339 | C | 213 239-0503 | 2778 |
| Kim & Cami Productions Inc. | 2339 | E | 323 584-1300 | 2780 |
| LAT LLC. | 2339 | E | 323 233-3017 | 2785 |
| Patterson Kincaid LLC. | 2339 | E | 323 584-3559 | 2798 |
| Rotax Incorporated. | 2339 | E | 323 589-5999 | 2805 |
| Tempted Apparel Corp. | 2339 | D | 323 589-2999 | 2814 |
| Vxb & Orfwid Inc. | 2339 | E | 213 222-0030 | 2821 |
| W & W Concept Inc. | 2339 | D | 323 803-3090 | 2822 |
| National Corset Supply House (PA). | 2341 | D | 323 261-0265 | 2833 |
| Selectra Industries Corp. | 2341 | E | 323 581-8500 | 2834 |
| Streets Ahead Inc. | 2387 | E | 323 277-0860 | 2885 |
| Anaya Brothers Cutting LLC. | 2389 | D | 323 582-5758 | 2889 |
| Rebecca International Inc. | 2395 | E | 323 973-2602 | 2999 |
| J & H Production. | 2396 | E | 323 261-6600 | 3010 |
| Sandberg Furniture Mfg Co Inc (PA). | 2511 | C | 323 582-0711 | 3456 |
| A Rudin Inc (PA). | 2512 | D | 323 589-5547 | 3464 |
| Yen-Nhai Inc. | 2512 | E | 323 584-1315 | 3495 |
| Marspring Corporation. | 2515 | D | 310 484-6849 | 3533 |
| Tempo Industries Inc. | 2515 | C | 415 552-8074 | 3544 |
| Paper Surce Converting Mfg Inc. | 2621 | E | 323 583-3800 | 3793 |
| Crown Carton Company Inc. | 2653 | E | 323 582-3053 | 3837 |
| Packaging Corporation America. | 2653 | D | 323 263-7581 | 3873 |
| Southland Box Company. | 2653 | C | 323 583-2231 | 3888 |
| Great American Packaging. | 2673 | E | 323 582-2427 | 3968 |
| Norman Paper and Foam Co Inc. | 2673 | E | 323 582-7132 | 3974 |
| Princess Paper Inc. | 2676 | E | 323 588-4777 | 4003 |
| Viva Holdings LLC (PA). | 2678 | F | 818 243-1363 | 4024 |
| Tagtime Usa Inc. | 2679 | E | 323 587-1555 | 4053 |
| Corporate Graphics Intl Inc. | 2752 | D | 323 826-3440 | 4574 |
| Superior Lithographics Inc. | 2752 | D | 323 263-8400 | 4774 |
| The Ligature Inc (HQ). | 2752 | E | 323 585-6000 | 4784 |
| Advanced Chemical Technology. | 2819 | E | 800 527-9607 | 5066 |
| Joes Plastics Inc. | 2821 | E | 323 771-8433 | 5172 |
| Continental Vitamin Co Inc. | 2834 | D | 323 581-0176 | 5408 |
| Peerless Materials Company. | 2842 | E | 323 266-0313 | 5925 |
| Evonik Corporation. | 2899 | D | 323 264-0311 | 6283 |
| Exxon Mbil - Rfnery Dist Plant. | 2911 | F | 323 586-5329 | 6337 |
| Aoclsc Inc. | 2992 | E | 562 776-4000 | 6386 |
| Demenno/Kerdoon Holdings. | 2992 | E | 323 268-3387 | 6390 |
| Sewing Collection Inc (PA). | 3053 | D | 323 264-2223 | 6467 |
| A&A Global Imports LLC (PA). | 3089 | D | 888 315-2453 | 6692 |
| Edris Plastics Mfg Inc. | 3089 | E | 323 581-7000 | 6816 |
| Geo Plastics. | 3089 | E | 323 277-8106 | 6840 |
| Home Concepts Products Inc. | 3089 | E | 866 981-0500 | 6855 |
| Makabi 26 Inc. | 3089 | F | 323 588-7666 | 6901 |
| Norton Packaging Inc. | 3089 | E | 323 588-6167 | 6937 |
| Nuconic Packaging LLC. | 3089 | E | 323 588-9033 | 6941 |
| Rplanet Erth Los Angles Hldngs. | 3089 | D | 833 775-2638 | 7014 |
| Sol-Pak Thermoforming Inc. | 3089 | E | 323 582-3333 | 7033 |
| Tom York Enterprises Inc. | 3089 | E | 323 581-6194 | 7055 |
| G & G Quality Case Co Inc. | 3161 | D | 323 233-2482 | 7130 |
| Isabelle Handbag Inc. | 3171 | E | 323 277-9888 | 7145 |
| Berney-Karp Inc. | 3269 | D | 323 260-7122 | 7286 |
| Calportland Company. | 3273 | F | 800 272-1891 | 7413 |
| National Cement Company Inc. | 3273 | E | 323 923-4466 | 7473 |
| Pabco Building Products LLC. | 3275 | C | 323 581-6113 | 7528 |
| Charman Manufacturing Inc. | 3317 | F | 213 489-7000 | 7662 |
| Nucor Warehouse Systems Inc (HQ). | 3317 | C | 323 588-4261 | 7668 |
| Global Truss America LLC. | 3354 | D | 323 415-6225 | 7739 |

# GEOGRAPHIC SECTION

## VISTA, CA

| Company | SIC | EMP | PHONE | ENTRY# |
|---|---|---|---|---|
| Bodycote Usa Inc. | 3398 | A | 323 264-0111 | 7881 |
| Kai USA Ltd. | 3421 | E | 323 589-2600 | 7937 |
| Progressive Frame & Fabg Co. | 3441 | F | 323 589-9933 | 8204 |
| Ajax Forge Company (PA) | 3462 | F | 323 582-6307 | 8772 |
| Luppen Holdings Inc (PA) | 3469 | E | 323 581-8121 | 8861 |
| Certified Steel Treating Corp. | 3471 | E | 323 583-8711 | 8939 |
| Atlas Galvanizing LLC | 3479 | E | 323 587-6247 | 9051 |
| Kennedy Name Plate Co. | 3479 | E | 323 585-0121 | 9085 |
| S S Schaffer Co Inc. | 3541 | F | 323 560-1430 | 9569 |
| Angelus Machine Corp Intl. | 3542 | E | 323 583-2171 | 9579 |
| Punch Press Products Inc. | 3544 | D | 323 581-7151 | 9644 |
| Flowserve Corporation. | 3561 | B | 323 584-1890 | 9921 |
| Westaire Engineering Inc. | 3585 | F | 323 587-3347 | 10528 |
| J F Duncan Industries Inc (PA) | 3589 | D | 562 862-4269 | 10567 |
| Bender Ccp Inc (PA) | 3599 | C | 323 232-2371 | 10744 |
| Brentwood Appliances Inc. | 3639 | E | 323 266-4600 | 11416 |
| La Spec Industries Inc. | 3646 | F | 323 588-8746 | 11540 |
| Unirex Corp. | 3674 | E | 323 589-4000 | 12781 |
| Westgate Mfg Inc. | 3699 | D | 323 826-9490 | 13332 |
| Team USA (PA) | 3711 | F | 323 826-9888 | 13389 |
| US Radiator Corporation (PA) | 3714 | E | 323 826-0965 | 13601 |
| Evergreen Industries Inc (DH) | 3821 | D | 323 583-1331 | 14336 |
| Mahar Manufacturing Corp (PA) | 3942 | E | 323 581-9988 | 15731 |
| UPD INC. | 3942 | D | 323 588-8811 | 15736 |
| Labeltex Mills Inc (PA) | 3965 | C | 323 582-0228 | 15912 |
| Two Lads Inc (PA) | 3965 | E | 323 584-0064 | 15921 |
| R Planet Earth LLC | 4953 | C | 213 320-0601 | 16361 |
| E B Bradley Co (PA) | 5072 | E | 323 585-9917 | 16752 |
| Kafco Sales Company. | 5084 | E | 323 588-7141 | 16822 |
| Strategic Materials Inc. | 5093 | F | 323 415-0166 | 16963 |
| Rggd Inc (PA) | 5099 | E | 323 581-6617 | 16985 |
| Romex Textiles Inc (PA) | 5131 | E | 213 749-9090 | 17068 |
| Urgent Gear Inc. | 5136 | F | 213 741-9926 | 17083 |
| Double Zero Inc (PA) | 5137 | E | 323 234-6000 | 17089 |
| Lymi Inc (PA) | 5137 | D | 844 701-0139 | 17095 |
| New Pride Corporation. | 5137 | E | 323 584-6608 | 17096 |
| Runway Liquidation LLC (HQ) | 5137 | E | 323 589-2224 | 17099 |
| The Timing Inc. | 5137 | E | 323 589-5577 | 17104 |
| Eastland Corporation. | 5147 | E | 323 261-5388 | 17161 |
| Pontrelli & Larricchia Ltd. | 5147 | E | 323 583-6690 | 17163 |
| Rancho Foods Inc. | 5147 | D | 323 585-0503 | 17165 |
| Sweetener Products Inc (PA) | 5149 | E | 323 234-2200 | 17218 |
| Cherokee Chemical Co Inc (PA) | 5169 | E | 323 265-1112 | 17241 |
| Norman Fox & Co. | 5169 | E | 323 973-4900 | 17248 |
| Anns Trading Company Inc. | 5199 | E | 323 585-4702 | 17284 |
| Kaiser Foundation Hospitals. | 5712 | C | 323 264-4310 | 17521 |
| Modernica Inc (PA) | 5712 | E | 323 826-1600 | 17522 |
| Good Fellas Industries Inc. | 5719 | D | 323 924-9495 | 17534 |
| Huxtables Kitchen Inc. | 5812 | D | 323 923-2900 | 17584 |
| Vie De France Yamazaki Inc. | 5812 | A | 323 582-1241 | 17611 |
| American Elc Components Inc. | 7629 | F | 323 771-4888 | 19174 |
| R A Reed Electric Company (PA) | 7694 | E | 323 587-2284 | 19231 |
| Superior Electric Mtr Svc Inc. | 7694 | E | 323 583-1040 | 19234 |

## VICTORVILLE, CA - San Bernardino County

| Company | SIC | EMP | PHONE | ENTRY# |
|---|---|---|---|---|
| Cwp Cabinets Inc. | 1751 | C | 760 246-4530 | 488 |
| Mars Petcare Us Inc. | 2047 | D | 760 261-7900 | 1107 |
| Reyes Coca-Cola Bottling LLC | 2086 | E | 760 241-2653 | 1954 |
| Graco Childrens Products Inc. | 2514 | B | 770 418-7200 | 3504 |
| Gatehouse Media LLC | 2711 | E | 760 241-7744 | 4121 |
| Church & Dwight Co Inc. | 2841 | F | 609 613-1551 | 5873 |
| Newell Brands Inc. | 3089 | E | 760 246-2700 | 6929 |
| Daikin Comfort Tech Mfg LP | 3585 | B | 760 955-7770 | 10495 |
| General Electric Company. | 3721 | E | 760 530-5200 | 13665 |
| Excel Scientific LLC. | 5049 | E | 760 246-4545 | 16600 |
| Comav LLC (PA) | 5088 | E | 760 523-5100 | 16918 |
| Focus Language Intl Inc. | 7389 | F | 800 374-5444 | 19091 |

## VILLA PARK, CA - Orange County

| Company | SIC | EMP | PHONE | ENTRY# |
|---|---|---|---|---|
| Manufactured Solutions LLC. | 3999 | E | 714 548-6915 | 16177 |

## VISALIA, CA - Tulare County

| Company | SIC | EMP | PHONE | ENTRY# |
|---|---|---|---|---|
| Anchor-41 Construction LLC. | 1542 | F | 559 740-7776 | 363 |
| CM Construction Services Inc (PA) | 1542 | E | 559 735-9556 | 366 |
| AFP Advanced Food Products LLC | 2026 | E | 559 651-1737 | 824 |
| California Dairies Inc (PA) | 2026 | D | 559 625-2200 | 828 |
| AFP Advanced Food Products LLC | 2032 | E | 559 627-2070 | 847 |
| Kruse Pet Holdings LLC (HQ) | 2047 | E | 559 302-4880 | 1106 |
| Diamond Crystal Brands Inc. | 2099 | E | 559 651-7782 | 2184 |
| Corrwood Containers. | 2449 | E | 559 651-0335 | 3369 |
| Kaweah Container Inc (HQ) | 2653 | E | 559 651-7846 | 3863 |
| Nexgen Container LLC. | 2653 | D | 559 553-7500 | 3868 |
| Pacific Southwest Cont LLC. | 2653 | E | 559 651-5500 | 3872 |
| Sorma USA LLC. | 2673 | B | 559 651-1269 | 3980 |
| Celebration West Inc. | 2752 | C | | 4545 |
| J-M Manufacturing Company Inc. | 2821 | E | 559 651-2100 | 5168 |
| Milk Specialties Company. | 2834 | E | 559 732-1220 | 5555 |
| Pace International LLC. | 2842 | F | 559 651-4877 | 5923 |
| US Cotton LLC. | 2844 | D | 559 651-3015 | 6051 |
| Edeniq Inc. | 2869 | D | 559 302-1777 | 6142 |
| Biagro Western Sales Inc. | 2879 | E | 559 635-4784 | 6193 |
| Trical Inc. | 2879 | E | 559 651-0736 | 6208 |
| Tempo Plastic Co. | 3086 | E | 559 651-7711 | 6666 |
| Polymerpak LLC. | 3089 | C | 559 651-1965 | 6973 |
| Pacific Coast Supply LLC | 3275 | E | 559 651-2185 | 7530 |
| R Lang Company. | 3442 | D | 559 651-0701 | 8287 |
| Kawneer Company Inc. | 3446 | C | 559 651-4000 | 8632 |
| Bluescope Buildings N Amer Inc. | 3448 | C | 559 651-5300 | 8656 |
| Spraying Devices Inc. | 3523 | F | 559 734-5555 | 9383 |
| Screw Conveyor Pacific Corp. | 3535 | C | 559 651-2131 | 9493 |
| Serpa Packaging Solutions LLC | 3565 | D | 559 651-2339 | 10030 |
| Tomra Sorting Inc. | 3569 | E | 877 402-1755 | 10118 |
| Voltage Multipliers Inc (PA) | 3674 | C | 559 651-1402 | 12796 |
| Powers Holdings Inc. | 3679 | E | 559 651-2222 | 13064 |
| Hellwig Products Company Inc. | 3714 | D | 559 734-7451 | 13513 |
| Premier Trailer Mfg Inc. | 3799 | E | 559 651-2212 | 14132 |
| CCS Manufacturing Inc. | 3999 | F | 559 786-8489 | 16112 |
| Gary W Gray. | 3999 | E | 559 750-8462 | 16133 |
| Guardian Fire Service Inc. | 5999 | F | 559 651-0919 | 17706 |
| Central Valley Presort Inc. | 7331 | D | 559 906-2003 | 17796 |
| Visalia Electric Motor Sp Inc. | 7694 | E | 559 651-0606 | 19236 |
| Neighborhood Mennonite. | 8661 | E | 559 732-9107 | 19369 |

## VISTA, CA - San Diego County

| Company | SIC | EMP | PHONE | ENTRY# |
|---|---|---|---|---|
| Bellissimo Distribution LLC. | 2032 | E | 760 292-9100 | 849 |
| Baked In The Sun. | 2051 | C | 760 591-9045 | 1165 |
| J&L Eppig Brewing LLC | 2082 | F | 760 295-2009 | 1436 |
| Pure Project LLC | 2082 | D | 760 552-7873 | 1456 |
| Great Western Malting Co. | 2083 | E | 360 991-0888 | 1468 |
| Javo Beverage Company Inc. | 2087 | D | 760 560-5286 | 2011 |
| Tacupeto Chips & Salsa Inc. | 2096 | F | 760 597-9400 | 2105 |
| Thirty Three Threads Inc (PA) | 2329 | E | 877 486-3769 | 2648 |
| Architctral Mllwk Slutions Inc. | 2431 | F | 760 510-6440 | 3109 |
| Earthlite LLC (DH) | 2514 | D | 760 599-1112 | 3502 |
| Killion Industries Inc (PA) | 2541 | E | 760 727-5102 | 3661 |
| Astro Converters Inc (PA) | 2677 | E | 800 752-5003 | 4007 |
| Precision Litho Inc. | 2752 | E | 760 727-9400 | 4729 |
| Advanced Web Offset Inc. | 2759 | D | 760 727-1700 | 4837 |
| Golden Rule Bindery Inc. | 2789 | E | 760 471-2013 | 5011 |
| J & D Laboratories Inc. | 2833 | B | 760 734-6800 | 5246 |
| Bachem Americas Inc. | 2834 | E | 888 422-2436 | 5353 |
| Captek Midco Inc. | 2834 | D | 760 734-6800 | 5389 |
| American Peptide Company Inc. | 2836 | E | 408 733-7604 | 5792 |
| Grifols Usa LLC. | 2836 | D | 760 931-8444 | 5834 |
| Mindera Corp. | 2836 | E | 858 810-6070 | 5849 |
| All One God Faith Inc. | 2841 | D | 760 599-4010 | 5870 |
| All One God Faith Inc (PA) | 2841 | C | 844 937-2551 | 5871 |
| Revlon Inc. | 2844 | D | 619 372-1379 | 6031 |
| Allied Coatings Inc. | 2851 | F | 800 630-2375 | 6067 |
| San Group Biotech Usa Inc. | 2879 | E | 760 599-8855 | 6206 |
| American General Tool Group. | 3011 | E | 760 745-7993 | 6404 |
| Watkins Manufacturing Corp. | 3088 | B | 760 598-6464 | 6688 |
| Distinctive Plastics Inc. | 3089 | D | 760 599-9100 | 6805 |
| Diversified Plastics Inc. | 3089 | E | 760 598-5333 | 6807 |
| J A English II Inc. | 3089 | E | 760 598-5333 | 6869 |
| Nubs Plastics Inc. | 3089 | E | 760 598-2525 | 6940 |
| Predator Motorsports Inc. | 3089 | E | 760 734-1749 | 6979 |
| Prime Plastic Products Inc. | 3089 | F | 760 734-3900 | 6982 |
| Oceanside Glasstile Company (PA) | 3253 | B | 760 929-4000 | 7270 |
| Kammerer Enterprises Inc. | 3281 | D | 760 560-0550 | 7540 |
| Monster Tool LLC. | 3423 | C | 760 477-1000 | 7960 |
| Aztec Technology Corporation (PA) | 3441 | E | 760 727-2300 | 8098 |
| McCain Manufacturing Inc. | 3441 | D | 760 295-9290 | 8178 |
| Solatube International Inc (DH) | 3442 | D | 888 765-2882 | 8291 |
| Protec Arisawa America Inc. | 3443 | E | 760 599-4800 | 8329 |
| AP Precision Metals Inc. | 3444 | E | 619 628-0003 | 8377 |
| Innovative Metal Products Inc. | 3444 | F | 760 734-1010 | 8474 |
| Versaform Corporation. | 3444 | D | 760 599-4477 | 8608 |
| Diversified Tool & Die. | 3469 | E | 760 598-9100 | 8837 |
| J-Mark Manufacturing Inc. | 3469 | E | 760 727-6956 | 8854 |
| West Coast Pvd Inc. | 3471 | E | 714 822-6362 | 9032 |
| Dig Corporation. | 3523 | E | 760 727-0914 | 9349 |
| Western Cactus Growers Inc. | 3524 | E | 760 726-1710 | 9402 |
| Sherline Products Incorporated. | 3541 | E | 760 727-5181 | 9571 |
| Addition Manufacturing Technologies CA Inc. | 3542 | E | 760 597-5220 | 9575 |
| Flotron. | 3544 | E | 760 727-2700 | 9623 |

Employee Codes: A=Over 500 employees, B=251-500
C=101-250, D=51-100, E=20-50, F=10-19, G=1-9

## VISTA, CA

| Company | SIC | EMP | PHONE | ENTRY# |
|---|---|---|---|---|
| Resers Fine Foods Inc | 3556 | E | 503 643-6431 | 9813 |
| Asml Us Inc | 3559 | B | 760 443-6244 | 9833 |
| Rxsafe LLC | 3559 | D | 760 593-7161 | 9897 |
| Accutek Packaging Equipment Co (PA) | 3565 | E | 760 734-4177 | 10009 |
| Rec Inc | 3569 | F | 760 727-8006 | 10109 |
| Apem Inc (HQ) | 3577 | E | 978 372-1602 | 10321 |
| Applied Membranes Inc | 3589 | C | 760 727-3711 | 10536 |
| Enaqua (DH) | 3589 | F | 760 599-2644 | 10557 |
| Hydrocomponents & Tech Inc | 3589 | F | 760 598-0189 | 10564 |
| Yanchewski & Wardell Entps Inc | 3589 | D | 760 754-1960 | 10615 |
| Henry Machine Inc | 3599 | F | | 10869 |
| Router Works Inc | 3599 | F | 760 599-9280 | 11092 |
| Stines Machine Inc | 3599 | F | 760 599-9955 | 11125 |
| Vista Industrial Products Inc | 3599 | C | 760 599-5050 | 11179 |
| Western Cnc Inc | 3599 | D | 760 597-7000 | 11191 |
| Zettler Magnetics Inc | 3612 | E | 949 831-5000 | 11232 |
| Ddh Enterprise Inc (PA) | 3643 | D | 760 599-0171 | 11449 |
| Exit Light Co Inc | 3646 | F | 877 352-3948 | 11530 |
| Blisslights LLC | 3648 | E | 888 868-4603 | 11586 |
| M Klemme Technology Corp | 3651 | E | 760 727-0593 | 11672 |
| Raveon Technologies Corp | 3663 | E | 760 444-5995 | 11929 |
| Outsource Manufacturing Inc | 3674 | D | 760 795-1295 | 12627 |
| Plansee USA LLC | 3674 | D | 760 438-9090 | 12633 |
| Csi Technologies Inc | 3675 | F | 760 682-2222 | 12816 |
| Apem Inc | 3679 | D | 760 598-2518 | 12914 |
| AZ Displays Inc | 3679 | E | 949 831-5000 | 12919 |
| Flux Power Holdings Inc (PA) | 3691 | C | 877 505-3589 | 13141 |
| Blisslights Inc | 3699 | E | 888 868-4603 | 13215 |
| Dutek Incorporated | 3699 | E | 760 566-8888 | 13236 |
| Nology Engineering Inc | 3714 | F | 760 591-0888 | 13549 |
| Carbon By Design LLC | 3728 | E | 760 643-1300 | 13806 |
| Nighthawk Flight Systems Inc | 3812 | E | 760 727-4900 | 14228 |
| Sandel Avionics Inc | 3812 | E | 760 727-4900 | 14298 |
| Sandel Avionics Inc (PA) | 3812 | E | 760 727-4900 | 14299 |
| Leica Biosystems Imaging Inc (HQ) | 3826 | C | 760 539-1100 | 14683 |
| Machine Vision Products Inc (PA) | 3827 | E | 760 438-1138 | 14797 |
| Mitchell Instruments Co Inc | 3829 | F | 760 744-2690 | 14902 |
| Biofilm Inc | 3841 | D | 760 727-9030 | 15009 |
| Carol Cole Company | 3841 | C | 888 360-9171 | 15035 |
| Surgistar Inc (PA) | 3841 | E | 760 598-2480 | 15271 |
| Djo Holdings LLC (DH) | 3842 | E | 760 727-1280 | 15334 |
| Vision Quest Industries Inc | 3842 | C | 949 261-6382 | 15427 |
| Conamco SA De CV | 3843 | D | 760 586-4356 | 15443 |
| Amron International Inc (PA) | 3949 | D | 760 208-6500 | 15779 |
| Aza Industries Inc (PA) | 3949 | E | 760 500-0440 | 15783 |
| Efgp Inc | 3949 | F | 760 692-3900 | 15806 |
| Rayzist Photomask Inc (PA) | 3955 | D | 760 727-8561 | 15900 |
| Wolfpack Inc | 3993 | E | 760 736-4500 | 16069 |
| Integrated Mfg Solutions LLC | 3999 | E | 760 599-4300 | 16152 |
| Watkins Manufacturing Corp (HQ) | 3999 | C | 760 598-6464 | 16268 |
| Tempo Communications Inc (PA) | 4813 | D | 800 642-2155 | 16323 |
| Ultra Communications Inc | 4813 | E | 760 652-0011 | 16324 |
| Phoenix Wheel Company Inc | 5013 | E | 760 598-1960 | 16389 |
| American Faucet Coatings Corp | 5023 | E | 760 598-5895 | 16420 |
| California Breakers Inc (PA) | 5063 | E | 760 598-1528 | 16648 |
| Swarco McCain Inc (DH) | 5084 | C | 760 727-8100 | 16848 |
| Apical Industries Inc | 5088 | D | 760 724-5300 | 16915 |
| Eliel & Co | 5136 | E | 760 877-8469 | 17073 |
| Altman Specialty Plants LLC (PA) | 5193 | A | 800 348-4881 | 17278 |
| Lee-Mar Aquarium & Pet Sups | 5199 | D | 760 727-1300 | 17299 |
| Coromega Company Inc | 5499 | E | 760 599-6088 | 17425 |
| Bni Publications Inc | 5942 | E | 760 734-1113 | 17637 |
| International Lottery & Totalizator Systems Inc | 7371 | E | 760 598-1655 | 17935 |
| Interntnal Lttery Ttlztor Syst | 7371 | E | 760 598-1655 | 17936 |
| Amkom Design Group Inc | 7389 | E | 760 295-1957 | 19071 |
| Systems Engineering & MGT Co (PA) | 8711 | E | 760 727-7800 | 19423 |
| Leidos Inc | 8731 | C | 858 826-9090 | 19460 |

## WALNUT, CA - Los Angeles County

| Company | SIC | EMP | PHONE | ENTRY# |
|---|---|---|---|---|
| Settlers Jerky Inc | 2013 | E | 909 444-3999 | 666 |
| Pepsico Inc | 2086 | E | 909 718-8229 | 1926 |
| Imperfect Foods Inc (HQ) | 2099 | D | 510 595-6683 | 2237 |
| Ninas Mexican Foods Inc | 2099 | E | 909 468-5888 | 2298 |
| Charades LLC | 2389 | C | 626 435-0077 | 2893 |
| Diamond Collection LLC | 2389 | E | 626 435-0077 | 2897 |
| Diana Did-It Designs Inc | 2389 | E | 970 226-5062 | 2898 |
| Southcoast Cabinet Inc (PA) | 2434 | E | 909 594-3089 | 3270 |
| SW Fixtures Inc | 2541 | F | 909 595-2506 | 3673 |
| DC Locker Inc | 2542 | F | 909 480-0066 | 3684 |
| All Strong Industry (usa) Inc (PA) | 2591 | E | 909 598-6494 | 3715 |
| 1perfectchoice | 2599 | F | 909 594-8855 | 3731 |
| Golden Applexx Co Inc | 2759 | E | 909 594-9788 | 4882 |
| Nu-Health Products Co | 2833 | E | 909 869-0666 | 5257 |
| Oyewan Inc | 2844 | E | 909 869-6200 | 6015 |
| Physicans Formula Holdings Inc (HQ) | 2844 | E | 626 334-3395 | 6021 |
| Enzyme Corporation | 2869 | E | 415 638-9595 | 6144 |
| Essentra International LLC | 2891 | A | 708 315-7498 | 6227 |
| 10 Day Parts Inc | 3089 | E | 951 279-4810 | 6689 |
| AMS Plastics Inc (PA) | 3089 | E | 619 713-2000 | 6716 |
| 2nd Source Wire & Cable Inc | 3312 | D | 714 482-2866 | 7602 |
| Tree Island Wire (USA) Inc (DH) | 3315 | C | 909 594-7511 | 7656 |
| Cast Parts Inc (HQ) | 3324 | C | 909 595-2252 | 7683 |
| Pengcheng Aluminum Enterprise Inc USA | 3354 | E | 909 598-7933 | 7745 |
| Sea Shield Marine Products Inc | 3363 | E | 909 594-2507 | 7821 |
| Western Hardware Company | 3429 | F | 909 595-6201 | 8037 |
| Edro Engineering LLC (DH) | 3544 | E | 909 594-5751 | 9619 |
| Fairway Injection Molds Inc | 3544 | D | 909 595-2201 | 9622 |
| Niron Inc | 3544 | F | 909 598-1526 | 9638 |
| Amergence Technology Inc | 3559 | E | 909 859-8400 | 9826 |
| In Win Development USA Inc | 3572 | E | 909 348-0588 | 10246 |
| Prophecy Technology LLC | 3577 | F | 909 598-7998 | 10424 |
| Tri-Net Technology Inc | 3577 | D | 909 598-8818 | 10446 |
| Trane US Inc | 3585 | E | 626 913-7913 | 10519 |
| Crush Master Grinding Corp | 3599 | E | 909 595-2249 | 10793 |
| Mjc America Ltd (PA) | 3634 | E | 888 876-5387 | 11411 |
| US Energy Technologies Inc | 3646 | E | 714 617-8800 | 11565 |
| Excellence Opto Inc (PA) | 3647 | E | 909 468-0550 | 11572 |
| Soderberg Manufacturing Co Inc | 3647 | D | 909 595-1291 | 11576 |
| Disc Replicator Inc | 3652 | F | 909 385-0118 | 11728 |
| Simple Solar Industries LLC | 3674 | E | 844 907-0705 | 12710 |
| Racing Power Company | 3714 | E | 909 468-3690 | 13565 |
| Aero Pacific Corporation | 3728 | C | 714 961-9200 | 13743 |
| Shore Western Manufacturing | 3826 | E | 626 357-3251 | 14717 |
| Total Resources Intl Inc (PA) | 3842 | E | 909 594-1220 | 15418 |
| Jakks Pacific Inc | 3944 | E | 909 594-7771 | 15755 |
| Hupa International Inc | 3949 | E | 909 598-9876 | 15823 |
| Loungefly LLC | 3961 | E | 818 718-5600 | 15905 |
| Infinity Watch Corporation | 3993 | E | 626 289-9878 | 15987 |
| Cal Southern Packg Eqp Inc | 5084 | F | 909 598-3198 | 16808 |
| Madaco Safety Products Inc | 5099 | F | 909 614-1756 | 16979 |
| Kleverness Incorporated | 5734 | F | 213 559-2480 | 17554 |
| Identigraphix Inc | 7336 | E | 909 468-4741 | 17831 |
| Gremlin Inc | 7372 | D | 408 214-9885 | 18363 |
| Zumen Inc | 7372 | F | 564 444-6964 | 18957 |

## WALNUT CREEK, CA - Contra Costa County

| Company | SIC | EMP | PHONE | ENTRY# |
|---|---|---|---|---|
| Hofmann Construction Co (PA) | 1531 | E | 925 478-2000 | 350 |
| Cytosport Inc | 2023 | C | 707 751-3942 | 753 |
| Bell-Carter Olive Packing Co (PA) | 2033 | E | 209 549-5939 | 880 |
| Basic American Inc (PA) | 2034 | D | 800 227-4050 | 945 |
| Andre-Boudin Bakeries Inc | 2051 | E | 925 935-4375 | 1156 |
| Contra Costa Newspapers Inc (DH) | 2711 | A | 925 935-2525 | 4098 |
| Diablo Country Magazine Inc | 2721 | E | 925 943-1111 | 4247 |
| Institutional Real Estate Inc (PA) | 2741 | E | 925 933-4040 | 4418 |
| Blue Tees Enterprises LLC | 2759 | E | 949 702-0564 | 4851 |
| Vertosa Inc | 2833 | E | 510 550-5850 | 5280 |
| Diablo Clinical Research Inc | 2834 | E | 925 930-7267 | 5427 |
| Tbdx Inc | 3556 | E | 415 225-1391 | 9820 |
| Carros Sensors Systems Co LLC | 3829 | B | 925 979-4400 | 14855 |
| Dreyers Grnd Ice Cream Hldngs (DH) | 5143 | C | 510 652-8187 | 17128 |
| Del Monte Foods Inc (HQ) | 5149 | C | 925 949-2772 | 17186 |
| Dreyers Grand Ice Cream Inc (DH) | 5812 | C | 510 594-9466 | 17577 |
| Joroda Inc (PA) | 5812 | E | 925 930-0122 | 17589 |
| Golden Rain Foundation (PA) | 6531 | D | 925 988-7700 | 17742 |
| Autoclerk Inc | 7371 | F | 925 284-1005 | 17884 |
| Innosys Incorporated | 7371 | E | 510 594-1034 | 17929 |
| Advisor Software Inc (PA) | 7372 | E | 925 299-7782 | 18024 |
| Domico Software | 7372 | F | 510 841-4155 | 18248 |
| Exadel Inc (PA) | 7372 | A | 925 363-9510 | 18303 |
| Forensic Logic Inc | 7372 | E | 415 810-2114 | 18319 |
| Issio Solutions Inc | 7372 | E | 888 994-7746 | 18448 |
| Seal Software Incorporated (HQ) | 7372 | F | 650 938-7325 | 18772 |
| Skuid Inc | 7372 | D | 800 515-2535 | 18794 |
| Vantiq Inc (PA) | 7372 | E | 650 346-1114 | 18910 |

## WALNUT GROVE, CA - Sacramento County

| Company | SIC | EMP | PHONE | ENTRY# |
|---|---|---|---|---|
| Wilcox Brothers Inc | 3523 | D | 916 776-1784 | 9396 |

## WASCO, CA - Kern County

| Company | SIC | EMP | PHONE | ENTRY# |
|---|---|---|---|---|
| Sunnygem LLC (PA) | 2033 | C | 661 758-0491 | 930 |
| Primex Farms LLC (PA) | 2068 | E | 661 758-7790 | 1364 |
| Certis USA LLC | 2879 | E | 661 758-8471 | 6195 |

## WATERFORD, CA - Stanislaus County

| Company | SIC | EMP | PHONE | ENTRY# |
|---|---|---|---|---|
| Riddle Ranches Inc | 0173 | E | 209 874-9784 | 41 |
| Foster Poultry Farms | 2015 | B | 209 394-7901 | 683 |

# GEOGRAPHIC SECTION
## WESTMINSTER, CA

| | SIC | EMP | PHONE | ENTRY# |
|---|---|---|---|---|
| Roberts Ferry Nut Company Inc | 2064 | E | 209 874-3247 | 1323 |

### WATSONVILLE, CA - Santa Cruz County

| | SIC | EMP | PHONE | ENTRY# |
|---|---|---|---|---|
| Granite Rock Company (PA) | 1442 | D | 831 768-2000 | 314 |
| Granite Construction Inc (PA) | 1622 | B | 831 724-1011 | 385 |
| Del Mar Food Products Corp | 2033 | D | 831 722-3516 | 882 |
| S Martinelli & Company | 2033 | E | 831 768-3958 | 923 |
| S Martinelli & Company | 2033 | E | 831 768-3958 | 924 |
| Nordic Naturals Inc | 2077 | C | 800 662-2544 | 1386 |
| HA Rider & Sons | 2086 | E | 831 722-3882 | 1893 |
| La Rosa Tortilla Factory Inc | 2099 | E | 831 728-5332 | 2258 |
| Laselva Beach Spice Co Inc | 2099 | F | 831 724-4500 | 2261 |
| Mizkan America Inc | 2099 | D | 831 728-2061 | 2281 |
| S Martinelli & Company (PA) | 2099 | D | 831 724-1126 | 2344 |
| S Martinelli & Company | 2099 | E | 831 724-1126 | 2345 |
| Noah Pharmaceuticals Inc | 2833 | E | 707 631-0921 | 5253 |
| Nordic Naturals Mfg Inc | 2833 | E | 800 662-2544 | 5254 |
| Threshold Enterprises Ltd | 2833 | E | 831 425-3955 | 5273 |
| Boyer Inc | 2873 | E | 831 724-0123 | 6170 |
| Annieglass Inc (PA) | 3229 | F | 831 761-2041 | 7189 |
| Pulse Shower Spas Inc | 3261 | E | 831 724-7300 | 7279 |
| Monterey Structural Steel Inc | 3441 | E | 831 768-1277 | 8191 |
| Cryowest Inc | 3443 | E | 831 786-9721 | 8314 |
| Stalfab Inc | 3556 | E | 831 786-1600 | 9817 |
| Sierrathermal Inc (DH) | 3567 | E | 831 763-0113 | 10059 |
| Printworx Inc | 3577 | E | 831 722-7147 | 10423 |
| Heatwave Labs Inc | 3671 | E | 831 722-9081 | 12033 |
| Eagle Tech Manufacturing Inc | 3823 | E | 831 768-7467 | 14407 |
| Elecraft Incorporated | 3825 | E | 831 763-4211 | 14515 |
| Sage Instruments Inc | 3825 | D | 831 761-1000 | 14583 |
| Trufocus Corporation | 3844 | F | 831 761-9981 | 15510 |
| Sv Labs Corporation (PA) | 5122 | D | 831 722-9526 | 17053 |
| DLa Colmena Inc | 5411 | E | 831 724-4544 | 17376 |

### WEED, CA - Siskiyou County

| | SIC | EMP | PHONE | ENTRY# |
|---|---|---|---|---|
| Cg Roxane LLC | 2086 | F | 530 225-1260 | 1877 |
| Sanders Prcsion Tmber Flling I (PA) | 2411 | E | 530 938-4120 | 3054 |

### WEST COVINA, CA - Los Angeles County

| | SIC | EMP | PHONE | ENTRY# |
|---|---|---|---|---|
| Ola Nation LLC | 2335 | E | 310 256-0638 | 2712 |
| Interspace Battery Inc (PA) | 3356 | E | 626 813-1234 | 7763 |
| Macdonald Carbide Co | 3544 | E | 626 960-4034 | 9633 |
| Baatz Enterprises Inc | 3711 | E | 323 660-4866 | 13342 |
| R & D Nova Inc | 3845 | E | 951 781-7332 | 15574 |
| Saint Jseph Communications Inc (PA) | 7812 | E | 626 331-3549 | 19296 |

### WEST HILLS, CA - Los Angeles County

| | SIC | EMP | PHONE | ENTRY# |
|---|---|---|---|---|
| Flavor Producers LLC (PA) | 2087 | E | 661 257-3400 | 2006 |
| Pharmavite LLC (DH) | 2833 | B | 818 221-6200 | 5261 |
| Aerojet Rocketdyne De Inc | 2869 | C | 818 586-9629 | 6123 |
| Jj Acquisitions LLC | 3069 | E | 818 772-0100 | 6505 |
| Source Photonics Usa Inc (PA) | 3674 | C | 818 773-9044 | 12726 |

### WEST HOLLYWOOD, CA - Los Angeles County

| | SIC | EMP | PHONE | ENTRY# |
|---|---|---|---|---|
| Mananalu Inc | 2086 | E | 805 222-0046 | 1902 |
| 402 Shoes Inc | 2341 | E | 323 655-5437 | 2826 |
| Pro Tour Memorabilia LLC | 2499 | E | 424 303-7200 | 3423 |
| Dedon Inc | 2511 | F | 310 388-4721 | 3438 |
| Rtmh Inc (PA) | 2512 | F | 323 651-2202 | 3489 |
| Clique Brands Inc | 2721 | E | 310 623-6916 | 4240 |
| Philip B Inc | 2833 | E | 888 376-8236 | 5263 |
| Capricor | 2834 | E | 310 423-2104 | 5387 |
| Cosmo International Corp | 2844 | D | 310 271-1100 | 5962 |
| Philip B Botanicals Products | 2844 | F | 202 759-0650 | 6020 |
| Speed Ventures | 3644 | E | 323 461-4795 | 11482 |
| Chase-Durer Ltd (PA) | 3873 | F | 310 550-7280 | 15676 |
| Fountainhead Industries | 3999 | E | 310 248-2444 | 16132 |
| Paul Ferrante Inc | 3999 | E | 310 854-4412 | 16196 |
| J Robert Scott Inc (PA) | 5131 | C | 310 680-4300 | 17062 |
| Ficto Holdings LLC | 7371 | F | 424 250-2400 | 17921 |
| Cedars-Sinai Medical Center | 8062 | E | 310 423-5641 | 19324 |

### WEST SACRAMENTO, CA - Yolo County

| | SIC | EMP | PHONE | ENTRY# |
|---|---|---|---|---|
| Vss International Inc (HQ) | 1611 | D | 916 373-1500 | 384 |
| AEP Span Inc | 1761 | E | 916 372-0933 | 510 |
| Farmers Rice Cooperative | 2044 | D | 916 373-5500 | 1077 |
| Nor-Cal Beverage Co Inc | 2086 | E | 916 371-1700 | 1906 |
| Better Meat Co | 2099 | F | 916 893-8777 | 2140 |
| Traditions Prepared Meals LLC | 2099 | E | 916 534-4937 | 2378 |
| Icon Apparel Group LLC | 2231 | E | 916 372-4266 | 2447 |
| Cosmo Import & Export LLC | 2514 | E | 916 209-5500 | 3500 |
| Tk Classics LLC | 2514 | E | 916 209-5500 | 3514 |
| Global Steel Products Corp | 2542 | E | 510 652-2060 | 3690 |
| International Paper Company | 2621 | D | 916 371-4634 | 3781 |
| Leo Lam Inc | 2752 | E | 925 484-3690 | 4675 |
| Redstone Print & Mail Inc | 2752 | C | 925 335-9090 | 4753 |
| Tackett Volume Press Inc | 2752 | E | 916 374-8991 | 4778 |
| Taylor Communications Inc | 2761 | E | 916 340-0200 | 4992 |
| Environmental Science US LLC | 2834 | C | 800 331-2867 | 5433 |
| Origin Materials Inc (PA) | 2836 | E | 916 231-9329 | 5852 |
| Nuseed Americas Inc (HQ) | 2879 | E | 800 345-3330 | 6204 |
| Richard K Gould Inc | 2899 | E | 916 371-5943 | 6321 |
| Talco Foam Inc (PA) | 3069 | F | 916 492-8840 | 6542 |
| Arcadia Inc | 3355 | E | 916 375-1478 | 7756 |
| Carter Group (PA) | 3441 | E | 916 373-0148 | 8119 |
| ECB Corp | 3444 | E | 916 492-8900 | 8438 |
| Crown Equipment Corporation | 3537 | E | 916 373-8980 | 9515 |
| Odenberg Inc | 3556 | E | 916 371-0700 | 9809 |
| Tri-C Manufacturing Inc | 3559 | E | 916 371-1700 | 9905 |
| Heco Inc | 3566 | F | 916 372-5411 | 10040 |
| Bullseye Leak Detection Inc | 3599 | E | 916 760-8944 | 10757 |
| Rocket Composites Inc | 3599 | E | 916 873-8840 | 11086 |
| Siemens Industry Inc | 3822 | E | 916 553-4444 | 14369 |
| Sign Technology Inc | 3993 | E | 916 372-1200 | 16038 |
| Scoggan Company Inc (PA) | 5013 | E | 916 371-3984 | 16399 |
| Clark - Pacific Corporation (PA) | 5032 | B | 916 371-0305 | 16471 |
| Sacramento Stucco Co | 5032 | E | 916 372-7442 | 16483 |
| Nor-Cal Beverage Co Inc (PA) | 5181 | E | 916 372-0600 | 17259 |
| Quad/Graphics Inc | 7311 | E | 916 371-9500 | 17782 |
| Premier Print & Mail Inc | 7331 | F | 916 503-5300 | 17801 |
| North Valley Fleet Svcs Inc (PA) | 7538 | F | 916 374-8850 | 19161 |
| Eurofins Envmt Tstg Nthrn Cal | 8734 | E | 916 373-5600 | 19502 |
| Novate Solutions Inc (PA) | 8748 | E | 866 668-2830 | 19567 |

### WESTLAKE VILLAGE, CA - Ventura County

| | SIC | EMP | PHONE | ENTRY# |
|---|---|---|---|---|
| Dole Holding Company LLC | 0179 | A | 818 879-6600 | 45 |
| Welbilt Inc | 1389 | E | 310 339-1555 | 292 |
| Soy Sauce Productions LLC | 2035 | E | 818 213-1092 | 993 |
| Dole Packaged Foods LLC (HQ) | 2037 | A | 800 232-8888 | 1003 |
| Opolo Vineyards Inc | 2084 | F | 805 238-9593 | 1698 |
| Americon | 2521 | E | 805 987-0412 | 3560 |
| Omics Group Inc | 2721 | B | 650 268-9744 | 4282 |
| Network Television Time Inc | 2741 | E | 877 468-8899 | 4438 |
| Earth Print Inc | 2752 | F | 818 879-6050 | 4599 |
| Odcombe Press (nashville) | 2752 | E | 615 793-5414 | 4711 |
| Akeso Health Sciences LLC | 2833 | F | 818 865-1046 | 5228 |
| Innocoll Biotherapeutics NA | 2834 | D | 484 406-5200 | 5494 |
| Kythera Biopharmaceuticals Inc | 2834 | C | 818 587-4500 | 5533 |
| Mannkind Corporation | 2834 | B | 818 661-5000 | 5541 |
| Capsida Biotherapeutics Inc (PA) | 2836 | E | 805 410-2673 | 5813 |
| Sugar Foods LLC (HQ) | 2869 | E | 805 396-5000 | 6162 |
| Interntional Photo Plates Corp | 3471 | E | 805 496-5031 | 8974 |
| Hydrodex LLC | 3589 | E | 800 218-8813 | 10565 |
| Baltic Ltvian Unvrsal Elec LLC | 3651 | E | 818 879-5200 | 11642 |
| Sunbritetv LLC (DH) | 3663 | F | 805 214-7250 | 11954 |
| Inphi International Pte Ltd | 3674 | E | 805 719-2300 | 12490 |
| Carros Sensors Americas LLC | 3679 | C | 805 267-7176 | 12932 |
| Energy Vault Inc (HQ) | 3691 | E | 805 852-0000 | 13135 |
| Ventura Aerospace Inc | 3728 | F | 818 540-3130 | 13987 |
| Rantec Microwave Systems Inc (PA) | 3812 | D | 818 223-5000 | 14282 |
| Erp Power (PA) | 3825 | E | 805 517-1300 | 14519 |
| Caldera Medical Inc (PA) | 3841 | D | 818 879-6555 | 15024 |
| Implant Direct Sybron Intl LLC (HQ) | 3843 | D | 818 444-3000 | 15458 |
| Gamebreaker Inc (PA) | 3949 | E | 818 224-7424 | 15816 |
| Vitavet Labs Inc | 3999 | E | 818 865-2600 | 16264 |
| Jri Inc | 5065 | E | 818 706-2424 | 16711 |
| Baxter Healthcare Corporation | 5122 | C | 805 372-3000 | 17028 |
| Ruby Ribbon Inc | 5137 | E | 650 449-4470 | 17098 |
| Cadillac Motor Div Area | 5511 | C | 805 373-9575 | 17437 |
| Toller Enterprises Inc (PA) | 5551 | E | 805 374-9455 | 17480 |
| Jafra Cosmetics Intl Inc (DH) | 5999 | D | 805 449-3000 | 17709 |
| Cforia Software LLC | 7372 | E | 818 871-9687 | 18162 |
| Facefirst LLC | 7372 | E | 805 482-8428 | 18305 |
| Srax Inc (PA) | 7372 | D | 323 205-6109 | 18830 |
| Rvl Packaging Inc | 7389 | E | 818 735-5000 | 19124 |
| Thousand Oaks Prtg & Spc Inc | 7389 | C | 818 706-8330 | 19139 |

### WESTLEY, CA - Stanislaus County

| | SIC | EMP | PHONE | ENTRY# |
|---|---|---|---|---|
| Just Tomatoes Inc | 0723 | E | 209 894-5371 | 82 |

### WESTMINSTER, CA - Orange County

| | SIC | EMP | PHONE | ENTRY# |
|---|---|---|---|---|
| Maintech Resources Inc | 1796 | E | 562 804-0664 | 550 |
| Einstein Noah Rest Group Inc | 2022 | C | 714 847-4609 | 712 |
| Freshsource North Inc | 2033 | F | 805 878-6567 | 888 |
| Nguoi Viet Vtnamese People Inc (PA) | 2711 | E | 714 892-9414 | 4169 |
| American Pacific Plastic Fabricators Inc | 2821 | F | 714 891-3191 | 5135 |

Employee Codes: A=Over 500 employees, B=251-500
C=101-250, D=51-100, E=20-50, F=10-19, G=1-9

# WESTMINSTER, CA

| | SIC | EMP | PHONE | ENTRY# |
|---|---|---|---|---|
| New Technology Plastics Inc | 2821 | E | 562 941-6034 | 5182 |
| Intertrade Industries Ltd | 3089 | D | 714 894-5566 | 6865 |
| Tru-Form Plastics Inc | 3089 | E | 310 327-9444 | 7061 |
| Bodycote Thermal Proc Inc | 3398 | E | 714 893-6561 | 7878 |
| Tolemar LLC | 3641 | E | 657 200-3840 | 11434 |
| B/E Aerospace Inc | 3728 | C | 714 896-9001 | 13795 |
| Thompson Industries Ltd | 3728 | C | 310 679-9193 | 13973 |
| Lexor Inc | 3999 | D | 714 444-4144 | 16169 |
| Neighborhood Steel LLC (HQ) | 5051 | E | 714 236-8700 | 16625 |
| Minh Phung Incorporated | 5149 | E | 714 379-0606 | 17196 |

## WHITEWATER, CA - Riverside County

| | SIC | EMP | PHONE | ENTRY# |
|---|---|---|---|---|
| Whitewater Rock & Sup Co Inc | 5032 | E | 760 325-2747 | 16488 |

## WHITTIER, CA - Los Angeles County

| | SIC | EMP | PHONE | ENTRY# |
|---|---|---|---|---|
| Russ Bassett Corp | 2511 | C | 562 945-2445 | 3454 |
| Johnson Controls Inc | 2531 | E | 562 698-8301 | 3629 |
| JC Window Fashions Inc | 2591 | E | 909 364-8888 | 3722 |
| Tube-Tainer Inc | 2655 | E | 562 945-3711 | 3911 |
| Pasadena Newspapers Inc | 2711 | F | 562 698-0955 | 4179 |
| D & R Screen Printing Inc | 2752 | E | 562 458-6443 | 4582 |
| Ss Whittier LLC | 2752 | E | 562 698-7513 | 4770 |
| A F E Industries Inc (PA) | 2759 | F | 562 944-6889 | 4831 |
| Coastal Tag & Label Inc | 2759 | D | 562 946-4318 | 4861 |
| Messer LLC | 2813 | E | 562 903-1290 | 5054 |
| Epmar Corporation | 2851 | E | 562 946-8781 | 6084 |
| AC Products Inc | 2891 | E | 714 630-7311 | 6215 |
| Sfrlc Inc | 3069 | E | 562 693-2776 | 6537 |
| Jason Incorporated | 3291 | E | 562 921-9821 | 7554 |
| Miller Castings Inc (PA) | 3324 | B | 562 695-0461 | 7691 |
| Rasmussen Iron Works Inc | 3433 | D | 562 696-8718 | 8075 |
| Fred R Rippy Inc | 3469 | E | 562 698-9801 | 8844 |
| Allblack Co Inc | 3471 | E | 562 946-2955 | 8914 |
| Quaker City Plating | 3471 | C | 562 945-3721 | 9001 |
| Cryostar USA LLC | 3561 | D | 562 903-1290 | 9918 |
| Compu Aire Inc | 3585 | E | 562 945-8971 | 10491 |
| Rahn Industries Incorporated (PA) | 3585 | E | 562 908-0680 | 10512 |
| Medlin and Son Engrg Svc Inc | 3599 | E | 562 464-5889 | 10970 |
| Miller Castings Inc | 3599 | E | 562 695-0461 | 10982 |
| Hedman Manufacturing (PA) | 3714 | E | 562 204-1031 | 13512 |
| Trans-Dapt California Inc | 3714 | E | 562 921-0404 | 13589 |
| Gulfstream Aerospace Corp GA | 3721 | C | 562 907-9300 | 13669 |
| Cameron Technologies Us LLC | 3823 | E | 562 222-8440 | 14393 |
| Harris Organs Inc | 3931 | E | 562 693-3442 | 15718 |
| Exiton Inc | 3993 | E | 562 699-1122 | 15974 |
| Fusion Sign & Design Inc | 3993 | E | 562 946-7545 | 15980 |
| Indio Products Inc (PA) | 5049 | E | 323 720-1188 | 16601 |
| Main Electric Supply Co LLC | 5063 | E | 323 753-5131 | 16660 |
| General Transistor Corporation (PA) | 5065 | E | 310 578-7344 | 16703 |
| Eps Corporate Holdings Inc | 5074 | F | 562 698-7774 | 16766 |
| Oncor Corp | 5122 | E | 562 944-0230 | 17043 |
| US Donuts & Yogurt | 5812 | F | 562 695-8867 | 17610 |
| Eurton Electric Company Inc | 7694 | E | 562 946-4477 | 19229 |

## WILDOMAR, CA - Riverside County

| | SIC | EMP | PHONE | ENTRY# |
|---|---|---|---|---|
| Fcp Inc (PA) | 3448 | D | 951 678-4571 | 8666 |

## WILLIAMS, CA - Colusa County

| | SIC | EMP | PHONE | ENTRY# |
|---|---|---|---|---|
| Morning Star Packing Co LP | 2033 | E | 530 473-3600 | 906 |
| Tamaki Rice Corporation | 2044 | E | 530 473-2862 | 1084 |
| Bar Ale Inc (PA) | 2048 | E | 530 473-3333 | 1120 |

## WILLITS, CA - Mendocino County

| | SIC | EMP | PHONE | ENTRY# |
|---|---|---|---|---|
| Northern Aggregates Inc | 1422 | E | 707 459-3929 | 300 |
| Willits Redwood Company Inc | 2421 | E | 707 459-4549 | 3091 |
| Windsor Willits Company | 2431 | D | 707 459-8568 | 3206 |
| Microphor Inc | 3261 | E | 707 459-5563 | 7278 |
| Westinghouse A Brake Tech Corp | 3261 | E | 707 459-5563 | 7281 |
| Advanced Mfg & Dev Inc | 3444 | C | 707 459-9451 | 8363 |
| Magnetic Coils Inc | 3677 | D | 707 459-5994 | 12844 |

## WILLOWS, CA - Glenn County

| | SIC | EMP | PHONE | ENTRY# |
|---|---|---|---|---|
| Rumiano Cheese Co | 2022 | C | 530 934-5438 | 732 |
| Sierra Nevada Cheese Co Inc (PA) | 2022 | D | 530 934-8660 | 739 |
| Calplant I LLC | 2493 | E | 530 361-0003 | 3406 |
| Calplant I Holdco LLC (PA) | 2493 | E | 530 570-0542 | 3407 |
| Johns Manville Corporation | 3296 | D | 530 934-6243 | 7577 |

## WILMINGTON, CA - Los Angeles County

| | SIC | EMP | PHONE | ENTRY# |
|---|---|---|---|---|
| Juanitas Foods | 2032 | C | 310 834-5339 | 861 |
| Cfwf Inc | 2092 | C | 310 221-6280 | 2050 |
| J Deluca Fish Company Inc | 2092 | E | 310 221-6500 | 2055 |
| Air Liquide Electronics US LP | 2813 | A | 310 549-7079 | 5037 |
| California Sulphur Company | 2819 | E | 562 437-0768 | 5076 |
| Royal Adhesives & Sealants LLC | 2899 | E | 310 830-9904 | 6322 |
| Valero Ref Company-California | 2911 | A | 562 491-6754 | 6357 |
| Paramount Forge Inc | 3462 | E | 323 775-6803 | 8784 |
| Wilmington Instrument Co Inc (PA) | 3825 | F | 310 834-1133 | 14600 |
| West Coast Aerospace Inc (PA) | 3965 | E | 310 518-3167 | 15923 |
| Icpk Corporation | 5141 | D | 310 830-8020 | 17115 |
| Coordnted Wire Rope Rgging Inc (HQ) | 5251 | E | 310 834-8535 | 17353 |
| American Soccer Company Inc (PA) | 5699 | C | 310 830-6161 | 17508 |

## WILTON, CA - Sacramento County

| | SIC | EMP | PHONE | ENTRY# |
|---|---|---|---|---|
| Champion Installs Inc | 2434 | F | 916 627-0929 | 3231 |

## WINDSOR, CA - Sonoma County

| | SIC | EMP | PHONE | ENTRY# |
|---|---|---|---|---|
| Sonoma-Cutrer Vineyards Inc (DH) | 0172 | E | 707 528-1181 | 31 |
| Windsor Oaks Vineyards LLP | 2084 | E | 707 433-4050 | 1830 |
| Nieco Corporation | 3589 | D | 707 838-3226 | 10587 |
| Staubli Electrical Connectors Inc (DH) | 3678 | F | 707 838-0530 | 12897 |
| Denbeste Manufacturing Inc | 3713 | E | 707 838-1407 | 13407 |
| Micro-Vu Corp California (PA) | 3827 | E | 707 838-6272 | 14800 |
| Luthiers Mercantile Intl Inc | 5961 | F | 707 433-1823 | 17666 |

## WINNETKA, CA - Los Angeles County

| | SIC | EMP | PHONE | ENTRY# |
|---|---|---|---|---|
| World Class Cheerleading Inc | 3949 | E | 877 923-2645 | 15878 |

## WINTERS, CA - Yolo County

| | SIC | EMP | PHONE | ENTRY# |
|---|---|---|---|---|
| Pavestone LLC | 3281 | E | 530 795-4400 | 7543 |
| Buckhorn Cafe Inc (PA) | 5812 | D | 530 795-1319 | 17566 |

## WOODLAKE, CA - Tulare County

| | SIC | EMP | PHONE | ENTRY# |
|---|---|---|---|---|
| Country Plastics Inc | 3089 | F | 559 597-2556 | 6782 |
| US Tower Corp (PA) | 3441 | E | 785 524-9966 | 8238 |

## WOODLAND, CA - Yolo County

| | SIC | EMP | PHONE | ENTRY# |
|---|---|---|---|---|
| Olam West Coast Inc | 2033 | C | 530 473-4290 | 913 |
| Pacific Coast Producers | 2033 | C | 530 662-8661 | 916 |
| Culinary Farms Inc | 2034 | E | 916 375-3000 | 950 |
| Bay State Milling Company | 2041 | E | 530 666-6565 | 1057 |
| Western Foods LLC | 2041 | C | 530 601-5991 | 1068 |
| Farmers Rice Cooperative | 2044 | D | 530 666-1691 | 1076 |
| Farmers Rice Cooperative | 2044 | E | 530 666-1691 | 1078 |
| Gold River Mills LLC (PA) | 2044 | E | 530 661-1923 | 1079 |
| California Sugars LLC | 2062 | E | 800 333-9666 | 1294 |
| Boundary Bend Inc | 2079 | E | 844 626-2726 | 1392 |
| Pure Nature Foods LLC | 2096 | E | 530 723-5269 | 2100 |
| Bright People Foods Inc (PA) | 2099 | E | 530 669-6870 | 2148 |
| Cache Creek Foods LLC | 2099 | D | 530 662-1764 | 2151 |
| Cfarms Inc | 2099 | E | 916 375-3000 | 2161 |
| Pgp International Inc (DH) | 2099 | C | 530 662-5056 | 2321 |
| Palletmasters LLC | 2448 | F | 510 715-1242 | 3354 |
| Johnstons Trading Post Inc | 2449 | E | 530 661-6152 | 3373 |
| Skyline Homes Inc | 2451 | C | 530 666-0974 | 3389 |
| Acme Bag Co Inc (PA) | 2674 | E | 530 662-6130 | 3989 |
| Gleason Industries | 2679 | D | 800 488-3471 | 4040 |
| Mediatech Inc | 2834 | E | 530 666-9868 | 5549 |
| Hygieia Biological Labs | 2836 | E | 530 661-1442 | 5838 |
| Mediatech Inc | 2836 | E | 530 666-9825 | 5847 |
| Mediatech Inc | 2836 | E | 530 666-9868 | 5848 |
| Metal Sales Manufacturing Corp | 3444 | E | 707 826-2653 | 8505 |
| Watts Regulator Co | 3491 | C | 530 666-2493 | 9163 |
| American International Mfg Co | 3523 | E | 530 666-2446 | 9338 |
| Crist Group Inc | 3559 | E | 530 661-0700 | 9844 |
| Ames Fire Waterworks | 3625 | D | 530 666-2493 | 11306 |
| Communications & Pwr Inds LLC | 3671 | E | 530 662-7553 | 12028 |
| Dfc Inc (PA) | 3721 | D | 530 669-7115 | 13649 |
| Blue Sea Resources Inc | 3792 | E | 530 666-1442 | 14118 |
| Bentec Medical | 3841 | D | 530 406-3333 | 15004 |
| Bentec Medical Opco LLC | 3841 | D | 530 406-3333 | 15005 |
| Gerlinger Fndry Mch Works Inc | 5051 | F | 530 243-1053 | 16620 |
| Yolo Ice & Creamery Inc | 5143 | F | 530 662-7337 | 17133 |
| Liberty Packing Company LLC (PA) | 5148 | D | 209 826-7100 | 17170 |
| Tremont Group Incorporated | 5191 | D | 530 662-5442 | 17275 |
| The Morning Star Company (PA) | 7363 | D | 530 666-6600 | 17870 |
| CPI Econco Division | 7629 | D | 530 662-7553 | 19175 |
| Woodside Electronics Corp | 7699 | D | 530 666-9190 | 19291 |
| City of Woodland | 9224 | E | 530 661-5860 | 19577 |

## WOODLAND HILLS, CA - Los Angeles County

| | SIC | EMP | PHONE | ENTRY# |
|---|---|---|---|---|
| Shadow Security App Inc | 1731 | F | 310 388-9371 | 469 |
| Legacy Epoch LLC | 2048 | D | 844 673-7305 | 1135 |
| Gold Coast Baking Company LLC | 2051 | F | 818 575-7280 | 1213 |
| Gold Coast Baking Company LLC (PA) | 2051 | D | 818 575-7280 | 1214 |
| Pascal Patisserie | 2051 | F | 818 712-9375 | 1236 |

# GEOGRAPHIC SECTION

## ZAMORA, CA

| | SIC | EMP | PHONE | ENTRY# |
|---|---|---|---|---|
| Western Bagel Baking Corp. | 2051 | E | 818 887-5451 | 1254 |
| Weider Health and Fitness | 2087 | B | 818 884-6800 | 2032 |
| Second Generation Inc. | 2339 | D | | 2806 |
| Advanstar Communications Inc | 2721 | F | 818 593-5000 | 4226 |
| La Parent Magazine (PA) | 2721 | F | 818 264-2222 | 4271 |
| Valley Business Printers Inc. | 2752 | D | 818 362-7771 | 4801 |
| Graham Webb International Inc (HQ) | 2844 | D | 760 918-3600 | 5982 |
| National Diversified Sales Inc (HQ) | 3089 | C | 559 562-9888 | 6926 |
| Silgan Can Company | 3411 | C | 818 348-3700 | 7925 |
| Silgan Containers Corporation (DH) | 3411 | D | 818 710-3700 | 7926 |
| Silgan Containers LLC (HQ) | 3411 | D | 818 710-3700 | 7927 |
| Silgan Containers Mfg Corp (DH) | 3411 | D | 818 710-3700 | 7931 |
| Hillside Capital Inc. | 3663 | C | 650 367-2011 | 11865 |
| Alliant Tchsystems Oprtons LLC | 3812 | F | 818 887-8185 | 14138 |
| Northrop Grumman Systems Corp. | 3812 | C | 818 715-2597 | 14239 |
| Northrop Grumman Systems Corp. | 3812 | A | 818 715-4040 | 14269 |
| Northrop Grumman Systems Corp. | 3812 | B | 818 715-4854 | 14271 |
| King Nutronics LLC | 3823 | E | 818 887-5460 | 14429 |
| Panavision International LP (HQ) | 3861 | B | 818 316-1080 | 15659 |
| Lucent Diamonds Inc. | 3915 | E | 424 781-7127 | 15710 |
| Sun-Mate Corp. | 3944 | F | 818 700-0572 | 15769 |
| IDS Inc. | 4724 | D | 866 297-5757 | 16304 |
| Ev Ray Inc. | 5023 | E | 818 346-5381 | 16423 |
| Wham-O Inc. | 5092 | D | 818 963-4200 | 16954 |
| Talon International Inc (PA) | 5131 | C | 818 444-4100 | 17072 |
| Armani Trade LLC. | 5199 | E | 310 849-0067 | 17285 |
| Panavision Inc (PA) | 7359 | A | 818 316-1000 | 17860 |
| Citrusbyte LLC. | 7371 | E | 888 969-2983 | 17897 |
| Javanan Inc. | 7371 | E | 310 741-0011 | 17937 |
| Apex Communications Inc (DH) | 7372 | F | 818 379-8400 | 18048 |
| Blackline Inc (PA) | 7372 | A | 818 223-9008 | 18109 |
| Intuit Inc. | 7372 | D | 818 436-7800 | 18430 |
| Invotech Systems Inc. | 7372 | F | 818 461-9800 | 18441 |
| Real Software Systems LLC (PA) | 7372 | E | 818 313-8000 | 18725 |
| Texican Inc. | 7372 | E | 310 384-7000 | 18875 |
| Thq Inc. | 7372 | A | 818 591-1310 | 18881 |
| TI Limited LLC (PA) | 7372 | D | 323 877-5991 | 18884 |
| Limsons It Services LLC. | 7379 | E | 323 988-5546 | 19040 |
| Mventix Inc (PA) | 7389 | D | 818 337-3747 | 19107 |
| Information Forecast Inc. | 8742 | E | 818 888-4445 | 19530 |

## WOODSIDE, CA - San Mateo County

| | SIC | EMP | PHONE | ENTRY# |
|---|---|---|---|---|
| Thomas Fogarty Winery LLC | 2084 | E | 650 851-6777 | 1782 |
| Solara Health Inc. | 7372 | E | 650 270-4500 | 18808 |

## YORBA LINDA, CA - Orange County

| | SIC | EMP | PHONE | ENTRY# |
|---|---|---|---|---|
| Aseptic Technology LLC. | 2033 | C | 714 694-0168 | 876 |
| Nasco Gourmet Foods Inc. | 2033 | D | 714 279-2100 | 907 |
| Beckers Fabrication Inc. | 2672 | E | 714 692-1600 | 3946 |
| C4 Litho LLC. | 2752 | E | 714 259-1073 | 4540 |
| Printegra Corp. | 2761 | D | 714 692-2221 | 4991 |
| Precise Aerospace Mfg LLC | 3089 | E | 951 898-0500 | 6978 |
| Corrpro Companies Inc. | 3331 | E | 562 944-1636 | 7703 |
| Infrared Dynamics Inc. | 3433 | E | 714 572-4050 | 8070 |
| Boyd Corporation (PA) | 3441 | E | 714 533-2375 | 8106 |
| Euroline Steel Windows. | 3442 | D | 877 590-2741 | 8265 |
| Wagner Plate Works West Inc (PA) | 3443 | E | 562 531-6050 | 8351 |
| Radiation Protection & Spc Inc. | 3444 | F | 714 771-7702 | 8552 |
| Progressive Marketing Pdts Inc. | 3448 | D | 714 888-1700 | 8681 |
| Alpha Omega Swiss Inc. | 3451 | E | 714 692-8009 | 8716 |
| Specialty Motions Inc. | 3562 | E | 951 735-8722 | 9955 |
| Ixi Technology Inc. | 3571 | E | 714 221-5000 | 10171 |
| Zet-Tek Precision Machining (PA) | 3599 | F | 714 777-8770 | 11200 |
| Romac Supply Co Inc. | 3613 | D | 323 721-5810 | 11249 |
| Filter Concepts Incorporated. | 3677 | E | 714 545-7003 | 12839 |
| Gunjoy Inc. | 3679 | E | 714 289-0055 | 12991 |
| American HX Auto Trade Inc. | 3711 | D | 909 484-1010 | 13338 |
| Engineering Jk Aerospace & Def. | 3728 | E | 714 499-9092 | 13837 |
| Inflight Warning Systems Inc. | 3728 | F | 714 993-9394 | 13873 |
| Carefusion Corporation. | 3841 | D | 800 231-2466 | 15032 |
| Pdma Ventures Inc. | 3843 | E | 714 777-8770 | 15476 |
| Jondo Ltd (HQ) | 3861 | D | 714 279-2300 | 15645 |
| B&K Precision Corporation (PA) | 5063 | E | 714 921-9095 | 16644 |
| Sid-Mar Inc. | 5943 | F | 213 626-8121 | 17641 |
| Sesa Inc (PA) | 7336 | E | 714 779-9700 | 17839 |
| Enterprise Security Inc (PA) | 7382 | D | 714 630-9100 | 19055 |
| Omni Optical Products Inc. | 7699 | E | 714 692-1400 | 19273 |
| Tom Ponton Industries Inc. | 8742 | F | 714 998-9073 | 19544 |

## YOUNTVILLE, CA - Napa County

| | SIC | EMP | PHONE | ENTRY# |
|---|---|---|---|---|
| Cosentino Signature Wineries. | 2084 | E | 707 921-2809 | 1519 |
| Domaine Chandon Inc (DH) | 2084 | D | 707 944-8844 | 1540 |
| Dominus Estate Corporation. | 2084 | F | 707 944-8954 | 1541 |
| Jessup Cellars Inc. | 2084 | F | 707 944-8523 | 1636 |
| Lady Family Wines | 2084 | F | 707 944-8642 | 1657 |
| Newton Vineyard LLC. | 2084 | C | 707 204-7410 | 1690 |
| Treasury Wine Estates Americas. | 2084 | F | 707 312-0081 | 1792 |
| Twin Peaks Winery Inc. | 2084 | D | 707 944-8642 | 1806 |

## YREKA, CA - Siskiyou County

| | SIC | EMP | PHONE | ENTRY# |
|---|---|---|---|---|
| Custom Crushing Industries Inc. | 1221 | E | 530 842-5544 | 112 |
| Timber Products Co Ltd Partnr. | 2435 | D | 530 842-2310 | 3289 |
| Shasta Forest Products Inc. | 2499 | E | 530 842-2787 | 3427 |
| Gatehouse Media LLC. | 2711 | E | 530 842-5777 | 4119 |
| Nor-Cal Products Inc (DH) | 3494 | C | 530 842-4457 | 9190 |
| Ozotech Inc (PA) | 3589 | F | 530 842-4189 | 10590 |

## YUBA CITY, CA - Sutter County

| | SIC | EMP | PHONE | ENTRY# |
|---|---|---|---|---|
| Valley View Foods Inc. | 2033 | D | 530 673-7356 | 935 |
| Sacramento Packing Inc. | 2034 | B | 530 671-4488 | 962 |
| Sunsweet Growers Inc (PA) | 2034 | A | 800 417-2253 | 970 |
| California Olive and Vine LLC. | 2079 | F | 530 763-7921 | 1394 |
| Valley Fine Foods Company Inc. | 2099 | C | 530 671-7200 | 2385 |
| Big Hill Log & Rd Bldg Co Inc (PA) | 2411 | E | 530 673-4155 | 3043 |
| Siller Brothers Inc (PA) | 2411 | E | 530 673-0734 | 3057 |
| Unity Forest Products Inc. | 2431 | E | 530 671-7152 | 3201 |
| Paperboard Packaging Corp. | 2671 | D | 530 671-9000 | 3933 |
| Amcor Flexibles LLC. | 2759 | D | 530 671-9000 | 4839 |
| Mathews Ready Mix LLC. | 3273 | E | 530 671-2400 | 7470 |
| Orchard Machinery Corp Disc (PA) | 3523 | D | 530 673-2822 | 9374 |
| Yuba Cy Wste Wtr Trtmnt Fcilty. | 3589 | E | 530 822-7698 | 10617 |
| Tri Counties Trucking. | 3713 | E | 530 692-5388 | 13433 |

## YUCAIPA, CA - San Bernardino County

| | SIC | EMP | PHONE | ENTRY# |
|---|---|---|---|---|
| Hi-Desert Publishing Company. | 2711 | E | 909 795-8145 | 4129 |
| Merrimans Incorporated. | 3441 | E | 909 795-5301 | 8182 |
| Sorenson Engineering Inc (PA) | 3451 | C | 909 795-2434 | 8731 |
| Technical Resource Industries (PA) | 3643 | E | 909 446-1109 | 11473 |
| B B G Management Group (PA) | 5145 | E | 909 797-9581 | 17139 |

## YUCCA VALLEY, CA - San Bernardino County

| | SIC | EMP | PHONE | ENTRY# |
|---|---|---|---|---|
| Hi-Desert Publishing Company (HQ) | 2711 | D | 760 365-3315 | 4130 |
| R3 Performance Products Inc. | 3714 | F | 760 909-0846 | 13563 |
| Catalyst Development Corp. | 7372 | E | 760 228-9653 | 18151 |

## ZAMORA, CA - Yolo County

| | SIC | EMP | PHONE | ENTRY# |
|---|---|---|---|---|
| Matchbook Wine Company. | 0172 | E | 530 662-1032 | 21 |